WHO'S WHO
1983

WHO WAS WHO

Seven volumes containing the biographies removed from WHO'S WHO each year on account of death, with final details and date of death added. Also a Cumulated Index to the seven volumes giving name, years of birth and death, and the volume in which each entry is to be found.

A CUMULATED INDEX 1897-1980

ADAM & CHARLES BLACK : LONDON

WHO'S WHO
1983

AN
ANNUAL BIOGRAPHICAL DICTIONARY

ONE HUNDRED AND THIRTY-FIFTH
YEAR OF ISSUE

ADAM AND CHARLES BLACK
LONDON

PUBLISHED BY A. & C. BLACK (PUBLISHERS) LIMITED
35 BEDFORD ROW LONDON WC1

———

COPYRIGHT © 1983 A. & C. BLACK (PUBLISHERS) LTD

"WHO'S WHO" IS A REGISTERED TRADE MARK
IN THE UNITED KINGDOM

ISBN 0–7136–2280–6

———

The United States
ST. MARTIN'S PRESS, NEW YORK

Australia
EDWARD ARNOLD (AUSTRALIA) LTD, CAULFIELD EAST, VICTORIA

New Zealand
BOOK REPS (NEW ZEALAND) LTD, AUCKLAND

Canada
THOMAS NELSON & SONS LTD,
SCARBOROUGH, ONTARIO

Southern Africa
BOOK PROMOTIONS (PTY) LTD, CLAREMONT, CAPE TOWN

West Indies
C. B. C. (TRINIDAD) LTD

Far East
BOOKS FOR ASIA LTD, SINGAPORE, KUALA LUMPUR,
HONG KONG, BANGKOK

Japan
BOOKS FOR JAPAN LTD, TOKYO

COMPUTED AND TYPESET BY
COMPUTAPRINT LIMITED LONDON

PRINTED IN GREAT BRITAIN BY BUTLER & TANNER LTD, FROME & LONDON

CONTENTS

PREFACE

The first edition of *Who's Who* was published in 1849. It consisted of an Almanack, followed by 39 lists of ranks and appointments and the names of those holding them. As might be expected there were lists of Peers, Members of the House of Commons, Archbishops, Bishops and Judges. Additionally, however, there were the names of the Governor and Board of Directors of the Bank of England, of British Ministers abroad, of the Directors of the East India Company and of the officers (including the actuaries) of the life and fire assurance companies in London.

In 1897 substantial changes were made to the nature and content of the book. The range of lists had by now been expanded to include, amongst others, the Police Commissioners, the officers of the principal railways, the members of the London School Board and the Crown Agents – together with the editors of significant newspapers and magazines whose names, the editor noted, were "given here, not for contributors, but that the public may know who lead public opinion." The major change, however, was the addition of a section of biographies in which details were given of the lives of some five and a half thousand leading figures of the day.

The book had, by this early date, set the pattern it has followed to this day, aiming to list those who, through their careers, affect the political, economic, scientific and artistic life of the country: the first invitations to prepare biographies for the 1897 edition were sent to such people. That origin explains the nature of *Who's Who*: it places its emphasis on careers whilst giving opportunity for the inclusion of family and other individual details, such as the recreations which have become a distinctive feature of the book.

Once established, the essential character of *Who's Who* has been consistently maintained. It seeks to be a detailed, comprehensive and accurate reference book of those people whose lives are of particular interest, whether because they decide our destinies, spend our money, influence our taste or because they are especially prominent in their fields – the arts, education, medicine, sport, the trade unions . . .

An invitation to appear in *Who's Who* has, on occasion, been thought of as conferring distinction; that is the last thing it can do. It recognises distinction and influence. The attitude of the present editorial board remains that of the editor of the 1897 edition, who stated in his preface that the book seeks to recognise people "whether their prominence is inherited, or depending upon office, or the result of ability which singles them out from their fellows in occupations open to every educated man or woman".

EDITORS' NOTE

Some occurrences of a date later than November 1982, when this edition had to go to press, could not be recorded in the relevant entries; a number of these, of the most general interest, are listed in a supplement preceding the first page of the biographies. The names in the second part of the supplement of those who received titles gazetted in the New Year Honours List, 1983, include some who have as yet no entry in the body of the book. The obituary, on pages *47–51*, includes the deaths reported up to mid-November 1982.

A proof of each entry is posted to its subject every year for personal revision, but this cannot be sent unless an address is recorded. It should be noted that the numbers given of the children of a marriage are, unless otherwise indicated, those of the sons and daughters now living; also, that it is the practice to print the names of London clubs unaccompanied by the word London. Forenames printed within brackets are those which the subject of the entry does not commonly use. While every care is taken to ensure accuracy, neither the publishers nor the printers can admit liability for any loss incurred through misprint or other circumstances.

It cannot be stated too emphatically that inclusion in *Who's Who* has never at any time been a matter for payment or of obligation to purchase the volume.

A

A	Anti-Aircraft; Automobile Association; Architectural Association; Augustinians of the Assumption	**ACS**	American Chemical Society; Additional Curates Society
AA	Amateur Athletic Association; American Accounting Association	**ACSEA**	Allied Command South East Asia
AAAL	American Academy of Arts and Letters (*now see* AAIL)	**ACSM**	Associate, Camborne School of Mines
AA&QMG	Assistant Adjutant and Quartermaster-General	**ACT**	Australian Capital Territory; Australian College of Theology; Associate, College of Technology
AAAS	American Association for Advancement of Science	**ACTT**	Association of Cinematograph, Television and Allied Technicians
AACCA	Associate, Association of Certified and Corporate Accountants (*now see* ACCA)	**ACTU**	Australian Council of Trade Unions
AACE	Association for Adult and Continuing Education	**ACU**	Association of Commonwealth Universities
AAF	Auxiliary Air Force (*now see* RAuxAF)	**ACWA**	Associate, Institute of Cost and Works Accountants (*now see* ACMA)
AAG	Assistant Adjutant-General	**AD**	Dame of the Order of Australia; *Anno Domini*
AAI	Associate, Chartered Auctioneers' and Estate Agents' Institute (*now* (after amalgamation) *see* ARICS)	**ADAS**	Agricultural Development and Advisory Service
AAIL	American Academy and Institute of Arts and Letters	**ADB**	Asian Development Bank
AAM	Association of Assistant Mistresses in Secondary Schools	**ADB/F**	African Development Bank/Fund
AAMC	Australian Army Medical Corps	**ADC**	Aide-de-camp
A&AEE	Aeroplane and Armament Experimental Establishment	**ADCM**	Archbishop of Canterbury's Diploma in Church Music
AASA	Associate, Australian Society of Accountants	**AD Corps**	Army Dental Corps, *now* RADC
AASC	Australian Army Service Corps	**ADC (P)**	Personal Aide-de-camp to HM The Queen
AAUQ	Associate in Accountancy, University of Queensland	**Ad eund**	*Ad eundem gradum;* and *see under* a e g
AB	Bachelor of Arts (US); able-bodied seaman	**ADFManc**	Art and Design Fellow, Manchester·
ABA	Amateur Boxing Association; Antiquarian Booksellers' Association; American Bar Association	**ADFW**	Assistant Director of Fortifications and Works
ABC	Australian Broadcasting Commission	**ADGB**	Air Defence of Great Britain
ABCA	Army Bureau of Current Affairs	**ADGMS**	Assistant Director-General of Medical Services
ABCC	Association of British Chambers of Commerce	**ADH**	Assistant Director of Hygiene
ABCFM	American Board of Commissioners for Foreign Missions	**Adjt**	Adjutant
ABIA	Associate, Bankers' Institute of Australasia	**ADJAG**	Assistant Deputy Judge Advocate General
ABINZ	Associate, Bankers' Institute of New Zealand	**ADK**	Order of Ahli Darjah Kinabalu (Malaysia)
ABNM	American Board of Nuclear Medicine	**Adm.**	Admiral
Abp	Archbishop	**ADMS**	Assistant Director of Medical Services
ABPsS	Associate, British Psychological Society	**ADOS**	Assistant Director of Ordnance Services
ABRC	Advisory Board for the Research Councils	**ADP**	Automatic Data Processing
ABS	Associate, Building Societies' Institute (*now see* ACBSI)	**ADS&T**	Assistant Director of Supplies and Transport
ABSI	Associate, Boot and Shoe Institute	**Adv.**	Advisory; Advocate
ABSM	Associate, Birmingham and Midland Institute School of Music	**ADVS**	Assistant Director of Veterinary Services
ABTAPL	Association of British Theological and Philosophical Libraries	**ADWE&M**	Assistant Director of Works, Electrical and Mechanical
AC	Companion of the Order of Australia; *Ante Christum* (before Christ)	**AE**	Air Efficiency Award (changed 1975)
ACA	Associate, Institute of Chartered Accountants	**AEA**	Atomic Energy Authority; Air Efficiency Award (*now see* AE)
Acad.	Academy	**AEAF**	Allied Expeditionary Air Force
ACARD	Advisory Council for Applied Research and Development	**AEC**	Agriculture Executive Council; Army Educational Corps (*now see* RAEC)
ACAS	Advisory, Conciliation and Arbitration Service; Assistant Chief of the Air Staff	**AEF**	Amalgamated Union of Engineering and Foundry Workers; American Expeditionary Forces
ACBSI	Associate, Chartered Building Societies Institute	**aeg**	*ad eundem gradum* (to the same degree—of the admission of a graduate of one university to the same degree at another without examination)
ACC	Association of County Councils	**AEGIS**	Aid for the Elderly in Government Institutions
ACCA	Associate, Association of Certified Accountants	**AEI**	Associated Electrical Industries
ACCM	Advisory Council for the Church's Ministry	**AEM**	Air Efficiency Medal
ACCS	Associate, Corporation of Secretaries (formerly of Certified Secretaries)	**AER**	Army Emergency Reserve
ACDS	Assistant Chief of Defence Staff	**AERE**	Atomic Energy Research Establishment (Harwell)
ACE	Association of Consulting Engineers	**AEt., AEtat.**	*AEtatis* (aged)
ACF	Army Cadet Force	**AEU**	Amalgamated Engineering Union
ACFA	Army Cadet Force Association	**AFA**	Amateur Football Alliance
ACG	Assistant Chaplain-General	**AFAIAA**	Associate Fellow, American Institute of Aeronautics and Astronautics
ACGI	Associate, City and Guilds of London Institute	**AFC**	Air Force Cross; Association Football Club
ACGS	Assistant Chief of the General Staff	**AFCAI**	Associate Fellow, Canadian Aeronautical Institute
ACIArb	Associate, Chartered Institute of Arbitrators	**AFD**	Doctor of Fine Arts (US)
ACII	Associate, Chartered Insurance Institute	**AFHQ**	Allied Force Headquarters
ACIS	Associate, Institute of Chartered Secretaries and Administrators (*formerly* Chartered Institute of Secretaries)	**AFIA**	Associate, Federal Institute of Accountants (Australia)
ACIT	Associate, Chartered Institute of Transport	**AFIAS**	Associate Fellow, Institute of Aeronautical Sciences (US) (*now see* AFAIAA)
ACLS	American Council of Learned Societies	**AFICD**	Associate Fellow, Institute of Civil Defence
ACMA	Associate, Institute of Cost and Management Accountants	**AFIMA**	Associate Fellow, Institute of Mathematics and its Applications
ACNS	Assistant Chief of Naval Staff	**AFM**	Air Force Medal
ACommA	Associate, Society of Commercial Accountants (*now see* ASCA)	**AFOM**	Associate, Faculty of Occupational Medicine
ACOS	Assistant Chief of Staff	**AFRAeS**	Associate Fellow, Royal Aeronautical Society (*now see* MRAeS)
ACP	Association of Clinical Pathologists; Associate, College of Preceptors; African/Caribbean/Pacific	**AFV**	Armoured Fighting Vehicles
ACPO	Association of Chief Police Officers		

66 This country is lucky enough to enjoy the richest music life of any in the world. Sadly, though, it has a poor record in providing for the very musicians who make this possible. Conditions are poor and hours are long in order to maintain a decent standard of living. There is no pay for missed working days caused by sickness or family misfortune and few can look forward to a pension. The Musicians Benevolent Fund does invaluable work to improve this situation, but it could do even more with your help. By supporting the Fund you can personally thank the musicians who have created and are creating the musical wealth of this country. 99

SIR GEORG SOLTI

Please send a donation, large or small.
**Philip Cranmer, Chairman,
MUSICIANS BENEVOLENT FUND,
16 Ogle Street, London W1P 7LG.**

Attorney-General
ARD Advisory Group for Aerospace Research and Development
H Australian General Hospital
(Artistes Graphiques Internationales; Associate, Institute of Certificated Grocers
RA Army Group Royal Artillery
GM Associate, Guildhall School of Music
A Area Health Authority; American Hospitals Association; Associate, Institute of Health Service Administrators
A(T) Area Health Authority (Teaching)
Q Army Headquarters
WC Associate, Heriot-Watt College, Edinburgh
ad interim
Associate, Institute of Actuaries; American Institute of Architects; Association of International Artists
A American Institute of Aeronautics and Astronautics
L Associate Member, International Institute of Arts and Letters
rb Associate, Institute of Arbitrators (*now see* ACIArb)
S Associate Surveyor Member, Incorporated Association of Architects and Surveyors
Associate, Institute of Bankers
D Associate, Institute of British Decorators
P Associate, Institute of British Photographers
Agricultural Improvement Council; Associate of the Institute of Chemistry (later ARIC, MRIC; *now see* MRSC)
A Associate Member, Commonwealth Institute of Accountants; Association Internationale des Critiques d'Art
C All-India Congress Committee
E Associate, Institution of Civil Engineers
PA American Institute of Certified Public Accountants
S Associate, Institute of Chartered Shipbrokers
TA Associate, Imperial College of Tropical Agriculture
E Associate, Institution of Electrical Engineers
Australian Imperial Forces
Adjutant-Inspector-General
A Associate, Insurance Institute of America
nfSc Associate, Institute of Information Scientists
Associate, Institute of Linguists
A Associate, Institute of Landscape Architects (*now see* ALI)
ocoE Associate, Institution of Locomotive Engineers
M Associate, Institution of Metallurgists (*now see* MIM)
ME American Institute of Mechanical Engineers
MarE Associate, Institute of Marine Engineers
stM Associate Member, Institute of Marketing
stP Associate, Institute of Physics
stPI Associate, Institute of Patentees and Inventors
rodE Associate, Institution of Production Engineers
QS Associate Member, Institute of Quantity Surveyors
RTE Associate, Institution of Road Transport Engineers
Associate, Institute of Statisticians (*now see* MIS)
A Associate, Incorporated Secretaries' Association
tructE Associate, Institution of Structural Engineers
AG Assistant Judge Advocate General
EX Association of Jewish Ex-Service Men and Women
Knight of the Order of Australia
C Associate, King's College (London)
A Associate, Library Association
Alabama (US)
AA Associate, Library Association of Australia
AM Associate, London Academy of Music and Dramatic Art
CD Associate, London College of Divinity
CM Associate, London College of Music
CS Authors Lending and Copyright Society
FSEA Allied Land Forces South-East Asia
I Argyll Light Infantry; Associate, Landscape Institute
LC Association for Literary and Linguistic Computing
P Australian Labor Party
PSP Association of Learned and Professional Society Publishers
S Associate, Linnaean Society
a Alberta
Albert Medal; Member of the Order of Australia; Master of Arts (US); Alpes Maritimes
MA Association of Metropolitan Authorities; Assistant Masters Association; Associate of the Museums Association; Australian Medical Association
b. Ambulance; Ambassador
BIM Associate Member, British Institute of Management
BritIRE Associate Member, British Institution of Radio Engineers (*now see* AMIERE)
C Association of Municipal Corporations
CT Associate, Manchester College of Technology
EME Association of Mining Electrical and Mechanical Engineers
et Associate of Metallurgy (Sheffield University)
F Australian Military Forces
GOT Allied Military Government of Occupied Territory
IAE Associate Member, Institution of Automobile Engineers
IAgrE Associate Member, Institution of Agricultural Engineers
ICE Associate Member, Institution of Civil Engineers (*now see* MICE)
IChemE Associate Member, Institution of Chemical Engineers
IE(Aust) Associate Member, Institution of Engineers, Australia
IED Associate Member, Institution of Engineering Designers
IEE Associate Member, Institution of Electrical Engineers (*now*

see MIEE)
AMIE(Ind) Associate Member, Institution of Engineers, India
AMIERE Associate Member, Institution of Electronic and Radio Engineers
AMIH Associate Member, Institute of Housing
AMIMechE Associate Member, Institution of Mechanical Engineers (*now see* MIMechE)
AMIMinE Associate Member, Institution of Mining Engineers
AMIMM Associate Member, Institution of Mining and Metallurgy
AMInstBE Associate Member, Institution of British Engineers
AMInstCE Associate Member, Institution of Civil Engineers (*now see* MICE)
AmInstEE American Institute of Electrical Engineers
AMInstR Associate Member, Institute of Refrigeration
AMInstT Associate Member, Institute of Transport (*now see* ACIT)
AMInstTA Associate Member, Institute of Traffic Administration
AMINucE Associate Member, Institution of Nuclear Engineers
AMIStructE Associate Member, Institution of Structural Engineers
AMN Ahli Mangku Negara (Malaysia)
AMP Advanced Management Program
AMRINA Associate Member, Royal Institution of Naval Architects
AMS Assistant Military Secretary; Army Medical Services
AMTE Admiralty Marine Technology Establishment
ANA Associate National Academician (America)
ANAF Arab Non-Arab Friendship
Anat. Anatomy; Anatomical
ANC African National Congress
ANECInst Associate, NE Coast Institution of Engineers and Shipbuilders
ANGAU Australia New Guinea Administrative Unit
Anon. Anonymously
ANU Australian National University
ANZAAS Australian and New Zealand Association for the Advancement of Science
AO Officer of the Order of Australia; Air Officer
AOA Air Officer in charge of Administration
AOC Air Officer Commanding
AOC-in-C Air Officer Commanding-in-Chief
AOD Army Ordnance Department
AOER Army Officers Emergency Reserve
APA American Psychiatric Association
APD Army Pay Department
APEX Association of Professional, Executive, Clerical and Computer Staffs
APHA American Public Health Association
APM Assistant Provost Marshal
APMI Associate, Pensions Management Institute
APS Aborigines Protection Society
APsSI Associate, Psychological Society of Ireland
APSW Association of Psychiatric Social Workers
APT&C Administrative, Professional, Technical and Clerical
APTC Army Physical Training Corps
AQ Administration and Quartering
AQMG Assistant Quartermaster-General
AR Associated Rediffusion (Television)
ARA Associate, Royal Academy
ARACI Associate, Royal Australian Chemical Institute
ARAD Associate, Royal Academy of Dancing
ARAeS Associate, Royal Aeronautical Society
ARAM Associate, Royal Academy of Music
ARAS Associate, Royal Astronomical Society
ARBA Associate, Royal Society of British Artists
ARBC Associate, Royal British Colonial Society of Artists
ARBS Associate, Royal Society of British Sculptors
ARC Architects' Registration Council; Agricultural Research Council; Aeronautical Research Council
ARCA Associate, Royal College of Art; Associate, Royal Canadian Academy
ARCamA Associate, Royal Cambrian Academy of Art
ARCE Academical Rank of Civil Engineer
Archt Architect
ARCM Associate, Royal College of Music
ARCO Associate, Royal College of Organists
ARCO(CHM) Associate, Royal College of Organists with Diploma in Choir Training
ARCPsych Associate Member, Royal College of Psychiatrists
ARCS Associate, Royal College of Science
ARCST Associate, Royal College of Science and Technology (Glasgow)
ARCUK Architects' Registration Council of the United Kingdom
ARCVS Associate, Royal College of Veterinary Surgeons
ARE Associate, Royal Society of Painter-Etchers and Engravers; Arab Republic of Egypt
ARELS Association of Recognised English Language Schools
ARIAS Associate, Royal Incorporation of Architects in Scotland
ARIBA Associate, Royal Institute of British Architects (*now see* RIBA)
ARIC Associate, Royal Institute of Chemistry (later MRIC; *now see* MRSC)
ARICS Professional Associate, Royal Institution of Chartered Surveyors
ARINA Associate, Royal Institution of Naval Architects
Ark Arkansas (US)
ARLT Association for the Reform of Latin Teaching
ARMS Associate, Royal Society of Miniature Painters

RP   Air Raid Precautions
RPS   Associate, Royal Photographic Society
RRC   Associate, Royal Red Cross
RSA   Associate, Royal Scottish Academy
RSCM   Associate, Royal School of Church Music
RSM   Associate, Royal School of Mines
RTC   Associate, Royal Technical College (Glasgow) (now see ARCST)
RVIA   Associate, Royal Victoria Institute of Architects
RWA   Associate, Royal West of England Academy
RWS   Associate, Royal Society of Painters in Water-Colours
S   Anglo-Saxon
SA   Associate Member, Society of Actuaries; Associate of Society of Actuaries (US); Australian Society of Accountants; Army Sailing Association
SAA   Associate, Society of Incorporated Accountants and Auditors
SAM   Associate, Society of Art Masters
S&TS of SA Associated Scientific and Technical Societies of South Africa
SBAH   Association for Spina Bifida and Hydrocephalus
SC   Administrative Staff College, Henley
SCA   Associate, Society of Company and Commercial Accountants
SCAB   Armed Services Consultant Approval Board
ScW   Association of Scientific Workers (now see ASTMS)
SD   Armament Supply Department
SE   Amalgamated Society of Engineers (now see AUEW)
SH   Action on Smoking and Health
SIAD   Associate, Society of Industrial Artists and Designers
SIA(Ed)   Associate, Society of Industrial Artists (Education)
SLE   American Society of Lubrication Engineers
SLEF   Associated Society of Locomotive Engineers and Firemen
SLIB (Aslib) Association of Special Libraries and Information Bureaux
SM   Association of Senior Members
SME   American Society of Mechanical Engineers; Association for the Study of Medical Education
SO   Air Staff Officer
SSC   Accounting Standards Steering Committee
SSET   Association of Supervisory Staffs, Executives and Technicians (now see ASTMS)
AssocISI   Associate, Iron and Steel Institute
AssocMCT   Associateship of Manchester College of Technology
AssocMIAeE Associate Member, Institution of Aeronautical Engineers
AssocRINA   Associate, Royal Institution of Naval Architects
AssocSc   Associate in Science
Asst   Assistant
ASTC   Administrative Service Training Course
ASTMS   Association of Scientific, Technical and Managerial Staffs
Astr.   Astronomy
ATA   Air Transport Auxiliary
ATAE   Association of Tutors in Adult Education
ATAF   Allied Tactical Air Force
ATC   Air Training Corps
ATCDE   Association of Teachers in Colleges and Departments of Education (now see NATFHE)
ATCL   Associate, Trinity College of Music, London
ATD   Art Teacher's Diploma
ATI   Associate, Textile Institute
ATII   Associate Member, Institute of Taxation
ato   Ammunition Technical Officer
ATS   Auxiliary Territorial Service (now see WRAC)
ATTI   Association of Teachers in Technical Institutions (now see NATFHE)
ATV   Associated TeleVision
AUA   American Urological Association
AUCAS   Association of University Clinical Academic Staff
AUEW   Amalgamated Union of Engineering Workers
AUEW(TASS) Amalgamated Union of Engineering Workers (Technical and Supervisory Section)
AUS   Army of the United States
AUT   Association of University Teachers
AVCC   Australian Vice-Chancellors' Committee
AVD   Army Veterinary Department
AVLA   Audio Visual Language Association
AVR   Army Volunteer Reserve
AWA   Anglian Water Authority
AWRE   Atomic Weapons Research Establishment
aws   Graduate of Air Warfare Course

B

b   born; brother
BA   Bachelor of Arts
BAAB   British Amateur Athletic Board
BAAL   British Association for Applied Linguistics
BAAS   British Association for the Advancement of Science
BAB   British Airways Board
BAC   British Aircraft Corporation
BACM   British Association of Colliery Management
BAe   British Aerospace
B&FBS   British and Foreign Bible Society

BAFO   British Air Forces of Occupation
BAFTA   British Academy of Film and Television Arts
BAG   Business Art Galleries
BAI   *Baccalarius in Arte Ingeniaria* (Bachelor of Engineering)
BAIE   British Association of Industrial Editors
BALPA   British Air Line Pilots' Association
BAO   Bachelor of Art of Obstetrics
BAOR   British Army of the Rhine (formerly on the Rhine)
BAOS   British Association of Oral Surgeons
BAppSc(MT) Bachelor of Applied Science (Medical Technology)
BARC   British Automobile Racing Club
Bart or Bt Baronet
BAS   Bachelor in Agricultural Science
BASc   Bachelor of Applied Science
BASW   British Association of Social Workers
Batt.   Battery
BBA   British Bankers' Association
BB&CIRly   Bombay, Baroda and Central India Railway
BBB of C   British Boxing Board of Control
BBC   British Broadcasting Corporation
BBM   Bintang Bakti Masharakat (Public Service Star) (Singapore)
BBS   Bachelor of Business Studies
BC   Before Christ; British Columbia
BCC   British Council of Churches
BCE (Melb) Bachelor of Civil Engineering (Melbourne)
BCh or BChir Bachelor of Surgery
BCL   Bachelor of Civil Law
BCMS   Bible Churchmen's Missionary Society
BCOF   British Commonwealth Occupation Force
BCom   Bachelor of Commerce
BComSc   Bachelor of Commercial Science
BCS   Bengal Civil Service
BCURA   British Coal Utilization Research Association
BCYC   British Corinthian Yacht Club
BD   Bachelor of Divinity
Bd   Board
BDA   British Dental Association
Bde   Brigade
BDS   Bachelor of Dental Surgery
BDSc   Bachelor of Dental Science
BE   Bachelor of Engineering; British Element
BEA   British East Africa; British European Airways; British Epilepsy Association
BEAMA   British Electrical and Allied Manufacturers' Association
BE&A   Bachelor of Engineering and Architecture (Malta)
BEAS   British Educational Administration Society
BEC   Business Education Council
BEc   Bachelor of Economics
BEd   Bachelor of Education
Beds   Bedfordshire
BEE   Bachelor of Electrical Engineering
BEF   British Expeditionary Force; British Equestrian Federation
BEM   British Empire Medal
BEME   Brigade Electrical and Mechanical Engineer
BEO   Base Engineer Officer
Berks   Berkshire
BFI   British Film Institute
BFMIRA   British Food Manufacturing Industries Research Association
BFPO   British Forces Post Office
BGS   Brigadier General Staff
Bhd   Berhad
BHRCA   British Hotels, Restaurants and Caterers' Association
BHS   British Horse Society
BICC   British Insulated Callender's Cables
BICERA   British Internal Combustion Engine Research Association
BIF   British Industries Fair
BIFU   Banking Insurance and Finance Union
BIM   British Institute of Management
BIR   British Institute of Radiology
BIS   Bank for International Settlements
BISF   British Iron and Steel Federation
BISFA   British Industrial and Scientific Film Association
BISPA   British Independent Steel Producers Association
BISRA   British Iron and Steel Research Association
BJ   Bachelor of Journalism
BJSM   British Joint Services Mission
BKSTS   British Kinematograph, Sound and Television Society
BL   Bachelor of Law
BLA   British Liberation Army
BLE   Brotherhood of Locomotive Engineers; Bachelor of Land Economy
BLESMA   British Limbless Ex-Servicemen's Association
BLitt   Bachelor of Letters
BM   British Museum; Bachelor of Medicine; Brigade Major; British Monomark
BMA   British Medical Association
BMEO   British Middle East Office
BMet   Bachelor of Metallurgy
BMEWS   Ballistic Missile Early Warning System
BMH   British Military Hospital
BMJ   British Medical Journal
Bn   Battalion
BNAF   British North Africa Force

NC Brasenose College
NEC British National Export Council
NFL British Nuclear Fuels Ltd
NOC British National Oil Corporation; British National Opera Company
OAC British Overseas Airways Corporation
omCS Bombay Civil Service
omSC Bombay Staff Corps
oT Board of Trade
ot. Botany; Botanical
OTB British Overseas Trade Board
p Bishop
PA British Paediatric Association
Pharm Bachelor of Pharmacy
PIF British Printing Industries Federation
PsS British Psychological Society
R British Rail
r. Branch
RA Brigadier Royal Artillery; British Rheumatism & Arthritis Association
RB British Railways Board
RCS British Red Cross Society
RE Building Research Establishment
rig. Brigadier
ritIRE British Institution of Radio Engineers (*now see* IERE)
RNC Britannia Royal Naval College
RS British Road Services
S Bachelor of Surgery; Bachelor of Science
SA Bachelor of Scientific Agriculture; Birmingham Small Arms
SAA British South American Airways
SAP British South Africa Police
SC British Steel Corporation; Bengal Staff Corps
Sc Bachelor of Science
ScA Bachelor of Science in Agriculture
Sc (Dent) Bachelor of Science in Dentistry
SE Bachelor of Science in Engineering (US)
SF British Salonica Force
SI British Standards Institution
SJA British Show Jumping Association
SocSc Bachelor of Social Science
SRA British Ship Research Association
ST Bachelor of Sacred Theology
T Bachelor of Teaching
t Baronet; Brevet
TA British Tourist Authority (*formerly* British Travel Association)
TC British Transport Commission
TCV British Trust for Conservation Volunteers
Th Bachelor of Theology
tss Baroness
UAS British Universities Association of Slavists
UPA British United Provident Association
VA British Veterinary Association
VM Blessed Virgin Mary
VMS Bachelor of Veterinary Medicine and Surgery
ucks Buckinghamshire
WI British West Indies
WM British War Medal

C

C) Conservative; 100
Child; cousin
CA Central America; County Alderman; Chartered Accountant (Scotland and Canada)
CAA Civil Aviation Authority
CAB Citizens' Advice Bureau
CACTM Central Advisory Council of Training for the Ministry (*now see* ACCM)
CALE Canadian Army Liaison Executive
Cambs Cambridgeshire
CAMC Canadian Army Medical Corps
CAMRA Campaign for Real Ale
CAMW Central Association for Mental Welfare
Cantab Of Cambridge University
CARE Cottage and Rural Enterprises
CARIFTA Caribbean Free Trade Area
CAS Chief of the Air Staff
CASI Canadian Aeronautics and Space Institute
Cav. Cavalry
CAWU Clerical and Administrative Workers' Union
CB Companion of the Bath
CBC County Borough Council
CBCO Central Board for Conscientious Objectors
CBE Commander of the Order of the British Empire
CBI Confederation of British Industry
CBIM Companion, British Institute of Management
CBS Columbia Broadcasting System
CBSA Clay Bird Shooting Association
CBSI Chartered Building Societies Institute
CC Companion of the Order of Canada; City Council; County Council; Cricket Club; Cycling Club; County Court

CCAB Consultative Committee of Accountancy Bodies
CCAHC Central Council for Agricultural and Horticultural Co-operation
CCBE Commission Consultative des Barreaux de la Communauté Européenne
CCC Corpus Christi College; Central Criminal Court; County Cricket Club
CCF Combined Cadet Force
CCFM Combined Cadet Forces Medal
CCG Control Commission Germany
CCH Cacique's Crown of Honour, Order of Service of Guyana
CChem Chartered Chemist
CCHMS Central Committee for Hospital Medical Services
CCJ Council of Christians and Jews
CCPR Central Council of Physical Recreation
CCRA Commander Corps of Royal Artillery
CCRE Commander Corps of Royal Engineers
CCRSigs Commander Corps of Royal Signals
CCS Casualty Clearing Station; Ceylon Civil Service
CCTA Commission de Coopération Technique pour l'Afrique
CD Canadian Forces Decoration; Commander of the Order of Distinction (Jamaica); Civil Defence
CDEE Chemical Defence Experimental Establishment
CDipAF Certified Diploma in Accounting and Finance
Cdre Commodore
CDS Chief of the Defence Staff
CDU Christliche Demokratische Union
CE Civil Engineer
CEDEP Centre Européen d'Education Permanente
CEE Communauté Economique Européenne
CEF Canadian Expeditionary Force
CEGB Central Electricity Generating Board
CEI Council of Engineering Institutions
CEIR Corporation for Economic and Industrial Research
CEMA Council for the Encouragement of Music and the Arts
CEMS Church of England Men's Society
CEN Comité Européen de Normalisation
CEng Chartered Engineer
Cento Central Treaty Organisation
CERL Central Electricity Research Laboratories
CERN Organisation (*formerly* Centre) Européenne pour la Recherche Nucléaire
CET Council for Educational Technology
CETS Church of England Temperance Society
CF Chaplain to the Forces
CFA Canadian Field Artillery
CFE Central Fighter Establishment
CFR Commander of Federal Republic of Nigeria
CFS Central Flying School
CGA Community of the Glorious Ascension
CGH Order of the Golden Heart of Kenya (1st class)
CGIA Insignia Award of City and Guilds of London Institute
CGLI City and Guilds of London Institute
CGM Conspicuous Gallantry Medal
CGRM Commandant-General Royal Marines
CGS Chief of the General Staff
CH Companion of Honour
Chanc. Chancellor; Chancery
Chap. Chaplain
ChapStJ Chaplain of Order of St John of Jerusalem (*now see* ChStJ)
CHAR Campaign for the Homeless and Rootless
CHB Companion of Honour of Barbados
ChB Bachelor of Surgery
Ch. Ch. Christ Church
Ch. Coll. Christ's College
CHE Campaign for Homosexual Equality
CHM Chevalier of Honour and Merit (Haiti)
(CHM) *See under* ARCO(CHM), FRCO(CHM)
ChM Master of Surgery
Chm. Chairman
CHSC Central Health Services Council
ChStJ Chaplain of Order of St John of Jerusalem
CI Imperial Order of the Crown of India; Channel Islands
CIA Chemical Industries Association; Central Intelligence Agency
CIAD Central Institute of Art and Design
CIAgrE Companion, Institution of Agricultural Engineers
CIAL Corresponding Member of the International Institute of Arts and Letters
CIArb Chartered Institute of Arbitrators
CIBS Chartered Institution of Building Services
CICHE Committee for International Co-operation in Higher Education
CID Criminal Investigation Department
CIDEC Conseil International pour le Développement du Cuivre
CIE Companion of the Order of the Indian Empire; Confédération Internationale des Etudiants
CIFRS Comité International de la Rayonne et des Fibres Synthétiques
CIGRE Conférence Internationale des Grands Réseaux Electriques
CIGS Chief of the Imperial General Staff (*now see* CGS)
CIIA Canadian Institute of International Affairs
CIM China Inland Mission
CIMarE Companion, Institute of Marine Engineers
CIMGTechE Companion, Institution of Mechanical and General

Technician Engineers
C-in-C Commander-in-Chief
CINCHAN Allied Commander-in-Chief Channel
CIOB Chartered Institute of Building
CIPFA Chartered Institute of Public Finance and Accountancy
CIPL Comité International Permanent des Linguistes
CIPM Companion, Institute of Personnel Management
CIR Commission on Industrial Relations
CIRIA Construction Industry Research and Information Association
CIS Institute of Chartered Secretaries and Administrators (*formerly* Chartered Institute of Secretaries); Command Control Communications and Information Systems
CISAC Confédération Internationale des Sociétés d'Auteurs et Compositeurs
CIT Chartered Institute of Transport; California Institute of Technology
CIU Club and Institute Union
CIV City Imperial Volunteers
CJ Chief Justice
CJM Congregation of Jesus and Mary (Eudist Fathers)
CL Commander of Order of Leopold
cl *cum laude*
Cl. Class
CLA Country Landowners' Association
CLit Companion of Literature (Royal Society of Literature Award)
CLJ Commander, Order of St Lazarus of Jerusalem
CLP Constituency Labour Party
CLRAE Conference of Local and Regional Authorities of Europe
CM Member of the Order of Canada; Congregation of the Mission (Vincentians); Master in Surgery; Certificated Master; Canadian Militia
CMA Canadian Medical Association
CMAC Catholic Marriage Advisory Council
CMB Central Midwives' Board
CMF Commonwealth Military Forces; Central Mediterranean Force
CMG Companion of St Michael and St George
CMLJ Commander of Merit, Order of St Lazarus of Jerusalem
CMM Commander, Order of Military Merit (Canada)
CMO Chief Medical Officer
CMP Corps of Military Police
CMS Church Missionary Society
CMT Chaconia Medal of Trinidad
CNAA Council for National Academic Awards
CNR Canadian National Railways
CNRS Centre National du Recherche Scientifique
CO Commanding Officer; Commonwealth Office (from Aug. 1966) (*see also* FCO); Colonial Office (before Aug. 1966); Conscientious Objector
Co. County; Company
C of E Church of England
C of S Chief of Staff
COI Central Office of Information
CoID Council of Industrial Design (*now* Design Council)
Co.L or Coal.L Coalition Liberal
Col Colonel
Coll. College; Collegiate
Colo Colorado (US)
Col-Sergt Colour-Sergeant
Com Communist
Comd Command
Comdg Commanding
Comdr Commander
Comdt Commandant
COMEC Council of the Military Education Committees of the Universities of the UK
COMET Committee for Middle East Trade
Commn Commission
Commnd Commissioned
CompAMEME Companion, Association of Mining Electrical and Mechanical Engineers
CompICE Companion, Institution of Civil Engineers
CompIEE Companion, Institution of Electrical Engineers
CompIERE Companion, Institution of Electronic and Radio Engineers
CompIMechE Companion, Institution of Mechanical Engineers
CompTI Companion of the Textile Institute
Comr Commissioner
Comy-Gen. Commissary-General
CON Commander, Order of the Niger
Conn Connecticut (US)
Const. Constitutional
COPA Comité des Organisations Professionels Agricoles de la CEE
COPEC Conference of Politics, Economics and Christianity
Corp. Corporation; Corporal
Corr. Mem. or Fell. Corresponding Member or Fellow
COS Chief of Staff; Charity Organization Society
COSA Colliery Officials and Staffs Association
CoSIRA Council for Small Industries in Rural Areas
COSSAC Chief of Staff to Supreme Allied Commander
COTC Canadian Officers' Training Corps
Co.U or Coal.U Coalition Unionist

CP Central Provinces; Cape Province
CPA Commonwealth Parliamentary Association; Chartered Patent Agent; Certified Public Accountant (Canada) (*now see* CA)
CPAS Church Pastoral Aid Society
CPC Conservative Political Centre
CPL Chief Personnel and Logistics
CPM Colonial Police Medal
CPR Canadian Pacific Railway
CPRE Council for the Protection of Rural England
CPSA Civil and Public Services Association
CPSU Communist Party of the Soviet Union
CPU Commonwealth Press Union
CQSW Certificate of Qualification in Social Work
CR Community of the Resurrection
cr created or creation
CRA Commander, Royal Artillery
CRAeS Companion, Royal Aeronautical Society
CRASC Commander, Royal Army Service Corps
CRC Cancer Research Campaign; Community Relations Council
CRCP(C) Certificant, Royal College of Physicians of Canada
CRE Commander, Royal Engineers; Commission for Racial Equality; Commercial Relations and Exports
Cres. Crescent
CRMP Corps of Royal Military Police
CRO Commonwealth Relations Office (before Aug. 1966; *now see* CO and FCO)
CS Civil Service; Clerk to the Signet
CSA Confederate States of America
CSB Bachelor of Christian Science
CSC Conspicuous Service Cross; Congregation of the Holy Cross
CSCA Civil Service Clerical Association (*now see* CPSA)
CSCE Conference on Security and Cooperation in Europe
CSD Civil Service Department; Cooperative Secretaries Diploma
CSEU Confederation of Shipbuilding and Engineering Unions
CSG Companion of the Order of the Star of Ghana
CSI Companion of the Order of the Star of India
CSIR Commonwealth Council for Scientific and Industrial Research (*now see* CSIRO)
CSIRO Commonwealth Scientific and Industrial Research Organization (Australia)
CSO Chief Scientific Officer; Chief Signal Officer; Chief Staff Officer
CSP Chartered Society of Physiotherapists; Civil Service of Pakistan
CSS Companion of Star of Sarawak
CSSp Holy Ghost Father
CSSR Congregation of the Most Holy Redeemer (Redemptorist Order)
CStJ Commander of the Order of St John of Jerusalem
CSU Christlich-Soziale Union in Bayern
CSV Community Service Volunteers
CTA Chaplain Territorial Army
CTB College of Teachers of the Blind
CTC Cyclists' Touring Club
CText Chartered Textile Technologist
CTR (Harwell) Controlled Thermonuclear Research
CU Cambridge University
CUAC Cambridge University Athletic Club
CUAFC Cambridge University Association Football Club
CUBC Cambridge University Boat Club
CUCC Cambridge University Cricket Club
CUF Common University Fund
CUHC Cambridge University Hockey Club
CUP Cambridge University Press
CURUFC Cambridge University Rugby Union Football Club
CV Cross of Valour (Canada)
CVO Commander of the Royal Victorian Order
CWA Crime Writers Association
CWS Co-operative Wholesale Society

D

D Duke
d Died; daughter
DA Diploma in Anaesthesia; Diploma in Art
DAA&QMG Deputy Assistant Adjutant and Quartermaster-General
DAAG Deputy Assistant Adjutant-General
DA&QMG Deputy Adjutant and Quartermaster-General
DACG Deputy Assistant Chaplain-General
DAD Deputy Assistant Director
DADMS Deputy Assistant Director of Medical Services
DADOS Deputy Assistant Director of Ordnance Services
DADQ Deputy Assistant Director of Quartering
DADST Deputy Assistant Director of Supplies and Transport
DAG Deputy Adjutant-General
DAgr Doctor of Agriculture
DAMS Deputy Assistant Military Secretary
DandAD Design and Art Directors Association
DAppSc Doctor of Applied Science
DAQMG Deputy Assistant Quartermaster-General
DASc Doctor in Agricultural Sciences
DATA Draughtsmen's and Allied Technicians' Association (*now see*

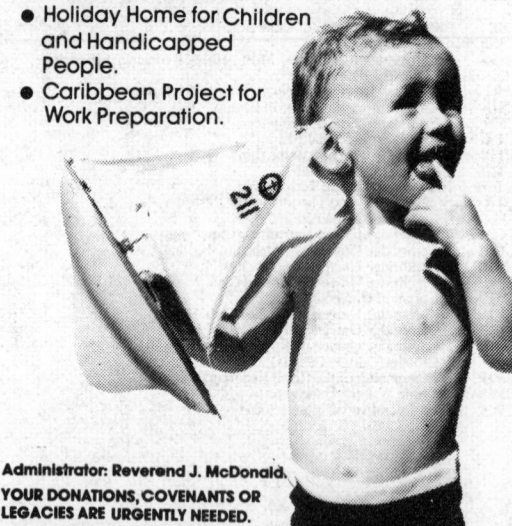

	AUEW (TASS))		CAM Foundation
·BA	Doctor of Business Administration	DipCC	Diploma of the Central College
·BE	Dame Commander Order of the British Empire	DipCD	Diploma in Civic Design
·C	District Council; District of Columbia (US)	DipCE	Diploma in Civil Engineering
·CAe	Diploma of College of Aeronautics	DipEd	Diploma in Education
·CAS	Deputy Chief of the Air Staff	DipESL	Diploma in English as a Second Language
)CB	Dame Commander of the Bath	DipEth	Diploma in Ethnology
)CG	Deputy Chaplain-General	DipFE	Diploma in Further Education
)CGRM	Department of the Commandant General Royal Marines	DipLA	Diploma in Landscape Architecture
)CGS	Deputy Chief of the General Staff	DipM	Diploma in Marketing
)Ch	Doctor of Surgery	DipPA	Diploma of Practitioners in Advertising (*now see* DipCAM)
)CH	Diploma in Child Health	DipTA	Diploma in Tropical Agriculture
)CIGS	Deputy Chief of the Imperial General Staff (*now see* DCGS)	DipT&CP	Diploma in Town and Country Planning
)CL	Doctor of Civil Law	DipTP	Diploma in Town Planning
)CLI	Duke of Cornwall's Light Infantry	DipTPT	Diploma in Theory and Practice of Teaching
)CM	Distinguished Conduct Medal	DistTP	Distinction in Town Planning
)CMG	Dame Commander of St Michael and St George	Div.	Division; Divorced
)CnL	Doctor of Canon Law	DJAG	Deputy Judge Advocate General
)CP	Diploma in Clinical Pathology; Diploma in Conservation of Paintings	DJStJ	Dame of Justice, Order of St John of Jerusalem (*now see* DStJ)
)CS	Deputy Chief of Staff; Doctor of Commercial Sciences	DJur	*Doctor Juris*
)CSO	Deputy Chief Scientific Officer	DK	Most Esteemed Family Order (Brunei)
)CT	Doctor of Christian Theology	DL	Deputy Lieutenant
)CVO	Dame Commander of Royal Victorian Order	DLC	Diploma Loughborough College
)D	Doctor of Divinity	DLES	Doctor of Letters in Economic Studies
)DL	Deputy Director of Labour	DLI	Durham Light Infantry
)DME	Deputy Director of Mechanical Engineering	DLitt or DLit	Doctor of Literature; Doctor of Letters
)DMI	Deputy Director of Military Intelligence	DLJ	Dame of Grace, Order of St Lazarus of Jerusalem
)DMS	Deputy Director of Medical Services	DLO	Diploma in Laryngology and Otology
)DMT	Deputy Director of Military Training	DM	Doctor of Medicine
)DNI	Deputy Director of Naval Intelligence	DMA	Diploma in Municipal Administration
)DO	Diploma in Dental Orthopaedics	DMD	Doctor of Medical Dentistry (Australia)
)DPR	Deputy Director of Public Relations	DME	Director of Mechanical Engineering
)DPS	Deputy Director of Personal Services	DMet	Doctor of Metallurgy
)DR	Deutsche Demokratische Republik	DMI	Director of Military Intelligence
)DRA	Deputy Director Royal Artillery	DMin	Doctor of Ministry
)DS	Doctor of Dental Surgery; Director of Dental Services	DMJ	Diploma in Medical Jurisprudence
)DSc	Doctor of Dental Science	DMO	Director of Military Operations
)DSD	Deputy Director Staff Duties	DMR	Diploma in Medical Radiology
)DSM	Defense Distinguished Service Medal	DMRD	Diploma in Medical Radiological Diagnosis
)DST	Deputy Director of Supplies and Transport	DMRE	Diploma in Medical Radiology and Electrology
)DWE&M	Deputy Director of Works, Electrical and Mechanical	DMRT	Diploma in Medical Radio-Therapy
)E	Doctor of Engineering	DMS	Director of Medical Services; Decoration for Meritorious Service (South Africa); Diploma in Management Studies
)EA	Department of Economic Affairs	DMT	Director of Military Training
)ecd	Deceased	DMus	Doctor of Music
)EconSc	Doctor of Economic Science	DNB	Dictionary of National Biography
)Ed	Doctor of Education	DNE	Director of Naval Equipment
)el	Delaware (US)	DNI	Director of Naval Intelligence
)eleg.	Delegate	DO	Diploma in Ophthalmology
)emU)	Democratic Unionist	DOAE	Defence Operational Analysis Establishment
)Eng	Doctor of Engineering	DObstRCOG	Diploma Royal College of Obstetricians and Gynaecologists
)enM	Docteur en Médicine	DOC	District Officer Commanding
)EOVR	Duke of Edinburgh's Own Volunteer Rifles	DocEng	Doctor of Engineering
)EP	Department of Employment and Productivity; European Progressive Democrats	DoE	Department of the Environment
)ep.	Deputy	DoI	Department of Industry
)ES	Department of Education and Science	DOL	Doctor of Oriental Learning
)èsL	Docteur ès lettres	Dom.	*Dominus*
)èsS	Docteur ès sciences	DOMS	Diploma in Ophthalmic Medicine and Surgery
)esRCA	Designer of the Royal College of Art	DOR	Director of Operational Requirements
)FA	Doctor of Fine Arts	DOS	Director of Ordnance Services
)FC	Distinguished Flying Cross	Dow.	Dowager
)FH	Diploma of Faraday House	DPA	Diploma in Public Administration; Discharged Prisoners' Aid
)FLS	Day Fighter Leaders' School	DPD	Diploma in Public Dentistry
)FM	Distinguished Flying Medal	DPEc	Doctor of Political Economy
)G	Dragoon Guards	DPed	Doctor of Pedagogy
)GAA	Distressed Gentlefolks Aid Association	DPH	Diploma in Public Health
)GAMS	Director-General Army Medical Services	DPh or DPhil	Doctor of Philosophy
)GMS	Dirctor-General of Medical Services	DPLG	Diplômé par le Gouvernement
)GMT	Director-General of Military Training	DPM	Diploma in Psychological Medicine
)GMW	Director-General of Military Works	DPR	Director of Public Relations
)GNPS	Director-General of Naval Personal Services	DPS	Director of Postal Services; Director of Personal Services; Doctor of Public Service
)GP	Director-General of Personnel	DQMG	Deputy Quartermaster-General
)GS	Diploma in Graduate Studies	Dr	Doctor
)GStJ	Dame of Grace, Order of St John of Jerusalem (*now see* DStJ)	DRAC	Director Royal Armoured Corps
)GU	Doctor of Griffith University	DRC	Diploma of Royal College of Science and Technology, Glasgow
)H	Doctor of Humanities	DRD	Diploma in Restorative Dentistry
)HA	District Health Authority	Dr ing	Doctor of Engineering (Germany)
)hc	Doctor *honoris causa*	Dr jur	Doctor of Laws
)HEW	Department of Health Education and Welfare (US)	DrŒcPol	*Doctor Œconomiæ Politicæ*
)HL	Doctor of Humane Letters; Doctor of Hebrew Literature	DRSAMD	Diploma of the Royal Scottish Academy of Music and Drama
)HM	Dean Hole Medal	DS	Directing Staff
)HMSA	Diploma in the History of Medicine (Society of Apothecaries)	DSA	Diploma in Social Administration
)HQ	District Headquarters	DSAO	Diplomatic Service Administration Office
)HSS	Department of Health and Social Security	DSC	Distinguished Service Cross
)IAS	Dublin Institute of Advanced Sciences	DSc	Doctor of Science
)IC	Diploma of the Imperial College	DScA	Docteur en sciences agricoles
)IG	Deputy Inspector-General	DSCHE	Diploma of the Scottish Council for Health Education
)IH	Diploma in Industrial Health	DScMil	Doctor of Military Science
)io.	Diocese	DSD	Director Staff Duties
)ipAD	Diploma in Art and Design	DSIR	Department of Scientific and Industrial Research (later SRC;
)ipAe	Diploma in Aeronautics		
)ipBS	Diploma in Fine Art, Byam Shaw School		
)ipCAM	Diploma in Communications, Advertising and Marketing of		

	now see SERC)
DSLJ	Dato Seri Laila Jasa Brunei
DSM	Distinguished Service Medal
DSNB	Dato Setia Negara Brunei
DSO	Companion of the Distinguished Service Order
DSocSc	Doctor of Social Science
DSP	Director of Selection of Personnel; Docteur en sciences politiques (Montreal)
dsp	*decessit sine prole* (died without issue)
DSS	Doctor of Sacred Scripture
Dss	Deaconess
DSSc	Doctor of Social Science (USA)
DST	Director of Supplies and Transport
DStJ	Dame of Grace, Order of St John of Jerusalem; Dame of Justice, Order of St John of Jerusalem
DTA	Diploma in Tropical Agriculture
DTD	Dekoratie voor Trouwe Dienst (Decoration for Devoted Service)
DTech	Doctor of Technology
DTH	Diploma in Tropical Hygiene
DTheol	Doctor of Theology
DThPT	Diploma in Theory and Practice of Teaching (Durham University)
DTI	Department of Trade and Industry
DTM&H	Diploma in Tropical Medicine and Hygiene
DU	Doctor of the University
DUniv	Doctor of the University
DUP	Docteur de l'Université de Paris
DVH	Diploma in Veterinary Hygiene
DVM	Doctor of Veterinary Medicine
DVMS	Doctor of Veterinary Medicine and Surgery
DVR	Diploma in Veterinary Radiology
DVSc	Doctor of Veterinary Science
DVSM	Diploma in Veterinary State Medicine

E

E	East; Earl
e	eldest
EAA	Edinburgh Architectural Association
EAHY	European Architectural Heritage Year
EAP	East Africa Protectorate
EAW	Electrical Association for Women
EBC	English Benedictine Congregation
Ebor	*(Eboracensis)* of York
EBU	European Broadcasting Union
EC	Etoile du Courage (Canada); East Central (postal district); European Commission; Emergency Commission
ECA	Economic Co-operation Administration
ECAFE	Economic Commission for Asia and the Far East (*now see* ESCAP)
ECE	Economic Commission for Europe
ECGD	Export Credits Guarantee Department
ECLA	Economic Commission for Latin America
ECSC	European Coal and Steel Community
ECU	English Church Union
ED	Efficiency Decoration; Doctor of Engineering (US); European Democrat
EdB	Bachelor of Education
EDC	Economic Development Committee
EdD	Doctor of Education
Edin.	Edinburgh
Edn	Edition
EDP	Executive Development Programme
Educ	Educated
Educn	Education
EEC	European Economic Community; Commission of the European Communities
EEF	Engineering Employers' Federation; Egyptian Expeditionary Force
EETPU	Electrical Electronic Telecommunication & Plumbing Union
EETS	Early English Text Society
EFTA	European Free Trade Association
eh	ehrenhalber (honorary)
EI	East Indian; East Indies
EICS	East India Company's Service
E-in-C	Engineer-in-Chief
EIS	Educational Institute of Scotland
EIU	Economist Intelligence Unit
ELBS	English Language Book Society
ELSE	European Life Science Editors
EM	Edward Medal; Earl Marshal
EMBO	European Molecular Biology Organisation
EMS	Emergency Medical Service
Ency. Brit.	Ecyclopaedia Britannica
Eng.	England
Engr	Engineer
ENO	English National Opera
ENSA	Entertainments National Service Association
ENT	Ear, Nose and Throat
EOPH	Examined Officer of Public Health
EORTC	European Organisation for Research on Treatment of Cancer

EPP	European People's Party
er	elder
ER	Eastern Region (BR)
ERA	Electrical Research Association
ERC	Electronics Research Council
ERD	Emergency Reserve Decoration (Army)
ESA	European Space Agency
ESCAP	Economic and Social Commission for Asia and the Pacific
ESRO	European Space Research Organization (*now see* ESA)
E-SU	English-Speaking Union
ETH	Eidgenössische Technische Hochschule
ETUC	European Trade Union Confederation
EUDISED	European Documentation and Information Service for Education
Euratom	European Atomic Energy Community
EUW	European Union of Women
Ext	Extinct

F

FA	Football Association
FAA	Fellow, Australian Academy of Science; Fleet Air Arm
FAAAS	Fellow, American Association for the Advancement of Science
FACC	Fellow, American College of Cardiology
FACCA	Fellow, Association of Certified and Corporate Accountants (*now see* FCCA)
FACCP	Fellow, American College of Chest Physicians
FACD	Fellow, American College of Dentistry
FACDS	Fellow, Australian College of Dental Surgeons (*now see* FRACDS)
FACE	Fellow, Australian College of Education
FACI	Fellow, Australian Chemical Institute (*now see* FRACI)
FACMA	Fellow, Australian College of Medical Administrators (*now see* FRACMA)
FACOG	Fellow, American College of Obstetricians and Gynæcologists
FACP	Fellow, American College of Physicians
FACR	Fellow, American College of Radiology
FACS	Fellow, American College of Surgeons
FACVT	Fellow, American College of Veterinary Toxicology
FAGO	Fellowship in Australia in Obstetrics and Gynaecology
FAGS	Fellow, American Geographical Society
FAHA	Fellow, Australian Academy of the Humanities
FAI	Fellow, Chartered Auctioneers' and Estate Agents' Institute (now (after amalgamation) *see* FRICS); Fédération Aéronautique Internationale
FAIA	Fellow, American Institute of Architects
FAIAA	Fellow, American Institute of Aeronautics and Astronautics
FAIAS	Fellow, Australian Institute of Agricultural Science
FAIEx	Fellow, Australian Institute of Export
FAIFST	Fellow, Australian Institute of Food Science and Technology
FAIM	Fellow, Australian Institute of Management
FAIP	Fellow, Australian Institute of Physics
FAMS	Fellow, Ancient Monuments Society
FANY	First Aid Nursing Yeomanry
FANZCP	Fellow, Australian and New Zealand College of Psychiatrists (*now see* FRANZCP)
FAO	Food and Agriculture Organization
FAPA	Fellow, American Psychiatric Association
FAPHA	Fellow, American Public Health Association
FAPI	Fellow, Australian Planning Institute (*now see* FRAPI)
FAPS	Fellow, American Phytopathological Society
FARELF	Far East Land Forces
FAS	Fellow, Antiquarian Society; Fellow, Nigerian Academy of Science
FASA	Fellow, Australian Society of Accountants
FASc	Fellow, Indian Academy of Sciences
FASCE	Fellow, American Society of Civil Engineers
FASSA	Fellow, Academy of the Social Sciences in Australia
FAustCOG	Fellow, Australian College of Obstetricians and Gynæcologists (*now see* FRACOG)
FBA	Fellow, British Academy; Federation of British Artists
FBCS	Fellow, British Computer Society
FBHI	Fellow, British Horological Institute
FBI	Federation of British Industries (*now see* CBI)
FBIA	Fellow, Bankers' Institute of Australasia
FBIM	Fellow, British Institute of Management (*now see* CBIM)
FBKSTS	Fellow, British Kinematograph, Sound and Television Society
FBOA	Fellow, British Optical Association
FBOU	Fellow, British Ornithologists' Union
FBritIRE	Fellow, British Institution of Radio Engineers (*now see* FIERE)
FBPsS	Fellow, British Psychological Society
FBS	Fellow, Building Societies Institute (*now see* FCBSI)
FBSI	Fellow, Boot and Shoe Institution
FBSM	Fellow, Birmingham School of Music
FC	Football Club
FCA	Fellow, Institute of Chartered Accountants; Fellow, Institute of Chartered Accountants in Australia

FCAI Fellow, New Zealand Institute of Cost Accountants; Fellow, Canadian Aeronautical Institute (*now see* FCASI)
FCAM Fellow, CAM Foundation
FCASI Fellow, Canadian Aeronautics and Space Institute
FCBSI Fellow, Chartered Building Societies Institute
FCCA Fellow, Association of Certified Accountants
FCCEA Fellow, Commonwealth Council for Educational Administration
FCCS Fellow, Corporation of Secretaries (*formerly* of Certified Secretaries)
FCEC Federation of Civil Engineering Contractors
FCGI Fellow, City and Guilds of London Institute
FCGP Fellow, College of General Practitioners (*now see* FRCGP)
FCH Fellow, Coopers Hill College
FChS Fellow, Society of Chiropodists
FCI Fellow, Institute of Commerce
FCIA Fellow, Corporation of Insurance Agents
FCIArb Fellow, Chartered Institute of Arbitrators
FCIB Fellow, Corporation of Insurance Brokers
FCIBS Fellow, Chartered Institution of Building Services
FCIC Fellow, Chemical Institute of Canada (*formerly* Canadian Institute of Chemistry)
FCII Fellow, Chartered Insurance Institute
FCIOB Fellow, Chartered Institute of Building
FCIPA Fellow, Chartered Institute of Patent Agents (*now see* CPA)
FCIS Fellow, Institute of Chartered Secretaries and Administrators (*formerly* Chartered Institute of Secretaries)
FCIT Fellow, Chartered Institute of Transport
FCM Faculty of Community Medicine
FCMA Fellow, Institute of Cost and Management Accountants
FCO Foreign and Commonwealth Office (departments merged Oct. 1968)
FCOG(SA) Fellow, South African College of Obstetrics and Gynæcology
FCommA Fellow, Society of Commercial Accountants (*now see* FSCA)
FCP Fellow, College of Preceptors
FCPath Fellow, College of Pathologists (*now see* FRCPath)
FCPS Fellow, College of Physicians and Surgeons
FCP(SoAf) Fellow, College of Physicians, South Africa
FCPSO(SoAf) Fellow, College of Physicians and Surgeons and Obstetricians, South Africa
FCRA Fellow, College of Radiologists of Australia (*now see* FRACR)
FCS Federation of Conservative Students
FCS or FChemSoc Fellow, Chemical Society (now absorbed into Royal Society of Chemistry)
FCSP Fellow, Chartered Society of Physiotherapy
FCSSA, FCS(SoAf) Fellow, College of Surgeons, South Africa
FCST Fellow, College of Speech Therapists
FCT Federal Capital Territory (*now see* ACT); Fellow, Association of Corporate Treasurers
FCTB Fellow, College of Teachers of the Blind
FCU Fighter Control Unit
FCWA Fellow, Institute of Cost and Works Accountants (*now see* FCMA)
FDS Fellow in Dental Surgery
FDSRCPS Glas Fellow in Dental Surgery, Royal College of Physicians and Surgeons of Glasgow
FDSRCS Fellow in Dental Surgery, Royal College of Surgeons of England
FDSRCSE Fellow in Dental Surgery, Royal College of Surgeons of Edinburgh
FEAF Far East Air Force
FEBS Federation of European Biochemical Societies
FEIS Fellow, Educational Institute of Scotland
FEng Fellow, Fellowship of Engineering
FES Fellow, Entomological Society; Fellow, Ethnological Society
FF Fianna Fáil; Field Force
FFA Fellow, Faculty of Actuaries (in Scotland)
FFARACS Fellow, Faculty of Anaesthetists, Royal Australian College of Surgeons
FFARCS Fellow, Faculty of Anaesthetists, Royal College of Surgeons of England
FFARCSI Fellow, Faculty of Anaesthetists, Royal College of Surgeons in Ireland
FFAS Fellow, Faculty of Architects and Surveyors, London
FFB Fellow, Faculty of Building
FFCM Fellow, Faculty of Community Medicine
FFDRCSI Fellow, Faculty of Dentistry, Royal College of Surgeons in Ireland
FFF Free French Forces
FFHom Fellow, Faculty of Homœopathy
FFI French Forces of the Interior; Finance for Industry
FFOM Fellow, Faculty of Occupational Medicine
FFPath, RCPI Fellow, Faculty of Pathologists of the Royal College of Physicians of Ireland
FFPS Fauna and Flora Preservation Society
FFR Fellow, Faculty of Radiologists (*now see* FRCR)
FG Fine Gael
FGA Fellow, Gemmological Association
FGGE Fellow, Guild of Glass Engineers
FGI Fellow, Institute of Certificated Grocers
FGS Fellow, Geological Society
FGSM Fellow, Guildhall School of Music

FGSMT Fellow, Guildhall School of Music (Music Therapy)
FHA Fellow, Institute of Health Service Administrators (*formerly* Hospital Administrators)
FHAS Fellow, Highland and Agricultural Society of Scotland
FHCIMA Fellow, Hotel Catering and Institutional Management Association
FHFS Fellow, Human Factors Society
FHKIE Fellow, Hong Kong Institution of Engineers
FHS Fellow, Heraldry Society
FH-WC Fellow, Heriot-Watt College (*now* University), Edinburgh
FIA Fellow, Institute of Actuaries
FIAA Fellow, Institute of Actuaries of Australia
FIAAS Fellow, Institute of Australian Agricultural Science
FIAA&S Fellow, Incorporated Association of Architects and Surveyors
FIAgrE Fellow, Institution of Agricultural Engineers
FIAI Fellow, Institute of Industrial and Commercial Accountants
FIAL Fellow, International Institute of Arts and Letters
FIAM Fellow, Institute of Administrative Management; Fellow, International Academy of Management
FIArb Fellow, Institute of Arbitrators (*now see* FCIArb)
FIArbA Fellow, Institute of Arbitrators of Australia
FIAS Fellow, Institute of Aeronautical Sciences (US) (*now see* FAIAA)
FIAWS Fellow, International Academy of Wood Sciences
FIB Fellow, Institute of Bankers
FIBD Fellow, Institute of British Decorators
FIBP Fellow, Institute of British Photographers
FIBiol Fellow, Institute of Biology
FIBScot Fellow, Institute of Bankers in Scotland
FIC Fellow, Institute of Chemistry (*now see* FRIC, FRSC)
FICA Fellow, Commonwealth Institute of Accountancy; Fellow, Institute of Chartered Accountants in England and Wales (*now see* FCA)
FICAI Fellow, Institute of Chartered Accountants in Ireland
FICD Fellow, Institute of Civil Defence; Fellow, Indian College of Dentists
FICE Fellow, Institution of Civil Engineers
FICeram Fellow, Institute of Ceramics
FICFor Fellow, Institute of Chartered Foresters
FIChemE Fellow, Institution of Chemical Engineers
FICI Fellow, Institute of Chemistry of Ireland; Fellow, International Colonial Institute
FICS Fellow, Institute of Chartered Shipbrokers; Fellow, International College of Surgeons
FICW Fellow, Institute of Clerks of Works of Great Britain
FIDCA Fellow, Industrial Design Council of Australia
FIDE Fédération Internationale des Echecs
FIE(Aust) Fellow, Institution of Engineers, Australia
FIED Fellow, Institution of Engineering Designers
FIEE Fellow, Institution of Electrical Engineers
FIEEE Fellow, Institute of Electrical and Electronics Engineers (NY)
FIEI Fellow, Institution of Engineering Inspection (*now see* FIQA)
FIEJ Fédération Internationale des Editeurs de Journaux et Publications
FIERE Fellow, Institution of Electronic and Radio Engineers
FIES Fellow, Illuminating Engineering Society (*now see* FIllumES)
FIExpE Fellow, Institute of Explosives Engineers
FIFA Fédération Internationale de Football Association
FIFE Fellow, Institution of Fire Engineers
FIFM Fellow, Institute of Fisheries Management
FIFor Fellow, Institute of Foresters (*now see* FICFor)
FIFST Fellow, Institute of Food Science and Technology
FIGasE Fellow, Institution of Gas Engineers
FIGCM Fellow, Incorporated Guild of Church Musicians
FIGD Fellow, Institute of Grocery Distribution
FIGO International Federation of Gynaecology and Obstetrics
FIH Fellow, Institute of Housing
FIHE Fellow, Institute of Health Education
FIHM Fellow, Institute of Housing Managers (*now see* FIH)
FIHospE Fellow, Institute of Hospital Engineering
FIHVE Fellow, Institution of Heating & Ventilating Engineers (*now see* FCIBS and MCIBS)
FIIA Fellow, Institute of Industrial Administration (*now see* FBIM and CBIM)
FIIC Fellow, International Institute for Conservation of Historic and Artistic Works
FIIM Fellow, Institution of Industrial Managers
FIInfSc Fellow, Institute of Information Scientists
FIInst Fellow, Imperial Institute
FIIP Fellow, Institute of Incorporated Photographers
FIIPE Fellow, Indian Institution of Production Engineers
FIL Fellow, Institute of Linguists
FILA Fellow, Institute of Landscape Architects (*now see* FLI)
FILLM Fédération Internationale des Langues et Litteratures Modernes
FIllumES Fellow, Illuminating Engineering Society
FIM Fellow, Institution of Metallurgists
FIMA Fellow, Institute of Mathematics and its Applications
FIMarE Fellow, Institute of Marine Engineers
FIMC Fellow, Institute of Management Consultants
FIMechE Fellow, Institution of Mechanical Engineers

FIGHT BACK AGAINST CANCER

It is good to remember that most people live their lives untouched by any form of cancer.

But as all too many are aware, cancer is something that casts its shadow far beyond those it directly affects. That is why so many people think it right to help the urgent work of the Imperial Cancer Research Fund.

From our discoveries in the past has come much of today's hope for sufferers. To go forward with our research for future alleviation, we ask *your* help in the present.

The main laboratories at Lincoln's Inn Fields

IMPERIAL CANCER RESEARCH FUND

Donations will be most gratefully received by The Appeals Secretary, Room 23, P.O. Box 123, Lincoln's Inn Fields, London WC2A 3PX

FIMGTechE	Fellow, Institution of Mechanical and General Technician Engineers
FIMH	Fellow, Institution of Materials Handling; Fellow, Institute of Military History
FIMI	Fellow, Institute of the Motor Industry
FIMinE	Fellow, Institution of Mining Engineers
FIMIT	Fellow, Institute of Musical Instrument Technology
FIMLS	Fellow, Institute of Medical Laboratory Sciences
FIMLT	Fellow, Institute of Medical Laboratory Technology *(now see FIMLS)*
FIMM	Fellow, Institute of Mining and Metallurgy
FIMS	Fellow, Institute of Mathematical Statistics
FIMT	Fellow, Institute of the Motor Trade *(now see FIMI)*
FIMTA	Fellow, Institute of Municipal Treasurers and Accountants *(now see IPFA)*
FIMunE	Fellow, Institution of Municipal Engineers
FIN	Fellow, Institute of Navigation *(now see FRIN)*
FInstAM	Fellow, Institute of Administrative Management
FInstB	Fellow, Institution of Buyers
FInstBiol	Fellow, Institute of Biology *(now see FIBiol)*
FInstD	Fellow, Institute of Directors
FInstE	Fellow, Institute of Energy
FInstF	Fellow, Institute of Fuel *(now see FInstE)*
FInstFF	Fellow, Institute of Freight Forwarders Ltd
FInstHE	Fellow, Institution of Highways Engineers
FInstLEx	Fellow, Institute of Legal Executives
FInstM	Fellow, Institute of Meat; Fellow, Institute of Marketing
FInstMC	Fellow, Institute of Measurement and Control
FInstMSM	Fellow, Institute of Marketing and Sales Management *(now see FInstM)*
FInstMet	Fellow, Institute of Metals (now part of Metals Society)
FInstP	Fellow, Institute of Physics
FInstPet	Fellow, Institute of Petroleum
FInstPI	Fellow, Institute of Patentees and Inventors
FInstPS	Fellow, Institute of Purchasing and Supply
FInstSM	Fellow, Institute of Sales Management
FInstW	Fellow, Institute of Welding
FInstWPC	Fellow, Institute of Water Pollution Control
FINucE	Fellow, Institution of Nuclear Engineers
FIOA	Fellow, Institute of Acoustics
FIOB	Fellow, Institute of Building *(now see FCIOB)*
FIOM	Fellow, Institute of Office Management *(now see FIAM)*
FIOP	Fellow, Institute of Printing
FIPA	Fellow, Institute of Practitioners in Advertising
FIPDM	Fellow, Institute of Physical Distribution Management
FIPHE	Fellow, Institution of Public Health Engineers
FIPlantE	Fellow, Institution of Plant Engineers *(now see FIIM)*
FIPM	Fellow, Institute of Personnel Management
FIPR	Fellow, Institute of Public Relations
FIProdE	Fellow, Institution of Production Engineers
FIQ	Fellow, Institute of Quarrying
FIQA	Fellow, Institute of Quality Assurance
FIQS	Fellow, Institute of Quantity Surveyors
FIRA(Ind)	Fellow, Institute of Railway Auditors and Accountants (India)
FIRE(Aust)	Fellow, Institution of Radio Engineers (Australia) *(now see FIREE (Aust))*
FIREE(Aust)	Fellow, Institution of Radio and Electronics Engineers (Australia)
FIRI	Fellow, Institution of the Rubber Industry *(now see FPRI)*
FIRTE	Fellow, Institute of Road Transport Engineers
FIS	Fellow, Institute of Statisticians
FISA	Fellow, Incorporated Secretaries' Association
FISE	Fellow, Institution of Sales Engineers; Fellow, Institution of Sanitary Engineers
FIST	Fellow, Institute of Science Technology
FISTC	Fellow, Institute of Scientific and Technical Communicators
FIStructE	Fellow, Institution of Structural Engineers
FISW	Fellow, Institute of Social Work
FITD	Fellow, Institute of Training and Development
FITE	Fellow, Institution of Electrical and Electronics Technician Engineers
FIW	Fellow, Welding Institute
FIWE	Fellow, Institution of Water Engineers *(now see FIWES)*
FIWES	Fellow, Institution of Water Engineers and Scientists
FIWM	Fellow, Institution of Works Managers *(now see FIIM)*
FIWPC	Fellow, Institute of Water Pollution Control
FIWSc	Fellow, Institute of Wood Science
FIWSP	Fellow, Institute of Work Study Practitioners *(now see FMS)*
FJI	Fellow, Institute of Journalists
FJIE	Fellow, Junior Institution of Engineers *(now see CIMGTechE)*
FKC	Fellow, King's College London
FKCHMS	Fellow, King's College Hospital Medical School
FLA	Fellow, Library Association
Fla	Florida (US)
FLAI	Fellow, Library Association of Ireland
FLAS	Fellow, Chartered Land Agents' Society *(now (after amalgamation) see FRICS)*
FLCM	Fellow, London College of Music
FLHS	Fellow, London Historical Society
FLI	Fellow, Landscape Institute
FLIA	Fellow, Life Insurance Association
FLS	Fellow, Linnaean Society
Flt	Flight

FM	Field-Marshal
FMA	Fellow, Museums Association
FMANZ	Fellow, Medical Association of New Zealand
FMF	Fiji Military Forces
FMS	Federated Malay States; Fellow, Medical Society; Fellow, Institute of Management Services
FMSA	Fellow, Mineralogical Society of America
FNA	Fellow, Indian National Science Academy
FNECInst	Fellow, North East Coast Institution of Engineers and Shipbuilders
FNI	Fellow, Nautical Institute; Fellow, National Institute of Sciences in India *(now see FNA)*
FNZIA	Fellow, New Zealand Institute of Architects
FNZIAS	Fellow, New Zealand Institute of Agricultural Science
FNZIC	Fellow, New Zealand Institute of Chemistry
FNZIE	Fellow, New Zealand Institution of Engineers
FNZIM	Fellow, New Zealand Institute of Management
FO	Foreign Office *(see also FCO)*; Field Officer; Flying Officer
FOIC	Flag Officer in charge
FPA	Family Planning Association
FPEA	Fellow, Physical Education Association
FPhS	Fellow, Philosophical Society of England
FPI	Fellow, Plastics Institute *(now see FPRI)*
FPMI	Fellow, Pensions Management Institute
FPRI	Fellow, Plastics and Rubber Institute
FPS	Fellow, Pharmaceutical Society; Fauna Preservation Society *(now see FFPS)*
FPhysS	Fellow, Physical Society
f r	fuori ruole
FRACDS	Fellow, Royal Australian College of Dental Surgeons
FRACGP	Fellow, Royal Australian College of General Practitioners
FRACI	Fellow, Royal Australian Chemical Institute
FRACMA	Fellow, Royal Australian College of Medical Administrators
FRACO	Fellow, Royal Australian College of Ophthalmologists
FRACOG	Fellow, Royal Australian College of Obstetricians and Gynaecologists
FRACP	Fellow, Royal Australasian College of Physicians
FRACR	Fellow, Royal Australasian College of Radiologists
FRACS	Fellow, Royal Australasian College of Surgeons
FRAD	Fellow, Royal Academy of Dancing
FRAeS	Fellow, Royal Aeronautical Society
FRAgS	Fellow, Royal Agricultural Societies *(ie of England, Scotland and Wales)*
FRAHS	Fellow, Royal Australian Historical Society
FRAI	Fellow, Royal Anthropological Institute
FRAIA	Fellow, Royal Australian Institute of Architects
FRAIB	Fellow, Royal Australian Institute of Building
FRAIC	Fellow, Royal Architectural Institute of Canada
FRAM	Fellow, Royal Academy of Music
FRAME	Fund for the Replacement of Animals in Medical Experiments
FRANZCP	Fellow, Royal Australian and New Zealand College of Psychiatrists
FRAPI	Fellow, Royal Australian Planning Institute
FRAS	Fellow, Royal Astronomical Society; Fellow, Royal Asiatic Society
FRASB	Fellow, Royal Asiatic Society of Bengal
FRASE	Fellow, Royal Agricultural Society of England
FRBS	Fellow, Royal Society of British Sculptors; Fellow, Royal Botanic Society
FRCGP	Fellow, Royal College of General Practitioners
FRCM	Fellow, Royal College of Music
FRCN	Fellow, Royal College of Nursing
FRCO	Fellow, Royal College of Organists
FRCO(CHM)	Fellow, Royal College of Organists with Diploma in Choir Training
FRCOG	Fellow, Royal College of Obstetricians and Gynaecologists
FRCP	Fellow, Royal College of Physicians, London
FRCPA	Fellow, Royal College of Pathologists of Australasia
FRCP&S (Canada)	Fellow, Royal College of Physicians and Surgeons of Canada
FRCPath	Fellow, Royal College of Pathologists
FRCP(C)	Fellow, Royal College of Physicians of Canada
FRCPE and FRCPEd	Fellow, Royal College of Physicians of Edinburgh
FRCPGlas	Fellow, Royal College of Physicians and Surgeons, Glasgow
FRCPI	Fellow, Royal College of Physicians of Ireland
FRCPS(Hon)	Hon. Fellow, Royal College of Physicians and Surgeons (Glasgow)
FRCPsych	Fellow, Royal College of Psychiatrists
FRCR	Fellow, Royal College of Radiologists
FRCS	Fellow, Royal College of Surgeons of England
FRCSE and FRCSEd	Fellow, Royal College of Surgeons of Edinburgh
FRCSGlas	Fellow, Royal College of Physicians and Surgeons of Glasgow
FRCSI	Fellow, Royal College of Surgeons of Ireland
FRCSE	Fellow, Royal College of Surgeons of Edinburgh
FRCSE	Fellow, Royal College of Surgeons (Denmark)
FRCvS	Fellow, Royal College of Veterinary Surgeons
FREconS	Fellow, Royal Economic Society
FREI	Fellow, Real Estate Institute (Australia)
FRES	Fellow, Royal Entomological Society of London

FRFPSG	Fellow, Royal Faculty of Physicians and Surgeons, Glasgow (*now see* FRCPGlas)
FRG	Federal Republic of Germany
FRGS	Fellow, Royal Geographical Society
FRGSA	Fellow, Royal Geographical Society of Australasia
FRHistS	Fellow, Royal Historical Society
FRHS	Fellow, Royal Horticultural Society
FRIAS	Fellow, Royal Incorporation of Architects of Scotland
FRIBA	Fellow, Royal Institute of British Architects (*and see* RIBA)
FRIC	Fellow, Royal Institute of Chemistry (*now see* FRSC)
FRICS	Fellow, Royal Institution of Chartered Surveyors
FRIH	Fellow, Royal Institute of Horticulture (NZ)
FRIN	Fellow, Royal Institute of Navigation
FRINA	Fellow, Royal Institution of Naval Architects
FRIPA	Fellow, Royal Institute of Public Administration (the Institute no longer has Fellows)
FRIPHH	Fellow, Royal Institute of Public Health and Hygiene
FRMCM	Fellow, Royal Manchester College of Music
FRMedSoc	Fellow, Royal Medical Society
FRMetS	Fellow, Royal Meteorological Society
FRMIA	Fellow, Retail Management Institute of Australia
FRMS	Fellow, Royal Microscopical Society
FRNCM	Fellow, Royal Northern College of Music
FRNS	Fellow, Royal Numismatic Society
FRPS	Fellow, Royal Photographic Society
FRPSL	Fellow, Royal Philatelic Society, London
FRS	Fellow, Royal Society
FRSA	Fellow, Royal Society of Arts
FRSAI	Fellow, Royal Society of Antiquaries of Ireland
FRSAMD	Fellow, Royal Scottish Academy of Music and Drama
FRSanI	Fellow, Royal Sanitary Institute (*now see* FRSH)
FRSC	Fellow, Royal Society of Canada; Fellow, Royal Society of Chemistry
FRSCM	Fellow, Royal School of Church Music
FRSE	Fellow, Royal Society of Edinburgh
FRSGS	Fellow, Royal Scottish Geographical Society
FRSH	Fellow, Royal Society for the Promotion of Health
FRSL	Fellow, Royal Society of Literature
FRSM or FRSocMed	Fellow, Royal Society of Medicine
FRSNZ	Fellow, Royal Society of New Zealand
FRSSAf	Fellow, Royal Society of South Africa
FRST	Fellow, Royal Society of Teachers
FRSTM&H	Fellow, Royal Society of Tropical Medicine and Hygiene
FRTPI	Fellow, Royal Town Planning Institute
FRTS	Fellow, Royal Television Society
FRVA	Fellow, Rating and Valuation Association
FRVC	Fellow, Royal Veterinary College
FRVIA	Fellow, Royal Victorian Institute of Architects
FRZSScot	Fellow, Royal Zoological Society of Scotland
FS	Field Security
fs	Graduate, Royal Air Force Staff College
FSA	Fellow, Society of Antiquaries
FSAA	Fellow, Society of Incorporated Accountants and Auditors
FSAE	Fellow, Society of Automotive Engineers
FSAIEE	Fellow, South African Institute of Electrical Engineers
FSAM	Fellow, Society of Art Masters
FSArc	Fellow, Society of Architects (merged with the RIBA 1952)
FSAScot	Fellow, Society of Antiquaries of Scotland
FSASM	Fellow, South Australian School of Mines
FSBI	Fellow, Savings Banks Institute
fsc	Foreign Staff College
FSCA	Fellow, Society of Company and Commercial Accountants
FSDC	Fellow, Society of Dyers and Colourists
FSE	Fellow, Society of Engineers
FSG	Fellow, Society of Genealogists
FSGT	Fellow, Society of Glass Technology
FSI	Fellow, Chartered Surveyors' Institution (*now see* FRICS)
FSIAD	Fellow, Society of Industrial Artists and Designers
FSLAET	Fellow, Society of Licensed Aircraft Engineers and Technologists
FSMA	Fellow, Incorporated Sales Managers' Association (later FInstMSM, *now see* FInstM)
FSMC	Freeman of the Spectacle-Makers' Company
FSS	Fellow, Royal Statistical Society
FSTD	Fellow, Society of Typographic Designers
FSVA	Fellow, Incorporated Society of Valuers and Auctioneers
FTCD	Fellow, Trinity College, Dublin
FTCL	Fellow, Trinity College of Music, London
FTI	Fellow, Textile Institute
FTII	Fellow, Institute of Taxation
FTP	Fellow, Thames Polytechnic
FTS	Fellow, Australian Academy of Technological Sciences; Flying Training School
FUCUA	Federation of University Conservative and Unionist Associations (*now see* FCS)
FUMIST	Fellow, University of Manchester Institute of Science and Technology
FWA	Fellow, World Academy of Arts and Sciences
FWACP	Fellow, West African College of Physicians
FWeldI	Fellow, Welding Institute
FWSOM	Fellow, Institute of Practitioners in Work Study, Organisation and Method (*now see* FMS)
FZS	Fellow, Zoological Society
FZSScot	Fellow, Zoological Society of Scotland (*now see* FRZSScot)

G

Ga	Georgia (US)
GA	Geologists' Association
GAPAN	Guild of Air Pilots and Air Navigators
GATT	General Agreement on Tariffs and Trade
GB	Great Britain
GBA	Governing Bodies Association
GBE	Knight or Dame Grand Cross Order of the British Empire
GBGSA	Association of Governing Bodies of Girls' Public Schools
GBSM	Graduate of Birmingham and Midland Institute School of Music
GC	George Cross
GCB	Knight Grand Cross of the Bath
GCFR	Grand Commander of the Federal Republic of Nigeria
GCH	Knight Grand Cross of Hanover
GCHQ	Government Communications Headquarters
GCIE	Knight Grand Commander of the Indian Empire
GCLJ	Grand Cross, St Lazarus of Jerusalem
GCM	Gold Crown of Merit (Barbados)
GCMG	Knight or Dame Grand Cross of St Michael and St George
GCON	Grand Cross, Order of the Niger
GCSG	Knight Grand Cross of the Order of St Gregory the Great
GCSI	Knight Grand Commander of the Star of India
GCStJ	Bailiff or Dame Grand Cross of the Order of St John of Jerusalem
GCVO	Knight or Dame Grand Cross of Royal Victorian Order
g d	grand-daughter
GDC	General Dental Council
Gdns	Gardens
GDR	German Democratic Republic
Gen.	General
Ges.	Gesellschaft
GFS	Girls' Friendly Society
g g d	great-grand-daughter
g g s	great-grandson
GHQ	General Headquarters
Gib.	Gibraltar
GIMechE	Graduate Institution of Mechanical Engineers
GL	Grand Lodge
GLC	Greater London Council
Glos	Gloucestershire
GM	George Medal; Grand Medal (Ghana)
GMBATU	General, Municipal, Boilermakers and Allied Trades Union
GmbH	Gesellschaft mit beschränkter Hoftung
GMC	General Medical Council; Guild of Memorial Craftsmen
GMIE	Grand Master of Indian Empire
GMSI	Grand Master of Star of India
GMWU	General and Municipal Workers' Union (*now see* GMBATU)
GNC	General Nursing Council
GOC	General Officer Commanding
GOC-in-C	General Officer Commanding-in-Chief
GOE	General Ordination Examination
Gov.	Governor
Govt	Government
GP	General Practitioner; Grand Prix
GPDST	Girls' Public Day School Trust
GPO	General Post Office
GQG	Grand Quartier Général (French GHQ)
Gr.	Greek
GRSM	Graduate of the Royal Schools of Music
GS	General Staff; Grammar School
g s	grandson
GSA	Girls' Schools Association
GSM	General Service Medal; Guildhall School of Music and Drama
GSMD	Guildhall School of Music and Drama
GSO	General Staff Officer
GTCL	Graduate, Trinity College of Music
GTS	General Theological Seminary (New York)
GUI	Golfing Union of Ireland
GWR	Great Western Railway

H

HA	Historical Association; Health Authority
HAA	Heavy Anti-Aircraft
HAC	Honourable Artillery Company
Hants	Hampshire
HARCVS	Honorary Associate, Royal College of Veterinary Surgeons
Harv.	Harvard
HBM	His (or Her) Britannic Majesty (Majesty's); Humming Bird Gold Medal (Trinidad)
hc	*honoris causa*
HCEG	Honourable Company of Edinburgh Golfers
HCF	Hon. Chaplain to the Forces
HCIMA	Hotel, Catering and Institutional Management Association

DEAF
FROM BIRTH

IT'S TIME SHE WAS LISTENED TO.

Discrimination is an ugly word. But it has to be said. Deaf people in Britain are shamefully treated.

We are denied educational opportunities. We find it especially hard to get jobs. Our British Sign Language is not officially recognised. Our access to information is strictly limited...

We have over 10,000 profoundly deaf members. They have to struggle to make themselves understood and they are increasingly impatient at being ignored. So we are speaking up for them. Helping to develop their communication skills. Promoting British Sign Language. Training more sign language interpreters. Running education and welfare schemes...

Our objectives: to give deaf people the same opportunities as everyone else. Nothing more, nothing less.
We have a long way to go yet. And to succeed we need your support.

Please help. With a donation, a covenant, a legacy. And with your concern right through the year.

WE ASK TO BE HEARD
The British Deaf Association
38, Victoria Place, Carlisle CA1 1HU.

IDA	Hawkesbury Diploma in Agriculture (Australia)
IDD	Higher Dental Diploma
IDipEd	Higher Diploma in Education
IE	His Excellency; His Eminence
IEC	Ecole des Hautes Etudes Commerciales
IEH	His Exalted Highness
IEIC	Honourable East India Company
IEICS	Honourable East India Company's Service
Ieir-pres.	Heir-presumptive
Ierts	Hertfordshire
IFARA	Honorary Foreign Associate of the Royal Academy
IFRA	Honorary Foreign Member of the Royal Academy
IG	Home Guard
IH	His (or Her) Highness; His Holiness: Member, Hesketh Hubbard Art Society
IHD	Doctor of Humanities (US)
IIH	His (or Her) Imperial Highness
IIM	His (or Her) Imperial Majesty
IJ	Hilal-e-Jurat (Pakistan)
ILD	Doctor of Humane Letters
ILI	Highland Light Infantry
IM	His (or Her) Majesty, or Majesty's
IMAS	His (or Her) Majesty's Australian Ship
IMC	Headmasters' Conference; Hospital Management Committee
IMCS	His (or Her) Majesty's Canadian Ship
IMHS	His (or Her) Majesty's Hospital Ship
IMI	His (or Her) Majesty's Inspector
IMOCS	His (or Her) Majesty's Overseas Civil Service
IMS	His (or Her) Majesty's Ship
IMSO	His (or Her) Majesty's Stationery Office
INC	Higher National Certificate
IND	Higher National Diploma
I of C	House of Commons
Ion.	Honourable; Honorary
IP	House Physician
IPk	Hilal-e-Pakistan
IQ	Headquarters
IQA	Hilal-i-Quaid-i-Azam
HR)	Home Rule
IRCA	Honorary Royal Cambrian Academician
IRH	His (or Her) Royal Highness
IRHA	Honorary Member of Royal Hibernian Academy
IRI	Honorary Member of Royal Institute of Painters in Water Colours
HROI	Honorary Member of Royal Institute of Oil Painters
HRSA	Honorary Member of Royal Scottish Academy
IRSW	Honorary Member of Royal Scottish Water Colour Society
IS	House Surgeon
HSE	Health and Safety Executive
HSH	His (or Her) Serene Highness
Hum.	Humanity, Humanities (Classics)
Hunts	Huntingdonshire
HVCert	Health Visitor's Certificate
Hy	Heavy

I

	Island
Ia	Iowa (US)
IA	Indian Army
IAC	Institute of Amateur Cinematographers
IADR	International Association for Dental Research
IAEA	International Atomic Energy Agency
IAF	Indian Air Force; Indian Auxiliary Force
IAHM	Incorporated Association of Headmasters
IAM	Institute of Advanced Motorists
IAMC	Indian Army Medical Corps
IAMTACT	Institute of Advanced Machine Tool and Control Technology
IAOC	Indian Army Ordnance Control
IAPS	Incorporated Association of Preparatory Schools
IARO	Indian Army Reserve of Officers
IAS	Indian Administrative Service
IASS	International Association for Scandinavian Studies
IATA	International Air Transport Association
IATUL	International Association of Technical University Libraries
IAU	International Astronomical Union
ib. or ibid.	Ibidem (in the same place)
IBA	Independent Broadcasting Authority; International Bar Association
IBG	Institute of British Geographers
IBRD	International Bank for Reconstruction and Development (World Bank)
i/c	In charge; in command
ICA	Institute of Contemporary Arts; Institute of Chartered Accountants in England and Wales
ICAA	Invalid Children's Aid Association
ICAI	Institute of Chartered Accountants in Ireland
ICAO	International Civil Aviation Organization
ICBS	Irish Christian Brothers' School
ICC	International Chamber of Commerce
ICCROM	International Centre for Conservation at Rome

ICD	*Iuris Canonici Doctor*; Independence Commemorative Decoration (Rhodesia)
ICE	Institution of Civil Engineers
ICED	International Council for Educational Development
Icel.	Icelandic
ICF	International Federation of Chemical and General Workers' Unions
ICFC	Industrial and Commercial Finance Corporation
ICFTU	International Confederation of Free Trade Unions
IChemE	Institution of Chemical Engineers
ICI	Imperial Chemical Industries
ICL	International Computers Ltd
ICM	International Confederation of Midwives
ICMA	Institute of Cost and Management Accountants
ICOM	International Council of Museums
ICOMOS	International Council of Monuments and Sites
ICRC	International Committee of the Red Cross
ICS	Indian Civil Service
ICSID	International Council of Societies of Industrial Design
ICSS	International Committee for the Sociology of Sport
ICSU	International Council of Scientific Unions
ICT	International Computers and Tabulators Ltd *(now see* ICL)
Id	Idaho (US)
IDA	International Development Association
IDB	Internal Drainage Board
IDC	Imperial Defence College *(now see* RCDS); Inter-Diocesan Certificate
idc	Completed a Course at, or served for a year on the Staff of, the Imperial Defence College *(now see* rcds)
IDS	Institute of Development Studies
IEE	Institution of Electrical Engineers
IEEE	Institute of Electrical and Electronics Engineers (NY)
IEETE	Institution of Electrical and Electronic Technician Engineers
IEME	Inspectorate of Electrical and Mechanical Engineering
IERE	Institution of Electronic and Radio Engineers
IES	Indian Educational Service; Institution of Engineers and Shipbuilders in Scotland
IExpE	Institute of Explosives Engineers
IFAC	International Federation of Automatic Control
IFC	International Finance Corporation
IFIP	International Federation for Information Processing
IFL	International Friendship League
IFLA	International Federation of Library Associations
IFPI	International Federation of the Phonographic Industry
IFS	Irish Free State; Indian Forest Service
IG	Instructor in Gunnery
IGasE	Institution of Gas Engineers
IGPP	Institute of Geophysics and Planetary Physics
IGS	Independent Grammar School
IGU	International Geographical Union; International Gas Union
IHA	Institute of Health Service Administrators
IHVE	Institution of Heating and Ventilating Engineers *(now see* CIBS)
IIM	Institution of Industrial Managers
IIMT	International Institute for the Management of Technology
IInfSc	Institute of Information Scientists
IIS	International Institute of Sociology
IISS	International Institute of Strategic Studies
ILEA	Inner London Education Authority
ILEC	Inner London Education Committee
Ill	Illinois (US)
ILO	International Labour Office; International Labour Organisation
ILP	Independent Labour Party
ILR	International Labour Review
IM	Individual Merit
IMA	International Music Association; Institute of Mathematics and its Applications
IMCO	Inter-Governmental Maritime Consultative Organization
IMEA	Incorporated Municipal Electrical Association
IMechE	Institution of Mechanical Engineers
IMEDE	Institut pour l'Etude des Méthodes de Direction de l'Entreprise
IMF	International Monetary Fund
IMGTechE	Institution of Mechanical and General Technician Engineers
IMinE	Institution of Mining Engineers
IMMLEP	Immunology of Leprosy
IMMTS	Indian Mercantile Marine Training Ship
Imp.	Imperial
IMS	Indian Medical Service; Institute of Management Services
IMTA	Institute of Municipal Treasurers and Accountants *(now see* CIPFA)
IMU	International Mathematical Union
IMunE	Institution of Municipal Engineers
IN	Indian Navy
Inc.	Incorporated
INCA	International Newspaper Colour Association
Incog.	Incognito
Ind.	Independent; Indiana (US)
INSEA	International Society for Education through Art
INSEAD (Insead)	Institut Européen d'Administration des Affaires
Insp.	Inspector
Inst.	Institute
Instn	Institution
InstnMM	Institution of Mining and Metallurgy

THE LEONARD CHESHIRE FOUNDATION

Leonard Cheshire House,
26-29 Maunsel Street, London SW1P 2QN. Telephone: 01-828 1822
Patron: Her Majesty The Queen
Founder: Group Captain G. L. Cheshire, V.C., O.M., D.S.O., D.F.C.
(Regd. Charity No. 218186)

Cheshire Homes provide residential care for physically or mentally handicapped adults and children, hostels for ex-psychiatric rehabilitation and attendant care schemes for disabled people living in their own homes. The United Kingdom section of the Foundation currently consists of 75 Homes and Hostels and there are 147 Homes in 45 countries overseas. It is estimated that in excess of 5,000 people are being cared for by the Foundation as a whole; yet the need is so great that no one would claim that this more than scratches the surface of the problem. Every year many hundreds of applicants are turned away in the UK alone, and money is urgently required for the enormous amount of work which remains to be done.

Donations, covenants and legacies may be given to the Foundation for the Trustees to use wherever the needs are greatest; or, if preferred, they can be given for any Home specified by the donor, or to your local Cheshire Home.

Lend Me Your Ears

Without hearing you cannot get far. If you were also blind, life would be finished. *How wrong you are!* A modest office in Peterborough is the National Headquarters of the only organisation of its kind in the world, the National Deaf-Blind Helpers' League.

Formed and controlled by people who can neither see nor hear, it started from nothing in 1928 and, today, it is the recognised Authority on this double disability – internationally consulted. You can lose sight and hearing in a day through accident or illness. If you did, you would come to us to find out what other men and women have done about it.

The League brings new hope – practical help and understanding friendship to all deaf-blind people. It depends entirely upon voluntary contributions. Do you think such a Body is worth your support? If so, write to the:

NATIONAL DEAF-BLIND HELPERS' LEAGUE,
(Registered under the Charities Act, 1960 No: 206871)
**18 Rainbow Court, Paston Ridings, Peterborough, PE4 6UP.
Telephone: Peterborough (0733) 73511**

astT	Institute of Transport
OB	Institute of Building (now see CIOB)
ODE	Imperial Order of the Daughters of the Empire
of M	Isle of Man
OGT	International Order of Good Templars
OM	Isle of Man; Indian Order of Merit
OOF	Independent Order of Odd-fellows
OP	Institute of Painters in Oil Colours
oW	Isle of Wight
PCS	Institution of Professional Civil Servants
PFA	Member or Associate, Chartered Institute of Public Finance and Accountancy
PI	International Press Institute
PlantE	Institution of Plant Engineers (now see IIM)
PM	Institute of Personnel Management
PPF	International Planned Parenthood Federation
PPS	Institute of Physics and The Physical Society
ProdE	Institution of Production Engineers
PS	Indian Police Service; Indian Political Service; Institute of Purchasing and Supply
PU	Inter-Parliamentary Union
RA	Irish Republican Army
RAD	Institute for Research on Animal Diseases
RC	Industrial Reorganization Corporation
REE(Aust)	Institution of Radio and Electronics Engineers (Australia)
RI	Institution of the Rubber Industry (now see PRI)
RO	International Refugee Organization
RTE	Institute of Road Transport Engineers
s	Island(s)
S	International Society of Sculptors, Painters and Gravers
SC	Imperial Service College, Haileybury; Indian Staff Corps
SCO	Independent Schools Careers Organisation
SE	Indian Service of Engineers
SI	International Statistical Institute
SIS	Independent Schools Information Service
SM	Incorporated Society of Musicians
SME	International Society for Musical Education
SMRC	Inter-Services Metallurgical Research Council
SO	Imperial Service Order; International Standards Organization
STC	Iron and Steel Trades Confederation; Institute of Scientific and Technical Communicators
STD	Imperial Society of Teachers of Dancing
StructE	Institution of Structural Engineers
T	Indian Territory (US)
TA	Independent Television Authority (now see IBA)
tal. or It.	Italian
TB	Industry Training Board
TC	International Trade Centre
TCA	Independent Television Companies Association Ltd
TF	International Transport Workers' Federation
TN	Independent Television News
TO	International Trade Organization
TV	Independent Television
UA	International Union of Architects
UB	International Union of Biochemistry
UC	Inter-University Council for Higher Education Overseas (now see IUPC)
UCN	International Union for the Conservation of Nature and Natural Resources
UCW	International Union for Child Welfare
UGS	International Union of Geological Sciences
UHPS	International Union of the History and Philosophy of Science
UP	Association of Independent Unionist Peers
UPAC	International Union of Pure and Applied Chemistry
UPAP	International Union of Pure and Applied Physics
UPC	Inter-University and Polytechnic Council for Higher Education Overseas
UPS	International Union of Physiological Sciences
VS	International Voluntary Service
W	Isle of Wight
WES	Institution of Water Engineers and Scientists
WGC	Imperial War Graves Commission
WM	Institution of Works Managers (now see IIM)
WPC	Institute of Water Pollution Control
WSOM	Institute of Practitioners in Work Study Organisation and Methods (now see IMS)
WSP	Institute of Work Study Practitioners (now see IMS)
Y	Imperial Yeomanry
Z	I Zingari

J

A	Judge Advocate
ACT	Joint Association of Classical Teachers
AG	Judge Advocate General
as	James
CB	Juris Canonici Bachelor (Bachelor of Canon Law)
CS	Journal of the Chemical Society
CD	Juris Canonici Doctor (Doctor of Canon Law)
CI	Junior Chamber International
CL	Licentiate of Canon Law

JCO	Joint Consultative Organisation (of ARC, MAFF, and Department of Agriculture and Fisheries for Scotland)
JD	Doctor of Jurisprudence
JDipMA	Joint Diploma in Management Accounting Services
JG	Junior Grade
JInstE	Junior Institution of Engineers (now see IMGTechE)
jls	Journals
JMN	Johan Mangku Negara (Malaysia)
Joh. or Jno.	John
JP	Justice of the Peace
Jr	Junior
jsc	Qualified at a Junior Staff Course, or the equivalent, 1942–46
JSD	Doctor of Juristic Science
JSLS	Joint Services Liaison Staff
JSM	Johan Setia Mahkota (Malaysia)
JSPS	Japan Society for the Promotion of Science
jssc	Joint Services Staff Course
jt, jtly	joint, jointly
JWS or jws	Joint Warfare Staff
JUD	Juris Utriusque Doctor, Doctor of Both Laws (Canon and Civil)
Jun.	Junior
Jun. Opt.	Junior Optime

K

Kans	Kansas (US)
KAR	King's African Rifles
KBE	Knight Commander Order of the British Empire
KC	King's Counsel
KCB	Knight Commander of the Bath
KCC	Commander of Order of Crown, Belgium and Congo Free State
KCH	King's College Hospital; Knight Commander of Hanover
KCHS	Knight Commander of the Holy Sepulchre
KCIE	Knight Commander of the Indian Empire
KCL	King's College London
KCMG	Knight Commander of St Michael and St George
KCSA	Knight Commander, Military Order of the Collar of St Agatha of Paterna
KCSG	Knight Commander of St Gregory
KCSI	Knight Commander of the Star of India
KCSS	Knight Commander of St Silvester
KCVO	Knight Commander of the Royal Victorian Order
KDG	King's Dragoon Guards
KEH	King Edward's Horse
KG	Knight of the Order of the Garter
KGStJ	Knight of Grace, Order of St John of Jerusalem (now see KStJ)
KH	Knight of Hanover
KHC	Hon. Chaplain to the King
KHDS	Hon. Dental Surgeon to the King
KHNS	Hon. Nursing Sister to the King
KHP	Hon. Physician to the King
KHS	Hon. Surgeon to the King; Knight of the Holy Sepulchre
K-i-H	Kaisar-i-Hind
KJStJ	Knight of Justice, Order of St John of Jerusalem (now see KStJ)
KLJ	Knight, St Lazarus of Jerusalem
KM	Knight of Malta
KORR	King's Own Royal Regiment
KOSB	King's Own Scottish Borderers
KOYLI	King's Own Yorkshire Light Infantry
KP	Knight of the Order of St Patrick
KPM	King's Police Medal
KRRC	King's Royal Rifle Corps
KS	King's Scholar
KSC	Knight of St Columba
KSG	Knight of St Gregory the Great
KSLI	King's Shropshire Light Infantry
KSS	Knight of St Silvester
KStJ	Knight of Order of St John of Jerusalem
KStJ(A)	Associate Knight of Justice, Order of St John of Jerusalem
KT	Knight of the Order of the Thistle
Kt or Knt	Knight
Ky	Kentucky (US)

L

(L)	Liberal
LA	Los Angeles; Literate in Arts; Liverpool Academy
La	Louisiana (US)
(Lab)	Labour
LAC	London Athletic Club
LAMDA	London Academy of Music and Dramatic Art
LAMSAC	Local Authorities' Management Services and Computer Committee
LAMTPI	Legal Associate Member, Town Planning Institute
L-Corp. or Lance-Corp.	Lance-corporal

Aggie had a concern for sailors in 1876 which is still necessary today

Many changes have taken place inside and outside the Royal Navy over the last 100 years. The size of the fleet and number of sailors have reduced dramatically. But the moral dangers a young sailor faces today are probably as great as those of last century.

Aggie Weston founded the Sailors' Rest in 1876, later to be given the "Royal" accolade by Queen Victoria, to provide a safe haven in British ports for our sailors, when the only other other places of entertainment open to them were the beer halls. She welcomed them in, whatever their creed or lack of one, whether they were drunk or sober and she treated them with a combination of Christian charity and gentle humour which bound them to her. And through her many a sailor found the joy of a Christian life.

Today the Centres offer a more modern environment with squash, badminton and other sporting activities, where a man or woman of the Services (or of foreign ones) can rest and relax. But the objectives are unchanged, the welcome is as warm as ever it was and the chance is still there for a sailor to find his way to our Lord Jesus Christ.

Our work is not funded either by the Navy or by any other official agency.
We rely on the generosity of your giving and your prayers.

If you would like to know more about our work please write to:

THE GENERAL SECRETARY,
THE ROYAL SAILORS' RESTS,
2B SOUTH STREET,
GOSPORT, HANTS. PO12 1ES.

Royal Sailors' Rests

ncs	Lancashire
ARSP	Language Assessment, Remediation and Screening Procedure
C	London Broadcasting Company
	Cross of Leo
AD	London Certificate in Art and Design (University of London)
C	London County Council (*now see* GLC)
h	Licentiate in Surgery
J	Lord Chief Justice
L	Licentiate of Canon Law
P	Licentiate, College of Preceptors
ST	Licentiate, College of Speech Therapists
	Liberal and Democratic
iv	Licentiate in Divinity
S	Licentiate in Dental Surgery
V	Local Defence Volunteers
A	Local Education Authority
PRA	British Leprosy Relief Association
sL	Licencié ès lettres
H	Light Horse
HD	*Literarum Humaniorum Doctor* (Doctor of Literature)
	Light Infantry; Long Island
BER	Ligue des Bibliothèques Européennes de Recherche
cMed	Licentiate in Medicine
eut	Lieutenant
ncs	Lincolnshire
OB	Licentiate, Institute of Building
t.	Literature; Literary
tD	Doctor of Literature; Doctor of Letters
t.Hum.	*Literae Humaniores* (Classics)
ttD	Doctor of Literature; Doctor of Letters
	Lord Justice
LA	Lady Literate in Arts
LB	Bachelor of Laws
LCM	Licentiate, London College of Music
LD	Doctor of Laws
LL	Licentiate in Laws
LM	Master of Laws
M	Licentiate in Midwifery
MBC	Lady Margaret Boat Club
MCC	Licentiate, Medical Council of Canada
Med	Licentiate in Medicine
MR	London Midland Region (BR)
MS	London, Midland and Scottish Railway; London Missionary Society
MSSA	Licentiate in Medicine and Surgery, Society of Apothecaries
MRTPI	Legal Member, Royal Town Planning Institute
Nat)	Liberal National
NER	London and North Eastern Railway
OB	Location of Offices Bureau
of C	Lines of Communication
PTB	London Passenger Transport Board (*now see* LTE)
RAD	Licentiate, Royal Academy of Dancing
RAM	Licentiate, Royal Academy of Music
RCP	Licentiate, Royal College of Physicians, London
RCPE	Licentiate, Royal College of Physicians, Edinburgh
RCPI	Licentiate, Royal College of Physicians of Ireland
RCS	Licentiate, Royal College of Surgeons of England
RCSE	Licentiate, Royal College of Surgeons, Edinburgh
RCSI	Licentiate, Royal College of Surgeons in Ireland
RFPS(G)	Licentiate, Royal Faculty of Physicians and Surgeons, Glasgow
RIBA	Licentiate, Royal Institute of British Architects (*now see* RIBA)
SA	Licentiate, Society of Apothecaries
SE	London School of Economics and Political Science
SHTM	London School of Hygiene and Tropical Medicine
SO	London Symphony Orchestra
t	Lieutenant; Light
T	London Transport; Licentiate in Teaching
TA	Lawn Tennis Association
TB	London Transport Board (*now see* LTE)
TCL	Licentiate of Trinity College of Music, London
t-Col	Lieutenant-Colonel
TE	London Transport Executive
t-Gen.	Lieutenant-General
Th	Licentiate in Theology
U)	Liberal Unionist
UOTC	London University Officers' Training Corps
WT	London Weekend Television
XX	Septuagint

M

	Marquess; Member; Monsieur
	married
A	Master of Arts; Military Assistant
AA	Manufacturers' Agents Association of Great Britain
AAF	Mediterranean Allied Air Forces
AAT	Member, Association of Accounting Technicians
ACE	Member, Australian College of Education; Member, Association of Conference Executives

MACI	Member, American Concrete Institute
MACM	Member, Association of Computing Machines
MACS	Member, American Chemical Society
MAEE	Marine Aircraft Experimental Establishment
MAF	Ministry of Agriculture and Fisheries
MAFF	Ministry of Agriculture, Fisheries and Food
MAI	*Magister in Arte Ingeniaria* (Master of Engineering)
MAIAA	Member, American Institute of Aeronautics and Astronautics
MAICE	Member, American Institute of Consulting Engineers
MAIChE	Member, American Institute of Chemical Engineers
Maj.-Gen.	Major-General
Man	Manitoba (Canada)
MAO	Master of Obstetric Art
MAOT	Member, Association of Occupational Therapists
MAOU	Member, American Ornithologists' Union
MAP	Ministry of Aircraft Production
MAPsS	Member, Australian Psychological Society
MArch	Master of Architecture
Marq.	Marquess
MASAE	Member, American Society of Agricultural Engineers
MASCE	Member, American Society of Civil Engineers
MASME	Member, American Society of Mechanical Engineers
Mass	Massachusetts (US)
Math.	Mathematics; Mathematical
MATSA	Managerial Administrative Technical Staff Association
MAusIMM	Member, Australasian Institute of Mining and Metallurgy
MB	Medal of Bravery (Canada); Bachelor of Medicine
MBA	Master of Business Administration
MBASW	Member, British Association of Social Workers
MBCS	Member, British Computer Society
MBE	Member, Order of the British Empire
MBFR	Mutual and Balanced Force Reductions (negotiations)
MBHI	Member, British Horological Institute
MBIM	Member, British Institute of Management (*now see* FBIM)
MBKSTS	Member, British Kinematograph, Sound and Television Society
MBOU	Member, British Ornithologists' Union
MBritIRE	Member, British Institution of Radio Engineers (*now see* MIERE)
MBS	Member, Building Societies Institute (*now see* MCBSI)
MC	Military Cross
MCAM	Member, CAM Foundation
MCB	Master in Clinical Biochemistry
MCBSI	Member, Chartered Building Societies Institute
MCC	Marylebone Cricket Club; Metropolitan County Council
MCD	Master of Civic Design
MCE(Melb)	Master of Civil Engineering (Melbourne University)
MCFP	Member, College of Family Physicians (Canada)
MCh or MChir	Master in Surgery
MChE	Master of Chemical Engineering
MChemA	Master in Chemical Analysis
MChOrth	Master of Orthopaedic Surgery
MCIBS	Member, Chartered Institution of Building Services
MCIOB	Member, Chartered Institute of Building
M.CIRP	Member, International Institution for Production Engineering Research
MCIT	Member, Chartered Institute of Transport
MCL	Master in Civil Law
MCMES	Member, Civil and Mechanical Engineers' Society
MCom	Master of Commerce
MConsE	Member, Association of Consulting Engineers
MCP	Member of Colonial Parliament; Master of City Planning (US)
MCPA	Member, College of Pathologists of Australia (*now see* MRCPA)
MCPath	Member, College of Pathologists (*now see* MRCPath)
MCPS	Member, College of Physicians and Surgeons
MCS	Madras Civil Service; Malayan Civil Service
MCSEE	Member, Canadian Society of Electrical Engineers
MCSP	Member, Chartered Society of Physiotherapy
MCT	Member, Association of Corporate Treasurers
MD	Doctor of Medicine; Military District
Md	Maryland (US)
MDC	Metropolitan District Council
MDes	Master of Design
MDS	Master of Dental Surgery
Me	Maine (US)
ME	Mining Engineer; Middle East; Master of Engineering
MEAF	Middle East Air Force
MEC	Member of Executive Council; Middle East Command
MEc	Master of Economics
MECAS	Middle East Centre for Arab Studies
Mech.	Mechanics; Mechanical
MECI	Member, Institute of Employment Consultants
Med.	Medical
MEd	Master of Education
MEF	Middle East Force
MEIC	Member, Engineering Institute of Canada
MELF	Middle East Land Forces
Mencap	Royal Society for Mentally Handicapped Children and Adults
MEng	Master of Engineering
MEO	Marine Engineering Officer
MEP	Member of the European Parliament
MetR	Metropolitan Railway

The Malcolm Sargent Cancer Fund for Children

Patron
H. R. H. THE PRINCESS OF WALES

The Fund was launched on March 26, 1968 as a lasting and practical memorial to the much-loved British musician whose name it bears.

Parents have written:—

"Dear Sir or Madam,

I'm sorry to address you so formally, but we don't know who you are, apart from the fact that you seem like a guardian angel. I'm writing to thank you from both of us for the grant you allowed us for travelling expenses to see our daughter, Kate. Although we were told our application would probably be accepted, we never dreamt the reward would be so substantial. We had been wondering how much longer we could continue to see her every day and now we don't need to worry for the time being".

Cancer is a dreaded word at any age, but doubly so at an age when life has little more than begun.

When the blow of the initial diagnosis strikes, parents are distraught and confused. They often need financial help to enable them to meet the needs of the child's illness. The Malcolm Sargent Cancer Fund for Children aims to provide this help and to provide it quickly, to relieve at least one of the many early anxieties with which the parents are afflicted.

Demands on the Fund's resources are for ever on the increase. Over 700 new cases are accepted by the Fund each year and grants are given for warm clothing, help with heating bills, beds and bedding, nourishing foods, convalescent holidays, etc.

PLEASE help this special Fund to continue its practical work by making a Deed of Covenant, a donation or by a legacy.

Applications for Deeds of Covenant Forms and donations should be addressed to the Fund's administrative offices:
6 Sydney Street   London SW3 6PP
Telephone: 01-352 6884

Thank you.

etSoc	Metals Society (formed by amalgamation of Institute of Metals and Iron and Steel Institute)	MInstP	Member, Institute of Physics
EXE	Military Engineering Experimental Establishment	MInstPet	Member, Institute of Petroleum
FA	Master of Fine Arts	MInstPI	Member, Institute of Patentees and Inventors
FC	Mastership in Food Control	MInstPkg	Member, Institute of Packaging
FCM	Member, Faculty of Community Medicine	MInstPS	Member, Institute of Purchasing and Supply
FGB	Miners' Federation of Great Britain	MInstR	Member, Institute of Refrigeration
FH	Master of Foxhounds	MInstRA	Member, Institute of Registered Architects
FOM	Member, Faculty of Occupational Medicine	MInstT	Member, Institute of Transport
GA	Major-General in charge of Administration	MInstTM	Member, Institute of Travel Managers in Industry and Commerce
GC	Machine Gun Corps		
GDS RCS	Member in General Dental Surgery, Royal College of Surgeons	MInstW	Member, Institute of Welding (now see MWeldI)
		MINucE	Member, Institution of Nuclear Engineers
GGS	Major-General, General Staff	MIOB	Member, Institute of Building (now see MCIOB)
GI	Member, Institute of Certificated Grocers	MIOM	Member. Institute of Office Management (now see MIAM)
GO	Master General of the Ordnance; Master of Gynaecology and Obstetrics	MIPA	Member, Institute of Practitioners in Advertising
		MIPlantE	Member, Institution of Plant Engineers (now see MIIM)
gr	Monsignor	MIPM	Member, Institute of Personnel Management
HA	Member of House of Assembly	MIPR	Member, Institute of Public Relations
HCIMA	Member, Hotel Catering and Institutional Management Association	MIProdE	Member, Institution of Production Engineers
		MIQ	Member, Institute of Quarrying
HK	Member of the House of Keys	MIRE	Member, Institution of Radio Engineers (now see MIERE)
HR	Member of the House of Representatives	MIREE(Aust)	Member, Institution of Radio and Electronics Engineers (Australia)
HRA	Modern Humanities Research Association		
HRF	Mental Health Research Fund	MIRT	Member, Institute of Reprographic Technicians
I	Military Intelligence	MIRTE	Member, Institute of Road Transport Engineers
IAeE	Member, Institute of Aeronautical Engineers	MIS	Member, Institute of Statisticians
IAgrE	Member, Institution of Agricultural Engineers	MIS(India)	Member, Institution of Surveyors of India
IAM	Member, Institute of Administrative Management	MISI	Member of Iron and Steel Institute (now part of Metals Society)
IAS	Member, Institute of Aeronautical Science (US) (now see MAIAA)	Miss	Mississippi (US)
		MIStructE	Member, Institution of Structural Engineers
IBF	Member, Institute of British Foundrymen	MIT	Massachusetts Institute of Technology
IBritE	Member, Institution of British Engineers	MITA	Member, Industrial Transport Association
IBS	Member, Institute of Bankers in Scotland	MITE	Member, Institution of Electrical and Electronics Technician Engineers
ICE	Member, Institution of Civil Engineers		
ICEI	Member, Institution of Civil Engineers of Ireland	MITT	Member, Institute of Travel and Tourism
ICFor	Member, Institute of Chartered Foresters	MIWES	Member, Institution of Water Engineers (now see MIWES)
ich	Michigan (US)	MIWES	Member, Institution of Water Engineers and Scientists
IChemE	Member, Institution of Chemical Engineers	MIWM	Member, Institution of Works Managers (now see MIIM)
ICS	Member, Institute of Chartered Shipbrokers	MIWPC	Member, Institute of Water Pollution Control
IDPM	Member, Institute of Data Processing Management	MIWSP	Member, Institute of Work Study Practitioners (now see MMS)
IE(Aust)	Member, Institution of Engineers, Australia		
IED	Member, Institution of Engineering Designers	MJI	Member, Institute of Journalists
IEE	Member, Institution of Electrical Engineers	MJIE	Member, Junior Institution of Engineers (now see MIGTechE)
IEEE	Member, Institute of Electrical and Electronics Engineers (NY)		
		MJr	Magister Juris
IEI	Member, Institution of Engineering Inspection	MJS	Member, Japan Society
IE(Ind)	Member, Institution of Engineers, India	ML	Licentiate in Medicine; Master of Laws
IERE	Member, Institution of Electronic and Radio Engineers	MLA	Member of Legislative Assembly; Modern Language Association; Master in Landscape Architecture
IES	Member, Institution of Engineers and Shipbuilders, Scotland		
IEx	Member, Institute of Export	MLC	Member of Legislative Council
IExpE	Member, Institute of Explosives Engineers	MLitt	Master of Letters
IFF	Member, Institute of Freight Forwarders	Mlle	Mademoiselle (Miss)
IFor	Member, Institute of Foresters (now see MICFor)	MLM	Member, Order of the Legion of Merit (Rhodesia)
IGasE	Member, Institution of Gas Engineers	MLO	Military Liaison Officer
IGeol	Member, Institution of Geologists	MM	Military Medal
IH	Member, Institute of Housing	MMA	Metropolitan Museum of Art
IHM	Member, Institute of Housing Managers (now see MIH)	MMB	Milk Marketing Board
IHVE	Member, Institution of Heating and Ventilating Engineers (now see MCIBS)	MME	Master of Mining Engineering
		Mme	Madame
IIA	Member, Institute of Industrial Administration (now see FBIM)	MMechE	Master of Mechanical Engineering
		MMet	Master of Metallurgy
IIM	Member, Institute of Industrial Managers	MMGI	Member, Mining, Geological and Metallurgical Institute of India
IInfSc	Member, Institute of Information Sciences		
IL	Member, Institute of Linguists	MMM	Member, Order of Military Merit (Canada)
il.	Military	MMS	Member, Institute of Management Services
ILGA	Member, Institute of Local Government Administrators	MMSA	Master of Midwifery, Society of Apothecaries
ILocoE	Member, Institution of Locomotive Engineers	MN	Merchant Navy
IM	Member, Institution of Metallurgists	MNAS	Member, National Academy of Sciences (US)
IMarE	Member, Institute of Marine Engineers	MNECInst	Member, North-East Coast Institution of Engineers and Shipbuilders
IMC	Member, Institute of Management Consultants		
IMechE	Member, Institution of Mechanical Engineers	MNI	Member, Nautical Institute
IMGTechE	Member, Institution of Mechanical and General Technician Engineers	MNSE	Member, Nigerian Society of Engineers
		MO	Medical Officer; Military Operations
IMI	Member, Institute of the Motor Industry	Mo	Missouri (US)
IMinE	Member, Institution of Mining Engineers	MoD	Ministry of Defence
IMM	Member, Institution of Mining and Metallurgy	Mods	Moderations (Oxford)
IMunE	Member, Institution of Municipal Engineers	MOF	Ministry of Food
in.	Ministry	MOH	Medical Officer(s) of Health
IN	Member, Institute of Navigation (now see MRIN)	MOI	Ministry of Information
inn	Minnesota (US)	Mon	Monmouthshire
InstAM	Member, Institute of Administrative Management	Mont	Montana (US); Montgomeryshire
InstBE	Member, Institution of British Engineers	MOP	Ministry of Power
InstCE	Member, Institution of Civil Engineers (now see FICE)	MoS	Ministry of Supply
InstD	Member, Institute of Directors	Most Rev.	Most Reverend
InstE	Member, Institute of Energy	MoT	Ministry of Transport
InstEnvSci	Member, Institute of Environmental Sciences	MP	Member of Parliament
InstF	Member, Institute of Fuel (now see MInstE)	MPA	Master of Public Administration
InstGasE	Member, Institution of Gas Engineers	MPBW	Ministry of Public Building and Works
InstHE	Member, Institution of Highway Engineers	MPH	Master of Public Health
InstM	Member, Institute of Marketing	MPP	Member, Provincial Parliament
InstMC	Member, Institute of Measurement and Control	MPS	Member, Pharmaceutical Society
InstME	Member, Institution of Mining Engineers	MR	Master of the Rolls; Municipal Reform
InstMet	Member of the Institute of Metals (now part of Metals Society)	MRAC	Member, Royal Agricultural College
		MRACP	Member, Royal Australasian College of Physicians

MRACS	Member, Royal Australasian College of Surgeons
MRAeS	Member, Royal Aeronautical Society
MRAIC	Member, Royal Architectural Institute of Canada
MRAS	Member, Royal Asiatic Society
MRC	Medical Research Council
MRCA	Multi-Role Combat Aircraft
MRCGP	Member, Royal College of General Practitioners
MRCOG	Member, Royal College of Obstetricians and Gynaecologists
MRCP	Member, Royal College of Physicians, London
MRCPA	Member, Royal College of Pathologists of Australia
MRCPE	Member, Royal College of Physicians, Edinburgh
MRCPGlas	Member, Royal College of Physicians and Surgeons, Glasgow
MRCPI	Member, Royal College of Physicians of Ireland
MRCPsych	Member, Royal College of Psychiatrists
MRCS	Member, Royal College of Surgeons of England
MRCSE	Member, Royal College of Surgeons, Edinburgh
MRCSI	Member, Royal College of Surgeons in Ireland
MRCVS	Member, Royal College of Veterinary Surgeons
MRES, MREmpS	Member, Royal Empire Society
MRI	Member, Royal Institution
MRIA	Member, Royal Irish Academy
MRIAI	Member, Royal Institute of the Architects of Ireland
MRIC	Member, Royal Institute of Chemistry (now see MRSC)
MRIN	Member, Royal Institute of Navigation
MRINA	Member, Royal Institution of Naval Architects
MRSanI	Member, Royal Sanitary Institute (see MRSH)
MRSC	Member, Royal Society of Chemistry
MRSH	Member, Royal Society for the Promotion of Health
MRSL	Member, Order of the Republic of Sierra Leone
MRSM, MRSocMed	Member, Royal Society of Medicine
MRST	Member, Royal Society of Teachers
MRTPI	Member, Royal Town Planning Institute
MRUSI	Member, Royal United Service Institution
MRVA	Member, Rating and Valuation Association
MS	Master of Surgery; Master of Science (US)
MS, MSS	Manuscript, Manuscripts
MSA	Master of Science, Agriculture (US); Mineralogical Society of America
MSAE	Member, Society of Automotive Engineers (US)
MSAICE	Member, South African Institution of Civil Engineers
MSAInstMM	Member, South African Institute of Mining and Metallurgy
MS&R	Merchant Shipbuilding and Repairs
MSAutE	Member, Society of Automobile Engineers
MSC	Manpower Services Commission; Missionaries of the Sacred Heart; Madras Staff Corps
MSc	Master of Science
MScD	Master of Dental Science
MSE	Master of Science in Engineering (US)
MSH	Master of Stag Hounds
MSIAD	Member, Society of Industrial Artists and Designers
MSINZ	Member, Surveyors' Institute of New Zealand
MSIT	Member, Society of Instrument Technology (now see MInstMC)
MSM	Meritorious Service Medal; Madras Sappers and Miners
MSocSc	Master of Social Sciences
MSR	Member, Society of Radiographers
MSTD	Member, Society of Typographic Designers
Mt	Mount, Mountain
MT	Mechanical Transport
MTA	Music Trades Association
MTAI	Member, Institute of Travel Agents
MTB	Motor Torpedo Boat
MTCA	Ministry of Transport and Civil Aviation
MTD	Midwife Teachers' Diploma
MTEFL	Master in the Teaching of English as a Foreign or Second Language
MTh	Master of Theology
MTPI	Member, Town Planning Institute (now see MRTPI)
MTS	Master of Theological Studies
MusB	Bachelor of Music
MusD	Doctor of Music
MusM	Master of Music
MV	Merchant Vessel, Motor Vessel (naval)
MVO	Member, Royal Victorian Order
MVSc	Master of Veterinary Science
MWA	Mystery Writers of America
MWeldI	Member, Welding Institute
MWSOM	Member, Institute of Practitioners in Work Study Organisation and Methods (now see MMS)

N

N)	Nationalist; Navigating Duties
N	North
n	Nephew
NA	National Academician (America)
NAACP	National Association for the Advancement of Colored People

NAAFI	Navy, Army and Air Force Institutes
NAAS	National Agricultural Advisory Service
NABC	National Association of Boys' Clubs
NACRO	National Association for the Care and Resettlement of Offenders
NADFAS	National Association of Decorative and Fine Arts Societies
NAHA	National Association of Health Authorities
NALGO (Nalgo)	National and Local Government Officers' Association
NAMCW	National Association for Maternal and Child Welfare
NAMH	MIND (National Association for Mental Health)
NAMMA	NATO MRCA Management Agency
NAPT	National Association for the Prevention of Tuberculosis
NASA	National Aeronautics and Space Administration (US)
NAS/UWT	National Association of Schoolmasters/Union of Women Teachers
NATCS	National Air Traffic Control Services
NATFHE	National Association of Teachers in Further and Higher Education (combining ATCDE and ATTI)
NATO	North Atlantic Treaty Organisation
Nat. Sci.	Natural Sciences
NATSOPA	National Society of Operative Printers, Graphical and Media Personnel (formerly of Operative Printers and Assistants)
NAYC	National Association of Youth Clubs
NB	New Brunswick
NBA	North British Academy
NBC	National Book Council (now see NBL); National Broadcasting Company (US)
NBL	National Book League
NBPI	National Board for Prices and Incomes
NC	National Certificate; North Carolina (US)
NCA	National Certificate of Agriculture
NCB	National Coal Board
NCCI	National Committee for Commonwealth Immigrants
NCCL	National Council for Civil Liberties
NCDAD	National Council for Diplomas in Art and Design
NCLC	National Council of Labour Colleges
NCU	National Cyclists' Union
NDA	National Diploma in Agriculture
NDak	North Dakota (US)
ndc	National Defence College
NDD	National Diploma in Dairying; National Diploma in Design
NDH	National Diploma in Horticulture
NDIC	National Defence Industries Council
NE	North-east
NEAC	New English Art Club
NEAF	Near East Air Force
Neb	Nebraska (US)
NEBSS	National Examinations Board for Supervisory Studies
NEC	National Executive Committee
NECCTA	National Educational Closed Circuit Television Association
NECInst	North-East Coast Institution of Engineers and Shipbuilders
NEDC	National Economic Development Council; North East Development Council
NEDO	National Economic Development Office
NEL	National Engineering Laboratory
NERC	Natural Environment Research Council
Nev	Nevada (US)
New M	New Mexico (US)
NFC	National Freight Consortium (formerly Corporation, then Company)
NFER	National Foundation for Educational Research
NFS	National Fire Service
NFT	National Film Theatre
NFU	National Farmers' Union
NFWI	National Federation of Women's Institutes
NGO	Non-Governmental Organisation(s)
NH	New Hampshire (US)
NHBC	National House-Building Council
NHS	National Health Service
NI	Northern Ireland; Native Infantry
NIAB	National Institute of Agricultural Botany
NIACRO	Northern Ireland Association for the Care and Resettlement of Offenders
NIAE	National Institute of Agricultural Engineering
NICG	Nationalised Industries Chairmen's Group
NICS	Northern Ireland Civil Service
NID	Naval Intelligence Division; National Institute for the Deaf; Northern Ireland District
NIESR	National Institute of Economic and Social Research
NIH	National Institutes of Health (US)
NILP	Northern Ireland Labour Party
NJ	New Jersey (US)
NL	National Liberal
NLF	National Liberal Federation
NNOM	Nigerian National Order of Merit
Northants	Northamptonshire
Notts	Nottinghamshire
NP	Notary Public
NPFA	National Playing Fields Association
NPk	Nishan-e-Pakistan
NPL	National Physical Laboratory
NRA	National Rifle Association; National Recovery Administration

THE
CHEST, HEART AND STROKE
ASSOCIATION

Patron: HER MAJESTY THE QUEEN
President: H.R.H. The Duke of Kent

We Care about people who suffer from

ASTHMA | CORONARY THROMBOSIS | LUNG CANCER
EMPHYSEMA | STROKE | TUBERCULOSIS
CHRONIC BRONCHITIS | ANGINA | HYPERTENSION

and other conditions of the chest and heart. We do all we can to help.
PLEASE HELP US by sending a donation, taking out a Deed of
Covenant or remembering us in your Will

The Association works throughout the United Kingdom for the prevention of Chest, Heart and Stroke illnesses and to help those who suffer from them. This is done by a continuing programme of Research, Rehabilitation, Health Education, Counselling and Welfare services.

We sponsor research projects concentrating on Chronic Bronchitis, Asthma, Emphysema and Stroke. We also sponsor schemes using voluntary workers to help Stroke patients with speech and language difficulties. By 1982 these schemes were active in 42 districts with 2,500 volunteers helping over 1,000 patients.

In the field of Health Education, we produce publications advising on the prevention of Chest, Heart and Stroke illnesses and giving patients a fuller understanding of their disabilities. In 1981 we responded to over 27,000 requests for help and advice from people suffering from these illnesses, as compared with some 12,000 dealt with in 1978.

We also, on the advice of Social Workers, make Welfare grants to individuals, mainly for fuel bills— for which we receive an ever increasing number of applications—visits to hospitals and convalescent holidays. In 1981 we helped over 1,200 individuals in this way. With greater resources the Association could help many more people.

WILL YOU HELP?

THE CHEST, HEART AND STROKE ASSOCIATION
TAVISTOCK HOUSE NORTH, TAVISTOCK SQUARE,
LONDON WC1H 9JE. 01-387 3012
and 52, North Castle Street, Edinburgh EH2 3LT.
031-225 6527

Chairman: The Rt. Hon. Lord Hill of Luton, MD. Director General: Sir Ernest Sidey, KBE, CB, MD

Reg. Charity No. 211015

NRD	National Registered Designer
NRDC	National Research Development Corporation
NRPB	National Radiological Protection Board
NRR	Northern Rhodesia Regiment
NS	Nova Scotia; New Style in the Calendar (in Great Britain since 1752); National Society; National Service
	Graduate of Royal Naval Staff College, Greenwich
NSA	National Skating Association
NSAIV	Distinguished Order of Shaheed Ali (Maldives)
NSMHC	National Society for Mentally Handicapped Children *(now see* Mencap)
NSPCC	National Society for Prevention of Cruelty to Children
NSRA	National Small-bore Rifle Association
NSSF	Novice, Society of St Francis
NSTC	Nova Scotia Technical College
NSW	New South Wales
NT	New Testament; Northern Territory (Australia); National Theatre; National Trust
NTDA	National Trade Development Association
NUAAW	National Union of Agricultural and Allied Workers
NUBE	National Union of Bank Employees *(now see* BIFU)
NUFLAT	National Union of Footwear Leather and Allied Trades
NUGMW	National Union of General and Municipal Workers *(now see* GMWU)
NUHKW	National Union of Hosiery and Knitwear Workers
NUI	National University of Ireland
NUJ	National Union of Journalists
NUM	National Union of Mineworkers
NUPE	National Union of Public Employees
NUR	National Union of Railwaymen
NUT	National Union of Teachers
NUTG	National Union of Townswomen's Guilds
NUTN	National Union of Trained Nurses
NUU	New University of Ulster
NW	North-west
NWFP	North-West Frontier Province
NWP	North-Western Province
NWT	North-Western Territories
NY	New York
NYC	New York City
NYO	National Youth Orchestra
NZ	New Zealand
NZEF	New Zealand Expeditionary Force
NZIA	New Zealand Institute of Architects

O

O	Ohio (US)
o	only
OA	Officier d'Académie
O & E	Operations and Engineers (US)
O & M	organisation and method
O & O	Oriental and Occidental Steamship Co.
OAS	Organisation of American States; On Active Service
OAU	Organisation for African Unity
ob	died
OBE	Officer, Order of the British Empire
OBI	Order of British India
OC	Officer of the Order of Canada (equivalent to former award SM)
o c	only child
OC and o/c	Officer Commanding
OCA	Old Comrades Association
OCDS, ocds Can	Overseas College of Defence Studies (Canada)
OCF	Officiating Chaplain to the Forces
OCSC	Oxford and Cambridge Shakespeare Society
OCTU	Officer Cadet Training Unit
OD	Officer of the Order of Distinction (Jamaica)
ODA	Overseas Development Administration
ODI	Overseas Development Institute
ODM	Ministry of Overseas Development
OE	Order of Excellence (Guyana)
OECD	Organization for Economic Co-operation and Development
OEEC	Organization for European Economic Co-operation *(now see* OECD)
OFEMA	Office Française d'Exportation de Matériel Aéronautique
OFM	Order of Friars Minor (Franciscans)
OFMCap	Order of Friars Minor Capuchin (Franciscans)
OFMConv	Order of Friars Minor Conventual (Franciscans)
OFR	Order of the Federal Republic (Nigeria)
OFS	Orange Free State
OFT	Office of Fair Trading
OHMS	On His (or Her) Majesty's Service
o i/c	Officer in charge
OJ	Order of Jamaica
OL	Officer of the Order of Leopold
OLM	Officer of Legion of Merit (Rhodesia)
OM	Order of Merit
OMI	Oblate of Mary Immaculate
OMM	Officer, Order of Military Merit (Canada)
ON	Order of the Nation (Jamaica)
Ont	Ontario

OON	Officer of the Order of the Niger
OP	*Ordinis Praedicatorum*: of the Order of Preachers (Dominican); Observation Post
OPCON	Operational Control
OPCS	Office of Population Censuses and Surveys
OR	Order of Rorima (Guyana); Operational Research
ORC	Orange River Colony
Ore	Oregon (US)
ORGALIME	Organisation de Liaison des Industries Mécaniques et Electriques
ORS	Operational Research Society
ORSL	Order of the Republic of Sierra Leone
ORT	Organization for Rehabilitation by Training
ORTF	Office de la Radiodiffusion et Télévision Française
o s	only son
OSA	Order of St Augustine (Augustinian); Ontario Society of Artists
OSB	Order of St Benedict (Benedictine)
OSFC	Franciscan (Capuchin) Order
O/Sig	Ordinary Signalman
OSNC	Orient Steam Navigation Co.
o s p	*obiit sine prole*
OSRD	Office of Scientific Research and Development
OSS	Office of Strategic Services
OStJ	Officer of Order of St John of Jerusalem
OSUK	Ophthalmological Society of the United Kingdom
OT	Old Testament
OTC	Officers' Training Corps
OTL	Officer of the Order of Toussaint L'Ouverture (Haiti)
OU	Oxford University; Open University
OUAC	Oxford University Athletic Club
OUAFC	Oxford University Association Football Club
OUBC	Oxford University Boat Club
OUCC	Oxford University Cricket Club
OUDS	Oxford University Dramatic Society
OUP	Oxford University Press; Official Unionist Party
OURC	Oxford University Rifle Club
OURFC	Oxford University Rugby Football Club
Oxon.	Oxfordshire; of Oxford

P

PA	Pakistan Army; Personal Assistant
Pa	Pennsylvania (US)
PAA	President, Australian Academy of Science
pac	passed the final examination of the Advanced Class, The Military College of Science
PACE	Protestant and Catholic Encounter
PAg	Professional Agronomist
P&O	Peninsular and Oriental Steamship Co.
P&OSNCo.	Peninsular and Oriental Steam Navigation Co.
PASI	Professional Associate, Chartered Surveyors' Institution *(now see* ARICS)
PBS	Public Broadcasting Service
PC	Privy Councillor; Police Constable; Perpetual Curate; Peace Commissioner (Ireland); Progressive Conservative (Canada)
pc	*per centum* (in the hundred)
PCC	Parochial Church Council
PCMO	Principal Colonial Medical Officer
PdD	Doctor of Pedagogy (US)
PDSA	People's Dispensary for Sick Animals
PE	Procurement Executive
PEI	Prince Edward Island
PEN	Poets, Playwrights, Editors, Essayists, Novelists (Club)
PEng	Registered Professional Engineer (Canada)
PEP	Political and Economic Planning *(now see* PSI)
PER	Professional and Executive Register
PEST	Pressure for Economic and Social Toryism
PETRAS	Polytechnic Educational Technology Resources Advisory Service
PF	Procurator-Fiscal
pfc	Graduate of RAF Flying College
PFE	Program for Executives
PGA	Professional Golfers' Association
PGCE	Post Graduate Certificate of Education
PH	Presidential Order of Honour (Botswana)
PHAB	Physically Handicapped & Able-bodied
PhB	Bachelor of Philosophy
PhC	Pharmaceutical Chemist
PhD	Doctor of Philosophy
Phil.	Philology, Philological; Philosophy, Philosophical
PhL	Licentiate of Philosophy
PhM	Master of Philosophy (USA)
PhmB	Bachelor of Pharmacy
Phys.	Physical
PIARC	Permanent International Association of Road Congresses
PIB	Prices and Incomes Board (see NBPI)
PICAO	Provisional International Civil Aviation Organization (now ICAO)
pinx.	(He) painted it
PIRA	Paper Industries Research Association
Pl.	Place; Plural

PLA	Port of London Authority
plc, PLC	public limited company
Plen.	Plenipotentiary
PLP	Parliamentary Labour Party
PMG	Postmaster-General
PMN	Panglima Mangku Negara (Malaysia)
PMO	Principal Medical Officer
PMRAFNS	Princess Mary's Royal Air Force Nursing Service
PMS	Presidential Order of Meritorious Service (Botswana); President Miniature Society
PNBS	Panglima Negara Bintang Sarawak
PNEU	Parents' National Educational Union
PNG	Papua New Guinea
PNP	People's National Party
PO	Post Office
POB	Presidential Order of Botswana
POMEF	Political Office Middle East Force
Pop.	Population
POW	Prisoner of War; Prince of Wales's
PP	Parish Priest; Past President
Pp	Pages
PPCLI	Princess Patricia's Canadian Light Infantry
PPE	Philosophy, Politics and Economics
PPInstHE	Past President, Institution of Highway Engineers
PPIStructE	Past President, Institution of Structural Engineers
PPITB	Printing and Publishing Industry Training Board
PPRA	Past President of the Royal Academy
PPRBA	Past President of the Royal Society of British Artists
PPRBS	Past President, Royal Society of British Sculptors
PPRE	Past President of the Royal Society of Painter-Etchers and Engravers
PPRTPI	Past President Royal Town Planning Institute
PPS	Parliamentary Private Secretary
PPSIAD	Past President of the Society of Industrial Artists and Designers
PQ	Province of Quebec
PRA	President of the Royal Academy
PRBS	President, Royal Society of British Sculptors
PRCS	President of the Royal College of Surgeons
PRE	President of the Royal Society of Painter-Etchers and Engravers
Preb.	Prebendary
PrEng.	Professional Engineer
Pres.	President
PRHA	President of the Royal Hibernian Academy
PRI	President of the Royal Institute of Painters in Water Colours; Plastics and Rubber Institute
PRIA	President of the Royal Irish Academy
Prin.	Principal
PRO	Public Relations Officer; Public Records Office
Proc.	Proctor; Proceedings
Prof.	Professor
PROI	President of the Royal Institute of Oil Painters
PRORM	Pay and Records Office, Royal Marines
Pro tem	*Pro tempore* (for the time being)
Prov.	Provost; Provincial
Prox.	*Proximo* (next)
Prox.acc.	*Proxime accessit* (next in order of merit to the winner, or a very close second)
PRS	President of the Royal Society; Performing Right Society Ltd
PRSA	President of the Royal Scottish Academy
PRSE	President of the Royal Society of Edinburgh
PRSH	President of the Royal Society for the Promotion of Health
PRSW	President of the Royal Scottish Water Colour Society
PRUAA	President of the Royal Ulster Academy of Arts
PRWA	President, Royal West of England Academy
PRWS	President of the Royal Society of Painters in Water Colours
PS	Pastel Society; Paddle Steamer
ps	passed School of Instruction (of Officers)
PSA	Property Services Agency
psa	Graduate of RAF Staff College
psc	Graduate of Staff College († indicates Graduate of Senior Wing Staff College)
PSD	Petty Sessional Division
PSGB	Pharmaceutical Society of Great Britain
PSI	Policy Studies Institute
PSIAD	President of the Society of Industrial Artists and Designers
PSM	Panglima Setia Mahkota (Malaysia)
psm	Certificate of Royal Military School of Music
PSMA	President of Society of Marine Artists
PSNC	Pacific Steam Navigation Co.
PSO	Principal Scientific Officer; Personal Staff Officer
PSSC	Personal Social Services Council
PTA	Passenger Transport Authority; Parent-Teacher Association
PTE	Passenger Transport Executive
Pte	Private (soldier)
ptsc	passed Technical Staff College
Pty	Proprietary
PUP	People's United Party
PVSM	Param Vishishc Seva Medal (India)
PWD	Public Works Department
PWO	Prince of Wales's Own

Q

Q	Queen
QAIMNS	Queen Alexandra's Imperial Military Nursing Service
QALAS	Qualified Associate Chartered Land Agents' Society (n~ (after amalgamation) *see* ARICS)
QARANC	Queen Alexandra's Royal Army Nursing Corps
QARNNS	Queen Alexandra's Royal Naval Nursing Service
QBD	Queen's Bench Division
QC	Queen's Counsel
QCVSA	Queen's Commendation for Valuable Service in the Air
QFSM	Queen's Fire Service Medal for Distinguished Service
QGM	Queen's Gallantry Medal
QHC	Queen's Honorary Chaplain
QHDS	Queen's Honorary Dental Surgeon
QHNS	Queen's Honorary Nursing Sister
QHP	Queen's Honorary Physician
QHS	Queen's Honorary Surgeon
Qld	Queensland
Qly	Quarterly
QMAAC	Queen Mary's Army Auxiliary Corps
QMC	Queen Mary College (London)
QMG	Quartermaster-General
QOOH	Queen's Own Oxfordshire Hussars
Q(ops)	Quartering (operations)
QPM	Queen's Police Medal
Qr	Quarter
QRIH	Queen's Royal Irish Hussars
QRV	Qualified Valuer, Real Estate Institute of New South Wale
QS	Quarter Sessions
qs	RAF graduates of the Military or Naval Staff College
QSM	Queen's Service Medal (NZ)
QSO	Queen's Service Order (NZ)
QUB	Queen's University, Belfast
qv	*quod vide* (which see)

R

(R)	Reserve
RA	Royal Academician; Royal Artillery
RAAF	Royal Australian Air Force
RAAMC	Royal Australian Army Medical Corps
RAC	Royal Automobile Club; Royal Agricultural College Royal Armoured Corps
RACGP	Royal Australian College of General Practitioners
RAChD	Royal Army Chaplains' Department
RACI	Royal Australian Chemical Institute
RACOG	Royal Australian College of Obstetricians and Gynaeco~ ogists
RACP	Royal Australasian College of Physicians
RACS	Royal Australasian College of Surgeons; Royal Arsen~ Co-operative Society
RADA	Royal Academy of Dramatic Art
RADAR	Royal Association for Disability and Rehabilitation
RADC	Royal Army Dental Corps
RAE	Royal Australian Engineers; Royal Aircraft Establishment
RAEC	Royal Army Educational Corps
RAeS	Royal Aeronautical Society
RAF	Royal Air Force
RAFA	Royal Air Force Association
RAFO	Reserve of Air Force Officers (*now see* RAFRO)
RAFRO	Royal Air Force Reserve of Officers
RAFVR	Royal Air Force Volunteer Reserve
RAI	Royal Anthropological Institute
RAIA	Royal Australian Institute of Architects
RAIC	Royal Architectural Institute of Canada
RAM	(Member of) Royal Academy of Music
RAMC	Royal Army Medical Corps
RAN	Royal Australian Navy
R&D	Research and Development
RANR	Royal Australian Naval Reserve
RANVR	Royal Australian Naval Volunteer Reserve
RAOC	Royal Army Ordnance Corps
RAPC	Royal Army Pay Corps
RARDE	Royal Armament Research and Development Establishmen~
RARO	Regular Army Reserve of Officers
RAS	Royal Astronomical Society; Royal Asiatic Society
RASC	Royal Army Service Corps (*now see* RCT)
RASE	Royal Agricultural Society of England
RAuxAF	Royal Auxiliary Air Force
RAVC	Royal Army Veterinary Corps
RB	Rifle Brigade
RBA	Member Royal Society of British Artists
RBC	Royal British Colonial Society of Artists
RBK&C	Royal Borough of Kensington and Chelsea
RBS	Royal Society of British Sculptors
RBSA	Royal Birmingham Society of Artists
RBY	Royal Bucks Yeomanry
RC	Roman Catholic

A	Member Royal Canadian Academy of Arts; Royal College of Art; Royal Cambrian Academy *(now see RCamA)*
AC	Royal Canadian Armoured Corps
AF	Royal Canadian Air Force
amA	Member Royal Cambrian Academy
AS	Royal Central Asian Society *(now see RSAA)*
DS	Royal College of Defence Studies
s	Completed a Course at, or served for a year on the Staff of, the Royal College of Defence Studies
GP	Royal College of General Practitioners
HA	Royal Canadian Horse Artillery
HM	Royal Commission on Historical Monuments
M	Royal College of Music
N	Royal Canadian Navy; Royal College of Nursing
NC	Royal Corps of Naval Constructors
NR	Royal Canadian Naval Reserve
NVR	Royal Canadian Naval Volunteer Reserve
O	Royal College of Organists
OG	Royal College of Obstetricians and Gynaecologists
P	Royal College of Physicians, London
Path	Royal College of Pathologists
PE and RCPEd	Royal College of Physicians of Edinburgh
PI	Royal College of Physicians of Ireland
PGlas	Royal College of Physicians and Surgeons, Glasgow
R	Royal College of Radiologists
S	Royal College of Surgeons of England; Royal Corps of Signals; Royal College of Science
SE and RCSEd	Royal College of Surgeons of Edinburgh
SI	Royal College of Surgeons in Ireland
T	Royal Corps of Transport
VS	Royal College of Veterinary Surgeons
•	Rural Dean; Royal Navy Reserve Decoration
	Road
A	Royal Defence Academy
C	Rural District Council
F	Royal Dublin Fusiliers
I	Royal Designer for Industry (Royal Society of Arts)
S	Royal Dublin Society
	Royal Engineers; Fellow of Royal Society of Painter-Etchers and Engravers
ar-Adm.	Rear-Admiral
conS	Royal Economic Society
g. Prof.	Regius Professor
gt	Regiment
ME	Royal Electrical and Mechnical Engineers
PC	Regional Economic Planning Council
RO	Royal Engineers Reserve of Officers
S	Royal Empire Society *(now Royal Commonwealth Society)*
s.	Resigned; Reserve; Resident; Research
v.	Reverend; Review
FA	Royal Field Artillery
FC	Royal Flying Corps *(now RAF)*; Rugby Football Club
FN	Registered Fever Nurse
FPS(G)	Royal Faculty of Physicians and Surgeons, Glasgow*(now see RCPGlas)*
FR	Rassemblement des Français pour la République
FU	Rugby Football Union
GA	Royal Garrison Artillery
GI	Royal Glasgow Institute of the Fine Arts
GJ	Royal Green Jackets
GN	Registered General Nurse
GS	Royal Geographical Society
GSA	Royal Geographical Society of Australasia
HA	Royal Hibernian Academy; Royal Horse Artillery; Regional Health Authority
HAS	Royal Highland and Agricultural Society of Scotland
HB	Regional Hospital Board
HF	Royal Highland Fusiliers
HG	Royal Horse Guards
HistS	Royal Historical Society
HR	Royal Highland Regiment
HS	Royal Horticultural Society; Royal Humane Society
I	Member Royal Institute of Painters in Water Colours; Rhode Island
IA	Royal Irish Academy
IAM	Royal Irish Academy of Music
IAS	Royal Incorporation of Architects in Scotland
IASC	Royal Indian Army Service Corps
IBA	Royal Institute of British Architects; *also* Member of the Institute
IBI	Rotary International in Great Britain and Ireland
IC	Royal Irish Constabulary; Royal Institute of Chemistry *(now see RSC)*
ICS	Royal Institution of Chartered Surveyors
IE	Royal Indian Engineering (College)
IF	Royal Inniskilling Fusiliers
IIA	Royal Institute of International Affairs
IM	Royal Indian Marines
IN	Royal Indian Navy
INA	Royal Institution of Naval Architects
IPA	Royal Institute of Public Administration
IPH&H	Royal Institute of Public Health and Hygiene
IrF	Royal Irish Fusiliers
RLSS	Royal Life Saving Society
RM	Royal Marines; Resident Magistrate
RMA	Royal Marine Artillery; Royal Military Academy Sandhurst *(now* incorporating Royal Military Academy, Woolwich)
RMB	Rural Mail Base
RMC	Royal Military College Sandhurst *(now see RMA)*
RMCS	Royal Military College of Science
RMedSoc	Royal Medical Society, Edinburgh
RMetS	Royal Meteorological Society
RMFVR	Royal Marine Forces Volunteer Reserve
RMIT	Royal Melbourne Institute of Technology
RMLI	Royal Marine Light Infantry
RMN	Registered Mental Nurse
RMO	Resident Medical Officer(s)
RMPA	Royal Medico-Phychological Association
RMS	Royal Microscopical Society; Royal Mail Steamer; Royal Society of Miniature Painters
RN	Royal Navy; Royal Naval
RNAS	Royal Naval Air Service
RNAY	Royal Naval Aircraft Yard
RNC	Royal Naval College
RNCM	(Member of) Royal Northern College of Music
RNEC	Royal Naval Engineering College
RNIB	Royal National Institute for the Blind
RNID	Royal National Institute for the Deaf
RNLI	Royal National Life-boat Institution
RNR	Royal Naval Reserve
RNS	Royal Numismatic Society
RNT	Registered Nurse Tutor
RNUR	Régie Nationale des Usines Renault
RNVR	Royal Naval Volunteer Reserve
RNVSR	Royal Naval Volunteer Supplementary Reserve
RNZAC	Royal New Zealand Armoured Corps
RNZAF	Royal New Zealand Air Force
RNZIR	Royal New Zealand Infantry Regiment
RNZN	Royal New Zealand Navy
RNZNVR	Royal New Zealand Naval Volunteer Reserve
ROC	Royal Observer Corps
ROF	Royal Ordnance Factories
R of O	Reserve of Officers
ROI	Member Royal Institute of Oil Painters
RoSPA	Royal Society for the Prevention of Accidents
(Rot.)	Rotunda Hospital, Dublin (after degree)
RP	Member Royal Society of Portrait Painters
RPC	Royal Pioneer Corps
RPMS	Royal Postgraduate Medical School
RPO	Royal Philharmonic Orchestra
RPS	Royal Photographic Society
RRC	Royal Red Cross
RRE	Royal Radar Establishment
RRS	Royal Research Ship
RSA	Royal Scottish Academician; Royal Society of Arts; Republic of South Africa
RSAA	Royal Society for Asian Affairs
RSAF	Royal Small Arms Factory
RSAI	Royal Society of Antiquaries of Ireland
RSAMD	Royal Scottish Academy of Music and Drama
RSanI	Royal Sanitary Institute *(now see RSH)*
RSC	Royal Society of Canada; Royal Society of Chemistry; Royal Shakespeare Company
RSCM	Royal School of Church Music
RSCN	Registered Sick Children's Nurse
RSE	Royal Society of Edinburgh
RSF	Royal Scots Fusiliers
RSFSR	Russian Socialist Federated Soviet Republic
RSGS	Royal Scottish Geographical Society
RSH	Royal Society for the Promotion of Health
RSL	Royal Society of Literature; Returned Services League of Australia
RSM	Royal School of Mines
RSM or RSocMed	Royal Society of Medicine
RSMA	Royal Society of Marine Artists
RSNC	Royal Society for Nature Conservation
RSO	Rural Sub-Office; Railway Sub-Office; Resident Surgical Officer
RSPB	Royal Society for Protection of Birds
RSPCA	Royal Society for Prevention of Cruelty to Animals
RSSAILA	Returned Sailors, Soldiers and Airmen's Imperial League of Australia *(now see RSL)*
RSSPCC	Royal Scottish Society for Prevention of Cruelty to Children
RSW	Member Royal Scottish Water Colour Society
RTE	Radio Telefís Eireann
Rt Hon.	Right Honourable
RTO	Railway Transport Officer
RTPI	Royal Town Planning Institute
RTR	Royal Tank Regiment
Rt Rev.	Right Reverend
RTS	Religious Tract Society; Royal Toxophilite Society; Royal Television Society
RTYC	Royal Thames Yacht Club
RU	Rugby Union
RUC	Royal Ulster Constabulary
RUI	Royal University of Ireland
RUKBA	Royal United Kingdom Beneficent Association

RUR	Royal Ulster Regiment
RUSI	Royal United Services Institute for Defence Studies *(formerly* Royal United Service Institution)
RVC	Royal Veterinary College
RWA (RWEA)	Member, Royal West of England Academy
RWAFF	Royal West African Frontier Force
RWF	Royal Welch Fusiliers
RWS	Member of Royal Society of Painters in Water Colours
RYA	Royal Yachting Association
RYS	Royal Yacht Squadron
RZSScot	Royal Zoological Society of Scotland

S

(S)	(in Navy) Paymaster
S	Succeeded; South; Saint
s	Son
SA	South Australia; South Africa; Société Anonyme
SAAF	South African Air Force
SACEUR	Supreme Allied Commander (Europe)
SACLANT	Supreme Allied Commander Atlantic
SACSEA	Supreme Allied Command, SE Asia
SA de CV	sociedad anónima de capital variable
SADF	Sudanese Auxiliary Defence Force
SADG	Société des Architectes Diplômés par le Gouvernement
SAE	Society of Automobile Engineers (US)
SAMC	South African Medical Corps
Sarum	Salisbury
SAS	Special Air Service
Sask	Saskatchewan
SASO	Senior Air Staff Officer
SATRO	Science and Technology Regional Organisation
SB	Bachelor of Science (US)
SBAC	Society of British Aerospace Companies *(formerly* Society of British Aircraft Constructors)
SBStJ	Serving Brother, Order of St John of Jerusalem
SC	Star of Courage (Canada); Senior Counsel (Eire, Guyana, South Africa); South Carolina (US)
sc	Student at the Staff College
SCAO	Senior Civil Affairs Officer
SCAPA	Society for Checking the Abuses of Public Advertising
SCAR	Scientific Committee for Antarctic Research
ScD	Doctor of Science
SCF	Senior Chaplain to the Forces; Save the Children Fund
Sch.	School
SCL	Student in Civil Law
SCM	State Certified Midwife; Student Christian Movement
SCONUL	Standing Conference of National and University Libraries
Sculpt.	Sculptor
SDA	Social Democratic Alliance
SDak	South Dakota (US)
SDB	Salesian of Don Bosco
SDF	Sudan Defence Force; Social Democratic Federation
SDLP	Social Democratic and Labour Party
SDP	Social Democratic Party
SE	South-east
SEAC	South-East Asia Command
SEALF	South-East Asia Land Forces
SEATO	South-East Asia Treaty Organization
Sec.	Secretary
SEE	Society of Environmental Engineers
SEN	State Enrolled Nurse
SERC	Science and Engineering Research Council
SESO	Senior Equipment Staff Officer
SFInstE	Senior Fellow, Institute of Energy
SFInstF	Senior Fellow, Institute of Fuel *(now see* SFInstE)
SFTA	Society of Film and Television Arts *(now see* BAFTA)
SFTCD	Senior Fellow, Trinity College Dublin
SG	Solicitor-General
SGA	Member Society of Graphic Art
SGBI	Schoolmistresses' and Governesses' Benevolent Institution
Sgt	Sergeant
SHA	Secondary Heads Association; Special Health Authority
SHAEF	Supreme Headquarters, Allied Expeditionary Force
SHAPE	Supreme Headquarters, Allied Powers, Europe
SHHD	Scottish Home and Health Department
SIAD	Society of Industrial Artists and Designers
SIB	Shipbuilding Industry Board
SICOT	Société Internationale de Chirurgie Orthopédique et de Traumatologie
SID	Society for International Development
SIMA	Scientific Instrument Manufacturers' Association of Great Britain
SIME	Security Intelligence Middle East
SIMG	*Societas Internationalis Medicinae Generalis*
SinDrs	Doctor of Chinese
SITA	Société Internationale de Télécommunications Aéronautiques
SITPRO	Simplification of International Trade Procedures
SJ	Society of Jesus (Jesuits)
SJAB	St John Ambulance Brigade
SJD	Doctor of Juristic Science

SL	Serjeant-at-Law
SLA	Special Libraries Association
SLAET	Society of Licensed Aircraft Engineers and Technologists
SLAS	Society for Latin-American Studies
SLP	Scottish Labour Party
SM	Medal of Service (Canada) *(now see* OC); Master of Scien Officer qualified for Submarine Duties
SMA	Society of Marine Artists *(now see* RSMA)
SME	School of Military Engineering
SMIEEE	Senior Member of Institute of Electrical and Electron Engineers (NY)
SMIRE	Senior Member Institute of Radio Engineers (New York)
SMMT	Society of Motor Manufacturers and Traders Ltd
SMN	Seri Maharaja Mangku Negara (Malaysia)
SMO	Senior Medical Officer; Sovereign Military Order
SMPTE	Society of Motion Picture and Television Engineers (US)
SMRTB	Ship and Marine Requirements Technology Board
SNAME	Society of Naval Architects and Marine Engineers (US)
SNCF	Société Nationale des Chemins de Fer Français
SNP	Scottish National Party
SNTS	Society for New Testament Studies
SO	Staff Officer
SOAS	School of Oriental and African Studies
Soc.	Society
SocCE(France)	Société des Ingénieurs Civils de France
SODEPAX	Committee on Society, Development and Peace
SOE	Special Operations Executive
SOGAT	Society of Graphical and Allied Trades
sowc	Senior Officers' War Course
sp	*sine prole* (without issue)
SP	Self-Propelled (Anti-Tank Regiment)
SPAB	Society for the Protection of Ancient Buildings
SPCK	Society for Promoting Christian Knowledge
SPD	Salisbury Plain District
SPDK	Seri Panglima Darjal Kinabalu
SPG	Society for the Propagation of the Gospel *(now see* USPG)
SPk	Sitara-e-Pakistan
SPMB	Seri Paduka Makhota Brunei
SPMO	Senior Principal Medical Officer
SPNC	Society for the Promotion of Nature Conservation *(now s* RSNC)
SPRC	Society for Prevention and Relief of Cancer
sprl	société de personnes à responsabilité limitée
SPSO	Senior Principal Scientific Officer
SPTL	Society of Public Teachers of Law
Sq.	Square
SQA	Sitara-i-Quaid-i-Azam
Sqdn, Sqn	Squadron
SR	Special Reserve; Southern Railway; Southern Region (B Representative Council
SRC	Science Research Council *(now see* SERC); Student
SRHE	Society for Research into Higher Education
SRN	State Registered Nurse
SRNA	Shipbuilders and Repairers National Association
SRO	Supplementary Reserve of Officers
SRP	State Registered Physiotherapist
SRY	Sherwood Rangers Yeomanry
SS	Saints; Straits Settlements; Steamship
SSA	Society of Scottish Artists
SSAFA, SS&AFA	Soldiers', Sailors', and Airmen's Families Assoc ation
SSC	Solicitor before Supreme Court (Scotland); Sculptors Socie of Canada
SSEB	South of Scotland Electricity Board
SSEES	School of Slavonic and East European Studies
SSJE	Society of St John the Evangelist
SSM	Society of the Sacred Mission
SSO	Senior Supply Officer
SSRC	Social Science Research Council
SStJ	Serving Sister, Order of St John of Jerusalem
St	Street; Saint
STB	*Sacrae Theologiae Baccalaureus* (Bachelor of Sacre Theology)
STC	Senior Training Corps
STD	*Sacrae Theologiae Doctor* (Doctor of Sacred Theology)
STh	Scholar in Theology
Stip.	Stipend; Stipendiary
STL	*Sacrae Theologiae Lector* (Reader or a Professor of Sacre Theology)
STM	*Sacrae Theologiae Magister* (Master of Sacred Theology)
STP	*Sacrae Theologiae Professor* (Professor of Divinity, old for of DD)
STRIVE	Society for Preservation of Rural Industries and Villag Enterprises
STSO	Senior Technical Staff Officer
Supp. Res.	Supplementary Reserve (of Officers)
Supt	Superintendent
Surg.	Surgeon
Surv.	Surviving
SW	South-west
SWET	Society of West End Theatre
SWIA	Society of Wildlife Artists
SWPA	South West Pacific Area
Syd.	Sydney

T

	Telephone; Territorial
	Telegraphic Address; Territorial Army
A	Territorial Army Association
&VRA	Territorial Auxiliary and Volunteer Reserve Association
F	Tactical Air Force
AFA	Territorial and Auxiliary Forces Association
AVR	Territorial and Army Volunteer Reserve
NS	Territorial Army Nursing Service
NU	Tanganyika African National Union
RO	Territorial Army Reserve of Officers
S	Torpedo and Anti Submarine Course
	Order of the Trinity Cross (Trinidad and Tobago)
CB	Test and County Cricket Board
D	Trinity College, Dublin (University of Dublin, Trinity College)
F	Temporary Chaplain to the Forces
PA	Town and Country Planning Association
	Territorial Efficiency Decoration; Efficiency Decoration (T&AVR) (since April 1967); (Teachta Dala) Member of the Dail, Eire
D	Tubercular Diseases Diploma
AC	Technical Educational Advisory Council
C	Technician Education Council
ch(CEI)	Technician
M	Territorial Efficiency Medal
MA	Telecommunications Engineering Manufacturers' Association
mp.	Temperature; Temporary
ng (CEI)	Technician Engineer
nn	Tennessee (US)
olD	Doctor of Theology
ES	Times Educational Supplement
ET	Teacher of Electrotherapy
ex	Texas (US)
F	Territorial Force
FR	Territorial Force Reserve
GEW	Timber Growers England and Wales Ltd
GO	Timber Growers' Organisation (now see TGEW)
GWU	Transport and General Workers' Union
HELEP	Therapy of Leprosy
HES	Times Higher Education Supplement
hL	Theological Licentiate
hSchol	Scholar in Theology
IMS	The Institute of Management Sciences
LS	Times Literary Supplement .
MMG	Teacher of Massage and Medical Gymnastics
NC	Theatres National Committee
OSD	Tertiary Order of St Dominic
P	Transvaal Province
PI	Town Planning Institute (now see RTPI)
ans.	Translation; Translated
ransf.	Transferred
RC	Thames Rowing Club
RE	Telecommunications Research Establishment (now see RRE)
RH	Their Royal Highnesses
rin.	Trinity
RRL	Transport and Road Research Laboratory
SB	Trustee Savings Bank
c	passed a Territorial Army Course in Staff Duties
SD	Tertiary of St Dominic
UC	Trades Union Congress
V	Television
YC	Thames Yacht Club (now see RTYC)

U

)	Unionist
	Uncle
AE	United Arab Emirates
AR	United Arab Republic
AU	Universities Athletic Union
C	University College
CCA	Universities Central Council on Admissions
CET	Universities Council for Education of Teachers
CH	University College Hospital (London)
CL	University College London
CLA	University of California at Los Angeles
CNS	Universities' Council for Non-academic Staff
CNW	University College of North Wales
CS	University College School
CW	University College of Wales; Union of Communication Workers
DC	Urban District Council
DF	Union Defence Force
DR	Ulster Defence Regiment; Union des Démocrates pour la Vème République (now see RFR)

UEA	University of East Anglia
UED	University Education Diploma
UEFA	Union of European Football Associations
UF	United Free Church
UGC	University Grants Committee
UJD	*Utriusque Juris Doctor*, Doctor of both Laws (Doctor of Canon and Civil Law)
UK	United Kingdom
UKAC	United Kingdom Automation Council
UKAEA	United Kingdom Atomic Energy Authority
UKISC	United Kingdom Industrial Space Committee
UKLF	United Kingdom Land Forces
UKSLS	United Kingdom Services Liaison Staff
UMIST	University of Manchester Institute of Science and Technology
UN	United Nations
UNA	United Nations Association
UNCAST	United Nations Conference on the Applications of Science and Technology
UNCIO	United Nations Conference on International Organisation
UNCSTD	United Nations Conference on Science and Technology for Development
UNCTAD (Unctad)	United Nations Commission for Trade and Development
UNDP	United Nations Development Programme
UNDRO	United Nations Disaster Relief Organisation
UNECA	United Nations Economic Commission for Asia
UNEP	United Nations Environment Programme
UNESCO (Unesco)	United Nations Educational, Scientific and Cultural Organisation
UNFAO	United Nations Food and Agriculture Organisation
UNFICYP	United Nations Force in Cyprus
UNHCR	United Nations High Commissioner for Refugees
UNICEF (Unicef)	United Nations Children's Fund (*formerly* United Nations International Children's Emergency Fund)
UNIDO	United Nations Industrial Development Organisation
UNIDROIT	Institut International pour l'Unification du Droit Privé
UNIPEDE	Union Internationale des Producteurs et Distributeurs d'Energie Electrique
UNISIST	Universal System for Information in Science and Technology
UNITAR	United Nations Institute of Training and Research
Univ.	University
UNRRA	United Nations Relief and Rehabilitation Administration
UNRWA	United Nations Relief and Works Agency
UNSCOB	United Nations Special Commission on the Balkans
UP	United Provinces; Uttar Pradesh; United Presbyterian
UPGC	University and Polytechnic Grants Committee
UPNI	Unionist Party of Northern Ireland
URC	United Reformed Church
URSI	Union Radio-Scientifique Internationale
US	United States
USA	United States of America
USAAF	United States Army Air Force
USAF	United States Air Force
USAID	United States Agency for International Development
USAR	United States Army Reserve
USC	University of Southern California
USDAW	Union of Shop Distributive and Allied Workers
USMA	United States Military Academy
USN	United States Navy
USNR	United States Naval Reserve
USPG	United Society for the Propagation of the Gospel
USPHS	United States Public Health Service
USS	United States Ship
USSR	Union of Soviet Socialist Republics
UTC	University Training Corps
(UU)	Ulster Unionist
(UUUC)	United Ulster Unionist Coalition
(UUUP)	United Ulster Unionist Party
UWIST	University of Wales Institute of Science and Technology
UWT	Union of Women Teachers

V

V	Five (Roman numerals); Version; Vicar; Viscount; *Vice*
v	*Versus* (against)
v or vid.	*Vide* (see)
Va	Virginia (US)
VAD	Voluntary Aid Detachment
V&A	Victoria and Albert
VAT	Value Added Tax
VC	Victoria Cross
VCAS	Vice-Chief of the Air Staff
VCDS	Vice-Chief of the Defence Staff
VCNS	Vice-Chief of Naval Staff
VD	Royal Naval Volunteer Reserve Officers' Decoration (now VRD); Volunteer Officers' Decoration; Victorian Decoration
VDC	Volunteer Defence Corps
Ven.	Venerable (of an Archdeacon)
Very Rev.	Very Reverend (of a Dean)
Vet.	Veterinary

VG   Vicar-General
VHS   Hon. Surgeon to Viceroy of India
VIC   Victoria Institute of Colleges
Vice-Adm.   Vice-Admiral
Visc.   Viscount
VM   Victory Medal
VMH   Victoria Medal of Honour (Royal Horticultural Society)
Vol.   Volume; Volunteers
VP   Vice-President
VPP   Volunteer Political Party
VQMG   Vice-Quartermaster-General
VR   *Victoria Regina* (Queen Victoria)
VRD   Royal Naval Volunteer Reserve Officers' Decoration
VSO   Voluntary Service Overseas
Vt   Vermont (US)
(VUP)   Vanguard Unionist Party

WNO   Welsh National Opera
WO   War Office
Worcs   Worcestershire
WOSB   War Office Selection Board
WR   West Riding; Western Region (BR)
WRAC   Women's Royal Army Corps
WRAF   Women's Royal Air Force
WRNS   Women's Royal Naval Service
WRVS   Women's Royal Voluntary Service
WS   Writer to the Signet
WSPU   Women's Social and Political Union
WUS   World University Service
WVa   West Virginia (US)
WVS   Women's Voluntary Services *(now see* WRVS)
WWF   World Wildlife Fund
Wyo   Wyoming (US)

W

W   West
WA   Western Australia
WAAF   Women's Auxiliary Air Force *(now see* WRAF)
Wash   Washington State (US)
WCC   World Council of Churches
W/Cdr   Wing Commander
WEA   Workers' Educational Association; Royal West of England
              Academy
WES/PNEU   Worldwide Education Service of Parents' National
              Educational Union
WEU   Western European Union
WFSW   World Federation of Scientific Workers
WFTU   World Federation of Trade Unions
WHO   World Health Organization
WhSch   Whitworth Scholar
WI   West Indies; Women's Institute
Wilts   Wiltshire
Wis   Wisconsin (US)
Wits   Witwatersrand
WJEC   Welsh Joint Education Committee
WLA   Women's Land Army
WLF   Women's Liberal Federation
Wm   William
WMO   World Meteorological Organization

X

X   Ten (Roman numerals)

Y

y   youngest
YC   Young Conservative
YCNAC   Young Conservatives National Advisory Committee
Yeo.   Yeomanry
YHA   Youth Hostels Association
YMCA   Young Men's Christian Association
Yorks   Yorkshire
yr   younger
yrs   years
YVFF   Young Volunteer Force Foundation
YWCA   Young Women's Christian Association

Z

ZANU   Zimbabwe African National Union

OBITUARY

Deaths notified from mid-November 1981 to mid-November 1982

Adair, Arthur Robin, CVO, MBE, 26 Dec. 1981.
Adam, Colin Gurdon Forbes, CSI, 12 Nov. 1982.
Adams, Sir Maurice Edward, KBE, 23 Jan. 1982.
Addington, 5th Baron; James Hubbard, 26 June 1982.
Addleshaw, Very Rev. George William Outram, 14 June 1982.
Aitken, Dr Janet Kerr, CBE, 21 April 1982.
Aitken, Air Vice-Marshal (Robert) Stanley, CB, CBE, MC, AFC, 21 Jan. 1982.
Allan, John Arthur Briscoe, CMG, 30 Nov. 1981.
Allen, Arthur Cecil   [*Deceased.*
Allen, Rt Rev. Geoffrey Francis, DD, 8 Nov. 1982.
Allen, Prof. George Cyril, CBE, FBA, 31 July 1982.
Allen, James Godfrey Colquhoun, CMG, 12 Nov. 1982.
Alty, Thomas, 2 May 1982.
Alvin, Juliette Louise, 30 Sept. 1982.
Amoroso, Prof. Emmanuel Ciprian, CBE, TC, FRS, 30 Oct. 1982.
Ansett, Sir Reginald Myles, KBE, 23 Dec. 1981.
Armer, Sir (Isaac) Frederick, KBE, CB, MC, 15 Nov. 1982.
Armstrong, Rev. Canon Claude Blakeley, 18 Oct. 1982.
Askey, Arthur Bowden, CBE, 16 Nov. 1982.
Aston, Sir Christopher Southcote, KCVO, 25 Jan. 1982.

Bacon, Sir Edmund Castell, 13th and 14th Bt, KG, KBE, TD, 30 Sept. 1982.
Badel, Alan, 19 March 1982.
Bader, Group Captain Sir Douglas Robert Steuart, CBE, DSO, DFC, 4 Sept. 1982.
Baker, Richard St Barbe, OBE, 9 June 1982.
Balmain, Pierre Alexandre, 29 June 1982.
Banwell, Sir (George) Harold, 10 April 1982.
Barker, Brig. Lewis Ernest Stephen, CBE, DSO,MC, 13 Dec. 1981.
Barlas, Sir Richard Douglas, KCB, OBE, 10 Nov. 1982.
Barnby, 2nd Baron; Francis Vernon Willey, CMG, CBE, MVO, 30 April 1982 (*ext*).
Barnes, Harold William   [*Deceased.*
Barnes, Sir Harry Jefferson, CBE, 31 May 1982.
Bastin, Brig. David Terence, CBE, TD, 23 July 1982.
Battle, Richard John Vulliamy, MBE, 26 May 1982.
Bednall, Maj-Gen.Sir (Cecil Norbury) Peter, KBE, CB, MC, 28 May 1982.
Beecham, Sir Adrian Welles, 3rd Bt, 4 Sept. 1982.
Bell, Sir Ronald McMillan, QC, MP, 27 Feb. 1982.
Bellamy, Dr Lionel John, CBE, 9 May 1982.
Beovich, Most Rev. Matthew, DD   [*Deceased.*
Bergman, Ingrid, 29 Aug. 1982.
Berry, Prof. Harry, 29 April 1982.
Bingham, Robert Porter, CMG, 29 May 1982.
Birley, Sir Robert, KCMG, 22 July 1982.
Biron, Sir (Moshe Chaim Efraim) Philip, 31 Dec. 1981.
Bishop, William Thomas, CBE, 16 Jan. 1982.
Blackburn, (Evelyn) Barbara   [*Deceased.*
Blackley, Travers Robert, CMG, CBE, 18 Feb. 1982.
Blakenham, 1st Viscount; John Hugh Hare, PC, OBE, VMH, 7 March 1982.
Blanco White, Amber, OBE, 26 Dec. 1981.
Blelloch, Ian William, CMG, 25 March 1982.
Boase, Alan Martin, 7 Nov. 1982.
Bodley Scott, Sir Ronald, GCVO, 12 May 1982.
Bolton, Sir George Lewis French, KCMG, 2 Sept. 1982.
Bolton, Captain Sir Ian Frederick Cheney, 2nd Bt, KBE, 12 Jan. 1982 (*ext*).
Borwick, Lt-Col Sir Thomas Faulkner, CIE, DSO, 12 Dec. 1981.
Boulton, Edward Henry Brooke, MC, 26 April 1982.
Boulton, Major Sir Edward John, 2nd Bt, 10 Aug. 1982.
Bourne, Baron (Life Peer); Geoffrey Kemp Bourne, GCB, KBE, CMG, 26 June 1982.
Boutwood, Rear-Adm. Laurence Arthur, CB, OBE, 29 July 1982.
Bowater, Sir Ian Frank, GBE, DSO, TD, 1 Oct. 1982.
Bower, Sir Frank, CBE, 1 Sept. 1982.
Bowring, Edgar Rennie, 6 April 1982.
Boyle, Rev. (John) Desmond, SJ, 12 Oct. 1982.
Bradley, Air Marshal Sir John Stanley Travers, KCB, CBE, 6 Jan. 1982.
Branson, Col Sir Douglas Stephenson, KBE, CB, DSO, MC, TD, 23 Nov. 1981.
Brezhnev, Leonid Ilyich, 10 Nov. 1982.
Bridgeman, 2nd Viscount; Robert Clive Bridgeman, KBE, CB, DSO, MC, 17 Nov. 1982.
Brooke, Maj.-Gen. Frank Hastings, CB, CBE, DSO, 25 Jan. 1982.
Brooke, Lt-Col Ralph, OBE, 16 Aug. 1982.
Brown, Rev. Canon Oscar Henry, CIE, OBE, 11 March 1982.
Browne, Brig. Dominick Andrew Sidney, CBE, 9 Sept. 1982.
Brunner, Sir Felix John Morgan, 3rd Bt, 2 Nov. 1982.

Brunskill, Brig. George Stephen, CBE, MC, 10 Nov. 1982.
Brunt, Robert Nigel Bright, CBE, 1 Jan. 1982.
Bull, Amy Frances, CBE, 6 Aug. 1982.
Bullough, Prof. Geoffrey, FBA, 12 Feb. 1982.
Burntwood, Baron (Life Peer); Julian Ward Snow, 24 Jan. 1982.
Bushe-Fox, Patrick Loftus, CMG, 2 June 1982.
Butler of Saffron Walden, Baron (Life Peer); Richard Austen Butler, KG, CH, PC, 8 March 1982.
Butler, Lionel Harry, 26 Nov. 1981.
Byford, Donald, CBE, 23 Nov. 1981.

Cadbury, Jocelyn Benedict Laurence, MP, 31 July 1982.
Cadbury, Laurence John, OBE, 5 Nov. 1982,
Campbell, Alan Johnston, CMG, 5 March 1982.
Canham, Erwin Dain, 3 Jan. 1982.
Cardwell, Sir David, KCB, 19 June 1982.
Carew, Major Robert John Henry, MC, 15 Nov. 1982.
Carlyon, Thomas Symington, CMG, OBE, 14 March 1982.
Carnock, 3rd Baron; Erskine Arthur Nicolson, DSO, 2 Oct. 1982.
Caroe, Sir Olaf Kirkpatrick, KCSI, KCIE, 23 Nov. 1981.
Carr, Edward Hallett, CBE, FBA, 3 Nov. 1982.
Carr, Brig. William Greenwood, CVO, DSO, 27 Jan. 1982.
Carritt, (Hugh) David (Graham), 3 Aug. 1982.
Carter, Edward Julian, 5 June 1982.
Carter, Harry Graham, OBE, 10 March 1982.
Carter, Malcolm Ogilvy, CIE, MC, 26 April 1982.
Cassie, Arnold Blatchford David, CBE, 16 March 1982.
Cavalcanti, Alberto de Almeida, 23 Aug. 1982.
Cazalet, Vice-Adm. Sir Peter Grenville Lyon, KBE, CB, DSO, DSC, 17 Feb. 1982.
Cecil-Wright, Air Cdre John Allan Cecil, AFC, TD, AE, 14 July 1982.
Chambers, Sir (Stanley) Paul, KBE, CB, CIE, 23 Dec. 1981.
Champion, Rev. Sir Reginald Stuart, KCMG, OBE, 9 Oct. 1982.
Chaplin, 3rd Viscount; Anthony Freskyn Charles Hamby Chaplin, 18 Dec. 1981 (*ext*).
Chapman, Very Rev. Clifford Thomas, 25 May 1982.
Charnley, Sir John, CBE, FRS, 5 Aug. 1982.
Cheever, John, 18 June 1982.
Cherniavsky, Mischel, 21 Feb. 1982.
Chetwynd, Sir George Roland, CBE, 2 Sept. 1982.
Childs, Leonard, CBE, 31 March 1982.
Chilston, 3rd Viscount; Eric Alexander Akers-Douglas, 10 April 1982.
Chilver, Prof. Guy Edward Farquhar, 7 Sept. 1982.
Chitty, Letitia, 29 Sept. 1982.
Chloros, Prof. Alexander George, 15 Nov. 1982.
Clarke, Sir Frederick Joseph   [*Deceased.*
Clarke, Gerald Bryan, CMG, ISO   [*Deceased.*
Cleall, Ven. Aubrey Victor George, 6 May 1982.
Clemitson, Rear-Adm. Francis Edward, CB, 27 Nov. 1981.
Cockburn, Claud, 15 Dec. 1981.
Cocker, Sir William Wiggins, OBE, 21 July 1982.
Cohen, Sir Jack, OBE, 7 Feb. 1982.
Coles, Captain Arthur Edward, RD, RNR, 8 Feb. 1982.
Collett, Rear-Adm. George Kempthorne, CB, DSC, 11 May 1982.
Collins, Norman Richard, 6 Sept. 1982.
Colville, Maj.-Gen. Edward Charles, CB, DSO, 10 Jan. 1982.
Compton, Eric Henry, CVO, 2 April 1982.
Condliffe, Prof. John Bell, Hon. KCMG, 23 Dec. 1981.
Coney, Rev. Canon Harold Robert Harvey, 6 Sept. 1982.
Corbett, Lt-Gen. Thomas William, CB, MC, 28 Dec. 1981.
Cordeaux, Lt-Col John Kyme, CBE, 4 Jan. 1982.
Cornish, Rt Rev. John Vernon Kestell, 26 Jan. 1982.
Cornwallis, 2nd Baron; Wykeham Stanley Cornwallis, KCVO, KBE, MC, 4 Jan. 1982.
Couchman, Dame Elizabeth May Ramsay, DBE, 18 Nov. 1982.
Courage, Edward Raymond, CBE, 3 July 1982.
Cox, Sir Christopher William Machell, GCMG, 6 July 1982.
Crawford, Hugh Adam, RSA, 2 March 1982.
Crawford, James, CBE, 15 July 1982.
Cresswell, William Foy, CBE, 21 Dec. 1981.
Cromwell, 6th Baron; David Godfrey Bewicke-Copley, 18 Aug. 1982.
Crossley, Prof. Eric Lomax, 13 June 1982.
Cudmore, Derek George, CBE, 20 Dec. 1981.
Cumming, Lt-Col Sir Ronald Stuart, TD, 17 Nov. 1982.
Cundiff, Major Frederick William, 7 Aug. 1982.
Curzon, Sir Clifford Michael,CBE, 1 Sept. 1982.

Dalling, Sir Thomas, 23 May 1982.
Dannatt, Sir Cecil, OBE, MC, 18 Dec. 1981.
Dannay, Frederic, 3 Sept. 1982.
Davies, Dr David Lewis, CBE, 24 Oct. 1982.
Davies, Eryl Oliver, 31 May 1982.

Davies, Rev. Canon George Colliss Boardman, DD, 21 April 1982.
Davies, Harold Haydn, CB, MC, 13 July 1982.
Davies, Ifor, MP, 6 June 1982.
Dawes, Charles Ambrose William, MC, 12 Jan. 1982.
Deacon, Lt-Col Edmund Henry, 20 Oct. 1982.
Dearnley, Gertrude, 14 March 1982.
de Clifford, 26th Baron; Edward Southwell Russell, OBE, TD, 3 Jan. 1982.
de Freitas, Rt Hon. Sir Geoffrey Stanley, PC, KCMG, 10 Aug. 1982.
Dempsey, James, MP, 12 May 1982.
de Normann, Sir Eric, KBE, CB, 25 Jan. 1982.
Deshmukh, Sir Chintaman Dwarkanath, CIE, 2 Oct. 1982.
Dickson, Dr David, CB, 4 Feb. 1982.
Dickson, Ian Anderson, WS, 10 April 1982.
Dillon, 21st Viscount; Charles Henry Robert Dillon, 15 Sept. 1982.
Dixey, Sir Frank, KCMG, OBE, FRS, 1 Nov. 1982.
Dobbie, Mitchell Macdonald, CB, 30 Oct. 1982.
Dodds, Gladys Helen, 5 Sept. 1982.
Dods, Sir Lorimer Fenton, MVO   [Deceased.
Dollar, Jean Marguerite, 20 April 1982.
Doubleday, John Gordon, OBE, 27 April 1982.
Douglas, Prof. David Charles, FBA, 12 Sept. 1982.
Downman, Prof. Charles Beaumont Benoy, 4 Jan. 1982.
Doyle, Brig. Richard Stanislaus, CBE, 15 Jan. 1982.
Driver, His Honour Major Arthur Robert   [Deceased.
Drummond-Wolff, Henry, 8 Feb. 1982.
Duncan, Ronald Frederick Henry, 3 June 1982.
Dunlop, Roy Leslie, CMG, 7 Dec. 1981.
Durlacher, Sir Esmond Otho, 28 May 1982.

Eddie, Sir George Brand, OBE   [Deceased.
Edwards, Air Cdre Sir Hughie Idwal, VC, KCMG, CB, DSO, OBE, DFC, 5 Aug. 1982.
Edwards, Prof. Kenneth Charles, CBE, 7 May 1982.
Elliott, Ralph Edward, 23 Dec. 1981.
Ellis, Sir Thomas Hobart, 12 Dec. 1981.
Elmhirst, Air Marshal Sir Thomas Walker, KBE, CB, AFC, 6 Nov. 1982.
Eshelby, Prof. John Douglas, FRS, 10 Dec. 1981.
Estcourt, Maj.-Gen. Edward Noel Keith, DSO, OBE, 26 May 1982.
Euwe, Dr Machgielis, 26 Nov. 1981.
Evans of Hungershall, Baron (Life Peer); Benjamin Ifor Evans, 28 Aug. 1982.
Evans, Vice-Adm. Sir Charles Leo Glandore, KCB, CBE, DSO, DSC, 27 Dec. 1981.
Evans, Evan Stanley, CBE, 27 Aug. 1982.
Evans, Dr Luther Harris, 23 Dec. 1981.
Evans, William Edis Webster, 5 March 1982.
Everington, Geoffrey Devas, QC, 23 Feb. 1982.

Fairbank, Alfred John, CBE, 14 March 1982.
Fairbanks, Maj.-Gen. Cecil Benfield, CB, CBE, 5 March 1982.
Fairhurst, William Albert, CBE, 13 March 1982.
Fairman, Prof. Herbert Walter, 16 Nov. 1982.
Fassbinder, Rainer Werner, 10 June 1982.
Fell, Captain William Richmond, CMG, CBE, DSC, RN, 28 Nov. 1981.
Fellowes, Brig. Reginald William Lyon, CBE, MC, 17 July 1982.
Fidge, Sir (Harold) Roy   [Deceased.
Fife, Charles Morrison, CB, 14 March 1982.
Finch, Maj.-Gen. Lionel Hugh Knightley, CB, DSO, OBE, 23 Oct. 1982.
Finlay, John Euston Bell, CB, OBE, TD, 6 Nov. 1982.
Finn, Donovan Bartley, CMG, 1 Nov. 1982.
Fisher, Prof. Charles Alfred, 7 Jan. 1982.
Fitton, James, RA, 2 May 1982.
Fitzmaurice, Sir Gerald Gray, GCMG, QC, 7 Sept. 1982.
Flett, Sir Martin Teall, KCB, 25 Feb. 1982.
Florence, Prof. Philip Sargant, Hon. CBE, 29 Jan. 1982.
Follett, Sir David Henry, 11 May 1982.
Fonda, Henry, 12 Aug. 1982.
Forbes, Charles Harington Gordon, CBE, 8 Nov. 1982.
Forsyth-Thompson, Aubrey Denzil, CMG, CVO, CBE, 13 June 1982.
Foster, Sir John Galway, KBE, QC, 1 Feb. 1982.
Foxon, Prof. George Eric Howard, 16 Nov. 1982.
Fraser, Thomas Cameron, CB, MBE, TD, 6 Oct. 1982.
Freeman, Captain Spencer, CBE, 27 May 1982.
Freud, Anna, CBE, 9 Oct. 1982.
Frisby, Maj.-Gen. Richard George Fellowes, CB, CBE, DSO, MC, 7 Feb. 1982.
Frome, Sir Norman Frederick, CIE, DFC, 29 Oct. 1982.
Fryars, Sir Robert Furness   [Deceased.

Gage, 6th Viscount; Henry Rainald Gage, KCVO, 27 Feb. 1982.
Galbraith, Hon. Sir Thomas Galloway Dunlop, KBE, MP, 2 Jan. 1982.
Gale, Gen. Sir Richard Nelson, GCB, KBE, DSO, MC, 29 July 1982.
Gamble, Sir David Arthur Josias, 4th Bt, 9 Jan. 1982.
Gardiner-Hill, Dr Harold, MBE, 25 March 1982.
Garland, Ailsa Mary, (Mrs John Rollit Mason), 5 Nov. 1982.
Garlick, Rev. Canon Wilfrid, 29 Oct. 1982.
Gattie, Maj.-Gen. Kenneth Francis Drake, DSO, MC, 24 Aug. 1982.
Gavey, Dr Clarence John, 7 Sept. 1982.
Geake, Maj.-Gen. Clifford Henry, CB, CBE, 30 July 1982.
George, Herbert Horace, CB, MC, 25 Oct. 1982.
Giauque, Prof. William Francis, 29 March 1982.
Gibbons, Sir John Edward, 8th Bt, 20 Sept. 1982.
Gibbs-Smith, Prof. Charles Harvard, 3 Dec. 1981.

Gielgud, Val Henry, CBE, 30 Nov. 1981.
Gill, Air Cdre Hon. Thomas Francis, (Frank), CBE, DSO, 1 March 1982.
Gill-Carey, Chapple, 21 Dec. 1981.
Glenday, Dorothea Nonita, 18 May 1982.
Glover, Sir Douglas, TD, 15 Jan. 1982.
Goldmann, Dr Nahum, 29 Aug. 1982.
Gosling, Sir Arthur Hulin, KBE, CB, 8 Aug. 1982.
Goulding, Sir (William) Basil, 3rd Bt, 16 Jan. 1982.
Gower-Jones, Ven. Geoffrey, 5 Nov. 1982.
Grady, John William, 8 April 1982.
Graham, Prof. John Macdonald, CBE, 7 April 1982.
Graham, Sir Richard Bellingham, 10th Bt, OBE, 29 Jan. 1982.
Graner, Most Rev. Lawrence L., CSC, DD, 21 April 1982.
Grant, Sir James Monteith, KCVO, 1 Dec. 1981.
Gray, Stephen Alexander Reith, 12 May 1982.
Greaves, Maj.-Gen. Charles Granville Barry, CB, CBE, 4 June 1982.
Greaves, Sir (William) Western, KBE, 8 July 1982.
Greenwood of Rossendale, Baron (Life Peer); Arthur William James Greenwood, (Anthony Greenwood), PC, 12 April 1982.
Greenwood, Prof. John Neill   [Deceased.
Gresford Jones, Rt Rev. Edward Michael, KCVO, DD, 7 March 1982.
Gretton, 2nd Baron; John Frederic Gretton, OBE, 26 March 1982.
Grüneberg, Prof. Hans, FRS, 23 Oct. 1982.
Guidotti, Gastone, 28 March 1982.
Guild, Surgeon Captain William John Forbes, CBE, RN, 23 June 1982.
Guildford, Bishop of; Rt Rev. David Alan Brown, 13 July 1982.
Guiringaud, Louis de, 15 April 1982.
Gwynne-Jones, Allan, CBE, DSO, RA, 5 Aug. 1982.

Haine, Reginald Leonard, VC, MC, 12 June 1982.
Haldane, Archibald Richard Burdon, CBE, 18 Oct. 1982.
Halliday, Frank Ernest, 26 March 1982.
Hallstein, Prof. Walter, 29 March 1982.
Halsey, Reginald John, CMG, 13 Jan. 1982.
Hamilton, Captain Sir Robert William Stirling-, 12th Bt, RN, 14 Feb. 1982.
Hamilton, William Aitken Brown, CMG, 14 May 1982.
Hammond, Maj.-Gen. Arthur Verney, CB, DSO, 15 Jan. 1982.
Hammond, Stanley Alfred Andrew, CMG   [Deceased.
Hanbury Tenison, Marika, 24 Oct. 1982.
Harding, Maj.-Gen. Reginald Peregrine, CB, DSO, 27 Dec. 1981.
Harding, Rosamond Evelyn Mary, 6 May 1982.
Hardman, Air Chief Marshal Sir (James) Donald Innes, GBE, KCB, DFC, 2 March 1982.
Hare, Prof. Patrick James, 5 April 1982.
Harland, Prof. Sydney Cross, FRS, 8 Nov. 1982.
Harlock, Maj.-Gen. Hugh George Frederick, CBE   [Deceased.
Harris, Dr Kenneth Edwin   [Deceased.
Hart, Sir George Charles, KBE, BEM   [Deceased.
Hartwell, Lady; Pamela Margaret Elizabeth Berry, 7 Jan. 1982.
Hartwell, Sir Charles Herbert, CMG, 31 Aug. 1982.
Haughton, Dr Sidney Henry, FRS, 24 May 1982.
Hawton, Sir John Malcolm Kenneth, KCB, 7 Jan. 1982.
Haycocks, Prof. Norman, CBE, 30 March 1982.
Headlam-Morley, Kenneth Arthur Sonntag, OBE, 28 Oct. 1982.
Heathcoat Amory, Sir William, 5th Bt, DSO, 27 Aug. 1982.
Heawood, Geoffrey Leonard, 9 April 1982.
Heckle, Arnold, CMG, 18 Jan. 1982.
Heinze, Prof. Sir Bernard Thomas, AC, 10 June 1982.
Hemingford, 2nd Baron; Dennis George Ruddock Herbert, 19 June 1982.
Hendel, Prof. Charles William, 12 Nov. 1982.
Henderson, Keith, OBE, 24 Feb. 1982.
Henriques, Sir Cyril George Xavier, QC (Jamaica), 18 June 1982.
Hensby, Frederick Charles, OBE, 6 April 1982.
Herbert, Major George, MBE, 16 June 1982.
Herchenroder, Sir (Marie Joseph Barnabe) Francis, QC (Mauritius), 9 April 1982.
Heron-Maxwell, Sir Patrick Ivor, 9th Bt, 18 Aug. 1982.
Herring, Lt-Gen. Hon. Sir Edmund Francis, KCMG, KBE, DSO, MC, ED, QC (Victoria), 5 Jan. 1982.
Herring, Dame Mary Ranken, DBE   [Deceased.
Hill, Sir Ian George Wilson, CBE, TD, 5 May 1982.
Hill, Sir (John) Denis (Nelson), 5 May 1982.
Hillingdon, 5th Baron; Patrick Charles Mills, MC, TD, 1 Sept. 1982 (ext).
Him, George, RDI, 4 April 1982.
Hines, Robert Henry, 26 March 1982.
Hinkson, Pamela, 26 May 1982.
Hodgkin, Thomas Lionel, 25 March 1982.
Hogger, Rear-Adm. Henry Charles, CB, DSC, 22 July 1982.
Holbeche, Brian Harry, CBE, 17 Feb. 1982.
Holden, Sir Michael Herbert Frank, CBE, ED, 11 March 1982.
Holdsworth, Max Ernest, OBE, TD, 22 July 1982.
Holland, Sir Jim Sothern, 2nd Bt, TD, 25 Dec. 1981.
Holloway, Stanley, OBE, 30 Jan. 1982.
Honywood, Col Sir William Wynne, 10th Bt, MC, 10 Aug. 1982.
Hood, Maj.-Gen. Ernest Lionel Ouseley, CB, 13 June 1982.
Hopkins, Prof. Harry Geoffrey, 4 Jan. 1982.
Horsfall Turner, Harold, CBE, 26 Dec. 1981.
Hoskyns-Abrahall, Rt Rev. Anthony Leigh Egerton, 1 May 1982.
Houstoun-Boswall, Sir Thomas, 7th Bt, 16 May 1982.
Howard, John Melbourne, 10 Aug. 1982.
Howell, Dorothy, 12 Jan. 1982.

Howells, Gilbert Haywood, 29 July 1982.
Hughes, Prof. Emmet John, 20 Sept. 1982.
Hulme, Alfred Clive, VC, 3 Sept. 1982.
Humphreys, Sir Kenneth Owens   [*Deceased.*
Hunt, Sir Joseph Anthony, MBE, 11 April 1982.
Hunt, Reginald Heber, 13 Sept. 1982.
Hunter Blair, Peter, FBA, 9 Sept. 1982.
Hurst, Leonard Henry, CBE, 25 Nov. 1981.
Hutchison, Isobel Wylie, 20 Feb. 1982.
Huxham, Henry William Walter, CB, CBE, 24 Sept. 1982.

Inchiquin, 17th Baron of; Phaedrig Lucius Ambrose O'Brien, 20 May 1982.
Inverforth, 3rd Baron; (Andrew Charles) Roy Weir, 6 June 1982.
Ispahani, Mirza Abol Hassan, 18 Nov. 1981.

Jackman, Frank Downer, CMG   [*Deceased.*
Jackson, Prof. Derek Ainslie, OBE, DFC, AFC, FRS, 20 Feb. 1982.
Jackson, Sir Donald Edward, 18 Nov. 1981.
Jackson, Harvey, 19 Sept. 1982.
Jacobs-Larkcom, Eric Herbert Larkcom, CBE, 28 May 1982.
Jakobson, Prof. Roman, 18 June 1982.
James, Robert Leoline, CBE, 14 May 1982.
James, William Thomas, OBE, 4 Sept. 1982.
Janner, Baron (Life Peer); Barnett Janner, 4 May 1982.
Jardine, Christopher Willoughby, CB, 3 Nov. 1982.
Jarrett, Norman Rowlstone, CMG, 21 June 1982.
Jarvis, Ven. Alfred Clifford, 21 Nov. 1981.
Jennings, (Richard Edward) Christopher, MBE, 25 July 1982.
Jeritza, Maria, 10 July 1982.
Johnson, Dame Celia, (Dame Celia Fleming), DBE, 25 April 1982.
Johnson, Sir William Clarence, CMG, CBE, 9 March 1982.
Johnson-Marshall, Sir Stirrat Andrew William, CBE, 16 Dec. 1981.
Johnston, Peter Hope, CMG, 17 Feb. 1982.
Jones, David Prys, 6 Feb. 1982.
Jordan, Most Rev. Anthony, OMI, 4 March 1982.
Joseph, Sir Maxwell, 22 Sept. 1982.
Joslin, Maj.-Gen. Stanley William, CB, CBE, 6 Oct. 1982.
Joyce, Alec Houghton, CIE, CBE, 23 May 1982.
Joyce, John Hall, 28 Feb. 1982.
Jukes, Ernest Martin, CBE, QC, 23 April 1982.

Karmel, David, CBE, QC, 31 May 1982.
Kellar, Alexander James, CMG, OBE, 8 Nov. 1982.
Kenyon, Alec Hindle, 16 Oct. 1982.
Ker, Neil Ripley, CBE, FBA, 23 Aug. 1982.
Kermack, Stuart Grace, CBE   [*Deceased.*
Keswick, Sir John Henry, KCMG, 5 July 1982.
Keynes, Sir Geoffrey Langdon, Hon. FBA, 5 July 1982.
King, Laurence Edward, OBE, 9 Dec. 1981.
Kinmonth, Prof. John Bernard, 16 Sept. 1982.
Kirchner, Bernard Joseph, CBE, 18 Jan. 1982.
Kirkman, Gen. Sir Sidney Chevalier, GCB, KBE, MC, 5 Nov. 1982.
Kirwan-Taylor, Harold George, 2 Dec. 1981.
Kitchin, John Leslie Harlow, CB, 24 Jan. 1982.
Kitto, Prof. Humphrey Davy Findley, FBA, 21 Jan. 1982.
Kodicek, Egon Hynek, CBE, FRS, 27 July 1982.
Konovalov, Prof. Sergey, 12 Feb. 1982.
Kraay, Colin Mackennal, FBA, 27 Jan. 1982.
Krebs, Sir Hans Adolf, FRS, 22 Nov. 1981.
Kyle, Elisabeth, (Agnes Mary Robertson Dunlop), 23 Feb. 1982.

Lambart, Julian Harold Legge, 11 Oct. 1982.
Lambert, Richard Stanton, 27 Nov. 1981.
Lambert, Dr Royston James, 25 Oct. 1982.
Lamborn, Harry George, MP, 21 Aug. 1982.
Lambrick, Hugh Trevor, CIE, 31 Aug. 1982.
Lamont, William Dawson, 9 Nov. 1982.
Lamplough, Maj.-Gen. Charles Robert Wharram, CBE, DSC, 28 Nov. 1981.
Langker, Sir Erik, OBE, 3 Feb. 1982.
Langton, Bernard Sydney, CBE, 21 Jan. 1982.
Larkin, Alfred Sloane, CIE, 3 Jan. 1982.
Lazell, Henry George Leslie, 17 Nov. 1982.
Lean, Air Vice-Marshal Daniel Alexander Ronald, OBE, QHDS, 24 Aug. 1982.
Leclerc, Maj.-Gen. Pierre Edouard, CBE, MM, ED, CD, 27 May 1982.
Lee Potter, Air Marshal Sir Patrick Brunton, KBE, 5 Jan. 1982.
Leslie, Doris, (Lady Fergusson Hannay), 30 May 1982.
Lévis Mirepoix, Antoine, Duc de   [*Deceased.*
Lewis, David John, 6 May 1982.
Lewis, Eric William Charles, CB, 31 Dec. 1981.
Leyland, Norman Harrison, 23 Nov. 1981.
Lind-Smith, His Honour Gerard Gustave, 3 Feb. 1982.
Lipscomb, Maj.-Gen. Christopher Godfrey, CB, DSO, 16 Jan. 1982.
Lissack, Victor Jack, 20 Dec. 1981.
Lister, Lt-Col Harry Laidman, OBE, TD, 2 Nov. 1982.
Lister-Kaye, Sir John Christopher Lister, 7th Bt, 15 May 1982.
Livingston, Air Marshal Sir Philip Clermont, KBE, CB, AFC, 13 Feb. 1982.
Lloyd, John Owen, CBE, 28 Aug. 1982.
Lloyd, Prof. (William) Arnold de Gorges, 4 July 1982.
Lloyd Webber, William Southcombe, CBE, 29 Oct. 1982.
Logsdon, Geoffrey Edward, CBE, TD, 11 July 1982.

Long, Ernest, CBE, 12 Oct. 1982.
Longden, Maj.-Gen. Harry Leicester, CB, CBE, 13 Dec. 1981.
Lord, Maj.-Gen. Wilfrid Austin, CB, CBE, 10 Jan. 1982.
Lott, Prof. Frank Melville, CBE, 16 May 1982.
Lovett, Maj.-Gen. Osmond de Turville, CB, CBE, DSO, 17 Oct. 1982.
Lowe, Arthur, 15 April 1982.
Lowther, Lt-Col Sir William Guy, 5th Bt, OBE, 7 May 1982.
Lunt, Rt Rev. Francis Evered, 27 May 1982.

MacArthur, (David) Wilson   [*Deceased.*
Macaulay, Lt-Col Archibald Duncan Campbell, OBE, 11 Oct. 1982.
McBeath, Rear-Adm. John Edwin Home, CB, DSO, DSC, 28 March 1982.
McComb, James Ellis, CBE, DFC, 4 Aug. 1982.
McCombs, Hon. Sir Terence Henderson, OBE, ED, 6 Nov. 1982.
McConnell, Gerard Hamilton, CB, 2 April 1982.
McConnell, William Samuel, 25 Feb. 1982.
McCrone, Robert Watson, MC, 5 April 1982.
McDonald, Sir Alexander Forbes, 5 Dec. 1981.
McElhone, Frank, MP, 22 Sept. 1982.
McGill, Air Vice-Marshal Frank Scholes, CB   [*Deceased.*
MacGregor, Sir Colin Malcolm, 6 Sept. 1982.
McIntyre, Sir Laurence Rupert, AC, CBE, 21 Nov. 1981.
McKee, William Desmond, CBE, 28 Jan. 1982.
Mackenzie, Alexander, OBE, 8 May 1982.
Mackessack, Lt-Col Kenneth, 18 Oct. 1982.
Mackie, John Leslie, FBA, 12 Dec. 1981.
McLaren, John Watt, 28 Oct. 1982.
McLaughlan, Roy James Philip, CMG, CVO, 15 April 1982.
Maclean, Brig. Gordon Forbes, CBE, MC, 6 May 1982.
MacLeay, His Honour Oswell Searight, 25 Aug. 1982.
MacLeish, Archibald, 20 April 1982.
McLellan, David, CMG, ED, 5 Oct. 1982.
McLellan, James Kidd, CBE, QPM   [*Deceased.*
McLeod, Maj.-Gen. Minden Whyte-Melville, CB, CBE, DSO, 17 Dec. 1981.
McMeekan, Brig. Gilbert Reader, CB, DSO, OBE, 25 Aug. 1982.
Macmillan, Donald, OBE, TD, 10 April 1982.
Macpherson, James, 1 March 1982.
Maddox, Sir George Henry, KBE, 27 March 1982.
Madgwick, Sir Robert Bowden, OBE   [*Deceased.*
Maguinness, Prof. William Stuart, 17 Nov. 1982.
Mahon, Sir Gerald MacMahon, 6 April 1982.
Maingot, Rodney, TC, 3 Jan. 1982.
Malley, Cecil Patrick   [*Deceased.*
Malvern, Harry Ladyman, CBE, 11 May 1982.
Mann, Frederick George, FRS, 29 March 1982.
Marriott, John Hayes, CB, OBE, 1 Sept. 1982.
Marsh, Dame Ngaio, DBE, 18 Feb. 1982.
Marshall, Sir Geoffrey, KCVO, CBE, 9 Aug. 1982.
Marshall, Hedley Herbert, CMG, QC (Nigeria), 27 April 1982.
Marshall, Prof. Thomas Humphrey, CMG, 29 Nov. 1981.
Martin, Prof. Nicholas Henry, TD, 13 Dec. 1981.
Martin, Olaus Macleod, CIE, 28 Dec. 1981.
Mason, Michael Henry, 18 Oct. 1982.
Masterman, Sir Christopher Hughes, CSI, CIE, 16 Feb. 1982.
Matheson, Prof. Arthur Alexander, QC (Scot.), 22 Dec. 1981.
Mathews, Henry Mends, CIE, 5 April 1982.
Maxwell, Maurice William, 13 July 1982.
Mendès France, Pierre, 18 Oct. 1982.
Merchant, Vivien, 3 Oct. 1982.
Meyer, Sir Oscar Gwynne, OBE, ED   [*Deceased.*
Michelmore, Maj.-Gen. Sir (William) Godwin, KBE, CB, DSO, MC, TD, 25 Oct. 1982.
Michie, Charles Watt, CMG, OBE, 20 March 1982.
Millbourn, Sir (Philip) Eric, CMG, 17 April 1982.
Miller, Gerald Cedar, MC, 3 June 1982.
Miller, Robert Sydney, CCH   [*Deceased.*
Milne-Watson, Sir (David) Ronald, 2nd Bt, 15 June 1982.
Milnes Coates, Sir Robert Edward James Clive, 3rd Bt, DSO, 9 May 1982.
Milward, John Frederic, 3 Oct. 1982.
Mitchell, Dr Robert Lyell, 7 Feb. 1982.
Mollan, Maj.-Gen. Francis Robert Henry, CB, OBE, MC, 28 Feb. 1982.
Molyneux, John Anthony, (Tony), 12 Sept. 1982.
Monck, 6th Viscount; Henry Wyndham Stanley Monck, OBE, 21 June 1982.
Monroe, Hubert Holmes, QC, 5 June 1982.
Moon, Prof. Harold Philip, 26 March 1982.
Moore, Prof. Stanford, 23 Aug. 1982.
More, Kenneth Gilbert, CBE, 12 July 1982.
Morgan, Alun Michael, CMG, 3 Dec. 1981.
Morgan, Rev. Irvonwy, 24 Sept. 1982.
Morrell, William Bowes, 11 Dec. 1982.
Morris, Sir Cedric Lockwood, 9th Bt, 8 Feb. 1982.
Morris, His Honour Gwyn Rhys Francis, QC, 18 Jan. 1982.
Morris, Harry Frank Grave, CMG, 31 May 1982.
Morris, Sir (Thomas) Gwilym, CBE, QPM, 18 May 1982.
Morris, Sir Willie, KCMG, 13 April 1982.
Morrison, Alexander, CBE, 18 May 1982.
Mulligan, Col Hugh Waddell, CMG, 26 July 1982.
Mumford, Lawrence Quincy, 15 Aug. 1982.
Murison, Maj.-Gen. Charles Alexander Phipps, CB, CBE, MC   [*Deceased.*
Murray, Angus, MC, 23 Aug. 1982.

Musgrave, Clifford, OBE, 15 Sept. 1982.
Mutch, Dr Nathan, 3 June 1982.
Myer, Dame (Margery) Merlyn Baillieu, DBE, 3 Sept. 1982.

Nesbitt, Cathleen Mary, CBE, 2 Aug. 1982.
Netherthorpe, 2nd Baron; James Andrew Turner, 4 Nov. 1982.
Nevill, Lord Rupert Charles Montacute, CVO, 18 July 1982.
Neville, Lt-Col Sir (James) Edmund (Henderson), 2nd Bt, MC, 24 June 1982.
Newman-Morris, Sir Geoffrey, ED   [*Deceased.*
Nicholson, Sir Arthur William, OBE   [*Deceased.*
Nicholson, Ben, OM, 6 Feb. 1982.
Nightingale, Percy Herbert, CMG, 26 Nov. 1981.
Noble, Comdr Rt Hon. Sir Allan Herbert Percy, PC, KCMG, DSO, DSC, 17 Nov. 1982.
Noble, Col Sir Arthur, KBE, CB, DSO, TD, 26 Feb. 1982.
Noel-Baker, Baron (Life Peer); Philip John Noel-Baker, PC, 8 Oct. 1982.
Normand, Sir Charles William Blyth, CIE, 25 Oct. 1982.
Norrington, Sir Arthur Lionel Pugh, 21 May 1982.
Northbourne, 4th Baron; Walter Ernest Christopher James, 17 June 1982.

Oman, Charles Chichele, 26 Jan. 1982.
O'Neill, Denis Edmund, CB, 22 Dec. 1981.
Opie, Peter Mason, 5 Feb. 1982.
Owen, Prof. Gwilym Ellis Lane, FBA, 10 July 1982.
Owen, Ronald Allan, 29 April 1982.

Parent, Most Rev. Charles Eugène, 2 June 1982.
Pargiter, Baron (Life Peer); George Albert Pargiter, CBE, 16 Jan. 1982.
Park, William, OBE, 2 March 1982.
Parker, (Richard) Eric, 1 April 1982.
Parker, Rt Rev. William Alonzo, 28 April 1982.
Parks, Sir Alan Guyatt, 3 Nov. 1982.
Parry, Prof. Clive, 10 Sept. 1982.
Parry, Prof. John Horace, CMG, MBE, 25 Aug. 1982.
Partridge, Sir (Ernest) John, KBE, 4 June 1982.
Pasley, Sir Rodney Marshall Sabine, 4th Bt, 25 July 1982.
Peacock, (John) Roydon, 28 March 1982.
Pearce, William Harvey, CBE, 3 Jan. 1982.
Pears, Harold Snowden; His Honour Judge Pears, 14 June 1982.
Pearson, Sir Neville Arthur, 2nd Bt, 6 Nov. 1982 (*ext*).
Peart, Prof. Donald Richard, 26 Nov. 1981.
Peart, Ernest Grafford, CD, 23 April 1982.
Peate, Dr Iorwerth Cyfeiliog, 19 Oct. 1982.
Pelletier, Wilfrid, CC, CMG, 9 April 1982.
Pennell, Montague Mattinson, CBE, FRS, 30 Dec. 1981.
Pennycuick, Rt Hon. Sir John, PC, 14 Jan. 1982.
Perham, Dame Margery, DCMG, CBE, FBA, 19 Feb. 1982.
Perowne, Maj.-Gen. Lancelot Edgar Connop Mervyn, CB, CBE, 24 March 1982.
Pert, Maj.-Gen. Claude Ernest, CB, CVO, DSO, 14 March 1982.
Peterkin, Ishbel Allan, 14 June 1982.
Peters, Sir Rudolph Albert, MC, FRS, 29 Jan. 1982.
Philipson-Stow, Sir Edmond Cecil, 4th Bt, MBE, 14 June 1982.
Phillips, Maj.-Gen. Charles George, CB, DSO, MC, 1 May 1982.
Phillips, Prof. Frank Coles, 11 Sept. 1982.
Phillips, Rev. Canon John Bertram, DD, 21 July 1982.
Phillips, John George Crispin, QC, Sept. 1982.
Phillips, Hon. Sir (John) Raymond, MC; Hon. Mr Justice Phillips, 2 Aug. 1982.
Pigott, Major Sir Berkeley, 4th Bt, 9 May 1982.
Pinckney, Charles Percy, 20 Feb. 1982.
Pitchforth, (Roland) Vivian, RA, 6 Aug. 1982.
Pollock, James Huey Hamill, CMG, OBE, 14 March 1982.
Popham, Margaret Evelyn, CBE, 25 April 1982.
Porbandar, Maharaja of; Lt-Col HH Maharaja Rana Saheb, Shri Sir Natwarsinhji Bhavsinhji, KCSI, 4 Oct. 1982.
Postan, Sir Michael Moïssey, FBA, 12 Dec. 1981.
Powell, Arthur Geoffrey, 4 May 1982.
Powell, Edward, CBE, 16 Nov. 1982.
Praz, Mario, Hon. KBE, 23 March 1982.
Preston, Col Rupert Lionel, CBE, 2 Nov. 1982.
Price, Gwilym Ivor, 26 Nov. 1981.
Price, Very Rev. Robert Peel, 26 Dec. 1981.
Price, William Thomas, CBE, MC, 17 Jan. 1982.
Primrose, William, CBE, 1 May 1982.
Pringle, Prof. John William Sutton, MBE, FRS, 2 Nov. 1982.
Pritchard, Sir Fred Eills, MBE, 10 Aug. 1982.
Pryor, Norman Selwyn, 29 July 1982.

Rambert, Dame Marie, (Dame Marie Dukes), DBE, 12 June 1982.
Ranasinha, Sir Arthur Godwin, CMG, CBE   [*Deceased.*
Randall, Sir Richard John, 15 Nov. 1982.
Randell, Dr John Bulmer, 30 April 1982.
Ransome, Maj.-Gen. Robert St George Tyldesley, CB, CBE, MC, 5 Nov. 1982.
Reader, (William Henry) Ralph, CBE, 13 May 1982.
Reed, Sir Reginald Charles, CBE, 17 Aug. 1982.
Rees-Reynolds, Col Alan Randall, CBE, TD, 13 April 1982.
Reid-Adam, Randle, CBE, 14 March 1982.
Rice, George Ritchie, CMG, OBE, 14 Feb. 1982.
Richardson, Arthur   [*Deceased.*
Richardson, Prof. Harold Owen Wilson, 4 March 1982.

Riding, George Albert, 3 Feb. 1982.
Ritchie-Calder, Baron (Life Peer); Peter Ritchie Ritchie-Calder, CBE, 31 Jan. 1982.
Roberts, Maj.-Gen. Frank Crowther, VC, DSO, OBE, MC, 12 Jan. 1982.
Roberts, Rev. Harold, 4 Oct. 1982.
Robertson, Alexander Thomas Parke Anthony Cecil, (Alec Robertson), MBE, 18 Jan. 1982.
Robertson, George Paterson, 4 Jan. 1982.
Robson, Prof. John Michael, 18 Feb. 1982.
Robson, Sir Lawrence William, 24 Aug. 1982.
Rodger, Prof. Alec, (Thomas Alexander Rodger), 15 Feb. 1982.
Rogers, Ven. Evan James Gwyn, 30 March 1982.
Roome, Rear-Adm. Henry Stewart, CBE, 21 Dec. 1981.
Root, Frederick James, CB, 2 Nov. 1982.
Roper, Maj.-Gen. Henry Ernest, CB, 13 July 1982.
Rose, Dame Hilda Nora, DBE, 18 July 1982.
Rose, Captain Sir Philip Humphrey Vivian, 3rd Bt, 14 March 1982.
Roskill, Captain Stephen Wentworth, CBE, DSC, FBA, RN, 4 Nov. 1982.
Ross, Prof. Allan Dawson, 6 Sept. 1982.
Ross, Col Walter John Macdonald, CB, OBE, MC, TD, 29 July 1982.
Routley, Rev. Erik Reginald, 8 Oct. 1982.
Rowell, Sir (Herbert Babington) Robin, CBE, AFC, 19 Dec. 1981.
Roy, Sir Asoka Kumar, 27 May 1982.
Rushton, Frederick Alan, 25 Sept. 1982.
Ruthnaswamy, Prof. Miriadas, CIE   [*Deceased.*
Ruthven of Freeland, Lady, 11th in line; Bridget Helen Monckton, (The Dowager Viscountess Monckton of Brenchley), CBE, 17 April 1982.

Samuels, Albert Edward, 19 June 1982.
Satterly, Air Vice-Marshal Harold Vivian, CB, CBE, DFC, 28 Apr. 1982.
Saville, (Leonard) Malcolm, 30 June 1982.
Schaeffer, Prof. Claude Frederic Armand, 25 Aug. 1982.
Schuster, Sir George Ernest, KCSI, KCMG, CBE, MC, 5 June 1982.
Scicluna, Sir Hannibal Publius, MBE, 21 Dec. 1981.
Scott, Sir Robert Heatlie, GCMG, CBE, 26 Feb. 1982.
Scott, Group Captain Roy Charles Edwin, CBE, MVO, AFC, 2 July 1982.
Searle, Humphrey, CBE, 12 May 1982.
Sender, Ramón José, 15 Jan. 1982.
Sephton, Ven. Arthur, 22 March 1982.
Seton, Sir Claud Ramsay Wilmot, MC, 3 Sept. 1982.
Seward, Sir Eric John, KBE, 30 Nov. 1981.
Seymour, Richard, CMG, CBE, 3 June 1982.
Shakerley, Sir Geoffrey Peter, CBE, MC, TD, 6 March 1982.
Sharp, Ven. Richard Lloyd, 4 July 1982.
Shaw, Anne Gillespie, (Mrs J. H. Pirie), CBE, 4 Feb. 1982.
Shewell-Cooper, Wilfred Edward, MBE, 21 Feb. 1982.
Shirley, Air Vice-Marshal Sir Thomas Ulric Curzon, KBE, CB, 17 Jan. 1982.
Showering, Sir Keith Stanley, 23 March 1982.
Siddeley, John Tennant Davenport, (3rd Baron Kenilworth), 26 Dec. 1981.
Sieff, Joseph Edward, 3 Nov. 1982.
Silverman, Herbert A.   [*Deceased.*
Simpson, Sir (John) Cyril (Finucane), 3rd Bt, 21 Dec. 1981 (*ext*).
Slater, Arthur Edward, CBE, 21 Sept. 1982.
Slocum, Captain Frank Alexander, CMG, OBE, RN, 22 May 1982.
Smith, Frederick William, CMG, MC   [*Deceased.*
Smith, Rt Rev. Thomas Geoffrey Stuart, 8 Dec. 1981.
Snaith, Rev. Norman Henry, DD, 4 March 1982.
Soloveytchik, George Michael de, 14 Oct. 1982.
Soper, Dr Frederick George, CBE, FRSNZ, 1 Jan. 1982.
Southborough, 3rd Baron; Francis John Hopwood, 4 Feb. 1982.
Southwell, Sir (Charles Archibald) Philip, CBE, MC, 30 Nov. 1981.
Spearman, Sir Alexander Cadwallader Mainwaring, 5 April 1982.
Spector, Prof. Walter Graham, 7 Jan. 1982.
Speed, Marjorie Jane, OBE, 22 Oct. 1982.
Spenser-Wilkinson, Sir Thomas Crowe, 28 Jan. 1982.
Spinks, Dr Alfred, CBE, FRS, 11 Feb. 1982.
Springall, Prof. Harold Douglas, 2 Nov. 1982.
Sprott, Rt Rev. John Chappell, DD, 11 Nov. 1982.
Stafford, Jack, CB, 24 Sept. 1982.
Stanier, Prof. Roger Yate, FRS, 29 Jan. 1982.
Steen, Dr Robert Elsworth, 12 Dec. 1981.
Stein, John Alan, CIE, 16 Jan. 1982.
Stephen, Sir Alastair Edward, 4 Aug. 1982.
Stephenson, Lt-Col Sir (Henry) Francis (Blake), 2nd Bt, OBE, TD, 14 Aug. 1982.
Stewart, Sir Jocelyn Harry, 12th Bt, 3 March 1982.
Stock, Allen Lievesley, 4 Aug. 1982.
Stockman, Henry Watson, CBE, 27 June 1982.
Stopford, Rear-Adm. Frederick Victor, CBE, 19 Jan. 1982.
Strachan, Lt-Col Henry, VC, MC, 1 May 1982.
Strang, Prof. Barbara Mary Hope, (Prof. Lady Strang), 12 April 1982.
Strange, 15th Baron; John Drummond, 13 April 1982.
Stratheden and Campbell, 4th Baron; Alastair Campbell, CBE, 12 Dec. 1981.
Strong, Maj.-Gen. Sir Kenneth William Dobson, KBE, CB, 11 Jan. 1982.
Strutt, Hon. Charles Richard, 11 Dec. 1981.
Stuart, Rt Rev. Cyril Edgar, 23 Aug. 1982.
Surridge, Brewster Joseph, CMG, OBE, 4 Jan. 1982.

Sutton, Peter John, 20 June 1982.
Swart, Hon. Charles Robberts, DMS, 16 July 1982.
Swinnerton, Frank Arthur, 6 Nov. 1982.
Syers, Sir Cecil George Lewis, KCMG, CVO, 4 Dec. 1981.
Sykes, Sir Charles, CBE, FRS, 29 Jan. 1982.
Synnott, Pierce Nicholas Netterville, CB, 23 Oct. 1982.

Tanner, Norman Cecil, 12 Oct. 1982.
Tarver, Maj.-Gen. Charles Herbert, CB, CBE, DSO, 13 May 1982.
Tati, Jacques, (Jacques Tatischeff), 4 Nov. 1982.
Taylor, Ven. Edward, 24 Oct. 1982.
Taylor, Gordon Rattray, 7 Dec. 1981.
Taylor, Thomas Whiting, 26 Nov. 1981.
Teelock, Sir Leckraz, CBE, 4 May 1982.
Tempest, Margaret Mary, (Lady Mears), 23 July 1982.
Thacker, Charles, CBE, 26 May 1982.
Theorell, Dr (Axel) Hugo (Teodor), 15 Aug. 1982.
Thom, James Robert, 13 Dec. 1981.
Thomas, Ivor Owen, 11 Jan. 1982.
Thompson, John Crighton, CB, CBE, 13 July 1982.
Thomson, George Ewart, 25 Nov. 1981.
Thuillier, Lt-Col Henry Shakespear, DSO, 25 March 1982.
Tillett, Emmie Muriel, 16 May 1982.
Tiltman, Brig. John Hessell, CMG, CBE, MC, 10 Aug. 1982.
Townley, Frank, 8 March 1982.
Townley, Reginald Colin, CMG, 3 May 1982.
Tredennick, Prof. (George) Hugh (Percival Phair), 31 Dec. 1981.
Tsibu Darku, Nana Sir, OBE, 12 April 1982.
Tuck, Sir Raphael Herman, 1 July 1982.
Tull, Thomas Stuart, CBE, DSO, 21 April 1982.
Turner, Francis McDougall Charlewood, MC, DFC, 18 Jan. 1982.
Tweddle, Sir William, CBE, TD, 23 Oct. 1982.
Twining, Gen. Nathan Farragut, DSM, DFC, 29 March 1982.

Unwin, Nora Spicer, 5 Jan. 1982.
Urgüplü, Ali Suad Hayri, 26 Dec. 1981.
Urton, Sir William Holmes Lister, MBE, TD, 25 Feb. 1982.
Usher, Brig. Thomas Clive, CBE, DSO, 17 Nov. 1982.

Vaughan, David Wyamar, CBE, 6 July 1982.
Veasey, Brig. Harley Gerald, DSO, 4 Oct. 1982.
Vickers, Sir (Charles) Geoffrey, VC, 16 March 1982.
Vidor, King Wallis, 1 Nov. 1982.
Villiers, Alan John, DSC, 3 March 1982.
Vines, Prof. Howard William Copland, 13 Sept. 1982.
von Frisch, Dr Karl, 12 June 1982.

Wackett, Sir Lawrence James, DFC, AFC, 18 March 1982.
Wadley, Walter Joseph Durham, CMG, 1 May 1982.
Walker, Prof. Gilbert James, 5 Aug. 1982.
Walker-Okeover, Col Sir Ian Peter Andrew Monro, 3rd Bt, DSO, TD, 20 Feb. 1982.
Wallace, Very Rev. Alexander Ross, 26 Aug. 1982.
Wansbrough-Jones, Sir Owen Haddon, KBE, CB, 10 March 1982.
Warburg, Sir Siegmund George, 18 Oct. 1982.

Wardle, Ven. Walter Thomas, 12 Feb. 1982.
Warren, Alec Stephen, CMG, 20 March 1982.
Waterlow, Sir Thomas Gordon, 3rd Bt, CBE, 8 Aug. 1982.
Waterman, Sir Ewen McIntyre, 23 Oct. 1982.
Watkins, Mary Gwendolen, 20 Dec. 1981.
Way, Rt Rev. Wilfrid Lewis Mark, 30 July 1982.
Webber, Sir William James Percival, CBE, 12 April 1982.
Weekley, Charles Montague, 30 Jan. 1982.
Weiner, Prof. Joseph Sidney, 13 June 1982.
Weiss, Peter Ulrich, 10 May 1982.
Westall, Rt Rev. Wilfrid Arthur Edmund, 22 Feb. 1982.
Wheatcroft, Edward Lewis Elam, 27 March 1982.
Whitaker, (Edgar) Haddon, OBE, 5 Jan. 1982.
White, Maj.-Gen. (Percival) Napier, CB, CBE, 20 Aug. 1982.
White, Prof. Robert George, 17 Sept. 1982.
Whitehouse, Cyril John Arthur, OBE, 3 May 1982.
Whitelock, Prof. Dorothy, CBE, FBA, 14 Aug. 1982.
Whitney, John Hay, Hon. CBE, 8 Feb. 1982.
Widdess, Rev. Canon Arthur Geoffrey, 17 July 1982.
Williams, Maj.-Gen Arthur Nicholl, CBE, 4 June 1982.
Williams, Prof. Charles Harold, 8 Dec. 1981.
Williams, Sir Charles Henry Trelease, (Sir Harry), CBE, 13 Jan. 1982.
Williams, Sir John Francis, 31 March 1982.
Williams, William Penry   [*Deceased.*
Williamson, John, 4 April 1982.
Williamson, Air Vice-Marshal Peter Greville Kaye, CB, CBE, DFC, 8 Oct. 1982.
Willis, John Robert, CB, MC, 18 Sept. 1982.
Willis, Comdr William John Adlam, CBE, MVO, CGM, KPM, RN, 22 June 1982.
Wilson, Robert Graham, MBE, 8 July 1982.
Wilson, Very Rev. Prof. Robert John, DD   [*Deceased.*
Wilson, Sir Roy Mickel, QC, 12 April 1982.
Wilson, William Joseph Robinson, CMG, 20 July 1982.
Wise, Rear-Adm. Cyril Hubert Surtees, CB, MBE, 14 May 1982.
Witt, Sir John Clermont, 26 April 1982.
Wood, Maj.-Gen. George Neville, CB, CBE, DSO, MC, 14 Jan. 1982.
Wood, Prof. Hubert Lyon-Campbell, 16 Aug. 1982.
Wood, James Maxwell, (Max Wood), OBE, 26 Oct. 1982.
Wood, William Walter, 14 July 1982.
Woods, George David, 20 Aug. 1982.
Woods, Maj.-Gen. Thomas Frederic Mackie, CB, OBE, 25 Sept. 1982.
Woodward, (Winifred) Joan, 24 Nov. 1981.
Wrangham, Cuthbert Edward, CBE, 10 Feb. 1982.
Wright, Prof. John Nicholson, 3 June 1982.
Wright, Sir Robert Brash, DSO, OBE, 4 Dec. 1981.
Wrigley, Dr Fred, CBE, 29 April 1982.
Wrisberg, Lt-Gen.Sir (Frederick) George, KBE, CB, 26 Feb. 1982.
Wyeth, Paul James Logan, 28 June 1982.
Wynne-Eyton, Selena Frances, CBE, 1 July 1982.
Wynne Finch, Col John Charles, CBE, MC, 15 May 1982.
Wynne-Jones, Baron (Life Peer); William Francis Kenrick Wynne-Jones, 8 Nov. 1982.

Zaimis, Prof. Eleanor, 3 Oct. 1982.

WHO'S WHO 1983

THE ROYAL FAMILY

THE SOVEREIGN

	Born
Her Majesty Queen Elizabeth II	21 Apr. 1926

Succeeded her father, King George VI, 6 February 1952.

Married 20 Nov. 1947, H R H The Duke of Edinburgh (*now* H R H The Prince Philip, Duke of Edinburgh), *b* 10 June 1921; *s* of H R H Prince Andrew of Greece (*d* 1944) and of H R H Princess Andrew of Greece (*d* 1969), *g g-d* of Queen Victoria.

Residences: Buckingham Palace, London, SW1; Windsor Castle, Berkshire; Sandringham House, Norfolk; Balmoral Castle, Aberdeenshire.

SONS AND DAUGHTER OF HER MAJESTY

H R H The Prince of Wales (Prince Charles Philip Arthur George)	14 Nov. 1948

Married 29 July 1981, Lady Diana Frances (*now* H R H The Princess of Wales), *b* 1 July 1961; *y d* of 8th Earl Spencer, *qv,* and has issue—

H R H PRINCE WILLIAM OF WALES (PRINCE WILLIAM ARTHUR PHILIP LOUIS) . . .	21 June 1982

Office: Buckingham Palace, London, SW1; Highgrove, Doughton, Tetbury, Gloucestershire GL8 8TG.

H R H The Prince Andrew (Albert Christian Edward)	19 Feb. 1960
H R H The Prince Edward (Antony Richard Louis)	10 Mar. 1964
H R H The Princess Anne (Elizabeth Alice Louise), Mrs Mark Phillips	15 Aug. 1950

Married 14 Nov. 1973, Mark Anthony Peter Phillips, *qv,* and has issue—

PETER MARK ANDREW PHILLIPS	15 Nov. 1977
ZARA ANNE ELIZABETH PHILLIPS	15 May 1981

Office: Buckingham Palace, SW1; Gatcombe Park, Minchinhampton, Stroud, Gloucestershire GL6 9AT.

SISTER OF HER MAJESTY

H R H The Princess Margaret, Countess of Snowdon	21 Aug. 1930

Married 6 May 1960, Antony Charles Robert Armstrong-Jones (*now* 1st Earl of Snowdon, *qv*) (marriage dissolved, 1978) and has issue—

DAVID ALBERT CHARLES ARMSTRONG-JONES (VISCOUNT LINLEY, *qv*)	3 Nov. 1961
SARAH FRANCES ELIZABETH ARMSTRONG-JONES (LADY SARAH ARMSTRONG-JONES)	1 May 1964

Residence: Kensington Palace, W8 4PU.

MOTHER OF HER MAJESTY

Her Majesty Queen Elizabeth The Queen Mother	4 Aug. 1900

Married 26 April 1923 (as Lady Elizabeth Bowes-Lyon, *d* of 14th Earl of Strathmore), H R H The Duke of York (Prince ALBERT), who succeeded as KING GEORGE VI, 11 Dec. 1936; he died 6 Feb. 1952.

Residences: Clarence House, St. James's, SW1; Royal Lodge, Windsor Great Park, Berkshire; Castle of Mey, Caithness-shire.

WIDOWS OF UNCLES OF HER MAJESTY

H R H Princess Alice, Duchess of Gloucester, 3rd *d* of 7th Duke of Buccleuch. . . . 25 Dec. 190●

Married 6 Nov. 1935, H R H The Duke of Gloucester (Prince Henry William Frederick Albert), *b* 31 March 1900; he died 10 June 1974. They had issue—

H R H PRINCE WILLIAM HENRY ANDREW FREDERICK, *b* 18 Dec. 1941; *d* 28 Aug. 1972.

H R H THE DUKE OF GLOUCESTER (PRINCE RICHARD ALEXANDER WALTER GEORGE) *(see below).*

Residences: Kensington Palace, W8 4PU; Barnwell Manor, Peterborough, PE8 5PJ.

The Duchess of Windsor (Wallis Warfield), *d* of Teakle Wallis Warfield, Baltimore, Maryland. 19 June 189●

Married 3 June 1937, H R H The Duke of Windsor (Prince Albert Edward Christian George Andrew Patrick David), *b* 23 June 1894; he died 28 May 1972.

Residence: 4 Route du Champ d'Entraînement, 75016 Paris.

COUSINS OF HER MAJESTY

Child of H R H The Duke of Gloucester and of H R H Princess Alice Duchess of Gloucester *(see above).*

H R H The Duke of Gloucester (Prince Richard Alexander Walter George) . . . . 26 Aug. 194●

Married 8 July 1972, Birgitte van Deurs, *d* of Asger Preben Wissing Henriksen, and has issue—

ALEXANDER PATRICK GREGERS RICHARD (EARL OF ULSTER, *qv*) . . . . . 24 Oct. 197●

DAVINA ELIZABETH ALICE BENEDIKTE (LADY DAVINA WINDSOR) . . . . 19 Nov. 197●

ROSE VICTORIA BIRGITTE LOUISE (LADY ROSE WINDSOR) . . . . . 1 Mar. 198●

Residences: Kensington Palace, W8 4PU; Barnwell Manor, Peterborough, PE8 5PJ.

Children of H R H The Duke of Kent (Prince George Edward Alexander Edmund, *b* 20 Dec. 1902, *d* 25 Aug. 1942) and H R H Princess Marina, Duchess of Kent (*b* 13 Dec. 1906, *d* 27 Aug. 1968), *y d* of late Prince Nicolas of Greece.

H R H The Duke of Kent (Prince Edward George Nicholas Patrick) . . . . . 9 Oct. 193●

Married 8 June 1961, Katharine, *b* 22 Feb. 1933, *o d* of Sir William Worsley, 4th Bt, and has issue—

GEORGE PHILIP NICHOLAS (EARL OF ST ANDREWS, *qv*) . . . . . . 26 June 196●

NICHOLAS CHARLES EDWARD JONATHAN (LORD NICHOLAS WINDSOR) . . . 25 July 197●

HELEN MARINA LUCY (LADY HELEN WINDSOR) . . . . 28 Apr. 196●

Residences: York House, St James's Palace, SW1; Anmer Hall, King's Lynn, Norfolk, PE31 6RW.

H R H Prince Michael George Charles Franklin . . . . 4 July 194●

Married 30 June 1978, Baroness Marie-Christine von Reibnitz, *d* of Baron Günther Hubertus von Reibnitz, and has issue—

FREDERICK MICHAEL GEORGE DAVID LOUIS (LORD FREDERICK WINDSOR) . . . 6 Apr. 197●

GABRIELLA MARINA ALEXANDRA OPHELIA (LADY GABRIELLA WINDSOR) . . . 23 Apr. 198●

Residences: Kensington Palace, W8 4PU; Nether Lypiatt Manor, Stroud, Gloucestershire GL6 7LS.

H R H Princess Alexandra, the Hon. Mrs Angus Ogilvy . . . . . . 25 Dec. 193●

Married 24 April 1963, Hon. Angus James Bruce Ogilvy, *qv*, and has issue—

JAMES ROBERT BRUCE OGILVY . . . . 29 Feb. 196●

MARINA VICTORIA ALEXANDRA OGILVY . . . . 31 July 196●

Residence: Thatched House Lodge, Richmond, Surrey; *office:* 22 Friary Court, St James's Palace, SW1.

INDEX TO ADVERTISERS

SUPPLEMENT

TO WHO'S WHO 1983

Part I of this Supplement contains a selection of the alterations too late for inclusion in the body of the book, noted up to late December 1982.

Part II of the Supplement contains a selection of names included in the New Year Honours List, 1983.

SUPPLEMENT : PART I

ABERNETHY, William Leslie. *Address:* 6 Ballakeyll, Colby, Isle of Man. *T:* Port St Mary 832792.

ADAM, General Sir Ronald Forbes, 2nd Bt. Died 26 Dec. 1982. *See p* 10 for heir.

ADAMSON, Prof. Colin. Rector, The Polytechnic of Central London, 1970–July 1983.

ADAMSON, Norman Joseph. *Address:* Whiteways, White Lane, Guildford, Surrey GU4 8PS. *T:* Guildford 65301.

ALLEN, Prof. Percival. Professor of Geology, University of Reading, 1952–82, now Emeritus.

ALSTEAD, Stanley. *Address:* Glenholme, Glen Road, Dunblane, Perthshire.

APPLEYARD, Leonard Vincent. Financial Counsellor, Paris, 1979–82.

ARDAGH AND CLONMACNOIS, Bishop of, (RC). *See infra* Daly.

ARGOV, Shlomo. Ambassador of Israel to the Court of St James's, 1979–82. *Address:* 6 Hagdud Haivri, Jerusalem, Israel.

ARMITAGE, Air Vice-Marshal Michael John. Deputy Chief of the Defence Staff (Intelligence), since 1983, in the rank of Air Marshal.

ASHTON, Rt. Rev. Leonard James. Bishop in Cyprus and The Gulf, 1976–83.

ASHWORTH, Prof. William. *Address:* Flat 14, Wells Court, Wells Road, Ilkley LS29 9LG. *T:* Ilkley 603157.

ATHERTON, Alan Royle. Principal Establishment Officer, Property Services Agency, since 1982.

ATKIN, Alec Field. Managing Director, Marketing, Aircraft Group, British Aerospace, 1981–82.

ATKINSON, Michael William. Counsellor, Peking, 1980–82.

AUSTEN-SMITH, Air Marshal Sir Roy (David). A Gentleman Usher to HM the Queen, since 1982.

AYERS, John Gilbert. Keeper, Far Eastern Department, Victoria and Albert Museum, 1970–82.

AYLMER, 12th Baron. Died Dec. 1982. *See p* 88 for heir.

AZNAM, Raja Tan Sri bin Raja Haji Ahmad. Malaysian High Commissioner in London, 1979–82. *Address:* c/o Ministry of Foreign Affairs, Kuala Lumpur, Malaysia.

BAILEY, Alan Marshall. Deputy Secretary, Industry, HM Treasury, since 1982.

BAKER, Martyn Murray. Counsellor, Civil Aviation and Shipping, Washington, 1978–82.

BARLTROP, Roger Arnold Rowlandson. CVO 1982.

BARRATT, Francis Russell. Deputy Secretary, HM Treasury, 1973–82.

BAUER, Prof. Peter Thomas. Baron (Life Peer), *cr* 1982.

BEARSTED, Viscount. Chairman, 1928 Investment Trust Ltd., 1948–82.

BECKETT, John Michael. Chairman, Woolworth Holdings plc, since 1982. *Address:* (office) 242 Marylebone Road, NW1 6JL.

BELL, Stewart Edward. Sheriff Principal of Grampian, Highland and Islands, since 1983.

BENN, Timothy John. Chairman, Benn Brothers plc, 1981–82.

BENTLEY, John Ransome. Resigned as Chairman, Intervision Video (Holdings) Ltd, Oct. 1982.

BENTON, Peter Faulkner, *T:* 01-432 4949.

BILLAM, John Bertram Hardy. Legal Adviser and Deputy Secretary, 1976–82, part-time Assessor, since 1982, Department of Employment.

BINNEY, Marcus Hugh Crofton. *Address:* c/o Country Life, King's Reach Tower, Stamford Street, SE1.

BINNING, Kenneth George Henry. Director of Government Relations, NEI, and Director, NEI International, since 1983.

BIRCH, Robert Edward Thomas. Director General, Federation Against Copyright Theft, since 1982. *Address:* Federation Against Copyright Theft, St Margarets House, 19–23 Wells Street, W1P 3FP.

BIRLEY, Derek. Vice-Chancellor designate, Proposed University of Ulster, since 1982.

BLACKER, Captain Derek Charles. *Address:* Smithenhayes Farm, Luppitt, near Honiton, Devon EX14 0TR. *T:* Honiton 41842.

BLACKSTONE, Dr Tessa Ann Vosper. Professor of Educational Administration in the University of London at the Institute of Education, 1978–83; Deputy Education Officer (Resources), Inner London Education Authority, from May 1983.

BLAIR, Claude. Keeper, Department of Metalwork, Victoria and Albert Museum, 1972–82.

BLOFELD, John Christopher Calthorpe; His Honour Judge Blofeld. A Circuit Judge, since 1982.

BOLAND, Frederick Henry. Chancellor, Dublin University, Trinity College, 1964–82.

BOORMAN, Henry Roy Pratt. Chairman, 1970–82, President, since 1982, Kent Messenger Group.

BORLEY, Lester. Director, National Trust for Scotland, from July 1983. *Address:* National Trust for Scotland, 5 Charlotte Square, Edinburgh.

BOULTON, Sir William (Whytehead). *London address:* 37 Rutland Gate, SW7. *T:* 01-581 2938.

BOURN, John Bryant. Deputy Secretary, Northern Ireland Office, since 1982. *Address:* Stormont Castle, Belfast BT4 3ST.

BOURNE, (Rowland) Richard. Deputy Director, The Commonwealth Institute, since 1983.

BOYD, Sir John (McFarlane). A Governor of the BBC, since 1982.

BRAGG, Stephen Lawrence. Extraordinary Fellow, Wolfson College, Cambridge, since 1982.

*The current edition contains no entry under this name.

BREWER, Rear-Adm. George Maxted Kenneth. *Address:* c/o National Westminster Bank Ltd, 2 West Street, Portcheste Fareham, Hants.

BRIDGEMAN, 2nd Viscount. Died 17 Nov. 1982. *See p* 268 for heir.

BRIGGS, Rear-Adm. Thomas Vallack. *Address:* c/o 630 Colonial Road, Guildford, Conn, USA.

BRODRICK, His Honour Norman John Lee. A Circuit Judge, 1967–82.

BROOKE, Sir George Cecil Francis, 3rd Bt. Died 27 Dec. 1982. *See p* 282 for heir.

BROOKE TURNER, Alan. Ambassador to Finland, since 1982.

BROWN, Alan Winthrop. Under Secretary, Energy Conservation Division, Department of Energy, since 1982.

BROWN, Maj.-Gen. James. Director General, Ordnance Services, 1980–83.

BROWN, (John) Michael. Ambassador to Costa Rica and to Nicaragua, 1979–82.

BROWNLOW, James Hilton. HM Inspector of Constabulary for Eastern England, since 1983.

BRUHN, Erik Belton Evers. Artistic Director, National Ballet of Canada, from summer 1983.

BRUNNER, Sir Felix John Morgan, 3rd Bt. *See* Obituary and *p* 302 for heir.

BRUTON, John (Gerard). Minister for Industry and Energy, Ireland, since Dec. 1982.

BULLER, Prof. Arthur John. *Address:* Lockhall, Cow Lane, Steeple Aston, Oxon OX5 3SG. *T:* Steeple Aston 47502.

BULPITT, Cecil Arthur Charles, (Philip Bulpitt). Chairman, Cambridge Developments Ltd, since 1982.

BURGESS, Claude Bramall. Minister for Hong Kong Commercial Relations with the European Communities and the Memb States, 1974–82. *Address:* 75 Chester Row, SW1. *T:* 01-730 8758.

BURNS, Sir Wilfred. Deputy Chairman, Local Government Boundary Commission for England, since 1982.

BYFORD, Lawrence. HM Chief Inspector of Constabulary, since 1983.

CAINES, John. Deputy Secretary, Central Policy Review Staff, Cabinet Office, since 1983.

CALLAN, Prof. Harold Garnet. Professor of Natural History, St Salvator's College, St Andrews, 1950–82, now Emeritus.

CAMPBELL, Ian Macdonald. Vice-Chairman, 1980–83, Part-time Member, since 1983, British Railways Board; Chairman Scottish Board, British Rail, since 1983.

CAMPOS, Roberto de Oliveira. Brazilian Ambassador to the Court of St James's, 1975–82; Senator, House of Congress, Brazil since 1982. *Address:* 140 Francisco Otaviano, Ipanema, Rio de Janeiro, Brazil.

CAREY, Sir Peter (Willoughby). Permanent Secretary, Department of Industry, 1976–83.

CARSON, John. Member (UU) for Belfast North, Northern Ireland Assembly, since 1982.

CARTER, Dorothy Ethel Fleming, (Jane). Under Secretary, Head of Energy Conservation Division, Department of Energy 1979–82.

CARTER, John Somers. *Address:* 58 Falmouth Road, Truro, Cornwall TR1 2HR. *T:* Truro 78711.

CASSIDI, Adm. Sir (Arthur) Desmond. Commander-in-Chief, Naval Home Command, since 1982.

CAULCOTT, Thomas Holt. Only *Address:* 43 Lee Crescent, Birmingham B15 2BJ. *T:* 021-235 2000.

CHESTERMAN, Sir Ross. Master, College of Craft Education, since 1982.

CLARK, Ian Robertson. Joint Managing Director, Britoil, since 1982.

CLARK, Sir Robert (Anthony). Chairman, UDS Group, since 1982.

CLEDWYN OF PENRHOS, Baron. Leader of the Opposition, House of Lords, since 1982.

CLUSKEY, Frank. Minister for Trade and Commerce, Ireland, since 1982.

COCKCROFT, Sir Wilfred Halliday. Chairman and Chief Executive, Secondary Examinations Council, since 1983. *Address* (office) Room 5/12, Department of Education and Science, York Road, SE1; 197 Hammersmith Grove, W6.

COLLINS, (James) Gerard. Minister for Foreign Affairs, Ireland, Feb.–Dec. 1982.

COLLINS, Margaret Elizabeth. Matron-in-Chief, Queen Alexandra's Royal Naval Nursing Service, 1980–83.

COOK, David Somerville. Member (Alliance) for Belfast South, Northern Ireland Assembly, since 1982.

COOK, Norman Charles. Hon. Curator, Wells Museum, Somerset, 1972–82.

CORISH, Brendan. TD Wexford, 1945–82.

COTTON, William Frederick, (Bill Cotton). Managing Director, Direct Broadcasting by Satellite, BBC, since 1983.

COUZENS, Sir Kenneth (Edward). Permanent Under Secretary of State, Department of Energy, since 1983.

*COX, Mrs Caroline Anne. Baroness (Life Peer), *cr* 1982. Director, Nursing Education Research Unit, Chelsea College University of London.

CRANE, Sir James (William Donald). HM Chief Inspector of Constabulary, 1979–82; Member, Parole Board, since 1983.

CROFT, Ivor John. Head of Home Office Research and Planning Unit, 1981–83.

CROWSON, Richard Borman. Counsellor, Hong Kong Commercial Affairs, Washington, 1977–82.

CULLIMORE, Charles Augustine Kaye. Counsellor and Head of Chancery, New Delhi, 1979–82.

CURRIE, (Joseph) Austin. Member (SDLP) for Fermanagh and South Tyrone, Northern Ireland Assembly, since 1982.

DALBY, Dr (Terry) David (Pereira). Reader in West African Languages, School of Oriental and African Studies, University o London, 1967–83, retired. *Address:* c/o Department of Africa, School of Oriental and African Studies, WC1E 7HP.

DALY, Most Rev. Cahal Brendan. Bishop of Ardagh and Clonmacnois, (RC), 1967–82; Bishop of Down and Connor since 1982.

DAVIES, Gwilym Prys. Baron (Life Peer), *cr* 1982.

DAVIES, Richard Harries. Treasurer to the Duke of Edinburgh, since 1982.

DAWE, Roger James. Chief Executive, Training Division, Manpower Services Commission, since 1982.

DAWSON, Hon. Sir Daryl Michael. KBE 1982; Justice of the High Court of Australia, since 1982. *Address:* High Court o Australia, Canberra, ACT, Australia.

DAY, Bernard Maurice. Assistant Under-Secretary of State (Supply and Organisation) (Air), Ministry of Defence, since 1982.

de BEER, Esmond Samuel. *Address:* 65 Century Court, Grove End Road, NW8.

DELL, Rt. Hon. Edmund. Chairman, Guinness Peat Group, 1979–82.

DICKENSON, Lt-Col Charles Royal. *Address:* 4600 Gatlin Oaks Lane, Orlando, Florida 32806, USA.

DINSDALE, Richard Lewis. *Address:* 15 Rivermount Gardens, Guildford, Surrey GU2 5DN.

DONKIN, Alexander Sim. Counsellor (Administration), UK Mission to UN, and Deputy Consul-General, New York, 1977–82.

DONOVAN, Prof. Desmond Thomas. Yates-Goldsmid Professor and Head of Department of Geology, University College London, 1966-82; Hon. Curator, Wells Museum, since 1982. *Address:* 8 Cathedral Green, Wells, Som BA5 2UE.

DOWN AND CONNOR, Bishop of, (RC). *See supra* Daly and *infra* Philbin.

UGDALE, Sir William (Stratford), Bt. Chairman, National Water Council, 1982–Sept. 1983.

UNLEATH, Baron. Member (Alliance) for North Down, Northern Ireland Assembly, since 1982.

UNSTAN, Hon. Donald Allan. Chairman, Victorian Tourist Commission, since 1982.

UTTON, Ralph Stawell. Succeeded cousin as 8th Baron Sherborne, 1982.

ARLE, Arthur Frederick. President, Boyden Consulting Group Ltd, 1974–82; management and economic consultant, since 1983. Only *Address:* PO Box 752, Niagara-on-the-Lake, Ont L0S 1J0, Canada.

BERLE, Adm. Sir James (Henry Fuller). Commander-in-Chief, Naval Home Command, and Flag ADC to the Queen, 1981–82; retired 1983. *Address:* c/o RUSI, Whitehall, SW1A 2ET.

CCLES, Hon. John Dawson. Member, Commonwealth Development Corporation, since 1982.

LLIS, Sir John (Rogers). Dean, London Hospital Medical College, 1968–82.

NGLISH, Sir David. Editor, Mail on Sunday, June–Oct. 1982.

VANS, Robert. Managing Director, Supplies, British Gas Corporation, since 1983. *Address:* British Gas Corporation, Rivermill House, 52 Grosvenor Road, SW1V 3JL.

ALETAU, 'Inoke Fotu. High Commissioner for Tonga in London, 1972–82. *Address:* c/o Ministry of Foreign Affairs, Nuku'alofa, Tonga, SW Pacific.

ARTHING, Richard Bruce Crosby. *Address:* Flat 4, 2/3 Ovington Gardens, SW3. *T:* 01-581 7088.

AULKNER, John Richard Hayward. Drama Director, Arts Council of Great Britain, 1977–82.

EARN, Patrick Robin. Royal College of Defence Studies, since 1982.

RMSTON-WILLIAMS, Peter. Deputy Chairman, Woolworth Holdings plc, since 1982.

SHER, Alan Wainwright. Member, British Airways Board, 1972–82.

ITZGERALD, Garret. Taoiseach (Prime Minister of Ireland), since Dec. 1982.

RAGA-IRIBARNE, Manuel. Leader of the Opposition, Spanish Cortes, since 1982.

RANCKLIN, Comdr (Mavourn Baldwin) Philip. Lord-Lieutenant of Nottinghamshire, 1972–83.

RANKLIN, Michael David Milroy. Permanent Secretary, Ministry of Agriculture, Fisheries and Food, since 1983.

RASER, Angus McKay. Chairman, Board of Customs and Excise, since 1983.

REEMAN, Raymond. Aldrichian Praelector in Chemistry, Oxford University, since 1982.

ALLACHER, John. Baron (Life Peer), *cr* 1982. Parliamentary Secretary to the Co-operative Union.

ARRETT, Terence. Counsellor (Science and Technology), Bonn, 1978–82.

EROSA, Peter Norman. Under Secretary, Rural Affairs, Department of the Environment, 1981–82.

IBBS, Stephen. Chairman, Turner & Newall, 1979–82.

IELGUD, Maina. Artistic Director, Australian Ballet, since 1983. *Address:* c/o Australian Ballet, 11 Mount Alexander Road, Flemington, Vic. 3010, Australia.

IFFARD, (Charles) Sydney (Rycroft). Deputy Under-Secretary of State, Foreign and Commonwealth Office, since 1982.

IMSON, George Stanley. Sheriff Principal of Grampian, Highland and Islands, 1975–82.

LOVER, Lt-Gen. Sir James (Malcolm). Deputy Chief of Defence Staff (Intelligence), 1981–82.

ORING-MORRIS, Rex. Counsellor and Consul-General, Stockholm, 1979–82.

RAHAM, Sir Charles Spencer Richard. Lord-Lieutenant of Cumbria, since 1983.

RANT, Alexander (Marshall). Artistic Director, National Ballet of Canada, 1976–summer 1983.

REENHILL OF HARROW, Baron. Member, Security Commission, 1973–82.

RIFFITH, Edward Michael Wynne. Member, Agricultural Research Council, 1973–82.

ROSS, John Jacob. Deputy Chairman, Jan.–Dec. 1982, Editorial Consultant, since 1982, Weidenfeld (Publishers) Ltd.

ROVES, Ronald Edward. Chairman, Meyer International PLC, since 1982.

UNN, Prof. Sir John (Currie). *Address:* 32 Beaconsfield Road, Glasgow G12 0NY. *T:* 041-357 2001.

URDON, John Bertrand. John Humphrey Plummer Professor of Cell Biology, University of Cambridge, from Sept. 1983.

ALL, Dame Catherine (Mary). *Address:* Barnsfield, Barnsfield Lane, Buckfastleigh, Devon TQ11 0NP. *T:* Buckfastleigh 2504.

AMILTON, Sir James (Arnot). Permanent Under-Secretary of State, Department of Education and Science, 1976–May 1983.

AMMOND, Eric Albert Barratt. General Secretary elect, Electrical, Electronic, Telecommunication and Plumbing Union.

ANCOCK, David John Stowell. Permanent Secretary, Department of Education and Science, since 1983.

ARDING, Wilfrid Gerald. *Address:* Bridge Cottage, High Street, Farningham, Dartford DA4 0DW. *T:* Farningham 862733.

ARMAN, Hon. Sir Jeremiah Le Roy; Hon. Mr Justice Harman. Kt 1982; a Judge of the High Court of Justice, Chancery Division, since 1982.

ARRIS, Martin Richard. Director, 1977–82, Deputy Chairman, 1979–82, Reckitt and Colman plc.

AUGHEY, Charles James. Taoiseach (Prime Minister of Ireland), Feb.–Dec. 1982; Leader of the Opposition, since 1982.

AYES, Sir Brian (David). Permanent Secretary, Department of Industry, since 1983. *Address:* Department of Industry, 123 Victoria Street, SW1E 6RB.

AZAN, John Boris Roderick; His Honour Judge Hazan. A Circuit Judge, since 1982.

EDDY, Brian Huleatt. Regional Co-ordinator and Resettlement Officer, British Refugee Council, 1979–82.

ELMORE, Roy Lionel. *Address:* 83 Chishill Road, Heydon, Royston, Herts SG8 8PN. *T:* Royston 838570.

ENDERSON, James Ewart. Managing Director, Mastiff Electronic Systems Ltd, since 1982. *Address:* Mastiff Electronic Systems Ltd, Randalls Road, Leatherhead, Surrey KT22 7RX.

ENHAM, John Alfred; His Honour Judge Henham. A Circuit Judge, since 1983.

INE, Air Vice-Marshal Patrick Bardon. Air Marshal, 1983; Commander-in-Chief designate, RAF Germany, and Commander designate, 2nd Allied Tactical Air Force.

OBDAY, Sir Gordon (Ivan). President of the Council, Nottingham University, 1973–82.

OBKIRK, Michael Dalgliesh. Assistant Under-Secretary of State, Ministry of Defence, 1980–82.

OLLAND-MARTIN, Robert George, (Robin). Hon. Deputy Treasurer, Conservative and Unionist Party, 1979–82; Consultant, Newmarket Company (1981) Ltd, since 1982.

OPKINS, (Richard) Julian. *Address:* Flat 9, 5 Bina Gardens, SW5.

ORNBY, Richard Phipps. Chairman, Halifax Building Society, from May 1983.

HOWLETT, Air Vice-Marshal Neville Stanley. *Address:* Milverton, Bolney Trevor Drive, Lower Shiplake, Oxon RG9 3PG.
HUME, John. Member (SDLP) for Londonderry, Northern Ireland Assembly, since 1982.
HUMPHREYS, Kenneth William. *Address:* 94 Metchley Lane, Harborne, Birmingham B17 0HS. *T:* 021-427 2785.
HUTCHISON, (Joseph) Douglas. Director, Ranks Hovis McDougall Ltd, 1956–83.
HYDE, John Bean. Chief Executive, Charterhouse Group, since 1982.

IBBOTT, Alec. Counsellor and Head of Chancery, Khartoum, 1979–82.
INSKIP, John Hampden; His Honour Judge Inskip. A Circuit Judge, since 1982.
IRWIN, Dr Michael Henry Knox. Medical Director, United Nations, UNICEF and UN Development Programme, since 1982.

JACKSON, Edward Francis. Director, Oxford University Institute of Economics and Statistics, and Professorial Fellow of St
    Antony's College, Oxford, 1959–82.
JAMIESON, Hon. Donald Campbell. Canadian High Commissioner to the United Kingdom, since 1983. *Address:* 1 Grosvenor
    Square, W1.
JARDINE, Brig. Sir Ian Liddell, 4th Bt. Died 25 Nov. 1982. *See p* 1170 for heir.
JONES, Emlyn Bartley. Director General, The Sports Council, 1978–83.
JONES, Francis Edgar. *Address:* Hornby House, 5 Latchmoor Avenue, Gerrards Cross, Bucks SL9 8LJ. *T:* Gerrards Cross
    885319.
JONES, (Thomas) Philip. Chairman, Electricity Council, since 1983.
JOSEPHS, Wilfred. *Address:* Flat 6, 1 Mornington Crescent, NW1.
JOWITT, Juliet Diana Margaret. *Address:* Thorpe Lodge, Littlethorpe, Ripon, N Yorks HG4 3LU.

KAYE, Sir Emmanuel. *Address:* Hartley Place, Hartley Wintney, Hants RG27 8HT.
KENDALL, William Leslie. Secretary General, Council of Civil Service Unions, 1976–83.
KENNEDY, Air Marshal Sir Thomas (Lawrie). Air Member for Personnel, since 1983. *Address:* Ministry of Defence (Air),
    Whitehall, SW1A 2HB.
KILFEDDER, James Alexander. Member (Ulster Popular Unionist) for North Down, and Presiding Officer, Northern Ireland
    Assembly, since 1982.
KILGOUR, Dr John Lowell. Director, Prison Medical Services, Home Office, since 1982.
KIMBERLEY AND KURUMAN, Bishop of. *See infra* Swartz.
KINAHAN, Maj.-Gen. Oliver John. Paymaster-in-Chief and Inspector of Army Pay Services, 1979–83.
KINCH, Anthony Alec. Head of Division for European Regional Development Fund operations, EEC, since 1982.
KINLOCH, Sir Alexander Davenport, 12th Bt. Died 22 Nov. 1982. *See p* 1257 for heir.
KNIGHT, Air Vice-Marshal Michael William Patrick. Air Member for Supply and Organisation, since 1983, in the rank of Air
    Marshal. *Address:* Ministry of Defence (Air), Main Building, Whitehall, SW1.
KNOX, Prof. Henry Macdonald. *Address:* 9 Elliot Gardens, Clinton, Edinburgh EH14 1EH. *T:* 031-441 6283.
KORNBERG, Prof. Sir Hans (Leo). Master of Christ's College, Cambridge, since 1982.

LAVERS, Patricia Mae. *Address:* Horse Pond Sluice, Delf Street, Sandwich, Kent.
LAWSON, John Alexander Reid. President, Royal College of General Practitioners, since 1982.
LAWTHER, Prof. Patrick Joseph. Professor of Environmental and Preventive Medicine, University of London, at St
    Bartholomew's Hospital Medical College, 1968–82, and at London Hospital Medical College, 1976–82.
LEE, Maj.-Gen. Patrick Herbert. Director General, Electrical and Mechanical Engineering (Army), 1979–83.
LEWIN, Admiral of the Fleet Sir Terence Thornton. Baron Lewin (Life Peer), of Greenwich in Greater London, Nov. 1982.
LEIGH-PEMBERTON, Robert, (Robin Leigh-Pemberton). Governor, Bank of England, from July 1983.
LISTER, Thomas Liddell. Under Secretary, Scottish Development Department, 1977–82.
LITTLER, (James) Geoffrey. Second Permanent Secretary (Overseas Finance Sector), HM Treasury, since 1983.
LLEWELYN-DAVIES OF HASTOE, Baroness. Opposition Chief Whip, House of Lords, 1979–82.
LLOYD, Leslie. General Manager, Western Region, British Rail, 1976–82. *Address:* 73 The Fairway, Burnham, Bucks.
LOCH, 3rd Baron. Died 15 Dec. 1982. *See p* 1365 for heir.
LOCKWOOD, Baroness. Chairman, Equal Opportunities Commission, 1975–83.
LOVELOCK, Sir Douglas Arthur. First Church Estates Commissioner, since 1983.
LYNCH, Rt. Hon. Sir Phillip (Reginald). MHR, Australia, 1966–82.

McCLELLAND, George Ewart. Solicitor, Department of Employment, since 1982.
McGRATH, John Peter. *Address:* c/o 7:84 Theatre Co., 58 Queen Street, Edinburgh EH2 3NS.
McINTOSH, Andrew Robert. Baron (Life Peer), *cr* 1982.
MACKENZIE, Keith Roderick Turing. Secretary, Royal and Ancient Golf Club of St Andrews, 1967–Sept. 1983.
MACKWORTH-YOUNG, (Gerard) William. *Address:* Fisherton Mill, Fisherton de la Mere, Wylye, Wilts. *T:* Wylye 246.
MacLEOD, Hugh Roderick. Chairman, Scottish Board, British Railways, 1980–83.
McNEILL, Peter Grant Brass. Sheriff of Lothians and Borders at Edinburgh, since 1982. *Address:* Sheriffs' Chambers, Sheriff
    Court House, Lawnmarket, Edinburgh EH1 2NS. *T:* 031-226 7181.
MAIS, Francis Thomas. Permanent Secretary, Department of Manpower Services, Northern Ireland, 1981–82.
MALMESBURY, Earl of. Lord-Lieutenant and Custos Rotulorum of Hampshire, 1973–82.
MARDON, Lt-Col John Kenric La Touche. Director, Bristol & West Building Society, retired 1982.
MARCHANT, Ven. George John Charles. Archdeacon of Auckland and Canon Residentiary, Durham Cathedral, 1974–Easter
    1983.
MARSHALL, Alexander Badenoch. Chairman, Commercial Union Assurance plc, since 1983.
MARSHALL, Frank Graham. Science and Technology Councellor, Tokyo, 1980–82.
MARSHALL, Sir Robert Braithwaite. Chairman, National Water Council, 1978–82.
MASON, Sir (Basil) John. Director-General of the Meteorological Office, 1965–Aug. 1983.
MATTHEWS, Paul Taunton. Vice-Chancellor, Bath University, 1976–Aug. 1983.
MAUGHAN, Air Vice-Marshal Charles Gilbert. General Secretary, The Royal British Legion, 1978–83; an Independent Panel

Inspector, Department of the Environment, since 1983. *Address:* Little Askett, Askett, Aylesbury, Bucks HP17 9LT.

MELLISH, Rt. Hon. Robert Joseph. MP Bermondsey, 1946–82 (Lab 1946–82, Ind. 1982). *Address:* London Docklands Development Corporation, West India House, Millwall Dock, E14 9TJ.

MENDOZA-ACOSTA, Vice-Adm. Felix. Venezuelan Ambassador to the Court of St James's, 1979–82. *Address:* c/o Ministry of Foreign Affairs, Carácas, Venezuela.

MERRISON, Sir Alexander Walter. Chairman, Association of Commonwealth Universities, 1982–83.

MIDDLETON, Peter Edward. Permanent Secretary, HM Treasury, since 1983.

MONAHAN, James Henry Francis. *Address:* 42 Castelnau, SW13. *T:* 01-748 7287.

MONCKTON, Hon. Christopher Walter. Special Adviser to the Prime Minister's Policy Unit (Home Affairs), since 1982.

MORTON, (Robert) Alastair (Newton). Also Chairman, Guinness Peat Group, since 1982.

MOTTRAM, Maj.-Gen. John Frederick. Major-General Training and Reserve Forces Royal Marines, 1980–83.

MOUNT EDGCUMBE, 7th Earl of. Died 9 Dec. 1982. *See p* 1608 for heir.

MYRDAL, Prof. (Karl) Gunnar. *Address:* Svalnäs Allé 12B, 18263 Djursholm, Sweden.

NEAL, Michael David. Headmaster, Cranborne Chase School, 1969–83.

NESS, Air Marshal Sir Charles. Air Member for Personnel, 1980–83.

NETHERTHORPE, 2nd Baron. *See* Obituary and *p* 1639 for heir.

NEWSAM, Richard William. *Address:* 2 Clarendon Road, St Heliers, Auckland, New Zealand.

NICOL, Mrs Olive Mary Wendy. Baroness (Life Peer), *cr* 1982. Member, Cambridge City Council.

NOAKES, Philip Reuben. *Address:* Little St Mary's, Uplyme, Lyme Regis, Dorset DT7 3XH. *T:* Axminster 33371.

NOLAN, Hon. Sir Michael Patrick; Hon. Mr Justice Nolan. Kt 1982; a Justice of the High Court, Queen's Bench Division, since 1982.

NORMAN, Sir Arthur (Gordon). Deputy Chairman, Thomas Tilling Ltd, since 1982.

O'BRIEN, Sir David Edmond, 6th Bt. Died 26 Nov. 1982. *See p* 1675 for heir.

OHLSON, Sir Eric James. *Address:* 9 Park Edge, Harrogate HG2 8JU.

O'LEARY, Michael. TD (FG) for Dublin South West, since 1982.

O'NEILL, Rt. Hon. Phelim Robert Hugh. Succeeded father as 2nd Baron Rathcavan, 1982.

OSOLA, (Victor) John, (Väinö Juhani). Group Chief Executive, Redman Heenan International plc, 1979–82.

OWEN, Peter Francis. Under Secretary, Rural Affairs, Department of the Environment, since 1982.

PAIBA, Denis Anthony; His Honour Judge Paiba. A Circuit Judge, since 1982.

PALMER, Andrew Eustace. Head of Falkland Islands Department, Foreign and Commonwealth Office, since 1982.

PALMER, John. A Deputy Secretary, Department of Transport, since 1982.

PARKER, (Thomas) John. Chairman, Harland and Wolff, since 1983. *Address:* Harland and Wolff Ltd, Belfast BT3 9DU.

PARRY-EVANS, Air Vice-Marshal David. Air Officer Commanding No 1 Group, RAF Strike Command, since 1983.

PARSONS, Sir Anthony (Derrick). Special Adviser to the Prime Minister, since 1982.

PEARCE, Hon. Richard Bruce Holroyd; His Honour Judge Pearce. A Circuit Judge, since 1982.

PEART, Baron. Leader of the Opposition in the House of Lords, 1979–82.

PERCIVAL-PRESCOTT, Westby William. Keeper and Head of Picture Department, National Maritime Museum, 1977–83.

PHALP, Geoffrey Anderson. *Address:* 19 Norfolk Road, Edgbaston, Birmingham B15 3PZ. *T:* 021-454 2616.

PHILBIN, Most Rev. William J. Bishop of Down and Connor, 1962–82.

PILE, Col Sir Frederick Devereux, 3rd Bt. Brother, Sir John Devereux Pile, died 13 Dec. 1982; heir now *nephew* Anthony John Devereux Pile [*b* 7 June 1947; *m* 1977, Jennifer Clare Youngman; one *s*].

PITFIELD, (Peter) Michael. CVO 1982; Clerk of the Privy Council and Secretary to the Cabinet, Canada, 1975–79 and 1980–82.

PLATT OF WRITTLE, Baroness. Chairman, Equal Opportunities Commission, from May 1983.

PONSONBY OF SHULBREDE, Baron. Chief Opposition Whip, House of Lords, since 1982.

POPE, Geoffrey George. Deputy Controller and Adviser (Research and Technology), Ministry of Defence, since 1982.

POPHAM, Maj.-Gen. Christopher John. Director, British Atlantic Committee, since 1982.

POPLE, John Anthony. *Address:* Carnegie-Mellon University, 4400 Fifth Avenue, Pittsburgh, Pa 15213, USA.

POTTER, John Herbert. Counsellor (Administration), Bonn, 1981–82.

POTTER, Sir (Joseph) Raymond (Lynden). Chairman, Halifax Building Society, 1974–May 1983.

PRICE, Geoffrey Alan. Chief Executive, County Council of Hereford and Worcester, since 1983. *Address:* County Hall, Spetchley Road, Worcester WR5 2NP.

PUGH, John Stanley. Editor, Liverpool Echo, 1978–82.

QUINTON, Anthony Meredith. Baron (Life Peer), *cr* 1982.

RAGLAN, Baron. Chairman, Cwmbran New Town Development Corporation, 1970–83.

RAMSAY, Patrick George Alexander. Controller, BBC Scotland, 1979–82.

RATHCAVAN, 1st Baron. Died 28 Nov. 1982. *See supra* O'Neill.

RAWLINSON, Sir Anthony (Keith). Permanent Secretary, Department of Trade, since 1983.

REECE, (Edward Vans) Paynter; His Honour Judge Reece. A Circuit Judge, since 1982.

REID, Robert Basil. Also a Vice-Chairman, British Railways Board, since 1983.

RESTREPO-LONDOÑO, Andrés. Colombian Ambassador to the Court of St James's, 1981–82. *Address:* Calle 8012 A-44, Bogotá, Colombia.

REYNTIENS, Nicholas Patrick. *Address:* Ilford Bridges Farm, Close Stocklinch, Ilminster, Som. *T:* Ilminster 2241.

RICHARDS, David Gordon. *Address:* Eastleach House, Eastleach, Glos GL7 3NW. *T:* Southrop 416.

RICHARDSON, Rt. Hon. Gordon (William Humphreys). Governor of the Bank of England, 1973–June 1983.

RITCHIE, Horace David. Dean, London Hospital Medical College, since 1982.

ROBERTS, Christopher William. Chief Executive, British Overseas Trade Board, since 1983.

ROBERTS, John Lewis. Assistant Under-Secretary of State (International and Industrial Policy), Ministry of Defence, since 1982.

ROBERTS, Rear-Adm. John Oliver. Director General, British Printing Industries Federation, 1981–83.

ROBERTSON, Rear-Adm. Ian George William. *Address:* Moons Oast, Barcombe Road, Piltdown, Sussex TN22 3XG. *T:* Newick 2279.

ROGERS, Hugh Charles Innes. Vice-Chairman, Bristol and West Building Society, retired 1982.

RUPERT'S LAND, Bishop of. *See infra* Valentine.

RUSSELL, George. Managing Director and Chief Executive, British Alcan Aluminium, since 1982.

SANDILANDS, Sir Francis (Edwin Prescott). Chairman, Commercial Union Assurance Co., 1972–83.

SCOTT, Sir James Walter. Lord-Lieutenant of Hampshire, since 1982.

SEIGNORET, Eustace Edward. High Commissioner for Trinidad and Tobago in London, 1977–82. *Address:* c/o Ministry for External Affairs, Queen's Park West, Port of Spain, Trinidad and Tobago, WI.

SHAW, John Dennis Bolton. *Address:* West Beeches, Ashurst Wood, W Sussex RH19 3RQ.

SHEERIN, John Declan; His Honour Judge Sheerin. A Circuit Judge, since 1982.

SHEPHERD, Geoffrey Thomas. Chairman, Midlands Electricity Board, 1972–82; management and engineering consultant, since 1982. *T:* Pershore 553076.

SHERBORNE, 7th Baron. Died 25 Dec. 1982. *See supra* Dutton.

SILK, Ven. (Robert) David. Also Team Rector, Holy Spirit, Leicester, since 1982.

SINDALL, Adrian John. Head of South America Department, Foreign and Commonwealth Office, since 1982.

SKINGSLEY, Air Vice-Marshal Anthony Gerald. Commandant, Royal Air Force Staff College, Bracknell, since 1983.

SMITH, Prof. (Francis) Graham. Astronomer Royal, since 1982.

SPENCER-SILVER, Prof. Peter Hele. S. A. Courtauld Professor of Anatomy in the University of London, 1974–82.

SPENDLOVE, Peter Roy. Deputy High Commissioner, Sri Lanka, 1981–82.

SPOONER, Sir James (Douglas). Chairman, Morgan Crucible, since 1983.

STANFORD, (William) Bedell. Chancellor, Dublin University, Trinity College, since 1982.

STEWART, Sir High Charlie Godfray, Bt. *Address:* Cottesbrook, Sandy Pluck Lane, Bentham, near Cheltenham, Glos.

STEWART, Kenneth Hope. Director of Research, Meteorological Office, 1976–82.

SUMNER, His Honour (William) Donald (Massey). A Circuit Judge (formerly Judge of County Courts), 1961–82.

SWARTZ, Rt. Rev. George Alfred. A Bishop Suffragan of Cape Town, 1972–83; Bishop of Kimberley and Kuruman since 1983.

TAYLOR, Sir Francis, (Sir Frank Taylor). Baron (Life Peer), *cr* 1982.

TAYLOR, Sir John Aked. Baron (Life Peer), *cr* 1982.

TAYLOR, Sir Robert (Mackinlay). Chairman, Thomas Tilling Ltd, 1976–May 1983.

TERRY, Sir George (Walter Roberts). Chief Constable of Sussex, 1973–May 1983. *Address:* c/o National Westminster Bank, 173 High Street, Lewes, Sussex BN7 1XD.

THOMPSON, (William) Pratt. Director, AIDCOM International, and Chairman, AIDCOM Technology, and Vice-Chairman, Trimtech, since 1982.

TINKER, Prof. Hugh Russell. Professor of Politics, University of Lancaster, 1977–82, now Emeritus.

TOMBS, Sir Francis (Leonard). Chairman, Turner & Newall, since 1982.

TONKIN, Hon. David Oliver. Premier, Treasurer, Minister of State Development and Minister of Ethnic Affairs, Government of South Australia, 1979–82.

TRENCH, Sir Peter (Edward). Chairman, Y. J. Lovell (Holdings) plc, 1972–83.

TURNER, Richard. *Address:* Flat 3, Western Field, Manor Road, Sidmouth, Devon EX10 8RR. *T:* Sidmouth 3805.

UNGER, Michael Ronald. Editor, Liverpool Echo, since 1982.

UTIGER, Ronald Ernest. Chairman, British Aluminium Co. Ltd, 1979–82; Director, British Alcan Aluminium, since 1982.

UVAROV, Dame Olga. Hon. Secretary, Research Defence Society, 1978–82.

VALENTINE, Rt. Rev. Barry. Bishop of Rupert's Land, 1979–82.

WADDS, Mrs Jean Casselman. Member, Royal Commission on Economic Union and Development Prospects for Canada, since 1983. *Address:* (office) Vanguard Building, Slater Street, Ottawa, Ont, Canada.

WADE, John Charles. Lord-Lieutenant of Cumberland, later Cumbria, 1968–83.

WADSWORTH, Vivian Michael. Chairman, Harland and Wolff, Belfast, 1981–82.

WALEY, (Andrew) Felix; His Honour Judge Waley. A Circuit Judge, since 1982.

WALLROCK, John. Chairman, Minet Holdings Ltd, 1972–82.

WATERLOW, Prof. John Conrad. Professor of Human Nutrition, London School of Hygiene and Tropical Medicine, 1970–82.

WATSON, Gerald Walter. Under Secretary, HM Treasury.

WENHAM, Brian George. Director of Programmes, BBC Television, since 1983.

WIGRAM, Rev. Canon Sir Clifford Woolmore, Bt. Vicar of Marston St Lawrence with Warkworth, 1945–83, also of Thenford, 1975–83.

WILCOX, Malcolm George. *Address:* c/o Midland Bank plc, Poultry, EC2P 2BX.

WILL, Ronald Kerr. Deputy Keeper of Her Majesty's Signet, 1975–83.

WILLIAMS, Rev. John Herbert. Deputy Chaplain General, Home Office Prison Department, 1974–83.

WILSON, John Warley; His Honour Judge John Wilson. A Circuit Judge, since 1982.

WILSON, Roy Vernon. Director, Eastern Region, Property Services Agency, Department of the Environment, 1980–82.

WISE, Baron. *Address:* Martlets, Blakeney, Norfolk NR25 7NP.

YATES, Alfred. Director, National Foundation for Educational Research in England and Wales, 1972–83.

ZACHAROV, Prof. Vasili, (Basil). Director, University of London Computing Centre, 1978–82, and Professor of Computer Studies, 1979–82.

ZILKHA, Selim Khedoury. Resigned as Director, Habitat Mothercare, Nov. 1982.

SUPPLEMENT : PART II

A SELECTION OF NAMES IN THE NEW YEAR HONOURS LIST
31 DECEMBER 1982

ADAMS, Richard Borlase. CBE 1983.
AGNEW, Sir Robert David Garrick. Kt 1983. For service to industry and commerce in Australia.
ANGLESEY, Marchioness of. DBE 1983.
ARMSTRONG, Sir Robert (Temple). GCB 1983.
*ASTON, Sir Harold George. Kt 1983. For service to industry in Australia.
ATKINSON, Sir Robert. Kt 1983.
AUCKLAND (NZ), Bishop of (RC). CBE 1983.

BAILEY, Sir Brian Harry. Kt 1983.
*BALDERSTONE, Sir James Schofield. Kt 1983. For service to primary industry and commerce in Australia.
BARING, Hon. Sir John Francis Harcourt. Kt 1983.
BARNETT, Joseph Anthony. CBE 1983.
BATES, Air Vice-Marshal David Frank. CB 1983.
BELSTEAD, Baron. PC 1983.
*BENNETT, Lt-Gen. Sir Phillip Harvey. KBE 1983. Chief of the General Staff, Australia.
BETHEL, David Percival. CBE 1983.
BEVAN, Peter Gilroy. CBE 1983.
BIRD, Richard Herries. CB 1983.
BIRTWISTLE, Maj.-Gen. Archibald Cull. CB 1983.
*BLACKBURN, Hon. Sir Richard Arthur; Hon. Mr Justice Blackburn. Kt 1983. For service to law in Australia.
BLELLOCH, John Niall Henderson. CB 1983.
BOOTH, Sir Christopher Charles. Kt 1983.
BOWETT, Prof. Derek William. CBE 1983.
BRIDGES, Baron. KCMG 1983.
BRISBANE, Archbishop of. KBE 1983.
*BROWN, Sir Douglas Denison. Kt 1983. For political service.
BUNCH, Sir Austin Wyeth. Kt 1983.
BUTLER, Sir Clifford Charles. Kt 1983.

CAINES, John. CB 1983.
CAMERON, Marshal of the Royal Air Force Sir Neil. Baron (Life Peer), cr 1983.
CAREY, D(avid) M(acbeth) M(oir). CBE 1983.
CARRICK, Roger John. CMG 1983.
CASSIDI, Adm. Sir (Arthur) Desmond. GCB 1983.
CHOUFFOT, Geoffrey Charles. CBE 1983.
CHRISTOFAS, Sir Kenneth Cavendish. KCMG 1983.
COCKCROFT, Sir Wilfred Halliday. Kt 1983.
COLE, Sir (Alexander) Colin. KCVO 1983.
COLLINS, Margaret Elizabeth. CBE 1983.
CONRAN, Sir Terence Orby. Kt 1983.
COWAN, James Robertson. CBE 1983.
CROMARTIE, (Ronald) Ian (Talbot). CMG 1983.
CUMMING, (John) Alan. CBE 1983.
CUNNINGHAM, David. CB 1983.
*CUTHBERTSON, Sir Harold Alexander. Kt 1983. For service to industry and the community in Australia.

DAKERS, Lionel Frederick. CBE 1983.
DAVIES, Ian Leonard. CB 1983.
DODD, William Atherton. CMG 1983.
DUNCAN, Stanley Frederick St Clare. CMG 1983.
DUNCAN, Sir William Barr McKinnon. Kt 1983.
DUNLEAVY, Philip. CBE 1983.

EADEN, Maurice Bryan. CBE 1983.

EBURNE, Sir Sidney Alfred William. Kt 1983.
EZRA, Sir Derek. Baron (Life Peer), cr 1983.

*FINK, Prof. Peter Thomas. CB 1983. For public service, Australia.
FITZPATRICK, James Bernard. CBE 1983.
*FLETCHER, Sir Leslie. Kt 1983. For political and public service.
FRANKLAND, (Anthony) Noble. CB 1983.
FREEDMAN, Charles. CB 1983.
FROST, Albert Edward. CBE 1983.

GARDNER, Sir Edward Lucas. Kt 1983.
GARNETT-ORME, Ion. CBE 1983.
GILBERT, Air Vice-Marshal Joseph Alfred. CB 1983.
GOULDING, Marrack Irvine. CMG 1983.
GOW, Gen. Sir (James) Michael. GCB 1983.
GRANT, Sir (John) Anthony. Kt 1983.
GREGSON, Peter Lewis. CB 1983.
GRENSIDE, Sir John Peter. Kt 1983.

HAINING, Thomas Nivison. CMG 1983.
HALL, David. CBE 1983.
HANDLEY, Prof. Eric Walter. CBE 1983.
HARDIE, (Charles) Jeremy (Mawdesley). CBE 1983.
HARDING, Sir George William. KCMG 1983.
HARDING, Air Marshal Sir Peter Robin. KCB 1983.
*HELE, Sir Ivor Thomas Henry. Kt 1983. For service to the arts in Australia.
HERBERT, Vice-Adm. Sir Peter Geoffrey Marshall. KCB 1983.
HILLIER, Sir Harold George. Kt 1983.
HODDINOTT, Prof. Alun. CBE 1983.
HOLME, Richard Gordon. CBE 1983.
HORDERN, Sir Michael Murray. Kt 1983.
HOUGHTON, Prof. John Theodore. CBE 1983.

IRVINE, John Ferguson. CB 1983.
IVENS, Michael William. CBE 1983.
IVINS, Prof. John Derek. CBE 1983.

JEFFS, Kenneth Peter. CMG 1983.
*JEPHCOTT, Hon. Sir Bruce Reginald. Kt 1983. For services to politics and the community in Papua New Guinea.
JOHNSTON, Ven. William Francis. CB 1983.
*JONES, Sir John Lewis. KCB 1983.

*KENNEDY-GOOD, Sir John. KBE 1983. For service to local government and the community, New Zealand.
KENNON, Vice-Adm. Sir James Edward Campbell. KCB 1983.
KERRY, Sir Michael James. KCB 1983.
KNOWELDEN, Prof. John. CBE 1983.
KOLTAI, Ralph. CBE 1983.
*KRAMER, Dame Leonie Judith. DBE 1983. For service to literature and the public service, Australia.

LAJTHA, Prof. Laszlo George. CBE 1983.
LANE, David Neil. CMG 1983.
LANE, Sir David William Stennis Stuart. Kt 1983.
LAWS, Richard Maitland. CBE 1983.

*The current edition contains no entry under this name.

*LEONARD, Sir Reginald Byron. Kt 1983. For service to the
  community in Australia.
 LEWIN, (George) Ronald. CBE 1983.
 LEWIS, Sir Kenneth. Kt 1983.
 LIAO POON-HUAI, Hon. Donald. CBE 1983.
 LLEWELLYN, David Walter. CBE 1983.
 LLOYD, Dr Brian Beynon. CBE 1983.
*LOGAN, Sir Raymond Douglas. Kt 1983. For service to the
  cattle industry and the community in Queensland.
 LOUISY, Rt. Hon. Allan. CBE 1983.
 LOVE, Prof. Philip Noel. CBE 1983.
 LUSH, Christopher Duncan. CMG 1983.

 McCOLL, Colin Hugh Verel. CMG 1983.
 McCOLL, Ian. CBE 1983.
*McCUSKER, Sir James Alexander. Kt 1983. For service to
  building societies in Western Australia.
*MACFARLANE, Sir Norman Somerville. Kt 1983.
  Chairman and Managing Director, Macfarlane Group
  (Clansman) PLC; for services to industry and the arts.
 MACKENZIE, Rear-Adm. David John. CB 1983.
 MACREADY, Sir Nevil (John Wilfred), Bt. CBE 1983.
 MANZIE, (Andrew) Gordon. CB 1983.
 MARA, Rt. Hon. Ratu Sir Kamisese Kapaiwai Tuimacilai.
  GCMG 1983.
 MARSHALL, Sir Peter Harold Reginald. KCMG 1983.
 MAVOR, Michael Barclay. CVO 1983.
 MILLER, Dr Jonathan Wolfe. CBE 1983.
 MOORE, Rt. Hon. Sir Philip (Brian Cecil). GCVO 1983.
 MOTTRAM, Maj.-Gen. John Frederick. CB 1983.
 NABARRO, Sir John David Nunes. Kt 1983.
 NAPIER, Maj.-Gen. Lennox Alexander Hawkins. CB 1983.
 NURSAW, James. CB 1983.
 NUTTGENS, Patrick John. CBE 1983.

 O'HARA, Rear-Adm. Derek. CB 1983.
*OLEWALE, Hon. Sir Niwia Ebia. Kt 1983. For services to
  politics and government in Papua New Guinea.

 PARKES, Sir Edward Walter. Kt 1983.
 PERCIVAL, Rt. Hon. Sir Ian. PC 1983.
*PETTIGREW, Sir Russell Hilton. Kt 1983. For services to
  the transport industry in New Zealand.
 PINDLING, Rt. Hon. Sir Lynden Oscar. KCMG 1983.
 PIPER, Sir David Towry. Kt 1983.
 PRITCHARD, Sir John Michael. Kt 1983.
 PUTTNAM, David. CBE 1983.

 RANKIN, James Deans. CBE 1983.
 RAYNER, Sir Derek George. Baron (Life Peer), *cr* 1983.
 REDFERN, Philip. CB 1983.
 RICHARDSON, Rt. Hon. Gordon William Humphreys.
  Baron (Life Peer), *cr* 1983.
 RIDLEY, Rt. Hon. Nicholas. PC 1983.
 RING, Prof. James. CBE 1983.
 ROBERTS, Sir David Arthur. KBE 1983.
 ROBINSON, Rt. Hon. Sir Kenneth. Kt 1983.

 ROBSON, John Adam. CMG 1983.
 ROSE, Clifford Alan. CBE 1983.

 SANDERS, Donald Neil. CB 1983.
 SANKEY, John Anthony. CMG 1983.
 SIMONS, (Alfred) Murray. CMG 1983.
 SINCLAIR, Maj.-Gen. George Brian. CB 1983.
*SIVEWRIGHT, Col Robert Charles Townsend. CB 1983.
  Vice-Chairman, Council of Territorial Auxiliary an
  Volunteer Reserve Associations.
 SKINGSLEY, Air Vice-Marshal Anthony Gerald. CB 1983
 SMITH, Sir Dudley (Gordon). Kt 1983.
 SNEDDON, Hutchison B. CBE 1983.
*SPEIGHT, Hon Sir Graham Davies. Kt 1983. Judge of th
  High Court of New Zealand, 1966–82.
 SPRAGGS, Rear-Adm. Trevor Owen Keith. CB 1983.
 STEEL, Prof. Robert Walter. CBE 1983.
 STEWART, Sir James Douglas. Kt 1983.
 STEWART, Lt-Col Robert Christie. CBE 1983.
 STORMONTH DARLING, Sir James Carlisle. Kt 1983.
 STUART, Ven. Herbert James. CB 1983.
 SUGDEN, Sir Theodore Morris. Kt 1983.

 TEMPLE, Sir John Meredith. Kt 1983.
 TERRY, Air Chief Marshal Sir Peter (David George). GCI
  1983.
 THOMASON, Prof. George Frederick. CBE 1983.
 THOMSON, Sir Adam. Kt 1983.
 TILLOTSON, Maj.-Gen. Henry Michael. CB 1983.
 TRYTHALL, Maj.-Gen. Anthony John. CB 1983.

 URQUHART, James Graham. CVO 1983.
 UVAROV, Dame Olga. DBE 1983.

 VICKERS, Lt-Gen. Sir Richard Maurice Hilton. KCE
  1983.

 WADE-GERY, Sir Robert Lucian. KCMG 1983.
 WALLACE, Charles William. CMG 1983.
*WALTERS, Sir Frederick Donald. Kt 1983. For politica
  and public service.
 WARD, Michael Phelps. CBE 1983.
 WATSON, Roy William. CBE 1983.
 WHITE, Prof. John Edward Clement Twarowski. CBE
  1983.
 WHITMORE, Clive Anthony. CVO 1983.
 WILLIAMS, Hon. Sir Edward (Stratten). KCMG 1983.
*WILLIAMS, Maj.-Gen. Robin Guy. CB 1983. Chief o
  General Staff, New Zealand.
 WILLIAMS, Walter Gordon Mason. CB 1983.
 WILLMOTT, Prof. John Charles. CBE 1983.
 WOODFIELD, Sir Philip John. KCB 1983.

 YOUDE, Sir Edward. GCMG 1983.
*YOUNG, Senator the Hon. Sir Harold William. KCMG
  1983. For parliamentary service, Australia.

A

AARON, Richard Ithamar, MA, DPhil; FBA 1955; Professor of Philosophy, University College of Wales, Aberystwyth, 1932-69; *b* 6 Nov. 1901; *s* of William and Margaret Aaron, Ynystawe, Swansea; *m* Rhiannon, *d* of Dr M. J. Morgan, Aberystwyth; two *s* three *d*. *Educ*: Ystalyfera Grammar School; Cardiff University College; Oriel College, Oxford. Fellow, Univ. of Wales, 1923; Lectr at Swansea, 1926; Chm., Central Adv. Coun. for Educn (Wales), 1946-52; Mem., Coun. for Wales, 1956-63 (Chm., 1960-63); Chm. Library Advisory Council (Wales), 1965-72; Mem. Gen. Advisory Council, BBC, 1962-73, and TV Research Council, 1963-69; Mem. Council, National Library of Wales, 1953-73; Vice-Chm., Coleg Harlech Residential Coll.; Chm., Pembroke and Cardigan Agricultural Wages Cttee, 1962-73. Vis. Prof. in Philosophy, Yale Univ., US, 1952-53 (Fell. of Pierson Coll.). Pres., Mind Assoc., 1955-56; Pres., Aristotelian Society, London, 1957-58. Hon. DLitt Wales, 1973. *Publications:* The Nature of Knowing, 1930; Hanes Athroniaeth, 1932; An Early Draft of Locke's Essay (with Jocelyn Gibb), 1936; John Locke, 1937, 3rd rev. edn 1971; The Limitations of Locke's Rationalism, in Seventeenth Century Studies, 1938; Our Knowledge of Universals, Annual Philosophical Lecture to British Academy, 1945; The Theory of Universals, 1952, 2nd rev. edn 1967; The True and the Valid, Friends of Dr Williams's Library Lecture, 1954; Knowing and the Function of Reason, 1971; Editor, Efrydiau Athronyddol, 1938-68; contributor to Mind, Proc. Arist. Soc., Philosophy, Mod. Lang. Rev., Llenor, etc. *Address:* Garth Celyn, Aberystwyth, Dyfed. *T:* 3535.

AARONS, Sir Daniel (Sidney), Kt 1970; OBE 1966; MC 1917 and Bar, 1918; retired; *b* 1 Aug. 1885; *s* of Solomon Aarons and Hannah Hart; *m* 1925, Jessie Chaddock Stronach; no *c*. *Educ*: North Broken Hill Public School. Joined Vacuum Oil Co. Australia in West Australia, 1903; enlisted AIF, 1915, 16th Infantry Battalion; returned 1920 and joined Head Office of Company, Melbourne; transf. to Sydney as Gen. Man. NSW, 1935; retd 1947. Foundn Mem., Liberal Party of Australia, 1945; subseq. Chm. of Finance Cttee; Treas. 1969. Past Pres., Legacy Club of Sydney; Mem. Federal Council, Legacy Clubs of Australia; Past Pres., Civic Reform Assoc. (local govt). *Recreations:* lawn bowls; formerly rowing (Mem. King's Cup 8-oared Crew WA 1912), lacrosse (Player Man., WA Interstate Lacrosse Team, 1912) and golf. *Address:* Australian Club, 165 Macquarie Street, Sydney, NSW 2000, Australia. *T:* 221 1533. *Club:* Australian (Sydney).

AARONSON, Graham Raphael; QC 1982; *b* 31 Dec. 1944; *s* of late John Aaronson and of Dora Aaronson (*née* Franks); *m* 1967, Linda Esther Smith; two *s* one *d*. *Educ*: City of London Sch.; Trinity Hall, Cambridge (Thomas Waraker Law Schol.; MA). Called to the Bar, Middle Temple, 1966; practised Revenue law, 1968-73 and 1978-. Founder, Standford Grange residential rehabilitation centre for ex-offenders, 1974; Man. Dir, Worldwide Plastics Development, 1974-77. *Publication:* contrib. Chitty on Contracts, 23rd edn 1968. *Recreations:* photography, sitting in the sun and staring at the sea and sometimes swimming under it. *Address:* Queen Elizabeth Building, Temple, EC4Y 9BS. *T:* 01-353 9076.

AARVOLD, His Honour Sir Carl (Douglas), Kt 1968; OBE 1945; TD 1950; DL; Recorder of London, 1964-75; *b* 7 June 1907; *s* of late O. P. Aarvold and late J. M. Aarvold, West Hartlepool, County Durham; *m* 1934, Noeline Etrenne Hill, Denton Park, Yorks; three *s*. *Educ*: Durham Sch.; Emmanuel College, Cambridge (Hon. Fellow, 1976). Called to the Bar, Inner Temple, 1932; North Eastern Circuit. Master of the Bench, Inner Temple, 1959. Recorder of Pontefract, 1951-54; a Judge of the Mayor's and City of London Court, 1954-59; Common Serjeant, City of London, 1959-64; Chm., City of London QS, 1969-71. Chm., Inner London Probation Cttee, 1965-75; Pres., Central Council of Probation Cttees, 1968-75; Chm., Home Sec.'s Adv. Bd on Restricted Patients, 1978-81. Chairman: RAC, 1978-81; Statutory Cttee, Pharmaceutical Soc., 1981-. DL Surrey, 1973. Hon. LLD Dalhousie, 1962; Hon. DCL Durham, 1965. Pres., Lawn Tennis Assoc., 1962-81. *Recreations:*

golf, tennis, gardening. *Address:* The Coach House, Crabtree Lane, Westhumble, Dorking, Surrey. *T:* Dorking 882771.

ABBADO, Claudio; Music Director, La Scala, Milan, since 1968; Principal Conductor, Vienna Philharmonic Orchestra, since 1971; *b* 26 June 1933; *m* ; two *s* one *d*. *Educ*: Conservatorio G. Verdi, Milan; Musical Academy, Vienna. Guest Conductor of principal orchestras in Europe and America: conductor at principal festivals and opera houses, 1961-. Musical Dir, European Community Youth Orch., 1977-; Principal Conductor, LSO, 1979-. Sergei Koussewitzky Prize, Tanglewood, 1958; Dimitri Mitropoulos Prize, 1963; Mozart-Medaille, Mozart-Gemeinde, Vienna, 1973; winner of major international prizes for recordings (Diapason, Deutscher Schalplatten-Preis, Grand Prix du Disque, Grammy, USA, etc), 1965-. *Address:* Piazzetta Bossi 1, 20121 Milan, Italy.

ABBOT, Dermot Charles Hyatt, CB 1959; Assistant Under-Secretary of State, Department of Health and Social Security, 1968-69 (Under-Secretary, Ministry of Pensions and National Insurance, 1955-66, Ministry of Social Security, 1966-68); retired 1969; *b* 8 Sept. 1908; *e s* of late Reginald Arthur Brame Abbot and late Sarah Ethel Abbot; *m* 1947, Elsie Myrtle Arnott (*see* Dame Elsie Abbot). *Educ*: High School, Newcastle-under-Lyme; High School, Southend-on-Sea; University College, London. Post Office, 1929-40 and 1945-49; transferred to Ministry of Pensions and National Insurance, 1949. *Recreations:* gardening, fishing, travel. *Address:* 4 Constable Close, NW11. *T:* 01-455 9413. *Club:* Royal Automobile.

ABBOT, Dame Elsie (Myrtle), DBE 1966 (CBE 1957); Third Secretary, HM Treasury, 1958-67; *b* 3 Sept. 1907; *d* of Leonard and Frances Tostevin, Streatham, London; *m* 1st, 1938, E. A. Arnott, *s* of R. E. Arnott, Pontypridd; one *s* one *d*; 2nd, 1947, D. C. H. Abbot, *qv*. *Educ*: Clapham County Secondary School; St Hugh's College, Oxford. 1st Class Hons Modern History, 1929; 1st Class Hons Philosophy, Politics and Economics, 1930. Entered Administrative Class of Home Civil Service, 1930; Post Office, 1930-47; transferred to HM Treasury, 1947. *Address:* 4 Constable Close, NW11. *T:* 01-455 9413.

ABBOTT, Sir Albert (Francis), Kt 1981; CBE 1974; Mayor, City of Mackay, Queensland, since 1970; *b* Marvel Loch, WA, 10 Dec. 1913; *s* of late Albert Victor and Diana Abbott; *m* 1941, Gwendoline Joyce Maclean; two *s* four *d*. *Educ*: Mount Martin and Mackay State Schs, Qld. Served RAAF, 1941-45. Sugar cane farmer, 1950-; has given twenty years service to sugar industry organisations. Member: Picture, Theatre and Films Commn, 1975-; Qld Local Govt Grants Commn, 1977-. Returned Services League of Australia: Mem., 1946-; Pres., Mackay Sub-Br., 1960-65; Dist Pres., Mackay, 1965-74; Pres., Qld State, 1974-. Pres., N Qld Local Govt Assoc., 1975-. Mem., Mackay Rotary Club. Governor, Utah Foundn, 1975-. *Recreations:* golf, tennis, racing. *Address:* 86 Kippen Street, Mackay, Qld 4740, Australia. *Clubs:* United Services (Brisbane); RSL Ex-Services, Bowls, Golf, Trotting, Turf, Amateur Race, Diggers Race, Legacy (all in Mackay).

ABBOTT, Anthony Cecil, MC 1945; RDI 1972; RIBA; Senior Designer, BBC Television, since 1962 (Designer, 1954-62); *b* 21 Aug. 1921; *s* of Col Albert Leigh Abbott, MC, and Alice Elizabeth Abbott. *Educ*: Dulwich Coll.; Architectural Assoc. (AADip Hons). Served Army, 1939-45 (Captain). AA, 1946-51; Architects' Dept, LCC; private practice, designing new Kuwait, 1952-54. *Work includes*: opera: Billy Budd, 1966; Rigoletto, La Bohème, Faust, 1968; Otello, 1969; *drama*: Horror of Darkness, 1964; Brothers Karamazov, Poet Game, 1965; The Idiot, Somerset Maugham, 1984, Out of the Unknown, Ross, 1966; Richard II, Beyond the Sunrise, 1968; Rembrandt, Vortex, 1969; St Joan, The Tempest, Somerset Maugham, 1970; Traitor, The General's Day, Sextet, 1971; Oh Fat White Woman, The Grievance, The Merchant of Venice, Lady Windermere's Fan, 1972; Caucasian Chalk Circle, Loyalties, Secrets, An Imaginative Woman (film), Twelfth Night, 1973; The Applecart, Forget-Me-Not-Lane, Savages, 1974; A Story to Frighten the Children (film), Look Back in Anger, 1975; 84, Charing Cross Road, A Picture of Dorian Gray, Abide with Me (film), Rogue Male (film), 1976;

Heartbreak House, She Fell Amongst Thieves (film), 1977; Beaux Stratagem, Richard II, Julius Caesar, 1978; Crime and Punishment, 1979; Dr Jekyll and Mr Hyde, The Crucible, The Fatal Spring, 1980; Timon of Athens, 1981; *theatre work includes:* Hotel in Amsterdam, Time Present, This Story is Yours, Look Back in Anger, 1968; Fidelio (opera), The Marquise, So What About Love, 1969; The Entertainer, 1974; The Exorcism, 1975. Awards: Guild of TV Directors and Producers: Designer of the Year, for The Idiot, 1984, Billy Budd, 1966; Pye Colour Award: Best Colour Prodn, for Otello, 1969; Soc. of Film and TV Arts: Designer of the Year, for Vortex, Rembrandt, 1970. *Recreations:* gardening, travel. *Address:* 4 The Hamlet, Champion Hill, SE5 8AW.

ABBOTT, Arthur William, CMG 1956; CBE 1949; FRHistS; *b* 5 Feb. 1893; *s* of late William Henry Abbott, Southampton, sometime President, Hampshire Law Society; *m* 1926, Kathleen, *d* of Richard Way; one *s. Educ:* Blundell's School, Tiverton. Entered Crown Agents' Office, 1912; served European War, 1914–18, Hampshire Regt, North Russia, 1917–19; Secretary, East African Currency Board, 1930–38; Head of Department, 1938; Establishment Officer, 1948; Secretary to the Crown Agents (for oversea governments and administrations), 1954–58. *Publications:* History of the Crown Agents (printed for private circulation, 1960); review and magazine articles. *Address:* Frithys Orchard, West Clandon, Surrey. *T:* Guildford 222565.

ABBOTT, Hon. Douglas Charles, PC (Can.) 1945; QC 1939; BCL (McGill); Hon. LLD, Hon. DCL; Justice of the Supreme Court, Canada, 1954–73; *b* Lennoxville, PQ, 29 May 1899; *s* of Lewis Duff Abbott and Mary Jane Pearce; *m* 1925, Mary Winifred Chisholm (*d* 1980); two *s* one *d*; *m* 1981, Elizabeth Peters. *Educ:* Bishop's College; McGill University; Dijon University, France. Elected to House of Commons, 1940; re-elected, 1945, 1949 and 1953. Minister of National Defence for Naval Services, April 1945; Minister of National Defence (Army), Aug. 1945; Min. of Finance, Canada, 1946–54. Practised law in Montreal with firm of Robertson, Abbott, Brierley and O'Connor. Chancellor, Bishop's Univ., 1958–68. *Recreations:* fishing, curling, golf. *Address:* 45 Lakeway Drive, Ottawa K1L 5A9, Canada. *TA:* Ottawa Canada. *T:* 746-6271. *Clubs:* University, Royal Montreal Curling (Montreal); Rideau (Ottawa).

ABBOTT, Rev. Eric Symes, KCVO 1966; DD (Lambeth); MA Cantab and Oxon (by incorporation); Dean of Westminster, 1959–74; *b* 26 May 1906; *s* of William Henry and Mary Abbott, Nottingham. *Educ:* Nottingham High School; Jesus College, Cambridge. Curate, St John's, Smith Square, Westminster, 1930–32; Chaplain, King's College, London, 1932–36; Chaplain to Lincoln's Inn, 1935–36; Warden of the Scholae Cancellarii, Lincoln, 1936–45; Canon and Prebendary of Lincoln Cathedral, 1940–60. Dean of King's College, London, 1945–55; Warden of Keble College, Oxford, 1956–60; Chaplain to King George VI, 1948-52, and to the Queen, 1952–59; an Extra Chaplain to the Queen, 1974–. Chaplain and Sub-Prelate, Order of St John of Jerusalem, 1969–. Freeman, City of Westminster, 1973. FKC, London, 1946–; Hon. Fellow: Keble Coll., Oxford, 1960; Jesus Coll., Cambridge, 1966. Hon. DD London, 1966. *Address:* 17 Vincent Square, SW1. *Club:* Athenæum.

ABBOTT, James Alan, PhD; Manager and Director of Research, Koninklijk/Shell Laboratorium, Amsterdam, Shell Research BV, since 1981; *b* 2 Dec. 1928; *s* of George Oswald and Eva Abbott; *m* 1954, Rita Marjorie Galloway; one *s* one *d. Educ:* Ilkeston Grammar School; University of Nottingham (BSc, PhD). Post-doctoral research, Univ. of Durham, 1952–53; served Royal Air Force, 1953–56 (Flt Lt RAF Technical Coll., Henlow). Shell companies, UK and Holland, 1956–; Dir, Shell Research Ltd, Sittingbourne Research Centre, 1980-81. *Publications:* papers in Trans Faraday Soc., Proc. Royal Society. *Recreations:* farming, golf. *Address:* Thick Withins, Hollinsclough, Buxton, Derbyshire SK17 0RD. *T:* Longnor 361.

ABBOTT, Morris Percy; Chairman and Chief Executive, The Hogg Robinson Group Ltd, since 1977; *b* 3 May 1922; *s* of Harry Abbott and Agnes Maud Breeze; *m* 1944, Marjorie Leven; one *s* one *d. Educ:* Rothesay Academy. MIBS. Bank of Scotland, 1939-49. Served War as Pilot, 1941-46; Flight Lieut, RAF; seconded to US Navy at Pensacola Naval Air Station, Florida. Senior Executive with National Bank of India (now Grindlays Bank) in India and East Africa, 1949-59. Managing Director: Credit Insurance Assoc. Ltd, 1969; Hogg Robinson & Gardner Mountain Ltd, 1971; Hogg Robinson Group Ltd: Group Man. Dir, 1973; Chief Exec., 1974–; Chm., 1977–. *Recreations:* music, golf, tennis, sailing. *Address:* Flat 6, Macartney House, Chesterfield Walk, SE10; Castlemans, Sedlescombe, Battle, Sussex. *T:* Sedlescombe 501. *Clubs:* City of London, Caledonian; Royal and Ancient Golf, Prestwick Golf, Rye Golf, Royal Calcutta Golf.

ABBOTT, Sir Myles (John), Kt 1964; Chief Justice of Bermuda, 1961-71; *b* 27 Feb. 1906; *s* of Edmund Rushworth Abbott, 13 Victoria Street, London, Solicitor; *m* 1st, 1932, Grace Ada Jeffery; one *d*; 2nd, 1960, Dorothy Anne Campbell, *widow* of Robert Currie Campbell. *Educ:* King's Sch., Canterbury. Admitted Solicitor, 1929; Partner, Chas Rogers Sons & Abbott, 1930. 2nd Lieut 9th Middlesex Regt. (TA), 1933. Selected for appointment to Colonial Legal Service, 1935; Lieut 9th Middx Regt and transferred to TARO, 1936; Asst Crown Solicitor, Hong Kong, 1936; called to the Bar, 1940; Official Receiver and Registrar of Trade Marks, Hong Kong, 1941. Served War of 1939-45 (prisoner); released, 1945. President, High Court of Ethiopia, Oct. 1946–Oct. 1949; Puisne Judge, Nigeria, 1950-55; Judge of High Court of Lagos, 1955-57; Federal Justice of Federal Supreme Court of Nigeri 1957-61. *Publications:* (ed) West African Court of Appeal Reports, 1946-4 (ed) Federal Supreme Court Reports, Nigeria, Vol. 4, 1959, 1960. *Address* 36 Mizzen-Top, Warwick 7-20, Bermuda. *T:* Bermuda 22658. *Club:* Nava and Military.

ABBOTT, Roderick Evelyn; Director, Directorate-General of External Relations, EEC Commission, Brussels; *b* 16 April 1938; *e s* of Stuart Evely Abbott, OBE; *m* 1963, Elizabeth Isobel McLean; three *d. Educ:* Rugby Sch Merton Coll., Oxford. Board of Trade, 1962-68 (Private Sec. to Pres. of Bo
 1965-66; seconded to DEA, 1966-68); UK Mission to UN, Geneva, 1968-7 Foreign Office, London, 1971-73; EEC, 1973-75; EEC Delegation, Geneva 1975-79; EEC, 1980-. *Recreation:* travel. *Address:* c/o EEC Commission Berlaymont (DG I), 1049 Brussels, Belgium. *Club:* Royal Commonwealt Society.

ABBOTT, Ronald William, CBE 1979; FIA, ASA, FPMI; Consultar Partner, Bacon & Woodrow, Consulting Actuaries, since 1982 (Senic Partner, 1972-81); Chairman, Occupational Pensions Board, since 198 (Deputy Chairman, 1973-82); *b* 18 Jan. 1917; *s* of late Edgar Abbott and Susa Mary Ann Abbott; *m* 1st, 1948, Hilda Mary Hampson (*d* 1972), *d* of lat William George Clarke and Emily Jane Clarke; two *d*; 2nd, 1973, Barbar Constance, *d* of late Gilbert Hugh Clough and of Harriet Clough. *Educ:* S Olave's and St Saviour's Grammar Sch. FIA 1946; FPMI 1976. Actuaria Assistant: Atlas Assce Co., 1934-38; Friends Provident & Century Life Office 1938-46; Sen. Actuary, Bacon & Woodrow, 1946, Partner 1948. Mem., Depu Cttee on Property Bonds and Equity Linked Life Assce, 1971-73. Mem Council: Inst. of Actuaries, 1966-74 (Hon. Treasurer, 1971-73); Indust. Soc 1964-; Pensions Management Inst., 1977-81 (Vice-Pres., 1978-80) *Publications:* contrib. to Jl of Inst. of Actuaries. *Recreation:* music. *Address* 21 The Byway, Sutton, Surrey. *T:* 01-642 3910. *Club:* Royal Automobile

ABDELA, Jack Samuel Ronald, TD 1948; QC 1966; **His Honour Judg Abdela;** a Circuit Judge, Central Criminal Court (formerly Deput Chairman, Inner London Quarter Sessions), since 1970; *b* 9 Oct. 1913; *s* o Joseph and Dorothy Abdela, Manchester; *m* 1942, Enid Hope Russell, *y d* o Edgar Dodd Russell, London; one *s* (and one *s* decd). *Educ:* Manchester Gram Sch.; Milton Sch., Bulawayo; Fitzwilliam House, Cambridge (MA). Calle to the Bar, Gray's Inn, 1935. 2nd Lieut, Lancashire Fusiliers (TA), 1938 Lieut-Col. Comdt 55 Div. Battle School, 1943; 7th Bn Royal Welch Fusilier NW Europe, 1944-46; Major, Inns of Court Regt. (TA), 1946-52. Liverymar The Worshipful Company of Painter-Stainers. *Recreations:* swimming tennis, gardening. *Address:* 4 South Square, Gray's Inn, WC1R 5PH. 1 01-405 3627; Central Criminal Court, EC4; Goldingtons, Sarratt, Herts. 7 Chorleywood 4593. *Club:* Savage.

ABDUL JAMIL RAIS, Tan Sri Dato', PMN; Chairman, Penang Po Commission, since 1971; High Commissioner for Malaysia in the UK 1967-71; *b* 14 Jan. 1912; *s* of Abdul Rais and Saodah; *m* ; four *s* six *d* (an one *s* decd). *Educ:* Clifford Sch.; Jesus Coll., Oxford. Joined Govt service 1932; State Sec., Perlis, 1951-52; State Financial Officer, Selangor, 1954-55 State Sec., Selangor, 1955-56; Chief Minister, Selangor, 1957-59; Sec. to Treasury, 1961-64; Chief Sec. to Malaysian Govt and Sec. to Cabinet, 1964-67 *Recreations:* golf, tennis. *Address:* Penang Pot Commission, Penang Malaysia.

ABDUL RAHMAN PUTRA, Tunku (Prince), CH 1961; Order of th National Crown, Malaysia; Kedah Order of Merit; Secretary General, Islami Conference of Foreign Ministers, 1969-73; Prime Minister of Malaysia 1963-70; Chairman, Star Publications, Penang; *b* 8 Feb. 1903; *m* 3rd, 1939 Puan Sharifah Rodziah binti Syed Alwi Barakbah; one *s* one *d* (both by 1s wife); one *s* three *d* (all adopted). *Educ:* Alor Star; Bangkok; St Catharine' Coll., Cambridge (Research Fellow, 1980); Inner Temple, London (Hor Master, 1971). Joined Kedah State Civil Service, 1931, District Officer During the occupation, when the Japanese returned Kedah to Siam, he serve as Supt of Educn and Dir of Passive Defence until the reoccupation, Sept 1945; opposed British Govt fusion of States and Colonies to form the Malayar Union and took a leading part in formation of United Malays Nationa Organisation (UMNO); when the Malayan Union gave way to the Federatio of Malaya in 1949, he became Chairman of UMNO in Kedah; after being called to Bar (Inner Temple), he returned to Kedah and was seconded to Federal Legal Dept as a Dep. Public Prosecutor, 1949; President of UMNO 1951; resigned from CS and a year later was apptd an unofficial Mem. Federa Executive and Legislative Councils; leader of the Alliance Party (UMNO Malayan Chinese Association, Malayan Indian Congress), 1954; Mem., Federa Legislative Council, 1955-73; became Chief Minister and Minister of Hom Affairs; in reshuffle of 1956 also took portfolio of Minister for Interna Defence and Security; was also Chm. Emergency Ops Council which decide on policy in fighting Malayan Communist Party; headed Alliance deleg. t London to negotiate Independence for the Federation, Dec. 1955; afte Independence on 31 Aug. 1957, became Prime Minister and Minister o External Affairs and continued to be Chm. Emergency Ops Council; resigne as Prime Minister in Feb. 1959 to prepare for general elections in Aug.; becam Prime Minister for second time, Aug. 1959, and in Sept. initiated Min. o Rural Development; became also Minister of Ext. Affairs, Nov. 1960, an Minister of Information and Broadcasting, June 1961; Prime Minister Federation of Malaya, until it became Malaysia, 1963; became Prime Ministe for third time, April 1964, following Gen. Elections in States of Malaya, also Minister of External Affairs and Minister of Culture, Youth and Sports. Attended Prime Ministers' Conferences in London, May 1960 and March 1961; Head of mission to London to discuss and agree in principle proposed formation of Federation of Malaysia, Nov. 1961; Head of second mission to London on formation of Malaysia, July 1962; attended Prime Ministers' Confs, London, 1965, 1966. Apptd Chancellor, Univ. Malaya, 1962. Pres., Football Assoc. of Malaya; Pres., Asian Football Confedn; Vice-Pres. (for life), Royal Commonwealth Society. Dr of Law, Univ. of Malaya; Hon. LLD: Araneta Univ., 1958; Cambridge Univ., 1960; Univ. of Sydney, 1960; Univ. of Saigon, 1961; Aligarh Muslim Univ., 1962; Univ. Sains, Malaysia, 1975; Hon. DLitt, Seoul National Univ., 1965; Hon. DCL Oxford, 1970. Holds various foreign Orders. *Publications:* Mahsuri (imaginary play of Malaya; performed on stage in North Malaya throughout 1941; filmed in Malaya, 1958); Raja Bersiong (filmed 1966). *Relevant publication:* Prince and Premier (Biography) by Harry Miller, 1959. *Recreations:* golf, football, tennis, walking, swimming, racing, motor-boating, photography (both cine and still); collector of ancient weapons, particularly the Malay kris. *Address:* 1 Jalan Tunku, Kuala Lumpur, Malaysia; 16 Ayer Rajah Road, Penang, Malaysia.

ABDULLAH bin Ali, Datuk; Director, Guthrie Ropel Berhad, since 1979; *b* Johore State, 31 Aug. 1922; *m* Datin Badariah binti Haji Abdul Aziz; two *s* two *d. Educ:* Raffles Coll., Singapore; ANU, Canberra. Entered Johore Civil Service, 1949, later Malayan Civil Service; with Independence of Malaysia joined Malaysian Foreign Service; served in India, Australia, Indonesia, Thailand, and as Head of Mission in Ethiopia, Morocco; Chief of Protocol and Dep. Sec.-Gen. (Admin and Gen Affairs), Min. of Foreign Affairs, Kuala Lumpur, 1969-71; High Comr to Singapore, 1971-74; Ambassador to Fed. Rep. of Germany, 1975; High Comr in London and Ambassador to Ireland, 1975-79. Has attended many foreign confs, incl. UNO in NY. Holds Orders: Panglima Setia DiRaja (Order of the Sovereign of Malaysia); Dato Paduka Mahkota Johore (Order of Crown of Johore, Malaysia); Kesatria Mangku Negara (Order of Upholder of Realm, Malaysia); Order of Sacred Heart (Japan). *Address:* c/o Guthrie Ropel Berhad Ltd, PO Box 900, Singapore 1027; 1 Jalan Setiajaya, Damansara Heights, Kuala Lumpur, Malaysia.

ABDY, Sir Valentine (Robert Duff), 6th Bt *cr* 1850; *b* 11 Sept. 1937; *s of* Sir Robert Henry Edward Abdy, 5th Bt, and Lady Diana Bridgeman (*d* 1967), *e d* of 5th Earl of Bradford; *S* father, 1976; *m* 1971, Mathilde Coche de la Ferté; one *s. Educ:* Eton. *Heir: s* Robert Etienne Eric Abdy, *b* 22 Feb. 1978. *Address:* 39 rue de Turenne, 75003 Paris, France; Newton Ferrers, Callington, Cornwall. *Clubs:* Travellers', Jockey (Paris).

ABEL-SMITH, Prof. Brian; Professor of Social Administration, University of London, at the London School of Economics, since 1965; *b* 6 Nov. 1926; *s of* late Brig.-Gen. Lionel Abel-Smith. *Educ:* Haileybury Coll.; Clare Coll., Cambridge. MA, PhD, 1955. Served Army: Private 1945; commissioned Oxford and Bucks Light Inf., 1946; Mil. Asst to Dep. Comr, Allied Commn for Austria (Capt.), 1947-48. Res. Fellow, Nat. Inst. of Economic and Social Res., collecting economic evidence for Guillebaud Cttee (cost of NHS), 1953-55. LSE: Asst Lectr in Social Science, 1955; Lectr, 1957; Reader in Social Administration, University of London, 1961. Assoc. Prof., Yale Law Sch., Yale Univ., 1961. Consultant and Expert Adv. to WHO on costs of med. care, 1957-; Consultant: to Social Affairs Div. of UN, 1959, 1961; to ILO, 1967; Special Adviser: to Sec. of State for Social Services, 1968-70, 1974-78; to Sec. of State for the Environment, 1978-79; Adviser to Comr for Social Affairs, EEC, 1977-80. Member: SW Metrop. Reg. Hosp. Bd, 1956-63; Cent. Health Services Coun. Sub-Cttee on Prescribing Statistics, 1960-64; Sainsbury Cttee (Relationship of Pharmaceut. Industry with NHS), 1965-67; Long-term Study Group (to advise on long-term devel of NHS), 1965-68; Hunter Cttee (Functions of Medical Administrators), 1970-72; Fisher Cttee (Abuse of Social Security Benefits), 1971-73. Chm., Chelsea and Kensington HMC, 1961-62; Governor: St Thomas' Hosp., 1957-68; Maudsley Hosp. and Inst. of Psychiatry, 1963-67. Hon. MD Limburg, 1981. *Publications:* (with R. M. Titmuss) The Cost of the National Health Service in England and Wales, 1956; A History of the Nursing Profession, 1960; (with R. M. Titmuss) Social Policy and Population Growth in Mauritius, 1961; Paying for Health Services (for WHO), 1963; The Hospitals, 1800-1948, 1964; (with R. M. Titmuss et al.) The Health Services of Tanganyika, 1964; (with K. Gales) British Doctors at Home and Abroad, 1964; (with P. Townsend) The Poor and the Poorest, 1965; (with R. Stevens) Lawyers and the Courts, 1967; An International Study of Health Expenditure (for WHO), 1967; (with R. Stevens) In Search of Justice, 1968; (with M. Zander and R. Brooke) Legal Problems and the Citizen, 1973; People Without Choice, 1974; Value for Money in Health Services, 1976; Poverty Development and Health Policy, 1978; National Health Service: the first thirty years, 1978; (with P. Grandjeat) Pharmaceutical Consumption, 1978; (with A. Maynard) The Organisation, Financing and Cost of Health Care in the European Community, 1979; Sharing Health Care Costs, 1980; pamphlets for Fabian Soc., 1953-; articles. *Recreations:* skiing, swimming. *Address:* London School of Economics, Houghton Street, WC2. *T:* 01-405 7686.

ABEL SMITH, Vice-Adm. Sir (Edward Michael) Connolly, GCVO 1958 (KCVO 1954; CVO 1946); CB 1951; RN retd; Extra Equerry to the Queen since 1952; *b* 3 Dec. 1899; 2nd *s* of Eustace Abel Smith, Longhills, Lincoln, and Aileen Geta, *d* of Col. John A. Connolly, VC, Coldstream Guards; *m* 1932, Lady Mary Elizabeth Carnegie, *d* of 10th Earl of Southesk; one *s* one *d. Educ:*

Royal Naval Colleges, Osborne and Dartmouth. Mid. HMS Princess Royal, 1915; Qualified Pilot, 1924; Comdr 1933; Naval Equerry to the King, 1939; Capt. 1940; HMS Biter, 1942; Naval Attaché, British Embassy, Washington, DC, 1944-46; HMS Triumph, 1947; Naval ADC to the King, 1949; Rear-Adm. 1949; Vice-Controller (Air), Chief of Naval Air Equipment and Chief Naval Representative, Min. of Supply, 1950; Vice-Adm. 1952; Flag Officer, Royal Yachts, 1953-58. JP 1958. HM Lieutenant for Selkirk, 1958-74. Grand Cross of St Olav, 1955. *Recreations:* hunting, shooting. *Address:* Ashiestiel, Galashiels, Scotland. *T:* Clovenfords 214. *Clubs:* Naval and Military, Buck's.

ABEL SMITH, Henriette Alice, (Lady Abel Smith), DCVO 1977 (CVO 1964); JP; a Lady-in-Waiting to the Queen (formerly as HRH Princess Elizabeth) since 1949; *b* 6 June 1914; *d* of late Comdr Francis Charles Cadogan, RN, and late Ruth Evelyn (*née* Howard, *widow* of Captain Gardner Sebastian Bazley); *m* 1st, 1939, Sir Anthony Frederick Mark Palmer, 4th Bt (killed in action, 1941); one *s* one *d* ; 2nd, 1953, Sir Alexander Abel Smith, KCVO, TD (*d* 1980); one *s* one *d.* JP Tunbridge Wells 1955, Gloucestershire 1971. *Address:* The Garden House, Quenington, Cirencester, Glos. *T:* Coln St Aldwyns 231.
See also Sir T. S. Bazley, Bt, Sir C. M. Palmer, Bt.

ABEL SMITH, Col Sir Henry, KCMG 1961; KCVO 1950; DSO 1945; DL; late Royal Horse Guards; Governor of Queensland, 1958-66; Administrator, Australian Commonwealth, during part of 1965; *b* 8 March 1900; *er s* of late Francis Abel Smith and Madeline St Maur, *d* of late Rev. Henry Seymour; *m* 1931, Lady May Cambridge, *o surv. c* of Earl of Athlone, KG, PC, GCB, GCMG, GCVO, DSO, FRS (*d* 1957), and Princess Alice, Countess of Athlone, VA, GCVO, GBE (*d* 1981); one *s* two *d. Educ:* RMC, Sandhurst. Entered RHG, 1919; Capt. 1930; Major, 1934; Temp. Lieut-Col 1941; Lieut-Col 1944; Acting Colonel, Corps of Household Cavalry, 1946; retired, 1950. ADC to Earl of Athlone, Governor-General of S Africa, 1928-31. DL Berks 1953. KStJ 1958; Hon. LLD Univ. of Queensland, 1962. Hon. Air Cdre, RAAF, 1966. *Recreations:* hunting, shooting, fishing, polo. *Address:* Barton Lodge, Winkfield, Windsor, Berks. *T:* Winkfield Row 882632. *Club:* Turf.

ABELES, Sir (Emil Herbert) Peter, Kt 1972; Deputy Chairman, Managing Director and Chief Executive, Thomas Nationwide Transport Ltd, Australia, and associated companies, since 1967; Joint Managing Director, since 1980 and Joint Chairman, since 1981, Ansett Transport Industries Ltd; *b* 25 April 1924; *s* of late Alexander Abel and of Mrs Anna Deakin; *m* 1969, Katalin Ottilia (*née* Fischer); two *d. Educ:* Budapest. Scrap metal industry, Hungary; emigrated to Australia, Sept. 1949; formed Alltrans Pty Ltd, 1950. Director: Seatainer Terminals Ltd; Acme World Wide Shipping Pty Ltd; Speedy Communications Pty Ltd; Thomas Nationwide Transport Ltd Group; Ansett Transport Industries Ltd Group; Bliss Welded Products Ltd; Business Telecommunications Services Pty Ltd; Union Shipping Group Ltd. *Recreations:* swimming, bridge. *Address:* TNT Management Pty Ltd, Tower 1, 10th Floor, TNT Plaza, Lawson Square, Redfern, NSW 2016, Australia. *Clubs:* Carlton; Royal Automobile of Australia, Royal Motor Yacht, Tattersalls, Australian Jockey.

ABELL, Sir Anthony (Foster), KCMG 1952 (CMG 1950); Gentleman Usher of the Blue Rod, in the Order of St Michael and St George, 1972-79; *b* 11 Dec. 1906; 2nd *s* of late G. F. Abell, JP, Foxcote Manor, Andoversford, Glos; unmarried. *Educ:* Repton; Magdalen Coll., Oxford. Joined Colonial Admin. Service, Nigeria, 1929. Resident, Oyo Province, Nigeria, 1949; Governor and C-in-C, Sarawak, 1950-59; High Commissioner, Brunei, 1950-58. Family Order of Brunei (First Class), 1954. *Address:* Gavel House, Wherwell, Andover, Hants. *Clubs:* MCC, Royal Over-Seas League, Bath.
See also Sir George Abell.

ABELL, Charles, OBE 1948; CEng, Hon. FRAeS; Consultant, British Airways Overseas Division, 1974-77; *b* 1 Dec. 1910; *s* of late Major George Henry Abell and Muriel Abell (*née* Griesbach); *m* 1st, 1939, Beryl Anne Boyce (*d* 1973); one *s* ; 2nd, 1976, M. A. Newbery. *Educ:* Sherborne Sch. Imperial Airways, 1934-39; BOAC 1939-74: Manager No 3 Line, 1946-51; Dep. Operations Dir (Engineering), 1951-55; Chief Engineer, 1955-68; Engineering Dir, 1968-74; Board Mem., 1972-74; Chm., British Airways Engine Overhaul Ltd, 1972-74. Hon FRAeS (Pres., 1976-77; Vice-Pres., 1972-74); Hon. FSLAET (Pres. 1973-74). British Silver Medal for Aeronautics, RAeS, 1957. *Recreation:* sailing. *Address:* Five Oaks, Woodlands Road West, Virginia Water, Surrey. *T:* Wentworth 2560. *Clubs:* Cruising Association; Royal Lymington Yacht; Royal Western Yacht.

ABELL, David; *see* Abell, J. D.

ABELL, Sir George (Edmond Brackenbury), KCIE 1947 (CIE 1946); OBE 1943; Hon. LLD (Aberdeen), 1947; Director, Portals Holdings Ltd, 1968-76; President, Council, Reading University, 1969-74; *b* 22 June 1904; *s* of late G. F. Abell, JP, Foxcote Manor, Andoversford, Glos; *m* 1928, Susan Norman-Butler; two *s* one *d. Educ:* Marlborough; Corpus Christi Coll., Oxford (Hon. Fellow, 1971-). Joined Indian Civil Service, 1928; Private Sec. to the Viceroy, 1945-47. Advisor, 1948-52, Director, 1952-64, Bank of England; First Civil Service Comr, 1964-67. Rhodes Trustee, 1949-74 (Chm., 1969-74). Mem. Council, 1955-77, Chm., 1974-77, Marlborough Coll. *Address:* Whittonditch

House, Ramsbury, Wilts. *T:* Marlborough 20449. *Clubs:* Oriental, MCC.
See also Sir Anthony Abell.

ABELL, (John) David; Chairman and Chief Executive, Suter Electrical, since 1981; *b* 15 Dec. 1942; *s* of Leonard Abell and Irene (*née* Anderson); *m* 1967, Anne Janette Priestley (marr. diss. 1977); three *s* ; *m* 1981, Sandra Dawn Abell (*née* Atkinson); one *s* one *d. Educ:* Univ. of Leeds (BAEcon); London School of Economics (Dip. Business Admin). Assistant to Cash and Investment Manager, Ford Motor Co., 1962-65; Asst. Treasurer's Office, AEI, 1965-67; British Leyland: joined Central Staffs as Financial Analyst, 1968-69; Manager, Investments and Banking, 1969-70; Exec. Chm., Prestcold, 1970-72; Corporation Treasurer, 1972; First Nat. Finance Corp., Nov. 1972-Aug. 1973; re-joined British Leyland as Man. Dir, Leyland Australia, 1974-75; Group Man. Dir, Leyland Special Products, 1975; Man. Dir, BL Commercial Vehicles, Chm. and Man. Dir, Leyland Vehicles Ltd, 1978-81. *Recreations:* walking, riding, swimming, the stock market. *Address:* c/o Suter plc, The Priory, Market Place, Grantham, Lincs NG31 6LJ.

ABERCONWAY, 3rd Baron, *cr* 1911, of Bodnant; **Charles Melville McLaren,** Bt 1902; JP; President, John Brown & Co. Ltd (Chairman, 1953-78); Chairman, English China Clays Ltd; Deputy Chairman: Sun Alliance & London Insurance Ltd, since 1978; Westland Aircraft Ltd, since 1979; Director, National Westminster Bank Ltd; Commissioner-General, International Garden Festival of Liverpool 1984, since 1982; President, Royal Horticultural Society, since 1961; *b* 16 April 1913; *e s* of 2nd Baron Aberconway, CBE, LLD and Christabel (*d* 1974), *y d* of Sir Melville Macnaghten, CB; *S* father, 1953; *m* 1st, 1941, Deirdre Knewstub (marr. diss. 1949); one *s* two *d* ; 2nd, 1949, Ann Lindsay Bullard, *o d* of Mrs A. L. Aymer, New York City; one *s. Educ:* Eton; New Coll., Oxford. Barrister, Middle Temple, 1937. Served War of 1939-45, 2nd Lieut RA. JP Denbighshire 1946; High Sheriff of Denbighshire 1950. *Recreations:* gardening, travel, motoring. *Heir: s* Hon. Henry Charles McLaren [*b* 26 May 1948; *m* 1981, Sally, *yr d* of Captain C. N. Lentaigne; one *d*] *Address:* 25 Egerton Terrace, SW3; Bodnant, Tal-y-cafn, North Wales.
See also K. R. M. Carlisle.

ABERCORN, 5th Duke of, *cr* 1868; **James Hamilton;** Lord of Paisley, 1587; Lord of Abercorn, 1603; Earl of Abercorn and Lord of Hamilton, Mountcastle and Kilpatrick, 1606; Baron of Strabane, 1617; Viscount of Strabane, 1701; Viscount Hamilton, 1786; Marquess of Abercorn, 1790; Marquess of Hamilton, 1868; Bt 1660; company director; *b* 4 July 1934; *er s* of 4th Duke of Abercorn, and of Lady Mary Kathleen Crichton (Dowager Duchess of Abercorn, GCVO); *S* father, 1979; *m* 1966, Anastasia Alexandra, *e d* of late Lt-Col Harold Phillips, Checkendon Court, Reading; two *s* one *d. Educ:* Eton Coll.; Royal Agricultural Coll., Cirencester, Glos. Joined HM Army, Oct. 1952; Lieut, Grenadier Guards. MP (UU) Fermanagh and South Tyrone, 1964-70. Member: Council of Europe, 1968-70; European Economic and Social Cttee, 1973-78. Pres. Royal UK Beneficent Assoc., 1979-. High Sheriff of Co. Tyrone, 1970. *Recreations:* shooting, water ski-ing. *Heir: s* Marquess of Hamilton, *qv. Address:* Barons Court, Omagh, Northern Ireland BT78 4EZ. *T:* Newtownstewart 61470. *Club:* Turf.

ABERCROMBIE, Prof. David; Professor of Phonetics, Edinburgh University, 1964-80, now Emeritus Professor; *b* 19 Dec. 1909; *e s* of Lascelles Abercrombie, FBA, and Catherine Abercrombie; *m* 1944, Mary, *d* of Eugene and Mary Marble, Carmel, Calif; no *c. Educ:* Leeds Grammar Sch.; Leeds Univ.; University Coll., London; Sorbonne. Asst Lectr in English, LSE, 1934-38; Dir of Studies, Inst. of English Studies, Athens, 1938-40; Lectr in English: Cairo Univ., 1940-45; LSE, 1945-47; Lectr in Phonetics, Leeds Univ., 1947-48; Edinburgh Univ.: Lectr in Phonetics, 1948-51; Sen. Lectr 1951-57; Reader, 1957-63. Lectr in Linguistics and Phonetics, Glasgow Univ., 1980-81. *Publications:* Isaac Pitman: a Pioneer in the Scientific Study of Language, 1937; Problems and Principles in Language Study, 1956; English Phonetic Texts, 1964; Studies in Phonetics and Linguistics, 1965; Elements of General Phonetics, 1967. *Address:* 13 Grosvenor Crescent, Edinburgh EH12 5EL. *T:* 031-337 4864. *Clubs:* Scottish Arts, New (Edinburgh).

ABERCROMBIE, Nigel James; free-lance writer; *b* 5 Aug. 1908; 2nd *s* of late Lieutenant-Colonel A. W. Abercrombie; *m* 1931, Elisabeth Brownlees; one *s* one *d. Educ:* Haileybury; Oriel College, Oxford. BA 1929; DPhil 1933; MA 1934. Lecturer in French, Magdalen College, Oxford, 1931-36; Paget Toynbee Prize, 1934; Professor of French and Head of Mod. Lang. Dept, University College, Exeter, 1936-40. Entered Secretary's Department, Admiralty, 1940; Asst Sec., 1942; Under-Secretary, 1956; Cabinet Office, 1962-63; Sec.-Gen., 1963-68, Chief Regional Advr, 1968-73, Arts Council of Great Britain. Editor, Dublin Review, 1953-55. *Publications:* The Origins of Jansenism, 1936; St Augustine and French Classical Thought, 1938, repr. 1972; editions of Le Misanthrope and Tartuffe, 1938; Life and Work of Edmund Bishop, 1959; The Arts in the South-East, 1974; Artists and Their Public, 1975; Cultural Policy in the United Kingdom, 1982; contrib. to: Times Anthology of Detective Stories, 1972; New Stories I, 1976; The State and the Arts, 1980; Studies in Sussex Church History, 1981; Challoner and his Church, 1981; articles and reviews in theological, historical and literary periodicals. *Recreations:* The 3 R's. *Address:* 32 Springett Avenue, Ringmer, Lewes, E Sussex BN8 5HE. *T:* Ringmer 813029.
See also J. L. Gardner.

ABERCROMBIE, Robert James, CMG 1964; General Manager, Bank of New South Wales, 1962-64, retired; *b* 9 July 1898; *s* of P. M. Abercrombie Whitburn, Scotland; *m* 1924, Dorothy, *d* of H. F. Oldham; two *d. Educ:* Sydney Grammar School; Scotch Coll., Melbourne. Chairman, Consultative Council of Export Payments Insurance Corporation, 1958-64; Chairman Australian Bankers' Assoc., 1964. *Recreation:* golf. *Address:* 1 Hillside Avenue, Vaucluse, NSW 2030, Australia. *Clubs:* Union (Sydney); Australian Athenæum (Melbourne).

ABERCROMBY, Sir Ian George, 10th Bt *cr* 1636, of Birkenbog; *b* 30 June 1925; *s* of Robert Ogilvie Abercromby (*g s* of 5th Bt); *S* kinsman, 1972; *m* 1st, 1950, Joyce Beryl, *d* of Leonard Griffiths; 2nd, Fanny Mary, *d* of late Dr Graham Udale-Smith; one *d* ; 3rd, 1976, Diana Marjorie, *d* of H. G. Cockell and *widow* of Captain Ian Charles Palliser Galloway. *Educ:* Lancing Coll. Bloxham Sch. *Heir:* none. *Address:* c/o National Westminster Bank, 224 King's Road, SW3; Tynte Park, Dunlavin, Co. Wicklow, Eire; El Amador Marbella, Spain. *Clubs:* Ski Club of Great Britain; Kandahar; Real Nautico (Tenerife).

ABERDARE, 4th Baron, *cr* 1873, of Duffryn; **Morys George Lyndhurst Bruce,** PC 1974; Chairman of Committees, House of Lords, since 1976; Prior for Wales, Order of St John; *b* 16 June 1919; *s* of 3rd Baron Aberdare, GBE and Margaret Bethune (*née* Black); *S* father 1957; *m* 1946, Maud Helen Sarah, *o d* of Sir John Dashwood, 10th Bt, CVO; four *s. Educ:* Winchester; New College, Oxford (MA). Welsh Guards, 1939-46. Minister of State, DHSS 1970-74; Minister Without Portfolio, 1974. Chm., Albany Life Assurance Co Ltd, 1975-. Chairman: The Football Trust, 1979-; Ye Olde Cheshire Cheese, President: Welsh Nat. Council of YMCAs; Kidney Res. Unit for Wales Foundn; Tennis and Rackets Assoc.; British Assoc. of Physical Trng; Nat. Assoc. of League of Hospital Friends. Bailiff Grand Cross, OStJ, 1974. *Publications:* The Story of Tennis, 1959; Willis Faber Book of Tennis and Rackets, 1980. *Recreations:* real tennis and rackets. *Heir: s* Hon. Alastair John Lyndhurst Bruce [*b* 2 May 1947; *m* 1971, Elizabeth Mary Culbert, *d* of John Foulkes; one *s* one *d*]. *Address:* 32 Elthiron Road, SW6 4BW. *T:* 01-736 0825. *Clubs:* Lansdowne, MCC, Queen's.

ABERDEEN, Bishop of, (RC), since 1977; **Rt. Rev. Mario Joseph Conti;** *b* Elgin, Moray, 20 March 1934; *s* of Louis Joseph Conti and Josephine Quintilia Panicali. *Educ:* St Marie's Convent School and Springfield, Elgin; Blairs Coll., Aberdeen; Pontifical Gregorian Univ. (Scots College), Rome. PhL 1955, STL 1959. Ordained, Rome, 1958; Curate, St Mary's Cathedral, Aberdeen, 1959-62; Parish Priest, St Joachim's, Wick and St Anne's, Thurso (joint charge), 1962-77. *Recreations:* music, art, book browsing, TV, travel, swimming. *Address:* 156 King's Gate, Aberdeen AB2 6BR. *T:* Aberdeen 39154.

ABERDEEN, Provost of (St Andrew's Cathedral); *see* Howard, Very Rev. Donald.

ABERDEEN AND ORKNEY, Bishop of, since 1978; **Rt. Rev. Frederick Charles Darwent;** *b* Liverpool, 20 April 1927; *y s* of Samuel Darwent and Edith Emily Darwent (*née* Malcolm); *m* 1949, Edna Lilian (*d* 1981), *o c* of David Waugh and Lily Elizabeth Waugh (*née* McIndoe); twin *d. Educ:* Warbreck Sch., Liverpool; Ormskirk Grammar Sch., Lancs; Wells Theological Coll., Somerset. Followed a Banking career, 1943-61 (War service in Far East with Royal Inniskilling Fusiliers, 1945-48). Deacon 1963; priest 1964, Diocese of Liverpool; Curate of Pemberton, Wigan, 1963-65 (in charge of St Francis, Kitt Green, 1964-65); Rector of: Strichen, 1965-71; New Pitsligo, 1965-78; Fraserburgh, 1971-78; Canon of St Andrew's Cathedral, Aberdeen, 1971; Dean of Aberdeen and Orkney, 1973-78. Hon. LTh, St Mark's Inst. of Theology, 1974. *Recreations:* amateur stage (acting and production), music (especially jazz); calligraphy. *Address:* Bishop's Lodge, 15 Morningfield Road, Aberdeen AB2 4AP. *T:* Aberdeen 34765. *Clubs:* Rotary International; Club of Deir (Aberdeens).

ABERDEEN AND ORKNEY, Dean of; *see* Adamson, Very Rev. A. C.

ABERDEEN AND TEMAIR, 5th Marquess of, *cr* 1916; **Archibald Victor Dudley Gordon;** Bt of Nova Scotia, 1642; Earl of Aberdeen, Viscount Formartine, Lord Haddo, Methlic, Tarves and Kellie, 1682, Peerage of Scotland; Viscount Gordon, 1814, and Earl of Haddo, 1916, Peerage of UK; writer and broadcaster; *b* 9 July 1913; *s* of 3rd Marquis of Aberdeen and Temair, DSO, and Cécile Elizabeth (*d* 1948), *d* of George Drummond, Swaylands, Penshurst, Kent; *S* brother, 1974; unmarried. *Educ:* Harrow. An assistant secretary, Council for the Protection of Rural England, 1936-40, joined BBC Monitoring Service, April 1940; BBC Talks Dept (Radio) 1946-72; Producer of The Week in Westminster, and of party political and election broadcasts (radio), 1946-66; Editor, Radio Documentaries and Talks, 1967-72. Independent. *Publication:* (as Archie Gordon) Towers, 1979. *Heir-pres.: b* Lord Alastair Ninian John Gordon [*b* 20 July 1920; *m* 1950, Anne, *d* of late Lt-Col Gerald Barry, MC; one *s* two *d*]. *Address:* Haughley Grange, Stowmarket, Suffolk IP14 3QT.

ABERDEEN AND TEMAIR, Marchioness of; (Beatrice Mary) June Gordon, MBE 1971; DL; Musical Director and Conductor, Haddo House Choral Society, since 1945; *d* of Arthur Paul Boissier, MA, and Dorothy Christina Leslie Smith; *m* 1939, David George Ian Alexander Gordon (later 4th Marquess of Aberdeen and Temair, CBE, TD) (*d* 1974); two adopted *s* two adopted d. Educ: Southlands School, Harrow; Royal Coll. of Music. GRSM, ARCM. Teacher of Music, Bromley High School for Girls, 1936-39. Director of Haddo House Choral Soc. and Arts Centre, 1945-. Chairman: Scottish Children's League, 1969-; NE Scotland Music School, 1975-; Adv. Council, Scottish Opera, 1979-; Chm. (local), Adv. Cttee, Aberdeen Internat. Festival of Music and the Performing Arts, 1980-. Governor: Gordonstoun Sch., 1971-; Royal Scottish Acad. of Music and Drama, 1979. FRCM 1967. DStJ 1977. DL Aberdeenshire, 1971. Hon. LLD Aberdeen, 1968. Publications: contribs to Aberdeen Univ. Jl, RCM magazine. Address: Haddo House, Aberdeen AB4 0ER. T: Tarves 216. Club: Naval & Military.

ABERDEEN, David du Rieu, FRIBA, MRTPI; Architect (Private Practice); b 13 Aug. 1913; s of David Aberdeen and Lilian du Rieu; m 1940, Phyllis Irene Westbrook (née Buller), widow; two step c. Educ: privately; Sch. of Architecture, London Univ. (BA Hons, Arch.). RIBA Donaldson Medallist, 1934; RIBA Alfred Bossom Research Fell., 1946-47. Works include: Brabazon Hangars, Filton, for Bristol Aeroplane Co.; TUC Headquarters, London, won in open architectural competition, 1948 (RIBA London Architecture Bronze Medal, 1958); 13-storey point block flats, New Southgate; housing for Basildon and Harlow New Towns. Architect for: new headquarters in City for Swiss Bank Corp.; redevelopment of Paddington Gen. Hosp.; New Gen. Market Hall, Shrewsbury; Swiss Centre, cultural and trade Headquarters, Leicester Square; First National City Bank of NY, London Office. Lectr, Atelier of Advanced Design, Sch. of Architecture, London Univ., 1947-53. Publications: contrib. to architectural press. Address: 20 Green Moor Link, N21; 19 Bloomsbury Square, WC1A 2NS.

ABERDOUR, Lord; John Stewart Sholto Douglas; b 17 Jan. 1952; s and heir of 22nd Earl of Morton, qv. Educ: Dunrobin Castle School. Studied Agriculture, Aberdeen Univ. Address: Haggs Farm, Kirknewton, Midlothian.

ABERGAVENNY, 5th Marquess of, cr 1876; John Henry Guy Nevill, KG 1974; OBE 1945; JP; Baron Abergavenny, 1450; Earl of Abergavenny and Viscount Nevill, 1784; Earl of Lewes, 1876; Lt-Col late Life Guards; Lord-Lieutenant of East Sussex, since 1974 (Vice-Lieutenant of Sussex, 1970-74); Chancellor, Order of the Garter, since 1977; b 8 Nov. 1914; er s of 4th Marquess and Isabel Nellie (d 1953), d of James Walker Larnach; S father, 1954; m 1938, Patricia (see Marchioness of Abergavenny); three d (and one s one d decd). Educ: Eton; Trinity Coll., Cambridge. Joined Life Guards, 1936; served War of 1939-45 (despatches, OBE); Lt-Col, retired 1946; Hon. Col, Kent & Co. of London Yeomanry, 1948-62. Director: Massey-Ferguson Holdings Ltd; Lloyds Bank Ltd; Lloyds Bank UK Management; Lloyds Bank SE Regional Bd (Chm.); Whitbread Investment Co. Trustee, Ascot Authority, 1953-; HM Representative at Ascot, 1972-; President: Royal Assoc. of British Dairy Farmers, 1955 and 1963; Assoc. of Agriculture, 1961-63; Royal Agric. Soc. of England, 1967 (Dep. Pres. 1968, 1972); Hunters' Improvement Soc., 1959; British Horse Soc., 1970-71; Vice-Chm., Turf Bd, 1967-68; Mem. Nat. Hunt Cttee, 1942 (Senior Steward, 1953 and 1963); Mem. Jockey Club, 1952. Member: E Sussex CC, 1947-54 (Alderman 1954-62); E Sussex Agric. Cttee, 1948-54. JP Sussex, 1948; DL Sussex, 1955. KStJ 1976 (Pres. Council, Order of St John, Sussex, 1975). Heir: nephew Guy Rupert Gerard Nevill [b 29 March 1945; s of Lord Rupert Nevill, CVO (d 1982); m 1982, Lady Beatrix Lambton, d of A. C. F. Lambton, qv]. Address: (seat) Eridge Park, Tunbridge Wells, East Sussex. T: Tunbridge Wells 27378; Flat 2, 46 Pont Street, SW1. T: 01-581 3967. Club: White's.
See also Earl of Cottenham.

ABERGAVENNY, Marchioness of; Mary Patricia Nevill, DCVO 1981 (CVO 1970); Lady of the Bedchamber to the Queen since 1966 (an Extra Lady of the Bedchamber, 1960-66); b 20 Oct. 1915; d of late Lt-Col John Fenwick Harrison, Royal Horse Guards, and Hon. Margery Olive Edith, d of 3rd Baron Burnham, DSO; m 1938, Marquess of Abergavenny, qv; three d (and one s one d decd). Address: Eridge Park, Tunbridge Wells, East Sussex; Flat 2, 46 Pont Street, SW1.

ABERNETHY, William Leslie, CBE 1972; FCA, IPFA; Managing Trustee, Municipal Mutual Insurance Ltd, since 1973, and Director of associated companies; Comptroller of Financial Services, Greater London Council, 1972-73 (Treasurer, 1964-72) and Chief Financial Officer, Inner London Education Authority, 1967-73; b 10 June 1910; s of Robert and Margaret Abernethy; m 1937, Irene Holden; one s. Educ: Darwen Grammar Sch., Lancs. Hindle & Jepson, Chartered Accts, Darwen, 1925-31; Borough Treasurer's Dept, Darwen, 1931-37; Derbyshire CC, Treasurer's Dept, 1937-48 (Dep. Co. Treas., 1944-48); 1st Treas., Newcastle upon Tyne Regional Hosp. Bd, 1948-50. LCC: Asst Comptroller, 1950-56; Dep. Comptroller, 1956-64; Comptroller, Sept. 1964-Mar. 1965. A Vice-Pres., Roy. Inst. of Public Admin (Chm. Exec. Coun., 1959-60). Mem. Council, IMTA, 1966-73. Publications: Housing Finance and Accounts (with A. R. Holmes), 1953; Internal Audit in Local Authorities and Hospitals, 1957; Internal Audit in the Public Boards, 1957; contribs professional jls. Address: Kia Cottage, Four Roads, Port St Mary, Isle of Man. T: Port St Mary 834191.

ABINGDON, Earl of; see Lindsey and Abingdon, Earl of.

ABINGER, 8th Baron, cr 1835; James Richard Scarlett, DL; Lt-Col, late Royal Artillery; farmer and company director; b 28 Sept. 1914; er s of 7th Baron and Marjorie (d 1965), 2nd d of John McPhillamy, Blair Athol,

Bathurst, NSW; S father, 1943; m 1957, Isla Carolyn, o d of late Vice-Adm. J. W. Rivett-Carnac, CB, CBE, DSC; two s. Educ: Eton; Magdalene College, Cambridge (MA 1952). India, France, Airborne Corps, and attached RAF; RNXS, 1968. DL Essex, 1968. CStJ. Heir: s Hon. James Harry Scarlett, b 28 May 1959. Address: Clees Hall, Bures, Suffolk. T: Bures 227 227. Clubs: Carlton, Cavalry and Guards, Royal Automobile.
See also Hon. J. L. C. Scarlett.

ABNEY-HASTINGS, family name of Countess of Loudoun.

ABOU-SEÉDA, Hassan A. H.; Order of Merit, First Class (Egypt), 1979; Star of Honour (Egypt) and King Abdel Aziz Alsaud Order, First Class (for performance during 1973 October War), 1973; Order of Liberation (Egypt), 1957; fourteen military medals; Ambassador of the Arab Republic of Egypt to the Court of St James's, since 1980; b 13 Oct. 1930; s of Aly Hassan Abou-Seéda and Fatimah Salamah; m 1973, Sohair A. A. el-Etriby; one s. Educ: Military College, Cairo (BA mil. sciences, MA mil. sciences). Fellow: Higher War Studies College; Nasser Academy. Military service with promotion all through command structure of Egyptian Armed Forces, 1949-79: Division Commander, 1971; Commander of an army, 1976; Chief of Military Operations and Dep. Chief of Staff of Armed Forces, 1978. Ambassador in Foreign Ministry, 1979. Publications: several research papers on the 1973 October War and on military strategy (Egypt). Recreations: reading (strategy, economics and history), chess, painting, tennis. Address: Embassy of the United Arab Republic of Egypt, 26 South Street, W1. T: 01-499 2401; 14 Sarayah el-Azbakeyah, off Mohamed Farid, Down Town Cairo. T: Cairo 911 644. Clubs: Royal Automobile; Gezirah, Armed Forces Officers', Tahrir (Cairo).

ABOYADE, Prof. Ojetunji, CON 1977; PhD; Professor of Economics, University of Ibadan, 1966-75 and since 1978; b 9 Sept. 1931; s of Mr and Mrs Aboyade, Awe, Oyo, Nigeria; m 1961, Olabimpe (see Odubanjo); two s two d. Educ: The University, Hull (Groves Prize, Best Perf. Econs Dept, 1957; BSc Hons Econs 1st Cl.); Pembroke Coll., Cambridge (PhD 1960). Govt Scholar, 1953-60. Res. Asst, Nigerian National Income Accounts, Fed. Office of Statistics, Lagos, 1958-59; University of Ibadan, Nigeria: Lectr, Grade II and I, 1960-64; Sen. Lectr, 1964-66; Head, Dept of Econs, 1966-71; Dean of Social Sciences, 1972-74; Vice-Chancellor and Professor, Univ. of Ife, 1975-78. Head, National Econ. Planning, Fed. Govt of Nigeria (Econ. Develt), 1969-70. Vis. Asst Prof. and Res. Fellow, Dept of Econs, Univ. of Mich, Ann Arbor, 1963-64; Vis. Consultant (Econ.), World Bank, USA, 1971-72. Editor, Nigerian Jl of Economic and Social Studies, 1961-71. Pres., Nigerian Econ. Soc., 1973-74; Member: Bd of Trustees, Internat. Food Policy Research Inst., USA; Internat. Assoc. for Res. and Income, 1964-; Council, Assoc. of Commonwealth Univs; Chm., Tech. Cttee on Revenue Allocation, 1977. Publications: Foundations of an African Economy: a study of investment and growth in Nigeria, 1967 (USA); Issues in the Development of an African Economy, 1976 (Nigeria); chapters in and essay contribs to books, and articles in professional jls, 1961-75. Recreations: hobbies include farming. Address: Department of Economics, University of Ibadan, Ibadan, Nigeria.

ABOYNE, Earl of; Granville Charles Gomer Gordon; b 4 Feb. 1944; s and heir of 12th Marquess of Huntly, qv; m 1972, Jane Elizabeth Angela, d of late Col Alistair Gibb and Lady McCorquodale of Newton; one s two d. Educ: Gordonstoun. Heir: s Lord Strathavon and Glenlivet, b 26 July 1973. Address: Aboyne Castle, Aberdeenshire. T: Aboyne 2118.
See also Baron Cranworth.

ABRAHAM, Sir Edward (Penley), Kt 1980; CBE 1973; FRS 1958; MA, DPhil (Oxon); Fellow of Lincoln College, Oxford, 1948-80, Honorary Fellow, since 1980; Professor of Chemical Pathology, Oxford, 1964-80; b 10 June 1913; s of Albert Penley Abraham and Mary Abraham (née Hearn); m 1939, Asbjörg Harung, Bergen, Norway; one s. Educ: King Edward VI School, Southampton; The Queen's College, Oxford (1st cl. Hons Sch. of Natural Science), Hon. Fellow 1973. Rockefeller Foundation Travelling Fellow at Universities of Stockholm (1939) and California (1948). Ciba lecturer at Rutgers University, NJ, 1957; Guest lecturer, Univ. of Sydney, 1960; Reader in Chemical Pathology, Oxford, 1960-64; Rennebohm Lecturer, Univ. of Wisconsin, 1966-67; Squibb Lectr, Rutgers Univ., 1972. Hon. Fellow: Linacre Coll., Oxford, 1976; Lady Margaret Hall, Oxford, 1978; Wolfson Coll., Oxford, 1982. Royal Medal, Royal Soc., 1973; Mullard Prize and Medal, Royal Soc., 1980; Scheele Medal, Swedish Academy of Pharmaceut. Sciences, 1975; Chemical Soc. Award in Medicinal Chemistry, 1975. Hon. DSc Exeter, 1980. Publications: Biochemistry of Some Peptide and Steroid Antibiotics, 1957; Biosynthesis and Enzymic Hydrolysis of Penicillins and Cephalosporins, 1974; contribs to: Antibiotics, 1949; The Chemistry of Penicillin, 1949; General Pathology, 1957, 4th edn 1970; Cephalosporins and Penicillins, Chemistry and Biology, 1972; scientific papers on the biochemistry of natural products, incl. penicillins and cephalosporins. Recreations: walking, ski-ing. Address: Badger's Wood, Bedwells Heath, Boars Hill, Oxford. T: Oxford 735395. Club: Athenæum.

ABRAHAM, Gerald Ernest Heal, CBE 1974; MA; FBA 1972; FTCL; President, Royal Musical Association, 1970-74; b 9 March 1904; s of Ernest and Dorothy Mary Abraham; m 1936, Isobel Patsie Robinson; one d. Asst Editor, Radio Times, 1935-39; Dep. Editor, The Listener, 1939-42; Director of Gramophone Dept, BBC, 1942-47; James and Constance Alsop Prof. of Music, Liverpool Univ., 1947-62; BBC Asst Controller of Music, 1962-67;

Music Critic, The Daily Telegraph, 1967-68; Ernest Bloch Prof. of Music, Univ. of Calif (Berkeley), 1968-69. Chairman, Music Section of the Critics' Circle, 1944-46. Editor, Monthly Musical Record, 1945-60; Editor, Music of the Masters (series of books); General Editor: The History of Music in Sound (gramophone records and handbooks); New Oxford History of Music; Chm., Early English Church Music Cttee, 1970-80; Mem. Editorial Cttee, Musica Britannica. President, International Society for Music Education, 1958-61; Dep. Chm. Haydn Institute (Cologne), 1961-68; Mem. Directorium, Internat. Musicological Soc., 1967-77; Corr. Mem., Amer. Musicological Soc., 1980; Governor, Dolmetsch Foundn, 1970-73. Hon. RAM 1970. Hon. DMus: Dunelm, 1961; Liverpool, 1978; Southampton, 1979; Hon. Dr of Fine Arts, California (Berkeley), 1969. Publications: This Modern Stuff, 1933; Nietzsche, 1933; Studies in Russian Music, 1935; Tolstoy, 1935; Masters of Russian Music (with M. D. Calvocoressi), 1936; Dostoevsky, 1936; A Hundred Years of Music, 1938; On Russian Music, 1939; Chopin's Musical Style, 1939; Beethoven's Second-Period Quartets, 1942; Eight Soviet Composers, 1943; Tchaikovsky, 1944; Rimsky-Korsakov, 1945; Design in Music, 1949; Slavonic and Romantic Music, 1968; The Tradition of Western Music, 1974; The Concise Oxford History of Music, 1979; (ed, with Dom Anselm Hughes) New Oxford History of Music, Vol. III (Ars Nova and the Renaissance), 1960; (ed) New Oxford History of Music, Vol. IV (The Age of Humanism), 1968. Recreations: walking, languages, military history. Address: The Old School House, Ebernoe, near Petworth, West Sussex. T: North Chapel 325.

ABRAHAM, Louis Arnold, CB 1956; CBE 1950; b 26 Nov. 1893; y s of late William Abraham, MP: West Limerick, 1885-92; North East Cork, 1893-1910; Dublin (Harbour), 1910-15; m 1921, Irene (d 1974), yr d of late Frederick George Kerin, Ennis, County Clare. Educ: Owen's School, London; Peterhouse, Cambridge (Exhibr) (1st cl. Hist. Tripos, pt 2, 1920). Pres., Cambridge Union, 1920. Asst Clerk, House of Commons, 1920; called to the Bar (certif. of honour), 1928; Pres., Hardwicke Soc., 1928; Senior Clerk, House of Commons, 1932; Clerk of Private Bills, 1945-52; Examr of Petitions for Private Bills and Taxing Officer, 1946-52; Principal Clerk of Committees, 1952-58. Publications: (with S. C. Hawtrey) A Parliamentary Dictionary, 1956; Defamation as Contempt of Parliament, in, Wicked, Wicked Libels, 1972; (ed) Palgrave's Chairman's Handbook, 1964. Address: 13 Lushington Road, Eastbourne, East Sussex BN21 4LG. T: Eastbourne 32223.

ABRAHAM, Maj.-Gen. (Sutton) Martin (O'Heguerty), CB 1973; MC 1942 and Bar, 1943; Secretary, Bedford College, University of London, since 1976; b 26 Jan. 1919; s of Capt. E. G. F. Abraham, CB, late Indian Civil Service, and Ruth Eostre Abraham; m 1950, Iona Margaret, d of Sir John Stirling, KT, MBE; two s one d. Educ: Durnford; Eton; Trinity Coll., Cambridge (BA Modern Languages). Commissioned in RA, 1939; transf. to 12th Royal Lancers, 1941; Egypt, 1941; Armoured Car Troop Leader, desert campaigns; Armoured Car Sqdn 2nd-in-Comd, Italian campaign, Sangro Valley, Rimini, Po Valley; accepted surrender of Trieste (Sqdn Ldr); Mil. Asst to C-in-C Austria, and accompanied him to BAOR, 1946; psc 1948; Mem. Chiefs of Staff Secretariat, 1949-52; Sqdn Ldr 12th Lancers, Malaya, 1953-54; Mem. Staff Coll. Directing Staff, 1955-57; 2nd-in-Comd 12th Lancers, 1957-58; CO 12th Lancers, 1958-62 (Cyprus, 1959-60); Asst Mil. Sec., Southern Comd, 1960-62; GSO1, Staff Coll. (Minley Div.), 1960-62; Comdr RAC (Brig.), 1st Brit. Corps, Germany, 1964-66; idc 1967; Dir, Combat Develt (Army), MoD, 1968-71; Chief of Jt Services Liaison Orgn, BAOR, 1971-73; Mil. Adviser to Arms Control and Disarmament Res. Unit and Western Organisations Dept, FCO, 1973-76. Col, 9/12 Royal Lancers, 1978-82. Recreations: painting, reading, sundry practical country pursuits and chores, shooting. Address: c/o C. Hoare & Co., 37 Fleet Street, EC4. T: 01-353 4522. Club: Cavalry and Guards.

ABRAHAMS, Allan Rose, CMG 1962; b 29 Nov. 1908; s of late Mr and Mrs Frank Abrahams; m 1948, Norma Adeline Neita; one s two d. Educ: Jamaica College, Jamaica. Joined Civil Service, 1927; Permanent Secretary, Ministry of Communications and Works, Jamaica, 1955-64, retired. Recreation: gardening. Address: 20 Widcombe Road, Kingston 6, Jamaica. T: 78214. Club: Kingston (Kingston, Jamaica).

ABRAHAMS, Anthony Claud Walter; Governor since 1966, and Chairman since 1978 of the Harpur Trust (the Bedford Charity); b 16 June 1923; s of late Rt Hon. Sir Sidney Abrahams, QC, and of Ruth Bowman; m 1950, Laila Myking; two s one d; m 1982, Elizabeth, d of late Comdr A. E. Bryant, RN. Educ: Bedford Sch.; Emmanuel Coll., Cambridge (MA). Barrister-at-law. Served War: Wavell Cadet, Bangalore, 1942-43; commnd 3/12 Royal Bn, Frontier Force Regt, 1943-45; India, N Africa, Italy, Greece (despatches). Called to the Bar, Middle Temple, 1951; practised Midland Circuit, 1951-64; Founder, Centre for British Teachers, 1964, Dir, 1973-; Man. Dir, Colchester and Bedford English Study Centres, 1968-. Liveryman, Worshipful Co. of Glaziers. Recreations: Rugby, cricket, golf, Rugby fives, English language learning. Address: Goldsmith Building, Temple, EC4Y 7BL. T: 01-353 7913. Clubs: Garrick, MCC, Jesters.

ABRAHAMS, Sir Charles (Myer), KCVO 1970; Deputy Chairman and Joint Managing Director, Aquascutum and associated companies, until 1982, now President; b 25 April 1914; s of late Isidor and Eva Abrahams; m 1940, Luisa (née Kramer); two d. Educ: Westminster School. Hon. President, Friends of the Duke of Edinburgh's Award Scheme, 1975-; Vice-President: Nightingale House, Home for Aged Jews, 1971-; British Paraplegic Sports

Soc., 1976-80. Freeman, City of London, 1981. Served War of 1939-45 i Italy, Flt-Lt RAFVR. OStJ 1977. Recreations: golf and sculpture. Address 188 Coombe Lane West, Kingston-upon-Thames, Surrey. T: 01-942 3379 Clubs: Coombe Hill Golf (Surrey); Sunningdale Golf (Berks).

ABRAHAMS, Gerald Milton, CBE 1967; Chairman and Managing Director Aquascutum Group, plc, since 1947; b 20 June 1917; s of late Isidor Abrahams m 1st, 1946, Doris, d of Mark Cole, Brookline, Mass, USA; two d; 2nd, 1972 Marianne Wilson, d of David Kay, London. Educ: Westminster Sch. Serve War of 1939-45, Major HAC, RHA, in Greece and W Desert. Member Council, FBI, 1962-65, CBI, 1965-; British Menswear Guild (Chm., 1959-61 1964-66); Clothing Export Council (Chm., 1966-70; Vice-Pres., 1970-) Clothing Manufacturers Fedn of GB (Chm., 1965-66); BNEC Cttee fo Exports to Canada, 1965-70; Econ. Develt Cttee for Clothing Industry 1966-69; North American Adv. Gp, BOTB, 1978-. FRSA 1972; CBIM 1973 Recreation: golf. Address: 100 Regent Street, W1A 2AQ. T: 01-734 6090 Club: Buck's.

ABRAMS, Mark Alexander, PhD; Director of Research Unit, Age Concern since 1976; b 27 April 1906; s of Abram Abrams and Anne (née Jackson); m 1st, 1931, Una Strugnell (marr. diss. 1951); one s one d; 2nd, 1951, Jean Bird one d. Educ: Latymer Sch., Edmonton; London Sch. of Economics, Univ. o London. Fellow, Brookings Institute, Washington, DC, 1931-33; Research Department, London Press Exchange, 1933-39; BBC Overseas Dept, 1939-41 Psychological Warfare Board and SHAEF, 1941-46; Man. Dir, then Chm. Research Services Ltd, 1946-70; Dir, Survey Res. Unit, SSRC, 1970-76. Mem Metrication Bd, 1969-79. Mem. Council, PSI, 1978-; Vis. Fellow, Science Policy Research Unit, Sussex Univ., 1976-. Member: Exec. Council, Austrian Soc. for Social Sci. Res.; Business Educn Council, 1974-77; Council, Brighton Polytechnic, 1977-. Publications: Condition of the British People, 1911-1946 1947; Social Surveys and Social Action, 1951; Beyond Three Score and Ten 1980. Recreation: listening to music. Address: 12 Pelham Square, Brighton East Sussex. T: Brighton 684537. Clubs: Reform, Civil Service.

ABRAMS, Dr Michael Ellis, FRCP; Senior Principal Medical Officer (Under Secretary), Department of Health and Social Security, since 1979; b 17 Sept. 1932; s of late Sam Philip and Ruhamah Emmie Abrams; m 1962 Rosalind J. Beckman; four c. Educ: King Edward's Sch., Birmingham; Univ of Birmingham (BSc 1st Cl. Anat. and Physiol. 1953; MB ChB Distinction in Medicine 1956). FRCP 1972; MFCM (Founder Mem.) 1972. Ho. Officer posts in United Birmingham Hosps, 1957-58; Univ. Research Fellow, Dep of Exp. Pathology, Univ. of Birmingham, and Medical Registrar, Queen Elizabeth Hosp., Birmingham, 1959; Medical Registrar and MRC Clinica Res. Fellow, Queen Elizabeth Hosp., Birmingham, 1959-62; MRC Clin. Res Fellow, Dept of Medicine, Guy's Hosp., London, 1962-63; Rockefeller Travelling Fellow, Cardiovascular Res. Inst., Univ. of California Med Centre, San Francisco, 1963-64; Lectr/Sen. Lectr and Hon. Cons. Phys., Guy's Hosp., 1964-75; Dir, Inter-Deptl Laboratory, Guy's Hosp., 1971-75; DHSS SMO, 1975-78; PMO, 1978-79. Hon. Cons. Phys. Emeritus, Guy's Hosp. and Hon. Lectr in Medicine, Guy's Hosp. Med. Sch. President, Section of Measurement in Medicine, RSM, 1981-; Chm., Computer Cttee, RCP, 1981- Publications: (ed) Medical Computing Progress and Problems, 1970; (ed) Spectrum 71, 1971; (ed) The Computer in the Doctor's Office, 1980; articles on biomedical computing, pulmonary surfactant and glucose tolerance in diabetes. Recreations: reading, gardening, beachcombing. Address: 97 Wood Vale, N10 3DL. T: 01-883 2392.

ABRAMSON, Sidney, CMG 1979; retired from Department of Trade (Under Secretary, 1972-81); b 14 Sept. 1921; s of Jacob and Rebecca Abramson; m 1st, 1946, Lerine Freedman (marr. diss. 1958); two s; 2nd, 1960, Violet Eller Eatly. Educ: Emanuel Sch., London; Queen's Coll. Oxford. Recreations music, gardening, writing. Address: 75a Holden Road, N12. T: 01-445 1264.

ABSE, Dr Dannie; Specialist in charge of chest clinic, Central Medical Establishment, London, since 1954; writer; b 22 Sept. 1923; s of Rudolph Abse and Kate (née Shepherd); m 1951, Joan (née Mercer); one s two d. Educ: St Illtyd's Coll., Cardiff; University Coll., Cardiff; King's Coll., London Westminster Hosp., London. MRCS, LRCP. First book of poems accepted for publication, 1946. Qualified at Westminster Hosp., 1950; RAF, 1951-54 Sqdn Ldr; Sen. Fellow of the Humanities, Princeton Univ., 1973-74. Pres. Poetry Soc., 1978-. Publications: poetry: After Every Green Thing, 1948 Walking Under Water, 1952; Tenants of the House, 1957; Poems, Golders Green, 1962; A Small Desperation, 1968; Funland and other Poems, 1973 Collected Poems, 1977; Way Out in the Centre, 1981; prose: Ash on a Young Man's Sleeve, 1954; novels: Some Corner of an English Field, 1957; O. Jones O. Jones, 1970; autobiography: A Poet in the Family, 1974; plays: House on Cowards, (first prod.) Questors Theatre, Ealing, 1960; The Dogs of Pavlov (first prod.) Questors, 1969; Pythagoras, (first prod.) Birmingham Rep. Th. 1976; Gone in January, (first prod.) Young Vic, 1978. Recreations: chess bowls, watching Cardiff City FC. Address: 85 Hodford Road, NW11; Green Hollows, Craig-yr-Eos Road, Ogmore-by-Sea, Glamorgan, South Wales. See also Leo Abse.

ABSE, Leo; MP (Lab) Pontypool, since Nov. 1958; b 22 April 1917; s of Rudolph and Kate Abse; m 1955, Marjorie (née Davies); one s one d. Educ: Howard Gardens High School; London School of Economics. Solicitor; senior partner of Cardiff law firm; Sponsor or Co-sponsor of Private Members Acts

relating to divorce, homosexuality, family planning, legitimacy, widows' damages, industrial injuries and congenital disabilities; initiated anti-Windscale Commons debates, 1978; led Labour anti-devolution campaign in Wales, 1979; Member: Home Office Adv. Cttee on adoption, 1972; Home Office Adv. Cttee on the Penal System, 1968; Select Cttee on Abortion, 1975-76; Council of Inst. for the Study and Treatment of Delinquency; Trustee, Clinic of Psychotherapy; Chairman: Welsh Parly Party, 1976; Select Cttee on Welsh Affairs, 1980 (first Chm.); Cardiff City Labour Party, 1952-53; Mem., Cardiff City Council, 1955-58; contested Cardiff North, 1955. *Publication:* Private Member: a psychoanalytically orientated study of contemporary politics, 1973. *Address:* 54 Strand-on-the-Green, W4 3PD. *T:* 01-994 1166.
See also D. Abse.

BUBAKAR, Prof. Iya; Minister of Defence, Nigeria, 1980-82; *b* 14 Dec. 1934; *s* of Buba Abubakar, Wali of Mubi, and Fatima Abubakar; *m* 1963, Ummu; one *s* three *d*. *Educ:* Univ. of Ibadan (BSc London (External)); Cambridge Univ. (PhD). FRAS, FIMA. Ahmadu Bello Univ., Zaria, Nigeria: Prof. of Maths, 1967-75, 1978-; Dean, Faculty of Science, 1968-69, 1973-75; Vice-Chancellor, 1975-78. Visiting Professor: Univ. of Michigan, 1965-66; City Univ. of New York, 1971-72. Chm., Natural Sciences Reg. Council of Nigeria, 1972-75. Mem., Nigerian Univs Commn, 1968-73. Dir, Central Bank of Nigeria, 1972-75. Hon. DSc Univ. of Ife, 1977. *Publications:* Entebbe Modern Mathematics, 1970; several research papers on mathematics in internat. jls. *Recreations:* chess, golf, horse riding. *Address:* Department of Mathematics, Ahmadu Bello University, Zaria, Nigeria. *T:* 0632-2691.

CHEBE, Prof. Chinua; author; Professor of English, University of Nigeria, Nsukka, 1973-81; *b* 16 Nov. 1930; *s* of Isaiah and Janet Achebe; *m* 1961, Christiana Okoli; two *s* two *d*. *Educ:* Univ. of Ibadan. Nigerian Broadcasting Corp.: Talks Producer, 1954; Controller, 1959; Dir, 1961-66. Rockefeller Fellowship, 1960; Unesco Fellowship, 1963; Prof. of English, Univ. of Massachusetts, 1972-75; Prof. of English, Univ. of Connecticut, Storrs, 1975-76. Chairman: Soc. of Nigerian Authors, 1966; Assoc. of Nigerian Authors, 1982-. Member of Council, Univ. of Lagos, 1966. Neil Gunn Internat. Fellowship, Scottish Arts Council, 1975; Hon. Fellow: Modern Language Assoc. of America, 1975; Amer. Acad. and Inst. of Arts and Letters, 1982. Editor, Okike, 1971-. Hon. DLitt: Dartmouth Coll., 1972; Southampton, 1975; Ife, 1978; DUniv Stirling, 1975; Hon. LLD Prince Edward Island, 1976; Hon. DHL Massachusetts, 1977. Jock Campbell New Statesman Award, 1965; Commonwealth Poetry Prize, 1972. Nigerian Nat. Merit Award, 1979; Order of the Fed. Repub. (Nigeria), 1979. *Publications:* Things Fall Apart, 1958; No Longer at Ease, 1960; Arrow of God, 1964; A Man of the People, 1966; Beware Soul-brother (poems), 1971; (jtly) The Insider, 1972; Girls at War, 1972; Morning Yet on Creation Day (essays), 1975; *for children:* Chike and the River, 1966; (jt) How the Leopard Got its Claws, 1971; The Flute, 1978; The Drum, 1978. *Recreation:* music. *Address:* PO Box 53, Nsukka, Nigeria.

CHESON, family name of **Earl of Gosford.**

CHESON, Prof. (Ernest) Donald; Professor of Clinical Epidemiology, University of Southampton, and Hon. Consultant Physician, Royal South Hants Hospital, since 1968; Director, Medical Research Council Unit in Environmental Epidemiology, since 1979; *b* 17 Sept. 1926; *s* of Malcolm King Acheson, MC, MD, and Dorothy Josephine Rennoldson; *m* Barbara Mary Castle; one *s* five *d*. *Educ:* Merchiston Castle Sch., Edinburgh; Brasenose Coll., Oxford (Theodore Williams Schol. in pathology, 1946; MA, DM); Middlesex Hospital (Sen. Broderip Schol. in Med., Surg. and Pathol., 1950). FRCP; FFCM. Sqdn Leader, RAF Med. Br., 1953-55. Medical Practitioner, 1951; various clinical posts at Middlesex Hosp.; Radcliffe Trav. Fellow of University Coll., Oxford, 1957-59; Medical Tutor, Nuffield Dept of Medicine, Radcliffe Infirmary, Oxford, 1960; Dir, Oxford Record Linkage Study and Unit of Clin. Epidemiology, 1962; May Reader in Medicine, 1965; Fellow, Brasenose Coll., Oxford, 1968; Foundation Dean, Faculty of Med., Southampton Univ., 1968-78. Member: Wessex Regional Hosp. Bd, 1968-74; Hampshire AHA (Teaching) 1974-78; Chm., SW Hants and Southampton DHA, 1981-; Member: Adv. Cttee on Asbestos, Health and Safety Exec., 1978; Royal Commn on Environmental Pollution, 1979-; UGC, 1982-; Chairman: Slow Virus Group, DHSS, 1979-80; Primary Health Care Inner London Gp, DHSS, 1980-81. R. Samuel McLaughlin Vis. Prof., McMaster Univ., 1977; King's Fund Travelling Fellow, NZ Postgrad. Med. Fedn, 1979; Lectures: inaugural Adolf Streicher Meml, Stoke-on-Trent, 1978; Walter Hubert, British Assoc. for Cancer Res., 1981; Christie Gordon, Univ. of Birmingham, 1982. Examiner in Community Medicine: Univ. of Aberdeen, 1971-74; Univ. of Leicester, 1981-82; Examiner in Medicine, Univ. of Newcastle upon Tyne, 1975. Mem., Assoc. of Physicians of GB and Ire, 1965- (Pres. 1979); MFOM 1982. *Publications:* Medical Record Linkage, 1967; Multiple Sclerosis, a reappraisal, 1966; Medicine, an outline for the intending student, 1970; scientific papers on epidemiology of cancer and chronic disease, medical education and organisation of medical care. *Recreations:* family, gardening, music, fishing. *Address:* MRC Unit in Environmental Epidemiology, South Block, Southampton General Hospital, Southampton SO9 4XY. *Club:* Athenæum.
See also R. M. Acheson.

ACHESON, Prof. Roy Malcolm, ScD, DM; FRCP, FFCM; Professor of Community Medicine, University of Cambridge, since 1976; Fellow, Churchill College, Cambridge, since 1976; *b* 18 Aug. 1921; *s* of Malcolm King Acheson, MC, MD and Dorothy Rennoldson; *m* 1950, Fiona Marigo O'Brien; two *s* one *d*. *Educ:* Merchiston Castle Sch., Edinburgh; TCD (MA, ScD); Brasenose Coll., Oxford (MA, DM); Radcliffe Infirmary, Oxford. FRCP 1973; FFCM 1972. Clin. and res. posts, Radcliffe Infirmary and Univ. of Oxford; Rockefeller Trav. Fellow, Western Reserve and Harvard Univs, 1955-56; Radcliffe Trav. Fellow, University Coll., Oxford, 1955-57; Lectr in Social Med., Univ. of Dublin, 1955-59; FTCD, 1957-59; Sen. Lectr, then Reader in Social and Preventive Med., Guy's Hosp. Med. Sch. and London Sch. of Hygiene and Trop. Med., 1959-62; Yale University: Associate Prof. of Epidemiology, 1962; Prof. of Epidemiology, 1964-72; Fellow, Jonathan Edwards Coll., 1966-75; London Sch. of Hygiene and Tropical Medicine: Commonwealth Fund Sen. Trav. Fellow in Med., 1968-69; Dir, Centre for Extension Trng in Community Med., 1972-76. Hon. Cons. in Community Med., NE Thames RHA (formerly NE Metrop. RHB), 1972-76, E Anglian RHA, 1976-; Prof. of Health Service Studies, Univ. of London, 1974-76. Samuel R. McLaughlin Vis. Prof. in Med., McMaster Univ., Hamilton, Ont, 1976. Member: Exec. Cttee and Council, Internat. Epidemiol Soc., 1964-75; Expert Cttee, Methods in Chronic Disease Epidemiol, WHO, 1966; Exec. Cttee, GMC, 1979-; Educn Cttee, GMC, 1979-. Cons., Argentina, Colombia, Guatemala, Venezuela, WHO, 1965-. Mem. Bd, 1974-, Sec. to Examrs, 1974-77, and Mem., numerous other cttees, Faculty of Community Med. Hon. MA Yale, 1964. *Publications:* (ed) Comparability in International Epidemiology, 1965; Seminars in Community Medicine: (ed with L. Aird) I: Sociology, 1976; (ed with L. Aird and D. J. Hall) II: Health Information, Planning and Monitoring, 1971. *Recreations:* tennis, golf (when time permits); meditating in the bath. *Address:* Department of Community Medicine, New Addenbrooke's Hospital, Hills Road, Cambridge CB2 2QQ. *T:* Cambridge 45171. *Clubs:* Queen's, United Oxford & Cambridge University.
See also E. D. Acheson.

ACHONRY, Bishop of, (RC), since 1977; **Most Rev. Thomas Flynn,** DD; *b* 8 July 1931; *s* of Robert and Margaret Flynn. *Educ:* St Nathy's, Ballaghaderreen; Maynooth College. BD, LPh, MA. Diocesan Religious Inspector of Schools, 1957-64; teaching in St Nathy's College, Ballaghaderreen, 1964-73; President and Headmaster of St Nathy's Coll., 1973-77. DD 1977. *Recreations:* gardening, fishing, golf. *Address:* St Nathy's, Ballaghaderreen, Co. Roscommon, Eire. *T:* Ballaghaderreen 21.

ACKERMAN, Myron, CBE 1972 (Hon.); Chairman, Tuscan Clothing Co. Ltd; Director: Atlas Avenue Ltd; d'Avenza spa, Carrara, Italy; *b* 21 Sept. 1913; *s* of late Simon Ackerman and late May Krones Ackerman; *m* 1954, Marjorie Molyneux Jacob; no *c*. *Educ:* Yale Univ. Hon. Freeman, Borough of Crewe, 1973. *Address:* Steward's Cottage, Combermere, near Whitchurch, Salop SY13 4AJ. *T:* Burleydam 665. *Clubs:* American; Yale (New York).

ACKERMANN, Georg K., *see* Kahn-Ackermann.

ACKERS, James George; Chairman, Ackers Jarrett Leasing Ltd, since 1982; Chairman, West Midlands Regional Health Authority, since 1982; *b* 20 Oct. 1935; *s* of James Ackers and Vera Harriet Ackers (*née* Edwards); *m* 1st, 1959, Judith Ann Locket; one *s* two *d*; 2nd 1972, Enid Lydia Silverthorne. *Educ:* Oundle Sch., Northants; LSE. Bsc(Econ). Man. Dir, 1963-, Chm., 1974-, Ackers Jarrett Ltd; Vice Pres., Michael Doud Gill & Associates, Washington, DC, 1968-71. Pres., Walsall Chamber of Industry and Commerce, 1978; Chairman: West Midlands Chambers of Industry and Commerce, 1980-82; Dep. Chm., Assoc. of British Chambers of Commerce, 1982- (Chm., Economic and Industrial Cttee, 1981-); Member: Cttee of Inquiry into Civil Service Pay, 1981-; Monopolies and Mergers Commn, 1981-. Chm., Fedn of Univ. Conservative Assocs, 1958; Vice-Chm., Bow Group, 1962-63. *Address:* 5 Wrekin Court, Walsall Road, Sutton Coldfield, West Midlands B74 4QN; 21A Greycoat Gardens, Greycoat Street, SW1. *Club:* Carlton.

ACKLAND, Joss, (Sidney Edmond Jocelyn); actor; *b* 29 Feb. 1928; *s* of Major Norman Ackland, Journalist, Daily Telegraph and Morning Post, and Ruth Izod; *m* 1951, Rosemary Jean Kirkcaldy, actress; one *s* five *d* (and one *s* decd). *Educ:* Cork GS; Dame Alice Owens Sch.; Central Sch. of Speech Training and Dramatic Art. *Plays:* The Hasty Heart, Aldwych, 1945; The Rising Sun, Arts, 1946; Dir, Winterset, 20th Century, 1946; Shakespeare Fest., Stratford-on-Avon, 1947; various try-out plays at Irving, Q, and Watergate Theatres, and toured, with Easy Money, in Germany, 1948; acted for Anthony Hawtrey, Embassy, Buxton and Croydon; then Arts Council tour, first Pitlochry Fest.; tours, and Repertory at Windsor, Chesterfield and Coventry. Went, with family, to Malawi, Central Africa, to work as a tea planter, 1954. S Africa: acting, directing, script writing and disc-jockeying, 1955-57; returned to England and joined Oxford Playhouse Co., 1957. Old Vic Co.: (incl. tours of America, Canada, USSR, Yugoslavia and Poland) Falstaff, Toby Belch, Caliban, Pistol, etc, 1958-61; Associate Dir, Mermaid Theatre: casting, choosing plays, Dir, Plough and the Stars, and playing numerous leading rôles, 1961-63. In 1963 his house burnt down so concentrated on television and did not return to theatre until 1965. Leading rôles on London stage: The Professor, in The Professor, 1966; Jorrocks, in Jorrocks, 1967; Hotel in Amsterdam, 1968-69; Come As You Are, 1969-70; Brassbound, in Captain Brassbound's Conversion, 1971; The Collaborators, 1973; Mitch, in A Streetcar Named Desire, 1974; Frederick, in A Little Night Music, 1975-76;

The Madras House, 1977; Juan Perón, in Evita, 1978; Falstaff, in Henry IV pts 1 and 2, RSC, opening of Barbican Theatre, 1982; tours: Petruchio, in The Taming of the Shrew, 1977; Sir, in The Dresser; Gaev in The Cherry Orchard, Chichester, 1981. *Films:* Seven Days to Noon, 1949; Crescendo, 1969; The House that Dripped Blood, Villain, 1970; The Happiness Cage, England Made Me, 1971; Penny Gold, The Little Prince, The Black Windmill, S-P-Y-S, The Three Musketeers, 1973; Great Expectations, One of our Dinosaurs is Missing, 1974; Operation Daybreak, Royal Flash, 1975; The Silver Bears, 1976; The End of Civilisation as we know it, The Greek Tycoon, Someone is killing the Great Chefs of Europe, 1977; Saint Jack, The Apple, Rough Cut, 1978. Numerous appearances on TV, incl. The Bankrupt, The Widower, Access to the Children, Country Matters, The Lie, Kipling, The Crezz, Tinker, Tailor, Soldier, Spy, Constance Kent, The Stinker, Closing Ranks, Elizabeth Alone, Escape to the West, Thicker than Water. *Recreations:* his children, writing, painting. *Club:* Garrick.

ACKLAND, Rodney; Playwright; *b* 18 May 1908; *m* 1952, Mab (*d* 1972), *d* of Frederick Lonsdale. First play, Improper People, Arts, 1929; Marionella, Players, 1930; Dance With No Music, Arts and Embassy, 1931; Strange Orchestra, Embassy and St Martin's, 1932; Ballerina, adapted from Lady Eleanor Smith's novel, Gaiety, 1933; Birthday, Cambridge, 1934; The Old Ladies, adapted from Sir Hugh Walpole's novel, New and St Martin's, 1935; After October, Criterion and Aldwych, 1936; Plot Twenty-One, Embassy, 1936; The White Guard, adapted from the Russian play by Michael Bulgakov, Phœnix, 1938; Remembrance of Things Past, Globe, 1938; Sixth Floor, adapted from the French play by Alfred Gehri, St James's, 1939; The Dark River, Whitehall, 1943; Crime and Punishment, adapted from Dostoevsky, New, 1946; (with Robert G. Newton) Cupid and Mars, Arts, 1947; Diary of a Scoundrel, based on a comedy by Ostrovsky, Arts, 1949; Before the Party, adapted from Somerset Maugham's short story, St Martin's, 1949, revived, Queen's and Apollo, 1980; The Pink Room, Lyric, Hammersmith, 1952; A Dead Secret, Piccadilly, 1957; adapted Farewell, Farewell, Eugene, Garrick, 1959. *Publications:* Improper People; Dance With No Music; Strange Orchestra; The Old Ladies; Birthday; After October; The Dark River; Crime and Punishment; Cupid and Mars; Diary of a Scoundrel; Before the Party; Farewell, Farewell, Eugene; The Celluloid Mistress (autobiography); The Other Palace. *Address:* c/o Eric Glass Ltd, 28 Berkeley Square, W1X 6HD.

ACKNER, Rt. Hon. Sir Desmond (James Conrad), Kt 1971; PC 1980; **Rt. Hon. Lord Justice Ackner;** a Lord Justice of Appeal, since 1980; *b* 18 Sept. 1920; *s* of Dr Conrad and Rhoda Ackner; *m* 1946, Joan, *d* of late John Evans, JP, and widow of K. B. Spence; one *s* two *d. Educ:* Highgate Sch.; Clare Coll., Cambridge (MA). Served in RA, 1941–42; Admty Naval Law Br., 1942–45. Called to Bar, Middle Temple, 1945; QC 1961; Recorder of Swindon, 1962–71; Judge of Courts of Appeal of Jersey and Guernsey, 1967–71; a Judge of the High Court of Justice, Queen's Bench Div., 1971–80; Presiding Judge, Western Circuit, 1976–79. Mem. Gen. Council of Bar, 1957–61, 1963–70 (Hon. Treas., 1964–66; Vice-Chm., 1966–68; Chm., 1968–70); Bencher Middle Temple, 1965; Mem. Senate of the Four Inns of Court, 1966–70 (Vice-Pres., 1968–70); Pres., Senate of the Inns of Court and the Bar, 1980–. Chm., Law Adv. Panel, British Council, 1980–. Hon. Mem., Canadian Bar Assoc., 1973–. *Recreations:* swimming, sailing, gardening, theatre. *Address:* 7 Rivermill, 151 Grosvenor Road, SW1. *T:* 01-821 8068; Browns House, Sutton, near Pulborough, West Sussex. *T:* Sutton (Sussex) 206. *Club:* Birdham Yacht.

ACKRILL, Prof. John Lloyd, FBA 1981; Professor of the History of Philosophy, Oxford University, since 1966; *b* 30 Dec. 1921; *s* of late Frederick William Ackrill and Jessie Anne Ackrill; *m* 1953, Margaret Walker Kerr; one *s* three *d. Educ:* Reading School; St John's Coll., Oxford (Scholar) (1940–41 and 1945–48). War service (Royal Berks Regt and GS, Capt.), 1941–45. Assistant Lecturer in Logic, Glasgow Univ., 1948–49; Univ. Lectr in Ancient Philosophy, Oxford, 1951–52; Fellow and Tutor, Brasenose Coll., 1953–66. Mem., Inst. for Adv. Study, Princeton, 1950–51, 1961–62; Fellow Coun. of Humanities, and Vis. Prof., Princeton Univ., 1955, 1964. *Publications:* Aristotle's *Categories* and *De Interpretatione* (trans. with notes), 1963; Aristotle's Ethics, 1973; Aristotle the Philosopher, 1981; articles in philos. and class. jls. *Address:* 22 Charlbury Road, Oxford. *T:* 56098.

ACKROYD, Dame (Dorothy) Elizabeth, DBE 1970; MA, BLitt (Oxon); Chairman, Patients Association, since 1978; *d* of late Major Charles Harris Ackroyd, MC. *Educ:* privately; St Hugh's Coll., Oxford. Min. of Supply, 1940–42, 1946–49, 1951–52 (Under-Sec., 1952); Min. of Prodn, 1942–45; BoT, 1945–46, 1955–61; Commonwealth Fund Fell., 1949–50; Dir of Steel and Power Div., Economic Commn for Europe, 1950–51; UK Delegn to High Authority of ECSC, 1952–55; MoT, 1961–63; Dir, Consumer Council, 1963–71. Chairman: Bloodstock and Racehorse Industries Confedn Ltd, 1977–78; Cinematograph Films Council, 1981– (Mem., 1970–); SE Electricity Consultative Council, 1972–; Indep. Mem., Council for the Securities Industry, 1978–; Vice-Pres., Consumers' Assoc., 1970–; Member: PO Users' Nat. Council, 1970–; Seeboard, 1972–; Bedford Coll. Council, 1970–; Horserace Totalisator Bd, 1975–; Waltham Forest Community Health Council, 1974–; Council, RSA, 1975–81; Exec. Cttee, Nat. Council for Voluntary Organisations, 1980–; Governor, Birkbeck Coll., 1973–; Vice-Chm., London Voluntary Service Council, 1977–; Pres., Patients' Assoc., 1971–78; Hon. Treasurer, Pedestrians' Assoc. for Road Safety, 1971–. *Address:* 73 St James's Street, SW1A 1PH. *T:* 01-493 6686.

ACKROYD, Sir John (Robert Whyte), 2nd Bt *cr* 1956; Chairman ar Managing Director, Ackroyd Underwriting Agencies Ltd, since 1978; *b* March 1932; *s* of Sir Cuthbert Lowell Ackroyd, 1st Bt, and Joyce Walla (*d* 1979), *d* of Robert Whyte; *S* father, 1973; *m* 1956, Jennifer Eilee MacLeod, *d* of H. G. S. Bishop; two *s* two *d. Educ:* Bradfield Coll.; Worceste Coll., Oxford (BA 1955, MA 1958). Commissioned RA, 1951; Sword o Honour, Mons Officer Cadet Sch., 1951; served in Jordan, 1951–52. Oxfo Univ., 1952; Steward, OUDS, 1954. Lloyd's, 1955–68, re-elected 1981; join Engineer Planning & Resources Ltd, 1968–75. Hon. Secretary, The Pilgrin of Gt Britain, 1966; Mem. Gen. Council, Victoria League for Commonweal Friendship, 1973. Mem. Council, Royal Coll. of Music, 1981–. Churc Warden, St Mary-le-Bow, Cheapside, and The Church of All Hallows. FZ 1970. Freeman of the City of London; Liveryman Carpenters' Co. *Publicatio* (ed) Jordan, 1978 (to commemorate Silver Jubilee of HM King Hussein o Jordan). *Recreations:* music, theatre. *Heir: er s* Timothy Robert Why Ackroyd, *b* 7 Oct. 1958. *Address:* 43 Lansdowne Crescent, Holland Park, W1 2NN. *T:* 01-727 5465. *Clubs:* Green Room; (Life Mem.) Union Socie (Oxford).

ACKROYD, Rev. Prof. Peter Runham, MA, PhD Cantab, BD, MTh, D London; Samuel Davidson Professor of Old Testament Studies, University o London, 1961–82, now Emeritus Professor; *b* 15 Sept. 1917; *s* of Jabez Robe Ackroyd and Winifred (*née* Brown); *m* 1940, Evelyn Alice Nutt, BS (Manch.), *d* of William Young Nutt; two *s* three *d. Educ:* Harrow Count School for Boys; Downing and Trinity Colleges, Cambridge. Ope Exhibition in Modern Languages, Downing Coll., Cambridge, 1935; Mo and Med. Langs Tripos, Pt I, 1936, Pt II, 1938; BDHons London, 194 Stanton Student, Trin. Coll., Cambridge, 1941–43; Dr Williams's Tru Exhibnr, 1941; MTh London, 1942; PhD Cambridge, 1945; DD Londo 1970. Minister of: Roydon Congregational Church, Essex, 1943–47; Balhar Congregational Church, London, 1947–48; Lectr in Old Testament an Biblical Hebrew, Leeds Univ., 1948–52; Cambridge University: Univ. Lec in Divinity, 1952–61; Select Preacher, 1955; Mem. Council of Senate, 1957–6 Hulsean Lectr, 1960–62; Select Preacher, Oxford, 1962; Dean of Faculty o Theology, King's Coll., London, 1968–69; FKC 1969; Mem. Senate, Londo Univ., 1971–79; Dean, Univ. Faculty of Theology, 1976–80. Vis. Professo Lutheran Sch. of Theology, Chicago, 1967 and 1976; Univ. of Toronto, 197 Univ. of Notre Dame, Indiana, 1982; Lectures: Selwyn NZ, 1970; Ethel M Wood, 1982; (first) Walter S. Williams, Denver, 1982. External Examine Belfast, Bristol, Durham, Cambridge, Edinburgh, Leeds, Nottingham, Exete West Indies. Ordained Deacon, 1957; Priest, 1958. Hon. Curate, Holy Trinity Cambridge, 1957–61. Proctor in Convocation, Cambridge Univ., 1960–6 Hon. Sec., Palestine Exploration Fund, 1962–70. Pres., Soc. for Old Testamer Study, 1972; Chm. Council, British Sch. of Archaeology in Jerusalem, 1979 Hon. DD St Andrews, 1970. *Publications:* Freedom in Action, 1951; Th People of the Old Testament, 1959, new edn 1981; Continuity, 1962; The Ol Testament Tradition, 1963; Exile and Restoration, 1968; Israel under Babylo and Persia, 1970; 1 & 2 Chronicles, Ezra, Nehemiah, Ruth, Jonah, Maccabee 1970; 1 Samuel (Cambridge Bible Commentary), 1971; I & II Chronicle Ezra, Nehemiah (Torch Bible Commentary), 1973; 2 Samuel, 1977; Doors o Perception, 1978; articles and reviews in various learned jls, dictionaries, etc *trans lations:* E. Würthwein's The Text of the Old Testament, 1957; I Köhler's Hebrew Man, 1957, repr. 1973; O. Eissfeldt's The Old Testamen An Introduction, 1965; *editor:* Bible Key Words, 1961–64; Society for Ol Testament Study Book List, 1967–73; Palestine Exploration Quarterly, 1971 *joint editor:* SCM Press OT Library, 1960–; Cambridge Bible Commentary 1961–79; SCM Studies in Biblical Theol., 1962–77; Words and Meaning Essays presented to D. W. Thomas, 1968; Cambridge History of the Bible vol. I, 1970; Oxford Bible Series, 1979–; Cambridge Commentaries: Jewis and Christian Writings of the period 200 BC to AD 200, 1979–. *Recreation* reading, music. *Address:* 19 Gayfere Street, SW1P 3HP. *T:* 01-222 297 Lavender Cottage, Middleton, Suffolk IP17 3NQ. *T:* Saxmundham 73458

ACLAND, Sir Antony (Arthur), KCMG 1982 (CMG 1976); KCVO 197 HM Diplomatic Service; Permanent Under-Secretary of State, Foreign an Commonwealth Office, and Head of the Diplomatic Service, since 1982; 12 March 1930; *s* of Brig. P. B. E. Acland, *qv* ; *m* 1956, Clare Anne Verdo two *s* one *d. Educ:* Eton; Christ Church, Oxford (MA 1956). Joine Diplomatic Service, 1953; ME Centre for Arab Studies, 1954; Dubai, 195 Kuwait, 1956; FO, 1958–62; Asst Private Sec. to Sec. of State, 1959–62; U Mission to UN, 1962–66; Head of Chancery, UK Mission, Geneva, 1966–6 FCO, 1968, Hd of Arabian Dept, 1970–72; Principal Private Sec. to Foreig and Commonwealth Sec., 1972–75; Ambassador to Luxembourg, 1975–77, t Spain, 1977–79; Deputy Under-Sec. of State, FCO, 1980–82. *Address:* c/ Foreign and Commonwealth Office, SW1. *Club:* Brooks's.
See also Maj.-Gen. Sir J. H. B. Acland.

ACLAND, Sir Antony Guy, 5th Bt *cr* 1890; *b* 17 Aug. 1916; *s* of Captai Sir Hubert Guy Dyke Acland, 4th Bt, DSO, RN, and Lalage Mary Kathlee (*d* 1961), *e d* of Captain John Edward Acland; *S* father, 1978; *m* 1st, 193 Avriel Ann Wingfield-Stratford (*d* 1943); one *d* ; 2nd, 1944, Margaret Joa Rooke; one *s* one *d. Educ:* Winchester; RMA, Woolwich. Served RA 1937–58: War of 1939–45, France, 1939–40; specialised in Anti-Aircraf Instructor, Fire Control; Instructor in Gunnery, Military Coll. of Scienc 1948–49; retired as Major, 1958. Joined Saunders-Roe on Rock Development and Trials, 1958; projects included Black Knight and Blac Arrow research rockets; retired, 1967. *Heir: s* Major Christopher Guy Dyk Acland, RA [*b* 24 March 1946; *m* 1971, Christine Mary Carden, *y d* of D

J. W. B. Waring; two s]. *Address:* Sunny Bank, Totland Bay, Isle of Wight. *T:* Freshwater 2085.

ACLAND, Maj.-Gen. Sir John (Hugh Bevil), KCB 1980; CBE 1978; farmer; Director of Liaison Research, Allied Breweries, since 1982; *b* 26 Nov. 1928; *s* of Brig. Peter Acland, *qv* ; *m* 1953, Myrtle Christian Euing, *d* of Brig. and Mrs Alastair Crawford, Auchentroig, Stirlingshire; one *s* one *d*. *Educ:* Eton. Enlisted Scots Guards, 1946; commnd, 1948; served with 1st or 2nd Bn in Malaya, Cyprus, Egypt, Germany, Kenya, Zanzibar and NI, 1949-70; Equerry to the Duke of Gloucester, 1957; Staff Coll., 1959; Bde Major, 4th Guards Armoured Bde, 1964-66; CO 2nd Bn Scots Guards, 1968-71; Col GS ASD, MoD, 1971-74; BGS, MoD, 1975; Comd Land Forces and Dep. Comd British Forces Cyprus, 1976-78; GOC South West Dist, 1978-81; Comd Monitoring Force, Southern Rhodesia, and Military Advr to the Governor, 1979-80. Hon. Col, Exeter Univ. OTC, 1980. *Publications:* articles in British Army Review and other jls. *Recreations:* fishing, shooting, gardening. *Address:* Feniton Court, Honiton, Devon.
See also Sir Antony Acland.

ACLAND, Brigadier Peter Bevil Edward, OBE 1945; MC 1941; TD; Vice-Lord-Lieutenant of Devon, 1962-78; *b* 9 July 1902; *s* of late Col A. D. Acland, CBE; *m* 1927, Susan Bridget Barnett, *d* of late Canon H. Barnett; two *s*. *Educ:* Eton; Christ Church, Oxford. Sudan Political Service, 1924-40. Served War of 1939-45: Abyssinia, Western Desert, Ægean (wounded, despatches). Comd Royal Devon Yeomanry, 1947-51, Hon. Col, 1953; Chairman, Devon AEC, 1948-58; Member, National Parks Commission, 1953-60; Chairman, Devon T&AFA, 1960. DL Devon, 1948; High Sheriff for Devon, 1961; JP 1962. 4th Class Order of the Nile; Greek War Cross. *Address:* Little Court, Feniton, Honiton, Devon.
See also Sir A. A. Acland, Maj.-Gen. Sir J. H. B. Acland.

ACLAND, Sir Richard Thomas Dyke, 15th Bt, *cr* 1644; *b* 26 Nov. 1906; *e s* of Rt Hon. Sir Francis Acland, 14th Bt, MP; *S* father, 1939; *m* 1936, Anne Stella Alford; three *s*. *Educ:* Rugby; Balliol Coll., Oxford. MP (L) Barnstaple Div. Devon, 1935-45; contested: Torquay Div., 1929; Barnstaple, 1931; Putney, 1945; MP (Lab) Gravesend Division of Kent, 1947-55. Sen. Lectr, St Luke's College of Educn, Exeter, 1959-74. Second Church Estates Commissioner, 1950-51. *Publications:* Unser Kampf, 1940; The Forward March, 1941; What it will be like, 1943; How it can be done, 1943; Public Speaking, 1946; Nothing Left to Believe?, 1949; Why So Angry?, 1958; Waging Peace, 1958; We Teach Them Wrong: religion and the young, 1963; (with others) Sexual Morality: three views, 1965; Curriculum or Life, 1966; Moves to the Integrated Curriculum, 1967; The Next Step, 1974. *Heir:* *s* John Dyke Acland [*b* 13 May 1939; *m* 1961, Virginia, *d* of Roland Forge; two *s* one *d*]. *Address:* Sprydon, Broadclyst, Exeter. *T:* Broadclyst 412.

A'COURT; *see* Holmes a'Court.

ACTON, 3rd Baron, *cr* 1869, of Aldenham, Salop; **John Emerich Henry Lyon-Dalberg-Acton;** Bt 1643; CMG 1963; MBE 1945; TD 1949; Hereditary Duke of Dalberg; Patrician of Naples; Major RA, TA; Chairman: British and Continental Holdings (Insurance Brokers) Ltd; Wood Acton Ltd; Trustee, Cold Comfort Farm Society, since 1967; *b* 15 Dec. 1907; *e s* of 2nd Baron Acton, KCVO, and Dorothy (*d* 1923), *d* of late T. H. Lyon, Appleton Hall, Cheshire; *S* father, 1924; *m* 1931, Daphne Strutt, *o d* of 4th Baron Rayleigh, FRS, and late Mary Hilda, 2nd *d* of 4th Earl of Leitrim; five *s* five *d*. *Educ:* Downside; RMC Sandhurst; Trinity Coll., Cambridge. Served War of 1939-45, Italy; Major, Shropshire Yeo. (MBE). Partner, Barham & Brooks, Mem. Birmingham Stock Exchange, 1936-47; emigrated S Rhodesia, 1947; Dir, Amal. Packaging Industries Ltd, 1950-67; Chm. and Man. Dir, API (Rhodesia) Ltd, Central Africa Paper Sacks Ltd, 1951-67; Director: Canadian Overseas Packaging Industries Ltd, 1962-65; Monterrey Packaging (Zambia) Ltd, 1964-67; Rhodesian Bd Standard Bank Ltd, 1958-67; Discount Co. of Rhodesia Ltd, 1960-67; East African Packaging, Jamaica Packaging Ltd, Caribbean Packaging Ltd, to 1965; Old Mutual Fire and General Insurance (Rhodesia) Ltd, to 1967; Chairman: Colcom Ltd, 1959-67; Rhodesian Insurances Ltd, Wright Dean (Rhodesia) Ltd, to 1967. Pres., Rhodesian Royal Agricl Show Soc., 1960-64; qualified Judge of Jersey cattle and pigs; Chairman: Gwebi Agricl Coll., 1958-62; Chibero Agricl Coll., 1960-65 (resigned on illegal declaration of independence); Mem. African Farm Develt Cttee, 1964-67; Chm., BRCS Rhodesia Council Br., 1962-68 (Life Mem. BRCS, 1966); Founding Chm., National (non-racial) Club, Salisbury, 1962; served SR Legal Aid and Welfare Cttee (detainees), 1965-67. Patron, Rhodesian Coll. of Music, to 1967. Chm., Mashonaland Owners and Trainers Assoc., 1956-57; Steward, Mashonaland Turf Club, 1957-67. Emigrated to Swaziland, 1967. Chairman: NEOPAC (Swaziland) Ltd, 1968-70; Swaziland Bd, Standard Bank Ltd, 1968-70; Dir, Swaziland Building Soc., 1968-70. Dir, Swaziland Br., BRCS, 1967-70; Founding Chm., Tattersalls Swaziland, 1969. Retired to Majorca, 1971. *Recreations:* music, bridge, roulette. *Heir:* *s* Hon. Richard Gerald Lyon-Dalberg-Acton [*b* 30 July 1941; *m* 1st, 1965, Hilary Juliet Sarah Cookson (*d* 1973); one *s* ; 2nd, 1974, Judith (writer), *d* of Hon. R. S. G. Todd, *qv*. *Educ:* St George's Coll., Salisbury, Rhodesia; Trinity Coll., Oxford (BA Hist. 1963). Called to Bar, Inner Temple, 1976. Dir, Coutts & Co., 1970-74]. *Address:* Ca-Na Rosalinda, Pollensa, Mallorca. *T:* 531071. *Clubs:* Royal Commonwealth Society; British American (Palma).

ACTON, Sir Harold (Mario Mitchell), Kt 1974; CBE 1965; author; *b* 5 July 1904; *s* of Arthur Mario Acton and Hortense Mitchell, La Pietra, Florence.

Educ: Eton Coll.; Christ Church, Oxford (BA). FRSL. Lectr in English Literature, National University of Peking and Peking Normal College, 1933-35. Lived for seven years in Peking, devoting much time to Chinese Classical Theatre. Served in RAF during War of 1939-45, chiefly in Far East. Grand Officer, Republic of Italy; Kt of the Constantinian Order. *Publications:* Aquarium, 1923; An Indian Ass, 1925; Five Saints and an Appendix, 1927; Humdrum, 1928; Cornelian, 1928; This Chaos, 1930; The Last Medici, 1932, new edn 1958; (in collab.) Modern Chinese Poetry, 1936; (in collab.) Famous Chinese Plays, 1937; Peonies and Ponies, 1941; Glue and Lacquer, 1941 (Four Cautionary Tales, 1947, reprint of former); Memoirs of an Aesthete, 1948; Prince Isidore, 1950; The Bourbons of Naples, 1956; The Last Bourbons of Naples, 1961; Florence (an essay), 1961; Old Lamps for New, 1965; More Memoirs of an Aesthete, 1970; Tit for Tat, 1972; Tuscan Villas, 1973; Nancy Mitford: a memoir, 1975; (in collab.) The Peach Blossom Fan, 1976; The Pazzi Conspiracy, 1979; The Soul's Gymnasium (short stories), 1982. *Recreations:* jettatura, hunting the Philistines. *Address:* La Pietra, Florence, Italy. *T:* 496-156. *Club:* Savile.

ACTON, William Antony; *b* 8 April 1904; *o s* of late William Walter Acton, Wolverton Hall, Pershore, Worcs; *m* 1932, Joan, *o c* of late Hon. Francis Geoffrey Pearson; one *d*. *Educ:* Eton; Trinity College, Cambridge. HM Treasury, 1939-45. Managing Director, Lazard Bros & Co. Ltd, 1945-53; Director: The National Bank Ltd, 1945-70 (Chm., 1964-70); Bank of London and South America Ltd, 1953-70; Standard Bank Ltd, 1953-70; Ottoman Bank, 1953-58; Bank of London and Montreal Ltd, 1959-64; Bank of West Africa Ltd, 1954-70; Bank of Ireland, 1966-70; National Commercial Bank of Scotland, 1967-70; National and Commercial Banking Group Ltd, 1969-70; The Whitehall Trust, 1945-70. High Sheriff, County of London, 1955. *Recreation:* travelling. *Address:* Poste Restante, Corfu, Greece. *T:* Corfu 91-236. *Club:* White's.
See also Sir H. H. T. Dawson, Bt.

ACUTT, Sir Keith (Courtney), KBE 1962 (CBE 1957); Deputy Chairman, Anglo-American Corporation of South Africa Ltd, retired 1982; Director, de Beers Consolidated Mines Ltd and several other finance and mining companies; *b* 6 Oct. 1909; *s* of late Guy Courtney Acutt. *Educ:* in South Africa. Served War of 1939-45 (despatches, 1944). *Address:* 44 Main Street, Johannesburg, South Africa. *T:* 838-8111.

ADAIR, Maj.-Gen. Sir Allan (Henry Shafto), 6th Bt, *cr* 1838; GCVO 1974 (KCVO 1967; CVO 1957); CB 1945; DSO 1940; MC; DL; JP; Lieutenant of HM Bodyguard of the Yeomen of the Guard, 1951-67; *b* 3 Nov. 1897; *o s* of Sir R. Shafto Adair, 5th Bt and Mary (*d* 1950), *d* of Henry Anstey Bosanquet; *S* father, 1949; *m* Enid, *d* of late Hon. Mrs Dudley Ward; three *d* (one *s* killed in action, 1943). *Educ:* Harrow. Grenadier Guards, 1916-41; commanded 3rd Battalion, 1940; Comdr 30 Guards Brigade, 1941; Comdr 6 Guards Brigade, 1942; Comdr Guards Armoured Division 1942-45; retired pay, 1947. Colonel of the Grenadier Guards, 1961-74. DL for Co. Antrim; JP for Suffolk. Governor of Harrow School, 1947-52. Dep. Grand Master, United Grand Lodge of Freemasons, 1969-76. *Recreations:* shooting, golf. *Address:* 55 Green Street, W1. *T:* 01-629 3860; Holy Hill, Strabane, Co. Tyrone. *Clubs:* Turf, Cavalry and Guards.
See also Brig. Sir J. L. Darell, Bt.

ADAM, Hon. Sir Alexander Duncan Grant (known as Hon. Sir Alistair Adam), Kt 1970; MA, LLM; Judge, Supreme Court of Victoria, 1957-74; *b* Greenock, Scotland, 30 Nov. 1902; *s* of late Rev. Prof. Adam and of Mrs D. S. Adam; *m* 1930, Nora Laver; one *s* two *d*. *Educ:* Scotch Coll., Melbourne; Melbourne Univ. Associate to Mr Justice Starke, 1927-28; Victorian Bar, 1928-57; Independent Lecturer in Real Property, Melbourne Univ., 1932-51; Defence Dept, 1942-45; QC 1950; Member Council: Melbourne Univ., 1957-69; Nat. Museum of Victoria, 1962-74. *Publications:* contributor to learned jls. *Recreation:* bowls. *Address:* 39 Walsh Street, Balwyn, Vic. 3103, Australia. *T:* 801524. *Clubs:* Australian (Melbourne); Deepdene Bowling.

ADAM, Colin Gurdon Forbes, CSI 1924; *b* 18 Dec. 1889; *y s* of Sir Frank Forbes Adam, 1st Bt; *m* 1920, Hon. Irene Constance Lawley, *o c* of 3rd Baron Wenlock; two *s* one *d* (and one *s* decd). *Educ:* King's Coll., Cambridge (BA). Entered Indian Civil Service, 1912; Asst Collector and Magistrate, Poona, 1913-15; Under-Sec. to Government of Bombay, 1919; Private Sec. to Governor of Bombay, 1920; Dep. Sec. to Govt, 1925; retired, 1927; District Comr for Special Area of Durham and Tyneside, 1934-39; Chairman, Yorkshire Conservative Newspaper Co., 1960-65. Served Indian Army Reserve of Officers, 1915-18; Indian Expeditionary Force, Mesopotamia and Palestine, 1916-18. DL Kingston upon Hull, 1958-66. *Publication:* Life of Lord Lloyd, 1948. *Address:* The Grange, Elvington, York YO4 5AD. *T:* Elvington 493.
See also Gen. Sir R. F. Adam.

ADAM, Gordon Johnston, PhD; Member (Lab) Northumbria, European Parliament, since 1979; *b* 28 March 1934; *s* of John Craig Adam and Deborah Armstrong Johnston; *m* 1973, Sarah Jane Seely; one *s*. *Educ:* Leeds Univ. (BSc Hons, PhD). CEng, MIMinE. Mining Engr, NCB, 1959-79. Mem., Whitley Bay Bor. Council, 1971-74; Mem. 1973-80, and Dep. Leader 1975-80, North Tyneside Metrop. Bor. Council (Chm., 1973-74); Mayor, 1974-75). Chm., Whitley Bay Playhouse Theatre Trust, 1975-80; Member: Northern Econ. Planning Council, 1974-79; Northern Arts Gen. Council, 1975-; Northern Sinfonia Management Cttee, 1978-. Parly Labour Candidate: Tynemouth,

1966; Berwick-upon-Tweed, Nov. 1973 (by-election), and Feb. 1974. *Recreation:* gardening. *Address:* 2 Queens Road, Whitley Bay, Tyne and Wear. *T:* Whitley Bay 528616; (office) Newgate Chambers, Newgate Street, Newcastle upon Tyne NE1 1RE. *T:* 329944.

ADAM, Madge Gertrude, MA, DPhil; FRAS; University Lecturer (Astronomy), Department of Astrophysics, University Observatory, Oxford, 1947-79; Research Fellow of St Hugh's College, 1957-79, now Emeritus Fellow; *b* 6 March 1912; 2nd *d* of late John Gill Simpson and late Gertrude Adam; unmarried. *Educ:* Municipal High School, Doncaster; St Hugh's College, Oxford (Scholar). Research Scholar, Lady Margaret Hall, 1935-37; Junior British Scholarship, 1936-37; Assistant Tutor of St Hugh's College and Research Assistant at Oxford University Observatory, 1937; lately Fellow and Tutor, St Hugh's College. *Publications:* papers in Monthly Notices of Royal Astronomical Society from 1937. *Address:* c/o Department of Astrophysics, South Parks Road, Oxford OX1 3RQ; 17 Dovehouse Close, Upper Wolvercote, Oxford OX2 8BG.

ADAM, Robert Wilson, (Robin); a Managing Director, since 1975, Deputy Chairman, since 1981, British Petroleum Co. Ltd; *b* 21 May 1923; *s* of R. R. W. Adam; *m* 1957, Marion Nancy Scott. *Educ:* Fettes, Edinburgh. Royal Scots, 1942; commnd RIASC 1942; served in India and Burma (Major). Chartered Accountant 1950. Joined British Petroleum Co. Ltd, 1950; Pres., BP North America Inc. New York, 1969-72; Director: BP Trading Ltd, 1973-75; The Standard Oil Co. (Sohio), 1972-76 and 1978-; General Accident, 1980-; Chm., BP Canada Incorporated, 1981-. *Recreation:* golf. *Address:* 25 Onslow Square, SW7. *Clubs:* Caledonian, MCC.

ADAM, General Sir Ronald Forbes, 2nd Bt, *cr* 1917; GCB 1946 (KCB 1941; CB 1939); DSO 1918; OBE 1919; late RA; Hon. LLD (Aberdeen). Hon. Fellow, Worcester College, Oxford; President, United Nations Association; *b* 30 Oct. 1885; *e s* of Sir Frank Forbes Adam, 1st Bt, and Rose Frances (*d* 1944), *d* of C. G. Kemball, late Judge, High Court, Bombay; *S* father, 1926; *m* 1915, Anna Dorothy (*d* of late F. I. Pitman; three *d. Educ:* Eton; RMA, Woolwich. Served European War (France and Flanders, Italy), 1914-18 (despatches, DSO, OBE); GSO1, Staff College, Camberley, 1932-35; GSO1, War Office, 1935-36; Deputy Director of Military Operations, War Office, 1936; Commander Royal Artillery, 1st Division, 1936-37; Commandant of Staff College, Camberley, 1937; Deputy Chief of Imperial General Staff, 1938-39; Commanding 3rd Army Corps, 1939-40; General Officer Commanding-in-Chief, Northern Command, 1940-41; Adjutant-General to the Forces, 1941-46; General, 1942; retired pay, 1946. Col Comdt of RA and of Army Educational Corps, 1940-50; Col Comdt Royal Army Dental Corps, 1945-51 (Representative, 1950). President: MCC, 1946-47; Library Assoc., 1949; Nat. Inst. of Adult Education, 1949-64; Chairman: Linoleum Working Party, 1946; Nat. Inst. Industrial Psychology, 1947-52; Council, Inst. of Education, London Univ., 1948-67; Mem., Miners Welfare Commn, 1946-52; Chm. and Dir-Gen., British Council, 1946-54; Executive Board UNESCO, 1950-54, Chm., 1952-54; Principal, Working Men's Coll., 1956-61. *Heir: n* Christopher Eric Forbes Adam [*b* 12 Feb 1920; *m* 1957, Patricia Ann Wreford, *y d* of late John Neville Wreford Brown]. *Address:* Carylls Lea, Faygate, Sussex RH12 4SJ. *Clubs:* Athenæum, Naval and Military.

See also C. G. F. Adam, Sir P. D. Proctor.

ADAM SMITH, Janet (Buchanan), (Mrs John Carleton), OBE 1982; author and journalist; *b* 9 Dec. 1905; *d* of late Very Rev. Sir George Adam Smith, Principal of Aberdeen Univ. and late Lady Adam Smith; *m* 1st, 1935, Michael Roberts (*d* 1948); three *s* one *d;* 2nd, 1965, John Carleton (*d* 1974). *Educ:* Cheltenham Ladies' College (scholar); Somerville College, Oxford (exhibitioner). BBC, 1928-35; Asst Editor, The Listener, 1930-35; Asst Literary Editor, New Statesman and Nation, 1949-52, Literary Editor, 1952-60. Virginia Gildersleeve Vis. Prof., Barnard Coll., New York, 1961 and 1964. Trustee, National Library of Scotland, 1950-. Pres., Royal Literary Fund, 1976-. Hon. LLD Aberdeen, 1962. *Publications:* Poems of Tomorrow (ed), 1935; R. L. Stevenson, 1937; Mountain Holidays, 1946; Life Among the Scots, 1946; Henry James and Robert Louis Stevenson (ed) 1948; Collected Poems of R. L. Stevenson (ed), 1950; Faber Book of Children's Verse (ed), 1953; Collected Poems of Michael Roberts (ed), 1958; John Buchan: a Biography, 1965; John Buchan and his World, 1979. *Recreation:* mountain walking. *Address:* 55 Lansdowne Road, W11. *T:* 01-727 9324. *Club:* Alpine (Vice-Pres., 1978-80).

See also Baron Balerno.

ADAMI, Edward F.; *see* Fenech-Adami, E.

ADAMS, Rt. Rev. Albert James; *see* Barking, Bishop Suffragan of.

ADAMS, Alec Cecil Stanley, CMG 1960; CBE 1952; HM Diplomatic Service, retired; *b* 25 July 1909; *e s* of late Stanley A. Adams. *Educ:* King's School, Canterbury; Corpus Christi Coll., Cambridge. One of HM Vice-Consuls in Siam, 1933; served in Portuguese East Africa (acting Consul at Beira, June 1936-Feb. 1937); local rank 2nd Secretary, Bangkok Legation, 1937; Acting Consul, Sourabaya, 1938; Bangkok Legation, 1939-40; Foreign Office, Ministry of Information, 1940; Consul, in Foreign Office, 1945; Bangkok, 1946, Acting Consul-General and Chargé d'Affaires, 1948; Consul, Cincinnati, 1949; HM Chargé d'Affaires in Korea, 1950; HM Consul-General at Houston, Texas, 1953-55; Counsellor and Consul-General at HM Embassy,

Bangkok, 1956-62; Deputy Commissioner-General for South East Asia 1962-63; Political Advisor to C-in-C (Far East) at Singapore, 1963-67; retirec 1967. *Address:* Flat 513, 97 Southampton Row, WC1B 4HH. *Club.* Travellers'.

ADAMS, Air Vice-Marshal Alexander Annan, CB 1957; DFC 1944; *b* 14 Nov. 1908; *s* of Capt. Norman Anderson Adams, Durham; *m* 1933, Eileen Mary O'Neill; one *s* (one *d* decd). *Educ:* Beechmont, Sevenoaks; Bellerive Switzerland; Austria. Commnd RAF, 1930; 54 Fighter Sqdn, 1931-32; 604 Aux. Sqdn, Hendon, 1933-35; CFS, 1935; Asst Air Attaché, Berlin, Brussels The Hague, Berne, 1938-40; Ops, Air Min., 1940; British Embassy Washington, 1941-42; in comd 49 (Lancaster) Sqdn, 1943-44; RAF Staff Coll., 1945; Head of RAF Intelligence, Germany, 1946-48; in comd RAF Binbrook, 1948-50; NATO Standing Gp, Washington, DC, 1951-53; idc 1954; Air Attaché, Bonn, 1955; Min. of Defence, 1956; Chief of Staff, Far East Air Force, 1957-59. Hawker Siddeley Aviation, 1961-66. Dir, Mental Health Trust and Res. Fund, later Mental Health Foundn, 1970-77. Comdr Order of Orange Nassau, 1950. *Recreations:* golf, painting. *Address:* High Meadow, Hollow Brook Road, Oldwick, PO Box 332, New Jersey 08858, USA. *Club.* Royal Air Force.

ADAMS, Allen; MP (Lab) Paisley, since 1979; computer analyst; *b* Feb. 1946. *Educ:* Camphill High Sch., Paisley; Reid-Kerr Technical Coll., Paisley. Former Mem., Strathclyde Reg. Council, to 1980; Vice-Chm., Strathclyde Social Services Council, 1969-. *Address:* House of Commons, SW1; 76 Murray Street, Paisley.

ADAMS, Prof. Anthony Peter, FFARCS; Professor of Anaesthetics in the University of London, at Guy's Hospital Medical School, since 1979; *b* 17 Oct. 1936; *s* of H. W. J. Adams and W. L. Adams; *m* 1973, Veronica Rosemary John; three *s* one *d. Educ:* Epsom College; London Univ. MB BS, PhD; DA MRCS; LRCP. Wellcome Res. Fellow, RPMS, 1964-66; Consultant Anaesthetist and Clinical Lectr, Nuffield Dept of Anaesthetics, Univ. of Oxford, 1968-79. *Publications:* Principles and Practice of Blood Gas Analysis, 1979, 2nd edn 1982; contribs to medical jls. *Recreations:* badger watching. English castles, history, tennis, croquet. *Address:* Department of Anaesthetics. Guy's Hospital Medical School, London Bridge, SE1 9RT. *T:* 01-407 7600. *Club:* Halifax House (Oxford).

ADAMS, Bernard Charles; architect; consultant to architects Messrs Steel, Coleman and Davis; *b* 29 Oct. 1915; *s* of late Charles Willoughby Adams and Emily Alice (*née* Ambrose); *m* 1942, Marjorie Barrett Weller; two *d* (and one *d* decd). *Educ:* King James I Sch., Newport, IoW. ARIBA 1948, FRIBA 1968. TA, 1938-39; served 1939-41, 57 (Wessex) HAA Regt, RA; commissioned 1941; served 1941-46, 107 HAA Regt RA, France (Normandy), Belgium, Holland, Germany; Captain RA (despatches). Sen. Architect, Derbs CC, 1951-54; Asst County Architect, Kent CC, 1954-59; Dep. County Architect, Herts CC, 1959-60; County Architect, Somerset CC, 1960-80. Mem. Council, RIBA, 1963-69 and 1970- (Vice-Pres., 1970-72; Chm., S-W Regional Council, 1972-74); Chm., Structure of the Profession Study, RIBA, 1976-79; Mem., Nat. Consultative Council for Building and Civil Engrg Industries, 1974-80; Pres., County Architects' Soc., 1973-74 (Vice-Pres., 1971-73); Pres., Soc. of Ch. Architects of Local Authorities (founded 1974), 1975-76 (Sen. Vice-Pres., 1974-75); Architect Adviser to ACC, 1971-80; Mem., Bd of Architectural Studies, Bristol Univ., 1964-74; Founder Chm., Architects' Cttee, Consortium for Method Building, 1961-68. Founder Mem., Taunton Theatre Trust, 1972. RIBA Architecture Award, 1970, and Commendation, 1974; Heritage Year Award (EAHY), 1975; Civic Trust Awards, 1962, 1968, 1971, and Commendation, 1965. FRSA 1972. *Publications:* contrib. Jl of RIBA and other jls. *Recreations:* arts, music, theatre, travel, languages. *Address:* Meadowside, Wild Oak Lane, Trull, Taunton, Somerset TA3 7JT. *T:* Taunton 72485.

ADAMS, Prof. Colin Wallace Maitland, MD, DSc; FRCP, FRCPath; Sir William Dunn Professor of Pathology, Guy's Hospital Medical School, since 1965; *b* 17 Feb. 1928; *s* of Sidney Ewart Adams and Gladys Alethea Fletcher Adams; *m* 1953, Anne Brownhill; one *s. Educ:* Oundle School; Christ's College, Cambridge. Sir Lionel Whitby Medal, Cambridge Univ., 1959-60; MD Cantab, 1960; DSc London, 1967. FRCP 1977; FRCPath 1975. Visiting Scientist, National Institutes of Health, Bethesda, USA, 1960-61. *Publications:* Neurohistochemistry, 1965; Vascular Histochemistry, 1967; Research on Multiple Sclerosis, 1972; (jtly) Multiple Sclerosis, Pathology, Diagnosis and Treatment, 1982; papers on arterial diseases, neuropathology and microscopical chemistry in medical and biological journals. *Address:* The Knoll, Westview Drive, Rayleigh, Essex. *T:* Rayleigh 776489.

ADAMS, Air Commodore Cyril Douglas, CB 1948; OBE 1942; retired; *b* 18 Sept. 1897; British; *m* 1927, D. M. Le Brocq (*d* 1957), Highfield, Jersey; one *s* one *d; m* 1968, Mrs K. E. Webster, NZ. *Educ:* Parkstone Grammar School. Served European War in Army, 1915-18, Egypt, Palestine; Commissioned RFC, 1918; Flying Instructor, 1918-25; Staff Duties, Iraq Command, 1925-27; Staff and Flying Duties, Halton Comd, 1928-35; CO 15 Sqdn, 1936-38; HQ Bomber Comd, 1938; CO 38 Sqdn, 1938-39; Sen. Officer i/c Administration, No 3 Group, 1939-40; Station Comdr, Kemble, Oakington, Abingdon, 1940-44; Base Comdr, Marston Moor and North Luffenham, 1944-45; India Command, AOA, AHQ, 1945-46; Base Comdr, Bombay, 1946; AOC No 2 Indian Group, 1946-47 (despatches 6 times, OBE (immediate award for gallantry)); Air Officer Commanding No 85 Group,

BAFO, 1948–49; retired, 1949. *Recreations:* represented: RAF (Rugby, cricket, athletics); Hampshire (Rugby); Dorset and minor counties (cricket); keen golfer. *Address:* 6 Solent Pines, Whitby Road, Milford-on-Sea, Lymington, Hants. *T:* Milford-on-Sea 3754.

ADAMS, Ernest Victor, CB 1978; Deputy Secretary and Commissioner, Inland Revenue, 1975–81; *b* 17 Jan. 1920; *s* of Ernest and Amelia Adams; *m* 1943, Joan Bastin, Halesworth, Suffolk; one *s* one *d. Educ:* Manchester Grammar Sch.; Keble Coll., Oxford (MA). HM Forces, RA, 1940–45. Inland Revenue Dept, 1947; Sen. Inspector of Taxes, 1956; Principal Inspector of Taxes, 1961; Sen. Principal Inspector of Taxes, 1966; Dep. Chief Inspector of Taxes, 1969. *Address:* Whitehill, Reades Lane, Sonning Common, Oxon. *T:* Kidmore End 723243; 34 Sloane Court West, Chelsea, SW3. *T:* 01-730 6482.

ADAMS, Frank Alexander, CB 1964; Member, Public Health Laboratory Service Board, 1968–79; *b* 9 July 1907; *m* 1928, Esther Metcalfe; two *d. Educ:* Selhurst Grammar Sch.; London School of Economics, Univ. of London. HM Inspector of Taxes, 1928; Assistant Secretary, Board of Inland Revenue, 1945; Counsellor (Economic and Financial), UK Delegation to OEEC, Paris, 1957–59; Director, Civil Service Pay Research Unit, 1960–63; Under-Sec. (Finance) and Accountant-General, Min. of Health, 1963–67. *Address:* 6 Magpie Way, Winslow, Buckingham. *T:* Winslow 3848. *Clubs:* Climbers'; Swiss Alpine (Geneva).

ADAMS, Frederick Baldwin, Jr; Director, Pierpont Morgan Library, 1948–69, now Emeritus; *b* 28 March 1910; *s* of Frederick B. Adams and Ellen Walters Delano; *m* 1st, 1933, Ruth Potter; 2nd, 1941, Betty Abbott; four *d*; 3rd, 1969, Marie-Louise de Croy. *Educ:* St Paul's Sch.; Yale Univ. (BA). Empl. Air Reduction Co. Inc., 1933–48. President: New-York Historical Soc., 1963–71; Bd Governors, Yale University Press, 1959–71; Assoc. Internationale de Bibliophilie; Trustee, Yale Univ., 1964–71; Fellow: Amer. Acad. Arts and Sciences; Amer. Philosophical Soc.; Amer. Antiquarian Soc.; Mass. Historical Soc.; Mem., Phi Beta Kappa. Hon. degrees: LittD: Hofstra Coll., 1959; Williams Coll., 1966; DFA, Union Coll., 1959; MA, Yale Univ., 1965; LHD, New York Univ., 1966. Chevalier, Légion d'Honneur, 1950; Comdr, Order of the Crown of Belgium, 1979. *Publications:* Radical Literature in America, 1939; One Hundred Influential American Books (with Streeter and Wilson), 1947; To Russia with Frost, 1963; contrib. to books and jls in bibliography, printing, collecting. *Address:* 208 rue de Rivoli, 75001 Paris, France. *Clubs:* Athenæum, Roxburghe; Century, Grolier (NY).

ADAMS, Hervey Cadwallader, RBA 1932; FRSA 1951; landscape painter; lecturer on art; *b* Kensington, 1903; *o s* of late Cadwallader Edmund Adams and Dorothy Jane, *y d* of Rev. J. W. Knight; *m* 1928, Iris Gabrielle, *y d* of late F. V. Bruce, St Fagans, Glamorgan; two *s. Educ:* Charterhouse. Studied languages and singing in France and Spain, 1922–26; studied painting under Bernard Adams, 1929. Art Master, Tonbridge Sch., 1940–63. *Publications:* The Student's Approach to Landscape Painting, 1938; Art and Everyman, 1945; Eighteenth Century Painting, 1949; Nineteenth Century Painting, 1949; The Adventure of Looking, 1949. *Address:* Pummel, Houndscroft, near Stroud, Glos.

ADAMS, Prof. James Whyte Leitch; Professor of Education, University of Dundee (formerly Queen's College), 1955–80, now Emeritus; *b* 7 Nov. 1909; *o s* of Charles and Helen Adams, Stirling; *m* 1939, Isobel Margaret, ARIBA, *d* of Robert Gordon, Fraserburgh; one *s* two *d. Educ:* Arbroath High School; St Andrews University; Oxford University. Harkness Scholar, St Andrews, 1928; Guthrie Scholar, 1931; 1st cl. hons Classics, 1932; Marshall Prizeman, Miller Prizeman, Lewis Campbell Medallist, etc; Waugh Scholar, Exeter Coll., Oxford, 1932; 1st cl. Classical Mods, 1934; 1st cl. Lit. Hum., 1936; Craven Fellowship, 1936; Dipl. in Educn, St Andrews Univ., 1937. Teacher of Classics, Golspie Senior Secondary Sch., 1937–39; Educn Officer (Scotland), BBC, 1939–47; RAF Education Service, 1942–45; HM Inspector of Schools, 1947–50; Lecturer in Humanity, Aberdeen University, 1950–55. *Publications:* various contributions, especially on Renaissance Latin Poetry. *Recreations:* golf and "brither" Scots. *Address:* Red Cottage, 80 Forthill Road, Broughty Ferry, Dundee. *T:* Dundee 78138.

ADAMS, Sir John (Bertram), Kt 1981; CMG 1962; FRS 1963; Engineer, European Organisation for Nuclear Research (CERN); *b* 24 May 1920; *s* of John A. Adams and Emily Searles; *m* 1943, Renie Warburton; one *s* two *d. Educ:* Eltham College; Research Laboratory, Siemens. Telecommunications Research Establishment, Swanage and Malvern, 1940–45; Atomic Energy Research Establishment, Harwell, 1945–53; European Organisation for Nuclear Research (CERN), Geneva, 1953, Dir of Proton Synchrotron Division, 1954–60; Director-Gen., CERN, 1960–61; Director, Culham Laboratory, AEA, Oxford, 1960–67; Controller, Min. of Technology, 1965–66; Member: Council for Scientific Policy, 1965–68; Board, UKAEA, 1966–69; Adv. Council on Technology, 1966–69; Dir-Gen., 300 GeV Accelerator Project, CERN, 1969–75; Executive Dir-Gen., CERN, 1976–80. Fellow, Wolfson College, Oxford, 1966 (MA), Emeritus Fellow 1981. Guthrie Lecturer, Phys. Soc., 1965. DSc *hc:* Univ. of Geneva, 1960; Birmingham Univ., 1961; Univ. of Surrey, 1966; Univ. of Strathclyde, 1978; Univ. of Milan, 1980. Röntgen Prize, Univ. of Giessen, 1960; Duddell Medal, Physical Soc., 1961; Leverhulme Medal, Royal Soc., 1972; Faraday Medal, IEE, 1977; Royal Medal, Royal Soc., 1977. *Publications:* contributions to Nature, Nuovo Cimento, etc. *Recreations:* swimming, ski-ing. *Address:* (home) Champ

Rosset, 1297 Founex VD, Switzerland; (office) European Organisation for Nuclear Research (CERN), 1211 Geneva 23, Switzerland.

ADAMS, John Crawford, MD, MS, FRCS; Honorary Consulting Orthopædic Surgeon, St Mary's Hospital, London; Civil Consultant in Orthopædic Surgery, Royal Air Force; Member, Council, Journal of Bone and Joint Surgery (formerly Production Editor). MB, BS 1937; MRCS 1937; LRCP 1937; FRCS 1941; MD (London) 1943; MS (London) 1965. Formerly: Chief Asst, Orthopædic and Accident Dept, London Hosp.; Orthopædic Specialist, RAFVR; Resident Surgical Officer, Wingfield-Morris Orthopædic Hosp., Oxford. FRSM; Fellow, British Orthopædic Assoc. (Hon. Sec., 1959–62; Vice-Pres., 1974–75). *Publications:* Outline of Orthopædics, 1956, 9th edn 1981; Outline of Fractures, 1957, 7th edn 1978; Ischio-femoral Arthrodesis, 1966; Arthritis and Back Pain, 1972; Standard Orthopædic Operations, 1976, 2nd edn 1980; Recurrent Dislocation of Shoulder (chapter in Techniques in British Surgery, ed Maingot), 1950; Associate Editor and Contributor Operative Surgery (ed Rob and Smith); contributions to the Journal of Bone and Joint Surgery, etc. *Address:* 36 Chester Close North, NW1.

ADAMS, John Douglas Richard; Registrar of Civil Appeals, since 1982; *b* 19 March 1940; *o s* of late Gordon Arthur Richard Adams and of Marjorie Ethel Adams (née Ongley; now Mrs Bettany); *m* 1966, Anne Easton Todd, *o d* of late Robert Easton Todd and late Mary Ann Margaret Todd (née Isaac); two *d. Educ:* Watford Grammar School; Durham Univ. (LLB 1963). Called to Bar, Lincoln's Inn, 1967. Lecturer: Newcastle Univ., 1963–71; University College London, 1971–78; also practised at Revenue Bar until 1978; Special Comr of Income Tax, 1978–82. Hon. Lecturer, St Edmund Hall, Oxford, 1978–. *Publication:* (with J. Whalley) The International Taxation of Multinational Enterprises, 1977. *Recreations:* music, walking, dining. *Address:* Royal Courts of Justice, Strand, WC2A 2LL.

ADAMS, Prof. John Frank, MA, ScD; FRS 1964; Lowndean Professor of Astronomy and Geometry, Cambridge University, since 1970; Fellow of Trinity College, Cambridge; *b* 5 Nov. 1930; *m* 1953, Grace Rhoda, BA, BD, AAPSW, MBASW; one *s* three *d. Educ:* Bedford School; Trinity College, Cambridge; The Institute for Advanced Study, Princeton. Junior Lecturer, Oxford, 1955–56; Research Fellow, Trinity College, Cambridge, 1955–58; Commonwealth Fund Fellow, 1957–58; Assistant Lecturer, Cambridge, and Director of Studies in Mathematics, Trinity Hall, Cambridge, 1958–61; Reader, Manchester, 1962–64; Fielden Prof. of Pure Mathematics, Manchester Univ., 1964–71. *Publications:* Stable Homotopy Theory, 1964; Lectures on Lie Groups, 1969; Algebraic Topology, 1972; Stable Homotopy and Generalised Homology, 1974; Infinite Loop Spaces, 1978; papers in mathematical jls. *Recreations:* walking, climbing. *Address:* 7 Westmeare, Hemingford Grey, Huntingdon PE18 9BZ.

ADAMS, Rear-Adm. John Harold, CB 1967; MVO 1957; Director General of British Paper and Board Industry Federation, since 1974; *b* Newcastle-on-Tyne, 19 Dec. 1918; *m* 1st, 1943, Mary Parker (marr. diss. 1961); one *s* decd; 2nd, 1961, Ione Eadie, MVO; two *s* two *d. Educ:* Glenalmond. Joined Navy, 1936; Home Fleet, 1937–39; Western Approaches, Channel and N Africa, 1939–42 (despatches); Staff Capt. (D), Liverpool, 1943–45; Staff Course, Greenwich, 1945; jssc 1949; Comdr, HM Yacht Britannia, 1954–57; Asst Dir, Underwater Weapons Matériel Dept, 1957–58; Capt. (SM) 3rd Submarine Sqdn, HMS Adamant, 1958–60; Captain Supt, Underwater Detection Estab., Portland, subseq. Admty Underwater Weapons Estab., 1960–62; idc 1963; comd HMS Albion, 1964–66; Asst Chief of Naval Staff (Policy), 1966–68; retd 1968. Lieut 1941; Lieut-Comdr 1949; Comdr 1951; Capt. 1957; Rear-Adm. 1966. Dir, Paper and Paper Products Industry Training Bd, 1968–71; Dir, Employers' Federation of Papermakers and Boardmakers, 1972–73. Chm. Governors, Cheam Sch. *Recreations:* shooting, fishing, photography. *Address:* The Oxdrove House, Burghclere, Newbury, Berks. *T:* Burghclere 385. *Club:* Army and Navy.

ADAMS, John Kenneth; Editor of Country Life, 1958–73; Editorial Director, Country Life Ltd, 1959–73; *b* 3 June 1915; *o c* of late Thomas John Adams and late Mabel Adams (née Jarvis), Oxford; *m* 1944, Margaret, *o c* of late Edward Claude Fortescue, Banbury, Oxon. *Educ:* City of Oxford Sch.; Balliol Coll., Oxford. Asst Master, Stonyhurst Coll., 1939–40; served with RAFVR, 1940–41 (invalided); Asst Master, Wellington Coll., 1941–44; attached to Manchester Guardian as Leader-writer, 1942–44; Leader-writer, The Scotsman, 1944–46; joined editorial staff of Country Life, 1946; Asst Editor, 1952; Deputy Editor, 1956; Editor, 1958; Editorial Director, 1959. *Recreations:* gardening, ornithology, travel. *Address:* 95 Alleyn Park, West Dulwich, SE21. *T:* 01-693 1736. *Club:* Athenæum.

ADAMS, Rt. Hon. John Michael Geoffrey Manningham, PC 1977; QC; MP Barbados Labour Party, since 1966; Prime Minister of Barbados, since 1976; *b* 24 Sept. 1931; *s* of late Sir Grantley Adams, CMG, QC, and Grace Adams; *m* 1962, Genevieve, *d* of Philip Turner, *qv;* two *s. Educ:* Harrison Coll., Barbados; Magdalen Coll., Oxford (MA, PPE). Barrister-at-Law, Gray's Inn. Producer, BBC London, 1958–62; Polit. Party Sec., Barbados Labour Party, 1965–69; Leader of Opposition, 1971–76. Mem., Scotia No 340 SC (Roll of the Grand Lodge of Scotland) (Past Master, etc), and of other Masonic Lodges. *Recreations:* gardening, philately; watching, reading and writing about cricket. *Address:* (home) 14 Walkers Terrace, Gun Hill, St

George, Barbados; (office) Prime Minister's Office, Bridgetown, Barbados. *Club:* Union (Bridgetown).

ADAMS, John Nicholas William B.; *see* Bridges-Adams.

ADAMS, John Roderick Seton; a Recorder of the Crown Court, since 1980; *b* 29 Feb. 1936; *s* of George Adams and Winifred (*née* Wilson); *m* 1965, Pamela Bridget, *e d* of Rev. D. E. Rice, MC; three *s*. *Educ:* Whitgift Sch., Croydon; Trinity Coll., Cambridge. BA (Hons) Classics and Law, 1959, MA 1963. Commnd, Seaforth Highlanders, 1955-56; Parachute Regt, TA, 1959-66. Legal Adviser in industry, 1960-66; Sec., Media Computer Services Ltd, 1966. Called to the Bar, Inner Temple, 1962; began practice at the Bar, 1967; Dep. Circuit Judge, 1978-80. *Recreations:* music, fishing, growing old roses. *Address:* 78 South Croxted Road, Dulwich, SE21. *T:* 01-670 4130; 6 Pump Court, Temple, EC4. *T:* 01-353 2510.

ADAMS, (John) Roland, QC 1949; *b* 24 July 1900; *s* of late Alfred Courthope Adams and Sabina Newberry; *m* 1st, 1924, Ruth (marr. diss. 1946), *d* of late David Schlivek, merchant, Woonsocket, RI; no *c* ; 2nd, 1946, Violet, *d* of late Sir Francis Hanson, London; no *c*. *Educ:* Charterhouse; New College, Oxford. Hon. Exhibitioner of New College, 1919; BA 1922; MA 1926. Barrister, Inner Temple, 1925; Master of the Bench, Inner Temple, 1957. Essex County Council, 1930-39; Vice-Chm., Essex Rivers Catchment Bd, 1935-39. Major, The Essex Regt, 1939-45; GSO3, War Office, 1939-40; DAAG, War Office, 1940-42; specially employed, 1942-45. Member, panel of Lloyd's arbitrators in salvage cases, 1950; appeal arbitrator, 1974; a Dep. Chm., Essex QS, 1950-56, Chairman, 1956-71. *Recreation:* staying at home. *Address:* Little Gubbions, Gubbions Hall Farm, Great Leighs, Chelmsford, Essex. *T:* Great Leighs 248.

ADAMS, Major Kenneth Galt, CVO 1979; Comino Fellow of the Royal Society of Arts, since 1979; *b* 6 Jan. 1920; *s* of William Adams, OBE, and Christina Elisabeth (*née* Hall); unmarried. *Educ:* Doncaster Grammar Sch.; Staff Coll., Camberley (psc 1953). MA Lambeth; CBIM, FMS, FRSA, FCIT. Served RASC, 1940-59: War Service, ME and N Africa; DADST WO, 1946-48; DAA&QMG, Aldershot, 1952; DAQMG HQ Northern Comd, 1954-56; Sen. Instr, RASC Officers Sch., 1956-59; Manager, Proprietors of Hay's Wharf Ltd, and dir of several cos in that gp, 1960-66; Exec. Dir, Proprietors of Hay's Wharf Ltd, 1966-70; St George's House, Windsor Castle: Dir of Studies, 1969-76; Comino Fellow, 1976-79; Associate Fellow, 1979-82. Chairman: Indust. Christian Fellowship, 1977-; S London Indust. Mission, 1975-76; Vice Chairman: Archbishops' Council on Evangelism, 1965-77; Southwark Cathedral Council, 1967-70; Member: Indust. Cttee, Bd for Social Responsibility of C of E, 1973-81; Bldg EDC, NEDC, 1977-81; Prof. Standards Cttee, BIM, 1976-81; Dept of Employment's Services Resettlement Cttee for SE England, 1967-77; Trustee, Industrial Trng Foundn, 1980-. *Publications:* papers on business ethics and attitudes to industry in Britain. *Recreations:* reading, gardening. *Address:* 7 Datchet Road, Windsor, Berks SL4 1QB. *T:* Windsor 69708. *Club:* Army and Navy.

ADAMS, Mary Grace, (Mrs Vyvyan Adams), OBE 1953; *b* Hermitage, Berks; *o d* of late Catherine Elizabeth Mary and Edward Bloxham Campin; *m* 1925, S. Vyvyan T. Adams (*d* 1951), sometime MP for W Leeds; one *d*. *Educ:* Godolphin Sch.; University Coll., Cardiff (1st class Hons BSc); Newnham Coll., Cambridge. 1851 Res. Scholar and Bathurst Student, Univ. of Cambridge, 1921-25; Lectr and Tutor under Cambridge Extra-Mural Board and Board of Civil Service Studies, and broadcaster, 1925-30; joined staff of BBC, 1930; Producer, BBC TV, 1936-39; Dir, Home Intelligence, Min. of Information, 1939-41; N Amer. Broadcasting, 1942-45; Head of Talks and Current Affairs, 1945-54; Asst to Controller of Television Programmes, BBC, 1954-58, retired. Member, ITA, 1965-70; Dep. Chm., Consumers' Assoc., 1958-70. Chm., Telephone Users Assoc. Vice-Chairman: Nat. Council for the Unmarried Mother and her Child; Soc. for Anglo-Chinese Understanding. Member: Women's Group on Public Welfare; Council, Nat. Assoc. for Mental Health; Design Panel, British Railways Board; BMA Planning Unit. Trustee: Res. Inst. for Consumer Affairs; Galton Foundn; Anglo-Chinese Educational Inst. *Publications:* papers on genetical cytology; Talks on Heredity; (ed) various symposia. *Recreation:* children. *Address:* 10 Regent's Park Road, NW1. *T:* 01-485 8324.

ADAMS, Surg. Rear-Adm. Maurice Henry, CB 1965; MB, BCh, DOMS; *b* 16 July 1908; *s* of Henry Adams and Dorothea (*née* Whitehouse); *m* 1938, Kathleen Mary (*née* Hardy); one *s* two *d*. *Educ:* Campbell Coll.; Queen's University, Belfast. MB, BCh, 1930. RN Medical Service 1933; HMS Cornwall, 1934; HMS Barham, 1936; Central Air Medical Board, 1940; HMS Activity, 1942; RN Hospital, Haslar, 1944; Med. Dept, Admiralty, 1946; RN Hospital: Malta, 1950; Chatham, 1952; MO i/c Trincomalee, 1957; Med. Dept, Admiralty, 1958; Medical Officer-in-Charge, Royal Naval Hosp., Malta, 1963; QHS, 1963-66; retd 1966. *Recreations:* sailing, golf. *Address:* Canberra, Rock, Cornwall.

ADAMS, Norman (Edward Albert), RA 1972 (ARA 1967); ARCA 1951; artist (painter and ceramic sculptor); Professor of Fine Art and Director of King Edward VII School, University of Newcastle, since 1981; *b* 9 Feb. 1927; *s* of Albert Henry Adams and Winifred Elizabeth Rose Adams; *m* 1947, Anna Theresa; two *s*. *Educ:* Royal Coll. of Art. Head of Sch. of Painting, Manchester Coll. of Art and Design, 1962-70; Lectr, Leeds Univ., 1975-. Exhibitions in most European capitals, also in America (New York,

Pittsburgh); Retrospective exhibns, Royal College of Art, 1969, Whitechapel Gall. Paintings in collections of: most British Provincial Art Galleries; Tate Gall., London; Nat. Galls, New Zealand; work purchased by: Arts Coun. of Gt Brit.; Contemp. Art Soc.; Chantrey Bequest; various Educn Authorities. Murals at: Broad Lane Comprehensive Sch., Coventry; St Anselm's Church, S London; Our Lady of Lourdes, Milton Keynes. Decor for ballets, Covent Garden and Sadler's Wells. *Publications:* Alibis and Convictions, 1978; A Decade of Painting, 1971-81, 1981. *Address:* Butts, Horton-in-Ribblesdale, Settle, North Yorks. *T:* Horton-in-Ribblesdale 284.

ADAMS, Sir Philip (George Doyne), KCMG 1969 (CMG 1959); Director, Ditchley Foundation, 1977-82; *b* 17 Dec. 1915; *s* of late George Basil Doyne Adams, MD, and of Arline Maud Adams (*née* Dodgson); *m* 1954, Hon (Mary) Elizabeth Lawrence, *e d* of Baron Trevethin and Oaksey (3rd and 1st Baron respectively); two *s* two *d*. *Educ:* Lancing Coll.; Christ Church, Oxford. Entered Foreign Service, 1939; served at: Beirut, 1939; Cairo, 1941; Jedda, 1945; FO, 1947; First Sec., 1948; Vienna, 1951; Counsellor, Khartoum, 1954; Beirut, 1956; FO, 1959; Chicago, 1963; Ambassador to Jordan, 1966-70; Asst Under-Sec., FCO, 1970; Dep. Sec., Cabinet Office, 1971-72; Ambassador to Egypt, 1973-75. Member: Board, British Council, 1977-82; Marshall Aid Commem. Commn, 1979-. *Address:* 78 Sussex Square, W2; The Malt House, Ditchley, Enstone, Oxford. *Club:* Brooks's.

ADAMS, Richard Borlase; Chief Executive, Peninsular & Oriental Steam Navigation Co., 1981-June 1983 (Director, 1970, Deputy Managing Director, 1974, Managing Director, 1979); *b* 9 Sept. 1921; *s* of James Elwin Cokayne Adams and Susan Mercer Porter; *m* 1951, Susan Elizabeth Lambert; two *s* one *d*. *Educ:* Winchester Coll.; Trinity Coll., Oxford, 1940. War service, Rifle Bde, 1940-46 (Major). Mackinnon Mackenzie Gp of Cos, Calcutta, New Delhi and Hongkong, 1947-63; Chm., Islay Kerr & Co. Ltd, Singapore, 1963-66; British India Steam Navigation Co.: Dir, 1966; Man. Dir, 1969; Chm., 1970. Dir, Clerical, Medical & General Life Assurance Soc., 1975. *Recreations:* gardening, tennis, golf. *Address:* Beacon House, Bethersden, Ashford, Kent TN26 3AE. *T:* Bethersden 247. *Club:* Oriental.

ADAMS, Richard George; author; *b* 10 May 1920; *s* of Evelyn George Beadon Adams, FRCS, and Lilian Rosa Adams (*née* Button); *m* 1949, Barbara Elizabeth Acland; two *d*. *Educ:* Bradfield Coll., Berks; Worcester Coll., Oxford (MA, Mod. Hist.). Entered Home Civil Service, 1948; retd as Asst Sec., DoE, 1974. Writer-in-residence: Univ. of Florida, 1975; Hollins Univ., Virginia, 1976. Pres., RSPCA, 1980-82. Carnegie Medal, 1972; Guardian Award for Children's Literature, 1972. Hon. FRSL 1975. *Publications:* Watership Down, 1972 (numerous subseq. edns in various languages; filmed 1978); Shardik, 1974; Nature through the Seasons, 1975 (filmed 1982); The Tyger Voyage, 1976; The Ship's Cat, 1977; The Plague Dogs, 1977; Nature Day and Night, 1978; The Girl in a Swing, 1980; The Iron Wolf, 1980. *Recreations:* folk-song, chess, country pursuits, fly-fishing, travel. *Address:* 26 Church Street, Whitchurch, Hants. *Club:* MCC.

ADAMS, Richard John Moreton G.; *see* Goold-Adams.

ADAMS, Robert; Sculptor and Designer; works in wood, stone, bronze, steel; *b* 5 Oct. 1917; *s* of Arthur Adams; *m* 1951, Patricia Devine; one *d*. *Educ:* Northampton School of Art. Instructor, Central School of Arts and Crafts, London, 1949-60. One man exhibitions: Gimpel Fils, London, 1947-; Galerie Jeanne Bucher, Paris, 1949; Passedoit Gall., New York, 1950; Victor Waddington Gall., Dublin, 1955; Douglas Coll., NJ, USA, 1955; Galerie Parnass, Wuppertal, Germany, 1957; Nebelung Galerie, Düsseldorf, 1957; Galerie Vertiko, Bonn, 1957; Museum am Ostwall, Dortmund, 1957; Bertha Schaefer Gall., New York, 1963; Northampton, Sheffield, Newcastle and London, 1971 Gimpel-Hanover Gall., Zurich, 1980; Lister Gall., Perth, WA, 1981; Gimpel & Weitenhofer, 1981. International Biennales: São Paulo, Brazil, 1950-57; Antwerp, 1951-53; Venice, 1952; Holland Park, London, 1954-57; Battersea Park, 1961; Venice, 1962; 7th Tokyo, 1963; work in British Sculpture in the 'Sixties' exhibn, Tate Gall., 1965; Internat. Sculpture Sonsbeek, 1966; Fest. of London, 1968; Open Air Sculpture, Edinburgh, 1970. Various Arts Council and British Council travelling exhibns in Europe, USA and Japan. Works in permanent collections: Arts Council; British Council; Tate Gallery; Museums of Modern Art: New York, Rome and Turin; New York Public Library; São Paulo Museum; Univ. of Michigan, Ann Arbor; and many private collections. Commissions include sculptures for: Kings Heath Sch., Northampton; Sconce Hills Secondary Sch., Newark; The State Theatre, Gelsenkirchen; LCC Comprehensive Sch., Eltham; Hull City Centre; P & O Liner Canberra; Sekers Showroom, London; BP Building, Moorgate; Gatwick Airport; Maths Building, UCL; Kings Well, NW3; Fire Services Trng Coll. Glos; Williams & Glyn's Bank, London. *Address:* Rangers Hall, Great Maplestead, Halstead, Essex. *T:* Hedingham 60142.

ADAMS, Roland; *see* Adams, J. R.

ADAMS, Sherman; Chairman and Chief Executive Officer, Loon Mountain Corporation, since 1980 (President, 1966-80); *b* 8 Jan. 1899; *s* of Clyde H. Adams and Winnie Marion (*née* Sherman); *m* 1923, Rachel Leona White; one *s* three *d*. *Educ:* Dartmouth College (Montgomery Fellow, 1980). Graduated, 1920; Manager, timberland and lumber operations, The Parker-Young Co., Lincoln, NH, 1928-45. Mem., New Hampshire House of Representatives, 1941-44; Chm. Cttee on Labor, 1941-42; Speaker of House, 1943-44; mem., 79th Congress, 2nd New Hampshire Dist; Gov. of New Hampshire, 1949-53;

Chief of White House Staff, Asst to President of US, 1953–58, resigned. Chairman: Conf. of New England Govs, 1951–52; Mt Washington Commn, 1969–. Director (life), Northeastern Lumber Mfrs Assoc., New England Council. Served with US Marine Corps, 1918. First Robert Frost Award, Plymouth State Coll., 1970. Holds several hon. degrees. *Publications:* First Hand Report, 1961 (Gt Brit. 1962); articles in Life, American Forests, Appalachia, 1958–70. *Recreations:* golf, fishing, ski-ing. *Address:* Pollard Road, Lincoln, New Hampshire 03251, USA.

ADAMS, Mrs Vyvyan; *see* Adams, Mary Grace.

ADAMS, William James, CMG 1976; HM Diplomatic Service; Assistant Under-Secretary of State, Foreign and Commonwealth Office, since 1980; *b* 30 April 1932; *s* of late William Adams and late Norah (*née* Walker); *m* 1961, Donatella, *d* of late Andrea Pais-Tarsilia; two *s* one *d*. *Educ:* Shrewsbury Sch.; Queen's Coll., Oxford. HM Forces, 1950–51. Foreign Office, 1954; 3rd Sec., Bahrain, 1956; Asst Political Agent, Trucial States, 1957; FO, 1958; 2nd Sec., 1959; Manila, 1960; 1st Sec. and Private Sec. to Minister of State, FO, 1963; 1st Sec. (Information), Paris, 1965–69; FCO, 1969; Counsellor, 1971; Head of European Integration Dept (2), FCO, 1971–72; seconded to Economic Commn for Africa, Addis Ababa, 1972–73; Counsellor (Developing Countries), UK Permanent Representation to EEC, 1973–77; Head of Chancery and Counsellor (Economic), Rome, 1977–80. *Address:* c/o Foreign and Commonwealth Office, SW1A 2AL.

ADAMS-SCHNEIDER, Rt. Hon. Lancelot Raymond; PC 1980; Ambassador of New Zealand to the United States, since 1982; *b* Wellington, NZ, 11 Nov. 1919; *s* of A. A. Adams; *m* 1945, Shirley Lois, *d* of L. A. Brunton; two *s* one *d*. *Educ:* Mt Albert Grammar School. Served War of 1939–45, NZ Medical Corps. Formerly Gen. Manager of department store, Taumarunui; Mem. Borough Council and Pres., Chamber of Commerce, Taumarunui; Exec. Member, NZ Retailers' Fedn. Vice-Chm. of Nat. Party in Waitomo electorate; Mem. S Auckland Div. Exec.; MP for Hamilton, 1959–69, for Waikato, 1969–81; Minister of Broadcasting, and Assistant to Minister of Customs, 1969; Minister of Customs, Asst Minister of Industries and Commerce, 1969–72; Minister of Health, Social Security and Social Welfare, Feb.–Nov. 1972; Opposition Spokesman on Health and Social Welfare, 1972–75, and on Industry, Commerce and Customs, 1974–75; Minister of Trade and Industry, 1975–81. *Address:* New Zealand Embassy, 37 Observatory Circle NW, Washington, DC 20008, USA.

ADAMSON, Very Rev. Alexander Campbell; Dean of Aberdeen and Orkney, since 1978; Rector of St Thomas Aboyne with St Kentigern, Ballater, with pastoral care of St Margaret's, Braemar, since 1979; *b* 21 June 1921; *s* of David Watson Adamson and Margaret Kinnaird Rae Adamson; *m* 1959, Betty Reeves (*d* 1980); one *s* one *d*. *Educ:* Petershill Public School, Glasgow; Albert Secondary School, Glasgow; Lichfield Theological Coll.. Staffs. Served RAF, 1941–46. Employed Glasgow Welfare Dept, 1946–48; Executive Officer, Nat. Assistance Bd, 1948–57; professional footballer, 1948–51; worked on Philmont Ranch, New Mexico, 1954. Deacon, Wakefield, Yorks, 1959; priest, Pontefract, Yorks, 1960; Curate, Pontefract Parish Church, 1959—62; Vicar of Honley with Brockholes, 1962–69; Royal Army Chaplaincy Dept, 1962–68; Rector of St John the Evangelist, Aberdeen, 1969–79. Canon, St Andrew's Cathedral, Aberdeen, 1973; Synod Clerk of Aberdeen and Orkney, 1976. Actors' Union Chaplain, His Majesty's Theatre, 1969–; Grampian Area Scout Chaplain, 1972–; Member: Religious Adv. Cttee, Scouts, Scotland, 1972–; Adv. Cttee to Royal Mission to Deep Sea Fishermen, 1973–; Adv. Cttee, Prince's Trust, 1975–; Religious Adv. Cttee, Grampian TV, 1978–. *Recreations:* Theatre, Scout movement, sport, and the three R's: reading, 'riting and reconciliation. *Address:* Glenmoriston, 7 Invercauld Road, Ballater, Aberdeenshire. *T:* Ballater 55726.

ADAMSON, Sir Campbell; *see* Adamson, Sir W. O. C.

ADAMSON, Prof. Colin, DSc; Rector, The Polytechnic of Central London, since 1970; *b* 23 Nov. 1922; British; *m* 1946, Janet Marjory Conyers; one *s* one *d*. *Educ:* Pocklington Sch., Yorks. BSc 1947, MSc(Eng.) 1952, London; DSc Manchester, 1961. REME (Capt.), 1942–46. Asst Lectr, then with A. Reyrolle & Co. (power systems analysis), 1946–52; Sen. Lectr, then Reader, in Electrical Power Systems Engrg, UMIST, 1952–61; Chm., Dept of Electrical Engineering and Electronics, Univ. of Manchester Institute of Science and Technology, 1961–70. Mem., Conférence Internationale des Grands Réseaux Electriques; Chm. of Consultants, Educational Overseas Services, 1975–; Chm. of Panel 1 (and Mem. Council), British Calibration Service, 1969–. Mem., Exec. Cttee, Inter-Univ. Council for Service Overseas, 1972–; Mem., Bd of Trustees, Ecole Supérieure Interafricaine d'Electricité, Abidjan, 1979–; UN Team leader for Yarmouk Univ. of Technology, Jordan, 1978–. Vis. Professor: Univ. of Roorkee, India, 1954–55; Univs of Washington and Wisconsin, 1959; Middle East Techn. Univ., Ankara, 1967–68; Univ. of Technology, Baghdad, 1975–. Cons. Editor, Internat. Jl of Electrical Engrg Educn. *Publications:* (jtly) High Voltage Direct Current Power Transmission, 1960; High Voltage DC Power Convertors and Systems, 1963; University Perspectives, 1970; UNESCO reports: Higher Technical Education (Egypt), 1972; Alternative University Structures (UK), 1973, 3rd edn 1977; Technical Higher Education (Iraq), 1974; Post-secondary Education for Persons Gainfully-employed, 1976 and 1977; contribs to Proc. IEE and other learned jls. *Recreations:* yachting, oriental science and technology. *Address:* 309 Regent Street, W1R 8AL. *Clubs:* Athenæum; Royal Mersey Yacht.

ADAMSON, Estelle Inez Ommanney, OBE 1962; Director of Nursing, St Thomas' Hospital, London, 1965–70, retired; *b* 21 May 1910; *d* of late R. O. Adamson, MA, MD, and late Evelyn Mary Ommanney. *Educ:* Benenden School, Cranbrook, Kent. Nurse training, St Thomas' Hosp., 1932–35; Sister, etc, St Thomas' Hosp., 1936–43; Asst Matron, King Edward VII Sanatorium, Midhurst, Sussex, 1943–45; Secretary, Nursing Recruitment Service, Nuffield Provincial Hospitals Trust, Scotland, 1946–51; Matron, Western General Hosp., Edinburgh, 1951–65. *Address:* 19 Millers Close, Goring-on-Thames, Oxon.

ADAMSON, Norman Joseph, CB 1981; QC (Scot.) 1979; Legal Secretary to the Lord Advocate and First Parliamentary Draftsman for Scotland, since 1979; *b* 29 Sept. 1930; *o s* of Joseph Adamson, wine and spirit merchant, and Lily Thorrat, Glasgow; *m* 1961, Patricia Mary, *er d* of Walter Scott Murray Guthrie and Christine Gillies Greenfield, Edinburgh; four *d*. *Educ:* Hillhead High Sch., Glasgow; Glasgow Univ. MA (Hons Philosophy and Economics) 1952; LLB 1955; Faculty of Advocates, Scotland, 1957; called to English Bar, Gray's Inn, 1959. Army Legal Aid (Civil) (UK), 1956–57; practice at Scottish Bar, 1957–65; Standing Jun. Counsel, Bible Board, 1962; Standing Jun. Counsel, MoD (Army), 1963–65; Hon. Sheriff Substitute, 1963–65; Parly Draftsman and Legal Sec., Lord Advocate's Dept, London, 1965–. Elder of the Church of Scotland. *Recreations:* music, theatre. *Address:* 6 Wildoaks, Acacia Road, Staines, Mddx TW18 1BY. *T:* Staines 50319. *Clubs:* Royal Over-Seas League (London and Edinburgh), College (Glasgow).

ADAMSON, Rt. Rev. Mgr. Canon Thomas; Canon, Liverpool Metropolitan Cathedral, since 1950; Parish Priest of St Clare's, Liverpool, since 1945; *b* 30 Sept. 1901; *s* of George and Teresa Adamson, Alston Lane, near Preston. *Educ:* St Edward's College, Liverpool; Upholland College; Oscott College, Birmingham; Gregorian University, Rome. Ordained Priest, 1926; Beda College, Rome, 1926–28; Private Secretary to Archbishop of Liverpool, 1928–45; Privy Chamberlain to Pope Pius XI, 1932; Domestic Prelate to the Pope, 1955; Vicar General to Archbishops of Liverpool, 1955–65; Protonotary Apostolic to the Pope, 1966. *Address:* St Clare's Presbytery, Arundel Avenue, Liverpool L17 2AU. *T:* 051-733 2374.

ADAMSON, Sir (William Owen) Campbell, Kt 1976; Chairman: Abbey National Building Society, since 1978; Renold Ltd, since 1982 (Director, since 1976; Deputy Chairman, 1981–82); Director: Imperial Group Ltd, since 1976; Lazard Bros & Co. Ltd, Doulton & Co. Ltd, since 1977; Tarmac plc, since 1980; *b* 26 June 1922; *o s* of late John Adamson, CA; *m* 1945, Gilvray (*née* Allan); two *s* two *d*. *Educ:* Rugby Sch.; Corpus Christi Coll., Cambridge. Royal Inst. of Internat. Affairs, 1944–45; Baldwins Ltd as Management Trainee, 1945; successive managerial appts with Richard Thomas & Baldwins Ltd and Steel Co. of Wales Ltd, 1947–69; Gen. Man. i/c of construction and future operation of Spencer Steelworks, Llanwern; Dir, Richard Thomas & Baldwins Ltd, 1959–69, seconded as Dep. Under-Sec. of State, and Co-ordinator of Industrial Advisers, DEA, 1967–69; Dir-Gen., CBI, 1969–76. Member: BBC Adv. Cttee, 1964–67 and 1967–75; SSRC (on formation), 1965–69; NEDC, 1969–76; Council, Industrial Soc.; Design Council, 1971–73; Council, Iron and Steel Inst.. 1960–72; Iron and Steel Industry Delegn to Russia, 1956, and to India, 1968; Vice-Chm., National Savings Cttee for England and Wales, 1975–77. Vis. Fellow: Lancaster Univ., 1970; Nuffield Coll., Oxford, 1971–79. Governor, Rugby Sch., 1979–. *Publications:* various technical articles. *Recreations:* brass rubbing, tennis, music, arguing. *Address:* 11 St Augustine's House, Bloomburg Street, SW1V 2RG.

ADCOCK, Sir Robert (Henry), Kt 1950; CBE 1941; retired as Clerk of County Council, Lancashire (1944–60), also as Clerk of the Peace for Lancashire and Clerk of the Lancashire Lieutenancy; *b* 27 Sept. 1899; *s* of late Henry Adcock, Polesworth, Warwicks; *m* Mary, *d* of late R. K. Wadsworth, Handforth Hall, Cheshire; one *s* two *d*. *Educ:* Atherstone, Warwicks. Asst Solicitor, Manchester, 1923; Asst Solicitor and Asst Clerk of the Peace, Notts CC, 1926; Senior Asst Solicitor, Manchester, 1929; Deputy Town Clerk, Manchester, 1931; Town Clerk, Manchester, 1938. DL Lancs, 1950–74. *Recreation:* golf. *Address:* Summer Place, Rock End, Torquay, Devon. *T:* 22775.

See also R. W. Adcock.

ADCOCK, Robert Wadsworth; DL; Chief Executive and Clerk, Essex County Council, since 1976; *b* 29 Dec. 1932; *s* of Sir Robert Adcock, *qv; m* 1957, Valerie Colston Robins; one *s* one *d*. *Educ:* Rugby Sch. Solicitor. Asst Solicitor, Lancs CC, 1955–56; Asst Solicitor, Manchester City Council, 1956–59; Sen. Solicitor, Berks CC, 1959–63; Asst Clerk, later Dep. Clerk, Northumberland CC, 1963–70; Dep. Chief Exec., Essex CC, 1970–76. DL Essex 1978. *Recreations:* gardening, ornithology. *Address:* The Christmas Cottage, Great Sampford, Saffron Walden, Essex. *T:* Great Sampford 363. *Club:* Law Society.

ADDERLEY, family name of **Baron Norton.**

ADDINGTON, family name of **Viscount Sidmouth.**

ADDINGTON, 6th Baron *cr* 1887; **Dominic Bryce Hubbard;** *b* 24 Aug. 1963; *s* of 5th Baron Addington and of Alexandra Patricia, *yr d* of late Norman Ford Millar; *S* father, 1982. *Heir: b* Hon. Michael Walter Leslie Hubbard, *b* 6 July 1965. *Address:* 9/11 Chalk Hill Road, Norwich NR1 1SL.

ADDIS, Sir John (Mansfield), KCMG 1973 (CMG 1959); HM Diplomatic Service, retired; Supernumerary Fellow, Wolfson College, Oxford, since 1982 (Senior Research Fellow in Contemporary Chinese Studies, 1975-82); *b* 11 June 1914; 5th *s* and 12th *c* of late Sir Charles and Lady Addis. *Educ:* Rugby School; Christ Church, Oxford. 3rd Sec., Foreign Office, 1938; with Allied Force HQ (Mediterranean), 1942-44; Junior Private Sec. to Prime Minister (Mr Attlee), 1945-47; 1st Sec., Nanking, 1947-50, Peking, 1950; Counsellor, Peking, 1954-57; Counsellor in the Foreign Office, 1957-60; Ambassador to Laos, 1960-62; Fellow at Harvard Centre for Internat. Affairs, 1962-63; Ambassador to the Philippines, 1963-70; Senior Civilian Instructor, IDC, later Royal Coll. of Defence Studies, 1970-71; Ambassador to China, 1972-74 (Chargé d'Affaires, Jan.-March 1972). Member: Expert Adv. Council, Percival David Foundn of Chinese Art, 1977-; Adv. Council, V&A Museum, 1977-79; a Trustee, British Museum, 1977-; Pres., Oriental Ceramic Soc., 1974-77. *Publications:* Chinese Ceramics from Datable Tombs, 1978; Chinese Porcelain from the Addis Collection, 1979. *Address:* Woodside, Frant, Tunbridge Wells TN3 9HW. *T:* Frant 202; Wolfson College, Oxford. *T:* Oxford 55605; 7D Pont Street, SW1X 9EJ. *T:* 01-235 7784. *Club:* Boodle's.

See also Sir Dallas Bernard, Bt.

ADDISON, family name of Viscount Addison.

ADDISON, 3rd Viscount *cr* 1945 of Stallingborough; **Michael Addison**; Baron Addison 1937; *b* 12 April 1914; 2nd *s* of 1st Viscount Addison, KG, PC, MD, FRCS, and Isobel McKinnon (*d* 1934), *d* of late Archibald Gray; *S* brother, 1976; *m* 1936, Kathleen Amy, *d* of Rt Rev. and Rt Hon. J. W. C. Wand, PC, KCVO, and late Amy Agnes Wiggins; one *s* two *d*. *Educ:* Hele's School, Exeter; Balliol Coll., Oxford. BA (PPE) 1935, MA 1965. Min. of Labour, 1935; War Damage Commission, 1940. Served RAFVR, 1941-45, FO Intell. Branch. War Damage Commn and Central Land Bd, 1945-51; Min. of Supply/Aviation, 1951-63; HM Treasury, 1963-65; Sen. Lectr, Polytechnic of Central London (School of Management Studies), 1965-76; retired, 1976. Member: Royal Inst. of Public Administration; Assoc. of Teachers of Management. *Recreation:* gardening. *Heir: s* Hon. William Matthew Wand Addison [*b* 13 June 1945; *m* 1970, Joanna Mary, *e d* of late J. I. C. Dickinson; one *s* two *d*]. *Address:* Old Stables, Maplehurst, Horsham, West Sussex. *T:* Lower Beeding 298. *Club:* Oxford Union Society.

ADDISON, Prof. Cyril Clifford, PhD, DSc (Dunelm); FRS 1970; FInstP; FRSC; Professor of Inorganic Chemistry, University of Nottingham, 1960-78, Dean of Faculty of Pure Science, 1968-71, Leverhulme Emeritus Fellow, 1978; *b* 28 Nov. 1913; *s* of late Edward Thomas Addison and Olive Clifford; *m* 1939, Marjorie Whineray Thompson; one *s* one *d*. *Educ:* Workington and Millom Grammar Schools, Cumberland; University of Durham (Hatfield College). Scientific Officer, British Launderers' Research Assoc., 1936-38; Lectr, Harris Inst., Preston, 1938-39; Ministry of Supply, Chemical Inspection Dept, 1939-45; Chemical Defence Research Establ., 1945; Univ. of Nottingham: Lectr, 1946; Reader in Inorganic Chemistry, 1952. Lectures: Corday-Morgan, CA Africa, 1969; Liverside, 1976; Dist. Vis. Prof., Auburn Univ., Alabama, 1979-80. Member: Chemical Soc. Council, 1954-57 (Pres. 1976-77); Inst. of Chemistry Council, 1948-51 and 1962-65 (Vice-Pres., 1965-67). Hon. DSc: Dunelm, 1977; Warwick, 1979. *Publications:* numerous papers in Jl Chemical Soc., Trans. Faraday Soc., etc. *Recreations:* mountain walking, gardening. *Address:* Department of Chemistry, The University, Nottingham. *T:* Nottingham 56101.

ADDISON, Air Vice-Marshal Edward Barker, CB 1945; CBE 1942 (OBE 1938); MA; CEng, FIEE; RAF, retired; *b* 4 Oct. 1898; *m* 1926, Marie-Blanche Marguerite Rosain; one *s* one *d*. *Educ:* Sidney Sussex Coll., Cambridge. Served European War, 1915-18, RFC and RAF; Cambridge Univ., 1918-21; BA (Cantab), 1921; MA (Cantab), 1926; Ingénieur Diplomé de l'Ecole Supérieure d'Electricité, Paris, 1927; re-commissioned RAF, 1921; retd from RAF, 1955; Dir and Div. Manager, Redifon Ltd, 1956-63, retd; Director, Intercontinental Technical Services Ltd, 1964-75, retd; Consultant to Vocational Guidance Assoc., 1966-72. AMIEE 1933; MIEE 1941; FIEE 1966. Commander of US Legion of Merit, 1947. *Address:* 7 Hall Place Drive, Weybridge, Surrey. *T:* Weybridge 47450.

ADDISON, Kenneth George, OBE 1978; Director, since 1971 and Deputy Chief General Manager, since 1976, Sun Alliance & London Insurance Group; *b* 1 Jan. 1923; *s* of Herbert George Addison and Ruby (*née* Leathers); *m* 1945, Maureen Newman; one *s* one *d*. *Educ:* Felixstowe Grammar Sch. LLB London. Served RAF, 1942-46. Joined Alliance Assurance Co. Ltd, 1939; various subsequent appts; Asst Sec., Law Fire Insurance Office, 1960-64; Gen. Manager, Sun Alliance & London Insurance Group, 1971. Director: Fire Insurers' Res. & Testing Orgn; Fire Protection Assoc.; Insurance Technical Bureau; Chairman: Internat. Oil Insurers; Management Cttee, Associated Insurers (British Electricity). Chm., Hearing Aid Council, 1971-78. FCIS; FCII (Pres., 1980); FCIArb (Pres., 1968-69). *Publications:* papers on insurance and allied subjects. *Recreations:* swimming, carpentry, gardening. *Address:* Ockley, 13 Hillcroft Avenue, Purley, Surrey. *T:* 01-660 2793.

ADDISON, Dr Philip Harold, MRCS, LRCP; Hon. Consulting Secretary, The Medical Defence Union, since 1974 (Secretary, 1959-74); *b* 28 June 1909; 2nd *s* of late Dr Joseph Bartlett Addison and Mauricia Renée Addison; *m* 1934, Mary Norah Ryan; one *s* one *d*. *Educ:* Clifton Coll., Bristol; St Mary's Hosp. Medical Sch. MRCS, LRCP 1933; Gold Medallist, Military Medicine and

Bronze Medallist Pathology, Army Medical Sch., Millbank, SW1, 1935; Permanent Commission, IMS, 1935; served Burma Campaign, 1943-4 (despatches). Chm., Ethical Cttee of Family Planning Assoc., 1956-60; Vice-Pres., Medico-Legal Soc., 1965-74. *Publications:* Professional Negligence, in Compendium of Emergencies, 1971; The Medico-Legal Aspects of General Anaesthesia, in, Clinical Practice of General Anaesthesia 1971; contrib. Brit. Med. Jl, Irish Med. Jl, Proc. R.Soc.Med, Medico-Legal Jl, Lancet. *Recreations:* fishing, golf, bridge. *Address:* Red-Wyn-Byn Monkmead Lane, West Chiltington, Pulborough, West Sussex. *T:* West Chiltington 3047. *Clubs:* East India, Devonshire, Sports and Public Schools; Shark Angling Club of Gt Britain; West Sussex Golf; BMA Bridge (Founder Mem.).

ADDISON, Sir William (Wilkinson), Kt 1974; JP; DL; Chairman of Council, The Magistrates' Association, 1970-76; *b* Mitton, WR Yorks, 4 April 1905; *s* of Joseph Addison, Bashall Eaves; *m* 1929, Phoebe, *d* of Robert Dean Rimington, WR Yorks. Verderer of Epping Forest, 1957-. Chm., Epping Petty Sessions, 1955-, combined Epping and Ongar Petty Sessions, 1968-76; Magistrates' Assoc.: Mem. Coun., 1959-76; Dep. Chm. of Coun., 1966-70; Chm., Treatment of Offenders Cttee, 1961-68; Chm. Exec. Cttee, 1968-75; Member: Hill Hall Prison Board of Visitors, 1955-70; Chelmsford Prison 1958-77; Bullwood Hall Borstal, 1962-76; Home Sec.'s Adv. Coun. on Probation and After-Care, 1964-67; Lord Chancellor's Adv. Coun. on Trng of Magistrates, 1964-73; Magistrates' Courts Rule Cttee, 1968-74; Council Commonwealth Magistrates Assoc., 1970-75; Assessor to Deptl Cttee on Liquor Licensing, 1971. Member: Court, Univ. of Essex, 1965-; Coun., Essex Archaeological Soc., 1949-71 (Pres., 1964-67); Adv. Council, Univ. of Cambridge Inst. of Criminology, 1972-78; Pres. or Chm. of several bodies connected with local history and the preservation of antiquities in Essex, inc. Victoria County History. JP 1949, DL 1973, Essex. FSA 1965; FRHistS 1965. *Publications:* Epping Forest, 1945; The English Country Parson, 1947; Essex Heyday, 1949; Suffolk, 1950; Worthy Dr Fuller, 1951; English Spas, 1951; Audley End, 1953; English Fairs and Markets, 1953; Thames Estuary, 1953; In the Steps of Charles Dickens, 1955; Wanstead Park, 1973; Essex Worthies, 1973; Portrait of Epping Forest, 1977; Understanding English Place-Names, 1978; Understanding English Surnames, 1978; The Old Roads of England, 1980; Local Styles of the English Parish Church, 1982. *Recreation:* exploring the English countryside for evidence of local history. *Address:* Ravensmere, Epping, Essex. *T:* Epping 73439.

ADDLESHAW, His Honour John Lawrence; a Circuit Judge (formerly County Court Judge), 1960-75; *b* 30 Oct. 1902; *s* of Harold Pope Addleshaw, Solicitor and Mary Gertrude (*née* Shore), Manchester; unmarried. *Educ:* Shrewsbury School; University College, Oxford (BA). Called to the Bar, Inner Temple, 1925. Auxiliary Air Force, 1939-45. *Recreations:* golf, walking. *Address:* 3 College House, Southdowns Road, Bowdon, Altrincham, Cheshire WA14 3DZ. *T:* 061-928 2139. *Club:* Clarendon (Manchester).

ADEANE, family name of Baron Adeane.

ADEANE, Baron *cr* 1972 (Life Peer), of Stamfordham; **Michael Edward Adeane**, PC 1953; GCB 1968 (KCB 1955; CB 1947); GCVO 1962 (KCVO 1951; MVO 1946); Royal Victorian Chain, 1972; MA; FSA; Extra Equerry to the Queen, since 1972; Chairman, Royal Commission on Historical Monuments, since 1972; Member, British Library Board, since 1972; *b* 30 Sept. 1910; *s* of late Capt. H. R. A. Adeane, Coldstream Guards (killed in action, 1914), and Hon. Victoria Eugenie Baige (*d* 1969); *m* 1939, Helen Chetwynd-Stapylton; one *s* (*and d decd*). *Educ:* Eton; Magdalene Coll., Cambridge (1st Cl. Hons Historical Tripos Part II); Hon. Fellow 1971. 2nd Lieut Coldstream Guards, 1931; ADC to Governor-General of Canada, 1934-36; Major, 1941; Lieut-Col 1942. Served War of 1939-45: with 2nd Bn Coldstream Guards. 1940-42; on Joint Staff Mission, Washington, 1942-43; 5th Bn Coldstream Guards, 1943-45; in NW Europe from 1944 (wounded, despatches). Page of honour to King George V; Equerry and Asst Private Sec. to King George VI, 1937-52, to the Queen, 1952-53; Private Sec. to the Queen and Keeper of HM's Archives, 1953-72. Lieut-Col (R of O) 1954. Director: Phoenix Assurance Co. Ltd, 1972-80; Banque Belge Ltd, 1972-80; Royal Bank of Canada, 1972-80; The Diners Club Ltd, 1976-82. Governor, Wellington College, 1960-81. *Recreations:* shooting and fishing. *Address:* 22 Chelsea Square, SW3 6LF. *T:* 01-352 3080; Mosshead Cottage, Kildrummy, Alford, Aberdeenshire. *T:* Kildrummy 261. *Clubs:* Brooks's, Beefsteak, Pratt's.

See also Hon. G. E. Adeane.

ADEANE, Hon. (George) Edward; Private Secretary and Treasurer to HRH the Prince of Wales, since 1979 and Treasurer to TRH the Prince and Princess of Wales, since 1981; *b* 4 Oct. 1939; *s* of Baron Adeane, *qv*. *Educ:* Eton; Magdalene College, Cambridge (MA). Called to Bar, Middle Temple, July 1962. *Address:* B4 Albany, Piccadilly, W1. *T:* 01-734 9410.

ADEBO, Simeon Olaosebikan, (Chief), The Okanlomo of Egbaland, CFR 1979; CMG 1959; Chairman, National Institute for Policy and Strategic Studies, since 1979; *b* 5 Oct. 1913; *s* of late Chief Adebo, the Okanlomo of Itoko, Abeokuta; *m* 1941, Regina Abimbola, *d* of Chief D. A. Majekodunmi, Abeokuta; three *s* one *d*. *Educ:* St Peter's Sch., Ake, Abeokuta; Abeokuta Grammar Sch.; King's Coll., Lagos, Nigeria. BA Hons (London) 1939; LLB Hons (London) 1946. Called to Bar, Gray's Inn, 1949. Accountant in trg, Nigerian Rly, 1933; Admin. Officer Cadet, Nigerian Govt, 1942; Asst Fin. Sec. to Govt of Nigeria, 1954; Western Nigeria: Admin. Officer, Class I, 1955;

Perm. Sec., Min. of Finance, 1957; Perm. Sec. to Treasury and Head of Civil Service, 1958; Head of Civil Service and Chief Secretary to Government, 1961; Permanent Representative of Nigeria at UN and Comr-Gen. for Economic Affairs, 1962-67; UN Under-Secretary-General and Exec. Dir of UNITAR, 1968-72. Chm., Nat. Universities Commn of Nigeria, 1975-77. Member: Nigeria Soc.; Soc. for Internat. Develt. Hon. LLD: Western Michigan, 1963; Nigeria, Nsukka, 1965; Fordham, 1966; Lincoln, 1966; Beaver Coll., 1966; Ife, 1968; Ibadan, 1969; Columbia, 1971; Ahmadu Bello (Nigeria), 1973; Open Univ., 1975; Lagos, Nigeria, 1978; Hon. DCL, Union Coll., 1965. *Publication:* (with Sir Sydney Phillipson) Report on the Nigerianisation of the Nigerian Civil Service, 1953. *Recreations:* tennis and cricket. *Address:* c/o PO Box 139, Abeokuta, Nigeria. *Clubs:* Royal Commonwealth Society; Abeokuta Sports.

ADELAIDE, Archbishop of, and Metropolitan of South Australia, since 1975; **Most Rev. Keith Rayner;** *b* 22 Nov. 1929; *s* of Sidney and Gladys Rayner, Brisbane; *m* 1963, Audrey Fletcher; one *s* two *d. Educ:* C of E Grammar Sch., Brisbane; Univ. of Queensland. BA 1951; PhD 1964. Deacon, 1953; Priest, 1953. Chaplain, St Francis' Theol Coll., Brisbane, 1954; Mem., Brotherhood of St John, Dalby, 1955-58; Vice-Warden, St John's Coll., Brisbane, 1958; Rotary Foundn Fellow, Harvard Univ., 1958-59; Vicar, St Barnabas', Sunnybank, 1959-63; Rector, St Peter's, Wynnum, 1963-69; Bishop of Wangaratta, 1969-75. Pres., Christian Conference of Asia, 1977-81; Chm., International Anglican Theological and Doctrinal Commission, 1980-. *Recreation:* tennis. *Address:* Bishop's Court, North Adelaide, SA 5006, Australia.

ADELAIDE, Archbishop of, (RC), since 1971; **Most Rev. James William Gleeson,** AO 1979; CMG 1958; DD 1957; FACE 1967; *b* 24 Dec. 1920; *s* of John Joseph and Margaret Mary Gleeson. *Educ:* St Joseph's Sch., Balaklava, SA; Sacred Heart Coll., Glenelg, SA. Priest, 1945; Inspector of Catholic Schs, 1947-52; Dir of Catholic Education for South Australia, 1952-58; Auxiliary Bishop to the Archbishop of Adelaide, and Titular Bishop of Sesta, 1957-64; Coadjutor Archbishop of Adelaide and Titular Archbishop of Aurusuliana, 1964-71. Episcopal Chm., Young Catholic Students Movement of Australia, 1958-65. *Address:* Archbishop's House, 91 West Terrace, Adelaide, SA 5000, Australia. *T:* 51.3551.

ADELSTEIN, Abraham Manie, MD; FRCP; FFCM; Visiting Professor, London School of Hygiene and Tropical Medicine, since 1981; *b* 28 March 1916; *s* of Nathan Adelstein and Rosa Cohen; *m* 1942, Cynthia Gladys Miller; one *s* one *d. Educ:* Univ. of Witwatersrand. MB, ChB, MD. SAMC, 1941-45; Health Officer (res. and medical statistics), SA Railways, 1947-61; Sen. Lectr, Univ. of Manchester, 1961-67; OPCS, 1967-81 (SPMO and Chief Medical Statistician, 1975-81). *Publications:* Thesis on Accident Proneness, 1950; papers in scientific jls on the distribution and aetiology of various diseases (diseases of heart, nervous system, respiratory system, cancer, accidents) and of methods of collecting, analysing and publishing national statistics. *Address:* 21 Dunstan Road, NW11 8AG. *T:* 01-455 9983.

ADEMOLA, Rt. Hon. Sir Adetokunbo (Adegboyega), GCON 1972; CFR 1963; PC 1963; KBE 1963; Kt 1957; Chancellor, University of Nigeria, since 1975; *b* 1 Feb. 1906; *e s* of late Sir Ladapo Ademola, Alake of Abeokuta, KBE, CMG; *m* 1939, Kofoworola, *yr d* of late Eric Olawolu Moore, CBE; three *s* two *d. Educ:* King's Coll., Lagos, Nigeria; Selwyn Coll., Cambridge. Attached to Attorney-General's Chambers, Lagos, Nigeria, 1934-35; Assistant Secretary, Secretariat, Southern Provinces, Nigeria, 1935-36; private law practice, Nigeria, 1936-39; Magistrate, Nigeria, 1939; served on commn for Revision of Courts Legislation, Nigeria, 1948; served on commn to enquire into Enugu (Nigeria) disturbances, 1949; Puisne Judge, Nigeria, 1949; Chief Justice, Western Region, Nigeria, 1955-58; Chief Justice of Nigeria, 1958-72. Deputy Chm., United Bank for Africa, 1972-74. Hon. Bencher, Middle Temple, 1959-. Chairman: Commonwealth Foundn, 1978-; Adv. Cttee on Conventions and Regulations of the ILO (Mem., 1962-); Member: Internat. Commn of Jurists, 1961- (now Hon. Mem.); Internat. Olympic Cttee, 1963-. Hon. LLD Ahmadu Bello, Nigeria, 1962; Hon. DSc Benin, 1972. *Recreations:* golf, horse racing. *Address:* The Close, Adetokunbo Ademola Street, Victoria Island, Lagos, Nigeria. *T:* Lagos 52219. *Clubs:* Island, Metropolitan, Yoruba Tennis (Lagos); Ibadan Recreation, Ibadan (Ibadan).

ADEY, (Arthur) Victor; Director: Ampex Corporation (USA), since 1973; Motability and Motability Finance Ltd, since 1978; *b* 2 May 1912; *s* of Arthur Frederick and Pollie Adey; *m* 1936, Kathleen Mary Lewis; one *s* one *d. Educ:* Wolverhampton Secondary Sch. Articled clerk, Crombie, Lacon & Stevens, 1928; Office Manager and Accountant, Attwoods Factors Ltd, 1933; Branch Man., Mercantile Union Guarantee Corp., 1937; Man. Dir, Mercantile Credit Co. of Ireland Ltd, 1949; Mercantile Credit Co. Ltd: Dir, Bd of Management, 1955; Director, 1957-; Man. Dir, 1964; Dep. Chm. and Man. Dir, 1973; Chm. and Man. Dir, 1975-77; Chm., 1977-80; Dir, Barclays Bank UK Management Ltd, 1975-79. *Recreations:* shooting, fishing. *Address:* Rosemount, Burtons Lane, Chalfont St Giles, Bucks HP8 4BN. *T:* Little Chalfont 2160.

ADIE, Jack Jesson, CMG 1962; BA (Oxon); *b* 1 May 1913; *s* of late P. J. Adie; *m* 1940, Patricia McLoughlin; one *s* two *d. Educ:* Shrewsbury Sch.; Magdalen Coll., Oxford. Entered Colonial Administrative Service, 1938; served in Zanzibar, 1938-48 (on military service, 1940-42 in Kenya Regt, KAR and Occupied Territory Administration), posts included: Private Sec. to The Sultan, Private Sec. to British Resident and Sen. Asst Sec.; seconded to

Colonial Office, 1949-51, as Principal; Asst Sec., Kenya, 1951; Sec. for Educn and Labour, Kenya, 1952; Sec. for Educn, Labour and Lands, Kenya, 1954; acted as Minister for Educn, Labour and Lands, Kenya, Sept. 1955-Feb. 1956; Chief Sec., Barbados, 1957; Perm. Sec. for Forest Development, Game and Fisheries, Kenya, April-Dec. 1958; for Agriculture, Animal Husbandry and Water Resources, and Chm. African Land Development Bd, Dec. 1958-July 1959; for Housing, and Chm. Central Housing Bd, Nov. 1959-April 1960; for Housing, Common Services, Probation and Approved Schools, April 1960-April 1961; for Labour and Housing, 1961-62; acted as Minister for Labour and Housing, Jan.-April 1962; Perm. Sec. for Labour, 1962-63; retd from HMOCS, Jan 1964; Temp. Principal, Min. of Overseas Develt, 1964-69. Brilliant Star of Zanzibar, 4th class, 1947. *Address:* 3 Braemar, Kersfield Road, Putney, SW15.

ADIE, Ven. Michael Edgar; Archdeacon of Lincoln, since 1977; Vicar of Morton with Hacconby, since 1976; *b* 22 Nov. 1929; *s* of Walter Granville Adie and Kate Emily Adie (*née* Parrish); *m* 1957, Anne Devonald Roynon; one *s* three *d. Educ:* Westminster School; St John's Coll., Oxford (MA). Assistant Curate, St Luke, Pallion, Sunderland, 1954-57; Resident Chaplain to the Archbishop of Canterbury, 1957-60; Vicar of St Mark, Sheffield, 1960-69; Rural Dean of Hallam, 1966-69; Rector of Louth, 1969-76. *Recreations:* gardening, walking, sneezing. *Address:* Morton Vicarage, near Bourne, Lincs. *T:* Morton 239.

ADISESHIAH, Dr Malcolm Sathianathan; Member of Parliament, Rajya Sabha, since 1978; Vice-Chancellor, University of Madras, 1975-78; Director, Institute of Development Studies, Madras, 1971-78, now Chairman and Fellow; *b* 18 April 1910; *s* of Varanasi Adiseshiah and Nesammah Adiseshiah; *m* 1951, Sanchu Pothan. *Educ:* Univ. of Madras (MA); LSE, London Univ. (PhD). Lectr in Econs, St Paul's Coll., Calcutta, 1931-36; Prof. of Econs, Madras Christian Coll., 1944-46; Associate Gen. Sec., World Univ. Service, Geneva, 1946-48; Unesco, Paris: Dep. Dir, Dept of Exchange of Persons, 1948-50; Dir, Dept of Tech. Assistance, 1950-54; Asst Dir-Gen., 1954-63; Dep. Dir-Gen., 1963-76. *Publications:* Demand for Money, 1938; Agricultural Development, 1941; Rural Credit, 1943; Planning Industrial Development, 1944; Non-political UN, 1964; Economics of Indian and Industrial Natural Resources, 1966; Education and National Development, 1967; Adult Education, 1968; Let My Country Awake, 1970; It is Time to Begin, 1972; Techniques of Perspective Planning, 1973; Plan Implementation Problems and Prospects for the Fifth Plan, 1974; Science in the Battle against Poverty, 1974; Literacy Discussion, 1976; Towards a Functional Learning Society, 1976; Backdrop to Learning Society: educational perspectives for Tamil Nadu, 1977; Adult Education faces Inequality, 1980; Mid Year Review of the Economy, 1978-; Madras Development Seminar Series, 1971-. *Address:* 21 Cenotaph Road, Madras-600018, India. *T:* Madras 440144.

ADLER, Larry, (Lawrence Cecil Adler); mouth organist; *b* 10 Feb. 1914; *s* of Louis Adler and Sadie Hack; *m* 1st, 1938, Eileen Walser (marr. diss. 1961); one *s* two *d* ; 2nd, 1969, Sally Cline (marr. diss. 1977); one *d. Educ:* Baltimore City Coll. Won Maryland Harmonica Championship, 1927; first stage appearance, 1928 (NY); first British appearance, 1934 (in C. B. Cochran's Streamline revue); first appearance as soloist with Symphony Orchestra, Sydney, Australia, 1939; jt recital tours with dancer Paul Draper, US, 1941-49; soloist with NY Philharmonic and other major US Orchestras, also orchestras in England, Japan and Europe; war tours for Allied Troops, 1943, 1944, 1945; Germany, 1947, 1949; Korea (Brit. Commonwealth Div.), 1951; Israel (Six Day War), 1967; (Yom Kippur War), 1973; articles and book reviews in Sunday Times, New Statesman, Spectator, New Society; numerous TV One Man Shows; soloist, Edinburgh Festival, playing first performance of unpublished Gershwin quartet (MS gift to Adler from I. Gershwin, 1963; works composed for Adler by: Dr Ralph Vaughan Williams, Malcolm Arnold, Darius Milhaud, Arthur Benjamin, Gordon Jacob and others. *Compositions:* film scores: Genevieve; King and Country; High Wind in Jamaica; The Great Chase, etc; TV scores: Midnight Men (BBC serial); various TV plays and documentaries; music for TV commercials, children's records, stage plays, etc; concert music: Theme and Variations; Camera III; One Man Show, From Hand to Mouth, Edinburgh Festival, 1965 (other festivals, 1965-). *Publications:* How I Play, 1937; Larry Adler's Own Arrangements, 1960; Jokes and How to Tell Them, 1963. *Recreations:* tennis, journalism, cycling, conversation. *Address:* c/o Michael Bakewell, 118 Tottenham Court Rd, W1.

ADLEY, Robert James; MP (C) Christchurch and Lymington, since 1974 (Bristol North East, 1970-74); Director and Marketing Consultant, Commonwealth Holiday Inns of Canada Ltd; Director, Brookgauge Ltd; *b* 2 March 1935; *s* of Harry and Marie Adley; *m* 1961, Jane Elizabeth Pople; two *s. Educ:* Falconbury; Uppingham. Lived and worked in: Malaya, Singapore, Thailand; established Pearl & Dean (Thailand) Ltd, 1956; Sales Director, May Fair Hotel, 1960-64. Chairman: Parly Tourism Cttee; British-Jordanian Parly Gp; British-Chinese Parly Gp; Pres., Western Area Young Conservatives, 1972; Vice-Chm., Wessex Cons. Mems Gp. Mem. Nat. Council, British Hotels, Restaurants and Caterers Assoc. Mem., Railway Correspondence and Travel Soc.; Founder and First Chm., Brunel Soc.; Trustee, Brunel Engineering Centre Trust; Patron, SS Great Britain Project. *Publications:* Hotels, the Case for Aid, 1966; One Man, No Vote, 1976; A Policy for Tourism, 1977; British Steam in Cameracolour 1962-68, 1979; Take It or Leave It, 1980; In Search of Steam, 1981; The Call of Steam, 1982. *Recreations:* railway photography, railway enthusiast. *Address:* Woodend

House, Lymington, Hants. *T:* 01-219 5036. *Clubs:* Carlton; Royal Lymington Yacht.

ADMANI, Dr Haji Abdul Karim, JP; Consultant Physician, Sheffield Area Health Authority (Teaching), since 1970; Hon. Clinical Lecturer in Medicine, Sheffield University Medical School, since 1972; *b* 19 Sept. 1937; *s* of late Haji Abdul Razzak Admani (Electrical Engr in India), and of Hajiani Rahima Admani; *m* 1968, Seema (*née* Robson; Nursing Dir); one *s* one *d*. *Educ:* Gujarat Univ., India (BSc 1st Cl. Hons 1956); Karachi Univ., Pakistan (MB, BS 1962). DTM&H 1963; MRCPE (Neurology), 1967; FRCPE 1979. Sec. Med. Div., Northern Dist, Sheffield, 1972-75; Mem. Dist Med. Cttee, N Dist, 1975-; Area Rep. and Mem. Exec. Cttee, BMA, Sheffield, 1975-; Mem., Sheffield AHA, 1977-; County Med. Officer, S Yorks Br., Red Cross. Mem. GMC, 1979-. President: Muslim Council of Sheffield, Rotherham and dist, 1977- (Chm., 1970-76); Sheffield and N Reg., Pakistan Med. Soc. in UK, 1972-; Anglo-Asian Soc., Sheffield, 1973-; Union of Pakistani Orgns in UK and Europe, 1979- (Sen. Vice Pres., 1978-79). Chm., Islamic Centre Man. Cttee, Sheffield, 1973-; Vice-Chairman: Overseas Doctors' Assoc. in UK, 1975- (Chm. Post-grad. Med. Sub-Cttee, 1975; Chm. S Yorks Div., 1976-; Chm., Int., Advice and Welfare Centre, 1977-); National Org. of Afro-Asian-Caribbean People in UK, 1977; Sheffield Cttee of Racial Equality. Member: Exec. Cttee, Standing Conf. of Pakistani Orgs in UK, 1976- (Chm. Standing Conf., 1974-76); Asian Action Cttee (National), 1976; Exec. Cttee, Sheffield Community Relations Council, 1974-76; Adv. Council, IBA for Radio Hallam, Sheffield, 1975-; National Cttee for Campaign against Rickets and Osteomalacia, 1980- (Chm., Sheffield Cttee, 1981-); Central Cttee for Hosp. Med. Services in UK, 1979-. Pres., Sheffield Stroke Club, 1977. Member: British Geriatric Soc.; Medico-Chirurgical Soc. Sheffield; Abbeydale Rotary Club, Sheffield; BMA; Collegiate Cttee of Edinburgh; Magistrates' Assoc. JP City of Sheffield, 1974. *Recreations:* tennis, cricket, chess, football, golf, table tennis. *Address:* 1 Derriman Glen, Silverdale Road, Sheffield S11 9LQ. *T:* Sheffield 360465.

ADORIAN, Paul; consulting engineer; *b* 29 Nov. 1905; *s* of Dr Emil Adorian; *m* 1932, Lilian A. Griffiths; two *s* one *d*. *Educ:* City and Guilds (Eng) Coll., London. Joined Rediffusion as development engineer, 1932; retd 1970, as Man. Dir; Dep. Chm., Wembley Stadium 1960-70; Dir, British Electric Traction, 1960-70; Dir and advisor, Resource Sciences Corp., Tulsa, Oklahoma and subs. co. Williams Bros Engineering Ltd, 1970-80. Member, Bd of Governors, British Film Inst., 1964-72. Past Pres., IERE. FCGI. *Publications:* several technical papers and lectures on electronics in general, flight simulation and distribution of broadcast sound and television programmes in particular. *Recreations:* lawn tennis (umpired Drobny-Patty match, also Drobny-Rosewall final, at Wimbledon), industrial archæology. *Address:* The Mill House, Gibbons Mill, near Billingshurst, West Sussex. *T:* Rudgwick 2477. *Club:* Athenæum.

ADRIAN, family name of **Baron Adrian.**

ADRIAN, 2nd Baron, *cr* 1955, of Cambridge; **Richard Hume Adrian,** MD; FRS 1977; Professor of Cell Physiology, University of Cambridge, since 1978; Master of Pembroke College, since 1981; *b* 16 Oct. 1927; *o s* of 1st Baron Adrian, OM, FRS, FRCP, and Hester Agnes, DBE 1965 (*d* 1966), *o d* of late Hume C. and Dame Ellen Pinsment, DBE, Birmingham; *S* father, 1977; *m* 1967, Lucy Caroe, MA, PhD. *Educ:* Swarthmore High Sch., USA; Westminster Sch.; Trinity Coll., Cambridge (MA). MB, BChir Cantab. UCH, 1951; National Service, RAMC, 1952-54; Univ. of Cambridge: G. H. Lewes Student, Physiol Lab., 1954; Univ. Demonstr, 1956; Fellow, Corpus Christi Coll., 1956; Univ. Lectr, 1961; Reader in Exptl Biophysics, 1968; Fellow of Churchill Coll., 1961-81. Trustee, British Museum, 1979-. Docteur *hc* Poitiers, 1975. *Publications:* articles in Jl of Physiol. *Recreations:* sailing, skiing. *Address:* The Master's Lodge, Pembroke College, Cambridge CB2 1RF. *T:* Cambridge 352241; Umgeni, Cley, Holt, Norfolk.

ADRIEN, Sir J. F. M. L.; *see* Latour-Adrien.

ADSHEAD, Mary; engaged on painting a series of house portraits; *m* 1929, Stephen Bone (*d* 1958). Trained at Slade School under Prof. Henry Tonks. Mural paintings in public and private buildings; illustrations, designs for GPO stamps. Chief works: murals in: Restaurant at Luton Hoo; St Peter's Church, Vauxhall Estate, Luton; Civic Centre, Plymouth; Town Hall, Totnes; Commonwealth Inst.; Messrs Costain & Sons; The Post House, Leicester.

AGA KHAN (IV), His Highness Prince Karim, granted title His Highness by the Queen, 1957, granted title His Royal Highness by the Shah of Iran, 1959; *b* 13 Dec. 1936; *s* of late Prince Aly Salomon Khan, and of Princess Joan Aly Khan (marr. diss. 1949) (*née* Hon. Joan Barbara Yarde-Buller, *e d* of 3rd Baron Churston, MVO, OBE); became Aga Khan, spiritual leader and Imam of Ismaili Muslims all over the world, on the death of his grandfather, Sir Sultan Mohamed Shah, Aga Khan III, GCSI, GCIE, GCVO, 11 July 1957; *m* 1969, Sarah Frances Crichton-Stuart, *o d* of Lt-Col A. E. Croker Poole; two *s* one *d*. *Educ:* Le Rosey, Switzerland; Harvard University (BA Hons). Leading owner and breeder of race horses in UK, 1981; won 1981 Derby (Shergar), 1982 Prix de l'Arc de Triomphe (Akiyda). Commander, Ordre du Mérite Mauritanien, 1960; Grand Croix de l'Ordre National de la Côte d'Ivoire, 1965; de la Haute-Volta, 1965; Malgache, 1966; Grand Croix de l'Ordre du Croissant Vert des Comores, 1966; Grand Cordon de l'Ordre du Tadj de l'Empire d'Iran, 1967; Nishan-I-Imtiaz, Pakistan, 1970; Cavaliere di

Gran Croce della Republica Italiana, 1977; Doctor of Laws (*hc*): Peshawar Univ., Pakistan, 1967; Sind Univ., Pakistan, 1970. *Recreations:* tennis, ski-ing. *Address:* Aiglemont, 60270 Gouvieux, France.

AGA KHAN, Prince Sadruddin; United Nations High Commissioner for Refugees, 1965-77; Founding Member and President, Groupe de Bellerive; Consultant to the Secretary-General of the UN, 1978; *b* 17 Jan. 1933; *s* of His late Highness Sir Sultan Mohamed Shah, Aga Khan III, GCSI, GCIE, GCVO and of Andrée Joséphine Caron; *m* 1957, Nina Sheila Dyer (marr. diss., 1962); *m* 1972, Catherine Aleya Sursock. *Educ:* Harvard Univ. (BA); Harvard Grad. Sch. Arts and Sciences; Centre of Middle Eastern Studies. Unesco Consultant for Afro-Asian Projects, 1958; Head of Mission and Adviser to UN High Comr for Refugees, 1959-60; Unesco Special Consultant to Dir-Gen., 1961; Exec. Sec., Internat. Action Cttee for Preservation of Nubian Monuments, 1961; UN Dep. High Comr for Refugees, 1962-65. Mem., World Wildlife Fund. Hon. Citizen Geneva, 1978. UN Human Rights Award, 1978; Hammarsköld Medal, German UN Assoc., 1979. Grand Cross: Order of St Silvestro (Papal), 1963; Order of Homayoun (Iran), 1967; Order of the Royal Star of Great Comoro (Comoro Is), 1970; Order of the Two Niles (First Class) Sudan, 1973; Commander's Cross with Star, Order of Merit of Polish People's Republic, 1977; Commandeur de la Légion d'Honneur (France), 1979. *Publications:* Lectures on refugee problems delivered to RSA and Acad. Internat. Law, The Hague. *Recreations:* Islamic art, sailing, ski-ing, photography, travel. *Address:* Château de Bellerive, 1245 Collonge-Bellerive, Canton of Geneva, Switzerland. *Clubs:* Travellers' (Paris); Knickerbocker (New York).

AGAR, family name of **Earl of Normanton.**

AGER, Rear-Adm. Kenneth Gordon, CB 1977; retired Royal Navy 1977; *b* 22 May 1920; *s* of Harold Stoddart Ager and Nellie Maud (*née* Tate); *m* 1944, Muriel Lydia Lanham; one *s* one *d*. *Educ:* Dulwich Central Sch. and Royal Navy. Called up for War Service, RN, 1940; Sub Lt (Special Br.) RNVR, 1943; Lieut (Electrical) RN, 1944; Weapons and Elect. Engr; Comdr (WE) 1958; Captain (E) 1966; Fleet Weapons and Elect. Engr Officer, 1969-71; Sen. Officers' War Course, 1971-72; CSO (Eng) to Flag Off. Scotland and NI, and Captain Fleet Maintenance, Rosyth, 1972-75; Rear-Adm. (E) 1975; Flag Off., Admiralty Interview Bd, 1975-77. *Recreations:* golf, reading. *Address:* South View, Washington Road, Storrington, West Sussex RH20 4DE. *Club:* Royal Naval and Royal Albert Yacht (Portsmouth).

AGHNIDES, Thanassis; Chairman Advisory Committee on Administrative and Budgetary Questions of UNO, 1946-64; *b* Nigdé, Asia Minor, 1889; *s* of Prodromos and Anastasia Aghnides. *Educ:* Superior National Greek Coll., Phanar, Istanbul; Anatolia Coll. (Asia Minor); Univ. of Istanbul; University of Paris. Directed Greek Press Bureau at Greek Legation, London, 1918-19; worked for League of Nations, 1919-42; Dir of Disarmament Section, 1930, and Under Secretary-General of the League, 1939; Secretary of Disarmament Conference, 1932-34; Secretary-General Montreux Conference concerning the Straits, May 1936; Secretary-General Conference for the suppression of Egyptian Capitulations, 1937; Secretary-General Nyon Conference for the suppression of piracy in the Mediterranean, 1937; Permanent Under-Secretary for Foreign Affairs in Greek Cabinet, 1942-43; Greek Ambassador to the Court of St James's, 1942-47; Greek Delegate to San Francisco Conference on International Organisation, 1945; Chief Delegate for General on Preparatory Commission of UNO; Chm. 6th Committee, on organisation of UNO Secretariat, Dec. 1945; Delegate to the 1st Assembly of UNO; Rapporteur of its 5th Cttee (on organisation), Jan. 1946; rep. Greece on Security Council when it dealt with question of presence of British troops in Greece, 1-6 Feb. 1946; Chairman Greek Deleg. to Gen. Assembly of UNO, Oct.-Dec. 1946; Chm. Cttee on Admin of UNESCO, Feb.-April 1948. Member Curatorium Acad. of Internat. Law of The Hague, 1948-68. *Recreation:* music. *Address:* 3 Avenue Bertrand, Geneva, Switzerland. *T:* 463602. *Club:* Brooks's.

AGLEN, Anthony John, CB 1957; FRSE; Her Majesty's Government special representative on international fisheries questions, since 1972; *b* 30 May 1911; 2nd *s* of late Sir Francis A. Aglen, GCMG, KBE, Alyth, Perthshire; *m* 1946, Audrey Louise Murray, *o d* of late Andrew E. Murray, WS, Edinburgh; one *s* one *d*. *Educ:* Marlborough; Trinity Coll., Cambridge (Scholar). First Class Mathematical Tripos, Part I, 1931, and Part II 1933, BA 1933. Entered Civil Service (Scottish Office), 1934; Private Secretary to successive Secretaries of State for Scotland, 1939-41; Assistant Secretary, Scottish Home Dept, 1942; Under-Sec., 1953; Dep. Sec., 1956-60; Jt Dep. Sec., Dept of Agric. and Fisheries for Scotland, 1960-71, also Fisheries Sec. for Scotland, 1946-71. President, North East Atlantic Fisheries Commission, 1963-66. *Recreations:* gardening, fishing. *Address:* Birkhill, Earlston, Berwickshire. *T:* Earlston 307. *Club:* New (Edinburgh).

AGLIONBY, Francis John; His Honour Judge Aglionby; a Circuit Judge, since 1980; *b* 17 May 1932; *s* of Francis Basil and Marjorie Wycliffe Aglionby; *m* 1967, Susan Victoria Mary Vaughan; one *s* one *d*. *Educ:* Charterhouse; Corpus Christi Coll., Oxford (MA). Barrister, Inner Temple, 1956, Bencher, 1976; a Recorder of the Crown Court, 1975-80. Chancellor of Diocese of Birmingham, 1971-; also of Portsmouth, 1978-. Held Home Office enquiry into Horserace Totalisator Bd's bets transmissions procedures, 1979. *Recreations:* variable. *Address:* 36 Bark Place, W2 4AT. *T:* 01-229 7303. *Club:* Brooks's.

GNELLI, Dr Giovanni; industrialist; car manufacturer, Italy; Chairman: Fiat, since 1966; Istituto Finanziario Industriale, since 1959; IFI International, Luxembourg; Agnelli Foundation, since 1968; *b* Turin, Italy, 12 March 1921; *s* of Edoardo Agnelli, and *g s* of Giovanni Agnelli, founder of Fabbrica Italiana Automobili Torino (FIAT); *m* 1953, Princess Marella Caracciolo di Castagneto; one *s* one *d. Educ:* Turin. DrJur, Univ. of Turin, 1943. Member Board: SKF, Göteborg; Eurafrance, Paris; Mediobanca; Credito Italiano; Assonime; Unione Industriale di Torino; Member: Internat. Adv. Cttee, Chase Manhattan Bank, NY; Internat. Indust. Conf., San Francisco. Member: Exec. Cttee, Trilateral Commn, Paris; Groupe des Présidents des Grandes Entreprises Européennes, Bruxelles. Governor, Atlantic Inst. for Internat. Affairs, Paris. Mayor, Villar Perosa, 1945-80. *Address:* 10 Corso Marconi, Turin, Italy. *T:* 65651.

GNEW, Sir Anthony Stuart; *see* Agnew, Sir J. A. S.

GNEW OF LOCHNAW, Sir Crispin Hamlyn, 11th Bt *cr* 1629; Chief of the Name and Arms of Agnew; Advocate; Unicorn Pursuivant to Lord Lyon King of Arms, since 1981; *b* 13 May 1944; *s* of (Sir) Fulque Melville Gerald Noel Agnew, 10th Bt and of Swanzie, *d* of late Major Esmé Nourse Erskine, CMG, MC; *S* father, 1975; *m* 1980, Susan, *yr d* of J. W. Strang Steel, Logie, Kirriemuir, Angus. *Educ:* Uppingham; RMA, Sandhurst. Leader: Army Expedn to E Greenland, 1968; Jt Services Expedn to Chilean Patagonia, 1972-73; Army Expedn to Api, NW Nepal, 1980; Major RARO (retired 1981), late Royal Highland Fusiliers; Slains Pursuivant of Arms to the Lord High Constable of Scotland, 1978-81. Member: RN Expedn to E Greenland, 1966; Jt Services to Elephant Island (Antarctica), 1970-71; Army Nuptse Expedn, 1975; Jt British and Royal Nepalese Army Everest Expedn, 1976 (reached the South Col). Mem. Cttee, Heraldry Soc. of Scotland, 1978- (Chm., 1981-). *Publications:* articles in Scotsman, Sunday Standard and other magazines, and in legal and heraldic jls. *Recreations:* mountaineering, sailing (Yacht Oran na Mara), heraldry. *Heir:* cousin Andrew David Quentin Agnew, PhD [*b* 31 Dec. 1929; *m* 1957, Shirley, *d* of late James Arnold Smithson; three *s*]. *Address:* 6 Palmerston Road, Edinburgh EH9 1TN. *Clubs:* Alpine, Alpine Ski.

GNEW, Sir Geoffrey (William Gerald), Kt 1973; Chairman, Thos Agnew & Sons, Ltd (Fine Art Dealers), 1965-82; *b* 11 July 1908; *er s* of late Charles Gerald Agnew and Olive May (*née* Danks); *m* 1934, Hon. Doreen Maud Jessel, *y d* of 1st Baron Jessel, CB, CMG; two *s* one *d. Educ:* Eton (Oppidan Scholar, 1923; Hon. Fellow, 1976); Trinity College, Cambridge (BA 1930; MA 1971); Munich. Joined Thos Agnew & Sons (Fine Art Dealers), 1931, a Managing Director, 1937-. Assistant master (History), Eton College, 1939-45. Chairman, Evelyn (Agnew) Nursing Home, Cambridge, 1955-81, Pres., 1981-. A Permanent Steward, 1955- and a Vice-Pres., 1968-, Artists' General Benevolent Institution; President, Fine Art Provident Institution, 1963-66; Chairman: St George's Arts Trust, King's Lynn, 1966-73; Society of London Art Dealers, 1970-74; Friends of the Courtauld Institute, 1970-; Vice-Pres., Guildhall of St George, King's Lynn, 1975-. *Publications:* Agnew's 1817-1967, 1967; various broadcasts on art published in the Listener. *Recreations:* works of art, travel, gardening. *Address:* Flat 3, 6 Onslow Square, SW7. *T:* 01-589 8536; Egmere Farm House, Walsingham, Norfolk. *T:* Walsingham 247. *Clubs:* Brooks's, Garrick.

GNEW, Sir Godfrey; *see* Agnew, Sir W. G.

GNEW, Sir (John) Anthony Stuart, 4th Bt, *cr* 1895; *b* 25 July 1914; *s* of Sir John Stuart Agnew, 3rd Bt, TD, DL, and Kathleen (*d* 1971), *d* of late I. W. H. White, Leeds; *S* father, 1957. *Educ:* privately in Switzerland. *Heir:* *b* Major George Keith Agnew, TD [*b* 25 Nov. 1918; *m* 1948, Anne Merete Louise, *yr d* of Baron Johann Schaffalitzky de Muckadell, Fyn, Denmark; two *s*]. *Address:* c/o Blackthorpe Farm, Rougham, Bury St Edmunds, Suffolk.

GNEW, Commander Sir Peter (Garnett), 1st Bt *cr* 1957; *b* 1900; *s* of late C. L. Agnew; *m* 1928, Enid Frances, *d* of late Henry Boan, Perth, Western Australia, and widow of Lt Col O. Marescaux; one *s. Educ:* Repton. Entered Royal Navy, 1918; ADC to Governor of Jamaica, 1927-28; retired, 1931; returned to service at sea, Aug. 1939 (despatches). MP (C) Camborne Div. of Cornwall, 1931-50; PPS to Rt Hon. Walter Runciman, President of Board of Trade, 1935-37, and to Rt Hon. Sir Philip Sassoon, First Commissioner of Works, 1937-39; an Assistant Government Whip, May-July, 1945; a Conservative Whip, Aug. 1945-Feb. 1950; contested (C) Falmouth and Camborne Div., Feb. 1950; MP (C) South Worcs, 1955-66. Member of House of Laity Church Assembly, 1935-65; a Church Comr for England, 1948-68; Trustee, Historic Churches Preservation Trust, 1968-. Chm., Iran Society, 1966-73; Internat. Pres., European Centre of Documentation and Information, 1974-76. Order of Homayoun (Iran), 1973; Kt Grand Cross, Order of Civil Merit (Spain), 1977. *Recreation:* travelling. *Heir:* *s* Quentin Charles Agnew-Somerville [*b* 8 March 1929; *m* 1963, Hon. April, *y d* of 15th Baron Strange; one *s* two *d. Educ:* RNC Dartmouth]. *Address:* 2 Smith Square, SW1P 3HS. *T:* 01-222 7179. *Clubs:* Carlton, Buck's.

GNEW, Peter Graeme, MBE 1946; BA; Deputy Chairman, Bradbury Agnew & Co. Ltd (Proprietors of Punch), since 1969; *b* 7 April 1914; *s* of late Alan Graeme Agnew; *m* 1937, Mary Diana (*née* Hervey); two *s* two *d. Educ:* Kingsmead, Seaford; Stowe School; Trinity College, Cambridge. Student Printer, 1935-37. Joined Bradbury Agnew & Co. Ltd, 1937. RAFVR

1937. Served War of 1939-45; Demobilised, 1945, as Wing Commander. *Recreations:* sailing, gardening. *Address:* Roscaddon, Manaccan, near Helston, Cornwall TR12 6JH. *T:* Manaccan 223.

AGNEW, Rudolph Ion Joseph; Chairman, since 1983, and Group Chief Executive, since 1978, Consolidated Gold Fields PLC; *b* 12 March 1934; *s* of Rudolph John Agnew and Pamela Geraldine (*née* Campbell); *m* 1980, Whitney Warren. *Educ:* Downside School. Commissioned officer, 8th King's Royal Irish Hussars, 1953-57. Joined Consolidated Gold Fields, 1957; Dep. Chm., 1978-82. FBIM; Fellow of the Game Conservancy. *Recreation:* shooting. *Address:* 49 Moorgate, EC2R 6BQ. *Club:* Cavalry and Guards.

AGNEW, Spiro Theodore, (Ted); *b* Baltimore, Md, 9 Nov. 1918; *s* of Theodore S. Agnew and Margaret Akers; *m* 1942, Elinor Isabel Judefind; one *s* three *d. Educ:* Forest Park High Sch., Baltimore; Johns Hopkins Univ.; Law Sch., Univ. Baltimore (LLB). Served War of 1939-45 with 8th and 10th Armd Divs, 1941-46, company combat comdr in France and Germany (Bronze Star). Apptd to Zoning Bd of Appeals of Baltimore County, 1957 (Chm., 1958-61); County Executive, Baltimore County, 1962-66; Governor of Maryland, 1967-68; Vice-President of the United States, 1969-73. Republican. With Pathlite Inc., Crofton, Md, 1974-. *Publication:* The Canfield Decision, 1976. *Recreations:* golf, tennis. *Address:* c/o Playboy Press, 919 North Michigan Avenue, Chicago, Ill 60611, USA. *Club:* Whitemarsh Tennis and Recreation Center (Bourie, Md).

AGNEW, Stanley Clarke, CEng, FICE; Chief Engineer, Scottish Development Department, since 1976; *b* 18 May 1926; *s* of Christopher Gerald Agnew and Margaret Eleanor Agnew (*née* Clarke); *m* 1950, Isbell Evelyn Parker (*née* Davidson); two *d. Educ:* Royal Belfast Academical Instn; Queen's Univ., Belfast (BSc Civil Eng., 1947). FIWE, FIPHE; Hon. FIWPC. Site Engr, Farrans Ltd, 1947-50; Asst Engr, Fife CC, 1950-52; Site Agent, R. J. McLeod (Contractors) Ltd, 1952-53; Sen. Asst Engr, Dumfries CC, 1953-57; Resident Engr, Blyth & Blyth, 1957-59; Engr to Dungannon and Clogher RDCs, 1959-62; Eng. Inspector, Scottish Develt Dept, 1962-68, Dep. Chief Engr, 1968-75. *Recreations:* golf, photography, motoring, gardening. *Address:* Duncraig, 52 Blinkbonny Road, Edinburgh EH4 3HX. *T:* 031-332 4072. *Clubs:* Royal Commonwealth Society; Murrayfield Golf (Edinburgh).

AGNEW, Sir (William) Godfrey, KCVO 1965 (CVO 1953); CB 1975; Chairman, Lady Clare Ltd, since 1970; Director: Sun Life Assurance Society Ltd, since 1974; Sun Life Properties Ltd, since 1980; *b* 11 Oct. 1913; *o s* of late Lennox Edelsten Agnew and Elsie Blyth (*née* Nott), Tunbridge Wells; *m* 1st, 1939, Ruth Mary (*d* 1962), *e d* of late Charles J. H. O'H. Moore, CVO, MC, and late Lady Dorothie Moore; three *s* three *d*; 2nd, 1965, Lady (Nancy Veronica) Tyrwhitt, *widow* of Adm. Sir St John Reginald Joseph Tyrwhitt, 2nd Bt, KCB, DSO, DSC; two step *s* one step *d. Educ:* Tonbridge. Solicitor, 1935; entered Public Trustee Office, 1936. Served RA and Surrey and Sussex Yeomanry, 1939-46; Major, 1945. Senior Clerk, Privy Council Office, 1946-51; Clerk of the Privy Council, 1953-74 (Deputy Clerk, 1951-53); Dep. Sec., Cabinet Office, 1972-74. Director: Seaway Shipping Agencies Ltd, 1971-80; Seaway Holdings Ltd, 1971-80; Artagen Properties Ltd, 1976-80; Consultant, CEI, 1974-79. Chairman, Sembal Trust, 1967-73. Mem., Bd of Hon. Tutors, Council of Legal Educn, Univ. of WI, 1973-. Hon. FIMechE, 1968; Hon. FIMunE, 1974; Hon. FCIBS, 1975. *Address:* Pinehurst, South Ascot, Berks. *T:* Ascot 20036. *Clubs:* Army and Navy; Swinley Forest Golf; Littlestone-on-Sea Golf; Rye Golf.

See also Sir J. M. H. Pollen, Bt, Sir Reginald Tyrwhitt, Bt.

AGRA, Archbishop of, (RC), since 1956; Most Rev. Dominic Romuald Athaide, DD; OFMCap; *b* Bandra, India, 7 Feb. 1909. *Educ:* Holland; France; Pontifical Gregorian University, Rome. Priest, 1932. Lecturer in Philosophy and Theology, Quilon, India, 1937. Missionary, Aden, 1940; subsequently Director of St Joseph's High School, and Parish Priest, Aden. Member Order of Friars Minor (Capuchins). Member: Standing Cttee, Catholic Bishops' Conf. of India; CBCI Commn for Dialogue with other faiths. *Address:* Cathedral House, Wazirpura Road, Agra 282003, UP, India. *T:* 7-24-07. *TA:* Cathedral.

AH-CHUEN, Sir Moi Lin Jean (Etienne), Kt 1980; Minister of Local Government, Mauritius, 1969-76; Chairman: Chue Wing & Co. Ltd, since 1977; Oceania Travel Agents Ltd, since 1977; The Mauritius Union Assurance Co. Ltd, since 1977; *b* 22 Feb. 1911; *s* of Jean Georges Ah-Chuen and Li Choi; *m* 1929, Jeanne Hau Man Mui; five *s* six *d. Educ:* De La Salle School; Chinese High Sch., Mauritius. Mem., Mauritius Legislative Assembly, 1948-76. Member: Delegn of Mauritius Govt to UN, 1974, 1976; Commonwealth Parly Assoc., Mauritius Br., 1948-. Founder (Chm. and Man. Dir), ABC Store (Chue Wing & Co. Ltd), 1931-68; Dir, Chinese Daily News, 1942-. Alternately Pres. and Vice-Pres., Chinese Chamber of Commerce, 1942-64; a Founder Mem. and Vice-Chm., Mauritius Union Assurance Co. Ltd, 1948-; a Founder Mem., 1955 and alternately Pres. and Vice-Pres., 1955-68, Associated Traders (Import and Export) Co. Ltd. Pres., Chinese Cultural Centre, 1968-; mem. or past-mem., various other social and charitable organisations. *Recreations:* reading, bridge, travelling, TV and cinema, theatre, concerts, sports. *Address:* 5 Reverend Lebrun Street, Rose Hill, Mauritius. *T:* 4-3804. *Clubs:* Mauritius Turf, Chinese Traders (Mauritius).

AHERN, Most Rev. John; *see* Cloyne, Bishop of, (RC).

AHMAD, Khurshid; Chairman, Institute of Policy Studies, Islamabad, Pakistan, since 1979; Chairman, Board of Trustees, Islamic Foundation, Leicester; *b* 23 March 1934; three *s* two *d. Educ:* Karachi Univ. (LLB; MA Economics; MA Islamic Studies); Leicester Univ. Dir-Gen., Islamic Foundn, 1973-78; Federal Minister for Planning and Devel and Dep. Chm., Planning Commn, Govt of Pakistan, 1978-79. *Publications:* Essays on Pakistan Economy, (Karachi) 1958; An Analysis of Munir Report, (Lahore) 1958; ed, Studies in the Family Law of Islam, (Karachi) 1960; ed, The Quran: an Introduction, (Karachi) 1966; The Prophet of Islam, (Karachi) 1967; Principles of Islamic Education, (Lahore) 1970; Fanaticism, Intolerance and Islam, (Lahore) 1970; Islam and the West, (Lahore) 1972; The Religion of Islam, (Lahore) 1973; Islam: Basic Principles and Characteristics, (Leicester, Islamic Foundn) 1974; Family Life in Islam, (Leicester, Islamic Foundn) 1974; ed, Islam: Its Meaning and Message, (London, Islamic Council of Europe) 1976; Islamic Perspectives: Studies in honour of Maulana Mawdudi, (Islamic Foundn) 1979; The Quran: Basic Teachings, (Islamic Foundn) 1979; contrib. The Third World's Dilemma of Development, Non-Aligned Third World Annual, (USA) 1970. *Recreations:* travelling, reading. *Address:* 1 Croft Drive, Wigston, Leicester LE8 1HD. *T:* Leicester 886422; Institute of Policy Studies, House No 3, Street No 56, Shalimar 6/4, Islamabad, Pakistan.

AICKIN, Hon. Sir Keith Arthur, KBE 1976; **Hon. Mr Justice Aickin;** Justice of High Court of Australia, since 1976; *b* Melbourne, 1 Feb. 1916; *s* of J. L. Aickin, Belfast, Ireland; *m* 1952, Elizabeth May, *d* of S. W. Gullett; one *s* one *d. Educ:* Church of England Grammar Sch., Melbourne; Univ. of Melbourne (LLM). Associate to Justice Dixon, High Court of Aust., 1939-41; Third Sec., Aust. Legation, Washington, DC, 1942-44; Legal Adviser, European Regional Office, UNRRA, 1944-48; in Legal Dept, UN, NY, 1948; Melbourne Bar, 1949-76. QC Vic 1957, Tas. 1959, NSW 1967. Mem., Interim Council, La Trobe Univ., 1966, Council, 1967-73. Director: Mayne Nickless Ltd, 1958-76; P&O Aust Ltd, 1969-76; Comalco Ltd, 1970-76; BHP Co. Ltd, 1971-76. *Address:* High Court of Australia, Canberra, ACT, Australia; 41 Marne Street, South Yarra, Vic. 3141, Australia. *Clubs:* Melbourne, Australian (Melbourne); Frankston Golf.

AIERS, David Pascoe, CMG 1971; HM Diplomatic Service, retired; High Commissioner in Malta, 1979-82; *b* 19 Sept. 1922; *s* of late George Aiers and Sarah Adshead; *m* 1948, Pauleen Victoria Brittain-Jones; one *s* one *d. Educ:* Stationers' Company's Sch.; Trinity Coll., Oxford. Royal Artillery, 1942-46; Third Sec., Warsaw, 1946-48; FO, 1948; Second Sec., Copenhagen, 1951-53, Buenos Aires, 1953-55; FO, 1955; First Sec. (Commercial), Manila, 1958-62; First Sec. and Head of Chancery, Ankara, 1962-65; Counsellor and Head of Chancery, Political Adviser's Office, Singapore, 1965-68; Head of SW Pacific Dept, FCO, 1968-71; Minister, Canberra, 1971-75; High Comr to Sri Lanka, and Ambassador to the Republic of Maldives, 1976-79. *Address:* c/o Barclays Bank Ltd, 230 Kentish Town Road, NW5. *Clubs:* Royal Automobile, Royal Commonwealth Society.

AIKEN, Frank; Member, Dáil Eireann for County Louth, 1923-73; Tánaiste (Deputy Prime Minister) in the Government of Ireland, 1965-69; *b* Camlough, Co. Armagh, 13 Feb. 1898; *y s* of James Aiken and Mary McGeeny; *m* 1934, Maud Davin; two *s* one *d. Educ:* Christian Brothers' Secondary Schools, Newry. Joined Irish Volunteers, 1913; Captain, Camlough Co., IRA, 1918; Comdt, Camlough Bn, IRA, 1919; Vice-Brig., Newry Bde, IRA, 1920; Comdt, 4th Northern Div., IRA, 1921; Chief of Staff, IRA, 1923. Secretary, Camlough Br., Gaelic League, 1914; Secretary, Sinn Fein Organisation, S Armagh, 1917. Military Service Medal (with Bar). Local and CCs, 1920. Minister for: Defence, Ireland, 1932-39; Lands and Fisheries, June-Nov. 1936; Co-ordination of Defensive Measures, 1939-45; Finance, 1945-48; External Affairs, 1951-54 and 1957-69; Agriculture, March-May 1957. Leader, Irish Delegn to Council of Europe, 1969. Hon. LLD: NUI; St John's Univ., Jamaica, New York; Dublin Univ. Military Service Medal with Bar. Grand Cross: Pian Order; Order of Merit of Federal Republic of Germany; Belgian Order of Crown. Grand Officer with plaque, Order of St Charles. *Address:* Dúngaoithe, Sandyford, Co. Dublin.

AIKEN, Joan Delano, (Mrs Julius Goldstein); writer of historical, mystery and children's novels, plays and poetry; *b* 4 Sept. 1924; *d* of Conrad Potter Aiken and Jessie McDonald; *m* 1st, 1945, Ronald George Brown (*d* 1955); one *s* one *d*; 2nd, 1976, Julius Goldstein. *Educ:* Wychwood Sch., Oxford. Inf. Officer, subseq. Librarian, UN London Inf. Centre, 1943-49; Features Editor, Argosy magazine, 1955-60; Copy-writer, J. Walter Thompson London office, 1960-61; time thereafter devoted to writing. Mem., Soc. of Authors. Guardian Award for Children's Literature, 1969; Lewis Carroll Award, 1970. *Publications:* (most also published in USA and as paperbacks): The Silence of Herondale, 1964; The Fortune Hunters, 1965; Trouble with Product X, 1966 (Beware of the Bouquet, USA 1966); Hate Begins at Home, 1967 (Dark Interval, USA 1967); The Ribs of Death, 1967 (The Crystal Crow, USA 1968); The Windscreen Weepers (stories), 1969; The Embroidered Sunset, 1970; The Butterfly Picnic, 1970 (A Cluster of Separate Sparks, USA 1972); Died on a Rainy Sunday, 1972; Voices in an Empty House, 1975; Castle Barebane, 1976; Last Movement, 1977; The Five-Minute Marriage, 1977; The Smile of the Stranger, 1978; A Touch of Chill (horror stories), 1979; The Lightning Tree, 1980 (The Weeping Ash, USA); The Girl from Paris, 1982; The Way to Write for Children, 1982; A Whisper in the Night, 1982; *for children:* (many also published in USA): All You've Ever Wanted (stories), 1953; More Than You Bargained For (stories), 1955; The Kingdom and the Cave, 1960; The Wolves of Willoughby Chase, 1962; Black Hearts in Battersea, 1964; Night Birds on Nantucket, 1966; The Whispering Mountai 1968; A Necklace of Raindrops (stories), 1968; A Small Pinch of Weath (stories), 1969; Night Fall, 1969; Armitage, Armitage, Fly Away Hor (stories), USA 1970; Smoke From Cromwell's Time, USA 1970; The Cuck Tree, 1971; The Kingdom Under the Sea (folktales), 1971; The Green Fla (fantasy and horror stories), USA 1971; A Harp of Fishbones (stories), 197 Winterthing (play), USA 1972; The Mooncusser's Daughter (play), US 1973; Winterthing & The Mooncusser's Daughter, 1973; Midnight is a Plac 1974; Arabel's Raven, USA 1974; Tales of Arabel's Raven, 1974; Not Wh You Expected (stories), USA 1974; Tale of a One-Way Street (stories), 197 The Skin Spinners (poems), USA 1976; A Bundle of Nerves (horror storie 1976; The Angel Inn (trans. from French), 1976; The Faithless Lollybi (stories), 1977; Mice and Mendelson, 1978; Go Saddle the Sea, 1978; Stre (play), USA 1978; Arabel and Mortimer, 1979; The Shadow Guests, 1980; T Stolen Lake, 1981. *Recreations:* listening to music, looking at art, trave reading, gardening, walking, talking to friends. *Address:* The Hermitage, Ea Street, Petworth, West Sussex GU28 0AB. *T:* Petworth 42279. *Clul* Writers' Guild, Crime Writers' Association, PEN; Mystery Writers America.

AIKEN, Air Chief Marshal Sir John (Alexander Carlisle), KCB 1973 (C 1967); Director General of Intelligence, Ministry of Defence, 1978-81; *b* Dec. 1921; *s* of Thomas Leonard and Margaret Aiken; *m* 1948, Pamela Ja (*née* Bartlett); one *s* one *d. Educ:* Birkenhead School. Joined RAF, 194 Fighter Sqdns, Europe and Far East, 1942-45; Fighter Comd, 1946-47; CF 1948; Staff of RAF Coll., Cranwell, 1948-50; OC Univ. of Birmingham Ai Sqdn, 1950-52; Staff Coll., 1953; HQ Fighter Comd, 1954-55; OC 29 Fighte Sqdn, 1956-57; jssc 1958; Headquarters AF North, 1958-60; Air Min., 1960-6 Station Comdr, RAF Finningley, 1963-64; Air Cdre Intelligence, Min. o Defence, 1965-67; idc 1968; Dep. Comdr, RAF, Germany, 1969-71; Dir-Ger Training, RAF, 1971-72; Head of Economy Project Team (RAF), 1972-7 AOC-in-C, NEAF, Comdr British Forces Near East, and Administrato Sovereign Base Areas, Cyprus, 1973-76; Air Member for Personnel, 1976-7 *Recreations:* ski-ing, music. *Club:* Royal Air Force.

AIKMAN, Colin Campbell, PhD; Director, New Zealand Institute o International Affairs, since 1979; *b* 24 Feb. 1919; *s* of Colin Campbell Aikma and Bertha Egmont Aikman (*née* Harwood); *m* 1952, Betty Alicia, *d* of F Y. James; three *d* (one *s* decd). *Educ:* Palmerston North Boys' High Sch Victoria University Coll., Wellington, NZ (LLM); London Sch. o Economics (PhD). Law Clerk in Legal Offices, 1935-41; Barrister an Solicitor of Supreme Court of New Zealand, 1940-41; Personal Asst to A Secretary, Air Dept (NZ), 1942-43; Prime Minister's Dept and Dept o External Affairs (Legal Adviser, 1949-55), 1943-55; Mem. NZ Delgn to Sa Francisco Conf., 1945; Prof. of Jurisprudence and Constitutional Law Victoria Univ. of Wellington (Dean of Law Faculty, 1957-59, 1962-67 1955-68; Mem. Council, NZ Inst. of Internat. Affairs (Nat. Pres., 1960-63 1955-; Advr to NZ Govt on Constitutional Develt of Cook Is, Wester Samoa and Niue, 1956-68, 1975; Vice-Chancellor, The Univ. of the Sout Pacific, Suva, Fiji, 1968-74; NZ High Comr to India, accredited also t Bangladesh and Nepal, 1975-78. Member: Council of Volunteer Servic Abroad (Inc.) (Chm. 1962-65), 1962-68; NZ Nat. Commn for UNESCC 1957-65; Univ. of Waikato Academic Cttee, Council and Professorial Bc 1963-66; (Chm.) Nat. Adv. Council on Teacher Trng, 1963-68; Law Revisio Commn and Public and Administrative Law Reform Cttee, 1966-68; Adv Cttee on External Aid and Develt, 1980-. Trustee, Norman Kirk Meml Trus 1979-. Queen's Silver Jubilee Medal. *Publications:* (co-author): A Report t Members of the Legislative Assembly of the Cook Islands on Constitutiona Development, 1963; New Zealand, The Development of its Laws an Constitution (ed Robson), 1967 (2nd edn); New Zealand's Record in th Pacific Islands in the Twentieth Century (ed Angus Ross), 1969; contribs t NZ Internat. Review. *Recreations:* golf, cricket, carpentry. *Address:* 2 Korokoro Road, Petone, New Zealand. *Clubs:* Wellington; Wellington Gol (Heretaunga).

AILESBURY, 8th Marquess of, *cr* 1821; **Michael Sydney Cedric Brudenell Bruce;** Bt 1611; Baron Brudenell 1628; Earl of Cardigan 1661; Baron Bruc 1746; Earl of Ailesbury 1776; Earl Bruce 1821; Viscount Savernake 1821; 30t Hereditary Warden of Savernake Forest; Lt RHG, 1946; Member Londo Stock Exchange since 1954; *b* 31 March 1926; *e s* of 7th Marquess of Ailesbur and Joan (*d* 1937), *d* of Stephen Salter, Ryde, Isle of Wight; *S* father, 1974 *m* 1st, 1952, Edwina Sylvia de Winton (from whom he obtained a divorce 1961), *yr d* of Lt-Col Sir (Ernest) Edward de Winton Wills, 4th Bt, *qv* ; one *s* two *d*; 2nd, 1963, Juliet Adrienne (marr. diss. 1974), *d* of late Hilar Lethbridge Kingsford and of Mrs Latham Hobrow, Hove; two *d* ; 3rd, 1974 Mrs Caroline Elizabeth Romilly, *d* of O. F. M. Wethered, RN retd, DL, JP *Educ:* Eton. *Heir: s* Earl of Cardigan, *qv. Address:* Bel Au Vent, St Lawrence Jersey. *Club:* Sloane.

AILSA, 7th Marquess of, *cr* 1831; **Archibald David Kennedy,** OBE 1979 Baron Kennedy, 1452; Earl of Cassillis, 1509; Baron Ailsa (UK), 1806; *b* Dec. 1925; *s* of 6th Marquess of Ailsa and Gertrude Millicent (*d* 1957), *d* o Gervas Weir Cooper, Wordwell Hall, Bury St Edmunds; *S* father 1957; *m* 1954, Mary, 7th *c* of John Burn, Amble; two *s* one *d. Educ:* Nautical Coll. Pangbourne. Scots Guards, 1943-47; Royal Northumberland Fusiliers, 1950 52. National Trust for Scotland, 1953-56. Territorial Army, 1958-68; Hon Col, Ayrshire Battalion ACF, 1980-. Patron, Isle of Man Railway Soc., 1978- Chm., Scottish Assoc. of Boys Clubs, 1978-. *Recreations:* walking, motoring modelling, sailing. *Heir: s* Earl of Cassillis, *qv. Address:* Blanefield, Kirkoswald, Ayrshire KA19 8HH. *Clubs:* Carlton; New (Edinburgh); Royal Yacht Squadron.

ILWYN, 4th Baron *cr* 1921; **Carol Arthur Fellowes**, TD 1946; *b* 23 Nov. 1896; 4th *s* of 1st Baron Ailwyn, PC, KCVO, KBE, 2nd *s* of 1st Baron de Ramsey, and Hon. Agatha Eleanor Augusta Jolliffe, *d* of 2nd Baron Hylton; *S* brother, 1976; *m* 1936, Caroline (Cudemore), *d* of late Maynard Cowan, Victoria, BC; one adopted step *d. Educ:* Royal Naval Colls, Osborne and Dartmouth. Lieut, 3rd and 2nd Norfolk Regt., 1916-19; served in Mesopotamia, 1917-19. Subsequently fruit farmer; Agent to Earl of Strafford, 1930-52. Formed 334 (Barnet) AA Company, RE (T), 1937; served War as Major RA (T) comdg 334 Co. and on staff of Anti-Aircraft Command, 1939-44. Asst Sec., RASE, 1952-59; Sec., Norfolk Club, Norwich, 1964-69; Trustee, Lord Wandsworth Coll., 1955-72; Governor, Felixstowe Coll., 1960-74 (Chm., 1966-72). Late JP Herts and Middlesex. *Heir:* none. *Address:* The Cottage, Gissing, Diss, Norfolk. *T:* Tivetshall 221. *Club:* (Hon. Member) Norfolk (Norwich).

INLEY, Sir (Alfred) John, Kt 1957; MC 1940; Chief Justice, Kenya, 1963-68; retired; Chairman of Industrial Tribunals, 1972-76; *b* 10 May 1906; *o s* of late Rev. A. Ainley, Cockermouth, Cumb; *m* 1935, Mona Sybil Wood (*d* 1981); *s* two *d. Educ:* St Bees Sch.; Corpus Christi, Oxford. Called to Bar, 1928; Magistrate, Gold Coast, 1935; Crown Counsel (Gold Coast), 1936; Puisne Judge, Uganda, 1946-55; Chief Justice of Eastern Region, Nigeria, 1955-59; Combined Judiciary of Sarawak, N Borneo and Brunei, 1959-62. Served War of 1939-45, West African Forces, E Africa and Burma. *Address:* Horrock Wood, Watermillock, Penrith, Cumbria.

INLEY, David Geoffrey, CEng, FIMechE, FRAeS; Deputy Director (Projects and Research), Military Vehicles and Engineering Establishment, Chertsey, since 1978; *b* 5 July 1924; *s* of Cyril Edward and Constance Ainley; *m* 1st, 1948, Dorothy Emily (*née* Roberts); one *s* one *d* ; 2nd, 1959, Diana Margery Hill (*née* Sayles); one *d. Educ:* Brentwood Sch., Essex; Queen Mary Coll., London Univ. (BSc, 1st Cl. Hons). Engine Dept, RAE, Farnborough, 1943-44; Power Jets (R&D) Ltd, 1944-46; National Gas Turbine Estabt, Pyestock, 1946-66; idc 1967; Dir of Engine Develt, MoD (Procurement Exec.), 1968-78. George Stephenson Research Prize, IMechE, 1953. *Publications:* contrib. books and learned jls on gas turbine technology. *Recreations:* golf, listening to music, painting. *Address:* Picket Post, 37 Cedar Road, Farnborough, Hants GU14 7AU. *T:* Farnborough (Hants) 511792.

INLEY, Eric Stephen; Under-Secretary, Department of the Environment (formerly Ministry of Transport), 1968-75; *b* 15 Sept. 1918; *s* of late Captain Eric E. Ainley and Dorothy Ainley (*née* Sharp); *m* 1946, Pamela, *d* of late Mr and Mrs Philip G. Meadows; two *s. Educ:* Giggleswick Sch.; Trinity Coll., Cambridge (BA, Classics and English; MA); Open Univ., 1977- (BA 1981). Served War of 1939-45: RA, RIASC, and Civil Affairs (Malaya), 1940-46. Asst Principal, Min. of Civil Aviation, 1948; Principal, 1950; Civil Air Adviser and Attaché, Singapore and Far East, 1955-58; Asst Sec., Min. of Transport, 1960; seconded as the Traffic Manager, GLC, 1965-67. *Publications:* Mathematical Puzzles, 1978; puzzles and verses in New Scientist, M500, Vox Latina. *Recreations:* mathematics, golf. *Address:* 8 Poynder Place, Hilmarton, near Calne, Wilts. *T:* Hilmarton 650. *Club:* N Wilts Golf.

INLEY, Sir John; *see* Ainley, Sir A. J.

INSCOW, Robert Morrison; Under Secretary and Principal Finance Officer, Overseas Development Administration, Foreign and Commonwealth Office, since 1980; *b* 3 June 1936; *s* of Robert M. Ainscow and Hilda Ainscow (*née* Cleminson); *m* 1965, Faye Bider; one *s* one *d. Educ:* Salford Grammar School; Liverpool Univ. (BA Econ Hons). Statistician: Govt of Rhodesia and Nyasaland, 1957-61; UN Secretariat, New York, 1961-65 and 1966-68; Dept of Economic Affairs, London, 1965-66. Ministry of Overseas Development: Economic Adviser, 1968-70; Senior Economic Adviser, 1971-76; Head, South Asia Dept, 1976-79. Under Secretary, FCO (ODA), 1979. *Address:* 32 Basing Hill, NW11. *T:* 01-455 7343.

INSWORTH, Sir David; *see* Ainsworth, Sir T. D.

INSWORTH, Sir (Thomas) David, 4th Bt *cr* 1916; *b* 22 Aug. 1926; *s* of Sir Thomas Ainsworth, 2nd Bt, and Marie Eleanor (May) (*d* 1969), *d* of Compton Charles Domvile; *S* half-brother, 1981; *m* 1957, Sarah Mary, *d* of late Lt-Col H. C. Walford; two *s* two *d. Educ:* Eton. Formerly Lt 11th Hussars. *Recreations:* shooting, fishing. *Heir: s* Anthony Thomas Hugh Ainsworth, *b* 30 March 1962. *Address:* Ballyneale House, Ballingarry, Co. Limerick; 80 Elm Park Gardens, SW10. *Club:* Cavalry and Guards.

IRD, Captain Alastair (Sturgis), CVO 1977 (MVO 1969); Comptroller to Queen Elizabeth the Queen Mother since 1974; *b* 14 Jan. 1931; *s* of Col Malcolm Aird; *m* 1963, Fiona Violet, MVO 1978, *d* of Lt-Col Ririd Myddelton, *qv. Educ:* Eton; RMA Sandhurst. Commnd 9th Queen's Royal Lancers, 1951; served in BAOR; Adjt 9th Lancers, 1956-59; retd from Army, 1964. Equerry to Queen Elizabeth the Queen Mother, 1960; Asst Private Sec. to the Queen Mother, 1964. *Recreations:* shooting, fishing, golf. *Address:* 31B St James's Palace, SW1A 1BA. *T:* 01-839 6700.

AIRD, Sir (George) John, 4th Bt *cr* 1901; Chairman and Managing Director, Sir John Aird & Co Ltd, since 1969; *b* 30 Jan. 1940; *e s* of Sir John Renton Aird, 3rd Bt, MVO, MC, and of Lady Priscilla Aird, *yr d* of 2nd Earl of Ancaster; *S* father, 1973; *m* 1968, Margaret, *yr d* of Sir John Muir, Bt, *qv* ; one *s* two *d. Educ:* Eton; Oxford Univ.; Harvard Business Sch. MICE. Trainee, Sir Alexander Gibb & Partners, 1961-65; Manager, John Laing & Son Ltd, 1967-69. *Recreations:* farming, hunting. *Heir: s* James John Aird, *b* 12 June 1978. *Address:* Grange Farm, Evenlode, Moreton-in-Marsh, Glos GL56 0NT. *T:* Moreton-in-Marsh 50607. *Club:* White's.

AIRD, Ronald, MC 1942; TD; Secretary Marylebone Cricket Club, 1952-62, retired; *b* 4 May 1902; 2nd *s* of late Malcolm R. Aird; *m* 1925, Viola Mary (*d* 1965), *d* of late Sir Godfrey Baring, Bt; one *d. Educ:* Eton; Clare College, Cambridge. Stock Exchange, 1924-26; Assistant Secretary, MCC, 1926-52; President: MCC, 1968-69; Hampshire CCC, 1971. *Recreations:* cricket, rackets, real tennis, golf, National Hunt racing. *Address:* West Down House, Yapton, West Sussex. *T:* Yapton 551140. *Clubs:* Oriental, MCC.

AIREDALE, 4th Baron, *cr* 1907; **Oliver James Vandeleur Kitson**, Bt, *cr* 1886; Deputy Chairman of Committees, House of Lords, since 1961; Deputy Speaker, House of Lords, since 1962; *b* 22 April 1915; *o s* of 3rd Baron Airedale, DSO, MC, and Sheila Grace (*d* 1935), *d* of late Frank E. Vandeleur, London; *S* father, 1958; unmarried. *Educ:* Eton; Trinity College, Cambridge. Is Major, The Green Howards. Called to the Bar, Inner Temple, 1941. *Heir:* none. *Address:* (seat) Ufford Hall, Stamford, Lincs.

AIREY OF ABINGDON, Baroness *cr* 1979 (Life Peer), of Abingdon in the County of Oxford; **Diana Josceline Barbara Neave Airey**; *b* 7 July 1919; *d* of late Thomas A. W. Giffard, MBE, JP, and late Angela Erskine Giffard (*née* Trollope); *m* 1942, Airey Middleton Sheffield Neave, DSO, OBE, MC (assassinated, March 1979), MP Abingdon; two *s* one *d. Educ:* privately and abroad. Quartermaster, RAF Hospital, 1939; later with Foreign Office and Polish Ministry of Information, London. Then, in politics with her husband. Trustee: Nat. Heritage Meml Fund, 1980-; Dorney Wood Trust, 1980-. Freedom, City of London, 1980. *Recreations:* reading, theatre, opera. *Address:* House of Lords, SW1.

AIREY, Sir Lawrence, KCB 1978 (CB 1976); Chairman of the Board of Inland Revenue, since 1980; *b* 10 March 1926; *s* of late Lawrence Clark Airey and Isabella Marshall Pearson; *m* 1953, Patricia Anne, *d* of late Edward George Williams and Mary Selway; two *s* one *d. Educ:* Newcastle Royal Grammar Sch.; Peterhouse, Cambridge. Entered Civil Service, 1949; General Register Office, 1949-56; Cabinet Office, 1956-58; HM Treasury, 1958-79: Under-Sec., 1969-73; Dep. Sec., 1973-77; Second Perm. Sec., 1977-79. Research Fellow, Nuffield Coll., Oxford, 1961-62. Mem., Bd of British Nat. Oil Corp., 1976-77. *Recreations:* collecting books; music. *Address:* 41 Fairdene Road, Coulsdon, Surrey. *T:* Downland 54191.

AIREY, Lt-Gen. Sir Terence (Sydney), KCMG 1951; CB 1944; CBE 1943 (OBE 1941); psc; retired; *b* 9 July 1900; *s* of late Sydney Airey, Orchard Cottage, Holbrook, Suffolk; *m* 1934, Constance Hedley (marr. diss. 1947); one *s* ; *m* 1947, Bridget Georgiana, *d* of late Col the Hon. Thomas Vesey. 2nd Lieutenant Durham Light Infantry, 1919; Eastern Arab Corps and HQ Sudan Defence Force, 1929-36; Capt. 1933; Major 1938; Temp. Lieut-Col 1940; War Subst. Lieut-Col; Col 1945; Temp. Maj.-Gen. 1944; Brig. Sept. 1945; Maj.-Gen. 1947; Lieut-Gen. 1952. Served War of 1939-45 (despatches, OBE, CBE, CB): Acting Deputy Supreme Allied Commander, Italy, 1946; Allied Commander and Military Gov., British-US Zone of Free Territory, Trieste, 1947-51; Assistant Chief of Staff, Supreme HQ, Allied Powers, Europe, 1951-52; Commdr, British Forces, Hong-Kong, 1952-54; representative Col Light Inf. Bde, 1954-55; retd 1954. Col The Durham Light Infantry, 1952-56. Commander, Order of Merit (US); Officer, Légion d'Honneur, and Croix de Guerre (France). *Address:* Fritton Old Rectory, Fritton, near Norwich, Norfolk. *T:* Hempnall 214.

AIRLIE, 13th Earl of, *cr* 1639 (*de facto* 10th Earl, 13th but for the Attainder); **David George Coke Patrick Ogilvy**, DL; Baron Ogilvy of Airlie, 1491; Captain late Scots Guards; *b* 17 May 1926; *e s* of 12th (*de facto* 9th) Earl of Airlie, KT, GCVO, MC, and of Lady Alexandra Marie Bridget Coke, *d* of 3rd Earl of Leicester, GCVO; *S* father, 1968; *m* 1952, Virginia Fortune Ryan, Moorland Farm, Newport, RI, USA; three *s* three *d. Educ:* Eton. Lieutenant Scots Guards, 1944; serving 2nd Battalion Germany, 1945; Captain, ADC to High Comr and C-in-C Austria, 1947-48; Malaya, 1948-49; resigned commission, 1950. Ensign, Queen's Body Guard for Scotland, Royal Company of Archers, 1975-. Chm., Schroders plc, 1977-; Dep. Chm., Gen. Accident Fire & Life Assurance Corp. Ltd., 1975-; Chm., Ashdown Investment Trust Ltd, to 1982; Director: J. Henry Schroder Wagg & Co. Ltd, 1961- (Chm., 1973-77); Scottish & Newcastle Breweries Ltd; Royal Bank of Scotland, 1980-. Treasurer, Scouts Assoc. DL Angus, 1964. *Heir: s* Lord Ogilvy, *qv. Address:* Cortachy Castle, Kirriemuir, Angus, Scotland. *T:* Cortachy 231; 5 Swan Walk, Chelsea SW3 4JJ.
See also Hon. Angus Ogilvy, Sir Hereward Wake.

AISHER, Sir Owen (Arthur), Kt 1981; Founder Member, Marley Ltd, 1934, Chairman, 1945-82, now Life President, Marley plc; *b* 28 May 1900; *s* of late Owen Aisher, Branksome Park, Poole; *m* 1921, Ann Allingham; two *s* two *d.* Mem. Court of Paviors; Pres., RYA, 1970-75; has had many successes in off-shore racing, inc. Fastnet Race, 1951; was elected Yachtsman of the Year,

1958. *Recreations:* sailing, fishing, shooting. *Address:* Faygate, South Godstone, Surrey. *Clubs:* Reform, City Livery; Royal Thames Yacht; RORC (Adm. 1969-75); Ranelagh Sailing; Little Ship (Pres.); Royal Southern Yacht (Hamble); Royal Yacht Squadron, Royal London Yacht, Island Sailing (Adm.) (Cowes); Bembridge Sailing; Royal Motor Yacht (Poole); New York YC, Seawanhaka Corinthian Yacht (USA); Royal St George Yacht (Eire).

AITCHISON, Sir Charles (Walter de Lancey), 4th Bt, *cr* 1938; *b* 27 May 1951; *er s* of Sir Stephen Charles de Lancey Aitchison, 3rd Bt, and (Elizabeth) Anne (Milburn), *er d* of late Lt-Col Edward Reed, Ghyllheugh, Longhorsley, Northumberland; *S* father 1958. Lieut, 15/19th The King's Royal Hussars, 1974; RARO 1974-78. *Recreations:* motor sport, shooting. *Heir: b* (Stephen) Edward Aitchison [*b* 27 March 1954; *m* 1978, Mrs Harriet N. Thomson, *yr d* of late Dr Henry Miller; one *s*]. *Address:* Howden Dene, Corbridge, Northumberland. *Clubs:* Cavalry and Guards; Northern Counties.
   See also R. A. Cookson.

AITCHISON, Craigie (Ronald John), ARA 1978; painter; *b* 13 Jan. 1926; *yr s* of late Rt Hon. Lord Aitchison, PC, KC, LLD. *Educ:* Scotland; Slade Sch. of Fine Art. British Council Italian Govt Scholarship for painting, 1955; Edwin Austin Abbey Premier Scholarship, 1965; Lorne Scholarship, 1974-75. One-man Exhibitions: Beaux Arts Gall., 1959, 1960, 1964; Marlborough Fine Art (London) Ltd, 1968; Compass Gall., Glasgow, 1970; Basil Jacobs Gall., 1971; Rutland Gall., 1975; Knoedler Gall., 1977; Kettle's Yard Gall., Cambridge, 1979; Serpentine Gall. (major retrospective, 1953-81), 1981-82. Exhibited: Galouste Gulbenkian Internat. Exhibn, 1964; Il Tempo del imagine, 2nd Internat. Biennale, Bologna, 1967; Modern British Painters, Tokyo, Japan, 1969; 23rd Salon Actualité de l'Esprit, Paris, 1975. Pictures in public collections: Tate Gall., Arts Council, Contemp. Art Soc., Scottish National Gall. of Modern Art, and Nat. Gall. of Melbourne, Australia. 1st Johnson Wax Prize, Royal Acad., 1982. *Address:* 33 St Mary's Gardens, SE11. *T:* 01-582 3708; Montecastelli San Gusme, Siena, Italy.

AITHRIE, Viscount; Andrew Victor Arthur Charles Hope; *b* 22 May 1969; *s* and *heir* of Earl of Hopetoun, *qv.*

AITKEN, family name of Beaverbrook Barony.

AITKEN, Sir Arthur Percival Hay, (Sir Peter Aitken), Kt 1968; *b* 2 Oct. 1905; *e s* of late Canon R. A. Aitken, Great Yarmouth; *m* 1937, Ursula Wales, *d* of Herbert Wales, MB; one *s* one *d. Educ:* Norwich Gram. Sch.; Trinity Coll., Oxford. Formerly: Man. Dir Textile Machinery Makers Ltd, 1949, Chm. 1960; Dep. Chm., Stone-Platt Industries Ltd; Director: Norwich General Trust (Chm.); Norwich Union Insurance Group; Norwich Union Life Insurance Soc.; Norwich Union Fire Insurance Soc.; Scottish Union and National Insurance Co.; Maritime Insurance Co. Chm., BNEC's Australia Cttee, 1966-69; Bd Mem., Commonwealth Develt Corp., 1960-69. *Recreations:* golf, fishing. *Address:* The Lodge, Alde House Drive, Aldeburgh, Suffolk IP15 5EE. *T:* Aldeburgh 3450. *Clubs:* Royal Thames Yacht; Aldeburgh Golf, Aldeburgh Yacht.

AITKEN, Ian Hugh, CBE 1964; Deputy Secretary, Institution of Civil Engineers, since 1974; *b* 4 Dec. 1919: *y s* of late James Maven Aitken and Anne Stevenson Aitken (*née* Lowe); *m* 1944, Sheila Agnes Hamilton, *d* of late F. A. Green, Arusha, Tanzania; one *s* one *d. Educ:* Greenock High Sch. Served War in 51st (Highland) Div. and 11th (E African) Div., in France, Belgium, Western Desert and E Africa, 1939-44. HMOCS, Kenya, 1944, Tanganyika, 1944-47, Kenya, 1947; Dep. Principal Immigration Officer, 1952; Principal Immigration Officer and Passport Control Officer, Colony and Protectorate of Kenya, 1960; retired after acting as Adviser on Immigration and related matters to independent Kenya Govt, 1964. Gen. Management, British Uralite Gp, 1964-70; Admin. Sec., Royal Soc. of Medicine, 1971-74. *Recreations:* most games, music. *Address:* 22 Pitfield Drive, Meopham, Kent. *T:* Meopham 812350. *Clubs:* Royal Commonwealth Society, MCC; Nairobi (Kenya).

AITKEN, Ian Levack; Political Editor, The Guardian, since 1975; *b* 19 Sept. 1927; *s* of George Aitken and Agnes Levack Aitken; *m* 1956, Dr Catherine Hay Mackie, *y d* of late Maitland Mackie, OBE; two *d. Educ:* King Alfred Sch., Hampstead; Regent Street Polytechnic; Lincoln Coll., Oxford (BA PPE); LSE. Served Fleet Air Arm, 1945-48. HM Inspector of Factories, 1951; Res. Officer, CSEU, 1952; Industrial Reporter, Tribune, 1953-54; Industrial Reporter, subseq. Foreign Correspondent and Political Correspondent, Daily Express, 1954-64; political staff, The Guardian, 1964-. *Recreation:* music. *Address:* 52A North Hill, N6. *T:* 01-340 5914. *Clubs:* Garrick, Wig and Pen.
   See also Baron John-Mackie, Baron Mackie of Benshie, Sir M. Mackie.

AITKEN, Prof. John Thomas; Professor of Anatomy, University College, London, 1965-80; *b* 6 May 1913; *s* of David and Helen Aitken; *m* 1941, Doreen Violet Whitaker; two *s* two *d. Educ:* High School, Glasgow; Grammar School, Hull; Glasgow University. MB, ChB 1936, MD 1950. University College, London, 1940-80. *Publications:* Manual of Human Anatomy (in collab.); Essential Anatomy (in collab.); papers on regeneration of nerves and muscles, in various jls. *Recreation:* gardening. *Address:* Woodpeckers Cottage, Sway Road, Brockenhurst, Hants SO4 7RX. *T:* Lymington 22493.

AITKEN, Sir (John William) Max, 2nd Bt, *cr* 1916; DSO 1942; DFC 194 President, Express (formerly Beaverbrook) Newspapers Ltd, since 19 (Chairman, 1968-77); former Director, Trafalgar House Ltd; Associat Television Ltd; *b* Montreal, 15 February 1910; *e s* of 1st Baron Beaverbroc (Bt 1916), PC, ED, CD; *S* father, 1964; disclaimed the barony, 11 June 196 *m* 1st, 1939, Cynthia Monteith (who obtained a divorce, 1944); 2nd, 194 Mrs Jane Lindsay (who obtained a divorce, 1950); two *d;* 3rd, 1951, Viol *d* of Sir Humphrey de Trafford, 4th Bt, MC; one *s* one *d. Educ:* Westminste Pembroke Coll., Cambridge. Joined RAuxAF, 1935. Served War of 1939-4 RAF (despatches, DSO, DFC, Czech War Cross); day fighter pilot durin Battle of Britain; comd night fighter squadron, 1941-42; Group Capt. comc Strike Mosquito Wing, Norwegian waters, 1943. MP (C) Holborn, 1945-5 President, Newspaper Press Fund, 1965-. Chancellor, Univ. of Ne Brunswick, Fredericton, NB, 1966-81. Hon. LLD, New Brunswick, 196 *Recreations:* Cambridge Assoc. Football Blue, 1930, 1931; golf, sailing. *Hei s* Hon. (as heir to disclaimed barony) Maxwell William Humphrey Aitke [*b* 29 Dec. 1951; *m* 1974, Susan Angela More O'Ferrall; two *s* one *d*]. *Addres* 46 Chelsea Square, SW3. *T:* 01-351 0116. *Clubs:* White's, Buck's, Roy Yacht Squadron.

AITKEN, Jonathan William Patrick; MP (C) Thanet East since Feb. 197 *b* 30 Aug. 1942; *s* of late Sir William Aitken, KBE and of Hon. Lady Aitke MBE, JP; *m* 1979, Lolicia Olivera, *d* of Mr and Mrs O. Azucki, Zürich; or *s* two *d. Educ:* Eton Coll.; Christ Church, Oxford. MA Hons Law. Priva Sec. to Selwyn Lloyd, 1964-66; Foreign Corresp., London Evening Standar 1966-71; Man. Dir, Slater Walker (Middle East) Ltd, 1973-75; Chm., Aitke Hume Ltd, 1981-; Dir, TV-AM Ltd, 1981-. Mem., Select Cttee o Employment, 1979-. *Publications:* A Short Walk on the Campus, 1966; Th Young Meteors, 1967; Land of Fortune: A Study of Australia, 1969; Official Secret, 1970; articles in Spectator, Sunday Telegraph, Sydney Mornin Herald, Washington Post, etc. *Recreations:* squash, ski-ing, marathon running *Address:* 8 Lord North Street, SW1. *Clubs:* Pratt's, Turf, Beefsteak.

AITKEN, Sir Max; *see* Aitken, Sir J. W. M.

AITKEN, Sir Peter; *see* Aitken, Sir A. P. H.

AITKEN, Sir Robert (Stevenson), Kt 1960; MD (New Zealand), DPh (Oxford); FRCP, FRACP; DL; retired; *b* NZ; *s* of late Rev. James Aitker *m* 1929, Margaret G. Kane; one *s* two *d. Educ:* Gisborne High Schoo Gisborne, NZ; University of Otago, Dunedin, NZ; Oxford. Medica Qualification in New Zealand, 1922; Rhodes Scholar, Balliol College Oxford, 1924-26; attached to Medical Unit, The London Hospital, 1926-3 Reader in Medicine, British Post-Graduate Medical School, Univ. of Londor 1935-38; Regius Prof. of Medicine, Univ. of Aberdeen, 1939-48; Vice Chancellor, Univ. of Otago, Dunedin, NZ, 1948-53; Vice-Chancellor, Univ of Birmingham, 1953-68. Vice-Chm. Association of the Britis Commonwealth, 1955-58; Dep. Chm., UGC, 1968-73; Chairman: Committe of Vice-Chancellors and Principals, 1958-61; Birmingham Repertory Theatre 1962-74. DL Co. Warwick, 1967, West Midlands, 1974. Hon. FRCPE; Hor FDSRCS; Hon. DCL Oxford; Hon. LLD: Dalhousie, Melbourne, Panjab McGill, Pennsylvania, Aberdeen, Newfoundland, Leicester, Birminghan Otago; Hon. DSc: Sydney, Liverpool. *Publications:* papers in medical an scientific journals. *Address:* 6 Hintlesham Avenue, Birmingham B15 2PH *Club:* Athenæum.

AITKEN, Thomas Patrick Howie; Chairman, Gill & Duffus Group Ltd 1979-82; *b* 2 July 1925; *s* of James Howie Aitken and Leslie Henrietta Aitken *m* 1953, Rosemary (*née* Decosmo); one *s* two *d. Educ:* Munro Coll., Jamaica WI. Served RAF, 1943-46. Gill & Duffus Group Ltd: Dir, Gill & Duffus Lt (renamed Gill & Duffus Group Ltd, 1972), 1965-76; Man. Dir, 1976-78; Dep Chm., 1978-79. Dir, Gill & Duffus Inc., 1959-80 (Vice-Pres. 1954-62, Pres 1963-80); Pres., Gill & Duffus Holdings Inc., 1980-82; Dir, I.C.P. Cocoa Inc. 1972-80. Cocoa Merchants Assoc.: Sec., 1961; Vice-Pres., 1962-63; Pres. 1964-65; Dir, 1966. Director: Futures Industry Assoc. Inc., 1972-77 (Vice Chm. 1974-75); New York Cocoa Exchange, 1971-78 (Vice-Chm. 1972-74 Chm. 1974-76). *Recreations:* usual country pastimes. *Clubs:* India Hous (New York); National Golf Links of America (Southampton, Long Island).

AITKEN, Rt. Rev. William Aubrey; *see* Lynn, Bishop Suffragan of.

AJAYI, Prof. Jacob Festus Ade; Professor of History, University of Ibadan since 1963; *b* 26 May 1929; *s* of Chief E. Ade Ajayi and late Mrs C. Bolajokc Ajayi; *m* 1956, Christie Aduke Martins; one *s* four *d. Educ:* University College, Ibadan; University College, Leicester; Univ. of London; BA, PhL (London). Research Fellow, Inst. of Historical Research, London, 1957-58 Lectr, Univ. of Ibadan, 1958-62, Sen. Lectr, 1962-63; Dean, Faculty of Arts 1964-66; Asst to Vice-Chancellor, 1966-68. Fellow, Centre for Advanced Study in the Behavioural Sciences, Stanford, Calif, 1970-71; Vice-Chancellor Univ. of Lagos, 1972-78. Member: UN University Council, 1974-80 (Chm 1976-77); Nat. Archives Cttee, Nigeria, 1961-72; Nat. Antiquities Commn Nigeria, 1970-74; Exec. Council, Internat. African Inst. London, 1971- (Chm 1975-); Exec. Bd, Assoc. of African Univs, 1974-; Pres., Historical Soc. o Nigeria, 1972-; Pres., Internat. Congress of African Studies, 1978-. Hon. LLD Leicester, 1975. Fellow, Hist. Soc. of Nigeria, 1980. *Publications:* Milestone in Nigerian History, 1962; (ed, with Ian Espie) A Thousand Years of Wes African History, 1964; (with R. S. Smith) Yoruba Warfare in the Nineteenth

Century, 1964; Christian Missions in Nigeria: the making of a new elite, 1965; (ed, with Michael Crowder) A History of West Africa, vol. I, 1972; vol. II, 1974; (ed jtly) The University of Ibadan, 1948-73; contribs to Jl Historical Soc. of Nigeria, Jl of African History, etc. *Recreations:* dancing, tennis. *Address:* History Department, University of Ibadan, Nigeria.

KEHURST, Maj.-Gen. John Bryan, CBE 1976; Commandant, The Staff College, Camberley, since 1982; *b* 12 Feb. 1930; *s* of late Geoffrey and of Doris Akehurst; *m* 1955, Shirley Ann, *er d* of late Major W. G. Webb, MBE, and of Ethel Webb; one *s* one *d* decd. *Educ:* Cranbrook Sch.; RMA, Sandhurst. Commnd Northamptonshire Regt, 1949; Malay Regt (despatches), 1952-55; Adjt, 5th Northamptonshire Regt (TA), 1959-60; Staff Coll., Camberley, 1961; Brigade Major, 12 Infantry Bde Gp, 1962-64; Instructor, Staff Coll., Camberley, 1966-68; commanded 2nd Royal Anglian Regt, 1968-70; Directing Staff, IDC/RCDS, 1970-72; Comdt, Jun. Div., Staff Coll., 1972-74; Comdr, Dhofar Bde, Sultan of Oman's Armed Forces, 1974-76; Dep. Mil. Sec. (A), MoD (Army), 1976-79; GOC 4th Armoured Div., BAOR, 1979-81. Dep. Col, Royal Anglian Regt, 1981-. Governor, Harrow Sch., 1982-. Order of Oman, 3rd Class (mil.), 1976. *Publication:* We Won a War, 1982. *Recreations:* golf, trout fishing. *Address:* Dresden Cottage, 46 Vicarage Street, Warminster, Wilts BA12 8JF. *Clubs:* Army and Navy; Wentworth Golf.

KERLOF, Prof. George Arthur, PhD; Cassel Professor of Economics, London School of Economics and Political Science, since 1978; *b* 17 June 1940; *s* of Gosta C. Akerlof and Rosalie C. Akerlof; *m* 1978, Janet Yellen. *Educ:* Yale Univ. (BA 1962); MIT (PhD 1966). Fellowships: Woodrow Wilson, 1962-63; National Science Co-op., 1963-66; Fulbright, 1967-68; Guggenheim, 1973-74. Univ. of Calif, Berkeley: Asst Prof. of Econs, 1966-70; Associate Prof., 1970-77; Prof., 1977-78. Vis. Prof., Indian Statistical Inst., New Delhi, 1967-68. Sen. Economist, Council of Econ. Advisors, USA, 1973-74; Vis. Economist, Bd of Governors of Fed. Reserve System, USA, 1977-78. *Publications:* contrib. American Econ. Rev., Econ. Jl, Qly Jl Econs, Jl Polit. Econ., Rev. of Econ. Studies, Internat. Econ. Rev., Jl Econ. Theory, Indian Econ. Rev., and Rev. of Econs and Stats. *Address:* London School of Economics and Political Science,Houghton Street, WC2A 2AE. *T:* 01-405 7686. *Club:* Piggy (Center Harbor, NH, USA).

KERS-DOUGLAS, family name of **Viscount Chilston.**

KERS-JONES, David, CMG 1978; Hong Kong Government Secretary for City and New Territories, since 1973; *b* 14 April 1927; *s* of Walter George and Dorothy Jones; *m* 1951, Jane Spickernell; one *d* (one *s* decd). *Educ:* Worthing High Sch.; Brasenose Coll., Oxford (MA). British India Steam Navigation Co., 1945-49. Malayan Civil Service (studied Hokkien and Malay), 1954—57; Hong Kong Civil Service, 1957-. Vice-Pres. Hong Kong Football Assoc., 1967-. *Recreations:* painting, gardening, walking, music. *Address:* Island House, Taipo, New Territories, Hong Kong. *Clubs:* Oriental, Royal Over-Seas League; Hong Kong (Hong Kong).

KHTAR, Prof. Muhammad, FRS 1980; Professor of Biochemistry, Southampton University, since 1973; *b* 23 Feb. 1933; *m* 1963, Monika E. Schurmann; two *s. Educ:* Punjab Univ., Pakistan (MSc 1st class 1954); Imperial College, London (PhD, DIC 1959). Research Scientist, Inst. for Medicine and Chemistry, Cambridge, Mass, USA, 1959-63; University of Southampton: Lecturer in Biochemistry, 1963-66; Senior Lectr, 1966-68; Reader, 1968-73. Member: Chemical Soc. of GB; American Chemical Soc.; Biochemical Soc. of GB. Sitara-I-Imtiaz (Pakistan), 1981. *Publications:* numerous works on: enzyme mechanisms; synthesis and biosynthesis of steroids and porphyrins; biochemistry of vision; synthesis of anti-microbial compounds. *Address:* Department of Biochemistry, University of Southampton, Southampton SO9 3TU. *T:* Southampton 559122, ext. 8338.

KINKUGBE, Prof. Oladipo Olujimi, CON 1979; Officier de l'Ordre National de la République de Côte d'Ivoire, 1981; MD, DPhil; FRCP, FWACP, FAS; Professor of Medicine, University of Ibadan, Nigeria, since 1968; *b* 17 July 1933; *s* of Chief David Akinbobola and Chief (Mrs) Grace Akinkugbe; *m* 1965, Dr Folasade Modupeore Dina; two *s. Educ:* Univs of Ibadan, London (MD), Liverpool (DTM&H) and Oxford (DPhil). FRCP 1968; FWACP 1975; FAS 1980. House Phys., London Hosp., 1958; House Surg., King's Coll. Hosp., London, 1959; Commonwealth Res. Fellow, Balliol Coll. and Regius Dept of Medicine, Oxford, 1962-64; Head of Dept of Medicine, 1972, Dean of Medicine, 1970-74, and Chm., Cttee of Deans, 1972-74, Univ. of Ibadan; Vice-Chancellor: Univ. of Ilorin, 1977-78 (Principal, 1975-77); Ahmadu Bello Univ., Zaria, 1978-79. Rockefeller Vis. Fellow, US Renal Centres, 1966; Vis. Fellow in Medicine, Univs of Manchester, Cambridge and London, 1969; Vis. Prof. of Medicine, Harvard Univ., 1974-75; Vis. Fellow, Balliol Coll., Oxford, 1981-82. Adviser on Postgrad. Med. Educn to Fed. Govt of Nigeria, 1972-75; Member: Univ. Grants Commn, Uganda Govt; OAU Scientific Panels on Health Manpower Develt; internat. socs of hypertension, cardiology, and nephrology; Med. Res. Soc. of GB; Scientific Adv. Panel, CIBA Foundn; WHO Expert Adv. Panels on Cardiovascular Diseases, 1973-78. *Publications:* High Blood Pressure in the African, 1972; (ed) Priorities in National Health Planning, 1974; (ed) Cardiovascular Disease in Africa, 1976; papers on hypertension and renal disease in African, Eur. and Amer. med. jls, and papers on med. and higher educn. *Recreations:* music, gardening. *Address:* Department of Medicine,

University of Ibadan, Ibadan, Nigeria. *T:* 400550. *Clubs:* Rotary International; Dining (Ibadan).

ALAM, Hon. Anthony Alexander; Member of Legislative Council, 1925-59, and 1963-73; Director: Alam Homes Pty Ltd; Alam Stores Pty Ltd; Mala Homes Pty Ltd; Latec Ltd; *b* Wallsend, NSW, 23 Jan. 1898; parents born Republic Lebanon; *m* ; no *c. Educ:* De La Salle College, Armidale, NSW. King George V Silver Jubilee Medal; Merit of Lebanon; Commander Nichan Iftikar; King George VI Coronation Medal; Commander Toile Noir; Chevalier, Legion of Honour; Commander Order Cedars (Liban); Queen Elizabeth Coronation Medal; Grand Cross; Order of Torsani; Order of St Mark; Grand Officer, Order of Phoenix, Greece. *Recreations:* bowls, billiards, tennis, motoring, horse-racing. *Address:* 69 Bradleys Head Road, Mosman, NSW 2088, Australia. *Club:* Commercial Travellers' (Sydney).

ALANBROOKE, 3rd Viscount *cr* 1946; **Alan Victor Harold Brooke;** Baron Alanbrooke, 1945; *b* 24 Nov. 1932; *s* of 1st Viscount Alanbrooke, KG, GCB, OM, GCVO, DSO, and Benita Blanche (*d* 1968), *d* of Sir Harold Pelly, 4th Bt; *S* half-brother, 1972. *Educ:* Harrow; Bristol Univ. (BEd Hons 1976). Qualified teacher, 1975. Served Army, 1952-72; Captain RA, retired. *Heir:* none.

ALBEE, Edward; American dramatist; *b* 12 March 1928. *Publications:* plays: The Zoo Story, 1959; The Death of Bessie Smith, 1960; The Sandbox, 1961; The American Dream, 1961; Who's Afraid of Virginia Woolf?, 1962; (adapted from Carson McCullers' novella) The Ballad of the Sad Café, 1963; Tiny Alice, 1964; (adapted from the novel by James Purdy) Malcolm, 1965; A Delicate Balance, 1966 (Pulitzer Prize, 1967); (adapted from the play by Giles Cooper) Everything in the Garden, 1967; Box and Quotations from Chairman Mao Tse-Tung, 1968; All Over, 1972; Seascape, 1975 (Pulitzer Prize, 1975); Listening, 1975; Counting the Ways, 1976; The Lady from Dubuque, 1978; Lolita (adapted from V. Nabakov), 1979. *Address:* 14 Harrison Street, New York, NY 10015, USA.

ALBEMARLE, 10th Earl of, *cr* 1696; **Rufus Arnold Alexis Keppel;** Baron Ashford, 1696; Viscount Bury, 1696; *b* 16 July 1965; *s* of Derek William Charles Keppel, Viscount Bury (*d* 1968), and Marina, *yr d* of late Count Serge Orloff-Davidoff; *S* grandfather, 1979. *Heir:* uncle Hon. Walter Arnold Crispian Keppel, DSC [*b* 6 Dec. 1914; *m* 1941, Aline Lucy, *d* of late Brig.-Gen. John Harington, CB, CMG, DSO; two *s* one *d*]. *Address:* Piazza di Bellosguardo 10, 50124 Florence, Italy.

ALBEMARLE, Countess of, (Diana Cicely), DBE 1956; Chairman: Development Commission, 1948-74; The Drama Board, 1964-78; *b* 6 Aug. 1909; *o c* of John Archibald Grove; *m* 1931, 9th Earl of Albemarle, MC (*d* 1979); one *d. Educ:* Sherborne Sch. for Girls. Norfolk County Organiser, WVS, 1939-44. Chairman: Exec. Cttee, Nat. Fedn of Women's Institutes, 1946-51; Departmental Cttee on Youth Service, 1958-60; Nat. Youth Employment Council, 1962-68. Vice-Chm., British Council, 1959-74. Member: Arts Council, 1951; Royal Commn on Civil Service, 1954; Harkness Fellowship Cttee of Award, 1963-69; UGC, 1956-70; Standing Commn on Museums and Galleries, 1958-71; English Local Govt Boundary Commn, 1971-77; Youth Develt Council, 1960-68; Council, Univ. of E Anglia, 1964-72. Life Trustee, Carnegie UK Trust (Chm., 1977-82); Trustee of: The Observer until 1977; Glyndebourne Arts Trust, 1968-80. RD Councillor, Wayland, Norfolk, 1935-46. Hon. DLitt Reading, 1959; Hon. DCL Oxon, 1960; Hon. LLD London, 1960. *Recreations:* gardening, reading. *Address:* Seymours, Melton, Woodbridge, Suffolk. *T:* Woodbridge 2151.
See also Sir Hew Hamilton-Dalrymple.

ALBERT, Sir Alexis (François), Kt 1972; CMG 1967; VRD 1942; Chairman and Governing Director, J. Albert & Son Pty Ltd, Sydney, since 1962; Chairman, The Australian Broadcasting Company Pty Ltd, Sydney; *b* 15 Oct. 1904; *s* of late M. F. and M. E. Albert, Sydney; *m* 1934, Elsa K. R. (decd), *d* of late Capt. A. E. Lundgren, Sydney; three *s. Educ:* Knox College, Sydney; St Paul's College, University of Sydney. BEc 1930. Director: Amalgamated Television Services Pty Ltd, 1955-; Australasian Performing Right Association Ltd, 1946-76. Underwriting Member of Lloyd's, 1944-74; President, Royal Blind Soc. of NSW, 1962-78; Fellow of Council, St Paul's Coll., Univ. of Sydney, 1965-; Council, Nat. Heart Foundn of Aust., NSW Div. 1959-. RANR, 1918-49; Lt-Comdr, retd. Hon. ADC to Governors of NSW, 1937-57. CStJ 1980 (OStJ 1976). *Recreations:* swimming, yachting. *Address:* 25 Coolong Road, Vaucluse, NSW 2030, Australia; (office) 139 King Street, Sydney, NSW 2000. *T:* 232 2144. *Clubs:* Naval and Military; Australian, Union (Sydney); Royal Sydney Golf, Royal Sydney Yacht Squadron (Commodore 1971-75); New York Yacht.

ALBERT, Carl (Bert); Speaker, US House of Representatives, 1970-76; Member, Third Oklahoma District, 1947-76 (Democratic Whip, 1955-62; Majority Leader, 1962-71); *b* 10 May 1908, McAlester, Oklahoma; *s* of Ernest Homer and Leona Ann (Scott) Albert; *m* 1942, Mary Sue Greene Harmon; one *s* one *d. Educ:* Univ. of Oklahoma (AB 1931); Oxford Univ. (Rhodes Scholar, BA 1933, BCL 1934). Served US Army, 1941-46. Admitted Oklahoma Bar, 1935; Legal Clerk, Fed. Housing Admin, 1935-37; attorney and accountant, Sayre Oil Co., 1937-38; legal dept, Ohio Oil Co., 1939-40. Practised law: Oklahoma City, 1938; Mattoon, Ill, 1938-39; McAlester, Oklahoma, 1946-47. Bronze Star, 1945. *Recreation:* reading. *Address:* Route two, McAlester, Oklahoma 74501, USA.

ALBERY, Sir Donald (Arthur Rolleston), Kt 1977; Former Chairman and Managing Director, The Wyndham Theatres Ltd, Donmar Productions Ltd and associated companies and Piccadilly Theatre Ltd; Director, Anglia Television Ltd, 1958–78; Chairman, Theatres' National Committee, 1974–78; *b* London, 19 June 1914; *s* of late Sir Bronson Albery and Una Gwen, *d* of T. W. Rollaston; *m* 1935, Rubina McGilchrist (decd); one *s*; *m* 1946, Heather Boys (marr. diss. 1974); two *s* one *d*; *m* 1974, Nobuko Uenishi. *Educ:* Alpine Coll., Switzerland. Gen. Man., Sadler's Wells Ballet, 1941–45; Dir and Administrator, London's Festival Ballet, 1965–68; Life Trustee, Royal Ballet Benevolent Fund. Has presented or jtly presented plays: The Living Room, 1953; Birthday Honours, 1953; I Am a Camera, The Living Room (NY, with Gilbert Miller), 1954; The Remarkable Mr Pennypacker, Lucky Strike, Waiting for Godot, 1955; The Waltz of the Toreadors, Gigi, Grab Me a Gondola, 1956; Zuleika, Tea and Sympathy, Dinner With the Family, Paddle Your Own Canoe, 1957; The Potting Shed, George Dillon, Irma La Douce (NY, 1960), 1958; The Rose Tattoo, A Taste of Honey (NY, 1960), The Hostage (NY, 1960), The Complaisant Lover, One to Another, The Ring of Truth, The World of Suzie Wong, Make Me an Offer, 1959; Fings Ain't Wot They Used T' Be, A Passage to India, Call It Love, The Art of Living, Oliver! (NY, 1963; tour, 1965), The Tinker, 1960; The Miracle Worker, Breakfast for One, Sparrers Can't Sing, Beyond the Fringe (NY, 1962), Celebration, Bonne Soupe, 1961; Not to Worry, Blitz!, Semi-Detached, Fiorello!, 1962; Licence to Murder, The Perils of Scobie Prilt (tour), A Severed Head (NY, 1964), The Time of the Barracudas (US), 1963; The Fourth of June, The Poker Session, Who's Afraid of Virginia Woolf?, A Little Winter Love (tour), Entertaining Mr Sloane (NY, 1965), Instant Marriage, Carving a Statue, The Diplomatic Baggage, Portrait of a Queen, Jorrocks, The Prime of Miss Jean Brodie, 1966; Mrs Wilson's Diary, Spring and Port Wine, The Restoration of Arnold Middleton, 1967; The Italian Girl, Man of La Mancha, 1968; Conduct Unbecoming (NY, 1970; Australia, 1971), 1969; It's a Two Foot Six Inches Above the Ground World, Mandrake, Poor Horace, 1970; Popkiss, 1972; Very Good Eddie, The Thoughts of Chairman Alf, 1976. *Address:* 31 Avenue Princesse Grace, Monte Carlo, Monaco. *T:* 507082. *Club:* Garrick.

ALBRECHT, Ralph Gerhart; American lawyer, barrister and international legal consultant; *b* Jersey City, NJ, 11 Aug. 1896; *s* of J. Robert Albrecht and Gertrude A. F. Richter; *m* 1936, Aillinn, *d* of late William Elderkin Leffingwell, Watkins Glen, NY; one *s*. *Educ:* Pennsylvania Univ. (AB); Harvard Univ. (JD). Admitted to Bar of NY, 1924, US Supreme Court, 1927; senior partner, Peaslee, Albrecht & McMahon, 1931–61, counsel to firm, 1961; gen. practice, specializing in foreign causes and internat. law. Special Dep. Attorney-Gen. of New York, 1926; Special Asst to US Attorney-Gen., 1945; Mem. US War Crimes Commn and trial special counsel in Prosecution of Major Nazi War Criminals, before Internat. Mil. Tribunal, Nuremberg, 1945–46, prosecuted Hermann Goering; counsel to German steel, coal and chem. industries in decartelization procs before Allied High Commn for Germany, 1950–53. Mem. Republican County Cttee, NY Co., 1933–35; Harvard Univ. Overseers' Visiting Cttee to Faculty of Germanic Langs and Lits, 1949–63. Apprentice Seaman, USN Res. Force, 1918; served with Sqdn A (101st Cavalry, NY Nat. Guard), 1924–30; Comdr USNR, on active duty, 1941–45; Naval Observer, American Embassy, London, 1942 (letter of commendation from Chief of Naval Ops); Asst Dir OSS (War Crimes), 1945. Member: NY City Bar Assoc.; Amer. Bar Assoc.; Amer. Soc. of Internat. Law (Donor of Manley O. Hudson Gold Medal Award; Chm., Medal Cttee, 1958–78); Internat. Bar Assoc.; International Law Assoc.; World Peace Through Law Center (Cttee on Conciliation and Mediation of Disputes). Fellow: Nat. Audubon Society; Massachusetts Audubon Soc.; Amer. Geog. Soc., etc. Delegate, First Internat. Congress Comparative Law, The Hague, 1932. Republican; Mason. *Publications:* (with Prof. Walter B. Pitkin) Studies for Vocational Guidance of Recent School and College Graduates; contrib. Peter Markham's (pseud.) America Next, 1940. *Address:* 520 East 86th Street, New York, NY 10028, USA. *Clubs:* University, Harvard, Pilgrims of the US, Squadron A (all in NY).

ALBROW, Desmond; Assistant Editor, Sunday Telegraph, since 1976; *b* 22 Jan. 1925; *er s* of Frederick and Agnes Albrow; *m* 1950, Aileen Mary Jennings; one *s* three *d*. *Educ:* St Bede's Grammar Sch., Bradford; Keble Coll., Oxford (MA). On the Editorial Staff of the Yorkshire Observer, 1950–51, Manchester Guardian, 1951–56, Daily Telegraph, 1956–60; Sunday Telegraph, 1960–66: Chief Sub-Editor, News Editor, and Night Editor; Editor, Catholic Herald, 1966–71; Features Editor, Sunday Telegraph, 1971–76. *Recreations:* drinking in moderation and talking to excess; watching other people cultivate their gardens. *Address:* Totyngton Cottage, Victoria Road, Teddington, Mddx. *T:* 01-979 4220.

ALBU, Austen Harry, BSc (Eng.); FCGI, CEng; *b* London, 21 Sept. 1903; *s* of Ferdinand and Beatrice Rachel Albu; *m* 1st, 1929, Rose (*d* 1956), *d* of Simon Marks, Newcastle; two *s*; 2nd, 1958, Dr Marie Jahoda, *qv*. *Educ:* Tonbridge School; City and Guilds College (Imperial College of Science and Technology). Works Manager, Aladdin Industries, Greenford, 1930–46. Dep. Pres., Govtl Sub-Commn, CCG, 1946–47. Dep. Dir, British Institute of Management, Feb.–Nov. 1948. MP (Lab) Edmonton, 1948–Feb. 1974; Minister of State, Dept of Economic Affairs, 1965–67. Fellow, Imp. Coll. of Science and Technology. DUniv Surrey, 1966. *Address:* 17 The Crescent, Keymer, Sussex BN6 8RB.

ALBU, Sir George, 3rd Bt, *cr* (UK) 1912, of Grosvenor Place, City of Westminster, and Johannesburg, Province of Transvaal, South Africa; farmer;

b 5 June 1944; *o s* of Major Sir George Werner Albu, 2nd Bt, and Kathlee Betty (*d* 1956), *d* of Edward Charles Dicey, Parktown, Johannesburg; *S* fathe 1963; *m* 1969, Joan Valerie Millar, London; two *d*. *Recreations:* horse racin tennis, golf. *Heir:* none. *Address:* Glen Hamish Farm, PO Box 62, Richmon Natal, 3780, South Africa. *T:* Richmond (Natal) 287. *Clubs:* Victor (Pietermaritzburg, Natal); Richmond Country (Richmond, Natal).

ALBU, Marie, (Mrs A. H. Albu); *see* Jahoda, Prof. Marie.

ALCOCK, Prof. Leslie; Professor of Archaeology, University of Glasgov since 1973; *b* 24 April 1925; *o s* of Philip John Alcock and Mary Ethel (*n* Bagley); *m* 1950, Elizabeth A. Blair; one *s* one *d*. *Educ:* Manchester Gramma Sch.; Brasenose Coll., Oxford. BA 1949, MA 1950. Supt of Exploration, De, of Archaeology, Govt of Pakistan, 1950; Curator, Abbey House Museun Leeds, 1952; Asst Lectr, etc, UC Cardiff, 1953. Prof. of Archaeology, U Cardiff, 1973. Member: Ancient Monuments Bd, Scotland, 1974–; Roy Commn on Ancient and Historical Monuments of Scotland, 1977–. Vice-Pres Council for British Archaeology, 1974–77; Pres., Cambrian Archaeologic Assoc., 1982. FSA 1957; FRHistS 1969; FRSE 1976; Hon. Fellow, Univ. c Mississippi, 1969; Mem., Medieval Academy of America, 1973. *Publication* Dinas Powys, 1963; Arthur's Britain, 1971; Cadbury/Camelot, 1972; article and reviews in British and Amer. jls. *Recreations:* mountaineering; baroqu and jazz music. *Address:* 29 Hamilton Drive, Hillhead, Glasgow G1 8DN.

ALDAM, Jeffery Heaton, CBE 1980; MC 1945; County Education Office Hampshire, since 1973; *b* 11 Nov. 1922; *s* of William and Clara Ellen Aldan *m* 1950, Editha Hilary Mary (*née* Preece); two *s* two *d*. *Educ:* Chesterfiel Grammar Sch.; Trinity Coll., Cambridge (MA); Harvard Univ. (AM). Serve 13th/18th Royal Hussars (QMO), 1942–45. Admin. Asst, Asst Educn Office then Sen. Asst Educn Officer, Norfolk CC, 1949–56; Dep. County Educ Officer, NR Yorks CC, 1957–62; Chief Educn Officer, East Suffolk CC 1962–71; County Educn Officer, (former) Hampshire CC, 1972–7: *Recreations:* reading, walking, gardening. *Address:* Derrymore, 71 Andove Road, Winchester, Hampshire SO22 6AU. *T:* Winchester 3594.

ALDENHAM, 5th Baron *cr* 1896, and **HUNSDON OF HUNSDON,** 3r Baron *cr* 1923; **Antony Durant Gibbs;** *b* 18 May 1922; *s* of 4th Baron an Beatrix Elinor (*d* 1978), *d* of Herbert Paul; *S* father, 1969; *m* 1947, Mar Elizabeth, *o d* of late Walter Parkyns Tyser; two *s* one *d* (and one *s* decd) *Educ:* Eton; Christ Church, Oxford. RNVR, 1940–46. Antony Gibbs & Son Ltd, 1947 (Chile, 1948–51); Dir, 1954; Dir, Antony Gibbs Holdings Ltc 1972–80. Master, Merchant Taylors' Co., 1977. *Recreations:* shooting, fishing sailing. *Heir:* s Hon. Vicary Tyser Gibbs [*b* 9 June 1948; *m* 1980, Josephin Nicola, *er d* of John Fell, Lower Bourne, Farnham, Surrey]. *Address:* Rimpto Manor, Yeovil, Somerset BA22 8AE. *Clubs:* Pratt's; MCC; Royal Yach Squadron (Cowes).

See also Sir C. H. Villens.

ALDER, Lucette, (Mrs Alan Alder); *see* Aldous, Lucette.

ALDER, Michael; Controller, English Regional Television, Britis Broadcasting Corporation, since 1977; *b* 3 Nov. 1928; *s* of Winifred Mille and late Thomas Alder; *m* 1955, Freda, *d* of late John and Doris Hall; tw *d*. *Educ:* Ranelagh Sch., Bracknell, Berks; Rutherford Coll., Newcastle-upon Tyne. Newcastle Evening Chronicle, 1947–59; BBC North-East: Chief New Asst, Newcastle; Area News Editor, Newcastle; Representative, NE England 1959–69; Head of Regional Television Development, BBC, 1969–77 *Recreations:* gardening, fishing, walking, country pursuits. *Address:* Inglefor 14 Danford Lane, Solihull, West Midlands B91 1QD. *T:* 021-705 1537.

ALDERSON, Brian Wouldhave; Senior Lecturer, (on Children's Literatur and the Book Trade), Polytechnic of North London, since 1965; Children' Books Editor, The Times, since 1967; *b* 19 Sept. 1930; *s* of John Willian Alderson and Helen Marjory (*née* Hogg), *m* 1953. Valerie Christine (*né* Wells); three *s* (and two *s* decd). *Educ:* Ackworth Sch.; University Colleg of the South-West, Exeter (BA Hons). Work in the book trade, 1952–63 Tutor-librarian, East Herts Coll. of Further Educn, 1963–65. *Publication* *translations:* Hürlimann, Three Centuries of Children's Books in Europe 1967; Grimm, Popular Folk Tales, 1978; *edited:* The Juvenile Library 1966–74; The Colour Fairy Books, by Andrew Lang, 1975–; Children's Book in England, by F. J. Harvey Darton, 1982. *Recreations:* bibliography dale-walking. *Address:* 67 High Road, Wormley, Broxbourne, Herts EN1 6JJ. *T:* Hoddesdon 63851.

ALDERSON, John Cottingham, CBE 1981; QPM 1974; Chief Constable o Devon and Cornwall, 1973–82; *b* 28 May 1922; *e s* of late Ernest Cottinghan Alderson and Elsie Lavinia Rose; *m* 1948, Irené Macmillan Stirling; one *s Educ:* Barnsley Elem. Schs and Techn. College. Called to Bar, Middl Temple. British Meml Foundn Fellow, Australia, 1956; Extension Certif. i Criminology, Univ. of Leeds. CBIM. Highland LI, 1938–41 (Corp.); Arm Phys. Trng Corps, N Africa and Italy, 1941–46 (Warrant Officer). Wes Riding Constabulary as Constable, 1946; Police Coll., 1954; Inspector, 1955 Sub-Divisional Comd, 1960; Sen. Comd Course, Police Coll., 1963–64; Dep Chief Constable, Dorset, 1964–66; Metropolitan Police, Dep. Comdr (Admin and Ops), 1966; 2nd-in-comd No 3 Police District, 1967; Dep. Asst Comr (Trng), 1968; Comdt, Police Coll., 1970; Asst Comr (Personnel and Trng) 1973. Consultant on Human Rights to Council of Europe, 1981–. Member

BBC Gen. Adv. Council, 1971–78; Royal Humane Soc. Cttee, 1973; Pres., Royal Life-Saving Soc., 1974–78. Fellow Commoner, Corpus Christi Coll., Cambridge, 1982; Fellow, Inst. of Criminology, Cambridge, 1982; Gwilym Gibbon Res. Fellow, Nuffield Coll., Oxford, 1982–83. Hon. LLD Exeter, 1979. *Publications:* (contrib.) Encyclopedia of Crime and Criminals, 1960; (ed jtly) The Police We Deserve, 1973; Policing Freedom, 1979; articles in professional jls and newspapers. *Recreations:* reading, writing, keeping fit. *Club:* Royal Over-Seas League.

ᴌDERSON, Dr Michael Rowland; Chief Medical Statistician, Office of Population Censuses and Surveys, since 1981; *b* 8 June 1931; *s* of Christopher Rowland and Phyllis Maud Alderson; *m* 1955, Dorothy Carter; two *d. Educ:* Epsom Coll.; Guy's Hospital. MD; FFCM; DPH etc. Prof. of Medical Information Science, Southampton Univ., 1970–75; Prof. of Epidemiology, Inst. of Cancer Research, 1975–81. *Publications:* Central Government Routine Health Statistics, 1974; An Introduction to Epidemiology, 1976; Health Surveys and Related Studies, 1979; International Mortality Statistics, 1981; Prevention of Cancer, 1982. *Recreation:* sailing. *Address:* 8 Westgate Street, Southampton SO1 0AY. *T:* Southampton 31804.

ᴌDERTON, John; actor (stage, films, television); *b* Gainsborough, Lincs, 27 Nov. 1940; *s* of Gordon John Alderton and Ivy Handley; *m* 1st, Jill Browne (marr. diss.); 2nd, Pauline Collins, *qv* ; two *s* one *d. Educ:* Kingston High Sch., Hull. *Stage:* 1st appearance (Rep.) Theatre Royal, York, in Badger's Green, 1961; cont. Rep.; 1st London appearance, Spring and Port Wine, Mermaid (later Apollo), 1965. Royal Shakespeare Company: Dutch Uncle, Aldwych, 1969; The Night I chased the Women with an Eel, Comedy, 1969; Punch and Judy Stories, Howff, 1973; Judies, Comedy, 1974; The Birthday Party, Shaw, 1975; Confusions (4 parts), Apollo, 1976; Rattle of a Simple Man, Savoy, 1980; *films:* (1962-): incl. Duffy, Hannibal Brooks, Zardoz, All Creatures Great and Small, Please Sir; *television:* series: Please Sir, No Honestly, My Wife Next Door, P. G. Wodehouse, The Upchat Line, Thomas and Sarah, and various plays. *Address:* c/o Nems Management Ltd, 29-31 King's Road, SW3. *Clubs:* Garrick, Green Room, Lord's Taverners.

ᴌDINGTON, 1st Baron, *cr* 1962; **Toby (Austin Richard William) Low;** PC 1954; KCMG 1957; CBE 1945 (MBE 1944); DSO 1941; TD and clasp, 1950; DL; Chairman: Sun Alliance and London Insurance plc; Westland Aircraft plc; Deputy Chairman, GEC plc; Director: Citicorp; Lloyds Bank plc; Warden, Winchester College, since 1979; Barrister-at-Law; *b* 25 May 1914; *s* of Col Stuart Low, DSO (killed at sea by enemy action, Dec. 1942), and of late Hon. Mrs Spear; *m* 1947, Araminta Bowman, *e d* of late Sir Harold MacMichael, GCMG, DSO; one *s* two *d. Educ:* Winchester; New Coll., Oxford (Hon. Fellow 1976). Called to the Bar, 1939. TA; 2nd Lieut 1934; Brig. BGS 5 Corps Italy, Aug. 1944–June 1945; served Greece, Crete, Egypt, Libya, Tunisia, Sicily, Italy, Austria (DSO, MBE, CBE, Croix de guerre avec palmes, Commander of Legion of Merit, USA); Hon. Col 288 LAA Regt RA (TA), 1947–59. MP (C) Blackpool North, 1945–62; Parliamentary Secretary, Ministry of Supply, 1951–54; Minister of State, Board of Trade, 1954–57; Dep. Chm., Cons. Party Organisation, Oct. 1959–63. Chm., Grindlays Bank Ltd, 1964–76. Chairman: Port of London Authority, 1971–77; Jt Special Cttee on Ports Industry, 1972. Chm., Cttee of Management, Inst. of Neurology, 1962–80; Chm., BBC Gen. Adv. Council, 1971–78. Fellow, Winchester Coll. DL Kent, 1973. *Recreation:* golf. *Heir: s* Hon. Charles Harold Stuart Low, *b* 22 June 1948. *Address:* Flat R, 45 Eaton Square, SW1W 9BD. *T:* 01-235 3425; Knoll Farm, Aldington, Kent. *T:* Aldington 292. *Clubs:* Beefsteak, Carlton.

ᴌDINGTON, Sir Geoffrey (William), KBE 1965 (OBE 1946); CMG 1958; HM Diplomatic Service, retired; *b* 1 June 1907; *s* of late Henry William Aldington; *m* 1932, Roberta Finch; two *d. Educ:* City of London School; Magdalen Coll., Oxford. Student Interpreter, China Consular Service, 1929; Vice-Consul (Grade I), China, 1931; Vice-Consul, Peking, 1931–33; Private Secretary to HM Minister, Peking, 1933–35; Foreign Office, 1936–37; Acting Consul, Chungking, 1937–39; Consul, Tsingtao, 1939–41; seconded to Min. of Information, 1943–45; Actg Consul-Gen., Hankow, 1945–46; Suptg Consul, Shanghai, 1946–47; Foreign Office, 1947–50; Political Adviser to Hong Kong Govt, 1950–53; Consul-Gen. Zagreb, Yugoslavia, 1954–56; Consul-General at Philadelphia, Pa, USA, 1956–61; HM Ambassador to Luxembourg, 1961–66; also Consul-General, Luxembourg, 1962–66. *Recreations:* tennis, riding, reading. *Address:* Rustlings, 4 Tudor Close, Barnmeadow Lane, Great Bookham, Surrey. *T:* Bookham 54088. *Clubs:* Phyllis Court (Henley); Hong Kong (Hong Kong); Racquet (Philadelphia, USA).
See also S. J. G. Semple.

ᴌDINGTON, John Norman, BSc, PhD; FRIC; FInstP; CEng; FIEE; Chairman, Royal Worcester Ltd, 1974–75 (Director, 1968–75); *b* 2 March 1905; *s* of Allen Aldington, Preston, Lancashire; *m* 1930, Edna, *d* of late John James Entwisle; one *s. Educ:* Balshaws Grammar Sch., Leyland; Harris Inst., Preston. Joined Siemens Electric Lamps and Supplies Ltd, 1923; Head of Laboratories, 1935; Dir of Research, 1948; Dir of the firm, 1948; Dir Alfred Graham & Co. Ltd, 1950; Man. Dir of Siemens Bros & Co. Ltd, 1955; former Man. Dir and Vice-Chm., AEI Ltd; former Director: LEW Ltd; Sub. Cables Ltd; Welwyn Electric Co. Ltd; Worcester Industrial Ceramics Ltd; Worcester Royal Porcelain Co. Ltd. Fellow and Past Pres., Illuminating Engrg Soc.; Mem. Amer. Illum. Engrg Soc., 1950; Chm. of Light Sources Secretariat, Internat. Commn on Illumination, 1945–54; Mem. various BSI Cttees. Part-time Lectr Harris Inst., Preston, 1928–38; Gov., Preston Grammar Sch.,

1950–55; JP Duchy of Lancaster, 1953–55. MRI 1958. Leon Gaster Meml Award, IES, 1945 and 1947; Crompton Award, IEE, 1949; Gold Medal, IES, 1970. *Publications:* The High Current Density Mercury Vapour Arc, 1944 (thesis, London Univ. Library); numerous papers, particularly on light sources and kindred devices, and on high current discharges and xenon gas arc. *Recreations:* gardening and golf. *Address:* The Turn, Townside, Haddenham, Bucks. *T:* Haddenham 291145. *Club:* Athenæum.

ALDISS, Brian Wilson; writer; critic; *b* 18 Aug. 1925; *s* of Stanley and Elizabeth May Aldiss; *m* 1965, Margaret Manson; one *s* one *d,* and one *s* one *d* by previous *m. Educ:* Framlingham Coll.; West Buckland School. Royal Signals, 1943–47; book-selling, 1947–56; writer, 1956–; Literary Editor, Oxford Mail, 1958–69. Pres., British Science Fiction Assoc., 1960–64. Editor, SF Horizons, 1964-. Chairman, Oxford Branch Conservation Soc., 1968–69; Vice Pres., The Stapledon Soc., 1975–; Jt Pres., European SF Cttees, 1976–79; Society of Authors: Mem., Cttee of Management, 1976–78, Chm., 1978; Chm., Cultural Exchanges Cttee, 1979–; Mem., Arts Council Literature Panel, 1978–80; Pres., World SF, 1982-. Observer Book Award for Science Fiction, 1956; Ditmar Award for Best Contemporary Writer of Science Fiction, 1969; first James Blish Award, for SF criticism, 1977; Pilgrim Award, 1978. *Publications:* The Brightfount Diaries, 1955; Space, Time and Nathaniel, 1957; Non-Stop, 1958 (Prix Jules Verne, 1977); Canopy of Time, 1959; The Male Response, 1961; Hothouse, 1962 (Hugo Award, 1961); Best Fantasy Stories, 1962; The Airs of Earth, 1963; The Dark Light Years, 1964; Introducing SF, 1964; Greybeard, 1964; Best SF Stories of Brian W. Aldiss, 1965; Earthworks, 1965; The Saliva Tree, 1966 (Nebula Award, 1965); Cities and Stones: A Traveller's Jugoslavia, 1966; An Age, 1967; Report on Probability A, 1968; Farewell, Fantastic Venus!, 1968; Intangibles Inc. and other Stories, 1969; A Brian Aldiss Omnibus, 1969; Barefoot in the Head, 1969; The Hand-Reared Boy, 1970; The Shape of Further Things, 1970; The Moment of Eclipse, 1971 (BSFA Award, 1972); A Soldier Erect, 1971; Brian Aldiss Omnibus II, 1971; Billion Year Spree: a history of science fiction, 1973 (Special BSFA Award, 1974; Eurocon Merit Award, 1976); Frankenstein Unbound, 1973; The Eighty-Minute Hour, 1974; (ed) Space Opera, 1974; (ed) Space Odysseys: an Anthology of Way-Back-When Futures, 1975; (ed) Hell's Cartographers, 1975; (ed) Evil Earths, 1975; Science Fiction Art: the fantasies of SF, 1975 (Ferrara Silver Comet, 1977); (ed with H. Harrison) Decade: the 1940s, 1976; (ed with H. Harrison) Decade: the 1950s, 1976; The Malacia Tapestry, 1976; (ed) Galactic Empires, vols 1 and 2, 1976; (ed with H. Harrison) The Year's Best Science Fiction No 9, 1976; Brothers of the Head, 1977; Last Orders, 1977; (ed with H. Harrison) Decade: the 1960's, 1977; A Rude Awakening, 1978; Enemies of the System, 1978; (ed) Perilous Planets, 1978; This World and Nearer Ones, 1979; New Arrivals, Old Encounters, 1979; Life in the West, 1980; Moreau's Other Island, 1980; Helliconia, 1982. *Recreation:* thinking about China. *Address:* 16 Moreton Road, Oxford.

ALDOUS, Alan Harold; Director of Sixth Form Studies, Longsands School, St Neots, since 1976; *b* 14 Nov. 1923; *m* ; one *s* one *d,* and one step *s. Educ:* Ilford County High Sch. for Boys; Jesus Coll., Oxford (MA). Royal Signals and Royal West African Frontier Force, 1943–46. Oxford Univ., 1942 and 1946–49; Asst Master, St Dunstan's Coll., Catford, 1949–54; Asst Master, Merchant Taylors' Sch., Crosby, 1954–59; Headmaster: King's Sch., Pontefract, 1959–70; Leeds Grammar Sch., 1970–75. *Recreations:* music, walking. *Address:* Casterbridge, Madeley Court, Hemingford Grey, Huntingdon, Cambs PE18 9DF. *T:* St Ives 66153.

ALDOUS, Lucette; Prima Ballerina, The Australian Ballet, since 1971; Master Teacher, Australian Ballet School, since 1979; Senior Adjudicator, National Eisteddfods, since 1979; *b* 26 Sept. 1938; *d* of Charles Fellows Aldous and Marie (*née* Rutherford); *m* 1972, Alan Alder; one *d. Educ:* Toronto Public Sch., NSW; Brisbane Public Sch., Qld; Randwick Girls' High Sch., NSW. Awarded Frances Scully Meml Schol. (Aust.) to study at Royal Ballet Sch., London, 1955; joined Ballet Rambert, 1957, Ballerina, 1958–63; Ballerina with: London Fest. Ballet, 1963–66; Royal Ballet, 1966–71. Rep. Australia, 1st Internat. Ballet Competition, Jackson, Miss, USA, 1979; Guest, Kirov Ballet and Ballet School, Leningrad, 1975–76. Guest appearances: Giselle, with John Gilpin, NY, 1968; Lisbon, 1969; with Rudolf Nureyev, in Don Quixote: Aust., 1970, NY, Hamburg and Marseilles, 1971; Carmen, Johannesburg, 1970; The Sleeping Beauty: E Berlin, 1970, Teheran, 1970, 1975; partnered Edward Villela at Expo '74, Spokane, USA. *Television:* title rôle, La Sylphide, with Fleming Flindt, BBC, 1960. *Films:* as Kitri, in Don Quixote, with Rudolf Nureyev and Robert Helpmann, Aust., 1972; The Turning Point, 1977. *Recreations:* music, reading, gardening, breeding Burmese cats.

ALDOUS, William, QC 1976; *b* 17 March 1936; *s* of Guy Travers Aldous, QC; *m* 1960, Gillian Frances Henson; one *s* two *d. Educ:* Harrow; Trinity Coll., Cambridge (MA). Barrister, Inner Temple, 1960. *Recreations:* hunting, tennis. *Address:* Layham Lodge, Layham, near Ipswich, Suffolk. *T:* Hadleigh 823143.

ALDRED, Cyril, FRSE 1978; *b* 19 Feb. 1914; 3rd *s* of late Frederick Aldred and Lilian Ethel (*née* Underwood); *m* 1938, Jessie Kennedy Morton; one *d. Educ:* Sloane Sch.; King's Coll. and Courtauld Art Inst., Univ. of London (BA). Asst Keeper, Royal Scottish Museum, 1937; Scottish Educn Dept, 1939. Served War, RAF (Signals), 1942–46. Associate Curator, Dept of Egyptian Art, Metropolitan Museum of Art, New York, 1955–56; Mem. Cttee, Egypt Exploration Soc., 1959–76; Keeper, Dept of Art and Archaeology, Royal Scottish Museum, Edinburgh, 1961–74. *Publications:* The Development of

Ancient Egyptian Art, 1952; The Egyptians, 1961; Egypt to the End of the Old Kingdom, 1965; Akhenaten, a New Study, 1968; Jewels of the Pharaohs, 1971; Akhenaten and Nefertiti, 1973; Tutankhamun, Craftsmanship in Gold in the Reign of the King, 1979; Egyptian Art in the Days of the Pharaohs, 1980; scripts for BBC programmes, Tutankhamun's Egypt, 1972, etc; chapters in: History of Technology; Cambridge Ancient History (2nd edn); Egypte (Univers des Formes); numerous articles on Ancient Egyptian art and archaeology in scientific periodicals. *Recreations:* composing light verse, gardening. *Address:* 4a Polwarth Terrace, Edinburgh EH11 1NE. *T:* 031-229 2845. *Club:* Scottish Arts (Edinburgh).

ALDRIDGE, Frederick Jesse; Member, Public Health Laboratory Service Board, since 1977; Under-Secretary and Controller of Supply, Department of Health and Social Security, 1968–75; *b* 13 Oct. 1915; *s* of late Jesse and Clara Amelia Aldridge; *m* 1940, Grace Hetty Palser; two *d*. *Educ:* Westminster City Sch. Clerical Off., Air Min., 1933; Exec. Off., Min. of Health, 1935; RAF, 1940–46; Acct-General's Div., Min. of Health: Asst Acct-Gen., 1956; Dep. Acct-Gen., 1958; Asst Sec. for Finance and Dep. Acct-Gen., 1964; Asst Sec., Food, Health and Nutrition, also Civil Defence, 1966. *Recreation:* music. *Address:* High Trees, 17 Tanglewood Close, Croydon CR0 5HX. *T:* 01-656 3623.

ALDRIDGE, (Harold Edward) James; author; *b* 10 July 1918; *s* of William Thomas Aldridge and Edith Quayle Aldridge; *m* 1942, Dina Mitchnik; two *s*. With Herald and Sun, Melbourne, 1937–38; Daily Sketch, and Sunday Dispatch, London, 1939; subsequently Australian Newspaper Service and North American Newspaper Alliance (war correspondent), Finland, Norway, Middle East, Greece, USSR, until 1945; also correspondent for Time and Life, Teheran, 1944. Rhys Meml Award, 1945; Lenin Peace Prize, 1972. *Publications:* Signed With Their Honour, 1942; The Sea Eagle, 1944; Of Many Men, 1946; The Diplomat, 1950; The Hunter, 1951; Heroes of the Empty View, 1954; Underwater Hunting for Inexperienced Englishmen, 1955; I Wish He Would Not Die, 1958; Gold and Sand (short stories), 1960; The Last Exile, 1961; A Captive in the Land, 1962; The Statesman's Game, 1966; My Brother Tom, 1966; The Flying 19, 1966; (with Paul Strand) Living Egypt, 1969; Cairo: Biography of a City, 1970; A Sporting Proposition, 1973; The Marvellous Mongolian, 1974; Mockery in Arms, 1974; The Untouchable Juli, 1975; One Last Glimpse, 1977; Goodbye Un-America, 1979. *Recreations:* underwater, trout fishing, hunting, etc. *Address:* 21 Kersley Street, SW11. *Club:* British Sub-Aqua.

ALDRIDGE, James; see Aldridge, Harold Edward James.

ALDRIDGE, John Arthur Malcolm, RA 1963 (ARA 1954); painter; Assistant at The Slade School of Fine Art, 1949–67, Lecturer (part-time), 1967–70; *b* 26 July 1905; *s* of Major John Bartelott Aldridge, DSO, RHA, and Margaret Jessica (*née* Goddard); *m* 1st, 1940, Cecilia Lucie Leeds Brown (*née* Saunders) (marr. diss. 1970); no *c*; 2nd, 1970, Margareta Anna Maria Cameron (*née* Bajardi). *Educ:* Uppingham Sch.; Corpus Christi Coll., Oxford (MA). London, 1928–33; Essex, 1933–. Served, 1941–45, Army (N Africa and Italy, 1943–45). Member of 7 and 5 Soc.; Exhibitions at Leicester Galleries, 1933, 1936, 1940, 1947; exhibited Royal Acad. 1948 onwards. Pictures acquired by: Nat. Portrait Gallery; Royal Acad. of Arts, Tate Gallery, Min. of Works, Italian Min. of Education, Aberdeen, Leeds, Manchester, Newport, Northampton, British Council, Contemporary Art Society. *Publications:* Illustrations: The Life of the Dead (text by Laura Riding), 1933; Adam was a Ploughman (text by C. Henry Warren), 1948. *Recreation:* gardening. *Address:* The Place House, Great Bardfield, Essex. *T:* Great Dunmow 810275.

ALDRIDGE, Michael William ffolliott; actor; *b* 9 Sept. 1920; *s* of Dr Frederick James Aldridge and Kathleen M. M. Aldridge; *m* 1947, Kirsteen Rowntree; three *d*. *Educ:* Watford Grammar Sch.; Gresham's Sch., Holt, Norfolk. Served RAF, 1940–46 (Flight-Lieut). First professional appearance in French without Tears, Palace Theatre, Watford, 1939; in rep. at Bristol, Blackpool, Sunderland, Sheffield, Bradford and Amersham, 1939–40; first London appearance in This Way to the Tomb, Garrick, 1946; toured with Arts Council Midland Theatre Co., 1946–48; title rôle in Othello, Nottingham, 1948, Embassy, 1949; with Birmingham Rep., 1949; Old Vic Co. at New Theatre, 1949–50: Love's Labour's Lost, She Stoops to Conquer, The Miser, Hamlet; with Arts Council Midland Theatre Co., 1950; Bristol Old Vic, 1951–52: title rôle in Macbeth, Two Gentlemen of Verona, Of Mice and Men; Chichester Festival, 1966–69, 1971–72. London appearances include: Escapade, St James's, Strand, 1953–54; Salad Days, Vaudeville, 1954; Free As Air, Savoy, 1957; Moon for the Misbegotten, Arts, 1960; Vanity Fair, Queen's, 1962; The Fighting Cock, Duke of York's, 1966; Heartbreak House, Lyric, 1967; The Cocktail Party, Wyndham's, Haymarket, 1968; The Magistrate, Cambridge, 1969; Bequest to the Nation, Haymarket, 1970; Reunion in Vienna, Piccadilly, 1972; Absurd Person Singular, Criterion, 1973; The Tempest, RSC at The Other Place, 1974; Jeeves, Her Majesty's, 1975; Lies, Albery, 1975; The Bed before Yesterday, Lyric, 1976; Rosmersholm, Haymarket, 1977; The Old Country, Queen's, 1978; Bedroom Farce, Nat. Theatre at The Prince of Wales, 1978; The Last of Mrs Cheyney, Cambridge, 1980; Noises Off, Lyric, Hammersmith and Savoy, 1982. Films include, 1946–: Nothing Venture; Bank Holiday Luck; The North Sea Bus; Murder in the Cathedral; A Life for Ruth; Chimes at Midnight; The Public Eye. Television plays and serials include: The Man in Room 17; Happy and Glorious; Bleak House; Sense and Sensibility; Fall of Eagles; Love for Lydia; Tinker, Tailor, Soldier, Spy; Love in a Cold Climate; Voyage Round My Father. Mem., BAFTA. *Recreation:* sailin *Address:* 11 Crooms Hill, Greenwich, SE10 8ER. *Club:* Little Ship.

ALDRIN, Dr. Edwin E., Jr; President, Research and Engineering Consulta Inc., since 1972; *b* Montclair, NJ, USA, 20 Jan. 1930; *s* of late Col Edwin Aldrin, USAF retd, Brielle, NJ, and Marion Aldrin (*née* Moon); two *s* o *d* of former marriage. *Educ:* Montclair High Sch., Montclair, NJ (grad.); U Mil. Academy, West Point, NY (BSc); Mass Inst. of Technology (DSc Astronautics). Received wings (USAF), 1952. Served in Korea (66 comb missions) with 51st Fighter Interceptor Wing. Aerial Gunnery Instr, Nellis A Force Base, Nevada; attended Sqdn Officers Sch., Air Univ., Maxwell A Force Base, Alabama; Aide to Dean of Faculty, USAF Academy; Flt Com with 36th Tactical Fighter Wing, Bitburg, Germany. Subseq. assigned Gemini Target Office of Air Force Space Systems Div., Los Angeles, Ca later transf. to USAF Field Office, Manned Spacecraft Center. One of 3 group of astronauts named by NASA, Oct. 1963; served as back up pil Gemini 9 Mission and prime pilot, Gemini 12 Mission (launched into spa with James Lovell, 11 Nov. 1966), a 4 day 59 revolution flight which broug Gemini Program to successful close; he established a new record f extravehicular activity and obtained first pictures taken from space of a eclipse of the sun; also made a rendezvous with the previously launched Ager later assigned to 2nd manned Apollo flight, as back-up command modu pilot; Lunar Module Pilot, Apollo 11 rocket flight to the Moon; first lun landing with Neil Armstrong, July 1969; left NASA to return to USAF Commandant, Aerospace Res. Pilots Sch., Edwards Air Force Base, Cal 1971; retired USAF 1972. Mem., Soc. of Experimental Test Pilots; FAIA Tau Beta Pi, Sigma Xi. Further honours include Presidential Medal Freedom, 1969; Air Force DSM with Oak Leaf Cluster; Legion of Merit; A Force DFC with Oak Leaf Cluster; Air Medal with 2 Oak Leaf Clusters; ar NASA DSM, Exceptional Service Medal, and Group Achievement Awar Various hon. memberships and hon. doctorates. *Publication:* Return to Ear (autobiography), 1973. *Recreations:* athletics, scuba diving, etc.

ALEC-SMITH, Col Rupert Alexander, TD 1950; FSA; Lord-Lieutenant Humberside, since 1980; *b* 5 Sept. 1913; *o s* of late Alexander Alec-Smit OBE, Wawne Lodge, Hull; *m* 1952, Suzette Genevieve, *e d* of James Watso Holyrood House, Hedon, Yorks; one *d*. *Educ:* Eastern Interned Horsle Smith & Co. Ltd, timber importers, 1932, Dir 1945–78. Served War 1939–45: temp. Lt-Col Green Howards (TA); Hon. Col 20th (N and Ridings) Bn Mobile Defence Corps, 1956–59; Mem. E Riding TA Assoc 1947–68 (Vice-Chm. 1961–65); Mem. Yorks TA&VRA, 1968–74; Vice-Pre; Yorks and Humberside TA & VRA, 1980–; Pres., Regtl Council Yorl Volunteers, 1982–83. Hon. Brother, Kingston upon Hull Trinity House, 195 Patronage Trustee, living of Holy Trinity, Kingston upon Hull, 1963; Patror Kingston upon Hull Conservative Fedn, 1970–75; Georgian Soc. for E Yorl Founder, 1937; Hon. Sec., 1937–74; Pres., 1975; Mem. Exec. Cttee, Georgia Group, 1953; Mem. Yorks Regional Cttee, National Trust, 1969. Pres., Hu and E Riding Inst. for the Blind, 1980. Kingston upon Hull: Mem. Cit Council, 1947–74 (leader Conservative Gp, 1955–70); Sheriff, 1949–5 Alderman, 1968–74 (Hon. Alderman, 1978–); Lord Mayor, 1970–71; Ho Freeman, 1973; JP 1950; DL ER Yorks and City and County of Kingsto upon Hull, 1958; JP and DL Humberside, 1974, High Sheriff 1975, Vic Lord-Lieutenant, 1975–80. FSA 1975. Hon. DLitt Hull, 1979. KStJ 198 *Publications:* A Catalogue Raisonné of the Corporation Plate and Insignia the City and County of Kingston upon Hull, 1973. *Recreation:* looking buildings. *Address:* Winestead, Hull HU12 0NN. *T:* Patrington 30297.

ALEIXANDRE, Vicente; Spanish writer; *b* Seville, 26 April 1898; *s* of Ciril Aleixandre Ballester and Elvira Merlo Garciía de Pruneda. *Educ:* Univ. Madrid (Law degree; diploma in Business Admin.). Associate Prof., Centra Sch. of Commerce, Madrid, 1919–21; worked for Ferrocarriles Andaluce 1921–25. Teacher of Business Terminology, Residencia de Estudiantes, 192 contrib., La Semana Financiera. Member: Royal Spanish Acad.; Hispanic Soc of America; Monde Latin Acad., Paris; Corresponding Member: Arts Acad Malaga; Scis and Arts Acad., Puerto Rico; Hispano-American Acad., Bogot Hon. Fellow, Profs of Spanish Assoc., USA. Nat. Prize for Literature, 193 Spanish Critics Prize, 1962, 1974; Nobel Prize for Literature, 1977. Gran Cross of Order of Carlos III, 1977. *Publications:* Ambito, 1928; Espadas com Labios, 1932; Pasión de la Tierra, 1935; La Destrucción o el Amor, 193 Sombra del Paraíiso, 1944; Mundo a Solas, 1950; Vida del Poeta: el amor la poesíia, 1950; Poemas Paradisíiacos, 1952; Nacimiento Ultimo, 195 Historia del Corazón, 1954; Algunos Carácteres de la Nueva Poesíia Español 1955; Ocho Poemas de Aleixandre, 1955; Mis Poemas Mejores, 1957; Lc Encuentros, 1958; Poemas Amorosos, 1960; Poesíias Completas, 1960; Picasso 1961; Antigua Casa Madrileña, 1961; En Un Vasto Dominio, 1962; Maríia Gorda, Retratos con Nombre, 1965; Presencias, 1965; Dos Vidas, 1967; Obra Completas, 1968; Poemas de la Consumación, 1968; Antologíia del Mar y 1 Noche, 1971; Poesíia Superrealista, 1971; Sonido de la Guerra, 1971; Diálogc del Conocimiento, 1974; Antología Total, 1976. *Address:* Vicente Aleixand 3, Madrid 3, Spain.

ALEPOUDELIS, Odysseus; see Elytis, Odysseus.

ALEXANDER, family name of **Baron Alexander of Potterhill,** of Ea **Alexander of Tunis,** and of **Earl of Caledon.**

ALEXANDER OF POTTERHILL, Baron *cr* 1974 (Life Peer), of Paisle **William Picken Alexander,** Kt 1961; LHD, PhD, MEd, MA, BSc, FBP;

General Secretary, Association of Education Committees (England, Wales, Northern Ireland, Isle of Man and Channel Islands), 1945-77; *b* 13 Dec. 1905; *y s* of Thomas and Joan Alexander; *m* 1949, Joan Mary, *d* of Robert and Margaret Williamson; one *s* (and one *s* decd). *Educ:* Paisley Grammar School; Glasgow Univ. Schoolmaster in Scotland, 1929-31; Asst Lectr in Education, Glasgow Univ., 1931-32; Rockefeller Research Fellow, 1932-33; Deputy Director of Education, Walthamstow, 1934-35; Director of Education, Margate, 1935-39, Sheffield, 1939-44. Joint Sec. to Management Panel of Burnham Committees and Associated Committees negotiating salaries of teachers, 1945-73. Hon. DLitt Leeds, 1977. *Publications:* Intelligence, Concrete and Abstract, 1935; The Educational Needs of Democracy, 1940; A Performance Scale for the Measurement of Technical Ability, 1947; A Parents' Guide to the Education Act, 1944, 1947; Education in England, 1953; Towards a new Education Act, 1969, etc. *Recreations:* golf and contract bridge. *Address:* 3 Moor Park Gardens, Pembroke Road, Moor Park, Herts HA6 2LF. *T:* Northwood 21003. *Club:* Moor Park Golf (Herts).

ALEXANDER OF TUNIS, 2nd Earl *cr* 1952; **Shane William Desmond Alexander**; Viscount, 1946; Baron Rideau, 1952; Lieutenant Irish Guards, retired, 1958; *b* 30 June 1935; *e s* of 1st Earl Alexander of Tunis, KG, PC, GCB, OM, GCMG, CSI, DSO, MC, and Lady Margaret Diana Bingham (Countess Alexander of Tunis), GBE, DStJ, DL (*d* 1977), *yr d* of 5th Earl of Lucan, PC, GCVO, KBE, CB; *S* father, 1969; *m* 1981, Hon. Davina Woodhouse, *y d* of 4th Baron Terrington, *qv*; one *d*. *Educ:* Ashbury Coll., Ottawa, Canada; Harrow. A Lord in Waiting (Govt Whip), 1974. Liveryman, Mercers Company. *Heir: b* Hon. Brian James Alexander, *b* 31 July 1939. *Address:* Winkfield Lodge, Windsor Forest, Berks. *T:* Winkfield Row 2240.

ALEXANDER, Sir Alexander Sandor, (Sir Alex), Kt 1974; Chairman, J. Lyons and Company, since 1979; Vice-Chairman, Allied-Lyons plc, since 1982; Director: Inchcape Insurance Holdings Ltd; Marchwiel plc; Tate & Lyle plc; Unigate plc; *b* 21 Nov. 1916; *m* 1946, Margaret Irma; two *s* two *d*. *Educ:* Charles Univ., Prague. Dir, 1954-69, Man. Dir and Chief Exec., 1967-69, Chm. 1969, Ross Group Ltd; Chm., Imperial Foods Ltd, 1969-79; Dir, Imperial Group Ltd (formerly Imperial Tobacco Group Ltd), 1969-79. Director: National Westminster Bank Ltd, South East Region; Ransomes, Sims & Jefferies plc; Dep. Chm., British United Trawlers, 1969-81. Chm., Theatre Royal (Norwich) Trust Ltd; Trustee, 1975-, Vice Chm., 1978-, Glyndebourne Arts Trust; Trustee, Charities Aid Foundn, 1979-; Friend of RCP, 1982-. President: Processors and Growers Research Orgn, 1978-82; British Food Export Council, 1973-76; Member: Eastern Gas Bd, 1963-72; Agric. Econ. Develt Cttee, 1974-78; Governor, British Nutrition Foundn. Chm., Appeals Cttee, Brit. Red Cross Soc. (Norfolk Branch), 1958-74. FBIM; FRSA. Mem. Court, UEA. High Sheriff, Norfolk, 1976. *Recreations:* tennis, shooting, painting, opera, ballet. *Address:* Westwick Hall, Westwick, Norwich. *T:* Swanton Abbot 664.

ALEXANDER, Sir Charles G(undry), 2nd Bt *cr* 1945; MA, AIMarE; Chairman, Alexander Shipping Co. Ltd; *b* 5 May 1923; *s* of Sir Frank Alexander, 1st Bt, and Elsa Mary (*d* 1959), *d* of late Charles Collett, 1st Bt; *S* father 1959; *m* 1st, 1944, Mary Neale, *o c* of S. R. Richardson; one *s* one *d*; 2nd, 1979, Eileen Ann Stewart. *Educ:* Bishop's Stortford College; St John's College, Cambridge. Served War as Lieut, RN, 1943-46. Chm., Governors Care Ltd; Dep. Chm., Houlder Bros and Co. Ltd; Director: Furness-Houlder Insurance Ltd; Furness-Houlder (Reinsurance Services) Ltd; Inner London Region, National Westminster Bank Ltd; formerly Dir, Hull, Blyth & Co. Ltd (Chm., 1972-75). Chm., Bd of Governors, Bishop's Stortford College. Mem. Court of Common Council, 1969; Alderman (Bridge Ward), 1970-76. *Recreation:* farming. *Heir: s* Richard Alexander [*b* 1 Sept. 1947; *m* 1971, Lesley Jane, *d* of Frederick William Jordan, Bishop's Stortford; two *s*]. *Address:* 53 Leadenhall Street, EC3. *T:* 01-481 2020; Bells Farm, East Sutton, near Maidstone, Kent. *T:* Sutton Valence 2410. *Club:* Royal Automobile.

ALEXANDER of Ballochmyle, Sir Claud Hagart-, 3rd Bt, *cr* 1886 of Ballochmyle; DL; *b* 6 Jan. 1927; *s* of late Wilfred Archibald Alexander (2nd *s* of 2nd Bt) and Mary Prudence, *d* of late Guy Acheson; *S* grandfather, 1945; assumed additional surname of Hagart, 1949; *m* 1959, Hilda Etain, 2nd *d* of Miles Malcolm Acheson, Ganges, BC, Canada; two *s* two *d*. *Educ:* Sherborne; Corpus Christi Coll., Cambridge (BA 1948). DL Ayrshire, 1973. *Heir: s* Claud Hagart-Alexander, *b* 5 Nov. 1963. *Address:* Kingencleugh House, Mauchline, Ayrshire KA5 5JL. *T:* Mauchline 50217. *Club:* New (Edinburgh).

ALEXANDER, Sir Darnley (Arthur Raymond), Kt 1974; CBE 1963; CFR 1979; Chairman, Nigerian Law Reform Commission, since 1979; *b* Castries, St Lucia, 28 Jan. 1920; *e s* of late Pamphile Joseph Alexander, MBE, and late Lucy Alexander; *m* 1943, Mildred Margaret King (*d* 1980); one *s* one *d*. *Educ:* St Mary's Coll., St Lucia; University Coll., London (LLB). Called to Bar, Middle Temple, 1942. Served in: legal service, Jamaica, WI, and Turks and Caicos Is, 1944-57; legal service, Western Nigeria, 1957-63; Solicitor-Gen. 1960; QC 1961; Judge, High Court of Lagos (later Lagos State), 1964-69; Chief Justice: South Eastern State of Nigeria, 1969-75; Fed. Repub. of Nigeria, 1975-79. Member: Nigerian Body of Benchers (Past Chm. and Life Mem.); Nigerian Soc. of Internat. Law, 1968-; Nigerian Inst. of Internat. Affairs, 1979-. *Publications:* Report of Inquiry into Owegbe Cult, 1966; Report of Inquiry into Examination Leakages, 1969. *Recreations:* cricket, football, table-tennis, swimming, reading. *Address:* (office) Nigerian Law

Reform Commission, Secretariat Complex, Ikoyi, PO Box 60008, Lagos, Nigeria; (home) 18 Osborne Road, Ikoyi, Lagos, Nigeria. *T:* 681080.

ALEXANDER, Maj.-Gen. David Crichton, CB 1976; Commandant, Scottish Police College, since 1979; *b* 28 Nov. 1926; *s* of James Alexander and Margaret (*née* Craig); *m* 1957, Diana Joyce (Jane) (*née* Fisher); one *s* two *d* and one step *s*. *Educ:* Edinburgh Academy. Joined RM, 1944; East Indies Fleet; 45 Commando, Malaya, Malta, Canal Zone, 1951-54; Parade Adjt, Lympstone, 1954-57; Equerry and Acting Treasurer to Duke of Edinburgh, 1957-60; psc 1960; Directing Staff, Staff Coll., Camberley, 1962-65; 45 Commando (2IC), Aden, 1965-66; Staff of Chief of Defence Staff, incl. service with Sec. of State, 1966-69; CO 40 Commando, Singapore, 1969-70; Col GS to CGRM, 1970-73; ADC to the Queen, 1973-75; RCDS 1974; Comdr, Training Gp RM, 1975-77. Dir-Gen., English-Speaking Union, 1977-79. Governor, Corps of Commissionaires, and Mem., Admin. Bd, 1978-; Mem., Civil Service Final Selection Bd, 1978-. Dir, Edinburgh Acad., 1980-. Freeman, City of London; Liveryman, Painter Stainers' Co., 1978. *Recreations:* fishing, gardening, golf. *Address:* Tulliallan Castle, Kincardine, Alloa, Clackmannanshire FK1O 4BE. *Club:* Army and Navy.

ALEXANDER, Sir Desmond William Lionel C.; *see* Cable-Alexander.

ALEXANDER, Sir Douglas (Hamilton), 2nd Bt, *cr* 1921; *b* 6 June 1900; *e s* of Sir Douglas Alexander, 1st Bt, and Helen Hamilton (*d* 1923), *d* of George Hamilton Gillespie, Hamilton; *S* father, 1949. *Educ:* Appleby College; Phillips Exeter Academy; Princeton University. BA 1921. The Singer Manufacturing Company, 1922; Secretary of the Company, 1946; now retired. *Heir: nephew* Prof. Douglas Alexander [*b* 9 Sept. 1936; *m* 1958, Marylon Scatterday; two *s*]. *Address:* 118 Palmers Hill Road, Stamford, Conn 06902, USA.

ALEXANDER, Duncan Hubert David, CBE 1980 (OBE 1959); TD; DL; MA; Consultant, Stephenson & Alexander, Chartered Surveyors, Chartered Auctioneers and Estate Agents, Cardiff; *b* 15 June 1911; *e c* of late Hubert G. and Edith Alexander; *m* 1937, Dorothy Evelyn, 3rd *d* of late Edmund L. Hann; three *d*. *Educ:* Sherborne School, Dorset; Trinity College, Cambridge (MA). Family business of Stephenson & Alexander, 1933- (except War Service, RA, 1939-45; served as G2 RA Combined Ops, then Germany). Mem., 1960-80, Dep. Chm., 1973-80, Cwmbran New Town Corporation. National Pres. of Chartered Auctioneers' and Estate Agents' Institute, 1964-65; Member, Housing Corporation, 1964-74. Indep. Mem., Lord Nugent's MoD Lands Rev. Cttee, 1971-73. Hon. Col, Glamorgan Army Cadet Force, 1975-82. DL 1958, High Sheriff 1960, Glamorgan. *Recreations:* golf, gardening. *Address:* Star House, Capel Llanilterne, Glamorgan. *T:* Pentyrch 890332; (business) 5 High Street, Cardiff. *T:* Cardiff 40244. *Clubs:* MCC; Cardiff and County (Cardiff) (Trustee); Royal Porthcawl Golf.

ALEXANDER, Henry Joachim, Dr phil, Dr jur Breslau; Member, Conseil Fédéral, Fédération Internationale des Communautés d'Enfants, Trogen, since 1980 (Secrétaire Général Adjoint, 1960-67; Chairman, UK Section, 1960-70; Vice-Pres., 1967-71); *b* 4 Jan. 1897; *s* of Bruno and Lisbeth Alexander-Katz; *m* 1st, 1925, Hilda (*née* Speyer) (*d* 1974); two *s*; 2nd, 1975, Amalia Cornelia (*née* Amato). *Educ:* Gymnasium Augustum Germany; Univs of Göttingen and Breslau. Member, Berlin Bar, 1925-37. Member, European Service of BBC, 1942-56; Vice-Chm. and Trustee, Assoc. of Broadcasting Staff, 1952-54 (Chm., Foreign Langs Panel, 1952-55). Chm., British Pestalozzi Children's Village Assoc., 1947-57; Chm. Pestalozzi Children's Village Trust, 1957-62 (Exec. Vice-Pres., 1962-63); Mem. Council, Pestalozzi Children's Village Foundation, Trogen, Switzerland, 1954-77; Mem. Exec. Cttee, Lifeline, an Internat. Refugee Organisation; 1965-72; Mem. Residential Care Assoc., 1965-, and Chm. of its Internat. Cttee, 1965-70. Hon. Mem., Mark Twain Soc., USA, 1977. *Publication:* International Trade Mark Law, 1935. *Recreations:* music, hill walking. *Address:* Hildings, Pett, Hastings, East Sussex. *T:* Pett 3055.

ALEXANDER, Sir (John) Lindsay, Kt 1975; MA; Chairman, Lloyds Bank International, since 1980 (Director, since 1975; Deputy Chairman, 1979-80); Deputy Chairman, Lloyds Bank Ltd, since 1980 (Director since 1970); Chairman, Overseas Containers Holdings Ltd, since 1976 (Director since 1971); Director: British Petroleum Co. Ltd, since 1975; Ocean Transport and Trading Ltd, since 1955; Jebsens Drilling Ltd, since 1980; Hawker Siddeley Ltd, since 1981; *b* 12 Sept. 1920; *e s* of Ernest Daniel Alexander and Florence Mary Mainsmith; *m* 1944, Maud Lilian, 2nd *d* of Oliver Ernest and Bridget Collard; two *s* one *d*. *Educ:* Alleyn's Sch.; Brasenose Coll., Oxford (Thomas Wall Schol.; Hon. Fellow 1977). Royal Engineers, 1940-45 (Capt.); served Middle East and Italy. Man. Dir, The Ocean Steam Ship Co. Ltd, later Ocean Transport and Trading Ltd, 1955-71, Chm. 1971-80. Chairman: Liverpool Port Employers' Assoc., 1964-67; Cttee, European Nat. Shipowners' Assocs, 1971-73; Vice-Chm., Nat. Assoc. of Port Employers, 1965-69; President: Chamber of Shipping of UK, 1974-75 (Vice-Pres., 1973-74); Gen. Council, British Shipping 1974-75. Hon. Mem., Master Mariners' Co., 1974-. FCIT (MInstT 1968); FBIM 1972. JP Cheshire, 1965-75. Comdr, Royal Order of St Olav, Norway. *Recreations:* gardening, music, photography. *Address:* Lloyds Bank International Ltd, 40/66 Queen Victoria Street, EC4P 4EL. *T:* 01-248 9822. *Club:* Brooks's.

ALEXANDER, Prof. John Malcolm; Professor and Head of Department of Mechanical Engineering, University College of Swansea, University of

Wales, since 1978; *b* 14 Oct. 1921; *s* of Robert Henry Alexander and Gladys Irene Lightfoot Alexander (*née* Domville); *m* 1946, Margaret, *d* of F. A. Ingram; two *s. Educ:* Ipswich Sch.; City and Guilds Coll. (Imperial Coll., London Univ.). DSc (Eng) London; PhD; FCGI; FICE; FIMechE; FIProdE; FIM; FEng; FRSA. Practical trng, Ransomes Sims & Jefferies Ltd, Ipswich, 1937–42; REME commn, 1942–47; res. in plasticity and applied mechanics, City and Guilds Coll., 1950–53; Head of Metal Deformation Section, Aluminium Labs Ltd, 1953–55; Head of Mech. Engrg Res. Labs and Nuclear Reactor Mechanical Design, English Electric, 1955–57; Reader in Plasticity, Univ. of London, 1957–63; Prof. of Engrg Plasticity, Univ. of London, 1963–69; Prof. of Applied Mechanics, Imp. Coll., Univ. of London, 1969–78. Chm., Applied Mechanics Gp, IMechE, 1963–65; Mem., Collège Internationale Recherche et Production, 1965–; Vice-President: Inst. of Metals, 1968–71; Inst. of Sheet Metal Engrg, 1979–; Chm. Board of Studies in Civil and Mech. Engrg, Univ. of London, 1966–68. Governor: Reigate Grammar Sch., 1964–67; Ipswich Sch., 1977–. Chm., British Cold Forging Gp, 1973–79; Pres., Forming Gp, Collège International Recherche et Production, 1979–; Chm., Stemmos Ltd, 1980–; Associate, John West Associates, 1980–. Engrg Adviser, Van Nostrand, 1964–; Series Editor, Ellis Horwood Ltd, 1970–; Mem. Editorial Board: Jl Strain Analysis, 1965–71; Internat. Jl Mech. Sciences, 1968–; Internat. Jl Machine Tool Design and Research, 1973–; Metals Technology, 1976–; Mem. Adv. Bd, Jl Mech. Working Tech., 1976–. Joseph Bramah Medal, IMechE, 1970. *Publications:* Advanced Mechanics of Materials, Manufacturing Properties of Materials, 1963; Hydrostatic Extrusion, 1971; Strength of Materials, 1980; papers to Royal Soc., IMechE, Iron and Steel Inst., Inst. Metals, Metals Soc. *Recreations:* music, gardening, swimming, squash. *Address:* Killan View, Dunvant Road, Three Crosses, Swansea SA4 3NU. *T:* Gowerton 873068. *Clubs:* Athenæum, Army and Navy.

ALEXANDER, Jonathan James Graham, DPhil; FSA 1981; Reader, History of Art Department, University of Manchester, since 1973; *b* 20 Aug. 1935; *s* of Arthur Ronald Brown and Frederica Emma Graham (who *m* 2nd, Boyd Alexander); *m* 1974, Mary Davey; one *s. Educ:* Magdalen Coll., Oxford (BA, MA, DPhil). Assistant, Dept of Western MSS, Bodleian Library, Oxford, 1963–71; Lecturer, History of Art Dept, Manchester Univ., 1971–73. Lyell Reader in Bibliography, Univ. of Oxford, 1982–83. *Publications:* (with Otto Pächt) Illuminated Manuscripts in the Bodleian Library, Oxford, 3 vols, 1966, 1970, 1973; (with A. C. de la Mare) Italian Illuminated Manuscripts in the Library of Major J. R. Abbey, 1969; Norman Illumination at Mont St Michel *c* 966–1100, 1970; The Master of Mary of Burgundy, A Book of Hours, 1970; Italian Renaissance Illuminations, 1977; Insular Manuscripts 6th–9th Century, 1978; The Decorated Letter, 1978; articles in Burlington Magazine, Arte Veneta, Pantheon, etc. *Recreations:* music, gardening. *Address:* 8 Pine Road, West Didsbury, Manchester M20 0UY. *T:* 061-445 1025.

ALEXANDER, Sir Kenneth (John Wilson), Kt 1978; BSc (Econ.); FRSE 1978; Principal and Vice-Chancellor, Stirling University, since 1981; *b* Edinburgh, 14 March 1922; *o s* of late William Wilson Alexander; *m* 1949, Angela-May, *d* of late Capt. G. H. Lane, RN; one *s* four *d. Educ:* George Heriot's Sch., Edinburgh; Sch. of Economics, Dundee. Research Asst, Univ. of Leeds, 1949–51; Lectr, Univ. of Sheffield, 1951–56; Lectr, Univ. of Aberdeen, 1957–62; Dean of Scottish Business Sch., 1973–75 (Chm., Acad. Exec. Cttee, 1972–73); Prof. of Econs, Strathclyde Univ., 1963–80, on leave of absence, 1976–80; Chm., Highlands and Islands Develt Bd, 1976–80. Umpire, N Derbyshire District Conciliation Bd, 1963; Mem. Adv. Cttee on University of the Air, 1965; Director: Fairfields (Glasgow) Ltd, 1966–68; Upper Clyde Shipbuilders Ltd, 1968–71; Chm., Govan Shipbuilders, 1974–76; Dir, Glasgow Chamber of Commerce, 1969–73; Economic Consultant to Sec. of State for Scotland, 1968–; Chm., Cttee on Adult Educn in Scotland, 1970–73; Member: Exec. Cttee, Scottish Council (Develt and Industry), 1968–; (part-time) Scottish Transport Gp, 1969–76; SSRC, 1975–76; Scottish Develt Agency, 1975–; Technical Change Centre, 1981–. Governor, Newbattle Abbey Coll., 1967–73; President: Section F, British Assoc., 1974; Saltire Soc., 1975–. CBIM 1980. Hon. LLD CNAA, 1976; DUniv Stirling, 1977. *Publications:* The Economist in Business, 1967; Productivity Bargaining and the Reform of Industrial Relations, 1969; (with C. L. Jenkins) Fairfields, a study of industrial change, 1971; (ed) The Political Economy of Change, 1976; articles in Oxford Econ. Papers, Quarterly Jl of Econ., Scottish Jl of Pol. Econ., Economica, Yorkshire Bulletin Economics, and other jls. *Recreation:* Scottish antiquarianism. *Address:* 1 Airthrey Castle Yard, Stirling.

ALEXANDER, Sir Lindsay; *see* Alexander, Sir J. L.

ALEXANDER, Rt. Rev. Mervyn Alban Newman; *see* Clifton, Bishop of, (RC).

ALEXANDER, Michael Charles; writer; *b* 20 Nov. 1920; *s* of late Rear-Adm. Charles Otway Alexander and Antonia Geermans; *m* 1963, Sarah Wignall (marr. diss.); one *d. Educ:* Stowe; RMC, Sandhurst; Oflag IVC, Colditz. Served War: DCLI; 5 (Ski) Bn Scots Gds; 8 Commando (Layforce); HQ 13 Corps (GSO 3); Special Boat Section; (POW, 1942–44); 2nd SAS Regt; War Office (Civil Affairs). Intergovtl Cttee on Refugees, 1946; Editorial Dir, Common Ground Ltd, 1946–50. Located Firuzkoh, Central Afghanistan, 1952; Himalayan Hovercraft Expedn, 1972; Yucatan Straits Hovercraft Expedn, 1975; Upper Ganges Hovercraft Expedn, 1980. Dir, Acorn Productions Ltd, 1977–. Mem., London Library. FZS, FRGS, FRAI. *Publications:* The Privileged Nightmare (with Giles Romilly), 1952 (republ. as Hostages at Colditz, 1975); Offbeat in Asia, 1953; The Reluctant

Legionnaire, 1955; The True Blue, 1957; Mrs Fraser on the Fatal Shore, 1972; Discovering the New World, 1976; Omai: Noble Savage, 1977; Queen Victoria's Maharajah, 1980. *Address:* 48 Eaton Place, SW1. *T:* 01-235 2724; Skelbo House, Dornoch, Sutherland. *T:* Golspie 3180.

ALEXANDER, Michael O'Donel Bjarne, CMG 1982; HM Diplomatic Service; HM Ambassador at Vienna since 1982; *b* 19 June 1936; *s* of late Cone Hugh O'Donel Alexander, CMG, CBE, and Enid Constance Crichton Neate; *m* 1960, Traute Krohn; two *s* one *d. Educ:* Foyle Coll., Londonderry; Ha Sch., Hampstead; St Paul's Sch.; King's Coll., Cambridge (Schol.); Harkness Fellow (Yale and Berkeley) 1960–62. MA (Cantab), AM (Yale). Royal Navy 1955–57. Entered HM Foreign (later Diplomatic) Service, 1962; Moscow 1963–65; Office of Political Adviser, Singapore, 1965–68; FCO, 1968–72; Ass Private Sec. to Secretary of State (Rt Hon. Sir Alec Douglas-Home, MP, an Rt Hon. James Callaghan, MP) 1972–74; Counsellor (Conf. on Security an Co-operation in Europe) and later Head of Chancery, UK Mission, Geneva 1974–77; Dep. Head, 1977–78, Head, 1978–79, Personnel Operations Dep FCO; Private Sec. (Overseas Affairs) to the Prime Minister (Rt Hon Margaret Thatcher, MP), 1979–81. Former Public Schools', British Universities' and National Junior Foil Champion; fenced for Cambridge Univ., 1957–60 (Captain, 1959–60); English Internat., 1958; Silver Medallis (Epée Team) Olympic Games, 1960; Gold Medallist, US Championships 1961; Captained England, 1963. Represented Cambridge in Field Event Match with Oxford, 1959–60. *Recreations:* reading history; watching o participating in sport of any kind. *Address:* c/o Foreign and Commonwealt' Office, SW1. *Clubs:* Athenæum, Epée, All England Fencing; Hawk (Cambridge).

ALEXANDER, Nell Haigh; President of Baptist Union, Great Britain and Ireland (first woman so appointed), 1978–79; *b* 24 Feb. 1915; *d* of Williar Henry and Grace Caroline Fowler; *m* 1938, Arthur Alexander; one *s. Educ* Higher Grade (Central) Girls' Sch., Cambridge. Nat. Chm., Women's Work Baptist Union, 1971–76; Representative for Europe, Baptist World Allianc (Women's Dept). *Recreations:* classical music, reading, theatre, church drama poetry. *Address:* 86 Thornton Road, Cambridge. *T:* Cambridge 276368.

ALEXANDER, Sir Norman (Stanley), Kt 1966; CBE 1959. Professor o Physics: Raffles Coll., Singapore, 1936–49; Univ. of Malaya, Singapore 1949–52; University Coll., Ibadan, Nigeria, 1952–60; Vice-Chancellor Ahmadu Bello Univ., Nigeria, 1961–66.

ALEXANDER, Richard Thain; MP (C) Newark, since 1979; *b* 29 June 1934 *s* of Richard Rennie Alexander and Gladys Alexander; *m* 1966, Valerie Ann one *s* one *d. Educ:* Dewsbury Grammar Sch., Yorks; University Coll. London (LLB Hons). Articled with Sir Francis Hill, Messrs Andrew & Co., Lincoln 1957–60; Asst Solicitor, Messrs McKinnell, Ervin & Holmes, Scunthorpe 1960–64; Sole Principal and Sen. Partner, Messrs Jones, Alexander & Co Retford, 1964–. *Recreations:* tennis, bowls, horse riding, a little squash *Address:* 28 Union Street, Retford, Notts. *Clubs:* Farmers'; Newark Conservative.

ALEXANDER, Rear-Adm. Robert Love, CB 1964; DSO 1943; DSC 1944 *b* 29 April 1913; *o s* of Captain R. L. Alexander, Edinburgh; *m* 1936, Margaret Elizabeth, *o d* of late George Conrad Spring, and Mrs Maurice House; on *s* four *d. Educ:* Merchiston Castle; Royal Naval College, Dartmouth. Joine RNC, 1927; Cadet HMS Repulse, 1930; Midshipman HMS Kent, 1931–33 Sub-Lieut, qualified in submarines, 1935. Served throughout War of 1939–4. in submarines; first command HMS H32, 1940; later commands: HMS Proteus 1942; HMS Truculent, 1942–44; HMS Tuna, 1945. Second in command an in temp. command HMS Glory, Korean War, 1951–52; in command Firs Destroyer Squadron, 1957; Imperial Defence College, 1959; in command HMS Forth and 1st Submarine Squadron, 1960; Captain Submarines an Minesweepers, Mediterranean, and NATO Commander Submarines Mediterranean, HMS Narvik, 1960–62. Vice Naval Deputy to the Supreme Allied Commander Europe, 1962–65. Lieut 1936; Comdr 1946; Capt. 1952 Rear-Adm. 1962; retd, 1965. *Address:* Beeches Croft, Fyning Lane, Rogate Petersfield, Hants. *T:* Rogate 368.

ALEXANDER, Robert Scott, QC 1973; *b* 5 Sept. 1936; *s* of late Samuel James and of Hannah May Alexander; *m* ; two *s* one *d* (and one *s* decd). *Educ* Brighton Coll.; King's Coll., Cambridge. BA 1959, MA 1963. Called to Bar Middle Temple, 1961; Bencher, 1979. Pres., King's Coll. Assoc., 1980–81 *Address:* 1 Brick Court, Temple, EC4. *T:* 01-583 0777.

ALEXANDER, Walter Ronald; Chairman, Walter Alexander plc, since 197 (Managing Director, 1973–79); *b* 6 April 1931; *s* of Walter Alexander and Katherine Mary Turnbull; *m* 1st, 1956, Rosemary Anne Sleigh (marr. diss 1975); two *s* two *d* ; 2nd, 1979, Mrs Lorna Elwes, *d* of Lydia Duchess o Bedford. *Educ:* Loretto Sch.; Cambridge Univ. (MA Hons). Chm. and Man Dir, Tayforth Ltd, 1961–71; Chm., Scottish Automobile Co. Ltd, 1971–73 Director: Scotcros plc, 1965– (Chm., 1973–82); Investors Capital Trust plc 1967–; Clydesdale Bank plc, 1971–; Great Northern Investment Trust plc 1973–; Dawson Internat. plc, 1979–. Chm., Scottish Appeals Cttee, Police Dependants' Trust, 1974–81; Pres., Public Schs Golfing Soc., 1973–79; Chm. PGA, 1982–; Governor, Loretto Sch., 1961–. Scottish Free Enterprise Award 1977. *Recreation:* golf. *Address:* Ryland Lodge, Dunblane, Perthshire FK15 0HY. *T:* Dunblane 823351. *Clubs:* Royal and Ancient Golf (Captain

1980-81); Hon. Company of Edinburgh Golfers; Prestwick Golf; Royal St George's Golf.

LEXANDER, William Gemmell, MBE 1945; Chairman, W. H. Stott & Co. Ltd, since 1979 (Director since 1968); *b* 19 Aug. 1918; *s* of Harold Gemmell Alexander and Winifred Ada Alexander (*née* Stott); *m* 1945, Janet Rona Page Alexander (*née* Elias); four *s* one *d. Educ:* Tre Arddur Bay Sch.; Sedbergh Sch.; Oxford Univ. (MA). Served War of 1939-45 (despatches, war stars and clasps): Driver Mechanic, 2nd Lieut, Lieut, Capt., Maj.; served in France, S Africa, Eritrea, Egypt, Middle East, Sicily, Italy, Algeria, NW Europe. HM Overseas Civil Service, 1946-59: Gilbert and Ellice Is, 1946-51; Mauritius, 1951-55; Cyprus, 1955-59; Man., Cooperative Wholesale Soc., Agricultural Dept, 1960-63; Dir, Internat. Cooperative Alliance, 1963-68; Dir-Gen., RoSPA, 1968-74; County Road Safety Officer, W Yorks MCC, 1974-78. Mem., BSI Quality Assurance Council, 1975-. Clerk, Dent Parish Council, 1980-. AMBIM 1963. *Recreations:* all sports and walking. *Address:* Cross House, Dent, Cumbria LA10 5TF. *T:* Dent 228. *Club:* Royal Commonwealth Society.

LEXANDER-SINCLAIR of Freswick, Maj.-Gen. David Boyd, CB 1981; Commandant, Staff College, 1980-82; *b* 7 May 1927; *s* of late Comdr M. B. Alexander-Sinclair of Freswick, RN and late Avril N. Fergusson-Buchanan; *m* 1958, Ann Ruth, *d* of late Lt-Col Graeme Daglish; two *s* one *d. Educ:* Eton (King's Scholar). Commnd into Rifle Bde, 1946, served in Germany, Kenya, Cyprus; ADC to GOC South Malaya District and Maj.-Gen. Bde of Gurkhas, 1950-51; psc 1958; Bde Major, 6th Inf. Bde Gp, 1959-61; GSO2 (Dirg Staff) Staff Coll., 1963-65; comdg 3rd Bn Royal Green Jackets, 1967-69; MoD, 1965-67 and 1969-71; Comdr, 6th Armd Bde, 1971-73; Student, RCDS, 1974; GOC 1st Division, 1975-77; COS, UKLF, 1978-80. *Address:* c/o Midland Bank Ltd, 69 Pall Mall, SW1Y 5EY.

LEXANDER-SINCLAIR, John Alexis Clifford Cerda, SMOM, FRSA, RMS; Executive Chairman, British Visual Artists Rights Society, 1981, 1982; Chairman, Human Rights Trust, since 1974 (Founder and Chairman, 1969, Vice-Chairman, 1971-73); Vice-Chairman: Anti-Slavery Society and Committee for Indigenous People, since 1971 (Committee Member, since 1965); British Institute of Human Rights, since 1971; Deputy Secretary General, International League for Animal Rights, Paris, since 1978; Chairman, Art Registration Committee, since 1969; *b* 22 Feb. 1906; *s* of Col C. H. Alexander, Jacob's Horse, and Donna Lyta Alexander dei Marchesi della Cerda; *m* 1st, 1927, Baroness von Gottberg (decd); one *d*; 2nd, 1933, Stella Tucker; one *s* one *d*; 3rd, 1950, Simonne de Rougemont (*née* Vion); 4th, 1965, Maureen Dover (*née* Wood); one step *s. Educ:* Charterhouse; Goettingen and Munich Univs. Entered HM Foreign Service, 1928; served in China as Vice-Consul and Consul; despatches (Admiralty) 1938; Founder and Mem., Chinese Industrial Co-operatives, 1940-41; Liaison Free French Headquarters, Far East, 1941 (POW Shanghai, 1942); served in Washington as 1st Sec. of Embassy, 1943; seconded to UNRRA, London and Paris, 1944 (Mem., Cabinet Particulier, French Minister, Refugees, Deportees, and PoWs, Paris); CCG as Controller (Col) Economic Plans, 1945; 1st Sec. UK Delegation, UN, NY, 1946, 1947, 1948; Vice-Chm. UNICEF, 1946, 1947; Sec. Gen. UK Delegation Geneva Red Cross Conf., 1949; served UN, NY, 1950; Dir UN Office of High Comr for refugees, Geneva, 1951-52; transf. UN High Comr for Refugees Rep. (local rank Minister), Rome, 1953-55; European Dir (Paris), International Rescue Cttee, NY, 1957-58; UN Tech. Assistance Adviser to Min. of Finance, Govt of Thailand, Jan.-Feb. 1959, to Nat. Iranian Oil Co., Tehran, Iran, 1959-60; Head of Oil Industry Labour Re-deployment Unit, 1960; Manpower Expert, FAO (UN Special Fund) in the Rif, Morocco, 1961-62. Founder Mem., Hansard Soc. for Parliamentary Govt, 1944; Executive Sec. Liberal International, London, 1963-64; Hon. Campaign Dir, UK Cttee for Human Rights Year, 1967, 1968, 1969; Member: Cttee, Internat. Social Service, 1972; Cttee, League Against Cruel Sports, 1974-81; Dir, Animal Welfare Year, 1976; Vice-Pres., British Assoc. of Former UN Civil Servants, 1978-81. Knight of Magistral Grace, British Assoc. of SMO Malta, 1957. Distinguished Service Award (Internat. Rescue Cttee), 1959. Life Member, Fellow 1965, RSA; Mem., Royal Soc. of Miniature Painters, Sculptors and Gravers, 1971; Hon. Mem. Exec. Cttee, UK Section, Association Internationale des Arts Plastiques et Graphiques, 1977. *Address:* 5 Aysgarth Road, Dulwich Village, SE21 7JR. *T:* 01-733 1666; The Clink, Goodings, Woodlands St Mary, Newbury RG16 7BD. *T:* Great Shefford 450; 56 Boulevard Richard Lenoir, 75011 Paris, France. *T:* Paris 805 3588. *Club:* Athenæum.

ALFORD, Ven. John Richard; Archdeacon of Halifax, since 1972; *b* 21 June 1919; *s* of Walter John and Gertrude Ellen Alford. *Educ:* Fitzwilliam House, Cambridge (History Tri. Pts 1 and 2, BA 1941, MA 1947); Cuddesdon College, Oxford. Deacon 1943, priest 1944, Wakefield; Curate, St Paul, King Cross, Halifax, 1943-47; Curate, Wakefield Cathedral, 1947-50; Tutor, Wells Theological College, 1950-56; Priest Vicar, Wells Cathedral, 1950-56; Vice-Principal, The Queen's College, Birmingham, 1956-67; Exam. Chaplain to Bp of Kimberley and Kuruman, 1961-65; Domestic Chaplain, Director of Ordinands, and Exam. Chaplain to Bp of Chester, 1967-72; Vicar of Shotwick, Chester, 1967-72; Hon. Canon of Chester Cathedral, 1969-72, Emeritus, 1972; Canon Residentiary of Wakefield Cathedral, 1972-; Examining Chaplain to Bp of Wakefield, 1972-. Mem., General Synod of C of E, 1980-; Vice-Pres., CEMS, 1980-. *Recreations:* music, walking. *Address:* Flat A, 5 South Parade, Wakefield WF1 1LR. *T:* Wakefield 378532. *Club:* Royal Over-Seas League.

ALFRED, (Arnold) Montague; Second Permanent Secretary, and Chief Executive, Property Services Agency, Department of the Environment, since 1982; *b* 21 March 1925; *s* of Reuben Alfred and Bessie Alfred (*née* Arbesfield); *m* 1947, Sheila Jacqueline Gold; three *s. Educ:* Central Foundation Boys' Sch.; Imperial Coll., London: London Sch. of Economics. Head of Economics Dept, Courtaulds Ltd, 1953-69; Director, CELON Div., Courtaulds Ltd, 1964-69; Dir, BPC Ltd, 1969-81; Chairman: BPC Publishing Ltd, 1971-81; Caxton Publishing Holdings Ltd, 1971-81. *Publications:* Discounted Cash Flow (jointly), 1965; Business Economics (jointly), 1968. Numerous articles in: Accountant, Textile Jl, Investment Analyst, etc. *Recreation:* active in Jewish community affairs. *Address:* Department of the Environment, 2 Marsham Street, SW1P 3EB.

ALFVÉN, Prof. Hannes Olof Gösta, PhD; Professor of Plasma Physics, Royal Institute of Technology, Stockholm, 1963-73; *b* Sweden, 30 May 1908; *s* of Johannes Alfvén and Anna-Clara Romanus; *m* 1935, Kerstin Erikson, *d* of Rolf E. and Maria Uddenberg. *Educ:* Univ. of Uppsala (PhD 1934). Prof. of Theory of Electricity, 1940-45 and of Electronics, 1945-63, Royal Inst. of Technology, Stockholm. Prof., Univ. of California at San Diego, 1967. Pres., Pugwash Confs on Science and World Affairs, 1967-72; Member: Bd of Dirs, Swedish Atomic Energy Co., 1956-68; Science Adv. Council of Swedish Govt, 1961-67. Member: Swedish Acad. of Sciences; several foreign acads incl. Royal Society, London, 1980, Acad. of Sciences of the USSR, Nat. Acad. of Sciences, Washington, DC. Hon. DSc Oxon, 1977. Awarded Gold Medal of Royal Astronomical Soc. (Gt Britain), 1967; Nobel Prize for Physics, 1970; Lomonosov Medal, 1971; Franklin Medal, 1971. *Publications:* Cosmical Electrodynamics, 1948; On the Origin of the Solar System, 1956; Cosmical Electrodynamics: Fundamental Principles (jointly), 1963; World-Antiworlds (Eng. trans.), 1966; (as Olof Johannesson) The Tale of the Big Computer (Eng. trans.), 1968; Atom, Man and the Universe (Eng. trans.), 1969; (with Kerstin Alfvén) M70-Living on the Third Planet, 1971; (with G. Arrhenius) Evolution of the Solar System NASA SP-345, 1976; Cosmic Plasma, 1981; papers in physics and astrophysics. *Address:* c/o Department of Plasma Physics, Royal Institute of Technology, S-100 44 Stockholm, Sweden; University of California, San Diego, EE & CS, C-014, La Jolla, Calif 92093, USA.

ALGAR, Claudius Randleson, JP; barrister-at-law; *b* 18 May 1900; *s* of Claudius G. Algar; *m* 1930, Constance, *d* of Edgar Tucker, Carmarthen; one *s. Educ:* Highgate School. Barrister-at-law, Inner Temple, 1925. Dep. Chm., Wilts QS, 1945-71. Member of the Corporation of London, 1930-48. JP Wiltshire, 1941. *Address:* Rye Hill, Longbridge Deverill, Warminster, Wilts. *T:* Maiden Bradley 316.

ALGOMA, Bishop of, since 1975; **Rt. Rev. Frank Foley Nock,** DD; *b* 27 Feb. 1916; *s* of David Nock and Esther Hambidge; *m* 1942, Elizabeth Hope Adams; one *s* one *d. Educ:* Trinity Coll., Toronto (BA, BD). Curate, St Matthew's, Toronto, 1940-42; Incumbent, Christ Church, Korah, Sault Ste Marie, 1942-45; Rector: Bracebridge, St Thomas', 1945-48; Church of the Epiphany, Sudbury, 1948-57; St Luke's Cathedral, 1957-74; Dean of Algoma, 1957-74. Chancellor, Thorneloe Univ., Sudbury, 1974-; Director: Sault Ste Marie & Dist Gp Health Assoc.; Community Concerts Assoc.; Mem., Sault Ste Marie Rotary Club. Hon. DD Toronto, 1957; Hon. STD Thorneloe, 1980. *Recreations:* music, golfing, cross country skiing. *Address:* 134 Simpson Street, Sault Ste Marie, Ontario P6A 3V4, Canada. *T:* 705-256-7379.

ALHEGELAN, Sheikh Faisal Abdul Aziz; Order of King Abdulaziz, Saudi Arabia; Saudi Arabian Ambassador to the United States of America, since 1979; *b* 7 Oct. 1929; *s* of Sheikh Abdulaziz Alhegelan and Fatima Alissa; *m* 1961, Nouha Tarazi; three *s. Educ:* Faculty of Law, Fouad Univ., Cairo. Min. of Foreign Affairs, 1952-54; Saudi Arabian Embassy, Washington, USA, 1954-58; Chief of Protocol, Jeddah, 1958-60; Polit. Adviser to the King, 1960-61; Ambassador to: Spain, 1961-68; Venezuela and Argentina (concurrently), 1968-75; Denmark, 1975-76; Court of St James's, 1976-79. Gran Cruz, Isobel la Catolica, Spain; Gran Cordon Orden del Libertador, Venezuela; Grande Official, Orden Rio Branco, Brazil. *Address:* Royal Embassy of Saudi Arabia, 1520 18th Street, NW, Washington, DC 20036, USA.

ALISON, Rt. Hon. Michael James Hugh; PC 1981; MP (C) Barkston Ash since 1964; Minister of State, Department of Employment, since 1981; *b* 27 June 1926; *m* 1958, Sylvia Mary Haigh; two *s* one *d. Educ:* Eton; Wadham Coll., Oxford. Coldstream Guards, 1944-48; Wadham Coll., Oxford, 1948-51; Lazard Bros & Co. Ltd, 1951-53; London Municipal Soc., 1954-58; Conservative Research Dept, 1958-64. Parly Under-Sec. of State, DHSS, 1970-74; Minister of State, Northern Ireland Office, 1979-81. *Address:* House of Commons, SW1A 0AA.

ALISON, William Andrew Greig, FLA; Director of Libraries, City of Glasgow, 1975-81; *b* 23 Oct. 1916; *m* 1942, Jessie Youngson Henderson; two *d. Educ:* Daniel Stewart's Coll., Edinburgh. Edinburgh Public Libraries, 1935-62: Assistant, 1935-46; Librarian, Fine Art Dept, 1946-55; Branch Librarian, 1955-61; Librarian, Scottish and Local History Depts, 1961-62; Glasgow City Libraries, 1962-81: Supt of District Libraries, 1962-64; Depute City Librarian, 1964-74; City Librarian, 1974-75. Served War, Royal Air Force, 1940-46. President: Scottish Library Assoc., 1975; Library Assoc., 1979 (also Mem. Council, 1979-82; Chm., Library Assoc. Publishing, 1981-); Member: British Library Adv. Council, 1979-82; Nat. Library of Scotland Library Co-operation Cttee, 1974-81. Church of Scotland elder and session clerk. Silver Jubilee Medal, 1977. *Recreations:* travel, philately. *Address:* St Mawgan, 103 Mossgiel Road, Glasgow G43 2BY. *T:* 041-632 6036.

AL-KHALIFA, Shaikh Abdul-Rahman Faris; Ambassador of the State of Bahrain to the Court of St James's, since Nov. 1980; *b* 24 Feb. 1942; *s* of Shaikh Faris bin Khalifa Al-Khalifa and Shaikha Latifa Rashid Al-Khalifa; *m* 1969, Shaikha Latifa Salman Al-Khalifa; one *s* four *d*. *Educ:* Bahrain; Univ. of Cairo (BSc Economics and Commercial Subjects). Member of the Ruling Family of the State of Bahrain. *Address:* 98 Gloucester Road, SW7 4AU. *T:* 01-370 6213. *Clubs:* Royal Automobile; Hurlingham, Hampstead Golf.

ALLAIRE, Paul Arthur; Managing Director, Rank Xerox Limited, since 1980; *b* 21 July 1938; *s* of late Arthur E. Allaire and of Mrs G. P. Murphy; *m* 1963, Kathleen Buckley; one *s* one *d*. *Educ:* Worcester Polytechnic Inst., USA (BS Elect. Eng.); Carnegie-Mellon Univ., USA (MS Industrial Admin). Engineer, Univac, 1960-62; Project Manager, General Electric, 1962-64; Manager Financial Planning and Pricing, Xerox Corp., 1966-70; Financial Controller, Rank Xerox Ltd, 1970-73; Xerox Corporation: Dir, Internat. Finance, 1973-74; Dir, Internat. Ops, 1974-75; Rank Xerox Ltd: Chief Staff Officer, 1975-79; Dep. Man. Dir, 1979-80. Bd Mem., American Chamber of Commerce, 1980-. *Recreations:* horse riding, tennis. *Address:* 9 Chester Terrace, NW1. *T:* 01-486 4368.

ALLAM, Peter John; Architect Principal in private practice of Peter Allam, Chartered Architect, Dollar; *b* 17 June 1927; *er s* of late Leslie Francis Allam and Annette Farquharson (*née* Lawson); *m* 1961, Pamela Mackie Haynes; two *d*. *Educ:* Royal High Sch., Edinburgh; Glasgow Sch. of Architecture. War service, 1944-48, Far East; commnd in Seaforth Highlanders, 1946. Architectural trng, 1948-53. Bahrain Petroleum Co., Engrg Div., 1954-55; Asst in private architectural practices, 1956-64; Principal, own practice, 1964-68 and 1971-78; Partner in private practice of Haswell-Smith & Partners, Edinburgh, 1978-79; Director, Saltire Soc., 1968-70; Dir of Sales, Smith & Wellstood Ltd, Manfg Ironfounders, 1979-81. ARIBA 1964; Associate, RIAS, 1964. *Recreations:* study and practice of conservation, both architectural and natural; music, riding, Rugby. *Address:* 8 Town Burnside, Dollar, Clackmannanshire FK14 7EW. *T:* Dollar 2850.

ALLAN, Andrew Norman; Director of Programmes, since 1978 and Deputy Managing Director, since 1982, Tyne Tees Television Ltd; *b* 26 Sept. 1943; *s* of Andrew Allan and Elizabeth (*née* Davison); *m* 1978, Joanna Forrest; one *s* one *d*, and two *d* of a former marriage. *Educ:* Birmingham Univ. (BA). Presenter, ABC Television, 1965-66; Producer: Thames Television, 1966-69; ITN, 1970; Thames TV, 1971-75; Head of News, Thames TV, 1976-78. *Recreations:* reading, dining. *Address:* The Old Post House, Hedley on the Hill, Stocksfield, Northumberland NE43 7SW. *T:* Stocksfield 2434.

ALLAN, Sir Anthony James Allan H.; *see* Havelock-Allan.

ALLAN, (Charles) Lewis (Cuthbert), MA, CEng, FICE, FIEE, FBIM; Chairman, South of Scotland Electricity Board, 1967-73 (Deputy Chairman, 1964-67); Member, North of Scotland Hydro-Electric Board, 1967-73; *b* 22 July 1911; *s* of Charles W. Allan, Edinburgh, and Isabella H. Young; *m* 1938, Kathleen Mary Robinson, Chesterfield, Derbyshire; one *s* three *d*. *Educ:* Merchiston Castle School, Edinburgh; Pembroke College, Cambridge (Mechanical Sciences Tripos). Bruce Peebles & Co. Ltd, Edinburgh, 1933-35; Balfour Beatty & Co. Ltd, 1935-38; Central Electricity Board, 1938-41; Ipswich Corp. Electric Supply and Transport Dept, 1941-44; North of Scotland Hydro-Electric Board, 1944-63 (Chief Electrical and Mechanical Engineer, 1954-63). *Publications:* articles in the electrical technical press and for World Power Conference. *Recreations:* gardening, walking, fishing, piping, Church work. *Address:* Kil Modan, North Connel, Argyll PA37 1RE.

ALLAN, Colin Faulds, CB 1976; Chief Planning Inspector (Director of Planning Inspectorate), Department of the Environment, 1971-78; *b* Newcastle upon Tyne, 1917; *s* of late Jack Stanley and Ruth Allan; *m* 1940, Aurea, 2nd *d* of Algernon Noble, Hexham; one *s* one *d*. *Educ:* Royal Grammar Sch., Newcastle upon Tyne; King's Coll. (Newcastle), Durham Univ. DipArch, ARIBA, DipTP (Distinction), FRTPI. Capt., RA, 1940-45; served in Iraq, India, Burma (despatches). Chief Asst to Dr Thomas Sharp, Planning Consultant, 1945-47; Area Planning Officer, Cumberland and Staffs CC, 1947-57; joined Housing and Planning Inspectorate, 1957; Chief Housing and Planning Inspector, DoE (formerly Min. of Housing and Local Govt), 1967-71. *Recreations:* walking, bird-watching, reading, eighteenth-century wineglasses. *Address:* Fieldfares, Chinthurst Lane, Shalford, Guildford, Surrey. *T:* Guildford 61528.

ALLAN, Sir Colin (Hamilton), KCMG 1977 (CMG 1968); OBE 1959; FRAI 1950; Her Majesty's Overseas Civil Service, retired; *b* 23 Oct. 1921; *yr s* of late John Calder Allan, Cambridge, NZ; *m* 1955, Betty Dorothy, *e d* of late A. C. Evans, Brisbane, Australia; three *s*. *Educ:* Hamilton High Sch., NZ; Christchurch College, Canterbury Univ., NZ; Magdalene College, Cambridge. Military Service, NZ, 1942-44. Cadet, Colonial Admin. Service, British Solomon Is, 1945; District Comr, Western Solomons, 1946; District Comr, Malaita, 1950; Special Lands Comr, 1953; Sen. Asst Sec., Western Pacific High Commn, 1957; Asst Resident Comr, New Hebrides, 1959, British Resident Comr, 1966-73; Governor and C-in-C, Seychelles, 1973-76, and Comr, British Indian Ocean Territory, 1973-76; Governor, Solomon Is, and

High Comr for Western Pacific, 1976-78. Delegate: Seychelles Constitution Conf., 1975, 1976; Solomon Is Constitutional Conf., 1977. Vis. Fellow Australian Nat. Univ., Research Sch. of Pacific Studies, 1979. Mem., Lepros Trust Bd (NZ), 1980-. Commandeur, l'Ordre Nationale du Mérite (France 1966. *Publications:* Land Tenure in the British Solomon Islands Protectorat 1958; papers on colonial administration. *Recreations:* malacology, reading Th Times. *Address:* Glen Rowan, 17 Sale Street, Howick, Auckland, Nev Zealand. *Club:* Royal Commonwealth Society.

ALLAN, George Alexander, MA; Headmaster, Robert Gordon's Colleg Aberdeen, since 1978; *b* 3 Feb. 1936; *s* of William Allan and Janet Peters (*n* Watt); *m* 1962, Anne Violet Veevers; two *s*. *Educ:* Daniel Stewart's Coll Edinburgh; Edinburgh Univ. (MA 1st Cl. Hons Classics; Bruce of Grangehi Scholar, 1957). Classics Master, Glasgow Acad., 1958-60; Daniel Stewart College: Classics Master, 1960-63; Head of Classics, 1963-73; Housemaster 1966-73; Schoolmaster Fellow, Corpus Christi Coll., Cambridge, 1972; Dep Headmaster, Robert Gordon's Coll., 1973-77. Governor, Welbeck Coll 1980-. *Recreations:* golf, gardening, music. *Address:* 24 Woodend Roac Aberdeen AB2 6YH. *T:* Aberdeen 321733. *Club:* East India, Devonshi Sports and Public Schools.

ALLAN, Gordon Buchanan, TD 1950; Chartered Accountant; *b* 11 Aug 1914; *s* of late Alexander Buchanan Allan, MIMechE, and Irene Lilian Allan Glasgow; *m* 1971, Gwenda Jervis Davies, *d* of late John William and Elizabet Davies, Porthcawl, Glam. *Educ:* Glasgow Academy; High Sch. of Glasgow Glasgow Univ. Mem. Inst. Chartered Accountants (Scot.), 1937 Commissioned into Royal Signals (TA), 1938. Served War of 1939-4! DAAG, GHQ, India, 1945, (Major). Director: George Outram & Co. Ltc 1960-75 (Dep. Man. Dir and Financial Dir, 1970-75); Holmes McDougall Ltc 1966-72. Mem. Press Council, 1969-74. Vice-Pres., Scottish Daily Newspape Soc., 1970, Pres. 1971-73; Dir, Glasgow Chamber of Commerce, 1971-7! Member: UK Newsprint Users' Cttee, 1972-75; Council, CBI, 1972-74 Finance Cttee, RIIA, 1975-77; Merchants' House of Glasgow, 1975-. Mem Bd, Bield Housing Assoc. Ltd, 1978-. Governor, The Queen's College Glasgow, 1976-. *Recreations:* music, golf, hill-walking. *Address:* 3 Wincheste Court, Glasgow G12 0JN. *T:* 041-334 2353. *Clubs:* Royal Scottis Automobile (Glasgow); Windyhill Golf (Bearsden).

ALLAN, Rt. Rev. Hugh James Pearson; *see* Keewatin, Bishop of.

ALLAN, Ian; Chairman, Ian Allan Group Ltd, since 1962; *b* 29 June 1922; of George A. T. Allan, OBE, and Mary Louise (*née* Barnes); *m* 1947, Molli Eileen (*née* Franklin); two *s*. *Educ:* St Paul's Sch. Joined Southern Railwa Co., 1939. Founded Ian Allan Ltd, Publishers, 1945; other cos co-ordinate into Ian Allan Group Ltd, 1962. Chm., Dart Valley Light Railway Ltd, 1976 Governor, Christ's Hosp., 1944-. Almoner, 1980-; Governor, King Edward Sch., Witley (Bridewell Royal Hosp.), 1975-. Vice Pres., Transport Trus 1979-; Mem., TUCC for London, 1982-. *Publications:* compiled and edite many books on railways and transport subjects, 1939-. *Recreation* swimming, touring, miniature railways. *Address:* Terminal House, Shepperto TW17 8AS. *T:* Walton-on-Thames 28950; The Jetty, Middleton-on-Sea Bognor Regis, W Sussex. *T:* Middleton-on-Sea 3378.

ALLAN, James Nicholas, CBE 1976; High Commissioner in Mauritius, sinc 1981; *b* 22 May 1932; *s* of Morris Edward Allan and late Joan Bach; *m* 196 Helena Susara Crouse; one *s* one *d*. *Educ:* Gresham's Sch.; London Sch. c Economics. HM Forces, 1950-53. Asst Principal, CRO, 1956-58; Third, late Second Sec., Cape Town/Pretoria, 1958-59; Private Sec. to Parly Under-Sec 1959-61; First Secretary: Freetown, 1961-64; Nicosia, 1964; CRO, later FCO 1964-68; Head of Chancery, Peking, 1969-71; Luxembourg, 1971-73 Counsellor, seconded to Northern Ireland Office, Belfast, 1973-7! Counsellor, FCO, 1976; Head of Overseas Inf. Dept., FCO, 1978-8 (Governor's Staff, Salisbury, Dec. 1979-March 1980). *Address:* c/o Foreig and Commonwealth Office, SW1. *Club:* Athenæum.

ALLAN, Commissioner Janet Laurie; retired 1957; *b* 20 March 1892; *d* c Thomas Alexander Allan, chemist, Strathaven, Scotland. *Educ:* in Scotland Entered Salvation Army Training Coll., 1911; commissioned as sergeant t the College, 1912; opened Salvation Army work in Castle Douglas, Scotland 1913; returned to Training College as a Brigade Officer, 1915; Home Office at Training Coll., 1918; with "Calypso" Party sailed to India (Sout Travancore, South India), 1921; returned to England, 1929, and appointed t slum and goodwill work in British Isles; returned to India; served i Travancore, Calcutta, and Eastern India; also Madras and Telegu country a Territorial Comdr; Territorial Comdr of Western India, 1951-54; Territoria Comdr of Southern India, 1954-57, Salvation Army. Leader Salvation Arm Women's Social Work, Great Britain and Ireland, 1947; Comr, 1951. *Address* Glebelands, 1 Grove Hill Road, SE5 8DF.

ALLAN, John Clifford, RCNC; Director, Manpower, Dockyards, 1975-79 *b* 3 Feb. 1920; *s* of James Arthur and Mary Alice Allan; *m* 1947, Dorothy Mar (*née* Dossett); two *d*. *Educ:* Royal Naval Coll., Greenwich. Entered Roya Corps of Naval Constructors, 1945; service at HM Dockyards: Portsmoutl Chatham, Devonport, Gibraltar, Singapore, 1950-75; Chief Constructo Chief Executive Dockyard HQ, 1967-69, Asst Dir, 1969, Dir, 1975 *Recreations:* tennis, squash. *Address:* New Morney, Lansdown Road, Bath Avon BA1 5TD. *T:* Bath 315237.

LLAN, John Gray, CBE 1975; Legal Adviser and Solicitor to the Crown Estate Commissioners, 1961–77; *b* 10 Nov. 1915; *s* of late John Allan, CB, FSA, FBA, LLD, and Ida Mary (*née* Law). *Educ:* Charterhouse; Oriel College, Oxford. Called to Bar, Middle Temple, 1940. War Service, 1940–46: The Black Watch, GSO2 (War Office and Allied Land Headquarters, Melbourne), 1942–46. Legal Branch, Min. of Agriculture, Fisheries and Food, 1946–57. Deputy Legal Adviser, Crown Estate Office, 1957. *Recreations:* golf, bridge. *Address:* 5 Rheidol Terrace, N1. *T:* 01-226 7616. *Club:* Boodles.

LLAN, Lewis; *see* Allan, C. L. A.

LLAN, William Nimmo, CMG 1948; MC 1917; FICE; engineering consultant; *b* 10 Nov. 1896; *s* of late Rev. W. G. Allan, MA, BD, Callander, Perthshire; *m* 1932, Mary Helen Burnett, *o d* of late Rev. T. Burnett Peter, MA, BD, Callander, Perthshire; two *s. Educ:* George Watson's Boys' College, Edinburgh. Served European War, 1914–19, 9th (Ser.) Bn The Gordon Highlanders, Captain (MC). BSc(Eng) Glasgow Univ., 1921. AMICE 1923, MICE 1944, FICE. Engineer with Kassala Cotton Co., Sudan, 1924; Irrigation Dept of Sudan Govt, 1927; Asst Director, 1941; Director, 1944; Irrigation Consultant to Sudan Govt, 1946–69; Consultant to FAO of UNO, Rome, 1959–67. *Address:* St Petroc's Cottage, Bread Street, Ruscombe, Stroud, Glos GL6 6EQ. *T:* Stroud 3941.

LLAN, William Roderick Buchanan; Editorial Consultant to Ommific; *b* 11 Sept. 1945; *s* of James Buchanan Allan and Mildred Pattenden; *m* 1973, Gillian Gail Colgan; two *s. Educ:* Stowe; Trinity Coll., Cambridge (BA Hons History, 1966). Joined staff of The Connoisseur, 1972, Editor 1976–80. Author of five radio plays with nineteenth century historical themes. *Publications:* contrib. to several books dealing with British history; contrib. to History Today, The Connoisseur, and Antique Collector. *Recreations:* military history, cooking. *Address:* 54 South Western Road, St Margaret's, Twickenham, Mddx. *T:* 01-891 0974.

LLANBRIDGE, Hon. Lord; William Ian Stewart; a Senator of the College of Justice in Scotland, since 1977; *b* 8 Nov. 1925; *s* of late John Stewart, FRIBA, and Mrs Maysie Shepherd Service or Stewart, Drimfearn, Bridge of Allan; *m* 1955, Naomi Joan Douglas, *d* of late Sir James Boyd Douglas, CBE, and of Lady Douglas, Barstibly, Castle Douglas; one *s* one *d. Educ:* Loretto; Glasgow and Edinburgh Univs. Sub-Lt, RNVR, 1944–46. Called to the Bar, 1951; QC (Scot.) 1965; Advocate-Depute, 1959–64; Mem., Criminal Injuries Compensation Bd, 1969–70; Home Advocate-Depute, 1970–72; Solicitor-General for Scotland, 1972–74; Temp. Sheriff-Principal of Dumfries and Galloway, Apr.–Dec. 1974. Mem., Criminal Injuries Compensation Bd, 1976–77. *Address:* 60 Northumberland Street, Edinburgh EH3 6JE. *T:* 031-556 2823. *Clubs:* New (Edinburgh); RNVR (Glasgow).

LLANSON-WINN, family name of **Baron Headley.**

LLARD, Sir Gordon (Laidlaw), Kt 1981; President, Royal Victorian Eye and Ear Hospital, 1964–80, now Vice President; *b* 7 Aug. 1909; *m* 1935, Cherry Singleton; one *s. Educ:* Scotch Coll., Melbourne. FCA; FCA (NZ). Joined Flack & Flack, later Price Waterhouse & Co., 1927; Partner, and a Sen. Partner, in Australia and NZ, 1942–74. Chairman: Australian Motor Industries Ltd; Grindlay Aust. Ltd. Mem., Gen. Council, Inst. of Chartered Accountants in Australia, 1962–70 (Victorian Chm., 1962–64). *Recreations:* golf, tennis, gardening. *Address:* 4 St Martins Close, Kooyong, Vic 3144, Australia. *Clubs:* Melbourne, Australian (Melbourne); Royal Melbourne Golf.

LLARD, General Jean Victor, CC (Canada) 1968; CBE 1946; DSO 1943 (Bars 1944, 1945); ED 1946; CD 1958; Chief of Canadian Defence Staff, 1966–69; Representative of the Province of Quebec in New York, Sept. 1969–June 1970; now engaged in business as a consultant in industrial promotion; *b* Nicolet, PQ, 12 June 1913; *s* of late Ernest Allard and Victorine Trudel; *m* 1939, Simone, *d* of Gustave Piche, OBE; two *d. Educ:* St Laurent Coll., Montreal; St Jerome Coll., Kitchener, Ont. Joined Three Rivers Regt, 1933; Capt., 1938; Major, 1939; War of 1939–45: Co. of London Yeomanry, 1940–41; Canadian Army Staff Coll., Kingston, 1941–42 (Instructor, 1942); 5th Canadian Armoured Div.; second in command: Régt de la Chaudière; Royal 22e Regt, 1943 (Italy); Lt-Col 1944; CO Royal 22e Regt; Brig. 1945; Comd 6th Canadian Infantry Brigade, 1945 (Holland); Military Attaché Canadian Embassy, Moscow, 1945–48; Comd Eastern Quebec Area, 1948–50; idc 1951; Vice Quarter-Master Gen., Canada, 1952; Comdr, 25th Canadian Infantry Brigade Group, in Korea, 1953; Comdr 3rd Canadian Infantry Brigade, 1954; Comd Eastern Quebec Area, 1956; Maj.-Gen. 1958; Vice Chief of the General Staff, Canada, 1958; Comdr 4th Division, BAOR, 1961–63 (first Canadian to command a British Div.); Maj.-Gen. Survival, Ottawa, 1963; Lt-Gen. 1964; Chief of Operational Readiness, Canada, 1964–65; Comdr, Mobile Command, Canada, Oct. 1965–June 1966; General, 1966; Col Comdt, 12 Regt Blindé du Canada. Member: Royal Canadian Military Inst.; Royal 22e Regt Assoc.; La Régie du 22e; Royal Canadian Air Force Assoc.; Royal Canadian Naval Service Assoc.; Cercle Universitaire d'Ottawa; Chm. Bd of Governors, Ottawa Univ., 1966–69, Member Bd, 1969–. Hon. DSS Laval, 1958; Hon. LLD: Ottawa, 1959; St Thomas, 1966; St Mary's, Halifax, 1969; Hon. DScMil RMC Canada, 1970. FRSA. Bronze Lion (Netherlands), 1945; Légion d'Honneur and Croix de Guerre (France), 1945; Legion of Merit (US), 1954. Kt of Magistral Grace, Sovereign and Military Order of Malta, 1967. *Recreations:* golf, music, fishing, hunting. *Address:* 3265 Boulevard du Carmel, Trois-Rivieres, Quebec, Canada. *Clubs:* Quebec Garrison, KI-8-EB Gulf; Maskety Fish and Game.

ALLARDICE, William Arthur Llewellyn; His Honour Judge Allardice; DL; a Circuit Judge since 1972 (Midland and Oxford Circuit); *b* 18 Dec. 1924; *s* of late W. C. Allardice, MD, FRCSEd, JP, and late Constance Winifred Allardice; *m* 1956, Jennifer Ann, *d* of G. H. Jackson, Cape Town; one *s* one *d. Educ:* Stonyhurst Coll.; University Coll., Oxford (MA). Open Schol., Classics, 1942; joined Rifle Bde, 1943, commnd 1944; served with 52nd LI, Europe and Palestine, 1945; Oxford, 1946–48; called to Bar, Lincoln's Inn, 1950; practised Oxford Circuit, 1950–71. DL Staffs, 1980. *Recreations:* local history, matters equestrian. *Address:* c/o Courts Administrator, Stafford. *T:* Stafford 55219.

ALLASON, Lt-Col James Harry, OBE 1953; *b* 6 Sept. 1912; *s* of late Brigadier-General Walter Allason, DSO (*m* 1946, Nuala Elveen (marr. diss. 1974), *d* of late J. A. McArevey, Foxrock, Co. Dublin; two *s. Educ:* Haileybury; RMA, Woolwich. Commissioned RA, 1932; transferred 3rd DG, 1937; War Service India and Burma, 1939–44; retired 1953. Member Kensington Borough Council, 1956–65. Contested (C) Hackney Central, General Election, 1955; MP (C) Hemel Hempstead, 1959–Sept. 1974; PPS to Sec. of State for War, 1960–64. *Recreations:* ski-ing, sailing. *Address:* 82 Ebury Mews, SW1. *T:* 01-730 1576. *Clubs:* White's; Royal Yacht Squadron.

ALLAUN, Frank; MP (Lab), East Salford, since 1955; *b* 27 Feb. 1913; *s* of Harry and Hannah Allaun; *m* 1941, Lilian Ball; one *s* one *d. Educ:* Manchester Grammar Sch. BA (Com); ACA. Town Hall Correspondent, and later Industrial Correspondent, Manchester Evening News; Northern Industrial Correspondent, Daily Herald; Editor, Labour's Northern Voice, 1951–67. Mem., NUJ; formerly Mem. AEU and Shop Assistants' Union; National Chm. Labour Action for Peace; helped organise first Aldermaston march. Vice-Pres. Assoc. of Public Health Inspectors. PPS to the Secretary of State for the Colonies, Oct. 1964–March 1965, resigned. Mem., Labour Party National Executive, 1967–, Dep. Chm., 1977–78, Chm., 1978–79. *Publications:* Stop the H Bomb Race, 1959; Heartbreak Housing, 1966; Your Trade Union and You, 1950; No Place Like Home, 1972; The Wasted £30 Billions, 1975; Questions and Answers on Nuclear Weapons; numerous broadcasts. *Recreations:* walking, swimming. *Address:* 1 South Drive, Manchester M21 2DX. *T:* 061-881 7547.

ALLAWAY, Percy Albert, CBE 1973; FEng; Director, EMI Ltd, 1965–81; Chairman, EMI Electronics Ltd, 1968–81; Member, Executive Management Board, THORN EMI Ltd, 1980–81, Consultant, since 1981; *b* 22 Aug. 1915; *s* of Albert Edward Allaway and Frances Beatrice (*née* Rogers); *m* 1959, Margaret Lilian Petyt. *Educ:* Southall Technical College. FEng 1980, FIProdE, FIERE, FIQA. Trained EMI Ltd, 1930–35, returned 1940; Man. Dir, 1961–81, Chm., 1969–81, EMI Electronics Ltd; Chairman: EMI-Varian Ltd, 1969–81; EMI-MEC Ltd, 1968–81; Director: Nuclear Enterprises Ltd, 1961–81; SE Labs (EMI) Ltd, 1967–81. Pres., EEA, 1969–70 (former Mem. Council). Chm., Defence Industries Quality Assurance Panel, 1971–78; Past Chm. and Hon. Mem., NCQR; Member: Nat. Electronics Council, 1965–80; Raby Cttee, 1968–69; Parly and Scientific Cttee, 1976–; Pres., IERE, 1975; a Vice-Pres., and Mem. Council: Inst. of Industrial Managers; IQA; Member: Bd and Exec. Cttee, CEI, 1974–78 (Vice-Chm., 1979–80, Chm., 1980–81); Design Council, 1978–80; PO Engrg Adv. Cttee, 1977–81. Mem. Bd, Industrial Inst., and Mem., Court and Council, Brunel Univ. Liveryman, Worshipful Co. of Scientific Instrument Makers. CompIEE. FRSA. DTech (hc) Brunel, 1973. *Address:* Kroller, 54 Howards Wood Drive, Gerrards Cross, Bucks. *T:* Gerrards Cross 85028.

ALLCHIN, Rev. Canon Arthur Macdonald; Residentiary Canon of Canterbury Cathedral since 1973; *b* 20 April 1930; *s* of late Dr Frank Macdonald Allchin and Louise Maude Allchin. *Educ:* Westminster Sch.; Christ Church, Oxford (BLitt, MA); Cuddesdon Coll., Oxford. Curate, St Mary Abbots, Kensington, 1956–60; Librarian, Pusey House, Oxford, 1960–69; Visiting Lecturer: General Theological Seminary, NY, 1967 and 1968; Catholic Theological Faculty, Lyons, 1980; Warden, Community of Sisters of Love of God, Oxford, 1967–. Editor, Sobornost, 1960–77; Jt Editor, Christian, 1975–. Hon. DD Bucharest Theol Inst., 1977. *Publications:* The Silent Rebellion, 1958; The Spirit and the Word, 1963; (with J. Coulson) The Rediscovery of Newman, 1967; Ann Griffiths, 1976; The World is a Wedding, 1978; The Kingdom of Love and Knowledge, 1979; The Dynamic of Tradition, 1981; The Taste of Liberty, 1982; contrib. Studia Liturgica, Irenikon, Theology, Eastern Churches Review. *Recreations:* music, poetry, walking in hill country. *Address:* 12 The Precincts, Canterbury CT1 2EH. *T:* 0227 63060.

See also F. R. Allchin.

ALLCHIN, Frank Raymond, PhD; FBA 1981; Fellow of Churchill College, since 1963, and Reader in Indian Studies, since 1972, University of Cambridge; *b* 9 July 1923; *s* of Frank MacDonald Allchin and Louise Maude Wright; *m* 1951, Bridget Gordon; one *s* one *d. Educ:* Westminster Sch.; Regent Street Polytechnic; Sch. of Oriental and African Studies, London Univ. (BA, PhD 1954); MA Cantab. Lectr in Indian Archaeology, SOAS, 1954–59; Univ. Lectr in Indian Studies, Cambridge, 1959–72. Jt Dir, Cambridge Univ. (British) Archaeol Mission to Pakistan, 1975–. Consultant: UNESCO, 1969, 1972, 1975; UNDP, 1971. Chm., Broads Tours, Wroxham,

Ltd, 1975- (Dir, 1964-). *Publications:* Piklihal Excavations, 1960; Utnur Excavations, 1961; Neolithic Cattle Keepers of South India, 1963; Kavitavali, 1964; The Petition to Rām, 1966; (with B. Allchin) Birth of Indian Civilization, 1968; (with N. Hammond) The Archaeology of Afghanistan, 1978; (with D. K. Chakrabarti) Sourcebook of Indian Archaeology, vol. 1, 1979; (with B. Allchin) The Rise of Civilization in India and Pakistan, 1982; contribs to learned journals. *Recreations:* gardening, brewing. *Address:* Westgate House, 3 Orwell Road, Barrington, Cambridge CB2 5SE. *T:* Cambridge 870494.

See also Rev. Canon A. M. Allchin.

ALLCOCK, John Gladding Major, CB 1964; *b* 20 July 1905; *o s* of Rev. William Gladding Allcock, MA (TCD), and Ada Allcock (*née* Hall); *m* 1936, Eileen, *d* of Dr Ll. A. Baiss, OBE, Swanage, Dorset; one *s* one *d. Educ:* St Paul's School; Jesus College, Cambridge. Classical Tripos Cl. II in Pts I and II, BA 1927; MA 1931. Asst Master: Exeter School, 1927-28; Liverpool College, 1928-35. HM Inspector of Schools, 1935. Awarded Commonwealth Fund Fellowship, 1939. War Service in Admiralty, 1939-44. Divisional Inspector (NW Div.), 1949; Chief Inspector for Educational Developments, 1959-66, retired. *Recreations:* music, theatre, foreign travel. *Address:* Russet Cottage, Corfe Castle, Dorset. *T:* Corfe Castle 480574.

ALLCROFT, Sir Philip Magnus-; see Magnus-Allcroft, Sir Philip.

ALLDAY, Coningsby, CBE 1971; BSc (Hons); Managing Director, British Nuclear Fuels Ltd, since 1971; Member, UKAEA, since 1976; *b* 21 Nov. 1920; *s* of late Esca and Margaret Allday; *m* 1945, Iris Helena Adams; one *s* one *d. Educ:* Solihull Sch.; BSc (Hons) Chemistry, London. CEng, FIChemE, 1979. ICI, 1939-59; UKAEA, 1959-71: Chief Chemist, Technical Dir, Commercial Dir, Dep. Man. Dir. *Recreations:* gardening, music. *Address:* British Nuclear Fuels Ltd, Risley, Warrington, Cheshire. *Club:* East India, Devonshire, Sports and Public Schools.

ALLDIS, Air Cdre Cecil Anderson, CBE 1962; DFC 1941; AFC 1956; RAF (retd); Secretary-General, The Air League, since 1982; *b* 28 Sept. 1918; 2nd *s* of John Henry and Margaret Wright Alldis, Birkenhead; *m* 1942, Jeanette Claire Tarrant, *d* of Albert Edward Collingwood and Aida Mary Tarrant, Johannesburg; no *c. Educ:* Birkenhead; Emmanuel Coll., Cambridge (MA). Served War, 1939-45 (despatches, DFC): Pilot, Wing Comdr, RAF, Bomber Command. Asst Air Attaché, Moscow, 1947-49; Flying and Staff appts, RAF, 1949-59; Dir of Administrative Planning, Air Ministry, 1959-62; Air Attaché, Bonn, 1963-66. Retd from RAF and entered Home Civil Service, 1966; MoD, 1966-69; seconded to HM Diplomatic Service, 1969; Counsellor (Defence Supply), HM Embassy, Bonn, 1969-80; retired from Home Civil Service, 1980. In retirement, raises funds for Peter Le Marchant Trust for the Disabled. *Recreations:* golf, fishing. *Address:* Tudor Cottage, Oxshott Way, Cobham, Surrey. *T:* Cobham 6092. *Club:* Naval and Military.

ALLDIS, John; conductor; *b* 10 Aug. 1929; *s* of William James and Nell Alldis; *m* 1960, Ursula Margaret Mason; two *s. Educ:* Felsted School; King's Coll., Cambridge (MA). ARCO. Formed John Alldis Choir, 1962; formed and conducted London Symphony Chorus, 1966-69; Conductor, London Philharmonic Choir, 1969-82; Joint Chief Conductor, Radio Denmark, 1971-77; Conductor, Groupe Vocal de France, 1979-. FGSM 1976; Fellow, Westminster Choir Coll., Princeton, NJ, 1978. *Address:* 3 Wool Road, Wimbledon, SW20 0HN. *T:* 01-946 4168.

ALLDRITT, Walter, JP; Regional Secretary, National Union of General and Municipal Workers, in Liverpool, North Wales, and Northern Ireland, since Oct. 1970; *b* 4 July 1918; *s* of late Henry and Bridget Alldritt; *m* 1945, Mary Teresa, *d* of W. H. McGuinness; four *s* one *d. Educ:* St Francis de Sales; Liverpool University (WEA). Served with HM Forces, 1939-46. Trade Union Officer. MP (Lab) Scotland Div. of Liverpool, June 1964-Feb. 1971. Member various public bodies. Councillor 1955, JP 1958, Liverpool. *Address:* 104 Longmeadow Road, Knowsley, Prescot, Merseyside. *T:* 051-546 5703.

ALLEGRO, John Marco; author; *b* 17 Feb. 1923; *s* of late John Marco Allegro and Mabel Jessie (*née* Perry); *m* 1948, Joan Ruby Lawrence; one *s* one *d. Educ:* Wallington County Grammar Sch.; Univ. of Manchester. Royal Navy, 1941-46; Manchester Univ. 1947-52; BA 1st cl. Hons Oriental Studies, 1951; MA 1952; Bles Hebrew Prize, 1950; Scarborough Sen. Studentship, 1951-54; Leverhulme Research Award, 1958; Oxford Univ. (Magdalen), research in Hebrew dialects, 1952-53; University of Manchester: Lectureship in Comparative Semitic Philology and in Hebrew, 1954-62; Lectr in Old Testament and Intertestamental Studies, 1962-70. Brit. rep. on Internat. editing team for Dead Sea Scrolls, Jerusalem, 1953-; Adviser to Jordanian Govt on Dead Sea Scrolls, 1961-; Trustee and Hon. Sec. of Dead Sea Scrolls Fund, 1962-70. Organiser and leader of archaeological expedns to Jordan, 1959-. Popular lectr and broadcaster on archaeological subjects. TV films include: Dead Sea Scrolls, BBC, 1957; Search in the Kidron, BBC, 1963; The Mystery of the Dead Sea Scrolls, BBC, 1981. *Publications:* The Dead Sea Scrolls (Pelican), 1956 (revised edn 1964); The People of the Dead Sea Scrolls, 1958; The Treasure of the Copper Scroll, 1960 (revised edn 1964); Search in the Desert, 1964; The Shapira Affair, 1964; Discoveries in the Judæan Desert, V, 1968; The Sacred Mushroom and the Cross, 1970; The End of a Road, 1970; The Chosen People, 1971; Lost Gods, 1977; The Dead Sea Scrolls and the Christian Myth, 1979; All Manner of Men, 1982; articles in learned jls on Semitic philology. *Recreations:* fell walking, sketching. *Address:* 5 Ballahane

Close, Port Erin, Isle of Man. *T:* Port Erin 833879. *Club:* Explorers' (Ne York).

See also Baron Croham.

ALLEN, family name of **Barons Allen of Abbeydale, Allen of Fallowfie'** and **Croham.**

ALLEN OF ABBEYDALE, Baron *cr* 1976 (Life Peer), of the City Sheffield; **Philip Allen,** GCB 1970 (KCB 1964; CB 1954); Member, Securi Commission, since 1973; *b* 8 July 1912; *yr s* of late Arthur Allen and Lou Tipper, Sheffield; *m* 1938, Marjorie Brenda Coe. *Educ:* King Edward V Sch., Sheffield; Queens' Coll., Cambridge (Whewell Schol. in Internat. La' 1934; Hon. Fellow 1974). Entered Home Office, 1934; Offices of W Cabinet, 1943-44; Commonwealth Fellowship in USA, 1948-49; Depu Chm. of Prison Commn for England and Wales, 1950-52; Asst Under Se of State, Home Office, 1952-55; Deputy Sec., Min. of Housing and Loc Govt, 1955-60; Deputy Under-Sec. of State, Home Office, 1960-62; Secon Sec., HM Treasury, 1963-66; Permanent Under-Sec. of State, Home Offic 1966-72. Chairman: Occupational Pensions Bd, 1973-78; Nat. Council c Social Service, 1973-77; Gaming Bd for GB, 1977- (Mem., 1975). Membe Royal Commissions: on Standards of Conduct in Public Life, 1974-76; c Civil Liability and Compensation for Personal Injury, 1973-78; Mem tribunal of inquiry into Crown Agents, 1978-82. Chief Counting Office EEC Referendum, 1975. *Address:* Holly Lodge, Englefield Green, Surre TW20 0JP. *T:* Egham 32291.

ALLEN OF FALLOWFIELD, Baron *cr* 1974 (Life Peer), of Fallowfiel **Alfred Walter Henry Allen,** CBE 1967; General Secretary, Union of Sho Distributive & Allied Workers, 1962-79; a Crown Estate Commissioner, sine 1965; *b* Bristol, 7 July 1914; *m* 1940, Ruby Millicent Hounsell; one *s* one *Educ:* East Bristol Sch. RAF (Sergeant), 1940-45. Apptd Area Organiser, Na Union Distributive & Allied Workers, 1946; Nat. Officer, Union of Sho Distributive & Allied Workers, 1951. Member: Gen. Council of TU(1962-79 (Chm., 1973-74); Industrial Arbitration Bd, 1973-; Governmen Ctee of Inquiry into Statutory Smallholdings, 1963; Council of th Manchester Business Sch.; NEDC, 1963-79; CIR, 1969-70; British Airpor Authority, 1976-82; Cttee to Review the Functioning of Financia Institutions, 1977-80; Central Lancashire Develt Corp., 1978-; Cttee o Enforcement Powers, Inland Revenue and Customs and Excise Depts, 1980 Chairman: EDC for Chemical Industry, 1975-81; TUC Economic Cttee 1975-79; Governor, BBC, 1976-82. Dir Industrial Training Service, 1974-8(*Recreations:* reading, theatre, gardening, cricket. *Address:* 83 Manley Road Sale, Cheshire. *T:* 061-973 3058.

ALLEN, Hon. Alfred Ernest, CMG 1973; JP; President, Associated Truste Savings Banks of New Zealand, 1976-78 (Vice-President, 1974-76) Chairman, Blinded Servicemen's Trust Board, since 1961; *b* Onehunga, N2 20 May 1912; 4th *s* of Ernest Richard Allen and Harriet May Allen; *m* 193 Nancy, 3rd *d* of Frederick Arthur Cutfield and Ethel Cutfield; one *s* thre *d. Educ:* numerous primary schs; Auckland Grammar School. Farm han 1927; farming on own account from 1933. Served War of 1939-45, 24 Bn NZEF, Middle East (Sgt-Major). MP Franklin, NZ, 1957-72; Junior Gov Whip, 1963-66; Chief Govt Whip, 1966-69; Chm. of Cttees and Deput Speaker, 1969-71; Speaker, House of Representatives, 1972. Is a Freemason (Past Master). Mem., Auckland Electric Power Bd, 1948-77 (Chm., 195€ 1957 and 1958). Pres., Bd of Trustees, Auckland Savings Bank, 1973-7 (Vice-Pres., 1972-73). *Recreations:* bowls, horse racing; formerly Rugb football (Country Union Rep.), tennis. *Address:* 32 Carlton Crescen Maraetai Beach, Auckland, New Zealand. *T:* Beachlands 6595. *Clubs:* Frankli (Pukekohe); Returned Servicemen's (Franklin); (Hon. Mem.) Bellamy' (Wellington).

ALLEN, Anthony Kenway, OBE 1946; **His Honour Judge Allen;** a Circui Judge, since 1978; *b* 31 Oct. 1917; *s* of Charles Valentine Allen and Edit Kenway Allen; *m* 1975, Maureen Murtough. *Educ:* St George's Coll Weybridge, Surrey; St John's Coll., Cambridge (BA Hons); Freiburg an Grenoble Univs. Served War, RAF Special Intelligence, 1939-45 (Win Comdr). Called to the Bar, Inner Temple, 1947. *Recreations:* gardening walking, music. *Address:* 73 Downswood, Epsom Downs, Surrey. *T:* Burg Heath 50017.

ALLEN, Arnold Millman, CBE 1977; Member for Finance an Administration, since 1976, Deputy Chairman, since 1981, and Chie Executive, since 1982, UKAEA; *b* 30 Dec. 1924; *s* of Wilfrid Millman an Edith Muriel Allen; *m* 1947, Beatrice Mary Whitaker; three *s* one *d. Educ* Hackney Downs Sec. Sch.; Peterhouse, Cambridge (Scholar). Entered HM Treasury, 1945; Private Sec. to Financial Secretary, 1951-52; Principal, HM Treasury, 1953-55; Private Sec. to Chm. of UKAEA (Lord Plowden) 1956-57; HM Treasury, 1958; Dir of Personnel and Admin., Development an Engineering Group (subseq. Reactor Group), UKAEA, 1959-63; Gen Manager, British Waterways Bd, 1963-68, and Mem. of Bd 1965-68 Personnel Officer, 1968-69, Personnel and Programmes Officer, 1970 Secretary and Mem. for Administration, 1971, UKAEA. *Address:* Duntisl Cottage, Duntish, Dorchester, Dorset. *T:* Buckland Newton 258. *Club* Athenæum.

ALLEN, Dr Clabon Walter; Professor of Astronomy at University College London University, 1951-72, now Emeritus Professor; *b* 28 Dec. 1904; *s o*

J. B. Allen and A. H. Allen; *m* 1937, Rose M. Smellie; five *s*. *Educ*: Perth High School; University of Western Australia. DSc (WA), 1935. Assistant at Commonwealth Observatory, Canberra, 1926-51. Solar Eclipse Expeditions, 1936, 1940, 1954, 1955 and 1959; Hackett Research Studentship, 1935-37. *Publications*: Astrophysical Quantities, 1955, 3rd rev. edn 1973; Hiking from Early Canberra, 1977; papers in Monthly Notices of Royal Astronomical Soc., Astro-physical Jl, Memoirs of Commonwealth Observatory, etc. *Address*: Mount Stromlo Observatory, Canberra, ACT 2600, Australia.

ALLEN, Colin Mervyn Gordon, CBE 1978; General Manager, Covent Garden Market Authority, since 1967; *b* 17 April 1929; *s* of late Cecil G. Allen and late Gwendoline L. Allen (*née* Hutchinson); *m* 1953, Patricia, *d* of late William and Doris Seddon; two *s* one *d*. *Educ*: King Edward's Sch., Bath. FInstPS. Naval Store Dept, Admiralty, 1948-56; National Coal Board: London HQ, 1956-59; Area Stores Officer, NE Div., 1959-64; Covent Garden Market Authority: Planning Officer, 1964-66; Asst Gen. Man., 1967. Pres., Assoc. of Wholesale Markets within Internat. Union of Local Authorities, 1972-78. Chm., Vauxhall Cross Amenity Trust. *Publications*: various papers on horticultural marketing and allied topics, and on supply and logistics matters. *Recreation*: archaeology. *Address*: 10 Whitecroft Way, Beckenham, Kent BR3 3AG. *T*: 01-650 0787.

ALLEN, Sir Denis; *see* Allen, Sir W. D.

ALLEN, Rev. Derek William; Vicar of St Saviour and St Peter's, Eastbourne, since 1976; *b* 2 Nov. 1925. *Educ*: Exeter College; Oriel College, Oxford. Curate of Christ the Saviour, Ealing, 1952-54. Tutor, 1954-56, Chaplain, 1956-60, St Stephen's House, Oxford. Asst Chaplain, Pembroke College, Oxford, 1955-60, Sub-Warden, King's College Hostel and Lecturer in Theology, King's College, London, 1960-62; Principal, St Stephen's House, Oxford, 1962-74; Warden, Community of St Mary the Virgin, Wantage, 1966-80. *Publications*: Articles in: Theology, Church Quarterly Review, Internat. Rev. of Missions, Lambeth Essays on Unity, Sobornost. *Address*: The Vicarage, Spencer Road, Eastbourne, Sussex BN21 4PA. *T*: 22317.

ALLEN, Prof. Deryck Norman de Garrs; Professor of Applied Mathematics in the University of Sheffield, 1955-80, now Emeritus; Warden of Ranmoor House, 1968-82; *b* 22 April 1918; *s* of Leonard Lincoln Allen and Dorothy Allen (*née* Asplin). *Educ*: King Edward VII School, Sheffield; Christ Church, Oxford. Messrs Rolls Royce, 1940; Research Asst to Sir Richard Southwell, FRS, 1941; Lectr in Applied Mathematics at Imperial Coll., London, 1945; Visiting Prof. in Dept of Mechanical Engineering, Massachusetts Inst. of Technology, 1949; Reader in Applied Mathematics at Imperial Coll. in Univ. of London, 1950. Pro-Vice-Chancellor, Sheffield Univ., 1966-70; Chm., Jt Matriculation Bd, 1973-76. *Publications*: Relaxation Methods, 1954 (US); papers on Applied Maths and Engineering Maths in: Proc. Royal Soc.; Philosophical Trans. of Royal Soc.; Quarterly Jl of Mechanics and Applied Maths; Jl of Instn of Civil Engineers. *Recreation*: travel. *Address*: 18 Storth Park, Fulwood Road, Sheffield S10 3QH. *T*: Sheffield 308751.

ALLEN, Donald George, CMG 1981; Deputy Parliamentary Commissioner for Administration (Ombudsman), since 1982, on transfer from HM Diplomatic Service; *b* 26 June 1930; *s* of Sidney George Allen and Doris Elsie (*née* Abercombie); *m* 1955, Sheila Isobel Bebbington; three *s*. *Educ*: Southall Grammar School. Foreign Office, 1948; HM Forces, 1949-51; FO, 1951-54; The Hague, 1954-57; 2nd Sec. (Commercial), La Paz, 1957-60; FO, 1961-65: 1st Sec. 1962; Asst Private Sec. to Lord Privy Seal, 1961-63 and to Minister without Portfolio, 1963-64; 1st Sec., Head of Chancery and Consul, Panama, 1966-69; FCO, 1969-72; Counsellor on secondment to NI Office, Belfast, 1972-74; Counsellor and Head of Chancery, UK Permanent Delegn to OECD, Paris, 1974-78; Inspector, 1978-80; Dir, Office of Parly Comr, 1980-82. *Recreations*: squash, tennis, golf. *Address*: Church House, Great Smith Street, SW1P 3BW; 99 Parkland Grove, Ashford, Mddx TW15 2JF. *T*: Ashford 55617. *Club*: Royal Automobile.

ALLEN, Sir Donald (Richard), Kt 1954; OBE 1944; MC and Bar 1917; Clerk to Trustees of London Parochial Charities, 1930-65; *b* 31 Aug. 1894; *s* of Thomas Allen and Elizabeth (*née* Willett); *m* 1918, Irene Dora Andrews (*d* 1965); one *s* one *d*. *Educ*: William Morris School, Walthamstow. Served European War, RFA, 1914-18; Ministry of Health, 1919-25; Assistant Clerk, London Parochial Charities, 1925: Barrister-at-Law, Inner Temple, 1928; Mem. Cttee on Charitable Trusts, 1950-52. *Publication*: History City Parochial Foundation, 1951. *Address*: Sprigg's Court, Epping, Essex. *Club*: Reform.

ALLEN, Fergus Hamilton, CB 1969; ScD, MA, MAI, FICE; Consultant, Boyden International Ltd, since 1982; First Civil Service Commissioner, Civil Service Department, 1974-81; *b* 3 Sept. 1921; *s* of Charles Winckworth Allen and Marjorie Helen, *d* of F. J. S. Budge; *m* 1947, Margaret Joan, *d* of Prof. M. J. Gorman; two *d*. *Educ*: Newtown Sch., Waterford; Trinity Coll., Dublin. ScD 1966. Asst Engineer, Sir Cyril Kirkpatrick and Partners, 1943-48; Port of London Authority, 1949-52; Asst Director, Hydraulics Research Station, DSIR, 1952-58; Dir of Hydraulics Research, DSIR, 1958-65; Chief Scientific Officer, Cabinet Office, 1965-69; Civil Service Comr, 1969-74; Scientific and Technological Advr, CSD, 1969-72. Instn Civil Engrs: Telford Gold Medal, 1958; Mem. Council, 1962-67, 1968-71. *Publications*: papers in technical journals; poems. *Address*: Dundrum, Wantage Road, Streatley, Berks RG8 9LB. *T*: Goring 873234. *Club*: Athenæum.

ALLEN, Francis Andrew; His Honour Judge Francis Allen; a Circuit Judge, since 1979; *b* 7 Dec. 1933; *s* of Andrew Eric Allen and Joan Elizabeth Allen; *m* 1961, Marjorie Pearce; one *s* three *d*. *Educ*: Solihull School; Merton College, Oxford. MA. 2nd Lieut, Highland Light Infantry, 1957; called to the Bar, Gray's Inn, 1958. A Recorder of the Crown Court, 1978-79. *Recreation*: walking. *Address*: 116 Oxford Road, Moseley, Birmingham B13 9SQ. *T*: 021-449 1270. *Club*: Mountain Bothies Association (Scottish Highlands).

ALLEN, Frank Graham; Clerk of the Journals, House of Commons, since 1975; *b* 13 June 1920; *s* of Percy and Gertrude Allen; *m* 1947, Barbara Caulton; one *s* one *d*. *Educ*: Shrewsbury Sch. (Schol.); Keble Coll., Oxford (Exhibr, BA). 7th Bn Worcs Regt, 1940-46, India, 1942-44. Asst Clerk, House of Commons, 1946; Principal Clerk, 1973. Silver Jubilee Medal, 1977. *Address*: March Mount, Haddon Road, Chorleywood, Herts. *T*: 01-260 2709.

ALLEN, Prof. Sir Geoffrey, Kt 1979; PhD; FRS 1976; FInstP; Head of Research, PLC, since 1981; Director, Unilever PLC and NV, since 1982; *b* 29 Oct. 1928; *s* of John James and Marjorie Allen; *m* 1973, Valerie Frances Duckworth; one *d*. *Educ*: Clay Cross Tupton Hall Grammar Sch.; Univ. of Leeds (BSc, PhD). FInstP 1972; FPRI 1974. Postdoctoral Fellow, Nat. Res. Council, Canada, 1952-54; Lectr, Univ. of Manchester, 1955-65, Prof. of Chemical Physics, 1965-75; Prof. of Polymer Science, 1975-76, Prof. of Chemical Technology, 1976-81, Imperial Coll. of Science and Technology; Vis. Fellow, Robinson Coll., Cambridge, 1980-. Mem., Science Research Council, 1976, Chm., 1977-81. Hon. MSc Manchester; DUniv Open, 1981. *Publications*: papers on chemical physics of polymers in Trans Faraday Soc., Polymer. *Recreations*: walking, talking and eating. *Address*: 16 Burghley Road, Wimbledon, SW19 5BH. *T*: 01-947 7459. *Club*: Athenæum.

ALLEN, Rt. Rev. Geoffrey Francis, DD; *b* 25 August 1902; 2nd *s* of late John Edward Taylor Allen, Holt House, Mobberley, Cheshire, and Mabel Saunders; *m* 1932, Madeline, *d* of Rev. R. J. S. Gill, Tadworth, Surrey. *Educ*: Rugby (Scholar); University College, Oxford (Scholar); Ripon Hall, Oxford (1st Class Philosophy, Politics, and Economics, 1924; 2nd Class Theology, 1926). Liverpool Intercollegiate Secretary of the Student Christian Movement, 1926; Curate of St Saviour's, Liverpool, 1927; Chaplain of Ripon Hall, Oxford, 1928; Fellow and Chaplain of Lincoln College, Oxford, 1930-35; Union Theological College, Canton, 1935; Deputy Provost, Birmingham Cathedral, 1941; Sec. National Christian Council of China and Chaplain to British Embassy, Chungking, 1942-44; Archdeacon of Birmingham, 1944-47; Bishop in Egypt, 1947-52; Principal of Ripon Hall, Oxford, 1952-59; Bishop of Derby, 1959-69. *Publications*: Tell John, 1932 (part author); He that Cometh, 1932; Christ the Victorious, 1935; The Courage to be Real, 1938; Law with Liberty, 1942; The Theology of Missions, 1943. Contributor, The Churches and Christian Unity (ed R. J. W. Bevan), 1963. *Recreations*: the company of our friends, our garden. *Address*: The Knowle, Deddington, Oxford OX5 4TB. *T*: Deddington 38225. *Club*: English-Speaking Union.

ALLEN, George Oswald Browning, CBE 1962; TD 1945; *b* 31 July 1902; *s* of late Sir Walter M. Allen, KBE. *Educ*: Eton; Trinity College, Cambridge. GSO1, War Office, 1944-45. Member of London Stock Exchange. Cricket: Eton XI, 1919-21; Cambridge Univ., 1922-23; represented England in 25 Test Matches; Captain *v* India, 1936, *v* Australia, 1936-37, *v* West Indies, 1948; Chm. Selection Cttee, 1955-61; Chm. MCC cricket sub cttee, 1956-63; President, MCC, 1963-64; Treasurer, 1964-76. Legion of Merit (USA). *Recreations*: cricket, golf. *Address*: 4 Grove End Road, NW8. *T*: 01-286 4601. *Club*: White's.

ALLEN, Godfrey; *see* Allen, W. G.

ALLEN, Hamish McEwan; Head of Administration Department, House of Commons, since 1981; *b* 7 Sept. 1920; *s* of late Ernest Frank Allen and Ada Florence Allen (*née* Weeks); *m* 1951, Peggy Joan Fifoot; one *s*. *Educ*: City of Bath Sch.; Portsmouth Southern Secondary Sch. Served RAF, 1941-46. Air Ministry: Clerical Officer, 1938; Exec. Officer, 1948; House of Commons: Asst Accountant, 1959; Dep. Accountant, 1962; Head of Estabs Office, 1968. *Address*: 124 Ridge Langley, South Croydon, Surrey CR2 0AS.

ALLEN, (Harold) Norman (Gwynne), CBE 1965; retired 1977; *b* 30 April 1912; *yr s* of Harold Gwynne Allen and Hilda Margaret Allen (*née* Langley), Bedford; *m* 1938, Marjorie Ellen (*née* Brown); one *s* three *d*. *Educ*: Westminster Sch.; Trinity Coll., Cambridge, BA 1933, MA 1936, Cantab; FEng, FICE, FIMechE, FRINA, FIMarE, FIProdE. Engrg trng, John Samuel White & Co. Ltd, Cowes, John Brown & Co. Ltd, Clydebank, and in Merchant Navy, 1933-37; W. H. Allen Sons & Co. Ltd, Bedford: progressive staff appts, 1937-43; Dir 1943-77; Techn. Dir 1945-52; Jt Man. Dir 1952-; Dep. Chm. 1962-70; Chm. 1970-77; Amalgamated Power Engrg Ltd, Bedford: Techn. Dir 1968-70; Dep. Chm. 1970-77. Belliss & Morcom Ltd, Birmingham, 1968-77. Mem. Bedfordshire CC, 1947-50. Mem. Council: British Internal Combustion Engrg Res. Assoc., 1952-60 (Chm. 1953-54); British Hydromechanics Res. Assoc., 1947-59; IMechE, 1952-70 (Vice-Pres. 1959-65, Pres. 1965); Mem. Adv. Cttee, Nat. Engrg Lab., 1971-73 (Mem. Steering Cttee 1962-68); Mem. British Transport Commn Res. Adv. Council, 1958-60; Vice-Chm. of Council, Mander Coll., Bedford, 1958-74; Governor, Coll. of Aeronautics, Cranfield, 1955-69 (Vice-Chm. 1962-69); Charter Pro-Chancellor, Cranfield Inst. of Technology, 1969-75; Mem. Bd, Council of Engrg Instns, 1964-66; Mem. Exec. Bd, BSI, 1970-76. Provost, Buffalo

Hunt of Manitoba, 1960. Dir, Son et Lumière, Woburn Abbey, 1957. Hon. DSc Bath, 1967; Hon. DSc Cranfield, 1977. *Publications:* papers in jls of IMarE, S African IMechE, Engrg Inst. Canada, IMechE. *Recreations:* sailing, gardening (FRHS), countryside (Mem. Nat. Trust), magic (Mem. Magic Circle). *Address:* Gwylfa, Bontddu, Dolgellau, Gwynedd. *T:* Bontddu 230. *Clubs:* United Oxford & Cambridge University; Island Sailing.

ALLEN, Prof. Harry Cranbrook, MC 1944; Professor of American Studies, 1971-80, now Emeritus, and Dean of the School of English and American Studies, 1974-76, University of East Anglia; *b* 23 March 1917; *s* of Christopher Albert Allen and Margaret Enid (*née* Hebb); *m* 1947, Mary Kathleen Andrews; one *s* two *d. Educ:* Bedford School; Pembroke College, Oxford (Open Scholar; 1st cl. hons Modern History; MA). Elected Fellow, Commonwealth Fund of New York, 1939 (held Fellowship, Harvard Univ., Jan.-Sept. 1946). Served War of 1939-45, with Hertfordshire and Dorsetshire Regts, in France and Germany (Major); comdt 43rd Division Educational Coll., June-Nov. 1945. Fellow and Tutor in Modern History, Lincoln College, Oxford, 1946-55; Commonwealth Fund Prof. of American History, University Coll., 1955-71, and Dir, Inst. of United States Studies, 1966-71, Univ. of London; Senior Research Fellow, Austr. Nat. Univ., Canberra, and Visiting Scholar, Univ. of California, Berkeley, 1953-54; Schouler Lecturer, The Johns Hopkins University, April 1956; American Studies Fellow, Commonwealth Fund of New York, 1957, at the University of Virginia; Vis. Mem., Inst. for Advanced Study, Princeton, NJ, 1959; Vis. Professor: Univ. of Rochester, New York, 1963; Univ. of Michigan, Ann Arbor, 1966. Member: Dartmouth Royal Naval College Review Cttee, 1958, Naval Education Adv. Cttee, 1960-66; Academic Planning Board, Univ. of Essex, 1962; Chm., British Assoc. for American Studies, 1974-77; Pres., European Assoc. for American Studies, 1976-80. *Publications:* Great Britain and the United States, 1955; Bush and Backwoods, 1959; The Anglo-American Relationship since 1783, 1960; The Anglo-American Predicament, 1960; The United States of America, 1964; Joint Editor: British Essays in American History, 1957; Contrast and Connection, 1976. *Recreation:* travel. *Address:* 10 Lime Kiln Road, Tackley, Oxon OX5 3BW. *Club:* Athenæum.

ALLEN, Jack, DSc, LLD; FICE; FRSE; Professor of Engineering, Aberdeen University, 1946-69; *b* 19 Sept. 1905; *s* of late John and Phoebe Annie Allen, Heywood; *m* 1933, Elizabeth (*d* 1979), *d* of late Samuel and Frances Hall, Heaton Park, Lancs. *Educ:* Elton Council School; Bury Grammar School; Manchester University, BSc (First Class Hons in Engineering) 1926; Vulcan Research Fellow, 1928-29; Asst Lecturer, 1929-35, Lecturer, 1935-43; DSc 1939; Senior Lecturer, 1943-46 (Manchester Univ.). Engaged on investigations of Severn Barrage Scheme, Liverpool Bay training walls, proposed Humber Bridge, improvement of rivers Mersey, Dee and Parrett, Scapa Flow causeways (all as Asst to Prof. A. H. Gibson); flood relief in river Great Ouse, harbour developments at Dundee and Aberdeen, spillways on hydro-electric schemes, etc. MICE 1946; FRSE 1951 (Vice-Pres., 1964-67). James Forrest Lecturer, Institution of Civil Engineers, 1947. Member: Hydraulics Research Bd (DSIR), 1946-53, 1957-61, 1962-65; Hydraulics Research Station Steering Cttee, 1965-68; Research Advisory Council, British Transport Commn, 1957-64; Academic Advisory Council, Univs of St Andrews and Dundee, 1964-66; Chm., Res. Adv. Gp, British Transport Docks Bd, 1968-81. Hon. LLD Manchester, 1968; Hon. DSc Aberdeen, 1975. *Publications:* Scale Models in Hydraulic Engineering, 1947; many papers in Jl ICE, Phil. Mag., etc. *Address:* 4 Finches Gardens, Lindfield, Sussex RH16 2PA.

ALLEN, James Godfrey Colquhoun, CMG 1956; Secretary, Nigeria Timber Association, 1961-69, retired; re-employed as Head of Social Welfare Services, 1972-76, Adviser Field Administration 1976, and General Director, 1977, Rivers State Rural Development Association, Port Harcourt, Nigeria, retired finally, 1978; *b* 26 May 1904; *s* of Dr J. D. C. Allen and F. D. L. Allen (*née* Beckett), Bath; *m* 1982, Patricia George. *Educ:* Blundell's Sch.; Ecole Supérieure de Commerce, Lausanne; Univ. of Munich. Asst Master, Alleyn Court School, Westcliff-on-Sea, 1926. Cadet, Nigerian Administrative Service, 1926; Asst District Officer and District Officer, 1929-45 (Major, Nigeria Regt, 1942-43); Resident, 1947; Senior Resident, 1953. Anglo-French Cameroons Boundary Commissioner, 1937-39; Nigerian Rep. with Free French, Douala, 1940; Chief Censor and Chief of Military Intelligence, Nigeria, 1940-41; W African Liaison Officer with Free French forces in Equatorial Africa, 1942-43; Political Sec. to Resident Minister, W Africa, 1943; Dep. Commissioner of the Colony, Lagos, 1946-52; Senior Resident, Rivers Province, Nigeria, 1952-56. Director of Administration, Nigerian Broadcasting Corporation, 1957-61. Mem. Bath Preservation Trust. Coronation Medal, 1953. *Publications:* A Native Court Handbook, 1955; The Organisation and Procedure of Local Government Councils, 1956. *Recreations:* golf, music. *Address:* 39 Lyncombe Hill, Bath, Avon BA2 4PQ. *T:* Bath 334826. *Club:* Royal Commonwealth Society.

ALLEN, Janet Rosemary; Headmistress of Benenden School, Kent, since 1976; *b* 11 April 1936; *d* of John Algernon Allen and Edna Mary Allen (*née* Orton). *Educ:* Cheltenham Ladies' Coll.; University Coll., Leicester; Hughes Hall, Cambridge. BA London 1958; CertEd Cambridge 1959. Asst Mistress, Howell's Sch., Denbigh, North Wales, 1959: Head of History Dept, 1961; in charge of First Year Sixth Form, 1968; Housemistress, 1968 and 1973-75. *Recreations:* music, drama. *Address:* Benenden School, Cranbrook, Kent TN17 4AA. *T:* Benenden 592.

ALLEN, Prof. John Anthony, PhD, DSc; FIBiol; FRSE; Director, University Marine Biological Station, Millport, Isle of Cumbrae, since 1976; *s* of George Leonard John Allen and Dorothy Mary Allen; *m* 1952, Marion Ferguson Crow; one *s* one *d. Educ:* High Pavement Sch., Nottingham; London Univ. (PhD, DSc). FIBiol 1969; FRSE 1968 (Mem. Council, 1970-73). Served in Sherwood Foresters, 1945-46, and RAMC, 1946-48. Asst Lectr, Univ. of Glasgow, 1951-54; John Murray Student, Royal Soc., 1952-54; Lectr/Sen. Lectr in Zool., then Reader in Marine Biol., Univ. of Newcastle upon Tyne, 1954-76. Post Doctoral Fellow and Guest Investigator, Woods Hole Oceanographic Instn, USA, 1965-81; Vis. Prof., Univ. of Washington, 1968, 1970, 1971; Royal Soc. Vis. Prof., Univ. of West Indies, 1976. Member: NERC, 1977- (Chm., Univ. Affairs Cttee, 1978-); Council, Scottish Marine Biol. Assoc., 1977-; Council, Marine Biol Assoc. UK, 1981-; Life Sciences Cttee, CNAA, 1981-. *Publications:* 70 papers on decapod crustacea and molluscs, and deep sea benthos, in learned jls. *Recreations:* travel, appreciation of gardens, pub-lunching. *Address:* Bellevue, Millport, Isle of Cumbrae, Scotland. *T:* Millport 260.

ALLEN, Very Rev. John Edward; Provost of Wakefield, since 1982; *b* 9 June 1932; *s* of Rev. Canon Ronald and Mrs Isabel Allen; *m* 1957, Eleanor (*née* Prynne); one *s* three *d. Educ:* Rugby; University Coll., Oxford (MA); Fitzwilliam Coll., Cambridge (BA); Westcott House. Colonial Service, Kenya, 1957-62; Sales and Marketing, Kimberly-Clark Ltd, 1962-66; Theological College, 1966-68; Curate, Deal, Kent, 1968-71; Senior Chaplain to Univ. of Bristol and Vicar of St Paul's, Clifton, 1971-78; Vicar of Chippenham, Wilts, 1978-82. *Recreations:* walking, fishing and people. *Address:* The Cathedral Vicarage, Margaret Street, Wakefield, West Yorkshire WF1 2DQ. *T:* Wakefield 72402.

ALLEN, Prof. John Frank, FRS 1949; Professor of Natural Philosophy in the School of Physical Sciences, University of St Andrews, 1947-78, now Emeritus; *b* 16 May 1908; *s* of late Prof. Frank Allen, FRSC; *m* 1933, Elfriede Hiebert (marr. diss. 1951); one *s. Educ:* Public schools of Winnipeg, Canada. BA (University of Manitoba, 1928), MA (University of Toronto, 1930), PhD (University of Toronto, 1933). Bursar, Student and Fellow of National Research Council of Canada, 1930-33; Fellow of National Research Council of USA, 1933-35; Research Assistant, Royal Society Mond Laboratory, Cambridge, 1935-44; MA Cantab, 1936; Lecturer in Physics, Univ. of Cambridge and Fellow and Lecturer of St John's College, Cambridge, 1944-47. Hon. DSc Manitoba, 1979. *Publications:* numerous scientific papers and articles, mainly on experimental low temperature physics. *Recreations:* scientific cinefilms, golf. *Address:* 2 Shorehead, St Andrews, Fife. *T:* St Andrews 72717.
See also W. A. Allen.

ALLEN, Maj.-Gen. John Geoffrey Robyn, CB 1976; Lay Observer attached to Lord Chancellor's Department, since 1979; *b* 19 Aug. 1923; *s* of R. A. Allen and Mrs Allen (*née* Youngman); *m* 1959, Ann Monica (*née* Morford); one *s* one *d. Educ:* Haileybury. Commissioned KRRC, 1942; trans. RTR, 1947; Bt Lt-Col, 1961; Lt-Col, CO 2 RTR, 1963; Mil. Asst (GSO1) to CGS, MoD, 1965; Brig., Comd 20 Armd Bde, 1967; IDC, 1970; Dir of Operational Requirements 3 (Army), MoD, 1971; Maj.-Gen., Dir-Gen., Fighting Vehicles and Engineer Equipment, MoD, 1973-74; Dir, RAC, 1974-76; Sen. Army Directing Staff, RCDS, 1976-78; retired 1979. Col Comdt, RTR, 1976-80. Mem., Adv. Cttee on Legal Aid, 1979-. *Recreation:* dinghy sailing. *Address:* Waney Edges, Fitzroy Road, Fleet, Hants. *T:* Fleet 4570. *Club:* Army and Navy.

ALLEN, John Piers, OBE 1979; *b* 30 March 1912; *s* of Percy Allen and Marjorie Nash; *m* 1937; two *s; m* 1945; two *s* two *d. Educ:* Aldenham Sch. Old Vic Theatre, 1933-35; Victor Gollancz Ltd, 1936-37; London Theatre Studio, 1937-39; RNVR, 1940-45; Dir, Glyndebourne Children's Theatre, 1945-51; writer-producer, BBC, 1951-61; HM Inspector of Schs, 1961-72 Principal, Central School of Speech and Drama, 1972-78. Vis. Prof. of Drama, Westfield Coll., Univ. of London, 1979-; Vis. Lectr, Centre for Arts, City Univ., 1979-. Vice-Chm., British Theatre Assoc., 1978-; Chm., Accreditation panels, Nat. Council of Drama Trng and Council of Dance Educn and Trng 1979-82; Mem., CNAA Dance and Drama Panels, 1979-82. *Publications* Going to the Theatre, 1949; Great Moments in the Theatre, 1949; Masters of British Drama, 1957; Masters of European Drama, 1962; Drama in Schools 1978; Theatre in Europe, 1981; (ed) Three Medieval Plays, 1956. *Address:* 13 Rotherwick Road, NW11 7DG. *T:* 01-455 4419.

ALLEN, Prof. John Robert Lawrence, DSc; FRS 1979; Professor o Geology, University of Reading, since 1972; *b* 25 Oct. 1932; *s* of George Eustace Allen and Alice Josephine (*née* Formby); *m* 1960, Jean Mary (*née* Wood); four *s* one *d. Educ:* St Philip's Grammar Sch., Birmingham; Univ of Sheffield (BSc, DSc). Academic career in University of Reading, 1959- FGS 1955. Lyell Medal, Geolog. Soc., 1980. *Publications:* Current Ripple 1968; Physical Processes of Sedimentation, 1970; Sedimentary Structure 1982; numerous contribs to professional jls. *Recreations:* music, opera *Address:* 17c Whiteknights Road, Reading RG1 5SY. *T:* Reading 64621.

ALLEN, Prof. Joseph Stanley; (first) Professor and Head of Department c Town and Country Planning, University of Newcastle upon Tyne (formerl King's College, Durham University), 1946-63 (developing first Universit Degree Course in Town and Country Planning); Senior Partner, J. S. Aller

Architects & Town Planning Consultants; *b* 15 March 1898; *s* of late Harry Charles Allen and of Elizabeth S. Allen; *m* 1931, Guinevere Mary Aubrey Pugh (*d* 1974); one *s* one *d* ; *m* 1977, Meryl, *d* of late Charles and Eveline Watts. *Educ:* Liverpool Collegiate School; Liverpool University; post-graduate study in USA. RIBA Athens Bursar. Head, Leeds School of Architecture, 1933–45; founded Leeds Sch. of Town and Country Planning, 1934. Vice-Chm. RIBA Bd of Architectural Education and Chm. Recognised Schools Cttee, 1943–45; Member of Council RIBA, 1943–50; Pres. Royal Town Planning Institute, 1959–60 (Vice-Pres. 1957–59). Architect and Town Planning Consultant for hospitals, churches, neighbourhood units, university and industrial undertakings. Consultant, Snowdonia National Park, 1957–74; Member, North of England Regional Advisory Committee, Forestry Commission, 1951–74; Member Diocesan Committees for Care of Churches: Ripon, Newcastle and York Dioceses. Hon. DLitt Heriot-Watt, 1978. *Publications:* (with R. H. Mattocks): Report and Plan for West Cumberland; Report and Plan for Accrington (Industry and Prudence), 1950. Founder-Editor, Planning Outlook (founded 1948); contrib. to professional journals on architecture and town and country planning. *Recreations:* motoring and walking in the countryside, music, breeding Welsh ponies. *Address:* Bleach Green Farm, Ovingham, Northumberland. *T:* Prudhoe 32340.

LLEN, Sir Kenneth; *see* Allen, Sir William Kenneth G.

LLEN, Prof. Kenneth William; Professor of Nuclear Structure, since 1963, and Head of Department of Nuclear Physics, 1976–79 and since 1982, University of Oxford; Fellow of Balliol College, since 1963, Estates Bursar, since 1980; *b* 17 Nov. 1923; *m* 1947, Josephine E. Boreham; two *s*. *Educ:* Ilford County High School; London University (Drapers' Scholar); St Catharine's College, Cambridge University. PhD (Cantab) 1947. Physics Division, Atomic Energy of Canada, Chalk River, 1947–51; Leverhulme Research Fellow and Lecturer, Liverpool University, 1951–54; Deputy Chief Scientist, UKAEA, 1954–63. Mem., Nuclear Physics Bd, SRC, 1970–73. *Publications:* contribs to Proc. Physical Soc., Physical Review, Review of Scientific Instruments, Nature, etc. *Recreations:* music, chess. *Address:* Ridgeway, Lincombe Lane, Boars Hill, Oxford.

LLEN, Mark Echalaz, CMG 1966; CVO 1961; Member of Joint Inspection Unit, United Nations, since 1978; *b* 19 March 1917; *s* of late Lancelot John Allen and of Eleanor Mary (*née* Carlisle); *m* 1948, Elizabeth Joan, *d* of late Richard Hope Bowdler and Elsie (*née* Bryning); two *s* one *d* (and one *d* decd). *Educ:* Charterhouse; Christ Church, Oxford (MA). Appointed Asst Principal, Dominions Office, 1939. Served War of 1939–45 in Western Desert, Sicily and Italy. Dublin, 1945; Bombay, 1948; United Nations, New York, 1953; Madras, 1960; New Delhi, 1961; Diplomatic Service Inspector, 1964; Dep. Chief of Administration, DSAO, 1966; Minister (Econ. and Social Affairs), UK Mission to UN, New York, 1968; Ambassador to Zaïre and Burundi, 1971, and to Congo Republic, 1973; Permanent UK Rep. to Disarmament Conf., Geneva, 1974–77, retired from Diplomatic Service, 1977. *Address:* 26 chemin du Pommier, 1218 Grand Saconnex, Geneva.

LLEN, Sir Milton (Pentonville), Kt 1972; OBE 1964; Governor, St Kitts/Nevis/Anguilla, 1972–75 (Acting Governor, 1969–Aug. 1972); *b* St Kitts, WI, 22 June 1888; *m* 1937, Annie Matilda (*née* Locker), MBE (*d* 1979); no *c*. *Educ:* (primary) Palmetto Point, St Kitts; then (for tailoring) studied at David Mitchell designing and cutting Academy, NY (diploma). Worked at trade of tailor until the Depression, 1929. Nominated Member, 1957, Speaker, 1962, House of Assembly, St Kitts. Patron: St Kitts Cricket Assoc.; St Kitts Net Ball Assoc.; Boy Scouts Assoc. KStJ 1974. *Publication:* Chosen Poems (a collection), (New York) 1945. *Recreations:* reading, music, gardening; interested in Arts Festival of Basseterre (one of his chosen poems set to music for a choir, by Dr Leon Forrester, FRCO). *Address:* The Fortlands, Basseterre, St Kitts, West Indies.

LLEN, Norman; *see* Allen, H. N. G.

LLEN, Prof. Percival, FRS 1973; Professor of Geology, University of Reading, since 1952; Head of Geology Department; Director, Sedimentology Research Laboratory since 1965; *b* 15 March 1917; *s* of late Norman Williams Allen and Mildred Kathleen Hoad; British; *m* 1941, Frances Margaret Hepworth, BSc; three *s* one *d*. *Educ:* Brede Council Sch.; Rye Grammar School; University of Reading. BSc 1939, PhD 1943, Reading. Univ. Demonstrator, 1942–45, Univ. Asst Lectr, 1945–46, Reading; University Demonstrator, 1946–47, Univ. Lectr, 1947–52, Cambridge; Dean of Science Faculty, Reading, 1963–66. Vis. Prof., Univ. of Kuwait, 1970. Served War of 1939–45. In Royal Air Force, 1941–42. Sedgwick Prize, Univ. of Cambridge, 1952; Daniel Pidgeon Fund, Geological Soc. of London, 1944; Leverhulme Fellowships Research Grant, 1948, 1949. Hon. Member: American Soc. of Economic Paleontologists and Mineralogists; Bulgarian Geological Soc.; Geologists' Assoc.; Internat. Assoc. of Sedimentologists; For. Fellow, Indian Nat. Sci. Acad., 1979; Geological Soc. of London: Mem. Council, 1964–67; Lyell Medal, 1971; Pres., 1978–80; Royal Society: Mem. Council, 1977–79; a Vice-Pres., 1977–79; Chm., Expeditions Cttee, 1974–; British Nat. Cttee for Geology, 1982–. Member: Natural Environment Res. Council, 1971–74 and Royal Soc. Assessor, 1977–80; Adv. Panel, UNDP Project on Nile Delta, 1972–; UNESCO/UNDP Geology Consultant, India, 1976–77. UK Editor, Sedimentology, 1961–67. Chm., Org. Cttees: VII Internat. Sedimentological Congress, 1967; first European Earth and Planetary Physics Colloquium, 1971; first Meeting European Geological Socs, 1975.

Sec.-Gen., Internat. Assoc. Sedimentologists, 1967–71; Algerian Sahara Glacials Expedn, 1970; Sec., Philpots Quarry Ltd. *Publications:* papers in various scientific journals. *Recreations:* chess, natural history, gardening. *Address:* Orchard End, Hazeley Bottom, Hartley Wintney, Hants RG27 8LU.

ALLEN, Sir Peter (Christopher), Kt 1967; MA, BSc (Oxor); Advisory Director, New Perspective Fund, since 1973; *b* Ashtead, Surrey, 8 Sept. 1905; *s* of late Sir Ernest King Allen and Florence Mary (*née* Gellatly); *m* 1st, 1931, Violet Sylvester Wingate-Saul (*d* 1951); two *d*; 2nd, 1952, Consuelo Maria Linares Rivas. *Educ:* Harrow; Trinity Coll., Oxford (Hon. Fellow 1969). Joined Brunner, Mond & Co., Ltd, 1928; Chm., Plastics Div. of ICI Ltd, 1948–51 (Man. Dir, 1942–48); Pres. and Chm., ICI of Canada Ltd, 1961–68; Chm., ICI Ltd, 1968–71 (Dir, 1951–63, a Dep. Chm., 1963–68); Dir, British Nylon Spinners Ltd, 1954–58; Pres., Canadian Industries Ltd, 1959–62, Chm., 1962–68; Director: Royal Trust Co., Canada, 1961–64; Bank of Montreal, 1968–75; BICC, 1971–81. Vice-President: Inst. of Manpower Studies, 1968–76; Manufacturing Chemists' Assoc., USA, 1961–62 (Dir, 1959–62); Mem. and Vice-Chairman: Council of Assoc. of Brit. Chem. Manufacturers, 1963–65; Bd of Dirs, Société de Chimie Industrielle, 1968; Chm., Chem. Ind. Assoc., 1966–67; President: Plastics Inst., 1950–52; Brit. Plastics Fedn, 1965; Univ. of Manchester Inst. of Sci. and Technology, 1968–71; Vice-Pres., British Assoc. for Commercial and Industrial Educn, 1969–; Mem. of Council, CBI, 1965–67. Chm., BNEC, 1970–71 (Mem., 1964–67); Chm., Cttee for Exports to Canada, 1964–67); Mem., British Overseas Trade Bd, 1972–75. Governor, Nat. Coll. of Rubber Technology, 1964–68; Member: Court, British Shippers' Council, 1968–70; Export Council for Europe, 1962–65; Overseas Development Inst. Council, 1963–64; Iron and Steel Holding and Realisation Agency, 1963–67; NEDC for Chemical Industry, 1964–67; Commonwealth Export Council, 1964–67; Industrial Policy Group, 1969–71. Pres., Transport Trust, 1967–. FBIM 1968; FInstD 1969; FRGS 1980. Hon. Member: Chemical Industries Assoc., 1968– (Pres., 1965–67; Mem. Council, 1967–68); Canadian Chemical Producers' Assoc., 1962–. Chm., Anglo-Spanish Soc., 1973–80. Trustee, Civic Trust, 1970–76. Governor, Harrow School, 1969–. Freeman, City of London, 1978. Knight Grand Cross, Spanish Order of Civil Merit, 1981. *Publications:* The Railways of the Isle of Wight, 1928; Locomotives of Many Lands, 1954; On the Old Lines, 1957; (with P. B. Whitehouse) Narrow Gauge Railways of Europe, 1959; (with R. A. Wheeler) Steam on the Sierra, 1960; (with P. B. Whitehouse) Round the World on the Narrow Gauge, 1966; (with Consuelo Allen) The Curve of Earth's Shoulder, 1966; (with A. B. MacLeod) Rails in the Isle of Wight, 1967; Famous Fairways, 1968; Play the Best Courses, 1973; (with P. B. Whitehouse) Narrow Gauge the World Over, 1976. *Recreations:* foreign travel, railways, golf, writing. *Address:* Telham Hill House, near Battle, E Sussex. *Clubs:* Carlton; Royal and Ancient; Royal Cinque Ports, Rye, Royal St George's; Oxford and Cambridge Golfing Soc.; Augusta National (Ga, USA); Pine Valley (NJ, USA).

ALLEN, Sir Richard (Hugh Sedley), KCMG 1960 (CMG 1953); retired; *b* 3 Feb. 1903; *s* of late Sir Hugh Allen, GCVO; *m* 1945, Juliet Home Thomson; one step *s* (and one *s* decd). *Educ:* Royal Naval Colleges, Osborne and Dartmouth; New College, Oxford. Junior Asst Sec., Govt of Palestine, 1925–27. Entered Foreign Office and Diplomatic Service, 1927; Second Sec., 1932; First Sec., 1939; Counsellor, 1946; Minister, British Embassy, Buenos Aires, 1950–54; Minister to Guatemala, 1954–56; British Ambassador to Burma, 1956–62. *Publications:* Malaysia: Prospect and Retrospect, 1968; A Short Introduction to the History and Politics of Southeast Asia, 1970; Imperialism and Nationalism in the Fertile Crescent, 1974. *Recreation:* sailing. *Address:* 37 Boulevard Guist'hau, 44000 Nantes, France. *T:* (40) 20-55-07. *Clubs:* Athenæum, Royal Automobile; Royal Naval Sailing Association, Itchenor Sailing.

ALLEN, Brig. Ronald Lewis, CBE 1970 (OBE 1956); General Manager, Building Societies' Staff College, Ware, since 1971; *b* 2 April 1916; *s* of W. J. Allen and M. B. Allen (*née* Lewis); *m* 1st, 1945, Jirina Georgette (*née* Valachova) (marr. dis. 1952); one *d* ; 2nd, 1956, Christine Maude (*née* Scott); one *s* one *d. Educ:* privately; Univ. of South Wales and Monmouthshire. BSc Hons London 1939. Scientist, Safety in Mines Research Bd; Birmingham Univ., 1939; Imperial Chemical Industries, 1939. War of 1939–45: commissioned, RAOC, 1940; served UK, 1940–42; MEF, 1942–44 (despatches, 1943); CMF, 1944–45. Egypt, 1949–50; USA, 1951–52; Cyprus, 1960–61; BAOR, 1961–62; Principal Ammunition Technical Officer, 1962–66; Comdr Ammunition Organisation and Chief Inspector, Land Service Ammunition, 1966–67; Dep. Comdr, Base Organisation RAOC, and Head of Inventory Systems Develt, 1967–71. Mem., Acceptable Risk Working Party, Council for Sci. and Soc., 1977. Mem., E Herts DC (Chairman: A & R Cttee; Computer WP; Organisational WP). FRIC 1962 (ARIC 1939); MBIM 1967; Fellow Brit. Computer Soc. 1969. Queen's Commendation for Brave Conduct, 1964. *Recreations:* bridge, music, astrophysics, conservation, computers. *Address:* Building Societies Training College, Fanhams Hall, Ware, Herts SG12 7PZ; Thorn Knoll, Aston, Herts.

ALLEN, Rowland Lancelot, CB 1968; Principal Assistant Treasury Solicitor, 1963–69, retired; *b* 17 Feb. 1908; *s* of Rowland Allen and Maud Annie Allen (*née* Bacon); *m* 1934, Elizabeth Ethel (*née* Lewis); two *s* one *d. Educ:* Eton College. Called to the Bar, Inner Temple, 1931; Public Trustee Office, 1934; Treasury Solicitor's Dept, 1940; Foreign Compensation Commission, 1950–53; Treasury Solicitor's Dept, 1953. *Recreation:* golf. *Address:* Herries, Crastock, Woking, Surrey GU22 0QT. *T:* Brookwood 2312.

ALLEN, Sir Roy George Douglas, Kt 1966; CBE 1954 (OBE 1946); MA, DSc (Econ.); FBA 1952; Professor of Statistics, University of London, 1944-73, now Professor Emeritus; Consultant, Royal Commission on Civil Liability, 1974-78; *b* 3 June 1906; *er s* of G. H. Allen, Worcester; *m* 1936; two *s* one *d. Educ:* Royal Grammar School, Worcester; Sidney Sussex College, Cambridge (Wrangler, 1927; Hon. Fellow, 1971); DSc (Econ.) London, 1943; Assistant and later Lecturer in Statistics, London School of Economics, 1928-39; Reader in Economic Statistics, Univ. of London, 1939-44; Statistician, HM Treasury, 1939-41; Dir of Records and Statistics, British Supply Council, Washington, 1941-42; British Dir of Research and Statistics, Combined Production and Resources Board, Washington, 1942-45; Statistical Adviser, HM Treasury, 1947-48; Consultant, UN Statistical Office, 1949-50 and 1952. Visiting Professor, Univ. of California, 1958-59. Member: Air Transport Licensing Bd, 1960-72; Civil Aviation Authority, 1972-73; Cttee of Inquiry on Decimal Currency, 1962-63; Chm., Impact of Rates Cttee, 1963-65; Mem. Research Council, DSIR, 1964-65; Mem., SSRC, 1967-70. Hon. Fellow, LSE, 1977. Hon. DSc (Soc. Sci.) Southampton, 1970. Guy Medal (Gold), Royal Statistical Soc., 1979. *Publications:* Family Expenditure (with Sir Arthur Bowley), 1935; Mathematical Analysis for Economists, 1938; Statistics for Economists, 1949; International Trade Statistics (with J. Edward Ely), 1953; Mathematical Economics, 1956; Basic Mathematics, 1962; Macroeconomic Theory, 1967; Index Numbers in Theory and Practice, 1975; Introduction to National Accounts Statistics, 1980; articles in economic and statistical journals. *Address:* 11 The Limes, Linden Gardens, W2. *T:* 01-727 9979; Greyfriars (South), South Green, Southwold, Suffolk. *T:* Southwold 723307.

ALLEN, Thomas; singer; *b* 10 Sept. 1944; *s* of Thomas Boaz Allen and Florence Allen; *m* 1968, Margaret Holley; one *s. Educ:* Robert Richardson Grammar Sch., Ryhope; Royal College of Music. ARCM. Welsh Nat. Opera, 1969-72; Principal Baritone, Royal Opera, Covent Garden, 1972-78; appearances include: Glyndebourne Fest. Opera; English Opera Group; Paris Opera; Florence; Teatro Colon, Buenos Aires; Met. Opera, NY; Hamburg; BBC TV (The Gondoliers, The Marriage of Figaro); all major orchestras and various concert engagements abroad. Major roles include: Figaro in Barber of Seville; Figaro and the Count in Marriage of Figaro; Paolo Albiani in Simon Boccanegra; Papageno in The Magic Flute; Billy Budd; Marcello in La Bohême; Belcore in l'Elisir d'Amore; Sid in Albert Herring; Tarquinius in Rape of Lucretia; Guglielmo in Così fan Tutte; Demetrius in A Midsummer Night's Dream; Valentin in Faust; Dr Falke in Die Fledermaus; King Arthur; The Count in Voice of Ariadne; Silvio in Pagliacci; Pelléas in Pelléas and Mélisande; Germont in La Traviata; title rôle in Don Giovanni, and many others. *Recreations:* gardening, golf, sailing, reading, ornithology. *Address:* c/o John Coast, 1 Park Close, Knightsbridge, SW1X 7PQ.

ALLEN, Walter Ernest, author and literary journalist; *b* Birmingham, 23 Feb. 1911; 4th *s* of Charles Henry Allen and Annie Maria Thomas; *m* 1944, Peggy Yorke, 3rd *d* of Guy Lionel Joy and Dorothy Yorke Maundrell, Calne, Wilts; two *s* two *d. Educ:* King Edward's Grammar School, Aston, Birmingham; Birmingham University. Assistant Master, King Edward's Grammar School, Aston, Birmingham, 1934; Visiting Lecturer in English, State University of Iowa, USA, 1935; Features Editor, Cater's News Agency, Birmingham, 1935-37; Assistant Technical Officer, Wrought Light Alloys Development Assoc., 1943-45. Asst Literary Editor, New Statesman, 1959-60, Literary Editor, 1960-61. Margaret Pilcher Vis. Prof. of English, Coe Coll., Iowa, 1955-56; Visiting Professor of English: Vassar College, New York, 1963-64; Univ. of Kansas, 1967; Univ. of Washington, 1967; Prof. of English, New Univ. of Ulster, 1967-73; Berg Prof. of English, New York Univ., 1970-71; Vis. Prof. of English, Dalhousie Univ., Halifax, NS, 1973-74; C. P. Miles Prof. of English, Virginia Polytechnic Inst. and State Univ., 1974-75. FRSL. *Publications:* Innocence is Drowned, 1938; Blind Man's Ditch, 1939; Living Space, 1940; Rogue Elephant, 1946; The Black Country, 1946; Writers on Writing, 1948; Arnold Bennett, 1948; Reading a Novel, 1949; Dead Man Over All, 1950; The English Novel A Short Critical History, 1954; Six Great Novelists, 1955; All in a Lifetime, 1959; Tradition and Dream, 1964; George Eliot, 1964; The Urgent West: an Introduction to the Idea of the United States, 1969; Transatlantic Crossing: American visitors to Britain and British visitors to America in the nineteenth century, 1971; The Short Story in English, 1981; As I Walked Down New Grub Street, 1981. *Address:* 6 Canonbury Square, N1. *T:* 01-226 7085.

ALLEN, W(alter) Godfrey, MA; FSA, FRIBA; Hon. DLitt (Oxford), 1963; Surveyor of the Fabric of St Paul's Cathedral, 1931-56; Consulting Architect to Southwark Cathedral, 1932-55, to Exeter Cathedral, 1942-52, to Gloucester Cathedral since 1953; architect in private practice; *b* 21 Oct. 1891; *s* of Walter Allen and Frances Baker; *m* 1931, Phyllis Seyler Gill (*d* 1973). *Educ:* Berkhampstead Sch.; Slade Sch.; King's Coll., London. Articled, later Asst to Sir Mervyn Macartney; Sec. to Commn of architects and engrs apptd in 1921 to investigate and report on condition of St Paul's Cathedral, Asst Architect to the Dean and Chapter, 1925-31. Member: Royal Commn on Historical Monuments (Eng.), 1952-60; Exec. Cttee of Wren Soc., 1933-43; Advisory Panel of Specialist Architects, Historic Churches Preservation Trust (London Region); Chairman Church Roofing Committee set up by Central Council for the Care of Churches and Society for the Protection of Ancient Buildings, 1952; Commander of St Paul's Watch, 1939-45; Prime Warden Goldsmiths' Co., 1951-53; Master of Art Workers' Guild, 1953-54; Hon. Mem., City and Guilds of London Inst. A Governor, Westminster Sch., 1951-70. *Works include:* restoration of St Bride's, Fleet Street; St Giles, Cripplegate; St Mary

Abchurch; St Dunstan-in-the-West; St James, Louth; St James's Chapel, Exet Cathedral; Chapter-House, St Paul's Cathedral; Sheldonian Theatre; O Ashmolean Building and Radcliffe Camera, Oxford. *Publications:* T Preservation of St Paul's Cathedral, RIBA Jl; A Survey of Views of St Pau Cathedral; numerous articles. *Recreation:* walking. *Address:* Morden Colleg Blackheath, SE3 0PW.

ALLEN, Walter John Gardener; Controller, Capital Taxes Office (former Estate Duty Office), Inland Revenue, 1974-78; *b* 8 Dec. 1916; *s* of late Joh Gardiner Allen and late Hester Lucy Allen, Deal, Kent; *m* 1944, Irene, *d* late John Joseph and Sarah Henderson, Lisburn, N Ireland; one *s* one *d. Edu* Manwoods, Sandwich; London Univ. (LLB). Entered Inland Revenue, 193 Served RAF, 1940-46 (Flying Officer). FGS. *Recreations:* amateur geologi; gardening. *Address:* 43 The Chase, Eastcote, Pinner, Mddx HA5 1SH. *T* 01-868 7101.

ALLEN, William Alexander, CBE 1980; RIBA; Chairman, Bickerdike Alle Partners, architects; *b* 29 June 1914; *s* of late Professor Frank Allen, FRSC *m* 1938, Beatrice Mary Teresa Pearson; two *s* one *d. Educ:* public schools Winnipeg; University of Manitoba. Royal Architectural Inst. of Canac Silver Medal, 1935. Univ. Gold Medal in Architecture, 1936. Appointed t Building Research Station, Watford, 1937; Chief Architect, Bldg Res. St 1953-61; Principal of the Architectural Assoc. School of Architecture, 196 66. Member Council RIBA, 1953-72 (Chairman various committees ARIBA 1937; FRIBA 1965; Chm., Fire Research Adv. Cttee, 1973 President: Institute of Acoustics, 1975-76; Ecclesiastic Arch. Assoc., 1980. Ho Associate NZIA, 1965. Hon. LLD Manitoba, 1977. Commander, Ordem d Mérito, Portugal, 1972. *Publications:* (with R. Fitzmaurice) Soun Transmission in Buildings, 1939. Papers, etc, on scientific and technical aspec of architecture, professionalism, and modern architectural history ar education. *Recreations:* writing, drawing, music. *Address:* 4 Ashley Clos Welwyn Garden City, Herts AL8 7LH. *T:* Welwyn Garden 24178. *Clu* Athenæum.

See also Prof. J. F. Allen.

ALLEN, Sir (William) Denis, GCMG 1969 (KCMG 1958; CMG 1950); C 1955; HM Diplomatic Service, retired; *b* 24 Dec. 1910; *s* of John Allen; *a* 1939, Elizabeth Helen (*née* Watkin Williams); one *s. Educ:* Wanganui, Ne Zealand; Cambridge. HM Diplomatic Service, 1934-69; Deput Commissioner General for South East Asia, 1959-62; Ambassador to Turke 1963-67; Dep. Under-Sec., Foreign Office (later FCO), 1967-69. *Addres* Stockland, Honiton, Devon.

ALLEN, Sir William (Guilford), Kt 1981; Chairman, family group companies; *b* 22 April 1932; *s* of Sir William Guilford Allen, CBE, and Mor Maree Allen; *m* 1959, Elaine Therese Doyle; two *s* one *d. Educ:* Downlan Coll., Toowoomba, Qld. In grazing industry, Merino sheep; Principa Historic Malvern Hills Registered Merino Stud; stud Shorthorn cattle breede Commercial broadcasting industry; Mem. Bd of Dirs, Qantas. Treasurer, Na Party, Qld. Councillor, Longreach Shire. *Recreation:* aviation. *Addres* Bexley, Longreach, Qld 4730, Australia. *T:* Longreach 723; Toorak Hous Hamilton, Brisbane, Qld 4007, Australia. *T:* Brisbane 2624111. *Club* Brisbane, Tattersalls, Royal Queensland Golf, Longreach, Queensland Tu Brisbane Amateur Turf (Brisbane).

ALLEN, Sir (William) Kenneth (Gwynne), Kt 1961; DL; *b* 23 May 190 *er s* of Harold Gwynne Allen and Hilda Allen, Bedford; *m* 1931, Eleanc Mary (*née* Eeles); one *s* one *d. Educ:* Westminster Sch.; Univ. of Neuchâte Switzerland. Started as engineering pupil, Harland & Wolff Ltd, Glasgow an Belfast; subsequently at W. H. Allen, Sons & Co. Ltd, Bedford; Dir, 1937-7 Man. Dir, 1946-70, Chm., 1955-70, W. H. Allen, Sons & Co. Ltd; Chm Amalgamated Power Engineering, 1968-70; Director: Whessoe Ltd, 1954-6! Electrolux, 1970-78. Chm., Brit. Internal Combustion Engine Manufacture Assoc., 1955-57; Pres., British Engineers' Assoc., 1957-59 (now Britis Mechanical Engineering Fedn); Chm., BEAMA, 1959-61; Pres., Engineerin Employers' Fedn, 1962-64; Chm., Labour and Social Affairs Cttee of CB 1965-67. FIMarE; MRINA; MIBritishE. Freeman of City of Londo Liveryman, Worshipful Company of Shipwrights. Mem. Beds CC, 1945-5! High Sheriff Beds, 1958-59; DL Beds, 1978. *Address:* Manor Close, Aspl Guise, Milton Keynes, Bedfordshire MK17 8HZ. *T:* Milton Keyne 583161.

ALLEN, William Maurice; Executive Director, Bank of England, 1964-7 *b* 16 April 1908; *s* of David Allen. *Educ:* Dulwich College; London Schoc of Economics. Army 1940-45. Asst Dir of Research, International Monetar Fund, 1947-49; Adviser, Bank of England, 1950-64. Fellow of Balliol Col Oxford, 1931-48; Visiting Fellow Nuffield Coll., Oxford, 1954-62. Ho Fellow, LSE, 1963. Governor, LSE, 1951. *Address:* Bank of England, EC. *Club:* Reform.

ALLEN, Maj.-Gen. William Maurice, FCIT; Director General of Transpo and Movements (Army), since 1981; *b* 29 May 1931; *s* of William James All and Elizabeth Jane Henrietta Allen; *m* 1955, Patricia Mary (*née* Fletcher); on *d* decd. *Educ:* Dunstable Sch. Associate FInstPet 1965; FCIT 1972; FIPDM Commnd RASC, 1950; RCT, 1965; regtl and staff appts, Korea, Cypru Germany and UK; Student, Staff Coll., Camberley, 1961; Instructor, Stac Coll., Camberley and RMCS Shrivenham, 1968-70; Student, RCDS, 197 Asst Comdt, RMA Sandhurst, 1979-81. Pres., Army Caving Assoc., 1982

Mem. Council, IAM, 1982-. Associate, St George's House. Freeman, City of London, 1981; Mem., Guild of Freemen of City of London; Hon. Liveryman and Mem. Ct, Worshipful Co. of Carmen, 1981. *Recreations:* economics, trout fishing, squash, gardening, rough shooting. *Address:* c/o Williams & Glyn's Bank Ltd, Holts Farnborough Branch, Lawrie House, 31-37 Victoria Road, Farnborough, Hants GU14 7PA. *Clubs:* City Livery, Royal Over-Seas League; Bristol Channel Yacht (Swansea).

ALLEN, Prof. William Sidney, MA, PhD (Cantab); FBA 1971; Professor of Comparative Philology in the University of Cambridge, and Fellow of Trinity College, since 1955; *b* 18 March 1918; *er s* of late W. P. Allen and of Ethel (*née* Pearce); *m* 1955, Aenea, *yr d* of late Rev. D. McCallum and Mrs McCallum, Invergordon. *Educ:* Christ's Hosp.; Trinity Coll., Cambridge (Classical Scholar); Porson Scholarship, 1939. War of 1939-45: RTR and General Staff (Int) (despatches). Lecturer in Phonetics, 1948-51, and in Comparative Linguistics, 1951-55, School of Oriental and African Studies, Univ. of London. Dialect research in India, 1952; Fellow of Rockefeller Foundation, USA, 1953; Brit. Council visitor, Univ. of W Indies, 1959. Linguistic Soc. of America's Professor, 1961; Collitz Professor, Linguistic Institute, USA, 1962. Pres., Philological Soc., 1965-67. Hon. Fellow, Soc. for Cycladic Studies (Athens), 1977. *Publications:* Phonetics in Ancient India, 1953; On the Linguistic Study of Languages (inaugural lecture), 1957; Sandhi, 1962; Vox Latina, 1965; Vox Graeca, 1968; Accent and Rhythm, 1973; articles on general and comparative linguistics, phonetics, metrics and classical, Indian and Caucasian Languages, Aegean cartography. *Address:* 24 Sherlock Road, Cambridge CB3 0HR. *T:* Cambridge 356739; 65621.

ALLEN, Woody; writer, actor, director; *b* Brooklyn, 1 Dec. 1935; *s* of Martin and Nettie Konigsberg; *m* 1966, Louise Lasser (marr. diss.). TV script writer, 1953-64, and appeared as a comedian in nightclubs and on TV shows. Sylvania Award, 1957. *Plays:* (writer) Don't Drink the Water, 1966; (writer and actor) Play It Again Sam, 1969 (filmed 1972). *Films:* (writer and actor) What's New Pussycat?, 1965; (actor) Casino Royale, 1967; (writer, actor and director): What's Up Tiger Lily?, 1966; Take the Money and Run, 1969; Bananas, 1971; Everything You Always Wanted to Know About Sex But Were Afraid to Ask, 1972; Sleeper, 1973; Love and Death, 1975; The Front, 1976; Annie Hall (Academy Award), 1977; Manhattan, 1979; Stardust Memories, 1980; (writer and director) Interiors, 1978. *Publications:* Getting Even, 1971; Without Feathers, 1975; Side Effects, 1981; contribs to New Yorker, etc. *Address:* c/o United Artists Corporation, 729 7th Avenue, New York City, NY 10019, USA.

ALLEN-JONES, Air Vice-Marshal John Ernest, CBE 1966; Director of RAF Legal Services, 1961-70, retired; *b* 13 Oct. 1909; *s* of Rev. John Allen-Jones, Llanyblodwel Vicarage, Oswestry; *m* 1st, 1937, Margaret Rix (*d* 1973), Sawbridgeworth; one *s* two *d*; 2nd, 1973, Diana Gibbons. *Educ:* Rugby; Worcester Coll., Oxford (MA). Solicitor (Honours), 1934; Partner with Vaudrey, Osborne & Mellor, Manchester. Joined RAF, 1939. Air Vice-Marshal, 1967. Gordon-Shepherd Memorial Prizeman, 1963. *Recreations:* tennis, bridge. *Address:* Hartfield, Duton Hill, Dunmow, Essex. *T:* Great Easton 554.

ALLENBY, family name of **Viscount Allenby.**

ALLENBY, 2nd Viscount, *cr* 1919, of Megiddo and of Felixstowe; **Dudley Jaffray Hynman Allenby;** late 11th Hussars; *b* 8 Jan. 1903; *e s* of late Capt. Frederick Claude Hynman Allenby, CBE, RN, JP; *S* uncle 1936; *m* 1st, 1930, Mary (marr. diss. 1949), *d* of Edward Champneys, Otterpool Manor, Kent; one *s*; 2nd, 1949, Mrs Daisy Neame, CStJ. *Educ:* Eton; RMC, Sandhurst. Joined 11th Hussars, 1923; served in India, 1923-26; Adjutant, 11th Hussars, 1926-30; Instructor, Royal Military College, Sandhurst, 1930-34; Captain, 1936; served Egypt, 1934-37; Adjutant, Army Fighting Vehicles School, 1937-40; Major, 1938; 2nd in Command Royal Gloucestershire Hussars, 1940-42; Lt-Col 2nd Derbyshire Yeomanry, 1942; retd (Lt-Col) 1946. *Heir:* *s* Lt-Col Hon. Michael Jaffray Hynman Allenby, The Royal Hussars [*b* 20 April 1931; *m* 1965, Sara Margaret Wiggin; one *s*]. *Address:* Parsonage Farm, Westwell, Ashford, Kent. *T:* Ashford 24783. *Club:* Cavalry and Guards.

ALLENBY, Rt. Rev. (David Howard) Nicholas; Assistant Bishop, Diocese of Worcester since 1968; Chaplain, St Oswald's Almshouses, Worcester, since 1973; *b* 28 Jan. 1909; *s* of late William Allenby. *Educ:* Kelham Theological College. MA (Lambeth), 1957. Deacon, 1934; Priest, 1935. Curate of St Jude, West Derby, Liverpool, 1934-36; Tutor, Kelham Theological College and Public Preacher, Diocese of Southwell, 1936-44; Rector of Averham with Kelham, 1944-57; Proctor in Convocation, Southwell, 1950-57; Editor of Diocesan News and Southwell Review, 1950-55; Hon. Canon of Southwell, 1953-57, Canon Emeritus, 1957-62; Personal Chaplain to Bishop of Southwell, 1954-57; Rural Dean of Newark, 1955-57; Provincial of Society of Sacred Mission in Australia, 1957-62; Commissary, Melanesia, 1958-62; Warden of Community of Holy Name, City and Diocese of Melbourne, 1961-62; Bishop of Kuching, 1962-68; Commissary, Kuching, 1969. Mem., Southwell RDC, 1944-52. *Publication:* Pray with the Church, 1937 (jointly). *Recreations:* reading, painting, cooking. *Address:* Chaplain's House, St Oswald's Close. The Tything, Worcester WR1 1HR. *T:* Worcester 22922. *Club:* Royal Commonwealth Society.

LLENDALE, 3rd Viscount, *cr* 1911; **Wentworth Hubert Charles Beaumont,** DL; Baron, 1906; *b* 12 Sept. 1922; *e s* of 2nd Viscount Allendale,

KG, CB, CBE, MC, and Violet (*d* 1979), *d* of Sir Charles Seely, 2nd Bt; *S* father 1956; *m* 1948, Hon. Sarah Ismay, 2nd *d* of 1st Baron Ismay, KG, PC, GCB, CH, DSO; three *s. Educ:* Eton. RAFVR, 1940; Flight-Lieutenant 1943; ADC to Viceroy of India, 1946-47. DL Northumberland, 1961. *Heir:* *s* Hon. Wentworth Peter Ismay Beaumont [*b* 13 Nov. 1948; *m* 1975, Theresa Mary, *d* of F. A. More O'Ferrall; one *s* one *d. Address:* Bywell Hall, Stocksfield on Tyne, Northumberland. *T:* Stocksfield 3169; Allenheads, Hexham, Northumberland. *T:* Allenheads 205. *Clubs:* Turf, White's; Northern Counties (Newcastle upon Tyne).

See also Earl of Carlisle.

ALLERTON, 3rd Baron of Chapel Allerton, *cr* 1902; **George William Lawies Jackson;** Squadron-Leader Auxiliary Air Force, retired; late Lieutenant Coldstream Guards; *b* 23 July 1903; *s* of 2nd Baron and Katherine Louisa (*d* 1956), *y d* of W. W. Wickham, JP, of Chestnut Grove, Boston Spa; *S* father, 1925; *m* 1st, 1926, Joyce (who obtained a divorce, 1934; *d* 1953), *o c* of late J. R. Hatfeild, Thorp Arch Hall, Yorks; (one *s* decd); 2nd, 1934, Mrs Hope Aline Whitelaw; 3rd, 1947, Anne, *er d* of late James Montagu, Skippetts, nr Basingstoke; one *d. Educ:* Eton; RMC, Sandhurst. *Recreations:* shooting, golf. *Address:* Loddington Hall, Leicestershire LE7 9XE. *T:* Belton 220. *Clubs:* White's, Turf, Pratt's.

ALLERTON, Reginald John, CBE 1964; FRICS, FIH; retired 1963; *b* 20 June 1898; 3rd *s* of late Robert Sterry Allerton, Lowestoft, and Mary Maria (*née* Bailey); *m* 1924, Dorothy Rose Saunders; one *s. Educ:* Lowestoft Grammar School. Entered Local Government Service, 1915; on Active Service with RNVR, 1917-19. Various urban and borough appointments until 1926; Chief Architectural and Building Asst, Reading Borough Council, 1926-30; Estates Surveyor, City of Norwich, 1930-39; Housing Manager and Sec., City of Bristol, 1939-51; Housing Manager, City of Birmingham, 1951-54; Director of Housing to the London County Council, 1954-63. Pres., Inst. of Housing, 1949-50, 1960-61. Apptd (by Minister of Housing and Local Govt) as Vice-Pres., Surrey and Sussex Rent Assessment Panel, 1965-71. Served on Govt Cttees on Housing and Immigration, and Housing in Greater London (Sir Milner Holland Cttee); Founder Mem., Hanover Housing Assoc. *Publications:* many papers and lectures to professional societies and conferences dealing mainly with municipal housing work. *Recreations:* gardening, fishing. *Address:* 10 Mill Mead, Wendover, Bucks. *T:* Wendover 622691.

ALLEY, Ronald Edgar; Keeper of the Modern Collection, Tate Gallery, London, since 1965; *b* 12 March 1926; *s* of late Edgar Thomas Alley; *m* 1955, Anthea Oswell (now painter and sculptor, as Anthea Alley); two *d. Educ:* Bristol Grammar School; Courtauld Institute of Art, London University. Tate Gallery staff as Asst Keeper II, 1951-54; Deputy Keeper, 1954-65. Member: Museum Board, Cecil Higgins Art Gallery, Bedford, 1957-; Art Cttee, Ulster Museum, Belfast, 1962-; Art Panel of Arts Council, 1963-70. *Publications:* Tate Gallery: Foreign Paintings, Drawings and Sculpture, 1959; Gauguin, 1962; William Scott, 1963; Ben Nicholson, 1963; Francis Bacon (with Sir John Rothenstein), 1964; British Painting since 1945, 1966; Picasso's "Three Dancers" 1967; Barbara Hepworth, 1968; Recent American Art, 1969; Abstract Expressionism, 1974; Catalogue of the Tate Gallery's Collection of Modern Art, other than works by British Artists, 1981. *Recreation:* ornithology. *Address:* 61 Deodar Road, SW15. *T:* 01-874 2016. *Club:* Institute of Contemporary Arts.

ALLEYNE, Captain Sir John (Meynell), 4th Bt *cr* 1769; DSO 1918; DSC; RN retired; *b* 11 Aug. 1889; *s* of Reynold Alleyne, *e s* of 3rd Bt and Susanna, *d* of late John Meynell of Meynell Langley, Derbyshire; *S* grandfather, 1912; *m* 1920, Alice Violet, *d* of late James Campbell, and Mrs Campbell, 12 Cornwall Gardens, SW; one *s* two *d*. Served European War; was navigator of HMS Vindictive when sunk to block Ostend Harbour, May 1918 (severely wounded); retired list, 1936. Served War of 1939-45. *Heir:* *s* Rev. John Olpherts Campbell Alleyne, [*b* 18 Jan. 1928; *m* 1968, Honor Irwin; one *s* one *d*]. *Address:* Greenacres, Seamans Lane, Minstead, Lyndhurst, Hants. *T:* Cadnam 3235. *Club:* Naval and Military.

ALLHUSEN, Major Derek Swithin, DL; farmer; Standard Bearer, HM's Body Guard of Honourable Corps of Gentlemen at Arms, since 1981; *b* 9 Jan. 1914; 2nd *s* of late Lt-Col F. H. Allhusen, CMG, DSO, Fulmer House, Fulmer, Bucks; *m* 1937, Hon. Claudia Violet Betterton, *yr d* of 1st and last Baron Rushcliffe, PC, GBE (*d* 1949); one *s* one *d* (and one *s* decd). *Educ:* Eton; Chillon Coll., Montreux, Switzerland; Trinity Coll., Cambridge. Lieut, 9th Queen's Royal Lancers, 1935. Served War of 1939-45: France, 1940 (wounded), North Africa, Italy (Silver Star Medal of USA, 1944); Major 1942; 2 i/c 1945-47; retired, 1949. One of HM's Body Guard of Hon. Corps of Gentlemen at Arms, 1963-. Chm., Riding for the Disabled, Norwich and Dist. Gp, 1968- (Vice-Pres., Eastern Region); President: Royal Norfolk Agric. Assoc., 1974; Nat. Pony Soc., 1982; Cambridge Univ. Equestrian Club; Norfolk Schs Athletic Assoc.; SE Norfolk Primary Schs Assoc.; Member: Farriers' Registration Council; British Horse Soc. Council; Governing Body, Langley Sch. Freeman, City of London; Hon. Freeman, Worshipful Co. of Saddlers and Farriers, 1969. High Sheriff, 1958, DL 1969, Norfolk. *Recreations:* riding, shooting, skiing. Represented GB: Winter Pentathlon Olympic Games, 1948; Equestrianism European Championships Three-Day Event, 1957, 1959, 1965, 1967, 1969 (Winners of Team Championship, 1957, 1967, 1969); Olympic Games, Mexico, 1968 (Gold Medal, Team; Silver Medal, Individual); lent his horse Laurieston to British Olympic Equestrian Team, Munich, 1972 (individual and team Gold Medals). *Address:* Manor

House, Claxton, Norwich, Norfolk. *T:* Thurton 228; Flat 1, 22 St James's Square, SW1. *T:* 01-839 3390. *Club:* Cavalry and Guards.

ALLIBONE, Thomas Edward, CBE 1960; FRS 1948; DSc Sheffield; External Professor of Electrical Engineering, University of Leeds, 1967-79, now Emeritus; Visiting Professor of Physics, City University, since 1971; *b* 11 Nov. 1903; *s* of Henry J. Allibone; *m* 1931, Dorothy Margery, *d* of Frederick Boulden, BSc, MEng, MIMechE; two *d. Educ:* Central Sch., Sheffield (Birley Scholar); Sheffield Univ. (Linley Scholar); Gonville and Caius Coll., Cambridge (Wollaston Scholar). PhD Sheffield; PhD Cantab. 1851 Exhibition Sen. Student, Cavendish Laboratory, Cambridge, 1926-30; i/c High-Voltage Laboratory, Metropolitan-Vickers Electrical Co., Manchester, 1930-46; Director: Res. Laboratory, AEI, Aldermaston, 1946-63; AEI (Woolwich) Ltd, 1948-63; Scientific Adviser, AEI, 1963; Chief Scientist, Central Electricity Generating Bd, 1963-70. Mem., British Mission on Atomic Energy, Berkeley, Calif, and Oakridge, Tenn, 1944-45; Visitor: BISRA, 1949-55; ASLIB, 1955-62. Lectures: Faraday, 1946, 1956; Royal Instn Christmas, 1959; Wm Menelaus, 1959; Bernard Price, 1959; Trotter Patterson, 1963; Fison Memorial, 1963; Royal Soc. Rutherford Memorial, 1964 and 1972; Baird Memorial, 1967; Melchett, 1970. President: Section A, British Assoc., 1958; EIBA, 1958-59; Inst. of Information Scientists, 1964-67. Vice-President: Inst. of Physics, 1948-52; Royal Instn, 1955-57, 1970-72. Chm., Res. Cttee, British Electrical and Allied Industries Res. Assoc., 1955-62. Member: Council, British Inst. of Radiology, 1935-38; Council, IEE, 1937-40, 1946-49, 1950-53; Cttee, Nat. Physical Laboratory, 1950-60; Govt Cttee on Copyright, 1951; DSIR (Mem., Industrial Grants Cttee, 1950-58); Council, Physical Soc., 1953-56; Council, Southern Electricity Bd, 1953-62; Adv. Council, Science Museum; Adv. Council, RMC; Adv. Court, AEA; Nuclear Safety Adv. Council, Min. of Power, 1959-. Trustee, British Museum, 1968-74. Governor, Downe House, 1959-69; Chm. Governors, Reading Technical Coll., 1959-68. Mem., Worshipful Co. of Broderers, 1967-. FInstP; FEng; FIEE; Fellow, Amer. Inst. of Electrical Engineers. Hon. DSc: Reading, 1960; City, 1970; Hon. DEng Sheffield, 1969. Röntgen Medal, British Inst. of Radiology; Thornton and Cooper Hill Medals, IEE; Melchett Medal, Inst. of Fuel. *Publications:* The Release and Use of Nuclear Energy, 1961; Rutherford: Father of Nuclear Energy (Rutherford Lecture 1972), 1973; The Royal Society and its Dining Clubs, 1975; Lightning: the long spark, 1977; papers on high voltage and transient electrical phenomena, fission and fusion. *Recreations:* photography, travel, gardening, philately. *Address:* York Cottage, Lovel Road, Winkfield, Windsor, Berks. *T:* Winkfield Row 884501.

ALLIGHAN, Garry; Journalist and Author; Principal, Premier School of Journalism, Johannesburg, 1963-73; *b* 16 Feb. 1900; *s* of George and Catherine Allighan, Wickford, Essex; *m* ; one *s* one *d. Educ:* St James School, Enfield; Enfield Grammar School. Naval service in European War; joined Luton News, 1919; Assistant Editor John Bull, 1921-25; Feature Editor Toronto Evening Telegram, 1925-28; Feature Writer Daily Express, 1928-31; Radio Editor Evening Standard, 1931-39; War Correspondent Toronto Star, 1939-41; News Editor Daily Mirror, 1941-44; Industrial Editor Daily Mail, 1944-46; MP (Lab) Gravesend Div. of Kent, 1945-47. Has also acted as Press Consultant to Advertising Assoc. and Radio Manufacturers Assoc. *Publications:* Priceless Treasure (Canada), 1926; Romance of the Talkies, 1929; Reith of the BBC, 1937; De Valera Revealed (USA), 1937; The First Thirteen, 1941; Curtain-Up on South Africa, 1960; Verwoerd-The End, 1961; The Welensky Story, 1962; Four Bonnets to Golgotha, 1963; The 65th Defendant, 1963; The Moving Finger, 1964; Forward into the Past, 1976. *Recreations:* motoring and photography. *Address:* 717 The Mariston, Claim Street, Johannesburg, South Africa.

ALLINSON, Sir Leonard; *see* Allinson, Sir W. L.

ALLINSON, Air Vice-Marshal Norman Stuart, CB 1946; DL; retired; *b* 19 April 1904; *s* of late Rev. H. C. W. Allinson, Hinxhill, Kent; *m* 1928, Florence Muriel Hall (*d* 1975); one *s* one *d. Educ:* Trent Coll.; RAF, Cranwell. Served with No 13 Sqdn, 1924-29; in HMS Hermes, 1930-32; Dept of Air Member of Personnel, 1933-35; RAF Staff Coll., 1936; comd No 269 Sqdn, 1937-38; HQ Coastal Comd, 1938-39; served War of 1939-45, Armament duties, Air Min. and MAP, 1940-41; HQ Army Co-operation Comd, 1942; served in Middle East, 1943-45, on planning duties, as AOC No 212 Group and Force 438 and as Dep. SASO, HQ Middle East; Dir of Operational Trng, Air Min., 1945-47; Imperial Defence Coll., 1948; AOC Rhodesian Air Trng Group, Bulawayo, S Rhodesia, 1949-51; Director-General of Manning, 1951-52; Director-General of Personnel I, 1953-54; Air Officer i/c Administration, Flying Training Command, 1954-56; retired, 1956. DL Essex, 1964. *Recreation:* sailing. *Address:* Dene House, Layer de la Haye, Colchester, Essex. *Club:* Royal Air Force.

ALLINSON, Sir (Walter) Leonard, KCVO 1979 (MVO 1961); CMG 1976; HM Diplomatic Service; High Commissioner in Kenya, since 1982; *b* 1 May 1926; *o s* of Walter Allinson and Alice Frances Cassidy; *m* 1951, Margaret Patricia Watts; three *d* (of whom two are twins). *Educ:* Friern Barnet Grammar Sch.; Merton Coll., Oxford. First class in History, 1947; MA. Asst Principal, Ministry of Fuel and Power (Petroleum Div.), 1947-48; Asst Principal, later Principal, Min. of Education, 1948-58 (Asst Private Sec. to Minister, 1953-54); transf. CRO, 1958; First Sec. in Lahore and Karachi, 1960-62, Madras and New Delhi, 1963-66; Counsellor and Head of Political Affairs Dept, March 1968; Dep. Head, later Head, of Permanent Under

Secretary's Dept, FCO, 1968-70; Counsellor and Head of Chancery subsequently Deputy High Comr, Nairobi, 1970-73; RCDS, 1974; Diplomatic Service Inspectorate, 1975; Dep. High Comr and Minister, New Delhi, 1975-77; High Comr, Lusaka, 1978-80; Asst Under-Sec. of State (Africa), 1980-82. Mem. Council, Royal African Soc. *Address:* c/o Foreign and Commonwealth Office, SW1. *Clubs:* Travellers'; Nairobi (Nairobi); Ndola (Zambia).

ALLIOTT, John Downes, QC 1973; a Recorder of the Crown Court, since 1972; *b* 9 Jan. 1932; *er s* of late Alexander Clifford Alliott and Ena Kathleen Alliott (*née* Downes); *m* 1957, Patsy Jennifer, *d* of late Gordon Beckley Willson; two *s* one *d. Educ:* Charterhouse; Peterhouse, Cambridge (Scholar BA). Coldstream Guards, 1950-51; Peterhouse, 1951-54; called to Bar, Inner Temple, 1955, Bencher 1980. Dep. Chm., E Sussex QS, 1970-71. *Recreations:* rural pursuits, France and Italy, military history. *Address:* (chambers) 1 Crown Office Row, Temple, EC4Y 7HH. *T:* 01-353 1801; (home) Park Stile, Lovel Hill Lane, Langley, Slough SL3 6DE. *T:* Iver 652745.

ALLISON, Charles Ralph, MA; Secretary, Lord Kitchener National Memorial Fund; Headmaster of Brentwood School, 1945-65; *b* 26 May 1903; *s* of Harry A. Allison, FCA, and Gertrude Wolfsberger; *m* 1930, Winifred Rita, *d* of A. C. Williams; two *s* one *d. Educ:* Caterham Sch.; University Coll., London; St Catharine's College, Cambridge (Exhibitioner). Assistant Master, Worksop College, 1928; Malvern College, 1929-36; English Tutor, Stowe School, 1936-38; Headmaster of Reigate Grammar School, 1938-40 and Alleyn's School, 1940-45. Formerly Mem. Cttee, Headmasters' Conf. (Vice-Chm. 1965). Governor: Sidney Perry Foundation (Chm.); Lindisfarn Coll., Ruabon, 1954-81; Brentwood Sch.; Stowe Sch., 1965-80. Vice-Chm Commonwealth Youth Exchange Cttee, 1970-72; Vice-Pres., Eastern Region UNA, 1965-. Mem., Nat. Commn for UNESCO, 1954-65; UK Delegate to Gen. Confs, 1958 and 1960. Member: Cttee, Governing Bodies' Assoc., 1972-79, 1980-; Essex Education Cttee, 1967-74. Reader in the Parish of St Mary's, Great Warley. *Address:* Barn Meadow, Great Warley, near Brentwood, Essex. *T:* Brentwood 214211. *Club:* East India, Devonshire, Sports and Public Schools.

ALLISON, Air Cdre Dennis; Commandant, Central Flying School, since 1979; *b* 15 Oct. 1932; *m* 1964, Rachel Anne Franks; one *s* four *d. Educ:* RAF Halton; RAF Coll., Cranwell. Commnd, 1954; No 87 Sqdn, 1955-58; cf 1958; Flying Instructor and Coll. Adjt, RAF Coll., 1958-61; CO, RAF Sharjah, 1961-62; Indian Jt Services Staff Coll., 1965; MoD Central Staffs, 1968-70; ndc, 1973; MoD Central Staffs, 1973-74; CO, RAF Coningsby, 1974-76; Canadian Nat. Defence Coll., 1977; MoD Central Staffs, 1978-79. *Recreations:* bridge, golf. *Address:* The Old Forge, Castle Bytham, Grantham, Lincs NG33 4RG. *T:* Castle Bytham 372. *Club:* Royal Air Force.

ALLISON, Rt. Rev. Oliver Claude, CBE 1971; Travelling Secretary, Sudan Church Association, since 1974; *b* Stafford, 1908; *s* of Rev. W. S. Allison. *Educ:* Dean Close School, Cheltenham; Queens' College and Ridley Hall Cambridge. BA 1930; MA 1934. Deacon, 1932; Priest, 1933; Curate of Fulwood, 1932-36; Curate of St John, Boscombe, and Jt Sec. Winchester Dioc Council of Youth, 1936-38; CMS Miss. at Juba, Dio. Sudan, 1938-47; Ass Bp in the Sudan, 1948-53; Bishop in the Sudan, 1953-74. *Publications:* Pilgrim Church's Progress, 1966; Through Fire and Water, 1976. *Address:* Gloucester Avenue, Bexhill-on-Sea, East Sussex TN40 2LA. *Club:* Royal Commonwealth Society.

ALLISON, Ralph Victor, CMG 1967; retired industrialist, Australia; *b* 20 Feb. 1900; *s* of late Albert John and Edith Victoria Allison; *m* 1923, Myrtle Ellen Birch; two *d. Educ:* public and night schools, Milang, SA. General Store, A. H. Landseer Ltd: Milang, 1916-19; Adelaide, 1919-26; R. J. Finlayson Ltd Adelaide: Company Sec., 1926-39; Dir, 1939-64; Man. Dir, 1954-64; Chm Dirs of subsidiaries, 1954-64. Mem. Council: Royal Agric. and Hort. Soc. o SA, 1937-72 (Exec. Mem. 8 yrs); SA Chamber of Manufactures, 1948- (Pres 1962, 1963); Chamber of Commerce and Industry SA Inc. (also Mem. Exec Cttee). Mem. SA Dairy Bd, 1957-. Pres. Aust. Chamber of Manufactures 1964; Mem. Aust. Export Devell Council, 1964-68; Director, Australian Export Promotions Ltd and various other Australian cos until 1966. Mem. many Aust. Commonwealth Cttees. *Recreations:* formerly tennis and bowls latterly golf. *Address:* 18 Taylor Terrace, Rosslyn Park, SA 5072, Australia. *T:* 31.2538. *Club:* Commonwealth (SA).

ALLISON, Roderick Stuart; Under-Secretary, Department of Employment since 1977; *b* 28 Nov. 1936; *s* of Stuart Frew Allison and Poppy (*née* Hodges); *m* 1968, Anne Sergeant; one *s* one *d. Educ:* Manchester Grammar Sch.; Balliol Coll., Oxford. Entered Ministry of Labour, 1959; Private Sec. to Perm. Sec. 1963-64; Principal, 1964; Civil Service Dept, 1969-71; Asst Sec., Dept of Employment, 1971. *Recreations:* playing with children, rough gardening, music. *Address:* c/o Department of Employment, Caxton House, Tothill Street, SW1.

ALLISON, Ronald William Paul, CVO 1978; Managing Director, Ronald Allison & Associates Ltd, since 1978; Controller of Sport and Outside Broadcasts, Thames Television, since 1980; *b* 26 Jan. 1932; *o s* of Percy Allison and Dorothy (*née* Doyle); *m* 1956, Maureen Angela Macdonald; two *d. Educ:* Weymouth Grammar Sch.; Taunton's Sch., Southampton. Reporter Hampshire Chronicle, 1952-57; Reporter, BBC, 1957-67; freelance broadcaster, 1968-69; special correspondent, BBC, 1969-73; Press Sec. to

Queen, 1973-78; regular presenter and commentator, Thames TV, 1978-. *Publications:* Look Back in Wonder, 1968; The Queen, 1973; Charles, Prince of our Time, 1978; The Country Life Book of Britain in the Seventies, 1980. *Recreations:* photography, painting, watching football. *Address:* 36 Ormond Drive, Hampton, Mddx. *T:* 01-979 1912. *Clubs:* Garrick; Stage Golf Soc.; Old Tauntonians (Southampton).

ALLISON, Rt. Rev. Sherard Falkner, MA, DD, LLD; *b* 19 Jan. 1907; *s* of Reverend W. S. Allison; *m* 1936, Ruth Hills; one *s* two *d* (and one *s* decd). *Educ:* Dean Close School, Cheltenham; Jesus Coll., Cambridge (Scholar); Ridley Hall, Cambridge. 1st Cl. Classical Tripos, Parts I and II; 2nd Class Theological Tripos, Part I and Jeremie Septuagint Prize; Curate of St James', Tunbridge Wells, 1931-34; Chaplain of Ridley Hall, Cambridge, and Examining Chaplain to Bishop of Bradford, 1934-36; Vicar of Rodbourne Cheney, Swindon, 1936-40; Vicar of Erith, 1940-45; Principal of Ridley Hall, Cambridge, 1945-50; Bishop of Chelmsford, 1951-61; Bishop of Winchester, and Prelate of the Most Noble Order of the Garter, 1961-74. Examining Chaplain to Bishop of Rochester, 1945, and to Bishop of Ely, 1947; Select Preacher: Univ. of Cambridge, 1946, 1955, 1962; Univ. of Oxford, 1953-55, 1963; Proctor in Convocation, Diocese of Ely, 1949. Hon. Fellow, Jesus College, Cambridge, 1963. DD, Lambeth, 1951; Hon. DD: Occidental Coll., Los Ángeles, 1959; Wycliffe Coll., Toronto, 1959; Hon. STD, Church Divinity Sch. of the Pacific, 1959; Hon. LLD: Sheffield, 1960; Southampton, 1974. *Publication:* The Christian Life, 1938 (Joint). *Recreations:* sailing, water-colour sketching, bird watching, gardening. *Address:* Winton Lodge, Alde Lane, Aldeburgh, Suffolk.

ALLNUTT, Ian Peter, OBE; MA; Representative of the British Council in Mexico, 1973-77; *b* 26 April 1917; *s* of Col E. B. Allnutt, CBE, MC, and Joan C. Gainsford; *m* 1946, Doreen Louise Lenagan; four *d*. *Educ:* Imperial Service Coll., Windsor; Sidney Sussex Coll., Cambridge. HM Colonial Service, 1939-46, Nigeria, with break, 1940-45, for service in World War II, Nigeria Regt, RWAFF (despatches). Officer of the British Council with service in Peru, E Africa, Colombia, Argentina, Malta, London and Mexico, 1946-77. OBE 1976; Insignia of Aztec Eagle, 1975. *Recreations:* all kinds of water sports, mountains, the arts. *Address:* Karen Cottage, Boulters Lane, Maidenhead, Berks SL6 8TJ. *T:* Maidenhead 20499. *Club:* Leander (Henley).

ALLOTT, Prof. Antony Nicolas, JP; Professor of African Law, in the University of London, since 1964; *b* 30 June 1924; *s* of late Reginald William Allott and Dorothy Allott (*née* Dobson); *m* 1952, Anna Joan Sargant, *d* of Tom Sargant, *qv*, and Marie Cerny; two *s* two *d*. *Educ:* Downside Sch.; New Coll., Oxford. Lieut Royal Northumberland Fusiliers and King's African Rifles, 1944-46. BA Oxon (1st class Hons Jurisprudence), 1948; PhD London 1954. Lecturer in African Law, School of Oriental and African Studies, London, 1948-60; Reader in African Law, Univ. of London, 1960-64. Hon. Director, Africa Centre, 1963-66; Pres., African Studies Assoc. of UK, 1969-70 (past Hon. Treas.); Vice-Pres., Internat. African Law Assoc., 1967. Académicien associé, Académie Internat. de Droit Comparé; Corresponding Mem., Académie Royale des Sciences d'Outre-Mer, Belgium. Vice-Chm., Governing Body, Plater Coll., Oxford; Governor, St Bartholomew's Hosp. Med. Sch. Member: Senate, Univ. of London; Council, Commonwealth Magistrates Assoc. JP Middlesex 1969. *Publications:* Essays in African Law, with special reference to the Law of Ghana, 1960; (ed) Judicial and Legal Systems in Africa, 1962, 2nd edn 1970; New Essays in African Law, 1970; The Limits of Law, 1980; articles in legal and other jls. *Recreations:* music, gardening, silviculture. *Address:* School of Oriental and African Studies, Malet Street, WC1E 7HP.

See also R. M. Allott, Prof. N. E. S. McIntosh.

ALLOTT, Air Cdre Molly Greenwood, CB 1975; *b* 28 Dec. 1918; *d* of late Gerald William Allott. *Educ:* Sheffield High Sch. for Girls (GPDST). Served War of 1939-45: joined WAAF, 1941; served in: Egypt, Singapore, Germany. Staff of AOC-in-C: RAF Germany, 1960-63; Fighter Command, 1963-66; Training Command, 1971-73; Dir, WRAF, 1973-76. ADC 1973-76; Nat. Chm., Girls' Venture Corps, 1977-82; Member: Council, Union Jack Club, 1977-; Main Grants Cttee, RAF Benevolent Fund, 1977-. FBIM. *Recreations:* travel, decorative arts. *Address:* c/o Midland Bank Ltd, High Street, Lymington SO4 9ZP. *Clubs:* Royal Air Force, Royal Lymington Yacht.

ALLOTT, Robin Michael; Under-Secretary, Establishment Personnel Division, Departments of Industry and Trade, 1978-80; *b* 9 May 1926; *s* of Reginald William Allott and Dorothy (*née* Dobson). *Educ:* The Oratory Sch., Caversham; New Coll., Oxford; Sheffield Univ. Asst Principal, BoT, 1948; UK Delegn to OECD, Paris, 1952; Private Sec. to Sec. for Overseas Trade, 1953; Principal, Office for Scotland, Glasgow, 1954; UK Delegn to UN Conf. on Trade and Develt, Geneva, 1964; Asst Sec., BoT, 1965; Counsellor, UK Delegn to EEC, Brussels, 1971; sabbatical year, New Coll., Oxford, 1974-75; Dept of Industry (motor industry), 1975; Under-Sec., Dept of Trade, 1976. *Publications:* The Physical Foundation of Language, 1973; The Natural Origin of Languages, 1982. *Recreations:* reading Marcus Aurelius, studying the relation of language and perception, computer programming. *Address:* 21 Headland Avenue, Seaford, East Sussex. *T:* Seaford 892609.

See also A. N. Allott.

ALLPORT, Denis Ivor; Chairman, since 1979, and Chief Executive, since 1977, Metal Box Ltd (Managing Director, 1977-79, Deputy Chairman, 1979);

b 20 Nov. 1922; *s* of late A. R. Allport and of E. M. Allport (*née* Mashman); *m* 1949, Diana (*née* Marler); two *s* one *d*. *Educ:* Highgate School. Served War, Indian Army, 1941-46; joined Metal Box Ltd, 1946; various appts in UK, Singapore and Pakistan; Man. Dir, Metal Box Co. of India, 1969-70; Director: Metal Box Overseas Ltd, 1970-74; Metal Box Ltd, 1973; Beecham Gp Ltd, 1981-. Mem., Nat. Enterprise Bd, 1980-. FBIM 1977. *Recreations:* golf, cricket. *Address:* Elm Place, Mumbery Hill, Wargrave, Reading, Berks RG10 8EE. *T:* Wargrave 3007. *Club:* MCC.

ALLSOP, Peter Henry Bruce; Chairman, Associated Book Publishers, since 1976; *b* 22 Aug. 1924; *s* of late Herbert Henry Allsop and of Elsie Hilpern (*née* Whitaker); *m* 1950, Patricia Elizabeth Kingwell Bown; two *s* one *d*. *Educ:* Haileybury; Caius Coll., Cambridge (MA). Called to Bar, Lincoln's Inn, 1948. Temp. Asst Principal, Air Min., 1944-48; Barrister in practice, 1948-50; Sweet & Maxwell: Editor, 1950-59; Dir, 1960-64; Man. Dir, 1965-73; Chm., 1974-80; Dir, Associated Book Publishers, 1963, Asst Man. Dir, 1965-67, Man. Dir, 1968-76. Dir, Yale University Press, 1981-. Mem. Council, Publishers Assoc., 1969-81 (Treasurer, 1973-75, 1979-81; Pres., 1975-77; Vice-Pres., 1977-78); Mem. Printing and Publishing Industry Trng Bd, 1977-79; Chairman: Software Scis Teleordering Ltd, 1978-; Management Cttee Book House Training Centre, 1980-. Chm., Supplementary Benefits Appeal Tribunal, 1982- (Mem., 1979-). Mem., St Albans City Council, 1955-68. FRSA. Editor, later Editor-in-Chief: Current Law, 1952-; Criminal Law Review, 1954-. *Publications:* (ed) Bowstead's Law of Agency, 11th edn, 1951. *Recreations:* gardening, hill walking, theatre, dinghy cruising, farming. *Address:* Manor Farm, Charlton Mackrell, Somerton, Somerset. *T:* Charlton Mackrell 3650. *Clubs:* Garrick, Farmers'.

ALLSOPP, family name of **Baron Hindlip.**

ALLSOPP, Bruce; *see* Allsopp, H. B.

ALLSOPP, Prof. Cecil Benjamin, MA, PhD, DSc; FInstP; Professor of Physics Applied to Medicine, University of London at Guy's Hospital Medical School, 1953-70, now Emeritus; Consultant Physicist Emeritus to Guy's Hospital; *b* 2 Sept. 1904; *m* 1935, Ivy Kathleen Johns; one *s* one *d*. *Educ:* Emmanuel College, Cambridge; University of Frankfurt-am-Main. MA, Cambridge, 1930; PhD, Cambridge, 1932; DSc, London, 1951. Pres., British Institute of Radiology, 1963-64; Silvanus Thompson Memorial Lectr, 1965. *Publications:* Absorption Spectrophotometry (with F. Twyman, FRS), 1934. Papers in Proc. of the Royal Soc., Jl of the Chemical Soc., Trans of the Faraday Soc., British Journal of Radiology, British Journal of Experimental Pathology, Cancer Research, etc. *Address:* 40 Queen Edith's Way, Cambridge CB1 4PW.

ALLSOPP, (Harold) Bruce, BArch, DipCD, FSA, MRTPI; Chairman, Oriel Press Ltd, since 1962; Director, Routledge & Kegan Paul Books Ltd, since 1974; *b* Oxford, 4 July 1912; *s* of Henry Allsopp and Elizabeth May Allsopp (*née* Robertson); *m* 1935, Florence Cyrilla Woodroffe; two *s*. *Educ:* Manchester Grammar Sch.; Liverpool School of Architecture. BArch (1st Cl. Hons), Liverpool, 1933; Rome Finalist, 1934; Diploma in Civic Design 1935; ARIBA 1935; AMTPI 1936; FRIBA 1955; FSA 1968. Asst Architect in Chichester and London, 1934-35; Lecturer, Leeds Coll. of Art, 1935-40. War Service 1940-46, N Africa, Italy, Captain RE. Lecturer in Architecture, Univ. of Durham, 1946; Sen. Lecturer, 1955; Sen. Lecturer, Univ. of Newcastle upon Tyne, 1963, Dir of Architectural Studies, 1965-69; Sen. Lecturer in History of Architecture, 1969-73; Reader, 1973-77. Chairman: Soc. of Architectural Historians of GB, 1959-65; Independent Publishers Guild, 1971-73; Master, Art Workers Guild, 1970; Pres., Northern Fedn of Art Socs, 1980. *Publications:* Art and the Nature of Architecture, 1952; Decoration and Furniture, Vol. 1 1952, Vol. 2 1953; A General History of Architecture, 1955; Style in the Visual Arts, 1957; Possessed, 1959; The Future of the Arts, 1959; A History of Renaissance Architecture, 1959; The Naked Flame, 1962; Architecture, 1964; To Kill a King, 1965; A History of Classical Architecture, 1965; Historic Architecture of Newcastle upon Tyne, 1967; Civilization, the Next Stage, 1969; The Study of Architectural History, 1970; Modern Architecture of Northern England, 1970; Inigo Jones on Palladio, 1970; Romanesque Architecture, 1971; Ecological Morality, 1972; Towards a Humane Architecture, 1974; Return of the Pagan, 1974; Cecilia, 1975; Inigo Jones and the Lords A'Leaping, 1975; A Modern Theory of Architecture, 1977; Appeal to the Gods, 1980; Should Man Survive?, 1982; (with Ursula Clark): Architecture of France, 1963; Architecture of Italy, 1964; Architecture of England, 1964; Photography for Tourists, 1966; Historic Architecture of Northumberland, 1969; Historic Architecture of Northumberland and Newcastle, 1977; English Architecture, 1979; (with U. Clark and H. W. Booton): The Great Tradition of Western Architecture, 1966; articles in Encyclopedia Americana, Jl of RSA, etc; Presenter, TV films, including Fancy Gothic, 1974; The Bowes Museum, 1977; Country Houses and Landscape of Northumberland, 1979. *Recreations:* piano and harpsichord, gardening. *Address:* Woodburn, 3 Batt House Road, Stocksfield, Northumberland NE43 7QZ. *T:* Stocksfield 2323; Stocksfield Studio, Stocksfield, Northumberland NE43 7NA. *T:* Stocksfield 3065. *Clubs:* Athenæum, Arts.

ALMENT, Sir (Edward) Anthony (John), Kt 1980; FRCOG; Consultant Obstetrician and Gynaecologist, Northampton, since 1960; *b* 3 Feb. 1922; *s* of Edward and Alice Alment; *m* 1946, Elizabeth Innes Bacon. *Educ:* Marlborough Coll.; St Bartholomew's Hosp. Med. Coll. MRCS, LRCP 1945; FRCOG 1967 (MRCOG 1951); FRCPI 1980 (Hon. FRCPI, 1979). Served

RAFVR, 1947-48. Trng appointments: St Bartholomew's Hosp., 1945-46 and 1954-60; Norfolk and Norwich Hosp., 1948; Queen Charlotte's Hosp. and Chelsea Hosp. for Women, 1949-50; London Hosp., 1951-52. Royal Coll. of Obstetricians and Gynaecologists: Mem. Council, 1961-67; Hon. Sec., 1968-73; Pres., 1978-81. Chm., Cttee of Enquiry into Competence to Practise, 1973-76; Member: Oxford Reg. Hosp. Bd, 1968-74 (Chm., Med. Adv. Cttee, 1972-74); Oxford RHA, 1973-75; Central Midwives Bd, 1967-68. Examiner: RCOG; Univs of Cambridge, Leeds and Dar-es-Salaam. Hon. Fellow, Amer. Assoc. of Obstetricians and Gynaecologists, 1973 (Joseph Price Oration, 1973); Hon. FRCPEd, 1981. *Publications:* Competence to Practise, 1976; contrib. to med. jls. *Recreations:* wine, fishing, engineering, church architecture. *Address:* Winston House, Boughton, Northampton NN2 8RR. *T:* Northampton 842317.

ALPHAND, Hervé; Grand Officier, Légion d'Honneur, 1968; *b* 1907; *s of* Charles Hervé and Jeanne Alphand; *m* 1958, Nicole Merenda (*d* 1979). *Educ:* Lycée Janson de Sailly; Ecole des Sciences Politiques. Inspector of Finances and Dir Dept of Treaties, Min. of Commerce, 1937-38; Financial Attaché to Embassy, Washington, 1940-41; Dir of Economic Affairs for French National Cttee in London, 1941-44; Director-General, Economic, Financial and Technical Affairs (Min. of Foreign Affairs), 1945; French Ambassador to OEEC; French Dep. to Atlantic Council, 1950, and Mem. NATO Perm. Council, 1952-54; Ambassador: to UN, 1955-56; to USA, 1956-65; Secretary-General, Min. of Foreign Affairs, France, 1965-73. *Publication:* L'étonnement d'être, 1978. *Address:* 122 rue de Grenelle, 75007 Paris, France.

ALPORT, family name of **Baron Alport.**

ALPORT, Baron, *cr* 1961, of Colchester (Life Peer); **Cuthbert James McCall Alport,** PC 1960; TD 1949; DL; *b* 22 March 1912; *o s of* late Prof. Arthur Cecil Alport, MD, FRCP, and of Janet, *y d of* James McCall, Dumfriesshire; *m* 1945, Rachel Cecilia, *o d of* late Lt-Col R. C. Bingham, CVO, DSO, and late Dorothy Louisa Pratt; *one s two d. Educ:* Haileybury; Pembroke Coll., Cambridge. MA History and Law; Pres., Cambridge Union Society, 1935. Tutor Ashridge Coll., 1935-37. Barrister-at-Law, Middle Temple. Joined Artists Rifles, 1934. Served War of 1939-45: Hon. Lieut-Col; Director Conservative Political Centre, 1945-50. MP (C) Colchester division of Essex, 1950-61; Chairman Joint East and Central African Board, 1953-55; Governor, Charing Cross Hospital, 1954-55. Asst Postmaster-General, Dec. 1955-Jan. 1957; Parliamentary Under-Secretary of State, Commonwealth Relations Office, 1957-59; Minister of State, Commonwealth Relations Office, Oct. 1959-March 1961; British High Commissioner in the Federation of Rhodesia and Nyasaland, 1961-63; Mem. of Council of Europe, 1964-65; British Govt Representative to Rhodesia, June-July 1967. A Dep. Speaker, House of Lords, 1971-. Adviser to the Home Secretary, 1974-. Chm., New Theatre Trust, 1970-; Pres., Minories Art Gall., Colchester, 1978-. Life Governor, Haileybury Coll. Master, Skinners' Co., 1969-70. Pro-Chancellor, City Univ., 1972-79. High Steward of Colchester, 1967-; DL Essex 1974. Hon. DCL City Univ., 1979. *Publications:* Kingdoms in Partnership, 1937; Hope in Africa, 1952; The Sudden Assignment, 1965. *Address:* The Cross House, Layer de la Haye, Colchester, Essex. *T:* Layer de la Haye 217. *Clubs:* Pratt's, Farmers'.

AL-SABAH, Shaikh Saud Nasir; Ambassador of Kuwait to the United States of America, since 1981; *b* 3 Oct. 1944; *m* 1962, Shaikha Awatif Al-Sabah; *two s two d.* Barrister-at-law, Gray's Inn. Entered Legal Dept, Min. of Foreign Affairs, Kuwait. Representative of Kuwait: to 6th Cttee of UN Gen. Assembly, 1969-74; to Seabed Cttee of UN, 1969-73; Vice-Chm., Delegn of Kuwait to Conf. of Law of the Sea, 1974-75; Rep. of Delegn to Conf. of Law of Treaties, 1969; Ambassador to London, Norway, Sweden and Denmark, 1975-80. *Address:* Embassy of Kuwait, 2940 Tilden Street NW, Washington, DC 20008, USA.

AL-SHAWI, Hisham Ibrahim; Ambassador of the Republic of Iraq to Austria, since 1982; *b* Baghdad, 16 March 1931; *s of* Ibrahim Al-Shawi and Najia Al-Shawi; *m* 1966, Hadia Al-Atia; *one s one d. Educ:* Baghdad (High Sch. Certif., Lit. Section, 1948); Amer. Univ. of Beirut (BA with Distinction Pol. Science, 1952); Univ. of Oxford (BLitt Internat. Relations, 1956). Asst Prof. and Head of Dept of Politics, Univs of Baghdad and Al-Mustansyria, 1958-70; Dean, Coll. of Law and Politics, Mustansyria Univ., 1970-72; Ambassador, Min. of Foreign Affairs, 1972; Perm. Rep. at UN, Geneva, 1972; Minister of Higher Educn and Scientific Res., 1972-74; Minister of State, 1974-75; Minister of State for For. Affairs, 1975-76; Ambassador, Min. of For. Affairs, 1976-77; Perm. Rep. at UN, New York, 1977; Head, Diwan of Presidency of Republic, 1977-78; Ambassador, Min. of For. Affairs, 1978; Ambassador to UK, 1978-81. First President: Iraqi Political Science Assoc.; Iraqi UN Assoc.; Mem., UN Sub-Commn on Prevention of Racial Discrimination and Protection of Minorities, 1972-74; Rep. on Commn on Human Rights, 26th and 30th Sessions. *Publications:* From the Essence of the Matter: a collection of articles, 1966; The Art of Negotiation, 1967; An Introduction in Political Science, 1967 (new edn 1978). *Recreations:* horse riding, hunting. *Address:* Embassy of the Republic of Iraq, Johannesgasse 26, A-1010 Vienna, Austria. *Club:* Iraqi Hunting (Iraq).

ALSTEAD, Stanley, CBE 1960; MD, FRCP; Professor Emeritus, Regius Chair of Materia Medica, University of Glasgow; formerly Senior Visiting Physician, Stobhill Hospital, Glasgow; *b* 6 June 1905; *s of* late Robert Alstead, OBE, and Anne Alstead; *m* 1932, Nora (*d* 1980), 2nd *d of* late M. W. Sowden and late Nell Sowden; *one s. Educ:* Wigan Grammar Sch.; Liverpool Univ.

Held various appts in north of England, Glasgow and Inverness. Appointee Pollok Lecturer in Pharmacology, Univ. of Glasgow, 1932, and became interested in clinical aspects of subject; Regius Prof. of Materia Medica and Therapeutics, Univ. of Glasgow, 1948-70. Hon. Prof., Univ. of East Afric (Makerere University Coll.) and Hon. Physician to Kenyatta Nat. Hosp Nairobi, Kenya, 1965-66. Served War of 1939-45, in RAMC as medical specialist to 5 CCS in Tunisia and Sicily, and in Belgium and Egypt as Office in Charge of Med. Div. 67 Gen. Hosp. and 63 Gen. Hosp. with rank of Lt-Col (despatches). MD Liverpool (N. E. Roberts Prize); FRCP; FRCPGlas FRCPE; FRSE. Pres. RFPSG (now RCPSGlas), 1956-58 (Hon. Fellow 1979). Member: British Pharmacopœia Commn, 1953-57; Standing Jt Cttee on Classification of Proprietary Preparations; Commn. on Spiritual Healing (General Assembly of Church of Scotland). Jt Editor, Textbook of Medical Treatment. *Publications:* papers in med. jls on results of original research in clinical pharmacology. *Recreations:* gardening, music (violin) and reading poetry. *Address:* 33 Ochlochy Park, Dunblane, Perthshire. *Clubs:* College RASC (Glasgow).

ALSTON, (Arthur) Rex; freelance broadcaster and journalist with The Daily Telegraph and The Sunday Telegraph; BBC Commentator, 1943-61, retired *b* 2 July 1901; *e s of* late Arthur Fawssett Alston, Suffragan Bishop o Middleton, and late Mary Isabel Alston; *m* 1932, Elspeth, *d of* late Sir Stewar Stockman and Lady Stockman; *one s one d. Educ:* Trent College; Clar College, Cambridge. Assistant Master, Bedford School, 1924-41. Joined BBC Jan. 1942. *Publications:* Taking the Air, 1950; Over to Rex Alston, 1953; Tes Commentary, 1956; Watching Cricket, 1962. *Recreations:* golf, gardening *Address:* Ryders, Oakwood Hill, Dorking, Surrey RH5 5NB. *T:* Oakwood Hill 410. *Clubs:* East India, Devonshire, Sports and Public Schools, MCC.

ALSTON, Rt. Rev. Mgr. Joseph Leo; Parish Priest, Sacred Heart Church Ainsdale, Southport, since 1972; *b* 17 Dec. 1917; *s of* Benjamin Alston and Mary Elizabeth (*née* Moss). *Educ:* St Mary's School, Chorley; Upholland College, Wigan; English Coll., Rome; Christ's College, Cambridge. Priest 1942; Licentiate in Theology, Gregorian Univ., Rome, 1942; BA (1st Cla Hons Classics) Cantab 1945. Classics Master, Upholland Coll., Wigan 1945-52, Headmaster, 1952-64; Rector, Venerable English Coll., Rome 1964-71. Chm., Liverpool RC Ecumenism Commn, 1977-. *Recreation* music. *Address:* 483 Liverpool Road, Ainsdale, Southport, Merseyside. *T* Southport 77527.

ALSTON, Rex; *see* Alston, A. R.

ALSTON, Robert John; HM Diplomatic Service; Counsellor, UK Delegation to NATO, Brussels, since 1981; *b* 10 Feb. 1938; *s of* Arthur William Alston and Rita Alston; *m* 1969, Patricia Claire Essex; *one s one d. Educ:* Ardingly Coll.; New Coll., Oxford (BA Mod. Hist.). Third Sec., Kabul, 1963; Eastern Dept, FO, 1966; Head of Computer Study Team, FCO, 1969; First Seco (Econ.), Paris, 1971; First Sec. and Head of Chancery, Tehran, 1974; Ass Head, Energy Science and Space Dept, FCO, 1977; Head, Joint Nuclear Unit FCO, 1978. *Recreations:* gardening, reading, listening to music. *Address:* c/ Foreign and Commonwealth Office, SW1.

ALSTON, Dr Robin Carfrae; Consultant in Bibliography to the British Library, since 1977; Editor-in-Chief, 18th Century Short Title Catalogue since 1978; *b* 29 Jan. 1933; *s of* Wilfred Louis Alston; *m* 1957, Joanna Dorothy Ormiston; *two s one d. Educ:* Rugby Sch.; Univs of British Columbia (BA) Oxford (MA), Toronto (MA) and London (PhD). Teaching Fellow University Coll., Toronto, 1956-58; Lectr, New Brunswick Univ., 1958-60 Lectr in English Lit., Leeds Univ., 1964-76. Jt Editor Leeds Studies in English and Leeds Texts and Monographs; Editor Studies in Early Modern English Jt Editor, The Direction Line, 1976-; Editor, The Eighteenth Century, 1982- Founder, Chm. and principal Editor, Scolar Press Ltd, 1966-72; Founder, Janu Press, devoted to original art prints, 1973. Mem. Adv. Cttee, British Library 1975-. Mem. Organising Cttee, 18th Century Short Title Catalogue, 1976- Mem. Council, Bibliographical Soc., 1967- (Vice-Pres., 1978-); Founding Mem. Council, Ilkley Literature Festival. *Publications:* An Introduction to Old English, 1961 (rev. edn 1966); A Catalogue of Books relating to the English Language (1500-1800) in Swedish Libraries, 1965; English Language and Medieval English Literature: a Select Reading-List for Students, 1966; A Bibliography of the English Language from the Invention of Printing to the Year 1800: Vol. I, 1965; Vols V and VIII, 1966; Vols VII and IV, 1967; Vol II, 1968; Vol. VI, 1969; Vol. III, 1970; Vol. IX, 1971; Vol. X, 1972; Vol. XI 1978; Alexander Gil's Logonomia Anglica (1619): a translation into Modern English, 1973; (jtly) The Works of William Bullokar, Vol. I, 1966; English Studies (rev. edn of Vol. III, Cambridge Bibl. Eng. Lit.), 1968; English Linguistics 1500-1800: a Collection of Texts in Facsimile (365 vols), 1967-72 European Linguistics 1500-1700: a Collection of Texts in Facsimile (12 vols) 1968-72; A Checklist of the works of Joseph Addison, 1976; Bibliography MARC and ESTC, 1978; numerous articles, etc. *Recreations:* music photography. *Address:* Starveall, Aldworth, near Reading, Berks. *Club* Grolier (NY).

ALSTON-ROBERTS-WEST, Lt-Col George Arthur; *see* West.

AL-TAJIR, Mohamed Mahdi; Ambassador of the United Arab Emirates to the Court of St James's, since 1972, and France, 1972-77; *b* 26 Dec. 1931; *m* 1956, Zohra Al-Tajir; *five s one d. Educ:* Al Tajir Sch., Bahrain; Preston Grammar Sch., Lancs, England. Dir, Dept of Port and Customs, Govt of

Bahrain, 1955-63; Dir, Dept of HH the Ruler's Affairs and Petroleum Affairs, 1963-; Director: Nat. Bank of Dubai Ltd, 1963-; Dubai Petroleum Co., 1963-; Dubai Nat. Air Travel Agency, 1966-; Qatar-Dubai Currency Bd, 1965-73; United Arab Emirates Currency Bd, 1973-; Dubai Dry Dock Co., 1973-; Chm., S Eastern Dubai Drilling Co., 1968-. Hon. Citizen of State of Texas, USA, 1963. *Address:* Embassy of the United Arab Emirates, 30 Prince's Gate, SW7. *T:* 01-581 1281.

LTAMONT, Earl of; Jeremy Ulick Browne; *b* 4 June 1939; *s* of 10th Marquess of Sligo, *qv* ; *m* 1961, Jennifer June, *d* of Major Derek Cooper, Dunlewey, Co. Donegal, and Mrs C. Heber Percy, Pophleys, Radnage; five *d. Educ:* St Columba's College, Eire; Royal Agricultural College, Cirencester. *Address:* Westport House, Co. Mayo, Éire.

LTHORP, Viscount; Charles Edward Maurice Spencer; *b* 20 May 1964; *s* and *heir* of 8th Earl Spencer, *qv. Educ:* Maidwell Hall; Eton College. Page of Honour to HM the Queen, 1977-79. *Address:* Althorp, Northampton NN7 4HG.

LTMAN, Lionel Phillips, CBE 1979; Chairman and Chief Executive, Emray plc Group, since 1978; *b* 12 Sept. 1922; *s* of late Arnold Altman and Catherine Phillips; *m* 1977, Jan Mary (*née* Borrodell); two *d* (and one *s* by a previous marriage). *Educ:* University Coll. and Business Sch., also in Paris. FIMI; FInstM; MIPR. Served war, 1942-46, special intelligence duties, War Office and Political Intelligence Dept, FO (UK and Far East). Director: Carmo Holdings Ltd, 1947-63; Sears Holdings Motor Gp, 1963-72; C. & W. Walker Holdings Ltd, 1974-77; Chairman and Chief Executive: Joint Garage Holdings Ltd, 1972-; Pre-Divisional Investments Ltd, 1972-. Chm., Motor Industry Educnl Consultative Council Industry Working Party, producing Altman Report on recruitment and training, 1968. Mem., Nat. Council, Motor Agents Assoc., 1965- (Pres., 1975-77); Vice-Pres., and Mem. Council, Inst. of Motor Industry, 1970-78. Chairman: Publicity Club of London, 1961-62; Industry Taxation Panel, 1977-; Member: Council, CBI, 1977-; CBI Industrial Policy Cttee, 1979-; Dun & Bradstreet Industry Panel, 1982-. Freeman: City of London, 1973; City of Glasgow, 1974; Liveryman and Hon. Treas., Coachmakers' and Coach Harness Makers' Co.; Burgess Guild Brother, Cordwainers' Co. *Publications:* articles and broadcasts. *Address:* (office) 61 Grosvenor Street, W1X 9DA. *T:* 01-493 3371; (home) The Cottage, Amersham Way, Little Chalfont, Bucks HP6 6SF.

LTMAN, Robert; film director; *b* Kansas City, 20 Feb. 1925; *m* 3rd, Kathryn Altman; one *s* and one adopted *s* and two *s* one *d* by previous marriages). *Educ:* Univ. of Missouri. Served US Army, 1943-47. Industrial film maker, Calvin Co., Kansas City, 1950-57. Television writer, producer and director, 1957-65. Films directed: That Cold Day in the Park, 1969; M*A*S*H*, 1970 (Grand Prix, Cannes, 1970); Brewster McCloud, 1971; McCabe and Mrs Miller, 1971; Images, 1972; The Long Goodbye, 1973; Thieves Like Us, 1974; California Split, 1974; Nashville, 1975; Buffalo Bill and the Indians, 1976; 3 Women, 1977; A Wedding, 1978; Quintet, 1979; A Perfect Couple, 1979; Health, 1979; Popeye, 1980; produced: Welcome to LA, 1977; The Late Show, 1977; Remember My Name, 1978; Rich Kids, 1979. *Address:* c/o Lion's Gate Films, 1861 South Bundy Drive, Los Angeles, CA 90025, USA.

LTON, David Patrick; MP (L) Edge Hill Division of Liverpool, since March 1979; *b* 15 March 1951; *s* of Frederick and Bridget Alton. *Educ:* Edmund Campion Sch., Hornchurch; Christ's College of Education, Liverpool. Elected to Liverpool City Council as Britain's youngest-ever City Councillor, 1972; Deputy Leader of the Council and Housing Chairman, 1978; Vice-Pres., AMA, 1979-. MP (L) Liverpool, Edge Hill (by-election), with a 32 per cent swing, March 1979 (youngest member of that parliament); re-elected (gen. election), May 1979; Liberal Party spokesman on the environment and race relations, 1979-. National President, Nat. League of Young Liberals. *Recreations:* theatre, reading, walking. *Address:* 45 Onslow Road, Edge Hill, Liverpool L6 3BA. *T:* 051-260 8792. *Club:* Edge Hill Liberal (Liverpool).

LTON, Euan Beresford Seaton, MBE 1945; MC 1943; Under Secretary, Department of Health and Social Security, 1968-76; *b* 22 April 1919; *y* *s* of late William Lester St John Alton and Ellen Seaton Alton; *m* 1953, Diana Margaret Ede; one *s* one *d. Educ:* St Paul's Sch.; Magdalen Coll., Oxford. Served with Army, 1939-45; Major RA. Admin. Officer, Colonial Service and HM OCS, Gold Coast and Ghana, 1946-58; Admin. Officer, Class 1, 1957. Entered Civil Service as Asst Principal, Min. of Health, 1958; Principal, 1958; Asst Sec., 1961; Under Sec., 1968. *Recreations:* sailing, walking. *Address:* The Old School, Church Lane, Brantham, Manningtree, Essex CO11 1QA. *T:* Manningtree 3419. *Clubs:* Royal Commonwealth Society, Cruising Association; Stour Sailing (Manningtree).

LTRINCHAM, Barony of, *cr* 1945, of Tormarton; title disclaimed by 2nd Baron. *Heir to barony:* Hon. Anthony Ulick David Dundas Grigg [*b* 12 Jan. 1934; *m* 1965, Eliane de Miramon; two *s* one *d*].

LVAREZ, Alfred; author; with The Observer, since 1956 (Poetry Editor, 1956-66); *b* London, 1929; *s* of late Bertie Alvarez and Katie Alvarez (*née* Levy); *m* 1st, 1956, Ursula Barr (marr. diss. 1961); one *s* ; 2nd, 1966, Anne Adams; one *s* one *d. Educ:* Oundle Sch.; Corpus Christi Coll., Oxford. BA (Oxon) 1952, MA 1956. Sen. Research Schol., CCC, Oxon, and Research Schol. of Goldsmiths' Company, 1952-53, 1954-55. Procter Visiting

Fellowship, Princeton, 1953-54; Vis. Fellow of Rockefeller Foundn, USA, 1955-56, 1958; gave Christian Gauss Seminars in Criticism, Princeton, and was Lectr in Creative Writing, 1957-58; D. H. Lawrence Fellowship, New Mexico, 1958; Drama Critic, The New Statesman, 1958-60. Visiting Prof.: Brandeis Univ., 1960; New York State Univ., Buffalo, 1966. Vachel Lindsay Prize for Poetry (from Poetry, Chicago), 1961. *Publications:* The Shaping Spirit (US title, Stewards of Excellence), 1958; The School of Donne, 1961; The New Poetry (ed and introd), 1962; Under Pressure, 1965; Beyond All This Fiddle, 1968; Lost (poems), 1968; Penguin Modern Poets, No 18, 1970; Apparition (poems), 1971; The Savage God, 1971; Beckett, 1973; Hers, 1974; Hunt, 1978; Autumn to Autumn and Selected Poems, 1978; Life After Marriage, 1982. *Recreations:* rock-climbing, poker, music. *Address:* c/o The Observer, 8 St Andrew's Hill, EC4. *Club:* Climbers'.

ALVAREZ, Prof. Luis W.; Professor of Physics, University of California, Berkeley, since 1945; *b* 13 June, 1911; *s* of late Dr Walter C. Alvarez and Harriet Smyth; *m* 1st, 1936, Geraldine Smithwick; one *s* one *d* ; 2nd, 1958, Janet Landis; one *s* one *d. Educ:* University of Chicago. SB 1932, PhD 1936. Radiation Lab., Univ. of California, 1936-; MIT Radiation Lab., 1940-43; Metallurgical Lab., Univ. of Chicago, 1943-44; Los Alamos Sci. Lab., 1944-45; Associate Dir, Lawrence Rad. Lab., 1954-59. Pres., Amer. Physical Soc., 1969; Member: Nat. Acad. of Sciences; Nat. Acad. of Engineering; Am. Phil. Soc.; Am. Acad. of Arts and Sciences; Assoc. Mem., Institut d'Égypte. Awarded: Collier Trophy, 1946; John Scott Medal, 1953; US Medal for Merit, 1947; Einstein Medal, 1961; Pioneer Award, AIEEE, 1963; Nat. Medal of Science, 1964; Michelson Award, 1965; Nobel Prize in Physics, 1968. Nat. Inventors' Hall of Fame, 1978. Hon. ScD: Chicago, 1967; Carnegie-Mellon, 1968; Kenyon, 1969; Notre Dame, 1976; Ain Shams Univ., Cairo, 1979. *Publications:* more than 100 contributions to Physics Literature, largely in Nuclear Physics and High Energy Physics; 22 US Patents, largely in Electronics and Optics. *Recreations:* flying, golf, music. *Address:* (business) Lawrence Radiation Laboratory, University of California, Berkeley, Calif 94720, USA. *T:* 415-486 4400; (home) 131 Southampton Avenue, Berkeley, Calif 94707, USA. *T:* 415-525-0590. *Clubs:* Bohemian (San Francisco); Faculty (Berkeley); Miravista Golf (El Cerrito).

ALVEY, John, CB 1980; Senior Director, Technology, British Telecommunications (formerly Post Office), since 1980; *b* 19 June 1925; *s* of George C. V. Alvey and Hilda E. Alvey (*née* Pellatt); *m* 1955, Celia Edmed Marson; three *s. Educ:* Reeds Sch.; London Univ.; BSc (Eng), DipNEC. CEng, FIEE. London Stock Exchange, to 1943. Royal Navy, 1943-46; Royal Naval Scientific Service, 1950; Head of Weapons Projects, Admiralty Surface Weapons Estabt, 1968-72; Dir-Gen. Electronics Radar, PE, MoD, 1972-73; Dir-Gen., Airborne Electronic Systems, PE, MoD, 1974-75; Dir, Admiralty Surface Weapons Estabt, 1976-77; Dep. Controller, R&D Estabts and Res. C, and Chief Scientist (RAF), MoD, 1977-80. *Recreations:* reading, Rugby, small-bore rifle shooting, theatre going. *Address:* 9A St Omer Road, Guildford, Surrey. *T:* Guildford 63859.

ALVINGHAM, 2nd Baron, *cr* 1929, of Woodfold; **Maj.-Gen. Robert Guy Eardley Yerburgh,** CBE 1978 (OBE 1972); *b* 16 Dec. 1926; *s* of 1st Baron and Dorothea Gertrude (*d* 1927), *d* of late J. Eardley Yerburgh; *S* father 1955; *m* 1952, Beryl Elliott, *d* of late W. D. Williams; one *s* one *d. Educ:* Eton. Commissioned 1946; Coldstream Guards 1947; served UK, Palestine, Farelf; Head of Estabt, CDS, 1972-75; Dep. Dir, Army Staff Duties, 1975-78; Dir of Army Quartering, 1978-81, retired. *Heir: s* Captain Hon. Robert Richard Guy Yerburgh, 17th/21st Lancers [*b* 10 Dec. 1956; *m* 1981, Vanessa, *yr* *d* of Captain Duncan Kirk]. *Address:* Bix Hall, Henley-on-Thames, Oxfordshire.

ALWYN, William, CBE 1978; composer; Professor of Composition, Royal Academy of Music, 1926-55; *b* Northampton, 1905. *Educ:* Northampton Sch.; Royal Acad. of Music. FRAM 1936; Collard Fellow, Worshipful Company of Musicians, 1938; Chm. of Composers' Guild of Gt Britain, 1949, 1950 and 1954; Fellow, British Film Acad., 1958. Hon. DMus Leicester, 1982. *Works:* Five Orchestral Preludes (Proms., 1927); Divertimento for Flute (Internat. Contemp. Music Festival, New York, 1940); Concerto Grosso No I (commnd by BBC, 1942); Symphony No I (Cheltenham Festival, 1950, London, 1953); Concerto Grosso No II (LSO and Proms, 1951); Festival March (commnd by Arts Council for Festival of Britain, 1951); Symphonic Prelude, The Magic Island (Hallé Concerts, 1953); Symphony No II (Hallé Concerts, Manchester, 1953, BBC, Festival Hall, 1954); Lyra Angelica, Concerto for Harp Proms, 1954; Autumn Legend, for cor anglais and strings (Cheltenham Festival and Proms, 1955); Symphony No III (commnd by BBC, 1956); Elizabethan Dances (commnd by BBC, Festival Hall, 1957); Symphony No IV (Promenade Concerts, 1959); Overture: Derby Day (commnd by BBC, Proms, 1960); Concerto Grosso No III (commnd by BBC, Proms, 1964); Sinfonietta for Strings (commnd by Cheltenham Festival, 1970); Hydriotaphia, Symphony No V (commnd by Arts Council for Norwich Triennial Festival, 1973); Miss Julie, 2-act opera, 1976; String Quartet no 2 (Aldeburgh Fest., 1976). *Film Music* since 1936 includes: Odd Man Out, The Way Ahead, The True Glory, World of Plenty, The Magic Box, etc. *Publications: orchestral:* 5 symphonies, 3 concerti grossi, Oboe Concerto, Festival March, The Magic Island, Sinfonietta, Suite; Harp Concerto (Lyra Angelica); *chamber music:* Rhapsody for Piano Quartet, String Quartet in D Minor, Sonata alla Toccata for Piano, Divertimento for Solo Flute, Fantasy-Waltzes for Piano, 12 Preludes for Piano; String Trio; Movements for Piano; Sonata for Clarinet and Piano; Mirages for baritone and piano; Naiades for flute and harp; Concerto for Flute and eight wind-instruments, 1980; *song cycles:* A Leave-Taking, 1979; Invocations, 1979; Seascapes (for soprano, treble recorder and piano), 1980. *Publications:* Ariel to Miranda in Adam Internat. Review, 1968; Anthology of 20th Century French Poetry, 1969; Winter in Copenhagen, 1971; Daphne, 1972; The World in my Mind, 1975; The Prayers and Elegies of Francis Jammes (trans. from French), 1979. *Address:* Lark Rise, Blythburgh, Suffolk. *T:* Blythburgh 331. *Clubs:* Savile; Island Sailing (Cowes).

AMALDI, Prof. Edoardo, PhD; Italian physicist; Professor of General Physics, University of Rome, since 1937; *b* Carpaneto, Piacenza, 5 Sept. 1908; *s* of Ugo Amaldi and Luisa Basini; *m* 1933, Ginestra Giovene; two *s* one *d. Educ:* Rome Univ. Dr of Physics, 1929. Sec.-Gen., European Org. for Nuclear Research, 1952-54; Pres., Internat. Union of Pure and Applied Physics, 1957-60; President: Istituto Nazionale di Fisica Nucleare, 1960-65; Council, CERN, 1970-71; Fellow: Acad. Naz. dei Lincei; Acad. Naz. dei XL; Foreign member: Royal Soc. of Sciences, Uppsala; Acad. of Sciences, USSR; Amer. Philos. Soc.; Amer. Acad. of Arts and Sciences; Nat. Acad. of Sciences, USA; Royal Acad., Netherlands; Acad. Leopoldina; Royal Instn of GB; Royal Society, London; Royal Acad. Sweden, 1968; Real Acad. Ciencias, Spain. Hon. DSc: Glasgow, 1973; Oxford, 1974. *Publications:* The production and slowing down of neutrons, 1959; contributor many papers on atomic, molecular and nuclear physics to learned jls. *Address:* Istituto di Fisica, Città Universitaria, Piazzale Aldo Moro, 00185 Rome, Italy; (home) Viale Parioli 50, 00197 Rome.

AMAN, family name of **Baron Marley.**

AMBARTSUMIAN, Victor; Hero of Socialist Labour (twice); Order of Lenin (five times); Order of Labour Red Banner (four times); President, Academy of Sciences of Armenian Soviet Socialist Republic, USSR, since 1947; *b* 18 Sept. 1908; *m* 1931, Vera Ambartsumian; two *s* two *d. Educ:* Univ. of Leningrad. Lecturer in Astronomy, 1931-34, Prof. of Astrophysics, 1934-44, Univ. of Leningrad; Prof. of Astrophysics, Univ. of Erevan, 1944-. Full Mem., Academy of Sciences of USSR, 1953-. Pres., Internat. Council of Scientific Unions, 1968-72. Hon. Dr of Science: Univs of Canberra, 1963; Paris, 1965; Liege, 1967; Prague, 1967; Torun, 1973; Foreign Member of Academies of Science: Washington, Paris, Rome, Vienna, Berlin, Amsterdam, Copenhagen, Sofia, Stockholm, Boston, New York, New Delhi, Cordoba, Prague, Budapest; Foreign Member of Royal Society, London. *Publications:* Theoretical Astrophysics, 1953 (in Russian; trans. into German, English, Spanish, Chinese); about 100 papers in learned jls. Editor of jl, Astrofizika. *Address:* Academy of Sciences of Armenian SSR, Barekamutyan Street 24, Erevan, Armenia, USSR.

AMBLER, Eric, OBE 1981; novelist and screenwriter; *b* 28 June 1909; *s* of Alfred Percy and Amy Madeleine Ambler; *m* 1st, 1939, Louise Crombie; 2nd, 1958, Joan Harrison. *Educ:* Colfe's Grammar Sch.; London Univ. Apprenticeship in engineering, 1927-28; advertisement copywriter, 1929-35; professional writer, 1936-. Served War of 1939-45: RA, 1940; commissioned, 1941; served in Italy, 1943; Lt-Col, 1944; Asst Dir of Army Kinematography, War Office, 1944-46, when released. US Bronze Star, 1946. Wrote and produced film, The October Man, 1947 and resumed writing career. Screenplays include: The Way Ahead, 1944; The October Man, 1947; The Passionate Friends, 1948; Highly Dangerous, 1950; The Magic Box, 1951; Gigolo and Gigolette, in Encore, 1952; The Card, 1952; Rough Shoot, 1953; The Cruel Sea, 1953; Lease of Life, 1954; The Purple Plain, 1954; Yangtse Incident, 1957; A Night to Remember, 1958; Wreck of the Mary Deare, 1959; Love Hate Love, 1970. *Publications:* The Dark Frontier, 1936; Uncommon Danger, 1937; Epitaph for a Spy, 1938; Cause for Alarm, 1938; The Mask of Dimitrios, 1939; Journey into Fear, 1940; Judgment on Deltchev, 1951; The Schirmer Inheritance, 1953; The Night-comers, 1956; Passage of Arms, 1959; The Light of Day, 1962; The Ability to Kill (essays), 1963; (ed and introd) To Catch a Spy, 1964; A Kind of Anger, 1964 (Edgar Allan Poe award, 1964); Dirty Story, 1967; The Intercom Conspiracy, 1969; The Levanter, 1972 (Golden Dagger award, 1973); Doctor Frigo, 1974 (MWA Grand Master award, 1975); Send No More Roses, 1977; The Care of Time, 1981; numerous short stories, magazine and newspaper articles. *Address:* Avenue Eugène Rambert 20, 1815 Clarens, Switzerland. *Clubs:* Garrick, Savile.

AMBLER, Harry, OBE 1963; QPM 1955; Chief Constable, City of Bradford Police, 1957-73; *b* 27 June 1908; *m* 1934, Kathleen Freda Muriel Mitchell; one *d. Educ:* Hanson Secondary Sch., Bradford; Oulton Sch., Liverpool. Joined City of Bradford Police as a Constable, 1930; Inspector, 1940; Staff Officer to HM Inspector of Constabulary, 1941-43; Superintendent, 1943; Asst and Dep. Chief Constable, 1952; Chief Constable, 1957. Hon. MA Bradford, 1973. Police Long Service and Good Conduct Medal, 1952; Coronation Medal, 1953. *Address:* 854 Leeds Road, Bramhope, near Leeds LS16 9ED. *T:* Leeds 673765.

AMBO, Rt. Rev. George Somboba; *see* Popondetta, Bishop of.

AMBROSE, Prof. Edmund Jack, MA (Cantab), DSc (London); Professor of Cell Biology, University of London, Institute of Cancer Research, 1967-76, now Emeritus Professor; Staff of Chester Beatty Research Institute, Institute of Cancer Research: Royal Cancer Hospital since 1952; *b* 2 March 1914; *s* of Alderman Harry Edmund Ambrose and Kate (née Stanley); *m* 1943, Andrée (née Huck), Seine, France; one *s* one *d. Educ:* Perse Sch., Cambridge; Emmanuel Coll., Cambridge. Wartime research for Admiralty on infra-red

detectors, 1940-45; subseq. research on structure of proteins using infra-r radiation at Courtauld Fundamental Research Laboratory. Formei Convener of Brit. Soc. for Cell Biology. Formerly Special Adviser in Cano to Govt of India at Tata Meml Centre, Bombay. Special Adviser in Lepro: Foundn for Med. Res., Bombay (awarded St Elizabeth Meml Medal, Orc of St John, Paris, 1981 for leprosy work). Pres., Internat. Cell Tissue a Organ Culture Group. Research on structure of proteins, on structure normal and cancer cells, and on characteristics of surface of cancer cells, c biology and microbiology of leprosy, using labelled metabolites. *Publicatio* Cell Electrophoresis, 1965; The Biology of Cancer, 1966, 2nd edn 1975; T Cancer Cell *in vitro*. 1967; (jtly) Cell Biology, 1970, rev. edn 197 publications on Protein Structure and Cell Biology, in Proc. Royal So biological jls. *Recreation:* sailing. *Address:* Institute of Cancer Researd Royal Cancer Hospital, Fulham Road, SW3 6BJ. *Club:* Royal Bomb Yacht.

AMBROSE, James Walter Davy; Judge, Supreme Court Singapore, 1958-(*b* 5 Dec. 1909; *s* of Samuel Ambrose; *m* 1945, Theresa Kamala Ambrose; *c. Educ:* Free Sch., Penang; Oxford Univ. Asst Official Assignee, Singapor 1936; Police Magistrate and Asst District Judge, Malacca, 1940; Registra Superior Court, Malacca, 1945; Dep. Public Prosecutor, 1946; Sen. A: Registrar, Supreme Courts of Ipoh, Penang, and Kuala Lumpur, 1947-5 President, Sessions Court, Penang, 1953; Acting District Judge and Fii Magistrate, Singapore, 1955; Official Assignee, Public Trustee, and Comr Estate Duties, Singapore 1957. *Address:* Block B, Apartment B306, Bradde Hill, Singapore 2057.

AMERS, Maj.-Gen. John Henry, OBE 1941; *b* 8 July 1904; *s* of John Amei *m* 1933, Muriel Henrietta Ethel Haeberlin; one *d. Educ:* Christ's Hospit. Royal Military Acad., Woolwich; Cambridge Univ. Commissioned 2i Lieut into Royal Engineers, 1925. Served War of 1939-45, E Africa, Midc East and Italy. Col 1951; Brig. 1955; Maj.-Gen. 1958. Served HQ, BCO Japan, 1947-48; Chief Engineer, Salisbury Plain District, 1951-54; Depu Director of Works, BAOR, 1955-57; Director of Fortification and Worl 1958-59; retired, 1959. *Address:* c/o Lloyds Bank Ltd, Cox's and King Branch, 6 Pall Mall, SW1Y 5NH. *Club:* Royal Commonwealth Society

AMERY, Rt. Hon. Julian, PC 1960; MP (C) Brighton Pavilion since 196 *b* 27 March 1919; *s* of late Rt Hon. Leopold Amery, PC, CH; *m* 195 Catherine, *d* of Rt Hon. Harold Macmillan, *qv*; one *s* three *d. Edu* Summerfields; Eton; Balliol Coll., Oxford. War Corresp. in Spanish Civ War, 1938-39; Attaché HM Legation, Belgrade, and on special missions Bulgaria, Turkey, Roumania and Middle East, 1939-40; Sergeant in RA 1940-41; commissioned and transferred to army, 1941; on active servic Egypt, Palestine and Adriatic, 1941-42; liaison officer to Albanian resistan movement, 1944; served on staff of Gen. Carton de Wiart, VC, Mr Churchil personal representative with Generalissimo Chiang Kai-Shek, 1945. Conteste Preston in Conservative interest, July 1945; MP (C) Preston North, 1950-(Delegate to Consultative Assembly of Council of Europe, 1950-53 and 195 Member Round Table Conference on Malta, 1955. Parly Under-Sec. of Sta and Financial Sec., War Office, 1957-58; Parly Under-Sec. of State, Coloni Office, 1958-60; Sec. of State for Air, Oct. 1960-July 1962; Minister Aviation, 1962-64; Minister of Public Building and Works, June-Oct. 197 Minister for Housing and Construction, DoE, 1970-72; Minister of Stal FCO, 1972-74. Kt Comdr, Order of Phoenix, Greece; Grand Cordon, Ord of Scanderbeg, Albania; Order of Oman, first class. *Publications:* Sons of th Eagle, 1948; The Life of Joseph Chamberlain: vol. IV, 1901-3: At the Heig of his Power, 1951; vols V and VI, 1901-14: Joseph Chamberlain and the Tar Reform Campaign, 1969; Approach March (autobiog.), 1973; articles National Review, Nineteenth Century and Daily Telegraph. *Recreatio* ski-ing, mountaineering, travel. *Address:* 112 Eaton Square, SW1. *T:* 01-2: 1543, 01-235 7409; Forest Farm House, Chelwood Gate, Sussex. *Clul* White's, Beefsteak, Carlton, Buck's.

AMES, Mrs Kenneth; *see* Gainham, S. R.

AMHERST, family name of **Earl Amherst.**

AMHERST, 5th Earl, *cr* 1826; **Jeffery John Archer Amherst,** MC 191 Baron Amherst of Montreal, 1788; Viscount Holmesdale, 1826; Major, la Coldstream Guards; Manager, External Affairs, BEA, 1946; later Director Associated Companies, retd, Dec. 1966; Hon. Commission as Wir Commander, RAF, 1942; *b* 13 Dec. 1896; *e s* of 4th Earl and Hon. Eleanc Clementina St Aubyn (*d* 1960), *d* of 1st Baron St Levan; *S* father, 1927. *Edu* Eton; RMC Sandhurst. Served European War, 1914-18, with Coldstrea Guards (MC); placed on RARO 1921; recalled 1940, served Middle Ea: 1940-44. Reportorial Staff, New York Morning World, 1923-2 Commercial Air Pilot and General Manager Air Line Company, 1929-39; A Air Adviser to British Railways, 1945-46. Dir, BEA associated cos, 1946-6 *Publication:* Wandering Abroad (autobiog.), 1976. *Clubs:* Cavalry ar Guards, Travellers', Pratt's, Garrick.

AMHERST OF HACKNEY, 4th Baron *cr* 1892; **William Hugh Amher** Cecil; Director, E. A. Gibson Shipbrokers Ltd; *b* 28 Dec. 1940; *s* of 3rd Barc Amherst of Hackney, CBE, and of Margaret Eirene Clifton, *d* of la Brig.-Gen. Howard Clifton Brown; *S* father, 1980; *m* 1965, Elisabeth, *d* Hugh Humphrey Merriman, DSO, MC, TD, DL; one *s* one *d. Educ:* Eto

Heir: s Hon. Hugh William Amherst Cecil, *b* 1968. *Address:* Hazel Hall, Peaslake, Surrey. *Clubs:* Royal Yacht Squadron, Royal Ocean Racing.

AMIES, (Edwin) Hardy, CVO 1977; RDI 1964; FRSA 1965; Dressmaker by Appointment to HM The Queen; Director Hardy Amies Ltd, since 1946; Design Consultant to Hepworths Ltd, since 1960, and to manufacturers in the EEC, USA, Canada, Australia, New Zealand, Japan and Argentina; *b* 17 July 1909; *s* of late Herbert William Amies and Mary (*née* Hardy). *Educ:* Brentwood. Studied languages in France and Germany, 1927-30; trainee at W. & T. Avery Ltd, Birmingham, 1930-34; managing designer at Lachasse, Farm Street, W1, 1934-39. War Service, 1939-45: joined Intelligence Corps, 1939, becoming Lt-Col and head of Special Forces Mission to Belgium, 1944; founded dressmaking business, 1946; opened Hardy Amies' Boutique Ltd, 1950. Chairman, Incorporated Society of London Fashion Designers, 1959-60 (Vice-Chm., 1954-56). Awards: Harper's Bazaar, 1962; Caswell-Massey, 1962, 1964, 1968; Ambassador Magazine, 1964; Sunday Times Special Award, 1965. Officier de l'Ordre de la Couronne (Belgium), 1946. *Publications:* Just So Far, 1954; ABC of Men's Fashion, 1964. *Recreations:* lawn tennis, gardening, opera. *Address:* 29 Cornwall Gardens, SW7; Hardy Amies Ltd, 14 Savile Row, W1. *T:* 01-734 2436. *Clubs:* Queen's, Buck's.

AMIS, Kingsley, CBE 1981; author; *b* 16 April 1922; *o c* of William Robert and Rosa Amis; *m* 1st, 1948, Hilary Ann, *d* of Leonard Sidney and Margery Bardwell; two *s* one *d* ; 2nd, 1965, Elizabeth Jane Howard, *qv. Educ:* City of London School; St John's, Oxford (Hon. Fellow, 1976). Served in Army, 1942-45. Lectr in English, University Coll. of Swansea, 1949-61; Fellow of Peterhouse, Cambridge, 1961-63. *Publications:* A Frame of Mind (verse), 1953; Lucky Jim (novel), 1954, filmed, 1957; That Uncertain Feeling (novel), 1955, filmed (Only Two Can Play), 1962; A Case of Samples (verse), 1956; I Like it Here (novel), 1958; Take a Girl Like You (novel), 1960; New Maps of Hell (belles-lettres), 1960; My Enemy's Enemy (short stories), 1962; One Fat Englishman (novel), 1963; The James Bond Dossier (belles-lettres), 1965; The Egyptologists (novel), with Robert Conquest, 1965; The Anti-Death League (novel), 1966; A Look Round the Estate (poems), 1967; (as Robert Markham) Colonel Sun (novel), 1968; I Want it Now (novel), 1968; The Green Man (novel), 1969; What Became of Jane Austen? (belles-lettres), 1970; Girl, 20 (novel), 1971; On Drink, 1972; The Riverside Villas Murder (novel), 1973; Ending Up (novel), 1974; (ed) G. K. Chesterton selected stories, 1972; (ed) Tennyson, 1972; Rudyard Kipling and his World, 1975; The Alteration, 1976; (ed) Harold's Years, 1977; Jake's Thing (novel), 1978; (ed) The New Oxford Book of Light Verse, 1978; (ed) The Faber Popular Reciter, 1978; Collected Poems 1944-1979, 1979; Russian Hide-and-Seek (novel), 1980; Collected Short Stories, 1980; (ed) The Golden Age of Science Fiction, 1981. *Recreations:* music, thrillers, television. *Address:* c/o Jonathan Clowes, 22 Prince Albert Road, NW1 7ST. *Club:* Garrick.

AMLOT, Roy Douglas; barrister; Senior Prosecuting Counsel to the Crown at the Central Criminal Court, since 1981; *b* 22 Sept. 1942; *s* of Douglas Lloyd Amlot and Ruby Luise Amlot; *m* 1969, Susan Margaret (*née* McDowell); two *s. Educ:* Dulwich Coll. Called to the Bar, Lincoln's Inn, 1963. Second Prosecuting Counsel to the Inland Revenue, Central Criminal Court and London Crown Courts, 1974; First Prosecuting Counsel to the Crown, Inner London Crown Court, 1975; Jun. Prosecuting Counsel to the Crown, Central Criminal Court, 1977. *Publication:* (ed) 11th edn, Phipson on Evidence. *Recreations:* skiing, squash, music. *Address:* 6 King's Bench Walk, Temple, EC4Y 7DR. *T:* 01-583 0410. *Clubs:* Lansdowne, Dulwich.

AMOORE, Rt. Rev. Frederick Andrew; Provincial Executive Officer, Church of the Province of South Africa, since 1982; *b* 6 June 1913; *s* of Harold Frederick Newnham Amoore and Emily Clara Amoore, Worthing; *m* 1948, Mary Dobson; three *s. Educ:* Worthing Boys' High Sch.; University of Leeds. BA (Hons Hist) Leeds, 1934. Curate of: Clapham, London, 1936; St Mary's, Port Elizabeth, S Africa, 1939; Rector of St Saviour's, E London, S Africa, 1945; Dean of St Albans Cathedral, Pretoria, 1950; Exec. Officer for Church of Province of S Africa, 1962-67; Bishop of Bloemfontein, 1967-82. *Recreations:* music, italic script. *Address:* Bishopscourt, Claremont, CP, 7700, South Africa.

AMOROSO, Prof. Emmanuel Ciprian, CBE 1969; TC 1977; FRS 1957; FRCP; FRCS; FRCOG; FRCPath; FInstBiol; DSc(London), PhD, MD, BCh, BAO; Professor Emeritus, Royal Veterinary College, University of London, since 1968. *Educ:* University Coll., Dublin (Grad. in Medicine, 1st cl. Hons and 1st place in all examinations in Science and Medicine); Kaiser Wilhelm Inst. für Zellforschung, Berlin; Albert-Ludwigs Univ., Freiburg; University Coll., London. McArdle Medal in Surgery and a travelling fellowship in science at NUI, 1929; then appointed to staff of Royal Veterinary College, 1935; Prof. of Physiology, Univ. of London, 1948-68; Special Prof., Dept of Physiol. and Environmental Studies, Sch. of Agric., Nottingham Univ., 1973-82. Privy Council Rep., Houghton Poultry Res. Station, 1956-63; Vis. Prof., Washington Univ., St Louis, 1958, 1961; Royal Soc. Leverhulme Visiting Professor: Univ. of Chile, 1968-69; Univ. of Nairobi, 1975-76; Vis. Prof., Univ. of Guelph, Ont, 1977, 1978; T. L. Pawlett Scholar, Univ. of Sydney, 1970-71. Treas., Soc. for Endocrinology and Jl Endocrinol. Ltd, 1955-60, Chm., 1960-65; Chm., 2nd Internat. Congress of Endocrinology, London, 1964; Trinidad and Tobago Rep., Commonwealth Scientific Cttee, 1968-; Mem., Biol Scis Cttee, IPPF, 1968-; Mem., Scientific Adv. Cttee, Brit. Egg Mkting Bd, 1963-70. Chm. Council, Jl Reprodn and Fertility Ltd, 1968-76 (Chm., Adv. Cttee, 1969-71; Chm. Exec. Cttee,

1971-76). Lectures: Univ. Voordtrachten, Rijksuniv., Gent, 1953; Goldwin Smith, Cornell, 1954; Holme, UCL, 1956; Keibel, Free Univ., Berlin, 1957; Josiah Macey, Harvard, 1958; Ingleby, Birmingham, 1958; Leo Loeb, Washington Univ., St Louis, 1958; Terry, Washington Univ., St Louis, 1961; Liebig, Univ. of Geissen, 1964; Darwin, Eugenics Soc., 1967; Sir James Mackenzie Oration, Burnley, 1970; J. Y. Simpson Oration, RCOG, 1971; Keith Entwhistle, Univ. of Cambridge, 1972; Woolridge, Brit. Vet. Assoc., 1976; E. H. W. Wilmott, Univ. of Bristol, 1979; William Dick, Edinburgh Univ., 1979; Shear Jones, RCVS, 1979.Hon. ARCVS 1959; Fellow: Royal Veterinary Coll., 1969; UCL, 1970. Hon. ScD NUI, 1963; Hon. DSc: Illinois, 1967; Nottingham, 1970; West Indies, 1971; Guelph, 1979; Hon DVetMed Santiago, 1967; Hon. Member: Soc. for Endocrinology, 1965; Soc. for Study of Fertility, 1965; Phys. Soc., 1976; Anat. Soc., 1976. *Prizes,* NUI: Botany, Zoology, Chemistry, Physics, 1923; Anatomy, Physiology, 1925; Pathology, Pharmacology, Materia Medica and Therapeutics, 1927; Medicine, Surgery and Obstetrics, 1929; Mary Marshall Medalist, Soc. Study of Fertility, 1972; Ludwig-Schunk Prize, Justus-Liebig Univ., Giessen, 1977; Henry Dale Medal, Soc. for Endocrinol., 1981; Carl G. Hartman Award, Soc. for Study of Reprodn, 1982. *Publications:* The Physiology of the Domestic Fowl, 1965; Protein Utilization by Poultry, 1967; Reproduction in the Female Mammal, 1967; chapter on Placentation in 3rd edn of Marshall's Physiology of Reproduction, 1952; papers in Phil. Trans and Proc. Roy. Soc., Jl of Physiol., Jl of Anat. *Recreations:* travel, languages, Westerns, Association football, cricket. *Address:* Agricultural Research Council Institute of Animal Physiology, Babraham, Cambridge CB2 4AT. *T:* Cambridge 832312; 29 Derwent Close, Cherry Hinton Road, Cambridge CB1 4DY. *T:* Cambridge 47825.

AMORY, Sir Ian H.; *see* Heathcoat Amory.

AMOS, Air Comdt Barbara Mary D.; *see* Ducat-Amos.

AMOS, Francis John Clarke, CBE 1973; BSc (Soc); DipArch, SPDip, ARIBA, PPRTPI; Chief Executive, Birmingham City Council, 1973-77; Senior Fellow, University of Birmingham, since 1977; *b* 10 Sept. 1924; *s* of late Frank Amos, FALPA (Director, H. J. Furlong & Sons, Ltd, London), and Alice Mary Amos; *m* 1956, Geraldine Mercy Sutton, JP, BSc (Econ), MRTPI; one *s* one *d* (and one *d* decd). *Educ:* Alleyns Sch., and Dulwich Coll., London; Sch. of Architecture, The Polytechnic, London (DipArch); Sch. of Planning and Regional Research, London (SPDip); LSE and Birkbeck Coll., Univ. of London (BSc(Soc). Served War: Royal Corps of Signals, 1942-44; RIASC, 1944-47. Harlow Devel Corp, 1951; LCC, Planning Div., 1953-58; Min. of Housing and Local Govt, 1958-59 and 1962-63; Adviser to Imperial Ethiopian Govt, 1959-62; Liverpool Corp. City Planning Dept, 1962-73, Chief Planning Officer 1966-74; Chairman: Planning Sub-Cttee, Merseyside Area Land Use/Transportation Study, 1967-73; Working Gp, Educnl Objectives in Urban and Regional Planning, Centre for Environmental Studies, 1970-72. Member: Exec. Cttee, Internat. Centre for Regional Planning and Develt, 1954-59; various Cttees, Liverpool Council of Social Services, 1965-72; Exec. Cttee, Town and Country Planning Summer Sch., 1969-70; Planning, Architecture and Bldg Studies Sub-Cttee, UGC, 1968-74; Community Work Gp of Calouste Gulbenkian Foundn, 1970-82; Constitution Cttee, Liverpool Community Relations Council, 1970-73; Planning and Transport Res. Adv. Council, DoE, 1971-77; Town and Country Planning Council and Exec. Cttee, 1972-74; Adv. Cttee, Bldg Res. Estabt, 1972-77 (Chm., Planning Cttee, 1972-80); SSRC Planning and Human Geography and Planning Cttees, 1972-76; Social Studies Sub-Cttee, UGC, 1974-76; W Midlands Economic Planning Council, 1974-77; Environmental Bd, DoE, 1975-78; Trustee, Community Projects Foundn, 1978-; Council of Management, Action Resource Centre, 1978-; Study Commn on Family, 1978-; Arts Council Regional Cttee, 1979-; Exec. Cttee, Watt Cttee on Energy, 1980-; Planning Cttee, CNAA. Part-time Prof. of Planning Practice and Management, Univ. of Nottingham, 1979-. External Examiner in Planning: Univs of: Liverpool, 1967-70; Newcastle, 1968-71; Aston (Birmingham), 1970-71; Queen's (Belfast), 1972-74; Heriot-Watt, 1972-74; Nottingham, 1973-76; UCL 1975-77; Sheffield, 1979-; Glasgow, 1979-; Polytechnics of: Leeds, 1967-68; Central London, 1967-70; Birmingham, 1975-; Liverpool, 1977-. Since 1977, has acted as adviser to govts in aid programmes: India (ODA); Tanzania (ODA); Turkey (OECD); Venezuela (IBRD); Kenya, Pakistan and Zimbabwe (UN). Mem., County Exec. Cttee, Scout Assoc., 1977-. Mem., Court, Univ. of Nottingham, 1975-77. Adviser to AMA Social Services Cttee, 1974-77; Chm., W Midlands Area, Nat. Assoc. of CAB, 1978-. Pres., Royal Town Planning Inst., 1971-72 (AMPTI, 1955; Fellow 1967; Hon. Sec., 1979-); Architect RIBA, 1951. FRSA 1977. Freeman of City of London, 1968. *Publications:* Education for Planning (CES Report), 1973; various reports on Liverpool incl.: Annual Reviews of Plans, Study of Social Malaise; RTPI Report on Future of Planning; (part) City Centre Redevelopment; articles on Planning and Management in Local Govt in various professional jls. *Recreations:* travel; unsystematic philately and unskilled building. *Address:* Grindstones, 20 Westfield Road, Edgbaston, Birmingham B15 3QG. *T:* 021-454 5661.

AMPLEFORTH, Abbot of; *see* Griffiths, Rt. Rev. M. A.

AMPTHILL, 4th Baron *cr* 1881; **Geoffrey Denis Erskine Russell;** Deputy Chairman of Committees, House of Lords, since 1980; *b* 15 Oct. 1921; *s* of 3rd Baron Ampthill, CBE, and Christabel, Lady Ampthill (*d* 1976); *S* father, 1973; *m* 1st, 1946, Susan Mary (marr. diss. 1971), *d* of late Hon. Charles John Frederic Winn; two *s* one *d* (and one *s* decd); 2nd, 1972, Elisabeth Anne Marie, *d* of late Claude Henri Gustave Mallon. *Educ:* Stowe. Irish Guards, 1941–46; 2nd Lt 1941, Captain 1944. Gen. Manager, Fortnum and Mason, 1947–51; Chairman, New Providence Hotel Co. Ltd, 1951–64; Dir, United Newspapers plc, 1981–. Managing Director of theatre owning and producing companies, 1953–. Dir, Leeds Castle Foundn, 1980–. *Heir: s* Hon. David Whitney Erskine Russell [*b* 27 May 1947; *m* 1980, April McKenzie Arbon, *y d* of Paul Arbon, New York; one *d*]. *Address:* 20 Cathcart Road, SW10 9NN. *T:* 01-352 4666.

AMRITANAND, Rt. Rev. Joseph; Bishop of Calcutta, 1970–82; *b* Amritsar, 17 Feb. 1917; *m* ; one *s* one *d. Educ:* District Board School, Toba Tek Singh, Punjab; Forman Christian Coll., Lahore, Punjab Univ. (BA); Bishop's College, Calcutta; Wycliffe Hall, Oxford. Deacon 1941, priest 1943; Missionary-in-charge of CMS Mission Field, Gojra, 1946–48; Bishop of Assam, 1949–62; Bishop of Lucknow, 1962–70; translated, after inauguration of Church of North India, Nov. 1970; first Bishop of Durgapur, 1972–74.

AMULREE, 2nd Baron, *cr* 1929; Basil William Sholto Mackenzie, KBE 1977; MD; FRCP; Liberal Whip, House of Lords, 1955–77; Chairman, Attendance Allowance Board, 1970–76; *b* 25 July 1900; *o s* of 1st Baron and Lilian (*d* 1916), *e d* of late W. H. Bradbury; *S* father, 1942. *Educ:* Lancing Coll.; Gonville and Caius Coll., Cambridge (MA 1925); Paris; University Coll. Hosp. MRCS, LRCP 1925; MRCP 1928; MD Cantab 1936; FRCP 1946. Asst Pathologist: University Coll. Hosp., 1929–31; Royal Northern Hosp., 1931–36; MO, Min. of Health, 1936–50; Physician, University Coll. Hosp., 1949–66. President: London Co. Div., British Red Cross, 1945–60; Assoc. of Occupational Therapists, 1956–60; Soc. of Chiropodists, 1963; Assoc. of Welfare Officers, 1960–68; British Geriatric Soc., 1949–65. Chm., Invalid Meals for London, 1956–59 (Mem. Inner London Area Adv. Cttee, 1965–75). Chm. Bd of Governors, London Medical Gp, 1968. Vice-Chm., Chadwick Trust, 1955–56. Member: Nat. Radium Commn, 1942–48; (professional) Assoc. of Water Engineers; Royal Inst. of Health. Hon. Mem. Faculty of Radiologists; Hon. FRGCP. Star of Ethiopia (1st class), 1952. *Publications:* Adding Life to Years; Min. of Health Report on Public Health and Medical Subjects, No 89; various articles in periodicals. *Recreation:* walking. *Heir:* none. *Address:* Cranbrook Lodge, Cranbrook, Kent. *Club:* Reform.

AMWELL, 2nd Baron *cr* 1947, of Islington; Frederick Norman Montague; *b* 6 Nov. 1912; *o s* of 1st Baron Amwell, CBE, and Constance (*d* 1964), *d* of James Craig; *S* father, 1966; *m* 1939, Kathleen Elizabeth Fountain; one *s* one *d. Educ:* Highbury Grammar School; Northampton Coll. of Technology. Aircraft Design Engineer (Apprenticeship in 1930), now retired. AFRAeS. *Heir: s* Hon. Keith Norman Montague, BSc, CEng, MICE, AMInstHE, FGS [*b* 1 April 1943; *m* 1970, Mary, *d* of Frank Palfreyman, Potters Bar, Herts; two *s*]. *Address:* 34 Halliford Road, Sunbury-on-Thames, Mddx. *T:* Sunbury-on-Thames 85413.

AMYOT, René, QC; Chairman, Air Canada, since 1981; *b* 1 Nov. 1926; *m* 1954, Monique Boutin; two *s* two *d. Educ:* Collège des Jésuites, Québec (BA 1946); Laval Univ. Law Sch. (LLL 1949); Harvard Univ. Grad. Sch. of Business Admin (MBA 1951). QC Canada, 1965. Vice President and Director: Imperial Life Assurance Co. of Canada; The Northern Life Assurance Co. of Canada; Director and Secretary: Fidusco Ltd; Canadian Helicopters; Ligistec Corp.; Director: Rothmans of Pall Mall Canada Ltd (Chm., Audit Cttee); Dome Mines Ltd (Mem., Audit Cttee); Sigma Mines (Quebec) Ltd (Mem., Audit Cttee); Dome Petroleum Ltd; Gaz Provincial du Nord de Québec Inc.; Northern Quebec Finance Co.; Innotech Aviation Ltd; Société immobilière du Canada (Vieux Port de Québec) Inc. (Mem. Exec. Cttee and Sec.). Consul of Belgium for Quebec City, 1966–. *Recreations:* farming, skiing, tennis, swimming. *Address:* c/o Air Canada, 1 Place Ville-Marie, Montreal, PQ H3B 3P7, Canada. *Clubs:* Quebec Garrison (Quebec City); Toronto (Toronto).

ANCASTER, 3rd Earl of, *cr* 1892; Gilbert James Heathcote-Drummond-Willoughby, KCVO 1971; TD; DL; Baron Willoughby de Eresby, 1313; Baron Aveland, 1856; Lord-Lieutenant of County of Lincoln, 1950–75; *b* 8 Dec. 1907; *s* of 2nd Earl of Ancaster, GCVO, and late Eloise, *e d* of W. L. Breese, New York; *S* father 1951; *m* 1933, Hon. Nancy Phyllis Louise Astor (*d* 1975), *o d* of 2nd Viscount Astor; one *d* (one *s* decd). *Educ:* Eton; Magdalene Coll., Cambridge (MA). Served War of 1939–45: Leicestershire Yeomanry and Major RA (wounded, despatches). MP (C) Rutland and Stamford, 1933–50; summoned to the Upper House of Parliament as Baron Willoughby de Eresby, 1951; Lord Great Chamberlain of England, 1950–52. Nat. Pres., BLESMA, 1956–. JP 1937, CC 1950, Alderman, 1954, Kesteven; DL 1947-50, 1977-, Co. Lincoln. KStJ 1957. *Heir:* (to Barony of Willoughby de Eresby): *d* Lady Nancy Jane Marie Heathcote-Drummond-Willoughby, *b* 1 Dec. 1934; (to Baronetcy) (Gilbert) Simon Heathcote, *qv. Address:* Grimsthorpe, Bourne, Lincs. *T:* Edenham 222; Drummond Castle, Crieff. *T:* Muthill 321.
See also Earl of Dalhousie.

ANCHORENA, Dr Manuel de; Argentine Ambassador to the Court of St James's, 1974–76; *b* 3 June 1933; *s* of Norberto de Anchorena and Ena Arrotea; *m* 1st, 1955, Elvira Peralta Martinez (*d* 1977); three *s* one *d* ; 2nd, 1978, Anne Margaret Clifford. *Educ:* Univ. of Buenos Aires. Doctorate in Law, Buenos Aires, 1955. Landowner, politician, and historian. *Publications:* several articles contrib. to jl of Inst. of Historic Investigation, Argentina; articles on wild life and natural preservation. *Recreations:* polo, tennis, squash, fencing. *Address:* Estancia La Corona, Villanueva 7225, F.C. Roca, Provincia de Buenos Aires,

Argentina. *Clubs:* Hurlingham, Royal Automobile; Circulo de Caza Mayo (Buenos Aires) (former Pres.).

ANCRAM, Earl of; Michael Andrew Foster Jude Kerr; MP (C) Edinburgh South, since 1979; advocate; *b* 7 July 1945; *s* and *heir* of 12th Marquess o Lothian, *qv* ; *m* 1975, Lady Jane Fitzalan-Howard, *y d* of 16th Duke o Norfolk, KG, PC, GCVO, GBE, TD, and of Lavinia Duchess of Norfolk *qv*; two *d. Educ:* Ampleforth; Christ Church, Oxford (BA); Edinburgh Univ (LLB). Advocate, Scottish Bar, 1970. MP (C) Berwickshire and East Lothian Feb.–Sept. 1974; Chm., Cons. Party in Scotland, 1980- (Vice-Chm., 1975–80) Mem., Select Cttee on Energy, 1979-. *Recreations:* ski-ing, photography folksinging. *Address:* 6 Ainslie Place, Edinburgh; Monteviot, Jedburgh Scotland. *T:* 031-226 3147. *Clubs:* Turf; New (Edinburgh).

ANDERSEN, Valdemar Jens, CMG 1965; OBE 1960 (MBE 1955); VRI 1962; Resident Commissioner, Gilbert and Ellice Islands Colony, 1962-70 retired; *b* 21 March 1919; 2nd *s* of Max Andersen, Maraenui, NZ; *m* 1946 Alison Leone, 2nd *d* of G. A. Edmonds, Remuera, Auckland, NZ; one *s* one *d. Educ:* Napier Boys High Sch. NZ; Auckland University Coll. (BSc). Lieut RNZNVR, 1940–46; Lieut, RANVR, 1947-62. British Solomon Islands Protectorate: Administrative Officer, 1947; Class A, Administrative Officer 1954; Secretary Protectorate Affairs, 1958. *Recreations:* drama, poetry gardening. *Address:* McKinney Road, Warkworth, New Zealand.

ANDERSON, family name of Viscount Waverley.

ANDERSON, Maj.-Gen. Alistair Andrew Gibson, CB 1980; Director Communications and Electronics Security Group, Government Communications Headquarters, since 1980; *b* 26 Feb. 1927; *s* of Lt-Col John Gibson Anderson and Margaret Alice (*née* Scott); *m* 1953, Dr Margaret Grace Smith; one *s* two *d. Educ:* George Watson's Boys Coll., Edinburgh University Coll. of SW of England, Exeter (Short Univ. Course, 1944); Staff Coll., Camberley; Jt Services Staff Coll., Latimer. Enlisted 1944; commnd Royal Corps of Signals, 1946; comd 18 Signal Regt, 1967–69; Defence Ops Centre, 1969-72; staff of Signal Officer-in-Chief, 1972-74; Comdt, Sch. of Signals, 1974–76; Signal Officer-in-Chief (Army), 1977–80, retired. Co Comdt, Royal Corps of Signals, 1980-. *Recreations:* hill walking, sailing gardening. *Club:* Army and Navy.
See also Sir J. E. Anderson.

ANDERSON, Anthony John; QC 1982; Barrister; *b* 12 Sept. 1938; *s* of A Fraser Anderson and Margaret Anderson; *m* 1970, Fenja Ragnhild Gunn *Educ:* Harrow; Magdalen Coll., Oxford. MA. 2nd Lieut, The Gordor Highlanders, 1957–59. Called to the Bar, Inner Temple, 1964. *Recreation* golf. *Address:* 2 Mitre Court Buildings, Temple, EC4. *T:* 01-353 4844; 33 Abinger Road, Bedford Park, W4. *T:* 01-994 2857. *Club:* Garrick.

ANDERSON, Dr Arthur John Ritchie, MRCS, MRCGP; General Medical and Hospital Practitioner, Trainer, since 1961; Leader, Hertfordshire County Council, since 1977; *b* 19 July 1933; *s* of Dr John Anderson and Dorothy Mary Anderson; *m* 1959, Janet Edith Norrish; two *s* one *d. Educ:* Bromsgrove Sch. Downing Coll., Cambridge; St Mary's Hospital Medical Sch. MA, MB BChir (Cantab). LRCP; DCH; DObstRCOG. Various hospital posts, 1958–61 Hemel Hempstead RDC, 1967-74, Vice-Chm., 1970-74; Councillor Hertfordshire CC, 1973-. Member: NW Thames Regional Health Authority 1978-; Regional Manning Council for South East, 1977-79. President Hertfordshire Branch, BMA, 1973-74. Member, various governing bodies o primary, secondary, further and higher educn instns. *Publications:* numerous articles, mainly in periodicals. *Recreations:* writing, hockey, walking. *Address* Leaside, Rucklers Lane, King's Langley, Herts WD4 9NQ. *T:* King's Langley 62884. *Club:* Herts 100.

ANDERSON, Campbell McCheyne; Managing Director, The Burmah Oi plc, since 1982; *b* 17 Sept. 1941; *s* of Allen Taylor Anderson and Ethe Catherine Rundle; *m* 1965, Sandra Maclean Harper; two *s* one *d. Educ:* The Armidale Sch., NSW, Aust.; Univ. of Sydney (BEcon). AASA. Trainee and General Administration, Boral Ltd, Australia, 1962-69; Gen. Manager/Man Dir, Reef Oil NL, Australia, 1969-71; Asst Chief Representative, Burmah Oi Australia Ltd, 1972; Corporate Development, Burmah Oil Incorporated, New York, 1973; Corporate Development, 1974; Finance Director and Group Planning, Burmah Oil Trading Ltd, UK, 1975; Special Projects Dir, 1976 Shipping Dir, 1978, Industrial Dir, 1979, Burmah Oil Co. Ltd. *Recreations* golf, swimming, horse-racing, shooting. *Address:* Cox's Hall, Stanford-in-the Vale, Oxfordshire SN7 8NQ. *T:* Stanford-in-the-Vale 248. *Clubs:* Oil Industries; Frilford Heath Golf; Australian; Royal Sydney Golf; Australia Jockey; Elanora Country (NSW).

ANDERSON, Carl David, PhD; Professor of Physics, California Institute o Technology, 1930–76, now Emeritus; Chairman, Division of Physics Mathematics and Astronomy, 1962-70; *b* 3 Sept. 1905; *s* of Carl David Anderson and Emma Adolfina Ajaxson; *m* 1946, Lorraine Bergman; two *s Educ:* California Institute of Technology. BS 1927, PhD 1930. War activitie on projects, 1941-45; Presidential Certificate of Merit, 1945. Has conducted research on X-rays, gamma rays, cosmic rays, elementary particles, etc Member: Nat. Acad. of Sciences; Amer. Philosoph. Soc.; Amer. Acad. of Art and Sciences. Gold Medal, Amer. Inst., City of NY, 1935; Nobel prize in Physics, 1936; Elliott Cresson Medal of the Franklin Inst., 1937; John Ericsson

Medal of Amer. Soc. of Swedish Engineers, 1960, etc. Holds hon. degrees. *Address:* California Institute of Technology, Pasadena, Calif 91109, USA.

NDERSON, Rear-Adm. (Charles) Courtney, CB 1971; Flag Officer, Admiralty Interview Board, 1969-71, retired; *b* 8 Nov. 1916; *s* of late Lt-Col Charles Anderson, Australian Light Horse, and Mrs Constance Powell-Anderson, OBE, JP; *m* 1940, Pamela Ruth Miles; three *s. Educ:* RNC, Dartmouth. Joined RN, 1930. Served War of 1939-45: in command of Motor Torpedo Boats, Destroyers and Frigates. Naval Intelligence, 1946-49 and 1955-57; Commanded HMS Contest, 1949-51; Comdr, 1952; BJSM, Washington, 1953-55; Capt., 1959; Naval Attaché, Bonn, 1962-65; Director, Naval Recruiting, 1966-68; ADC to Queen, 1968; Rear-Adm., 1969. Editor, The Board Bulletin, 1971-78. *Publications:* The Drum Beats Still, 1951. Numerous articles and short stories. *Recreations:* gardening, do-it-yourself. *Address:* Coomb Cottage, Charlton, near Malmesbury, Wilts.

ANDERSON, Lt-Col Charles Groves Wright, VC 1942; MC; Member House of Representatives, for Hume, New South Wales, 1949-51 and 1955-61; grazier; *b* Capetown, South Africa, 12 Feb. 1897; *s* of A. G. W. Anderson; *m* 1931, Edith M. Tout; two *s* two *d*. Served European War, 1914-18 (MC), KAR, E Africa. Served War of 1939-45 (VC, POW), 2nd AIF, Malaya. *Recreation:* motoring. *Address:* 119 Mugga Way, Canberra, ACT 2603, Australia.

ANDERSON, Courtney; *see* Anderson, (Charles) Courtney.

ANDERSON, Rev. David; Principal Lecturer in Religious Studies, Hertfordshire College of Higher Education (formerly Wall Hall College), Aldenham, Herts, since 1974 (Senior Lecturer, 1970-74); *b* 30 Oct. 1919; *s* of William and Nancy Anderson, Newcastle upon Tyne; *m* 1953, Helen Finlay Robinson, 3rd *d* of Johnson and Eleanor Robinson, Whitley Bay, Northumberland; one *s* two *d. Educ:* Royal Grammar Sch. Newcastle upon Tyne; Selwyn Coll., Cambridge. Served in RA, 1940-42, Intelligence Corps, 1942-46, Lieut. Deacon, 1949, Priest; 1950; Curate of parish of St Gabriel, Sunderland, 1949-52; Tutor of St Aidan's Coll., Birkenhead, 1952-56; Warden of Melville Hall, Ibadan, Nigeria, 1956-58; Principal of: Immanuel Coll., Ibadan, Nigeria, 1958-62; Wycliffe Hall, Oxford, 1962-69. Examining Chaplain: to Bishop of Liverpool, 1969-75; to Bishop of St Albans, 1972-80. *Publications:* The Tragic Protest, 1969; Simone Weil, 1971; contrib: Religion and Modern Literature, 1975; William Golding: some critical considerations, 1978; The Passion of Man, 1980. *Recreations:* listening to music, hi-fi gramophones. *Address:* Hertfordshire College of Higher Education, Aldenham, Watford, Herts.

ANDERSON, David Colville, VRD 1947, and Clasp, 1958; QC (Scotland) 1957; *b* 8 Sept. 1916; *yr s* of late J. L. Anderson of Pittormie, Fife, solicitor and farmer, and late Etta Colville; *m* 1948, Juliet, *yr d* of late Hon. Lord Hill Watson, MC, LLD; two *s* one *d. Educ:* Trinity Coll., Glenalmond; Pembroke Coll., Oxford; Edinburgh Univ. BA (Hons) Oxford 1938; LLB (Distinction) 1946. Thow Scholar, Maclagan Prizeman, Dalgety Prizeman, Edinburgh Univ. Lecturer in Scots Law, Edinburgh Univ., 1947-60; Advocate, 1946; Standing Junior Counsel to Ministry of Works, 1954-55, and to War Office, 1955-57. Contested (C) Coatbridge and Airdrie, 1955, and East Dunbartonshire, 1959; MP (C) Dumfries, Dec. 1963-Sept. 1964. Solicitor-General for Scotland, 1960-64; Vice-Chairman, Commissioners of Northern Lighthouses, 1963-64; Hon. Sheriff-Substitute, Lothians and Peebles, 1965-; Chm., Industrial Tribunals (Scotland), 1971-72; Chief Reporter for Public Inquiries and Under Sec., Scottish Office, 1972-74. Joined RNVR, 1935. In VIII awarded Ashburton Shield, Bisley, 1933 (Trinity Coll., Glenalmond; schools event); Inter-Services XX at Bisley, 1936-38. Served War of 1939-45 in destroyers (despatches); Lieut 1940; Egerton Prizeman in Naval Gunnery, 1943; Gunnery Officer, Rosyth Escort Force, 1943-45; Norway, 1945; Lt-Comdr 1948. King Haakon VII Liberty Medal, 1946. *Relevant Play:* The Case of David Anderson QC by John Hale (Manchester, and Traverse Theatre, Edinburgh, 1980; Lyric Studio Hammersmith, 1981). *Address:* 8 Arboretum Road, Edinburgh EH3 5PD. *T:* 031-552 3003. *Club:* New (Edinburgh).

ANDERSON, David Fyfe, MD, ChB, FRCOG, FRCPGlas; Muirhead Professor of Obstetrics and Gynæcology, University of Glasgow, 1946-70, now Emeritus Professor; Obstetric Surgeon, Royal Maternity Hospital, Glasgow; Gynæcological Surgeon, Royal Infirmary, Glasgow; *b* 8 June 1904; *o s* of David Fyfe Anderson and Mary Ann Mackay, Viewfield, Strathaven, Lanarkshire; *m* 1945, Elizabeth Rose, 2nd *d* of W. F. McAusland, Wyndyknowe, Scottstounhill, Glasgow; three *s* one *d. Educ:* Strathaven Academy (Dux); High Sch. of Glasgow (Dux, Modern Side); Univ. of Glasgow (Gardiner Bursary); Johns Hopkins Univ. MB, ChB (Commendation), Univ. of Glasgow, 1926; McCunn Research Scholar, 1929-31; MRCOG 1932; FRFPSG 1935; MD (Hons) 1935; FRCOG 1940; Rockefeller Travelling Fellowship 1935-36; FRSM; FRCPGlas 1964; Fellow of Glasgow Obstetrical and Gynæcological Soc. and of Edinburgh Obstetrical Soc.; formerly Examiner to Central Midwives Board for Scotland; lately Professor of Midwifery and Diseases of Women at Anderson College of Medicine, Glasgow. Freeman of City of Glasgow. Member of Incorporations of: Barbers, Bonnetmakers and Dyers, and Tailors (Ex-Deacon). OStJ 1973. *Publications:* Medical papers and verse. *Address:* 55 Kingston Road, Bishopton, Renfrewshire PA7 5BA. *T:* Bishopton 2403.

ANDERSON, David Heywood, CMG 1982; HM Diplomatic Service; Legal Counsellor, Foreign and Commonwealth Office, since 1982; Barrister-at-Law; *b* 14 Sept. 1937; *s* of late Harry Anderson; *m* 1961, Jennifer Ratcliffe; one *s* one *d. Educ:* King James' Grammar Sch., Almondbury. LLB (Leeds); LLM (London). Called to Bar, Gray's Inn, 1963. Asst Legal Adviser, FCO, 1960-69; Legal Adviser, British Embassy, Bonn, 1969-72; Legal Counsellor, FCO, 1972-79; Legal Adviser, UK Mission to UN, NY, 1979-82. *Recreations:* reading, gardening. *Address:* c/o Foreign and Commonwealth Office, King Charles Street, SW1.

ANDERSON, Prof. David Steel; Emeritus Professor of Accounting and Business Method, Edinburgh University; *b* 27 Oct. 1902; *s* of David Anderson and Jessie Marian Steel; *m* 1931, Cicely Bouskell Hockin (*d* 1980); one *s. Educ:* Viewpark School; George Watson's College, Edinburgh. Mem. Soc. of Accountants in Edinburgh, 1925; private practice as Chartered Accountant, 1927-29; joined firm of Wallace & Somerville, Edinburgh, as partner, 1929; retired partner of Whinney Murray & Co, 1973. External Examiner in Accounting, Faculty of Law, Edinburgh Univ., 1938-41; Mem. Gen. Examining Bd, Chartered Accountants of Scotland, 1939; Mem. Council Soc. of Accountants in Edinburgh, 1942-46; Mem. Advisory Cttee, Gen. Examining Bd, Inst. of Chartered Accountants of Scotland, 1937-57; Mem. Council Inst. of Chartered Accountants of Scotland, 1955-57, Vice-Pres., 1966, President, 1967-68. Hon. MA (Edinburgh Univ.), 1957. *Recreations:* golf, fishing. *Address:* Napier House, 8 Colinton Road, Edinburgh EH10 5DS. *T:* 031-447 3130. *Club:* Caledonian (Edinburgh).

ANDERSON, Brig. David William, CBE 1976 (OBE 1972); Chief Executive, North East Fife District Council, since 1982; *b* 4 Jan. 1929; *s* of David Anderson and Frances Anderson; *m* 1954, Eileen Dorothy Scott; one *s* two *d. Educ:* St Cuthbert's Grammar Sch., Newcastle on Tyne; RMA, Sandhurst. Black Watch, 1946; RMA, Sandhurst, 1947; commnd HLI, 1948; served ME and Malaya; RHF, Staff Coll., Trucial Oman Scouts, Sch. of Inf., I RHF, Germany, and HQ NORTHAG, 1959-66; Instr, Staff Coll., 1967-69; CO I RHF, Scotland, N Ireland, Singapore, 1969-72; Colonel GS: MoD, 1972-73; HQ Dir of Inf., 1974; Comdr, 3 Inf. Bde, N Ireland, 1975-76; Comdt, Sch. of Infantry, 1976-79; Comdr, Highlands, 1979-81, Comdr 51 Highland Bde, 1982; ADC to the Queen, 1981-82. Hon. Col, Aberdeen Univ. OTC, 1982-. FBIM 1981. *Recreations:* restoring old houses, walking. *Address:* c/o Royal Bank of Scotland, 18 South Methven Street, Perth.

ANDERSON, Prof. Declan John; Professor of Oral Biology, University of Bristol, since 1966; *b* 20 June 1920; *s* of Arthur John Anderson and Katherine Mary Coffey; *m* 1947, Vivian Joy Dunkerton; four *s* three *d. Educ:* Christ's Hospital; Guy's Hospital Medical School, Univ. of London. BDS (London) 1942; LDSRCS 1943, BSc 1946, MSc 1947, PhD 1955. Prof. of Physiology, Univ. of Oregon, USA, 1957-58; Prof. of Physiology in Relation to Dentistry, Univ. of London, 1963-66. *Publications:* Physiology for Dental Students, 1952; scientific papers in professional jls. *Recreations:* silversmithing, forging, music. *Address:* 7 Worcester Terrace, Bristol BS8 3JW.

ANDERSON, Donald; MP (Lab) Swansea East, since Oct. 1974; barrister-at-law; *b* 17 June 1939; *s* of David Robert Anderson and Eva (*née* Mathias); *m* 1963, Dr Dorothy Trotman, BSc, PhD; three *s. Educ:* Swansea Grammar Sch.; University Coll. of Swansea. 1st cl. hons Modern History and Politics, Swansea, 1960. Barrister; called to Bar, Inner Temple, 1969. Member of HM Foreign Service, 1960-64: Foreign Office, 1960-63; 3rd Sec., British Embassy, Budapest, 1963-64; lectured in Dept of Political Theory and Govt, University Coll., Swansea, 1964-66. MP (Lab) Monmouth, 1966-70; Mem. Estimates Cttee, 1966-69; Vice-Chm., Welsh Labour Group, 1969-70; PPS to Min. of Defence (Administration), 1969-70; PPS to Attorney General, 1974-79; Chairman: Parly Lab. Party Environment Gp, 1974-; Welsh Lab. Gp, 1977-78; Select Cttee on Welsh Affairs, 1981- (Mem., 1980-). Councillor, Kensington and Chelsea, 1971-75. Pres., Gower Soc., 1976-78. Methodist local preacher. *Recreations:* church work, walking and talking. *Address:* House of Commons, SW1; Lamb Building, Temple, EC4.

ANDERSON, Prof. Donald Thomas, PhD, DSc, FRS 1977; Professor of Biology, University of Sydney, since 1972; *b* 29 Dec. 1931; *s* of Thomas and Flora Anderson; *m* 1960, Joanne Trevathan (*née* Claridge). *Educ:* King's Coll., London Univ. Lectr in Zoology, Sydney Univ., 1958-61; Sen. Lectr, 1962-66; Reader in Biology, 1967-71. Clarke Medal, Royal Soc. of NSW, 1979. *Publication:* Embryology and Phylogeny, of Annelids and Arthropods, 1973; papers in zool. jls. *Recreations:* gardening, photography. *Address:* 52 Spruson Street, Neutral Bay, NSW 2089, Australia. *T:* (home) 929.7583; (office) 692.2438.

ANDERSON, Prof. Ephraim Saul, CBE 1976; FRCP, FRS 1968; Director, Enteric Reference Laboratory, Public Health Laboratory Service, 1954-77; *b* 1911; *e s* of Benjamin and Ada Anderson, Newcastle upon Tyne; *m* 1959, Carol Jean (*née* Thompson) (marr. diss.); three *s. Educ:* Rutherford Coll., and King's Coll. Med. Sch. (Univ. of Durham), Newcastle upon Tyne. MB, BS 1934; MD Durham, 1953; Dip.Bact. London, 1948; Founder Fellow, Royal Coll. of Pathologists, 1963. GP, 1935-39; RAMC, 1940-46; Pathologist, 1943-46; Registrar in Bacteriology, Postgrad. Med. Sch., 1946-47; Staff, Enteric Reference Lab., 1947-52, Dep. Dir, 1952-54. WHO Fellow, 1953; FIBiol 1973; FRCP 1975. Chm., Internat. Fedn for Enteric Phage Typing of Internat. Union of Microbiol. Socs, 1966- (Jt Chm., 1958-66); Dir, Internat. Ref. Lab. for Enteric Phage Typing of Internat. Fedn for Enteric Phage

Typing, 1954-77; Dir, Collab. Centre for Phage Typing and Resistance of Enterobacteria of WHO, 1960-; Mem., WHO Expert Adv. Panel for Enteric Diseases. Vis. Prof., Sch. of Biol Sciences, Brunel Univ., 1973-77. Lectures: Almroth Wright, Wright-Fleming Inst. of Microbiol., 1967; Holme, UCH, 1970; Cutter, Sch. of Public Health, Harvard, 1972; Marjory Stephenson Meml, Soc. for Gen. Microbiol., 1975. Hon. DSc Newcastle, 1975. *Publications:* contrib. to: The Bacteriophages (Mark Adams), 1959; The World Problem of Salmonellosis (Van Oye), 1964; numerous articles on bacteriophage typing and its genetic basis, microbial ecology, transferable drug resistance, its evolution, and epidemiology. *Recreations:* music, photography. *Address:* 10 Rosecroft Avenue, NW3 7QB.

ANDERSON, Eric; see Anderson, W. E. K.

ANDERSON, Sir Ferguson; see Anderson, Sir W. F.

ANDERSON, Dame Frances Margaret; see Anderson, Dame Judith.

ANDERSON, George David, CMG 1967; HM Diplomatic Service, retired; *b* 11 Sept. 1913; *m* 1950, Audrey Rowena Money; one *d. Educ:* King Edward VII Gram. Sch., King's Lynn; Emmanuel Coll., Cambridge. National Association of Boys' Clubs, 1935-37; Macgregor and Co., Rangoon, Burma, 1937-41. Army Service, Burma Rifles, 1941-44; Combined Services Detailed Interrogation Centre (India), 1944-46. Min. of Food, 1946; CRO, 1947. Office of British High Commission in New Delhi and Calcutta, 1947-51; British Embassy, Dublin, 1957-60; Dep. High Comr, Ceylon, 1961-66; Diplomatic Service, 1964; Head of Chancery, British High Commn, Lagos, Nigeria, 1967-69; British High Comr in Botswana, 1969-73. *Recreations:* music, gardening and the enjoyment of retirement. *Address:* c/o Grindlay's Bank Ltd, 13 St James's Square, SW1. *T:* (home) 01-650 4613. *Club:* Royal Commonwealth Society.

ANDERSON, Rev. Prof. George Wishart, FRSE 1977; FBA 1972; Professor of Old Testament Literature and Theology, 1962-68, of Hebrew and Old Testament Studies, 1968-82, University of Edinburgh; *b* 25 Jan. 1913; *s* of George Anderson and Margaret Gordon Wishart; *m* 1st, 1941, Edith Joyce Marjorie Walter (decd); one *s* one *d*; 2nd, 1959, Anne Phyllis Walter. *Educ:* Arbroath High Sch.; Univs of St Andrews, Cambridge, Lund. United Coll., St Andrews: Harkness Scholar; MA 1st Cl. Hons Classics, 1935. Fitzwilliam House and Wesley House, Cambridge: 1st Cl. Theol Tripos Part I, 1937; 2nd Cl. Theol Tripos Part II, 1938; BA 1937; MA 1946. Asst Tutor, Richmond Coll., 1939-41. Chaplain, RAF, 1941-46; Tutor in OT Lang. and Lit., Handsworth Coll., 1946-56; Lecturer in OT Lit. and Theol., Univ. of St Andrews, 1956-58; Prof. of OT Studies, Univ. of Durham, 1958-62. Hon. Sec., Internat. Organization of Old Testament Scholars, 1953-71 (Pres., 1971-74); Mem. Editorial Bd of Vetus Testamentum, 1950-75; Editor, Book List of Soc. for OT Study, 1957-66; President, Soc. for OT Study, 1963; Hon. Sec. (Foreign Correspondence), Soc. for OT Study, 1964-74; Charles Ryder Smith Meml Lectr, 1964; Fernley-Hartley Lectr, 1969; Speaker's Lectr in Biblical Studies, Univ. of Oxford, 1976-80; Henton Davies Lectr, 1977. Hon. DD St Andrews, 1959; Hon. TeolD Lund, 1971. Burkitt Medal for Biblical Studies, British Acad., 1982. *Publications:* He That Cometh (trans. from Norwegian of S. Mowinckel), 1956; A Critical Introduction to the Old Testament, 1959; The Ras Shamra Discoveries and the Old Testament (trans. from Norwegian of A. S. Kapelrud, US 1963, UK 1965); The History and Religion of Israel, 1966; (ed) A Decade of Bible Bibliography, 1967; (ed) Tradition and Interpretation, 1979; articles in: The Old Testament and Modern Study (ed H. H. Rowley), 1951; The New Peake Commentary (ed M. Black and H. H. Rowley), 1962; The Cambridge History of the Bible, Vol. I (ed P. R. Ackroyd and C. F. Evans), 1970, and in various learned jls. *Recreations:* reading, music, walking. *Address:* 51 Fountainhall Road, Edinburgh EH9 2LH.

ANDERSON, Rev. Hector David, MVO 1951; MA, BD; Chaplain to the Queen, 1955-77; *b* 16 Aug. 1906; *s* of Rev. David Anderson, LLD, Dublin; *m* 1931, Muriel Louise Peters; one *s. Educ:* The Abbey, Tipperary; Trinity Coll., Dublin. Schol. 1928, BA Mods 1929, MA 1932, BD 1949. Curate, Shirley, Croydon, 1930-33; St Michael's, Chester Square, SW1, 1933-39; CF, Sept. 1939-42; Domestic Chaplain to King George VI, 1942-52, to the Queen, 1952-55; Rector: Sandringham, 1942-55; Lutterworth, 1955-61; Swanage, 1961-69. *Address:* Adare, The Hyde, Langton Matravers, Swanage, Dorset. *T:* Swanage 3206.

ANDERSON, H(ector) John, FRCP; Physician, St Thomas' Hospital, since 1948, Governor since 1968; Physician, Lambeth Hospital, South Western Hospital and French Hospital; *b* Central Provinces, India, 5 Jan. 1915; *s* of H. J. Anderson; *m* 1st, 1940, Frances Pearce (marr. diss.), *er d* of Rev. W. P. Putt; one *s* one *d*; 2nd, 1956, Pauline Mary, *d* of A. Hammond; one *d. Educ:* Exeter Sch.; St Catharine's Coll., Cambridge; St Thomas' Hospital. MA, MB (Cantab), FRCP 1950. Medical Registrar and Res. Asst Physician, St Thomas' Hospital, 1941 and 1942. Hon. Lt-Col RAMC; served MEF, 1944-47. Kitchener Scholar; Mead Prizeman, St Thomas' Hospital; Murchison Scholar, RCP, 1942; Goulstonian Lectr, RCP, 1951; Examiner: MB London; Medicine, Conjoint Bd, London and England; RCP. Mem. AHA, Lambeth, Southwark, Lewisham Area (T). Member: Assoc. of Physicians of Gt Britain; Thoracic Soc.; FRSoc.Med. *Publications:* Brim of Day, 1944; contrib. to medical literature. *Address:* 5 Coombe Rise, Kingston Hill, Surrey; 3 Upper

Wimpole Street, W1. *T:* 01-935 5873; 102 Lambeth Road, SE1. *T:* 01-92 1533.

ANDERSON, Rev. Prof. Hugh, MA, BD, PhD, DD; Professor of New Testament Language, Literature and Theology, University of Edinburgh since 1966; *b* 18 May 1920; *s* of Hugh Anderson and Jeannie Muir; *m* 194? Jean Goldie Torbit; one *s* one *d* (and one *s* decd). *Educ:* Galston Sch Kilmarnock Acad.; Univ. of Glasgow (MA (Hons Classics and Semitic Lang I), BD (Dist. New Testament); PhD); post-doctoral Fellow, Univs of Oxfor and Heidelberg. Chaplain, Egypt and Palestine, 1945-46; Lectr in Ol Testament, Univ. of Glasgow, 1946-51; Minister, Trinity Presb. Churc Glasgow, 1951-57; A. B. Bruce Lectr, Univ. of Glasgow, 1954-57; Prof. o Biblical Criticism, Duke Univ., N Carolina, 1957-66. Dir, Postgrad. Studie in Theology, Univ. of Edinburgh, 1968-72; Select Preacher, Oxford Univ 1970; Haskell Lectr, Oberlin Coll., Ohio, 1971; McBride Vis. Prof. o Religion, Bryn Mawr Coll., Pa, 1974-75; Vis. Prof. of Religion, Meredit Coll., N Carolina, 1982; James A. Gray Lectr, Duke Univ., N Carolina, 1982 Scholar-in-res., Florida Southern Coll., Lakeland, Fla, 1983. Convener of Cl of Scotland's Special Commn on Priorities of Mission in 70s and 80s, 1969-7? Chm., Internat. Selection Council for Albert Schweitzer Internat. Prizes 1972-. Hon. DD Glasgow, 1970. *Publications:* Psalms I-XLV, 1951; Historian of Israel, 1957; Jesus and Christian Origins, 1964; The Inter-Testamenta Period in The Bible and History (ed W. Barclay), 1965; (ed with W. Barclay The New Testament in Historical and Contemporary Perspective, 1965; Jesus 1967; The Gospel of Mark, 1976; Commentary on 3 and 4 Maccabee Doubleday Pseudepigrapha Vol., 1982; contribs to Religion in Life Interpretation, Scottish Jl of Theology, Expos. Times. *Recreations:* golf gardening, music. *Address:* 5 Comiston Springs Avenue, Edinburgh EH1 NT6. *T:* 031-447 1401. *Clubs:* Greek (Edinburgh); Luffness Golf (Lothian).

ANDERSON, Hugh Fraser, MA, FRCS; Urological Surgeon, St George' Hospital, London, 1948-76, now Emeritus; Honorary Archivist, St George' Hospital, since 1976; late Surgeon, West Park Hospital, Epsom; *b* 19 Apr 1910; *s* of late William Thomson Anderson and late Madeline Bertha (né Grubb); *m* 1942, Nancy Singleton; one *s* one *d. Educ:* King William's Coll I of M; Gonville and Caius Coll., Cambridge (Open Exhibition, 1929); S George's Hospital (Anne Selina Fernee Exhibition, 1932). MA (Cantab) 1939 MB, BCh (Cantab) 1935; LRCP 1935; FRCS 1940. Allingham Prize i Surgery, St George's Hospital, 1938. Served War of 1939-45 (Major, RAMC (despatches). Examiner in Surgery: Univ. of London, 1958; Univ. of Basrah 1973; Univ. of Lagos, 1975-80; Member: Court of Examiners, RCS, 1966 Med. Appeals Tribunal, 1975; Assoc. of Surgeons; British Association o Urological Surgeons; International Soc. of Urology. *Publications:* articles o urological subjects and the infected hand in learned journals and textbook *Recreations:* golf, railways, gardening. *Address:* 13 Durrington Park Road Wimbledon, SW20 8NU. *T:* 01-946 2114. *Clubs:* MCC Ski Club of Grea Britain; Walton Heath Golf, St Enodoc Golf (Rock, Cornwall).

ANDERSON, James Frazer Gillan, CBE 1979; JP, DL; Convener, Central Regional Council, Scotland, since 1974; *b* 25 March 1929; *m* 1956, Ma Harley; one *s* one *d. Educ:* Maddiston Primary Sch.; Graeme High Sch Falkirk. Member: Stirling CC, 1958-75 (Convener, 1971-75); Central Regional Council, 1974-; Health and Safety Commission, 1974-80. OSt *Recreations:* gardening, walking. *Address:* 23 California Road, Maddiston, b Falkirk. *T:* Polmont 715875. *Club:* British Legion (Polmont).

ANDERSON, Prof. Sir (James) Norman (Dalrymple), Kt 1975; OB (mil.) 1945 (MBE 1943); BA 1930, LLB 1931, MA 1934, LLD 1955 (Cantab) Hon. DD St Andrews 1974; FBA 1970; QC 1974; Professor of Oriental Law in the University of London, 1954-75, now Emeritus Professor; Director c the Institute of Advanced Legal Studies in the University of London, 1959-76 *b* 29 Sept. 1908; *s* of late William Dalrymple Anderson; *m* 1933, Patrici Hope, *d* of A. Stock Givan; one *s* and two *d* decd. *Educ:* St Lawrence Coll Ramsgate; Trinity Coll., Cambridge (Senior Scholar). 1st Class, Law Tripc Parts I and II (distinction in Part I); 1st Class LLB. Called to the Bar, Gray' Inn, 1965. Missionary, Egypt General Mission, 1932; served War of 1939-4 in Army as Arab Liaison Officer, Libyan Arab Force, 1940 (Capt.); Sec. fo Sanusi Affairs, Civil Affairs Branch, GHQ, MEF, 1941 (Major); Sec. for Ara Affairs, 1943 (Lieut-Col); Political Sec., 1943; Chief Sec. (Col), 1944; Lect in Islamic Law, Sch. of Oriental and African Studies, 1947; Reader in Orienta Laws in Univ. of London, 1951-53; Hd of Dept of Law, SOAS, 1953-71, nov Hon. Fellow, SOAS; Dean of Faculty of Laws, Univ. of London, 1965-69 President, Soc. of Public Teachers of Law, 1968-69. Chm. UK Nat. Cttee c Comparative Law, 1957-59; Vice-Chm. Internat. African Law Assoc.; Visitin Prof., Princeton Univ. and New York Univ. Law Sch., 1958; Harvard Lav Sch., 1966; Mem., Denning Cttee on Legal Education for Students fron Africa, 1960. Conducted survey of application of Islamic Law in Britis African possessions for Colonial Office, 1950-51. President: BCMS; CPAS Scripture Union, 1975-80; Victoria Inst. First Chairman, House of Laity in Gen. Synod of Church of England, 1970-79 (Mem., 1970-80; Mem. forme Church Assembly, 1965-70); Anglican delegate to the World Council c Churches; Examining Chaplain to the Bishop of London. Hon. Fellow Wheaton Coll., 1969. Libyan Order of Istiqlal, Class II, 1959. *Publication* Al-'Aql wa'l Iman (in Arabic), 1939; Islamic Law in Africa, 1954; Islamic Lav in the Modern World, 1959; Into the World: The Need and Limits c Christian Involvement, 1968; Christianity: the witness of history, 196S Christianity and Comparative Religion, 1970; Morality, Law and Grac

(Forwood Lectures), 1972; A Lawyer among the Theologians, 1973; Law Reform in the Muslim World, 1976; Issues of Life and Death, 1976; Liberty, Law and Justice (Hamlyn Lectures), 1978; The Mystery of the Incarnation (Bishop John Prideaux Lectures), 1978; The Law of God and the Love of God, 1980; God's Word for God's World, 1981; Editor: The World's Religions, 1950, 4th edn 1975; Changing Law in Developing Countries, 1963; Family Law in Asia and Africa, 1968; numerous articles in periodicals. *Address:* 9 Larchfield, Gough Way, Cambridge. *T:* Cambridge 358778. *Club:* Athenæum.

ANDERSON, John, CB 1956; CBE 1950; CEng, FIEE; retired as Chief Scientist, Admiralty Surface Weapons Establishment, Portsmouth, 1961; *b* 29 Aug. 1896; *s* of John Anderson, Beith, Ayrshire; *m* 1928, Isabella Mary Morton Crerar (*d* 1975); no *c. Educ:* Spiers Sch., Beith, Ayrshire; Royal Technical Coll., Glasgow (Diploma). Joined RN Scientific Service, 1918; Chief Scientist: HM Underwater Detection Establishment, Portland, 1943-51; Admiralty Signal and Radar Establishment, Portsmouth, 1951. American Medal of Freedom, 1946. *Address:* Blue Hills, Denbigh Road, Haslemere, Surrey. *T:* Haslemere 3575.

ANDERSON, Prof. John, MD, FRCP; Professor of Medicine, King's College Hospital Medical School, since 1964; *b* 11 Sept. 1921; *s* of James and Margaret Anderson; *m* 1952, Beatrice May Venner; three *s. Educ:* Durham Univ. BA Hons, Dunelm (Mod. Hist.) 1942; MB, BS Hons, 1950; BSc Hons, 1952 (Physiology); MA (Mod. Hist.), MD. Served War, Lt, RA (Field) (Ayrshire Yeomanry), 1940-45. MRC Fellow in Clin. Med., Univ. Coll. Hosp., London, 1952-55; Rockefeller Travelling Fellowship, 1956-57; Reader in Medicine, King's Coll. Hosp. Med. Sch., Med. Unit, 1962-65. Mem., Med. Research Soc. FRCP 1962; FBCS 1969; FIBiol 1977. *Publications:* A New Look at Medical Education, 1965; Information Processing of Medical Records, 1970; articles in Lancet and BMJ, on: nutron activation, medical computing, cancer, endocrinology, med. educn. *Recreations:* shooting, sailing, fishing. *Address:* 14 Styles Way, Park Langley, Beckenham, Kent. *T:* (office) 01-274 6222. *Club:* University (Durham).

ANDERSON, General Sir John (D'Arcy), GBE 1967 (CBE 1945); KCB 1961 (CB 1957); DSO 1940; *b* 23 Sept. 1908; *s* of late Major Reginald D'Arcy Anderson, RGA, and Norah Anderson (*née* Gracey), Ballyhossett, Downpatrick, Co. Down; *m* 1937, Elizabeth, *d* of late Augustus M. Walker. *Educ:* Winchester; New Coll., Oxford (MA). 2nd Lieut 5th Royal Inniskilling Dragoon Guards, 1929; served War of 1939-45, France, Middle East and Italy (wounded, despatches twice); GOC 11th Armoured Div., BAOR, 1955-56. Chief of Staff, Headquarters Northern Army Group and BAOR, 1956-58; Director, RAC, WO, 1958-59; Dir-Gen. of Military Training, 1959-61; DCIGS, 1961-63; Military Sec. to: Sec. of State for War, 1963-64; Min. of Defence, 1964-65. Commandant IDC, 1966-68; Col 5th Royal Inniskilling Dragoon Guards, 1962-67; Col Comdt, RAEC, 1964-70; Col Comdt, UDR, 1969-79 (Rep., 1969-77); Hon. Col: Oxford Univ. OTC, 1961-67; Queen's Univ., Belfast, OTC, 1964-75. ADC General to the Queen, 1966-68. Pro-Chancellor, QUB, 1969-80. Mem., Commonwealth War Graves Commn, 1963-71. Mem., Army Museums Ogilby Trust; Vice-Pres. Sandes Soldiers' and Airmen's Homes; Deputy Pres., ACF Assoc. (NI). DL Co. Down 1969-80, High Sheriff Co. Down 1974. Hon. LLD QUB, 1980. Grand Officer, Order of the Crown (Belgium), 1963. Grand Officer, Order of Leopold (Belgium), 1966. *Recreation:* painting. *Address:* 36 Whitelands House, Cheltenham Terrace, SW3 4QY. *T:* 01-730 6887. *Club:* Cavalry and Guards.

ANDERSON, Maj.-Gen. Sir John (Evelyn), KBE 1971 (CBE 1963); CEng, FIEE; CBIM; *b* 28 June 1916; *e s* of Lt-Col John Gibson Anderson, Christchurch, NZ, and Margaret (*née* Scott), Edinburgh; *m* 1944, Jean Isobel, *d* of Charles Tait, farmer, Aberdeenshire; one *s* one *d. Educ:* King's Sch., Rochester; RMA, Woolwich. Commissioned in Royal Signals, 1936; Lt-Col 1956; Col 1960; Brig. 1964; Maj.-Gen. 1967; Signal Officer in Chief (Army), MoD, 1967-69; ACDS (signals), 1969-72. Col Comdt, Royal Corps of Signals, 1969-74. Hon. Col 71st (Yeomanry) Signal Regt TAVR, 1969-76; Hon. Col Women's Transport Corps (FANY), 1970-76. Dir Gen., NATO Integrated Communications System Management Agency, 1977-81. *Recreation:* fishing. *Address:* The Beeches, Amport, Andover, Hampshire. *Clubs:* Army and Navy, Flyfishers'.
See also Maj.-Gen. A. A. G. Anderson.

ANDERSON, Prof. John Kinloch, FSA; Professor of Classical Archaeology, University of California, Berkeley, since 1958; *b* 3 Jan. 1924; *s* of late Sir James Anderson, KCIE, and of Lady Anderson; *m* 1954, Esperance, *d* of Guy Batham, Dunedin, NZ; one *s* two *d. Educ:* Trinity Coll., Glenalmond; Christ Church, Oxford (MA). Served War, in Black Watch (RHR) and Intelligence Corps, 1942-46 (final rank, Lieut). Student, British Sch. at Athens, 1949-52; Lecturer in Classics, Univ. of Otago, NZ, 1953-58. FSA 1976. *Publications:* Greek Vases in the Otago Museum, 1955; Ancient Greek Horsemanship, 1961; Military Theory and Practice in the Age of Xenophon, 1970; Xenophon, 1974; articles and reviews in Annual of British Sch. at Athens, Jl of Hellenic Studies, etc. *Recreations:* gardening, riding. *Address:* 1020 Middlefield Road, Berkeley, California 94708, USA. *T:* Berkeley 841-5335.

ANDERSON, Sir John (Muir), Kt 1969; CMG 1957; Commissioner of State Savings Bank of Victoria, since 1962, Chairman of Commissioners, 1967; *b* 14 Sept. 1914; *s* of John Weir Anderson; *m* 1949, Audrey Drayton Jamieson;

one *s* one *d. Educ:* Brighton Grammar Sch.; Melbourne Univ. 2/6th Commando Co., 1941; Lieut, 1st Australian Parachute Bn, 1944; served SE Asia, 1941-45. Established John M. Anderson & Co. Pty Ltd, Manufacturers, Agents and Importers, 1951; Managing Director, King Oscar Fine Foods Pty Ltd. Pres. of Liberal and Country Party of Victoria, 1952-56 (Treasurer, 1957-61, 1978-80). Comr, Melbourne Harbour Trust, 1972-. Trustee, Melbourne Exhibn, 1960, Chm. of Trustees, 1968. *Recreations:* swimming, fishing. *Address:* 25 Cosham Street, Brighton, Vic 3186, Australia. *T:* 92-4790.

ANDERSON, Professor John Neil; (first) Professor of Dental Prosthetics, since 1964, Dean of Dentistry, 1972-76, 1980-82, University of Dundee; *b* 11 Feb. 1922; *s* of late Mr and Mrs J. Anderson, Sheffield; *m* 1945, Mary G. Croll; one *s* one *d. Educ:* High Storrs Gram. Sch., Sheffield; Sheffield Univ. Asst Lectr, Sheffield Univ., 1945-46; Lectr, Durham Univ., 1946-48; Lectr, Birmingham Univ., 1948-52; Sen. Lectr, St Andrews Univ., 1952-64. External Examiner, Univs of Malaya, Baghdad, Newcastle upon Tyne, Bristol, Birmingham, Liverpool, RCSI. *Publications:* Applied Dental Materials, 5th edn, 1976; (with R. Storer) Immediate and Replacement Dentures, 1966, 1966, 3rd edn, 1981; contribs to leading dental jls. *Recreations:* music, gardening, carpentry. *Address:* The Bensil, Carnoustie, Angus, Scotland. *T:* Carnoustie 52133.

ANDERSON, Prof. John Russell, CBE 1980; Professor of Pathology at the Western Infirmary, Glasgow University, since 1967; *b* 31 May 1918; *s* of William Gregg Anderson and Mary Gordon Adam; *m* 1956, Audrey Margaret Shaw Wilson; two *s* two *d. Educ:* Worksop Coll.; St Andrews Univ. BSc (St Andrews) 1939, MB, ChB (St Andrews) 1942, MD (St Andrews) 1955; MRCP 1961; FRCPGlas 1965; FRCPath 1966; FRSE 1968. RAMC, 1944-47 (Emergency Commn). Lecturer and Senior Lecturer in Pathology, Glasgow Univ., 1947-65; George Holt Prof. of Pathology, Liverpool Univ., 1965-67. Rockefeller travelling fellowship in Medicine, at Rochester, NY, 1953-54. Pres., RCPath, 1978 (Vice-Pres., 1975). Hon. LLD Dundee, 1981. *Publications:* Autoimmunity, Clinical and Experimental (jtly), 1967; Muir's Textbook of Pathology (jtly), 9th edn 1972, 10th edn 1976; various papers on immunopathology in scientific jls. *Recreations:* squash, ski-ing, gardening. *Address:* Pathology Department, Western Infirmary, Glasgow G11 6NT. *T:* 041-339 8822.

ANDERSON, Prof. John Stuart, FRS 1953; MA, PhD, MSc; Professor of Inorganic Chemistry, Oxford University, 1963-75, now Emeritus; *b* 9 Jan. 1908; *m* 1935, Joan Taylor; one *s* three *d.* Formerly Dep. Chief Scientific Officer, Chemistry Div., Atomic Energy Research Establishment, Harwell, Berks; Prof. of Inorganic and Physical Chemistry and Head of the Dept of Chemistry, Univ. of Melbourne, Australia, 1954-59; Director of the National Chemical Laboratory (Department of Scientific and Industrial Research), Teddington, 1959-63. Pres., Dalton Div. of Chemical Soc., 1974-76. Hon. Fellow, Indian Acad. of Sciences, 1978. Hon. DSc Bath, 1979. Davy Medal, Royal Soc., 1973. *Address:* Edward Davies Chemical Laboratory, University College of Wales, Aberystwyth, Dyfed; The Cottage, Abermagwr, near Aberystwyth, Dyfed SY23 4AR.

ANDERSON, Josephine, (Mrs Ande Anderson); *see* Barstow, J.

ANDERSON, Dame Judith, DBE 1960; (Dame Frances Margaret Anderson); Actress; *b* Adelaide, South Australia, 10 Feb. 1898; *d* of James Anderson Anderson and Jessie Saltmarsh; *m* 1937, Prof. B. H. Lehman (marr. diss. 1939); *m* 1946, Luther Greene (marr. diss. 1950). *Educ:* Norwood High Sch., South Australia. Started Theatre with Julius Knight; toured Australia and America, 1918; has played in: The Dove, 1925; Behold the Bridegroom, 1927; Strange Interlude, 1930; Mourning becomes Electra, 1931; Come of Age, 1934; The Old Maid, 1935; Hamlet, 1936; Macbeth (London), 1937; Family Portrait, 1939; Three Sisters, 1942; Medea (New York, 1947-48; toured America, 1948-49; Paris Internat. Drama Festival, 1955); The Seagull, Edin. Fest., 1960, Sept. at Old Vic; The Oresteia, 1966; Hamlet, 1970. *Films:* Rebecca, Edge of Darkness, Laura, King's Row, Spectre of the Rose, The Red House, Pursued, Tycoon, Cat on a Hot Tin Roof, Macbeth, Don't Bother to Knock, A Man Called Horse; TV: The Chinese Prime Minister, 1974. *Recreation:* gardening.

ANDERSON, Sir Kenneth, KBE 1962 (CBE 1946); CB 1955; *b* 5 June 1906; *s* of Walter Anderson, Exmouth; *m* 1932, Helen Veronica Grose; one *s* one *d. Educ:* Swindon Secondary Sch.; Wadham Coll., Oxford (MA). Entered India Office, 1928; Asst Sec., 1942; Dep. Financial Adviser to British Military Governor, Germany, 1947-48; Imperial Defence Coll., 1949; Under-Sec., HM Treasury, 1950-51; Dep. Director-General, 1954-66 and Comptroller and Accountant-General, 1952-66, GPO. Officer, Order of Orange-Nassau, 1947. *Address:* 7 Milton Close, N2 0QH. *T:* 01-455 8701. *Club:* United Oxford & Cambridge University.

ANDERSON, Hon. Sir Kenneth (McColl), KBE 1972; Kt 1970; Senator for New South Wales, Australia, 1953-75; Government Leader in the Senate, 1968-72; Commonwealth Minister for Health, 1971-72; *b* 11 Oct. 1909; *m* ; one *d.* MLA, NSW, for Ryde, 1950-53; Minister for Customs and Excise, 1964-68 (Actg Minister for Civil Aviation, 1966; Actg PMG, 1967); Minister for Supply, 1968-71. Alderman, Ryde Municipal Council, and Mayor of Ryde, 1949-50; Mem., Cumberland CC, 1949-50. Member: Cttee of Disputed Returns and Qualifications, 1953-62; Standing Cttee on Public Works,

1956-64; Jt Cttee on New and Permanent Parliament House, 1967; Standing Cttee on Standing Orders, 1968-72; Chm., Senate Select Cttee to consider problems of Road Safety, 1960. Served with 2nd AIF, Lieut, 8 Div. Signals, Malaya (PoW). *Recreation:* bowls. *Address:* 80 East Parade, Eastwood, NSW, Australia. *Clubs:* National, Union, Ryde RSL.

ANDERSON, Hon. Sir Kevin (Victor), Kt 1980; Judge of the Supreme Court of Victoria, since 1969; *b* 4 Sept. 1912; *s* of Robert Victor Anderson and Margaret Anderson (*née* Collins); *m* 1942, Claire Margaret Murphy; six *d. Educ:* Xavier Coll., Kew; Melbourne Univ. (LLB). Victorian Crown Law Dept, 1929-42: Courts Branch, 1929-35; Professional Asst, Crown Solicitor's Office, 1935-42; Lt, RAN, 1942-46; Victorian Bar, 1946-69; QC (Victoria) 1962. Chm., Bd of Inquiry into Scientology, 1963-65. Chm., Victorian Bar Council, 1966-67; Treasurer, Australian Law Council, 1966-68. Kt, Australian Assoc. of SMO of Malta, 1979. *Publications:* Stamp Duties in Victoria, 1949, 2nd edn 1968; joint author: Price Control, 1947; Landlord and Tenant Law, 1948, 3rd edn 1958; Victorian Licensing Law, 1952; Victoria Police Manual, 1956, 2nd edn 1969; Workers' Compensation, 1958, 2nd edn 1966; (ed) Victorian Law Reports, 1956-69. *Recreations:* yachting, woodworking. *Address:* 12 Power Avenue, Toorak, Victoria 3142, Australia. *T:* 03-202901. *Clubs:* Australian, Victoria Racing, Royal Automobile of Victoria, Celtic, West Brighton, Blairgowrie Yacht Squadron (all Melbourne).

ANDERSON, Lindsay (Gordon); film and theatre director; *b* 17 April 1923; 2nd *s* of late Maj.-Gen. A. V. Anderson and Estelle Bell Sleigh. *Educ:* Cheltenham Coll.; Wadham Coll., Oxford. Associate Artistic Director, Royal Court Theatre, 1969-75. Governor, British Film Institute, 1969-70. *Films include:* Wakefield Express, 1953; Thursday's Children (with Guy Brenton), 1954; O Dreamland, 1954; Every Day Except Christmas, 1957; This Sporting Life, 1963; The White Bus, 1966; Raz, Dwa, Trzy (The Singing Lesson), for Warsaw Documentary Studio, 1967; If . . . ., 1968 (Grand Prix, Cannes Fest., 1969); O Lucky Man!, 1973 (Film Critics' Guild award for best film of 1973); In Celebration, 1974; Britannia Hospital, 1982. *Productions in theatre:* The Waiting of Lester Abbs, 1957; The Long and the Short and the Tall; Progress to the Park; Jazzetry; Serjeant Musgrave's Dance, 1959; The Lily White Boys; Billy Liar; Trials by Logue, 1960; The Fire-Raisers, 1961; The Diary of a Madman, 1963; Andorra, 1964; Julius Caesar, 1964; The Cherry Orchard, 1966; first Polish production of Inadmissible Evidence (Nie Do Obrony), Warsaw, 1966; In Celebration, 1969; The Contractor, 1969; Home (also NY), 1970; The Changing Room, 1973; The Farm, 1974; Life Class, 1974; What the Butler Saw, 1975; The Sea Gull, 1975; The Bed Before Yesterday, 1975; The Kingfisher, 1977 (NY, 1978); Alice's Boys, 1978; Early Days, 1980; Hamlet, 1981. *Television play:* The Old Crowd, 1979. Editor, film quarterly, Sequence, 1947-51. *Publications:* Making a Film, 1952; About John Ford, 1981; contrib. to Declaration, 1957. *Address:* 9 Stirling Mansions, Canfield Gardens, NW6.

ANDERSON, Marian, (Mrs Orpheus H. Fisher); American contralto; *b* Philadelphia, Pa, 17 Feb. 1902; *m* 1943, Orpheus H. Fisher. *Educ:* Philadelphia; New York; Chicago; and in Europe. MusD Howard Univ., 1938. Singing career began in 1924; 1st prize at Lewisohn Stadium competition, New York, 1925. Has made numerous tours in the United States, Europe, Japan, Israel, India, Pakistan, Korea, etc. Ulrica in Verdi's The Masked Ball, Metropolitan Opera House, New York, 1955. US Delegate to UN, 1958. Has made many recordings. Holds numerous American and other hon. doctorates; Bok Award, 1940. Finnish decoration, 1940; Litteris et Artibus Medal, Sweden, 1952; Yukusho Medal, Japan, 1953; Gimbel Award, 1958; Gold Medal, US Inst. of Arts and Sciences, 1958; US Presidential Medal of Freedom, 1963; Congressional Gold Medal, 1978. *Publication:* My Lord, What a Morning, 1957. *Address:* Danbury, Conn 06810, USA.

ANDERSON, Brig. Hon. Dame Mary Mackenzie; *see* Pihl, Brig. Hon. Dame M. M.

ANDERSON, Vice Adm. Sir Neil Dudley, KBE 1982 (CBE 1976); CB 1979; Chief of Defence Staff (NZ), since 1980; *b* 5 April 1927; *s* of Eric Dudley Anderson and Margaret Evelyn (*née* Craig); *m* 1951, Barbara Lillias Romaine Wright; two *s. Educ:* Hastings High Sch.; BRNC. Joined RNZN, 1944; trng and sea service with RN, 1944-49; Korean War Service, 1950-51; qual. as navigation specialist; Navigator: HMS Vanguard, 1952-53; HMNZS Lachlan, 1954; HMS Saintes, 1958-59; Commanding Officer, HMNZS: Taranaki, 1961-62; Waikato, 1968-69; Philomel, 1969-70; Dep. Chief of Def. Staff, 1976-77; Chief of Naval Staff, 1977-80. Lieut 1949, Lt-Comdr 1957, Comdr 1960, Captain 1968, Cdre 1972, Rear Adm. 1977, Vice Adm. 1980. *Recreations:* golf, fishing. *Address:* 36 Beauchamp Street, Karori, Wellington, New Zealand. *T:* 766 257. *Club:* Wellington (Wellington, NZ).

ANDERSON, Sir Norman; *see* Anderson, Sir J. N. D.

ANDERSON, Prof. Philip Warren; Joseph Henry Professor of Physics, Princeton University, New Jersey, since 1975; Consulting Director, Physical Research Laboratory, Bell Telephone Laboratories, NJ, since 1976 (Member of Staff, 1949-76); *b* 13 Dec. 1923; *s* of Prof. H. W. Anderson and Mrs Elsie O. Anderson; *m* 1947, Joyce Gothwaite; one *d. Educ:* Harvard Univ. BS 1943; MA 1947; PhD 1949, Harvard. Naval Res. Lab., Washington, DC, 1943-45 (Chief Petty Officer, USN). Fulbright Lectr, Tokyo Univ., 1952-53; Overseas Fellow, Churchill Coll., Cambridge, 1961-62; Vis. Prof. of Theoretical Physics, Univ. of Cambridge, 1967-75, and Fellow of Jesus College,

Cambridge, 1969-75, Hon. Fellow, 1978-; Cherwell-Simon Mem Lectureship, Oxford, 1979-80. Member: Amer. Acad. of Arts and Sciences 1966; Nat. Acad. of Sciences, US, 1967; For. Mem., Royal Society, London 1980. O. E. Buckley Prize, Amer. Phys. Soc., 1964; Dannie Heinemann Prize Akad. Wiss. Göttingen, 1975; (jtly) Nobel Prize for Physics, 1977; Guthri Medal, Inst. of Physics, 1978. Hon. DSc, Illinois, 1978. *Publications:* Concept in Solids, 1963; numerous articles in scholarly jls. *Recreations:* go (Japanese game), rank sho-dan, walking. *Address:* Millbrook Road, New Vernon, N 07976, USA.

ANDERSON, Reginald, CMG 1974; Chairman, A. B. Jay Ltd; *b* 3 Nov. 192 *s* of late Herbert Anderson and late Anne Mary (*née* Hicks); *m* 1945, Audre Gabrielle Williams; two *d. Educ:* Palmers, Grays, Essex. Cabinet Office 1938-40. Served War, RAF, Flt Lt, 1941-46. Ministry of: Supply, 1947-5 Supply Staff, Australia, 1957-59; Aviation, 1960-67; Counsellor, Britis Embassy, Washington, 1967-70; Asst Under-Sec. of State, 1970-76, Dep Under-Sec. of State, 1976-81, MoD. *Recreations:* tennis, badminton, gol *Address:* Reynosa, Heronway, Shenfield, Essex. *T:* Brentwood 213077. *Clut* Royal Air Force.

ANDERSON, Robert Bernerd; lawyer and statesman, United States Chairman, Robert B. Anderson & Co. Ltd; *b* Burleson, Texas, 4 June 191(*s* of Robert Lee Anderson and Elizabeth (*née* Haskew); *m* 1935, Ollie Ma Anderson; two *s. Educ:* Weatherford Coll., Texas; Univ. of Texas (LLB) Admitted to Texas Bar, and began law practice, Fort Worth, Texas, 193 elected to Texas legislature, 1932; Asst Attorney-Gen., Texas, 1932; Prof. c Law, Univ. of Texas, 1933; State Tax Commr, Texas, 1934; Racing Commn Texas, 1934; Member State Tax Board, 1934; Chm. and Executive Directo Texas Unemployment Commn, 1936; Gen. Counsel for the Waggoner Estat (oil and ranching), 1937-40 (Gen. Man., 1941-53). Secretary of US Navy 1953-54; Dep. Secretary of Defense, 1954-55; Secretary of the Treasury 1957-61. Chm., American Gas & Chemical Co. Ltd; Director: Pan America World Airways; Intercontinental Trailsea Corp.; Fed-Mart Corp.; Energ Clinic Corp.; NRX Technologies Inc.; Partner, Anderson & Pendleton. Mem Texas Bar Assoc.; Associate of Bar of City of New York. *Address:* 630 Fift Avenue, Suite 950, New York, NY 10111, USA.

ANDERSON, Robert Geoffrey William; Keeper, Department c Chemistry, Science Museum, London, since 1980; *b* 2 May 1944; *er s* c Herbert Patrick Anderson and Kathleen Diana Anderson (*née* Burns); *m* 197: Margaret Elizabeth Callis Lea; one *s. Educ:* Woodhouse Sch., London; S John's Coll., Oxford (Casberd exhibitioner) (BSc, MA, DPhil). Assistan Keeper: Royal Scottish Museum, 1970-75; Science Museum, 1975-78; Dep Keeper, Wellcome Museum of History of Medicine, and Sec., Adv. Counci Science Museum, 1978-80. Sec., Royal Scottish Soc. of Arts, 1973-75; Mem Council: Soc. for History of Alchemy and Chemistry, 1978-; Gp fc Scientific, Technological and Medical Collections, 1979-; British Soc. Histor of Science, 1981-; Pres., Scientific Instrument Commn, IUHPS, 1982-. Mem Editorial Bd, Annals of Science, 1981-. *Publications:* The Mariner's Astrolabe 1972; Edinburgh and Medicine, 1976; (ed) The Early Years of the Edinburg Medical School, 1976; The Playfair Collection and the Teaching of Chemistr at the University of Edinburgh, 1978; (contrib.) The History of Technology Vol. VI, ed T. I. Williams, 1978; Science in India, 1982. *Recreation:* book *Address:* 19 Stanley Road, Oxford. *T:* Oxford 725203.

ANDERSON, Robert (Woodruff); playwright; *b* NYC, 28 April 1917; *s* c James Hewston Anderson and Myra Esther (*née* Grigg); *m* 1st, 1940, Phylli Stohl (*d* 1956); 2nd, 1959, Teresa Wright (marr. diss. 1978). *Educ:* Phillir Exeter Acad.; Harvard Univ. AB 1939, MA 1940. Served USNR, 1942-4 (Lt); won prize (sponsored by War Dept) for best play written by serviceman, Come Marching Home, 1945, subseq. prod, Univ. of Iowa an Blackfriars Guild, NY. Rockefeller Fellowship, 1946; taught playwriting American Theatre Wing Professional Trng Prog., 1946-50; organized an taught Playwright's Unit, Actors Studio, 1955; Writer in Residence, Univ of N Carolina, 1969; Faculty, Univ. of Iowa Writers' Workshop, 197(Member: Playwrights Co., 1953-60; Bd of Governors, American Playwright Theatre, 1963-; Council, Dramatists Guild, 1954- (Pres., 1971-73); Nev Dramatists Cttee, 1950-60 (Pres., 1955-57); Fac., Salzburg Seminar i American Studies, 1968; Vice-Pres., Authors' League of America; Chm Harvard Bd of Overseers' Cttee to visit the Performing Arts, 1970-76. Wrot and adapted plays for TV and Radio. Elected to Theater Hall of Fame, 198 *Plays:* Eden Rose, 1948; Love Revisited, 1952; Tea and Sympathy, 1953; A Summer Long, 1954; Silent Night, Lonely Night, 1959; The Days Betwee 1965; You Know I Can't Hear You When the Water's Running (four sho plays), 1967; I Never Sang For My Father, 1968; Solitaire/Double Solitair 1971; Free and Clear, 1981; *Screenplays:* Tea and Sympathy, 1956; Until The Sail, 1957; The Nun's Story, 1959; The Sand Pebbles, 1965; I Never Sang Fc My Father, 1970 (Writers Guild Award for Best Screenplay, 1971); Th Patricia Neal Story, TV, 1981; *novels:* After, 1973; Getting Up and Goin Home, 1978. *Recreations:* photography, tennis. *Address:* Roxbury, Con 06783 USA. *Clubs:* Harvard, Century Association, Coffee House (New Yor City).

ANDERSON, Roy Arnold; Chairman of the Board, Lockheed Corporation since 1977; *b* Ripon, Calif, 15 Dec. 1920; *s* of Carl Gustav Anderson an Esther Marie Johnson; *m* 1948, Betty Leona Boehme; two *s* two *d. Edu* Ripon Union High Sch.; Humphreys Sch. of Business; Stanford Univ. A 1947; MBA 1949; Phi Beta Kappa; CPA. Served War, USNR, 1942-4

Westinghouse Electric Corporation: Manager, Factory Accounting, 1952-56; Lockheed Missiles and Space Co.: Manager, Accounting and Finance, and Dir, Management Controls, 1956-65; Lockheed Georgia Co.: Dir of Finance, 1965-68; Lockheed Corporation: Asst Treas., 1968-69; Vice-Pres. and Controller, 1969-71; Sen. Vice-Pres., Finance, 1971-75; Vice-Chm. of Board, also Chief Financial and Admin. Officer, 1975-77. Director of cos in California. *Recreation:* tennis. *Address:* c/o Lockheed Corporation, PO Box 551, Burbank, California 91520, USA. *T:* (213) 847-6452; (office) 2655 N Hollywood Way, Burbank, California 91520, USA.

ANDERSON, Thomas, CBE 1972; MD, FRCPE, FRCPGlas, FFCM; Henry Mechan Professor of Public Health, University of Glasgow, 1964-71, retired (Professor of Infectious Diseases, 1959-64); *b* 7 Dec. 1904; *e s* of Thomas Anderson and Mary (*née* Johnstone); *m* 1935, Helen Turner Massey (*d* 1974), one *s* three *d. Educ:* The High Sch. of Glasgow; Glasgow Univ. (MB, ChB 1928; MD, Hons and Bellahouston Gold Medal, 1945); MRCPE 1934; FRCPE 1940; FRCPGlas 1947. Dep. Phys., Ruchill Hosp., 1933-41; Phys. Supt, Knightswood Hosp., 1941-47; Sen. Lectr, subseq. Reader, Infectious Diseases, Glasgow Univ., 1947-59. Mem., Industrial Injuries Adv. Council, 1971-77. Formerly Consultant in Infectious Diseases to Western Region of Scotland. Founder, Scottish-Scandinavian Conf. on Infectious Disease. Hon. Member: Soc. for Study of Infectious Disease; Royal Medico-Chirurgical Soc., Glasgow; Swedish Med. Assoc.; Soc. for Social Med.; Section of Epidemiology and Preventive Med., RSM. *Publications:* various, on Infectious Diseases, in med. scientific jls. *Recreation:* bowls. *Address:* Braeside, Brodick, Isle of Arran KA27 8AF.

ANDERSON, Walter Charles, CBE 1968; Solicitor; General Secretary, National and Local Government Officers Association, 1957-73; Member, IBA, 1973-78; *b* 3 Dec. 1910; *s* of William Walter John Anderson and Mary Theresa McLoughlin; *m* 1941, Doris Jessie Deacon; two *s. Educ:* Bootle Grammar Sch. and Wigan Grammar Sch.; Liverpool Univ. (LLB). Articled Clerk, J. W. Wall & Co., Solicitors, Bootle, Liverpool, 1930-33; Asst Solicitor, Bootle, 1933-34; Dep. Town Clerk, Heywood, 1934-37; Asst Solicitor, Nalgo, 1937-41; Royal Air Force, 1941-45; Legal Officer, Nalgo, 1945-50; Dep. Gen. Sec., Nalgo, 1950-57; Mem., Gen. Council of TUC, 1965-73. Member: Fulton Cttee on Civil Service Recruitment, Structure, Management and Training, 1966-68; Nat. Insurance Adv. Cttee, 1970-74; Industrial Injuries Adv. Council, 1970-74; Nat. Inst. of Econ. and Social Res., 1970-76; Industrial Arbitration Bd, Workpeople's Rep., 1972; Royal Commn on Civil Liability and Compensation for Personal Injury, 1973-78. *Publication:* Simonds' Local Government Superannuation Act, 1937 (rev. and ed) 1947. *Recreations:* sport, gardening. *Address:* 1 The Comyns, Bushey, Watford WD2 1HN. *T:* 01-950 3708.

ANDERSON, (William) Eric (Kinloch), MA, BLitt, DLitt; Headmaster of Eton College, since 1980; *b* 27 May 1936; *er s* of W. J. Kinloch Anderson, Edinburgh; *m* 1960, Poppy, *d* of W. M. Mason, Skipton; one *s* one *d. Educ:* George Watson's Coll.; Univ. of St Andrews (MA; Hon. DLitt); Balliol Coll., Oxford (BLitt). Asst Master: Fettes Coll., 1960-64, 1966-67; Gordonstoun, 1964-66; Housemaster, Arniston House, Fettes Coll., 1967-70; Headmaster: Abingdon Sch., 1970-75; Shrewsbury Sch., 1975-80. Pres., Edinburgh Sir Walter Scott Club, 1981. *Publications:* The Written Word, 1964; (ed) The Journal of Sir Walter Scott, 1972; essays and articles. *Recreations:* golf, fishing. *Address:* The Cloisters, Eton College, Windsor, Berks.

ANDERSON, Professor Sir (William) Ferguson, Kt 1974; OBE 1961; David Cargill Professor of Geriatric Medicine, University of Glasgow, 1965-79; *b* 8 April 1914; *s* of James Kirkwood Anderson, Capt. 7th Scottish Rifles (killed on active service Gaza 1917) and late Sarah Barr Anderson; *m* 1940, Margaret Battison Gebbie; one *s* two *d. Educ:* Merchiston Castle Sch.; Glasgow Academy; Glasgow Univ. (MB Hons 1936; MD Hons 1942, with Bellahouston Gold Medal). FRFPSG 1939 (now FRCPG); FRCPE 1961; FRCP 1964; FRCPI 1975; FRCP (C) 1976. Med. Registrar, Univ. Med. Clinic, 1939-41; Army Service, 1941-46, Major (Med. Specialist). Sen. Lectr, Dept of Materia Medica and Therapeutics, Univ. of Glasgow, and Asst Phys., Univ. Med. Clinic, Stobhill Hosp., Glasgow, 1946-49; Sen. Univ. Lectr, Medical Unit, also Hon. Cons. Phys., Cardiff Royal Infirmary, 1949-52; Physician in Geriatric Medicine, Stobhill Gen. Hosp., Adviser in Diseases of Old Age and Chronic Sickness, Western Reg. Hosp. Bd, Scotland, 1952-74. Mem., adv. panel on organization of medical care, WHO, 1973-. Fogarty Internat. Scholar, Nat. Inst. on Aging, Bethesda, 1979. President: RCPGlas, 1974-76; British Geriatric Soc., 1975-78; BMA, 1977-78. Chairman, Scottish Retirement Council; Hon. Chairman: St Mungo's Old Folks' Club, Glasgow; European Clin. Sect., Internat. Assoc. Gerontology. Fellow, Australasian Coll. of Technologists, 1971; Hon. Fellow, Amer. Coll. of Physicians, 1980. St Mungo Prize, Glasgow, 1968. KStJ 1974. *Publications:* Practical Management of the Elderly, 1967, 3rd edn 1976; Current Achievements in Geriatrics (ed with Dr B. Isaacs), 1964; articles on Geriatric Medicine and Preventive aspects of Geriatrics in current med. jls. *Recreation:* walking. *Address:* Strathallan, Blanefield, Glasgow G63 9AU. *T:* Blanefield 70862. *Clubs:* University Staff, Royal Scottish Automobile (Glasgow).

ANDERTON, (Cyril) James, CBE 1982; QPM 1977; Chief Constable, Greater Manchester Police Force, since 1976 (Deputy Chief Constable, 1975); *b* 24 May 1932; *o s* of late James Anderton and late Lucy Anderton (*née* Occleshaw); *m* 1955, Joan Baron; one *d. Educ:* St Matthew's Church Sch., Highfield; Wigan Grammar Sch. Certif. Criminology, Manchester Univ.,

1960; Sen. Comd Course, Police Coll., 1967. Corps of Royal Mil. Police, 1950-53; Constable to Chief Inspector, Manchester City Police, 1953-67; Chief Supt, Cheshire Constab., 1967-68; Asst Chief Constable, Leicester and Rutland Constab., 1968-72; Asst to HM Chief Inspector of Constab. for England and Wales, Home Office, London, 1972-75; Dep. Chief Constable, Leics Constabulary, 1975. Crown Courts Adv. Cttee, Manchester Circuit, 1976-; Mem. Adv. Cttee, Law Dept, Manchester Polytechnic, 1976-. Lecture Tour of Far East and SE Asia for FCO, 1973; UK Govt Deleg., European Regional Meeting of 5th UN Congress on Prevention of Crime and Treatment of Offenders, Budapest, 1974; Vis. Lectr, Police Coll.; Chm. Governing Council, British Coll. of Accordionists, 1972-77, Vice-Pres., 1977-. President: Leics Bn, Boys' Bde, 1972-76; Manchester NSPCC League of Pity, 1979-; Christian Police Assoc., 1979-81; Mem., Manchester Adv. Bd, Salvation Army, 1977-; County Dir, St John Amb. Assoc., Greater Manchester, 1976-; Vice-President: Manchester YMCA, 1976-; Adelphi Lads' Club, Salford, 1979. CBIM 1980; Hon. FBCA 1976. Member: RSCM; Corps of Royal Mil. Police Assoc. Mancunian of The Year, 1980. OSTJ 1978. *Publications:* contrib. Police Review and Police Jl. *Recreations:* home and family. *Address:* Greater Manchester Police Force, Police Headquarters, Chester House, Boyer Street, Manchester M16 ORE. *Clubs:* Royal Commonwealth Society, Special Forces; Manchester Luncheon (Manchester).

ANDERTON, James, CBE 1966 (OBE 1956); CEng, MIMinE; *b* 3 Nov. 1904; *s* of Richard and Rebecca Anderton; *m* 1st, 1931, Margaret Asbridge (*d* 1945); no *c* ; 2nd, 1949, Lucy Mackie; no *c. Educ:* Wigan and District Mining and Technical Coll. Manager of various collieries. On nationalisation of mining industry in 1947 became Asst Agent for a group of collieries in St Helens, Lancs; later made Prod. Man., St Helens Area, N Western Div.; Area Gen. Man., St Helens Area, 1949; Dep. Chm., Scottish Div., NCB, 1958. Chm., North Western Div., NCB, 1961-67. Dir, Gullick Ltd, Wigan, 1967-. Hon. MIMinE, 1968. Medal, Instn of Mining Engineers, 1965. Alfried Krupp von Bohlen und Halbach Prize for Energy Research, 1979. *Recreation:* golf. *Address:* The Knoll, Mere Road, Newton-le-Willows, Merseyside. *T:* Newton-le-Willows 5901.

ANDERTON, James; *see* Anderton, C. J.

ANDOVER, Viscount; Alexander Charles Michael Winston Robsahm Howard; *b* 17 Sept. 1974; *s* and *heir* of 21st Earl of Suffolk and Berkshire, *qv.*

ANDRESKI, Prof. Stanislav Leonard; Professor of Sociology and Head of Department of Sociology, University of Reading, since 1964; *b* 18 May 1919; two *s* two *d. Educ:* Secondary sch. in Poznan, 1928-37; Univ. of Poznan (Faculty of Economics and Jurisprudence), 1938-39; London Sch. of Economics, 1942-43. Military service in Polish Army (with exception of academic year 1942-43), 1937-38 and 1939-47 (commissioned, 1944). Lectr in Sociology, Rhodes Univ., SA, 1947-53; Sen. Research Fellow in Anthropology, Manchester Univ., 1954-56; Lectr in Economics, Acton Technical Coll., London, 1956-57; Lectr in Management Studies, Brunel Coll. of Technology, London, 1957-60; Prof. of Sociology, Sch. of Social Sciences, Santiago, Chile, 1960-61; Sen. Res. Fellow, Nigerian Inst. of Social and Economic Research, Ibadan, Nigeria, 1962-64. Vis. Prof. of Sociology and Anthropology, City Coll., City Univ. of New York, 1968-69; Vis. Prof. of Sociology, Simon Frazer Univ., Vancouver, 1976-77. *Publications:* Military Organization and Society (Internat. Library of Sociology and Social Reconstruction), 1954 (2nd aug. edn, 1968, USA, 1968, paperback, 1969); Class Structure and Social Development (with Jan Ostaszewski and others), (London), 1964 (in Polish); Elements of Comparative Sociology (The Nature of Human Society Series), 1964, Spanish edn 1972; The Uses of Comparative Sociology (American edn of the foregoing), 1965, paperback 1969; Parasitism and Subversion: the case of Latin America, 1966 (NY, 1967, rev. edn 1968, etc; Buenos Aires (in Spanish with a postscript), 1968; paperback edn, London, 1970); The African Predicament: a study in pathology of modernisation, 1968 (USA, 1969); Social Sciences as Sorcery, 1972, Spanish edn 1973, German edn 1974, French edn 1975, Italian edn 1977; Prospects of a Revolution in the USA, 1973; The Essential Comte, 1974; Reflections on Inequality, 1975; Editor: Herbert Spencer, Principles of Sociology, 1968; Herbert Spencer, Structure, Function and Evolution, 1970; contribs to: A Dictionary of the Social Sciences (UNESCO); A Dictionary of Sociology (ed D. Mitchell); Brit. Jl of Sociology; Japanese Jl of Sociology; The Nature of Fascism (ed S. Woolf); Science Jl, Man, European Jl of Sociology, etc. *Recreations:* sailing, boat building. *Address:* University of Reading, Reading, Berks. *T:* Reading 875123.

ANDREW, Most Rev. Agnellus Matthew, DD; (His Excellency the Most Reverend Agnellus Andrew); Bishop of Numana; Executive Head, Vatican Commission for Communication, since 1980; *b* 27 May 1908; *s* of Hugh Andrew and Mary Andrew (*née* Burns). *Educ:* Jesuit College, Garnet Hill; London Univ. Entered Franciscan Order, 1925; ordained priest, 1932; parish, missionary and retreat work, Manchester, 1932-55; Asst Chaplain, Manchester Univ., 1939-42. Began broadcasting career, 1942; Roman Catholic Adviser, BBC, 1946; attended BBC Staff College, 1946 and 1956; Assistant to Head of Religious Broadcasting, BBC, Director and Producer, 1955-67; Adviser to IBA, 1968-75; TV Commentator for many Papal and national occasions. President: Internat. Catholic Assoc. for Radio and Television (UNDA), 1968-80; Catholic Media Council, 1979-; Chairman, Churches' Advisory

Cttee for Local Broadcasting, 1977–; Founder (1955) and Director, Nat. Catholic Radio and TV Centre, Hatch End, 1955–80, now Director Emeritus and Trustee. DD, Gregorian Univ., Rome, 1980. *Publications:* numerous contribs to media and religious jls. *Recreation:* music (founded the Greyfriars Players, choral and orchestral society). *Address:* Palazzo San Carlo, Vatican City; St Ninian's, Oakleigh Road, Hatch End, Middlesex. *Clubs:* BBC, KSC.

ANDREW, Dr Christopher Maurice, FRHistS; Fellow since 1967, and Senior Tutor since 1981, Corpus Christi College, Cambridge; *b* 23 July 1941; *s* of Maurice Viccars Andrew and Freda Mary (*née* Sandall); *m* 1962, Jennifer Ann Alicia Garratt; one *s* two *d*. *Educ:* Norwich Sch.; Corpus Christi Coll., Cambridge (MA, PhD). FRHistS 1976. Res. Fellow, Gonville and Caius Coll., Cambridge, 1965–67; Dir of Studies in History, Corpus Christ Coll., Cambridge, 1967–81; Univ. Lectr in History, 1972–. Ext. Examr in History, NUI, 1977–. Editor, The Historical Journal, 1976–. *Publications:* Théophile Delcassé and the making of the Entente Cordiale, 1968; The First World War: causes and consequences, 1970 (vol. 19 of Hamlyn History of the World); (with A. S. Kanya-Forstner) France Overseas: the First World War and the climax of French imperial expansion, 1981; broadcasts and articles on mod. history and internat. relations. *Address:* 67 Grantchester Meadows, Cambridge CB3 9JL. *T:* Cambridge 353773.

ANDREW, Dr Colin, FIMechE; Managing Director, Maxseal Ltd, Bristol, since 1982; Hon. Professor, Bristol University, since 1982; *b* 22 May 1934; *s* of Arnold Roy and Kathleen Andrew; *m* 1952, Ruth E. Probert; two *s* two *d*. *Educ:* Bristol Grammar Sch.; Christ's Coll., Cambridge Univ. MA; PhD. Res. Engr, Rolls-Royce, 1955–58; research, Cambridge, 1958–60; Develt Engr, James Archdale & Co., 1960–61; Bristol University: Lectr, 1961–68; Reader, 1968–71; Prof. of Applied Mechanics, 1971–82. Chm., Engrg Processes Cttee, SERC, 1981–. *Publications:* papers in scientific jls. *Address:* 13 Hill Burn, Bristol BS9 4RH. *T:* Bristol 621150.

ANDREW, Prof. Edward Raymond, MA, PhD, ScD (Cambridge); FInstP; FRSE; Lancashire-Spencer Professor of Physics, University of Nottingham, since 1964; Dean of Faculty of Science, 1975–78; *b* Boston, Lincs, 27 June 1921; *o s* of late Edward Richard Andrew and Anne Andrew; *m* 1948, Mary Ralph Farnham (*d* 1965); two *d*; *m* 1972, Eunice Tinning. *Educ:* Wellingborough Sch.; Christ's (Open Scholarship) and Pembroke Coll, Univ. of Cambridge. Scientific Officer, Royal Radar Establishment, Malvern, 1942–45; Cavendish Laboratory, Cambridge, 1945–48; Stokes Student, Pembroke Coll., Cambridge, 1947–49; Commonwealth Fund Fellow, Harvard Univ., 1948–49; Lectr in Natural Philosophy, Univ. of St Andrews, 1949–54; Prof. of Physics, University of Wales, Bangor, 1954–64. Vis. Prof. of Physics, Univ. of Florida, 1969–70. Pres., Groupement Ampère, 1974–80, Hon. Pres., 1980–; Chm., Standing Conf. of Profs of Physics, 1976–79; Mem. Council, European Physical Soc., 1976–79; Chm., British Radio Spectroscopy Gp, 1981– (Founder-Chm., 1956–59). Hon. DSc Univ. of Turku, 1980. *Publications:* Nuclear Magnetic Resonance, 1955; scientific papers in learned jls. *Recreation:* travel. *Address:* Department of Physics, University of Nottingham, University Park, Nottingham. *T:* Nottingham 56101.

ANDREW, Rev. Sir (George) Herbert, KCMG 1963; CB 1956; Assistant Curate of Edenbridge, Kent; *b* 19 March 1910; *s* of James Andrew and Harriet Rose, Woodley, Cheshire; *m* 1936, Irene Jones; two *s* two *d*. *Educ:* Godley Sch.; Manchester Grammar Sch.; Corpus Christi Coll., Oxford (MA). Patent Office (Asst Examiner), 1931; Transf. to Board of Trade headquarters, 1938; Asst Sec., 1945; Second Secretary: (General) 1955–60, (Overseas) 1960–63, Bd of Trade; Mem., UK delegn to Common Market Conf., 1961–63; Deputy Secretary, Ministry of Education, during 1963, Permanent Secretary, 1963–64; Permanent Under-Sec. of State for Education and Science, 1964–70. Hon. Fellow, Corpus Christi Coll., Oxford, 1965. *Recreations:* walking, talking. *Address:* 18 Stangrove Road, Edenbridge, Kent. *T:* Edenbridge 862569.

ANDREW, Herbert Henry, QC 1982; Barrister-at-law; a Recorder of the Crown Court, since 1978; *b* 26 July 1928; *s* of Herbert Henry Andrew and Nora Andrew (*née* Gough); *m* 1966, Annette Josephine Colbert; two *s* two *d*. *Educ:* Preston Grammar Sch.; Queens' Coll., Cambridge (BA). Called to the Bar, Gray's Inn, 1952; practised on Northern Circuit, 1953–. *Recreation:* fell walking. *Address:* Peel House, 5/7 Harrington Street, Liverpool L2 9QA. *T:* 051-236 4321. *Club:* Liverpool Racquet.

ANDREW, Robert John, CB 1979; Deputy Under Secretary of State, Home Office, since 1976; *b* 25 Oct. 1928; *s* of late Robert Young Andrew; *m* 1963, Elizabeth, *d* of late Walter de Courcy Bayley; two *s*. *Educ:* King's College Sch., Wimbledon; Merton Coll., Oxford (MA). Intelligence Corps, 1947–49. Joined Civil Service, 1952: Asst Principal, War Office, Principal, 1957; Min. of Defence, 1963; Asst Sec., 1965; Defence Counsellor, UK Delegn to NATO, 1967–70. Private Sec. to Sec. of State for Defence, 1971–73; Under-Sec., CSD, 1973–75; Asst Under-Sec. of State, MoD, 1975–76. Conservator of Wimbledon and Putney Commons. Governor, King's College Sch. *Recreations:* gardening, carpentry. *Address:* 3 Camp View, Wimbledon Common, SW19 4UL. *T:* 01-947 2732.

ANDREW, Sydney Percy Smith, FRS 1976; FEng, FIChemE, MIMechE; ICI Senior Research Associate, Group Manager, Catalysts and Chemicals Research, 1963–76; *b* 16 May 1926; *s* of Harold C. Andrew and Kathleen M. (*née* Smith). *Educ:* Barnard Castle Sch.; King's Coll., Durham Univ. (Open

Schol.; BSc); Trinity Hall, Cambridge (Schol. and Prizeman; MA). Joined IC Billingham Div., 1950; Chemical Engrg Res., 1951; Plant Engr, 1953; Section Manager: Reactor Res., 1955; Process Design, 1959. Chm., Res. Cttee IChemE. Hon. DSc Leeds, 1979. *Publications:* Catalyst Handbook, 1970 various papers in chemical engrg and applied chemistry. *Recreations:* archaeology, ancient and medieval history. *Address:* 83 Hutton Avenue Hartlepool TS26 9PR. *T:* Hartlepool 75329.

ANDREWES, Antony, MBE 1945; FBA 1957; Wykeham Professor of Ancient History, Oxford, 1953–77; Fellow of New College, Oxford, 1946–77 Hon. Fellow, since 1978; *b* 12 June 1910; *s* of late P. L. Andrewes; *m* 1938 Alison Blakeway (*née* Hope); two *d*. *Educ:* Winchester; New College Oxford. Fellow of Pembroke Coll., Oxford, 1933-46. Intelligence Corps 1941–45. Comdr of Order of Phœnix, Greece, 1978. *Publications:* (with R Meiggs) revised edition of Sir George Hill's Sources for Greek History, 1951 The Greek Tyrants, 1955; The Greeks, 1967; (with K. J. Dover) Vol. IV o A. W. Gomme's Historical Commentary on Thucydides, 1970, Vol. V, 1981 articles in Classical Quarterly, etc. *Address:* 13 Manor Place, Oxford. *T* Oxford 48807.

ANDREWES, Sir Christopher (Howard), Kt 1961; FRS 1939; Deputy Director, National Institute for Medical Research, 1952–June 1961 (Member of Scientific Staff from 1927) and in charge of World Influenza Centre (WHO) until June 1961; *b* 7 June 1896; *s* of late Sir Frederick William Andrewes, MD, FRS and Phyllis Mary Hamer; *m* 1927, Kathleen Helen Lamb; three *s*. *Educ:* Highgate Sch.; St Bartholomew's Hospital. Surgeon Sub-Lt (RNVR), 1918-19; MRCS, LRCP, 1921, MB BS London (Univ Gold Medal), 1921, MD London (Univ. Gold Medal), 1922, MRCP, 1923 FRCP, 1935; House Physician and Asst to Medical Unit St Bartholomew's Hospital, 1921-23 and 1925-26; Assistant Resident Physician, Hospital of the Rockefeller Institute, New York City, 1923-25; William Julius Mickle Fellowship, Univ. of London, 1931; Oliver-Sharpey Lectureship, Royal Coll. of Physicians, 1934; Bisset-Hawkins Medal, RCP, 1947; Stewart Prize, BMA 1952; Robert Koch Gold Medal, 1979; Hon LLD Aberdeen 1963; Hon. MD Lund, 1968. *Publications:* Viruses of Vertebrates, 1964, 4th edn (with H. G Pereira and P. Wildy) 1978; The Common Cold, 1965; Viruses and Evolution (Huxley lecture), 1966; Natural History of Viruses, 1967; The Lives of Wasps and Bees, 1969; Viruses and Cancer, 1970. *Recreation:* natural history especially entomology. *Address:* Overchalke, Coombe Bissett, Salisbury Wilts. *T:* Coombe Bissett 201.

ANDREWES, Edward David Eden; Deputy Chairman and Managing Director, Tube Investments Ltd, 1972-75; *b* Portmadoc, 4 Oct. 1909; *s* of Edward and Norah Andrewes; *m* 1935, Katherine Sheila, *d* of Brig. W. B G. Barne, CBE, DSO; one *s* two *d*. *Educ:* Repton Sch.; Oriel Coll., Oxford (BA). Admitted Solicitor, 1935. Joined Tube Investments Ltd, 1935. Former Dir, Maen Offeren Slate Quarry Co. Ltd. Trustee, Cheshire Foundn, 1976-80 Legion of Merit (USA). *Recreations:* gardening, hunting, shooting, fishing *Address:* Stockton House, Worcester WR6 6UT. *T:* Eardiston 272. *Club* Boodle's.

ANDREWS; see Burt-Andrews.

ANDREWS, (Arthur) John (Francis), CBE 1970; Chairman, Clark Equipment Ltd, UK, 1962-73; Deputy Chairman, Clark Equipment Co. AG Zürich, 1963-73; Chairman, All Wheel Drive Ltd, 1954-73; *b* 15 May 1906 *s* of Arthur Andrews and Gertrude Ellen Andrews (*née* Francis); *m* 1936, Elsy Maud (*née* Johns); one *d*. *Educ:* Malvern; Paris. Development Engineer, AC Cars Ltd, 1926; Chief Purchasing Manager, Gardner Diesel Engines, 1935 *Recreations:* sailing, golf. *Address:* Junipers, Haytor, Newton Abbot, South Devon TQ13 9XY. *T:* Haytor 362. *Clubs:* Royal Automobile, Royal Thames Yacht; Royal Motor Yacht (Poole); Berkshire Golf (Ascot); Ferndown Golf (Ferndown); Isle of Purbeck Golf; Parkstone Golf.

ANDREWS, Dame Cicily; see West, Dame Rebecca.

ANDREWS, David Roger Griffith, CBE 1981; Chairman and Chief Executive, Land Rover-Leyland Ltd, since 1982; *b* 27 March 1933; *s* of C. H. R. Andrews and G. M. Andrews; *m* 1963, Dorothy Ann Campbell; two *s* one *d*. *Educ:* Abingdon Sch.; Pembroke Coll., Oxford (MA). ACMA, CBIM. Pirelli-General, 1956-59; Ford Motor Company, 1960-69: Controller Product Engrg, 1965-66; Transmission and Chassis Div., 1967; European Sales Ops, 1967-69; Asst Controller, Ford of Europe, 1969; BLMC: Controller 1970; Finance Dir, Austin Morris, 1971-72; Man. Dir, Power and Transmission Div., 1973-75; British Leyland Ltd: Man. Dir, Leyland International, 1975-77 Exec. Vice Chm., BL Ltd, 1977-82; Chm., Leyland Gp and Land Rover Gp 1981-82. Member: CBI Council, 1981-; Exec. Cttee, SMMT, 1981-; Open Univ. Visiting Cttee, 1982-. FRSA. *Recreations:* reading, sailing, model making. *Address:* 35/38 Portman Square, W1H 0HQ.

ANDREWS, Derek Henry, CBE 1970; Deputy Secretary, Ministry of Agriculture, Fisheries and Food, since 1981; *b* 17 Feb. 1933; *s* of late Henry Andrews and Emma Jane Andrews; *m* 1956, Catharine May (*née* Childe) (*c* 1982); two *s* one *d*. *Educ:* LSE. BA (Hons) 1955. Ministry of Agriculture, Fisheries and Food: Asst Principal, 1957; Asst Private Sec. to Minister of Agriculture, Fisheries and Food, 1960-61; Principal, 1961; Asst Sec., 1968; Private Sec. to Prime Minister, 1966-70; Harvard Univ., USA, 1970-71;

Under-Sec., 1973. *Address:* Flat 5, 24 Morden Road, Blackheath, SE3. *T:* 01-852 7734.

ANDREWS, Éamonn, CBE; Television Compère; Broadcaster; Writer; *b* 19 Dec. 1922; *s* of William and Margaret Andrews; *m* 1951, Gráinne Bourke; one *s* two *d. Educ:* Irish Christian Brothers, Synge Street, Dublin. Radio Eireann broadcaster (boxing commentaries, general sports commentating, interview programmes, etc.), 1941-50; first broadcast for the BBC, 1950; first appeared on BBC Television, 1951; BBC programmes included: What's My Line?, This Is Your Life, Sports Report, Crackerjack, Playbox; also boxing commentaries, variety, interview and general sports programmes. Chm. Radio Eireann Statutory Authority, charged with establishment of television in Ireland, 1960-66; joined ABC Television, 1964, Thames Television, 1968; ITV programmes include: This Is Your Life, Today, Time for Business. Former All-Ireland Amateur Junior Boxing Champion (Middle Weight). Knight of St Gregory, 1964. Hon. CBE 1970. *Publications:* The Moon is Black (play), 1941; This Is My Life (autobiog.), 1963; Surprise of Your Life, 1978; articles for magazines and newspapers. *Recreations:* walking and talking. *Address:* Windsor House, Heathfield Gardens, Chiswick, W4 4ND. *Clubs:* Irish, Royal Automobile.

ANDREWS, Brig. George Lewis Williams, CBE 1960; DSO 1944; *b* 1 July 1910; *o s* of Captain C. G. W. Andrews, The Border Regt (killed in action, 1914) and of late Mrs Diana Gambier-Parry (*née* Norrington); *m* 1938, Marianne, *d* of late Carl Strindberg, Stockholm and late Fru Greta Winbergh (*née* Skjöldebrand); one *s. Educ:* Haileybury; Sandhurst. Commissioned 2nd Lieut, The Seaforth Highlanders, 1930; active service, Palestine, 1936. Served War of 1939-45; BEF, 1939, MEF, 1941-43, BLA, 1944-45; Comd 2nd Bn The Seaforth Highlanders, 1943-45. Comd 1st Bn Seaforth Highlanders, 1953-54; Comd 152nd Highland Infantry Brigade (TA), 1954-57; Assistant Commandant, RMA Sandhurst, 1957-60. Hon. Col, 2nd Bn 51st Highland Volunteers, 1975-79. Lieut-Col, 1953; Colonel, 1955; Hon. Brig., 1960; psc 1940; jssc 1948. Chevalier, Order of Leopold, Belgium, 1945; Croix de Guerre with palm, Belgium, 1945. *Address:* West Kingsteps, Nairn, Scotland. *T:* Nairn 53231.

ANDREWS, Lt-Col Harold Marcus E.; *see* Ervine-Andrews.

ANDREWS, Harry (Fleetwood), CBE 1966; Actor since 1933; *b* 10 Nov. 1911. *Educ:* Tonbridge; Wrekin Coll. With Liverpool Repertory, 1933-35. Played Horatio in Hamlet, New York 1936; John Gielgud's Season, 1937; served War of 1939-45 (despatches); with Old Vic, 1945-49; Bolingbroke, Mirabel, Warwick in St Joan; Shakespeare Memorial Theatre; Wolsey, Macduff Brutus, Bolingbroke in Henry IV Pts I and II, 1949-51; Enobarbus, Buckingham, Kent, 1953; Othello, Claudius, 1956; Menenius in Coriolanus, 1959; Casanova in Camino Real, Phoenix, 1957; Henry VIII, Old Vic, 1958; Allenby in Ross, Haymarket, 1960; Rockhart in The Lizard on the Rock, Phoenix, 1962; Ekhart in Baal, Phoenix, 1963; Crampton in You Never Can Tell, Haymarket, 1966; Lear, Royal Court, 1971; Ivan in The Family, Haymarket, 1978; Serebryakov in Uncle Vanya, Haymarket, 1982. *Films:* Red Beret, Helen of Troy, Alexander the Great, Hill in Korea, Moby Dick, St Joan, Dreyfus, Ice Cold in Alex, Solomon and Sheba, Question of Larceny, Circle of Deception, The Best of Enemies, The Inspector, Barabbas, Reach for Glory, Nine Hours to Rama, 55 Days at Peking, The Snout, The Best of Everything, The Hill, The Agony and the Ecstasy, The Sands of Kalahari, Modesty Blaise, The Deadly Affair, The Jokers, The Long Duel, A Dandy in Aspic, The Charge of The Light Brigade, The Night They Raided Minsky's, The Southern Star, The Seagull, A Nice Girl Like Me; Too Late The Hero; The Gaunt Woman; Entertaining Mr Sloan; I want what I want; Burke and Hare; Country Dance; Wuthering Heights; Nicholas and Alexandra; The Nightcomers; The Ruling Class; Man of La Mancha; Theatre of Blood; The Mackintosh Man; Man at the Top; Jacob and Esau; The Bluebird; Sky Riders; The Passover Plot; The Prince and the Pauper; Equus; The Four Feathers; Superman—the Movie; The Titanic; The Captain; The Curse of King Tutankhamen (Earl of Carnarvon). *Television:* Leo Tolstoy; An Affair of Honour; Edward VII; Clayhanger series; The Garth People; Valley Forge; Two Gentle People, adapted from Graham Greene; A Question of Faith; A Question of Guilt; Constance Kent; Closing Ranks; 7 Dials Mystery; The Sound Machine; Tales of the Unexpected; A. J. Wentworth, BA. *Recreations:* cricket, tennis, sailing, gardening. *Address:* Church Farm Oast, Salehurst, Robertsbridge, E Sussex; Flat 7, 1 Bryanston Square, W1.

ANDREWS, Harry Thomson; Director, Welkom GM Co. (Anglo-American Corp. of South Africa); *b* Capetown, South Africa, 11 Dec. 1897; *s* of late H. Andrews, Capetown; *m* 1926, R. D. Williams, Pretoria. *Educ:* Observatory High Sch., Capetown; Marist Brothers' Coll., Capetown; Univ. of Pretoria. Served European War, 1917-19, in France, South African Signals, RE. Advocate, Supreme Court (Transvaal), 1927; Political Secretary South Africa House, London, 1930-35; Accredited Representative of Union of South Africa to League of Nations, Geneva, 1936-40; Asst Sec. for Defence, Pretoria; Under-Sec. for External Affairs, Pretoria; Head of South Africa Govt Supply Mission to USA, 1942-45; Ambassador of South Africa to USA, 1945-49; Permanent Representative of SA to United Nations, 1945-49; South African Ambassador to France, 1949-57; Minister to Switzerland, 1954-56. Member French-Commonwealth War Graves Commission, 1954-57. Vice-Pres., S Africa Foundn, 1977. *Recreation:* golf. *Address:* 214 Bretton Woods, Killarney, Johannesburg, 2193, S Africa. *Clubs:* Kimberley (Kimberley);

Rand, Bryanston Country (Johannesburg); West Province Sports (Cape Town).

ANDREWS, James Roland Blake F.; *see* Fox-Andrews.

ANDREWS, John; *see* Andrews, Arthur John Francis.

ANDREWS, John Hayward; Agent General for Queensland, since 1981; *b* 9 Nov. 1919; *s* of James Andrews and Florence Elizabeth Andrews; *m* 1947; one *s* one *d* (and one *s* decd). *Educ:* Univ. of Queensland (BEc). FIE(Aust); FAIM; DipT&CP; DipCE. Served Royal Aust. Engineers, 1940-45. Local Govt City Engineer, Wagga Wagga and Tamworth, NSW, 1946-60; Deputy Commissioner, Main Roads Dept, Queensland, 1961-78; Administrator, Gold Coast City, 1978-79; private practice, 1979-81. *Recreations:* golf, painting, walking. *Address:* 7/5 Carlton Gardens, SW1. *T:* 01-836 3224. *Clubs:* Royal Automobile (Hon. Member), East India, Devonshire, Sports and Public Schools; Indooroopilly Golf (Queensland).

ANDREWS, Rt. Hon. Sir John (Lawson Ormrod), PC (Northern Ireland) 1957; KBE 1974; DL; Senator, 1964-72; Minister and Leader in the Senate, Northern Ireland, 1964-72; *b* 15 July 1903; *o s* of late Right Hon. John Miller Andrews, CH, DL, LLD, MP, Maxwell Court, Comber, Co. Down, and Jessie, *er d* of Joseph Ormrod, Morelands, Heaton, Bolton; *m* 1928, Marjorie Elaine Maynard James (*d* 1980), *d* of Alfred Morgan James, The Fields, Newport, Mon; three *s* one *d. Educ:* Mourne Grange Preparatory Sch., Kilkeel, Co. Down; Shrewsbury. Served apprenticeship to flax spinning trade and joined family firm, John Andrews & Co. Ltd, Comber, 1922; now Chm. and Man. Dir. Northern Ireland Government: MP (U) Mid-Down, 1953-64; Minister of Health and Local Govt, 1957-61; Minister of Commerce, 1961-63; Minister of Finance, 1963-64; Dep. Prime Minister, 1970-72. President, Ulster Unionist Council, 1969-73. DL Co. Down, N Ireland, 1961. *Recreation:* yachting (Commodore Strangford Lough Yacht Club). *Address:* Maxwell Court, Comber, Co. Down. *T:* Comber 872263. *Club:* Royal Ulster Yacht.

ANDREWS, Air Vice-Marshal John Oliver, CB 1942; DSO 1917; MC; idc; *b* 20 July 1896; *s* of John Andrews, Waterloo, Lancs; *m* 1923, Bertha, *d* of Wilfred Bisdée, Hambrook, Glos; two *s.* Lieut Royal Scots; seconded RFC, 1914; served France, 1914-18; S Russia, 1919; India, 1920 (MC and bar, Montenegrin Silver Medal for bravery, DSO, despatches thrice); transferred to RAF, 1919; retired, 1945.

ANDREWS, Julie (Elizabeth); Actress; *b* 1 Oct. 1935; *m* 1st, Anthony J. Walton (marr. diss. 1968); one *d*; 2nd, 1969, Blake Edwards; one step *s* one step *d*, and two adopted *d. Educ:* Woodbrook Girls' Sch., Beckenham and private governess. Appeared in The Boy Friend, Broadway, New York, 1954; My Fair Lady: New York, 1956, London, 1958; Camelot, New York, 1960. *Films:* (Walt Disney) Mary Poppins, 1963 (Academy Award, 1964); Americanisation of Emily, 1964; Sound of Music, 1964; Hawaii, 1965; Torn Curtain, 1966; Thoroughly Modern Millie, 1966; Star, 1967; Darling Lili, 1970; The Tamarind Seed, 1973; "10", 1980; Little Miss Marker, 1980; S.O.B., 1981; Victor/Victoria, 1982. *TV:* The Julie Andrews Hour, 1972-73. *Publication:* (as Julie Andrews Edwards) Mandy, 1972; Last of the Really Great Whangdoodles, 1973. *Recreations:* boating, ski-ing, riding. *Address:* c/o Elaine Greene Ltd, 31 Newington Green, N16.

ANDREWS, Rev. Canon Leonard Martin, CVO 1946; MBE; MC 1917; Rector of Stoke Climsland, Cornwall, 1922-68; Chaplain to the Queen, 1952-69 (to King Edward VIII, 1936, and to King George VI, 1936-52); Hon. Canon of Truro since 1932; *b* 24 Sept. 1886. *Educ:* Queens' Coll., Cambridge. BA 1909; MA 1921; Deacon, 1909; Priest, 1910; Rector of Brewarrina, NSW, 1913-14; Vice-Principal Brotherhood of the Good Shepherd, NSW, 1914-15; Temp. CF, 1914-19; Chaplain at Khartoum, 1920-22; Rural Dean of Trigg Major, 1929-32. *Publication:* Canon's Folly, 1974. *Address:* Climsland, Downderry, Torpoint, Cornwall PL11 3LW.

ANDREWS, Raymond Denzil Anthony, MBE 1953; VRD 1960; Senior Partner, Andrews, Downie & Kelly, Architects, since 1960; *b* 5 June 1925; *s* of Michael Joseph Andrews, BA, and Phylis Marie Andrews (*née* Crowley); *m* 1958, Gillian Whitlaw Small, BA; one *s* one *d. Educ:* Highgate Sch.; Christ's Coll., Cambridge; University Coll. London (DipArch, DipTP); Univ. of Michigan (MArch). RIBA. Lieut, Royal Marines, 1943-46; RM Reserve, 1948-68 (Major). King George VI Meml Fellow of English-Speaking Union of US, 1954-55; Chm., London Region, RIBA, 1968-72; Vice-Pres., RIBA, 1972-74, 1978-81; Pres., Architectural Assoc., 1975-77. Civic Trust Award, 1971 and 1978; 1st Prize, Royal Mint Square Housing Competition, GLC, 1974. Order of Al Rafadain (Iraq), 1956. *Recreation:* sailing. *Address:* 6 Addison Avenue, W11 4QR. *T:* 01-602 7701. *Club:* Bosham Sailing.

ANDREWS, Stuart Morrison; Head Master of Clifton College, since 1975; *b* 23 June 1932; *s* of William Hannaford Andrews and Eileen Elizabeth Andrews; *m* 1962, Marie Elizabeth van Wyk; two *s. Educ:* Newton Abbot Grammar Sch.; St Dunstan's Coll.; Sidney Sussex Coll., Cambridge (MA). Nat. service with Parachute Bde, 1952-53. Sen. History Master and Librarian, St Dunstan's Coll., 1956-60; Chief History Master and Librarian, Repton Sch., 1961-67; Head Master, Norwich Sch., 1967-75. Chm., Direct-grant Sub-cttee of Headmasters' Conf., 1974-75. Editor, Conference. *Publications:* Eighteenth-century Europe, 1965; Enlightened Despotism, 1967; Methodism and Society, 1970; articles in various historical jls. *Recreations:* walking, writing. *Address:* Headmaster's House, Clifton College, Bristol BS8 3HT. *T:* Bristol 735613. *Clubs:* East India, Devonshire, Sports and Public Schools; Clifton (Bristol).

ANDREWS, William Denys Cathcart, CBE 1980; WS; Partner, Shepherd & Wedderburn, WS, Edinburgh, since 1962; *b* 3 June 1931; *s* of Eugene Andrews and Agnes Armstrong; *m* 1955, May O'Beirne; two *s* two *d. Educ:* Girvan High Sch.; Worksop Coll.; Edinburgh Univ. (BL). Served RASC, 1950-52. Law Society of Scotland: Mem. Council, 1972-81; Vice Pres., 1977-78; Pres., 1978-79. Examr in Conveyancing, Edinburgh Univ., 1974-77. Pt-time Mem., Lands Tribunal for Scotland, 1980-. *Recreation:* gardening. *Address:* Hillend House, Lothianburn, Edinburgh EH10 4YS. *T:* 031-445 2767. *Club:* New (Edinburgh).

ANDREWS, Winifred Agnes, (Mrs F. S. Andrews), CBE 1976; Area Nursing Officer, Wolverhampton Area Health Authority, since 1974; *b* 20 Jan. 1918; *d* of Isaac and Winifred Jones; *m* 1961, Frederick S. Andrews. *Educ:* Bargoed Grammar Sch., Bargoed, Glam. SRN, RFN, SCM, HV Cert. Supervisor of Midwives, Birmingham, 1954-72; Dir of Nursing Services, Wolverhampton, 1972-74. Member: W Midlands Regional Health Authority, 1973-; Central Health Services Council, 1974-; Standing Nursing and Midwifery Adv. Cttee, 1974; President: Royal Coll. of Midwives, 1975-81; ICM, 1978-; Sec., British Commonwealth Nurses and Midwives Meml Fund, 1978-. *Recreations:* gardening, music. *Address:* 9 Frankley Avenue, Halesowen, West Midlands B62 0EH. *T:* 021-422 3140.

ANDRIESSEN, Dr Frans, (Franciscus H. J. J.), Kt, Order of Dutch Lion; Officer, Order of Orange-Nassau; LLD; Member of the European Commission, since 1981 (responsible for competition policy); *b* Utrecht, 2 April 1929; *m* ; four *c. Educ:* Univ. of Utrecht (LLD). Served at Catholic Housing Institute, latterly as Director, 1954-72. Member: Provincial Estates of Utrecht, 1958-67; Lower House of the States-General, initially as specialist in housing matters, 1967-77; Chairman, KVP party in Lower House, 1971-77; Minister of Finance, 1977-79; Member, Upper House of States-General (Senate), 1980. *Address:* Commission of the European Communities, 200 rue de la Loi, 1049 Brussels, Belgium.

ANDRUS, Francis Sedley, MVO 1982; Beaumont Herald of Arms Extraordinary, since 1982; *b* 26 Feb. 1915; *o s* of late Brig.-Gen. Thomas Alchin Andrus, CMG, JP, and of Alice Loveday Parr; unmarried. *Educ:* Wellington Coll.; St Peter's Hall (now Coll.), Oxford (MA). Entered College of Arms as Member of Staff, 1938; Bluemantle Pursuivant of Arms, 1970-72; Lancaster Herald of Arms, 1972-82. *Address:* 8 Oakwood Rise, Longfield, near Dartford, Kent DA3 7PA. *T:* Longfield 5424.

ANFINSEN, Dr Christian Boehmer; Professor of Biology, Johns Hopkins University, since 1982; *b* Monessen, Pa, 26 March 1916; *s* of Christian Boehmer Anfinsen and Sophie (*née* Rasmussen); *m* 1941, Florence Bernice Kenenger; one *s* two *d*; *m* 1979, Libby Esther Shulman. *Educ:* Swarthmore Coll. (BA); Univ. of Pennsylvania (MS); Harvard (PhD). Amer.-Scand. Foundn Fellow, Carlsberg Lab., Copenhagen, 1939; Sen. Cancer Res. Fellow, Nobel Inst. Medicine, Stockholm, 1947; Asst Prof. of Biological Chemistry, Harvard Medical Sch., 1948-50; Head of Lab. of Cellular Physiology and Metabolism, Nat. Heart Inst., Bethesda, Md, 1950-62; Prof. of Biochemistry, Harvard Med. Sch., 1962-63; Head of Lab. of Chem. Biol., Nat. Inst. of Arthritis, Metabolism and Digestive Diseases, Bethesda, 1963-82. Rockefeller Fellow, 1954-55; Guggenheim Fellow, Weizmann Inst., Rehovot, Israel, 1958. Mem., Bd of Governors, Weizmann Inst., Rehovot, 1960-. Member: Amer. Soc. of Biol Chemists (Pres., 1971-72); Amer. Acad. of Arts and Scis; Nat. Acad. of Scis; Royal Danish Acad.; Washington Acad. of Scis; Fedn Amer. Scientists (Vice-Chm., 1958-59, and 1974-75). Hon. DSc: Swarthmore, 1965; Georgetown, 1967; Pennsylvania, 1973; NY Med. Coll.; Gustavus Adolphus Coll., 1975; Brandeis, 1977; Providence Coll., 1978. (Jtly) Nobel Prize for Chemistry, 1972. *Publication:* The Molecular Basis of Evolution, 1959. *Address:* Department of Biology, Johns Hopkins University, Baltimore, Md 21218, USA.

ANFOM, Emmanuel E.; *see* Evans-Anfom.

ANGEL, Gerald Bernard Nathaniel Aylmer; Registrar of the Family Division of the High Court, since 1980; *b* 4 Nov. 1937; *s* of late Bernard Francis and Ethel Angel; *m* 1968, Lesley Susan Kemp; three *s* one *d* (and one *s* decd). *Educ:* St Mary's Sch., Nairobi. Served Kenya Regt, 1956-57. Called to Bar, Inner Temple, 1959; Advocate, Kenya, 1960-62; practice at Bar, 1962-80. *Publications:* ed, Industrial Tribunals Reports, 1966-78. *Recreations:* reading, walking, joinery. *Address:* 9 Lancaster Avenue, SE27 9EL. *T:* 01-670 7184.

ANGELES, Victoria de los; *see* de los Angeles.

ANGELL-JAMES, John, CBE 1967; MD, FRCP, FRCS; Hon. Consulting Surgeon in Otolaryngology, United Bristol Hospitals, since 1966; *b* 23 Aug. 1901; *s* of Dr John Angell James, MRCS, LRCP and Emily Cornwell (*née* Ashwin), Bristol; *m* 1930, Evelyn Miriam Everard, *d* of Francis Over and Ada Miriam Everard, Birmingham; one *s* two *d. Educ:* Bristol Grammar Sch.; Univ. of Bristol; London Hosp.; Guy's Hosp. MB ChB 1st Cl. Hons 1924, Bristol; MBBS London (Hons) 1924; MD 1927; FRCS 1928; FRCP 1965.

Res. appts, 1924-28, Bristol and London; Hon. ENT Registrar, Bristol Royal Infirmary, 1928-29; Hon. ENT Surg., Bristol Children's Hosp., 1928-48; Cons. ENT Surg., 1948-66; Hon. Asst ENT Surg., later Hon. ENT Surg., Bristol Royal Infirmary, 1929-48; Clin. Tutor, Univ. of Bristol, 1928-55, Lectr and Head of Dept of Otolaryngology, 1955-66; Cons. ENT Surg., United Bristol Hosps, 1948-66. Lt-Col RAMC, 1942-46; Adviser in Otorhinolaryngol., MEF, 1945. Hunterian Prof., RCS, 1962; Semon Lectr in Laryngol., Univ. of London, 1965; James Yearsley Lectr, 1966; Sir William Wilde Meml Lectr, Irish Otolaryngol. Soc., 1966; Vis. Lectr, Univs of Toronto, Vermont, Cornell, Baylor and Chicago. Royal Soc. of Medicine: Former Fellow, Hon. FRSM 1976; Hon. Mem., Sections of Laryngol. (Pres., 1955) and otology. Member: SW Laryngolog. Assoc. (Chm. 1956); Brit. Medical Assoc. (Pres. Sect. of Otolaryngol., 1959; Chm. Bristol Div., 1966-67; Pres., Bath, Bristol and Som Br., 1968-69); Bristol Med.-Chirurg. Soc. (Pres. 1961); Visiting Assoc. of ENT Surgs of GB, 1948 (Pres. 1965-66); Brit. Assoc. of Otolaryngologists, 1942 (Pres. 1966-69); Collegium Oto-Rhino-Laryngologicum Amicitiae Sacrum, 1948 (Councillor, 1966-74; Pres., 1974); Barany Soc.; Pres., Otolaryngological Res. Soc., 1978. Extern. Examr, Univ. of Manchester, 1964. Hon. Member: Irish Otolaryngol. Soc.; S Africa Soc. of Otolaryngol.; Corresp. Mem., Deutsche Gesellschaft für Hals-Nasen-Ohren-Heilkunde Kopf-und Hals-Chirurgie. Hon. FRCSE 1971; Jobson Horne Prize, BMA, 1962; Colles Medal, RCSI, 1963; Dalby Prize, RSM, 1963; W. J. Harrison Prize in Laryngology, RSM, 1968. Pres., Gloucester Soc., 1977. Chm. Editorial Cttee, Clinical Otolaryngology. *Publications:* Chapters in: British Surgical Practice, 1951; Diseases of the Ear, Nose and Throat, 1952 (2nd edn 1966); Ultrasound as a diagnostic and surgical tool, 1964; Clinical Surgery, 1966; Ménière's Disease, 1969; Family Medical Guide, 1980; articles in learned jls in Eng., USA, Canada, Germany and Sweden. *Recreations:* farming; shooting. *Address:* Sundayshill House, Falfield, near Wotton-under-Edge, Glos; (consulting rooms) Litfield House, Clifton Down, Bristol BS8 3LS. *T:* Bristol 33483. *Club:* Sesame.

ANGLESEY, 7th Marquess of, *cr* 1815; **George Charles Henry Victor Paget;** Baron Paget, of Beau Desert, 1549; Earl of Uxbridge, 1784; Bt 1730; Vice-Lieutenant of Anglesey, since 1960; *b* 8 Oct. 1922; *o s* of 6th Marquess of Anglesey, GCVO, and Lady Victoria Marjorie Harriet Manners (*d* 1946), *d* of 8th Duke of Rutland; *S* father, 1947; *m* 1948, Elizabeth Shirley Vaughan Morgan (*see* Marchioness of Anglesey); two *s* three *d. Educ:* Wixenford, Wokingham; Eton Coll. Major, RHG, 1946. Div. Dir, Wales, Nationwide Building Soc., 1973-. President: Anglesey Conservative Assoc.; Nat. Museum of Wales, 1962-68; Friends of Friendless Churches. Treasurer, Danilo Dolci Trust (Britain). Vice-Chairman: Welsh Cttee, Nat. Trust; Member: Historic Buildings Council for Wales, 1953- (Chm., 1977-); Royal Fine Art Commn, 1965-71; Redundant Churches Fund, 1969-78; Council, Soc. of Army Historical Research; Trustee: Nat. Portrait Gall., 1979-; Nat. Heritage Memorial Fund, 1980-. FSA 1952; FRSL 1969; Hon. FRIBA, 1971; FRHistS, 1975. Cdre, Royal Welsh Yacht Club, 1948. Anglesey: CC, 1951-67; JP, 1959-68; DL, 1960. Hon. Fellow, Royal Cambrian Acad. Lord of the Manor of Burton-upon-Trent; Freeman of the City of London. *Publications:* (ed) The Capel Letters, 1814-1817, 1955; One-Leg: the Life and Letters of 1st Marquess of Anglesey, 1961; (ed) Sergeant Pearman's Memoirs, 1968; (ed) Little Hodge, 1971; A History of the British Cavalry, 1816-1919, vol I, 1973, vol. II, 1975, vol. III, 1982. *Recreations:* gardening, music. *Publ: s* Earl of Uxbridge, *qv. Address:* Plâs-Newydd, Llanfairpwll, Anglesey. *T:* Llanfairpwll 714330.

ANGLESEY, Marchioness of; (Elizabeth) Shirley Vaughan Paget, CBE 1977; Member, Independent Broadcasting Authority, since 1976; *b* 4 Dec. 1924; *d* of late Charles Morgan, novelist, and of Hilda Vaughan, *qv* ; *m* 1948, Marquess of Anglesey, *qv* ; two *s* three *d. Educ:* Francis Holland Sch., London; St James', West Malvern; Kent Place Sch., USA. Personal Secretary to Gladwyn Jebb, FO, until marriage. Dep. Chm., Prince of Wales Cttee, 1970-80. Member: Civic Trust for Wales, 1967-76; Arts Council, 1972-81 (Chm., Welsh Arts Council, 1975-81); Royal Commn on Environmental Pollution, 1973-79; Museums and Galls Commn, 1981-; Radioactive Waste Management Adv. Cttee, 1981-; Chairman: Nat. Federation of Women's Institutes, 1966-69; Drama and Dance Adv. Cttee, British Council, 1981-; Vice-Chm., Govt Working Party on Methods of Sewage Disposal, 1969-70. Hon. LLD Wales, 1977. *Address:* Plâs-Newydd, Llanfairpwll, Gwynedd. *T:* Llanfairpwll 714330.
See also R. H. V. C. Morgan.

ANGLIN, Prof. Douglas (George); Professor of Political Science, Carleton University, Ottawa, Canada, since 1958; *b* Toronto, Canada, 16 Dec. 1923; *s* of George Chambers Anglin, MD, and Ruth Cecilia Cale, MD; *m* 1948, Mary Elizabeth Watson; two *d. Educ:* Toronto Univ.; Corpus Christi and Nuffield Colls, Oxford Univ. BA Toronto; MA, DPhil Oxon. Lieut, RCNVR, 1943-45. Asst (later Associate) Prof. of Polit. Sci. and Internat. Relations, Univ. of Manitoba, Winnipeg, 1951-58; Associate Prof. (later Prof.), Carleton Univ., 1958. Vice-Chancellor, Univ. of Zambia, Lusaka, Zambia, 1965-69; Associate Research Fellow, Nigerian Inst. of Social and Economic Research, Univ. of Ibadan, Ibadan, Nigeria, 1962-63; Research Associate, Center of Internat. Studies, Princeton Univ., 1969-70; Pres., Canadian Assoc. of African Studies, 1973-74. *Publications:* The St Pierre and Miquelon Affair of 1941: a study in diplomacy in the North Atlantic quadrangle, 1966; Zambia's Foreign Policy: studies in diplomacy and dependence, 1979; edited jointly: Africa: Problems and Prospects 1961; Conflict and Change in Southern Africa, 1978; Canada, Scandinavia and Southern Africa, 1978; articles on Internat. and African affairs in a variety of learned jls. *Address:* Carleton University, Colonel By Drive, Ottawa, Ontario K1S 5B6, Canada.

ANGLIN, Eric Jack; HM Diplomatic Service; Consul-General, Melbourne, since 1979; *b* 9 Aug. 1923; *m* 1954, Patricia Farr; three *s.* Joined Foreign Service (subseq. Diplomatic Service), 1948; FO, 1948-52; HM Missions in: Damascus, 1952-56; Rangoon, 1956-59; Madrid, 1960-64; FO, 1964-67; La Paz, 1967-70; Khartoum, 1970-72; Inspector, Diplomatic Service, FCO, 1973-76; Buenos Aires, 1976-78; Chargé d'Affaires and Consul-Gen., Santiago, 1978-79. *Recreations:* sailing and auctions. *Address:* c/o Foreign and Commonwealth Office, SW1.

ANGLISS, Dame Jacobena Victoria Alice, DBE 1975 (CBE 1949); Chairman, William Angliss Charitable Trust; *b* 23 May 1897; *d* of Francis Grutzner, Thomastown, Vic, Australia; *m* 1919, Hon. Sir William Charles Angliss (*d* 1957). Chairman: Bluff Downs Pastoral Co., Miranda Downs Pty Ltd; Dir, Investors Pty Ltd; Trustee, William Angliss Estate. Pres., Astra Chamber Music Soc.; Dir, Aust. Nat. Memorial Theatre. *Recreations:* gardening, music. *Address:* Harcourt Street, Hawthorne, Melbourne, Vic 3122, Australia. *Clubs:* Lyceum, Alexandra (Melbourne).

ANGUS, Col Edmund Graham, CBE 1944; MC; TD; DL; JP; Chairman, George Angus & Co. Ltd, Newcastle upon Tyne 1933-64, later President; *b* 9 June 1889; *s* of Col W. M. Angus, CB; *m* 1922, Bridget E. I. Spencer (*d* 1973); one *s* one *d* (and two *s* decd, of whom *e s* was presumed killed in action, Anzio, Italy, 1944). *Educ:* Felsted Sch. Joined George Angus & Co. Ltd, 1906. Commissioned in Volunteer Forces (RA). Served in firm's Boston office, 1910-11, mobilised Aug. 1914; served in France and Flanders with 50th Div. Artillery till Feb. 1919; demobilised with rank of Major; rejoined G. Angus & Co. Ltd, Dir. 1920. Rejoined TA 1920; commanded 74th Northumbrian Field Regt, 1925-32; subst. Col with effect, 1929. FRSA 1974. DL Co. Durham, 1945; JP Northumberland, 1948. KStJ 1966. *Recreation:* horticulture. *Address:* Ravenstone, Corbridge, Northumberland NE45 5RZ. *T:* Corbridge 2122.

ANGUS, Rev. (James Alexander) Keith, TD; Minister of Braemar and Crathie Parish Churches, since 1979; Domestic Chaplain to the Queen, since 1979; *b* 16 April 1929; *s* of late Rev. Walter C. S. Angus and late Margaret I. Stephen; *m* 1956, Alison Jane Daly; one *s* one *d. Educ:* High School of Dundee; Univ. of St Andrews (MA). National Service, Army, 1947-49; served with TA, 1950-76; Captain RA (TA), 1955; Chaplain to 5, KOSB (TA), 1957-67, to 154 Regt, RCT (V), 1967-76. Assistant Minister, The Cathedral, Glasgow, 1955-56; Minister: Hoddam Parish Church, 1956-67; Gourock Old Parish Church, 1967-79. Convener, Gen. Assembly's Cttee on Chaplains to HM Forces, 1981–. *Recreations:* fishing, hill walking. *Address:* The Manse of Crathie, Crathie, near Ballater, Aberdeenshire AB3 5UL. *T:* Crathie 208. *Clubs:* New (Edinburgh); Royal Gourock Yacht.

ANGUS, Brig. (hon.) Tom Hardy, DSO 1938; psc†; fs; late Indian Army; *b* 22 May 1899; *s* of late J. B. Angus and M. S. D. Hardy; *m* 1954, Lilian Maud, *er d* of late John Emil and Ada Hyort. *Educ:* privately; RMC, Sandhurst. First Commission, 1918; Joined 45th Rattray's Sikhs, now 3rd Bn 11th Sikh Regt (Rattray's Sikhs), 1918; Regimental duty until 1932; Staff Coll., Quetta, 1932-33; RAF Staff Coll., Andover, 1935; Brigade Major, 1st Infantry Brigade, Abbottabad, NWFP, 1936-40; served Waziristan (DSO); Instructor (GSO2) Staff Coll., Quetta, 1940; Brig. Gen. Staff, Ceylon, 1942; Commander 51 Indian Infantry Brigade, 1943-44; DDMT, GHQ, India, 1945; Director of Air, India, 1946-47; retired 1948. *Recreation:* golf. *Address:* c/o Lloyds Bank Ltd, St Mary Street, Weymouth, Dorset. *Club:* Royal Dorset Yacht (Weymouth).

ANNALY, 5th Baron *cr* 1863; **Luke Robert White;** Partner, W. Greenwell & Co., Members of London Stock Exchange; *b* 15 March 1927; *o s* of 4th Baron Annaly and Lady Annaly (formerly Lady Lavinia Spencer); *S* father, 1970; *m* 1st, 1953, Lady Marye Pepys (marr. diss. 1957; she *d* 1958); one *s* ; 2nd, 1960, Jennifer Carey (marr. diss. 1967); two *d. Educ:* Eton. RAF, 1944-48; RAuxAF, 1948-51; Flying Officer (601 Sqdn). Livery, Haberdashers' Company; Freeman of City of London, 1953. *Recreations:* cricket, golf, theatre. *Heir: s* Hon. Luke Richard White [*b* 29 June 1954. *Educ:* Eton; RMA Sandhurst. Commnd Royal Hussars, 1974-78, RARO]. *Address:* Welches, Bentley, Farnham, Surrey. *T:* Bentley (Hants) 22107. *Clubs:* Turf, Royal Air Force, Pratt's, MCC; Hawks (Cambridge).

ANNAMUNTHODO, Sir Harry, Kt 1967; FRCS, FACS; Professor of Surgery, University Kebangsaan, since 1980; *b* 26 April 1920; *s* of George Annamunthodo and Rosaline (*née* Viapree); *m* 1953, Margaret Pullman; one *s* three *d. Educ:* Queen's Coll., Guyana; London Hospital Medical Coll. MB, BS London, 1946; DTM&H, 1947; FRCS, 1951; FACS, 1961. Lectr in Surg., Univ. of the W Indies, 1955-57; Sen. Lectr in Surg., UWI, 1957-61; Prof. and Head of Dept of Surg., UWI, 1961-80, now Professor Emeritus. Rockefeller Research Fellow, 1959-60; Hunterian Prof., Royal Coll. of Surgeons, 1960. *Publications:* (Co-author) Lymphogranuloma Venereum, 1962; papers on: various cancers and diseases of stomach, rectum, etc in British and American Med. Jls. *Recreation:* horticulture. *Address:* Department of Surgery, University Kebangsaan, PO Box 2418, Jalan Raja Muda, Kuala Lumpur, Malaysia.

ANNAN, family name of **Baron Annan.**

ANNAN, Baron, *cr* 1965 (Life Peer); **Noël Gilroy Annan,** OBE 1946; Chairman, Board of Trustees, National Gallery, since 1980 (Trustee, since 1978); *b* 25 Dec. 1916; *s* of late James Gilroy Annan; *m* 1950, Gabriele, *d* of Louis Ferdinand Ullstein, Berlin; two *d. Educ:* Stowe Sch.; King's Coll., Cambridge (Exhibitioner and Scholar). Served War of 1939-45: WO, War Cabinet Offices, and Military Intelligence, 1940-44; France and Germany, 1944-46; GSO1, Political Div. of British Control Commn, 1945-46. University of Cambridge: Fellow of King's Coll., 1944-56, 1966; Asst Tutor, 1947; Lectr in Politics, 1948-66; Provost of King's Coll., 1956-66; Provost of University Coll., London, 1966-78; Vice-Chancellor, Univ. of London, 1978-81. Romanes Lectr, Oxford, 1965. Chairman: Departmental Cttee on Teaching of Russian in Schools, 1960; Academic Planning Bd, Univ. of Essex, 1965-70; Cttee on Future of Broadcasting, 1974-77, report published 1977. Member: Academic Adv. Cttee, Brunel Coll., 1966-73; Academic Planning Bd, Univ. of East Anglia, 1964-71; Public Schools Commn, 1966-70. Chm., Enquiry on the disturbances in Essex Univ. (report published 1974). Sen. Fellow Eton Coll., 1956-66. Governor: Stowe Sch., 1945-66; Queen Mary Coll., London, 1956-60. Trustee: Churchill Coll., 1958-76; British Museum, 1963-80. Dir, Royal Opera House, Covent Garden, 1967-78; Gulbenkian Foundation: Mem., Arts Cttee, 1957-64; Chm., Educn Cttee, 1971-76. FRHistS; Fellow, Berkeley Coll., Yale, 1963; Hon. Fellow, UCL, 1968. For. Hon. Mem., Amer. Acad. of Arts and Sciences, 1973. Hon. DLitt: York, Ontario, 1966; New York, 1981; DUniv Essex, 1967; Hon. LLD Pennsylvania, 1980, Le Bas Prize, 1948; Diamond Jubilee Medal, Inst. of Linguists, 1971. Comdr, Royal Order of King George I of the Hellenes (Greece), 1962. *Publications:* Leslie Stephen: his thought and character in relation to his time, 1951 (awarded James Tait Black Memorial Prize, 1951); The Intellectual Aristocracy (in Studies in Social History, a tribute to G. M. Trevelyan, 1956); Kipling's Place in the History of Ideas (in Kipling's Mind and Art, 1964); The Curious Strength of Positivism in English Political Thought, 1959; Roxburgh of Stowe, 1965; articles in Victorian Studies and other periodicals. *Recreation:* writing English prose. *Address:* 16 St John's Wood Road, NW8 8RE. *Club:* Brooks's.

ANNAND, John Angus; Under Secretary, Welsh Office, since 1975; *b* 13 May 1926; *s* of James Annand and Lilias Annand (*née* Smith); *m* 1971, Julia Dawn Hardman. *Educ:* Hillhead High Sch., Glasgow; Glasgow Univ. (MA, 1st Cl. Hons); Brasenose Coll., Oxford (MLitt). Lecturer: Univ. of Ceylon; Univ. of South Australia, 1951-53; Asst Dir, Civil Service Commn, 1953-57; Principal, 1957, Asst Sec., 1967, HM Treasury; Civil Service Dept, 1968; Welsh Office, 1971; Under Sec., Health and Social Work Dept, Welsh Office, 1975; Economic Planning Gp, 1978. *Address:* c/o Welsh Office, Cathays Park, Cardiff CF1 3NQ.

ANNAND, Richard Wallace, VC 1940; DL; Personnel Officer at Finchale Abbey Training Centre for the Disabled, near Durham, 1948-79; late Captain Durham Light Infantry (RARO); *b* 5 Nov. 1914; *s* of Lt-Comdr Wallace Moir Annand, Royal Naval Division (killed Gallipoli 1915), and late Dora Elizabeth Chapman, South Shields; *m* 1940, Shirley Osborne, JP 1957. *Educ:* Pocklington, East Yorks. Staff of National Provincial Bank, 1933-37; commissioned in RNVR 1933 (Tyne and London Divisions); transferred to Durham Light Infantry, Jan. 1938; served in France and Belgium, 1939-40 (wounded, VC). Invalided, Dec. 1948. Hon. Freeman Co. Borough of South Shields, 1940; Hon. Representative of The Officers' Assoc.; DL Co. of Durham, 1956. *Recreations:* Rugby football, golf; interest: general welfare of the deafened. *Address:* Springwell House, Whitesmocks, Durham City DH1 4LL. *Club:* County (Durham).

ANNENBERG, Walter H., KBE (Hon.) 1976; US Ambassador to the Court of St James's, 1969-74; *b* 13 March 1908; *s* of M. L. Annenberg; *m* 1951, Leonore Cohn; one *d. Educ:* Peddie Sch.; Univ. of Pennsylvania. President, Triangle Publications Inc., Philadelphia, Pa; Publisher: Seventeen Magazine; TV Guide; Daily Racing Form. Holds foreign decorations. *Address:* Llanfair Road, Wynnewood, Pa 19096, USA; 250 King of Prussia Road, Radnor, Pa 19088, USA. *Clubs:* White's; Racquet, Rittenhouse (Philadelphia); Lyford Cay (Bahamas); National Press (Washington, DC); Swinley Forest Golf.

ANNESLEY, family name of **Earl Annesley** and **Viscount Valentia.**

ANNESLEY, 10th Earl *cr* 1789; **Patrick Annesley;** Baron Annesley, 1758; Viscount Glerawly, 1766; *b* 12 August 1924; *e s* of 9th Earl Annesley, and of Nora, *y d* of late Walter Harrison; *S* father, 1979; *m* 1947, Catherine, *d* of John Burgess, Edinburgh; four *d. Heir: b* Hon. Philip Harrison Annesley [*b* 29 March 1927; *m* 1951, Florence Eileen, *o d* of late John Arthur Johnston]. *Address:* 35 Spring Rise, Egham, Surrey.

ANNETT, David Maurice, MA; Headmaster of King's School, Worcester, 1959-79; *b* 27 April 1917; *s* of late M. W. Annett and Marguerite, *d* of Rev. W. M. Hobson; *m* 1953, Evelyn Rosemary, *d* of late M. W. Gordon, Headmaster of Wrekin Coll., and *widow* of R. E. Upcott; one *d* (one step-*s* two step-*d*). *Educ:* Haileybury Coll.; Queens' Coll., Cambridge. Head of Classical Dept at Oundle Sch., 1939-53, and Housemaster, 1948-53; Headmaster of Marling Sch., Stroud, 1953-59. Served with 27th Field Regt, RA, in India and Burma (Capt.), 1941-45. *Address:* The Old Shop, Whitbourne, Worcester WR6 5SR. *T:* Knightwick 21727.

ANNIGONI, Pietro, RP; Italian painter; artist in oil, tempera, etching and fresco; *b* Milan, 7 June 1910; *s* of Ricciardo Annigoni, engineer; *m* 1st, Anna

Maggini (d 1969); one s one d; 2nd, 1976, Rosa Segreto. Educ: Accademia delle Belle Arti, Florence. Member of: Accademia di S Luca, Rome; Accademia delle Arti del Disegno, Florence; Academy of Design, New York. Portraits exhibited: (at Nat. Portrait Gallery) The Queen, 1970; (at Royal Academy, London) The Queen (for the Fishmongers' Company), 1955, Dame Margot Fonteyn, 1956, The Duke of Edinburgh (for the Fishmongers' Company), 1957, Maharanee of Jaipur, 1958. Other works: Portrait of Princess Margaret, 1958; The Immaculate Heart of Mary, 1962; The Last Supper, fresco in San Michele Arcangelo, Ponte Buggianese, 1974-75; Glory of St Benedict, fresco at Montecassino, 1978; Scenes of St Benedict's life, fresco in dome of Montecassino Cathedral, 1980-81; frescoes in Basilica del Santo, Padova, 1981-82. Permanent collections showing his works include: Uffizi (Print Room), Florence; Galleria Arte Moderna, Milan; Frescoes: S Martino, Florence; Madonna del Consiglio, Pistoia; Basilica of S Lorenzo, Florence. Exhibitions include: Wildenstein Gall., London, 1954; Royal Academy, 1956; Wildenstein, NY, 1957; Galleries of Fedn of British Artists, 1961; retrospective exhbn, New York and San Francisco, 1969; Arts Unlimited Gall., London, 1971. Has also exhibited in Rome, Turin, Paris, Florence, Milan, etc. Publication: (autobiog.) An Artist's Life, 1977. Address: Borgo degli Albizi 8, Florence, Italy.

ANNING, Raymon Harry, CBE 1982; QPM 1975; HM Inspector of Constabulary for England and Wales, since 1979; b 22 July 1930; s of Frederick Charles Anning and Doris Mabel Anning (née Wakefield); m 1949, Beryl Joan Boxall; one s one d. Educ: Richmond and East Sheen Grammar School. Army (East Surrey Regt and Royal Military Police), 1948-50. Metropolitan Police, 1952-79: Constable to Chief Supt, Divisions and Headquarters, 1952-69; Officer i/c Anguilla Police Unit, W Indies, 1969; Chief Supt i/c Discipline Office, New Scotland Yard, 1970-72; Commander i/c A 10 (Complaints Investigation) Branch, NSY, 1972-75; seconded to Hong Kong Govt, 1974; Dep. Asst Commissioner C (CID) Dept, 1975-78; Inspector of Metropolitan Police (Dep. Asst Comr), 1979. Graduate of Nat. Exec. Inst., FBI Academy, Quantico, Virginia, USA, 1979. Recreations: boating, walking, gardening. Address: Hayes House, The Hayes, Cardiff, Wales CF1 2DU.

ANNIS, David, MD; FRCS; Director, Bioengineering Unit, Department of Surgery, University of Liverpool, since 1969; Science and Engineering Research Council Senior Fellow, since 1981; b 28 Feb. 1921; s of Harold and Gertrude Annis; m 1948, Nesta Roberts; three s one d. Educ: Manchester Grammar Sch.; Univ. of Liverpool. ChM 1953, MD 1959; FRCS 1946. Res. Fellow in Exptl Surgery, Mayo Clinic, Minn., 1949-51. Liverpool University: Sen. Lectr in Surgery, 1951-54; Dir of Studies, Surg. Sci., 1964-69; Consultant Gen. Surgeon, Royal Liverpool Hosp., 1954-81. Member: Biomaterials Sub-Cttee, SRC, 1978-80; Physiolog. Systems and Disorders Bd, MRC, 1980-. Mem. Ct of Examrs, RCS, 1963-69; Examiner in Surgery, Univs of Leeds, Glasgow, Cardiff, Dundee, Liverpool and Lagos. Member, Editorial Committee: Bioengineering Jl, 1980-; British Jl of Surgery, 1965-80. Publications: contribs to: Wells and Kyle, Scientific Foundations of Surgery, 1967, 3rd edn 1982; Cuschieri, Moosa and Giles, Companion to Surgical Practice, 1982; papers on surgical and med. bioengrg subjects in learned jls. Recreation: countryside. Address: Little Hey, Dibbinsdale Road, Bromborough, Merseyside L63 0HQ. T: 051-334 3422.

ANNIS, Francesca; actress; b 1945. Theatre: Royal Shakespeare Company: Romeo and Juliet, 1976; Troilus and Cressida, 1976; Luciana in Comedy of Errors, 1976; Natalya in A Month in the Country, Nat. Theatre, 1981. Films: Penny Gold, 1972; Macbeth, 1973. Television: A Pin to see the Peepshow, 1973; Madame Bovary, 1975; Stronger than the Sun, 1977; The Ragazza, 1978; Lillie (series), 1978. Address: c/o Dennis Selinger, ICM, 22 Grafton Street, W1.

ANNIS, Philip Geoffrey Walter; Deputy Director, National Maritime Museum, since 1979; b 7 Feb. 1936; s of Walter and Lilian Annis; m 1967, Olive, d of Mr & Mrs E. W. A. Scarlett; one s. Educ: Sale Grammar Sch.; Kelsick Grammar Sch., Ambleside; Manchester Univ. FSA 1973; FRHistS 1975. Served RA, 1957-59. Board of Inland Revenue, 1959-62. Joined National Maritime Museum, 1962; Head of Museum Services, 1971. Mem., British Sub-Cttee, Internat. Commn for Maritime History, 1980-. Publications: Naval Swords, 1970; (with Comdr W. E. May) Swords For Sea Service, 1970; articles on the history of naval uniform. Recreations: gardening, walking. Address: c/o National Maritime Museum, Greenwich SE10 9NF. T: 01-858 4422.

ANOUILH, Jean; French dramatic author; b Bordeaux, 23 June 1910; s of François Anouilh and Marie-Magdeleine Soulue; m 1953, Nicole Lançon; one s two d. Educ: Collège Chaptal; Univ. of Paris. Plays include: L'Ermine, 1934 (prod Nottingham, 1955, as The Ermine); Y'avait un prisonnier, 1935; Le Voyageur sans bagages, 1937; Le Bal des Voleurs, 1938 (prod London, 1952, as Thieves' Carnival); La Sauvage, 1938 (prod London, 1957, as Restless Heart); Cavalcade d'Amour, 1941; Le Rendez-vous de Senlis, 1942: Léocadia, 1942 (prod London, 1954, as Time Remembered); Eurydice, 1942 (prod London as Point of Departure, 1950); Humulus le Muet (in collaboration with Jean Aurenche), 1945; Oreste, 1945; Antigone, 1946 (prod London, 1949); Jézébel, 1946; Roméo et Jeannette, 1946 (prod London, 1949, as Fading Mansion); Médée, 1946; L'Invitation au château, 1948 (prod London, 1950, 1968, as Ring Round the Moon); Ardèle ou la Marguerite, 1949; La Répétition, ou l'amour puni, 1950 (prod Edinburgh Festival 1957, and

London, 1961); Colombe, 1950 (prod London, 1951); La Valse des toréadors, 1952 (prod London, 1956); L'Alouette, 1953 (prod London, 1955, as The Lark); Ornifle, 1955; L'Hurluberlu, 1959 (prod Chichester and London, 1966, as The Fighting Cock); La Foire d'Empoigne, 1960; Becket (prod London, 1961); La Grotte, 1961 (prod London, 1965, as The Cavern); Poor Bitos (prod London, 1963-64); Le Boulanger, la Boulangère et le Petit Mitson, 1968; Cher Antoine, 1969; Les Poissons Rouges, 1969; Ne Réveillez Pas, Madame, 1970; Tu étais si gentil quand tu étais petit, 1974; L'arrestation, 1975; Le Scénario, 1976; Chers Zoiseaux, 1976; Vive Henri IV, 1977; La Culotte, 1978; Le Nombril, 1981. Films include: Monsieur Vincent (awarded Grand Prix du Cinéma Français); Pattes blanches; Caprice de Caroline, etc. Address: c/o Les Editions de la Table Ronde, 40 rue du Bac, 75007 Paris, France.

ANSCOMBE, Gertrude Elizabeth Margaret, FBA 1967; Professor of Philosophy, University of Cambridge, since 1970; Fellow, New Hall, Cambridge, since 1970; b 1919; d of Allen Wells Anscombe and Gertrude Elizabeth Anscombe (née Thomas); m 1941, Prof. Peter Thomas Geach, qv; three s four d. Educ: Sydenham High Sch.; St Hugh's Coll., Oxford (Schol.); Newnham Coll., Cambridge. 2nd cl. Hon. Mods 1939, 1st cl. Greats 1941, Oxford. Research studentships, Oxford and Cambridge, 1941-44; research fellowships, Somerville Coll., Oxford, 1946-64; Fellow, Somerville Coll., 1964-70, Hon. Fellow, 1970-; Hon. Fellow, St Hugh's Coll., Oxford, 1972. For. Hon. Mem., Amer. Acad. of Arts and Sciences, 1979. Ehrenkreuz Pro Litteris et Artibus (Austria). Publications: Intention, 1957; An Introduction to Wittgenstein's Tractatus, 1959; (with Peter Geach) Three Philosophers, 1961; Collected Papers: 1, Parmenides to Wittgenstein, 2, Metaphysics and the Philosophy of Mind, 3, Ethics, Religion and Politics, 1981; translator and co-editor of posthumous works of Ludwig Wittgenstein. Address: New Hall, Cambridge.

ANSELL, Dr Barbara Mary, CBE 1982; Consultant Physician (Rheumatology), Canadian Red Cross Memorial Hospital, Taplow, since 1962; Head of Division of Rheumatology, Clinical Research Centre, Northwick Park Hospital, Harrow, since 1976; b 30 Aug. 1923. Educ: Kings High Sch. for Girls, Warwick; Birmingham Univ. (MD 1969). MRCP 1951, FRCP 1967. Former Mem., Cttee for the Review of Medicines. Member: British Assoc. for Rheumatism and Rehabilitation (former Mem. Council); Arthritis and Rheumatism Council (former Chm., Educn Cttee); Heberden Soc. (Past Pres.). Hon. Member: Amer. Coll. of Physicians; American, Australian, Finnish, French, German and South African Rheumatism Associations; Spanish Soc. of Rheumatology. Editor, Medicine, 1974, 1976, 1978-79. Publications: (ed) Clinics in Rheumatic Diseases, 1976; (ed jtly) Surgical Management of Juvenile Chronic Polyarthritis, 1978; Rheumatic Disorders in Childhood, 1980. Recreations: travelling, cooking. Address: Dumgoyne, Templewood Lane, Stoke Poges, Bucks SL2 4BG. T: Fulmer 2321. Club: Royal Society of Medicine.

ANSELL, Sir Michael Picton, Kt 1968; CBE 1951; DSO 1944; DL; First President/Chairman, British Equestrian Federation, 1972-76; Show Director, Royal International Horse Show, and Horse of the Year Show, 1949-75; b 26 March 1905; s of Lieut-Col G. K. Ansell and K. Cross; m 1st, 1936, Victoria Jacintha Fleetwood Fuller (d 1969); two s one d; 2nd, 1970, Eileen (née Stanton) (d 1971), widow of Maj.-Gen. Roger Evans, CB, MC. Educ: Wellington; RMC Sandhurst. Gazetted 5th Royal Inniskilling Dragoon Guards, 1924, Col. 1957-62. War of 1939-45: Lieut-Col to command 1st Lothian & Border Yeo., 1940 (severely wounded and prisoner, 1940); discharged disabled, 1944. Chairman: British Show Jumping Assoc., 1945-64, 1970-71 (Pres., 1964-66); (first) British Horse Soc., 1963-72 (Hon. Dir, British Horse Soc., 1952-73). Yeoman, Worshipful Co. of Saddlers, 1963; Freeman: Worshipful Co. of Farriers, 1962, Worshipful Co. of Loriners, 1962. Mem. Council, St Dunstan's, 1958- (a Vice-Pres., 1970, Vice-Chm., 1975-77, Pres., 1977-). DL 1966, High Sheriff 1967, Devon. Chevalier, Order of Leopold, Belgium, 1932; Commander's Cross, Order of Merit, German Federal Republic, 1975; Olympic Order, Silver, IOC, 1977. Publications: Soldier On (autobiog.), 1973; Riding High, 1974; Leopold, the Story of My Horse, 1980. Recreations: show jumping (International, 1931-39), polo International, fishing. Address: Pillhead House, Bideford, N Devon. T: Bideford 2574. Club: Cavalry and Guards.

ANSON, family name of **Earl of Lichfield.**

ANSON, Viscount; Thomas William Robert Hugh Anson; b 19 July 1978; s and heir of Earl of Lichfield, qv.

ANSON, Vice-Adm. Edward Rosebery, FRAeS 1982; Chief of Staff to C-in-C Fleet, since 1982; b 11 May 1929; s of Ross Rosebery Anson and Ethel Jane (née Green); m 1960, Rosemary Anne Radcliffe; one s one d. Educ: Prince of Wales Sch., Nairobi, Kenya; BRNC, Dartmouth; Empire Test Pilots Sch., Farnborough (grad. 1957). Served, 1953-64: Naval Air Sqdns, and 700X and 700Z Flts (Blackburn Aircraft Ltd, 1959-61); comd HMS Eskimo, 1964-66; Commander (Air): RNAS Lossiemouth, 1967-68; HMS Eagle, 1969-70; comd Inter Service Hovercraft Trials Unit, 1971; Naval and Air Attaché, Tokyo and Seoul, 1972-74; comd HMS Juno and Captain F4, 1974-76; comd HMS Ark Royal, 1976-78; Flag Officer, Naval Air Command, 1979-82. Recreations: walking, golf, tennis, photography. Address: c/o Lloyds Bank Ltd, High Street, Yeovil, Somerset.

ANSON, John, CB 1981; Economic Minister, British Embassy, Washington, and UK Executive Director, IMF and IBRD, since 1980; *b* 3 Aug. 1930; *yr s* of Sir Edward Anson, 6th Bt, and of Dowager Lady Anson; *m* 1957, Myrica Fergie-Woods; two *s* two *d. Educ:* Winchester; Magdalene Coll., Cambridge. Served in HM Treasury, 1954-68; Financial Counsellor, British Embassy, Paris, 1968-71; Asst Sec., 1971-72, Under-Sec., 1972-74, Cabinet Office; Under-Sec., 1974-77, Dep. Sec., 1977-79, HM Treasury. *Address:* 18 Church Road, Barnes, SW13 9HN. *T:* 01-748 5079.
See also Sir Peter Anson, Bt.

ANSON, Malcolm Allinson; Chairman, Wessex Water Authority, since 1982; Member, National Water Council, since 1982; Director, National Westminster Bank Ltd, since 1981; *b* 23 April 1924; *s* of Sir (George) Wilfrid Anson, MBE, MC, and Dinah Maud Lilian Anson (*née* Bourne); *m* 1950, Isabel Alison Valerie Lothian, *d* of late Sir Arthur Lothian, KCIE, CSI; three *s* one *d. Educ:* Winchester; Trinity College, Oxford (MA). War Service, Royal Horse Artillery, 1943-46. Joined Imperial Tobacco Co. (of GB & Ireland) Ltd, 1948; Dir, 1968; Dep. Chm., Imperial Gp Ltd, 1979-80, Chm. 1980-81. Dir, Bristol Waterworks Co., 1981-82. Chairman: Bristol Assoc. of Youth Clubs, 1963-71; Endeavour Training, 1969-76. Pres., Colston Res. Soc., 1982-83. Dir, Oxford Univ. Business Summer Sch., 1966; Chm., Careers Adv. Bd, Bristol Univ., 1971-; Vice-Chm., Clifton Coll. Council, 1978-; Dir, Ullswater Outward Bound Mountain Sch., 1971-. High Sheriff of Avon, 1977-78. Master, Society of Merchant Venturers, Bristol, 1979-80. *Recreations:* ski-ing, sailing, shooting, golf. *Address:* Hill Court, Congresbury, Bristol BS19 5AD. *T:* Yatton 832117. *Club:* Cavalry and Guards.

ANSON, Rear-Adm. Sir Peter, 7th Bt, *cr* 1831; CB 1974; CEng, FIERE; Divisional Manager, Satellites, Marconi Space and Defence Systems Ltd, since 1977; *b* 31 July 1924; *er s* of Sir Edward R. Anson, 6th Bt, and Alison, *o d* of late Hugh Pollock; *S* father 1951; *m* 1955, Elizabeth Audrey, *o d* of late Rear-Adm. Sir Philip Clarke, KBE, CB, DSO; two *s* two *d. Educ:* RNC, Dartmouth. Joined RN 1938; Lieut 1944. Served War of 1939-45, HMS Prince of Wales, HMS Exeter. Lieut-Comdr, 1952; Comdr 1956. Commanding Officer, HMS Alert, 1957-58; Staff of RN Tactical Sch., Woolwich, 1959-61; Commanding Officer, HMS Broadsword, 1961-62; Captain, 1963; Director Weapons, Radio (Naval), 1965-66 (Dep. Director, 1963-65); CO HMS Naiad and Captain (D) Londonderry Squadron, 1966-68; Captain, HM Signal School, 1968-70; Commodore, Commander Naval Forces Gulf, 1970-72; ACDS (Signals), 1972-74, retired 1975. Chm., UK Industrial Space Cttee, 1980-82. FIERE 1972. Mem., Inst. of Advanced Motorists. *Heir: s* Philip Roland Anson, *b* 4 Oct. 1957. *Address:* Rosefield, Rowledge, Farnham, Surrey. *T:* Frensham 2724. *Club:* Pratt's.
See also John Anson.

ANSTEY, Edgar, MA, PhD; Deputy Chief Scientific Officer, Civil Service Department, and Head of Behavioural Sciences Research Division, 1969-77; *b* 5 March 1917; British; *s* of late Percy Lewis Anstey and Dr Vera Anstey; *m* 1939, Zoë Lilian Robertson; one *s. Educ:* Winchester Coll.; King's Coll, Cambridge. Assistant Principal, Dominions Office, 1938; Private Sec. to Duke of Devonshire, 1939. 2nd Lieut Dorset Regt, 1940; Major, War Office (DSP), 1941. Founder-Head of Civil Service Commission Research Unit, 1945; Principal, Home Office, 1951; Senior Principal Psychologist, Min. of Defence, 1958; Chief Psychologist, Civil Service Commn, 1964-69. *Publications:* Interviewing for the Selection of Staff (with Dr E. O. Mercer), 1956; Staff Reporting and Staff Development, 1961; Committees-How they work and how to work them, 1962; Psychological Tests, 1966; The Techniques of Interviewing, 1968; (with Dr C. A. Fletcher and Dr. J. Walker) Staff Appraisal and Development, 1976; An Introduction to Selection Interviewing, 1978; articles in Brit. Jl of Psychology, Occupational Psychology, etc. *Recreations:* fell-walking, surfing, golf, bridge. *Address:* Sandrock, Higher Tristram, Polzeath, Wadebridge, Cornwall PL27 6TF. *T:* Trebetherick 3324. *Club:* Royal Commonwealth Society.

ANSTEY, Edgar (Harold Macfarlane), OBE 1969; Documentary Film Producer, Lecturer and Critic; *b* 16 Feb. 1907; *s* of Percy Edgar Macfarlane Anstey and Kate Anstey (*née* Clowes); *m* 1949, Daphne Lilly, Canadian film-maker; one *s* one *d. Educ:* Watford Grammar Sch. Empire Marketing Board Film Unit, 1931; associated with Grierson group in develt of sociological and scientific documentaries, 1931-; organised Shell Film Unit, 1934; March of Time: London Dir of Productions, later Foreign Editor, NY, 1936-38. Produced wartime films for Ministries and Services, 1940-46. Film planning and prod. for BOAC, for oil industry in Venezuela and for CO in WI, 1946-49; rep. short films on Cinematograph Films Council, 1947-49; org. and acted as producer-in-charge, British Transport Films, 1949-74. Formerly film critic of The Spectator; regular mem., BBC Radio programme The Critics. Chairman: Brit. Film Acad., 1956; and again (with Soc. of Film and Television Arts), 1967; Pres., Internat. Scientific Film Assoc., 1961-63; Mem. Council RCA, 1963-74 (Sen. Fellow, 1970); led British cultural delegns to USSR, 1964, 1966; Pres., British Industrial and Scientific Film Assoc., 1974-81 (Chm., 1969-70); Chm., Children's Film Foundn Production Cttee, 1981-; Governor, British Film Inst., 1965-75. Hon. Fellow, British Kinematograph Soc., 1974. *Notable films include:* Housing Problems, 1935; Enough to Eat?, 1936; Journey into Spring, 1957 (British Film Acad. and Venice Award); Terminus, 1961 (British Film Acad. and Venice Award); Between the Tides, 1958 (Venice Award); Wild Wings, 1965 (Hollywood Oscar). *Publication:* The Development of Film Technique in Britain (Experiment in the Film),

1948. *Recreations:* formerly football, tennis and walking, now mental exercising with students of Temple University. *Address:* 6 Hurst Close, Hampstead Garden Suburb, NW11. *T:* 01-455 2385. *Club:* Savile.

ANSTEY, Brig. Sir John, Kt 1975; CBE 1946; TD; DL; President and Chairman, National Savings Committee, 1975-78 (a Vice-Chairman, 1968-75); retired as Chairman and Managing Director, John Player & Sons; Director, Imperial Tobacco Co., Ltd, 1949-67; *b* 3 Jan. 1907; *s* of late Major Alfred Anstey, Matford House, Exeter, Devon; *m* 1935, Elizabeth Mary, *d* of late William Garnett, Backwell, Somerset; one *s* one *d. Educ:* Clifton; Trinity Coll., Oxford. Served War of 1939-45: N Africa, France, SEAC (despatches); Lt-Col 1944; Brig. 1944. Mem. Council, Nottingham Univ. (Treasurer, 1979-81; Pro-Chancellor, 1981-); Member: (part-time) East Midlands Gas Board, 1968-72; Univ. Authorities Panel, 1979-. Governor, Clifton Coll. Mem. Council, The Queen's Silver Jubilee Appeal, 1976. High Sheriff of Nottinghamshire, 1967; DL Notts 1970. Hon. LLD Nottingham, 1975. Legion of Honour; Croix de Guerre (France); Legion of Merit (USA). *Address:* West Wing, Norwood Park, Southwell, Notts NG25 0PB.

ANSTEY, Sidney Herbert; HM Diplomatic Service, retired; Consul-General, Atlanta, 1968-70; *b* 4 June 1910; *m* 1937, Winifred Mary Gray; three *s* one *d.* Foreign Office, 1940-49; Vice-Consul, Nantes, 1950; First Sec. and Consul, Port-au-Prince, 1951; Belgrade, 1952; Vienna, 1953; Dep. Finance Officer, Foreign Office, 1957; First Sec., Paris, 1960, Counsellor, 1963; Consul, Bilbao, 1965; Consul-Gen., Bilbao, 1966. *Address:* 17 Hambledon Hill, Epsom, Surrey. *T:* Epsom 25989.

ANSTRUTHER, Sir Ralph (Hugo), 7th Bt, *cr* 1694; KCVO 1976 (CVO 1967); MC 1943; DL; Equerry to the Queen Mother since 1959, also Treasurer, since 1961; *b* 13 June 1921; *o s* of late Capt. Robert Edward Anstruther, MC, The Black Watch, *o s* of 6th Bt; *S* grandfather, 1934. *Educ:* Eton; Magdalene Coll., Cambridge (BA). Major, RARO Coldstream Gds. Served Malaya, 1950 (despatches). Mem. Queen's Body Guard for Scotland (Royal Co. of Archers). DL Fife, 1960, Caithness-shire, 1965. *Heir: cousin,* Ian Fife Campbell Anstruther, Capt. late Royal Corps of Signals [*b* 11 May 1922; *m* 1st, 1951, Honor (marr. diss., 1963), *er d* of late Capt. Gerald Blake, MC; one *d* ; 2nd, 1963, Susan Margaret Walker, *e d* of H. St J. B. Paten; two *s* three *d*]. *Address:* Balcaskie, Pittenweem, Fife; Watten, Caithness.
See also Sir T. D. Erskine.

ANSTRUTHER - GOUGH - CALTHORPE, Brig. Sir Richard (Hamilton), 2nd Bt *cr* 1929; CBE 1946 (OBE 1940); DL; JP, CA; Croix de Guerre, 1947; Hon. LLD Birmingham 1950; MA (Cantab); *b* 28 March 1908; *o s* of Sir FitzRoy Anstruther-Gough-Calthorpe, 1st Bt; *S* father 1957; *m* 1939, Nancy Moireach (*d* 1976), *o d* of late Vernon Austen Malcolmson, MA, JP, Aston Bury, Stevenage, Herts; two *s* (and one *s* decd). *Educ:* Harrow; Magdalene Coll., Cambridge (MA). 2nd Lieut Royal Scots Greys, 1930, Captain, 1938. Served War of 1939-45, Norway and Middle East; Dep. Director Military Operations, War Office, 1944-47; retd 1947. Director: Rowton Hotels Ltd, 1958-79; Lloyds Bank Ltd, 1972-78. CC 1949, JP 1950, DL 1955, CA 1956, Chm. CC 1967-74, Hants; Chm., Hants Local Govt Reorganisation Jt Cttee, 1972-73. *Heir: g s* Euan Hamilton Anstruther-Gough-Calthorpe, *b* 22 June 1966. *Address:* Elvetham Farm House, Hartley Wintney, Hants. *T:* Hartley Wintney 2117. *Clubs:* Royal Yacht Squadron; Warwickshire County Cricket.
See also Baron Luke.

ANSTRUTHER-GRAY, family name of **Baron Kilmany.**

ANTCLIFFE, Kenneth Arthur; Director of Education, City of Liverpool, since 1975. *Address:* Education Offices, 14 Sir Thomas Street, Liverpool. *T:* 051-236 5480.

ANTHONY, Metropolitan, of Sourozh; Head of the Russian Orthodox Patriarchal Church in Great Britain and Ireland (Diocese of Sourozh); *né* André Borisovich Bloom; *b* Lausanne, Switzerland, 19 June 1914; *o c* of Boris Edwardovich Bloom (Russian Imperial Diplomatic Service) and Xenia Nikolaevna Scriabin (sister of the composer Alexander Scriabin). *Educ:* Lycée Condorcet and Sorbonne, Paris. Dr of Med., Sorbonne, 1943. Army service, med. corps French Army and Resistance, 1939-45. Gen. Practitioner, 1945-49. Took monastic vows, 1943; Priest, Russian Orthodox Church in Paris, 1948; Chaplain to Fellowship of St Alban and St Sergius, London, 1949-50; Vicar, Russian Orthodox Church of St Philip, London, 1950; apptd Hegumen, 1953, Archimandrite, 1956; consecrated Bishop of Sergievo, Suffragan Bishop, Exarchate of Western Europe, 1957; Archbishop of Sourozh, 1960, acting Exarch, 1962-65; Metropolitan of Sourozh and Exarch of the Patriarch of Moscow and All Russia in Western Europe, 1965-74. Member: Ecumenical Commn of Russian Orthodox Church; Central Cttee and Christian Medical Commn of World Council of Churches, 1968. Hulsean Preacher, Cambridge, 1972-73; Preacher, Lambeth Conf., 1978; Firth Lectures, Nottingham Univ., 1982; Eliot Lectures, Kent Univ., 1982; Constantinople Lecture, 1982. Médaille de Bronze de la Société d'encouragement au bien (France), 1945; Browning Award (for spreading of the Christian gospel), USA, 1974. Orders of: St Vladimir 1st Cl. (Russia), 1962; St Andrew (Ecumenical Patriarchate), 1963; St Sergius (Russia), 1977. Lambeth Cross, 1975. Hon. DD (Aberdeen), 1973. *Publications:* Living Prayer, 1965; School for Prayer, 1970; God and Man, 1971; Meditations on a Theme, 1972; Courage to Pray, 1973. *Address:* Russian Orthodox Cathedral, Ennismore Gardens, SW7. *T:* 01-584 0096.

ANTHONY, C. L.; see Smith, Dodie.

ANTHONY, Rt. Hon. Douglas; see Anthony, Rt Hon. J. D.

ANTHONY, Evelyn; author; *b* 3 July 1928; *d* of Christian Stephens and Elizabeth (*née* Sharkey); *g g d* of Henry Stephens, inventor of Stephens Ink; *m* 1955, Michael Ward Thomas; four *s* two *d*. *Educ:* Convent of Sacred Heart, Roehampton. *Publications:* Imperial Highness, 1953; Curse Not the King, 1954; Far Fly the Eagles, 1955; Anne Boleyn, 1956 (US Literary Guild Award); Victoria, 1957 (US Literary Guild Award); Elizabeth, 1959; Charles the King, 1961; Clandara, 1963; The Heiress, 1964; Valentina, 1965; The Rendezvous, 1967; Anne of Austria, 1968; The Legend, 1969; The Assassin, 1970; The Tamarind Seed, 1971; The Poellenberg Inheritance, 1972; The Occupying Power, 1973 (Yorkshire Post Best Novel); The Malaspiga Exit, 1974; The Persian Ransom, 1975; The Silver Falcon, 1977; The Return, 1978; The Grave of Truth, 1979; The Defector, 1980; The Plumed Serpent, 1981; Albatross, 1982. *Recreations:* racing (National Hunt), three-day eventing with her children, riding, gardening, going to sale rooms, preferably Christie's. *Address:* c/o M. Ward Thomas, Selection Trust Building, Mason's Avenue, EC2.

ANTHONY, Rt. Hon. (John) Douglas, CH 1982; PC 1971; MEC 1963; MP, Parliament of Australia, since 1957; Leader, National Country Party of Australia (formerly Australian Country Party), since 1971; Deputy Prime Minister, and Minister for Trade and Resources, since 1975; *b* 31 Dec. 1929; *s* of late H. L. Anthony; *m* 1957, Margot Macdonald Budd; two *s* one *d*. *Educ:* Murwillumbah Primary and High Schs, The King's Sch., Parramatta; Queensland Agricultural Coll. (QDA). Minister for Interior, 1964; Dep. Leader, Australian Country Party, 1966-71; Minister for Primary Industry, 1967-71; Dep. Prime Minister and Minister for Trade and Industry, 1971-72; Minister for Overseas Trade, Minerals and Energy, Nov.-Dec. 1975. *Recreations:* golf, tennis, fishing, swimming. *Address:* Parliament House, Canberra, ACT 2600, Australia. *T:* 733296. *Club:* Union (Sydney).

ANTHONY, Sir Mobolaji B.; see Bank-Anthony.

ANTHONY, Ronald Desmond; Chief Inspector of Nuclear Installations and Director, Hazardous Installations Group, Health and Safety Executive, since 1981; *b* 21 Nov. 1925; *s* of William Arthur Anthony and Olive Frances Anthony (*née* Buck); *m* 1948, Betty Margaret Croft; four *d*. *Educ:* Chislehurst and Sidcup Grammar School; City and Guilds Coll., Imperial Coll. of Science and Technology (BSc, ACGI). CEng, FIMechE, MRAeS. Vickers Armstrongs (Supermarine), 1950; Nuclear Power Plant Co., 1957; Inspectorate of Nuclear Installations, 1960; Deputy Chief Inspector, 1973; Dir, Safety Policy Div., Health and Safety Exec., 1977. *Publications:* papers in technical journals. *Recreations:* gardening, golf. *Address:* 3 Mereside, Orpington, Kent BR6 8ET. *T:* Farnborough (Kent) 57565.

ANTHONY, Vivian Stanley; Headmaster, Colfe's School, London, since 1976; *b* 5 May 1938; *s* of Captain and Mrs A. S. Anthony; *m* 1969, Rosamund Anne MacDermot Byrn; one *s* one *d*. *Educ:* Cardiff High Sch.; LSE (1st Div. 2nd Cl. Hons BSc Econs); Fitzwilliam Coll., Cambridge (DipEd); Merton Coll., Oxford (schoolmaster student). Asst Master, Leeds Grammar Sch., 1960-64; Asst Master and Housemaster, Tonbridge Sch., 1964-69; Lectr in Educn, Univ. of Leeds, 1969-71; Dep. Headmaster, The King's Sch., Macclesfield, 1971-76. Asst Examr, Econ. Hist., London Univ., 1964-71; Asst Examr, Econs, Oxford and Cambridge Bd, 1970-76, Chief Examr (Awarder), Econs, 1976-; Ext. Examr, Educn, Univs of Manchester, 1972-75, Birmingham, 1975-78, and Lancaster, 1977-79. Chm., Econs Assoc., 1974-77; Mem., Schools Council Social Science Cttee, 1976-79; elected Headmasters' Conf., 1980-. *Publications:* Monopoly, 1968, 3rd edn 1976; Overseas Trade, 1969, 4th edn 1981; Banks and Markets, 1970, 3rd edn 1979; (contrib.) The Teaching of Economics in Secondary Schools, 1970; Objective Tests in A Level Economics, 1971, 2nd edn 1974; (contrib.) Curriculum Development in Secondary Schools, 1973; (contrib.) Control of the Economy, 1974; Objective Tests in Introductory Economics, 1975, 3rd edn 1983; History of Rugby Football at Colfe's, 1980; articles in Economics. *Recreations:* choral singing (Thomas Tallis Society, Dyfed Choir), Rugby football, squash, tennis. *Address:* Lincoln Lodge, Pines Road, Bickley, Kent BR1 2AA. *T:* 01-852 2283. *Clubs:* East India, Devonshire, Sports and Public Schools, Old Colfeians Association.

ANTICO, Sir Tristan, Kt 1973; Managing Director, Pioneer Concrete Services Ltd; Company Director; *b* 25 March 1923; *s* of Terribile Giovani Antico and Erminia Bertin; *m* 1950, Dorothy Brigid Shields; three *s* four *d*. *Educ:* Sydney High Sch. Began career as Accountant; subseq. became Company Secretary, Melocco Bros; Founder of Pioneer Concrete Services Ltd. Knighthood awarded for services to industry and the community in New South Wales. Comdr, Order of Star of Solidarity (Italy), 1967. *Recreations:* horse racing, yachting, boating. *Address:* 161 Raglan Street, Mosman, NSW 2088, Australia. *T:* 969 4070. *Clubs:* Tattersall's, Australian Jockey, Sydney Turf, American National, Royal Sydney Yacht Squadron, Royal Motor Yacht Squadron (all in Sydney).

ANTON, Alexander Elder, CBE 1973; FRSE 1977; FBA 1972; Full-time Member, Scottish Law Commission, since 1973 (part-time Member, 1966-73); *b* 1922; *m* 1949, Doris May Lawrence; one *s*. *Educ:* Aberdeen Univ. (MA, LLB with dist.). Solicitor, 1949; Lectr, Aberdeen, 1953-59; Prof. of Jurisprudence,

Univ. of Glasgow, 1959-73. Literary Dir, Stair Soc., 1960-66. *Publications:* Private International Law, 1967; (co-ed) Amos and Walton's Introduction to French Law, 3rd edn, 1966; contribs to legal and historical jls. *Recreation:* hill walking. *Address:* 41 Braid Farm Road, Edinburgh EH10 6LE.

ANTONIO; see Ruiz Soler, Antonio.

ANTONIONI, Michelangelo; Film Director; *b* Ferrara, Italy, 29 Sept. 1912; *s* of Ismaele and Elisabetta Roncagli; *m* (marr. diss.). *Educ:* degree in Economics and Commerce, Univ. of Bologna. Formerly an Asst Dir, Film Critic to newspapers, and Script Writer. Films directed include: 8 documentaries, etc, 1943-50; subseq. long films: Cronaca di un Amore, 1950; one episode in Amore in Città, 1951; I Vinti, 1952; La Signora Senza Camelie, 1953; Le Amiche, 1955; Il Grido, 1957; L'Avventura, 1959-60; La Notte, 1961; L'Eclisse, 1962; Il Deserto Rosso, 1964; one episode in I Tre Volti, 1965; Blow-Up, 1967; Zabriskie Point, 1969; Chung Kuo-China, 1972; The Passenger, 1974; Il Mistero di Oberwald, 1979; Identificazione di una Donna, 1981. *Recreations:* collecting blown glass, tennis, ping-pong. *Address:* Via Vincenzo Tiberio 18, Rome, Italy.

ANTRIM, 14th Earl of, *cr* 1620; **Alexander Randal Mark McDonnell;** Viscount Dunluce; Keeper of Conservation, Tate Gallery, since 1975 (Restorer, 1965-75); *b* 3 Feb. 1935; *er s* of 13th Earl of Antrim, KBE, and of Angela Christina, *d* of Sir Mark Sykes, 6th Bt; *S* father, 1977 (but continues to be known as Viscount Dunluce); *m* 1963, Sarah Elizabeth Anne (marr. diss. 1974), 2nd *d* of St John Harmsworth; one *s* two *d*; *m* 1977, Elizabeth, *d* of Michael Moses Sacher, *qv*; one *d*. *Educ:* Downside; Christ Church, Oxford; Ruskin Sch. of Art. Restorer, the Ulster Museum, 1969-71. *Recreations:* painting, vintage cars. *Heir: s* Hon. Randal Alexander St John McDonnell, *b* 2 July 1967. *Address:* Glenarm Castle, Glenarm, Co. Antrim, N Ireland. *T:* Glenarm 229; 35 Durand Gardens, Stockwell, SW9. *Club:* Beefsteak.

ANTROBUS, Maurice Edward, CMG 1943; OBE 1938; *b* 20 July 1895; *er s* of late Sir Reginald Antrobus and late Dame Edith Antrobus, DBE; *m* 1929, Betty (*d* 1982), *er d* of late Sir Llewelyn Dalton; two *s*. *Educ:* Winchester; Trinity Coll., Cambridge (Exhibitioner). BA 1920; served European War, 1914-19, KRRC (wounded twice); Asst Principal, Colonial Office, 1920; Private Sec. to Governor of Ceylon, 1927-30; Principal Dominions Office, 1930; Political Sec., Office of UK High Comr in Union of S Africa, 1935-39; Asst Sec., Colonial Office, 1939; Principal Sec., Office of UK Representative to Eire, 1939-41; Official Sec., Office of UK High Comr in Commonwealth of Australia, 1941-44; Official Sec., Office of UK High Commissioner in New Zealand, 1944-45; Asst Sec., Commonwealth Relations Office, 1945; retd 1955. *Recreations:* golf, gardening. *Address:* Yaffles, Ashdown Road, Forest Row, East Sussex RH18 5BN. *T:* Forest Row 2159. *Club:* Royal Ashdown Forest Golf (Forest Row).

ANTROBUS, Sir Philip Coutts, 7th Bt, *cr* 1815; *b* 10 April 1908; *s* of late Geoffrey Edward Antrobus and Mary Atherstone, *d* of Hilton Barber, JP, Halesowen, Cradock, Cape Province; *S* cousin, 1968; *m* 1st, 1937, Dorothy Margaret Mary (*d* 1973), *d* of late Rev. W. G. Davis; two *s* one *d*; 2nd, 1975, Doris Primrose, *widow* of Ralph Dawkins. Served War, 1939-45 (POW). *Heir: s* Edward Philip Antrobus [*b* 28 Sept. 1938; *m* 1966, Janet, *d* of Philip Sceales; one *s* two *d*]. *Address:* West Amesbury House, West Amesbury, near Salisbury, Wilts.

ANWAR, Mohamed Samih; Order of the Republic, 2nd Class (Egypt), 1958; Order of Merit, 1st Class (Egypt), 1968; *b* 10 Dec. 1924; *s* of Ahmed Fouad Anwar and Aziza Tewfik; *m* 1953, Omayma Soliman Hazza; one *s* one *d*. *Educ:* Cairo Univ. (Bachelor of Law, 1945). Min. of Justice, 1946-54; First Sec., Min. of Foreign Affairs, 1954; apptd to Egyptian Embassies in Moscow, 1957, and London, 1963; Ambassador to Kuwait, 1966; Under Sec., Min. of Foreign Affairs, 1968; Ambassador to Iran, 1970; Minister of State for Foreign Affairs, 1974; Ambassador to UK, 1975-79. Order of Hamayon, 1st Cl. (Iran), 1974; Order of the Flag (Yugoslavia), 1970. *Recreations:* rowing, tennis. *Address:* Ministry of Foreign Affairs, Cairo, Egypt. *Clubs:* Royal Automobile, Hurlingham; Al Ahly (Cairo).

ANWYL, Shirley Anne, (Mrs R. H. C. Anwyl); see Ritchie, S. A.

ANWYL-DAVIES, Marcus John, MA, QC 1967; **His Honour Judge Anwyl-Davies;** a Circuit Judge, since 1972; *b* 11 July 1923; *s* of late Thomas Anwyl-Davies and of Kathleen Beryl Anwyl-Davies (*née* Oakshott); *m* 1954, Eva Hilda Elisabeth Paulson (marr. diss. 1974); one *s* one *d*. *Educ:* Harrow Sch.; Christ Church, Oxford. Royal Artillery, including service with Hong Kong and Singapore RA, 1942-47 (despatches 1945). Called to Bar, Inner Temple, 1949. Legal Assessor, GMC and GDC, 1969-72; Liaison Judge to Herts Magistrates, 1972. Vice-Pres., Herts Magistrates' Assoc., 1975. Resident Judge, St Albans Crown Court, 1977. *Recreations:* farming, photography. *Club:* Reform.

ANYAOKU, Eleazar Chukwuemeka, (Emeka); Ndichie Chief Adazie of Obosi; Deputy Secretary-General of the Commonwealth, since 1978 (Assistant Secretary-General, 1975-77); *b* 18 Jan. 1933; *s* of late Emmanuel Chukwuemeka Anyaoku, Ononukpo of Okpuno Ire, Obosi, Nigeria, and Cecilia Adiba (*née* Ogbogu); *m* 1962, Ebunola Olubunmi, *yr d* of late barrister Olusola Akanbi Solanke, of Abeokuta, Nigeria; three *s* one *d*. *Educ:* Merchants of Light Sch., Oba; Univ. of Ibadan (Schol.), Nigeria; courses at

Cambridge and Inst. of Public Admin (London); also at Cavillam Inst. (France). Management Trainee, and later Regional Asst, Commonwealth Develt Corp., in London and Lagos, 1959-62. Joined Nigerian Diplomatic Service, 1962; served as Mem. Nigerian Permanent Mission to the UN, New York, 1963-66; seconded to Commonwealth Secretariat as Asst Dir, 1966-71, and Dir, 1971-75, Internat. Affairs Div. Served as Secretary: Review Cttee on Commonwealth inter-governmental organisations, June-Aug., 1966; Commonwealth Observer Team for Gibraltar Referendum, Aug.-Sept., 1967; Anguilla Commn, WI, Jan.-Sept. 1970; (Dep. Conf. Sec.) Meeting of Commonwealth Heads of Govt, in London, 1969, and Singapore, 1971; (Conf. Sec.) Meeting of Commonwealth Heads of Govt, Ottawa, 1973, Jamaica, 1975. Vice-Pres., Royal Commonwealth Society, London, 1975- (Dep. Chm., 1972); Mem., Cttee of Management, London University's Inst. of Commonwealth Studies, 1972-; Chm., Africa Centre, London, 1977-82 (Director, 1971-77); Mem. Council, Overseas Develt Inst., 1979-. *Recreations:* tennis, athletics, swimming, reading. *Address:* Commonwealth Secretariat, Marlborough House, Pall Mall, SW1. *T:* 01-839 3411; Orimili, Obosi, Nigeria. *Clubs:* Royal Commonwealth Society, Africa Centre, Travellers'; Metropolitan (Lagos).

AOTEAROA, Bishop of, since 1981; **Rt. Rev. Whakahuihui Vercoe,** MBE 1970; *b* 4 June 1928; *s* of Joseph and Wyness Vercoe; *m* 1951, Dorothy Eivers; three *s. Educ:* Torere Primary; Feilding Agricultural High School; College House Theological Coll.; Canterbury Univ. Curate, St John's Church, Feilding, 1951-53; Priest-in-Charge, Wellington Pastorate, 1953-54; Pastor: Wairarapa, 1954-57; Rangitikei, 1957-61; Chaplain: Armed Forces, Malaya, 1961-64; Papakura Military Camp, 1964-65; ANZAC Brigade, Vietnam, 1968-69; Burnham Mil. Camp, 1965-71; Principal, Te Waipounamu Girls' School, 1971-76; Vicar: Ohinemutu Pastorate, 1976-78; Te Rohe o Whakaari, 1978-81; Archdeacon of Tairawhiti and Vicar-General to Bishopric of Aotearoa, 1978-81. *Recreations:* Rugby, golf, reading, tennis, cricket, fishing. *Address:* PO Box 146, Rotorua, New Zealand. *T:* (home) 479-241, (office) 86-093.

APEL, Dr Hans Eberhard; Social-democratic Member of Bundestag, since 1965 (Deputy-Chairman of Group, 1969-72); *b* Hamburg, 25 Feb. 1932; *m* 1956, Ingrid Schwingel; two *d. Educ:* Hamburg Univ. Diplom-Volkswirt, 1957, Dr.rer.pol, 1960. Apprentice in Hamburg export and import business, 1951-54; Sec., Socialist Group in European Parlt, 1958-61; Head of Economics, Finance and Transportation Dept of European Parlt, 1962-65. Chm., Bundestag Cttee on Transportation, 1969-72. Mem. Nat. Bd, Social-democratic Party (SPD), 1970-; Parly Sec. of State, Min. for Foreign Affairs, 1972-74; Federal Minister of Finance, 1974-78, of Defence, 1978-82. *Publications:* Edwin Cannan und seine Schüler (Doct. Thesis), 1961; Raumordnung der Bundesrepublik, in: Deutschland 1975, 1964; Europas neue Grenzen, 1964; Der deutsche Parlamentarismus, 1968; Bonn, den . . ., Tagebuch eines Bundestagsabgeordneten, 1972. *Recreations:* sailing, soccer. *Address:* Bundeshaus, Görresstrasse 15, 5300 Bonn, Federal Republic of Germany.

APPEL, Karel Christian; Netherlands Artist (Painter); *b* 25 April 1921; *s* of Jan Appel and Johanna Chevallier. *Educ:* Royal Academy of Art, Amsterdam. Began career as artist in 1938. Has had one-man exhibitions in Europe and America including the following in London: Inst. of Contemporary Art, 1957; Gimpel Fils, 1959, 1960, 1964. UNESCO Prize, Venice Biennale, 1953; Lissone Prize, Italy, 1958; Acquisition Prize, Sao Paulo Biennale, Brazil, 1959; Graphique Internat. Prize, Ljubljana, Jugoslavia, 1959; Guggenheim National Prize, Holland, 1961; Guggenheim International Prize, 1961. *Publications:* Illustrations: De Blijde en Onvoorziene Week, by Hugo Claus, 1950; Atonaal, by Simon Vinkenoog, 1951; De Ronde Kant van de Aarde, by Hans Andreus, 1952; Het Bloed Stroomt Door, by Bert Schierbeek, 1954; Haine, by E. Looten, 1954; Cogne Ciel, by E. Looten, 1954; Rhapsodie de ma Nuit, by E. Looten, 1958; Unteilbare Teil, by André Frénaud, 1960; Een Dier Heeft een Mens Getekend, by B. Schierbeek, 1961. *Address:* c/o Galérie Statler, 51 rue de Seine, Paris, France.

APPLEBY, Brian John, QC 1971; a Recorder of the Crown Court, since 1972; *b* 25 Feb. 1930; *s* of Ernest Joel and Gertrude Appleby; *m* 1958, Rosa Helena (*née* Flitterman); one *s* one *d. Educ:* Uppingham; St John's Coll., Cambridge (BA). Called to Bar, Middle Temple, 1953; Bencher, 1980. Dep. Chm., Notts QS, 1970-71. Mem., Nottingham City Council, 1955-58 and 1960-63. District Referee, Nottinghamshire Wages Conciliation Board, NCB, 1980-. *Recreations:* watching good football (preferably Nottingham Forest). Mem. Club Cttee, 1965-, Vice-Chm., 1972-75, Chm., 1975-78); swimming, reading and enjoying, when possible, company of wife and children. *Address:* The Poplars, Edwalton Village, Notts. *T:* Nottingham 232814.

APPLEBY, Maj.-Gen. David Stanley, CB 1979; MC 1943; TD 1950; Director of Army Legal Services, 1976-78, retired; *b* 4 Dec. 1918; *s* of Stanley Appleby and Mabel Dorothy Mary (*née* Dickson); *m* 1942, Prudence Marianne Chisholm; one *s* one *d* (and one *s* decd). *Educ:* St Peter's School. Barrister, Middle Temple, 1951. Rifleman, London Rifle Bde (TA), 1938; 2nd Lieut, Royal Fusiliers (TA), 1939; Army Legal Services, 1950-; Captain, 1950; Maj.-Gen. 1976. *Recreations:* sailing, military and other history. *Address:* Two Acres, Beechwood Lane, Burley, Ringwood, Hants. *Clubs:* Naval & Military; Island Sailing (Cowes).

APPLEBY, Douglas Edward Marrison; farmer and stockbreeder; retired as Managing Director, The Boots Co. Ltd; *b* 17 May 1929; *s* of late Robert Appleby, MSc and Muriel (*née* Surtees); *m* 1952, June (*née* Marrison), company director; one *s* one *d. Educ:* Durham Johnston Sch.; Univ. of Nottingham. BSc London, BSc Nottingham, 1950. Chartered Accountant, 1957. Commissioned, RAF, 1950-54. Moore, Stephens & Co., Chartered Accountants, London, 1954-57; Distillers Co. Ltd, 1957-58; Corn Products Co., USA, 1959-63; Wilkinson Sword Ltd, 1964-68; The Boots Co Ltd, 1968-81 (Finance Dir, 1968-72, Man. Dir, 1973-81). Member Council: Inst. Chartered Accountants, 1971-75; Loughborough Univ., 1973-75; CBI, 1977-81; Regional Dir, Nat. Westminster Bank, 1979-. *Recreations:* mathematics, flat and National Hunt racing. *Address:* Pond Farm, Upper Broughton, Melton Mowbray, Leics.; West Drums, by Brechin, Angus.

APPLEBY, (Lesley) Elizabeth, (Mrs Michael Kenneth Collins), QC 1979; barrister-at-law; *b* 12 Aug. 1942; *o d* of Arthur Leslie Appleby and late Dorothy Evelyn Appleby (*née* Edwards); *m* 1978, Michael Kenneth Collins; one *s. Educ:* Dominican Convent, Brewood, Staffs; Wolverhampton Girls' High Sch.; Manchester Univ. (LLB Hons). Called to Bar, Gray's Inn, 1965 (Richardson Schol.); *ad eundem* Lincoln's Inn, 1975; in practice at Chancery Bar, 1966-; Member, Senate of Inns of Court and Bar, 1977-80, 1981-82. *Recreations:* hunting, sailing, swimming, music, golf, gardening. *Address:* 4/5 Gray's Inn Square, Gray's Inn, WC1R 5AY. *T:* 01-404 5252; 32 Pembroke Road, W8. *T:* 01-602 4141; King's Lea, King's Saltern Road, Lymington, Hants. *T:* Lymington 76569. *Club:* Royal Lymington Yacht.

APPLEBY, Dom Raphael; National Co-ordinator for RC Chaplains in Higher Education, since 1980; *b* 18 July 1931; *s* of Harold Thompson Appleby and Margaret Morgan. *Educ:* Downside; Christ's Coll., Cambridge (MA). Downside novitiate, 1951. Housemaster at Downside, 1962-75, Head Master, 1975-80. National Chaplain to Catholic Students' Council, 1974. *Recreations:* books, music. *Address:* Downside Abbey, Bath BA3 4RJ.

APPLEBY, Robert, CBE 1969; Chairman, Black & Decker Ltd, 1956-75 (Managing Director, 1956-72); *b* 1913; *s* of Robert James Appleby; *m* 1957, Elisabeth Friederike (*d* 1975), *d* of Prof. Eidmann. *Educ:* Graham Sea Training and Engineering Sch., Scarborough. Dep. Chm., Black & Decker Manufacturing Co., Maryland, 1968-72. Mem., Post Office Bd, 1972-73. CEng, FIProdE; FBIM.

APPLETON, Rt. Rev. George, CMG 1972; MBE 1946; *b* 20 Feb. 1902; *s* of Thomas George and Lily Appleton; *m* 1929, Marjorie Alice (*d* 1980), *d* of Charles Samuel Barrett; one *s* two *d. Educ:* County Boys' School, Maidenhead; Selwyn Coll., Cambridge; St Augustine's Coll., Canterbury. BA Cantab 1924 (2nd Cl. Math. Trip. pt 1, 1st Cl. Theological Trip. pt I); MA 1929. Deacon, 1925; Priest, 1926. Curate, Stepney Parish Church, 1925-27; Missionary in charge SPG Mission, Irrawaddy Delta, 1927-33; Warden, Coll. of Holy Cross, Rangoon, 1933-41; Archdeacon of Rangoon, 1943-46; Director of Public Relations, Government of Burma, 1943-46; Vicar of Headstone, 1947-50; Sec., Conf. of Brit. Missionary Societies, 1950-57; Rector of St Botolph, Aldgate, 1957-62; Archdeacon of London and Canon of St Paul's Cathedral, 1962-63; Archbishop of Perth and Metropolitan of W Australia, 1963-69; Archbishop in Jerusalem and Metropolitan, 1969-74. Buber-Rosenzweig Medal, Council of Christians and Jews, 1975. *Publications:* John's Witness to Jesus, 1955; In His Name, 1956; Glad Encounter, 1959; On the Eightfold Path, 1961; Daily Prayer and Praise, 1962; Acts of Devotion, 1963; One Man's Prayers, 1967; Journey for a Soul, 1974; Jerusalem Prayers, 1974; The Word is the Seed, 1976; The Way of a Disciple, 1979; The Practice of Prayer, 1980; Glimpses of Faith, 1982; Praying with the Bible, 1982. *Address:* 112A St Mary's Road, Oxford OX4 1QF.

APPLEYARD, Leonard Vincent; HM Diplomatic Service; Financial Counsellor, British Embassy, Paris, since 1979; *b* 2 Sept. 1938; *s* of Thomas William Appleyard; *m* 1964, Elizabeth Margaret West; two *d. Educ:* Read School, Drax, W Yorks; Queens' Coll., Cambridge (MA). Foreign Office, 1962; Third Secretary, Hong Kong, 1964; Second Secretary, Peking, 1966; Second, later First, Secretary, Foreign Office, 1969; First Secretary, Delhi 1971, Moscow 1975; HM Treasury, 1978. *Recreations:* music, reading, tennis. *Address:* c/o Foreign and Commonwealth Office, SW1; British Embassy, Paris. *Club:* Brooks's.

APPLEYARD, Raymond Kenelm, PhD; Director-General for Information Market and Innovation, Commission of the European Communities, since 1981; *b* 5 Oct. 1922; *s* of late Maj.-Gen. K. C. Appleyard, CBE, TD, DL, and Monica Mary Louis; *m* 1947, Joan Greenwood; one *s* two *d. Educ:* Rugby; Cambridge. BA 1943, MA 1948, PhD 1950. Instructor, Yale Univ., 1949-51; Fellow, Rockefeller Foundn, California Inst. of Technology, 1951-53; Research Officer, Atomic Energy of Canada Ltd, 1953-56; Sec., UN Scientific Cttee on effects of atomic radiation, 1956-61; Dir, Biology Div., Commn of European Atomic Energy Community, 1961-73; Dir-Gen. for Scientific and Tech. Information and Information Management, EEC Commn, 1973-80; Exec. Sec., European Molecular Biology Organisation, 1965-73; Sec., European Molecular Biology Conf., 1969-73. Hon. Dr.med Ulm, 1977. *Publications:* contribs to: Nature, Jl Gen. Microbiol., Genetics. *Recreations:* bridge, tennis, squash. *Address:* 200 rue de la Loi, 1049 Brussels, Belgium; Bâtiment Jean Monnet, Plateau du Kirchberg, Luxembourg. *Club:* Athenæum.

ap ROBERT, Hywel Wyn Jones; His Honour Judge ap Robert; a Circuit Judge, since 1975; *b* 19 Nov. 1923; *s* of Rev. Robert John Jones, BA, BD and Mrs Jones (*née* Evans); *m* 1956, Elizabeth Davies; two *d. Educ:* Cardiff High Sch.; Corpus Christi Coll., Oxford (MA). War Service, FO and Intell. Corps. 1942-46, in Britain and India. Called to Bar, Middle Temple, 1950. A Recorder of the Crown Court, 1972-75; Stipendiary Magistrate, Cardiff, later S Glamorgan, 1972-75. Contested (Plaid Cymru) Cardiganshire, 1970. Hon. Mem., Gorsedd of the Bards, 1973. *Recreations:* Welsh literature, classical and modern languages. *Address:* Law Courts, Cardiff. *Clubs:* Cardiff and County (Cardiff); Bristol Channel Yacht (Swansea).

APSLEY, Lord; Allen Christopher Bertram Bathurst; *b* 11 March 1961; *s* and *heir* of 8th Earl Bathurst, *qv. Address:* Cirencester Park, Cirencester, Glos GL7 2BT.

APTHORP, John Dorrington; Executive Chairman, Bejam Group plc, since 1968; *b* 25 April 1935; *s* of Eric and Mildred Apthorp; *m* 1959, Jane Frances Arnold; three *s* one *d. Educ:* Aldenham School. FIBM 1977; FInstD 1978; FIGD 1981. Sub-Lieut RNVR, 1953-55. Family business, Appypak, 1956-68; started Bejam Group, 1968-. Guardian Young Business Man of Year, 1974. Liveryman, Butchers' Company, 1974-. Commandeur d'Honneur pour Commanderie du Bontemps de Medoc et des Graves, 1977. *Recreations:* shooting, wine. *Address:* The Field House, Newlands Avenue, Radlett, Herts WD7 8EL. *T:* Radlett 5201. *Club:* St Hubert's.

AQUILECCHIA, Prof. Giovanni; Professor of Italian, University of London, since 1970; *b* Nettuno, Rome, 28 Nov. 1923; *s* of late Gen. Vincenzo Aquilecchia and Maria L. Filibeck; *m* 1951, Costantina M. Bacchetta (marr. diss. 1973); two *s* one *d. Educ:* Liceo T. Tasso, Rome; Univ. of Rome. Dott. Lett., 1946, Diploma di Perfezionamento in Filologia Moderna, 1948, Univ. of Rome. Asst in Italian, Univ. of Rome, 1946-49; Boursier du Gouvernement Français at Collège de France, Univ. of Paris, 1949-50; British Council Scholar, Warburg Inst., Univ. of London, 1950-51; Asst, Dept of Italian Studies, Univ. of Manchester, 1951-53; Asst Lectr in Italian, University Coll., London, 1953-55, Lectr, 1955-59; Libero Docente di Letteratura Italiana, Univ. of Rome, 1958-; Reader in Italian, Univ. of London, at University Coll., 1959-61; Prof. of Italian Lang. and Lit., Univ. of Manchester, 1961-70. Corr. Fellow, Arcadia, 1961. MA (Manchester) 1965. *Publications:* Giordano Bruno, 1971; Schede di italianistica, 1976; critical editions of: Giordano Bruno: La Cena de le Ceneri, 1955; Due Dialoghi sconosciuti, 1957; Dialoghi Italiani, 1958, repr. 1972; Praelectiones geometricæ e Ars deformationum, 1964; De la causa, principio et uno, 1973; Pietro Aretino: Sei Giornate, 1969, 2nd edn with Introduction, 1975, reprint 1980; Giovanni Villani: Cronica con le continuazioni di Matteo e Filippo, 1979; (co-editor) Collected essays on Italian Language and Literature, 1971; contrib.: Atti dell'Accad. Nazionale Lincei, Atti e Memorie dell'Arcadia, Bull. dell'Accad. della Crusca, Bull. John Rylands Library, Cultura Neolatina, Dizionario Biografico degli Italiani, Enciclopedia Dantesca, Encyclopædia Britannica, English Miscellany, Giornale storico della letteratura italiana, Lingua Nostra, Storia della cultura veneta, Studi Secenteschi, Studi Tassiani, etc. *Address:* Department of Italian, Bedford College, Regent's Park, NW1.

ARAGON, Louis; Chevalier de la Légion d'Honneur, 1981; poet; novelist; essayist; *b* 3 Oct. 1897; *m* 1939, Elsa Triolet (*née* Kagan). *Educ:* Faculty of Medicine, Paris Univ. Served European War, 1914-18, Infantry; War of 1939-45, Tank Div., 1939-40 (prisoner, escaped to unoccupied France); one of leaders of intellectual Resistance. Co-founder, 1919, and leader since 1924 of former Surrealist Movement, now Socialistic Realism Movement; founder, 1935, and Sec. of Internat. Assoc. of Writers for Defence of Culture; founder, 1944, and co-director, Editeurs français réunis; Vice-Pres., Assoc. des Ecrivains Combattants, 1945-60. Editor: Les Lettres Françaises, 1944-; Ce Soir, Paris, 1950; Member: Cttee of Dirs, Europe review; Nat. Cttee of Authors, 1958-; Goncourt Academy, 1967-68. Mem., French Communist Party Central Cttee. *Publications:* poems: Feu de joie, 1920; Le mouvement perpétuel, 1925; La grande gaîté; Persécuté persécuteur; Hourra l'Oural, 1934; Le crève-coeur, 1941; Les yeux d'Elsa, 1942; Brocéliande; Le Musée Grévin; La Diane Française, 1945; Les yeux et la mémoire, 1954; Elsa, 1959; Le fou d'Elsa, 1963; *novels:* Anicet ou le panorama, 1921; Le libertinage; Le paysan de Paris, 1926 (trans. as Paris Peasant, 1971); Les cloches de Bâle, 1933; Les beaux quartiers, 1936 (awarded Prix Renardot); Les voyageurs de l'Impériale, 1942; Aurélien, 1945; La Semaine Sainte, 1958 (trans. as Holy Week, 1961); La mise à mort, 1965; Blanche ou l'oubli, 1967; Henri Matisse, 1972; *history:* Histoire de l'URSS de 1917-60; (with A. Maurois) Histoire parallèle des USA et de l'URSS, 1962; *essays:* La lumière de Stendhal, 1954; Litterature sovietique, 1955; Traité du style; Les aventures de Télémaque; Pour un réalisme socialiste; La culture et les hommes; Chroniques du Bel-Canto; Matisse ou comme il vous plaira; *translations:* La chasse au Snark by Lewis Carroll, 1928; Cinq sonnets de Pétrarque, 1947. *Address:* 56 rue de Varenne, 75007 Paris, France; 78730 Saint-Arnoult-en-Yvelines, France.

ARAIN, Shafiq, MP (Uganda); Minister without Portfolio, President's Office, and High Commissioner for Uganda to London, since 1980; *b* 20 Nov. 1933; *s* of Din Mohd Arain; *m* 1966, Maria Leana Godinho; one *s* two *d. Educ:* Government Sch., Kampala; Regent's Polytechnic, London; Nottingham Univ. MP (UPC), 1962-71; Member, E African Legislative Assembly, 1963-71; E African Minister for Common Market and Economic Affairs, later E African Minister for Communications, Research and Social Services; Chairman: Minimum Wages Commission, 1964; Statutory Commn on

Cooperative Movement, 1967. Uganda's Delegate to UN General Assembly 1965-66; Leader, Uganda Delegn to Canada and CPA Conf., Trinidad an Tobago, 1969. Member, Governing Council, Univ. of Dar es Salaam, 1967-6 Chm., Commonwealth Parly Assoc., Uganda Br., 1969-70. Pres., Uganda Cricket Assoc., 1968-69. Left for exile in London following coup in 197 returned to Uganda, 1979; elections were held in Dec. 1980. *Recreations:* gol walking, reading. *Address:* Uganda House, Trafalgar Square, WC2. *T:* 01-83 1866. *Clubs:* Uganda, Royal Commonwealth Society; Hurlingham Wentworth Golf.

ARBER, Prof. Werner; Professor of Molecular Microbiology, Basl University, since 1971. Discovered restriction enzymes at Geneva in 1960' Nobel Prize in Physiology or Medicine (jointly), 1978. *Address:* Departmen of Microbiology, Biozentrum der Universität Basel, 70 Klingelbergstrasse CH 4056, Basel, Switzerland.

ARBUTHNOT, Andrew Robert Coghill; Chairman, Arbuthnot Insuranc Services Ltd, since 1968; Director, Sun Alliance and London Insurance Ltd since 1970; *b* 14 Jan. 1926; *s* of Robert Wemyss Muir Arbuthnot and Mar Arbuthnot (*née* Coghill); *m* 1952, Audrey Dutton-Barker; one *s* one *d. Edu* Eton. Served 1944-47, Captain, Scots Guards, wounded. Dir, Arbuthno Latham & Co. Ltd, 1953-82; Chm. and Chief Exec., Arbuthnot Lathan Holdings, 1974-82. Contested (C) Houghton-le-Spring, 1959. Ordaine Deacon, 1974; Priest, 1975; Licensed to officiate, Farnham Deanery, 1978-82 Holy Trinity Church, Brompton, 1982-. *Recreations:* water colour painting walking. *Address:* Monksfield House, Tilford, Farnham, Surrey GU10 2AI *T:* Runfold 2233.

ARBUTHNOT, Sir Hugh Fitz-Gerald, 7th Bt, *cr* 1823; late Temporar Captain Welsh Guards; *b* 2 Jan. 1922; *s* of Brig.-Gen. Sir Dalrympl Arbuthnot, 5th Bt, CMG, DSO, and Alice Maude (*d* 1969), *d* of Hugl Arbuthnot; *S* brother 1944; *m* 1st, 1949, Elizabeth K. (*d* 1972), *e d* of Squa Ldr G. G. A. Williams, Curral Hall, Tenbury Wells; two *s* one *d* ; 2nd, 1977 Julia Grace, *d* of Lt-Col F. G. Peake, Hawkslee, St Boswells. *Educ:* Etor MFH: Ludlow Hounds, 1948-52; Cotswold Hounds, 1952-64; Duke o Buccleuch's Hounds, 1964-76; Jedforest Hounds, 1977-82. *Heir:* s Keit Robert Charles Arbuthnot [*b* 23 Sept. 1951; *m* 1982, Anne, *yr d* of Brig. Pete Moore]. *Address:* Brundeanlaws, Jedburgh, Roxburghshire.

ARBUTHNOT, Sir John (Sinclair-Wemyss), 1st Bt *cr* 1964; MBE 1944 TD 1951; Chairman, Folkestone and District Water Co.; Director, Th Ecclesiastical Insurance Office plc; Underwriting Member of Lloyd's; *b* 1 Feb. 1912; *s* of late Major K. W. Arbuthnot, the Seaforth Highlanders; *m* 1943 Margaret Jean, *yr d* of late Alexander G. Duff; two *s* three *d. Educ:* Etor Trinity Coll., Cambridge. MA Hons in Nat. Sciences. Served throughout Wa of 1939-45, in RA, Major (wounded); Dep. Inspector of Shell, 1942-45; hon pac 1944; TARO, 1948-62. Prospective Conservative candidate, Don Valley Div. of Yorks, 1934-35, Dunbartonshire, 1936-45, Dover Div. of Kent 1945-50, contesting elections in 1935 and 1945. MP (C) Dover Div. of Kent 1950-64; PPS to Parly Sec., Min. of Pensions, 1952-53, to Minister of Pensions 1953-56, and to Minister of Health, 1956-57; a Chm. of Committees and a Temporary Chm. of the House, 1958-64; Second Church Estates Comr 1962-64; Church Comr for England and Mem., Bd of Governors, 1962-7 (Dep Chm., Assets Cttee, 1966-77); Mem., Church Assembly and Gen. Synoc of Church of England, 1955-75, Panel of Chairmen, 1970-72; Trustee Lambeth Palace Library, 1964-77; Chm., Archbp of Canterbury's Commn to inquire into the organisation of the Church by dioceses in London and the SE of England, 1965-67. Member: Crathorne Cttee on Sunday Observance 1961-64; Hodson Commn on Synodical Government for the Church of England, 1964-66; Parliamentary Chm., Dock & Harbour Authorities Assoc. 1962-64; Member: Public Accounts Cttee, 1955-64; Standing Cttee, Ross Inst. 1951-62; Council, Ceylon Assoc., 1951-62; Cttee, South Indian Assoc. 1951-62. Member Parliamentary Delegations: to the Iron and Stee Community, 1955; to West Africa, 1956; to USA, 1957; to The West Indies 1958; to Zanzibar, Mauritius and Madagascar, 1961; Leader of Parliamentary Delegation to Bulgaria, 1963. A Vice Pres., Trustee Savings Banks Assoc. 1962-76; in business in tea industry concerned with India and Ceylon, 1934-74 Chm., Estates & Agency Holdings Ltd, 1955-70; Joint Hon. Sec. Assoc. o British Chambers of Commerce, 1953-59. *Recreation:* gardening. *Heir:* s William Reierson Arbuthnot, *b* 2 Sept. 1950. *Address:* Poulton Manor, Ash Canterbury, Kent CT3 2HW. *T:* Ash 812516; 7 Fairholt Street, SW7 1EG *T:* 01-589 1727. *Clubs:* Carlton, Royal Commonwealth Society.

ARBUTHNOTT, family name of Viscount of Arbuthnott.

ARBUTHNOTT, 16th Viscount of, *cr* 1641; **John Campbell Arbuthnott**, DSC 1945; Lord-Lieutenant Grampian Region (Kincardineshire), since 1977 Director: Northern Area, Clydesdale Bank, since 1975; Aberdeen and Northern Marts, since 1973; Scottish Widows' Fund and Life Assuranc Society, since 1978 (Deputy Chairman, since 1982); Scottish Northern Investment Trust, since 1979; *b* 26 Oct. 1924; *e s* of 15th Viscount o Arbuthnott, CB, CBE, DSO, MC, and Ursula Collingwood; *S* father, 1966 *m* 1949, Mary Elizabeth Darley (*née* Oxley); one *s* one *d. Educ:* Fettes Coll. Gonville and Caius Coll., Cambridge. Served RNVR (Fleet Air Arm), 1942-46; Near and Far East, British Pacific Fleet, 1945. Cambridge University 1946-49 (Estate Management), MA 1967. Chartered Surveyor and Land Agent; Agricultural Land Service, 1949-55; Land Agent (Scotland), The Nature Conservancy, 1955-67; Member: Countryside Commn for Scotland

1967-71; Aberdeen Univ. Court, 1978-; Chm., Red Deer Commn, 1969-75; President: Wildfowlers Assoc. of GB and Ireland, 1973-; The Scottish Landowners' Fedn, 1974-79 (Convener, 1971-74); Royal Zool Soc. of Scotland, 1976-; Scottish Agricl Orgn Soc., 1980-; Dep. Chm., Nature Conservancy Council, 1980-, Chm., Adv. Cttee for Scotland, 1980-. FRSA. *Recreations:* countryside activities, historical research. *Heir: s* Master of Arbuthnott, *qv. Address:* Arbuthnott House, by Laurencekirk, Kincardineshire, Scotland. *T:* Inverbervie 226. *Clubs:* Army and Navy, Farmers'; New (Edinburgh).

ARBUTHNOTT, Master of; Hon. John Keith Oxley Arbuthnott; *b* 18 July 1950; *s* and *heir* of 16th Viscount of Arbuthnott, *qv; m* 1974, Jill Mary, *er d* of Captain Colin Farquharson; one *s* two *d. Educ:* Fettes College; Aberdeen Univ. *Address:* Kilternan, Arbuthnott, Laurencekirk, Kincardineshire AB3 1NA. *T:* Inverbervie 203.

ARBUTHNOTT, Hugh James; HM Diplomatic Service; Head of Chancery, Paris, since 1980; *b* 27 Dec. 1936; *m:* three *s.* Joined Foreign (subseq. Diplomatic) Service, 1960; 3rd Sec., Tehran, 1962-64; 2nd, later 1st Sec., FO, 1964-66; Private Sec., Minister of State for Foreign Affairs, 1966-68; Lagos, 1968-71; 1st Sec. (Head of Chancery), Tehran, 1971-74; Asst, later Head of European Integration Dept (External), FCO, 1974-77; Counsellor (Agric. and Econ.), Paris, 1978-80. *Publication:* (ed with G. Edwards) Common Man's Guide to the Common Market, 1979. *Address:* c/o Foreign and Commonwealth Office, SW1.

ARBUTHNOTT, Robert; British Council Representative for the German Federal Republic and West Berlin, since 1981; *b* 28 Sept. 1936; *s* of late Archibald Arbuthnott, MBE, ED, and of Barbara Joan (*née* Worters); *m* 1962, Sophie Robina (*née* Axford); one *s* two *d. Educ:* Sedbergh Sch. (scholar); Emmanuel Coll., Cambridge (exhibnr; BA Mod Langs, MA). Nat. service, 1955-57 (2nd Lieut The Black Watch RHR). British Council, 1960-: Karachi, 1960-62; Lahore, 1962-64; London, 1964-67; Representative, Nepal, 1967-72; London Inst. of Education, 1972-73; Representative, Malaysia, 1973-76; Director, Educational Contracts Dept, 1976-77; Controller, Personnel and Staff Recruitment Div., 1978-81. *Recreations:* music-making, the arts, sport. *Address:* Foundry Cottage, Foundry Lane, Haslemere, Surrey GU27 2QF. *T:* Haslemere 4343. *Club:* United Oxford & Cambridge University.

ARCHDALE, Sir Edward (Folmer), 3rd Bt, *cr* 1928; DSC 1943; Captain, RN, retired; *b* 8 Sept. 1921; *s* of Vice-Adm. Sir Nicholas Edward Archdale, 2nd Bt, CBE, and Gerda *(d* 1969), 2nd *d* of late F. C. Sievers, Copenhagen; *S* father 1955; *m* 1954, Elizabeth Ann Stewart (marr. diss. 1978), *d* of late Maj-Gen. Wilfrid Boyd Fellowes Lukis, CBE; one *s* two *d. Educ:* Royal Naval Coll., Dartmouth. Joined Royal Navy, 1935; served War of 1939-45 (despatches, DSC). *Recreation:* civilization. *Heir: s* Nicholas Edward Archdale, *b* 2 Dec. 1965. *Address:* 11 West Hill Park, Winchester, Hants.

ARCHER, Albert, MBE 1980; President, Institution of Environmental Health Officers, since 1979; Member, Royal Commission on Environmental Pollution, since 1981; *b* 7 March 1915; *s* of Arthur Archer and Margaret Alice Norris; *m* 1st, 1939; two *s*; 2nd, 1975, Peggy, *widow* of John F. Marsh; two step *s. Educ:* Manchester Grammar Sch.; Manchester Coll. of Technology. Fellow, Instn of Environmental Health Officers, 1961. Chief Public Health Inspector, Bor. of Halesowen, 1943-73; City of Birmingham: Senior Environmtl Protection Officer, 1973-75; Dep. City Environmtl Officer, 1975-76; City Environmtl Officer, 1976-80. Hon. Res. Fellow, Dept of Chemistry, Univ. of Aston in Birmingham, 1980-. Mem., govt working parties on air pollution. *Publications:* articles on air pollution in technical jls. *Recreation:* watching cricket. *Address:* 8 Portland Drive, Stourbridge, West Midlands DY9 0SD. *T:* Hagley 883366.

ARCHER, Sir Archibald, Kt 1982; CMG 1961; grazier; company director; *b* 10 Jan. 1902; *s* of late Robert Stubbs Archer and Alice Manon Archer, Gracemere Station, Queensland; *m* 1930, Sarah Beatrice Cameron Crombie, *er d* of late Donald Charles Cameron Crombie and Mildred Ida Lloyd Crombie, Greenhills Station, Longreach, Qld; one *s* two *d. Educ:* Church of England Grammar Sch., Sydney, NSW, Australia. Land Consultant to Qld Govt, 1961-63. Dep. Chm., Picture Theatre and Films Commn, 1972-76 (Mem., 1957-76); Vice-Pres., Royal National Assoc., 1961-80, Pres., 1980-; President: Australian Agricl Socs, 1975-76; Qld Electoral Commn, 1971-72, 1977-; City of Brisbane, Electoral Wards Commn, 1972. Pres., Royal Geog. Soc. Qld, 1971-72, Fellow, 1972. *Address:* 23 Sefton Avenue, Clayfield, Queensland 4011, Australia. *T:* Brisbane 2623375. *Clubs:* Queensland (Brisbane); Australasian Pioneers (Sydney).

ARCHER, Gen. Sir (Arthur) John, KCB 1976; OBE 1964; Chief Executive, Royal Hong Kong Jockey Club, since 1980; *b* 12 Feb. 1924; *s* of Alfred and Mildred Archer, Fakenham; *m* 1950, Cynthia Marie, *d* of Col Alexander and Eileen Allan, Swallowcliffe, Wilts; two *s. Educ:* King's Sch., Peterborough; St Catharine's Coll., Cambridge. Entered Army, 1943; commnd 1944; regular commn Dorset Regt, 1946; psc 1956; jssc 1959; GSO1 3rd Div., 1963-65; CO 1 Devon and Dorset Regt, 1965-67; Comdr Land Forces Gulf, 1968-69; idc 1970; Dir of Public Relations (Army), 1970-72; Comdr 2nd Div., 1972-74; Dir of Army Staff Duties, 1974-76; Comdr British Forces Hong Kong, 1976-78 and Lt-Gen. Brigade of Gurkhas, 1977-78; C-in-C, UKLF, 1978-79. CBIM. Col, Devonshire and Dorset Regt, 1977-79. *Recreations:* light

aviation and gliding. *Address:* Royal Hong Kong Jockey Club, Sports Road, Happy Valley, Hong Kong. *Club:* Army and Navy.

ARCHER, Bruce; *see* Archer, L. B.

ARCHER, Sir Clyde Vernon Harcourt, Kt 1962; Judge of the Court of Appeal, Bahamas, 1971-75; *b* 12 Nov. 1904. *Educ:* Harrison Coll., Barbados; Cambridge Univ. Barrister-at-Law, Gray's Inn; clerk to the Attorney-General, Barbados, 1930; police magistrate Barbados, 1935; Judge, Bridgetown Petty Debt Court, 1938; Legal Draftsman, Trinidad and Tobago, 1944; Solicitor-General, Trinidad and Tobago, 1953; Puisne Judge, Trinidad and Tobago, 1954; Chief Justice of the Windward Islands and Leeward Islands, 1958; a Federal Justice, WI, 1958-62. *Publication:* (jointly) Revised Edition of the Laws of Barbados, 1944. *Address:* 40 Graeme Hall Terrace, Christchurch, Barbados.

ARCHER, Frank Joseph, RE 1960 (ARE 1940); RWS 1976 (ARWS 1972); ARCA 1937; Head of School of Fine Art, Kingston Polytechnic, Kingston upon Thames (formerly Kingston College of Art), 1962-73, retired; *b* 30 June 1912; *s* of Joseph and Alberta Archer; *m* 1939, Celia Cole; one *s* one *d. Educ:* Eastbourne Grammar Sch.; Eastbourne Sch. of Art; Royal Coll. of Art. ARCA 1937; Rome Scholar, Engraving, 1938; British Sch. at Rome, 1938. Paintings bought by numerous local authorities and private collectors. *Address:* 2 Owls Castle Cottages, Cottenden Road, Stonegate, Wadhurst, E Sussex. *T:* Ticehurst 200082.

ARCHER, Maj.-Gen. Gilbert Thomas Lancelot, CB 1960; FRCPI; retired; *b* 6 April 1903; *s* of Gilbert Archer, Dublin, Ireland, and Kate Archer (*née* Lamb); *m* 1928, Catherine, *d* of Edward O'Malley, Louisburgh, Westport, Co. Mayo, Ireland; two *s* one *d. Educ:* St Andrews Coll., Dublin; Dublin Univ. (TCD). MB 1926; Lieut RAMC, 1928; Major, 1937; Deputy Asst Dir of Pathology, China Command, 1937-40; Asst Dir of Pathology, West Africa, 1943-45; Reader in Pathology, Royal Army Medical Coll., 1946-48; Asst Dir of Pathology, Middle East Land Forces, 1949-52; MRCPI, 1953; Officer Commanding David Bruce Laboratories, 1952-53; QHS 1953-61; Dir of Pathology and Consulting Pathologist to the Army, 1953-61; Brig., 1956; Major-General, 1958; FRCPI 1958. *Publications:* Articles on bacteriology, immunity, etc., in Jl of the RAMC, Brit. Med. Jl, etc. *Address:* 7 Nutley Avenue, Ballsbridge, Dublin, Eire.

See also J. M. Archer.

ARCHER, Graham Robertson; HM Diplomatic Service; Counsellor, Pretoria, since 1982; *b* 4 July 1939; *s* of late Henry Robertson Archer and Winifred Archer; *m* 1963, Pauline Cowan; two *d. Educ:* Judd School, Tonbridge. Joined Commonwealth Relations Office, 1962; British High Commission, New Delhi, 1964; Vice Consul, Kuwait, 1966; CRO (later FCO), 1967; Second Secretary (Commercial), Washington, 1970; First Secretary: FCO, 1972; Wellington, NZ, 1975; FCO, 1979. *Recreations:* listening to music, gardening, hill walking. *Address:* c/o Foreign and Commonwealth Office, SW1; 218 Crown Avenue, Waterkloof, Pretoria, South Africa. *T:* 46-3811.

ARCHER, Mrs Jean Mary; Under-Secretary, Ministry of Agriculture, Fisheries and Food, since 1973; *b* 24 Aug. 1932; *e d* of late Reginald R. and D. Jane Harvey, Braiseworth Hall, Tannington, Suffolk; *m* 1954, G. Michéal D. Archer, MB, BChir, FFARCS, *er s* of Gen. G. T. L. Archer, *qv* ; two *d. Educ:* Fleet House, Felixstowe; St Felix Sch., Southwold; Newnham Coll., Cambridge. MA Econs 1954. Asst Principal, Min. of Agriculture, 1954; Private Sec. to successive Perm. Secs, MAFF, 1956-59; Principal 1960; Sec., Reorganisation Commn for Eggs, 1967; Asst Sec. 1968; Under-Sec. i/c Food Policy Gp, MAFF, 1973; Under-Sec., Dept of Prices and Consumer Protection, 1974-76; returned to MAFF, as Under-Sec., Milk and Marketing Group, 1976; Under-Sec., Meat, Poultry and Eggs Div., 1980. *Recreations:* travel, music, tennis, watching sport, swimming administration (Team Man., Chelsea/Kensington Swimming Club; Hon. Sec., Swimmers' Parents' and Supporters' Assoc.). *Address:* 51 Sussex Street, SW1. *T:* 01-828 6296; Friary Cottage, Mendlesham, Suffolk. *T:* Mendlesham 395. *Club:* Hurlingham.

See also Sir A. J. D. McCowan.

ARCHER, Jeffrey Howard; author and politician; *b* 15 April 1940; *s* of William Archer and Lola Archer (*née* Cook); *m* 1966, Mary Weeden; two *s. Educ:* by his wife since leaving Wellington Sch., Somerset; Brasenose Coll., Oxford. Athletics Blues, 1963-65, Gymnastics Blue, 1965, Pres. OUAC 1965; ran for Great Britain (very slowly); Oxford 100 yards record, 1966. Mem. GLC for Havering, 1966-70; MP (C) Louth, Dec. 1969-Sept. 1974. Mem. Exec., British Theatre Museum. Pres., Somerset AAA, 1973; Chm., Cambridge RFC, 1981-. FRSA 1973. *Publications:* Not a Penny More, Not a Penny Less, 1975; Shall We Tell the President?, 1977; Kane and Abel, 1979; A Quiver Full of Arrows, 1980; The Prodigal Daughter, 1982. *Recreations:* theatre, watching Somerset play cricket (represented Somerset CCC in charity match, 1981). *Address:* 93 Albert Embankment, SE1; The Old Vicarage, Grantchester. *Clubs:* MCC; Louth Working Men's.

ARCHER, Sir John; *see* Archer, Sir A. J.

ARCHER, John Francis Ashweek, QC 1975; a Recorder of the Crown Court since 1974; *b* 9 July 1925; *s* of late George Eric Archer, FRCSE, and late Frances Archer (*née* Ashweek); *m* 1960, Doris Mary Hennessey. *Educ:*

Winchester Coll., 1938-43; New Coll., Oxford, 1947-49 (BA 1949). Served War of 1939-45, 1944-47; Lieut RA, 1948. Called to Bar, Inner Temple, 1950. *Recreations:* motoring, bridge. *Address:* 22a Connaught Square, W2. *T:* 01-262 9406.

ARCHER, John Norman; Managing Director, International Tanker Owners Pollution Federation Ltd, since 1979; *b* 27 Feb. 1921; *s* of Clifford Banks Archer and Grace Archer; *m* 1952, Gladys Joy (*née* Barnes); one step *d. Educ:* Wandsworth School. Served with RA, 1939-46 (Major). Entered Civil Service, Board of Educn, 1937; Asst Principal 1947, Principal 1949, Min. of Educn; attended Admin. Staff Coll., Henley, 1960; Asst Sec. (Joint Head, Architects and Buildings Br.), 1962; technical assistance assignments etc educn, Nigeria, Yugoslavia, Tunisia, 1961-63; Asst Sec., Treasury, O&M Div., 1964; Civil Service Department: Asst Sec., Management Services Development Div., 1968; Under-Sec., Management Services, 1970; Under-Sec., Marine Div., DTI, later Dept of Trade, 1972-79. Member: Cttee of Management, RNLI; Council, Marine Soc. *Recreations:* lawn tennis, bridge, watching cricket. *Address:* 1 Dacre Court, Tite Street, SW3. *T:* 01-352 2898. *Clubs:* All England Lawn Tennis, Hurlingham, MCC.

ARCHER, Prof. (Leonard) Bruce, CBE 1976; DrRCA; CEng, MIMechE; Head of Department of Design Research, Royal College of Art, since 1968; *b* 22 Nov. 1922; *s* of Leonard Castella Archer and Ivy Hilda Archer; *m* 1950, Joan Henrietta Allen; one *d. Educ:* Henry Thornton Sch., London; City Univ., London. MIED, ASIA(Ed). Served, Scots Guards, 1941-44. City Univ. 1946-50. Various posts in manufacturing industry, 1950-57; Lectr, Central Sch. of Art and Design, London, 1957-60; Guest Prof., Hochschule für Gestaltung, Ulm, 1960-61; Research Fellow, later Prof., Royal Coll. of Art, 1961-. Various public appointments in design, educn and industrial and scientific policy, 1968-; Member: Design Council, 1972-80; Science Policy Foundn, 1979-; Council, Assoc. of Art Instns, 1980-; Chm., Confedn of Art and Design Assocs, 1981-. Director: Design into Industry Exhibition and Conference Ltd, 1981-; Gore Projects Ltd, 1982-; Design Research Innovation Centre Ltd, 1982-. Mem. Council, Brunel Univ., 1978-. *Publications:* varied, on the theory and practice of research, design, develt and educn. *Recreations:* music, the theatre. *Address:* 43 Avenue Road, N6 5DF. *T:* 01-404 5011.

ARCHER, Dr Mildred Agnes, (Mrs W. G. Archer), OBE 1979; in charge of Prints and Drawings Section, India Office Library, London, 1954-80; *b* 28 Dec. 1911; *d* of V. A. Bell, MBE; *m* 1934, William George Archer (*d* 1979); one *s* one *d. Educ:* St Hilda's College, Oxford. MA, DLitt (Oxon). Art historian (British period, India); resided India, 1934-47; revisited India (study tours), 1966, 1972, 1976, 1981-82. *Publications:* Patna Painting, 1947; (with W. G. Archer) Indian Painting for the British, 1955; Tippoo's Tiger, 1959; Natural History Drawings in the India Office Library, 1962; Indian Miniatures and Folk Paintings, 1967; Indian Architecture and the British, 1968; British Drawings in the India Office Library (2 vols), 1969; Indian Paintings from Court, Town and Village, 1970; Company Drawings in the India Office Library, 1972; Artist Adventurers in Eighteenth Century India, 1974; Indian Popular Painting, 1977; India and British Portraiture, 1770-1825, 1979; (with John Bastin) The Raffles Drawings in the India Office Library, 1979; Early Views of India, 1980; (with T. Falk) Indian Miniatures in the India Office Library, 1981; articles in Country Life, Apollo, Connoisseur, History Today, Geographical Mag. *Recreations:* grandchildren, gardening, travel. *Address:* 18A Provost Road, Hampstead, NW3 4ST. *T:* 01-722 2713; 5 Frog Meadow, Dedham, Colchester, Essex. *T:* Colchester 323099.

ARCHER, Rt. Hon. Peter (Kingsley), PC 1977; QC 1971; MP (Lab) Warley West, since 1974 (Rowley Regis and Tipton, 1966-74); a Recorder of the Crown Court, since 1982; *b* 20 Nov. 1926; *s* of Cyril Kingsley Archer and May (*née* Baker); *m* 1954, Margaret Irene (*née* Smith); one *s. Educ:* Wednesbury Boys' High Sch.; LSE; University Coll., London (Fellow 1978). Called to Bar, Gray's Inn, 1952; Bencher, 1974; commenced practice, 1953. PPS to Attorney-Gen., 1967-70; Solicitor General, 1974-79; Opposition front bench spokesman on legal affairs, 1979-. UK Deleg. to UN Gen. Assembly (Third Cttee), 1969. Chm., Amnesty International (British Section), 1971-74; Chm., Parly Gp for World Govt, 1970-74; Chm., Soc. of Labour Lawyers, 1971-74; Vice-Chm., Anti-Slavery Soc., 1970-74; Mem., Exec. Cttee, Fabian Soc., 1974- (Chm., 1980-). *Publications:* The Queen's Courts, 1956; ed Social Welfare and the Citizen, 1957; Communism and the Law, 1963; contrib. Trends in Social Welfare, 1965; contrib. Atkins, Court Forms, 1965; (with Lord Reay) Freedom at Stake, 1966; contrib. The International Protection of Human Rights, 1967; Human Rights, 1969; (jtly) Purpose in Socialism, 1973; The Role of the Law Officers, 1978. *Recreations:* music, writing, talking. *Address:* 5 Penn Close, Chorleywood, Herts.

ARCHIBALD, Barony of, *cr* 1949, of Woodside, Glasgow; title disclaimed by 2nd Baron; *see under* Archibald, George Christopher.

ARCHIBALD, George Christopher, FRSC 1979; Professor of Economics, University of British Columbia, since 1970; *b* 30 Dec. 1926; *s* of 1st Baron Archibald, CBE, and Dorothy Holroyd Edwards (*d* 1960); *S* father, 1975, as 2nd Baron Archibald, but disclaimed his peerage for life; *m* 1st, 1951, Liliana Barou (marr. diss. 1965); 2nd, 1971, Daphne May Vincent. *Educ:* Phillips Exeter Academy, USA; King's Coll., Cambridge (MA); London Sch. of Economics (BSc Econ.). Served in Army, 1945-48, Captain RAEC. Formerly: Prof. of Economics, Univ. of Essex; Lectr in Economics, Otago Univ. and LSE; Leon Fellow, London Univ. Fellow, Econometric Soc., 1976.

Publications: (ed) Theory of the Firm, 1971; (with R. G. Lipsey) Introduction to a Mathematical Treatment of Economics, 1973. *Address:* c/o Department of Economics, University of British Columbia, Vancouver, BC V6T 1Y2 Canada.

ARCHIBALD, Dr Harry Munro, CB 1976; MBE 1945; Deputy Chief Medical Officer (Deputy Secretary), Department of Health and Social Security, 1973-77; *b* 17 June 1915; *s* of James and Isabella Archibald unmarried. *Educ:* Hillhead High Sch.; Univ. of Glasgow. MB, ChB 1938 DPH 1956. War Service: RAMC, 1940-43; IMS/IAMC, 1943-46; Lt-Col Italian Campaign (despatches). Colonial Medical Service, Nigeria, 1946-62 Senior Specialist (Malariologist), 1958; Principal Med. Officer, Prevent Services, N Nigeria, 1960; Med. Officer, Min. of Health, 1962; Sen. Med Off., 1964; Principal Med. Off., DHSS, 1970; Sen. Principal Med. Off., 1972 Mem. Bd, Public Health Laboratory Service, 1975-77. Fellow, Faculty of Community Medicine, 1973. *Recreation:* travel. *Address:* 1 Camborne House Camborne Road, Sutton, Surrey. *T:* 01-643 1076. *Club:* Caledonian.

ARCHIBALD, James Montgomery, MBE 1945; JP; Chairman and Managing Director, James Archibald & Associates Ltd, since 1963; film producer, writer and director; *b* 3 April 1920; *s* of Brig. Gordon King Archibald, DSO, and Helen Archibald; *m* 1956, Sheila Elizabeth Maud Stafford; two *s. Educ:* Westminster Sch.; Merton Coll., Oxford (MA). Rep Oxford Univ., Foil and Epée, 1939. Served War, 1939-45: Private 1939 Lt-Col 1944 (mentioned in despatches, 1943). Anglo-Iranian Oil Co., 1946-49; Rank Org., 1950-56; Dir, J. Walter Thompson Ltd, 1956-63; Chm. Academy Sound & Vision Ltd, 1980-82. Gen. Comr of Income Tax, St Martin's in the Fields, 1961; Chm. Comrs of Income Tax, St Martin's in the Fields and Charing Cross, 1974. Chairman: Nat. Music Council of GB, 1974-80, Vice-Pres., 1980-; Arts Panel, Inst. of Dirs; Member: Exec. Cttee, Assoc. for Business Sponsorship of the Arts; BAFTA; Royal Television Soc.; British Film & TV Producers' Assoc. Governor: BFI, 1976-79; Loughborough Coll. of Art and Design, 1972-80; Trinity Coll. of Music; Yehudi Menuhin's Live Music Now, 1979- (Chm., 1979-80). Member: Ct, Worshipful Co. of Bowyers (Master, 1982-83); Worshipful Co. of Musicians (Pres., Livery Club, 1981-82). JP Inner London, 1967. FRSA, Hon. FTCL. 67 Internat. Awards for films. OStJ 1977. *Address:* 35 Morpeth Mansions, Morpeth Terrace, SW1P 1EU. *T:* 01-828 9691; 1 The Coastguards, Thorpeness, Leiston, Suffolk. *T:* Aldeburgh 2922. *Clubs:* Brooks's, Royal Thames Yacht; Myrmidon (Oxford).

ARCHIBALD, Liliana; EEC Adviser to Lloyd's and to the British Insurance Brokers Association, since 1978; International Affairs Adviser to Lloyd's, since 1981; Adviser to International Group of Protection & Indemnity Clubs, since 1980; *b* 25 May 1928; *d* of late Noah and Sophie Barou; *m* 1951, George Christopher Archibald (marr. diss. 1965). *Educ:* Kingsley Sch.; Geneva University. Univ. Lectr, Otago Univ., 1952-55; Director: Const & Co. Ltd, 1955-73; Credit Consultants Ltd, 1957-73; Adam Brothers Contingency Ltd, 1970-; Head of Division (Credit Insurance and Export Credit), EEC, 1973-77. Member of Lloyd's, 1973-. *Publications:* (trans. and ed) Peter the Great, 1958; (trans. and ed) Rise of the Romanovs, 1970; contrib. Bankers Magazine. *Recreations:* driving fast cars, ski-ing, gardening. *Address:* 21 Langland Gardens, NW3 6QE.

See also A. Kennaway.

ARCTIC, Bishop of The, since 1974; **Rt. Rev. John Reginald Sperry;** *b* 2 May 1924; *s* of William Reginald Sperry and Elsie Agnes (*née* Priest); *m* 1952, Elizabeth Maclaren; one *s* one *d* (and one *d* decd). *Educ:* St Augustine's Coll., Canterbury; King's Coll., Halifax (STh). Deacon, 1950; priest, 1951; St Andrew's Mission, Coppermine, NWT, 1950-69; Canon of All Saints' Cathedral, Aklavik, 1957-59; Archdeacon of Coppermine, 1959-69; Rector of St John's, Fort Smith, NWT, 1969-73; Rector of Holy Trinity, Yellowknife, NWT, 1974. Hon. DD; Coll. of Emmanuel, St Chad, 1974; Wycliffe Coll., Toronto, 1979. *Publications:* translations into Copper Eskimo: Canadian Book of Common Prayer (1962), 1969; Four Gospels and Acts of the Apostles, 1972. *Address:* 1 Dakota Court, Yellowknife, Northwest Territories, X1A 2A4, Canada. *T:* 403-873-4517.

ARCULUS, Sir Ronald, KCMG 1979 (CMG 1968); KCVO 1980; HM Diplomatic Service; Ambassador to Italy, since 1979; *b* 11 Feb. 1923; *s* of late Cecil and of Ethel L. Arculus; *m* 1953, Sheila Mary Faux; one *s* one *d. Educ:* Solihull; Exeter Coll., Oxford (BA). 4th Queen's Own Hussars (now Queen's Royal Irish Hussars), 1942-45 (Captain). Joined HM Diplomatic Service, 1947; FO, 1947; San Francisco, 1948; La Paz, 1950; FO, 1951; Ankara, 1953; FO, 1957; Washington, 1961; Counsellor, 1965; New York, 1965-68; IDC, 1969; Head of Science and Technology Dept, FCO, 1970-72; Minister (Economic), Paris, 1973-77; Ambassador and Permt Leader, UK Delegn to UN Conf. on Law of the Sea, 1977-79. *Recreations:* travel, music and fine arts. *Address:* c/o Lloyds Bank Ltd, Guards and Cavalry Section, 6 Pall Mall, SW1. *Club:* Army and Navy.

ARDAGH AND CLONMACNOIS, Bishop of, (RC), since 1967; **Most Rev. Cahal Brendan Daly;** *b* 1917. *Educ:* St Malachy's, Belfast; Queen's Univ., Belfast (BA Hons, Classics, MA); St Patrick's, Maynooth (DD); Institut Catholique, Paris (LPh). Ordained, 1941. Lecturer in Scholastic Philosophy, Queen's Univ., Belfast, 1946-62; Reader, 1962-67; consecrated Bishop, 1967. *Publications:* Morals, Law and Life, 1962; Natural Law Morality Today, 1965; Violence in Ireland and Christian Conscience, 1973; Theologians and the

Magisterium, 1977; Peace the Work of Justice, 1979; chapters in: Prospect for Metaphysics, 1961; Intellect and Hope, 1968; New Essays in Religious Language, 1969; Understanding the Eucharist, 1969. *Address:* St Michael's, Longford, Ireland. *T:* Longford 6432.

ARDEE, Lord; John Anthony Brabazon; *b* 11 May 1941; *e s* of 14th Earl of Meath, *qv; m* 1973, Xenia Goudime; one *s* two *d. Educ:* Harrow. Page of Honour to the Queen, 1956-57. Served Grenadier Guards, 1959-62. *Heir: s* Hon. Anthony Jaques Brabazon, *b* 30 Jan. 1977. *Address:* Furnace House, Rathdrum, Co. Wicklow, Ireland.

ARDEN, Rt. Rev. Donald Seymour, CBE 1981; Priest-in-charge of St Margaret's Church, Uxbridge, and an Assistant Bishop of Willesden, since 1981; *b* 12 April 1916; *s* of Stanley and Winifred Arden; *m* 1962, Jane Grace Riddle; two *s. Educ:* St Peter's Coll., Adelaide; University of Leeds (BA); College of the Resurrection, Mirfield. Deacon, 1939; Priest, 1940. Curate of: St Catherine's, Hatcham, 1939-40; Nettleden with Potten End, 1941-43; Asst Priest, Pretoria African Mission, 1944-51; Director of Usuthu Mission, Swaziland, 1951-61; Bishop of Nyasaland, 1961 (name of diocese changed, when Nyasaland was granted independence, July 1964); Bishop of Malaŵi, 1964-71, of Southern Malaŵi, 1971-81; Archbishop of Central Africa, 1971-80. *Publication:* Out of Africa Something New, 1976. *Recreations:* photography, farming. *Address:* 72 Harefield Road, Uxbridge UB8 1PL. *T:* Uxbridge 39055.

ARDEN, John; playwright; *b* 26 Oct. 1930; *s* of C. A. Arden and A. E. Layland; *m* 1957, Margaretta Ruth D'Arcy; four *s* (and one *s* decd). *Educ:* Sedbergh Sch.; King's Coll., Cambridge; Edinburgh Coll. of Art. Plays produced include: All Fall Down, 1955; The Life of Man, 1956; The Waters of Babylon, 1957; Live Like Pigs, 1958; Serjeant Musgrave's Dance, 1959; Soldier, Soldier, 1960; The Happy Haven, 1960; Wet Fish, 1962; The Workhouse Donkey, 1963; Ironhand, 1963; Armstrong's Last Goodnight, 1964; Left-Handed Liberty, 1965; The True History of Squire Jonathan and his Unfortunate Treasure, 1968; The Bagman, 1970; Pearl, 1978; To Put It Frankly, 1979; Don Quixote, 1980; with Margaretta D'Arcy: The Business of Good Government, 1960; Ars Longa Vita Brevis, 1964; Friday's Hiding, 1966; The Royal Pardon, 1966; The Hero Rises Up, 1968; Island of the Mighty, 1972; The Ballygombeen Bequest, 1972; The Non-Stop Connolly Cycle, 1975; Vandaleur's Folly, 1978; The Little Gray Home in the West, 1978. *Publications:* To Present the Pretence (essays), 1977; Silence Among the Weapons (novel), 1982. *Recreations:* antiquarianism, mythology. *Address:* c/o Margaret Ramsay Ltd, 14 Goodwin's Court, WC2.

ARDWICK, Baron *cr* 1970 (Life Peer), of Barnes; **John Cowburn Beavan;** Member of European Parliament, 1975-79; *b* 1910; *s* of late Silas Beavan and Alderman Emily Beavan, JP; *m* 1934, Gladys (*née* Jones); one *d. Educ:* Manchester Grammar Sch. Blackpool Times, 1927; Evening Chronicle, Manchester, 1928; Manchester Evening News, 1930; London staff, Manchester Evening News, 1933; News Editor, Manchester Evening News, Manchester, 1936; Asst Editor, Londoner's Diary, Evening Standard, and leader writer, 1940; News Editor and Chief Sub, Observer, 1942; Editor, Manchester Evening News; Dir, Manchester Guardian and Evening News Ltd, 1943; London Editor, Manchester Guardian, 1946; Asst Dir, Nuffield Foundation, 1955; Editor, Daily Herald, 1960-62; Political Adviser to the Daily Mirror Group, 1962-76; Mem. Editorial Bd, The Political Quarterly, 1978-; Chm., Press Freedom Cttee, Commonwealth Press Union, 1980-. Chm., Industrial Sponsors, 1975-. Sec., British Cttee, Internat. Press Inst., 1972-76. *Address:* 10 Chester Close, SW13. *T:* 01-789 3490. *Clubs:* Garrick, Roehampton.

ARGENT, Eric William, FCA; FCBSI; Director, Anglia Building Society (formerly Anglia, Hastings & Thanet), since 1978 (Joint General Manager, 1978-81); *b* 5 Sept. 1923; *s* of Eric George Argent and Florence Mary Argent; *m* 1949, Pauline Grant; two *d. Educ:* Chiswick Grammar Sch. FCA 1951. War Service, 1942-47. With City Chartered Accountants, 1940-42 and 1947-51; with London Banking House, Antony Gibbs & Sons Ltd, 1951-59; Hastings & Thanet Building Society, 1959-: Sec. and Chief Accountant, 1962; Dep. Gen. Man., 1964; Gen. Man. and Sec., 1966; Dir and Gen. Man., 1976. *Recreations:* reading, gardening, walking. *Address:* New House, Whiston, Northampton. *T:* Northampton 891342. *Club:* English-Speaking Union.

ARGENT, Malcolm; Secretary of British Telecommunications, since 1981; *b* 14 Aug. 1935; *s* of Leonard James and Winifred Hilda Argent; *m* 1961, Mary Patricia Addis Stimson; one *s* one *d. Educ:* Palmer's Sch., Grays, Essex. General Post Office, London Telecommunications Region: Exec. Officer, 1953-62; Higher Exec. Officer, 1962-66; Principal, PO Headquarters, 1966-70; Private Sec., Man. Dir, Telecommunications, 1970-74; Personnel Controller, External Telecommun. Exec., 1974-75; Dir, Chairman's Office, PO Central Headquarters, 1975-77; Dir, Eastern Telecommun. Region, 1977; Secretary of the Post Office, 1978-81. FBIM 1980. *Recreations:* tennis, gardening. *Address:* 12A Ash Court, Forest View, Chingford, E4 7AR.

ARGENTINA AND EASTERN SOUTH AMERICA, Bishop in, since 1975; **Rt. Rev. Richard Stanley Cutts;** Archbishop of Canterbury's Commissary in the Falkland Islands, since 1978; *b* 17 Sept. 1919; *s* of Edward Stanley and Gabrielle Cutts; *m* 1960, Irene Adela Sack; one *s* three *d. Educ:* Felsted School, Essex. Asst Curate, SS Peter and Paul, Godalming, 1951-56; Director of St Cyprian's Mission, Etalaneni and Priest-in-Charge Nkandhla Chapelry, Zululand, 1957-63; Director, Kambula Mission District, 1963-65;

Rector, St Mary's, Kuruman and Director, Kuruman Mission District, 1965-71; Archdeacon of Kuruman, 1969-71; Dean of Salisbury, Rhodesia, 1971-75. *Address:* 25 de Mayo 282, Buenos Aires, Argentina.

ARGOV, Shlomo; Ambassador of Israel to the Court of St James's, since 1979; *b* 1929; *m* Hava Argov; one *s* two *d. Educ:* Georgetown Univ., USA (BSc Pol. Science); London School of Economics (Internat. Relns) (MSc Econ). Israel Defence Force, 1947-50; Prime Minister's Office, Jerusalem, 1955-59; Consul General of Israel, Lagos, 1959-60; Counsellor, Accra, 1960-61; Consul, Consulate General of Israel, New York, 1961-64; Dep. Director, United States Div., Min. of Foreign Affairs, Jerusalem, 1965-68; Minister, Embassy of Israel, Washington, 1968-71; Ambassador of Israel, Mexico, 1971-74; Asst Dir Gen. (Dir of Israel Information Services), Min. of Foreign Affairs, Jerusalem, 1974-77; Ambassador of Israel, Netherlands, 1977-79. *Address:* Embassy of Israel, 2 Palace Green, W8. *T:* 01-937 8050.

ARGYLE, Major Michael Victor, MC 1945; QC 1961; **His Honour Judge Argyle;** a Circuit Judge (formerly an Additional Judge of the Central Criminal Court), since 1970; *b* 31 Aug. 1915; *e s* of late Harold Victor Argyle and Elsie Marion, Repton, Derbyshire; *m* 1951, Ann Norah, *d* of late Charles Newton, and of Mrs V. Jobson, Duffield, Nr Derby; three *d. Educ:* Shardlow Hall, Derbyshire; Westminster Sch.; Trinity Coll., Cambridge (MA). Served War of 1939-45: with 7th QO Hussars in India, ME and Italy (immediate MC), 1939-47. Called to Bar, Lincoln's Inn, 1938, Bencher, 1967; resumed practice at Bar, 1947 (Midland Circuit); Recorder of Northampton, 1962-65, of Birmingham, 1965-70; Dep. Chm., Holland QS, 1965-71; Lay Judge, Arches Court, Province of Canterbury, 1968-. General Elections, contested (C) Belper, 1950, and Loughborough, 1955. *Publications:* (ed) Phipson on Evidence, 10th edn. *Recreations:* chess, boxing. *Address:* The Red House, Fiskerton, near Southwell, Notts. *Clubs:* Carlton, Cavalry and Guards, Kennel.

ARGYLL, 12th Duke of, *cr* 1701 (Scotland), 1892 (UK); **Ian Campbell;** Marquess of Lorne and Kintyre; Earl of Campbell and Cowal; Viscount Lochow and Glenyla; Baron Inveraray, Mull, Morvern, and Tiry, 1701; Baron Campbell, 1445; Earl of Argyll, 1457; Baron Lorne, 1470; Baron Kintyre, 1633 (Scotland); Baron Sundridge, 1766; Baron Hamilton of Hameldon, 1776; Bt 1627; 36th Baron and 46th Knight of Lochow; Celtic title, Mac Cailein Mhor, Chief of Clan Campbell (from Sir Colin Campbell, knighted 1280); Hereditary Master of the Royal Household, Scotland; Hereditary High Sheriff of the County of Argyll; Admiral of the Western Coast and Isles; Keeper of the Great Seal of Scotland and of the Castles of Dunstaffnage, Dunoon, and Carrick and Tarbert; *b* 28 Aug. 1937; *e s* of 11th Duke of Argyll, TD, and Louise (*d* 1970), *o d* of Henry Clews; *S* father, 1973; *m* 1964, Iona Mary, *d* of Captain Sir Ivar Colquhoun, *qv* ; one *s* one *d. Educ:* Le Rosey, Switzerland; Glenalmond; McGill Univ., Montreal. Captain (retd) Argyll and Sutherland Highlanders. Member, Queen's Body Guard for Scotland, the Royal Company of Archers. KStJ 1975. *Heir: s* Marquess of Lorne, *qv. Address:* Inveraray Castle, Inveraray, Argyll. *T:* Inveraray 2275. *Clubs:* White's; New (Edinburgh).

ARGYLL AND THE ISLES, Bishop of, since 1977; **Rt. Rev. George Kennedy Buchanan Henderson,** MBE 1974; *b* 5 Dec. 1921; *s* of George Buchanan Henderson and Anna Kennedy Butters; *m* 1950, Isobel Fergusson Bowman. *Educ:* Oban High School; University of Durham (BA, LTh). Assistant Curate, Christ Church, Glasgow, 1943-48; Priest in Charge, St Bride's, Nether Lochaber, 1948-50; Chaplain to Bishop of Argyll and The Isles, 1948-50; Rector, St Andrew's, Fort William, 1950-77; Canon, St John's Cathedral, Oban, 1960; Synod Clerk, 1964-73; Dean of Argyll and The Isles, 1973-77. JP of Inverness-shire, 1963-; Hon. Sheriff, 1977-; Provost of Fort William, 1962-75; Hon. Burgess of Fort William, 1973. *Address:* Bishop's House, Alma Road, Fort William, Inverness-shire PH33 6HD.

ARGYLL AND THE ISLES, Bishop of, (RC), since 1968; **Rt. Rev. Colin MacPherson;** *b* Lochboisdale, South Uist, 5 Aug. 1917; *e s* of Malcolm MacPherson and Mary MacPherson (*née* MacMillan). *Educ:* Lochboisdale School; Daliburgh H. G. School; Blairs Coll., Aberdeen; Pontificium Athenæum Urbanum, Rome. Bachelor of Philosophy 1936; Bachelor of Theology 1938; Licentiate of Theology 1940 (Rome). Assistant Priest, St Columba's Cathedral, Oban, 1940-42. Parish Priest: Knoydart, 1942-51; Eriskay, 1951-56; Benbecula, 1956-66; Fort William, 1966-68. Hon. LLD, Univ. of St Francis Xavier, Canada, 1974. *Address:* Bishop's House, Esplanade, Oban, Argyll. *T:* Oban 2010.

ARGYLL AND THE ISLES, Dean of; *see* Wilson, Very Rev. I. G. MacQ.

ARGYRIS, Prof. John, DScEng, DE Munich; Professor of Aeronautical Structures in the University of London, at Imperial College of Science and Technology, 1955-75, Visiting Professor 1975-80, now Emeritus Professor; Director of Institute for Statics and Dynamics, Stuttgart, since 1959; *b* 19 Aug. 1916; *s* of Nicolas and Lucie Argyris; *m* 1953, Inga-Lisa (*née* Johansson); one *s. Educ:* 3rd Gymnasium, Athens; Technical Universities, Athens, Munich and Zurich. With J. Gollnow u. Son, Stettin, Research in Structures, 1937-39; Royal Aeronautical Soc., Research and Technical Officer, 1943-49; Univ. of London, Imperial Coll. of Science and Technology, Dept of Aeronautics: Senior Lecturer, 1949; Reader in Theory of Aeronautical Structures, 1950. Corres. Mem., Acad. of Scis, Athens, 1973; Hon. Fellow, Groupe pour l'Avancement des Méthodes Numériques de l'Ingenieur, Paris, 1974; Hon. FCGI, 1976; Hon. Dott Ing Genoa; Hon. dr.tech Trondheim. Silver Medal, RAeS, 1971; Von Kármán Medal, Amer. Soc. of Civil Engrs, 1975; Copernicus Medal, Polish Acad. of Scis, 1979; Gold Medal, Land Baden-Württemberg, 1980; Hon. Prof., Northwestern Polytechnical Univ., Xian, Shaanxi, PR of China, 1980; Timoshenko Medal, ASME, 1981. Editor, Jl of Computer Methods in Applied Mechanics and Engineering, 1972-. *Publications:* Handbook of Aeronautics, Vol. I, 1952: Energy Theorems and Structural Analysis, 1960; Modern Fuselage Analysis and the Elastic Aircraft, 1963; Recent Advances in Matrix Methods of Structural Analysis, 1964; Introduction into the Finite Element Method, vols I and II, 1982; articles and publications in Ingenieur Archiv, Reports and Memoranda of Aeronautical Research Council, Journal of Royal Aeronautical Society and Aircraft Engineering, CMAME, etc; over 280 scientific publications. *Recreations:* reading, music, hiking, archæology. *Address:* Institut für Statik und Dynamik, 27 Pfaffenwaldring, D-7 Stuttgart, Federal Republic of Germany. *T:* 010-49711 6853594; c/o Department of Aeronautics, Imperial College, Prince Consort Road, SW7. *Club:* English-Speaking Union.

ARIAS, Dame Margot Fonteyn de, (Margot Fonteyn), DBE 1956 (CBE 1951); Prima Ballerina Assoluta; President of the Royal Academy of Dancing, since 1954; Chancellor of Durham University, since 1982; *b* 18 May 1919; *m* 1955, Roberto E. Arias, *qv.* Hon. degrees: LittD Leeds; DMus London and Oxon; LLD Cantab; DLitt Manchester; LLD Edinburgh. Benjamin Franklin Medal, RSA, 1974; Internat. Artist Award, Philippines, 1976; Hamburg Internat. Shakespeare Prize, 1977. Order of Finnish Lion, 1960; Order of Estacio de Sa, Brazil, 1973; Chevalier, Order of Merit of Duarte, Sanchez and Mella, Dominican Republic, 1975. *Publications:* Margot Fonteyn, 1975; A Dancer's World, 1978; The Magic of Dance, 1980 (BBC series, 1979). *Address:* c/o Royal Opera House, Covent Garden, WC2.

ARIAS, Roberto Emilio; *b* 1918; *s* of Dr Harmodio Arias (President of Panama, 1932-36) and Rosario Guardia de Arias; *m*; one *s* two *d*; *m* 1955, Margot Fonteyn (see Dame Margot Fonteyn de Arias). *Educ:* Peddie Sch., New Jersey, USA; St John's Coll., Cambridge. Called to the Bar, Panama, 1939; Fifth Circuit, Court of Appeals, US, 1941; Editor, El Panama-America, 1942-46; Counsellor to Panama Embassy, Chile, 1947; Publisher, La Hora, 1948-68; Delegate to UN Assembly, New York, 1953; Panamanian Ambassador to the Court of St James's, 1955-58, 1960-62; Elected Dep. to the Nat. Assembly of Panama, Oct. 1964-Sept. 1968. *Address:* PO Box 6-1140, Eldorado, Panama, Republic of Panama.

ARIAS-SALGADO Y MONTALVO, Fernando; Spanish Ambassador to the Court of St James's, since 1981; Barrister-at-Law; *b* 3 May 1938; *s* of Gabriel Arias-Salgado y Cubas and Maria Montalvo Gutierrez; *m* 1969, Maria Isabel Garrigues Lopez-Chicheri; one *s* one *d*. *Educ:* Univ. of Madrid. Mem., Illustrious Coll. of Lawyers of Madrid. Entered Diplomatic Sch., 1963; Sec., Permanent Rep. of Spain to UN, 1966; Advr, UN Security Council, 1968-69; Asst Dir Gen., Promotion of Research, 1971, Asst Dir Gen., Internat. Co-operation, 1972, Min. of Educn and Science; Legal Advr (internat. matters), Legal Dept, Min. of Foreign Affairs, 1973; Counsellor, Spanish Delegn to Internat. Court of Justice, 1975; Tech. Sec. Gen., Min. of Foreign Affairs, 1976; Dir Gen., Radiotelevisión Española, 1977. Comendador: Orden de Isabel la Católica; Orden del Merito Civil; Orden de San Raimundo de Peñafort; Caballero, Orden de Carlos III. *Address:* Spanish Embassy, 24 Belgrave Square, SW1. *T:* 01-235 8363.

ARIFIN, Dr Sjahabuddin; Indonesian Ambassador to the Court of St James's, since 1981; *b* 3 March 1928; *m* Siti Asiah; three *s*. *Educ:* Universität Bern, Switzerland (Dr of Econs, Rechts- und Wirtschafts- Wissenschaftliche Fakultät). Indonesian Embassy, Bern, Switzerland, 1951-57; Econ. Expert, Dept of Foreign Affairs, Jakarta, 1957-62; Lectr, Sch. of Econs, Pajajaran Univ., Bandung, 1960-62; Counsellor, Indonesian Embassy, Washington, USA, 1962-63; Ambassador to Iran, 1963-67; Dept of Foreign Affairs, Jakarta: Head of Directorate, Econ. Multilateral Co-operation, 1967-71; Dir Gen., Foreign Econ., Social and Cultural Relations, 1971-77; Sec. Gen., 1977-81. *Recreations:* reading, walking, golf. *Address:* Nusantara, Bishops Grove, The Bishops Avenue, N2 0BP. *T:* 01-455 8154. *Clubs:* Highgate Golf; Jakarta Golf (Indonesia).

ARKELL, John Heward, CBE 1961; TD; MA; CBIM, FIPM; Senior Associate, Kramer International Ltd, since 1980; Director of Administration, BBC, 1960-70; Chairman, Air Transport and Travel Industry Training Board, 1970-80; Director, UK Provident Institution, 1971-80; *b* 20 May 1909; *s* of Rev. H. H. Arkell, MA, and Gertrude Mary Arkell; *m* 1st, 1940, Helen Birgit Huitfeldt; two *s* one *d*; 2nd, 1956, Meta Bachke Grundtvig (marr. diss.) one *s*. *Educ:* Dragon Sch.; Radley Coll.; Christ Church, Oxford (MA). Sir Max Michaelis (Investment) Trust, 1931-37. Asst Sec., CPRE, 1937-39, Mem. of Exec. Cttee, 1945-75, Vice-Chm., 1967-74, Vice-Pres., 1975-. Commissioned Territorial Officer, KRRC 1939; served War of 1939-45; demobilised 1945, Major. Personnel Manager, J. Lyons, 1945-49; BBC: Controller, Staff Admin, 1949-58; Dir, Staff Admin, 1958-60. Dir, The Boots Co. Ltd, 1970-79. Lay Mem., Nat. Industrial Relations Ct, 1972-74. Lectr on indust. subjects; occasional indpe. management consultancies include P&O and Coates Group of Cos (Dir, 1970-76). Founder and Exec. Pres., and former Gen. Hon. Sec., then Chm., Christ Church (Oxford) United Clubs (Community Centre, SE London), 1932-. Chm. Council, British Institute of Management, 1972-74 (Fellow, 1964-, now Companion; Vice-Chm., 1966-72; Chm. Exec. Cttee,

1966-69; Vice Pres., 1974-); Chm. BIM/CBI Educl Panel, 1971-72; Dir, BIM Foundn, 1976-81; Member Council: CBI, 1973-75; Industry for Management Educn, 1971-; Foundn for Management Educn, 1971-75; National Trust 1971-; Adv. Council, Business Graduates Assoc., 1973-; Action Resource Centre, 1975-; Chm., Cttee of British Council of Churches responsible for report on further educn of young people, 1960-61; Member: Finance Cttee C of E Bd of Finance, 1960-68; CS Deptl Cttee to consider application o Fulton Report to Civil Service, 1968-70; Final Selection Bd, CS Commn 1978-81. Trustee, Visnews, 1960-69; Vis. Fellow, Administrative Staff Coll 1971-; Governor, Radley Coll., 1965-70; Chm., Radley Coll. War Mem Cttee, 1968-. FRSA. *Publications:* composer of light music; contrib. to jls o management and indust. subjects. *Recreations:* walking, swimming, music *Address:* Pinnocks, Fawley, near Henley-on-Thames, Oxon. *T:* Henley 301? Glen Cottage, Ringstead Bay, Dorchester, Dorset. *T:* Warmwell 85268(. *Clubs:* Savile; Leander.

ARKFELD, Most Rev. Leo; see Madang, Archbishop of, (RC).

ARLOTT, John; see Arlott, L. T. J.

ARLOTT, (Leslie Thomas) John, OBE 1970; wine correspondent an general writer, The Guardian; topographer; former broadcaster; *b* Basingstoke 25 Feb. 1914; *s* of late William John and Nellie Jenvey Arlott; *m* 1st, Daw: Rees; one *s* (and one *s* decd); 2nd, Valerie France (*d* 1976); one *s* (one *d* decd) 3rd, 1977, Patricia Hoare. *Educ:* Queen Mary's Sch., Basingstoke. Clerk in Mental Hospital, 1930-34; Police (Detective Sergeant), 1934-45; Produce BBC, 1945-50; General Instructor, BBC Staff Training School, 1951-53 Contested (L) Epping Division, Gen. Election, 1955 and 1959. President Cricketers' Assoc., 1968-; Hampshire Schools Cricket Assoc., 1966-80. Hon MA Southampton, 1973. Sports Journalist of 1979 (British Press Award) Sports Personality of 1980 (Soc. of Authors' Pye Radio Award); Spor Presenter of the Year, 1980 (TV and Radio Industries Club Award). DUniv Open, 1981. *Publications:* (with G. R. Hamilton) Landmarks, 1943; Of Perio and Place (poems), 1944; Clausentum (poems), 1945; First Time In Americ (anthology), 1949; Concerning Cricket, 1949; How to Watch Cricket, 1949 Maurice Tate, 1951; Concerning Soccer, 1952; (ed) Cricket (Pleasures of Lif series), 1953; The Picture of Cricket, 1955; English Cheeses of the South an West, 1956; Jubilee History of Cricket, 1965; Vintage Summer, 1967; (wit Sir Neville Cardus) The Noblest Game, 1969; Fred: portrait of a fast bowler 1971; The Ashes, 1972; Island Camera: the Isles of Scilly in the photograph of the Gibson family, 1973; The Snuff Shop, 1974; (ed) The Oxfor Companion to Sports and Games, 1975; (with Christopher Fielden Burgundy, Vines and Wines, 1976; Krug: House of Champagne, 1977; (wit' Patrick Eagar) An Eye for Cricket, 1979; Jack Hobbs: a profile of the master 1981. *Recreations:* watching cricket, drinking wine, talking, sleeping collecting aquatints, engraved glass, and wine artefacts. *Address:* c/o Th Guardian, 119 Farringdon Road, EC1R 3ER. *Clubs:* National Liberal, MCC (Hon. Life Mem., 1980); Master's; Forty, Hampshire CCC.

ARMAGH, Archbishop of, and Primate of All Ireland, since 1980; Mos Rev. John Ward Armstrong; *b* 30 Sept. 1915; *s* of John and Elizabeth Armstrong, Belfast; *m* 1941, Doris Winifred, *d* of William J. Harrison, PC and Florence Harrison, Dublin; two *s* two *d* (and one *d* decd). *Educ:* Belfas Royal Academy; Trinity College, Dublin, BA, Respondent, 1938; Toplad Memorial Prize, Past. Theol Pr. and Abp. King's Prize (2) 1937; Biblical Greel Prize and Downes Prize (1) 1938; 1st Class Hons Hebrew, 1936 and 1937; 1s Class Divinity Testimonium, 1938; BD 1945; MA 1957 (SC). Deacon, the Priest, All Saints, Grangegorman, 1938; Hon. Clerical Vicar, Christ Churcl Cathedral, 1939; Dean's Vicar, St Patrick's Cathedral, 1944; Prebend. o Tassagard, St Patrick's Cathedral, 1950; Rector of Christ Church, Leeson Park 1951; Dean of St Patrick's Cathedral, Dublin, 1958-68; Bishop of Cashel an Emly, Waterford and Lismore, 1968-77 (when diocese reorganised), o Cashel, Waterford, Lismore, Ossory, Ferns and Leighlin (known as Bishop o Cashel and Ossory), 1977-80. Wallace Lecturer, TCD, 1954-65; Dean o Residences, University College, Dublin, 1954-63. Vice-Pres. Boys' Brigade 1963-73. Trustee, Nat. Library of Ireland, 1964-74; Member: British Counci of Churches, 1966-80; Anglican Consultative Council, 1971-81. Hon. DI Trinity Coll. Dublin, 1981. *Publication:* contrib. to Church and Eucharist-an Ecumenical Study (ed Rev. M. Hurley, SJ), 1966. *Recreations:* carpentering and bird-watching. *Address:* The See House, Cathedral Close, Armagh, Co Armagh BT61 7EE. *T:* 522851. *Clubs:* Friendly Brothers of St Patrick, Kildar Street and University (Dublin).

ARMAGH, Archbishop of, (RC), and Primate of All Ireland, since 1977 His Eminence Cardinal Tomás Séamus O'Fiaich; *b* Crossmaglen, 3 Nov 1923; *s* of Patrick Fee and Annie Fee (née Caraher). *Educ:* Cregganduff Publi Elem. School; St Patrick's Coll., Armagh; St Patrick's Coll., Maynooth; S Peter's Coll., Wexford; University Coll., Dublin; Catholic Univ. of Louvain BA (Celtic Studies) 1943, MA (Early Irish History) 1950 (NUI); LicScHis 1952 (Louvain). Ordained, Wexford, 1948; Curate, Moy, Co. Tyrone 1952-53; St Patrick's College, Maynooth: Lectr in Modern History, 1953-59 Prof. of Modern History, 1959-74; Pres., 1974-77. Cardinal, 1979. Chairman Govt Commn on Restoration of the Irish Language, 1959-63; Irish Languag Advisory Council, 1965-68; Pres., Soc. of Irish-speaking Priests, 1955-67 Treas., Catholic Record Soc. of Ireland, 1954-74; Editor, Jl of Armagh Historical Soc. and other jls. *Publications:* Gaelscrinte i gCéin, 1960; Iris Cultural Influence in Europe, 1967; Imeacht na nIarlaíi, 1972; Má Nuad, 1972 Art MacCumhaigh, 1973; St Columbanus in his own words, 1974; Olive

Plunkett: Ireland's New Saint, 1975; Aifreann Ceolta Tíre, 1977; Art Mac Bionaid, 1979. *Address:* Ara Coeli, Armagh, Ireland. *T:* Armagh 522045.

ARMAGH, Auxiliary Bishop of, (RC); *see* Lenny, Most Rev. Francis.

ARMAGH, Dean of; *see* Crooks, Very Rev. J. R. M.

ARMER, Sir (Isaac) Frederick, KBE 1954; CB 1945; MC 1918; *b* 1891; 2nd *s* of William and Gwenllian Armer; *m* 1925, Elsie Maude Neale; one *s* two *d. Educ:* Welsh University Coll., Cardiff. BSc (Hons). Served European War, 1914-19. Entered Civil Service Sept. 1919 as Assistant Principal; Sec. Royal Commission on London Squares, 1928; Assistant Sec., 1938; Chm. Welsh Board of Health, 1940-44; Under Sec., Min. of Health, 1946, Dep. Sec., 1951-56; Chm., Board of Control, 1952-60. *Address:* Picketston Cottage, Flemingston, Barry, South Glam.

ARMIDALE, Bishop of, since 1976; **Rt. Rev. Peter Chiswell;** *b* 18 Feb. 1934; *s* of Ernest and Florence Ruth Chiswell; *m* 1960, Betty Marie Craik; two *s* one *d. Educ:* Univ. of New South Wales (BE); Moore Theological College (BD London, Th. Schol.). Vicar of Bingara, 1961-68; Vicar of Gunnedah, 1968-76; Archdeacon of Tamworth, 1971-76. *Address:* Bishopscourt, Armidale, NSW, Australia. *T:* 067-724555.

ARMITAGE, Sir Arthur (Llewellyn), Kt 1975; MA, LLB, LLD; Vice-Chancellor, and Professor of Common Law, Victoria University of Manchester, 1970-80, now Professor Emeritus; Chairman, Social Security Advisory Committee, since 1980; *b* 1 Aug. 1916; *m* 1940, Joan Kenyon Marcroft; two *d. Educ:* Oldham Hulme Grammar Sch.; Queens' Coll., Cambridge. Law Tripos 1936; LLB 1937; Commonwealth Fund Fellow, Yale Univ., USA, 1937-39; called to the Bar, 1940, Inner Temple. Served Army, 1940-45, KRRC and 2nd Army, temp. Major. Fellow Queens' Coll., Cambridge, 1945-58; Asst Tutor, 1945; Tutor, 1946; Senior Tutor, 1957; President, 1958-70; Hon. Fellow, 1970. University Lectr in Law, 1947-70; Vice-Chancellor, Univ. of Cambridge, 1965-67, Dep. Vice-Chancellor, 1967-70. Dep. Chm. QS, Co. Huntingdon, 1963-65, Co. Huntingdon and Peterborough, 1965-71. Mem. and Chm., Wages Councils, 1955-70; Chairman: Trustee Savings Bank Arbitration Tribunal, 1964-78; Cttee on Pay of Postmen, 1964; Adv. Cttee on Trng and Supply of Teachers, 1973-79; British Cttee of Award of Commonwealth Fund, 1969-74; Cttee of Vice-Chancellors and Principals of Univs of UK, 1974-76; Cttee on Political Activities of Civil Servants, 1976-78; Cttee on Lorries, People and the Environment (Report, 1981); Member: Departmental Cttee on Summary Trial of Minor Offences, 1954-55; Chm.'s Panel Industrial Ct, 1962-74; Agric. Wages Bd for England and Wales, 1967-72 (Chm., 1968-72); Nat. Adv. Council on Training of Magistrates, 1964-70; UGC, 1967-70; Lord Chancellor's Cttee on Legal Educn, 1967-71; NI Cttee on Legal Educn, 1973-74; UNESCO Adv. Mission for Develt of Univ. of W Indies, 1964; Standing Adv. Cttee on Grants to Students, 1961-65; Council, ACU, 1972-80 (Vice-Chm., 1979-80); Inter-Univ. Council for Higher Educn Overseas, 1972-81 (Dep. Chm., 1978-80); Adv. Council on the Penal System, 1976-78; Council for the Securities Industry, 1980-. Pres., Soc. of Public Teachers of Law, 1967-68; Trustee, Henry Fund, 1961-70; Mem., Council of Management, Chatsworth House Trust, 1981-; Chm. Governors, Leys Sch., Cambridge, 1971-. Hon. Bencher, Inner Temple. JP City of Cambridge, 1950-70. Hon. LLD: Manchester, 1970; Belfast, 1980; Liverpool, 1981; Birmingham, 1981. Order of Andrés Bello 1st Class (Venezuela), 1968. *Publications:* Case Book on Criminal Law (with J. W. C. Turner), 1952, 1958, 1964; Jt Editor Clerk and Lindsell on Torts, 1954, 1961, 1969, 1975. *Address:* Rowley Lodge, Kermincham, near Holmes Chapel, Cheshire. *Club:* Athenæum.

ARMITAGE, Edward, CB 1974; Comptroller-General, Patent Office and Industrial Property and Copyright Department, Department of Trade (formerly Trade and Industry), 1969-77; *b* 16 July 1917; *s* of Harry and Florence Armitage; *m* 1940, Marjorie Pope; one *s* two *d. Educ:* Huddersfield Coll.; St Catharine's Coll., Cambridge. Patent Office, BoT: Asst Examr 1939; Examr 1944; Sen. Examr 1949; Principal Examr 1960; Suptg Examr 1962; Asst Comptroller 1966. Governor, Centre d'Etudes Internationales de la Propriété Industrielle, Strasbourg, 1975-. *Recreations:* tennis, bridge, gardening. *Address:* Lynwood, Lascot Hill, Wedmore, Somerset. *T:* Wedmore 712079.

See also Peter Armitage.

ARMITAGE, Maj.-Gen. Geoffrey Thomas Alexander, CBE 1968 (MBE 1945); *b* 5 July 1917; *s* of late Lt-Col H. G. P. Armitage and late Mary Madeline (*née* Drought); *m* 1949, Monica Wall Kent (*widow, née* Poat); one *s* one step *d. Educ:* Haileybury Coll.; RMA, Woolwich (Sword of Honour). Commissioned Royal Artillery, 1937. Served War of 1939-45 (despatches, MBE), BEF, Middle East, Italy, NW Europe. Transferred to Royal Dragoons (1st Dragoons), 1951, comd 1956-59; Instructor (GSO1), IDC, 1959-60; Col GS, War Office, 1960-62; Comdt RAC Centre, 1962-65; Chief of Staff, HQ1 (BR) Corps, 1966-68; Dir, Royal Armoured Corps, 1968-70; GOC Northumbrian Dist, 1970-72; retd 1973. Dir, CLA Game Fair, 1974-80. *Recreations:* writing, some field sports. *Address:* Clyffe, Tincleton, near Dorchester, Dorset. *Clubs:* Army and Navy, Kennel.

ARMITAGE, Henry St John Basil, CBE 1978 (OBE 1968); HM Diplomatic Service, retired; Middle East consultant; Director: Société Commissionaire et Financière, Geneva; SCF Finance Ltd, London; Honorary Secretary to British/Saudi Arabian Parliamentary Group; *b* 5 May 1924; *s* of Henry John Armitage and late Amelia Eleanor Armitage; *m* 1956, Jennifer Gerda Bruford, *d* of Prof. W. H. Bruford, *qv* ; one *s* one *d. Educ:* St Bede's and Bradford Grammar Schs; Lincoln Christ's Hosp.; Trinity Coll., Cambridge. Served Army, 1943-49; Arab Legion, 1946; British Mil. Mission to Saudi Arabia, 1946-49. Mil. Adviser to Saudi Arabian Minister of Defence, 1949-51; Desert Locust Control, Kenya and Aden Protectorates, 1952; in mil. service of Sultan of Muscat and Oman in Oman and Dhofar, 1952-59; Resident Manager, Gen. Geophysical Co. (Houston), Libya, 1959-60; Oil Conslt, Astor Associates, Libya, 1960-61; Business conslt, Beirut, 1962; joined HM Diplomatic Service, 1962; First Secretary (Commercial): Baghdad, 1963-67; Beirut, 1967-68; First Sec., Jedda, 1968 and 1969-74; Consul Gen. and Counsellor, Dubai, 1974-78. Mem., Editl Adv. Bd, 8 Days, 1978-79. *Recreations:* reading, travel. *Address:* The Old Vicarage, East Horrington, Wells, Somerset. *Club:* Travellers'.

ARMITAGE, Prof. John Vernon, PhD; Principal, College of St Hild and St Bede, Durham, since 1975; *b* 21 May 1932; *s* of Horace Armitage and Evelyn (*née* Hauton); *m* 1963, Sarah Catherine Clay; two *s. Educ:* Rothwell Grammar Sch., Yorks; UCL (BSc, PhD); Cuddesdon Coll., Oxford. Asst Master: Pontefract High Sch., 1956-58; Shrewsbury Sch., 1958-59; Lectr in Maths, Univ. of Durham, 1959-67; Sen. Lectr in Maths, King's Coll., London, 1967-70; Prof. of Mathematical Educn, Univ. of Nottingham, 1970-75; Special Prof., Nottingham Univ., 1976-79. Chm., Math. Instruction Sub-Cttee, Brit. Nat. Cttee for Maths, Royal Soc., 1975-78. *Publications:* A Companion to Advanced Mathematics (with H. B. Griffiths), 1969; papers on theory of numbers in various jls. *Recreations:* railways, cricket and most games inexpertly. *Address:* The Principal's House, Leazes Lane, Durham DH1 1TB. *T:* Durham 63741.

ARMITAGE, Kenneth, CBE 1969; sculptor; *b* 18 July 1916; *m* 1940. Studied at Slade Sch., London, 1937-39. Served War of 1939-45 in the Army. Teacher of Sculpture, Bath Academy of Art, 1946-56. Regular one-man exhibitions, Gimpel Fils, London, since 1952, and New York since 1954, the last at Paul Rosenberg & Co., 1958; Marlborough Fine Art London, 1962, 1965; Arts Council Exhibn touring 10 English cities, 1972-73; Gall. Kasahara, Osaka, 1974, 1978 and Fuji Telecasting Gall., Tokyo, and Gal. Humanite, Nagoya; Stoke-on-Trent City Mus. and Art Gall., 1981; Sala Mendoza, Caracas, Venezuela, 1982. Gregory Fellowship in sculpture, Leeds Univ., 1953-55; Guest Artist: Caracas, Venezuela, 1963; City of Berlin, 1967-69. Work shown in: Exhibn of Recent Sculpture in British Pavilion at 26th Venice Biennale, 1952; Internat. Open-Air Exhibns of sculpture in Antwerp, London, Sonsbeek, Varese, and Sydney; British Council Exhibns of sculpture since 1952, which have toured Denmark, Germany, Holland, Norway, Sweden, Switzerland, Canada, USA, and S America; New Decade Exhibn, Museum of Modern Art, New York, 1955; British Section of 4th Internat. São Paulo Biennial, Brazil, 1957; 5th Internat. Exhibn of Drawings and Engravings, Lugano, 1958 (prize-winner); British Pavilion at 29th Venice Biennale, 1958; Art since 1945, Kassel Exhibition, 1959; work in British Sculpture in the 'Sixties' exhibition, Tate Gallery, 1965; Internat. Open-air Exhibn, Hakone, Japan, 1969, 1971; 24 English Sculptors, Burlington House, 1971; Jubilee sculpture exhibn, Battersea Park, 1977. Work represented in: Victoria and Albert Museum, Tate Gallery; Museum of Modern Art, New York; Musée D'Art Moderne, Paris; Galleria Nazionale d' Arti Moderne, Rome, and other galleries throughout the world. *Address:* 22a Avonmore Road, W14 8RR. *T:* 01-603 5800.

ARMITAGE, Air Vice-Marshal Michael John, CBE 1975; Director of Service Intelligence, since 1982; *b* 25 Aug. 1930; *m* 1970, Gretl Renate Steinig; two *s. Educ:* Newport Grammar Sch., IW; Halton Apprentice; RAF Coll., Cranwell. psc 1965, jssc 1970, rcds 1975. Commnd 1953; flying and staff appts, incl. 28 Sqn, Hong Kong, and No 4 and No 1 Flying Trng Schools; Personal Staff Officer to Comdr Second Allied Tactical Air Force, 1966; OC 17 Sqdn, 1967-70; Stn Comdr, RAF Luqa, Malta, 1972-74; Dir Forward Policy, Ministry of Defence (Air Force Dept), 1976-78; Dep. Comdr, RAF Germany, 1978-80; Senior RAF Mem., RCDS, 1980-81. *Publications:* (jtly) Air Power in the Nuclear Age, 1982; contrib. prof. jls. *Recreations:* military history, game shooting, reading. *Address:* c/o Lloyds Bank, 6 Pall Mall, SW1. *Club:* Royal Air Force.

ARMITAGE, Prof. Peter; Professor of Biomathematics, and Fellow, St Peter's College, University of Oxford, since 1976; *b* 15 June 1924; *s* of Harry and Florence Armitage, Huddersfield; *m* 1947, Phyllis Enid Perry, London; one *s* two *d. Educ:* Huddersfield Coll.; Trinity Coll., Cambridge. Wrangler, 1947; MA Cambridge, 1952; PhD London, 1951; Ministry of Supply, 1943-45; National Physical Laboratory, 1945-46; Mem. Statistical Research Unit of Med. Research Council, London Sch. of Hygiene and Trop. Med., 1947-61; Prof. of Medical Statistics, Univ. of London, 1961-76. Hon. Sec., Royal Statistical Society, 1958-64; President: Biometric Soc., 1972-73; Royal Statistical Soc., 1982-; Mem., International Statistical Institute, 1961. Editor, Biometrics, 1980-. *Publications:* Sequential Medical Trials, 1960, 2nd edn 1975; Statistical Methods in Medical Research, 1971; papers in statistical and medical journals. *Recreation:* music. *Address:* 71 High Street, Drayton, Abingdon, Oxon OX14 4JW. *T:* Drayton (Abingdon) 763.

See also Edward Armitage.

ARMITAGE, Sir Robert (Perceval), KCMG 1954 (CMG 1951); MBE 1944; MA; *b* 21 Dec. 1906; *s* of late F. Armitage, CIE; *m* 1930, Gwladys Lyona, *d* of late Lt-Col H. M. Meyler, CBE, DSO, MC, Croix de Guerre; two *s. Educ:* Winchester; New Coll. District Officer, Kenya Colony, 1929; Sec. to

Mem. for Agriculture and Natural Resources, 1945; Administrative Sec., 1947; Under Sec., Gold Coast, 1948; Financial Sec., 1948; Min. for Finance, Gold Coast, 1951-53; Governor and C-in-C, Cyprus, 1954-55; Governor of Nyasaland, 1956-61, retired. Trustee of the Beit Trust, 1963–. KStJ 1954. *Recreations:* golf and gardening. *Address:* Suite 24, Great Maytham Hall, Rolvenden, Kent TN17 4NE. *T:* Rolvenden 279. *Club:* Royal Commonwealth Society.

ARMITAGE, (William) Kenneth; *see* Armitage, Kenneth.

ARMOUR, Mary Nicol Neill, RSA 1958 (ARSA 1940); RSW 1956; RGI 1977 (Vice-President, 1982); Teacher of Still Life, Glasgow School of Art, 1952-62, retd; *b* 27 March 1902; *d* of William Steel; *m* 1927, William Armour, RSA, RSW, RGI (*d* 1979). *Educ:* Glasgow Sch. of Art. Has exhibited at Royal Academy, Royal Scottish Academy, Soc. of Scottish Artists, and Royal Glasgow Institute. Work in permanent collections: Glasgow Municipal Gallery; Edinburgh Corporation; Art Galleries of Aberdeen, Perth, Dundee, Newport, Paisley, Greenock and Victoria (Australia). Hon. LLD Glasgow, 1980. *Recreations:* weaving, gardening. *Address:* 2 Gateside, Kilbarchan, Renfrewshire. *T:* Kilbarchan 2873.

ARMSON, Rev. Canon John Moss; Principal, Edinburgh Theological College, since 1982; *b* 21 Dec. 1939; *s* of Arthur Eric Armson and Edith Isobel Moss. *Educ:* Wyggeston Sch.; Selwyn Coll., Cambridge (MA); St Andrews Univ. (PhD); College of the Resurrection, Mirfield. Curate, St John Notting Hill, 1966; Chaplain and Fellow, Downing Coll., Cambridge, 1969; Chaplain, 1973-77, Vice-Principal, 1977-82, Westcott House, Cambridge. *Recreation:* gardening. *Address:* Edinburgh Theological College, Rosebery Crescent, EH12 5JT. *T:* 031-337 3838.

ARMSTRONG, 3rd Baron *cr* 1903, of Bamburgh and Cragside; **William Henry Cecil John Robin Watson-Armstrong;** *b* 6 March 1919; *s* of 2nd Baron Armstrong and Zaida Cecile (*d* 1978), *e d* of Cecil Drummond-Wolff; *S* father, 1972; *m* 1947, Baroness Maria-Teresa du Four Chiodelli Manzoni, *o c* of late Mme Ruegger (*see* Paul J. Ruegger); one adopted *s* one adopted *d*. *Educ:* Eton; Trinity College, Cambridge. An Underwriting Member of Lloyd's. Served War of 1939-45, Captain Scots Guards. *Heir:* none. *Address:* 1 Mount Vernon, Hampstead, NW3; Bamburgh Castle, Northumberland. *Club:* Brooks's.

ARMSTRONG, Andrew Clarence Francis, CMG 1959; Permanent Secretary, Ministry of Mines and Power, Federation of Nigeria, retired; *b* 1 May 1907; *s* of E. R. C. Armstrong, FSA, MRIA, Keeper of Irish Antiquities and later Bluemantle Pursuivant, Herald's Coll., and Mary Frances, *d* of Sir Francis Cruise; *cousin* and *heir-pres.* to Sir Andrew St Clare Armstrong, 5th Bt, *qv*; *m* 1st, 1930, Phyllis Marguerite (*d* 1930), *e d* of Lt-Col H. Waithman, DSO; 2nd, 1932, Laurel May, *d* of late A. W. Stuart; one *s* (and one *s* decd). *Educ:* St Edmund's Coll., Old Hall, Ware; Christ's Coll., Cambridge; BA. Colonial Administrative Service : Western Pacific, 1929; Nigeria, 1940. *Recreation:* golf. *Address:* 15 Ravenscroft Road, Henley-on-Thames, Oxon. *T:* Henley-on-Thames 77635. *Clubs:* Phyllis Court, Temple Golf.

ARMSTRONG, Sir Andrew St Clare, 5th Bt *cr* 1841; *b* 20 Dec. 1912; *s* of Sir Nesbitt William Armstrong, 4th Bt, and Clarice Amy, *d* of John Carter Hodkinson, Maryborough, Victoria, Australia; *S* father 1953. *Educ:* Waitaki; Wellesley Coll. Served War of 1939-45 with RAE, 2nd AIF. *Heir:* cousin Andrew Clarence Francis Armstrong, *qv*.

ARMSTRONG, Anne Legendre; Member, Board of Directors: General Motors, First City Bancorporation of Texas, General Foods, Halliburton Company, since 1977; Boise Cascade Corporation, since 1978; *b* New Orleans, Louisiana, 27 Dec. 1927; *d* of Armant Legendre and Olive Martindale; *m* 1950, Tobin Armstrong; three *s* two *d*. *Educ:* Foxcroft Sch., Middleburg, Va; Vassar Coll., NY (BA). Deleg. Nat. Conventions, 1964, 1968 and 1972; Mem. Republican Nat. Cttee, 1968-73 (Co-Chm., 1971-73); Counselor to the President, with Cabinet rank, 1972-74; Ambassador to the Court of St James's, 1976-77. Co-Chm., Reagan/Bush Campaign, 1980. Lectr in Diplomacy, Chm. Adv. Bd, Vice-Chm. Exec. Bd, Center for Strategic and Internat. Studies, Georgetown Univ., 1977–. Dir, Atlantic Council, 1977–; Member: Council on Foreign Relations, 1977–; Congressional Awards Bd, 1980-81; Chairman: E-SU of the US, 1977-80; President's Foreign Intell. Adv. Bd, 1981–. Trustee: Southern Methodist Univ., 1977–; Economic Club of NY, 1978-81; Guggenheim Foundn, 1980–. Mem. President's Council, Tulane Univ., 1977-80; Citizen Regent, Smithsonian Instn, 1978–; Mem., Visiting Cttee, John F. Kennedy Sch. of Govt, Harvard Univ., 1978-82. Hon. Mem., City of London Br., Royal Soc. of St George, 1978. Phi Beta Kappa. Hon. LLD: Bristol, 1976; Washington and Lee, 1976; Williams Coll., 1977; St Mary's Univ., 1978; Tulane, 1978; Hon. LHD Mt Vernon Coll., 1978. Gold Medal, Nat. Inst. Social Scis, 1977. Josephine Meredith Langstaff Award, Nat. Soc. Daughters of British Empire in US, 1978; Republican Woman of the Year Award, 1979; Texan of the Year Award, 1981. *Address:* Armstrong Ranch, Armstrong, Texas 78338, USA. *Club:* Pilgrims.

ARMSTRONG, Prof. Arthur Hilary, MA Cantab; FBA 1970; Emeritus Professor, University of Liverpool, since 1972; Visiting Professor of Classics and Philosophy, Dalhousie University, Halifax, Nova Scotia, since 1972; *b* 13 Aug. 1909; *s* of the Rev. W. A. Armstrong and Mrs E. M. Armstrong (*née* Cripps); *m* 1933, Deborah, *d* of Alfred Wilson and Agnes Claudia Fox Pease;

two *s* two *d* (and one *d* decd). *Educ:* Lancing Coll.; Jesus Coll., Cambridge Asst Lectr in Classics, University Coll., Swansea, 1936-39; Professor c Classics, Royal University of Malta, Valletta, 1939-43; Classical VIth Form Master, Beaumont Coll., Old Windsor, Berks, 1943-46; Lectr in Latin University Coll., Cardiff, 1946-50; Gladstone Professor of Greek, Univ. c Liverpool, 1950-72. Killam Sen. Fellow, Dalhousie Univ., 1970-7 *Publications:* The Architecture of the Intelligible Universe in the Philosoph of Plotinus, 1940, repr. 1967; An Introduction to Ancient Philosophy, 194 (American edn, 1949, 4th edn, 1965); Plotinus, 1953 (American edn, 1963) Christian Faith and Greek Philosophy (with R. A. Markus), 1960 (America edn, 1964); Plotinus I-III (Loeb Classical Library), 1966-67; Cambridg History of Later Greek and Early Mediæval Philosophy (Editor and par author), 1967, repr. 1970; St Augustine and Christian Platonism, 1968 Plotinian and Christian Studies, 1979; contribs to Classical Qly, Mind, J Hellenic Studies, Jl Theological Studies, Downside Review, etc. *Recreation* travel, gardening. *Address:* The Hollins, Whitton, near Ludlow, Shropshir SY8 3AE. *T:* Ludlow 890241.

ARMSTRONG, Brig. Charles Douglas, CBE 1945; DSO 1940; MC 1919 late East Surrey Regiment; *b* 11 June 1897; *s* of late C. F. Armstrong, Kital Kenya Colony; *m* 1935, Sylvia Holden Earl Bailey; one *s* three *d*. *Educ* Cheltenham Coll.; RMC, Sandhurst. Served European War (wounded twice MC): France, 1916-18; North Russia, Mesopotamia, 1920-21; NWF Indi 1930-31; War of 1939-45 (wounded twice, DSO, Africa Star, CBE): France 1939-40; N Africa, 1943; Jugoslavia, 1943-44. Retired 1948. *Addres* Rushetts, Old Green Lane, Camberley, Surrey GU15 4LG. *T:* Camberle 21028. *Club:* Special Forces.

ARMSTRONG, Christopher Wyborne, OBE 1943; farming in Kenya sinc 1959; *b* 9 May 1899; *s* of Rt Hon. H. B. Armstrong, Dean's Hill, Armagh *m* 1956, Hilde Ingeburg Kolz, Lübeck; one *s* one *d*. *Educ:* Winchester; Trinit Coll., Cambridge (MA). Lieutenant RFA, BEF, France, 1918; Burmah Oi Co., Burma, 1922-39; Royal Engineers, BEF, France, 1939-40; Burmah Oi Co., Burma, 1940-42; Member, House of Representatives, Burma, 1942 Controller of Petroleum Industry, Burma, 1942; AQMG, MEF, Egypt 1942-43; GHQ, India, 1944-45; Commissioner, Magwe Division, Burma 1945-46; farming in Kenya, 1947-54 and 1959-. MP (UU) Co. Armagh 1954-59. Mem., UK delegn to Council of Europe and WEU, 1957-59 *Address:* Kwetu Farm, Gilgil, Kenya. *Club:* United Oxford & Cambridg University.

ARMSTRONG, Rev. Canon Claude Blakeley, MA, BD; Canon residentiar of Worcester, 1947-70, Canon Emeritus 1970; Vice-Dean and Treasurer 1965-70; *b* 31 Oct. 1889; *e s* of late Rev. J. B. Armstrong, MA; *m* 1914, Hester (*d* 1968), *d* of late Sir Samuel Dill, LittD; one *d*. *Educ:* St Stephen's Greer School and Trinity Coll., Dublin (First Classical Scholar). Senior Moderator in Classics and Philosophy; Fellowship prizeman; Vice-Chancellor's prizeman and Medallist. Lieut, OTC, 1914-18; Observer Officer, ROC, 1940-45 Deputy for the Professor of Greek, Queen's Univ. Belfast, 1913-14 Headmaster of Cork Grammar Sch., 1914-19; Warden of St Columba's Coll. Rathfarnham, 1920-33; Headmaster of St Andrew's Coll., Grahamstown, SA 1934-38; Rector of Clannaborough, near Exeter, 1940-43; Rector of Clyst S George, 1943-47; Lectr in Classics, University Coll. of the South-West Exeter, 1940-47. Pres. Irish Schoolmasters Assoc., 1929; Pres. Exeter Clerica Soc., 1942; Vice-Pres. Classical Assoc. (Chm. Council). Examining Chaplain to the Bishop of Worcester, and Director of Training, 1948; Warden Worcester Ordination Coll., 1952-64; Founder, Worcester Ordination Coll. 1965. Editor, Veritas (for Anglican Assoc.). *Publications:* The Persians of Aeschylus translated into English verse; Outline of Western Philosophy, 1964 Foundations Unshaken, 1966; Creeds and Credibility, 1969; Autumn Leaves 3 vols, (light verse), 1979, 1980, 1981; contributor to Reviews and Punch Editor Sir S. Dill's Roman Society in Gaul in the Merovingian Age. *Address* 12a College Green, Worcester. *T:* Worcester 25837. *Club:* Kildare Street and University (Dublin).

ARMSTRONG, Rt. Hon. Ernest, PC 1979; MP (Lab) North West Durham since 1964; *b* 12 Jan. 1915; *s* of John and Elizabeth Armstrong; *m* 1941, Hannah P. Lamb; one *s* one *d*. *Educ:* Wolsingham Grammar Sch. Schoolmaster 1937-52; Headmaster, 1952-64. Chm., Sunderland Educn Cttee, 1960-65. Ass Govt Whip, 1967-69; Lord Comr, HM Treasury, 1969-70; an Opposition Whip, 1970-73; Parly Under-Sec. of State, DES, 1974-75, DoE, 1975-79 Dep. Chm., Ways and Means and Dep. Speaker, 1981-. Vice-Pres., Methodist Conf., 1974-75. *Recreation:* walking. *Address:* Penny Well, Witton-le-Wear Bishop Auckland, Co. Durham. *T:* Witton-le-Wear 397.

ARMSTRONG, Francis William, CB 1977; MVO 1953; *b* 11 July 1919; *s* of late W. T. Armstrong, Gravesend, Kent; *m* 1st, 1945, Brenda Gladys de Wardt (*d* 1967); one *d* ; 2nd, 1969, Muriel Ernestine Hockaday, MBE. *Educ* King's Sch., Rochester; Brasenose Coll., Oxford (Open Scholarship in Classics) (MA). Served War of 1939-45: RA (commissioned, 1940); Western Desert, India, Burma. Asst Principal, War Office, 1947; Private Sec. to Permanent Under-Sec., War Office, 1948-50; Principal Private Sec. to Sec. of State for War, 1957-60; Director of Finance, Metropolitan Police, 1968-69 Asst Under-Sec. of State, MoD, 1969-72; Under Sec., Cabinet Office, 1972-74; Dep. Sec., N Ireland Office, 1974-75; Dep. Sec., MoD, 1975-77 retired 1977. Comr, Royal Hospital, Chelsea, 1977-. *Recreations:* walking cricket, reading. *Address:* 50 Nork Way, Banstead, Surrey. *T:* Burgh Heath 54602. *Clubs:* Royal Commonwealth Society, Kent CCC.

RMSTRONG, Jack; see Armstrong, J. A.

RMSTRONG, Rt. Rev. John, CB 1962; OBE 1942; Assistant Bishop in the Diocese of Exeter; *b* 4 Oct. 1905; *y s* of late John George and Emily Armstrong; *m* 1942, Diana Gwladys Prowse, *widow* of Lieut Geoffrey Vernon Prowse, and 2nd *d* of late Admiral Sir Geoffrey Layton, GBE, KCB, KCMG, DSO; one step *s. Educ:* Durham School and St Francis Coll., Nundah, Brisbane, Qld. LTh, 2nd Class Hons, Australian College of Theology, 1932. Ordained 1933; Mem. Community of Ascension, Goulburn, 1932-33; Curate, St Martin, Scarborough, 1933-35; Chaplain RN, HMS Victory, 1935; Courageous, 1936-39; 6th Destroyer Flotilla, 1939-41 (despatches 1940); RM Div., 1941-43; Commando Group, 1943-45; HMS Nelson, 1945; Sen. Naval Chaplain, Germany, 1946-48; Excellent, 1948-50; RM Barracks, Portsmouth, 1950-53; Indomitable, 1953; RN Rhine Sqdn, 1953-54; HMS Vanguard, 1954; Tyne, 1954; HM Dockyard, Malta, and Asst to Chaplain of the Fleet, Mediterranean, 1955-57; HMS Bermuda, 1957-59; RM Barracks, Portsmouth, 1959-60; Chaplain of the Fleet and Archdeacon of the Royal Navy, 1960-63; Bishop of Bermuda, 1963-68; Vicar of Yarcombe, Honiton, 1969-73. QHC, 1958-63. Life Mem., Guild of Freemen of City of London. *Address:* Foundry Farm, Yarcombe, Honiton, Devon EX14 9AZ. *T:* Chard 3332. *Club:* Naval and Military.

RMSTRONG, John Anderson, CB 1980; OBE 1945; TD 1945; Master of the Court of Protection, 1970-82; *b* 5 May 1910; *s* of W. A. Armstrong; *m* 1938, Barbara, *d* of Rev. W. L. Gantz; two *d* (and one *s* decd). *Educ:* Wellington Coll.; Trinity Coll., Cambridge. BA 1931, MA 1943. Called to Bar, Lincoln's Inn, 1936. City of London Yeomanry, RHA(T), 1931-40. Served War: Lt-Col Comdg 73 Light AA Regt, 1940-45 (Normandy, 1944). Practice at Chancery Bar, 1946-70; Bencher, Lincoln's Inn, 1969. *Recreations:* gardening, walking, fishing, golf. *Address:* 62 Chelsea Park Gardens, SW3 6AE. *T:* 01-352 0369; Dacre Cottage, Penrith, Cumbria CA11 0HL. *T:* Pooley Bridge 224. *Club:* Brooks's.

RMSTRONG, John Archibald, (Jack); Chief Executive Officer, 1973-82, and Chairman, 1974-82, Imperial Oil Ltd; *b* Dauphin, Manitoba, 24 March 1917. *Educ:* Univ. of Manitoba (BSc Geol.); Queen's Univ. at Kingston (BSc Chem. Engrg). Worked for short time with Geol Survey of Canada and in mining industry; joined Imperial Oil Ltd as geologist, Regina, 1940; appts as: exploration geophysicist, western Canada, and with affiliated cos in USA and S America; Asst Reg. Manager, Producing Dept, 1949; Asst Co-ordinator, Producing Dept of Standard Oil Co. (NJ), New York; Gen. Man., Imperial's Producing Dept, Toronto, 1960; Dir, 1961; Dir resp. for Marketing Ops, 1963-65; Exec. Vice-Pres., 1966, Pres. 1970, Chief Exec. officer, 1973, Chm., 1974. Dir, Royal Bank of Canada; Vice Chm., Bd of Trustees of Fraser Inst.; Member: Exec. Bd, Internat. Chamber of Commerce; British-North American Cttee; Canadian-Amer. Cttee; Conf. Bd Inc. Chm. Adv. Cttee, Sch. of Business Admin, Univ of Western Ontario, 1980-. Hon. LLD: Winnipeg, 1978; Calgary, 1980. *Address:* 111 St Clair Avenue W, Toronto, Ont M5W 1K3, Canada.

RMSTRONG, Most Rev. John Ward; see Armagh, Archbishop of, and Primate of All Ireland.

RMSTRONG, Rt. Rev. Mervyn, OBE 1946; Adviser on Industry to the Archbishop of York, and Assistant Bishop of York, 1964-70, retired; *b* 10 Mar. 1906; *o s* of Rev. Evan Armstrong and Sarah Armstrong; *m* 1st, 1933, Charlotte Stewart (*d* 1961), *y d* of Rev. A. Irvine-Robertson, DD, Clackmannan; 2nd, 1963, Mrs Barbara Newborn, *widow* of G. R. Newborn, Epworth. *Educ:* Balliol Coll. Oxford. In business in China, 1928-37; ordained 1938; served War of 1939-45 as Chaplain, RNVR, 1940-43; Adviser on Seamen's Welfare, Min. of War Transport and Dir of Seamen's Welfare, Govt of India, 1944-45; Vicar of Margate, 1946-49; Chaplain to Archbishop of Canterbury, 1949-51; Archdeacon of Stow and Rector of Epworth and Wroot, 1951-54; Provost of Leicester, 1954-58; Bishop Suffragan of Jarrow, 1958-64. *Address:* Glen Brathay, Skelwith Fold, Ambleside, Cumbria LA22 0HT. *T:* Ambleside 3249.

RMSTRONG, Prof. Neil A.; Chairman, Cardwell International Ltd, since 1980; formerly NASA Astronaut (Commander, Apollo 11 Rocket Flight to the Moon; first man to step on to the Moon, 20 July 1969, Edwin Aldrin being the second); *b* Wapakoneta, Ohio, USA, 5 Aug. 1930; *s* of Stephen and Viola Armstrong, Wapakoneta; *m* 1956, Janet Shearon, Evanston, Ill, *d* of Mrs Louise Shearon, Pasadena, Calif; two *s. Educ:* High Sch., Wapakoneta, Ohio; Univ. of Southern California (MS); Purdue Univ. (BSc). Pilot's licence obtained at age of 16. Served in Korea (78 combat missions) being a naval aviator, 1949-52. He joined NASA's Lewis Research Center, 1955 (then NACA Lewis Flight Propulsion Lab.) and later transf. to NASA High Speed Flight Station (now Flight Research Center) at Edwards Air Force Base, Calif, as an aeronautical research pilot for NACA and NASA; in this capacity, he performed as an X-15 project pilot, flying that aircraft to over 200,000 feet and approximately 4,000 miles per hour; other flight test work included piloting the X-1 rocket airplane, the F-100, F-101, F-102, F-104, F5D, B-47, the paraglider, and others; as pilot of the B-29 "drop" aircraft, he participated in the launches of over 100 rocket airplane flights. Selected as an astronaut by NASA, Sept. 1962; served as backup Command Pilot for Gemini 5 flight; as Command Pilot for Gemini 8 mission, launched 16 March 1966; he performed the first successful docking of 2 vehicles in space; served as backup Command Pilot for Gemini 11 mission; assigned as backup Comdr for Apollo

VIII Flight, 1969; Dep. Associate Administrator of Aeronautics, Space HQ, Washington, 1970-71; University Prof. of Aerospace Engrg, Univ. of Cincinnati, 1971-79. Director: Gates Learjet Corp.; Cincinnati Gas and Electric Co.; 5th 3rd Bank of Cincinnati; Taft Broadcasting Co.; Marathon Oil Corp.; Cincinnati Milacron; UAL Inc. Mem., Nat. Acad. of Engrg. Chm., Bd of Trustees, Cincinnati Museum of Natural History. Fellow, Soc. of Experimental Test Pilots; FRAeS. Honours include NASA Exceptional Service Medal, and AIAA Astronautics Award for 1966; RGS Gold Medal, 1970. Presidential Medal for Freedom, 1969. *Recreation:* soaring (FAI gold badge). *Address:* Cardwell International Ltd, 31 North Broadway, Lebanon, Ohio 45036, USA.

ARMSTRONG, Robert George, CBE 1972; MC 1946; TD 1958; Deputy Director and Controller, Savings Bank, Department for National Savings, 1969-74, retired (Deputy Director and Controller, Post Office Savings Bank, 1964); *b* 26 Oct. 1913; *s* of late George William Armstrong; *m* 1947, Clara Christine Hyde; one *s* one *d. Educ:* Marylebone Grammar Sch.; University Coll., London. Post Office Engineering Dept, 1936-50. Served War of 1939-45, Royal Signals. Principal, PO Headquarters, 1950; Asst Sec., 1962; Dep. Dir of Savings, 1963; Under-Sec., 1972. *Address:* Barryleigh, Wheelers Lane, Brockham, Betchworth, Surrey. *T:* Betchworth 3217.

ARMSTRONG, Sir Robert (Temple), KCB 1978 (CB 1974); CVO 1975; Secretary of the Cabinet, since 1979, Permanent Secretary to Management and Personnel Office, and Joint Head of the Home Civil Service, since 1981; *b* 30 March 1927; *o s* of Sir Thomas (Henry Wait) Armstrong, *qv*.; *m* 1953, Serena Mary Benedicta, *er d* of Sir Roger Chance, 3rd Bt, *qv*; two *d. Educ:* Dragon Sch., Oxford; Eton; Christ Church, Oxford. Asst Principal, Treasury, 1950-55; Private Secretary to: Rt Hon. Reginald Maudling, MP (when Economic Sec. to Treasury), 1953-54; Rt Hon. R. A. Butler, CH, MP (when Chancellor of the Exchequer), 1954-55; Principal, Treasury, 1955-57; Sec., Radcliffe Cttee on Working of Monetary System, 1957-59; returned to Treasury as Principal, 1959-64; Sec., Armitage Cttee on Pay of Postmen, 1964; Asst Sec., Cabinet Office, 1964-66; Sec. of Kindersley Review Body on Doctors' and Dentists' Remuneration and of Franks Cttee on Pay of Higher Civil Service, 1964-66; Asst Sec., Treasury, 1967-68; Jt Princ. Private Sec. to Rt Hon. Roy Jenkins, MP (Chancellor of the Exchequer), 1968; Under Secretary (Home Finance), Treasury, 1968-70; Principal Private Sec. to Prime Minister, 1970-75; Dep. Sec., 1973; Dep. Under-Sec. of State, Home Office, 1975-77, Permt Under Sec. of State, 1977-79. Sec., Bd of Dirs, Royal Opera House, Covent Garden, 1968-; Member: Governing Body, RAM, 1975-; Cttee of Management, Royal Philharmonic Soc., 1975-; Rhodes Trust, 1975-. Fellow of Eton Coll., 1979-. *Recreations:* music, gardening. *Address:* Cabinet Office, SW1. *Clubs:* Athenæum, Brooks's.

ARMSTRONG, Sheila Ann; soprano; *b* 13 Aug. 1942. *Educ:* Hirst Park Girls' Sch., Ashington, Northumberland; Royal Academy of Music, London. Debut Sadler's Wells, 1965 Glyndebourne, 1966, Covent Garden, 1973. Sings all over Europe, Far East, N and S America; has made many recordings. K. Ferrier and Mozart Prize, 1965; Hon. RAM 1970, FRAM 1973. Hon. MA Newcastle, 1979. *Recreations:* interior decoration, collecting antique keys, swimming, driving.

ARMSTRONG, Sir Thomas Henry Wait, Kt 1958; MA, DMus; FRCM; Hon. FRCO, Hon. RAM; Principal, Royal Academy of Music, 1955-68; Organist of Christ Church, Oxford, 1933-55; Student of Christ Church, 1939-55; Student Emeritus, 1955; Hon. Student, 1981; Choragus of the University and University lecturer in music, 1937-54; Conductor of the Oxford Bach Choir and the Oxford Orchestral Society; Musical Director of the Balliol Concerts; Trustee, The Countess of Munster Musical Trust; *b* 15 June 1898; *o s* of A. E. Armstrong, Peterborough, Northants; *m* 1926, Hester (*d* 1982), 2nd *d* of late Rev. W. H. Draper; one *s* one *d. Educ:* Choir Sch., Chapel Royal, St James's; King's Sch., Peterborough; Keble Coll., Oxford; Royal Coll. of Music. Organist, Thorney Abbey, 1914; sub-organist, Peterborough Cathedral, 1915; Organ Scholar, Keble Coll., Oxford 1916, Hon. Fellow, 1955; served in RA, BEF, France, 1917-19; sub-organist, Manchester Cathedral, 1922; organist, St Peter's, Eaton Square, 1923; organist of Exeter Cathedral, 1928. Cramb Lectr in music, Univ. of Glasgow, 1949. Vice-President, Bruckner-Mahler Chorale, 1970. *Compositions:* various, the larger ones remain unpublished. *Publications:* include choral music, songs and church music, together with many occasional writings on music. *Address:* The Old Rectory, Newton Blossomville, near Turvey, Beds MK43 8AL. *Club:* Garrick.

See also Sir R. T. Armstrong.

ARMSTRONG-JONES, family name of Earl of Snowdon.

ARMYTAGE, Captain Sir John Lionel, 8th Bt *cr* 1738; *b* 23 Nov. 1901; *s* of Brig.-Gen. Sir George (Ayscough) Armytage, 7th Bt, CMG, DSO, and Aimée (*d* 1955), 3rd *d* of Sir Lionel Milborne Swinnerton-Pilkington, 11th Bt; *S* father 1953; *m* 1st, 1927, Evelyne Mary Jessamine (marr. diss., 1946); *d* of Edward Herbert Fox, Adbury Park, Newbury; one *s* one *d*; 2nd, 1949, Maria Margarete, *o d* of Paul Hugo Tenhaeff, Bruenen, Niederrhein; one *d. Educ:* Eton; Royal Military Coll., Sandhurst. Joined King's Royal Rifle Corps, 1921; retired owing to ill-health, 1940. *Heir: s* John Martin Armytage, *b* 26 Feb. 1933. *Address:* (seat) Kirklees Park, Brighouse, West Yorks. *T:* Brighouse 713016. *Clubs:* Naval and Military, Oriental.

ARMYTAGE, Rear-Adm. Reginald William, GC (AM 1928); CBE 1959; retired; *b* 18 May 1903; *s* of Sir George Ayscough Armytage, 7th Bart, CMG, DSO, Kirklees Park, Brighouse; *m* 1928, Sylvia Beatrice Staveley; three *s. Educ:* Osborne and Dartmouth. Entered Royal Navy, 1917. Served in HMS: Royal Oak, 1921; Capetown, 1922-24; Emergency Destroyers, 1925; Warspite, 1926-28 (Albert Medal 1928). Qualified in Gunnery, 1929. Served HMS: Devonshire, 1930-32; Mackay, 1932-34; Frobisher, 1935. Took up Naval Ordnance Design, Experiment and Inspection Duties, 1935; Head of Gun Design and Senior Naval Representative at Armament Design Estab., 1946; Deputy Chief Inspector of Naval Ordnance, 1949; Chief Inspector of Naval Ordnance, 1956; Vice-Pres. (Naval), Ordnance Board, 1959; President of The Ordnance Board, 1961-62. *Address:* The Malt House, Downton, Wilts.

ARMYTAGE, Prof. Walter Harry Green; Professor of Education, University of Sheffield, 1954-82, now Emeritus Professor; Gerald Read Professor of Education, Kent State University, Ohio, 1982; *b* 22 Nov. 1915; *e s* of Walter Green Armytage and Harriet Jane May Armytage; *m* 1948, Lucy Frances Horsfall; one *s. Educ:* Redruth County School; Downing Coll., Cambridge. 1st Cl. Hist. Trip. 1937, Cert. in Educ., 1938. History Master, Dronfield Grammar Sch., 1938-39; served War of 1939-45 (despatches); Captain, London Irish Rifles. Univ. of Sheffield: Lectr, 1946; Sen. Lectr, 1952; Pro-Vice-Chancellor, 1964-68. Visiting Lecturer: Univ. of Michigan, USA, 1955, 1959, 1961, 1963, 1975; Newcastle, NSW, 1977; Lectures: Ballard-Matthews, University Coll. of North Wales, 1973; Cantor, RSA, 1969; Hawkesley, IMechE, 1969; S. P. Thompson, IEE, 1972; Galton, Eugenics Soc., 1974; Clapton, Leeds Univ., 1979. Hon. DLitt: NUU, 1977; Hull, 1980. *Publications:* A. J. Mundella 1825-1897; The Liberal Background of the Labour Movement, 1951; Thomas Hughes: The Life of the Author of Tom Brown's Schooldays, 1953 (with E. C. Mack); Civic Universities: Aspects of a British Tradition, 1955; Sir Richard Gregory: his Life and Work, 1957; A Social History of Engineering, 1961; Heavens Below: Utopian Experiments in England, 1560-1960, 1962; Four Hundred Years of English Education, 1964; The Rise of the Technocracy, 1965; The American Influence on English Education, 1967; Yesterday's Tomorrows: A Historical Survey of Future Societies, 1968; The French Influence on English Education, 1968; The German Influence on English Education, 1969; The Russian Influence on English Education, 1969. *Recreations:* walking, gardening. *Address:* 3 The Green, Totley, Sheffield, South Yorks. *T:* Sheffield 362515. *Clubs:* National Liberal; University Staff (Sheffield).

ARNDT, Ulrich Wolfgang, MA, PhD; FRS 1982; Member, Scientific Staff of Medical Research Council Laboratory of Molecular Biology, Cambridge, since 1962; *b* 23 April 1924; *o s* of E. J. and C. M. Arndt; *m* 1958, Valerie Howard, *e d* of late Maj.-Gen. F. C. Hilton-Sergeant, CB, CBE, QHP; three *d. Educ:* Dulwich Coll.; King Edward VI High Sch., Birmingham; Emmanuel Coll., Cambridge (MA, PhD). Metallurgy Dept, Birmingham Univ., 1948-49; Davy-Faraday Laboratory of Royal Instn, 1950-63; Dewar Fellow of Royal Instn, 1957-61; Univ. of Wisconsin, Madison, 1956; Institut Laue-Langevin, Grenoble, 1972-73. *Publications:* (with B. T. M. Willis) Single Crystal Diffractometry, 1966; (with A. J. Wonacott) The Rotation Method in Crystallography, 1977; papers in scientific jls. *Recreations:* walking, reading. *Address:* 28 Barrow Road, Cambridge CB2 2AS. *T:* Cambridge 350660.

ARNELL, Richard Anthony Sayer; Hon. FTCL; composer; conductor; film maker; Principal Lecturer, Trinity College of Music, since 1981 (Teacher of Composition, 1949-81); *b* 15 Sept. 1917; *s* of late Richard Sayer Arnell and of Helène Marie Sherf; *m* 1981, Audrey Millar Paul. *Educ:* The Hall, Hampstead; University Coll. Sch., NW3; Royal Coll. of Music. Music Consultant, BBC North American Service, 1943-46; Lectr, Royal Ballet Sch., 1958-59. Editor, The Composer, 1961-64; Chairman: Composers' Guild of GB, 1965, 1974-75; Jt Cttee, Songwriters' and Composers' Guilds, 1977-; Young Musicians' Symph. Orch. Soc., 1973-75. Vis. Lectr (Fulbright Exchange), Bowdoin Coll., Maine, 1967-68; Vis. Prof. Hofstra Univ., New York, 1968-70. Music Dir and Board Mem., London Internat. Film Sch., 1975- (Chm., Film Sch. Trust, 1981-); Music Dir, Ram Filming Ltd, 1980-; Dir, Organic Sounds Ltd, 1982-. Composer of the Year 1966 (Music Teachers Assoc. Award). Compositions include: 5 symphonies; 2 concertos for violin; concerto for harpsichord; concerto for piano; 5 string quartets; 2 quintets; piano trio; piano works; songs; cantatas; organ works; music for string orchestra, wind ensembles, brass ensembles, song cycles; electronic music. *Opera:* Love in Transit; Moonflowers. *Ballet scores:* Punch and the Child, for Ballet Soc., NY, 1947; Harlequin in April, for Arts Council, 1951; The Great Detective, for Sadler's Wells Theatre Ballet, 1953; The Angels, for Royal Ballet, 1957; Giselle (Adam) re-orchestrated, for Ballet Rambert, 1965. *Film Scores:* The Land, 1941; The Third Secret, 1963; The Visit, 1964; The Man Outside, 1966; Topsail Schooner, 1966; Bequest for a Village, 1969; Second Best, 1972; Stained Glass, 1973; Wires Over the Border, 1974; Black Panther, 1977; Antagonist, 1980; Dilemma, 1981. *Other works:* Symphonic Portrait, Lord Byron, for Sir Thomas Beecham, 1953; Landscapes and Figures, for Sir Thomas Beecham, 1956; Petrified Princess, puppet operetta, for BBC, 1959; Robert Flaherty, Impression for Radio Eireann, 1960; Musica Pacifica for Edward Benjamin, 1963; Festival Flourish, for Salvation Army, 1965; 2nd piano concerto, for RPO, 1967; Overture, Food of Love, for Portland Symph. Orch., 1968; My Ladye Greene Sleeves, for Hofstra Univ., 1968; Nocturne: Prague, 1968; I Think of all Soft Limbs, for Canadian Broadcasting Corp., 1971; Astronaut One, 1973; Life Boat Voluntary, for RNLI, 1974; Call, for

LPO, 1980. *Address:* c/o Composers' Guild of Great Britain, 10 Stratfo Place, W1. *Club:* Savage.

ARNEY, Frank Douglas, CBE 1959; *b* 4 Feb. 1899; *s* of Frank Charles Arne *m* 1925, Mildred, *d* of W. J. Dallin; three *s. Educ:* Grammar Sch., Brist Formerly: General Manager, Port of Bristol Authority, for 16 years until re Oct. 1961; Part-time Chm. British Waterways Board, Dec. 1962-June 196 Mem., National Ports Council, 1963-71. *Recreations:* fly fishing, go *Address:* Glenleven, Northumbria Drive, Henleaze, Bristol. *T:* Brist 628810.

ARNOLD, Prof. Denis Midgley, FBA 1976; Heather Professor of Musi University of Oxford, since 1975; *b* 15 Dec. 1926; *m* 1951, Elsie Millice Dawrant; two *s. Educ:* Sheffield Univ. (MA, BMus). ARCM. Queen's Univ Belfast: Lectr in Music, Extra-Mural Studies, 1951-60; Reader in Musi 1960-64; Sen. Lectr in Music, Hull Univ., 1964-69; Prof. of Musi Nottingham Univ., 1969-75. Mem. Council, Internat. Musicological Asso 1977-. Pres., Royal Musical Assoc., 1978-. Foreign Mem., Accademia d Lincei, 1976. Hon. RAM; Hon. DMus: Belfast, 1980, Sheffield, 1980; FRCI 1981. Galileo Prize, 1977. Jt Editor, Music and Letters, 1976-80. *Publicatio* Monteverdi, 1963; Marenzio, 1965; Monteverdi's Madrigals, 1967; (ed wi N. Fortune) Monteverdi Companion, 1969; Beethoven Companion, 197 Giovanni Gabrieli, 1974; Giovanni Gabrieli and Venetian music of the Hig Renaissance, 1980; Monteverdi's Church Music, 1982; articles in Music ar Letters, Musical Qly, Monthly Musical Record, Brass Qly, Musical Tim Galpin Soc. Jl, Rivista Musicale Italiana. *Address:* Faculty of Music, Oxfoi University, St Aldate's, Oxford, OX1 1DB. *T:* Oxford 47069.

ARNOLD, Mrs Elliott; *see* Johns, Glynis.

ARNOLD, Rt. Rev. George Feversham, DD; *b* 30 Dec. 1914; *s* of Arno Feversham and Elsie Mildred Arnold; *m* 1940, Mary Eleanor Sherma Holmes; one *s* one *d. Educ:* Univ. of King's Coll., Halifax, NS (LTh 193 BD 1944); Dalhousie Univ. (BA 1935, MA 1938). Rector: Louisbour 1938-41; Mahone Bay, 1941-50; St John's, Fairview, 1950-53; Windso 1953-58; Clerical Sec. and Diocesan Registrar, 1958-67; Exam. Chaplain Bishop of Nova Scotia, 1947-70; Hon. Canon of All Saints Cathedra 1959-63, Canon, 1963-67; Bishop Suffragan of Nova Scotia, 1967-75, Bisho Coadjutor, May-Sept. 1975; Bishop of Nova Scotia, 1975-79. Hon. Di King's Coll., Halifax, 1968. *Recreation:* yachting. *Address:* 56 Holmes H Road, Hantsport, NS B0P 1P0, Canada.

ARNOLD, Rt. Hon. Sir John Lewis, Kt 1972; PC 1979; **Rt. Hon. M Justice Arnold;** a Judge of the High Court, Family Division, since 197 President of Family Division, since 1979; *b* 6 May 1915; *s* of late A. L. Arnol and E. K. Arnold; *m* 1940, Alice Margaret Dorothea (*née* Cookson) (mar diss., 1963); one *s* one *d; m* 1963, Florence Elizabeth, *d* of H. M. Hagu Montreal; one *s* two *d. Educ:* Wellington Coll.; abroad. Called to Bar, Midd Temple, 1937; served War of 1939-45 in Army (despatches, 1945); resume practice at Bar, 1946; QC 1958; Chm. Bar Council, 1970-72, Chm., Pla Variety Rights Tribunal for proceedings in England and Wales, 1969-7 *Recreations:* cricket, travel. *Address:* Royal Courts of Justice, WC2; Litt Horse Leas, Bradfield, Berks. *T:* Bradfield 442; 8 Mimosa Street, SW6. 01-736 8686.

ARNOLD, Very Rev. John Robert; Dean of Rochester, since 1978; *b* 1 No 1933; *s* of John Stanley and Ivy Arnold; *m* 1963, Livia Anneliese Franke; or *s* two *d. Educ:* Christ's Hospital; Sidney Sussex Coll., Cambridge (MA Westcott House Theol Coll. Curate of Holy Trinity, Millhouses, Sheffiel 1960-63; Sir Henry Stephenson Fellow, Univ. of Sheffield, 1962-63; Chapla and Lectr, Univ. of Southampton, 1963-72; Secretary, Board for Mission an Unity, General Synod of the Church of England, 1972-78; Hon. Canon c Winchester Cathedral, 1974-78; Mem., General Synod, 1980-. Order of Sai Vladimir (Russian Orthodox Church), 1977. *Publications:* (trans.) Eucharist Liturgy of Taizé, 1962; contribs to Theology, Crucible. *Recreations:* musi European languages and literature. *Address:* The Deanery, The Precinc Rochester, Kent ME1 1TG. *T:* Medway 44023. *Club:* Christ's Hospital.

ARNOLD, Rt. Rev. Keith Appleby; *see* Warwick, Bishop Suffragan of.

ARNOLD, Malcolm, CBE 1970; composer; *b* 21 Oct. 1921; *s* of William ar Annie Arnold, Northampton; *m* ; two *s* one *d. Educ:* Royal Coll. of Musi London (Schol., 1938). Principal Trumpet, London Philharmonic Orchestr 1941-44; served in the Army, 1944-45; Principal Trumpet, Londc Philharmonic Orchestra, 1945-48; Mendelssohn Schol. (study in Italy), 194 Coronation Ballet, Homage to the Queen, performed Royal Opera Hous 1953. Awarded Oscar for music for film Bridge on the River Kwai, 195 Bard of the Cornish Gorsedd, 1969. Hon. DMus Exeter, 1970; Hon. RAM *Publications:* symphonies: No 1, 1949; No 2, 1953; No 3, 1957; No 4, 196 No 5, 1961; No 6, 1967; No 7, 1973; No 8, 1978; Symphony for Bra Instruments, 1979; other works: Beckus the Dandipratt, overture, 1943; Ta O'Shanter, overture, 1955; Peterloo, overture, 1967; twenty seven concerto five ballets; two one-act operas; two string quartets; brass quintet; vocal, chor and chamber music. *Recreations:* reading and foreign travel. *Address:* c/ Faber Music, 3 Queen Square, WC1N 3AU.

ARNOLD, Dr Richard Bentham; Director, Association of the Britis Pharmaceutical Industry, since 1977; *b* 29 Aug. 1932; *s* of George Benjamn and Alice Arnold; *m* 1956, Margaret Evelyn Racey; one *s* one *d. Educ:* Stamford Sch.; King Edward VII Sch., King's Lynn; Nottingham Univ. BSc, PhD. Joined May & Baker Ltd, 1959; Commercial Manager, Pharmaceuticals Div., 1974-76; Dir Designate, Assoc. of British Pharmaceutical Industry, 1976. *Recreations:* golf, fishing, bird watching. *Address:* Long Rough, Grange Close, Ingrave, Brentwood, Essex. *T:* Brentwood 810740. *Club:* Reform.

ARNOLD, Thomas Richard; MP (C) Hazel Grove, since Oct. 1974; *b* 25 Jan. 1947; *s* of Thomas Charles Arnold and Helen Breen. *Educ:* Bedales Sch.; Le Rosey, Geneva; Pembroke Coll., Oxford (MA). Theatre producer; Mem., Soc. of West End Theatre. Contested (C): Manchester Cheetham, 1970; Hazel Grove, Feb. 1974; PPS to Sec. of State for NI, 1979-81, to Lord Privy Seal, FCO, 1981-. *Address:* House of Commons, SW1A 0AA. *T:* 01-219 4096. *Clubs:* Carlton, Royal Automobile.

ARNOLD, Vere Arbuthnot, CBE 1970; MC 1945; TD 1953; JP; DL; Chairman, Ross T. Smyth & Co. Ltd, since 1957; *b* 23 May 1902; *s* of Rev. H. A. Arnold, Wolsingham Rectory, Co. Durham; *m* 1928, Joan Kathleen, *d* of C. J. Tully, Wairarapa, NZ; one *s* one *d. Educ:* Haileybury Coll.; Jesus Coll., Cambridge (BA). Ross T. Smyth & Co. Ltd, 1924, Director, 1931; President Liverpool Corn Trade Association, 1947-48 and 1951-52; Chairman: Liverpool Grain Storage and Transit Co. Ltd; Runcorn Develt Corp., 1964-74. Served War of 1939-45 as Major (MC, TD). JP County of Chester, 1949; High Sheriff, Cheshire, 1958; DL Cheshire, 1969. *Recreations:* shooting, fishing. *Address:* Ardmore, Great Barrow, near Chester. *T:* Tarvin 40257.

ARNOLD-BAKER, Charles, OBE 1966; Deputy Chairman, Eastern Traffic Commissioners, since 1978; Consultant Lecturer, City University, since 1978; Secretary, National Association of Local Councils, 1953-78; *b* 25 June 1918; *s* of Baron Albrecht v. Blumenthal and Alice Wilhelmine (*née* Hainsworth); *m* 1943, Edith (*née* Woods); one *s* one *d. Educ:* Winchester Coll.; Magdalen Coll., Oxford. BA 1940. Called to Bar, Inner Temple, 1948. Army (Private to Captain), 1940-46. Admty Bar, 1948-52; Mem., Royal Commn on Common Lands, 1955-58; Mem. European Cttee, Internat. Union of Local Authorities, 1960-78; a Deleg. to European Local Govt Assembly, Strasbourg, 1960-78. Gwylim Gibbons Award, Nuffield Coll., Oxford, 1959. King Haakon's Medal of Freedom (Norway), 1945. *Publications:* Norway (pamphlet), 1946; Everyman's Dictionary of Dates, 1954; Parish Administration, 1958; New Law and Practice of Parish Administration, 1966; The 5000 and the Power Tangle, 1967; The Local Government Act 1972, 1973; Local Council Administration, 1975, 2nd rev. edn 1981; The Local Government, Planning and Land Act 1980, 1981; many contribs to British and European local govt and legal jls. *Recreations:* travel, history, writing, music, cooking, journalism, wine and doing nothing. *Address:* Top Floor, 2 Paper Buildings, Inner Temple, EC4. *T:* 01-353 3490. *Club:* Union (Oxford).

ARNOTT, Sir Alexander John Maxwell, 6th Bt *cr* 1896, of Woodlands, Shandon, Co. Cork; *b* 18 Sept. 1975; *s* of Sir John Robert Alexander Arnott, 5th Bt, and of Ann Margaret, *d* of late T. A. Farrelly, Kilcar, Co. Cavan; *S* father, 1981. *Heir: b* Andrew John Eric Arnott, *b* 20 June 1978. *Address:* Ashtown House, Castleknock, Co. Dublin, Ireland.

ARNOTT, Most Rev. Felix Raymond, CMG 1981; MA (Oxon); ThD; MACE; Honorary Chaplain in Venice, since 1980; *b* Ipswich, Suffolk, 8 March 1911; *s* of late Richard Girling Arnott, Ipswich; *m* 1938, Anne Caroline, *d* of W. A. P. Lane, Kingston Gorse, Sussex; two *s* two *d. Educ:* Ipswich Sch.; Keble Coll., Oxford; Cuddesdon Theol Coll. Curate, Elland, Yorks, 1934-38; Exam. Chaplain, Bp of Wakefield, 1936-39; Vice-Prin., Cheshunt, 1938; Warden, St John's Coll., Brisbane, 1939-46; Warden, St Paul's Coll., Univ. of Sydney, 1946-63; Lectr i/c of Ecclesiastical History, Univ. of Sydney, 1951-63; a Co-Adjutor Bishop of Melbourne, 1963-70; Archbishop of Brisbane and Metropolitan of Queensland, 1970-80. Member: Monash Univ. Council, 1964-70; Anglican-Roman Catholic Internat. Cttee, 1969-81; Queensland Univ. Senate, 1971-80. Comr, Royal Commn on Human Relations, Australia, 1974-. A Founder of Blake Prize for Religious Art, 1951. *Publications:* The Anglican Via Media in the Seventeenth Century, 1948; contribs to learned jls. *Recreations:* walking, music. *Address:* Dorsoduro 870, 30123 Venezia, Italy. *Clubs:* Melbourne, Royal Automobile (Victoria); Australian (Sydney); Queensland (Brisbane).

ARNOTT, Prof. James Fullarton, TD and bar 1952; Professor of Drama, Glasgow University, 1973-79, now Emeritus Professor; *b* 29 April 1914; *s* of late Hezekiah Merricks Arnott and Susannah Willock Fullarton; *m* 1945, Martha Lawrence Miller (*née* Grant); one *s. Educ:* Ardrossan Acad.; Glasgow Univ. (MA); Merton Coll., Oxford (MLitt); Peterhouse, Cambridge. Asst Lectr in English Lang., University Coll. of Hull, 1938; Glasgow University: Asst in Eng. Lit., 1939; Lectr, 1944; Sen. Lectr, 1962; first Head of Drama Dept, 1966; Reader, 1971. Rockefeller Fellow, 1950; Gillespie Vis. Prof., Coll. of Wooster, Ohio, 1959-60; Fellow, Folger Shakespeare Library, 1964; British Acad. Overseas Fellow, 1978; Fellow, Huntington Libr., 1978; Vis. Prof., Arizona State Univ., 1981-82. Chm., Standing Cttee of Univ. Drama Depts, 1976-79; Pres., Internat. Fedn for Theatre Res., 1976-79. Member: Coll. of Drama Cttee, Royal Scottish Acad. of Music, 1949 (Governor, 1965-81); Bd, Glasgow Citizens' Theatre, 1970-76; Bd, Scottish Ballet, 1970-; Scottish Arts Council, 1972-79 (Chm., Drama Cttee, 1976-79); Council, British Theatre Institute, 1975-80 (Hon. Vice-Chm., 1980-); Bd, Third Eye Centre, 1975-80; Arts Council of GB, 1977-79; UK Nat. Commn for Unesco, 1980-81; Bd, Scottish Theatre Co., 1980- (Chm., 1980-81). Chairman: J. D.

Fergusson Art Foundn, 1978-81; British Liaison Cttee of Internat. Theatre Organisations, 1979-; Exec. Cttee, British Centre of Internat. Theatre Inst., 1980-; Bd, Internat. Assoc. of Margaret Morris Movement, 1979-; Trustee, Theatres Trust, 1980-. Editor, Theatre Research International (formerly Theatre Research/Recherches Théâtrales), 1964-81. FR.SAMD 1979. *Publications:* English Theatrical Literature 1559-1900 (with J. W. Robinson), 1970; Sale Catalogues of the Libraries of Eminent Persons: actors, 1973. *Recreation:* directing plays. *Address:* 1 Huntly Gardens, Glasgow G12 9AS. *T:* 041-339 8494. *Clubs:* Lansdowne; College (Glasgow).

ARNOTT, Sir Melville; *see* Arnott, Sir W. M.

ARNOTT, Sir (William) Melville, Kt 1971; TD (and clasps) 1944; MD; FRCP; FRCPE, FRSE, FRCPath; British Heart Foundation Professor of Cardiology, University of Birmingham, 1971-74, now Emeritus; Physician, United Birmingham Hospitals, since 1946; *b* 14 Jan. 1909; *s* of Rev. Henry and Jeanette Main Arnott; *m* 1938, Dorothy Eleanor, *er d* of G. F. S. Hill, Edinburgh; one *s. Educ:* George Watson's Coll., Edinburgh; Univ. of Edinburgh. MB, ChB (Hons), 1931, BSc (1st Cl. Hons Path.), 1934, MD (Gold Medal and Gunning Prize in Path.), 1937, Edinburgh; McCunn Res. Schol. in Path., 1933-35, Crichton Res. Schol. in Path., 1935, Shaw Macfie Lang Res. Fellow, 1936-38, Edinburgh. MD Birmingham, 1947. 2nd Lieut RA, 1929; TA 1929-39; War of 1939-45, served as specialist physician; five years foreign service (Siege of Tobruk; despatches, NW Europe); Lt-Col 1942. Asst Physician, Edinburgh Municipal Hosps, 1934-36; Hon. Asst Physician: Church of Scotland Deaconess Hosp., Edinburgh, 1938-46; Edinburgh Royal Infirmary, 1946. Dir, Post-grad. studies in Medicine, Edinburgh Univ., 1945-46; William Withering Prof. of Medicine, Univ. of Birmingham, 1946-71. Consultant Adviser in Research to W Midlands RHA, 1974-79. Associate Examr in Medicine, London Univ., 1948-49; Examr in Medicine, to Univs of Cambridge, 1950-56, London, 1951-54, Wales, 1954-57, Queen's, Belfast, 1956-59, Edinburgh, 1959-62, Leeds, 1959-62, St Andrews, 1961-63, Oxford, 1961-68, Newcastle, 1964-67, Manchester, 1964-70, Singapore, 1965, East Africa, 1965, Malaysia, 1973, NUI, 1975-77. Member: UGC, 1954-63; MRC, 1965-69; Council, University Coll. of Rhodesia, 1964-70; UGC Hong Kong, 1966-75; Home Office Cttee (Brodrick) on Death Registration and Coroners, 1965-71; Tropical Medicine Res. Bd, 1967-71. Dep. Pres., First Internat. Conf. on Med. Educn, 1953. Editor, Clinical Science, 1953-58, and Mem., Ed. Bd of Brit. Jl of Social Medicine. RCPE: Mem., 1933; Fellow, 1937; John Matheson Shaw Lectr, 1958; Cullen Prize, 1958. RCP: Mem., 1947; Fellow, 1951; Mem. Council, 1954-56; Oliver-Sharpey Lectr, 1955; Examr for Membership, 1957-66; Croonian Lectr, 1963; Censor, 1969-71; Sen. Vice-Pres., and Sen. Censor, 1973. Foundation Fellow, Royal Coll. of Pathologists. FRMedSoc 1929 (late Senior Pres.); Hon. FRCP(C), 1957; Hon. FACP, 1968 (Lilly Lectr, 1968). Member: Assoc. of Physicians; Physiological Soc.; Pathological Soc.; Med. Res. Soc.; Cardiac Soc.; Thoracic Soc.; Internat. Soc. of Internal Medicine. Sir Arthur Sims Commonwealth Trav. Prof. of Medicine, 1957. Lectures: Frederick Price, Trinity Coll., Dublin, 1959; Hall, Cardiac Soc. of Aust. and NZ, 1962; Henry Cohen, Hebrew Univ. of Jerusalem, 1964; Alexander Brown Meml, Univ. of Ibadan, 1972; John Snow, Soc. of Anaesthetists, 1973. Pres., Edinburgh Harveian Soc., 1955. Research: Originally into experimental path. of renal hypertension and peripheral vascular disease; at present, into physiology and path. of cardio-respiratory function. Hon. DSc Edinburgh, 1975; Hon. LLD: Rhodesia, 1976; Dundee, 1976. *Publications:* some 50 scientific papers, principally in Lancet, Jl of Physiol., Jl of Path., Brit. Jl of Social Medicine, Edinburgh Med. Jl, etc. *Recreation:* travel. *Address:* 40 Carpenter Road, Edgbaston, Birmingham B15 2JJ. *T:* 021-440 2195. *Club:* Naval and Military.

ARON, Prof. Raymond Claude Ferdinand; Officier de la Légion d'Honneur; author; President, comité éditorial, l'Express; Columnist, Figaro, 1947-77; *b* Paris, 14 March 1905; *m* 1933, Suzanne Gauchon; two *d* (and one *d* decd). *Educ:* Ecole Normale Supérieur and Sorbonne, Paris. Lectr, Univ. of Cologne, 1931; French Academic House, Berlin, 1931-33; Lycée du Havre, 1933-34; Centre Documentation sociale ENS, 1934-39; Maître de Conférences, Univ. of Toulouse, 1939; Editor, La France Libre, in London, 1940-44; Columnist, Combat, 1946-47; Professor of Sociology at Sorbonne, 1955-68; Prof. at Ecole Pratique des Hautes Etudes, 1960; Prof. at Coll. de France, 1970-78. Several hon. doctorates from foreign univs, 1958-; For. Hon. Mem., Amer. Acad. of Arts and Sciences, Boston, 1962; Mem., Académie des Sciences Morales et Politiques, Paris, 1963; Mem., Philosophical Soc., Philadelphia, 1967; Corres. Fellow, British Acad., 1970; Hon. Fellow, LSE, 1974; Hon. LittD Cambridge, 1981. Mem., Acad. Royale de Belgique, 1977. Goethe Prize, 1979; Tocqueville Prize, 1979; Aujourd'hui Prize, 1982. *Publications:* Introduction à la philosophie de l'histoire, 1938 (Introduction to the Philosophy of History, 1961); Le grand schisme, 1948; Les guerres en chaîne, 1951 (Century of Total War, 1954); L'Opium des intellectuels, 1955 (Opium of the Intellectuals, 1957); Espoir et peur du siècle, 1957 (Part III trans. as On War: atomic weapons and global diplomacy, 1958); Diversity of Worlds, 1957; La tragédie algérienne, 1957; Immuable et changeante, 1959 (France: steadfast and changing, 1960); La société industrielle et la guerre, 1959; Dimensions de la conscience historique, 1960 (parts trans. in Evidence and Inference, 1959, and The Dawn of Universal History, 1961); France: the new republic, 1960; Imperialism and Colonialism, 1960; Paix et guerre entre les nations, 1962 (Peace and War, 1967); Dix-huit leçons sur la société industrielle, 1963 (Eighteen Lectures on Industrial Society, 1968); Le grand débat, 1963 (The Great Debate: theories of nuclear strategy, 1965); (ed) World

Technology and Human Destiny, 1963; La lutte de classes, 1964; Démocratie et totalitarisme, 1965 (Democracy and Totalitarianism, 1968); Trois essais sur la société industrielle, 1966 (The Industrial Society, 1967); Les étapes de la pensée sociologique, 1967 (Main Currents in Sociological Thought: I, Montesquieu, Comte, Marx, Tocqueville, the sociologist and the revolution of 1848, 1965; II, Durkheim, Pareto, Weber, 1968); De Gaulle, Israël et les juifs, 1968 (De Gaulle, Israel and the Jews, 1969); La révolution introuvable, 1968 (The Elusive Revolution: anatomy of a student revolt, 1970); Les désillusions du progrès, 1969 (Progress and Disillusion, 1968); Etudes politiques, 1972; République impériale, 1973 (The Imperial Republic, 1975); Histoire et Dialectique de la Violence, 1973 (History and the Dialectic of Violence, 1975); Penser la Guerre, Clausewitz, vol. I, L'Age européen, vol. II, L'Age planétaire, 1976; Plaidoyer pour l'Europe décadente, 1977 (In Defense of Decadent Europe); Le spectateur engagé, 1982. *Address:* 87 Boulevard Saint-Michel, 75005 Paris, France.

ARONSON, Geoffrey Fraser, CB 1977; part time consultant to Law Commission; Legal Adviser and Solicitor to Ministry of Agriculture, Fisheries and Food, to Forestry Commission, and to (EEC) Intervention Board for Agricultural Produce, 1974-79; *b* 17 April 1914; *er s* of late Victor Rees Aronson, CBE, KC, and Annie Elizabeth Aronson (*née* Fraser); *m* 1940, Marie Louise, *e d* of late George Stewart Rose-Innes; one *s* two *d. Educ:* Haileybury. Solicitor (Honours) 1936. Legal Dept, Min. of Agriculture and Fisheries, 1938; served War of 1939-45, Flying Control Officer, RAFVR; promoted Asst Solicitor, MAFF, 1960; Under-Sec. (Principal Asst Solicitor), 1971, when chiefly concerned with UK accession to EEC. *Recreations:* travel, gardening, fishing. *Address:* Cedars Cottage, Church Street, Epsom, Surrey KT17 4QB. *T:* Epsom 22431; Little Thatch, Child Okeford, Blandford Forum, Dorset. *T:* Child Okeford 860089. *Clubs:* Royal Commonwealth Society, Royal Automobile.

ARONSON, Hazel Josephine, (Mrs John A. Cosgrove); Sheriff of Glasgow and Strathkelvin at Glasgow, since 1979; *b* 12 Jan. 1946; *d* of late Moses Aron Aronson and Julia Tobias; *m* 1967, John Allan Cosgrove, dental surgeon; one *s* one *d. Educ:* Glasgow High Sch. for Girls; Univ. of Glasgow (LLB). Advocate at the Scottish Bar. Admitted to Fac. of Advocates, 1968; Standing Junior Counsel to Dept of Trade, 1977-79. *Recreations:* rearing children, foreign travel, opera, reading, cooking and dieting. *Address:* 14 Gordon Terrace, Edinburgh EH16 5QR. *T:* 031-667 8955.

ARRAN, 8th Earl of, *cr* 1762; **Arthur Kattendyke Strange David Archibald Gore;** Bt 1662; Viscount Sudley, Baron Saunders, 1758; Earl of Arran of the Arran Islands, Co. Galway, 1762; Baron Sudley (UK) 1884; journalist; broadcaster on radio and television; *b* 5 July 1910; *s* of 6th Earl of Arran, KP, PC(Ire.), and Maud, *o d* of Baron Huyssen van Kattendijke; *S* brother, 1958; *m* 1937, Fiona Bryde, *d* of Sir Iain Colquhoun, 7th Bt, of Luss, KT, DSO; one *s* (and one *s* decd). *Educ:* Eton; Balliol Coll., Oxford. Assistant Press Attaché, British Legation, Berne, 1939-40; Attaché, British Embassy, Lisbon, 1941-42; Deputy Dir, Overseas General Div., MOI, 1943-45; Dir of Secretariat, Central Office of Information, 1945-49. Introduced in House of Lords: Sexual Offences Bill (now Act) (3 times); Badger Protection Bill (now Act). Director, Daily Mail and General Trust Ltd, to 1981. Chm., Children's Country Holidays Fund; Hon. Treasurer of Moorfields Eye Hospital. *Publications:* Lord Arran Writes, 1964; columnist, Evening News; contributions to Encounter, Punch, The Observer, Manchester Guardian, Daily Mail and Evening Standard. *Recreations:* shooting and tennis. *Heir: s* Viscount Sudley, *qv. Address:* Pimlico House, Hemel Hempstead, Herts. *Club:* Beefsteak.

ARRAU, Claudio; Concert Pianist; *b* Chillan, Chile, 6 Feb. 1903; *m* ; two *s* one *d.* Gave first recital at Santiago at age of 5; musical education in Europe financed by Chilean Govt; studied at Stern Konservatorie Berlin, under Martin Krause; won Liszt Prize 1919, 1920 (not awarded in 45 years), Schulhoff prize, Ibach prize (1917), and in 1927, first place in Geneva International Congress of Pianists. Has appeared in US, Canada, England, France, Holland, Italy, Germany, Scandinavia, Russia, South America, Mexico, Cuba, Hawaii, South Africa, Australia, Israel, Japan, NZ, Iceland, Hong Kong, Singapore, Ceylon and Bombay. Chile has named two streets in his honour. Cycle performances include: all keyboard works of Bach in 12 recitals, Berlin, 1935; all Beethoven Sonatas, 8 recitals, Berlin, Buenos Aires, Santiago; all Beethoven Sonatas, Diabelli Variations, (first BBC broadcast from London, 1952), all Beethoven, NY Season, 1953-54, 1962; renowned also for Chopin, Schumann, Brahms, Liszt. Decorations from France, Germany, Mexico, Chile. *Address:* c/o ICM Artist Ltd, 40 West 57 Street, New York, NY 10019, USA.

ARRINDELL, Sir Clement Athelston, Kt 1982; Governor, St Kitts-Nevis, since 1981; *b* Basseterre, 19 April 1931. *Educ:* privately; St Kitts-Nevis Grammar Sch. (Island Scholar). Called to the Bar, Lincoln's Inn, 1958. Post-grad. studies; in practice as barrister and solicitor, 1959-66; Acting Magistrate, 1964-66; Magistrate, 1966-78; Judge, WI Associated States Supreme Court, 1978-81. *Recreations:* piano-playing, classical music, gardening. *Address:* Government House, Basseterre, St Kitts, West Indies. *T:* 2315/2260.

ARROW, Kenneth Joseph; Professor of Economics and Operations Research, Stanford University, since 1979; *b* 23 Aug. 1921; *s* of Harry I. and Lillian Arrow; *m* 1947, Selma Schweitzer; two *s. Educ:* City College (BS in Social

Science 1940); Columbia Univ. (MA 1941, PhD 1951). Captain, US AAF, 1942-46. Research Associate, Cowles Commn for Research in Economics, Univ. of Chicago, 1947-49; Actg Asst Prof., Associate Prof. and Prof. of Economics, Statistics and Operations Research, Stanford Univ., 1949-68; Prof. of Econs, later University Prof., Harvard Univ., 1968-79. Staff Mem., US Council of Economic Advisers, 1962. Consultant, The Rand Corp., 1948-. Fellow, Churchill Coll., Cambridge, 1963-64, 1970, 1973. Member: Inst. of Management Sciences (Pres., 1963); Nat. Acad. of Sciences; Amer. Inst. of Medicine; Amer. Philosoph. Soc.; Econometric Soc. (Pres., 1956); Fellow: Amer. Acad. of Arts and Sciences; Amer. Assoc. for Advancement of Science (Chm., Section K, 1982); Dist. Fellow: Amer. Econ. Assoc. (Pres., 1972); Western Econ. Assoc. (Pres., 1980-81); Corresp. Fellow, British Acad., 1976; Foreign Hon. Mem., Finnish Acad. of Sciences. John Bates Clark Medal, American Economic Assoc., 1957; Nobel Meml Prize in Economic Science, 1972. Hon. LLD: Chicago, 1967; City Univ. of NY, 1972; Hon. Dr Soc. and Econ. Sciences, Vienna, 1971; Hon. ScD Columbia, 1973; Hon. DSocSci, Yale, 1974; Hon. Dr: Paris, 1974; Hebrew Univ. of Jerusalem, 1975; Helsinki, 1976. *Publications:* Social Choice and Individual Values, 1951, 2nd edn 1963; (with S. Karlin and H. Scarf) Studies in the Mathematical Theory of Inventory and Production, 1958; (with M. Hoffenberg) A Time Series Analysis of Interindustry Demands, 1959; (with L. Hurwicz and H. Uzawa) Studies in Linear and Nonlinear Programming, 1959; Aspects of the Theory of Risk Bearing, 1965; (with M. Kurz) Public Investment and the Rate of Return, and Optimal Fiscal Policy, 1971; Essays in the Theory of Risk-Bearing, 1971; (with F. Hahn) General Competitive Analysis, 1972; The Limits of Organization, 1974; (with L. Hurwicz) Studies in Resource Allocation Processes, 1977. *Address:* Department of Economics, Stanford University, Calif 94305, USA.

ARROWSMITH, Sir Edwin (Porter), KCMG 1959 (CMG 1950); *b* 23 May 1909; *s* of late Edwin Arrowsmith and of Kathleen Eggleston Arrowsmith (*née* Porter); *m* 1936, Clondagh, *e d* of late Dr W. G. Connor; two *d. Educ:* Cheltenham Coll.; Trinity Coll., Oxford (MA). Assistant District Commissioner, Bechuanaland Protectorate, 1932; in various District posts, Bechuanaland Protectorate, 1933-38; Commissioner, Turks and Caicos Islands, BWI, 1940-46; Administrator, Dominica, BWI, 1946-52; Resident Commissioner, Basutoland, 1952-56; Governor and Commander-in-Chief, Falkland Islands, 1957-64, and High Commissioner, British Antarctic Territory, 1962-64; Dir of Overseas Services Resettlement Bureau, 1965-79. Mem. Council, St Dunstan's, 1965-. Chm., Royal Commonwealth Soc. for the Blind, 1970-. Pres., Freshwater Biol Assoc., 1977-. *Recreation:* flyfishing. *Address:* 25 Rivermead Court, SW6 3RU. *T:* 01-736 4757. *Clubs:* Flyfishers', Hurlingham, Royal Commonwealth Society.

ARROWSMITH, Pat; pacifist and socialist; Editorial Assistant at Amnesty International, since 1971; *b* 2 March 1930; *d* of late George Ernest Arrowsmith and late Margaret Vera (*née* Kingham); *m* Mr Gardner, 11 Aug. 1979, separated 11 Aug. 1979; homosexual partnership with Wendy Butlin, 1962-76. *Educ:* Farringtons; Stover Sch.; Cheltenham Ladies' Coll.; Newnham Coll., Cambridge (BA history); Univ. of Ohio; Liverpool Univ. (Cert. in Social Science). Has held many jobs, incl.: Community Organizer in Chicago, 1952-53; Cinema Usherette, 1953-54; Social Caseworker, Liverpool Family Service Unit, 1954; Child Care Officer, 1955 and 1964; Nursing Asst, Deva Psychiatric Hosp., 1956-57; Reporter for Peace News, 1965; Gardener for Camden BC, 1966-68; Researcher for Soc. of Friends Race Relations Cttee, 1969-71; Case Worker for NCCL, 1971; and on farms, as waitress in cafes, in factories, as a toy demonstrator, as a 'temp' in numerous offices, as asst in children's home, as newspaper deliverer and sales agent, as charperson, as bartender, and in a holiday camp. Organizer for Direct Action Cttee against Nuclear War, Cttee of 100 and Campaign for Nuclear Disarmament, 1958-68; gaoled 10 times as political prisoner, 1958-77 (adopted twice as Prisoner of Conscience by Amnesty International); awarded Holloway Prison Green Band, 1964; awarded Girl Crusaders knighthood, 1940. Contested: Fulham, 1966 (Radical Alliance) and 1970 (Hammersmith Stop the SE Asia War Cttee), on peace issues; Cardiff South East (Independent Socialist), 1979. Member: War Resisters' Internat. Troops Out Movement; Campaign for Nuclear Disarmament; Anti Nazi League; Labour Party; TGWU. *Publications:* Jericho (novel), 1965; Somewhere Like This (novel), 1970; To Asia in Peace, 1972; The Colour of Six Schools, 1972; Breakout (poems and drawings from prison), 1975; On the Brink (anti-war poems), 1981; The Prisoner (novel), 1982. *Recreations:* water colour painting (has held and contrib. exhibns), swimming, writing poetry. *Address:* 132c Middle Lane, N8. *T:* 01-340 2661. *Club:* Gateways.

ARTHINGTON-DAVY, Humphrey Augustine, MVO 1977; OBE 1965; HM Diplomatic Service, retired; High Commissioner to Tonga, 1973-80, and Western Samoa, 1973-77; *b* 1920. *Educ:* Eastbourne Coll.; Trinity Coll., Cambridge. Indian Army, 1941; Indian Political Service, 1946; Civil Service of Pakistan, 1947; CRO, 1958; British Representative in the Maldives, 1960; Deputy High Commissioner: Botswana, 1966; Mauritius, 1968; Tonga, 1970. *Recreation:* travel. *Address:* c/o Grindlays Bank, 13 St James's Square, SW1; PO Box 56, Nuku' Alofa, Tonga, South Pacific. *Club:* Naval and Military.

ARTHUR, family name of **Baron Glenarthur.**

ARTHUR, Allan James Vincent, MBE 1948; DL; Vice Lord-Lieutenant of Essex, since 1978; *b* 16 Sept. 1915; *s* of late Col Sir Charles Arthur, MC, VD, and of Lady (Dorothy Grace) Arthur; *m* 1940, Joan Deirdre Heape (marr. diss. 1948); *m* 1949, Dawn Rosemary Everil, *d* of Col F. C. Drake; two *s* two *d*. *Educ:* Rugby Sch.; Magdalene Coll., Cambridge (MA). Indian Civil Service (Punjab), 1938-47; SDO, Murree, Kasur; Dep. Comr, Attock, Multan; Sudan Political Service, 1949-54; District Comr, Khartoum, Shendi; Dep. Governor, Northern Province; J. V. Drake and Co. Ltd, Sugar Brokers, 1954-60; Woodhouse, Drake, and Carey Ltd, Commodity Merchants, 1960-75 (Chm., 1972-75). Member, Chelmsford Borough Council, 1973-79, Mayor, 1977-78; Governor: Chigwell Sch., 1972-; Brentwood Sch., 1973-; London Hosp. Med. Coll., 1956-74. Member: Bd of Visitors, HM Prison, Chelmsford, 1973-79; Council, Univ. of Essex, 1980-. High Sheriff, 1971-72, DL 1974, Essex. *Publication:* contrib. to The District Officer in India, 1930-47, 1980. *Recreations:* swimming, shooting. *Address:* Mount Maskall, Boreham, Chelmsford CM3 3HW. *T:* Chelmsford 467776. *Clubs:* Oriental; Hawks (Cambridge).

ARTHUR, Hon. Sir Basil (Malcolm), 5th Bt, *cr* 1841; MP (Lab) for Timaru, New Zealand, since 1962; Minister of Transport, and Minister in charge of State Insurance Office, New Zealand, 1972-75; *b* 18 Sept. 1928; *o s* of Sir George Malcolm Arthur, 4th Bt, and Doris Fay, *y d* of Joseph Wooding, JP, Woodland Grange, Woodbury, Geraldine, New Zealand; *S* father 1949; *m* 1950, Elizabeth Rita, *d* of late Alan Wells, Wakefield, Nelson, New Zealand; one *s* two *d*. *Heir:* *s* Stephen John Arthur [*b* 1 July 1953; *m* Carolyn Margaret Rita, *d* of Burney Lawrence Diamond, Cairns, Queensland; one *s* two *d*]. *Address:* Seadown, No 3 RD, Timaru, New Zealand.

ARTHUR, Prof. Donald Ramsay, MSc, PhD, DSc; Professor and Head of Department of Zoology, King's College, London University, 1963-80, now Emeritus Professor; Director of Studies, School of Human Environmental Studies, 1975-79, and since 1981; FKC 1972; *b* 1 May 1917; *s* of Henry and Rachel Arthur; *m* 1945, Iris Doreen (*née* Gingell); one *d*. *Educ:* Amman Valley Gram. Sch.; UCW, Aberystwyth. School Master, Brockley Co. Sch., London, 1938-39; Scientist, Royal Ordnance Factory, 1939-42; Sen. Entomologist, University Coll. South Wales (working under grant from ARC), 1943-47; Sen. Biology Master, City of Cardiff High Sch., 1947-48; King's Coll., London: Lectr in Zoology, 1948-59; Leverhulme Research Award, 1954-55; Reader in Zoology, 1959-63; Dean, Faculty of Science, 1968-70; Consultant: US Naval Med. Res. Unit, Cairo, 1955-62; Environmental Resources Ltd, 1972; TEST (Transport and Environment Studies), 1970-. Univ. of Rhodesia, 1962; Vis. Res. Fellow, Tick Res. Unit, Rhodes Univ., 1972; Mem. Council, Brit. Soc. Parasitol., 1962-64; Chm., Bd of Studies in Zoology, Univ. of London, 1965-67; Mem. Bd of Studies (as other person), 1981-; Vis. Prof., Queen Mary Coll., Univ. of London, 1981-; Pres., London Branch of Assoc. for Science Educn, 1965-66; Member: Exec. Cttee and Finance and Admin. Cttee, Field Studies Council, 1963-72; Council of Environmental Educn, 1968-72; Editorial Bd, Parasitology, 1964-; Editorial Bd, Internat. Jl of Environmental Sciences, 1970-; Council, John Cass Coll., 1965-69; Delegacy, King's Coll., 1970-76; Finance Cttee, King's Coll., 1970-77; Cleaner Thames Consultative Cttee, 1968-72; Adv. Cttee of Pollution by oil of the sea, 1970-72; Council, Instn of Environmental Sciences, 1970-79. Editor, Biological Science Texts, 1966-. President: London Old Aberystwythians, 1967-68; London Carms Soc., 1970-71. FIBiol, 1965; FRSA 1981. *Publications:* Ticks: a Monograph of the Ixodoidea, Pt V, 1960; Ticks and Disease, 1962; (ed) Aspects of Disease Transmission by Ticks, 1962; British Ticks, 1963; Ticks of the Genus Ixodes in Africa, 1965; (ed) Looking at Animals Again, 1966; Survival: Man and his Environment, 1969; (ed with J. D. Carthy) Oil Pollution and Littoral Organisms, 1968; Joint Editor, Symposium vol., 2nd Internat. Acarological Congress, 1969; Adv. Editor, Encyclopaedia of Zoology, 1970; chapter (with I. Birtwell) in Aquatic Oligochaeta Biology, 1980; papers in Parasitology, Jl Parasitology, Proc. Zool. Soc., Bulletin Entomological Research, etc. *Recreation:* Rugby football. *Address:* 57 Rushgrove Avenue, NW9. *T:* 01-205 6375.

ARTHUR, Sir Geoffrey (George), KCMG 1971 (CMG 1963); HM Diplomatic Service, retired; Master of Pembroke College, Oxford, since 1975; *b* 19 March 1920; *s* of G. J. Arthur; *m* 1946, Margaret, *d* of late T. A. Woodcock, OBE; no *c*. *Educ:* Ashby de la Zouch Grammar Sch.; Christ Church, Oxford. Served in Army, 1940-45. Joined HM Foreign Service, 1947. Served in: Baghdad, 1948-50; Ankara, 1950-53; Foreign Office, 1953-55; Bonn, 1956-58; Cairo, 1959-63; Counsellor in Foreign Office, 1963-67; Ambassador to Kuwait, 1967-68; Asst Under-Sec. of State, FCO, 1968-70; Political Resident in the Persian Gulf, 1970-72; Visiting FCO Fellow, St Antony's Coll., Oxford, 1972-73; Dep. Under-Sec. of State, FCO, 1973-75. Dir, 1975-79, Special Advr to Bd, 1980-, British Bank of the Middle East. *Address:* Master's Lodgings, Pembroke College, Oxford. *T:* Oxford 43482. *Clubs:* United Oxford & Cambridge University, Beefsteak.

ARTHUR, Prof. Geoffrey Herbert; Clinical Professor, Faculty of Veterinary Science and Animal Resources, King Faisal University, Dammam, Saudi Arabia, since Jan. 1980; *b* 6 March 1916; *s* of William Gwyn Arthur and Ethel Jessie Arthur; *m* 1948, Lorna Isabel Simpson; four *s* one *d*. *Educ:* Abersychan Secondary Sch.; Liverpool Univ. BVSc 1939; MRCVS 1939; MVSc 1945; DVSc 1957; FRCVS 1957. Lectr in Veterinary Medicine, Liverpool Univ., 1941-48; Reader in Veterinary Surgery, Royal Veterinary Coll., 1949-51; Reader in Veterinary Surgery and Obstetrics, Univ. of London, 1952-65; Prof. of Veterinary Obstetrics and Diseases of Reproduction, Univ. of London, 1965-73; Prof. and Head of Dept of Vet. Surgery, Bristol Univ., 1974-79.

Examiner to Univs of Cambridge, Dublin, Edinburgh, Glasgow, Liverpool, London, Reading, Bristol and Ceylon. Visiting Professor: Univ. of Khartoum, 1964; Pahlavi Univ., 1976; Nairobi Univ., 1979. *Publications:* Wright's Veterinary Obstetrics, including Diseases of Reproduction, 3rd edn, 1964; Veterinary Reproduction and Obstetrics, 4th edn, 1975; papers on medicine and reproduction in Veterinary Record, Veterinary Jl, Jl of Comparative Pathology, Jl Reprod. Fert., Equine Vet. Jl and Jl Small Animal Pract. (Editor). *Recreations:* observing natural phenomena and experimenting. *Address:* Fallodene, Stone Allerton, Axbridge, Som BS26 2NH.

ARTHUR, James Stanley, CMG 1977; HM Diplomatic Service; British High Commissioner in Bridgetown, 1978-82, also British High Commissioner (non-resident) to Dominica, 1978-82, to St Lucia and St Vincent, 1979-82, to Grenada, 1980-82, to Antigua and Barbuda, 1981-82, and concurrently British Government Representative to West Indies Associated State of St Kitts-Nevis; *b* 3 Feb. 1923; *s* of Laurence and Catherine Arthur, Lerwick, Shetland; *m* 1950, Marion North; two *s* two *d*. *Educ:* Trinity Academy, Edinburgh; Liverpool Univ. (BSc). Scientific Civil Service, 1944-46; Asst Principal, Scottish Educn Dept, 1946; Min. of Educn/Dept of Educn and Science, 1947-66: Private Sec. to Parly Sec., 1948-50; Principal Private Sec. to Minister, 1960-62; Counsellor, FO, 1966; Nairobi, 1967-70; Dep. High Comr, Malta, 1970-73; High Comr, Suva, 1974-78, and first High Comr (non-resident), Republic of Nauru, 1977-78. *Recreations:* golf, music. *Address:* The Bank of Scotland, 57-60 Haymarket, SW1Y 4QY. *Clubs:* Travellers', Royal Commonwealth Society.

ARTHUR, Maj.-Gen. (John) Norman (Stewart); Director of Personal Services (Army), Ministry of Defence, since 1983; *b* 6 March 1931; *s* of Col Evelyn Stewart Arthur and Mrs E. S. Arthur (*née* Burnett-Stuart); *m* 1960, Theresa Mary Hopkinson; one *s* one *d* (and one *s* decd). *Educ:* Eton Coll.; RMA, Sandhurst. rcds, jssc, psc. Commnd Royal Scots Greys, 1951; commanded: Royal Scots Dragoon Guards, 1972-74 (despatches, 1974); 7th Armoured Bde, 1976-77; GOC 3rd Armoured Div., 1980-82. Member: Royal Co. of Archers, Queen's Body Guard for Scotland; British Olympic Team, Equestrian Three-Day Event, 1960-. *Recreations:* field and country sports and pursuits, horsemanship, military history. *Address:* c/o Lloyds Bank, Cox's & King's Branch (Gds & Cav.), 6 Pall Mall, SW1Y 5NH. *Clubs:* Cavalry and Guards; Caledonian Hunt.

ARTHUR, John Rhys, DFC 1944; JP; **His Honour Judge Arthur;** a Circuit Judge, since 1975; *b* 29 April 1923; *s* of late John Monar Arthur and Eleanor Arthur; *m* 1951, Joan Tremearne Pickering; two *s* one *d*. *Educ:* Mill Hill; Christ's Coll., Cambridge (MA). Commnd RAF, 1943, demobilised 1946. Cambridge, 1946-48; called to Bar, Inner Temple, 1949. Dep. Chm., Lancs County QS, 1970-71; a Recorder, 1972-75. JP Lancs 1970. *Address:* Orovales, Caldy, Wirral L48 1LP. *T:* 051-625 8624. *Clubs:* MCC, Old Millhillians; Racquet, Athenæum (Liverpool).

ARTHUR, Maj.-Gen. Norman; *see* Arthur, Maj.-Gen. J. N. S.

ARTHUR, Peter Bernard; Deputy Chairman and Chairman of the Sub-Committees of Classification, Lloyd's Register of Shipping, since 1976; *b* 29 Aug. 1923; *s* of Charles Frederick Bernard Arthur and Joan (*née* Dyer); *m* 1954, Irène Susy (*née* Schüpbach); one *s* two *d*. *Educ:* Oundle Sch. Commnd 1943; Mahratta LI, 1943-47 (mentioned in despatches, Italy, 1945); RA, 1947-53. Underwriting Mem. of Lloyd's, 1954-; Mem. Cttee, Lloyd's Register of Shipping, and Vice-Chm., Sub-Cttees of Classification, 1967. Dir, Bolton Steam Shipping Co. Ltd, 1958-; Chairman: London Deep Sea Tramp Shipowners' Assoc., 1970-71; Deep Sea Tramp Sect., Chamber of Shipping of UK, 1972-73; Mem., London Gen. Shipowners Soc., 1965-. *Recreations:* golf, music, gardening. *Address:* Oak Lodge, Peter Avenue, Oxted, Surrey RH8 9LG. *T:* Oxted 2962. *Clubs:* City of London; Tandridge Golf.

ARTHUR, Rt. Rev. Robert Gordon; *b* 17 Aug. 1909; *s* of George Thomas Arthur and Mary Arthur; *m* Marie Olive Cavel Wheen; two *s* two *d*. *Educ:* Launceston and Devonport High Schs, Tasmania; Queen's Coll., Univ. of Melbourne. MA (Hons) 1932. Rector of: Berridale, NSW, 1950-53; St John's, Canberra, ACT, 1953-60; Wagga Wagga, NSW, 1960-61; Archdeacon of Canberra, 1953-60; Asst Bp of Canberra and Goulburn, 1956-61; Bishop of Grafton, NSW, 1961-73; Rector of St Philip's, Canberra, 1973-74; Priest-in-charge of Bratton, Wilts, 1975-78, and Rural Dean of Heytesbury, 1976-78; Hon. Asst Bishop of Sheffield, 1978-80. *Address:* 4 Berry Street, Downer, Canberra, ACT 2602, Australia.

ARTHURE, Humphrey George Edgar, CBE 1969; MD, FRCS, FRCOG; Consulting Obstetric and Gynæcological Surgeon: Charing Cross Hospital; Queen Charlotte's Hospital; Mount Vernon Hospital. MRCS, LRCP 1931; MB, BS 1933; FRCS 1935; MD London 1938; FRCOG 1950 (Hon. Sec. 1949-56; Vice-Pres. 1964-67); FRSM (Pres., Section of Obstetrics and Gynæcology, 1969); co-opted Mem. Council, RCS 1960; Pres., West London Medico-Chirurgical Soc., 1964; Formerly: Chm., Central Midwives Board, and Adviser, Obstetrics and Gynæcology, DHSS; Mem., Standing Maternity and Midwifery Advisory Cttee; Resident Obstetric Medical Officer and Obstetrical Registrar, Charing Cross Hospital; Resident Medical Officer, Chelsea Hospital for Women. Served War of 1939-45, temp. Lt-Col, RAMC. *Publications:* Simpson Oration, 1972; (jtly) Sterilisation, 1976; contribs med. jls. *Address:* 12 Eyot Green, Chiswick Mall, W4 2PT. *T:* 01-994 7698.

ARTIS, Prof. Michael John; Professor of Economics, Manchester University, since 1975; *b* 29 June 1938; *s* of Cyril John and Violet Emily Artis; *m* 1961, Lilian Gregson (now separated); two *d*. *Educ:* Baines Grammar Sch., Poulton-le-Fylde, Lancs; Magdalen Coll., Oxford. BA Hons (PPE) Oxon. Assistant Research Officer, Oxford Univ., 1959; Lectr in Economics, Adelaide Univ., 1964; Lectr and Sen. Lectr in Economics, Flinders Univ., 1966; Research Officer and Review Editor, Nat. Inst. of Economic and Social Research, London, 1967; Prof. of Applied Economics, Swansea Univ. Coll., 1972. *Publications:* Foundations of British Monetary Policy, 1964; contribs on economics, economic policy to books and learned jls. *Recreations:* cycling, walking. *Address:* 15 Manchester Road, Knutsford, Cheshire WA16 0LY. *T:* Knutsford 3204.

ARTON, Major A. T. B.-; *see* Bourne-Arton.

ARTRO MORRIS, John Evan; a Registrar of the Supreme Court, Family Division, since 1977; *b* 17 Feb. 1925; *s* of Tudor and Mabel Artro Morris; *m* 1961, Karin Ilse Alide Russell; two *s*. *Educ:* Liverpool Coll.; The Queen's Coll., Oxford. BA Oxon. Served RN, 1943-47. Called to the Bar, Middle Temple, 1952. *Recreations:* D-I-Y, Rugby (spectator), rough shooting, fishing. *Address:* 6 Billing Street, SW10 9UR. *T:* 01-352 5249. *Club:* London Welsh RFC.

ARTUS, Ronald Edward; Secretary and Group Chief Investment Manager, Prudential Corporation Ltd, since 1979; Chief Investment Manager, Prudential Assurance Co. Ltd, since 1982 (Joint Secretary and Chief Investment Manager, 1975-82); Chairman: Prutec Ltd, since 1980; Prudential Portfolio Managers Ltd, since 1981; *b* 8 Oct 1931; *s* of late Ernest and of Doris Artus; *m* 1956, Brenda Margaret, *d* of late Sir Norman Touche, Bt, and Eva, Lady Touche (*née* Cameron); three *s* one *d*. *Educ:* Sir Thomas Rich's Sch., Gloucester; Magdalen Coll., Oxford (MA, 1st Cl. PPE). Joined Prudential, 1954; Head of Economic Intelligence Dept, 1958-71; Sen. Asst Investment Manager, 1971-73; Dep. Investment Manager, 1973-75; Dir various cos, Prudential Gp. Director: Keyser Ullmann Holdings Ltd, 1972-80; Charterhouse Gp Ltd, 1980-; Celltech Ltd, 1980-. Member: City Capital Markets Cttee, 1982-; Accounting Standards Cttee, 1982-. Hon. Fellow, Soc. of Investment Analysts, 1980- (Mem. Council, 1964-76; Chm., 1973-75). *Publications:* contrib. various jls on economic and investment matters. *Recreations:* cricket, music, collecting English watercolours, farm labour. *Address:* 142 Holborn Bars, EC1N. *T:* 01-405 9222.

ARUNDEL AND BRIGHTON, Bishop of, (RC), since 1977; **Rt. Rev. Cormac Murphy-O'Connor;** *b* 24 Aug. 1932; *s* of late Dr P. G. Murphy-O'Connor and Ellen (*née* Cuddigan). *Educ:* Prior Park Coll., Bath; English Coll., Rome; Gregorian Univ. PhL, STL. Ordained Priest, 1956. Asst Priest, Portsmouth and Fareham, 1957-66; Sec. to Bp of Portsmouth, 1966-70; Parish Priest, Parish of the Immaculate Conception, Southampton, 1970-71; Rector, English College, Rome, 1971-77. Chm., Bishops' Cttee for Europe, 1978-; Mem., Sacred Congregation for Catholic Educn, 1978-. *Recreations:* music, sport. *Address:* St Joseph's Hall, Storrington, Pulborough, Sussex RH20 4HE. *Club:* Athenæum.

ARUNDEL AND SURREY, Earl of; Edward William Fitzalan-Howard; *b* 2 Dec. 1956; *s* and *heir* of 17th Duke of Norfolk, *qv*. *Educ:* Ampleforth Coll., Yorks; Lincoln Coll., Oxford. *Recreations:* ski-ing, motor-racing, shooting, farming. *Address:* Arundel Castle, Sussex. *T:* Arundel 882173; Carlton Towers, Yorks. *T:* Goole 860 243; Bacres House, Hambleden, Henley-on-Thames. *T:* Hambleden 350.

ARUNDELL; *see* Monckton-Arundell, family name of Viscount Galway.

ARUNDELL, Dennis Drew, OBE 1978; (formerly D. D. Arundel); actor, composer, producer, writer for theatre, radio, films and television, since 1926; *b* 22 July 1898; *s* of Arundel Drew Arundel and Rose Lucy Campbell. *Educ:* Tonbridge Sch.; St John's Coll., Cambridge. Lieut, RGA, 1917-19 (gassed, 1918). St John's Coll., 1919-29 (Sizarship, 1917; Strathcona Studentship, 1922); BA (Classics) 1922, MusB 1923, MA 1924. Fellow of St John's Coll., Cambridge, 1923-29; Lecturer in Music and English Drama, Deputy Organist St John's, 1924. First appeared on professional stage at Lyric, Hammersmith, 1926; subseq. joined Old Vic Company, playing Trofimov in A Month in the Country, Lucio in Measure for Measure, and has since taken many parts, inc. first Lord Peter Wimsey, Manningham in Gaslight; directed and composed music for plays in West End theatres, films, radio and television. Chief Producer, RCM Opera Sch., 1959-73 (Crees Lectr, RCM, 1970; FRCM 1969); Resident Opera Producer and Coach, Royal Northern Coll. of Music, Manchester, 1974. Chm., Internat. Jury of Singing, Jeunesses Musicales, Belgrade, 1972. As an opera director his work has been especially with Sadler's Wells and the BBC; producer of over 50 operas; translator of some 15 operas; arr. Purcell's Indian Queen for Opera da Camera, 1973; directed both operas and plays in Australia, 1956, 1975 and Finland, 1947, 1952, 1957 (scene from 1952 production of Hamlet inc. in centenary prog. of Helsinki Nat. Theatre, 1973). Lecture to Soc. of Theatre Research, 1971. *Publications:* Henry Purcell, 1927 (in German, 1929); (ed) King Arthur, Purcell Soc. edn, 1928; Dryden and Howard, 1929; The Critic at the Opera, 1957 (repr. NY, with subtitle Contemporary Comments on Opera in London over Three Centuries, 1980); The Story of Sadler's Wells, 1965 (new edn as The Story of Sadler's Wells, 1633-1977, 1978); Introduction to Le Nozze di Figaro and Cosi fan Tutte (Cassell Opera Guides), 1971; (ed) Congreve's Semele, 1925; (trans.) Morax

and Honegger's King David, 1929; (trans.) Weinberger's Schwanda the Bagpiper, 1946; (trans.) Claudel's and Honegger's Jeanne d'Arc au Bûcher, 1939; (trans.) Monteverdi's Il Combattimento di Tancredi e Clorinda, 1974; Sibelius's Kullervo, 1974; various musical compositions and musical articles. *Recreation:* operatic research. *Address:* 21 Lloyd Square, WC1. *T:* 01-837 2942.

ARUNDELL, Brig. Sir Robert (Duncan Harris), KCMG 1950 (CMG 1947); OBE 1943; retired as Governor and Commander-in-Chief, Barbados (1953-59) (Acting Governor-General and C-in-C, The West Indies, 1959); Zanzibar Delimitation Commissioner, 1962; *b* Lifton, Devon, 22 July 1904; *s* of late C. H. Arundell; *m* 1929, Joan, *d* of late Capt. J. A. Ingles, RN; one *s*. *Educ:* Blundell's Sch.; Brasenose Coll., Oxford. Colonial Administrative Service, Tanganyika Territory, 1927; seconded Colonial Office, 1935-37; Sec. Nyasaland Financial Commission, 1937-38; Tanganyika Territory, 1938-39; Assistant Chief Sec. Uganda, 1939; Army, Civil Affairs, 1941-45; served War of 1939-45 in Middle East and East Africa (despatches, OBE); Chief Civil Affairs Officer MEF (Brig.), 1944-45; British Resident Mem. in Washington of Caribbean Commission, 1946-47; Governor and C-in-C, Windward Islands, 1948-53. KStJ 1952. *Address:* Wakehill, Ilminster, Somerset. *Club:* East India, Devonshire, Sports and Public Schools.

ARUP, Sir Ove (Nyquist), Kt 1971; CBE 1953; FEng, FICE, FIStructE, MICEI; MSocCE(France); Founder, Ove Arup Partnerships; *b* Newcastle upon Tyne, 16 April 1895; *s* of Jens Simon Johannes Arup and Mathilde B. Nyquist; *m* 1925, Ruth Sœrensen; one *s* two *d*. *Educ:* Preparatory Sch., Hamburg, Germany; Public Sch., 1909; Univ. of Copenhagen, Denmark. MIngF (Medlem Ingeniør Forening), Copenhagen. Designer Christiani & Nielsen, GmbH, Hamburg, 1922-23, transf. to London 1923; Designer, 1923-25, Chief Designer, 1925-34, Christiani & Nielsen, Ltd, London; Director and Chief Designer, J. L. Kier & Co., Ltd, London, 1934-38; Consulting Engineer for: schools, flats, air raid shelters, industrial projects, marine work (Air Min.); Director: Arup Designs, Ltd; Arup & Arup, Ltd; Pipes, Ltd, 1938-45; Senior Partner: Ove Arup & Partners, Consulting Engineers, 1949; Arup Associates, 1963. Chm. Soc. of Danish Civil Engineers in Gt Britain and Ireland, 1955-59; Visiting Lectr, Harvard Univ., 1955; Alfred Bossom Lectr, RSA, 1970; Maitland Lecture, IStructE, 1968. RIBA Royal Gold Medal for Architecture for 1966; Gold Medal, IStructE, 1973. Hon. DSc: Durham, 1967; Heriot-Watt, 1976; City Univ., 1979; Hon. ScD East Anglia, 1968; Hon. Dr Tekniske Hojskole, Lyngby, Denmark, 1974. Fellow Amer. Concrete Inst., 1975. Commander (First Class), Order of the Dannebrog, 1975 (Chevalier, 1965). *Publications:* Design, Cost, Construction and Relative Safety of Trench, Surface, Bomb-proof and other Air Raid Shelters, 1939; Safe Housing in War-Time, 1941; various contribs to technical jls. *Recreations:* music and reading. *Address:* 6 Fitzroy Park, Highgate, N6. *T:* 01-340 3388. *Clubs:* Athenæum; Danish.

ARVILL, Robert; *see* Boote, R. E.

ASAAD, Prof. Fikry Naguib M.; *see* Morcos-Asaad.

ASFA WOSSEN HAILE SELLASSIE, HIH Merd Azmatch; GCMG (Hon.) 1965; GCVO (Hon.) 1930; GBE (Hon.) 1932; Crown Prince of Ethiopia, since 1930; *b* 27 July 1916; *e s* and *heir* of late Emperor Haile Sellassie, KG, and Empress Menen; *m* 1st, Princess Wallata Israel; one *d* decd; 2nd, Princess Madfariash Wark Abebe; one *s* three *d*. *Educ:* privately; Liverpool Univ. Governor of Wollo province; Mem., Crown Council. Fought in Italo-Ethiopian War, 1935-36. Grand Cross: Légion d'Honneur; Belgian Order of Leopold; Order of the Netherlands; Order of Rising Sun, Japan; Order of White Elephant, Siam. *Heir:* s Prince Zara Yacob, *b* 18 Aug. 1953. *Address:* 82 Portland Place, W1.

ASH, Prof. Eric Albert, FRS 1977; Pender Professor and Head of Department of Electronic and Electrical Engineering, University College London, since 1980; *b* 31 Jan. 1928; *s* of Walter and Dorothea Ash; *m* 1954, Clare (*née* Babb); five *d*. *Educ:* University College Sch.; Imperial Coll. of Science and Technology. BSc(Eng), PhD, DSc, FCGI, DIC. FIEE; FIEEE; FInstP; FEng 1978. Research Fellow: Stanford Univ., Calif, 1952-54; QMC, 1954-55; Res. Engr, Standard Telecommunication Laboratories Ltd, 1955-63; Sen. Lectr, 1963-65, Reader, 1965-67, Prof., 1967-, Dept of Electronic and Electrical Engrg, UCL. Member: Royal Soc. cttees; Council, IEE; Exec. Bd, Fellowship of Engrg, 1981-. Manager and Vice-Pres., Royal Instn, 1980-. *Publications:* patents; papers on topics in physical electronics in various engrg and physics jls. *Recreations:* music, skiing, swimming. *Address:* 11 Ripplevale Grove, N1 1AE. *T:* 01-607 4989.

ASH, Maurice Anthony, BSc (Econ); Chairman, Dartington Hall Trust, since 1972; Chairman of Executive, Town and Country Planning Association, since 1969; Chairman, Green Alliance, since 1978; *b* 31 Oct. 1917; *s* of Wilfred Cracroft and Beatrice Ash; *m* 1947, Ruth Whitney Elmhirst, *o d* of late Leonard Knight and Dorothy Whitney Elmhirst; three *d* (one *s* decd). *Educ:* Gresham's Sch., Holt; LSE; Yale. Served War of 1939-45, armoured forces in Western Desert, Italy, Greece (despatches 1944). Mem. Executive, TCPA, 1956-; Trustee, Dartington Hall and Dir associated companies, 1964-; Mem., SW Regional Economic Planning Council, 1965-68. Founder, Harlow Arts Trust. Mem., Henry Moore Foundn, 1980-. *Publications:* The Human Cloud, 1962; Who are the Progressives Now?, 1969; Regions of Tomorrow, 1969; A Guide to the Structure of London, 1972; Green Politics, 1980; articles on land use, education, international relations. *Recreation:* applying Wittgenstein. *Address:* Sharpham House, Ashprington, Totnes, Devon TQ9 7UT. *T:* Harbertonford 216. *Club:* Reform.

ASH, Raymond; Director, Business Statistics Office, since 1977; *b* 2 Jan. 1928; *s* of late Horace Ash and Gladys Ash; *m* 1947, Mavis Claire (*née* Wootton); two *s* one *d. Educ:* Wolverhampton Grammar Sch. Civil Service, 1949-: professional statistician, 1957-, with experience at various levels of seniority in health, labour, overseas trade, and business statistics. *Publications:* contrib. learned jls. *Recreations:* Rotary, bridge, country walks. *Address:* 20 Taliesin Close, Rogerstone, Newport, Gwent. *T:* Newport 895470.

ASH, Rear-Admiral Walter William Hector, CB 1962; WhSch; CEng; FIEE; *b* Portsmouth, Hants, 2 May 1906; *s* of Hector Sidney and Mabel Jessy Ash; *m* 1932, Louisa Adelaide Salt, Jarrow-on-Tyne; three *d. Educ:* City & Guilds Coll., Kensington; Royal Naval Coll., Greenwich. Whitworth Scholar, 1926; John Samuel Scholar, 1927. Asst Elect. Engr, Admiralty (submarine design), 1932-37; Elect. Engr, Admiralty (battleship design), 1937-39; Fleet Elect. Engr, Staff C-in-C Med., 1939-40; Supt Elect. Engr, Admiralty (supply and prod.), 1940-45; Supt Elect. Engr, HM Dockyard, Hong Kong, 1945-48; Supt Elect. Engr, Admiralty Engineering Lab., 1948-49; Comdr RN, HMS Montclare, 1950-51; Capt. RN, Admiralty (weapon control design), 1951-54; Capt. RN, Elect. Engr Manager, HM Dockyard, Devonport, 1954-58; Capt. RN, Ship Design Dept, Admiralty, 1959-60; Rear-Adm. 1960; subseq. Ship Dept Directorate, Admty, retd Aug. 1963. Vis. Lectr in electrical machinery design, RN Coll., Greenwich, 1934-37. Chairman IEE, SW Sub Centre, 1957-58. ADC to the Queen, 1958-60. *Recreations:* golf, music (piano and organ). *Address:* Saltash, 14 Beacon Drive, Highcliffe-on-Sea, Christchurch, Dorset BH23 5DH. *T:* Highcliffe 5261.

ASH, Rear-Adm. William Noel, CB 1977; MVO 1959; Secretary, Defence Press and Broadcasting Committee, since 1980; *b* 6 March 1921; *s* of late H. Arnold Ash, MRCS, LRCP; *m* 1951, Pamela, *d* of late Harry C. Davies, Hawkes Bay, NZ; one *s* one *d. Educ:* Merchant Taylors' School. Joined RN, 1938; HM Yacht Britannia, 1955-58; Captain 1965; Canadian NDC, 1965-66; Staff of SACLANT (NATO), 1966-69; Cabinet Office, 1969-71; comd HMS Ganges, 1971-73; Rear-Adm. 1974; Dir of Service Intelligence, 1974-77, retired. *Address:* 7 Wonford Road, Exeter, Devon. *T:* Exeter 58751. *Club:* Royal Commonwealth Society.

ASHBEE, Paul; Archaeologist, University of East Anglia, since 1969; *b* 23 June 1918; *s* of Lewis Ashbee and Hannah Mary Elizabeth Ashbee (*née* Brett); *m* 1952, Richmal Crompton Lamburn Disher; one *s* one *d. Educ:* sch. in Maidstone, Kent; Univ. of London; Univ. of Leicester (MA). Post-grad. Dip. Prehistoric Archaeology, London. Royal W Kent Regt and REME, 1939-46; Control Commn for Germany, 1946-49; Univ. of London, Univ. of Bristol (Redland Coll.), 1949-54; Asst Master and Head of History, Forest Hill Sch., 1954-68. Excavation of prehistoric sites, mostly barrows both long and round for then Min. of Works, 1949-; Co-dir with R. L. S. Bruce-Mitford of BM excavations at Sutton-Hoo, 1964-69. Mem. Council and Meetings Sec., Prehistoric Soc., 1960-74; Sec. (Wareham Earthwork), British Assoc. Sub-Cttee for Archaeological Field Experiment, 1961-; one-time Sec., Neolithic and Bronze Age Cttee, Council for British Archaeology; Mem. Royal Commn on Historical Monuments (England), 1975-; Mem., Area Archaeological Adv. Cttee (DoE) for Norfolk and Suffolk, 1975-79. Pres., Cornwall Archæol Soc., 1976-80, Vice-Pres., 1980-; Chm., Scole Cttee for E Anglian Archaeology, 1979-. FSA 1958. *Publications:* The Bronze Age Round Barrow in Britain, 1960; The Earthen Long Barrow in Britain, 1970; Ancient Scilly, 1974; The Ancient British, 1978; chapter in Sutton Hoo, Vol. I, 1976; numerous papers, articles and reviews in Archaeologia, Antiquaries Jl, Archaeological Jl, Proc. Prehistoric Soc., Antiquity, Cornish Archaeology, Arch. Cantiana, Proc. Dorset Arch. and Nat. Hist. Soc., Proc. Hampshire FC, Wilts Archaeol Magazine, Yorks Arch. Jl, etc. *Recreations:* East Anglia historical architecture, bibliophilia, dog ownership. *Address:* The Old Rectory, Chedgrave, Norfolk NR14 6ND; University of East Anglia, Norwich NR4 7TJ. *T:* Loddon 20595.

ASHBOURNE, 3rd Baron, *cr* 1885; **Edward Russell Gibson,** CB 1950; DSO 1943; Vice-Admiral, retired; *b* 1 June 1901; *s* of Hon. Edward Graves Mayne Gibson (3rd *s* of 1st Baron Ashbourne) and Mary Philips Greg; *S* uncle, 1942; *m* 1929, Reta Frances Manning, *e d* of E. M. Hazeland of Hong Kong; one *s* one *d. Educ:* Osborne; Dartmouth; Caius Coll., Cambridge. Entered Osborne, 1915; Midshipman, 1917; served in HMS Superb, Dreadnought, Monarch, in War of 1914-18; Lieut, 1922; specialised in submarines, 1925; Commander 1934; served on staff of Admiral of the Fleet Sir Dudley Pound in Mediterranean, 1938-39; Capt., 1939; served War of 1939-45 (DSO, Legion of Merit, US); served on staff of Adm. Sir Max Horton, 1940-42; Sicily Assault (DSO), 1943; commanded HMS Ariadne (Legion of Merit, US), 1943-45; commanded 3rd Submarine Flotilla, 1945; served on Naval Staff at Admiralty, 1946-47; commanded HMS Mauritius, 1947-48; Rear-Adm., 1948; Naval Representative on Military Staff Cttee, UN, 1949-50; Flag Officer, Gibraltar, and Admiral Supt, HM Dockyard, Gibraltar, 1950-52; Vice-Adm. 1952; retired list, 1952. JP Co. of Devon, 1955. County Pres., St John Ambulance Brigade for Devon, 1963. OStJ 1964. *Heir:* s Lieut-Comdr Hon. Edward Barry Greynville Gibson, RN, retired [*b* 28 Jan. 1933; *m* 1967, Yvonne Georgina, *d* of late Major G. W. Ham; three *s*]. *Address:* 56 Chiltley Way, Liphook, Hampshire. *Club:* Army and Navy.

ASHBROOK, 10th Viscount, *cr* 1751 (Ire.); **Desmond Llowarch Edward Flower,** KCVO 1977; MBE 1945; DL; Baron of Castle Durrow, 1733; Member of Council of Duchy of Lancaster, 1957-77; *b* 9 July 1905; *o s* of 9th Viscount and late Gladys, *d* of late Gen. Sir George Wentworth A. Higginson, GCB, GCVO; *S* father, 1936; *m* 1934, Elizabeth, *er d* of late Capt. John Egerton-Warburton, and of late Hon. Mrs Waters; two *s* one *d. Educ:* Eton; Balliol Coll., Oxford (BA 1927). Served War of 1939-45, RA. Formerly a Chartered Accountant. JP, 1946-67, DL 1949-, Vice-Lieutenant, 1961-67, Cheshire. *Heir:* s Hon. Michael Llowarch Warburton Flower [*b* 9 Dec. 1935; *m* 1971, Zoë Engleheart, *y d* of late F. H. A. Engleheart; two *s* one *d*]. *Address:* Woodlands, Arley, Northwich, Cheshire.

ASHBURNHAM, Captain Sir Denny Reginald, 12th Bt *cr* 1661; Captain South Staffordshire Regiment; *b* 24 March 1916; *o* surv. *s* of Sir Fleetwood Ashburnham, 11th Bt, and Elfrida, *d* of late James Kirkley, JP, Cleadon Park, Co. Durham; *S* father 1953; *m* 1946, Mary Frances, *d* of Major Robert Pascoe Mair, Wick, Udimore, Sussex; two *d* (one *s* decd). *Heir: g s* James Fleetwood Ashburnham, *b* 17 Dec. 1979. *Address:* Little Broomham, Guestling, Hastings, East Sussex.

ASHBURTON, 6th Baron, *cr* 1835; **Alexander Francis St Vincent Baring,** KG 1969; KCVO 1961; JP; DL; Lord Lieutenant and Custos Rotulorum, Hampshire and Isle of Wight, 1960-73 (Vice-Lieutenant, 1951-60); High Steward of Winchester, 1967-78; Receiver-General to the Duchy of Cornwall, 1961-74; *b* 7 April 1898; *o s* of 5th Baron and Hon. Mabel Edith Hood (*d* 1904), *d* of 4th Viscount Hood; *S* father, 1938; *m* 1924, Hon. Doris Mary Thérèse Harcourt (*d* 1981), *e d* of 1st Viscount Harcourt; two *s. Educ:* Eton; Royal Military Coll. Lieut The Greys, 1917-23; Flt-Lt AAF, 1939, retd as Group Captain, 1944. Director: Baring Brothers & Co. Ltd, 1962-68 (Managing Director, 1928-62); Alliance Assurance, 1932-68; Pressed Steel Co. Ltd, 1944-66; Mem. London Cttee, Hongkong & Shanghai Banking Corp., 1935-39. Treasurer, King Edward VII Hospital Fund for London, 1955-64, Governor, 1971-76; Trustee: King George's Jubilee Trust, 1949-68; Chantrey Bequest, 1963-81; St Cross Hospital of Noble Poverty, Winchester, 1961-81. Chm., Hampshire and IoW Police Authy, 1961-71. President: Hampshire and IoW Territorial Assoc., 1960-67 (Mem., 1951-60); Eastern Wessex Territorial Assoc., 1968-70. CC 1945, CA 1955, JP 1951, DL 1973, Hants. KStJ 1960. *Heir:* s Hon. John Francis Harcourt Baring, *qv. Address:* Itchen Stoke House, Alresford, Hants. *T:* Alresford 2479. *Clubs:* Lansdowne; Hampshire County (Winchester).

ASHBY, family name of **Baron Ashby.**

ASHBY, Baron *cr* 1973 (Life Peer), of Brandon, Suffolk; **Eric Ashby,** Kt 1956; FRS 1963; DSc London, MA Cantab; DIC; Chancellor, Queen's University, Belfast, since 1970; Fellow of Clare College, Cambridge, 1958, Life Fellow since 1975; *b* 1904; *s* of Herbert Charles Ashby, Bromley, Kent, and Helena Chater; *m* 1931, Elizabeth Helen Farries, Castle-Douglas, Scotland; two *s. Educ:* City of London Sch.; Imperial Coll. of Science, Univ. of London; Univ. of Chicago. Demonstrator at Imperial Coll., 1926-29; Commonwealth Fund Fellow in Univ. of Chicago and Desert Laboratory of Carnegie Institution, 1929-31; Lectr, Imperial Coll. of Science, 1931-35; Reader in Botany, Bristol Univ., 1935-37; Prof. of Botany, Univ. of Sydney, Australia, 1938-46; Harrison Prof. of Botany and Dir of Botanical Labs, Univ. of Manchester, 1946-50; Pres. and Vice-Chancellor, Queen's Univ., Belfast, 1950-59; Master of Clare College, Cambridge, 1959-75; Vice-Chancellor, Univ. of Cambridge, 1967-69. Chm., Aust. National Research Council, 1940-42; Chm., Professorial Board, Univ. of Sydney, 1942-44; Mem., Power Alcohol Committee of Enquiry, 1940-41; conducted enquiry for Prime Minister into enlistment of scientific resources in war, 1942; Trustee, Aust. Museum, 1942-46; Dir, Scientific Liaison Bureau, 1942-43; Counsellor and Chargé d'Affaires at Australian Legation, Moscow, USSR, 1945-46; Member of: Advisory Council on Scientific Policy, 1950-53; Nuffield Provincial Hospitals Trust, 1951-59; Advisory Council on Scientific and Industrial Research, 1954-60; Chairman: Scientific Grants Cttee, DSIR, 1955-56; Postgraduate Grants Cttee, DSIR, 1956-60; Northern Ireland Adv. Council for Education, 1953-58; Adult Education Cttee 1953-54; Cttee of Award of Commonwealth Fund, 1963-69 (Member, 1956-61); Royal Commn on Environmental Pollution, 1970-73; Member: Univ. Grants Cttee, 1959-67; Commonwealth Scholarship Commn, 1960-69; Council of Royal Soc., 1964-65; Governing Body, Sch. of Oriental and African Studies, Univ. of London, 1965-70; Chm., Commn for post-secondary and higher education in Nigeria, 1959-61; Chm., working party on pollution control in connection with UN conf. on the Environment, Stockholm, June 1972. Vice-Chm. Assoc. of Univs of Brit. Commonwealth, 1959-61; Pres., Brit. Assoc. for the Advancement of Science, 1963. Walgreen Prof., Michigan, 1975-77; Lectures: Godkin, Harvard Univ., 1964; Whidden, McMaster Univ., 1970; Bernal, Royal Soc., 1971; Prof-at-large, Cornell Univ., 1967-72; Trustee: Ciba Foundation, 1966-79; British Museum, 1969-77; Fellow: Imperial Coll. of Science; Davenport Coll., Yale Univ.; Hon. Fellow, Clare Hall; Hon. FRSE; Hon. FRIC. Hon. Foreign Mem., Amer. Acad. of Arts and Sciences. Hon. LLD: St Andrews; Aberdeen; Belfast; Rand; London; Wales; Columbia; Chicago; Michigan; Windsor; Western Australia; Manchester; Johns Hopkins; Liverpool; Hon. ScD Dublin; Hon. DSc: NUI; Univ. of Nigeria; Southampton; Hon. DLitt: W Ont; Sydney; Hon. DPhil Tech. Univ. Berlin; Hon. DCL East Anglia; Hon. DHL: Yale; Utah. Jephcott Medal, RSM, 1976. Order of Andrés Bello, first class, Venezuela, 1974. *Publications:* papers on aspects of experimental botany and on education; Environment and Plant Development, translated from German,

1931; German-English Botanical Terminology (with Elizabeth Helen Ashby), 1938; Food Shipment from Australia in Wartime; Challenge to Education, 1946; Scientist in Russia, 1947 (German trans., 1950); Technology and the Academics, 1958 (Japanese trans., 1963; Spanish trans, 1970); Community of Universities, 1963; African Universities and Western Tradition, 1964 (French trans. 1964); Universities: British, Indian, African (with Mary Anderson), 1966 (Spanish trans. 1972); Masters and Scholars, 1970; (with Mary Anderson) The Rise of the Student Estate, 1970; Any Person, Any Study, 1971; (with Mary Anderson) Portrait of Haldane, 1974; Reconciling Man with the Environment, 1978. *Recreations:* chamber music, mountain walking. *Address:* Norman Cottage, Manor Road, Brandon, Suffolk IP27 0LG.
See also M. F. Ashby.

ASHBY, Francis Dalton, OBE 1975; Director, National Counties Building Society, since 1980; *b* 20 Jan. 1920; *s* of late John Frederick Ashby and late Jessie Ashby; *m* 1948, Mollie Isabel Mitchell; one *s* two *d*. *Educ:* Watford Grammar Sch. Diploma in Govt Admin. War Service, Royal Signals, 1940-46: POW, Far East, 1942-45. National Debt Office: Exec. Officer, 1938; Asst Comptroller and Estabt Officer, 1966-76; Comptroller-General, 1976-80, retired. *Recreations:* dinghy sailing, walking. *Address:* Moorfield, Carpenters Wood Drive, Chorleywood, Herts.

ASHBY, Rt. Rev. Godfrey William Ernest Candler; *see* St John's (Transkei and S Africa), Bishop of.

ASHBY, Prof. Michael Farries, FRS 1979; Professor of Engineering Materials, University of Cambridge, since 1973; *b* 20 Nov. 1935; *s* of Lord Ashby, *qv*; *m* 1962, Maureen Ashby; two *s* one *d*. *Educ:* Campbell Coll., Belfast; Queens' Coll., Cambridge (BA, MA, PhD). Post-doctoral work, Cambridge, 1960-62; Asst, Univ. of Göttingen, 1962-65; Asst Prof., Harvard Univ., 1965-69; Prof. of Metallurgy, Harvard Univ., 1969-73. Mem., Akad. der Wissenschaften zu Göttingen, 1980-. Hon. MA Harvard, 1969. Editor, Acta Metallurgica, 1974-. *Recreations:* music, design. *Address:* 51 Maids Causeway, Cambridge CB5 8DE. *T:* Cambridge 64741.

ASHCOMBE, 4th Baron, *cr* 1892; **Henry Edward Cubitt;** late RAF; Chairman, Cubitt Estates Ltd; *b* 31 March 1924; *er s* of 3rd Baron Ashcombe; *S* father, 1962; *m* 1955, Ghislaine (marr. diss. 1968), *o d* of Cornelius Willem Dresselhuys, Long Island, New York; *m* 1973, Hon. Virginia Carington, *yr d* of Baron Carrington, *qv* ; *m* 1979, Mrs Elizabeth Dent-Brocklehurst. *Educ:* Eton. Served War of 1939-45, RAF. Consul-General in London for the Principality of Monaco, 1961-68. *Heir:* cousin Alick John Archibald Cubitt [*b* 10 Aug. 1927; *m* 1st, 1956, Rosemary Priscilla (*d* 1957), *er d* of T. C. Gouldsmith; 2nd, 1961, Jennifer Faith, *yr d* of late Lt-Col William Henry Ewart Gott, CB, CBE, DSO, MC; two *d*]. *Address:* Denbies, Dorking, Surrey. *Club:* White's.
See also Earl of Harrington.

ASHCROFT, Charles Neil; Clerk and Chief Executive, Derbyshire County Council, since 1979; *b* 27 Aug. 1937; *s* of Charles and Maggie Ashcroft; *m* 1962, Irene Riding; one *s*. *Educ:* Hutton Grammar Sch., near Preston. CIPFA. Lancashire County Council, 1954-58; Wigan County Borough Council, 1958-66; Liverpool City Council, 1966-69; Derbyshire County Council: Chief Accountant, 1969-72; Asst Clerk, 1972-74; Dep. Clerk, 1974-79. *Recreations:* shooting, motoring, modern history. *Address:* Lumb Lane, Darley Dale, Matlock, Derbyshire. *T:* Darley Dale 2210.

ASHCROFT, David, TD 1957; MA Cantab; Headmaster, Cheltenham College, 1959-78; *b* 20 May 1920; *s* of late A. H. Ashcroft, DSO; *m* 1949, Joan Elizabeth Young; two *s* three *d*. *Educ:* Rugby Sch.; Gonville and Caius Coll., Cambridge. War Service, 1940-46 (despatches). Asst Master, Rossall Sch., 1946-50; Asst Master, Rugby Sch., 1950-59. *Address:* London House, Ashton Keynes, Swindon, Wilts. *T:* Cirencester 861319.

ASHCROFT, James Geoffrey; Assistant Under Secretary of State, General Finance, Ministry of Defence, since 1976; *b* 19 May 1928; *s* of James Ashcroft and Elizabeth (*née* Fallingham); *m* 1953, Margery (*née* Barratt); one *s*. *Educ:* Cowley Sch., St Helens; Peterhouse, Cambridge. BA (Hons Hist.). Min. of Supply, 1950-59; Min. of Aviation, 1959-61, 1964-65; Min. of Defence, 1961-64, 1965-68, 1970-73; Inst. of Strategic Studies, 1968-70; Under-Sec., Pay Board, 1973-74; Asst Under Sec. of State, Management Services, PE, 1974-76. *Publications:* papers on international collaboration in military logistics. *Recreation:* golf. *Address:* 39 Hill Rise, Hinchley Wood, Esher, Surrey KT10 0AL. *T:* 01-398 5637.

ASHCROFT, Ven. Lawrence; retired as Archdeacon of Stow and Vicar of Burton-on-Stather (1954-62); *b* 1901; *s* of Lawrence Ashcroft; *m* 1927, Barbara Louise Casson; two *s* three *d*. *Educ:* University Coll., Durham; Lichfield Theological Coll. Deacon, 1926; Priest, 1927; Curate of Ulverston, 1926-29, of Egremont, 1929-30; District Sec., Brit. and Foreign Bible Society, 1930-33; Vicar of St Saviour's, Retford, 1934-40; Chaplain to the Forces (Emergency Commission), 1940-43; Rector of St Michael Stoke, Coventry, 1943; Rural Dean of Coventry, 1949; Hon. Canon of Coventry, 1952; Hon. Canon of Lincoln, 1954; Chaplain to British Embassy, Oslo, 1967, Luxembourg, 1968; Rector, St Philip's, Antigua, 1969, Manvers St Crispin, Toronto, 1970-. *Address:* c/o Lloyds Bank Ltd, St Helier, Jersey, Channel Islands.

ASHCROFT, Dame Peggy, (Edith Margaret Emily), DBE 1956 (CBE 1951); actress; Director, Royal Shakespeare Co., since 1968; *b* 22 Dec. 1907; *d* of William Worsley Ashcroft and Violet Maud Bernheim; *m* 1st, 1929, Rupert Hart-Davis (marr. diss.; he was knighted, 1967); 2nd, 1934, Theodore Komisarjevsky (marr. diss.); 3rd, 1940, Jeremy Hutchinson, QC, now Lord Hutchinson of Lullington (marr. diss., 1966); one *s* one *d*. *Educ:* Woodford Sch., Croydon; Central Sch. of Dramatic Art. Member of the Arts Council, 1962-64. Ashcroft Theatre, Croydon, named in her honour, 1962. First appeared as Margaret in Dear Brutus, Birmingham Repertory Theatre, 1926; parts include: Bessie in One Day More, Everyman, Eve in When Adam Delved, Wyndham's, 1927, Mary Bruin in The Land of Heart's Desire, Hester in The Silver Cord, 1928; Constance Neville in She Stoops to Conquer, Naomi in Jew Süss, 1929; Desdemona in Othello with Paul Robeson, 1930; Fanny in Sea Fever, 1931; Cleopatra, Imogen, Rosalind, etc, at Old Vic and Sadler's Wells, 1932; Juliet at New, 1935; Nina in Seagull, New, 1936; Portia, Lady Teazle, and, Irina in Three Sisters, Queen's, 1937-38; Yeliena in White Guard and Viola, Phoenix, 1938-39; Cecily Cardew in The Importance of Being Earnest, 1939-40, and Dinah in Cousin Muriel, 1940, both at Globe; revival of Importance of Being Earnest, Phoenix, 1942; Catherine in The Dark River, Whitehall, 1943; Ophelia, Titania, Duchess of Malfi, Haymarket Repertory Season, 1944-45; Evelyn Holt in Edward my Son, His Majesty's, 1947; Catherine Sloper in The Heiress, Haymarket, 1949; Beatrice and Cordelia, Memorial Theatre, Stratford-on-Avon, 1950; Viola, Electra and Mistress Page, Old Vic 1950-51; Hester Collyer in the Deep Blue Sea, Duchess, 1952; Cleopatra, Stratford-on-Avon and Princes, 1953; title-rôle, Hedda Gabler, Lyric, Hammersmith and Westminster, 1954; Beatrice in Much Ado About Nothing, Stratford Festival Company, 1955 (London, provinces and continental tour); Miss Madrigal in The Chalk Garden, Haymarket, 1956; Shen Te in The Good Woman of Setzuan, Royal Court, 1956; Rosalind, Imogen, Cymbeline, Stratford-on-Avon, 1957; Julia Rajk in Shadow of Heroes, Piccadilly, 1958; Stratford-on-Avon Season, 1960: Katharina in The Taming of the Shrew; Paulina in The Winter's Tale; The Hollow Crown, Aldwych, 1961; title rôle in The Duchess of Malfi, Aldwych, 1961; Emilia in Othello, Stratford-on-Avon, 1961, also Madame Ranevskaya in the Cherry Orchard, subseq. Aldwych; Margaret of Anjou in Henry VI and Margaret in Edward IV, also Margaret in Richard III, Stratford-on-Avon, 1963, Aldwych, 1964; Mme Arkadina in The Seagull, Queen's, 1964; Mother in Days in the Trees, Aldwych, 1966; Mrs Alving in Ghosts, 1967; A Delicate Balance, Aldwych, 1969; Beth in Landscape, Aldwych, 1969; Katharine of Aragon in Henry VIII, Stratford-on-Avon, 1969; The Plebeians Rehearse the Uprising, Aldwych, 1970; The Lovers of Viorne, Royal Court, 1971 (Evening Standard Best Actress award, 1972); All Over, Aldwych, 1972; Lloyd George Knew My Father, Savoy, 1972; Beth in Landscape, Flora in A Slight Ache, Ashcroft Theatre, foreign tour and Aldwych, 1973; The Hollow Crown, tour in US, 1973; John Gabriel Borkman, National, 1975; Happy Days, National, 1975, 1977; Old World, Aldwych, 1976; Watch on the Rhine, Edinburgh Fest. and National, 1980; Family Views, National, 1981; All's Well that Ends Well, Stratford-on-Avon, 1981, Barbican, 1982. Entered films 1933; subsequent films include: The Wandering Jew, The Thirty-nine Steps, The Nun's Story (played Mother Mathilde), Hullabaloo over Georgie and Bonnie's Pictures, 1979. Queen Victoria for BBC Radio, 1973; Queen Mary in Edward and Mrs Simpson, ITV series, 1978; television plays include: Caught on a Train, BBC2, 1980; Cream in My Coffee, LWT, 1980. King's Gold Medal, Norway, 1955; Hon. DLitt: Oxford, 1961; Leicester, 1964; Warwick, 1974; Hon. DLit London, 1965; Hon LittD Cantab, 1972. Hon. Fellow, St Hugh's College, Oxford, 1964. Comdr, Order of St Olav, Norway, 1976. *Address:* Manor Lodge, Frognal Lane, NW3.

ASHCROFT, Philip Giles; Solicitor, British Telecommunications, since 1981; *b* 15 Nov. 1926; *s* of Edmund Samuel Ashcroft and Constance Ruth Ashcroft (*née* Giles); *m* 1968, Kathleen Margaret Senior; one *s*. *Educ:* Royal Grammar Sch., Newcastle upon Tyne; Durham Univ. Admitted solicitor, 1951. Joined Treasury Solicitor's Dept, 1955; Asst Legal Adviser, Land Commn, 1967; Asst Treasury Solicitor, 1971; Under-Sec. (Legal), DTI, 1973; Legal Adviser, Dept of Energy, 1974-80; Dep. Solicitor to the Post Office, 1980-81. *Recreations:* reading, listening to music, walking. *Address:* 3 Julian Close, Woking, Surrey GU21 3HD. *T:* Woking 71383.

ASHE, Sir Derick (Rosslyn), KCMG 1978 (CMG 1966); HM Diplomatic Service, retired 1979; Ambassador and Permanent UK Representative to Disarmament Conference, Geneva, 1977-79 and Permanent Head of UK Delegation to UN Special Session on Disarmament, New York, 1977-78; *b* 20 Jan. 1919; *s* of late Frederick Allen Ashe and late Rosalind Ashe (*née* Mitchell); *m* 1957, Rissa Guinness, *d* of late Capt. Hon. Trevor Tempest Parker, DSC, Royal Navy (retd) and Mrs Parker; one *s* one *d*. *Educ:* Bradfield Coll.; Trinity Coll., Oxford. HM Forces, 1940-46 (despatches 1945). Second Sec., Berlin and Frankfurt-am-Main, 1947-49; Private Sec. to Permanent Under-Sec. of State for German Section of FO, 1950-53; First Sec., La Paz, 1953-55; FO, 1955-57; First Sec. (Information), Madrid, 1957-61; FO, 1961-62; Counsellor and Head of Chancery: Addis Ababa, 1962-64; Havana, 1964-66; Head of Security Dept, FCO (formerly FO), 1966-69; Minister, Tokyo, 1969-71; Ambassador to: Romania, 1972-75; Argentina, 1975-77. Knight of the Order of Orange-Nassau (with swords), 1945. *Recreations:* riding, antiques. *Address:* Dalton House, Hurstbourne Tarrant, Andover, Hants. *T:* Hurstbourne Tarrant 276. *Clubs:* White's, Travellers', Beefsteak.

ASHE LINCOLN, Fredman; *see* Lincoln, F. A.

ASHENHEIM, Sir Neville (Noel), Kt 1963; CBE 1958; Leader of Government Business in the Senate and Minister without Portfolio, Jamaica, 1967-72; b 18 Dec. 1900; s of Lewis Ashenheim and Estelle Lillian de Cordova; m 1926, Leonie Vivienne Delevante; three s. *Educ:* Jamaica Coll.; Munro Coll.; Wadham Coll., Oxford. BA 1922, MA 1943. Admitted Solicitor of Supreme Court, 1926, and joined father's firm of Milholland, Ashenheim & Stone. HM's Jamaican Ambassador to the USA, 1962-67. Chairman: "The Gleaner" Company, 1946-67 (newspaper in Caribbean founded by his forbears in 1834); Jamaica Industrial Development Corporation, 1952-57; Caribbean Cement Co., 1965-73; Caribbean Steel Co., 1965-73; Wray & Nephew Gp Ltd (formerly Consolidated Internat. Corporation), 1958-73; Internat. Corp.; Standard Life Assurance Co. (Jamaican Branch), 1958-61, 1967-71; Jamaica Housing Devett Co., 1957-62. Director: Lascelles de Merado & Co. Ltd; Henriques Brothers Ltd, 1950-73; West Indies Glass Co. Ltd, 1961-73. Hon. DHL Hebrew Union Coll., 1964. *Address:* Apartment B5, Roxdene, Pitts Bay Road, Pembroke, Bermuda. *Clubs:* Jamaica, Liguanea, St Andrew, Kingston Cricket, Jamaica Jockey (all in Jamaica); Royal Bermuda Yacht.

ASHERSON, Nehemiah, MA Cape; MB, BS London; FRCS, LRCP; FZS, etc; Fellow International College of Surgeons; Hon. Fellow Surgical Academy, Madrid; Associate, Royal Institute of Chemistry, 1919; Hon. Cons. Surgeon, The Royal National (Central London) Throat, Nose, and Ear Hospital (late Member of Board of Governors, 1948-49-50-58); late Hon. Secretary to the Medical Council; Lecturer to the Institute of Otology and Laryngology (Member Academic Board); Teacher in Oto-laryngology in the University of London; Consulting Surgeon for Diseases of the Ear, Nose, and Throat to the NE, NW and SE regional hospital boards, including the Queen Elizabeth Hospital for Children; FRSocMed (Hon. Fellow, former Pres., Section of Laryngology; Member Council, Section History of Medicine; late Member Council Section Otology, and Library Committee); Trustee (Hon. Fellow, former Pres., Hunterian Society); formerly Hon. Treasurer, BMA, St Marylebone Division, and Mem. Ethical Cttee; Fellow and Hon. Librarian, late Councillor, Medical Society of London; b 1897; s of Isaac Asherson; m; one s one d. *Educ:* South African Coll.; Univ. of Cape Town (Entrance Scholar); University Coll. and Hospital, London; postgraduate study in speciality in London and Vienna. Medallist in Chemistry; exhibitioner at the BA examination; Jamieson Scholar at MA; Alexander Bruce Gold Medallist in Surgery and Liston Gold Medal in Surgical Pathology, University Coll. Hosp.; Geoffrey Duveen Travelling Scholar of the Univ. of London in Oto-rhino Laryngology; late Harker Smith Cancer (radium) Registrar and Casualty Surgical Officer at University Coll. Hosp.; Chief Asst to the Royal Ear Hosp., University Coll. Hosp.; Chief Asst to the Ear, Nose, and Throat Dept of the Bolingbroke Hosp., etc; Late: Ear Consultant to Army Medical Boards; Surgeon Emergency Medical Service, 1939-45; Consulting Surgeon to LCC and to the Charterhouse Rheumatism Clinic. Hunterian Prof., RCS, 1942. Mem. Royal Instn (Visitor, 1969-71). Mem., Apothecaries Soc. *Publications:* Diagnosis and Treatment of Foreign Bodies in the Upper Food and Respiratory Passages, 1932; Acute Otitis and Mastoiditis in General Practice, 1934; Chronic Ear Discharge (Otorrhœa) and its complications, 1936; Otogenic Cerebellar Abscess, Hunterian Lecture, 1942; Identification by Frontal Sinus Prints, 1965; The Deafness of Beethoven, 1965; Bibliography of G. J. Du Verney's Traité de l'Organe de l'Ouïe, 1683 (first scientific treatise on the ear), 1979; communications in Jl of Laryngology, of the Royal Society of Medicine, in The Lancet and in medical journals on subjects relating to the speciality. *Recreations:* numismatics, book collecting. *Address:* 21 Harley Street, W1. *T:* 01-580 3197; Green Shutters, East Preston, West Kingston, West Sussex. *Clubs:* Reform, Savage.

ASHFORD, (Albert) Reginald, CMG 1962; Assistant Secretary, Board of Customs and Excise, 1952-73; b 30 June 1914; s of Ernest Ashford; m 1946, Mary Anne Ross Davidson, d of Thomas Davidson; one s. *Educ:* Ealing Grammar Sch.; London Sch. of Economics. UK Delegate to and many times chm. of numerous internat. conferences on reduction of trade barriers and simplification of customs formalities, 1946-60. *Recreations:* local amenity and welfare societies, walking, gardening. *Address:* Piper's Lawn, 21 Frogmore Close, Hughenden Valley, High Wycombe, Bucks. *T:* Naphill 2440.

ASHFORD, George Francis, OBE 1945; retired; b 5 July 1911; s of G. W. Ashford and L. M. Redfern; m 1950, Eleanor Vera Alexander; two s. *Educ:* Malvern Coll.; Trinity Hall, Cambridge; Birmingham Univ. Served War of 1939-45, Army, N Africa and Italy (despatches 1944). Distillers Co. Ltd, 1937-67: Solicitor, 1937; Legal Adviser, 1945; Dir, 1956; Management Cttee, 1963-67; Dir, BP Co. Ltd, 1967-73; Man. Dir, 1969-73; Dir, Albright & Wilson Ltd, 1973-79. Mem., Monopolies and Mergers Commn, 1973-80. Pres., British Plastics Fedn, 1966-67; Vice-President: Soc. of Chemical Industry, 1966-69; Chem. Ind. Assoc., 1967-70. Mem. Economic Policy Cttee for Chemical Industry, 1967-74; Chm., Working Party on Industrial Review, 1973. *Recreation:* gardening. *Address:* The Old House, Sonning, Berks. *T:* Reading 692122. *Club:* Royal Automobile.

ASHFORD, Ven. Percival Leonard; Chaplain General of Prisons, Home Office, since 1981; Archdeacon to the Prison Service, and Chaplain to the Queen, since 1982; b 5 June 1927; s of late Edwin and Gwendoline Emily Ashford; m 1955, Dorothy Helen Harwood; two s. *Educ:* Kemp Welch Sch., Poole; Bristol Univ.; Tyndale Hall Theol Coll., Bristol. Asst Curate, St Philip and St James, Ilfracombe, 1954; Curate-in-Charge, Church of Good Shepherd, Aylesbury, 1956; Vicar, St Olaf's, Poughill, Bude, 1959; HM Prison Service: Asst Chaplain, Wormwood Scrubs, 1965; Chaplain: Risley Remand Centre,

1966; Durham, 1969; Wandsworth, 1971; Winchester, 1975; SW Reg. Chaplain of Prisons, 1977. *Recreations:* choral and classical music, reading, golf. *Address:* Home Office Prison Department, Portland House, Stag Place, SW1. *T:* 01-828 9848. *Club:* City Livery (via Sion College).

ASHFORD, Reginald; see Ashford, A. R.

ASHFORD, William Stanton, OBE 1971; HM Diplomatic Service, retired; b 4 July 1924; s of Thomas and May Ashford; m 1957, Rosalind Anne Collett; two s. *Educ:* Winchester Coll.; Balliol Coll., Oxford. Served RAF, 1943-47; Air Ministry, 1948; Commonwealth Relations Office, 1961; Director of British Information Services, Sierra Leone, 1961, Ghana, 1962; Acting Consul-General, Tangier, 1965; Regional Information Officer, Bombay, 1966; Head of Chancery, British Government Office, Montreal, 1967; seconded to Northern Ireland Office, 1972; FCO, 1974; Consul-General, Adelaide, 1977; High Comr, Vanuatu, 1980-82. *Recreations:* music, gardening, swimming, reading. *Address:* c/o Lloyds Bank Ltd, Fore Street, Bodmin, Cornwall PL31 2HP. *T:* Bodmin 3434.

ASHIOTIS, Costas; High Commissioner of Cyprus in London, 1966-79; Cyprus Ambassador to Denmark, Sweden, Norway and Malta, 1966-79; b 1908; m. *Educ:* Pancypriant Gymnasium, Nicosia; London Sch. of Economics. Journalist and editor; joined Govt Service, 1942; Asst Comr of Labour, 1948; Dir-Gen., Min. of Foreign Affairs, 1960. Mem. Cyprus delegns to UN and to internat. confs. Retired from Foreign Service, 1979. MBE 1952. *Publications:* Labour Conditions in Cyprus during the War Years, 1939-45; literary articles. *Address:* c/o Ministry of Foreign Affairs, Nicosia, Cyprus.

ASHKENAZY, Vladimir; concert pianist; b Gorky, Russia, 6 July 1937; m 1961, Thorunn Johannsdottir, d of Jouan Tryggvason, Iceland; two s three d. *Educ:* Central Musical Sch., Moscow; Conservatoire, Moscow. Studied under Sumbatyan; Lev Oborin class, 1955: grad 1960. Internat. Chopin Comp., Warsaw, at age of 17 (gained 2nd prize); won Queen Elizabeth Internat. Piano Comp., Brussels, at age of 18 (gold medal). Joint winner (with John Ogdon) of Tchaikovsky Piano Comp., Moscow, 1962. London debut with London Symph. Orch. under George Hurst, and subseq, solo recital, Festival Hall, 1963. Principal Guest Conductor, Philharmonia Orchestra, 1982-. Has played in many countries. Makes recordings. Hon. RAM 1972. Icelandic Order of the Falcon, 1971. *Address:* Sonnenhof 4, 6004 Lucerne, Switzerland.

ASHLEY, Lord; Anthony Nils Christian Ashley-Cooper; b 24 June 1977; s and heir of Earl of Shaftesbury, qv.

ASHLEY, Bernard Albert, FSIAD; Chairman, Laura Ashley Ltd, since 1954 (Ashley, Mountney Ltd, 1954-68, name changed to Laura Ashley Ltd, 1968); b 11 Aug. 1926; s of Albert Ashley and Hilda Maud Ashley; m 1949, Laura Mountney; two s two d. *Educ:* Whitgift Sch., Croydon, Surrey. Army commission, 1944; Royal Fusiliers, 1944-46, seconded 1 Gurkha Rifles, 1944-45. Incorporated Ashley, Mountney Ltd, 1954. Chm., Assoc. Laura Ashley Companies Overseas. *Recreations:* sailing, flying. *Address:* 32 rue de Namur, Brussels, Belgium. *Clubs:* Royal Thames Yacht (Southampton), Army Sailing Association.

ASHLEY, Cedric, PhD; Director, Motor Industry Research Association, since 1977; b 11 Nov. 1936; s of Ronald Ashley and Gladys Fincher; m 1st, 1960, Pamela Jane Turner (decd); one s; 2nd, 1965, (Marjorie) Vivien Gooch; one s one d. *Educ:* King Edward's Sch., Birmingham; Mech. Engrg Dept, Univ. of Birmingham (BSc 1958, PhD 1964). FIMechE 1978. Rolls-Royce Ltd, Derby, 1955-60; Univ. of Birmingham, 1960-73: ICI Res. Fellow, 1963; Lectr, 1966; Internat. Technical Dir, Bostrom Div., Universal Oil Products Ltd, 1973-77. Mem. and Chm. of internat. standards orgns, and BSI cttees and working groups, 1968-. Chairman: SEE, 1970-72; RAC Tech. Cttee, 1980-. Member: Noise Adv. Council, 1977-81; SMMT Technical Bds, 1977-; Board, Assoc. Ind. Contract Res. Orgns, 1977- (Vice-Pres., 1981-82); Coventry and District Engineering Employers Assoc., 1978-; Board, Automobile Div., IMechE, 1978-; Court, Cranfield Inst. of Technol., 1977-. Cementation Muffelite Award, SEE, 1968; Design Council Award, 1974. TA, 1959-68. *Publications:* (contrib.) Infrasound and Low Frequency Vibration, ed Tempest, 1976; papers on electro-hydraulics, vehicle ride, and effect of vibration and shock on man and buildings, in learned jls. *Recreations:* travel, reading. *Address:* The Old Rectory, Church Walk, Bilton, Rugby. *T:* Rugby 816776. *Clubs:* Royal Automobile, Anglo-Belgian.

ASHLEY, Rt. Hon. Jack, CH 1975; PC 1979; MP (Lab) Stoke-on-Trent, South, since 1966; b 6 Dec. 1922; s of John Ashley and Isabella Bridge; m 1951, Pauline Kay Crispin; three d. *Educ:* St Patrick's Elem. Sch., Widnes, Lancs; Ruskin Coll., Oxford; Gonville and Caius Coll., Cambridge. Labourer and cranedriver, 1936-46; Shop Steward Convener and Nat. Exec. Mem., Chemical Workers' Union, 1946; Scholarship, Ruskin Coll., 1946-48 and Caius Coll., 1948-51 (Chm. Cambridge Labour Club, 1950; Pres. Cambridge Union, 1951); BBC Radio Producer, 1951-57; Commonwealth Fund Fellow, 1955; BBC Senior Television Producer, 1957-66; Mem., General Advisory Council, BBC, 1967-69, 1970-74. PPS to Sec. of State, DHSS, 1974-76. Mem., Lab. Party Nat. Exec. Cttee, 1976-78. Councillor, Borough of Widnes, 1945. *Publication:* Journey into Silence, 1973. *Address:* House of Commons, SW1A 0AA.

ASHLEY, Maurice Percy, CBE 1978; b 4 Sept. 1907; s of Sir Percy Ashley, KBE, and Lady Ashley (née Hayman); m 1935, Phyllis Mary Griffiths; one s one d. Educ: St Paul's Sch., London; New Coll., Oxford (History Scholar). 1st Class Hons Modern History; DPhil Oxon; DLitt Oxon, 1979. Historical Research Asst to Sir Winston Churchill, 1929-33; Editorial Staff, The Manchester Guardian, 1933-37; Editorial Staff, The Times, 1937-39; Editor, Britain Today, 1939-40. Served in Army, 1940-45 (Major, Intelligence Corps). Deputy Editor, The Listener, 1946-58, Editor, 1958-67; Research Fellow, Loughborough Univ. of Technology, 1968-70. Pres. Cromwell Association, 1961-77. Publications include: Financial and Commercial Policy under the Cromwellian Protectorate, 1934 (revised, 1962); Oliver Cromwell, 1937; Marlborough, 1939; Louis XIV and the Greatness of France, 1946; John Wildman: Plotter and Postmaster, 1947; Mr President, 1948; England in the Seventeenth Century, 1952, rev. edn, 1976; Cromwell's Generals, 1954; The Greatness of Oliver Cromwell, 1957 (revised 1967); Oliver Cromwell and the Puritan Revolution, 1958; Great Britain to 1688, 1961; The Stuarts in Love, 1963; Life in Stuart England, 1964; The Glorious Revolution of 1688, 1966 (revised, 1968); Churchill as Historian, 1968; A Golden Century, 1598-1715, 1969; (ed) Cromwell: great lives observed, 1969; Charles II: the man and the statesman, 1971; Oliver Cromwell and his World, 1972; The Life and Times of King John, 1972; The Life and Times of King William I, 1973; A History of Europe 1648-1815, 1973; The Age of Absolutism 1648-1775, 1974; A Concise History of the English Civil War, 1975; Rupert of the Rhine, 1976; General Monck, 1977; James II, 1978; The House of Stuart, 1980; A Short History of the People of England, 1982; Recreations: bridge, gardening. Address: 34 Wood Lane, Ruislip, Mddx HA4 6EX. T: Ruislip 35993. Club: Reform.

ASHLEY-COOPER, family name of Earl of Shaftesbury.

ASHLEY-SMITH, Jonathan, PhD; Keeper, Department of Conservation, Victoria and Albert Museum, since 1977; b 25 Aug. 1946; s of Ewart Frist and Marian Tanfield Ashley-Smith; m 1967, Diane Louise (née Wagland); one s. Educ: Sutton Valence Public Sch.; Bristol Univ. (BSc (Hons), PhD). Post-doctoral research, Cambridge Univ., 1970-72; Victoria and Albert Museum, 1973-. Member: UK Inst. for Conservation, 1974- (Mem., Exec Cttee, 1978-; Vice-Chm., 1980-); Crafts Council, 1980-; Conservation Cttee, Crafts Council, 1978-; Council for Care of Churches Conservation Cttee, 1978-. Publications: articles in learned jls on organometallic chemistry, spectroscopy and scientific examination of art objects. Recreations: loud music, good beer. Address: Victoria and Albert Museum, Exhibition Road, SW7 2RL. T: 01-589 6371.

ASHMOLE, Professor Bernard, CBE 1957; MC; MA, BLitt; Hon. FRIBA, FBA; Hon. Fellow of Lincoln College, Oxford, 1980; Hon. Fellow, University College, London, 1974; Hon. Fellow, Hertford College, Oxford, 1961; b Ilford, 22 June 1894; 2nd s of late William Ashmole and Caroline Wharton Tiver; m 1920, Dorothy Irene, 2nd d of late Everard de Peyer, Newent Court, Glos; one s two d. Educ: Forest; privately; Hertford Coll., Oxford (Classical Scholar). 11th Royal Fusiliers, 1914-18; Craven Fellow, and Student of the British schools at Athens and Rome, 1920-22; Asst Curator of Coins, Ashmolean Museum, 1923-25; Director of the British Sch. at Rome, 1925-28; Florence Bursar, RIBA, 1937; Hon. Member of the Archæological Institute of America, 1940; RAF 1940-45, Adjutant of 84 Sqdn in Greece, Iraq, Western Desert, Sumatra and India (despatches twice, Hellenic Flying Cross). Yates Professor of Archæology, University of London, 1929-48; Keeper of Greek and Roman Antiquities, British Museum, 1939-56; Lincoln Professor of Classical Archæology, Univ. of Oxford, 1956-61, and Fellow of Lincoln Coll., Oxford, 1956-80; Geddes-Harrower Professor of Greek Art and Archæology, Univ. of Aberdeen, 1961-63; Visiting Professor in Archæology, Univ. of Yale, 1964. Rhind Lectr, 1952; Myres Memorial Lectr, Oxford, 1961; Norton Lectr, Archæological Inst. of America, 1963; Wrightsman Lectr, New York, 1967. Hon. LLD Aberdeen, 1968. Hon. Fellow, Archaeol Soc. of Athens, 1978. Kenyon Medal, British Acad., 1979; Cassano Medal, Taranto, 1980. Publications: Catalogue of Ancient Marbles at Ince Blundell, 1929; Greek Sculpture and Painting (with Beazley), 1932, repr. 1966; The Ancient World (with Groenewegen-Frankfort), 1967; Olympia: sculptures of the temple of Zeus (with Yalouris and Frantz), 1967; Architect and Sculptor in Classical Greece, 1972; articles on Greek sculpture in the Journal of Hellenic Studies and other periodicals. Address: 5 Tweed Green, Peebles. T: Peebles 21154. Club: Athenæum.

ASHMOLE, (Harold) David; Senior Principal, Sadler's Wells Royal Ballet, since 1978; b 31 Oct. 1949; s of Richard Thomas Ashmole and Edith Ashmole. Educ: Sandye Place, Beds; Royal Ballet Sch. Solo Seal, Royal Acad. of Dancing; ARAD. Joined Royal Ballet Co., 1968; Soloist, 1972; Principal, 1975; transf. to Sadler's Wells Royal Ballet, 1976. Appeared in: Dame Alicia Markova's Master Classes, BBC Television, 1980; Maina Gielgud's Steps, Notes and Squeaks, Aberdeen Internat. Festival, 1981. Guest appearances with Scottish Ballet and in Japan, Germany, S Africa and France. Roles include: (choreography by Ashton): Cinderella, The Two Pigeons, Daphnis and Chloe, La Fille Mal Gardée, Les Rendezvous, The Dream, Lament of the Waves; (Balanchine): Apollo, Prodigal Son, Serenade, The Four Temperaments, Agon; (Bintley): Night Moves, Homage to Chopin; (Cranko): Pineapple Poll, The Taming of the Shrew; (Darrell): The Nutcracker, Swan Lake, The Tales of Hoffmann; (de Valois): Checkmate, The Rake's Progress; (Fokine): Les Sylphides, Petrushka; (Hynd): Papillon; (MacMillan): Concerto, Elite Syncopations, Romeo and Juliet, Quartet; (Massine): La Boutique Fantasque;

(Nureyev): Raymonda, La Bayadère; (Nijinska): Les Biches; (Robbins): Dances at a Gathering, Requiem Canticles; (Seymour): Intimate Letters: (Samsova): Paquita; (Tetley): Gemini; (van Manen): Grosse Fugue; (Wright): Giselle, Swan Lake, Summertide, Coppélia. Recreations: Moorcroft pottery collection, gardening, Welsh property estate, shooting, fishing. Address: c/o Sadler's Wells Theatre, Sadler's Wells Royal Ballet, Rosebery Avenue, N1.

ASHMORE, Prof. Alick, CBE 1979; Director, Daresbury Laboratory, Science Research Council, 1970-81; b 7 Nov. 1920; s of Frank Owen Ashmore and Beatrice Maud Swindells; m 1947, Eileen Elsie Fuller; two s three d. Educ: King Edward VII Sch., Lytham; King's Coll., London. Experimental Officer, RRDE, Malvern, 1941-47; Lecturer in physics, University of Liverpool, 1947-59; Queen Mary Coll., London: Reader in experimental physics, 1960-64; Prof. of Nuclear Physics, 1964-70, also Head of Physics Dept, 1968-70. Publications: research publications on nuclear and elementary-particle physics in Proc. Phys. Soc., Nuclear Physics, Physical Review. Recreations: walking, camping. Address: 60 Marina Village, Preston Brook, Runcorn, Cheshire WA7 3BQ. T: Runcorn 718459.

ASHMORE, Admiral of the Fleet Sir Edward (Beckwith), GCB 1974 (KCB 1971; CB 1966); DSC 1942; Director, Racal Electronics Ltd, since 1978; b 11 Dec. 1919; er s of late Vice-Admiral L. H. Ashmore, CB, DSO and late Tamara Vasilevna Shutt, Petrograd; m 1942, Elizabeth Mary Doveton Sturdee, d of late Rear-Admiral Sir Lionel Sturdee, 2nd Bt, CBE; one s one d (and one d decd). Educ: RNC, Dartmouth. Served HMS Birmingham, Jupiter, Middleton, 1938-42; qualified in Signals, 1943; Staff of C-in-C Home Fleet, Flag Lieut, 4th Cruiser Sqdn, 1944-45; qualified Interpreter in Russian, 1946; Asst Naval Attaché, Moscow, 1946-47; Squadron Communications Officer, 3rd Aircraft Carrier Squadron, 1950; Commander 1950; comd HMS Alert, 1952-53; Captain 1955; Captain (F) 6th Frigate Sqdn, and CO HMS Blackpool, 1958; Director of Plans, Admiralty and Min. of Defence, 1960-62; Commander British Forces Caribbean Area, 1963-64; Rear-Adm., 1965; Asst Chief of the Defence Staff, Signals, 1965-67; Flag Officer, Second-in-Command, Far East Fleet, 1967-68; Vice-Adm. 1968; Vice-Chief, Naval Staff, 1969-71; Adm. 1970; C-in-C Western Fleet, Sept.-Oct. 1971; C-in-C, Fleet, 1971-74; Chief of Naval Staff and First Sea Lord, 1974-77; First and Principal Naval Aide-de-Camp to the Queen, 1974-77; CDS, Feb.-Aug. 1977. Governor, Suttons Hosp. in Charterhouse. Recreations: usual. Address: South Cottage, Headley Down, Hants. Club: Naval and Military.
See also Vice-Adm. Sir P. W. B. Ashmore, Sir Francis Sykes, Bt.

ASHMORE, Vice-Adm. Sir Peter (William Beckwith), KCB 1972 (CB 1968); KCVO 1980 (MVO (4th Class) 1948); DSC 1942; Master of HM's Household, since 1973; Extra Equerry to the Queen, since 1952; b 4 Feb. 1921; yr s of late Vice-Adm. L. H. Ashmore, CB, DSO and late Tamara Vasilevna Shutt, Petrograd; m 1952, Patricia Moray Buller, o d of late Admiral Sir Henry Buller, GCVO, CB and of Lady Hermione Stuart; one s three d. Educ: Yardley Court; RN Coll., Dartmouth. Midshipman, 1939. Served War of 1939-45, principally in destroyers (despatches); Lieut, 1941; Equerry (temp.) to King George VI, 1946-48; Extra Equerry, 1948; Comdr, 1951; Captain, 1957; Deputy Director, RN Staff Coll., Greenwich, 1957; Captain (F) Dartmouth Training Squadron, 1960-61; Imperial Defence Coll., 1962; Admiralty, Plans Division, 1963; Rear-Adm. 1966; Flag Officer, Admiralty Interview Board, 1966-67; Chief of Staff to C-in-C Western Fleet and to NATO C-in-C Eastern Atlantic, 1967-69; Vice-Adm. 1969; Chief of Allied Staff, NATO Naval HQ, S Europe, 1970-72, retired 1972. Recreations: fishing, golf.
See also Adm. of the Fleet Sir E. B. Ashmore.

ASHMORE, Prof. Philip George; Professor of Physical Chemistry, The University of Manchester Institute of Science and Technology, 1963-81, now Professor Emeritus; b 5 May 1916; m 1943, Ann Elizabeth Scott; three s one d. Educ: Emmanuel Coll., Cambridge. Fellow, Asst Tutor and Dir of Studies of Natural Sciences, Emmanuel Coll., Cambridge, 1949-59; Lecturer in Physical Chem., Univ. of Cambridge, 1953-63; Fellow and Tutor to Advanced Students, Churchill Coll., Cambridge, 1959-63. Vice-Principal Acad. Affairs, UMIST, 1973, 1974. Mem., Adv. Cttee on Dangerous Substances, HSE, 1978-; Course Consultant, Open Univ., 1981-. Publications: The Catalysis and Inhibition of Chemical Reactions, 1963; (ed) Reaction Kinetics, 1975; RIC Monographs for Teachers: No 5 and No 9; many papers in: TFS, International Symposium on Combustion, Jl of Catalysis. Address: 30 Queen Edith's Way, Cambridge CB1 4PN. T: Cambridge 248225.

ASHTON, family name of Baron Ashton of Hyde.

ASHTON OF HYDE, 2nd Baron cr 1911; Thomas Henry Raymond Ashton, DL, JP; Major, late 1st Royal Gloucestershire Hussars, RAC, TA; Joint Master, Heythrop, 1934-36, sole Master, 1936-48, Joint Master, 1948-52; b 2 Oct. 1901; s of 1st Baron and Eva Margaret (d 1938) d of J. H. James Kingswood, Watford, Herts; S father, 1933; m 1925, Marjorie Nell, d of late Hon. Marshall Brooks; one s (two d decd). Educ: Eton; New Coll., Oxford (MA). DL 1957, JP 1944, Gloucestershire. Recreations: hunting, shooting, deerstalking. Heir: s Hon. Thomas John Ashton [b 19 Nov. 1926; m 1957, Pauline Trewlove, er d of late Lieut-Col R. H. L. Brackenbury, Yerdley House, Long Compton, Shipston-on-Stour; two s two d]. Address: Broadwell Hill, Moreton-in-Marsh, Glos. T: Stow-on-the-Wold 30626. Club: Boodle's.

ASHTON, Anthony Southcliffe; Director, Provincial Insurance Co., since 1974; *b* 5 July 1916; *s* of late Prof. Thomas Southcliffe Ashton, FBA, and of Mrs Marion Hague Ashton; *m* 1939, Katharine Marion Louise Vivian; two *d. Educ:* Manchester Grammar Sch.; Hertford Coll., Oxford (MA). Economist, Export Credits Guarantee Dept, 1937. Served War of 1939-45, as driver and Lt-Col, RASC. Asst Financial Editor, Manchester Guardian, 1945; Dep. Asst Dir of Marketing, NCB, 1947; Manager, various depts of Vacuum Oil Co. (later Mobil Oil Co.), 1949; attended Advanced Management Programme, Harvard Business Sch., 1961; Treasurer, and later Finance Director, Esso Petroleum Co., 1961; Mem. Bd (Finance and Corporate Planning), Post Office Corp., 1970-73. Dir, Tyzack and Partners Ltd, 1974-79. Member: Shipbuilding Industry Bd, 1967-71; Council of Manchester Business Sch., 1968-81; Dir, Oxford Univ. Business Summer Sch., 1974 (Mem., Steering Cttee, 1978-81). Trustee: PO Pension Fund, 1975-; Tyzack Employee Trust, 1979-. Vice-Pres., Hertford Coll. Soc., 1977-. *Address:* Quarry Field, Stonewall Hill, Presteigne, Powys LD8 2HB. *T:* Presteigne 447.

ASHTON, Sir (Arthur) Leigh (Bolland), Kt 1948; Director and Secretary, Victoria and Albert Museum, 1945-55, retired; *b* London, 20 Oct. 1897; *o s* of late A. J. Ashton, KC, Recorder of Manchester; *m* 1952, Mrs Madge Garland. *Educ:* Horris Hill; Winchester; Balliol Coll., Oxford, BA (war degree). Served European War, Lieut RGA, 1916-19. Victoria and Albert Museum: Asst Keeper (2nd class), Dept of Architecture and Sculpture, 1922-25; Dept of Textiles, 1925-31; Dept of Ceramics, 1931-37; Keeper of Special Collections, 1937, Secretary of the Advisory Council, 1935, and Asst to Dir, 1937; Asst Keeper, 1st class, 1932; Keeper (1st class) 1938. Mem. Committee, City Companies Exhibition, 1927; Asst Dir International Exhibition of Persian Art, RA, 1931; Executive Committee and arranger of the Exhibition of Chinese Art, RA, 1935-36; Executive Committee, Exhibition of 17th Century Art, RA, 1937; Dir, Exhibition of the Arts of India and Pakistan, RA, 1947-48; loaned to Ministry of Information, April 1939; Officer i/c Finance, 1939; Dep.-Dir of Foreign Division, 1940; Director of Neutral Countries Division, 1941; Dir of British Information Office, Istanbul, 1942, and head of Press Office, HM Embassy, Ankara, with rank of Counsellor. Comdr of the Dannebrog. *Publications:* Introduction to the History of Chinese Sculpture, 1922; Samplers, 1927; Memoirs of the Prince de Ligne, 1928; Chinese Art (with Basil Gray), 1935; Chinese Art (with others), 1935; (ed) Commemoration Catalogue of Chinese Exhibition, 1936; (ed) Commemorative Catalogue of the Exhibition of the Arts of India and Pakistan, 1950; numerous articles and lectures on the decorative arts. *Recreations:* music, the theatre, travel, bridge.

ASHTON, Ellis, MBE 1975; variety artiste, stage director and touring manager, since 1947; now theatre historian, lecturer, broadcaster; *b* Whiston, Liverpool, 1 Dec. 1919; *s* of Joseph and Beatrice Ashton; *m* 1957, Margaret Mitchell, speciality dancer; one *s* one *d. Educ:* Holy Trinity, Liverpool; Army Formation Coll. Various positions before the War; served War, Scots Guards and Personnel Selection Staff, 1939-47. Chm., British Music Hall Soc.; Patron, Cinema Theatre Assoc.; Pres., National Assoc. of Theatrical, Television and Kine Employees, 1982. Founder Member: Theatres' Trust; British Theatre Inst. Exec. Member: Actors' Church Union; Entertainment Artistes Benevolent Fund. Member: Theatres Adv. Council; Variety Adv. Cttee; Radio and Television Safeguards Cttee. Life Member: National Trust; Ancient Monuments Soc.; Victorian Soc.; British Archaeol Assoc.; Royal Archaeol Inst.; Picture Palace Preservation Soc. Governor, Ruskin Coll., Oxford; Vice-Pres., Ruskin Fellowship, London. FRSA; FLS, FZS, FRGS. *Publications:* contrib. books on the theatre; contrib. The Stage, and The Call Boy. *Recreation:* preserving the British way of life. *Address:* 1 King Henry Street, N16. *T:* 01-254 4209.

ASHTON, Sir Frederick (William Mallandaine), OM 1977; CH 1970; Kt 1962; CBE 1950; Founder-choreographer to the Royal Ballet (Principal Choreographer, 1933-70, and Director, 1963-70); *b* Guayaquil, Ecuador, 17 Sept. 1904; *s* of George Ashton and Georgiana Fulcher. *Educ:* The Dominican Fathers, Lima, Peru; Dover Coll., Dover. With Ballet Rambert, 1926-33, as dancer and choreographer; Ida Rubinstein Company, Paris, 1929-30. Best known ballets: Les Patineurs, Apparitions, Horoscope, Symphonic Variations, Façade, Wedding Bouquet, Scènes de Ballet, Cinderella (first English choreographer to do a 3-act ballet), Illuminations, Sylvia, Romeo and Juliet, Ondine, La Fille Mal Gardée, Les Deux Pigeons, Marguerite and Armand, The Dream, Sinfonietta, Jazz Calendar, Enigma Variations, Walk to the Paradise Garden, Birthday Offering, A Month in the Country, Rhapsody, etc. Film: The Tales of Beatrix Potter (choreography, and appeared as Mrs Tiggywinkle), 1971. Served in Royal Air Force during War as Flight Lieut. Queen Elizabeth II Coronation Award, Royal Academy of Dancing, 1959. Freedom of City of London, 1981. Hon. DLitt: Durham, 1962; East Anglia, 1967; Hon. DMus: London, 1970; Hull, 1971; Oxon, 1976. Legion of Honour (France), 1960; Order of Dannebrog (Denmark), 1964. *Relevant publications:* Frederick Ashton: a Choreographer and his Ballets, by Z. Dominic and J. S. Gilbert, 1971; Frederick Ashton and his Ballets, by David Vaughan, 1977. *Recreation:* dancing. *Address:* Royal Opera House, Covent Garden, WC2.

ASHTON, Joseph William; MP (Lab) Bassetlaw Division of Notts since Nov. 1968; journalist; *b* 9 Oct. 1933; *s* of Arthur and Nellie Ashton, Sheffield; *m* 1957, Margaret Patricia Lee; one *d. Educ:* High Storrs Grammar Sch.; Rotherham Technical Coll. Engineering Apprentice, 1949-54; RAF National Service, 1954-56; Cost Control Design Engineer, 1956-68; Sheffield City

Councillor, 1962-69. PPS to Sec. of State for Energy, formerly Sec. of State for Industry, 1975-76; an Asst Govt Whip, 1976-77; Opposition Spokesman on Energy, 1979-81. Columnist for: Sheffield Star, 1970-75, 1979-80; Labour Weekly, 1971-; Daily Star, 1979-. *Publications:* Grass Roots, 1977; A Majority of One (stage play), 1981. *Recreations:* watching Sheffield Wednesday, reading, do-it-yourself, motoring. *Address:* 16 Ranmoor Park Road, Sheffield. *T:* Sheffield 301763. *Clubs:* Foundry Working Men's (Sheffield); Doncaster Road Working Men's (Langold); various Miners' Institutes, etc.

ASHTON, Kenneth Bruce; General Secretary, National Union of Journalists, since 1977; *b* 9 Nov. 1925; *s* of late Harry Anstice Ashton and of Olive May Ashton; *m* 1955, Amy Anne, *d* of late John Baines Sidebotham and of Amy Sidebotham; four *s. Educ:* Latymer Upper School. Served Army, 1942-46. Reporter: Hampstead and Highgate Express, 1947-50; Devon and Somerset News, Mansfield Reporter, Sheffield Star, 1950-58; Sub-Editor, Sheffield Telegraph, Daily Express, London and Daily Mail, Manchester, 1958-75. Nat. Exec. Cttee Mem., NUJ, 1968-75, Pres., 1975, Regional Organiser, 1975-77. Member: TUC Printing Industries' Cttee, 1975-; Printing and Publishers' Industry Training Bd, 1977-; British Cttee, Journalists in Europe, 1980; consultative Mem., Press Council, 1977-80. Deported from S Africa, Jan. 1981. *Recreation:* gliding. *Address:* Acorn House, 314 Gray's Inn Road, WC1X 8DP. *T:* 01-278 7916. *Clubs:* Manchester Press (Pres. 1971); Derbyshire and Lancashire Gliding.

ASHTON, Sir Leigh; *see* Ashton, Sir A. L. B.

ASHTON, Rt. Rev. Leonard (James), CB 1970; Bishop in Cyprus and The Gulf, since 1976, Episcopal Church in Jerusalem and the Middle East; Episcopal Canon, St George's Cathedral, Jerusalem, 1976; Hon. Canon and Prebendary of St Botolph, Lincoln Cathedral, 1969-73, Canon Emeritus since 1973; *b* 27 June 1915; *s* of late Henry Ashton and Sarah Ashton (*née* Ing). *Educ:* Tyndale Hall, Bristol. Ordained, Chester, 1942; Curate, Cheadle, 1942-45; Chap. RAF, 1945-; N Wales, 1945; AHQ Malaya and Singapore, 1946; BC Air Forces, Japan, 1947-48; Halton, 1948-49; Feltwell, 1949-50; Chap. and Lectr, RAF Chap. Sch., Cheltenham, 1950-53; Sen. Chap., AHQ Iraq, 1954-55; RAF Coll., Cranwell, 1956-60; Br. Forces Arabian Peninsular and Mid. East Command, 1960-61; Asst Chap. Chief, Trng Commands, 1962-65; Res. Chap., St Clement Danes, Strand, 1965-69; Chaplain-in-Chief, (with relative rank of Air Vice-Marshal) RAF, and Archdeacon of RAF, 1969-73; QHC, 1967-73; Asst Bishop in Jerusalem, 1974-76. ChStJ 1976. *Recreations:* gardening, photography. *Address:* 60 Lowndes Avenue, Chesham, Bucks. *T:* Chesham 2952; 5A John Clerides Street, PO Box 2075, Nicosia, Cyprus. *Clubs:* Royal Air Force, Royal Commonwealth Society.

ASHTON, Prof. Norman (Henry), CBE 1976; DSc (London); FRS 1971; FRCP, FRCS; FRCPath; Professor of Pathology, University of London, 1957-78, now Emeritus; Director, Department of Pathology, Institute of Ophthalmology, University of London, 1948-78; Consultant Pathologist, Moorfields Eye Hospital, 1948-78; *b* 11 Sept. 1913; 2nd *s* of Henry James and Margaret Ann Ashton. *Educ:* West Kensington Sch.; King's Coll. and Westminster Hosp. Med. Sch., Univ. of London. Westminster Hospital: Prize in Bacteriology, 1938; Editor Hosp. Gazette, 1939-40; House Surg., House Phys., Sen. Casualty Officer and RMO, 1939-41. Asst Pathologist, Princess Beatrice Hosp., 1939; Dir of Pathology, Kent and Canterbury Hosp., and Blood Transfusion Officer of East Kent, 1941. Lieut-Col RAMC, Asst Dir of Pathology and Officer i/c Central Pathological Lab., Middle East, 1946. Pathologist to the Gordon Hosp., 1947; Reader in Pathology, Univ. of London, 1953; Fellow in Residence, Johns Hopkins Hosp., Baltimore, 1953, and Visiting Prof. there, 1959. Emeritus Fellow, Leverhulme Trust. Vis. Research Fellow, Merton Coll., Oxford, 1980. Lectures: Walter Wright, 1959; Banting, 1960; Clapp (USA), 1964; Proctor (USA), 1965; Bradshaw (RCP), 1971; Montgomery, 1973; Edward Nettleship Prize for Research in Ophthalmology, 1953; BMA Middlemore Prize, 1955; Proctor Medal for Research in Ophthalmology (USA), 1957; Doyne Medal (Oxford), 1960; William Julius Mickle Fellow, Univ. London, 1961; Bowman Medal, 1963; Donder's Medal, 1967; Wm Mackenzie Memorial Medal, 1967; Gonin Medal, 1978; 1st Jules Stein Award, USA, 1981. Chm., Fight for Sight Appeal; Trustee, Sir John Soane's Museum, 1977-82. Member, Board of Governors: Moorfields Eye Hosp., 1963-66 and 1975-78; Hosp. for Sick Children, Gt Ormond St, 1977-80; Royal Nat. Coll. for the Blind, 1977-; Member: Brit. Nat. Cttee for Prevention of Blindness, 1973-78; Royal Postgrad. Med. Sch. Council, 1977-80; Council, RCPath, 1963-66 and 1976-78 (Founder Fellow); Governing Body, Brit. Postgrad. Med. Fedn, 1966-, and Cent. Acad. Council, 1957-78 (Chm., 1967-70); Council, RSM, 1971-79, and Exec. Cttee, 1976-81; Med. Adv. Bd, British Retinitis Pigmentosa Soc.; Pathological Soc. of Great Britain and Ireland; European Assoc. for Study of Diabetes; Chapter Gen. and Hosp. Cttee of St John; Oxford Ophthalmological Congress; Medical Art Soc.; Member, Cttee of Management: Inst. of Ophthalmology, 1953-78; Inst. of Child Health, 1960-65; Cardio-Thoracic Inst., 1972-78; Inst. of Rheumatology, 1973-77. President: Ophth. Sect., RSM, 1972-74; Assoc. of Clinical Pathologists, 1978-79; Ophth. Soc. of UK, 1979-81; Chm., Brit. Diab. Assoc. Cttee on Blindness in Diabetes, 1967-70. Fellow, Inst. of Ophthalmology. Hon. Life Mem., British Diabetic Association; Life Pres. European Ophth. Pathology Soc.; Pres. Brit. Div. Internat. Acad. of Pathology, 1962. Hon. Member: Assoc. for Eye Research; Hellenic Ophth. Soc.; British Div., Internat. Acad. of Pathology; Gonin Club. Hon. Fellow: RSocMed; Coll. of Physicians, Philadelphia; Amer. Acad. Ophthal. and

Otolaryng. Mem. Ed. Bd, Brit. Jl Ophthalmology, 1963-78, and Jl Histopathology. FRSocMed; Liveryman and Mem. Court of Assistants, Soc. of Apothecaries of London. Freeman, City of London. Hon. DSc Chicago. KStJ. *Publications:* contrib. to books and numerous scientific articles in Jl of Pathology and Bacteriology, Brit. Jl of Ophthalmology, and Amer. Jl of Ophthalmology. *Recreations:* painting, gardening. *Address:* 2 The Cloisters, Westminster Abbey, SW1. *T:* 01-222 4982. *Clubs:* Athenæum, Garrick.

ASHTON, Rev. Canon Patrick Thomas, MVO; Chaplain to the Queen, since 1955; *b* 27 July 1916; *s* of Lieut-Col S. E. Ashton, OBE; *m* 1942, Mavis St Clair Brown, New Zealand; three *d* (one *s* decd). *Educ:* Stowe; Christ Church, Oxford (MA); Westcott House, Cambridge. Served War of 1939-45 as Captain, Oxfordshire Yeomanry; Curate, St Martin-in-the-Fields, 1947-51; Rector of All Saints, Clifton, Beds, 1951-55; Rector of Sandringham with West Newton and Appleton, and Domestic Chaplain to the Queen, 1955-70; Rector: Sandringham Gp of Eight Parishes, 1963-70; Swanborough Team of Parishes, 1970-73; Priest-in-charge of Avebury with Winterbourne Monkton and Berwick Bassett, 1974-77; Rector, Upper Kennet team of Parishes, 1975-77; a Canon of Salisbury Cathedral, 1975; Rural Dean of Marlborough, 1976-77. *Address:* Field Cottage, Bottlesford, Pewsey, Wilts. *T:* Woodborough 340.

ASHTON, Prof. Robert, PhD; Professor of English History, University of East Anglia, since 1963; *b* 21 July 1924; *s* of late Joseph and late Edith F. Ashton; *m* 1946, Margaret Alice Sedgwick; two *d. Educ:* Magdalen Coll. Sch., Oxford; University Coll., Southampton (1942-43, 1946-49); London Sch. of Economics (1949-52). BA 1st Cl. hons (London) 1949; PhD (London) 1953; Asst Lecturer in Economic History, Univ. of Nottingham, 1952; Lecturer, 1954; Senior Lecturer, 1961; Vis. Associate Prof. in History, Univ. of California, Berkeley, 1962-63; Prof. of English History, 1963, and Dean of Sch. of English Studies, 1964-67, Univ. of East Anglia. Vis. Fellow, All Souls Coll., Oxford, 1973-74; James Ford Special Lectr in History, Oxford, 1982. FRHistS 1960. *Publications:* The Crown and the Money Market, 1603-1640, 1960; Charles I and the City, in Essays in the Economic and Social History of Tudor and Stuart England in honour of R. H. Tawney (ed F. J. Fisher), 1961; James I by his Contemporaries, 1969; The Civil War and the Class Struggle, in The English Civil War and After 1642-1658 (ed R. H. Parry), 1970; The English Civil War: Conservatism and Revolution 1603-49, 1978; The City and the Court 1603-1643, 1979; articles in learned periodicals. *Recreations:* music, looking at old buildings, wine. *Address:* The Manor House, Brundall, Norwich NR13 5JY. *T:* Norwich 713368.

ASHTON, Roy; a Recorder of the Crown Court, since 1979; barrister-at-law; *b* 20 Oct. 1928; *s* of Charles and Lilian Ashton; *m* 1954, Brenda Alice Dales; one *s* one *d. Educ:* Boston Grammar Sch.; Nottingham Univ. (LLB Hons). National Service, Directorate of Legal Services, RAF, 1951-53. Called to the Bar, Lincoln's Inn, 1954. Dep. Chairman, Agricultural Land Tribunal, 1978-. *Recreations:* reading, chess, film collecting. *Address:* The White House, 100 Chaul End Road, Caddington, Bedfordshire LU1 4AS. *T:* Luton 413660. *Club:* Northampton and County.

ASHTON HILL, Norman, MBE (mil.) 1945; TD; Consultant since 1981, Ashton Hill Bond, Solicitors and Commissioners for Oaths (Principal Partner, 1948-81); *b* 1 March 1918; *s* of Sydney and Marguerite Ashton Hill, Bewdley, Worcs; *m* 1971, Ireina Hilda Marie; (one *s* two *d* by former *m*). *Educ:* Uppingham Sch.; Birmingham Univ. (LLB Hons). Served War, 1939-45: commnd 2nd Lieut TA, 1939; BEF, BLA, BAOR; Staff Coll. (psc), mentioned in despatches; NW Europe War Crimes, 1945-46; Hon. Lt-Col, Royal Warwickshire Regt. Enrolled Gibraltar Bar, 1971. Chm., Radio Trent Ltd, 1973-79; Dir, 1971-78, Vice-Chm., Bonser Engrg Ltd, 1972-78. Director: Lunn Poly (formerly Sir Henry Lunn Ltd) (Vice-Chm., 1974-58); Eagle Aviation Ltd, and Cunard Eagle Airways Ltd and Group, 1952-68; North Midland Construction Co. Ltd, 1971-; Morgan Housing Co. Ltd and Group, 1962-81; Derby Music Finance Ltd, 1978-; Cooper & Roe Ltd, 1979-80; Savings & Investment Bank Ltd, 1979-. Chairman: Air Transport Cttee, ABCC, 1958- (a Vice-Pres. ABCC, 1977-); Air Transp. Cttee, British National Chamber of Internat. Chamber of Commerce, 1970-. Mem., Air Transport Users Cttee, 1976- (Dep. Chm., 1978-80; Chm., 1980-); CRAeS 1980. NSPCC: Hon. Vice-Pres., and formerly Hon. Gen. and Cases Sec., Nottingham Br.; Mem. Central Exec. Cttee, 1955-80, Vice-Chm. 1974-80; Hon. Vice-Pres. Hon. Vice-Consul for Norway, Notts, 1955-80. Assistant, Glaziers Co., 1978-. FRSA. Kt (1st Cl.), Order of St Olav, Norway, 1972. *Recreations:* gardening, shooting. *Address:* Middle Garth, Crosby, IoM. *T:* Douglas (IoM) 851650; (office) 5 Hill Street, Douglas, IoM. *T:* Douglas (IoM) 27111. *Club:* Royal Aero.

ASHTOWN, 6th Baron *cr* 1800; **Christopher Oliver Trench;** *b* 23 March 1931; *s* of Algernon Oliver Trench (*d* 1955) (*g g s* of 2nd Baron) and Muriel Dorothy (*d* 1954), *d* of Frank Thorne, Weston-super-Mare; *S* kinsman, 1979. *Recreation:* study of the philosophy of Gurdjeff and Ouspensky. *Heir: cousin* Cosby Patrick Musgrave Trench [*b* 14 Jan. 1915; *m* 1956, Julia Violetta May, *widow* of Frank Louis Whiting and *d* of late Frank Porch]. *Address:* 131 Stinson Street, Hamilton, Ontario, Canada.

ASHWELL, Major Arthur Lindley, DSO 1916; OBE 1946; TD 1926; DL; late 8th Battalion Sherwood Foresters; *b* 19 Jan. 1886; *o s* of Arthur Thomas Ashwell, solicitor, Nottingham; *m* 1932, Sylvia Violet (*d* 1980), *widow* of Harold Gallatly, MC, and *d* of Philip Scratchley. *Educ:* Lambrook, Bracknell;

Winchester Coll. Served European War, 1915 (wounded thrice, despatches, DSO). DL Notts, 1941. *Address:* Flat 3, 19 The Vale, SW3. *Clubs:* Naval and Military, Royal Automobile.

ASHWORTH, Prof. Graham William, CBE 1980; Professor of Urban Environmental Studies, University of Salford, since 1973; Director, University of Salford Environmental Institute, since 1978; *b* 14 July 1935; *s* of Frederick William Ashworth and Ivy Alice Ashworth; *m* 1960, Gwyneth Mai Morgan-Jones; three *d. Educ:* Devonport High Sch., Plymouth; Univ. of Liverpool (Master of Civic Design, BArch). RIBA, PPRTPI, FRSA, MInst EnvSci. LCC (Hook New Town Project), 1959-61; consultancy with Graeme Shankland, 1961-64; architect to Civic Trust, 1964-65; Dir, Civic Trust for North-West, 1965-73. Member: Skeffington Cttee on Public Participation in Planning, 1969; North-West Adv. Council of BBC, 1970-75 (Chm.); NW Economic Planning Council (and Sub-gp Chm.), 1968-79; Countryside Commn, 1974-77; Merseyside Urban Develt Corp., 1981-. Governor, Northern Baptist Coll., 1966-82; Pres., Royal Town Planning Inst., 1973-74; Chairman: Exec. Cttee, Civic Trust for North-West, 1973-; Instn of Environmental Sciences, 1980-82; Dir, Campaign to promote Univ. of Salford, 1981-. Editor, Internat. Jl of Environmental Educn, 1981-. *Publication:* An Encyclopædia of Planning, 1973. *Recreations:* gardening, painting, church and social work. *Address:* Manor Court, Manor Farm, Samlesbury Hall, Preston New Road, Preston PR5 0UP. *Club:* National Liberal.

ASHWORTH, Sir Herbert, Kt 1972; Chairman Nationwide Building Society (formerly Co-operative Permanent Building Society), 1970-82 (Deputy-Chairman, 1968-70); *b* 30 Jan. 1910; *s* of Joseph Hartley Ashworth; *m* 1936, Barbara Helen Mary, *d* of late Douglas D. Henderson; two *s* one *d. Educ:* Burnley Grammar Sch.; London Univ. (grad. econ. and law). General Manager, Portman Building Soc., 1938-50; General Manager, Co-operative Permanent Building Soc., 1950-61; Director and General Manager, Hallmark Securities Ltd, 1961-66. Dep. Chm., 1964-68, Chm., 1968-73, Housing Corp. Dir, The Builder Ltd, 1975-80. Chm., Surrey and W Sussex Agricl Wages Cttee, 1974-. Vice-President: Building Socs Assoc.; Building Socs Inst.; Metropolitan Assoc. of Building Socs. *Publications:* Housing in Great Britain, 1951; Building Society Work Explained, (current edn) 1977; The Building Society Story, 1980. *Address:* 8 Tracery, Park Road, Banstead, Surrey SM7 3DD. *T:* Burgh Heath 52608.

ASHWORTH, Ian Edward; Circuit Administrator, Western Circuit, Lord Chancellor's Office, since 1970; *b* 3 March 1930; *s* of William Holt and Cicely Ashworth, Rochdale; *m* Pauline, *er d* of Maurice James and Gladys Heddle, Westcliff-on-Sea; two *s* one *d. Educ:* Manchester Grammar Sch.; The Queen's Coll., Oxford (BCL, MA). Admitted Solicitor, 1956; Asst Solicitor, Rochdale, 1956-58; Dep. Town Clerk, Dep. Clerk of Peace, Canterbury, 1958-63; Town Clerk, Clerk of Peace, Deal, 1963-66; Town Clerk, Rugby, 1966-70. *Recreations:* music, painting, gardening. *Address:* 5 St Hilary Close, Stoke Bishop, Bristol BS9 1DA. *T:* Bristol 685236. *Club:* United Oxford & Cambridge University.

ASHWORTH, James Louis, FIMechE, FIEE, ARTC (Salford); Full-Time Member for Operations, Central Electricity Generating Board, 1966-70, retired; *b* 7 March 1906; *s* of late James and late Janet Ashworth; *m* 1931 Clara Evelyn Arnold; one *s* two *d. Educ:* Stockport Grammar Sch.; Salford Royal Coll. of Technology. Apprenticeship with Mirrlees, Bickerton & Day Ltd, Stockport (Diesel Oil Engine Manufrs), 1924-29; Metro-Vickers Electrical Co. Ltd, 1929; Manchester Corp. Elec. Dept, Stuart Street Gen. Stn, 1930-32; Hull Corp. Elec. Dept, 1932-35; Halifax Corp. Elec. Dept, 1935-40; Mersey Power Co. Ltd, Runcorn, 1940-48; British Elec. Authority, N West: Chief Generation Engr (O), 1948-57; Dep. Divisional Controller, 1957-58; Central Elec. Gen. Bd, N West, Merseyside and N Wales Region: Dep. Regional Dir, 1958-62; Regional Dir, 1962-66. *Recreations:* gardening, photography, travel, reading. *Address:* Chase Cottage, 23 The Chase, Reigate, Surrey. *T:* Redhill 61279.

ASHWORTH, Brig. John Blackwood, CBE 1962; DSO 1944; DL; retired 1965; *b* 7 Dec. 1910; *s* of Lieut-Col H. S. Ashworth, Royal Sussex Regt (killed in action, 1917) and late Mrs E. M. Ashworth; *m* 1946, Eileen Patricia, *d* of late Major H. L. Gifford (Royal Ulster Rifles) and of Lady Gooch; one *d. Educ:* Wellington Coll.; RMC, Sandhurst. Commissioned Royal Sussex Regt, 1930; Instructor RMC, 1938; War of 1939-45 (despatches twice); OC Training Centre, 1942; OC 1/5 Queen's Royal Regt (wounded, DSO), 1944; GSO1, War Office, 1944; OC 4/5 Royal Sussex, 1945; OC 1st Royal Sussex, 1946; GSO1, Brit. Middle East Office, 1947; AMS War Office, 1948; OC 1st Royal Sussex, 1951; Comdt Joint Sch. of Chemical Warfare, 1954; Commander 133rd Inf. Bde (TA), 1957; Director of Military Training, War Office, 1959-62; Inspector of Boys' Training, War Office, 1962-65. ADC to the Queen, 1961-65. Col The Royal Sussex Regt, 1963-66; Dep. Col, The Queen's Regt (Royal Sussex), 1967-68. DL Sussex 1972. OStJ 1950. Grand Officer, Order of House of Orange, 1967. *Address:* West Common Drive, Hayward's Heath, West Sussex RH16 2AN. *T:* Hayward's Heath 452371.

ASHWORTH, John Michael, DSc; FIBiol; Vice-Chancellor, University of Salford, since 1981; *b* 27 Nov. 1938; *s* of late Jack Ashworth and late Constance Mary Ousman; *m* 1963, Ann Knight; one *s* three *d. Educ:* West Buckland Sch., N Devon; Exeter Coll., Oxford (MA, DSc); Leicester Univ. (PhD). FIBiol 1974. Dept of Biochemistry, Univ. of Leicester: Res. Demonstr, 1961-63;

Lectr, 1963-71; Reader, 1971-73; Prof. of Biology, Univ. of Essex, 1974-79 (on secondment to Cabinet Office, 1976-79); Under-Sec., Cabinet Office, 1979-81 and Chief Scientist, Central Policy Review Staff, 1976-81. Harkness Fellow of Commonwealth Fund, NY, at Brandeis Univ. and Univ. of Calif, 1965-67. Colworth Medal, Biochem. Soc., 1972. *Publications:* Cell Differentiation, 1972; (with J. Dee) The Slime Moulds, 1976; over 50 pubns in prof. jls on biochem., genet., cell biolog. and educnl topics. *Recreation:* sailing. *Address:* University of Salford, Salford M5 4WT. *Club:* Wivenhoe Sailing (Wivenhoe).

ASHWORTH, Peter Anthony Frank; Director, Leeds Permanent Building Society, since 1971 (President, 1978); *b* 24 Aug. 1935; *s* of Peter Ormerod and Dorothy Christine Ashworth; *m* 1964, Elisabeth Crompton; one *s* one *d*. *Educ:* Leeds Grammar School. Articled to Hollis & Webb, Chartered Surveyors, Leeds (now Weatherall, Hollis & Gale), 1953-56; Partner, 1961-80. FRICS; ACIArb. *Recreations:* golf, gardening. *Address:* The Spinney, Garth Avenue, Collingham, Wetherby LS22 5BJ. *T:* Collingham Bridge 72172. *Clubs:* Leeds, Alwoodley Golf (Leeds).

ASHWORTH, Piers, QC 1973; a Recorder of the Crown Court, since 1974; *b* 27 May 1931; *s* of Tom and Mollie Ashworth; *m* 1st, 1959, Iolene Jennifer (marr. diss. 1978), *yr d* of W. G. Foxley; three *s* one *d*; 2nd, 1980, Elizabeth, *er d* of A. J. S. Aston. *Educ:* Christ's Hospital; Pembroke Coll., Cambridge (scholar). Commnd Royal Signals, 1951. BA (Cantab) 1955; Harmsworth Law Scholar, 1956; called to Bar, Middle Temple, 1956; Midland and Oxford circuit. *Recreations:* sailing, squash, tennis, bridge. *Address:* Meadow Cottage, Goring Heath, Reading RG8 7TA. *T:* Checkendon 681368; 2 Harcourt Buildings, Temple, EC4Y 9DB. *T:* 01-583 9020.

ASHWORTH, Prof. William; Professor of Economic and Social History, University of Bristol, 1958-82, Pro-Vice-Chancellor, 1975-78; *b* 11 March 1920; *s* of Harold and Alice Ashworth; unmarried. *Educ:* Todmorden Grammar Sch.; London Sch. of Economics and Political Science. Served 1941-45, RAPC and REME. BSc (Econ.) 1946; PhD 1950. Research Assistant, London Sch. of Economics and Political Science, 1946-47; on staff of Cabinet Office (Historical Section), 1947-48; Assistant Lecturer and Lecturer in Economic History, London Sch. of Economics and Political Science, 1948-55; Reader in Economic History in the Univ. of London, 1955-58. Dean, Faculty of Social Sciences, Univ. of Bristol, 1968-70. *Publications:* A Short History of the International Economy, 1952 (revised 1962, 1975); Contracts and Finance (History of the Second World War: UK Civil Series), 1953; The Genesis of Modern British Town Planning, 1954; An Economic History of England, 1870-1939, 1960; contributor to: London, Aspects of Change, ed by Centre for Urban Studies, 1964; Victoria County History of Essex, 1966; The Study of Economic History, ed N. B. Harte, 1971. Articles and reviews in Economic History Review and other jls. *Address:* 91 High Kingsdown, Bristol BS2 8ER. *T:* Bristol 423771.

ASIMOV, Prof. Isaac, PhD; Professor of Biochemistry, University of Boston, since 1979; author; *b* 2 Jan. 1920; *s* of Judah Asimov and Anna Rachel (*née* Berman); *m* 1st, 1942, Gertrude Blugerman; one *s* one *d*; 2nd, 1973, Dr Janet Jeppson. *Educ:* Columbia Univ. (BS 1939, MA 1941, PhD 1948, all in chemistry). Joined faculty of Boston Univ. Sch. of Medicine, 1949; retd from academic labors, 1958, but retained title. First professional sale of short story, 1938; first book published, 1950; 250th book published, 1982. *Publications:* 228 books, including: I, Robot, 1950; The Human Body, 1963; Asimov's Guide to Shakespeare, 1970; Asimov's Guide to Science, 1972; Murder at the ABA, 1976; The Collapsing Universe, 1977; In Memory Yet Green (autobiog., vol. 1), 1979; A Choice of Catastrophes, 1979; In Joy Still Felt (autobiog., vol. 2), 1980; In the Beginning, 1981. *Recreation:* a man's work is his play: my recreation is writing. *Address:* 10 West 66th Street, New York, NY 10023, USA. *T:* 212-362-1564.

ASIROGLU, Vahap; Turkish Ambassador to the Court of St James's, 1978-81; *b* Karamürsel, 1916; *m*; one *c*. *Educ:* Galatasaray High Sch.; Istanbul Univ. (Faculty of Law). Third Sec., Second Political Dept, Min. of Foreign Affairs, 1943-46; successively, Third, Second, First Sec., Turkish Embassy, Prague, 1946-51; First Sec., Dept of Internat. Economic Affairs, MFA, 1951-53; First Sec. and Counsellor, Turkish Perm. Mission to UN, 1953-59; Asst Dir Gen., Dept of Internat. Econ. Affairs, MFA, 1959-60; Asst Dir Gen. and Dir Gen., Personnel and Admin. Dept, MFA, 1960; Dir Gen., UN and Internat. Instns Dept, MFA, 1960-62; Asst Perm. Rep., Turkish Perm. Mission to UN, 1962-65; Turkish Ambassador: to Copenhagen, 1965-68; to Jakarta, 1968-71; Sec. Gen., Reg. Cooperation for Develt (a reg. org. between Turkey, Iran and Pakistan), 1971-74; Sen. Counsellor, MFA, 1974; Director General: Dept of Consular Affairs, MFA, 1974-75; Dept of Cultural Affairs, MFA, 1975-76; Asst Sec. Gen. for Inf. and Cultural Affairs, MFA, 1976. Mem., UN Human Rights Commn, 1953-56; Turkish Rep., ICAO Conf., Montreal, 1956-57; Head of Turkish Delegn, GATT Conf., Tokyo, 1959; Asst Chm., Conf. on Immunities and Diplomatic Relns, Vienna, 1961; Chm., Fifth Commn, UN Gen. Assembly, 1967. *Address:* c/o Ministry of Foreign Affairs, Ankara, Turkey.

ASKE, Rev. Sir Conan, 2nd Bt *cr* 1922; Assistant Curate of St John-in-Bedwardine, Worcester, 1972-80; *b* 22 April 1912; *s* of Sir Robert William Aske, 1st Bt, TD, QC, LLD, and Edith (*d* 1918), *d* of Sir Walter Herbert Cockerline; *S* father 1954; *m* 1st, 1948, Vera Faulkner (*d* 1960); 2nd, 1965, Rebecca, *d* of Hugh Grant, Wick, Caithness. *Educ:* Rugby; Balliol Coll.,

Oxford. TA, London Irish Rifles, 1939; served, 1939-49, with East York Regt, Sudan Defence Force, Somalia Gendarmerie. Major, Civil Affairs Officer, Reserved Area of Ethiopia and The Ogaden, 1949-51; Schoolmaster, Hillstone, Malvern, 1952-69; Asst Curate, Hagley, Stourbridge, 1970-72. *Heir:* *b* Robert Edward Aske [*b* 21 March 1915; *m* 1940, Joan Bingham, *o d* of Captain Bingham Ackerley, Cobham; one *s*]. *Address:* 167 Malvern Road, Worcester WR2 4NN. *T:* Worcester 422817.

ASKEW, Barry Reginald William; journalist, broadcaster and public relations consultant; *b* 13 Dec. 1936; *s* of late Reginald Ewart Askew and Jane Elizabeth Askew; *m* 1st, 1958, June Roberts (marr. diss. 1978), *d* of Vernon and late Betty Roberts; one *s* one *d*; 2nd, 1980, Deborah Parker, *d* of Harold and Enid Parker. *Educ:* Lady Manners Grammar Sch., Bakewell, Derbys. Trainee reporter upwards, Derbyshire Times, 1952-57; Reporter and sub-ed., Sheffield Telegraph, 1957-59; reporter, feature writer and broadcaster, Raymonds News Agency, Derby, 1959-61; Editor, Matlock Mercury, 1961-63; Industrial Correspondent, Asst Ed., Dep. Ed., Sheffield Telegraph, later Morning Telegraph, Sheffield, 1964-68; Associate Ed., The Star, Sheffield, 1968; Editor, 1968-81, Dir, 1978-81, Lancashire Evening Post; Editor, News of the World, 1981. Presenter and anchor man: ITV, 1970-81; BBC Radio 4, 1971-72; BBC 1, 1972; BBC 2, 1972-76. Mem., Davies Cttee to reform hosp. complaints procedures in UK, 1971-73. Campaigning Journalist of 1971, IPC Nat. Press Awards; Journalist of 1977, British Press Awards; Crime Reporter of 1977, Witness Box Awards. *Recreations:* Rugby, chess, reading military history, golf. *Address:* Rose Cottage, Whittle Hill, Woodplumpton, near Preston, Lancs. *Clubs:* London Press; Preston Grasshoppers RF.

ASKEW, Herbert Royston, QC 1955; BSc; MICE; *e s* of late Leonard Askew; *m* 1st, 1919, Christiana Rachel (decd), *o d* of late C. Wolryche Dixon, Great Roke, Witley, Surrey; one *d* (one *s* killed on active service, 1942; and one *d* decd); 2nd, 1948, Dorothy Beatrice, *o d* of late J. Gale Wilson, Aberdour, Fife. *Educ:* Alleyn's Sch., Dulwich; London Univ. Served European War 1914-18, Capt. Middlesex Regt and Royal Tank Corps. Called to the Bar, Middle Temple, 1926; Master of the Bench, 1963. Mem. Kensington Borough Council, 1931-39. Served War of 1939-45, Lieut-Col, Gen. List (GSO1). *Address:* 24 Palace Court, W2. *T:* 01-727 6033.

ASKEW, John Marjoribanks Eskdale, CBE 1974; *b* 22 Sept. 1908; *o s* of late William Haggerston Askew, JP, Ladykirk, Berwicks, and Castle Hills, Berwick-on-Tweed; *m* 1st, 1933, Lady Susan Egerton (marr. diss., 1966), 4th *d* of 4th Earl of Ellesmere, MVO; one *s* one *d*; *m* 1976, Priscilla Anne, *e d* of late Algernon Ross-Farrow. *Educ:* Eton; Magdalene Coll., Cambridge (BA). Lieut 2 Bn Grenadier Guards, 1932; Capt. 1940; Major 1943. Royal Company of Archers, Queen's Body Guard for Scotland. Convener: Berwicks CC, 1961; Border Regional Council, 1974. *Address:* Ladykirk, Berwicks. *T:* Berwick 82229; Castle Hills, Berwick-on-Tweed. *Clubs:* Boodle's; New (Edinburgh).
See also Baron Faringdon, Duke of Sutherland.

ASKEW, Rev. Canon Reginald James Albert; Principal of Salisbury and Wells Theological College since 1974; *b* 16 May 1928; *s* of late Paul Askew and Amy Wainwright; *m* 1953, Kate, *yr d* of late Rev. Henry Townsend Wigley; one *s* two *d*. *Educ:* Harrow; Corpus Christi Coll., Cambridge (MA); Lincoln Theological College. Curate of Highgate, 1957-61; Tutor and Chaplain of Wells Theol Coll., 1961-65, Vice-Principal 1966-69; Priest Vicar of Wells Cath., 1961-69; Vicar of Christ Church, Lancaster Gate, London, 1969-73; Canon of Salisbury Cathedral and Prebendary of Grantham Borealis, 1975-. *Publication:* The Tree of Noah, 1971. *Recreations:* music, gardening, cricket. *Address:* 19 The Close, Salisbury, Wilts. *T:* Salisbury 4223.

ASKEY, Arthur Bowden, CBE 1981 (OBE 1969); theatrical artiste; *b* 6 June 1900; *s* of Samuel Askey, Liverpool, and Betty Askey (*née* Bowden), Knutsford, Cheshire; *m* 1925, Elizabeth May Swash (*d* 1974); one *d*. *Educ:* Liverpool Institute. Liverpool Education Offices, 1916-24; concert parties, pantomimes, broadcasts, London and Provincial Concerts, 1924-38. *Films:* Band Waggon, Charlie's Big-Hearted Aunt, The Ghost Train, I Thank You, Back-Room Boy, King Arthur was a Gentleman, Miss London Ltd, Bees in Paradise, 1939-44; The Love Match; Ramsbottom Rides Again; Make Mine a Million; Friends and Neighbours. *Broadcast Series:* Band Waggon, 1938-39, and 1971; Big's Broadcast, 1940; Big Time, 1942; Forever Arthur, 1945; How Do You Do, 1949; Arthur's Inn, 1952; Hello, Playmates, 1954; Askey Galore, 1957; The Arthur Askey Show, 1958. *Television Series:* Before Your Very Eyes, 1953, 1955, 1956, 1957; Living it up, 1958; Arthur's Treasured Volumes, 1960; The Arthur Askey Show, 1961; Raise Your Glasses, 1962. *London Theatres:* The Boy Who Lost His Temper, Garrick, 1937, Cambridge, 1938; Band Waggon, London Palladium, 1939; Jack and Jill, Palace, 1941, His Majesty's, 1942; The Love Racket, Victoria Palace, Prince's and Adelphi, 1944-45; Follow the Girls, His Majesty's, 1945-47; Cinderella, London Casino, 1948; The Kid from Stratford, Prince's, Winter Garden, 1948-49; Goody Two Shoes, London Casino, 1950; Bet Your Life, London Hippodrome, 1951-52; The Love Match, Palace, 1953-54; Babes in the Wood, Golders Green, 1954; Babes in the Wood, Streatham Hill, 1955; Humpty Dumpty, Golders Green Hippodrome, 1956; Robinson Crusoe, Palladium, 1957; Dick Whittington, Golders Green Hippodrome, 1958; Dick Whittington, Streatham Hill Theatre, 1959-60; Cinderella, Golders Green Hippodrome, 1961-62; *Pantomime:* Robin Hood, Coventry Theatre, 1963-64; Babes in the Wood, Wimbledon, 1966-67; Sleeping Beauty, Wimbledon, 1969-70; Cinderella, Manchester, 1970-71; Cinderella, Nottingham, 1971-72; Cinderella,

Birmingham, 1972-73; Babes in the Wood, Richmond, 1973-74; Cinderella, Bournemouth, 1974-75; Babes in the Wood, Bristol, 1975-76; Cinderella, Richmond, 1976-77; Jack and the Beanstalk, Richmond, 1977-78, Birmingham, 1978-79, Richmond, 1979-80; Aladdin, Richmond, 1981-82. London Palladium: Aladdin, 1964-65; Babes in the Wood, 1965-66; Robinson Crusoe, 1967-68; Jack and the Beanstalk, 1968-69. Royal Command Performance (Palladium), 1946, 1948, 1952, 1954, 1955, 1957, 1968, 1972, 1978, 1980; Command Performance (Manchester), 1959. Australian tour, 1949-50; various radio and television broadcasts and provincial variety tours. Summer seasons: Blackpool, Bournemouth, Southsea, Margate, Shanklin, Hastings, Rhyl, Torquay, Eastbourne, etc. Pres., Stage Golfing Soc. Variety Club of GB Special Award, 1978. Jubilee Medal, 1977. *Publication:* Before Your Very Eyes (autobiog.), 1975. *Recreations:* reading, music, watching sport, reminiscing. *Club:* Savage.

ASKONAS, Brigitte Alice, PhD; FRS 1973; Head of Division of Immunology, MRC, National Institute for Medical Research, London, since 1977; *b* 1 April 1923; *d* of late Charles F. Askonas and Rose Askonas. *Educ:* McGill Univ., Montreal (BSc, MSc); Cambridge Univ. (PhD). Research student, Sch. of Biochemistry, Univ. of Cambridge, 1949-52; Immunology Div., NIMR, 1953-; Dept of Bacteriology and Immunology, Harvard Med. Sch., Boston, 1961-62; Basel Inst. for Immunology, Basel, Switzerland, 1971-72. Hon. Member: Amer. Soc. of Immunology; Soc. française d'Immunologie. *Publications:* contrib. scientific papers to various biochemical and immunological jls and books. *Recreations:* art, travel. *Address:* 23 Hillside Gardens, N6 5SU. *T:* 01-348 6792.

ASKWITH, Hon. Betty Ellen, FRSL; *b* 26 June 1909; *o d* of late Baron Askwith, KCB, KC, LLD, and Lady Askwith, CBE; *m* 1950, Keith Miller Jones (*d* 1978). *Educ:* Lycée Français, London; North Foreland Lodge, Broadstairs. *Publications:* First Poems, 1928; If This Be Error, 1932; Poems, 1933; Green Corn, 1933; Erinna, 1937; Keats, 1940; The Admiral's Daughters, 1947; A Broken Engagement, 1950; The Blossoming Tree, 1954; The Tangled Web, 1960; A Step Out of Time, 1966; Lady Dilke, 1969; Two Victorian Families, 1971; The Lytteltons, 1975; A Victorian Young Lady, 1978; Piety and Wit: Harriet Countess Granville 1785-1862, 1982; with Theodora Benson: Lobster Quadrille, 1930; Seven Basketfuls, 1932; Foreigners, 1935; Muddling Through, 1936; How to Be Famous, 1937. *Translations:* The Tailor's Cake, 1947; A Hard Winter, 1947; Meeting, 1950. *Recreation:* reading Victorian novels. *Address:* 9/105 Onslow Square, SW7. *T:* 01-589 7126.

ASLIN, Elizabeth Mary; art historian; *b* 23 March 1923; *d* of Charles Herbert Aslin and Ethel Fawcett Aslin. *Educ:* various schools; Slade Sch. of Fine Art, Univ. of London. Res. Asst, Circulation Dept, V & A Museum, 1947; Asst Keeper i/c, Bethnal Green Museum, 1964-68; Asst Dir, V & A Museum, 1968-74; Keeper i/c, Bethnal Green Museum, 1974-81. Member: Victorian Soc.; Decorative Arts Soc. FRSA. *Publications:* Nineteenth Century English Furniture, 1962; The Aesthetic Movement: Prelude to Art Nouveau, 1969. *Recreations:* drawing, etching, travel. *Address:* 11 Fulmar Close, Hove, East Sussex BN3 6NW. *T:* Brighton 508467.

ASPIN, Norman, CMG 1968; HM Diplomatic Service, retired; Adviser and Secretary, East Africa Association, since 1981; *b* 9 Nov. 1922; *s* of Thomas and Eleanor Aspin; *m* 1948, Elizabeth Irving; three *s.* *Educ:* Darwen Grammar Sch.; Durham Univ. (MA). War Service, 1942-45, Lieut RNVR. Demonstrator in Geography, Durham Univ., 1947-48; Asst Principal, Commonwealth Relations Office, 1948; served in India, 1948-51; Principal, Commonwealth Relations Office, 1952; served in Federation of Rhodesia and Nyasaland, 1954-57; British Deputy High Commissioner in Sierra Leone, 1961-63; Commonwealth Relations Office, 1963-65; British Embassy, Tel Aviv, 1966-69; IDC 1970; Head of Personnel Policy Dept, FCO, 1971-73; Under-Sec., FCO, 1973-76; Comr, British Indian Ocean Territory, 1976; British High Comr in Malta, 1976-79; Asst Under-Sec. of State, FCO, 1979-80. *Recreations:* sailing, tennis. *Address:* Mounsey Bank, Dacre, Cumbria CA11 0HL. *Club:* Naval.

ASPINALL, Wilfred; Parliamentary and Industrial Relations Consultant; Executive Director, Managerial, Professional & Staff Liaison Group, since 1978; Consultant, Royal Insurance Branch Managers Association, since 1980; Vice-President, Confédération International des Cadres (and Member Comité Directeur at CIC Bureau), since 1979; *b* 14 Sept. 1942; *s* of late Charles Aspinall and Elizabeth Aspinall; *m* 1973, Judith Mary, *d* of late Leonard James Pimlott and Kathleen Mary Pimlott; one *d.* *Educ:* Poynton Secondary Modern; Stockport Coll. for Further Educn. Staff, National Provincial Bank Ltd, 1960-69; Asst Gen. Sec., National Westminster Staff Assoc., 1969-75; Dep. Sec. (part-time), Council of Bank Staff Assocs, 1969-75; Mem., Banking Staff Council, 1970-77; Gen. Sec., Confedn of Bank Staff Assocs, 1975-79; Admin. Sec., Nationwide Bldg Soc. Staff Assoc., 1979; Gen. Sec., Halcrow Staff Assoc., 1979; Consultant, Nat. Unilever Managers Assoc., 1979-81. Member: N Herts DHA, 1981-; Hammersmith Special Health Authority, 1981-. *Recreations:* motoring, photography, mem. of Round Table (Chm., London West End 1980-82), fund raising for charity, social protection of individuals, travel—particularly to places of historical interest, social affairs and political history. *Address:* Fig Tree Cottage, Preston, near Hitchin, Herts. *T:* Hitchin 56664; Tavistock House, Tavistock Square, WC1. *Clubs:* Lighthouse, London West End Round Table.

ASPINALL, William Briant Philip, OBE 1945; Headmaster, Queen School, HQ Northern Army Group, Rheindahlen, 1960-72, retired; *b* 1912 *s* of William Pryce Aspinall and Ethel Eleanor (*née* Ravenscroft); *m* 1s Aileen, *d* of Major R. FitzGerald; one *s* ; 2nd, Phyllis, *d* of Leopold Hill. *Educ* Royal Masonic Sch.; St John's Coll., Cambridge; Headmaster, Sutton Valenc Sch., 1950-53; Windsor Sch., Hamm, BAOR, 1953-58; King Richard Sch Cyprus, 1959. *Recreations:* cricket, hockey, golf, etc. *Address:* Baker's Farn House, Goudhurst, Kent. *Clubs:* MCC; Rye Golf.

ASPINWALL, Jack Heywood; MP (C) Kingswood, since 1979; compan director; *b* Feb. 1933; *m* Brenda Jean Aspinwall. *Educ:* Prescot Gramma School, Lancs; Marconi College, Chelmsford. Served RAF, 1949-56. Directo investment co. Mem., Avon County Council. Contested (L) Kingswood, Fet and Oct. 1974. *Address:* House of Commons, SW1A 0AA; 154 Bath Roac Willsbridge, Bristol.

ASPRAY, Rodney George, FCA; Chief Executive Officer, Norwei Cooperative Society, since 1969; *b* 1934. Secretary, Manchester and Salfor Cooperative Society, 1965-69; Director: Cooperative Bank Ltd, 1980- Cooperative Wholesale Soc. Ltd, 1980-. Mem., Monopolies and Merge Commn, 1975-81. FCA 1960. *Address:* Kambara, 4 Green Lane, Highe Poynton, Cheshire.

ASPREY, Algernon; independant consultant and designer; *b* 2 June 1912 of George Kenneth Asprey and Charlotte Esta Asprey; *m* 1939, Beatrice (*né* Bryant); one *s* two *d.* *Educ:* Bowden House Prep. Sch., Seaford; Charterhouse Sch. of Art, Regent Street Polytechnic, London. Served War, 1940-4C commnd Scots Guards, Captain. Joined Asprey of Bond Street, 1933; wit Aspreys, 1946-71, when own business, Algernon Asprey, formed; re-appointe Dir, Asprey & Co. Ltd, 1979-81; Chm., Algernon Asprey (Furnishing) Ltd 1971-81. Chairman: Purchase Tax Cttee in post war years to disbandmen Guards Club, 1960-65. Pres., Bond Street Assoc., 1968-81 (Chm., 1965-68] Mem. Cttee, Friends of Royal Acad. Prime Warden, Worshipful Co. c Goldsmiths, 1977-78. *Recreations:* painting, sailing, golf. *Address:* 34 Trevo Square, Knightsbridge, SW7 1DY. *T:* 01-589 2465. *Clubs:* Buck's, Cavalr and Guards.

ASQUITH, family name of **Earl of Oxford and Asquith.**

ASQUITH, Viscount; Raymond Benedict Bartholomew Michae Asquith; HM Diplomatic Service; Foreign and Commonwealth Office, sinc 1980; *b* 24 Aug. 1952; *er s* and *heir* of 2nd Earl of Oxford and Asquith, *qv m* 1978, Mary Clare, *e d* of Francis Pollen; one *s* one *d.* *Educ:* Ampleforth Balliol College, Oxford. *Heir:* *s* Hon. Mark Julian Asquith, *b* 13 May 1979 *Address:* Manor House, Mells, Frome, Somerset.

ASSHETON, family name of **Baron Clitheroe.**

ASTAIRE, Fred; actor, motion pictures; *b* 10 May 1899; *s* of F. E. Astaire an Ann Geilus; *m* 1933, Phyllis Livingston Potter (*d* 1954); two *s* one *d* ; *m* 198C Robyn Smith. *Educ:* private. Stage musical comedy-vaudeville until 1933 then motion pictures. First appearance in London, 1923, in Stop Flirting American and English successes: Lady Be Good, Funny Face, The Ban Waggon, Gay Divorce. *Films:* Flying Down to Rio, Top Hat, Roberta, Ga Divorce, Follow the Fleet, Swingtime, Shall We Dance?, Story of Vernon an Irene Castle, Holiday Inn, Ziegfeld Follies, Blue Skies, Easter Parade, Th Barkleys of Broadway, Three Little Words, Let's Dance, Daddy Longleg: Funny Face, Silk Stockings, On the Beach, The Pleasure of His Company Finian's Rainbow, The Midas Run, A Run on Gold, The Towering Infernc Un Taxi Mauve, Ghost Story. *Television Shows:* An Evening with Fre Astaire, 1958; Another Evening with Fred Astaire, 1959; Astaire Time, 196C The Fred Astaire Show, 1968; Family Upside Down, 1978. *Publicatio* Autobiography, Steps in Time, 1959. *Recreations:* golf, thoroughbred racing *Address:* Beverly Hills, California 90210, USA. *Clubs:* Racquet and Tennis The Brook, Lamb's (New York).

ASTBURY, Sir George, Kt 1966; JP; *b* 10 May 1902; 2nd *s* of Thoma Astbury, Longton, Stoke-on-Trent; *m* 1930, Nellie (decd), 2nd *d* of Albe Bagnall, Sandford Hill, Longton; two *s.* *Educ:* St James's, Longton. Retire as Co-operative Soc. Insurance Agent. Former Mem. Nat. Wages Bd c Co-op. Union. CC 1937, JP 1938, CA 1951, Hon. Alderman 1974, Cheshire *Address:* West Winds, Strawberry Roundabout, Backford, near Chester.

ASTBURY, Norman Frederick, CBE 1968; MA, ScD Cantab, CEng, FIEF FInstP, FRSA; Director, British Ceramic Research Association, 1960-73; *b* Dec. 1908; *y c* of William and Clara Astbury, Normacot, Staffs; *m* 1933, Nor Enid (*d* 1979), *yr d* of William and Mary Wilkinson; three *s* one *d.* *Edu* Longton High Sch.; St John's Coll., Cambridge (Scholar and Prizeman National Physical Laboratory, 1929-39; HM Anti-Submarine Experimenta Establishment, 1939-45; Dir of Research, J. Sankey & Sons Ltd and Gues Keen & Nettlefold Ltd, 1945-49; Prof. of Applied Physics, NSW Univ. o Technology, 1949-51; Prof. of Physics, Univ. of Khartoum, 1951-56; Roya Aircraft Establishment, 1956-57; Dep. Dir of Research, Brit. Ceram. Researc Assoc., 1957-60. Pres., Brit. Ceram. Soc., 1969; Member: Coun. Inst. of Physic and Phys. Soc., 1963-66; Nat. Coun. for Technological Awards, 1958-64 Coun. for Nat. Academic Awards, 1964-66; Inter-services Metallurgica Research Coun., 1962-64; Joint Services Non-metallic Materials Researc Board, 1964-69; Chm. Cttee of Directors of Research Assocs, 1964-66

Vice-Pres., Parly and Sci. Cttee, 1965-68; Mem., Construction Res. Adv. Council, DoE (formerly MPBW), 1968-71. *Publications:* Industrial Magnetic Testing, 1952; Electrical Applied Physics, 1956; numerous papers in scientific jls. *Recreations:* music, model railways. *Address:* 85 Atlantic Way, Westward Ho!, Devon. *T:* Bideford 5482. *Clubs:* Athenæum; Federation (Stoke-on-Trent).

ASTELL HOHLER, Thomas Sidney, MC 1944; Chairman, King & Shaxson Ltd, since 1965 (Partner since 1946); Chairman of associated companies; *b* 1919; *s* of late Lt-Col Arthur Preston Hohler, DSO and late Mrs Stanley Barry, Long Crendon Manor, Bucks; granted name and arms of Astell in lieu of name and arms of Hohler, by Royal Licence, 1978; *m* 1952, Jacqueline, *d* of late Marquis de Jouffroy d'Abbans, Chateau d'Abbans, Doubs, France; one *d. Educ:* Eton. 2nd Lieut SRO Grenadier Guards, 1939; Major 1944; served in: France; N Africa, 1942; Italy, 1943-44. Dir, Henry Sotheran Ltd; Chm., London Discount Market Assoc., 1972. Liveryman, Grocers' Co., 1956. *Recreations:* farming, shooting. *Address:* 59 Eaton Square, SW1W 9BG. *T:* 01-235 4751; Wolverton Park, Basingstoke, Hants. *T:* Kingsclere 298200. *Clubs:* Brooks's, City of London.
See also Earl of Erroll, H. A. F. Hohler.

ASTILL, Michael John; barrister; a Recorder of the Crown Court, since 1980; *b* 31 Jan. 1938; *s* of Cyril Norman Astill and Winifred Astill; *m* 1968, Jean Elizabeth, *d* of Dr J. C. H. Mackenzie; three *s* one *d. Educ:* Blackfriars School, Laxton, Northants. Admitted solicitor, 1962; called to the Bar, Middle Temple, 1972. *Recreations:* music, gardening, sport. *Address:* Colborough House, Halstead, Tilton-on-the-Hill, Leics. *T:* Tilton 608.

ASTLEY, family name of **Baron Hastings.**

ASTLEY, Sir Francis Jacob Dugdale, 6th Bt, *cr* 1821; Head of Classics Department, The Atlantic College, St Donat's Castle, Glamorgan, 1962-69, retired; *b* 26 Oct. 1908; *s* of Rev. Anthony Aylmer Astley (6th *s* of 2nd Bt); *S* kinsman 1943; *m* 1934, Brita Margareta Josefina Nyström, Stockholm; one *d. Educ:* Marlborough; Trinity Coll., Oxford. Sen. Lectr, University Coll. of Ghana, 1948-61. *Heir:* none. *Address:* 16 Doulton Mews, Lymington Road, NW6 1XY. *T:* 01-435 9945.

ASTON, Bishop Suffragan of, since 1982; **Rt. Rev. Michael Humphrey Dickens Whinney;** *b* 8 July 1930; *s* of late Humphrey Charles Dickens Whinney and Evelyn Lawrence Revell Whinney (*née* Low); great-great-grandson of Charles Dickens; *m* 1958, Veronica (*née* Webster); two *s* one *d. Educ:* Charterhouse; Pembroke Coll., Cambridge (BA 1955, MA 1958); Ridley Hall, Cambridge. National Service commission, RA, 1949 (served in 5th Regt, RHA and Surrey Yeo. Queen Mary's Regt). Articled clerk to Chartered Accountants, Whinney Smith & Whinney (now Ernst Whinney), 1950-52. Curate, Rainham Parish Church, Essex, 1957-60; Head, Cambridge University Mission Settlement, Bermondsey, 1960-67, Chaplain, 1967-72; Vicar, St James' with Christ Church, Bermondsey, 1967-73; Archdeacon and Borough Dean of Southwark, 1973-82. *Address:* 60 Handsworth Wood Road, Birmingham B20 2DT. *T:* 021-554 5129.

ASTON, Archdeacon of; *see* Cooper, Ven. J. L.

ASTON, Prof. Peter George, DPhil; Professor of Music since 1974, Dean, School of Fine Arts and Music, since 1981, University of East Anglia; *b* 5 Oct. 1938; *s* of late George William Aston and Elizabeth Oliver Smith; *m* 1960, Elaine Veronica Neale; one *s. Educ:* Tettenhall Coll.; Birmingham Sch. of Music (GBSM); Univ of York (DPhil); FTCL, ARCM. Lectr in Music, 1964-72, Sen. Lectr, 1972-74, Univ. of York. Dir, Tudor Consort, 1958-65; Conductor: English Baroque Ensemble, 1968-70; Aldeburgh Festival Singers, 1975-. Chm., Eastern Arts Assoc. Music Panel, 1976-81; Gen. Editor, UEA Recording Series, 1979-. FRSA 1980. *Compositions:* two song cycles, chamber music, choral and orchestral works, church music, opera. *Publications:* George Jeffreys and the English Baroque, 1970; The Music of York Minster, 1972; Sound and Silence (jtly), 1970, German edn 1972, Italian edn 1979; (ed) The Collected Works of George Jeffreys, 3 vols, 1977; contrib. to internat. music jls. *Recreations:* Association football, cricket, bridge, chess. *Address:* University of East Anglia, Music Centre, School of Fine Arts and Music, University Plain, Norwich NR4 7TJ. *T:* Norwich 56161. *Club:* Athenæum.

ASTON, Hon. Sir William (John), KCMG 1970; JP; Speaker, House of Representatives, Australia, 1967-73; MP for Phillip, 1955-61, 1963-72; Chairman, Kolotex Holdings Ltd; Director, Neilson McCarthy & Partners; *b* 19 Sept. 1916; *s* of Harold John Aston and Dorothea (*née* McKeown); *m* 1941, Beatrice Delaney Burrett; one *s* two *d. Educ:* Randwick Boys' High School. Mayor of Waverley, 1952-53. Dep. Govt Whip, 1959-61 and 1963-64; Chief Govt Whip, 1964-67; Trustee, Parlt Retiring Allowances, 1964-67; Mem. and Dep. Chm., Joint Select Cttee on New and Perm. Parlt House, 1965-72; Chairman: House of Reps Standing Orders Cttee, 1967-72; Joint House Cttee, 1967-72; Library Cttee, 1967-72; Joint Cttee on Broadcasting of Parly Proceedings, 1967-72; Jt Chm., Inter-Parliamentary Union (Commonwealth of Aust. Br.) and Commonwealth Parly Assoc. (Aust. Br.), 1967-72; Leader, Aust. Delegn to IPU Conf., Ottawa, 1964; Convenor and Chm., First Conf. of Aust. Presiding Officers, 1968; rep. Australia at: opening of Zambian Parlt Bldg; Funeral of Israeli Prime Minister Eshkol and IPU Symposium, Geneva, 1968; Conf. of Commonwealth Presiding Officers, Ottawa, 1969, New Delhi,

1971; opened Aust. House, Mt Scopus, Univ. of Israel, 1971; led Parly delegn to Turkey, Yugoslavia, UK and to Council of Europe, 1971. JP NSW 1954. Korean Order of Distinguished Service Merit (1st Class), 1969. *Recreations:* cricket, golf, football, fishing, bowls. *Address:* 55 Olola Avenue, Vaucluse, NSW 2030, Australia. *T:* 337-5992. *Clubs:* Royal Automobile of Australia (Sydney); Waverley Bowling.

ASTOR, family name of **Viscount Astor** and **Baron Astor of Hever.**

ASTOR, 4th Viscount, *cr* 1917, of Hever Castle; Baron *cr* 1916; **William Waldorf Astor;** *b* 27 Dec. 1951; *s* of 3rd Viscount Astor; *S* father 1966; *m* 1976, Annabel Sheffield, *d* of T. Jones; two *s* one *d. Educ:* Eton Coll. *Recreation:* shooting. *Heir:* *s* Hon. William Waldorf Astor, *b* 18 Jan. 1979. *Address:* Ginge Manor, Wantage, Oxon. *Clubs:* White's, Turf.

ASTOR OF HEVER, 2nd Baron *cr* 1956, of Hever Castle; **Gavin Astor;** Director, Alliance Assurance Co. Ltd, 1954; *b* 1 June 1918; *e s* of 1st Baron Astor of Hever, and Lady Violet Mary Elliot (*d* 1965), *y d* of 4th Earl of Minto, KG, PC, GCSI, GCMG, GCIE, and *widow* of Lord Charles Mercer Nairne, 2nd *s* of 5th Marquess of Lansdowne; *S* father, 1971; *m* 1945, Lady Irene Haig, *d* of late Field Marshal Earl Haig, KT, GCB, OM, GCVO, KCIE; two *s* three *d. Educ:* Eton; New Coll., Oxford. Served with The Life Guards, 1940-46. Director: C. Townsend Hook Ltd, 1954-65; Reuters Ltd, 1955-61; Electrolux Ltd, 1959-70; Monotype Corp. Ltd, 1952-73; Chm., The Times Publishing Co. Ltd, 1959-66 (Dir, 1952-66); Co-Chief Proprietor of The Times, 1964-66; Pres., Times Newspapers Ltd, 1967-81; Dir, Times Newspapers Holdings Ltd, 1981-. Commonwealth Press Union: Chm. Council, 1959-72; Pres., 1972-81; Hon. Life Mem., 1981; Chairman: 9th Commonwealth Press Conf., India and Pakistan, 1961; 10th Conf., West Indies, 1965; 11th Conf., UK, 1970; 12th Conf., SE Asia, 1974; 13th Conf., Canada, 1978; Exec. Cttee, Pilgrims Soc. of Gt Britain, 1967-77 (Pres., 1977-82); Central Council, Royal Commonwealth Soc., 1972-75. President: Kent Magistrates Assoc.; Kent County Cttee, TAVR Assoc.; Kent Cttee, Army Benevolent Fund; Kent Branch, Country Landowners' Assoc.; Kent Voluntary Service Council; Kent Assoc. of Youth Clubs; Council of Order of St John for Kent; Nat. Vice Pres., Royal British Legion (Pres., Kent Council). Master of Guild of St Bride's Ch., Fleet St, 1970-78. Seneschal of Canterbury Cathedral, 1973-82. Mem. Ct of Assts, Goldsmiths' Company, 1973- (Prime Warden, 1981-82). High Sheriff 1955-56, DL 1956-62, Sussex; DL 1966, JP 1973, Lord-Lieutenant and Custos Rotulorum, 1972-82, Kent. FRSA 1965. KStJ 1974. *Heir:* *s* Hon. John Jacob Astor [*b* 16 June 1946; *m* 1970, Fiona Diana, *d* of Captain R. E. L. Harvey; three *d*]. *Address:* Tillypronie, Tarland, Aberdeenshire. *T:* Tarland 238. *Club:* White's.
See also Hon. H. W. and Hon. John Astor, Marquess of Lansdowne.

ASTOR, Hon. (Francis) David (Langhorne); Editor of The Observer, 1948-75; Director, The Observer, 1976-81; *b* 5 March 1912; *s* of 2nd Viscount Astor and Nancy, Viscountess Astor, CH, MP (*d* 1964); *m* 1st, 1945, Melanie Hauser; one *d* ; 2nd, 1952, Bridget Aphra Wreford; two *s* three *d. Educ:* Eton; Balliol, Oxford. Yorkshire Post, 1936. Served War of 1939-45, with Royal Marines, 1940-45. Foreign Editor of the Observer, 1946-48. Croix de Guerre, 1944. *Publication:* (with V. Yorke) Peace in the Middle East: super powers and security guarantees, 1978. *Address:* 9 Cavendish Avenue, St John's Wood, NW8 9JD. *T:* 01-286 0223; Manor House, Sutton Courtenay, Oxon. *T:* Sutton Courtenay 221. *Clubs:* Athenæum, Boodle's.

ASTOR, Hon. Hugh Waldorf, JP; Director: Hambro's Bank; Phœnix Assurance; Winterbottom Trust Ltd; *b* 20 Nov. 1920; *2nd s* of 1st Baron Astor of Hever; *m* 1950, Emily Lucy, *d* of Sir Alexander Kinloch, 12th Bt, *qv* ; two *s* three *d. Educ:* Eton; New Coll., Oxford. Served War of 1939-45; Intelligence Corps, Europe and SE Asia (Lieut-Col). Joined The Times as Asst Middle East Correspondent, 1947; elected to Board of The Times, 1956; Dep. Chm., 1959, resigned 1967 on merger with Sunday Times; Chm., The Times Book Co. Ltd, 1960, resigned 1967 on merger with Sunday Times. Chairman: Times Trust, 1967; Trust Houses Forte Council, 1971 (Mem. Council, 1962); Dep. Chm., Olympia Ltd, 1971-73. Dep. Chm., Middlesex Hosp., 1965-74; Governor: Bradfield Coll.; Peabody Trust (Chm., Peabody Donation Fund, 1981); Hon. Treasurer: Franco-British Soc., 1969-76; Marine Biol Assoc. UK, 1968-78; has served on Council or governing body of: RNLI; RYA; RORC; Air League. Mem. Ct of Assts, Fishmongers' Co. (Prime Warden, 1976-77). In partnership with Sir William Dugdale participated in air races, London-Sydney 1969, London-Victoria 1971. JP Berks, 1963; High Sheriff of Berks, 1963. *Recreations:* sailing, flying, shooting, diving. *Address:* Folly Farm, Sulhamstead, Berks. *T:* Reading 302326; 14 Culross Street, W1. *T:* 01-629 4601. *Clubs:* Brooks's, Buck's, Pratt's; Royal Yacht Squadron, Royal Ocean Racing.
See also Baron Astor of Hever, Hon. John Astor.

ASTOR, Hon. John; a Director, TPC (Investments) Ltd; *b* 26 Sept. 1923; *3rd s* of 1st Baron Astor of Hever; *m* 1950, Diana Kathleen Drummond; two *s* one *d. Educ:* Summerfields, Hastings; Eton Coll. RAFVR, 1942-45. Berkshire County Council, 1953-74; Alderman, 1960; Chairman, Education Cttee, 1961-66. Vice-Chm., South Berkshire Conservative Assoc., 1958 until 1963, when adopted as candidate. MP (C) Newbury, 1964-Feb. 1974. *Recreations:* fishing, shooting. *Address:* Kirby House, Inkpen, Berks. *T:* Inkpen 284. *Clubs:* Buck's; Royal Yacht Squadron.
See also Baron Astor of Hever, Hon. H. W. Astor.

ASTOR, Major Hon. Sir John (Jacob), Kt 1978; MBE 1945; DL; Major, Life Guards; *b* 29 Aug. 1918; 4th *s* of 2nd Viscount Astor; *m* 1st, 1944, Ana Inez (marr. diss. 1972), *yr d* of Señor Dr Don Miguel Carcano, KCMG, KBE; one *s* one *d*; 2nd, 1976, Susan Sheppard, *d* of Major M. Eveleigh. *Educ:* Eton; New Coll., Oxford. Served War of 1939–45 (MBE, Legion of Honour, French Croix de Guerre). Contested (C) Sutton Div. of Plymouth, 1950; MP (C) Sutton Div. of Plymouth, 1951–Sept. 1959. PPS to Financial Sec. of Treasury, 1951–52. Chairman: Governing Body of Nat. Inst. of Agricultural Engineering, 1963–68; Agric. Res. Council, 1968–78; NEDC for Agricultural Industry, 1978–. Member: Horserace Totalisator Bd, 1962–68; Horserace Betting Levy Bd, 1976–80. Steward of Jockey Club, 1968–71. DL 1962, JP, Cambs, 1960–74. *Address:* Hatley Park, Hatley St George, Sandy, Beds. *T:* Gamlingay 50266. *Clubs:* White's, Royal Automobile.

ASTWOOD, Hon. Sir James (Rufus), Kt 1982; JP; **Hon. Mr Justice Astwood;** Chief Justice of Bermuda, since 1977; *b* 4 Oct. 1923; *s* of James Rufus Astwood, Sr, and late Mabel Winifred Astwood; *m* 1952, Gloria Preston Norton; one *s* two *d*. *Educ:* Berkeley Inst., Bermuda; Univ. of Toronto, Canada. Called to the Bar, Gray's Inn, London, Feb. 1956; admitted to practice at Jamaican Bar, Oct. 1956; joined Jamaican Legal Service, 1957; Dep. Clerk of Courts, 1957–58; Clerk of Courts, Jamaica, 1958–63; Stipendiary Magistrate and Judge of Grand Court, Cayman Islands (on secondment from Jamaica), 1958–59; Resident Magistrate, Jamaica, 1963–74; Puisne Judge, Jamaica, during 1971 and 1973; retd from Jamaican Legal Service, 1974. Sen. Magistrate, Bermuda, 1974–76; Solicitor General, 1976–77; Acting Attorney General, during 1976 and 1977; Acting Dep. Governor for a period in 1977. Has served on several cttees, tribunals and bds of enquiry, both in Bermuda and Jamaica. *Recreations:* golf, cricket, photography, reading, bridge, travel, cycling. *Address:* (home) Clifton, Middle Road, Devonshire, Bermuda; (office) Chief Justice's Chambers, Supreme Court, Bermuda. *Clubs:* Kingston Cricket (Kingston, Jamaica); Castle Harbour Golf, Royal Hamilton Amateur Dinghy, Coral Beach and Tennis (Bermuda).

ASTWOOD, Lt-Col Sir Jeffrey (Carlton), Kt 1972; CBE 1966; OBE (mil.) 1946; ED 1942; Speaker of House of Assembly, Bermuda, 1968–72, retired; *b* 5 Oct. 1907; *s* of late Jeffrey Burgess Astwood, Neston, Bermuda, and Lilian Maude (*née* Searles); *m* 1928, Hilda Elizabeth Kay (*née* Onions); one *s* one *d*. *Educ:* Saltus Grammar School, Bermuda. Served local TA, 1922–60; retired as Lt-Col, having commanded since 1943. House of Assembly, Bermuda, 1948–72; Minister of Agriculture, of Immigration and Labour, of Health; Member of Exec. Council; Dep. Speaker, 1957–68. Pres., Exec. Cttee, Sandys Grammar Sch., 1950–57 (Chm. Trustees, 1950–); Chm., St James' Church Vestry. President: Atlantic Investment and Development Co. Ltd; J. B. Astwood & Son Ltd; Belfield-in-Somerset Ltd; Brewer Distributors Ltd; Aberfeldy Nurseries Ltd. *Recreations:* theatre, horticulture. *Address:* Greenfield, Somerset, Bermuda. *T:* (business) Hamilton 1.1283; (home) Somerset 4.1729. 4.8180. *Clubs:* No 10; Royal Bermuda Yacht, Sandys Boat.

ATCHERLEY, Sir Harold Winter, Kt 1977; Chairman: Police Negotiating Board, since 1982 (Deputy Chairman, 1982); Tyzack & Partners, since 1979; Member, Top Salaries Review Body, since 1971; *b* 30 Aug. 1918; *s* of L. W. Atcherley and Maude Lester (*née* Nash); *m* 1946, Anita Helen (*née* Leslie) (legal separation, 1978), *widow* of Sub Lt W. D. H. Eves, RN; one *s* two *d*. *Educ:* Gresham's Sch.; Heidelberg and Geneva Univs. Joined Royal Dutch Shell Gp, 1937. Served War: Queen's Westminster Rifles, 1939; commissioned Intelligence Corps, 1940; served 18th Infty Div., Singapore; PoW, 1942–45. Rejoined Royal Dutch Shell Gp, 1946: served Egypt, Lebanon, Syria, Argentina, Brazil, 1946–59. Personnel Co-ordinator, Royal Dutch Shell Group, 1964–70, retd. Recruitment Advisor to Ministry of Defence, 1970–71. Dir, British Home Stores Ltd, 1973–. Chm., Armed Forces Pay Review Body, 1971–82; Member: Nat. Staff Cttee for Nurses and Midwives, 1973–77; Cttee of Inquiry into Remuneration of Members of Local Authorities, 1977. Mem., Management Cttee, Toynbee Hall, 1979–. Empress Leopoldina Medal (Brazil), 1958. *Recreations:* music, skiing, good food. *Address:* Conduit House, The Green, Long Melford, Suffolk. *T:* Sudbury 310897.

ATHA, Bernard Peter; Principal Lecturer in Business Studies, Huddersfield Technical College, since 1973; *b* 27 Aug. 1928; *s* of Horace Michael Atha and Mary Quinlan; unmarried. *Educ:* Leeds Modern Sch.; Leeds Univ. (LLB Hons). Barrister-at-law, Gray's Inn. Commn, RAF, 1950-52. Variety artist on stage; Mem. Equity; films incl. Kes, and Family Life; TV plays. Elected Leeds City Council, 1957; Chm., Watch Cttee and Leisure Services Cttee; Chm., Leeds Educn Cttee. Parly Candidate (Lab) Penrith and the Border, 1959, Pudsey, 1964. Pres., Leeds Coop. Soc.; Director: Leeds Grand Theatre and Leeds Playhouse; English Opera North. Member: Ministerial Working Party on Sport and Recreation, 1974; Arts Council, 1979–82; Chm., Yorks and Humberside Reg. Sports Council, 1966–81; Vice-Chm., Sports Council, 1976–80; Chairman: Nat. Water Sports Centre; UK Sports Assoc. for People with Mental Handicap. Governor, Sports Aid Foundn. FRSA. *Recreations:* dilettante involvement in variety of sports; music, ballet, travel. *Address:* 25 Moseley Wood Croft, Leeds 16, West Yorks. *T:* Leeds 672485.

ATHABASCA, Bishop of, since 1975; **Rt. Rev. Frederick Hugh Wright Crabb,** DD; Metropolitan of Rupert's Land, 1977–82; *b* Luppitt, Devon, 24 April 1915; *s* of William Samuel and Florence Mary Crabb; *m* 1946, Alice Margery Coombs; two *s* two *d*. *Educ:* Luppitt Parochial Sch.; Univ. of London (St John's Hall, Highbury, London). BD Lond. (1st Cl. Hons); ALCD

(1st Cl. Hons). Asst Curate, St James', West Teignmouth, Devon, 1939-4 Asst Priest, St Andrew's, Plymouth, 1941-42; Missionary at Akot, S Suda 1942-44; Principal, Bishop Gwynne Divinity Sch., S Sudan, 1944-51; Vic Principal, London Coll. of Divinity, 1951-57; Principal, Coll. of Emmanue and St Chad, Saskatoon, Sask., 1957-67; Assoc. Priest, Christ Church, Calgar Alberta, 1967-69; Rector, St Stephen's Church, Calgary, 1969-75. Men Governing Council, Athabasca Univ., 1982-. Hon. DD: Wycliffe Col Toronto, 1960; St Andrew's Coll., Saskatoon, 1967; Coll. of Emmanuel an St Chad, Saskatoon, 1979. *Recreations:* gardening, mountain hiking. *Addre* Box 279, Peace River, Alberta T0H 2X0, Canada. *T:* 1-403-624-2419.

ATHAIDE, Most Rev. D. R.; *see* Agra, Archbishop of, (RC).

ATHERTON, Alan Royle; Controller, PSA Supplies, Department of th Environment, since 1981; *b* 25 April 1931; *s* of Harold Atherton and Hild (*née* Royle); *m* 1959, Valerie Kemp; three *s* one *d*. *Educ:* Cowley Sch., S Helens; Sheffield Univ. (BSc (Hons Chem.)). ICI Ltd, 1955-58; DSIR: Sen Scientific Officer, 1959-64, Private Sec. to Permanent Sec., 1960-64; Principa Sci. Officer, Road Res. Lab., 1964-65; Principal, Min. of Housing and Loca Govt, 1965-70; Asst Sec., Ordnance Survey, 1970-74; Under-Sec., DoE, 1975- *Recreation:* walking. *Address:* Riverside, East Mill, Fordingbridge, Hants SP 2JS. *T:* Fordingbridge 52231. *Club:* Royal Commonwealth Society.

ATHERTON, David; Music Director, San Diego Symphony Orchestra, since 1980; Principal Guest Conductor, from Sept. 1983, Royal Liverpoo Philharmonic Orchestra (Principal Conductor and Artistic Adviser, 198C Aug. 1983); Artistic Director and Conductor, London Stravinsky Festiva since 1979, performing complete works of Stravinsky; *b* 3 Jan. 1944; *s* o Robert and Lavinia Atherton; *m* 1970, Ann Gianetta Drake; one *s* two *o Educ:* Cambridge Univ. (MA). LRAM, LTCL. Repetiteur, Royal Oper House, Covent Garden, 1967-68; Founder and Musical Dir, Londo Sinfonietta, 1967-73; Resident Conductor, Royal Opera House, 1968-79 Became youngest conductor in history of Henry Wood Promenade Concer at Royal Albert Hall, and also at Royal Opera House, 1968; Royal Festiva Hall debut, 1969; from 1970 performances in Europe, Middle East, Far Eas Australasia, N America. Adapted and arranged Pandora by Roberto Gerhar for Royal Ballet, 1975. Conductor of the year award (Composers' Guild o GB), 1971; Edison award, 1973; Grand Prix du Disque award, 197 Koussevitzky Award, 1981. *Publications:* (ed) The Complete Instrumental an Chamber Music of Arnold Schoenberg and Roberto Gerhard, 1973; (ec Pandora and Don Quixote Suites by Roberto Gerhard, 1973; contrib., Tl Musical Companion, 1978, The New Grove Dictionary, 1981. *Recreation* travel, squash, theatre. *Address:* c/o Harold Holt Ltd, 31 Sinclair Road, W1 0NS.

ATHOLL, 10th Duke of, *cr* 1703; **George Iain Murray;** DL; Lord Murra of Tullibardine, 1604; Earl of Tullibardine, Lord Gask and Balquhidder, 160€ Earl of Atholl, 1629; Marquess of Atholl, Viscount Balquhidder, Lor Balvenie, 1676; Marquess of Tullibardine, Earl of Strathtay, Earl c Strathardle, Viscount Glenalmond, Viscount Glenlyon, 1703—all in th peerage of Scotland; Representative Peer for Scotland in the House of Lord 1958-63; *b* 19 June 1931; *s* of Lieut-Col George Anthony Murray, OBE Scottish Horse (killed in action, Italy, 1945), and Hon. Mrs Angela Campbel Preston, (*d* 1981), *d* of 2nd Viscount Cowdray (she *m* 2nd, 1950, Robei Campbell-Preston of Ardchattan, *qv*); *S* kinsman 1957. *Educ:* Eton; Chri Church, Oxford. Director: Westminster Press (Chm., 1974-); BPM Holding Pearson Longman Ltd, 1975-. Convener, Scottish Landowners Fedn, 1976-7 (Vice-Convener, 1971-76); Chm., RNLI, 1979- (Dep. Chm., 1972-79 Member: Cttee on the Preparation of Legislation, 1973-75; Exec. Cttee, Na Trust for Scotland (Vice-Pres., 1977-); Red Deer Commn. DL Perth an Kinross, 1980. *Heir:* cousin Arthur Stewart Pakington Murray, *b* 9 Sept. 189¢ *Address:* Blair Castle, Blair Atholl, Perthshire. *T:* Blair Atholl 212; 3 Marlborough Hill, NW8. *Clubs:* Turf, White's; New (Edinburgh).

ATIYAH, Michael Francis, MA, PhD Cantab; FRS 1962; Royal Societ Research Professor, Mathematical Institute, Oxford, and Professorial Fellov of St Catherine's College, Oxford, since 1973; *b* 22 April 1929; *e s* of lat Edward Atiyah and Jean Levens; *m* 1955, Lily Brown; three *s*. *Educ:* Victori Coll., Egypt; Manchester Grammar Sch.; Trinity Coll., Cambridge. Researc Fellow, Trinity Coll., Camb., 1954-58, Hon. Fellow, 1976; First Smith's Prize 1954; Commonwealth Fund Fellow, 1955-56; Mem. Inst. for Advanced Study Princeton, 1955-56, 1959-60, 1967-68; Asst Lectr in Mathematics, 1957-58 Lectr 1958-61, Univ. of Cambridge; Fellow Pembroke Coll., Cambridge 1958-61; Reader in Mathematics, Univ. of Oxford, and Professorial Fellov of St Catherine's Coll., Oxford, 1961-63; Savilian Prof. of Geometry, an Fellow of New College, Oxford, 1963-69; Prof. of Mathematics, Inst. fc Advanced Study, Princeton, NJ, 1969-72. Visiting Lecturer, Harvard, 1962-6 and 1964-65. Mem. Exec. Cttee, Internat. Mathematical Union, 1966-74 President: London Mathematical Soc., 1975-77; Mathematical Assoc., 1981-82 Foreign Member: Amer. Acad. of Arts and Scis; Swedish Royal Acad Leopoldina Acad.; Nat. Acad. of Scis, USA; Acad. des Sciences, France; Roya Irish Acad. Hon. DSc: Bonn; Warwick, Durham, St Andrew's, Dublin. Field Medal, Internat. Congress of Mathematicians, Moscow, 1966; Royal Meda Royal Soc., 1968; De Morgan Medal, London Mathematical Soc., 198C Antonio Feltrinelli Prize for mathematical sciences, Accademia Nazionale d Lincei, Rome, 1981. *Publications:* papers in mathematical journals *Recreation:* gardening. *Address:* Mathematical Institute, 24-29 St Gile Oxford OX1 3LB. *T:* Oxford 54295; Shotover Mound, Headington, Oxfor

T: Oxford 62359.
See also P. S. Atiyah.

ATIYAH, Prof. Patrick Selim, DCL; FBA 1978; Professor of English Law, Oxford University, since 1977; *b* 5 March 1931; *s* of Edward Atiyah and D. J. C. Levens; *m* 1951, Christine Best; four *s. Educ:* Woking County Grammar Sch. for Boys; Magdalen Coll., Oxford (MA 1957, DCL 1974). Called to the Bar, Inner Temple, 1956. Asst Lectr, LSE, 1954-55; Lectr, Univ. of Khartoum, 1955-59; Legal Asst, BoT, 1961-64; Fellow, New Coll., Oxford, 1964-69; Professor of Law: ANU, 1970-73; Warwick Univ., 1973-77; Visiting Prof., Univ of Texas, 1979; Lionel Cohen Lectr, Hebrew Univ., Jerusalem, 1980; Oliver Wendell Holmes Lectr, Harvard Law Sch., 1981. General Editor, Oxford Jl of Legal Studies. *Publications:* The Sale of Goods, 1957 (6th edn 1980); Introduction to the Law of Contract, 1961 (3rd edn 1981); Vicarious Liability, 1967; Accidents, Compensation and the Law, 1970 (3rd edn 1980); The Rise and Fall of Freedom of Contract, 1979; Promises, Morals and Law, 1981; articles in legal jls. *Recreations:* gardening, cooking. *Address:* St John's College, Oxford; The Old Rectory, Middleton Stoney, Oxon. *T:* Middleton Stoney 317.
See also M. F. Atiyah.

ATKIN, Alec Field, CBE 1978; FEng, FIMechE, FRAeS; Managing Director, Marketing, Aircraft Group, British Aerospace, since 1981; *b* 26 April 1925; *s* of Alec and Grace Atkin; *m* 1948, Nora Helen Darby (marr. diss. 1982); two *s* one *d. Educ:* Riley High Sch.; Hull Technical Coll. (DipAe); Hull Univ. (BSc Hons). FIMechE 1955; FRAeS 1952. English Electric Co., Preston: Aerodynamicist, 1950; Dep. Chief Aerodyn., 1954; Head of Exper. Aerodyns, 1957; Asst Chief Engr, then Proj. Manager, 1959; Warton Div., British Aircraft Corporation Ltd: Special Dir, 1964; Dir, 1970; Asst Man. Dir, 1973-75; Dep. Man. Dir, 1975-76; Man. Dir, 1976-77; Man. Dir (Mil.), Aircraft Gp of British Aerospace, and Chm., Warton, Kingston-Brough and Manchester Divs, 1978-81. FRSA. *Recreation:* sailing. *Address:* Grange Cottage, 19 London Road, Holybourne, Alton, Hants. *T:* Alton 82113; British Aerospace, Richmond Road, Kingston, Surrey. *T:* 01-546 7741. *Clubs:* Royal Automobile; Ribble Cruising (Lytham, Lancs).

ATKINS, Prof. Sir Hedley (John Barnard), KBE 1967; DM, MCh, FRCS, FRCP; Emeritus Professor of Surgery, University of London; formerly Director of the Department of Surgery, Guy's Hospital; *b* 30 Dec. 1905; *s* of Col Sir John Atkins, KCMG, KCVO, FRCS; *m* 1933, Gladwys Gwendolen, *e d* of Frank Harding Jones; two *s. Educ:* Rugby; Trinity Coll., Oxford; Guy's Hospital. War of 1939-45 (despatches): Temp. Lieut-Col RAMC, 1941. Surgeon to Guy's Hosp., 1936; Hunterian Professor, RCS, 1936; Examiner in Surgery at: Cambridge Univ., 1947; London Univ., 1948; Durham Univ., 1950; Univ. of The W Indies 1960; Member: Court of Examiners, RCS, 1950, Council, 1952; Gen. Dental Council, 1954; Gen. Medical Council, 1955; Central Health Services Council, 1956; Dean of the Institute of Basic Med. Sciences, 1957-62; Clinical Research Bd. Med. Research Council, 1959; Pres. Surgical Research Soc., 1960. Visiting Professor: Johns Hopkins Hosp., 1947; UCLA, 1954; Univ. of California, 1956; Univ. of Miami, 1972; Sims Commonwealth Travelling Prof., 1961. Lectures: Syme Oration, Brisbane, 1961; Bradshaw, RCS, 1965; Astor, Middlesex Hosp., 1970; Cavendish, W London Med. Chir. Soc., 1970; Gideon de Laune, Soc. of Apothecaries, 1970; Hunterian Orator, RCS, 1971; Macewen, Glasgow, 1972; First Leah Lederman, RSM, 1973; Purvis Oration, 1975. Mem. Med. Advisory Cttee of British Council, 1962; Chm., MRC working party, on Tristan da Cunha, 1962; Mem. Med. Consultative Cttee of Nuffield Provincial Hosps Trust, 1962; Chm., Med. Res. Council Cttee on Uses of High Oxygen Tension, 1963, and on Gastric Hypothermia, 1963; Mem., Med. Research Council, 1963; Thomas Vicary Lecturer, Royal Coll. of Surgeons, 1964; Examr in Surgery, at Birmingham Univ., 1964; Vice-Chm., Standing Med. Adv. Cttee (of Central Health Services Council), 1964; Chairman: (MRC) Cttee on Endolymphatic Therapy, 1965; Jt Bd, Clinical Nursing Studies, 1969-; Med. Bd, St John, 1969. Chm. Council, Queen Elizabeth Coll., Univ. of London, 1969-. President: Med. Soc. of London, 1972; RSM, 1971-72 (Hon. Fellow, 1974; Pres., Section of Measurement in Medicine, 1965); RCS, 1966-69 (Vice-Pres. 1964-66). Governor, Strangeways Research Laboratory, Cambridge, 1968. Hon. FACS, 1956; Hon. FRACS, 1961; Hon. FCS (So. Af.), 1968; Hon. FRCS Glas., 1971; Hon. FRCP&S (Can.) 1969; Hon. FDSRCS 1972; Hon. Fellow: Trinity Coll., Oxford, 1968; Queen Elizabeth Coll., Univ. of London, 1968; Assoc. of Surgeons of GB and Ireland, 1973; American Surgical Assoc., 1966; New England Surgical Soc. Thomas and Edith Dixon Medal, 1965. Hon. DSc: East Anglia, 1968; Kent, 1971. KStJ 1968. *Publications:* After-Treatment, 1942; (author of Biographical introduction) Hilton's Rest and Pain, 1950; (ed) Tools of Biological Research, 1959; The Surgeon's Craft, 1965; Down, the Home of the Darwins, 1974; Memoirs of a Surgeon, 1977; numerous articles in med. jls. *Recreation:* gardening. *Address:* Down House, Downe, Kent BR6 7JT. *Clubs:* Athenæum; Vincent's (Oxford), Harlequins.

ATKINS, Henry St J., DSc; President, University College, Cork, 1954-63, retired; *b* 19 March 1896; *s* of Patrick Atkins and Agnes Egan, Cork; *m* 1929, Agnes E. O'Regan (*d* 1960), MB, BCh; one *s* one *d. Educ:* Christian Brothers, North Monastery, Cork; University Coll., Cork. BSc (Math. Science) 1915; post-grad. scholar, MSc 1923. Prof. of Pure Maths, University Coll., Cork, 1936-54; Registrar, 1943-54. Hon. DSc 1955. MRIA, 1957. *Recreations:* golf, fishing. *Address:* Knockrea Park, Cork. *T:* Cork 32448. *Clubs:* National University of Ireland; Cork City and County (Cork).

ATKINS, Rt. Hon. Humphrey Edward Gregory, PC 1973; MP (C) Spelthorne since 1970 (Merton and Morden, Surrey, 1955-70); *b* 12 Aug. 1922; *s* of late Capt. E. D. Atkins, Nyeri, Kenya Colony; *m* 1944, Margaret, *d* of Sir Robert Spencer-Nairn, 1st Bt; one *s* three *d. Educ:* Wellington Coll. Special entry cadetship, RN, 1940; Lieut RN, 1943; resigned, 1948. PPS to Civil Lord of the Admiralty, 1959-62; Hon.. Sec. Conservative Parly Defence Cttee, 1965-67; Opposition Whip, 1967-70; Treasurer of HM Household and Dep. Chief Whip, 1970-73; Parly Sec. to the Treasury and Govt Chief Whip, 1973-74; Opposition Chief Whip, 1974-79; Secretary of State for N Ireland, 1979-81; Lord Privy Seal, 1981-82. Underwriting Mem. of Lloyd's. Vice-Chm., Management Cttee, Outward Bound Trust, 1966-70. *Address:* House of Commons, SW1. *Club:* Brooks's.

ATKINS, John Spencer, DSO 1945; TD; DL; President, Atkins Brothers (Hosiery) Ltd; *b* 28 Oct. 1905; 3rd *s* of late Col E. C. Atkins, CB, DL; *m* 1936, Monica Lucy Standish; one *s* two *d. Educ:* Uppingham Sch. DL Leics 1946. *Address:* White House, Ullesthorpe, Lutterworth, Leics. *T:* Leire 209274. *Club:* Naval and Military.

ATKINS, Leonard B. W.; *see* Walsh Atkins.

ATKINS, Robert James; MP (C) Preston North, since 1979; *b* 5 Feb. 1946; *s* of late Reginald Alfred and of Winifred Margaret Atkins; *m* 1969, Dulcie Mary (*née* Chaplin); one *s* one *d. Educ:* Highgate School. Councillor, London Borough of Haringey, 1968-77; Vice-Chm., Greater London Young Conservatives, 1969-70, 1971-72. Contested (C) Luton West, Feb. 1974 and Oct. 1974 general elections. Jt Sec., Cons. Defence and Aviation Cttees; Vice-Pres., Cons. Trade Unionists. *Recreations:* wine, old churches, cricket. *Address:* 29c Haringey Park, Hornsey, N8 9JD. *T:* 01-348 5316. *Clubs:* Middlesex County Cricket, Lords and Commons Cricket.

ATKINS, Ronald Henry; *b* Barry, Glam, 13 June 1916; *s* of Frank and Elizabeth Atkins; *m* ; three *s* two *d. Educ:* Barry County Sch.; London Univ. (BA Hons). Teacher, 1949-66 (latterly Head, Eng. Dept, Halstead Sec. Sch.); Lectr, Accrington Coll. of Further Educn, 1970-74. Member: Braintree RDC, 1952-61; Preston Dist Council, 1974-76, 1980-. Contested (Lab) Lowestoft, 1964; MP (Lab) Preston North, 1966-70 and Feb. 1974-1979. *Recreations:* jazz, dancing, walking. *Address:* 38 James Street, Preston, Lancs. *T:* Preston 51910.

ATKINS, Sir William Sydney Albert, Kt 1976; CBE 1966; FEng, FICE, FIStructE; Chairman: W. S. Atkins & Partners, since 1951; W. S. Atkins & Partners (Ethiopia) Ltd, since 1963; W. S. Atkins Group Ltd, since 1971; W. S. Atkins & Associates Pty Ltd, since 1971; W. S. Atkins (Overseas Projects) Ltd, since 1973; W. S. Atkins International, since 1973; W. S. Atkins Group Consultants, 1975-78; Sir William Atkins & Partners, since 1977; *b* 6 Feb. 1902; 2nd *s* of Robert Edward and Martha Atkins; *m* 1928, Elsie Jessie, *d* of Edward and Hilda Barrow, Hockley, Essex; two *d. Educ:* Coopers' Sch.; London Univ. (BSc). Chief Engr, Smith Walker Ltd, 1928; Founder and Man. Dir, London Ferro-Concrete Co. Ltd, 1935, Chm. 1937; Founder and Chm., R. E. Eagan Ltd, 1945; Founder and Sen. Partner, W. S. Atkins & Partners, 1938; Founder and Partner, Round Pond Nurseries, 1943. Member, London Chamber of Commerce. Fellow, UCL. CInstMC; Hon. FInstW. Hon. Freeman, Borough of Epsom and Ewell. *Publications:* many technical papers. *Recreations:* gardening and horticultural research, swimming. *Address:* Chobham Place, Chobham, near Woking, Surrey GU24 8TN. *T:* Chobham 8867.

ATKINSON, Sir Alec; *see* Atkinson, Sir J. A.

ATKINSON, Prof. Anthony Barnes; Professor of Economics, London School of Economics and Political Science, since Jan. 1980; *b* 4 Sept. 1944; *s* of Norman Joseph Atkinson and Esther Muriel Atkinson; *m* 1965, Judith Mary (*née* Mandeville); two *s* one *d. Educ:* Cranbrook Sch.; Churchill Coll., Cambridge (MA). Fellow, St John's Coll., Cambridge, 1967-71; Prof. of Econs, Univ. of Essex, 1971-76; Prof. and Hd of Dept of Political Economy, UCL, 1976-79. Vis. Prof. MIT, 1973. Mem., Royal Commn on Distribution of Income and Wealth, 1978-79. Fellow, Econometric Soc., 1975. Editor, Jl of Public Economics, 1972-. *Publications:* Poverty in Britain and the Reform of Social Security, 1969; Unequal Shares, 1972; The Tax Credit Scheme, 1973; Economics of Inequality, 1975; (with A. J. Harrison) Distribution of Personal Wealth in Britain, 1978; (with J. E. Stiglitz) Lectures on Public Economics, 1980; Social Justice and Public Policy, 1982; articles in Rev. of Econ. Studies, Econ. Jl, Jl of Public Econs, Jl of Econ. Theory. *Address:* 33 Hurst Green, Brightlingsea, Colchester, Essex. *T:* Colchester 302253.

ATKINSON, Arthur Kingsley Hall; Chief Executive, Intervention Board for Agricultural Produce, since 1980; *b* 24 Dec. 1926; *er s* of Arthur Hall Atkinson and Florence (*née* Gerrans). *Educ:* Priory Sch., Shrewsbury; Emmanuel Coll., Cambridge (MA). RAF, 1948; MAFF: Asst Principal 1950; Private Sec. 1953; Principal 1956; Asst Sec. 1965; Under Sec., 1973; Cabinet Office, 1976-78; MAFF, 1978-80. *Recreations:* travel, music, gardening. *Address:* Massey's Pightle, Woodcote, Oxon RG8 0PH. *T:* Checkendon 680344.

ATKINSON, Brooks; *see* Atkinson, J. B.

ATKINSON, Colin Ronald Michael; Headmaster, Millfield School, Somerset, since 1971 (Acting Headmaster, 1969-70), Governor since 1977; *b* 23 July 1931; *s* of R. and E. Atkinson; *m* 1957, Shirley Angus; two *s* one *d*. *Educ:* Hummersknott, Darlington, Co. Durham; Durham Univ. (BA); Queen's Univ., Belfast (BA); Loughborough Coll. of Educn; MEd, Univ. of Bath, 1977. Served 5th Fusiliers (Northumberland) in Kenya, 1954-56. The Friends' School, Great Ayton, 1956-58; Haughton School, Darlington, 1958-60; Millfield, 1960-. West of England Hockey and Chief Divl coach, 1965-69; Founder and former Mem.: Nat. Hockey Coaching Cttee; Nat. Cricket Coaching Cttee, 1967-71; Chm., Phys. Educn Cttee of Schools Council, 1974-79; former Minister for Sport and Recreation's Nominee for SW Council for Sport and Recreation. Director: McArthur Steel Export Co.; HTV Ltd; Hillside Prop. Co.; Hon. Dir, Millfield Enterprises Ltd. Chm., Edington Sch., Somerset. President: Somerset CCC; Somerset Schools Cricket Assoc. *Publications:* An Experiment in Closed Circuit TV at Millfield School, 1970; various articles. *Recreations:* County Representation in five sports; Captain Somerset CCC XI, 1965-67 and County Hockey XI, 1963-65. *Address:* Millfield School, Street, Somerset. *T:* Street 42291. *Clubs:* East India, MCC, Free Foresters, I Zingari.

ATKINSON, David Anthony; MP (C) Bournemouth East, since Nov. 1977; *b* 24 March 1940; *s* of late Arthur Joseph Atkinson and of Joan Margaret Atkinson (*née* Zink); *m* 1968, Susan Nicola Pilsworth; one *s* one *d*. *Educ:* St George's Coll., Weybridge; Coll. of Automobile and Aeronautical Engrg, Chelsea. Diplomas in Auto. Engrg and Motor Industry Management. Member: Southend County Borough Council, 1969-72; Essex CC, 1973-78. Mem., Council of Europe, 1979-. PPS to Rt Hon. Paul Channon, MP (Minister of State, Civil Service Dept, 1979-81, Minister for the Arts, 1981-). Chm., Young Conservative Orgn, 1970-71. *Recreations:* mountaineering, art and architecture, travel. *Address:* House of Commons, SW1.

ATKINSON, Air Marshal Sir David William, KBE 1982; FFCM; QHP 1977; Director-General, RAF Medical Services, since 1981; *b* 29 Sept. 1924; *s* of late David William Atkinson and of Margaret Atkinson; *m* 1948, Mary (*née* Sowerby); one *s*. *Educ:* Edinburgh Univ. (MB, ChB 1948). DPH and DIH, London; FFCM 1976; MFOM 1978. Joined RAF, 1949; med. officer appts, UK, Jordan and Egypt, 1949-63; Student, RAF Staff Coll., 1963-64; SMO, RAF Brüggen, Germany, 1964-67; Dep. PMO, HQ Air Support Comd, 1967-70; PMO, HQ Brit. Forces Gulf, Bahrain, 1970-71; OC RAF Hosp., Wegberg, Germany, 1971-73; Dir of Health and Research (RAF), 1974-78; PMO, RAF Strike Command, 1978-81. *Publication:* (jtly) Double Crew Continuous Flying Operations: a study of aircrew sleep patterns, 1970. *Recreations:* walking, shooting, reading, looking at pictures. *Address:* 39 Brim Hill, N2. *Club:* Royal Air Force.

ATKINSON, Sir Frederick John, (Sir Fred Atkinson), KCB 1979 (CB 1971); Visiting Professor of Economics, Bradford University; Hon. Fellow of Jesus College, Oxford, since 1979; *b* 7 Dec. 1919; *s* of George Edward Atkinson and of late Elizabeth Sabina Cooper; *m* 1947, Margaret Grace Gibson; two *d*. *Educ:* Dulwich Coll.; Jesus Coll., Oxford; Hon. Fellow, Jesus Coll., 1979. Lectr, Jesus and Trinity Colls, Oxford, 1947-49; Economic Section, Cabinet Office, 1949-51; British Embassy, Washington, 1952-54; HM Treasury, 1955-62; Economic Adviser, Foreign Office, 1962-63; HM Treasury, 1963-69 (Dep. Dir, Economic Section, Treasury, 1965-69); Controller, Economics and Statistics, Min. of Technology, 1970; Chief Econ. Adviser, DTI, 1970-73; an Asst Sec.-Gen., OECD, Paris, 1973-75; Dep. Sec. and Chief Econ. Advr, Dept of Energy, 1975-77; Chief Economic Adviser, HM Treasury, and Head of Govt Econ. Service, 1977-79. *Recreation:* reading. *Address:* 26 Lee Terrace, Blackheath, SE3. *T:* 01-852 1040; Tickner Cottage, Aldington, Kent. *T:* Aldington 514.

ATKINSON, Harry Hindmarsh, PhD; Under Secretary, Director (Astronomy, Space and Radio, and Nuclear Physics), Science Research Council, since 1979; *b* 5 Aug. 1929; *s* of late Harry Temple Atkinson and Constance Hindmarsh Atkinson (*née* Shields); *m* 1958, Anne Judith Barrett; two *s* one *d*. *Educ:* Nelson Coll., Nelson, NZ; Canterbury University Coll., NZ (BSc, sen. schol.; MSc (1st cl. Hons)), 1948-52. Asst Lectr, Physics, CUC, 1952-53; Research Asst, Cornell Univ., USA, 1954-55; Corpus Christi Coll. and Cavendish Laboratory, Cambridge Univ., 1955-58 (PhD); Sen. Research Fellow, AERE, Harwell, 1958-61; Head, General Physics Group, Rutherford Laboratory, 1961-69; Staff Chief Scientific Adviser, Cabinet Office, 1969-72; Dep. Chief Scientific Officer and Head of Astronomy, Space and Radio Division, SRC, 1972-78. UK Deleg. to Council, ESA, 1974-, Vice Chm. of Council, 1981-; UK Mem. of Bd, Anglo-Aust. Telescope, 1979-. *Publications:* papers on various branches of physics. *Recreations:* sailing, walking, talking. *Address:* Smoke Acres, Faringdon Road, Abingdon OX14 1BD. *T:* Abingdon 20560. *Club:* Athenæum.

ATKINSON, Prof. James; Consultant Professor with Evangelical Anglican Research Centre, Latimer House, Oxford, since 1981; *b* 27 April 1914; *s* of Nicholas Ridley Atkinson and Margaret (*née* Hindhaugh); *m* 1939, Laura Jean Nutley (decd); one *s* one *d*. *Educ:* Tynemouth High Sch.; Univ. of Durham. MA 1939, MLitt 1950 Durham; DrTheol, Münster, Germany, 1955. Curate, Newcastle upon Tyne, 1937; Precentor, Sheffield Cath., 1941; Vicar, Sheffield, 1944; Fellow, Univ. of Sheffield, 1951; Canon Theologian: Leicester, 1954-70; Sheffield, 1971-; Reader in Theology, Univ. of Hull, 1956; Vis. Prof., Chicago, 1966; Prof. of Biblical Studies, Univ. of Sheffield, 1967-79. Examining Chaplain to: Bp of Leicester, 1968-79; Bp of Derby, 1978-.

Member: Anglican-Roman Catholic Preparatory Commission, 1967-; Gen. Synod of Church of England, 1975-80; Marriage Commn, 1976-78. Pres., Soc. for Study of Theology, 1978-80; Mem., Acad. Internat. des Sciences Religieuses, 1980-. *Publications:* Library of Christian Classics, Vol. XVI 1962; Rome and Reformation, 1965; Luther's Works, Vol. 44, 1966; Luther and the Birth of Protestantism, 1968; The Reformation, Paternoster Church History, Vol. 4, 1968; The Trial of Luther, 1971; contribs to learned jls, also essays and parts of books. *Recreations:* gardening, music. *Address:* Leach House, Hathersage, Derbyshire. *T:* Hope Valley 50570.
See also Robert Atkinson.

ATKINSON, Sir John Alexander, (Sir Alec Atkinson), KCB 1978 (CB 1976); DFC 1943; Member, Panel of Chairmen, Civil Service Selection Board, since 1979; *b* 9 June 1919; *yr s* of late Rev. R. F. Atkinson and late Harriet Harrold Atkinson, BSc (*née* Lowdon); *m* 1945, Marguerite Louise Pearson; one *d*. *Educ:* Kingswood Sch.; Queen's Coll., Oxford. Served in RAF, 1939-45. Asst Prin., 1946, Prin., 1949, Min. of Nat. Insce; Cabinet Office, 1950-52; Prin. Private Sec. to Minister of Pensions and Nat. Insce, 1957-58. Asst Sec., 1958; Under-Sec., Min. of Social Security, later DHSS, 1966-73; Dep. Sec., DHSS, 1973-76, Second Perm. Sec., 1977-79. Mem., Occupational Pensions Bd, 1981-. *Address:* Bleak House, The Drive, Belmont, Sutton, Surrey. *T:* 01-642 6479. *Club:* United Oxford & Cambridge University.

ATKINSON, Sir (John) Kenneth, Kt 1953; retired as Chief Valuer, Valuation Office, Board of Inland Revenue (1951-66); *b* 21 May 1905; *2nd s* of late James Oswald and Jane Atkinson, Liverpool; *m* 1930, Ellen Elsie Godwin Dod (*d* 1975); one *d*. *Educ:* The Leys, Cambridge. Joined Valuation Office, 1928; Deputy Chief Valuer, 1950. Fellow of the Royal Institution of Chartered Surveyors. *Recreation:* Rugby football. *Address:* Clouds, High Park Avenue, East Horsley, Leatherhead, Surrey. *T:* East Horsley 3103.

ATKINSON, (Justin) Brooks; US journalist and writer; retired as Staff Writer, New York Times; *b* Melrose, Massachusetts, USA, 28 Nov. 1894; *s* of Jonathan H. Atkinson and Garafelia Taylor; *m* 1926, Oriana Torrey MacIlveen; one step *s*. *Educ:* Harvard Univ. (AB). Reporter, Springfield Daily News, 1917; Teacher of English, Dartmouth Coll., 1917-18; Boston Evening Transcript, Reporter and Asst Drama Critic, 1919-22; New York Times, 1922-65: Editor Book Review, 1922-25; Drama Critic, 1925-42; War Correspondent, China, 1942-44; Correspondent in Russia, 1945-46; Drama Critic, 1946-60; retd, 1965. Pulitzer Prize for Journalism, 1947. Hon. LHD Williams College, Mass, 1941; Hon. LLD: Adelphi Coll., NY; Pace Coll., NY, 1961; Franklin and Marshall Coll., 1962; Brandeis Univ. 1965; Clark Univ. 1966; Washington Coll., 1966; Dartmouth Coll., 1975. *Publications:* Skyline Promenades, 1925; Henry Thoreau, the Cosmic Yankee, 1927; East of the Hudson, 1931; Cingalese Prince, 1935; Once Around the Sun, 1951; Tuesdays and Fridays, 1963; Brief Chronicles, 1966; Broadway, 1970; This Bright Land, 1972; (with Al Hirschfeld) The Lively Years, 1973; (ed) Walden and other writings of Henry David Thoreau, 1937; (ed) Complete Essays and other writings of Ralph Waldo Emerson, 1940; (ed) Sean O'Casey Reader, 1968. *Address:* Durham, NY 12422, USA.

ATKINSON, Sir Kenneth; *see* Atkinson, Sir J. K.

ATKINSON, Leonard Allan, CMG 1963; *b* 6 Dec. 1906; *s* of L. Atkinson; *m* 1933, Annie R., *d* of A. E. Wells; one *s* two *d*. *Educ:* Wellington Coll. and Victoria Univ. of Wellington, New Zealand. Joined Customs Dept, 1924, Inspector, Public Service Commission, 1941-44; Sec., 1944-47; Asst Comr, 1947-54; Commission Member, 1954-58; Chm., 1958-62; Chm., State Services Commission, NZ, 1963-66. *Recreation:* bowls. *Address:* 181 The Parade, Island Bay, Wellington, NZ. *Club:* Wellington (NZ).

ATKINSON, Maj.-Gen. Sir Leonard Henry, KBE 1966 (OBE 1945); *b* 4 Dec. 1910; *s* of A. H. Atkinson; *m* 1939, Jean Eileen, *d* of C. A. Atchley, OBE; one *s* three *d*. *Educ:* Wellington Coll., Berks; University Coll., London (Fellow, 1977). BSc (Eng) 1932; commnd in RAOC, 1933; transf. to REME, 1942; Comdr REME (Lieut-Col) Guards Armd Div. (NW Europe), 1943-45; DDEME (Col) Brit. Airborne Corps, India, 1945; Staff Coll., Quetta, 1945-46; served in Far East, UK and WO, 1946-50; JSSC, 1950-51; GSO1, REME Trg Centre, 1951-53; DDEME (Col) HQ 1st Corps (Germany) 1953-55; DDEME (Brig.). WO, 1956-58; Comdt (Brig.) REME Training Centre and Commander Berkshire Dist, 1958-63; Dir (Maj.-Gen.), Electrical and Mechanical Engineering, Army, 1963-66; Col Comdt, REME, 1967-72. Man. Dir, Harland Simon, 1970-72; Director: Harland Engineering, 1966-69; Simon Equipment, 1966-69; Weir Engineering Industries, 1970-74; United Gas Industries, 1972-76; C. & W. Walker Ltd, 1974-77; Bespoke Securities 1974-; Emray, 1978-. Chairman: Christopher Gold Associates, 1976-; DTI Cttee on Terotechnology, 1970-75; Council of Engineering Instns, 1974-75 (Vice-Chm., 1973); Technology Transfer Associates Ltd, 1980-; Vice Chm. Southern Regional Council for Further Educn, 1978-. Member: Court of Bradford Univ., 1968-76; Court of Cranfield Inst. of Technology, 1975-77; Governor, Reading Coll. of Technology, 1968-. FIMechE; FIEE; FIGasE; FIERE (past Pres.); Hon. MIPlantE. Liveryman, Turners' Company, 1966-. *Address:* Pound Cottage, Silchester, Reading, Berks. *T:* Basingstoke 881220. *Club:* Naval and Military.

ATKINSON, Leslie, CMG 1965; OBE 1961; Managing Director, Leslie Atkinson Pty Ltd, 1960; Member of Export Development Council, Sydney, 1959; *b* 11 Jan. 1913; *s* of J. Atkinson; *m* 1935, Ellen, *d* of J. Kinsey; one *s* one d. *Educ:* Wollongong Technical Sch. Controller, Nock and Kirby Ltd, 1943-49, Associate Dir, 1949-53; Dir and General Manager, Carr and Elliott, 1953-59. Pres., Sydney Junior Chamber of Commerce, 1946-47; Vice-Pres. and Hon. Treasurer, Sydney Chamber of Commerce, 1949-53, Pres., 1953-54, 1957-58; Vice-Pres., Associated Chambers of Commerce of the Commonwealth of Australia, 1956-57 (Pres., 1964-65). Mem. of Standing Cttee, NSW Methodist Conference, 1957-62. *Address:* 11 Kyle Parade, Kyle Bay, NSW 2221, Australia.

ᴀTKINSON, Mary; *see under* Hardwick, Mollie.

ᴀTKINSON, **Michael William**, MBE 1970; HM Diplomatic Service; Counsellor, Peking, since 1980; *b* 11 April 1932; *m* 1963, Veronica Bobrovsky; two *s* one d. *Educ:* Purley County Grammar School; Queen's College, Oxford (BA Hons). Served FO, Vientiane, Buenos Aires, British Honduras, Madrid; FCO 1975; NATO Defence Coll., 1976; Counsellor, Budapest, 1977-80. *Address:* c/o Foreign and Commonwealth Office, King Charles Street, SW1.

ᴀTKINSON, **Norman**; MP (Lab) Haringey, Tottenham, since 1974 (Tottenham, 1964-74); *b* 25 March 1923; *s* of George Atkinson, Manchester; *m* 1948, Irene Parry. *Educ:* elementary and technical schs. Member of Manchester City Council, 1945-49. Chief Design Engineer, Manchester University, 1957-64. Contested (Lab) Wythenshawe, 1955, Altrincham and Sale, 1959. Treasurer, Labour Party, 1976-81. *Recreations:* walking, cricket, football. *Address:* House of Commons, SW1.

ᴀTKINSON, Reay; *see* Atkinson, W. R.

ᴀTKINSON, **Prof. Richard John Copland**, CBE 1979; MA; FSA 1946; Professor of Archaeology, University College, Cardiff, since 1958; *b* 22 Jan. 1920; *e s* of Roland Cecil Atkinson and Alice Noel Herbert Atkinson (née Wright); *m* 1st, 1942, Hester Renée Marguerite Cobb (d 1981); three *s* ; 2nd, 1981, Judith Marion O'Kelly. *Educ:* Sherborne School; Magdalen College, Oxford. Asst Keeper, Department of Antiquities, Ashmolean Museum, Oxford, 1944-49; Lectr in Prehistoric Archæology, Univ. of Edinburgh, 1949-58; Dep. Principal, UC Cardiff, 1970-74. Member: Ancient Monuments Board for Wales, 1959-; Cttee of Enquiry into Arrangements for Protection of Field Monuments, 1966-68; Science-Based Archaeology Cttee, SRC, 1977-81; Royal Commission: on Ancient Monuments (Wales) 1963-; on Historical Monuments (England), 1968-; UGC, 1973-82 (Vice Chm., 1976-77; Chm., Arts Sub-cttee, 1978-82). Vice-President: Prehistoric Society, 1963-67; Council for British Archæology, 1970-73 (Hon. Sec., 1964-70); Dir, BBC Silbury Hill project, 1967-69. *Publications:* Field Archæology, 1946; Stonehenge, 1956; Stonehenge and Avebury, 1959; Archæology, History and Science, 1960. Articles in archæological journals. *Recreations:* archæology, wood-work and wine. *Address:* The Old Rectory, Wenvoe, S Glamorgan CF5 6AN. *Clubs:* Athenæum, United Oxford & Cambridge University.

ᴀTKINSON, **Robert**, DSC 1941; RD 1947; Chairman: British Shipbuilders, since 1980; Aurora Holdings, Sheffield, since 1972; *b* 7 March 1916; *s* of Nicholas and Margaret Atkinson; *m* 1st, 1941, Joyce Forster (d 1973); one *s* one d ; 2nd, 1977, Margaret Hazel Walker. *Educ:* London Univ. (BSc(Eng) Hons). MIMechE, CEng. Served War 1939-45 (DSC 1941 and two Bars, 1st, 1943, 2nd, 1944, mentioned in Despatches, 1943). Managing Director: Wm Doxford, 1957-61; Tube Investments (Eng), 1961-67; Unicorn Industries, 1967-72. *Publications:* The Design and Operating Experience of an Ore Carrier Built Abroad, 1957; The Manufacture of Doxford Crankshafts, 1960; Some Crankshaft Failures: Investigation into Causes and Remedies, 1960; technical papers. *Recreations:* salmon fishing, walking. *Address:* 16 Ivy Park Court, Sheffield S10 3LA; 3 Whitehall Court, SW1. *Club:* Royal Thames Yacht.

See also Prof. James Atkinson.

ᴀTKINSON, **William Christopher**; Stevenson Professor of Hispanic Studies in University of Glasgow, 1932-72; Director, Institute of Latin-American Studies, 1966-72; *b* Belfast, 9 Aug. 1902; *s* of Robert Joseph Atkinson; *m* 1928, Evelyn Lucy, d of C. F. Wakefield, Hampstead; one *s* three d. *Educ:* Univs of Belfast and Madrid. Lectr in Spanish at Armstrong Coll., Newcastle upon Tyne, 1926-32; Hon. Sec., Modern Humanities Research Assoc., 1929-36; Head of Spanish and Portuguese sections, Foreign Research and Press Service of Royal Institute of International Affairs, 1939-43; Visiting British Council Lecturer to Latin America, 1946, 1960, 1971; Hon. Prof. National Univ. of Colombia, 1946; Chm. 1st Scottish cultural delegation to USSR, 1954; Carnegie Research Fellow visiting US Univs, 1955; Member, Hispanic Society of America, 1955 (Corres. Mem., 1937); Rockefeller Fellow visiting Latin-American Univs, 1957; Visiting Prof. of Portuguese Studies, University Coll. of Rhodesia and Nyasaland, 1963. Commander, Order of Prince Henry the Navigator, Portugal, 1972. *Publications:* Spain, A Brief History, 1934; The Lusiads of Camoens, 1952; The Remarkable Life of Don Diego, 1958; A History of Spain and Portugal, 1960; The Conquest of New Granada, 1961; The Happy Captive, 1977; contributions to Encyclopædia Britannica, learned periodicals and reviews, and to composite works on Spanish and Portuguese studies. *Recreations:* travel and tramping. *Address:* 39 Manse Road, Bearsden, Glasgow. *T:* 041-942 0368.

ᴀTKINSON, **(William) Reay**; Under Secretary, since 1978, and Regional Director, North Eastern Region, since 1981, Department of Industry; *b* 15

March 1926; *s* of William Edwin Atkinson and Lena Marion (née Haselhurst); *m* ; one *s* two d. *Educ:* Gosforth Grammar Sch., Newcastle upon Tyne; King's Coll., Durham Univ.; Worcester Coll., Oxford. Served RNVR, 1943-46. Entered Civil Service as Inspector of Taxes, 1950; Principal, 1958, Asst. Sec., 1965; Secretaries Office, Inland Revenue, 1958-61 and 1962-69; Asst Sec., Royal Commn on the Press, 1961-62; Civil Service Dept, 1969; Under Sec., and Dir, Central Computer Agency, CSD, 1973-78. *Recreations:* fell walking, music. *Address:* High Dryburn, Garrigill, near Alston, Cumbria CA9 3EJ.

ATTENBOROUGH, **David Frederick**, CBE 1974; broadcaster and traveller; *b* 8 May 1926; *s* of late Frederick Levi Attenborough; *m* 1950, Jane Elizabeth Ebsworth Oriel; one *s* one d. *Educ:* Wyggeston Grammar Sch. for Boys, Leicester; Clare Coll., Cambridge (Hon. Fellow, 1980). Served in Royal Navy, 1947-49. Editorial Asst in an educational publishing house, 1949-52; joined BBC Television Service as trainee producer, 1952; undertook zoological and ethnographic filming expeditions to: Sierra Leone, 1954; British Guiana, 1955; Indonesia, 1956; New Guinea, 1957; Paraguay and Argentina, 1958; South West Pacific, 1959; Madagascar, 1960; Northern Territory of Australia, 1962; the Zambesi, 1964; Bali, 1969; Central New Guinea, 1971; Celebes, Borneo, Peru and Colombia, 1973; Mali, British Columbia, Iran, Solomon Islands, 1974; Nigeria, 1975; Controller, BBC-2, BBC Television Service, 1965-68; Dir of Programmes, Television, and Mem., Bd of Management, BBC, 1969-72. Writer and presenter, BBC series: Tribal Eye, 1976; Life on Earth, 1979. Mem., Nature Conservancy Council, 1973-. Trustee: WWF Internat., 1979-; British Museum, 1980-. Special Award, Soc. of Film and TV Arts, 1961; Silver Medal, Zool Soc. of London, 1966; Silver Medal, Royal Television Soc., 1966; Desmond Davis Award, Soc. of Film and Television Arts, 1970; Cherry Kearton Medal, RGS, 1972; BAFTA Fellowship Award, 1980. Hon. DLitt: Leicester, 1970; City, 1972; London, 1980; Birmingham, 1982; Hon. DSc: Liverpool, 1974; Heriot-Watt, 1978; Sussex, 1979; Bath, 1981; Ulster, Durham, 1982; Hon. LLD: Bristol, 1977; Glasgow, 1980; DUniv Open Univ., 1980. Hon. Fellow: Manchester Polytechnic, 1976; UMIST, 1980. *Publications:* Zoo Quest to Guiana, 1956; Zoo Quest for a Dragon, 1957; Zoo Quest in Paraguay, 1959; Quest in Paradise, 1960; Zoo Quest to Madagascar, 1961; Quest under Capricorn, 1963; The Tribal Eye, 1976; Life on Earth, 1979. *Recreations:* music, tribal art, natural history. *Address:* 5 Park Road, Richmond, Surrey.

See also Sir R. S. Attenborough.

ATTENBOROUGH, **James**, CMG 1915; TD; Colonel (retired) TF; solicitor; *b* 7 Aug. 1884; *e s* of Stanley J. Attenborough, 30 Clarges Street, Piccadilly; *m* 1915, Phyllis, d of late Edwin J. Layton. *Educ:* Rugby. Served European War, 1914-18 (CMG) and War of 1939-45; commanded 9th Batt. Royal Fusiliers (TF) and Halton Camp RAF. *Recreations:* shooting and golf. *Address:* The Old Rectory, Great Mongeham, near Deal, Kent. *Clubs:* East India, Devonshire, Sports and Public Schools; Royal St George's (Sandwich).

ATTENBOROUGH, **John Philip**, CMG 1958; CBE 1953 (OBE 1946); retired; *b* 6 Nov. 1901; *s* of late Frederick Samuel and Edith Attenborough; *m* 1947, Lucie Blanche Woods, y d of late Rev. J. R. and Mrs Prenter and widow of late Dr P. P. Murphy; one step s. *Educ:* Manchester Grammar Sch.; Corpus Christi Coll., Oxford (MA). Superintendent of Education, Northern Nigeria, 1924-30; Lecturer and Senior Inspector, Education Dept, Palestine, 1930-37; Dir of Education, Aden, 1937-46; Deputy Dir of Education, Palestine, 1946-48; Asst Educational Adviser, Colonial Office, 1948; Dir of Education, Tanganyika, 1948-55; Mem. for Social Services, Tanganyika, 1955-57; Min. for Social Services, Tanganyika, 1957-58; Consultant: UNICEF, 1963-65; UNESCO, 1967; Devon, CC, 1961-68; Mem. SW Regional Hosp. Bd, 1965-71. Pres. Torbay Conservative Assoc., 1967-79. *Address:* 21 Thorncliff Close, Torquay, Devon. *T:* Torquay 27291.

ATTENBOROUGH, **Peter John**; Headmaster of Charterhouse, since 1982; *b* 4 April 1938; *m* 1967, Alexandra Deirdre Campbell Page; one *s* one d. *Educ:* Christ's Hospital; Peterhouse, Cambridge. BA Classics 1960, MA 1964. Asst Master, Uppingham Sch., 1960-75 (Housemaster, Senior Classics Master); Asst Master, Starehe Boys' Centre, Nairobi, 1966-67; Headmaster, Sedbergh Sch., 1975-81. Freeman, City of London, 1965. *Address:* Charterhouse, Godalming, Surrey.

ATTENBOROUGH, **Philip John**; publisher; Chairman: Hodder & Stoughton Ltd and Hodder & Stoughton Holdings Ltd, since 1975; Lancet Ltd, since 1977; *b* 3 June 1936; *er s* of John Attenborough, CBE, and Barbara (née Sandle); *m* 1963, Rosemary, y d of Dr W. B. Littler, qv ; one *s* one d. *Educ:* Rugby; Trinity Coll., Oxford. Christmas postman (parcels), 1952-54; Nat. Service, Sergeant 68th Regt RA, Oswestry, 1956; lumberjack, Blind River, Ont, 1957; joined Hodder & Stoughton, 1957: Export Manager, 1960; Dir, 1963; Sales Dir, 1969. Publishers Association: Mem. Council, 1976- (Treasurer, 1981-82; Vice-Pres., 1982-83; Pres., 1983-); Leader, delegn of Brit. publishers to China, 1978; Chm., Book Develt Council, 1977-79; Mem. British Council (Publishers Adv. Panel), 1977-. Liveryman, Skinners Co., 1970. *Recreations:* trout and coarse fishing, playing golf and tennis, watching cricket. *Address:* Coldhanger, Seal Chart, near Sevenoaks, Kent. *T:* Sevenoaks 61516. *Clubs:* Garrick, MCC; Kent CC, Rye Golf, Wildernesse.

ATTENBOROUGH, **Sir Richard (Samuel)**, Kt 1976; CBE 1967; actor, producer and director; *b* 29 Aug. 1923; *s* of late Frederick L. Attenborough; *m* 1945, Sheila Beryl Grant Sim; one *s* two d. *Educ:* Wyggeston Grammar

Sch., Leicester. Leverhulme Schol. to Royal Acad. of Dramatic Art, 1941 (Bancroft Medal). First stage appearance as Richard Miller in Ah Wilderness, Intimate Theatre, Palmers Green, 1941. West End début as Ralph Berger in Awake and Sing, Arts Theatre, 1942; The Little Foxes, Piccadilly Theatre, 1942; Brighton Rock, Garrick, 1943. Joined RAF 1943; seconded to RAF Film Unit, 1944, and appeared in Journey Together; demobilised, 1946. Returned to Stage, Jan. 1949, in The Way Back (Home of the Brave), Westminster; To Dorothy, a Son, Savoy, 1950 (transf. to Garrick, 1951); Sweet Madness, Vaudeville, 1952; The Mousetrap, Ambassadors, 1952-54; Double Image, Savoy, 1956-57, St James's, 1957; The Rape of the Belt, Piccadilly, 1957-58. First film appearance in In Which We Serve, 1942; other film appearances include: School for Secrets, The Man Within, Dancing With Crime, Brighton Rock, London Belongs to Me, The Guinea Pig, The Lost People, Boys in Brown, Morning Departure, Hell is Sold Out, The Magic Box, Gift Horse, Father's Doing Fine, Eight O'Clock Walk, The Ship That Died of Shame, Private's Progress, The Baby and the Battleship, Brothers in Law, The Scamp, Dunkirk, The Man Upstairs, Sea of Sand, Danger Within, I'm All Right Jack, Jet Storm, SOS Pacific; The Angry Silence (also co-prod), 1959; The League of Gentlemen, 1960; Only Two Can Play, All Night Long, 1961; The Dock Brief, The Great Escape, 1962; Séance On a Wet Afternoon (also prod; Best actor, San Sebastian Film Fest. and British Film Acad.), The Third Secret, 1963; Guns at Batasi, 1964 (Best actor, British Film Acad.); The Flight of the Phœnix, 1965; The Sand Pebbles, Dr Dolittle, 1966 (both Hollywood Golden Globe); The Bliss of Mrs Blossom, 1967; Only When I Larf, 1968; The Last Grenade, A Severed Head, David Copperfield, Loot, 1969; 10 Rillington Place, 1970; Ten Little Indians, Rosebud, Brannigan, Conduct Unbecoming, 1974; The Chess Players, 1977; The Human Factor, 1979; produced: Whistle Down the Wind, 1961; The L-Shaped Room, 1962; directed: Oh! What a Lovely War, 1968 (16 Internat. Awards incl. Hollywood Golden Globe and SFTA UN Award); Young Winston, 1972 (Hollywood Golden Globe); A Bridge Too Far, 1976 (Evening News Best Drama Award); Magic, 1978; dir. and prod., Gandhi, 1980-81. Formed: Beaver Films with Bryan Forbes, 1959; Allied Film Makers, 1960; Chm., Goldcrest Films, 1981-; Dir, Goldcrest Films & Television, 1981-; Dep. Chm., Channel Four Television, 1980-; Chm., Capital Radio, 1973-. Member: British Actors' Equity Assoc. Council, 1949-73; Cinematograph Films Council, 1967-73; Arts Council of GB, 1970-73; Young Vic Bd, 1974-; Chairman: RADA, 1970- (Mem. Council, 1963-); Actor's Charitable Trust, 1956-; Combined Theatrical Charities, 1964-; Governor, Nat. Film Sch., 1970-81; Governor and Chm., BFI, 1982-; Vice-Pres., BAFTA (formerly SFTA), 1971- (Chm., 1969-70); Trustee, Tate Gall., 1976-. Pres., Muscular Dystrophy Gp of GB, 1971- (Vice Pres., 1962-71). Dir, Chelsea Football Club, 1969-. Pro-Chancellor, Sussex Univ., 1970-. Hon. DLitt: Leicester, 1970; Kent, 1981; Hon. DCL Newcastle, 1974. Recreations: listening to music, collecting paintings, watching football. Address: Old Friars, Richmond Green, Surrey. Clubs: Garrick, Beefsteak, Green Room.

See also D. F. Attenborough.

ATTERTON, David Valentine, CBE 1981; PhD; FEng; FIM; Chairman, Foseco Minsep Ltd, since 1979; b 13 Feb. 1927; s of Frank Arthur Shepherd Atterton and Ella Constance (née Collins); m 1948, Sheila Ann McMahon; two s one d. Educ: Bishop Wordsworth's Sch., Salisbury; Peterhouse, Cambridge. MA, PhD Cantab. Post-doctorate research, Cambridge, 1950-52; joined Foundry Services Ltd, 1952; Managing Director: Foseco Ltd, 1966; Foseco Minsep Ltd, 1969. Dep. Chm., Associated Engineering Ltd, 1979- (Dir 1972-); Director: Finance Corp. for Industry Ltd and Finance for Industry Ltd, 1974-; IMI Ltd, 1976-; Barclays Bank UK Ltd, 1982-. Chm., NEDO Iron and Steel Sector Working Party, 1977-; Member: Bd of Governors, United World Coll. of the Atlantic, 1968- (Chm., 1973-79); Adv. Council for Applied R&D, 1982-; Pres., Birmingham Chamber of Commerce and Industry, 1974-75. Publications: numerous scientific papers in learned jls. Recreations: cartography, notaphilia, astronomy, photography. Address: The Tan House, Lapworth, Solihull, West Midlands B94 6JZ. T: Lapworth 2902.

ATTLEE, family name of Earl Attlee.

ATTLEE, 2nd Earl, cr 1955; **Martin Richard Attlee**; Viscount Prestwood, 1955; Owner of Prestwood Publicity, since 1967; b 10 Aug. 1927; o s of 1st Earl Attlee, KG, PC, OM, CH, FRS, and Violet Helen (d 1964), d of H. E. Millar; S father, 1967; m 1955, Anne Barbara, er d of late James Henderson, CBE, Bath, Somerset; one s one d. Educ: Millfield Coll.; Southampton University Coll. (now Southampton Univ.). Served in Merchant Navy, 1945-50. Active Mem. Hon. Artillery Company, 1951-55. Asst PRO, Southern Region, British Rail, 1970-76. MIPR 1964. Publication: Bluff Your Way in PR, 1971. Recreations: cars, carpentry. Heir: s Viscount Prestwood, qv. Address: 125 Hendon Lane, N3 3PR. Clubs: Press, Pathfinders'.

ATTLEE, Air Vice-Marshal Donald Laurence, CB 1978; MVO 1964; fruit farmer, since 1977; b 2 Sept. 1922; s of Major Laurence Attlee; m 1952, Jane Hamilton Young; one s two d. Educ: Haileybury. Pilot trng in Canada, 1942-44; Flying Instructor, 1944-48; Staff, Trng Comd, 1949-52; 12 Sqdn, 1952-54; Air Ministry, Air Staff, 1954-55; RAF Staff Coll., 1955; 59 Sqdn, 1957-59; CO, The Queen's Flight (W/Cdr), 1960-63; HQ, RAF Germany, 1964-67; CO, RAF Brize Norton, 1968-69; IDC, 1970; MoD Policy Staff, 1971-72; Dir of RAF Recruiting, 1973-74; Air Cdre, Intell., 1974-75; AOA Trng Comd, 1975-77, retired. Recreations: genealogy, Do-it-Yourself, gardening. Address: Jerwoods, Culmstock, Cullompton, Devon. T: Hemycock 680317. Club: Royal Air Force.

ATTWELL, Ven. Arthur Henry; Archdeacon of Westmorland and Furne since 1978; Director, Carlisle Diocesan Training Institute, since 1978; b 5 Au 1920; s of Henry John and Kate Attwell. Educ: Wilson School, Readin Leeds Univ. (BA 1941); College of the Resurrection, Mirfield. MTh Londo 1958, MA London, 1972. Deacon 1943, priest 1944; Curate of St Georg Wolverton, 1943-45; Curate of Wigan, 1945-51; Sub-warden of St Pau Coll., Grahamstown, S Africa, 1951-52; Dean of Kimberley, S Afric 1952-60; Rector of Workington, Cumberland, 1960-72; Hon. Canon Carlisle, 1964-72, 1978-; Rural Dean of Cockermouth and Workingto 1966-70; Canon Residentiary of Carlisle Cathedral, 1972-78; Vicar of St John's, Windermere, 1978-82. Proctor in Convocation, 1965-; Exar Chaplain to Bishop of Carlisle, 1972-. Recreation: travel. Address: Fairfiel Oxenholme, Kendal, Cumbria LA9 7RF. T: Kendal 26275.

ATTWOOD, Thomas Jaymril; Chairman: Cargill, Attwood and Thom Ltd, Management Consultancy Group, since 1965; Post Office Users' Nation Council, since 1982; b 30 March 1931; s of George Frederick Attwood ar Avril Sandys (née Cargill, NZ); m 1963, Lynette O. E. Lewis; one s one Educ: Haileybury and Imperial Service Coll.; RMA Sandhurst; Harvard Gra Sch. of Business Admin; INSEAD, Fontainebleau. Pres., Internat. Consultan Foundn, 1978-81. Conducted seminars for UN Secretariat, European Comm and World Council of Churches, 1970-80; presented papers to Eur. To Management Symposium Davos, Internat. Training Conf. and to Wor Public Relations Conf. Publications: (jtly) Bow Group pubn on Unite Nations, 1961; contrib. to reference books, incl. Systems Thinking, Innovatio in Global Consultation, Handbook of Management Development, an Helping Across Cultures. Recreations: travel, music, City of London, cricke Address: 8 Teddington Park, Teddington, Mddx TW11 8DA. T: 01-977 809 Clubs: City Livery, Eccentric, MCC.

ATWELL, Sir John (William), Kt 1976; CBE 1970; FEng; FIMechE, FRS Chairman, Omega Software Ltd, since 1982; b 24 Nov. 1911; s of Willia Atwell and Sarah Workman; m 1945, Dorothy Hendry Baxter, d of J. F Baxter and Janet Muir; no c. Educ: Hyndland Secondary Sch., Glasgow Royal Technical Coll., Glasgow (ARTC); Cambridge Univ. (MSc). Genera Management, Stewarts and Lloyds Ltd, 1939-54; Dir 1955-61, Man. D 1961-68, G. & J. Weir Ltd; Dir, The Weir Group Ltd, 1961-74, and Chm Engineering Div., 1968-74; Mem., BRB (Scottish), 1975-81. Chm., Scottis Offshore Partnership, 1975-81; Director: Anderson Strathclyde Ltd, 1975-7 Govan Shipbuilders Ltd, 1975-79. Mem., Bd of Royal Ordnance Factorie 1974-79. Chm., Requirements Bd for Mechanical Engineering and Machir Tools, DTI, 1972-76. Member: University Grants Cttee, 1965-69; NED(Mech. Eng Cttee, 1969-74; Court, Strathclyde Univ., 1967- (Chm., 1975-80 Council, RSE, 1974- (Treas., 1977-82; Pres., 1982-); Exec. Cttee, Scottis Council of Develt and Industry, 1972-77; Adv. Council for Applied R&L 1976-80; Scottish Hosps Res. Trust, 1972-; Council, Scottish Business Sch 1972-80. Vice-Pres., IMechE, 1966-73, Pres., 1973-74; Vice-Chm., 1977-78 Chm., 1978-79, CEI. Hon. LLD Strathclyde, 1973. Recreation: golf. Addres Elmfield, Buchanan Drive, Rutherglen, Glasgow. T: 041-647 1824. Club Caledonian; New (Edinburgh); Western (Glasgow).

ATWILL, Sir (Milton) John (Napier), Kt 1979; Deputy Chairman: Davi Jones Ltd, since 1975 (Board Member, since 1971); D. J.'s Properties Ltd, sin 1976; Director: Waugh & Josephson Holdings Ltd, since 1965; Nation Mutual Life Association of Australasia Ltd (NSW), since 1973; Bushell Holdings Ltd, since 1975; Federal President of Liberal Party, since 1975; b 1 Jan. 1926; s of Milton Spencer Atwill and Isabella Caroline Atwill; m 1955 Susan Playfair; two d. Educ: Cranbrook Sch., Sydney; Geelong Church o England Grammar Sch.; Jesus Coll., Cambridge (MA). Called to the Ba Gray's Inn, 1953, NSW Bar, 1953. President, NSW Division, Liberal Party of Australia, 1970-75; Hon. Treas., 1968-69. Recreations: cricket, tennis Address: 5 Fullerton Street, Woollahra, NSW 2025, Australia. T: (02 32-1570. Clubs: Australian, Union, Royal Sydney Golf, Elanora Countr Melbourne.

AUBREY, Henry M. W.; see Windsor-Aubrey.

AUBREY, John Melbourn, CBE 1979; Consultant, since 1982; b 5 Marc 1921; s of Melbourn Evans Aubrey and Edith Maria Aubrey; m 1949, Judit Christine Fairbairn; two s two d (and one s decd). Educ: St Paul's Sch.; Corpu Christi Coll., Cambridge (Mech. Sciences Tripos). FCIPA 1952. Armstron Siddeley Motors Ltd, 1942-43; RE, 1943-47; Tootal Broadhurst Lee Co 1947-49; Gill Jennings and Every, Chartered Patent Agents, 1949-55 Courtaulds Ltd, 1955-81. Chm., Baptist Insurance Co. Ltd, 1980- (Dir, 1971-) Mem. Council, Baptist Union of GB and Ireland, 1970-. Recreation gardening, tennis, swimming, skiing. Address: 52 Kenilworth Road Leamington Spa. T: Leamington Spa 24463. Clubs: United Oxford & Cambridge University, Ski of GB; Coventry Aeroplane.

AUBREY-FLETCHER, Sir John (Henry Lancelot), 7th Bt cr 1782; a Recorder of the Crown Court, 1972-74; Metropolitan Magistrate, 1959-71 b 22 Aug. 1912; s of Major Sir Henry Aubrey-Fletcher, 6th Bt, CVO, DSO and Mary Augusta (d 1963), e d of Rev. R. W. Chilton; S father, 1969; m 1939, Diana Fynvola, d of late Lieut-Col Arthur Egerton, Coldstream Guards and late Mrs Robert Bruce; one s (one d decd). Educ: Eton; New Coll. Oxford. Called to Bar, 1937. Served War of 1939-45, Grenadier Guards, reaching rank of temp. Lieut-Col and leaving Army with rank of Hon. Major Dep. Chm., Bucks Quarter Sessions, 1959-71. High Sheriff, Bucks, 1961. Heir.

s Henry Egerton Aubrey-Fletcher [b 27 Nov. 1945; m 1976, Roberta Sara, d of Major Robert Buchanan, Blackpark Cottage, Evanton, Ross-shire, and Mrs Ogden White; three s]. *Address:* The Gate House, Chilton, Aylesbury, Bucks. *T:* Long Crendon 347.
See also Hon. R. O. Stanley.

AUCHINCLOSS, Louis Stanton; author; Partner, Hawkins Delafield and Wood, NYC, since 1957 (Associate, 1954-57); *b* NY, 27 Sept. 1917; *s of* J. H. Auchincloss and P. Stanton; *m* 1957, Adèle Lawrence; three s. *Educ:* Groton Sch.; Yale Univ.; Univ. of Virginia (LLB). Lieut USNR; served, 1941-45. Admitted to NY Bar, 1941; Associate Sullivan and Cromwell, 1941-51. Mem. Exec. Cttee, Assoc. of Bar of NY City. Pres., Museum of City of NY, 1967; Trustee, Josiah Macy Jr Foundn. Mem., Nat. Inst. of Arts and Letters. *Publications:* The Indifferent Children, 1947; The Injustice Collectors, 1950; Sybil, 1952; A Law for the Lion, 1953; The Romantic Egoists, 1954; The Great World and Timothy Colt, 1956; Venus in Sparta, 1958; Pursuit of the Prodigal, 1959; The House of Five Talents, 1960; Reflections of a Jacobite, 1961; Portrait in Brownstone, 1962; Powers of Attorney, 1963; The Rector of Justin, 1964; Pioneers and Caretakers, 1966; The Embezzler, 1966; Tales of Manhattan, 1967; A World of Profit, 1969; Second Chance: tales to two generations, 1970; Edith Wharton, 1972; I come as a thief, 1972; Richelieu, 1972; The Partners, 1974; A Writer's Capital, 1974; Reading Henry James, 1975; The Winthrop Covenant, 1976; The Dark Lady, 1977; The Country Cousin, 1978; The House of the Prophet, 1980; The Cat and the King, 1981; Watch Fires, 1982; pamphlets on American writers. *Address:* 1111 Park Avenue, New York, NY 10028, USA; (office) 67 Wall Street, New York, NY 10005. *Club:* Century Association (NY).

AUCKLAND, 9th Baron (*cr* Irish Barony, 1789; British 1793); **Ian George Eden;** insurance consultant; Non-executive Director, C. J. Sims & Co. Ltd; *b* 23 June 1926; *s* of 8th Baron Auckland; *S* father 1957; *m* 1954, Dorothy Margaret, *d* of H. J. Manser, Eastbourne; one *s* two *d. Educ:* Blundell's Sch. Royal Signals, 1945-48; 3/4 County of London Yeomanry (Sharpshooters) (TA), 1948-53. Underwriting Mem. of Lloyd's, 1956-64. Vice-Pres., Royal Society for Prevention of Accidents; Mem., New Zealand Soc. Past Master, Broderers' Co. *Recreations:* music, theatre, tennis and walking. *Heir:* s Hon. Robert Ian Burnard Eden, *b* 25 July 1962. *Address:* Tudor Rose House, 30 Links Road, Ashtead, Surrey. *T:* Ashtead 74393. *Clubs:* City Livery, St Stephen's Constitutional.

AUCKLAND (Dio. Durham), **Archdeacon of;** *see* Marchant, Ven. G. J. C.

AUCKLAND (NZ), Bishop of; *see* New Zealand, Primate and Archbishop of.

AUCKLAND (NZ), Bishop of, (RC), since 1974; **Most Rev. John Mackey.** *Educ:* Auckland Univ. (MA, DipEd); Notre Dame Univ., USA (PhD). Formerly Professor in Theological Faculty, National Seminary of Mosgiel, Dunedin. *Publications:* The Making of a State Education System, 1967; Reflections on Church History, 1975. *Address:* Bishop's House, 36 New Street, Ponsonby, PO Box 47255, Auckland 1, New Zealand. *T:* 764-244.

AUCKLAND (NZ), Assistant Bishop of; *see* Buckle, Rt Rev. E. G.

AUDLAND, Christopher John, CMG 1973; Director-General for Energy, Commission of the European Communities, since 1981; *b* 7 July 1926; *s* of late Brig. Edward Gordon Audland, CB, CBE, MC, and Violet Mary, *d* of late Herbert Shepherd-Cross, MP; *m* 1955, Maura Daphne Sullivan; two *s* one *d. Educ:* Winchester Coll. RA, 1944-48 (Temp. Capt.). Entered Foreign (subseq. Diplomatic) Service, 1948; has served in: Bonn; British Representation to Council of Europe; Washington; UK Delegn to Common Market negotiations, Brussels, 1961-63; Buenos Aires; FCO, 1968-70; Counsellor (Head of Chancery), Bonn, 1970-73. Mem., UK Delegn to Four-Power negotiations on Berlin, 1970-72; Dep. Sec. Gen., EEC, 1973-81. *Address:* (office) Commission des Communautés Européennes, 200 rue de la Loi, Bruxelles 1049, Belgium. *T:* Brussels 2351959; (home) 5 avenue des Lauriers, Brussels 1150, Belgium. *T:* Brussels 7313467. *Club:* United Oxford & Cambridge University.

AUDLEY, 25th Baron *cr* 1312-13; **Richard Michael Thomas Souter;** Director, Graham Miller & Co. Ltd; *b* 31 May 1914; *s* of Sir Charles Alexander Souter, KCIE, CSI (*d* 1958) and Lady Charlotte Dorothy Souter (*née* Jesson) (*d* 1958); *S* kinswoman, Baroness Audley (24th in line), 1973; *m* 1941, Pauline, *d* of D. L. Eskell; three *d. Educ:* Uppingham. Fellow, CILA. Military Service, 1939-46; Control Commission, Germany, 1946-50. Insurance Broker until 1955; Loss Adjuster, 1955-. *Recreations:* shooting, gardening. *Heir:* three co-heiresses. *Address:* Friendly Green, Cowden, near Edenbridge, Kent TN8 7DU. *T:* Cowden 682.

AUDU, Dr Ishaya Shu'aibu, FRCPE; Minister of External Affairs, Federal Republic of Nigeria, since 1979; *b* 1 March 1927; *s* of Malam Bulus Audu and Malama Rakiya Audu; *m* 1958, Victoria Abosede Ohiorhenuan; two *s* five *d. Educ:* Ibadan and London Univs. House Officer, Sen. House Officer, Registrar in Surgery, Medicine, Obstetrics and Gynæcology and Pædiatrics, King's Coll. Hosp., London and Univ. Coll. Hosp., Ibadan, 1954-58; postgrad. studies, UK, 1959-60; Specialist Physician, Pædiatrician to Govt of Northern Nigeria and Personal Physician to Premier of North Region Govt, 1960-62;

Lectr to Associate Professorship in Pæds, Univ. of Lagos Med. Sch., 1962-66; Vis. Res. Associate Prof., Univ. of Rochester Med. Sch., NY, 1964-65; Dep. Chm., Lagos Univ. Teaching Hosp. Man. Bd and Mem. Council, Univ. Lagos Med. Coll., 1962-66; Mem. Senate, Lagos Univ., 1963-66; Vice-Chancellor, Ahmadu Bello Univ., 1966-1975; Prof. of Medicine, 1967-77; Sen. Medical Officer, Ashaka Cement Co. Ltd, 1977-79. Hon. LHD Ohio, 1968; Hon DSc Nigeria, 1971; Hon. LLD Ibadan, 1973; FMC (Pæd) Nigerian Med. Council; FRSocMed. *Publications:* contribs to learned jls. *Recreations:* walking, table tennis. *Address:* Ministry of External Affairs, Republic Building, Marina, Lagos, Nigeria.

AUDUS, Prof. Leslie John, MA, PhD, ScD Cantab; FLS, FInstBiol; Hildred Carlile Professor of Botany, Bedford College, University of London, 1948-79; *b* 9 Dec. 1911; English; *m* 1938, Rowena Mabel Ferguson; two *d. Educ:* Downing Coll., Cambridge Univ. Downing Coll. Exhibitioner, 1929-31; Frank Smart Research Student (Cambridge Univ.), 1934-35; Lecturer in Botany, University Coll., Cardiff, 1935-40. Served War of 1939-45: RAFVR (Technical, Radar, Officer), 1940-46; PoW South Pacific, 1942-45. Scientific Officer, Agricultural Research Council, Unit of Soil Metabolism, Cardiff, 1946-47; Monsanto Lecturer in Plant Physiology, University Coll., Cardiff, 1948. Recorder, 1961-65, Pres., 1967-68, Section K, British Assoc. for the Advancement of Science. Vis. Prof. of Botany: Univ. of California, Berkeley, 1958; Univ. of Minnesota, Minneapolis, 1965; Vice-Pres. Linnean Soc. of London, 1959-60; Life Mem. New York Academy of Sciences, 1961. Editor, Journal Exp. Botany, 1965-74. *Publications:* Plant Growth Substances, 1953, 3rd edn 1972; (ed) The Physiology and Biochemistry of Herbicides, 1964; (ed) Herbicides: physiology, biochemistry and ecology, 1976; original research on plant respiration, hormones, responses to gravity, soil micro-biology in relation to pesticides, etc in Annals of Botany, New Phytologist, Nature, Journal of Experimental Botany, Weed Research, etc. *Recreations:* music, photography. *Address:* 38 Belmont Lane, Stanmore, Middlesex HA7 2PT.

AUERBACH, Charlotte, FRS 1957; PhD, DSc; FRSE; Professor of Genetics in the University of Edinburgh (Institute of Animal Genetics), 1967, Emeritus 1969 (Lecturer, 1947-57; Reader, 1957-67). Has done pioneering work on the chemical induction of mutations. Hon. Mem., Genetics Soc., Japan, 1966; Foreign Mem., Kongelige Danske Videnskabernes Selskab, 1968; Foreign Associate, Nat. Acad. of Sciences, USA, 1970. Hon. Dr Leiden, 1975; Hon. ScD Dublin, 1977; Hon. ScD Cambridge, 1977. Darwin Medal, Royal Soc., 1976. *Publications:* Genetics in the Atomic Age, 1956; The Science of Genetics, 1961; Mutation Pt 1-Methods, 1962; Heredity, 1965; Mutation Research, 1976; papers in various general journals. *Address:* Institute of Animal Genetics, The University, West Mains Road, Edinburgh EH9 1SN.

AUERBACH, Frank Helmuth; painter, draughtsman; *b* 29 April 1931; *s* of Max Auerbach, lawyer, and Charlotte Norah Auerbach; *m* 1958, Julia Wolstenholme; one *s. Educ:* privately; St Martin's Sch. of Art; Royal Coll. of Art. *One-man exhibitions:* Beaux Arts Gallery, 1956, 1959, 1961, 1962, 1963; Marlborough Fine Art, 1965, 1967, 1971, 1974, 1977; Marlborough-Gerson, New York, 1969; Villiers, Sydney, Australia, 1972; Bergamini, Milan, 1973; Univ. of Essex, 1973; Mun. Gall. of Modern Art, Dublin, 1974; Marlborough, Zurich, 1976; Anthony D'Offay, London; Arts Council Retrospective, Hayward Gall., 1978; Edinburgh, 1978; NY, 1979, 1982. *Mixed exhibitions:* Carnegie International, Pittsburgh, 1958, 1962; Dunn International, Fredericton, 1963; Gulbenkian International, Tate Gallery, 1964; European Painting in the Seventies, USA, 1976; Annual Exhbn, part I, Hayward Gall., 1977; Westkunst, Cologne, 1981; *Public collections:* Brit. Council; Brit. Museum; Tate Gallery, London; Metropolitan Museum, NY; Mus. of Modern Art, NY; National Gallery of Victoria, Melbourne; Nat. Galls of Australia and W Australia; Chrysler Museum, Provincetown, Mass; County Museum of LA, Calif; Univ. of Cincinnati; Aberdeen, Bedford, Edinburgh, Hartlepool, Huddersfield, Hull, Leeds, Leicester, Manchester, Nottingham, Oldham, Rochdale, Sheffield, Southampton Galls; Arts Council, Contemporary Art Soc., etc. *Address:* c/o Marlborough Fine Art, 6 Albemarle Street, W1X 3HF.

AUGER, Pierre Victor, Grand Officer, Legion of Honour; retired as Director-General European Space Research Organisation (ESRO); Professor, Faculty of Sciences, University of Paris, since 1937; *b* 14 May 1899; *s* of Victor E. Auger, Prof., Univ. of Paris, and Eugénie Blanchet; *m* 1921, Suzanne Motteau; two *d. Educ:* Ecole Normale Supérieure, Paris; Univ. of Paris. Université de Paris (Faculté des Sciences): Asst 1927; Chef de Travaux, 1932; Maître de Conférences, 1937. Research Associate, Univ. of Chicago, 1941-43; Head of Physics Div., joint Anglo-Canadian research project on atomic energy, 1942-44; Dir of Higher Education, Min. of Education, France, 1945-48; Mem. exec. Board of UNESCO, 1946-48; Membre du comité de l'Energie Atomique, France, 1946-48; Dir, Natural Sciences Dept, UNESCO, 1948-59; Special Consultant, UNO and UNESCO, 1959-60; Chm., French Cttee on Space Research, 1960-62. Mem., French Academy of Sciences, 1977. Feltrinelli International Prize, 1961; Kalinga Internat. Prize, 1972; Gaede-Langmuir Award, 1979. FRSA. *Publications:* Rayons cosmiques, 1941; L'Homme microscopique, 1952; Current Trends in Scientific Research, 1961; scientific papers on physics (X-rays, neutrons, cosmic rays), 1923-; papers on philosophy of science, 1949-. *Address:* 12 rue Emile Faguet, 75014 Paris, France. *T:* 540 96 34.

AUGUSTINE, Fennis Lincoln; High Commissioner for Grenada in London, since 1979; *b* 22 April 1932; *s* of late Mr Augustine and of Festina Joseph; *m*

1973, Oforiwa Augustine; one s one d. *Educ:* London Univ. (LLB); Ruskin Coll., Oxford (Labour Studies). Called to the Bar, Gray's Inn, 1972. *Recreations:* cricket, music. *Address:* 18 Langham Road, N15. *T:* 01-839 5922.

AULD, Margaret Gibson, MPhil, SRN, SCM; FRCN; Chief Nursing Officer, Scottish Home and Health Department, since 1977; *b* 11 July 1932; *d* of Alexander John Sutton Auld and late Eleanor Margaret Ingram. *Educ:* Glasgow; Cardiff High Sch. for Girls; Radcliffe Infirm., Oxford (SRN 1953); St David's Hosp., Cardiff; Queen's Park Hosp., Blackburn (SCM 1954). Midwife Teacher's Dipl., 1962; Certif. of Nursing Admin, 1966, MPhil 1974, Edinburgh. Queen's Park Hosp., Blackburn, 1953–54; Staff Midwife, Cardiff Maternity Hosp., 1955, Sister, 1957; Sister, Queen Mary Hosp., Dunedin, NZ, 1959–60; Deptl Sister, Cardiff Maternity Hosp., 1960–66; Asst Matron, Simpson Meml Maternity Pavilion, Edinburgh, 1966–68, Matron, 1968–73; Actg Chief Reg. Nursing Officer, S-Eastern Reg. Hosp. Bd, Edinburgh, 1973; Chief Area Nursing Off., Borders Health Bd, 1973–76. Member: Cttee on Nursing (Briggs), 1970–72; Maternity Services Cttee, Integration of Maternity Work (Tennent Report), 1972–73; Gen. Nursing Council (Scotland), 1973–76; Central Midwives Bd (Scotland), 1972–76. FRCN 1981. *Recreations:* reading, music, entertaining. *Address:* Staddlestones, Belwood Road, Milton Bridge, Penicuik, Midlothian. *T:* Penicuik 72858. *Club:* University of Edinburgh Staff (Edinburgh).

AULD, Robin Ernest, QC 1975; a Recorder of the Crown Court, since 1977; *b* 19 July 1937; *s* of late Ernest Auld; *m* 1963, Catherine Eleanor Mary, *er d* of late David Henry Pritchard; one s one d. *Educ:* Brooklands Coll.; King's Coll., Univ. of London (LLB 1st cl. Hons, PhD). Called to Bar, Gray's Inn, 1959 (Macaskie Schol., Lord Justice Holker Sen. Schol.); SE Circuit; Mem., Commn of Inquiry into Casino Gambling in the Bahamas, 1967; Prosecuting Counsel to Dept of Trade, 1969–75; called to N Ireland Bar, 1973; Chm., William Tyndale Schools' Inquiry, 1975–76; Dept of Trade Inspector, Ashbourne Investments Ltd, 1975–79; Legal Assessor, GMC and GDC, 1982–. Upper Warden, Woolmen's Co. *Address:* Lamb Building, Temple, EC4Y 7AS. *T:* 01-353 6701. *Clubs:* City Livery; Moor Park Golf.

AURIC, Georges; Grand Cross, Legion of Honour, 1981; Commander, Order of Academic Palms; French composer; General Administrator, Paris Opéra and Opéra Comique, 1962–68; *b* Lodève, 15 Feb. 1899; *m* 1930, Nora Vilter. *Educ:* Paris Conservatoire; Schola Cantorum, Paris. Co-founder Les Six movement, 1916. Mem. Acad. des Beaux-Arts, 1962–. Pres., CISAC, 1968–70. *Publications include:* Trois Interludes; Chandelles Romaines; Trio pour Hautbois; *ballet music:* Le Peintre et son Modèle, 1949; Phèdre, 1950; Chemin de Lumière, 1952; Coup de Feu, 1952; Tricolore, 1978; *opera:* Sous le Masque; *music for films:* Le Sang d'un Poète; A Nous la Liberte; Entrée des Artistes; L'Eternel Retour; La Belle et la Bête; La Symphonie Pastorale; Torrents; Ruy Blas; L'Aigle à Deux Têtes; Les Parents Terribles; Maya; Orphée: Caroline Chérie; La P . . . Respectueuse; La Fête à Henriette, etc. *Address:* 36 avenue Matignon, 75008 Paris, France.

AUSTEN-SMITH, Air Marshal Sir Roy (David), KBE 1979; CB 1975; DFC 1953; retired; *b* 28 June 1924; *m* 1951, Ann (*née* Alderson); two s. *Educ:* Hurstpierpoint College. Pilot trng, Canada, 1943–44; 41 Sqn (2 TAF), 1945; 33 Sqdn, Malaya, 1950–53; Cranwell, 1953–56; 73 Sqdn, Cyprus, 1956–59; Air Min., 1960–63; 57 Sqdn, 1964–66; HQ 2 ATAF, 1966–68; CO, RAF Wattisham; MoD, 1970–72; AOC and Comdt, RAF Coll., Cranwell, 1972–75; SASO Near East Air Force, 1975–76; Comdr British Forces, Cyprus, AOC Air HQ Cyprus and Administrator, Sovereign Base Areas, Cyprus, 1976–78; Hd of British Defence Staff, Washington, and Defence Attaché, 1978–81. *Recreation:* golf. *Address:* c/o National Westminster Bank, Swanley, Kent. *Club:* Royal Air Force.

AUSTERBERRY, Ven. Sidney Denham; Archdeacon of Salop, 1959–79, now Archdeacon Emeritus; *b* 28 Oct. 1908; *s* of late Mr and Mrs H. Austerberry; *m* 1934, Eleanor Jane Naylor; two s two d. *Educ:* Hanley High Sch.; Egerton Hall, Manchester. Curate, Newcastle-under-Lyme Parish Church, 1931–38; Vicar of S Alkmund, Shrewsbury, 1938–52; Vicar of Brewood, 1952–59; Hon. Clerical Sec., Lichfield Diocesan Conf., 1954–70; Rural Dean of Penkridge, 1958–59; Vicar of Great Ness, 1959–77. Hon. Canon, Lichfield Cathedral, 1968–79. *Address:* 6 Honeysuckle Row, Sutton Park, Shrewsbury. *T:* Shrewsbury 68080.

AUSTICK, David; Master bookseller, and publisher; *b* 8 March 1920; *m* 1944, Florence Elizabeth Lomath. Member: Leeds City Council (for W Hunslet), 1969–74; Leeds Metropolitan District Council (for Hunslet), 1974–75; W Yorkshire County Council (for Otley and Lower Wharfedale), 1974–. MP (L) Ripon, July 1973–Feb. 1974; Contested (L) Ripon, 1974, (L) Cheadle, 1979, (L) Leeds, European Parlt, 1979. Vice-Pres., Liberal Candidates' Assoc. Member: Electoral Reform Soc.; European Movement; Fellowship of Reconciliation. *Address:* Austick's Bookshops, 29 Cookridge Street, Leeds LS1 3AN; Cross Green, Otley, West Yorks. *Clubs:* National Liberal; Manchester Reform.

AUSTIN, Brian Patrick; HM Diplomatic Service; Deputy High Commissioner, Kaduna, since 1981; *b* 18 March 1938; *s* of Edward William Austin and Winifred Alice Austin; *m* 1968, Augusta Francisca Maria Lina; one *s* one d. *Educ:* St Olave's Grammar Sch.; Clare Coll., Cambridge. National Service, 1956–58. Joined CRO, 1961; Central African Office, 1962; Lagos,

1963; The Hague, 1966; First Sec., FCO, 1969; Montreal, 1973; FCO, 1978. *Recreation:* birdwatching. *Address:* c/o Foreign and Commonwealth Office SW1A 2AH.

AUSTIN, Prof. Colin Russell; Charles Darwin Professor of Animal Embryology, University of Cambridge, 1967–81; *b* 12 Sept. 1914; *s* of Ernest Russell Austin and Linda Mabel King; *m* 1941, Patricia Constance Jack; two s. *Educ:* Univ. of Sydney, Australia (BVSc 1936; DSc 1954). Mem. Research Staff, CSIRO, Australia, 1938–54; Mem. Scientific Staff of MRC, UK, 1954–64; Editor, Jl of Reproduction and Fertility, 1959–64; Head of Genetic and Developmental Disorders Research Program, Delta Regional Primate Research Center, and Prof. of Embryology, Tulane Univ., New Orleans, 1964–67. Editor: Reproduction in Mammals, 1972–; Biological Reviews, 1981–. Marshall Medal, Soc. for Study of Fertility, 1981. *Publications:* The Mammalian Egg, 1961; Fertilization, 1965; Ultrastructure of Fertilization, 1968; numerous research papers. *Recreations:* gardening, swimming, squash. *Address:* Manor Farm House, Toft, Cambridge. *T:* Comberton 2101.

AUSTIN, Hon. Jacob, (Jack), PC (Canada) 1981; QC (Canada) 1970; Member of the Senate, Canadian Parliament, since 1975; Minister of State in Federal Cabinet, since 1981; *b* 2 March 1932; *s* of Morris Austin and Clara Edith (*née* Chetner); *m* (marr. diss.); three d; *m* 1978, Natalie Veiner Freeman. *Educ:* Univ. of British Columbia (BA, LLB); Harvard Univ. (LLM). Barrister and Solicitor, BC and Yukon Territory. Asst Prof. of Law, Univ. of Brit. Columbia, 1955–58; practising lawyer, Vancouver, BC, 1958–63; Exec. Asst to Minister of Northern Affairs and Nat. Resources, 1963–65; contested (Liberal) Vancouver-Kingsway, Can. Federal Election, 1965; practising lawyer, Vancouver, BC, 1966–70; Dep. Minister, Dept of Energy, Mines and Resources, Ottawa, 1970–74; Principal Sec. to Prime Minister, Ottawa, May 1974–Aug. 1975. *Publications:* articles on law and public affairs in Canadian Bar Rev., Amer. Soc. of Internat. Law and other publns. *Recreations:* sailing, squash, reading, theatre. *Address:* Room 283-S, The Senate, Ottawa, Ontario K1A 0A4, Canada. *T:* (613) 992-1437. *Clubs:* Rideau (Ottawa); Cercle Universitaire d'Ottawa; University Club of Vancouver (Vancouver, BC); Metropolitan (NY).

AUSTIN, Professor Lloyd James; FBA 1968; Emeritus Fellow of Jesus College, Cambridge; Emeritus Professor of French; *b* 4 Nov. 1915; *s* of late J. W. A. Austin and late Mrs J. E. Austin (*née* Tymms), Melbourne, Australia; *m* 1939, Jeanne Françoise Guerin, Rouen, France; three s one d. *Educ:* Melbourne Church of England Grammar Sch.; Univ. of Melbourne; Univ. of Paris. French Government Scholar, Paris, 1937–40; Lecturer in French, Univ. of Melbourne, 1940–42. Active Service as Lieut (Special Branch) RANVR, SW Pacific area, 1942–45. Lecturer in French, Univ. of Melbourne, 1945–47; Lecturer in French, Univ. of St Andrews, 1947–51; Research work in Paris, 1951–55; Fellow of Jesus Coll., Cambridge, 1955–56, 1961–80; Professor of Modern French Literature, Univ. of Manchester, 1956–61; Lecturer in French, Univ. of Cambridge, 1961–66, Reader, 1966–67, Drapers Prof. of French, 1967–80; Librarian, Jesus Coll., Cambridge, 1965–68, 1972–73. Herbert F. Johnson Visiting Prof., Inst. for Research in the Humanities, Univ. of Wisconsin, 1962–63; Mem., Editorial Bd, French Studies, 1964–80, Gen. Editor, 1967–80, Mem. Adv. Bd, 1980–; Pres., Assoc. Internat. des Etudes Françaises, 1969–72 (Vice-Pres., 1966–69); Hon. Member: Soc. for French Studies, 1980–; Société d'Histoire Littéraire de la France, 1980; Mem., Acad. Royale de Langue et de Littérature Françaises de Belgique, 1980. Docteur *hc* Paris-Sorbonne, 1973. Prix Henri Mondor, Acad. française, 1981; Prix internat. des amitiés françaises, Soc. des Poètes français, 1982. Chevalier de l'Ordre des Arts et des Lettres, 1971; Officier de l'Ordre National du Mérite, 1976. *Publications:* Paul Bourget, 1940; Paul Valéry: Le Cimetière marin, 1954; L'Univers poétique de Baudelaire, 1956; ed (with E. Vinaver and G. Rees) Studies in Modern French Literature, presented to P. Mansell-Jones, 1961; ed (with H. Mondor) Les Gossips de Mallarmé, 1962; ed (with H. Mondor) Stéphane Mallarmé: Correspondance (1871–1885), 1965, (1886–1889), 1969, (1890–1891), 1973, (1892), 1981, (1893–1894), 1981, (1894–1895), 1982, (1896), 1982, (1897), 1983, (1897–1898), 1983; (ed) Baudelaire: L'Art romantique, 1968; contrib. to French Studies, Modern Languages, Modern Language Review, Forum for Modern Language Studies, Bulletin of the John Rylands Library, Mercure de France, Revue des Sciences Humaines, Revue d'Histoire littéraire de la France, Revue de littérature comparée, Romanic Review, Studi francesi, Synthèses, Revue de l'Université de Bruxelles, L'Esprit créateur, Comparative Literature Studies, Wingspread Lectures in the Humanities, Encyclopædia Britannica, Yale French Studies, Meanjin Quarterly, Australian Jl for French Studies, AUMLA, Quadrant, etc. *Recreations:* watching cricket, tennis, travel. *Address:* 2 Park Lodge, Park Terrace, Cambridge CB1 1JJ. *T:* 59630; Jesus College, Cambridge.

AUSTIN, Dame (Mary) Valerie (Hall), DBE 1979 (OBE 1952); JP; *b* London, 29 July 1900; *d* of Admiral Percival Henry Hall Thompson, CB, CMG, RN, and Helen Sydney Hall Thompson (*née* Deacon); *m* 1925, Ronald Albert Austin, MC; one s. *Educ:* Marsden College, New Zealand. Travelled with father, etc, to Australia, New Zealand, Malta, England; married Australia; lived on land at Eilyer, Mortlake, Vic. Vice Pres., Liberal Party, Victoria, for 30 years; Hon. Life Member: Red Cross, Australia; Victoria League; Victorian Family Council. Coronation Medal, 1953. *Address:* Flat 39, 11 Marne Street, South Yarra, Victoria 3141, Australia. *Clubs:* Alexandra (Melbourne); Barwon Heads Golf.

AUSTIN, Vice-Adm. Sir Peter (Murray), KCB 1976; Director, Avanova International Ltd, since 1980; *b* 16 April 1921; *er s* of late Vice-Adm. Sir Francis Austin, KBE, CB, and late Lady Marjorie Austin (*née* Barker); *m* 1959, Josephine Rhoda Ann Shutte-Smith; three *s* one *d*. *Educ:* RNC, Dartmouth. Cadet, Dartmouth, 1935. Served War of 1939-45: at sea in HMS Cornwall, 1939-40; destroyers, 1941-45. Qualif. as pilot in FAA, 1946; served in 807 Sqdn, 1947-49; CO 736 Sqdn, 1950-52; grad. from RAF Flying Coll., Manby, 1953; comd 850 Sqdn in HMAS Sydney, incl. Korea, 1953-54; Lt-Cmdr (Flying), HMS Bulwark, 1954-56; Comdr (Air), RNAS Brawdy, 1956-58; Comdr (Air), HMS Eagle, 1958-59; Captain, 1961; Captain F7 in HMS Lynx, 1963-65; CO, RNAS Brawdy, 1965-67; Staff of SACLANT, 1967-69; comd aircraft carrier, HMS Hermes, 1969-70; Rear-Adm., 1971; Asst Chief of Naval Staff (Ops and Air), 1971-73; Flag Officer, Naval Air Comd, 1973-76, retired; Vice-Adm., 1974. Operations Dir, Mersey Docks and Harbour Co., 1976-80. FBIM. *Recreations:* golf, ski-ing, squash, sailing, caravanning. *Address:* Dolphin Cottage, 93 The Parade, West Kirby, Wirral LA8 0RR.

AUSTIN, Richard, FRCM; Professor, 1946-76, Director of Opera, 1955-76, Royal College of Music; *b* 26 Dec. 1903; *s* of Frederic and Amy Austin; *m* 1935, Leily, *y d* of Col Wilfred Howell, CBE, DSO. *Educ:* Gresham's Sch., Holt; RCM; Munich. Conductor, Carl Rosa Opera Co., 1929; Musical Dir of the Bournemouth Corporation, 1934-40; Music Advisor Northern Command, 1941-45; Music Dir, New Era Concert Soc., 1947-57. Guest Conductor: Sadler's Wells, London and provincial orchestras, Holland, Belgium, Germany, Spain, Sweden, Switzerland, Finland, Yugoslavia, Czechoslovakia, Cuba, Mexico, South Africa, South America and USA. *Recreations:* squash, tennis. *Address:* Stubbles, Ashampstead, Berks. *T:* Compton 565. *Club:* Savage.

AUSTIN, Thomas Aitken, CMG 1949; LRCP, LRCS, LM (Ireland); DTM&H (Liverpool); DPH (Dublin); late Public Health Officer for East and Central Africa, UN World Health Organisation; *b* 1895. *Educ:* Derry Church Sch.; Royal Coll. of Surgeons, Dublin. Storey Memorial Gold Medal (Anatomy), De Renzy Centenary Prize, 1st place 1st class honours DPH, Royal Coll. of Surgeons, Dublin. Served War of 1939-45, 1939-40; Major. Appointed Zanzibar Protectorate, 1924; Nyasa, 1930; SMO, Tanganyika Territory, 1939; DMS: Nyasa, 1943; Uganda, 1946; PMO, Colonial Office, 1949. *Address:* 38 Sycamore Road, Mount Merrion, Blackrock, Co. Dublin.

AUSTIN, Dame Valerie; *see* Austin, Dame M. V. H.

AUSTIN, Sir William (Ronald), 4th Bt *cr* 1894; *b* 20 July 1900; *s* of Sir William Michael Byron Austin, 2nd Bt, and Violet Irene (*d* 1962), *d* of Alexander Fraser, Westerfield House, near Ipswich; *S* brother, 1981; *m* 1st, 1926, Dorothy Mary (*d* 1957), *d* of late L. A. Bidwell, FRCS; two *s*; 2nd, 1958, Mary Helen Farrell. *Heir: s* Michael Trescawen Austin [*b* 27 Aug. 1927; *m* 1951, Bridget Dorothea Patricia, *d* of late Francis Farrell; three *d*]. *Address:* Creagan, Appin, Argyll. *T:* Appin 213.

AUSTRALIA, Primate of; *see* Brisbane, Archbishop of.

AUSTRALIA, North-West, Bishop of, since 1981;**Rt. Rev. Gerald Bruce Muston;** *b* 19 Jan. 1927; 3rd *s* of Stanley John and Emily Ruth Muston; *m* 1951, Laurel Wright; one *s* one *d*. *Educ:* N Sydney Chatswood High School; Moore Theological College, Sydney. ThL (Aust. Coll. of Theology). Rector, Wallerawang, NSW, 1951-53; Editorial Secretary, Church Missionary Society (Aust.), 1953-58; Rector, Tweed Heads, NSW, 1958-61; Vicar, Essendon, Vic, 1961-67; Rural Dean of Essendon, 1963-67; Rector of Darwin, NT, and Archdeacon of Northern Territory, 1967-69; Federal Secretary, Bush Church Aid Society of Aust., 1969-71; Bishop Coadjutor, dio. Melbourne (Bishop of the Western Region), 1971-81. *Recreations:* golf, reading. *Address:* Bishop's House, 11 Mark Way, Tarcoola, Geraldton, WA 6530, Australia. *Clubs:* Melbourne, Royal Automobile of Victoria (Melbourne).

AUSTWICK, Prof. Kenneth, JP; Professor of Education, Bath University, since 1966; *b* 26 May 1927; *s* of Harry and Beatrice Austwick; *m* 1956, Gillian Griffin; one *s* one *d*. *Educ:* Morecambe Grammar Sch.; Sheffield Univ. BSc Maths, DipEd, MSc, PhD Sheffield. Fellow, Royal Statistical Soc.; FRSA. Schoolmaster, Bromsgrove, Frome and Scunthorpe, 1950-59; Lectr/Sen. Lectr, Sheffield Univ., 1959-65; Dep. Dir, Inst. of Educn, Reading Univ., 1965-66; Pro-Vice-Chancellor, Bath Univ., 1972-75. Vis. Lecturer: Univ. of BC, 1963; Univ. of Michigan, 1963; Univ. of Wits., 1967. Consultant, OECD, 1965; Adviser, Home Office, 1967-81; Chm., Nat. Savings SW Regional Educn, 1975-78. JP Bath 1970. *Publications:* Logarithms, 1962; Equations and Graphs, 1963; (ed) Teaching Machines and Programming, 1964; (ed) Aspects of Educational Technology, 1972; articles and contribs on maths teaching and educnl technology. *Recreations:* gardening, wine making. *Address:* Brook House, Combe Hay, near Bath. *T:* Combe Down 832541. *Club:* Royal Commonwealth Society.

AUSWILD, Sir James (Frederick John), Kt 1974; CBE 1970; FCA, FAIM; Chartered Accountant and Company Director, Australia; Commissioner of Rural Bank of New South Wales (now State Bank of New South Wales), 1961-81; *b* Canbelego, 12 April 1908; *s* of late James Auswild, Temora, and Janet Caroline Auswild (*née* Starr); *m* 1933, Kathleen, *d* of late M. Conway, Lake Cargelligo; two *d*. *Educ:* Temora High Sch. Principal of James F. J.

Auswild & Co., Business Consultants and Chartered Accountants, 1930-. Supervisor, Rural Reconstr. Bd, 1932-39. Mem., Advanced Educn Bd, NSW, 1969-74. Past Dir: Skandia Aust. Insurance Ltd, 1966-74; Glass Tougheners Pty Ltd, 1967-70. Governing Dir, Auswild Org., embracing 130 associated cos; Chairman, Austwide Corp. Pty Ltd and many private cos; Jt Chm. and Managing Dir, Preston Motors Holdings Ltd and Subsidiary Cos. Director: Boyded Pty Ltd; C. V. Holland Pty Ltd; Finance & Guarantee Co. Ltd; Rossfield House Pty Ltd; Auswild Securities Pty Ltd; Embassy Motel, Statesman Hotel Pty Ltd, Canberra; ACT Motors Pty Ltd; Holden Dealers, Canberra; Ambassador Hotel, Canberra; Cooma-Monaro Express Pty Ltd; Canberra Publishing & Printing Co. Pty Ltd; J. F. J. Auswild (Holdings) Pty Ltd; Auswild Properties Pty Ltd; Denman Estate Wines Pty Ltd; Fellow of Local Govt Auditors' Assoc. (FLGA), Aust. *Recreation:* yachting. *Address:* 609 New South Head Road, Rose Bay, Sydney, NSW 2029, Australia. *T:* 36.1711. *Clubs:* American National, Tattersall's, RMYC, CYC, AJC, STC (Sydney); Athenaeum (Melbourne).

AUTY, Richard Mossop, CBE 1978 (OBE 1968); retired; British Council Representative, France and Cultural Counsellor, British Embassy, Paris, 1976-80; *b* 29 Jan. 1920; *s* of Rev. Thomas Richard Auty and Mrs Edith Blanche Auty (*née* Mossop); *m* 1st, 1944, Noreen Collins (marr. diss. 1949); one *d*; 2nd, 1956, (Anne) Marguerite Marie Poncet; one *s* one *d*. *Educ:* Hanley High Sch.; LSE, Univ. of London (BScEcon). Research Officer: Planning Br., Min. of Agriculture and Fisheries, 1942-46; Bureau of Current Affairs, 1946-49; Lectr, Goldsmiths' Coll. and Morley Coll., 1947-49; British Council, 1949-80: Lectr, Milan, 1949-57; Head, Overseas Students Centre, London, 1957-61; Reg. Rep., S India, 1961-65; Cultural Attaché, Brit. Embassy, Budapest, 1965-68; Director: S Asia Dept, 1968-70; Personnel Dept, 1970-72; Controller, European Div., 1972-76. *Recreations:* literature, theatre, cinema. *Address:* 4 Thurlow Road, NW3. *T:* 01-435 8982.

AVEBURY, 4th Baron *cr* 1900; **Eric Reginald Lubbock;** Bt 1806; *b* 29 Sept. 1928; *s* of Hon. Maurice Fox Pitt Lubbock (6th *s* of 1st Baron) (*d* 1957), and Hon. Mary Katherine Adelaide Stanley (*d* 1981), *d* of 5th Baron Stanley of Alderley; *S* cousin, 1971; *m* 1953, Kina Maria, *d* of Count Joseph O'Kelly de Gallagh and Mrs I. D. Bruce; two *s* one *d*. *Educ:* Upper Canada Coll.; Harrow Sch.; Balliol Coll., Oxford (BA Engineering; boxing blue). Welsh Guards (Gdsman, 2nd Lieut), 1949-51; Rolls Royce Ltd, 1951-56; Grad. Apprentice; Export Sales Dept; Tech. Assistant to Foundry Manager. Management Consultant: Production Engineering Ltd, 1953-60; Charterhouse Group Ltd, 1960. MP (L) Orpington, 1962-70; Liberal Whip in House of Commons, 1963-70. Consultant, Morgan-Grampian Ltd, 1970-; Chm., Digico Ltd; Dir, C. L. Projects Ltd. President: Data Processing Management Assoc., 1972-75; Fluoridation Soc., 1972-; Conservation Soc., 1973-. Member: Council, Inst. of Race Relations, 1972-74; Royal Commn on Standards of Conduct in Public Life, 1974-76. MIMechE. *Recreations:* listening to music, reading. *Heir: s* Hon. Lyulph Ambrose Jonathan Lubbock, *b* 15 June 1954. *Address:* House of Lords, SW1.

AVELING, Alan John; Under Secretary, Director of Home Regional Services, Property Services Agency, Department of the Environment, since 1980; *b* 4 Jan. 1928; *s* of late Herbert Ashley Aveling and Ethel Aveling; *m* 1960, Stella May Reed; one *s* one *d*. *Educ:* Fletton Grammar Sch.; Rugby Technical Coll. CEng; FIEE, FIMechE, FCIBS. Air Min. Works Dir, Newmarket, 1951-52; RAF Airfield Construction, 2nd Allied Tactical Air Force, 1952-55; Air Min. HQ, 1955-61; Sen. Engr, War Office Works Dept, 1961-63; BAOR Services, Germany, MPBW, 1963-66; Directorate Personnel, MPBW, 1966-67; Superintending Engr, Overseas Defence and FCO Services, 1967-72; Reg. Works Officer, later Regional Dir, British Forces, Germany, PSA/DoE, 1972-76; Dir of Estate Management Overseas, 1976-78; Dir Eastern Region, PSA/DoE, 1978-80. *Recreations:* aviculture, skiing. *Address:* Running Hook, Peaslake, Guildford, Surrey. *T:* Shere 2499. *Club:* Royal Air Force.

AVERY, David Robert, OBE 1976; HM Diplomatic Service, retired; *b* 20 Oct. 1921; *o s* of late Percival John Avery and Mary Woodcock Avery; *m* 1948, Vera Andrews; one *s* one *d*. *Educ:* Plympton Grammar Sch., Devonport; Dockyard Technical Coll. Admiralty service in Sierra Leone, India and Ceylon, 1939-59. Lieut RNVR, 1943. Commonwealth Relations Office, 1960; First Secretary, Lagos, Nigeria, 1963-65; Consul, Basra, Iraq, 1966; FCO, 1967-71; First Sec., Nairobi, Kenya, 1972-76; FCO, 1976; Counsellor and Head of Claims Dept, FCO, 1978-80. *Recreations:* gardening, shooting. *Address:* Little Acre, 1 Woodland Way, Kingsgate, Broadstairs, Kent CT10 3QD. *T:* Thanet 602400. *Club:* Nairobi (Kenya).

AVERY, Gillian Elise, (Mrs A. O. J. Cockshut); writer; *b* 1926; *d* of Norman and Grace Avery; *m* 1952, A. O. J. Cockshut; one *d*. *Educ:* Dunottar Sch., Reigate. *Publications: children's fiction:* The Warden's Niece, 1957; Trespassers at Charlcote, 1958; James without Thomas, 1959; The Elephant War, 1960; To Tame a Sister, 1961; The Greatest Gresham, 1962; The Peacock House, 1963; The Italian Spring, 1964; The Call of the Valley, 1966; A Likely Lad (Guardian Award, 1972), 1971; Huck and her Time Machine, 1977; *adult fiction:* The Lost Railway, 1980; *non-fiction:* 19th Century Children: heroes and heroines in English children's stories (with Angela Bull), 1965; Victorian People in Life and Literature, 1970; The Echoing Green: memories of Regency and Victorian youth, 1974; Childhood's Pattern, 1975. Ed, Gollancz revivals of early children's books, 1967-70, and anthologies of stories and extracts from early children's books. *Recreations:* walking, growing vegetables, cooking. *Address:* 32 Charlbury Road, Oxford.

AVERY, James Royle, (Roy Avery); Headmaster, Bristol Grammar School, since 1975; *b* 7 Dec. 1925; *s* of Charles James Avery and Dorothy May Avery; *m* 1954, Marjorie Louise (*née* Smith); one *s* one *d*. *Educ:* Queen Elizabeth's Hosp., Bristol; Magdalen Coll., Oxford; Bristol Univ. MA Oxon, CertifEd Bristol; FRSA. Asst History Master, Bristol Grammar Sch., 1951-59; Sen. History Master, Haberdashers' Aske's Sch. at Hampstead, then Elstree, 1960-65; Head Master, Harrow County Boys' Sch., 1965-75. *Publications:* The Story of Aldenham House, 1961; The Elstree Murder, 1962; contrib. Dictionary of World History, 1973; articles, reviews in educnl jls. *Recreations:* ecumenical movement, American studies and international affairs, rugby, cricket, theatre, music, walking. *Address:* Headmaster's House, Bristol Grammar School, 7 Elton Road, Bristol BS8 1SJ. *T:* Bristol 737832.

AVERY, Percy Leonard; Chairman, staff side, Civil Service National Whitley Council, 1977-80; General Secretary, Association of Government Supervisors and Radio Officers, 1951-79; *b* 10 March 1915; *s* of Percy James Avery and Frances Elisabeth Avery; *m* 1940, Joan Mahala Breakspear; one *s* one *d* (and one *d* decd). *Educ:* Woolwich Polytechnic. Served War: Navigator, RAF Bomber Comd, 1941-45; Flt Lieut. Exec. Sec., Internat. Fedn of Air Traffic Electronics Assoc., 1972-79. Member: Kent Area Health Authority, 1973-; MoD Management Review Body, 1975-76; Civil Service Pay Rev. Board, 1978-79; CS Deptl Whitley Councils (various), 1949-77. Dir of Admin, British Karate Bd, 1979-; Treasurer, English Karate Council, 1981-. Governor, Ruskin Coll; Mem., Kent Age Concern, 1980-. *Recreations:* athletics, Rugby, music, gardening. *Address:* Ben Edor, Woodchurch, near Tenterden, Kent. *T:* Woodchurch 339.

AVERY, Roy; *see* Avery, J. R.

AVERY JONES, Sir Francis; *see* Jones, Sir F. A.

AVES, Dame Geraldine (Maitland), DBE 1977 (CBE 1963; OBE 1946); *b* 22 Aug. 1898; *er d* of Ernest Aves, MA, FSS, and Eva Mary (*née* Maitland). *Educ:* Frognal Sch., Hampstead; Newnham Coll., Cambridge (MA; Hon. Fellow, 1981). Education Dept, LCC: Sch. Care Organiser, 1924-38; assisting planning and develt of war-time evacuation services, 1938-41; Ministry of Health, Chief Welfare Officer and Head of Welfare Divn, 1941-63. Seconded: to UNRRA as Chief Child Care Consultant (Europe), 1945-46; to Home Office, to initiate child care training, 1947-48; various assignments to UN Headqrs, in field of family and child welfare and to direct UN Seminars for European Region, 1949-69. Governor, Nat. Inst. for Social Work Training, 1961-71; Mem. Council for Training in Social Work, 1962-72; Associate Fellow, Newnham Coll., 1962-65 and 1966-69. Chairman: Adv. Council of Nat. Corp. for the Care of Old People, 1965-72 (Vice-Pres. 1981-); Cttee of Enquiry into Voluntary Workers in the Social Services, 1966-69 (Report: The Voluntary Worker in the Social Services, 1969); N Islington Welfare Centre, 1977-81 (Pres., 1981-). Pres., Newnham College Roll, 1969-72. Mem., London Diocesan Synod and Bishop's Council, 1971-79; Vice-Chm., London Diocesan Bd for Social Responsibility, 1979-; Founder Mem., Governing Body, The Volunteer Centre, 1973- (Vice-Pres., 1977-); Chairman: Working Party that produced PIVOT (People Involved in Volunteer Organisation and Tasks), published 1976; Prep. Cttee, 1977, Bd of Dirs, 1980-, The Harington Scheme (horticultural trng centre for mentally handicapped); Highgate Cemetery Trust, 1977-81; serves on several local environmental and parochial organisations. *Recreation:* birdwatching. *Address:* 24 North Grove, Highgate Village, N6 4SL. *T:* 01-340 1685. *Club:* University Women's.

AVGHERINOS, George, QC 1982; *b* Poti, Georgia, Caucasus, 6 Jan. 1906; *s* of Homer and Eftichia Avgherinos; *m* 1944, Beatrice Eleanor, *d* of Oscar and Mabel Siewert; one *s*. *Educ:* St Paul's School; Brasenose Coll., Oxford. MA, BCL. Served RAF, 1941-46, Administration. Harmsworth Scholarship, Middle Temple, 1929; called to the Bar, Middle Temple, 1932; Barstow Scholarship, 1932; Bencher, Middle Temple, 1964. *Publications:* (ed jtly) Landlord and Tenant Act 1927, 3rd edn 1949; (jtly) Leasehold Property (Temporary Provisions) Act 1951, 1951; (jtly) Housing Repairs and Rents Act 1954, 1954; (ed jtly) Rent and Mortgage Interest Restrictions, 23rd edn, 1956. *Recreations:* music, braille. *Address:* Flat 5, 1 Linden Gardens, W2 4HA.

AVON, 2nd Earl of, *cr* 1961; **Nicholas Eden,** OBE 1970; TD 1965; ADC; DL; a Lord in Waiting (Government Whip), and spokesman for the arts, environment and transport, since 1980; *b* 3 Oct. 1930; *o surv. s* of 1st Earl of Avon, KG, PC, MC, and Beatrice Helen (*d* 1957), *d* of Hon. Sir Gervase Beckett, 1st Bt; *S* father, 1977. *Educ:* Eton. Served with KRRC, 1949-51; ADC to the Governor-Gen. of Canada, 1952-53; served in Queen Victoria's Rifles (TA), 1953-61; on amalgamation, served in Queen's Royal Rifles (TA), 1961-67; 4th (Volunteer) Bn, Royal Green Jackets, 1967-70; Major, 1959; Lt-Col, 1965; Col, TAVR, 1972-75; Hon. Col. ACF, NE Sector Greater London, 1970; Vice-Chm., Greater London TA&VRA, 1976-81. ADC (TA) to the Queen, 1978-. An Opposition Whip, 1978-79; Parly deleg. to N Atlantic Assembly, 1979-80. Master, Salters' Co., 1979-80. DL Greater London, 1973. *Recreations:* lawn tennis, Eton fives. *Address:* House of Lords, SW1. *Club:* All England Lawn Tennis.

AVONSIDE, Rt. Hon. Lord; Ian Hamilton Shearer, PC 1962; a Senator of the College of Justice in Scotland since 1964; *b* 6 Nov. 1914; *s* of Andrew Shearer, OBE, and Jessie Macdonald; *m* 1st, 1942; one *s* one *d*; 2nd, 1954, Janet

Sutherland Murray (*see* Lady Avonside). *Educ:* Dunfermline High Sch. Glasgow Univ.; Edinburgh Univ. MA Glasgow, 1934; LLB Edinburgh, 1937 Admitted to Faculty of Advocates, 1938; QC (Scotland) 1952. Served War of 1939-45, RA; Major; released 1946, Emerg. R of O. Standing Counsel: to Customs and Excise, Bd of Trade and Min. of Labour, 1947-49; to Inland Revenue, 1949-51; to City of Edinburgh Assessor, 1949-51; Junior Lega Assessor to City of Edinburgh, 1951; Sheriff of Renfrew and Argyll, 1960-62 Lord Advocate, 1962-64. Mem., Lands Valuation Court, 1964 (Chm., 1975-) Chm. Nat. Health Service Tribunal, Scotland, 1954-62; Mem. Scottish Cttee of Coun. on Tribunals, 1958-62; Chm. Scottish Valuation Advisory Coun. 1965-68; Mem., Scottish Univs Cttee of the Privy Council, 1971-. Pres., Stair Soc., 1975-. *Publications:* Purves on Licensing Laws, 1947; Acta Dominorum Concilii et Sessionis, 1951. *Recreation:* golf. *Address:* The Mill House Samuelston, East Lothian. *T:* Haddington 2396. *Clubs:* Garrick; New (Edinburgh).

AVONSIDE, Lady; Janet Sutherland Shearer, OBE 1958; Scottish Governor, BBC, 1971-76; *b* 31 May 1917; *d* of William Murray, MB, ChB, and Janet Harley Watson; *m* 1953, Ian Hamilton Shearer, Rt Hon. Lord Avonside, *qv. Educ:* St Columba's Sch., Kilmacolm; Erlenhaus, Baden Baden; Univ. of Edinburgh. LLB, Dip. of Social Science. Asst Labour Officer (Scot.), Min. of Supply, 1941-45; Sec. (Scot.), King George's Fund for Sailors, 1945-53; Hon. Sec. (Scot.), Federal Union and United Europe, 1945-64 Scottish Delegate: Congress of Europe, 1947; Council of Europe, Strasburg, 1949. Contested (C), elections: Maryhill, Glasgow, 1950; Dundee East, 1951; Leith, 1955. Lectr in Social Studies, Dept of Educational Studies, Univ. of Edinburgh, 1962-70. *Recreation:* gardening. *Address:* The Mill House, Samuelston, East Lothian, Scotland. *T:* Haddington 2396. *Clubs:* Caledonian (Associate Mem.); New (Edinburgh).

AWAD, Muhammad Hadi; Ambassador of The People's Democratic Republic of Yemen to Tunisia and Permanent Representative to The Arab League, since 1980; *b* 5 May 1934; Yemeni; *m* 1956, Adla; one *s* three *d*. *Educ:* Murray House Coll. of Educn. DipEd, Certif. Social Anthrop. Edinburgh. Teacher, 1953-59; Educn Officer, 1960-62; Chief Inspector of Schs, 1963-65; Vice-Principal, As-Shaab Coll., 1965-67; Perm. Rep. to Arab League, Ambassador to UAR and non-resident Ambassador to Sudan, Lebanon, Libya and Iraq, 1968-70; Perm. Sec., Min. of For. Affairs, 1970-73; Ambassador to London, 1973-80, to Sweden and Spain, 1974-80, to Denmark, Portugal and the Netherlands, 1975-80. *Recreation:* photography. *Address:* Embassy of The People's Democratic Republic of Yemen, Tunis, Tunisia.

AWAK, Shehu, OFR 1981; High Commissioner for Nigeria in the UK, since 1981; *b* Awak, 14 May 1932; *m* 1953, A'ishatu Shehu Awak; four *s* six *d*. *Educ:* Nigerian Coll.; Manchester Univ. (DCPA 1966); London Sch. of Economics. ASTC IV, Zaria, 1961. Nigerian Foreign Service: Admin. Officer, 1961-70; actg Perm. Sec., 1970-73; Perm. Sec., 1973-78; Sec. to Mil. Govt, 1978-79, and Head of CS, 1978-81, Bauchi State. *Recreations:* table tennis, walking, gaming. *Address:* (office) 9 Northumberland Avenue, WC2N 5BX. *T:* 01-839 2037; (home) 15A Kensington Palace Gardens, W8. *T:* 01-221 3734.

AWDRY, Daniel (Edmund), TD; DL; *b* 10 Sept. 1924; *s* of late Col Edmund Portman Awdry, MC, TD, DL, Coters, Chippenham, Wilts, and Mrs Evelyn Daphne Alexandra Awdry, JP (formerly French); *m* 1950, Elizabeth Cattley; three *d*. *Educ:* Winchester Coll. RAC, OCTU, Sandhurst, 1943-44 (Belt of Honour). Served with 10th Hussars as Lieut, Italy, 1944-45; ADC to GOC 56th London Div., Italy, 1945; Royal Wilts Yeo., 1947-62; Major and Sqdn Comdr, 1955-62. Qualified Solicitor, 1950. Mayor of Chippenham, 1958-59; Pres., Southern Boroughs Assoc., 1959-60. MP (C) Chippenham, Wilts, Nov. 1962-1979; PPS to Minister of State, Board of Trade, Jan.-Oct. 1964; PPS to Solicitor-Gen., 1973-74. Director: BET Omnibus Services, 1966-80; Sheepbridge Engineering, 1968-79; Rediffusion Ltd, 1973-; Colonial Mutual Life Assurance Ltd, 1974-. DL Wilts, 1979. *Recreations:* cricket (Mem. Free Foresters and Butterflies), chess. *Address:* Old Manor, Beanacre, near Melksham, Wilts. *T:* Melksham 702315.

AXELROD, Julius, PhD; Chief, Section on Pharmacology, Laboratory of Clinical Science, National Institute of Mental Health, USA, since 1955 (Acting Chief, Jan.-Oct. 1955); *b* NYC, 30 May 1912; *s* of Isadore Axelrod, Michaliev, Poland, and Molly Liechtling, Striej, Poland (formerly Austria); *m* 1938, Sally (*née* Taub); two *s*. *Educ:* George Washington Univ., Wash., DC (PhD); New York Univ. (MA); New York City Coll. (BS). Lab. Asst Dept Bacteriology, NY Univ. Med. Sch., 1933-35; Chemist, Lab. Industrial Hygiene, 1935-46; Res. Associate, Third NY Univ.; Research Div., Goldwater Memorial Hosp., 1946-49; Nat. Heart Inst., NIH: Associate Chemist, Section on Chem. Pharmacology, 1949-50; Chemist, 1950-53; Sen. Chemist, 1953-55. Jt Nobel Prize for Physiology-Medicine, 1970; Mem., Nat. Academy of Sciences, 1971; Fellow, Amer. Acad. of Arts and Sciences; Senior Mem., Amer. Inst. of Medicine, 1979. For. Mem., Royal Society, 1979. Hon. LLD: George Washington, 1971; College City, NY, 1972; Hon. DSc: Chicago, 1966; Med. Coll., Wisconsin, 1971; New York, 1971; Pennsylvania Coll. of Med., 1973; Doctor *hc* Panama, 1972. Winner of 15 awards; holds 23 hon. lectureships; Member: 13 editorial boards; 5 Sci. Adv. Cttees. *Publications:* (with Richard J. Wurtman and Douglas E. Kelly) The Pineal, 1968; numerous original papers and contribs to jls in Biochem., Pharmacol. and Physiology. *Recreations:* reading and listening to music. *Address:* 10401 Grosvenor Place, Rockville, Maryland 20852, USA. *T:* (301) 493-6376.

AXFORD, Dr William Ian; Vice-Chancellor, Victoria University of Wellington, New Zealand, since 1982; *b* 2 Jan. 1933; *s* of John Edgar Axford and May Victoria Axford; *m* 1955, Catherine Joy; two *s* two *d*. *Educ*: Univ. of Canterbury, NZ (MSc Hons, ME Dist.); Univ. of Manchester (PhD); Univ. of Cambridge. NZ Defence Science Corps, 1957–63; seconded to Defence Res. Bd, Ottawa, 1960–62; Associate Prof. of Astronomy, 1963–66, Prof. of Astronomy, 1966–67, Cornell Univ. Ithaca, NY; Prof. of Physics and Applied Physics, Univ. of Calif at San Diego, 1967–74; Dir, Max-Planck-Institut für Aeronomie, Lindau, W Germany, 1974–82. *Publications*: about 150 articles in scientific jls on aspects of space physics and astrophysics. *Address*: 11 Kinross Street, Wellington, New Zealand.

AXISA, John Francis, MBE 1950; *b* 20 Nov. 1906; *s* of late Emmanuel Axisa and Vincenzina (*née* Micallef); *m* 1939, Ariadne Cachia; three *s* one *d*. *Educ*: St Paul's Sch., Malta and privately. Joined Malta Civil Service, 1927; Dir of Emigration, 1947–56; Dir of Technical Education, 1956–59; Dir of Emigration, Labour and Social Welfare, 1959–60; Under-Sec., 1960–61; Commissioner-Gen. for Malta in London, 1961–64; Malta's first High Commissioner on Malta's Independence, 1964–69; Ambassador of Malta to: France, 1966–69; Fed. Republic of Germany, 1967–69; Libya, 1966–68; Belgium, 1967–68; Netherlands, 1968–69. *Recreations*: carpentry, fishing, reading. *Address*: Godolphin, San Anton, Attard, Malta, GC. *Club*: Union (Malta).

AXTON, Henry Stuart, FCA; Deputy Chairman since 1971, and Managing Director since 1963, Brixton Estate Ltd; *b* 6 May 1923; *s* of Wilfrid George Axton and Mary Louise Laver; *m* 1947, Constance Mary Godefroy; one *d*. *Educ*: Rock Ferry. RMC, Sandhurst, commissioned 1942; served: N Africa, Royal Tank Regt, NW Europe, Fife and Forfar Yeo.; wounded three times, invalided out, 1945. Articles, G. E. Holt & Son; Chartered Accountant 1948. Treas., United Sheffield Hosps and other hosp. appts, 1948–55; Company Sec., Midland Assurance, 1955–61; Brixton Estate, 1961–; Chm., Investment Cos in Australia, Belgium, France Germany, USA; Mem. Council, British Property Fedn, 1974–. Member: Council, St George's Hosp. Med. Sch., 1969– (Chm. 1977–, Dep. Chm. 1974); St George's New Hosp. Bldg Cttee, 1969– (Chm. 1972–); Governor: Nuffield Nursing Homes Trust, 1968– (Chm. 1976–; Dep. Chm. 1975); BUPA, 1969–80; Medical Centre, 1970–82 (Chm. 1973–82); St George's Hosp., 1970–74, Special Trustee, 1974–77. *Recreations*: sailing, music. *Address*: Invermark, Oxted, Surrey RH8 0EJ. *T*: Oxted 2935. *Clubs*: Royal Thames Yacht, Royal Ocean Racing.

AXWORTHY, Geoffrey (John); Artistic Director of Sherman Theatre, University College, Cardiff, since 1970; *b* Plymouth, England, 10 Aug. 1923; *s* of William Henry Axworthy and Gladys Elizabeth Kingcombe; *m* 1st, 1951, Irene Dickinson (*d* 1976); two *s* one *d*; 2nd, 1977, Caroline Griffiths. *Educ*: Exeter Coll., Oxford (MA). On staff of: Univ. of Baghdad 1951–56; Univ. of Ibadan, Nigeria, 1956–67. First Director, Univ. of Ibadan Sch. of Drama, 1962–67. Principal, Central School of Speech and Drama, London, 1967–70. Founded Univ. of Ibadan Travelling Theatre, 1961. *Address*: Monkton House, Marine Parade, Penarth, South Glamorgan, S Wales. *T*: Cardiff 703360.

AYALA, Jaime Z. de; *see* Zobel de Ayala.

AYCKBOURN, Alan; playwright; Director of Productions, Stephen Joseph Theatre-in-the-Round, Scarborough; *b* 12 April 1939; *s* of Horace Ayckbourn and Irene Maude (*née* Worley); *m* 1959, Christine Helen (*née* Roland); two *s*. *Educ*: Haileybury. Worked in repertory as Stage Manager/Actor at Edinburgh, Worthing, Leatherhead, Oxford, and with late Stephen Joseph's Theatre-in-the-Round Co., at Scarborough. Founder Mem., Victoria Theatre, Stoke-on-Trent, 1962. BBC Radio Drama Producer, Leeds, 1964–70. Has written numerous full-length plays, mainly for Theatre-in-the-Round Co., 1959–. London productions: Mr Whatnot, Arts, 1964; Relatively Speaking, Duke of York's, 1967; How the Other Half Loves, Lyric, 1970; Time and Time Again, Comedy, 1972 (televised 1976); Absurd Person Singular, Criterion, 1973 (Evening Standard Drama Award, Best Comedy, 1973); The Norman Conquests (Trilogy), Globe, 1974 (Evening Standard Drama Award, Best Play; Variety Club of GB Award; Plays and Players Award) (televised, 1977); Jeeves (musical, with Andrew Lloyd Webber), Her Majesty's, 1975; Absent Friends, Garrick, 1975; Confusions, Apollo, 1976; Bedroom Farce, Nat. Theatre, 1977 (televised 1980); Just Between Ourselves, Queen's, 1977 (Evening Standard Drama Award, Best Play) (televised, 1978); Ten Times Table, Globe, 1978; Joking Apart, Globe, 1979 (Plays and Players Award); Sisterly Feelings, Nat. Theatre, 1980; Taking Steps, Lyric, 1980; Suburban Strains, Round House, 1981; Season's Greetings, Apollo, 1982; Way Upstream, Nat. Theatre, 1982. Scarborough: Making Tracks (musical with Paul Todd), 1981; Intimate Exchange, 1982. Hon. DLitt Hull, 1981. *Publications*: The Norman Conquests, 1975; Three Plays (Absurd Person Singular, Absent Friends, Bedroom Farce), 1977; Joking Apart and Other Plays (Just Between Ourselves, Ten Times Table), 1979; Sisterly Feelings, 1981; Taking Steps, 1981. *Recreations*: music, reading, cricket, films. *Address*: c/o Margaret Ramsay Ltd, 14a Goodwin's Court, St Martin's Lane, WC2N 4LL. *T*: 01-240 0691. *Club*: Garrick.

AYER, Sir Alfred (Jules), Kt 1970; FBA 1952; Wykeham Professor of Logic in the University of Oxford, and Fellow of New College, Oxford, 1959–78, Hon. Fellow, 1980; Fellow of Wolfson College, Oxford, since 1978; *b* 29 Oct. 1910; *s* of late Jules Louis Cyprien Ayer; *m* 1932, Grace Isabel Renée Lees; one *s* one *d*; *m* 1960, Alberta Constance Chapman (Dee Wells); one *s*. *Educ*:

Eton Coll. (scholar); Christ Church, Oxford (scholar; Hon. Student, 1979). 1st class Lit. Hum. 1932; MA 1936; Lecturer in Philosophy at Christ Church, 1932–35; Research Student, 1935–44; Fellow of Wadham Coll., Oxford, 1944–46, Hon. Fellow, 1957; Dean, 1945–46; Grote Professor of the Philosophy of Mind and Logic, 1946–59, and Dean of the Arts Faculty, 1950–52, Univ. of London; Hon. Fellow, UCL, 1979. Visiting Prof. at: NY Univ., 1948–49; City Coll., New York, 1961–62; Surrey Univ., 1978–; Lectures: William James, Harvard, 1970; John Dewey, Columbia, 1970; Gifford, St Andrews, 1972–73. Mem., Central Advisory Council for Education, 1963–66; President: Independent (formerly Agnostics) Adoption Soc., 1965–; Humanist Assoc., 1965–70; Modern Languages Assoc., 1966–67. Chm., Booker Prize Cttee, 1978. Hon. Mem. Amer. Acad. of Arts and Sciences 1963; For. Mem., Royal Danish Acad. of Sciences and Letters, 1976. Dr *hc* Univ. of Brussels, 1962; Hon. DLitt: East Anglia, 1972; London, 1978; Trent, Ontario, 1980. Chevalier de la Légion d'Honneur, 1977; Order of Cyril and Methodius, 1st cl. (Bulgaria), 1977. Enlisted in Welsh Guards, 1940; commissioned, 1940; Capt. 1943. Attaché at HM Embassy, Paris, 1945. *Publications*: Language, Truth and Logic, 1936 (revised edn 1946); The Foundations of Empirical Knowledge, 1940; Thinking and Meaning (Inaugural Lecture), 1947; (ed with Raymond Winch) British Empirical Philosophers, 1952; Philosophical Essays, 1954; The Problem of Knowledge, 1956; (ed) Logical Positivism, 1959; Privacy (British Academy lecture), 1960; Philosophy and Language (Inaugural lecture), 1960; The Concept of a Person and Other Essays, 1963; Man as a Subject for Science (Auguste Comte Lecture), 1964; The Origins of Pragmatism, 1968; (ed) The Humanist Outlook, 1968; Metaphysics and Common Sense, 1969; Russell and Moore: the analytical heritage, 1971; Probability and Evidence, 1972; Russell, 1972; Bertrand Russell as a Philosopher (British Acad. Lecture), 1973; The Central Questions of Philosophy, 1974; Part of my Life, 1977; Perception and Identity (Festschrift with reply to critics), 1979; Hume, 1980; articles in philos. and lit. jls. *Address*: 51 York Street, W1H 1DF. *T*: 01-402 0235. *Clubs*: Athenæum, Garrick, Beefsteak.

AYERS, Herbert Wilfred, CB 1951; CBE 1948; retired; Under Secretary for Finance and Accountant-General, Ministry of National Insurance, 1948–53; *b* 22 May 1889; *s* of Joseph Drake Ayers; *m* Ethel M. Pitcher (decd); two *s*. Entered Civil Service, 1905; Ministry of Labour, 1913–44; joined Ministry of National Insurance, Dec. 1944 (Deputy Accountant-General). *Recreation*: philately. *Address*: 3158 Mallbridge Crescent, Malton, Ontario L4T 2C6, Canada.

See also J. G. Ayers.

AYERS, John Gilbert; Keeper, Far Eastern Department, Victoria and Albert Museum, since 1970; *b* 27 July 1922; *s* of H. W. Ayers, *qv*; *m* 1957, Bridget Elspeth Jacqualine Fanshawe; one *s* two *d*. *Educ*: St Paul's Sch.; St Edmund Hall, Oxford. Served in RAF, 1941–46 (Sgt). Asst Keeper, Dept of Ceramics, Victoria and Albert Museum, 1950, Dep. Keeper 1963. *Publications*: The Seligman Collection of Oriental Art, II, 1964; The Baur Collection; Chinese Ceramics, I–IV, 1968–74; (with R. J. Charleston) The James A. de Rothschild Collection: Meissen and Oriental Porcelain, 1971; Oriental Ceramics, The World's Great Collections: Victoria and Albert Museum (Tokyo), 1975; (with J. Rawson) Chinese Jade throughout the Ages, exhbn catalogue, 1975; (with D. Howard) China for the West, 2 vols, 1978; (with D. Howard) Masterpieces of Chinese Export Porcelain, 1980. *Address*: 3 Bedford Gardens, W8 7ED. *T*: 01-229-5168.

AYKROYD, Sir Cecil William, 2nd Bt, *cr* 1929; *b* 23 April 1905; *e s* of Sir Frederic Alfred Aykroyd, 1st Bt and late Lily May, *e d* of Sir James Roberts, 1st Bt, LLD, of Strathallan Castle, Perthshire, and Fairlight Hall, near Hastings; *S* father 1949; unmarried. *Educ*: Charterhouse; Jesus Coll., Cambridge. BA 1926. Dir, Nat. Provincial Bank Ltd, 1958–69 (Dir Bradford and District Bd, 1946–69). *Recreations*: fishing and shooting. *Heir*: *b* Bertram Aykroyd [*b* 17 Sept. 1915; *m* 1st, 1938, Margot (marr. diss. 1947), *er d* of late Leonard Graham Brown, FRCS; one *s* one *d*; 2nd, 1949, Catalina, *o d* of late Henry Marchington; two *s* one *d*]. *Address*: Birstwith Hall, near Harrogate, North Yorks. *T*: Harrogate 770250.

AYKROYD, Sir William Miles, 3rd Bt *cr* 1920; MC 1944; *b* 24 Aug. 1923; *s* of Sir Alfred Hammond Aykroyd, 2nd Bt, and Sylvia Ambler Aykroyd (*née* Walker), *widow* of Lieut-Col Foster Newton Thorne; *S* father, 1965. *Educ*: Charterhouse. Served in 5th Royal Inniskilling Dragoon Guards, Lieut, 1943–47. Dir, Hardy Amies Ltd, 1950–69. *Heir*: *cousin* Michael David Aykroyd [*b* 14 June 1928; *m* 1952, Oenone Gillian Diana, *o d* of Donald George Cowling, MBE; one *s* three *d*]. *Address*: Buckland Newton Place, Dorchester, Dorset. *T*: Buckland Newton 259. *Club*: Boodle's.

AYLEN, Rear-Adm. Ian Gerald, CB 1962; OBE 1946; DSC 1942; CEng; FIMechE; *b* 12 Oct. 1910; *s* of late Commander A. E. Aylen, RN and Mrs S. C. M. Aylen; *m* 1937, Alice Brough Maltby; one *s* two *d*. *Educ*: Blundell's, Tiverton. RNE Coll., Keyham, 1929–33; served in HMS Rodney; Curacoa; Galatea, 1939–40; Kelvin, 1940–42; 30 Assault Unit, 1945; Cossack; Fleet Engineer Officer, Home Fleet, 1957–58; CO HMS Thunderer, RNE Coll., 1958–60; Rear-Admiral, 1960; Admiral Superintendent, HM Dockyard, Rosyth, 1960–63; Dep. Sec., Instn Mechanical Engineers, 1963–65; Asst Sec., Council of Engineering Instns, 1966–71, retired 1971. *Address*: Tracey Mill Barn, Honiton, Devon. *Club*: St Stephen's Constitutional.

AYLESFORD, 11th Earl of; **Charles Ian Finch-Knightley**, JP; Baron Guernsey, 1703; Lord-Lieutenant of West Midlands, since 1974; *b* 2 Nov. 1918; *er s* of 10th Earl of Aylesford; *S* father, 1958; *m* 1946, Margaret Rosemary Tyer; one *s* two *d. Educ:* Oundle. Lieut RSF, 1939; Captain Black Watch, 1947. Regional Dir, Birmingham and W Midlands Bd, Lloyds Bank, 1982-. Mem., Water Space Amenity Commn, 1973-. County Comr for Scouts, 1949-74, Patron 1974-. JP 1948, DL 1954, Vice-Lieutenant 1964-74, Warwicks. KStJ 1974. *Recreations:* wild life and nature conservation. *Heir: s* Lord Guernsey, *qv. Address:* Packington Old Hall, Coventry, West Midlands CV7 7HG. *T:* (home) Meriden 23273; (office) Meriden 22274. *Club:* Warwickshire CC (President, 1980-).

AYLESTONE, Baron *cr* 1967 (Life Peer), of Aylestone; **Herbert William Bowden**; PC 1962; CH 1975; CBE 1953; Chairman, Independent Broadcasting Authority (formerly Independent Television Authority), 1967-75; *b* 20 Jan. 1905; *m* 1928, Louisa Grace, *d* of William Brown, Cardiff; one *d.* RAF, 1941-45. MP (Lab) S Leicester, 1945-50, S-W Div. of Leicester, 1950-67. PPS to Postmaster-Gen., 1947-49; Asst Govt Whip, 1949-50; a Lord Comr of the Treasury, 1950-51; Dep. Chief Oppn Whip, 1951-55; Chief Oppn Whip, 1955-64; Lord Pres. of the Council and Leader of the House of Commons, 1964-66; Secretary of State for Commonwealth Affairs, 1966-67; joined SDP, 1981, Leader of SDP in House of Lords, 1981-. *Address:* c/o House of Lords, SW1.

AYLING, Peter William, BSc, CEng, FRINA; Secretary, Royal Institution of Naval Architects, since 1967; *b* 25 Sept. 1925; *s* of late William Frank and Edith Louise Ayling; *m* 1949, Sheila Bargery; two *s* two *d. Educ:* Royal Dockyard Sch., Portsmouth; King's Coll., Univ. of Durham (BSc). Shipwright apprentice, HM Dockyard, Portsmouth, 1942-47; King's Coll., Univ. of Durham, 1947-50; Research and Principal Research Officer, British Ship Research Assoc., London, 1950-65; Principal Scientific Officer, Ship Div., Nat. Physical Laboratory, Feltham (now Nat. Maritime Inst.), 1965-67. *Publications:* papers on ship strength and vibration, Trans RINA, NECInst and IESS. *Recreations:* music, gardening, walking, motoring. *Address:* Royal Institution of Naval Architects, 10 Upper Belgrave Street, SW1X 8BQ. *T:* 01-235 4622; (home) Oakmead, School Road, Camelsdale, Haslemere, Surrey. *T:* Haslemere 4474.

AYLING, Air Vice-Marshal Richard Cecil, CB 1965; CBE 1961 (OBE 1948); Adjudicator, Immigration Appeals, since 1970; *b* 7 June 1916; *s* of A. C. Ayling, LDS, Norwood, London; *m* 1st, 1941, Patricia Doreen Wright (*d* 1966); one *s* one *d* ; 2nd, 1971, Virginia, *d* of Col Frank Davis, Northwood; two *d. Educ:* Dulwich Coll. No 3(F) Sqdn, 1936-39. Served RNZAF, 1940-43; Comd No 51 Sqdn (Bomber Comd), 1944; Station Comdr, Bomber Comd, 1944-45; Staff Coll., 1945. Staff of Central Bomber Estabt, 1946-48; Air Staff (Plans) Far East, 1948-50; Air Min. (OR1 and Dep. Dir Policy Air Staff), 1951-54; Station Comdr, Bomber Comd, 1954-58; Asst Chief of Defence Staff, Min. of Defence, 1958-59; Dir of Organisation (Estabts), Air Min., 1960-61; SASO, Flying Training Command, 1962-65; Min. of Defence, 1965-66; AOA, RAF Air Support (formerly Transport) Comd, 1966-69; retd, 1969. *Recreations:* ski-ing, sailing, gardening. *Address:* Buckler's Spring, Buckler's Hard, Beaulieu, Hants. *T:* Buckler's Hard 204. *Clubs:* various yacht clubs and sailing associations.

AYLMER, family name of **Baron Aylmer**.

AYLMER, 12th Baron *cr* 1718; **Hugh Yates Aylmer**; Bt 1662; retired; *b* 5 Feb. 1907; *s* of Arthur Lovell Aylmer (*d* 1961) and Georgina Henrietta Emmeline (*d* 1936), *d* of Lt-Col J. F. Sweeny; *S* kinsman, 1977; *m* 1939, Althea, *e d* of late Lt-Col John Talbot; one *d. Educ:* Minneapolis, Minnesota, USA. General business career; sales, purchasing and management; retired, 1971. *Recreations:* badminton, shooting, hunting and varied outdoor sports. *Heir: cousin* Michael Anthony Aylmer [*b* 27 March 1923; *m* 1950, Countess Maddalena Sofia Maria Gabriella Cecilia Stefania Francesca, *d* of late Count Arbeno Attems di Santa Croce; one *s* one *d*]. *Address:* 601-1159 Beach Drive, Victoria, BC V8S 2N2, Canada.

AYLMER, Sir Fenton Gerald, 15th Bt, *cr* 1622; *b* 12 March 1901; *s* of Sir Gerald Evans-Freke Aylmer, 14th Bt, and Mabel Howard, *d* of late Hon. J. K. Ward, MLC, Province of Quebec; *S* father, 1939; *m* 1928, Rosalind Boultbee, *d* of J. Percival Bell, Hamilton, Ont; one *s* one *d. Educ:* Lower Canada Coll., Montreal; Bishop's Coll. Sch., Lennoxville. *Heir: s* Richard John Aylmer [*b* 23 April 1937; *m* 1962, Lise Demers; one *s* one *d*]. *Address:* 29 Church Hill, Westmount, Quebec H3Y 2Z8, Canada.

AYLMER, Dr Gerald Edward, FBA 1976; Master of St Peter's College, Oxford, since 1978; *b* 30 April 1926; *s* of late Captain E. A. Aylmer, RN, and Mrs G. P. Aylmer (*née* Evans); *m* 1955, Ursula Nixon; one *s* one *d. Educ:* Winchester; Balliol Coll., Oxford (MA, DPhil). Jane Eliza Proctor Vis. Fellow, Princeton Univ., NJ, USA, 1950-51; Jun. Res. Fellow, Balliol Coll., Oxford, 1951-54; Asst Lectr in History, Univ. of Manchester, 1954-57, Lectr, 1957-62; Prof. of History and Head of Dept of History, Univ. of York, 1963-78. Vis. Mem., Inst. for Advanced Study, Princeton, 1975. Mem., Royal Commn on Historical Manuscripts, 1978-. Mem., Editorial Bd, History of Parliament, 1969-. *Publications:* The King's Servants, 1961 (2nd edn 1974); (ed) The Diary of William Lawrence, 1962; The Struggle for the Constitution, 1963 (5th edn 1975); (ed) The Interregnum, 1972 (2nd edn 1974); The State's Servants, 1973; (ed) The Levellers in the English

Revolution, 1975; (ed with Reginald Cant) A History of York Minster, 197[?] articles and revs in learned jls. *Address:* Canal House, St Peter's Colleg[?] Oxford OX1 2DL. *T:* Oxford 48436, 40554.

AYNSLEY, George Ayton, CMG 1956; CBE 1949; *b* 2 May 1896; *e s* [?] George Morrison Thomas Aynsley and Annie Sarah Jones Aynsley (*n[?]* Ayton); *m* 1920, Margaret Studdy Oliver; one *d. Educ:* Rutherford Coll[?] Newcastle upon Tyne. Colonial Office, 1912-13; Crown Agents for Colonie[?] 1913-15; joined London Scottish, 1915; served France, Balkans, Egypt an[?] Palestine, 1916-19; Min. of Pensions, 1919-20; Mercantile Marine Dept, B[?] of Trade, 1920-23; Customs and Excise, 1923-39; Establishment Officer, Mi[?] of Information, 1939-44; recruited personnel for Allied Commission [?] Austria, and Control Commission for Germany, 1944-45; administration c[?] Commissions under War Office, 1945, Control Office for Germany an[?] Austria, 1946-47, and Foreign Office, 1947. Head of Personnel Dept, Foreig[?] Office (German Section), 1947-56; Establishment Officer, British Council fc[?] Aid to Refugees (Hungarian Dept), 1956-57 (reception and administration c[?] refugees from Hungary). Coronation Medal, 1953. *Recreations:* golf, bowl[?] *Address:* 9 The Grove, St Margarets, Twickenham, Middlesex. *T:* 01-89[?] 8556.

AYOUB, John Edward Moussa, FRCS; Consulting Surgeon, Moorfields Ey[?] Hospital, since 1973 (Surgeon, 1950-73); Consulting Ophthalmic Surgeon[?] London Hospital, since 1973 (Surgeon, 1947-73); Consulting Ophthalm[?] Surgeon, Royal Masonic Hospital, since 1973 (Consultant, 1967-73[?] Consulting Ophthalmic Surgeon, Royal Navy; *b* 7 Sept. 1908; British; *i* 1939, Madeleine Marion Coniston Martin; one *s* one *d. Educ:* St Paul's Sch[?] Lincoln Coll., Oxford; St Thomas' Hospital. BM, BCh Oxon 1933; FRC[?] 1935. Fellow, and past Vice-Pres. Section of Ophthalmology, RSM; Pa[?] Mem. Council, Faculty of Ophthalmologists (Vice-Pres., 1959-). Served Wa[?] of 1939-45, Surg. Lieut-Comdr RNVR, specialist in ophthalmology. Visitin[?] consultant ophthalmologist to Western Memorial Hosp., Newfoundland[?] 1974-. *Publications:* contributions to medical journals. *Recreations:* gardening[?] bell-ringing. *Address:* 1 Royal Connaught Square, Alderney, Channel Islands[?] *Clubs:* Leander; Royal Cruising.

AYRTON, Norman Walter; international theatre and opera director; *i* London, 25 Sept. 1924. Served War of 1939-45, RNVR. Trained as an acto[?] at Old Vic Theatre School under Michael Saint Denis, 1947-48; joined Ol[?] Vic Company, 1948; repertory experience at Farnham and Oxford, 1949-5[?] on staff of Old Vic Sch., 1949-52; rejoined Old Vic Company for 195[?] Festival Season; opened own teaching studio, 1952; began dramatic coachin[?] for Royal Opera House, Covent Garden, 1953; apptd Asst Principal c[?] London Academy of Music and Dramatic Art, 1954; taught at Shakespear[?] Festival, Stratford, Ont, and Royal Shakespeare Theatre, Stratford-upon[?] Avon, 1959-62; apptd GHQ Drama Adviser to Girl Guide Movemen[?] 1960-74; Principal, LAMDA, 1966-72; Dean, World Shakespeare Stud[?] Centre, Bankside, 1972. *Director:* Artaxerxes, for Handel Opera Soc., Camde[?] Festival, 1963; La Traviata, Covent Garden, 1963; Manon, Covent Garder[?] 1964; Sutherland-Williamson Grand Opera Season, in Australia, 196[?] Twelfth Night at Dallas Theatre Center, Texas, 1967; The Way of the Worl[?] NY, 1976; Lakmé, Sydney Opera, 1976; *Guest Director:* Australian Counc[?] for Arts, Sydney and Brisbane, 1973; Loeb Drama Center, Harvard (an[?] teacher), 1974; Faculty, Juillard Sch., NY, 1974-; Melbourne Theatre Co[?] 1974-; Nat. Inst. of Dramatic Art, Sydney, 1974; Vancouver Opera Assoc[?] 1975-; Sydney Opera House, 1976-81, 1983; Williamstown Festival, USA[?] 1977; Hartford Stage Co. and Amer. Stage Fest., 1978-; Missouri Rep[?] Theatre, 1980-81; Nat. Opera Studio, London, 1980-81; Resident Stag[?] Director: Amer. Opera Center, NY, 1981-; Australian Opera, 1981-8[?] *Recreations:* reading, music, travel. *Address:* 40A Birchington Road[?] NW6.

AZIKIWE, Rt. Hon. Nnamdi, PC 1960; LLD, DLitt, MA, MSc; Ndichi[?] Chief Owelle of Onitsha, 1973; (First) President of the Federal Republic o[?] Nigeria, 1963-66; Governor-General and Commander-in-Chief of Nigeria[?] 1960-63; *b* Zungeru, Northern Nigeria, 16 Nov. 1904; *s* of Obededor[?] Chukwuemeka and Rachel Chinwe Azikiwe; *m* 1936, Flora Ogbenyanu[?] Ogoegbunam, *d* of Chief Ogoegbunam, the Adazia of Onitsha (Ndichi[?] Chief); three *s* one *d. Educ:* CMS Central Sch., Onitsha; Methodist Boys[?] High Sch., Lagos; Storer Coll., Harpers Ferry, W Va, USA; Howard Univ[?] Washington, DC; Lincoln Univ., Pa; Univ. of Pennsylvania. Overseas Fellow[?] Inst. Journalists, London, 1962 (Mem., 1933-). Editor-in-Chief, Africa[?] Morning Post, Accra, 1934-37; Editor-in-Chief, West African Pilot, 1937-4[?] Correspondent for Associated Negro Press, 1944-47; Gen. Sec., Nat. Counci[?] of Nigeria and the Cameroons, 1944-46 (Pres., 1946-60); Correspondent fo[?] Reuter's, 1944-46; Chm. African Continental Bank Ltd, 1944-53. MLC[?] Nigeria, 1947-51; Mem. Foot Commission for Nigerianisation of Civi[?] Service, 1948. Leader of Opposition in the Western House of Assembly[?] 1952-53; Mem. Eastern House of Assembly, 1954-59; MHR 1954; Ministe[?] Eastern Nigeria, 1954-57; Leader, Educational Missions to UK and USA, fo[?] establishment of Univ. of Nigeria, 1955 and 1959; Premier of Eastern Nigeri[?] 1954-59; Pres., Exec. Council of Govt of E Nigeria, 1957-59; President o[?] Senate of Federation, Jan.-Nov. 1960. Ndichie Chief Ozizani Obi of Onitsh[?] 1963-72. Chm., Provisional Council of Univ. of Nigeria, 1960-61; Chancello[?] of Univ. of Nigeria, 1961-66, of Univ. of Lagos, 1970-76. Jt Pres., Anti[?] Slavery Soc. for Human Rights, London, 1970- (Vice-Pres., 1966-69). (Life[?] FREconS; (Life) FRAI; (Life) Mem. British Association for Advancement o[?] Science; Member: American Soc. of International Law; America[?]

Anthropological Assoc. Pres. numerous sporting assocs and boards, 1940-60; Mem., Nigerian Olympic Cttee, 1950-60. Hon. DCL Liberia, 1969; Hon. DSc Lagos, 1972. KStJ 1960-66. *Publications:* Renascent Africa; Political Blueprint of Nigeria; Economic Reconstruction of Nigeria; Meditations: A Collection of Poems; Treasury of West African Poetry; My Odyssey, 1971, etc. *Recreations:* athletics, boxing, cricket, soccer, swimming, tennis, reading. *Address:* Onuiyi Haven, PO Box 7, Nsukka, Nigeria.

ZIZ, Suhail Ibne; international management consultant, since 1981; *b* Bangladesh (then India), 3 Oct. 1937; *s* of Azizur Rahman and Lutfunnessa Khatoon; *m* 1960, Elizabeth Ann Pyne, Dartmouth, Devon; two *d. Educ:* Govt High Sec. Sch., Sylhet; Murarichand Coll., Dacca Univ., Sylhet (Intermed. in Science, 1954); Jt Services Pre-Cadet Trng Sch., Quetta; Cadet Trng Sch., PNS Himalaya, Karachi; BRNC, Dartmouth (Actg Sub-Lieut 1958); (mature student) Kingston upon Thames Polytechnic and Trent Polytech., Nottingham (Dipl. in Man. Studies, 1970); (ext. student) London Univ. (BScEcon Hons 1972); (internal student) Birkbeck Coll., London Univ., (MScEcon 1976). FBIM. Sub-Lieut and Lieut, Pakistan Navy Destroyers/Mine Sweeper (Exec. Br.), 1954-61. Personnel and indust. relations: Unilever (Pakistan); Royal Air Force; Commn on Indust. Relations, London; Ford Motor Co. (GB); Mars Ltd, 1963-78; Dir of Gen. Services Div., CRE, 1978-81. Permanently living in England, 1966-. Leading Mem., Bangladesh Movement in UK, 1971. Member: Exec., Standing Conf. of Asian Orgs in UK, 1972-; N Metropol. Conciliation Cttee, Race Relations Bd, 1971-74; Exec., Post Conf. Constituent Cttee, Black People in Britain—the Way Forward, 1975-76; Adv. Cttee to Gulbenkian Foundn on Area Resource Centre and Community Support Forum, 1976-81; Exec., Nottingham and Dist Community Relations Council, 1975-78; Exec., Fedn of Bangladesh Assocs, UK and Europe, 1972-76; Dept of Employment Race Relations Employment Adv. Gp, 1977-78; BBC Asian programme Adv. Cttee, 1977-81; Industrial Tribunals, 1977-; Jt Trustee, United Action-Bangladesh Relief Fund, 1971-; Founder Mem., Bangladesh Econ. Soc., UK, 1975-78; Exec., Nat. Org. of African, Asian and Caribbean Peoples, 1976-77; Home Sec.'s Standing Adv. Council on Race Relations, 1976-78; Labour Econ. Finance Taxation Assoc., 1973-; Cambridge Econ. Soc., 1973-79. Trustee, Brixton Neighbourhood Assoc., 1979-. Deeply interested in community and race relations and believes profoundly that future health of Brit. society depends on achieving good race relations. *Recreations:* travelling, seeing places of historical interest, meeting people, reading (*eg* political economy). *Address:* 126 St Julian's Farm Road, West Norwood, SE27 0RR. *T:* 01-670 6027. *Club:* Royal Air Force.

ZNAM, Raja Tan Sri bin Raja Haji Ahmad; Malaysian High Commissioner in London, since 1979; *b* Taiping, 21 Jan. 1928; *s* of Raja Haji Ahmad and Hajjah Zainab; *m* 1954, Tengku Puan Sri Zailah Btd T. Zakaria; one *s* two *d. Educ:* King Edward VII Coll., Taiping; Malay Coll., Kuala Kangsar; Univ. of Malaya in Singapore. Joined Malayan Civil Service 1953, Foreign Service 1956; Second Sec., Bangkok, 1957; First Sec., Cairo, 1960-62; Principal Asst Sec., Min. of Foreign Affairs, 1962-65; Dep. Perm. Rep to UN, 1965-68; High Comr in India, 1968-71; Ambassador to Japan, 1971-74, to USSR, Bulgaria, Hungary, Mongolia, Poland and Romania, 1974-77, to France, Morocco, Portugal and Spain, 1977-79. *Recreations:* reading, golf. *Address:* Malaysian High Commission, 45 Belgrave Square, SW1X 8QT. *T:* 01-245 9221/5.

B

ABCOCK, Horace Welcome; Astronomer, Mount Wilson Observatory, 1946-80; *b* 13 Sept. 1912; *s* of Harold D. Babcock and Mary G. (*née* Henderson); *m* 1st, 1940; one *s* one *d*; 2nd, 1958, Elizabeth M. Aubrey; one *s. Educ:* California Institute of Technology (BS); Univ. of California (PhD). Instructor, Yerkes and McDonald Observatories, 1939-41; Radiation Laboratory, Mass Inst. of Tech., 1941-42; Calif Inst. of Tech., 1942-45; Staff Mem., Mount Wilson Observatory, 1946-51; Astronomer, Mount Wilson and Palomar Observatories, 1951-80, Asst Dir, 1957-63, Associate Dir, 1963-64, Dir, 1964-78. Founded Las Campanas Observatory, Chile, of Carnegie Instn, Washington, 1968. Elected to: National Acad. of Sciences, 1954 (Councillor, 1973-76); American Acad. of Arts and Sciences, 1959; American Philosophical Soc., 1966; Corres. Mem., Société Royale des Sciences de Liège, 1968; Associate, Royal Astronomical Soc., 1969; Member: American Astronomical Soc.; Astronomical Soc. of the Pacific; Internat. Astronomical Union. Hon. DSc Univ. of Newcastle upon Tyne, 1965. US Navy Bureau of Ordnance Development Award, 1945; Eddington Gold Medal, RAS, 1958; Henry Draper Medal of the National Acad. of Sciences, 1957; Bruce Medal, Astronomical Soc. of the Pacific, 1969; Gold Medal, RAS, 1970. *Publications:* scientific papers in Astrophysical Jl, Publications of the Astronomical Soc. of the Pacific, Jl of Optical Soc. of America, etc, primarily on magnetic fields of the stars and sun, astrophysics, diffraction gratings, and astronomical instruments. *Address:* Mount Wilson and Las Campanas Observatories, Carnegie Institution of Washington, 813 Santa Barbara Street, Pasadena, California 91101, USA. *T:* (213) 577-1122.

BABER, Hon. Ernest George; Hon. Mr. Justice Baber; Judge of the Supreme Court of Hong Kong, since 1973; *b* 18 July 1924; *s* of late Walter Averette Baber and Kate Marion (*née* Pratt); *m* 1960, Dr Flora Marion, *y d* of late Dr Raymond Bisset Smith and Mrs Jean Gemmell Bisset Smith (*née* Howie); one *s* two *d. Educ:* Brentwood; Emmanuel Coll., Cambridge (MA, LLB). Served RN, 1942-47 (Lieut (S)). Called to Bar, Lincoln's Inn, 1951. Resident Magistrate, Uganda, 1954-62; Magistrate and President of Tenancy Tribunal, Hong Kong, 1962; Senior Magistrate, 1963-67; District Judge, 1967-73. *Recreations:* children, music, walking. *Address:* Supreme Court, Hong Kong. *Clubs:* Naval; Hong Kong, United Services Recreation, Ladies Recreation (Hong Kong).

BABINGTON, Anthony Patrick; His Honour Judge Babington; a Circuit Judge, since 1972; *b* 4 April 1920; 2nd *s* of late Oscar John Gilmore Babington, MAI, AMICE, Monkstown, Co. Cork. *Educ:* Reading Sch. Served with Royal Ulster Rifles and Dorset Regt, 1939-45 (wounded twice); Croix de Guerre with Gold Star (France), 1944. Called to the Bar, Middle Temple, 1948; Bencher, 1977; South Eastern Circuit; Prosecuting Counsel to Post Office, SE Circuit (South), 1959-64; Metropolitan Stipendiary Magistrate, 1964-72. Mem., Home Office Working Party on Bail, 1971-73. Mem., Nat. Exec. Cttee, Internat. PEN English Centre, 1979-. *Publications:* No Memorial, 1954; The Power to Silence, 1968; A House in Bow Street, 1969; The English Bastille, 1971; The Only Liberty, 1975. *Recreations:* music, theatre, reading. *Address:* 3 Gledhow Gardens, South Kensington, SW5 0BL. *T:* 01-373 4014; Thydon Cottage, Chilham, near Canterbury, Kent. *T:* Chilham 300. *Club:* Garrick.

BABINGTON, Ven. Richard Hamilton; Archdeacon of Exeter and Canon Residentiary of Exeter Cathedral, 1958-70, Archdeacon Emeritus, 1970; Treasurer of Exeter Cathedral, 1962-70; retired; *b* 30 Nov. 1901; *s* of Very Rev. R. Babington; *m* 1926, Evelyn Ruth Montgomery; two *s* two *d. Educ:* Malvern; Keble Coll., Oxford. Curate of Banstead, 1925; Vicar of West End, Southampton, 1929; Vicar of St Mary-le-Tower, Ipswich, 1942; Hon. Canon of St Edmundsbury, 1947. *Recreations:* gardening, trout fishing. *Address:* 2 Beauvale Close, Ottery St Mary, Devon EX11 1AA.

BABINGTON, Robert John, DSC 1943; QC (NI) 1965; **His Honour Judge Babington;** appointed County Court Judge for Fermanagh and Tyrone, 1978; *b* 9 April 1920; *s* of David Louis James Babington and Alice Marie (*née* McClintock); *m* 1952, Elizabeth Bryanna Marguerite Alton; *d* of Dr E. H. Alton, Provost of Trinity College, Dublin; two *s* one *d. Educ:* St Columba's Coll., Rathfarnham, Dublin; Trinity Coll., Dublin (BA). Called to the Bar, Inn of Court of NI, 1947. MP North Down, Stormont, 1968-72. *Recreations:* golf, bird-watching. *Address:* Royal Courts of Justice, Chichester Street, Belfast BT1 3JF. *Clubs:* Royal Over-Seas League; Tyrone County (Omagh); Fermanagh County (Enniskillen); Royal Belfast Golf.

BABINGTON, William, CBE 1972; QFSM 1969; Chief Officer, Kent County Fire Brigade, 1966-76, retired; *b* 23 Dec. 1916; *s* of William and Annie Babington; *m* 1940, Marjorie Perdue Le Seelleur; one *d. Educ:* King Edward's Grammar Sch., Birmingham. Addtl Supt of Police, Assam, India, 1942-44; Instructor, Fire Service Coll., 1951-53; Divl Officer, Hampshire Fire Service, 1954-59; Asst Chief Officer, Suffolk and Ipswich Fire Service, 1959-62; Dep. Chief Officer, Lancashire Fire Brigade, 1962-66. *Recreations:* sailing, travel. *Address:* Alpine Cottage, Grouville, Jersey, CI. *T:* Jersey 52737.

BABINGTON SMITH, Michael James, CBE 1945; Consultant, Williams & Glyn's Bank Ltd (late Deputy Chairman); Chairman, London Committee of Ottoman Bank, 1975-82; Director of other companies; Brigadier R of O (TA); *b* 20 March 1901; *e s* of Sir Henry Babington Smith, GBE, KCB, CH, and Lady Elisabeth Mary Bruce; *m* 1943, Jean Mary Meade, *yr d* of late Admiral Hon. Sir Herbert Meade-Fetherstonhaugh, GCVO, CB, DSO; one *s* two *d. Educ:* Eton; Trinity Coll., Cambridge. Director: Bank of England, 1949-69; Bank for International Settlements, 1965-74; Compagnie Financière de Suez, 1957-74. Sheriff of London, 1953 and 1962. *Recreations:* fishing, shooting, etc. *Address:* Flat 6, 20 Embankment Gardens, SW3 4LW. *T:* 01-352 2854. *Club:* Brooks's.
See also J. H. Hemming.

BACHE, Andrew Philip Foley; HM Diplomatic Service; Counsellor and Head of Chancery, Tokyo, since 1981; *b* 29 Dec. 1939; *s* of Robert Philip Sidney Bache and Jessie Bache; *m* 1963, Shân Headley; two *s* one *d. Educ:* Shrewsbury Sch.; Emmanuel Coll., Cambridge (MA). Joined HM Diplomatic Service, 1963; 3rd Sec., Nicosia, 1964-66; Treasury Centre for Admin. Studies, 1966; 2nd Sec., Sofia, 1966-68; FCO, 1968-71; 1st Sec., Lagos, 1971-74; FCO, 1974-78; 1st Sec. (Commercial), Vienna, 1978-81. *Recreations:* diverse, including history, ornithology, fine arts, squash, tennis, cricket and logging. *Address:* c/o Foreign and Commonwealth Office, King Charles Street, SW1. *Club:* MCC.

BACK, Mrs J. H.; *see* Harrison, Kathleen.

BACK, Kenneth John Campbell, MSc, PhD; Vice-Chancellor, James Cook University of North Queensland, since 1970; *b* 13 Aug. 1925; *s* of J. L. Back; *m* 1950, Patricia, *d* of R. O. Cummings; two *d. Educ:* Sydney High Sch.; Sydney Univ. (MSc, PhD). Res. Bacteriologist, Davis Gelatine (Aust) Pty Ltd, 1947-49; Queensland University: Lectr in Bacteriology, 1950-56; Sen. Lectr in Microbiology, 1957-61; Actg Prof. of Microbiology, 1962; Warden,

University Coll of Townsville, Queensland, 1963-70. Hon. DSc Queensland, 1982. *Publications:* papers on microbiological metabolism. *Recreations:* golf, bridge, sailing. *Address:* James Cook University of North Queensland, Post Office, James Cook University, Qld 4811, Australia; 15 Yarrawonga Drive, Townsville, Qld 4810. *Clubs:* Queensland (Brisbane); North Queensland (Townsville).

BACK, Patrick, QC 1970; a Recorder of the Crown Court, since 1972; *b* 23 Aug. 1917; *s* of late Ivor Back, FRCS, and Barbara Back (*née* Nash). *Educ:* Marlborough; Trinity Hall, Cambridge. Captain, 14th Punjab Regt, 1941-46. Called to Bar, 1940; Bencher, Gray's Inn, 1978. commenced practice, Western Circuit, 1948; Dep. Chm., Devon QS, 1968. *Recreation:* fly-fishing. *Address:* Paddock Edge, Broadwindsor, Dorset. *T:* Broadwindsor 644; 3 Paper Buildings, Temple, EC4; Flat 3, Marquess House, 74 Marquess Road, N1. *T:* 01-226 0991.

BACK, Ronald Eric George; Senior Director, Network, British Telecom, since 1979; *b* 20 April 1926; *s* of George Ernest Back and Margery A. (*née* Stupples); *m* 1949, Beryl Gladys Clark. *Educ:* Ashford Grammar School; Northampton Polytechnic. CEng; FIEE. Joined Post Office as engineering trainee, 1942; Asst Engineer on plant protection, 1949; Exec. Engineer, civil engineering projects, 1951-60; Sen. Exec. Engineer, microwave link provision, 1960-65; Asst Staff Engineer and Staff Engineer, Satellite Earth Station design and provision, 1965-72; Dep. Dir Engineering, Network Planning, 1972-76; Dir, Service Dept, 1976-79. *Recreations:* breeding and exhibiting Airedale terriers (International Judge). *Address:* High Oaks, Lamberhurst, Kent TN3 8EP. *T:* Lamberhurst 890317.

BACKETT, Prof. Edward Maurice; Foundation Professor of Community Health, University of Nottingham, 1969-81; *b* 12 Jan. 1916; *o s* of late Frederick and Louisa Backett; *m* 1940, Shirley Paul-Thompson; one *s* two *d*. *Educ:* University Coll., London; Westminster Hospital. Operational Research with RAF; Nuffield Fellow in Social Medicine; Research Worker, Medical Research Council; Lecturer, Queen's Univ., Belfast; Senior Lecturer, Guy's Hospital and London Sch. of Hygiene and Tropical Medicine; Prof. and Head of Dept of Public Health and Social Medicine, Univ. of Aberdeen, 1958-69. *Publications:* papers in scientific journals. *Recreations:* swimming, walking, sailing. *Address:* Flat 1, 23/24 Chalcot Road, NW1 8LN. *T:* 01-722 1751.

BACKHOUSE, Jonathan; retired; *b* 16 March 1907; 2nd *s* of late Lieut-Col M. R. C. Backhouse, DSO, TD, and of Olive Backhouse; *m* 1934, Alice Joan Woodroffe; two *s* one *d*. *Educ:* RNC Dartmouth. Served War of 1939-45, Royal Artillery. Merchant Bank, 1924-28; Stock Exchange, 1928-50; Merchant Bank, 1950-70. *Recreations:* shooting, etc. *Address:* Breewood Hall, Great Horkesley, Colchester, Essex. *T:* Colchester 271260. *Club:* Royal Thames Yacht.

BACKHOUSE, Sir Jonathan Roger, 4th Bt, *cr* 1901; Director, W. H. Freeman & Co. Ltd, Publishers; *b* 30 Dec. 1939; *s* of Major Sir John Edmund Backhouse, 3rd Bt, MC, and Jean Marie Frances, *d* of Lieut-Col G. R. V. Hume-Gore, MC, The Gordon Highlanders; *S* father, 1944. *Educ:* Oxford. *Heir: b* Oliver Richard Backhouse, [*b* 18 July 1941; *m* 1970, Gillian Irene, *o d* of L. W. Lincoln, Northwood, Middx]. *Address:* c/o Lloyds Bank, 39 Piccadilly, W1.

BACON, family name of **Baroness Bacon.**

BACON, Baroness *cr* 1970 (Life Peer), of Leeds and Normanton; **Alice Martha Bacon,** PC 1966; CBE 1953; DL; *d* of late County Councillor B. Bacon, miner. *Educ:* Elementary Schs, Normanton, Yorks; Normanton Girls' High Sch.; Stockwell Training Coll.; external student of London Univ. Subsequently schoolmistress. MP (Lab) NE Leeds, 1945-55, SE Leeds, 1955-70; Minister of State: Home Office, 1964-67; Dept of Educn and Science, 1967-70. Mem. National Executive Cttee of Labour Party, 1941-70; Chm., Labour Party, 1950-51. DL W Yorkshire 1974. Hon. LLD Leeds, 1972. *Address:* 53 Snydale Road, Normanton, West Yorks. *T:* Wakefield 893229.

BACON, Francis; artist; *b* Dublin, 1909. One-man exhibitions: Hanover Gall., London, 1949, 1950, 1951, 1952 (after travelling in S Africa and Kenya), 1954, 1957; Durlacher Gall., New York, 1953; Galerie Rive Droite, Paris, 1957; Galleria D'Arte Galatea, Turin; Galleria Dell' Ariete, Milan; Galleria Obelisco, Rome, 1958; Marlborough Fine Art Gall., London, 1960; Tate Gall., 1962; Grand Palais, Paris, 1971; Metropolitan Museum, NY, 1975; Galérie Claud Bernard, 1977. Exhibitions etc: Beaux Arts Gall., London, 1953; (rep. Great Britain, with Ben Nicholson and Lucien Freud) 27th Venice Biennale, 1954; Hanover Gall., and in New York, 1954; Inst. of Contemporary Arts, London, 1955 (retrospective); New Decade Show, Museum of Modern Art, New York, 1955; New London Gall., 1963, 1965; Solomon Guggenheim Museum, New York, 1963; Gallerie Maeght, Paris, 1966; Marlborough Fine Art, 1967; Marlborough-Gerson Gall., New York, 1968; Kunsthalle, Düsseldorf, 1972. Travelling exhibitions: Mannheim, Turin, Zürich, Amsterdam, 1962; Hamburg, Stockholm, Dublin, 1965. Important works include: triptychs: Three Studies for Figures at the Base of a Crucifixion, 1944; Crucifixion, 1962; Sweeney Agonistes, 1967; single oils: Painting, 1946; Man with Dog, 1953; Study after Velazquez's portrait of Pope Innocent X, 1953; Two Figures, 1953; Study for portrait of Van Gogh II, 1957; Portrait of Isabel Rawsthorne standing in a street in Soho, 1967. Paintings acquired by: Tate Gall.; Arts

Council; Aberdeen, Belfast and Leeds Museums; Nat. Galls of Adelaide a Canberra; Museums in Berlin, Bochum, Düsseldorf, Hamburg, Hanov Mannheim, Munich and Stuttgart; CNAC, Paris; MOMA, NY; Amsterda Rotterdam, Stockholm etc. Rubens Prize, 1966; Prize, Carnegie In Pittsburgh, 1967. *Address:* c/o Marlborough Fine Art, 6 Albemarle Str W1X 3HF.

BACON, Francis Thomas, OBE 1967; FRS 1973; FEng, 1976; consultant fuel cells, retired; *b* 21 Dec. 1904; 2nd *s* of T. W. Bacon, Ramsden H Billericay; *m* 1934, Barbara Winifred, *y d* of G. K. Papillon, Manor Hou Barrasford; one *s* one *d* (and one *s* decd). *Educ:* Eton Coll.; Trinity Co Cambridge. MIMechE 1947. With C. A. Parsons & Co. Ltd, Newcastle-c Tyne, 1925-40 (i/c production of silvered glass reflectors, 1935-3 experimental work on hydrogen/oxygen fuel cell at King's Coll., London, v Merz & McLellan, 1940-41; Temp. Exper. Off. at HM Anti-Submar Experimental Estbt, Fairlie, 1941-46; exper. work on hydrogen/oxygen f cell at Cambridge Univ., 1946-56 (for ERA); Consultant to: NRDC on f cells at Marshall of Cambridge Ltd, 1956-62; Energy Conversion L Basingstoke, 1962-71; Fuel Cells Ltd, AERE, 1971-72. British Assoc. Lectu 1971; Bruno Breyer Meml Lecture and Medal, Royal Aust. Chem. Inst., 19 S. G. Brown Award and Medal (Royal Soc.), 1965; British Silver Med (RAeS), 1969; Churchill Gold Medal, Soc. of Engineers, 1972; Melch Medal, Inst. of Fuel, 1972; Vittorio de Nora Diamond Shamrock Award a Prize, Electrochemical Soc. Inc., 1978. Hon. DSc Newcastle upon Tyne, 198 *Publications:* chapter 5 in Fuel Cells (ed G. J. Young), 1960; chapter 4 in Fu Cells (ed W. Mitchell), 1963; papers on fuel cells for World Power Con Royal Instn, Nature, two UN Confs, Amer. Inst. of Chem. Eng., Inst. of Fu Electrochimica Acta, Royal Soc. *Recreations:* hill walking, mus photography, gardening. *Address:* Trees, 34 High Street, Little Shelfo Cambridge CB2 5ES. *T:* Cambridge 843116. *Club:* Athenæum.

BACON, Prof. George Edward, MA, DSc Cantab, PhD London; Profes of Physics, University of Sheffield, 1963-81, now Emeritus; *b* 5 Dec. 19 *s* of late George H. Bacon and Lilian A. Bacon, Derby; *m* 1945, Enid Trip one *s* one *d*. *Educ:* Derby Sch.; Emmanuel Coll., Cambridge (Open and Se Schol.). Air Ministry, Telecommunications Research Estabt, 1939-46. De Chief Scientific Officer, AERE, Harwell, 1946-63. FInstP. *Publicatio* Neutron Diffraction, 1955; Applications of Neutron Diffraction Chemistry, 1963; X-ray and Neutron Diffraction, 1966; Neutron Physi 1969; Neutron Scattering in Chemistry, 1977; The Architecture of Soli 1981; many scientific pubns on X-ray and neutron crystallographic studies Proc. Royal Society, Acta Cryst., etc. *Recreations:* gardening, photograph travel. *Address:* Windrush Way, Guiting Power, Cheltenham GL54 5US

BACON, Sir Nicholas Hickman Ponsonby, 14th Bt of Redgrave, *cr* 161 and 15th Bt of Mildenhall, *cr* 1627; Premier Baronet of England; *b* 17 M 1953; *s* of Sir Edmund Castell Bacon, 13th and 14th Bt, KG, KBE, TD a of Priscilla Dora, *d* of Col Sir Charles Edward Ponsonby, 1st Bt, TD; *S* fathe 1982; *m* 1981, Susan, *d* of Raymond Dinnis, Edenbridge, Kent. *Educ:* Eto Dundee Univ. (MA). Barrister-at-law, Gray's Inn. A Page of Honour to t Queen, 1966-69. *Heir: cousin* Anthony Walter Bacon, *b* 10 March 19 *Address:* Raveningham Hall, Norfolk. *Club:* Pratt's.

BACON, Sir Ranulph Robert Maunsell, Kt 1966; KPM 1953; Consulta International Intelligence Inc., USA, since 1981 (Director, 1970-81); *b* 6 Au 1906; *s* of late Arthur Ranulph and Hester Mary (*née* Ayles), Westgate-o Sea; *m* 1932, Alfreda Violet (*née* Annett); one *d* decd. *Educ:* Tonbridge Sc Queens' Coll., Cambridge (BA). Joined Metropolitan Police, 192 Metropolitan Police Coll., 1935 (Baton of Honour); seconded to Provo Service, 1940; Capt. 1940, Major 1941, Lieut-Col 1941; all service was Middle East; Dep. Provost Marshal, Ninth Army, 1942; seconded to Colon Police Service, 1943; Dep. Inspector-Gen., 1943, Inspector-Gen., 1944-4 Ceylon Police; Chief Constable of Devon, 1947-61; Asst Comr, Met. Polic 1961-66; Dep. Comr New Scotland Yard, 1966. Dir, Securicor Ltd, 1966-8 Mem., Gaming Board, 1968-75. President: Gun Trade Assoc., 1972-7 Shooting Sports Trust, 1972-77. CStJ 1964. *Address:* 3 Royal Court, 8 King Gardens, Hove, Sussex BN3 2PF. *T:* Brighton 732396. *Club:* United Oxfor & Cambridge University.

BACON, Sir Sidney (Charles), Kt 1977; CB 1971; BSc(Eng); FEn FIMechE, FIProdE, FTP; Managing Director, Royal Ordnance Factorie 1972-79; Deputy Chairman, Royal Ordnance Factories Board, 1972-79; *b* Feb. 1919; *s* of Charles and Alice Bacon. *Educ:* Woolwich Polytechni London Univ. Military Service, 1943-48, Capt. REME. Royal Arsena Woolwich, 1933-58; Regional Supt of Inspection, N Midland Regio 1958-60; Asst Dir, ROF, Nottingham, 1960-61; Director, ROF: Leed 1961-62; Woolwich, 1962-63; Birtley, 1965; idc, 1964; Dir of Ordnan Factories, Weapons and Fighting Vehicles, 1965-66; Dep. Controller, ROF 1966-69; Controller, ROFs, 1969-72. Dir, Short Brothers Ltd, 1980-. Pre IProdE, 1979. *Recreations:* golf, listening to music. *Address:* 228 Erith Roa Bexleyheath, Kent. *Clubs:* Shooters Hill Golf; Royal Cinque Ports Golf.

BADCOCK, Maj.-Gen. John Michael Watson, CB 1976; MBE 1969; D Chief Appeals Officer, Cancer Research Campaign, 1978-82; *b* 10 Nov. 192 *s* of late R. D. Badcock, MC, JP and Mrs J. D. Badcock; *m* 1948, Gilli Pauline (*née* Attfield); one *s* two *d*. *Educ:* Sherborne Sch.; Worcester Coll Oxford. Enlisted in ranks (Army), 1941; commnd Royal Corps of Signa

1942; war service UK and BAOR; Ceylon, 1945-47; served in UK, Persian Gulf, BAOR and Cyprus; Comdr 2 Inf. Bde and Dep. Constable of Dover Castle, 1968-71; Dep. Mil. Sec., 1971-72; Dir of Manning (Army), 1972-74; Defence Advr and Head of British Defence Liaison Staff, Canberra, 1974-77; retired. psc, jssc, idc. Col Comdt, Royal Signals, 1974-80; Master of Signals, 1982-; Hon. Col, 31 (London) Signal Regt (Volunteers), T&AVR, 1978-. Chm., SE TA&VRA, 1979-. DL Kent, 1980. *Recreations:* Rugby football, cricket, hockey, most field sports less horsemanship. *Address:* Palmer's Lodge, Petham, Canterbury, Kent CT4 5RL. *T:* Petham 248. *Club:* Army and Navy.

ADDELEY, Hermione; actress; *b* Broseley, Shropshire, 13 Nov. 1908; *d* of late W. H. Clinton-Baddeley and Louise Bourdin; *m* 1st, 1928, Hon. David Tennant (marr. diss., 1939); one *s* one *d*; 2nd, Captain J. H. Willis, MC. *Educ:* privately. Appeared on London stage in La Boîte à Joujoux, Court Theatre, 1918; 1919-23; Makebelieve, Lyric, Hammersmith, 1920; West End parts; early success as Florrie Small in The Likes of Her, St Martin's, 1923; Punchbowl revue, Palace, 1924; joined the Co-Optimists, London Pavilion, 1925; continuous appearances in West End theatres in varied plays, including The Greeks had a Word for It; Nine Sharp; Rise Above It; Sky High; Brighton Rock; one and a half years entertaining the troops; A La Carte; Grand National Night; Fallen Angels; Far East and Middle East tour in Cabaret, 1955-56; A Taste of Honey, US tour, 1961-62; The Milk Train Doesn't Stop Here Any More, (New York) 1963; The Killing of Sister George, St Martin's, 1966; The Threepenny Opera, Prince of Wales, 1972. Debut on Commercial Television, 1956; constant appearances in film and TV, 1957-61. *US TV:* Julia (Golden Globe Award, 1976); Mrs Naugutuck in Maude (comedy series) (Emmy nomination, 1976). *Films include:* Caste; Kipps; It Always Rains on Sunday; Brighton Rock; No Room at the Inn; Quartet; Passport to Pimlico; Scrooge; The Belles of St Trinian's; Midnight Lace; Room at the Top (Oscar nomination); Mary Poppins; The Unsinkable Molly Brown; Marriage on the Rocks; Harlow; Do Not Disturb; The Black Windmill. *Recreations:* swimming, reading, entertaining. *Address:* c/o Eric Glass Ltd, 28 Berkeley Square, W1X 6HD.

See also Sir H. A. C. Rumbold, Bt.

ADDELEY, Sir John (Wolsey Beresford), 4th Bt *cr* 1922; *b* 27 Jan. 1938; *s* of Sir John Beresford Baddeley, 3rd Bt, and of Nancy Winifred, *d* of late Thomas Wolsey; *S* father, 1979; *m* 1962, Sara Rosalind Crofts; three *d*. *Educ:* Bradfield College, Berks. FCA. Qualified as Chartered Accountant, 1961; Deloitte Haskins & Sells, 1961-65; Baddeley Bros (London) Ltd, 1966-69; Burmah Oil Co. Ltd, 1969-70; Court Line Ltd, 1971-73; Babcock & Wilcox Ltd, 1973-77; Spillers International Ltd, 1978-79. *Recreations:* inland waterways, tennis, squash. *Heir: cousin* Mark David Baddeley, *b* 10 May 1921. *Address:* 41 School Hill, Storrington, Sussex. *T:* Storrington 2423.

ADDELEY, Very Rev. William Pye, BA; Dean Emeritus of Brisbane, 1981; *b* 20 March 1914; *s* of W. H. Clinton-Baddeley and Louise Bourdin, Shropshire; *m* 1947, Mary Frances Shirley, *d* of Col E. R. C. Wyatt, CBE, DSO; one *d*. *Educ:* Durham Univ.; St Chad's Coll., Durham; Cuddesdon Coll., Oxford. Deacon, 1941; Priest, 1942; Curate of St Luke, Camberwell, 1941-44; St Anne, Wandsworth, 1944-46; St Stephen, Bournemouth, 1946-49; Vicar of St Pancras (with St James and Christ Church from 1954), 1949-58; Dean of Brisbane, 1958-67; Rector of St James's, Piccadilly, 1967-80; RD of Westminster (St Margaret's), 1974-79; Commissary to: Archbishop of Brisbane, 1967-; Bishop of Wangaratta, 1970-; Bishop, Archbishop of Papua New Guinea, 1972-80; Bishop of Newcastle, NSW, 1976-. Member: London Diocesan Synod, 1970-80; Bishop of London's Council, 1975-80. Chaplain: Elizabeth Garrett Anderson Hospital, London, 1949-59; St Luke's Hostel, 1952-54; Qld Univ. Anglican Soc., 1960-64; St Martin's Hosp., Brisbane, 1960; London Companions of St Francis, 1968-80; Lord Mayor of Westminster, 1968-69 and 1974-75; Actors' Church Union, 1968-70; Royal Acad. of Arts, 1968-80. Hon. Chaplain to: Archbishop of Brisbane (Diocesan Chaplain, 1963-67); Union Soc. of Westminster, 1972-80. President: Brisbane Repertory Theatre, 1961-64; Qld Ballet Co., 1962-67; Qld Rep. Elizabethan Theatre Trust, 1963-67; Dir, Australian Elizabethan Theatre Trust, 1965-67; Mem. Council of Management, Friends of Royal Academy, 1978-; Chairman: Diocesan Radio and Television Council, 1961-67; weekly television Panel "Round Table", 1962-66; monthly television Panel "What Do YOU Think", 1960-67. Governor: Burlington Sch., 1967-76; Archbishop Tenison's Sch., 1967-80; Chairman: Assoc. for Promoting Retreats, 1967-80; Malcolm Sargent Cancer Fund for Children, 1968-; Cttee for Commonwealth Citizens in China, 1970-73; Mem. Council, Metropolitan Hosp. Sunday Fund, 1968-78; Vice-Pres., Cancer Relief Appeal, 1977-. Life Governor of Thomas Coram Foundation, 1955-. Mem. Chapter-Gen., OStJ, 1974-. ChStJ 1971 (SBStJ 1959). *Recreations:* theatre, music, photography. *Address:* Cumberland House, Woodbridge, Suffolk IP12 4AH. *Clubs:* East India, Devonshire, Sports and Public Schools, Carlton, Arts.

ADDILEY, Prof. Sir James, Kt 1977; PhD, DSc; FRS 1961; FRSE 1962; Professor of Chemical Microbiology since 1977, and Director, Microbiological Chemistry Research Laboratory, since 1975, University of Newcastle upon Tyne; SERC Senior Research Fellow, and Fellow of Pembroke College, University of Cambridge, since 1981; *b* 15 May 1918; *s* of late James Baddiley and Ivy Logan Cato; *m* 1944, Hazel Mary, *yr d* of Wesley Wilfrid Townsend and Ann Rayner Townsend (*née* Kilner); one *s*. *Educ:* Manchester Grammar Sch.; Manchester University (BSc 1941, PhD DSc 1953; Sir Clement Royds Meml Schol., 1942, Beyer Fellow,

1943-44); MA Cantab 1981. Imperial Chemical Industries Fellow, University of Cambridge, 1945-49; Swedish Medical Research Council Fellow, Wenner-Grens Institute for Cell Biology, Stockholm, 1947-49; Mem. of Staff, Dept of Biochemistry, Lister Institute of Preventive Medicine, London, 1949-55; Rockefeller Fellowship, Mass. Gen. Hosp., Harvard Med. Sch., 1954; Prof. of Organic Chem., King's Coll., Univ. of Durham, 1955-77 (later Univ. of Newcastle upon Tyne); Head of Sch. of Chemistry, Newcastle upon Tyne Univ., 1968-78. Member: Council, Chemical Soc., 1962-65; Cttee, Biochemical Soc., 1964-67; Council, Soc. of Gen. Microbiol., 1973-75; SERC (formerly SRC), 1979-81 (Mem., Enzyme Chem. and Technol Cttee, 1972-75, Biol Scis Cttee, 1976-79; Mem., Science Bd, 1981-); Council, Royal Soc., 1977-79; Editorial Boards, Biochemical Preparations, 1960-70, Biochimica et Biophysica Acta, 1970-77. Karl Folkers Vis. Prof. in Biochem., Illinois Univ., 1962; Tilden Lectr, Chem. Soc., 1959; Special Vis. Lectr, Dept of Microbiology, Temple Univ., Pa, 1966; Leeuwenhoek Lectr, Royal Society, 1967; Pedler Lectr, Chem. Soc., 1978; Endowment Lectr, Bose Inst., Calcutta, 1980. Hon. Mem., Amer. Soc. Biol Chem. Hon. DSc Heriot Watt, 1979. Meldola Medal, RIC, 1947; Corday-Morgan Medal, Chem. Soc., 1952; Davy Medal, Royal Soc., 1974. *Publications:* numerous in Journal of the Chemical Society, Nature, Biochemical Journal, etc; articles in various microbiological and biochemical reviews. *Recreations:* photography, music. *Address:* Department of Biochemistry, University of Cambridge, Tennis Court Road, Cambridge CB2 1QW. *T:* Cambridge 51781; Bay Tree House, 45 High Street, Balsham, Cambs CB1 6DJ. *T:* Cambridge 893055.

BADEN-POWELL, family name of **Baron Baden-Powell.**

BADEN-POWELL, 3rd Baron, *cr* 1929, of Gilwell; **Robert Crause Baden-Powell;** Bt, *cr* 1922; Chief Scouts Commissioner, 1965-82; *b* 15 Oct. 1936; *s* of 2nd Baron and Carine Crause Baden-Powell (*née* Boardman); *S* father, 1962; *m* 1963, Patience Hélène Mary Batty (see Lady Baden-Powell). *Educ:* Bryanston (Blandford). Pres., West Yorks Scout Council, 1972-; Vice-Pres., Scout Assoc., 1982- (Mem. Council, 1965-; Mem. Cttee of Council, 1972-78). *Recreations:* model making, scouting. *Heir: b* Hon. David Michael Baden-Powell [*b* 11 Dec. 1940; *m* 1966, Joan Phillips, *d* of H. W. Berryman, Melbourne, Australia; three *s*]. *Address:* Chapel Farm, Ripley, Woking, Surrey GU23 6NE. *T:* Ripley 2262.

BADEN-POWELL, Lady; Patience Hélène Mary Baden-Powell; Chief Commissioner, The Girl Guides Association, since 1980; President, Commonwealth Youth Exchange Council, since 1982; *b* 27 Oct. 1936; *d* of Mr and Mrs D. M. Batty, Zimbabwe; *m* 1963, Baron Baden-Powell, *qv. Educ:* St Peter's Diocesan Sch., Bulawayo. Internat. Comr, Girl Guides Assoc., 1975-79. Mem., Adv. Bd for GB, Imperial Life Assurance Co. of Canada. Vice-Pres., Alone in London Service; Patron: National Playbus Assoc.; Woodlarks Camp Site for the Disabled; Surrey Antiques Fair. *Address:* Chapel Farm, Ripley, Woking, Surrey GU23 6NE. *T:* Ripley 2262; The Girl Guides Association, 17-19 Buckingham Palace Road, SW1W 0PT. *T:* 01-834 6242.

BADENOCH, Alec William, MA, MD, ChM, FRCS; *b* 23 June 1903; *s* of late John Alexander Badenoch, chartered accountant, Banff; *m* 1942, Jean McKinnell, MB, ChB (Edinburgh), *d* of late Alexander Brunton; two *s* (and one *s* decd). *Educ:* Banff Academy; Aberdeen Univ. Pres. Student Representation Council of Scotland, 1926. Served RAFVR, 1937-45, as Temp. Wing Comdr, i/c Surgical Divs, RAF Hosps Rauceby, Wroughton and St Athan; Surgeon: Royal Hosp. of St Bartholomew, 1947-68; St Peter's Hosp. for Stone and other Urological Diseases, 1946-68; Visiting Urologist: Royal Masonic Hosp., 1950-70; King Edward VII's Hosp. for Officers, 1947-77; Visiting Professor: Cairo, 1962; Dallas, Texas, 1967; Guest Lectr, Amer. Urological Assoc., 1968; Hon. Civilian Consultant in Urology to RAF. Hunterian Prof., RCS, 1948; Hon. Fellow, British Assoc. of Urological Surgeons (Pres., 1968-69; St Peter's Medal, 1974); Hon. FR.SocMed (Hon. Treasurer 1971-76, Hon. Mem. and Past Pres. Section of Urology); Hon. Fellow, Hunterian Soc. (Pres. 1949, Vice-Pres. and Orator, 1957); Chm., Editorial Bd, British Jl of Urology, 1969-72 (Treasurer, 1961-67); Member: BMA (Vice-Pres. Section of Urology, 1955); Internat. Soc. of Urology (Treas. London Congress, 1964, British Delegate, 1966-74; Hon. Fellow); (Founder Mem.) Cttee of Management, European Soc. of Urology, 1972; Council, RCS, 1963-71 (Patron, 1975); GMC, 1966-71; GDC, 1969-71. Mem., Bd of Governors, St Peter's Hosp. Gp, 1948-73; Chm., Management Cttee, Inst. of Urology, 1968-72. Hon. Mem. Peruvian, American and French Urological Assocs; Corresp. Mem., Mexican Urological Assoc. and Amer. Assoc. of Genito Urinary Surgeons. Founding Jt Editor, European JL of Urology, 1974-78. *Publications:* Manual of Urology, 1953, 2nd edn 1974; contrib. to British Surgery, Modern Operative Surgery, and Modern Trends in Urology. Articles in scientific jls. *Recreations:* gardening, music, swimming. *Address:* 123 Harley Street, W1N 1HE. *T:* 01-935 3881; Church Hayes, Lea, Malmesbury, Wilts. *T:* Malmesbury 2289. *Club:* Royal Air Force.

BADENOCH, John, DM; FRCP; Consultant Physician, Oxford Area Health Authority (Teaching); University Lecturer in Medicine, and Fellow of Merton College, Oxford University; *b* 8 March 1920; *s* of William Minty Badenoch, MB, and Ann Dyer Badenoch (*née* Coutts); *m* 1944, Anne Newnham, *d* of Prof. Lancelot Forster; two *s* two *d*. *Educ:* Rugby Sch.; Oriel College, Oxford. MA; DM 1952; FRCP 1959. Rockefeller Med. Studentship, Cornell Univ. Med. Coll., 1941. Res. Asst, Nuffield Dept of Clin. Medicine,

Oxford, 1949-56; Dir, Clin. Studies, Univ. of Oxford, 1954-65. Former Mem., Board of Governors of United Oxford Hosps; Mem. Board, Oxford AHA(T), 1974-. Royal College of Physicians: Pro-Censor and Censor, 1972-73; Sen. Censor and Sen. Vice-Pres., 1975-76; Goulstonian Lectr, 1960; Lumleian Lectr, 1977. Examiner in Medicine at various times for the Universities of: Oxford, Cambridge, Manchester, QUB and NUI. Member: Assoc. of Physicians of GB and Ireland; Med. Res. Soc.; British Soc. of Haematology; British Soc. of Gastroenterology. Liveryman, Soc. of Apothecaries. *Publications:* (ed jtly) Recent Advances in Gastroenterology, 1965, 2nd edn 1972; various papers in the field of gastroenterology and medicine. *Recreations:* reading, walking, natural history. *Address:* Grove House, Kybald Street, Oxford OX1 4ET.

BADGE, Peter Gilmour Noto; a Metropolitan Stipendiary Magistrate, since 1975; Chairman, Inner London Juvenile Panel, since 1979; Deputy Circuit Judge, since 1979; a Recorder of the Crown Court, since 1980; *b* 20 Nov. 1931; *s* of late Ernest Desmond Badge, LDS and Marie Benson Badge (*née* Clough); *m* 1956, Mary Rose Noble; four *d*. *Educ:* Univ. of Liverpool (LLB). National Service, 1956-58: RNVR, lower deck and commnd; UK, ME and FE; RNR, 1958-62. Solicitor, 1956; Mem., Solicitor's Dept, New Scotland Yard, 1958-61; Asst Solicitor and later Partner, 1961-75, Notary Public 1964-75, Kidd, Rapinet, Badge & Co.; Clerk to Justices, Petty Sessional Div. of Marlow, 1967-74; Lectr in Magisterial Law, Bucks Magistrates Courts Cttee, 1968-72; Sen. Solicitor to Comr and Detention Appeals Tribunal, NI, 1973-75. Mem., Cttee on Criminal Law, Law Soc., 1971-79. Contested (L) Windsor and Maidenhead, 1964. *Recreations:* sailing, skiing, fencing, music. *Address:* Thames Magistrates' Court, Aylward Street, E1. *Club:* Royal Dart Yacht.

BADGER, Sir Geoffrey Malcolm, Kt 1979; AO 1975; PhD, DSc, FRSC, FRACI, FACE, FAIM, FTS, FAA; Chairman, Australian Science and Technology Council, since 1977; *b* 10 Oct. 1916; *s* of J. McD. Badger; *m* 1941, Edith Maud, *d* of Henry Chevis. *Educ:* Geelong Coll.; Gordon Inst. of Technology; Univs of Melbourne, London, Glasgow. Instructor Lieut, RN, 1943-46. Finney-Howell Research Fellow, London, 1940-41; Research Chemist, ICI, 1941-43; Research Fellow, Glasgow, 1946-49. Univ. of Adelaide: Sen. Lectr, 1949-51; Reader, 1951-54; Prof. of Organic Chemistry, 1955-64, now Emeritus Professor; Dep. Vice-Chancellor, 1966-67; Vice-Chancellor, 1967-77; Res. Professor, 1977-79. Mem. Executive, CSIRO, 1964-65. President: Aust. Acad. of Science, 1974-78; Aust. and NZ Assoc. for Advancement of Science, 1979-80. *Publications:* Structures and Reactions of Aromatic Compounds, 1954; Chemistry of Heterocyclic Compounds, 1961; The Chemical Basis of Carcinogenic Activity, 1962; Aromatic Character and Aromaticity, 1969; (ed) Captain Cook, 1970; numerous papers in Jl Chem. Soc., etc. *Address:* 1 Anna Court, West Lakes, SA 5021, Australia. *T:* (08) 49-4594.

BADHAM, Douglas George, CBE 1975; JP; company director; Chairman, Economic Forestry Group, since 1981 (Deputy Chairman, 1980-81); Deputy Chairman, Welsh Development Agency, since 1980 (Member, since 1978); Lieutenant of Mid Glamorgan, since 1982; *b* 1 Dec. 1914; *s* of late David Badham, JP; *m* 1939, Doreen Spencer Phillips; two *d*. *Educ:* Leys Sch., Cambridge. CA. Exec. Dir, Powell Duffryn Gp, 1938-69; Chm., Nat. Health Service Staff Commn, 1972-75; Member: Wales and the Marches Telecommunications Bd, 1973-80; British Gas Corp., 1974-; Forestry Commn, S Wales Reg. Adv. Cttee, 1946-76 (Chm., 1973-76); Western Region Adv. Bd, BR, 1977-82; Welsh Council (Chm., Industry and Planning Panel), 1971-80; Nature Conservancy Council Adv. Cttee for Wales; Council, UWIST, 1975-80; Develt Corp. for Wales, 1965- (Chm., 1971-80). JP Glamorgan, 1962; DL Mid Glamorgan, 1975; High Sheriff Mid Glamorgan, 1976. *Recreations:* forestry, trout breeding. *Address:* Plas Watford, Caerphilly, Mid Glamorgan CF8 1NE. *T:* Caerphilly 882094. *Clubs:* Royal Automobile; Cardiff and County (Cardiff).

BADHAM, Leonard; Managing Director, J. Lyons & Company Ltd, since 1977; Director, Allied Breweries, since 1978; *b* 10 June 1923; *s* of John Randall Badham and Emily Louise Badham; *m* 1944, Joyce Rose Lowrie; two *d*. *Educ:* Wandsworth Grammar Sch. Commnd E Surrey Regt, 1943; Royal W Kent Regt, 5th Indian Div., 1944-46; SO II Stats, Burma Comd, 1946-47. J. Lyons & Co. Ltd: Management Trainee, 1939; Main Bd, 1965; Chief Comptroller, 1965; Tech. and Commercial Co-ordinator, 1967; Exec. Dir, Finance and Admin, 1970; Asst Gp Man. Dir, 1971; Dep. Gp Man. Dir, 1975. Fellow, Inst. of Admin. Management; FHCIMA; FBIM. *Recreations:* bridge, gardening. *Address:* 26 Vicarage Drive, East Sheen, SW14 8RX. *T:* 01-876 4373.

BADIAN, Ernst, FBA 1965; Professor of History, since 1971, John Moors Cabot Professor, since 1982, Harvard University; *b* 8 Aug. 1925; *s* of Joseph Badian and Sally (*née* Horinger), Vienna (later Christchurch, NZ); *m* 1950, Nathlie Anne (*née* Wimsett); one *s* one *d*. *Educ:* Christchurch Boys' High Sch.; Canterbury Univ. Coll., Christchurch, NZ; University Coll., Oxford (Chancellor's Prize for Latin Prose, 1950; Craven Fellow, 1950; Conington Prize, 1959). MA (1st cl. hons), NZ, 1946; LitD, Victoria, NZ, 1962. BA (1st cl. hons Lit. Hum.) Oxon, 1950; MA 1954; DPhil 1956. Asst Lectr in Classics, Victoria University Coll., Wellington, 1947-48; Rome Scholar in Classics, British Sch. at Rome, 1950-52; Asst Lectr in Classics and Ancient History, Univ. of Sheffield, 1952-54; Lectr in Classics, Univ. of Durham, 1954-65; Prof. of Ancient History, Univ. of Leeds, 1965-69; Prof. of Classics and History, State Univ. of NY at Buffalo, 1969-71. Vis. Professor: Univs of

Oregon, Washington and California (Los Angeles), 1961; Univ. of S Afr 1965, 1973; Harvard, 1967; State Univ. of NY (Buffalo), 1967-68; Heidelbe 1973; Univ. of California (Sather Prof.), 1976; Univ. of Colorado, 19 Univ. of Tel-Aviv, 1981; Martin Classical Lectr, Oberlin Coll., 19 lecturing visits to Australia, Canada, France, Germany, Holland, Israel, Ita NZ, Rhodesia, Switzerland, and S Africa. Fellow, Amer. Acad. of Arts Sciences, 1974; Corresponding Member: Austrian Acad. of Scis, 1975; Germ Archaeol Inst., 1981. Editor, Amer. Jl of Ancient History. *Publicatio Foreign Clientelae* (264-70 BC), 1958; Studies in Greek and Roman Histc 1964; Polybius (The Great Histories Series), 1966; Roman Imperialism in Late Republic, 1967 (2nd edn 1968); Publicans and Sinners, 1972; contribu Artemis-Lexikon, Encyc. Britannica, Oxf. Class. Dictionary and to classi and historical journals. *Recreations:* travelling, reading. *Address:* Departm of History, Harvard University, Cambridge, Mass 02138, USA.

BADMIN, Stanley Roy, RE 1935 (ARE 1931); (Hon. retired 1965); RW 1939 (ARWS 1932); ARCA 1927; *b* Sydenham, 18 April 1906; 2nd *s* Charles James and Margaret Badmin, Somersetshire; *m* 1st, 1929; one *s* o *d* ; 2nd, 1950, Mrs Rosaline Flew, widow of Dr R. Flew; one *d* one step *Educ:* private tutor; Royal College of Art. One man exhibns London, N York, Worthing; works bought by Liverpool, Manchester, Huddersfie Bradford, Birmingham, V & A Museum, Chicago Inst. of Art, South Lonc Galleries, Newport, Ashmolean, Worthing, Boston Museum, Lonc Museum, NY Metropolitan Museum, etc. *Publications:* Etched Pla Autolithoed Educational books; Village and Town, Trees in Britain and Fa Crops in Britain; colour prints; illustrations to: British Countryside in Colo Trees for Town & Country and Famous Trees; Shell Guide to Trees a Shrubs; The Seasons (by Ralph Wightman); Trees of Britain (Sunday Time Readers' Digest Publications; Royles Publications. *Recreations:* painting a gardening. *Address:* Streamfield, Bignor, Pulborough, West Sussex. *T:* Sutt (Sussex) 229.

BAELZ, Very Rev. Peter Richard; Dean of Durham, since 1980; *b* 27 J 1923; 3rd *s* of Eberhard and Dora Baelz; *m* 1950, Anne Thelma Clea Harding; three *s*. *Educ:* Dulwich Coll.; Cambridge Univ. BA 1944, MA 19 BD 1971; DD Oxon 1979. Asst Curate: Bournville, 1947-50; Sherbor 1950-52; Asst Chap. Ripon Hall, Oxford, 1952-53; Rector of Wisha Birmingham, 1953-56; Vicar of Bournville, 1956-60; Fellow and Dean, Je Coll., Cambridge, 1960-72; University Lectr in Divinity, Cambridge, 196 72; Canon of Christ Church and Regius Prof. of Moral and Pasto Theology, Univ. of Oxford, 1972-79. Hulsean Lectr, 1965-66; Bampton Lec 1974. *Publications:* Prayer and Providence, 1968; Christian Theology a Metaphysics, 1968; The Forgotten Dream, 1975; Ethics and Belief, 1977; De God Answer Prayer?, 1982; contributor to: Traditional Virtues Reassess 1964; Faith, Fact and Fantasy, 1964; The Phenomenon of Christian Beli 1970; Christianity and Change, 1971; Christ, Faith and History, 1972; Christianity Credible, 1981; God Incarnate: story and belief, 1981; Choices Childlessness (ed), 1982. *Recreations:* walking, motoring. *Address:* T Deanery, Durham DH1 3EQ. *T:* Durham 47500.

BAER, Jack Mervyn Frank; Managing Director, Hazlitt, Gooden & Fc since 1973; *b* 29 Aug. 1924; *yr s* of late Frank and Alix Baer; *m* 1st, 19 Jean St Clair (marr. diss 1969; she *d* 1973), *o c* of late L. F. St Clair and Evel Synnott; one *d* ; 2nd, 1970, Diana Downes Baillieu, *yr d* of Aubrey Cla Robinson and Mollie Panter-Downes, *qv* ; two step *d*. *Educ:* Bryanston; Sla Sch. of Fine Art, University Coll., London. Served RAF (Combined Op 1942-46. Joined Hazlitt Gallery as Partner, 1948, Man. Dir, 1957, Chr 1960-82. Chm., Fine Arts and Antiques Export Adv. Cttee to Dept of Tra 1971-73 (Vice-Chm., 1969-71). Pres., Fine Art Provident Institution, 1972- Chm., Soc. of London Art Dealers, 1977-80 (Vice Chm. 1974-7 *Publications:* numerous exhibition catalogues; articles in various *Recreation:* drawing. *Address:* 9 Phillimore Terrace, W8. *T:* 01-937 68 *Clubs:* Brooks's, Buck's, Beefsteak.

BAGGE, Sir John (Alfred Picton), 6th Bt *cr* 1867; ED; DL; *b* 27 Oct. 19 *e s* of Sir Picton Bagge, 5th Bt, CMG, and Olive Muriel Mary (*d* 1965), of late Samuel Mendel; *S* father, 1967; *m* 1939, Elizabeth Helena (Lena), of late Daniel James Davies, CBE, Comr for Newfoundland in London; thr *s* three *d*. *Educ:* Eton and abroad. Served Inns of Court Regt, 1936- commnd into Cheshire Yeo., 1939; served War of 1939-45, Palestine, Suda Liberation Campaign of Ethiopia; Major 1941; GSO 2, Brit. Mil. Mission Ethiopia, 1941-44; GSO 2, HQ, E Africa Comd Liaison with French, 194 Mil. Asst to Brit. Comdr Allied Control Commn for Bulgaria, 1944-45; GS 2, War Office, 1945. KStJ 1975; Chm. Council of St John in Norfolk, 1969-80. Vice-Chm., W Norfolk DC, 1973-76, Chm., 1976-77; High Sher of Norfolk, 1977; DL Norfolk, 1978. *Recreations:* shooting, ski-ing and wa ski-ing. *Heir: s* (John) Jeremy (Picton) Bagge [*b* 21 June 1945; *m* 1979, Sara *d* of late James Armstrong; one *s*. Chartered Accountant, 1968]. *Addre* Stradsett Hall, Kings Lynn, Norfolk. *T:* Fincham 215. *Club:* Allsor (Norfolk).

BAGGLEY, Charles David Aubrey, CBE 1980; MA; Headmaster of Bolt School since 1966; *b* 1 Feb. 1923; *s* of A. C. and M. Baggley, Bradford, Yor *m* 1949, Marjorie Asquith Wood, *d* of M. H. Wood, Harrogate; one *s* o *d*. *Educ:* Bradford Grammar Sch.; King's Coll., Cambridge (1942 a 1945-47) (Exhibitioner in Classics, Scholar in History; Class I, Part II Historical Tripos, 1947; BA 1947, MA 1952). Temp. Sub. Lieut, RNV 1942-45. History Master, Clifton Coll., 1947-50; Head of History Sic

Dulwich Coll., 1950-57; Headmaster, King Edward VII Sch., Lytham, 1957-66. Chm., HMC, 1978. Member: Bolton Civic Trust; Bolton Branch, Historical Assoc.; Bolton Rotary Club. FRSA. *Recreations:* walking, gardening, reading. *Address:* Leverhouse, Greenmount Lane, Bolton, Lancs BL1 5JF. *T:* Bolton 40202 (school), Bolton 40607 (home).

AGIER, Gordon Alexander Thomas; MP (Lab) Sunderland South since 1964; *b* July 1924; *m* 1949, Violet Sinclair; two *s* two *d*. *Educ:* Pendower Secondary Technical Sch., Newcastle upon Tyne. Signals Inspector, British Railways; Pres., Yorks District Council, NUR, 1962-64. Mem. of Keighley Borough Council, 1956-60; Mem. of Sowerby Bridge Urban Council, 1962-65. PPS to Home Secretary, 1968-69. *Address:* House of Commons, SW1; Rahana, Whickham Highway, Dunston, Gateshead, Durham.

AGLEY, Desmond; professional novelist since 1962; *b* Kendal, 29 Oct. 1923; *s* of John Bagley and Hannah Marie Bagley (*née* Whittle); *m* 1960, Joan Margaret (*née* Brown). *Educ:* spottily, mainly by reading and travel. British Aircraft Industry, 1940-46. Travelled overland to Africa, 1947; worked in: Uganda, 1947; Kenya, 1948; Rhodesia, 1949; S Africa, 1950-64; variety of jobs incl. nightclub photographer, film scenario writer; freelance journalist from 1956, contrib. S African press; travels extensively. Member: Soc. Authors; Crime Writers' Assoc.; Mystery Writers of America; Writers' Guild (US). *Publications:* The Golden Keel, 1963; High Citadel, 1965; Wyatt's Hurricane, 1966; Landslide, 1967; The Vivero Letter, 1968; The Spoilers, 1969; Running Blind, 1970 (adapted as BBC serial, 1979); The Freedom Trap, 1971; The Tightrope Men, 1973; The Snow Tiger, 1975; The Enemy, 1977; Flyaway, 1978; Bahama Crisis, 1980; Windfall, 1982; work trans. into many languages. *Recreations:* sailing, travel, military history, reading, recreational mathematics, computer programming. *Address:* Catel House, Les Rohais de haut, St Andrew, Guernsey, CI. *T:* Guernsey 54345. *Clubs:* Detection; Royal Channel Islands Yacht (Guernsey); Aero (Johannesburg); Antarctic Press (McMurdo Sound).

AGNALL, Frank Colin, CBE 1950; Commercial Director, Imperial Chemical Industries Ltd, 1965-70, also Finance Director, 1967-68; Director, African Explosives and Chemical Industries Ltd, 1965-70; *b* 6 Nov. 1909; *s* of late Francis Edward Bagnall, OBE and Edith Bagnall; *m* 1st, 1933, Ethel Hope (*née* Robertson) (killed by enemy action, 1941), Blechingley; 2nd, Rona (*née* Rooker Roberts) (marr. diss.), Belmont, Mill Hill; one *s* one *d*; 3rd, Christine (*née* Gerrard), Westhill, Ledbury. *Educ:* Repton; Brasenose Coll., Oxford (MA); Dept of Business Administration, London Sch. of Economics. ICI Ltd, 1932-38; Urwick, Orr and Partners, 1938-40. War Office, 1940-42; British Nylon Spinners: Dir and Gen.-Man., 1944-45, Man. Dir, 1945-64; Non-Exec. Dir, ICI, 1964. Mem., Oxford Univ. Appts Cttee, 1948-69; Governor, Ashridge Coll., 1958-70; Chm. Regular Forces Resettlement Cttee for Wales, 1968-68. Life Governor, University Coll. of S Wales and Monmouthshire (Pres., 1963-68); Chm. Wales Business Training Cttee, 1946-49; Founder Mem., BIM (Mem. Council, 1949-52); Dir Oxford Univ. Business Summer Sch., 1954; Mem. Govt Cttee of Enquiry into Electricity Supply Industry, 1954-55; Chm. SW Reg. Council, FBI, 1956-57; Mem. Air Transport Licensing Bd, 1960-64; Chm. Man-Made Fibres Producers Cttee, 1961-65; Vice-Pres. British Man-Made Fibres Fedn, 1965-70 (Chm. 1963-65); Pres. Textile Inst., 1964-65. Hon. LLD, Wales, 1969. OStJ. *Address:* Vermont, Budleigh Salterton, Devon. *T:* Budleigh Salterton 3068. *Club:* Boodle's.
See also R. M. Bagnall.

AGNALL, Kenneth Reginald, QC 1973; a Deputy Judge of the Crown Court, since 1975; *b* 26 Nov. 1927; *s* of Reginald and Elizabeth Bagnall; *m* 1st, 1955, Margaret Edith Wall; one *s* one *d*; 2nd, 1963, Rosemary Hearn; one *s* one *d*. *Educ:* King Edward VI Sch., Birmingham; Univ. of Birmingham. LLB (Hons). Served Royal Air Force; Pilot Officer, 1947, Flt Lt, 1948. Called to the Bar, Gray's Inn, 1950. Chairman: Hurstwood Timber Co. Ltd, 1972-79; Zestime Ltd, 1979-; Anglo-American Real Property Inst., 1980-82. Freeman, City and Corp. of London, 1972; Freeman and Liveryman, Barber-Surgeons' Co., 1972. *Publications:* Guide to Business Tenancies, 1956; Atkins Court Forms and Precedents (Town Planning), 1973; (with K. Lewison) Development Land Tax, 1978. *Recreations:* yachting, motoring, travel. *Address:* 11 King's Bench Walk, Temple, EC4Y 7EQ. *T:* 01-353 2484. *Clubs:* Royal Thames Yacht; Wentworth Golf.

AGNALL, Gen. Sir Nigel (Thomas), KCB 1981; CVO 1978; MC 1950 and Bar 1953; C-in-C BAOR and Commander, Northern Army Group, from July 1983; *b* 10 Feb. 1927; *s* of Lt-Col Harry Stephen Bagnall and Marjory May Bagnall; *m* 1959, Anna Caroline Church; two *d*. *Educ:* Wellington Coll. Joined Army, 1945; commnd Green Howards, 1946; Palestine, 1946-48, 5th Airborne Div.; Malaya, 1949-53, Green Howards; GSO1 (Intell.), Dir of Borneo Ops, 1966-67; comd 4/7 Royal Dragoon Guards, NI and BAOR, 1967-69; Sen. Directing Staff (Army), Jt Services Staff Coll., 1970; comd Royal Armoured Corps HQ1 (Br.) Corps, 1970-72; Defence Fellow, Balliol Coll., Oxford, 1972-73; Sec., Chief of Staff Cttee, 1973-75; GOC 4th Div., 1975-77; ACDS (Policy), MoD, 1978-80; Comdr, 1 (Br.) Corps, 1980-83. Col Comdt, APTC, 1981-. *Recreations:* country pursuits. *Address:* HQ BAOR, BFPO 40.

AGNALL, Richard Maurice, MBE 1945; Deputy Chairman, Tube Investments Ltd, 1976-81, Managing Director, 1974-81, Director, 1969-81; *b* 20 Nov. 1917; *s* of late Francis Edward Bagnall, OBE and Edith Bagnall; *m* 1946, Irene Pickford; one *s* one *d*. *Educ:* Repton. Served War, 1939-45: RA,

Shropshire Yeomanry, 1939-43 (despatches); Bde Major, 6 AGRA Italy, 1943-45. Joined Tube Investments Ltd, 1937. Chm., Round Oak Steel Works Ltd, 1976-81 (Dir, 1974-81). Bronze Star, USA, 1945. *Recreations:* golf, gardening, photography. *Address:* Oak House Farm, Himbleton, Droitwich, Worcs. *Club:* MCC.
See also F. C. Bagnall.

BAGNALL, Rt. Rev. Walter Edward, DD; *b* 1903. *Educ:* Masonic School, Dublin, Ireland; University of Western Ontario; Huron College, London, Ont. BA, Univ. of Western Ontario, 1927; Licentiate in Theology, Huron Coll., 1927. Deacon, 1927; Priest, 1928; Curate of All Saints, Windsor, Ont, 1927-28; Incumbent of St Mark's, London, Ont, 1928-30; Rector of St John's, Preston, Ont, Canada, 1930-36; Rural Dean of Waterloo, Ont, 1932-36; Rector of All Saints, Hamilton, Ont, 1936-40; Rector of St George's, St Catharine's, Ont, 1940-47; Canon of Niagara, 1944-47; Dean of Niagara and Rector of Ch. Ch. Cathedral, Hamilton, 1947-49; Bishop of Niagara, 1949-73. Hon. degrees: DD Univ. of Western Ontario, 1949; DD Trinity Coll., Toronto, 1953; DCL Bishops Univ., Lennoxville, 1956; LLD McMaster Univ., 1959. *Address:* 252 James Street North, Hamilton, Ont, Canada.

BAGNOLD, Brig. Ralph Alger, OBE 1941; FRS 1944; Consultant on movement of sediments by wind and water, since 1956; Fellow of Imperial College, University of London, since 1971; *b* 3 April 1896; *s* of late Col A. H. Bagnold, CB, CMG: *m* 1946, Dorothy Alice, *d* of late A. E. Plank; one *s* one *d*. *Educ:* Malvern College; Royal Military Academy, Woolwich; Gonville and Caius Coll., Cambridge. Commission RE, 1915; Capt, 1918; transferred Royal Corps of Signals, 1920; Major, 1927; retired, 1935. Served European War, Western Front, 1915-18 (despatches); North-West Frontier of India, 1930 (despatches). Organised and led numerous explorations in Libyan Desert and elsewhere, 1925-32; Founder's Medal of Royal Geographical Soc., 1935. Called up, 1939. Raised and commanded Long Range Desert Group in Middle East, 1940-41 (despatches); Deputy Signal-Officer-in-Chief, Middle East, 1943-44; released from Army Service, 1944. G. K. Warren Prize, US Acad. of Sciences, 1969; Penrose Medal, Geolog. Soc. of America, 1970; Wollaston Medal, Geolog. Soc. of London, 1971; Sorby Medal, Internat. Assoc. of Sedimentologists, 1978. *Publications:* Libyan Sands, 1935; Physics of Blown Sand and Desert Dunes, 1941; papers, etc, on deserts, hydraulics, and beach formation. *Recreations:* exploration, research. *Address:* Rickwoods, Mark Beech, near Edenbridge, Kent. *T:* Cowden 516.

BAGOT, family name of **Baron Bagot.**

BAGOT, 9th Baron *cr* 1780; **Heneage Charles Bagot;** Bt 1627; *b* 11 June 1914; *s* of Charles Frederick Heneage Bagot (*d* 1939) (4th *s* of *g s* of 1st Baron) and of Alice Lorina, *d* of Thomas Farr; S half-brother, 1979; *m* 1939, Muriel Patricia Moore, *y d* of late Maxwell James Moore Boyle; one *s* one *d*. *Educ:* Harrow. Formerly Major, 6th Gurkha Rifles. *Recreations:* shooting, skiing, sailing. *Heir:* s Hon. Charles Hugh Shaun Bagot, *b* 23 Feb. 1944. *Address:* Hillcot House, Bitterley, Ludlow, Salop. *Clubs:* Army and Navy, Alpine Ski; Himalayan.

BAILEY, family name of **Baron Glanusk.**

BAILEY, Alan Marshall, CB 1982; Deputy Secretary, Central Policy Review Staff, Cabinet Office, since 1981; *b* 26 June 1931; *s* of John Marshall Bailey and Muriel May Bailey; *m* 1st, 1959, Stella Mary Scott (marr. diss. 1981); three *s*; 2nd, 1981, Shirley Jane Barrett. *Educ:* Bedford Sch.; St John's and Merton Colls, Oxford (MA, BPhil). Harmsworth Senior Scholarship, 1954; Harkness Commonwealth Fellowship, USA, 1963-64. Principal Private Sec. to Chancellor of the Exchequer, 1971-73; Under-Sec., HM Treasury, 1973-78, Dep. Sec., 1978. *Address:* 118 Tarnwood Park, SE9. *T:* 01-850 3620.

BAILEY, Brian Harry, OBE 1976; JP; Chairman: South Western Regional Health Authority, since 1975; Health Education Council, since 1983; Chairman, Television South West Ltd, since 1980; *b* 25 March 1923; *s* of Harry Bailey and Lilian (*née* Pulfer); *m* 1948, Nina Olive Sylvia (*née* Saunders); two *d*. *Educ:* Lowestoft Grammar Sch. RAF, 1941-45. SW Dist Organisation Officer, NALGO, 1951-82; SW Reg. Sec., TUC, 1968-81. Member: Somerset CC, 1966-; SW Econ. Pl;anning Council, 1969-79; Central Health Services Council, 1978-80; MRC, 1978-; Adv. Cttee on Severn Barrage, Dept of Energy, 1978-81; Business Educn Council, 1980-. Vice-Chm., BBC Radio Bristol Adv. Council, 1971-78; Mem., BBC West Reg. Adv. Council, 1973-78. Dir, Western Orchestral Soc. Ltd, 1982-. JP Somerset, 1964. *Recreations:* football, cricket and tennis (watching), music, fishing and golf (playing). *Address:* Runnerstones, 32 Stonegallows, Taunton, Somerset. *T:* Taunton 46265. *Club:* Wyvern (Taunton).

BAILEY, D(avid) R(oy) Shackleton, LittD; FBA 1958; Pope Professor of the Latin Language and Literature, Harvard University, since 1982; *b* 10 Dec. 1917; *y s* of late Rev. J. H. Shackleton Bailey, DD, and Rosamund Maud (*née* Giles); *m* 1967, Hilary Ann (marr. diss. 1974), *d* of Leonard Sidney and Margery Bardwell. *Educ:* Lancaster Royal Grammar Sch.; Gonville and Caius Coll., Cambridge. Fellow of Gonville and Caius Coll., 1944-55, Praelector, 1954-55; Fellow and Dir of Studies in Classics, Jesus Coll., Cambridge, 1955-64; Visiting Lecturer in Classics, Harvard Coll., 1963; Fellow and Dep. Bursar, Gonville and Caius Coll., 1964; Senior Bursar 1965-68; Univ. Lectr in Tibetan, 1948-68; Prof. of Latin, Univ. of Michigan, 1968-74; Prof. of Greek and Latin, Harvard Univ., 1975-82. Andrew V. V. Raymond Vis. Prof.,

State Univ. of NY at Buffalo, 1973-74; Vis. Fellow of Peterhouse, Cambridge, 1980-81; Nat. Endowment of Humanities Fellowship, 1980-81. Mem., Amer. Philosophical Soc., 1977. Fellow, Amer. Acad. of Arts and Sciences, 1979. Editor, Harvard Studies in Classical Philology, 1978. Charles J. Goodwin Award of Merit, Amer. Philol Assoc., 1978. *Publications:* The Śatapañcāśatka of Mātrceta, 1951; Propertiana, 1956; Towards a Text of Cicero, *ad Atticum*, 1960; Ciceronis Epistulae ad Atticum IX-XVI, 1961; Cicero's Letters to Atticus, Vols I and II, 1965; Vol. V, 1966, Vol. VI, 1967, Vols III and IV, 1968, Vol. VII, 1970; Cicero, 1971; Two Studies in Roman Nomenclature, 1976; Cicero: *Epistulae ad Familiares*, 2 vols, 1977; (trans.) Cicero's Letters to Atticus, 1978; (trans.) Cicero's Letters to his Friends, 2 Vols, 1978; Towards a Text of *Anthologia Latina*, 1979; Selected Letters of Cicero, 1980; Cicero: *Epistulae ad Q. Fratrem et M. Brutum*, 1981; Profile of Horace, 1982; articles in Classical and Orientalist periodicals. *Recreation:* cats. *Address:* Department of Classics, Harvard University, Cambridge, Mass 02138, USA.

BAILEY, David Royston, FRPS, FSIAD; photographer, film director; *b* 2 Jan. 1938; *s* of William Bailey and Agnes (*née* Green); *m* 1st, 1960, Rosemary Bramble; 2nd, 1967, Catherine Deneuve; 3rd, 1975, Marie Helvin. *Educ:* self taught. FRPS 1972; FSIAD 1975. Photographer for Vogue, 1959-; Dir of television commercials, 1966-, Dir of documentaries, 1968-; Proprietor and Co-Editor, Ritz, 1976-. Exhibitions: Nat. Portrait Gall., 1971; Photographers' Gall., 1973. *Publications:* Box of Pinups, 1964; Goodbye Baby and Amen, 1969; Warhol, 1974; Beady Minces, 1974; Papua New Guinea, 1975; Mixed Moments, 1976; Trouble and Strife, 1980; David Bailey's Book of Photography, 1981. *Recreations:* aviculture, photography, travelling, painting. *Address:* 177 Gloucester Avenue, NW1 8LA. *T:* 01-722 6615/4221.

BAILEY, Rev. Dr (Derrick) Sherwin; Non-residentiary Canon of Wells Cathedral and Prebendary of Ashill, since 1975; *b* 30 June 1910; *s* of William Thomas and Ellen Mary Bailey, Alcester, Warwicks; *m* 1st, 1939, Philippa Eleanor (*d* 1964), *d* of Capt. Philip James and Eleanor Frances Vandeleur Green; one *s* two *d*; 2nd, 1966, Morag Stuart Macdonald, MD, DPM. *Educ:* The Grammar Sch., Alcester, Warwks; Lincoln Theological Coll.; Edinburgh Univ. In business, 1928-40; ACII 1934; Linc. Theol Coll., 1940-42; Univ. of Edin., PhD 1947; DLitt, 1962; Fellow of Eugenics Soc., 1957-74. Deacon, 1942; Priest, 1943; Curate, Mablethorpe St Mary and Theddlethorpe St Helen with Theddlethorpe All Saints, 1942-44; Chaplain to Anglican students at Univ. and Colls of Edinburgh, and Curate of St John Evang., Edin., 1944-51; Anglican Lectr in Divinity, Moray House Trg Coll., Edin., 1948-51; Central Lectr, C of E Moral Welfare Counc., 1951-55; Actg Educ. Sec., 1954-55; Study Sec., 1955-59; Permission to officiate in Dio. B'ham, 1951-59; Rector of Lyndon with Manton, Martinsthorpe and Gunthorpe, 1959-62; Canon Residentiary of Wells Cathedral, 1962-74; Chancellor of Wells, and Prebendary of Litton, 1962-69; Precentor of Wells and Prebendary of Whitchurch, 1968-74. Select Preacher, Univ. of Camb., 1963. Examining Chaplain to Bishop of Bath and Wells, 1963-76. *Publications:* Sponsors at Baptism and Confirmation, 1952; Thomas Becon and the Reformation of the Church in England, 1952; The Mystery of Love and Marriage, 1952; Homosexuality and the Western Christian Tradition, 1955; Sexual Offenders and Social Punishment, 1956; The Man-Woman Relation in Christian Thought, 1959; Common Sense about Sexual Ethics, 1962; The Canonical Houses of Wells, 1982; (Joint-Author) Celibacy and Marriage, 1944; (ed) Wells Cathedral Chapter Act Book 1666-1683, 1973; (ed jtly) Le Neve, Fasti Ecclesiae Anglicanae Dioc. Bath and Wells V, 1979; contributor: They Stand Apart, 1955; The Human Sum, 1957; Die Religion in Geschichte und Gegenwart, 1959; Westminster Dict. of Christian Educ., 1961; Dictionary of Christian Ethics, 1967; Sexual Ethics and Christian Responsibility, 1970; Oxford Dictionary of the Christian Church, 1974; Medieval Art and Architecture at Wells and Glastonbury, 1981; also contrib. to: Theology; Journal of Ecclesiastical History; Church Quarterly Review; Scottish Jl of Theol.; London Quarterly and Holborn Review; The Churchman, etc. *Recreations:* chess, stamp collecting, railways. *Address:* 23 Kippax Avenue, Wells, Somerset BA5 2TT. *T:* Wells 75061.

BAILEY, Sir Derrick Thomas Louis, 3rd Bt, *cr* 1919; DFC; *b* 15 Aug. 1918; 2nd *s* of Sir Abe Bailey, 1st Bt, KCMG; *S* half-brother, 1946; *m* 1st, 1946, Katharine Nancy Stormonth Darling; four *s* one *d*; 2nd, 1980, Mrs Jean Roscoe. *Educ:* Winchester. Engaged in farming. *Recreations:* all sports, all games. *Heir:* s John Richard Bailey [*b* 11 June 1947; *m* 1977, Jane, *o d* of John Pearson Gregory; two *d*]. *Address:* Lappingford, Worminghall, Aylesbury, Bucks; Bluestones, Alderney, CI. *Club:* Rand (Johannesburg).

BAILEY, His Honour Desmond Patrick; a Circuit Judge (formerly Judge of County Courts), 1965-79; *b* 6 May 1907; 3rd *s* of Alfred John Bailey, Bowdon, Cheshire, and of Ethel Ellis Johnson; unmarried. *Educ:* Brighton Coll.; Queens' Coll., Cambridge (BA, LLB). Called to Bar, Inner Temple, 1931. Northern Circuit. Served War of 1939-45: Rifle Brigade, Lancashire Fusiliers, Special Operations Executive, North Africa, Italy (Major). Recorder of Carlisle, 1963-65. *Recreations:* cricket, fishing, gardening. *Address:* Chaseley, Bowdon, Cheshire. *T:* 061-928 0059. *Club:* St James's (Manchester).

BAILEY, Sir Donald Coleman, Kt 1946; OBE 1944; JP; *b* 15 Sept. 1901; *s* of J. H. Bailey, Rotherham, Yorkshire; *m* 1st, Phyllis (*d* 1971), *d* of Charles Frederick Andrew, Wick, Bournemouth; one *s*; 2nd, 1979, Mrs Mildred Stacey. *Educ:* The Leys, Cambridge; Univ. of Sheffield (BEng). Posts:

Rowntree & Co. Ltd, York, Efficiency Dept; London Midland & Scott Rly, Civil Engineers Dept; City Engineer's Dept, Sheffield; Dir, Milit Engineering Experimental Estabt; Dean, RMCS, 1962-66. Hon. Fl FIStructE; MICE; Hon. Member: Instn of Royal Engrs; Inst. of En Designers. Hon. DEng Sheffield, 1946. JP Bournemouth, 1946. Comman of the Order of Orange-Nassau, 1947. *Recreation:* golf. *Address:* Ways Cottage, 10 Gordon Road, Highcliffe, Christchurch, Dorset BH23 5HN. Highcliffe 77550.

BAILEY, Air Vice-Marshal Dudley Graham, CB 1979; CBE 1970; Dep Managing Director, Services Sound and Vision (formerly Kiner Corporation, since 1980; *b* 12 Sept. 1924; *s* of P. J. Bailey and D. M. Bai (*née* Taylor); *m* 1948, Dorothy Barbara Lovelace-Hunt; two *d. Educ:* Chri Coll., Finchley; Teignmouth Grammar Sch. Pilot trng, Canada, 1943- Intell. Officer, Air HQ Italy, 1946-47 and HQ 23 Gp, 1948-49; Berlin Air 1949; Flt Comdr No 50 and 61 Sqdns, Lincolns, 1950-52; exchange dut USAF, B-36 aircraft, 1952-54; Canberra Sqdn: Flt Comdr, 1955; Sqdn Com 1956; Air Min., 1956-58; psc (m) 1959; OC No 57 (Victor) Sqdn, 1960- Air Warfare course, Manby, 1962; Wing Comdr Ops, HQ Air Forces Mid East, 1963-65; MoD Central Staffs, 1965-66; MoD (Air) Directorate of A Staff Plans, 1966-68; OC RAF Wildenrath, 1968-70; Sen. Personnel St Officer, HQ Strike Comd, 1970-71; Royal Coll. of Defence Studies, 19 Dir of Personnel (Air), RAF, 1972-74; SASO, RAF Germany, 1974-75; D Comdr, RAF Germany, 1975-76; Dir Gen., Personal Services (RAF), Mc 1976-80, retired. *Recreations:* music gardening. *Address:* Firs Corr Abbotswood, Speen, Aylesbury, Bucks. *T:* Hampden Row 462. *Club:* Ro Air Force.

BAILEY, Eric; Director, Plymouth Polytechnic, 1970-74, retired; *b* 2 N 1913; *s* of Enoch Whittaker Bailey, Overton Hall, Sandbach, Cheshire; 1942, Dorothy Margaret Laing, Stockport; one *s* one *d. Educ:* King's Sc Macclesfield; Manchester Univ. BSc Hons; CEng, FRIC, MIChemE; Dip Lectr, Stockport Coll. of Technology, 1936-41; Industrial Chemist, 1941- Lectr, Enfield Coll. of Technology, 1945-46; Vice-Principal, Technical Co Worksop, 1946-51; Principal: Walker Technical Coll., Oakengates, Sala 1951-59; Plymouth Coll. of Technology, 1959-69. *Recreations:* putti colour into gardens, photography, pursuing leisure and voluntary activiti *Address:* 3 St Bridget Avenue, Crownhill, Plymouth, Devon. *T:* Plymou 771426. *Club:* Rotary (Plymouth).

BAILEY, Harold, CMG 1960; Under-Secretary, Department of Trade a Industry, 1970-74, retired; *b* 26 Feb. 1914; *yr s* of late John Bailey a Elizabeth Watson, Preston, Lancashire; *m* 1946, Rosemary Margaret, *d* Harold and Irene Brown, Shotesham St Mary, Norfolk; two *s* one *d. Ed* Preston Grammar Sch.; Christ Church, Oxford. Asst Principal Air Ministr 1937; Principal, Min. of Aircraft Production, 1942; Served, Royal Air For 1942-45; Private Sec. to Minister of Supply and Aircraft Production, 1945- Asst Sec., 1947; Min. of Supply Rep. and Adviser (Defence Supplies) to U High Comr, Ottawa, 1953-55; Under-Secretary: Ministry of Supply, 19! BoT, 1958; British Senior Trade Comr in India, and Economic Adviser to British High Comr, 1958-63. *Address:* Hollies, Hurstbourne Tarrant, Har *T:* Hurstbourne Tarrant 976482.

BAILEY, Sir Harold (Walter), Kt 1960; FBA 1944; MA, W Aust.; M DPhil Oxon; Professor of Sanskrit, Cambridge Univ., 1936-67, Profess Emeritus, 1967; *b* Devizes, Wilts, 16 Dec. 1899. Was Lecturer in Irani Studies at Sch. of Oriental Studies. Member of: Danish Academy, 194 Norwegian Academy, 1947; Kungl. Vitterhets Historie och Antikvite Akademien, Stockholm, 1948; Governing Body, SOAS, Univ. of Londc 1946-70; L'Institut de France, Associé étranger, Académie des Inscriptions Belles-Lettres, 1968. President: Philological Soc., 1948-52; Royal Asia Society, 1964-67 (Gold Medal, RAS, 1972); Soc. for Afghan Studies, 1972-7 Soc. of Mithraic Studies (1971), 1975-; Chm., Anglo-Mongolian Sc 1979-81. Chm., Ancient India and Iran Trust, 1978-. FAHA 1971; Hc Fellow: SOAS, London Univ., 1963-; Queens' Coll., Cambridge, 1967; Catherine's Coll., Oxford, 1976. Hon. DLitt: W Aust., 1963; ANU, 197 Oxon, 1976; Hon. DD Manchester, 1979. *Publications:* in Bulletin of Sch. Oriental Studies, Journal of Royal Asiatic Soc., Zeitschrift der Deutsch Morgenländischen Gesellschaft, etc. Codices Khotaneses, 1938; Zoroastri Problems in the Ninth Century Books, 1943, 2nd edn 1971; Khotanese Te: I, 1945; Khotanese Buddhist Texts, 1951; Indoscythian Studies, Khotanes Texts II, 1953; III, 1956; IV, 1961; V, 1963; VI, 1967; Corpus inscriptionu iranicarum, Saka Documents, Portfolios I-IV, 1960-67; Saka Documents, te volume, 1968; Dictionary of Khotan Saka, 1979. *Address:* Queens' Colleg Cambridge.

BAILEY, Jack Arthur; Secretary, MCC, since 1974; Secretary, Internation Cricket Conference, since 1974; *b* 22 June 1930; *s* of Horace Arthur and El Winifred Bailey; *m* 1957, Julianne May Squier; one *s* two *d. Educ:* Chris Hospital; University Coll., Oxford (BA). Asst Master, Bedford Sch., 1958-(Reed Paper Group, 1960-67; Rugby Football Correspondent, Sund Telegraph, 1962-74; Asst Sec., MCC, 1967-74. *Recreations:* cricket (played f Essex and for Oxford Univ.), golf. *Address:* 20 Elm Tree Road, NW8. 01-286 6246. *Clubs:* Wig and Pen, MCC, Vincent's (Oxford).

BAILEY, James Vincent; Executive Director, Bank of England, 1964-69; 26 July 1908; *s* of R. H. Bailey; *m* 1946, Ida Hope Weigall; no *c. Edu* Malvern; Pembroke Coll., Oxford. Entered Bank of England, 1928; Depu

Chief Cashier, 1959-62; Chief Accountant, 1962-64. *Address:* Common Barn, Remenham, Henley-on-Thames, Oxon. *T:* Henley 2480.

AILEY, John; *see* Bailey, W. J. J.

AILEY, John Bilsland, CB 1982; Deputy Secretary, Treasury Solicitor's Department, since 1979; *b* 5 Nov. 1928; *o s* of late Walter Bailey and of Ethel Edith Bailey, FRAM (who *m* 2nd, Sir Thomas George Spencer); *m* 1952, Marion Rosemary (*née* Carroll); two *s* one *d. Educ:* Eltham Coll.; University Coll., London (LLB). Solicitor of Supreme Court. Legal Asst, Office of HM Treasury Solicitor, 1957; Sen. Legal Asst, 1962; Asst Treasury Solicitor, 1971; Principal Asst Treasury Solicitor, 1973; Under-Sec. (Legal), Dept of HM Procurator General and Treasury Solicitor, 1973-77; Legal Dir, Office of Fair Trading, 1977-79. *Recreations:* walking, reading, listening to music. *Address:* Sherwood Cottage, West Meon, Hampshire. *T:* West Meon 354; 01-834 1376. *Club:* Reform.

AILEY, John Everett Creighton, CBE 1947; Executive Chairman, Difco Laboratories (UK) Ltd, 1970-75; Chairman and Managing Director, Baird & Tatlock Group of Cos, 1941-69; *b* 2 Nov. 1905; *s* of late John Edred Bailey and late Violet Constance Masters; *m* 1928, Hilda Anne Jones; one *s* four *d. Educ:* Brentwood Sch. Peat Marwick Mitchell & Co., 1925-31; Director: Derbyshire Stone Ltd, 1959-69; Tarmac Derby Ltd, 1969-70; G. D. Searle & Co., 1969-70, and other companies. Mem., Admlty Chemical Adv. Panel, 1940-50; Pres. Scientific Instrument Manufacturers Assoc., 1945-50; Chm. Brit. Laboratory Ware Assoc., 1950-52, Pres., 1974-; Chm. Brit. Sci. Instr. Research Assoc., 1952-64 (Pres. 1964-71), first Companion, SIRA Inst.; Mem., Grand Council FBI, 1945-58; Mem. BoT Exhibns Adv. Cttee, 1957-65, and Census of Production Adv. Cttee, 1960-68. Formerly Special Member, Prices and Incomes Board. Master, 1957-58 and 1974-75, Worshipful Co. of Scientific Instrument Makers; Master, Worshipful Co. of Needlemakers, 1981-82; Freeman of City of London. Fellow, Inst. of Export; MRI; FBIM. *Recreation:* golf. *Address:* The Haven, Paternoster Row, Ottery St Mary, South Devon EX11 1DP. *Club:* Athenæum.

AILEY, Ven. Jonathan Sansbury; Archdeacon of Southend, since 1982; Bishop's Officer for Industry and Commerce, diocese of Chelmsford, since 1982; *b* 24 Feb. 1940; *s* of Walter Eric and Audrey Sansbury Bailey; *m* 1965, Susan Mary Bennett-Jones; three *s. Educ:* Quarry Bank High School, Liverpool; Trinity College, Cambridge (MA). Assistant Curate: Sutton, St Helens, Lancs, 1965-68; St Paul, Warrington, 1968-71; Warden, Marrick Priory Residential Youth Training Centre, 1971-76; Vicar of Wetherby, Yorks, 1976-82. *Address:* 144 Alexandra Road, Southend-on-Sea SS1 1HB. *T:* Southend 345175.

AILEY, Norman Stanley, CBE 1977; operatic and concert baritone; *b* 23 March 1933; *s* of Stanley and Agnes Bailey; *m* 1957, Doreen Simpson; two *s* one *d. Educ:* Rhodes Univ., S Africa; Vienna State Academy. BMus; Performer's and Teacher's Licentiate in Singing; Diplomas, opera, lieder, oratorio. Principal baritone, Sadler's Wells Opera, 1967-71; presently leading English-born Wagnerian baritone; regular engagements at world's major opera houses and festivals, including: La Scala, Milan; Royal Opera House, Covent Garden; Bayreuth Wagner Festival (first British Hans Sachs in Meistersinger, 1969); Vienna State Opera (first British Wanderer in Siegfried, 1976); Metropolitan Opera, NY; Paris Opera; Edinburgh Festival; Hamburg State Opera; Munich State Opera. BBC Television performances in Falstaff, La Traviata, The Flying Dutchman, Macbeth. Recordings include The Ring (Goodall); Meistersinger and Der Fliegende Holländer (Solti); Walküre (Klemperer), among others. Hon. RAM, 1981. *Recreations:* Mem., Baha'i world community; chess, notaphily, tropical fish, squash, golf. *Address:* Quarry Hangers, Spring Bottom, White Hill, Bletchingley, Surrey RH1 4QZ. *T:* Caterham 48271.

AILEY, Patrick Edward Robert; Director, Gatwick and Stansted Airports, British Airports Authority, since 1977; *b* 16 Feb. 1925; *s* of late Edward Bailey and Mary Elizabeth Bailey; *m* 1947, Rowena Evelyn Nichols; two *s* three *d. Educ:* Clapham Coll.; St Joseph's Coll., Mark Cross; LSE. BSc(Econ). MIPM; FCIT 1971. RAPC and RAEC (Captain), 1943-48; Labour Management, Min. of Supply and Army Department: ROF Glascoed, 1951-54; RAE Farnborough, 1954-58; RSAF Enfield, 1958-59; ROF Radway Green, 1959-61; ROFs Woolwich, 1961-66. British Airports Authority: Dep. Personnel Dir, 1966; Personnel Dir, 1970; Airport Services Dir, 1974. Mem., Air Transport and Travel Industry Trng Bd, 1971-76. *Address:* 17 Lucastes Lane, Haywards Heath, W Sussex. *Club:* Reform.

AILEY, Reginald Bertram, CBE 1976; Member, Employers' Panel, Industrial Tribunals in England and Wales, since 1977; *b* 15 July 1916; *s* of late George Bertram Bailey and Elizabeth Bailey, Ilford; *m* 1942, Phyllis Joan Firman; one *s* one *d. Educ:* Owen's School. Served War of 1939-45: RAPC, 1940-42; RE, 1942-46 (Captain). Entered Post Office as Exec. Officer, 1947; Higher Exec. Officer, 1947; Sen. Exec. Officer, 1948; Principal, 1950; Instructor, Management Trng Centre, 1957; Staff Controller, SW Region, 1958; Comdt, Management Trng Centre, 1962; Asst Sec., 1965; Dir, Wales and the Marches Postal Region, 1967; Dir, South-Eastern Postal Region, 1970-76. *Recreations:* walking, gardening, philately, old railway timetables. *Address:* 6 Wanderdown Road, Ovingdean, Brighton BN2 7BT. *T:* Brighton 35670.

BAILEY, Ronald William, CMG 1961; HM Diplomatic Service, retired; *b* 14 June 1917; *o s* of William Staveley and May Eveline Bailey, Southampton; *m* 1946, Joan Hassall, *d* of late A. E. Gray, JP, Stoke-on-Trent; one *s* one *d. Educ:* King Edward VI Sch., Southampton; Trinity Hall, Cambridge (Wootton Isaacson Scholar in Spanish). Probationer Vice-Consul, Beirut, 1939-41; HM Vice-Consul, Alexandria, 1941-45; Asst Oriental Sec., British Embassy, Cairo, 1945-48; Foreign Office, 1948-49; 1st Sec., British Legation, Beirut, 1949-52 (acted as Chargé d'Affaires, 1949, 1950 and 1951); 1st Sec., British Embassy, Washington, 1952-55; Counsellor, Washington, 1955-57; Khartoum, 1957-60 (acted as Chargé d'Affaires in each of these years); Chargé d'Affaires, Taiz, 1960-62; Consul-Gen., Gothenburg, 1963-65; Minister, British Embassy, Baghdad, 1965-67; Ambassador to Bolivia, 1967-71; Ambassador to Morocco, 1971-75. Vice-Pres., Soc. for Protection of Animals in N Africa; Vice-Pres., British-Moroccan Soc.; Mem. Council, Anglo-Arab Assoc. *Recreations:* walking, photography, gardening. *Address:* Redwood, Tennyson's Lane, Haslemere, Surrey. *T:* Haslemere 2800. *Club:* Oriental.

BAILEY, Rev. Dr Sherwin; *see* Bailey, Rev. Dr D. S.

BAILEY, Stanley Ernest, CBE 1980; QPM 1975; Chief Constable of Northumbria, since 1975; *b* 30 Sept. 1926; *m* 1954, Marguerita Dorothea Whitbread. Joined Metropolitan Police, 1947; Asst Chief Constable, Staffs, 1966; Dir, Police Res., Home Office, 1970-72; Dep. Chief Constable, Staffs, 1973-75. Chm., Cttee on Burglar Alarms, BSI, 1975-. OStJ 1981. *Recreations:* gardening, travel. *Address:* Police HQ, Ponteland, Newcastle-upon-Tyne NE20 0BL.

BAILEY, Thomas Aubrey, MBE 1959; Director, Peter Cox Ltd, Building Restoration Specialists (Member of SGB Group of Cos), 1970-76; *b* 20 Jan. 1912; *o s* of late Thomas Edward Bailey and Emma Bailey; *m* 1944, Joan Woodman, *d* of late John Woodman Hooper; one *s. Educ:* Adams' Grammar Sch., Newport, Shropshire; Regent Street Polytechnic Sch. of Architecture. Entered HM Office of Works, Ancient Monuments Br., 1935; Asst Architect, 1945-49; Architect, London and E Anglia, 1949-54; Sen. Architect in charge Ancient Monuments Br., Eng., Wales and Overseas, Min. of Public Building and Works, 1954-69; Architectural Adv. to Oxford Historic Bldgs Fund, 1963-69. Served on various cttees on stone decay and preservation; seconded to Sir Giles G. Scott, OM, RA, for Rebuilding of House of Commons, 1944-49. *Principal works:* Direction of MPBW Survey for Oxford Historic Bldg Appeal, 1957-62 and Cambridge Appeal, 1963; re-erection of fallen Trilithons at Stonehenge, 1958-64; Conservation of Claudian Aqueduct and Aurelian Wall, Brit. Embassy at Rome, 1957-69; etc. Resigned professional membership of RIBA and ARCUK, to enter specialised Bldg Industry, 1969. Mem. Conservation Cttee, for Council for Places of Worship, 1968; Mem. Council, Ancient Monuments Soc., 1970-. FSA 1957; FRSA 1969; Fellow of Faculty of Bldg, 1970. Freeman of City of London, 1967; Freeman and Liveryman, Worshipful Company of Masons, 1973. Hon. MA Oxon, 1963. *Publications:* (jointly) The Claudian Aqueduct in the Grounds of the British Embassy, Rome, 1966; many technical reports on conservation of Historic Monuments. *Recreations:* music, photography, travel, motoring. *Address:* 32 Anne Boleyn's Walk, Cheam, Sutton, Surrey SM3 8DF. *T:* 01-642 3185. *Club:* City Livery.

BAILEY, Wilfrid; Chairman, Southern Gas Region (formerly Southern Gas Board), 1969-75; Chartered Accountant; *b* 9 March 1910; *s* of late Harry Bailey and Martha Bailey (*née* Pighills); *m* 1934, Vera (*née* Manchester); two *s* one *d. Educ:* Keighley Grammar Sch. Borough Treasurer, Bexley BC, 1945-47; Chief Financial Officer, Crawley Development Corp., 1947-49; Gas Council: Southern Council, 1949-58; Secretary, 1958-61; Dep. Chm., Southern Gas Bd, 1961-69. FCA 1935; CBIM. *Recreations:* cricket, motoring, music, photography, gardening. *Address:* (home) Bramble Way, Clease Way, Compton Down, near Winchester. *T:* Twyford 713382.

BAILEY, (William) John (Joseph); journalist; *b* 11 June 1940; *s* of Ernest Robert Bailey and Josephine Smith; *m* 1963, Maureen Anne, *d* of James Gibbs Neenan and Marjorie Dorema Wrigglesworth; five *s* three *d. Educ:* St Joseph's, Stanford-le-Hope, Essex; Campion Hall, Jamaica; St George's Coll., Kingston, Jamaica; St Chad's Coll., Wolverhampton. Reporter: Southend Standard, Essex, and Essex and Thurrock Gazette, 1960-63; Northern Daily Mail, 1963-64; Chief Reporter, Billingham and Stockton Express, 1964-72; Sub-Editor, Mail, Hartlepool, 1972-75; Features Editor, Echo, Sunderland, 1975-. Member: Press Council, 1974-80; Complaints Cttee, 1974-77; Cttee for Evidence to Royal Commission on Press, 1975-76; Gen. Purposes Cttee, 1976-77; Secretariat Cttee, 1976-. Nat. Union of Journalists: Mem., Nat. Exec. Council, 1966-; Vice-Pres., 1972-73; Pres., 1973-74; Gen. Treasurer, 1975-. Provincial Journalist of the Year (jtly with Carol Roberton), British Press Awards, 1977 (commended, 1979). *Address:* 225 Park Road, Hartlepool, Cleveland TS26 9NG. *T:* Hartlepool 64577. *Club:* Press (Glasgow).

BAILIE, Rt. Hon. Robin John, PC (N Ire) 1971; Solicitor of the Supreme Court of Judicature, Northern Ireland, since 1961; *b* 6 March 1937; *m* 1961, Margaret F. (*née* Boggs); one *s* three *d. Educ:* Rainey Endowed Sch. Magherafelt, Co. Londonderry; The Queen's Univ. of Belfast (LLB). MP (N Ire) for Newtownabbey, 1969-72; Minister of Commerce, Govt of NI, 1971-72. *Recreations:* wine drinking, ski-ing, squash, golf, tennis. *Address:* 3 Ovington Square, SW3; 39a Malone Park, Belfast. *T:* Belfast 668085. *Club:* Ulster (Belfast).

BAILLIE, family name of **Baron Burton.**

BAILLIE, Alastair Turner; HM Diplomatic Service; Counsellor (Commercial), Caracas, since 1981; *b* 24 Dec. 1932; *s* of late Archibald Turner Baillie and Margaret Pinkerton Baillie; *m* 1st, 1965, Wilma Noreen Armstrong (marr. diss. 1974); one *s* ; 2nd, 1977, Irena Maria Gregor; one step *s* one step *d. Educ:* Dame Allan's Sch., Newcastle upon Tyne; Christ's Coll., Cambridge (BA). National Service, commissioned Queen's Own Cameron Highlanders, 1951-53. HMOCS: North Borneo, subseq. Sabah, Malaysia, 1957-67; joined HM Diplomatic Service, 1967; FCO, 1967-73; Consul (Commercial), Karachi, 1973-77; First Sec. and Head of Chancery, Manila, 1977-80; Counsellor, Addis Ababa, 1980-81. *Recreations:* vicarious sport, reading, travelling. *Address:* c/o Foreign and Commonwealth Office, SW1A 2AH. *Club:* Royal Commonwealth Society.

BAILLIE, Sir Gawaine George Hope, 7th Bt, of Polkemmet, *cr* 1823; *b* 8 March 1934; *s* of Sir Adrian Baillie, 6th Bt, and Hon. Olive Cecilia (*d* 1974), *d* of 1st Baron Queenborough, GBE; *S* father, 1947; *m* 1966, Margot, *d* of Senator Louis Beaubien, Montreal; one *s* one *d. Heir: s* Adrian Louis Baillie, *b* 26 March 1973. *Address:* Freechase, Warninglid, Sussex.

BAILLIE, Ian Fowler, CMG 1966; OBE 1962; Director, The Thistle Foundation, Edinburgh, 1970-81; *b* 16 Feb. 1921; *s* of late Very Rev. Principal John Baillie, CH, DLitt, DD, LLD and Florence Jewel (*née* Fowler); *m* 1951, Sheila Barbour (*née* Mathewson); two *s* one *d. Educ:* Edinburgh Acad,; Corpus Christi Coll., Oxford (MA). War service, British and Indian Armies, 1941-46. HM Overseas Civil Service (formerly Colonial Service), 1946-66: Admin. Officer (District Comr), Gold Coast, 1946-54; Registrar of Co-operative Socs and Chief Marketing Officer, Aden, 1955; Protectorate Financial Sec., Aden, 1959; Dep. British Agent, Aden, 1962; Brit. Agent and Asst High Comr, Aden, 1963; Dir, Aden Airways 1959-66; Sen. Research Associate and Administrative Officer, Agricultural Adjustment Unit, Dept of Agricultural Economics, Univ. of Newcastle upon Tyne, 1966-69. *Publication:* (ed with S. J. Sheehy) Irish Agriculture in a Changing World, 1971. *Recreation:* angling. *Address:* 4 Grange Loan Gardens, Edinburgh EH9 2EB. *T:* 031-667 2647.

BAILLIE, Dame Isobel, DBE 1978 (CBE 1951); Hon. MA (Manchester Univ.), 1950; RCM, RAM; Singer; *b* Hawick, Scotland; *m* 1918, H. L. Wrigley; one *d. Educ:* Dover Street High Sch. for Girls, Manchester. Appeared at all leading Festivals, including Three Choirs, Edinburgh, London, etc.; only British singer to appear with Toscanini on three occasions. Concerts with Sir Malcolm Sargent, Sir Adrian Boult, Sir Hamilton Harty, Sir Henry Wood, Bruno Walter, De Sabata, etc. Sang at Covent Garden in Orphée, and in Hollywood Bowl. Toured New Zealand twice; concerts in Malaya, 1948, South Africa, 1952, etc. Professor of Singing: Cornell Univ., USA, 1960-61; Royal Coll. of Music, London; Manchester Sch. of Music. Hon. DLitt Salford, 1977. *Address:* Flat 14, Pavilion Lodge, Edgbaston Drive, Old Trafford, Manchester M16 0JN. *T:* 061-860 6458. *Club:* VAD Ladies.

BAILLIE, John Strachan, CBE 1965; *b* 1896; *s* of William T. Baillie, Belfast; *m* 1926, Eileen Mary, *d* of Saxon J. Payne. *Educ:* Queen's Univ., Belfast (BComSc). Joined Harland and Wolff, Belfast, 1913, and (apart from service in RN, 1914-18) was with Co. throughout his career; transf. to Co.'s London Office, 1924; Asst Sec., Harland & Wolff, Belfast, 1937; London Manager, 1945; Dir 1947; Dep. Chm. 1958; Chm. 1962-65; Dir, Short Brothers & Harland Ltd, 1948-67; Dep. Chm. Brown Bros & Co. Ltd, 1962-67. Liveryman, Worshipful Co. of Shipwrights. Commander: Order of St Olav (Norway), 1960; Dannebrog (Denmark) 1964. *Address:* Merrydown, 12 Aldersey Road, Guildford, Surrey.

BAILLIE, William James Laidlaw, RSA 1979 (ARSA 1968); PRSW 1974 (RSW 1963); painter; Senior Lecturer in Drawing and Painting, Edinburgh College of Art, since 1968; Treasurer, Royal Scottish Academy, since 1980; *b* 19 April 1923; *s* of James and Helen Baillie; *m* 1961, Helen Gillon; one *s* two *d. Educ:* Dunfermline High Sch.; Edinburgh College of Art (Andrew Grant Schol., 1941-50; Dip. Drawing and Painting 1950). Studies interrupted by war service with Royal Corps of Signals, mainly in Far East, 1942-47. Taught in Edinburgh schools, 1951-60; Mem., Teaching Staff, Edin. College of Art, 1960-; Visiting Tutor, National Gallery of Canada Summer Sch., near Ottawa, 1955. Exhibits mostly in galleries in Scotland; first retrospective exhibn in Kirkcaldy Art Gallery, 1977. *Recreations:* music, travel. *Address:* 6A Esslemont Road, Edinburgh EH16 5PX. *T:* 031-667 1538.

BAILLIE-HAMILTON, family name of **Earl of Haddington.**

BAILLIEU, family name of **Baron Baillieu.**

BAILLIEU, 3rd Baron *cr* 1953, of Sefton, Australia and Parkwood, Surrey; **James William Latham Baillieu;** *b* 16 Nov. 1950; *s* of 2nd Baron Baillieu and Anne Bayliss, *d* of Leslie William Page, Southport, Queensland; *S* father, 1973; *m* 1974, Cornelia Masters Ladd, *d* of W. Ladd; one *s. Educ:* Radley College; Monash Univ., Melbourne (BEc 1977). Short Service Commission, Coldstream Guards, 1970-73. *Heir: s* Hon. Robert Latham Baillieu, *b* 2 Feb. 1979. *Address:* c/o Mutual Trust Pty Ltd, 360 Collins Street, Melbourne, Victoria 3000, Australia. *Club:* Boodle's.

BAIN, Prof. Andrew David, FRSE 1980; Walton Professor of Monetary a Financial Economics, University of Strathclyde, since 1977; *b* 21 March 19. *s* of Hugh Bain and Kathleen Eadie; *m* 1960, Anneliese Minna Frieda Krogg three *s. Educ:* Glasgow Academy; Christ's Coll., Cambridge. PhD Can 1963. Junior Res. Officer, Dept of Applied Econs, Cambridge Univ., 1958-4 Res. Fellow, Christ's Coll., Cambridge, 1960; Instructor, Cowles Foun Yale Univ., 1960-61; Lectr, Cambridge, 1961-66; Fellow, Corpus Chr Coll., Cambridge, 1962; on secondment to Bank of England, 1965-67; Pr of Econs, 1967-70, Hd of Econs Dept, 1967-71, Esmee Fairbairn Prof. Econs of Finance and Investment, 1970-77, Univ. of Stirling. Member: Ct to Review the Functioning of Financial Institutions, 1977-80; (part-tin Monopolies and Mergers Commn, 1981-. *Publications:* The Growth Television Ownership in the United Kingdom (monograph), 1964; 1 Control of the Money Supply, 1970; Company Financing in the UK, 19 The Economics of the Financial System, 1981; articles on demand analy: monetary policy and other subjects. *Address:* 7 Pathfoot Avenue, Bridge Allan, Stirlingshire. *T:* Bridge of Allan 832433. *Club:* Royal Commonwea Society.

BAIN, Cyril William Curtis, MC; DM Oxford; FRCP; Hon. Consulti Physician, Harrogate General Hospital; Past President BMA; *b* Thornfie Heaton Mersey, near Manchester, 5 June 1895; *e s* of late William Bain, M FRCP, and Ellen, *d* of late John Curtis, Rose Leigh, Heaton Chapel, ne Manchester; *m* 1930, Diana Alice, *y d* of late Lt-Col H. R. Pease, and g of late Joseph Robinson Pease, Hesslewood, near Hull; three *s* one *d. Edu* Bilton Grange, near Rugby; Wellington Coll.; Christ Church, Oxford; Thomas's Hospital, London. Served European War, 1914-18; gazetted to t Duke of Wellington's Regt 29 August 1914; Captain, 1916; Major, 191 served in Machine Gun Corps (despatches, MC); active service in France a Flanders, 1915-17; retired, 1918; Extra-ordinary member of the Card Society. *Publications:* Recent Advances in Cardiology (with C. F. T. Eas 5th edn, 1959; Incomplete Bundle Branch Block; Bilateral Bundle Bran Block; The Oesophageal Lead; Clinical Value of Unipolar Chest and Lir Leads, etc. *Recreation:* gardening. *Address:* Red Willows, The Belyars, Ives, Cornwall. *T:* Penzance 796298.

BAIN, Douglas John; Director, J. & P. Coats Ltd, since 1968; *b* 9 July 192 *s* of Alexander Gillan Bain and Fanny Heaford; *m* 1946, Jean Walla Fairbairn; three *d. Educ:* Pollokshields Secondary School; Royal Technic Coll. (now Strathclyde Univ.), Glasgow (DRTC). ATI. Royal Tech. Col 1941-43 and 1948-51. RAF, 1943-48. J. & P. Coats Ltd, 1951-: gradua trainee, 1951-55; overseas management, 1955-60; central management, 196 68; Director, 1968; seconded to Scottish Office (Scottish Econ. Planni Dept) as Under Sec., 1979-82. *Recreations:* golf, walking, geology, flyin Address: 18 Herries Road, Glasgow G41 4DF. *T:* 041-423 0458.

BAIN, Prof. George Sayers, DPhil; Professor of Industrial Relatio University of Warwick, since 1979; *b* 24 Feb. 1939; *s* of George Alexand Bain and Margaret Ioleen Bamford; *m* 1962, Carol Lynne Ogden White; o *s* one *d. Educ:* Univ. of Manitoba (BA Hons 1961, MA 1964); Oxford Un (DPhil 1968). Lectr in Econs, Univ. of Manitoba, 1962-63; Res. Fello Nuffield Coll., Oxford, 1966-69; Frank Thomas Prof. of Indust. Relatio UMIST, 1969-70; Dep. Dir, 1970-74, Dir, 1974-81, SSRC Industr Relations Res. Unit, Univ. of Warwick. Member: Res. Staff, Royal Comm on Trade Unions and Employers' Assocs (Donovan Commn), 1966-67; Mec Engrg Econ. Develt Cttee, NEDO, 1974-76; Cttee of Inquiry on Indu Democracy, Dept of Trade (Chm., Lord Bullock), 1975-76; Res. Sta Canadian Task Force on Labour Relations, 1968. Consultant, NBPI, 1967-6 acted as Consultant to Dept of Employment, and to the Manitoba and Cana Depts of Labour; frequently acts as arbitrator and mediator in indust. dispute *Publications:* Trade Union Growth and Recognition, 1967; The Growth White-Collar Unionism, 1970; (jtly) The Reform of Collective Bargaini at Plant and Company Level, 1971; (jtly) Social Stratification and Tra Unionism, 1973; (jtly) Union Growth and the Business Cycle, 1976; (jtly) Bibliography of British Industrial Relations, 1979; (jtly) Profiles of Unic Growth, 1980; contrib. prof. and learned jls. *Recreation:* ice skating. Addre 7 Northumberland Road, Leamington Spa CV32 6HE. *T:* Leamington Sp 24050.

BAIN, John Taylor, CBE 1975; JP; Director of Education, Glasgow, 1968-7 Lay Observer (Solicitors Act) in Scotland, since 1977; *b* 9 May 1912; *m* 194 Anne Nicoll Dewar; one *s* two *d. Educ:* St Andrews Univ. (BSc, MA Edinburgh Univ. (BEd). War service, RAF (Technical Br.), 1939-45. As Dir of Educn, Stirlingshire, 1947-49; Depute Dir of Educn, Glasgow, 1949-6 JP Glasgow, 1971. *Recreation:* golf. *Address:* 20 Essex Drive, Glasgow G 9NA. *T:* 041-959 2390.

BAIN, Kenneth Bruce Findlater; *see* Findlater, Richard.

BAIN, Mrs Margaret Anne; journalist; *b* 1 Sept. 1945; *d* of John and Pegg McAdam; *m* 1968, Donald Straiton Bain. *Educ:* Univs of Glasgow a Strathclyde. MA Glasgow 1967, BA Hons Strathclyde 1973. Asst Teache Our Lady's High, Cumbernauld, 1968-70; St Modan's High, Stirling: Speci Asst Teacher, 1970-73; Principal Teacher, Remedial Educn, 1973-74. M (SNP) East Dunbartonshire, Oct. 1974-1979. *Recreations:* the arts in gener folk music in particular. *Address:* 60 Galloway Terrace, West High Stree Kirkintilloch, Dunbartonshire.

BAINBRIDGE, Beryl, FRSL; actress, writer; *b* 21 Nov. 1934; *d* of Richard Bainbridge and Winifred Baines; *m* 1954, Austin Davies (marr. diss.); one *s* two *d. Educ:* Merchant Taylors' Sch., Liverpool; Arts Educational Schools, Ltd, Tring. FRSL 1978. *Plays:* Tiptoe Through the Tulips, 1976; The Warrior's Return, 1977; Its a Lovely Day Tomorrow, 1977; Journal of Bridget Hitler, 1981; Somewhere More Central (TV), 1981. *Publications:* A Weekend with Claud, 1967, revd edn 1981; Another Part of the Wood, 1968, rev. edn 1979; Harriet Said. . . ., 1972; The Dressmaker, 1973; The Bottle Factory Outing, 1974 (Guardian Fiction Award); Sweet William, 1975 (film, 1980); A Quiet Life, 1976; Injury Time, 1977 (Whitbread Award); Young Adolf, 1978; Winter Garden, 1980. *Recreations:* painting, sleeping. *Address:* 42 Albert Street, NW1 7NU. *T:* 01-387 3113.

BAINBRIDGE, Cyril; Assistant Managing Editor, The Times, since 1982; author and journalist; *b* 15 Nov. 1928; *o s* of late Arthur Herman Bainbridge and of Edith Bainbridge; *m* 1952, Barbara Hannah (*née* Crook); one *s* two *d. Educ:* privately (Negus Coll., Bradford). Served Army, staff of CGS, WO, 1947-49. Entered journalism as Reporter, Bingley Guardian, 1944-45; Telegraph and Argus, and Yorkshire Observer, Bradford, 1945-54; Press Assoc., 1954-63; joined The Times, 1963; Asst News Editor, 1967; Dep. News Editor, 1967-69; Regional News Editor, 1969-77; Managing News Editor, 1977-82. Vice-Pres., 1977-78, Pres., 1978-79, Inst. of Journalists; Mem., Press Council, 1980-. *Publications:* Taught With Care: a Century of Church Schooling, 1974; The Brontës and their Country, 1978; Brass Triumphant, 1980. *Recreations:* reading, brass bands, collecting old bookmarks. *Address:* 98 Mayfield Avenue, North Finchley, N12 9JE. *T:* 01-445 4178. *Club:* Press.

BAINBRIDGE, Maj.-Gen. Henry, CB 1948; CBE 1944; psc; retired; late Corps of Royal Engineers; *b* 1903. 2nd Lieut Royal Engineers, 1923. Served War of 1939-45, 1939-44 (despatches twice, CBE). Dir of Man-power Planning, War Office, 1949-52; Dep. QMG, War Office, 1952-55, retired 1955. *Address:* Brizlee, Hoe Lane, Peaslake, Surrey.

BAINES, Anthony Cuthbert, DLitt; FBA 1980; *b* 6 Oct. 1912; *s* of Cuthbert Edward Baines and Margaret Clemency Lane Poole; *m* 1960, Patricia Margaret Stammers. *Educ:* Westminster Sch. (KS); Christ Church Oxford; Royal College of Music. BA 1933, MA 1970, DLitt 1977, Oxon. Member, London Philharmonic Orchestra, 1935-39, 1946-49. Commissioned Royal Tank Regt, 1940-45. Associate Conductor, International Ballet Co., 1950-53; Member, Music Staff: Uppingham Sch., 1954-65; Dean Close Sch., 1965-70; Curator, Bate Collection of Historical Wind Instruments, Oxford Univ., 1970-80, retired. Fellow, University Coll., Oxford, 1974-80, retired. Editor, Galpin Society Jl, 1956-63 and 1970-. *Publications:* Woodwind Instruments and their History, 1957, 5th edn 1977; Bagpipes, 1960, 4th edn 1979; ed and contrib. Musical Instruments through the Ages, 1961, 6th edn 1978; Victoria and Albert Museum, Catalogue of Musical Instruments, vol. II, Non-Keyboard, 1968; European and American Musical Instruments, 1966, 2nd edn 1981; Brass Instruments, their History and Development, 1976, 3rd edn 1980. *Recreations:* folk music, wild birds. *Address:* 23 St Margaret's Road, Oxford OX2 6RX. *T:* Oxford 53813.

BAINES, Sir George G.; *see* Grenfell-Baines.

BAINES, Prof. John Robert, MA, DPhil; Professor of Egyptology, Oxford University and Fellow of Queen's College, Oxford, since 1976; *b* 17 March 1946; *o s* of late Edward Russell Baines and of Dora Margaret Jean (*née* O'Brien); *m* 1971, Jennifer Christine Ann, *e d* of S. T. Smith; one *s* one *d. Educ:* Winchester Coll.; New Coll., Linacre Coll., Worcester Coll., Oxford (BA 1967, MA, DPhil 1976). Lectr in Egyptology, Univ. of Durham, 1970-75; Laycock Student, Worcester Coll., Oxford, 1973-75; Vis. Prof., Univ. of Arizona, 1982; Fellow, Humboldt-Stiftung, 1982. *Publications:* (trans. and ed) H. Schäfer, Principles of Egyptian art, 1974; (with J. Málek) Atlas of ancient Egypt, 1980; (trans. and ed) E. Hornung, Conceptions of God in Ancient Egypt, 1982; articles in Acta Orientalia, Jl Egypt. Archaeol., Orientalia, Studien altägypt. Kultur, etc. *Address:* The Queen's College, Oxford.

BAINS, Lawrence Arthur, FCII; DL; Director: Bains Brothers Ltd; Crowland Leasings Ltd; Tower Timber Group Ltd, and associated companies; Chairman, Haringey District Health Authority, since 1981; *b* 11 May 1920; *s* of late Arthur Bains and Mabel (*née* Payn); *m* 1954, Margaret, *d* of late Sir William and Lady Grimshaw; two *s* one *d. Educ:* Stationers' Company's School. Served War, 1939-46: Middlesex Yeomanry, 1939; N Africa, 1940; POW, 1942, escaped, 1943. Member of Lloyd's. Hornsey Borough Council: Mem., 1949-65; Dep. Leader, 1958-64; Mayor, 1964-65; Council, London Borough of Haringey: Mem., 1964-74; Finance Chm., 1968-71; Greater London Council: Chm., 1977-78; Mem. for Hornsey/Haringey, 1967-81; Chm., South Area Planning Bd, 1970-73; Dep. Leader, Housing Policy Cttee, 1979-81; Chm., GLC/Tower Hamlets Jt Management Cttee, 1979-81; Mem., Lee Valley Regional Park Authority, 1968-81 (Chm., 1980-81). Liveryman, Worshipful Co. of Basketmakers. DL Greater London, 1978. *Recreation:* riding. *Address:* Crowland Lodge, 100 Galley Lane, Arkley, Barnet EN5 4AL. *T:* 01-440 3499. *Clubs:* City Livery, United Wards.

BAINS, Malcolm Arnold; JP, DL; Clerk of the Kent County Council and Clerk to the Lieutenancy of Kent, 1970-74; *b* 12 Sept. 1921; *s* of Herbert Bains, Newcastle-upon-Tyne; *m* 1st, 1942, Winifred Mayes Davies (marr. diss. 1961); three *s*; 2nd, 1968, Margaret Hunter. *Educ:* Hymers Coll.; Durham Univ.

(LLB (Hons)); Solicitor. Commnd as Pilot in RAF, 1942-46. Solicitor with Taunton and Sunderland and with Notts and Hants County Councils, 1946-55; Dep. Clerk of Hants County Council and Dep. Clerk of the Peace, 1955-60; Dep. Clerk of Kent County Council, 1960-70; Chm., Working Group which advised Secretary of State for Environment on future management of Local Authorities, 1971-73. Chm., Local Govt Review Bd of Victoria, 1978-79. Fellow, ANU and Advr to NSW Govt, 1977-78. Head of Norfolk Island Public Service, 1979-82. FRSA 1976. DL Kent 1976; JP Norfolk Is, 1980. *Publications:* The Bains Report, 1972; Principles and Processes of Management for New Local Authorities, 1974; Management Reform in English Local Government, 1978. *Recreations:* swimming, walking, travel. *Address:* 18 Royal Road, Teddington, Middlesex; PO Box 244, Norfolk Island, 2899, via Australia.

BAIRAMIAN, Sir Vahé (Robert), Kt 1959; *b* 30 Nov. 1900; 2nd *s* of Dr Bairamian, Cyprus; *m* 1934, Eileen Elsie Connelly; one *s. Educ:* English Sch., Nicosia, Cyprus; University Coll., London. Barrister-at-Law, Middle Temple, 1923. Served in the Courts and Land Registry, Cyprus, 1926-44; Legal Asst, Lands and Survey, Nigeria, 1944; Chief Registrar, Supreme Court, Nigeria, 1944; Magistrate, 1946; Puisne Judge, 1949; Senior Puisne Judge, High Court, Northern Region of Nigeria, 1955; Chief Justice, Sierra Leone, 1957-60; Justice, Supreme Court of Nigeria, 1960-68. Fellow UCL, 1963. Jubilee Medal, 1935; Coronation Medal, 1953. *Publications:* Editor, All Nigeria Law Reports of 1963, 1964, 1965 and 1966 (Supreme Court Judgments) (wrote a Synopsis of Criminal Procedure and Evidence in Nigeria based on them, and a Supplement for 1967-76 cases, with notes on interpretation of written law and appeals). *Address:* 36 The Crescent, Sandgate, Folkestone, Kent CT20 3EE. *T:* Folkestone 38240. *Club:* Royal Commonwealth Society.

BAIRD, Charles Fitz; Chairman and Chief Executive Officer, Inco Ltd, since 1980; *b* 4 Sept. 1922; *s* of George White and Julia (Fitz) Baird; *m* 1947, Norma Adele White; two *s* two *d. Educ:* Middlebury Coll. (BA); New York Univ. (Grad. Sch. of Bus. Admin); Harvard Univ. (Advanced Management Program). Standard Oil Co. (NJ), now Exxon, 1948-65: Dep. European Financial Rep., London, 1955-58; Asst Treas., 1958-62; Dir, Esso Standard SA Française, 1962-65; Asst Sec., Financial Man., US Navy, 1965-67, Under Secretary, 1967-69; Internat. Nickel Co. of Canada Ltd (Inco Ltd): Vice Pres. Finance, 1969-72, Sen. Vice Pres., 1972-76; Dir, 1974-; Vice Chm., 1976-77; Pres., 1977-80. Director: Bank of Montreal, 1975-; ICI Americas Inc., 1978-; Aetna Life and Casualty Co., 1981-. Member: Business Council on National Issues; British North-American Cttee; Council on Foreign Relations; Can. Inst. of Mining and Metallurgy; Canadian American Cttee. Hon. LLD Bucknell Univ. 1976. US Navy Distinguished Civilian Service Award, 1969. *Recreations:* tennis, platform tennis, golf. *Address:* Inco Ltd, 1 First Canadian Place, Toronto, Ontario M5X 1C4, Canada. *T:* (416) 361-7720. *Clubs:* Toronto, Queen's, Toronto Lawn Tennis (Toronto); The Links (New York City); Chevy Chase (Washington, DC); Short Hills (New Jersey).

BAIRD, Sir David Charles, 5th Bt of Newbyth, *cr* 1809; *b* 6 July 1912; *s* of late William Arthur Baird, of Lennoxlove, and Lady Hersey Baird; *m* 1st, 1938, Maxine Christine (marr. diss. 1960), *o c* of Rupert Darrell, New York; one *s*; 2nd, 1960, Maria Florine Viscart; one *d*]. *Address:* Summerhill, Hardgate, Castle Douglas, Kirkcudbright.

BAIRD, Sir Dugald, Kt 1959; MD, FRCOG, Hon. FRCPGlas, BSc, DPH; Belding Scholar, Association for Aid to Crippled Children, New York, 1966-71; Regius Professor of Midwifery in the University of Aberdeen, 1937-65, retired; formerly Obstetrician-in-Chief, Aberdeen Maternity Hospital and Visiting Gynæcologist, Aberdeen Royal Infirmary and Hon. Director, Obstetric Medicine Research Unit, Medical Research Council; *b* 16 Nov. 1899; *er s* of David Baird, MA, Gourock, Renfrewshire; *m* 1928, May Tennent (*see* Lady Baird); two *s* two *d. Educ:* Greenock Acad.; University of Glasgow; University of Strasbourg. Formerly with Glasgow Royal Maternity and Women's Hosp., Glasgow Royal Infirmary, and Glasgow Royal Cancer Hosp. Freedom of City of Aberdeen, 1966. Hon. LLD: Glasgow, 1959; Aberdeen, 1966; Hon. DSc: Manchester, 1962; Wales, 1966; Hon. DCL, Newcastle; DUniv Stirling, 1971. *Publications:* various papers on obstetrical and gynæcological subjects. *Recreation:* golf. *Address:* Manor House, Boswall Road, Edinburgh.

BAIRD, Lt-Gen. Sir James (Parlane), KBE 1973; MD, FRCP, FRCPEd; Medical Adviser, National Advice Centre for Postgraduate Education, since 1977; *b* 12 May 1915; *s* of Rev. David Baird and Sara Kathleen Black; *m* 1948, Anne Patricia Anderson; one *s* one *d. Educ:* Bathgate Academy; Univ. of Edinburgh. FRCPEd 1952, MD 1958, FRCP 1959. Commissioned, RAMC, 1939; Lt-Col 1956; Prof. of Military Medicine, Royal Army Medical Coll., 1965; Cons. Physician, BAOR, 1967; Dir of Medicine and Consulting Physician to the Army, 1969-71; Comdt and Dir of Studies, Royal Army Med. Coll., 1971-73; Dir Gen., Army Medical Services, 1973-77. QHP 1969. *Publication:* Tropical Diseases Supplement to Principles and Practice of Medicine, 1968. *Recreation:* golf. *Address:* 30 Stonehills Court, College Road, Dulwich, SE21 7LZ. *T:* 01-693 2735. *Club:* West Sussex Golf.

BAIRD, Sir James Richard Gardiner, 10th Bt *cr* 1695; MC 1945; *b* 12 July 1913; *er s* of Captain William Frank Gardiner Baird (killed in action 1914) (2nd *s* of 8th Bt) and Violet Mary (*d* 1947), *d* of late Richard Benyon Croft; *S* uncle, Sir James Hozier Gardiner Baird, 9th Bt, 1966; *m* 1941, Mabel Ann

(Gay), *d* of A. Algernon Gill; two *s* one *d. Educ:* Eton. Served War of 1939-45. Lieut, Royal Artillery, 1940; Captain, Kent Yeomanry, 1944. *Recreation:* shooting. *Heir: s* James Andrew Gardiner Baird [*b* 2 May 1946. *Educ:* Eton]. *Address:* 11 St Mary Abbots Court, W14. *T:* 01-603 7356.

BAIRD, Joyce Elizabeth Leslie; Joint General Secretary, Assistant Masters and Mistresses Association, since 1978; *b* 8 Dec. 1929; *d* of Dr J. C. H. Baird and Mrs J. E. Baird. *Educ:* The Abbey School, Reading; Newnham College, Cambridge (MA); secretarial training. Secretary to Sir Austin Robinson and editorial assistant, Royal Economic Soc., 1952-60; Senior Geography Mistress, Hertfordshire and Essex High School, Bishop's Stortford, 1961-77 (Dep. Head, 1973-75). President: Assoc. of Assistant Mistresses, 1976-77; Internat. Fedn of Secondary Teachers, 1981-. *Recreations:* walking, gardening, travel. *Address:* 26 Fulbrooke Road, Cambridge CB3 9EE. *T:* Cambridge 354909; 103 Clare Court, Judd Street, WC1H 9QP. *T:* 01-837 5822. *Club:* University Women's.

BAIRD, Lady, (May Deans), CBE 1962; National Governor of the BBC in Scotland, 1966-70; *b* 14 May 1901; *er d* of Matthew Tennent, Newton, Lanarks; *m* 1928, Sir Dugald Baird, *qv;* two *s* two d. *Educ:* Glasgow High Sch. for Girls; Glasgow Univ. BSc 1922; MB, ChB 1924. Hospital appts until marriage; social and local govt work, 1938-54; Chm. of Public Health Cttee, Aberdeen Town Council; Chm. NE Regional Hosp. Bd (Scotland), 1947-66. Freedom of City of Aberdeen, 1966. Hon. LLD Aberdeen Univ., 1958. *Address:* Manor House, 17 Boswall Road, Edinburgh.

BAIRD, Vice-Adm. Sir Thomas (Henry Eustace), KCB 1980; DL; *b* Canterbury, Kent, 17 May 1924; *s* of Geoffrey Henry and Helen Jane Baird; *m* 1953, Angela Florence Ann Paul, Symington, Ayrshire; one *s* one d. *Educ:* RNC, Dartmouth. Served HM Ships: Trinidad, in support of convoys to Russia, 1941, Midshipman; Bermuda, Russian convoys and landings in N Africa, and Orwell, Russian convoys and Atlantic escort force, 1942; Howe, E Indies, 1943, Sub-Lt; Rapid, E Indies, 1944 until VJ Day, Lieut; St James, Home Fleet, 1946; Ganges, Ratings' New Entry Trng, 1948; Plucky, Exec. Officer, mine clearance in Mediterranean, 1950; Lt Comdr 1952; Veryan Bay, Exec. Officer, W Indies and Falkland Is., 1953; O-in-C, Petty Officers' Leadership Sch., Malta, 1954; Exec. Officer, HMS Whirlwind, Home Fleet and Med., for Suez Op., 1956; Comd, HMS Acute, Dartmouth Trng Sqdn, 1958; Comdr 1959; Comd, HMS Ulysses, Home Fleet, 1960; Staff, C-in-C, Home Fleet, Northwood, 1961; Exec. Officer, Jt Anti-Sub. Sch., Londonderry, 1963; EO, HMS Bulwark, Far East, 1965; Ch. Staff Officer to Cdre, Naval Drafting, 1966; Captain 1967; Dep. Dir, Naval Equipment, Adm., Bath, 1967; Captain: Mine Countermeasures, Fishery Protection and HMS Lochinvar (comd), 1969; Comd, HMS Glamorgan, Far East, W Indies, S Amer., Med., and UK Waters, 1971; Captain of the Fleet, 1973; Rear Adm. 1976; Chief of Staff to C-in-C Naval Home Comd, 1976-77; Dir Gen., Naval Personal Services, 1978-79; Vice-Adm. 1979; Flag Officer Scotland and NI, 1979-82. DL Ayr and Arran, 1982. *Recreations:* cricket, golf, shooting, fishing. *Address:* Craigrethill, Symington, Ayrshire KA1 5QN. *Clubs:* Army and Navy; Prestwick Golf (Prestwick).

BAIRD, Dr Thomas Terence, CB 1977; Chief Medical Officer, Department of Health and Social Services, Northern Ireland, 1972-78, retired; *b* 31 May 1916; *s* of Thomas Baird, Archdeacon of Derry, and Hildegarde Nolan; *m* 1940, Joan Crosbie; two d. *Educ:* Haileybury Coll.; Queen's Univ. of Belfast. MB, BCh, BAO, 1939; DPH, 1947; FFCM (RCP), 1972; MRCPI 1973, FRCPI 1975; MRCPEd 1975; FFCM Ireland (Founder Fellow), 1977. Ho. Surg./Ho. Phys., North Lonsdale Hosp., Barrow-in-Furness, 1939-40. Served War, RNVR, 1940-46. Queen's Univ. of Belfast, DPH course, 1946-47. Berks CC: Asst MO, 1947-49; Dep. County MO and Dep. Principal Sch. MO, 1949-54. Welsh Bd of Health: MO, 1954-57; Sen. MO, 1957-62; Min. of Health and Local Govt, Northern Ireland: PMO, 1962-64; Dep. Chief MO, 1964-68; Min. of Health and Social Services, NI, Sen. Dep. Chief MO, 1968-72. Chairman: NI Med. Manpower Adv. Cttee; NI Adv. Cttee on infant mortality and handicaps. Member: GMC, 1973-79; Faculty of Medicine, QUB; NI Council for Postgrad. Med. Educn; Bd, Faculty of Community Medicine, RCPI. Chief Surgeon for Wales, St John Ambulance Bde, 1959-62. QHP 1974-77. CStJ 1959. *Publications:* (jtly) Infection in Hospital-a code of practice, 1971; papers in various learned jls. *Recreations:* fishing, forestry. *Address:* 2 Kensington Road, Belfast BT5 6NF. *T:* Belfast 798020; Port-a-Chapel, Greencastle, Co. Donegal. *T:* Greencastle 38. *Club:* Carlton.

BAIRD, William; Under Secretary, Scottish Home and Health Department, since 1978; *b* 13 Oct. 1927; *s* of Peter and Christina Baird, Airdrie; *m* 1954, Anne Templeton Macfarlane; two d. *Educ:* Airdrie Academy; Glasgow Univ. Entered Scottish Home Dept, 1952; Private Sec. to Perm. Under-Sec. of State, Scottish Office, 1957; Principal, Scottish Educn Dept, 1958-63; Private Sec. to Minister of State and successive Secs of State for Scotland, 1963-65; Asst Sec., Scottish Educn Dept, 1965-66; Dept of Agriculture and Fisheries for Scotland, 1966-71; Scottish Office Finance Div., 1971-73; Registrar General for Scotland, 1973-78. *Recreations:* reading, music, gardening. *Address:* 18 Lygon Road, Edinburgh EH16 5QB. *T:* 031-667 3054. *Club:* Royal Commonwealth Society.

BAIRSTO, Air Marshal Sir Peter (Edward), KBE 1981 (CBE 1973); CB 1980; AFC 1957; Deputy Commander-in-Chief, Strike Command, since 1981; *b* 3 Aug. 1926; *s* of late Arthur Bairsto and Beatrice (née Lewis); *m* 1947, Kathleen, (née Clarbour); two *s* one d. *Educ:* Rhyl Grammar Sch. Pilot, FAA,

1944-46; 1946-62: FO RAF Regt, Palestine, Aden Protectorate; Flying Instr, Fighter Pilot, Fighter Comd and Near East; Flight Comdr, 43 Sqdn, and Leader, RAF Aerobatic Team; Sqdn Comdr, 66 Sqdn; RAF Staff Coll.; Wing Comdr, Flying, Nicosia, 1963-64; Op. Requirements, MoD, 1965-67; JSSC Latimer, 1967; Instr, RAF Staff Coll., 1968-70; Stn Comdr, RAF Honington, 1971-73; Dir, Op. Requirements, MoD, 1974-77; AOC Training Units Support Command, 1977-79; Comdr, Northern Maritime Air Region, 1979-81. Queen's Commendation for Valuable Services in the Air, 1955 and 1960. CBIM. *Recreations:* golf, fishing, shooting, gardening. *Address:* Lucklaw House, Logie, by Cupar, Fife. *T:* Balmullo 870546. *Clubs:* Royal Air Force; New (Edinburgh).

BAKER, family name of **Baron Baker.**

BAKER, Baron *cr* 1977 (Life Peer), of Windrush, Gloucestershire; **John Fleetwood Baker,** Kt 1961; OBE 1941; FRS 1956; MA, ScD Cantab; DSc Wales; Hon. LLD Glasgow; Hon. DSc Leeds, Manchester, Edinburgh, Aston, Leicester, Salford, Cranfield, Lancaster, Bristol; Hon. DEng Liverpool; Hon. DS Ghent; Hon. FIMechE; Hon. ARIBA; Hon. FWeldI; Hon. Mem., Inst. of Royal Engineers; FICE; FIStructE; Associate MASCE; Fellow of Clare College, Cambridge, 1943; Director of Research and Development, IDC Group Ltd; Deputy Chairman, IDC Consultants Ltd; Director, IDC Project Management Consultants Ltd; *b* 19 March 1901; *s* of J. W. Baker, Wallasey and Emily C. Fleetwood; *m* 1928, Fiona Mary MacAlister (*d* 1979), *d* of late John Walker; two *d. Educ:* Rossall; Clare Coll., Cambridge (Scholar). Technical Asst, Design Dept, Royal Airship Works, 1925; Asst Lecturer, University Coll., Cardiff, 1926; Scientific Asst, Building Research Station, 1928; Technical Officer to Steel Structures Res. Cttee, 1931-36; Prof. of Civil Engineering, Bristol Univ., 1933-43; Prof. of Mechanical Sciences and Head of Dept of Engineering, Cambridge Univ., 1943-68, Prof. Emeritus, 1968. Chm. Council, Sch. of Physical Sciences, Cambridge Univ., 1945-72. Telford Gold Medal, 1932, Telford Premium, 1936 and 1953; Howard Quinquennial Medal and Prize, 1937; Ewing Medal, 1952; Inst. Lecture to Students, 1936-37. Unwin Memorial Lecture, 1961. Mem. of Council 1947-56, 1958-63, 1964-66. Vice-Pres., 1968-70, Inst. of Civil Engrs; Research Medal 1951, Instn Silver Medal 1951, Gold Medal 1953; Mem. of Council, 1936-39, Chm., Western Counties Br., 1935-39, Midland Lecture, 1971, Instn of Structural Engineers; Royal Medal, Royal Soc., 1970; Sir Alfred Herbert Paper, Instn of Production Engrs, 1973. Member: Civil Defence Research Cttee, 1939-1948; Scientific Adv. Com., Min. of Works, 1945-46; Adv. Council to Military Coll. of Science, 1947-52; UGC, 1953-63; Council, British Welding Res. Assoc.; Pres. Welding Inst., 1971-73 (Brooker Medal, 1977); Pres., British Assoc. for the Advancement of Science, 1975-76; Chm., Naval Educn Adv. Cttee, 1958-64; Consultant, Naval Constructional Research Establishment, Rosyth, 1948-63; Director: Technical Development Capital Ltd, 1962-74; John Brown & Co. Ltd, 1963-71; Cambridge Fender & Engineering Co. Ltd, 1964-74. Scientific Adviser, and in charge of Design and Development Section, Ministry of Home Security, ARP Dept, 1939-43; designer of Morrison indoor shelter, 1940. Founder Fellow, Fellowship of Engineering, 1976. Officier du Mérite pour la Recherche et l'Invention, Paris, 1964. *Publications:* Differential Equations of Engineering Science, 1929; Analysis of Engineering Structures, 1936, 4th edn, 1968; The Steel Skeleton, Vol 1, 1954, Vol. 2, 1956; Plastic designs of frames, Vol. 1, 1969; Enterprise versus Bureaucracy, 1978; numerous scientific and technical papers on Theory of Structures and Strength of Materials, etc. *Address:* 42 Crossways Gardens, Cambridge CB2 2JT. *T:* Cambridge 840152. *Club:* Athenæum.

BAKER, Prof. Alan, FRS 1973; Professor of Pure Mathematics, University of Cambridge, since 1974; Fellow of Trinity College, Cambridge, since 1964; *b* 19 Aug. 1939; *o c* of Barnet and Bessie Baker. *Educ:* Stratford Grammar Sch.; University Coll. London; Trinity Coll., Cambridge. BSc (London); MA, PhD (Cantab). Mem., Dept of Mathematics, UCL, 1964-65 and Fellow, UCL 1979; Research Fellow, 1964-68, and Dir of Studies in Mathematics, 1968-74 Trinity Coll., Cambridge; Mem., Dept of Pure Maths and Math. Statistics Univ. of Cambridge, 1966-; Reader in Theory of Numbers, 1972-74. Visiting Professor: Univs of Michigan and Colorado, 1969; Stanford Univ., 1974; Mem., Inst. for Advanced Study, Princeton, 1970; First Turán Lectr, J. Bolyai Math. Soc. Hungary, 1978. For. Fellow, Indian Nat. Sci. Acad., 1980. Fields Medal, Internat. Congress of Mathematicians, Nice, 1970; Adams Prize of Univ. of Cambridge, 1971-72. *Publications:* Transcendental Number Theory 1975; papers in various mathematical jls. *Recreations:* hiking, travel. *Address:* Trinity College, Cambridge. *T:* Cambridge 358201.

BAKER, Alex Anthony, CBE 1973; MD, MRCP, DPM; FRCPsych; Consultant Psychiatrist with special interest in the elderly to Gloucestershire Clinical Area, 1973-77, retired; *b* 22 March 1922; *m* 1944; two *s* two d. *Educ:* St Mary's Hosp. Med. Sch. Consultant Psychiatrist: Banstead Hosp., 1955; Mother and Baby Unit, Downview Hosp., 1958; St Mary Abbotts Hosp., 1967; Medical Administrator, Banstead Hosp., 1964; sometime Consultant to WHO; Sen. Principal Medical Officer, Dept of Health, 1968; Dir, NHS Hospital Adv. Service, 1969-73. *Publications:* (jtly) Psychiatric Services and Architecture, 1958; (jtly) Social Psychiatry; Psychiatric Disorders in Obstetrics, 1967; Comprehensive Psychiatric Care, 1976; chapters in sundry books; papers in numerous jls on research, psychiatric treatment, organisation of psychiatric services, etc. *Address:* Crest Cottage, Amberley, Stroud, Glos. *T:* Amberley 2585.

BAKER, Alexander Shelley, CB 1977; OBE 1958; DFC 1944; Assistant Under Secretary of State, Home Office, 1973-77, retired; *b* 5 June 1915; *s* of late Rev. William Shelley Baker and Mrs Winifred Baker, Staines and Stratford E15; *m* 1944, Cynthia, 2nd *d* of late Charles Mould, Great Easton, Leics; two *d. Educ:* West Ham Secondary School. Served RAF, 1939-65 (despatches, 1944; 2 citations French Croix de Guerre); comd Nos 4, 16, 37 and 224 Sqdns and RAF North Front Gibraltar; retd as Group Captain. Principal, Home Office, 1965; Asst Sec., 1969-73. Reader, Church of England. *Recreations:* gardening, bridge. *Address:* High View, Foxearth, near Sudbury, Suffolk. *T:* Sudbury 72548. *Club:* Royal Air Force.

BAKER, Alfreda Helen, MD; FRCS; Consulting Surgeon: to Elizabeth Garrett Anderson Hospital, 1937-68; to Hounslow Hospital, 1930-68; to Marie Curie Hospital, 1937-68; *b* 2 Oct. 1897; *d* of Alfred Rawlings and Hannah Mary Baker. *Educ:* Queen's Univ., Belfast. MB, BCh, QU Belfast, 1921 (hons); MD 1926 (Commendation); FRCS, Eng. 1927. Demonstrator of Anatomy, QU Belfast, 1922-24; House Surgeon, Royal Cancer Hosp., 1926; Riddel Research Fellow, Royal Free Hosp., 1924-26; Surgical Registrar, Elizabeth Garrett Anderson Hosp., 1930-33; Surgeon, EMS, 1939-45. Fellow Assoc. of Surgeons of Gt Brit. and Ire., 1950. *Publications:* original work published in: British Journal of Surgery; Lancet; British Journal of Obstetrics and Gynæcology, etc. *Recreations:* water colour painting, oil painting, photography, foreign travel. *Address:* Arkesden, Saffron Walden, Essex. *T:* Clavering 370.

BAKER, Allan; see Baker, J. F. A.

BAKER, Sir (Allan) Ivor, Kt 1972; CBE 1944; JP; DL; Chairman, Baker Perkins Holdings Ltd, 1944-75; *b* 2 June 1908; *s* of late Allan Richard Baker; *m* 1935, Josephine, *d* of late A. M. Harley, KC; three *s* one *d. Educ:* Bootham, York; King's Coll., Cambridge; Harvard, USA. Baker Perkins: Student apprentice, 1931; Director, 1935-; Jt Man. Dir., 1942-67; Chm., 1944-75. British Engineers' Assoc.: Mem. Council, 1943-68; Pres., 1960-61; Director Lloyds Bank Ltd, 1973-79; Lloyds Bank Eastern Region, 1953-73 (Chm., 1973-79); Mitchell Construction Holdings Ltd, 1963-. Member: Economic Planning Council for East Anglia, 1965-69; Peterborough Development Corp., 1968-78. JP 1954; High Sheriff, 1968-69, DL 1973, Cambridgeshire. *Recreations:* golf, gardening. *Address:* 214 Thorpe Road, Peterborough PE3 6LW. *T:* Peterborough 262437.

BAKER, Ann Maureen, (Mrs D. R. Baker); see Jenner, A. M.

BAKER, Anthony Baxter, JP; Regional Administrator, Northern Regional Health Authority, since 1973; *b* 12 June 1923; *s* of late Anthony Thurlbeck Baker and Robina Frances Jane (*née* Baxter); *m* 1st, 1946, Mary Margherita Patterson (*d* 1978); one *s* three *d*; 2nd, 1981, Judith Margaret Ayers, JP. *Educ:* Tynemouth High Sch.; Durham Univ. DPA; FHA. RAFVR, UK, Canada and Iceland, 1942-46. Admin. Asst, later Dep. Sec., SE Northumberland HMC, 1949-60; Asst Sec., later Principal Asst Sec., Newcastle Regional Hosp. Bd, 1960-73. JP Tynemouth 1965; Chm., North Tyneside PSD. *Recreations:* Rugby football (PP Percy Park RFC; Pres. Northumberland RFU), golf. *Address:* 59 Broadway, Tynemouth, North Shields NE30 2LJ. *T:* North Shields 574660.

BAKER, Anthony Castelli, MVO 1980; MBE 1975; HM Diplomatic Service, retired; *b* 27 Dec. 1921; *s* of late Alfred Guy Baker and of Luciana (*née* Castelli). *Educ:* Merchant Taylors' Sch., Northwood, Mddx. Served War: munitions worker, 1940-41; volunteered for RAFVR and served in UK, ME and Italy, 1941-46 (Flt Lieut). Joined HM Diplomatic Service, 1946; served in Rome and Paris, 1946-50; Third Sec., Prague, 1951; Hamburg, 1953; Vice-Consul, Milan, 1954; Third, later Second Sec., Athens, 1959; Second Sec., Beirut, 1963; First Sec., Cairo, 1965; Naples, 1968; Turin, 1970; First Sec. Commercial, Calcutta, 1972; Consul, Montreal, 1975; First Sec. Commercial, Port of Spain, 1976; Consul, Genoa, 1979-81. Officer, Order of Merit (Italy), 1980. *Recreations:* tennis, skiing, watching cricket, travelling, jazz music. *Address:* c/o Flat 2, 44 Elsworthy Road, NW3 3BU; Box 91, La Bisbal, Gerona, Spain. *Clubs:* Royal Air Force, MCC.

BAKER, Arthur John, CBE 1981; Principal, Brockenhurst Sixth Form College (formerly Brockenhurst Grammar School), since 1969; *b* 29 Nov. 1928; *s* of Arthur Reginald and Ruth Baker; *m* 1953, June Henrietta Dunham; one *s* two *d. Educ:* Southampton Univ. (BSc; DipEd). Mathematics Master, Hampton Grammar Sch., 1952-55; Dep. Head, Sunbury Grammar Sch., 1955-61; Headmaster, Christchurch Grammar Sch., 1961-69. *Recreations:* walking, gardening. *Address:* 93 New Forest Drive, Brockenhurst, Hampshire SO4 7QT. *T:* Lymington 23138.

BAKER, Prof. Arthur Lemprière Lancey, DSc (Eng), FICE, FIStructE, FACI; Professor of Concrete Structures and Technology, University of London (Imperial College), 1945-73, now Emeritus; *b* 16 Dec. 1905; *s* of late W. L. Baker, Exeter; *m* 1930, Lillian Hollings; two *d. Educ:* Queen Elizabeth's Sch., Crediton; University of Manchester. Asst Engineer, Mersey Tunnel, Edmund Nuttall, Sons & Co. Ltd, 1926-28; Dist Engineer, PWD, Nigeria, 1928-30; Asst Engineer, Christiani & Nielsen Ltd, 1930-33; Senior Design Engineer, Reinforcing Steel Co., Johannesburg, 1933-36; Senior Civil Engineer, Trinidad Leaseholds Ltd, 1936-45. Mem., BSI Cttee for the Structural Use of Concrete, 1970-; Hon. ACGI; Hon. DTech Bradford, 1971. *Publications:* Raft Foundations, 1937; Reinforced Concrete, 1949; The

Ultimate Load Theory Applied to the Design of Reinforced and Pre-stressed Concrete Frames, 1956; The Inelastic Space Frame, 1967; Limit State Design of Reinforced Concrete, 1970. *Address:* Department of Mechanical Engineering, Imperial College of Science and Technology, SW7 2BU. *T:* 01-589 5111.

BAKER, Cecil John; Chairman: Hunting Gate Group Ltd, since 1980; Alliance Building Society, since 1981; *b* 2 Sept. 1915; *s* of late Frederick William Baker and Mildred Beatrice Palmer; *m* 1st, 1942, Kathleen Cecilia Henning (marr. diss. 1965); one *s*; 2nd, 1971, Joan Beatrice Barnes; one *d. Educ:* Whitgift Sch.; LSE (LLB 1939; BSc(Econ) 1949); Inst. of Actuaries. FIA 1948; ACII 1937. Sec., Insurance Inst. of London, 1945-49; Investment Manager, London Assurance, 1950-64; Investment Consultant, Hambros Bank Ltd, 1964-74; Chairman: Pension Fund Property Unit Trust, 1966-; Charities Property Unit Trust, 1967-; Property Unit Trust for Public and General Superannuation Schemes, 1967-; Victory Insurance Co. Ltd, 1972-; Agricl Property Unit Trust for Pension Funds and Charities, 1976-; Victory Insurance Holdings Ltd, 1979-; Director: Abbey Life Assurance Co. Ltd, 1965-; Hampton Gold Mining Areas Ltd, 1972-; United Real Property Trust plc, 1982-. *Recreations:* golf, travel. *Address:* 73 Brook Street, W1Y 1YE. *T:* 01-499 7191.

BAKER, Charles A.; see Arnold-Baker.

BAKER, Colin Lewis Gilbert, CBE 1974; FCA; Director of companies; *b* 24 Aug. 1913; *m* 1942, Pauleen Denice Hartley; two *s* two *d. Educ:* Queen's Coll., Taunton. Professional accountancy, 1931-39. Served War, Somerset LI, Major, 1939-45. George Angus & Co. Ltd, 1945-73: Director, 1958-63; Dep. Chm., 1963-64; Chm., 1964-73; Exec. Dir, The Dunlop Co. Ltd (later Dunlop Holdings Ltd), 1968-73; Local Dir, Baring Bros & Co. Ltd, 1975-79. Mem., Companies Consultative Gp, DoT, 1972-80. Other interests include: Mem., Northern Regional Bd, Lloyds Bank (Chm., 1979-); Dir, Lloyds Bank UK Management Ltd; Commissaris, Royal Boskalis Westminster NV. Former Member: Northern Economic Planning Council (Chm. 1973-77); Northern Regional Council, CBI (Chm. 1972-73); Newcastle upon Tyne AHA (T), 1975-79. Gen. Comr of Income Tax, 1965-80. *Recreations:* fishing, gardening, going to cottage in Cornwall. *Address:* Lynton, Apperley Road, Stocksfield, Northumberland. *T:* Stocksfield 3454. *Club:* Army and Navy.

BAKER, Derek; see Baker, L. G. D.

BAKER, Hon. Francis Edward N.; see Noel-Baker.

BAKER, Geoffrey, QC 1970; **His Honour Judge Geoffrey Baker;** a Circuit Judge, since 1978; *b* 5 April 1925; *er s* of late Sidney and Cecilia Baker, Bradford; *m* 1948, Sheila (*née* Hill); two *s* one *d. Educ:* Bradford Grammar Sch.; Leeds Univ.; LLB (Hons). Called to Bar, Inner Temple, 1947. Recorder: of Pontefract, 1967-71; of Sunderland, 1971; a Recorder of the Crown Court, 1972-78. Mem. Cttee, Leeds and WR Medico-Legal Soc., 1980-. Mem., Standing Council, Convocation of Leeds Univ., 1980-; Pres., Leeds Univ. Law Graduates' Assoc., 1981-. *Recreations:* gardening, painting, photography. *Address:* 246 Lidgett Lane, Leeds LS17 6QH. *T:* Leeds 685181.

BAKER, Geoffrey Hunter, CMG 1962; HM Diplomatic Service, retired; *b* 4 Aug. 1916; *s* of late Thomas Evelyn Baker and Gladys Beatrice Baker (*née* Marsh); *m* 1963, Anita Wägeler; one *d. Educ:* Haberdashers' Aske's Hampstead Sch.; Royal Masonic Sch., Bushey, Herts; Gonville and Caius Coll., Cambridge (Scholar). Joined Consular Service, 1938; Vice-Consul at Hamburg, 1938, Danzig, 1939, Bergen, 1939; captured by German forces there, April 1940; Vice-Consul, Basra, 1942, Jedda, 1942; Foreign Office, 1945-47; First Sec., Rangoon, 1947-51, Tehran, 1951-52; FO, 1953-54; NATO Def. Coll., Paris, 1954; Consul-Gen., Hanoi, 1954-56; UK Delegation, UN, Nov. 1956-March 1957; Cabinet Office, 1957-60; UK Delegation to the European Free Trade Association, Geneva, 1960-66; Consul-General, Munich, 1966-71, Zagreb, 1971-74. Order of Merit (Bavaria), 1971. *Recreations:* tennis, sailing, reading, and listening to music. *Address:* 10 Leigh Road, Highfield, Southampton SO2 1EF. *Clubs:* United Oxford & Cambridge University; Cambridge University Cruising (Cambridge).

BAKER, Rt. Hon. Sir George (Gillespie), PC 1971; Kt 1961; OBE 1945; President of the Family Division (formerly of the Probate, Divorce and Admiralty Division) of the High Court of Justice, 1971-79, a Judge in the Division, 1961-79; *b* 25 April 1910; *s* of late Captain John Kilgour Baker, Stirling; *m* 1935, Jessie McCall Findlay; three *s. Educ:* Glasgow Academy; Strathallan Sch., Perthshire; Brasenose Coll., Oxford (Hon. Fellow; Sen. Hulme Schol.). Called to the Bar, Middle Temple, 1932 (Harmsworth Schol.); Bencher, Hon.; Lent Reader, 1975; Treasurer, 1976. Army, 1939-45; Queen's Own RWK 1939-40; commissioned The Cameronians (Scottish Rifles), 1940; DAAG War Office, 1941-42; AAG Allied Force HQ, 1942-44; Col. 'A' 15 Army Gp, 1945: AAG British War Crimes Executive, Nuremberg, 1945. Contested (C) Southall (Middlesex), 1945. Recorder: of Bridgnorth, 1946-51; of Smethwick, 1951-52; of Wolverhampton, 1952-61. Dep. Chm. QS, Shropshire, 1954-71. QC 1952, Leader of Oxford Circuit, 1954-61; Presiding Judge, Wales and Chester Circuit, 1970-71. Governor, Strathallan Sch., 1947-57, Hon. Governor, 1968-; Governor: Epsom Coll., 1958-72; Wycombe Abbey, 1972-82. Commissioner holding Government enquiry, Feb.-April 1956 into objections to proposed British Egg Marketing Scheme and for Kenya Government into pyrethrum industry, 1960; Chairman: (First) General Optical Council, 1959-61; Departmental Cttee on Mechanical Recording of

Court Proceedings, 1964-70; Statute Law Soc., 1980-. Hon. Mem., Canadian Bar Assoc. Hon. Fellow, Brasenose Coll., Oxford, 1966. Freeman, City of London, 1981. *Recreations:* golf, fishing. *Address:* Camrie, Overstream, Loudwater, Rickmansworth, Herts. *T:* Rickmansworth 77296. *Clubs:* Caledonian; Denham Golf (Captain 1967-68).
See also T. S. G. Baker.

BAKER, George William, CBE 1977 (OBE 1971); VRD 1952 (Clasp 1979); HM Diplomatic Service, retired; *b* 7 July 1917; *e s* of late George William Baker and of Lilian Turnbull Baker; *m* 1942, Audrey Martha Elizabeth, *e d* of Harry and Martha Day; two *d. Educ:* Chigwell Sch.; Hertford Coll., Oxford (Colonial Service Second Devonshire Course). London Div., RNVR, 1937-62; served War, RN, 1939-45. Colonial Admin. Service, Tanganyika, 1946-62: Asst Colonial Attaché, Washington (incl. service in UK Delegn to Trusteeship Council at UN), 1957; Defence Sec., Tanganyika, 1959; Head of Tanganyika Govt Information Dept, 1959-62; retd after Tanganyika Independence, 1962. Joined CRO, 1962; First Sec. (Information) and Dir of British Inf. Services, British High Commn, Freetown, 1962-65; served in FCO (Consular and Defence Depts), 1965-69; First Sec. and Head of Chancery, Kinshasa, 1969-72; Dep. British Govt Rep., St Vincent and Grenada, Windward Is, 1972-74; British Commissioner, Port Moresby, Papua New Guinea, 1974-75, High Comr to Papua New Guinea, 1975-77. Chm., E Sussex Cttee, VSO. A Vice-Pres., Royal African Soc., 1973-. Chm., Heathfield Cttee, Sussex Housing Assoc. for Aged; Mem., Waldron Cttee, Rye and Bexhill Cons. Assoc. Mem. Guild of Freemen of City of London. Freeman: City of London, 1980; Clockmakers' Co., 1981. *Publications:* official booklets and contribs to learned jls. *Recreations:* photography, fishing (Mem., Sussex Piscatorial Soc.), sailing, climbing, tennis, Rugby Union, cricket, flying, cabinet-making. *Address:* Siggswood, Waldron, near Heathfield, Sussex TN21 0RG. *T:* Heathfield 2847. *Clubs:* MCC; Scientific Exploration Society (Hon. Mem.; Foreign Affairs Advr).

BAKER, Howard Henry, Jr; US Senator from Tennessee, since 1967; Majority Leader in the Senate, since 1981 (Minority Leader, 1977-81); *b* 15 Nov. 1925; *s* of Howard H. Baker and Dora Ladd; *m* 1951, Joy Dirksen; one *s* one *d. Educ:* McCallie Sch.; Tulane Univ.; Univ. of Tennessee (LLB 1949). Served USNR, 1943-46. Formerly: Partner, Baker, Worthington, Barnett & Crossley, law firm; Chm. of Bd, First Nat. Bank, Oneida, Tenn. Co-Chm., Senate Select Cttee on Presidential Campaign Activities, and mem. other Senate cttees. Mem., Amer. Bar Assoc. *Address:* Senate Office Building, Washington, DC 20510, USA; (home) Huntsville, Tenn 37756, USA.

BAKER, Sir Humphrey D. B. S.; *see* Sherston-Baker.

BAKER, Maj.-Gen. Ian Helstrip, CBE 1977 (MBE 1965); Secretary, University College, London, since 1982; *b* 26 Nov. 1927; *s* of Henry Hubert Baker and Mary Clare (*née* Coles); *m* 1956, Susan Anne, *d* of Major Henry Osmond Lock; one *s* one *d* (and one *s* decd). *Educ:* St Peter's Sch., York; St Edmund Hall, Oxford. Commnd RA, 1948; served RA and RHA, 1948-55; transf. Royal Tank Regt, 1955; Staff Coll., 1959; DAAG 17 Gurkha Div., Malaya, 1960-62; commanded Parachute Sqdn RAC (C Sqdn 2nd Royal Tank Regt), 1963-65; Instr Staff Coll., at Bt Lt-Col, 1965; GSOI Chiefs of Staff Cttee, 1966-67; commanded 1st Royal Tank Regt, 1967-69; commanded 7th Armoured Bde, 1972-73; RCDS, 1974; Brig. Gen. Staff, HQ UKLF, 1975-77; Service Fellow, St Catharine's Coll., Cambridge, 1977; Asst Chief of Gen. Staff (Op. Requirements), 1978-80; General Officer Commanding, North East District, 1980-82. Col Comdt, Royal Tank Regt, 1981-. *Recreations:* skiing, sailing, outdoor pursuits. *Address:* c/o Barclays Bank, Dorchester, Dorset. *Club:* Army and Navy.

BAKER, Sir Ivor; *see* Baker, Sir A. I.

BAKER, Dame Janet (Abbott), DBE 1976 (CBE 1970); professional singer; Joint Artistic Director, King's Lynn Festival, since 1981; *b* 21 Aug. 1933; *d* of Robert Abbott Baker and May (*née* Pollard); *m* 1957, James Keith Shelley. *Educ:* The College for Girls, York; Wintringham, Grimsby. FRSA 1979. Daily Mail Kathleen Ferrier Award, 1956; Queen's Prize, Royal College of Music, 1959; Shakespeare Prize, Hamburg, 1971; Copenhagen Sonning Prize, 1979. Hon. DMus: Birmingham, 1968; Leicester, 1974; London, 1974; Hull, 1975; Oxon, 1975; Leeds, 1980; Hon. LLD Aberdeen, 1980. Hon. Fellow St Anne's Coll., Oxford, 1975. *Recreations:* reading, tennis, walking. *Address:* c/o Ibbs & Tillett Ltd, 450-452 Edgware Road, W2 1EG.

BAKER, John Arnold; His Honour Judge Baker; a Circuit Judge, since 1973; *b* Calcutta, 5 Nov. 1925; *s* of late William Sydney Baker, MC and Hilda Dora Baker (*née* Swiss); *m* 1954, Edith Muriel Joy Heward; two *d. Educ:* Plymouth Coll.; Wellington Sch., Somerset; Wadham Coll., Oxford (MA, BCL). Treas., Oxford Union, 1948. Admitted Solicitor, 1951; called to Bar, Gray's Inn, 1960. A Recorder, 1972-73. Chm., Nat. League of Young Liberals, 1952-53; contested (L: Richmond, 1959 and 1964; Dorking, 1970; Vice-Pres., Liberal Party, 1968-69; Chm., Liberal Party Exec., 1969-70. *Recreations:* music, boating. *Address:* 1 Rosemont Road, Richmond, Surrey. *T:* 01-940 6983.

BAKER, Rt. Rev. John Austin; *see* Salisbury, Bishop of.

BAKER, John B.; *see* Brayne-Baker.

BAKER, John Burkett, QC 1975; His Honour Judge J. Burkett Baker; a Circuit Judge, since 1978; *b* 17 Sept. 1931; *s* of Philip and Grace Baker; *m* 1955, Margaret Mary Smeaton; three *s* seven *d. Educ:* Finchley Catholic Grammar Sch.; White Fathers, Bishops Waltham; UC Exeter. LLB London. RAF, 1955-58. Called to Bar, Gray's Inn, 1957; practised from 1958. Prosecuting Counsel to Dept of Health and Social Security, 1969-75; Dep Chm., Shropshire QS, 1970-71; a Recorder of the Crown Court, 1972-78; Marriage Counsellor, Catholic Marriage Adv. Council (Chm., 1981-82). Pres., Barnet, Haringey and Hertsmere Marriage Guidance Council, 1982. *Address:* 43 The Ridgeway, Enfield, Mddx EN2 8PD.

BAKER, (John Frederic) Allan, CB 1957; FEng, FICE; Ministry of Transport, retired; *b* 5 Oct. 1903; *s* of late H. J. Baker; *m* 1927, Nancy Elizabeth Wells; one *d* (and one *s* decd). *Educ:* St Paul's Sch. After Local Authority experience in Middlesex, 1922-, joined Ministry of Transport, 1929; serving in Exeter, Bedford, Nottingham and London; apptd Divisional Road Engineer for Wales and Mon, at Cardiff, 1947, and Dep. Chief Engineer at Headquarters, 1953; Chief Engineer and Dir of Highway Engineering 1954-65. Member: Road Research Board, 1954-65; London Roads Cttee 1959; Traffic Signs Cttee, 1963; Cons. Adviser to Automobile Assoc., 1965-69. Past Chm., Road Engrg Industry Cttee of BSI; Vice-Pres., Internat. Exec Cttee of Permanent Internat. Assoc. of Road Congresses, 1960-72 and Pres d'Honneur, Brit. Nat. Cttee. Mem. Council, ICE, 1956-61, 1962-67. Founder Fellow, Fellowship of Engineering, 1976; Hon. FIMunE; Hon. FInstHE. Viva Shield and Gold Medal, Worshipful Co. of Carmen, (for pioneering the British Motorway system), 1967. *Address:* 36 Imber Close, Ember Lane, Esher Surrey. *T:* 01-398 3331.
See also B. D. Dance.

BAKER, Rt. Rev. John Gilbert Hindley; *b* 10 Oct. 1910; 3rd and *y s* of late Arthur Ernest Baker, MRCS, LRCP, and Agnes Flora Baker (*née* Hindley) Bromley, Kent; *m* 1st, 1941, Martha Levering Sherman (*d* 1976), *d* of late Rev. Arthur Sherman, STD and Mrs Martha Sherman, Wuchang, China and Ohio, USA; two *s* two *d* ; 2nd, 1980, Mrs Joan Rogers, widow of Rev. Dennis Rogers (Minister of Union Church, Hong Kong, 1965-77). *Educ:* Westminster Sch.; Christ Church, Oxford. Deacon, 1935; Priest, 1936. SCM Sec., London, 1932-34; Dio. of Hong Kong and S China, 1935-51; taught at Lingnan Univ., Canton, 1936-38; in Kunming, Yunnan, 1939-45; St John's Univ., Shanghai, 1947-49; Union Theol. Coll., Lingnan, 1949-51; Rector of Christ Church, Guilford, Conn, 1952-55; Gen. Sec., Church Assembly Overseas Coun., London, 1955-63; Vicar, St Nicholas Cole Abbey, London 1955-66; Actg Dir, Christian Study Centre, Hong Kong, 1966; Bishop of Hong Kong and Macao, 1966-81. *Publications:* The Changing Scene in China 1946 (US 1948); The Church on Asian Frontiers, 1963; St Nicholas Cole Abbey: a short history, 1964; (contrib.) All One Body, 1969; (contrib.) Yes to Women Priests, 1978; Bishop Speaking, 1981. *Recreations:* walking, swimming, listening to music. *Address:* Orchard End, Nower Road, Dorking Surrey RH4 3BY. *Club:* Royal Commonwealth Society.

BAKER, John Randal, MA, DPhil, DSc Oxon; FRS 1958; Emeritus Reader in Cytology, Oxford University (Reader, 1955-67); *b* 23 Oct. 1900; *y s* of Rear-Adm. Julian A. Baker, RN; *m* 1st, 1923, Inezita Davis; one *s* one *d* ; 2nd 1939, Mrs Helen Savage. *Educ:* New Coll., Oxford (1st Class in Honour Sch of Natural Science). Scientific expeditions to New Hebrides, 1922-23, 1927 1933-34; Joint editor Quarterly Journal of Microscopical Science, 1946-64 Professorial Fellow, New Coll., Oxford, 1964-67; Pres. Royal Microscopical Society, 1964-65, Hon. Fellow, 1968. Oliver Bird Medal for researches on chemical contraception, 1958. *Publications:* Sex in Man and Animals, 1926 Man and Animals in the New Hebrides, 1929; Cytological Technique, 1933 (5th edn, 1966); The Chemical Control of Conception, 1935; The Scientific Life, 1942; Science and the Planned State, 1945; Abraham Trembley of Geneva, 1952; Principles of Biological Microtechnique, 1958; Race, 1974 (German edn, Die Rassen der Menschheit, 1976); Julian Huxley: scientist and world citizen, 1978. *Address:* 45 Lakeside, North Oxford OX2 8JQ.

BAKER, John William; Member, Central Electricity Generating Board, since 1980; *b* 5 Dec. 1937; *s* of Reginald and Wilhelmina Baker; *m* 1st, 1962 Pauline (*née* Moore); one *s* ; 2nd, 1976, Gillian (*née* Bullen). *Educ:* Harrow Weald County Grammar Sch.; Oriel Coll., Oxford. Served Army, 1959-61 MoT, 1961-70; DoE, 1970-74; Dep. Chief Exec., Housing Corp., 1974-78 Sec., CEGB, 1979-80. *Recreations:* tennis, squash, bridge, music, theatre *Address:* 5 Old Acre, Pyrford, Woking, Surrey GU22 8XP. *T:* Byfleet 43215.

BAKER, Sir Joseph; *see* Baker, Sir S. J.

BAKER, Kenneth Wilfred; MP (C) St Marylebone since Oct. 1970; a Minister of State and Minister for Information Technology, Department of Industry, since 1981; Industrial Consultant; *b* 3 Nov. 1934; *s* of late W. M Baker, OBE and of Mrs Baker (*née* Harries); *m* 1963, Mary Elizabeth Gray-Muir; one *s* two *d. Educ:* St Paul's Sch.; Magdalen Coll., Oxford. Nat Service, 1953-55: Lieut in Gunners, N Africa; Artillery Instructor to Libyan Army. Oxford, 1955-58 (Sec. of Union). Served Twickenham Borough Council, 1960-62. Contested (C: Poplar, 1964; Acton, 1966; MP (C) Acton March 1968-70; Public Accounts Cttee, 1969-70; Parly Sec., CSD, 1972-74 PPS to Leader of Opposition, 1974-75; Mem. Exec., 1922 Cttee. Chm. Hansard Soc., 1978-81. Sec. Gen., UN Conf. of Parliamentarians on World Population and Development, 1978. *Publications:* I Have No Gun But I Can

Spit, 1980; (ed) London Lines, 1982. *Recreation:* collecting books. *Address:* House of Commons, SW1. *Clubs:* Athenæum, Carlton.

BAKER, (Leonard Graham) Derek, MA, BLitt; Head Master, Christ's Hospital, since 1979; *b* 21 April 1931; *s* of Leonard and Phoebe Caroline Baker; *m* 1970, Jean Dorothy Johnston; one *s* one *d. Educ:* Christ's Hospital; Oriel Coll., Oxford (1st Class Hons Modern History 1955, MA, BLitt). Captain, Royal Signals, 1950-52. Senior History Master, The Leys School, 1956-66; Lecturer in Medieval History, Univ. of Edinburgh, 1966-79. Editor, Ecclesiastical History Soc., 1969; Pres., British Sub-Commission, Commission Internationale d'Histoire Ecclesiastique Comparée, 1971. FRHistS 1969. *Publications:* Portraits and Documents, Vol. 1 1967, Vol. 2 1969; Partnership in Excellence, 1974; (ed) Studies in Church History, 7-17, 1970-80 (subsidia 1-2, 1978-79); numerous articles in historical jls. *Recreations:* singing; climbing, mountaineering, pot-holing, camping; good company; food and wine; travel. *Address:* The Head Master's House, Christ's Hospital, Horsham, Sussex RH13 7LS. *T:* Horsham 52547; 30 Dick Place, Edinburgh EH9 2JB. *T:* 031-667 5920. *Clubs:* National Liberal; Leander (Henley-on-Thames).

BAKER, Martyn Murray; Counsellor (Civil Aviation and Shipping), British Embassy, Washington, DC, since 1978; *b* 10 March 1944; *s* of Norman and Constance Baker; *m* 1970, Rosemary Caroline Holdich. *Educ:* Dulwich Coll.; Pembroke Coll., Oxford (MA). Asst Principal, Min. of Aviation, 1965-67; Asst Private Sec. to Minister of State, Min. of Technology, 1968-69; Private Sec. to Parly Under Secs of State, Min. of Technology, Min. of Aviation Supply, DTI, 1969-71; Principal 1971; Principal Private Sec. to Sec. of State for Trade, 1977-78; Asst Sec., Dept of Trade, 1978. *Address:* c/o Foreign and Commonwealth Office, SW1A 2AH.

BAKER, Maurice S.; Managing Director, F. W. Woolworth & Co. Ltd, 1967-71, retired; *b* 27 Jan. 1911; *s* of Sidney B. Baker and Ellen Elizabeth (*née* Airey); *m* 1st, 1935, Helen Johnstone (*née* Tweedie) (*d* 1977); one *s*; 2nd, 1978, Kirsten Randine (*née* Haugen). *Educ:* Lowestoft Grammar School. Trainee Manager, F. W. Woolworth & Co. Ltd, 1928; RAOC, 1940-46 (Major); rejoined company; Dir 1962. Officer, Legion of Merit (US), 1945. *Recreation:* bowls. *Address:* Ness Point, 7a Woodcote Park Avenue, Purley, CR2 3ND. *T:* 01-660 3718.

BAKER, Michael John David; a Recorder of the Crown Court, since 1980; *b* 17 April 1934; *s* of late Edward Baker and of Dulcie Baker; *m* 1958, Edna Harriet Lane; one *s* one *d. Educ:* Trinity Sch. of John Whitgift; Bristol Univ. (LLB Hons). Admitted solicitor, 1957. Flying Officer, RAF, 1957-60. Joined firm of Glanvilles, Wells & Way, Solicitors, Portsmouth, 1960; Partner, 1963-. Coroner, S Hampshire, 1973- (Asst Dep. Coroner, 1971; Dep. Coroner, 1972). Pres., Southern Coroners Soc., 1975-76; Mem. Council, Coroners Soc. of England and Wales, 1979-. *Recreations:* jogging, walking, tennis and cricket (playing and watching), the theatre, music (particularly choral singing). *Address:* The Drift, Park Crescent, Emsworth, Hants PO10 7NT. *T:* Emsworth 2748. *Clubs:* Law Society; Emsworth Sailing; Waterlooville Rotary; Hampshire CCC.

BAKER, Nicholas Brian; MP (C) North Dorset, since 1979; *b* 23 Nov. 1938; *m* 1970, Penelope Carol d'Abo; one *s* one *d* and one adopted *d. Educ:* Clifton Coll.; Exeter Coll., Oxford(MA). Partner in Frere Cholmeley, solicitors, WC2, 1973-. PPS to Min. of State for the Armed Forces, 1981-. *Publication:* Better Company: proposals for company law reform (Bow Gp), 1973. *Recreations:* squash, music, English countryside. *Address:* House of Commons, SW1. *Clubs:* Carlton; Wimborne and Blandford Conservative.

BAKER, Paul Vivian, QC 1972; *b* 27 March 1923; *er s* of Vivian Cyril Baker and Maud Lydia Baker; *m* 1957, Stella Paterson Eadie, *d* of William Eadie, MD; one *s* one *d. Educ:* City of London Sch.; University Coll., Oxford (BCL, MA). Called to Bar, Lincoln's Inn, 1950, Bencher, 1979. Editor, Law Quarterly Review, 1971-. *Recreations:* music, gardening. *Address:* 9 Old Square, Lincoln's Inn, WC2A 3SR. *T:* 01-405 0846. *Clubs:* Athenæum, Authors'.

BAKER, Prof. Peter Frederick, ScD; FRS 1976; Halliburton Professor and Head of Department of Physiology, King's College, London, since 1975; *b* 11 March 1939; *s* of F. T. Baker and D. E. Skelton; *m* 1966, Phyllis Light; one *s* three *d. Educ:* Lincoln Sch.; Emmanuel Coll., Cambridge (Scholar; BA Natural Sciences Tripos, Cl. 1, 1960; PhD 1964; ScD 1980). Univ. of Cambridge: Demonstrator in Physiol., 1963-66; Lectr in Physiol., 1966-74; Fellow, Emmanuel Coll., Cambridge, 1962-74. Guest Investigator, Rockefeller Univ., NY, 1964. Zoological Society of London: Scientific Medal, 1975; G. L. Brown Lectr, 1977; Wander Prize, 1981. *Publications:* Calcium Movement in Excitable Cells (with H. Reuter), 1975; papers on cell physiol. in Jl of Physiol. and other sci. jls. *Recreation:* natural history, the Loch Ness Monster. *Address:* Meadow Cottage, Bourn, Cambridge. *T:* Caxton 212.

BAKER, Peter Maxwell, QC 1974; a Recorder of the Crown Court, since 1972; *b* 26 March 1930; *s* of late Harold Baker and of Rose Baker; *m* 1954, Jacqueline Mary Marshall; three *d. Educ:* King Edward VII Sch., Sheffield; Exeter Coll., Oxford. MA Oxon. Called to Bar, Gray's Inn, 1956 (Holker Senior Exhibitioner); Junior, NE Circuit, 1960. *Recreations:* yachting, music, watching others garden. *Address:* 28 Snaithing Lane, Sheffield S10 3LG. *Club:* Sheffield (Sheffield).

BAKER, Richard Douglas James, OBE 1976; RD 1979; broadcaster and author; Presenter, Omnibus, BBC TV, since 1983; *b* Willesden, London, 15 June 1925; *s* of Albert and Jane Isobel Baker; *m* 1961, Margaret Celia Martin; two *s. Educ:* Kilburn Grammar Sch.; Peterhouse, Cambridge (MA). Served War, Royal Navy, 1943-46. Actor, 1948; Teacher, 1949; Third Programme Announcer, 1950-53; BBC TV Newsreader, 1954-82; Commentator for State Occasion Outside Broadcasts, 1967-70; TV Introductions to Promenade Concerts, 1960-; Panellist on BBC2's Face the Music, 1966-79; on Radio 4: Presenter of Start the Week with Richard Baker, 1970-; These You Have Loved, 1972-77; Baker's Dozen, 1978-. Columnist, Now! Magazine, 1979-80. Dir, Youth and Music; Mem., Exec. Cttee, Friends of Covent Garden; Vice-Pres., Internat. Voluntary Service 'Master Key' (Multiple Sclerosis Soc.). TV Newscaster of the Year (Radio Industries Club), 1972, 1974, 1979. FRSA. Hon. FLCM 1974; Hon. LLD Strathclyde, 1979. *Publications:* Here is the News (broadcasts), 1966; The Terror of Tobermory, 1972; The Magic of Music, 1975; Dry Ginger, 1977; Richard Baker's Music Guide, 1979; Mozart, 1982. *Recreations:* gardening, the gramophone. *Address:* c/o Bagenal Harvey Organisation, 15-19 Cavendish Place, W1A 9DL. *T:* 01-637 5541 (Agent). *Club:* Garrick.

BAKER, Richard Hugh; HM Diplomatic Service; Deputy High Commissioner, Ottawa, since 1982; *b* 22 Oct. 1935; *s* of Hugh Cuthbert Baker and Muriel Lovenda Baker (*née* Owens); *m* 1963, Patricia Marianne Haigh Thomas; one *s* three *d. Educ:* Marlborough Coll.; New Coll., Oxford. Army (2nd Lieut RA), 1954-56. Plebiscite Officer, UN Plebiscite, S Cameroons, 1960-61; joined Diplomatic Service, 1962; 3rd, later 2nd, then 1st Sec., Addis Ababa, 1963-66; Foreign Office, 1967; Private Sec. to Permanent Under-Sec. of State, Foreign Office (later FCO), 1967-70; 1st Sec. and Head of Chancery, Warsaw, 1970-72; FCO, 1973-76; RCDS 1977; Econ. and Financial Counsellor, and Dep. Head, UK Perm. Delegn to OECD, Paris, 1978-82. *Recreations:* music, painting, wind-surfing. *Address:* c/o Foreign and Commonwealth Office, SW1.

BAKER, Sir Rowland, Kt 1968; OBE 1946; RCNC; Director, Balrena Group; *b* 3 June 1908; *s* of Isaac and Lizzie Baker; *m* 1931, Frances Cornish; one *s* three *d*; *m* 1972, Barbara Mary Comley. *Educ:* RNC Greenwich. Assistant Constructor, HM Dockyards, 1933-39; Constructor, Admty, 1939-42; Supt of Landing Craft, 1942-46; Naval Constructor-in-Chief, Royal Canadian Navy, 1948-56; Technical Chief Exec., Dreadnought Project, 1958-63; Tech. Dir, Polaris Exec., MoD (Navy), 1963-68, retired. Medal of Freedom with Silver Palm (US), 1946. *Publications:* contribs to jls. *Recreations:* golf, bridge. *Address:* Newfield, Entry Hill, Bath. *T:* Bath 22452.

BAKER, Scott; *see* Baker, T. S. G.

BAKER, Sir (Stanislaus) Joseph, Kt 1958; CB 1947; retired as Receiver for the Metropolitan Police District and Courts (1952-60); *b* 7 March 1898; *s* of Henry G. Baker, Liverpool; *m* 1920, Eleonora White (*d* 1981); one *d* (and one *d* deced). *Educ:* St Francis Xavier Sch.; Liverpool Univ. BSc 1919, Hons 1920. Served European War, 1914-18, RE 1915-17; Royal Artillery, 1917-18. Local Government Board for Ireland, 1920; Chief Sec.'s Office, Dublin Castle, 1922; Irish Office, 1922; Home Office, 1924; Sec. to Privy Council Cttee on question of contributions to Imperial Funds from the Islands of Jersey, Guernsey and Man, 1925. Asst Under-Sec. of State, Home Office, 1941-52. Chairman: National Police Fund Advisory Council, 1946-52; Police Regional Services Cttee, 1945-48; Police Common Services Cttee, 1948-52; Mem. Board of Governors of Police Coll., 1947-52. Chm., Kenya Police Commission, 1953. *Address:* Camplehaye Hotel, Lamerton, Tavistock, Devon PL19 8QD.

BAKER, Stephen; Managing Director, British Electricity International, since 1978; *b* 27 March 1926; *s* of late Arthur and Nancy Baker; *m* 1950, Margaret Julia Wright; one *s* two *d. Educ:* Epsom Coll.; Clare Coll., Cambridge (MA). FIMechE. Engr Officer, RN, 1944-47; Apprentice, Davy United Engineering Co. Ltd, 1947-49; Works Engr, John Baker & Bessemer Ltd, 1949-51; Davy United Engrg Co. Ltd, 1951: Dir of Prodn, 1960; Gen. Man., 1961; Dir, Davy Ashmore Ltd, 1963; Dir of Ops, Davy-Ashmore Engrg Ltd, 1964; Chm. and Chief Exec. of Davy United Engrg Co. Ltd, Ashmore Benson Pease Ltd and Loewy Robertson Engrg Co. Ltd, 1968; Man. Dir, Kearney & Trecker Ltd, 1970; Co-ordinator of Industrial Advrs, Depts of Trade and Industry, 1974-78. *Recreations:* shooting, gardening. *Address:* 43A Heathfield Road, SW18.

BAKER, Very Rev. Thomas George Adames, MA; Dean of Worcester, since 1975; *b* 22 Dec. 1920; *s* of late Walter and Marion Baker, Southampton; unmarried. *Educ:* King Edward VI Sch., Southampton; Exeter Coll., Oxford; Lincoln Theological Coll. Curate of All Saints, King's Heath, Birmingham, 1944-47; Vicar of St James, Edgbaston, 1947-54; Sub-Warden of Lincoln Theological Coll., 1954-60; Principal of Wells Theological College and Prebendary of Combe II in Wells Cathedral, 1960-71; Archdeacon of Bath, 1971-75. Canon Theologian of Leicester Cathedral, 1959-66. Select Preacher, Univ. of Cambridge, 1963, Univ. of Oxford, 1973. Recognised Teacher, Bristol Univ., 1969-74. *Publications:* What is the New Testament?, 1969; Questioning Worship, 1977. *Recreation:* music. *Address:* The Deanery, College Green, Worcester. *T:* Worcester 23501.

BAKER, (Thomas) Scott (Gillespie); QC 1978; a Recorder of the Crown Court, since 1976; *b* 10 Dec. 1937; *s* of Rt Hon. Sir George Baker, *qv*; *m* 1973,

Margaret Joy Strange; two *s* one *d. Educ:* Haileybury; Brasenose Coll., Oxford. Called to the Bar, Middle Temple, 1961 (Astbury Schol.); Midland and Oxford Circuit. Mem. Senate, Inns of Court, 1977-. Mem., Chorleywood UDC, 1965-68. *Recreations:* golf, fishing. *Address:* Highlands, Woodrow, near Amersham, Bucks HP7 0QG. *T:* Amersham 7068. 1 Crown Office Row, Temple, EC4Y 7HH. *T:* 01-353 1801. *Clubs:* Caledonian, MCC; Denham Golf.

BAKER, Willfred Harold Kerton, TD; company director; *b* 6 Jan. 1920; *o s* of late W. H. Baker; *m* 1st, 1945, Kathleen Helen Sloan (*née* Murray Bisset); one *s* two *d*; 2nd, Jean Gordon Scott (*née* Skinner). *Educ:* Hardye's Sch.; Edinburgh Univ.; Cornell Univ., USA. Joined TA, and served War of 1939-45 (Major). Edinburgh Univ. (BSc Agriculture), 1946-49. MP (C) Banffshire, 1964-Feb. 1974. *Recreations:* golf, fishing, philately. *Address:* Tamarisk, 16 Stoke Gabriel Road, Galmpton, South Devon TQ5 0NQ. *T:* Churston 842832.

BAKER, Rt. Rev. William Scott, MA; Assistant Bishop, Diocese of Liverpool, since 1968; *b* 22 June 1902; *s* of late Rev. Canon William Wing Carew Baker, Vicar of Southill, Beds; unmarried. *Educ:* King's Coll. Choir Sch., Cambridge; Aldenham; King's Coll., Cuddesdon. Deacon, 1925; Priest, 1927; Chaplain of King's Coll., Cambridge, and Asst Curate of St Giles with St Peter's Church, Cambridge, 1925-32; Vicar of St John The Baptist's, Newcastle on Tyne, 1932-43; Examining Chaplain to Bishop of Wakefield, 1928-32; to Bishop of Newcastle, 1941-43; Proctor in Convocation for Diocese of Newcastle, 1943; Bishop of Zanzibar and Dar-es-Salaam, 1943-65, of Zanzibar and Tanga, 1965-68; Lectr, St Katherine's Coll., Liverpool, 1968-75. *Publication:* (contributor) The Parish Communion, 1937. *Address:* 11 Woolacombe Road, Liverpool L16 9JG. *T:* 051-722 5035.

BAKER, Wilson, FRS 1946; FRSC; BSc, MSc, PhD, DSc (Manchester); MA (Oxon.); retired; Alfred Capper Pass Professor of Organic Chemistry, University of Bristol, 1945-65 (Dean of the Faculty of Science, 1948-51; Emeritus Professor, University of Bristol, 1965); *b* 24 Jan. 1900; *yr s* of Harry and Mary Baker, Runcorn, Cheshire; *m* 1927, Juliet Elizabeth, *d* of Henry and Julia R. Glaisyer, Birmingham; one *s* two *d. Educ:* Liverpool Coll. Upper Sch.; Victoria Univ. of Manchester (Mercer Schol., Baeyer Fellow and Dalton Scholar). Asst Lecturer in Chemistry, Univ. of Manchester, 1924-27; Tutor in Chemistry, Dalton Hall, Manchester, 1926-27; Univ. Lecturer and Demonstrator in Chemistry, Univ. of Oxford, 1927-44; Fellow and Praelector in Chemistry, The Queen's Coll., Oxford, 1937-44. Vice-Pres. of the Chemical Society, 1957-60. *Publications:* numerous original papers on organic chemistry, dealing chiefly with the synthesis of natural products, the development of synthetical processes, compounds of abnormal aromatic type, organic inclusion compounds, and the preparation of large-ring compounds, and the chemistry of penicillin, published mainly in Journal of the Chemical Society; (with T. W. J. Taylor) 2nd Edition of Professor N. V. Sidgwick's The Organic Chemistry of Nitrogen, 1937. *Recreations:* walking, gardening, music, mineralogy. *Address:* Lane's End, Church Road, Winscombe, Avon. *T:* Winscombe 3112.

BAKER-BATES, Merrick Stuart; General Manager (Commercial), Cornes & Co., Tokyo, since 1982; *b* 22 July 1939; *s* of E. T. Baker-Bates, MD, FRCP, and Norah Stuart (*née* Kirkham); *m* 1963, Chrystal Jacqueline Goodacre; one *s* one *d. Educ:* Shrewsbury Sch.; Hertford Coll., Oxford (MA); College of Europe, Bruges. Asst Correspondent, Daily Telegraph, and Financial Times, Brussels, 1962-63; entered HM Diplomatic Service, 1963; 3rd, later 2nd Sec., Tokyo, 1963-68; 1st Secretary: FCO, 1968-73; (Inf.), Washington, 1973-76; (Commercial), Tokyo, 1976-79; Counsellor (Commercial), Tokyo, 1979-82. *Recreations:* photography, Japanese fencing, cycling. *Address:* 36-4 Kamiyama-Cho, Shibuya-Ku, Tokyo 150, Japan; 5 Crouchmans Close, SE26 6ST. *T:* 01-670 2602. *Club:* Brooks's.

BAKER-CARR, Air Marshal Sir John (Darcy), KBE 1962 (CBE 1951); CB 1957; AFC 1944; Controller of Engineering and Equipment, Air Ministry, 1962-64, retired; *b* 13 January 1906; *s* of late Brigadier-General C. D. Baker-Carr, CMG, DSO and Sarah Quinan; *m* 1934, Margery Dallas; no *c. Educ:* England and USA. Entered RAF as Pilot Officer, 1929; No 32 Fighter Sqdn 1930, Flying Officer; Flying Boats at home and overseas, 1931; Armament Specialist Course, 1934; Flight-Lieut; Armament and Air Staff appts, 1935-38; Sqdn Ldr, 1938; Armament Research and Development, 1939-45 (AFC); Wing Comdr, 1940; Gp Captain, 1942; Central Fighter Estab., 1946-47; Dep. Dir Research, Air Min., 1947-48; Air Cdre, 1948; Dir of Armament Research and Development, Min. of Supply, 1948-51 (CBE); idc 1952; Comdt RAF, St Athan, 1953-56; Senior Technical Staff Officer, HQ Fighter Command, RAF, 1956-59; Air Vice-Marshal, 1957; Air Officer Commanding, No 41 Group, Maintenance Command, 1959-61; Air Marshal, 1962. *Recreations:* sailing and carpentry. *Address:* Thatchwell Cottage, King's Somborne, Hants. *Club:* Royal Air Force Yacht (Hamble, Hants).

BAKER WILBRAHAM, Sir Richard, 8th Bt *cr* 1776; Director, J. Henry Schroder Wagg & Co. Ltd; *b* 5 Feb. 1934; *s* of Sir Randle Baker Wilbraham, 7th Bt, and Betty Ann, CBE (*d* 1975), *d* of W. Matt Torrens; *S* father, 1980; *m* 1962, Anne Christine Peto, *d* of late Charles Peto Bennett, OBE; one *s* three *d. Educ:* Harrow. Welsh Guards, 1952-54. J. Henry Schroder Wagg & Co. Ltd, 1954-. Trustee, Grosvenor Estate, 1981-. Governor, Harrow Sch., 1982-. *Recreations:* field sports. *Heir: s* Randle Baker Wilbraham, *b* 28 May 1963.

Address: 41 Carlyle Square, SW3 6HA. *T:* 01-352 5069; Rode Hall, Schola Green, Cheshire. *T:* Alsager 3237. *Clubs:* Brooks's, Pratt's.

BAKEWELL, Joan Dawson; broadcaster and writer; Arts Correspondent to BBC Television, since 1981; *b* 16 April 1933; *d* of John Rowlands and Ros Bland; *m* 1st, 1955, Michael Bakewell (marr. diss. 1972); one *s* one *d;* 2nd 1975, Jack Emery. *Educ:* Stockport High Sch. for Girls; Newnham Coll. Cambridge (BA History and Econs). *BBC Television incl:* Meeting Point 1964; The Second Sex, 1964; Late Night Line Up, 1965-72; The Youthful Eye 1968; Moviemakers at the National Film Theatre, 1971; Film 72, and Film 73 1972-73; For the Sake of Appearance, Where is Your God?, Who Cares?, and The Affirmative Way (series), 1973; Holiday '74, '75, '76, '77 and '78 (series) What's it all About? (2 series) and Time Running Out (series), 1974; The Shakespeare Business, The Brontë Business, and Generation to Generation (series), 1976; My Day with the Children, 1977; The Moving Line, 1979; Art UK: OK?, 1980. *ITV incl.* Sunday Break, 1962; Home at 4.30, 1964; (write and producer) Thank You, Ron (documentary), 1974; Fairest Fortune and Edinburgh Festival Report, 1974; Reports Action (4 series), 1976-78. *Radio* Away from it All, 1978-79; PM, 1979-. *Theatre:* Brontës: The Private Faces Edinburgh Fest., 1979. *Publications:* (with Nicholas Garnham) The New Priesthood: British television today, 1970; (with John Drummond) A Fine and Private Place, 1977; The Complete Traveller, 1977; journalism for Punch Radio Times; formerly Television Critic of The Times. *Recreations:* theatre travel, talk. *Address:* c/o A.D. Peters & Co. Ltd, 10 Buckingham Street WC2N 6BU. *T:* 01-839 2556.

BAKEWELL, Robert Donald, CMG 1952; JP; Chm. Australian Woolgrowers' Council, 1949-54 (Member, 1940-); Member Australian Wool Realization Commission, 1945-59; *b* 9 Sept. 1899; *s* of late E. H. Bakewell Adelaide; *m* 1929, Ydonea, *d* of Hylton Dale, Toorak; one *d. Educ:* Kyre Coll (now Scotch Coll.), Adelaide. Man. Dir Farnley Grazing Pty. Ltd, 1935-73 Pres., Graziers' Federal Council of Aust., 1948-49 (Mem. 1940-50); Pres. Graziers' Assoc. of Vic., 1943-46 (Mem. Council and Exec., 1937-, Trustee 1945-80); Mem. Exec. Chamber of Agric. of Vic., 1940-50 (Vice-Pres 1946-48); Graziers Rep., Primary Producers' Council of Aust., 1947-49; Mem Wool Industry Conference, 1963-70. *Recreation:* bowls. *Address:* 2 Parkview Parade, Benalla, Vic 3672, Australia. *T:* Benalla 62-3368. *Clubs* Australian (Melbourne); Adelaide (S Australia); Benalla (Victoria).

BALANCHINE, George Melitonovitch; Choreographer; Artistic director New York City Ballet Company, since 1948; *b* St Petersburg (now Leningrad), Russia, 22 Jan. 1904; *s* of Meliton Balanchivadze, composer, and Maria Vassiliev; became a citizen of the US. *Educ:* Imperial Academy of Dance, Imperial Academy of Music, St Petersburg. Left Russia on a European tour with the Soviet State Dancers, 1924, playing in Germany, England and France. Ballet-Master: for Serge Diaghilev, 1925-29; staged dances for Cole Porter production of Wake up and Dream, London, 1929; Maître de Balle at Royal Theatre, Copenhagen, 1930; with Boris Kochno organized Ballet de Théâtre de Monte Carlo, under patronage of Princess of Monaco, 1932 presented Les Ballets, 1933; went to US, 1933, and founded School of American Ballet, 1934 (Chm. of Faculty); Artistic director, Ballet Society New York, 1946; with Lincoln Kirstein as General director and himself as artistic director the New York City Ballet Company was started, 1948; it has subsequently made many tours in US and abroad. Has composed over 100 ballets and his choreography includes ballets in operas, musical comedies and films. Was guest of Grand Opera, Paris, 1947, and Sadler's Wells, London 1950. *Publications:* Balanchine's Complete Stories of the Great Ballets, 1954 (with Francis Mason) Festival of Ballet, 1978. *Address:* c/o School o American Ballet, Inc., NY State Theatre, NY 10023, USA.

BALCAZAR-MONZON, Dr Gustavo; Gran Cruz, Order of Boyaca Colombia; Orden del Mérito Militar, General José Maria Córdoba, Colombia Ciudades Confederadas Gran Cauca, Colombia; Senator of the Republic o Colombia, since 1962; *b* 10 Aug. 1927; *m* 1952, Bolivia Ramos de Balcázar two *d. Educ:* Universidad Javeriana, Bogotá, Colombia (Dr in Econ. an Jurid. Sciences). Municipal Civil Judge, Cali, 1949-51; Attorney of the City of Cali, 1951-52. Member, House of Representatives, 1958-62, President 1960; Governor of the Valle, 1962-64; Minister of Agriculture, 1964-65 President of the Senate, 1975; President Designate of the Republic, 1978-80 Colombian Ambassador to the Court of St James's, 1979-81. Member, Liberal Party Nat. Governing Body, 1970-71, 1974-77 and 1978; a Director of the Liberal Party, 1978. *Publications:* La Ciudad, el Urbanismo y el Impuesto de Valorización (The City, Urban Planning and the Tax for Increase in Value) 1950; La Reforma Tributaria de 1960 (The Tax Reform of 1960), 1961 several articles for the press. *Recreation:* apiculture. *Address:* Calle 10 Nort 9AN-10, Cali, Colombia; Senado de la República, Capitolio Nacional Bogotá, Colombia. *Clubs:* Royal Automobile, Travellers'; Le Ambassadors.

BALCHIN, John Alfred; General Manager, Stevenage Development Corporation, 1969-76, retired; *b* 8 Aug. 1914; *er s* of Alfred and Florence Balchin; *m* 1940, Elsie Dormer; one *s* two *d. Educ:* Sir Walter St John's Sch Battersea; Sir John Cass Coll., City of London. DPA (London), DMA, FCIS FIH. LCC Clerk's Dept, 1932-38; civil defence co-ordination work, 1938-45 to Housing Dept, 1946-65; Asst Dir (Housing Management), 1963; Sen. Ass Dir of Housing, GLC, 1965-69. Assoc. Sen. Lectr, for Housing Management and Administration, Brunel Univ., 1969-71. Member: Housing Services Adv Gp, DoE, 1976-80; North British Housing Assoc., 1976-. *Publications*

Housing: programming and development of estates, 1971, revd edn 1978; Housing Management: history, principles and practice, 1972; Housing Studies, 1st series, 1979, 2nd series, 1980, revd edn 1981; First New Town: an autobiography of the Stevenage Development Corporation, 1980. *Address:* Westwards, Perran Downs, Goldsithney, Cornwall TR20 9HL. *T:* Penzance 710449.

BALCOMBE, Hon. Sir (Alfred) John, Kt 1977; Hon. Mr Justice Balcombe; a Judge of the High Court of Justice, Family Division, since 1977; *b* 29 Sept. 1925; *er s* of Edwin Kesteven Balcombe; *m* 1950, Jacqueline Rosemary, *yr d* of late Julian Cowan; two *s* one *d. Educ:* Winchester (schol.); New Coll., Oxford (exhibnr). Served, 1943-47: Royal Signals; commnd 1945. BA 1949 (1st class Hons Jurisprudence), MA 1950. Called to Bar, Lincoln's Inn, 1950, Bencher 1977; QC 1969; practised at Chancery Bar, 1951-77; Mem., Gen. Council of the Bar, 1967-71. Chm., London Marriage Guidance Council, 1982-. Master, Worshipful Company of Tin Plate Workers, 1971-72. *Publications:* Exempt Private Companies, 1953; (ed) Estoppel, in Halsbury's Laws of England, 4th edn. *Address:* 6 Highbury Road, Wimbledon, SW19 7PR. *T:* 01-947 0980. *Club:* Garrick.

BALCOMBE, Frederick James, Lord Mayor of Manchester, 1974-75, Deputy Lord Mayor, 1975-76; *b* 17 Dec. 1911; *s* of late Sidney and late Agnes Balcombe; *m* 1st, 1936, Clarice (*née* Cassel) *d* 1949; two *s* (and two *c* decd); 2nd, 1956, Rhoda (*née* Jaffe); one *d. Educ:* St Anthony's RC Sch., Forest Gate; West Ham Secondary Central Sch., Stratford, London. Served War of 1939-45, RAF (commnd). Chm., family co. of insurance loss assessors; active in SDP. President: Manchester and District Fedn of Community Assocs; Manchester and District Allotments Council; Higher Blackley Community Assoc.; Vice-President: Blackley Prize Band; Blackley Football League; formerly Mem. Cttee and Hon. Treas., Crumpsall Hosp. League of Friends; connected with 199th Manchester Scout Gp. Mem. Manchester City Council, Crumpsall Ward, 1958, subseq. St Peter's Ward, now Collegiate Church Ward; served as Chm. Central Purchasing Cttee, Gen. and Parly (now Policy), Markets, Airports (Chm.), Parks and Finance Cttees (Dep. Chm.). Chm., Manchester Internat. Airport, 1975-79. Mem., Airport Owners' Assoc., 1979-. Founder, Hillel House, Manchester Univ. (Hon. Sec., 1958-68, now Sen. Life Vice-Pres.); Former Chm. of Governors, Coll. of Building, Manchester; Past Mem. Council, BBC Radio Manchester; Mem. Council, Manchester and Salford Police Authority, 1968-74; Mem., AMC Rating Cttee, 1973-74. Mem., Bd of Deputies of British Jews, 1956-64; Mem., Council, Manchester and Salford Jews, 1958- (Exec. Mem., 1963-68); Founder Mem., Manchester Jewish Blind Soc. (Hon. Sec. 13 years, now Vice-Pres.); Adjutant, Jewish Lads' Brigade and Club, Manchester, 1946-49, Chm. 1972-78; Governor, King David Schs, Manchester, 1954-; Vice-Pres., Fedn of Boys' Clubs; President: Manchester Cttee, Central British Fund; RAFA Manchester South, 1981-; Manchester City Swimming Club, 1981-. Founder Mem., Variety Club of Israel; Barker of Variety Club (Chm. Manchester Cttee, 1976). JP Manchester, 1967-82. Mem. Jewish Faith. Life long blood donor. *Recreations:* family, communal endeavour, swimming, walking. *Address:* 16 Spath Road, Didsbury, Manchester M20 8GA. *T:* 061-434 2555; (office) 061-228 3395.

BALCOMBE, Hon. Sir John; *see* Balcombe, Hon. Sir A. J.

BALCON, Dr Raphael, MD; FRCP, FACC; Consultant Cardiologist, National Heart and Chest Hospitals, London Chest Hospital, since 1970; *b* 26 Aug. 1936; *s* of Henry and Rhoda Balcon; *m* 1959, Elizabeth Ann Henry; one *d. Educ:* King's Coll., London; King's Coll. Hosp. Med. Sch. (MB, BS 1960, MD 1969). LRCP, MRCS 1960, MRCP 1965, FRCP 1977; FACC 1973. House Phys., Med. Unit, KCH, 1960; House Surg., KCH, Dulwich, 1960; House Phys., London Chest Hosp., 1961; Sen. House Officer, St Stephen's Hosp., 1962; Public Health Fellow in Cardiology, Wayne State Univ. Med. Sch., USA, 1963; British Heart Foundn Fellow, Dept of Cardiol., KCH, 1964, Med. Registrar 1965; Registrar, then Sen. Registrar, National Heart Hosp., 1966-70. Dean, Cardiothoracic Inst., 1976-80. Mem., British Cardiac Soc. *Publications:* contrib. books on cardiological subjects; papers in BMJ, Lancet, Brit. Heart Jl, Amer. Jl of Cardiol., Circulation, Eur. Jl of Cardiol., Acta Medica Scandinavica. *Recreations:* ski-ing, tennis, mountain walking. *Address:* 68 Gloucester Crescent, NW1 7EG. *T:* 01-267 2212.

BALDOCK, John Markham, VRD 1949; Lieutenant Commander RNVR 1948; Chairman Lenscrete Ltd, 1949; Director CIBA-GEIGY (UK) Ltd; *b* 19 Nov. 1915; *s* of late Captain W. P. Baldock, and Mrs H. Chalcraft; *m* 1949, Pauline Ruth Gauntlett; two *s. Educ:* Rugby Sch.; Balliol Coll., Oxford. Agric. degree, 1937. Served War of 1939-45, with Royal Navy, Atlantic, Mediterranean, Indian Ocean; Russian convoys, 1942-43. Lloyds, EC3, 1945. Joined Board of Lenscrete, 1946. MP (C) Harborough Div. of Leics, 1950-Sept. 1959, retd, also as Parl. Private Sec. to Rt Hon. D. Ormsby Gore (Minister of State, Foreign Office). Founder, Hollycombe steam collection and steam fair. *Recreations:* country life, sailing, steam engines, industrial archæology, theatre. *Address:* Hollycombe House, Liphook, Hants. *T:* Liphook 723233; 17 Aylesford Street, SW1; *T:* 01-821 8759. *Club:* Farmers'.

BALDRY, Prof. Harold Caparne, Emeritus Professor of Classics, University of Southampton; *b* 4 March 1907; *s* of William and Gertrude Mary Baldry, Nottingham; *m* 1934, Carina Hetley (*née* Pearson); one *s* two *d. Educ:* Nottingham High Sch.; Trinity Hall, Cambridge (Warr Schol., MA). Editor Cambridge Review, 1931. Educational Staff, Trinity Hall, Cambridge,

1931-34; Asst Lecturer in Classics, University Coll. of Swansea, 1934-35; Univ. of Cape Town: Lecturer in Classics, 1936-48, Prof. of Classics, 1948-54; Univ. of Southampton: Prof. of Classics, 1954-72; Dean of Faculty of Arts, 1959-62; Dep. Vice-Chancellor, 1963-66; Public Orator, 1959-67. Chm., Council of University Classical Depts, 1969-72; Pres., Orbilian Soc., 1970; Vice-Pres., Classical Assoc., 1972-; Mem., Arts Council of GB, 1973-78 (Chm. Regional Cttee, 1975-78); Chm., Southern Arts Assoc., 1972-74. Hon. DLitt Southampton, 1975. *Publications:* The Classics in the Modern World (an Inaugural Lecture), 1949; Greek Literature for the Modern Reader, 1951; Ancient Utopias (an Inaugural Lecture), 1956; The Unity of Mankind in Greek Thought, 1965; Ancient Greek Literature in its Living Context, 1968; The Greek Tragic Theatre, 1971; The Case for the Arts, 1981; articles and reviews in classical journals. *Address:* 19 Uplands Way, Highfield, Southampton. *T:* Southampton 555290.

BALDRY, Jack Thomas; Director, Purchasing and Supplies, Post Office, 1969-72; *b* 5 Oct. 1911; *s* of late John and Ellen Baldry; *m* 1936, Ruby Berenice (*née* Frost); three *d. Educ:* Framlingham Coll. Post Office: Asst Traffic Supt, 1930; Asst Surveyor, 1935; Asst Princ., 1940; Princ., 1947 (Private Sec. to PMG, 1950-53); Asst Sec., 1953; Dep. Dir, External Telecommunications, 1960; Dir of Personnel, 1967. Part-time Mem., VAT Appeals Tribunals. *Recreations:* tennis, farming, foreign travel. *Address:* Bruisyard Road, Badingham, Woodbridge IP13 8NA. *T:* Badingham 331.

BALDWIN, family name of Earl Baldwin of Bewdley.

BALDWIN OF BEWDLEY, 4th Earl *cr* 1937; Edward Alfred Alexander Baldwin; Viscount Corvedale, 1937; *b* 3 Jan. 1938; *o s* of 3rd Earl Baldwin of Bewdley and Joan Elspeth, *y d* of late C. Alexander Tomes, New York, USA; *S* father, 1976; *m* 1970, Sarah MacMurray, *er d* of Evan James, *qv;* three *s. Educ:* Eton; Trinity Coll., Cambridge (MA). *Heir: s* Viscount Corvedale, *qv. Address:* Manor Farm House, Upper Wolvercote, Oxford OX2 8AJ.

BALDWIN, Captain George Clifton, CBE 1966; DSC 1941 and Bar 1944; RN (retd); Member: Press Council, 1973-78; Press Council Appointments Commission, since 1978; *b* 17 Jan. 1921; *s* of late George and late Louisa Baldwin; *m* 1947, Hasle Mary MacMahon; three *s. Educ:* Sleaford Grammar Sch., Lincs; Hitchin Grammar Sch., Herts. Served War: joined RN, 1939, and trained as Pilot in Fleet Air Arm; in comd: 807 Sqdn, 1943; No 4 Naval Fighter Wing, 1944-45. Qual. at Empire Test Pilots' Sch., 1946; in comd, 800 Sqdn, 1952; Captain, RN, 1958; in comd, RN Air Station, Lossiemouth, 1961-62; IDC course, 1963; Dir, Naval Air Warfare, MoD, 1964-66; in comd, RN Air Station, Yeovilton, 1966-68; ADC, 1967; retd, 1968. Mem., Royal United Services Inst., 1968. Chm., Fleet Air Arm Officers' Assoc., 1973-78. *Publications:* articles in: Air Pictorial, Navy International, Embassy, etc. *Recreations:* gardening, tennis, swimming. *Address:* Three Greens, Level Mare Lane, Eastergate, Chichester, West Sussex. *T:* (home) Eastergate 3040; (office) Chichester 782559. *Club:* Naval and Military.

BALDWIN, Prof. Jack Edward, PhD; FRS 1978; Waynflete Professor of Chemistry and Fellow of Magdalen College, University of Oxford, since 1978; *b* 8 Aug. 1938; *s* of Frederick Charles Baldwin and Olive Frances Headland; *m* 1977, Christine Louise, *d* of William B. Franchi. *Educ:* Lewes County Grammar Sch.; Imperial Coll., London Univ. (BSc, DIC, PhD). ARCS. Asst Lectr in Chem., Imperial Coll., 1963, Lectr, 1966; Asst Prof. of Chem., Pa State Univ., 1967, Associate Prof., 1969; Associate Prof. of Chem., MIT, 1970, Prof., 1972; Daniell Prof. of Chem., King's Coll., London, 1972; Prof. of Chem., MIT, 1972-78. Chemical Society: Tilden Lectr, 1979; Simonsen Lectr, 1982; Corday Morgan Medal and Prize, 1975; Award in Synthetic Chemistry, 1979. *Publications:* res. pubns in Jl of Amer. Chem. Soc. and Jl of Chem. Soc. *Address:* Dyson Perrins Laboratory, South Parks Road, Oxford OX1 3QY. *T:* Oxford 57809.

BALDWIN, James (Arthur); Author; *b* Harlem, New York City, 2 Aug. 1924; *s* of David and Berdis Emma Baldwin. *Educ:* DeWitt Clinton High Sch., New York. Various non-literary jobs, 1942-45. Moved to Paris, 1948; lived in Europe until 1956. Active in civil rights movement in USA. Saxton Fellow, 1945; Rosenwald Fellow, 1948; Guggenheim Fellow, 1954; Nat. Inst. of Arts and Letters Award, and Partisan Review Fellow, 1956. Mem. Nat. Inst. of Arts and Letters, 1964. Martin Luther King Jr Award, City Coll. of Univ. of NY, 1978. DLitt, Univ. of British Columbia, 1963. *Publications:* novels: Go Tell It on the Mountain, 1953; Giovanni's Room, 1956; Another Country, 1962; Going to Meet the Man, 1965; Tell Me How Long the Train's Been Gone, 1968; If Beale Street Could Talk, 1974; Little Man, Little Man (with Yoran Cazac), 1975; The Devil Finds Work, 1976; Just Above my Head, 1979; *essays:* Notes of a Native Son, 1955; Nobody Knows My Name, 1961; The Fire Next Time, 1963; Nothing Personal (with Richard Avedon), 1964; No Name in the Street, 1971; (with Margaret Mead) A Rap on Race, 1971; (with Nikki Giovanni) A Dialogue, 1975; Evidence of Things not Seen, 1983; *plays:* The Amen Corner, 1955 (prod Saville, London, 1965); Blues for Mr Charlie, 1964; One Day when I was Lost, 1972; The Woman at the Well, 1972; essays and short stories in many jls and anthologies, 1946-. *Recreation:* American Negro music. *Address:* c/o Edward J. Acton Inc., 825 Third Avenue, New York, NY 10022, USA.

BALDWIN, John, OBE 1978; General Secretary, Amalgamated Union of Engineering Workers/Construction Section, since 1976; *b* 16 Aug. 1923; *s* of Stephen John Baldwin and Elizabeth (*née* Hutchinson); *m* 1945, Grace May

Florence (née Wilson); two d. Educ: Laindon High Road Sen. Sch., Essex. Boy service, RN, HMS Ganges, 1938; returned to civilian life, 1948; Steel Erector, CEU, 1950; played active part as Shop Steward and Site Convenor; elected full-time official, 1957; Asst Gen. Sec., AUEW/Construction Sect., 1969-76. Chm., Mechanical Handling Sector Working Party of NEDO; Member: Engrg Construction EDC, 1975-; Construction Equipment and Mobile Cranes Sector Working Party of NEDO; National Jt Council for the Engrg Construction Industry. Prominent Mem., Labour Party, 1962-. *Recreations:* most sports. *Address:* 7 Ridge Langley, Sanderstead, South Croydon, Surrey. *T:* 01-651 1643.

BALDWIN, Maj.-Gen. Peter Alan Charles; Deputy Director, Radio, Independent Broadcasting Authority, since 1979; *b* 19 Feb. 1927; *s* of Alec Baldwin and Anne Dance; *m* 1953, Judith Elizabeth Mace. *Educ:* King Edward VI Grammar Sch., Chelmsford. Enlisted 1942; commnd R Signals 1947; early service included Berlin, 1948-49 (during airlift), and Korean War, 1950; Staff Coll., 1960; JSSC, 1964; Borneo operations (despatches, 1967); Directing Staff, Staff Coll., 1967-69; Comdr, 13 Signal Regt, BAOR, 1969-71; Sec. for Studies, NATO Defence Coll., 1971-74; Comdr, 2 Signal Group, 1974-76; ACOS Jt Exercises Div., Allied Forces Central Europe, 1976-77; Maj.-Gen. and Chief Signal Officer, BAOR, 1977-79. *Recreations:* tennis, cricket, music, theatre. *Address:* c/o Lloyds Bank Ltd, 6 Pall Mall, SW1. *Club:* Army and Navy.

BALDWIN, Sir Peter (Robert), KCB 1977 (CB 1973); Permanent Secretary, Department of Transport, 1976-82; *b* 10 Nov. 1922; *s* of Charles Baldwin and Katie Baldwin (née Field); *m* 1951, Margaret Helen Moar; two *s. Educ:* City of London Sch.; Corpus Christi Coll., Oxford (Hon. Fellow, 1980). Foreign Office, 1942-45; Gen. Register Office, 1948-54; HM Treasury, 1954-62; Cabinet Office, 1962-64; HM Treasury, 1964-76; Principal Private Sec. to Chancellor of Exchequer, July 1966-Jan. 1968; Under-Sec., HM Treasury, 1968-72; Dep. Sec., HM Treasury, 1972-76; Second Permanent Sec., DoE, 1976. Chairman: Civil Service Sports Council, 1977- (Vice-Chm., 1974-77); St Catherine's Home and Sch., Ventnor, 1961-78; Vice Chm., PHAB. FRSA. *Recreations:* painting, watching cricket. *Address:* 123 Alderney Street, SW1. *T:* 01-821 7157. *Clubs:* Athenæum, Royal Over-Seas League.

BALERNO, Baron *cr* 1963, of Currie (Life Peer); **Alick Drummond Buchanan-Smith;** Kt 1956; CBE 1945 (OBE 1939); TD 1938; DL; MA, DSc; MSA Iowa; FRSE; FRSGS; Lecturer in Animal Genetics, University of Edinburgh, 1925-60, retired; *b* 9 Oct. 1898; *s* of late Very Rev. Sir George Adam Smith, DD, LLD, FBA, Principal of Aberdeen Univ., 1909-35 and of late Lilian, *d* of Sir George Buchanan, LLD, FRS; *m* 1926, Mary Kathleen (*d* 1947), *d* of late Captain George Smith of Pittodrie; four *s* one *d. Educ:* Glasgow Acad., Glenalmond; University of Aberdeen; Iowa State Univ. Lt-Col Comdg 5/7th, 5th and 9th Bns The Gordon Highlanders, TA, 1936-42; Brigadier and Dir Selection of Personnel, War Office, 1942-45; Col Comdg Edinburgh Univ. Contingent, OTC, 1945-53; Chm. Edinburgh, Lothians and Peebles TA & AFA, 1953-57. Pres. Scottish Unionist Assoc., 1955-56; Dep. Chm., Unionist Party in Scotland, 1960-63. Vice-Chm., Pigs Industry Develt Authority, 1957-69; Vice-Pres. Brit. Council of Churches, 1971-; Pres., Royal Scottish Geographical Soc., 1968-74. Hon. Mem., BVA, 1976. Mem., Edinburgh Univ. Court, 1961-68; Mem., Heriot-Watt Univ. Court, 1966-78 (Chm., 1966-72). Pres. Edinburgh Bn The Boys' Brigade, 1955-68. Hon. Col 5/6th Bn The Gordon Highlanders, 1958-61, of 3rd Bn, 1961. Hon. DSc Heriot-Watt, 1970. Hon. ARCVS, 1971. Iowa State Univ. Distinguished Achievement Citation, 1967. DL, Midlothian, 1975. *Publications:* papers on breeding of farm livestock, in various sci. jls. *Address:* House of Cockburn, Balerno, Midlothian EH14 7JD. *T:* 031-449 3737. *Clubs:* Caledonian; New (Edinburgh).
See also *Janet Adam Smith (Mrs John Carleton), Rt Hon. A. L. Buchanan-Smith.*

BALES, Kenneth Frederick; Regional Administrator, West Midlands Regional Health Authority, since 1973; *b* 2 March 1931; *s* of Frederick Charles Bales and Deborah Alice Bales; *m* 1958, Margaret Hazel Austin; two *s* one *d. Educ:* Buckhurst Hill Grammar Sch.; LSE; Univ. of Manchester. BScSoc; DipSocAdmin. Hosp. Sec., Newhall & Hesketh Park Hosps, 1958-62; Regional Trng Officer, Birmingham Regional Hosp. Bd, 1962-65; Regional Staff Officer, Birmingham Regional Staff Cttee, 1965-68; Group Sec., W Birmingham HMC, 1968-73. Associate, Inst. Health Service Administrators. *Recreations:* painting, sport. *Address:* 25 South Road, West Hagley, West Midlands DY9 0JT. *T:* Hagley 882550.

BALFE, Richard Andrew; Member (Lab) London South Inner, European Parliament, since 1979, and Labour spokesman on budgets; Director, Royal Arsenal Co-operative Society and associated companies, since 1978 (Political Secretary, 1973-79); *b* 14 May 1944; *s* of Dr Richard J. Balfe and Mrs Dorothy L. Balfe (née de Cann); *m* 1978, Vivienne Patricia Job; one *s. Educ:* Brook Comprehensive Sch., Sheffield; LSE (BSc Hons 1971). Fellow Royal Statistical Soc., 1972. Res. Officer, Finer Cttee on One Parent Families, 1970-73. Parly Candidate (Labour), Paddington South, 1970. Mem., GLC for Southwark/Dulwich, 1973-77; Chairman: Thamesmead New Town Cttee, 1973-75; GLC Housing Cttee, 1975-77. Mem. Exec. Cttee, Fabian Soc., 1981-. Mem. Ct of Governors, LSE, 1973-. *Publications:* Housing: a new Socialist perspective, 1976; Role and Problems of the Co-operative Movement in the 1980s (with Tony Banks), 1977. *Recreation:* collecting books and pamphlets

on political and social history topics. *Address:* 259 Barry Road, SE22 0JT. 7 (office) 01-299 0868; (home) 01-693 1748. *Club:* Peckham Labour.

BALFOUR, family name of **Earl of Balfour** and **Barons Balfour o Inchrye, Kinross** and **Riverdale.**

BALFOUR, 4th Earl of, *cr* 1922; **Gerald Arthur James Balfour;** Viscour Traprain 1922; JP; *b* 23 Dec. 1925; *er s* of 3rd Earl of Balfour and Jean (1981), 4th *d* of late Rev. Canon J. J. Cooke-Yarborough; *S* father, 1968; *i* 1956, Natasha Georgina, *d* of late Captain George Anton. *Educ:* Eton; HM Conway. Holds Master Mariner's certificate. Mem., E Lothian CC, 1960-75 JP East Lothian, 1970. Mem., Internat. Assoc. of Cape Horners, 1960. *Heir cousin* Eustace Arthur Goschen Balfour [*b* 26 May 1921; *m* 1st, 1946, Anno *d* of late Major Victor Yule; two *s*; 2nd, 1971, Mrs Paula Cuene-Grandidier *Address:* The Tower, Whittinghame, Haddington, Scotland. *Club:* English Speaking Union.

BALFOUR OF BURLEIGH, Lord *cr* 1607 (*de facto* 8th Lord, 12th but fc the Attainder); **Robert Bruce,** CEng, FIEE; Director: Bank of Scotland, sinc 1968; Scottish Investment Trust, since 1971; Chairman, Federation of Scottis Bank Employers, since 1977; President, Friends of Vellore, since 197: Treasurer, Royal Scottish Corporation, since 1967; *b* 6 Jan. 1927; *e s* of 11t Lord Balfour of Burleigh and Dorothy (*d* 1976), *d* of late R. H. Done; father, 1967; *m* 1971, Mrs Jennifer Brittain-Catlin, *d* of late E. S. Manasseh two *d.* Served RN, 1945-48, as Ldg Radio Electrician's Mate. Joined Englis Electric Co. Ltd, 1951; graduate apprentice, 1951-52; Asst Foreman, Heav Electrical Plant Dept, Stafford Works, 1952-54; Asst Superintendent, Heav Electrical Plant Dept, Netherton Works, Liverpool, 1954-57; Manage English Electric Co. of India (Pvt) Ltd, Madras, 1957-60; Dir and Ger Manager, English Electric Co. India Ltd, 1960-64; Dep. Gen. Manage English Electric Co. Ltd, Netherton, Liverpool, 1964-65, Gen. Manage 1965-66; Dir and Gen. Manager, D. Napier & Son Ltd, 1966-68; Chm., Vikin Oil Ltd, 1971-80. Chm., Scottish Arts Council, 1971-80. Mem., British Ra Scotland regl bd, 1982-. Forestry Comr, 1971-74. *Recreations:* musi climbing, woodwork. *Heir: d* Hon. Victoria Bruce, *b* 7 May 1973. *Addres.* Brucefield, Clackmannan, Scotland.
See also *G. J. D. Bruce.*

BALFOUR OF INCHRYE, 1st Baron *cr* 1945, of Shefford; **Harol Harington Balfour,** PC 1941; MC and Bar; *b* 1 Nov. 1897; *s* of Col N. F Balfour, OBE, Belton, Camberley, Surrey; *m* 1st, 1921, Diana Blanche (mar diss. 1946; she *d* 1982), *d* of Sir Robert G. Harvey, 2nd Bt; one *s*; 2nd, 1947 Mary Ainslie Profumo, *d* of late Baron Profumo, KC, and of Barone Profumo; one *d. Educ:* Chilverton Elms, Dover; RN Coll., Osborne. Joine 60th Rifles, 1914; attached RFC 1915; RAF 1918; served European Wa 1914-18 (MC and bar); RAF 1918-23; journalism and business since 192 contested (C) Stratford, West Ham, 1924; MP (C) Isle of Thanet, 1929-4! Parly Under-Sec. of State for Air, 1938-44; Minister Resident in West Afric 1944-45. President, Federation Chambers of Commerce of the British Empir 1946-49; President, Commonwealth and Empire Industries Association, 195€ 60; Part-time Member, Board of BEA, 1955-66; Chairman, BEA Helicopter Ltd, 1964-66. *Publications:* An Airman Marches, 1935; Wings ov€ Westminster, 1973; Folk, Fish and Fun, 1978. *Recreation:* fishing. *Heir: s* Hor Ian Balfour [*b* 21 Dec. 1924; *m* 1953, Josephine Maria Jane, *d* of late Mr an of the Hon. Mrs Morogh Bernard, Shankill, Co. Dublin; one *d*]. *Address:* En House, St Mary Abbot's Place, W8 6LS. *T:* 01-603 6231. *Clubs:* Carlto Pratt's.
See also *J. D. Profumo.*

BALFOUR, David, CBE 1960; DPhil; FIL; retired diplomat; free-lanc conference interpreter; *b* London, 20 Jan. 1903; *s* of Reginald Balfour an Charlotte Warre Cornish; *m* 1948, Louise Fitzherbert; one *d. Educ:* Orator Sch., Edgbaston; and at Angers, Prague, Salzburg, Rome, Athens. Graduat of Oriental Institute, Rome, and of Athens Univ. (1940); DPhil (Oxon), 197(On staff of the Institute of English Studies, Athens, 1939-41. Served War c 1939-45 in Army, 1941-43, GSO II, GHQ, Middle East Forces (despatches Entered HM Foreign Service, 1943, established 1946; served Cairo, Athen Foreign Office, Tel Aviv (Oriental Sec., 1949-50), Smyrna (Consul-Gene 1951-55), Genoa (Consul-Gen., 1955-60), and Geneva (Consul-Gen., 196(63); Interpreter and Translator, FO, 1963-68; retd 1968. Mem., Internat. Asso of Conf. Interpreters, 1969. *Recreations:* theology, byzantinology (especiall 14th and 15th century). *Publications:* critical editions of unedited works c Symeon of Thessalonica, 1979 and 1981, and of Gregory of Sinai, 198 *Address:* The Old Mill, Kingsclere, Hants. *T:* Kingsclere 298610.

BALFOUR, David Mathers, CBE 1970; MA; CEng, MICE; Director, R. N Douglas Construction Ltd, since 1975; Chairman, Balfour, Beatty & Co. Lt 1971-74 (Managing Director, 1966-72); *b* 11 Jan. 1910; *s* of late Georg Balfour, MP and Margaret (née Mathers); *m* 1938, Elisabeth, *d* of Joh Murdoch Beddall; two *s* one *d. Educ:* Shrewsbury Sch.; Pembroke Col Cambridge (MA). Served War of 1939-45, Lt-Col RE. Joined Balfou Beatty & Co. Ltd, as Civil Engineer, 1930 (Dir, 1942); Chairman: Powe Securities Corporation Ltd, 1971-74; Balfour Kilpatrick Ltd, 1971-72 (Di 1971-75); Exec. Dir, British Insulated Callender's Cables Ltd, 1970-72. Chm Export Gp for the Constructional Industries, 1963-65; Vice-Pres., Fedn Civil Engineering Contractors (Chm. 1966-67). *Recreations:* golf, shootin *Address:* Little Garnstone Manor, Seal, Sevenoaks, Kent. *T:* Sevenoaks 6122

Clubs: East India, Devonshire, Sports and Public Schools; Rye Golf (Rye); Wildernesse Golf (Sevenoaks).

BALFOUR, (Elizabeth) Jean, CBE 1981; FRSE 1980; FRSA 1981; FIFor; JP; Chairman, Countryside Commission for Scotland, 1972-82; *b* 4 Nov. 1927; 2nd *d* of late Maj.-Gen. Sir James Syme Drew, KBE, CB, DSO, MC, and late Victoria Maxwell, Munches; *m* 1950, John Charles Balfour, *qv*; three *s*. *Educ:* Edinburgh Univ. (BSc). Partner, Balbirnie Home Farms; Dir, A. & J. Bowen & Co. Ltd. Pres., Royal Scottish Forestry Soc., 1969-71; Mem., Fife CC, 1958-70; Chm., Fife County and City and Royal Burgh of Dunfermline Joint Probation Cttee, 1967-69; Governor, East of Scotland Coll. of Agriculture, 1958-; Member: Scottish Agric. Develt Council, 1972-77; Verney Working Party on Management of National Resources, 1971-72; Nature Conservancy Council, 1973-80; Oil Develt Council, 1973-78; Council, Scottish Agricultural Coll., 1974-; Scottish Economic Council, 1978-; Vice-Chm., Scottish Wildlife Trust, 1968-72; Chm., Regional Adv. Cttee, East (Scotland) Conservancy, Forestry Commn, 1976-. JP Fife, 1963. Hon. DSc St Andrews, 1977. *Recreations:* hill walking, fishing, painting, exploring arctic vegetation, shooting. *Address:* Kirkforthar House, Markinch, Fife KY7 6LS. *T:* Glenrothes 752233; Scourie, by Lairg, Sutherland. *Clubs:* Farmers', Royal Commonwealth Society; (Assoc. Mem.) New (Edinburgh).

BALFOUR, Rear-Adm. George Ian Mackintosh, CB 1962; DSC 1943; *b* 14 Jan. 1912; *yr s* of late Dr T. Stevenson Balfour, Chard, Som, and Mrs Balfour; *m* 1939, Pamela Carlyle Forrester, *y d* of late Major Hugh C. C. Forrester, DL, JP, Tullibody House, Cambus, and late Mrs Forrester; two *s* one *d. Educ:* Royal Naval Coll., Dartmouth. Served in China, 1930-32; South Africa, 1935-37. Commanded Destroyers for most of War of 1939-45, on various stations. Mediterranean, 1948, Far East, 1949-50, USA 1951-53, Captain (D) 2nd Destroyer Flotilla, 1956-58; Dir of Officer Appointments, 1958-59; Senior Naval Mem., Imperial Defence Coll., 1960-63; retired list, 1963. Chief Appeals Officer, Cancer Res. Campaign, 1963-77. *Address:* Westover, Farnham Lane, Haslemere, Surrey. *T:* 3876.

BALFOUR, Jean; *see* Balfour, E. J.

BALFOUR, Sir John, GCMG 1954 (KCMG 1947; CMG 1941); GBE 1959; *b* 26 May 1894; *s* of Charles Barrington Balfour, CB, Newton Don and Balgonie, and of Lady Nina Balfour; *m* 1933, Frances (CVO 1969; Lady-in-Waiting to HRH Princess Marina, Duchess of Kent, 1961-68), *d* of Prof. Alexander van Millingen, DD. *Educ:* Eton; New Coll., Oxford. Interned in Germany, 1914-18; 3rd Sec. in the Diplomatic Service or Foreign Office, 1919; served in Foreign Office, at HM Legations at Budapest, Sofia and Belgrade, and at HM Embassies at Madrid and Washington; IDC 1937; Minister in Lisbon, 1941-43; in Moscow, 1943-45; in Washington, 1945-48; Ambassador to Argentine Republic, 1948-51; Ambassador to Spain, 1951-54; retired from Foreign Service, 1954. UK Commissioner-Gen. to Brussels International Exhibition of 1958. Chairman: British and French Bank, 1959-69; United Bank for Africa, 1961-69. Officier de la Légion d'Honneur, 1972. *Address:* 38 Onslow Square, SW7. *T:* 01-584 1970. *Club:* Brooks's.

BALFOUR, John Charles, OBE 1978; MC 1943; JP; DL; Member, Fife Area Health Board, since 1981; *b* 28 July 1919; *s* of late Brig. E. W. S. Balfour, CVO, DSO, OBE, MC, and Lady Ruth Balfour, CBE; *m* 1950, (Elizabeth) Jean Drew (*see* (Elizabeth) Jean Balfour); three *s. Educ:* Eton Coll.; Trinity Coll., Cambridge (BA). Served war, Royal Artillery, 1939-45 (Major), N Africa and Europe. Member, Royal Company of Archers, Queen's Body Guard for Scotland, 1949-. Member: Inter-departmental Cttee on Children and Young Persons, Scotland (Chm., Lord Kilbrandon), 1961-64; Scottish Council on Crime, 1972-75; Chairman: Children's Panel, Fife County, 1970-75, Fife Region 1975-77; Scottish Assoc. of Youth Clubs, 1968-73. JP 1957, DL 1958, Fife. *Recreations:* shooting, fishing. *Address:* Kirkforthar House, Markinch, Glenrothes, Fife KY7 6LS. *T:* Glenrothes 752233. *Club:* New (Edinburgh).
See also P. E. G. Balfour.

BALFOUR, Michael John; Assistant Director, Bank of England, since 1980; *b* 17 Oct. 1925; *s* of Duncan and Jeanne Germaine Balfour; *m* 1951, Mary Campbell Penney, *d* of Maj.-Gen. Sir (William) Ronald Campbell Penney, KBE, CB, DSO, MC; two *s* one *d* (and *e s* decd). *Educ:* Eton Coll.; Christ Church, Oxford (MA Hons Modern Languages 1949). War service, RAF, 1944-47. Entered Bank of England, 1950: Senior Adviser, European affairs, 1973, Chief Adviser, 1976. Alternate Director, Bank for International Settlements, 1972-; Member, EEC Monetary Cttee, 1974-. Director, Balgonie Estates Ltd, 1955-. *Recreations:* music, fishing, tennis, boat-building, etc. *Address:* 40 Ladbroke Square, W11 3ND. *T:* 01-229 8013; Harrietfield, Kelso, Roxburghshire TD5 7SY. *T:* Kelso 2825. *Club:* Overseas Bankers'.

BALFOUR, Nancy, OBE 1965; Chairman, Contemporary Art Society, 1976-82; *b* 1911; *d* of Alexander Balfour and Ruth Macfarland Balfour. *Educ:* Wycombe Abbey Sch.; Lady Margaret Hall, Oxford (MA). Foreign Office Research Dept, 1941-45; BBC N American Service, 1945-48; Economist Newspaper, 1948-72: Asst Editor with responsibility for American Survey, 1954-72; Fellow, Inst. of Politics, Kennedy Sch. of Govt, Harvard Univ., 1973-74. Mem. Council, Royal Inst. of Internat. Affairs, 1963-; Hon. Treasurer, Contemporary Art Soc., 1971-76; Mem., Crafts Council, 1980-. *Recreations:* sightseeing, ancient and modern; viewing work by living artists. *Address:* 36E Eaton Square, SW1W 9DH. *T:* 01-235 7874. *Club:* Arts.

BALFOUR, Neil Roxburgh; Member (C) North Yorkshire, European Parliament, since 1979; Director, European Banking Co. Ltd, since 1974; *b* 12 Aug. 1944; *s* of Archibald Roxburgh Balfour and Lilian Helen Cooper; *m* 1st, 1969, HRH Princess Elizabeth of Yugoslavia; one *s*; 2nd, 1978, Serena Mary Churchill Russell; one *s* one *d. Educ:* Ampleforth Coll., Yorks; University Coll., Oxford Univ. (BA History); called to the Bar, Middle Temple, 1969. Baring Brothers & Co., 1968-74. *Publication:* Paul of Yugoslavia (biography), 1980. *Recreations:* bridge, writing, golf, tennis, shooting, fishing. *Address:* 24 The Little Boltons, SW10 9LP. *T:* 01-373 8092; Studley Royal, near Ripon, North Yorkshire. *Clubs:* Turf, Pratt's; Royal St George's (Sandwich).

BALFOUR, Peter Edward Gerald; Chairman and Chief Executive, Scottish & Newcastle Breweries Ltd; *b* 9 July 1921; *y s* of late Brig. Edward William Sturgis Balfour, CVO, DSO, OBE, MC and Lady Ruth Balfour, CBE, MB; *m* 1st, 1948, Grizelda Davina Roberta Ogilvy (marr. diss. 1967); two *s* one *d*; 2nd, 1968, Diana Rosemary Wainman; one *s* one *d. Educ:* Eton College. Scots Guards, 1940-54. Joined Wm McEwan & Co. Ltd, 1954. Director: Royal Bank of Scotland, 1971-; Scottish & Newcastle Breweries Ltd, 1961; British Assets Trust Ltd; Edinburgh American Assets Trust, 1962- (Chm., 1978-); First Charlotte Assets Trust (Chm., 1981); Royal Bank of Scotland Gp Ltd, 1978-. Chm., Scottish Council for Develt and Industry, 1978-. Mem., Hansard Soc. Commn on Electoral Reform, 1975-76. *Address:* Scadlaw House, Humbie, East Lothian. *T:* Humbie 252. *Clubs:* Cavalry and Guards; New (Edinburgh).
See also J. C. Balfour.

BALFOUR, Raymond Lewis, MVO 1965; HM Diplomatic Service; Counsellor, Kuwait, since 1979; *b* 23 April 1923; *s* of Henry James Balfour and Vera Alice (née Dunford); *m* 1955, Vanda Gaye Crompton. RMA Sandhurst, 1942; commnd RAC; served with IV Queen's Own Hussars, 1942-47. Diplomatic Service, 1947-; served at Munich, Beirut, Gdansk (Poland), Baghdad, Khartoum, Geneva, Damascus; Counsellor, Tripoli, 1976-79. Order of the Blue Nile, Sudan, 1965. *Recreations:* travel, gardening. *Address:* c/o Foreign and Commonwealth Office, SW1A 2AH.

BALFOUR, Richard Creighton, MBE 1945; retired; *b* 3 Feb. 1916; *s* of Donald Creighton Balfour and Muriel Fonçeca; *m* 1943, Adela Rosemary Welch; two *s. Educ:* St Edward's Sch., Oxford. FIB. Joined Bank of England, 1935; Agent, Leeds, 1961-65; Deputy Chief Cashier, 1965-70; Chief Accountant, 1970-75. Dir, Datasaab Ltd, 1975-81. Naval Service, Lt-Comdr RNVR, 1939-46. Pres., Royal National Rose Soc., 1973 and 1974; Chairman: 1976—The Year of the Rose; Internat. Rose Conf., Oxford, 1976; Vice-Pres. (Europe), World Fedn of Rose Socs (Chm., Classification Cttee); organiser and designer of the British Garden at Montreal Floralies, 1980. Liveryman, Worshipful Co. of Gardeners; Freeman, City of London. DHM 1974. *Publications:* articles in Rose Annual and many horticultural magazines. *Recreations:* roses, gardening, photography, dancing, sea floating, collecting rocks and hat pins, travel, watching sport. *Address:* Albion House, Little Waltham, Chelmsford, Essex CM3 3LA. *T:* Chelmsford 360410.

BALFOUR, Sir Robert George Victor FitzGeorge; *see* FitzGeorge-Balfour.

BALFOUR-LYNN, Dr Stanley; Director and Member of Corporate Executive Committee, AMI Inc., since 1977; Chairman, AMI (Europe) Ltd, since 1969; *b* 21 June 1922; *s* of John Balfour-Lynn and Yetta Selwyn; *m* 1952, Valerie Eker; three *s* one *d. Educ:* City of London Sch.; Guy's Hosp., London. MB, BS London; MRCS, LRCP. Prosector and Demonstr of Anatomy, RCS, 1949-51; RMO, Queen Charlotte's Maternity Hosp., 1951-52; Edgware Gen. Hosp.; Selly Oak Hosp.; Royal Northern Hosp.; Guy's Sector Hosp.; Bromley. Underwriting Mem. of Lloyd's, 1977-. Exec. Mem., Assoc. of Indep. Hosps (Chm., Acute Div.). FRSM. *Publications:* contrib. on parthenogenesis, Lancet. *Recreations:* scuba diving, flying, tennis, the NHS. *Address:* Flat F, 19 Hyde Park Gardens, W2. *T:* 01-723 3960; Hush Heath Manor, Goudhurst, Kent. *T:* Goudhurst 211312. *Clubs:* Variety Club of GB, MCC, Annabel's; Kidlington Flying.

BALFOUR-PAUL, (Hugh) Glencairn, CMG 1968; HM Diplomatic Service, retired; Director General, Middle East Association, 1978-79; Research Fellow, University of Exeter, since 1979; *b* 23 Sept. 1917; *s* of late Lt-Col J. W. Balfour Paul, DSO; *m* 1st, 1950, Margaret Clare Ogilvy (*d* 1971); one *s* three *d*; 2nd, 1974, Janet Alison Scott; one *s* one *d. Educ:* Sedbergh; Magdalen Coll., Oxford. Served War of 1939-45, Sudan Defence Force. Sudan Political Service, Blue Nile and Darfur, 1946-54; joined Foreign Office, 1955; Santiago, 1957; Beirut, 1960; Counsellor, Dubai, 1964; Dep. Political Resident, Persian Gulf, 1966; Counsellor, FO, attached St Antony's Coll., Oxford, 1968; Ambassador to Iraq, 1969-71; Ambassador to Jordan, 1972-75; Ambassador to Tunisia, 1975-77. *Recreations:* archaeology, modern poetry, carpentry. *Address:* Bradridge House, Diptford, Totnes, Devon. *T:* South Brent 3165.

BALGONIE, Lord; David Alexander Leslie Melville; *b* 26 Jan. 1954; *s* and heir of Earl of Leven and Melville, *qv*; *m* 1981, Julia Clare, *yr d* of Col I. R. Critchley, Lindores, Muthill, Perthshire. *Educ:* Eton. Captain Queen's Own Highlanders (GSM for N Ireland); RARO 1979. *Address:* Glenferness House, Nairn.

BALKWILL, Bryan Havell; conductor; Professor of Conducting, Indiana University, Bloomington, since 1977; *b* 2 July 1922; *s* of Arthur William Balkwill and Dorothy Silver Balkwill (*née* Wright); *m* 1949, Susan Elizabeth Roberts; one *s* one *d. Educ:* Merchant Taylors' Sch.; Royal Academy of Music. Asst Conductor, New London Opera Co., 1947-48; Associate Conductor, Internat. Ballet, 1948-49; Musical Director and Principal Conductor, London Festival Ballet, 1950-52; Music staff and subseq. Associate Conductor, Glyndebourne Opera, 1950-58; Musical Dir, Arts Council 'Opera For All', 1953-63; Resident Conductor, Royal Opera House, Covent Garden, 1959-65; Musical Director: Welsh Nat. Opera Company, 1963-67; Sadler's Wells Opera, 1966-69; free-lance opera and concert conducting in N America, Europe and GB, 1970-. Guest Conductor: Royal Opera House, Covent Garden, English Nat. Opera, Glyndebourne, Wexford Festival, Aldeburgh, RPO, LPO, BBC. Mem. Royal Philharmonic Society; FRAM. *Recreation:* open air. *Address:* 8 The Green, Wimbledon Common, SW19 5AZ. *T:* 01-947 4250.

BALL, Alan Hugh; Deputy Chairman, Lonrho Ltd, since 1982 and Director of associated companies (Chairman and Joint Managing Director, 1961-72; Executive Deputy Chairman, 1972-78); *b* 8 June 1924; *s* of late Sir George Joseph Ball, KBE and Mary Caroline Ball; *m* 1948, Eleanor Katharine Turner; two *s* one *d. Educ:* Eton. KRRC, 1943-47. Lonrho Ltd and associated cos, 1947-. *Recreations:* fishing, shooting. *Address:* The Old Mill, Ramsbury, Wilts. *T:* Ramsbury 266.

BALL, Air Marshal Sir Alfred (Henry Wynne), KCB 1976 (CB 1967); DSO 1943; DFC 1942; Vice-Chairman (Air), Council of Territorial, Auxiliary and Volunteer Reserve Association; Military Affairs Adviser, International Computers Ltd, since 1979; *b* 18 Jan. 1921; *s* of Captain J. A. E. Ball, MC, BA, BÉ; *m* 1942, Nan McDonald; three *s* one *d. Educ:* Campbell Coll., Belfast; RAF Coll., Cranwell; idc, jssc, psc, pfc. Served War of 1939-45 (Despatches twice; US Air Medal 1943); Sqdn Ldr 1942; Wing Comdr 1944; air operations, Lysanders, Spitfires, Mosquitoes; commanded: 4 Photo. Reconn. Unit; 682, 542, 540 and 13 Photo. Reconn. Sqdns in N Africa, UK, France and Middle East; E Africa, 1947; Bomber Comd, 1952; Gp Captain, Operations, BJSM, Washington, 1959; Comdr, Honington V Bomber Base, 1963-64; Air Cdre, Air Officer, Administration, Aden, 1965; IDC, 1967; Dir of Operations, (RAF), MoD, 1967-68; Air Vice-Marshal, 1968; ACOS, Automatic Data Processing Div., SHAPE, 1968-71; Dir-Gen. Organisation (RAF), 1971-75; Air Marshal, 1975; UK Rep., Perm. Mil. Deputies Gp, Cento, 1975-77; Dep. C-in-C, RAF Strike Command, 1977-78, retired 1979. Hon. Mem. British Computer Soc., 1974. *Recreation:* golf. *Address:* Tarshyne, Lambridge Wood Road, Henley-on-Thames, Oxon. *Clubs:* Royal Air Force; Phyllis Court (Henley), Huntercombe.

BALL, Anthony George, FInstM; Chief Executive and Group Managing Director, Henlys plc, since 1982; *b* 14 Nov. 1934; *s* of Harry Ball and Mary Irene Ball, Bridgwater; *m* 1957, Ruth Parry Davies; two *s* one *d. Educ:* Dr Morgan's Grammar Sch., Bridgwater. FIMI, ACIArb. Indentured engineering apprentice, Austin Motor Co., 1950-55; management trainee, 1955-57; sales representative, 1957-59; UK sales executive, 1959-62; responsible for launch of Mini, 1959; Commercial Vehicle Sales Manager, 1962-64, Car Sales Manager, 1964-66, Austin Motor Co.; Sales and Marketing Exec., British Motor Corp., 1966-67; Chm. and Man. Dir, Barlow Rand UK Motor Gp, 1967-78; Managing Director: Barlow Rand Ford, S Africa, 1971-73; Barlow Rand European Operations, 1973-78; Barlow Handling Ltd, 1975-78; returned to British Leyland as Man. Dir, Overseas Trading Operations, 1978; Director: Leyland Australia, Leyland S Africa, Leyland Kenya and all BL African subsids; Dep. Man. Dir, Austin Morris Ltd, 1979; Chm. and Man. Dir, BL Europe & Overseas, 1979-82; Director, 1979-82: BL Cars Ltd; Austin Morris Ltd; Rover Triumph Ltd; Jaguar Rover Triumph Inc. (USA); Harry Ball (Bridgwater) Ltd; Dir, Jaguar Cars Ltd, 1981-82. Chairman, Nuffield Press, 1978-80. Responsible for conducting BL's Buy British campaign and launch of the Austin Metro in 1980. Lectr and public speaker; TV and radio broadcasts on motoring and industrial subjects include: The Money Programme, Today, Top Gear, Going Places, World in Action, Focus, World at One. Freeman of City of London, 1980; Liveryman of Worshipful Co. of Coach Makers and Coach Harness Makers, 1980. Fellowship of Inst. of Marketing awarded 1981, for launch of the Metro and services to Brit. Motor Industry; Hon. Mem. CGLI, 1982, for services to technical and vocational educn. *Publications:* contribs to numerous industrial, management and marketing jls. *Recreations:* theatre, British military history, golf. *Address:* Blythe House, Grange Road, Bidford-on-Avon, Warwickshire B50 4BY. *T:* Bidford-on-Avon 778015. *Clubs:* Oriental, City Livery.

BALL, Arthur Beresford, OBE 1973; HM Diplomatic Service, retired; Consul-General, Perth, Western Australia, 1978-80; *b* 15 Aug. 1923; *s* of Charles Henry and Lilian Ball; *m* 1961, June Stella Luckett; one *s* two *d. Educ:* Bede Collegiate Boys' Sch., Sunderland. Joined HM Diplomatic Service, 1949: Bahrain, 1949; Tripoli, 1950; Middle East Centre for Arab Studies, 1952; Ramullah, 1953; Damascus, 1954; Foreign Office, 1957; Kuwait, 1959; HM Consul, New Orleans, 1963; Jedda, 1965; FO, 1967; São Paulo, 1969; Lisbon, 1972; Ankara, 1975. *Recreations:* sailing, philately, historical studies. *Address:* 15 Eccles Road, Holt, Norfolk NR25 6HJ.

BALL, Sir Charles (Irwin), 4th Bt *cr* 1911; *b* 12 Jan. 1924; *s* of Sir Nigel Gresley Ball, 3rd Bt, and of Florine Isabel, *d* of late Col Herbert Edwardes Irwin; *S* father, 1978; *m* 1950, Alison Mary, *d* of late Lt-Col Percy Holman

Bentley, MBE, MC; one *s* one *d. Educ:* Sherborne Sch. FCA 1960. Served RA, 1942-47. Chartered Accountant, 1950; Peat, Marwick, Mitchell & Co 1950-54; joined Robert, Benson, Lonsdale & Co. Ltd (now Kleinwort, Benson Ltd), 1954; Director: Kleinwort, Benson Ltd, 1964-76 (Vice-Chm., 1974-76) Kleinwort, Benson, Lonsdale Ltd, 1974-76; Kleinwort Benson Investmen Trust (Chm., 1974-76); Cadbury Schweppes Ltd, 1971-76; Chubb & Son Ltd 1971-76; Sun Alliance and London Insurance Ltd, 1971-; Telephone Renta. Ltd, 1971- (Vice-Chm., 1978-81, Chm., 1981-); Tunnel Holdings Ltd 1976-82; Barclays Bank Ltd, 1976-77 (Chm., Barclays Merchant Bank Ltd 1976-77); Rockware Group Ltd, 1978-; Peachey Property Corporation Ltd 1978- (Chm., 1981-). Mem., British Transport Docks Board, 1971-, Vice Chm., 1982-. Liveryman, 1960, Mem. Ct of Assts, 1979, Clockmakers' Co *Heir: s* Richard Bentley Ball, *b* 29 Jan. 1953. *Address:* Downlands, Seale, nea Farnham, Surrey GU10 1HB. *T:* Runfold 2415.

BALL, Christopher John Elinger, MA; Warden, Keble College, Oxford since 1980; *b* 22 April 1935; *er s* of late Laurence Elinger Ball, OBE, anc Christine Florence Mary Ball (*née* Howe); *m* 1958, Wendy Ruth Colyer, c of Cecil Frederick Colyer and Ruth Colyer (*née* Reddaway); three *s* three *d. Educ:* St George's School, Harpenden; Merton College, Oxfor (Harmsworth Scholar 1959). 1st Cl. English Language and Literature, 1959 Dipl. in Comparative Philology, 1962; MA Oxon, 1963. 2nd Lieut, Parachut Regt, 1955-56. Lectr in English Language, Merton Coll., Oxford, 1960-61 Lectr in Comparative Linguistics, Sch. of Oriental and African Studies (Univ of London), 1961-64; Fellow and Tutor in English Language, Lincoln Coll. Oxford, 1964-79 (Sen. Tutor and Tutor for Admissions, 1971-72; Bursar 1972-79; Hon. Fellow, 1981). Sec., Linguistics Assoc. of GB, 1964-67; Pres. Oxford Assoc. of University Teachers, 1968-70; Publications Sec. Philological Soc., 1969-75; Chairman: CNAA English Studies Bd, 1973-80 Linguistics Bd, 1977-82; Oxford Univ. English Bd, 1977-79; Jt Standing Ctte for Linguistics, 1979-82; Bd of National Adv. Body for Local Authority Higher Educn in England, 1982-. *Publications:* various contributions to philological and linguistic jls. *Address:* Keble College, Oxford. *T:* Oxfore 59201. *Club:* United Oxford & Cambridge University.

BALL, Denis William, MBE 1971; Headmaster of Kelly College since 1972 *b* 20 Oct. 1928; *er s* of William Charles Thomas and Dora Adelaide Ball Eastbourne; *m* 1972, Marja Tellervo Lumijärvi, *er d* of Osmo Kullervo anc Leila Tellervo Lumijärvi, Toijala, Finland; two *s* one *d. Educ:* Brunswick Sch. Tonbridge Sch. (Scholar); Brasenose Coll., Oxford (MA). Asst Master, The King's Sch., Canterbury, 1953-72 (Housemaster, 1954-72). Sub-Lt, RNR 1953; Lieut 1954; Lt-Comdr 1958. Trustee, Tavistock Sch., 1972-; Vice-Chm of Governors, St Michael's Sch., Tawstock Court, 1974-; Mem., Political anc PR Sub-Cttee, HMC, 1979-. *Recreations:* Elizabethan history, cryptography literary and mathematical puzzles, cricket, real tennis, squash (played for Oxford Univ. and Kent), golf. *Address:* Kelly College, Tavistock, Devor PL19 0HZ. *T:* Tavistock 3005. *Clubs:* East India, Devonshire, Sports anc Public Schools, MCC.

BALL, Sir George Thomas T.; *see* Thalben-Ball.

BALL, Dr Harold William; Keeper of Palæontology, British Museum (Natural History), since 1966; *b* 11 July 1926; *s* of Harold Ball and Florence (*née* Harris); *m* 1955, Patricia Mary (*née* Silvester); two *s* two *d. Educ* Yardley Gram. Sch.; Birmingham Univ. BSc 1947, PhD 1949, Birminghan Geologist, Nyasaland Geological Survey, 1949-51; Asst Lectr in Geology King's Coll., London, 1951-54; Dept of Palæontology, British Museum (Nat Hist.), 1954-: Dep. Keeper, 1965; Keeper, 1966. Adrian Vis. Fellow, Univ. of Leicester, 1972-77. Sec., 1968-72, Vice-Pres., 1972-73, Geological Soc. o London; Pres., Soc. for the Bibliography of Natural History, 1981-. Wollastor Fund, Geological Soc. of London, 1965. *Publications:* papers on the stratigraphy of the Old Red Sandstone and on the palæontology of the Antarctic in several scientific jls. *Recreations:* music, rhododendron species collecting early books on natural history and voyages. *Address:* Wilderbrook Dormans Park, East Grinstead, West Sussex. *T:* Dormans Park 426.

BALL, Prof. John Geoffrey, CEng; consultant metallurgist; Senior Researcl Fellow, Imperial College, University of London, since 1980, Professor o Metallurgy, 1956-80, now Emeritus; Head of Metallurgy Department, 1957 79; *b* 27 Sept. 1916; *s* of late I. H. Ball and late Mrs E. M. Ball; *m* 1941, Joar C. M., *d* of late Arthur Wiltshire, JP, Bournemouth. *Educ:* Wellington (Salop) High Sch.; Univ. of Birmingham. British Welding Res. Assoc. 1941-49; Sen. Metallurgist, 1945-49; AERE, Harwell, 1949-56; Head o Reactor Metallurgy, 1953-56. Min. of Tech. Visitor to British Non-Ferrou Metals Res. Assoc., 1962-72. Dean, Royal Sch. of Mines, Imperial Coll. 1962-65 and 1971-74; Dean, Faculty of Engineering, Univ. of London 1970-74. Chairman: Res. Bd, 1964-74, and Mem. of Council Br. Welding Res. Assoc., 1964-81; Engrg Physics Sub-Cttee, Aeronautical Res. Counci 1964-68; Metallurgy Bd, CNAA, 1965-71; Metallurgy and Materials Cttee and Univ. Science and Technology Bd, SRC, 1967-70; Engrg Bd, SRC 1969-71; Manpower Utilisation Working Party, 1967-; Mem., Light Wate Reactor Pressure Vessel Study Gp, Dept of Energy, 1974-77. Pres., Inst. o Welding, 1965-66. Member: Council, Instn of Metallurgists, 1951-56, 1958 (Pres., 1966-67); Council, Br. Nuclear Forum, 1964-71; Manpower Resource Cttee, 1965-; Council, Inst. of Metals, 1965; Council, Iron and Steel Inst. 1965; Council, City Univ., 1966-; Brain Drain Cttee, 1966-67; Public Enquir into loss of "Sea Gem", 1967; Materials and Structures Cttee, 1967-70 Technology Sub-Cttee of UGC, 1968-73. Governor, Sir John Cass Coll

1958-67. Hon. ARSM 1961. Brooker Medal, Welding Inst., 1979. *Recreations:* gardening, painting, travel. *Address:* 3 Sylvan Close, Limpsfield, Surrey. *T:* Oxted 3511.

BALL, Rev. Kenneth Vernon James, MA; *b* 10 July 1906; *s* of Vernon Arthur and Eveline Ball, Brighton; *m* 1939, Isabella Jane Armstrong, MB, ChB, *d* of Archibald Armstrong, JP, and Eleanor Elsie Armstrong, Strachur, Argyll; one *s* one *d. Educ:* The College, Swindon; Jesus Coll., Oxford; Wycliffe Hall, Oxford. Acting Headmaster, Busoga High Sch., Uganda, 1930-32; Curate, St Paul, Bedminster, 1932-35; Curate, Temple or Holy Cross Church, Bristol, 1935-38; Vicar, St Barnabas, Bristol, 1938-42; Vicar, St Leonard, Redfield, Bristol, 1942-47; Bishop of Liverpool's Special Service Staff, 1947-50; Vicar, St Nicholas, and Chap. St Bartholomew's Hosp., Rochester, 1950-59; Oriel Canon of Rochester Cath., 1955-59; Vicar of Leatherhead, Surrey, 1959-70; Rector of Piddlehinton, Dorset, 1970-72; retd. *Publication:* Spiritual Approach to Marriage Preparation, 1948. *Recreations:* rowing, walking, camping, singing. *Address:* 11 Manor Mead, Hindhead, Surrey. *T:* Hindhead 5428.

BALL, Rt. Rev. Michael Thomas; *see* Jarrow, Bishop Suffragan of.

BALL, Rt. Rev. Peter John; *see* Lewes, Bishop Suffragan of.

BALL, Robert Edward, CB 1977; MBE 1946; Chief Master of the Supreme Court of Judicature (Chancery Division), 1969-79 (Master, 1954-68); *b* 8 March 1911; *s* of James Ball, LLB, Purley, Surrey, and Mabel Louise (*née* Laver); *m* 1935, Edith Margaret Barbara, *d* of late Dr Patrick Edward Campbell; one *s* two *d* (and one *s* decd). *Educ:* Westminster Sch.; Lycée de Vendôme, France; Germany; London Univ. (LLB). Law Soc.'s Studentship, 1929. Admitted Solicitor, 1933; junior partner, James Ball & Son, 1933-46; served War, 1939-46; commissioned in Queen's Royal Regt, 1940; served KORR and in various staff appts, England, France and India; AA & QMG, Madras; released with rank of Lt-Col, 1946; formed practice of Potts and Ball, Chester and London, with Henry Potts, 1946. Mem. Council, Teilhard Centre for the Future of Man, 1971-. Formerly: Hon. Sec., Chester and North Wales Incorp. Law Soc.; Chm. Chester Insurance Tribunal, etc. *Publications:* The Law and the Cloud of Unknowing, 1976; The Crown, The Sages and Supreme Morality, 1982; contrib. to Study Notes of the Inst. of Moralogy, Chiba, Japan. *Recreations:* history, oriental studies, gardening. *Address:* 62 Stanstead Road, Caterham, Surrey. *T:* Caterham 43675. *Club:* Athenæum.

BALL, Prof. Robert James, MA, PhD; Principal, London Business School, since 1972; Chairman, Legal & General Group, since 1980; *b* 15 July 1933; *s* of Arnold James Hector Ball; *m* 1st, 1954, Patricia Mary Hart Davies (marr. diss. 1970); one *s* three *d* (and one *d* decd); 2nd, 1970, Lindsay Jackson (*née* Wonnacott); one step *s. Educ:* St Marylebone Grammar Sch.; The Queen's College, Oxford; Styring Schol.; George Webb Medley Junior Schol. (Univ. Prizeman), 1956. BA 1957 (First cl. Hons PPE), MA 1960; PhD Univ. of Pennsylvania, 1973. RAF 1952-54 (Pilot-Officer, Navigator). Research Officer, Oxford University Inst. of Statistics, 1957-58; IBM Fellow, Univ. of Pennsylvania, 1958-60; Lectr, Manchester Univ., 1960, Sen. Lectr, 1963-65; Prof. of Economics, London Business School, 1965-, Governor, 1969-, Dep. Principal, 1971-72. Director: Barclays Bank Trust Co. Ltd; Tube Investments Ltd; IBM UK Holdings Ltd; IBM UK Ltd; Ogilvy and Mather Ltd, 1969-71; Economic Models Ltd, 1971-72. Part-time Mem., Nat. Freight Corporation, 1973-77. Member: Cttee to Review National Savings (Page Cttee) 1971-73; Economics Cttee of SSRC, 1971-74; Cttee on Social Forecasting, SSRC, 1971-72; Cttee of Enquiry into Electricity Supply Industry (Plowden Cttee), 1974-75; Chm., Treasury Cttee on Policy Optimisation, 1976-78. Governor, NIESR, 1973-. Member Council: REconS, 1973-79; BIM, 1974- (Chm., Economic and Social Affairs Cttee, 1979-). Fellow, Econometric Soc., 1973; FBIM, 1974. *Publications:* An Econometric Model of the United Kingdom, 1961; Inflation and the Theory of Money, 1964; (ed) Inflation, 1969; (ed) The International Linkage of National Economic Models, 1972; Money and Employment, 1982; articles in professional jls. *Recreations:* fishing, chess. *Address:* 1 Sussex Place, Regent's Park, NW1 4SA. *T:* 01-723 8777; Cross Trees, Beacon Road, Kingswear, Devon. *T:* Kingswear 333. *Club:* Royal Dart Yacht.

ALLANTYNE, Alexander Hanson, CVO 1957; CBE 1963; HM Diplomatic Service, retired; Consultant, Organisation for Economic Co-operation and Development, 1971-80; *b* 27 Feb. 1911; *s* of late Dr Harold Sherman Ballantyne and Mrs Gladys Pauline Ballantyne; *m* 1944, Hélène Georgette Contoroussi; one *s* one *d. Educ:* Rugby; Christ's Coll., Cambridge. BA (Hons) Cantab. HM Consular Service, 1934. Vice-Consul: Bangkok, 1934-38; Valencia, 1938 and 1939; Tokyo, 1940-42; Antananarivo, 1942-45; Actg Consul-Gen. Antananarivo, 1945 and 1946; Foreign Office, 1946 and 1947; First Sec. (Commercial), Istanbul, 1947-50; Actg Consul-Gen, Istanbul, 1950 and 1951; Foreign Office, 1951 and 1952; First Sec. (Commercial), Bangkok, 1952-55; Counsellor (Commercial) and Consul-General, Copenhagen, 1956-60; Chargé d'Affaires, Ankara, 1962; Counsellor (Commercial), Ankara, 1960-64; Consul-General, Frankfurt-am-Main, 1964-69. Commander of the Dannebrog, 1957. *Publication:* French Clocks the World Over (translation of Tardy's La Pendule Française dans le Monde): vol. I, 1981; vols II and III, 1982; vol. IV, 1983. *Recreation:* music. *Address:* 2 Avenue Marie-Christine, 06 Nice, France.

BALLANTYNE, Colin Sandergrove, CMG 1971; photographer and director; Chairman, Performing Arts Collection of South Australia, since 1980; *b* 12 July 1908; *s* of James Fergusson Ballantyne, Adelaide; *m* 1934, Gwenneth Martha Osborne Richmond; one *s* two *d. Educ:* Adelaide High School. Directed: cycle Shakespeare plays, 1948-52; 100 contemporary plays, 1948-78; five major productions Adelaide Festival of Arts, 1960-68. Dir, Sheridan Theatre, 1962-72. Chm. Bd of Governors, State Theatre Co., 1972-78; Pres., Arts Council of Australia (SA), 1974-77 (Federal Dir, 1966-74). Hon. FIAP 1971. *Publications:* (plays) Harvest, 1936; The Ice-Cream Cart, 1962; Between Gunshots, 1964 (also Pacific Rape, unpublished). *Address:* 77 Kingston Terrace, North Adelaide, SA 5006, Australia. *T:* Adelaide 267 1138.

BALLANTYNE, Henry, CBE 1968; DL, JP; President, Henry Ballantyne & Sons Ltd, since 1981 (Chairman, 1977-81); *b* 27 Nov. 1912; *er s* of late Lieut-Col David Ballantyne, OBE, Barns Kirkton Manor, Peeblesshire; *m* 1938, Barbara Mary, *d* of late C. S. Gavin, Worthing; one *s* three *d. Educ:* Cheltenham Coll.; Pembroke Coll., Cambridge. Entered family business, D. Ballantyne Bros & Co. Ltd, 1937: Dir, 1937; Chm., 1940, also of subsid. cos; merged twelve Border woollen firms to form Scottish Worsteds & Woollens Ltd, 1968, new holding co. Henry Ballantyne & Sons Ltd formed 1977; Dir, Chagford Investment Hldgs Ltd and other cos. Pres., S of Scotland Chamber of Commerce, 1942-44; Pres., Nat. Assoc. of Scottish Woollen Manufrs, 1951-55; Member: BoT Adv. Cttee, 1961-67; Scottish Econ. Planning Cttee, 1965-68; Royal Commn on Local Govt in Scotland, 1967-69; Scottish Constitutional Cttee of Conservative Party, 1969-70; Scottish Woollen Publicity Council (Chm., 1974-80); Scottish Veterans' Garden City Assoc. (Chm., 1974-). Member of the Royal Company of Archers (Queen's Body Guard for Scotland). DL 1953, JP 1943, Peeblesshire. *Recreations:* shooting, yachting, gardening. *Address:* The Kirklands, Innerleithen, Peeblesshire. *T:* Innerleithen 392. *Clubs:* Lansdowne, Royal Ocean Racing; Leander (Henley-on-Thames).

BALLARAT, Bishop of, since 1975; **Rt. Rev. John Hazlewood;** *b* 19 May 1924; *s* of George Harold Egerton Hazlewood and Anne Winnifred Edeson; *m* 1961, Dr Shirley Shevill; two *s. Educ:* Nelson Coll., New Zealand; King's Coll., Cambridge (BA 1948, MA 1952); Cuddesdon Coll., Oxford. Deacon 1949, priest 1950, Australia. Asst Curate: SS Michael and All Angels, Camberwell, 1949-50, 1953-55; St Jude, Randwick, Sydney, 1950-51; Holy Trinity, Dubbo, NSW, 1951-53; Vice-Principal, St Francis Coll., Brisbane, 1955-60; Asst Lectr in Ecclesiastical History, Univ. of Queensland, 1959-60; Dean of Rockhampton, Qld, 1960-68; Dean of Perth, WA, 1968-75. *Recreations:* travelling, music, gardening, reading, theatre, art. *Address:* Bishopscourt, 454 Wendouree Parade, Ballarat, Victoria 3355, Australia. *T:* 053-392370. *Clubs:* Melbourne, Naval and Military (Melbourne); Ballarat.

BALLARAT, Bishop of, (RC), since 1971; **Most Rev. Ronald Austin Mulkearns,** DD, DCL; *b* 11 Nov. 1930. *Educ:* De La Salle Coll., Malvern; Corpus Christi Coll., Werribee; Pontifical Lateran Univ., Rome. Ordained, 1956; Coadjutor Bishop, 1968-71. *Address:* 340 Wendouree Parade, Ballarat, Victoria 3350, Australia.

BALLARD, Ven. Arthur Henry; Archdeacon of Manchester and Canon Residentiary of Manchester Cathedral, 1972-80; *b* 9 March 1912; 3rd *s* of Alfred and Lillian Ballard; *m* 1943, Phyllis Marion, *d* of Walter East, Theydon Bois, Essex; two *s. Educ:* privately; St John's Coll., Univ. of Durham (Van Mildert Scholar). BA (with distinction) 1938; DipTh. 1939; MA 1941. Deacon 1939; Curate of Walthamstow, 1939-43; Rector of Broughton, Manchester, 1943-46; Rector of All Saints, Stand, Manchester, 1946-72. Rural Dean of Radcliffe and Prestwich, 1952-67; Hon. Canon of Manchester, 1958-66; Archdeacon of Rochdale, 1966-72. Mem., Gen. Synod of CofE, 1972-80. *Recreations:* restoration of clocks, antique furniture, paintings. *Address:* 30 Rathen Road, Withington, Manchester M20 9GH. *T:* 061-445 4703. *Club:* Manchester.

BALLARD, Prof. Clifford Frederick; Professor Emeritus in Orthodontics, University of London; Hon. Consultant, Eastman Dental Hospital, London; *b* 26 June 1910; *s* of Frederick John Ballard and Eliza Susannah (*née* Wilkinson); *m* 1937, Muriel Mabel Burling; one *s* one *d. Educ:* Kilburn Grammar Sch.; Charing Cross Hosp. and Royal Dental Hospital. LDS 1934; MRCS, LRCP 1940. Hd of Dept of Orthodontics, Inst. of Dental Surgery, British Post-Grad. Med. Fedn, Univ. of London, 1948-72; Prof. of Orthodontics, London Univ., 1956-72; Dental Surgeon, Victoria Hosp. for Children, SW3, 1948-64, Tooting, 1964-71. Pres. of Brit. Soc. for the Study of Orthodontics, 1957, Senior Vice-Pres., 1963, 1964; Mem. Council of Odontological Section of Royal Society Med., 1954-56, 1959-62 (Sec., 1957, Vice-Pres., 1969-72); Mem. Board, Faculty of Dental Surgery. RCS, 1966-74. FDS 1949; Diploma in Orthodontics, 1954 (RCS); FFDRCS Ire., 1964. Charles Tomes Lectr, RCS, 1966; Northcroft Memorial Lectr, Brit. Soc. for Study of Orthocorties, 1967. Hon. Life Mem., British Dental Assoc., 1982; Hon. Member: British Soc. for Study of Orthodontics; Israel Orthodontic Soc.; NZ Orthodontic Soc.; European Orthodontic Soc.; Membre d'Honneur, Société Française d'Orthopédie Dento-faciale. Colyer Gold Medal, RCS, 1975. *Publications:* numerous contributions to learned journals, 1948-. *Recreations:* golf, gardening. *Address:* Winnards Perch, Ridge, Wareham, Dorset BH20 5BQ. *T:* Wareham 3346.

BALLARD, Geoffrey Horace, CBE 1978; JP; Managing Director: G. H. Ballard (Farms) Ltd; G. H. Ballard (Leasing) Ltd; Chairman, M.S.F. (Meats) Ltd; Vice-Chairman: M.S.F. Ltd; Woodbury Growers Ltd; *b* 21 May 1927; *s* of Horace and Mary Catherine Ballard; *m* 1948, Dorothy Sheila Bache; two *s* one *d. Educ:* Hanley Castle Grammar Sch. Farming with father at Home Farm, Abberley, 1943; Maesllwch Castle Estates: Cowman, 1947, Bailiff, 1948; in partnership with father and brother at Home Farm, 1950; farming, on own account, at Old Yates Farm, Abberley, 1953; Nuffield Farming Schol. to USA, 1965. Chm., W Midlands Reg. panel for Agric., 1972-80. Chm., Worcestershire County NFU, 1967. JP 1967-. *Recreations:* sailing, shooting. *Address:* Old Yates, Abberley, Worcester WR6 6AT. *T:* Great Witley 307. *Clubs:* Farmers'; Dale Sailing (Dyfed); Astley and District Farmers Discussion (Worcs).

BALLARD, Ronald Alfred; Head of Technical Services of the Central Computers and Telecommunications Agency, HM Treasury (formerly Civil Service Department), since 1980; *b* 17 Feb. 1925; *s* of Joseph William and Ivy Amy Ballard; *m* 1948, Eileen Margaret Edwards; one *d. Educ:* Univ. of Birmingham (BSc (Hons) Physics). National Service, RN, 1945-47. Admiralty Surface Weapons Establishment, Portsmouth: Scientific Officer, then Sen. Scientific Officer, Research and Development Seaborne Radar Systems, 1948-55; Application of Computers to Naval Comd and Control Systems, 1955-69; PSO, 1960, responsibilities for Action Data Automation (ADA), on HMS Eagle and destroyers; SPSO, to Head Computer Systems and Techniques in Civil Service Dept (Central Computers Agency in 1972), 1969; Head of Central Computers Facility, 1972-76; DCSO, to Head Technical Services Div. of Central Computers Agency, 1977; CSO(B), 1980-. *Address:* Central Computer and Telecommunications Agency, Riverwalk House, 157-161 Millbank, SW1P 4RT.

BALLENTYNE, Donald Francis; HM Diplomatic Service; Counsellor, East Berlin, since 1982; *b* 5 May 1929; *s* of late Henry Q. Ballentyne and Frances R. MacLaren; *m* 1950, Elizabeth Heywood, *d* of Leslie A. Heywood; one *s* one *d. Educ:* Haberdashers' Aske's Hatcham Sch. FO, 1950-53; Berne and Ankara, 1953-56; Consul: Munich, 1957; Stanleyville, 1961; Cape Town, 1962; First Secretary: Luxembourg, 1965-69, Havana, 1969-72; FCO, 1972-74; Counsellor (Commercial), The Hague, 1974-78, Bonn, 1978-81. *Recreation:* sailing. *Address:* c/o Foreign and Commonwealth Office, SW1.

BALME, Prof. David Mowbray, CMG 1955; DSO 1943; DFC 1943; MA; Professor of Classics, Queen Mary College, London University, 1964-78, retired; *b* 8 Sept. 1912; *s* of late Harold Balme, OBE, MD, FRCS; *m* 1936, Beatrice Margaret Rice; four *s* one *d. Educ:* Marlborough; Clare Coll., Cambridge. Res. Student, Clare Coll. and Univ. of Halle, Germany, 1934-36; Lecturer, Reading Univ., 1936-37; Research Fellow, Clare Coll., Cambridge, 1937-40; Fellow of Jesus Coll., 1940. Served with No 207 (Bomber) Squadron, 1943; Comd Nos 227 and 49 Squadrons, 1945. Tutor of Jesus Coll., 1945-47; Senior Tutor, 1947-48; University Lecturer in Classics, 1947-48; Principal, University College of Ghana, 1948-57; Reader in Classics, Queen Mary Coll., London, 1957-64. Vis. Prof., Princeton Univ., 1973. Hon. LLD Lincoln, Pa, 1955; Hon. LittD Ghana, 1970. *Publications:* Aristotle's De Partibus Animalium, I, 1972; articles in classical journals on Greek Philosophy. *Recreations:* music, foxhunting. *Address:* Gumley, near Market Harborough, Leics. *T:* Kibworth 2762.

BALMER, Sir Joseph (Reginald), Kt 1965; JP; Retired Insurance Official; *b* 22 Sept. 1899; *s* of Joseph Balmer; *m* 1927, Dora, *d* of A. Johnson; no *c. Educ:* King Edward's Grammar Sch., Birmingham. North British and Mercantile Insurance Co. Ltd, 1916-60; National Chairman Guild of Insurance Officials, 1943-47. Pres. Birmingham Borough Labour Party, 1946-54; elected to Birmingham City Council, 1945, 1949, 1952; Alderman 1952-74; Chairman Finance Cttee, 1955-64; Lord Mayor of Birmingham, 1954-55; Hon. Alderman, 1974; City Magistrate, 1956. Hon. Life Mem. Court, Birmingham Univ.; formerly Governor, King Edward VI Schs, Birmingham; Member or ex-member various cttees. Served European War, 1914-18, overseas with RASC and Somerset Light Infantry. *Recreations:* gardening, woodwork and reading. *Address:* 26 Stechford Lane, Ward End, Birmingham B8 2AN. *T:* 021-783 3198.

BALMFORTH, Ven. Anthony James; Archdeacon of Bristol, since 1979; *b* 3 Sept. 1926; *s* of Joseph Henry and Daisy Florence Balmforth; *m* 1952, Eileen Julia, *d* of James Raymond and Kitty Anne Evans; one *s* two *d. Educ:* Sebright School, Wolverley; Brasenose Coll., Oxford (BA 1950, MA 1951); Lincoln Theological Coll. Army service, 1944-48. Deacon 1952, priest 1953, dio. Southwell; Curate of Mansfield, 1952-55; Vicar of Skegby, Notts, 1955-61; Vicar of St John's, Kidderminster, Worcs, 1961-65; Rector of St Nicolas, King's Norton, Birmingham, 1965-79; Hon. Canon of Birmingham Cathedral, 1975-79; RD of King's Norton, 1973-79; Examining Chaplain to: Bishop of Birmingham, 1978-79; Bishop of Bristol, 1981-. Hon. Canon of Bristol Cathedral, 1979-. *Recreations:* cricket, gardening. *Address:* 10 Great Brockeridge, Westbury-on-Trym, Bristol BS9 3TY. *T:* Bristol 622438.

BALNIEL, Lord; Anthony Robert Lindsay; *b* 24 Nov. 1958; *s* and *heir* of 29th Earl of Crawford and 12th of Balcarres, *qv. Educ:* Eton Coll.; Univ. of Edinburgh. *Address:* 107 Frognal, NW3.

BALOGH, family name of **Baron Balogh.**

BALOGH, Baron *cr* 1968 (Life Peer), of Hampstead; **Thomas Balogh,** MA, Dr rer. pol. Budapest; Hon. Dr econ. Budapest, 1979; Dr *hc* econ. York Univ., Toronto, 1980; Fellow Emeritus of Balliol College, Oxford, 1973; *b* Budapest, 2 Nov. 1905; *e s* of Emil Balogh; *m* 1945, Penelope (marr. diss. 1970), *widow* of Oliver Gatty, sometime Fellow of Balliol; two *s* one *d* one step-*d* ; *m* 1970, Catherine Storr; three step-*d. Educ:* The Gymnasium of Budapest Univ.; Univs of Budapest, Berlin, Harvard. Fellow of Hungarian Coll., Berlin, 1927; Rockefeller Fellow, 1928-30; League of Nations, 1931; economist in the City, 1931-39; National Institute of Economic Research, 1938-42; Oxford Univ. Institute of Statistics, 1940-55; Special Lecturer, 1955-60; Fellow of Balliol Coll., Oxford, 1945-73; Reader in Econs, Oxford Univ., 1960-73; Leverhulme Fellow, Oxford, 1973-76; Senior Research Associate, Queen Elizabeth House, Oxford, 1979-. Visiting Prof., Minnesota and Wisconsin, 1951; Delhi and Calcutta, 1955. Consultant: Reserve Bank of Australia, 1942-64; UNRRA Mission to Hungary, 1946; Govt of Malta, 1955-57, of Jamaica, 1956, 1961-62; Food and Agricultural Organisation of UN, 1957-59, 1961-62; UN Economic Commn for Latin America, 1960; Government of India Statistical Inst., 1960, 1971; Greece, 1962; Mauritius, 1962-63; UN Special Fund, 1964, 1970, 1971; OECD, 1964; Turkey, Peru, 1964. Member, Economic and Financial Cttee of the Labour Party, 1943-64, 1971-; Mem. and acting Chm., Minerals Cttee, Min. of Fuel and Power, 1964-68; Economic Advr to Cabinet, 1964-67; Consultant to Prime Minister, 1968; Minister of State, Dept of Energy, 1974-75. Dep. Chm., BNOC, 1976-78, Economic Adviser, 1978-79. Chm., Fabian Soc., 1970. Fellow, New York Univ., 1969; Fellow, W. Wilson Center, Washington, 1976. Hon. Res. Fellow, UCL, 1980-81. Mem., Hungarian Acad. of Science. *Publications:* Hungarian Reconstruction and the Reparation Question, 1946; Studies in Financial Organisation, 1946; Dollar Crisis, 1949; Planning through the Price Mechanism, 1950; (with D. Seers) The Economic Future of Malta (Valetta), 1955; Planning and Monetary Organisation in Jamaica, 1956; The Economic Problem of Iraq, 1957; The Economic Development of the Mediterranean (as Head of a Research team), 1957; Economic Policy and Price Mechanism, 1961; Development Plans in Africa, 1961; (with M. Bennett) Sugar Industry in Mauritius; Unequal Partners, 2 vols, 1963; Planning for Progress, 1963; Economics of Poverty, 1966; Labour and Inflation, 1970; Fact and Fancy: an essay in monetary reform, 1973; (co-author): Economics of Full Employment, 1945; War Economics, 1947; Foreign Economic Policy for the US; Fabian International and Colonial Essays; The Establishment, 1960; Crisis in the Civil Service, 1968; Keynes College Essays, 1976, 1978, 1980; (co-author) Crisis of Capitalism, 1978; The Irrelevance of Conventional Economics, 1982; papers in Economic Journal, Bulletin of Oxford Institute of Statistics, etc. *Address:* The Cottage, Christmas Common, Watlington, Oxon. *Club:* Reform.

BALSTON, Antony Francis; a Recorder of the Crown Court, since 1980; Partner in Herington Willings & Penry Davey, Solicitors of Hastings, since 1967; *b* 18 Jan. 1939; *s* of Comdr E. F. Balston, DSO, RN, and D. B. L. Balston (*née* Ferrers); *m* 1966, Anne Marie Judith Ball; two *s* one *d. Educ:* Downside; Christ's Coll., Cambridge (MA). Served Royal Navy, 1957-59; Univ. of Cambridge, 1959-62; admitted Solicitor, 1966. *Recreation:* gardening. *Address:* Elmside, Northiam, Rye, East Sussex TN31 6NS. *T:* Northiam 2270.

BALTIMORE, Prof. David, PhD; Professor of Biology, Massachusetts Institute of Technology, since 1972; American Cancer Society Professor of Microbiology, since 1973; Director, Whitehead Institute, since 1982; *b* New York, 7 March 1938; *s* of Richard and Gertrude Baltimore; *m* 1968, Alice Huang; one *d. Educ:* Swarthmore Coll.; Rockefeller Univ. Postdoctoral Fellow, MIT, 1963-64; Albert Einstein Coll. of Med., NY, 1964-65; Research Associate, Salk Inst., La Jolla, Calif, 1965-68; Associate Prof., MIT, 1968-72 FAAAS 1980. Member: Nat. Acad. of Scis, 1974; Amer. Acad. of Arts and Scis, 1974. Eli Lilly Award in Microbiology and Immunology, 1971; US Steel Foundn Award in Molecular Biology, 1974; (jtly) Nobel Prize for Physiology or Medicine, 1975. *Address:* Center for Cancer Research, Massachusetts Institute of Technology, Cambridge, Mass 02139, USA.

BAMBERG, Harold Rolf, CBE 1968; Chairman, Bamberg Group Ltd and other companies, including Eagle Aircraft Services Ltd; *b* 17 Nov. 1923; *m* 1957, June Winifred Clarke; one *s* two *d* (and one *s* one *d* of a former marriage). *Educ:* Fleet Sch.; William Ellis Sch., Hampstead. FRSA. *Recreations:* polo, shooting, bloodstock breeding. *Address:* Harewood Park Sunninghill, Berks.

BAMBOROUGH, John Bernard; Principal of Linacre College, Oxford, since 1962; Pro-Vice-Chancellor, Oxford University, since 1966; *b* 3 Jan. 1921; *s* of John George Bamborough; *m* 1947, Anne, *d* of Olav Indrehus, Indrehus Norway; one *s* one *d. Educ:* Haberdashers' Aske's Hampstead Sch. (Scholar) New College, Oxford (Scholar). 1st Class, English Language and Literature 1941; MA 1946. Service in RN, 1941-46 (in Coastal Forces as Lieut RNVR afterwards as Educ. Officer with rank of Instructor Lieut, RN). Junior Lectr New Coll., Oxford, 1946; Fellow and Tutor, Wadham Coll., Oxford 1947-62 (Dean, 1947-54; Domestic Bursar, 1954-56; Sen. Tutor, 1957-61 Univ. Lectr in English, 1951-62; Mem. Hebdomadal Council, Oxford Univ 1961-79. Hon. Fellow, New Coll., Oxford, 1967. Editor, Review of Englis Studies, 1964-78. *Publications:* The Little World of Man, 1952; Ben Jonson 1959; (ed) Pope's Life of Ward, 1961; Jonson's Volpone, 1963; The Alchemis 1967; Ben Jonson, 1970. *Address:* 40 St Giles', Oxford. *T:* 59886. *Club* United Oxford & Cambridge University.

BAMFIELD, Clifford, CB 1981; Under Secretary, Civil Service Department, 1974–80; *b* 21 March 1922; *s* of G. H. Bamfield. *Educ:* Wintringham Grammar Sch., Grimsby. Served War, RNVR, 1941–46. Customs and Excise: Clerical Officer, 1939; Exec. Officer, 1946; Private Sec. to Chm., 1959–61; Principal, 1961; Asst Sec., 1967; Under Sec., Comr and Dir of Estabs, 1973. *Address:* 15 The Linkway, Sutton, Surrey SM2 5SE. *T:* 01-642 5377. *Club:* Army and Navy.

BAMFORD, Anthony Paul; Chairman and Managing Director, J. C. Bamford Group, since 1976; *b* 23 Oct. 1945; *s* of Joseph Cyril Bamford, *qv* ; *m* 1974, Carole Gray Whitt; two *s* one *d. Educ:* Ampleforth Coll.; Grenoble Univ. Joined JCB on shop floor, 1962; led company's only takeover so far, Chaseside Engineering, 1968; launched JCB's French company and received a Young Exporter of the Year award for the achievement, 1972. Young Businessman of the Year, 1979. *Recreations:* riding, farming. *Address:* c/o J. C. Bamford Excavators Ltd, Rocester, Uttoxeter, Staffs ST14 5JP. *T:* Rocester 590312. *Clubs:* Lighthouse, British Racing Drivers'.

BAMFORD, Prof. Clement Henry, FRS 1964; MA, PhD, ScD Cantab; CChem, FRSC; Honorary Research Fellow, Bioengineering and Medical Physics Unit, University of Liverpool, since 1980; Campbell Brown Professor of Industrial Chemistry, University of Liverpool, 1962–80, now Emeritus Professor; *b* 10 Oct. 1912; *s* of Frederic Jesse Bamford and Catherine Mary Bamford (*née* Shelley), Stafford; *m* 1938, Daphne Ailsa Stephan, BSc Sydney, PhD Cantab, of Sydney, Australia; one *s* one *d. Educ:* St Patrick's and King Edward VI Schs, Stafford; Trinity Coll., Cambridge (Senior Scholar). Fellow, Trinity Coll., Cambridge, 1937; Dir of Studies in Chemistry, Emmanuel Coll., Cambridge, 1937. Joined Inter-Services Research Bureau, 1941; joined Fundamental Research Laboratory of Messrs Courtaulds Ltd, at Maidenhead, 1945; head of laboratory, 1947–62; Liverpool University: Dean, Faculty of Science, 1965–68; Pro-Vice-Chancellor, 1972–75. Member: Council, Chem. Soc., 1972–75; Council, Soc. Chem. Ind., 1974–75. Pres., British Assoc. Section B (Chemistry), 1975–76; Vice-Pres., 1977–81, Pres., 1981–, Macromolecular Div., Internat. Union of Pure and Applied Chemistry. Vis. Professor: Kyoto Univ., 1977; Univ. of NSW, 1981. Mem. Edit. Bd, Polymer, 1958–. Hon. DSc Bradford, 1980. Meldola Medal, Royal Inst. of Chemistry, 1941; Macromolecules and Polymers Award, Chemical Soc., 1977. *Publications:* Synthetic Polypeptides (with A. Elliott and W. E. Hanby), 1956; The Kinetics of Vinyl Polymerization by Radical Mechanisms (with W. G. Barb, A. D. Jenkins and P. F. Onyon), 1958; (ed with C. F. H. Tipper) Comprehensive Chemical Kinetics (series), 1969–; papers on physical chemistry and polymer science in learned journals. *Recreations:* music, especially playing violin in string quartets, hill walking, gardening. *Address:* Broom Bank, Tower Road, Prenton, Birkenhead, Merseyside L42 8LH. *T:* 051-608 3979.

BAMFORD, Joseph Cyril, CBE 1969; formerly Chairman and Managing Director: J. C. Bamford Excavators Ltd; JCB Farms Ltd; JCB Research Ltd; JCB Sales Ltd; JCB Service; JCB Earthmovers Ltd; *b* 21 June 1916; *m* 1941, Marjorie Griffin; two *s. Educ:* St John's, Alton, Staffs; Stonyhurst Coll. Founded J. C. Bamford Excavators Ltd, 1945; more than seventy per cent of total production now goes to export market. *Recreations:* yacht designing, landscaping, landscape gardening. *Address:* 16 Rue de Bourg, CH 1003 Lausanne, Switzerland.

See also A. P. Bamford.

BAMFORD, Louis Neville Jules; Legal Executive with Margetts & Ritchie, Solicitors, Birmingham, since 1960; Chairman, West Midlands County Council, since 1981; *b* 2 July 1932; *s* of Neville Barnes Bamford and Elise Marie Bamford; unmarried. *Educ:* local schools in Birmingham. Elected Mem. (Lab) Birmingham CC, 1971 (Mem., Airport Police Cttee); elected Birmingham DC, 1974 (Mem., Land and Finance Cttees); elected W Midlands CC; Chm., Legal and Parly Cttee, 1974–77; formerly Member: Police Cttee and No 4 Dist Police Authorities Cttee; Finance, Fire, and Personnel and Admin Cttees. *Recreations:* football, cricket, reading, music (classical and jazz). *Address:* County Hall, 1 Lancaster Circus, Queensway, Birmingham B4 7DJ.

BAMPFYLDE, family name of **Baron Poltimore.**

BANANA, Rev. Canaan Sodindo; President of Zimbabwe, since 1980; *b* 5 March 1936; *s* of Aaron and Jese Banana; *m* 1961, Janet Mbuyazwe; three *s. Educ:* Mzinyati Mission; Tegwani High Sch.; Epworth Theol Coll., Salisbury; Wesley Theol Seminary, Washington, DC; Univ. of SA. MTS Hons, Wesley Theol Seminary; BTh Univ. of SA; Dip. Urban & Industrial Mission, Kansai Industrial Centre, Japan. Methodist Minister and Manager of Schools: Wankie Area, 1963–64; Plumtree Area, 1965–66 (Sch. Chaplain); Methodist Minister, Fort Viet Area, 1967–68; Methodist Minister, Bulawayo and Chm., Bulaway Council of Churches, 1969–70; resigned from Methodist Church over differences regarding WCC aid to liberation gps, 1971; with Mambo Press as Promotion Officer for Moto, Catholic newspaper, 1971; Deputy Pres., ANC, 1971–73; Chaplain, American Univ., 1973–75; Publicity Sec., People's Movement Internal Co-ordinating Cttee, ZANU, 1976–77. Chm., Southern Africa Contact Gp, 1970–73; Mem., Adv. Cttee, WCC, 1970–80. *Publications:* The Zimbabwe Exodus, 1974; The Gospel According to the Ghetto, 1974, 3rd edn 1980; The Woman of my Imagination, 1980; various articles. *Recreations:* tennis, volley ball, football, music. *Address:* State House, Box 368, Salisbury, Zimbabwe. *T:* Salisbury 26666.

BANBURY, family name of **Baron Banbury of Southam.**

BANBURY OF SOUTHAM, 3rd Baron *cr* 1924, of Southam; **Charles William Banbury;** Bt 1902; *b* 29 July 1953; *s* of 2nd Baron Banbury of Southam and of Hilda Ruth, *d* of late A. H. R. Carr; *S* father, 1981. *Educ:* Eton College. *Heir:* none. *Address:* The Mill, Fossebridge, Glos.

BANBURY, (Frederick Harold) Frith; Theatrical director, producer and actor; *b* 4 May 1912; *s* of Rear-Adm. Frederick Arthur Frith Banbury and Winifred (*née* Fink); unmarried. *Educ:* Stowe Sch.; Hertford Coll., Oxford; Royal Academy of Dramatic Art. First stage appearance in "If I Were You", Shaftesbury Theatre, 1933; for next 14 years appeared both in London and Provinces in every branch of theatre from Shakespeare to revue. Appearances included: Hamlet, New Theatre, 1934; Goodness How Sad, Vaudeville, 1938; (revue) New Faces, Comedy, 1939; Uncle Vanya, Westminster, 1943; Jacobowsky and the Colonel, Piccadilly, 1945; Caste, Duke of York's, 1947. During this time he also appeared in numerous films including The Life and Death of Colonel Blimp and The History of Mr Polly, and also on the television screen. Since 1947 he has devoted his time to production and direction, starting with Dark Summer at Lyric, Hammersmith (later transferred St Martin's), 1947; subseq. many, in both London and New York, including The Holly and the Ivy, Duchess, 1950; Waters of the Moon, Haymarket, 1951; The Deep Blue Sea, Duchess, 1951, and Morosco, New York, 1952; A Question of Fact, Piccadilly, 1953; Marching Song, St Martin's, 1954; Love's Labour's Lost, Old Vic, 1954; The Diary of Anne Frank, Phoenix, 1956; A Dead Secret, Piccadilly, 1957; Flowering Cherry, Haymarket, 1957, and Lyceum, New York, 1959; A Touch of the Sun, Saville, 1958; The Ring of Truth, Savoy, 1959; The Tiger and the Horse, Queen's, 1960; The Wings of the Dove, Lyric, 1963; The Right Honourable Gentleman, Billy Rose, New York, 1965; Howards End, New, 1967; Dear Octopus, Haymarket, 1967; Enter A Free Man, St Martin's, 1968; A Day In the Death of Joe Egg, Cameri Theatre, Tel Aviv, 1968; Le Velet, Théâtre de la Renaissance, Paris, 1968; On the Rocks, Dublin Theatre Festival, 1969; My Darling Daisy, Lyric, 1970; The Winslow Boy, New, 1970; Captain Brassbound's Conversion, Cambridge, 1971; Reunion in Vienna, Chichester Festival, 1971, Piccadilly, 1972; The Day After the Fair, Lyric, 1972, Shubert, Los Angeles, 1973; Glasstown, Westminster, 1973; Ardèle, Queen's, 1975; On Approval, Canada and SA, 1976, Vaudeville, 1977; directed in Australia, Kenya, USA, 1978–79; Motherdear, Ambassadors, 1980; Dear Liar, Mermaid, 1982. *Recreation:* playing the piano. *Address:* 4 St James's Terrace, Prince Albert Road, NW8. *T:* 01-722 8481.

BANBURY, Frith; see Banbury, Frederick Harold F.

BANCROFT, family name of **Baron Bancroft.**

BANCROFT, Baron *cr* 1982 (Life Peer), of Coatham in the county of Cleveland; **Ian Powell Bancroft,** GCB 1979 (KCB 1975; CB 1971); former Head of the Home Civil Service and Permanent Secretary to the Civil Service Department, retired November 1981; *b* 23 Dec. 1922; *s* of A. E. and L. Bancroft; *m* 1950, Jean Swaine; two *s* one *d. Educ:* Coatham Sch.; Balliol Coll., Oxford (Scholar; Hon. Fellow 1981). Served Rifle Brigade, 1942–45. Entered Treasury, 1947; Private Secretary: to Sir Henry Wilson Smith, 1948–50; to Chancellor of the Exchequer, 1953–55; to Lord Privy Seal, 1955–57; Cabinet Office, 1957–59; Principal Private Sec. to successive Chancellors of the Exchequer, 1964–66; Under-Sec., HM Treasury, 1966–68, Civil Service Dept, 1968–70; Dep. Sec., Dir Gen. of Organization and Establishments, DoE, 1970–72; a Comr of Customs and Excise, and Dep. Chm. of Bd, 1972–73; Second Permanent Sec., CSD, 1973–75; Permanent Sec., DoE, 1975–77. Dir, Rugby Portland Cement Co. Ltd. Vis. Fellow, Nuffield Coll., Oxford, 1973–81; Chm. Council, Mansfield Coll. Oxford. Governor and Mem. Bd of Management, Royal Hosp. and Home for Incurables. *Address:* 4 Melrose Road, West Hill, SW18. *Club:* United Oxford & Cambridge University.

BAND, Robert Murray Niven, MC 1944; QC 1974; **His Honour Judge Band;** a Circuit Judge, since 1978; *b* 23 Nov. 1919; *s* of Robert Niven Band and Agnes Jane Band; *m* 1948, Nancy Margery Redhead; two *d. Educ:* Trinity Coll., Glenalmond; Hertford Coll., Oxford (MA). Served in Royal Artillery, 1940–46. Called to the Bar, Inner Temple, 1947; Junior Treasury Counsel in Probate Matters, 1972–74; Chm. Family Law Bar Assoc., 1972–74; a Recorder of the Crown Court, 1977–78. Chm., St Teresa's Hosp., Wimbledon. *Recreations:* the countryside, gardens, old buildings, treen. *Address:* Well Farm, Banstead, Surrey. *T:* Burgh Heath 52288.

BANDA, Hastings Kamuzu, MD, (**His Excellency Ngwazi Dr H. Kamuzu Banda**); President of Malaŵi since 1966, Life President, 1971; Chancellor, University of Malaŵi, since 1965; Life President, Malaŵi Congress Party; *b* 14 May 1906. *Educ:* Meharry Medical Coll., Nashville, USA (MD); Universities of Glasgow and Edinburgh. Further degrees: BSc, MB, ChB, LRCSE; and several hon. degrees awarded later. Practised medicine in Liverpool and on Tyneside during War of 1939–45 and in London, 1945–53. Returned to Africa, 1953, and practised in Gold Coast. Took over leadership of Nyasaland African Congress in Blantyre, 1958, and became Pres.-Gen.; was imprisoned for political reasons, 1959; unconditionally released, 1960; Minister of Natural Resources and Local Government, Nyasaland, 1961–63; Prime Minister of Malaŵi (formerly Nyasaland), 1963–66. *Address:* Office of the President, Lilongwe, Malaŵi.

BANDARANAIKE, Mrs Sirimavo; Member of Parliament of Sri Lanka, 1960-80; Prime Minister of Sri Lanka (Ceylon until 1972), 1960-65, and 1970-77, also Minister of Defence and Foreign Affairs, of Planning and Economic Affairs, and of Plan Implementation; President, Sri Lanka Freedom Party, since 1960; *b* 17 April 1916; *d* of Barnes Ratwatte, Ratemahatmaya of Ratnapura Dist, Mem. of Ceylon Senate; *m* 1940, Solomon West Ridgeway Dias Bandaranaike (*d* 1959), Prime Minister of Ceylon, 1956-59; one *s* two d. *Educ:* Ratnapura Ferguson Sch.; St Bridget's Convent, Colombo. Assisted S. W. R. D. Bandaranaike in political career. Campaigned for Sri Lanka Freedom Party in election campaigns, March and July 1960. Formerly Pres. and Treasurer, Lanka Mahila Samiti. Prime Minister of Ceylon, also Minister of Defence and External Affairs, 1960-65; Minister of Information and Broadcasting, 1964-65; Leader of the Opposition, 1965-70. Ceres Medal, FAO, 1977. *Address:* Horagolla, Nittambuwa, Sri Lanka.

BANERJEE, Rabindra Nath, CSI 1946; CIE 1938; Chairman, Union Public Service Commission, India, 1949-55, retired; *b* 1 Feb 1895; *s* of late Haradhan Banerjee; *m* Manisha (*d* 1953) *d* of late Lieut-Col Upendra Nath Mukerjee, IMS; one *s* one d. *Educ:* Calcutta Univ. (MA 1915); Emmanuel Coll., Cambridge (BA 1918). Entered Indian Civil Service, 1920; Registrar Co-operative Societies and Dir Of Industries, Central Provinces and Berar, 1929-33; Vice-Chm. Provincial Banking Enquiry Cttee, 1929; Sec. to Govt, Central Provinces and Berar, Revenue Dept, 1933; Sec. to Govt, CP and Berar, Local Self-Government Dept, 1936; Mem. CP and Berar Legislative Council, 1929-36; Sec. to the Governor, CP and Berar, 1937; Commissioner, 1941; Commissioner of Food Supply, 1943; Sec. to Govt of India, Commonwealth Relations Dept and Min. of Home Affairs, 1944-48. Mem. Council of State (India), 1944, 1945, 1947; MLA (India), 1946. Mem. of Cttee of Experts of International Labour Organisation, 1956-58. *Address:* 17 Friends' Colony, Mathura Road, New Delhi, India. *T:* New Delhi 630220.

BANGHAM, Alec Douglas, FRS 1977; MD; Research Worker, Agricultural Research Council, Institute of Animal Physiology, Babraham, 1952-82 and Head, Biophysics Unit, 1971-82; *b* 10 Nov. 1921; *s* of Dr Donald Hugh and Edith Bangham; *m* 1943, Rosalind Barbara Reiss; three *s* one d. *Educ:* Bryanston Sch.; UCL and UCH Med. Sch. (MD). Captain, RAMC, 1946-48. Lectr, Dept of Exper. Pathology, UCH, 1949-52; Principal Scientific Officer, 1952-63, Senior Principal Scientific Officer (Merit Award), 1963-82, ARC, Babraham. Fellow, UCL, 1981-. *Publications:* contrib. Nature, Biochim. Biophys. Acta, and Methods in Membrane Biol. *Recreations:* horticulture, photographic arts, sailing. *Address:* 17 High Green, Great Shelford, Cambridge. *T:* Cambridge 843192.

BANGOR, 7th Viscount *cr* 1781; **Edward Henry Harold Ward;** Baron, 1770; free-lance journalist (as Edward Ward); *b* 5 Nov. 1905; *s* of 6th Viscount Bangor, PC (Northern Ireland), OBE and Agnes Elizabeth (*d* 1972), 3rd *d* of late Dacre Hamilton of Cornacassa, Monaghan; *S* father, 1950; *m* 1st, 1933, Elizabeth (who obtained a divorce, 1937), *e d* of T. Balfour, Wrockwardine Hall, Wellington, Salop; 2nd, 1937, Mary Kathleen (marr. diss. 1947), *d* of W. Middleton, Shanghai; 3rd, 1947, Leila Mary (marr. diss. 1951; she died, 1959), *d* of David R. Heaton, Brookfield, Crownhill, S Devon; one *s* ; 4th, 1951, Mrs Marjorie Alice Simpson, *d* of late Peter Banks, St Leonards-on-Sea; one *s* one d. *Educ:* Harrow; RMA, Woolwich. Formerly Reuter's correspondent in China and the Far East; BBC War Correspondent in Finland, 1939-40, ME, 1940-41, and Foreign Correspondent all over world, 1946-60. *Publications:* 1940 Despatches from Finland, 1946; Give Me Air, 1946; Chinese Crackers, 1957; The New Eldorado, 1957; Oil is Where They Find It, 1959; Sahara Story, 1962; Number One Boy, 1969; I've Lived like a Lord, 1970. With his wife, Marjorie Ward: Europe on Record, 1950; The US and Us 1951; Danger is Our Business, 1955. *Heir: s* Hon. William Maxwell David Ward [*b* 9 Aug. 1948; *m* 1976, Mrs Sarah Bradford]. *Address:* 59 Cadogan Square, SW1. *T:* 01-235 3202. *Clubs:* Savile, Garrick.

BANGOR, Dean of; *see* Rees, Very Rev. J. I.

BANHAM, Mrs Belinda Joan, CBE 1977; JP; Chairman: Paddington and North Kensington Health Authority, since 1981; Kensington and Chelsea and Westminster Family Planning Committee, since 1979 (Member, since 1972); *b* 1917; *d* of Col Charles Unwin and Winifred Unwin; *m* 1939, Terence Middlecott Banham; two *s* two d. *Educ:* privately; West Bank Sch.; Brussels. BSc (Hons) London; Dip. Social Studies London. SRN. Ward and Departmental Sister, Theatre Sister, Night Sister, 1939-51; work in theory and practice, The Problem of the Problem Family, 1954-67; Member, SW Regional Hosp. Board, 1965-74; Chairman: Cornwall and Isles of Scilly HMC, 1967-74; Cornwall and Isles of Scilly AHA, 1974-77. Director, then Hon. Director, Disabled Living Foundn, 1977-. Member, MRC, 1980-; Chm., Standing Cttee on Use of Medical Records for Research (MRC), 1982-. JP Cornwall, later Inner London, 1972. *Publication:* (jtly) (paper) Systems Science in Health Care (NATO Conf., Paris, 1977). *Recreations:* tennis, botany, gardening, theatre; special interest: social deprivation, social deviance, use of operational research in Health Service Management, and resource allocation. *Address:* Ponsmaen, St Feock, Truro, Cornwall TR3 6OG. *T:* Truro 862 275; 70 Vandon Court, Petty France, SW1. *T:* 01-222 0067.

BANHAM, Prof. (Peter) Reyner; Professor of Art History, University of California at Santa Cruz, since 1980; *b* 2 March 1922; *m* 1946, Mary Mullett; one *s* one d. *Educ:* King Edward VI Sch., Norwich; Courtauld Institute of

Art, London. BA 1952, PhD 1958. Bristol Aeroplane Co., 1939-45. Editorial Staff, Architectural Review, 1952-64; Sen. Lectr, University Coll., London 1964, Reader in Architecture, 1967, Prof. of History of Architecture, 1969-76 Chm., Dept of Design Studies, State Univ. of NY at Buffalo, NY, 1976-80 Research Fellow, Graham Foundation (Chicago), 1964-66. Prix Jean Tschumi 1975. *Publications:* Theory and Design in the First Machine Age, 1960; Guide to Modern Architecture, 1962; The New Brutalism, 1966; Architecture of the Well-tempered Environment, 1969; Los Angeles, 1971; (ed) The Asper Papers, 1974; The Age of the Masters: a Personal View of Architecture, 1975 Megastructure, 1976. *Recreations:* indistinguishable from daily interests in architecture and design. *Address:* Porter College, University of California a\ Santa Cruz, Santa Cruz, Calif 95064, USA.

BANISTER, Stephen Michael Alvin; Secretary, British and Foreign School Society, since 1978; Director, Taylor and Francis Ltd, since 1978; Editor Transport Reviews, since 1981; *b* 7 Oct. 1918; *s* of late Harry Banister and Idwen Banister (*née* Thomas); *m* 1944, Rachel Joan Rawlence; four *s. Educ:* Eton; King's Coll., Cambridge (MA). With Foreign Office, 1939-45; Home Guard (Major, 1944). Asst Principal, Min. of Civil Aviation, 1946; Principal. 1947; Private Sec. to six successive Ministers of Transport and Civil Aviation. 1950-56; Asst Sec., Min. of Transport and BoT, 1956-70; Under Sec., DoE. 1970-76, Dept of Transport, 1976-78. UK Shipping Delegate, UNCTAD, 1964. Mem., Nat. Insurance Tribunal, Kingston upon Thames, 1979-. *Compositions:* (amateur) for singers, including Bluebeard. *Recreations:* countryside, walking, singing (particularly in opera); formerly cricket (Cambridge Crusader); played for CU *v* Australians, 1938. *Address.* Bramshaw, Lower Farm Road, Effingham, Surrey KT24 5JJ. *T:* Bookham 52778.

BANK-ANTHONY, Sir Mobolaji, KBE 1963 (OBE 1956); Company Director, Lagos, Nigeria; *b* 11 June 1907; *e s* of Alfred Bank-Anthony and Rabiatu Aleshinloye Williams, Lagos; *m* 1935, Olamide Adeshigbin. *Educ:* Methodist Boys' High Sch., Lagos; CMS Gram. Sch., Lagos; Ijebu-Ode Gram. Sch. Postal Clerk in Nigerian P & T Dept, 1924; course in Palm Oil cultivation methods, in England, 1931-33, when returned Nigeria, and gradually built up extensive business, opening stores in many parts of Lagos Dir of some leading local companies. Fellow of Royal Commonwealth Society; FRSA, FInstD. Stella della Solidarieta (Italy), 1957. *Recreations:* working, reading, newspapers, dancing. *Address:* Executive House, 2a Oil Mill Street, Lagos, Nigeria. *T:* Lagos 24660, 24669; Fountainpen House, 29 Okotie-Eboh Street, Ikoyi, Lagos, Nigeria. *T:* Lagos 21900 and 21363. *Clubs.* Royal Automobile (London); Rotary, Metropolitan, Island, Lagos Race. Lagos Motor, Lagos Amateur Cricket, Yoruba Tennis, Skal, Lodge Academic (Lagos).

BANKS, family name of **Baron Banks.**

BANKS, Baron *cr* 1974 (Life Peer), of Kenton in Greater London; **Desmond Anderson Harvie Banks,** CBE 1972; President, Liberal European Action Group, since 1971; Deputy Liberal Whip, House of Lords, since 1977; *b* 23 Oct. 1918; *s* of James Harvie Banks, OBE and Sheena Muriel Watt; *m* 1948 Barbara Wells; two *s. Educ:* Alpha Prep. Sch.; University College Sch. Served with KRRC and RA, 1939-46, Middle East and Italy (Major); Chief Public Relations Officer to Allied Mil. Govt, Trieste, 1946. Joined Canada Life Assce Co., subseq. Life Assoc. of Scotland; life assce broker from 1959; Dir, Tweddle French & Co. (Life & Pensions) Ltd, 1973-. Liberal Party: Pres., 1968-69 Chm. Exec., 1961-63 and 1969-70; Dir of Policy Promotion, 1972-74; Chm Res. Cttee, 1966; Hon. Sec., Home Counties Liberal Fedn, 1960-61; Chm. Working Party on Machinery of Govt, 1977-74; Mem., For. Affairs and Social Security Panels, 1961-; Hon. Sec., Liberal Candidates Assoc., 1947-52 contested (L): Harrow East, 1950; St Ives, 1955; SW Herts, 1959. Vice-Chm. Liberal Party Standing Cttee, 1973-79; Liberal spokesman on social services 1977-; Vice-Chairman: European Atlantic Gp, 1979-; British Council European Movement, 1979-. Elder, United Reformed Church. *Publications* Clyde Steamers, 1947, 2nd edn 1951; numerous political pamphlets *Recreations:* pursuing interest in Gilbert and Sullivan opera and in Clyde rive steamers; reading. *Address:* Lincoln House, The Lincolns, Little Kingshill Great Missenden, Bucks HP16 0EH. *T:* Great Missenden 6164. *Club:* National Liberal.

BANKS, Alan George; HM Diplomatic Service, retired; *b* 7 April 1911; *s* of George Arthur Banks and Sarah Napthen; *m* 1946, Joyce Frances Telford Yates; two *s. Educ:* Preston Gram. Sch. Served in HM Forces, 1939-43; a\ Consulate-Gen., Dakar, 1944-45; Actg Consul, Warsaw, 1945-48; HM Vice-Consul: Bordeaux, 1948-50; Istanbul, 1950-52; Zagreb, 1952-55; FO, 1955-58 HM Consul, Split, 1958-60; 1st Sec. and Consul, Madrid, 1960-62; 1st Sec. FO, 1962-67; Consul-General, Alexandria, 1967-71. *Recreations:* classica music, gardening, photography. *Address:* Ferney Field, Parkgate Road Newdigate, Dorking, Surrey. *T:* Newdigate 434. *Club:* MCC.

BANKS, A(rthur) Leslie, MA Cantab; MD London; FRCP; DPH; Barrister at-Law (Lincoln's Inn); Professor of Human Ecology, Cambridge, 1949-71 now Emeritus; Fellow, Gonville and Caius College; *b* 12 Jan. 1904; *o s* of late A. C. and E. M. F. Banks; *m* 1933, Eileen Mary (*d* 1967), *d* of Sidney Barrett Arkley, Herts; two *s. Educ:* Friern Barnet Gram. Sch.; Middlesex Hospital and Medical Sch. Resident hospital appointments, including house-surgeon resident officer to special depts and acting Registrar, Middlesex Hosp. 1926-28; Locum tenens and asst in general practice, Asst Medical Officer, Gen

Post Office, EC1, 1928-34; Divisional Medical Officer, Public Health Dept, LCC (duties included special public health enquiries and slum clearance), 1934-37; Min. of Health, 1937-49; seconded as Medical Officer of Health to City of Newcastle, 1946. Formerly Principal Medical Officer, Min. of Health. First Viscount Bennett prize, Lincoln's Inn, for essay on the Jurisdiction of the Judicial Cttee of the Privy Council. Member: WHO Expert Advisory Panel on Organisation of Med. Care, 1972-76; Hon. Society of Lincoln's Inn; Middlesex Hosp. Club. FRSocMed. *Publications:* Social Aspects of Disease, 1953; (ed) Development of Tropical and Sub-tropical Countries, 1954; (with J. A. Hislop) Health and Hygiene, 1957; (with J. A. Hislop) Art of Administration, 1961; private and official papers on medical and social subjects. *Address:* 4 Heycroft, Eynsham, Oxford. *T:* Oxford 880791.

BANKS, Colin; Founder Partner, Banks and Miles, graphic designers, London and Amsterdam, since 1958; Director, John Marshbank Ltd, publishers; *b* 16 Jan. 1932; *s* of William James Banks and late Ada Jenny (*née* Hood); *m* 1961, Caroline Grigson, PhD; one *s* (one *d* decd). Prodn Editor (with John Miles) of Which? and other Consumers' Assoc. magazines, 1964-. Design Consultant to: Zool Soc., 1962- (FZS); British Council, 1968-; E Midlands Arts Assoc., 1974-; English National Opera, 1975-76; Direct Election Campaign, European Parlt, 1978; (new visual identity for) Post Office: Royal Mail, Telecommunications, etc, 1972-; British Telecom., 1980. Designer/Design Adviser to: Commn for Racial Equality; London Transp.; Central Clearing Banks; other instns and commercial cos. Exhibitions: London, Amsterdam, Glasgow, Brussels, Kyoto. Vice-Pres., SIAD, 1974-76. Mem. Council, Design and Industries Assoc. Lectured in Europe, Japan, SE Asia, USA. FRSA. Heinrick Mann Medals for art editorship, Cambridge History series, 1971. *Publications:* Social Communication, 1979; contrib. jls, London and USA. *Recreation:* India. *Address:* 1 Tranquil Vale, Blackheath, SE3 0BU. *T:* 01-318 1131; Little Town Farmhouse, Wilts. *Clubs:* Arts; Double Crown, Wynkyn de Worde.

BANKS, Air Cdre Francis Rodwell, CB 1946; OBE 1919; RAF (retired); *b* 22 March 1898; *s* of late Bernard Rodwell and Frances Emily Banks; *m* 1925, Christine Constance Grant Langlands; two *d*. *Educ:* Christ's Coll., London, N. Served in two wars, 1914-19 in Navy and 1939-46 in RAF. Between the two wars specialised in the development of aviation engines and their fuels with The Associated Ethyl Co.; responsible in the recent war successively for the production, the research and development of aero engines, including gas turbines, at MAP. Principal Dir of Engine Research and Development, Min. of Supply, 1952-53; Dir, The Bristol Aeroplane Co., 1954-59; Dir, Hawker Siddeley Aviation Ltd, 1954-59, now Engrg Consultant. Pres. RAeS, 1969. CEng; Hon. CGIA; Hon. FRAeS; Hon. FAIAA; FIMechE; FInstPet. *Publications:* I Kept No Diary, memoirs, 1978; technical papers on aviation engines and their fuels. *Recreation:* golf. *Address:* 5a Albert Court, SW7. *T:* 01-584 2740. *Club:* Royal Air Force.

BANKS, Frank David, FCA; Managing Director, Agribusiness Division, Tate & Lyle Ltd, since 1981; *b* 11 April 1933; *s* of Samuel and Elizabeth Banks; *m* 1st, 1955, Catherine Jacob; one *s* two *d*; 2nd, 1967, Sonia Gay Coleman; one *d*. *Educ:* Liverpool Collegiate Sch.; Carnegie Mellon Univ. (PFE). British Oxygen Co. Ltd, 1957-58; Imperial Chemical Industries Ltd, 1959-62; English Electric Co. Ltd, 1963-68; Finance Dir, Platt International Ltd, 1969-71; Industrial Advr, DTI, 1972-73; Constructors John Brown Ltd, 1974-80. *Recreations:* music, history. *Address:* Enterprise House, Holmesdale Road, Bromley, Kent.

BANKS, Mrs Gillian Theresa; Under Secretary, Department of Health and Social Security, since 1981; *b* 7 Feb. 1933; *d* of Percy and Enid Brimblecombe; *m* 1960, John Anthony Gorst Banks; one *s* two *d*. *Educ:* Walthamstow Hall Sch., Sevenoaks; Lady Margaret Hall, Oxford (BA). Asst Principal, Colonial Office, 1955; Principal, Treasury, 1966; Asst Sec., DHSS, 1972. *Recreation:* hill walking. *Address:* 16 Chalcot Square, NW1 8YA. *T:* 01-722 3962.

BANKS, James Dallaway, MA; seconded to Regional and Planning Division, Department of Health and Social Security, 1973-75, retired 1975; *b* 3 Jan. 1917; *s* of late Dr Cyril Banks; *m* 1942, Winifred Holt (*d* 1982); one *s* one *d* (and one *s* decd). *Educ:* Nottingham High Sch.; St John's Coll., Cambridge. BA 1938, MA 1943. Indian Civil Service, 1939-47. Dep. House Governor, King's Coll. Hosp., 1947-53; House Governor: Royal Marsden Hospital 1953-59; The Hospital for Sick Children, Great Ormond Street, 1959-60; Sec. to Bd of Governors, KCH, Denmark Hill, 1960-73. Vis. Fellow, Computer Studies Gp, Univ. of Southampton, 1978-. *Address:* 8 Newenham Road, Lymington, Hants. *T:* Lymington 74999. *Club:* Lymington Town Sailing.

BANKS, Sir Maurice (Alfred Lister), Kt 1971; *b* 11 Aug. 1901; *s* of Alfred Banks, FRCS and Elizabeth Maud (*née* Davey); *m* 1933, Ruth Hall, Philadelphia, USA; one *s* two *d*. *Educ:* Westminster Sch.; Manchester Univ., Coll. of Technology. BSc Tech., FRIC, MIChemE. Coal Research Fellowship under DSIR, 1923; joined Anglo Persian Oil Co., 1924. British Petroleum: a Man. Dir, 1960; a Dep. Chm., 1965; retd from BP, 1967. Chairman: Adv. Council on Calibration for Min. of Technology, 1965-66; Adv. Cttee on Hovercraft for Min. of Technology, 1967-68; Chairman BoT Departmental Cttee to enquire into Patent Law and Procedure, 1967-70; Chm., Laird Gp Ltd, 1970-75. *Recreations:* golf, gardening. *Address:* Beech Coppice, Kingswood, Surrey. *T:* Mogador 2270. *Clubs:* Athenæum; Walton Heath Golf.

BANKS, Richard Alford, CBE 1965; *b* 11 July 1902; *s* of William Hartland Banks, Hergest Croft, Kington, Hereford; *m* 1st, 1937, Lilian Jean (*d* 1974), *d* of Dr R. R. Walker, Presteigne, Radnorshire; two *s* one *d*; 2nd, 1976, Rosamund Gould. *Educ:* Rugby; Trinity Coll., Cambridge (BA). Dir of Imperial Chemical Industries Ltd, 1952-64; Chm. of the Industrial Training Council, 1962-64; Mem., Water Resources Bd, 1964-74. JP Hereford, 1963-73. *Recreations:* arboriculture, gardening and travel. *Address:* Ridgebourne, Kington, Herefordshire.

BANKS, Robert George; MP (C) Harrogate, since Feb. 1974; *b* 18 Jan. 1937; *s* of George Walmsley Banks, MBE, and Olive Beryl Banks (*née* Tyler); *m* 1967, Diana Margaret Payne Crawfurd; four *s* one *d* (of whom one *s* one *d* are twins). *Educ:* Haileybury. Lt-Comdr RNR. Jt Founder Dir, Antocks Lairn Ltd, 1963-67; Partner, Breckland Securities, investment co. Mem., Alcohol Educn and Res. Council, 1982-. Mem., Paddington BC, 1959-65. PPS to Minister of State and to Under-Sec. of State, FCO, 1979-82. Member: Council of Europe, 1977-81; WEU, 1977-81; N Atlantic Assembly, 1981-. Jt Sec., Cons. Defence Cttee, 1976-79; Vice-Chairman: All-Party Tourism Gp, 1979-; All-Party Anglo-Sudan Gp, 1982- (Sec., 1978-82). Introd Licensing (Alcohol Educn and Res.) Act, 1981. *Publication:* (jtly) Britain's Home Defence Gamble, 1979. *Recreations:* travel, farming, architecture. *Address:* House of Commons, SW1A 0AA.

BANKS, Captain William Eric, CBE 1943; DSC; RN retired; *b* 17 July 1900; *er s* of late Walter Banks; *m* 1937, Audrey Steel; two *s*. *Educ:* University Coll. Sch. Joined Navy in 1918; retired list, 1952. *Address:* 2 College Yard, Gloucester. *Club:* Naval and Military.

BANNENBERG, Jon, RDI 1978; AMRINA; *b* Australia, 8 July 1929; *s* of Henryk and Kay Bannenberg; *m* 1960, Beaupré Robinson; two *s*. *Educ:* Canterbury High Sch., Sydney; Sydney Conservatorium of Music. RDI (Motor Yacht Design) 1978. Designed: 'Siècle d'Elégance' Exhibn, Louvre, Paris, 1959; CINOA Exhibn, V&A Museum, London, 1960; Motor and Sail Boat Designs include: Queen Elizabeth 2, 1967; Tiawana, Tamahine, 1968; Carinthia V, Anemos II, 1969; Benedic, 1970; Carinthia VI, Arjuna, Aetos, 1971; Blue Lady, Yellowbird, Firebird, Heron 21, 1972; Stilvi, Pegasus III, 1973; My Gail, Xiphas, Mediterranean Sky, 1974; Boule Dogue, Southern Breeze, 1975; Solitaire, 1976; Majestic, 1977; Rodis Island, Nabila, Cimba, 1979; My Gail II, Nahema, 1981. Member, RYA. *Recreations:* running, swimming, sailing, music, Polynesian and Pacific history. *Address:* 35 Carlyle Square, Chelsea, SW3. *T:* 01-352 6129.

BANNER, Mrs Delmar; *see* Vasconcellos, J. de.

BANNER, Sir George Knowles H.; *see* Harmood-Banner.

BANNERMAN, Lt-Col Sir Donald Arthur Gordon, 13th Bt, *cr* 1682; *b* 2 July 1899; *s* of Lt-Col Sir Arthur D'Arcy Gordon Bannerman, KCVO, CIE, 12th Bt and of late Virginia Emilie Bannerman; *S* father 1955; *m* 1932, Barbara Charlotte, *d* of late Lieut-Col A. Cameron, OBE, IMS; two *s* twin *d*. *Educ:* Harrow; Royal Military Coll., Sandhurst; commissioned into Queen's Own Cameron Highlanders, 1918; served in N Russian Campaign, 1919; 1st Class Interpreter (Russian), 1925; served with 1st and 2nd Bns of his Regt in Egypt and India, 1931-34 and 1936-39; served War of 1939-45: with 4th Indian Div. and in MEF, 1940-43; in NW Europe, 1944, attached to US 9th Army, in closing stages of fighting, and then for 3 yrs with Control Commission as Senior Control Officer; retired from Army as Lieut-Col, 1947. On staff of Gordonstoun Sch., 1948-52, of Fettes Coll., 1952-69. *Publications:* Bannerman of Elsick: a short family history, 1975; Random Recollections, 1980. *Recreations:* gardening, walking, reading. *Heir: s* Alexander Patrick Bannerman [*b* 5 May 1933; *m* 1977, Joan Mary Wilcox]. *Address:* 11 Learmonth Place, Edinburgh EH4 1AX. *T:* 031-332 1076.

BANNISTER, Grace, JP; Lord Mayor of Belfast, 1981-82; *d* of William H. Collim and Grace (*née* Johnston); *m* 1948, John Bannister; one *d*. *Educ:* Park Parade Sch. Belfast County Borough Council, later City Council: Councillor, 1965-; Dep. Lord Mayor, 1975-77; High Sheriff, 1979; Chm., Parks and Cemeteries Cttee, 1969-72 (Dep. Chm., 1966-69, 1972-73); Dep. Chm., Parks and Recreation Cttee, 1973-78; Chm., Parks Cttee, 1978-; Member: Improvement, Educn, Town Planning and Traffic Special Cttees, 1965-73; Gen. Purposes Cttee, 1969-73; Gen. Purposes and Finance Cttee, 1978-81; Leisure Centres/Services Cttee, 1976-81. Member: Belfast, Holywood and Castlereagh Jt Bd, 1969-73; Belfast Educn and Library Area Board, 1973-81. JP Belfast, 1965. *Recreations:* welfare, community work, knitting, pottery, music, school management committees. *Address:* 34 Grand Parade, Belfast BT5 5HH. *T:* Belfast 57879.

BANNISTER, Sir Roger (Gilbert), Kt 1975; CBE 1955; DM (Oxon); FRCP; Consultant Physician: National Hospital for Nervous Diseases, Queen Square, WC1; Department of Nervous Diseases, St Mary's Hospital, W2; Consultant Neurologist, Western Ophthalmic Hospital, NW1; Chairman, Hon. Consultants, King Edward VII Convalescent Home for Officers, Osborne; *b* 23 March 1929; *s* of late Ralph and of Alice Bannister, Harrow; *m* 1955, Moyra Elver, *d* of late Per Jacobsson, Chairman IMF; two *s* two *d*. *Educ:* City of Bath Boys' Sch.; University Coll. Sch., London; Exeter and Merton Colls, Oxford; St Mary's Hospital Medical Sch., London. Amelia Jackson Studentship, Exeter Coll., Oxford, 1947; BA (hons) Physiology, Junior Demonstrator in Physiology, Harmsworth Senior Scholar, Merton

Coll., Oxford, 1950; Open and State Schol., St Mary's Hosp., 1951; BSc Thesis in Physiology, 1952; MRCS, LRCP, 1954; BM, BCh Oxford, 1954; DM Oxford, 1963. William Hyde Award for research relating physical education to medicine; MRCP 1957. Junior Medical Specialist, RAMC, 1958; Radcliffe Travelling Fellowship, at Harvard, USA, 1962-63. Pres. of National Fitness Panel, NABC, 1956-59. Mem. Council, King George's Jubilee Trust, 1961-67; Pres., Sussex Assoc. of Youth Clubs, 1972-79; Chm., Res. Cttee, Adv. Sports Council, 1965-71; Mem., Min. of Health Adv. Cttee on Drug Dependence, 1967-70; Chm., Sports Council, 1971-74; Pres., Internat. Council for Sport and Physical Recreation, 1976-. Chadwick Trust Lectr, 1972. Winner Oxford v Cambridge Mile, 1947-50; Pres. OUAC, 1948; Capt. Oxford & Cambridge Combined American Team, 1949; Finalist, Olympic Games, Helsinki, 1952; British Mile Champion, 1951, 1953, 1954; World Record for One Mile, 1954; British Empire Mile title and record, 1954; European 1500 metres title and record, 1954. Hon. FUMIST, 1974; Hon. Fellow, Exeter Coll., Oxford. Hon. LLD Liverpool, 1972; Hon. DLitt Sheffield, 1978. Hans-Heinrich Siegbert Prize, 1977. *Publications:* First Four Minutes, 1955; (ed) Brain's Clinical Neurology, 5th edn, 1978; papers on physiology of exercise, heat illness and neurological subjects. *Recreation:* cycling. *Address:* 16 Edwardes Square, W8. *T:* 01-603 9903; Churchfield, Lyminster, Sussex. *Clubs:* Athenæum; Vincent's (Oxford).

BANNON, John Kernan, ISO 1969; Director of Services, Meteorological Office, 1973-76; *b* 26 April 1916; *s* of Frederick J. Bannon, Clerk in Holy Orders and Eveline Bannon, Muckamore, NI; *m* 1947, Pauline Mary Roch Thomas, Pembroke; one *s* one *d*. *Educ:* Royal Sch., Armagh; Emmanuel Coll., Cambridge (Braithwaite Batty Scholar). BA (Wrangler) 1938. Technical Officer, Meteorological Office, 1938; commnd RAFVR, 1943-46 (Temp. Sqdn Ldr); Met. Office, 1946-76; idc 1963. *Publications:* some official scientific works; articles in meteorological jls. *Recreations:* walking, gardening. *Address:* 18 Courtenay Drive, Emmer Green, Reading RG4 8XH. *T:* Reading 473696.

BANTOCK, Prof. Geoffrey Herman; Emeritus Professor of Education, University of Leicester, 1975; *b* 12 Oct. 1914; *s* of Herman S. and Annie Bantock; *m* 1950, Dorothy Jean Pick; no *c*. *Educ:* Wallasey Grammar Sch.; Emmanuel Coll., Cambridge. BA 1936, MA 1942, Cantab. Taught in grammar schs, training coll.; Lectr in Educn, University Coll. of Leicester, 1950-54; Reader in Educn, University Coll., Leicester, later Univ. of Leicester, 1954-64; Prof. of Educn, 1964-75; Leverhulme Emeritus Fellow, 1976-78. Vis. Prof., Monash Univ., Melbourne, 1971. *Publications:* Freedom and Authority in Education, 1952 (2nd edn 1965); L. H. Myers: a critical study, 1956; Education in an Industrial Society, 1963 (2nd edn 1973); Education and Values, 1965; Education, Culture and the Emotions, 1967; Education, Culture and Industrialization, 1968; T. S. Eliot and Education, 1969 (paperback 1970); Studies in the History of Educational Theory: Vol. I, Artifice and Nature 1350-1765, 1980; Dilemmas of the Curriculum, 1980; The Parochialism of the Present, 1981. *Recreations:* music, art, foreign travel. *Address:* c/o The University, Leicester.

BANTOCK, John Leonard; Assistant Under Secretary of State, Home Office, since 1976; *b* 21 Oct. 1927; *s* of Edward Bantock and Agnes Bantock; *m* 1947, Maureen McKinney; two *s*. *Educ:* Colfe's Grammar Sch., SE13; King George V Sch., Southport, Lancs; LSE, London Univ. (LLB 1951). Unilever Ltd, 1943-45; Army, 1945-48 (Staff Captain); Colonial Office, 1951-52; Inland Revenue, 1952-69; Secretariat, Royal Commn on Constitution, 1969-73; Cabinet Office, 1973-76; Sec., Cttee of Privy Counsellors on Recruitment of Mercenaries, 1976. *Address:* 1 Heathcote Road, St Margarets, Twickenham, Mddx TW1 1RX. *T:* 01-892 2972.

BANTON, Prof. Michael Parker, PhD, DSc; JP; Professor of Sociology, University of Bristol, since 1965; *b* 8 Sept. 1926; *s* of Francis Clive Banton and Kathleen Blanche (née Parkes); *m* 1952, Rut Marianne (née Jacobson), Luleà; two *s* two *d*. *Educ:* King Edward's Sch., Birmingham; London Sch. of Economics. BSc Econ. 1950; PhD 1954; DSc 1964. Midn, then Sub-Lieut RNVR, 1945-47. Asst, then Lecturer, then Reader, in Social Anthropology, University of Edinburgh, 1950-65; Dir, SSRC Res. Unit on Ethnic Relations, 1970-78; Visiting Professor: MIT, 1962-63; Wayne State Univ., Detroit, 1971; Univ. of Delaware, 1976; ANU, 1981; Duke Univ., 1982. Editor, Sociology, 1966-69. Pres., Section N, British Assoc. for the Advancement of Science, 1970-71; Mem., Vetenskaps-societeten, Lund, Sweden, 1972; Member: Royal Commn on Criminal Procedure, 1978-80; Royal Commn on Bermuda, 1978; Mem., SW Regl Hosp. Board, 1966-70. JP Bristol, 1966. FRSA 1981. *Publications:* The Coloured Coun., 1955; West African City, 1957; White and Coloured, 1959; The Policeman in the Community, 1964; Roles, 1965; Race Relations, 1967; Racial Minorities, 1972; Police-Community Relations, 1973; (with J. Harwood) The Race Concept, 1975; The Idea of Race, 1977. *Address:* 9 Canynge Road, Bristol BS8 3JZ. *T:* Bristol 36459.

BANWELL, Derick Frank, CBE 1978; Chairman: BCAR (Homes) Ltd, since 1979; BCAR (Housing) Ltd, since 1979; *b* 19 July 1919; *s* of Frank Edward Banwell; *m* 1945, Rose Kathleen Worby; two *s* one *d*. *Educ:* Kent Coll., Canterbury. Admitted as Solicitor, 1947; Asst Solicitor, Southend-on-Sea Co. Borough Coun., 1947-48; Sen. Asst Solicitor, Rochdale Co. Borough Coun., 1948-51; Chief Common Law Solicitor, City of Sheffield, 1951-56; Sen. Asst Solicitor, 1956-59, Asst Town Clerk, 1959-60, Southend-on-Sea Co. Borough Coun.; Dep. Town Clerk and Dep. Clerk of the Peace, Swansea Co. Borough Council, 1960-64; Gen. Manager, Runcorn Develt Corp., 1964-78. Sec.,

Church Bldgs Cttee, United Reformed Church, 1978-. *Recreations:* history, music, model railways. *Address:* 57 Broad Street, Canterbury, Kent.

BÁNYÁSZ, Dr Rezső; Order of Merit for Labour, 1955; Hungarian Ambassador to the Court of St James's, since 1981; *b* 9 Jan. 1931; *m* 1951, Irén Horváth; two *s*. *Educ:* Univ. of Budapest. Foreign Editor, "Magyar Ifjusàg" (Hungarian Youth) daily, "Népszava" (People's Voice) daily, 1950-61 entered Min. of Foreign Affairs, 1961; First Sec., Press Attaché, Stockholm, 1962-68; Counsellor and Dep. Head of Press Dept, Budapest, 1968-70, Head of Press Dept, 1970-72; Sen. Counsellor and Dep. Perm. Rep. of Hungary to UN, NY, 1972-76; Vice-Chm., Hungarian Delegn to Belgrade Meeting of CSCE, 1977; Head, Press Dept, 1978-81. Commenda da Orden do Infante D. Henrique (Portugal), 1979. *Recreation:* gardening. *Address:* 35 Eaton Place, SW1. *T:* 01-235 4048/7191.

BARBACK, Ronald Henry; Consultant, Confederation of British Industry; *b* 31 Oct. 1919; *s* of late Harry Barback and Winifred Florence (née Norris); *m* 1950, Sylvia Chambers; one *s* one *d*. *Educ:* Woodside Sch., Glasgow; Univ. Coll., Nottingham (BScEcon); Queen's and Nuffield Colls, Oxford (MLitt). Asst Lectr in Econs, Univ. of Nottingham, 1946-48; Lectr in Econs, subseq. Sen. Lectr, Canberra University Coll., Australia, 1949-56; Univ. of Ibadan (formerly University Coll., Ibadan): Prof. of Econs and Social Studies, 1956-63; Dean, Faculty of Arts, 1958-59; Dean, Faculty of Econs and Social Studies, 1959-63; Dir, Nigerian (formerly W African) Inst. of Social and Econ. Res., 1956-63; Sen. Res. Fellow, Econ. Res. Inst., Dublin, 1963-64; Prof. of Econs, TCD, 1964-65; Univ. of Hull: Prof. of Econs, 1965-76; Dean, Faculty of Social Sciences and Law, 1966-69; Head, Dept of Econs and Commerce, 1971-74. Dep. Econ. Dir and Head, Econ. Res., CBI, 1977-81 Nigeria: Mem., Ibadan Univ. Hosp. Bd of Management, 1958-63; Mem., J. Econ. Planning Cttee, Fedn of Nigeria, 1959-61; Sole Arbitrator, Trade Disputes in Ports and Railways, 1958; Chm., Fed. Govt Cttee to advise on fostering a share market, 1959. UK Official Delegate, FAO meeting on investment in fisheries, 1970; Mem., FAO mission to Sri Lanka, 1975, Consultant, Div. of Fisheries, Europ. Commn Directorate-Gen. of Agriculture, 1974. Commonwealth Scholarships Commn Adviser on Econs 1971-76; Mem., Schools Council Social Sciences Cttee, 1971-80; Chm., Sch. Council Econs and Business Studies Syllabus Steering Gp, 1975-77. Member Hull and Dist Local Employment Cttee, 1966-73; N Humberside Dis Manpower Cttee, 1973-76; CNAA Business and Management Studies Bd 1978-; Ct, Brunel Univ., 1979-; Editorial Bd, Bull. of Economic Research (formerly Yorks Bull. of Social and Economic Research), 1965-76 (Jt Editor 1966-67); Editorial Adv. Bd, Applied Economics, 1969-80. Editor Humberside Statistical Bull., nos 1-3, 1974, 1975, 1977. Specialist adviser House of Lords Select Cttee on the European Communities, 1980-. *Publications:* (contrib.) The Commonwealth in the World Today, ed J. Eppstein, 1956; (ed with Prof. Sir Douglas Copland) The Conflict of Expansion and Stability, 1957; (contrib.) The Commonwealth and Europe (EfU), 1960; The Pricing of Manufactures, 1964; (contrib.) Insurance Markets of the World, ed M. Grossmann 1964; (contrib.) Webster's New World Companion to English and American Literature, 1973; Forms of Co-operation in the British Fishing Industry, 1976; (with M. Breimer and A. F. Haug) Development of the East Coast Fisheries of Sri Lanka, 1976; contrib. New Internat. Encyc., FAO Fisheries Reports, and jls. *Recreations:* walking, music *Address:* 14a Calverley Park Gardens, Tunbridge Wells, Kent TN1 2JN. *T:* Tunbridge Wells 33290. *Club:* Royal Commonwealth Society.

BARBARA, Hon. Agatha; President of the Republic of Malta, since 1982; *b* 11 March 1923. *Educ:* Government Grammar School. School teacher, 1945; entered politics, 1946; first woman Member of Parliament, 1947; became first woman Minister, in Labour Govt, 1955, as Minister of Education; also Minister of Educn, 1971-74; Minister of Labour, Culture, and Welfare 1974-81. Was Acting Prime Minister on various occasions, and elected President of the Republic, 16 Feb. 1982. *Recreations:* philately, classical and modern music. *Address:* The Palace, San Anton, Republic of Malta. *T:* 40354.

BARBER, family name of **Baron Barber.**

BARBER, Baron *cr* 1974 (Life Peer), of Wentbridge; **Anthony Perrinot Lysberg Barber,** PC 1963; TD; Chairman, Standard Chartered Bank plc, since 1974; a Government Director, British Petroleum, since 1979; *b* 4 July 1920; *s* of John Barber, CBE, Doncaster; *m* 1950, Jean Patricia, *d* of Milton Asquith, Wentbridge, Yorks; two *d*. *Educ:* Retford Grammar Sch.; Oriel Coll., Oxford Univ. (PPE, MA) (Hon. Fellow 1971). Served War of 1939-45, commnd in Army (Dunkirk); seconded to RAF as pilot, 1940-45 (despatches, prisoner of war, 1942-45, took Law Degree with 1st Class Hons while POW escaped from Poland, prisoner of the Russians). Barrister-at-law, Inner Temple, 1948 (Inner Temple Scholarship). MP (C): Doncaster, 1951-64, Altrincham and Sale, Feb. 1965-Sept. 1974; PPS to the Under-Sec. of State for Air, 1952-55; Asst Whip, 1955-57; a Lord Comr of the Treasury, 1957-58; PPS to the Prime Minister, 1958-59; Economic Sec. to the Treasury, 1959-62; Financial Sec. to the Treasury, 1962-63; Minister of Health and Mem. of the Cabinet, 1963-64; Chancellor of the Duchy of Lancaster, June-July 1970; Chancellor of the Exchequer, 1970-74. Chm., Conservative Party Organisation, 1967-70. *Address:* Standard Chartered Bank plc, 10 Clement's Lane, EC4. *T:* 01-623 7500. *Club:* Carlton.
See also N. J. L. Barber.

BARBER, Alan Theodore, MA (Oxon); Headmaster of Ludgrove Preparatory School, Wokingham, Berks, 1937-73, retired; *b* 17 June 1905; *s* of Harold Priestman Barber, Todwick House, Todwick, Yorks; *m* 1937, Dorothy Shaw; one *s* two *d. Educ:* Shrewsbury Sch.; Queen's Coll., Oxford. BA 1929; Triple Blue, captained cricket and football XIs, Oxford; captained Yorks County Cricket XI, 1929 and 1930; played football regularly for Corinthians. Asst master, Ludgrove, 1930. *Recreations:* golf, cricket, Eton Fives. *Address:* The Garden Cottage, Ludgrove, Wokingham, Berks. *T:* Wokingham 782639. *Clubs:* Sports, MCC; Berkshire Golf (Bagshot).

BARBER, Derek Coates; Environment Consultant to Humberts, Chartered Surveyors, since 1972; Chairman, Countryside Commission, since 1981; *b* 17 June 1918; *s* of Thomas Smith-Barber and Elsie Coates. *Educ:* Royal Agricl Coll., Cirencester (MRAC; Gold Medal, Practical Agriculture). Served War: invalided, Armed Forces, 1942. Farmed in Glos Cotswolds; Dist Adv. Officer, National Agricl Adv. Service, MAFF, 1946-57; County Agricl Advisor, Glos, 1957-72. Chm., BBC's Central Agricl Adv. Cttee, 1974-80 (*ex officio* Mem., BBC's Gen. Adv. Council, 1972-80). Royal Soc. for Protection of Birds: Mem., 1970-75, Chm., 1976-81, Council; Chm., Educn Cttee, 1972-75; Vice-Pres., 1982; Pres., Glos Naturalists' Soc., 1981-; Founder Mem., 1969, Vice-Pres., 1981-, Farming and Wildlife Gp of landowning, farming and wildlife conservation bodies. Associate Mem., Guild of Agricl Journalists, 1981. Bledisloe Gold Medal for Distinguished Service to UK Agriculture, 1967; RSPB Gold Medal, 1982. Silver Jubilee Medal, 1977. *Publications:* (with Keith Dexter) Farming for Profits, 1961, 2nd edn 1967; (with J. G. S. and Frances Donaldson) Farming in Britain Today, 1969, 2nd edn 1972; (ed) Farming with Wildlife, 1971; A History of Humberts, 1980; contrib. farming and wildlife conservation jls. *Recreations:* birds, wildlife conservation, farming, hill walking. *Address:* The Manor Farm, Stanley Pontlarge, Winchcombe, Glos GL54 5HD. *T:* Winchcombe 602394. *Club:* Farmers'.

BARBER, Hon. Sir (Edward Hamilton) Esler, Kt 1976; Puisne Judge, Supreme Court of Victoria, Australia, 1965-77; *b* Hamilton, Vic., 26 July 1905; *s* of late Rev. John Andrew Barber and Maggie Rorke; *m* 1954, Constance, *d* of Captain C. W. Palmer; one *s* one *d. Educ:* Hamilton Coll., Victoria; Scots Coll., Sydney; Scotch Coll., Melbourne; Melbourne Univ. Barrister-at-law, 1929; QC (Vic.) 1955, Tas. 1956; Judge, County Court, Vic., 1957-65; Actg Judge, 1964-65. Chm., Royal Commn into Failure of King's Bridge, 1962-63; Dep. Chm. Parole Bd, Vic., Nov. 1969-77; Mem. Council of Legal Educn, 1968-77; Chm., Royal Commn into West Gate Bridge Disaster, 1970-71; Chm., Bd of Inquiry into causes and origins of bush and grass fires in Vic. during Jan.-Feb. 1977, 1977-. *Publications:* articles on Matrimonial Law, incl. Divorce—the Changing Law, 1968. *Address:* 1 St George's Court, Toorak, Vic. 3142, Australia. *T:* 24-5104. *Club:* Australian (Melbourne).

BARBER, Hon. Sir Esler; *see* Barber, Hon. Sir E. H. E.

BARBER, Dr James Peden, JP; Master, Hatfield College, Durham, since 1980; *b* 6 Nov. 1931; *s* of John and Carrie Barber; *m* 1955, Margaret June (*née* McCormac); three *s* one *d. Educ:* Liverpool Inst. High Sch.; Pembroke Coll., Cambridge (MA, PhD); The Queen's Coll., Oxford. Served RAF, 1950-52 (Pilot Officer). Colonial Service, Uganda: Dist Officer, subseq. Asst Sec. to Prime Minister and Clerk to the Cabinet, 1956-63; Lectr, Univ. of NSW, Australia, 1963-65; Lectr in Govt, Univ. of Exeter, 1965-69 (seconded to University Coll. of Rhodesia, 1965-67); Prof. of Political Science, Open Univ., 1969-80. Mem. RIIA; Part-time Dir, Chatham House study, Southern Africa in Conflict, 1979-81. JP Bedford, 1977-80. *Publications:* Rhodesia: the road to rebellion, 1967; Imperial Frontier, 1968; South Africa's Foreign Policy, 1973; European Community: vision and reality, 1974; The Nature of Foreign Policy, 1975; Who Makes British Foreign Policy?, 1977; The West and South Africa, 1982. *Recreations:* choral music, all kinds of sport, walking the dog. *Address:* Kingsgate House, Bow Lane, Durham DH1 3ER. *T:* Durham 48651. *Club:* Royal Commonwealth Society.

BARBER, Rear-Adm. John L.; *see* Lee-Barber.

BARBER, John Norman Romney; company director; *b* 22 April 1919; *s* of George Ernest and Gladys Eleanor Barber; *m* 1941, Babette Chalu; one *s. Educ:* Westcliff. Served with Army, 1939-46 (Capt.). Min. of Supply, 1946-55 (Princ.). Joined Ford Motor Co. Ltd, 1955, Finance Dir, 1962; Chm., Ford Motor Credit Co. Ltd, 1963; Dir, Henry Ford & Son Ltd, Cork, 1963; Dir Autolite Motor Products Ltd, 1963; Finance Dir, AEI Ltd, 1965; Chm., Telephone Cables Ltd, 1967; Dir of Finance and Planning, 1968-71, Dep. Man. Dir, 1971-73, Dep. Chm. and Man. Dir, 1973-75, British Leyland Motor Corp. Ltd; Chairman, 1973-75: British Leyland International Ltd; Leyland Innocenti, SpA; Leyland Motor Corp. of Australia Ltd; Director: Leyland España SA; Automóviles de Turismo Motor Ingleses SA; NZ Motor Corp. Ltd; British Leyland Motors Inc.; Metalurgica de Santa Ana SA; Chairman: Pullmaflex International Ltd, 1976-79; Aberhurst Ltd, 1976-; A. C. Edwards Engineering Ltd, 1976-81; Cox & Kings Financial Services Ltd, 1980-; C & K Executive Search Ltd, 1980-; C & K Consulting Group Ltd, 1982-; C & K Marketing Ltd, 1982-; Director: Acrow Ltd, 1977-; Good Relations Group Ltd, 1979-; Amalgamated Metal Corp. Ltd, 1980-81; Spear & Jackson International Ltd, 1980-; Twinprint Ltd, 1981-; Economists Advisory Group Ltd, 1981-; Deputy Chairman: Cox & Kings Ltd, 1980-81; John E. Wiltshier & Co. Ltd, 1980- (Dir, 1979-). Mem., Royal Commn on Medical Educn, 1965-68; Chm., Adv. Cttee to BoT on Investment Grants, 1967-68; Mem.,

Adv. Council for Energy Conservation, 1974-75. Vice Pres., SMMT, 1974-76. FBIM; Mem. Council BIM, 1967-71. *Publications:* papers on management subjects in various jls. *Recreations:* motor sport, forestry, photography. *Address:* High Walls, Claremont Drive, Esher, Surrey KT10 9LU. *Clubs:* British Automobile Racing, British Racing and Sports Car.

BARBER, Noël John Lysberg; author; *b* 9 Sept. 1909; *s* of John Barber, CBE, and Danish-born 'Musse' Barber (*née* Lysberg); *m* 1st, 1938, Helen Whichello, in Singapore; 2nd, 1954, Countess de Feo of Florence; one *s* one *d. Educ:* erratically, briefly, terminated by attack of lockjaw at age of fourteen. After unsuccessful attempts to write books and articles, became professional journalist in the 1930s with Yorkshire Post group, then Daily Express, Manchester; after travelling world by tramp steamer, became editor, Malaya Tribune, Singapore, 1937-38; travels in China, Siberia, Russia, 1938-39; Editor, Overseas Daily Mail, London, 1940. RAF navigator, 1942-45. Légion d'Honneur, 1945. Editor and Man. Dir, Continental Daily Mail, Paris, 1945-53; paintings exhibited at Salon d'Hiver, Paris, 1950-53; Foreign Correspondent, Daily Mail, 1953-65; wounded, Morocco, during French N African war, 1954; wounded, Hungarian Uprising, 1956; first Briton to reach South Pole since Captain Scott, 1957. Organized and appeared in Assignment Unknown, series of TV documentary travelogues, 1959-60; Foreign Manager, then Syndication Manager and Dir, Associated Newspapers Ltd, 1962-73. Ridder of Danneborg, Denmark, 1948. Jordanian Order of Merit, 1961. *Publications:* (after 19 full-length books had been rejected) Newspaper Reporting, 1936; How Strong is America, 1941; The Menace of Japan, 1942; Trans-Siberian, 1943; Prisoner of War, 1944; Fires of Spring, 1952; Strangers in the Sun, 1952; Distant Places, 1956; A Handful of Ashes, 1957; The White Desert, 1958; From the Land of Lost Content, 1960; Life with Titina, 1961; Conversations with Painters, 1964; The Black Hole of Calcutta, 1965; Sinister Twilight, the Fall of Singapore, 1968; The War of the Running Dogs, 1971; Lords of the Golden Horn, 1973; Seven Days of Freedom, 1974; The Week France Fell, 1976; The Natives were Friendly, an autobiography, 1977; The Singapore Story, 1979; The Fall of Shanghai, 1979; *Juveniles:* Adventures at Both Poles, 1958; Let's Visit the USA, 1960; *Novel:* Tanamera, 1981; *In partnership:* Hitler's Last Hope (with Ernest Phillips) 1942; Cities (with Rupert Croft-Cooke) 1946; An Island to Oneself (with Tom Neale) 1966. *Recreations:* writing, music, painting, travel, tennis, bridge, watching cricket. *Address:* 312a King's Road, SW3. *T:* 01-352 2828. *Clubs:* Carlton, Savage, Press, International Lawn Tennis of Great Britain.
See also Baron Barber.

BARBER, Ven. Paul Everard; Archdeacon of Surrey, since 1980; Hon. Canon of Guildford, since 1980; *b* 16 Sept. 1935; *s* of Cecil Arthur and Mollie Barber; *m* 1959, Patricia Jayne Walford; two *s* two *d* (one *s* decd). *Educ:* Sherborne School; St John's Coll., Cambridge (BA 1958, MA 1966); Wells Theological College. Deacon 1960, priest 1961, dio. Guildford; Curate of St Francis, Westborough, 1960-66; Vicar: Camberley with Yorktown, 1966-73; St Thomas-on-The Bourne, Farnham, 1973-80; Rural Dean of Farnham, 1974-79. General Synod, 1979; Member, Council of College of Preachers, 1969-. *Recreations:* diocesan clergy cricket, theatre. *Address:* Tarawera, 71 Boundstone Road, Rowledge, Farnham, Surrey GU10 4AT. *T:* Frensham 3987.

BARBER, Sir William (Francis), 2nd Bt *cr* 1960; TD; JP; *b* 20 Nov. 1905; *yr* and *o* surv. *s* of Sir (Thomas) Philip Barber, 1st Bt, DSO, TD, JP, DL, and of Beatrice Mary (*d* 1962), *d* of Lieut-Col W. Ingersoll Merritt; *S* father, 1961; *m* 1st, 1936, Diana Constance (marr. diss. 1978), *d* of late Lieut-Col Thomas Owen Lloyd, CMG, Minard Castle, Argyll; one *s* one *d*; 2nd, 1978, Jean Marie, widow of Dr H. C. Nott, Adelaide, S Australia. *Educ:* Eton Coll. South Nottinghamshire Hussars Yeomanry (Commnd, 1924). Royal Horse Artillery; served in Palestine, Egypt, North Africa, NW Europe; Lieut-Col 1947. Hon. Col, South Nottinghamshire Hussars Yeomanry, 1961-66. JP Notts, 1952; High Sheriff, Notts., 1964. *Heir:* s (Thomas) David Barber [*b* 18 Nov. 1937; *m* 1st, 1972, Amanda Mary (*née* Rabone) (marr. diss. 1976), widow of Maj. Michael Healing; one *s*; 2nd, 1978, Jeannine Mary Boyle, *d* of Captain T. J. Gurney; one *s*]. *Address:* Lamb Close, Eastwood, Notts. Dunmaglass, Aberarder, Invernessshire.

BARBER, Prof. William Joseph, Hon. OBE 1981; Professor of Economics, Wesleyan University, Middletown, Conn, USA, since 1965; *b* 13 Jan. 1925; *s* of Ward Barber; *m* 1955, Sheila Mary Marr; three *s. Educ:* Harvard Univ. (AB); Balliol Coll., Oxford. BA, 1st Cl. Hons, 1951, MA 1955; DPhil (Nuffield Coll.) 1958. Served War, US Army, 1943-46. Lectr in Econs, Balliol Coll., Oxford, 1956; Dept of Economics, Wesleyan Univ., USA, 1957- (Asst Prof., 1957-61; Associate Prof., 1961-65; Prof., 1965-; Andrews Prof., 1972-). Research Associate: Oxford Univ. Inst. of Economics and Statistics, 1962-63; Twentieth Century Fund, South Asian Study, 1961-62. Amer. Sec., Rhodes Scholarship Trust, 1970-80. *Publications:* The Economy of British Central Africa, 1961; A History of Economic Thought, 1967; contributor to Asian Drama: an inquiry into the poverty of nations (with Gunnar Myrdal and others), 1968; British Economic Thought and India 1600-1858, 1975; (jtly) Exhortation and Controls: the search for a wage-price policy, 1975; Energy Policy in Perspective, 1981; contribs to professional jls. *Address:* 306 Pine Street, Middletown, Conn, USA. *T:* 203-346-2612.

BARBIERI, Margaret Elizabeth; Senior Principal, Sadler's Wells Royal Ballet, since 1974; *b* 2 March 1947; *d* of Ettore Barbieri and Lea Barbieri. *Educ:* Convent High Sch., Durban, S Africa. Trained with Iris Manning and

Brownie Sutton, S Africa; Royal Ballet Sen. Sch., 1963; joined Royal Ballet, 1965; Principal, 1970. Gypsy Girl, Two Pigeons, 1966; 1st Giselle, Covent Garden, 1968; 1st Sleeping Beauty, Leeds, 1969; 1st Swan Lake, Frankfurt, 1977; 1st Romeo and Juliet, Covent Garden, 1979. Other roles with Royal Ballet: La Fille mal Gardée, Two Pigeons, The Dream, Façade, Wedding Bouquet, Rendezvous (Ashton); Lady and the Fool, Card Game, Pineapple Poll (Cranko); The Invitation, Solitaire, (Summer) The Four Seasons (MacMillan); Checkmate, The Rake's Progress (de Valois); Grosse Fugue, Tilt (van Manen); Lilac Garden (Tudor); Fête Etrange (Howard); Grand Tour (Layton); Summer Garden (Hynd); Game Piano (Thorpe), 1978; Cinderella (Killar), 1978; Cinderella (Rodrigues), 1979; Papillon, The Taming of the Shrew, 1980; Coppélia, Les Sylphides, Raymonda Act III, Spectre de la Rose; La Vivandière, 1982. Roles created: Knight Errant (Tudor), 1968; From Waking Sleep (Drew), 1970; Ante-Room (Cauley), 1971; Oscar Wilde (Layton), 1972; Sacred Circles and The Sword (Drew), 1973; The Entertainers (Killar), 1974; Charlotte Brontë (Hynd), 1974; Summertide (Wright), 1977. Recreated Pavlova's Dragonfly Solo, 1977. Travelled with Royal Ballet to Australia, Egypt, Far East, France, Germany, Greece, Holland, Israel, Italy, New Zealand, Portugal, Spain, Switzerland, Yugoslavia; guest appearances, USA, Germany, S Africa, France, Norway, Czechoslovakia. TV Appearances in: Spectre de la Rose; Grosse Fugue; Giselle; Coppelia; Checkmate; Markova master classes. *Recreations:* music (classical), theatre, gardening. *Address:* 19 Merton Avenue, Chiswick, W4 1TA. *T:* 01-995 6554.

BARBOUR, Very Rev. Prof. Robert Alexander Stewart, MC 1945; Professor of New Testament Exegesis, University of Aberdeen, 1971-82; Master of Christ's College, Aberdeen, 1977-82; Chaplain-in-Ordinary to the Queen, since 1976; Dean of the Chapel Royal in Scotland, since 1981; Prelate of the Priory of Scotland of the Order of St John, since 1977; *b* 11 May 1921; *s* of George Freeland Barbour and Helen Victoria (*née* Hepburne-Scott); *m* 1950, Margaret Isobel Pigot; three *s* one *d. Educ:* Rugby Sch.; Balliol Coll., Oxford (MA 1946); Univ. of St Andrews (BD 1952); Yale Univ. (STM 1953). Sec., Edinburgh Christian Council for Overseas Students, 1953-55; Lectr and Sen. Lectr in NT Lang., Lit. and Theol., Univ. of Edinburgh, 1955-71. Moderator, Gen. Assembly of Church of Scotland, 1979-80. Hon. Sec., Studiorum Novi Testamenti Societas, 1970-77. Chm. Governors, Rannoch Sch., 1973-79. Hon. DD St Andrews, 1979. *Publications:* The Scottish Horse 1939-45, 1950; Traditio-Historical Criticism of the Gospels, 1972; What is the Church for?, 1973; articles in various jls. *Recreations:* music, walking, forestry. *Address:* Fincastle, Pitlochry, Perthshire PH16 5RJ. *T:* Pitlochry 3209. *Club:* New (Edinburgh).

BARBOUR, Walworth; US Ambassador to Israel, 1961-73; *b* 4 June 1908; *s* of Samuel Lewis Barbour and Clara Hammond; unmarried. *Educ:* Harvard Coll. USA. Vice Consul, Naples, 1932; Athens, 1933; Baghdad, 1936; Sofia, 1939; Dip. Sec., Cairo, 1941; Athens, 1944; Dept of State, Washington, 1945-49; Minister, Moscow, 1949-51; Dept of State, Washington, 1951-55; Deputy Asst Sec. of State for European Affairs, 1954-55; American Minister, London, 1955-61. Hon. Fellow, Weizmann Inst. of Sci., 1970. Hon. PhD: Tel Aviv, 1971; Hebrew Univ. of Jerusalem, 1972; Hon. LLD Dropsie, Pa, 1973. *Recreation:* golf. *Address:* 14 Grapevine Road, Gloucester, Mass 01930, USA. *Clubs:* American; Swinley Forest (Surrey); Chevy Chase (Md, USA).

BARCLAY, Alexander, CBE 1957; ARCS, FRSC; Keeper, Department of Chemistry and Photography, Science Museum, S Kensington, 1938-59; retired; *b* 25 July 1896; *o s* of late Alexander Barclay; *m* 1921, Irene Margaret (*d* 1973), *y d* of late Frank Carrington Falkner, Wisbech. *Educ:* Berkhamsted Sch.; Royal College of Science. Served European War with Special Gas Brigade, RE, 1916-17; invalided, 1917; Postal Censorship Research Dept, 1918; entered Science Museum, 1921; Asst Keeper, 1930; Board of Education, 1940 and 1943; Postal Censorship, 1944-45. Hon. Member Royal Photographic Soc.; Mem. of Nat. Film Library Cttee, British Film Institute, 1938-55. *Publications:* Official Handbooks to the Chemistry Collections, Science Museum, 1927-37; various papers in scientific journals. *Address:* Towers End, Walberswick, Southwold, Suffolk. *T:* Southwold 722146.

BARCLAY, Christopher Francis Robert, CMG 1967; *b* 8 June 1919; *s* of late Captain Robert Barclay, RA (retired) and late Annie Douglas Dowdeswell Barclay (*née* Davidson); *m* 1st, 1950, Clare Justice Troutbeck (marr. diss., 1962); two *s* one *d* ; 2nd, 1962, Diana Elizabeth Goodman; one *s* one *d. Educ:* Eton Coll.; Magdalen Coll., Oxford (MA). 2nd Lieut The Rifle Bde, 1940; Capt. 1942; Major 1943; served in Egypt; Middle East Centre of Arab Studies, Jerusalem, 1944-45; Political Officer, Northern Iraq, 1945; Asst Information Officer, Brit. Embassy, Baghdad, 1946. Joined Foreign Office, 1946; Second Sec., British Embassy, Cairo, 1947; First Sec., Foreign Office, 1950; Brit. Embassy, Bonn, 1953; FO, 1956; Regional Information Officer, Beirut, 1960; FO, 1961; Counsellor and Head of Information Research Dept, 1962-66; Head of Personnel Dept (Training and General), FCO, 1967-69; Asst Sec., CSD, 1969-73, DoE, 1973-76; Sec., Govt Hospitality Fund, 1976-80. Mem. Council, City Univ., 1976. Warden, Saddlers' Co., 1980. *Recreations:* fishing, gardening. *Address:* 88 Redcliffe Gardens, SW10. *T:* 01-373 1677.

BARCLAY, Sir Colville Herbert Sanford, 14th Bt, *cr* 1668; Painter; *b* 7 May 1913; *s* of late Rt Hon. Sir Colville Adrian de Rune Barclay, 3rd *s* of 11th Bt, and Sarita Enriqueta, *d* of late Herbert Ward; *S* uncle, 1930; *m* 1949, Rosamond Grant Renton Elliott; three *s. Educ:* Eton, Trinity Coll., Oxford. Third Sec., Diplomatic Service, 1937-41; enlisted in Navy, Nov. 1941; Sub-Lieut RNVR 1942; Lieut 1943; Lieut Commander 1945; demobilised,

1946. Exhibitor: Royal Academy, RBA, London Group, Bradford City and Brighton Art Galleries. Chm. Royal London Homoeopathic Hospital, 1970-74 (Vice-Chm., 1961-65; Chm., League of Friends, 1974-). *Publications:* articles in botanical jls. *Recreations:* gardening, plant-hunting. *Heir: s* Robert Colraine Barclay [*b* 12 Feb. 1950; *m* 1980, Lucilia Saboia, *y d* of Carlos Saboia de Albuquerque, Rio de Janeiro; one *s*]. *Address:* Pitshill, Petworth, West Sussex. *T:* Lodsworth 341. *Club:* Brooks's.

BARCLAY, Hugh Maben; Clerk of Standing Committees, House of Commons, since 1976; *b* 20 Feb. 1927; *s* of late William Barclay, FRCS, and Mary Barclay; *m* 1956, Hilda Johnston; one *s* one *d. Educ:* Fettes Coll., Edinburgh (exhbnr); Gonville and Caius Coll., Cambridge (schol.). Served Royal Artillery, 1948. House of Commons: Asst Clerk, 1950; Sen. Clerk, 1955; Dep. Principal Clerk, 1967; Principal Clerk, 1976. *Address:* 37 Stockwell Green, SW9. *T:* 01-274 7375.

BARCLAY, Peter Maurice; Partner, Beachcroft Hyman Isaacs, Solicitors, since 1974; *b* 6 March 1926; *s* of George Ronald Barclay and Josephine (*née* Lambert); *m* 1953, Elizabeth Mary Wright; one *s* two *d. Educ:* Bryanston Sch.; Magdalene Coll., Cambridge (MA). Served RNVR, 1944-46. Admitted Solicitor, 1952; Senior Partner, Beachcroft & Co., 1964-74. Chairman, National Inst. for Social Work, 1973-; Trustee, Joseph Rowntree Memorial Trust, 1972-; Governor, Bryanston Sch., 1972-. Chm., Cttee on Roles and Tasks of Social Workers, 1981-82. *Recreations:* gardening, painting, golf. *Address:* 112 Albert Street, NW1 7NE. *T:* 01-485 6429.

BARCLAY, Sir Roderick (Edward), GCVO 1966 (KCVO 1957; CVO 1953); KCMG 1955 (CMG 1948); HM Diplomatic Service, retired; Director: Slough Estates, since 1969; Barclays Bank SA, 1969-79 (Chairman, 1970-74); Barclays Bank International, 1971-77; Banque de Bruxelles, 1971-77; *b* 22 Feb. 1909; *s* of late J. Gurney Barclay and Gillian (*née* Birkbeck); *m* 1934, Jean Cecil, *d* of late Sir Hugh Gladstone; one *s* three *d. Educ:* Harrow; Trinity Coll., Cambridge. Entered Diplomatic Service, 1932. Served at HM Embassies at Brussels, Paris, Washington and in FO; Counsellor in FO 1946; Principal Private Sec. to Sec. of State for Foreign Affairs, 1949-51; Asst Under-Sec. of State, 1951; Dep. Under-Sec. of State, 1953-56; HM Ambassador to Denmark, 1956-60; Adviser on European Trade Questions, Foreign Office, and Dep. Under-Sec. of State for Foreign Affairs, 1960-63; Ambassador to Belgium, 1963-69. Knight Grand Cross of the Dannebrog (Denmark) and of the Couronne (Belgium). *Publication:* Ernest Bevin and the Foreign Office 1932-69, 1975; contrib. Country Life, etc. *Recreations:* shooting, fishing. *Address:* Great White End, Latimer, Bucks. *T:* Little Chalfont 2050. *Club:* Brooks's.

See also A. E. Palmer.

BARCLAY, Yvonne Fay, (Mrs William Barclay); *see* Minton, Y. F.

BARCROFT, Prof. Henry, FRS 1953; MA; MD; FRCP; Professor of Physiology, St Thomas's Hospital Medical School, London, 1948-71, Emeritus since 1971; a Wellcome Trustee, 1966-75; *b* 18 Oct. 1904; *s* of late Sir Joseph Barcroft, CBE, FRS; *m* 1933, Bridget Mary, *d* of late A. S. Ramsey; three *s* one *d. Educ:* Marlborough Coll.; King's Coll. Cambridge; Exhibitioner, 1923. Natural Science Tripos Class I, Parts I and II; Harold Fry and George Henry Lewes studentships at Cambridge, 1927-29; Gedge Prize, 1930; Harmsworth Scholar, St Mary's Hospital, London, 1929-32; Lectr in Physiology, University Coll., London, 1932-35; Dunville Prof. of Physiology, Queen's Univ., Belfast, 1935-48. Arris and Gale Lectr, RCS, 1945; Bertram Louis Abrahams Lectr, RCP, 1960; Robert Campbell Meml Orator, Ulster Med. Soc., 1975; Bayliss-Starling Meml Lectr, Physiological Soc., 1976; Vis. Prof., Univ. of Adelaide, 1963. Chairman: Editorial Bd, Monographs of Physiological Soc., 1957-65; Research Defence Soc., 1968-71, Sec. 1972-77, Vice-Pres., 1978-. Hon. Member: Academic Adv. Cttee, Loughborough Coll. of Technology, 1964-66; Société Française d'Angiologie; Japanese Coll. of Angiology; Czechoslovak Med. Soc. J. E. Purkinje. Hon. DSc Univ. Western Australia, 1963; Hon. MD Leopold-Franzens Univ., Innsbruck, 1969. Hon. DSc QUB, 1975. Pro meritis médaille in silver, Karl Franzens Univ., Graz. *Publications:* (with H. J. C. Swan) Sympathetic Control of Human Blood Vessels, 1953; papers in the Journal of Physiology. *Recreations:* sailing and golf. *Address:* 73 Erskine Hill, NW11 6EY. *T:* 01-458 1066. *Club:* Athenæum.

BARD, Dr Basil Joseph Asher, CBE 1968; Chairman, New Product Management (NPM) Group, since 1977; Director, Technology and Innovations Exchange, since 1981; *b* London, 20 Aug. 1914; *s* of late Abram Isaac Bard and Anita Bard; *m* 1942, Ena Dora Birk; three *s. Educ:* Owen's Sch.; RCS (Imperial Coll.). BSc(Chem.), ARCS 1934, DIC (Chem. Engrg and Fuel Technology) 1935, PhD (Chem. Constitution of Coal) 1936, London; Bar Finals (1st cl. hons) and Studentship, Coun. of Legal Educn, 1937; called to Bar, Gray's Inn (Birkenhead and William Shaw Schol.), 1938. Practised at Bar, 1938-39; Legal Dept, Coal Commn, 1939-41; Explosives Prodn Dept, Min. of Supply, 1941-43; Materials Dept, Min. of Aircraft Production, 1943-45; Depts of Industrial Res., Educn, Design, etc, FBI, 1945-49; NRDC, 1950-74; in turn, Commercial Man., Techn. Dir, Exec. Dir, and Chief Exec., Dept of Applied Science; Mem., NRDC, 1956-73, Man. Dir, 1971-73; Exec. Dir, First National Finance Corp., 1974-76; Chm., Birmingham Mint Ltd, 1977-81. Founder and Chm., 1968, subsequently Vice-Pres., UK Licensing Execs Soc. (awarded Gold Medal 1973). Consultant to UNIDO, 1972-74; Member: Management Cttee, Science Policy Foundn;

Council, Foundn for Sci. and Technol., 1982-; has served on various Govt Cttees. President: Anglo-Jewish Assoc., 1977-; Jewish Meml Council, 1982. *Publications*: (ed) Industry and Research, 1947; (ed) The Patent System, 1975; various articles on science, technology, patents, industry, commerce and their inter-relationships. *Recreations*: music, bridge, chess, social life. *Address*: 23 Mourne House, Maresfield Gardens, Hampstead, NW3 5SL. *T*: 01-435 5340; c/o NPM Group, 63 Lincoln's Inn Fields, Holborn, WC2. *T*: 01-404 5414. *Club*: Athenæum.

BARDEEN, Prof. John; Professor of Physics and Electrical Engineering, University of Illinois, 1951-75, now Emeritus; *b* Madison, Wisconsin, 23 May 1908; *s* of Dr Charles R. Bardeen and Althea Bardeen (*née* Harmer); *m* 1938, Jane Maxwell; two *s* one *d*. *Educ*: Univ. of Wisconsin; Princeton Univ. BS 1928, MS 1929, Univ. of Wisconsin; PhD 1936, Princeton Univ. Geophysicist, Gulf Research and Development Corp., Pittsburgh, Pa, 1930-33; Junior Fellow, Soc. of Fellows, Harvard Univ., 1935-38; Asst Prof. of Physics, Univ. of Minnesota, 1938-41; Physicist, Naval Ordnance Laboratory, Washington, DC, 1941-45; Research Physicist, Bell Telephone Laboratories, Murray Hill, NJ, 1945-51. Foreign Member: Royal Soc., 1973; Indian Nat. Sci. Acad., 1976; Japan Acad., 1977. Holds hon. doctorates. Nobel Prize for Physics: (with W. H. Brattain and W. Shockley), 1956; (with L. N. Cooper and J. R. Schrieffer), 1972; National Medal of Science, 1965; Presidential Medal of Freedom, 1977. *Publications*: articles on solid state physics, including semi-conductors, metals, superconductivity in Physical Review and other periodicals and books. *Address*: 55 Greencroft, Champaign, Illinois, USA. *T*: Champaign 352-6497.

BARDEN, Prof. Laing, PhD, DSc; FICE; Director, Newcastle upon Tyne Polytechnic, since 1978; *b* 29 Aug. 1931; *s* of Alfred Eversfield Barden and Edna (*née* Laing); *m* 1956, Nancy Carr; two *s* one *d*. *Educ*: Washington Grammar Sch.; Durham Univ. (BSc, MSc). R. T. James & Partners, 1954-59. Liverpool Univ., 1959-62 (PhD); Manchester Univ., 1962-69 (DSc); Strathclyde Univ., 1969-74; Newcastle Polytechnic, 1974-. *Publications*: contribs to Geotechnique, Proc. ICE, Jl Amer. Soc. CE, Qly Jl Eng. Geol. *Recreations*: cricket, soccer, snooker. *Address*: 7 Grasmere, Cleadon, Tyne and Wear SR6 7QF. *T*: Boldon 361383.

BARDER, Brian Leon; HM Diplomatic Service; Ambassador to Ethiopia, since 1982; *b* 20 June 1934; *s* of Harry and Vivien Barder; *m* 1958, Jane Maureen Cornwell; one *s* two *d*. *Educ*: Sherborne; St Catharine's Coll., Cambridge (BA). 2nd Lieut, 7 Royal Tank Regt, 1952-54. Colonial Office, 1957; Private Sec. to Permanent Under-Sec., 1960-61; HM Diplomatic Service, 1965; First Secretary, UK Mission to UN, 1964-68; FCO, 1968-70; First Sec. and Press Attaché, Moscow, 1971-73; Counsellor and Head of Chancery, British High Commn, Canberra, 1973-77; Canadian Nat. Defence Coll., Kingston, Ontario, 1977-78; Head of Central and Southern, later Southern African Dept, FCO, 1978-82. *Recreations*: music, squash. *Address*: c/o Foreign and Commonwealth Office, SW1. *Clubs*: United Oxford & Cambridge University, Royal Commonwealth Society.

BARDSLEY, Andrew Tromlow; JP; Principal, Westgate Development Consultancy, since 1980; *b* 7 Dec. 1927; *o s* of Andrew and Gladys Ada Bardsley; *m* 1954, June Patricia (*née* Ford); one *s* one *d*. *Educ*: Ashton-under-Lyne Grammar Sch.; Manchester Coll. of Art. CEng, FIMunE, FInstHE, FBIM. Royal Navy, 1947-49. Entered Local Govt (Municipal Engrg), 1950; various appts leading to Borough Engr and Surveyor, Worksop MB, 1962-69; Director of Technical Services: Corby New Town, 1969-71; Luton CBC, 1971-73; Gen. Manager and Chief Exec., Harlow Develt Corp., 1973-80. JP Essex, 1975. *Publications*: papers on engrg and associated matters incl. housing and town centre re-development. *Recreations*: golf, music, gardening, most spectator sports. *Address*: Westgate House, The High, Harlow, Essex. *T*: Harlow 441318.

BARDSLEY, Rt. Rev. Cuthbert Killick Norman, CBE 1952; DD 1957; *b* 28 March 1907; *yr s* of late Canon J. U. N. Bardsley and Mabel Killick; *m* 1972, Ellen Mitchell. *Educ*: New Coll., Oxford. Curate of All Hallows, Barking by the Tower, 1932-34; Rector of Woolwich, 1940-44; Provost of Southwark Cathedral, 1944-47. Suffragan Bishop of Croydon, 1947-56; Bishop of Coventry, 1956-76. Hon. Canon in Canterbury Cathedral, 1948-56; Archbishop of Canterbury's Episcopal Representative with the three Armed Forces, 1948-56; Hon. Chaplain Siemens Bros, 1943-46; Proctor in Convocation, 1945-46. Select Preacher, University of Cambridge, 1958. ChStJ 1976. Hon. DLitt Warwick Univ., 1976. *Publications*: Bishop's Move, 1952; Sundry Times, Sundry Places, 1962; Him We Declare, 1967; I Believe in Mission, 1970. *Recreations*: golf, sketching. *Address*: Grey Walls, Berkeley Road, Cirencester, Gloucestershire GL7 1TY.

BARENBOIM, Daniel; pianist and conductor; Musical Director, Orchestre de Paris, since 1975; *b* Buenos Aires, 15 Nov. 1942; *s* of Enrique Barenboim and Aida Barenboim (*née* Schuster); *m* 1967, Jacqueline du Pré, *qv*. *Educ*: Santa Cecilia Acad., Rome; studied with his father; coached by Edwin Fischer, Nadia Boulanger, and Igor Markevitch. Debut as pianist with: Israel Philharmonic Orchestra, 1953; Royal Philharmonic Orchestra, 1956; Berlin Philharmonic Orchestra, 1963; NY Philharmonic Orchestra, 1964; tours include: Australia, 1958, 1962; South America, 1960; Far East, 1962; regular appearances at Edinburgh, Lucerne, Prague and Salzburg Festivals. Beethoven Medal, 1958; Paderewski Medal, 1963; subsequently other awards. *Address*: c/o Harold Holt Ltd, 134 Wigmore Street, W1.

BARFETT, Ven. Thomas; Archdeacon of Hereford and Canon Residentiary of Hereford Cathedral, 1977-82, now Emeritus; Prebendary of Colwall and Treasurer, 1977-82; Chaplain to the Queen, since 1975; *b* 2 Oct. 1916; *s* of Rev. Thomas Clarence Fairchild Barfett and Dr Mary Deborah Barfett, LRCP, LRCS, MA; *m* 1945, Edna, *d* of Robert Toy; one *s* one *d*. *Educ*: St John's Sch., Leatherhead; Keble Coll., Oxford (BA 1938; MA 1942); Wells Theol Coll. Ordained deacon, Portsmouth, 1939; priest, 1940; Curate: Christ Church, Gosport, 1939-44; St Francis of Assisi, Gladstone Park, London, 1944-47; St Andrew Undershaft with St Mary Axe, City of London, 1947-49; Asst Sec., London Diocesan Council for Youth, 1944-49; Vicar, St Paul, Penzance, dio. of Truro, 1949-55; Rector of Falmouth, 1955-77; Officiating Chaplain, 1102 Marine Craft Unit, RAF, 1957-75; Sec., Truro Diocesan Conf., 1952-67; Proctor in Convocation, dio. of Truro, 1958-76; Hon. Canon, Truro, 1964-77. Chm., House of Clergy, and Vice-Pres., Truro Diocesan Synod, 1970-76; Mem., Gen. Synod, 1977-82. Chaplain to lay Sheriff, City of London, 1976-77. Church Comr, 1975-82; Mem. C of E Central Bd of Finance, 1969-77, Pensions Board, 1973-. Freeman, City of London, 1973; Freeman and Liveryman, Scriveners Co., 1976. Sub ChStJ, 1971 (Asst ChStJ, 1963). Silver Jubilee Medal, 1977. *Publication*: Trebarfoote: a Cornish family, 1975. *Recreations*: heraldry, genealogy. *Address*: Treberveth, 57 Falmouth Road, Truro, Cornwall TR1 2HL. *T*: Truro 3726. *Club*: United Oxford & Cambridge University.

BARFORD, Sir Leonard, Kt 1967; Deputy Chairman, Horserace Totalisator Board, 1974-77 (Member, 1973-77); Chief Inspector of Taxes, Board of Inland Revenue, 1964-73; Commissioner of Inland Revenue, 1970-73; *b* 1 Aug. 1908; *s* of William and Ada Barford, Finsbury Park; *m* 1939, Betty Edna Crichton, Plymouth; two *s*. *Educ*: Dame Alice Owen's Sch.; St Catharine's Coll., Cambridge Univ. (Exhibitioner in History). Asst Inspector of Taxes, 1930; Administrative Staff Coll., Henley, 1948; President, Assoc. of HM Inspectors of Taxes, 1951-53; Principal Inspector of Taxes, 1953; Senior Principal Inspector of Taxes, 1957; Deputy Chief Inspector, 1960. *Publication*: (jointly) Essay on Management in Tax Offices, 1950. *Recreations*: badminton, tennis, chess, bridge. *Address*: Harley House, 79 Sutton Road, Seaford, East Sussex. *T*: Seaford 893364. *Club*: Civil Service.

BARING, family name of **Baron Ashburton,** of **Earl of Cromer,** of **Baron Howick of Glendale,** of **Baron Northbrook,** and of **Baron Revelstoke.**

BARING, Sir Charles Christian, 2nd Bt, *cr* 1911; JP; DL; *b* 16 Dec. 1898; *s* of Sir Godfrey Baring, 1st Bt, KBE, DL, and Eva Hermione Mackintosh of Mackintosh (*d* 1934); *S* father 1957; *m* 1948 Jeanette (Jan), *d* of Henry Charles Daykin. *Educ*: Eton. Served European War: Lieut Coldstream Guards, 1917-18 (severely wounded); War of 1939-45: Major Coldstream Guards, 1940-45; Political Warfare Executive, 1943-44; Staff, AFHQ, Italy, War Office, 1944-45. Attaché, HM Legation, Warsaw, 1922-23; Cunard White Star Ltd, 1933-36; HM Prison Service, 1936-38; Probation Officer: West London Magistrates' Court, 1938-40; Central Criminal Court, 1945-46; Inspector, Probation Branch Home Office, 1946-49; Colonial Service: Warden of Prisons, Bermuda, 1949-53. Member, Cttee of Management, RNLI (Vice-Pres., 1972). JP Isle of Wight County, 1956; DL Co. Southampton subseq. IoW, 1962; Chm. of Justices, IoW Petty Sessional Div., 1962-70. *Recreations*: golf, swimming, walking. *Heir*: nephew (Charles) Peter Baring [*b* 24 May 1939; *m* 1st, 1964, Sarah (marr. diss. 1974), *d* of late Col William Gill Withycombe; two *d*; 2nd, 1976, Susannah Jane, *d* of Dr W. E. Smith; one *d*]. *Address*: 4 Sandlands, Seaview, Isle of Wight.

BARING, Hon. John Francis Harcourt, CVO 1980; Chairman, Baring Brothers & Co. Ltd, since 1974 (a Managing Director, 1955-74); Receiver-General of Duchy of Cornwall, since 1974; *b* 2 Nov. 1928; *er s* and *heir* of 6th Baron Ashburton, *qv*; *m* 1955, Susan Mary Renwick, *e d* of 1st Baron Renwick, KBE, and Mrs John Ormiston; two *s* two *d*. *Educ*: Eton (Fellow, 1982); Trinity Coll., Oxford (MA). Director: Trafford Park Estates Ltd, 1964-77; Pye Holdings Ltd, 1966-79; Outwich Ltd, Johannesburg, 1967-77; Dep. Chm., Royal Insurance Co. Ltd, 1975- (Dir, 1964-); Chm., Outwich Investment Trust Ltd, 1968-; Director: Dunlop Holdings Ltd, 1981-; British Petroleum, 1982-. Vice-Pres., British Bankers' Assoc., 1977-; Pres., Overseas Bankers' Club, 1977-78. Chm., Accepting Houses Cttee, 1977-81; Chm., Cttee on Finance for Industry, NEDC, 1980-. Mem., British Transport Docks Bd, 1966-71; Mem. Council, CBI, 1976-80 (Mem. President's Cttee, 1976-79). Rhodes Trustee, 1970; Trustee, Nat. Gall., 1981-. Hon. Fellow, Hertford Coll., Oxford, 1976. *Address*: Lake House, Northington, Alresford, Hants SO24 9TG. *T*: Alresford 4293; Flat 7, 34 Bryanston Square, W1H 7LQ. *Clubs*: Pratt's, Flyfishers'.

BARING, Sir Mark, KCVO 1980 (CVO 1970); JP; General Commissioner for Income Tax, since 1966; Executive Chairman, King Edward VII's Hospital for Officers, since 1969; *b* 9 June 1916; *yr s* of late Hon. Windham Baring and Lady Gweneth Cavendish, 3rd *d* of 8th Earl of Bessborough; *m* 1949, Victoria Winifred Russell, *d* of late Col R. E. M. Russell, CVO, CBE, DSO; two *d*. *Educ*: Eton Coll.; Trinity Coll., Cambridge. Served War of 1939-45, Grenadier Guards; in Italy and UK; Mil. Liaison Officer HM Embassy, Rome, 1945-46 (Major 1945); retd 1946. Man. Dir, Seccombe Marshall and Campion Ltd, Discount Brokers, 1950-76. JP, Inner Area of London, 1963. Treasurer, Inst. of Urology, 1969-74; Mem. Bd of Governors, St Peter's Hosp., 1970-74; Governor, The Peabody Trust, 1971; Mem. Council, Baring Foundn, 1975-; Chm., Assoc. of Independent Hosps; Pres., St Marylebone Housing Assoc.,

1956-77. High Sheriff, Greater London, 1976-77. *Recreations:* tennis, bridge. *Address:* 18 Thurloe Square, SW7. *T:* 01-589 8485. *Clubs:* Brooks's, White's.

BARING, Lady Rose (Gwendolen Louisa), DCVO 1972 (CVO 1964); Extra Woman of the Bedchamber to the Queen, since 1973; *b* 23 May 1909; *er d* of 12th Earl of Antrim and of Margaret, *y d* of late Rt Hon. J. G. Talbot; *m* 1933, Francis Anthony Baring (killed in action, 1940); two *s* one *d*. Woman of the Bedchamber to the Queen, 1953-73. *Address:* 43 Pembroke Square, W8.

BARK, Evelyn (Elizabeth Patricia), CMG 1967; OBE 1952; retired as Director International Affairs Department of British Red Cross (1950-66); *b* 26 Dec. 1900; *e d* of late Frederick William Bark. *Educ:* privately. On staff of Swedish Match Co. (at home and abroad) until 1939, when joined British Red Cross. Served War, 1939-44, VAD (Stars of 1939-45, of France, and of Germany; Defence Medal, and War Medal, 1939-45). Foreign Relations Officer, 1944-48. Commissioner, NW Europe, 1948-49; Foreign Relations and Relief Adviser, 1950 (title later changed to Dir International Affairs). Serving Sister of St John's, 1953; British Red Cross Certificate First Class, 1966. *Publication:* No Time to Kill, 1960. *Recreations:* reading, music, nordic languages. *Address:* 4 Milton Mansions, Queen's Club Gardens, W14. *T:* 01-385 2181. *Club:* VAD Ladies'.

BARKE, James Allen; Director, Falcon Engineering Co., since 1972; *b* 16 April 1903; *s* of James E. Barke and Emma Livsey; *m* 1st, 1937, Doris Marian Bayne (*d* 1952); two *s* one *d*; 2nd, 1953, Marguerite Amy Sutcliffe (*née* Williams) (*d* 1968); one *step d*. *Educ:* Birley Street Central Sch.; Manchester Coll. of Technology. Mather & Platt and general engineering experience, 1922-32; joined Ford Motor Co., 1932; Buyer, Purchase Dept, 1939; Chief Buyer (Tractors), 1947; Manager, Leamington Foundry, 1948; Executive Dir and General Manager, Briggs Motor Bodies Ltd, 1953; Ford Motor Co.: Dir, Product Divs, 1959; Asst Man. Dir, 1961; Man. Dir, 1962; Chief Exec. Officer and Man. Dir, 1963; Vice-Chm., 1965-68; Dir, De La Rue Company Ltd, 1970-73. *Recreations:* golf, rock climbing, walking, reading. *Address:* Thurlestone, Mill Green, Ingatestone, Essex. *Club:* Oriental.

BARKER, family name of **Baroness Trumpington.**

BARKER, Alan; *see* Barker, William A.

BARKER, Sir Alwyn (Bowman), Kt 1969; CMG 1962; BSc, BE; CEng, FIEAust; Chairman, Kelvinator Australia Ltd, 1967-80 (Managing Director, 1952-67); *b* 5 Aug. 1900; *s* of late A. J. Barker, Mt Barker, South Australia; *m* 1926, Isabel Barron Lucas, *d* of late Sir Edward Lucas; one *d* (one *s* decd). *Educ:* St Peter's Coll., Adelaide; Geelong C of E Grammar Sch.; Univ. of Adelaide. British Thomson Houston Co. Ltd, England, 1923-24; Hudson Motor Car Co., Detroit, 1924-25; Production Manager, Holden's Motor Body Builders Ltd, Adelaide, 1925-30; Works Manager, Kelvinator Aust. Ltd, Adelaide, 1931-40; Gen. Man., Chrysler Aust. Ltd, Adelaide, 1940-52; Chm., Municipal Tramways Trust SA, 1953-68; Dep. Chm., Australian Mineral Foundn; Dir, public companies. Mem. Faculty of Engineering, Univ. of Adelaide, 1937-66 (Lectr in Industrial Engineering, 1929-53). Chm., Industrial Develt Adv. Council, 1968-70; Fellow, Internat. Acad. of Management; Member: Manufacturing Industries Adv. Council, 1958-72; Res. and Develt Adv. Cttee, 1967-72. Hon. Fellow Australian Inst. of Management (Federal Pres., 1952-53, 1959-61; Pres. Adelaide Div., 1952-54); Pres., Australian Council, Inst. of Prodn Engrs, 1970-72. John Storey Meml Medal, 1965; Jack Finlay Nat. Award, 1964. *Publications:* Three Presidential Addresses, 1954; William Queale Memorial Lecture, 1965. *Recreations:* pastoral. *Address:* 51 Hackney Road, Hackney, SA 5069, Australia. *T:* 42.2838. *Club:* Adelaide.

BARKER, Arthur Vincent, CBE 1974 (OBE 1955); FCIT; Scottish Chartered Accountant; financial planning consultant; *b* 10 Nov. 1911; *e s* of late Arthur and Susannah Mary Barker; *m* 1936, Dorothy Drew; one *d*. *Educ:* Whitley and Monkseaton High Sch.; London Sch. of Economics. Qual. as CA, 1934; with Price Waterhouse & Co., 1934-35; with NAAFI in Middle East and UK, 1935-62 (Jt Gen. Man., 1955); Asst Gen. Man., Southern Region, British Railways, and Mem., Southern Railway Bd, 1962; Asst Gen. Man., London Midland Region, British Railways, and Mem., LMR Bd, 1965; Chairman: Shipping and Internat. Services Div., British Railways, 1968-69; British Rail Hovercraft, 1970-71; British Transport Hotels Ltd, 1968-74; Mem., British Railways Bd, 1968-74. *Recreation:* fly-fishing. *Address:* 25 West Mount, The Mount, Guildford, Surrey GU2 5HL. *T:* Guildford 39524.

BARKER, Audrey Lilian; writer; *b* 13 April 1918; *d* of Harry and Elsie Barker. *Educ:* County secondary schools in Beckenham, Kent and Wallington, Surrey. Editorial office, Amalgamated Press, 1936; Publisher's reader, Cresset Press, 1947; BBC, 1949-78. Atlantic Award in Literature, 1946; Somerset Maugham Award, 1947; Cheltenham Festival of Literature Award, 1962; SE Arts Creative Book Award, 1981. FRS 1970; Mem. Exec. Cttee, PEN. *Publications:* Innocents, 1947; Apology for a Hero, 1950; Novelette, 1951; The Joy-Ride, 1963; Lost Upon the Roundabouts, 1964; A Case Examined, 1965; The Middling, 1967; John Brown's Body, 1969; Femina Real, 1971; A Source of Embarrassment, 1974; A Heavy Feather, 1978; Life Stories, 1981. *Address:* 103 Harrow Road, Carshalton, Surrey.

BARKER, Barry, MBE 1960; FCIS; Secretary and Chief Executive, Institute of Chartered Secretaries and Administrators (formerly Chartered Institute of Secretaries), since 1976; *b* 1929; *s* of late Francis Walter Barker and of Amy Barker; *m* 1954, Dr Vira Dubash; two *s*. *Educ:* Ipswich Sch.; Trinity Coll., Oxford (MA Class. Greats). FBIM. Secretary: Bombay Chamber of Commerce and Industry, 1956-62; The Metal Box Co. of India Ltd, 1962-67. Dir, Shipbuilding Industry Bd, 1967-71; Consultant at Dept of Industry, 1972; Sec., Pye Holdings Ltd, 1972-76. *Recreations:* the theatre and the arts. *Address:* Worsted Barrows, Babraham, Cambridge CB2 4AX. *T:* Cambridge 833298. *Club:* Oriental.

BARKER, Rt. Rev. Clifford Conder; *see* Whitby, Bishop Suffragan of.

BARKER, David, QC 1976; a Recorder of the Crown Court, since 1974; *b* 13 April 1932; *s* of Frederick Barker and Amy Evelyn Barker; *m* 1957, Diana Mary Vinson Barker (*née* Duckworth); one *s* three *d*. *Educ:* Sir John Deane's Grammar Sch., Northwich; University Coll., London; Univ. of Michigan. 1st cl. hons LLB London; LLM Michigan. RAF, 1956-59. Called to Bar, Inner Temple, 1954; practised Midland and Oxford Circuit; Mem., Senate of Inns of Court and the Bar, 1981-. Contested (Lab) Runcorn, 1955. *Recreations:* gardening, walking, sailing. *Address:* Nanhill, Woodhouse Eaves, Leics. *T:* Woodhouse Eaves 890224; Goldsmith Building, Temple, EC4. *T:* 01-353 7881. *Club:* Northampton and County (Northampton).

BARKER, Prof. David (Faubert), MA, DPhil, DSc; Professor of Zoology, University of Durham, since 1962; *b* 18 Feb. 1922; *s* of Harold and Doreen Barker; *m* 1st, 1945, Kathleen Mary Frances Pocock; three *s* two *d*; 2nd, 1978, Patricia Margaret Drake; one *s* one *d*. *Educ:* Bryanston Sch.; Magdalen Coll., Oxford. DSc 1972. Senior Demy of Magdalen Coll., 1946; Leverhulme Research Scholar, Royal Coll. of Surgeons, 1946; Demonstrator in Zoology and Comparative Anatomy, Univ. of Oxford, 1947; DPhil 1948; Rolleston Prizeman, 1948; Prof. of Zoology, Univ. of Hong Kong, 1950-62; led scientific expeditions to Tunisia, 1950, North Borneo, 1952; Dean of Faculty of Science, Hong Kong, 1959-60; Public Orator, Hong Kong, 1961. *Publications:* (Founder) Editor, Hong Kong Univ. Fisheries Journal, 1954-60; Editor, Symposium on Muscle Receptors, 1962; scientific papers, mostly on muscle innervation. *Address:* Department of Zoology, Science Laboratories, South Road, Durham. *T:* Durham 64971.

BARKER, Dennis Albert; Hon. Mr Justice Barker; Justice of Appeal, Hong Kong, since 1981; *b* 9 June 1926; *s* of J. W. and R. E. Barker; *m* 1949, Daphne (*née* Ruffle); one *s* one *d* (and one *d* decd). *Educ:* Nottingham High Sch.; The Queen's Coll. Oxford (Jodrell Schol.). Flying Officer, RAFVR, 1944-47. 1st cl. hons (Jurisprudence), Oxon, 1949; 1st cl. Certif. of Honour and Studentship, Bar Finals, 1950; Harmsworth Law Schol., 1950; Eldon Law Schol., 1950; called to the Bar, Middle Temple, 1950, Bencher, 1975. Mem. Midland Circuit; Dep. Chm., Bucks QS, 1963-71; QC 1968; a Recorder of the Crown Court, 1972-79. Former Mem., Criminal Injuries Compensation Bd. *Recreations:* golf, flying. *Address:* Supreme Court, Hong Kong. *Club:* Hong Kong (Hong Kong).

BARKER, Edward, OBE 1966; QPM 1961; Chief Constable of Sheffield and Rotherham Constabulary, 1967-72; *b* 1 Nov. 1909; *s* of George and Gertrude Barker; *m* 1935, Clare Garth; one *d*. *Educ:* The Grammar School, Malton. Joined Preston Borough Police, 1931; transf. Lancs Constabulary, 1938; Inspector/Chief Inspector, Comdt of Constabulary Trng Sch., 1946-51; Supt 1954; Vis. Lectr to Bermuda Police, 1955; Chief Supt 1956; Asst Comdt, Police Coll., Bramshill, 1956-57; Chief Constable: Bolton Borough Police, 1957; Sheffield City Police, 1964. Police Long Service and Good Conduct Medal, 1953. SBStJ. *Recreations:* golf, gardening, watching field sports. *Address:* 21 Woodstock Road, Aberdeen. *Clubs:* Royal Over-Seas League; Deeside Golf.

BARKER, Eric Leslie; Author and Entertainer; *b* 20 Feb. 1912; *s* of Charles and Maude Barker; *m* 1936, Pearl Hackney; one *d*. *Educ:* Whitgift Sch. Character actor Birmingham, Oxford and Croydon Repertory Theatres, 1932-33; Comedian, also sketch and lyric writer, Charlot revues, Windmill, and Prince of Wales Theatre, 1933-38. Author and star of radio series: Howdyfolks, 1939-40; Navy Mixture, 1944-45; Merry-Go-Round, 1945-49; Just Fancy, 1950-62; Passing Parade, 1957; Barker's Folly, 1958; Law and Disorder, 1960. Lieut RNVR, 1940-45. Author and star of television series: Eric Barker Half Hour, 1952-55; Absolutely Barkers, 1963. *Films:* Brothers-in-Law (British Film Acad. Award); Clean Sweep; Blue Murder at St Trinians; Happy Is The Bride; Carry on, Sergeant; Eye Spy; Bachelor of Hearts; Right, Left and Centre; Carry on, Constable; Dentist in the Chair; Raising the Wind; The Fast Lady; Those Magnificent Men in their Flying Machines; Doctor in Clover; Maroc 7. *Publications:* short stories, 3 novels, 1931-33; The Watch Hunt, 1931; Day Gone By, 1932; Steady Barker (Autobiog.), 1956; Golden Gimmick, 1958. *Recreations:* antiques, photography, gardening, history, cricket, swimming. *Address:* c/o Lloyds Bank, Faversham, Kent.

BARKER, Gen. Sir Evelyn Hugh, KCB 1950 (CB 1944); KBE 1945 (CBE 1940); DSO 1918; MC; *b* 22 May 1894; *y s* of late Maj.-Gen. Sir George Barker, KCB, and late Hon. Lady Barker; *m* 1923, Violet Eleanor, *y d* of T. W. Thornton of Brockhall, near Weedon, Northants; one *s*. *Educ:* Wellington Coll.; RM Coll., Sandhurst. Joined KRRC, 1913; Capt. 1916; Bt-Maj. 1929; Major 1930; Bt Lt-Col 1934; Lt-Col 1936; Bt-Col 1937; Col

1938; Maj.-Gen., 1941; Lt-Gen., 1944; General, 1948. Served European War, 1914-18, France, Salonica, and South Russia; GSO3, 1917; Bde-Major, 1917; despatches, DSO, MC; GSO3 (War Office), 1919; Brigade-Major 8th Infantry Brigade, 1931-33; commanded 2nd Bn KRRC, 1936-38; commanded 10th Infantry Brigade, 1938-40; commanded 54th Div. 1941-42, and 49th (West Riding) Div. 1943-44; commanded 8 Corps, 1944-April 1946; commanded British Troops in Palestine and Transjordan, 1946; ADC General to the King, 1949-50; GOC-in-C Eastern Command, 1947-50; retd 1950. Col Comdt 2nd Bn KRRC, 1946-56; Hon. Col Loyal Suffolk Hussars (Yeomanry), 1946-50; Hon. Col, Beds Yeo., 1951-60; Hon. Col Herts and Beds Yeo., 1961-62. DL, Beds, 1952-67. Cmdr, Legion of Honour; Croix de Guerre (with palm) France; Silver Medal, Italy; O St Stanislas, Russia; Grand Cross of Dannebrog, Denmark. *Address:* Park House, Bromham, Bedford. *T:* Oakley 2332.

BARKER, George Granville; writer; *b* 26 Feb. 1913; *s* of George Barker and Marion Frances Barker (*née* Taaffe); *m* 1964, Elspeth Langlands. *Educ:* Marlborough Road London County Council Sch., Chelsea. Prof. of English Literature at Imperial Tohoku Univ., Japan, 1939; visited America, 1940; returned to England, 1943; lived in Rome, 1960-65. Arts Fellow York Univ., 1966-67; Vis. Prof., Florida Internat. Univ., 1974. *Publications:* Thirty Preliminary Poems, 1933; Alanna Autumnal, 1933; Poems, 1935; Janus, 1935; Calamiterror, 1937; Lament and Triumph, 1940; Eros in Dogma, 1944; News of the World, 1950; The Dead Seagull, 1950; The True Confession of George Barker, 1950; A Vision of Beasts and Gods, 1954; Collected Poems, 1930-55, 1957; The True Confession of George Barker, Book II, 1957; Two Plays, 1958; The View from a Blind I, 1962; Dreams of a Summer Night, 1966; The Golden Chains, 1968; Essays, 1970; Runes & Rhymes & Tunes & Chimes, 1970; To Aylsham Fair, 1970; At Thurgarton Church, 1970; Poems of Places and People, 1971; The Alphabetical Zoo, 1972; In Memory of David Archer, 1973; Dialogues etc, 1976; Villa Stellar, 1978. *Address:* Bintry House, Itteringham, Aylsham, Norfolk. *T:* Saxthorpe 240.

BARKER, Harold; retired; Keeper, Department of Conservation and Technical Services, British Museum, 1975-79; Member: Council for Care of Churches, 1976-81; Crafts Council, 1979-80; *b* 15 Feb. 1919; *s* of William Frampton Barker and Lily (*née* Pack); *m* 1942, Everilda Alice Whittle; one *s* one *d. Educ:* City Secondary Sch., Sheffield; Sheffield Univ. (BSc). Experimental Asst, 1940, Experimental Officer, 1942, Chemical Inspectorate, Min. of Supply; British Museum: Experimental Officer, Research Lab., 1947; Sen. Experimental Officer, 1953; Chief Experimental Officer, 1960; Principal Scientific Officer, 1966; Acting Keeper, 1975. *Publications:* papers on radiocarbon dating and scientific examination of antiquities in various jls. *Recreations:* music, walking, cinematography. *Address:* 27 Westbourne Park, Falsgrave, Scarborough, N Yorks YO12 4AS. *T:* Scarborough 70967.

BARKER, Sir Harry Heaton, KBE 1978 (CBE 1972; OBE 1964); JP; New Zealand Journalist; chairman various organisations; *b* Nelson, NZ, 18 July 1898; *s* of J. H. Barker; *m* 1926, Anita (MBE), *d* of H. Greaves; no *c. Educ:* Wellington and Auckland; New Plymouth Boys' High Sch. Served NZEF, 1917-19. Entered journalism, working with NZ Herald and country newspapers, 1916-17, 1919-23; Gisborne Herald: joined, 1923; sub-editor, 1926; Leader Writer, Associate Editor, 1930; Editor, 1935-43, resigned. Mayor of Gisborne, 1950; re-elected, 1953, 1956, 1959, 1962, 1965, 1968, 1971, 1974. Contested Gisborne seat, 1943, 1946. Member: Cook Hospital Board, 1944-71; King George V Health Camps Federation Board, 1953-69; Exec., Dist Roads Council, 1953-78; East Coast Planning Council, 1972-77. Chairman: Barrington Miller Educnl Trust, 1950-77; Gisborne Airport Cttee, 1958-77; cttee organising nat. celebration, Cook Bicentenary celebration, 1969. Executive, NZ Municipalities Assoc., and Dir, Municipalities Insurance Co., 1959-69. Knighted for services to the City of Gisborne, NZ, and local government. *Recreations:* reading, writing, gardening. *Publications:* To-Days and Yesterdays, 1978; political articles. *Address:* 218 Harris Street, Gisborne, New Zealand. *T:* 6405. *Club:* Victoria League.

BARKER, Hugh Purslove; Chairman, 1956-71 and Managing Director, 1945-71, Parkinson Cowan Group; Chairman, Boosey & Hawkes Ltd, 1974-79; Vice-President, British Institute of Management, since 1962 (Chairman, 1960-62); *b* 11 March 1909; *s* of Arthur Henry Barker and Florence Barker (*née* Saich); *m* 1935, Joye Frances Higgs (decd); two *s* one *d* ; *m* Kathleen Mary Miles (decd); *m* Rosemary Ursula Meyer. *Educ:* Oundle Sch. Mech. Engr Apprenticeship (concurrently studied Engineering, Accountancy and Law), Waygood-Otis Ltd, 1927-31; private mfg business, 1931-35; Cons. Engr, A. H. Barker & Partners, 1935-39. Min of Munic. Bldg Cos. Min. of Aircraft Prodn (Dep. Dir Instrument Prodn), 1940-44. Part-time Mem., British Railways Bd, 1962-67 (British Transport Commn, 1951-62); Chm., EDC for the Rubber Industry, 1968-71. Mem., Royal Commn on Assizes, 1967-70. CEng; FIEE; FIMechE; FInstGasE; FIHVE; FCIT; CBIM. *Publications:* papers and articles to Technical Institutes and press, on engineering subjects, and to financial and econ. press on management. *Recreations:* fishing, music. *Address:* 7 Stopham House, Stopham, Pulborough, W Sussex RH20 1EA. *T:* Fittleworth 619. *Club:* Carlton.

BARKER, Air Vice-Marshal John Lindsay, CB 1963; CBE 1946; DFC 1945; RAF (Retired); *b* 12 Nov. 1910; *s* of Abraham Cockroft Barker and Lilian Alice (*née* Woods); *m* 1948, Eleanor Margaret Hannah; one *s. Educ:* Trent Coll., Derbys; Brasenose Coll., Oxford. Called to the Bar, Middle Temple, 1947. RAFO, 1930, RAF, 1933. Served War of 1939-45: France,

1939-40; N Africa, 1942-44; Bomber Command, 1944-45; Far East, 1945-48; Egypt, 1950-53; Air Attaché, Rome, 1955-58; Cmdr Royal Ceylon Air Force, 1958-63. Air Vice-Marshal, 1959. Retd, 1963. Order of Merit, Italy, 1958. *Recreations:* golf, photography, sailing. *Address:* Ravensbourne, Ravensbourne Lane, Stoke Fleming, Dartmouth, Devon TQ6 0QR. *Club:* Royal Air Force.

BARKER, John Michael Adrian; His Honour Judge Barker; a Circuit Judge, since 1979; *b* 4 Nov. 1932; *s* of Robert Henry Barker and Annie Robson Barker (*née* Charlton); *m* 1971, Gillian Marsha (*née* Greenstone). *Educ:* Marist Coll., Hull; Univs of Sheffield and Hull. BSc, LLB. Called to Bar, Middle Temple, 1959. Schoolmaster, Stonyhurst Coll., 1957-59; Lectr in Law, Univ. of Hull, 1960-63. A Recorder of the Crown Court, 1974-79. Mem., Hull CC, 1965-71. *Publications:* articles in Conveyancer and Property Lawyer, Solicitors' Jl and Solicitor. *Recreations:* music, cricket. *Address:* 86 Davenport Avenue, Hessle, North Humberside. *T:* Hull 648909. *Club:* Lansdowne.

BARKER, Nicolas John; Head of Conservation, British Library Reference Division, since 1976; Editor, Book Collector, since 1965; *b* 6 Dec. 1932; *s* of Sir Ernest Barker, FBA, and Olivia Stuart Horner; *m* 1962, Joanna Mary Sophia Nyda Cotton; two *s* three *d. Educ:* Westminster Sch.; New Coll., Oxford (MA). With Bailliere, Tindall & Cox, 1959 and Rupert Hart-Davis, 1959; Asst Keeper, National Portrait Gallery, 1964; with Macmillan & Co. Ltd, 1965; with OUP, 1976. President: Amici Thomae Mori, 1978-; Double Crown Club, 1980-81; Pres., Bibliographical Soc., 1981-; Member: Publication Bd of Dirs, RNIB, 1969-; London Library Cttee, 1971-; BBC and ITV Appeals Adv. Cttee, 1977-; Nat. Trust Arts Panel, 1979-; Trustee, The Pilgrim Trust, 1977-. *Publications:* The Publications of the Roxburghe Club, 1962; The Printer and the Poet, 1970; Stanley Morison, 1972; (ed) Essays and Papers of A. N. L. Munby, 1977; (ed) The Early Life of James McBey: an autobiography, 1883-1911, 1977; Bibliotheca Lindesiana, 1977; The Oxford University Press and the Spread of Learning 1478-1978, 1978; A Sequel to an Enquiry, 1982. *Address:* 22 Clarendon Road, W11. *T:* 01-727 4340. *Clubs:* Garrick, Beefsteak.

BARKER, Paul; Editor of New Society since 1968; *b* 24 Aug. 1935; *s* of Donald and Marion Barker; *m* 1960, Sally, *e d* of James and Marion Huddleston; three *s* one *d. Educ:* Hebden Bridge Grammar Sch.; Calder High Sch.; Brasenose Coll., Oxford (Hulme Exhibr), BA 1958, MA 1970. Intell. Corps (commn), 1953-55. Lecteur, Ecole Normale Supérieure, Paris, 1958-59; The Times, 1959-64; New Society, staff writer, 1964; The Economist, 1964-65; New Society, Assistant Editor, 1965-68. Reviewer for The Times, Guardian, Radio Three. *Publications:* (ed) A Sociological Portrait, 1972; (ed) One for Sorrow, Two for Joy, 1972; (ed) The Social Sciences Today, 1975; (ed) Arts in Society, 1977; (ed) The Other Britain, 1982. *Recreation:* driving along an empty motorway to a baroque church, with the radio on. *Address:* 26 Patshull Road, NW5. *T:* 01-485 8861.

BARKER, Richard Philip; Headmaster, Sevenoaks School, since 1981; *b* 17 July 1939; *s* of late Philip Watson Barker and Helen May Barker; *m* 1966, Imogen Margaret Harris; two *s* one *d. Educ:* Repton; Trinity Coll., Cambridge (MA 1962); Bristol Univ. (Cert. Ed. 1963). Head of Geography, Bedales Sch., 1963-65; Dir, A level business studies project, 1966-73; Lectr, Inst. of Education, London Univ., 1973-74; Housemaster, Marlborough Coll., 1973-81. *Publications:* (ed) Understanding Business Series, 1976-81. *Recreations:* fishing, sailing, travelling. *Address:* Headmaster's House, Sevenoaks School, Kent TN13 1HU. *T:* Sevenoaks 55133.

BARKER, Ronald Hugh, PhD, BSc; CEng, FIEE, FIMechE; Deputy Director, Royal Armament Research and Development Establishment, 1965-75, retired; *b* 28 Oct. 1915; *s* of E. W. Barker and L. A. Taylor; *m* 1943, W. E. Hunt; two *s. Educ:* University of Hull. Physicist, Standard Telephones and Cables, 1938-41; Ministry of Supply, 1941-59; Dep. Dir, Central Electricity Research Laboratories, 1959-62; Technical Dir, The Pullin Group Ltd, 1962-65. *Publications:* various, on servomechanisms and control systems. *Address:* Cró Madra, St Monica's Road, Kingswood, Surrey KT20 6HA. *T:* Burgh Heath 55489.

BARKER, Ronnie, (Ronald William George Barker), OBE 1978; actor; *b* 25 Sept. 1929; *s* of Leonard and Edith Barker; *m* 1957, Joy Tubb; two *s* one *d. Educ:* Oxford High Sch. Started acting career, Aylesbury Rep. Co., 1948. *Plays (West End):* Mourning Becomes Electra, 1955; Summertime, 1955; Listen to the Wind, 1955; Double Image, 1956; Camino Real, 1957; Lysistrata, 1958; Irma la Douce, 1958; Platanov, 1960; On the Brighter Side, 1961; Midsummer Night's Dream, 1962; Real Inspector Hound, 1968; The Two Ronnies, Palladium, 1978. *Films include:* Robin and Marian, 1975; Picnic, 1975; Porridge, 1979. *Television: series:* Seven Faces of Jim, 1965; Frost Report, 1966-67; Hark at Barker, 1968-69; Six Dates with Barker, 1970; The Two Ronnies, 9 series, 1971-; Porridge, 1974, 1975, 1976, 1977; Open All Hours, 1976; Going Straight, 1978. Awards: Variety Club, 1969, 1974, 1980; SFTA, 1971; Radio Industries Club, 1973, 1974, 1977, 1981; Water Rats, 1975; British Acad. Award, 1975, 1977, 1978; Royal Television Society's award for outstanding creative achievement, 1975; Sun Awards, 1975, 1977. *Publications:* Book of Bathing Beauties, 1974; Book of Boudoir Beauties, 1975; It's Goodnight From Him, 1976; Sauce, 1977; Gentlemen's Relish, 1979; Sugar and Spice, 1981. *Recreations:* writing song lyrics, collecting postcards.

BARKER, Susan Vera; see Cooper, Susie.

BARKER, Prof. Theodore Cardwell, PhD, FRHistS; Professor of Economic History, University of London, since 1976; *b* 19 July 1923; *s* of Norman Humphrey Barker and Louie Nettleton Barker; *m* 1955, Joy Marie (Judith) Pierce. *Educ:* Cowley Sch., St Helens; Jesus Coll., Oxford (MA); Manchester Univ. (PhD). FRHistS 1963. Econ. History staff, LSE, 1953-64; first Prof. of Econ. and Social Hist., Univ. of Kent at Canterbury, 1964-76. Chairman: Management Cttee, Inst. of Historical Res., London Univ., 1977-; Hist. Bd, CNAA, 1977-81; British National Cttee, Internat. Historical Congress, 1978-; Management Cttee, London Univ. Business History Unit, 1979-; Oral Hist. Soc., 1973-76. Mem. Council, RHistS, 1967-70 and 1974-77; Central Bureau, Internat. Historical Congress, 1981-; Hon. Sec., Econ. Hist. Soc., 1960-. *Publications:* A Merseyside Town in the Industrial Revolution (with J. R. Harris), 1954; A History of the Girdlers Company, 1957; Pilkington Brothers and the Glass Industry, 1960; (with R. H. Campbell, Peter Mathias and B. S. Yamey) Business History, 1960, 2nd edn 1970; (with R. M. Robbins) A History of London Transport: Vol. I, 1963, Vol. II, 1974; (ed with J. C. McKenzie and John Yudkin) Our Changing Fare: two hundred years of British food habits, 1966; (with B. W. E. Alford) A History of the Worshipful Company of Carpenters, 1968; (ed) The Long March of Everyman, 1974; (with M. J. Hatcher) A History of British Pewter, 1974; (with C. I. Savage) An Economic History of Transport, 1975; The Glassmakers, 1977; The Transport Contractors of Rye, 1982; (ed with Michael Drake) The Population Factor, 1982. *Recreations:* walking, motoring. *Address:* Minsen Dane, Brogdale Road, Faversham, Kent ME13 8YA. *T:* Faversham 3523. *Club:* Reform.

BARKER, Thomas Christopher; HM Diplomatic Service, retired; Curator, Scottish National War Memorial, Edinburgh; *b* 28 June 1928; *s* of late Rowland Francis Barker and Kathleen Maude Barker (*née* Welch); *m* 1960, Griselda Helen Cormack; two *s* one *d. Educ:* Uppingham (Schol.); New Coll., Oxford (Schol.). MA, Lit Hum, 1952. 2nd Lt, 1st Bn, The Worcestershire Regt, 1947-48. HM Foreign (non Diplomatic) Service, 1952; Third Sec., Paris, 1953-55; Second Sec., Baghdad, 1955-58; FO, 1958-62; First Sec., Head of Chancery and Consul, Mexico City, 1962-67; FO, 1967-69; Counsellor and Head of Chancery, Caracas, 1969-71; FCO, 1971-75; seconded as Under Sec., NI Office, Belfast, 1976. *Address:* Hillhead of Dunkeld, Dunkeld, Perthshire PH8 0BA. *T:* Dunkeld 522.

BARKER, Sir William, KCMG 1967 (CMG 1958); OBE 1949; Bowes Professor of Russian, University of Liverpool, 1969-76, now retired; *b* 19 July 1909; *s* of Alfred Barker; *m* 1939, Margaret Beirne; one *s* one *d. Educ:* Universities of Liverpool and Prague. Employed in Foreign Office, 1943; First Sec., Prague, 1945; Foreign Service Officer, Grade 7, Senior Branch of Foreign Service, 1946; Chargé d'Affaires, Prague, 1947; transferred Moscow, Aug. 1947; granted rank of Counsellor, Dec. 1948; Grade 6, 1950; Counsellor, Oslo, 1951, also Chargé d'Affaires; Consul-Gen., Boston, Mass, Sept. 1954; Counsellor, Washington, 1955; Minister, Moscow, 1960-63; Fellow, Center for Internat. Affairs, Harvard Univ., 1963-64. Asst Under-Sec. of State, FO, 1965-66; British Ambassador to Czechoslovakia, 1966-68. *Address:* 53 Eshe Road North, Liverpool L23 8UE.

BARKER, (William) Alan; Head Master, University College School, Hampstead, 1975-82, retired from ill-health; *b* 1 Oct. 1923; 2nd *s* of late T. L. Barker, Edinburgh and Beaconsfield and I. N. Barker, Salisbury, Zimbabwe; *m* 1954, Jean Alys (*see* Baroness Trumpington); one *s. Educ:* Rossall Sch.; Jesus Coll., Cambridge (scholar). Lieut Royal Artillery, 69 (WR) Field Regt, NW Europe; wounded, 1944. 1st cl. Hons Hist. Tripos Pt I, 1946, Pt II, 1947; BA 1946, MA 1948. Asst Master, Eton Coll., 1947-53; Commonwealth Fund Fellow, Yale Univ., 1951-52, MA (Yale) 1952. Fellow Queens' Coll., Cambridge, and Dir Studies in History, 1953-55; Asst Master, Eton Coll., 1955-58; Headmaster, The Leys School, 1958-75. Governor: Rossall Sch.; St Felix Sch.; Mem. Eton UDC, 1956-59; Councillor, Cambs and I of Ely, 1959-70, Alderman 1970-74. Select Preacher, Oxford Univ., 1966; Paul M. Angle Meml Lectr, Chicago, 1978. *Publications:* (jt) A General History of England 1688-1950, 2 vols, 1952, 1953; Religion and Politics (1558-1642), 1957; The Civil War in America, 1961, repr. US 1974, UK 1977; (contrib.) The Rebirth of Britain, 1964. *Recreations:* bridge, American history, learning to depend on women. *Address:* Luckboat House, 52 King Street, Sandwich, Kent CT13 9BL. *T:* Sandwich 613007; 25 Laxford House, Cundy Street, SW1. *T:* 01-730 4016. *Clubs:* East India, Devonshire, Sports and Public Schools; MCC; Pitt (Cambridge); Elizabethan (Yale).

BARKING, Bishop Suffragan of, 1975-30 April 1983; Rt. Rev. Albert James Adams; *b* 9 Nov. 1915; *s* of James and Evelyn Adams, Rayleigh, Essex; *m* 1943, Malvena Jones; three *s. Educ:* Brentwood Sch.; King's Coll., London; Community of St Andrew, Whittlesford, Cambridge. Ordained Deacon, 1942; Priest, 1943; Curate of Walkley, Sheffield, 1942-44; Succentor, 1944, Precentor, 1945-47, Sheffield Cathedral. Rector of Bermondsey, 1947-55; Rural Dean of Bermondsey, 1954-55; Rector of: Stoke Damerel, Devonport, 1955-63; Wanstead, 1963-71. Sub-Dean, Wanstead and Woodford, 1968-69; Asst Rural Dean, Redbridge, 1970-71; Archdeacon of West Ham, 1970-75. *Address:* 670 High Road, Buckhurst Hill, Essex. *T:* 01-505 1372.

BARKLEY, Brenda Edith, (Mrs Harry Barkley); see Ryman, B. E.

BARKLEY, Rev. Prof. John Montieth; Principal, Union Theological College, Belfast, 1978-81; *b* 16 Oct. 1910; *s* of Rev. Robert James Barkley, BD, and Mary Monteith; *m* 1936, Irene Graham Anderson; one *d. Educ:* Magee Univ. Coll. Derry; Trinity Coll., Dublin; The Presbyterian Coll., Belfast. BA 1934, MA 1941, BD 1944, PhD 1946, DD 1949, Trinity Coll., Dublin; BA 1952, MA 1953, Queen's Univ., Belfast. Thompson Memorial Prizeman in Philosophy, 1934; Larmour Memorial Exhibitioner in Theology, 1944; Paul Memorial Prizeman in History, 1953; Carey Lecturer, 1954-56; Lecturer in Ecclesiastical History, Queen's Univ., Belfast, 1951-54; Prof. in Ecclesiastical Hist., 1954-79, Vice-Principal, 1964-76, Principal, 1976-78, Presbyterian Coll., Belfast, until amalgamated with Magee Coll. to form Union Theological Coll. FRHistS. Ordained, Drumreagh Presbyterian Church, 1935; installed in II Ballybay and Rockcorry, 1939; installed in Cooke Centenary, Belfast, 1949. *Publications:* Handbook on Evangelical Christianity and Romanism, 1949; Presbyterianism, 1951; Westminster Formularies in Irish Presbyterianism, 1956; History of the Presbyterian Church in Ireland, 1959; Weltkirchenlexikon (arts), 1960; History of the Sabbath School Society for Ireland, 1961; The Eldership in Irish Presbyterianism; The Baptism of Infants, 1963; The Presbyterian Orphan Society, 1966; Worship of the Reformed Church, 1966; St Enoch's 1872-1972, 1972; (ed) Handbook to Church Hymnary, 3rd edn, 1979; articles in Scottish Journal of Theology, Verbum Caro, Biblical Theology, Dictionary of Worship. *Recreations:* bowls, golf. *Address:* 14 Clonallon Park, Belfast BT4 2BZ.

BARKSHIRE, Robert Hugh, CBE 1968; *b* 24 Oct. 1909; *yr s* of late Lt-Col Charles Robert Barkshire, OBE; *m* 1934, Emily Blunt, *er d* of A. S. Blunt, Bedford; one *s. Educ:* King's Sch., Bruton. Bank of England, 1927-55: Private Sec. to the Governor (C. F. Cobbold, later Lord Cobbold), 1949-53; Sec. to Cttee of London Clearing Bankers, British Bankers' Assoc., Bankers' Clearing House, and Mem., various inter-Bank Cttees, 1955-70; Hon. Sec., Meetings of Officers of European Bankers' Assocs, 1959-72; Gen. Comr of Income Tax for City of London, 1969-78; Governor, NIESR, 1970-78. FIB 1960. Freeman, City of London. *Address:* The Boat House, Fowey, Cornwall PL23 1BH. *T:* Fowey 3389. *Club:* Royal Fowey Yacht.

BARKWORTH, Peter Wynn; actor, since 1948; *b* 14 Jan. 1929; *s* of Walter Wynn Barkworth and Irene May Barkworth. *Educ:* Stockport Sch.; Royal Academy of Dramatic Art. Folkestone and Sheffield Repertory Cos, 1948-51. West End plays include: A Woman of No Importance, Savoy, 1953; Roar Like a Dove, Phoenix, 1957-60; The School for Scandal, Haymarket, 1962; Crown Matrimonial, Haymarket, 1972; Donkeys' Years, Globe, 1976; Can You Hear Me at the Back?, Piccadilly, 1979; A Coat of Varnish, Haymarket, 1982. Television serials: The Power Game, 1966; Manhunt, 1969; Telford's Change, 1979; Winston Churchill: the wilderness years, 1981. Awards: Best Actor, BAFTA, 1974 and 1977; Royal TV Soc. and Broadcasting Press Guild, 1977 (both 1977 awards for Professional Foul). *Publication:* About Acting, 1980. *Recreations:* walking, gardening, music, looking at paintings. *Address:* 47 Flask Walk, NW3 1HH. *T:* 01-794 4591. *Club:* British Academy of Film and Television Arts.

BARLAS, Sir Richard (Douglas), KCB 1977 (CB 1968); OBE 1943; Clerk of the House of Commons, 1976-79; *b* 19 May 1916; *s* of E. D. M. Barlas and Elena Barlas (*née* Kenyon); *m* 1940, Ann, *d* of Canon R. W. Porter; three *s. Educ:* Westminster; Christ Church, Oxford. War Service, 1939-45, R.A.F. Asst Clerk, House of Commons, 1946; Senior Clerk, 1947. Called to the Bar, Middle Temple, 1949. Fourth Clerk at the Table, House of Commons, 1959; Second Clerk Asst, 1962; Clerk Asst, 1974. *Recreations:* inland waterways, travel, gardening. *Address:* Walnut House, Ticehurst, E Sussex. *Club:* Royal Air Force.

BARLEY, Prof. Maurice Willmore, MA; Professor of Archaeology, University of Nottingham, 1971-74, now Emeritus; *b* 19 Aug. 1909; *s* of late Levi Baldwin and Alice Barley, Lincoln; *m* 1934, Diana, *e d* of late A. E. Morgan; two *s* one *d. Educ:* Lincoln Sch.; Reading Univ. (BA). Asst Lectr, UC Hull, 1935-40; Mins of Information and Labour, 1940-45; Adult Educn Dept, Nottingham, 1946-62; Classics Dept, Nottingham, 1962-74. Sec. 1954-64, Pres. 1964-67, Council for British Archaeology; Vice-Pres., Soc. of Antiquaries, 1965-68; Mem. Royal Commn Hist. Monuments, 1966-76. FSA. *Publications:* Parochial Documents of the East Riding, 1939; Lincolnshire and the Fens, 1952 (repr. 1972); Documents relating to Newark on Trent, 1955; The English Farmhouse and Cottage, 1961; The House and Home, 1963 (repr. 1971); Guide to British Topographical Collections, 1974; The Plans and Topography of Medieval Towns in England and Wales, 1975; European Towns, their Archaeology and early History, 1977; contrib. Agrarian History of England vol. V, Antiquaries Jl and other learned jls. *Address:* 60 Park Road, Chilwell, Nottingham. *T:* Nottingham 257501. *Club:* Athenæum.

BARLOW, Sir Christopher Hilaro, 7th Bt, *cr* 1803; architect; *b* 1 Dec. 1929; *s* of Sir Richard Barlow, 6th Bt, AFC, and Rosamund Sylvia, *d* of late F. S. Anderton (she *m* 2nd, 1950, Rev. Leonard Haslet Morrison, MA); *S* father, 1946; *m* 1952, J. C. de M. Audley, *e d* of J. E. Audley, Bahamas; one *s* two *d* (and one *s* decd). *Educ:* Eton; McGill Univ., Montreal. BArch. MRAIC. Past Pres., Newfoundland Architects' Assoc. Lt Governor's Silver Medal, 1953. *Heir: s* Crispian John Edmund Audley Barlow, Inspector, Royal Hong Kong Police, *b* 20 April 1958. *Address:* 18 Winter Avenue, St John's, Newfoundland.

BARLOW, David John; The Secretary, BBC, since 1981; *b* 20 Oct. 1937; *s* of Ralph and Joan Barlow; *m* 1981, Sanchia Béatrice Oppenheimer; three *s* of previous marr. *Educ:* Leighton Park Sch.; The Queen's Coll., Oxford; Leeds Univ. MA, DipEd (Oxon); DipESL (Leeds). British Council, 1962-63; BBC, 1963-: Producer, African Service; Schools Broadcasting, 1965-67; Programme Organiser, Hindi, Tamil, Nepali and Bengali Service, 1967-70; Further Educn Radio, 1970-71; UNESCO, British Council Consultancies, 1970-73; Head of Liaison Internat. Relations, 1974-76; Chief Asst Regions, 1977-79; Gen. Sec., ITCA, 1980-81. *Recreations:* photography, bird watching, mountain walking, book collecting. *Address:* 11 Courtland Road, Oxford. *T:* Oxford 770835.

BARLOW, Donald Spiers Monteagle, MS London; FRCS; Consulting Surgeon: Hospitals for Diseases of the Chest, since 1971 (Consultant Surgeon 1947-71); Southend Group of Hospitals, since 1970 (Consultant Surgeon 1936-70); Luton Group of Hospitals, since 1970 (Consultant Surgeon 1940-70); Italian Hospital, since 1970 (Hon. Consultant Thoracic Surgeon 1955-70); Penrose-May Surgical Tutor to the Royal College of Surgeons of England, since 1969 (Surgical Tutor, 1962-69); *b* 4 July 1905; *s* of late Leonard Barlow, MIEE, and Katharine Barlow; *m* 1934, Violet Elizabeth (*née* Maciver); one *s* three *d* (and one *d* decd). *Educ:* Whitgift Sch.; University Coll. Hospital and Medical Sch. MRCS, LRCP 1927; MB, BS London 1928; MS London 1930; FRCS 1930. Formerly: RMO, Wimbledon Hosp., 1927; House Phys., UCH, 1928; House Surg., UCH, 1929; Ho. Surg., Norfolk and Norwich Hosp., 1930-31; Resident Asst Surg., West London Hosp., 1931-35; Surg. Registrar London Lock Hosp., 1936; Research work at UCL, 1936-37; Hon. Surg., St John's Hosp., Lewisham, 1937-47; Cons. Thoracic Surg., LCC, 1945-48. Teacher, 1964-67, Lectr, 1967-71, Inst. of Diseases of the Chest, Univ. of London. Chm., S Beds Div., BMA, 1971-72. Coronation Medal, 1953. *Publications:* contribs to: Progress of Clinical Surgery, 1960 (ed Rodney Smith); Operative Surgery, 2nd edn 1969 (ed Rob and Smith). Many publications in learned jls mostly concerning diseases of oesophagus, chest and abdomen. Also 3 reports (Ceylon Govt White Papers), 1952, 1954, 1967. *Recreations:* golf (Captain, Harpenden Golf Club, 1971-72, Pres., 1976-79), painting. *Address:* Deacons Field, High Elms, Harpenden, Herts. *T:* Harpenden 3400.

See also Prof. H. E. M. Barlow, Michael Miller.

BARLOW, Prof. Frank, MA, DPhil; FBA 1970; FRSL 1971; Professor of History and Head of Department, University of Exeter, 1953-76, now Emeritus Professor; *b* 19 April 1911; *e s* of Percy Hawthorn and Margaret Julia Barlow; *m* 1936, Moira Stella Brigid Garvey; two *s*. *Educ:* Newcastle High Sch.; St John's Coll., Oxford. Open Schol., St John's Coll., Oxford, 1929; 1st Cl. Hons Sch. of Modern History, 1933; Bryce Student, 1933; Oxford Senior Student, 1934.; BLitt, 1934; Fereday Fellow, St John's Coll., Oxford, 1935-38; DPhil 1937. Asst Lecturer, University Coll., London, 1936-40; War service in the Army, 1941-46, commissioned into Intelligence Corps, demobilised as Major; Lecturer 1946, Reader 1949, Dep. Vice-Chancellor, 1961-63, Public Orator, 1974-76, University of Exeter. Hon. DLitt Exon, 1981. *Publications:* The Letters of Arnulf of Lisieux, 1939; Durham Annals and Documents of the Thirteenth Century, 1945; Durham Jurisdictional Peculiars, 1950; The Feudal Kingdom of England, 1955; (ed and trans.) The Life of King Edward the Confessor, 1962; The English Church, 1000-1066, 1963; William I and the Norman Conquest, 1965; Edward the Confessor, 1970; (with Martin Biddle, Olof von Feilitzen and D. J. Keene) Winchester in the Early Middle Ages, 1976; The English Church 1066-1154, 1979. *Recreation:* gardening. *Address:* Middle Court Hall, Kenton, Exeter. *T:* Starcross 890438.

BARLOW, Sir (George) William, Kt 1977; BSc Tech, FEng, FIMechE, FIEE; Chairman, THORN EMI Engineering Group, since 1980; Director: Royal Worcester, since 1976; Inmos International, since 1980; BICC, since 1980; *b* 8 June 1924; *s* of Albert Edward and Annice Barlow; *m* 1948, Elaine Mary Atherton (*née* Adamson); one *s* one *d*. *Educ:* Manchester Grammar Sch.; Manchester Univ. (Kitchener Schol., Louis Atkinson Schol.; BSc Tech. 1st cl. Hons Elec. Engrg, 1944). Served as Elec. Lt, RNVR, 1944-47. Various appts, The English Electric Co. Ltd (in Spain, 1952-55, Canada, 1958-62); Gen. Manager, Liverpool and Netherton, 1964-67; Managing Director: English Electric Domestic Appliance Co. Ltd, 1965-67; English Electric Computers Ltd, 1967-68. Gp Chief Exec., 1969-77, Chm., 1971-77, Ransome Hoffman Pollard Ltd. Chm., Post Office, 1977-80. Member: Industrial Develt Adv. Bd, 1972-79; Electronics EDC, 1981-; Council, IEE, 1969-72 (Vice-Pres., 1978-80); Council, IMechE, 1971-74; Engineering Industries Council, 1975-77; National Electronics Council, 1982-; Pres., IWM, 1976-77; Chm., Ferrous Foundries Adv. Cttee, 1975-78; Chm., Ball & Roller Bearings Manufacturers' Assoc., 1975-76; Independent Mem., Electrical Engrg EDC, 1975-76; Pres., Fedn of European Bearing Manufacturers, 1977; Vice Pres., City and Guilds of London Inst., 1982-. Chm., Design Council, 1980-. Governor, London Business Sch., 1979-. Freeman, City of London. Liveryman, Worshipful Company of Glaziers. CBIM 1971. Hon. FUMIST, 1978; Hon. DSc Cranfield, 1979. *Recreation:* golf. *Address:* 2 Neville Drive, N2 0QR. *Clubs:* Army and Navy, Brooks's; Hampstead Golf, Royal Birkdale Golf.

BARLOW, Prof. Harold Everard Monteagle, BSc (Eng.) London, PhD (Sci.), London; FRS 1961; FIEEE; FIEE; MIMechE; Emeritus Professor of Electrical Engineering, University College, London (Pender Professor, 1950-67); *b* Highbury, 15 Nov. 1899; *s* of late Leonard Barlow, MIEE, and Katharine Monteagle, Glasgow; *m* 1931, Janet Hastings, *d* of the late Rev. J. Hastings Eastwood, BA; three *s* one *d*. *Educ:* Wallington Grammar School; City & Guilds Engineering College; University College, London. Sub-Lieut. RNVR 1917-19; Student at University College, London, 1919-23; Practical engineering training with East Surrey Ironworks and Barlow & Young Ltd, 1923-25; Member of Academic Staff, Faculty of Engineering, UCL, 1925-67 (absent from University on War Service, Sept. 1939-Oct. 1945). Joined staff of Telecommunications Research Establishment, Air Ministry, to deal with Radar development, Sept. 1939; Superintendent, Radio Dept, RAE, 1943-45. Fellow of University College, 1946, Prof. of Elec. Engineering, 1945-50; Dean of Engineering Faculty, and Mem. UCL Cttee, 1949, 1961. Mem. of: Radar and Signals Advisory Bd, Min. of Supply, 1947; Scientific Advisory Council, Min. of Supply, 1949; Radio Research Bd, DSIR, 1948 and 1960; London Regional Advisory Council and of Academic Bd for Higher Technological Educn, 1952-67; Academic Council, Univ. of London, 1953-55; BBC Scientific Advisory Committee, 1953-76; Governor, Woolwich Polytechnic, 1948; Dir, Marconi Instruments, 1963. Member of Council of IEE, 1955-58 and 1960-; awarded Kelvin Premium, J. J. Thomson Premium, Oliver Lodge and Fleming Premium of IEE; Faraday Medal, 1967; Mem. Council, IERE, 1973-76. FCGI 1969. For. Mem., Polish Acad. of Science, 1966; Hon. Mem., Japanese Inst. of Electronics and Communications Engineers, 1973; For. Associate, US Nat. Acad. of Engineering, 1979. Chm., British Nat. Cttee for Radio Science, 1968; Mem., Nat. Electronics Council, 1969-. Dellinger Gold Medal, Internat. Radio Union, 1969; Harold Hartley Medal, Inst. of Measurement and Control, 1973; Mervin J. Kelly Award, IEEE, 1975. Hon. DSc Heriot-Watt, 1971; Hon. DEng Sheffield, 1973. *Publications:* Micro-waves and Wave-guides, 1947; (with A. L. Cullen) Micro-Wave Measurements, 1950; (with J. Brown) Radio Surface Waves, 1962; many scientific papers. *Recreations:* sailing, walking, reading. *Address:* 13 Hookfield, Epsom, Surrey. *T:* Epsom 21586; University College, Gower Street, WC1. *T:* 01-387 7050. *Club:* Athenæum.

See also D. S. M. Barlow.

BARLOW, Prof. Horace Basil, FRS 1969; Royal Society Research Professor, Physiological Laboratory, Cambridge University, since 1973; *b* 8 Dec. 1921; *s* of Sir (James) Alan (Noel) Barlow, 2nd Bt, GCB, KBE (*d* 1968), and of Nora Barlow (*née* Darwin); *m* 1st, 1954, Ruthala (marr. diss., 1970), *d* of Dr M. H. Salaman, *qv* ; four *d* ; 2nd, 1980, Miranda, *d* of John Weston Smith. *Educ:* Winchester; Trinity Coll., Cambridge. Research Fellow, Trinity Coll., 1950-54, Lectr, King's Coll., Cambridge, 1954-64. Demonstrator and Asst Dir of Research, Physiological Lab., Cambridge, 1954-64; Prof. of Physiological Optics and Physiology, Univ. of Calif, Berkeley, 1964-73. *Publications:* several, on neurophysiology of vision in Jl of Physiology, and elsewhere. *Address:* Physiological Laboratory, Cambridge CB2 3EG.

See also Sir T. E. Barlow, Bt.

BARLOW, Sir John (Denman), 2nd Bt, *cr* 1907; JP for Cheshire; Consultant, Thomas Barlow and Bro., Manchester and London; Emeritus Director, Manchester Chamber of Commerce; Chairman: various Rubber Plantation Companies; United Kingdom Falkland Islands Committee; *b* 15 June 1898; *er s* of Sir John Barlow, 1st Bt, and Hon. Anna Maria Heywood Denman (*d* 1965), *sister* of 3rd Baron Denman, PC, GCMG, KCVO; *S* father, 1932; *m* 1928, Hon. Diana Helen Kemp, *d* of 1st Baron Rochdale, CB, and *sister* of 1st Viscount Rochdale, *qv* ; three *s* one *d*. Contested (L) Northwich Division of Cheshire, 1929; MP (Nat Lib) Eddisbury Division of Cheshire, 1945-50; contested (U and Nat Lib) Walsall Div. of Staffordshire, 1950; MP (C) Middleton and Prestwich Division of Lancashire, 1951-66. Led CPA Mission to Malaya, 1959; led Parly Mission to new Malaysian Parlt, taking gift of Speaker's chair, 1963; Chm., Cons. Trade and Industries Cttee, 1955-60. Vice-Chm., Cotton Bd, 1940; Director: Union Bank of Manchester, 1932-40; Barclays Bank Ltd (Manchester Local Bd), 1940-73; Calico Printers Assoc., 1952-68; The Falklands Islands Co. Mem. Council, RASE, 1942-53. *Recreations:* hunting, polo, shooting. *Heir: s* John Kemp Barlow [*b* 22 April 1934; *m* 1962, Susan, *er d* of Col Sir Andrew Horsbrugh-Porter, *qv* ; four *s*]. *Address:* Bradwall Manor, Sandbach, Cheshire. *T:* Sandbach 2036. *Club:* Brooks's.

BARLOW, Roy Oxspring; solicitor; a Recorder of the Crown Court, since 1975; *b* 13 Feb. 1927; *s* of George and Clarice Barlow; *m* 1957, Kathleen Mary Roberts; two *s* one *d*. *Educ:* King Edward VII Sch., Sheffield; Queen's Coll., Oxford; Sheffield Univ. (LLB). Local Government, 1952-62; solicitor in private practice, 1962-. *Recreations:* farming, walking, reading. *Address:* The Cottage, Oxton Rakes, Barlow, Sheffield S18 5TH. *T:* Sheffield 890652.

BARLOW, Thomas Bradwall; merchant banker; director of rubber, insurance and other public companies; Joint Senior Consultant in Thomas Barlow & Bro. Ltd, London and Manchester; *b* 7 March 1900; 2nd *s* of Sir John Emmott Barlow, 1st Bt; *m* 1943, Elizabeth Margaret, *d* of Hon. B. G. Sackville-West; one *s* one *d*. Chairman: Br. Assoc. of Straits Merchants, 1937; Rubber Trade Assoc., 1942-43; Rubber Growers' Assoc., 1945-46; British Assoc. of Malaysia, 1965; Highlands & Lowlands Para Rubber Co. Ltd; Chersonese (F.M.S.) Estates Ltd. Farming. *Recreations:* hunting, steeplechasing, and travelling. *Address:* Thornby House, Northampton. *T:* Northampton 740214. *Clubs:* Brooks's, City of London, Hurlingham.

BARLOW, Sir Thomas (Erasmus), 3rd Bt *cr* 1902; DSC 1945; DL; *b* 23 Jan. 1914; *s* of Sir Alan Barlow, 2nd Bt, GCB, KBE, and of Nora, *d* of late Sir Horace Darwin, KBE; *S* father, 1968; *m* 1955, Isabel, *d* of late Dr T. M. Body, Middlesbrough, Yorks; two *s* two *d*. *Educ:* Winchester College. Entered RN as cadet, 1932; qualified Submarines, 1937; served in Submarines in Atlantic, Mediterranean, Indian Ocean and Far East during War of 1939-45; Naval

Staff Course, 1946; Joint Services Staff Course, 1947, Commander, 1950. British Joint Services Mission, Washington, 1950-53; Captain 1954; Imperial Defence Coll., 1957; Chief Staff Officer to Flag Officer Submarines, 1960-62; Commodore, HMS Drake, Devonport, 1962-64; retired, 1964. Now farms at Wendover, Bucks. Pres. Chiltern Hills Agricultural Assoc., 1968; actively concerned in Wildlife and Countryside Conservation: Royal Soc. for Nature Conservation; Berks, Bucks and Oxfordshire Naturalists' Trust; Charles Darwin Foundn for Galapogos Is. DL Bucks, 1977. *Recreations:* bird watching, the countryside. *Heir: s* James Alan Barlow, *b* 10 July 1956. *Address:* Boswells, Wendover, Bucks. *T:* Wendover 622119. *Clubs:* Athenæum, Savile. *See also Prof. H. B. Barlow.*

BARLOW, Sir William; *see* Barlow, Sir G. W.

BARLTROP, Roger Arnold Rowlandson; HM Diplomatic Service; High Commissioner to Fiji and (non-resident) to Republic of Nauru and to Tuvalu, since 1982; *b* 19 Jan. 1930; *s* of late Ernest William Barltrop, CMG, CBE, DSO, and Ethel Alice Lucy Barltrop (*née* Baker); *m* 1962, Penelope Pierrepont Dalton; two *s* two *d. Educ:* Solihull Sch.; Leeds Grammar Sch.; Exeter Coll., Oxford. BA (Hons). Served RN, 1949-50, RNVR/RNR, 1950-64 (Lt-Comdr 1962). Asst Principal, CRO, 1954-56; Second Sec., New Delhi, 1956-57; Private Sec. to Parly Under-Sec. of State and Minister of State, CRO, 1957-60; First Sec., E Nigeria, 1960-62; Actg Dep. High Comr, W Nigeria, 1962; First Sec., Salisbury, Rhodesia, 1962-65; CO and FO, later FCO, 1965-69; First Sec. and Head of Chancery, Ankara, 1969-70; Dep. British Govt Rep., WI Associated States, 1971-73; Counsellor and Head of Chancery, Addis Ababa, 1973-77; Head of Commonwealth Coordination Dept, FCO, 1978-82. *Recreations:* sailing, genealogy, opera. *Address:* c/o Foreign and Commonwealth Office, SW1A 2AH. *Club:* Royal Commonwealth Society.

BARNA, Prof. Tibor, CBE 1974; Professor of Economics, University of Sussex, since 1962; Member, Monopolies and Mergers Commission, 1963-78; *b* 1919. *Educ:* London School of Economics. Lecturer, London School of Economics, 1944; Official Fellow, Nuffield College, Oxford, 1947; senior posts in UN Economic Commission for Europe, 1949; Assistant Director, National Institute of Economic and Social Research, London, 1955. *Publications:* Redistribution of Income through Public Finance in 1937, 1945; Investment and Growth Policies in British Industrial Firms, 1962; Agriculture towards the Year 2000, 1979; European Process Plant Industry, 1981; papers in Jl Royal Statistical Soc., Economic Jl, European Econ. Review. *Address:* Beanacre, Westmeston, Hassocks, West Sussex. *T:* Hassocks 2384.

BARNARD, 11th Baron, *cr* 1698; **Harry John Neville Vane,** TD 1960; Landowner; Lord-Lieutenant and Custos Rotulorum of County Durham, since 1970; *b* 21 Sept. 1923; *er s* of 10th Baron Barnard, CMG, OBE, MC, TD, and Sylvia Mary, *d* of Herbert Straker; *S* father, 1964; *m* 1952, Lady Davina Mary Cecil, CStJ, *e d* of 6th Marquess of Exeter, KCMG; one *s* four *d. Educ:* Eton. Served War of 1939-45, RAFVR, 1942-46 (Flying Officer, 1945). Northumberland Hussars (TA), 1948-66; Lt-Col Commanding, 1964-66. Vice-Pres., N of England TA&VRA, 1970 and 1977-, Pres., 1974-77. Hon. Col, 7 Bn The Light Infantry, 1979-. County Councillor, Durham, 1952-61. Member: Durham Co. AEC, 1953-72 (Chm., 1970-72); N Regional Panel, MAFF, 1972-76; CLA Council, 1950-80; Dir, NE Housing Assoc., 1964-77; President: Farmway Ltd, 1965-; Durham Co. Br. BRCS, 1969-; Durham Co. Br., CLA, 1965-; Durham Co. St John Council, 1971-; Durham Co. Scout Assoc., 1972-; Durham Co. Br. RBL, 1973-. DL Durham, 1956, Vice-Lieutenant, 1969-70; JP Durham, 1961. Joint Master of Zetland Hounds, 1963-65. KStJ 1971. *Heir: s* Hon. Henry Francis Cecil Vane, *b* 11 March 1959. *Address:* (Residence) Selaby, Gainford, Darlington, Co. Durham DL2 3HF. *T:* Darlington 730206; (Seat) Raby Castle, Staindrop, Darlington, Co. Durham. *Clubs:* Brooks's; Durham County (Durham); Northern Counties (Newcastle upon Tyne).

BARNARD, Sir (Arthur) Thomas, Kt 1958; CB 1954; OBE 1946; Director-General of Inspection, Ministry of Supply, 1956-58, retired; *b* 28 Sept. 1893; *s* of late Arthur Barnard; *m* 1921, Grace, *d* of William Magerkorth, Belvedere, Kent. *Educ:* Erith Technical Coll. Is a Chartered Civil Engineer. Chief Superintendent, Royal Ordnance Factories, Woolwich, 1951-55; Dep. Dir-Gen., Royal Ordnance Factories, Adelphi, London, 1955-56. *Address:* Kentmere, 26 Heathfield, Chislehurst, Kent BR7 6AE.

BARNARD, Prof. Christiaan Neethling, MD, MMed, PhD; Professor of Surgical Science, Cape Town University, since 1968; *b* 8 Nov. 1922; *s* of Adam Hendrik Barnard and Maria Elizabeth Barnard (*née* De Swart); *m* 1st, 1948, Aletta Gertruida Louw (marr. diss. 1970); one *s* one *d*; 2nd, 1970, Barbara Maria Zoellner (marr. diss. 1982); two *s. Educ:* Beaufort West High Sch.; Univs of Cape Town and Minnesota. MB, ChB 1946, MD 1953, Cape Town; MS, PhD 1958, Minnesota. Private practice, Ceres, CP, 1948-51; Sen. Resident MO, City Hosp., Cape Town, 1951-53; subseq. Registrar, Groote Schuur Hosp.; Registrar, Surgery Dept, Cape Town Univ.; Charles Adams Meml Schol. and Dazian Foundn Bursary for study in USA; US Public Health Grant for further res. in cardiac surgery; Specialist Cardio-Thoracic Surgeon, Lectr and Dir of Surg. Res., Cape Town Univ. and Groote Schuur Hosp., 1958; Head of Cardio-Thoracic Surgery, Cape Town Univ. Teaching Hosps, 1961; Assoc. Prof., Cape Town Univ., 1962. Oppenheimer Meml Trust Bursary for overseas study, 1960. Performed world's first human heart transplant operation, 3 Dec. 1967, and world's first double-heart transplant,

25 Nov. 1974. Holds numerous hon. doctorates, foreign orders and award hon. citizenships and freedoms, medallions, etc; Dag Hammarskjöld Interna Prize and Peace Prize, Kennedy Foundn Award, Milan Internat. Prize fc Science, etc; hon. fellow or member various colleges, societies, etc. FAC 1963; Fellow NY Cardiological Soc. 1965; FACC 1967. *Publications:* (wit V. Schrire) Surgery of Common Congenital Cardiac Malformations, 196 One Life, 1969; Heart Attack: You Don't Have to Die, 1971; The Unwante 1974; South Africa: Sharp Dissection, 1977; In The Night Season, 1977; Be Medicine, 1979; Good Life—Good Death, 1980; numerous contribs to me jls. *Recreations:* viticulture, ornithology, farming. *Address:* Department Cardiac Surgery, Medical School, Observatory, Cape Town, South Africa. ? 551358.

BARNARD, Prof. Eric Albert, PhD; FRS 1981; Rank Professor Physiological Biochemistry, since 1976, Chairman, Division of Life Science since 1977, and Head of Department of Biochemistry, since 1979, Imperia College, University of London; *b* 2 July 1927; *m* 1956, Penelope J. Henness two *s* two *d. Educ:* Davenant Foundn Sch.; King's Coll., London. BSc, Ph 1956. King's College, London: Nuffield Foundn Fellow, 1956-59; Asst Lect 1959-60; Lectr, 1960-64. State University of New York at Buffalo: Associa Prof. of Biochemical Pharmacol., 1964-65; Prof. of Biochemistry, 1965-7 Head of Biochemistry Dept, 1969-76. Rockefeller Fellow, Univ. of Cali Berkeley, 1960-61; Guggenheim Fellow, MRC Lab. of Molecular Biol Cambridge, 1971. Vis. Prof., Univ. of Marburg, Germany, 1965; Vis. Scientis Inst. Pasteur, France, 1973. Member: Amer. Soc. Biol Chemists; Internat. So Neurochem; Committee Member: MRC; CNRS. Josiah Macy Facult Scholar Award, USA, 1975; Medal of Polish Acad. of Scis, 1980. *Publication* editor of four scientific books; mem., editorial bds of four scientific j numerous papers in learned jls. *Recreation:* the pursuit of good claret. *Addres* 32 Campden Grove, W8. *T:* 01-937 1606.

BARNARD, Surg. Rear Adm. Ernest Edward Peter, QHP 1980; DPhi FFCM; Surgeon Rear Admiral, Institute of Naval Medicine, and Dean Naval Medicine, since 1982; *b* 22 Feb. 1927; *s* of Lionel Edward Barnard an Ernestine (*née* Lethbridge); *m* 1955, Dr Joan Barnard (*née* Gunn); one *s* or *d. Educ:* schools in England and Australia; Univ. of Adelaide; St Mary's Hosp Univ. of London (MB, BS 1955); St John's Coll., Univ. of Oxford (studen 1966-68; DPhil 1969). MRCS, LRCP 1955; MFOM 1979; FFCM 1980. Afte house appts, joined RN, 1956; served, 1957-76: HMS Bulwark, Reclaim an Dolphin; RN Physiol Lab.; RN Med. Sch.; Inst. of Naval Medicine; Dept c Med. Dir Gen. (Naval); exchange service with US Navy at Naval Med. Re Inst., Bethesda, Md, 1976-78; Inst. of Naval Medicine, 1978-80; Dep. Mec Dir Gen. (Naval), 1980-82. FRSM 1962. *Publications:* papers on underwate medicine and physiology. *Recreations:* gardening, literature, photography *Address:* c/o Barclay's Bank, 12 The Square, Wickham, Hants PO17 5JQ

BARNARD, Prof. George Alfred, MA, DSc; Emeritus Professor c Mathematics, University of Essex; statistical consultant to variou organisations; *b* 23 Sept. 1915; *s* of Frederick C. and Ethel C. Barnard; *m* 1s 1942, Helen J. B. Davies; three *s*; 2nd, 1949, Mary M. L. Jones; one *s. Edu* Sir George Monoux Grammar Sch., Walthamstow; St John's Coll Cambridge. Math. Trip., Pt III, 1936, Res. Studentship, St John's Coll., sper at Grad. Sch. Princeton, NJ, USA, 1937-39. Plessey Co., Ilford, as Matl Consultant, 1940-42; Ministry of Supply Adv. Unit, 1942-45; Maths Dep Imperial Coll., London: Lectr, 1945-47; Reader in Math. Statistics, 1948-5 Professor, 1954-66; Prof. of Mathematics, Univ. of Essex, 1966-75; Prof. c Statistics, Univ. of Waterloo, 1975-81. Visiting Professor: Yale, 1966; Univ of Waterloo, 1972-73; Univ. of Nottingham, 1975-77. Member: UGC 1967-72; Computer Bd, 1970-72; SSRC, 1971-74. Royal Statistical Society Council Mem. and Vice-Pres., 1952, 1962, Pres. 1971-72 (Chm. Res. Sect 1958; Guy Medal in Silver, 1958, in Gold, 1975); Mem. Internat. Statistica Inst., 1952; Statistical Adviser, Brit. Standards Instn (with Prof. E. S. Pearson) 1954; Chm. Inst. of Statisticians, 1960-62; President: Operational Res. Soc 1962-64; Inst. of Mathematics and its Applications, 1970-71; Fellow: Amer Statistical Assoc.; Inst. of Mathematical Statistics; Amer. Assoc. fc Advancement of Science. *Publications:* (ed) The Foundations of Statistica Inference, 1962; papers in Jl Royal Statistical Society; Technometric Biometrika. *Recreations:* viola playing, boating. *Address:* Mill House, Hurs Green, Brightlingsea, Essex. *T:* Brightlingsea 2388.
See also Prof. D. E. C. Wedderburn.

BARNARD, Captain Sir George (Edward), Kt 1968; Deputy Master c Trinity House, 1961-72; *b* 11 Aug. 1907; 2nd *s* of Michael and Alice Louis Barnard; *m* 1940, Barbara Emma Hughes (*d* 1976); one *s.* Apprenticed at sea 1922; 1st Command, Blue Star Line, 1945. Elder Brother of Trinity House 1958-. Trustee, Nat. Maritime Museum, 1967-74; Treasurer, Internat. Asso of Lighthouse Authorities, 1961-72; Hon. Sec., King George's Fund fc Sailors, 1967-75; first Chm., Nautical Inst., 1972-73, Pres., 1973-75, Fellow 1975; Mem. Cttee of Management, RNLI, 1972-. FRSA 1969. *Recreatio* gardening. *Address:* Warden, Station Road, Much Hadham, Herts SG10 6AX *T:* Much Hadham 3133.

BARNARD, Howard Clive, MA, BLitt Oxon; MA (Educ), DLit Londor FCP, FTCL; Professor of Education, Reading University, 1937-51; Emeritu since 1951; *b* City of London, 7 June 1884; Freeman of the City and Mem of the Goldsmiths' Co. by patrimony; *s* of late Howard Barnard, journalis *m* Edith Gwendolen (*d* 1956), *d* of late John Wish, Civil Servant; one *s* on *d. Educ:* University Coll. Sch., London; Brasenose Coll., Oxford (Sen. Hulm

Scholar); London Sch. of Economics; King's Coll., London (Advanced Student); also studied in France and Germany. Asst Master at Manchester, Ramsgate, and Bradford; Headmaster, Grammar Sch., Gillingham, Kent; Examiner at various times to Univs of Oxford, Cambridge, London, Durham, Birmingham, Liverpool, Manchester, Leeds, Sheffield, Wales, Nottingham and Hull, the Civil Service Commission, the LCC, the Coll. of Preceptors, etc. Hon. DLitt Reading, 1974. *Publications:* The Little Schools of Port-Royal; The Port-Royalists on Education (source-book); The French Tradition in Education; Madame de Maintenon and Saint-Cyr; Fénelon on Education; Girls at School under the Ancien Régime; Education and the French Revolution (also Italian edn); A History of English Education from 1760 (also Hindi edn); Were those the Days?; A Clowder of Cats; An Introduction to Teaching; Principles and Practice of Geography Teaching; Observational Geography and Regional Survey; The Expansion of the Anglo-Saxon Nations (ed); A Handbook of British Educational Terms (with Prof. J. A. Lauwerys); and numerous school books. *Recreations:* walking, organ-playing. *Address:* c/o The School of Education, University of Reading, Whiteknights, Reading, Berks RG6 2AH.

BARNARD, Hon. Lance Herbert, AO; *b* 1 May 1919; *s* of Hon. H. C. Barnard and M. M. Barnard (*née* McKenzie); *m* 2nd, 1962, Jill Denise Carstairs, *d* of Senator H. G. J. Cant; one *s* two *d* (and one *d* decd); also one *d* by a former marriage. *Educ:* Launceston Technical Coll. Served War, overseas, AIF 9th Div., 1940. Formerly teacher, Tasmanian Educn Dept. Elected to House of Representatives as Member for Bass, 1954, 1955, 1958, 1961, 1963, 1966, 1969, 1972, 1974. From Dec. 1972: Minister of Defence, Navy, Army, Air, Supply, Postmaster-Gen.; Labour and National Service, Immigration, Social Services, Repatriation, Health, Primary Industry, National Development, and of the Interior. Dep. Leader, Federal Parliamentary Labor Party, 1967–72; Deputy Prime Minister, 1973–74; Minister for Defence (Navy, Army, Air and Supply), 1973–75. Australian Ambassador to Sweden, Norway and Finland, 1975–78. Captain, Aust. Cadet Corps, post War of 1939–45. State Pres., Tasmanian Br., Aust. Labor Party; Tasmanian deleg., Federal Exec., Aust. Labor Party. *Publication:* Labor's Defence Policy, 1969. *Recreations:* bowls, golf, swimming. *Address:* 8 Lantana Avenue, Launceston, Tasmania 7250, Australia. *Clubs:* South Launceston Rotary, East Launceston Bowling, Launceston Workingmen's (Launceston).

BARNARD, Sir Thomas; *see* Barnard, Sir A. T.

BARNARD, Thomas Theodore, MC; MA Oxon; PhD Cantab; *b* 31 Aug. 1898; *e s* of late T. H. Barnard, banker, Bedford; *m* 1924, Gillian Sarah (*d* 1961), *d* of late Lieut-Col Hon. A. S. Byng, DSO; one *s* two *d*. *Educ:* Eton, Christ Church, Oxford; King's Coll., Cambridge. Lieut, Coldstream Guards, 1917–19; Prof. of Social Anthropology, and Dir of the Sch. of African Life and Languages, University of Cape Town, 1926–34. Rejoined Coldstream Guards, 1940–45, Capt., Guards Depôt. VMH 1965. *Address:* Furzebrook, Wareham, Dorset. *Club:* Cavalry and Guards.

BARNEBY, Lt-Col Henry Habington, TD 1946; retired from HM Forces 1955; Vice Lord-Lieutenant of Hereford and Worcester, 1974–77; *b* 19 June 1909; *er s* of Richard Hicks Barneby, Longworth Hall, Hereford; *m* 1st, 1935, Evelyn Georgina Heywood; 2nd, 1944, Angela Margaret Campbell (*d* 1979); four *s* one *d* (and one *s* decd). *Educ:* Radley Coll.; RMC Sandhurst. QALAS 1939. 2nd Lieut KSLI 1929, retd 1935; Lieut Hereford Regt TA 1936; commanded: Hereford Regt (TA), 1945–46; Hereford LI (TA), 1947–51; Jamaica Bn, 1951–53; regranted commn in KSLI as Major, 1947; retd 1955. Mem., Herefordshire T&AFA, 1955–68; Mem., W Midlands T&AVR, 1968–77. Member: Hereford RDC, 1955–67 (Chm., 1964–67); Dore and Bredwardine RDC, 1966–73; S Herefordshire RDC, 1973–76. DL Herefordshire 1958, Vice Lieut, 1973–74, JP 1960–79, High Sheriff 1972. *Address:* Llanerch-y-Coed, Dorstone, Herefordshire. *T:* Clifford 215.

BARNES, family name of **Baron Gorell.**

BARNES, Alan Robert, CBE 1976; JP; Headmaster, Ruffwood School, Kirkby, Liverpool, since 1959; *b* 9 Aug. 1927; *s* of Arthur Barnes and Ida Barnes; *m* 1951, Pearl Muriel Boughton; one *s* (and one *s* decd). *Educ:* Enfield Grammar Sch.; Queens' Coll., Cambridge (MA). National Service, RAEC. Wallington County Grammar Sch., 1951–55; Churchfields Sch., West Bromwich, 1955–59. Pres., Headmasters' Assoc., 1974, Treas., 1975–77; Chm., Jt Four Secondary Assocs, 1978; Treas., Secondary Heads Assoc., 1978–82; Vice-Chm., British Educn Management and Admin Soc., 1980–82. JP Knowsley, Merseyside, 1967. *Publications:* (contrib.) Going Comprehensive (ed Halsall), 1970; (contrib.) Management and Headship in the Secondary School (ed Jennings), 1978; contrib. to: HMA Rev., Education, BEAS Jl. *Recreations:* bridge, cricket. *Address:* 16 Oaktree Road, St Helens, Merseyside. *T:* St Helens 28073.

BARNES, Dame (Alice) Josephine (Mary Taylor), (Dame Josephine Warren), DBE 1974; FRCP, FRCS, FRCOG; Consulting Obstetrician and Gynaecologist, Charing Cross Hospital and Elizabeth Garrett Anderson Hospital; President, Women's National Cancer Control Campaign, since 1974 (Chairman 1969–72; Vice-President, 1972–74); *b* 18 Aug. 1912; *er d* of late Rev. Walter W. Barnes, MA(Oxon), and Alice Mary Ibbetson, FRCO, ARCM; *m* 1942, Sir Brian Warren, *qv* (marr. diss. 1964); one *s* two *d*. *Educ:* Oxford High Sch.; Lady Margaret Hall, Oxford (Hon. Fellow, 1980);

University College Hosp. Med. Sch. 1st class Hons Physiology, Oxford, BA 1934, MA, BM, BCh 1937, DM 1941. University College Hospital: Goldschmid Scholar; Aitchison Scholar; Tuke Silver Medal; Fellowes Silver Medal; F. T. Roberts Prize; Suckling Prize. Various appointments at UCH, Samaritan Hosp., Queen Charlotte's Hosp., and Radcliffe Infirmary, Oxford; Dep. Academic Head, Obstetric Unit, UCH, 1947–52; Surgeon, Marie Curie Hosp., 1947–67. Medical Women's Federation: Hon. Sec., 1951–57; Pres., London Assoc., 1958–60; Pres., 1966–67. Royal Society of Medicine: Mem. Council, 1949–50; Pres., Sect. of Obstetrics and Gynaecology, 1972–73; Hon. Editor, Sect. of Obstetrics, 1951–71. President: W London Medico-Chirurgical Soc., 1969–70; Nat. Assoc. of Family Planning Doctors, 1976–; Obstetric Physiotherapists Assoc., 1976–; BMA, 1979–80 (Pres.-elect, 1978–79); Union Professionelle Internationale de Gynécologie et d'Obstétrique, 1977–79; Royal Medical Benevolent Soc., 1982–. Examiner in Obstetrics and Gynaecology: Univ. of London; RCOG; Examining Bd in England, Queen's Univ., Belfast; Univ. of Oxford; Univ. of Kampala. Member: Council, Med. Defence Union; Royal Commn on Med. Educn, 1965–68; Council, RCOG, 1965–71 (Jun. Vice-Pres., 1972–74, Sen. Vice-Pres., 1974–75); MRC Cttee on Analgesia in Midwifery; Min. of Health Med. Manpower Cttee; Medico-Legal Soc.; Population Investigation Cttee, Eugenics Soc.; Cttee on the Working of the Abortion Act, 1971–73; Standing Med. Adv. Cttee, DHSS, 1976–80; Council, Advertising Standards Authority, 1980–; Vice-Pres., Nat. Union of Townswomen's Guilds, 1979–; Pres., Nat. Assoc. of Family Planning Nurses, 1980–. Mem. of Honour, French Gynaecological Soc., 1945; Hon. Member: Italian Soc. of Obstetrics and Gynaecology, 1979; Nigerian Soc. of Gynaecology and Obstetrics, 1981; Corresp. Mem., Royal Belgian Soc. of Obstetricians and Gynaecologists, 1949. Governor: Charing Cross Hosp.; Chelsea Coll. of Science and Technology; Member Council: Benenden Sch.; Bedford Coll. Lectures: Fawcett, Bedford Coll., 1969; Rhys-Williams, Nat. Birthday Trust, 1970; Winston Churchill Meml, Postgrad. Med. Centre, Canterbury, 1971; Bartholomew Mosse, Rotunda Hosp., Dublin, 1975; Simpson Oration, RCOG, 1977; Annual, Liverpool Med. Instn, 1979; Sophia, Univ. of Newcastle upon Tyne, 1980. Hon. FRCPI 1977; Hon. Fellow, Edinburgh Obstetrical Soc., 1980. Hon. MD: Liverpool, 1979; Southampton, 1981; Hon. DSc Leicester, 1980. Commandeur du Bontemps de Médoc et des Graves, 1966. *Publications:* Gynaecological Histology, 1948; The Care of the Expectant Mother, 1954; Lecture Notes on Gynaecology, 1966; (ed, jtly) Scientific Foundations of Obstetrics and Gynaecology, 1970; Essentials of Family Planning, 1976; numerous contribs to med. jls, etc. *Recreations:* music, gastronomy, motoring, foreign travel; formerly hockey (Oxford Univ. Women's Hockey XI, 1932, 1933, 1934). *Address:* 8 Aubrey Walk, W8 7JG. *T:* 01-727 9832.

See also F. W. I. Barnes, M. G. J. Neary.

BARNES, Arthur Chapman, CMG 1936; BSc (Hons); CChem, FRSC; Sugar Consultant; *b* 1891. *Educ:* Deacon's School, Peterborough; Municipal College of Technology and Victoria Univ., Manchester. Entered Survey Dept, East Africa Protectorate, 1914; agricultural chemist, Nigeria, 1923; Asst Director of Agriculture, Zanzibar, 1927; Director of Agriculture, Fiji, 1929; Director of Agriculture and Island Chemist, Jamaica, 1933; General Manager West Indies Sugar Co. Ltd, 1938; seconded for duty as Director of Research for The Sugar Manufacturers' Association (of Jamaica), Ltd, 1947; Technical Consultant, S African Cane Growers Assoc., 1958; retired 1972. *Publications:* Agriculture of the Sugar-cane, 1953; The Sugar Cane, 1964, 2nd edn, 1974. *Address:* 8 Newlands, Musgrave Road, Durban, Natal, South Africa.

BARNES, Clive Alexander, CBE 1975; Associate Editor and Chief Drama and Dance Critic, New York Post, since 1977; New York Correspondent of The Times, since 1970; *b* London, 13 May 1927; *s* of Arthur Lionel Barnes and Freda Marguerite Garrat; *m* 1958, Patricia Winckley; one *s* one *d*. *Educ:* King's Coll., London; St Catherine's Coll., Oxford. Served RAF, 1946–48. Admin. Officer, Town Planning Dept, LCC, 1952–61; concurrently freelance journalist; Chief Dance Critic, The Times, 1961–65; Exec. Editor, Dance and Dancers, Music and Musicians, and Plays and Players, 1961–65; a London Correspondent, New York Times, 1963–65, Dance Critic, 1965–77, Drama Critic (weekdays only), 1967–77. Knight of the Order of Dannebrog (Denmark), 1972. *Publications:* Ballet in Britain since the War, 1953; (ed, with others) Ballet Here and Now, 1961; Frederick Ashton and his Ballets, 1961; Dance Scene, USA (commentary), 1967; (ed with J. Gassner) Best American Plays, 6th series, 1963–67, 1971, and 7th series, 1974; (ed) New York Times Directory of the Theatre, 1973; contribs to jls, inc. Punch, The New Statesman, The Spectator, The New Republic. *Recreations:* eating, drinking, walking, theatregoing. *Address:* 450 West End Avenue, New York, NY 10024, USA. *Club:* Century (NY).

BARNES, Very Rev. Cyril Arthur; Dean of Moray, Ross and Caithness, since 1980; *b* 10 Jan. 1926; *s* of Reginald William and Mary Adeline Barnes; *m* 1951, Patricia Patience Allen. *Educ:* Penistone Grammar School; Edinburgh Theological Coll. King's Own Scottish Borderers, 1944–47. Curate, St John's, Aberdeen, 1950–53; Rector, St John's, Forres, 1953–55; Priest-in-Charge, Wentbridge, Yorks, 1955–58; Vicar, St Bartholomew's, Ripponden with St John's, Rishworth, 1958–65; also St John's, Thorpe, 1966–67; Rector, Christ Church, Huntly with St Marnan's, Aberchirder, 1967–, also Holy Trinity, Keith, 1974–; Canon of Inverness Cathedral, 1971–80; Synod Clerk, 1977–80. *Recreations:* gardening, do-it-yourself. *Address:* The Rectory, Provost Street, Huntly, Aberdeenshire. *T:* Huntly 2667.

BARNES, Daniel Sennett, CBE 1977; CEng, FIEE; Managing Director, Bracknell Division British Aerospace Dynamics Group (formerly Sperry Gyroscope), since 1982; Managing Director, Sperry Gyroscope, 1971-82; Director: Sperry Trustees Ltd, since 1971; Sperry AG Switzerland, since 1979; *b* 13 Sept. 1924; *s* of Paula Sennett Barnes and John Daniel Barnes; *m* 1955, Jean A. Steadman; one *s. Educ:* Dulwich Coll.; Battersea Polytechnic (BScEng, 1st Cl. Hons). Apprenticeship at Philips, 1941-46; served REME, 1946-48; Battersea Polytechnic, 1948-51; Sperry Gyroscope, 1951-82: Dir of Engineering, 1962-68; Manager, Defence Systems, 1968-70; Gen. Manager, 1970-71. Pres., Electronic Engrg Assoc., 1981-82. *Recreations:* sailing, joinery, music and ballet, gardening. *Address:* Zenda, 9 Eastwick Road, Burwood Park, Walton-on-Thames, Surrey KT12 5AW. *T:* Walton-on-Thames 28042.

BARNES, David Michael William, QC 1981; *b* 16 July 1943; *s* of David Charles Barnes and Florence Maud Barnes; *m* 1970, Susan Dorothy Turner; three *s. Educ:* Monmouth Sch.; Wadham Coll., Oxford. Called to Bar, Middle Temple, 1965. Hon. Research Fellow, Lady Margaret Hall, Oxford, 1979. *Publications:* Leasehold Reform Act 1967, 1967; Hill and Redman's Law of Landlord and Tenant, 15th edn 1970, 16th edn 1976. *Recreations:* walking, crime fiction. *Address:* 64 Alleyn Park, SE21 8SF. *T:* 01-670 6969.

BARNES, Sir Denis (Charles), KCB 1967 (CB 1964); Director: Glynwed Ltd; General Accident, Fire & Life Assurance Corporation, since 1976; President, Manpower Society, since 1976; *b* 15 Dec. 1914; *s* of Frederick Charles Barnes; *m* 1938, Patricia Abercrombie. *Educ:* Hulme Gram. Sch., Manchester; Merton Coll., Oxford. Postmaster, Merton Coll., Oxford, 1933-37. BA, 1st Cl. Mod. History, 1936; PPE 1937. Entered Min. of Labour, 1937; Private Sec. to Minister of Labour, 1945-47; Dep. Sec., Min. of Labour, 1963, Permanent Sec. 1966; Permanent Sec., Dept of Employment, 1968-73; Chairman: Manpower Services Commn, 1974-76; Member: Council, Manchester Business Sch., 1975; Council, Zoological Soc. of London, 1978. FIPM 1974. Commonwealth Fellowship, 1953. *Publication:* Governments and Trade Unions, 1980. *Address:* The Old Inn, 30 The Street, Wittersham, Kent. *T:* Wittersham 528. *Club:* Savile.

BARNES, Edward Campbell; Head of Children's Programmes, BBC Television, since 1978; *b* 8 Oct. 1928; *s* of Hubert Turnbull Barnes and Annie Mabel Barnes; *m* 1950, Dorothy Smith; one *s* two *d. Educ:* Wigan Coll. British Forces Network, Vienna, 1946-49; stage management, provincial and West End theatre, 1949-55; BBC Television: studio management, 1955-62; Producer, Blue Peter, 1962-70; Dep. Head of Children's Progs, 1970-78, incl.: original Editor, John Craven's Newsround; Producer: Blue Peter Royal Safari with Princess Anne; 6 series of Blue Peter Special Assignments. *Publications:* 18 Blue Peter Books and 8 Blue Peter Mini Books, 1964-79; 6 Blue Peter Special Assignment Books, 1973-75; Blue Peter Royal Safari, 1971; Petra: a dog for everyone, 1977; numerous articles for nat. press. *Recreations:* cricket, ballet, opera, walking. *Address:* 50 Hill House Road, SW16 2AQ. *T:* 01-769 0323; Carn Mallows, Rinsey, Cornwall. *T:* Germoe 3381. *Club:* BAFTA.

BARNES, Eric Cecil, CMG 1954; Colonial Administrative Service; Provincial Commissioner, Nyasaland, 1949-55, retired; *b* 1899; *m* 1950, Isabel Margaret Lesley, MBE, *d* of late Mrs Isabel Wauchope; one *s* one *d. Educ:* Bishop Cotton's Sch., Simla; Bedford Sch. and Cadet Coll., Quetta, India. Indian Army, 1917-23; Administrative Service, Nyasaland, 1925. Deputy Provincial Commissioner, 1946. *Address:* 9 Riverdale Close, Fordingbridge, Hants. *T:* Fordingbridge 53860.

BARNES, Hon. Eric Charles; Hon. Mr Justice Barnes; High Court Judge, Hong Kong, since 1981; *b* 12 Sept. 1924; *m* 1st, Estelle Fay Barnes (*née* Darnell); five *s* one *d* ; 2nd, 1978, Judianna Wai Ling Barnes (*née* Chang). *Educ:* Univ. of Queensland (LLB). *Recreations:* tennis, racing (horse), sports. *Address:* 2B Eastview, 3 Cox's Road, Kowloon, Hong Kong. *T:* 3-679221. *Clubs:* United Services Recreation, Kowloon Cricket, Royal Hong Kong Jockey (Hong Kong).

BARNES, Sir (Ernest) John (Ward), KCMG 1974; MBE (mil.) 1946; HM Diplomatic Service, retired; *b* 22 June 1917; *er s* of Rt Rev. Ernest William Barnes, 3rd Bishop of Birmingham, and Adelaide, *d* of Sir Adolphus Ward, Master of Peterhouse, Cambridge; *m* 1948, Cynthia Margaret Ray (JP E Sussex), *d* of Sir Herbert Stewart, CIE, *qv;* two *s* three *d. Educ:* Dragon Sch., Oxford; Winchester; Trinity Coll., Cambridge. Classical Tripos, Pts I and II, Class I; Porson Scholar, 1939. Royal Artillery, 1939-46 (Lt-Col, MBE, US Bronze Star). HM Foreign Service, 1946; served Washington, Beirut, Bonn and Harvard Univ. (Center for International Affairs); Ambassador to Israel, 1969-72; Ambassador to the Netherlands, 1972-77. Director: Alliance Investment Co., 1977-; Whiteaway Laidlaw Ltd, 1979-. *Publication:* Ahead of his Age, 1979. *Address:* Hampton Lodge, Hurstpierpoint, Sussex; 20 Thurloe Place Mews, SW7. *Clubs:* Athenæum, Beefsteak, Brooks's; MCC.

BARNES, Francis Walter Ibbetson; a full-time Chairman, Industrial Tribunals, since 1976; *b* 10 May 1914; *s* of late Rev. Walter W. Barnes, MA (Oxon) and Alice Mary Ibbetson, FRCO, ARCM; *m* 1st, 1941, Heather Katherine (marr. diss. 1953), *d* of Frank Tamplin; two *s* ; 2nd, 1955, Sonia Nina (Nina Walker, pianist), *d* of late Harold Higginbottom; two *s* one *d. Educ:* Dragon Sch., Oxford; Mill Hill Sch.; Balliol Coll., Oxford. BA Jurisprudence (Hons), Oxford, 1937; MA 1967. Called to Bar, Inner Temple, 1938. Profumo Prize, Inner Temple, 1939. Served War, 1939-46 in Army

(Middlesex Regt) and Home Office and Military Fire Services; Sen. Company Officer NFS and Capt. comdg military Fire Fighting Co. on BLA; later Staff Capt., JAG (War Crimes Section). Functioned as Judge Advocate and Prosecutor in various trials of war criminals in Germany. Recorder of Smethwick, 1964-66; Dep. Chm., Oxfordshire QS, 1965-71; Recorder of Warley, 1966-71, Hon. Recorder, 1972; a Recorder of the Crown Court, 1972-76. Life Governor, Mill Hill Sch., 1939-; Mem., Dame Henrietta Barnett Bd (Educl Trust), 1951-. Elected to Bar Council, 1961. Bar Council's rep. (observer) on Cons. cttee of Lawyers of the Common Market countries. 1962-71; contrib. to Common Market Law Review. Union Internat. des Avocats: Mem. Council, 1964-; Rapporteur Général at Vienna Congress, 1967; Rapporteur National at Paris Congress, 1971. *Recreations:* music, gardening, motoring. *Address:* 93 Ebury Bridge Road, SW1; 42 St Martin's Approach, Ruislip, Mddx. *T:* Ruislip 37326; Southernhay, Diptford, S Devon.

See also Dame A. J. M. T. Barnes.

BARNES, James Edwin; Under-Secretary, Small Firms and Regional Development Grants, Department of Industry, 1974-75; retired; *b* 23 Nov. 1917; *s* of James Barnes and Kate (*née* Davies); *m* 1943, Gloria Parkinson; two *s* one *d. Educ:* King Edward VI Sch., Nuneaton. Joined Civil Service as Executive Officer, War Office, 1936; Higher Executive Officer, Min. of Supply, 1942; Sen. Exec. Officer 1945, Principal, 1946, Asst Sec. 1952; Under-Secretary: Min. of Aviation, 1964-66; BoT, 1966-70; DTI, 1970-74. Coronation Medal, 1953. *Address:* 12 Encombe, Sandgate, Folkestone, Kent CT20 3DE. *T:* Folkestone 38142.

BARNES, James Frederick, CB 1982; Deputy Controller, Establishments Resources and Personnel, Ministry of Defence, since 1982; *b* 8 March 1932; *s* of Wilfred and Doris M. Barnes; *m* 1957, Dorothy Jean Drew; one *s* two *d. Educ:* Taunton's Sch., Southampton; Queen's Coll., Oxford. BA 1953, MA 1957; CEng, FIMechE, FRAeS. Bristol Aeroplane Co. (Engine Div.), 1953; Min. of Supply, Nat. Gas Turbine Estabt: Sci. Officer 1955; Sen. Sci. Off. 1957; Principal Sci. Off. 1962; Sen. Principal Sci. Off. (Individual Merit) 1965; Min. of Aviation Supply, Asst Dir, Engine R&D, 1970; seconded to HM Diplomatic Service, Counsellor (Science and Technology), British Embassy, Washington, 1972; Under-Sec., MoD, 1974; Dir Gen. Res. (C), MoD (Procurement Exec.), 1974-77; Dep. Dir (Weapons), RAE, 1978-79; Dep. Chief Scientific Adviser (Projs), MoD, 1979-82. James Clayton Fund Prize, IMechE, 1964. *Publications:* contrib. books and learned jls on mech. engrg, esp. gas turbine technology, heat transfer and stress analysis. *Recreation:* making things. *Address:* Scientific Staff, Ministry of Defence, Main Building, Whitehall, SW1A 2HB.

BARNES, Sir James George, Kt 1976; MBE (mil.); JP; Mayor of Dunedin, New Zealand, 1968-77; sharebroker; *b* Dunedin, NZ; *s* of Richard R. Barnes; *m* 1938, Elsie, *d* of James D. Clark; one *d. Educ:* King Edward Technical High Sch. Served War, RNZAF 75 Sqdn, 1940-46 (POW, 1942-45). Mem., Dunedin City Council, 1947-53 and 1959-80 (Dep. Mayor 1951-53 and 1959-68); MP, 1951-57. Exec. Mem.: Otago Peninsula Trust; NZ Fedn for the Blind; Chm., Bd of Ocean Beach Domain. Past Pres., Otago Savings Bank. Chm. or Dir, Sch. Bds and Youth orgs. NZ mile champion, 1932; NZ Cross Country Champion, 1933; Manager NZ Empire Games Team, 1950; Asst Man., NZ Olympic Team, 1956; Past Pres., NZ AAA; Mem. Otago AAA; Mem. NZ Trotting Conf. (Pres., 1979-80); Sen. Vice Pres., Aust. Trotting Council, 1977-80; Exec. Mem., World Trotting Congress, 1980; Past Pres., Forbury Park Trotting Club. CStJ 1979. *Recreations:* golf, trotting. *Address:* 35 Cliffs Road, Dunedin, New Zealand; PO Box 221, Dunedin.

BARNES, Sir John; see Barnes, Sir E. J. W.

BARNES, Prof. John Arundel, DSC 1944; FBA 1981; Professor of Sociology, University of Cambridge, and Fellow of Churchill College, since 1969; *b* Reading, 9 Sept. 1918; *s* of T. D. and M. G. Barnes, Bath; *m* 1942, Helen Frances, *d* of Charles Bastable; three *s* one *d. Educ:* Christ's Hosp.; St John's Coll., Cambridge; Balliol Coll., Oxford. Fellow, St John's Coll., Cambridge, 1950-53; Simon Research Fellow, Manchester Univ., 1951-53; Reader in Anthropology, London Univ., 1954-56; Prof. of Anthropology, Sydney Univ., 1956-58; Prof. of Anthropology, Inst. of Advanced Studies, ANU, Canberra, 1958-69; Overseas Fellow, Churchill Coll., Cambridge, 1965-66. *Publications:* Marriage in a Changing Society, 1951; Politics in a Changing Society, 1954; Inquest on the Murngin, 1967; Sociology in Cambridge, 1970; Three Styles in the Study of Kinship, 1971; Social Networks, 1972; The Ethics of Inquiry in Social Science, 1977; Who Should Know What?, 1979. *Address:* Churchill College, Cambridge CB3 0DS. *T:* Cambridge 61200.

BARNES, Dame Josephine; see Barnes, Dame A. J. M. T.

BARNES, Sir Kenneth, KCB 1977 (CB 1970); Permanent Secretary, Department of Employment, 1976-82; *b* 26 Aug. 1922; *s* of Arthur and Doris Barnes, Accrington, Lancs; *m* 1948, Barbara Ainsworth; one *s* two *d. Educ:* Accrington Grammar Sch.; Balliol Coll., Oxford. Entered Ministry of Labour, 1948; Asst Sec., 1963; Under-Sec., Cabinet Office, 1966-68; Dep. Sec., Dept of Employment, 1968-75. *Address:* Hill House, 35 Pilgrim's Way, Reigate, Surrey. *T:* Reigate 45237. *Club:* United Oxford & Cambridge University.

BARNES, Kenneth James, CBE 1969 (MBE 1964); Advisor (Finance), Directorate General for Development, Commission of the European Communities, since 1982; *b* 8 May 1930; *s* of late Thomas Arthur Barnes and Ethel Maude Barnes; *m* 1st, 1953, Lesley Dawn Grummett Wright (*d* 1976); two *s* one *d* ; 2nd, 1981, Anna Elisabeth Gustaf Maria Vanoorlé. *Educ:* Dover Coll.; St Catharine's Coll., Cambridge (Crabtree exhibnr; MA); London Univ. MBIM. Pilot Officer, RAF, 1949-50; Flying Officer, RAFVR, 1950-53. Administrative Officer, HMOCS Eastern Nigeria, 1954-60; Asst Sec., Min. of Finance, Malawi, 1960-64, Sen. Asst Sec., 1965, Dep. Sec., 1966, Permanent Sec., 1967-71; Asst Sec., British Steel Corp., 1971-73; EEC: Principal Administrator, Directorate-Gen. for Develt, 1973-75; Head of Div. for Ind. Co-operation, Trade Promotion and Regional Co-operation, 1976-78; Hd of Div. for Caribbean, Indian and Pacific Oceans, 1979-80; Advr (Political), 1981-82. *Recreations:* reading, esp. history, listening to music, mediaeval fortifications. *Address:* Commission of the European Communities, 200 rue de la Loi, B1049 Brussels, Belgium. *T:* (office) Brussels 2355970; (home) 735 57 31. *Club:* Travellers'.

BARNES, Michael Cecil John; marketing consultant; *b* 22 Sept. 1932; *s* of late Major C. H. R. Barnes, OBE and of Katherine Louise (*née* Kennedy); *m* 1962, Anne Mason; one *s* one *d*. *Educ:* Malvern; Corpus Christi Coll., Oxford. MP (Lab) Brentford and Chiswick, 1966-Feb. 1974; an Opposition Spokesman on food and food prices, 1970-71; Chairman: Parly Labour Party Social Security Group, 1969-70; ASTMS Parly Cttee, 1970-71; Jt Hon. Sec., Labour Cttee for Europe, 1969-71; Mem., Public Accounts Cttee, 1967-74. Contested (Lab): Wycombe, 1964; Brentford and Isleworth, Feb. 1974; Mem. Labour Party, 1957-79; helped form SDP, 1981. Member: Council of Management, War on Want, 1972-77; Nat. Consumer Council, 1975-80; Arts Council Trng Cttee, 1977-; Energy Commn, 1977-79; Internat. Cttee of Nat. Council for Voluntary Organisations, 1977-; Advertising Standards Authority, 1979-; Chairman: UK Adv. Cttee on EEC Action Against Poverty Programme, 1975-76; Notting Hill Social Council, 1976-79; Electricity Consumers' Council, 1977-; West London Fair Housing Gp Ltd, 1980-; Vice Chm., Bangabandhu Soc., 1980-; Organising Secretary: Gulbenkian Foundn Drama Trng Inquiry, 1974-75; Music Trng Inquiry, 1976-77; Sec., Nat. Council for Drama Trng, 1976-; Chm., Hounslow Arts Trust, 1974-; Trustee, Project Hand Trust, 1974-77; Governor, Internat. Musicians Seminar, Prussia Cove, 1978-81. *Recreations:* lawn tennis, walking, swimming, reading. *Address:* 45 Ladbroke Grove, W11. *T:* 01-727 2533.

BARNES, Peter; dramatist; *b* 10 Jan. 1931; *s* of Frederick and Martha Barnes; *m* 1958, Charlotte (*née* Beck). *Educ:* Stroud Grammar Sch. Plays: Sclerosis, 1965; The Ruling Class, 1968; Leonardo's Last Supper, 1969; Noonday Demons, 1969. Adapted and co-directed: Wedekind's Lulu, 1970; The Bewitched, 1974; adapted and directed: Feydeau's The Purging, 1976; Wedekind's The Singer, 1976; Jonson's Bartholomew Fair, 1978; Marston's Antonio, 1979; Wedekind's The Devil Himself, 1980; adapted Jonson's The Devil is an Ass, 1977; directed: For All Those Who Get Despondent, 1977; Laughter!, 1978; Somersaults, 1981. *Publications:* The Ruling Class, 1969; Leonardo's Last Supper, 1970; Noonday Demons, 1970; Lulu, 1971; The Bewitched, 1974; The Frontiers of Farce, 1976; Laughter!, 1978; The Collected Plays, 1981. *Address:* 7 Archery Close, Connaught Street, W2 2BE. *T:* 01-262 9205.

BARNES, Peter Robert, CB 1982; Deputy Director of Public Prosecutions, 1977-82; *b* 1 Feb. 1921; *s* of Robert Stanley Barnes and Marguerite (*née* Dunkels); *m* 1955, Pauline Belinda Hannen; two *s* one *d*. *Éduc:* Eton Coll.; Trinity Coll., Cambridge (BA). Called to Bar, Inner Temple, 1947. Dir. of Public Prosecutions: Legal Asst, 1951; Sen. Legal Asst, 1958; Asst Solicitor, 1970; Asst Director, 1974; Principal Asst Dir, 1977. *Recreations:* golf, tennis, ski-ing, conjuring. *Address:* Woodhurst, Hydestile, Godalming, Surrey GUB 4AY. *Club:* Boodle's.

BARNES, Dr Robert Sandford; Principal, Queen Elizabeth College, Kensington, London University, since 1978; *b* 8 July 1924; *s* of William Edward Barnes and Ada Elsie Barnes (*née* Sutherst); *m* 1952, Julia Frances Marriott Grant; one *s* three *d*. *Educ:* Univ. of Manchester. BSc 1948, MSc 1959, DSc 1962. Radar Research, Admiralty Signals Estab., Witley, Surrey, 1944-47; AERE, Harwell: Metallurgical Research, 1948-62; Head of Irradiation Branch, 1962-65; Vis. Scientist, The Science Center, N Amer. Aviation Co., Calif, 1965; Head of Metallurgy Div., AERE, Harwell, 1966-68; Dep. Dir, BISRA, 1968-69; Dir, BISRA, 1969-70; Dir R&D, British Steel Corp., 1970-75; Chief Scientist, BSC, 1975-78. Technical Adviser: Bd of BOC International Ltd, 1979-; Bd of BOC Ltd, 1978-79. Chm., Ruthner Continuous Crop Systems Ltd, 1976-78. Member: CBI Res. and Technol. Cttee, 1968-75; Adv. Council on R&D for Iron and Steel, 1970-75; European Industrial Res. Management Assoc., 1970 (Vice-Pres., 1974-78); Parly and Scientific Cttee, 1970-80; Council, Welding Inst., 1970-75; Council, Instn of Metallurgists, 1970-75 and 1979- (Vice Pres., 1979; Sen. Vice Pres., 1982); Council, Metals Soc., 1974-80 (Chairman: Coordinating Cttee, 1976-78, Executive Cttee, 1976-80); Materials Science and Technology Cttee, SRC, 1975-79; Chm., European Nuclear Steel-making Club, 1973-76; UK Representative: Commn de la Recherche Technique Sidérurgique, 1972-78; Conseil d'Association Européenne pour la Promotion de la Recherche Technique en Sidérurgie, 1972-78; Adv. Council on Energy Conservation, Industry Group, 1977-78; Council, Backpain Assoc., 1979-. Lectures: Hatfield Meml, Iron and Steel Inst., 1973; John Player, IMechE, 1976. Hon. Mem. Council, Iron and Steel Inst., 1969-73. Governor, Sheffield Polytechnic,

1968-72; Member: Court of Univ. of Surrey, 1968-80; Collegiate Council, Univ. of London, 1978; Jt Finance and Gen. Purposes Cttee, Univ. of London, 1978-; Senate, Univ. of London, 1980-. Rosenhain Medallist, Inst. of Metals, 1964. FInstP 1961, FIM 1965, FRSA 1976. CEng 1977. *Publications:* chapters in specialist books of science; scientific papers in various learned jls. *Recreations:* family yachting, gardening. *Address:* Queen Elizabeth College, Campden Hill Road, Kensington, W8 7AH. *T:* 01-939 5411; (home) Pigeon Forge, Daneshill, The Hockering, Woking, Surrey. *T:* Woking 61529. *Club:* Athenæum.

BARNES, Roland, CBE 1970; BSc, MB, ChB, FRCS, FRCSE, FRCSGlas; Professor of Orthopaedic Surgery, University of Glasgow, 1959-72, now Professor Emeritus; *b* 21 May 1907; *y s* of Benjamin Barnes and Mary Ann Bridge, Accrington, Lancs.; *m* 1938, Mary Mills Buckley; one *s* two *d*. *Educ:* University of Manchester. BSc 1927; MB, ChB 1930; Medical and Surgical Clinical prizes. Usual resident appointments; Resident Surgical Officer, Manchester Royal Infirmary, 1934-35; Dickinson Travelling Scholar, Univ. of Manchester, 1935-36; visited orthopaedic clinics in USA; Fellow, Hospital for Ruptured and Crippled, New York. Chief Asst to Sir Harry Platt, Bt, Orthopaedic Department, Royal Infirmary, Manchester, 1937-39; Surgeon in Charge of Orthopædic and Peripheral Nerve Injury Centre, EMS Hospital, Winwick, Lancs, 1940-43. Past Pres., British Orthopædic Assoc.; Hon. Mem. French, Finnish, German and S African Orthopædic Assocs; Corresp. Mem. Amer. Orthopædic Assoc. *Publications:* papers on injuries of the peripheral nerves and spine, fractures of neck of femur, and on tumours of bone. *Recreation:* gardening. *Address:* 35 Boclair Road, Bearsden, Glasgow. *T:* 041-942 2699.

BARNES, Sir William Lethbridge G.; *see* Gorell Barnes.

BARNES, Prof. Winston Herbert Frederick, MA (Oxon); Professor Emeritus, Universities of Manchester and Liverpool; *b* 30 May 1909; *er s* of Frederick Charles and Martha Lilley Barnes; *m* 1938, Sarah, *d* of late Thomas David Davies; two *d*. *Educ:* Manchester Grammar Sch.; Corpus Christi Coll., Oxford (Hugh Oldham Scholar, Haigh Scholar). 1st Cl., Classical Hon. Mods. 1930; 1st Cl., Lit. Hum. 1932; John Locke Scholar in Mental Philosophy, Oxford, 1932; Sen. Demy, Magdalen Coll., Oxford, 1933-34. Asst Lecturer in Philosophy, 1936-39; Lecturer 1939-41, Univ. of Liverpool; served in RAFVR, 1941-42; Temporary Principal, Ministry of Supply, 1942-45; Prof. of Philosophy, Univ. of Durham (Durham Colls) 1945-59; Prof. of Moral Philosophy, Univ. of Edinburgh, 1959-63, Gifford Lectr in Natural Theology, 1968-69, 1969-70; Vice-Chancellor, Univ. of Liverpool, 1963-69; Vis. Prof. of Philosophy, Univ. of Auckland, NZ, 1970; Sir Samuel Hall Prof. of Philosophy, Manchester Univ., 1970-73. Pres., Mind Assoc., 1948. Mem. Planning Bd, Independent Univ., 1970-73; Mem. Council, University Coll. at Buckingham, 1973-78 (Hon. Fellow, 1979). Hon. DCL Durham, 1964. *Publications:* The Philosophical Predicament, 1950; contributions to Mind, Philosophy, Aristotelian Society Proceedings. *Recreations:* walking, swimming. *Address:* 7 Great Stuart Street, Edinburgh EH3 7TP. *T:* 031-226 3158.

BARNETSON, Maj.-Gen. James Craw, CB 1965; OBE 1945; Director of Medical Services, BAOR, December 1964-66, retired; *b* 26 July 1907; *s* of Dr R. B. Barnetson; *m* 1935, Sylvia Joan Milner Moore; three *s*. *Educ:* Edinburgh Academy; Edinburgh Univ. (MB, ChB). Staff Coll., Camberley, 1942; ADMS, AFHQ, 1942-43; ADMS, 6th Armd Div., 1943-46, ADMS, Scot. Comd, 1946-47; Asst DGAMS, War Office, 1947-50; Joint Staff Coll., Latimer, 1950; ADMS, 11th Armd Div., 1951; ADMS, Plans, SHAPE, 1951-53; OC Commonwealth Mil. Hosp., Japan, 1953-54; ADMS, GHQ, E Africa, 1954-57; ADMS, 6 Armd Div., 1958-59; Comdt Field Trg Centre, HQ, AER, RAMC, 1959-60; DDMS, Northern Comd, 1960-61; Dep. DGAMS, 1961-64. QHP 1961-66. Col Comdt, RAMC, 1968-72. OStJ 1965. *Recreations:* golf and fishing. *Address:* The Old Cottage, Wardley Green, Milland, West Sussex. *T:* Milland 371.

BARNETT, Christopher John Anthony; a Recorder of the Crown Court, since 1982; *b* 18 May 1936; *s* of Richard Adrian Barnett and Phyllis Barnett (*née* Cartwright); *m* 1959, Sylvia Marieliese (*née* Pritt); two *s* one *d*. *Educ:* Repton Sch., Derbyshire; College of Law, London. Called to the Bar, Gray's Inn, 1965. District Officer (Kikuyu Guard) and Kenya Government Service, 1955-60; a District Officer in HM Overseas Civil Service, serving in Kenya, 1960-62; in practice as barrister, 1965-. *Recreations:* cricket, lawn tennis. *Address:* 53 North Hill, Colchester CO1 1QA. *T:* Colchester 72756. *Club:* Norfolk (Norwich).

BARNETT, Colin Michael; Regional Secretary, North-West Regional Council of the Trades Union Congress, since 1976; Divisional Officer, North-West Division of the National Union of Public Employees, since 1971; *b* 27 Aug. 1929; *s* of Arthur Barnett and Kathleen Mary Barnett; *m* 1953, Margaret Barnett (marr. diss. 1980); one *s* one *d*; lives with Hilary Carolyn Hodge, PhD. *Educ:* St Michael's Elem. Sch., Southfields; Wandsworth Grammar Sch.; London Sch. of Econs and Polit. Science; WEA classes. Area Officer, NUPE, 1959, Asst Divl Officer 1961. Secretary: NW Peace Council, 1979-; NW Cttee Against Racism, 1980. Organised People's March for Jobs, 1981. *Recreations:* walking, reading, promotion of socialism. *Address:* 14 Elm Grove, Eccleston Park, Prescot, Merseyside L34 2AX. *T:* 051-426 4045; (office) Civic House, 131 Katherine Street, Ashton under Lyne. *T:* 061-339 2796. *Clubs:* White Horse Social (Ashington); Labour (Kirkby).

BARNETT, Correlli (Douglas); author; Keeper of the Archives, and a Fellow, Churchill College, Cambridge, since 1977; Teaching Fellow in Defence Studies, Cambridge University, since 1980; *b* 28 June 1927; *s* of D. A. Barnett; *m* 1950, Ruth Murby; two *d. Educ:* Trinity Sch., Croydon; Exeter Coll., Oxford. Second class hons, Mod. Hist. with Mil. Hist. and the Theory of War as a special subject; MA 1954. Intell. Corps, 1945-48. North Thames Gas Bd, 1952-57; Public Relations, 1957-63. Vice-Pres., E Arts Assoc., 1978- (Chm. Literature Panel, and Mem. Exec. Cttee, 1972-78); Pres., East Anglian Writers; Member: Organising Cttee, Inter-Univ. Seminar on Armed Forces and Society; Council, RUSI, 1973; Cttee, London Library, 1977-79 and 1982-. Leverhulme Res. Fellowship, 1976; Winston Churchill Meml Lectr, Switzerland, 1982. FRSL. *Publications:* The Hump Organisation, 1957; The Channel Tunnel (with Humphrey Slater), 1958; The Desert Generals, 1960; The Swordbearers, 1963; Britain and Her Army, 1970 (RSL award, 1971); The Collapse of British Power, 1972; Marlborough, 1974; Bonaparte, 1978; The Great War, 1979; (historical consultant and writer to) BBC Television series: The Great War, 1963-64; The Lost Peace, 1965-66; The Commanders, 1972-73; reviews Mil. Hist. for The Sunday Telegraph; contrib. to: The Promise of Greatness (a symposium on the Great War), 1968; Governing Elites (a symposium), 1969; Decisive Battles of the Twentieth Century, 1976; The War Lords, 1976. *Recreations:* gardening, interior decorating, idling, eating, mole-hunting. *Address:* Catbridge House, East Carleton, Norwich. *T:* Mulbarton 410.

BARNETT, Air Chief Marshal Sir Denis Hensley Fulton, GCB 1964 (KCB 1957; CB 1956); CBE 1945; DFC 1940; RAF, retired; Member for Weapons Research and Development, Atomic Energy Authority, 1965-72; *b* 11 Feb. 1906; *y s* of late Sir Louis Edward Barnett; *m* 1939, Pamela, *y d* of late Sir Allan John Grant; one *s* two *d. Educ:* Christ's Coll., NZ; Clare Coll., Cambridge (BA 1929, MA 1935). Perm. Commn, RAF, 1929; Flt Lieut, 1934; Sqdn Ldr 1938; comd 84 Sqdn, Shaibah, 1938. Served War of 1939-45; Sqdn Comdr, Stn Comdr and G/C Ops, Bomber Comd, 1939-44; Dep. Dir Bomber Ops, Air Min., 1944; Dep. SASO at HQ Bomber Comd, 1945; Actg Wing Cdr, 1940; Gp Capt., 1941; Air Cdre, 1945; Dir of Ops at Air Min., 1945-46; Air Staff, India, 1946-47; Jt Services Staff Coll., 1948; Comdt Central Bomber Estabt, 1949; Dir of Ops Air Min., 1950-52; idc, 1952; Representative of UK Chiefs of Staff at HQ, UN Command, Tokyo, 1952-54; AOC, No. 205 Group, Middle East Air Force, 1954-56; Commandant, RAF Staff Coll., Bracknell, 1956; Commander Allied Air Task Force, Near East, 1956; Air Secretary, Air Ministry, 1957-59; AOC-in-C, RAF Transport Command, 1959-62; Air Officer Commanding-in-Chief, RAF Near East; Commander, British Forces Cyprus, and Administrator of the Sovereign Base Areas, 1962-64; Subst. Air Commodore, 1950; Air Vice-Marshal, 1953; Air Marshal, 1959; Air Chief Marshal, 1962. Comdr, US Legion of Merit, 1954; French Légion d'Honneur (Commandeur) and Croix de Guerre, 1958. *Recreations:* fishing, shooting. *Address:* River House, Rushall, Pewsey, Wilts SN9 6EN.

See also J. S. Peel.

BARNETT, Guy; *see* Barnett, N. G.

BARNETT, Dame Henrietta; *see* Barnett, Dame M. H.

BARNETT, Rt. Hon. Joel, PC 1975; JP; MP (Lab) Heywood and Royton Division of Lancashire, since 1964; Chairman, Public Accounts Committee, since 1979; *b* 14 Oct. 1923; *s* of Louis and Ettie Barnett, both of Manchester; *m* 1949, Lillian Goldstone; one *d. Educ:* Derby Street Jewish Sch.; Manchester Central High Sch. Certified accountant. Served RASC and British Military Govt in Germany. Mem. of Prestwich, Lancs, Borough Council, 1956-59; JP Lancs 1960; Hon. Treas. Manchester Fabian Society, 1953-65. Contested (Lab) Runcorn Div. of Cheshire, Oct. 1959. Member: Public Accounts Cttee, 1965-71; Public Expenditure Cttee, 1971-74; Select Cttee on Tax Credits, 1973-74; Chm. Parly Labour Party Economic and Finance Group, 1967-70 and 1972-74 (Vice-Chm., 1966-67); Opposition Spokesman on Treasury matters, 1970-74; Chief Sec. to the Treasury, 1974-79 (Cabinet Mem., 1977-79). Hon. Visiting Fellow, Univ. of Strathclyde, 1980-. *Publication:* Inside the Treasury, 1982. *Recreations:* walking, conversation and reading; good food. *Address:* Flat 92, 24 John Islip Street, SW1; 7 Hillingdon Drive, Whitefield, Manchester M25 7QQ.

BARNETT, Joseph Anthony, OBE 1975; Representative, British Council, Tokyo, from Sept. 1983; *b* 19 Dec. 1931; *s* of Joseph Edward Barnett and Helen Johnson; *m* 1960, Carolina Johnson Rice; one *s* one *d. Educ:* St Albans Sch.; Pembroke Coll., Cambridge (BA (Hons) English and Psychology); Edinburgh Univ. (Diploma in Applied Linguistics). Served Army, 1950-51 (2nd Lieut). Teaching, Aylesford House, St Albans, 1954-55; Unilever Ltd, 1955-58; apptd British Council, 1958; Asst Educn Officer, Dacca, Pakistan, 1958; trng at Sch. of Applied Linguistics, Edinburgh Univ., 1960; Educn Officer, Dacca, 1961; seconded to Inst. of Educn, London Univ., 1963; Head, English Language Teaching Inst., London, 1964; Dir of Studies, Regional Inst. of English, Bangalore, India, 1968; Representative, Ethiopia, 1971; Controller, English Language Teaching Div., 1975; Representative, Brazil, 1978-82. *Publications:* (jtly) Getting on in English, 1960; Success with English (language laboratory materials), Books 1-3, 1966-69. *Recreation:* sport (tennis, cricket, riding). *Address:* The Thatch, Stebbing Green, Dunmow, Essex. *T:* Stebbing 352.

BARNETT, Kenneth Thomas, CB 1979; a Deputy Secretary, Department of the Environment, 1976-80; *b* 12 Jan. 1921; *yr s* of late Frederick Charles Barnett and Ethel Barnett (*née* Powell); *m* 1943, Emily May Lovering; one *d. Educ:* Howard Gardens High Sch., Cardiff. Entered Civil Service (Min. of Transport), 1937; Sea Transport Office, Port Said, 1951-54; Asst Sec., 1961; Under-Sec., Cabinet Office (on secondment), 1971-73; Under-Sec., DoE, 1970-76. *Recreations:* gardening, watching Rugby football. *Address:* The Stone House, Frith End, Bordon, Hants. *T:* Bordon 2856.

BARNETT, Dame (Mary) Henrietta, DBE 1958 (CBE 1956; OBE 1950); Director of the Women's Royal Air Force, 1956-60; *b* 16 Feb. 1905; *d* of Col George Henry Barnett, 60th Rifles, Glympton Park, Woodstock, Oxon. *Educ:* Heathfield, Ascot. Joined Women's Auxiliary Air Force in 1939. *Address:* Hoggrove House, Park Street, Woodstock, Oxon. *T:* Woodstock 811502.

BARNETT, (Nicolas) Guy; MP (Lab) Greenwich, since July 1971; *b* 23 Aug. 1928; *s* of late B. G. Barnett; *m* 1967, Daphne Anne, *d* of Geoffrey William Hortin, JP; one *s* one *d. Educ:* Highgate; St Edmund Hall, Oxford. Teacher Queen Elizabeth Gram. Sch., 1953-59; Friends Sch., Kamusinga, Kenya, 1960-61. Famine Relief Sec., Christian Council of Kenya, 1962; on staff VSO, 1966-69; Chief Educn Officer, Commonwealth Inst., 1969-71. Contested (Lab) NR Yorks (Scarborough and Whitby Div.), 1959; MP (Lab) S Dorset Div., Nov. 1962-Sept. 1964; PPS to Minister for Local Govt and Planning, 1974-75; Parly Under-Sec. of State, DoE, 1976-79; Junior opposition spokesman on overseas development, 1980-81; on European and Community affairs, 1981-; Member: Parly Select Cttee on Race Relations and Immigration, 1972-74; Public Accts Cttee, 1975. Mem., European Parl., 1975-76. Parly Adviser, Soc. of Civil Servants, 1973-76. Mem., Gen. Adv. Council of BBC, 1973-76; Trustee, Nat. Maritime Museum, 1974-79. *Publication:* By the Lake, 1964. *Recreations:* music, walking. *Address:* 3 Westcombe Park Road, SE3. *Club:* Royal Commonwealth Society.

BARNETT, Sir Oliver (Charles), Kt 1968; CBE 1954 (OBE 1946); QC 1956; *b* 7 Feb. 1907; *er s* of Charles Frederick Robert Barnett, 2nd Lieut Gloucestershire Regt (TA) (killed in action, 1915), and late Cicely Frances Barnett (*née* Cornish); *m* 1945, Joan, *o surv c* of Capt. W. H. Eve, 13th Hussars (killed in action, 1917), *o s* of late Rt Hon. Sir Harry Trelawney Eve, a Judge of the High Court. *Educ:* Eton. Called to Bar, Middle Temple, 1928; Bencher, Middle Temple, 1964, Oxford Circuit; Central Criminal Court Sessions; Dep. Chm., Somerset QS, 1967-71. Dir of Public Prosecutions Office, 1931; Legal Asst, Judge Advocate General's Office, 1934; Second Deputy Judge Advocate, 1937; First Deputy Judge Advocate, 1938; RAF 1939-47 (OBE); Wing Comdr (RAFVR); Asst Judge Advocate Gen. (RAF) 1942-47; Asst Judge Advocate Gen. (Army and RAF), 1947-54; Deputy Judge Advocate Gen. (Army and RAF) BAOR, BTA and 2nd TAF, 1953-54; Vice Judge Advocate Gen., 1955-62; Judge Advocate Gen., 1963-68. *Address:* The Almonry, Stogumber, Taunton, Somerset. *T:* Stogumber 291. *Clubs:* Brooks', Pratt's.

BARNETT, Richard David, CBE 1974; MA, DLitt; FBA 1962; FSA; b Acton, 23 Jan. 1909; *o s* of late Lionel David Barnett, CB; *m* 1948, Barbara Joan, *d* of Ralph Pinto; two *s* one *d. Educ:* St Paul's Sch., London; Corpus Christi Coll., Cambridge. Student of British Sch. of Archaeology at Athens, 1930-32; Asst Keeper, Dept of Egyptian and Assyrian Antiquities, British Museum, 1932; Dep. Keeper, 1953; Keeper, Dept of Western Asiatic Antiquities, 1955-74. Vis. Prof., Hebrew Univ., Jerusalem, 1974-75. Sec. British Sch. of Archaeology at Athens, 1933-35; Pres. Jewish Historical Society of England, 1959-61. Corr. Mem., Greek Archaeological Soc.; Ordinary Fellow, German Archaeological Inst., 1961. Served War of 1939-45: Admiralty 1939-40; Foreign Office, 1940-42; Intelligence Officer, RAF, 1942-46, Egypt, Syria, Libya, Turkey. *Publications:* (ed) Treasures of London Temple, 1951; (with Sir L. Woolley) British Museum Excavations at Carchemish, Vol. III, 1952; Catalogue of Nimrud Ivories in the British Museum, 1957, 2nd edn 1975; (trans.) The Jewish sect of Qumran and the Essenes (by J. Dupont-Sommer), 1954; Assyrian Palace Reliefs, 1960; (with M. Falkner) The Sculptures of Tiglath-pileser III, 1962, 2nd edn, 1970; Illustrations of Old Testament History, 1966, 2nd edn 1977; (ed) The Sephardi Heritage, 1971; (ed) Catalogue of the Jewish Museum, London, 1974; (with Amleto Lorenzini) Assyrian Sculpture, 1976; The Sculptures of Ashurbanipal, 1976; articles on archaeology and Anglo-Jewish history in various learned jls. *Address:* 14 Eldon Grove, NW3 5PT. *T:* 01-794 2066.

BARNETT, William Evans; barrister; a Recorder of the Crown Court, since 1981; *b* 10 March 1937; *s* of late Alec Barnett and Esmé (*née* Leon); *m* 1970, Lucinda Jane Gilbert, MA, ARCM; two *s. Educ:* Repton; Keble Coll., Oxford (BA Jurisprudence, 1961; MA 1965). National Service, RCS, 1956-58. Called to the Bar, Inner Temple, 1962; Major Scholarship, Inner Temple, 1962. *Recreations:* golf, photography, gardening. *Address:* Carleon, 55 Croham Manor Road, South Croydon, Surrey CR2 7BJ. *T:* 01-688 9559; 12 King's Bench Walk, Temple, EC4Y 7EL. *T:* 01-583 0811. *Club:* Addington Golf.

BARNEWALL, family name of **Baron Trimlestown.**

BARNEWALL, Sir Reginald Robert, 13th Bt, *cr* 1622; cattle breeder and orchardist at Mount Tamborine; *b* 1 Oct 1924; *o s* of Sir Reginald Aylmer Barnewall, 12th Bt and of Jessie Ellen, *d* of John Fry; *S* father 1961; *m* 1st

1946, Elsie Muriel (d 1962), d of Thomas Matthews-Frederick, Brisbane; three d (one s decd); 2nd, 1962, Maureen Ellen, d of William Joseph Daly, South Caulfield, Vic; one s. *Educ:* Xavier Coll., Melbourne. Served War of 1939-45, overseas with Australian Imperial Forces. Served with Citizen Military Forces Unit, Royal Australian Armoured Corps, 1948-56. Managing Dir, Southern Airlines Ltd of Melbourne, 1953-58; Operation Manager, Polynesian Airlines, Apia, Western Samoa, 1958-62; Managing Dir, Orchid Beach (Fraser Island) Pty Ltd, 1962-71; Dir, Island Airways Pty Ltd, Pialba, Qld, 1964-68; owner and operator, Coastal-Air Co. (Qld), 1971-76; Dir and Vice-Chm., J. Roy Stevens Pty Ltd, to 1975. *Heir:* s Peter Joseph Barnewall, b 26 Oct. 1963. *Address:* Mount Tamborine, Queensland 4272, Australia. *Clubs:* United Service (Brisbane); RSL (Surfers Paradise).

BARNSLEY, Alan Gabriel; see Fielding, Gabriel.

BARNSLEY, Thomas Edward, OBE 1975; FCA; a Managing Director, Tube Investments Ltd, 1974-82; b 1 Sept. 1919; s of Alfred E. Barnsley and Ada F. Nightingale; m 1947, Margaret Gwyneth Llewellin; one s one d. *Educ:* Wednesbury Boys' High Sch. ACMA. Friends' Ambulance Unit, 1940-45. Price Waterhouse Peat & Co., South America, 1948-49; Asst Sec., 1958-62, Group Financial Controller, 1962-65, Tube Investments Ltd; Chm. and Man. Dir, Raleigh Industries Ltd, 1968-74. *Recreations:* gardening, cycling. *Address:* Old Rectory, Cossington, near Leicester LE7 8UU. *T:* Sileby 2623.

BARNSLEY, (William) Edward, CBE 1945; Designer and maker of furniture and building woodwork; Adviser in woodwork design, Loughborough Training College, 1938-60; Consultant in Furniture Design to Rural Industries Bureau, 1945-60; b 7 Feb. 1900; s of Sidney Howard Barnsley, Sapperton, Cirencester; m 1925, Tatiana, d of late Dr Harry Kellgren; one s one d. *Educ:* Bedales. Retrospective exhibition, 60 Years of Designing and Making, at Fine Arts Society Gallery, London, and then at Holburne of Menstrie Museum, Bath, 1982. Work includes Throne and Prie-Dieu for Archbishop, Canterbury Cathedral; practically all work still in private or public use; examples in V & A Museum and Melbourne Art Gall., Australia. *Address:* Froxfield, Petersfield, Hants. *T:* Hawkley 233.

BARNSTAPLE, Archdeacon of; see Herniman, Ven. R. G.

BARNWELL, Col Ralph Ernest, CBE 1943; retired; b 20 Jan. 1895; s of late E. F. Barnwell, Rugby; m 1927, Lilian Katharine Oliphant, d of late C. R. Bradburne, Official Solicitor to the Supreme Court of Judicature; one d (one s decd). *Educ:* Rugby Sch. HAC 1914; 2nd Lieut Royal Warwicks Regt 1914; served in France in European War, 1914-18 (despatches); Capt. 1923; Adjutant, 7th Bn Royal Warwicks Regt, 1924-27; Staff Coll., Camberley, 1928-29; Staff Capt., War Office, 1930-32; GSO Weapon Training, Eastern Command, 1932-34; Bt Major 1935; Major, 1938; DAAG Lahore District, 1937-39; Lieut-Col 1939; DAA and QMG (France), 1939; AQMG 2nd Corps (France), 1940; Asst Adjutant-Gen., War Office, 1940-45; Col (temp.) 1941; retd pay 1945; Commandant, Duke of York's Royal Military Sch., 1945-53. *Recreation:* painting. *Address:* Woodrow House, Fifehead Neville, Sturminster Newton, Dorset. *T:* Hazelbury Bryan 297. *Club:* Army and Navy.

BARODA, Maharaja of; see Gaekwad, Lt-Col F. P.

BARON, Alexander; Writer; b 4 Dec. 1917; s of Barnet Baron and Fanny Levinson; m 1960, Delores Salzedo; one s. *Educ:* Hackney Downs Sch., London. Asst Editor, The Tribune, 1938-39. Served War of 1939-45, Army. Editor, New Theatre, 1946-49. *Publications:* novels: From the City, From the Plough, 1948; There's No Home, 1950; Rosie Hogarth, 1951; With Hope, Farewell, 1952; The Human Kind, 1953; The Golden Princess, 1954; Queen of the East, 1956; Seeing Life, 1958; The Lowlife, 1963; Strip Jack Naked, 1966; King Dido, 1969; The In-Between Time, 1971; Gentle Folk, 1976; Franco is Dying, 1977; also film scripts and television plays. *Address:* 30 Cranbourne Gardens, NW11. *T:* 01-455 8352. *Club:* PEN.

BARON, Colin; Director General, Research (General) and Assistant Chief Scientific Adviser (Research), Ministry of Defence, 1977-81; b 20 May 1921; s of John Henry Baron and Dorothy May (née Crumpler); m 1961, Anita Veronica Hale; one s one d by former marriage. *Educ:* Carlton Grammar Sch., Bradford; Univ. of Leeds (BSc Hons 1941, MSc 1947). Scientific Civil Service, 1941-81; Royal Radar Estabt, Malvern: radar trials and res., 1941-57; weapon systems assessment, 1957-66; RAE, Farnborough: Head, Weapons Res. Gp, 1966-70; Head, Avionics Dept, 1970-74; Head, Flt Systems Dept, 1974-76; Dir Gen., Weapons Res., MoD, 1976-77. *Publications:* contribs to Jl IEE and Jl Applied Physics. *Recreations:* gardening, badminton, economics. *Address:* Tanglewood, Vicarage Lane, The Bourne, Farnham, Surrey. *T:* Farnham 721433. *Club:* Civil Service.

BARR, A. W. Cleeve, CBE 1972; retired 1980; b 1910; s of Albert John Barr and Ellen (née Cleeve); m 1st, 1935, Edith M. Edwards, BA (d 1965); one s one d (and one s decd); 2nd, 1966, Mrs Mary W. Harley (widow). *Educ:* Borlase, Marlow; Liverpool Univ. Private offices (Charles Holden and Paul Mauger); Herts CC (schools) and LCC (housing). Dep. Housing Architect, LCC, 1956-57; Development Architect, Ministry of Education, 1957-58; Chief Architect, Min. of Housing and Local Govt, 1959-64. Dir, Nat. Building Agency, 1964-77 (Man. Dir, 1967-77); Dir, Nat. Building Agency

Film Unit, 1977-80; Vice-Pres., UK Housing Trust, 1981-. Hon. Sec. RIBA, 1963-65. *Address:* 72 Eastwick Road, Walton-on-Thames, Surrey KT12 5AR.

BARR, David; a Metropolitan Stipendiary Magistrate, since 1976; b 15 Oct. 1925; s of late Walter and of Betty Barr; m 1960, Ruth Weitzman; one s one d. *Educ:* Haberdashers' Aske's Hampstead Sch.; Brookline High Sch., Boston, USA; Edinburgh Univ.; University Coll., London (LLB). Royal Navy, 1943-47. Solicitor, 1953; private practice, 1953-76 (Partner, Pritchard Englefield & Tobin). JP Inner London Area, 1963-76; Chm., Inner London Juvenile Panel, 1969-76; Dep. Chm., N Westminster PSD, 1968-76. Manager, Finnart House Sch., Weybridge, 1955-81, Trustee 1973-. *Recreations:* book collecting, bridge. *Address:* Highbury Corner Magistrates' Court, Holloway Road, N7. *Clubs:* Garrick, MCC.

BARR, Rev. Prof. James, MA, BD, DD; FBA 1969; Regius Professor of Hebrew, Oxford University, and Student of Christ Church, since 1978; b 20 March 1924; s of Rev. Prof. Allan Barr, DD; m 1950, Jane J. S. Hepburn, MA; two s one d. *Educ:* Daniel Stewart's Coll., Edinburgh; Edinburgh Univ. (MA 1948, BD 1951); MA 1976, BD DD 1981, Oxon. Served War of 1939-45 as pilot in RNVR (Fleet Air Arm), 1942-45. Minister of Church of Scotland, Tiberias, Israel, 1951-53; Prof. of New Testament Literature and Exegesis, Presbyterian Coll., Montreal, 1953-55; Prof. of Old Testament Literature and Theology, Edinburgh Univ., 1955-61; Prof. of Old Testament Literature and Theology, Princeton Theological Seminary, 1961-65; Prof. of Semitic Languages and Literatures, Manchester Univ., 1965-76; Oriel Prof. of the Interpretation of Holy Scripture, and Fellow of Oriel Coll., Oxford Univ., 1976-78 (Hon. Fellow, 1980). Visiting Professor: Hebrew Univ., Jerusalem, 1973; Chicago Univ., 1975, 1981; Strasbourg Univ., 1975-76; lectured in Princeton Univ., 1962-63; in Union Theol. Seminary, New York, 1963; Lectures: Currie, Austin Theol. Seminary, Texas, 1964; Guggenheim Memorial Fellowship for study in biblical semantics, 1965; Cadbury, Birmingham Univ., 1969; Croall, Edinburgh Univ., 1970; Grinfield, on the Septuagint, Oxford Univ., 1974-78; Firth, Nottingham Univ., 1978; Sprunt, Richmond, Va, 1982; Sanderson, Ormond Coll., Melbourne, 1982. Editor: Jl of Semitic Studies, 1965-76; Oxford Hebrew Dictionary, 1974-80. President: Soc. for OT Studies, 1973; British Assoc. for Jewish Studies, 1978. FRAS 1969. Hon. Fellow, SOAS, 1975. Hon. DD: Knox Coll., Toronto, 1964; Dubuque, 1974; St Andrews, 1974; Hon. MA Manchester, 1969. Corresp. Mem., Göttingen Acad. of Sciences, 1976; Mem., Norwegian Acad. of Science and Letters, 1977. *Publications:* The Semantics of Biblical Language, 1961; Biblical Words for Time, 1962; Old and New in Interpretation, 1966; Comparative Philology and the Text of the Old Testament, 1968; The Bible in the Modern World, 1973; Fundamentalism, 1977; The Typology of Literalism, 1979; Explorations in Theology 7: The Scope and Authority of the Bible, 1980; Holy Scripture: Canon, Authority, Criticism, 1983; articles in Semitic and biblical journals. *Recreation:* bird watching. *Address:* 6 Fitzherbert Close, Iffley, Oxford OX4 4EN. *T:* Oxford 772741.

BARR, Kenneth Glen; Sheriff of South Strathclyde, Dumfries and Galloway at Dumfries, since 1976; b 20 Jan. 1941; o s of Rev. Gavin Barr and Mrs Catherine McLellan Barr (née McGhie); m 1970, Susanne Crichton Keir. *Educ:* Ardrossan Acad.; Royal High Sch.; Edinburgh Univ. (MA, LLB). Admitted to Faculty of Advocates, 1964. *Address:* Sheriff Court House, Dumfries DG1 2AN.

BARR, Prof. Murray Llewellyn, OC (Canada) 1968; FRS 1972; Professor of Anatomy, University of Western Ontario, 1949-79, now Emeritus Professor; b 20 June 1908; Canadian; m 1934, Ruth Vivian King; three s one d. *Educ:* Univ. of Western Ontario (BA, MD, MSc). FRSC 1958; FRCP(C) 1964; FACP 1965; FRCOG 1972. Served War of 1939-45 as MO, RCAF (Wing Comdr). Univ. of Western Ontario: Instructor in Anatomy, 1936-45; Associate Prof. of Anatomy, 1945-49 (Chm., Dept of Anatomy, 1951-67). Hon. Degrees: LLD Queen's, 1963; LLD Toronto, 1964; Drmed Basel, 1966; LLD Alberta, 1967; LLD Dalhousie, 1968; LLD Saskatchewan, 1973; DSc Western Ontario, 1974. *Publications:* The Human Nervous System: an anatomical viewpoint, 1972, 3rd edn 1979; A Century of Medicine at Western, 1977; numerous scientific papers. *Address:* 430 Old Wonderland Road, London, Ontario, Canada N6K 3R2. *T:* (519) 471-5618. *Club:* Harvey (London, Ont.).

BARR, His Honour Judge Reginald Alfred; a Circuit Judge (formerly Judge of County Courts), since 1970; b 21 Nov. 1920; s of Alfred Charles Barr; m 1946, Elaine, 3rd d of James William Charles O'Bala Morris, Llanstephan, Carmarthenshire. *Educ:* Christ's Hospital; Trinity Coll., Oxford (MA). Served War, 1941-46, Middle East and Burma. Called to Bar, Middle Temple, 1954; Standing Counsel to Registrar of Restrictive Trading Agreements, 1962-70. Mem. Review Bd for Govt Contracts, 1969-70. *Address:* 42 Bathurst Mews, Hyde Park, W2. *T:* 01-262 5731.

BARR, William Greig, DL; Rector, Exeter College, Oxford, 1972-82; b 10 June 1917; s of late William S. Barr, Glasgow; m 1954, Helen Georgopoulos; two s. *Educ:* Sedbergh Sch.; Magdalen Coll., Oxford. Stanhope Prize; 1938; 1st cl., Hon. Sch. of Modern History, 1939. Served War, 1939-45: Lt-Col, Royal Devon Yeomanry. Fellow of Exeter Coll., Oxford, 1945-72; Sub-Rector, 1947-54; Sen. Tutor, 1960-66. Lectr in Modern History, Univ. of Oxford, 1949-72. Hon. Treas., Oxford Univ. Rugby Football Club, 1948-73; Jun. Proctor, 1951-52. A Rhodes Trustee, 1975-. Visiting Prof. of Hist., Univ.

of South Carolina, 1968. Governor: Brighton Coll.; Plymouth Coll.; Sedbergh Sch.; Trustee, Uppingham Sch. DL Oxon 1974. *Address:* 24 Northmoor Road, Oxford. *T:* Oxford 58253.

BARR YOUNG, Gavin Neil; a Recorder of the Crown Court, since 1979; *b* 14 Aug. 1939; *s* of Dr James Barr Young and Elsie Barr Young (*née* Hodgkinson); *m* 1969, Barbara Elizabeth Breckon; two *d. Educ:* Loretto Sch., Musselburgh; Leeds Univ. (LLB). Called to the Bar, Gray's Inn, 1963; Member, North Eastern Circuit, 1964- (North Eastern Circuit Junior, 1968). *Recreations:* gardening, music, sailing. *Address:* 2 Park Square, Leeds LS1 2NE. *T:* Leeds 33277; 4 Paper Buildings, Temple, EC4. *T:* 01-353 8408. *Club:* Leeds (Leeds).

BARRACK, William Sample, Jr; Chairman and Chief Executive Officer, Texaco Ltd, London, since 1980; *b* 26 July 1929; *s* of William Sample Barrack and Edna Mae Henderson; *m* 1953, Evelyn Irene Ball; one *s* one *d. Educ:* Pittsburgh Univ. BSc (Engr) 1950. FInstPet 1981. Comdr, USN, 1950-53. Joined Texaco Inc., 1953; marketing and management positions in USA, 1953-67; in Europe, 1967-71; Vice-President: in NY, 1971-80; Marketing Dept, Europe, 1971-76; Producing Dept, Eastern Hemisphere, 1976-77; Personnel and Corporate Services Dept, 1977-80. Former Director: Deutsche Texaco AG; Aramco; Texaco Canada Inc.; Texaco Ltd; Texaco Philanthropic Foundn. Governor: Foreign Policy Assoc.; US Naval War College Foundn. *Address:* Texaco Ltd, 1 Knightsbridge Green, SW1 7QJ.

BARRACLOUGH, Geoffrey; *b* 10 May 1908; *e s* of late Walter and Edith M. Barraclough. *Educ:* Bootham Sch., York; Oriel Coll., Oxford; Univ. of Munich. Bryce Research Student, 1931; Rome Scholar, British Sch. at Rome, 1931; Fellow of Merton Coll., Oxford, 1934; Fellow and Lectr, St John's Coll., Cambridge, 1936; Univ. Lectr, Cambridge, 1937; Foreign Office, 1940; RAFVR, 1942-45; Prof. of Mediæval History, University of Liverpool, 1945-56. Research Prof. of Internat. History, University of London, 1956-62; Prof. of History, Univ. of California, 1965-68; Springer Prof. of History, Brandeis Univ., 1968-70; Chichele Prof. of Modern History, and Fellow of All Souls Coll., Oxford Univ., 1970-73. Arnold Bernhard Vis. Prof., Williams Coll., Mass, 1982; Eric Voegelin Vis. Prof., Munich Univ., 1983. President: Historical Assoc., 1964-67; Internat. Soc. Sci. Council, Gp of Twenty, 1975-. Hon. Mem., Austrian Inst. Historical Research. *Publications:* Public Notaries and the Papal Curia, 1934; Papal Provisions, 1935; Mediæval Germany, 1938; The Origins of Modern Germany, 1946; Factors in German History, 1946; The Mediæval Empire, 1950; The Earldom and County Palatine of Chester, 1953; History in a Changing World, 1955; Early Cheshire Charters, 1957; (ed) Social Life in Early England, 1960; European Unity in Thought and Action, 1963; An Introduction to Contemporary History, 1964; The Mediæval Papacy, 1968; (ed) Eastern and Western Europe in the Middle Ages, 1970; The Crucible of Europe, 1976; Management in a Changing Economy, 1976; Atlante della Storia 1945-1975, 1977; Main Trends in History, 1979; (ed) Times Atlas of World History, 1978; Turning Points in World History, 1979; From Agadir to Armageddon, 1982; (ed) Times Concise Atlas of World History, 1982; (with R. F. Wall) Survey of International Affairs, 1955-56; Survey of International Affairs, 1956-58; Survey of International Affairs, 1958-60.

BARRACLOUGH, Henry, CVO 1976 (MVO 1958); *b* 10 Aug. 1894; *s* of late Henry Barraclough, Shipowner, West Hartlepool; *m* 1922, Ethel Mary, *d* of Wilkinson Dix Sunderland; two *s. Educ:* Giggleswick Sch. On leaving school joined staff of Lambert Bros Ltd, Newcastle on Tyne office, 1911. Served European War, 1914-18, Durham LI, retiring as Capt.; served in Mesopotamia and NW Persia, 1916-19. Silver Line Ltd: Treasury Dir, 1940-48; Chm. and Man. Dir, 1948-60. Chairman, Prince of Wales Dry Dock Co., Swansea, Ltd, 1943-65 (Dir of the company, 1931-66); Dir, Dene Shipping Co. Ltd from formation until 1970 (Chm., 1941-66), and of other cos; Mem. of Lloyd's. Chm. London General Shipowners' Soc., 1946-47; Dep. Chm. and Chm. of Sub-Cttees of Classification of Lloyd's Register of Shipping, 1949-50. Chm. Governors, The "Cutty Sark" Soc., from foundation to 1976. Liveryman of Worshipful Company of Shipwrights. *Address:* Cotehow, Martindale, Penrith, Cumbria. *T:* Pooley Bridge 521.

BARRACLOUGH, Air Chief Marshal Sir John, KCB 1970 (CB 1969); CBE 1961; DFC 1942; AFC 1941; FRSA, FIPM, FBIM, MIPR; Gentleman Usher to the Sword of State, since 1980; Vice-Chairman, Commonwealth War Graves Commission, since 1981 (Commissioner since 1974); Vice-Chairman Editorial Board, NATO's Fifteen Nations, since 1981 (Editorial Director, 1978-81); *b* 2 May 1918; *s* of late Horatio and Marguerite Maude Barraclough; *m* 1946, Maureen (*née* McCormack), niece of George Noble, Count Plunkett; one *d. Educ:* Cranbrook Sch. Service Artists' Rifles, 1935-38. Commissioned RAF, 1938. Air Vice-Marshal, 1964; Air Marshal, 1970; Air Chief Marshal, 1973. Served Near, Middle and Far East; first single-engined jet flight to S Africa, 1957. On staffs of Central Flying Sch. and IDC, 1949-54; Station Commander, RAF Biggin Hill and Middleton St George, 1954-58; Dir of Public Relations, Air Ministry, 1961-64; AOC No 19 Group, and NATO Air Comdr, Central Sub-Area, Eastern Atlantic Comd, 1964-67; Harvard Business Sch., 1967; AOA, Bomber Command, 1967-68; AOA, Strike Comd, 1968-70; Vice-Chief of Defence Staff, 1970-72; Air Secretary, 1972-74; Comdt, Royal Coll. of Defence Studies, 1974-76, retired. Hon. Air Cdre, No 3 (County of Devon) Maritime HQ Unit, RAuxAF, 1979-. Mem., RAF Training and Educn Adv. Bd, 1976-79; Vice Chm., Air League Council, 1977-81; Vice-Chm., British Export Finance Adv. Council, 1982- (Mem.,

1981-); Chm., RUSI Council, 1977-80, Vice-Pres., 1980-; Pres., West Devon Area, St John Ambulance. Past Pres., RAF Modern Pentathlon Assoc. *Publications:* (jtly) The Third World War, 1978; contrib. to The Third World War: the untold story, 1982; contribs to professional jls. *Recreations:* sailing, country pursuits. *Address:* c/o Barclays Bank, 11 Newgate Street, EC1. *Club:* Boodle's, Royal Air Force; Royal Western Yacht.

BARRACLOUGH, Sir Kenneth (James Priestley), Kt 1978; CBE 1965 (OBE 1945); TD; JP; Chief Metropolitan Magistrate 1975-78, retired; *b* 1907; *s* of Herbert Barraclough, Leeds; *m* 1931, Gladys Evelyn, *d* of Charles Henderson, Liverpool and Rio de Janeiro; two *s d. Educ:* Oundle Sch.; Clare Coll., Cambridge. Barrister, Middle Temple, 1929 (Master of the Bench 1975), North Eastern Circuit; Inns of Court Regt, TA, 1938; Col 1945. HQ 21st Army Group (despatches). Metropolitan Magistrate, 1954; Dep. Chm. Appeals Cttee, Hampshire QS, 1957-62; Chm., HO Poisons Board, 1958-76; Member: Adv. Cttee on Drug Dependence, 1966-70; Adv. Council on the Misuse of Drugs, 1972-73; Medicines Commn, 1969-75. JP Hampshire, 1957. *Address:* 18 Fitzroy Road, Fleet, Hants.

BARRAN, Sir David Haven, Kt 1971; Chairman, Midland Bank Ltd, 1980-82 (Deputy Chairman, 1975-80); *b* 23 May 1912; *s* of Sir John Barran, 2nd Bt and Alice Margarita (*née* Parks); *m* 1944, Jane Lechmere Macaskie; four *s* three *d. Educ:* Winchester; Trinity Coll., Cambridge. BA 1934. Joined Asiatic Petroleum Co., 1934; served in Egypt, Palestine, Sudan, India, 1935-46; Pres., Asiatic Petroleum Corp., New York, 1958; Managing Dir, Royal Dutch/Shell Group, 1961-72; Chm., Shell Oil Co., 1970-72; Director: Shell Transport and Trading Co. Ltd, 1961-73 (Dep. Chm., 1964-67; Chm. 1967-72; Man. Dir, 1964-73); General Accident Insurance; BICC; Glaxo Hldgs. Chairman: CBI Cttee on Inflation Accounting, 1973-74; Adv. Cttee on Appt of Advertising Agents, 1975-78 (Mem., 1973-78); Ct of Governors, Administrative Staff Coll., 1971-76; Governor, Centre for Environmental Studies, 1972-75. Comdr, Order of Oranje Nassau, 1971; Comdr, Order of Merit, Fed. Repub. of Germany, 1980. *Recreations:* gardening, shooting, embroidery. *Address:* Shell Centre, SE1 7NA; 36 Kensington Square, W8. *T:* 01-937 5664; Brent Eleigh Hall, Suffolk. *T:* Lavenham 247202. *Club:* River (New York).

BARRAN, Sir John (Napoleon Ruthven), 4th Bt *cr* 1895; Head of Viewdata Unit, Central Office of Information, since 1978; *b* 14 Feb. 1934; *s* of Sir John Barran Leighton Barran, 3rd Bt, and Hon. Alison Mary (*d* 1973), 3rd *d* of 9th Baron Ruthven, CB, CMG, DSO; *S* father, 1974; *m* 1965, Jane Margaret, *d* of Sir Stanley Hooker, *qv*; one *s* one *d. Educ:* Heatherdown Sch., Ascot; Winchester Coll. National Service, 1952-54, Lieut, 5th Roy. Inniskilling Dragoon Guards, served Canal Zone. Asst Account Executive: Dorland Advertising Ltd, 1956-58; Masius & Fergusson Advertising Ltd, 1958-61; Account Executive Ogilvy, Benson & Mather (New York) Inc., 1961-63; Overseas TV News Service, COI, 1964; First Sec. (Information), British High Commission, Ottawa, 1965-67; Central Office of Information: Home Documentary Film Section, 1967-72; Overseas TV and Film News Services, 1972-75; TV Commercials and Fillers Unit, 1975-78. Mem. Council, Assoc. of Viewdata Inf. Providers. *Recreations:* entertaining, gardening. *Heir: s* John Ruthven Barran, *b* 10 Nov. 1971. *Address:* 17 St Leonard's Terrace, SW3. *T:* 01-730 2801; The Hermitage, East Bergholt, Suffolk.

BARRATT, Francis Russell, CB 1975; Deputy Secretary, HM Treasury, since 1973; *b* 16 Nov. 1924; *s* of Frederick Russell Barratt; *m* 1st, 1949, Jane Mary Sherborne (marr. diss. 1978); three *s;* 2nd, 1979, Josephine Nora Harrison (*née* McCririck). *Educ:* Durban High Sch., SA; Clifton; University Coll., Oxford. War Service, 1943-46; Captain, Intelligence Corps, 1946. Asst Principal, HM Treasury, 1949; Principal, 1953; First Sec., UK High Commission, Karachi, 1956-58; Asst Sec., 1962, Under Sec., 1968, HM Treasury. *Recreations:* reading, golf, music. *Address:* 8 Arlington Avenue, N1 *T:* 01-359 1747.

BARRATT, Gilbert Alexander; Master of the Supreme Court, Chancery Division, since 1980; *b* 1930; *s* of Arthur Walter Barratt and Frances Erskine Barratt (*née* Scott); *m* 1964, Fiona MacDermott; one *s* one *d. Educ:* Winchester; New Coll., Oxford. BA Modern History. Qualified as Solicitor 1957; Partner: Stitt & Co., 1960-63; Thicknesse & Hull, 1963-67; Lee Bolton & Lee, 1967-78; Winckworth & Pemberton, 1978-80. *Recreation:* travel. *Address:* The Old School, Clungunford, Craven Arms, Shropshire. *Club:* Travellers'.

BARRATT, Herbert George Harold, OBE 1966; General Secretary, Confederation of Shipbuilding and Engineering Unions, 1957-70; *b* 12 Jan. 1905; *m* 1926; one *s* three *d. Educ:* Vicarage Street Church of England Sch. Nuneaton. Nuneaton Borough Councillor, 1945-47; Mem. Nat. Cttee AEU, 1943-48; Delegate to USSR, 1946. Chm. Nuneaton Labour Party, 1944-46 Coventry Dist. Cttee AEU, 1943-49; Shop Steward Convener, Daimler Motors, 1940-49; Appeals Board Assessor during war years; Nat. Insurance Tribunal Assessor; elected Nat. Organiser AEU, 1949-57. Formerly Member: Gas Adv. Council; Shipbuilding and Ship repairing Council; Nat. Adv. Council for the Motor Manufacturing Industry; Motor Industry Joint Labour Council; British Railways Productivity Council; Econ. Develt Cttee for Mech. Engrg Industry; Econ. Develt Cttee for Electrical Engrg Industry Econ. Develt Cttee for Motor Manufacturing Industry; Industrial Training Board, Engrg; Industrial Training Board, Shipbuilding; British Productivity team to Swedish Shipyards, 1959; visited German Federal Railways, 1960

Exchange Leader Scheme visitor to USA, 1961; Vice-Chm., Sub-Cttee on Programme and Planning, Metal Trades Cttee, ILO, Geneva, 1965. *Recreation:* gardening. *Address:* 34 Collington Park Crescent, Bexhill-on-Sea, East Sussex TN39 3RF. *T:* Bexhill-on-Sea 216646.

BARRATT, Sir Lawrence (Arthur), (Sir Lawrie Barratt), Kt 1982; FCIS; Chairman and Managing Director, Barratt Developments plc, and subsidiary companies, since 1962; *b* Newcastle, 1927; *m*; two *s*. Built first house, 1953; founded Barratt Developments, as a private co., 1958. *Address:* Barratt Developments, Wingrove House, Ponteland Road, Newcastle upon Tyne NE5 3DP.

BARRATT, Michael Fieldhouse; communications consultant; broadcaster on radio and television; Chairman: Commercial Video Ltd, since 1981; Michael Barratt Ltd, since 1977; Director: United Media Finance Ltd, since 1981; Travel and Leisure Communications Ltd, since 1982; *b* 3 Jan. 1928; *s* of late Wallace Milner Barratt and Doris Barratt; *m* 1st, 1952, Joan Francesca Warner (marr. diss.); three *s* three *d*; 2nd, 1977, Dilys Jane Morgan; two *s*. *Educ:* Rossall and Paisley Grammar Sch. Entered journalism, Kemsley Newspapers, 1945; Editor, Nigerian Citizen, 1956; *television:* Reporter, Panorama, 1963; Presenter: 24 Hours, 1965-69; Nationwide, 1969-77; Songs of Praise, 1977-; *radio:* Question-Master, Gardeners' Question Time, 1973-79. Mem. Cttee, Yorks and Humberside School Broadcast Assoc., 1975. Rector, Aberdeen Univ., 1973. Hon. LLD Aberdeen, 1975. FRHS. *Publications:* Michael Barratt, 1973; Michael Barratt's Down-to-Earth Gardening Book, 1974; Michael Barratt's Complete Gardening Book, 1977; Golf with Tony Jacklin, 1978. *Recreations:* golf, cricket, listening. *Address:* 108 Cromwell Road, SW7 4ES. *T:* 01-370 4391. *Club:* Lord's Taverners.

BARRATT, Prof. Michael George; Professor of Mathematics, Northwestern University, Illinois, since 1974; *b* 26 Jan. 1927; *e s* of George Bernard Barratt and Marjorie Holloway Barratt (*née* Oldham); *m* 1952, Jenepher Hudson; one *s* four *d*. *Educ:* Stationers' Company's Sch.; Magdalen Coll., Oxford. Junior Lecturer, Oxford Univ., 1950-52; Fellow, Magdalen Coll., Oxford, 1952-56; Lectr, Brasenose Coll., Oxford, 1955-59; Sen. Lectr and Reader, 1959-63, Prof. of Pure Maths, 1964-74, Manchester Univ. Vis. Prof., Chicago Univ., 1963-64. *Publications:* Papers in Mathematical Jls. *Address:* Department of Mathematics, Northwestern University, Evanston, Ill 60201, USA.

BARRATT, Richard Stanley, CBE 1981; QPM 1974; HM Inspector of Constabulary, since 1978; *b* 11 Aug. 1928; *s* of Richard Barratt and Mona Barratt; *m* 1952, Sarah Elizabeth Hale; one *s* two *d*. *Educ:* Saltley Grammar Sch., Birmingham. CBIM. Birmingham City Police (Constable to Chief Inspector), 1949-65; Dir, Home Office Crime Prevention Centre, Stafford, 1963; seconded to Home Office (Res. and Develt), 1964; Sen. Comd Course, Police Coll., 1964; Supt, Cheshire Constab., 1965; Chief Supt, 1966; Asst Chief Constable, Manchester City Police, 1967; Asst Chief Constable, Manchester and Salford Police, 1968, Dep. Chief Constable, 1972; Dep. Chief Constable, Greater Manchester Police, 1974; Chief Constable, S Yorks Police, 1975-78. OStJ 1978. *Recreations:* reading, gardening. *Address:* Loddon House, Basing View, Basingstoke, Hants RG21 2JT. *T:* Basingstoke 51106.

BARRATT-BOYES, Sir Brian (Gerald), KBE 1971 (CBE 1966); Surgeon-in-Charge, Cardio-Thoracic Surgical Unit, Greenlane Hospital, Auckland, since 1964; Hon. Senior Cardio-Thoracic Surgeon, Mater Misericordiae Hospital, Auckland, since 1966; *b* 13 Jan. 1924; *s* of Gerald Cave Boyes and Edna Myrtle Boyes (*née* Barratt); *m* 1949, Norma Margaret Thompson; five *s*. *Educ:* Wellington Coll.; Univ. of Otago. MB, ChB 1946; FRACS 1952; FACS 1960; ChM 1962. Lectr in Anatomy, Otago Univ. Med. Sch., 1947; House Surg. and Registrar, Wellington Hosp., 1948-50; Surgical Registrar and Pathology Registrar, Palmerston North Hosp., 1950-52; Fellow in Cardio-Thoracic Surgery, Mayo Clinic, USA, 1953-55; Nuffield Trav. Fellowship UK (Bristol Univ.), 1956; Sen. Cardio-Thoracic Surg., Greenlane Hosp., 1957. Hon. Prof. of Surgery, Auckland Univ., 1971. R. T. Hall Prize for Distinguished Cardiac Surgery in Austr. and NZ, 1966. FRSNZ 1970. Hon. FACS 1977. *Publications:* Heart Disease in Infancy: diagnosis and surgical treatment, 1973; numerous in med. jls throughout the world. *Recreations:* farming, trout fishing. *Address:* 3 Omana Avenue, Epsom, Auckland 3, New Zealand. *T:* 689-414; (consulting rooms) 102 Remuera Road, Auckland 5. *T:* 500176. *Club:* Northern (Auckland).

BARRAULT, Jean-Louis; Officer of the Legion of Honour; actor, director, producer; Director: Odéon-Théâtre de France, 1959-68; Théâtre des Nations, Paris, 1965-67, and since 1971; *b* Vésinet, France, 8 Sept. 1910; *m* Madeleine Renaud, *qv*. *Educ:* public sch., Paris; Collège Chaptal. Taught at Collège Chaptal, 1931; Atelier Dramatic Sch. and Theatre (schol.), 1931-35; formed experimental theatrical company. Served War of 1939-40. With Comédie-Française as producer-director, 1940-46. At instigation of French Govt formed company with Madeleine Renaud, Marigny Theatre. Has appeared at Venice; Edinburgh Festival, 1948 and 1957; St James's Theatre, London, 1951; Palace Theatre, London, 1956, etc.; produced Duel of Angels, Apollo, 1958; World Theatre Season, Aldwych, 1965, 1968; toured Western Europe, S America, Canada, and US. Films include: Les Beaux Jours, Hélène, Les Perles de la couronne, La Symphonie fantastique, Les Enfants du Paradis, D'Hommes à hommes, Versailles, Chappaqua, Le Puritain, La route de Varennes. *Publications:* Une Troupe et ses auteurs, 1950; Reflections on the Theatre (autobiography), 1951; Rabelais, 1971 (prod, Paris 1968-69, tours in Japan and USA, 1969, London 1971); Memories for Tomorrow: the memoirs of

Jean-Louis Barrault, 1974; articles in theatrical publications. *Address:* 18 avenue du Président Wilson, 75116 Paris, France.

BARRE, Raymond; Chevalier de la Légion d'Honneur, Chevalier de l'Ordre National du Mérite agricole, Officier des Palmes Académiques; Grand Croix de l'Ordre National du Mérite, 1977; Deputé from Rhône, French National Assembly; *b* Saint-Denis, Réunion, 12 April 1924; *s* of René Barre and Charlotte Déramond; *m* 1954, Eve Hegedüs; two *s*. *Educ:* Lycée Leconte-de-Lisle, Saint-Denis-de-la-Réunion; Faculté de Droit, Paris; Institut d'Etudes Politiques, Paris. Professor at Faculté de Droit et des Sciences Economiques: Caen, 1950; Paris (Chair of Political Economy), 1963-; Professor at Institut d'Etudes Politiques, Paris, 1961-. Director of Cabinet of Mr J.-M. Jeanneney (Minister of Industry), 1959-62; Member: Cttee of Experts (Comité Lorain) studying financing of investments in France, 1963-64; Gen. Cttee on Economy and Financing of Fifth Plan, 1966; Vice-Chm., Commn of European Communities (responsible for Economic and Financial Affairs), 1967-72; Minister of Foreign Trade, Jan. 1976; Prime Minister, Aug. 1976-1981; elected to National Assembly, from Rhône, 1978. Mem. Gen. Council, Banque de France, 1973; Chm. Cttee for studying Housing Financing Reform, 1975-76. *Publication:* Economie Politique, 1955, and 1974. *Address:* 4-6 avenue Emile-Acollas, 75007 Paris, France.

BARRER, Prof. Richard Maling, FRS 1956; PhD Cantab; DSc (NZ); ScD Cantab; FRSC (FRIC 1939); Hon. ARCS, 1959; Professor of Physical Chemistry, Imperial College of Science and Technology, University of London, 1954-76, now Emeritus; Head of Department of Chemistry, 1955-76; Dean of the Royal College of Science, 1964-66; *b* 16 June 1910; *s* of T. R. Barrer, 103 Renall Street, Masterton, New Zealand; *m* 1939, Helen Frances Yule, Invercargill, NZ; one *s* three *d*. *Educ:* Canterbury University Coll., NZ (MSc); Clare Coll., Cambridge (1851 Exhibition Scholar). PhD Cantab, 1935; DSc NZ, 1937; ScD Cantab, 1948. Major Research Student, 1935-37, Research Fellow, 1937-39, Clare Coll.; Head of Chemistry Dept, Technical Coll., Bradford, 1939-46; Reader in Chemistry, London Univ., 1946-49; Prof. of Chemistry, Aberdeen Univ., 1949-54. Member Council: Faraday Soc., 1952-55; Chemical Soc., 1956-59, 1974-; Royal Institute of Chemistry, 1961-64; Soc. of Chemical Industry, 1965-68. Governor, Chelsea Coll. of Sci. and Technol., 1960-. Hon. FRSNZ 1965; Hon. DSc Bradford, 1967. *Publications:* Diffusion in and through Solids, 1941; Zeolites and Clay Minerals as Sorbents and Molecular Sieves, 1978; research papers in British and foreign scientific journals. *Recreations:* tennis and interest in athletics. Full Blue for cross-country running, 1934. *Address:* Flossmoor, Orpington Road, Chislehurst, Kent. *Clubs:* Hawks (Cambridge); Achilles.

BARRÈRE, Prof. Jean-Bertrand Marie; Croix de Guerre (France), 1940; Légion d'Honneur, 1969; Professor of French Literature, University of Cambridge, 1954-82, now Emeritus Professor; Fellow of St John's College, Cambridge, 1957; *b* 15 Dec. 1914; *s* of Alexandre Barrère and Marie-Claire Lavigne; *m* 1941, Micheline, *d* of Henri Cousin and Inès Dumontier; three *s* three *d*. *Educ:* Lycées Buffon and Louis-le-Grand; Ecole Normale Supérieure and Sorbonne, Paris. MA; Agrégé des Lettres; Docteur ès Lettres. Served War: Sous-Lieut, 32e Régiment d'Infanterie, 1939-40; 1re Armée Française, 1945; Lieut 1945; Capitaine de réserve, 1954; Capitaine Honoraire, 1967. Teacher of French and Classics, Lycée d'Amiens, 1940-42; Asst Lectr on French Literature, Sorbonne, 1942-46; Lectr on French Literature, Institut Français, London, 1946-49; Lectr on French Literature, Univ. of Lyons, 1949-50; appointed Prof. of French Literature, Univ. of Lyons, 1950; seconded as Prof. of French Literature, Ibrahim Univ., Cairo, 1950-52; Prof. at Lyons, 1952-54. *Publications:* Explications françaises, 1946; La Fantaisie de Victor Hugo, 3 vols, 1949, 1960, 1950, rev. edn 1973; Hugo, l'homme et l'œuvre, 1952; Romain Rolland par lui-même, 1955; Le Regard d'Orphée, 1956; La Cure d'amaigrissement du roman, 1964; Critique de chambre, 1964; Un Carnet des Misérables, 1965; Victor Hugo devant Dieu, 1965; Victor Hugo à l'œuvre, 1966; Romain Rolland, l'âme et l'art, 1966; L'Idée de Goût, 1972; Ma Mère qui boite, 1975; L'Echange poétique, 1977; Claudel, le destin et l'œuvre, 1979. *Recreations:* painting, violin. *Address:* Coleby, 31 Storey's Way, Cambridge.

BARRETT, Sir Arthur George, Kt 1942; *b* Geelong, 7 May 1895; *s* of A. O. and F. M. Barrett, Melbourne; *m* 1922, Jean Beatrice, *d* of late E. S. Mair, Melbourne; two *d*. *Educ:* Melbourne Church of England Grammar Sch. Served European War, AIF, 1916-19; Lord Mayor of Adelaide, 1937-41; Alderman, Adelaide City Council, 1941-53; retired. Formerly Wing Comdr Air Training Corps RAAF. Former Chairman: Red Cross Soc., Adelaide; Nat. Heart Foundation, Adelaide. *Address:* 210 Stanley Street, North Adelaide, South Australia 5006, Australia. *T:* 267.1171. *Club:* Adelaide (Adelaide).

BARRETT, Prof. (Arthur) Michael, PhD; Professor of Pharmacology and Head of Department, Leeds University, since 1970; *b* 1 April 1932; *s* of Arthur Cowley Barrett and late Doris Annie Barrett; *m* 1960, Patricia Lillian Harris; one *s* one *d*. *Educ:* Cheltenham Grammar Sch.; Sch. of Pharmacy, Univ. of London (BPharm 1st Cl. Hons, PhD). Cleveland, Ohio, Rotary Foundn Fellow, Western Reserve Univ., 1956-57; Asst Lectr in Pharmacology, 1958-59, Lectr, 1959-61, Sch. of Pharmacy, London Univ.; Res. Pharmacologist, Pharmaceuticals Div., ICI Ltd, 1961-70; Head of Pharmacology, Organon Internat. BV, 1970. Pro Vice Chancellor, Leeds Univ., 1979-81. Chm., Leeds Eastern Health Authority, 1981-; Vice-Chm., Kirklees AHA, 1978-79 (Mem., 1974-79); Mem., Gen. Sales List Cttee, Medicines Commn, DHSS, 1971-74; Assessor to Inquiry on LD50 Test, Home

Office, 1977-79. Sec. Gen., Internat. Union for Pharmacology, 1981-; Member: British Pharmacol Soc., 1963- (Meetings Sec., 1977-79; Gen. Sec., 1980-82); Soc. for Endocrinology, 1959-. *Publications:* The Pharmacology of Beta-adrenoceptor blockade, 1975; papers in pharmacol and endocrinol jls. *Recreations:* models, gardening, music. *Address:* Pennygate, Micklefield Lane, Rawdon, Leeds LS19 6BA. *T:* Leeds 506133.

BARRETT, Rev. Prof. Charles Kingsley, DD; FBA 1961; Professor of Divinity, Durham University, 1958-82; *b* 4 May 1917; *s* of Rev. F. Barrett and Clara (*née* Seed); *m* 1944, Margaret E. Heap, Calverley, Yorks; one *s* one *d. Educ:* Shebbear Coll.; Pembroke Coll., Cambridge; Wesley House, Cambridge. DD Cantab. 1956. Asst Tutor, Wesley Coll., Headingley, 1942; Methodist Minister, Darlington, 1943; Lecturer in Theology, Durham Univ., 1945. Hewett Lecturer (USA), 1961; Shaffer Lecturer (Yale), 1965; Delitzsch Lectr, Münster, 1967; Cato Lecturer (Australia), 1969; Tate-Willson Lectr, Dallas, 1975; McMartin Lectr, Ottawa, 1976; Sanderson Lectr, Melbourne, 1983. Vice-Pres., British and Foreign Bible Soc.; Pres., Studiorum Novi Testamenti Societas, 1973; Hon. Mem., Soc. of Biblical Literature, USA. Hon. DD: Hull, 1970; Aberdeen, 1972; Hon. DrTheol Hamburg, 1981; Burkitt Medal for Biblical Studies, 1966. *Publications:* The Holy Spirit and the Gospel Tradition, 1947; The Gospel according to St John, 1955, 2nd edn 1978; The New Testament Background: Selected Documents, 1956; Biblical Preaching and Biblical Scholarship, 1957; The Epistle to the Romans, 1957; Westcott as Commentator, 1959; Yesterday, Today and Forever: The New Testament Problem, 1959; Luke the Historian in Recent Study, 1961; From First Adam to Last, 1962; The Pastoral Epistles, 1963; Reading Through Romans, 1963; History and Faith: the Story of the Passion, 1967; Jesus and the Gospel Tradition, 1967; The First Epistle to the Corinthians, 1968; The Signs of an Apostle, 1970; Das Johannesevangelium und das Judentum, 1970; The Prologue of St John's Gospel, 1971; New Testament Essays, 1972; The Second Epistle to the Corinthians, 1973; The Fourth Gospel and Judaism, 1975; (ed) Donum Gentilicium, 1978; Essays on Paul, 1982; Essays on John, 1982; contributions to learned journals and symposia in Britain, the Continent, and USA. *Address:* 8 Princes Street, Durham DH1 4RP. *T:* Durham 61340.

BARRETT, David, MLA since 1960; Leader of the Official Opposition, British Columbia, 1970-72 and since 1975; Premier and Minister of Finance, Province of British Columbia, Canada, 1972-75; *b* Vancouver, 2 Oct. 1930; *s* of Samuel Barrett and Rose (*née* Hyatt); father a business man in East Vancouver, after war service; *m* 1953, Shirley Hackman, West Vancouver; two *s* one *d. Educ:* Britannia High Sch., Vancouver; Seattle Univ.; St Louis Univ. BA(Phil) Seattle, 1953; Master of Social Work, St Louis, 1956. Personnel and Staff Trng Officer, Haney Correctional Inst., 1957-59; also gained experience in a variety of jobs. Elected: MLA for Dewdney, Sept. 1960 and 1963; to re-distributed riding of Coquitlam 1966, 1969 and 1972; Vancouver East, by-election 1976, 1979; New Democratic Party Leader, June 1970 (first Social Democratic Govt in history of Province). Dr of Laws, *hc,* St Louis Univ., 1974. *Address:* Legislative Buildings, Victoria, British Columbia V8V 1X4, Canada. *T:* 387-5571.

BARRETT, Lt-Gen. Sir David William S.; *see* Scott-Barrett.

BARRETT, Denis Everett; a Special Commissioner of Income Tax, 1967-71; *b* 7 Jan. 1911; *o s* of late Walter Everett Barrett, London, and Julia Barrett (*née* MacCarthy), Cork; *m* 1947, Eilish (*d* 1974), *y d* of late William and Margaret Phelan, Co. Laois; one *s* two *d. Educ:* Wimbledon Coll.; London Univ. Entered Inland Revenue Dept, 1930; Asst Sec., 1948. *Address:* 2 Hayes Court, Sunnyside, Wimbledon, SW19 4SH. *T:* 01-946 6615.

BARRETT, Sir Dennis Charles T.; *see* Titchener-Barrett.

BARRETT, Edmond Fox, OBE 1981; HM Diplomatic Service; Consul-General, Bilbao, since 1981; *b* 24 Aug. 1928; *s* of late Edmond Henry Barrett and Ellen Mary Barrett (*née* Fox); *m* 1959, Catherine Wendy Howard (*née* Slater). *Educ:* St Brendan's Coll., Bristol. Dominions Office, 1946; Royal Navy, 1947-49; CRO, 1949-50; Karachi, 1950-52; New Delhi, 1952-54; CRO, 1954-55; Admiralty, 1955-60; Foreign Office, 1960-63; Bucharest, 1963-65; Rio de Janeiro, 1965-68; Boston, 1968-70; Mexico City, 1971-73; FCO, 1973-76; Santo Domingo, 1976-79; Tehran, 1979-81. *Recreations:* reading, golf, gardening. *Address:* c/o Foreign and Commonwealth Office, SW1. *Club:* Royal Commonwealth Society.

BARRETT, Edwin Cyril Geddes, CMG 1958; MA; *b* 15 Feb. 1909; *s* of late Lieut-Col C. C. J. Barrett, CSI, CIE, IA, and late Mrs Mabel Ada Barrett (*née* Geddes); *m* 1936, Eleanor Nelson Raymond (*d* 1970); one *s. Educ:* Marlborough Coll.; Jesus Coll., Cambridge. Cadet, Malayan Civil Service, 1931; many appts in Malaya and Borneo, 1931-42. Military Service, 1942-45. Resumed duty in the Malayan CS, 1946; Chief Registration Officer, Fedn of Malaya, 1949; Pres. Municipal Council, Kuala Lumpur, 1951; Comr for Resettlement of Special Constables in Civil Life, Fedn of Malaya, 1952; Acting British Adviser, Perak, 1953; British Adviser, Kedah, 1953; left Malaya on abolition of appt, 1957; Lectr in Malay, SOAS, Univ. of London, 1957-71. *Recreation:* walking dogs. *Address:* 12 Well Walk, Hampstead, NW3.

BARRETT, Ernest; Chairman, Henry Barrett & Sons Ltd, since 1982 (Joint Managing Director, 1968-82); Chairman: Steel Stockholding Division, Henry Barrett & Sons Ltd, since 1967; Henry Lindsay Ltd, since 1974; *b* 8 April 1917; *s* of Ernest Barrett and Marian Conyers; *m* 1940, Eileen Maria Peel; one *d.*

Educ: Charterhouse. Joined Henry Barrett & Sons Ltd, Bradford, 1934. Served War, RA, and commissioned, 1940; served in Mediterranean Theatre, with 1st Army, 1943-46 (despatches, 1944); Major 1945. Apptd Dir, Henry Barrett & Sons Ltd, 1946. Pres., Nat. Assoc. of Steel Stockholders, 1977-79 (Chm., Yorks Assoc., 1964-66; Vice-Pres., 1975-77); Pres., Engineering Industries Assoc., 1971 (Chm. Yorks Region, 1960-65; Vice-Pres. of Assoc., 1965-71). *Recreations:* badminton, gardening. *Address:* West Ghyll, Victoria Avenue, Ilkley, W Yorks. *T:* Ilkley 609294.

BARRETT, Jack Wheeler, CBE 1971; Chairman, Cole Group plc, since 1979 (Director, 1978); *b* 13 June 1912; *s* of John Samuel Barrett, Cheltenham; *m* 1935, Muriel Audley Read; two *s* two *d. Educ:* Cheltenham Grammar Sch.; Imperial Coll., Univ. of London. BSc, PhD, CChem, FRSC, FEng, FIChemE. Chief Chemist, London Essence Co. Ltd, 1936-41; joined Monsanto Chemicals Ltd, 1941; Dir of Research, 1955-71; Dir, Monsanto Ltd, 1955-78; Chm., Info-line Ltd, 1976-80. President: IChemE, 1971-72; Chem. Soc., 1974-75; IInfSc, 1976-79; ICSU Abstracting Bd, 1974-77; Chm., Chemical Divl Council, BSI, 1973-79; Mem., British Library Bd, 1973-79. Fellow, Imperial Coll., London, 1977. *Publications:* articles in Jl Chem. Soc., Chemistry and Industry, Jl ASLIB, Chemistry in Britain. *Recreation:* gardening. *Address:* 195 Latymer Court, Hammersmith Road, W6 7JQ. *T:* 01-748 7080; West Manor House, Bourton-on-the-Water, Cheltenham, Glos GL54 2AP. *T:* Bourton-on-the-Water 20296. *Club:* Athenæum.

BARRETT, Prof. Michael; *see* Barrett, Prof. A. M.

BARRETT, Stephen Jeremy, CMG 1982; HM Diplomatic Service; Assistant Under-Secretary of State, Foreign and Commonwealth Office, since 1981; *b* 4 Dec. 1931; *s* of late W. P. Barrett and Dorothy Barrett; *m* 1958, Alison Mary Irvine; three *s. Educ:* Westminster Sch.; Christ Church, Oxford (MA). FO, 1955-57; 3rd, later 2nd Sec., Political Office with Middle East Forces, Cyprus, 1957-59; Berlin, 1959-62; 1st Sec., FO, 1962-65; Head of Chancery, Helsinki, 1965-68; 1st Sec., FCO, 1968-72; Counsellor and Head of Chancery, Prague, 1972-74; Head of SW European Dept, FCO, later Principal Private Sec. to Foreign and Commonwealth Sec., 1975; Head of Science and Technology Dept, FCO, 1976-77; Fellow, Center for Internat. Affairs, Harvard, 1977-78; Counsellor, Ankara, 1978-81; Head of British Interests Section, Tehran, 1981. *Recreations:* climbing small mountains, reading. *Address:* c/o Foreign and Commonwealth Office, SW1. *Clubs:* Travellers', Hurlingham; Keene Valley Country.

BARRETT, William Spencer, FBA 1965; Fellow of Keble College, Oxford, 1952-81 and Tutor in Classics, 1939-81; Reader in Greek Literature, University of Oxford, 1966-81; *b* 29 May 1914; *o s* of William Barrett and Sarah Jessie Barrett (*née* Robbins); *m* 1939, Georgina Margaret Elizabeth, *e d* of William and Alma Georgina Annie Hill; one *s* one *d. Educ:* Derby Sch. Christ Church, Oxford (Scholar). Ireland and Craven Schol. 1933; 1st Class Classical Hon. Mods, 1934; Gaisford Prize for Greek Verse, 1934; de Paravicini Schol., 1934; 1st Class Lit. Hum., 1937; Derby Schol., 1937; Charles Oldham Prize, 1938. Lectr, Christ Church, Oxford, 1938-39; Lectr, Keble Coll. 1939-52; Librarian, 1946-66; Univ. Lectr in Greek Literature, 1947-66; Sub Warden, Keble Coll., 1968-76. Temp. Civilian Officer, Admty (Naval Intelligence Div.), 1942-45. *Publications:* (ed) Euripides, Hippolytos, 1964; Sophocles, Niobe (in Papyrus Fragments of Sophocles, ed R. Carden), 1974; articles in learned jls. *Address:* Sumner House, 108 Mill Street, Kidlington, Oxford. *T:* Kidlington 3170.

BARRETT-LENNARD, Rev. Sir Hugh (Dacre), 6th Bt *cr* 1801; Priest, London Oratory; *b* 27 June 1917; *s* of Sir Fiennes Cecil Arthur Barrett-Lennard (*d* 1963) and Winifrede Mignon (*d* 1969), *d* of Alfred Berlyn; cousin, 1977. *Educ:* Radley College, Berks; Pontifical Beda College, Rome. Teaching, 1936. Served War of 1939-45, NW Europe (despatches); enlisted London Scottish, Jan. 1940; commissioned 2nd Lt, Oct. 1940; Captain Essex Regt, 1945. Entered Brompton Oratory, 1946; ordained Priest in Rome, 1950. *Recreations:* on Isle of Eigg, Hebrides. *Heir: cousin* Richard Fynes Barrett Lennard, *b* 6 April 1941. *Address:* The Oratory, South Kensington, SW7 2RW. *T:* 01-589 4811.

BARRIE, Derek Stiven Maxwelton, OBE 1969 (MBE 1945); FCIT; *b* 1 Aug. 1907; *s* of John Stiven Carruthers Barrie and Dorothea Barrie; *m* 1936, Kathleen Myrra Collins; one *s* one *d. Educ:* Apsley House, Clifton; Tonbridge Sch. London and provincial journalism (Daily Graphic, Allied Newspapers etc), reporter and sub-editor, 1924-32; joined LMS Railway, 1932; on return from war service, rejoined LMS, 1946; PRO Railway Exec., 1948; Chief PRO British Transport Commn, 1956; Asst Sec.-Gen., BTC, 1958; Asst Gen. Man., York, 1961; Chm., British Railways (Eastern) Bd, and Gen. Man., British Railways Eastern Region, 1968-70. Mem. Council, Inst. of Transport, 1968. Served with Royal Engineers, 1941-46; Hon. Col 74 Movement Control Regt, RE and RCT, 1961-67; Major, Engr. and Rly Staff Corps (RE & AVR), 1967, Lt-Col 1968-73. Bronze Star Medal (US), 1945. OStJ 1964. *Publications:* A Regional History of the Railways of Great Britain, vol. 1: South Wales, 1980; numerous railway historical books and monographs, contribs various transport jls, 1928-. *Recreations:* railways, authorship, country life. *Address:* 1 Norman Close, Castlegate, Pickering, N Yorks YO18 7AZ. *T:* Pickering 73580.

BARRIE, Sir Walter, Kt 1958; Chairman of Lloyd's, 1953, 1954, 1957, 1958; Director: Jos. W. Hobbs Ltd; Westminster Bank Ltd, 1958-68; Ulster Bank

1964-72; *b* 31 May 1901; *y s* of late Right Hon. H. T. Barrie, MP, DL, JP, and late Katie Barrie; *m* 1927, Noele Margaret (*d* 1968), *d* of G. J. Furness, JP; two *s. Educ:* Coleraine; Merchiston Castle, Edinburgh; Gonville and Caius Coll., Cambridge. Entered Lloyd's, 1926; first served on Cttee of Lloyd's, 1946; Deputy-Chm. of Lloyd's, 1951, 1952. Lloyd's Gold Medal, 1958. Pres. Insurance Inst. of London, 1955-56; Vice-Pres., Chartered Insurance Inst., 1957, 1958, 1959, Dep. Pres. 1961. Pres. 1962-63. *Recreation:* golf. *Address:* Compton Elms, Pinkneys Green, Maidenhead, Berks SL6 6NR. *T:* Maidenhead 27151.

BARRINGTON, family name of Viscount Barrington.

BARRINGTON, 11th Viscount *cr* 1720; **Patrick William Daines Barrington;** Baron Barrington, 1720; Baron Shute (UK) 1880 (sits as Baron Shute); *b* 29 Oct. 1908; *s* of Hon. Walter Bernard Louis Barrington (*d* 1959); *S* uncle, 1960. *Educ:* Eton; Magdalen Coll., Oxford (BA). Called to the Bar, Inner Temple, 1940. Late 2nd Lieut, RA. Formerly Hon. Attaché, HBM's Embassy, Berlin, and sometime in Foreign Office. *Heir:* none.

BARRINGTON, Sir Alexander (Fitzwilliam Croker), 7th Bt *cr* 1831; retired; *b* 19 Nov. 1909; *s* of Sir Charles Burton Barrington, 5th Bt, and Mary Rose (*d* 1943), *d* of Sir Henry Hickman Bacon, 10th and 11th Bt; *S* brother, 1980. *Educ:* Castle Park, Dalkey, Co. Dublin; Shrewsbury School; Christ Church, Oxford. Director of various private companies, 1932-39. Served in Army as Captain, Intelligence Corps, 1939-42; prisoner of war, Singapore and Thailand, 1942-45. Book publishers' executive, editor and production manager, 1946-72. *Recreations:* gardening, travel, Viennese music. *Heir:* cousin John William Barrington, Major retd, Royal Irish Fusiliers [*b* 20 Oct. 1917; *m* 1948, Annie Wetten; two *s* one *d*]. *Address:* 11 Tedworth Square, SW3 4DU.

BARRINGTON, Prof. Ernest James William, FRS 1967; Professor of Zoology, Nottingham University, 1949-74, now Emeritus; *b* 17 Feb. 1909; *o s* of late William Benedict and Harriet Barrington; *m* 1943, Muriel Catherine Anne Clinton; one *s* one *d. Educ:* Christ's Hosp.; Oriel Coll., Oxford (Organ Scholar). ARCO 1926; LRAM 1927; BA (Oxford), 1931; BSc 1934; MA 1936; DSc 1947. Lectr in Zoology, Univ. Coll., Nottingham, 1932, Head of Zoology Dept, 1934, Reader, 1945; Dep. Vice-Chancellor, 1956-59; Public Orator, 1964-70. Rockefeller Foundation Fellow in Comparative Physiology at McGill Univ., 1939, and Harvard Univ., 1940; Buell Gallagher Vis. Prof., City Coll., New York, 1966; Royal Soc. Leverhulme Vis. Prof., Univ. of Buenos Aires, 1970; Vis. Prof., Univ. of São Paulo, 1972. European Editor, General and Comparative Endocrinology, 1960-74. Mem. Council, Royal Society, 1970-72, a Vice-Pres., 1971-72; Pres., Inst. of Biology, 1980-82. Hon DSc Nottingham, 1975. Frink Medal, Zoological Soc. of London, 1976. Membre d'honneur, European Soc. for Comparative Endocrinology, 1974. *Publications:* Introduction to General and Comparative Endocrinology, 1963, 2nd edn, 1975; Hormones and Evolution, 1964; The Biology of Hemichordata and Protochordata, 1965; Zoological Editor, Contemporary Biology Series, 1966; Invertebrate Structure and Function, 1967, 2nd edn, 1979; The Chemical Basis of Physiological Regulation, 1968; Perspectives in Endocrinology (Jt Editor with C. B. Jørgensen), 1968; (Jt Editor with M. Hamburgh) Hormones in Development, 1972; (ed) Trends in Comparative Endocrinology, 1975; (ed) Hormones and Evolution, vols 1 and 2, 1979; Environmental Biology, 1980; papers on chordate morphology and physiology in various jls. *Recreation:* music. *Address:* Cornerways, 2 St Margaret's Drive, Alderton, Tewkesbury, Glos GL20 8NY. *T:* Alderton 375.

BARRINGTON, Sir Kenneth (Charles Peto), Kt 1973; *b* 27 Aug. 1911; *er s* of C. W. Barrington; *m* 1938, Eileen Doris Stone; one *d. Educ:* St Paul's School. FCA. Joined Morgan Grenfell & Co. Ltd, Merchant Bankers, 1929; Naval Service, 1939-46; Chartered Accountant, 1952; Director: Morgan Grenfell & Co. Ltd, 1961-76; Morgan Grenfell Holdings Ltd, 1971-76 (Mem., Internat. Adv. Council, 1980-); English & New York Trust plc; Ultramar plc. *Address:* Hall Land, Slinfold, Horsham, West Sussex. *T:* Slinfold 790250.

BARRINGTON, Nicholas John, CMG 1982; CVO 1979; HM Diplomatic Service; Head of British Interests Section, Tehran, since 1981; *b* 23 July 1934; *s* of late Eric Alan Barrington and Mildred (*née* Bill). *Educ:* Repton; Clare Coll., Cambridge (MA 1957). HM Forces, RA, 1952-54. Joined Diplomatic Service, 1957; Tehran (language student), 1958; Oriental Sec. Kabul, 1959; FO, 1961; 2nd Sec., UK Delegn to European Communities, Brussels, 1963; 1st Sec., Rawalpindi, 1965; FO, 1967; Private Sec. to Permanent Under Sec., Commonwealth Office, April 1968; Asst Private Sec. to Foreign and Commonwealth Sec., Oct. 1968; Head of Chancery, Tokyo, 1972-75 (promoted Counsellor and for a period apptd Chargé d'Affaires, Hanoi, 1973); Head of Guidance and Information Policy (subsequently Information Policy) Dept, FCO, 1976-78; Counsellor, Cairo, 1978-81. 3rd Cl., Order of the Sacred Treasure, Japan, 1975. *Recreations:* theatre, drawing, prosopography. *Address:* c/o Foreign and Commonwealth Office, King Charles Street, SW1; 33 Gilmerton Court, Trumpington, Cambridge. *Clubs:* Athenæum, Royal Commonwealth Society.

BARRINGTON-WARD, Rev. Canon Simon; General Secretary, Church Missionary Society, since 1975; Hon. Canon of Derby Cathedral, since 1975; *b* 27 May 1930; *s* of Robert McGowan Barrington-Ward and Margaret Adele Barrington-Ward; *m* 1963, Jean Caverhill Taylor; two *d. Educ:* Eton;

Magdalene Coll., Cambridge (MA). Lektor, Free Univ., Berlin, 1953-54; Westcott House, Cambridge, 1954-56; Chaplain, Magdalene Coll., Cambridge, 1956-60; Asst Lectr in Religious Studies, Univ. of Ibadan, 1960-63; Fellow and Dean of Chapel, Magdalene Coll., Cambridge, 1963-69; Principal, Crowther Hall, Selly Oak Colls, Birmingham, 1969-74. FRAI. *Publications:* contributor to: Christianity in Independent Africa (ed Fasholé Luke and others), 1978; Today's Anglican Worship (ed C. Buchanan), 1980; Renewal—An Emerging Pattern, by Graham Pulkingham and others, 1980. *Address:* 62 Park House Gardens, Twickenham, Mddx TW1 2DE. *T:* 01-892 4852.

BARRITT, Sir David (Thurlow), Kt 1969; BSc, FEng, FIChemE; Chairman, Cammell Laird, 1971-79; *b* 17 Oct. 1903; *er s* of late David Webster Barritt and Rachel Barritt; *m* 1931, Hilda Marshall Creyke; one *s. Educ:* High Sch., Newcastle-under-Lyme, Staffs; N Staffs Polytechnic. Chairman: Simon Engineering Ltd, 1963-70; Twyfords Holdings Ltd, 1969-71; Davy International, 1970-73. Chm. Govs, The Newcastle-under-Lyme Endowed Schs, Newcastle, Staffs, 1962-72. SFInstE; Vice-Pres., IChemE 1974. MUniv Keele, 1981. *Publications:* papers in technical jls. *Recreations:* golf, music, gardening, photography. *Address:* 7 Castle Rise, Prestbury, Cheshire SK10 4UR. *T:* Prestbury 829716.

BARRITT, Rev. Gordon Emerson, OBE 1979; Principal, National Children's Home, since 1969; *b* 30 Sept. 1920; *s* of Norman and Doris Barritt; *m* 1947, Joan Mary Alway; two *s* one *d. Educ:* William Hulme's Grammar Sch., Manchester; Manchester Univ.; Cambridge Univ. (Wesley House and Fitzwilliam Coll.). Served War, RAF, 1942-45 (despatches). Methodist Minister: Kempston Methodist Church, Bedford, 1947-52; Westlands Methodist Church, Newcastle-under-Lyme, 1952-57; Chaplain, Univ. of Keele, 1953-57. Treasurer, Nat. Council of Voluntary Child Care Organisations (Chm., 1970-72); Member: Home Office Adv. Council on Child Care, 1968-71; Nat. Children's Bureau; Brit. Assoc. of Social Workers; Internat. Union for Child Welfare; UK and Internat. Cttees; Council of Selly Oak Colls, Birmingham. *Publications:* The Edgworth Story, 1972; (ed) Many Pieces—One Aim, 1975; (ed) Family Life, 1979; Residential Care, 1979; contrib.: Caring for Children, 1969; Giving Our Best, 1982. *Recreations:* music, do-it-yourself. *Address:* (office) National Children's Home, 85 Highbury Park, N5 1UD. *T:* 01-226 2033; (residence) 10 Cadogan Gardens, Grange Park, N21 1ER. *T:* 01-360 8687.

BARRON, Sir Donald (James), Kt 1972; DL; Chairman, Midland Bank Ltd, since 1982 (Director, since 1972; Vice-Chairman, 1981-82); *b* 17 March 1921; *o s* of Albert Gibson Barron and Elizabeth Macdonald, Edinburgh; *m* 1956, Gillian Mary, *o d* of John Saville, York; three *s* two *d. Educ:* George Heriot's Sch., Edinburgh; Edinburgh Univ. (BCom). Member, Inst. Chartered Accountants of Scotland. Joined Rowntree Mackintosh Ltd, 1952; Dir, 1961; Vice-Chm., 1965; Chm., 1966-81. Director: Finance for Industry Ltd, 1979-; Finance Corp. for Industry Ltd, 1979-; Canada Life Assurance Co. of GB Ltd, 1980-; Canada Life Unit Trust Managers Ltd, 1980-; Canada Life Assurance Co., Toronto, 1980-; FFI (UK Finance) Ltd, 1980-; Industrial and Commercial Finance Corp. Ltd, 1980-. Dir, BIM Foundn, 1977-80 and Mem. Council, BIM, 1978-80; Trustee, Joseph Rowntree Memorial Trust, 1966-73, 1975- (Chm., 1981-); Treasurer, York Univ., 1966-72; Member: Council of CBI, 1966-81 (Chm., CBI Educn Foundn, 1981-); SSRC, 1971-72; UGC, 1972-81; Council, PSI, 1978-; Council, Inst. of Chartered Accountants of Scotland, 1980-. DL N Yorks (formerly WR Yorks and City of York), 1971. *Recreations:* golf, tennis, boating, gardening. *Address:* Greenfield, Sim Balk Lane, Bishopthorpe, York YO2 1QH. *T:* York 705675; 143 Whitehall Court, SW14 2EL. *Clubs:* Athenæum; Yorkshire (York).

BARRON, Douglas Shield, CIE 1945; Chairman, Godfrey Phillips, India, Ltd, retired 1973; *b* 18 March 1904; *s* of Thomas Barron; *m* 1934, Doris Katherine (*d* 1970), *o d* of late Henry Deakin; no *c. Educ:* Holgate Grammar Sch.; Corpus Christi Coll., Cambridge. Joined Indian Civil Service, 1926; retired, 1948. *Address:* Eyeworth Lodge, Fritham, Lyndhurst, Hants SO4 7HJ. *T:* Cadnam 2256. *Club:* Bombay Yacht.

BARRON, Prof. John Penrose, MA, DPhil, FSA; Professor of Greek Language and Literature, University of London, since 1971, and Head of Department of Classics, King's College London, since 1972; *b* 27 Apr. 1934; *s* of George Barron and Minnie Leslie Marks; *m* 1962, Caroline Mary, *d* of late W. D. Hogarth, OBE; two *d. Educ:* Clifton Coll.; Balliol Coll., Oxford (Hon. Exhibnr). 1st Cl., Class. Hon. Mods, 1955; Lit. Hum., 1957; MA 1960, DPhil 1961; Thomas Whitcombe Greene Prizeman, 1955, and Scholar, 1957; Barclay Head Prizeman, 1959; Cromer Prize, British Academy, 1963. Asst Lectr in Latin, Bedford Coll., 1959-61, and Lectr, 1961-64; Lectr in Archaeology, University Coll. London, 1964-67; Reader in Archaeology and Numismatics, Univ. of London, 1967-71; Dean, Faculty of Arts, Univ. of London, 1976-80; Mem. Senate, 1977-81, Mem. Academic Council, 1977-81; Public Orator, 1978-81. Vis. Mem., Inst. for Advanced Study, Princeton, 1973. Blegen Distinguished Vis. Res. Prof., Vassar Coll., NY, 1981. *Publications:* Greek Sculpture, 1965 (new and rev. edn 1981); Silver Coins of Samos, 1966; articles in Classical Quarterly, Jl of Hellenic Studies, Bulletin of Inst. of Classical Studies, etc. *Recreations:* travel, homes and gardens. *Address:* King's College, Strand, WC2R 2LS. *T:* 01-836 5454. *Club:* Athenæum.

BARRON, Rt. Rev. Patrick Harold Falkiner; *b* 13 Nov. 1911; *s* of Albert Harold and Mary Isabel Barron; *m* 1942, Kathleen May Larter; two *s* one *d.* *Educ:* King Edward VII Sch., Johannesburg; Leeds Univ. (BA); College of the Resurrection, Mirfield. Curate: Holy Redeemer, Clerkenwell, London, 1938-40; Boksburg, S Africa, 1940-41; CF (S African), 1941-46; Rector: Zeerust, S Africa, 1946-50; Potchefstroom, 1950-51; Blyvooruitzicht, 1951-55. St Cyprian's Mission, Johannesburg, 1956-59; Archdeacon of Germiston, 1957-58; Dean of Johannesburg, 1959-64; Bishop Suffragan of Cape Town, 1965-66; Bishop of George, 1966-77. *Recreation:* gardening. *Address:* E37 Edingight, Duke Road, Rondebosch, Cape Town, South Africa. *T:* 69.1820.

BARRON, (Thomas) Robert, CBE 1980; FCIT; Member, British Railways Board, 1978-81; *b* 27 Dec. 1918; *s* of late Robert and Florence May Barron; *m* 1942, Constance Lilian Bolter; one *s* three *d.* *Educ:* Dame Allan's Sch., Newcastle-on-Tyne; King's Coll., Durham Univ. BA Hons (Economics, 1st cl.). Served RA and 1st Airborne Div., 1940-46. Joined LNER as Traffic Apprentice, 1946; Asst Gen. Manager, London Midland Region, 1966, Western Region, 1967; British Railways Board: Dir Management Staff, 1970; Controller of Corporate Planning, 1972; Dir of Planning and Investment, 1977. Exec. Dir, Channel Tunnel, 1981-82. Mem., NW Economic Planning Council, 1965-67. *Recreations:* music, fishing, watching sport. *Address:* 8 Pigeonwick, Harpenden, Herts. *T:* Harpenden 62792.

BARRONS, John Lawson; Director, since 1972, and Managing Director, since 1976, Westminster Press; *b* 10 Oct. 1932; *s* of late William Cowper Barrons, MBE and Amy Marie Barrons (*née* Lawson); *m* 1957, Caroline Anne, *d* of late George Edward Foster; three *s.* *Educ:* Caterham Sch. Nat. Service, 1st Bn Northamptonshire Regt, 1952-54. Journalist, UK and USA, 1950-57; Gen. Manager, Nuneaton Observer, 1957; Managing Editor, Northampton Chronicle & Echo, 1959; General Manager: Edinburgh Evening News, 1961; Westminster Press, 1965-76. Director: Southern Publishing Co., 1968-; Pearson Longman, 1979-; President: Westminster (Florida) Inc., 1980-; Westminster (Jacksonville) Inc., 1982-; Alternate Dir, BPM Hldgs, 1982-. Dir, Evening Newspaper Advertising Bureau, 1978-81 (Chm. 1979-80); Founder Dir, Reg. Newspaper Advertising Bureau, 1980- (Chm. 1982-). Mem. Council, Printing Industry Res. Assoc., 1978- (a Vice-Chm. 1979-); Mem. Bd of Management, Internat. Electronic Publishing Res. Centre, 1981-. Newspaper Society: Mem., Industrial Relations Cttee, 1964-; Chm., Newsprint Cttee, 1975-80; Mem., Council, 1975-; Pres., 1981-82; Commonwealth Press Union: Mem., Council, 1970-; Trustee, Journalists' Trng and Educn Trust, 1974-. *Recreations:* hockey, tennis, gardening, fishing. *Address:* Upmeads, 7 The Drive, Chorleywood, Herts WD3 4EA. *Club:* Flyfishers'.

BARROW, Rt. Hon. Errol Walton, PC 1969; MP (Democratic Labour Party), Barbados; *b* 21 Jan. 1920; *s* of late Reginald Grant Barrow, LTh, DD, and of Ruth Barrow (*née* O'Neal); *m* 1945, Carolyn Plaskett; one *s* one *d.* *Educ:* Harrison Coll., Barbados; LSE (BSc); Hon. Fellow 1975. Royal Air Force, 1940-47. Barrister, Lincoln's Inn, 1949. Elected House of Assembly, Barbados, 1951; Minister of Finance, 1961-76; Premier, 1961; Prime Minister, 1966-76. Founder Mem., Democratic Labour Party, 1955, Chm. 1958-76. Hon. LLD: McGill, 1966; Sussex. *Recreations:* sailing, flying, diving, tennis. *Address:* PO Box 125, Bridgetown, Barbados.

BARROW, Prof. Geoffrey Wallis Steuart, FBA 1976; Sir William Fraser Professor of Scottish History and Palæography, University of Edinburgh, since 1979; *b* Headingley, Leeds, 28 Nov. 1924; *s* of late Charles Embleton Barrow and Marjorie, *d* of Donald Stuart; *m* 1951, Heather Elizabeth, *d* of James McLeish Lownie; one *s* one *d.* *Educ:* St Edward's Sch., Oxford; Inverness Royal Acad.; St Andrews Univ.; Pembroke Coll., Oxford. FRSE 1977. Lecturer in History, University Coll., London, 1950-61; Prof. of Mediaeval Hist., King's Coll., Univ. of Durham, later Univ. of Newcastle upon Tyne, 1961-74; Prof. of Scottish History, Univ. of St Andrews, 1974-79. Ford's Lectr, Univ. of Oxford, 1977. *Publications:* Feudal Britain, 1956; Acts of Malcolm IV, King of Scots, 1960; Robert Bruce and the Community of the Realm of Scotland, 1965; Acts of William I, King of Scots, 1971; Kingdom of the Scots, 1973; (ed) The Scottish Tradition, 1974; The Anglo-Norman Era in Scottish History, 1980; Kingship and Unity, 1981; contrib. Scottish Historical Review, etc. *Recreation:* hill walking. *Address:* University of Edinburgh, Edinburgh EH8 9YW.

BARROW, John Frederick; HM Diplomatic Service, retired; *b* 28 Dec. 1918; *s* of Frederick William and Caroline Barrow; *m* 1947, Mary Roberta Young; two *d.* *Educ:* King Edward VII Sch., King's Lynn. Home Civil Service, 1936-39; war service in British and Indian Armies, 1939-46 (Major); rejoined Home Civil Service, 1946; Treasury, 1952-62; FCO, 1962; service overseas at Delhi, Kuala Lumpur, Jesselton, Prague, Washington, Hong Kong; retired as Counsellor, 1977. *Address:* 3 Tomkyns, Hillside Street, Hythe, Kent.

BARROW, Captain Sir Richard John Uniacke, 6th Bt *cr* 1835; *b* 2 Aug. 1933; *s* of Sir Wilfrid John Wilson Croker Barrow, 5th Bt and (Gwladys) Patricia (*née* Uniacke); *S* father 1960; *m* 1961, Alison Kate (marr. diss. 1974), *yr d* of late Capt. Russell Grenfell, RN, and of Mrs Lindsay-Young; one *s* two *d.* *Educ:* Abbey Sch., Ramsgate; Beaumont Coll., Old Windsor. Commnd 2nd Lieut Irish Guards, 1952; served: Germany, 1952-53; Egypt, 1953-56; Cyprus, 1958; Germany, 1959-60; retired, 1960; joined International

Computers and Tabulators Ltd; resigned 1973. *Heir: s* Anthony John Grenfel Barrow, *b* 24 May 1962.

BARROWCLOUGH, Anthony Richard, QC 1974; a Recorder of th Crown Court, since 1972; *b* 24 June 1924; *m* 1949, Mary Agnes Pery-Knox Gore; one *s* one *d.* *Educ:* Stowe; New Coll., Oxford. Served RNVR, 1943-4 (Sub-Lieut and later Lieut). Called to the Bar, Inner Temple, 1949, Benche 1982. Part-time Member, Monopolies Commn, 1966-69. *Recreation:* countr pursuits. *Address:* 60 Ladbroke Grove, W11; The Old Vicarage, Winsford near Minehead, Somerset.

BARRY, Daniel; Deputy Secretary, Department of Education for Norther Ireland, since 1980; *b* 4 March 1928; *s* of William John Graham Barry an Sarah (*née* Wilkinson); *m* 1951, Florence (*née* Matier); two *s* one *d.* *Educ* Belfast Mercantile Coll. FCIS, FSCA. Local Government Officer with variou NI Councils, 1944-68; Town Clerk, Carrickfergus Borough Council, 1968 73; Asst Sec. (Roads), Dept of the Environment for NI, 1973-76, Dep. Sec 1976-80. *Recreations:* golf, gardening, tobacco producing, wine making.

BARRY, (Donald Angus) Philip, CBE 1980 (OBE 1969); HM Chie Inspector of Prisons for Scotland, since 1980; *b* 18 Sept. 1920; *s* of John an Dorothy Barry; *m* 1942, Margaret Orr; five *s* one *d.* *Educ:* The Abbey Sch Fort Augustus. Army Service, 1939-46: Captain Gordon Highlanders, 51s (Highland) Div., N Africa, Sicily; Family Business, 1946-, Man. Dir, 1963- Cruz de Caballero del Orden de Isabel La Católica (Spain), 1980. *Address:* S Andrew's House, Edinburgh EH1 3DE. *Club:* University Staf (Edinburgh).

BARRY, Sir Edward; *see* Barry, Sir L. E. A. T.

BARRY, Edward Norman, CB 1981; Under Secretary, Northern Irelan Office, 1979-81, retired 1981; *b* 22 Feb. 1920; *s* of Samuel and Matilda (*né* Legge); *m* 1952, Inez Anna (*née* Elliott); one *s* two *d.* *Educ:* Bangor Gramma Sch. Northern Ireland Civil Service: Department of Finance: Establishmen Div., 1940-51; Works Div., 1951-60; Treasury Div., 1960-67; Establishmen Officer, 1967-72; Min. of Home Affairs, 1972-74; Asst Sec., N Ireland Office 1974-79. *Recreations:* golf, Irish Football Association Ltd (Hon. Treasurer) *Address:* Allied Irish Banks Ltd, 697/703 Upper Newtownards Road Dundonald, Belfast.

BARRY, Sir (Lawrence) Edward (Anthony Tress), 5th Bt *cr* 1899; Baro de Barry in Portugal *cr* 1876; *b* 1 Nov. 1939; *s* of Sir Rupert Rodney Franci Tress Barry, 4th Bt, MBE, and Diana Madeline (*d* 1948), *o d* of R. O'Brie Thompson; *S* father, 1977; *m* 1968, Fenella Hoult; one *s* one *d.* *Educ* Haileybury. Formerly Captain, Grenadier Guards. *Heir: s* William Ruper Philip Tress Barry, *b* 13 Dec. 1973. *Address:* 3 Sunnyside Cottages, Warehorn Road, Ham Street, Kent. *T:* Ham Street 2454.

BARRY, Michael, (James Barry Jackson); OBE 1956; Principal, Londo Academy of Music and Dramatic Art, 1973-78, retired; *b* 15 May 1910; *s* o A. G. and Helen Jackson; *m* 1st, 1934, Judith Gick (marr. diss. 1947); one *d* 2nd, 1948, Rosemary Crosbie (*d* 1968); one *d* ; 3rd, 1973, Pamela Corbett Studied farming and horticulture in Glos and Herts. Studied for theatre a RADA (Baliol Holloway Award, Best Diploma Performance, 1930) anc subsequently as actor, stage-manager, designer and producer at th Northampton, Birmingham, Hull and Croydon Repertory Theatres before working in London. Appointed BBC television producer, 1938. Served Roya Marine Brigade Landing-Craft and as AMS, RM Office, 1939-45 (Major) Producer and writer, BBC television drama and documentary, 1946-5 (Programmes included: The Silence of the Sea, I Want to be a Doctor Promise of Tomorrow, The Passionate Pilgrim, Shout Aloud Salvation); Heac of Drama, BBC Television, 1952-61; Programme Controller, Irish Television 1961-63; prod The Wars of the Roses (TV), 1966; Prof. of Drama and Dep Head, Stanford Univ., Calif, 1968-72. Literary Adviser, Council of Repertory Theatres, 1964-67; Dir, Manchester Royal Exchange Theatre (formerly 196 Theatre), 1972-. Member: Drama Panel, Arts Council, 1955-68; Council RADA, 1966-69; Nat. Council Drama Training, 1976-78; Governing Body Wimbledon Sch. of Art, 1976-78. Desmond Davis Award, SFTA, 1961 *Publication:* (selected) The Television Playwright, 1960. *Address:* 5 Clarence Gardens, Brighton, East Sussex. *Club:* Savile.

BARRY, Rev. Noel Patrick, OSB; Headmaster of Ampleforth College 1964-79; *b* 6 Dec. 1917; 2nd *s* of Dr T. St J. Barry, Wallasey, Cheshire. *Educ* Ampleforth Coll.; St Benet's Hall, Oxford. Housemaster, Ampleforth Coll. 1954-64. Chairman: Conference of Catholic Colleges, 1973-75; HMC, 1975 *Address:* Ampleforth Abbey, York. *T:* Ampleforth 224.

BARRY, Norman, OBE 1978; SRN, RMN, RMPA; Divisional Nursing Officer (Mental Illness), South District, Kensington, Chelsea and Westminste Area Health Authority, 1975-77 retired (based at Banstead Hospital) Chairman, General Nursing Council, 1974-76; *b* 30 July 1916; *s* of Edward and Annie Barry; *m* 1940, Winifred McGowan; two *d.* *Educ:* Houghton-le Spring Intermed. Sch. Graylingwell Hosp.: completed Mental Nurse trng 1939; Staff Nurse, 1939; served RAMC, 1940-47; Staff Nurse, Graylingwel Hosp., 1947-50; qual. SRN, Lambeth Hosp., 1951; Graylingwell Hosp. Charge Nurse, 1951, Night Supt, 1953; Sen. Asst Chief Male Nurse, Park Prewett Hosp., 1954; Banstead Hosp.: Dep. Chief Male Nurse, 1955, Chie Male Nurse, 1960, Chief Nursing Officer, 1972. Gen. Nursing Council: Mem.

1970– (Mem. Mental Nurses Cttee, Dec. 1960–); Vice-Chm., 1972–74; Mem. DHSS and Nat. Assoc. for Mental Health gps examining care of patients in mental hosps; Chm., Nat. Assoc. Chief and Prin. Nursing Officers. *Recreation:* reading (lay reader, All Saints Church, Banstead). *Address:* 130 Winkworth Road, Banstead, Surrey SM7 2QT. *T:* Burgh Heath 57376.

BARRY, Philip; *see* Barry, D. A. P.

BARRY, Sir Philip Stuart M.; *see* Milner-Barry.

BARRY, Maj.-Gen. Richard Hugh, CB 1962; CBE 1953 (OBE 1943); retired; *b* 9 Nov. 1908; *s* of Lieut-Col Alfred Percival Barry and Helen Charlotte (*née* Stephens); *m* 1st, 1940, Rosalind Joyce Evans (*d* 1973); one *s* two *d* ; 2nd, 1975, Elizabeth Lucia Middleton. *Educ:* Winchester; Sandhurst. 2nd Lieut Somerset LI, 1929; Staff Coll., Camberley, Capt., 1938; served War of 1939–45; BEF, SOE, AFHQ, Algiers. Military Attaché, Stockholm, 1947; Deputy Chief of Staff Western Europe Land Forces, 1948; Dir, Standing Group, NATO, 1952; Chief of Staff, HQ British Troops in Egypt, 1954–56; Imperial Defence Coll., 1957; Standing Group Representative, North Atlantic Council, 1959–62; retired, 1962. Maj.-Gen. 1959. Africa Star, 1943; 1939–45 Star; Defence, Victory Medals, 1945. *Recreation:* hunting. *Address:* Little Place, Farringdon, Alton, Hants GU34 3EH. *T:* Tisted 216. *Club:* Army and Navy.

BARSTOW, Josephine, (Mrs Ande Anderson); opera singer, free-lance since 1971; *b* Sheffield, 27 Sept. 1940; *m* 1969, Ande Anderson; no *c. Educ:* Birmingham Univ. (BA). Debut with Opera for All, 1964; studied at London Opera Centre, 1965–66; Opera for All, 1966; Glyndebourne Chorus, 1967; Sadler's Wells Contract Principal, 1967–68, sang Cherubino, Euridice, Violetta; Welsh Nat. Opera: Contract Principal, 1968–70, sang Violetta, Countess, Fiordiligi, Mimi, Amelia, Simon Boccanegra; Don Carlos, 1973; Jenufa, 1975; Peter Grimes, 1978; Tatyana in Onegin, 1980; Covent Garden: Helena, world première, Tippett's The Knot Garden, 1970 (recorded 1974); Falstaff, 1975; Glyndebourne: Lady Macbeth (for TV), 1972; Idomeneo, 1974; Fidelio, 1981; Coliseum: Der Rosenkavalier, 1975; Salome, 1975; Don Carlos, 1976; Tosca, 1976; Forza del Destino, 1978; Aida, 1979; Fidelio, 1980; Arabella, 1980; The Flying Dutchman, 1982; has sung all parts in Hoffman, Emilia Marty (Makropulos Case), Natasha (War and Peace) and Traviata, Sadler's Wells; Alice in Falstaff, Aix-en-Provence Festival, 1971; Nitocris in Belshazzar, Geneva, 1972; Jeanne, British première, Penderecki's The Devils, 1973; Marguerite, world première, Crosse's The Story of Vasco, 1974; Fidelio, Jenufa, Scottish Opera, 1977; Gayle, world première, Tippett's The Ice Break, 1977; US debut as Lady Macbeth, Miami, 1977; Musetta in La Bohème, NY Met., 1977; Salome, Staatsoper, East Berlin, 1979 (Critics Prize); Abigaille in Nabucco, Miami, 1981; debut in Chicago as Lady Macbeth, 1981; new prod. of Jenufa, Cologne, 1981; sings in other opera houses in USA, Canada and Europe. *Recreation:* country cottage where grows all own vegetables and endless flowers. *Address:* c/o John Coast, 1 Park Close, Knightsbridge, SW1X 7PQ.

BARSTOW, Stan; writer; *b* 28 June 1928; *s* of Wilfred Barstow and Elsie Gosney; *m* 1951, Constance Mary Kershaw; one *s* one *d. Educ:* Ossett Grammar Sch. Employed in Engineering Industry, 1944–62, mainly as Draughtsman. Best British Dramatisation, Writers' Guild of GB, 1974; Royal TV Soc. Writers' Award, 1975. Hon. MA Open Univ., 1982. *Television:* dramatisations: A Raging Calm, 1974; South Riding, 1974; Joby, 1975; The Cost of Loving, 1977; Travellers, 1978; A Kind of Loving (from A Kind of Loving, The Watchers on the Shore, The Right True End), 1982; *Publications:* A Kind of Loving, 1960; The Desperadoes, 1961; Ask Me Tomorrow, 1962; Joby, 1964; The Watchers on the Shore, 1966; A Raging Calm, 1968; A Season with Eros, 1971; The Right True End, 1976; A Brother's Tale, 1980; A Kind of Loving: The Vic Brown Trilogy, 1982; *plays:* Listen for the Trains, Love, 1970; An Enemy of the People (ad. Ibsen), 1978; (with Alfred Bradley): Ask Me Tomorrow, 1966; A Kind of Loving, 1970; Stringer's Last Stand, 1972. *Address:* Goring House, Goring Park Avenue, Ossett, West Yorks. *T:* Wakefield 273362.

BART, A. S.; *see* Schwarz-Bart.

BART, Lionel; composer, lyricist and playwright; *b* 1 Aug. 1930. Wrote lyrics for Lock Up Your Daughters, 1959; music and lyrics for Fings Ain't Wot They Used T'be, 1959; music, lyrics and book for Oliver!, 1960; music, lyrics and direction of Blitz!, 1962; music and lyrics of Maggie May, 1964; music of Lionel, 1977. Has also written several film scores and many individual hit songs. *Films:* Serious Charge; In the Nick; Heart of a Man; Let's Get Married; Light up the Sky; The Tommy Steele Story; The Duke Wore Jeans; Tommy the Toreador; Sparrers Can't Sing; From Russia with Love; Man in the Middle; Oliver; The Optimists. Ivor Novello Awards as a song writer: three in 1957; four in 1959; two in 1960. Variety Club Silver Heart as Show Business Personality of the Year, 1960. Broadway, USA; Tony (Antoinette Perry) Award, etc (for Oliver!), best composer and lyricist, 1962. *Address:* c/o Patricia Macnaughton, MLR, 194 Old Brompton Road, SW5. *T:* 01-373 1161.

BARTELL, Lt-Col (Hon.) Kennèth George William, CBE 1977; FIB; Past President, British Chambers of Commerce in Continental Europe; Past President (twice) and Honorary Vice-President, British Chamber of Commerce, France; Director: ICL (France) International Computers, SA,

since 1976; Wimpey France SA, Builders and Engineers, since 1978; *b* 5 Dec. 1914; *s* of William Richard Aust Bartell and Daisy Florence (*née* Kendall); *m* 1955, Lucie Adèle George. *Educ:* Cooper's Company's Sch. BCom London. Westminster Bank Ltd, London, 1933. Served war, RAOC: France, 1939–40, Egypt and Middle East, 1940–46 (despatches twice); demobilised Hon. Lt-Col. Westminster Bank Ltd, London, 1946–49; Westminster Foreign Bank Ltd: Paris, 1950–51; Lyons, 1952–53; Bordeaux, 1954–55; Manager, State Commercial Bank, Rangoon, Burma, 1955–59; Man., then Chief Man., Westminster Foreign Bank, Paris, 1960–74; Gen. Man., Internat. Westminster Bank Ltd, France, 1974–76, retired. Freeman: Coopers' Co.; City of London, 1981. *Recreations:* sylviculture, swimming, bridge, dancing. *Address:* (principal) 5 avenue Saint-Honore-d'Eylau, Paris 75116, France. *T:* 553-69-48; (country) Baucis, rue Charles Gounod, Lozère-sur-Yvette 91120, France. *T:* 010-03-94. *Clubs:* Army and Navy, Royal Automobile; Cercle de l'Union Interalliée (Paris).

BARTER, John (Wilfred); JP; Chartered Secretary; Management and Financial Consultant; Chairman, Ealing and Acton Building Society, since 1975; *b* 6 Oct. 1917; *s* of late W. F. Barter; *m* 1st, 1941, Joan Mackay (*d* 1973); two *s* one *d* ; 2nd, 1974, Jessica Crabtree. *Educ:* Royal Pinner Sch. Contested (C) East Ham South, 1951; MP (C) Ealing North, 1955–64; PPS to Minister of Health, 1957; PPS to Parly Sec., Min. of Power, 1958–60. Middlesex County Council: Mem., 1949; Alderman, 1961–65; Leader of Majority Party, 1962–63; Vice-Chm., 1963–64; last Chm., 1964–65. Chm. subseq. Pres., Middlesex County Assoc., 1964–76. JP Greater London, Middlesex, 1974.

BARTHOLOMEW, John Eric, OBE 1976, (Eric Morecambe); actor comedian; *b* 14 May 1926; *m* 1952, Joan Dorothy Bartlett; one *s* one *d* (and one adopted *s*). *Educ:* Euston Road Elementary Sch., Morecambe. First double act (with E. Wise), at Empire Theatre, Liverpool, 1941; first broadcast, 1943; BBC television series, 1955; BBC TV and ATV series, 1961–; joined Thames TV, 1978. Best Light Entertainment Award, BAFTA (formerly SFTA) 1963, 1971, 1972, 1973, 1974, 1977. A Vice-Pres., Luton Town Football Club (Dir, 1969-75). Pres., Lord's Taverners', 1977–79. Freeman, City of London, 1976. Hon. DLitt Lancaster, 1977. *Films:* The Intelligence Men, 1964; That Riviera Touch, 1965; The Magnificent Two, 1966. *Publications:* (with E. Wise) Eric and Ernie: an autobiography of Morecambe and Wise, 1973; (with E. Wise) The Best of Morecambe and Wise, ed E. Braben, 1975; (with E. Wise) The Morecambe and Wise Special, 1977; (with E. Wise) Bring Me Sunshine, 1978; Mr Lonely (novel), 1981; (with E. Wise) There's No Answer to That, 1981; The Reluctant Vampire (for children), 1982. *Recreations:* fishing, bird-watching, photography. *Address:* 235/241 Regent Street, W1A 2JT. *T:* 01-734 8851.

BARTINGTON, Dennis Walter, CB 1950; *b* 12 May 1901; *s* of late Walter Bartington; *m* 1934, Margaret Christina Skinner. *Educ:* Dulwich Coll.; Trinity Coll., Cambridge (Sen. Schol., MA). Inland Revenue, 1923; Department of Scientific and Industrial Research, 1925; War Office, 1926-39; Asst Sec., Ministry of Supply, 1939, Principal Asst Sec., 1942; Under-Sec., 1947-59. Min. of Aviation, 1959-61; retired, 1961. *Address:* Kingsfield, 19 Orchard Way, Esher, Surrey KT10 9DY. *T:* Esher 63918. *Club:* United Oxford & Cambridge University.

BARTLE, Ronald David; a Metropolitan Stipendiary Magistrate since 1972; a Deputy Circuit Judge, since 1975; *b* 14 April 1929; *s* of Rev. George Clement Bartle and Winifred Marie Bartle; *m* 1963, Barbara Gloria Teleri Dawn Bartle (*née* Williams) (marr. diss. 1980); one *s* one *d* ; *m* 1981, Hisako (*née* Yagi). *Educ:* St John's Sch., Leatherhead; Jesus Coll., Cambridge (MA). Called to Bar, Lincoln's Inn, 1954. Contested (C) Islington North, 1958 and 1959. A Chm., Inner London Juvenile Courts, 1975-79. Liveryman, Basketmaker's Co., 1976. Freeman, City of London, 1976 (Mem., Guild of Freemen, 1979); Mem., Royal Soc. of St George. *Publication:* Introduction to Shipping Law, 1958. *Recreations:* music, reading, swimming. *Address:* Bow Street Magistrates' Court, WC2E 7AS. *Clubs:* Garrick, Lansdowne.

BARTLEET, Rt. Rev. David Henry; *see* Tonbridge, Bishop Suffragan of.

BARTLETT, Lt-Col Sir Basil Hardington, 2nd Bt, *cr* 1913; MA (Cantab); dramatic author; *b* 15 Sept. 1905; *s* of late Hardington Arthur Bartlett, *e s* of 1st Bt and Irene (*d* 1974), *d* of Prof. Henry Robinson; *S* grandfather, 1921; *m* 1937, Mary (marr. diss. 1960), *o d* of late Sir Ian Malcolm, KCMG; three *d. Educ:* Repton; Corpus Christi Coll., Cambridge. Served War of 1939-45 (wounded, despatches); Lt-Col, Intelligence Corps. Drama script supervisor, BBC, Television, 1952-55. *Publications:* My First War, 1940; Next of Kin, 1944. *Plays:* This Seat of Mars, 1938; The Intruder, 1939; The Jersey Lily, produced Gate Theatre, 1940; Less than Kind, 1947; A Fish in the Family, 1947. *Heir:* *b* Henry David Hardington Bartlett, MBE [*b* 18 March 1912; *m* 1936, Katherine Rosemond (marr. diss.), *d* of Lt-Col W. H. Stanbury; three *s*]. *Clubs:* Garrick, Beefsteak.

BARTLETT, Charles; *see* Bartlett, Harold Charles.

BARTLETT, Charles Vernon Oldfeld; *see* Bartlett, Vernon.

BARTLETT, (Harold) Charles, ARCA 1949; RE 1961 (ARE 1950); RWS 1970 (ARWS 1959); painter and printmaker; *b* Grimsby, 23 Sept. 1921; *s* of Charles Henry and Frances Kate Bartlett; *m* ; one *s. Educ:* Eastbourne

Grammar Sch.; Eastbourne Sch. of Art; Royal College of Art. First one man exhibition in London, 1960. *Recreations:* music, sailing. *Address:* St Andrews, Fingringhoe, near Colchester, Essex. *T:* Rowhedge 406.

BARTLETT, Henry Francis, CMG 1975; OBE 1964; Executive Officer, Utah Foundation, Brisbane, since 1976; painter; HM Diplomatic Service, retired; *b* 8 March 1916; *s* of F. V. S. and A. G. Bartlett, London; *m* 1940, A. D. Roy. *Educ:* St Paul's Sch.; Queen's Coll., Oxford; Ruskin Sch. of Drawing; Univ. of California (Commonwealth Fellow). Min. of Inf., 1940–45; Paris, 1944–47; Vice-Consul Lyons, 1948–49; FO, 1949–50; Vice-Consul, Szczecin, 1950; Second, later First, Sec., Warsaw, 1951-53; FO, 1953-55; First Sec. (Commercial), Caracas, 1955–60; First Sec. (Inf.), Mexico City, 1960-63; Consul, Khorramshahr, 1964–67; Dep. High Comr, Brisbane, 1967–69; Counsellor, Manila, 1969–72 (Charge d'Affaires, 1971); Ambassador to Paraguay, 1972–75. Hon. Prof., Nat. Univ. of Asunción, 1975. Exhibitions of painting: Paris, 1947; London, 1950; Caracas, 1957, 1959; Mexico City, 1962; Brisbane 1969, 1978, 1981. Represented: Commonwealth Art Bank; Queensland and S Aust. State Galleries; Brisbane Colleges of Advanced Educn. Trustee: Queensland Art Gallery, 1977–; Qld Cultural Centre Trust, 1980–. *Address:* c/o Utah Foundation, PO Box 279, Brisbane, Qld 4001, Australia; 14 Bowen Place, 341 Bowen Terrace, New Farm, Qld 4005, Australia.

BARTLETT, John Vernon, CBE 1976; MA; FEng, FICE, FASCE, FIE Aust.; Consulting Engineer; Senior Partner and Chairman, Mott, Hay & Anderson; *b* 18 June 1927; *s* of late Vernon F. Bartlett and Olga Bartlett (*née* Testrup); *m* 1951, Gillian, *d* of late Philip Hoffmann, Sturmer Hall, Essex; four *s*. *Educ:* Stowe; Trinity Coll., Cambridge. Served 9th Airborne Squadron, RE, 1946-48. Engineer with John Mowlem & Co. Ltd, 1951-57; joined staff of Mott, Hay & Anderson, 1957; Partner, 1966–. Vice-Pres., ICE, 1979– (Mem. Council, 1974-77); Chm., British Tunnelling Soc., 1977-79. Telford Gold Medal, (jointly) 1971, 1973; S. G. Brown Medal, Royal Soc., 1973. FRSA 1975. Mem. Council, Fellowship of Engrg, 1982. *Publications:* Tunnels: Planning Design and Construction (with T. M. Megaw), vol. 1, 1981, vol. 2, 1982; contrib. various papers to ICE, ASCE, etc. *Recreation:* sailing. *Address:* c/o Mott, Hay & Anderson, 20/26 Wellesley Road, Croydon, Surrey CR9 2UL. *T:* 01-686 5041. *Clubs:* St Stephens; Hawks (Cambridge); Harlequin Football; Royal Engineers Yacht.

BARTLETT, Prof. Maurice Stevenson, FRS 1961; MA Cambridge, DSc London; Professor of Bio-mathematics in the University of Oxford, 1967-75, now Emeritus; *b* 18 June 1910; *s* of W. S. Bartlett, Scrooby; *m* 1957, Sheila, *d* of C. E. Chapman; one *d*. *Educ:* Latymer Upper Sch.; Queens' Coll., Cambridge. Wrangler, 1932; Rayleigh Prize, 1934. Asst Lectr in Statistics, University Coll., London, 1933-34; Statistician, Imperial Chemical Industries, Ltd, 1934-38; Lectr in Mathematics, Univ. of Cambridge, 1938-47. National Service, Min. of Supply, 1940-45. Visiting Prof. of Mathematical Statistics, Univ. of North Carolina, 1946; Prof. of Mathematical Statistics, Univ. of Manchester, 1947-60; Prof. of Statistics, Univ. of London (University Coll.), 1960-67. Mem. Internat. Statistical Institute, 1949, Hon. Mem., 1980; President: Manchester Statistical Soc., 1959-60; Biometric Soc. (Brit. Reg.), 1964-66; Internat. Assoc. Statistics Phys. Sci., 1965-67; Royal Statistical Society, 1966-67. Hon. DSc: Chicago, 1966; Hull, 1976. Gold Medal, Royal Statistical Soc., 1969; Weldon Prize and Medal, Oxford, 1971. *Publications:* An Introduction to Stochastic Processes, 1955; Stochastic Population Models in Ecology and Epidemiology, 1960; Essays in Probability and Statistics, 1962; Probability, Statistics and Time, 1975; Statistical Analysis of Spatial Pattern 1976; papers on statistical and biometrical theory and methodology. *Address:* Priory Orchard, Priory Avenue, Totnes, Devon TQ9 5HR.

BARTLETT, Prof. Neil, FRS 1973; FRSC; Professor of Chemistry, University of California, Berkeley, since 1969, and Principal Investigator, Materials and Molecular Research Division, Lawrence Berkeley Laboratory, since 1969; *b* Newcastle upon Tyne, 15 Sept. 1932; *s* of Norman Bartlett and Ann Willins Bartlett (*née* Voak), both of Newcastle upon Tyne; *m* 1957, Christina I., *d* of J. W. F. Cross, Guisborough, Yorks; three *s* one *d*. *Educ:* Heaton Grammar Sch., Newcastle upon Tyne; King's Coll., Univ. of Durham, Newcastle upon Tyne. BSc 1954, PhD 1958. Senior Chemistry Master, The Duke's Sch., Alnwick, Northumberland, 1957-58; Mem. Faculty (Dept of Chemistry), Univ. of British Columbia, 1958-66; Prof. of Chemistry, Princeton Univ., and Scientist, Bell Telephone Laboratories, Murray Hill, NJ, USA, 1966-69. For. Associate, Nat. Acad. of Sciences, USA, 1979. Member: Deutsche Akademie der Naturforscher Leopoldina, 1969; Der Akademie der Wissenschaften in Göttingen, 1977; Amer. Chem. Soc., Amer. Soc. for Advancement of Science, etc. Sigma Xi. Visiting Miller Prof., Univ. of Calif, Berkeley, 1967-68; Brotherton Vis. Prof., Univ. of Leeds, 1981, etc. Hon. DSc: Univ. of Waterloo, Canada, 1970; Colby Coll. Maine, USA, 1972; Univ. of Newcastle, 1981; Dr *hc* Univ. of Bordeaux, 1976. Fellow: Amer. Acad. of Arts and Scis, 1977; Chem. Inst. of Canada; Chem. Soc. (London). Corday-Morgan Medal and Prize of Chem. Soc., 1962; Robert A. Welch Award, 1976; Medal of Inst. Jožef Stefan, Ljubljana, 1980; various overseas awards and prizes, 1965–. *Publications:* The Chemistry of the Monatomic Gases, 1975; scientific papers to: Jl of Chem. Soc., Inorganic Chem., etc; Mem. various editorial advisory bds in Gt Britain, France and USA. *Recreations:* water colour painting; walking in high country; gardening. *Address:* 6 Oak Drive, Orinda, Calif 94563, USA. *T:* (415) 254 5322; Chemistry Dept, University of California, Berkeley, Calif 94720, USA. *T:* (business) (415) 642-7259.

BARTLETT, Peter Geoffrey, FRIBA; Partner, Bartlett & Gray, Chartere Architects/Surveyors, Nottingham, since 1951; *b* Bristol, 15 May 1922; *s* o Percy Bartlett, FRIBA, and Daisy Bartlett (*née* Eungblut); *m* 1944, Joa Trevor Lees; one *s*. *Educ:* Nottingham High Sch.; Nottingham Sch. o Architecture, 1939-40 and 1946-49 (Governor's Prize 1949). DipArch. LDV 1939-40. Served War, Pilot, RAF, 1940-46 (Bomber, Middle East an Transport Commands). Lectr, Sch. of Architecture, Nottingham, and Ass Architect, Dudding and Thornely, 1949-51. (With Colin Gray) RIBA Bronz Medal (for Notts, Derbys, Lincs), 1958-61; Civic Trust Awards an Commendations in 1960, 1965, 1968, 1969; Craftmanship Awards in J Midlands, 1967, 1968; Competitions: (Jt winners) Brit. Columbia Lumbe Manufrs Assoc. of Canada for Housing of Timber Construction, 1958; Specia Collective Insts for the Physically Handicapped, Kuwait, Arabia, 196 original research into: timber constr. in Canada, 1958; pre-cast concrete const in Denmark, 1958; Bldgs in hot climates in Kuwait, 1962. RIBA Part I Examr, Univ. of Nottingham, 1975-78; Mem., Court of Governors, Univ. c Nottingham, 1975-; Mem. Council, RIBA, 1973-76; Mem. Press Counci 1973-76; Past Pres., Nottingham and Derby Soc. of Architects. FRSA Liveryman, Guild of Air Pilots and Air Navigators; Freeman, City of Londor Papal Cross (for services to architecture), 1981. Qual. Flying Instr, Gps A an B; Mem. Flying Trng Cttee of Brit. Light Aviation Centre, 1966-68; Bd c Trade Examr for Private Pilot's Licence, 1967-69. *Recreations:* inlan waterways, gardening. *Address:* (home) The Pantiles, Mill Road, Elston, nea Newark, Notts. *T:* East Stoke 241; (office) Bartlett & Gray, DipArch F/FRIBA, 14-16 Bridgford Road, West Bridgford, Nottingham NG2 6AF *T:* Nottingham 866434/8. *Club:* Sherwood Flying (Nottingham) (Hon. Lif Mem.).

BARTLETT, Vernon, CBE 1956; author; *b* Westbury, Wilts, 30 April 1894 *s* of late T. O. Bartlett, Swanage; *m* 1st, Marguerite van den Bemden (*d* 1966) two *s*; 2nd, 1969, Eleanor Needham Ritchie. *Educ:* Blundell's, Tivertor Travelled abroad, 1911-14; European War, 1914-16; joined staff of Dail Mail, 1916; Reuter's Agency, 1917; Paris Peace Conference for Reuter's, an later, for Daily Herald; joined staff of The Times, 1919; special corresponden of that paper in Switzerland, Germany, Poland, 1919-20; Correspondent i Rome, 1921-22; London Director of the League of Nations, 1922-32 broadcast regularly on foreign affairs, 1928-34 and during the war; Staff o News Chronicle, 1934-54; Political Commentator for the Straits Times Singapore, 1954-61; SE Asia Correspondent for Manchester Guardian (nov The Guardian), 1954-61. MP (Ind Prog) Bridgwater Div. of Som. 1938-50 Mem. of UN Advisory Cttee of Information Experts, 1948. *Publication:* some twenty-eight books including: Calf Love, 1929; (with R. C. Sherriff Journey's End, 1930; Nazi Germany Explained, 1933; This is My Life, 1937 Tomorrow Always Comes, 1943; East of the Iron Curtain, 1950; Struggle fo Africa, 1953; And Now, Tomorrow, 1960; Tuscan Retreat, 1964; A Boo about Elba, 1965; Introduction to Italy, 1967; The Past of Pastimes, 1969; Th Colour of their Skin, 1969; Tuscan Harvest, 1971; Central Italy, 1972 Northern Italy, 1973; I Know What I Liked, 1974. *Recreation:* meeting an making friends. *Address:* Middle Barn, Rimpton, Yeovil, Somerset BA2 8AB. *T:* Marston Magna 850708. *Clubs:* Garrick, Beefsteak.

BARTON, Arthur Edward Victor, CBE 1936 (OBE 1933); *b* 26 Aug. 1892 *s* of Arthur Moore Barton and Margaret (*née* Bourke); *m* 1st, 1919, Mega Lewis (*d* 1960), *d* of Anthony Matthews, Liverpool; one *s* one *d*; 2nd, 1962 Aileen, widow of Ronald S. Lonergan, Mexico City and London. *Educ* Manchester Grammar Sch. Imperial Customs and Excise Service, 1912; Ass to Chief of Customs, Kenya and Uganda, 1919; Comptroller Customs an MLC, Br. Guiana, 1924; Collector General and MLC, Jamaica, 1927 Collector of Customs and Excise and MLC, Trinidad and Tobago, 1929 MEC, 1936; Mem. West Indies Cricket Board of Control, 1938-39 Comptroller of Customs and Mem. of Legislative Council, Nigeria, 1939-44 retired from Colonial Service, 1944; Sec. to the West India Cttee, 1949-61 Mem. Council, Football Assoc., 1952-70. *Address:* 64 Seabright, West Parade Worthing, W Sussex BN11 3QU. *T:* Worthing 33935. *Clubs:* Roya Commonwealth Society; Queen's Park Cricket (Port of Spain); Britis Caribbean Association.

BARTON, Sir Charles Newton, Kt 1974; OBE; ED; BE; Hon. FIEAus FAIM; FTS 1978; Chairman: Port of Brisbane Authority, 1977-79 Queensland Local Government Grants Commission, 1977-79; *b* 5 July 1907 *s* of J. Barton, Maryborough, Qld; *m* 1935, Enid, *d* of W. Wetherell. *Educ* Maryborough Boys' Grammar Sch.; Queensland Univ. (BE Civil Consulting Engr, Mackay, 1935-59; Comr of Main Roads, Qld, 1960-68 Co-ordinator-Gen., Qld, 1969-76. Served War, AIF, 1940-41; 2/15th Bi (PW), Europe, 1941-45. CO, 31 Bn, CMF, 1948-52, 42 Bn, 1952-57; Hor Col, Kennedy Regt, 1958-60; Aust. Cadet Corps, N Comd, 1962-66; Qle Univ. Regt, 1966-73. Peter Nicol Russel Medal, 1978. *Recreations* gardening, fishing. *Address:* 78 Jilba Street, Indooroopilly, Queensland 4068 Australia. *Clubs:* Queensland, Johnsonian, United Service, Mackay (all i Qld).

BARTON, Sir Derek Harold Richard, Kt 1972; FRS 1954; FRSE 1976 Directeur, Institut de Chimie des Substances Naturelles, Gif-sur-Yvette, since 1978; *b* 8 Sept. 1918; *s* of William Thomas and Maude Henrietta Barton; *n* 1st, 1944, Jeanne Kate Wilkins; one *s*; 2nd, 1969, Christiane Cognet. *Educ* Tonbridge Sch.; Imperial Coll., Univ. of London (Fellow, 1980). BSc Hor (1st Class) 1940; Hofmann Prizeman; PhD (Organic Chemistry) 1942; DS London 1949. Research Chemist: on Govt project, 1942-44. Albright an

Wilson, Birmingham, 1944-45; Asst Lectr, Dept of Chemistry, Imperial Coll., 1945-46, ICI Research Fellow, 1946-49; Visiting Lectr in Chemistry of Natural Products, Harvard Univ., USA, 1949-50; Reader in Organic Chemistry, Birkbeck Coll., 1950, Prof. of Organic Chemistry, 1953-55; Regius Prof. of Chemistry, Glasgow Univ., 1955-57; Prof. of Organic Chem., 1957-70, Hofmann Prof. of Organic Chem., 1970-78, Imperial Coll.; Emeritus Prof. of Organic Chem., Univ. of London, 1978. Arthur D. Little Vis. Prof., MIT, 1958; Karl Folkers Vis. Prof., Univs of Illinois and Wisconsin, 1959; Cecil H. and Ida Green Vis. Prof., Univ. of British Columbia, 1977; Firth Vis. Prof. in Chemistry, Univ. of Sheffield, 1978. Lectures: Tilden, Chem. Soc., 1952; Max Tischler, Harvard Univ., 1956; First Simonsen Memorial, Chem. Soc., 1958; Falk-Plaut, Columbia Univ., 1961; Aub, Harvard Med. Sch., 1962; Renaud, Michigan State Univ., 1962; Inaugural 3 M's, Univ. of Western Ontario, 1962; 3 M's, Univ. of Minnesota, 1963; Hugo Müller, Chem. Soc., 1963; Pedler, Chem. Soc., 1967; Sandin, Univ. of Alberta, 1969; Robert Robinson, Chem. Soc., London, 1970; Bakerian, Royal Society, 1970; Bose Endowment, Bose Inst., Calcutta, 1972; Stieglitz, Chicago Univ., 1974; Bachmann, Michigan, 1975; Woodward, Yale, 1975; First Smissman, Kansas, 1976; Benjamin Rush and Priestley, Pennsylvania State Univ., 1977; Romanes, Edinburgh, 1979; (first) Hirst, St Andrews Univ., 1980. President: Section B, British Assoc. for the Advancement of Science, 1969; Organic Chemistry Div., Internat. Union of Pure and Applied Chemistry, 1969; Perkin Div., Chem. Soc., 1971; Pres., Chem. Soc., 1973-74. Mem., Council for Scientific Policy, 1965-. Hon. Member: Sociedad Quimica de Mexico, 1969; Belgian Chem. Soc., 1970; Chilean Chem. Soc., 1970; Polish Chem. Soc., 1970; Pharmaceutical Soc. of Japan, 1970; Royal Acad. Exact Scis, Madrid, 1971; Acad. of Pharmaceutical Scis, USA, 1971; Danish Acad. Scis, 1972; Argentinian Acad. Scis, 1973; Societa Italiana per il Progresso delle Scienze, 1976; Chem. Soc. of Japan, 1982; Corresp. Mem., Argentinian Chem. Soc., 1970; Foreign Member: Acad. das Ciencias de Lisboa, 1971; Academia Nazionale dei Lincei, Rome, 1975; Foreign Hon. Mem. American Academy of Arts and Sciences, 1960; Foreign Associate: Nat. Acad. of Sciences, USA, 1970; l'Académie des Sciences, Institute de France, 1978. Hon. Fellow: Deutsche Akad. der Naturforscher Leopoldina, 1967; Birkbeck Coll., 1970; ACS Centennial Foreign Fellow, 1976. Hon. DSc: Montpellier Univ., 1962; Dublin, 1964; St Andrews, Columbia NYC, 1970; Coimbra, 1971; Oxon, Manchester, 1972; South Africa, 1973; City, 1975; Hon. Dr: La Laguna, 1975; Univ. of Western Virginia, 1975; Univs of Valencia, Sheffield, Western Ontario, Metz, 1979. Harrison Memorial Prize, Chem. Soc., 1948; First Corday-Morgan Medallist, Chemical Soc., 1951; Fritzsche Medal, Amer. Chem. Soc., 1956; First Roger Adams Medal, Amer. Chem. Soc., 1959; Davy Medal, Royal Society, 1961; Nobel Prize for Chemistry (jointly), 1969; First award in Natural Product Chemistry, Chem. Soc. of London, 1971; Longstaff Medal, Chem. Soc., 1972; B. C. Law Gold Medal, Indian Assoc. for Cultivation of Science, 1972; Medal, Soc. of Cosmetic Chem. of GB, 1972; Royal Medal, Royal Soc., 1972; Second Centennial of Priestly Chemistry Award, Amer. Chem. Soc., 1974; Medal of Union of Sci. Workers, Bulgaria, 1978; Univ. of Sofia Medal, 1978; Acad. of Scis, Bulgaria Medal, 1978; Copley Medal, Royal Soc., 1980; Hanbury Meml Medal, PSGB, 1981. Order of the Rising Sun (2nd class), Japan, 1972; Chevalier, Légion d'Honneur, 1974. Publications: numerous, in Journal of Chemical Society. Address: Institut de Chimie des Substances Naturelles, 91190 Gif-sur-Yvette, France.

BARTON, Maj.-Gen. Eric Walter, MBE 1966; BSc, FBIM, FRGS; Director of Military Survey, since 1980; b 27 April 1928; s of Reginald John Barton and Dorothy (née Bradfield); m 1963, Margaret Ann, d of Reginald Tunstall Jenkins, Selsey; two s. Educ: St Clement Danes Sch., London; Royal Military Coll. of Science (BScEng 1955). Dip. in Photogrammetry, UCL, 1960. FBIM 1979; FRGS 1979. Commnd RE, 1948; served Mid East, 1948-50; Arab Legion, 1951-52; seconded to Dir, Overseas Surveys, E Africa, 1957-59; Sen. Instr, Sch. of Mil. Survey, 1961-63; OC 13 Fd Survey Sqdn, Aden, 1965-67; Dir, Surveys and Prodn, Ordnance Survey, 1977-80. Major 1961, Lt-Col 1967, Col 1972, Brig. 1976, Maj.-Gen. 1980. Col Comdt, RE, 1982-. Member: Council, Photogrammetric Soc., 1979-; Nat. Cttee for Photogrammetry, 1979-; Council, RGS, 1980-; Nat. Cttee for Geography, 1981-. Recreations: swimming, water sports, ski-ing, numismatics. Address: Directorate of Military Survey, Elmwood Avenue, Feltham, Mddx TW13 7AE. Club: Army and Navy.

BARTON, Maj.-Gen. Francis Christopher, CB 1966; CBE 1964; b 17 Jan. 1916; s of Rev. John Bernard Barton, Elphinstone House, Hastings; m 1939, Olivia Mary Darroll-Smith; two d. Educ: Haileybury Coll. 2nd Lieut, Royal Marines, 1934; Lieut-Col, 1956; Brig., 1961; Maj.-Gen., 1964. Comd 45 Commando, RM, 1958-60; Comd 3 Commando Brigade, RM, 1962-63; Comdt, Joint Warfare Establishment, Old Sarum, 1964-66; retired, 1966. Voluntary Help Organiser, Royal Victoria Hospitals, Bournemouth, 1967-80; Chm., Standing Conf., Voluntary Help Organisers, 1971-72. Address: Moorcroft, Blissford, Fordingbridge, Hants.

BARTON, John Bernard Adie, CBE 1981; Associate Director, Royal Shakespeare Company, since 1964; b 26 Nov. 1928; s of late Sir Harold Montague Barton and Joyce Wale; m 1968, Anne Righter. Educ: Eton Coll.; King's Coll., Cambridge (BA, MA). Fellow, King's Coll., Cambridge, 1954-60 (Lay Dean, 1956-59). Joined Royal Shakespeare Company, 1960; Associate Dir, 1964. Has adapted texts and directed or co-directed many plays for Royal Shakespeare Company, including: The Taming of the Shrew, 1960; The Hollow Crown, 1961; The Art of Seduction, 1962; The Wars of the Roses, 1963-64; Henry IV, Parts I and II, and Henry V, 1964-66; Love's

Labour's Lost, 1965; Coriolanus and All's Well That Ends Well, 1967; Julius Caesar and Troilus and Cressida, 1968; Twelfth Night and When Thou Art King, 1969; Measure for Measure and The Tempest, 1970; Richard II, Henry V, and Othello, 1971; Richard II, 1973; King John, Cymbeline, and Dr Faustus, 1974; Perkin Warbeck, 1975; Much Ado About Nothing, The Winter's Tale, and Troilus and Cressida, 1976; A Midsummer Night's Dream, Pillars of the Community, 1977; The Way of the World, The Merchant of Venice, Love's Labour's Lost, 1978; The Greeks, 1979; Hamlet, 1980; The Merchant of Venice, Titus Andronicus and The Two Gentlemen of Verona, 1981; La Ronde, 1982. Publications: The Hollow Crown, 1962 (and 1971); The Wars of the Roses, 1970. Recreations: travel, chess, work. Address: Hillborough Manor, near Bidford-on-Avon, Alcester, Warwickshire. T: Bidford-on-Avon 2275.

BARTON, Margaret, LRAM; writer; b 1897; y d of Thomas Lloyd Barton and Fanny Roberta Isaacs. Educ: St Paul's Girls' Sch.; Royal Academy of Music. Publications: Tunbridge Wells, 1937; Garrick, 1948; (with Sir Osbert Sitwell) Sober Truth, 1930; Victoriana, 1931; Brighton, 1935. Address: 8 Rutland House, Marloes Road, W8.

BARTON, Sidney James; Part-time Member, London Transport Executive, 1969-76; Additional Chairman, National Health Service Appeal Tribunals, South West Thames/Wessex Regions, since 1974; b 5 March 1909; s of James George Barton and Emily Hannah Jury; m 1933, Lorna Beatrice Mary Williams; one s one d. Educ: Elliott Sch., Wandsworth. Laboratory Technician, Metropolitan Asylums Board and LCC, 1927-34; appointed a full-time Officer, National Union of Public Employees, 1934, National Officer, 1962-73. Mem. Exec. Cttee, London Labour Party, 1950-78; Vice-Chm., Greater London Regional Council, Labour Party, 1969-74. Former Member: General Council, Nurses and Midwives Council; Ancillary Staffs Council; Professional and Technical Staffs Council for the Health Services; TUC Local Govt and Nurses Advisory Cttees; Chm., London Trades Council, 1970-74 (Vice-Chm., 1952-70); Former Member: Surrey County Council (1945-49); Sutton and Cheam Borough Council (1945-48); Surrey Exec. Council for Health Services (1947-54); Epsom Group Hosp. Management Cttee and Long Grove Hosp. Management Cttee; South West Metropolitan Regional Hosp. Bd Farming Adv. Cttee. JP 1955; Alderman LCC 1953-65 (Chm. Public Control Cttee, 1954-59); Chm., LCC, 1959-60 (Chm., Primary and Secondary Schools Sub-Cttee, 1960-61); Vice-Chm. General Purposes Cttee, 1961-65. Alderman London Borough of Sutton, 1964-68. Chm., Governors, Garratt Green Comprehensive Sch. 1958-67, 1970-78 (Vice-Chm., 1967-70); Governor, Hosp. for Sick Children, Great Ormond Street, 1969-75. Member: Met. Regional Exams Bd for Cert. of Secondary Educn, 1964-72; London and Home Counties Regional Advisory Council for Technological Educn, 1965-73; Heathrow Airport London Consultative Cttee. Order of Homayoun Class III (Iran), 1959; Grand Cross of Order Al Merito (Peru), 1960; Comdr Legion of Honour (France), 1960. Address: 14 Chatsworth Road, Cheam, Surrey. T: 01-644 9222. Club: Ewhurst Bowls (Vice-Pres.).

BARTON-CHAPPLE, Dorothy, (Mrs Derek Barton-Chapple); see Tutin, Dorothy.

BARTOSIK, Rear-Adm. Josef C., CB 1968; DSC 1943; b 20 July 1917; m 1st, 1943, Cynthia Pamela Bowman; three s one d; 2nd, 1969, Jeannine Scott (née Bridgeman). Joined Polish Navy, 1935; served in Polish destroyers under British operational control, 1939-46; transf. to RN, 1948; commanded: HMS Comus, 1955-56; HMS Scarborough and 5th Frigate Sqn, 1960-61; HMS Seahawk (RN Air Station Culdrose), 1962-63, HMS London, 1964-65; Rear-Adm. 1966; Asst Chief of Naval Staff (Ops), 1966-68; retired 1968. Coordinating Dir, European Jt Org., Australia Europe Container Service and Australia NZ Europe Container Service, 1969-81, retired 1981. Recreation: picture framing. Address: 33 Cheval Place, SW7.

BARTTELOT, Lt-Col Sir Brian Walter de Stopham, 5th Bt, cr 1875; psc; Commanding Officer, 1st Battalion Coldstream Guards, since 1982; b 17 July 1941; s of Lt-Col Sir Walter de Stopham Barttelot, 4th Bt, and Sara Patricia (who m 2nd, 1965, Comdr James Barttelot, RN retd), d of late Lieut-Col H. V. Ravenscroft; S father, 1944; m 1969, Hon. Mary Angela Fiona Weld Forester, y d of 7th Baron Forester, and of Marie Louise Priscilla, CStJ, d of Sir Herbert Perrott, 6th Bt, CH, CB; four d. Educ: Eton, RMA, Sandhurst. Temp. Equerry to HM the Queen, 1970-71; Camberley Staff Coll., 1974; GSO2, Army Staff Duties Directorate, MoD, 1975-76; Second in comd, 2nd Bn, Coldstream Guards, 1977-78; Mil. Sec. to Maj.-Gen. comdg London Dist and Household Div., 1978-81; GSO1, MoD, 1981-82. Heir: b Robin Ravenscroft Barttelot, b 15 Dec. 1943. Address: Keepers, Stopham, Pulborough, W Sussex RH20 1EB. T: Fittleworth 347. Clubs: Cavalry and Guards, Pratt's, Farmers', Buck's.

BARWICK, David Robert, CBE 1976; QC 1977; Governor of British Virgin Islands, since 1982; b 20 Oct. 1927; s of Jack Barwick and Kathleen Barwick (née Gould); m 1951, Margaret (née Funnell); one s two d. Educ: Christchurch Boys' High Sch.; Univ. of New Zealand (LLB). Barrister and Solicitor of the Supreme Court of New Zealand. Private practice, NZ, 1953-56; Asst Attorney-General, Judicial Comr, British Solomon Islands, 1956-62; Judge of the High Court of Western Pacific, Gilbert and Ellice Islands, 1962-67; Parliamentary Draftsman, Solicitor-General, Secretary for Justice, Actg Attorney-General, Malawi, 1967-76; Attorney-General: Solomon Islands, 1976; Cayman Islands, 1976-82. Recreations: painting, conchology, music, golf. *Address:* Government House, Tortola, British Virgin Islands. *T:* 43400. *Club:* Royal Commonwealth Society.

BARWICK, Rt. Hon. Sir Garfield (Edward John), AK 1981; GCMG 1965; Kt 1953; PC 1964; QC (Australia); Chief Justice of Australia, 1964-81; *b* 22 June 1903; *s* of late Jabez Edward Barwick and Lilian Grace Ellicott; *m* 1929, Norma Mountier Symons; one *s* one d. *Educ:* Fort Street Boys' High Sch., Sydney; University of Sydney, BA 1923; LLB (Hons) 1926; Hon. LLD Sydney, 1972. New South Wales Bar, 1927; KC 1941; Victorian Bar, 1945; KC (Vic) 1945; Queensland Bar, 1958; QC Queensland, 1958. Practised extensively in all jurisdictions: Supreme Court, High Court of Australia and Privy Council. Pres. NSW Bar Assoc., 1950-52 and 1955-56; Attorney-Gen. Commonwealth of Australia, Dec. 1958-Feb. 1964; Minister for External Affairs, Dec. 1961-April 1964. Judge ad hoc, Internat. Court of Justice, 1973-74. President: Law Council of Australia, 1952-54; Australian Inst. of Internat. Affairs, 1972-. Hon. Bencher, Lincoln's Inn, 1964. Leader: Australian Delegation, SEATO Council, Bangkok, 1961, Paris, 1963; UN Delegation, 1960, 1962-64; Australian Delegation to ECAFE, Manila, 1963; Australian Delegation, ANZUS, Canberra, 1962, Wellington, 1963. Chancellor, Macquarie Univ., 1967-78. Pres., NSW Inst. for Deaf and Blind Children, 1976-. *Recreations:* fishing, yachting. *Address:* Mundroola, 133 George Street, Careel Bay, Sydney, NSW, Australia. *Clubs:* Australian (Sydney); Melbourne (Melbourne); Royal Yacht Squadron; Royal Sydney Yacht Squadron.

BARYSHNIKOV, Mikhail; Artistic Director, since 1980, and Principal Dancer, 1974-78 and since 1980, American Ballet Theater; *b* 28 Jan. 1948; *s* of Nicolai Baryshnikov and Alexandra (*née* Kisselov). *Educ:* Ballet Sch. of Riga, Latvia; Kirov Ballet Sch., Leningrad. Soloist, Kirov Ballet Co., 1969-74; Principal Dancer, NY City Ballet, 1978-79. Guest Artist, 1974-, with: Royal Ballet; National Ballet of Canada; Hamburg Ballet; Ballet Victoria, Aust.; Stuttgart Ballet; Alvin Ailey Dance Co., and Eliot Feld Ballet, New York; Spoleto Festival. Repertoire includes: Shadowplay (Tudor); Le Jeune Homme et la Morte (Petit); Sacré du Printemps (Tetley); Prodigal Son, Apollo, Theme and Variations (Balanchine); Afternoon of a Faun (Robbins); Romeo and Juliet, Wild Boy (MacMillan); Configurations (Choo San Goh); Les Patineurs (Ashton); Spectre de la Rose, Le Pavillon d'Armide, Petrouchka (Fokine); Santa Fe Saga (Feld); La Sylphide, La Bayadère, Coppélia, La Fille mal gardée (Bournonville); Swan Lake (Sergeyev and Bruhn); The Nutcracker, Don Quixote (own choreography). Works created: Medea (Butler), 1975; Push Comes to Shove, and, Once More Frank (Tharp), Connotations on Hamlet (Neumeier), Pas de Duke (Ailey), Other Dances (Robbins), 1976; Variations on America (Feld), 1977; Rubies (Balanchine), Opus Nineteen (Robbins), 1979. Gold Medal: Varna Competition, Bulgaria, 1966; 1st Internat. Ballet Comp., Moscow, 1968 (also awarded Nijinsky Prize by Paris Acad. of Dance); Dance Magazine Award, NYC, 1978. *Film:* The Turning Point, 1978. *Publication:* (with Charles Engell France, photographs by Martha Swope) Baryshnikov at Work, 1976. *Recreation:* fishing. *Address:* c/o Edgar Vincent Associates, 145 East 52nd Street, Suite 804, New York, NY 10022, USA. *T:* (212) 752-3020.

BARZEL, Dr Rainer C.; Federal Minister for Inter. German Affairs, Federal Republic of Germany, since 1982; *b* 20 June 1924; *s* of Dr Candidus Barzel, Senior Asst Master, and Maria Barzel. *Educ:* studied Jurisprudence and Political Economy, Univ. of Cologne (Referendar, Dr jur.). With Govt of North Rhine-Westphalia, 1949-; Member of the German Federal Parliament, 1957; Federal Minister in the Adenauer Govt, for all-German affairs, Dec. 1962-Oct. 1963; Chairman: Cttee on Economic Affairs, German Fed. Parlt, 1977-79; Cttee on Foreign Affairs, 1980-82. Coordinator for German-French cooperation, Feb.-Dec. 1980. Chm., CDU, 1971-73 and Chm., CDU/CSU Group in German Federal Parlt, 1964-73. Pres., German-French Inst., 1980-. *Publications:* (all publ. in Germany): Die geistigen Grundlagen der politischen Parteien, 1947; Die deutschen Parteien, 1952; Gesichtspunkte eines Deutschen, 1968; Es ist noch nicht zu spät, 1976; Auf dem Drahtseil, 1978; Das Formular, 1979. *Recreation:* skating. *Address:* Bundeshaus, 5300 Bonn, Germany.

BARZUN, Jacques; University Professor Emeritus, Columbia University; *b* 30 Nov. 1907; *s* of Henri Barzun and Anna-Rose Martin; *m* 1936, Mariana Lowell (*d* 1979); two *s* one *d* ; *m* 1980, Marguerite Davenport. *Educ:* Lycée Janson de Sailly; Columbia Univ. Instructor in History, Columbia Univ., 1929; Research Fellow, American Council of Learned Socs, 1933-34; Columbia University: Asst Prof., 1938; Associate Prof., 1942; Prof. of History, 1945-75; University Prof., 1967; Dean of Grad. Faculties, 1955-58; Dean of Faculties and Provost, 1958-67. Director: American Friends of Cambridge Univ.; Council for Basic Educn; Peabody Inst.; NY Soc. Library; Mem. Adv. Council, Univ. Coll. at Buckingham. Membre Associé de l'Académie Delphinale, Grenoble, 1952; Member: Amer. Acad. of Arts and Letters, USA (President, 1972-75, 1977-79); Amer. Acad. of Arts and Sciences; American Historical Assoc.; FRSA, USA (Benjamin Franklin Fellow). Seth Low Prof. of History, Columbia Univ., 1960; Extraordinary Fellow, Churchill Coll., Cambridge, 1961-. Literary Advisor, Charles Scribner's Sons Ltd, 1975-. Chevalier de la Légion d'Honneur. *Publications:* The French Race: Theories of its Origin, 1932; Race: A Study in Superstition, 1937 (revd, 1965); Of Human Freedom, 1939 (revd, 1964); Darwin, Marx, Wagner, 1941 (revd, 1958); Teacher in America, 1945 (revd, 1981); Berlioz and the Romantic Century, 1950 (4th edn 1982); Pleasures of Music, 1951, rev. edn 1977; Selected Letters of Byron, 1953 (2nd edn 1957); Nouvelles Lettres de Berlioz, 1954, 2nd edn 1974; God's Country and Mine, 1954; Music in American Life, 1956; The Energies of Art, 1956; The Modern Researcher (with Henry F.

Graff), 1957, 3rd edn 1977; The House of Intellect, 1959 (2nd edn 1961) Classic, Romantic and Modern, 1961; Science: The Glorious Entertainmen 1964; (ed) Follett's Modern American Usage, 1967; The American University 1968 (2nd edn 1970); (with W. H. Taylor) A Catalogue of Crime, 1971, rev edn 1973; On Writing, Editing and Publishing, 1971; Berlioz's Evenings wit the Orchestra, 1956, 2nd edn 1973; The Use and Abuse of Art, 1974; Clio an the Doctors, 1974; Simple and Direct, 1975; contrib. to leading US journals *Address:* Charles Scribner's Sons, 597 Fifth Avenue, New York, NY 10017 USA. *T:* 486-4041. *Clubs:* Athenæum, Authors'; Century (New York).

BASARAH, Air Chief Marshal Saleh; Indonesian Ambassador to the Cour of St James's, 1978-81; *b* 14 Aug. 1928; *m* 1955, Sartini Kartina; two *s* thre d. *Educ:* Air Force Staff and Command College. Sqdn Comdr, 1960; AO fc Operation No 001 Trng Wing, 1963; Actg Wing Comdr, CO Wing, No 00 Trng Wing, 1964-66; Dir of Operation Air HQ, 1966-68; Comdr, Fift Regional Air Comd, 1966-69; Comdr, Air Force Special Troop Comc 1967-69; Asst CoS for Operation, 1969-70; CoS, Deptl Affairs, Dept o Defence and Security, 1970-73; CoS of Air Force, 1973-77. 11 Medals an Satya Lencana Orders of Merit. *Recreations:* golf, soccer, boxing. *Address:* c/ Department of Defence, Jakarta, Indonesia.

BASHFORD, Humphrey John Charles, MA; Headmaster, Hessle Hig School, 1964-81, retired; *b* 5 Oct. 1920; *s* of late Sir Henry Bashford, MD FRCP, and late Margaret Eveline Sutton; *m* 1942, Alyson Margaret Liddle two *s* three d. *Educ:* Sherborne Sch.; Clare Coll., Cambridge. MA Cambridg 1950. Served War of 1939-45: commissioned 2nd Bn Oxford Bucks LI, 194 GSO3 HQ Airborne Corps 1944-46. Senior History Master, Leys Sch Cambridge, 1947; Part-time Tutor, WEA, 1950; Headmaster Wellingborough Sch., 1956-64. *Recreations:* gardening, fly-fishing. *Addres* 16 Main Street, Hotham, York.

BASING, 4th Baron *cr* 1887; **George Lutley Sclater-Booth;** *b* 7 Dec. 1903 *s* of Hon. Charles Lutley Sclater-Booth (*d* 1931) (2nd *s* of 1st Baron) and Elle Geraldine (*d* 1957), *y d* of George Jones, Mitton Manor, Staffs; *S* cousin, 1969 *m* 1st, 1938, Jeannette (marr. diss. 1944; she *d* 1957), *d* of late N. B. MacKelvie New York; one *s* ; 2nd, 1951, Cynthia, *widow* of Carl H. Beal, Los Angeles and *d* of late Charles W. Hardy, Salt Lake City, Utah. *Educ:* Winchester *Heir: s* Hon. Neil Lutley Sclater-Booth [*b* 16 Jan. 1939; *m* 1967, Patricia Ann *d* of G. B. Whitfield; two *s*]. *Address:* PO Box 301, Pebble Beach, California USA.

BASINGSTOKE, Bishop Suffragan of, since 1977; **Rt. Rev. Michae Richard John Manktelow;** Residentiary Canon of Winchester Cathedra since 1977; *b* 23 Sept. 1927; *s* of late Sir Richard Manktelow, KBE, CB, an late Helen Manktelow; *m* 1966, Rosamund Mann; three d. *Educ:* Whitgif School, Croydon; Christ's Coll., Cambridge (MA 1952); Chicheste Theological Coll. Deacon 1953, priest 1954, Lincoln; Asst Curate of Bosto Lincs, 1953-57; Chaplain of Christ's Coll., Cambridge, 1957-61; Chaplain o Lincoln Theological Coll., 1961-64, Sub-Warden, 1964-66; Vicar c Knaresborough, 1966-73; Rural Dean of Harrogate, 1972-77; Vicar of S Wilfrid's, Harrogate, 1973-77; Hon. Canon of Ripon Cathedral, 1975-77 *Publication:* Forbes Robinson: Disciple of Love, 1961. *Recreations:* music walking. *Address:* 1 The Close, Winchester, Hants SO23 9LS. *T:* Wincheste 69374.

BASINGSTOKE, Archdeacon of; *see* Nash, Ven. T. G.

BASINSKI, Zbigniew Stanislaw, DPhil, DSc; FRS 1980; FRSC; Principa Research Officer and Head of Crystal Plasticity (Division of Physics National Research Council of Canada; *b* Wolkowysk, Poland, 28 April 1928 *s* of Antoni Basinski and Maria Zofia Anna Hilferding Basinska; *m* 1952 Sylvia Joy Pugh; two *s*. *Educ:* Lyceum of Krzemieniec, Poland; Polish Arm Cadet Sch., Camp Barbara, Palestine, 1943-47; Univ. of Oxford (BSc, MA DPhil, DSc). Research Asst, Univ. of Oxford, 1951-54; Staff Member, Dep of Mech. Engrg (Cryogenic Lab.), Massachusetts Inst. of Technol., 1954-56 Nat. Res. Council of Canada, 1956-. Ford Distinguished Vis. Prof., Carnegi Inst. of Technol., Pittsburgh, USA, 1964-65; Commonwealth Vis. Prof., Univ of Oxford, Fellow of Wolfson Coll., Oxford, 1969-70; Adjunct Prof. Carleton Univ., Ottawa, 1975-77, 1981-; Overseas Fellow, Churchill Coll Cambridge, 1980-81. *Publications:* over 60 original research papers, mainl related to crystal defects and the mechanical properties of metals, in learne jls. *Recreations:* computer design, the stock market, vineculture, winemaking flying, general reading. *Address:* 108 Delong Drive, Ottawa, Ontario K1 7E1, Canada. *T:* (613) 7468227. *Clubs:* Oxford Union, Halifax Hous (Oxford).

BASNETT, David; General Secretary, General and Municipal Worker Union, since 1973 (National Industrial Officer, General and Municipa Workers', 1960-72); *b* 9 Feb. 1924; British; *m* 1956, Kathleen Joan Molyneaux two *s*. *Educ:* Quarry Bank High School, Liverpool. Served War of 1939-45 RAF. Trade Union Official, 1948. Mem. TUC General Council, 1966- Chm., 1977-78. Numerous committees of enquiry including: Roya Commission on Penal Reform; Commission on the Constitution, 1969-71 Royal Commn on the Press, 1974-77. Mem., NEDC, 1973-; Mem., Nationa Enterprise Bd, 1975-79 (and of Organising Cttee, 1975). *Address:* Thorn House, Ruxley Ridge, Claygate, Esher, Surrey. *T:* Esher 62081.

BASOV, Prof. Nikolai Gennadievich; Orders of Lenin, 1967, 1969, 1972, 1975; Hero of Socialist Labour, 1969; Physicist, USSR; Member of the Praesidium of the Academy of Sciences of USSR, since 1967; Deputy of USSR Supreme Soviet, since 1974; Director of the P. N. Lebedev Physical Institute, Moscow, since 1973 (Vice-Director, 1958-72), also Head of the Laboratory of Quantum Radiophysics; Professor, Moscow Institute of Physical Engineers; *b* 1922; *s* of Prof. Gennady Fedorovich Basov and Zinaida Andreevna Molchanova; *m* 1950, Ksenia Tikhonovna Nazarova Basova; two *s*. *Educ:* secondary; Kiev Military-medical Sch.; Institute of Physical Engineers, Moscow. Joined the P. N. Lebedev Physical Institute, 1948. Pres., All-Union Soc., Znanie, 1978; Vice-Pres., Exec. Council, WFSW, 1976. Editor: Priroda (Nature), Popular Sciences Magazine; Soviet Jl of Quantum Electronics. Corresponding Mem. USSR Acad. of Sciences, 1962; Academician, 1966. Fellow, Optical Soc. of America, 1974 (Mem. 1972); Member: Acad. of Sciences of GDR, 1967; German Acad. of Natural Scis, Leopoldina, 1971; Bulgarian Acad. of Scis, 1974; Swedish Royal Acad. of Engineering Sciences, 1975; Polish Acad. of Scis, 1977; Czechoslovakian Acad. of Scis, 1977 (Gold Medal, 1975). Hon. Dr: Polish Mil.-Tech. Acad., 1972; Jena Univ., 1974; Prague Polytechnic Inst., 1975; Pavia Univ., 1977. Awarded Lenin Prize, 1959; Nobel Prize for Physics (jointly with Prof. A. M. Prokhorov of the P. N. Lebedev Physical Institute, Moscow, and Prof. C. H. Townes of MIT Cambridge, Mass, USA), 1964; A. Volta gold medal, Italian Physical Soc., 1977. *Address:* P. N. Lebedev Physical Institute, Academy of Sciences of the USSR, Lenin Prospekt 53, Moscow, USSR.

BASS, Harry Godfrey Mitchell, CMG 1972; HM Diplomatic Service, retired; *b* 26 Aug. 1914; *s* of late Rev. Arthur Edward Bass and Mildred Bass; *m* 1948, Monica Mary, *d* of late Rev. H. F. Burroughs (and eponym of the orchid *Oncidium flexuosum* x *Rodriguezia fragrans*); two *s* one *d*. *Educ:* Marlborough Coll.; Gonville and Caius Coll., Cambridge; St John's Coll., Oxford (BA (Oxon) 1937, MA (Cantab) 1940). British Museum, Dept of Egyptian and Assyrian Antiquities, 1939; Admiralty, 1940; Dominions Office, 1946; Asst Sec., Office of UK High Commissioner, Australia, 1948-51; Mem. of Secretariat, Commonwealth Economic Conference, 1952 and Meeting of Commonwealth Prime Ministers, 1953; Counsellor, Office of UK High Commissioner, Calcutta, 1954-57; Dep. UK High Commissioner, Federation of Rhodesia and Nyasaland, 1959-61; British Minister (Pretoria and Cape Town) in the Republic of S Africa, 1961-62; seconded to Central African Office, 1963-64; British Dep. High Commissioner, Ibadan, 1965-67; Head of Consular Dept, FCO, 1967-70; High Comr in Lesotho, 1970-73. Chapter Clerk, St George's Chapel, Windsor, 1974-77. Silver Jubilee Medal, 1977. *Recreations:* birdwatching, walking. *Address:* Tyler's Mead, Reepham, Norfolk NR10 4LA.

BASS, Rear-Adm. Paul Eric, CB 1981; CEng, FIMechE, MIMarE; *b* 7 March 1925; *s* of C. H. P. Bass, Ipswich; *m* 1948, Audrey Bruce Tomlinson; one *s*. *Educ:* Northgate School, Ipswich; Royal Naval Engineering Coll., Keyham. Served as Midshipman in HM Ships Cambrian, Mauritius, Premier and Rodney; Lieut in Belfast, Phoebe and Implacable; Lt Comdr in Ulysses; Comdr in Lion and Tiger; Naval Staff Course, 1962; Captain, Weapons Trials, 1969-72; NATO Defense Course, 1972-73; Asst Chief of Staff (Intelligence), SACLANT, 1973-75; Dir, Naval Manning and Training (Engineering), 1975-78; Flag Officer, Portsmouth and Port Admiral, Portsmouth, 1979-81, retired 1981. *Recreations:* sailing, fishing, swimming, golf. *Address:* c/o National Westminster Bank Ltd, 68 Palmerston Road, Southsea, Hants PO5 3PN. *Clubs:* Royal Yacht Squadron; Royal Naval Sailing Association; Royal Naval and Royal Albert Yacht (Portsmouth).

BASSETT, Douglas Anthony; Director, National Museum of Wales, since 1977; *b* 11 Aug. 1927; *s* of Hugh Bassett and Annie Jane Bassett; *m* 1955, Elizabeth Menna Roberts; three *d*. *Educ:* Llanelli Boys' Grammar Sch.; University Coll. of Wales, Aberystwyth. Asst Lectr and Lectr, Dept of Geology, Glasgow Univ., 1952-59; Keeper, Dept of Geology, Nat. Museum of Wales, 1959-77. Member: Water Resources Bd, 1965-73; Nature Conservancy Council (and Chm., Adv. Cttee for Wales), 1973-; Secretary for State for Wales, Celtic Sea Adv. Cttee, 1974-79; Ordnance Survey Rev. Cttee, 1978-79; Founder Mem. and first Chm., Assoc. of Teachers of Geology, 1967-68; Chm., Royal Soc. Cttee on History of Geology, 1972-. Dir, Nat. Welsh-American Foundn, 1980-. Hon. Professorial Fellow, University Coll., Cardiff. *Publications:* Bibliography and Index of Geology and Allied Sciences for Wales and the Welsh Borders, 1897-1958, 1961; A Source-book of Geological, Geomorphological and Soil Maps for Wales and the Welsh Borders (1800-1966), 1967; contribs to various geological and earth science jls. *Recreations:* bibliography, chronology. *Address:* 58 Ely Road, Llandaff, Cardiff CF5 2JG.

BASSETT SMITH, (Newlands) Guy, CVO 1977; Consultant, Blundell-Permoglaze Holdings Ltd, 1975-81; *b* 14 July 1910; *s* of Guy Burroughs Smith and Elizabeth Hawkins; *m* 1939, Barbara, *d* of Clement Lionel Tyrer. Joined Dunlop Rubber Co. Ltd, 1927. Served War, Army, 1940-46; passed Staff Coll., Camberley, 1943; Staff appt, 8th Army in Italy, 1944; demobilised 1946, with rank of Lt-Col. Rejoined Dunlop Ltd; General Manager: Dunlop Chem. Products Ltd, 1946-60; Dunlop Footwear Ltd, 1960-69, Dir, 1960-69; Man. Dir, Blundell-Permoglaze Holdings Ltd, 1970; Chm., Blundell Eomite Paints Ltd, Bombay, 1971-76. Chm., British Rubber Adhesive Mfrs Assoc., 1958-60; Council Member: Fedn of British Rubber Mfrs, 1951-60; Inst. of British Carriage and Automobile Mfrs, 1958-77 (Fellow, 1958). Mem. Council, Liverpool Sch. of Tropical Med., 1962. Hon. Trustee, Duke of Edinburgh

Award Scheme, 1971- (Liaison Officer, 1956-71); Sec., English Tennis and Racquets Assoc., 1972-76. Freeman, City of London, 1980. *Recreations:* fishing, youth work, local municipal affairs. *Address:* Upper Derculich, by Strathtay, Pitlochry, Perthshire PH9 0LR. *Clubs:* Boodle's, Queen's; New (Edinburgh).

BASTEN, Sir Henry (Bolton), Kt 1966; CMG 1947; MA Oxon and Adelaide; University of Adelaide, 1953-67, Vice-Chancellor, 1958-67. Formerly Chairman and General Manager, Singapore & Penang Harbour Boards. Investigated conditions in Australian ports for Commonwealth Government, 1951-52, report published, 1952. Chm., Aust. Univs Commn, 1968-71. Hon. DLitt Flinders Univ. (S Australia), 1967. *Address:* 13 Holmes Cresent, Campbell, ACT 2601, Australia.

BASTIN, Prof. John Andrew, MA, PhD; FRAS; Professor, since 1971, and Head of Department of Physics, 1975-80, Queen Mary College, London University; *b* 3 Jan. 1929; *s* of Lucy and Arthur Bastin; *m* 1959, Wendy Susan Jacobsen; one *s* one *d*. *Educ:* George Monoux Grammar Sch., London; Corpus Christi Coll., Oxford. MA, PhD. Univ. of Ibadan, Nigeria, 1952-56; Univ. of Reading, 1956-59; Queen Mary Coll., Univ. of London, 1959-. Initiated a group in far infrared astronomy at Queen Mary College, 1960-70. *Publications:* papers on far infrared astronomy and lunar evolution. *Recreations:* English water colours, Renaissance and Baroque music, tennis, skiing. *Address:* 3 Hambrook Close, Chilham, Canterbury, Kent. *T:* Chilham 634.

BATCHELOR, Alfred Alexander Meston, MA; Headmaster, Temple Grove School, Heron's Ghyll, near Uckfield, 1935-57; *b* 8 March 1901; *s* of late Rev. Canon A. W. Batchelor, and late Agnes Lowe; *m* 1949, Thelma Williams (*d* 1973). *Educ:* Temple Grove; Charterhouse (Scholar); Christ Church, Oxford (Holford Exhibitioner). Hon. Mods 1922; Lit. Hum. 1924; Senior Asst Master, The Old Ride, Bournemouth, 1926-30; Joint Headmaster, St Christopher's, near Bath, 1930-35; Private Holiday Tutor to the late Duke of Connaught, 1929-34. *Publications:* Cradle of Empire, 1981; contributor to Country Life, Punch, BBC, The Times, etc. *Recreations:* natural history, music. *Address:* Hundred End, Fairwarp, near Uckfield, East Sussex. *T:* Nutley 2151.

BATCHELOR, G(eorge) F(rederick) Grant, MB, ChB, LRCP, FRCS; retired as consulting surgeon; *b* 6 April 1902; *s* of Robert and Margaret Grant Batchelor; *m* 1944, Helen Elspeth Mackintosh (*d* 1976), *d* of late Lieut-Col C. H. Simpson, Harrogate. *Educ:* Dundee High Sch.; St Andrews Univ. MB, ChB (St Andrews), 1923; MRCS, LRCP, 1925; FRCS, 1926; Asst Surgeon, West London Hospital, 1929; Hounslow Hospital, 1930; Surgeon: Wembley Hospital, 1930; West London Hospital, 1935; EMS, London, 1939-42; Lieut-Col, RAMC, 1942. Consulting Surgeon, Charing Cross Hosp., 1972. *Recreations:* golf; shooting. *Address:* Apartado 45, 8600 Lagos, Algarve, Portugal. *Club:* Constitutional.

BATCHELOR, George Keith, FRS 1957; Professor of Applied Mathematics, University of Cambridge, since 1964, and Head of Department of Applied Mathematics and Theoretical Physics, since 1959; *b* Melbourne, 8 March 1920; *s* of George Conybere Batchelor and Ivy Constance Batchelor (*née* Berneye); *m* 1944, Wilma Maud Rätz, MBE; three *d*. *Educ:* Essendon and Melbourne High Schs; University of Melbourne. BSc 1940, MSc 1941, University of Melbourne; PhD 1948, Adams Prize, 1951, University of Cambridge; Research Officer, Aeronautical Research Laboratory, Melbourne, 1940-44; Fellow of Trinity Coll., Cambridge, 1947-; Lecturer, University of Cambridge, 1948-59; Reader in Fluid Dynamics, Univ. of Cambridge, 1959-64. Chairman: European Mechanics Cttee, 1965-; Nat Cttee for Theoretical and Applied Mechanics, 1967-72. Editor, Cambridge Monographs on Mechanics and Applied Mathematics, 1953-; Editor, Journal of Fluid Mechanics, 1956-. Mem., Royal Soc. of Sciences, Uppsala, 1972. Foreign Hon. Member: Amer. Acad. of Arts and Scis, 1959; Polish Acad of Scis, 1974. Dr hc: Univ. of Grenoble, 1959; Tech. Univ. of Denmark, 1974. *Publications:* The Theory of Homogeneous Turbulence, 1953; An Introduction to Fluid Dynamics, 1967; various papers on fluid mechanics in journals devoted to physical science. *Address:* Cobbers, Conduit Head Road, Cambridge. *T:* Cambridge 356387.

BATCHELOR, Sir Ivor (Ralph Campbell), Kt 1981; CBE 1976; FRCPE, FRCPsych, DPM, FRSE; Professor of Psychiatry, University of Dundee, 1967-82; Consultant Psychiatrist to Dundee general and psychiatric hospitals; *b* 29 Nov. 1916; *s* of Ralph C. L. Batchelor, FRCSE, FRCPE, and Muriel (*née* Shaw); *m* 1941, Honor Wallace Williamson; one *s* three *d*. *Educ:* Edinburgh Academy; Edinburgh Univ. MB ChB. Sqdn Ldr, RAFVR, 1941-46. Asst Phys. and Dep. Phys. Supt, Royal Edinburgh Hosp., and Sen. Lectr in Psychiatry, Univ. of Edinburgh, 1947-56; Phys. Supt, Dundee Royal Mental Hosp., 1956-62; Prof. of Psychiatry, Univ. of St Andrews, 1962-67. Member: Gen. Nursing Council for Scotland (Chm. Educn Cttee), 1964-71; Standing Med. Adv. Cttee, Scot., 1967-74; Adv. Cttee on Med. Research, Scotland, 1969-73; Scottish Council for Postgraduate Med. Educn, 1970-79; Chief Scientist Cttee, Scotland, 1973-82. Mem., Med. Services Review (Porritt) Cttee, 1958-62; Chm., Cttee on Staffing Mental Deficiency Hosps, 1967-70; Member: Cttee on Nursing (Briggs Cttee), 1970-72; Cttee on the Working of the Abortion Act (Lane Cttee), 1971-74; MRC (Chm. Clinical Research Bd, 1973-74, Chm. Neuro-Sciences Bd, 1974-75), 1972-76; Royal Commn on the Nat. Health Service, 1976-79; Indep. Sci. Cttee on Smoking and Health, 1980-; UK Central Council for Nursing, Midwifery and Health

Visiting, 1980-; MRC Health Services Research Panel, 1981-. *Publications:* Aviation Neuro-Psychiatry, 1945; Henderson and Gillespie's Textbook of Psychiatry, 8th edn 1956 and subseq. edns to 10th edn 1969; contribs to med. jls. *Address:* 38 Seafield Road, Broughty Ferry, Dundee DD5 3AN. *T:* Dundee 77955. *Club:* Athenæum.

BATCHELOR, Prof. (John) Richard; Professor of Tissue Immunology, Royal Postgraduate Medical School, Hammersmith Hospital, since 1979; *b* 4 Oct. 1931; *s* of B. W. Batchelor, CBE and Mrs C. E. Batchelor; *m* 1955, Moira Ann (*née* McLellan); two *s* two *d*. *Educ:* Marlborough Coll.; Emmanuel Coll., Cambridge; Guy's Hospital, London. MB, BChir Cantab, 1955; MD Cantab 1965. Nat. Service, RAMC, 1957-59; Dept of Pathology, Guy's Hospital: Res. Fellow, 1959-61; Lectr and Sen. Lectr, 1961-67. Prof. of Transplantation Research, RCS, 1967; Dir, McIndoe Res. Unit, Queen Victoria Hosp., East Grinstead, 1967-78. Mem. Court, Skinners' Company. Hon. Sec., then Vice-Pres. (E Hemisphere), Transplantation Soc., 1976-80; Member Council: British Kidney Patients' Assoc., 1975-; Nat. Kidney Res. Fund, 1979-. European Editor, Transplantation, 1964-. *Publications:* scientific articles upon tissue transplantation research in various special jls. *Recreations:* sailing; tennis; walking. *Address:* Little Ambrook, Nursery Road, Walton-on-the-Hill, Tadworth, Surrey. *T:* Tadworth 2028.

BATCHELOR, John Stanley, FRCS; Orthopaedic Surgeon, Guy's Hospital, 1946-70, retired; *b* 4 Dec. 1905; *s* of Dr Ferdinand Stanley Batchelor and Florence Batchelor; *m* 1934, Marjorie Blanche Elvina Rudkin; two *s* one *d*. *Educ:* Christ's Coll., Christchurch, NZ; Otago Univ.; Guy's Hospital. MRCS, LRCP 1931; FRCS 1934. Pres., Section of Orthopaedics, R.SocMed, 1958-59; British Orthopaedic Assoc.: Hon. Treas. 1960-65; Hon. Sec. 1964; Vice-Pres. 1967-68; Pres. 1970-72. *Publications:* contribs to med. jls. *Recreations:* golf, walking, antiques. *Address:* 51 Ruston Avenue, Rustington, West Sussex.

BATCHELOR, Richard; *see* Batchelor, J. R.

BATE, Ven. Alban F., MA; DCnL; Archdeacon of St John, 1949-63, retired; Rector of St Paul's Church, St John, New Brunswick, 1936-63, retired; *b* 12 May 1893; *s* of Rev. William John Bate and Alice C. McMullen; *m* 1919, Norah F. Warburton, Charlottetown, PEI; two *s* five *d*. *Educ:* Rothesay Collegiate Sch.; Dalhousie, Superior Sch.; University of King's Coll., Nova Scotia, (made Hon. Fellow 1939), BA, 1914; Divinity Testamur, 1916; MA, 1918; Deacon, 1916; Priest, 1917; Curate of Cathedral, Fredericton, 1916-19; Asst at Parish Church, Fredericton, 1919-20; Rector of Fredericton 1920-36 and Archdeacon of Fredericton, 1932-36; Canon of Christ Church Cathedral, Fredericton, 1946; Chaplain of the Legislature of Province of New Brunswick, 1925-35; Chaplain 7th Machine Gun Bn, 1927; 1936; Chaplain, St George's Soc., 1939-42; Pres. Rotary Club of Fredericton, 1928-29; Saint John, 1941-42. DCnL (King's Univ. Halifax) 1955. *Recreation:* gardening. *Address:* 351 Charlotte Street West, Saint John, NB E2M 1Y7, Canada. *Clubs:* Rotary, Canadian (St John, NB).

BATE, Sir David (Lindsay), KBE 1978 (CBE 1968); Chief Judge, Benue and Plateau States of Nigeria, 1975-77; Senior Puisne Judge, High Court of Justice, Northern States of Nigeria, 1968-75 (Puisne Judge 1957-68); *b* 3 March 1916; *m* 1948, Thadeen June, *d* of late R. F. O'Donnell Peet; two *s*. *Educ:* Marlborough; Trinity Coll., Cambridge. Called to Bar, Inner Temple, 1938. Commissioned, Royal Artillery, 1939 and served, Royal Artillery, 1939-46. Entered Colonial Legal Service, 1947; Crown Counsel, Nigeria, 1947-52; Senior Crown Counsel, Nigeria, 1952-54; Senior Crown Counsel, Northern Nigeria 1954-56; Solicitor-Gen., Northern Nigeria, 1956. *Recreations:* shooting, fishing. *Address:* 4029 Lanchaster Road, RR2, Duncan, British Columbia, Canada. *Club:* Flyfishers'.

BATE, Henry, OBE 1971; Vice-Chairman of Press Council, 1960-75; founder member, 1953-75; *b* 14 Oct. 1899; *m* 1st, 1926, Annie Stonehewer (marr. diss.); one *s*; 2nd, 1949, May Abbott. Journalist, provincial newspapers in Brecon, Cardiff, Aberystwyth, 1918-22; Evening Chronicle, Manchester, 1922-45 (Industrial Corresp. 1933-45); Daily Telegraph, Fleet Street, 1945-70 (Architectural Reporter 1959-70). Mem., Nat. Union of Journalists Appeals Tribunal, 1976-80 (Mem. Exec. Council, 1946-76; Nat. Pres., 1952-53; Trustee 1956-76); Mem. Exec. Cttee, Internat. Fedn of Journalists, 1957-60; Mem. Newspaper Mergers Panel, Monopolies Commn, 1965-73. *Address:* 48 Berwyn Road, Richmond, Surrey. *Club:* Press.

BATE, Sir (Walter) Edwin, Kt 1969; OBE 1955; Barrister, Solicitor and Notary Public, Hastings, New Zealand, since 1927; *b* 12 March 1901; *s* of Peter and Florence Eleanor Bate; *m* 1925, Louise Jordan; two *s* one *d*. *Educ:* Victoria Univ., Wellington. LLM (first class hons), 1922. Admitted Barrister and Solicitor, 1922; practised: Taumarunui, NZ, 1923; Hastings, NZ, 1927. Mayor, City of Hastings, NZ, 1953-59; Chm., Hawke Bay Hosp. Bd, 1941-74; Pres., Hosp. Bds Assoc. of NZ, 1953-74; Pres., Associated Trustee Savings Banks of NZ, 1968 and 1969. OStJ 1961. Grand Master of Freemasons in NZ, 1972-74. *Recreations:* fishing, gardening. *Address:* PO Box 749, Hastings, New Zealand. *T:* 777448.

BATE, Prof. Walter Jackson; Kingsley Porter University Professor, Harvard University, since 1980; *b* 23 May 1918; *s* of William George Bate. *Educ:* Harvard Univ. AB 1939, PhD 1942. Harvard University: Associate Prof. of English, 1949-55; Prof. of English, 1955-62; Chm., Dept of English, 1955-62; Abbott Lawrence Lowell Prof. of the Humanities, 1962-80. Corresp. Fellow,

British Acad., 1978. Member: Amer. Acad. of Arts and Sciences; Amer. Philosophical Soc.; Cambridge Scientific Soc. Christian Gauss Award, 1956, 1964, 1970; Pulitzer Prize for Biography, 1964, 1978; Nat. Book Award, 1978; Nat. Book Critics Award, 1978. *Publications:* Stylistic Development of Keats, 1945; From Classic to Romantic, 1946; Criticism: The Major Texts, 1952; The Achievement of Samuel Johnson, 1955; Prefaces to Criticism, 1959; Yale Edition of Samuel Johnson, Vol. II, 1963, Vols III-V, 1969; John Keats, 1963-Coleridge, 1968; The Burden of the Past and The English Poet, 1971; Samuel Johnson, 1977. *Recreation:* farming. *Address:* 3 Warren House, Cambridge, Mass, USA. *Club:* Saturday (Boston, Mass).

BATE, Maj.-Gen. William, CB 1974; OBE 1963; DL; Secretary to the Council of TAVR Associations, since 1975 (Deputy Secretary, 1973-75); *b* 6 June 1920; *s* of S. Bate, Warrington; *m* 1946, Veronica Mary Josephine (*née* Quinn); two *s* two *d*. Commnd, 1941; war service in Burma, 1941-46 (despatches); Senior Instructor, RASC Officers Sch., 1947-50; Co. Comd 7th and 11th Armoured Divs, 1951-53; psc 1954; DAA&QMG Q (Ops), WO 1955-57; jssc 1957; Admin. Staff Coll., Henley, 1958; Directing Staff, Staff Coll., Camberley, 1958-60; AA&QMG, Ops and Plans, HQ BAOR, 1961-63; CO, 2 Div. Column, BAOR, 1963-65; Col GS, Staff Coll., Camberley, 1965-67; Brig. Q (Maint.), MoD, 1967-68; ADC to the Queen, 1969; idc 1969; Dir of Admin. Planning (Army), 1970; Dir of Movements (Army), MoD, 1971-73. Col Comdt, RCT, 1974-; Hon. Col, 163 Movement Control Regt, RCT(V), TAVR, 1974-79. FCIT 1967. DL Surrey, 1980. *Recreations:* cricket, tennis. *Address:* Netherbury, Belton Road, Camberley, Surrey. *T:* Camberley 63529. *Clubs:* East India, Devonshire, Sports and Public Schools, MCC.

BATE, Dame Zara (Kate), DBE 1968; *b* 10 March; *d* of Sidney Herbert Dickens; *m* 1st, 1935, Captain James Fell; three *s*; 2nd, 1946, Rt Hon. Harold Edward Holt, PC, CH (*d* 1967), Prime Minister of Australia; 3rd, 1969, Hon. Henry Jefferson Percival Bate, MHR. *Educ:* Ruyton and Toorak Coll Director: John Stafford & Co.; Colebrook Estates. Chm. Bd, St Laurent Melbourne. Hon. Dr Lit and Hum, Ewha Women's Univ., Seoul, Korea 1967. Coronation Medal, 1953. *Recreations:* tennis, reading, spear fishing. *Address:* 18 Millicent Avenue, Toorak, Victoria 3142, Australia. *T:* 24. 1128.

BATE-SMITH, Dr Edgar Charles, CBE 1963; FLS 1959; Hon. FIFST; ScD; Director, Low Temperature Research Station, Cambridge, 1947-65, retired; *b* 24 Aug. 1900; *s* of Albert Edward Smith and Avis Ellen Jenkinson; *m* 1934, Margaret Elizabeth Bate Hardy; one *s*. *Educ:* Wellingborough Sch.; Manchester Univ.; Gonville and Caius Coll., Cambridge. Mem., Soc. of Chemical Industry Food Group Cttee, 1939-41, 1956-60; (Jubilee Memorial Lectr, 1962-63); formerly Mem. Council, Inst. of Food Science and Technology; Pres., Cambridge Philosophical Soc., 1953-55; Chm., Phytochemical Soc. (formerly Plant Phenolics Group), 1958-60. *Publications:* Food Science (with T. N. Morris), 1952. Papers in scientific jls on post-mortem physiology of muscle, chemistry and taxonomy of plants. *Recreations:* plants and animals; sketching. *Address:* c/o Institute of Animal Physiology, Babraham, Cambridge.

BATELY, Prof. Janet Margaret, (Mrs L. J. Summers); Professor of English Language and Medieval Literature, King's College, University of London, since 1977; *b* 3 April 1932; *d* of Alfred William Bately and Dorothy Maud Bately (*née* Willis); *m* 1964, Leslie John Summers, sculptor; one *s*. *Educ:* Greenhead High Sch., Huddersfield; Westcliff High Sch. for Girls; Somerville Coll., Oxford (Shaw Lefevre Scholar). BA 1st cl. hons English 1954, Dip. in Comparative Philology (with distinction) 1956, MA 1958. Asst Lectr in English, Birkbeck Coll., Univ. of London, 1955-58, Lectr, 1958-69, Reader 1970-76. Sir Israel Gollancz Meml Lectr, British Acad., 1978. Mem. Council, EETS, 1981-. *Publications:* The Old English Orosius, 1980; The Literary Prose of King Alfred's Reign: Translation or Transformation, 1980; contribs to: England Before the Conquest, 1971; Saints, Scholars and Heroes (ed M. H. King and W. M. Stevens), 1979; Medium Aevum, Rev. of English Studies, Anglia, English Studies, Classica et Mediaevalia, Scriptorium, Studies in Philology, Mediev. Arch., Notes and Queries, Archaeologia, Anglo-Saxon England, The Dickensian, Jl Soc. of Archivists. *Recreations:* music, gardening. *Address:* 86 Cawdor Crescent, W7 2DD. *T:* 01-567 0486.

BATEMAN, Sir Cecil (Joseph), KBE 1967 (MBE 1944); Chairman, G. Heyn & Sons Ltd, since 1971; Director: Nationwide Building Society, since 1970 Allied Irish Banks, 1970-80; Allied Irish Investment Bank Ltd, 1971-80; *b* 6 Jan. 1910; *s* of Samuel and Annie Bateman; *m* 1938, Doris M. Simpson; one *s* one *d*. *Educ:* Queen's Univ., Belfast. Served War of 1939-45, Royal Artillery (Major). Entered NI Civil Service, Nov. 1927. Dir of Establishments, Min. of Finance, 1958-63; Sec. to Cabinet and Clerk of Privy Council of N Ireland, 1963-65; Permanent Sec., Min. of Finance, and Head of Northern Ireland Civil Service, 1965-70. *Recreations:* golf, reading. *Address:* 60 Knocklofty Park, Belfast 4, N Ireland. *T:* Belfast 650818. *Club* Shandon Park Golf.

BATEMAN, Sir Charles Harold, KCMG 1950 (CMG 1937); MC; *b* Portsmouth, 4 Jan. 1892; *s* of late Charles Bateman; *m* 1940, Bridget Mary *d* of late Michael Kavanagh, Co. Wicklow. *Educ:* London Univ. (BA) Sorbonne, Paris. Served European War, 1914-18, with 2nd London Reg (Royal Fusiliers), Gallipoli and France; Royal Artillery, France and Belgium (MC, twice wounded); entered Diplomatic Service, 1920; Third Sec.

Santiago, Chile; Foreign Office, 1924; First Sec., 1929; transferred Bagdad, 1932; Acting Counsellor, 1935; Counsellor, Lisbon, 1937; Minister at Cairo, 1938; transferred Foreign Office, 1940; Minister to Mexico, 1941-44, Ambassador, 1944-47; Asst Under Sec., Foreign Office, 1948-50; British Ambassador to Poland, 1950-52; retired, 1952. *Address:* Amesbury Abbey, Amesbury, Wiltshire.

BATEMAN, Sir Geoffrey (Hirst), Kt 1972; FRCS; Surgeon, Ear, Nose and Throat Department, St Thomas' Hospital, London, 1939-71; *b* 24 Oct. 1906; *s* of Dr William Hirst Bateman, JP, Rochdale, Lancs; *m* 1931, Margaret, *d* of Sir Samuel Turner, Rochdale; three *s* one *d. Educ:* Epsom Coll.; University Coll., Oxford. Theodore Williams Schol. in Anat., Oxford Univ., 1926; BA Oxon, Hons sch. Physiol., 1927; Epsom schol. to King's Coll. Hosp., 1927; BM, BCh Oxon, 1930; FRCS, 1933; George Herbert Hunt Trav. Schol., Oxford Univ., 1933. RAFVR, Wing Comdr, 1939-45. Mem., Bd Governors, St Thomas' Hosp., 1948; Mem. Collegium Otolaryngologica Amicitiæ Sacrum, 1949; Hon. Corr. Mem. Amer. Laryngological Assoc., 1960; Past Mem. Council, RCS; Editor, Jl of Laryngology and Otology, 1961-77; Formerly Hon. Cons. on Oto-rhino-laryngology to the Army; Cons. Adviser in Otolaryngology, Dept of Health and Social Security. Pres., British Assoc. of Otolaryngologists, 1970-71 (Vice-Pres., 1967-70). Hon. FRSM 1978. *Publications:* Diseases of the Nose and Throat (Asst Editor to V. E. Negus, 6th edn), 1955; contributor various jls, etc. *Recreations:* golf, fishing. *Address:* Thorney, Graffham, Petworth, West Sussex GU28 0QA. *T:* Graffham 314.

See also Sir R. M. Bateman.

BATEMAN, Leslie Clifford, CMG 1965; FRS 1968; Secretary-General, International Rubber Study Group, since 1976; *b* 21 March 1915; *s* of Charles Samuel Bateman; *m* 1st, 1945, Marie Louise Pakes (*d* 1967); two *s*; 2nd, 1973, Mrs Eileen Joyce Jones (*née* Henwood). *Educ:* Bishopshalt Sch., Uxbridge; University Coll., London. BSc, 1st cl. Hons Chem., 1935; PhD and Ramsey Memorial Medal, 1938; DSc 1955; Fellow, 1974. Oriel Coll., 1940-41; Chemist, Natural Rubber Producers Research Assoc., 1941-53; Dir of Research, 1953-62; Controller of Rubber Res., Malaysia, 1962-74; Chm., Internat. Rubber R&D Board, 1962-74. Hon. DSc: Malaya, 1968; Aston, 1972. Colwyn Medal, 1963, and Jubilee Foundn Lectr, 1971, Inst. of Rubber Industry. Hon. PSM, Malaysia, 1974. *Publications:* (ed and contrib.) The Chemistry and Physics of Rubber-like Substances, 1963; numerous scientific papers in Jl Chem. Soc., etc, and articles on technical-economic status of natural rubber and its developments. *Recreations:* cricket, golf and other outdoor pursuits. *Address:* 3 Palmerston Close, Welwyn Garden City, Herts. *T:* Welwyn Garden 22391.

BATEMAN, Mary-Rose Christine, MA; Headmistress, Perse School for Girls, Cambridge, since 1980; *b* 16 March 1935; *d* of Comdr G. A. Bateman, RN, and Mrs G. A. Bateman. *Educ:* The Abbey, Malvern Wells, Worcs; St Anne's Coll., Oxford (MA); CertEd Cambridge. Assistant English Mistress: Westonbirt Sch., Tetbury, Glos, 1957-60; Ashford Sch., Kent, 1960-61; Lady Eleanor Holles Sch., Mddx, 1961-64; Head of English Department: Westonbirt Sch., Glos, 1964-69; Brighton and Hove High Sch., GPDST, 1969-71; Headmistress, Berkhamsted School for Girls, Herts, 1971-80. *Address:* 27 Leys Road, Cambridge CB4 2AR. *T:* Cambridge 315373.

BATEMAN, Sir Ralph (Melton), KBE 1975; MA Oxon; Chairman, Stothert and Pitt, since 1977; Deputy Chairman: Rea Brothers, since 1979 (Director since 1977); Furness Withy, since 1979 (Director since 1978); Deputy Chairman, Crosby Woodfield, since 1980; Vice-President, Confederation of British Industry, since 1976 (Deputy President, 1973-74, President, 1974-76); *b* 15 May 1910; 3rd *s* of William Hirst Bateman, MB, BCh, and of Ethel Jane Bateman, Rochdale, Lancs.; *m* 1935, Barbara Yvonne, 2nd *d* of Herbert Percy Litton and Grace Vera Litton, Heywood Lancs.; two *s* two *d. Educ:* Epsom Coll.; University Coll., Oxford. Turner & Newall Ltd: joined as management trainee, 1931; held various directorships in Group, 1942-76; Dir, 1957; Dep. Chm., 1959; Chm., 1967-76. Mem., NEDC, 1973-76. Mem. Council, Manchester Business Sch., 1972-76; Vice-Pres., Ashridge Management Coll.; Chm. of Council, University Coll. at Buckingham, 1976-79; Member Court: Manchester Univ.; Salford Univ. FCIS, CBIM; FRSA 1970. Hon. DSc Salford, 1969. *Recreations:* family and social affairs. *Address:* 2 Bollin Court, Macclesfield Road, Wilmslow, Cheshire. *T:* Wilmslow 530437. *Club:* Carlton.

See also Sir G. H. Bateman.

BATEMAN, Richard George Saumarez La T.; *see* La Trobe-Bateman.

BATES, Alan (Arthur); actor; *b* 17 Feb. 1934; *m* 1970, Victoria Ward; twin *s. Educ:* Herbert Strutt Grammar Sch., Belper, Derbyshire; RADA. *Theatre:* English Stage Co. (Royal Court Theatre, London): The Mulberry Bush; Cards of Identity; Look Back in Anger; The Country Wife; In Celebration; London (West End): Long Day's Journey into Night; The Caretaker; The Four Seasons; Hamlet; Butley, London and NY (Evening Standard Best Actor award, 1972; Antoinette Perry Best Actor award, 1973); Poor Richard, NY; Richard III and The Merry Wives of Windsor, Stratford, Ont.; Venice Preserved, Bristol Old Vic; Taming of the Shrew, Stratford-on-Avon, 1973; Life Class, 1974; Otherwise Engaged, Queen's, 1975; The Seagull, Duke of York's, 1976; Stage Struck, Vaudeville, 1979. *Films:* The Entertainer, Whistle Down the Wind, A Kind of Loving, The Running Man, The Caretaker, Zorba the Greek, Nothing but the Best, Georgie Girl, King of Hearts, Far from the Madding Crowd, The Fixer (Oscar nomination), Women in Love, The Three Sisters (National Theatre Co.), A Day in the Death of Joe Egg, The Go-Between, Second Best (also prod.), Impossible Object, Butley, In Celebration, Royal Flash, An Unmarried Woman, The Shout, The Rose, Nijinsky, Quartet, The Return of the Soldier. *Television:* various plays; Plaintiff and Defendant, Two Sundays, The Collection, 1977; The Mayor of Casterbridge, 1978; Very Like a Whale, 1980; The Trespasser, 1980; A Voyage Round my Father, 1982. *Recreations:* swimming, squash, driving, riding, water skiing, reading. *Address:* c/o Michael Linnit, Chatto & Linnit Ltd, Globe Theatre, Shaftesbury Avenue, W1.

BATES, Alfred; researcher and presenter, BBC television, since 1980; *b* 8 June 1944; *s* of Norman and Alice Bates; single. *Educ:* Stretford Grammar Sch. for Boys; Manchester Univ. (BSc); Corpus Christi Coll., Cambridge. Lectr in Maths, De La Salle Coll. of Educn, Middleton, 1967-74. MP (Lab) Bebington and Ellesmere Port, Feb. 1974-1979; PPS to Minister of State for Social Security, 1974-76; Asst Govt Whip, 1976-79; a Lord Comr, HM Treasury, 1979. *Recreation:* cricket umpiring. *Address:* 34 Brooks Road, Old Trafford, Manchester M16 9QR.

BATES, Allan Frederick, CMG 1958; *b* 15 July 1911; *s* of John Frederick Lawes and Ethel Hannah Bates; *m* 1937, Ena Edith, *d* of John Richard Boxall; three *s. Educ:* Woolwich Central Sch.; London Univ. Qualified as Certified Accountant, 1938; practised in London, 1938-44. Joined Colonial Service (now Overseas Civil Service), 1944; Deputy Comptroller Inland Revenue, Cyprus, 1944-48; Comptroller Inland Revenue, Cyprus, 1948-52; Financial Secretary: Cyprus, 1952-60; Mauritius, 1960-64; Man. Dir, Develt Bank of Mauritius, 1964-70; Financial Advr (IMF) to Govt of Bahamas, 1971-75; Budget Advr (IMF) to Govt of Lesotho, 1975-76. Accounts Adviser, British Exec. Service Overseas, to Govt of Belize, 1982. Fellow Inst. of Taxation 1950; Mem., Inst. of Directors. *Recreation:* painting, carving. *Address:* 5 Redford Avenue, Coulsdon, Surrey. *T:* 01-660 7421. *Club:* Royal Commonwealth Society.

BATES, Sir Darrell; *see* Bates, Sir J. D.

BATES, Air Vice-Marshal David Frank; Air Officer Administration, HQ RAF Support Command, 1979-82; *b* 10 April 1928; *s* of late S. F. Bates, MusB, FRCO, and N. A. Bates (*née* Story); *m* 1954, Margaret Winifred (*née* Biles); one *s* one *d. Educ:* Warwick Sch.; RAF Coll., Cranwell. Commnd, 1950; served Egypt, Innsworth, UKSLS Australia, HQ Transport Comd, RAF Technical Coll., Staff Coll., Lyneham, El Adem, Staff Coll., Jt Services Staff Coll., Innsworth, and RCDS, 1950-73; Stn Comdr, Uxbridge, 1974-75; Dir of Personnel Ground, 1975-76; Dir of Personnel Management (ADP), 1976-79. Pres., Adastrian Cricket Club, 1977-. *Recreations:* cricket, most sports, gardening, model railways. *Address:* c/o Lloyds Bank Ltd, 73 Parade, Leamington Spa, Warwicks CV32 4BB. *Clubs:* Royal Air Force, MCC.

BATES, Prof. Sir David (Robert), Kt 1978; MSc; DSc; FRS 1955; MRIA; Regents' Fellow, Smithsonian Institution, 1982-83; *b* Omagh, Co. Tyrone, N Ireland, 18 Nov. 1916; *s* of late Walter Vivian Bates and of Mary Olive Bates; *m* 1956, Barbara Bailey Morris; one *s* one *d. Educ:* Royal Belfast Academical Institution; Queen's Univ., Belfast; University Coll., London. Engaged at Admiralty Research Laboratory, 1939-41, and at Mine Design Department, 1941-45; Lecturer in Mathematics, University Coll., London, 1945-50; Consultant at US Naval Ordnance Test Station, Inyokern, Calif., 1950; Reader in Physics, University Coll., London, 1951; Queen's Univ., Belfast: Prof. of Applied Mathematics, 1951-68; Prof. of Theoretical Physics, 1968-74; Research Prof., 1976-82. Chm., Adv. Bd Postgrad. Awards, NI Dept of Educn, 1974-82. Vice-Pres., RIA, 1976-77. Chapman Meml Lectr, Univ. of Colorado, 1973. Vice-Pres., Alliance Party of NI, 1971. Hon. Foreign Mem., Amer. Acad. of Arts and Scis, 1974; Associate Mem., Royal Acad., Belgium, 1979. Hon. DSc: Ulster, 1972; NUI, 1975; Hon ScD Dublin, 1979; Hon. LLD Glasgow, 1979. Hughes Medal, Royal Soc., 1970; Chree Medal, Inst. Physics, 1973; Gold Medal, Royal Astron. Soc., 1977. *Publications:* papers in geophysical and physical journals. Editor-in-Chief, Planetary and Space Science. *Recreations:* reading and listening to radio. *Address:* Harvard-Smithsonian Center for Astrophysics, 60 Garden Street, Cambridge, Mass 02138, USA. *T:* (617) 495-4403.

BATES, Sir Dawson; *see* Bates, Sir J. D.

BATES, Maj.-Gen. Sir (Edward) John (Hunter), KBE 1969 (OBE 1952); CB 1965; MC 1944; Director, Thomson Regional Newspapers, 1969-77; *b* 5 Dec. 1911; *s* of Ernest Bates, FRIBA; *m* 1947, Sheila Ann Norman; two *s* two *d. Educ:* Wellington Coll.; Corpus Christi Coll., Cambridge. BA 1933; MA 1963. Commissioned, 1932; Pre-war service in UK and Malaya; War Service in Africa, Middle East, Sicily, Italy and Greece; Senior Army Instructor, JSSC, 1954-57; Student, IDC, 1958; CRA, 2 Div., 1959; CCRA 1 (British) Corps, 1960-61; Dir, RA, War Office, 1961-64; Comdt of RMCS, 1964-67; Dir, Royal Defence Acad., 1967-68. Special Comr, Duke of York's Royal Military Sch., 1972-. Col Comdt, RA 1966-76. Mem. Ct of Assts, 1972-, Warden, 1977, Master, 1979, Worshipful Co. of Haberdashers. Chm., RUSI, 1976-78. *Recreations:* fishing, shooting. *Address:* Seymours Oast, Leeds, near Maidstone, Kent. *T:* Maidstone 861275. *Clubs:* Army and Navy; Rye Golf.

See also Hon. Sir J. D. Waite.

BATES, Eric; Chairman, Midlands Electricity Board, 1969-72; *b* 1 Nov. 1908; *s* of late John Boon Bates and late Edith Anne Bates; *m* 1933, Beatrice, *d* of late William Henry Herapath and late Beatrice Herapath; one *s* two *d.* Trained Ilford Elec. Dept.; Asst, County of London Elec. Supply Co., 1929-32; Consumers' Engr: West Kent Electric Co., 1933-36; Isle of Thanet Elec. Supply Co., 1937-42; Elec. Engr, Kennedy & Donkin, 1942-44; Consumers' Engr, Luton Elec. Dept, 1944-48; Sect. Head, Eastern Elec. Bd, 1948-49; Dep. Chief Commercial Officer, Eastern Elec. Bd, 1949-57; North Eastern Electricity Board: Chief Commercial Officer, 1957-62; Dep. Chm., 1962-67; Chm., 1967-69. *Publications:* contribs to Proc. IEE. *Recreation:* golf. *Address:* 24 Grange Road, Broadstairs, Kent.

BATES, Sir Geoffrey Voltelin, 5th Bt, *cr* 1880; MC 1942; *b* 2 Oct. 1921; *s* of Major Cecil Robert Bates, DSO, MC (3rd *s* of 2nd Bt) and Hylda, *d* of Sir James Heath, 1st Bt; *S* uncle, 1946; *m* 1st, 1945, Kitty Kendall Lane (*d* 1956); two *s*; 2nd, 1957, Olivia Gwyneth Zoë (*d* 1969) *d* of Capt. Hon. R. O. FitzRoy (now 2nd Viscount Daventry, *qv*); one *d* (and one *d* decd); 3rd, 1971, Mrs Juliet Eleanor Hugolyn Whitelocke-Winter, *widow* of Edward Colin Winter and *d* of late Comdr G. C. A. Whitelocke, RN retd, and of Mrs S. H. Whitelocke, Cerrigllwydion Hall, Denbigh. *Educ:* Radley. High Sheriff, Flintshire, 1969. *Recreations:* hunting, shooting, fishing. *Heir: s* Edward Robert Bates, *b* 4 July 1946. *Address:* Gyrn Castle, Llanasa, near Holywell, Clwyd. *T:* Prestatyn 3500. *Club:* Cavalry and Guards.

BATES, Harry Stuart, CSI 1947; *b* 16 March 1893; *s* of late Albert Bates, Congleton, Cheshire; *m* 1920, *d* of late William Hammond Walker, Congleton, Cheshire; two *s* one *d. Educ:* Denstone; St Catharine's Coll., Cambridge (BA). Served in British and Indian Armies 1914-19. Joined Indian Civil Service, 1920: Collector, Settlement Offr and Manager, Balrampur Estate, 1926-42; Comr, 1942-45; Mem., Bd of Revenue, UP, 1945-47; retired, 1949. Employed Colonial Office, 1948-57. *Address:* Rowhurst Cottage, Milford-on-Sea, Hants. *T:* Milford 2906.

BATES, James P. M.; *see* Martin-Bates.

BATES, Maj.-Gen. Sir John; *see* Bates, Maj.-Gen. Sir E. J. H.

BATES, Sir John (David), Kt 1969; CBE 1962; VRD; Australian Consul-General in New York, 1970-73; *b* 1 March 1904; *s* of H. W. Bates, Plymouth, Devon; *m* 1930, Phyllis Helen Muller; one *s. Educ:* Plymouth. Joined sea staff of Orient Line, 1925; transf. to shore staff, in Australia, 1929; RANVR, 1932-57, Comdr; Gen. Manager in Australia of Orient Line, 1954-60; Dep. Chm., P & O Lines of Australia, 1960-67; Chm., Hon. Bd of Australian Nat. Travel Assoc., 1956-67; Chm. Australian Tourist Commn, 1967-69. Federal Pres., Navy League of Australia, 1950-56; Trustee, Art Gallery of NSW, 1962-70; Lay Member, Trade Practices Tribunal, 1968-70. *Recreations:* reading, walking. *Address:* 18 Southern Cross Gardens, 2 Spruson Street, Neutral Bay, NSW 2089, Australia. *Club:* Union (Sydney).

BATES, Sir (John) Dawson, 2nd Bt, *cr* 1937; MC 1943; Area Land Agent for the National Trust; *b* 21 Sept. 1921; *o s* of Sir (Richard) Dawson Bates, 1st Bt, PC, and Muriel (*d* 1972), *d* of late Sir Chas. Cleland, KBE, MVO, LLD; *S* father, 1949; *m* 1953, Mary Murray, *o d* of late Lieut-Col Joseph M. Hoult, Norton Place, Lincoln; two *s* one *d. Educ:* Winchester; Balliol. BA 1949. FRICS. Served War of 1939-45, Major, Rifle Brigade (MC). *Heir: s* Richard Dawson Hoult Bates, *b* 12 May 1956. *Address:* Eaton Hastings Grange, Faringdon, Oxon.

BATES, Sir (Julian) Darrell, Kt 1966; CMG 1956; CVO 1954; *b* 10 Nov. 1913; *y s* of late E. Stuart Bates; *m* 1944, Susan Evelyn June Sinclair; two *s* one *d. Educ:* Sevenoaks Sch.; Keble Coll., Oxford. Entered Colonial Service, Tanganyika Territory, 1936; served King's African Rifles (despatches), 1940-43; seconded Colonial Office, 1944-46; Officer Administering the Government, Seychelles, 1950-51; Deputy Chief Secretary, Somaliland Protectorate, 1951-53; Colonial Sec., Gibraltar, 1953-64, Permanent Sec., 1964-68. *Publications:* A Fly Switch from the Sultan, 1961; The Shell at My Ear, 1961; The Mango and the Palm, 1962; A Longing for Quails, 1964; Susie, 1964; A Gust of Plumes, 1972; The Companion Guide to Devon and Cornwall, 1976; The Abyssinian Difficulty, 1979. *Address:* Mellinpons, St Buryan, Cornwall. *Club:* Travellers'.

BATES, Merrick Stuart B.; *see* Baker-Bates.

BATES, Ralph; *b* Swindon, Wilts, 3 Nov. 1899; *s* of Henry Roy and Mabel Stevens Bates; *m* 1940, Eve Salzman; one *s. Educ:* Swindon and North Wilts. Secondary Sch. After service in 16th Queen's Royal West Surreys, 1917-19, worked in Great Western Railway Factory at Swindon; in Spain, 1930-37; took active part in Republican politics in Spain; began literary career in 1933 as consequence of unemployment; Capt. in the Spanish Loyalist Army and in the International Brigade, Madrid sector, 1936-37; lecture tour in USA 1937-38; one year resident in Mexico, 1938-39; Adjunct Prof. of Literature, New York Univ. 1948-68, now Professor Emeritus of Literature. *Publications:* Sierra, 1933; Lean Men, 1934, Schubert, 1934, The Olive Field, 1936; Rainbow Fish, 1937; The Miraculous Horde, 1939; The Fields of Paradise, 1941; The Undiscoverables, 1942; The Journey to the Sandalwood Forest, 1947; The Dolphin in the Wood, 1949. *Recreations:* small boating, music. *Address:* 37 Washington Square West, New York, NY 10011, USA. *T:* (212) 254-4149.

BATES, Stewart Taverner, QC 1970; a Recorder of the Crown Court, since 1981; *b* 17 Dec. 1926; *s* of John Bates, Greenock; *m* 1950, Anne Patricia, *d* of David West, Pinner; two *s* four *d. Educ:* Univs of Glasgow and St Andrews; Corpus Christi Coll., Oxford. Called to Bar, Middle Temple, 1954, Bencher, 1975; Mem., Bar Council, 1962-66. Mem., Cttee of Management. Inst. of Urology, Univ. of London, 1978-. *Recreations:* theatre, sailing, ski-ing. *Address:* The Grange, Horsington, Templecombe, Somerset BA8 0EF. *T:* Templecombe 70521. *Club:* Garrick.

BATES, William Stanley, CMG 1971; HM Diplomatic Service, retired Ambassador to Korea, 1975-80; *b* 7 Sept. 1920; *m* 1970, Suzanne Elston. *Educ:* Christ's Hospital; Corpus Christi Coll., Cambridge. Asst Principal, Colonial Office, 1948; Principal, 1951; Commonwealth Relations Office, 1956; Canberra, 1956-59; Asst Sec., 1962. British Deputy High Commissioner, Northern Nigeria, 1963-65; Imperial Defence Coll., 1966; Head of Communications Dept, FCO, 1967-70; High Comr in Guyana, 1970-75. *Address:* 38 Onslow Square, SW7 3NS.

BATESON; *see* de Yarburgh-Bateson, family name of Baron Deramore.

BATESON, Andrew James, QC 1971; *b* 29 June 1925; *m* 1954, Janette Mary Poupart (*d* 1970); one *s* three *d. Educ:* Eton. Called to the Bar, Middle Temple, 1951; Bencher, 1977. *Recreations:* shooting, fishing, gardening. *Address:* 10 South Square, Grays Inn, Holborn, WC1; Bracken House, Beechwood Avenue, Weybridge, Surrey. *Club:* Garrick.

BATESON, Air Vice-Marshal Robert Norman, CB 1964; DSO 1943 and Bar, 1944; DFC 1940; idc; jssc; psa; *b* 10 June 1912; *s* of late George Rowland Bateson; *m* 1st, 1942, Elizabeth Lindsay Davidson (*d* 1975); 2nd, 1976, Margaret Graham Craig. *Educ:* Watford Grammar Sch. Joined RAF 1936. Served War of 1939-45. Asst Chief of Air Staff, Operational Requirements, Air Min., 1959-61; Air Officer Comdg No. 12 Group, Fighter Comd. 1961-62; SASO, Fighter Comd, 1963-67. ADC to the Queen, 1958-60. Air Cdre, 1958; actg Air Vice-Marshal, 1959; Air Vice-Marshal, 1960. Dutch Flight Cross, 1943; Order of Dannebrog, 1944. *Recreations:* squash, tennis, sailing, motor sport. *Address:* Cleave Cottage, Weir Quay, Bere Alston, Yelverton, Devon. *T:* Tavistock 840366. *Clubs:* Royal Air Force; Weir Quay Yacht.

BATH, 6th Marquess of, *cr* 1789; **Henry Frederick Thynne,** Bt 1641; Viscount Weymouth and Baron Thynne, 1682; Major Royal Wiltshire Yeomanry; JP; *b* 26 Jan. 1905; *o surv. s* of 5th Marquess, KG, PC, CB and Violet Caroline (*d* 1928), *d* of Sir Charles Mordaunt, 10th Bt; *S* father, 1946; *m* 1st, 1927, Hon. Daphne (marr. diss., 1953; she *m* 2nd, 1953, Major A. W. Fielding, DSO), *er d* of 4th Baron Vivian, DSO; two *s* one *d* (and one *s* decd); 2nd, 1953, Mrs Virginia Penelope Tennant, *d* of late Alan L. R. Parsons; one *d. Educ:* Harrow; Christ Church, Oxford. MP (U) Frome Division, Som., 1931-35. Served War of 1939-45 (wounded). Chm., Football Pools Panel, 1973- (Vice-Chm., 1968-72). Life-long interest in forestry; Longleat has some of the best private woodland in the country. *Heir: s* Viscount Weymouth, *qv.* *Address:* Job's Mill, Warminster, Wilts BA12 8BB. *T:* Warminster 2279; Longleat, Warminster, Wilts. *Club:* White's.

See also D. R. Somerset.

BATH and WELLS, Bishop of, since 1975; **Rt. Rev. John Monier Bickersteth;** Clerk of the Closet to the Queen, 1979; *b* 6 Sept. 1921; *yr s* of late Rev. Canon Edward Monier Bickersteth, OBE; *m* 1955, Rosemary, *yr d* of late Edward and Muriel Cleveland-Stevens, Gaines, Oxted; three *s* one *d. Educ:* Rugby; Christ Church, Oxford; Wells Theol College. MA Oxon 1953. Captain, Buffs and Royal Artillery, 1941-46. Priest, 1951; Curate, St Matthew, Moorfields, Bristol, 1950-54; Vicar, St John's, Hurst Green, Oxted 1954-62; St Stephen's, Chatham, 1962-70; Hon. Canon of Rochester, 1968-70; Bishop Suffragan of Warrington, 1970-75. Chaplain and Sub-Prelate OStJ, 1977. Chairman: Royal Sch. of Church Music, 1977; Bible Reading Fellowship, 1978; Vice Chm., Central Bd of Finance of Church of England 1981. Mem., Marlborough Coll. Council, 1980. *Address:* The Palace, Wells, Somerset. *T:* Wells 72341.

BATH, Archdeacon of; *see* Burgess, Ven. J. E.

BATH, Alan Alfred; Director, Education and Training, Commission of the European Communities, 1973-80; *b* 3 May 1924; *s* of Alfred Edward Bath and Doris Ellen Lawson; *m* 1946, Joy Roselle Thornton (*d* 1979), *d* of George Jeune, St Saviour, Jersey; one *s* two *d. Educ:* Frays Coll., Uxbridge; Queen's Univ., Belfast (BSc Econ). RAF, 1942-46. Asst Lectr in Econs, QUB 1950-53; Admin. Officer, Assoc. of Univs of British Commonwealth, 1953-58; Imperial Coll., Univ. of London, 1958-62 (Develt Sec., 1960-62); Sec., Cttee of Vice-Chancellors and Principals of Univs of UK, 1964-73; Sec., UK Nat. Delego to Council of Europe Cttee for Higher Educn and Research, 1969-73. *Recreations:* music, sailing, gardening. *Address:* 12 Voltaire, Ennerdale Road, Kew Gardens, Surrey TW9 3PQ. *T:* 01-940 6577. *Club:* Athenæum.

BATHER, Elizabeth Constance, OBE 1946; retired as Chief Superintendent Metropolitan (Women) Police, (1946-60); *b* 11 Oct. 1904; *d* of late Rev. Arthur George Bather, MA, and Lilian Dundas Firth, Winchester. *Educ:* St Swithuns Sch., Winchester. Mem. Hampshire County Council, 1937-46 Served in WAAF, 1939-45; Group Officer, 1944-45. JP Winchester, 1937-46;

Councillor, Hartley Witney and Hart DCs, 1967-76. *Address:* Laburnham Cottage, Odiham, Hants.

BATHO, Edith Clara, MA, DLit (London); Principal, Royal Holloway College, University of London, 1945-62, retired; *b* 21 Sept. 1895; 3rd *d* of late William John Batho and Ellen Clara Hooton. *Educ:* Highbury Hill High Sch.; University Coll., London. BA (Hons English), 1915, MA 1920, DLit 1935; war work, 1916-18; on staff of Roedean Sch., 1918-19; Downe House Sch., 1919-21; Quain Student and Asst in English at University Coll., London, 1921; Fellow of University Coll., London, 1934; Reader in English Literature, University Coll., London, 1935-45. Visiting Prof., Univ. of Wisconsin, 1963. An active mem. British Fedn of Univ. Women. Hon. D de l'U Poitiers, 1962. *Publications:* The Ettrick Shepherd, 1927 (reprinted 1969); The Later Wordsworth, 1934 (reprinted, 1964); The Poet and the Past (Warton Lecture of the British Acad.), 1937; The Victorians and After (with Bonamy Dobrée), 1938; Chronicles of Scotland by Hector Boece, tr. Bellenden (ed for STS), Vol. I with R. W. Chambers, 1936, Vol. II with H. W. Husbands, 1941; A Wordsworth Selection, 1962; other articles and reviews. *Recreations:* travelling, languages, needlework. *Address:* 130 Wood Street, Barnet, Herts. *Clubs:* New Arts Theatre, English-Speaking Union.

BATHO, Sir Maurice Benjamin, 2nd Bt, *cr* 1928; Chairman and Managing Director, Ridgley (Huntingdon) Ltd and associated companies; *b* 14 Jan. 1910; *o surv. s* of Sir Charles Albert Batho, 1st Bt, and Bessie (*d* 1961), 4th *d* of Benjamin Parker, Oulton Broad, Suffolk; *S* father, 1938; *m* 1934, Antoinette, *o d* of Baron d'Udekem d'Acoz, Ghent; two *s* two *d. Educ:* Uppingham; Belgium. Served War of 1939-45: Lt-Col, KRRC. Jt Sub-Dir, Syrian Wheat Collection Scheme of Spears Mission, 1943; Adviser on Cereals Collection, Min. of Finance of Imp. Iranian Govt, 1944; Dep. Dir, Rice Procurement, Bengal, 1945; Managing Dir, Reed Paper & Board Sales Ltd, 1959, resigned 1965; formerly Director: Reed Paper & Board (UK) Ltd; London Paper Mills Co. Ltd; Empire Paper Mills Ltd; Reed Board Mills (Colthorp) Ltd; Reed Brookgate Ltd. *Recreation:* golf. *Heir:* s Peter Ghislain Batho [*b* 9 Dec. 1939; *m* 1966, Lucille Mary, *d* of Wilfrid F. Williamson; three *s*]. *Address:* Carlton Hall, Saxmundham, Suffolk. *T:* 2505. *Clubs:* Naval and Military, St Stephen's Constitutional.

BATHO, Walter James Scott; Under Secretary, Department of the Environment, since 1979; *b* 13 Nov. 1925; *er s* of Walter Scott Batho and Isabella Laidlaw Batho (*née* Common); *m* 1951, Barbara Kingsford; two *s* two *d. Educ:* Epsom County Grammar Sch.; Univ. of Edinburgh (MA Eng. Lit. and Lang.). Served War, RNVR, 1943-46. Air Min., 1950-53; WO, 1953-63 (Private Sec. to Perm. Under Sec. of State, 1956-57); MPBW, 1963-70; DoE, 1970-. *Recreations:* singing, reading, gardening. *Address:* Bushpease, Grays Lane, Ashtead, Surrey KT21 1BU. *T:* Ashtead 73471. *Club:* Naval.

BATHURST, family name of **Earl Bathurst** and **Viscount Bledisloe.**

BATHURST, 8th Earl, *cr* 1772; **Henry Allen John Bathurst,** DL; Baron Bathurst of Battlesden, Bedfordshire, 1712; Baron Apsley of Apsley, Sussex, 1771; Earl Bathurst of Bathurst, Sussex, 1772; Capt. Royal Gloucestershire Hussars (TA); TARO, 1959; *b* 1 May 1927; *s* of late Lord Apsley, DSO, MC, MP (killed on active service, 1942), and late Lady Apsley, CBE; *g s* of 7th Earl; *S* grandfather, 1943; *m* 1st 1959, Judith Mary (marr. diss. 1977), *d* of Mr and Mrs A. C. Nelson, Springfield House, Foulridge, Lancs; two *s* one *d* ; 2nd, 1978, Gloria, *widow* of David Rutherston and *o d* of Harold Edward Clarry, Vancouver, BC. *Educ:* Ridley Coll., Canada; Eton; Christ Church, Oxford, 1948-49. Late Lieut 10th Royal Hussars (PWO). Capt., Royal Glos. Hussars, TA, 1949-57. Hon. Sec. Agricultural Cttee (Conservative), House of Lords, 1957; a Lord-in-Waiting, 1957-61; Joint Parliamentary Under-Sec. of State, Home Office, 1961-July 1962. Governor, Royal Agricultural Coll.; Pres. Glos Branch CPRE. DL County of Gloucester, 1960. Chancellor, Primrose League, 1959-61. Member: CLA Council, 1965 (Chm., Glos Branch of CLA, 1968-71); Timber Growers' Organisation (TGO) Council, 1966; Pres., Royal Forestry Soc., 1976-78. *Heir:* s Lord Apsley, qv. *Address:* Cirencester Park, Cirencester, Glos GL7 2BT. *T:* Cirencester 3412. *Club:* White's.

BATHURST (NSW), Bishop of, since 1981; **Rt. Rev. Howell Arthur John Witt;** *b* 12 July 1920; *s* of Thomas Leyshon Witt and Harriet Jane Witt; *m* 1949, Gertrude Doreen Edwards; three *s* two *d. Educ:* Newport Sec. Sch.; Leeds Univ.; Coll. of the Resurrection, Mirfield. Deacon 1944; Priest 1945. Asst Curate of: Usk, Mon, 1944-47; St George's, Camberwell, 1948-49; Chaplain, Woomera, S Australia, 1949-54; Rector, St Mary Magdalene's, Adelaide, 1954-57; Priest in charge of Elizabeth, 1957-65; Missioner of St Peter's Coll. Mission, 1954-65; Bishop of North-West Australia, 1965-81. *Publication:* Bush Bishop (autobiography), 1980. *Recreations:* Rugby football coaching; script writing. *Address:* Bishopscourt, Bathurst, NSW 2795, Australia. *Club:* Public Schools (Adelaide).

BATHURST, (NSW), Bishop of, (RC), since 1963; **Rt. Rev. Albert Reuben Edward Thomas;** *b* Farnborough, Hants, 26 Oct. 1908; *s* of Albert Charles Thomas and Esperie Loreto Clarke. *Educ:* St Joseph's College, Hunter's Hill; St Columba's Coll., St Patrick's Coll., Manly. Diploma of Social Studies, Sydney Univ., 1944. Ordained, 1931. Asst Suburban Parishes, 1931-38; Diocesan Dir, Pontifical Missions, 1938-63, National Dir, 1944-70. Founder of Catholic Welfare Bureau, 1941. Initiated Australian National Pilgrimage, 1950-63; Hon. Chaplain of House of Lourdes, 1960; Foundation Chm. of St Vincent's Hospital Advisory Board, 1955; Chm. of Unity Movement for Christian Christmas, 1956-63. *Publication:* contrib. to Australian Encyclopaedia, on Catholic Missions and Welfare, 1958. *Address:* Bishop's House, Bathurst, NSW 2795, Australia.

BATHURST, Sir Frederick Peter Methuen Hervey-, 6th Bt, *cr* 1818; *b* 26 Jan. 1903; *s* of Sir Frederick Edward William Hervey-Bathurst, 5th Bt, DSO and Hon. Moira O'Brien, 2nd *d* of 14th Baron Inchiquin; *S* father 1956; *m* 1st, 1933, Maureen (marr. diss. 1956), *d* of Charles Gordon, Boveridge Park, Salisbury; one *s* one *d* ; 2nd, 1958, Mrs Cornelia Shepard Riker, *widow* of Dr John Lawrence Riker, Rumson, NJ, USA. *Educ:* Eton. Served War of 1939-45, Capt. Grenadier Guards. *Recreations:* sailing, riding, ski-ing, flying. *Heir:* s Frederick John Charles Gordon Hervey-Bathurst [*b* 23 April 1934; *m* 1957, Caroline Myrtle, *d* of Lieut-Col Sir William Starkey, 2nd Bt, and late Irene Myrtle Francklin; one *s* two *d*]. *Address:* Bellevue Avenue, Rumson, New Jersey 07760, USA. *T:* 842-0791. *Clubs:* Cavalry and Guards, Royal Ocean Racing.

BATHURST, Joan Caroline; *see* Petrie, J. C.

BATHURST, Maurice Edward, CMG 1953; CBE 1947; QC 1964; Judge, Arbitral Tribunal and Mixed Commission for the Agreement on German External Debts, since 1977; *b* 2 Dec. 1913; *o s* of late Edward John James Bathurst and Annie Mary Bathurst; *m* 1941, Dorothy (marr. diss. 1963), *d* of late W. S. Stevens, LDS, RCS; one *s* ; *m* 1968, Joan Caroline Petrie, *qv. Educ:* Haberdashers' Aske's, Hatcham; King's Coll., London; Gonville and Caius Coll., Cambridge; Columbia Univ. LLB, First Class Hons. (London), 1937; University Law Schol. (London), 1937; Post-Grad. Research Studentship (London), 1938; Bartle Frere Exhibitioner (Camb.), 1939; Tutorial Fellow (Chicago), 1939; Special Fellow (Columbia), 1940; LLM (Columbia), 1941; Hon. DCL (Sacred Heart, NB), 1946; PhD (Camb.), 1949; LLD (London), 1966. Solicitor of Supreme Court, 1938-56. Called to Bar, Gray's Inn, 1957; Master of the Bench, 1970; Master of the Library, 1978-81. Legal Adviser, British Information Services, USA, 1941-43; Legal Adviser, British Embassy, Washington, 1943-46 (First Sec., 1944; Counsellor, 1946); Legal Member, UK Delegation to United Nations, 1946-48; UK Representative, Legal Advisory Cttee, Atomic Energy Commission, 1946-48; Legal Adviser to British Chm., Bipartite Control Office, Frankfurt, 1949; Dep. Legal Adviser, CCG, 1949-51; Legal Adviser, UK High Commn, Germany, 1951-55; Judge, Supreme Court, British Zone, Germany, 1953-55; Legal Adviser, British Embassy, Bonn, 1955-57; British Judge, Arbitral Commn, Germany, 1968-69. Mem. UK Delegations to UNRRA; United Nations San Francisco Conference; Bermuda Civil Aviation Conference; PICAO; Washington Financial Talks; UN Gen. Assembly; FAO; WHO; Internat. Tin Study Group; UK-US Double Taxation Treaty Negotiations; London Nine-Power Conf.; Paris Conf. on W Eur. Union; NATO Status of Forces Conf., Bonn. Internat. Vice-Pres. UN League of Lawyers; Vice-Chm. Council, Brit. Inst. of International and Comparative Law; a Pres. of Arbitral Tribunals, Internat. Telecommunications Satellite Orgn, 1974-78. Member: Panel of Arbitrators, Internat. Centre for Settlement of Investment Disputes; UK Cttee, UNICEF; Ct of Assistants, Haberdashers' Co. (Fourth Warden, 1973-74; Second Warden, 1978-79; First Warden, 1979-80; Master, 1980-81); Editorial Cttee, British Yearbook of International Law; *ad eundem,* Inner Temple; Gen. Council of the Bar, 1970-71; Senate of Inns of Court, 1971-73; Council of Legal Educn, 1971-79; Senate of the Inns of Court and the Bar, 1974-77. Hon. Vis. Prof. in Internat. Law, King's Coll., London, 1967-77; Hon. Fellow, King's Coll., London. Chm. Governors, Haberdashers' Aske's Hatcham Schools, 1972-80. Pres., British Insurance Law Assoc., 1971-75. Freeman of the City of London and of the City of Bathurst, NB. *Publications:* Germany and the North Atlantic Community: A Legal Survey (with J. L. Simpson), 1956; (ed, jtly) Legal Problems of an Enlarged European Community, 1972; notes and articles in legal jls, etc., British and American. *Recreation:* theatre. *Address:* Airlie, The Highlands, East Horsley, Surrey. *T:* East Horsley 3269. *Club:* Garrick.

BATHURST NORMAN, George Alfred; Metropolitan Stipendiary Magistrate, since 1981; *b* 15 Jan. 1939; *s* of Charles Phipps Bathurst Norman and Hon. Doreen Albinia de Burgh Norman (*née* Gibbs); *m* 1973, Susan Elizabeth Ball; one *s* one *d. Educ:* Harrow Sch.; Magdalen Coll., Oxford (BA). Called to the Bar, Inner Temple, 1961; SE Circuit, 1962; Dep. Circuit Judge, 1975. Mem., Home Office Working Party on Coroners Rules, 1976-81. Mem., Gen. Council of the Bar, 1968-70. *Recreations:* wildlife, ornithology, cricket, travel. *Address:* Camberwell Green Magistrates' Court, D'Eynsford Road, SE5 7UP. *Club:* Anglo-Belgian.

BATSFORD, Sir Brian (Caldwell Cook), Kt 1974; *b* 18 Dec. 1910; *s* of late Arthur Caldwell Cook, Gerrards Cross, Bucks; assumed mother's maiden name of Batsford by Deed Poll 1946; *m* 1945, Joan (Wendy), *o d* of late Norman Cunliffe, DSc, of Oxford; two *d. Educ:* Repton Sch. Joined B. T. Batsford Ltd, Booksellers and Publishers, 1928; Chairman, 1952-74; President, 1974-77. Lectured in Canada under auspices Canadian National Council of Education, 1935, 1937; lectured in Scandinavia and Baltic States under auspices British Council, 1940. Hon. Sec. Empire Youth Sunday Cttee, 1938; Chm. Youth City Cttee of Enquiry, 1939. RAF, 1941-46. Contested Chelmsford Div. of Essex for Nat. Govt, 1945; MP (C) Ealing South, 1958-Feb. 1974; PPS to Minister of Works, 1959-60; Asst Govt Whip, 1962-64; Opposition Deputy Chief Whip, 1964-67. Chairman: Adv. Cttee on Works of Art in House of Commons, 1970; House of Commons Library Cttee, 1970-74.

Alderman, GLC, and Parly Rep. of GLC Majority Party, 1967-70; co-opted Mem., GLC Arts and Recreation Cttee, 1970-72. Pres., London Appreciation Soc., 1955. FRSA 1955, Mem. Council, 1967, Treasurer, 1971-73; Chm., RSA, 1973-75, Vice-Pres., 1975; FSIAD 1971. Mem., Post Office Stamp Adv. Cttee, 1967-80. Pres., Old Reptonian Soc., 1973; Mem., Governing Body, Repton Sch., 1973. Vice-Pres., Questors' Theatre, Ealing, 1978; Chm., Rye Conservation Soc., 1978. *Recreations:* painting, gardening. *Address:* Lamb House, Rye, Sussex. *T:* Rye 3763. *Club:* Pratt's.

BATT, Reginald Joseph Alexander; barrister; a Recorder of the Crown Court, since 1982; *b* 22 July 1920; *o s* of late Benjamin and Alice Harriett Batt; *m* 1951, Mary Margaret (*née* Canning), actress; one *d*. *Educ:* local authority schs; privately. Called to the Bar, Inner Temple, 1952. *Publications:* articles on law of real property and on landlord and tenant. *Recreations:* walking, tennis, antiques, music. *Address:* 6 King's Bench Walk, Temple, EC4Y 7DR. *T:* 01-583 0410.

BATTEN, Edith Mary, OBE 1948; Principal, William Temple College, 1950-66; *b* 1905, British. *Educ:* High Sch. for Girls, Southport; Liverpool Univ.; London School of Economics; St Anne's Coll., Oxford. BSc Liverpool; BSc (Econ) London; MA Oxon. Asst Industrial Personnel Officer; Sec. North West Ham Branch, Invalid Children's Aid Association; Sub-Warden, St Helen's Settlement, E15; Warden, Birmingham Settlement, 1933-38; JP City of Birmingham, 1937-38; Organising Sec. British Assoc. of Residential Settlements, 1938-42; Mem. Factory and Welfare Advisory Board to Min. of Labour, 1940-42; Min. of Labour and National Service, 1942-47. Res. Officer, Bd for Social Responsibility of Church Assembly, 1967-70. *Recreations:* reading, listening to music. *Address:* Guillard's Oak House, Midhurst, West Sussex. *Club:* Royal Commonwealth Society.

BATTEN, Jean Gardner, CBE 1936; *b* 1909; *d* of Capt. F. H. Batten, Dental Surg., Auckland, New Zealand. *Educ:* Cleveland House Coll., Auckland, NZ. Gained Private pilot's licence at London Aeroplane Club, 1930; commercial pilot's licence London, 1932; solo flight England-Australia (women's record) May 1934; solo flight Australia-England (first woman to complete return flight), April 1935; solo flight England-Argentina (first woman to make solo flight across South Atlantic Ocean to South America), Nov. 1935; world records established: England-Brazil 61 hrs 15 mins; fastest crossing of South Atlantic Ocean by air 13 hrs 15 mins; solo flight England-New Zealand 11 days 45 mins, Oct. 1936; first direct flight from England to Auckland, NZ; solo record England-Australia 5 days 21 hrs; record flight across Tasman Sea, Australia-New Zealand, 9hrs 29 mins; record solo flight Australia-England, 5 days 18 hrs 15 mins, Oct. 1937. Jean Batten Archive estbd RAF Museum, Hendon, 1972; Museum issued 13,000 Jean Batten Commemorative Covers which were flown over route to New Zealand by British Airways to mark 40th anniversary of first direct flight, 1976; 1981 Airliner of Britannia Airways named 'Jean Batten'. Invited to visit Auckland, NZ by Mus. of Transport and Technology to open new Pavilion, 1977. Officer of the Order of the Southern Cross, Brazil; Chevalier of the Legion of Honour, France; awarded Britannia Trophy, Royal Aero Club, 1935 and 1936; Harmon Trophy awarded by international vote, 1935, 1936 and 1937; Johnston Memorial Air Navigation Trophy, 1935; Challenge Trophy (USA), Women's International Association of Aeronautics, 1934, 1935 and 1936; Segrave Trophy, 1936; Coupe de Sibour, 1937; gold medals: Fédération Aéronautique Internationale; Royal Aero Club, Aero Club de France, Belgian Royal Aero Club, Académie des Sports, Royal Swedish Aero Club, Ligue International des Aviateurs, Aero Club of Argentine, Royal Danish Aeronautical Society, Royal Norwegian Aero Club, Aero Club of Finland. City of Paris Medal, 1971. Liveryman, Guild of Air Pilots and Air Navigators, 1978. Freeman, City of London, 1978. *Publication:* My Life, 1938, repr. as Alone in the Sky, 1979. *Recreations:* walking, swimming, music. *Address:* c/o Barclays Bank Ltd, 25 Charing Cross Road, WC2H 0HZ.

BATTEN, John Charles, MD, FRCP; Physician to the Queen, since 1974 (Physician to HM Royal Household, 1970-74), and Head of HM Medical Household, since 1982; Physician: Brompton Hospital, since 1959; King Edward VII Hospital for Officers, since 1968; King Edward VII Hospital, Midhurst, since 1969; Hon. Physician to: St Dunstan's, since 1960; St George's Hospital, since 1980; Consultant, King Edward VII Convalescent Home, IoW, since 1975; Chief Medical Referee, Confederation Life Assoc. of Canada, since 1974 (Deputy Chief Medical Referee, 1958-74); *b* 11 March 1924; *s* of late Raymond Wallis Batten, JP and of Gladys (*née* Charles); *m* 1950, Anne Mary Margaret, *d* of late John Oriel, CBE, MC; one *s* two *d* (and one *d* decd). *Educ:* Mill Hill School; St Bartholomew's Medical School. MB, BS 1946 London Univ.; MRCP 1950; MD London 1951; FRCP 1964. Junior appts, St George's Hosp. and Brompton Hosp., 1946-58. Surgeon Captain, Royal Horse Guards, 1947-49. Physician, St George's Hospital, 1958-79. Dorothy Temple Cross Research Fellow, Cornell Univ. Medical Coll., New York, 1954-55. Examiner in Medicine, London Univ., 1968; Marc Daniels Lectr, RCP, 1969. Member: Board of Governors, Brompton Hosp., 1966-69; St George's Hosp. Medical School Council, 1969; Management Cttee, King Edward VII Hosp. Fund; Council, R.SocMed, 1970; Royal College of Physicians: Censor, 1977-78; Senior Censor, 1980-81; Vice-Pres., 1980-81. *Publications:* contributions to medical books and journals. *Recreations:* music and sailing. *Address:* 7 Lion Gate Gardens, Richmond, Surrey. *T:* 01-940 3282.

BATTEN, Mark Wilfrid, RBA 1962; FRBS 1952 (ARBS 1950); Sculptor, direct carver in stone; *s* of Edward Batten; *m* 1933, Elsie May Owston Thorneloe (*d* 1961); one *d*. *Educ:* Chelsea Sch. of Art. Commenced to experiment individually with stone carving, 1927; exhibited only drawings and paintings until 1934; combined experiment in sculpture with learning craft of stone carving mainly in granite mason's yards in Cornwall; first exhibited sculpture, 1936; FRSA 1936. Collaborated with Eric Gill, 1939; first exhibited sculpture at Royal Academy, 1939. War service in Life Guards, 1940-45. Exhibited Paris Salon, 1949, and thereafter frequently at RA and many sculpture exhibitions in Paris, London and provincial cities. Many commissions for stone sculptures on public buildings; works in museums and art galleries. President, RBS 1956-61; Council, 1953-; Council, RBA, 1964, 1982. Société des Artistes Français: Gold Medal for Sculpture, 1977 (Silver Medal, 1952); Associate, 1970. Hon. Mem. National Sculpture Soc. of the USA, 1956; Syracuse Univ., USA, estab. Mark Batten Manuscripts Collection, 1965, also Wichita State Univ., 1971. *Publications:* Stone Sculpture by Direct Carving, 1957; Direct Carving in Stone, 1966; articles in art magazines. *Recreations:* country life, travel, contemplation of other men's sculptures. *Address:* Christian's River Studio, Dallington, Heathfield, East Sussex TN21 9NX. *Club:* Chelsea Arts.

BATTERBURY, Paul Tracy Shepherd, TD 1972 (Bar 1978); barrister-at-law; a Recorder of the Crown Court, since 1979; *b* 25 Jan. 1934; only *s* of Hugh Basil John Batterbury and Inez Batterbury; *m* 1962, Sheila Margaret, *d* of John Watson; one *s* one *d*. *Educ:* St Olave's Grammar Sch., Southwark; Univ. of Bristol (LLB). Served RAF, 1952-55. Called to Bar, Inner Temple, 1959; practising barrister, 1959-. TA (Royal Artillery): Major, 1975. Councillor: Chislehurst and Sidcup UDC, 1960-62; London Borough of Greenwich, 1968-71 (Chm., Housing Cttee, 1970-71). *Recreations :* TA, photography, walking, caravanning. *Address:* 3 Hare Court, Temple, EC4Y 7BJ. *T:* 01-353 3344. *Club:* Civil Service.

BATTERSBY, Prof. Alan Rushton, MSc, PhD, DSc, ScD; FRS 1966; Professor of Organic Chemistry, University of Cambridge, since 1969; Fellow of St Catharine's College, Cambridge; Director, FBC Ltd; *b* 4 March 1925; *s* of William and Hilda Battersby; *m* 1949, Margaret Ruth, *d* of Thomas and Annie Hart, Whaley Bridge, Cheshire; two *s*. *Educ:* Grammar Sch., Leigh; Univ. of Manchester (Mercer and Woodiwis Schol.); Univ. of St Andrews. MSc Manchester; PhD St Andrews; DSc Bristol; ScD Cantab. Asst Lectr in Chemistry, Univ. of St Andrews, 1948-53; Commonwealth Fund Fellow at Rockefeller Inst., NY, 1950-51 and at Univ. of Illinois, 1951-52; Lectr in Chemistry, Univ. of Bristol, 1954-62; Prof. of Organic Chemistry, Univ. of Liverpool, 1962-69. Mem. Council, Royal Soc., 1973-75. Mem. Deutsche Akademie der Naturforscher Leopoldina, 1967. Pres., Bürgenstock Conf., 1976. Mem. Exec. Council, Ciba Foundn, 1977-. Lectures: Treat Johnson, Yale, 1969; Pacific Coast, USA, 1971; Karl Folkers, Wisconsin, 1972; N-E Coast, USA, 1974; Andrews, NSW, 1975; Middle Rhine, 1976; Tishler, Harvard, 1978; August Wilhelm von Hoffmann, Ges. Deutscher Chem., 1979; Pedler, Chem. Soc., 1980-81; Rennebohm, Wisconsin, 1981; Kharasch, Chicago, 1982; Visiting Professor: Cornell Univ., 1969; Virginia Univ., 1971; Tohoku Univ., Japan, 1974; ANU, 1975; Technion, Israel, 1977; Univ. of Canterbury, NZ, 1980. Tilden Medal and Lectr, Chem. Soc., 1963; Hügo Müller Medal and Lectr, Chem. Soc., 1972; Paul Karrer Medal and Lectr, Univ. Zürich, 1977; Corday-Morgan Medal, Chem. Soc., 1959; Flintoff Medal, Chem. Soc., 1975; Davy Medal, Royal Soc., 1977; Chem. Soc. Award in Natural Product Chemistry, 1978. Hon. LLD St Andrews, 1977; Hon. DSc Rockefeller Univ., USA, 1977. *Publications:* papers in chemical jls, particularly Jl Chem. Soc. *Recreations:* music, camping, sailing and gardening. *Address:* University Chemical Laboratory, Lensfield Road, Cambridge CB2 1EW. *T:* Cambridge 66499.

BATTERSBY, Robert Christopher, MBE 1971; Member (C) Humberside, European Parliament, since 1979; *b* 14 Dec. 1924; *s* of late Major Robert Luther Battersby, MM, RFA, late Indian Army, and Dorothea Gladys (*née* Middleton); *m* 1st, 1949, June Scriven (marr. diss.); one *d* ; 2nd, 1955, Marjorie Bispham; two *s* one *d*. *Educ:* Firth Park Grammar Sch., Sheffield; Edinburgh Univ. (Gen. Sciences); Fitzwilliam House, Cambridge; Sorbonne; Toulouse Univ. BA Cantab (Hons Russian and Modern Greek) 1950; Cert. of Educn 1952; MA Cantab 1954; Cert. de Langue française, Toulouse, 1953; FIL 1958. Served Royal Artillery (Field) and Intelligence Corps, 1942-47 (Italian Campaign, Greece and Crete 1944, Central and Western Macedonia 1945-47); TA to 1952; Lieut RARO. With Dowsett Gp of shipbuilding and civil engrg cos on major distant water trawler and pre-stressed concrete plant export contracts, 1953-63; Manager, Eastern Trade Dept, Glacier Metal Co. Ltd, 1963-66; Sales Dir, Associated Engrg Export Services Ltd, 1966-71; Sales Dir, GKN Contractors Ltd, 1971-73. Responsible for negotiating and installing USSR, Polish, Czechoslovak and Romanian plain bearing industries, Polish diesel engine component industry, and several other metallurgical and machining plants in E Europe; Export, Financial and Commercial Adviser to various UK and USA cos. Mem. CBI and Soc. of British Engrs delegns to China, Poland, Yugoslavia and Singapore. Mem. Exec. Council, Russo-British Chamber of Commerce, and of London Chamber of Commerce Russian and Polish sections, 1968-73; Adviser to E European Trade Council, 1969-71. Principal Administrator: Credit and Investments Directorate-Gen., EEC Commn, Luxembourg, 1973-75; Agriculture Directorate-Gen., 1975-76; Fisheries Directorate-Gen., Brussels, 1976-79; Mem., first EEC Vice-Presidential delegn to Poland, 1977; Mem., European Parly Agriculture and Budgetary Control Cttees, 1979; Chm., Fisheries Working Gp, European

Parlt, 1979-; Vice-Pres., Eur. Parlt Delegn to China, 1981. Vice Pres., Yorkshire and Humberside Develt Assoc., 1980-. Occasional lectr at Farnham Castle on East/West trade, and in Poland and USSR on automotive component manufg technology; broadcaster. Member: RIIA; Royal Belgian Inst. for Foreign Affairs; Anglo-Hellenic Soc.; Belgian section, E-SU; British Cons. Assoc., Brussels; European Democrat Forum; Cons. Foreign Affairs Forum; European Atlantic Gp. Silver Medal for European Merit, Luxembourg, 1981. FBIM 1982. *Publications:* works in English and Russian on distant water trawler operation; articles on fishing technology, shipbuilding and East/West trade; translations from Greek, Russian and other languages. *Recreations:* politics, European and Oriental languages, history, opera, music, rowing, travel. *Address:* West Cross, Rockshaw Road, Merstham, Surrey RH1 3BZ. *T:* Merstham 3783; 203 rue Belliard, Brussels 1040, Belgium. *Club:* Carlton.

BATTISCOMBE, Christopher Charles Richard; HM Diplomatic Service; Commercial Counsellor, Cairo, since 1981; *b* 27 April 1940; *s* of Lt-Col Christopher Robert Battiscombe and Karin Sigrid (*née* Timberg); *m* 1972, Brigid Melita Theresa Lunn; one *s* one *d. Educ:* Wellington Coll.; New Coll., Oxford (BA Greats). Entered FO, 1963; ME Centre for Arabic Studies, Shemlan, Lebanon, 1963-65; Third/Second Sec., Kuwait, 1965-68; FCO, 1968-71; First Secretary: UK Delegn, OECD, Paris, 1971-74; UK Mission to UN, New York, 1974-78; Asst Head, Eastern European and Soviet Dept, FCO, 1978-80. *Recreations:* golf, skiing, tennis. *Address:* c/o Foreign and Commonwealth Office, SW1; 8 Gayton Road, NW3. *T:* 01-794 8778. *Club:* Moor Park Golf (Rickmansworth, Herts).

BATTISCOMBE, Mrs (Esther) Georgina, BA; FRSL 1964; author; *b* 21 Nov. 1905; *d* of late George Harwood, MP, Master Cotton Spinner, Bolton, Lancs, and Ellen Hopkinson, *d* of Sir Alfred Hopkinson, KC, MP, First Vice-Chancellor of Manchester Univ.; *m* 1932, Lt-Col Christopher Francis Battiscombe, OBE, FSA (*d* 1964), Grenadier Guards; one *d. Educ:* St Michael's Sch., Oxford; Lady Margaret Hall, Oxford. *Publications:* Charlotte Mary Yonge, 1943; Two on Safari, 1946; English Picnics, 1949; Mrs Gladstone, 1956; John Keble (James Tait Black Memorial Prize for best biography of year), 1963; Christina Rossetti (Writers and their Work), 1965; ed, with M. Laski, A Chaplet for Charlotte Yonge, 1965; Queen Alexandra, 1969; Shaftesbury, 1974; Reluctant Pioneer: The Life of Elizabeth Wordsworth, 1978; Christina Rossetti, 1981. *Recreations:* walking, looking at churches. *Address:* 3 Queen's Acre, King's Road, Windsor, Berks. *T:* Windsor 60460.

BATTISHILL, Anthony Michael William; Under Secretary, Inland Revenue, since 1982; *b* 5 July 1937; *s* of William George Battishill and Kathleen Rose Bishop; *m* 1961, Heather Frances Lawes; one *d. Educ:* Taunton Sch.; Hele's Sch., Exeter; London Sch. of Economics. BSc (Econs). 2nd Lieut, RAEC, 1958-60. Inland Revenue, 1960-63; HM Treasury, 1963-65; Inland Revenue, 1965-76, Asst Sec., 1970; Central Policy Review Staff, 1976-77; Principal Private Sec. to Chancellor of the Exchequer, HM Treasury, 1977-80; Under Sec., HM Treasury, 1980-82. *Recreations:* gardening, walking. *Address:* 4 Highfield Close, West Byfleet, Weybridge, Surrey KT14 6QR. *T:* Byfleet 40725.

BATTY, Peter Wright; television and film producer, director and writer; Chief Executive, Peter Batty Productions, since 1970; *b* 18 June 1931; *s* of Ernest Faulkner Batty and late Gladys Victoria Wright; *m* 1959, Anne Elizabeth Stringer; two *s* one *d. Educ:* Bede Grammar Sch., Sunderland; Queen's Coll., Oxford. Feature-writer, Financial Times, 1954-56; freelance journalist, 1956-58; Producer, BBC TV, 1958-64: mem. original Tonight team, other prodns incl. The Quiet Revolution, The Big Freeze, The Katanga Affair, Sons of the Navvy Man; Editor, Tonight, 1963-64; Exec. Producer and Associate Head of Factual Programming, ATV, 1964-68: prodns incl. The Fall and Rise of the House of Krupp (Grand Prix for Documentary, Venice Film Fest., 1965; Silver Dove, Leipzig Film Fest., 1965), The Road to Suez, The Suez Affair, Vietnam Fly-in, Battle for the Desert; freelance work for BBC TV and ITV, 1968-. Recent progs dir., prod and scripted incl. The Plutocrats, The Aristocrats, Battle for Cassino, Battle for the Bulge, Birth of the Bomb, Farouk: last of the Pharaohs, Operation Barbarossa, Superspy, Sunderland's Pride and Passion, A Rothschild and his Red Gold, Search for the Super, Spy Extraordinary, Story of Wine, World of Television, The Rise and Rise of Laura Ashley, The Gospel According to St Michael, Battle for Warsaw, Battle for Dien Bien Phu, Nuclear Nightmares and A Turn Up in a Million; contrib. World At War series. *Publication:* The House of Krupp, 1966. *Recreations:* walking, reading, listening to music. *Address:* Claremont House, Renfrew Road, Kingston, Surrey. *T:* 01-942 6304. *Club:* White Elephant.

BATTY, Mrs Ronald; *see* Foyle, C. A. L.

BATTY, Sir William (Bradshaw), Kt 1973; TD 1946; Chairman, Ford Motor Co. Ltd, 1972-75, retired (Managing Director, 1968-73); *b* 15 May 1913; *s* of Rowland and Nellie Batty; *m* 1946, Jean Ella Brice; one *s* one *d* (and one *s* decd). *Educ:* Hulme Grammar Sch., Manchester. Served War of 1939-45, RASC (Lt-Col). Apprentice toolmaker, Ford Motor Co. Ltd, Trafford Park, Manchester, 1930; Co. trainee, 1933; Press liaison, Advertising Dept, 1936; Service Dept, 1937; Tractor Sales Dept, 1945; Asst Man., Tractor Dept, 1948; Man., Tractor and Implement Product Planning, 1953; Man., Tractor Div., 1955; Gen. Man., Tractor Gp, 1961; Dir, Tractor Gp, 1963; Dir, Car and Truck Gp, 1964; Exec. Dir, 1963-75. Chairman: Ford Motor Credit

Co. Ltd, 1968 (Dir, 1963-); Automotive Finance Ltd, 1970-75; Director: Henry Ford & Son Ltd, Cork, 1965-75; Ford Lusitana SARL, Portugal, 1973-75. Mem., Engineering Industries Council, 1975-76. Pres., SMMT, 1975-76. Hon. LLD Manchester, 1976. FBIM. *Recreations:* golf, sailing, gardening. *Address:* Glenhaven Cottage, Riverside Road West, Newton Ferrers, South Devon. *Club:* Royal Western Yacht.

BATTYE, Maj.-Gen. (Retd) Stuart Hedley Molesworth, CB 1960; *b* 21 June 1907; *s* of late Lieut-Col W. R. Battye, DSO, MS, LRCP, Chev. de Légion d'Honneur, CStJ, and late M. St G. Molesworth; *m* 1940, Evelyn Désirée, *d* of late Capt. G. B. Hartford, DSO and bar, RN; one *s* two *d. Educ:* Marlborough Coll.; RMA, Woolwich; Cambridge Univ. (MA). Commissioned 2nd Lieut, RE, 1927; served with Bengal Sappers and Miners, India, 1930-44 (NW Frontier Campaign, 1930-31); Iraq, 1941-42; India, 1942-44; 21 Army Group, BLA, 1945-47; MELF, 1952-55; War Office, 1955; Dir of Movements, the War Office, 1958-61; Dir, Council for Small Industries in Rural Areas (formerly Rural Industries Bureau), 1963-73. FRSA 1963. *Publications:* contrib. to Blackwood's and RE Journal. *Recreations:* fishing, painting. *Address:* Sunninghill, Ascot, Berks. *Club:* Army and Navy.

See also Baron Hankey.

BAUDOUX, Most Rev. Maurice, STD, PhD, DèsL; *b* Belgium, 1902. *Educ:* Prud'homme convent, Saskatchewan; St Boniface College, Manitoba; St Joseph's Seminary, Alberta; Grand Seminary, Quebec. Priest, 1929; Curate then Pastor, Prud'homme, Sask; Domestic Prelate, 1944; First Bishop of Saint Paul in Alberta, 1948; Coadjutor-Archbishop of Saint Boniface, 1952; Archbishop of St Boniface, 1955-74. *Address:* c/o Archbishop's Residence, 151 Cathedral Avenue, St Boniface, Manitoba R2H 0H6, Canada.

BAUER, Prof. Peter Thomas, MA; FBA; Professor of Economics (with special reference to economic development and under-developed countries) in the University of London, at the London School of Economics, since 1960; Fellow of Gonville and Caius College, Cambridge, 1946-60, and since 1968; *b* 6 Nov. 1915; unmarried. *Educ:* Scholae Piae, Budapest; Gonville and Caius Coll., Cambridge. Reader in Agricultural Economics, University of London, 1947-48; University Lecturer in Economics, Cambridge Univ., 1948-56; Smuts Reader in Commonwealth Studies, Cambridge Univ., 1956-60. *Publications:* The Rubber Industry, 1948; West African Trade, 1954; The Economics of Under-developed Countries (with B. S. Yamey), 1957; Economic Analysis and Policy in Under-developed Countries, 1958; Indian Economic Policy and Development, 1961; (with B. S. Yamey) Markets, Market Control and Marketing Reform, 1968; Dissent on Development, 1972; Aspects of Nigerian Development, 1974; Equality, the Third World and Economic Delusion, 1981; articles on economic subjects. *Address:* London School of Economics and Political Science, Houghton Street, Aldwych, WC2. *Club:* Garrick.

BAUGHEN, Rt. Rev. Michael Alfred; *see* Chester, Bishop of.

BAUM, Prof. Michael, ChM; FRCS; Professor of Surgery, King's College Hospital Medical School, London, since 1980; *b* 31 May 1937; *s* of Isidor and Mary Baum; *m* 1965, Judith (*née* Marcus); one *s* two *d. Educ:* Univ. of Birmingham (MB, ChB; ChM). FRCS 1965. Lecturer in Surgery, King's College Hosp., 1969-72; Research Fellow, Univ. of Pittsburgh, USA, 1971-72; Reader in Surgery (Dep. Director), Welsh National Sch. of Medicine, Cardiff, 1972-78; Hon. Cons. Surgeon, King's College Hosp., 1978-80. *Publications:* Breast Cancer—The Facts, 1981; multiple pubns on breast cancer, cancer therapy, cancer biology and the philosophy of science. *Recreations:* painting, theatre, reading, philosophizing. *Address:* 22 Red Post Hill, SE24 9JQ. *T:* 01-733 6229. *Club:* Athenæum.

BAVERSTOCK, Donald Leighton; Executive Producer, Television, BBC Manchester, 1975-77; *b* 18 Jan. 1924; *s* of Thomas Philip Baverstock and Sarah Ann; *m* 1957, Gillian Mary, *d* of late Mrs Kenneth Darrell Waters (Enid Blyton); two *s* two *d. Educ:* Canton High Sch., Cardiff; Christ Church, Oxford (MA). Served with RAF, 1943-46; completed tour of operations Bomber Command, 1944; Instructor, Navigation, 1944-46. History Master, Wellington Coll., 1949. Producer, BBC General Overseas Service, 1950-54; Producer, BBC Television Service, 1954-57; Editor, Tonight Programme, 1957-61; Asst Controller, Television Programmes, BBC, 1961-63; Chief of Programmes BBC TV (1), 1963-65; Partner, Jay, Baverstock, Milne & Co., 1965-67; Dir of Programmes, Yorkshire TV, 1967-73; Man. Dir, Granada Video Ltd, 1974-75. *Address:* Low Hall, Middleton, Ilkley, Yorks. *T:* Ilkley 608037.

BAVIN, Alfred Robert Walter, CB 1966; Deputy Secretary, Department of Health and Social Security, 1968-73 (Ministry of Health, 1966-68); *b* 4 April 1917; *s* of late Alfred and late Annie Bavin; *m* 1947, Helen Mansfield; one *s* three *d. Educ:* Christ's Hosp.; Balliol Coll., Oxford. 1st cl. Hon. Mods 1937; 1st cl. Lit. Hum. 1939. Min. of Health, Asst Principal, 1939, Principal, 1946; Cabinet Office, 1948-50; Min. of Health, Principal Private Sec. to Minister, 1951; Asst Sec. 1952; Under-Sec. 1960. Nuffield Home Civil Service Travelling Fellowship, 1956. *Address:* 7 First Avenue, Felpham, Bognor Regis, W Sussex. *T:* Middleton-on-Sea 3073. *Clubs:* Athenæum, MCC.

BAVIN, Rt. Rev. Timothy John; *see* Johannesburg, Bishop of.

BAWDEN, Edward, CBE 1946; RA 1956 (ARA 1947); RDI 1949; Painter and Designer; Draughtsman; formerly a Tutor in the School of Graphic Design, Royal College of Art; *b* Braintree, Essex, 1903; *m* 1932, Charlotte (*d* 1970), *d* of Robert Epton, Lincoln; one *s* one *d. Educ:* Cambridge Sch. of Art; Royal Coll. of Art. As an Official War Artist he travelled in Middle East, 1940-45; visited Canada during 1949 and 1950 as a guest instructor at Banff Sch. of Fine Arts, Alberta. His work is represented in the Tate Gallery, London, and by water-colour drawings in several London, Dominion and provincial galleries; exhibitions: at Leicester Galleries, 1938, 1949, 1952; at Zwemmer Gallery, 1934, 1963; at Fine Art Soc., 1968, 1975, 1978, 1979; at Fitzwilliam Museum, 1978. Printmaker and graphic designer. He has designed and cut blocks for a series of wallpapers printed by Messrs Cole & Son, and has painted mural decorations for the SS Orcades and SS Oronsay, also for Lion and Unicorn Pavilion on South Bank site of Festival of Brtain. Trustee of Tate Gallery, 1951-58. Hon. Dr RCA; DUniv Essex; Hon. RE; *Illustrated books include:* The Histories of Herodotus, Salammbô, Tales of Troy and Greece, The Arabs, Life in an English Village. *Relevant publications:* "Edward Bawden" by J. M. Richards (Penguin Modern Painters); "Edward Bawden" by Robert Harling (English Masters of Black and White); "Edward Bawden": A Book of Cuts, 1978; "Edward Bawden" by Douglas Percy Bliss, 1979. *Address:* 2 Park Lane, Saffron Walden, Essex CB10 1DA.

BAWDEN, Nina Mary, (Mrs A. S. Kark), MA; FRSL; JP; novelist; *b* 19 Jan. 1925; *d* of Charles and Ellalaine Ursula May Mabey; *m* 1st, 1946, Henry Walton Bawden; two *s* ; 2nd, 1954, Austen Steven Kark, *qv*; one *d. Educ:* Ilford County High Sch.; Somerville Coll., Oxford (BA). Asst, Town and Country Planning Assoc., 1946-47. JP Surrey, 1968. Mem., ALCS. Pres., Soc. of Women Writers and Journalists. *Publications: novels:* Who Calls the Tune, 1953; The Odd Flamingo, 1954; Change Here for Babylon, 1955; Devil by the Sea, 1958, 2nd edn 1972 (abridged for children, 1976); The Solitary Child, 1956; Just Like a Lady, 1960; In Honour Bound, 1961; Tortoise by Candlelight, 1963; Under the Skin, 1964; A Little Love, a Little Learning, 1965; A Woman of My Age, 1967; The Grain of Truth, 1969; The Birds on the Trees, 1970; Anna Apparent, 1972; George beneath a Paper Moon, 1974; Afternoon of a Good Woman, 1976 (Yorkshire Post Novel of the Year, 1976); Familiar Passions, 1979; Walking Naked, 1981; *for children:* The Secret Passage; On the Run; The White Horse Gang; The Witch's Daughter; A Handful of Thieves; The Runaway Summer; Squib; Carrie's War; The Peppermint Pig (Guardian award, 1976); Rebel on a Rock, 1978; The Robbers, 1979; Kept in the Dark, 1982. *Recreations:* travelling, reading, garden croquet. *Address:* 22 Noel Road, N1. *T:* 01-226 2839. *Clubs:* Lansdowne; Ski Club of Great Britain, PEN, Society of Authors.

BAWN, Cecil Edwin Henry, CBE 1956; FRS 1952; BSc, PhD; Brunner Professor of Physical Chemistry in the University of Liverpool, 1969-Dec. 1973, now Emeritus (Grant-Brunner Professor of Inorganic and Physical Chemistry, 1948-69); *b* 6 Nov. 1908; British; *m* 1934, Winifred Mabel Jackson; two *s* one *d. Educ:* Cotham Grammar Sch., Bristol. Graduated, Univ. of Bristol, 1929; PhD in Chemistry (Bristol), 1932; Asst Lectr in Chemistry, Univ. of Manchester, 1931-34; Lectr in Chemistry, 1934-38; Lectr in Physical Chemistry, Univ. of Bristol, 1938-45; Reader in Physical Chemistry, 1945-49. During War of 1939-45 was in charge of a Physico-Chemical Section in Armament Research Dept, Min. of Supply. Mem., Univ. Grants Cttee, 1965-74. Swinburne Gold Medal, 1966. Hon. DSc: Bradford, 1966; Birmingham, 1968; Bristol, 1974. *Publications:* The Chemistry of High Polymers, 1948; papers in chemical journals. *Address:* Springfields, Stoodleigh, near Tiverton, Devon EX16 9PT. *T:* Oakford 220.

BAX, Rodney Ian Shirley, QC 1966; **His Honour Judge Bax;** a Circuit Judge, since 1973; *b* 16 Sept. 1920; *s* of late Rudolph Edward Victor Bax, Barrister, and of Shirley Winifred, *d* of Canon G. A. Thompson; *m* 1953, Patricia Anne, *d* of late Martin Stuart Turner, MC; one *s* one *d. Educ:* Bryanston Sch. (Scholar); Royal Coll. of Music (Exhibitioner). Served with Royal Fusiliers and Intelligence Corps, 1940-46 (Major GS). Called to Bar, Gray's Inn, 1947, Bencher, 1972; S Eastern Circuit. A Recorder, 1972-73. Mem., General Council of the Bar, 1961-65. Asst Comr, Boundary Commn for England, 1965-69. Comr, Central Criminal Court, 1971. Chm., Barristers' Benevolent Assoc., 1979– (Dep. Chm., 1974-79). Governor, Ashfold Sch. Trust, Bucks. *Recreations:* music, books. *Address:* 4 Jocelyn Road, Richmond, Surrey. *T:* 01-940 3395; Alderney, Channel Islands.

BAXANDALL, David Kighley, CBE 1959; Director of National Galleries of Scotland, 1952-70; *b* 11 Oct. 1905; *m* 1931, Isobel, *d* of Canon D. J. Thomas; one *s* twin *d. Educ:* King's Coll. Sch., Wimbledon; King's Coll., University of London. Asst Keeper, 1929-39, and Keeper of the Department of Art, 1939-41, National Museum of Wales. Served in RAF, 1941-45. Dir of Manchester City Art Galleries, 1945-52. *Publications:* Ben Nicholson, 1962; numerous articles, gallery handbooks, catalogues and broadcast talks. *Address:* 12 Darnaway Street, Edinburgh EH3 6BG. *T:* 031-225 1417.
See also M. D. K. Baxandall.

BAXANDALL, Prof. Michael David Kighley, FBA 1982; Professor of the History of the Classical Tradition, Warburg Institute, University of London, since 1981 (Reader, 1973-81); *b* 18 Aug. 1933; *o s* of David Baxandall, *qv*; *m* 1963, Katharina Simon; one *s* one *d. Educ:* Manchester Grammar Sch.; Downing Coll., Cambridge (MA); Univs of Pavia and Munich. Jun. Res. Fellow, Warburg Inst., 1959-61; Asst Keeper, Dept of Architecture and Sculpture, Victoria and Albert Museum, 1961-65; Lectr in Renaissance

Studies, Warburg Inst., 1965-73; Slade Prof. of Fine Art, Univ. of Oxford, 1974-75. *Publications:* Giotto and the Orators, 1971; Painting and Experience in Fifteenth-Century Italy, 1972; South German Sculpture 1480-1530 in the Victoria and Albert Museum, 1974; The Limewood Sculptors of Renaissance Germany, 1980. *Address:* The Warburg Institute, Woburn Square, WC1H 0AB.

BAXENDELL, Sir Peter (Brian), Kt 1981; CBE 1972; Chairman, Shell Transport and Trading Co., since 1979; Chairman, Committee of Managing Directors of Royal Dutch/Shell Group of Companies, since 1982; *b* 28 Feb. 1925; *s* of Lesley Wilfred Edward Baxendell and Evelyn Mary Baxendell (*née* Gaskin); *m* 1949, Rosemary (*née* Lacey); two *s* two *d. Educ:* St Francis Xavier's, Liverpool; Royal School of Mines, London (ARSM, BSc). Joined Royal Dutch/Shell Group, 1946; Petroleum Engr in Egypt, 1947, and Venezuela, 1950; Techn. Dir, Shell-BP Nigeria, 1963; Head of SE Asia Div., London, 1966; Man. Dir, Shell-BP Nigeria, 1969; Man. Dir, 1973-75, Chm., 1974-79, Shell UK; Man. Dir, Royal Dutch/Shell Gp of Cos, 1973; Chm., Shell Canada Ltd, 1980–; Dir, Shell Oil Co., USA, 1982–. FEng 1978. Hon. DSc Heriot-Watt 1982. *Publications:* articles on petroleum engrg subjects in scientific jls. *Recreations:* tennis, fishing. *Address:* Shell Centre, SE1 7NA. *T:* 01-934 2772.

BAXTER, Prof. Alexander Duncan, CEng; Research Consultant, since 1970; Director, de Havilland Engine Co. Ltd, 1958-63; Chief Executive Rocket Division and Nuclear Power Group, de Havilland Engine Co. Ltd, 1957-63; *b* 17 June 1908; *e s* of Robert Alexander and Mary Violet Baxter; *m* 1933, Florence Kathleen McClean; one *s* two *d. Educ:* Liverpool Institute High Sch.; Liverpool Univ. BEng (1st Cl. Hons MechEng) 1930; MEng 1933. Post-graduate pupil with Daimler Company, 1930-34; commissioned in RAFO, 1930-35; Research Engineer with Instn. of Automobile Engrs, 1934-35; Scientific Officer at RAE, Farnborough, 1935; engaged on aircraft propulsion and gas turbine research until 1947; Supt, Rocket Propulsion, RAE, 1947-50; Prof. of Aircraft Propulsion, Coll. of Aeronautics, Cranfield, 1950-57; Dep. Principal, Cranfield, 1954-57; Sen. Exec., Bristol Siddeley Engines Ltd, 1963-68, Bristol Engine Div. of Rolls Royce Ltd, 1968-70. Mem. Council: InstMechE, 1955-57; RAeS, 1953-70 (Vice-Pres, 1962-66, Pres., 1966-67). Served as member of many educnl bodies, incl.: jt Cttee on Higher Nat. Certificate in Engrg; RAF Educn Adv. Cttee; Aeronautical Board, CNAA; Board of CEI, 1962-69; various Govt advisory cttees. Member of Court: Univ. of Bristol; Cranfield Inst. of Technology. Hon. DSc Cranfield Inst. of Technology, 1980. FIMechE, FRAeS, FInstPet, Fellow, British Interplanetary Soc. *Publications:* various reports in government R & M series; papers in Proc. Instn Mech. Engineers and RAeS. *Recreations:* do-it-yourself, grandchildren, cine photography. *Address:* Glebe Cottage, Pucklechurch, Glos. *T:* Abson 2204.

BAXTER, Prof. James Thomson; William Dick Professor of Veterinary Medicine, Edinburgh University, since 1970; *b* Feb. 1925; *e s* of James T. Baxter and Victoria A. D. Montgomery; *m* 1951, Muriel Elizabeth Knox; two *s* one *d. Educ:* Trinity Academy, Edinburgh; Royal (Dick) Veterinary Coll., Edinburgh. MA(Dub), PhD(Dub); MRCVS; FIBiol; FRSH. Served War, Royal Navy, 1944-46. Gen. veterinary practice, 1950-52; Veterinary Officer, then Veterinary Research Officer, Min. of Agr., N Ireland, 1952-60; Lectr, Loughry Agr. Coll., 1955-60; Asst Lectr in Vet. Sci., Queen's Univ., Belfast, 1958-60; Prof. in Clinical Vet. Practices, Dublin Univ., 1960-70; Dir, Sch. of Veterinary Medicine, Dublin Univ., 1963-70. Mem. Council: Irish Grassland and Animal Production Assoc., 1961-70 (Pres. 1963-64); RCVS, 1962-70, 1978-82; Agricl Inst. (An Foras Taluntais), 1964-70. Mem., Irish Veterinary Council, 1962-70. Fellow, Trinity Coll., Dublin, 1965-70. Editor: Veterinary Science Communications, 1976-80; Veterinary Research Communications, 1980–. *Publications:* articles in vety and other jls. *Address:* 1 Wilton Road, Edinburgh EH16 5NX. *T:* 031-667 3055.

BAXTER, Jeremy Richard; Secretary of the Post Office, since 1982; *b* 20 Jan. 1929; *s* of late Andrew Paterson Baxter and late Ann Winifred Baxter; *m* 1965, Faith Elizabeth Graham; two *s* one *d. Educ:* Sedbergh Sch.; St John's Coll., Cambridge (BA Class. Tripos). Asst Principal, Post Office, 1952; Asst Private Sec. to Postmaster-Gen., 1956; Private Sec. to Asst Postmaster-Gen., 1957; Principal, Post Office, 1958; Principal, Treasury, 1964; Asst Sec., Post Office, 1967; Dir, Postal Personnel, 1971; Dir of Personnel, European Commn, 1973-81. *Recreation:* sailing. *Address:* Spring Grove Farm, Mursley, Milton Keynes MK17 0SA. *Club:* Travellers'.

BAXTER, John Lawson; *b* 25 Nov. 1939; *s* of John Lawson Baxter and Enid Maud Taggart; *m* 1967; three *s. Educ:* Trinity Coll., Dublin; Queen's Univ., Belfast; BA, BComm, LLM; LLM Tulane Univ., New Orleans. Solicitor. Mem. (U) N Ireland Assembly, for N Antrim, 1973-75; Minister of Information, N Ireland Executive, 1974. Chm. (part-time), Industrial Tribunals (NI), 1980–. *Recreations:* golf, fishing. *Address:* Beardiville, Cloyfin, Coleraine, N Ireland. *T:* Bushmills 31552.

BAXTER, Prof. Sir (John) Philip, KBE 1965 (OBE 1945); CMG 1959; PhD, FAA, FTS; Chairman, Sydney Opera House Trust, 1968-75; *b* 7 May 1905; *s* of John and Mary Netta Baxter; *m* 1931, Lilian May Baxter (*née* Thatcher); three *s* one *d. Educ:* University of Birmingham. BSc 1925, PhD 1928. University of Birmingham. Research Dir, ICI General Chemicals Ltd and Dir, Thorium Ltd, until 1949; Prof. Chem. Eng, NSW University of Technology, 1950; Vice-Chancellor, Univ. of NSW, 1953-69. Chm,

Australian Atomic Energy Commn, 1957-72. Fellow: Aust. Acad. of Science; Aust. Acad. of Technological Sciences. FRACI; MIE(Aust). Hon. LLD Montreal, 1958; Hon. DSc Newcastle, Queensland; NSW; Hon. DTech Loughborough, 1969. *Address:* 1 Kelso Street, Enfield, NSW 2136, Australia. *T:* 7474261.

BAXTER, John Walter, CBE 1974; Consultant, G. Maunsell & Partners (Partner, 1955, Senior Partner, 1959-80); *b* 4 June 1917; *s* of late J. G. Baxter and late D. L. Baxter (*née* Phelps); *m* 1941, Jessie, *d* of late T. Pimblott; one *d. Educ:* Westminster City Sch.; City and Guilds Engrg College. BSc(Eng), FCGI, FEng, FICE, FRSA. Civil Engineer: Trussed Concrete Steel Co. Ltd, 1936-41; Shell Refining Co. Ltd, 1941-52; Maunsell Posford & Pavry, 1952-55. Pres., ICE, 1976-77 (Vice-Pres., 1973-76, Mem. Council, 1963-68 and 1970-79); Vice-Chm., ACE, 1979-80, Chm., 1980-81. *Publications:* contrib. Proc. ICE. *Address:* The Down Side, Itchen Abbas, Hants. *Club:* Athenæum.

BAXTER, Prof. Sir Philip; *see* Baxter, Prof. Sir J. P.

BAXTER, Raymond Frederic, FRSA; broadcaster and writer; *b* 25 Jan. 1922; *s* of Frederick Garfield Baxter and Rosina Baxter (*née* Rivers); *m* 1945, Sylvia Kathryn (*née* Johnson), Boston, Mass; one *s* one *d. Educ:* Ilford County High Sch. Joined RAF, 1940; flew Spitfires with 65, 93 and 602 Sqdns, in UK, Med. and Europe. Entered Forces Broadcasting in Cairo, still as serving officer, 1945; civilian deputy Dir BFN BBC, 1947-49; subseq. short attachment West Region and finally joined Outside Broadcast Dept, London; with BBC until 1966; Dir, Motoring Publicity, BMC, 1967-68. Member Cttee of Management: RNLI, 1979-; Air League, 1980-. *Publications:* (with James Burke and Michael Latham) Tomorrow's World, Vol. 1, 1970, Vol. 2, 1971; Farnborough Commentary, 1980; film commentaries, articles and reports on motoring and aviation subjects, etc. *Recreations:* motoring, riding, boating. *Address:* The Old Rectory, Denham, Bucks. *Clubs:* British Racing Drivers, Eccentric, etc.

BAXTER, Prof. Rodney James, FRS 1982; FAA 1977; Professor in the Department of Theoretical Physics, Research School of Physical Sciences, Australian National University, since 1981; *b* 8 Feb. 1940; *s* of Thomas James Baxter and Florence A. Baxter; *m* 1968, Elizabeth Ann Phillips; one *s* one *d. Educ:* Bancroft's Sch., Essex; Trinity Coll., Cambridge; Australian National Univ. Reservoir Engineer, Iraq Petroleum Co., 1964-65; Research Fellow, ANU, 1965-68; Asst Prof., Mathematics Dept, Massachusetts Inst. of Technology, 1968-70; Fellow, ANU, 1970-81. Pawsey Medal, Aust. Acad. of Science, 1975; Boltzmann Medal, IUPAP, 1980. *Publications:* Exactly Solved Models in Statistical Mechanics, 1982; contribs to Proc. Royal Soc., Jl of Physics A, Physical Rev., Statistical Physics, Annals of Physics. *Recreation:* theatre. *Address:* Theoretical Physics IAS, Australian National University, Canberra 2600, Australia. *T:* (062) 492968.

BAXTER, Roger George, PhD; FRAS; Headmaster of Sedbergh School, since 1982; *b* 21 April 1940; *s* of Rev. Benjamin George Baxter and Gweneth Muriel Baxter (*née* Causer); *m* 1967, Dorothy Ann Cook; one *s* one *d. Educ:* Handsworth Grammar Sch., Birmingham; Univ. of Sheffield (BSc, PhD). Junior Research Fellow, Univ. of Sheffield, 1965-66, Lectr, Dept of Applied Mathematics, 1966-70; Asst Mathematics Master, Winchester Coll., 1970-81, Under Master, 1976-81. *Publications:* various papers on numerical studies in magnetoplasma diffusion with applications to the F-2 layer of the ionosphere. *Recreations:* opera, music, cooking. *Address:* Birksholme, Sedbergh, Cumbria LA10 5HQ. *T:* Sedbergh 20491.

BAXTER, Walter; author; *b* 1915. *Educ:* St Lawrence, Ramsgate; Trinity Hall, Cambridge. Worked in the City, 1936-39; served War of 1939-45, with KOYLI in Burma; afterwards, in India, ADC to General Slim, and on Staff of a Corps HQ during re-conquest of Burma. After completion of first novel, returned to India to work temporarily on a mission. *Publications:* Look Down in Mercy, 1951; The Image and The Search, 1953. *Address:* 119 Old Brompton Road, SW7.

BAXTER, William T., BCom Edinburgh; Professor of Accounting, London School of Economics, 1947-73, Hon. Fellow 1980; *b* 27 July 1906; *s* of W. M. Baxter and Margaret Threipland; *m* 1st, 1940, Marjorie Allanson (*d* 1971); one *s* one *d* ; 2nd, 1973, Leena-Kaisa Laitakari-Kaila. *Educ:* George Watson's Coll.; Univ. of Edinburgh. Chartered Accountant (Edinburgh), 1930; Commonwealth Fund Fellow, 1931, at Harvard Univ.; Lectr in Accounting, Univ. of Edinburgh, 1934; Prof. of Accounting, Univ. of Cape Town, 1937. *Publications:* Income Tax for Professional Students, 1936; The House of Hancock, 1945; Depreciation, 1971; Accounting Values and Inflation, 1975; Collected Papers on Accounting, 1979. *Address:* 1 The Ridgeway, NW11. *T:* 01-455 6810.

BAYDA, Hon. Edward Dmytro; Chief Justice of Saskatchewan, since 1981; *b* 9 Sept. 1931; *s* of Dmytro A. Bayda and Mary Bilinski; *m* 1953, Marie-Thérèse Yvonne Gagne; one *s* five *d. Educ:* Univ. of Saskatchewan (BA 1951, LLB 1953). Called to the Bar, Saskatchewan, 1954; QC (Sask) 1966. Judge, Court of Queen's Bench, 1972; Justice, Court of Appeal, 1974. KM 1975. *Addresses:* (home) 9 Turnbull Place, Regina, Sask S4S 4H2, Canada. *T:* 586-2126; (chambers) Court House, 2425 Victoria Avenue, Regina, Sask S4P 3E4. *T:* 565-5412.

BAYHAM, Viscount; James William John Pratt; *b* 11 Dec. 1965; *s* and *heir* of Earl of Brecknock, *qv.*

BAYLEY, Gordon Vernon, CBE 1976; FIA, FIMA, FSS, CBIM; Director, General Manager and Actuary, National Provident Institution, since 1964; *b* 25 July 1920; *s* of late Capt. Vernon Bayley, King's Regt, and Mrs Gladys Maud Bayley; *m* 1945, Miriam Allenby, *d* of late Frederick Walter Ellis and Miriam Ellis, Eastbourne; one *s* two *d. Educ:* Abingdon. Joined HM Forces, 1940; commissioned Royal Artillery, Major 1945. Asst Actuary, Equitable Life Assurance Soc., 1949; Partner, Duncan C. Fraser and Co. (Actuaries), 1954-57; National Provident Institution: Assistant Sec., 1957, Joint Sec. 1959. Mem., Occupational Pensions Bd, 1973-74. Mem., Cttee to Review the Functioning of Financial Institutions, 1977-80. Institute of Actuaries: Fellow, 1946; Hon. Sec., 1960-62; Vice-Pres., 1964-67; Pres., 1974-76; Chm., Life Offices Assoc., 1969-70 (Dep. Chm., 1967-68). Chm., Bd of Governors, Abingdon Sch., 1979-. *Publications:* contribs to Jl Inst. Actuaries, Jl Royal Statistical Soc. *Recreations:* tennis, ski-ing, sailing. *Address:* The Old Manor, Witley, Surrey. *T:* Wormley 2301. *Clubs:* English Speaking Union; Island Sailing; Sea View Yacht.

BAYLEY, Prof. John Oliver; Warton Professor of English Literature, and Fellow of St Catherine's College, University of Oxford, since 1974; *b* 27 March 1925; *s* of F. J. Bayley; *m* 1956, Jean Iris Murdoch, *qv. Educ:* Eton; New Coll., Oxford. 1st cl. hons English Oxon 1950. Served in Army, Grenadier Guards and Special Intell., 1943-47. Mem., St Antony's and Magdalen Colls, Oxford, 1951-55; Fellow and Tutor in English, New Coll., Oxford, 1955-74. *Publications:* In Another Country (novel), 1954; The Romantic Survival: A Study in Poetic Evolution, 1956; The Characters of Love, 1961; Tolstoy and the Novel, 1966; Pushkin: A Comparative Commentary, 1971; The Uses of Division: unity and disharmony in literature, 1976; An Essay on Hardy, 1978; Shakespeare and Tragedy, 1981. *Address:* Cedar Lodge, Steeple Aston, Oxford. *T:* Steeple Aston 40229.

BAYLEY, Mrs John Oliver; *see* Murdoch, J. I.

BAYLEY, Lt-Comdr Oscar Stewart Morris, RN retd; Accountant, John Lewis Partnership, since 1981; *b* 15 April 1926; *s* of late Rev. J. H. S. Bayley; *m* Pamela Margaret Harrison (one *s* one *d* by a former marriage). *Educ:* St John's Sch., Leatherhead; King James's Grammar Sch., Knaresborough. Called to Bar, Lincoln's Inn, 1959. Entered RN, 1944: Ceylon, 1956-58; Supply Off., HMS Narvik and Sqdn Supply Off., 5th Submarine Div., 1960-62; Sec. to Comdr British Forces Caribbean Area, 1962-65; retd from RN at own request, 1966. Legal Asst (Unfair Competition), The Distillers Co. Ltd, 1966-68; Clerk, Fishmongers' Co., 1968-73. Director: Anglers Co-operative Assoc. Trustee Co. Ltd; Seed Oysters (UK) Ltd. Clerk to Governors of Gresham's Sch., Holt; Hon. Sec., Salmon and Trout Assoc. and of Shellfish Assoc. of Great Britain; Vice-Chm., National Anglers' Council; Secretary: Atlantic Salmon Research Trust; City and Guilds of London Art Sch. Ltd, 1968-73; Nat. Assoc. of Pension Funds Investment Protection Cttee, 1974-75. Dir and Chief Sec., The Royal Life Saving Soc., 1976-78; Accountant, Hawker Siddeley Group, 1978-81. *Address:* 3 Ravendale, Spencer Road, Bromley, Kent BR1 3SX.

BAYLEY, Peter Charles; Berry Professor and Head of the Department of English, since 1978, and Warden of St Regulus Hall, University of St Andrews; *b* 25 Jan. 1921; *y s* of late William Charles Abell Bayley and Irene (*née* Heath); *m* 1951, Patience (marr. diss. 1980), *d* of late Sir George (Norman) Clark, and of Barbara, *e d* of W. B. Keen; one *s* two *d. Educ:* Crypt Sch., Gloucester; University Coll., Oxford (Sidgwick Exhibnr; MA 1st Cl. Hons English, 1947). Served RA and Intell. Corps, India, 1941-45. Jun. Fellow, University Coll., Oxon, 1947; Fellow and Praelector in English, 1949-72 (at various times Domestic Bursar, Tutor for Admissions, Librarian, Editor of University Coll. Record); Univ. Lectr in English, 1952-72; Proctor, 1957-58; Oxford Univ. Corresp., The Times, 1960-63; Master of Collingwood Coll., Univ. of Durham, 1971-78. Vis. Lectr, Yale Univ., and Robert Bates Vis. Fellow, Jonathan Edwards Coll., 1970; Brown Distinguished Vis. Prof., Univ. of the South, Sewanee, Tenn, 1978. Prepared Macbeth, 1977, Antony and Cleopatra, 1978, Brit. Council Recorded Seminars. *Publications:* Edmund Spenser, Prince of Poets, 1971; 'Casebook' on Spenser's The Faerie Queene, 1977; edited: Spenser, The Faerie Queene: Book II, 1965; Book I, 1966; Loves and Deaths: short stories by 19th century novelists, 1972; Poems of Milton, 1982; contributed to: Patterns of Love and Courtesy, ed Lawlor, 1966; English Poetry: select bibliographical guides, 1971. *Recreations:* nature and art. *Address:* Department of English, University of St Andrews, Fife.

BAYLIS, Clifford Henry, CB 1971; Clerk, The Worshipful Company of Shipwrights; *b* 20 March 1915; *s* of late Arthur Charles and Caroline Jane Baylis, Alcester, Warwicks; *m* 1st, 1939, Phyllis Mary Clark; two *s* ; 2nd, 1979, Margaret A. Hawkins. *Educ:* Alcester Grammar Sch.; Keble Coll., Oxford. Harrods Ltd, 1937-39. Served with HM Forces, 1940-46: Major RASC. Principal, Board of Trade, 1947; Asst Sec., UK Trade Commissioner, Bombay, 1955; Export Credits Guarantee Dept, 1963-66; Under-Sec., Board of Trade, 1966-67; Under-Sec., Min. of Technology, 1967-69; Controller, HM Stationery Office, and Queen's Printer of Acts of Parlt, 1969-74; Dir, Shipbuilders' and Repairers' Nat. Assoc., 1974-77. *Address:* 38 Cleaver Street, SE11 4DP. *T:* 01-587 0817. *Club:* Royal Automobile.

BAYLIS, Rear-Adm. Robert Goodwin, OBE 1963; CEng; FIEE; President, Ordnance Board, since 1981 (Vice-President, 1980–81); *b* 29 Nov. 1925; *s* of Harold Goodwin Baylis and Evelyn May (*née* Whitworth); *m* 1949, Joyce Rosemary Churchill; two *s* one *d*. *Educ*: Highgate Sch.; Edinburgh Univ.; Loughborough Coll.; RN Engrg Coll.; Trinity Coll., Cambridge. MA Cantab. MRAeS. Stoker, Small Vessels Pool, 1943; joined Royal Navy as Naval Airman (Second Class), 1943; commnd 1944; Accident Investigation Staff, Admiral (Air), 1946; graduate apprentice, Mullard Radio Valve Co., 1951; Equipment and Trials Section, HMS Ariel, 1951; Dep. Electrical Officer, HMS Newcastle, 1954; Gunnery Radar Div., Adm. Signal and Radar Estabt, 1956; Fleet Electrical Officer, Staff of C-in-C, S Atlantic and S America, 1958; Equipment and Trials Section, HMS Collingwood, 1961; Sqdn Weapons and Radio Officer, 20th Frigate Sqdn, 1961; Staff Weapons and Radio Officer, Comdr British Navy Staff, Washington, and Special Projects (Polaris), 1964; Trng Comdr, RN Weapons and Elec. Sch., HMS Collingwood, 1966; Defence Fellow, Southampton Univ., 1969; Asst Dir, Fleet Maintenance, Captain-in-Charge Ship Maintenance Authority, and Captain Reserve Ships Authority, 1971; Fleet Weapons Electrical Officer, Staff of C-in-C, Fleet, 1973; Captain, RNEC, Manadon, 1975; Adm. Interview Bd, 1978; Staff of Vice Chief of Defence Staff, 1979. Comdr 1961, Captain 1970, Rear-Adm. 1979. *Recreations:* tennis, sailing. *Address:* Ordnance Board, 375 Kensington High Street, W14 8QP.

BAYLISS, Frederic Joseph; Accountant General and Head of Economic and Social Division, Department of Employment, since 1977; *b* 15 April 1926; *s* of Gordon and Gertrude Bayliss; *m* 1948, Mary Provost; two *d*. *Educ:* Ashby de la Zouch Grammar Sch.; Hertford Coll., Oxford. PhD Nottingham 1960. RAF, 1944–47. Tutor in Economics, Oxford Univ. Tutorial Classes Cttee, 1950–57; Lectr in Industrial Relations, Dept of Adult Education, Univ. of Nottingham, 1957–65; Industrial Relations Advr, NBPI, 1965–69; Asst Sec., CIR, 1969–71; Sen. Economic Advr, Dept of Employment, 1971–73; Under Sec., Pay Board, 1973–74; Sec., Royal Commn on the Distribution of Income and Wealth, 1974–77. *Publications:* British Wages Councils, 1962; The Standard of Living, 1965. *Recreations:* gardening, walking. *Address:* 11 Deena Close, Queens Drive, W3 0HR. *T:* 01-992 1126. *Club:* Reform.

BAYLISS, Colonel George Sheldon, CB 1966; OBE 1945; TD 1941; DL; *b* 26 Dec. 1900; *s* of Francis and E. M. Bayliss, Walsall; *m* 1935, Margaret Muriel Williamson (*d* 1962), *widow* of Dr K. B. Williamson, MC, and *d* of J. S. Harker, Penrith; one *s* and one *step s*. *Educ:* Shrewsbury Sch. Joined TA, 2nd Lieut, 1921; Major 1926–40; Lieut-Col 1940–45 (despatches 4 times, 1941–45). Hon. Col 473 HAA Regt, 1947–53. DL Co. Stafford, 1953; Chm., Staffs T&AFA, 1959–65. Managing Dir, S B & N Ltd, Walsall, 1930–76, retired. Bronze Star (USA). *Address:* Littlefield House, Wall, Lichfield, Staffs WS14 0AU. *T:* Shenstone 480024.

BAYLISS, Sir Noel (Stanley), Kt 1979; CBE 1960; PhD, FRACI, FAA; Professor of Chemistry, University of Western Australia, 1938–71, Emeritus Professor, 1972; *b* 19 Dec. 1906; *s* of Henry Bayliss and Nelly Stothers; *m* 1933, Nellie Elise Banks; two *s*. *Educ:* Queen's Coll., Univ. of Melbourne (BSc 1927); Lincoln Coll., Oxford (BA 1930); Univ. of Calif, Berkeley (PhD 1933). FRACI 1942; FAA 1954. Victorian Rhodes Scholar, 1927–30; Commonwealth Fund (Harkness) Fellow, Univ. of Calif, 1930–33; Sen. Lectr in Chem., Univ. of Melbourne, 1933–37. Chm., Murdoch Univ. Planning Bd, 1970–73; Member: Australian Univs Commn, 1959–70; Hong Kong Univ. and Polytech. Grants Cttee, 1966–73. Hon. FACE 1965; Hon. DSc Univ. of WA, 1968; Hon. DUniv Murdoch Univ., 1975. *Publications:* over 70 original papers in scientific jls. *Recreations:* power boating, golf, music. *Address:* 104 Thomas Street, Nedlands, WA 6009, Australia. *T:* (09) 386 1453. *Clubs:* Weld (Perth, WA); Royal Perth Yacht, Nedlands Golf (WA).

BAYLISS, Sir Richard (Ian Samuel), KCVO 1978; MD, FRCP; Physician to the Queen, 1970–81, and Head of HM Medical Household, 1973–81; Consultant Physician, King Edward VII's Hospital for Officers, since 1964; Consulting Physician, Westminster Hospital, since 1981; Medical Director, Swiss Reinsurance Co.; Assistant Director, Medical Services Study Group, Royal College of Physicians; *b* 2 Jan. 1917; *o s* of late Frederick William Bayliss, Tettenhall, and late Muryel Anne Bayliss; *m* 1st, 1941, Margaret Joan Hardman (marr. diss. 1956); one *s* one *d*; 2nd, 1957, Constance Ellen, *d* of Wilbur J. Frey, Connecticut; two *s*; 3rd, 1979, Marina Rankin, *widow* of Charles Rankin. *Educ:* Rugby; Clare Coll., Cambridge; St Thomas' Hosp., London. MB, BChir Cambridge 1941; MRCS, LRCP 1941; MRCP 1942; MD Cambridge 1946; FRCP 1956. Casualty Officer, Ho.-Phys., Registrar, Resident Asst Phys., St Thomas' Hosp.; Off. i/c Med. Div., RAMC, India; Sen. Med. Registrar and Tutor, Hammersmith Hosp.; Rockefeller Fellow in Medicine, Columbia Univ., New York, 1950–51; Lectr in Medicine and Physician, Postgrad. Med. Sch. of London; Dean, Westminster Med. Sch., 1960–64; Physician to HM Household, 1964–70; Consultant Physician: Westminster Hosp., 1954–81; King Edward VII Hosp., Midhurst, 1973–82; Civilian Consultant in Medicine, RN, 1975–82. Hon. Sec., Assoc. of Physicians, 1958–63, Cttee 1965–68, Pres., 1980–81; Pres., Section of Endocrinology, RSM, 1966–68; Examr in Medicine, Cambridge and Oxford Univs; Examr, MRCP. Member: Bd of Governors, Westminster Hosp., 1960–64, 1967–74; Council, Westminster Med. Sch., 1960–75; Soc. for Endocrinology (Council, 1956–60); Brit. Cardiac Soc., 1952; Council, RCP, 1968–71; Bd of Advrs, Merck Inst. of Therapeutic Res., 1972–76; Dir, Provident Assoc. for Medical Care, Private Patients Plan, 1979–; Hon. Med. Adviser, Nuffield Nursing Home Trust, 1981–; Chm., Jt Liaison Cttee for

Indep. Health Care, 1979–. *Publications:* Practical Procedures in Clinical Medicine, 3rd edn. Various, in med. jls and textbooks, on endocrine, metabolic and cardiac diseases. *Recreations:* ski-ing, music, gardening. *Address:* 9 Park Square West, NW1 4LJ. *T:* 01-935 2071. *Club:* Garrick.

BAYLY, Vice-Adm. Sir Patrick (Uniacke), KBE 1968; CB 1965; DSC 1944, and 2 bars, 1944, 1951; Director, The Maritime Trust, since 1971; *b* 4 Aug. 1914; *s* of late Lancelot F. S. Bayly, Nenagh, Eire; *m* 1945, Moy Gourlay Jardine, *d* of Robert Gourlay Jardine, Newtonmearns, Scotland; two *d*. *Educ:* Aravon, Bray, Co. Wicklow; RN Coll., Dartmouth, Midshipman, 1932; Sub-Lieut, 1934; Lieut, 1935; South Africa, 1936; China station, 1938; Combined operations, 1941–44, including Sicily and Salerno; Lieut-Comdr 1944; HMS Mauritius, 1946; Comdr 1948, Naval Staff, 1948; Korean War 1952–53, in HMS Alacrity and Constance; Captain 1954, Naval Staff; Imperial Defence Coll., 1957; Capt. (D) 6th Destroyer Sqdn, 1958; Staff of SACLANT, Norfolk, Va, 1960; Chief of Staff, Mediterranean, 1962; Rear-Admiral, 1963; Flag Officer, Sea Training, 1963; Adm. Pres., RN Coll., Greenwich, 1965–67; Chief of Staff, COMNAVSOUTH, Malta, 1967–70; retd, 1970. Vice-Adm. 1967. US Legion of Merit, 1951. *Recreation:* golf. *Address:* Dunning House, Liphook, Hants.

BAYNE, John; Advocate; Sheriff of Glasgow and Strathkelvin, 1975–79; Sheriff (formerly Sheriff-Substitute) of Lanarkshire at Glasgow, 1959–74. *Address:* Winsford, 7 Milrig Road, Rutherglen G73 2NQ.

BAYNE, Nicholas Peter; HM Diplomatic Service; attached to Royal Institute of International Affairs (Chatham House), since 1982; *b* 15 Feb. 1937; *s* of late Captain Ronald Bayne, RN and of Elisabeth Ashcroft; *m* 1961, Diana Wilde; three *s*. *Educ:* Eton Coll.; Christ Church, Oxford (MA, DPhil). Entered Diplomatic Service, 1961; served at British Embassies in Manila, 1963–66, and Bonn, 1969–72; seconded to HM Treasury, 1974–75; Financial Counsellor, Paris, 1975–79; Head of Financial, later Economic Relations, Dept, FCO 1979–82. *Recreations:* reading, sightseeing. *Address:* c/o Foreign and Commonwealth Office, King Charles Street, SW1. *Club:* Travellers'.

BAYNE-POWELL, Robert Lane, CB 1981; Senior Registrar of the Family Division, High Court of Justice, 1976–82, retired (Registrar, 1964–76); *b* 10 Oct. 1910; 2nd *s* of William Maurice and Rosamond Alicia Bayne-Powell; *m* 1938, Nancy Geraldine (*d* 1979), *d* of late Lt-Col J. L. Philips, DSO; one *s* two *d*. *Educ:* Charterhouse; Trinity Coll., Cambridge (BA). Called to Bar, Middle Temple, 1935; Mem., Senate of Inns of Court and the Bar, 1978–81. Served War of 1939–45, Intell. Corps; Major 1944; Allied Commn for Austria 1945. Mem., Reviewing Cttee on Export of Works of Art, 1975–81; Hon Keeper of the Miniatures, Fitzwilliam Museum, Cambridge, 1980–. *Publication:* (special editor) Williams and Mortimer on Executors and Probate, 1970. *Recreations:* gardening, miniature collecting, wine-tasting. *Address:* The Mount, Borough Green, Sevenoaks, Kent. *T:* Borough Green 882045. *Club:* Athenæum.

BAYNES, Sir John (Christopher Malcolm), 7th Bt *cr* 1801; Lt-Col retd; Joint Proprietor, Lake Vyrnwy Hotel; *b* 24 April 1928; *s* of Sir Rory Malcolm Stuart Baynes, 6th Bt and Ethel Audrey (*d* 1947), *d* of late Edward Giles, CIE; *S* father, 1979; *m* 1955, Shirley Maxwell, *o d* of late Robert Allan Dodds; four *s*. *Educ:* Sedbergh School; RMA Sandhurst; Edinburgh Univ. (MSc). Commissioned Cameronians (Scottish Rifles), 1949; served Malaya, 1950–53 (despatches); Aden, 1966; Defence Fellow, Edinburgh Univ., 1968–69; comd 52 Lowland Volunteers (TAVR), 1969–72; retired, 1972. Order of the Sword 1st Class (Sweden), 1965. *Publications:* Morale, 1967; The Jacobite Rising of 1715, 1970; History of the Cameronians, Vol. IV, 1971; The Soldier in Modern Society, 1971; contribs to RUSI Jl, Purnell's History of First World War, and other military jls. *Recreations:* shooting, fishing, golf. *Heir: s* Christopher Rory Baynes, *b* 11 May 1956. *Address:* The Cottage, Lake Vyrnwy Hotel, via Oswestry, Salop SY10 0LY. *T:* Llanwddyn 244. *Clubs:* Army and Navy, Flyfishers'.

BAYNES, Pauline Diana, (Mrs F. O. Gasch); designer and book illustrator *b* 9 Sept 1922; *d* of Frederick William Wilberforce Baynes, CIE and Jessie Harriet Maud Cunningham; *m* 1961, Fritz Otto Gasch. *Educ:* Beaufront Sch. Camberley; Farnham Sch. of Art; Slade Sch. of Art. MSIA 1951. Mem. Women's Internat. Art Club, 1938. Voluntary worker, Camouflage Devel and Trng Centre, RE, 1940–42; Hydrographic Dept, Admty, 1942–45 Designed world's largest crewel embroidery, Plymouth Congregational Church, Minneapolis, 1970. Kate Greenaway Medal, Library Assoc., 1968 *Publications: illustrated:* Farmer Giles of Ham, and subseq. books and poster by J. R. R. Tolkien, 1949; The Lion, the Witch and the Wardrobe, and subseq Narnia books by C. S. Lewis, 1950; The Arabian Nights, 1957; The Puffin Book of Nursery Rhymes, 1963; Recipes from an Old Farmhouse, 1966 Dictionary of Chivalry, 1968; Snail and Caterpillar, 1972; A Companion to World Mythology, 1979; The Enchanted Horse, 1981; Frog and Shrew, 1981 numerous other children's books, etc. *Recreation:* going for walks with dogs *Address:* Rock Barn Cottage, Dockenfield, Farnham, Surrey. *T:* Headley Down 713306.

BAYNHAM, Dr Alexander Christopher; Deputy Director, Royal Signal and Radar Establishment, Malvern, since 1980; *b* 22 Dec. 1935; *s* of Alexander Baynham and Dulcie Rowena Rees; *m* 1961, Eileen May Wilson; two *s* one *d*. *Educ:* Marling Sch.; Reading Univ. (BSc); Warwick Univ. (PhD); Royal Coll. of Defence Studies (rcds). Joined Royal Signals and Radar Estab

Malvern, 1955; rejoined, 1961 (univ. studies, 1958-61); Head, Optics and Electronics Gp, 1976; RCDS, 1978; Scientific Adviser to Asst Chief Adviser on Projects, 1979. *Publications:* Plasma Effects in Semi-conductors, 1971; assorted papers in Jl of Physics, Jl of Applied Physics and in Proc. Phys. Soc. *Recreations:* church activities, music. *Address:* Royal Signals and Radar Establishment, St Andrews Road, Great Malvern, Worcs WR14 3PS.

BAYNHAM, Tom, CBE 1975 (OBE 1964); County Councillor, South Yorkshire CC, 1973-81 (Chairman, 1973, 1974, 1975); *b* 12 Aug. 1904; *s* of James Baynham and Elizabeth Baynham (*née* Heathcote); *m* 1926, Florence May (*née* Jones); one *s* two *d*. *Educ:* state school. Miner, 1918-69. Adwick Le Street UDC, 1939-74; W Riding CC, 1946-74; W Riding Health Exec. Council, 1948-74. Served on Mental Health Tribunal for approx. nine years to 1974; past Trade Union local official, also Safety Inspector. *Recreations:* reading, gardening. *Address:* 17 Willington Road, Skellow, Doncaster, South Yorkshire DN6 8JE. *T:* Doncaster 722226. *Clubs:* Carcroft Village; Skellow Grange Working Men's; Doncaster Trade Union and Labour; Hooton Pagnell.

BAYÜLKEN, Ümit Halûk; Secretary-General, Presidency of the Turkish Republic, since 1977; *b* 7 July 1921; *s* of Staff Officer H. Hüsnü Bayülken and Mrs Melek Bayülken; *m* 1952, Mrs Valihe Salci; one *s* one *d*. *Educ:* Lycée of Haydarpasa, Istanbul; Faculty of Political Science (Diplomatic Sect.), Univ. of Ankara. Joined Min. of For. Affairs, 1944; 3rd Sec., 2nd Political Dept; served in Private Cabinet of Sec.-Gen.; mil. service as reserve Officer, 1945-47; Vice-Consul, Frankfurt-on-Main, 1947-49; 1st Sec., Bonn, 1950-51; Dir of Middle East Sect., Ankara, 1951-53; Mem. Turkish Delegn to UN 7th Gen. Assembly, 1952; Political Adviser, 1953-56, Counsellor, 1956-59, Turkish Perm. Mission to UN; rep. Turkey at London Jt Cttee on Cyprus, 1959-60; Dir-Gen., Policy Planning Gp, Min. of Foreign Affairs, 1960-63; Minister Plenipotentiary, 1963; Dep. Sec.-Gen. for Polit. Affairs, 1963-64; Sec.-Gen. with rank of Ambassador, 1964-66; Ambassador to London, 1966-69, to United Nations, 1969-71; Minister of Foreign Affairs, 1971-74; Secretary-General, Cento, 1975-77. Mem., Turkish Delegns to 8th-13th, 16th-20th Gen. Assemblies of UN; rep. Turkey at internat. confrs, 1953-66; Leader of Turkish Delegn: at meeting of For. Ministers, 2nd Afro-Asian Conf., Algiers, 1965. Univ. of Ankara: Mem., Inst. of Internat. Relations; Lectr, Faculty of Polit. Scis, 1963-66. Hon. Gov., Sch. of Oriental and African Studies, London. Isabel la Catolica (Spain), 1964; Grand Cross of Merit (Germany), 1965; Hon. GCVO, 1967; Sitara-i-Pakistan (Pakistan), 1970; Star, Order One (Jordan), 1972; Sirdar-i-Ali (Afghanistan), 1972. *Publications:* lectures, articles, studies and essays on subject of minorities, Cyprus, principles of foreign policy, internat. relations and disputes. *Recreations:* music, painting, reading. *Address:* Cumhurbaskanligi Genel Sekreteri, Ankara, Turkey. *Clubs:* Hurlingham, Travellers', Royal Automobile.

BAZALGETTE, Rear-Adm. Derek Willoughby, CB 1976; Principal, Netley Waterside House, since 1977; *b* 22 July 1924; *yr s* of late H. L. Bazalgette; *m* 1947, Angela Hilda Vera, *d* of late Sir Henry Hinchliffe, JP, DL; four *d*. *Educ:* RNC Dartmouth. Served War of 1939-45; specialised in Gunnery, 1949; HMS Centaur, 1952-54; HMS Birmingham, 1956-58; SO 108th Minesweeping Sqdn and in comd HMS Houghton, 1958-59; HMS Centaur, 1963-65; Dep. Dir Naval Ops, 1965-67; comd HMS Aurora, 1967-68; idc 1969; Chief Staff Officer to Comdr British Forces Hong Kong, 1970-72; comd HMS Bulwark, 1972-74; Admiral President, RN Greenwich, 1974-76; Comdr 1958; Captain 1965; Rear-Adm. 1974. ADC 1974. HQ Comr for Water Activities, Scout Assoc., 1976. Freeman, City of London, 1976. *Address:* The Glebe House, Newtown, Fareham, Hants. *Club:* Lansdowne.

BAZELL, Prof. Charles Ernest; Professor of General Linguistics, School of Oriental and African Studies, University of London, 1957-77; *b* 7 Dec. 1909; *s* of Charles Thomas Bazell. *Educ:* Berkhamsted Sch.; Wadham Coll., Oxford; Fellow of Magdalen Coll., Oxford 1934-42; Prof. of English Language and General Linguistics, Univ. of Istanbul, 1942-57. *Publications:* Linguistic Form, 1953; articles and reviews for Archivum Linguisticum, Word, Acta Linguistica, etc. *Address:* c/o Lloyds Bank, 23 Old Woking Road, West Byfleet, Surrey.

BAZIN, Germain René Michel; Officier, Légion d'Honneur; Commandeur des Arts et des Lettres; Conservateur en chef honoraire du Musée du Louvre, since 1971; Professeur honoraire à L'Ecole du Louvre, since 1971; Research Professor Emeritus, York University, Toronto; Membre de l'Institut, 1975; *b* Paris, 1907; *s* of Charles Bazin, Industrialist and engineer of Ecole Centrale de Paris, and J. Laurence Mounier-Pouthot; *m* 1947, Countess Heller de Bielotzerkowka. *Educ:* Ste Croix de Neuilly; Ste Croix d'Orléans; Collège de Pontlevoy; Sorbonne. D ès L; Lic. en Droit; Dipl. Ecole du Louvre. Served French Infantry (Capt.), 1939-45. Prof., Univ. Libre de Bruxelles, since 1934; joined staff of Louvre, 1937; Conservateur en chef du Musée du Louvre, 1951-71; Professeur de muséologie, Ecole du Louvre, 1942-71; lecturer and writer; responsible for more than 30 exhibitions of paintings in France and elsewhere; his books are translated into English, German, Spanish, Italian, Japanese, Portuguese, Yugoslav, Hebrew, Swedish, Dutch, Rumanian, Czech, Danish. Corresponding Mem. of many Academies. Grand Officier, Ordre Léopold, Belgium; Grand Officier, Couronne, Belgium; Commandeur, Mérite, République d'Italie; Officier: Ordre de Santiago, Portugal; Star of the North, Sweden; Cruzeiro do Sul, Brazil, etc. Dr *hc:* Univ. of Rio de Janiero; Villanova, Pa, Univ. *Publications:* Mont St Michel, 1933; Le Louvre, 1935, rev. edn 1980; Les primitifs français, 1937; La peinture italienne aux XIVe et

XVe siècles, 1938; Memling, 1939; De David à Cézanne, 1941; Fra Angelico, 1941; Corot, 1942; Le crépuscule des images, 1946; L'Epoque impressioniste, 1947; Les grands maîtres de la peinture hollandaise, 1950; Histoire générale de l'art, 1951; L'Architecture religieuse baroque au Brésil, 1956-58; Trésors de la peinture au Louvre, 1957; Musée de l'Ermitage: écoles étrangères, 1957; Trésors de l'impressionisme au Louvre, 1958; A gallery of Flowers, 1960; Baroque and Rococo, 1964; Message de l'absolu, 1964; Aleijadinho, 1963; Francesco Messina, 1966; Le Temps des Musées, 1967; La Scultura francese, 1968; Destins du baroque, 1968; La peinture d'avant garde, 1969; Le Monde de la sculpture, 1972 (trans. as Sculpture in the World, 1968); Manet, 1972; Langage des styles, 1976; Les Palais de la Foi, 1980; L'Univers impressioniste, 1981; numerous articles in principal reviews and French periodicals and foreign art journals of Europe and America. *Recreation:* Swimming. *Address:* 23 quai Conti, 75006 Paris, France. *Clubs:* Army and Navy, Carlton, East India, Devonshire, Sports and Public Schools; Cercle de l'Union, Fondateur de la Maison de l'Amérique Latine (Paris).

BAZIRE, Rev. Canon Reginald Victor; Archdeacon and Borough Dean of Wandsworth, 1973-75; an Honorary Canon of Southwark, 1959-67 and since 1975; *b* 30 Jan. 1900; *s* of Alfred Arsène Bazire and Edith Mary (*née* Reynolds); *m* 1927, Eileen Crewsdon Brown; two *s*. *Educ:* Christ's Hospital. Missionary, China Inland Mission, 1922-45; Vicar, St Barnabas, Clapham Common, 1949-67; Rural Dean of Battersea, 1953-66; Archdeacon of Southwark, 1967-73. Proctor in convocation: 1959-64, 1970-. *Address:* 7 Grosvenor Park, Bath BA1 6BL. *T:* Bath 317100.

BAZLEY, Rt. Rev. Colin Frederick; *see* Chile, Bishop of.

BAZLEY, Sir Thomas Stafford, 3rd Bt, *cr* 1869; *b* 5 Oct. 1907; *s* of Captain Gardner Sebastian Bazley, DL, *o s* of 2nd Bt (*d* 1911) and Ruth Evelyn (*d* 1962), *d* of late Sir E. S. Howard (she *m* 2nd, Comdr F. C. Cadogan, RN, retd; he *d* 1970); *S* grandfather, 1919; *m* 1945, Carmen, *o d* of late J. Tulla; three *s* two *d*. *Educ:* Harrow; Magdalen Coll., Oxford. *Heir:* *s* Thomas John Sebastian Bazley, *b* 31 Aug. 1948. *Address:* Eastleach Folly, near Hatherop, Cirencester, Glos. *T:* Cirencester 75333.
See also H. A. Abel Smith.

BB; *see* Watkins-Pitchford, D. J.

BEACH; *see* Hicks-Beach, family name of Earl St Aldwyn.

BEACH, Gen. Sir (William Gerald) Hugh, GBE 1980 (OBE 1966); KCB 1976; MC 1944; Warden, St George's House, Windsor Castle, since 1981; Vice Lord-Lieutenant for Greater London, since 1981; Chief Royal Engineer, since 1982; *b* 20 May 1923; *s* of late Maj.-Gen. W. H. Beach, CB, CMG, DSO; *m* 1951, Estelle Mary (*née* Henry); three *s* one *d*. *Educ:* Winchester; Peterhouse, Cambridge (MA; Hon. Fellow 1982). Active service in France, 1944 and Java, 1946; comd: 4 Field Sqn, 1956-57; Cambridge Univ. OTC, 1961-63; 2 Div. RE, 1965-67; 12 Inf. Bde, 1969-70; Defence Fellow, Edinburgh Univ. (MSc), 1971; Dir, Army Staff Duties, MoD, 1971-74; Comdt, Staff Coll., Camberley, 1974-75; Dep. C-in-C, UKLF, 1976-77; Master-Gen. of the Ordnance, 1977-81. Colonel Commandant: REME, 1976-81; RPC, 1976-80; RE, 1977-; Hon. Colonel, Cambridge Univ. OTC, TAVR, 1977-. DL Greater London, 1981. CBIM; FRSA. *Recreations:* sailing, ski-ing. *Address:* The Ropeway, Beaulieu, Hants. *T:* Beaulieu 612269. *Clubs:* Farmers'; Royal Lymington Yacht.

BEACH, Surgeon Rear-Adm. William Vincent, CB 1962; OBE 1949; MRCS; LRCP; FRCSE; Retd; *b* 22 Nov. 1903; *yr s* of late William Henry Beach; *m* 1931, Daphne Muriel, *yr d* of late Eustace Ackworth Joseph, ICS; two *d*. *Educ:* Seaford Coll.; Guy's Hospital, London. Joined RN Medical Service, 1928. Served War of 1939-45 as Surgical specialist in Hospital ships, Atlantic and Pacific Fleets. Surgical Registrar, Royal Victoria Infirmary, Newcastle upon Tyne; Senior Specialist in Surgery, RN Hospitals, Chatham, Haslar, Malta, Portland; Senior Medical Officer, RN Hospital, Malta; Medical Officer i/c RN Hospital, Portland; Sen. Medical Officer, Surgical Division, RN Hospital, Haslar; Medical Officer in charge of Royal Naval Hospital, Chatham, and command MO on staff of C-in-C the Nore Command, 1960-61; MO i/c RN Hospital, Malta, and on staff of C-in-C, Mediterranean and as Medical Adviser to C-in-C, Allied Forces, Mediterranean, 1961-63. Surg. Rear-Admiral, 1960. QHS 1960. Senior Surgeon i/c Shaw Savill Passenger Liners, 1966-75. Fellow, Assoc. of Surgeons of Great Britain and Ireland, 1947, Senior Fellow, 1963. *Publications:* Urgent Surgery of the Hand, 1940; Inguinal Hernia-a new operation, 1946; The Treatment of Burns, 1950. *Recreations:* shooting, fishing. *Address:* Cherrytree Cottage, Easton, Winchester. *T:* Itchen Abbas 222. *Club:* Naval and Military.

BEACHAM, Prof. Arthur, OBE 1961; MA, PhD; Deputy Vice-Chancellor, Murdoch University, Western Australia, 1976-79 (Acting Vice-Chancellor, 1977-78); *b* 27 July 1913; *s* of William Walter and Maud Elizabeth Beacham; *m* 1938, Margaret Doreen Moseley (*d* 1979); one *s* one *d*. *Educ:* Pontywaun Grammar Sch.; University Coll. of Wales (BA 1935); Univ. of Liverpool (MA 1937); PhD Belfast 1941. Jevons Res. Student, Univ. of Liverpool, 1935-36; Leon Res. Fellow, Univ. of London, 1942-43; Lectr in Economics, Queen's Univ. of Belfast, 1938-45; Sen. Lectr, University Coll. of Wales, 1945-47; Prof. of Indust. Relations, University Coll., Cardiff, 1947-51; Prof. of Economics, University Coll. of Wales, Aberystwyth, 1951-63; Vice-Chancellor, Univ. of Otago, Dunedin, New Zealand, 1964-66; Gonner Prof.

of Applied Econs, Liverpool Univ., 1966–75. Chairman: Mid-Wales Industrial Devclt Assoc., 1957–63; Post Office Arbitration Tribunal, 1972–73; Member: Advisory Council for Education (Wales), 1949–52; Transp. Consultative Cttee for Wales, 1948–63 (Chm. 1961–63); Central Transp. Consultative Cttee, 1961–63; Economics Cttee of DSIR, 1961–63; North West Economic Planning Council, 1966–74; Merseyside Passenger Transport Authority, 1969–71; Council, Royal Economic Soc., 1970–74. Hon. LLD Otago, 1969; Hon. DUniv Murdoch, 1982. *Publications:* Economics of Industrial Organisation, 1948 (5th edn 1970); Industries in Welsh Country Towns, 1950. Articles in Econ. Jl, Quarterly Jl of Economics, Oxford Econ. Papers, etc. *Recreations:* golf, gardening. *Address:* 35 Hogarth Way, Bateman, WA 6155, Australia.

BEACHCROFT, Thomas Owen; Author; Chief Overseas Publicity Officer, BBC, 1941–61; *b* 3 Sept. 1902; *s* of Dr R. O. Beachcroft, Dir of Music at Clifton Coll., and Nina Cooke, Beckley Grove, Oxfordshire; *m* 1926, Marjorie Evelyn Taylor (*d* 1978); one *d*. *Educ:* Clifton Coll.; Balliol Coll., Oxford. Scholarship, Balliol. Joined BBC 1924; subsequently in Messrs. Unilevers Advertising Service; rejoined BBC 1941. *Publications: fiction:* A Young Man in a Hurry, 1934; You Must Break Out Sometimes, 1936; The Man Who Started Clean, 1937; The Parents Left Alone, 1940; Collected Stories, 1946; Asking for Trouble, 1948; Malice Bites Back, 1948; A Thorn in The Heart, 1952; Goodbye Aunt Hesther, 1955; (with Lowes Luard) Just Cats, 1936; Calling All Nations, 1942; British Broadcasting, 1946 (booklets about BBC); The English Short Story, 1964; The Modest Art, 1968; contributor of short stories and literary criticism to numerous publications throughout world, and to BBC. Gen. Editor British Council series Writers and their Work, 1949–54. *Recreations:* the arts in general; formerly track and cross-country running (represented Oxford against Cambridge at mile and half-mile). *Address:* The White Cottage, Datchworth Green, Herts SG3 6TL. *Club:* United Oxford & Cambridge University.

BEADLE, Prof. George Wells; President Emeritus and Professor of Biology Emeritus, University of Chicago; *b* Wahoo, Nebraska, 22 Oct. 1903; *s* of Chauncey E. Beadle and Hattie Albro; *m* 1st, 1928, Marion Cecile Hill (marr. diss., 1953); one *s*; 2nd, 1953, Muriel McClure Barnett; one step *s*. *Educ:* Univ. of Nebraska; Cornell Univ. BS 1926, MS 1927, Nebraska; MA Oxford, 1958; PhD Cornell, 1931. Teaching Asst, Cornell, 1926–27; Experimentalist, 1927–31; National Research Fellow, Calif. Institute of Technology, 1931–33; Research Fellow and Instructor, Calif. Institute of Technology, 1933–35; Guest Investigator, Institut de Biologie Physico-Chimique, Paris, 1935; Asst Prof. of Genetics, Harvard Univ., 1936–37; Prof. of Biology, Stanford Univ., 1937–46; Prof. of Biology and Chm. of the Division of Biology, California Institute of Technology, 1946–60, Acting Dean of Faculty, 1960–61; Univ. of Chicago: Pres., 1961–68, Emeritus, 1969. Trustee and Prof. of Biology, 1961–68; William E. Wrather Distinguished Service Prof., 1969–75. Research interests: genetics, cytology and origin of Indian corn (*Zea*); genetics and development of the fruit fly Drosophila; biochemical genetics of the bread mould Neurospora. Hon. Trustee, Univ. of Chicago, 1971–. Hon. DSc: Yale, 1947; Nebraska, 1949; Northwestern, 1952; Rutgers, 1954; Kenyon Coll., 1955; Wesleyan Univ., 1956; Oxford Univ., 1959; Birmingham Univ., 1959; Pomona Coll., 1961; Lake Forest Coll., 1962; Univ. of Rochester, Univ. of Illinois, 1963; Brown Univ., Kansas State Univ., Univ. of Pennsylvania, 1964; Wabash Coll., 1966; Syracuse, 1967; Loyola, 1970; Eureka Coll., 1972; Butler Univ., 1973; Hon. PhD: Gustavus Adolphus Coll.; Indiana State Univ., 1976; Hon. LLD: UCLA, 1962; Univ. of Miami, Brandeis Univ., 1963; Johns Hopkins Univ., Beloit Coll., 1966; Michigan, 1969; Hon. DHL: Jewish Theological Seminary of America, 1966; DePaul Univ., 1969; Univ. of Chicago, 1969; Canisius Coll., 1969; Knox Coll., 1969; Roosevelt Univ., 1971; Carroll Coll., 1971; DPubSer, Ohio Northern Univ., 1970. Pres., Chicago Horticultural Soc., 1968–71; Trustee: Museum of Sci. and Industry, Chicago, 1967–68; Nutrition Foundn, 1969–73. Member: Twelfth Internat. Congress of Genetics (Hon. Pres.), 1968; National Academy of Sciences (Mem. Council, 1969–72); American Philosophical Soc.; Amer. Assoc. of Adv. Sci. (Pres., 1946); Amer. Acad. of Arts and Sciences; Genetics Soc. of America (Pres., 1955); President's Sci. Adv. Cttee, 1960; Genetics Soc. (Gt Britain); Indian Soc. of Genetics and Plant Breeding; Inst. Lombardo di Scienze E Lettre; Sigma Xi. Hon. Member: Japan Acad.; Phi Beta Kappa. Royal Danish Academy of Sciences; Foreign Member: Royal Society 1960; Indian Nat. Science Acad. Lasker Award, American Public Health Association, 1950; Emil Christian Hansen Prize (Denmark), 1953; Albert Einstein Commemorative Award in Science, 1958; Nobel Prize for Medicine (jointly), 1958; National Award, American Cancer Soc., 1959; Kimber Genetics Award, National Academy of Sciences, 1959; Priestley Memorial Award, 1967; Donald Forsha Jones Award, 1972; (with Muriel B. Beadle) Edison Award for Best science book for youth, 1967. George Eastman Visiting Professor, University of Oxford, 1958–59. Trustee Pomona Coll., 1958–61. *Publications:* An Introduction to Genetics (with A. H. Sturtevant), 1939; Genetics and Modern Biology, 1963; The Language of Life (with Muriel Beadle), 1966. Technical articles in Cytology and Genetics. *Address:* 900 East Harrison Avenue, Apt D33, Pomona, Calif 91767, USA. *Clubs:* Chicago, Tavern (Chicago).

BEAGLEY, Thomas Lorne, CB 1973; Member, Dover Harbour Board, since 1980; *b* 2 Jan. 1919; *s* of late Captain T. G. Beagley, Royal Montreal Regt; *m* 1942, Heather Blanche Osmond; two *s* one *d*. *Educ:* Bristol Grammar Sch.; Worcester Coll., Oxford (MA). Served War: 2nd Lieut, Northamptonshire Regt, 1940; Lt-Col, AQMG (Movements), AFHQ, Italy, 1945. Joined Min. of Transport, 1946; Cabinet Office, 1951–52; Min. of Defence, 1952–54; UK Delegn to NATO, 1954–57; UK Shipping Rep., Far East, 1960–63; Asst Under-Sec. of State, Dept of Economic Affairs, 1966–68; Under-Sec., Min. of Transport, 1968–71; Dep. Sec., Transport Industries, DoE, 1972–76; Dep. Chief Exec., PSA, 1976–79. Mem., Nat. Ports Council, 1979–81. FCIT (Pres., 1977); Hon. FIRTE. *Recreations:* golf, galleries, gardening. *Address:* 3 Sheen Common Drive, Richmond, Surrey. *T:* 01-876 1216. *Clubs:* Travellers'; Richmond Golf, St Enodoc Golf.

BEAL, Anthony Ridley; Chairman, Heinemann Educational Books, since 1979; Managing Director, Heinemann Educational Books (International), since 1979; *b* 28 Feb. 1925; *s* of Harold and Nesta Beal; *m* 1958, Rosemary Jean Howarth; three *d*. *Educ:* Haberdashers' Aske's Hampstead School; Downing College, Cambridge (scholar); 1st class English Tripos 1948. RN, 1943–46; Lectr in English, Eastbourne Training Coll., 1949; joined William Heinemann, 1949; Dep. Man. Dir, Heinemann Educational Books, 1962–73, Man. Dir, 1973–79; Dir, Heinemann Group of Publishers, 1973–; Chairman: Heinemann Publishers (NZ), 1980–; Heinemann Publishers Australia Pty, 1981–. Chm., Educational Publishers' Council, 1980–83 (Vice-Chm., 1978–80); Mem. Council, Publishers' Assoc., 1982–. *Publications:* D. H. Lawrence: Selected Literary Criticism, 1956; D. H. Lawrence, 1961; contribs to books on literature, education and publishing. *Recreations:* reading maps, travelling, thinking while gardening. *Address:* 24 Loom Lane, Radlett, Herts. *T:* Radlett 4567. *Club:* Garrick.

BEALE, Evelyn Martin Lansdowne, FRS 1979; Technical Director: Scicon Consultancy International Ltd, since 1968; Scicon Computer Services Ltd, since 1975; Visiting Professor, Mathematics Department, Imperial College of Science and Technology, since 1967; *b* 8 Sept. 1928; *s* of late Evelyn Stewart Lansdowne Beale and Muriel Rebecca Beale, OBE; *m* 1953, Violette Elizabeth Anne (*née* Lewis); two *s* one *d*. *Educ:* Winchester Coll.; Trinity Coll., Cambridge (BA, DipMathStat). Member, Mathematics Gp, Admiralty Research Laboratory, 1950–61; Research Associate, Princeton Univ., 1958; posts in Scicon (originally known as CEIR), 1961–. Hon. Sec., Royal Statistical Soc., 1970–76; Chm., Mathematical Programming Soc., 1974–76. Silver Medal, ORS, 1980. *Publications:* Mathematical Programming in Practice, 1968, repr. 1976; papers in Jl of Royal Stat. Soc., Mathematical Programming, etc. *Address:* Scicon Computer Services Ltd, Brick Close, Kiln Farm, Milton Keynes, Bucks MK11 3EJ. *T:* Milton Keynes 565656.

BEALE, Prof. Geoffrey Herbert, MBE 1947; FRS 1959; PhD; Royal Society Research Professor, Edinburgh University, 1963–78; *b* 11 June 1913; *s* of Herbert Walter and Elsie Beale; *m* 1949, Betty Brydon McCallum (marr. diss. 1969); three *s*. *Educ:* Sutton County Sch.; Imperial Coll. of Science, London. Scientific Research Worker, John Innes Horticultural Institution, London, 1935–40. Served in HM Forces (1941–46). Research worker, department of Genetics, Carnegie Institute, Cold Spring Harbor, New York, 1947; Rockefeller Fellow, Indiana Univ., 1947–48; Lecturer, Dept of Animal Genetics, 1948–59, Reader in Animal Genetics, 1959–63, Edinburgh Univ. *Publications:* The Genetics of Paramecium aurelia, 1954; (with Jonathan Knowles) Extranuclear Genetics, 1978. *Address:* 23 Royal Terrace, Edinburgh EH7 5AH. *T:* 557 1329.

BEALE, Hon. Sir Howard; *see* Beale, Hon. Sir O. H.

BEALE, Josiah Edward Michael; Assistant Secretary, Department of Industry; *b* 29 Sept. 1928; *s* of late J. E. Beale and of Mrs P. A. Beale, Upminster, Essex; *m* 1958, Jean Margaret McDonald; two *d* (and one *d* decd). *Educ:* Brentwood Sch.; Jesus Coll., Cambridge. Entered Civil Service, 1950; Principal, Min. of Transport, 1956; Asst Sec., BoT later DoI, 1968–; British Govt Shipping Representative for Far East, Singapore, 1968–71. *Address:* 43 Shenfield Road, Brentwood, Essex.

BEALE, Hon. Sir (Oliver) Howard, KBE 1961; QC; Australian Ambassador to United States, 1957–64; formerly Barrister-at-Law, Member of Commonwealth Parliament and Cabinet Minister; *b* 1898; *s* of late Rev. Joseph Beale; *m* 1927, Margery Ellen Wood; one *s*. *Educ:* Sydney High Sch.; University of Sydney. BA 1921; LLB 1925. Called to NSW Bar and High Court of Australia, 1925; served War of 1939–45, RANVR, 1942–45. Elected MHR (L) Parramatta, 1946, re-elected, 1949, 1951, 1954, 1955; Mem. Commonwealth Parly. Public Works Cttee, 1947–49; Austr. Deleg., Internat. Bar Congress at The Hague, 1948; apptd KC 1950. Minister for Information and Minister for Transport (Menzies Govt), 1949–50; Chm., Austr. Transp. Adv. Council, 1949–50; Minister for Supply, 1950–58, including control of guided missiles research and Woomera Rocket Range, and atomic weapons research and Maralinga atomic testing ground; Minister i/c Austr. Aluminium Prod. Commn, 1950–58; Minister i/c Austr Atomic Energy Commn and Rum Jungle uranium project, 1950–56; Minister for Defence Prod., 1956–58, responsible for govt ordnance ammunition, explosives, chemicals, aircraft and engine factories; Actg Minister: for Immigration, 1951–52, 1953 and 1954; for Nat. Development, 1952–53; for Air, 1952; for Defence, 1957; Mem. Austr. Defence Council, 1950–58; Mem. Cabinet Defence Preparations Cttee and Cabinet Cttee on Uranium and Atomic Energy, 1950–58. Austr. rep., Anzus Council, Washington, 1958, 1959, Canberra, 1962; Leader, Austr. Delegn, Colombo Plan Conf., Seattle, 1958; Dep. Leader, Austr. Delegn to UN, New York, 1959; Dep. Leader, later Leader Austr. Delegn to Antarctic Conf., Washington, 1959; Austr. Deleg. SEATO Conf., Washington, 1959, 1960; Alt. Gov., Internat. Monetary Fund, 1960, 1962, 1963; Leader, Austr. Delegn, World Food Congress, Washington, 1963; State Visitor to Mexico and Chile, 1963; Woodward Lectr, Yale Univ., 1960; Dean of British Commonwealth

Diplomatic Corps, Washington, 1961-64; Pres., Arts Council of Australia, 1964-68. Dir of various corporations. Regents' Visiting Prof., Univ. of Calif., 1966; Marquette Univ., Wisconsin, 1967, 1969. Holds Hon. degrees. *Publication:* This Inch of Time: memoirs of politics and diplomacy, 1977. *Address:* 4 Marathon Road, Darling Point, Sydney, NSW 2027, Australia. *Clubs:* Union, Australasian Pioneers' (Sydney).

BEALE, Thomas Edward, CBE 1966; JP; Chairman, Beale's Ltd; *b* 5 March 1904; *s* of late Thomas Henderson Beale; London; *m* Beatrice May, *d* of William Steele McLaughlin, JP, Enniskillen; one *s. Educ:* City of London Sch. Mem. Bd, British Travel Assoc., 1950-70, Dep. Chm. 1965-70. Vice-Pres. and Fellow, Hotel and Catering Inst., 1949-71; Chm., Caterers' Assoc. of Gt Britain, 1949-52; Pres., Internat. Ho-Re-Ca (Union of Nat. Hotel, Restaurant & Caterers Assocs), 1954-64. Chm., Treasury Cttee of Enquiry, House of Commons Refreshment Dept, 1951. Master, Worshipful Co. of Bakers, 1955. Mem., Islington Borough Council, 1931-34; JP Inner London, 1950 (Chm. EC Div., Inner London Magistrates, 1970-73). FRSH 1957; FRSA 1968. Médaille d'Argent de Paris, 1960. *Recreation:* arboriculture. *Address:* West Lodge Park, Hadley Wood, Herts; Shoreacres, Banks Road, Sandbanks, Poole, Dorset. *Club:* Carlton.

BEALE, Sir William (Francis), Kt 1956; OBE 1945; *b* 27 Jan. 1908; *y s* of late George and Elizabeth Beale, Potterspury Lodge, Northants; *m* 1934, Dèva Zaloudek; one *s* one *d. Educ:* Downside Sch., Pembroke Coll., Cambridge. Joined Green's Stores (Ilford) Ltd, Dir, 1929-63 (Chm., 1950-63). Navy, Army and Air Force Institutes, UK, 1940-41, Dir, 1949-61 (Chm. 1953-61). EFI, GHQ West Africa, 1942-43; EFI, 21st Army Gp, 1944-46. *Recreations:* hunting, shooting; formerly Rugby football (Eastern Counties Cap, 1932). *Address:* The Old Rectory, Woodborough, Pewsey, Wilts. *Club:* Bath.

BEALES, Prof. Derek Edward Dawson, PhD; FRHistS; Professor of Modern History, University of Cambridge, since 1980; Fellow of Sidney Sussex College, Cambridge, since 1958; *b* 12 June 1931; *s* of Edward Beales and Dorothy Kathleen Beales (*née* Dawson); *m* 1964, Sara Jean (*née* Ledbury); one *s* one *d. Educ:* Bishop's Stortford Coll.; Sidney Sussex Coll., Cambridge (MA, PhD). Sidney Sussex College: Research Fellow, 1955-58; Tutor, 1961-70; Vice-Master, 1973-75; University Asst Lectr, Cambridge, 1962-65; Lectr, 1965-80. Vis. Lectr, Harvard Univ., 1965; Chairman, Faculty Board of History, Cambridge, 1979-81. Editor, Historical Journal, 1971-75. *Publications:* England and Italy 1859-60, 1961; From Castlereagh to Gladstone, 1969; The Risorgimento and the Unification of Italy, 1971; History and Biography, 1981; articles in learned jls. *Recreation:* music. *Address:* Sidney Sussex College, Cambridge. *T:* Cambridge 61501.

BEALES, Hugh Lancelot; Reader in Economic History in University of London, 1931-56; *b* 18 Feb. 1889; 3rd *s* of Rev. W. Beales; *m* ; two *s* one *d. Educ:* Kingswood Sch., Bath; University of Manchester. Lecturer in Economic History, University of Sheffield, 1919-26; Lecturer in Economic History, University of London (London Sch. of Economics), 1926-31. Visiting Prof., Columbia Univ., 1954-55, Harvard Univ., 1956, University of Washington, 1959, USA. Editorial Adviser, Penguin and Pelican Books, to 1945; Ed. of Agenda, a journal of reconstruction issued by London Sch. of Economics to 1945; mem. of Editorial Bd of Political Quarterly; Editor, Kingswood Books on Social History. Mem. of CS Arbitration Tribunal, 1955-65. Hon. Fellow, LSE, 1971. Hon. DLitt: Exeter, 1969; Sheffield, 1971; Hon. DrRCA, 1974. *Publications:* Industrial Revolution, 1929; Early English Socialists, 1932; Making of Social Policy (Hobhouse Lecture), 1945, etc. Contributor to Economic History Review and various periodicals. *Address:* 16 Denman Drive, NW11. *T:* 01-455 4091.

BEALEY, Prof. Frank William; Professor of Politics, University of Aberdeen, since 1964; *b* Bilston, Staffs, 31 Aug. 1922; *er s* of Ernest Bealey and Norah (*née* Hampton), both of Netherton, Dudley; *m* 1960, Sheila Hurst; one *s* two *d. Educ:* Hill Street Elem. Sch.; King Edward VI Grammar Sch., Stourbridge; London Sch. of Economics. Seaman in RN, 1941-46; Student, LSE, 1946-48; Finnish Govt Scholar, 1948-49; Research Asst for Passfield Trust, 1950-51; Extra-Mural Lectr, University of Manchester (Burnley Area), 1951-52; Lectr, University of Keele, 1952-64. Vis. Fellow, Yale, 1980. *Publications:* (with Henry Pelling) Labour and Politics, 1958; (with J. Blondel and W. P. McCann) Constituency Politics, 1965; The Social and Political Thought of the British Labour Party, 1970; The Post Office Engineering Union, 1976; (with John Sewel) The Politics of Independence, 1981; articles in academic jls. *Recreations:* reading poetry, eating and drinking, watching football and cricket, darts. *Address:* 355 Clifton Road, Aberdeen. *T:* Aberdeen 44689. *Club:* Economicals Association Football and Cricket.

BEAM, Jacob D.; US Ambassador to USSR, 1969-73; *b* Princeton, NJ, 24 March 1908; *s* of Jacob Newton Beam and Mary Prince; *m* 1952, Margaret Glassford; one *s. Educ:* Kent Sch., USA; Princeton Univ. (BA 1929); Cambridge Univ., England (1929-30). Vice-Consul, Geneva, 1931-34; Third Sec., Berlin, 1934-40; Second Sec., London, 1941-45; Asst Political Adviser, HQ, US Forces, Germany, 1945-47; Chief of Central European Div., Dept of State, 1947-49; Counsellor and Consul-Gen., US Embassy, Djakarta, 1949-51; Actg US Rep., UN Commn for Indonesia, 1951; Counsellor, Belgrade, 1951-52; Minister-Counsellor, US Embassy, Moscow, 1952-53 (actg head); Dep. Asst Sec. of State, 1953-57; US Ambassador to Poland, 1957-61; Asst Dir, Internat. Relations Bureau, Arms Control and Disarmament Agency, USA, 1962-66; US Ambassador to Czechoslovakia, 1966-68. Chm., US

Delegn to Internat. Telecomm. Union Plenipotentiary Conf., Malaga, 1973. Dir, Radio Free Europe, 1974-. LLB *hc* Princeton, 1970. *Publication:* Multiple Exposure, 1978. *Address:* 3129 'O' Street NW, Washington, DC 20007, USA. *Club:* Metropolitan (Washington, DC).

BEAMENT, Sir James (William Longman), Kt 1980; ScD; FRS 1964; Drapers' Professor of Agriculture and Head of the Department of Applied Biology, University of Cambridge, since 1969; Vice-President, Queens' College, Cambridge, since 1981; *b* 17 Nov. 1921; *o c* of late T. Beament, Crewkerne, Somerset; *m* 1962, Juliet, *y d* of late Prof. Sir Ernest Barker, Cambridge; two *s. Educ:* Crewkerne Grammar Sch.; Queens' Coll., Cambridge; London Sch. of Tropical Medicine. Exhibitioner, Queens' Coll., 1941; BA 1943; MA 1946; PhD London 1945; ScD Cantab 1960. Research Officer with Agricultural Research Council, Cambridge, 1946; Univ. Lectr, and Fellow and Tutor of Queens' Coll., Cambridge, 1961; Reader in Insect Physiology, 1966. Member: Adv. Bd for the Res. Councils, 1977; NERC, 1970-82 (Chm., 1977-80). Mem., Composers' Guild of Great Britain, 1967. Scientific Medal of Zoological Soc., 1963. *Publications:* many papers on insect physiology in scientific journals; Editor of several review volumes. *Recreations:* acoustics, playing the double-bass. *Address:* 19 Sedley Taylor Road, Cambridge CB2 2PW. *T:* 246045; Queens' College, Cambridge CB3 9ET. *T:* 65511. *Clubs:* Farmers'; Amateur Dramatic (Cambridge).

BEAMISH, family name of **Baron Chelwood.**

BEAMISH, Adrian John; HM Diplomatic Service; Counsellor (Economic), Bonn, since 1981; *b* 21 Jan. 1939; *s* of Thomas Charles Constantine Beamish and Josephine Mary (*née* Lee); *m* 1965, Caroline Lipscomb; two *d. Educ:* Christian Brothers' Coll., Cork; Prior Park Coll., Bath; Christ's Coll., Cambridge (BA); Università per gli Stranieri, Perugia; School of Oriental and African Studies, London Univ. Third, later Second Secretary, Tehran, 1963-66; Foreign Office, 1966-69; First Sec., UK Delegn, OECD, Paris, 1970-73; New Delhi, 1973-76; FCO, 1976-78; Counsellor, Dep. Head, Personnel Operations Dept, FCO, 1978-80. *Recreations:* people, books, plants. *Address:* c/o Foreign and Commonwealth Office, SW1.

BEAMISH, Air Vice-Marshal Cecil Howard, CB 1970; FDSRCS; Director of Dental Services, Royal Air Force, 1969-73; *b* 31 March 1915; *s* of Frank George Beamish, Coleraine; *m* 1955, Frances Elizabeth Sarah Goucher; two *s. Educ:* Coleraine Acad.; Queen's Univ., Belfast. Joined Royal Air Force, 1936; Group Capt., 1958; Air Cdre, 1968; Air Vice-Marshal, 1969. QHDS 1969-73. *Recreations:* Rugby football, golf, squash. *Address:* East Keal Manor, Spilsby, Lincs.

BEAMONT, Wing Comdr Roland Prosper, CBE 1969 (OBE 1953); DSO 1943, Bar 1944; DFC 1941, Bar 1943; DFC (US) 1946; FRAeS; author, aviation consultant; *b* 10 Aug. 1920; *s* of Lieut-Col E. C. Beamont and Dorothy Mary (*née* Haynes); *m* 1946, Patricia Raworth; three *d. Educ:* Eastbourne Coll. Commissioned in RAF, 1939; served War of 1939-45, Fighter Command, RAF, BEF, Battle of Britain (despatches), Battle of France and Germany. Attached as Test Pilot to Hawker Aircraft Ltd during rest periods, in 1941-42 and 1943-44; Experimental Test Pilot, Gloster Aircraft Co. Ltd, 1946; Chief Test Pilot, English Electric Co., 1947-61; Special Dir and Dep. Chief Test Pilot, BAC, 1961-64; Director and Manager, Flight Operations, BAC Preston, later British Aerospace, Warton Division, 1965-78; Dir of Flight Operations, Panavia, 1971-79. Events while Chief Test Pilot, English Electric Co. Ltd: 1st British pilot to fly at speed of sound (in USA), May 1948; 1st Flight of Britain's 1st jet bomber (the Canberra), May 1949; holder of Atlantic Record, Belfast-Gander, 4 hours 18 mins. Aug. 1951 and 1st two-way Atlantic Record, Belfast-Gander-Belfast, 10 hrs 4 mins Aug. 1952 (in a Canberra); first flight of P1, 1954 (Britain's first fully supersonic fighter); first British pilot in British aircraft to fly faster than sound in level flight, 1954, and first to fly at twice the speed of sound, Nov. 1958; first flight of Lightning supersonic all-weather fighter, 1957; first flight of TSR2, Sept. 1964 (Britain's first supersonic bomber). Britannia Trophy for 1953; Derry and Richards Memorial Medal, 1955; R. P. Alston Memorial Medal, RAeS, 1960; British Silver Medal for Aeronautics, 1965. Pres., Popular Flying Assoc., 1979-. Master Pilot and Liveryman, Guild of Air Pilots. DL Lancashire 1977-81. *Publications:* Phoenix into Ashes, 1968; Typhoon and Tempest at War, 1975; Testing Years, 1980. *Recreations:* sailing, fishing. *Address:* Cross Cottage, Pentridge, Salisbury, Wilts. *Club:* Royal Air Force.

BEAN, Basil; Chief Executive, Merseyside Development Corporation, since 1980; *b* 2 July 1931; *s* of Walter Bean and Alice Louise Bean; *m* 1956, Janet Mary Brown; one *d. Educ:* Archbishop Holgate Sch., York. Mem. CIPFA. York City, 1948-53; West Bromwich Borough, 1953-56; Sutton London Bor., 1957-62; Skelmersdale Develt Corp., 1962-66; Havering London Bor., 1967-69; Northampton Develt Corp., 1969-80 (Gen. Manager, 1977-80); overseas consultancies. *Publications:* financial and technical papers. *Recreations:* reading, walking, travel. *Address:* Triscombe, Church Brampton, Northampton. *T:* Northampton 843599. *Club:* Northampton and County (Northampton).

BEAN, Hugh (Cecil), CBE 1970; violinist (freelance); Professor of Violin, Royal College of Music, since 1954; *b* 22 Sept. 1929; *s* of Cecil Walter Claude Bean and Gertrude Alice Chapman; *m* 1963, Mary Dorothy Harrow; one *d. Educ:* Beckenham Grammar Sch. Studied privately, and at RCM, London (principal prize for violin) with Albert Sammons, 1938-57; Boise Trav. Schol.,

1952; at Brussels Conservatoire with André Gertler (double premier prix for solo and chamber music playing), 1952-53. National Service, Gren. Gds, 1949-51. Formerly Leader of Harvey Phillips String Orch. and Dennis Brain Chamber Orch.; Leader of Philharmonia and New Philharmonia Orch., 1957-67; Associate Leader, BBC Symph. Orch., 1967-69. Member: Bean-Parkhouse Duo; Music Gp of London. Has made solo commercial records, and has performed as soloist with many major orchestras. Hon. ARCM 1961, FRCM 1968. *Recreations:* design and construction of flying model aircraft; steam-driven passenger hauling model railways; gramophone record collection. *Address:* Rosemary Cottage, 30 Stone Park Avenue, Beckenham, Kent. *T:* 01-650 8774.

BEAN, Rev. Canon John Victor; Vicar, St Mary, Cowes, IoW, since 1966, and Priest-in-charge, All Saints, Gurnard, IoW, since 1978; Chaplain to the Queen, since 1980; *b* 1 Dec. 1925; *s* of Albert Victor and Eleanor Ethel Bean; *m* 1955, Nancy Evelyn Evans; two *s* one *d* (and one *d* died in infancy). *Educ:* local schools; Grammar Sch., Gt Yarmouth; Downing Coll., Cambridge (MA); Salisbury Theological Coll., 1948. Served War, RNVR, 1944-46; returned to Cambridge, 1946-48. Assistant Curate: St James, Milton, Portsmouth, 1950-55; St Peter and St Paul, Fareham, 1955-59; Vicar, St Helen's, IoW, 1959-66. Rural Dean of West Wight, 1968-73; Clergy Proctor for Diocese of Portsmouth, 1973-80; Hon. Canon, Portsmouth Cathedral, 1970-. *Recreations:* sailing, photography, keeping fit. *Address:* The Vicarage, Church Road, Cowes, Isle of Wight PO31 8HA. *T:* Cowes 292509. *Clubs:* Island Sailing (Cowes); Gurnard Sailing (Gurnard).

BEAN, Leonard, CMG 1964; MBE 1945; MA; Secretary, Southern Gas Region, 1966-79, retired; *b* 19 Sept. 1914; *s* of late Harry Bean, Bradford, Yorks, and late Agnes Sherwood Beattie, Worcester; *m* 1938, Nancy Winifred, *d* of Robert John Neilson, Dunedin, NZ; one *d*. *Educ:* Canterbury Coll., NZ; Queens' Coll., Cambridge. Served War of 1939-45: Major, 2nd NZ Div. (despatches, MBE). Entered Colonial Service, N Rhodesia, 1945; Provincial Comr, 1959; Perm. Sec. (Native Affairs), 1961; acted as Minister for Native Affairs and Natural Resources in periods, 1961-64; Permanent Secretary: to Prime Minister, 1964; also to President, 1964. Adviser to President, Zambia, 1964-66. *Recreations:* golf, gardening. *Address:* Squirrels Gate, 20 Ashley Park, Ringwood, Hants BH24 2HA. *T:* Ringwood 5262. *Clubs:* MCC; Bramshaw Golf.

BEAN, Robert E.; *b* 5 Sept. 1935. *Educ:* Rochester Mathematical Sch.; Medway Coll. of Technol. MIOB; AMBIM. Polytechnic Lectr. Joined Labour Party, 1950. Mem., Chatham Borough Council, 1958-74; formerly Member: Fabian Soc.; Co-operative party. Contested (Lab): Gillingham, 1970; Thanet East, Feb. 1974; MP (Lab) Rochester and Chatham, Oct. 1974-1979. Mem., Medway Borough Council, 1974-76. *Address:* 22 Horsted Way, Rochester, Kent ME1 2XY. *T:* Medway 42689.

BEAN, Thomas Ernest, CBE 1957; *b* 11 Feb. 1900; *s* of Arthur Charles Bean; *m* 1929, Eleanor Child; one *d*. Asst Circulation Manager, Manchester Guardian, 1928-44; General Manager: Hallé Concerts Soc., Manchester, 1944-51; Royal Festival Hall, London, 1951-65; Sec., London Orchestral Concert Bd, 1965-71. Austrian Order of Merit (Officer's Class), 1959. *Recreation:* gardening. *Address:* 5 Pixholme Court, Dorking, Surrey. *T:* Dorking 2900.

BEANEY, Alan; *b* 3 March 1905; *s* of John Beaney, New Silksworth, Co. Durham; *m* 1926, Mary Elizabeth, *d* of William Wass, New Silksworth, Co. Durham; one *s* two *d*. *Educ:* Elementary Sch.; NCLC. Mem. Dearne Urban District Council, 1938; County Councillor, WR Yorks, 1949; MP (Lab) Hemsworth Div. WR Yorks, 1959-Feb. 1974. Formerly Mem., Yorks Executive Cttee, National Union of Mineworkers. *Recreations:* hiking, fishing, reading. *Address:* 190 Houghton Road, Thurnscoe, Rotherham, W Yorks. *T:* Rotherham 893304. *Club:* Royal Automobile.

BEAR, Leslie William, CBE 1972; Editor of Official Report (Hansard), House of Commons, 1954-72; *b* 16 June 1911; *s* of William Herbert Bear, Falkenham, Suffolk; *m* 1st, 1932, Betsy Sobels (*d* 1934), Lisse, Holland; 2nd, 1936, Annelise Gross (*d* 1979), Trier, Germany; two *s*. *Educ:* Gregg Sch., Ipswich. Served War, 1943-44, Royal Air Force. Mem. of Official Reporting Staff, League of Nations, Geneva, 1930-36; joined Official Report (Hansard), House of Commons, 1936; Asst Ed., 1951. *Recreations:* ski-ing, gardening, chess. *Address:* Medleys, Ufford, Woodbridge, Suffolk. *T:* Eyke 358.

BEARD, Allan Geoffrey, CB 1979; Under Secretary, Department of Health and Social Security, 1968-79 (Ministry of Social Security 1966-68); *b* 18 Oct. 1919; *s* of late Major Henry Thomas Beard and Florence Mercy Beard; *m* 1945, Helen McDonagh; one *d*. *Educ:* Ormskirk Grammar Sch. Clerical Officer, Air Min., 1936; Exec. Off., Higher Exec. Off., Asst Principal, Assistance Board, 1938-47; Army Service, 1940-46 (Capt., RE); Principal, Nat. Assistance Board, 1950; Asst Sec., 1962. Governor of Motability, 1980. *Recreations:* music, gardening, do-it-yourself. *Address:* 51 Rectory Park, Sanderstead, Surrey CR2 9JR. *T:* 01-657 4197. *Club:* Royal Automobile.

BEARD, (Christopher) Nigel; Senior Consultant, Imperial Chemical Industries Ltd, since 1979; *b* 10 Oct. 1936; *o s* of Albert Leonard Beard, Castleford, Yorks, and Irene (*née* Bowes); *m* 1969, Jennifer Anne, *d* of T. B. Cotton, Guildford, Surrey; one *s* one *d*. *Educ:* Castleford Grammar Sch., Yorks; University Coll. London. BSc Hons, Special Physics. Asst Mathematics

Master, Tadcaster Grammar Sch., Yorks, 1958-59; Physicist with Englis Electric Atomic Power Div., working on design of Hinckley Point Nuclea Power Station, 1959-61; Market Researcher, Esso Petroleum Co., assessir future UK Energy demands and market for oil, 1961. MoD: Scientific Office later Principal Scientific Officer, in Defence Operational Analysis Estab (engaged in analysis of central defence policy and investment issues), 1961-6 and Supt of Studies pertaining to Land Ops; responsible for policy an investment studies related to Defence of Europe and strategic movement o the Army, Dec. 1968-72; Chief Planner, Strategy, GLC, 1973-74; Dir, Londo Docklands Develt Team, 1974-79. Mem., SW Thames RHA, 1978 Contested (Lab) Woking, 1979. FRSA. *Publication:* The Practical Use c Linear Programming in Planning and Analysis, 1974 (HMSO). *Recreation* reading history, walking, the theatre. *Address:* Lanquhart, The Ridgway Pyrford, Woking, Surrey. *T:* Byfleet 48630.

BEARD, Derek, CBE 1979; British Council Representative in Belgium, sinc 1981; *b* 16 May 1930; *s* of Walter Beard and Lily Beard (*née* Mellors); *m* 1s 1953, Ruth Davies (marr. diss. 1966); two *s*; 2nd, 1966, Renate Else, *d* of lat W. E. Kautz, Berlin and Mecklenburg; two *s*. *Educ:* Hulme Grammar Sch Oldham; Brasenose Coll., Oxford (MA, DipEd). Stand Grammar Sch Whitefield, 1954-56; HMOCS, Nyasaland, 1956-59; Asst Educn Officer, WI Yorks, 1959-61; Sen. Asst, Oxfordshire, 1961-63; British Council, Pakistar 1963-65; Producer, BBC Overseas Educnl Recordings Unit, 1965-66; Dir Appts, Services Dept, British Council, 1966-70; Dep. Rep., India, 1970-73 Controller, Educn and Science Div., British Council, 1973-77; Rep. i Germany, 1977-81. *Publications:* articles on educn and cultural relns *Recreations:* sculpture, music, travel. *Address:* Galilée Building, Avenu Galilée 5 (Boite 10), 1030 Brussels, Belgium. *Club:* Travellers'.

BEARD, Nigel; *see* Beard, C. N.

BEARD, Paul, OBE 1952; FRAM; FGSM; Professor of Violin, Guildha School of Music, retired 1968; *b* 4 Aug. 1901; *m* 1925, Joyce Cass-Smith; on *s* one *d*. *Educ:* Birmingham Oratory and St Philip's. Began violin playing a 4, being taught by father; first public appearance at 6; studied as Scholarship holder at RAM; appointed ARAM, 1921, and FRAM 1939; Principal 1s Violin of following Orchestras: City of Birmingham and Spa, Scarborough 1920-32; National of Wales, 1929; London Philharmonic, 1932-36; BB(Symphony Orchestra, 1936-62. *Recreations:* golf, gardening. *Address:* 8 Downs Wood, Epsom Downs, Surrey. *T:* Burgh Heath 50759.

BEARD, Paul Michael; a Recorder of Crown Courts since 1972; Barrister-at Law; *b* 21 May 1930; *s* of late Harold Beard, Sheffield; *m* 1959, Rhod. Margaret, *er d* of late James Henry Asquith, Morley, Yorks; one *s* one *d*. *Educ* The City Grammar Sch., Sheffield; King's Coll., London. LLB (Hons Commissioned RASC, 1949; served BAOR (Berlin), 1949-50. Called to Bar Gray's Inn, 1955; North-Eastern Circuit. Contested (C): Huddersfield East 1959; Oldham East, 1966; Wigan, Feb. and Oct. 1974; Doncaster, 1979; Chm. Brightside Conservative Assoc., 1961-68. *Recreations:* reading, walking *Address:* Flowerdale, Church Street, East Markham, near Newark, Notts. *T:* Tuxford 870074; 42 Bank Street, Sheffield S1 1EE. *T:* 20606/26826. *Club:* Sheffield (Sheffield).

BEARDS, Paul Francis Richmond; *b* 1 Dec. 1916; *s* of late Dr Clifford Beards and Dorothy (*née* Richmond); *m* 1950, Margaret Elizabeth, *y d* of late V. R. Aronson, CBE, KC; one *s* one *d*. *Educ:* Marlborough; Queen's Coll. Oxford (Open Scholar; 1st cl. hons Mod. Hist.). Entered Admin. Class o Home Civil Service, 1938; Asst Princ., War Office; served in Army, 1940-44 Principal War Office, 1945; Asst Private Sec. to successive Prime Ministers 1945-48; Princ. Private Sec. to successive Secs of State for War, 1951-54; Ass Sec., 1954; Imp. Def. Coll., 1961; Asst Under-Sec. of State, MoD, 1964-69 Comr for Administration and Finance, Forestry Commn, 1969; retd, 1970 Coronation Medal, 1953. *Recreations:* fishing, gardening, archæology *Address:* Thrale Cottage, Budleigh Salterton, Devon EX9 6EA. *T:* Budleigh Salterton 2084. *Club:* Royal Commonwealth Society.

BEARDSWORTH, Maj.-Gen. Simon John; Deputy Master General of the Ordnance, since 1981; *b* 18 April 1929; *s* of late Captain (S) Stanley Thoma Beardsworth, RN and Pearl Sylvia Emma (Biddy) Beardsworth (*née* Blake) *m* 1954, Barbara Bingham Turner; three *s*. *Educ:* RC Sch. of St Edmund' Coll., Ware; RMA Sandhurst; RMCS. BSc; FBIM. Commissioned Roya Tank Regt, 1949; Regtl service, staff training and staff appts, 1950-69; CC 1st RTR, 1970-72; Project Manager, Future Main Battle Tank, 1973-77 Student, Royal Naval War College, 1977; Dir of Projects, Armoured Fighting Vehicles, 1977-80; Dep. Comdt, RMCS, 1980-81. *Recreations:* game shooting, Pony Club Tetrathlon, horses, amateur dramatics, contemplating authorship. *Address:* Ministry of Defence, Main Building, Whitehall, SW1A 2HB. *T:* 01-218 6341. *Club:* Army and Navy.

BEARE, Robin Lyell Blin, MB, BS; FRCS; Hon. Consultant Plasti Surgeon: Queen Victoria Hospital, East Grinstead, since 1960; Brightor General Hospital and Brighton and Lewes Group of Hospitals, since 1960 Hon. Consulting Plastic Surgeon, St Mary's Hospital, London, since 1976 (Consultant Plastic Surgeon, 1959-76); *b* 31 July 1922; *s* of late Stanley Samue Beare, OBE, FRCS, and late Cecil Mary Guise Beare (*née* Lyell); *m* 1947 Iris Bick; two *s* two *d*. *Educ:* Radley (scholar). Middlesex Hosp. Medical Sch MB, BS (Hons) 1952 (dist. Surg.); FRCS (Eng) 1955. Served with RAF Bomber Command (Aircrew) 1940-46. Formerly Ho. Surg., Casualty Officer

Asst Pathologist and Surgical Registrar, The Middlesex Hosp., 1952-56. Surg. Registrar, Plastic Surgery and Jaw Injuries Centre, Queen Victoria Hosp., East Grinstead, 1957-60. Examr in gen. surgery for FRCS, 1972-78. Fellow Assoc. of Surgeons of Gt Britain and Ireland; Fellow Royal Society Med.; Mem. Brit. Assoc. of Plastic Surgeons; Mem. of Bd of Trustees, McIndoe Memorial Research Unit, E Grinstead; Hon. Mem. Société Française de Chirurgie Plastique et Reconstructive. *Publications:* various on surgical problems in BMJ, Amer. Jl of Surgery, etc. *Recreations:* fishing, shooting. *Address:* 149 Harley Street, W1N 2DE. *T:* 01-935 4444; Scraggs Farm, Cowden, Kent. *T:* Cowden 386.

BEARN, Prof. Alexander Gordon, MD; FRCP, FRCPEd, FACP; Professor of Medicine, Cornell University Medical College, since 1966 (Stanton Griffis Distinguished Medical Professor, 1976-79); Attending Physician, The New York Hospital, since 1966; Senior Vice President, Medical and Scientific Affairs, Merck Sharp and Dohme International, since 1979; *b* 29 March 1923; *s* of E. G. Bearn, CB, CBE; *m* 1952, Margaret, *d* of Clarence Slocum, Fanwood, NJ, USA; one *s* one *d. Educ:* Epsom Coll.; Guy's Hosp., London. Postgraduate Medical Sch. of London, 1949-51. Rockefeller Univ., 1951-66; Hon. Research Asst, University Coll. (Galton Laboratory), 1959-60; Prof. and Sen. Physician, Rockefeller Univ., 1964-66, Vis. and Adjunct Prof. 1966-; Chm., Dept of Medicine, Cornell Univ. Med. Coll., 1966-77; Physician-in-Chief, NY Hosp., 1966-77. Woodrow Wilson Foundn Vis. Fellow, 1979-80. Trustee, Rockefeller Univ.; Dir, Josiah Mary Jr Foundn. Mem. Editorial Bd, several scientific and med. jls. Lectures: Lowell, Harvard, 1958; Medical Research Soc., 1969; Lilly, RCP, 1973; Harvey, 1975; Lettsomian, Med. Soc., 1976. Macy Faculty Scholar Award, 1974-75. Alfred Benzon Prize, Denmark, 1979. Member: Nat. Acad. Science; Amer. Philosophical Soc.; Foreign Mem., Norwegian Acad. Science and Letters. Docteur *hc* Paris, 1975. *Publications:* articles on human genetics and liver disease, 1950-; (Co-Editor) Progress in Medical Genetics, Vol. 2, 1962-; (Associate Editor) Cecil and Loeb: Textbook of Medicine. *Recreations:* biography, travel. *Address:* 1225 Park Avenue, New York, NY 10028, USA. *T:* 534-2495. *Clubs:* Grolier, Knickerbocker, Century (NY).

BEARNE, Air Vice-Marshal Guy, CB 1956; *b* 5 Nov. 1908; *y s* of late Lieut-Col L. C. Bearne, DSO, AM; *m* 1933, Aileen Cartwright, *e d* of late H. J. Randall, Hove; one *s* two *d.* Commissioned RAF, 1929; served in various Bomber Sqdns, 1930-33; specialist armament course, 1933; armament duties, 1934-44; Bomber Command, 1944-45 (despatches twice); Staff Officer i/c Administration, RAF Malaya, 1946; Joint Services Staff Coll., 1947; Dep. Dir Organisation (Projects), 1947-49; Command of Central Gunnery Sch., 1949-51; SASO, Rhodesian Air Training Gp, 1951-52; AOC Rhodesian Air Training Gp, 1953; Dir of Organisation (Establishments), Air Ministry, 1954-56; Air Officer in Charge of Administration, Technical Training Command, 1956-61; retd, 1961. *Recreation:* golf. *Address:* 2 Mill Close, Hill Deverill, Warminster, Wilts BA12 7EE. *T:* Sutton Veny 533.

BEARSTED, 3rd Viscount, *cr* 1925, of Maidstone; **Marcus Richard Samuel,** TD 1945; DL; Baron, *cr* 1921; Bt *cr* 1903; Chairman: 1928 Investment Trust Ltd, since 1948; Samuel Properties Ltd and subsidiary companies, 1961-82; Hill Samuel & Co. (Jersey) Ltd, 1962-80; Negit SA, Luxembourg, 1966-82; Director: Hill Samuel Group Ltd, 1933-79 (formerly Chairman); Sun Alliance & London Insurance Group, 1949-80; Lloyds Bank Ltd and subsidiary companies, 1963-80; *b* 1 June 1909; *e s* of 2nd Viscount and Dorothea (*d* 1949), *e d* of late E. Montefiore Micholls; *S* father 1948; *m* 1st, 1947, Elizabeth Heather (marr. diss. 1966), *er d* of G. Firmston-Williams; one *d* (and one *d* decd); 2nd, 1968, Mrs Jean Agnew Somerville (*d* 1978), *d* of R. A. Wallace. *Educ:* Eton; New Coll., Oxford. Served War of 1939-45, Warwicks Yeomanry (Major), Middle East, Italy (wounded). Chm., Warwicks Hunt, 1960-69. Trustee and Chm. of Whitechapel Art Gallery, 1949-73. Chm., Bearsted Meml Hosp., 1948-; President: Jewish Home and Hosp. at Tottenham, 1948-; St Mary's Hosp. Med. Sch., 1964-80; Dep. Chm., St Mary's Hosp., Paddington, 1958-74; Vice-Chm., Tottenham Gp HMC, 1949-74; Board Member: Eastman Dental Hosp., 1970-75; Kensington, Chelsea and Westminster AHA, 1973-77; St John's Hosp. for Diseases of the Skin, 1975-78. Pres., Nat. Soc. for Epileptics, Chalfont Colony, 1960-; Jt Pres., Barkingside Jewish Youth Centre, 1969-. DL Warwicks, 1950. *Recreations:* fishing, tapestry. *Heir: b* Hon. Peter Montefiore Samuel, *qv. Address:* 3 Netherton Grove, SW10 9TQ. *T:* 01-730 2026; Upton House, Banbury, Oxon OX15 6HT. *T:* Edgehill 242. *Club:* White's.

BEASLEY, Michael Charles, IPFA, FCA, FCCA; County Treasurer, Royal County of Berkshire, since 1970; *b* 20 July 1924; *y s* of late William Isaac Beasley and Mary Gladys (*née* Williams), Ipswich, Suffolk; *m* 1955, Jean Anita Mary, *o d* of Reginald John Webber and Margaret Dorothy (*née* Rees), Penarth, S Glamorgan; one *s. Educ:* Northgate Grammar Sch., Ipswich. BScEcon London. Treasurer's Dept, East Suffolk County Council, 1940-48; served Royal Navy, 1943-46; Treasurer's Dept, Staffordshire CC, 1948-51; Educn Accountant, Glamorgan CC, 1951-54; Asst County Treasurer, Nottinghamshire CC, 1954-61; Dep. County Treasurer, Royal County of Berkshire, 1961-70. Examiner, CIPFA, 1963-66; Financial Adviser, Assoc. of County Councils and former County Councils Assoc., 1971-; Hon. Sec., 1972-80, Vice-Pres., 1980-81, Pres., 1981-82, Soc. of County Treasurers; Mem., Treasury Cttee on Local Authority Borrowing, 1972-; Member Council: Local Authorities Mutual Investment Trust, 1974-75; RIPA, 1976-. *Publications:* contribs to jls on local govt finance and computers. *Recreations:*

pottering and pondering. *Address:* Greenacre, Hyde End Road, Spencers Wood, Berkshire RG7 1BU. *T:* Reading 883868.

BEASLEY, Prof. William Gerald, CBE 1980; BA, PhD; FRHistS; FBA 1967; Professor of the History of the Far East, University of London, 1954-Sept. 1983; Head of Japan Research Centre, School of Oriental and African Studies, 1978-Sept. 1983; *b* 1919; *m* 1955, Hazel Polwin; one *s. Educ:* Magdalen Coll. Sch., Brackley; University Coll., London. Served War, 1940-46, RNVR. Lecturer, Sch. of Oriental and African Studies, University of London, 1947. Mem., 1961-68, British Chm., 1964-68, Anglo-Japanese Mixed Cultural Commn. Vice-Pres., British Acad., 1974-75, Treasurer, 1975-79. Hon. DLitt Hong Kong, 1978. *Publications:* Great Britain and the opening of Japan, 1951; Select Documents on Japanese foreign policy, 1853-1868, 1955; The Modern History of Japan, 1963; The Meiji Restoration, 1972. *Address:* School of Oriental and African Studies, University of London, WC1E 7HP. *T:* 01-637 2388.

BEASLEY-MURRAY, George Raymond, DD, PhD; *b* 10 Oct. 1916; *s* of George Alfred Beasley; *m* 1942, Ruth Weston; three *s* one *d. Educ:* City of Leicester Boys' Sch.; Spurgeon's Coll. and King's Coll., London; Jesus Coll., Cambridge (MA). BD 1941, MTh 1945, PhD 1952, DD 1964, London; DD McMaster, Canada, 1973. Baptist Minister, Ilford, Essex, 1941-48; Cambridge, 1948-50; New Testament Lectr, Spurgeon's Coll., 1950-56; New Testament Prof., Baptist Theological Coll., Rüschlikon, Zürich, 1956-58; Principal, Spurgeon's Coll., 1958-73; Buchanan-Harrison Prof. of New Testament Interpretation, Southern Baptist Theol Seminary, Louisville, Ky, 1973-80. Pres., Baptist Union of Great Britain and Ireland, 1968-69. *Publications:* Christ is Alive, 1947; Jesus and the Future, 1956; Preaching the Gospel from the Gospels, 1956; A Commentary on Mark Thirteen, 1957; Baptism in the New Testament, 1962; The Resurrection of Jesus Christ, 1964; Baptism Today and Tomorrow, 1966; Commentary on 2 Corinthians (Broadman Commentary), 1971; The Book of Revelation (New Century Bible), 1974. *Recreation:* music. *Address:* 193 Croydon Road, Beckenham, Kent BR3 3QH.

BEATON, Arthur Charles, CMG 1954; Assistant Area General Manager, North Staffs Area, West Midlands Division, National Coal Board, 1955-61; National Coal Board Civil Defence Organiser, 1961, retired 1967; *b* 22 Aug. 1904; *s* of Samuel and Alice Ellen Beaton; *m* 1935, Jessie, *d* of Albert and Sarah Burrow; one *s* one *d. Educ:* Leeds Grammar Sch.; Keble Coll., Oxford. BA Litt. Hum. (Oxon), 1927; MA (Oxon), 1935. Sudan Political Service, 1927; District Comr, 1937; Dep. Gov., Equatoria, 1947; Dir, Local Govt Branch, 1950; Dep. Civil Sec., 1952; Actg Civil Sec., 1953; Permanent Under Sec. Ministry of the Interior, Sudan Government, 1954. 4th Class, Order of the Nile, 1941. *Publications:* Handbook, Equatoria Province, 1952. Articles in Sudan Notes and Records on anthropological subjects. *Recreations:* gardening, reading. *Address:* 50 Chiltern Road, Sutton, Surrey SM2 5RD. *T:* 01-643 9893.

BEATON, Surg. Rear-Adm. Douglas Murdo, CB 1960; OBE 1940; retired as Medical Officer in Charge, RN Hospital, Plymouth, and Command Medical Officer, Plymouth Command (1957-60); *b* 27 May 1901; *s* of late Murdo Duncan Beaton, Kishorn, Ross-shire; *m* 1929, Violet, 2nd *d* of late David R. Oswald, MD, Kinross, Scotland; one *s* one *d. Educ:* Bristol Grammar Sch.; Edinburgh, Royal Colleges LDS 1923; LRCPE, LRCSE, LRFPS (Glas), 1924; Surg. Lieut Royal Navy, 1924; Surg. Comdr, 1936; Surg. Capt., 1948; Surg. Rear-Adm., 1957. Asst to Medical Dir-Gen., 1944-46; Medical Officer in Charge, HMHS Maine, 1947-48; MO i/c RN Sick Quarters, Shotley, 1949-51; Senior Medical Officer, Medical Section, RN Hospital, Plymouth, 1951-54; Asst to Medical Dir-Gen., Admiralty, 1954-57. QHP 1956-60; KStJ 1979. *Recreations:* golf, gardening, sailing. *Address:* Ardarroch, Auchterarder, Perthshire. *T:* Auchterarder 2329.

BEATON, Chief Inspector James Wallace, GC 1974; Chief Inspector, Metropolitan Police, since 1979; *b* St Fergus, Aberdeenshire, 16 Feb. 1943; *s* of J. A. Beaton and B. McDonald; *m* 1965, Anne C. Ballantyne; two *d. Educ:* Peterhead Acad., Aberdeenshire. Joined Metropolitan Police, 1962: Notting Hill, 1962-66; Sergeant, Harrow Road, 1966-71; Station Sergeant, Wembley, 1971-73; Royalty Protection Officer, 'A' Division, 1973; Police Officer to The Princess Anne, 1973-79; Police Inspector, 1974. Director's Honor Award, US Secret Service, 1974. *Recreations:* reading, keeping fit. *Address:* 12 Embry Way, Stanmore, Mddx HA7 3AZ. *T:* 01-954 5054.

BEATON, John Angus, CB 1975; solicitor; lately Director, Scottish Courts Administration (Deputy Director, 1972-74); *b* 24 July 1909; *s* of Murdoch Beaton, TD, ISO, Inverness, and Barbara Mackenzie Beaton (*née* Rose); *m* 1942, Margaret Florence McWilliam; two *s* one *d. Educ:* Inverness Royal Acad.; Edinburgh Univ. (BL). Scottish Office: Sen. Legal Asst, 1947; Asst Solicitor, 1960; Deputy Solicitor, 1966-72. Chm., Supplementary Benefit Appeals Tribunal, 1978-. Temporary Sheriff, 1979-81. Vice-Pres., 1960-63 and Hon. Mem., 1963-, Instn of Professional Civil Servants. *Publications:* Glossary of Scottish Legal Terms, 1980; Scots Law Terms and Expressions, 1982; articles in Encycl. of Scots Law and in legal jls. *Recreations:* reading, golf, fishing. *Address:* 2 Dryden Place, Edinburgh EH9 1RP. *T:* 031-667 3198. *Clubs:* Edinburgh University Staff (Edinburgh); Gullane Golf (East Lothian); New Golf (St Andrews).

BEATTIE, Hon. Sir Alexander (Craig), Kt 1973; **Hon. Mr Justice Beattie;** President, Industrial Commission of New South Wales, Australia, since 1966 (Member, 1955); *b* 24 Jan. 1912; *e s* of Edmund Douglas and Amie Louisa Beattie; *m* 1st, 1944, Joyce Pearl Alder (*d* 1977); two *s*; 2nd, 1978, Joyce Elizabeth de Groot. *Educ:* Fort Street High Sch., Sydney; Univ. of Sydney (BA, LLB). Admitted to NSW Bar, 1936. Served War of 1939-45: Captain, 2nd AIF, Royal Australian Armoured Corps, New Guinea and Borneo. Trustee, Royal Botanic Gardens and Govt Domain, Sydney, 1976-. *Recreations:* gardening, tennis. *Address:* 50 Phillip Street, Sydney, NSW 2000, Australia. *Club:* Australian (Sydney).

BEATTIE, Prof. Arthur James, FRSE 1957; Professor of Greek at Edinburgh University, 1951-81; Dean of the Faculty of Arts, 1963-65; *b* 28 June 1914, *e s* of Arthur John Rait Beattie. *Educ:* Montrose Academy; Aberdeen Univ.; Sidney Sussex Coll., Cambridge. Wilson Travelling Fellowship, Aberdeen, 1938-40. Served War, 1940-45; RA 1940-41; Int. Corps, 1941-45; Major GS02; despatches, 1945. Fellow and Coll. Lectr, Sidney Sussex Coll., 1946-51; Faculty Asst Lectr and Univ. Lectr in Classics, Cambridge, 1946-51. Chm. Governors, Morrison's Acad., Crieff, 1962-75; Governor, Sedbergh Sch., 1967-78. Comdr, Royal Order of the Phœnix (Greece), 1966. *Publications:* articles contributed to classical jls. *Recreations:* walking, bird-watching. *Club:* New (Edinburgh).

BEATTIE, Charles Noel, QC 1962; *b* 4 Nov. 1912; *s* of Michael William Beattie and Edith Beattie (*née* Lickfold); *m*; one *s* three *d*. *Educ:* Lewes Grammar Sch. LLB (London). Admitted a solicitor, 1938. Served War of 1939-45 (despatches), Capt. RASC. Called to the Bar, 1946; Bencher 1971. *Address:* 24 Old Buildings, Lincoln's Inn, WC2A 3UJ. *T:* 01-242 2744.

BEATTIE, Colin Panton, MA, MB, ChB, DPH; FRCPath; Professor of Bacteriology, University of Sheffield, 1946-67; now Emeritus Professor; *b* 11 Sept. 1902; *s* of James Beattie, MA, and Eleanor Anne Beattie; *m* 1937, May Hamilton Christison, BA, PhD; no *c*. *Educ:* Fettes Coll., Edinburgh; University of Edinburgh. House appointments in Royal Infirmary, Edinburgh, and Royal Northern Infirmary, Inverness, 1928-30; Asst in Bacteriology Dept., University of Edinburgh, 1930-32; Rockefeller Travelling Fellow, 1932-33; Lecturer in Bacteriology Dept, University of Edinburgh, 1933-37; Prof. of Bacteriology in The Royal Faculty of Medicine of Iraq and Dir of Govt Bacteriology Laboratory, Baghdad, 1937-46. *Publications:* various papers on bacteriological and parasitological subjects. *Recreation:* gardening. *Address:* 39 Stumperlowe Crescent Road, Sheffield S10 3PR. *T:* 302158.

BEATTIE, David; HM Diplomatic Service; Counsellor (Commercial), British Embassy, Moscow, since 1982; *b* 5 March 1938; *s* of George William David Beattie and Norna Alice (*née* Nicolson); *m* 1966, Ulla Marita Alha, *d* of Allan Alha and Brita-Maja (*née* Tuominen), Helsinki, Finland; two *d*. *Educ:* Merchant Taylors' Sch., Crosby; Lincoln Coll., Oxford (BA 1964, MA 1967). National Service, Royal Navy, 1957-59; Sub-Lieut RNR, 1959; Lieut RNR 1962-67. Entered HM Foreign (now Diplomatic) Service, 1963; FO, 1963-64; Moscow, 1964-66; FO, 1966-70; Nicosia, 1970-74; FCO, 1974-78; Counsellor, later Dep. Head, UK Delegn to Negotiations on Mutual Reduction of Forces and Armaments and Associated Measures in Central Europe, Vienna, 1978-82. *Recreations:* diplomacy, bridge, walking, history of the House of Stuart. *Address:* c/o Foreign and Commonwealth Office, SW1A 2AH. *Club:* Travellers'.

BEATTIE, Hon. Sir David (Stuart), GCMG 1980; GCVO 1981; Governor-General of New Zealand, since Nov. 1980; *b* Sydney, Australia, 29 Feb. 1924; *s* of Joseph Nesbitt Beattie; *m* 1950, Norma, *d* of John Macdonald; three *s* four *d*. *Educ:* Dilworth Sch.; Univ. of Auckland (LLB). Served War of 1939-45, Naval Officer. Barrister and Solicitor; President Auckland Dist Law Soc., 1964; QC 1965; Judge of Supreme Court, 1969-80; Chairman, Royal Commission on the Courts, 1977-78. Chairman, Sir Winston Churchill Memorial Trust Board, 1975-80. *Publications:* legal articles. *Address:* Government House, Wellington, New Zealand.

BEATTIE, Brigadier Joseph Hamilton, CBE 1945; DSO 1944; *b* 29 Sept. 1903; *s* of late Malcolm Hamilton Beattie and Maria Isabel Beattie; *m* 1938, Margaret Antonia, *er d* of J. R. Makeig-Jones, CBE, Budleigh Salterton, Devon; three *s* (and one *s* decd), three *d*. *Educ:* Royal Woolwich, 2nd Lieut RA, 1924; ADC to Viceroy of India, 1933-34; served Mohmand Campaign, NWF, India, 1935; served War of 1939-45: France, Belgium, Holland, Germany and Burma (despatches twice); Lieut-Col 1942, Brig. 1945; retd, 1956. *Recreations:* shooting, fishing. *Address:* San Anard, Zabbar, Malta.

BEATTIE, Thomas Brunton, CMG 1981; OBE 1968; HM Diplomatic Service; Counsellor, Foreign and Commonwealth Office, since 1981; *b* 17 March 1924; *s* of Joseph William Beattie and Jessie Dewar (*née* Brunton), Rutherglen; *m* 1956, Paula Rahkola; one *d*. *Educ:* Rutherglen Acad.; Pembroke Coll., Cambridge. MA. Served RAF, 1943-47. Jt Press Reading Service, British Embassy, Moscow, 1947; Finnish Secretariat, Helsinki, 1951; FO, 1954; Second Sec., Madrid, 1956; FO, 1960; First Sec., Athens, 1964; First Sec., later Counsellor, FCO, 1969; Rome, 1977. *Recreations:* hill walking, local Scottish history, music. *Address:* Cairnside, Kirkland of Glencairn, Moniaive, Dumfriesshire DG3 4HD. *Clubs:* Carlton, Travellers'; Royal Scottish Automobile (Glasgow).

BEATTIE, Prof. William, CBE 1963; Librarian, National Library of Scotland, 1953-70; Director, Institute for Advanced Studies in the Humanities Edinburgh University, 1972-80; *b* 27 Aug. 1903; *s* of William Beattie and Elizabeth Vallance; *m* 1932, Agnes Howie (*d* 1979), *d* of Henry Wood; two *d* (and one *d* decd). *Educ:* Jedburgh Grammar Sch.; George Watson's Coll. University of Edinburgh. Asst Librarian, University of Edinburgh, 1926-30 Keeper of Printed Books, National Library of Scotland, 1931-53. Visiting Fellow, Folger Library, 1957. Lyell Reader in Bibliography, University of Oxford, 1964-65. David Murray Lectr, Glasgow Univ., 1976. Chm., Standing Conference of National and University Libraries, 1964-67. Vice-Pres., 1963-75, Pres., 1975-77, Bibliographical Soc.; Pres., Scottish Soc. for Northern Studies, 1976-79. Hon. LLD St Andrews, 1957; Hon. LittD, Trinity Coll. Dublin, 1967; Hon. Prof., Univ. of Edinburgh, 1967. St Olav's Medal (Norway), 1977. *Publications:* The Chepman and Myllar Prints, The Taill o Rauf Coilyear (facsimiles, with introductions), 1950, 1966; (with H. W Meikle) selection of Robert Burns, 1946, rev. edn, 1972; selection of Border Ballads, 1952; articles in Edinburgh Bibliographical Soc. Transactions *Address:* 7 South Gillsland Road, Edinburgh EH10 5DE.

BEATTIE, William John Hunt Montgomery, MA Cantab; MD, FRCS FRCOG, FRCGP; Consultant Gynæcologist and Obstetric Surgeon, St Bartholomew's Hospital; Gynæcologist: Leatherhead Hospital; Florence Nightingale Hospital; retired. *Educ:* Cambridge Univ.; London Univ MRCS; LRCP 1927; BCh (Cantab) 1928; FRCS 1929; MB 1930; MD 1933 FRCOG 1942; Examiner: Central Midwives' Board; Univs. of Oxford Cambridge and London (Obst. and Gynæcol.); Conjoint Board (Midwifery and Gynæcol.). *Publications:* (jt) Diseases of Women by Ten Teachers, 1941 articles in medical journals. *Address:* Ivy Cottage, Reigate Heath, Surrey.

BEATTY, 3rd Earl *cr* 1919; **David Beatty;** Viscount Borodale of Wexford Baron Beatty of the North Sea and of Brooksby, 1919; *b* 21 Nov. 1946; *s* of 2nd Earl Beatty, DSC, and Dorothy Rita, *d* of late M. J. Furey, New Orleans USA; *S* father, 1972; *m* 1971, Ann, *d* of A. Please, Wokingham; one *s*. *Educ:* Eton. Heir: *s* Viscount Borodale, *qv*. *Address:* c/o House of Lords, SW1.

BEATTY, (Alfred) Chester; President, Selection Trust, since 1978, Chairman 1950-78; *b* 1907; *o s* of late Sir (Alfred) Chester Beatty and late Grace Madeline, *d* of Alfred Rickard, Denver, USA; *m* 1st, 1933, Pamela (marr. diss 1936; she *d* 1957), *o d* of Captain George Belas; one *d*; 2nd, 1937, Enid (marr diss. 1950), *d* of S. H. Groome, Golfe Juan, France; 3rd, 1953, Helen Gertrude widow of Roger Casalis de Pury. *Educ:* Eton; Trinity Coll., Cambridge Past-Pres., Overseas Mining Assoc.; Jt Master, Ashford Valley Foxhounds 1927-31, Master, 1931-53. FID. *Address:* Owley, Wittersham, Kent; 76 Park Street, W1. *Club:* Royal Yacht Squadron.

BEAUCHAMP, Sir Christopher Radstock Proctor-, 9th Bt *cr* 1744; solicitor with Gilbert H. Stephens & Sons, Exeter; *b* 30 Jan. 1935; *s* of Rev Sir Ivor Cuthbert Proctor-Beauchamp, 8th Bt, and Caroline Muriel, *d* of late Frank Densham; *S* father, 1971; *m* 1965, Rosalind Emily Margot, 3rd *d* of G. P. Wainwright, St Leonards-on-Sea; two *s* one *d*. *Educ:* Rugby; Trinity College, Cambridge (MA). Heir: *s* Charles Barclay Proctor-Beauchamp, *b* 7 July 1969. *Address:* The White House, Harpford, near Sidmouth, East Devon.

BEAUCHAMP, Sir Douglas Clifford (commonly known as Sir Peter), 2nd Bt, *cr* 1918; *b* 11 March 1903; *s* of Sir Frank Beauchamp, 1st Bt, and Mabel Constance (*d* 1957), *e d* of James Norman Bannon, Kent; *S* father 1950; *m* 1st, 1926, Nancy (who obtained a divorce, 1933), *o d* of Laurence E. Moss, Sydney, NSW; 2nd, 1933, Pamela Dorothy May Chandor (*d* 1971); 3rd, 1972 M. Elizabeth, widow of J. H. Tilbury. *Educ:* Eton. Heir: none. *Address:* The Pebbles, Budleigh Salterton, Devon. *T:* Budleigh Salterton 3197.

BEAUCHAMP, Sir Peter; *see* Beauchamp, Sir D. C.

BEAUCLERK, family name of **Duke of St Albans.**

BEAUFORT, 10th Duke of, *cr* 1682; **Henry Hugh Arthur FitzRoy Somerset,** KG 1937; PC 1936; GCVO 1930; JP; Royal Victorian Chain 1953; Baron Botetourt, 1305, confirmed, 1803; Baron Herbert of Raglan, Chepstow, and Gower, 1506; Earl of Worcester, 1514; Marquess of Worcester, 1642; late Royal Horse Guards; Hon. Colonel: Royal Gloucestershire Hussars, TA, 1925-69, T&AVR, 1969-71; A and C Squadrons, The Wessex Yeomanry, T&AVR, since 1972; *b* 4 April 1900; *o s* of 9th Duke and Louise Emily (*d* 1945), *d* of William H. Harford of Oldown. Almondsbury, Glos, and widow of Baron Carlo de Tuyll; *S* father, 1924; *m* 1923, Lady Mary Cambridge, *er d* of 1st Marquess of Cambridge. *Educ:* Eton: Sandhurst. Master of the Horse, 1936-78. Chancellor, Univ. of Bristol, 1966-70. High Steward: Bristol, 1925-; Gloucester, 1925-; Tewkesbury, 1948-. Lord Lieutenant of Co. of Gloucester and Bristol, 1931-74, Lord-Lieutenant of Gloucestershire, 1974-78. Received Freedom of City of Gloucester 1945. KStJ 1935. *Publications:* Fox Hunting, 1980; Memoirs, 1981. *Heir: cousin* David Robert Somerset, *qv*. *Address:* Badminton, Glos GL9 1DB. *TA:* Badminton. *Club:* Turf.

BEAUMAN, Wing Commander Eric Bentley; Librarian, Royal United Service Institution, 1952-57; *b* 7 Feb. 1891; *yr s* of late Bentley Martin Beauman; *m* 1940, Katharine Burgoyne, MA, *yr d* of late F. W. Jones; one *s*. *Educ:* Malvern Coll.; Geneva Univ.; Royal Aero Flying Certificate, 1913;

served European war, 1914-18: commnd RNAS Aug. 1914; Anti-Submarine patrols, Home and Aegean; Home Defence and flying instruction: comd seaplane stations at Dundee and Newhaven (despatches). Major, RAF 1918; psa 1922-23 (first course of RAF Staff College); psc 1929-30; instructor at RAF Staff Coll., 1932-33; retd, 1938; Air Ministry, 1938-51. War of 1939-45; RAF liaison officer with BBC. Expeditions: Mount Kamet, Himalaya, 1931; Coast Range of British Columbia, 1934 (paper to RGS on Coast Range Crossing); climbed the Matterhorn 5 times. Pres. Alpine Ski Club, 1933-35, Hon. Mem., 1978-; Hon. Librarian, Alpine Club, 1947-58. Vice-Pres. RAF Mountaineering Assoc. 1951-; Chm., Touring and Mountaineering Cttee of Ski Club of Gt Britain, 1952-54. Broadcasts on many occasions. *Publications:* compiled: Winged Words, 1941 (Book Soc. Choice); The Airmen Speak, 1941; (with Cecil Day Lewis) compiled: We Speak from the Air, 1942; Over to You, 1943; chapters in: Living Dangerously, 1936; Travellers' Tales, 1945; The Boys' Country Book, 1955; contributor to The Times, Guardian, Sunday Times, The Field, The Listener, National Review, The Geographical Magazine, Alpine Jl, RUSI Jl, British Ski Year Book, Dictionary of National Biography, Encyclopædia Britannica. *Recreations:* writing, reading, gardening. *Address:* 59 Chester Row, SW1W 8JL. *T:* 01-730 9038. *Clubs:* Alpine (elected 1920), Royal Air Force.

BEAUMONT, family name of **Viscount Allendale** and **Baron Beaumont of Whitley.**

BEAUMONT OF WHITLEY, Baron *cr* 1967 (Life Peer), of Child's Hill; **Timothy Wentworth Beaumont,** MA (Oxon); Managing Director, Holystone Productions Ltd, since 1974; *b* 22 Nov. 1928; *o s* of Major and Hon. Mrs M. W. Beaumont; *m* 1955, Mary Rose Wauchope; one *s* two *d* (and one *s* decd). *Educ:* Gordonstoun; Christ Church, Oxford; Westcott House, Cambridge. Asst Chaplain, St John's Cathedral, Hong Kong, 1955-57; Vicar, Christ Church Kowloon Tong, Hong Kong, 1957-59; Hon. Curate, St Stephen's Rochester Row, London, 1960-63; resigned orders, 1973. Editor: Prism, 1960-63 and 1964; New Outlook, 1964, 1972-74; Chm., Studio Vista Books Ltd, 1963-68; Proprietor of New Christian, 1965-70. Food Columnist, Illustrated London News, 1976-80. Asst Dir (Public Affairs), Make Children Happy, 1977-78; Co-ordinator, The Green Alliance, 1978-80. Liberal Party Organisation: Jt Hon. Treas., 1962-63; Chm., Liberal Publications Dept, 1963-64; Head of Org., 1965-66; Chm., Liberal Party's Org. Cttee, 1966; Chm., Liberal Party, 1967-68; Pres., Liberal Party, 1969-70; Vice-Chm., Liberal Party Exec. and Dir, Policy Promotion, 1980-; Liberal spokesman on education and the arts, House of Lords, 1968-78, 1980-; Alternate Mem., Assemblies of Council of Europe and WEU, 1973-77; Leader of Liberal Delegn, 1977-78, Vice-Chm., Liberal Gp, 1977-78; Dir of Policy Promotion, Liberal Party, 1980-. Pres., British Fedn of Film Socs, 1973-79. Chairman: Albany Trust, 1969-71; Inst. of Res. into Mental and Multiple Handicap, 1971-73; Exit, 1980-81. Mem., Exec. Cttee, British Council, 1974-78. *Publications:* (ed) Modern Religious Verse, 1965; ed and contrib., The Liberal Cookbook, 1972; (ed) New Christian Reader, 1974; (ed) The Selective Ego: the diaries of James Agate, 1976. *Address:* 1 Hampstead Square, NW3. *Clubs:* Beefsteak, National Liberal.

BEAUMONT, Christopher Hubert; a Recorder of the Crown Court, since 1981; *b* 10 Feb. 1926; *s* of Hubert and Beatrix Beaumont; *m* 1st, 1959, Catherine Sanders Clark (*d* 1971); two *s*; 2nd, 1972, Sara Patricia Magee; one *d. Educ:* West Monmouth Sch., Pontypool; Balliol Coll., Oxford (MA). Served RN, 1944-47 (Sub-Lieut RNVR). Called to Bar, Middle Temple, 1950. Asst Dep. Coroner, Inner West London, 1963-81. Dep. Chairman, Agricultural Land Tribunal, Eastern Area, 1979-. *Publications:* Law Relating to Sheriffs, 1968; Town and Country Planning Act 1968, 1969; Housing Act 1969, 1969; Town and Country Planning Acts 1971 and 1972, 1973; (with W. G. Nutley) Land Compensation Act 1973, 1973; (with W. G. Nutley) Community Land Act 1975, 1976. *Address:* Rose Cottage, Lower Eashing, Godalming, Surrey GU7 2QG. *T:* Godalming 6316; 2 Harcourt Buildings, Temple, EC4Y 9DB. *T:* 01-353 8415.

BEAUMONT, Sir George Howland Francis, 12th Bt, *cr* 1661; late Lieutenant 60th Rifles; *b* 24 Sept. 1924; *s* of 11th Bt and Renée Muriel, 2nd *d* of late Maj.-Gen. Sir Edward Northey, GCMG, CB; *S* father 1933; *m* 1949, Barbara Singleton (marr. annulled, 1951); *m* 1963, Henrietta Anne, *d* of late Dr A. Waymouth and of Mrs J. Rodwell, Riverside Cottage, Donnington, Berks; twin *d. Educ:* Stowe Sch. *Address:* Duntrune Nurseries, Deddington Mill, Deddington, Oxfordshire. *T:* Deddington 277. *Club:* Lansdowne.

BEAUMONT, Herbert Christopher, MBE 1948; **His Honour Judge Beaumont;** a Circuit Judge, since 1972; *b* 3 June 1912; *s* of late Gerald Beaumont, MC, and Gwendolene Beaumont (*née* Haworth); *m* 1940, Helen Margaret Gordon Smail, *d* of William Mitchell Smail; one *s* two *d. Educ:* Uppingham Sch.; Worcester Coll., Oxford. Indian Civil and Political Services, 1936-48; Foreign Office, 1948-52. Called to the Bar, Inner Temple, 1951; Metropolitan Magistrate, 1962-72. Chm. of the London Juvenile Courts, 1964; Dep. Chm., North Riding QS, 1966-71. Mem., Parole Bd, 1974-76. *Recreations:* travel in Europe, bridge. *Address:* Minskip Lodge, Boroughbridge, Yorks. *T:* Boroughbridge 2365. *Clubs:* Brooks's; Yorkshire (York).

See also G. M. Waller.

BEAUMONT, (John) Michael; Seigneur of Sark since 1974; *b* 20 Dec. 1927; *s* of late Lionel (Buster) Beaumont and Enid Beaumont (*née* Ripley); *m* 1956, Diana (*née* La Trobe-Bateman); two *s. Educ:* Loughborough Coll. (DLC). Aircraft Design Engr, 1952-70; Chief Techn. Engr, Beagle Aircraft, 1969-70; Design Engr, BAC GW Div., 1970-75. *Recreations:* theatre, music, gardening. *Heir: s* Christopher Beaumont, *b* 4 Feb. 1957. *Address:* La Seigneurie, Sark. *T:* Sark 2017.

BEAUMONT, Sir Richard Ashton, KCMG 1965 (CMG 1955); OBE 1949; HM Diplomatic Service, retired; Chairman, Arab-British Chamber of Commerce, since 1980; *b* 29 Dec. 1912; *s* of A. R. Beaumont, FRCS, Uppingham, and Evelyn Frances (*née* Rendle); *m* 1942, Alou, *d* of M. Camran, Istanbul; one *d. Educ:* Repton; Oriel Coll., Oxford. Joined HM Consular Service, 1936; posted Lebanon and Syria, 1936-41. Served War, 1941-44. Returned to Foreign Office, 1944; served in London, Iraq, Venezuela; Imperial Defence Coll., 1958; Head of Arabian Department, Foreign Office, 1959; Ambassador: to Morocco, 1961-65; to Iraq, 1965-67; Dep. Under-Sec. of State, FO, 1967-69; Ambassador to the Arab Republic of Egypt, 1969-72. Dir-Gen., Middle East Assoc., 1973-77; Chairman: Arab British Centre, 1976-77; Anglo-Arab Assoc., 1979-. Governor, SOAS, 1973-78. Trustee, Thomson Foundn, 1974-. *Recreation:* golf. *Address:* 14 Cadogan Square, SW1X 0JU. *Club:* United Oxford & Cambridge University.

BEAUMONT, William Anderson, OBE (mil.) 1961; AE 1953; Speaker's Secretary, House of Commons, since 1982; *b* 30 Oct. 1924; *s* of late William Lionel Beaumont and of Mrs E. Taverner; *m* 1946, Kythé, *d* of late Major K. G. Mackenzie, Victoria, BC; one *d. Educ:* Terrington Hall, York; Cranleigh Sch.; Christ Church, Oxford (MA, DipEd). Served RAF, Navigator, 1942-47, 355 Sqdn, 232 Sqdn, SEAC (Flt Lt); RAuxAF 3507 (Co. of Somerset) FCU, 1948-54; 3609 (W Riding) FCU, 1954-61 (Wing Comdr CO, 1958-61); Observer Comdr, No 18 (Leeds) Gp, Royal Observer Corps, 1962-75 (ROC Medal 1975). Asst Master, Bristol Grammar Sch., 1951-54; Beaumont and Smith Ltd, Pudsey, 1954-66, Man. Dir, 1958-66; Henry Mason (Shipley) Ltd, Man. Dir, 1966-76; Principal, Welsh Office, 1976-79; Asst Sec., Welsh Office, 1979-82. *Recreations:* inland waterways, reluctant gardening, walking. *Address:* Kelowna, St Hilary, S Glamorgan CF7 7DP. *T:* Cowbridge 3251. *Clubs:* Royal Air Force; United Services Mess (Cardiff).

BEAUMONT-DARK, Anthony Michael; MP (C) Birmingham, Selly Oak, since 1979; investment analyst; *b* Birmingham, 11 Oct. 1932; *s* of Leonard Cecil Dark; *m* 1959, Sheelagh Irene, *d* of R. Cassey; one *s* one *d. Educ:* Birmingham Coll. of Arts and Crafts; Birmingham Univ. Mem., Birmingham Stock Exchange, 1958-; Sen. Partner, Smith, Keen, Cutler; Director: Cope Allman Internat. Ltd; Wigham Poland (Midlands) Ltd; Nat. Exhibition Centre Ltd, 1971-73. Mem., Central Housing Adv. Cttee, DoE, 1970-76. Member: Birmingham City Council, 1956-67 (Alderman, 1967-74, Hon. Alderman, 1976); W Midlands CC, 1973- (Chm., Finance Cttee, 1977-). Contested (C) Birmingham, Aston, 1959, 1964. Trustee, Birmingham Copec Housing Trust, 1975-. *Address:* House of Commons, SW1; 124 Lady Byron Lane, Copt Heath, Solihull, Birmingham B93 9BA. *Club:* Carlton.

BEAUREPAIRE, Dame Beryl (Edith), DBE 1981 (OBE 1975); Convener, National Women's Advisory Council, Australia, since 1978; *b* 24 Sept. 1923; *d* of late E. L. Beddgood; *m* 1946, Ian Francis Beaurepaire, *qv* ; two *s. Educ:* Fintona Girls' Sch., Balwyn, Victoria; Univ. of Melbourne. ASO, WAAAF, 1942-45. Mem. Nat. Exec., YWCA Australia, 1969-77. Liberal Party of Australia: Chm., Victorian Women's Sect., 1973-76; Chm., Federal Women's Sect., 1974-76; Vice-Pres., Victorian Div., 1976-. Mem., Federal Women's Adv. Cttee Working Party, 1977. Chm., Bd of Management, Fintona Girls' Sch., 1973-. Jubilee Medal, 1977. *Recreations:* golf, swimming. *Address:* 124 Powlett Street, East Melbourne, Vic 3002, Australia. *T:* 419 2996. *Clubs:* Alexandra (Melbourne); Peninsula Country Golf (Frankston).

BEAUREPAIRE, Ian Francis, CMG 1967; Director, Dunlop Olympic Ltd, since 1980; Chairman, Olex Cables Ltd, since 1973; *b* 14 Sept. 1922; *s* of late Sir Frank and Lady Beaurepaire; *m* 1946, Beryl Edith Beddgood (*see* Dame Beryl Beaurepaire); two *s. Educ:* Carey Grammar Sch., Scotch Coll., Melbourne; Royal Melbourne Inst. of Technology. Served RAAF (Flying Officer), 1942-45. Man. Dir, Beaurepaire Tyre Service Pty Ltd, 1953-55; Gen. Man., The Olympic Tyre & Rubber Co. Pty Ltd, 1955-61; Chm., 1959-78, Man. Dir, 1959-75, Chief Exec., 1975-78, Exec. Chm., 1978-80, Olympic Consolidated Industries Ltd. Mem., Melbourne Underground Rail Loop Authority, 1971-, Chm., 1981-. Member: Melbourne City Council, 1956-75 (Lord Mayor of Melbourne, 1965-67); Management Cttee of Royal Victorian Eye and Ear Hosp., 1966-. *Recreations:* golf, grazing. *Address:* GPO Box 1492N, Melbourne, Victoria 3001, Australia. *Clubs:* Athenæum, Naval and Military, Melbourne (Melbourne); Peninsula Country Golf (Frankston).

BEAUVOIR, Simone de; French author; *b* Paris, 9 Jan. 1908; *d* of Georges Bertrand de Beauvoir and Françoise (*née* Brasseur). *Educ:* Institut Catholique; Institut Sainte-Marie; Univ. of Paris. Taught, 1931-43. President, Ligue du Droit des Femmes, 1974-. *Publications:* L'Invitée, 1943 (trans. She Came to Stay, 1949); Le Sang des autres, 1944 (trans. The Blood of Others, 1948); Pyrrhus et Cinéas (essay), 1945; Les Bouches Inutiles (play), 1945; Tous les hommes sont mortels, 1947 (trans. All Men are Mortal, 1955); Pour une morale de l'ambiguïté (essay), 1947; L'Amérique au jour le jour, 1948 (trans. America Day by Day, 1952); L'existentialisme et la sagesse des nations (essay), 1948; Le Deuxième Sexe, 1949: vol. I, Les faits et les mythes; vol. II, L'expérience vécue; Faut-il brûler Sade?, 1951 (trans. Must We Burn Sade?, 1963); Les Mandarins, 1954 (Prix Goncourt, 1954; trans. The Mandarins,

1957); Privilèges (essay), 1955; La longue marche (essay on China), 1957 (trans. The Long March, 1958); Mémoires d'une jeune fille rangée, 1958 (trans. The Memoirs of a Dutiful Daughter, 1959); La force de l'âge, 1960 (trans. The Prime of Life, 1963); Brigitte Bardot, 1960; (with G. Halimi) Djamila Boupacha, 1962; La force des choses, 1963 (trans. Force of Circumstance, 1965); Une mort très douce, 1964 (trans. A Very Easy Death, 1966); Les belles images, 1966; La femme rompue, 1968 (trans. The Woman Destroyed, 1969); L'âge de discrétion, 1968; La vieillesse, 1969 (trans. Old Age, 1972); Tout compte fait, 1972 (trans. All Said and Done, 1974); Quand prime le spirituel, 1979 (When Things of the Spirit Come First, 1982); La Cérémonie des adieux, 1981. *Address:* 11 bis rue Schoelcher, 75014 Paris, France.

BEAVAN, family name of **Baron Ardwick.**

BEAVEN, John Lewis, MVO 1974; HM Diplomatic Service; Consul-General, San Francisco, since 1982; *b* 30 July 1930; *s* of Charles and Margaret Beaven; *m* 1960, Jane Beeson (marr. diss.); one *s* one *d*; *m* 1975, Jean McComb Campbell. *Educ:* Newport (Gwent) High Sch. BoT, 1946; RAF, 1948-50; Asst Trade Comr, British High Commn, Karachi, 1956-60; Second Secretary (Commercial), British High Commn, Freetown, 1961-64; First Secretary (Commercial): British High Commn, Nicosia, 1964-66; Nairobi, 1966-68; FCO, 1969-72; Head of Chancery, British Embassy, Jakarta, 1972-74; Counsellor (Economic and Commercial), British High Commn, Lagos, 1975-77; Dep. Consul General (Commercial) and Dir, British Trade Develt Office, NY, 1978-82. *Recreations:* music, riding. *Address: c/o* Foreign and Commonwealth Office, SW1; Scannell Road, Ghent, NY 12075, USA. *T:* 518.392.2152. *Clubs:* Reform; Brook (New York).

BEAVERBROOK, Barony of (*cr* 1917, of Beaverbrook, New Brunswick and Cherkley, Surrey); title disclaimed by 2nd Baron; *see under* Aitken, Sir (John William) Max, 2nd Bt.

BEAVIS, David, CBE 1976; retired; Chairman, West Midlands Gas Region (formerly West Midlands Gas Board), 1968-77; Part-time Member, British Gas Corporation, 1973-77; *b* 12 Dec. 1913; *s* of David Beavis; *m* 1946, Vera, *d* of F. C. Todd; one *s* one *d*. *Educ:* Whitehill Secondary Sch.; Royal Technical Coll., Glasgow (now Strathclyde Univ.). Dep. Engineer and Manager, Helensburgh Town Council Gas Dept, 1935-41; Asst Engineer, Camb. Univ. and Town Gas Light Co., 1942-47; Dep. Engineer and Manager, Edin. Corp. Gas Dept, 1947-49; Divisional Gen. Man. Edin. and SE Div., and subseq. Area Manager, Scottish Gas Bd, 1949-64; Mem. Scottish Gas Bd, 1962-64; Dep. Chm., Eastern Gas Bd, 1964-68. President: Scottish Assoc. of Gas Managers, 1960-61; IGasE, 1967. *Publications:* technical papers presented to Engineering Instns. *Recreations:* technological education, golf, sailing. *Address:* 1 Sandal Rise, Solihull, West Midlands. *T:* 021-704 1819.

BEAVIS, Air Marshal Sir Michael (Gordon), KCB 1981; CBE 1977 (OBE 1969); AFC 1962; Air Officer Commanding-in-Chief, RAF Support Command, since 1981; *b* 13 Aug. 1929; *s* of Walter Erle Beavis and Mary Ann (*née* Sarjantson); *m* 1950, Joy Marion (née Jones); one *s* one *d*. *Educ:* Kilburn Grammar School. Joined RAF 1947; commnd 1949; served Fighter Comd Squadrons 1950-54, RNZAF 1954-56; flew Vulcan aircraft, Bomber Comd, 1958-62; Staff Coll., 1963; MoD, 1964-66; OC No 10 Squadron (VC10s), 1966-68; Group Captain Flying, Akrotiri, Cyprus, 1968-71; Asst Dir, Defence Policy, MoD, 1971-73; RCDS, 1974; RAF Germany, 1975-77 (SASO 1976-77); Dir Gen. RAF Training, 1977-80; Comdt, RAF Staff Coll, 1980-81. CBIM. *Recreation:* golf. *Address:* HQ RAF Support Command, RAF Brampton, Huntingdon, Cambs PE18 8QL. *Club:* Royal Air Force.

BEAZLEY, Peter George; Member (C) Bedfordshire, European Parliament, since 1979; *b* 9 June 1922; *s* of Thomas Alfred and Agnes Alice Mary Beazley; *m* 1945, Joyce Marion Sulman; one *s* two *d* (and one *d* decd). *Educ:* Highgate Sch.; St John Baptist Coll., Oxford. 2nd Cl. Final Hons PPE, MA Oxon. Captain, Rifle Brigade, served in N Africa, Italy, Austria, 1942-47. Joined ICI, 1947; Sales Manager, ICI Export Portugal, 1948-54; Sales Control Manager and International Marketing Manager, ICI Fibres Ltd, 1955-65; Gen. Man., ICI Europa Fibres, 1965-72; Member, ICI Europa Bd and ICI Fibres Bd, 1968-73; Director: ICI Italy, 1965-73; Finicisa Portugal; Vice-Pres., Alcudia Spain, 1971-73; Dep. Chm. and Jt Man. Dir, South African Nylon Spinners & Pan Textiles, 1973-76; Research Fellow, RIIA, 1977-78; retd from ICI 1978. *Publication:* The Role of Western Technology Transfer in the Development of the Soviet Union's Chemical Industry (with V. Sobeslavsky), 1979. *Recreations:* golf, gardening. *Address:* Rest Harrow, 14 The Combe, Ratton, Eastbourne, East Sussex BN20 9DB. *T:* Eastbourne 54460; 4 Bridgewater Court, Little Gaddesden, Herts. *T:* Little Gaddesden 3548. *Club:* Oriental.

BECHER, Major Sir William Fane Wrixon-, 5th Bt, *cr* 1831; MC 1943; Temp. Major, Rifle Brigade (SRO); *b* 7 Sept. 1915; *o s* of Sir Eustace W. W. Becher, 4th Bt, and Hon. Constance Gough-Calthorpe, *d* of 6th Baron Calthorpe; *S* father, 1934; *m* 1st, 1946, Vanda (marr. diss. 1960; she *m* 1962, Rear-Adm. Viscount Kelburn, now 9th Earl of Glasgow, *qv*), *d* of 4th Baron Vivian; one *s* one *d*; 2nd, 1960, Hon. Mrs Yvonne Mostyn. *Educ:* Harrow; Magdalene Coll., Cambridge. Served War of 1939-45; Western Desert and Tunisian Campaigns, 1940-43 (MC, wounded twice; taken prisoner at battle of Sidi Rezegh, Nov. 1941, and escaped); Italian Campaign, 1944; ADC to FM Lord Wilson, Supreme Allied Comdr Mediterranean. Member: British Boxing Bd of Control, 1961-82; Nat. Playing Fields Assoc., 1953-65 (Pres.,

Wiltshire Branch, NPFA, 1950-56). *Recreations:* golf and cricket (played cricket for Sussex, 1939, captained Wiltshire, 1949-53). *Heir: s* John William Michael Wrixon-Becher, *b* 29 Sept. 1950. *Address:* 16 Wilton Place, SW1. *Clubs:* MCC, White's; I Zingari.

BECK, Prof. Arnold Hugh William, BSc (Eng), MA; Professor of Engineering, since 1966, Head of Electrical Division, 1971-81, University of Cambridge; Fellow of Corpus Christi College, Cambridge, since 1962; Fellow of University College, London, since 1979; *y s* of Major Hugh Beck and Diana L. Beck; *m* 1947, Katharine Monica, *y d* of S. K. Ratcliffe; no *c*. *Educ:* Gresham's Sch., Holt; University Coll., London. Research Engr, Henry Hughes & Sons, 1937-41; seconded to Admty Signal Estab., 1941-45; Standard Telephones & Cables, 1947-58; Lectr, Cambridge Univ., 1958-64; Reader in Electrical Engrg, 1964-66. FIEEE 1959. *Publications:* Velocity Modulated Thermionic Tubes, 1948; Thermionic Valves, 1953; Space-charge Waves, 1958; Words and Waves, 1967; (with H. Ahmed) Introduction to Physical Electronics, 1968; Handbook of Vacuum Physics, Vol. 2, Parts 5 and 6, 1968; Statistical Mechanics, Fluctuations and Noise, 1976; papers in Jl IEE, Inst. Radio Engrs, etc. *Address:* 18 Earl Street, Cambridge. *T:* Cambridge 62997.

BECK, Sir Edgar (Charles), Kt 1975; CBE 1967; Chairman, John Mowlem & Company Ltd, 1961-79, President, since 1981; *b* 11 May 1911; *s* of Edgar Bee Beck and Nellie Stollard Beck (*née* Osborne); *m* 1933, Mary Agnes Sorapure (marr. diss. 1972); three *s* two *d*; *m* 1972, Anne Teresa Corbould. *Educ:* Lancing Coll.; Jesus Coll., Cambridge (MA). Joined John Mowlem & Co. Ltd as Engineer, 1933: Dir 1940; Man. Dir 1958. Director: Scaffolding Great Britain Ltd, 1942 (Chm., 1958-78); Builders' Accident Insce Ltd, 1959, Dep. Chm., 1969; Mem., ECGD Adv. Council, 1964-69; President, Fedn of Civil Engrg Contractors, 1971-75 (Chm., 1958-59); Chairman: Export Gp for the Constructional Industries, 1959-63; Brit. Hosps Export Council, 1964-75. Under-writing Mem. of Lloyd's, 1955-. FEng; FICE. *Recreations:* golf, salmon fishing. *Address:* 13 Eaton Place, SW1. *T:* 01-235 7455; Logierait House, Ballinluig, Perthshire. *T:* Ballinluig 228. *Clubs:* Buck's; Swinley Forest Golf.

BECK, James Henry John; Director of Industries and Farms, Prison Department, Home Office, 1976-80; *b* 5 April 1920; *s* of James Henry and Elizabeth Kate Beck; *m* 1942, Doris Peacock; two *d*. *Educ:* Polytechnic Secondary Sch., Regent Street, W1. Entered Home Office as Clerical Officer, 1937; HM Forces, 1939; returned to Home Office as Executive Officer, 1946; Higher Exec. Officer, 1950; Sen. Exec. Officer, 1958; Principal, 1963; Asst Sec., 1968. *Address:* Scarlet Oaks, Ridgway, Pyrford, Woking, Surrey GU22 8PN. *T:* Byfleet 46064.

BECK, Prof. (John) Swanson; Professor of Pathology, University of Dundee, since 1971; *b* 22 Aug. 1928; *s* of late Dr John Beck and Mary (*née* Barbour); *m* 1960, Marion Tudhope Paterson; one *s* one *d*. *Educ:* Glasgow Acad.; Univ. of Glasgow. BSc, MB, ChB, MD, FRCPG, FRCPE, FRCPath. Lectr in Pathology, Univ. of Glasgow, 1958-63; Sen. Lectr in Pathology, Univ. of Aberdeen, 1963-71. *Publications:* various papers in Jl of Pathology and other medical and scientific jls. *Recreations:* walking, gardening, sailing. *Address:* Morar, Hazel Avenue, Dundee DD2 1QD. *T:* Dundee 68606.

BECK, (Richard) Theodore, FRIBA, FSA, FRSA, MRTPI; architect; *b* 11 March 1905; *s* of Alfred Charles Beck and Grace Sophia Beck (*née* Reading); *m* 1950, Margaret Beryl Page; one *s* one *d*. *Educ:* Haileybury; Architectural Association Sch. Past Mem. Council, Royal Archaeological Inst.; Past Master: Broderers Company; Barber-Surgeons Company; Parish Clerks Co.; Mem. Court of Common Council, Corporation of London; Dep., Ward of Farringdon Within, 1978-; Sheriff, City of London, 1969-70; Dep. Chm., Central Criminal Court Extension Cttee. Former Dep. Governor, the Hon. the Irish Soc.; Chm., Governors, City of London Sch, 1971-75, Dep. Chm., 1976-; Chm., Schools Cttee, Corporation of London, 1977, Dep. Chm., 1978. Governor: Bridewell Royal Hosp.; King Edward's Sch., Witley; Christ's Hospital (Aldermanic Almoner); Reeves Foundn. Vicary Lectr, 1969; Prestonian Lectr, 1975. *Publication:* The Cutting Edge: early history of the surgeons of London, 1975. *Recreations:* golf, archaeology. *Address:* Blundens House, Upper Froyle, Alton, Hants. *T:* Bentley 3147. *Clubs:* East India, Devonshire, Sports and Public Schools, City Livery.

BECK, (Rudolph) Rolf, (Baron Rolf Beck); Chairman and Managing Director of Slip and Molyslip Group of Companies since 1939; *b* 25 March 1914; *s* of Baron Dr Otto Beck (famous industrialist and politician in Austrian and Hungarian Empire; also special Envoy and Representative in Switzerland of Emperor Franz Josef of Austria during 1914-18 War) and Baroness Margaret Beck; *m* 1st, 1944, Elizabeth Lesley Brenchley (marr. diss.), *d* of Captain Fletcher, RN; one *s*; 2nd, 1979, Countess Mariana von Rosen, *d* of Count and Countess Mörner, Bjorksund, Sweden. *Educ:* Theresanium Mil. Acad.; Univs of Geneva, Lausanne, Vienna. Degrees in Engrg and Chem. Whilst still at univ. took up racing and rally driving seriously in a Skoda car; became well known amateur driver, 1935; came to London as rep. of Skoda works to make Skoda cars in UK with 51 per cent British parts and labour and 49 per cent Czechoslovakian parts; outbreak of war ended this develt, 1938; founded Slip Products Ltd, 1939; discovered Milex (petrol economiser), 1940, and Dieslip (fuel additive of interest to the Admty and Min. of War Transport); apptd Adviser on gas producer research, 1940; acted as export adviser to Rolls Royce and toured USA twice. Formed cos: Slip Products and

Engrg, Slip Trading and Shipping also Slip Auto Sales and Engrg, 1948-49. Invented for automobiles or oil drilling: Molyslip (lubricant); Copaslip (compound), 1959. Founded: Slip Internat. Ltd; Molyslip Trading, 1961; Molyslip Holdings, 1964; Molyslip Chemicals Ltd, 1967; Molytex Internat., 1970; on 1 Nov. 1980 a 50/50 company formed between Molyslip Holdings Ltd and Jet-Lube Lubricants Ltd, Maidenhead, called Molyslip Internat. Sales Ltd. Introduced additives: Multiglide and Molyglide, 1972. Fellow of Scientific Exploration Soc.; FZS. *Recreations:* skiing, water skiing, shooting, sailing. *Heir: s* Stephen Rolf Beck, *b* 2 Dec. 1948. *Address:* Layham Hall, near Hadleigh, Suffolk IP7 5LE. *T:* Hadleigh 822137; Cap Davia, Marine de Davia, Ile Rousse, Corsica. *T:* Ile Rousse 600.625; 19 Empire House, Thurloe Place, SW7. *T:* 01-589 7570. *Clubs:* Royal Automobile; Royal Scottish Automobile; Royal Harwich Yacht; West Mersey Yacht; Hurlingham; Union Interalliée (Paris); Princeton (NY).

BECK, Swanson; *see* Beck, J. S.

BECKE, Mrs Shirley Cameron, OBE 1974; QPM 1972; Vice-Chairman, since 1976, Regional Administrator, London Region, 1974-79, Women's Royal Voluntary Service; *b* 29 April 1917; *er d* of late George L. Jennings, AMIGasE and Marion Jennings; *m* 1954, Rev. Justice Becke, MBE, TD, FCA; no *c. Educ:* privately; Ealing Co. Gram. Sch. Trained in Gas Engineering, 1935-40. Joined Metropolitan Police as Constable, 1941; served in various ranks; Woman Commander, 1969-74. OStJ 1975. *Recreations:* reading, keeping cats. *Address:* 51 St Pancras, Chichester, Sussex PO19 4LT. *T:* Chichester 784295.

BECKE, Lt-Col William Hugh Adamson, CMG 1964; DSO 1945; Personnel Officer, Gas and Fuel Corporation of Victoria, 1974-82; *b* 24 Sept. 1916; *er s* of late Brig.-Gen. J. H. W. Becke, CMG, DSO, AFC, and late Mrs A. P. Becke (*née* Adamson); *m* 1945, Mary Catherine, 3rd *d* of late Major G. M. Richmond, Kincairney, Murthly, Perthshire. *Educ:* Charterhouse; RMC Sandhurst. Commissioned in The Sherwood Foresters, 1937. British Military Mission to Greece, 1949-52; Asst Military Adviser to the High Commissioner for the UK in Pakistan, 1957-59; Military Attaché, Djakarta, 1962-64; retd 1966. Private Sec. and Comptroller to Governor of Victoria, 1969-74. *Address:* 3 Chambers Street, South Yarra, Vic 3141, Australia. *Clubs:* Army and Navy; Melbourne, Victoria Racing (Melbourne).

BECKERMAN, Wilfred, PhD, DPhil; Fellow of Balliol College, Oxford, since 1975; Reader in Economics, Oxford University, since 1978; *b* 19 May 1925; *s* of Morris and Mathilda Beckerman; *m* 1952, Nicole Geneviève Ritter (*d* 1979); one *s* two *d. Educ:* Ealing County Sch.; Trinity Coll., Cambridge (MA, PhD); MA, DPhil Oxon. RNVR, 1943-46. Trinity Coll., Cambridge, 1946-50; Lecturer in Economics, Univ. of Nottingham, 1950-52; OEEC and OECD, Paris, 1952-61; National Inst. of Economic and Social Research, 1962-63. Fellow of Balliol Coll., Oxford, 1964-69; Prof. of Political Economy, Univ. of London, and Head of Dept of Political Economy, UCL, 1969-75; The Economic Adviser to the Pres. of the Board of Trade (leave of absence from Balliol), 1967-69. Mem., Royal Commn on Environmental Pollution, 1970-73. Mem. Exec. Cttee, NIESR, 1973-. Elie Halévy Vis. Prof. Institut d'Etudes Politiques, Paris, 1977. Pres., Section F (Economics), BAAS, 1978. *Publications:* The British Economy in 1975 (with associates), 1965; International Comparisons of Real Incomes, 1966; An Introduction to National Income Analysis, 1968; (ed and contrib.) The Labour Government's Economic Record, 1972; In Defence of Economic Growth, 1974; Measures of Leisure, Equality and Welfare, 1978; (ed and contrib.) Slow Growth in Britain: causes and consequences, 1979; Poverty and the Impact of Income Maintenance Programmes, 1979; (with S. Clark) Poverty and the Impact of Social Security in Britain since 1961, 1982; articles in Economic Jl, Economica, Econometrica, Review of Economic Studies, Review of Economics and Statistics, etc. *Recreations:* various. *Address:* Balliol College, Oxford. *T:* Oxford 44784.

BECKETT, family name of **Baron Grimthorpe.**

BECKETT, Prof. Arnold Heyworth; Professor of Pharmacy, Chelsea College (University of London), since 1959; *b* 12 Feb. 1920; *m* 1st 1942, Miriam Eunice Webster; one *s* one *d* ; 2nd, Susan Yvonne Harris. *Educ:* Baines Grammar Sch., Poulton-le-Fylde; Sch. of Pharmacy and Birkbeck Coll., University of London, FPS 1942; BSc 1947; PhD 1950; DSc London, 1959. Head, Dept of Pharmacy, Chelsea Coll. of Sci. and Technology, 1959-79. Member: Council, Pharmaceutical Soc. of Gt Brit., 1965-; Med. Commn, Internat. Olympic Cttee, 1968-; British Olympic Assoc. Med. Commn; Chm., Bd of Pharmaceutical Sciences, Fédération Internat. Pharmaceutique, 1960-80; Pres., Pharmaceutical Soc. of GB, 1981-. Vis. Prof. to Univs, USA and Canada. Examr in Pharmaceut. Chem., Univs in UK, Nigeria, Ghana, Singapore. Pereira Medal, 1942; STAS Medal, Belg. Chem. Soc., 1962; Hanbury Meml Medal, 1974; Charter Gold Medal, 1977; Mem. of Olympic Order, Silver Medal, 1980. Hon DSc: Heriot-Watt Univ., 1976; Univ. of Uppsala, 1977. *Publications:* (co-author) Practical Pharmaceutical Chemistry, 1962; Part 1, 3rd edn, 1975, Part 2, 3rd edn, 1976; founder Co-editor, Jl of Medicinal Chemistry; research contribs to jls. *Recreations:* travel, sport, photography. *Address:* 16 Crestbrook Avenue, Palmers Green, N13.

BECKETT, Bruce Probart, FRIBA, FRTPI, FRIAS, FCIOB; Chief Architect, since 1967, and Director of Building, since 1978, Scottish Office; *b* 7 June 1924; *s* of J. D. L. Beckett and Florence Theresa (*née* Probart); *m*

1957, Jean McDonald; two *s* three *d* (incl. twin *s* and *d*). *Educ:* Rondebosch Boys' High Sch., Cape Town; Univ. of Cape Town (BArch with distinction, 1950); University Coll. London (Diploma in Town Planning, 1963). Active Service SA Navy, 1943; Midshipman, 1943; Sub-Lieut, 1944; seconded RN, 1944; Lieut, 1946. ARIBA 1950, FRIBA 1968; FRIAS 1968. Mem. Inst. S African Architects, 1950; FRTPI (AMTPI 1966); FIOB 1979. Private practice in S Africa, 1952-59, London, 1960. Sen. Architect, War Office, 1961; Superintending Grade Arch., Directorate-Gen. of Res. and Development, 1963-67. Dep. Leader, Timber Trade Mission to Canada, 1964. A Vice-Pres., RIBA, 1972-73, 1975-76, 1976-77; Hon. Librarian, 1976-78. Sec. of State for Scotland's nominee on ARCUK; Member Council: EAA, 1970-; RIAS, 1971-; RIBA, 1972-; Member: Sec. of State for Environment's Construction and Housing Adv. Council, 1968-79; Building Res. Estabt Adv. Cttees in England and Scotland, 1970-; York Adv. Cttee for continuing educn for building profession, 1975-80. Assessor to Scottish Cttee of Design Council, 1974-. *Publications:* papers on industrialised building, contract procedure, etc, in various jls; HMSO publications on Scottish housing, educational and health buildings. *Recreations:* sailing, walking. *Address:* 71 Ravelston Dykes Road, Edinburgh EH4 3NU. *T:* 031-337 7301. *Clubs:* New, Scottish Arts (Edinburgh); Western Province Sports (Kelvin Grove, Cape Town).

BECKETT, Maj.-Gen. Denis Arthur, CB 1971; DSO 1944; OBE 1960; *b* 19 May 1917; *o s* of late Archibald Beckett, Woodford Green, Essex; *m* 1946, Elizabeth (marr. diss. 1974), *er d* of late Col Guy Edwards, Upper Slaughter, Glos; one *s* ; *m* 1978, Nancy Ann Hitt. *Educ:* Forest Sch.; Chard Sch. Joined Hon. Artillery Co., 1939; commnd into Essex Regt, 1940; served in W. Africa, Middle East, Italy and Greece, 1940-45; DAA & QMG and Bde Major, Parachute Bdes, 1948-50; Instructor, RMA Sandhurst, 1951-53; Staff Coll., Camberley, 1953-56; Second in Comd 3rd Bn Para. Regt, 1956-58; comd 2nd Bn Para. Regt, 1958-60; jssc 1960-61; comd 19 Bde, 1961-63; idc 1964; DAG, BAOR, 1965-66; Chief of Staff, Far East Land Forces, 1966-68; Dir of Personal Services (Army), 1968-71, retired 1971. *Address:* 12 Wellington House, Eton Road, NW3. *Clubs:* Army and Navy, Lansdowne.

BECKETT, Prof. James Camlin, MA; Professor of Irish History, Queen's University of Belfast, 1958-75; *b* 8 Feb. 1912; 3rd *s* of Alfred Beckett and Frances Lucy Bushell. *Educ:* Royal Belfast Academical Instn; Queen's Univ., Belfast. History Master, Belfast Royal Academy, 1934; Lectr in Modern History, Queen's Univ., Belfast, 1945, Reader in Modern History, 1952. Fellow Commoner, Peterhouse, Cambridge, 1955-56; Cummings Lectr, McGill Univ., Montreal, 1976; Mellon Prof., Tulane Univ., New Orleans, 1977; Member: Irish Manuscripts Commn, 1959; Royal Commission on Historical Manuscripts, 1960. Hon. DLitt New Univ. of Ulster, 1979; Hon DLit Queen's Univ. of Belfast, 1980. FRHistS; MRIA. *Publications:* Protestant Dissent in Ireland, 1687-1780, 1948; Short History of Ireland, 1952; (ed with T. W. Moody) Ulster since 1800: a Political and Economic Survey, 1954; (ed with T. W. Moody) Ulster since 1800: a Social Survey, 1957; (with T. W. Moody) Queen's Belfast, 1845-1949, 1959; The Making of Modern Ireland 1603-1923, 1966; (ed with R. E. Glasscock) Belfast: the Origin and Growth of an Industrial City, 1966; (ed) Historical Studies VII, 1969; Confrontations, 1973; The Anglo-Irish Tradition, 1976; contrib. The Ulster Debate, 1972; articles, reviews, etc., in English Hist. Rev., History, Irish Hist. Studies and other jls. *Recreations:* chess, walking. *Address:* 19 Wellington Park Terrace, Belfast, N Ireland BT9 6DR. *Club:* Ulster (Belfast).

BECKETT, John Angus, CB 1965; CMG 1956; MA; Chairman, Press Offshore Group; Director, Total Oil Marine Ltd, since 1979; *b* 6 July 1909; *s* of late John Beckett, BA; *m* 1935, Una Joan, *yr d* of late George Henry Wright; one *s* two *d. Educ:* privately; Sidney Sussex Coll., Cambridge. BA 2nd Cl. Hons (Geog. Tripos); Mem., Cambridge Iceland Expedition, 1932. Schoolmaster, 1933-40; entered Civil Service, 1940; Principal Private Sec. to Minister of Fuel and Power, 1946-47; Asst Sec., Min. of Fuel and Power, 1947-59; Under-Sec., 1959 (Gas Div., 1959-64, Petroleum Div., 1964-72) Min. of Power, Min. of Technology, DTI; retired 1972. Chm., Petroleum Cttee of OEEC, 1948-50, 1955-59, 1965-72; Petroleum Attaché, British Embassy, Washington, 1950-53. Chm., William Press Production Systems Ltd, 1972. *Publication:* Iceland Adventure, 1934. *Recreations:* rowing, Rugby football, administration. *Address:* Tyle Cottage, Needlesbank, Godstone, Surrey RH9 8LN. *T:* Godstone 842295. *Clubs:* St Stephen's Constitutional; Arctic (Cambridge).

BECKETT, John Michael; Chairman, Paternoster Stores plc, since 1982; *b* 22 June 1929; *yr s* of H N. Beckett, MBE, and C. L. Beckett; *m* 1955, Joan Mary, *o d* of Percy and F. M. Rogerson; five *d. Educ:* Wolverhampton Grammar Sch.; Magdalen Coll., Oxford (BA 1953, MA 1957). Nat. Service and Reg. Commn RA, 1947-50; TA 1950-60. Called to Bar, Gray's Inn, 1954. Bar, 1954-55; Tootal Ltd, 1955-58; Tarmac Ltd, 1958-75; Dir, 1963-82 (non-exec., 1975-82); Chief Exec., British Sugar Corp. Ltd, 1975-82. Chairman: British Slag Fedn, 1967-69; Asphalt & Coated Macadam Assoc., 1971-73; Mem., Transport and Road Research Laboratory Adv. Cttee, 1972-80 (Chm., 1977-80). Chairman: British Sugar Bureau, 1978-81; UK Sugar Industries Assoc., 1978-. Hon. MIQ; FRSA; CBIM. *Address:* Belton House, Rutland LE15 9JZ. *T:* Belton 682. *Clubs:* Naval and Military, Special Forces.
See also Sir T. N. Beckett.

BECKETT, Margaret M., (Mrs L. A. Beckett); Principal Researcher, Granada TV, since 1979; *b* Jan. 1943; *m* 1979, Lionel A. Beckett. *Educ:* Notre Dame High Sch., Norwich; Manchester Coll. of Sci. and Technol. Formerly:

student apprentice, AEI, Manchester; exptl officer, Manchester Univ.; Labour Party res. asst; political adviser, Minister for Overseas Develt, 1974. Contested (Lab) Lincoln, Feb. 1974; MP (Lab) Lincoln, Oct. 1974-1979; PPS to Minister for Overseas Develt, 1974-75; Asst Govt Whip, 1975-76; Parly Under-Sec. of State, DES, 1976-79. Mem. NEC, Labour Party, 1980-81. Prospective Parly Cand., Derby S, 1981. *Address:* 16 Oaklands Road, Swinton, Lancs.

BECKETT, Sir Martyn Gervase, 2nd Bt, *cr* 1921; MC 1945; RIBA; Architect; *b* 6 Nov. 1918; *s* of Hon. Sir Gervase Beckett, 1st Bt, and Lady Marjorie Beckett (*d* 1964), *e d* of 5th Earl of Warwick; *S* father, 1937; *m* 1941, Hon. Priscilla Brett, *y d* of 3rd Viscount Esher, GBE; two *s* one *d. Educ:* Eton; Trinity Coll., Cambridge. Enlisted in Green Howards, 1939; commnd Welsh Guards, 1940; served War of 1939-45 (MC); Lieut (temp. Captain). DipArch 1951, ARIBA 1952. Built or reconstructed several country houses and housing estates, hotels, libraries etc; works to over 50 scheduled buildings and for National Trust. Architect to King's College Chapel, Cambridge, 1960- (internal alterations and renovations to the Chapel, 1968); Cons. arch. to Savoy Hotel Gp, 1981. Exhibited: RA, London, provinces; one man exhibn, Clarges Gall., 1980. Trustee: The Wallace Collection, 1972- (Chm. 1976-); British Museum, 1978-; Chm., Yorkshire Regional Cttee, Nat. Trust, 1980; Member: N York Moor Nat. Park Cttee, 1972-78; Council of Management, Chatsworth House Trust, 1981; President: Ryedale Br., CPRE, 1964-; Friends of York Art Gall., 1970-. Member of Lloyds. FRSA. *Recreations:* painting, photography, piano. *Heir: s* Richard Gervase Beckett [*b* 27 March 1944; *m* 1976, Elizabeth, *d* of Major Hugo and Lady Caroline Waterhouse; two *d*]. *Address:* 3 St Albans Grove, W8. *T:* 01-937 7834; Kirkdale Farm, Nawton, Yorks. *Clubs:* Brooks's, MCC.

BECKETT, Noel George Stanley; HM Diplomatic Service, retired; *b* 3 Dec. 1916; *s* of Captain J. R. Beckett, MC, and Ethel Barker; *m* 1948, Huguette Laure Charlotte Voos (*d* 1982); one *s* two *d. Educ:* Peterhouse, Cambridge. MA Hons Cantab 1938, BScEcon Hons London 1961. Mem., Inst. of Linguists. British Embassy, Paris, 1946; UK Commercial Rep., Frankfurt and Cologne, 1949; Lima, 1956; Bonn, 1959; British Embassy, Addis Ababa, 1963 and liaison officer with Econ. Commn for Africa; Sec., European Conf. on Satellite Communications, FO, 1965; British Embassy, Beirut, 1968; Consul-Gen., Casablanca, 1973-76. *Recreations:* oil painting, photography, reading, travel. *Address:* The Second House, South Drive, Dorking, Surrey. *T:* Dorking 882665. *Club:* Royal Commonwealth Society.

BECKETT, Samuel; author and playwright; *b* Dublin, 1906. *Educ:* Portora Royal School; Trinity Coll., Dublin (MA). Lectr in English, Ecole Normale Supérieure, Paris, 1928-30; Lectr in French, Trinity Coll., Dublin, 1930-32; from 1932 has lived mostly in France, in Paris since 1937. Nobel Prize for Literature, 1969. *Publications: verse:* Whoroscope, 1930; Echo's Bones, 1935; Collected Poems in English and French, 1977; *novels:* Murphy, 1938; Watt, 1944; Molloy, 1951 (Eng. trans. 1956); Malone meurt, 1952 (Eng. trans. Malone Dies, 1956); L'Innommable, 1953 (Eng. trans. 1960); Comment c'est, 1961 (Eng. trans 1964); Imagination Dead Imagine, 1966 (trans. from French by author); First Love, 1973; Mercier and Camier, 1974; Company, 1980; Ill Seen Ill Said, 1982; *short stories:* More Pricks than Kicks, 1934; Nouvelles et textes pour rien, 1955; Le Dépeupleur, 1971 (Eng. trans., The Lost Ones, 1972); Four Novellas, 1977; *plays:* En attendant Godot, 1952 (Eng. trans. Waiting for Godot, 1954); Fin de Partie, 1957 (Eng. trans. End Game); Krapp's Last Tape, 1959; La Dernière Bande, 1961; Happy Days, 1961; Play, 1963; Film, 1972; Breath and Other Short Plays, 1972; Not I, 1973; *radio plays:* All that Fall, 1957; Embers, 1959; Cascando, 1964; *TV plays:* Ghost Trio and . . . But the Clouds . . . , 1977. *Address:* c/o Faber & Faber Ltd, 24 Russell Square, WC1.

BECKETT, Sir Terence (Norman), Kt 1978; CBE 1974; Director General, Confederation of British Industry, since 1980; *b* 13 Dec. 1923; *s* of late Horace Norman Beckett, MBE and late Clarice Lillian (*née* Allsop); *m* 1950, Sylvia Gladys Asprey; one *d. Educ:* London Sch. of Econs. BScEcon, CEng, FEng, FIMechE, CBIM, FIMI. Captain REME, British Army (UK, India, Malaya), 1945-48; RARO, 1949-62. Company Trainee, Ford Motor Co. Ltd, 1950; Asst in office of Dep. Chm. and Man. Dir, 1951; Man., Styling, Briggs Motor Bodies Ltd (Ford subsid.), 1954; Admin Man., Engrg, Briggs, 1955; Manager: Product Staff, 1955; Product Planning Staff, 1961 (responsible for Cortina, Transit Van, 'D' series truck); Marketing Staff, 1963; Dir, Car Div., 1964; Exec. Dir, Ford Motor Co. Ltd, 1966 and Dir of Sales, 1968; Vice-Pres., European and Overseas Sales Ops, Ford of Europe Inc., 1969; Man. Dir and Chief Exec., 1974-80 and Chm., 1976-80, Ford Motor Co. Ltd; Chm., Ford Motor Credit Co. Ltd, 1976-80; Director: ICI, 1976-80; Automotive Finance Ltd, 1974-77. Member: NEDC, 1980-; Engineering Industries Council, 1975-80; BIM Council, 1976-77; CBI Council, 1976-80; Grand Council, Motor and Cycle Trades Benevolent Fund (BEN), 1976-80; SMMT Council and Exec. Cttee, 1974-80; Council, Automobile Div., IMechE, 1979-80; Vice Pres. and Hon. Fellow, Inst. of the Motor Industry, 1974-; Vice-Pres., Conference on Schs, Sci. and Technol., 1979-80; Chm., Governing Body, London Business Sch., 1980-; Mem. Court, Cranfield Inst. of Technology, 1977-; Governor, Nat. Inst. of Econ. and Social Res., 1978-; Governor and Mem. Corp., LSE, 1978-. Patron, MSC Award Scheme for Disabled People, 1979-80. Hambro Businessman of the Year Award, 1978; BIM Gold Medal, 1980. Hon. DSc: Cranfield, 1977; Heriot-Watt, 1981; Hon. Fellow Sidney Sussex Coll., Cambridge, 1981. *Recreations:* ornithology, music. *Address:* Confederation of British Industry, Centre Point, 103 New Oxford Street,

WC1. *Club:* Athenæum.
See also J. M. Beckett.

BECKETT, Veronica Evelyn; HM Diplomatic Service; Permanent United Kingdom Delegate to UNESCO, Paris, since 1981; *b* 25 April 1939; *d* of late Lt-Col Maurice George Beckett, KOYLI, and of Constance Mary Cavenagh-Mainwaring; *m* 1981, Alex James Sutherland. *Educ:* Royal Sch., Bath; London Univ. (BA); Southampton Univ. (MA). Joined HM Diplomatic Service, 1965 Second, later First Sec., Copenhagen, 1967-70; FCO, 1970-75; First Sec., New Delhi, 1975-78; FCO, 1978-80; Counsellor, 1981. *Address:* c/o Foreign and Commonwealth Office, SW1.

BECKETT, William Cartwright, CB 1978; LLM; Solicitor, Departments of Trade and Industry, since 1980; *b* 21 Sept. 1929; *s* of late William Beckett and Emily (*née* Cartwright); *m* 1st, 1956, Marjorie Jean Hoskin; two *s* ; 2nd, 1974 Lesley Margaret Furlonger. *Educ:* Salford Grammar Sch.; Manchester Univ (LLB 1950, LLM 1952). Called to Bar, Middle Temple, 1952. Joined Treasury Solicitor's Dept, 1956; Board of Trade, 1965; Asst Solicitor, DEP, 1969 Under-Sec., DTI, 1972; Dep.-Sec. 1977; Legal Secretary, Law Officers' Dept 1975-80. *Recreations:* music, golf. *Address:* Park House, Bradwell, near Braintree, Essex. *T:* Braintree 61109. *Club:* Reform.

BECKINGHAM, Charles Fraser; Professor of Islamic Studies, University of London, 1965-81 now Emeritus; *b* 18 Feb. 1914; *o c* of Arthur Beckingham, ARBA and Alice Beckingham, Houghton, Hunts; *m* 1st, 1946, Margery (*o* 1966), *o d* of John Ansell; one *d* ; 2nd, 1970, Elizabeth, *y d* of R. J. Brine (marr. diss. 1977). *Educ:* Grammar Sch., Huntingdon; Queens' Coll. Cambridge (scholar, Members' English prizeman, 1934). Dept of Printed Books, British Museum, 1936-46. Seconded to military and naval Intelligence 1942-46. Foreign Office, 1946-51; Lectr in Islamic History, Manchester Univ. 1951-55; Sen. Lectr, 1955-58; Prof. of Islamic Studies, 1958-65. Pres., Hakluyt Soc., 1969-72; Treas., Royal Asiatic Soc., 1964-67, Pres., 1967-70, 1976-79, Hon. Fellow, Sri Lanka Branch, 1978. Chm., St Marylebone Soc., 1980-. Jt Editor, 1961-64, Editor, 1965, Jl of Semitic Studies. *Publications:* contribs to Admiralty Handbook of Western Arabia, 1946; (with G. W. B. Huntingford) Some Records of Ethiopia, 1954; Introduction to Atlas of the Arab World and Middle East, 1960; (with G. W. B. Huntingford) A True Relation of the Prester John of the Indies, 1961; Bruce's Travels (ed and selected), 1964; The Achievements of Prester John, 1966; (ed) Islam, in Religion in the Middle East (ed A. J. Arberry), 1969; (with E. Ullendorff) The Hebrew Letters of Prester John, 1982; articles in learned jls. *Address:* 56 Queen Anne Street, W1M 9LA. *Club:* Travellers'.

BECKLAKE, Dr Ernest John Stephen; Keeper, Department of Electrical Engineering, Communications and Circulation, Science Museum, since 1980; *b* 24 June 1943; *s* of Ernest and Evelyn Becklake; *m* 1965, Susan Elizabeth (*née* Buckle), BSc; two *s. Educ:* Bideford Grammar Sch.; Exeter Univ. (BSc, PhD). Engr, EMI Electronics, Wells, 1967-69; Post-Doctoral Fellow, Victoria Univ., BC, Canada, 1969-70; Sen. Scientist, Marconi Space and Def. Systems, Frimley, 1970-72; Asst Keeper, Dept of Earth and Space Sciences, Science Mus., 1972-80. *Publications:* Man and the Moon, 1980; (series editor) Exploration and Discovery, 1980-; technical pubns in Electronics Letters, Jl of Physics D, Jl of British Interplanetary Soc., and Spaceflight. *Recreations:* gardening, golf, rugby. *Address:* Tree Wood, Robin Hood Lane, Sutton Green, Woking, Surrey. *T:* Woking 66931. *Club:* Worplesdon Golf (Woking).

BECKMAN, Michael David, QC 1976; *b* 6 April 1932; *s* of Nathan and Esther Beckman; *m* 1966, Sheryl Robin (*née* Kyle) (marr. diss.); two *d. Educ:* King's Coll., London (LLB (Hons)). Called to the Bar, Lincoln's Inn, 1954. *Recreations:* various and interesting. *Address:* Bullards, Widford, Herts. *T:* Much Hadham 2669; (chambers) 19 Old Buildings, Lincoln's Inn, WC2. *Club:* Tennis de Talloires.

BECKWITH, John Gordon, FBA 1974; FSA 1968; Keeper, Department of Architecture and Sculpture, Victoria and Albert Museum, 1974-79; *b* 2 Dec. 1918; *s* of late John Frederick Beckwith. *Educ:* Ampleforth Coll., York; Exeter Coll., Oxford (Loscombe Richards Exhibnr; Amelia Jackson Student). MA. Served with The Duke of Wellington's Regt, 1939-45. Victoria and Albert Museum: Asst Keeper, Dept of Textiles, 1948; Asst Keeper, Dept of Architecture and Sculpture, 1955, Dep. Keeper, 1958. Vis. Fellow of Harvard Univ. at Dumbarton Oaks Res. Library and Collection, Washington, DC, 1950-51; Visiting Professor: at Harvard Univ. (Fogg Museum of Art), 1964; at Univ. of Missouri, Columbia, Mo, 1968-69; Slade Prof. of Fine Art, Oxford Univ., 1978-79. Reynolds-Stephens Meml Lecture, RBS, 1965. Mem., Centre International des Etudes des Textils Anciens at Lyon, 1953-. *Publications:* The Andrews Diptych, 1958; Coptic Textiles, 1959; Caskets from Cordoba, 1960; The Art of Constantinople, 1961; The Veroli Casket, 1962; Coptic Sculpture, 1963; The Basilewsky Situla, 1963; Early Medieval Art, 1964; The Adoration of the Magi in Whalebone, 1966; Early Christian and Byzantine Art, Pelican History of Art, 1970; Ivory Carvings in Early Medieval England, 1972; Catalogue of Exhibition, Ivory Carvings in Early Medieval England 700-1200, 1974; contrib. Art Bulletin, Burlington Magazine, etc. *Recreation:* music. *Address:* Flat 12, 77 Ladbroke Grove, W11 2PF. *T:* 01-727 7277.

BECTIVE, Earl of; Thomas Michael Ronald Christopher Taylour; *b* 10 Feb. 1959; *s* and *heir* of 6th Marquis of Headfort, *qv. Educ:* Harrow; RAC

Cirencester. *Address:* Horsley Hall, Eccleshall, Stafford. *Clubs:* Lansdowne; Royal Dublin Society (Dublin).

BEDBROOK, Sir George (Montario), Kt 1978; OBE 1963; FRCS; FRACS; Senior Surgeon, Spinal Unit, Department of Paraplegia, Royal Perth Rehabilitation Hospital, since 1972; Senior Orthopaedic Consultant, Department of Orthopaedic Surgery, Royal Perth Hospital and Royal Perth Rehabilitation Hospital, since 1979 (Chairman, 1965-79); *b* 8 Nov. 1921; *s* of Arthur Bedbrook and Ethel (*née* Prince); *m* 1946, Jessie Violet (*née* Page); two *s* three *d*. *Educ:* University High Sch., Melbourne; Medical Sch., Univ. of Melbourne (MB BS (Hons) 1944, J. P. Ryan Schol. in Surgery, MS 1950). FRACS 1950; FRCS (England) 1951; DPRM (Sydney) 1970. Resident MO, Royal Melb. Hosp., Vic, 1944-45; Lectr in Anatomy, Univ. of Melb., Vic, 1946-50; Resident MO, Nat. Orthopaedic Hosp., London, 1951; Registrar, Orthopaedic Dept, Croydon Gp Hosps, 1951-53; private practice in Perth, WA, with Mr R. D. McKellar Hall, FRCS, FRACS (Mem. Orthopaedic Dept, Royal Perth Hosp.), 1953; began Paraplegic Service, Royal Perth Hosp., 1954; Sen. Surgeon and Head, Dept of Paraplegia, Royal Perth Rehabilitation Hosp., 1954-72, resigned. Vice Chairman: Nat. Adv. Council for the Handicapped; WA br., Australian Council for the Rehabilitation of the Disabled (ACROD); Pres., Internat. Med. Soc. of Paraplegia; Chm., W Australian Cttee, Internat. Year of Disabled Persons. Hon. FRCSE 1981; Hon. MD, WA, 1973. OStJ 1972. *Publications:* Care and Management of Spinal Cord Injuries, 1981; numerous (71) papers and contribs to medical and scientific jls, espec. relating to spinal injuries with paraplegia. *Recreations:* reading, music, travel, sports for the disabled. *Address:* (home) 29 Ulster Road, Floreat Park, WA 6014, Australia. *T:* 387.3582; (office) 13 Colin Grove, West Perth, WA 6005, Australia. *T:* 321.7543.

BEDBROOK, Jack Harry, CEng, FRINA; FBIM; RCNC; General Manager, HM Dockyard, Devonport, since 1979; *b* 8 Aug. 1924; *s* of Harry Bedbrook and Emma Bedbrook; *m* 1963, Janet Bedbrook; three *d*. *Educ:* Technical Coll., Portsmouth; RNC, Greenwich. Dir Gen. Ships Dept, Admiralty, 1946-51; Asst Constructor, Devonport, 1951-54; Dockyard Dept, Bath, 1954-56; Constructor, Gibraltar Dockyard, 1956-58; Admiralty Exptl Works, Haslar, 1958-62; Dir Gen. Ships Dept, 1962-65; Chief Constructor, Portsmouth, 1965-71; Project Manager, Rosyth, 1971-74; Prodn Manager, Devonport, 1974-77; Gen. Manager, HM Dockyard, Rosyth, 1977-79. *Recreations:* squash, sailing, gardening, music. *Address:* Laxtons, Cargreen Saltash, Cornwall. *T:* Saltash 4519.

BEDDALL, Hugh Richard Muir; Chairman, Muir Beddall & Co. Ltd, since 1964; Member of Lloyd's; *b* 20 May 1922; *s* of Herbert Muir Beddall and Jennie Beddall (*née* Fowler); *m* 1946, Monique Henriette (*née* Haefliger); three *s* one *d*. *Educ:* Stowe; Ecole de Commerce, Neuchatel, Switzerland. Employee of Muir Beddall & Co., 1939-41. Served War of 1939-45; Royal Marines, 2nd Lieut, 1941; subseq. Captain A Troop 45 RM Commando and No 1 Commando Bde HQ; demob., 1946. Employee, Muir Beddall, Mise & Cie, Paris, 1946-47; returned as employee of Muir Beddall & Co. Ltd, 1947; Dir, 1949; Dep. Chm., 1960; Chm., 1964. Chairman in Iver Stud. FCII. Director: Muir Beddall Boda & Co.; H. M. Beddall & Partners; Muir Beddall Mise & Cie, Paris. *Recreations:* shooting, fishing, racing. *Address:* Iver Lodge, Iver, Bucks. *T:* Iver 653007. *Clubs:* Buck's, East India, Devonshire, Sports and Public Schools; Denham Golf; Stoke Poges Golf.

BEDDARD, Dr Frederick Denys, CB 1974; Deputy Chief Medical Officer, Department of Health and Social Security, 1972-77, retired; *b* 28 Feb. 1917; *s* of late Rev. F. G. Beddard and late Mrs Emily Beddard; *m* 1942, Anne (*née* Porter); two *d*. *Educ:* Haileybury Coll.; St Mary's Hosp. Med. Sch., London Univ. MRCS, LRCP 1939; MB, BS 1940; FRCPE 1972; FFCM 1972. House Phys. and Surg., St Mary's, 1939-41; RAMC, 1941-45 (Lt-Col). St Mary's Hosp. and Brompton Hosp., 1946-49; SE Metrop. Reg. Hosp. Bd, 1950-55; SE Reg. Hosp. Bd (Scotland), 1955-57; NE Reg. Hosp. Bd (Scotland), 1957-68 (seconded to Dept of Health, New Zealand, 1967); Chief Medical Officer, Min. of Health and Social Services, NI, 1968-72. Short-term consultant, WHO, 1978-79. Governor, Charlotte Mason Coll. of Educn, Ambleside, 1981-. *Publications:* various contribs to Lancet, etc. *Recreations:* gardening, geology. *Address:* Birk Field, Staveley, Kendal, Cumbria LA8 9QU. *T:* Staveley 821454.

BEDDINGTON, Charles Richard; Metropolitan Magistrate, 1963-80; *b* 22 Aug. 1911; *s* of late Charles Beddington, Inner Temple, and Stella (*née* de Goldschmidt); *m* 1939, Dinbie, *d* of late Frederick Appleby Holt; two *s* one *d*. *Educ:* Eton (scholar); Balliol Coll., Oxford. Barrister, Inner Temple, 1934. Joined TA, 1939; served RA, 1939-45, Major. Practised at the Bar in London and on SE Circuit. Mem. Mental Health Review Tribunal (SE Metropolitan Area), 1960-63. *Recreations:* swimming, relaxing in the company of his family. *Address:* Rosehill, Cuckfield, Sussex RH17 5EU. *T:* Haywards Heath 54063; 1 Temple Gardens, Temple, EC4.

BEDDINGTON, Nadine Dagmar, MBE 1982; architect in own practice, since 1967; *d* of Frank Maurice Beddington and Mathilde Beddington. *Educ:* New Hall; Regent Polytechnic Sch. of Architecture. FRIBA (ARIBA 1940); FSIAD; FRSA. Asst in central and local govt, 1940-45; asst in private practice, 1945-55; Chief Architect to Freeman Hardy Willis/Trueform, 1957-67. Vice-Chm., Architects in Industry Group, 1965-67; Mem., RIBA Council, 1969-72, 1975-79, Vice-Pres., RIBA, 1971-72; Mem., ARCUK, 1969-82; Pres., Camberwell Soc., 1977-82; Fellow, Ancient Monuments Soc. Vice

Chm., Brixton and District Dog Training Club, 1974-82. Silver Jubilee Medal, 1977. *Publications:* Design for Shopping Centres, 1982; articles on shops, shopping centres, building maintenance, building legislation. *Recreations:* reading, riding, people, music, travel, dogs. *Address:* 17 Champion Grove, SE5 8BN; (office) 60 Welbeck Street, W1M 7HB. *T:* 01-486 7348/9. *Club:* Reform.

BEDDOE, Jack Eglinton, CB 1971; Chief Executive, Severn Trent Water Authority, 1974-77; *b* 6 June 1914; *s* of Percy Beddoe and Mabel Ellen Hook; *m* 1st, 1940, Audrey Alison Emelie (*d* 1954); two *s* one *d*; 2nd, 1957, Edith Rosina Gillanders. *Educ:* Hitchin Grammar Sch.; Magdalen Coll., Cambridge. Entered Ministry of Health, 1936; Principal Private Sec. to Minister of Health, 1948-51; to Minister of Housing and Local Government, 1951-53; Asst Sec., 1953; Under-Sec., Ministry of Housing and Local Government, 1961-65; Asst Under-Sec. of State, Dept of Economic Affairs, 1965-66; Chm., SE Planning Board, during 1966; Under-Sec., Min. of Housing and Local Govt, later DoE, 1966-74. *Address:* 32 Northfield End, Henley, Oxfordshire.

BEDDOES, Air Vice-Marshal John Geoffrey Genior, CB 1981; FRAeS; aviation consultant; *b* 21 May 1925; *s* of Algernon Geoffrey Beddoes and Lucy Isobel (*née* Collier); *m* 1948, Betty Morris Kendrick; three *s*. *Educ:* Wirral Grammar Sch., Bebington, Cheshire. Pilot training in Rhodesia and Egypt, 1943-45; No 114 Sqdn, Italy and Aden, Bostons and Mosquitos, 1945-46; No 30 Sqdn, Abingdon and Berlin Airlift, Dakotas, 1947-49; Central Flying Sch., 1949; Flying Instr, RAF Coll., Cranwell and Central Flying Sch., 1950-55; Flight Comdr, No 57 Sqdn, Canberras, 1955; Air Ministry, 1956-57; Flying Coll., 1958; Flt Comdr No 57 Sqdn, Victor Mk 1, 1959-61; sc Bracknell, 1962; OC No 139 (Jamaica) Sqdn, Victor Mk 2, 1963-64; Wing Comdr Ops HQ No 3 Gp, 1965-67; Directing Staff Coll. of Air Warfare, 1968-69; OC RAF Laarbruch, 1969-71; MoD Dep. Dir, Operational Requirements, 1971-73; HQ 2 ATAF Asst COS Offensive Operations, 1974-75; MoD Director of Operational Requirements, 1975-78; Dir Gen. Aircraft (2), MoD PE, 1978-80; retired RAF, 1981. FBIM. *Recreations:* music, cricket, DIY, golf, gardening. *Address:* White Stables, Stow Bedon, Norfolk NR17 1HP. *T:* Caston 524. *Clubs:* Royal Air Force, MCC.

BEDFORD, 13th Duke of, *cr* 1694; **John Robert Russell;** Marquess of Tavistock, 1694; Earl of Bedford, 1550; Baron Russell of Chenies, 1540; Baron Russell of Thornhaugh, 1603; Baron Howland of Streatham, 1695; *b* 24 May 1917; *er s* of 12th Duke and Louisa Crommelin Roberta (*d* 1960), *y d* of Robert Jowitt Whitwell; *S* father 1953; *m* 1st, 1939, Clare Gwendolen Hollway, *née* Bridgman (*d* 1945); two *s*; 2nd, Lydia (marr. diss., 1960), widow of Capt. Ian de Hoghton Lyle, 3rd *d* of 3rd Baron Churston and late Duchess of Leinster; one *s*; 3rd, 1960, Mme Nicole Milinaire, *d* of Paul Schneider. Coldstream Guards, 1939; invalided out, 1940. *Publications:* A Silver-Plated Spoon, 1959; (with G. Mikes) Book of Snobs, 1965; The Flying Duchess, 1968; (with G. Mikes) How to Run a Stately Home, 1971. *Heir: s* Marquess of Tavistock, *qv*. *Address:* 7 Rue Basse, MC 98000, Monaco. *Clubs:* Brooks's, Pratt's.

BEDFORD, Bishop Suffragan of, since 1981; **Rt. Rev. David John Farmbrough;** *b* 4 May 1929; 2nd *s* of late Charles Septimus and late Ida Mabel Farmbrough; *m* 1955, Angela Priscilla Hill; one *s* three *d*. *Educ:* Bedford Sch.; Lincoln Coll., Oxford (BA 1951, MA 1953); Westcott House, Cambridge, 1951-53. Deacon, 1953, priest, 1954; Curate of Bishop's Hatfield, 1953-57; Priest-in-charge, St John's, Hatfield, 1957-63; Vicar of Bishop's Stortford, 1963-74; Rural Dean of Bishop's Stortford, 1973-74; Archdeacon of St Albans, 1974-81. Mem., Gen. Synod, 1972-81. *Publications:* In Wonder, Love and Praise, 1966; Belonging, Believing, Doing, 1971. *Recreations:* sailing, gardening. *Address:* 168 Kimbolton Road, Bedford MK41 8DN. *T:* Bedford 57551.

BEDFORD, Archdeacon of; *see* Mayfield, Ven. C. J.

BEDFORD, Alfred William, (Bill), OBE 1961; AFC 1945; FRAeS; Divisional Marketing Manager, British Aerospace, since 1978; *b* 18 Nov. 1920; *m* 1941, Mary Averill; one *s*. *Educ:* Loughbourough College School, Leics. Electrical engineering apprenticeship, Blackburn Starling & Co. Ltd. RAF 1940-51: served Fighter Sqdns, 605 (County of Warwick) Sqdn, 1941; 135 Sqdn, 1941-44; 65 Sqdn, 1945. Qualified Flying Instructor, Upavon, 1945, and Instructor, Instrument Rating Examiner, until 1949; Graduate Empire Flying School all-weather course. Awarded King's Commendation, 1949; Graduate and Tutor, Empire Test Pilots' School, 1949-50; Test Pilot, RAE Farnborough, 1950-51; Experimental Test Pilot, Hawker Aircraft Ltd, 1951-56; Chief Test Pilot, Hawker Aircraft Ltd, 1956-63; Chief Test Pilot (Dunsfold); Hawker Siddeley Aviation Ltd, 1963-67; Sales Man., Hawker Siddeley Aviation, 1968-78. London-Rome and return world speed records, 1956. Made initial flight, Oct. 1960, on the Hawker P1127 (the World's first VTOL strike fighter), followed by first jet V/STOL operations of such an aircraft from an Aircraft Carrier (HMS Ark Royal) on 8 Feb. 1963; Harrier first flight, Aug. 1966. Holder Gliding Internat. Gold 'C' with two diamonds; held British and UK national gliding records of 257 miles and altitude of 21,340 ft (19,120 ft gain of height); awarded BGA trophies: de Havilland (twice), Manio, and Wakefield, 1950-51. Approved Air Registration Bd glider test pilot. Chm. and founder Mem., Test Pilots' Group, RAeS, 1964-66. Member SBAC Test Pilots' Soc., 1956-67. Member Society of Experimental Test Pilots. RAeS Alston Memorial Medal, 1959; Guild of Air Pilots and Air Navigators Derry Richards Memorial Medal, 1959-60; Segrave Trophy, 1963;

Britannia Trophy, 1964; Air League Founders Medal, 1967. *Recreations:* squash, sail-plane flying. *Address:* The Chequers, West End Lane, Esher, Surrey. *T:* Esher 62285. *Clubs:* Royal Air Force; Esher Squash.

BEDFORD, David; composer-in-residence, Queen's College, London, since 1969, teacher, 1968–80; *b* 4 Aug. 1937; *s* of Leslie Herbert Bedford, *qv*; *m* 1st, 1958, Maureen Parsonage; two *d*; 2nd, 1969, Susan Pilgrim; two *d*. *Educ:* Lancing College; Royal Acad. of Music; Trinity Coll. London (LTCL). Guy's Hosp. porter, 1956; teacher, Whitefield Sch., Hendon, 1965. ARAM. Mem. Exec. Cttee, Assoc. of Professional Composers. Numerous compositions, many commissioned by major London orchestras and BBC; numerous recordings. *Recreations:* squash, table tennis, astronomy, ancient history, philosophy. *Address:* 39 Shakespeare Road, Mill Hill, NW7 4BA. *T:* 01-959 3165. *Clubs:* Ridgeway Table Tennis, Mill Hill Squash.
See also S. J. R. Bedford.

BEDFORD, Eric, CB 1959; CVO 1953; Chief Architect, Ministry of Works, 1952–70 (Chief Architect, Directorate General of Works, Ministry of Public Building and Works, 1963–70). ARIBA 1933; Grissell Gold Medal of Royal Institute of British Architects, 1934. Was responsible for Ministry of Works decorations for the Coronation, 1953.

BEDFORD, Leslie Herbert, CBE 1956 (OBE 1942); retired as Director of Engineering, Guided Weapons Division, British Aircraft Corporation Ltd, 1968; *b* 23 June 1900; *s* of Herbert Bedford; *m* 1928, Lesley Florence Keitley Duff; three *s*. *Educ:* City and Guilds Engineering Coll., London (BSc); King's Coll., Cambridge (MA). Standard Telephones & Cables Ltd, 1924–31; Dir Research, A. C. Cossor Ltd, 1931–47; Chief TV Engr, Marconi's Wireless Telegraph Co. Ltd, 1947–48. Chief Engineer, GW Div., The English Electric Aviation Ltd, 1948–59; Dir, 1959–60. Mem., Council for Scientific and Industrial Research, 1961–. CEng, FCGI, FIEEE, MBritIRE, FIEE, FRAeS. Silver Medal (RAeS), 1963; Gold Medal, Société d'Encouragement pour la Recherche et l'Invention, 1967; Faraday Medal, 1968; Achievement Award, Scientific Instrument Makers' Soc., 1980. *Publications:* Articles in: Proc. Phys. Soc., Jl BritIRE, Jl RSA, Jl RAeS, Jl IEE, Wireless Engineer, Electronic and Radio Engineer, Electronic Technology. *Recreations:* music, sailing. *Address:* 82a Hendon Lane, N3. *T:* 01-346 1558.
See also D. Bedford, S. J. R. Bedford.

BEDFORD, Steuart John Rudolf; freelance conductor; Co-Artistic Director, English Music Theatre Co. since 1976; Artistic Director, English Sinfonia, 1981; *b* 31 July 1939; *s* of L. H. Bedford, *qv*; *m* 1st, 1969, Norma Burrowes, *qv*; 2nd, 1980, Celia, *e* *d* of Mr and Mrs G. R. Harding. *Educ:* Lancing Coll., Sussex; Royal Acad. of Music. Fellow, RCO; FRAM; BA. Artistic Dir, Aldeburgh Festival, 1974; Royal Acad. of Music, 1965; English Opera Gp, now English Music Theatre, 1967–. Debut at Metropolitan, NY, 1974 (Death in Venice); new prodn of The Marriage of Figaro, 1975. Has conducted regularly with English Opera Gp and Welsh National Opera; also at Royal Opera House, Covent Garden (operas incl. Owen Wingrave and Death in Venice, by Benjamin Britten, and Cosi Fan Tutte); also in Santa Fe, Buenos Aires, France, Belgium, Holland, Canada, Vienna, etc. *Recreations:* golf, gardening. *Address:* c/o Harrison Parrott Ltd, 12 Penzance Place, W11 4PA.
See also D. Bedford.

BEDFORD, Sybille, OBE 1981; author; *b* 16 March 1911; *d* of Maximilian von Schoenebeck and Elizabeth Bernard; *m* 1935, Walter Bedford. *Educ:* privately, in Italy, England and France. Career in writing and literary journalism. Vice-Pres., PEN, 1979. FRSL. *Publications:* The Sudden View, A Journey to Don Otavio, 1953, new edn 1982; A Legacy, 1956, 5th edn 1975, televised 1975; The Best We Can Do (The Trial of Dr Adams), 1958; The Faces of Justice, 1961; A Favourite of the Gods, 1962, new edn 1983; A Compass Error, 1968, new edn 1983; Aldous Huxley, a Biography, Vol I, 1973, Vol II, 1974. *Recreations:* wine, reading, travel. *Address:* c/o Messrs Coutts, 1 Old Park Lane, W1Y 4BS. *Club:* PEN.

BEDINGFELD, Sir Edmund; see Paston-Bedingfeld.

BEDINGFIELD, Christopher Ohl Macredie, TD 1968; QC 1976; a Recorder of the Crown Court, since 1972; *b* 2 June 1935; *s* of late Norman Macredie Bedingfield, Nantygroes, Radnorshire and of Mrs Macredie Bedingfield. *Educ:* Rugby; University Coll., Oxford (MA). Called to Bar, Gray's Inn, 1957; Wales and Chester Circuit. Commnd 2 Mon R; NS 24th Regt; Staff Captain TA, 1960–64; Coy Comdr 4 RWF, 1964–69; Lt-Col TAVR, 1973–76, Co. Comdt Denbigh and Flint ACF 1973, Clwyd ACF 1974–76 (resigned on appt as QC). *Recreations:* riding, squash. *Address:* 5 Essex Court, Temple, EC4. *T:* 01-353 2440; (residence) Nantygroes, near Knighton, Powys. *T:* Whitton 220. *Clubs:* Reform; BCYC (Swansea).

BEDSER, Alec Victor, CBE 1982 (OBE 1964); PR Consultant; *b* 4 July 1918; twin *s* of late Arthur and of Florence Beatrice Bedser. *Educ:* Monument Hill Secondary Sch., Woking. Served with RAF in UK, France (BEF), N Africa, Sicily, Italy, Austria, 1939–46. Joined Surrey County Cricket Club, as Professional, 1938; awarded Surrey CCC and England caps, 1946, 1st Test Match v India, created record by taking 22 wickets in first two Tests; toured Australia as Member of MCC team, 1946–47, 1950–51, 1954–55; toured S Africa with MCC, 1948–49; held record of most number of Test wickets (236), since beaten, 1953; took 100th wicket against Australia (first English bowler

since 1914 to do this), 1953; Asst Man. to Duke of Norfolk on MCC tour to Australia, 1962–63; Manager: MCC team to Australia, 1974–75; England team tour of Australia, 1979–80; Chm., England Cricket Selection Cttee, 1968–81 (Mem. 1961-). Founded own company (office equipment and supplies) with Eric Bedser, 1955. Freeman, City of London, 1968; Mem., Guild of Master Cleaners. *Publications:* (with E. A. Bedser) Our Cricket Story, 1951; Bowling, 1952; (with E. A. Bedser) Following On, 1954; Cricket Choice, 1981. *Recreations:* cricket, golf. *Address:* c/o Brengreen Holdings Ltd, 61 Cheapside, EC2. *Clubs:* MCC (Hon. Life), East India, Devonshire, Sports and Public Schools, Eccentric; Surrey County Cricket (Vice-Pres.); West Hill Golf.

BEEBY, Clarence Edward, CMG 1956; PhD; International Consultant, New Zealand Council for Educational Research, since 1969; *b* 16 June 1902; *s* of Anthony and Alice Beeby; *m* 1926, Beatrice Eleanor, *d* of Charles Newnham; one *s* one *d*. *Educ:* Christchurch Boys' High Sch.; Canterbury Coll., University of NZ (MA); University Coll., London; University of Manchester (PhD). Lectr in Philosophy and Education, Canterbury Univ. Coll., University of NZ, 1923–34; Dir, NZ Council for Educational Research, 1934–38; Asst Dir of Education, Education Dept, NZ, 1938–40; Dir of Education, NZ, 1940–60 (leave of absence to act as Asst Dir-Gen. of UNESCO, Paris, 1948–49); NZ Ambassador to France, 1960–63; Research Fellow, Harvard Univ., 1963–67; Commonwealth Visiting Prof., Univ. of London, 1967–68; Consultant: to Australian Govt in Papua and New Guinea, 1969; to Ford Foundn in Indonesia, 1970–77; to UNDP in Malaysia, 1976. Leader of NZ Delegs, to Gen. Confs of UNESCO, 1946, 1947, 1950, 1953, 1954, 1956, 1958, 1960, 1962. Hon. Counsellor of UNESCO, 1950; Mem., Exec. Bd, UNESCO, 1960–63 (Chm., Exec. Bd, 1963–64); Mem., Council of Consultant Fellows, Internat. Inst. for Educnl Planning, Paris, 1971–77. For. associate, US Nat. Acad. of Educn, 1981. Mackie Medal, ANZAAS, 1971. Hon. LLD Otago, 1969; Hon. LittD Wellington, 1970. Order of St Gregory (1st cl.), 1964. *Publications:* The Intermediate Schools of New Zealand, 1938; (with W. Thomas and M. H. Oram) Entrance to the University, 1939; The Quality of Education in Developing Countries, 1966; (ed) Qualitative Aspects of Educational Planning, 1969; Assessment of Indonesian Education: a guide in planning, 1978; articles in educational periodicals. *Recreations:* gardening, fishing, cabinet-making. *Address:* 73 Barnard Street, Wellington N2, New Zealand.

BEEBY, George Harry, CBE 1974; PhD, BSc, CEng, FIChemE, FRSC; Chairman, Inveresk Research Foundation, since 1977; *b* 9 Sept. 1902; *s* of George Beeby and Lucy Beeby (née Monk); *m* 1929, Helen Elizabeth Edwards; one *d*. *Educ:* Loughborough Grammar Sch.; Loughborough Coll. BSc Hons 1922; PhD 1924, London Univ. Various appts in rubber and chemical industries, 1924–; Chm., Thorium Ltd and Radiochemical Centre (later Amersham Internat.), 1949–57; Divisional Chm., ICI, 1954–57; Chm., British Titan Ltd, 1957–69. Chairman: EDC for Chemical Industry, 1964–67; Nat. Sulphuric Acid Assoc., 1963–65; British Standards Instn, 1967–70 (Dep. Pres. 1970–73). Pres., Soc. of Chemical Industry, 1970–72 (Vice-Pres., 1966–69); Vice-Pres., RoSPA, 1969–; Hon. Mem., Chemical Industries Assoc. Member: Robens Cttee on Safety and Health at Work, 1970; Parly and Sci. Cttee, 1971; Windeyer Cttee on lead poisoning, 1972. FRSA 1969. Hon. DTech Loughborough Univ. of Technology, 1969. Soc. of Chemical Industry Medal, 1973. *Publications:* contribs to various jls on industrial safety, industrial economics and business administration. *Recreations:* golf, racing. *Address:* The Laurels, Sandy Drive, Cobham, Surrey. *T:* Oxshott 2346. *Club:* Royal Automobile.

BEECH, Patrick Mervyn, CBE 1970; Controller, English Regions, BBC, 1969–72, retired; *b* 31 Oct. 1912; *s* of Howard Worcester Mervyn Beech and Stella Patrick Campbell; *m* 1st, 1935, Sigrid Gunnel Christenson (*d* 1959); two *d*; 2nd, 1960, Merle-Mary Barnes; one *d*. *Educ:* Stowe; Exeter Coll., Oxford. Joined BBC as Producer, West Region, 1935; News Editor, West Region, 1945; Asst Head of programmes, West Region, 1954; Controller, Midland Region, 1964–69. *Recreations:* photography, music, theatre. *Address:* Mill Bank, Cradley, near Malvern, Worcs. *T:* Ridgway Cross 234.

BEECHAM, John Stratford Roland, (4th Bt *cr* 1914, but does not use the title); a Minister in the Pentecostal Church; *b* 21 April 1940; *s* of Sir Adrian Welles Beecham, 3rd Bt and of Barbara Joyce, *d* of late Edward Cairn; *S* father, 1982. *Educ:* Winchester; Oxford Univ. *Heir:* *b* Robert Adrian Beecham [*b* 6 Jan. 1942; *m* 1969, Daphne Mattinson; one *s* one *d*]. *Address:* Shalom, Station Road, Shipston-on-Stour, Warwickshire. *T:* Shipston-on-Stour 61608.

BEECHER, Most Rev. Leonard James, CMG 1961; ARCS, MA, DD; *b* 21 May 1906; *er* *s* of Robert Paul and Charlotte Beecher; *m* 1930, Gladys Sybil Bazett (*d* 1982), *yr* *d* of late Canon Harry and Mrs Mary Leakey; two *s* one *d*. *Educ:* St Olave's Grammar Sch., Southwark; Imperial Coll. and London Day Trg Coll., University of London. ARCS 1926; BSc 1927; MA (London) 1937. DD Lambeth, 1962. Asst Master, Alliance High Sch., Kikuyu, Kenya, 1927–30; Missionary, Church Missionary Soc., Diocese of Mombasa, 1930–57; Unofficial Mem. of Legislative Council, Colony of Kenya, representing African interests, 1943–47; MEC of the Colony of Kenya, 1947–52; Asst Bishop of Mombasa, Kenya Colony, 1950–53; Archdeacon and Canon of the Diocese, 1945–53; Bishop of Mombasa, 1953–64; Archbishop of East Africa, 1960–70; Bishop of Nairobi, 1964–70; Archbishop Emeritus, 1970. *Publications:* (with G. S. B. Beecher) A Kikuyu-English Dictionary, 1933;

translator of parts of the Kikuyu Old Testament, 1939-49; Editor, Kenya Church Review, 1941-50. *Recreations:* recorded music, bird-watching, photography. *Address:* PO Box 21066, Nairobi, Kenya. *T:* Nairobi 567485.

BEECHING, family name of **Baron Beeching.**

BEECHING, Baron, *cr* 1965 (Life Peer); **Richard Beeching,** PhD; Director, Lloyds Bank Ltd, since 1965; *b* 21 April 1913; *s* of Hubert J. Beeching; *m* 1938, Ella Margaret Tiley. *Educ:* Maidstone Grammar Sch.; Imperial Coll. of Science and Technology, London. ARCS, BSc, 1st Cl. Hons; DIC; PhD London. Fuel Research Station, 1936; Mond Nickel Co. Ltd 1937; Armaments Design Dept, Min. of Supply, 1943; Dep. Chief Engineer of Armaments Design, 1946. Joined Imperial Chemical Industries, 1948, Dir, 1957-61 and 1965, Dep. Chm. 1966-68. Vice-Pres. ICI of Canada Ltd, 1953; Chm., Metals Div., ICI, 1955. Furness Withy & Co. Ltd: Dir, 1972-75; Chm., 1973-75; Chm., Redland Ltd, 1970-77. Member: Special Adv. Gp on BTC, 1960; NEDC, 1962-64; Top Salaries Review Body, 1971-75; Chairman: British Railways Bd, 1963-65; BTC, 1961-63. Chm., Royal Commn on Assizes and QS, 1966. First Pres., Inst. of Work Study Practitioners, 1967-72; Pres., RoSPA, 1968-73. Fellow, Imperial Coll.; CIMechE, FInstP; Hon. LLD London; Hon. DSc NUI. *Publication:* Electron Diffraction, 1936. *Address:* Little Manor, East Grinstead, West Sussex.

BEECK, Sir Marcus (Truby), Kt 1979; farmer and company director; *b* 28 Dec. 1923; 2nd *s* of Gustav Edwin Beeck and Martha Ellen (*née* Keast); *m* 1950, Léonie Pamela Dale Robertson, *y d* of Robert Robertson, retired grazier; one *s* two *d*. *Educ:* State Correspondence Sch., W Australia; Katanning State Sch., W Australia. Served War, RAAF, SW Pacific, 1942-45. Community service in many fields, including: Leader, Australian Materials and Equipment Trade Mission to Indonesia, 1974; Chm., Grain Pool of Western Australia, 1975-76; Pres., Royal Agricultural Soc. of Western Australia, 1975-77; Member: Australian Trade Exhibition and Mission to Moscow, 1976; 3-Man Western Australian Agricl Mission to Japan, 1978. Director, Westralian Farmers Co-operative Ltd. Queen's Silver Jubilee Medal, 1977. *Recreations:* flying, rifle shooting, golf, tennis. *Address:* Coyrecup, PO Box 110, Katanning, Western Australia 6317. *T:* East Katanning 222224. *Clubs:* Weld, West Australian (Perth); Katanning (Katanning).

BEEDHAM, Brian James; Foreign Editor, The Economist; *b* 12 Jan. 1928; *s* of James Victor Beedham and Nina Beedham (*née* Zambra); *m* 1960, Ruth Barbara Zollikofer. *Educ:* Leeds Grammar Sch.; The Queen's Coll., Oxford. RA, 1950-52. Asst Editor, Yorkshire Post, 1952-55; The Economist, 1955-, Washington correspondent, 1958-61. Commonwealth Fellowship, 1956-57. Fellow, Royal Geographical Society. *Recreations:* hillwalking, music, Kipling and Wodehouse. *Address:* 9 Hillside, SW19. *T:* 01-946 4454. *Clubs:* Travellers', Savile.

BEELEY, Sir Harold, KCMG 1961 (CMG 1953); CBE 1946; *b* 15 Feb. 1909; *s* of Frank Arthur Beeley; *m* 1st, 1933, Millicent Mary Chinn (marr. diss., 1953); two *d*; 2nd, 1958, Mrs Patricia Karen Brett-Smith; one *d*. *Educ:* Highgate; Queen's Coll., Oxford. 1st Cl. in Modern History, 1930. Asst Lectr in Modern History, Sheffield Univ., 1930-31; University Coll., London, 1931-35; Junior Research Fellow and Lecturer, Queen's Coll., Oxford, 1935-38; Lecturer in Charge of History Dept, University Coll., Leicester, 1938-39. Mem. of wartime organisation of Royal Institute of International Affairs, and subsequently of Foreign Office Research Dept, 1939-45. Mem. of Secretariat of San Francisco Conf. and of Preparatory Commission of UN, 1945; Sec. of Anglo-American Cttee of Enquiry on Palestine, 1946. Entered Foreign Service, 1946; Counsellor of Embassy, Copenhagen, 1949-50; Baghdad, 1950-53; Washington, 1953-55; Ambassador to Saudi Arabia, during 1955; Asst Under-Sec., Foreign Office, 1956-58; Dep. UK Representative to UN, New York, 1958-61; UK Representative, Disarmament Conf., Geneva, 1964-67; Ambassador to the United Arab Republic, 1961-64, 1967-69. Lectr in History, Queen Mary Coll., Univ. of London, 1969-75. Chm., Ibis Securities Ltd, 1979-. Pres., Egypt Exploration Soc., 1969-; Chairman: World of Islam Festival Trust, 1973-; Egyptian-British Chamber of Commerce, 1981-. *Address:* 2 Ormond Road, Richmond, Surrey. *Club:* Reform.

BEER, Prof. (Anthony) Stafford; International Consultant and Adviser in Cybernetics to Ernst and Whinney (Canada); Visiting Professor of Cybernetics at Manchester University (Business School), since 1969, also Adjunct Professor of Statistics and Operations Research at Pennsylvania University (Wharton School), 1972-81, and of Social Systems Sciences since 1981; *b* London, 25 Sept. 1926; *er s* of late William John and of Doris Ethel Beer; *m* 1st, 1947, Cynthia Margaret Hannaway; four *s* one *d*; 2nd, 1968, Sallie Steadman (*née* Child); one *s* two *d*. *Educ:* Whitgift Sch.; University Coll., London. MBA Manchester. Lieut, 9th Gurkha Rifles 1945; Captain, Royal Fusiliers 1947. Man. of Operational Res. and Prodn Controller, S. Fox & Co., 1949-56; Head of Op. Res. and Cybernetics, United Steel, 1956-61; Man. Dir, SIGMA Science in General Management Ltd and Dir, Metra International, 1961-66; Develt Dir, International Publishing Corp.; Dir, International Data Highways Ltd; Chm., Computaprint Ltd, 1966-69. Vis. Prof. of Gen. Systems, Open Univ., 1970-71; Scientific Dir, Project Cybersyn, Chile, 1971-73. Ex-Pres., Operational Res. Soc.; Ex-Pres., Soc. for Gen. Systems Res. (USA); Pres., World Orgn of Gen. Systems and Cybernetics, 1981-; Mem. UK Automation Council, 1957-69; Mem. Gen. Adv. Council of BBC, 1961-69. Silver Medal, Royal Swedish Acad. for Engrg Scis, 1958;

Lanchester Prize (USA) for Ops Res., 1966; McCulloch Award (USA) for Cybernetics, 1970. *Publications:* Cybernetics and Management, 1959; Decision and Control, 1966; Management Science, 1967; Brain of the Firm, 1972 (new edn, 1981); Designing Freedom, 1974; Platform for Change, 1975; Transit (poems), 1977; The Heart of Enterprise, 1979; chapters in numerous other books. *Recreations:* spinning, painting, poetry, classics, staying put. *Address:* Cwarel Isaf, Pont Creuddyn, Lampeter, Dyfed, Wales. *Club:* Athenæum.
See also I. D. S. Beer.

BEER, Ian David Stafford, MA; JP; Head Master of Harrow, since 1981; *b* 28 April 1931; *s* of late William Beer and Doris Ethel Beer; *m* 1960, Angela Felce, *d* of Col E. S. G. Howard, MC, RA; two *s* one *d*. *Educ:* Whitgift Sch.; (Exhibitioner) St Catharine's Coll., Cambridge. Second Lieut in 1st Bn Royal Fusiliers, 1950. House Master, Marlborough Coll., Wilts, 1957-61; Head Master: Ellesmere Coll., Salop, 1961-69; Lancing Coll., Sussex, 1969-81. Chairman: HMC Academic Cttee, 1977-79; HMC, 1980. Chm. Editorial Bd, Rugby Post, 1977-. JP Shropshire, 1963-69, JP W Sussex, 1970-81, JP Mddx, 1981-. *Recreations:* Rugby Football Union Cttee (formerly: played Rugby for England; CURFC (Capt.), Harlequins, Old Whitgiftians), swimming, reading, zoology, meeting people. *Address:* Peel House, Football Lane, Harrow-on-the-Hill, Mddx. *Clubs:* East India, Devonshire, Sports and Public Schools; Hawks (Cambridge).
See also A. S. Beer.

BEER, James Edmund; Director: Short Loan and Mortgage Co. Ltd; Short Loan (Leasing) Ltd; London Financial Futures Co. Ltd; *b* 17 March 1931; *s* of Edmund Huxtable Beer and Gwendoline Kate Beer; *m* 1953, Barbara Mollie (*née* Tunley); two *s* one *d*. *Educ:* Torquay Grammar School. IPFA, FRVA, MBCS, MBIM. Torquay Borough Council, 1951-54; Chatham, 1954-56; Wolverhampton, 1956-58; Doncaster, 1958-60; Chief Accountant, Bedford, 1960-62; Asst Borough Treas., Croydon, 1963-65; Dep. Treas., Leeds, 1965; Chief Financial Officer, Leeds, 1968; Dir of Finance, Leeds City Council, 1973-78. Mem. Local Govt Financial Exec., CIPFA, 1974-78; Financial Adviser to AMA, 1974-78; Treas., Soc. of Metropolitan Treasurers, 1974-78; Member: LAMSAC Computer Panel, 1972-78; Yorks and Humberside Develt Assoc. London Section, 1970-; Past Examr, CIPFA; Adviser on Rate Support Grant, AMA, 1974-78; Treas., Leeds Grand Theatre & Opera House Ltd, 1974-78; Governor, Leeds Musical Festival. *Publications:* contrib. professional jls. *Recreations:* golf, theatre, swimming, Rugby (past playing mem., Torquay Athletic RUFC). *Address:* 48 High Ash Avenue, Alwoodley, Leeds LS17 8RG. *T:* Leeds 683907.

BEER, Prof. János Miklós, DSc, PhD, FEng; Professor of Chemical and Fuel Engineering, Massachusetts Institute of Technology (MIT), since 1976; Programme Director for Combustion, MIT Energy Laboratory, since 1976; *b* Budapest, 27 Feb. 1923; *s* of Sándor Beér and Gizella Trismai; *m* 1944, Marta Gabriella Csató. *Educ:* Berzsenyi Dániel Gymnasium, Budapest; Univ. of Budapest (Dipl-Ing 1950). PhD (Sheffield), 1960, DSc(Tech) Sheffield 1967. Heat Research Inst., Budapest: Research Officer, 1949-52; Head, Combustion Dept, 1952-56; Princ. Lectr (part-time), University of Budapest, 1953-56; Research Engr, Babcock & Wilcox Ltd, Renfrew, 1957; Research Bursar, University of Sheffield, 1957-60; Head, Research Stn, Internat. Flame Research Foundn, Ijmuiden, Holland, 1960-63; Prof., Dept of Fuel Science, Pa State Univ., 1963-65; Newton Drew Prof. of Chemical Engrg and Fuel Technology and Head of Dept, Univ. of Sheffield, 1965-76; Dean, Faculty of Engineering, Univ. of Sheffield, 1973-75. Member: Adv. Council on R&D for Fuel and Power, DTI, later Dept of Energy, 1973-76; Adv. Bd, Safety in Mines Research, Dept of Energy, 1974-76; Clean Air Council, DoE, 1974-76; Bd of Directors, The Combustion Inst., Pittsburgh, USA, 1974-; Mem., Adv. Cttee, Italian Nat. Res. Council, 1974-. Gen. Superintendent of Research, Internat. Flame Research Foundn, 1971-. Australian Commonwealth Vis. Fellow, 1972; Fellow ASME, 1978 (Moody Award, 1964); FEng 1979. Editor, Fuel and Energy Science Monograph Series, 1966-. *Publications:* (with N. Chigier) Combustion Aerodynamics, 1972; (ed with M. W. Thring) Industrial Flames, 1972; (ed with H. B. Palmer) Developments in Combustion Science and Technology, 1974; (ed with N. Afgan) Heat Transfer in Flames, 1975; contribs to Nature, Combustion and Flame, Basic Engrg Jl, Amer. Soc. Mech. Engrg, Jl Inst. F, ZVDI, Internat. Gas Wärme, Proc. Internat. Symposia on Combustion, etc. *Recreations:* swimming, rowing, reading, music. *Address:* Department of Chemical Engineering, Massachusetts Institute of Technology, Cambridge, Mass 02139, USA. *T:* 617-253-6661.

BEER, Mrs Nellie, OBE 1957; JP; DL; Member of Manchester City Council, 1937-72 (Alderman 1964-72; Lord Mayor of Manchester, 1966); *b* 22 April 1900; *d* of Arthur Robinson and Nelly Laurie Robinson (*née* Hewitt); *m* 1927, Robert Beer (*d* 1977); one *d*. *Educ:* Ardwick Higher Grade Sch. Hon. MA Univ. of Manchester, 1978. JP Manchester, 1942; DL Lancs, 1970. *Address:* 6 Princes Avenue, Didsbury, Manchester. *T:* 061-445 6237.

BEER, Patricia, (Mrs J. D. Parsons); freelance writer; *b* 4 Nov. 1924; *yr d* of Andrew William and Harriet Beer, Exmouth, Devon; *m* 1964, John Damien Parsons. *Educ:* Exmouth Grammar Sch.; Exeter Univ. (BA, 1st cl. Hons English); St Hugh's Coll., Oxford (BLitt). Lecturer: in English, Univ. of Padua, 1947-49; British Inst., Rome, 1949-51; Goldsmiths' Coll., Univ. of London, 1962-68. *Publications:* poetry: Loss of the Magyar, 1959; The Survivors, 1963; Just Like The Resurrection, 1967; The Estuary, 1971; (ed) New Poems 1975, 1975; Driving West, 1975; (ed jtly) New Poetry 2, 1976; Selected Poems, 1980; *novel:* Moon's Ottery, 1978; *autobiog.:* Mrs Beer's

House, 1968; *criticism:* Reader, I Married Him, 1974; contrib. The Listener, London Review of Books. *Recreations:* travelling, cooking. *Address:* 1 Oak Hill Park, NW3. *T:* 01-435 2470.

BEER, Prof. Stafford; *see* Beer, Prof. A. S.

BEESLEY, Mrs Alec M.; *see* Smith, Dodie.

BEESLEY, Prof. Michael Edwin, PhD; Professor of Economics since 1965, and Director of Institute of Public Sector Management since 1978, London Business School; *b* 3 July 1924; *s* of late Edwin S. and Kathleen D. Beesley; *m* 1947, Eileen Eleanor Yard; *three s two d. Educ:* King Edward's Grammar Sch., Five Ways, Birmingham; Univ. of Birmingham (BCom Div. 1, 1945; PhD 1951). Lectr in Commerce, Univ. of Birmingham, 1951-60; Rees Jeffreys Res. Fellow, LSE, 1961-64; Sir Ernest Cassel Reader in Econs, with special ref. to transport, Univ. of London tenable at LSE, 1964-65. Vis. Associate Prof., Univ. of Pennsylvania, 1959-60; Vis. Prof., Harvard Univ., 1974; Vis. Prof. and Commonwealth Fellow: Univ. of BC, 1968; Macquarie Univ., Sydney, 1979-80. Dir, Transmark Ltd, 1979-. Chief Econ. Adviser, Min. of Transport, 1964-68; Special Adviser, Treasury and CS Cttee, Nationalised Industry Financing, 1981; formerly Member: Cttee on Road Pricing (Smeed Cttee); Cttee on Transport in London; Cttee on Transport Planning (Lady Sharp Cttee); Urban Motorways Inter-Deptl Cttee; Standing Adv. Cttee on Trunk Road Assessment (Sir George Leitch Cttee). Managing Editor, Jl of Transport Economics and Policy, 1975-. *Publications:* Urban Transport: studies in economic policy, 1973; (co-ed with D. C. Hague) Britain in the Common Market: a new business opportunity, 1974; (ed) Productivity and Amenity: achieving a social balance, 1974; (ed) Industrial Relations in a Changing World, 1975; (with T. C. Evans) Corporate Social Responsibility: a reassessment, 1978; Liberalisation of the Use of British Telecommunications Network: an independent economic enquiry, 1981. *Recreations:* music, table tennis, golf. *Address:* 59 Canons Drive, Edgware, Mddx HA8 7RG. *T:* 01-952 1320. *Club:* Reform.

BEESON, Prof. Paul Bruce, Hon. KBE 1973; FRCP; Professor of Medicine, University of Washington, since 1974; *b* 18 Oct. 1908; *s* of John Bradley Beeson, Livingston, Mont; *m* 1942, Barbara Neal, *d* of Ray C. Neal, Buffalo, NY; *two s one d. Educ:* Univ. of Washington, McGill Univ. Med. Sch. MD, CM, 1933. Intern, Hosp. of Univ. of Pa, 1933-35; Gen. practice of medicine, Wooster, Ohio, 1935-37; Asst Rockefeller Inst., 1937-39; Chief Med. Resident, Peter Bent Brigham Hosp., 1939-40; Instructor in Med., Havard Med. Sch., and Chief Phys., American Red Cross-Harvard Field Hosp. Unit, Salisbury, 1940-42; Asst and Assoc. Prof. of Med., Emory Med. Sch., 1942-46; Prof. of Med. Emory Med. Sch., 1946-52; Prof. of Med. and Chm. Dept of Med., Yale Univ., 1952-65; Nuffield Prof. of Clinical Med., Oxford Univ., and Fellow of Magdalen Coll., 1965-74, Hon. Fellow, 1975; Hon. Fellow RSM, 1976. Vis. Investigator, Wright-Fleming Inst., St Mary's Hosp., 1958-59. Pres., Assoc. Amer. Physicians, 1967; Master, Amer. Coll. of Physicians, 1970. Phillips Award, Amer. Coll. Physicians, 1975; Flexner Award, Assoc. Amer. Med. Colls, 1977. *Alumnus Summa Laude Dignatus,* Univ. of Washington, 1968; Hon. DSc: Emory Univ., 1968; McGill Univ., 1971; Yale Univ., 1975; Albany Med. Coll., 1975; Ohio Med. Coll., 1979. *Publications:* Edited: Cecil-Loeb Textbook of Medicine, 1959-82; Yale Journal Biology and Medicine, 1959-65; Journal Amer. Geriatric Soc., 1981-; numerous scientific publications relating to infectious disease, pathogenesis of fever, pyelonephritis and mechanism of eosinophilia. *Address:* 8262 Avondale Road, Redmond, Washington 98052, USA.

BEESON, Rev. Canon Trevor Randall; Canon of Westminster, since 1976; Rector of St Margaret's, Westminster, since 1982; Chaplain to the Speaker of the House of Commons, since 1982; *b* 2 March 1926; *s* of late Arthur William and Matilda Beeson; *m* 1950, Josephine Grace Cope; *two d. Educ:* King's Coll., London (AKC 1950); St Boniface Coll., Warminster. RAF Met Office, 1944-47. Deacon, 1951; Priest, 1952; Curate, Leadgate, Co. Durham, 1951-54; Priest-in-charge and subseq. Vicar of St Chad, Stockton-on-Tees, 1954-65; Curate of St Martin-in-the-Fields, London, 1965-71; Vicar of Ware, Herts, 1971-76. Treasurer, Westminster, 1978-82. Chaplain of St Bride's, Fleet Street, 1967-. Gen. Sec., Parish and People, 1962-64; Editor, New Christian, and Man. Dir, Prism Publications Ltd, 1965-70; European Corresp. of The Christian Century (Chicago), 1970-; Chm., SCM Press Ltd, 1978-. Hon. MA (Lambeth) 1976. *Publications:* New Area Mission, 1963; (jtly) Worship in a United Church, 1964; An Eye for an Ear, 1972; The Church of England in Crisis, 1973; Discretion and Valour: religious conditions in Russia and Eastern Europe, 1974; Britain Today and Tomorrow, 1978; Westminster Abbey, 1981. *Recreations:* cricket, travel. *Address:* 2 Little Cloister, Westminster Abbey, SW1.

BEESTON, Prof. Alfred Felix Landon, MA, DPhil; FBA 1965; Laudian Professor of Arabic, Oxford, 1956-78; Emeritus Fellow, St John's College, Oxford, 1978 (Fellow, 1955-78); *b* 1911; *o s* of Herbert Arthur Beeston and Edith Mary Landon. *Educ:* Westminster Sch.; Christ Church, Oxford. James Mew Arabic Scholarship, Oxford, 1934; MA (Oxford), 1936; DPhil (Oxford), 1937. Asst in Dept of Oriental Books, Bodleian Library, Oxford, 1935-40; Sub-Librarian and Keeper of Oriental Books, Bodleian Library, 1946-55. *Publications:* Descriptive Grammar of Epigraphic South Arabian, 1962; Baidáwi's Commentary on Sürah 12, 1963; Written Arabic, 1968; The Arabic Language Today, 1970; Selections from the Poetry of Baššār, 1977;

Samples of Arabic Prose, 1977; The 'Epistle on Singing Girls' of Jāhiz, 1980; many articles. *Address:* St John's College, Oxford OX1 3JP.

BEETHAM, Marshal of the Royal Air Force Sir Michael (James), GCB 1978 (KCB 1976); CBE 1967; DFC 1944; AFC 1960; FRAeS; Chief of the Air Staff, 1977-82; Air ADC to the Queen, 1977-82; *b* 17 May 1923; *s* of Major G. C. Beetham, MC; *m* 1956, Patricia Elizabeth Lane; *one s one d. Educ:* St Marylebone Grammar School. Joined RAF, 1941; pilot trng, 1941-42; commnd 1942; Bomber Comd: 50, 57 and 35 Sqdns, 1943-46; HQ Staff, 1947-49; 82 (Recce) Sqdn, E Africa, 1949-51; psa 1952; Air Min. (Directorate Operational Requirements), 1953-56; CO 214 (Valiant) Sqdn Marham, 1958-60; Gp Captain Ops, HQ Bomber Comd, 1962-64; CO RAF Khormaksar, Aden, 1964-66; idc 1967; Dir Ops (RAF), MoD, 1968-70; Comdt, RAF Staff Coll., 1970-72; ACOS (Plans and Policy), SHAPE, 1972-75; Dep. C-in-C, Strike Command, 1975-76; C-in-C RAF Germany, and Comdr, 2nd Tactical Allied Air Force, 1976-77. FRSA 1979; FRAeS 1982. *Recreations:* golf, tennis. *Address:* Lloyds Bank, Cox's & King's Branch, 6 Pall Mall, SW1. *Clubs:* Royal Air Force; Royal Mid-Surrey Golf.

BEETHAM, Roger Campbell, MVO 1976; HM Diplomatic Service; Counsellor (Economic and Commercial), New Delhi, since 1981; *b* 22 Nov. 1937; *s* of Henry Campbell and Mary Beetham; *m* 1965, Judith Mary Yorwerth Rees. *Educ:* Peter Symonds Sch., Winchester; Brasenose Coll., Oxford (MA). Entered HM Diplomatic Service, 1960; FO, 1960-62; UK Delegation to Disarmament Conference, Geneva, 1962-65; Washington, 1965-68; News Dept, FCO, 1969-72; Head of Chancery, Helsinki, 1972-76; FCO, 1976; seconded to European Commission, Brussels, as Spokesman of the President, Rt Hon. Roy Jenkins, 1977-80. Order of the White Rose of Finland, 1976. *Recreations:* oenology, cooking, travel, skiing. *Address:* c/o Foreign and Commonwealth Office, SW1; 64 Beaulieu Avenue, SE26.

BEEVOR, John Grosvenor, OBE 1945; *b* 1 March 1905; *s* of Henry Beevor, Newark-on-Trent, Notts; *m* 1st, 1933, Carinthia Jane (marr. diss., 1956), *d* of Aubrey and Caroline Waterfield, Aulla, Italy; *three s* ; 2nd, 1957, Mary Christine Grepe. *Educ:* Winchester; New Coll., Oxford. Solicitor, 1931-53, Slaughter and May, London, EC2. Served HM Army, 1939-45, RA and SOE. Adviser to British Delegation to Marshall Plan Conf., Paris, 1947; Mem. Lord Chancellor's Cttee on Private Internat. Law, 1952-53; Man. Dir, Commonwealth Development Finance Co. Ltd, 1954-56; Vice-Pres., Internat. Finance Corp., Washington, DC, 1956-64. Chairman: Doulton & Co., 1966-75; Tilbury Contracting Group, 1966-76; Lafarge Organisation Ltd, 1966-76; Director: Lafarge SA, 1969-80; Williams & Glyn's Bank Ltd, 1970-75; Glaxo Holdings Ltd, 1965-75. Member Councils: The Officers' Assoc.; Overseas Develt Inst. *Publications:* The Effective Board, a Chairman's View, 1975; SOE, Recollections and Reflections, 1981. *Address:* 51 Eaton Square, SW1W 9BE. *T:* 01-235 7987. *Club:* Special Forces.

BEEVOR, Miles; retired as Solicitor and Director of Companies; *b* 8 March 1900; 2nd *s* of Rowland Beevor; *m* 1st, 1924, Margaret Florence Platt (*d* 1934); *one s* (and *one d* decd); 2nd, 1935, Sybil Gilliat; *two s one d. Educ:* Winchester (Scholar); New Coll., Oxford (Scholar), BA 1921. Admitted a Solicitor, 1925. Served European War, 1914-18, in Army (RE Officer Cadet Battalion), 1918; War of 1939-45, RAFVR (Flt-Lieut Admin. and Special Duties Br.), 1941-43. Chief Legal Adviser, LNER, 1943-47; Actg Chief General Manager, LNER, 1947; Chief Sec. and Legal Adviser, British Transport Commission, 1947-51; Managing Dir, Brush Electrical Engineering Co. Ltd (which became The Brush Group Ltd), 1952-56; Deputy Chm. and Joint Managing Dir, 1956-57. *Recreations:* fishing, shooting. *Address:* 44 Mill Lane, Welwyn, Herts. *T:* Welwyn 5103.

BEEVOR, Sir Thomas Agnew, 7th Bt, *cr* 1784; *b* 6 Jan. 1929; *s* of Comdr Sir Thomas Beevor, 6th Bt, and of Edith Margaret Agnew (who *m* 2nd, 1944, Rear-Adm. R. A. Currie, *qv*); *S* father 1943; *m* 1st, 1957, Barbara Clare (marr. diss., 1965), *y d* of Capt. R. L. B. Cunliffe, RN (retd); *one s two d* ; 2nd, 1966, Carola, *d* of His Honour J. B. Herbert, MC; 3rd, 1976, Mrs Sally Bouwens, White Hall, Saham Toney, Norfolk. *Heir: s* Thomas Hugh Cunliffe Beevor, *b* 1 Oct. 1962. *Address:* Hargham Hall, Norwich.

BEEZLEY, Frederick Ernest; His Honour Judge Beezley; a Circuit Judge, since 1976; *b* 30 Jan. 1921; *s* of Frederick William Beezley and Lilian Isabel (*née* Markham); *m* 1969, Sylvia Ruth (*née* Locke). *Educ:* Acton County Sch. Served War, Royal Signals, Combined Operations, 1940-46. Called to Bar, Gray's Inn, 1947. *Recreations:* organ playing, sea angling. *Address:* c/o Crown Court, Norwich. *T:* Norwich 29859.

BEGG, Rt. Rev. Ian Forbes, MA, DD; *b* 12 Feb. 1910; *e s* of Rev. John Smith Begg and Elizabeth Macintyre; *m* 1949, Lillie Taylor Paterson. *Educ:* Aberdeen Grammar Sch.; Aberdeen Univ.; Westcott House, Cambridge. Deacon 1933; Priest 1934. Curate, St Paul's, Prince's Park, Liverpool, 1933-35; Priest-in-Charge of St Ninian's Episcopal Church, Seaton, Aberdeen, 1935-73; Dean, United Diocese of Aberdeen and Orkney, 1969-73; Bishop of Aberdeen and Orkney, 1973-77; Canon of St Andrew's Cathedral, Aberdeen, 1965. Chm., Church Guest Houses' Assoc., 1969-. Hon. DD Aberdeen, 1971. *Recreations:* fishing, gardening. *Address:* 430 King Street, Aberdeen. *T:* Aberdeen 632169.

BEGG, Robert William, CBE 1977; MA; CA; Partner, Mann Judd Gordon, Chartered Accountants, Glasgow, since 1951; *b* 19 Feb. 1922; *s* of late David

Begg, CA, FFA, and of Elizabeth Young Thomson; *m* 1948, Sheena Margaret Boyd; two *s. Educ:* Glasgow Univ. (MA 1942). Served Royal Navy, 1942-46, Lieut RNVR (despatches). Institute of Chartered Accountants of Scotland: Member, 1948; Students' Society, 1947-55: President, 1954-55; Examining Bd, 1952-58; Public Relations Cttee, 1968-74; Pres., Benevolent Assoc., 1973-75; Convener, Students' Affairs Cttee, 1979-; Mem. Glasgow Univ. General Council Business Cttee, 1973-76; Hon. Treasurer: Royal Philosophical Soc. of Glasgow, 1952-62; Royal Glasgow Inst. of Fine Arts, 1975-; Mem. Bd of Governors, Glasgow School of Art, 1955-77, Chm., 1970-76; Trustee, RIAS Hill House Trust, 1977-; Bd of Trustees, National Galleries of Scotland, 1974-, Chm., 1980-. *Recreation:* painting. *Address:* 142 St Vincent Street, Glasgow G2 5LD. *T:* 041-221 6991; (home) 3 Colquhoun Drive, Bearsden, Glasgow G61 4NQ. *T:* 041-942 2436. *Clubs:* Art (Glasgow); New (Edinburgh).

EGG, Admiral of the Fleet Sir Varyl (Cargill), GCB 1965 (KCB 1962; CB 1959); DSO 1952; DSC 1941; Governor and Commander-in-Chief of Gibraltar, 1969-73; *b* 1 Oct. 1908; *s* of Francis Cargill Begg and Muriel Clare Robinson; *m* 1943, Rosemary Cowan, CStJ; two *s. Educ:* St Andrews Sch., Eastbourne; Malvern Coll. Entered RN, special entry, 1926; Qualified Gunnery Officer, 1933; HMS Glasgow, 1939-40; HMS Warspite, 1940-43; Comdr Dec. 1942; Capt. 1947; commanded HM Gunnery Sch., Chatham, 1948-50; 8th Destroyer Flotilla, 1950-52; HMS Excellent, 1952-54; HMS Triumph, 1955-56; idc 1954; Rear-Adm. 1957; Chief of Staff to C-in-C Portsmouth 1957-58; Flag Officer Commanding Fifth Cruiser Squadron and Flag Officer Second-in-Command, Far East Station, 1958-60; Vice-Adm. 1960; a Lord Commissioner of the Admiralty and Vice-Chief of Naval Staff, 1961-63; Admiral, 1963; C-in-C, British Forces in the Far East, and UK Military Adviser to SEATO, 1963-65; C-in-C, Portsmouth, and Allied C-in-C, Channel, 1965-66; Chief of Naval Staff and First Sea Lord, 1966-68. KStJ 1969. PMN 1966. *Recreations:* fishing, gardening. *Address:* Copyhold Cottage, Chilbolton, Stockbridge, Hants. *Club:* Army and Navy.

EGIN, Menachem, MJr; Prime Minister, State of Israel, since June 1977; *b* Brest-Litovsk, Poland, 16 Aug. 1913; *s* of Ze'ev-Dov and Hassia Begin; *m* Aliza Arnold; one *s* two *d. Educ:* Mizrachi Hebrew Sch.; Polish Gymnasium (High Sch.); Univ. of Warsaw (MJ). Belonged to Hashomer Hatza'ir scout movement as a boy, joining Betar, the Zionist Youth Movement, when 16; head of Organization Dept of Betar for Poland, 1932; also delegated to Czechoslovakia to head movement there; returned to Poland, 1937, and after spell of imprisonment for leading demonstration against British policy in Eretz Israel became head of the movement in Poland, 1939. On outbreak of World War II, arrested by Russian NKVD and later confined in concentration camps in Siberia, 1941-42; subseq. released under Stalin-Sikorski agreement; joined Polish Army, 1942, his brigade being posted to Eretz Israel; after demobilization assumed comd of IZL, the National Military Organization, directing from underground headquarters operations against the British; met members of UN Inquiry Cttee and foreign press, secretly, to explain his movement's outlook. After estabt of State of Israel, 1948, he and his colleagues founded the Herut Movement and he headed that party's list of candidates for the Knesset; has been a member of the Knesset since the first elections; on eve of Six Day War, 1 June 1967, joined Govt of Nat. Unity, serving as Minister without Portfolio, until Aug. 1970; presented his Coalition to the Knesset, June 1977, winning necessary vote of confidence to become Prime Minister; re-elected Prime Minister following nat. elections, June 1981. Nobel Peace Prize (jtly, with Mohamed Anwar El-Sadat), 1978. *Publications:* White Nights (describing his wartime experience in Europe); The Revolt, trans. several languages; numerous articles. *Address:* Office of the Prime Minister, Jerusalem, Israel.

EHNE, Edmond Rowlands, CMG 1974; Managing Director, Pioneer Sugar Mills Ltd, Queensland, 1952-76; *b* 20 Nov. 1906; *s* of late Edmund Behne; *m* 1932, Grace Elizabeth Ricketts; two *s* one *d. Educ:* Bendigo Sch. of Mines; Brisbane Boys' Coll.; Univ. of Queensland. BSc and MSc (App.); ARACI. Bureau of Sugar Experiment Stations, 1930-48 (Director, 1947); Pioneer Sugar Mills Ltd, 1948-80. *Recreation:* bowls. *Address:* Craigston, 217 Wickham Terrace, Brisbane, Qld 4000, Australia. *T:* 221-5657. *Clubs:* Queensland, Johnsonian (both in Brisbane).

EHR, Norman Isaac, FRICS; Deputy Chief Valuer (Rating), since 1981; *b* 28 Sept. 1922; *s* of Moses and Sarah Behr; *m* 1950, Anne Laurette Hilton. *Educ:* Haberdashers' Aske's Sch.; College of Estate Management. Chartered Surveyor. Articled, De Groot & Co., 1939-42; served War, RAOC, REME, 1942-46; joined Valuation Office, 1948; District Valuer and Valuation Officer, Westminster, 1965-67, City of London, 1967-70; Superintending Valuer, 1970; Asst Chief Valuer, 1977. First Prize, Chartered Auctioneers and Estate Agents Inst., 1941; Wainwright Prize, Royal Instn of Chartered Surveyors, 1950. *Recreations:* opera, cooking, computers. *Address:* 43 Netherhall Gardens, NW3 5RL. *T:* 01-435 9391.

EHRMAN, Simon, FRCP; Consultant Emeritus in Neurology, Guy's Hospital; Consulting Physician, Moorfields, Eye Hospital; formerly Consulting Neurologist: Regional Neurosurgical Centre, Brook Hospital; Lewisham, Dulwich, St Giles', St Francis', St Leonard's, Bromley and Farnborough Hospitals; *s* of late Leopold Behrman; *m* 1940, Dorothy, *d* of late Charles Engelbert; two *s* two *d. Educ:* University Coll. and St Bartholomew's Hosp., London. BSc (Hons) London. 1925; MRCS Eng. 1928; MRCP London 1932. Member: Assoc. of British Neurologists; Ophthalmological Soc. of UK; Academic Bd of Inst of Ophthalmology,

University of London; FRSocMed. House Physician and Registrar, Hosp. for Nervous Diseases, Maida Vale, 1930-33; Registrar: Nat. Hosp., Queen Square, 1934-38; Dept of Nervous Diseases, Guy's Hosp., 1935-45. *Publications:* articles on neurology and neuro-ophthalmology. *Address:* 33 Harley Street, W1. *T:* 01-580 3388; The Dower House, Oxney, St Margaret's-at-Cliffe, Kent. *T:* Dover 852161.

BEIT, Sir Alfred Lane, 2nd Bt, *cr* 1924; Trustee of the Beit Trust; Trustee of Beit Fellowships for scientific research; *b* London, 19 Jan. 1903; *o* surv. *s* of 1st Bt and Lilian (*d* 1946), *d* of late T. L. Carter, New Orleans, USA; *S* father, 1930; *m* 1939. Clementine, 2nd *d* of late Major the Hon. Clement Mitford, DSO and Lady Helen Nutting. *Educ:* Eton; Christ Church, Oxford. Contested West Islington in LCC election 1928; South-East St Pancras (C) in general election, 1929; MP (U) St Pancras South-East, 1931-45. Pres., Wexford Fest. Opera; Mem., Board of Governors and Guardians, Nat. Gallery of Ireland. Hon. LLD Nat. Univ. of Ireland, 1979. *Heir:* none. *Address:* Russborough, Blessington, Co. Wicklow, Eire; Gordon's Bay, CP, S Africa. *Clubs:* Brooks's, Carlton; Kildare Street and University (Dublin); Civil Service (Cape Town); Muthaiga (Nairobi).

BEITH, Alan James; MP (L) Berwick-upon-Tweed since Nov. 1973; Liberal Chief Whip, since 1976, and spokesman on Education, since 1977; *b* 20 April 1943; *o s* of James and Joan Beith, Poynton, Ches; *m* 1965, Barbara Jean Ward; one *s* one *d. Educ:* King's Sch., Macclesfield; Balliol and Nuffield Colls, Oxford. BLitt, MA Oxon. Lectr, Dept of Politics, Univ. of Newcastle upon Tyne, 1966-73. Vice-Chm., Northumberland Assoc. of Parish Councils, 1970-71 and 1972-73; Jt Chm., Assoc. of Councillors, 1974-79; Member: Gen. Adv. Council of BBC, 1974-; Hexham RDC, 1969-74; Corbridge Parish Council, 1970-74; Tynedale District Council, 1973-74; BBC NE Regional Adv. Council, 1971-74; NE Transport Users' Consultative Cttee, 1970-74. Mem., House of Commons Commn, 1979-. UK Rep. to Council of Europe and WEU, 1976-. Methodist Local Preacher. *Publications:* chapter in The British General Election of 1964, ed Butler and King, 1965; articles in Public Administration Bull., Policy and Politics, New Society, Local Government Chronicle, District Councils Review, Parish Councils Review, etc. *Recreations:* walking, music, looking at old buildings. *Address:* West End Cottage, Whittingham, Alnwick, Northumberland. *T:* Whittingham 313. *Clubs:* National Liberal; Union Society (Oxford); Shilbottle Working Men's (Alnwick).

BEITH, Sir John, KCMG 1969 (CMG 1959); HM Diplomatic Service, retired; *b* 4 April 1914; *s* of late William Beith and Margaret Stanley, Toowoomba, Qld; *m* 1949, Diana Gregory-Hood, *d* of Sir John Little Gilmour, 2nd Bt; one *s* one *d* (and one *d* decd), (one step *s* one step *d*). *Educ:* Eton; King's Coll., Cambridge. Entered Diplomatic Service, 1937, and served in FO until 1940; 3rd Sec., Athens, 1940-41; 2nd Sec., Buenos Aires, 1941-45; served Foreign Office, 1945-49; Head of UK Permanent Delegation to the UN at Geneva, 1950-53; Head of Chancery at Prague, 1953-54; Counsellor, 1954; Counsellor and Head of Chancery, British Embassy, Paris, 1954-59; Head of Levant Dept, FO, 1959-61; Head of North and East African Dept, Foreign Office, 1961-63; Ambassador to Israel, 1963-65; an Asst Sec.-Gen., NATO, 1966-67; Asst Under-Sec. of State, FO, 1967-69; Ambassador to Belgium, 1969-74. *Recreations:* music, racing, tennis. *Address:* Dean Farm House, Winchester. *T:* Sparsholt 326. *Clubs:* White's, Anglo-Belgian.

BEITH, John William, CBE 1972; Director Special Duties, Massey Ferguson Holdings Ltd, 1971-74, retired; *b* 13 Jan. 1909; *s* of John William Beith and Ana Theresia (née Denk); *m* 1931, Dorothy (née Causbrook); two *s. Educ:* Spain, Chile, Germany; Llandovery Coll., S Wales. Joined Massey Harris (now Massey Ferguson), 1927, London; occupied senior exec. positions in Argentina, Canada, France and UK; Vice-Pres., Canadian parent co., 1963; Chm., Massey Ferguson (UK) Ltd, 1970. Pres., Agricl Engrs Assoc. Ltd, 1970. *Recreations:* ancient and contemporary history; follower of Rugby; swimming. *Address:* Torre Blanca, Cala Serena, Cala d'Or, Mallorca. *T:* Baleares 657830. *Club:* Oriental.

BEJART, Maurice (Jean); choreographer; Director, Twentieth Century Ballet Company, since 1959; *b* 1 Jan. 1927; *s* of Gaston and Germaine Berger. *Educ:* Lycée de Marseilles. Début as ballet dancer with Marseilles Opéra, 1945; International Ballet, 1949-50; Royal Opera, Stockholm, 1951-52; co-founded Les Ballets de l'Etoile, later Ballet-Théâtre de Paris, 1954 (Dir, 1954-59); Dir of Ballet, Théâtre Royal de la Monnaie, Brussels, 1959; Dir, Mudra sch., 1972-. Grand Prix National de la Musique, 1970; Prix Erasme de la danse, 1974. Chevalier des Arts et des Lettres. Principal works include: La Belle au Boa, Symphonie pour un homme seul, 1955; Orphée, 1958; Le sacre du printemps, 1960; The Tales of Hoffman, 1962; The Merry Widow, 1963; The Damnation of Faust, 1964; Ode à la joie (Beethoven's 9th Symphony), Romeo and Juliet, 1966; Messe pour le temps présent, 1967; Firebird, 1970; Nijinsky: clown de Dieu, Simmung, 1972; Le Marteau sans Maître, La Traviata, 1973; Pli selon Pli, Notre Faust, 1976; Rhapsodie, Ah vous dirai-je Mamam?, 1977; Gaîté Parisienne, 1980; Wien, Wien, nur du allein, 1982. *Publications:* Mathilde, ou le temps perdu (novel), 1963; La Reine Verte (play), 1963; L'autre chant de la danse, 1974. *Address:* Ballet du XXe Siècle, Théâtre de la Monnaie, 4 Rue Léopold, Brussels, Belgium.

BEKOE, Dr Daniel Adzei; Professor of Chemistry since 1974, and Vice-Chancellor since 1976, University of Ghana; President, International Council of Scientific Unions, since 1980; *b* 7 Dec. 1928; *s* of Aristocles Silvanus Adzete

Bekoe and Jessie Nadu (née Awuletey); *m* 1958, Theresa Victoria Anyisaa Annan; three *s* (and one *s* decd). *Educ:* Achimota Sch.; University Coll. of Gold Coast (BSc London); Univ. of Oxford (DPhil). Jun. Res. Asst, Univ. of Calif, LA, 1957-58; Univ. of Ghana (formerly University Coll. of Ghana): Lectr, 1958-63; Sen. Lectr, 1963-65; Associate Prof., 1965-74. Sabbatical year, Univ. of Calif, LA, 1962-63; Vis. Associate Prof., Univ. of Ibadan, 1966-67. Member: UN Univ. Council, 1980-; UN Adv. Cttee on Science and Technology for Develt, 1980-82. *Publications:* articles on molecular structures in crystallographic and chemical jls; gen. articles in Proc. Ghana Acad. of Arts and Sciences. *Recreations:* music, swimming, walking. *Address:* Vice-Chancellor's Office, University of Ghana, Legon, Accra, Ghana. *T:* Accra 74717.

BELAM, Noël Stephen; Regional Director, North-West, Department of Industry, 1975-79; *b* 19 Jan. 1920; *s* of Dr Francis Arthur Belam and Hilda Mary Belam; *m* 1948, Anne Coaker; one *s* one *d. Educ:* Cranleigh Sch.; St Edmund Hall, Oxford (MA). Royal Artillery (T/Captain), 1940-46. Board of Trade, 1947; Trade Comr, Karachi, 1955-58; Private Sec. to successive Ministers of State, BoT, 1961-63; Asst Sec., 1963; Principal Trade Comr, Vancouver, 1963-67; Board of Trade: Regional Controller NW Region, 1967-70; Asst Sec., London, 1970-75; Under Sec., 1975. *Recreations:* fishing, Dartmoor ponies. *Address:* Fore Stoke Farm, Holne, Newton Abbot, Devon TQ13 7SS. *T:* Poundsgate 394.

BELCH, Alexander Ross, CBE 1972; FRSE; FRINA; CBIM; Chairman: Associated British Engineering, since 1980; Jebsens Offshore Drilling Ltd, since 1980; Deputy Chairman, Jebsens Drilling Ltd, since 1980; *b* 13 Dec. 1920; *s* of Alexander Belch, CBE, and Agnes Wright Ross; *m* 1947, Janette Finnie Murdoch; four *d. Educ:* Morrison's Acad., Crieff, Perthshire; Glasgow Univ. (BSc Naval Arch. 1st Cl. Hons). Lithgows Ltd: Dir and Gen. Manager, 1954-59; Asst Man. Dir, 1959-64; Man. Dir, 1964-69; Scott Lithgow Ltd: Man. Dir, 1969-80; Chm., 1978-80; Director: Lithgows (Holdings) Ltd, 1972-; Lithgow Hotels Ltd, 1972-; Jebsens (UK) Ltd, and various other Jebsen Gp cos, 1973-; Gault Armstrong and Kemble Ltd, 1980-; YARD Ltd, 1980-. Mem., British Railways (Scottish) Board, 1979-. Pres., Shipbuilders and Repairers Nat. Assoc., 1974-76. Hon. LLD Strathclyde, 1978. *Address:* Altmacraig, Lyle Road, Greenock, Renfrewshire. *T:* Greenock 21124.

BELCHER, John Rashleigh, MS 1946; FRCS 1942; Consultant Thoracic Surgeon, NE Metropolitan Regional Hospital Board, since 1950; Surgeon, London Chest Hospital, since 1951; Thoracic Surgeon, Middlesex Hospital, since 1955; *b* 11 Jan. 1917; *s* of late Dr Ormonde Rashleigh Belcher, Liverpool; *m* 1940, Jacqueline Mary, *d* of late C. P. Phillips; two *s* one *d. Educ:* Epsom Coll.; St Thomas' Hosp. MB 1939; FRCS 1942; MS 1946; Resident appointments at St Thomas' Hospital, 1939-40. RAF, 1940-46: Medical Service; general duties and surgical specialist; Squadron Leader. Resident and Asst posts at St Thomas', Brompton, London Chest, and Middlesex Hosps; followed by consultant appointments; co-editor, Brit. Jl of Diseases of the Chest. Pres., Assoc. of Thoracic Surgeons, 1980; Member: Thoracic Soc.; Cardiac Soc.; Amer. Coll. of Chest Physicians. Toured: for British Council, Far East 1969, Cyprus and Greece 1973; for FCO, Indonesia 1971, Bolivia 1975; Yugoslavia 1977. Hunterian Prof., RCS, 1979. *Publications:* Thoracic Surgical Management, 1953; chapters in standard text-books; papers in British and foreign medical journals. *Recreations:* golf, ski-ing, photography. *Address:* 23 Hornton Court, Hornton Street, W8. *T:* 01-937 7006.

BELCHER, Ronald Harry, CMG 1958; Under-Secretary, Ministry of Overseas Development, 1965-75; *b* 5 Jan 1916; *s* of Harry Albert Belcher; *m* 1948, Hildegarde (née Hellyer-Jones); one *s. Educ:* Christ's Hosp., Horsham; Jesus Coll., Cambridge; Brasenose Coll., Oxford. BA (Hons Classics) Cantab 1937; Dipl. Class. Arch. Cantab 1938; BA Oxon 1938. Indian Civil Service, Punjab, 1939-48; Commonwealth Relations Office, 1948-65; seconded to Foreign Office for service in British Embassy, Washington, 1951-53; Private Sec., 1953-54; Asst Sec., 1954; Deputy High Commissioner for the UK in S Africa, 1956-59; Asst Under Sec. of State, CRO, 1960-61; British Dep. High Comr, Delhi, 1961-65. *Address:* Fieldview, Lower Road, Fetcham, Surrey. *Club:* Royal Commonwealth Society.

BELDAM, Hon. Sir (Alexander) Roy (Asplan), Kt 1981; Hon. Mr Justice Beldam; a Judge of the High Court of Justice, Queen's Bench Division, since 1981; *b* 29 March 1925; *s* of George William Beldam and Margaret Frew Shettle (formerly Beldam, née Underwood); *m* 1953, Elisabeth Bryant Farr; two *s* one *d. Educ:* Oundle Sch.; Brasenose Coll., Oxford. Sub-Lt, RNVR Air Branch, 1943-46. Called to Bar, Inner Temple, 1950; Bencher, 1977; QC 1969; a Recorder of the Crown Court, 1972-81. *Recreations:* sailing, cricket, naval history. *Address:* Royal Courts of Justice, Strand, WC2.

BELFAST, Earl of; Arthur Patrick Chichester; *b* 9 May 1952; *s* and *heir* of 7th Marquess of Donegall, *qv. Educ:* Harrow. Coldstream Guards. *Recreations:* hunting, shooting, fishing, knitting. *Address:* Dunbrody Park, Arthurstown, Co. Wexford, Eire.

BELFAST, Dean of; see Crooks, Very Rev. S. B.

BELFRAGE, Leif Axel Lorentz, GBE (Hon.), 1956; former Swedish Ambassador; *b* 1 Feb. 1910; *s* of J. K. E. Belfrage and G. U. E. Löfgren; *m* 1937, Greta Jering; one *s* three *d. Educ:* Stockholm University. Law degree, 1933. Practised law at Stockholm Magistrates Court; joined Min. of

Commerce, 1937; Dir, Swedish Clearing Office, 1940; Dir, war-time Swedi Trade Commn, 1943-45; entered Swedish Diplomatic Service, as Head Section in Commercial Dept, 1945; Commercial Counsellor, Swedi Embassy, Washington, 1946; Head of Commercial Dept, FO, Stockholi 1949-53; Dep. Under-Sec. of State, FO, 1953; Perm. Under-Sec. of State F 1956; Ambassador to Court of St James's, 1967-72; Ambassador and Head Swedish Delegn to OECD and UNESCO, 1972-76. Internat. Adv PKbanken, Stockholm, 1976-; Chm. Bd of Dirs, Marabou AB, Sundyber 1977-. Grand Cross, Order of North Star (Sweden). *Address:* Sturegatan 1 11436 Stockholm, Sweden.

BELHAM, David Ernest, CB 1975; Principal Assistant Solicitor (Und Secretary), Department of Employment, 1970-77, retired; *b* 9 Aug. 1914; *s* Ernest George Belham and Grace Belham (née Firth); *m* 1938, Eunice Moni (née Vine); two *s* two *d. Educ:* Whitgift Sch.; Law Society's Sch. of La Solicitor (Hons), 1937. Private practice, 1937-39. Served War, RAFV 1940-46. Entered Solicitor's Department, Min. of Labour, 1946; Asst Solicitc 1962. *Address:* 26 The Chase, Findon, Worthing, W Sussex BN14 0TT. Findon 3771.

BELHAVEN and STENTON, 13th Lord, *cr* 1647; Robert Anthor Carmichael Hamilton; farming; *b* 27 Feb. 1927; *o* *s* of 12th Lord; *S* fathe 1961; *m* 1st, 1952, Elizabeth Ann, *d* of late Col A. H. Moseley, Warrawe NSW; one *s* one *d*; 2nd, 1973, Rosemary Lady Mactaggart, only *d* of S Herbert Williams, 1st Bt, MP; one *d* (adopted). *Educ:* Eton. Commissione The Cameronians, 1947. Dir, Morton Develt Co. Ltd. *Recreations:* cookin dachshund minding. *Heir:* *s* Master of Belhaven, *qv. Address:* 37 Dorvi Crescent, W6. *T:* 01-748 5005. *Club:* Army and Navy.

BELHAVEN, Master of; Hon. Frederick Carmichael Arthur Hamilto *b* 27 Sept. 1953; *s* of 13th Lord Belhaven and Stenton, *qv* ; *m* 1981, Elizabe Anne, *d* of S. V. Tredinnick, Wisborough Green, Sussex. *Educ:* Eton. *Addre* 11 Markham Square, SW3.

BELL, Alexander Gilmour; Chief Reporter for Public Inquiries, Scotti Office, since 1979; *b* 11 March 1933; *s* of Edward and Daisy Bell; *m* 196 Mary Chisholm; four *s. Educ:* Hutcheson's Grammar Sch.; Glasgow Uni (BL). Admitted Solicitor, 1954. After commercial experience in Far East a in private practice, entered Scottish Office, as Legal Officer, 1967; Dep. Chi Reporter, 1973. *Recreations:* casual outdoor pursuits, choral music. *Addre* Woodend, Haddington, East Lothian EH41 4PE. *T:* Haddington 3514.

BELL, Alistair Watson; His Honour Judge Bell; a Circuit Judge, since 197 *b* Edinburgh, 31 March 1930; *s* of Albert William Bell and Alice Elizabe Watson; *m* 1957, Patricia Margaret Seed; one *s* two *d. Educ:* Lanark Gramm Sch.; George Watson's Coll.; Univs of Edinburgh (MA) and Oxford (M. BCL). 2nd Lieut RASC, 1955. Called to Bar, Middle Temple, 195 Harmsworth Scholar, 1956; entered practice, Northern Circuit, 1957; Recorder of the Crown Court, 1972-78. Contested (L) Chorley, 1964 ar Westmorland, 1966. *Recreation:* hill walking, with or without golf club *Address:* Oaklands, Whittingham Lane, Broughton, Preston, Lancs. *T:* Presto (Lancs) 863065. *Club:* Reform (Manchester).

BELL, Andrew Montgomery; Sheriff of South Strathclyde, Dumfries ar Galloway, since 1979; *b* 21 Feb. 1940; *s* of James Montgomery Bell and Mar Bell (née Cavaye), Edinburgh; *m* 1969, Ann Margaret Robinson; one *s* o *d. Educ:* Royal High Sch., Edinburgh; Univ. of Edinburgh (BL). Solicitc 1961-74; called to Bar, 1975. *Address:* 5 York Road, Trinity, Edinburgh EH 3EJ. *T:* 031-552 3859.

BELL, Archibald Angus, QC (Scot.) 1961; Sheriff of Glasgow ai Strathkelvin (formerly Lanark) at Glasgow, since 1973; *b* 13 April 1923; *c* of James Dunlop Bell, Solicitor, Ayrshire, and Katherine Rachel Gorde Miller; *m* 1949, Dorothy, *d* of Dr Pollok Donald, Edinburgh, and M Dorothy Donald; two *s. Educ:* The Leys Sch., Cambridge; Univ. of Andrews; Univ. of Glasgow. Served War, Royal Navy, 1941-45; Sub-Lie RNVR. MA, St Andrews, 1947; LLB, Glasgow, 1949; admitted to Facul of Advocates, 1949; Reporter, Court of Session Cases, 1952-55. Contested and U) Maryhill Div. of Glasgow, Gen. Elec., 1955. Standing Junior Couns in Scotland: to Board of Trade, 1955-57; to War Dept, 1957-61. Pres., Scotti Cricket Union, 1975. *Recreations:* watching the sun rise, getting fun out games. Formerly: hockey and cricket blue, St Andrews, and Pres. UAU ar Dramatic Soc. *Clubs:* Royal Scots (Edinburgh); MCC; Royal and Ancie (St Andrews); RNVR (Scotland).

BELL, Arthur; see Bell, E. A.

BELL, (Charles) Trevor; General Secretary, Colliery Officials and Staffs Are of the National Union of Mineworkers, since 1979; Member, Nation Executive Committee of the National Union of Mineworkers, since 1979; 22 Sept. 1927; *s* of Charles and Annie Bell; *m* 1974, Patricia Ann Tappi *Educ:* state schools; Technical Coll. (City and Guilds Engrg); Coleg Harlec N Wales (Trades Union scholarship, 1955). Craftsman in coal mini industry, 1941. Mem., Labour Party, 1946-. *Recreations:* gardening, spo *Address:* 25 Mallard Avenue, Sandal, Wakefield, West Yorks, WF2 6SH. Wakefield 250815. *Clubs:* Pontefract Labour; Painthorpe Country.

BELL, Sir Charles (William), Kt 1980; CBE 1968; Chairman of Coats Patons Ltd, 1967–75; *b* 4 June 1907; *s* of Herbert James Bell and Bertha Alice Bell (*née* Jones), Pen-y-Ffordd, Flintshire; *m* 1931, Eileen, *d* of Edwin James Hannaford, Eastham, Cheshire; three *s*. *Educ:* Chester City Grammar Sch.; Selwyn Coll., Cambridge (Open Exhibr). Joined Coats Patons Ltd, 1930; Dir, Central Agency Ltd (subsid. co.), 1934; Dir, J. & P. Coats Ltd, (Subsid. Co.), 1947; Man. Dir, J. & P. Coats Ltd, 1961; Dir, Coats Patons Ltd, 1961. Dep. Chm., and Nat. Treasurer, Scottish Conservative and Unionist Party, 1971–81. *Recreations:* shooting, fishing, golf. *Address:* The White Cottage, 19 Lennox Drive East, Helensburgh, Dunbartonshire. *T:* Helensburgh 4973. *Clubs:* Royal and Ancient (St Andrews); Royal Northern Yacht; Helensburgh Golf.

BELL, Donald L.; *see* Lynden-Bell.

BELL, Donald Munro; international concert and opera artist; freelance; Professor and Head of Vocal Department, University of Ottawa, since 1979; *b* 19 June 1934; one *s*. *Educ:* South Burnaby High Sch., BC, Canada. Made Wigmore Hall Debut, 1958, since when has sung at Bayreuth Wagner Festival, 1958, 1959, 1960; Lucerne and Berlin Festivals, 1959; Philadelphia and New York debuts with Eugene Ormandy, 1959; Israel, 1962; Russia Recital Tour, 1963; Glyndebourne Festival, 1963, 1973, 1974; with Deutsche Oper am Rhein, Düsseldorf, 1964–66; Scottish National Opera, 1974; Australian Tour (Musica Viva), 1980. Has made recordings. Arnold Bax Medal, 1955. *Address:* c/o AIM Ltd, 3/4 Albert Terrace, NW1 7SU.

BELL, Douglas Maurice, CBE 1972; Chairman and Chief Executive, Tioxide Group Ltd (formerly British Titan Ltd), 1973–78; Chairman, Tinsley Wire Industries Group, since 1981 (Director, since 1978); *b* Shanghai, China, 15 April 1914; *s* of Alexander Dunlop Bell; *m* 1947, Elizabeth Mary Edelsten; one *s* two *d*. *Educ:* The Edinburgh Academy; St Andrews Univ. War Dept, Chemist, Woolwich Arsenal, 1936. Imperial Chemical Industries: Dyestuffs Div., 1937–42; Regional Sales Manager, 1944–53; Billingham Dir, 1953; Billingham Man. Dir, 1955–57; Heavy Organic Chemicals Managing Dir, 1958–61; Chm. of European Council, Imperial Chemical Industries Ltd, 1960–65; Chief Executive, ICI (Europa) Ltd, 1965–72. Director: British Titan Products Ltd, 1968–78; Tioxide Australia Pty Ltd, 1973–78; Tioxide of Canada Ltd, 1973–78; Tioxide SA, 1973–78. Hon. Dir, NV Bekaert SA, 1979–. FBIM 1974; FRSA 1976; Soc. of Chemical Industry: Vice-Pres., 1975–76; Pres., 1976–78; Mem. Council, Chemical Industry Assoc., 1973–78. Member, Governing Board: British Sch. of Brussels, 1971–; Maison de la Chemie Française, 1972–. Hon. FIChemE, 1977. Hon. LLD St Andrews, 1977. Comendador de Numero de la Orden de Merito Civil (Spain), 1967; Commandeur, Ordre de Léopold II (Belgium), 1973. *Recreations:* sports and gardens. *Address:* Stocks Cottage, Church Street, West Chiltington, Sussex. *T:* West Chiltington 2284. *Clubs:* Anglo-Belgian; Cercle Royal Gaulois (Brussels); Royal Waterloo Golf, West Sussex Golf.

BELL, Edith Alice, OBE 1981; Chief Nursing Officer, Welsh Office, 1972–81; *b* 14 Sept. 1919; *d* of George and Alice Bell. *Educ:* Girls' Grammar Sch., Lancaster. SRN University Hosp., Leeds; SCM St Luke's Hosp., Bradford; Cert. Royal Medico Psychological Assoc., Westwood Hosp., Bradford; Registered Nurse, Mentally Subnormal, Aston Hall, Derby. Ward Sister, Aston Hall Hosp., Derby, 1941–43; Asst Matron, Royal Albert Hosp., Lancaster, 1943–46; Dep. Matron, Darenth Park Hosp., Dartford, 1946–48; Gp Matron, Foundation Gp HMC, London, 1948–60; Management Services Officer, SE RHB, Scotland, 1960–63; Chief Regional Nursing Officer, E Anglian RHB, 1963–72. WHO Fellowship, 1951. Past Member: Gen. Nursing Council, England and Wales; Nat. Council of Nurses; Standing Nursing Adv. Cttee; Services Cttee, Internat. Council of Nurses; Jt Bd, Clinical Nursing Studies; Council, Queen's Inst. of Dist Nursing Service; SW Metrop. RHB: Nursing, Research and Trng Cttees. Chairman: Mental Nurses Cttee; Jt Organizations; Reg. Nursing Officers Gp; Royal Coll. of Nursing Br. Mem., NHS Reorganization Steering Cttee. Hon. Sec., Mental Hosp. Matrons Assoc.; Pres., Inst. of Religion and Medicine. *Publications:* contribs to professional jls. *Recreations:* reading, travel, gardening, supporting ecumenical activities. *Address:* Tyla Teg, 51 Armdale Road, Newlands, Lancaster LA1 4JB.

BELL, (Edward) Percy, OBE 1974; Member for Newham South, Greater London Council, since 1973 (for Newham, 1964–73); *b* 3 April 1902; *m* 1932, Ethel Mary Bell. *Educ:* Rutherford Coll., Newcastle upon Tyne; King's Coll., London. Teacher in the service of West Ham County Borough, 1922–64; Headmaster, Shipman County Secondary School, West Ham, 1951–64. Chairman: Planning Cttee of GLC, 1973–74; Town Development Cttee, 1974–75; Docklands Jt Cttee, 1974–77. *Recreations:* foreign travel; local and national social history. *Address:* 151c Ham Park Road, E7 9LE. *T:* (private) 01-472 8897; (business) 01-633 5670.

BELL, (Ernest) Arthur, PhD; FLS, CChem, FRSC; Director, Royal Botanic Gardens, Kew, since 1981; *b* 20 June 1926; *s* of Albert Bell and Rachel Enid (*née* Williams), Gosforth, Northumberland; *m* 1952, Jean Swinton Ogilvie; two *s* one *d*. *Educ:* Dame Allan's Sch., Newcastle upon Tyne; Univ. of Durham (King's Coll., Newcastle upon Tyne) BSc; Trinity Coll., Univ. of Dublin (MA, PhD). CChem, FRIC (now FRSC) 1961. Res. Chemist, ICI, Billingham, 1946; Demonstr and holder of Sarah Purser Med. Res. Award, TCD, 1947; Asst to Prof. of Biochem., TCD, 1949; Lectr in Biochem., KCL, 1953; Reader in Biochem., Univ. of London, 1964–68; Prof. of Botany, Univ. of Texas, 1968; Prof. of Biology, London Univ., and Hd of Dept of Plant

Scis, KCL, 1972–81; FKC 1982. Sen. Foreign Scientist Fellow, Nat. Sci. Foundn, USA, and Vis. Prof. of Biol., Univ. of Kansas, 1966; Vis. Prof., Univ. of Sierra Leone, 1977; Vis. Commonwealth Fellow, Australia, 1980. *Publications:* contribs on plant biochem., chemotaxonomy, and chem. ecology to Phytochemistry, and Biochem. Jl. *Recreations:* walking, travel. *Address:* Royal Botanic Gardens, Kew, Richmond, Surrey.

BELL, Sir Ewart; *see* Bell, Sir W. E.

BELL, Prof. Frank, DSc, PhD; FRSC; FRSE; Professor of Chemistry, Heriot-Watt University (formerly College), Edinburgh, 1950–66 (now Emeritus); *b* 24 Dec. 1904; *o s* of Thomas Bell, Derby; *m* 1930, May Perryman; one *s* one *d*. *Educ:* Crypt Grammar Sch., Glos; Queen Mary Coll., University of London. Head of Science Dept, Blackburn Tech. Coll. 1935–41; Principal Lancaster Tech. Coll., 1941–46; Prof. of Chemistry, Belfast Coll. of Tech., 1947–50. *Publications:* original papers mainly in Journal of Chemical Soc. *Recreations:* numismatics, walking and field-club activities (Past Pres., Cotteswold Naturalists' Field Club; Past Pres., Edinburgh Natural History Soc.). *Address:* Hilcot, Finchcroft Lane, Prestbury, Cheltenham, Glos.

BELL, Sir Gawain (Westray), KCMG 1957; CBE 1955 (MBE mil. 1942); Secretary-General, South Pacific Commission, 1966–70; *b* 21 Jan. 1909; *s* of late William Westray Bell; *m* 1945, Silvia, *d* of Major Adrian Cornwell-Clyne; three *d*. *Educ:* Winchester; Hertford Coll., Oxford. Sudan Political Service, 1931; seconded to the Government of Palestine, 1938 (attached Palestine Police, DSP). 2nd Lt TA, 1929–32; Military Service in Middle East, 1941–45; Kaimakam (Col): Arab Legion, 1942–45; RARO, 1949–59. District Comr, Sudan Political Service, 1945–49; Dep. Sudan Agent, Cairo, 1949–51; Dep. Civil Sec., Sudan Government, 1953–54; Permanent Under-Sec., Ministry of the Interior, 1954–55; HM Political Agent, Kuwait, 1955–57; Governor, Northern Nigeria, 1957–62; Sec Gen., Council for Middle East Trade, 1963–64; engaged, with Sir Ralph Hone, as Constitutional Adviser to Govt of Fedn of S Arabia, 1965–66. Various missions to Arab world, 1970–. Chm., Exec. Cttee, LEPRA, 1972–; Member: Governing Body, SOAS, London Univ., 1971–81; part-time Chm., CS Selection Bds, 1972–77; Chapter Gen., Order of St John, 1964–66, 1970– (KStJ 1958). Order of Independence 3rd Class (Trans Jordan), 1944. *Recreations:* walking, riding, shooting, rifle shooting (Capt. Oxford Univ. 1931; shot for Sudan). *Address:* Hidcote Bartrim Manor, Chipping Campden, Glos. *T:* Mickleton 305. *Club:* Army and Navy.

BELL, Geoffrey Foxall, MC; MA; *b* 16 April 1896; *s* of late F. R. Bell, Burton-on-Trent; *m* 1926, Margaret, *d* of late R. Austin-Carewe, Montreal, Canada; three *s*. *Educ:* Repton; Balliol Coll., Oxford. Served in RFA, 1915–19; Asst Master, Upper Canada Coll. and Christ's Hospital; Headmaster, Trent Coll., Derbs, 1927–36; Headmaster, Highgate Sch., 1936–54. Retired from fruit farming, 1972. Oxford Univ. Cricket XI, 1919. *Publications:* Establishing a Fruit Garden, 1963; Seven Old Testament Figures (Bishop of London's Lent Book), 1968. *Address:* Widford, Haslemere, Surrey.

BELL, George Douglas Hutton, CBE 1965; FRS 1965; PhD; Director, Plant Breeding Institute, Cambridge, 1947–71, retired; a Vice President, Royal Society, 1976–78; *b* 18 Oct. 1905; *er s* of George Henry and Lilian Mary Matilda Bell; *m* 1934, Eileen Gertrude Wright; two *d*. *Educ:* Bishop Gore's Grammar Sch., Swansea; Univ. Coll. of North Wales, Bangor (BSc 1928); University of Cambridge. PhD 1931. Research Officer. Plant Breeding Inst., 1931; University Demonstrator, Cambridge, 1933, Lectr, 1944; Fellow of Selwyn Coll., Cambridge, 1944–54, Hon. Fellow, 1965. Research Medal, Royal Agricultural Soc. of England, 1956; Royal Society Mullard Medal, 1967. Hon. DSc: Reading Univ., 1968; Univ. Wales, 1968; Liverpool Univ., 1970; Hon. ScD Cambridge, 1978. Massey-Ferguson National Award, 1973. *Publications:* Cultivated Plants of the Farm, 1948; The Breeding of Barley Varieties in Barley and Malt, 1962; Cereal Breeding in Vistas in Botany, Vol. II, 1963; Phylogeny of Temperate Cereals in Crop Plant Evolution, 1965; papers on barley and breeding in Jl of Agricultural Science, etc. *Recreations:* natural history; theatre, music. *Address:* 6 Worts Causeway, Cambridge. *T:* Cambridge 247449.

BELL, Prof. George Howard, MD; FRCPGlas 1946; FRSE 1947; Symers Professor of Physiology in the University of Dundee (formerly Queen's College, Dundee), 1947–75, now Emeritus; Dean of The Faculty of Medicine, 1954–56 and 1963; *b* 24 Jan. 1905; *m* 1934, Isabella Margaret Thomson, MB, ChB; two *s*. *Educ:* Ayr Academy; Glasgow Univ. BSc 1929; MB (Hons) 1930; MD (Hons) 1943. House Physician, Royal Hosp. for Sick Children, 1930; Asst Lecturer in Physiology Dept, University of Glasgow, 1931–34; Lecturer in Physiology: Univ. of Bristol, 1934–35; Univ. of Glasgow, 1935–47. Mem. Physiological Soc., 1934–, and Sec., 1949–54; Mem. Inter-University Council for Higher Education Overseas, 1957–75; Mem. Eastern Regional Hospital Board, 1957–67 (Vice-Chm., 1966–67); Gen. Dental Council Visitor, 1960–62; Comr, Royal University of Malta, 1962–70. Hon. Fellow, Accademia Anatomico-Chirurgica, Perugia, 1959. *Publications:* (with D. Emslie Smith and C. R. Paterson) Textbook of Physiology, 10th edn, 1980; papers in Journal of Physiology, Journal of Endocrinology, Lancet, etc. *Address:* Duntulm, 80 Grove Road, Broughty Ferry, Dundee DD5 1LB. *T:* Dundee 78724.

BELL, Sir (George) Raymond, KCMG 1973; CB 1967; Vice-President, European Investment Bank, 1973–78, retired; Hon. Vice-President, European

Investment Bank, 1978; *b* 13 March 1916; *e s* of late William Bell and Christabel Bell (*née* Appleton); *m* 1944, Joan Elizabeth, *o d* of late W. G. Coltham and Christina Coltham; two *s* two *d. Educ:* Bradford Grammar Sch.; St John's Coll., Cambridge (Scholar). Entered Civil Service, Assistant Principal, 1938; Min. of Health, 1938; transf. Treasury, 1939; served War 1941-44, Royal Navy (Lieut RNVR). Principal, Civil Service, 1945; Asst Sec., 1951; Under-Sec., 1960; Dep. Sec., 1966; Dep. Sec. HM Treasury, 1966-72. Sec. (Finance), Office of HM High Commissioner for the UK in Canada, 1945-48; Counsellor, UK Permanent Delegn to OEEC/NATO, Paris, 1953-56; Principal Private Sec. to Chancellor of Exchequer, 1958-60. Mem. UK Delegation to Brussels Conference, 1961-62 and 1970-72. *Recreations:* music, reading, travel. *Address:* Quartier des Bories, Aouste-sur-Sye, 26400 Crest, Drôme, France. *T:* (75) 75 26 94. *Club:* Athenæum.

BELL, George Trafford, CMG 1961; OBE 1952; retired; *b* 9 March 1913; 2nd *s* of late George H. Bell and of Veronica Jessie Bell, Alderley Edge, Ches; *m* 1944, Eileen Patricia, *d* of late A. Geoffrey Southern, Wilmslow, Ches; two *s* one *d. Educ:* Sedbergh; St John's Coll., Cambridge. Apptd Admin. Offr, Tanganyika, 1936; Sen. Admin. Offr, 1954; Provincial Comr, 1958-62. *Recreations:* golf, fishing. *Address:* Dukenfield Grange, Mobberley, Knutsford, Cheshire WA16 7PT.

BELL, Griffin B.; Attorney-General, USA, 1977-79; *b* Americus, Georgia, 31 Oct. 1918; *s* of A. C. Bell and Thelma Pilcher; *m* 1943, Mary Foy Powell; one *s. Educ:* Southwestern Coll., Ga; Mercer Univ. (LLB *cum laude* 1948, LLD 1967). Served AUS, 1941-46, reaching rank of Major. Admitted to Georgia Bar, 1947; practice in Savannah and Rome, 1947-53. Partner in King and Spalding, Atlanta, 1953-59, 1976-77, 1979-, Managing Partner, 1959-61; United States Judge, 5th Circuit, 1961-76. Chairman: Atlanta Commn on Crime and Delinquency, 1965-66; CSCE, 1980. Mem., Vis. Cttee, Law Sch., Vanderbilt Univ.; Trustee, Mercer Univ.; Member: Amer. Law Inst.; Amer. Coll. of Trial Lawyers. *Address:* 3100 Habersham Road, NW Atlanta, Georgia 30305, USA.

BELL, Harry, OBE 1945; MA; MEd; Research Fellow, University of St Andrews, since 1972 (Research Scholar, 1967); *b* 11 April 1899; *s* of late John Nicol Bell, Aberdeen, and late Isabella Georgina Reith; *m* 1933, Sophia McDonald, *d* of late Alexander B. Fulton, Kilkerran, Newlands, Glasgow; two *s* one *d. Educ:* Robert Gordon's Coll.; Aberdeen Univ. (Kay Prize and Dey Scholarship); Clare Coll., Cambridge (Foundation Scholar); Glasgow Univ. (MEd). Served Army, 1917-19. Asst Master, Glasgow Academy, 1927-33; Rector of Elgin Academy, 1933-36; Rector of Dollar Academy, 1936-60. Scottish Educational Adviser Air Training Corps, 1941-45; Mem. of Scottish Youth Advisory Cttee, 1942-45; Pres. of Scottish Association of Headmasters, 1948. Adviser with UNESCO Delegation, Florence, 1950; Mem. of Advisory Council on Scottish Education, 1957-61. Fellow Internat. Inst. of Arts and Letters, 1960. *Publications:* English for Air Cadets; Stevenson's Travels and Essays; Thirteen Short Stories; Selected English Prose; Approach to English Literature; General Editor of Oxford Comprehension Course; articles on literary, historical and educational subjects. *Recreations:* reading, writing, walking. *Address:* Viewpark, 31 Lawhead Road East, St Andrews, Fife. *T:* St Andrews 72867. *Clubs:* Royal Over-Seas League; Scottish Mountaineering.

BELL, Ian Wright, CBE 1964; HM Diplomatic Service, retired; *b* Radlett, Herts, 21 Aug. 1913; *s* of late T. H. D. Bell; *m* 1940, Winifred Mary Ruth Waterfield, *y d* of late E. H. Waterfield, ICS; three *s. Educ:* Canford Sch.; St Peter's Hall, Oxford. Vice-Consul: Valparaiso, 1938; Montevideo, 1940; Foreign Office, 1946; First Sec., 1947; First Sec., Addis Ababa, 1949, Chargé d'Affaires, 1949, 1950, 1952 and 1953; Consul, Innsbruck, 1953; First Sec., Prague, 1954, Chargé d'Affaires, 1954 and 1956; Counsellor and Consul-Gen., Jedda, 1956; Counsellor and Official Sec., UK High Commission, Canberra, 1957; HM Consul-Gen., Lyons, 1960-65; Ambassador, Santo Domingo, 1965-69; Consul-Gen., Stuttgart, 1969-73. FRSA; FRGS. *Publications:* The Scarlet Flower (Poems), 1947; The Dominican Republic, 1981; reviews and articles in various periodicals. *Recreations:* painting, drama, music, walking. *Address:* Liveras House, Broadford, Skye. *Club:* Athenæum.

BELL, Very Rev. John, MM 1917; Dean Emeritus of Perth, WA; Dean, 1953-59, retired; *b* 11 Nov. 1898; *s* of Thomas and Isabella McCracken Bell; unmarried. *Educ:* Gair Sch., Dumfriesshire; privately; St John's Coll., Perth, WA. Deacon, 1926, Priest, 1928; Curate of Christ Church, Claremont, 1926-29; Rector of S Perth, 1929-32; Priest-in-Charge of Claremont, 1933, Rector, 1933-43; Canon of St George's Cathedral, Perth, 1938-44; Org. Sec. (for NSW) Austr. Bd of Missions, 1943-46; Dean of Armidale, 1946-48; Exam. Chap. to Bp of Armidale, 1946-48; Rector of Oddington with Adlestrop, Dio. Gloucester, 1948-52. *Publications:* This Way Peace, 1939; Many Coloured Glass, 1943; Facing the Week, 1947; For Comfort and Courage, 1958. *Recreation:* travel. *Address:* 22/8 Darley Street, South Perth, Western Australia 6151. *T:* 367-4434. *Club:* Weld (Perth, WA).

BELL, Rear-Adm. John Anthony, CB 1977; Education Secretary of the BBC, since 1979; *b* 25 Nov. 1924; *s* of Mathew Bell, Dundee, and Mary Ann Ellen Bell (*née* Goss), London; *m* 1946, Eileen Joan Woodman; three *d. Educ:* St Ignatius Coll., Stamford Hill; London Univ. BA, BSc, LLB. Barrister, Gray's Inn, 1970. RM 1943-45; Schoolmaster, RN, Instr Lt, Courses, Reserve Fleet, service with RAN, 1945-52; HMS Implacable, Theseus, Admiralty, HMS Excellent, 1952-59; HMS Centaur, RN Staff Course, Staff of

SACLANT, USA, Directing Staff, RN Staff Course, Western Fleet, 1959-69; Naval Educn Service, Dir, Dept of Naval Oceanography and Meteorology, 1969-75; Instr Captain 1969, Rear-Adm. 1975; Dir, Naval Education Service, 1975-78; Chief Naval Instructor Officer, 1978-79. Member: BEC Educn Cttee, 1975-; C&G Policy Cttee, 1975-79; TEC, 1976-79; Cert. of Extended Educn Cttee, DES, 1978-79. Governor, SOAS, 1978-. President: United Services Catholic Assoc.; RN Assoc., Gravesend, 1981-. *Recreations:* swimming, wines, travelling, France. *Address:* The Beild, Conifer Avenue, Hartley, Dartford, Kent DA3 8BX. *T:* Longfield 2485. *Club:* Hartley Country.

BELL, John Elliot; *b* 6 Nov. 1886; *e s* of late David Bell and Elizabeth Elliot; *m* 1924, Olga, *er d* of late Henry Banks and Elizabeth Ritchie, Edinburgh; one *s* one *d. Educ:* George Watson's Coll.; Edinburgh Univ. Vice-Consul at Paris, 1911; Boston, USA 1912; Leopoldville, Belgian Congo, 1913-14; Magallanes, Chile, 1915-19; Santo Domingo, 1920; Consul at Galveston, USA, 1920-23; Portland, Ore., 1923-29; Bahia, Brazil, 1930-32; Basle, 1932-34 Consul Gen. at Cologne, 1934-39; at Zurich, 1939-42; at Strasbourg, 1945-46 retired, 1947. *Recreations:* golf, riding. *Address:* 3175 Point Grey Road, Vancouver 8, BC, Canada. *T:* 731-3490.

BELL, John Geoffrey Y.; *see* Yates-Bell.

BELL, Sir John Lowthian, 5th Bt *cr* 1885; *b* 14 June 1960; *s* of Sir Hugh Francis Bell, 4th Bt and of Lady Bell (Mary Howson, MB, ChB, *d* of late George Howson, The Hyde, Hambledon); *S* father, 1970. *Recreations:* shooting, fishing, hunting. *Heir: b* David Hugh Bell, *b* 8 Oct. 1961. *Address:* Arncliffe Hall, Ingleby Cross, Northallerton, N Yorks.

BELL, Dr John Stewart, FRS 1972; Physicist, CERN, Geneva, since 1960 *b* 28 July 1928; *s* of John Bell and Annie (*née* Brownlee); *m* 1954, Mary Ross *Educ:* Technical High Sch., Belfast; Queen's Univ., Belfast (BSc); Univ. of Birmingham (PhD). AERE Harwell, 1949-60. *Publications:* various papers on electromagnetic, nuclear, elementary particle, and quantum theory. *Address:* CERN, 1211 Geneva 23, Switzerland.

BELL, Joseph, CBE 1953; Chief Constable, City of Manchester, 1943-58 retired; *b* 15 July 1899; *s* of late Joseph Bell; *m* 1926, Edith (*d* 1980), *d* o late Matthew Adamson; one *s* (one *d* decd). *Educ:* Alderman Wood Sch. Stanley, Co. Durham. Royal Naval Volunteer Reserve, 1917-19. Newcastle on Tyne City Police, 1919-33; Chief Constable, Hastings, 1933-41; Asst Chief Constable, Manchester, 1941-43. *Address:* Norwood, 246 Windlehurst Road Marple, Cheshire.

BELL, Joseph Denis Milburn; Chairman, North Western Electricity Board since 1976; *b* 2 Sept. 1920; *s* of John Bell, BEM, and Ann Bell; *m* 1949 Wilhelmina Maxwell Miller; one *s* one *d. Educ:* Bishop Auckland Gramma Sch.; St Edmund Hall, Oxford (MA). Served War, RAF, 1941-45. Contested (Lab) Canterbury, 1945. Lectr in Modern Econ. History, Univ. of Glasgow 1946; National Coal Board: Indust. Relations Dept, 1954; Dep. Indust Relations Dir, Durham Div., 1963; Electricity Council: Statistical Officer Indust. Relations Dept, 1966; Dep. Indust. Relations Adviser (Negotiating) 1967; Indust. Relations Adviser, 1972. *Publications:* Industrial Unionism: a critical analysis, 1949 (repr. in Trade Unions: selected readings, ed W. E. J McCarthy, 1972); (contrib.) The Scottish Economy (ed A. K. Cairncross) 1953; (contrib.) The System of Industrial Relations in Great Britain (ed A Flanders and H. A. Clegg), 1954; (contrib.) The Lessons of Public Enterprise (ed M. Shanks), 1963. *Address:* Rossways, Broad Lane, Hale, Altrincham Cheshire. *T:* 061-980 4451. *Club:* United Oxford & Cambridge University.

BELL, Prof. Kathleen Myra, CBE 1978; Professor of Social Studies in the University of Newcastle upon Tyne, since 1971; *b* 6 March 1920; *d* of late Walter Petty and late Myra Petty; *m* 1945, Rev. Jack Martin Bell; one *s* one *d. Educ:* St Joseph's Coll., Bradford; Univ. of Manchester (Prize in Public Admin. 1940). Asst Personnel Officer, later Trng Officer, Min. of Supply ROF, 1942-45; Tutor and Lectr in Univ. Depts of Extra-Mural Studies 1945-63; University of Newcastle upon Tyne: Lectr in Social Studies, 1963-67 Sen. Tutor, 1967-69; Sen. Lectr, 1969-71. Member: Lord Chancellor's Counci on Tribunals, 1963-81 (Ch. person, Cttee on Functions of the Council 1977-81); Social Admin. Cttee of Jt Univ. Council for Public and Socia Admin., 1965-; BBC Programmes Complaints Commn, 1978-81; Academic Adviser (apptd by Govt Chief Scientist) to DHSS Social Security Res. Policy Cttee, 1976-; Expert Adviser to OECD Directorate for Social Affairs and Educn, for their project, Role of Women in the Economy, 1976-77; Mem. AHA for N Tyneside, 1974-77; Mem., Davies Cttee on Hosp. Complaint Procedure, 1971-73; Member Editorial Board: Jl of Social Policy, 1971-78; J of Social Welfare Law, 1977-. *Publications:* Tribunals in the Social Services 1969; Disequilibrium in Welfare, 1973; Research Study on Supplementary Benefit Appeal Tribunals—Review of Main Findings, Conclusions and Recommendations, 1975; The Functions of the Council on Tribunals, 1980 various papers in Jl of Social Policy, Econ. and Social Admin, and other jls *Address:* Department of Social Policy, University of Newcastle upon Tyne NE1 7RU.

BELL, Leslie Gladstone, CEng, FRINA; RCNC; Director of Naval Ship Production, Ministry of Defence, 1977-79, retired; *b* 20 Oct. 1919; *s* of late John Gladstone Bell and Jessie Gray Bell (*née* Quigley); *m* 1963, Adriana

Agatha Jacoba van den Berg; one s one d. *Educ:* Portsmouth Dockyard Tech. Coll.; Royal Naval Engineering Coll., Keyham; Royal Naval Coll., Greenwich. Staff Constructor Cdr, Home Fleet, 1953-56; Aircraft Carrier Design, 1956-59; Chief Constructor, Weapon Development, 1959-67; IDC, 1968; Asst Dir, Submarine Design, 1969-72; Director, Submarine Project Team, 1972-77. *Recreations:* gardening, golf, music. *Address:* Haytor, Old Midford Road, Bath, Avon. *T:* Bath 833357. *Club:* Bath Golf.

ELL, Martin; Washington Correspondent, BBC TV News, since 1978; *b* 31 Aug. 1938; *s* of late Adrian Hanbury Bell and of Marjorie H. Bell; *m* 1971, Nelly Lucienne Gourdon; two d. *Educ:* The Leys Sch., Cambridge; King's Coll., Cambridge (MA). Reporter, BBC TV News, 1965-77; Diplomatic Correspondent, BBC TV News, 1977-78. Royal Television Society Reporter of the Year, 1977. *Address:* c/o BBC, CBS Building, 2020 M St NW, Washington, DC 20036, USA. *T:* 202-223-2050.

ELL, Percy; see Bell, E. P.

ELL, Prof. Peter Robert; Quain Professor of Botany and Head of Department of Botany and Microbiology, University College London, since 1978; *b* 18 Feb. 1920; *s* of Andrew and Mabel Bell; *m* 1952, Elizabeth Harrison; two s. *Educ:* Simon Langton School, Canterbury; Christ's Coll., Cambridge (MA 1949). University College London: Asst Lecturer in Botany, 1946; Lectr in Botany, 1949; Reader in Botany, 1967; Prof. of Botany, 1967. Visiting Professor: Univ. of California, Berkeley, 1966-67; Univ. of Delhi, India, 1970. British Council Distinguished Visitor, NZ, 1976; many other visits overseas, including exploration of Ecuadorian Andes. Vice-Pres., Linnean Soc., 1962-65; Mem. Biological Sciences Cttee, 1974-79 (Chm. Panel 1, 1977-79), SRC. *Publications:* Darwin's Biological Work, Some Aspects Reconsidered, 1959; (with C. F. Woodcock) The Diversity of Green Plants, 1968, 2nd edn 1971; (trans., with D. E. Coombe) Strasburger's Textbook of Botany, 8th English edn, 1976; scientific papers on botanical topics, particularly reproductive cells of land plants. *Recreation:* mountains. *Address:* 13 Granville Road, Barnet, Herts EN5 4DU. *T:* 01-449 9331.

ELL, Prof. Peter Robert Frank, MD; FRCS, FRCSGlas; Professor of Surgery, University of Leicester since 1974; *b* 12 June 1938; *s* of Frank and Ruby Bell; *m* 1961, Anne Jennings; one s two d. *Educ:* Univ. of Sheffield (MB, ChB Hons 1961; MD 1969). FRCS 1965; FRCSGlas 1968. Postgrad. surg. career in Sheffield hosps, 1961-65; Lectr in Surgery, Univ. of Glasgow, 1965-68; Sir Henry Wellcome Travelling Fellow, Univ. of Colorado, 1968-69; Consultant Surgeon and Sen. Lectr, Western Infirm., Glasgow, 1969-74. *Publications:* Surgical Aspects of Haemodialysis, 1974; Operative Arterial Surgery, 1982; pubns on vascular disease, transplantation and cancer in med. and surg. jls. *Recreations:* horticulture, oil painting, tennis (Mem., Leics Club). *Address:* Department of Surgery, Clinical Sciences Building, PO Box 65, Royal Infirmary, Leicester.

ELL, His Honour P(hilip) Ingress, TD 1950; QC 1952; a Circuit Judge (formerly Judge of County Courts), 1960-75; *b* 10 Jan. 1900; *s* of Geoffrey Vincent and Mary Ellen Bell; *m* 1933, Agnes Mary Eastwood; two s one d. *Educ:* Stonyhurst, Blackburn; Royal Naval College, Keyham; Queen's Coll., Oxford (BA Jurisprudence, BCL). Called to the Bar, Inner Temple, 1925. Cadet RN, 1918; Midshipman RN, 1918-20. Lieut TA, 1939; JAG Dept, 1941, Temp. Major, 1944. MP (C) Bolton East, 1951-60. *Publication:* Idols and Idylls, 1918. *Recreations:* golf; Capt., Oxford University Boxing Club, 1923. *Address:* Windlesham Manor, Crowborough, Sussex. *Club:* Carlton.

ELL, Prof. Quentin (Claudian Stephen), FRSA; FRSL; Emeritus Professor of the History and Theory of Art, Sussex University; painter, sculptor, potter, author, art critic; *b* 19 Aug. 1910; 2nd *s* of late Clive Bell and Vanessa Stephen; *m* 1952, Anne Olivier Popham; one s two d. *Educ:* Leighton Park. Exhibitions, 1935, 1947, 1949, 1972, 1977, 1981, 1982. Political warfare executive, 1941-43. Lectr in Art Education, King's Coll., Newcastle, 1952; Senior Lecturer, 1956; Prof. of Fine Art, University of Leeds, 1962-67 (Head of Dept of Fine Art, 1959); Slade Professor of Fine Art, Oxford Univ., 1964-65; Ferens Prof. of Fine Art, University of Hull, 1965-66; Prof. of History and Theory of Art, Sussex Univ., 1967-75. MA Dunelm, 1957. Regular contributor to Listener, 1951-. *Publications:* On Human Finery, 1947, rev. edn 1976; Those impossible English (with Helmut Gernsheim), 1951; Roger Montané, 1961; The Schools of Design, 1963; Ruskin, 1963; Victorian Artists, 1967; Bloomsbury, 1968; Virginia Woolf, a Biography, 2 vols, 1972 (James Tait Black Meml Prize; Duff Cooper Meml Prize); A New and Noble School, 1982. *Address:* Cobbe Place, Beddingham, Sussex. *T:* Glynde 201. *Club:* Reform.

ELL, Sir Raymond; see Bell, Sir G. R.

ELL, Robert Donald Murray, CB 1966; Chairman of Executive, Scottish Council of Social Service, since 1978; *b* 8 Oct. 1916; *s* of Robert William and Mary Caroline Bell; *m* 1941, Karin Anna Smith; one s one d. *Educ:* Christ's Hosp.; Clare Coll., Cambridge. First Class Honours, Natural Sciences Tripos (Physics), 1938. Joined Scottish Office, 1938. War of 1939-45: Royal Artillery, 1940-45 (Mil. Coll. of Science, Bury, 1943). Principal, Scottish Home Dept, 1946; Private Sec. to Sec. of State for Scotland, 1947-50; Under-Secretary in Scottish Depts, 1959-76. *Address:* Smeaton House, Inveresk, Musselburgh, Midlothian. *T:* 031-665 2940.

BELL, Prof. Robert Edward, CC (Canada) 1971; FRS 1965; FRSC 1955; Rutherford Professor of Physics, McGill University, Montreal, since 1960; Principal and Vice-Chancellor, McGill University, 1970-79; *b* 29 Nov. 1918; *s* of Edward Richardson Bell and Edith E. Rich, British Columbia; *m* 1947, Jeanne Atkinson; one d. *Educ:* Univ. of British Columbia (BA 1939, MA 1941); McGill Univ. (PhD 1948). Wartime Radar development, Nat. Research Council, Ottawa, 1941-45; Sen. Research Officer, Chalk River Nuclear Laboratories, 1946-56; seconded to Foster Radiation Lab., McGill Univ., 1952-56; Assoc. Prof. of Physics, 1956-60; Dir, Foster Radiation Lab., 1960-69; Vice-Dean for Physical Scis, 1964-67, Dean, Fac. of Grad. Studies and Research, 1969-70, McGill Univ. Visiting scientist, Copenhagen Univ. Inst. for Theoretical Physics, under Niels Bohr, 1958-59. President: Royal Society of Canada, 1978- (Sec., Section III (Science), 1962-64); Cdn Assoc. of Physicists, 1965-66. Fellow, American Physical Soc. Hon. DSc: Univ. of New Brunswick; Université Laval; Université de Montréal; Univ. of BC; McMaster Univ.; McGill Univ.; Carleton Univ., 1980; Hon. LLD: Univ. of Toronto; Concordia Univ.; Hon. DCL Bishop's Univ. *Publications:* contribs to books: Annual Reviews of Nuclear Science, 1954; Beta and Gamma Ray Spectroscopy, 1955; Alpha, Beta and Gamma Ray Spectroscopy, 1964; papers on nuclear physics and allied topics in scientific jls. *Address:* 363 Olivier Avenue, Westmount, Montreal, Quebec H3Z 2C8, Canada. *T:* (514) 935-3769.

BELL, Rodger, QC 1982; a Recorder of the Crown Court, since 1980; *b* 13 Sept. 1939; *s* of John Thornton Bell and Edith Bell; *m* 1969, Sylvia Claire Tatton Brown; one s three d. *Educ:* Brentwood Sch.; Brasenose Coll., Oxford (BA). Called to the Bar, Middle Temple, 1963. *Recreation:* running. *Address:* 14 Castello Avenue, SW15 6EA. *T:* 01-788 3857.

BELL, Dr Ronald Leslie, CEng, FIM, FInstP, FIAgrE; Director, National Institute of Agricultural Engineering, since 1977; *b* 12 Sept. 1929; *s* of Thomas William Alexander Bell and Annie (née Mapleston); *m* 1954, Eleanor Joy (née Lancaster); one s two d. *Educ:* The City School, Lincoln; Univ. of Birmingham (BSc, PhD). Research Fellow, Royal Radar Estabt, Malvern, 1954-57; Imperial College, Univ. of London: Lectr in Metallurgy, 1957-62; Reader in Metallurgy, 1962-65; University of Southampton: Prof. of Engrg Materials, 1965-77; Head of Dept of Mech. Engrg, 1968; Dean of Faculty of Engrg and Applied Scis, 1970-72; Dep. Vice Chancellor, 1972-76. Vis. Prof., Cranfield Inst. of Technology, 1979-. *Publications:* numerous papers in learned jls dealing with twinning and brittle fracture of metals, grain boundary sliding and creep in metals, dislocations in semi-conductors. *Recreations:* jogging, music, Association football, gardening. *Address:* The Garden House, Wrest Park, Silsoe, Beds MK45 4HR. *T:* Silsoe 60249.

BELL, Ronald Percy, MA; FRS 1944; FRSE 1968; FRSC; Professor of Chemistry, University of Stirling, 1967-75, now Emeritus; Hon. Research Professor of Chemistry, University of Leeds, 1976-82; *b* 1907; *s* of E. A. Bell, Maidenhead; *m* 1931, Margery Mary Mead; one s. *Educ:* County Boys' Sch., Maidenhead; Balliol Coll., Oxford. Bedford Lecturer in Physical Chemistry, Balliol Coll., 1932; Fellow of Balliol Coll., 1933 (Vice-Master, 1965); Hon. Fellow, 1967; Univ. Lecturer and Demonstrator, Oxford Univ., 1938; Univ. Reader, Oxford Univ., 1955. George Fisher Baker Lectr, Cornell Univ., 1958; Nat. Science Foundn Fellow, Brown Univ., 1964; Visiting Professor: Weizmann Inst. of Sci., Israel, 1973; Tech. Univ. of Denmark, Lyngby, 1976. President: Faraday Soc., 1956; Chemistry Section, British Assoc. Meeting, Durham, 1970; Vice-Pres. Chemical Soc., 1958 (Tilden Lectureship, 1941; Liversidge Lectureship, 1973-74; Spiers Meml Lectureship, 1975). Foreign Mem. Royal Danish Acad. of Arts and Sciences, 1962; Foreign Associate, Nat. Acad. of Sciences, USA, 1972; Foreign Hon. Mem., Amer. Acad. of Arts and Scis, 1974. Hon. LLD Illinois Inst. of Techn., 1965; Hon. DTech, Tech. Univ. of Denmark, 1969; Hon. DSc Kent, 1971; Hon. DUniv. Stirling, 1977. Leverhulme Emeritus Fellow, 1976. Meldola Medal, Inst. of Chemistry, 1936; Chem. Soc. Award in Kinetics and Mechanism, 1974. *Publications:* Acid-Base Catalysis, 1941; Acids and Bases, 1952, 2nd edn 1969; The Proton in Chemistry, 1959, 2nd edn 1973; The Tunnel Effect in Chemistry, 1980; papers in scientific journals. *Address:* Flat 5, Park Villa Court, Roundhay, Leeds LS8 1EB. *T:* Leeds 664236; Bowderbeck, Buttermere, Cumbria. *T:* Buttermere 226.

BELL, Stewart Edward; Advocate; Sheriff of Glasgow and Strathkelvin (formerly Sheriff of Lanarkshire at Glasgow), since 1961; *b* 4 Aug. 1919; *yr* *s* of late Charles Edward Bell, Shipowner, and Rosalind Stewart; *m* 1948, Isla, 2nd d of late James Spencer and Adeline Kelly; three d. *Educ:* Kelvinside Academy, Glasgow; Trinity Hall, Cambridge; Glasgow Univ. Trinity Hall, 1937-39 and 1946 (MA Cantab), Glasgow Univ., 1946-48 (LLB). Commissioned, Loyal Regt, 1939; served with 2nd Bn in Singapore and Malaya, 1940-42 (wounded, POW in Singapore and Korea, 1942-45). Admitted Advocate, 1948; practised: in Malacca, Malaya as Advocate and Solicitor, 1949-51; at Scottish Bar, 1951-61. *Recreation:* Highland bagpipe (Hon. Pipe-major, The Royal Scottish Pipers' Soc., 1975-77). *Address:* 23 Cleveden Drive, Glasgow G12 0SD. *T:* 041-339 3481. *Clubs:* Western (Glasgow); Caledonian (Edinburgh).

BELL, Trevor; see Bell, C. T.

BELL, Rev. Vicars, MBE 1964; author; Vicar of Clawton, and Rector of Tetcott with Luffincott, 1966-78; formerly Lecturer; *b* 24 Jan. 1904; *s* of W. A. Bell, Edinburgh; *m* 1926, Dorothy Carley. *Educ:* Radnor Sch., Redhill;

Reigate Grammar Sch.; Goldsmiths' Coll., King's Coll., Univ. of London. Asst master at Horley Boys' Council Sch., 1925; Headmaster: Spaldwick Council Sch., 1926; Little Gaddesden C of E Sch., 1929-63. *Publications*: Little Gaddesden: the story of an English Parish, 1949; Death Under the Stars, 1949; The Dodo, 1950; Two by Day and One by Night, 1950; Death has Two Doors, 1950; This Way Home, 1951; Death Darkens Council, 1952; On Learning the English Tongue, 1953; Death and the Night Watches, 1954; To Meet Mr Ellis, 1956; Death Walks by the River, 1959; That Night, a play for the Nativity, 1959; Orlando and Rosalind, three tales, 1960; Steep Ways and Narrow, 1963; The Flying Cat, 1964; (ed) Prayers for Every Day, 1965. *Address*: 20 Watts Road, Tavistock, Devon.

BELL, Walter (Fancourt), CMG 1967; *b* 7 Nov. 1909; *s* of Canon George Fancourt Bell; *m* 1948, Katharine Spaatz, Washington, DC, USA; no *c. Educ*: Tonbridge Sch. Barrister, Inner Temple. Vice-Consul (Acting): New York, 1935-40; Mexico City, 1940-41; New York, 1941-42; Foreign Office, London, 1942-45; 1st Sec., Brit. Embassy, Washington, DC, 1946-48; attached E Africa High Commn, Nairobi, Kenya, 1949-52; 1st Sec., Brit. High Commn, New Delhi, 1952-55; attached War Office, London, 1956-57; Adviser, Federal Govt, W Indies, 1957-60; attached Govt of Kenya, 1961-63; Counsellor, British High Commn, Nairobi, Kenya, 1963-67. US Medal of Freedom with Bronze Palm, 1946. *Recreations*: tennis, walking. *Address*: 6 Onslow Square, SW7. *Clubs*: Travellers'; Nairobi (Nairobi).

BELL, William Archibald Ottley Juxon; Member: Greater London Council for Chelsea, since 1970; Inner London Education Authority, since 1970; Chairman, Historic Buildings Committee, 1977-81; *b* 7 July 1919; *s* of Maj. William Archibald Juxon Bell and Mary Isabel Maude Bell (*née* Ottley); *m* 1947, Belinda Mary (*née* Dawson); three *s* three *d. Educ*: Eton; Trinity College, Oxford (MA(Hist.)). Temp. Captain, Welsh Guards, 1940-45. Entered HM Foreign Service, 1945; Political Private Sec. to Sir Terence Shone, UK High Comr in India, 1946-47; Sec. to Exec. Dirs, British S Africa Co., 1947-50; Partner and Dir, King & Shaxson Ltd (Bill-brokers), 1950-. Chm., Diocesan Bd of Finance for Oxon, 1973-76. Mem., UK Cttee for European Architectural Heritage Year, 1973-75. Chm., Heritage of London Trust, 1980-. High Sheriff, Oxon, 1978-79. *Recreations*: shooting, golf, music. *Address*: Cottisford House, near Brackley, Northants. *T*: Finmere 247; Langcliffe Hall, Settle, N Yorks. *T*: Settle 2556; 165 Cranmer Court, SW3. *T*: 01-589 1033. *Clubs*: White's, Pratt's.

BELL, William Bradshaw; Lord Mayor of Belfast, 1979-80; *b* 9 Oct. 1935; *s* of Robert Bell and Mary Ann Bell; *m* 1969, Leona Maxwell; one *s* three *d. Educ*: Fane Street Primary School, Belfast; Grosvenor High School, Belfast. Jt proprietor, retail motor accessory firm. Mem. for N Belfast, NI Constitutional Convention, 1975-76; Mem., Belfast City Council, 1976- (Unionist spokesman on housing 1976-79); Asst Treasurer, Ulster Unionist Council. *Recreations*: music, motoring, gardening. *Address*: 15 Coachman's Way, Hillsborough, Co. Down, Northern Ireland.

BELL, Sir (William) Ewart, KCB 1982 (CB 1978); Head of Northern Ireland Civil Service, since 1979 and Second Permanent Secretary, Northern Ireland Office, since 1981; *b* 13 Nov. 1924; *s* of late Rev. Dr Frederick G. Bell and late Margaret Jane Ewart; *m* 1957, Kathleen Ross Boucher; two *d. Educ*: Methodist Coll., Belfast; Wadham Coll., Oxford (MA). Asst Master, Cheltenham Coll., 1946-48; Northern Ireland Civil Service, 1948-; Min. of Health and Local Govt, 1948-52; Min. (later Dept) of Commerce, 1952-76; Asst Sec., 1963-70; Dep. Sec., 1970-73; Sec., 1973-76; Permanent Sec., Dept of Finance, 1976-79. *Recreations*: gardening, golf, Rugby football. *Address*: Stormont Castle, Belfast, N Ireland BT4 3ST. *T*: Belfast 63011.

BELL, Sir William H. D. M.; *see* Morrison-Bell.

BELL, William Lewis, CMG 1970; MBE 1945; Information Officer, University of Oxford, since 1977; *b* 31 Dec. 1919; *s* of Frederick Robinson Bell and Kate Harper Bell (*née* Lewis); *m* 1943, Margaret Giles; one *s* one *d. Educ*: Hymers Coll., Hull; Oriel Coll., Oxford. Served The Gloucestershire Regt (Major), 1940-46. Colonial Administrative Service, Uganda, 1946-63: Dep. Sec. to the Treasury, 1956-58; Perm. Sec., Min. of Social Services, 1958-63; Fellow, Economic Develt Inst., World Bank, 1958. Chm., Uganda National Parks, 1962; Pres., Uganda Sports Union, 1961-62. Director, Cox & Danks Ltd (Metal Industries Group), 1963-64. Sec. to the Governors, Westfield Coll., Univ. of London, 1964-65; seconded to ODA as Head of British Develt Div. in the Caribbean, 1966-72; UK Dir, Caribbean Develt Bank, 1970-72; Dir-Gen., Technical Educn and Training Org. for Overseas Countries, 1972-77. *Recreations*: cricket, writing, Caribbeana. *Address*: Greystones, Stanton St John, Oxon. *Club*: MCC.

BELL, William Rupert Graham, CB 1978; Under Secretary, Department of Industry, 1975-80; *b* 29 May 1920; *s* of Bradford Grammar Sch.; St John's Coll., Cambridge (Scholar). Served Royal Artillery, 1940-45 (despatches). Asst Principal, Min. of Fuel and Power, 1948; Principal, 1949; Asst Sec., 1959; Under-Sec., Min. of Power, 1966-70, DTI, 1970-72; Deputy Principal, Civil Service Coll., 1972-75. Imperial Defence Coll., 1965. *Address*: 47 Chiswick Staithe, Hartington Road, W4 3TP. *T*: 01-994 2545.

BELL DAVIES, Vice-Adm. Sir Lancelot (Richard), KBE 1977; Commandant, NATO Defence College, Rome, 1978-81; *b* 18 Feb. 1926; *s* of late Vice-Adm. R. Bell Davies, VC, CB, DSO, AFC, and Mrs Bell Davi Lee on Solent, Hants; *m* 1949, Emmeline Joan (*née* Molengraaff), Wassena Holland; one *s* two *d. Educ*: Boxgrove Preparatory Sch., Guildford; R Coll., Dartmouth. War of 1939-45: Midshipman, HMS Norfolk, 19 (Scharnhorst sunk); joined Submarines, 1944. First Command, HMS Subt 1953; subseq. commands: HMS Explorer, 1955; Comdr, HMS Leander, 19 Captain: HMS Forth, also SM7, 1967, and HMS Bulwark, 1972; Rear-Adr 1973. Ministry of Defence Posts: (Comdr) Naval Staff, 1960; (Captain) Nav Asst to Controller, 1964; Director of Naval Warfare, 1969; Comdr, Brit Naval Staff, Washington, and UK Rep. to Saclant, 1973-75; Supreme Alli Commander Atlantic's Rep. in Europe, 1975-78. CBIM (FBIM 197 *Recreations*: sailing, skiing, gardening. *Address*: Holly Hill Lodge, Barr Lane, Sarisbury Green, Southampton. *T*: Locks Heath 3131. *Clubs*: Naval a Military, Royal Yacht Squadron, Royal Naval Sailing Association.

BELLAIRS, Prof. Angus d'Albini; Emeritus Professor of Vertebra Morphology in the University of London, at St Mary's Hospital Medic School (Professor, 1970); *b* 11 Jan. 1918; *s* of late Nigel Bellairs and Kathle Bellairs (*née* Niblett); *m* 1949 (Madeline) Ruth (PhD, Professor Embryology at UCL), *d* of Trevor Morgan; one *d. Educ*: Stowe Sch.; Quee Coll., Cambridge (MA); University Coll. Hosp., London. DSc Londc MRCS, LRCP. Served War, RAMC, 1942-46; Major, Operational Resear SE Asia, 1944-46. Lectr in Anat. and Dental Anat., London Hosp. Med. Col 1946-51; Lectr in Anat., Univ. of Cambridge, 1951-53; St Mary's Hosp. Me Sch.: Reader in Anatomy, 1953-66, in Embryology, 1966-70. Vis. Prof. Zoology, Kuwait Univ., 1970. Scientific Fellow and Hon. Co. Herpetologist, Zoological Soc. of London; FLS 1941; FIBiol 197 *Publications*: Reptiles, 1957 (4th edition with J. Attridge, 1975); The Wo of Reptiles (with Richard Carrington), 1966; The Life of Reptiles, 196 contribs to zoological literature, mainly on reptiles. *Recreations*: natu history (especially reptiles and cats), modern fiction. *Address*: 7 Champi Grove, SE5. *T*: 01-274 1834.

BELLAMY, Rear-Adm. Albert John, CB 1968; OBE 1956; Depu Director, Polytechnic of the South Bank, 1970-80; *b* Upton-on-Severn, Feb. 1915; *s* of late A. E. Bellamy and late Mrs A. E. Bellamy; *m* 194 Dorothy Joan Lawson; one *s* one *d. Educ*: Hanley Castle Grammar Sc Downing Coll., Cambridge (Buchanan Exhibitioner). 1st cl. hons Pts I a II, Math. tripos. Asst master, Berkhamsted Sch., 1936-39. Joined RN, 193 as Instructor Lieut; Fleet Instr and Meteorological Officer, America and W 1948-50 (HMS Glasgow); Instr Comdr, 1950; Headmaster, RN Schs, Mal 1951-54; HMS Ark Royal, 1955-56; Dean of the College, RN Engineeri Coll., Manadon, Plymouth, 1956-60; Instr Capt., 1958; Staff of Dir, Nav Educn Service, 1960-63; Dir of Studies, RN Electrical, Weapons and Rad Engineering Sch., HMS Collingwood, 1963-65; Instr Rear-Adm., 1965; D Naval Educn Service and Hd of Instructor Branch, MoD, 1965-7 *Recreations*: gardening, show jumping. *Address*: The Cottage, Kingt Magna, Gillingham, Dorset. *T*: East Stour 668.

BELLAMY, Alexander (William); retired; Senior Legal Assistant, Coun on Tribunals, 1967-76 (temporary Legal Assistant, 1963-67); *b* Aug. 1909; 1931, Lena Marie Lauga Massy. *Educ*: Mill Hill Sch.; Clare Coll., Cambridg Called to Bar, Gray's Inn, 1934; practised at Bar, London, 1934-38; Magistra Straits Settlements and FMS, 1938; seconded as District Magistrate, Gc Coast, 1942; legal staff, Malaya Planning Unit, WO, 1944; Crown Counse Singapore, 1946; District Judge (Civil), Singapore, 1948; District Judge a 1st Magistrate, Singapore, 1952; actg Puisne Judge, Fed. of Malaya, 1953-5 Puisne Judge, Supreme Court, Nigeria, 1955; Actg Chief Justice, High Cou of Lagos and Southern Cameroons, 1959, 1960; Actg Chief Justice, Hi Court of Lagos, 1961; a Judge of High Court of Lagos and Southe Cameroons, 1955-62. *Address*: 212 Collingwood House, Dolphin Squa SW1.

BELLAMY, Basil Edmund, CB 1971; Under-Secretary, Department of Tra and Industry (formerly Board of Trade), 1965-74; *b* 9 Feb. 1914; *s* of Willia Henry and Mary Bellamy; *m* 1943, Sheila Mary Dolan; one *d. Educ*: Whitg Sch. Joined Board of Trade, 1932; Asst Dir, Min. of War Transport, 194 Asst Sec., Min. of Transport, 1951; Under-Sec., 1963-65. Joint Services Sta Coll., 1950; Imperial Defence Coll., 1957. *Address*: 52 Denmark Roa Wimbledon, SW19 4PQ.

BELLAMY, David James, PhD; FLS; FIBiol; botanist; writer and broadcast *b* 18 Jan. 1933; *s* of Thomas Bellamy and Winifred (*née* Green); *m* 19 Rosemary Froy; two *s* three *d. Educ*: London University: Chelsea Coll. Science and Technology (BSc); Bedford Coll. (PhD). Lectr, then Sen. Lec Dept of Botany, Univ. of Durham, 1960-80; Hon. Prof. of Adult a Continuing Educn, 1980-82. Presenter and script writer for television a radio programmes, BBC and ITV. Main series: Life in our Sea, 1970; Bellar on Botany, 1973; Bellamy's Britain, 1975; Bellamy's Europe, 1977; Botar Man, 1979; Up a Gum Tree, 1980; Backyard Safari, 1981; The Great Seaso 1982. *Publications*: Peatlands, 1974; Bellamy on Botany, 1974; Bellam Britain, 1975; Bellamy's Europe, 1977; Life Giving Sea, 1977; Botanic Ma 1978; Half of Paradise, 1979; The Great Seasons, 1981; Backyard Safari, 198 Discovering the Countryside with David Bellamy, vols I and II, 198 *Recreations*: children, ballet. *Address*: Mill House, Bedburn, Bish Auckland, Co. Durham.

ELLAMY, Prof. Edmund Henry, MA, PhD; Professor of Physics in the University of London, Westfield College, since 1960; *b* 8 April 1923; *s* of Herbert Bellamy and Nellie (*née* Ablett); *m* 1946, Joan Roberts; three *s. Educ:* Quarry Bank Sch., Liverpool; King's Coll., Cambridge. Lectr in Natural Philosophy, Univ. of Glasgow, 1951-59, Sen. Lectr, 1959-60. Mem., Nuclear Physics Board of Science Research Council, 1965-66. Visiting Prof., Univ. of Stanford, 1966-67. *Publications:* numerous scientific papers in Proc. Phys. Soc. and other journals. *Recreations:* skiing, squash, travel, football. *Address:* 7 Homefield Road, Radlett, Herts. *T:* Radlett 4677.

ELLEW, family name of **Baron Bellew.**

ELLEW; *see* Grattan-Bellew.

ELLEW, 7th Baron *cr* 1848; **James Bryan Bellew;** Bt 1688; *b* 5 Jan. 1920; *s* of 6th Baron Bellew, MC, and Jeanie Ellen Agnes (*d* 1973), *d* of late James Ormsby Jameson; *S* father, 1981; *m* 1st, 1942, Mary Elizabeth (*d* 1978), *d* of Rev. Edward Eustace Hill; two *s* one *d*; 2nd, 1978, Gwendoline, formerly wife of Major P. Hall and *d* of late Charles Redmond Clayton-Daubeny. Served War of 1939-45, Irish Guards (Captain). *Heir: s* Hon. Bryan Edward Bellew [*b* 19 March 1943; *m* 1968, Rosemary Sarah, *d* of Major Reginald Kilner Brasier Hitchcock; two *s*]. *Address:* Barmeath Castle, County Louth, S Ireland; 24 Dartmouth Place, W4.

ELLEW, Hon. Sir George (Rothe), KCB 1961; KCVO 1953 (CVO 1950; MVO 1935); Kt 1950; FSA 1948; Secretary of the Order of the Garter, 1961-74, Garter Principal King of Arms, 1950-61; Genealogist of the Order of the Bath, 1950-61; Genealogist Order of St John, 1951-61; Knight Principal of Imperial Society of Knights Bachelor, 1957-62 (Deputy Knight Principal, 1962-71); Inspector of Regimental Colours, 1957-61; *b* 13 Dec. 1899; *s* of late Hon. Richard Bellew and Gwendoline, *d* of William R. J. Fitzherbert Herbert-Huddleston of Clytha; *m* 1935, Ursula Kennard, *e d* of late Anders Eric Knös Cull, Warfield House, Bracknell; one *s. Educ:* Wellington Coll.; Christ Church, Oxford. Served War of 1939-45: Squadron Leader RAFVR, 1940-45 (despatches). Formerly Portcullis Pursuivant of Arms; Somerset Herald, 1926-50, and Registrar of the Coll. of Arms, 1935-46. KStJ 1951 (Mem. Chapter Gen., 1951-). *Address:* The Grange, Farnham, Surrey.

ELLINGER, Sir Robert (Ian), GBE 1967; Kt 1964; Chairman: Kinloch (PM) Ltd, 1946-75; National Savings Committee, 1970-75, and President, 1972-75; Director, Rank Organisation, since 1971; *b* Tetbury Glos, 10 March 1910; *s* of David Morgan Bellinger, Cardiganshire, and Jane Ballantine Deans, Edinburgh; *m* 1962, Christiane Marie Louise Janssens, Brussels; one *s* one *d. Educ:* Church of England sch. Elected Court of Common Council, 1953; Chm. City of London Freemen's Sch., 1957; Alderman for Ward of Cheap, 1958; Sheriff, City of London, 1962-63; Lord Mayor of London, 1966-67; one of HM Lieutenants, City of London, 1976-. Chairman: Panel for Civil Service Manpower Review, 1968-71; Adv. Cttee on Magistracy, City of London, 1968-76; Licensing Cttee, City of London; Finance Cttee, BBC; Governor, BBC, 1968-71; Trustee, St Paul's Cathedral Trust, 1977-; Dir, Arsenal Football Club. Chm., Danish Trade Adv. Bd, 1979. Past Master, Broderers' Company; Liveryman, Fletchers' Company. Hon. DSc City Univ., 1966. Gentleman Usher of the Purple Rod, Order of the British Empire, 1969-. Chm., Anglo-Danish Soc., 1976. KStJ 1966; Commandeur, Ordre de Léopold, cl. III (Belgium), 1963; Comdr, Royal Order of the Phoenix (Greece), 1963; Officier, Ordre de la Valeur Camerounaise (Cameroons), 1963; Knight Comdr of the Order of Dannebrog (Denmark), 1977. *Recreations:* tennis, football, music, motoring. *Address:* Penn Wood, Fulmer, Bucks. *T:* Fulmer 2029. *Club:* City Livery.

ELLINGHAM, Sir Noel (Peter Roger), 7th Bt (2nd creation) *cr* 1796; accountant; *b* 4 Sept. 1943; *s* of Sir Roger Carroll Patrick Stephen Bellingham, 6th Bt, and of Mary, *d* of late William Norman; *S* father, 1973; *m* 1977, Jane, *d* of late Edwin William and of Joan Taylor, Sale, Cheshire. *Heir: b* Anthony Edward Norman Bellingham, *b* 24 March 1947. *Address:* 20 Davenport Park Road, Davenport, Stockport, Cheshire. *T:* 061-483 7168. *Club:* 64 Society (Cheshire).

ELLIS, Bertram Thomas; Headmaster, The Leys School, Cambridge, since 1975; *b* 4 May 1927; *s* of Rev. Thomas J. Bellis and Mary A. Bellis; *m* 1952, Joan Healey; two *s. Educ:* Kingswood Sch., Bath; St John's Coll., Cambridge (Exhibr in Maths, MA). Rossall Sch., 1951-55; Highgate Sch., 1955-65; Headmaster, Daniel Stewart's Coll., 1965-72; Principal, Daniel Stewart's and Melville Coll., 1972-75. Chm., Scottish Educn Dept Cttee on Computers and the Schools (reports, 1969 and 1972); Member: Council, Inst. of Math., 1975-79; Educational Research Bd, SSRC, 1975-80. Governor: Queenswood Sch., 1980-; St John's Coll. Sch., 1981-. Pres., Mathematical Assoc., 1971-72. Schoolmaster Fellow, Balliol Coll., Oxford, 1963; FIMA 1964; FRSE 1972. *Recreation:* fell walking. *Address:* The Leys School, Cambridge CB2 2AD.

ELLOW, family name of **Baron Bellwin.**

ELLOW, Saul; American writer; *b* 10 June 1915; *s* of Abraham and Liza Gordon Bellow; three *s. Educ:* Univ. of Chicago; Northwestern Univ. Three one-act plays: Out From Under, Orange Soufflé, and The Wen, prod. London, 1966. Nobel Prize for Literature, 1976. Hon. DLitt, Northwestern Univ., 1962. *Publications:* Dangling Man, 1944 (reissued 1972); The Victim,

1947; The Adventures of Augie March, 1953; Seize the Day, 1956; Henderson the Rain King, 1959; Herzog, 1964; Mosby's Memoirs and Other Stories, 1969; Mr Sammler's Planet, 1970; Humboldt's Gift, 1975 (Pulitzer Prize 1976); To Jerusalem and Back, 1976; The Dean's December, 1982. Play: The Last Analysis, 1967. *Address:* University of Chicago, Chicago, Ill 60637, USA.

BELLOWS, James Gilbert; Editor, Los Angeles Herald Examiner, since 1978; *b* 12 Nov. 1922; *s* of Lyman Hubbard Bellows and Dorothy Gilbert Bellows; *m* 1950, Marian Raines (decd); three *d*; *m* 1964, Maggie Savoy (decd); *m* 1971, Keven Ryan; one *d. Educ:* Kenyon Coll. (BA, LLB). Columbus (Ga) Ledger, 1947; News Editor Atlanta (Ga) Jl, 1950-57; Asst Editor, Detroit (Mich.) Free Press, 1957-58; Managing Editor Miami (Fla) News, 1958-61; Exec. Editor (News Ops), NY Herald Tribune, 1961-62; Editor, 1962-66; associate Editor, Los Angeles Times, 1966-75; Editor, Washington Star, 1975-78. Member: Kenyon Review Adv. Bd; Amer. Soc. of Newspaper Editors. *Address:* 115 South Rockingham Avenue, Los Angeles, Calif. 90049, USA. *Club:* Bel-Air Country.

BELLWIN, Baron *cr* 1979 (Life Peer), of the City of Leeds; **Irwin Norman Bellow;** JP; Parliamentary Under Secretary of State, Department of the Environment, since 1979; *b* 7 Feb. 1923; *s* of Abraham and Leah Bellow; *m* 1948, Doreen Barbara Saperia; one *s* two *d. Educ:* Lovell Road; Leeds Grammar School; Leeds Univ. LLB. Leader, Leeds City Council, 1975-79; Vice-Chm. Assoc. of Metropolitan Authorities, 1978-79. JP Leeds, 1969. *Recreation:* golf. *Address:* Woodside Lodge, Ling Lane, Scarcroft, Leeds LS14 3HX. *T:* Leeds 892908. *Clubs:* Carlton; Moor Allerton Golf (Club Pres.).

BELMORE, 8th Earl of, *cr* 1797; **John Armar Lowry-Corry;** Baron Belmore, 1781; Viscount Belmore, 1789; *b* 4 Sept. 1951; *s* of 7th Earl of Belmore and Gloria Anthea, *d* of late Herbert Bryant Harker, Melbourne, Australia; *S* father 1960. *Educ:* Lancing; Royal Agricultural Coll., Cirencester. *Heir: kinsman* Frederick Henry Lowry-Corry [*b* 23 Dec. 1926; *m* 1949, Hon. Rosemary Diana Lavinia, *y d* of 2nd Viscount Plumer; two *s*]. *Recreation:* conservation. *Address:* Castle Coole, Enniskillen, Co. Fermanagh, N Ireland. *T:* Enniskillen 22368/4255. *Club:* Kildare Street and University (Dublin).

BELOE, Robert, CBE 1960; Liaison Officer between Anglican Communion and World Council of Churches, 1969-71; *b* 12 May 1905; *s* of late Rev. R. D. Beloe, Headmaster of Bradfield Coll., and of Clarissa, *d* of Rev. Prebendary J. T. Bramston, Winchester Coll.; *m* 1933, Amy (JP), *d* of Capt. Sir Frank Rose, 2nd Bt (killed in action, 1914) and of late Daphne, Lady Rose; one *s* two *d. Educ:* Winchester; Hertford Coll., Oxford. Asst Master: Bradfield, 1927-28; Eton, 1928-30; Reading elementary sch., 1930-31. Kent Education Office, 1931-34; Asst Education Officer, Surrey, 1934-39; Dep. Education Officer, 1939-40; Chief Education Officer, 1940-59; Sec. to Archbishop of Canterbury, 1959-69. Mem. of various commissions and departmental cttees, including Royal Commission on Marriage and Divorce, 1951-55; Mauritius Electoral Boundary Commission, 1957; Higher Agricultural Education Cttee, 1944-46; Secondary Sch. Examinations Council, 1947-64 (Chm. Cttee on Exams other than GCE, 1958-60, leading to establishment of Cert. of Secondary Educn); Hon. Consultant, CSE Sub-Cttee of Schools Council, 1964-78; Mem., Home Office Central Training Council for Child Care, 1947-53. Hon. Sec. County Education Officers Soc., 1958-59; Governor of Commonwealth Inst., 1949-67. Trustee of Duke of Edinburgh's Award Scheme, 1960-66. Secretary: Monckton Cttee on Admin of Church Comrs, 1963; Archbishop's Advisers on Needs and Resources, 1963-69; General Synod C of E: Mem., 1970-75; Mem., Standing Cttee, 1971-75. Hon DCL Kent, 1979. *Recreations:* gardening, travel. *Address:* The Hill House, Queen's Road, Richmond, Surrey.

See also Sir Julian Rose, Bt.

BELOFF, family name of **Baron Beloff.**

BELOFF, Baron *cr* 1981 (Life Peer), of Wolvercote in the County of Oxfordshire; **Max Beloff;** Kt 1980; MA, DLitt (Oxon); FBA 1973; FRHistS; FRSA; *b* 2 July 1913; *er s* of late Simon and Mary Beloff; *m* 1938, Helen Dobrin; two *s. Educ:* St Paul's Sch.; Corpus Christi Coll., Oxford (Scholar). Gibbs Schol. in Mod. Hist., 1934; 1st Cl. Hons, School of Modern History, 1935; Senior Demy, Magdalen Coll., Oxford, 1935. Junior Research Fellow, Corpus Christi Coll., 1937; Asst Lecturer in History, Manchester Univ., 1939-46; Nuffield Reader in Comparative Study of Institutions, Oxford Univ., 1946-56; Fellow of Nuffield Coll., 1947-57; Gladstone Prof. of Govt and Public Admin, Oxford Univ., 1957-74, now Professor Emeritus, and Fellow, All Souls Coll., 1957-74, Emeritus Fellow, 1980-; Supernumerary Fellow, St Antony's Coll., Oxford, 1975-82; Principal, University Coll. at Buckingham, 1974-79. War of 1939-45, Royal Corps of Signals, 1940-41. Governor, Haifa Univ.; Ex-Trustee and Ex-Librarian, Oxford Union Soc. Hon. LLD Pittsburgh, USA, 1962; Hon. DCL, Bishop's Univ. Canada, 1976; Hon. DLitt Bowdoin Coll., USA, 1976; Hon. DrUniv. Aix-Marseille III, 1978. *Publications:* Public Order and Popular Disturbances, 1660-1714, 1938; The Foreign Policy of Soviet Russia, Vol. 1, 1947, Vol. 2, 1949; Thomas Jefferson and American Democracy, 1948; Soviet Policy in the Far East, 1944-51, 1953; The Age of Absolutism, 1660-1815, 1954; Foreign Policy and the Democratic Process, 1955; Europe and the Europeans, 1957; The Great Powers, 1959; The American Federal Government, 1959; New Dimensions in Foreign Policy, 1961; The United States and the Unity of Europe, 1963; The Balance of Power, 1967; The Future of British Foreign Policy, 1969; Imperial

Sunset, vol. 1, 1969; The Intellectual in Politics, 1970; (with G. R. Peele) The Government of the United Kingdom, 1980; edited: The Federalist, 1948; Mankind and his Story, 1948; The Debate on the American Revolution, 1949; On the Track of Tyranny, 1959; L'Europe du XIXe et XXe siècle, 1960-67; (with V. Vale) American Political Institutions in the 1970's, 1975; articles in English, French, Italian and American journals. *Recreation:* watching cricket. *Address:* c/o House of Lords, SW1. *Club:* Reform.
See also Hon. Michael Beloff.

BELOFF, Hon. Michael Jacob, MA; QC 1981; barrister and writer; *b* 19 April 1942; *s* of Baron Beloff, *qv* ; *m* 1969, Judith Mary Arkinstall; one *s* one *d*. *Educ:* Dragon Sch., Oxford; Eton Coll. (King's Schol.; Captain of Sch. 1960); Magdalen Coll., Oxford (Demy; H. W. C. Davis Prizeman, 1962; BA Hist. (1st cl.) 1963, Law 1965; MA 1967). Pres., Oxford Union Soc., 1962; Oxford Union tour of USA, 1964. Called to the Bar, Gray's Inn, 1967 (Gerald Moody Schol., 1963; Atkin Schol., 1967). Lectr in Law, Trinity Coll., Oxford, 1965-66. Legal Correspondent: New Society, 1969-79; The Observer, 1979-. Hon. Mem., Internat. Athletes' Club. *Publications:* A Short Walk on the Campus (with J. Aitken), 1966; The Plateglass Universities, 1968; The Sex Discrimination Act, 1976; contrib. Halsbury's Laws of England, Encounter, Minerva, Irish Jurist, Political Qly, etc. *Recreation:* running marathons. *Address:* 58 Park Town, Oxford OX2 6SJ; Flat 6, 38/9 Redcliffe Road, SW10 9NJ; 2 Hare Court, Temple, EC4Y 7BH. *T:* 01-353 0076. *Clubs:* Reform; Vincent's (Oxford).

BELOFF, Nora; author and journalist; *b* 24 Jan. 1919. *Educ:* King Alfred Sch.; Lady Margaret Hall, Oxford. BA Hons History 1940. Polit. Intell. Dept, FO, 1941-44; British Embassy, Paris, 1944-45; reporter, Reuters News Agency, 1945-46; Paris corresp., The Economist, 1946-48; Observer corresp., Paris, Washington, Moscow, Brussels etc, 1948-78; political correspondent, 1964-76, roving correspondent, 1976-78. *Publications:* The General Says No, 1963; The Transit of Britain, 1973; Freedom under Foot, 1976; No Travel like Russian Travel, 1979 (US, as Inside the Soviet Union: myth and reality, 1980). *Address:* 11 Belsize Road, NW6 4RX. *T:* 01-586 0378.

BELPER, 4th Baron *cr* 1856; **Alexander Ronald George Strutt;** formerly Major, Coldstream Guards; *b* 23 April 1912; *s* of 3rd Baron and Hon. Eva Isabel Mary Bruce, 2nd *d* of 2nd Baron Aberdare (she *m* 2nd, 6th Earl of Rosebery); *S* father 1956; *m* 1940, Zara Sophie Kathleen Mary (marr. diss. 1949), *y d* of Sir Harry Mainwaring, 5th Bt; one *s*. *Educ:* Harrow. Served War with Coldstream Guards, 1939-44 (wounded). *Heir:* *s* Hon. Richard Henry Strutt [*b* 24 Oct. 1941; *m* 1966, Jennifer Vivian, *d* of late Capt. Peter Winser and of Mrs James Whitaker; one *s* one *d* ; *m* 1980, Judith Mary de Jonge, *d* of Mr and Mrs James Twynam, Kitemore House, Faringdon, Oxon]. *Address:* Kingston Hall, Nottingham.

BELSKY, Franta; sculptor; *b* Brno, 6 April 1921; *s* of Joseph Belsky, economist; *m* Margaret Owen (cartoonist Belsky). *Educ:* Acad. of Fine Arts, Prague; Royal Coll. of Art, London. ARCA, Hons Dip. 1950. Served War as gunner (France, 1940; Normandy, 1944; various decorations). Taught in art schs, 1950-55. FRBS (Mem. Council); Pres., Soc. of Portrait Sculptors, 1963-68; Governor, St Martin's Sch. of Art, 1967-. Work in Nat. Portrait Gall. and collections in Europe and USA, for numerous co. councils, industrial and private cos and educn authorities: Paratroop Memorial, Prague, 1947; Lt-Col Peniakoff (Popski), Ravenna, 1952; statue of Cecil Rhodes, 8′, Bulawayo, 1953; groups: Constellation, Colchester, 1953; Lesson, LCC housing develt, 1957-58; Triga, Knightsbridge, 1958; Joy-ride, Stevenage New Town Centre, 1958; Astronomer Herschel Memorial, 18′, Slough, 1969; Oracle, 18′, Temple Way House, Bristol, 1975 (RBS Sir Otto Beit Medal, 1976); Totem, 32′, Manchester Arndale Centre, 1975 (RBS Sir Otto Beit Medal, 1978); fountains: European Shell Centre, 30′, South Bank; Four Seasons, 17′, Yate; reliefs: Epicentre, Doncaster City Centre, 1965; Key West, Slough, 1966; Radiation, St Luke's Hosp., Guildford; a number of sculptured bulkheads in BR and P & O ships; 1978 Jean Masson Davidson Award for Dist. in Portrait Sculpture, portraits include: Queen Mother, Birmingham Univ.; Prince Philip and HM Queen, Nat. Portrait Gall.; Prince Andrew; statue of Sir Winston Churchill for Churchill Meml and Library in US, Fulton, Missouri, and bust in Churchill Archives, Cambridge; Harry S. Truman, Presidential Library, Independence, Mo and H. S. T. Dam, Osage River, Mo; Adm. Cunningham, Trafalgar Square; Lord Cottesloe, Nat. Theatre. Queen Mother 80th Birthday Crown coin. *Publications:* illus. and contrib. various books and jls. *Recreations:* ski-ing, gardening, amateur archaeology. *Address:* 12 Pembroke Studios, W8 6HX.

BELSTEAD, 2nd Baron, *cr* 1938; **John Julian Ganzoni;** Bt 1929; JP; Minister of State, Foreign and Commonwealth Office, since 1982; *b* 30 Sept. 1932; *o s* of 1st Baron Belstead and Gwendolen Gertrude Turner (*d* 1962); *S* father, 1958. *Educ:* Eton; Christ Church, Oxford. MA 1961. Parliamentary Under-Secretary of State: DES, 1970-73; NI Office, 1973-74; Home Office, 1979-82. Chm., Assoc. of Governing Bodies of Public Schools, 1974-79. JP Borough of Ipswich, 1962; DL Suffolk, 1979. *Heir:* none. *Address:* The Old Rectory, Great Bealings, near Woodbridge, Suffolk. *T:* Grundisburgh 278. *Clubs:* All England Lawn Tennis (Wimbledon); MCC.

BELTRAM, Geoffrey; Visiting Research Associate, London School of Economics, since 1981; Under-Secretary, Department of Health and Social Security, 1973-81; *b* 7 April 1921; *s* of George and Beatrice Dorothy Beltram; *m* 1945, Audrey Mary (*née* Harkett); one *s* one *d*. *Educ:* Dame Alice Owen's

School. Tax Officer, Inland Revenue, 1938; served in RAF, 1941-46; Exec Officer and Higher Exec. Officer, Min. of Town and Country Planning 1947-51; Asst Principal, Nat. Assistance Bd, 1951-55; Principal 1955-63; Ass Sec. 1963-73 (NAB 1963-66, Min. of Social Security 1966-68, DHS 1968-73). *Recreations:* literature, listening to music, opera, ballet, walking tennis. *Address:* 115 Abbots Gardens, East Finchley, N2 0JJ. *T:* 01-88 5776.

BEMROSE, Sir Max, (John Maxwell), Kt 1960; DL; Director, 1938-79, an Chairman, Bemrose Corporation Ltd, 1953-78; now retired; *b* 1 July 190 *y s* of late Dr Henry Howe Bemrose and late Mrs Bemrose; *m* 1933, Margare Le Mare; one adopted *s* and one adopted *d*. *Educ:* Derby Sch.; Brighton Coll Clare Coll., Cambridge. MA (Economics). Joined family firm, 192 Prospective Conservative Candidate for Derby, 1938; fought Gen. Election 1945; contested Watford Div., 1950; Chm. East Midlands Provincial Are Conservative & Unionist Assoc., 1957-61; Mem. Exec. and Gen. Purpose Cttee of Conservative Assoc.; Chm. Nat. Union of Conservative & Unioni Associations, 1964-65; Chm., Printing and Publishing Industry Training Bo 1972-77; Pres., British Fedn of Master Printers, 1967-68, 1971-72. D Derbyshire, 1967, High Sheriff of Derbyshire, 1969-70. *Recreation* swimming, music, gardening. *Address:* Hazelbrow, Duffield, Derbyshire. 7 Derby 840388. *Clubs:* Carlton, Lansdowne.

BEN-TOVIM, Atarah, (Mrs Douglas Boyd), MBE 1980 (for services t children's music); Founder and Artistic Director, Children's Concert Centr since 1975; *b* 1 Oct. 1940; *d* of Tsvi Ben-Tovim and Gladys Ben-Tovim; *n* 1976, Douglas Boyd; one *d*. *Educ:* Royal Acad. of Music, London. ARAN 1967. Principal Flautist, Royal Liverpool Philharmonic Orchestra, 1962-7 Founder and Trustee, Ben Tovim Children's Music Centre Trust, 1978 *Publications:* Atarah's Book (autobiog.), 1976, 2nd edn 1979; Atarah's Bar Kits (14 published), 1978-; Children and Music, 1979. *Recreations:* musi writing, France and the Mediterranean. *Address:* c/o Children's Conce Centre, 12-16 Regent Street, Haslingden, Rossendale, Lancs. *T:* Rossenda 29488.

BENABDELJALIL, Mohamed-Mehdi; Ambassador of the Kingdom c Morocco to the Court of St James's, since 1981; *b* 12 Jan. 1930; *m* 1962, M Kinza Abdelmalek Torres; two *s* one *d*. *Educ:* Imperial Coll., Rabat, Morocc Faculty of Law, Univ. of Paris; Inst. for Internat. Studies, and Inst. for Poli Studies, Paris. Formerly: Head of Cabinet of Minister i/c Negotiations; Hea of Cabinet of Minister of Interior; Head, Dept of Mines and Geolog Under-Sec. of State for Indust. Prodn and Mining; Gen. Sec., Min. of Nation Economy; Dir Gen., Bureau des Etudes et des Participations Industrielle successively Ambassador in Bonn, Tehran, and in Turkey and Afghanistan; la practice, Casablanca, 1973-80. Grand Cross: West Germany; Lebanon; Ira *Recreations:* sport, hunting. *Address:* Embassy of the Kingdom of Morocc 49 Queen's Gate Gardens, SW7 5NE. *T:* 01-581 5004.

BENACERRAF, Prof. Baruj; Fabyan Professor of Comparative Patholog and Chairman of the Department of Pathology, Harvard Medical Schoc since 1970; President, Sydney Farber Cancer Institute, Boston, since 1980; *b* 29 Oct. 1920; *m* 1943, Annette Dreyfus; one *d*. *Educ:* Lycée Janson, Par (BèsL 1940); Columbia Univ. (BS 1942); Medical Coll. of Virginia (M 1945). Served US Army, 1946-48. Intern, Queens Gen. Hosp., NY, 1945-4 Res. Fellow, Dept of Micro-biol., Coll. of Physicians and Surgeons, Columb Univ., 1948-49; Chargé de Recherches, CNRS, Hôpital Broussais, Par 1950-56; New York University School of Medicine: Asst Prof. of Patho. 1956-58; Assoc. Prof. of Pathol., 1958-60; Prof. of Pathol., 1960-68; Chie Lab. of Immunol., Nat. Inst. of Allergy and Infectious Diseases, NII Bethesda, 1968-70. Scientific Adv. WHO; Chm., Scientific Adv. Ctte Centre d'Immunologie de Marseille, CNRS-INSERM; Mem., Immunolog A Study Sect., NIH, 1965-69; Member Scientific Advisory Board: Trude Foundn, 1970-76; Mass Gen. Hosp., 1971-74. Associate Editor: Amer. Jl Pathology; Jl of Exptl Medicine. President: Amer. Assoc. of Immunologis 1973-74; Fedn of Amer. Socs for Exptl Biol., 1974-75; Internat. Union Immunol Socs, 1980-. Fellow, Amer. Acad. of Arts and Scis, 1972. Membe Nat. Acad. of Scis, 1973; Nat. Inst. of Med., 1981; Amer. Assoc. of Pathologis and Bacteriologists; Amer. Soc. for Exptl Pathol.; Soc. of Exptl Biol. ar Medicine; British Assoc. for Immunol.; French Soc. of Biol Chem.; Harve Soc.; NY Acad. of Scis. Lectures: R. E. Dyer, NIH, 1969; Harvey, 1971, 197 J. S. Blumenthal, Univ. of Minnesota, 1980. Hon. MD Geneva, 1980; Ho DSc: Virginia Commonwealth Univ., 1981; NY Univ., 1981. Rabbi Sh Shacknai Lectr and Prize, Hebrew Univ. of Jerusalem, 1974; T. Duckett Jor Meml Award, Helen Hay Whitney Foundn, 1976; Waterford Biomedic Science Award, 1980; (jtly) Nobel Prize for Physiology or Medicine, 198 *Publications:* (with D. Katz) Immunological Tolerance, 197 Immunogenetics and Immunodeficiency, 1975; (with D. Katz) The Role Products of the Histocompatibility Gene Complex in Immune Response 1976; Textbook of Immunology, 1979; 550 articles in professional journa *Recreations:* music, art collecting. *Address:* Department of Patholog Harvard Medical School, 25 Shattuck Street, Boston, Mass 02115, USA. 617.732.1971.

BENARROCH, Heather Mary, (Mrs E. J. Benarroch); *see* Harp Heather.

BENAUD, Richard, OBE 1961; international sports consultant, journalist a media representative; BBC and Channel Nine Network televisi commentator, since 1960; *b* 6 Oct. 1930; *s* of Louis Richard Benaud and Irene Benaud; *m* 1967, Daphne Elizabeth Surfleet; two *s* by previous marr. *Educ:* Parramatta High Sch. Captain, Australian Cricket Team, 28 Tests, played for Australia 63 Tests, Tours to England, 1953, 1956, 1961. *Publications:* Way of Cricket, 1960; Tale of Two Tests, 1962; Spin Me a Spinner, 1963; The New Champions, 1965; Willow Patterns, 1972. *Recreation:* golf. *Address:* 19/178 Beach Street, Coogee, NSW 2034, Australia. *T:* Sydney 665-6464.

BENCE, Cyril Raymond; *b* 26 Nov. 1902; *s* of Harris Bryant Bence; *m* 1st, 1926, Florence Maud Bowler (*d* 1974); one *s* one *d* ; 2nd, 1975, Mrs I. N. Hall (*née* Lewis). *Educ:* Pontywaen Sch.; Newport High Sch., Mon. Apprenticed to Ashworth Son & Co. Ltd of Dock Street, Newport, Mon, Weighing Machine Manufacturers; moved to Birmingham, 1937. Member of National Union of Scalemakers; Mem. of AEU; Mem. of Birmingham Trades Council, 1942-45; Pres. Witton Branch AEU. Contested (Lab) Handsworth Div. of Birmingham, at Gen. Elections of 1945 and 1950, and Bye-election Nov. 1950; MP (Lab) Dunbartonshire East, 1951-70. *Address:* Leda, Sweethay Close, Staplehay, Taunton, Som.
    See also V. L. Pearl.

BENDALL, David Vere, CMG 1967; MBE 1945; HM Diplomatic Service, retired; Director, Morgan Grenfell (Holdings) Ltd, since 1971; Chairman, Banque Morgan Grenfell en Suisse, since 1981; Deputy Chairman: Morgan Grenfell International Ltd, since 1974; Avon Cosmetics Ltd, since 1979; Comité Consultatif, Banque de l'Indochine et de Suez, since 1974; *b* 27 Feb. 1920; *s* of John Manley Bendall; *m* 1941, Eve Stephanie Merrilees Galpin; one *d*. *Educ:* Winchester; King's Coll., Cambridge. Served Grenadier Guards, 1940-46. Third Sec., Allied Force HQ, Caserta, 1946; Rome, 1947; FO, 1949; First Sec., Santiago, 1952; FO, 1955; seconded to NATO Secretariat, Paris 1957; FO, 1960; NATO Secretariat, Paris as Dep. Head, Economic and Finance Div. and Special Advisor on Defence Policy, 1962; Counsellor, 1962; Counsellor, Washington, 1965-69; Asst Under-Sec. of State for Western Europe, 1969-71. Chm., British Red Cross Soc., 1980- (Vice-Chm., 1979-80). *Recreations:* golf, tennis, languages. *Address:* 3 Eaton Terrace Mews, SW1. *T:* 01-730 4229; Ashbocking Hall, near Ipswich, Suffolk. *T:* Helmingham 262. *Club:* Boodle's.

BENDALL, Dr Eve Rosemarie Duffield; Chief Executive Officer, English National Board for Nursing, Midwifery and Health Visiting, since 1981; *b* 7 Aug. 1927; *d* of Col F. W. D. Bendall, CMG, MA, and Mrs M. L. Bendall, LRAM, ARCM. *Educ:* Malvern Girls' Coll.; London Univ. (MA, PhD); Royal Free Hosp. (SRN). Ward Sister, Dorset County Hosp., 1953-55; Night Supt, Manchester Babies' Hosp., 1955-56; Nurse Tutor: United Sheffield Hosps Sch. of Nursing, 1958-61; St George's Hosp., London, 1961-63; Principal, Sch. of Nursing, Hosp. for Sick Children, Gt Ormond Street, 1963-69. Registrar, GNC, 1973-77. *Publications:* (jtly) Basic Nursing, 1963, 3rd edn 1970; (jtly) A Guide to Medical and Surgical Nursing, 1965, 2nd edn 1970; (jtly) A History of the General Nursing Council, 1969; So You Passed, Nurse (research), 1975. *Recreations:* gardening, breeding Jersey cows. *Address:* c/o English National Board for Nursing, Midwifery and Health Visiting, Victory House, 170 Tottenham Court Road, W1P 0HA.

BENDALL, Vivian Walter Hough; MP (C) Redbridge, Ilford North, since March 1978; surveyor and valuer; *b* 14 Dec. 1938; *s* of late Cecil Aubrey Bendall and Olive Alvina Bendall (*née* Hough); *m* 1969, Ann Rosalind (*née* Jarvis). *Educ:* Coombe Hill House, Croydon; Broad Green Coll., Croydon. LRVA 1976, MRSH 1965. Mem. Croydon Council, 1964-78; Mem. GLC, 1970-73; Chm., Greater London Young Conservatives, 1967-68. Former Member: Central Council for Care of the Elderly; South Eastern Area Reg. Assoc. for the Blind; Mem., Dr Barnardo's New Mossford Home Fund Raising Cttee. Contested (C) Hertford and Stevenage, Feb. and Oct. 1974. *Recreation:* cricket. *Address:* (business) 25 Brighton Road, South Croydon, Surrey CR2 6EA. *T:* 01-688 0341. *Clubs:* Carlton; Essex County Cricket; Ilford Golf.

BENDER, Prof. Arnold Eric; Professor of Nutrition and Dietetics, University of London and Head of Department of Food Science and Nutrition, Queen Elizabeth College, since 1978 (Professor of Nutrition, 1971-78); *b* 24 July 1918; *s* of Isadore and Rose Bender; *m* 1941, Deborah Swift; two *s*. *Educ:* Liverpool Inst. High Sch.; Univ. of Liverpool (BSc Hons); Univ. of Sheffield (PhD). Research, Pharmaceutical Industry, 1940-45 and 1950-54; Lectr, Univ. of Sheffield, 1947-49; Research, Food Industry, 1954-64; Teaching and Research, Univ. of London, 1965-. Hon. Treasurer: Nutrition Soc., 1962-67; Royal Soc. British Nat. Cttee for Biochem., 1963-69, for Nutritional Scis, 1976-; Chairman: Food and Nutrition Gp, Royal Soc. of Health, 1968-70; Cttee on Toxicity of Chemicals in Food and the Environment, 1976-; UK Dept, Health Cttee on Medical Aspects of Food Policy, 1977-; Exec., Internat. Union of Food, Sci. and Technol., 1978-; Food Gp, Soc. of Chem. Industry, 1979; European Cttee for Co-operation in Sci. and Technol. (COST 91), 1980-. Hon. Sec., UK Council for Food Science and Technology, 1964-78. *Publications:* Dictionary of Nutrition and Food Technology, 1960, 5th edn 1982, Japanese edn 1965; Nutrition and Dietetic Foods, 1967, 2nd edn 1973; Value of Food, 1970, 3rd edn 1979, Spanish edn 1972; Facts of Food, 1975, Polish edn 1979; Food Processing and Nutrition, 1978, Japanese edn 1978; The Pocket Guide to Calories and Nutrition, 1979, Dutch, US, Italian and Spanish edns 1981; Nutrition for Medical Students, 1982; research papers and review articles in Brit. Jl of Nutrition, Biochem. Jl,

BMJ, and other professional jls, and reports. *Recreations:* writing, gardening. *Address:* 59 Perryn Road, W3 7LS. *T:* 01-743 6419.

BENDIGO, Bishop of, since 1975; **Rt. Rev. Oliver Spencer Heyward;** *b* Launceston, Tasmania, 16 March 1926; *s* of Harold and Vera Heyward; *m* 1952, Peggy Butcher; four *s*. *Educ:* Church Gram. Sch., Launceston; Univ. of Tasmania (BA Hons 1949); Oriel Coll., Univ. of Oxford (BA 1953, MA 1956); Cuddesdon Coll., Oxford. RAAF, 1944-46. Rhodes Scholar, 1949. Deacon 1953, priest 1954, dio. Chichester; Asst Curate, St Peter's, Brighton, 1953-56; Rector of Sorell, Tasmania, 1956-60; Rector of Richmond, Tasmania, 1960-62; Precentor, St David's Cathedral, Hobart, 1962-63; Warden, Christ Coll., Univ. of Tasmania, 1963-74. *Recreation:* gardening. *Address:* Bishopscourt, 40 Forest Street, Bendigo, Victoria 3550, Australia. *T:* 436093.

BENEY, Frederick William, CBE 1962; QC 1943; *b* 9 March 1884; *s* of late William Augustus Beney, JP, Beckenham, Kent; *m* Irene Constance, *e d* of Henry Ward-Meyer, Weybridge; two *s*. *Educ:* Mill Hill Sch.; New Coll., Oxford (MA). Called to Bar, Inner Temple, 1909, Bencher 1948. Legal Asst, War Office, 1914-20; Recorder of Norwich, 1944-59; Mem., Deptl Cttee on Alternative Remedies, 1944-46; Chm. Deptl Cttee on Nat. Insurance against Industrial Diseases, 1953-54; Commissioner, Central Criminal Court, 1959-64; Commissioner of Assize, SE Circuit, 1959; Western Circuit, 1961; retd from practice, 1961. BBC Broadcasting, 1961-66. Mem. Appeal Tribunal, Assoc. of British Travel Agents. *Publications:* contributions to legal journals. *Address:* Silverwood, 35 Ashley Drive, Walton-on-Thames, Surrey KT12 1JT. *T:* Walton-on-Thames 27047.

BENJAMIN, Prof. Bernard; Professor of Actuarial Science, The City University, London, 1973-75; now Visiting Professor; *b* 8 March 1910; *s* of Joseph and Lucy Benjamin; London; *m* 1937, May Pate, Horham, Suffolk; two *d*. *Educ:* Colfe Grammar Sch.; Sir John Cass Coll. (London University). BSc (Hons); PhD London. LCC, 1928; statistician Public Health Dept; 1940; served War, 1943-46, RAF; statistician, General Register Office, 1952; Chief Statistician, 1954; Dir of Statistics, Ministry of Health, 1963-65; Dir of Research and Intelligence, GLC, 1965-70; Dir of Statistical Studies, CS College, 1970-73; Hon. Cons. in Med. Stats to Army, 1966. Chm., Standing Cttee of Statistics Users, 1971-. Fellow: Inst. of Actuaries (a Vice-Pres. 1963; Pres., 1966-68; Gold Medal, 1975); Royal Statistical Soc. (Pres. 1970-71); Eugenics Soc. (Pres., 1982-). Hon. DSc City Univ., London. *Publications:* Social and Economic Factors in Mortality, 1965; Health and Vital Statistics, 1968; Demographic Analysis, 1969; The Population Census, 1970; (with H. W. Haycocks) The Analysis of Mortality and Other Actuarial Statistics, 1971; Statistics in Urban Administration, 1976; (ed) Medical Records, 1977; General Insurance, 1977; (with J. H. Pollard) The Analysis of Mortality and Other Actuarial Statistics, 1980; numerous medical and population statistical papers and contribs to Jl of Royal Statistical Society and Jl of Inst. of Actuaries. *Recreations:* gardening, painting (both kinds). *Address:* 39 Dale Wood Road, Orpington, Kent. *T:* Orpington 24092. *Club:* Athenæum.

BENJAMIN, Brooke; *see* Benjamin, T. B.

BENJAMIN, Louis; Chief Executive, Stoll Moss Theatres Ltd, since 1981 (The London Palladium, Theatre Royal, Drury Lane, Victoria Palace, Apollo, Her Majesty's, Lyric, Globe, Queen's, and Bristol Hippodrome); *b* 17 Oct. 1922; *s* of Benjamin and Harriet Benjamin; *m* 1954, Vera Doreen Ketteman; two *d*. *Educ:* Highbury County Sec. Sch. Served Second World War: RAC, India, Burma and Singapore. Joined Moss Empires Ltd, 1937; entered theatrical management as Second Asst Manager, London Palladium, 1945; Asst Man., then Box Office Man., Victoria Palace, 1948; Gen. Man., Winter Gardens, Morecambe, 1953; Pye Records: Sales Controller, 1959; Gen. Man., 1962; Man. Dir, 1963; Chm., Pye Records Gp, 1975-80; a Jt Man. Dir, ATV Corp., 1975; Mem., Exec. Bd, Associated Communications Corp.; Executive Director: ATV Licensing; Bermans & Nathans; Precision Records & Tapes; Precision Video. Vice Pres., Entertainment Artistes Benevolent Fund and presenter of Royal Variety Perf., annually, 1979-, and Children's Royal Variety Perf., annually, 1981-. Companion, Grand Order of Water Rats; Mem., Exec. Cttee, Variety Club of GB. *Address:* Cranbourn Mansions, Cranbourn Street, WC2H 7AG. *T:* 01-437 2274.

BENJAMIN, Pauline, (Mrs Joseph Benjamin); *see* Crabbe, Pauline.

BENJAMIN, Dr Ralph, CB 1980; DSc, PhD, BSc, FCGI, CEng, FIEE, FIERE; Chief Scientist, Government Communications Headquarters, since 1971; *b* 17 Nov. 1922; *s* of Charles Benjamin and Claire Benjamin (*née* Stern); *m* 1951, Kathleen Ruth Bull, BA; two *s*. *Educ:* in Germany and Switzerland; St Oswald's Coll., Ellesmere; Imperial Coll. of Science and Technology, London. DSc(Eng) London, 1970. Joined Royal Naval Scientific Service, 1944; Senior Scientific Officer, 1949; Principal Scientific Officer, 1952; Senior Principal Scientific Officer (Special Merit), 1955; Deputy Chief Scientific Officer (Special Merit), 1960; Head of Research and Deputy Chief Scientist, Admiralty Surface Weapons Establishment, 1961; Dir and Chief Scientist, Admiralty Underwater Weapons Estab., 1964-71, and Dir, Underwater Weapons R&D (Navy), 1965-71. Hon. consultant: Univ. of Illinois; US Office of Naval Research, 1956; IEE Marconi Premium, 1964; IERE Heinrich Hertz Premium, 1980; Council Mem., Brit. Acoustical Soc., 1971; Vis. Prof., Dept of Electrical and Electronic Engineering, Univ. of Surrey, 1973-80. FCGI 1982. *Publications:* Modulation, Resolution and Signal

Processing for Radar Sonar and Related Systems, 1966; contribs to various advisory cttees, working parties, symposia, etc; articles in Jls of Instn of Electrical Engineers and Inst. of Electronic and Radio Engineers, etc. *Recreations:* work, mountaineering, ski-ing, swimming, sailing, sub-aqua (qualified naval diving officer), canoeing, judo (black belt). *Address:* c/o Government Communications Headquarters, Cheltenham, Glos. *Club:* Athenæum.

BENJAMIN, Prof. (Thomas) Brooke, MEng, MA, PhD; FRS 1966; Sedleian Professor of Natural Philosophy, and Fellow of The Queen's College, University of Oxford, since 1979; *b* 15 April 1929; *s* of Thomas Joseph Benjamin and Ethel Mary Benjamin (*née* Brooke); *m* 1st, 1956, Helen Gilda-Marie Rakower Ginsburg (marr. diss. 1974); one *s* two *d;* 2nd, 1978, Natalia Marie-Thérèse Court; one *d. Educ:* Wallasey Grammar Sch.; University of Liverpool; Yale Univ. (USA); University of Cambridge. BEng (Liverpool) 1950; MEng. (Yale) 1952; PhD (Cantab) 1955; MA (Oxon) 1979. Fellow of King's Coll., Cambridge, 1955-64; Asst Dir of Research, University of Cambridge, 1958-67; Reader in Hydrodynamics, Univ. of Cambridge, 1967-70; Prof. of Maths, and Dir, Fluid Mechanics Res. Inst., Essex Univ., 1970-78. Chm., Mathematics Cttee, SRC, 1975-78. Editor, Journal of Fluid Mechanics, 1960-65; Consultant to English Electric Co., 1956-67. William Hopkins Prize, Cambridge Philosophical Soc., 1969. *Publications:* various papers on theoretical and experimental fluid mechanics. *Recreations:* music, poetry. *Address:* Mathematical Institute, 24-29 St Giles, Oxford OX1 3LB. *T:* Oxford 54295; 8 Hernes Road, Oxford OX2 7PU. *T:* Oxford 54439.

BENN, Anthony, OBE 1945; *b* 7 Oct. 1912; *s* of late Francis Hamilton Benn and Arta Clara Benn (*née* Boal); *m* 1943, Maureen Lillian Kathleen Benn (*née* Denbigh); two *s* four *d. Educ:* Harrow; Christ Church, Oxford. Scholar; 1st cl. Hon. Mods; 2nd cl. Greats. Oxford Univ. Cricket XI, 1935. Price & Pierce Ltd, 1935 (Director, 1947, Chm., 1956-72). Joined Surrey and Sussex Yeomanry, 1936. Served War of 1939-45 (OBE): Staff Coll., 1942; Instructor, Middle East Staff Coll., 1943. Comdr, Order of the Lion of Finland, 1958. *Recreations:* golf, shooting, travel.

BENN, Edward, CMG 1981; Minister (Defence Equipment), British Embassy, Washington, 1978-82, retired; *b* 8 May 1922; *s* of John Henry Benn and Alice (*née* Taylor); *m* 1947, Joan Taylor; one *d. Educ:* High Storrs Grammar Sch., Sheffield; Sheffield Univ. (BEng; 1st Cl. Hons Civil Engrg; Mappin Medal, 1943). Operational Research with Army, 1943-48; India and Burma, 1944-46 (Major); entered War Office, 1948; tank research, Supt Special Studies, and later Dep. Dir, Army Op. Res. Estabt, 1961; Asst Sci. Adviser to SACEUR, Paris, 1962-65; Dep. Chief Sci. Adviser, Home Office, 1966-68; Dir, Defence Policy, MoD, 1968-75; Under Sec. and Dep. Chief Scientist (RAF), MoD, 1975-78. *Recreation:* golf. *Address:* 37 Woodham Waye, Woking, Surrey GU21 5SJ. *Clubs:* MCC; West Byfleet Golf.

BENN, Edward Glanvill; Life President, Benn Brothers, plc, Publishers, since 1976, Chairman, 1945-76; *b* 1905; 2nd *s* of late Sir Ernest Benn, 2nd Bt, CBE; *m* 1931, Beatrice Catherine, MBE, *d* of Claude Newbald; one *s* one *d. Educ:* Harrow; Clare Coll., Cambridge. Served War of 1939-45, East Surrey Regt, 1940-45; Brigade Major, 138 Infantry Brigade, Italy, 1944 (despatches). Council Member: Nat. Advertising Benevolent Soc., 1937-61 (Trustee, 1951-80, and Pres. 1961-62); Advertising Assoc., 1951-67 (Hon. Treasurer 1960-65); Commonwealth Press Union, 1956- (Hon. Treasurer 1967-77, Hon. Life Mem. 1975; Astor Award, 1982); Vice Pres., Readers' Pension Cttee, 1950-; Life Vice Pres., Newspaper Press Fund, 1965- (Appeals Pres. 1971); Chm., Advertising Advisory Cttee, Independent Television Authority, 1959-64; Dir., Exchange Telegraph Co. Ltd, 1960-72 (Chm. 1969-72); Pres., Periodical Publishers Assoc. 1976-78. Master, Stationers' Company, 1977. Mackintosh Medal, 1967. *Address:* Crescent Cottage, Aldeburgh, Suffolk IP15 5HW.

See also Sir J. A. Benn.

BENN, Sir John Andrews, 3rd Bt, *cr* 1914; Consultant, Benn Brothers plc and Ernest Benn Ltd; *b* 28 Jan. 1904; *e s* of Sir Ernest Benn, 2nd Bt, CBE and Gwendolen, *d* of F. M. Andrews, Edgbaston; *S* father, 1954; *m* 1929, Hon. Ursula Helen Alers Hankey, *o d* of 1st Baron Hankey, PC, GCB, GCMG, GCVO, FRS; two *s* three *d. Educ:* Harrow; Princeton Univ., USA (Class of 1926 Achievement Award 1970); Gonville and Caius Coll., Cambridge. Toured Latin America, founding Industria Britanica to promote British export trade, 1931. Helped to get new industries to Crook, South-West Durham, depressed area, 1936-38. Served War of 1939-45, KOYLI. Contested Bradford N (Nat. C), General Election, 1945. Chm. and Man. Dir, UK Provident Instn, 1949-68; Chairman: Crosby Trust Management Ltd, 1958-61; Cincinnati Milacron Ltd, 1969-76; Founder, 1962, and former Chm., Technical Development Capital Ltd. Chairman: English-Speaking Union of the Commonwealth, 1969-72; Benn Charitable Foundn, 1972-80; Vice-Pres., Book Trade Benevolent Soc., 1974. Associate, Princeton Univ. Press, 1965; Pres., Princeton Club of London, 1969-70. *Publications:* Columbus-Undergraduate, 1928; A Merchant Adventurer in South America, 1931; Tradesman's Entrance, 1935; I Say Rejoice, 1942; Something in the City, 1959. *Recreations:* painting, swimming, reading. *Heir:* s James Jonathan Benn [*b* 27 July 1933; *m* 1960, Jennifer, *e d* of Dr Wilfred Howells; one *s* one *d. Educ:* Harrow]. *Address:* High Field, Limpsfield, Surrey.

See also E. G. Benn, T. J. Benn.

BENN, John Meriton, CB 1969; Pro-Chancellor, Queen's University, Belfast, since 1979, Senator, since 1973; *b* 16 July 1908; *s* of late Ernest and Emily Louise Benn, Burnley; *m* 1933, Valentine Rosemary, *d* of late William Seward, Hanwell; two *d. Educ:* Burnley Gram. Sch.; Christ's Coll. Cambridge (Scholar; Modern Languages Tripos, 1st Cl. Hons French, 2nd Cl. Hons German). Asst Master, Exeter Sch., 1931-34; Lektor, Halle Univ. Germany, 1934; Asst Master, Regent Street Polytechnic Secondary Sch., 1935, Inspector of Schs., Ministry of Education for Northern Ireland, 1935-44; Principal, 1944-51; Asst Sec., 1951-59; Senior Asst Sec., 1959-64; Permanent Sec., 1964-69; NI Comr for Complaints, 1969-73; Parly Comr for Administration, NI, 1972-73. Chm., NI Schools Exams Council, 1974-81. Hon. LLD QUB, 1972. *Publication:* Practical French Proses, 1935. *Recreations:* gardening, bell-ringing, amateur dramatics. *Address:* 7 Tudor Oaks, Holywood, Co. Down. *T:* Holywood 2817.

BENN, Captain Sir Patrick (Ion Hamilton), 2nd Bt *cr* 1920; Captain, Reserve of Officers, late Duke of Cornwall's Light Infantry; Major, Norfolk Army Cadet Force, 1960; *b* 26 Feb. 1922; *o s* of late Col Ion Bridges Hamilton Benn, JP (*o s* of 1st Bt), Broad Farm, Rollesby, Gt Yarmouth, and late Theresa Dorothy, *d* of late Major F. H. Blacker, Johnstown, Co. Kildare; *S* grandfather, 1961; *m* 1959, Edel Jørgine, *d* of late Col W. S. Løbach, formerly of The Royal Norwegian Army, Andenes, Vesteraalen; one *s* one *d* (both adopted). *Educ:* Rugby. Served War of 1939-45 (despatches); North Africa, Italy, Greece, 1941-45; Capt. 1943; served Korea, 1951-52; retd, 1955. *Recreations:* shooting, fishing. *Address:* Rollesby Hall, Great Yarmouth, Norfolk NR29 5DT. *T:* Great Yarmouth 740313.

BENN, Timothy John; Chairman, Benn Brothers plc, since 1981; *b* 27 Oct. 1936; *yr s* of Sir John Benn, Bt, *qv. Educ:* Harrow; Clare Coll., Cambridge (MA); Princeton Univ., USA; Harvard Business Sch., USA. FInstM. Benn Brothers Ltd: Board Member, 1961; Managing Director, 1972; Dep. Chm., 1976. Ernest Benn: Board Member, 1967; Managing Director, 1973; Chairman and Managing Director, 1974. *Recreations:* fishing, flytying, writing, toymaking. *Address:* 25 New Street Square, EC4A 3JA. *T:* 01-353 3212. *Club:* Flyfishers'.

BENN, Rt. Hon. Tony; PC 1964; MP (Lab) Bristol South East, Nov. 1950-60 and since Aug. 1963; *b* 3 April 1925; *er surv. s* of 1st Viscount Stansgate, DSO, DFC, PC, former Labour MP (*d* 1960); having unsuccessfully attempted to renounce his right of succession, 1955 and 1960, won a bye-election in May 1961 only to be prevented from taking seat; instigated Act to make disclaimer possible, and disclaimed title for life, 1963; *m* 1949, Caroline Middleton De Camp, MA; three *s* one *d.* Served: RAFVR, 1943-45; RNVR, 1945-46. Joined Labour Party, 1943; Mem., NEC, 1959-60, 1962- (Chm., 1971-72). Postmaster-Gen., 1964-66, recommended establishment of GPO as public corp. and founded Giro; Minister of Technology, 1966-70, assumed responsibility for Min. of Aviation, 1967 and Min. of Power, 1969; opposition spokesman on Trade and Industry, 1970-74; Sec. of State for Industry and Minister for Posts and Telecommunications, 1974-75; Sec. of State for Energy, 1975-79. *Publications:* The Privy Council as a Second Chamber, 1957; The Regeneration of Britain, 1964; The New Politics, 1970; Speeches, 1974; Arguments for Socialism, 1979; Arguments for Democracy, 1981; numerous pamphlets. *Address:* House of Commons, SW1A 0AA.

BENNER, Patrick, CB 1975; Deputy Secretary, Department of Health and Social Security, since 1976; *b* 26 May 1923; *s* of Henry Grey and Gwendolen Benner; *m* 1952, Joan Christabel Draper; two *d. Educ:* Ipswich Sch.; University Coll., Oxford. Entered Min. of Health as Asst Princ., 1949; Princ., 1951; Princ. Private Sec. to Minister, 1955; Asst Sec., 1958; Under-Sec., Min. of Health, 1967-68, DHSS 1968-72; Dep. Sec., Cabinet Office, 1972-76. *Address:* 44 Ormond Crescent, Hampton, Mddx TW12 2TH. *T:* 01-979 1099. *Club:* Royal Commonwealth Society.

BENNET, family name of **Earl of Tankerville.**

BENNETT, Alan; dramatist and actor; *b* 9 May 1934; *s* of Walter Bennett and Lilian Mary Peel; unmarried. *Educ:* Leeds Modern Sch.; Exeter Coll., Oxford. BA Modern History, 1957. Jun. Lectr, Modern History, Magdalen Coll. Oxford, 1960-62. Co-author and actor, Beyond the Fringe, Royal Lyceum, Edinburgh, 1960, Fortune, London, 1961 and Golden, NY, 1962; author and actor: On the Margin (TV series), 1966; Forty Years On, Apollo, 1968; *stage plays:* Getting On, Queen's, 1971; Habeas Corpus, Lyric, 1973; The Old Country, Queen's, 1977; Enjoy, Vaudeville, 1980; *BBC TV films:* A Day Out, 1972; Sunset Across the Bay, 1975; *TV Plays for LWT,* 1978-79: Doris and Doreen; The Old Crowd; Me! I'm Afraid of Virginia Woolf; All Day on the Sands; Afternoon Off; One Fine Day; *BBC TV plays:* A Little Outing, A Visit from Miss Prothero, 1977; Intensive Care, Say Something Happened, Our Winnie, Marks, A Woman of No Importance, Rolling Home, An Englishman Abroad, 1982. *Publications:* (with Cook, Miller and Moore) Beyond the Fringe, 1962; Forty Years On, 1969; Getting On, 1972; Habeas Corpus, 1973; The Old Country, 1978; Enjoy, 1980; Office Suite, 1981. *Address:* c/o Chatto & Linnit Ltd, Globe Theatre, Shaftesbury Avenue, W1. *T:* 01-439 4371.

BENNETT, Albert Joseph, CBE 1966; Secretary, National Health Service Staff Commission, 1972-75; *b* 9 April 1913; *er s* of late Albert James Bennett and late Alice Bennett, Stourbridge, Worcs; unmarried. *Educ:* King Edward VI Sch., Stourbridge; St John's Coll., Cambridge (MA) Mathematical Tripos

(Wrangler). Admin. Officer, LCC, 1936-39; Central Midwives Board: Asst Sec., 1939-45; Sec., 1945-47; Instructor Lieut, later Lt-Comdr, RN, 1940-45; Sec., NW Met. Regional Hosp. Bd, 1947-65; Principal Officer, NHS Nat. Staff Cttee, 1965-72; Under-Sec., DHSS, 1972-75, seconded as Sec., NHS Staff Commn. Member: Nat. Selection Cttee for Recruitment of Trainee Hospital Admin. Staff, 1955-64; Cttee of Inquiry into the Recruitment, Training and Promotion of Admin. and Clerical Staff in Hospital Service, 1962-63; Adv. Cttee on Hospital Engineers Training, 1967-72; Admin. Training Cttee, Cttee of Vice-Chancellors and Principals, 1970-72; Kensington and Chelsea and Westminster AHA(T) and Family Practitioner Cttee, 1977-. *Recreations:* walking, gardening. *Address:* 19 Garson House, Gloucester Terrace, W2 3DG. *T:* 01-262 8311.

BENNETT, Alexander; *see* Bennett, F. O. A. G.

BENNETT, Andrew Francis; MP (Lab) Stockport North since Feb. 1974; Teacher; *b* Manchester, 9 March 1939; *m* ; two *s* one *d. Educ:* Birmingham Univ. (BSocSc). Joined Labour Party, 1957; Member, Oldham Borough Council, 1964-74. Member, National Union of Teachers. Contested (Lab) Knutsford, 1970. Interested especially in social services and education. *Recreations:* photography, walking, climbing. *Address:* 28 Brownsville Road, Stockport SK4 4PF; House of Commons, SW1A 0AA.

BENNETT, Sir Arnold (Lucas), Kt 1975; QC (Aust.); Barrister-at-Law of Supreme Courts of Queensland, New South Wales and Victoria and of High Court of Australia, in private practice, since 1932; *b* 12 Nov. 1908; *s* of George Thomas Bennett and Celia Juliana Bennett (*née* Lucas); *m* 1st, 1934, Marjorie Ella May Williams (*d* 1942); two *s* two *d* ; 2nd, 1944, Nancy Margaret Mellor; one *s* three *d. Educ:* Brisbane Grammar Sch.; University of Queensland. Called to Bar, 1932, and except for a period of war service, has practised ever since in Australian Courts and in the Privy Council. Served War, AIF (2 service medals), 1939-45: Captain in Artillery; Lieut and Major, Sqdn Ldr 2/5 Aust. Armoured Regt, and as 2 i/c of 2/1 Ind. Light Tank Sqdn, and as 2 i/c and Actg CO, 2/7 Aust. Armoured Regt. KC (Qld), 1947 (automatically became KC in High Court of Aust.), Victoria, 1952, NSW, 1953. Served 2/14 Qld Mounted Inf., 1950-54. Has conducted cases in all jurisdictions increasingly in sphere of constitutional law. At present (1982-) opinion practice only, but serves in Qld Adv. Cttee on constitutional law and as Mem. Qld Treaties Commn. For over 40 yrs, Member: Barristers' Bd of Qld (Chm. 1957-80); Supreme Court Library Cttee, Qld; Incorp. Council of Law Reporting (Chm. 1957-79); Rotary International (Governor D260, now D960, 1972-73, in Qld's Fiftieth Rotary Year); (Chm.) Constitution and By-Laws Cttee, RI. Coronation Medal, 1953; Silver Jubilee Medal, 1977. *Publications:* Rotary in Queensland—an historical survey, 1980; articles in Australian Law Jl, Sunday Mail, Weekend Australian. *Recreations:* tennis, farming, golf, aviation. *Address:* 20 Markwell Street, Auchenflower, Brisbane, Qld 4066, Australia. *T:* (07) 371 3313; (home) Fairthorpe, 16 Bellevue Terrace, St Lucia, Brisbane, Qld 4067, Australia. *T:* (07) 370 8485. *Club:* Rotary (Pres., 1959-60) (Brisbane).
See also Air Vice-Marshal D. C. T. Bennett.

BENNETT, Charles John Michael, CBE 1974; FCA; Partner in Barton, Mayhew & Co., Chartered Accountants, 1937-71; *b* 29 June 1906; *e s* of late Hon. Sir Charles Alan Bennett and Constance Radeglance, *d* of Major John Nathaniel Still; *m* 1931, Audrey Thompson; two *d. Educ:* Clifton Coll.; Trinity Coll., Cambridge. Served with HM Forces, 1939-45. Member: Electricity Supply Companies Commn, 1959, in Hong Kong; Fiji Sugar Inquiry Commn, 1961; Commn of Inquiry (Sugar Industry) 1962, in Mauritius; Commn of Inquiry into Banana Industry of St Lucia, 1963; Commn of Inquiry (Chm.) into Sugar Industry and Agriculture of Antigua, 1965; Commn of Enquiry into Sugar Industry of Guyana, 1967; Cttee of Enquiry into the pricing of certain contracts for the overhaul of aero-engines by Bristol Siddeley Engines Ltd. Mem. of Council, Institute of Chartered Accountants, 1963-69. Part-time Mem., Commonwealth Development Corp., 1965-73, Dep. Chm. 1970-71, 1972-73; Independent Mem., NEDC for Chemical Industry, and Chm., Pharmaceuticals Working Party, 1969. Mem., E Anglian Regional Cttee of Nat. Trust, 1971-81. *Recreations:* golf, fishing. *Address:* 15 St Olave's Court, St Petersburgh Place, W2 4JY. *T:* 01-229 9554.

BENNETT, Sir Charles (Moihi), Kt 1975; DSO 1943; company director; President, New Zealand Labour Party, 1972-76; *b* 27 July 1913; *s* of Rt Rev. Frederick August Bennett, Bishop of Aotearoa, 1928-50, and Rangioue Bennett; *m* 1947, Elizabeth May Stewart. *Educ:* Univ. of New Zealand; Exeter Coll., Oxford. MA, DipSocSci, DipEd. Director of Maori Welfare, 1954-57; High Comr for New Zealand to Fedn of Malaya, 1959-63; Asst Sec., Dept of Maori Affairs, 1963-69. Mem., NZ Prisons Parole Bd, 1974-76. Hon. LLD Canterbury Univ. of NZ, 1973. Hon. Kt PMN (Malaysia), 1963. *Address:* Maketu, Bay of Plenty, New Zealand. *T:* Te Puke (NZ) 32010. *Club:* Officers' (Wellington).
See also Rt Rev. M. A. Bennett.

BENNETT, Daniel, JP; Chairman, Greater Manchester Council, 1976-77, retired; *b* 18 Jan. 1900; *s* of Daniel Bennett and Margaret Bennett; *m* 1923, Helen Holt Atherton; two *d. Educ:* elementary sch. Elected to Orrell UDC, 1946; served continuously until 1974 (Chm. 3 times); elected to Lancs CC, 1966; elected to Divnl Educn Exec., 1950, Chm., 1969-74; elected to Greater

Manchester CC, 1973, now retired. JP Lancs 1952. *Recreation:* bowling. *Address:* 56 Lodge Road, Orrell, Wigan, Lancs. *T:* Up Holland 622894.

BENNETT, Air Vice-Marshal Donald Clifford Tyndall, CB 1944; CBE 1943; DSO 1942; late Royal Air Force; Chairman and Managing Director, Fairthorpe Ltd, and other companies; consultant, director, etc.; *b* 14 Sept. 1910; *s* of G. T. Bennett, Brisbane, Queensland; *m* 1935, Elsa Gubler, Zürich; one *s* one *d.* Royal Australian Air Force; Royal Air Force; AOC the Pathfinder Force of RAF Bomber Command, war of 1939-45; resigned commission, 1945; Imperial Airways; Empire and Atlantic Air Route Development; holder of the world's long-distance seaplane record (Dundee, Scotland, to Alexandra Bay, South Africa); a founder as Flying Superintendent of the Atlantic Ferry organisation (later Ferry Command); MP (L) Middlesbrough West, 1945; Managing Director and Chief Exec., British South American Airways, 1945-48. Chairman: Exec. Cttee United Nations Assoc. of Gt Britain and N Ireland, 1946-49; Political Freedom Movement, 1964-; Nat. Council of Anti Common Mkt Organisations, 1973-76; Pres. Radar Assoc., 1952-55; Vice-Chm., British Anti-Common Market Campaign (formerly Safeguard Britain Campaign), 1947-; Patron: Pathfinder Assoc., 1947-; British League of Rights, 1970-. FRAeS. Oswald Watt Medallist, 1938, 1946; Johnston Memorial Trophy, 1937-38. Order of Alexander Nevsky, 1944. *Publications:* Complete Air Navigator, 1935, 7th edn. 1967; Air Mariner, 1937, 2nd edn 1943; Freedom from War, 1945; Pathfinder, 1958; Let us try Democracy, 1970. *Recreations:* tennis, ski-ing, car racing, sailing. *Address:* Fairthorpe, Denham, Uxbridge; Monte Carlo; Brisbane. *Club:* Royal Air Force.
See also Sir Arnold Bennett.

BENNETT, Air Vice-Marshal Erik Peter; Commander, Sultan of Oman's Air Force, since 1974; *b* 3 Sept. 1928; *s* of Robert Francis and Anne Myra Bennett. *Educ:* The King's Hospital, Dublin. Air Adviser to King Hussein, 1961-62; RAF Staff College, 1963; Jt Services Staff Coll., 1971. Order of Istiqlal (Jordan), 1960; Order of Oman, 1980. *Recreations:* riding, sailing. *Address:* PO Box 6803, Muscat. *Club:* Royal Air Force.

BENNETT, Sir Frederic (Mackarness), Kt 1964; MP (C) Torbay, since 1974 (Reading N, 1951-55; Torquay, Dec. 1955-1974); *b* 2 Dec. 1918; 2nd *s* of late Sir Ernest Bennett and Lady (Marguerite) Bennett; *m* 1945, Marion Patricia, *e d* of Cecil Burnham, OBE, FRCSE. *Educ:* Westminster. Served War of 1939-45, enlisted Middx Yeo., 1939; commissioned RA, 1940; Military Experimental Officer in Petroleum Warfare Dept, 1943-46, when released to reserve with rank of Major. Called to English Bar, Lincoln's Inn, 1946, Southern Rhodesian Bar, 1947. Visited Greece as guest of Greek Govt, 1947 and 1949, to observe Communist war there and children's refugee camps. Retained as diplomatic correspondent, Birmingham Post, Jan. 1950 until election to Parliament. Contested (C) Burslem, 1945, Ladywood Div. of Birmingham, 1950. PPS: to Under-Sec. of State, Home Office, 1953-55, to Minister of Supply, 1956-57, to Paymaster-Gen., 1957-59, and to Pres. of Bd of Trade, 1959-61. Leader, British Delegation to Council of Europe and WEU, 1979-. Chm., Foreign Affairs Res. Inst. Chm., Bank Credit Commerce International (Hong Kong); Director: Kleinwort Benson Europe SA; Arawak Trust Co. Ltd (Bahamas); Squibb A/S; Commercial Union Assurance Co. Ltd, West End and Exeter Bds; Arawak Trust (Caymans) Ltd; Gibraltar Building Soc. Lord of the Manor of Mawddwy. Comdr, Order of Phœnix, Greece, 1963; (Sithari) Star of Pakistan, 1st cl., 1964; Commander, Polonia Restituta, Poland, 1977; Order of Al-Istiqlal, 1st cl., Jordan, 1980. *Recreations:* shooting, fishing, ski-ing. *Address:* Cwmllecoediog, Aberangell, Powys. *T:* Cemmaes Road 430; Kingswear Castle, South Devon; 2 Stone Buildings, Lincoln's Inn, WC2. *Club:* Carlton.

BENNETT, (Frederick Onslow) Alexander (Godwyn), TD; Chairman: Whitbread & Co. Ltd, 1972-77; Whitbread Investment Co. Ltd, since 1977; *b* 21 Dec. 1913; *s* of Alfred Bennett, banker and Marjorie Muir Bremner; *m* 1942, Rosemary, *d* of Sir Malcolm Perks, 2nd Bt, and of Neysa Gilbert (*née* Cheney); one *s* four *d. Educ:* Winchester Coll.; Trinity Coll., Cambridge (BA). Commnd 2nd Bn London Rifle Bde TA, 1938; Lt-Col 1944, GSO1 SHAEF and 21 Army Gp (despatches). Joined Whitbread & Co. Ltd, 1935: Man. Dir, 1949; Dep. Chm., 1958; Chief Exec., 1967-75. Master, Brewers' Company, 1963-64; Chm., Brewers' Soc., 1972-74. US Bronze Star, 1944. *Recreations:* shooting, gardening, the countryside, music. *Address:* Grove House, Selling, Faversham, Kent ME13 9RN. *T:* Selling 250. *Clubs:* Brooks's, MCC.

BENNETT, Captain Geoffrey Martin, DSC 1944; RN retired; *b* 7 June 1909; *s* of late Rear-Adm. Martin Gilbert Bennett, and late Ella Esme Geraldine Bennett (*née* Hicks); *m* 1932, Rosemary Alys (*née* Béchervaise); two *s. Educ:* Royal Naval Coll., Dartmouth, 1923-26; Flag Lieut, Second Cruiser Squadron, Home Fleet, 1938-40; Fleet Signal Officer, S Atlantic, 1940-42; Signal Officer to Adm. Comdg Force H, 1943; Sig. Off. to Flag Officer Levant and E Med., 1943-44; Admlty, 1945-47; HMS Ajax, 1947-48; HMS St Bride's Bay, 1948-49; COHQ, 1949-51; Admiralty, 1951-53; Naval Attaché, Moscow, Warsaw and Helsinki, 1953-55; CSO to CINCHAN, 1956-58; City Marshal. Common Cryer and Serjeant-at-Arms (London), 1958-60. Secretary to Lord Mayor of Westminster, 1960-74; Vis. Lectr on War Studies, Univ. of Fredericton, NB, 1973. Gold Medal and Trench-Gascoigne Prize of RUSI, 1934, 1942 and 1943. FRHistS, 1963. Order of Orange Nassau, 1972. *Publications:* By Human Error, 1961; Coronel and Falklands, 1962; Cowans' War, 1963; Battle of Jutland, 1964; Charlie B: biography of Admiral Lord Beresford, 1968; Naval Battles of First World

War, 1968; Nelson the Commander, 1972; Battle of the River Plate, 1972; Loss of the 'Prince of Wales' and 'Repulse', 1973; Naval Battles of World War Two, 1975; Battle of Trafalgar, 1977; *novels*: (under Pseudonym "Sea-Lion"): Phantom Fleet, 1946; Sink Me the Ship, 1947; Sea of Troubles, 1947; Cargo for Crooks, 1948; When Danger Threatens, 1949; Invisible Ships, 1950; This Creeping Evil, 1950; Quest of John Clare, 1951; Diamond Rock, 1952; Meet Desmond Drake, 1952; Damn Desmond Drake!, 1953; Desmond Drake Goes West, 1956; Death in Russian Habit, 1958; Operation Fireball, 1959; Down Among the Dead Men, 1961; Death in the Dog Watches, 1962; also books for children; radio scripts, etc. *Address*: Stage Coach Cottage, 57 Broad Street, Ludlow, Shropshire SY8 1NH. *T*: Ludlow 3863.

BENNETT, Harry Graham, QC 1968; **His Honour Judge Bennett**; a Circuit Judge, since 1972; *b* 19 Sept. 1921; *s* of Ernest and Alice Mary Bennett, Cleckheaton, Yorks. *Educ*: Whitcliffe Mount Grammar Sch., Cleckheaton; King's Coll., London. Royal Artillery, 1943-47. Called to Bar, Gray's Inn, 1948. Recorder: Doncaster, 1966-68; York, 1968-71; Crown Court, 1972; Dep. Chm., ER of Yorks QS, 1964-71. Chm., Agricl Land Tribunal (N Area), 1967-72. *Address*: c/o Leeds Crown Court, Leeds LS2 7DG. *Club*: Leeds (Leeds).

BENNETT, Sir Hubert, Kt 1970; FRIBA; Architect in private practice; Architect to UNESCO Headquarters, Paris, since 1980; former Architect to the Greater London Council (formerly London County Council) and Superintending Architect of Metropolitan Buildings, 1956-71; *b* 4 Sept. 1909; *s* of late Arthur Bennett and Eleanor Bennett; *m* 1939, Louise F. C. Aldred; three *d*. *Educ*: Victoria University, Manchester, School of Architecture. Asst Lecturer, Leeds School of Architecture, 1933-35; Asst Lecturer, Regent Street Polytechnic Sch. of Architecture, 1935-40; Superintending Architect (Lands), War Dept, 1940-43; Borough Architect, Southampton, 1943-45; County Architect, W Riding of Yorks, 1945-56. Exec. Dir, English Property Corp. Ltd, 1971-79. Mem. of Council, RIBA, 1952-55, 1957-62, 1965-66, 1967-69; Hon. Treas. RIBA, 1959-62; Pres., W Yorks Soc. of Architects, 1954-66; Chm., Technical Panel, Standing Conf. on London Regional Planning, 1962-64; Member: Building Res. Bd, 1959-66; Timber Res. and Develt Assoc. Adv. Panel, 1965-68; Housing Study Mission from Britain to Canada, 1968. Dir, Help the Aged Housing Assoc. (UK) Ltd. Prof., Univ of NSW, 1973. Architect for the Hyde Park Corner-Marble Arch Improvement Scheme, Crystal Palace Recreational Centre and South Bank Arts Centre; RIBA Assessor, South Bank Competition, Vauxhall Cross, 1981. RIBA: Silver Medallist for Measured Drawings (Hon. Mention), 1932; Arthur Cates Prize, 1933; Sir John Soane Medallist, 1934; Neale Bursar, 1936; Godwin and Wimperis Bursar, 1948; RIBA London Architecture Bronze Medal, 1959; RIBA Bronze Medal, 1968. Royal Society of Arts Medal, 1934; Rome Scholarship Special Award, 1936; Min. of Housing and Local Govt Housing Medal, 1954, 1963, 1964, 1966, 1968; Civic Trust Awards; Sir Patrick Abercrombie Award (for planning project Thamesmead), Internat. Union of Architects, 1969; Fritz Schumacher Prize, 1970. Hon. Member: Architects in Industry Group; Inst. of Architects of Czechoslovakia; Soc. of Architects of Venezuela. *Address*: Shepherds Close, Munstead Park, Godalming, Surrey. *T*: Godalming 28828.

BENNETT, James; *b* 18 Dec. 1912; *s* of Samuel and Elizabeth Bennett; *m* 1st, 1936, Dorothy Maclaren (marr. diss. 1980); one *s* one *d*; 2nd, 1980, Lilian Alice Cook. *Educ*: Grove Street Primary and North Kelvinside Secondary Schs., Glasgow. Councillor, Glasgow, 1947-62. Magistrate, 1950-52, Police Judge, 1952-62, JP, 1962-73. MP (Lab) Bridgeton Div. of Glasgow, Nov. 1961-Feb. 1974; PPS to Sec. of State for Scotland, 1964-67. *Recreations*: reading, bowls, gardening. *Address*: 27 Shepley Court, 50 Aldrington Road, SW16 1TT.

BENNETT, Jill; actress; *b* Penang, SS, 24 Dec. 1931; *d* of Randle and Nora Bennett; *m* 1st, 1962, Willis Hall, *qv* (marr. diss., 1965); 2nd, 1968, John Osborne, *qv* (marr. diss. 1977). *Educ*: Tortington Park; Priors Field. Stratford-upon-Avon, 1949-50. First London appearance in Captain Carvallo, St James's Theatre, 1950; Iras in Anthony and Cleopatra, and Caesar and Cleopatra (Olivier Season), St James's, 1951; Helen Elliot in Night of the Ball, New, 1955; Masha in The Seagull, Saville, 1956; Sarah Stanham in The Touch of Fear, Aldwych, 1956; Isabelle in Dinner with the Family, New, 1957; Penelope in Last Day in Dream Land, Lyric, Hammersmith, 1959; Feemy Evans and Lavinia in Shaw double bill, Mermaid, 1961; Estelle in In Camera, Oxford Playhouse, 1962; Ophelia in Castle in Sweden, Piccadilly, 1962; Hilary and Elizabeth in double bill of Squat Betty and The Sponge Room, Royal Court, 1962; The Countess in A Patriot for Me, Royal Court, 1965; Anna Bowers in A Lily of Little India, St Martin's, 1965; Katrina in The Storm, and Imogen Parrott in Trelawney of the Wells, National, 1966; Pamela in Time Present, Royal Court (and later) Duke of York's, 1968 (won Evening Standard Award and Variety Club's Best Actress Award); Anna in Three Months Gone, Royal Court and Duchess, 1970; West of Suez, Royal Court and Cambridge, 1971; Hedda Gabler, Royal Court, 1972; Leslie in The Letter, Palace, Watford, 1973; Amanda in Private Lives, Globe, 1973; The End of Me Old Cigar, Greenwich, 1975; Loot, Royal Court, 1975; Watch It Come Down, National, 1976; Separate Tables, Apollo, 1977; The Aspern Papers, Chichester, 1978; The Eagle has Two Heads, The Man Who Came to Dinner, Chichester, 1979; Hamlet, Royal Court, 1980; The Little Foxes, Nottingham Playhouse, 1981. *Films include*: Lust for Life; The Nanny; The Criminal; The Charge of the Light Brigade; Inadmissible Evidence; Julius Caesar (Calpurnia); I Want What I Want; Quilp; Full Circle; For Your Eyes Only;

Britannia Hospital. Numerous TV appearances in classical works, etc *Recreations*: riding, water ski-ing, ski-ing, having holidays, collecting paintings. *Address*: 91 Regent Street, W1.

BENNETT, Joan, MA; Life Fellow of Girton College, Cambridge; Lecture in English, Cambridge University, 1936-64; *b* 26 June 1896; *d* of Arthu Frankau and of Julia Frankau (Frank Danby); *m* 1920, Henry Stanley Bennet (*d* 1972), FBA; one *s* three *d*. *Educ*: Wycombe Abbey; Girton Coll. Cambridge. Visiting Lectr in the University of Chicago, 1952, 1955, and 1958 Warton Lecturer (Brit. Acad.), 1958; Rose Mary Crawshay Prize (Brit Acad.), 1963. Fellow, Folger Library, 1961. *Publications*: Five Metaphysica Poets, 1965 (formerly Four Metaphysical Poets, 1934); Virginia Woolf; He Art as a Novelist, 1945, 2nd edn enl. 1964; George Eliot: Her Mind and her Art, 1948; Sir Thomas Browne, 1962; The Love Poetry of John Donn (chapter in Seventeenth Century Studies), 1938. *Address*: Church Rate Corner, Cambridge. *T*: Cambridge 353571.

See also C. F. Eccleshare, J. P. W. Gaskell.

BENNETT, Joan; Actress (films and plays); *b* 27 Feb. 1910; *d* of Richard Bennett and Adrienne Morrison; *m* 1st, 1926, John Fox (marr. diss., 1928; h *d* 1963); one *d*; 2nd, 1932, Gene Markey (marr. diss., 1936; he *d* 1980); one *d*; 3rd, 1940, Walter Wanger (marr. diss., at Juarez, Mexico, 1965; he *d* 1968) two *d*; *m* 1978, David Wilde. *Educ*: St Margaret's Sch., Waterbury, Conn. Mlle Lataple's, Versailles, France. *Films include*: (first film) Bulldog Drummond, 1929; Three Live Ghosts; Disraeli; Little Women; Pursuit o Happiness; Private Worlds; The Man in the Iron Mask; Margin for Error Woman in the Window; Man Hunt; Scarlet Street; Father of the Bride. *Play include*: (first play) Jarnegan, 1928; Bell, Book and Candle; We're no Angels Love Me Little; Butterflies are Free; Never too Late, Prince of Wales Theatre London, 1963. Has appeared on Television: (series) Too Young to go Steady Dark Shadows. *Publication*: The Bennett Playbill (with Lois Kibbee), 1970 *Recreation*: interior decorating. *Address*: 67 Chase Road, Scarsdale North NY 10583, USA.

BENNETT, John, MBE 1945; HM Senior Chief Inspector of Schools fo Scotland, 1969-73; *b* 14 Nov. 1912; *m* 1940, Johanne R. McAlpine, MA; two *s* one *d*. *Educ*: Edinburgh Univ. MA (first class hons) 1934. Schoolmaster unti 1951. Served War of 1939-45: Capt. REME, 79 Armd Div., 1940-46. HM Inspector of Schools, 1951. *Recreations*: mathematics, golf, bridge. *Address* 35 Cadzow Drive, Cambuslang, Glasgow G72 8NF. *T*: 041-641 1058.

BENNETT, John Sloman, CMG 1955; *b* 22 Nov. 1914; *y s* of late Ralph Bennett, FRCVS, and Constance Elkington; *m* 1955, Mary Fisher (*see* Mrs M. L. S. Bennett). *Educ*: Royal Liberty Sch., Romford; Magdalene Coll. Cambridge (Schol.). 1st cl. historical tripos, 1935. Entered Colonial Office 1936; seconded to Office of Minister of State in Middle East, 1944-45; Ass Sec., Colonial Office, 1946; Imperial Defence College, 1953; served Commonwealth Office, subsequently FCO, after merger of Colonial Office in 1966; retired 1976. *Address*: Rock Cottage, Thursley, Surrey. *Club*: United Oxford & Cambridge University.

BENNETT, Rt. Rev. Manu Augustus, CMG 1981; DD; *b* 10 Feb. 1916; of Rt Rev. F. A. Bennett, Bishop of Aotearoa, 1928-50, and Alice Rangioue Bennett; *m* 1944, Kathleen Clark; one *d*. *Educ*: Victoria Univ. Coll., Univ of Hawaii. BSc 1954. Deacon, 1939; Priest, 1940; Vicar of Tauranga, Te Puk Maori District, Dio. Waiapu, 1940-44; Chaplain to 2 NZEF, 1944-46; Pasto of Rangitikei South-Manawatu Pastorate, Dio. Wellington, 1946-52; Ass Vicar of Church of Holy Nativity, Honolulu, 1953-54; Pastor of Wellington Pastorate, 1952-57; Vicar of Ohinemutu Pastorate, Waikato, 1964-68; Bishop of Aotearoa, 1968-81. Nat. Council of Churches Chaplain, Dept of Justice Hon. DD Jackson Coll., 1964. *Address*: PO Box 115, Te Puke, New Zealand.

See also Sir C. M. Bennett.

BENNETT, Mrs Mary Letitia Somerville, MA; Principal, St Hilda' College, Oxford, 1965-80, Hon. Fellow 1980; Pro-Vice-Chancellor, Oxfor University, 1979-80; *b* 9 Jan. 1913; *o c* of Rt Hon. H. A. L. Fisher, OM, an Lettice Ilbert; *m* 1955, John Sloman Bennett, *qv*. *Educ*: Oxford High Sch Somerville Coll. (Schol.); 2nd Cl. Mods, 1st Cl. Lit. Hum.; Hon. Fellow 1977. Mary Ewart Travelling Schol., 1936-37; Jt Broadcasting Cttee, 1940-41 Transcription Service of BBC, 1941-45; Colonial Office, 1945-56. Mem Hebdomodal Council, Oxford Univ., 1973-79. Hon. Sec., Society for the Promotion of Roman Studies, 1960-. *Address*: Rock Cottage, Thursley Surrey. *Club*: University Women's.

BENNETT, Patrick, QC 1969; a Recorder of the Crown Court, since 1972 *b* 12 Jan. 1924; *s* of Michael Bennett; *m* 1951, Lyle Reta Pope; two *d*. *Educ* Bablake Sch., Coventry; Magdalen Coll., Oxford. State Scholar, 1941, MA BCL 1949. Served RNVR, 1943-46. Sub Lt. Called to Bar, Gray's Inn, 1949 Bencher 1976, Master of Students, 1980; Asst Recorder, Coventry, 1969-71 Dep. Chm., Lindsey QS, 1970-71. *Publication*: Assessment of Damages i Personal Injury and Fatal Accidents, 1980. *Recreations*: food, flying. *Address* (home) 22 Wynnstay Gardens, W8. *T*: 01-937 2110; 233 rue Nationale Boulogne sur Mer, France. *T*: 21 91 33 39; (professional) 2 Crown Office Row, Temple, EC4. *T*: 01-236 9337. *Clubs*: Hurlingham; Spartan Flying (Denham).

BENNETT, Peter Ward, OBE; Chairman, SLS Environetics International Ltd, since 1981; Director: Lloyds & Scottish Ltd, since 1979; THORN EMI Ltd, since 1977; Chairman, W. H. Smith & Son Ltd, 1977-82. *Address:* SLS Environetics International Ltd, 23 Eastcastle Street, W1. *T:* 01-580 1214.

BENNETT, Philip Hugh Penberthy, CBE 1972; FRIBA; Consultant, T. P. Bennett & Son, architects, since 1980 (Partner 1948-80, Senior Partner, 1967-80); *b* 14 April 1919; *o s* of late Sir Thomas Penberthy Bennett, KBE, FRIBA, and late Mary Langdon Edis; *m* 1943, Jeanne Heal; one *s* one *d. Educ:* Highgate Sch.; Emmanuel Coll., Cambridge (MA). Lieut (G) RNVR, 1940-46. Principal works: town centres at Bootle and Stratford (London); head offices for Norwich Union Insce Socs, Ford Motor Co. and other commercial cos; dept stores for United Africa Co. in Ghana and Nigeria, Bentalls (Kingston) and Fenwicks (Newcastle); extensions to Middlesex Hosp.; hostel for Internat. Students Trust; Cunard Internat. Hotel; flats for local authorities and private developers; buildings for airfield and dock develt. Chm., Building Regulations Adv. Cttee (DoE), 1965-77; former RIBA rep. on Jt Contracts Tribunal (Chm. 1973-78) and Nat. Jt Consultative Cttee (Chm. 1970); Mem. other cttees of RIBA and NEDO; Governor: Sch. of Building, 1952-72; Vauxhall Coll. of Further Educn, 1972-77; Member: Home Office Deptl Cttee enquiring into Fire Service, 1967-70; Adv. Council for Energy Conservation, 1974-76. *Publications:* Architectural Practice and Procedure, 1981; chapter on building, in Britain 1984, 1963; articles in Building, Financial Times, etc. *Recreations:* travel, drawing, theatre. *Address:* Grey Walls, Park Lane, Aldeburgh, Suffolk. *T:* Aldeburgh 2766.

BENNETT, Ralph Featherstone; *b* 3 Dec. 1923; *o s* of late Mr and Mrs Ralph J. P. Bennett, Plymouth, Devon; *m* 1948, Delia Marie, *o d* of late Mr and Mrs J. E. Baxter, Franklyns, Plymouth; two *s* two *d. Educ:* Plympton Grammar Sch.; Plymouth Technical Coll. Articled pupil to City of Plymouth Transport Manager, 1940-43; Techn. Asst, Plymouth City Transp., 1943-54; Michelin Tyre Co., 1954-55; Dep. Gen. Man., City of Plymouth Transp. Dept, 1955-58; Gen. Manager: Gt Yarmouth Transp. Dept, 1958-60; Bolton Transp. Dept, 1960-65; Manchester City Transp., 1965-68; London Transport Executive (formerly London Transport Board): Mem., 1968-71; Dep. Chm., 1971-78; Chief Exec., 1975-78; Chairman: London Transport Executive, 1978-80; London Transport International, 1976-80. Pres., Confedn of Road Passenger Transport, 1977-78; Vice-President: Internat. Union of Public Transport, 1978-; CIT, 1979-. CEng; FIMechE; FCIT; FRSA. *Address:* Buffers, Green Lane, Yelverton, South Devon. *T:* Yelverton 2153. *Club:* National Liberal.

BENNETT, Sir Reginald (Frederick Brittain), Kt 1979; VRD 1944; MA Oxon; BM, BCh, 1942; LMSSA 1937; DPM 1948; Grand Officer, Italian Order of Merit, 1977; company director and wine consultant; formerly psychiatrist; *b* 22 July 1911; *e s* of late Samuel Robert Bennett and Gertrude (*née* Brittain); *m* 1947, Henrietta, *d* of Capt. H. B. Crane, CBE, RN; one *s* three *d. Educ:* Winchester Coll.; New College, Oxford. Oxford Univ. Air Squadron, 1931-34; RNVR, 1934-46; Fleet Air Arm, Medical Officer and Pilot; torpedoed twice. St George's Hosp., SW1, 1934-37; Maudsley Hosp., SE5, 1947-49. MP(C) Gosport and Fareham, 1950-74, Fareham, 1974-79; PPS to Rt Hon. Iain Macleod, MP, 1956-63; Chairman: House of Commons Catering Sub-Cttee, 1970-74, 1976-79 (Dep. Chm., 1974-76); Anglo-Italian Parly Gp, 1971-79 (Hon. Sec. 1961-71); Parly and Scientific Cttee, 1959-62. Vice-Pres, Franco-British Parly Relations Cttee, 1973-79; Rapporteur on the Ocean Floor and Seabed, Inter-Parly Conf., The Hague, 1970; Leader, Parly Delegn to: Iceland 1965; European Parliament, Strasbourg, 1971; Conf. on Mediterranean Pollution, Rome, 1974 and Monaco, 1975; Détente Conf., Belgrade, 1977. Mem. Council, Internat. Inst. of Human Nutrition, 1975-. President: Brit. Launderers' Research Association, 1960-77; Southern Boroughs Assoc., 1950-73; Club Oenologique, 1976-77. Helmsman: Shamrock V, 1934-35; Evaine, 1936-38; Olympic Games (reserve), 1936; in British-American Cup Team, 1949 and 1953 in USA; various trophies since. Chairman: Amateur Yacht Research Soc., 1972-; World Sailing Speed Record Cttee, RYA, 1980- (Vice-Chm., 1979-80). Hon. Lieut-Col, Georgia Militia, 1960; Hon. Citizen of Atlanta, Ga, 1960. Commandeur du Bontemps-Médoc, 1959; Chevalier du Tastevin, 1970; Galant de la Verte Marennes; Chevalier de St Etienne, Alsace, 1971; Chevalier Bretvin (Muscadet), 1973. *Publications:* articles on wine, medicine, psychiatry, politics and yacht racing. *Recreations:* sailing, painting, foreign travel, basking in the sun, avoiding exercise. *Address:* 30 Strand-on-the-Green, W4. *Clubs:* White's; Anchorites; Imperial Poona Yacht (Cdre); Wykehamist Sailing (Cdre); Royal Colombo Yacht; Bembridge Sailing, etc.

BENNETT, Richard Rodney, CBE 1977; composer; Member of General Council, Performing Right Society, since 1975; *b* 29 March 1936; *s* of H. Rodney and Joan Esther Bennett. *Educ:* Leighton Park Sch., Reading; Royal Academy of Music. Works performed, 1953-, at many Festivals in Europe, S Africa, USA, Canada, Australia, etc. Has written music for numerous films including: Indiscreet; The Devil's Disciple; Only Two Can Play; The Wrong Arm of the Law; Heavens Above; Billy Liar; One Way Pendulum; The Nanny; Far from the Madding Crowd; Billion Dollar Brain; Secret Ceremony; The Buttercup Chain; Figures in a Landscape; Nicholas and Alexandra; Lady Caroline Lamb; Voices; Murder on the Orient Express (SFTA award, 1975; Academy Award Nomination, 1975; Ivor Novello award, PRS, 1976); Permission to Kill; Equus (BAFTA Nomination, 1978); Sherlock Holmes in New York; L'Imprecateur; The Brinks Job; Yanks (BAFTA Nomination, 1980); also the music for Television series, Hereward

the Wake; The Christians. Commissioned to write 2 full-length operas for Sadler's Wells: The Mines of Sulphur, 1965, A Penny for a Song, 1968; commnd to write opera for Covent Garden: Victory, 1970; (children's opera) All the King's Men, 1969; Guitar Concerto, 1970; Spells (choral work), 1975. *Publications include:* chamber music, orchestral music, educational music, song cycles, etc; articles for periodicals, about music. *Recreations:* cinema, modern jazz. *Address:* c/o Mrs Keys, London Management, Regent House, 235 Regent Street, W1.

BENNETT, Ronald Alistair, QC (Scotland) 1959; Sheriff-Principal of South Strathclyde, Dumfries and Galloway, since 1981; Vice-President for Scotland, Value Added Tax Tribunals, since 1977; *b* 11 Dec. 1922; *s* of Arthur George Bennett, MC and Edythe Sutherland; *m* 1950, Margret Magnusson, *d* of Sigursteinn Magnusson, Icelandic Consul-Gen. for Scotland; three *s* three *d. Educ:* Edinburgh Academy; Edinburgh Univ.; Balliol Coll., Oxford. MA, LLB Univ. of Edinburgh, 1942; Muirhead and Dalgety Prizes for Civil Law, 1942. Lieut, 79th (Scottish Horse) Medium Regt RA, 1943-45; Capt. attached RAOC, India and Japan, 1945-46. Called to Scottish Bar, 1947; Vans Dunlop Schol. in Scots Law and Conveyancing, 1948; Standing Counsel to Min. of Labour and National Service, 1957-59; Sheriff-Principal of Roxburgh, Berwick and Selkirk, 1971-74. Lectr in Mercantile Law: Edinburgh Univ., 1956-68; Heriot-Watt Univ., 1968-75. Chairman: Med. Appeal Tribunals (Scotland), 1971-; Agricultural Wages Bd for Scotland, 1973-; Local Govt Boundaries Commn for Scotland, 1974-; Northern Lighthouse Bd, April-Sept. 1974; Industrial Tribunals, (Scotland), 1977-. Arbiter, Motor Insurers' Bureau appeals, 1975-; Mem., Scottish Medical Practices Cttee, 1976-. *Publications:* Bennett's Company Law, 2nd edn, 1950; Fraser's Rent Acts in Scotland, 2nd edn 1952; Editor: Scottish Current Law and Scots Law Times Sheriff Court Reports, 1948-74; Court of Session Reports, 1976-. *Recreations:* shooting, swimming, reading, music, gardening. *Address:* Laxamyri, 46 Cammo Road, Barnton, Edinburgh EH4 8AP. *T:* 031-339 6111. *Club:* New (Edinburgh).

BENNETT, Sir Ronald (Wilfred Murdoch), 3rd Bt, *cr* 1929; *b* 25 March 1930; *o s* of Sir Wilfred Bennett, 2nd Bt, and Marion Agnes (OBE 1953), *d* of late James Somervell, Sorn Castle, Ayrshire, and step *d* of late Edwin Sandys Dawes; *S* father 1952; *m* 1st, 1953, Rose-Marie Audrey Patricia, *o d* of Major A. L. J. H. Aubépin, France and Co. Mayo, Ireland; two *d*; 2nd, 1968, Anne, *d* of late Leslie George Tooker. *Educ:* Wellington Coll.; Trinity Coll., Oxford. *Heir:* cousin Michael Bennett [*b* 15 Feb. 1924; *m* 1952, Jane Hazel Margaret, *d* of Brig. E. J. Todhunter, TD; one *s* two *d*]. *Clubs:* Kampala, Uganda (Kampala).

BENNETT, Roy Grissell, CMG 1971; Chairman, Maclaine Watson & Co. Ltd, London and Singapore, 1970-72 (Director, 1958-72), retired; Chairman: Pilkington (South East Asia) Private Ltd; Beder International and Beder Malaysia; Director, Vosper Pte Ltd, Warship Builders, Singapore; *b* 21 Nov. 1917. *Educ:* RMC Sandhurst. Served War of 1939-45, 17th/21st Lancers (Major). Joined J. H. Vavasseur & Co. Ltd, Penang, 1946; Director, 1949; joined Maclaine, Watson & Co. Ltd, Singapore 1952, Dir London Board 1958, Man. Dir, Eastern interests, 1960; Director Fibreglass Pilkington Ltd (Chm.), and other cos; retired from Singapore Internat. Chamber of Commerce (Chm. 1967-68, 1969-70); Singapore Chamber of Commerce Rubber Assoc. (Chm. 1960-63); Rubber Assoc. of Singapore (past Chm., Dep. Chm. 1966-72); Mem. Council, Singapore Anti-Tuberculosis Assoc.; Founder and Past Chm. Governors, United World Coll., SE Asia; Chm., Racehorse Spelling Station, Cameron Highlands, Malaysia; Patron, Nat. Kidney Foundn. MInstD. *Recreations:* economics, commercial, polo, racing, shooting, swimming, photography, motoring, safaris, camping, gardening, zoology, boating, reading, travelling, people especially of the East, social welfare. *Address:* Beder International, PO Box 49, Bukit Panjang, Singapore; 22 Jalan Perdana, Johore Baru, Malaysia. *T:* Johore Baru 24505. *Clubs:* Cavalry and Guards; Tanglin, Town, Turf (Dep. Chm.), Polo (Patron; Past Chm.), Foreign Correspondents' (Singapore); Turf, Polo (Penang).

BENNETT, Sir William Gordon, Kt 1955; Member of Glasgow Royal Exchange; Member of the Glasgow Trades House. Formerly a Magistrate and Member of Glasgow Corporation. Past President of the Scottish Unionist Association. Contested (C) Shettleston Division of Glasgow, July 1945. MP (C) Woodside Division of Glasgow, 1950-55. Served European War, 1914-18 (wounded); Officer in the Tank Corps. *Address:* 3 Hillside Road, Glasgow G43 1DE.

BENNETT, William John, OBE 1946; LLD; retired 1977; Consultant, Iron Ore Company of Canada, Montreal; Chairman: Phillips Canada Ltd; C. D. Howe Institute; Director: Canadian Reynolds Metals Co. Ltd; The Investors Group; Eldorado Nuclear Ltd; Canron Inc.; Cominco Ltd; Canadian Pacific Ltd; Peterson, Howell & Heather Canada Inc.; *b* 3 Nov. 1911; *s* of Carl Edward Bennett and Mary Agnes Downey; *m* 1936, Elizabeth Josephine Palleck; three *s* four *d. Educ:* University of Toronto (BA Hons). Private Sec., Minister of Transport, 1935-39; Chief Exec. Asst to Minister of Munitions and Supply, 1939-46; President: Atomic Energy of Canada Ltd, 1953-58; Canadian British Aluminium Co. Ltd, 1958-60. Eldorado Mining & Refining Ltd, 1946-58. Hon. LLD, Toronto Univ., 1955; Hon. Dr of Science, St Francis Xavier Univ., Antigonish, NS, 1956; Hon Dr of Laws, University of Ottawa, 1957. *Recreations:* ski-ing, music. *Address:* 1321 Sherbrooke Street West, Apt F41, Montreal, Quebec H3G 1J4, Canada. *Clubs:* Mount Royal, Canadian (Montreal).

BENNETT, Hon. William Richards, PC (Can.); Premier of British Columbia, since Dec. 1975; *b* 1932; *y s* late Hon. William Andrew Cecil Bennett, PC (Can.) and of Annie Elizabeth May, *d* of J. A. Richards, Edmonton, Alta; *m* Audrey; four *s*. Began a business career. Elected MP for Okanagan South (succeeding to a constituency which had been held by his father), 1973; Leader of Social Credit Group in Provincial House, 1973; formed Social Credit Govt after election of Dec. 1975. *Address:* Provincial House of Legislature, Victoria, BC V8V 4R3, Canada.

BENNEY, Prof. (Adrian) Gerald (Sallis), RDI 1971; goldsmith and silversmith; Professor of Silversmithing and Jewellery, Royal College of Art, since 1974; *b* 21 April 1930; *s* of late Ernest Alfred Benney and Aileen Mary Benney; *m* 1957, Janet Edwards; three *s* one *d*. *Educ:* Brighton Grammar Sch.; Brighton Coll. of Art (Nat. Dip. in Art); RCA (DesRCA). FSIAD 1975. Estabd 1st workshop, Whitfield Place, London, 1955; Consultant Designer, Viners Ltd, 1957-69; began designing and making Reading civic plate, 1963; discovered technique of texturing on silver, 1964; moved workshop to Bankside, London, 1969; began prodn of Beenham Enamels, 1970. Holds Royal Warrants of Appt to the Queen, the Duke of Edinburgh, Queen Elizabeth the Queen Mother and the Prince of Wales. Mem., Govt's Craft Adv. Cttee, 1972-77; Metalwork Design Advisor to Indian Govt (UP State), 1977-78; Mem., UK Atomic Energy Ceramics Centre Adv. Cttee, 1979-. Liveryman, 1964, and Mem., Court of Assistants, Worshipful Co. of Goldsmiths; Major Exhibn, Worshipful Co. of Goldsmiths, 1973. Hon. MA Leicester, 1963. *Recreations:* walking, barging, landscape gardening. *Address:* Beenham House, Beenham, Berks RG7 5LJ. *T:* Reading 744370. *Club:* Arts.

BENNION, Francis Alan Roscoe; writer and lecturer; *b* 2 Jan. 1923; *o s* of Thomas Roscoe Bennion, Liverpool; *m* 1st, 1951, Barbara Elisabeth Braendle (separated 1971, marr. diss. 1975); three *d*; 2nd, 1977, Mary Field. *Educ:* John Lyon's, Harrow; Balliol Coll., Oxford. Pilot, RAFVR, 1941-46. Gibbs Law Scholar, Oxford, 1948. Called to Bar, Middle Temple, 1951 (Harmsworth Scholar). Lectr and Tutor in Law, St Edmund Hall, Oxford, 1951-53; Office of Parly Counsel, 1953-65, and 1973-75; Dep. Parly Counsel, 1964; Parly Counsel, 1973-75; seconded to Govt of Pakistan to advise on drafting of new Constitution, 1956; seconded to Govt of Ghana to advise on legislation and drafting Constitution converting the country into a Republic, 1959-61. Sec., RICS, 1965-68; Governor, College of Estate Management, 1965-68. Co-founder and first Chm., Professional Assoc. of Teachers, 1968-72; Founder: Statute Law Soc., 1968 (Chm., 1978-79); Freedom Under Law, 1971; Towards One World, 1979; founder and first Chm., World of Property Housing Trust (later WPHT Housing Assoc.), 1968-72. *Publications:* Constitutional Law of Ghana, 1962; Professional Ethics: The Consultant Professions and their Code, 1969; Tangling with the Law, 1970; Consumer Credit Control, 1976-; Consumer Credit Act Manual, 1978, 2nd edn 1981; Statute Law, 1980, 2nd edn 1983. *Recreations:* creation. *Address:* 24 St Aubyns, Hove, East Sussex BN3 2TD. *Club:* MCC.

BENNITT, Mortimer Wilmot; *b* 28 Aug. 1910; *s* of Rev. F. W. and Honoria Bennitt. *Educ:* Charterhouse; Trinity Coll., Oxford. Entered Office of Works, 1934; Private Sec. to Sir Philip Sassoon, 1937-38. Served War of 1939-45: RAF, 1943-45. Under Sec., 1951; Dep. Dir, Land Commn, 1967-71; retired 1971. Chairman: Little Theatre Guild of Gt Britain, 1959-60; Tavistock Repertory Company, London, 1975-77. Patron of St Mary's, Bletchley. *Publication:* Guide to Canonbury Tower, 1980. *Recreation:* travel. *Address:* 3/5 Highbury Grove, N5. *T:* 01-226 5937. *Clubs:* United Oxford & Cambridge University, Tower Theatre.

BENSON, family name of **Baron Benson.**

BENSON, Baron *cr* 1981 (Life Peer), of Drovers in the County of W Sussex; **Henry Alexander Benson,** GBE 1971 (CBE 1946); Kt 1964; FCA; Partner, Coopers and Lybrand (formerly Cooper Brothers & Co.), Chartered Accountants, 1934-75; Adviser to the Governor of the Bank of England, since 1975; *b* 2 Aug. 1909; *s* of Alexander Stanley Benson and Florence Mary (*née* Cooper); *m* 1939, Anne Virginia Macleod; two *s* one *d*. *Educ:* Johannesburg, South Africa. ACA (Hons) 1932; FCA 1939. Commissioned Grenadier Guards, 1940-45; seconded from Army to Min. of Supply to advise on reorganisation of accounts of Royal Ordnance Factories, 1943-44, and in Dec. 1943 apptd Dir Ordnance Factories, to carry out reorganisation; apptd Controller of Building Materials, Min. of Works, 1945; Special appt to advise Minister of Health on housing production, 1945, and subseq. other appts, also Mem. Cttee (Wilson Cttee) to review work done on, and to make recommendations for further research into, processes for transformation of coal into oil, chemicals and gas, 1959-60. Mem. Crawley Development Corp., 1947-50; Mem. Royal Ordnance Factories Board, 1952-56; Dep. Chm. Advisory Cttee (Fleck Cttee) to consider organisation of National Coal Board, 1953-55. Dir Hudson's Bay Co., 1953-62 (Dep. Governor 1955-62); Director: Finance Corporation for Industry Ltd, 1953-79; Industrial and Commercial Finance Corp., 1974-79; Hawker Siddeley Gp, 1975-81; Council, Institute of Chartered Accountants, 1956-75 (Pres., 1966); Mem. Advisory Cttee on Legal Aid, 1956-60; Mem. Tribunal under Prevention of Fraud (Investments) Act 1939, 1957-75; Mem. Special Advisory Cttee to examine structure, finance and working of organisations controlled by British Transport Commission, 1960; apptd by Minister of Commerce, N Ireland, to investigate position of railways; to make recommendations about their future, and to report on effect which recommendations will have on transport system

of Ulster Transport Authority, 1961; apptd Chm. of a Cttee to examine possible economies in the shipping and ancillary services engaged in meat, dairy products and fruit trades of New Zealand, 1962; Mem. Cttee apptd by Chancellor of the Exchequer to investigate practical effects of introduction of a turnover tax, 1963. Chm., Royal Commn on Legal Services, 1976-79. Joint Comr to advise on integration of Nat. Assoc. of Brit. Manufrs, FBI, Brit. Employers' Confed., and on formation of a Nat. Industrial Organisation (CBI), 1963; Joint Inspector, Bd of Trade, to investigate affairs of Rolls Razor Ltd, 1964; Indep. Chm. of British Iron & Steel Fedn Development Co-ordinating Cttee, 1966; Indep. Chm., Internat. Accounting Standards Cttee (IASC), 1973-76; Member: Permanent Jt Hops Cttee, 1967-74; Dockyard Policy Bd, 1970-75; NCB team of inquiry into Bd's purchasing procedures, 1973; CBI Company Affairs Cttee, 1972; Dir, Finance for Industry Ltd, 1974-79; City Liaison Cttee, 1974-75; Chm., Exec. Cttee of Accountants' Jt Disciplinary Scheme to review cases involving public concern, 1979-; Vice-Pres., Union Européene des Experts Comptables économiques et financiers (UEC), 1969; Mem. Cttee to enquire into admin and organisation of MoD. Apptd by Nat. Trust as Chm. of adv. cttee to review management, organisation and responsibilities of Nat. Trust, 1967; apptd by Jt Turf Authorities as Chm. of The Racing Industry Cttee of Inquiry to make detailed study of financial structure and requirements of racing industry, 1967. Treasurer, Open Univ., 1975-79. Trustee, Times Trust, 1967-81. *Recreations:* shooting, golf, sailing. *Address:* 9 Durward House, 31 Kensington Court, W8 5BH. *T:* 01-937 4850. *Clubs:* Brooks's, Jockey; Royal Yacht Squadron.

BENSON, Sir Arthur (Edward Trevor), GCMG 1959 (KCMG 1954; CMG 1952); *b* 21 Dec. 1907; *s* of late Rev. Arthur H. Trevor Benson, Vicar of Ilam, Staffs, formerly of Castle Connell, Co. Limerick and of St Saviour's, Johannesburg, and Emily Maud Malcolmson, Woodlock, Portlaw, Co. Waterford, late of Hanson Mount, Ashbourne, Derbyshire; *m* 1933, Daphne Mary Joyce, *d* of late E. H. M. Fynn, Serui, near Hartley, S Rhodesia; two *d*. *Educ:* Wolverhampton Sch.; Exeter Coll., Oxford. Colonial Administrative Service; Cadet, N Rhodesia, 1932; seconded to Colonial Office, 1939; to Prime Minister's Office, 1940-42; to Cabinet Office, 1942-43; to Colonial Office, 1943-44; Northern Rhodesia, 1944-46; Administrative Sec., Uganda, 1946-49; Chief Sec., Central African Council, 1949-51; Chief Sec. to Govt of Nigeria, 1951-54; Governor of Northern Rhodesia, 1954-59. Hon. Fellow, Exeter Coll., Oxford, 1963. JP Devon, 1962-66. KStJ 1954. *Recreation:* fishing. *Address:* Combe Hill, Combe Raleigh, near Honiton, Devon.

BENSON, Christopher John, JP; FRICS; Vice-Chairman since 1977, Managing Director since 1976, MEPC plc; *b* 20 July 1933; *s* of Charles Woodburn Benson and Catherine Clara (*née* Bishton); *m* 1960, Margaret Josephine, OBE, JP, *d* of Ernest Jefferies Bundy; two *s*. *Educ:* Worcester Cathedral King's Sch.; Thames Nautical Trng Coll., HMS Worcester. FRICS. Director: MEPC plc, 1974-; House of Fraser plc, 1982-. Underwriting Mem. of Lloyds, 1979-; Member: Investment Cttee, British Petroleum Pension Trust, 1979-; West End Board, Sun Alliance and London Insurance Group. Pres., British Property Fedn, 1981-; Mem., Property Adv. Gp, 1982- (Mem., New Towns Adv. Sub-Gp, 1982-). Trustee, Chair of Land Valuation and Management, City Univ.; Trustee, Westminster Christmas Appeal. Mem. Council, Marlborough Coll., 1982-. JP City of London, 1981. Freeman, City of London, 1975. Liveryman: Worshipful Co. of Gold and Silver Wyre Drawers, 1975; Guild of Air Pilots and Air Navigators, 1981. *Recreations:* farming, aviation, swimming. *Address:* Pauls Dene House, Castle Road, Salisbury, Wilts SP1 3RY. *T:* Salisbury 22187. *Clubs:* Naval, Royal Automobile, City Livery.

BENSON, Rev. Sir (Clarence) Irving, Kt 1963; CBE 1960 (OBE 1951); DD; Superintendent of the Wesley Church Central Mission, Melbourne, 1926-67; *b* 1 Dec. 1897; *s* of Walter Benson; *m* 1st, 1919, Agnes Lyell (*d* 1947); three *d*; 2nd, 1967, Marjorie Featonby. *Educ:* Hull Technical Coll.; Hymers Coll. and Private Tutors for Ministry. DD 1939. Minister, Hamilton (Victoria) Circuit, 1916-17; Toorak, 1918-23; Brunswick, 1923-26. Bevan Lectr, 1933; Drew (USA) Lectr, 1944. Pres., Methodist Conf., 1943. Pres., Australian Reading Union; Vice-Pres., Library Association of Victoria; Pres. of Trustees, State Library of Victoria; Chm., Free Library Service Board. *Publications:* The Man with the Donkey; A Century of Victorian Methodism; The Craft of Prayer; The Craft of Finding God; contribs to the Melbourne Herald, 1924-79. *Recreations:* swimming, book collecting. *Address:* 25 Hoddle Street, Elsternwick, Victoria 3185, Australia. *Club:* Melbourne.

BENSON, Maj.-Gen. Edward Riou, CB 1952; CMG 1950; CBE 1945; *b* 4 April 1903; *yr s* of late Brig.-Gen. Riou Philip Benson, CB, CMG, Guildford, Surrey; *m* 1931, Isolda Mary Stuart, *d* of late Gen. Sir John Stuart Mackenzie Shea, GCB, KCMG, DSO; one *s* (one *d* deed). *Educ:* Cheltenham Coll.; RMA Woolwich, 2nd Lieut, Royal Field Artillery, 1923; Lieut, RA, 1925; Capt. 1936; Major 1940; Temp. Lieut-Col 1941; Temp. Brig. 1942; Col 1946; Maj.-Gen. 1951. Served War of 1939-45, North-West Europe, 1944-46. Dep. Dir Mil. Govt (BE), Berlin, 1948-50; Comdr 4 Anti-Aircraft Group, 1951-53; Chief of Staff, GHQ, Middle East Land Forces, 1954-57, retired. Col Commandant, Royal Artillery, 1960-65. *Address:* Well House, Aldermaston, Berks. *T:* Woolhampton 3347.

BENSON, Prof. Frank Atkinson, BEng, MEng (Liverpool); PhD, DEng (Sheffield); FIEE, FIEEE; DL; Professor and Head of Department of Electronic and Electrical Engineering, University of Sheffield, since 1967;

Pro-Vice Chancellor, 1972-76; *b* 21 Nov. 1921; *s* of late John and Selina Benson; *m* 1950, Kathleen May Paskell; two *s*. *Educ:* Ulverston Grammar Sch.; Univ. of Liverpool. Mem. research staff, Admty Signal Estab., Witley, 1943-46; Asst Lectr in Electrical Engrg, University of Liverpool, 1946-49; Lectr 1949-59, Sen. Lectr 1959-61, in Electrical Engrg, University of Sheffield; Reader in Electronics, University of Sheffield, 1961-67. DL South Yorks, 1979. *Publications:* Voltage Stabilizers, 1950; Electrical Engineering Problems with Solutions, 1954; Voltage Stabilized Supplies, 1957; Problems in Electronics with Solutions, 1958; Electric Circuit Theory, 1959; Voltage Stabilization, 1965; Electric Circuit Problems with Solutions, 1967; Millimetre and Submillimetre Waves, 1969; many papers on microwaves, gas discharges and voltage stabilization in learned jls. *Address:* 64 Grove Road, Sheffield S7 2GZ. *T:* Sheffield 363493.

BENSON, Horace Burford; *b* 3 April 1904; *s* of Augustus W. Benson and Lucy M. (*née* Jarrett); *m* 1930, Marthe Lanier; one *s* one *d*. Called to Bar, Gray's Inn, 1936; practised as Barrister, Seychelles Islands, 1936-46; District Magistrate, Ghana, 1946; Puisne Judge, Ghana, 1952-57; retired, 1957. Temp. Magistrate, Basutoland, 1958-60; Puisne Judge, Basutoland, Bechuanaland Protectorate and Swaziland, 1960-61; Chief Justice, Basutoland (now Lesotho), 1965; Puisne Judge, Malawi, 1967-69. *Recreations:* bowls, bridge. *Address:* c/o Barclays Bank Ltd, Tulse Hill, SE27.

BENSON, Rev. Sir Irving; *see* Benson, Rev. Sir C. I.

BENSON, Jeffrey; *see* Benson, W. J.

BENSON, Jeremy Henry; architect in private practice, (Benson & Benson F/ARIBA), since 1954; *b* 25 June 1925; *s* of late Guy Holford Benson and Lady Violet Benson; *m* 1951, Patricia Stewart; two *s* three *d*. *Educ:* Eton; Architectural Assoc. (AADipl.); FRIBA. Royal Engineers, 1944-47. Chm., Georgian Gp, 1980– (Mem., Exec. Cttee, 1967–); Vice-Chairman: Soc. for Protection of Ancient Buildings, 1971– (Mem. Exec. Cttee, 1959–); Joint Cttee of SPAB, GG, Victorian Soc., Civic Trust and Ancient Monuments Soc., 1972– (Mem., 1968–), and Chm. of its Tax Group; Member: Forestry Commn's Westonbirt Adv. Cttee, 1969–; Historic Buildings Council for England, 1974–; Adv. Cttee on Trees in the Royal Parks, 1977-80. *Recreation:* gardening. *Address:* Walpole House, Chiswick Mall, W4 2PS. *T:* 01-994 1611; Field Barn, Taddington, Temple Guiting, Cheltenham, Glos. *T:* Stanton 228. *Club:* Brooks's.

BENSON, Maj.-Gen. Peter Herbert, CBE 1974 (MBE 1954); Member of Panel of Fee-Paid Inspectors, Planning Inspectorate, Departments of Environment and Transport, since 1981; *b* 27 Oct. 1923; *s* of Herbert Kamerer Benson and Edith Doris Benson; *m* 1949, Diana Betty Ashmore; one *s* one *d*. *Educ:* Craig-y-Nos Sch., Swansea; Swansea Techn. Coll. FCIT. Joined Army, 1944; commnd into S Wales Borderers, 1945; transf. to RASC, 1948, and Royal Corps of Transport, 1965; served, Palestine, Cyprus, Malaya and Singapore (three times), Borneo, Africa and Australia; Comdr, 15 Air Despatch Regt, 1966-68; GSO1 (DS) Staff Coll., Camberley, and Australian Staff Coll., 1968-70; Col Q (Movements), MoD (Army), 1971-72; Comdr, 2 Transport Gp RCT (Logistic Support Force), 1972-73. Comdr, ANZUK Support Gp Singapore, Sen. British Officer Singapore, and Leader, UK Jt Services Planning Team, 1973-74; Chief Transport and Movements Officer, BAOR, 1974-76; Dir Gen. of Transport and Movements (Army) (formerly Transport Officer in Chief (Army)), MoD, 1976-78. Chm., Grants Cttee, Army Benevolent Fund. Col Comdt, RCT. *Recreations:* golf, fly-fishing, shooting.

BENSON, (William) Jeffrey, FIB; Director, since 1975 and a Deputy Chairman, 1983, National Westminster Bank plc; *b* 15 July 1922; *s* of Herbert Benson and Lilian (*née* Goodson); *m* 1947, Audrey Winifred Parsons; two *s*. *Educ:* West Leeds High Sch. FIB 1976. Served War, RAF, 1941-46. Joined National Provincial Bank Ltd, 1939; Asst Gen. Manager, 1965-68; National Westminster Bank: Reg. Exec. Dir, 1968-73; Gen. Man., Management Services Div., 1973-75; Dep. Chief Exec., 1975-77; Gp Chief Exec., 1978-82. Chm., Export Guarantees Adv. Council, 1982. *Recreations:* golf, swimming. *Address:* Auben, Spencer Walk, The Drive, Rickmansworth, Herts. *T:* Rickmansworth 78260. *Club:* Clifton (Bristol).

BENTALL, Hugh Henry, MB; FRCS; Professor of Cardiac Surgery, Royal Postgraduate Medical School of London, since 1965; Consultant Thoracic Surgeon, Hammersmith Hospital, since 1955; *b* 28 April 1920; *s* of Henry Bentall and of late Lilian Alice Greeno; *m* 1944, Jean, *d* of late Hugh Cameron Wilson, MD, FRCS; three *s* one *d*. *Educ:* Seaford Coll., Sussex; Medical Sch. of St Bartholomew's Hospital, London. RNVR, Surg Lieut, 1945-47. Lecturer in Thoracic Surgery, Postgraduate Medical Sch., London, 1959; Reader, 1962-65. *Publications:* books and papers on surgical subjects. *Recreation:* sailing. *Address:* Royal Postgraduate Medical School of London, Ducane Road, W12. *T:* 01-743 2030. *Clubs:* Naval; Cruising Association; Royal Naval Sailing Association (Portsmouth); Royal Air Force Yacht.

BENTALL, (Leonard Edward) Rowan, DL; President, Bentalls Ltd, since 1978 (Chairman, 1968-78 and Managing Director, 1963-78); *b* 27 Nov. 1911; *yr s* of late Leonard H. Bentall and Mrs Bentall; *m* 1937, Adelia E., *yr d* of late David Hawes and Mrs Hawes; three *s* two *d*. *Educ:* Aldro Sch.; Eastbourne Coll. Joined family business, 1930. Served War of 1939-45: joined East Surrey Regt, 1940; commissioned, Royal Welch Fusiliers, 1941; served Middle East,

N Africa, Sicily, Italy, France, Belgium, Holland, 231 (Malta) Inf. Bde; now Hon. Captain, Royal Welch Fusiliers. Bentalls: Dep. Chm., 1950; Merchandise Dir, 1946-63. Pres., Surrey Br., Inst. of Directors, 1979–. Trustee, New Victoria Hosp., Kingston upon Thames. Freeman of City of London, 1972. Pres., Steadfast Sea Cadet Corps. FRSA. DL, Greater London 1977, Rep. for Kingston-upon-Thames 1979. Cavaliere, Order Al Merito della Repubblica Italiana, 1971. *Publication:* My Store of Memories, 1974. *Recreations:* gardening, ornithology. *Address:* Hill House, Broughton, near Stockbridge, Hants. *Club:* Royal Automobile.

BENTHALL, Sir (Arthur) Paul, KBE 1950; FLS; Medal, Internationales Burgen Institut, 1978; *b* 25 Jan. 1902; *s* of Rev. Charles Francis Benthall and Annie Theodosia Benthall; *m* 1932, Mary Lucy, *d* of John A. Pringle, Horam, Sussex; four *s*. *Educ:* Eton; Christ Church, Oxford. Joined Bird & Co. and F. W. Heilgers & Co., Calcutta, 1924; partner (later dir) of both firms, 1934-53; Pres., Bengal Chamber of Commerce, and of Assoc. Chambers of Commerce of India, 1948 and 1950; Mem. Central Board, Imperial Bank of India, 1948 and 1950-53; Chm. All India Board of Technical Studies in Commerce and Business Administration, 1950-53; Pres. Royal Agri-Horticultural Society of India, 1945-47; Pres., UK Citizens' Assoc. (India), 1952. Chairman: Bird & Co. (London) Ltd, 1953-73; Amalgamated Metal Corporation Ltd, 1959-72; Director: Chartered Bank, 1953-72; Royal Insurance Co. and Associated Cos, 1953-72. *Publication:* The Trees of Calcutta, 1946. *Address:* Benthall Hall, Broseley, Salop. *T:* Telford 882254. *Clubs:* Oriental, Landsowne.

See also J. C. M. Benthall.

BENTHALL, Jonathan Charles Mackenzie; Director, Royal Anthropological Institute, since 1974; *b* Calcutta, 12 Sept. 1941; *s* of Sir Arthur Paul Benthall, *qv*; *m* 1975, Zamira, *d* of Yehudi Menuhin, *qv*; two *s* one step *s*. *Educ:* Eton (KS); King's Coll., Cambridge (MA). Sec., Inst. of Contemporary Arts, 1971-73. Mem., UK Child Care Cttee, Save the Children Fund, 1981-. Chevalier de l'Ordre des Arts et des Lettres (France), 1973. *Publications:* Science and Technology in Art Today, 1972; The Body Electric: patterns of western industrial culture, 1976; (ed) Ecology: the Shaping Enquiry, 1972; (ed) The Limits of Human Nature, 1973; (ed jtly) The Body as a Medium of Expression, 1975. *Address:* 212 Hammersmith Grove, W6 7HG. *Club:* Athenæum.

BENTHALL, Sir Paul; *see* Benthall, Sir A. P.

BENTINCK; *see* Cavendish-Bentinck, family name of Duke of Portland.

BENTLEY, Rev. Canon Geoffrey Bryan; Canon of Windsor, 1957-82; Hon. Canon, since 1982; *b* 16 July 1909; *s* of late Henry Bentley; *m* 1938, Nina Mary, *d* of late George Coombe Williams, Clerk; two *s* two *d*. *Educ:* Uppingham Sch.; King's Coll., Cambridge (Scholar); Cuddesdon Coll., Oxford. BA and Carus Greek Testament Prize, 1932; MA 1935. Ordained, 1933; Asst Curate, St Cuthbert's, Copnor, 1933-35; Tutor of Scholae Cancellarii, Lincoln, 1935-38; Lecturer, 1938-52; Priest Vicar of Lincoln Cathedral and Chaplain of Lincoln County Hosp., 1938-52; Proctor in Convocation, 1945-55; Rector of Milton Abbot with Dunterton, Dio. Exeter, 1952-57; Examg Chap. to Bp of Exeter, 1952-74; Commissary to Bp of SW Tanganyika, 1952-61; Canon of Windsor, 1957, Precentor, 1958-69, 1970-73, 1977, President, May-Dec. 1962, Feb.-July 1971 and Aug.-Nov. 1976, Steward 1969, 1975-76; Mem., Archbp's Group on Reform of Divorce Law, 1964; William Jones Golden Lectr., 1965; Scott Holland Lectr., 1966. *Publications:* The Resurrection of the Bible, 1940; Catholic Design for Living, 1940; Reform of the Ecclesiastical Law, 1944; God and Venus, 1964; Dominance or Dialogue?, 1965. *Address:* 5 The Cloisters, Windsor Castle, Berks SL4 1NJ. *T:* Windsor 63001. *Club:* National Liberal.

BENTLEY, Prof. George, FRCS; Professor of Orthopaedic Surgery, Institute of Orthopaedics, University of London, since 1982; *b* 19 Jan. 1936; *s* of George and Doris Bentley; *m* 1960, Ann Gillian Hutchings; two *s* one *d*. *Educ:* Rotherham Grammar Sch.; Sheffield Univ. (MB, ChB, ChM), FRCS 1964. House Surgeon, Sheffield Royal Infirmary, 1959-61; Lectr in Anatomy, Birmingham Univ., 1961-62; Surg. Registrar, Sheffield Royal Infirm., 1963-65; Sen. Registrar in Orthopaedics, Nuffield Orthopaedic Centre and Radcliffe Infirm., Oxford, 1967-69; Instructor in Orth., Univ. of Pittsburgh, USA, 1969-70; Lectr, 1970-71, Sen. Lectr and Reader in Orth., 1971-76, Univ. of Oxford; Prof. of Orth. and Accident Surgery, Univ. of Liverpool, 1976-82. *Publications:* (ed) 3rd edn vols I and II, Rob and Smith Operative Surgery—Orthopaedics, 1979; papers on arthritis, accident surgery and scoliosis in leading med. and surg. jls. *Recreations:* tennis, music. *Address:* Institute of Orthopaedics, Royal National Orthopaedic Hospital, 234 Great Portland Street, W1N 6AD. *T:* 01-387 5070.

BENTLEY, John Ransome; Chairman, Intervision Video (Holdings) Ltd; *b* 19 Feb. 1940; *m* 1st, 1960 (marr. diss. 1969); one *s* one *d*; 2nd, 1982, Katherine Susan, *d* of Gerald Percy and the Marchioness of Bute. *Educ:* Harrow Sch. *Recreation:* living.

BENTLEY, William, CMG 1977; HM Diplomatic Service; High Commissioner in Malaysia, since 1981; *b* 15 Feb. 1927; *s* of Lawrence and Elsie Jane Bentley; *m* 1950, Karen Ellen Christensen; two *s* three *d*. *Educ:* Bury High Sch.; Manchester Univ.; Wadham Coll., Oxford (1st cl. Mod. Hist.); Coll. of Europe, Bruges. HM Foreign (later Diplomatic) Service, 1952; 3rd (later 2nd) Sec., Tokyo, 1952-57; United Nations Dept, Foreign Office, 1957-60; 1st Sec., UK Mission to United Nations, 1960-63; Far Eastern Dept, FO, 1963-65; Head of Chancery, Kuala Lumpur, 1965-69; Dep. Comr-Gen., British Pavilion, Expo 70, Osaka, 1969-70; Counsellor, Belgrade, 1970-73; Head of Permanent Under-Sec.'s Dept, FCO, 1973-74; Head of Far Eastern Dept, FCO, 1974-76; Ambassador to the Philippines, 1976-81. *Recreations:* golf, skiing, fishing, shooting. *Address:* c/o Foreign and Commonwealth Office, SW1; 6 Landsdowne Close, SW20. *T:* 01-946 1985; Oak Cottage, Oak Lane, Crickhowell, Breconshire. *Clubs:* Brooks's; Roehampton.

BENTON, Gordon William, CIE 1946; *b* 25 March 1893; *s* of William Benton, Cannock, Staffs; *m* 1st, 1922, Ethel Beatrice (*d* 1971), *d* of George Mark Robinson; no *c* ; 2nd, 1973, Vera Alicia, *d* of P. W. J. J. Harman-Harris and *widow* of H. W. Trussler. *Educ:* Merchant Taylors' Sch. Joined Indian Police, 1912; Indian Army Reserve of Officers, 45th Rattray's Sikhs, Mesopotamia, 1917-19; lent to Govt of HEH the Nizam of Hyderabad for CID, and Dir-Gen., Police and Jails, 1926-33; Deputy Dir, Intelligence Bureau, Home Dept, Govt of India and Mem., two Cttees on aspects of Railway Police admin under the Govt of India Bill then under consideration in parlt, 1935-38; Deputy Inspector-General, Central Provinces and Berar, 1938; retd 1947. Indian Police Medal, 1940; King's Police Medal, 1945. *Address:* 21 Lodge Gardens, Alverstoke, Hants PO12 3PY. *Club:* East India, Devonshire, Sports and Public Schools.

BENTON, Kenneth Carter, CMG 1966; *b* 4 March 1909; *s* of William Alfred Benton and Amy Adeline Benton (*née* Kirton); *m* 1938, Peggie, *d* of Maj.-Gen. C. E. Pollock, CB, CBE, DSO; one *s* one step *s* (and one step *s* decd). *Educ:* Wolverhampton Sch.; London Univ. Teaching and studying languages in Florence and Vienna, 1930-37; employed British Legation, Vienna, 1937-38; Vice-Consul, Riga, 1938-40; 2nd Sec., British Embassy, Madrid, 1941-43; 2nd, later 1st Sec., Rome, 1944-48; FO, 1948-50; 1st Sec., Rome, 1950-53; 1st Sec., Madrid, 1953-56; FO, 1956-62; 1st Sec. and Consul, Lima, 1963-64; FO, 1964-66; Counsellor, Rio de Janeiro, 1966-68; retd from Diplomatic Service, 1968. *Publications:* Twenty-fourth Level, 1969; Sole Agent, 1970; Spy in Chancery, 1972; Craig and the Jaguar, 1973; Craig and the Tunisian Tangle, 1974; Death on the Appian Way, 1974; Craig and the Midas Touch, 1975; A Single Monstrous Act, 1976; The Red Hen Conspiracy, 1977. *Recreations:* writing, enamelling. *Address:* 2 Jubilee Terrace, Chichester, West Sussex PO19 1XL. *T:* Chichester 787148. *Club:* Detection.

BENTON, Peter Faulkner, MA, CBIM; Deputy Chairman, British Telecommunications, since 1981 (Managing Director, Post Office Telecommunications, since 1978); *b* 6 Oct. 1934; *s* of S. F. Benton and Mrs H. D. Benton; *m* 1959, Ruth, *d* of late R. S. Cobb, MC, and Mrs J. P. Cobb; two *s* three *d*. *Educ:* Oundle; Queens' Coll., Cambridge (MA Nat. Sciences). 2nd Lieut RE, 1953-55. Unilever Ltd, 1958-60; Shell Chemicals Ltd, 1960-63; Berger Jenson and Nicholson Ltd, 1963-64; McKinsey & Co. Inc., London and Chicago, 1964-71; Gallaher Ltd, 1971, Dir, 1973-77. Chairman: Saunders Valve Ltd, 1972-77; Mono Pumps Group, 1976-77; Heating, Ventilating, Air Conditioning and Refrigerating Equipment Sector Working Party, NEDO, 1976-79; Member: Electronics Industry EDC, 1980-; Econ. and Financial Policy Cttee, CBI, 1979-. Pres., Highgate Literary and Scientific Inst., 1981-; Vice-Pres., British Mech. Engrg Confedn, 1974-77. Royal Signals Instn Lectr, London, 1980. *Recreations:* reading, fishing, gardening, looking at buildings. *Address:* Northgate House, Highgate Hill, N6 5HD. *T:* 01-357 2222. *Clubs:* United Oxford & Cambridge University, The Pilgrims.

BENTON JONES, Sir Simon W. F.; *see* Jones.

BENYON, Thomas Yates; MP (C) Abingdon, since 1979; *b* 13 Aug. 1942; *s* of Thomas Yates Benyon and Ida Joan Walters; *m* 1968, Olivia Jane (*née* Scott Plummer); two *s* two *d*. *Educ:* Wellington Sch., Somerset; RMA, Sandhurst. Lieut, Scots Guards, 1963-67. Insurance Broker, 1967-71; Director of various companies, 1971-: commodity broking, leasing. Councillor, Aylesbury Vale DC, 1976-79. Contested (C): Huyton, Feb. 1974; Haringey (Wood Green), Oct. 1974. Sec., Health and Social Services Cttee; Mem., Social Services Select Cttee. Vice-Pres., Guidepost Trust (charity for mentally sick), 1975-; Mem., Nat. Council, New Horizon (charity for young at risk in London), 1974-. *Recreation:* hunting. *Address:* Old Rectory, Adstock, near Winslow, Bucks; 33 Marsham Court, Marsham Street, Westminster, SW1. *Club:* Brooks's.

BENYON, William Richard, DL; MP (C) Buckingham since 1970; *b* 17 Jan. 1930; *e s* of late Vice-Adm. R. Benyon, CB, CBE, and of Mrs. Benyon, The Lambdens, Beenham, Berkshire; *m* Elizabeth Ann Hallifax; two *s* three *d*. *Educ:* Royal Naval Coll., Dartmouth. Royal Navy, 1947-56; Courtaulds Ltd, 1956-64; Farmer, 1964-. PPS to Minister of Housing and Construction, 1972-74; Conservative Whip, 1974-76. Mem., Berks CC, 1964-74; JP 1962-78, DL 1970, Berks. *Address:* Englefield House, Englefield, near Reading, Berkshire. *T:* Reading 302221. *Clubs:* Boodle's, Pratt's, White's.

BERE, Rennie Montague, CMG 1957; retired; *b* 28 Nov. 1907; *s* of late Rev. M. A. Bere; *m* 1936, Anne Maree Barber; no *c*. *Educ:* Marlborough Coll.; Selwyn Coll., Cambridge (MA). Colonial Administrative Service, Uganda, 1930-55; Asst District Officer, 1930; District Officer, 1942; Provincial Commissioner, 1951-55. Commandant, Polish Refugee Settlements, 1943-44; Dir and Chief Warden, Uganda National Parks, 1955-60; Pres., Cornwall Naturalists-Trust, 1967-70. *Publications:* The Wild Mammals of Uganda,

1961; The African Elephant, 1966; Wild Animals in an African National Park, 1966; The Way to the Mountains of the Moon, 1966; Birds in an African National Park, 1969; Antelopes, 1970; Wildlife in Cornwall, 1971; Crocodile's Eggs for Supper, 1973; The Mammals of East and Central Africa, 1975; (with B. D. Stamp) The Book of Bude and Stratton, 1980; The Nature of Cornwall, 1982; articles (chiefly of mountaineering and wild life and anthropological interest) in Alpine Jl, Uganda Jl, Oryx, Animals, etc. *Recreations:* mountaineering; game and bird watching; cricket. *Address:* West Cottage, Bude, N Cornwall. *T:* Bude 2082. *Clubs:* Alpine, Royal Commonwealth Society; Uganda Kobs (past Pres.).

BERESFORD, family name of **Baron Decies** and **Marquess of Waterford.**

BERESFORD, His Honour Eric George Harold; a Circuit Judge (formerly Judge of County Courts), 1959-76; *b* 19 Nov. 1901; *s* of Henry Beresford, Sutton Coldfield; *m* 1930, Barbara Muriel, *d* of Wallace Edwin Marley, Sutton Coldfield; one *s* one *d*. *Educ:* King Edward's Sch., Birmingham; Emanuel Coll., Cambridge (MA, LLB). Called to Bar, Lincoln's Inn, 1926; practised on Midland Circuit. Chm., Licensed Premises Cttee, New Town of Redditch, 1965. *Recreations:* history and literature. *Address:* Saxbys, Rolvenden, Kent. *T:* Rolvenden 403.

BERESFORD, Prof. Maurice Warwick; Professor of Economic History, University of Leeds, since 1959; *b* 6 Feb. 1920; *s* of late H. B. Beresford and Mrs N. E. Beresford. *Educ:* Boldmere and Green Lane Elementary Schs; Bishop Vesey's Grammar Sch., Sutton Coldfield; Jesus Coll., Cambridge. Historical Tripos, Pt I class I, 1940, Pt II class I, 1941; MA 1945. On Staff of Birmingham Univ. Settlement, 1941-42; Sub-warden, Percival Guildhouse, Rugby, 1942-43; Warden, 1943-48; University of Leeds: Lecturer, 1948-55; Reader, 1955-59; Dean, 1958-60; Chm., Sch. of Economic Studies, 1965-68, 1971-72, 1981-83; Chm. of Faculty Bd, 1968-70. Harrison Vis. Prof. of History, Coll. of William and Mary, Virginia, 1975-76. Chairman: Yorks Citizens' Advice Bureaux Cttee, 1963-69; Parole Review Cttee, Leeds Prison, 1970-; Northern Area Inst. for Study and Treatment of Delinquency, 1973-78; Co-opted Mem., City of Leeds Probation Cttee, 1972-78; SSRC, Economic and Social History Cttee, 1972-75. Minister's nominee, Yorkshire Dales National Park Cttee, 1964-71; Member: Consumer Council, 1966-71; Hearing Aids Council, 1969-71; Royal Commn on Historical Monuments (England), 1979-. *Publications:* The Leeds Chambers of Commerce, 1951; The Lost Villages of England, 1954; History on the Ground, 1957; (with J. K. S. St Joseph) Medieval England: an Aerial Survey, 1958, rev. edn 1979; Time and Place, 1962; New Towns of the Middle Ages, 1967; (Ed, with G. R. J. Jones) Leeds and Its Region, 1967; (with J. G. Hurst) Deserted Medieval Villages, 1971; (with H. P. R. Finberg) English Medieval Boroughs, 1973; (with B. J. Barber) The West Riding County Council 1889-1974, 1979; Walks Round Red Brick, 1980; contribs to Economic History Review, Agricultural History Review, Medieval Archaeology, etc. *Recreations:* music, theatre, maps, delinquency. *Address:* 6 Claremont Avenue, Leeds LS3 1AT. *T:* Leeds 454563; 4 Southcot Place, Bath. *T:* Bath 319063.

BERESFORD-PEIRSE, Sir Henry Grant de la Poer, 6th Bt *cr* 1814; *b* 7 Feb. 1933; *s* of Sir Henry Campbell de la Poer Beresford-Peirse, 5th Bt, CB, and of Margaret, *d* of Frank Morison Seafield Grant, Knockie, Inverness-shire; *S* father, 1972; *m* 1966, Jadranka, *d* of Ivan Njerš, Zagreb, Yugoslavia; two *s*. Heir: *s* Henry Njerš de la Poer Beresford-Peirse, *b* 25 March 1969.

BERESFORD-STOOKE, Sir George; *see* Stooke.

BERESFORD-WEST, Michael Charles, QC 1975; a Recorder of the Crown Court, since 1975; *b* 3 June 1928; *s* of Arthur Charles and Ida Dagmar West; *m* 1956, Patricia Eileen Beresford; two *s* one *d*. *Educ:* St Peter's, Southbourne; Portsmouth Grammar Sch.; Brasenose Coll., Oxford (MA). Nat. Service, Intell. Corps, Middle East, SIME. Called to Bar, Lincoln's Inn, 1952; Western Circuit, 1953-65; SE Circuit, 1965; a Chm., Independent Schools Tribunal and Tribunal (Children's Act 1948), 1974. *Recreations:* swimming, lawn tennis, music. *Address:* Chilterns, 4 Furze Hill, Purley, Surrey. *T:* 01-660 3293; 10 King's Bench Walk, Temple, EC4Y 7DQ. *T:* 01-353 7202-4.

BERG, Rev. John J.; *see* Johansen-Berg.

BERG, Prof. Paul, PhD; Willson Professor of Biochemistry, Stanford University School of Medicine, since 1970; *b* New York, 30 June 1926; *m* Mildred Levy; one *s*. *Educ:* Pennsylvania State Univ. (BS); Western Reserve Univ. (PhD). Pre-doctoral and post-doctoral med. research, 1950-54; scholar in cancer research, American Cancer Soc., Washington Univ., 1954; Asst to Associate Prof. of Microbiology, Washington Univ., 1955-59; Stanford Univ. Sch. of Medicine: Associate Prof. of Biochem., 1959-60; Prof., Dept of Biochem., 1960, Chm. 1969-74; Non-resident Fellow, Salk Inst., 1973-. Editor, Biochemical and Biophysical Res. Communications, 1959-68; Member: NIH Study, Sect. on Physiol Chem.; Editorial Bd, Jl of Molecular Biology, 1966-69; Bd of Sci. Advisors, Jane Coffin Childs Foundn for Med. Res.; Adv. Bds to Nat. Insts of Health, Amer. Cancer Soc., Nat. Sci. Foundn, MIT and Harvard, 1970-80; Council, Nat. Acad. of Scis, 1979. Former Pres., Amer. Soc. of Biological Chemists; Foreign Member: Japan Biochem. Soc., 1978-; French Acad. of Scis, 1981-. Lectures: Harvey, 1972; Lynen, 1977; Weizmann Inst., 1977; Univ. of Pittsburgh, 1978; Priestly, Pennsylvania State

Univ., 1978; Shell, Univ. of California at Davis, 1978; Dreyfus, Northwestern Univ., 1979; Jesup, Columbian Univ., 1980; Karl-August-Förster, Univ. of Mainz, 1980; David Rivett Meml, CSIR, Melb., 1980. Hon. DSc: Rochester and Yale Univs, 1978; numerous awards include: Nat. Acad. of Scis, 1966, 1974; Amer. Acad. of Arts and Scis, 1966; Henry J. Kaiser, Stanford Univ. Sch. of Med., 1969, 1972; Dist, Alumnus, Pennsylvania State Univ.; V. D. Mattia Prize of Roche Inst. for Molec. Biol., 1972; Gairdner Foundn Award, Nobel Prize in Chemistry, New York Acad. of Scis and Albert Lasker Med. Res. awards, 1980. *Publications:* many scientific articles and reviews. *Address:* Stanford University Medical Center, Stanford, California 94305, USA.

BERGANZA, Teresa; singer (mezzo-soprano); *b* Madrid, Spain; *d* of Guillermo and Maria Ascension Berganza; *m* ; three *c.* Début in Aix-en-Provence, 1957; début in England, Glyndebourne, 1958; appeared at Glyndebourne, 1959; Royal Opera House, Covent Garden, 1959, 1960, 1963, 1964, 1976, 1977, 1979, 1981; Royal Festival Hall, 1960, 1961, 1962, 1967, 1971; appears regularly in Vienna, Milan, Aix-en-Provence, Holland, Japan, Edinburgh, Paris, Israel, America. Prizes: Lucretia Arana; Nacional Lírica, Spain; Lily Pons, 1976; Acad. Nat. du Disque Lyrique; USA record award; Harriet Cohen Internat. Music Award, 1974. Charles Cross (4 times); Grand Cross, Isabel la Católica, Spain. *Recreations:* music, books, the arts. *Address:* c/o Musicaglotz, 141 Boulevard Saint Michel, 75005 Paris, France. *T:* 33-1-3543833.

BERGEL, Prof. Franz, FRS 1959; DPhil. Nat. (Freiburg), PhD (London), DSc (London), CChem, FRSC, FIBiol; Professor Emeritus of Chemistry, University of London; Member, Institute of Cancer Research: Royal Cancer Hospital; *b* Vienna, 13 Feb. 1900; *s* of Moritz Martin Bergel and Barbara Betty Spitz; *m* 1939, Phyllis Thomas. *Educ:* Universities of Vienna and Freiburg im Breisgau. Head of Dept of Medical Chemistry, Inst. Chem., 1927-33, and Privatdoz., Univ. of Freiburg, 1929-33; research worker: Med. Chem. Dept, Univ. of Edinburgh, 1933-36; Lister Inst. of Preventive Med., Dept of Biochemistry, 1936-38; Dir of Research, Roche Products Ltd, Welwyn Garden City, 1938-52; Head, Chemistry Dept, Chester Beatty Res. Inst., 1952-66; Dean, Inst. Cancer Research, 1963-66. Hon. Lectr, Pharmacology Dept, Faculty of Medical Sciences. University Coll., London 1946-73; Consultant, Harvard Med. Sch. and Children's Cancer Research Foundn (now Sidney Farber Cancer Inst.), Boston, Mass, 1959-60, 1967-73; FRSM; FRSA 1957 (Life Mem., 1967-); Member: Soc. Chem. Ind.; Biochem. Soc.; Amer. Assoc. Adv. Sci. (Fellow); Brit. Pharm. Soc.; NY Acad. Sci. *Publications:* Chemistry of Enzymes in Cancer, 1961; All about Drugs, 1970; Today's Carcinochemotherapy, 1970; Alexander Haddow (biographical memoir), 1977; papers and reviews in chemical, biochemical and pharmacological journals. *Recreation:* sketching. *Address:* Magnolia Cottage, Bel Royal, Jersey, CI. *T:* Jersey 33688.

BERGER, John; author and art critic; *b* London, 5 Nov. 1926; *s* of late S. J. D. Berger, OBE, MC, and of Mrs Miriam Berger (*née* Branson). *Educ:* Central Sch. of Art; Chelsea Sch. of Art. Began career as a painter and teacher of drawing; exhibited at Wildenstein, Redfern and Leicester Galls, London. Art Critic: Tribune; New Statesman. Numerous TV appearances, incl.: Monitor; two series for Granada TV. Scenario: (with Alain Tanner) La Salamandre; Le Milieu du Monde; Jonas (New York Critics Prize for Best Scenario of Year, 1976). George Orwell Meml Prize, 1977. *Publications:* Marcel Frishman, 1958; A Painter of Our Time (novel), 1958; Permanent Red, 1960; trans. (with A. Bostock) Poems on the Theatre, by B. Brecht, 1960; The Foot of Clive (novel), 1962; Corker's Freedom (novel), 1964; The Success and Failure of Picasso, 1965; (with J. Mohr) A Fortunate Man: the story of a country doctor, 1967; Art and Revolution, 1969; Moments of Cubism and Other Essays, 1969; trans. (with A. Bostock) Return to My Native Land, by Aimé Césaire, 1969; Selected Essays and Articles: The Look of Things, 1972; G (novel), 1972 (Booker Prize 1972; James Tait Black Meml Prize, 1972); Ways of Seeing, 1972; The Seventh Man, 1975 (Prize for Best Reportage, Union of Journalists and Writers, Paris 1977); Poems in Voix, Maspero, Paris 1977; Pig Earth (fiction), 1979; About Looking (essays), 1980. *Address:* c/o Penguin Books, Harmondsworth, Mddx.

BERGER, Vice-Adm. Sir Peter (Egerton Capel), KCB 1979; MVO 1960; DSC 1949; Bursar and Fellow, Selwyn College, Cambridge, since 1981; *b* 11 Feb. 1925; *s* of late Capel Colquhoun Berger and Winifred Violet Berger (*née* Levett-Scrivener); *m* 1956, June Kathleen Pigou; three *d. Educ:* Harrow Sch. Served War of 1939-45: entered RN as a Cadet, 1943; Normandy and South of France landings in HMS Ajax, 1944; Sub-Lt, 1945; Lieut, 1946; Yangtse Incident, HMS Amethyst, 1949; Lt-Comdr, 1953; Comdr, 1956; Fleet Navigating Officer, Home Fleet, 1956-58; Navigating Officer, HM Yacht Britannia, 1958-60; Commanded HMS Torquay, 1962-64; Captain, 1964; Defence, Naval and Military Attaché, The Hague, 1964-66; commanded HMS Phoebe, 1966-68; Commodore, Clyde, 1971-73; Rear-Adm., 1973; Asst Chief of Naval Staff (Policy), 1973-75; COS to C-in-C Fleet, 1976-78; Flag Officer Plymouth, Port Admiral Devonport, Comdr Central Sub Area Eastern Atlantic and Comdr Plymouth Sub Area Channel, 1979-81, retired 1981. *Recreations:* shooting, fishing, history. *Address:* Linton End House, Linton Road, Balsham, Cambs CB1 6HA. *T:* Cambridge 892959.

BERGERSEN, Dr Fraser John, FRS 1981; Chief Research Scientist, Division of Plant Industry, CSIRO, Canberra, since 1972; *b* 26 May 1929; *s* of Victor E. and Arabel H. Bergersen; *m* 1952, Gladys Irene Heather; two *s* one *d. Educ:* Univ. of Otago, New Zealand (BSc, MSc (Hons)); Univ. of New Zealand

(DSc 1962). Bacteriology Dept, Univ. of Otago, 1952-54; Div. of Plant Industry, CSIRO, Canberra, Aust., 1954-, currently engaged full-time in scientific research in microbiology, with special reference to symbiotic nitrogen fixation in legume root-nodules. David Rivett Medal, CSIRO Officers' Assoc. 1968. *Publications:* Methods for Evaluating Biological Nitrogen Fixation, 1980; Root Nodules of Legumes: structure and functions, 1982; ninety articles and chapters in scientific journals and books. *Recreations:* music, gardening. *Address:* CSIRO Division of Plant Industry, PO Box 1600, Canberra City, ACT 2601, Australia. *T:* (062) 465098, (home) (062) 477413.

BERGIN, John Alexander, CB 1980; Deputy Secretary, Lord Chancellor's Department, 1977-80; *b* 25 May 1920; *s* of late B. A. G. and Mrs L. Bergin; *m* 1953, Pierrette Wack, MA. *Educ:* Varndean Sch., Brighton; St Catharine's Coll., Cambridge. BA Hons (Natural Science) 1947. REME, 1940-46 (T/Major, despatches). Asst Principal, Bd of Trade, 1948; HM Customs and Excise, 1954-56; Office of Chancellor, Duchy of Lancaster, 1960; Dept of Economic Affairs, 1964; IDC, 1966; Under-Sec., BoT, 1968-71; Principal Estabt and Finance Officer, Lord Chancellor's Dept, 1971-77. *Recreations:* photography; hybridising *Liliaceae, Amaryllidaceae. Address:* 15 Granard Avenue, SW15 6HH. *Club:* United Oxford & Cambridge University.

BERGMAN, (Ernst) Ingmar; Swedish film producer; Director, Royal Dramatic Theatre, Stockholm; director of productions on television; *b* Uppsala, 14 July 1918; *s* of a Chaplain to the Royal Court at Stockholm; *m* 1971, Mrs Ingrid von Rosen; (eight *c* by previous marriages). *Educ:* Stockholm Univ. Producer, Royal Theatre, Stockholm, 1940-42; Producer and script-writer, Swedish Film Co., 1940-44; Theatre Director: Helsingborg, 1944-46; Gothenburg, 1946-49; Malmö, 1952-1959. Produced: Hedda Gabler, Cambridge, 1970; Show, 1971. Films (British titles) produced include: Torment, 1943; Crisis, 1945; Port of Call, 1948; Summer Interlude, 1950; Waiting Women, 1952; Summer with Monika, 1952; Sawdust and Tinsel, 1953; A Lesson in Love, 1953; Journey into Autumn, 1954; Smiles of a Summer Night, 1955; The Seventh Seal, 1956-57; Wild Strawberries, 1957; So Close to Life, 1957; The Face, 1958; The Virgin Spring, 1960 (shown Edinburgh Fest., 1960); The Devil's Eye, 1961 (shown Edinburgh Fest., 1961); Through a Glass Darkly, 1961; Winter Light, 1962; The Silence, 1963; Now About all these Women, 1964 (first film in colour); Persona, 1967; Hour of the Wolf, 1968; Shame, 1968; The Rite, 1969; The Passion, 1970; The Fåro Document, 1970 (first documentary, shown Venice Fest., 1980); The Touch, 1971; Cries and Whispers, 1972 (NY Film Critics Best Film Award, 1972); Scenes from a Marriage, 1974 (BBC TV Series, 1975; published, 1975); Face to Face, 1976 (BBC TV Series, 1979); The Serpent's Egg, 1977; Autumn Sonata, 1978; From the Life of the Marionettes, 1981. Has gained several international awards and prizes for films; Goethe Prize, 1976; Great Gold Medal, Swedish Acad. of Letters, 1977. *Publication:* Four Stories, 1977.

BERGMAN, Ingmar; *see* Bergman, E. I.

BERGNER, Elisabeth; actress; *b* Vienna, 22 Aug. 1900; naturalised British subject, 1938; *m* Dr Paul Czinner. Early stage appearances in Austria, Switzerland and Germany included performances with Wedekind in Spring Awakening, Lulu and Schloss Wetterstein; Ophelia in Hamlet, Zürich; Rosalind in As You Like It, Vienna; Katherine in The Taming of the Shrew; Julie in Miss Julie; Viola in Twelfth Night; Juliet in Romeo and Juliet; Joan in Saint Joan, 1924; Mrs Cheyney in The Last of Mrs Cheyney, 1926; Tessa in The Constant Nymph, 1927 (all in Berlin). First London appearance as Gemma Jones in Escape Me Never, Apollo, 1933, NY, 1935; The Boy David, His Majesty's, 1936; The Two Mrs Carrolls, NY, 1943; Duchess of Malfi, NY, 1946; The Gay Invalid, Garrick, 1951; toured Germany and Austria in Long Day's Journey Into Night, 1957; First Love, United States, 1964; The Madwoman of Chaillot, Oxford, 1967. Films include: Der Evangelimann; Ariane, Fräulein Else, Escape Me Never, Dreaming Lips, Catherine the Great, Stolen Life, As You Like It, Pfingstausflug (Berlin Prize, 1969). Schiller Prize, 1963; Goldene Band, International Film Festival, Berlin, 1963 and 1965. Das Grosse Verdienstkreuz mit Stern, Germany; Ehrenmedaille der Bundeshaupstadt Wien, Austria. Daughter of Mark Twain, 1976. *Publication:* Elisabeth Bergner's unordentliche Erinnerungen. *Recreations:* walking, music. *Address:* 42 Eaton Square, SW1.

BERGONZI, Prof. Bernard; Professor of English, University of Warwick, since 1971; *b* 13 April 1929; *s* of late Carlo and Louisa Bergonzi; *m* 1960, Gabriel Wall; one *s* two *d. Educ:* Wadham Coll., Oxford (BLitt, MA). Asst Lectr in English, Manchester Univ., 1959-62, Lectr, 1962-66; Sen. Lectr, Univ. of Warwick, 1966-71, Pro-Vice-Chancellor, 1979-82. Vis. Lectr, Brandeis Univ., 1964-65; Vis. Prof., Stanford Univ., 1982. *Publications:* Descartes and the Animals (verse), 1954; The Early H. G. Wells, 1961; Heroes' Twilight, 1965; The Situation of the Novel, 1970; Anthony Powell, 1971; T. S. Eliot, 1972; The Turn of a Century, 1973; Gerard Manley Hopkins, 1977; Reading the Thirties, 1978; Years (verse), 1979; The Roman Persuasion (novel), 1981. *Recreations:* conversation, looking at pictures and buildings. *Address:* Department of English, University of Warwick, Coventry CV4 7AL. *T:* Coventry 24011.

BERIO, Luciano; composer; *b* 24 Oct. 1925; *s* of Ernesto Berio and Ada dal Fiume; *m* 1st, 1950, Cathy Berberian (marr. diss. 1964); one *d* ; 2nd, 1964, Susan Oyama (marr. diss. 1971); one *s* one *d* ; 3rd, 1977, Talia Pecker; two *s. Educ:* Liceo Classico, Oneglia; Conservatorio G. Verdi, Milan. Hon. degree in Composition, City Univ., 1979. Works include: Differences, 1958; Epifanie, 1959-63; Circles, 1960; Passaggio, 1962; Laborintus II, 1965; Sinfonia, 1968; Concerto for 2 pianos, 1972; Opera, 1969-74; Sequenzas for solo instruments; A-Ronne for five actors, 1974-75; Coro for chorus and orchestra, 1975-76; La Ritirata Notturna di Madrid, 1975; Ritorno degli Snovidenia, 1977; La Vera Storia, 1981. *Address:* Il Colombaio, Radicondoli (Siena), Italy.

BERIOZOVA, Svetlana; Ballerina; *b* 24 Sept. 1932; *d* of Nicolas and Maria Beriozoff (Russian); *m* 1959, Mohammed Masud Khan (marr. diss. 1974). *Educ:* New York, USA. Joined Grand Ballet de Monte Carlo, 1947; Metropolitan Ballet, 1948-49; Sadler's Wells Theatre Ballet, 1950-52; Sadler's Wells Ballet (now The Royal Ballet), 1952. Has created leading rôles in Designs for Strings (Taras), Fanciulla delle Rose (Staff), Trumpet Concerto (Balanchine), Pastorale (Cranko), The Shadow (Cranko), Rinaldo and Armida (Ashton), The Prince of the Pagodas (Cranko), Antigone (Cranko), Baiser de la Fée (MacMillan), Diversions (MacMillan), Persephone (Ashton), Images of Love (MacMillan). Classical Roles: Le Lac des Cygnes, The Sleeping Beauty, Giselle, Coppélia, Sylvia, Cinderella. Other rôles currently danced: Les Sylphides, The Firebird, The Lady and Fool, Checkmate, Fête Etrange, Ondine, Nutcracker. Has danced with The Royal Ballet in USA, France, Italy, Australia, S Africa, Russia, and as guest ballerina in Belgrade, Granada, Milan (La Scala), Stuttgart, Bombay, Nervi, Helsinki, Paris, Vienna, New Zealand, Zurich. Played the Princess in The Soldier's Tale (film), 1966. Has frequently appeared on television. *Relevant publications:* Svetlana Beriosova (by C. Swinson), 1956, Svetlana Beriosova (by A. H. Franks), 1958. *Recreation:* the arts. *Address:* c/o Royal Opera House, Covent Garden, WC2. *T:* 01-240 1200.

BERISAVLJEVIĆ, Živan; Member of the Presidency of the Central Committee of the League of Communists of Vojvodina, since 1981; *b* 19 Sept. 1935; *s* of Rajko and Ljubica Prodanović; *m* 1963, Slobodanka Koledin; two *d. Educ:* Belgrade Univ. Held leading political functions in Youth League of Socialist Republic of Serbia, 1955-62; Editor-in-Chief, Gledista magazine, 1962-65; held scientific, cultural, educational and press positions, Central Cttee of League of Communists of Serbia, 1962-67; Sec. for Educn, Science and Culture, Serbia, 1967-71; Official of Assembly, Serbia, 1971-72; Advr to Fed. Sec., 1972-74, Asst Fed. Sec., i/c press, information and cultural affairs, 1974-77, Yugoslav Fed. Secretariat for Foreign Affairs. Mem., Commn for Information and Propaganda, Exec. Cttee of Presidency of League of Communists of Yugoslavia, 1972-77; Yugoslav Ambassador to London, 1977-81. Formerly: Mem. Council, Museum of Contemporary Art, Belgrade; Mem. Federal Cttees for Information, and for Science and Culture. Several decorations. *Publications:* Democratisation of Society and the League of Communists, 1967; Cultural Action, 1972; Education between the Past and Future, 1973; many articles and papers in journals and newspapers. *Recreations:* tennis, football, walking. *Address:* c/o Rajko B., Lovćenska 4, Novi Sad, Yugoslavia. *Clubs:* Brooks's, Travellers', Hurlingham.

BERKELEY, Baroness (17th in line); (*cr* 1421; called out of abeyance, 1967); **Mary Lalle Foley-Berkeley;** *b* 9 Oct. 1905; *e d* of Col Frank Wigram Foley, CBE, DSO (*d* 1949), Royal Berks Regt, and Eva Mary Fitzhardinge, Baroness Berkeley; *S* mother, Baroness Berkeley (16th in line) (*d* 1964). *Heiress presumptive: sister* Hon. Cynthia Ella [*b* 31 Jan. 1909; *m* 1937, Brig. Ernest Adolphus Leopold Gueterbock; one *s*]. *Address:* Pickade Cottage, Great Kimble, Aylesbury, Bucks. *T:* Princes Risborough 3051.

BERKELEY, (Augustus Fitzhardinge) Maurice, CB 1975; MA; Chief Registrar of The High Court in Bankruptcy, 1966-75; Registrar of The Companies Court, 1957-75 and Clerk of the Restrictive Practices Court, 1965-75; *b* 26 Feb. 1903; *s* of late Dr Augustus Frederic Millard Berkeley and Anna Louisa Berkeley; *m* 1931, Elaine Emily, *d* of Adin Simmonds; no *c. Educ:* Aldenham Sch.; Pembroke Coll., Cambridge. Called to the Bar, Inner Temple, 1927. Served War of 1939-45, in The Welch Regiment, 1940-45; Temp. Lieut-Col; AAG, AG3d, War Office. Junior Counsel in Chancery Matters to Ministry of Agriculture, Fisheries and Food, The Commissioners of Crown Lands and the Forestry Commissioners, 1956-57. Bar Council, 1955-57. *Recreations:* watching cricket, travel, theatre, reading. *Address:* 3 Dr Johnson's Buildings, Inner Temple, EC4. *T:* 01-353 2448; Freshwell Cottage, Little Sampford, near Saffron Walden, Essex CB10 2QL. *T:* Great Sampford 244. *Club:* Garrick.
See also F. G. Berkeley.

BERKELEY, Frederic George; Master of the Supreme Court (Taxing Office), since 1971; *b* 21 Dec. 1919; *s* of late Dr Augustus Frederic Millard Berkeley and Anna Louisa Berkeley; *m* 1964, Gillian Eugenie Louise Depreux; one *s* two *d* and one step *s. Educ:* Aldenham Sch.; Pembroke Coll., Cambridge (MA). Admitted Solicitor, 1948. Served War of 1939-45, Leics Regt, Normandy (wounded); Major; DADAWS Allied Land Forces SE Asia, 1945-46. Partner in Lewis & Lewis (from 1964 Penningtons and Lewis & Lewis), 1951-70. Mem. No 1 (London) Legal Aid Area Cttee (later No 14), 1954-70, Vice-Chm. 1964-70, Chm. 1970. *Recreations:* reading, travel, gardening. *Address:* Tyrells End Farm, Eversholt, Milton Keynes MK17 9DS. *T:* Ridgmont 308.
See also A. F. M. Berkeley.

BERKELEY, Humphry John; writer and broadcaster; *b* 21 Feb. 1926; *s* of late Reginald Berkeley, author and playwright, former MP (L), and Mrs

Hildegarde Tinne. *Educ:* Dragon Sch., Oxford; Malvern; Pembroke Coll., Cambridge (Exhibitioner); BA 1947, MA 1963; Pres., Cambridge Union, 1948; Chm., Cambridge Univ. Conservative Assoc., 1948. Held various appointments at Conservative Political Centre, 1949-56; Dir Gen., UK Council of European Movement, 1956-57; Chairman of Coningsby Club 1952-55; Hon. Sec., Carlton Club Political Cttee, 1954-59. MP (C) Lancaster, 1959-66; Member, British Parly Delegn to Council of Europe and Council of WEU, 1963-66; personal representative of Colonial Secretary in constitutional talks in Seychelles, 1965; Hon. Sec., Cons. Parly West Africa Cttee, 1959-64; Hon. Sec., UN Parly Gp, 1962-64; joined Labour Party July 1970; contested (Lab) N Fylde, Oct. 1974. Prospective Parly Cand. (SDP), Hounslow, Chiswick, 1982. Director: Caspair Ltd; Island Developments Ltd Mem., Prince Philip's Cttee on Overseas Volunteers, 1966-70; Chm., UN A of GB and NI, 1966-70; Vice-Chm, Nat. Coordinating Cttee for 25th Anniversary of UN, 1970; Mem., UK Nat. Commn for Unesco, 1966-71. Hon. Treasurer, Howard League for Penal Reform, 1965-71; Mem. Governing Body, Inst. for Study of Internat. Relations, Sussex Univ., 1969-. *Publications:* The Power of the Prime Minister, 1968; Crossing the Floor 1972; The Life and Death of Rochester Sneath, 1974; The Odyssey of Enoch, a political memoir, 1977; The Myth that will not Die: the formation of the National Government 1931, 1978. *Address:* 3 Pages Yard, Church Street, Chiswick, W4 2PA. *Club:* Savile.

BERKELEY, Sir Lennox (Randal), Kt 1974; CBE 1957; composer; President; Performing Right Society, since 1975; Cheltenham Festival of Music, since 1977; *b* 12 May 1903; *o s* of Capt. Hastings George Fitzhardinge Berkeley, RN, and Aline Carla (*née* Harris); *m* 1946, Elizabeth Freda Bernstein; three *s. Educ:* Gresham's Sch., Holt; Merton Coll., Oxford. BA Oxford, 1926; Hon. DMus Oxford, 1970. Studied music in Paris under Nadia Boulanger, 1927-32. Returned to London, 1935; on staff of BBC Music Dept, 1942-45. Composition Professor, Royal Acad. of Music, 1946-68. Hon. Prof. of Music, Keele Univ., 1976-. Pres., Composers' Guild of Great Britain, 1975-. Vice-President: Bach Choir, 1978-; Western Orchestral Soc., 1978-; Cttee, Internat. Soc. of Authors and Composers, 1980-. Hon. Mem., Amer. Acad. and Inst. of Arts and Letters, 1980. Hon. Fellow, Merton Coll., Oxford, 1974. Awarded Collard Fellowship in Music, 1946; Cobbett Medal 1962; Ordre de Mérite Culturel, Monaco, 1967; KSG 1973. Composer of the Year Composer's Guild of GB, 1973. *Compositions include:* symphony orchestra: four symphonies; Divertimento; piano concerto; Concerto for Two Pianos; Flute Concerto; Suite: A Winter's Tale; Voices of the Night; orchestration of Poulenc's Flute Sonata; *chamber orchestra:* Violin Concerto; Partita; Windsor Variations; Dialogue for cello and chamber orchestra; Sinfonia Concertante for oboe and orchestra; *string orchestra:* Serenade; Antiphon; Suite; *vocal /choral music:* Four Poems of St Teresa of Avila for contralto and strings; Stabat Mater for soloists and ensemble; Missa Brevis; Batter My Heart for soprano, choir and chamber orchestra; Four Ronsard Sonnets for tenor and orchestra; Signs in the Dark for choir and strings; Magnificat for choir and orchestra; Three Latin Motets; Hymn for Shakespeare's Birthday; The Hill of the Graces; Judica Me; *chamber music:* many chamber works, including four string quartets; String Trio; Trio for horn, violin and piano; Sextet for clarinet, horn and string quartet; Oboe Quartet; Quintet for wind and piano; various piano works; many songs; *opera:* Nelson; A Dinner Engagement; Ruth; Castaway. *Recreations:* reading, walking. *Address:* 8 Warwick Avenue, W2. *T:* 01-262 3922.

BERKELEY, Maurice; *see* Berkeley, A. F. M.

BERKELEY MILNE, Alexander; *see* Milne.

BERKHOUWER, Cornelis; Chevalier, Order of the Netherlands Lion 1966; Member, European Parliament, since 1963, elected Member, since 1979; *b* Alkmaar, Holland, 19 March 1919; *m* 1966, Michelle Martel; one *s. Educ:* Amsterdam Univ. Dr of Law 1946. Barrister, High Court of Amsterdam, 1942. Pres., European Parliament, 1973-75, Vice-Pres., 1975-79. Grand Cross of Merit (Italy), 1974. *Publications:* Conversion of Void Legal Acts (thesis) 1946; Medical Responsibilities, 1951; Civil Responsibility for Illegal Publicity, 1954. *Recreations:* tennis, ancient literature, swimming bibliotheque, vinothèque, chess. *Address:* 56 Stationsweg, Heiloo, Netherlands. *Clubs:* National Liberal; de Witte (The Hague); Cercle Gaulois (Brussels).

BERKSHIRE, Archdeacon of; *see* Brown, Ven. J. E.

BERKSON, David Mayer; a Recorder of the Crown Court, since 1978; *b* 8 Sept. 1934; *s* of Louis Berkson and Regina Berkson (*née* Globe); *m* 1961, Pamela Anne (*née* Thwaite); one *d. Educ:* Birkenhead School. Called to the Bar, Gray's Inn, 1957. *Recreations:* tennis, caravanning. *Address:* 1 Exchange Flags, Liverpool L2 3XN. *T:* 051-236 7747. *Clubs:* Athenæum (Liverpool) Border and County (Carlisle); Oxton Cricket.

BERLIN, Irving; author and composer; *b* Russia, 11 May 1888; *s* of Moses Baline and Leah Lipkin; brought to USA, 1893; *m* 1st, 1913, Dorothy Goetz (*d* 1913); 2nd, 1926, Ellin, *d* of Clarence H. Mackay, NY; three *d. Educ:* public schools, NY City, for two years only. First song published, Marie From Sunny Italy, 1907; first complete Broadway score, Watch Your Step, 1914 Music Box Revue, 1921-24; Ziegfeld Follies, 1919, 1920, 1927. Pres. Irving Berlin Music Corp. Served as Sergt Infantry at Camp Upton, LI. Hon. Degrees, Bucknell, Temple, and Fordham Univs; Medal of Merit for This I*

The Army; awarded a special Gold Medal by Congress for God Bless America; Legion of Honour, France. Has composed about 800 songs, including: Alexander's Ragtime Band; Oh, How I Hate To Get Up In the Morning; When I Lost You; A Pretty Girl Is Like A Melody; Say It With Music; Always; Remember; Blue Skies; Easter Parade; Heat Wave; Isn't This A Lovely Day; Top Hat, White Tie and Tails; I've Got My Love To Keep Me Warm; White Christmas; This Is The Army, Mr Jones; Anything You Can Do; Doin' What Comes Natur'lly; The Girl That I Marry; There's No Business Like Show Business. Musicals (several of which have been filmed) include: As Thousands Cheer; Face The Music; Louisiana Purchase; Annie Get Your Gun; Miss Liberty; Call Me Madam; Mr President. US Medal of Freedom, 1977. *Address:* Irving Berlin Music Corp., 1290 Avenue of the Americas, New York City, USA. *Clubs:* Lambs, Friars.

BERLIN, Sir Isaiah, OM 1971; Kt 1957; CBE 1946; FBA 1957; MA; President of the British Academy, 1974-78; Fellow of All Souls College, Oxford; *b* 6 June 1909; *s* of Mendel and Marie Berlin; *m* 1956, Aline, *d* of Pierre de Gunzbourg. *Educ:* St Paul's Sch.; Corpus Christi Coll., Oxford. Lectr in Philosophy, New Coll., Oxford, 1932; Fellow: All Souls, 1932-38; New Coll., 1938-50; war service with Min. of Information, in New York, 1941-42, at HM Embassy in Washington, 1942-46, HM Embassy, Moscow, Sept. 1945-Jan. 1946; Fellow, All Souls Coll., Oxford, 1950-66, 1975-; Chichele Prof. of Social and Pol Theory, Oxford Univ., 1957-67; Pres., Wolfson Coll., Oxford 1966-Mar. 1975, Hon. Fellow, 1975. Mem. Cttee of Awards: Commonwealth (Harkness) Fellowships, 1960-64; Kennedy Scholarships, 1967-. Vice-Pres., British Academy, 1959-61; Pres. Aristotelian Soc., 1963-64. Mem., Academic Adv. Cttee., Univ. of Sussex, 1963-66. Visiting Professor: Harvard Univ., 1949, 1951, 1953, 1962; Bryn Mawr Coll., 1952; Chicago Univ., 1955; Princeton Univ., 1965; ANU, Canberra, 1975; Prof. of Humanities, City Univ. of NY, 1966-71. Lectures: Northcliffe, UCL, 1953; Mellon, Nat. Gall. of Art, Washington, DC, 1965; Danz, Washington Univ., 1971. Foreign Member: American Academy of Arts and Sciences; American Academy-Institute of Arts and Letters; American Philosophical Soc. Member, Board of Directors, Royal Opera House, Covent Garden, 1954-65, 1974-; a Trustee, Nat. Gall., 1975-. Governor, Univ. of Jerusalem; Pres., British Friends of the Univ. of Jerusalem. Hon. doctorates of the following universities: Hull, 1965; Glasgow, 1967; E Anglia, 1967; Brandeis (USA), 1967; Columbia, 1968; Cambridge, 1970; London, 1971; Jerusalem, 1971; Liverpool, 1972; Tel Aviv, 1973; Harvard, 1979; Sussex, 1979; Johns Hopkins, 1981; Northwestern, 1981; NY, 1982. Hon. Fellow: Corpus Christi Coll., Oxford; Wolfson Coll., Cambridge. *Publications:* Karl Marx, 1939, 4th edn 1978; Translation of First Love by I. S. Turgenev, 1950; The Hedgehog and the Fox, 1953, 4th edn 1979; Historical Inevitability, 1954; The Age of Enlightenment, 1956; Moses Hess, 1958; Two Concepts of Liberty, 1959; Mr Churchill in 1940, 1964; Four Essays on Liberty, 1969; Fathers and Children, 1972; Vico and Herder, 1976; Russian Thinkers, 1978; Concepts and Categories, 1978; Against the Current, 1979; Personal Impressions, 1980; translation of A Month in the Country by I. S. Turgenev, 1980. *Address:* All Souls College, Oxford. *Clubs:* Athenæum, Brooks's, Garrick; Century (New York).

BERMAN, Edward David, (ED Berman), MBE 1979; social entrepreneur, playwright, theatre director and producer; community activist; Founder and Artistic Director, Inter-Action, since 1968; *b* 8 March 1941; 2nd *s* of Jack Berman and Ida (*née* Webber); naturalized British citizen, 1976. *Educ:* Harvard (BA Hons); Exeter Coll., Oxford (Rhodes Schol.); Dept of Educnl Studies, Oxford (1978-). *Plays:* Freeze, 1966; Stamp, 1967; Super Santa, 1967; Sagittarius, 1968; Virgo, 1968; The Nudist Campers Grow and Grow, 1968; The Alien Singer, 1978; A Rosary for Israel, 1979; *director: theatre:* (premières) *inter alia* Dirty Linen (London and Broadway), 1976, and The Dogg's Troupe (15 minute) Hamlet, (ed) by Tom Stoppard, 1976 (also filmed, 1976); The Irish Hebrew Lesson, 1978 and Samson and Delilah, 1978, by Wolf Mankowitz; Dogg's Hamlet, Cahoot's Macbeth, 1979, by Tom Stoppard; Show Trial, 1981; *producer: theatre:* 125 stage premières for adults and 160 new plays for children, London, 1967-82; *maker of films:* (educational) The Head, 1971; Two Weeker, 1972; Farm in the City, 1977; Marx for Beginners Cartoon (co-prod., voice dir), 1978; *actor:* over 1200 performances as Prof. Dogg, Otto Première Check, Super Santa. Editor: 18 community arts and action handbooks, 1972-82; 2 anthologies of plays, 1976-78. Trustee and Founder, Inter-Action Trust, 1968; Director and Founder: Ambiance Lunch-Hour Th. Club, 1968; Prof. Dogg's Troupe for Children, 1968; Labrys Trust, 1969; Inter-Action Advisory Service, 1970; Infilms, 1970; The Almost Free Th., 1971; Inprint Publishing Unit, 1972; City Farm 1, 1972; Inter-Action Trust Ltd, 1974; Town and Country Inter-Action (Milton Keynes) Ltd, 1975; Ambiance Inter-Action Inc., 1976; Talacre Centre Ltd, 1977; Co-Founder: Inter-Action Housing Trust Ltd, 1970; NUBS, Neighbourhood Use of Bldgs and Space; Community Design Centre, 1974; Beginners Books Ltd, 1978; Inter-Action Housing Co-operative, 1978. Founder, Artistic Dir, BARC, British Amer. Rep. Co., 1978. Devised: Inter-Action Game Method, 1967; Super Santa, Father Xmas Union, 1967-82; Chairman: Save Piccadilly Campaign, 1971-80; Talacre Action Gp, 1972; Nat. Assoc. of Arts Centres, 1975-79; Dir, Islington Bus Co., 1974-76; Treas., Fair Play for Children Campaign, 1975-77; Founder: City Farm Movement, 1976; WAC—Weekend Arts Coll., 1979; co-founder: Sport-Space, 1976; FUSION—London and Commonwealth Youth Ensemble, 1981. Founder and Director: Internat. Inst. for Social Enterprise, 1980; Amer. Inst. for Social Enterprise, 1980; Country Wings, 1981. Part-time Adviser on voluntary organizations in inner cities to Sec. of State for the Environment, 1982-. As community artist: created 17 formats for participatory theatre, 1968-82; Community Media Van, 1973; Fun Art Loo, 1975; Community Cameos, 1977-82; MIY—Make It Yourself, 1978; RIY—Raise It Yourself, 1981. *Publication:* Prof. R. L. Dogg's Zoo's Who I and II, 1975. *Recreations:* solitude, conversation, work, music. *Address:* Inter-Action Housing Co-operative, 81 Willes Road, NW5. *T:* 01-267 9421. *Club:* Talacre Family Social.

BERMAN, Franklin Delow; Counsellor and Legal Adviser, UK Mission to the UN, New York, 1982; *b* 23 Dec. 1939; *s* of Joshua Zelic Berman and Gertrude (*née* Levin); *m* 1964, Christine Mary Lawler; two *s* three *d. Educ:* Rondebosch Boys' High Sch., Cape Town; Univ. of Cape Town; Wadham and Nuffield Colls, Oxford. BA, BSc Cape Town; MA Oxford. Rhodes Scholar, 1961; called to Bar (Middle Temple), 1966. HM Diplomatic Service, 1965: Asst Legal Adviser, FO, 1965; Legal Adviser: British Military Govt, Berlin, 1971; British Embassy, Bonn, 1972; Legal Counsellor, FCO, 1974. Chm., Diplomatic Service Assoc. 1979-. *Recreations:* walking, reading, music. *Address:* c/o Foreign and Commonwealth Office, SW1. *T:* 01-233 3000.

BERMAN, Lawrence Sam, CB 1975; Director of Statistics, Departments of Industry and Trade, since 1972; *b* 15 May 1928; *yr s* of Jack and Violet Berman; *m* 1954, Kathleen D. Lewis; one *s* one *d. Educ:* St Clement Danes Grammar Sch.; London Sch. of Economics. BSc (Econ) 1st cl. hons 1947; MSc (Econ) 1950. Res. Asst, LSE, 1947; Nuffield Coll., Oxford, 1948; Econ. Commn for Europe, 1949; Central Statistical Office: Asst Statistician 1952; Statistician 1955; Chief Statistician 1964; Asst Dir 1968. Editor, National Income Blue Book, 1954-60; Member: Council, Royal Statistical Soc., 1970-74 (Vice-Pres., 1973-74); Council Internat. Assoc. for Research in Income and Wealth; ISI. *Publications:* articles and papers in Jl of Royal Statistical Soc., Economica, Economic Trends, Statistical News, etc. *Recreations:* travel, theatre, gardening and other do-it-yourself activities. *Address:* 10 Carlton Close, Edgware, Mddx. *T:* 01-958 6938.

BERMANT, Chaim Icyk; author, since 1966; *b* 26 Feb. 1929; *s* of Azriel Bermant and Feiga (*née* Daets); *m* 1962, Judy Weil; two *s* two *d. Educ:* Queen's Park Sch., Glasgow; Glasgow Yeshiva; Glasgow Univ. (MA Hons; MLitt); London School of Economics (MScEcon). School-master, 1955-57; Economist, 1957-58; Television script writer, 1958-61; Journalist, 1961-66. *Publications:* Jericho Sleep Alone, 1964; Berl Make Tea, 1965; Ben Preserve Us, 1965; Diary of an Old Man, 1966; Israel, 1967; Swinging in the Rain, 1967; Troubled Eden, 1969; The Cousinhood, 1971; Here Endeth the Lesson, 1969; Now Dowager, 1971; Roses are Blooming in Picardy, 1972; The Last Supper, 1973; The Walled Garden, 1974; Point of Arrival, 1975; The Second Mrs Whitberg, 1976; Coming Home, 1976 (Wingate-Jewish Chronicle Book Award); The Squire of Bor Shachor, 1977; The Jews, 1978; Now Newman was Old, 1978; Belshazzar, 1979; (with Dr M. Weitzman) Ebla, 1979; The Patriarch, 1981; On the Other Hand, 1982. *Recreations:* walking, sermon-tasting. *Address:* c/o A. P. Watt, 26/28 Bedford Row, WC1R 4HL. *T:* 01-405 1057.

BERNACCHI, Michael Louis, CMG 1955; OBE 1952; *b* 5 May 1911; *s* of late Louis Charles Bernacchi, Physicist and Antarctic explorer, and late Winifred Edith Harris; *m* 1943, Elaine Chapman; one *s* one *d. Educ:* RN Colls Dartmouth and Greenwich; Magdalene Coll., Cambridge. Royal Navy, 1925-34; entered Colonial Service as Cadet, Fiji, 1936; District Commissioner, 1937; acting ADC to Governor of Fiji, 1939; served Royal Navy, 1940-44; Lieut Comdr RN (retd); transferred Malayan Civil Service, 1944; special duty, N Borneo, 1944; Military Administration N Borneo (Col), 1945-46; acting Chief Sec., N Borneo, 1946, Malaya, 1947-52; Class Ic Malayan Civil Service, 1951; (Perak Meritorious Service Medal, 1951); Resident Commissioner, Gilbert and Ellice Islands Colony, 1952-61, retd 1962. *Recreation:* reading. *Address:* 61 Leinster Road, Merivale, Christchurch 1, New Zealand. *Club:* Christchurch (NZ).

BERNAL-PEREIRA, Gen. Waldo; Bolivian Orders of: Merito Aeronautico; Guerrilleros Lanza; Merito Naval; Constancia Militar; Merito Aeronautico Civil; La Gran Orden de la Educación (Colombia); US Legion of Merit; Commander-in-Chief, Bolivian Air Force, since 1980; *b* 5 Dec. 1934; *s* of Romulo Bernal and Amalia Pereira; *m* Maria Antonieta Arze; three *s. Educ:* German Coll., Oruro, Bolivia; Military Aviation Coll.; Pilotage Course, USA; grad. as Pilot in Reese AFB, USA, 1958; Modern Meteorological Techniques Course at Chanute AFB, USA; Squadron Comd Course, Air Force Univ., Maxwell AFB, USA; Diploma, Comd and Mil. Staff, Buenos Aires, Argentina; Diploma Top Grade Nat. Studies, La Paz, Bolivia. Pilot Instructor, Air Force Mil. Coll., 1958; Pilot, Mil. Air Transport, 1959; Head of Operations, Aerial Fighter Gp, 1964; Head of Mil. Aeronaut. Polytechnic, 1966; Chief of Dept III, Aerial Comd Ops, 1970; Comdr, Air Transport Gp, 1972; Comdr, Mil. Aviation Coll., 1973; Head of Presidential COS, 1974; Minister of State for Education and Culture, Aug. 1974-Nov. 1976; Air Attaché, Bolivian Embassy, Washington, 1977; Comdr, Mil. Aviation Coll., 1978; Ambassador to Court of St James's, 1979-80. *Recreation:* tennis. *Address:* Avenida Julio C. Patiño No 665, Calacoto, Casilla No 345, La Paz, Bolivia; Comando General de la Fuerza Aérea Boliviana, Avenida Montes No 734, La Paz, Bolivia.

BERNARD, Sir Dallas (Edmund), 2nd Bt *cr* 1954; Director, Italian International Bank Ltd, since 1978; Chairman, National & Foreign Securities Trust Ltd, since 1981; *b* 14 Dec. 1926; *o s* of Sir Dallas Gerald Mercer Bernard, 1st Bt, and Betty (*d* 1980), *e d* of late Sir Charles Addis, KCMG; *S* father, 1975; *m* 1st, 1959, Sheila Robey (marr. diss. 1979); three *d*; 2nd, 1979, Mrs

Monica Montford, *d* of late James Edward Hudson; one *d. Educ:* Eton Coll.; Corpus Christi Coll., Oxford (MA). FCIS. Director: Morgan Grenfell (Holdings) Ltd, 1972-79; Morgan Grenfell & Co. Ltd, 1964-77; Dominion Securities Ltd, Toronto, 1968-79; Dreyfus Intercontinental Investment Fund NV, 1970-. Mem. Monopolies and Mergers Commn, 1973-79. *Heir:* none. *Address:* 7 Cresswell Gardens, SW5 0BJ. *T:* 01-373 9412. *Club:* Brooks's.

BERNARD, Joan Constance, MA, BD; FKC; Principal of Trevelyan College, University of Durham, and Honorary Lecturer in Theology, 1966-79; *b* 6 April 1918; *d* of late Adm. Vivian Henry Gerald Bernard, CB, and Eileen Mary Bernard. *Educ:* Ascham Sch., Sydney, NSW; St Anne's Coll., Oxford Univ. (BA Lit. Hum. 1940, MA 1943); King's Coll., London (BD 1961). War Service, ATS, 1940-46; Regtl duties, AA Comd, 1940-42; SO HQ AA Comd, 1942-44; SO Air Def. Div., SHAEF, 1944-45 (mentioned in despatches 1945); Special Projectile Ops Gp, July-Nov. 1945; SO HQ Northern Comd, 1945-46. Dep. Admin. Officer, NCB, 1946-50; Asst Sec., Educn, Music and Drama, NFWI, 1950-57; full-time student, 1957-61; Warden, Canterbury Hall, Univ. of London, and part-time Lectr, Dept of Theol., KCL, 1962-65; FKC 1976. Mem., Ordination Candidates' Cttee, ACCM, 1972-. Governor: Godolphin Sch., Salisbury, 1980-; St Saviour's Sch., Southwark, 1981-. *Recreations:* music (assisted John Tobin in Handel research for many years); mountaineering, photography. *Address:* 89 Rennie Court, Upper Ground, SE1.

BERNERS, Baroness (15th in line) *cr* 1455; **Vera Ruby Williams;** *b* 25 Dec. 1901; *d* of late Hon. Rupert Tyrwhitt, Major RA (5th *s* of Emma Harriet, Baroness Berners) and of Louise I. F. (*née* Wells); *S* cousin, 1950; *m* 1927, Harold Williams, Colonial Civil Service; two *d. Educ:* Ladies' Coll., Eastbourne; St Agnes' Sch., East Grinstead. *Co-heiresses: d* [Hon. Mrs Michael Kirkham, *b* (Pamela Vivian Williams) 30 Sept. 1929; *m* 1952; two *s* one *d*]; and *d* [Hon. Mrs Kelvin Pollock, *b* (Rosemary Tyrwhitt Williams) 20 July 1931; *m* 1959; two *s*]. *Address:* Ashwellthorpe, Charlton Lane, Cheltenham, Glos. *T:* Cheltenham 519595.

BERNEY, Sir Julian (Reedham Stuart), 11th Bt *cr* 1620; *b* 26 Sept. 1952; *s* of Lieut John Reedham Erskine Berney (killed on active service in Korea, 1952), Royal Norfolk Regt, and of Hon. Jean Davina (who *m* 2nd, P. W. Jesson), *d* of 1st Viscount Stuart of Findhorn, PC, CH, MVO, MC; *S* grandfather, 1975; *m* 1976, Sheena Mary, *yr d* of Ralph Day and Ann Gordon Day; one *s. Educ:* Wellington Coll.; North-East London Polytechnic. ARICS. *Recreation:* sailing. *Heir: s* William Reedham John Berney, *b* 29 June 1980. *Address:* Reeds House, 40 London Road, Nawdon, Essex CN9 6HE. *T:* Nawdon 53420. *Club:* Royal Ocean Racing.

BERNSTEIN, family name of **Baron Bernstein.**

BERNSTEIN, Baron *cr* 1969 (Life Peer), of Leigh; **Sidney Lewis Bernstein,** LLD; Chairman, Granada Group Ltd, 1934-79, President since 1979 (Granada Television, Granada Publishing, Granada Theatres, Granada TV Rental, Granada Motorway Services, Novello & Co.); *b* 30 Jan. 1899; *s* of Alexander and Jane Bernstein; *m* Sandra, *d* of Charles and Charlotte Malone, Toronto; one *s* two *d*. A founder, Film Society, 1924. Mem., Mddx CC, 1925-31. Films Adviser, Min. of Inf., 1940-45; Liaison, British Embassy, Washington, 1942; Chief Film Section, AFHQ N Africa, 1942-43; Chief, Film Section, SHAEF, 1943-45. Lectr on Film and Internat. Affairs, New York Univ. and Yale. Mem., Resources for Learning Cons. Cttee, Nuffield Foundn, 1965-72. Governor, Sevenoaks Sch., 1964-74. *Address:* 36 Golden Square, W1R 4AH; Coppings Farm, Leigh, Tonbridge, Kent TN11 8PN. *Club:* Garrick.

BERNSTEIN, Alexander; Chairman, Granada Group plc, since 1979; *b* 15 March 1936; *s* of late Cecil Bernstein and of Myra Ella, *d* of Lesser and Rachel Lesser; *m* 1962, Vanessa Anne, *d* of Alwyn and Winifred Mills; one *s* one *d. Educ:* Stowe Sch.; St John's Coll., Cambridge. Chm., Granada TV Rental Ltd, 1977- (Man. Dir, 1964-68); Director: Granada TV Ltd, 1970- (Jt Man. Dir, 1971-75; Dep. Chm., 1975-79); Barranquilla Investments, 1975-; Waddington Galleries, 1966-; Trustee: Civic Trust for the North-West, 1964-; Granada Foundn, 1968-. Dep. Chm., Royal Exchange Theatre, 1980-. Mem. Ct, Univ. of Salford, 1976-. Hon. DLitt Salford 1981. *Recreations:* modern art, ski-ing. *Address:* 36 Golden Square, W1R 4AH.

BERNSTEIN, Prof. Basil Bernard; Karl Mannheim Professor of Sociology of Education, since 1979, Head of Sociological Research Unit, since 1963, University of London; *b* 1 Nov. 1924; *s* of Percival and Julia Bernstein; *m* 1955, Marion Black; two *s. Educ:* LSE (BScEcon); UCL (PhD). Teacher, City Day Coll., Shoreditch, 1954-60; Hon. Research Asst, UCL, 1960-62; Sen. Lectr, Sociology of Educn, Univ. of London Inst. of Educn, 1963; Reader in Sociology of Educn, 1965; Prof., 1967. Hon. DLitt Leicester, 1974; Fil H Dr Univ. of Lund, 1980. *Publications:* Class Codes and Control, Vol. I 1971 (2nd edn 1974), Vol. II 1973, Vol. III 1975, revd edn 1977; (with W. Brandis) Selection and Control, 1974. *Recreations:* theatre, painting, conversation, etc. *Address:* 90 Farquhar Road, Dulwich, SE19 1LT. *T:* 01-670 6411.

BERNSTEIN, Ingeborg, (Inge); a Recorder of the Crown Court, since 1978; *b* 24 Feb. 1931; *d* of Sarah and Eli Bernstein; *m* 1967, Eric Geoffrey Goldrein; one *s* one *d. Educ:* Peterborough County School; St Edmund's College, Liverpool; Liverpool University. Called to the Bar, Inner Temple, 1952; practice on Northern Circuit. Chm., Mental Health Review Tribunal; Chm.

of local tribunals. *Recreations:* children and domesticity. *Address:* 54 Castle Street, Liverpool L2 7LQ. *T:* 051-236 4421.

BERNSTEIN, Leonard; conductor, composer, pianist, lecturer; *b* Lawrence, Mass, 25 Aug. 1918; *s* of Samuel J. and Jennie (Resnick) Bernstein; *m* 1951, Felicia Montealegre Cohn (*d* 1978); one *s* two *d. Educ:* Boston Latin Sch.; Harvard Univ.; Curtis Inst. of Music. Asst to Koussevitzky, Berkshire Music Center, 1942, Head of Conducting Dept, 1951-56; Asst Conductor, NY Philharmonic Orch., 1943-44; Conductor, NYC Symphony, 1945-48; Musical Adviser, Israel Philharmonic Orch., 1948-49; Prof. of Music, Brandeis Univ., 1951-56; Charles Eliot Norton Prof. of Poetry, Harvard Univ., 1973-74; co-conductor (with Dimitri Mitropoulos), NY Philharmonic Orch., 1957-58; Music Dir, NY Philharmonic Orch., 1958-69, now Laureate Conductor; Pres., English Bach Festival, 1977-. Has conducted all major orchestras of US and Europe in annual tours, 1944-; has toured N and S America, Europe, Near East, USSR and Japan with NY Philharmonic Orch. Holds decorations from: France, Italy, Finland, Chile and Austria. *Works include:* Clarinet Sonata, 1942; Symphony, No 1, Jeremiah, 1942; Song cycle (I Hate Music), 1943; Seven Anniversaries for Piano, 1943; Fancy Free, 1944; Hashkivenu, 1945; Facsimile, 1946; Five Pieces for Brass Instruments, 1947; Four Anniversaries for Piano, 1948; Symphony, No 2, The Age of Anxiety, 1949; Song Cycle (La Bonne Cuisine), 1949; songs, Afterthought and Silhouette, 1951; Trouble in Tahiti (one-act opera), 1952; Serenade (after Plato's Symposium) for violin solo, with string orch. and percussion, 1954; Symphony, No 3, Kaddish, 1963; Five Anniversaries for Piano, 1964; Chichester Psalms (a choral work with orchestra), 1965; Mass, a theatre piece for singers, players and dancers, 1971; Score for ballet, Dybbuk, 1974; Suite No 1 from Dybbuk, 1975; Seven Dances from Dybbuk, 1975; Songfest, 1977; scores for Broadway musicals including: On the Town, 1944, Wonderful Town, 1953, Candide, 1956, West Side Story, 1957; Score for Film, On the Waterfront, 1954. Has received Hon. Degrees from universities and colleges. *Publications:* The Joy of Music, 1959; Leonard Bernstein's Young People's Concerts for Reading and Listening, 1962; The Infinite Variety of Music, 1966; The Unanswered Question, 1973. *Address:* Amberson Productions, 1414 Avenue of the Americas, New York, NY 10019, USA.

BERNSTEIN, Ronald Harold, DFC 1944; QC 1969; a Recorder of the Crown Court, since 1974; *b* 18 Aug. 1918; *s* of late Mark and Fanny Bernstein; *m* 1955, Judy, *d* of David Levi, MS, and Vera Levi; three *s* one *d. Educ:* Swansea Grammar Sch.; Balliol Coll., Oxford. BA (Jurisprudence) 1939. Served in RA, 1939-46, and in 654 Air OP Sqdn, RAF, 1942-46. Commanded 661 Air OP Sqdn, RAuxAF, 1954-56. Called to the Bar, Middle Temple, 1948, Bencher, 1975. Mem., Gen. Council of the Bar, 1965-69; Mem., Law Commn Working Party on the Law of Landlord and Tenant, 1966-. *Publications:* (jointly) The Restrictive Trade Practices Act, 1956; Handbook of Rent Review, 1981; (Joint Editor) Foa, Landlord and Tenant, 8th edn, 1957. *Address:* (professional) 11 King's Bench Walk, Temple, EC4. *T:* 01-353 2484; *T:* (home) 01-340 9933. *Club:* Athenæum.

BERRIDGE, (Donald) Roy, CBE 1981; Chairman, South of Scotland Electricity Board, 1977-82 (Deputy Chairman, 1974-77); Director, Howden Group since 1982; *b* 24 March 1922; *s* of Alfred Leonard Berridge and Pattie Annie Elizabeth (*née* Holloway); *m* 1945, Marie (*née* Kinder); one *d. Educ:* King's Sch., Peterborough; Leicester Coll. of Art and Technology. FEng, FIMechE. Taylor, Taylor & Hobson Ltd, Leicester, 1940; James Gordon & Co., 1946; British Electricity Authority, 1948; seconded to AERE, Harwell, 1952; Reactor Design Engr, CEGB, 1962; Chief Generation Design Engr, 1964-70; Dir-Gen., Gen. Develt Constr. Div., CEGB, 1970-72; Dir of Engrg, SSEB, 1972-74. Member: N of Scotland Hydro-Electric Bd, 1977-82; Scottish Economic Council, 1977-; CBI (Scottish Council), 1977-82; Lloyds Register of Shipping (Scottish Cttee), 1980-. Mem. Board, Scottish Nat. Orchestra, 1982-. CBIM. *Address:* Whinfell, Broom Road, Newton Mearns, Glasgow G77 5DN. *T:* 041-639 1091.

BERRIEDALE, Lord; Alexander James Richard Sinclair; *b* 26 March 1981; *s* and *heir* of Earl of Caithness, *qv.*

BERRILL, Sir Kenneth, KCB 1971; Chairman, Vickers da Costa Ltd, since 1981; *b* 28 Aug. 1920; *m* 1950, June Phillips (marr. diss.); one *s* one *d* ; *m* 1977, Jane Marris. *Educ:* London Sch. of Economics; Trinity Coll., Cambridge. BSc(Econ) London; MA Cantab, 1949. Served War, 1939-45, REME. Economic Adviser to Turkey, Guyana, Cameroons, OECD, and World Bank. Univ. Lectr in Economics, Cambridge, 1949-69; Rockefeller Fellowship Stanford and Harvard Univs, 1951-52; Fellow and Bursar, St Catharine's Coll., Cambridge, 1949-62, Hon. Fellow, 1974; Prof., MIT, 1962; Fellow and First Bursar, King's Coll., Cambridge, 1962-69, Hon. Fellow, 1973; HM Treasury Special Adviser, 1967-69; Chm., UGC, 1969-73; Head of Govt Econ. Service and Chief Economic Advr, HM Treasury, 1973-74; Head of Central Policy Review Staff, Cabinet Office, 1974-80. Member: Council for Scientific Policy, 1969-72; Adv. Bd for Research Councils, 1972-77; Adv. Council for Applied R&D, 1977-80; Brit. Nat. Commn for UNESCO, 1967-70; Inter-Univ. Council, 1969-73; UGC, Univ. of S Pacific, 1972-; Council, Royal Economic Soc., 1972-; Adv. Bd, RCDS, 1974-80; Review Bd for Govt Contracts, 1981-. Governor: Administrative Staff Coll., Henley, 1969-; Overseas Develt Inst., 1969-73; Council, Open Univ., 1978-; Salford Univ., 1981-. Cambridge City Cllr, 1963-67. Director: General Funds Investment Trust, 1980-; Investing in Success Investment Trust, 1965-67; Ionian Bank, 1969-73; Robert Horne and Co. Ltd, 1982-; Dep. Chm.,

Universities' Superannuation Scheme, 1981-. Hon. Fellow: LSE, 1970; Chelsea Coll., London, 1973. Hon. LLD: Cambridge, 1974; Bath 1974; East Anglia 1975; Leicester 1975; DUniv Open, 1974; Hon. DTech Loughborough, 1974; Hon DSc Aston, 1974. Jephcott Lectr and Medallist, 1978. *Recreation:* ski-ing. *Address:* Vickers da Costa Ltd, Regis House, King William Street, EC4. *Clubs:* Climbers (Hon. Mem.); Himalayan; Cambridge Alpine.

ERRILL, Prof. Norman John, PhD, DSc; FRS 1952; FRSC; FAAAS; lately Strathcona Professor of Zoology, McGill University, Montreal; *b* 28 April 1903. *Educ:* Bristol Gram. Sch., Somerset, England; Bristol Univ.; London Univ. BSc Bristol; PhD, DSc London. FAAAS 1979. *Publications:* The Tunicata, 1951; The Living Tide, 1951; Journey into Wonder, 1953; Sex and the Nature of Things, 1954; The Origin of Vertebrates, 1955; Man's Emerging Mind, 1955; You and the Universe, 1958; Growth, Development and Pattern, 1962; Biology in Action, 1966; Worlds Apart, 1966; Life of the Oceans, 1967; The Person in the Womb, 1968; Developmental Biology, 1971; Development, 1976. *Address:* 410 Swarthmore Avenue, Swarthmore, Pa 19081, USA.

BERRIMAN, David, FIB; CBIM; Managing Director, Guinness Mahon & Co. Ltd, since 1973; Chairman: Bunzl Textile Holdings, since 1981 (Deputy Chairman, 1980); Satellite Television Ltd, since 1981; Director (non-executive): Cable and Wireless Ltd, since 1975; Telsat ag, since 1981; *b* 20 May 1928; *s* of late Algernon Edward Berriman, OBE and late Enid Kathleen Berriman (*née* Sutcliffe); *m* 1st, 1955, Margaret Lloyd (*née* Owen) (marr. diss. 1970); two *s*; 2nd, 1971, Shirley Elizabeth (*née* Wright). *Educ:* Winchester; New Coll., Oxford (MA, Dip. Econ. and Pol. Sc.); Harvard Business Sch. PMD course, 1961. First National City Bank of New York, 1952-56; Ford Motor Co. Ltd, 1956-60; AEI Hotpoint, 1960-63; Gen. Manager, United Leasing Corporation Ltd, 1963-64; Morgan Grenfell & Co. Ltd: Manager, 1964; Dir, 1968-73. Chm., Lewisham and N Southwark DHA, 1981-. Member: Bd of Trade's Interim Action Cttee for the Film Industry, 1977-; Govt review body on Harland and Wolff diversification, 1980-. Governor, Nat. Film School, 1977-. Chm., MacIntyre Schools Ltd (for mentally handicapped), 1978- (Governor, 1972). *Recreations:* golf, lawn tennis. *Clubs:* Royal Automobile, International Lawn Tennis; Wildernesse (Sevenoaks).

ERRY, family name of **Viscount Camrose, Baron Hartwell** and **Viscount Kemsley.**

BERRY, Alan Percival, FBIM; FITD; Barrister-at-Law; Director, Coventry & District Engineering Employers' Association, since 1963; *b* 1 Oct. 1926; *s* of Percy Berry and Winifred Berry; *m* 1952, Audrey Gwendolen, *d* of Douglas E. Spalton, Bramley; one *s* one *d. Educ:* Jesus Coll., Oxford (MA). DPA. Called to the Bar, Middle Temple, 1957. HM Factory Inspectorate, 1951-57; Sec., W of England Engrg Employers' Assoc., 1957-63. Dir, Midland Gp Trng Services Ltd, 1970-; Commissioner, Manpower Services Commn, 1976-79. Member: Coventry Educn Cttee, 1963-; CBI Midlands Council, 1972-; Council, Warwick Univ., 1974-; BBC Midlands Adv. Council, 1977-81 (Chm., 1979-81); BBC Gen. Adv. Council, 1979-81. Governor, Coventry (Lanchester) Polytechnic, 1970- (Chm., 1977-). OStJ 1968. *Publications:* Worker Participation: the European experience, 1974; Labour Relations in Japan, 1979. *Recreation:* sailing. *Address:* 50 Beverley Road, Leamington Spa, Warwicks. *T:* Leamington Spa 23262.

BERRY, Anthony Arthur; Chairman, Berry Bros & Rudd Ltd, since 1965; *b* 16 March 1915; *s* of Francis L. Berry and Amy Marie (*née* Freeman); *m* 1953, Sonia Alice, *d* of Sir Harold Graham-Hodgson, KCVO; one *s* one *d. Educ:* Charterhouse; Trinity Hall, Cambridge. Served War, RNVR, 1939-45, incl. 2½ yrs in the Mediterranean. Joined the wine trade on leaving Cambridge, 1936; rejoined family firm of Berry Bros & Rudd on completion of war service; Dir, 1946-. Worshipful Co. of Vintners: Liveryman, 1946; Mem. Court, 1972-; Master, 1980-81. *Recreations:* golf, walking. *Address:* (office) 3 St James's Street, SW1A 1EG. *T:* 01-930 1888; (home) 4 Cavendish Crescent, Bath, Avon BA1 2UG. *T:* Bath 22669. *Clubs:* Boodle's, MCC; Royal Wimbledon Golf; Royal St George's Golf (Sandwich).

BERRY, Hon. Anthony George; MP (C) Enfield, Southgate, since 1974 (Southgate, 1964-74); Comptroller of HM Household, since 1981; *b* 12 Feb. 1925; *y s* of 1st Viscount Kemsley, GBE; *m* 1st, 1954, Hon. Mary Cynthia Burke Roche (from whom he obtained a divorce, 1966), *er d* of 4th Baron Fermoy; one *s* three *d*; 2nd, 1966, Sarah Anne, *d* of Raymond Clifford-Turner, *qv*; one *s* one *d. Educ:* Eton; Christ Church, Oxford (MA). Served as Lieut, Welsh Guards, 1943-47. Asst Editor, Sunday Times, 1952-54; Editor, Sunday Chronicle, 1954; Dir, Kemsley Newspapers, 1954-59; Managing Dir, Western Mail and Echo Ltd, 1955-59. Dep. Chm., Leopold Joseph & Sons Ltd, 1962-79. PPS to Rt Hon. Peter Walker, Sec. of State, for the Environment, 1970-72, for Trade and Industry, 1972-74; Vice-Chm., Cons. Transport Cttee, 1969-70, 1974-75; Opposition Whip, 1975-79; Vice-Chamberlain of HM Household, 1979-81. Pres., Welsh Games Council, 1959-. JP Cardiff, 1961; High Sheriff, Glamorgan, 1962. CStJ. *Publication:* (jt editor) Conservative Oxford, 1949. *Address:* 1 Graham Terrace, SW1. *T:* 01-235 3801; Fox's Walk, Shurlock Row, Twyford, Berkshire. *Clubs:* Portland, White's; Cardiff and County (Cardiff).

BERRY, Prof. Colin Leonard, FRCPath; Professor of Morbid Anatomy, University of London, at The London Hospital Medical College, since 1976; *b* 28 Sept. 1937; *s* of Ronald Leonard Berry and Peggy-Caroline (*née* Benson); *m* 1960, Yvonne Waters; two *s. Educ:* privately; Charing Cross Hosp. Med.

Sch. (MB, BS; Governors' Clinical Gold Medal, Llewellyn Schol., Pierera Prize in Clinical Subjects, Steadman Prize in Path.); trained in Histopath., Charing Cross Hosp., 1962-64. MD, PhD (London). Lectr and Sen. Lectr, Inst. of Child Health, London, 1964-70; Reader in Pathology, Guy's Hosp. Med. Sch., 1970-76; Gillson Scholar, Worshipful Soc. of Apothecaries, 1967-68 and 1970-72; Arris and Gail Lectr, RCS, 1973. Mem., Toxicology Review Panel, WHO, 1976-; Vice-Chm., Cttee on Dental and Surgical Materials, 1979 (Chm., 1982-); Pres., Developmental Path. Soc., 1976-; Meetings Sec., ACP, 1979; Member: Scientific Sub-Cttee on Pesticides, MAFF; Adv. Commn on Pesticides, MAFF/DHSS, 1982-; Scientific Adv. Commn on Pesticides, EEC, 1981-. Asst Registrar, RCPath, 1981-. *Publications:* Teratology: trends and applications, 1975; Paediatric Pathology, 1981; contrib. Cardiac Pathology (Pomerance and Davies), 1975, and to other texts; numerous publns in LJl of Path., Circulation Res. and other path. jls. *Recreations:* sailing, shooting, pond building. *Address:* 1 College Gardens, Dulwich SE21 7BE. *T:* 01-299 0066. *Clubs:* Reform; Tollesbury Cruising (Essex).

BERRY, Prof. Francis; Emeritus Professor of English Language and Literature, Royal Holloway College, University of London, since 1980; *b* 23 March 1915; *s* of James Berry and Mary Augusta Jane Berry (*née* Ivens); *m* 1st, 1947, Nancy Melloney (*d* 1967), *d* of Cecil Newton Graham; one *s* one *d*; 2nd, 1970, Patricia, *d* of John Gordon Thomson (marr. diss. 1975); 3rd, 1979, Eileen, *d* of Eric Charles Lear. *Educ:* Hereford Cathedral Sch.; Dean Close Sch.; University Coll., Exeter. BA London (1st cl. hons); MA Exeter. Solicitor's articled clerk, 1931; University Coll., Exeter, 1937. War Service, 1939-46. University Coll., Exeter, 1946; successively Asst Lectr, Lectr, Sen. Lectr, Reader in English Literature, and Prof. of English Literature, Univ. of Sheffield, 1947-70; Prof. of English Lang. and Lit., Royal Holloway Coll., Univ. of London, 1970-80. Visiting Lectr: Carleton Coll., Minn, USA, 1951-52; University Coll. of the West Indies, Jamaica, 1957; Lectr for British Council, in India, 1966-67; W. P. Ker Lectr, Glasgow, 1979; Vis. Fellow, ANU, Canberra, 1979; Vis. Prof. of English, Univ. of Malawi, 1980-81. FRSL 1968. *Publications:* Gospel of Fire, 1933; Snake in the Moon, 1936; The Iron Christ, 1938; Fall of a Tower, 1942; Murdock and Other Poems, 1947; The Galloping Centaur, 1952, 2nd edn 1970; Herbert Read, 1953, 2nd edn 1961; An Anthology of Medieval Poems (ed), 1954; Poets' Grammar: time, tense and mood in poetry, 1958, 2nd edn, 1974; Morant Bay and other poems, 1961; Poetry and the Physical Voice, 1962; The Shakespeare Inset, 1965, 2nd edn 1971; Ghosts of Greenland, 1967; John Masefield: the Narrative Poet, 1968; (ed) Essays and Studies for the English Association, 1969; Thoughts on Poetic Time, 1972; I Tell of Greenland (novel), 1977; Contributor: Essays in Criticism; BBC Radio Three, ABC, etc. *Recreations:* devising outdoor games, walking, watching cricket. *Address:* 33 Lyndhurst Avenue, Sunbury on Thames, Mddx TW16 6QZ. *T:* Sunbury on Thames 61666.

BERRY, Dr James William; Director General Strategic Electronic Systems, Ministry of Defence (Procurement Executive), since 1979; *b* 5 Oct. 1931; *s* of Arthur Harold Berry and Mary Margaret Berry; *m* 1960, Monica Joan Hill; three *d. Educ:* St Mary's Coll., Blackburn; Municipal Technical Coll., Blackburn; Manchester Univ. (BSc); Leeds Univ. (PhD); CEng, FIEE. Royal Signals and Radar Estab., Malvern, 1956-60; Admiralty Surface Weapons Estab., Portsdown, 1960-76 (Head of Computer Div., 1972-76); Dir of Long Range Surveillance and Comd and Control Projs, MoD (PE), 1976-79. *Recreations:* music, walking, bird watching. *Address:* c/o Prospect House, 100 New Oxford Street, WC1. *Club:* Civil Service.

BERRY, John, CBE 1968; MA (Cantab); PhD (St Andrews); FRSE 1936; DL; Consultant on Water Impoundment Biology; Conservation and Fisheries Adviser to: North of Scotland Hydro-Electric Board, since 1968; South of Scotland Electricity Board, since 1973; Chairman, Interdepartmental Salmon Research Group (UK and Ireland), since 1971; *b* Edinburgh, 5 Aug. 1907; *o s* of late William Berry, OBE, DL, Tayfield, Newport, Fife; *m* 1936, Hon. Bride Fremantle, MA (Cantab), 3rd *d* of 3rd Baron Cottesloe, CB; two *s* one *d. Educ:* Eton; Trinity Coll., Cambridge. BA 1929 (Zoo. Chem. Phys. Pt I and Law Pt II); MA 1933; PhD 1935; Salmon research, Fishery Bd for Scotland, 1930-31; Biological Research Station, University Coll., Southampton, Research Officer, 1932-36 and Dir, 1937-39. Press Censor for Scotland, 1940-44; Biologist and Information Officer, North of Scotland Hydro-Electric Bd, 1944-49; Dir of Nature Conservation in Scotland, 1949-67. Pres. 1954-56, Vice-Pres. 1956-60, and Mem., 1966-72, Commn on Ecology, Internat. Union for Conservation of Natural Resources; UK rep., Exec. Bd, Internat. Wildfowl Research Bureau, 1963-72. Mem. Court, Univ. of Dundee, 1970-78; Vice-President: RZS Scotland, 1959-; Wildfowlers' Assoc. of GB and Ireland; Wildfowl Trust; Scottish Wildlife Trust. Hon. LLD Dundee, 1970. DL Fife, 1969. *Publications:* The Status and Distribution of Wild Geese and Wild Duck in Scotland, 1939; various papers and articles on fresh-water fisheries, hydro-electric development and ornithology. *Recreations:* wild geese, photography, music. *Address:* Tayfield, Newport-on-Tay, Fife DD6 8HA. *T:* Dundee 543118. *Club:* New (Edinburgh).

BERRY, Michael Francis; Director of Robert Fleming & Co. Ltd, Merchant Bankers, 1937-77; *b* 17 Oct. 1906; *e s* of C. Seager Berry and Constance, *d* of Rev. D. C. Cochrane; *m* 1939, Prudence *d* of C. G. Atha, Haverbrack House, Milnthorpe; one *d. Educ:* Eton; Hertford Coll., Oxford. Entered City, 1929; served War of 1939-45, Royal Artillery. A Crown Estate Commissioner, 1956-65. High Sheriff Northants 1973. *Publications:* A History of the Puckeridge Hunt, 1950; (with C. M. Floyd) A History of the

Eton College Hunt 1857-1968, 1969. *Recreations:* hunting, farming. *Address:* Benefield House, near Peterborough. *T:* Benefield 219. *Club:* Boodle's.

BERRY, Rt. Rev. Robert Edward Fraser; *see* Kootenay, Bishop of.

BERRY, Prof. Robert James, FRSE 1981; Professor of Genetics in the University of London, since 1974; *b* 26 Oct. 1934; *o s* of Albert Edward James Berry and Nellie (*née* Hodgson); *m* 1958, Anne Caroline Elliott, *d* of Charles Elliott and Evelyn Le Cornu; one *s* two *d*. *Educ:* Shrewsbury Sch.; Caius Coll., Cambridge (MA); University Coll. London (PhD; DSc 1976). Lectr, subseq. Reader, then Prof., in Genetics, at Royal Free Hospital Sch. of Medicine, 1962-78; Prof. of Genetics at University Coll. London, 1978-. Member: Board of Social Responsibility of the General Synod, 1976-; Natural Environment Research Council, 1981-; President, Linnean Soc., 1982-; Chm., Research Scientists' Christian Fellowship, 1968-. *Publications:* Teach Yourself Genetics, 1965, 3rd edn 1977; Adam and the Ape, 1975; Inheritance and Natural History, 1977; (jtly) Natural History of Shetland, 1980; ed, Biology of the House Mouse, 1981; Neo-Darwinism, 1982. *Recreations:* hill-walking (especially Munros), recovering. *Address:* Department of Zoology, University College London, Gower Street, WC1E 6BT. *T:* 01-387 7050.

BERRY, Dr Robert Langley Page, CBE 1979; Chairman, 1968-78, Deputy Chairman, 1978-79, Alcoa of Great Britain Ltd; *b* 22 Nov. 1918; *s* of Wilfred Arthur and Mabel Grace Berry; *m* 1946, Eleanor Joyce (*née* Cramp); one *s* one *d*. *Educ:* Sir Thomas Rich's Sch., Gloucester; Birmingham Univ. (BSc (Hons), PhD). Served war, Royal Engrs, 1939-45. ICI Metals Div., 1951-66, Director, 1960-66; Man. Dir, Impalco, 1966-68. Non-Exec. Dir, Royal Mint, 1981-. Dir, Nat. Anti-Waste Prog., 1976-80. President: Inst. of Metals, 1973; Aluminium Fedn, 1974. *Publications:* several, in scientific jls. *Recreations:* fly-fishing, gardening. *Address:* Waterloo Cottage, Waterloo Lane, Fairford, Glos GL7 4BP. *T:* Cirencester 712038. *Club:* Army and Navy.

BERRY, Air Cdre Ronald, CBE 1965 (OBE 1946); DSO 1943; DFC 1940 and Bar, 1943; RAF retired; Director of Control Operations, Board of Trade, 1965-68; *b* 3 May 1917; *s* of W. Berry, Hull; *m* 1940, Nancy Watson, Hessle, near Hull; one *d*. *Educ:* Hull Technical Coll. VR Pilot, Brough Flying Sch., 1937-39; 603 F Sqdn, Turnhouse/Hornchurch, 1939-41 (Battle of Britain); Sqdn Ldr, and CO 81 F Sqdn, North Africa, 1942; Wing Comdr, and CO 322 F Wing, North Africa, 1942-43; Camberley Army Staff Coll., 1944; CO, RAF Acklington, 1945-46; *jssc* 1955; various operational appts in Fighter and Bomber Comd; V Sqdn, 1957-59; Group Capt., Air Min. and HQ Bomber Comd, 1959. *Recreations:* motoring, gardening, flying. *Address:* Aldrian, Mereview Avenue, Hornsea, N Humberside HU18 IRR.

BERTHOIN, Georges Paul; Médaille militaire, Croix de Guerre, Médaille de la Résistance avec Rosette, France, 1945; Executive Member of the Trilateral Commission (Japan, N America, W Europe), since 1973, Chairman, since 1975; Honorary International Chairman, the European Movement, since 1981 (Chairman, 1978-81); *b* Nérac, France, 17 May 1925; *s* of Jean Berthoin and Germaine Mourgnot; *m* 1st, 1950, Ann White Whittlesey; four *d*; 2nd, 1965, Pamela Jenkins; two *s*. *Educ:* Grenoble Univ.; Ecole Sciences Politiques, Paris; Harvard Univ. Licencié ès Lettres (Philosophie), Licencié en Droit, Laureate for Economics (Grenoble). Lectr, McGill Univ., Montreal, 1948; Private Sec. to French Minister of Finance, 1948-50; Head of Staff of Superprefect of Alsace-Lorraine-Champagne, 1950-52. Joined High Authority of European Coal and Steel Community, and then Principal Private Sec. to its Pres. (Jean Monnet), 1952-53-55. Dep. Chief Rep. of ECSC in UK, 1956-67; Chargé d'Affaires for Commission of the European Communities (ECSC Euratom-Common Market), 1968; Principal Adviser to the Commission, and its Dep. Chief Rep. in London, 1969-70, Chief Representative, 1971-73. *Recreations:* art, theatre, walking, collecting objects. *Address:* 67 Avenue Niel, 75017 Paris, France.

BERTHON, Vice-Adm. Sir Stephen (Ferrier), KCB 1980; *b* 24 Aug. 1922; *s* of late Rear-Adm. C. P. Berthon, CBE and Mrs C. P. Berthon (*née* Ferrier); *m* 1948, Elizabeth Leigh-Bennett; two *s* two *d*. *Educ:* Old Malthouse, Swanage; RNC Dartmouth. Served War of 1939-45 at sea, Mediterranean, Atlantic, Russia; spec. communications, 1945-46; Flag Lieut Singapore, 1946-48; submarines, 1949-51; East Indies Flagship, 1951-52; HMS Mercury, 1952-54; Staff of Flag Officer Aircraft Carriers, 1954-56; Fleet Communications Officer Mediterranean, 1957-59; *jssc* 1959; Comdr HMS Mercury, 1959-61; Jt Planning Staff, 1961-64; Naval Attaché, Australia, 1964-66; Dir of Defence Policy, MoD, 1968-71; Cdre HMS Drake, 1971-73; Flag Officer Medway and Port Adm. Chatham, 1974-76; Asst Chief of Naval Staff (Op. Req.), 1976-78; Dep. Chief of Defence Staff (Operational Requirements), 1978-81; retired 1981. Jt MFH, Avon Vale Hunt, 1981-. *Recreations:* hunting, riding, gardening, walking, painting. *Address:* Stert House, Devizes, Wilts. *T:* Devizes 3713. *Club:* Army and Navy.

BERTHOUD, Sir Eric Alfred, KCMG 1954 (CMG 1945); MA; retired from HM Foreign Service, 1960; *b* 10 Dec. 1900; 2nd *s* of late Alfred E. Berthoud and Helene Berthoud; *m* 1927, Ruth Tilston, *d* of Sir Charles Bright, FRSE; two *s* two *d* (and one *s* decd). *Educ:* Gresham's Sch., Holt; Magdalen Coll., Oxford; MA. Demy; Hons in Natural Science; Goldsmith's Exhibnr. Anglo-Austrian Bank Ltd, London, 1922-26; Anglo-Iranian Oil Co. (BP) Ltd, 1926-39; served as board mem. in France, Holland and Germany, war time mandate, 1939-44, denial of oil to Axis. Commercial Sec. to HM Legation, Bucharest, 1939-41; Mem. British military and econ. mission to Soviet Union,

1941-42; Asst Sec., Min. of Fuel and Power (Petroleum Div.), 1942-44 Minister of State's Office, Cairo, 1942-43; Dir Economic Div., Allie Commission for Austria (British Element), 1944-46; Under-Sec., Petroleur Div., Min. of Fuel and Power, 1946-48; Asst Under-Sec., FO, 1948-52; HM Ambassador to Denmark, 1952-56, to Poland, 1956-60. Jt Chairman International Cttee setting up OEEC in Paris, 1948; Anglo-Polish Roun Table Confs, 1963-70. Chm. (part-time) Civil Service Selection Bd, 1963-68 Pres., Colchester Constituency Liberal Assoc., 1974-76. Member: Council 1962-73, and Court, Essex Univ.; Council, SSEES, London Univ., 1964-70 Mem. Internat. Council and Governor, Atlantic College, 1962-. Mem., Bd o Visitors, Chelmsford Prison, 1960-75; Pres. (formerly Chm.), Katherine Low Settlement, Battersea; Vice Chm., Sue Ryder Foundn, 1970-72. DL Essex 1969-. Knight Comdr's Cross with star, Order of Polonia Restituta, 1965 *Recreation:* international relations. *Address:* Gosfield Hall, Halstead, Esse CO9 1SF. *T:* Halstead 473844. *Club:* Brooks's.
See also M. S. Berthoud, R. G. Pentney.

BERTHOUD, Martin Seymour; HM Diplomatic Service; Consul-Genera Sydney, since 1982; *b* 20 Aug. 1931; *s* of Sir Eric Berthoud, *qv*; *m* 196 Marguerite Joan Richarda Phayre; three *s* one *d*. *Educ:* Rugby Sch.; Magdale Coll., Oxford (BA). Served with British Embassies in: Tehran, 1956-58 Manila, 1961-64; Pretoria/Cape Town, 1967-71; Tehran, 1971-73 Counsellor, Helsinki, 1974-77; Inspector, HM Diplomatic Service, 1977-79 Head of N. American Dept, FCO, 1979-81. Commander, Order of the Lior Finland, 1976. *Recreations:* squash, tennis, food and wine, photography bird-watching, fishing. *Address:* c/o Foreign and Commonwealth Office SW1A 2AH. *Club:* United Oxford & Cambridge University.

BERTIE, family name of **Earl of Lindsey and Abingdon.**

BERTRAM, Dr Christoph; Political and Foreign Editor, Die Zeit, since 1982 *b* 3 Sept. 1937; German national; *m* 1st, 1967, Renate Edith Bergemann (marri diss. 1980); 2nd, 1980, Ragnhild Lindemann. *Educ:* Free Univ. Berlin an Bonn Univ. (law); Institut d'Etudes Politiques, Paris (political science). Dr o Law 1967. Joined Internat. Inst. for Strategic Studies as Research Associate 1967, Asst Dir 1969-74, Dir, 1974-82; Mem. Planning Staff, West Germar Min. of Defence, 1969-70. *Publications:* (with Alastair Buchan *et al.*) Europe' Futures—Europe's Choices, 1969; Mutual Force Reductions in Europe: the political aspects, 1972; (ed, with Johan J. Holst) New Strategic Factors in th North Atlantic, 1977; Arms Control and Technological Change, 1979 *Recreations:* clocks, sailing. *Address:* Die Zeit, Pressehaus, Speersort, 200 Hamburg 1, West Germany. *Club:* Garrick.

BERTRAM, (Cicely) Kate, MA; PhD; JP; President, Lucy Cavendis College, Cambridge, 1970-79 (Tutor, 1965-70; Hon. Fellow, 1982); *b* 8 Jul 1912; *d* of late Sir Harry Ralph Ricardo, FRS; *m* 1939, Dr George Coli Lawder Bertram (Fellow and formerly Senior Tutor of St John's Coll Cambridge); four *s*. *Educ:* Hayes Court, Kent; Newnham Coll., Cambridge MA, PhD (Cantab), 1940. Jarrow Research Studentship, Girton Coll Cambridge, 1937-40. Mem. Colonial Office Nutrition Survey, in Nyasaland 1939; Adviser on Freshwater Fisheries to Govt of Palestine, 1940-43. Mem Council, New Hall, Cambridge, 1954-66; Associate of Newnham Coll. FLS JP Co. Cambridge, and Isle of Ely, 1959. *Publications:* 2 Crown Agents Reports on African Fisheries, 1939 and 1942; papers on African Fish, in zoological jls; papers and articles on Sirenia (with G.C.L. Bertram) *Recreations:* foreign travel, gardening. *Address:* Ricardo's, Graffham, nea Petworth, Sussex. *T:* Graffham 255. *Club:* English-Speaking Union.

BERTRAM, Prof. Douglas Somerville; Professor of Medical Entomolog and Director of Department of Entomology, London School of Hygiene an Tropical Medicine, 1956-76, now Emeritus; *b* 21 Dec. 1913; *s* of William R J. Bertram and Katherine Arathoon Macaskill, Glasgow, Scotland; *m* 1st, 1947 Louisa Menzies MacKellar (*d* 1956); two *d*; 2nd, 1973, Muriel Elizabeth (*né* Maas), widow of W. M. Drury. *Educ:* Hillhead High Sch., Glasgow; Univ of Glasgow. 1st cl. hons BSc (Zoology), 1935, PhD 1940, DSc 1964, Glasgow Univ.; FIBiol; Strang-Steel Scholar, Glasgow Univ., 1935-36. Demonstrator Dept of Zoology, Glasgow Univ., 1936-38; Lectr, Liverpool Sch. of Tropica Medicine, 1938-40, and 1946-48; Reader in Entomology, London Sch. o Hygiene and Tropical Medicine, 1948-56. Hon. Treasr, Royal Society o Tropical Medicine and Hygiene, 1960-73. Overseas work in East and Wes Africa, India and Ceylon, Central America periodically. Served War o 1939-45: Lieut to Major, Royal Army Medical Corps, Middle East, POW Germany, Army Sch. of Health Staff, 1945-46. *Publications:* scientific paper in Annals of Trop. Medicine and Parasitology, Transactions Royal Societ Tropical Medicine and Hygiene, Adv. Parasitology, Bulletin WHO, etc *Recreations:* gardening, painting, travel. *Address:* 33 Parkside Drive, Watford Herts WD1 3AS. *Club:* Royal Commonwealth Society.

BERTRAM, Kate; *see* Bertram, C. K.

BERTRAM, Robert David Darney; Partner, Dundas & Wilson, Clerks to the Signet, Edinburgh, since 1969; Member, Scottish Law Commission, sinc 1978; *b* 6 Oct. 1941; *s* of D. N. S. Bertram; *m* 1967, Patricia Joan Laithwaite two *s*. *Educ:* Edinburgh Academy; Oxford Univ. (MA); Edinburgh Univ (LLB (Hons), Berriedale Keith Prize). An Assistant Solicitor, Linklaters & Paines, London, 1968-69. Associate, Institute of Taxation, 1970. Examiner Law Society of Scotland, 1972-75. *Publications:* contribs to professional jls

Address: 25 Charlotte Square, Edinburgh EH2 4EZ. *T:* 031-225 1234. *Clubs:* Edinburgh University Staff; Scottish Arts.

BESCH, Anthony John Elwyn; opera and theatre director, since 1950; *b* 5 Feb. 1924; *s* of Roy Cressy Frederick Besch and Ann Gwendolen Besch. *Educ:* Rossall Sch., Lancs; Worcester Coll., Oxford (MA). Dir, opera and theatre, 1950-: Royal Opera House, Covent Garden; English Nat. Opera, London Coliseum; Scottish Opera; Welsh Nat. Opera; New Opera Co., London; Handel Opera Soc.; Edinburgh Festival; Wexford Festival; Deutsche Oper, Berlin; Royal Netherlands Opera; Théâtre de la Monnaie, Brussels; Teatro Colon, Buenos Aires; New York City Opera; San Francisco Opera; Canadian Opera Co.; Nat. Arts Centre, Canada; Australian Opera; State Opera, S Australia. *Recreation:* gardening. *Address:* 19 Church Lane, Aston Rowant, Oxfordshire. *Club:* Garrick.

BESLEY, Christopher; a Metropolitan Magistrate since 1964; *b* 18 April 1916; *s* of late C. A. Besley, Tiverton; *m* 1947, Pamela, *d* of Dr W. E. David, Sydney, Australia; four *s* two *d*. *Educ:* King's Coll., Wimbledon; King's Coll., London. Barrister, Gray's Inn, 1938. Served War of 1939-45, Devon Regt. *Address:* Queen Elizabeth Building, Temple, EC4; 15 Belvedere Avenue, SW19. *T:* 01-946 2184.

BESSBOROUGH, 10th Earl of, *cr* 1739, Earl (UK), *cr* 1937; **Frederick Edward Neuflize Ponsonby;** DL; Baron of Bessborough; Viscount Duncannon, 1723; Baron Ponsonby, 1749; Baron Duncannon (UK), 1834; *b* 29 March 1913; *s* of 9th Earl of Bessborough, PC, GCMG, and Roberte de Neuflize, GCStJ (*d* 1979), *d* of late Baron Jean de Neuflize; *S* father, 1956; *m* 1948, Mary, *d* of Charles A. Munn, USA; one *d*. *Educ:* Eton; Trinity Coll., Cambridge (MA). Contested W Div. Islington (Nat. Govt), 1935. Joined Sussex Yeomanry (TA), 1936; Sec., League of Nations High Commission for Refugees, 1936-39. Served War of 1939-45, France, Flanders and Dunkirk; ADC to Comdr, Canadian Corps; Experimental Officer (Capt.) Tank Gunnery; GSO2 (liaison) in West and North Africa; Second and subsequently First Sec., British Embassy, Paris, 1944-49. With Robert Benson, Lonsdale and Co. Ltd and Dir High Definition Films, Associated Broadcasting Development Co. Ltd, ATV, Glyndebourne Arts Trust; English Stage Co. Ltd, etc, 1950-63. Chairman of Governors: Dulwich College, 1972-73; British Soc. for Internat. Understanding, 1951-71; Chairman: International Atlantic Cttee, 1952-55; European Atlantic Group, 1954-61. Mem. of UK Parly Delegn to USSR, 1960. Parly Sec. for Science, Oct. 1963; Jt Parly Under-Sec. of State for Educn and Science, 1964; Cons. front bench spokesman on Science, Technology, Power, Foreign and Commonwealth Affairs, 1964-70; Minister of State, Min. of Technology, June-Oct. 1970. Dep. Chm., Metrication Board, 1969-70; Chm., Cttee of Inquiry into the Res. Assocs, 1972-73. Lectures throughout world on British sci. and ind.; Member: Parly and Scientific Cttee (Vice-Pres.); European Parliament, 1972-79 (Vice-Pres., 1973-76; Dep. Leader, European Cons. Gp, 1972-77; Mem. Cttees on Budgets, Energy, Research and Technology); House of Lords Select Cttees on European Communities and Science and Technology, 1979-; President: SE Assoc. of Building Socs; Men of the Trees; Chichester Cons. Assoc.; Chichester Festival Theatre Trust; British Theatre Assoc. DL West Sussex, 1977. OStJ; Chevalier Legion of Honour; MRI; FRGS. *Plays and publications:* Nebuchadnezzar (with Muriel Jenkins), 1939; The Four Men (after H. Belloc), 1951; Like Stars Appearing, 1953; The Noon is Night, 1954; Darker the Sky, 1955; Triptych, 1957; A Place in the Forest, 1958; Return to the Forest, 1962; articles, reviews. *Heir pres.: c* Arthur Mountifort Longfield Ponsonby [*b* 11 Dec. 1912; *m* 1939, Patricia (*d* 1952), *d* of Col Fitzhugh Lee Minnigerode, Va, USA; one *s* one *d*; *m* 1956, Princess Anne Marie Galitzine (marr. diss., 1963), *d* of late Baron Sir Rudolph Slatin Pasha; *m* 1963, Madeleine, *d* of Maj.-Gen. Laurence Grand, CB, CIE, CBE; two *s*]. *Address:* 4 Westminster Gardens, SW1. *T:* 01-828 5959; Stansted Park, Rowland's Castle, Hants. *T:* Rowlands Castle 2223. *Clubs:* Turf, Garrick, Beefsteak; Grolier (New York).
See also Lady M. B. M. Browne.

BESSELL, Peter Joseph; investment consultant and writer; *b* Bath, 24 Aug. 1921; *o s* of Joseph Edgar Bessell and Olive Simons Bessell (*née* Hawkins); *m* 1st, 1942, Joyce Margaret Thomas (*d* 1947), Bath; 2nd, Pauline Colledge (marr. diss. 1978), Saltford, Bristol; one *s* one *d*; 3rd, Diane, *o d* of Frederick and Doryce Miller, Yardley, Pa, USA. *Educ:* Lynwyd Sch., Bath. Min. of Information Lectr to HM and Allied Forces, 1943-45. Contested (L): Torquay, 1955 and by-election Dec. 1955; Bodmin, 1959; MP (L) Bodmin, 1964-70, retired; Member: Estimates Cttee, 1964-66, 1966-67; Parly Commn to S Vietnam, 1967; Select Cttees on Agriculture, 1967; Vehicle Excise Duty (Allegations), 1969; Procedure, 1964-65. Nat. Pres., Brotherhood Movement, 1967-68. Congregational Lay Preacher, 1939-70. Chm. and Dir, Milbest Publications Inc. *Publication:* Cover-up (The Jeremy Thorpe Affair), 1981. *Recreations:* music, reading, gardening. *Address:* PO Box 2145, Oceanside, California 92054, USA. *T:* (714) 722-3677.

BESSEY, Gordon Scott, CBE 1968; *b* 20 Oct. 1910; *s* of late Edward Emerson and Mabel Bessey, Great Yarmouth; *m* 1937, Cynthia (*d* 1966), *d* of late William and Mary Bird, Oxford; one *s* three *d*. *Educ:* Heath Sch., Halifax; St Edmund Hall, Oxford. BA 1932, Dip Ed 1933, MA 1937. Teaching: Keighley and Cheltenham, 1933-37; Admin. Asst, Surrey, 1937-39; Asst, later Dep. Educn Officer, Norfolk, 1939-45; Dep. Educn Officer, Somerset, 1945-49. Mem., Youth Service Development Council, 1960-67; Chm., Working Party on part-time training of Youth Leaders, 1961-62; Pres., Assoc. of Chief Educn Officers, 1963; Treas., Soc. of Educn Officers, 1971-74;

Chairman: Educnl Adv. Council of IBA (formerly ITA), 1970-74; County Educn Officers' Soc., 1969-70; Dir of Educn, Cumberland, 1949-74, Cumbria, 1974-75. Chairman: East Cumbria Community Health Council, 1974-79; Assoc. of Community Health Councils in England and Wales, 1977-79; Voluntary Action, Cumbria, 1975-. Hon. DCL Newcastle upon Tyne, 1970. *Recreations:* fishing, golf, fell-walking, ornithology. *Address:* 8 St George's Crescent, Carlisle. *T:* Carlisle 22253. *Club:* Border and County (Carlisle).

BEST, family name of **Baron Wynford.**

BEST, Alfred Charles, CBE 1962 (OBE 1953); DSc (Wales); Director of Services, Meteorological Office, 1960-66; *b* 7 March 1904; *s* of late Charles William Best, Barry, Glam; *m* 1932, Renée Margaret, *d* of late John Laughton Parry, Blaina, Mon; two *s*. *Educ:* Barry Grammar Sch.; University Coll., Cardiff. Professional Asst, Meteorological Office, 1926; appointments: Shoeburyness, 1926; Porton, 1928; Air Min., 1933; Malta, 1936; Larkhill, 1939; Air Min., 1940; Wing Comdr RAFVR, ACSEA, 1945; Air Min., 1945; Research, 1945-54; Meteorological Office Services, 1955-66. *Publications:* Physics in Meteorology, 1957; meteorological papers in jls. *Recreation:* photography. *Address:* Blaina, 10 Flintgrove, Bracknell, Berks. *T:* Bracknell 21772.

BEST, Edward Wallace, CMG 1971; JP; Deputy Chairman, Melbourne and Metropolitan Board of Works, 1975-79; *b* 11 Sept. 1917; *s* of Edward Lewis Best and Mary Best (*née* Wallace); *m* 1940, Joan Winifred Ramsay; three *d*. *Educ:* Trinity Grammar Sch. and Wesley Coll., Melbourne. Served War 6 years with AIF; 3½ years PoW (Lieut). Elected to Melbourne City Council, 1960; Lord Mayor of Melbourne, 1969-71; has served on numerous cttees: Electric Supply, Finance, Civic Square Bldg, Victoria Market Redevelopment Cttees; Melbourne and Metropolitan Bd of Works Finance and Publicity Cttee; Sidney Myer Music Bowl, 1967- (Chm. 1969); Victorian Olympic Park Cttee of Management, 1967-; Chm., Sports and Recreation Council to Victoria State Govt; Trustee for Olympic Park (Exec. Mem. on Vic. Olympic Cttee which applied for 1956 Melbourne Olympic Games); Mem. Publicity and Pentathlon Cttees at Melbourne Games); Chm., Exhibn Buildings, 1973-75; Melbourne Moomba Festival, 1969- (Pres. 1969-71); Lord Mayor's Holiday Camp, 1969- (Chm. 1969-71); associated 25 years with Lord Mayor's Fund, in an adv. capacity, for appeals; Mem. Cttee: Royal Agricultural Soc. Council, 1970-; Equestrian Fedn of Australia, 1965-75; Moonee Valley Racing Club, 1975-. Visited Edinburgh, Commonwealth Games, 1970 to present Melbourne's application for 1974 Commonwealth Games; Victorian Chm., 1972 Aust. Olympic Appeal, 1971-72, 1974 Commonwealth Games Appeal; Pres., XXth World Congress of Sports Medicine; Chm., Victorian Olympic Council, 1970-75. *Recreations:* racing, hunting, farming; athletics (rep. Australia at 1938 Empire Games; former Victorian champion sprinter). *Address:* 670 Orrong Road, Toorak, Vic 3142, Australia. *Clubs:* Australian, Bendigo Jockey, Melbourne Cricket, Moonee Valley Racing, Victorian Amateur Turf, Victoria Racing, Royal Automobile Club of Victoria.

BEST, Prof. Ernest; Professor of Divinity and Biblical Criticism, University of Glasgow, 1974-82, now Professor Emeritus; Dean of the Faculty of Divinity, 1978-80; *b* 23 May 1917; *s* of John and Louisa Elizabeth Best; *m* 1949, Sarah Elizabeth Kingston; two *d*. *Educ:* Methodist Coll., Belfast; Queen's Univ., Belfast (BA, MA, BD, PhD); Presbyterian Coll., Belfast. Asst Minister, First Bangor Presbyterian Church, 1943-49; Minister, Caledon and Minterburn Presbyt. Churches, 1949-63; Lectr (temp.), Presbyt. Coll., Belfast, 1953-54; Guest Prof., Austin Presbyt. Theol Seminary, Texas, 1955-57; Lectr in Biblical Lit. and Theol., St Andrews Univ., 1963-74 (Sen. Lectr 1971-74). Jt Editor, Biblical Theology, 1962-72; Associate Editor, Irish Biblical Studies, 1978-. *Publications:* One Body in Christ, 1955; The Temptation and the Passion, 1965; The Letter of Paul to the Romans, 1967; 1 Peter, 1971; 1 and 2 Thessalonians, 1972; From Text to Sermon, 1977; Text and Interpretation (ed jtly), 1979; Following Jesus, 1981; contrib. Biblica, Ecumenical Review, Expository Times, Interpretation, Jl Theol Studies, New Testament Studies, Novum Testamentum, Scottish Jl Theology, Catholic Biblical Qly, Zeit. neu. test. Wiss. *Recreations:* vegetable growing, golf. *Address:* Department of Divinity and Biblical Criticism, University of Glasgow, Glasgow G12 8QQ; 13 Newmile Gardens, St Andrews, Fife.

BEST, Prof. Geoffrey Francis Andrew; Professor of History in the School of European Studies, since 1974, Dean, since 1980, University of Sussex; *b* 20 Nov. 1928; *s* of Frederick Ebenezer Best and Catherine Sarah Vanderbrook (*née* Bultz); *m* 1955, Gwenllyan Marigold Davies; two *s* one *d*. *Educ:* St Paul's Sch.; Trinity Coll., Cambridge (MA, PhD). Army (RAEC), 1946-47; Choate Fellow, Harvard Univ., 1954-55; Fellow of Trinity Hall and Asst Lectr, Cambridge Univ., 1955-61; Lectr, Edinburgh Univ., 1961-66; Sir Richard Lodge Prof. of History, Edinburgh Univ., 1966-74. Vis. Prof., Chicago Univ., 1964; Vis. Fellow, All Souls Coll., Oxford, 1969-70; Lees Knowles Lectr, Cambridge, 1970; Fellow, Woodrow Wilson Internat. Centre, Washington, DC, 1978-79; Joanne Goodman Lectr, Univ. of Western Ontario, 1981. Mem. Council, British Red Cross Soc., 1981-. Jt Editor, Victorian Studies, 1958-68; Editor, War and Society Newsletter, 1973-. FRHistS 1977. *Publications:* Temporal Pillars, 1964; Shaftesbury, 1964; Bishop Westcott and the Miners, 1968; Mid-Victorian Britain, 1971; (ed) Church's Oxford Movement, 1971; (jt ed) War, Economy and the Military Mind, 1976; Humanity in Warfare, 1980; War and Society in Revolutionary Europe, 1982; Honour Among Men and Nations, 1982; contrib. various jls. *Recreations:* music, walking, Victorian arts and architecture. *Address:* c/o School of European Studies, University of Sussex, Brighton BN1 9QN.

BEST, Giles Bernard; His Honour Judge Best; a Circuit Judge, since 1975; *b* 19 Oct. 1925; *yr s* of late Hon. James William Best, OBE. *Educ:* Wellington Coll.; Jesus Coll., Oxford. Called to Bar, Inner Temple, 1951; Dep. Chm., Dorset QS, 1967-71; a Recorder, 1972-75. *Recreations:* walking, fishing, shooting. *Address:* Pitcombe, Little Bredy, Dorset.
   See also T. W. Best.

BEST, Keith (Lander), TD; MP (C) Anglesey, since 1979; *b* 10 June 1949; *s* of Peter Edwin Wilson Best and Margaret Louisa Best. *Educ:* Brighton Coll.; Keble Coll., Oxford (BA (Hons) Jurisprudence; MA). Assistant Master, Summerfields Sch., Oxford, 1967; called to the Bar, Inner Temple, 1971; Lectr in Law, 1973. Served: 289 Parachute Battery, RHA (V), 1970-76; with RM on HMS Bulwark, 1976. PPS to Sec. of State for Wales, 1981-. Councillor, Brighton Borough Council (Chm. Lands Cttee, Housing Cttee), 1976-80; Mem., Young Conservative Nat. Adv. Cttee, 1978. Founder Member: Two Piers Housing Co-operative, 1977-; Brighton Housing Trust, 1976-; school manager, Downs County First Sch. and Downs Middle Sch., 1976-. *Publications:* Write Your Own Will, 1978 (paperback); The Right Way to Prove a Will, 1980 (paperback); contrib. District Councils Rev. *Recreations:* parachuting, walking, photography, travel. *Address:* House of Commons, SW1. *T:* 01-219 4118. *Clubs:* Town House Royal Artillery Mess (Woolwich); Holyhead Conservative.

BEST, Rear-Adm. Thomas William, CB 1966; DL; *b* Hoshangabad, India, 1 Sept. 1915; *s* of late Hon. James William Best, OBE, and Florence Mary Bernarda (née Lees); *m* 1942, Brenda Joan, *d* of late F. A. Hellaby, MC, Auckland, New Zealand; two *s* one *d.* *Educ:* Farnborough Sch.; Royal Naval Coll., Dartmouth. Served in NZ Div. of RN (HMS Leander, 1937-41); War of 1939-45 (despatches); Qualified Gunnery Specialist, 1942. Korean War, 1951-52 (despatches); i/c HMS Barrosa, 1952-54; Dep. Dir Naval Ordnance, 1955-58; i/c HMS Ausonia, 1958-60; Capt. Supt, Admiralty Surface Weapons Establishment, 1961-64. ADC to the Queen, 1964; Flag Officer Gibraltar, 1964-66; retd 1967. Governor, Bryanston Sch., 1969-. Chm., Dorset County Branch NFU, 1976. Member: Royal Bath & West & Southern Counties Soc.; Dorset Naturalists' Trust; Small Industries Cttee for Dorset, CoSIRA, 1973-; West Dorset Beekeepers' Assoc.; Somerset Fruit Growers' Assoc. Dir, Norton Cider Growers' Assoc., 1977-; Governor, Nat. Fruit and Cider Inst., Long Ashton Res. Station, 1978-. DL Dorset, 1977. *Recreations:* beekeeping, fruit farming. *Address:* Hincknowle, Melplash, Bridport, Dorset. *T:* Netherbury 221. *Club:* Naval and Military.
   See also G. B. Best.

BEST-SHAW, Sir John (James Kenward), 9th Bt *cr* 1665; Commander (E) RN, retired; *b* 11 June 1895; *s* of Rev. Sir Charles J. M. Shaw, 8th Bt, and Louisa (*d* 1961), *d* of J. W. Bosanquet; *S* father, 1922; assumed the name and arms of Best by Royal Licence, 1956; *m* 1921, Elizabeth Mary Theodora, *e d* of Sir Robert Hughes, 12th Bt; three *s* four *d.* *Educ:* Cheam Sch., Sutton, Surrey; Royal Naval Colls, Osborne and Dartmouth. A lay guardian of the Sanctuary of Our Lady of Walsingham, 1931-78. Served with Royal Navy, Wars of 1914-18 and 1939-45. High Sheriff, Kent, 1961. Pres., Church Union, 1969-71. OStJ. *Heir: s* John Michael Robert Best-Shaw [*b* 28 Sept. 1924; *m* 1960, Jane Gordon, *d* of A. G. Guthrie, Hampton Court House, Farningham, Kent; two *s* one *d* (and *e s* decd)]. *Address:* Boxley Abbey, Sandling, Maidstone, Kent. *T:* Maidstone 52910. *Club:* Naval and Military.

BESTERMAN, Edwin Melville Mack, MD, MA, Cantab; FRCP; Consultant Cardiologist: St Mary's Hospital, London, since 1962; Paddington Green Children's Hospital, since 1972; Hon. Consultant Physician, Department of Medicine, Hammersmith Hospital, since 1981; *b* 4 May 1924; *s* of late Theodore Deodatus Nathaniel Besterman and Evelyn, *y d* of Arthur Mack, NY; *m* 1978, Perri Marjorie Burrowes, *d* of R. Burrowes, Kingston, Jamaica, WI; four *s* by previous marriage. *Educ:* Stowe Sch.; Trinity Coll., Cambridge; Guy's Hospital. BA (Cantab) 1943 (1st cl. hons Physiology); MB, BChir 1947; MRCP 1949; MD 1955 (Raymond Horton Smith Prize); FRCP 1967. Out-patient Officer, Guy's Hosp., 1947; House Physician, Post-graduate Medical Sch., Hammersmith, 1948; Registrar, Special Unit for Juvenile Rheumatism, Canadian Red Cross Memorial Hosp., Taplow, Berks, 1949-52; First Asst (Lectr), Inst of Cardiology and Nat. Heart Hosp., 1953-56; Sen. Registrar, Middlesex Hosp., 1956-62. Member: Brit. Cardiac Soc.; Faculty of History of Medicine and Pharmacy; British Pacing Group. *Publications:* contrib. to Paul Wood, Diseases of the Heart and Circulation, 3rd edn, 1968; articles on phonocardiography, pulmonary hypertension, atherosclerosis, blood platelet function, lipid fractions and drug trials in angina and hypertension in Brit. Heart Jl, Brit. Med. Jl, Lancet, Circulation, Atherosclerosis Research, etc. *Recreations:* photography, gardening, fishing, tennis, dogs. *Address:* 29 Harley Street, W1N 1DA. *T:* 01-580 9347; 32 Langbourne Avenue, N6. *T:* 01-348 9572. *Club:* Savile.

BESTOR, Arthur (Eugene); Professor of History, University of Washington, 1962-76, now Emeritus; *b* 20 Sept. 1908; *s* of Arthur Eugene and Jeanette Louise Lemon Bestor; *m* 1st, 1931, Dorothea Nolte (marr. diss.); 2nd, 1939, Anne Carr (*d* 1948); two *s* ; 3rd, 1949, Dorothy Alden Koch; one *s.* *Educ:* Yale Univ. PhB 1930; PhD 1938. Yale University: Instructor in English, 1930-31; Instructor in History, 1934-36; Teachers Coll., Columbia University: Associate in History, 1936-37; Asst Prof. of History, 1937-42;

Stanford University: Asst Prof. of Humanities, 1942-45; Associate Prof. of History, 1945-46; Lectr in American History, Univ. of Wisconsin, 1947 University of Illinois: Associate Prof. of History, 1947-51; Prof. of Histor 1951-62. Harold Vyvyan Harmsworth Prof. of American History, Oxfor 1956-57; Fulbright Vis. Prof., University of Tokyo, 1967. Editor-in-chie Chautauquan Daily, Chautauqua, NY, 1931-33. Fellow, Newberry Librar Chicago, Ill., 1946; John Simon Guggenheim Memorial Fellow, 1953-54 1961-62. President: Ill. State Historical Soc., 1954-55; Council for Basic Education, 1956-57; Pacific Coast Branch, Amer. Historical Assoc., 1976. M. (Oxon) by decree, 1956; LLD Lincoln Univ. (Pa), 1959. John Addison Porte Prize, Yale Univ., 1938; Albert J. Beveridge Award, Amer. Historical Assoc 1946. *Publications:* Chautauqua Publications, 1934; David Jacks of Monterey 1945; Education and Reform at New Harmony, 1948; Backwoods Utopia 1950; Educational Wastelands, 1953; The Restoration of Learning, 1955; Stal Sovereignty and Slavery (in Jl Ill State Historical Soc.), 1961; The America Civil War as a Constitutional Crisis (in Amer. Historical Review), 1964 Separation of Powers in the Realm of Foreign Affairs (in Seton Hall La Review), 1974; Respective Roles of Senate and President in the Making an Abrogation of Treaties (in Washington Law Review), 1979; jointly: Problem in American History, 1952, 3rd edn 1966; Three Presidents and Their Book 1955; The Heritage of the Middle West, 1958; Education in the Age of Science, 1959; Interpreting and Teaching American History, 1961; Th American Territorial System, 1973; contribs to Amer. Hist. Review, Jl of His of Ideas, William and Mary Quarterly, Encounter, Procs Amer. Philosophica Soc., American Scholar, Daedalus, Washington Law Review, New England Quarterly, Jl of Southern History, Harvard Educational Review, New Republic, Scientific Monthly, School and Society. *Recreations:* photography walking. *Address:* Department of History, DP-20, Smith Hall, University c Washington, Seattle, Washington 98195, USA; (home) 4553 55th Avenu NE, Seattle, Washington, 98105, USA. *Club:* Elizabethan (New Haven).

BESWICK, Baron, *cr* 1964 (Life Peer); **Frank Beswick,** PC 1968; JF Chairman, British Aerospace, 1976-80 (Chairman, Organising Committee 1975-76); *b* 1912; *m* Dora, *d* of Edward Plumb; one *s* one *d.* Joined RAF 1940; Transport Command (despatches). MP (Lab Co-op.) Uxbridge Div. c Middlesex, 1945-Oct. 1959. PPS to Under-Sec. of State for Air, 1946-49 Parly Sec., Min. of Civil Aviation, 1950-Oct. 1951. UK Govt Observer Bikini Tests, 1946; Delegate UN General Assembly, 1946. Formerly: Chm Parly Labour Party Civil Aviation Sub-Cttee; Chm., Co-operative Part Parly Group; a Lord-in-Waiting, 1965; Parly Under-Sec. of State in CC 1965-67; Captain, Hon. Corps of Gentlemen at Arms, and Govt Chief Whir House of Lords, 1967-70, Chief Opposition Whip, 1970-74; Minister of Stat for Industry, and Deputy Leader, House of Lords, 1974-75. Special Advise to Chm., British Aircraft Corp., 1970-74. Chm. Supervisory Bd, Airbu Industrie, 1978-80. Pres., British Air Line Pilots Assoc., 1978-82 (Vice-Pres 1965-77). Companion, RAeS, 1978. FRSA 1979. JP Co. of London, 1963 *Address:* 27 Margin Drive, SW19.

BESWICK, John Reginald, CBE 1973; FCIArb; FBIM; Director Genera British Ports Association, since 1980; *b* 16 Aug. 1919; *s* of Malcolm Hollano Beswick and Edythe Beswick (née Bednall); *m* 1943, Nadine Caruth Moor Pryde; one *s* two *d.* *Educ:* Manchester Grammar Sch.; Rossall Sch.; Trinit College, Cambridge (MA). Sub-Lt RNVR, 1940-42: anti submarine trawlers N and S Atlantic; Lt RNVR, 1942-46: submarines, home waters and Far Eas Called to Bar, Lincoln's Inn, 1947. Practised at Chancery Bar, 1947-51. Sec Mullard Ltd, 1951-62; Jt Sec., Philips Electrical Industries Ltd, 1953-62; Di Mullard Equipment Ltd, 1955-62; Dir, Soc. of Motor Manufrs & Traders Ltc 1963-79. Member: CBI Council, 1965-79; Council, Inst. of Advance Motorists, 1966-76. UK delegate, Bureau Permanent International de Constructeurs d'Automobiles, 1966-79. FCIArb 1978. FRSA 1954; FBIN 1982. Asst, Worshipful Co. of Coachmakers, 1973-79. *Recreations:* golt fly-fishing, reading. *Address:* Amberley, 11 Ferncroft Avenue, Hampstead NW3. *T:* 01-435 5706. *Clubs:* Naval and Military, Royal Automobile.

BETHE, Prof. Hans Albrecht, PhD; Professor of Theoretical Physics, Corne University, 1937-75, now Professor Emeritus; *b* Strassburg, Germany, 2 Jul 1906; *m* 1939, Rose Ewald; one *s* one *d.* *Educ:* Goethe Gymnasium, Frankfur on Main; Univs of Frankfurt and Munich. PhD Munich, 1928. Instructor i Theoretical Physics, Univs of Frankfurt, Stuttgart, Munich and Tübinger 1928-33; Lectr, Univs of Manchester and Bristol, England, 1933-35; Asst Prof Cornell Univ., Ithaca, 1935-37. Dir, Theoretical Physics Div. of Los Alamo Atomic Scientific Laboratory, 1943-46. Sabbatic leave to Cambridge Univ academic year, 1955-56. Mem., President's Science Adv. Cttee, 1956-59 Member: Nat. Acad. Sciences; Amer. Physical Soc.; Amer. Astron. Soc.; For Mem., Royal Society. Holds hon. doctorates in Science. US Medal of Meri 1946; Planck Medal, German Physical Soc., 1955; Eddington Medal, Roya Astronomical Soc., 1961; Enrico Fermi Award, US Atomic Energy Commr 1961; Nobel Prize for Physics, 1967. *Publications:* (jt author) Elementar Nuclear Theory, 1947; Mesons and Fields, 1955; Quantum Mechanics of One and Two-Electron Atoms, 1957; Intermediate Quantum Mechanics, 1964 contributions to: Handbuch der Physik, 1933, 1954; Reviews of Mod. Physics 1936-37; Physical Review. *Address:* Laboratory of Nuclear Studies, Corne University, Ithaca, NY 14853, USA.

BETHEL, David Percival; Director, Leicester Polytechnic, since 1973; *b* Bath 7 Dec. 1923; *m* 1943, Margaret Elizabeth, *d* of late Alexander Wriggleswort one *s* one *d.* *Educ:* King Edward VII Sch., Bath; Crypt Grammar Sch., Glou West of England Coll. of Art; Bristol Univ., 1946-51; NDD, ATD, FRSA

FSAE, FSIAD, ARWA. Served with RN, Far East, 1943-45. Lectr, Stafford Coll. of Art, 1951-56; Deputy Principal, Coventry Coll. of Art, 1956-65; Principal, Coventry Coll. of Art, 1965-69; Dep. Dir, Leicester Polytechnic, 1969-73. Pres., Nat. Soc. for Art Educn, 1965-66; Member: Nat. Adv. Cttee for Art Educn, 1965-71; Jt Summerson Coldstream Cttee, 1968-70; Chairman: CNAA Cttee for Art and Design (and Research Degrees Sub-Cttee), 1975-81; Cttee of Dirs of Polytechnics, 1978-80; Vice-Chm., Inter-Univs and Polytechnics Council for Higher Educn Overseas. Sometime Design Consultant to Massey Ferguson, Van Heusen, Monotype Corp., etc. British Council Adviser to Hong Kong Govt, 1971-; Member: Hong Kong UPGC, 1982-; World Council, INSEA; Council of Europe; The Design Council, 1980-; Trustee: Cyril Wood Meml Trust; Leicester Haymarket Theatre, 1979-. Paintings and prints in Glos. Libraries, Stafford Art Gallery, Coventry, RWA, private collections. Mem., Worshipful Co. of Frame-Work Knitters. Aust. Commonwealth Travelling Fellowship, 1979. Hon. LLD Leicester, 1982. *Recreations:* travel; study of art, design, architecture; archæology and music. *Address:* Leicester Polytechnic, PO Box 143, Leicester LE1 9BH. *Club:* Athenæum.

BETHEL, Martin; a Recorder of the Crown Court since 1979; *b* 12 March 1943; *o s* of late Rev. Ralph Bethel and of Enid Bethel; *m* 1974, Kathryn Denby; two *s* one *d*. *Educ:* Kingswood Sch.; Fitzwilliam Coll., Cambridge (MA, LLB). Called to the Bar, Inner Temple, 1965; North-Eastern Circuit (Circuit Junior, 1969). *Recreations:* family, music, travel, skiing, golf. *Address:* (chambers) 37 Park Square, Leeds LS1 2PD. *T:* Leeds 452702.

BETHELL, family name of **Barons Bethell** and **Westbury.**

BETHELL, 4th Baron *cr* 1922, of Romford; **Nicholas William Bethell;** Bt 1911; Member (C) European Parliament, since 1975, elected for London North-West, 1979; free-lance writer; *b* 19 July 1938; *s* of Hon. William Gladstone Bethell (*d* 1964) (3rd *s* of 1st Baron), and of Ann Margaret Bethell (*née* Barlow, now Thornycroft); *S* kinsman, 1967; *m* 1964, Cecilia Mary (marr. diss. 1971, she *d* 1977), *er d* of Prof. A. M. Honeyman, *qv*; two *s*. *Educ:* Harrow; Pembroke Coll., Cambridge. On editorial staff of Times Literary Supplement, 1962-64; a Script Editor in BBC Radio Drama, 1964-67. A Lord in Waiting (Govt Whip, House of Lords), June 1970-Jan. 1971. Vice-Chm., Political Cttee, European Parlt; Chm., Friends of Cyprus. *Publications:* Gomulka: his Poland and his Communism, 1969; The War Hitler Won, 1972; The Last Secret, 1974; Russia Besieged, 1977; The Palestine Triangle, 1979; *translations:* Six Plays, by Slawomir Mrozek, 1967; Elegy to John Donne, by Joseph Brodsky, 1967; Cancer Ward, by A. Solzhenitsyn, 1968; The Love Girl and the Innocent, by A. Solzhenitsyn, 1969; The Ascent of Mount Fuji, by Chingiz Aitmatov, 1975; dramatic works for radio and TV; occasional journalism. *Recreations:* poker, cricket. *Heir: s* Hon. James Nicholas Bethell, *b* 1 Oct. 1967. *Address:* 73 Sussex Square, W2 2SS. *T:* 01-402 6877. *Clubs:* Garrick, Pratt's.

BETHELL, Maj.-Gen. Donald Andrew Douglas Jardine; Warden, Sackville College, since 1981; *b* 6 Feb. 1921; *e s* of D. L. Bethell, Stourbridge, near Birmingham, and L. K. Bethell; *m* 1946, Pamela Mary Woosnam; two *s*. *Educ:* Sherborne Sch., Dorset. Commnd RA, 1940; Regimental Service, 1940-47; Staff and Regimental appts, 1947-66; CRA, 3rd Div., 1966-68; Dep. Commandant, Staff Coll., 1969-72; Pres., Regular Commissions Bd, 1972-75. Col Comdt, RA, 1978-. *Recreations:* sailing, fishing, golf, shooting. *Address:* Sackville College, East Grinstead, W Sussex. *T:* East Grinstead 26561; Yacht Acquest. *Club:* Royal Cruising.

BETHELL, Richard Anthony; Vice Lord-Lieutenant of Humberside since 1980; *b* 22 March 1922; *s* of late William Adrian Bethell and Cicely Bethell (*née* Cotterell); *m* 1945, Lady Jane Pleydell-Bouverie, *d* of 7th Earl of Radnor, KG, KCVO; two *s* two *d*. *Educ:* Eton. JP, ER Yorks, 1950; DL 1975, High Sheriff 1976-77, Humberside. *Address:* Rise Park, Hull HU11 5BL. *T:* Skirlaugh 62241.

BETHUNE, Sir Alexander Maitland Sharp, 10th Bt (NS), *cr* 1683; Managing Director: Copytec Services Ltd; Contoura Photocopying Ltd; *b* 28 March 1909; *o s* of late Alexander Bethune, JP, DL, of Blebo, Cupar, 9th Bt of Scotscraig, and Elisabeth Constance Carnegie (*d* 1935), 3rd *d* of Frederick Lewis Maitland Heriot of Ramornie, Fife; *S* father, 1917; *m* 1955, Ruth Mary, *d* of J. H. Hayes; one *d*. *Educ:* Eton; Magdalene Coll., Cambridge. *Recreations:* golf, nature, dyeline printing. *Address:* 21 Victoria Grove, W8.

BETHUNE, Hon. Sir (Walter) Angus, Kt 1979; pastoralist; *b* 10 Sept. 1908; *s* of Frank Pogson Bethune and Laura Eileen Bethune; *m* 1936, Alexandra P., *d* of P. A. Pritchard; one *s* one *d*. *Educ:* Hutchin's Sch., Hobart; Launceston Church of England Grammar Sch. Served War, RAAF Air Crew, Middle East, 1940-43. Member, Hamilton Municipal Council, 1936-56, resigned (Dep. Warden, 1955-56). MHA, Wilmot, Tasmania, 1946-75, resigned; Leader of Opposition, 1960-69; Premier and Treasurer, Tasmania, 1969-72. Leader of Liberal Party, 1960-72, resigned. President: Clarendon Children's Homes, 1977-; St John's Ambulance Brigade (Tasmania), 1979-. *Address:* Dunrobin, Ouse, Tasmania 7461, Australia. *Clubs:* Tasmanian; Naval, Military and Air Force; Royal Autocar of Tasmania.

BETJEMAN, Sir John, Kt 1969; CBE 1960; CLit 1968; poet and author; Poet Laureate, since 1972; *b* 1906; *s* of late E. E. Betjeman; *m* 1933, Penelope

Valentine Hester (author, as Penelope Chetwode, of Two Middle-aged Ladies in Andalusia, 1963, and Kulu, 1972), *d* of Field-Marshal Lord Chetwode, GCB, OM, GCSI; one *s* one *d*. *Educ:* Marlborough; Oxford. UK Press Attaché, Dublin, 1941-42; Admiralty, 1943. Mem., Royal Commn on Historical Monuments (England), 1970-76. A Governor of Pusey House, Church of England. Hon. Fellow: Keble Coll., Oxford, 1972; Magdalen Coll., Oxford, 1975. Hon. LLD Aberdeen; Hon. DLitt: Oxon, Reading, Birmingham, Exeter, City, Liverpool, Hull, Trinity Coll., Dublin; Hon. ARIBA. *Publications:* Mount Zion; Ghastly Good Taste, 1933, new edn 1971; Continual Dew; An Oxford University Chest; Shell Guides to Cornwall and Devon, and (with John Piper) Shropshire; Antiquarian Prejudice; Old Lights for New Chancels; Selected Poems, 1948 (Heinemann Award); First and Last Loves, 1952; A Few Late Chrysanthemums, 1954 (Foyle Poetry Prize); Collected Poems, 1958 (Duff Cooper Prize; Foyle Poetry Prize; Queen's Gold Medal for Poetry, 1960): Summoned By Bells (verse autobiography), 1960; High and Low (poems), 1966; A Nip in the Air (poems), 1974; (ed with John Piper): Buckinghamshire Guide, 1948; Berkshire Guide, 1949; (ed with late Geoffrey Taylor): An Anthology of Landscape Verse; English Love Poems; English Churches (with Basil Clarke), 1964; (ed) Pocket Guide to English Parish Churches, 1968; Victorian and Edwardian London, 1969; (with David Vaisey) Victorian and Edwardian Oxford from Old Photographs, 1971; A Pictorial History of English Architecture, 1972; London's Historic Railway Stations, 1972; (contrib.) Westminster Abbey, 1972; (with J. S. Gray) Victorian and Edwardian Brighton from Old Photographs, 1972; West Country Churches, 1973; (with A. L. Rowse) Victorian and Edwardian Cornwall, 1974; A Nip in the Air, 1974; Archie and the Strict Baptists, 1977; Church Poems, 1981; Uncollected Poems, 1982. *Address:* c/o John Murray Ltd, 50 Albemarle Street, W1X 4BD. *Club:* Beefsteak.

BETT, Michael, MA; Board Member for Personnel, British Telecommunications, since 1981; *b* 18 Jan. 1935; *s* of Arthur Bett and Nina Daniells; *m* 1959, Christine Angela Reid; one *s* two *d*. *Educ:* St Michael's Coll.; Aldenham Sch.; Pembroke Coll., Cambridge. FIPM, CBIM. Dir, Industrial Relations, Engrg Employers' Fedn, 1970-72; Personnel Dir, General Electric Co. Ltd, 1972-77; Dir of Personnel, BBC, 1977-81. Member: Pay Bd, 1973-74; Training Levy Exemption Referee, 1975-82; Civil Service Arbitration Tribunal, 1977-; Cttee of Inquiry into UK Prison Services, 1978-79. Mem., RTS. FRSA. *Recreations:* theatre, cooking, gardening. *Address:* The Spinney, Lodge Road, Bromley, Kent. *T:* 01-460 2846.

BETTLEY, F(rancis) Ray, TD 1945; MD; FRCP; Physician for Diseases of the Skin, Middlesex Hospital, London, 1946-74, now Emeritus; Physician, St John's Hospital for Diseases of the Skin, London, 1947-74, now Emeritus; formerly Dean, Institute of Dermatology, British Postgraduate Medical Federation; Lieutenant-Colonel RAMC, TARO; *b* 18 Aug. 1909; *yr s* of late Francis James Bettley; *m* 1951, Jean Rogers, 2nd *d* of late Archibald Barnet McIntyre; one *s* (one *d* decd), and one adopted *d*. *Educ:* Whitgift Sch., Croydon; University Coll., London; University Coll. Hosp. Medically qualified, 1932; MD 1935; FRCP 1948. Gazetted RAMC TA, 1932; Resident House-appointments, 1932-33; Radcliffe-Crocker Student (Vienna, Strasbourg), 1936; Hon. Dermatologist to Cardiff Royal Infirmary, 1937; various military hosps in UK and Middle East, 1939-44; Dermatologist and Venereologist, E Africa Comd, 1944-45. Malcolm Morris Lectr, 1959 and 1970; Watson Smith Lectr (RCP), 1960; Emeritus Mem., and former Pres., Brit. Assoc. of Dermatologists; Hon. or Corresp. Mem. of dermatological assocs of: Belgium, Denmark, France, Holland, India, Israel, Poland, USA, Venezuela. *Publications:* Skin Diseases in General Practice, 1949; Editor, British Jl of Dermatology, 1949-59; medical papers in various medical jls. *Recreation:* painting. *Address:* Friary House, St Michael's Road, Winchester, Hants. *Club:* Athenæum.

BETTS, Alan Osborn, PhD, MA, BSc, MRCVS; Principal and Dean, The Royal Veterinary College, University of London, since Oct. 1970; *b* 11 March 1927; *s* of A. O. and D. S. A. Betts; *m* 1952, Joan M. Battersby; one *s* one *d*. *Educ:* Royal Veterinary Coll.; Magdalene Coll., Cambridge. Asst in Gen. Practice, 1949; Animal Health Trust Research Scholar, 1950-52; Demonstrator, Univ. of Cambridge, 1952-56; Commonwealth Fund Fellow, Cornell Univ., USA, 1955-56; University Lectr, Cambridge, 1956-64; Prof. of Veterinary Microbiology and Parasitology, Univ. of London, 1964-70. Vice-Chm., Governing Body of Wye Coll., 1976-; Chm., Collegiate Council, Univ. of London, 1981-. Treasurer, RCVS, 1978-81. Member: Brit. Pharmacopoeia Commn, 1978-; EEC Adv. Cttee on Veterinary Trng, 1980-. Dalrymple-Champneys Cup and Medal of BVA, 1978. *Publications:* Viral and Rickettsial Infections of Animals, 1967; papers in microbiological and veterinary jls. *Recreations:* travel, gliding. *Address:* The Royal Veterinary College, Royal College Street, NW1 0TU. *T:* 01-387 2898; Lower Boycott, Stowe, Buckingham. *T:* Buckingham 3287. *Club:* Athenæum.

BETTS, Air Vice-Marshal (Charles) Stephen, CBE 1963; MA; Head of Control and Inspection Division, Agency for the Control of Armaments, WEU, Paris, since 1974; *b* 8 April 1919; *s* of H. C. Betts, Nuneaton; *m* 1st, 1943, Pauline Mary (deceased), *d* of Lt-Col P. Heath; two *d*; 2nd, 1964, Margaret Doreen, *d* of Col W. H. Young, DSO. *Educ:* King Edward's Sch., Nuneaton; Sidney Sussex Coll., Cambridge. Joined RAF 1941; Air Cdre 1966; Asst Comdt (Eng.), RAF Coll., Cranwell, 1971-72; Air Vice-Marshal 1972; AOC No 24 Group, RAF, 1972-73, retired 1974. *Recreations:* travel, music. *Address:* Agence pour le Contrôle des Armaments, UEO, 43 avenue du

Président-Wilson, 75116 Paris, France. *T:* 723 5432. *Club:* Royal Air Force.

BETTS, Rt. Rev. Stanley Woodley, CBE 1967; *b* 23 March 1912; *yr s* of Hubert Woodley and Lillian Esther Betts. *Educ:* Perse Sch.; Jesus Coll., Cambridge (MA 1937); Ridley Hall, Cambridge. Curate of St Paul's Cheltenham, 1935-38; Chaplain, RAF, 1938-47 (despatches); Sen. Chaplain of BAFO, Germany, 1946-47; Comdt, RAF Chaplains' Sch., Dowdeswell Court, 1947; Chaplain, Clare Coll., Cambridge, 1947-49; Chaplain, Cambridge Pastorate, 1947-56; Proctor in Convocation, 1952-59; Vicar of Holy Trinity Cambridge, 1949-56; Exam. Chaplain to Bishop of Southwell, 1947-56; Select Preacher to University of Cambridge, 1955; Suffragan Bishop of Maidstone, 1956-66; Archbishop of Canterbury's Episcopal Representative with the three Armed Forces, 1956-66; Dean of Rochester, 1966-77. Chairman: Bd of the Church Army, 1970-80; Council, Wadhurst Coll.; Vice-Pres., Lee Abbey. *Address:* 2 King's Houses, Old Pevensey, Sussex. *T:* Eastbourne 762421. *Club:* National.

BETTS, Stephen; see Betts, C. S.

BEVAN, family name of **Baroness Lee of Asheridge.**

BEVAN, (Andrew) David Gilroy; MP (C) Yardley (Birmingham), since 1979; Principal, A. Gilroy Bevan, Incorporated Valuers & Surveyors; *b* 10 April 1928; *s* of Rev. Thomas John Bevan and Norah Gilroy Bevan; *m* 1967, Cynthia Ann Villiers Boulstridge; one *s* three *d. Educ:* Woodrough's Sch., Moseley; King Edward VI Sch., Birmingham. Served on Birmingham City Council and later W Midlands County Council, 1959-80; past Mem., Finance and Gen. Purposes Cttee, and Policy and Priorities Cttee; past Chm., City Transport Cttee, W Midlands PTA and Transport and Highways Cttee. Member, House of Commons Committees: All Party Leisure and Recreation Industry (Jt Chm.); Urban Affairs and New Towns (Jt Sec.); Tourism. FIAA&S 1962 (Past Chm., W Midlands Br.); FRVA 1971; FSVA 1968 (Past Chm., W Midlands Br.); FFB 1972; FCIA 1954; MRSH 1957. *Recreations:* gardening, walking. *Address:* The Cottage, 12 Wentworth Road, Four Oaks Park, Sutton Coldfield, West Midlands B74 2SG. *T:* (home) 021-308 3292; (business) 021-308 6319. *Club:* Carlton.

See also P. G. Bevan.

BEVAN, Cecil Wilfrid Luscombe, CBE 1965; Principal, University College, Cardiff, since 1966; Vice-Chancellor, University of Wales, since 1981; *b* 2 April 1920; *s* of Benjamin Cecil Bevan and Maud Luscombe; *m* 1944, Elizabeth Bondfield, *d* of Henry Dale Bondfield; four *s. Educ:* University Coll. of Wales, Aberystwyth; University Coll., London. BSc Wales 1940; PhD London 1949; FRIC 1957; DSc London 1971. Served Royal Welch Fusiliers and Nigeria Regt, 1940-46 (despatches). Univ. of Exeter, 1949-53; Prof. and Head of Dept of Chemistry, Univ. of Ibadan, 1953-66, Vice Principal and Dep. Vice-Chancellor, 1960-64; Vice-Chancellor, Univ. of Wales, 1973-75. Member: Tropical Products Inst. Adv. Cttee, 1971-77; Council, University of Cape Coast, Ghana, 1967-74; Welsh Council, 1968-71; Chm., Conciliation Cttee of Wales and SW Race Rel. Bd, 1968-72; Governor Welbeck Coll.; Prof. Associé Univ. de Strasbourg, 1965. Fellow UCL, 1969. Hon. DSc, Univ. of Ibadan, 1973. *Publications:* papers, mainly in Jl of Chemical Soc., 1951-. *Recreation:* labouring. *Address:* University College, Cathays Park, Cardiff. *Clubs:* Athenæum, Royal Commonwealth Society; Cardiff and County.

BEVAN, Rear-Adm. Christopher Martin, CB 1978; Under Treasurer Gray's Inn, since 1980; *b* London, 22 Jan. 1923; *s* of Humphrey C. Bevan and Mary F. Bevan (*née* Mackenzie); *m* 1948, Patricia C. Bedford; one *s* three *d. Educ:* Stowe Sch., Bucks; Victoria Univ., Wellington, NZ. Trooper in Canterbury Yeoman Cavalry (NZ Mounted Rifles), 1941; joined RN as Ord. Seaman, 1942; served remainder of 1939-45 war, Mediterranean and N Atlantic; commissioned 1943; Comdr 1958; Captain 1967; Supt Weapons and Radio, Dockyard Dept, MoD (Navy), 1967-70; Asst Dir, Weapons Equipment (Surface), later, Captain Surface Weapons Acceptance, Weapons Dept, MoD (Navy), 1970-73; Dir, Naval Officer Appts (Engrs), 1973-76; ADC to the Queen, 1976; Rear-Adm. 1976; Flag Officer Medway and Port Adm. Chatham, 1976-78. *Recreations:* photography, theatre, music, gardening. *Address:* c/o Messrs C. Hoare and Co., 37 Fleet Street, EC4P 4DQ.

BEVAN, David Gilroy; see Bevan, A.D.G.

BEVAN, John Stuart; Secretary, National Advisory Body for Local Authority Higher Education, since 1982; *b* 19 Nov. 1935; *s* of Frank Oakland and Ruth Mary Bevan; *m* 1960, Patricia Vera Beatrice (*née* Joyce); two *s* two *d. Educ:* Eggar's Grammar Sch.; Jesus Coll., Oxford; S Bartholomew's Hosp. Med. Coll. MA, MSc; FInstP. Health Physicist, UK Atomic Energy Authority, 1960-62; Lectr, then Sen. Lectr in Physics, Polytechnic of the South Bank (previously Borough Polytechnic), 1962-73; Inner London Education Authority: Asst Educn Officer, then Sen. Asst Educn Officer, 1973-76; Dep. Educn Officer, 1977-79; Dir of Educn, 1979-82. Former Member, National Executive Committees: Nat. Union of Teachers; Assoc. of Teachers in Technical Instns (Pres., 1972-73). *Publications:* papers in various scientific jls in fields of nuclear physics, radiation physics, radiation protection. *Recreations:* Scouting (Asst Comr, Kent), mountaineering. *Address:* 4 Woodland Way, Bidborough, Tunbridge Wells, Kent TN4 0UX. *T:* Tunbridge Wells 27461.

BEVAN, Rt. Rev. Kenneth Graham; Assistant Bishop, Diocese of Wakefield, 1968-77; *b* 27 Sept. 1898; *s* of late Rev. James Alfred Bevan, MA; *m* 1927, Jocelyn Duncan Barber; three *d. Educ:* The Grammar Sch., Great Yarmouth; London Coll. of Divinity. Deacon, 1923; Priest, 1924; Curate of Holy Trinity Tunbridge Wells, 1923-25; Missionary, Diocese of Western China, 1925-36, Diocese of Eastern Szechwan, 1936-40; Bishop of Eastern Szechwan, 1940-50; Vicar of Woolhope, 1951-66; Rural Dean, Hereford (South) 1955-66; Prebendary de Moreton et Whaddon, Hereford Cathedral, 1956-66; Master of Archbishop Holgate's Hosp., Wakefield, 1966-77. *Address:* 12 Howard Link, Shipton Road, York YO3 6UU. *T:* York 51895.

BEVAN, Leonard; HM Diplomatic Service, retired; *b* 16 Nov. 1926; *s* of Richard (Dick) and Sarah Bevan; *m* 1st, 1953, Muriel Anne Bridger (*d* 1979); 2nd, 1981, Jeanette Elfreda Phillips. *Educ:* Swansea and Gowerton Grammar Schs; UCW, Aberystwyth (BA Hons). RAF, 1948-50. BoT, 1950 (Private Sec. to Parly Sec., 1952-54); UK Trade Comr: Karachi, 1954; Kuala Lumpur, 1957; Principal British Trade Comr and Econ. Adviser to High Comr, Accra, 1959; Nairobi, 1961; Commonwealth Office (later FCO), 1968; Counsellor (Econ. and Commercial), Canberra, 1970; Head, SW Pacific Dept, FCO, 1974; Counsellor (Economic), Brasilia, 1976-79. *Recreations:* bird spotting, clock repairing and restoring, flower gardening. *Address:* Waun Wen, Abercastle Road, Trefin, Dyfed. *T:* Croesgoch 570.

BEVAN, Sir Martyn Evan E.; see Evans-Bevan.

BEVAN, Peter Gilroy, MB, ChB; FRCS; Consultant Surgeon, Dudley Road Hospital, Birmingham, since 1958; Professor of Surgery and Postgraduate Medical Education, University of Birmingham, since 1981; *b* 13 Dec. 1922; *s* of Rev. Thomas John Bevan and Norah (*née* Gilroy); *m* 1949, Patricia Joan (*née* Laurie); one *s* one *d. Educ:* King Edward VI High Sch., Birmingham; Univ. of Birmingham Medical Sch. (MB, ChB 1946; ChM 1958). LRCP MRCS 1946, FRSC 1952. Served RAMC, BAOR, 1947-49 (Captain). Demonstrator in Anatomy, Univ. of Birmingham, 1949-51; Resident Surgical Officer, Birmingham Children's Hosp., 1954-55; Lectr in Surgery and Sen. Surgical Registrar, Queen Elizabeth Hosp., Birmingham, 1954-58; WHO Vis. Prof. of Surgery to Burma, 1969; Director, Board of Graduate Clinical Studies, Univ. of Birmingham, 1978-. Mem. Council, RCS, 1971-, Vice-Pres., 1980-; Fellow, Assoc. of Surgeons of Gt Britain, 1960-, Mem. Council, 1975-; Founder Chm., W Midlands Oncology Assoc., 1974-79; Vice-Pres., Brit. Assoc. of Surgical Oncology, 1975-78; Pres., Pancreatic Soc. of Gt Britain, 1977. EEC: UK representative: on Monospecialist Section of Surgery, 1975-; on Adv. Cttee on Medical Trng, 1980-. *Publications:* Reconstructive Procedures in Surgery, 1982; various surgical papers in BMJ, Brit. Jl Surgery, Lancet, Annals of RCS. *Recreations:* inland waterways, golf, photography. *Address:* 10 Russell Road, Moseley, Birmingham B13 8RD. *T:* 021-449 3055. *Club:* Edgbaston Golf (Birmingham).

See also A. D. G. Bevan.

BEVAN, Richard Thomas, MD; FRCP; Chief Medical Officer, Welsh Office, 1965-77, retired; *b* 13 Jan. 1914; *s* of T. Bevan, Bridgend; *m* 1940, Dr Beryl Bevan (*née* Badham); two *s* one *d. Educ:* Welsh Nat. Sch. of Medicine. MB, BCh 1939; DPH 1941; MD 1955; FRCP; FFCM. Resident Medical Officer, St David's Hosp., Cardiff; RAF, 1941-46; Lecturer, Welsh Nat. Sch. of Medicine, 1946-68; Deputy County MO, Glamorgan CC, 1948-62. QHP 1974-77. *Address:* 40 Richard Cooper Road, Shenstone, near Lichfield. *T:* Shenstone 481 070.

BEVAN, Timothy Hugh; Chairman, Barclays Bank Ltd, since 1981; Director: Barclays Bank International Ltd, since 1971; Commercial Union Assurance, since 1974; The Union Discount Company of London Ltd, since 1975; *b* 24 May 1927; *y s* of late Hugh Bevan and Pleasance (*née* Scrutton); *m* 1952, Pamela, *e d* of late Norman Smith and late Margaret Smith; two *s* two *d. Educ:* Eton. Lieut Welsh Guards. Called to Bar, 1950. Joined Barclays Bank Ltd, 1950; Vice-Chm., 1968-73; Dep. Chm., 1973-81; Chm., Barclays Bank UK Management Ltd, 1972-80. Chm., City Communications Centre, 1982-. Mem., Institut International d'Etudes Bancaires. *Recreations:* sailing, gardening. *Address:* 1 Sloane Street, SW1X 9LA. *Clubs:* Cavalry and Guards, Royal Ocean Racing; Royal Yacht Squadron.

BEVAN, Walter Harold, CBE 1977; FCIS; Chairman, Gateshead District Health Authority (formerly of Gateshead Area Health Authority), since 1977; *b* 22 May 1916; *s* of late Walter Bevan and Sarah (*née* Grainger); *m* 1958, Patricia Edna Sadler, *d* of late Sir Sadler Forster, CBE, DCL; twin *s* and *d. Educ:* Gateshead Sec. Sch. FCIS 1961. 5th Bn Royal Northumberland Fusiliers, TA, 1938-42; served War: commissioned RA; Arakan campaign, Burma, with 81st W African Div., 1942-46; 4/5 Bn Royal Northumberland Fusiliers, TA, 1947-52. Asst to Sec., North Eastern Trading Estates Ltd, 1937, Chief Accountant 1956; English Industrial Estates Corporation: Chief Accountant, 1960; Sec., 1966; Finance Dir and Sec., 1973; Chief Exec. and Chm., Management Bd, 1974-79. Governor, Gateshead Technical Coll., 1971-81. *Publications:* articles on industrial estates and distribution of industry. *Recreations:* public and voluntary services, angling, reading. *Address:* Cornerways, Lyndhurst Grove, Low Fell, Gateshead NE9 6AX. *T:* Low Fell 876827.

BEVERIDGE, Prof. Gordon Smith Grieve, FRSE; CEng, FIChemE; Professor of Chemical Engineering and Head of Department of Chemical and Process Engineering, University of Strathclyde, Glasgow, since 1971; *b* 28

Nov. 1933; *s* of Victor Beattie Beveridge and Elizabeth Fairburn Beveridge (*née* Grieve); *m* 1963, Geertruida Johanna Hillegonda Bruyn; two *s* one *d*. *Educ:* Inverness Royal Academy; Univ. of Glasgow (BSc, 1st Cl. Hons Chem. Engrg); Royal College of Science and Technology, Glasgow (ARCST 1st Cl. Hons Chem. Engrg); Univ. of Edinburgh (PhD). Asst Lectr, Univ. of Edinburgh, 1956-60; post-doctoral Harkness Fellow of Commonwealth Fund, New York, at Univ. of Minnesota, 1960-62; Vis. Prof., Univ. of Texas, 1962-64; Lectr, Univ. of Edinburgh and Heriot-Watt Univ., 1962-67; Sen. Lectr/Reader, Heriot-Watt Univ., 1967-71. Consultant to industry. Institution of Chemical Engineers: Fellow, 1969-; Vice-Pres., 1979-81; Exec. Cttee, 1981-; Hon. Librarian, 1977-; Member: Council, 1975-76, 1977-; Careers Cttee, 1965-73; Research Cttee, 1973-79; Engrg Practice Cttee, 1977-; Sen. Academics Cttee, 1967-; Technical Responses Bd, 1979-; Scottish Branch: Sec., 1963-71; Vice-Chm., 1972-74; Chm., 1974-76. Society of Chemical Industry, London: Mem. Council, 1978-; Chm. of W of Scotland Section, 1978-. Council of Engineering Institutions (Scotland): Member, 1977-; Vice-Chm., 1979-80; Chm., 1980-81; Organiser of 1981 Exhibn, Engineering in the '80s, Edinburgh. Council for National Academic Awards: Chemical, Instrumentation and Systems Engrg Bd, 1976-81: Vice-Chm., 1979-81; Engineering Bd, 1981-. Science Research Council, various committees: 1973-76, 1980-. Mem., Engineering Council, 1981-. Associate Editor, Computers and Chemical Engineering, 1974-. *Publications:* Optimization - theory and practice (with R. S. Schechter), 1970; multiple pubns in learned jls. *Recreations:* Scottish and Dutch history, family golf, hill-walking. *Address:* 76 Craigcrook Road, Edinburgh EH4 3PN. *T:* 031-336 4704. *Club:* Caledonian.

BEVERIDGE, John Caldwell, QC 1979; Recorder, Western Circuit, since 1975; *b* 26 Sept. 1937; *s* of William Ian Beardmore Beveridge, *qv*; *m* 1972, Frances Ann Clunes Grant Martineau. *Educ:* privately; Jesus Coll., Cambridge (MA, LLB). Called to the Bar, Inner Temple, 1963; Western Circuit; called to the Bar, NSW, 1975, QC (NSW), 1980. Partner, Beveridge & Forwood, Zurich. Conservative Mem., Westminster City Council, 1968-72. Freeman, City of London. Jt Master, Westmeath Foxhounds, 1976-79. *Recreations:* hunting, shooting, travelling. *Address:* 28 Arlington House, St James's, SW1. *T:* 01-493 3945; The Astor, Macquarie Street, Sydney, NSW, Australia. *Clubs:* Brooks's, Turf.

BEVERIDGE, William Ian Beardmore, MA, ScD Cantab; DVSc Sydney; Professor of Animal Pathology, Cambridge, 1947-75; Emeritus Fellow of Jesus College; *b* 1908; *s* of J. W. C. and Ada Beveridge; *m* 1935, Patricia, *d* of Rev. E. C. Thomson; one *s*. *Educ:* Cranbrook Sch., Sydney; St Paul's Coll., University of Sydney. ScD Cantab 1974. Research bacteriologist, McMaster Animal Health Laboratory, Sydney, 1931-37; Commonwealth Fund Service Fellow at Rockefeller Inst. and at Washington, 1938-39; Walter and Eliza Hall Inst. for Medical Research, Melbourne, 1941-46; Visiting Worker, Pasteur Inst., Paris, 1946-47; Vis. Prof., Ohio State Univ., 1953; Guest Lectr, Norwegian Veterinary Sch., 1955; first Wesley W. Spink Lectr on Comparative Medicine, Minnesota, 1971. Consultant: WHO, Geneva, 1964-79; Bureau of Animal Health, Canberra, 1979-81; Vis. Fellow, John Curtin Sch. of Med. Res., Aust. Nat. Univ., Canberra, 1979-81. Chm. Permanent Cttee of the World Veterinary Assoc., 1957-75. DVM (*hc*) Hanover, 1963; Hon. Associate RCVS, 1963; Life Fellow, Aust. Vet. Assoc., 1963; Hon. Member: British Veterinary Assoc., 1970; Amer. Vet. Med. Assoc., 1973; World Veterinary Congresses, 1975; Hon. Foreign Mem., Académie Royale de Médicine de Belgique, 1970; Foundation Fellow, Aust. Coll. Vet. Scientists, 1971; Mem., German Acad. for Scientific Research, Leopoldina, 1974; Hon. Dip., Hungarian Microbiological Assoc., Budapest, 1976. Karl F. Meyer Goldheaded Cane Award, 1971; Gamgee Gold Medal, World Vet. Assoc., 1975; Medal of Honour, French Nat. Cttee of World Vet. Assoc., 1976. *Publications:* The Art of Scientific Investigation, 1950; Frontiers in Comparative Medicine, 1972; Influenza: the last great plague, 1977; Seeds of Discovery, 1980; Viral Diseases of Farm Livestock, 1981; Bacterial Diseases of Ruminants, 1982; articles on infectious diseases of man and domestic animals and comparative medicine, in scientific jls. *Recreations:* bush-walking, skiing. *Address:* University House, PO Box 1535, Canberra City, ACT 2601, Australia.
See also J. C. Beveridge.

BEVERLEY, Vice-Adm. Sir (William) York (La Roche), KBE 1952 (CBE 1947); CB 1949; *b* 14 Dec. 1895; *s* of Major W. H. Beverley; *m* 1931, Maria Teresa Matilde (*d* 1957), *d* of Enrico Palazio, Santa-Margherita-Ligure, Italy; one *s* one *d* (and one *s* decd). *Educ:* Royal Naval Colls, Osborne and Dartmouth. Served throughout European War, 1914-18, and War of 1939-45; ADC to the King, 1947-48; Admiral Supt, Portsmouth, 1949-51; Vice-Adm., 1950; Dir of Dockyards, 1951-54, retired Dec. 1954. *Address:* c/o Grindlays Bank Ltd, 13 St James's Square, SW1Y 4LF.

BEVERTON, Raymond John Heaphy, CBE 1968; FRS 1975; FIBiol 1973; Programme Integrator for International Federation of Institutes for Advanced Study, since 1982; currently a Senior Research Fellow at University of Bristol, engaged on a study of change and adaptation in scientific research careers; *b* 29 Aug. 1922; *s* of Edgar John Beverton and Dorothy Sybil Mary Beverton; *m* 1947, Kathleen Edith Marner; three *d*. *Educ:* Forest Sch., Snaresbrook; Downing Coll., Cambridge (MA). Cambridge, 1940-42 and 1946-47. Joined Fisheries Research Lab. (MAFF), 1947; Dep. Dir, Fisheries Res., 1959-65; Sec., NERC, 1965-80. Hon. posts during research career: Chm., Comparative Fishing Cttee of ICES, 1957-62; Chm., Res. and Statistics Cttee of Internat.

Commn for Northwest Atlantic Fisheries, 1960-63. Member: MAFF Fisheries R & D Bd, 1972-79; NRPB, 1976-80; Council, Fisheries Soc. of British Isles. Vice-Pres., Freshwater Biological Assoc., 1980-. *Publications:* (with S. J. Holt) On the Dynamics of Exploited Fish Populations, 1957; papers on mathematical basis of fish population dynamics, theory and practice of fisheries conservation and various fisheries research topics. *Recreations:* fishing, sailing, golf, music. *Address:* 55 Sandown Avenue, Swindon SN3 1QQ. *T:* Swindon 25677.

BEVINGTON, Eric Raymond, CMG 1961; *b* 23 Jan. 1914; *s* of late R. Bevington and N. E. Bevington (*née* Sutton); *m* 1939, Enid Mary Selina (*née* Homer); one *s* one *d*. *Educ:* Monkton Combe Sch.; Loughborough Coll.; Queens' Coll., Cambridge. CEng, MIMechE. Cadet, HM Overseas Service, Gilbert and Ellice Islands, 1937; District Officer, Fiji, 1942; Sec., Commn of Enquiry into Cost of Living Allowances, Nigeria, 1945-46; Admin. Officer Cl I, Fiji, 1950; Asst Col Sec. (Devclt), Fiji, 1951; Devclt Comr, Brunei, 1954; Financial Sec., Fiji, 1958-61, Development Commissioner, 1962-63; Mem., Executive Council, Fiji, 1958-63; Senior Project Engineer, Wrigh Rain Ltd, 1964-67; Appeals Inspector, Min. of Housing and Local Govt, 1967-70; Sen. Housing and Planning Inspector, DoE, 1970-78. Mem., New Forest DC, 1979-May 1983. *Recreations:* golf, sailing, zymurgy. *Address:* Holmans Cottage, Bisterne Close, Burley, Hants. *T:* Burley 3316

BEVINS, Rt. Hon. John Reginald, PC 1959; *b* 20 Aug. 1908; *e s* of John Milton and Grace Eveline Bevins, Liverpool; *m* 1933, Mary Leonora Jones; three *s*. *Educ:* Dovedale Road and Liverpool Collegiate Schs. Served War of 1939-45; gunner, 1940; Major, RASC, 1944; MEF and Europe. Mem. Liverpool City Council, 1935-50. Contested West Toxteth Div., 1945, and Edge Hill (bye-election), 1947; MP (C) Toxteth Div. of Liverpool, 1950-64; PPS to the Minister of Housing and Local Government, 1951-53; Parliamentary Sec., Ministry of Works, 1953-57, Ministry of Housing and Local Govt, 1957-59; Postmaster-General, 1959-64. *Publication:* The Greasy Pole, 1965. *Address:* 37 Queen's Drive, Liverpool L18 2DT. *T:* 051-722 8484.
See also K. M. Bevins.

BEVINS, Kenneth Milton, CBE 1973; TD 1951; Director: Royal Insurance Co. Ltd, since 1970; British Aerospace plc, since 1981; *b* 2 Nov. 1918; *yr s* of late John Milton Bevins and Grace Eveline Bevins, Liverpool; *m* 1st, 1940, Joan Harding (*d* 1969); two *d*; 2nd, 1971, Diana B. Sellers, *y d* of Godfrey J. Sellers, Keighley. *Educ:* Liverpool Collegiate Sch. Joined Royal Insurance Co. Ltd, 1937. Served War, 1939-46: 136 Field Regt, RA, incl. with 14th Army in Burma, 1943-46 (Major). Sec., Royal Insurance Co. Ltd, 1957; Gen. Manager, 1963; Dep. Chief Gen. Manager, 1966; Chief Gen. Manager, 1970-80; Director: Trade Indemnity Co. Ltd, 1970-80 (Chm., 1975-80); Mutual & Federal Insurance Co. Ltd, 1971-80. Dir, Fire Protection Assoc., 1963-77 (Chm., 1966-68). Member: Jt Fire Research Organisation Steering Cttee, 1966-68; Home Secretary's Standing Cttee on Crime Prevention, 1967-73; Exec. Cttee, City Communications Centre, 1976-80; Bd, British Aerospace, 1980-81. Chm., British Insurance Assoc., 1971-73 (Dep. Chm., 1967-71). *Address:* Linton, The Drive, Sevenoaks, Kent. *T:* Sevenoaks 456909. *Clubs:* Oriental, Army and Navy.
See also Rt Hon. J. R. Bevins.

BEWICK, Herbert; barrister; *b* 4 April 1911; *s* of late James Dicker and Elizabeth Jane Bewick. *Educ:* Whitehill Secondary Sch., Glasgow; Royal Grammar Sch., Newcastle upon Tyne; St Catharine's Coll., Cambridge. Called to Bar, Gray's Inn, 1935. Recorder of Pontefract, 1961-67. Chm. of Industrial Tribunal (Newcastle upon Tyne), 1967-72. *Address:* 51 Westgate Road, Newcastle upon Tyne NE1 1SS. *T:* Newcastle 320541; 27 Mitchell Avenue, Jesmond, Newcastle upon Tyne NE2 3JY. *T:* Newcastle 811138.

BEWICKE-COPLEY; family name of Baron Cromwell.

BEWLEY, Edward de Beauvoir; Hon. Mr Justice Bewley; Judge of the High Court of Hong Kong, since 1980; *b* 12 March 1931; *s* of Harold de Beauvoir Bewley and Phyllis Frances Cowdy; *m* 1968, Mary Gwenefer Jones; one *s* three *d*. *Educ:* Shrewsbury School; Trinity College, Dublin. BA, LLB; Barrister at Law. Administrative Officer, Northern Rhodesia, 1956-59; English Bar, 1960-61; Resident Magistrate, Nyasaland, 1961-64; Magistrate, Hong Kong, 1964-76, District Judge, 1976-80. *Recreations:* golf, skiing, reading, music. *Address:* 11 Mansfield Road, The Peak, Hong Kong. *T:* 5-96111. *Clubs:* Hong Kong; Royal Irish Yacht (Dun Laoghaire), Royal Hong Kong Golf, Royal Hong Kong Jockey, Kowloon Cricket.

BEXON, Roger; Managing Director, British Petroleum Co. Ltd, since 1981; *b* 11 April 1926; *s* of late Macalister Bexon, CBE, and Nora Hope Bexon (*née* Jenner); *m* 1952, Lois Loughran Walling; one *s* one *d*. *Educ:* Denstone Coll. (schol.); St John's Coll., Oxford (MA); Tulsa Univ. (MS). Geologist and petroleum engineer with Trinidad Petroleum Development Co. Ltd, 1946-57; management positions with British Petroleum Co. Ltd, E Africa, 1958-59; Libya, 1959-60; Trinidad, 1961-64; London, 1964-66; Manager, North Sea Operations, 1966-68; General Manager, Libya, 1968-70; Regional Coordinator, Middle East, London, 1971-73; Gen. Manager, Exploration and Production, London, 1973-76; Managing Director, BP Exploration Co. Ltd, London, 1976-77; Dir and Sen. Vice Pres., Standard Oil Co., Cleveland, Ohio, USA, 1977-80. *Publications:* general and technical contribs to internat. jls on oil and energy matters. *Recreations:* reading, golf, Times crossword puzzles.

Address: c/o British Petroleum Co. Ltd, Britannic House, Moor Lane, EC2Y 9BU. *T:* 01-920 6021.

BEYFUS, Drusilla Norman; writer, editor, broadcaster; *d* of Norman Beyfus and Florence Noel Barker; *m* 1956, Milton Shulman, *qv* ; one *s* two *d. Educ:* Royal Naval Sch. Woman's Editor, Sunday Express, 1950; columnist, Daily Express, 1952-55; Associate Editor, Queen magazine, 1956; Home Editor, The Observer, 1963; Associate Editor, Daily Telegraph magazine, 1966; Editor, Brides and Setting Up Home magazine, 1972-79; Associate Editor, Vogue magazine, 1979-. TV and radio appearances, incl. Call My Bluff and talks programmes. *Publications:* (with Anne Edwards) Lady Behave, 1956 (rev. edn 1969); The English Marriage, 1968; The Brides Book, 1981; contrib. to Sunday Times, Picture Post, Punch, New Statesman. *Recreations:* walking, modern art, cooking. *Address:* 51G Eaton Square, SW1. *T:* 01-235 7162.

BEYNON, Ernest Geoffrey; Joint General Secretary, Assistant Masters and Mistresses Association, since 1979; *b* 4 Oct. 1926; *s* of Frank William George and Frances Alice Pretoria Beynon; *m* 1954, Denise Gwendoline Rees; two *s* one *d. Educ:* Borden Grammar Sch., Kent; Univ. of Bristol, 1944-47, 1949-50 (BSc (Hons Maths) 1947, CertEd 1950). National Service, Royal Artillery, 1947-49. Mathematics Master, Thornbury Grammar Sch., Glos, 1950-56; Mathematics Master and Sixth Form Master, St George Grammar Sch., Bristol, 1956-64; Asst Sec., Assistant Masters Assoc., 1964-78. *Publications:* many reports/pamphlets for AMA, incl. The Middle School System, Mixed Ability Teaching, Selection for Admission to a University. *Recreations:* family, work, canal boating, caravanning, walking, books. *Address:* (office) Gordon House, 29 Gordon Square, WC1H 0PX. *T:* 01-388 5861; (home) 3 Templewood, Welwyn Garden City, Herts AL8 7HT. *T:* Welwyn Garden City 21380.

BEYNON, Sir Granville; *see* Beynon, Sir W. J. G.

BEYNON, Ven. James Royston; Archdeacon of Winchester, 1962-73, now Emeritus; *b* 16 Sept. 1907; *s* of James Samuel and Catherine Beynon; *m* 1933, Mildred Maud Fromings; four *d. Educ:* St Augustine's Coll., Canterbury. LTh Durham. Ordained, 1931; Chaplain, Indian Eccl. Estabt, 1933; Senior Chaplain: Peshawar, 1941; Quetta, 1943; Archdeacon of Lahore, 1946-48; Vicar of Twyford, Winchester, 1948-73; Rural Dean of Winchester, 1958-62. Hon. CF, 1945. *Address:* 1511 Geary Avenue, London, Ontario, Canada.

BEYNON, Prof. John Herbert, DSc; FRS 1971; Royal Society Research Professor, University College Swansea, University of Wales, since 1974; *b* 29 Dec. 1923; British; *m* 1947, Yvonne Lilian (*née* Fryer); no *c. Educ:* UC Swansea, Univ. of Wales. BSc (1st cl. hons Physics); DSc; FInstP; CChem; FRSC. Experimental Officer, Min. of Supply, Tank Armament Research, 1943-47; ICI Ltd (Organics Div.), 1947-74; Associate Research Man. i/c Physical Chemistry, 1962-70; Sen. Res. Associate, 1966-74. Hon. Professorial Fellow, and Lectr in Chemistry, UC Swansea, 1967-74; Prof. of Chemistry, Purdue Univ., Indiana, 1969-75; Associate Prof. of Molecular Sciences, Univ. of Warwick, 1972-74; Vis. Prof., Univ. of Essex, 1973-74; Hon. Prof., Univ. of Warwick, 1977-. *Publications:* Mass Spectrometry and its Applications in Organic Chemistry, 1960; Mass and Abundance Tables for use in Mass Spectrometry, 1963; The Mass Spectra of Organic Molecules, 1968; Table of Ion Energies for metastable transitions in mass spectrometry, 1970; Metastable Ions, 1973; An Introduction to Mass Spectrometry, 1981; papers in Proc. Royal Soc., Nature, Jl Sci. Inst., Jl Applied Physics, Chem. Soc., JACS, Trans Faraday Soc., Int. Jl Mass Spectrom. and Ion Physics, Org. Mass Spectrom., Anal. Chem., etc. *Recreations:* photography, golf. *Address:* Royal Society Research Unit, University College Swansea, Singleton Park, Swansea SA2 8PP. *T:* Swansea 205678; 17 Coltshill Drive, Mumbles, Swansea SA3 4SN. *T:* Swansea 68718. *Club:* Athenæum.

BEYNON, Prof. Sir (William John) Granville, Kt 1976; CBE 1959; PhD, DSc; FRS 1973; Professor and Head of Department of Physics, University College of Wales, Aberystwyth, 1958-81, now Emeritus; *b* 24 May 1914; *s* of William and Mary Beynon; *m* 1942, Megan Medi, *d* of Arthur and Margaret James; two *s* one *d. Educ:* Gowerton Grammar Sch.; University Coll., Swansea. Scientific Officer, later Senior Scientific Officer, National Physical Laboratory, 1938-46; Lecturer, later Senior Lecturer in Physics, University Coll. of Swansea, 1946-58. Mem., SRC, 1976-80. Mem., Schools Council, 1965-76; Pres., 1972-75, Hon. Pres., 1981-, URSI; Hon. Professorial Fellow, UC Swansea, 1981-; Hon. DSc Leicester, 1981. *Publications:* (ed) Solar Eclipses and the Ionosphere, 1956; (ed) Proceedings Mixed Commission on the Ionosphere, 1948-58; numerous publications in scientific jls. *Recreations:* music, cricket, tennis, Rugby. *Address:* Caebryn, Caergôg, Aberystwyth. *T:* Aberystwyth 3947; Bryn Eithin, 103 Dunvant Road, Swansea. *T:* Swansea 23585.

BIBBY, Major Sir (Arthur) Harold, 1st Bt *cr* 1959; Kt 1956; DSO 1917; DL; LLD (Hon.) Liverpool; President, Bibby Line Ltd; *b* 18 Feb. 1889; *s* of late Arthur Wilson Bibby; *m* 1920, Marjorie, *d* of late Charles J. Williamson and late The Lady Royden; one *s* three *d* (and one *s* decd). *Educ:* Rugby. Served in RFA (TF), 1908-19; in France and Flanders, 1915-18 (despatches twice, DSO awarded on field of Cambrai). Senior Partner, Bibby Bros & Co., Shipowners and Bankers, 1935-73; Chm., Bibby Line Ltd, 1935-69, Pres., 1969; Director: Sea Insurance Co. Ltd, 1922-68 (Chm., 1930-56); Liverpool & London Steamship Protection & Indemnity Association, 1921-68; LNER, 1924-47; Martins Bank Ltd, 1929-67 (Chm., 1947-62); Suez Canal Co.,

1939-57; Member: Mersey Docks & Harbour Board, 1931-65; Governing Body of Rugby Sch., 1932-67; Chairman: Liverpool Steam Ship Owners Association, 1927 and 1958 (Centenary Year); Employers' Association of Port of Liverpool, 1938-47; Vice-Chm., National Assoc. of Port Employers 1941-47; Jt Vice-Chm., General Council of British Shipping, 1958-59. President: Training Ship Indefatigable (Chm., 1931-60); Liverpool Sailors Home (Chm., 1921-51); Liverpool Conservative Assoc., 1959-66; Northwic Conservative Association, 1960-74. DL, Chester, 1937; High Sheriff o Cheshire, 1934-35. Hon. Freeman, City of Liverpool, 1970. *Heir: s* Dere James Bibby, *qv. Address:* Tilstone Lodge, Tarporley, Cheshire CW 9HT.

BIBBY, Benjamin; *see* Bibby, J. B.

BIBBY, Dr Cyril; *b* 1914; *s* of William and Elizabeth Jane Bibby, Liverpool *m* 1936, Frances (Florence Mabel) Hirst, Mddx; two *s* two *d. Educ:* Liverpool Collegiate Sch.; Queens' Coll., Cambridge. Open Major Scholar in natura sciences, 1932; Coll. Prizeman, 1933; Icelandic expedn, 1934; BACantab, 1935. Physics and Chemistry Master, Oulton Sch., Liverpool, 1935-38; Scientific research, Univ. of Liverpool, 1935-40; MACantab, 1939; Sen. Biology Master Chesterfield Grammar Sch., 1938-40; MSc Liverpool, 1940. Educn Officer to Brit. Social Hygiene Council and then Central Council for Health Educn 1941-46; Tutor in Biol. (becoming Co-ordinator of Sciences and Sec. to Academic Bd), Coll. of S Mark and S John, London, 1946-59; educational and other research, 1947-59; Principal, Kingston upon Hull Coll. of Educn 1959-76; Pro-Dir, Hull Coll. of Higher Educn, 1976-78. Visiting Prof., Univ of Illinois, 1950; PhD London, 1955; Silver Medal of RSA, 1956. Visiting Lecturer at several Univs in USA (also investigatory visits for US Nat. Science Foundn, 1962). Delegate to many internat. congresses, etc., 1947-64. At various periods, Mem. Executive of: Internat. Union of Family Organisations Fraternité Mondiale; Assoc. of Teachers in Colls and Depts of Educn; Council of Christians and Jews; Eugenics Soc., Nat. Foundn for Educl Research; Soc for Research into Higher Educn; School Broadcasting Council of UK, etc Many political activities. FLS, 1942; FRSA, 1954. *Publications:* Evolution of Man and His Culture, 1938; Heredity, Eugenics and Social Progress, 1939 Experimental Human Biology, 1942; Simple Experiments in Biology, 1943 Sex Education, 1944; How Life is Handed On, 1946; Healthy and Happy 1948; Story of Birth, 1949; Healthy Day, 1949; Active Human Biology, 1950 Health Education, 1951; Healthy People, 1954; Human Body, 1955 Education in Racial and Intergroup Relations, 1957; T. H. Huxley, 1959 Race, Prejudice and Education, 1959; The First Fifty Years, 1964; Essence o T. H. Huxley, 1968; Biology of Mankind, 1968; T. H. Huxley on Education 1971; Scientist Extraordinary, 1972; The Art of the Limerick, 1978; papers in various scientific, health, educnl, political, sociological and gen. lit. jls. *Recreations:* reading, writing, walking, sun-bathing, film, theatre, travel *Address:* 11 Beech Grove, Beverley Road, Hull.

BIBBY, Derek James, MC 1945; Chairman, Bibby Line Ltd, since 1969; *b* 29 June 1922; *s* and *heir* of Major Sir (Arthur) Harold Bibby, 1st Bt, *qv; m* 1961, Christine Maud, *d* of late Rt. Rev. F. J. Okell, MA, DD, Bishop of Stockport; four *s* one *d. Educ:* Rugby; Trinity Coll., Oxford (MA). Served War, Army 1942-46. *Recreations:* shooting, gardening. *Address:* Willaston Grange Willaston, South Wirral L64 2UN. *T:* 051-327 4913. *Club:* Royal Commonwealth Society.

BIBBY, (John) Benjamin; Chairman, J. Bibby & Sons Ltd, 1970-78; *b* 19 April 1929; *s* of late J. P. and D. D. Bibby; *m* 1956, Susan Lindsay Paterson; two *s* one *d. Educ:* Oundle Sch.; St Catharine's Coll., Cambridge (MA). Called to the Bar, Gray's Inn. Has held various positions in J. Bibby & Sons Ltd, 1953-; Director, 1961-. Mem. Council, Univ. of Liverpool, 1978-81. JP Liverpool 1975-81. *Publication:* (with C. L. Bibby) A Miller's Tale, 1978. *Recreations:* sailing, squash. *Address:* Kirby Mount, Warwick Drive, West Kirby, Wirral, Merseyside. *T:* 051-625 8071. *Clubs:* Liverpool Racquet; West Kirby Sailing; Royal Mersey Yacht; Royal Anglesey Yacht.

BIBBY, Samuel Leslie, CBE 1947 (OBE 1945); DL; *b* 19 Jan. 1897; *s* of Samuel Gawith Bibby, Sutton, Surrey; *m* 1923, Eva Margaret Wood, *d* of Dr G. Benington Wood, Sandown, IoW; one *s* one *d* (and one *s* decd). *Educ:* Malvern. Served European War, 1915-19, Capt. RA(TA) (despatches). Col TA, 1943; Comd 6th (Leatherhead) Bn Surrey Home Guard, 1940-43; Comdt Surrey Army Cadet Force, 1943-49; Chm. Army Cadet Force Sports Council, 1940-49; Military Mem. Surrey T&AFA, 1940-49. DL 1955; High Sheriff of Surrey, 1959. *Address:* Foresters, Deans Lane, Walton-on-the-Hill, Tadworth, Surrey. *T:* Tadworth 2820. *Clubs:* Gresham, MCC.

BICESTER, 3rd Baron *cr* 1938, of Tusmore; Angus Edward Vivian Smith; *b* 20 Feb. 1932; *s* of Lt-Col Hon. Stephen Edward Vivian Smith (*d* 1952) (2nd *s* of 1st Baron) and Elenor Anderson, *d* of Edward S. Hewitt, New York City; *S* uncle, 1968. *Educ:* Eton. *Heir: b* Hugh Charles Vivian Smith, *b* 8 Nov. 1934.

BICKERSTETH, Rt. Rev. John Monier; *see* Bath and Wells, Bishop of.

BICKERTON, Frank Donald, CBE 1966; Director General, Central Office of Information, 1971-74; *b* 22 June 1917; *s* of F. M. Bickerton and A. A. Hibbert; *m* 1945, Linda Russell; two *s. Educ:* Liverpool Collegiate Sch. Min. of Health, in Public Relations Div., 1935-40. Served War, RNVR, 1940-45. Min. of National Insurance (later Min. of Pensions and Nat. Insurance),

1946-61: initially Asst Press Officer and in charge of Information Div., 1952-61; Chief Information Officer, Min. of Transport, 1961-68; Controller (Home), COI, 1968-71. *Recreations:* walking, gardening, cruising. *Address:* 6 Diana Close, Granville Rise, Totland, Isle of Wight.

BICKFORD SMITH, John Roger, TD 1950; Master of Supreme Court, Queen's Bench Division, since 1967; *b* 31 Oct. 1915; *er s* of late Leonard W. Bickford Smith, Camborne, Cornwall, For. Man., ICI, and of Anny Grete (*née* Huth); *m* 1st, 1939, Cecilia Judge Heath (marr. diss.), *er d* of W. W. Heath, Leicester; two *s* ; 2nd, 1972, Baronin Joaise Miranda et Omnes Sancti von Kirchberg-Hohenheim. *Educ:* Eton (King's Schol.); Hertford Coll., Oxford (Schol.). BA 1937; MA 1952. Commnd in Duke of Cornwall's LI (TA), 1939; served 1939-46: UK, India, Burma and Germany; AJAG (Major), 1942; Lieut-Col 1944. Called to Bar, Inner Temple, 1942. Practised at Common Law Bar in London and on Midland Circuit, 1946-67. *Publications:* The Crown Proceedings Act 1947, 1948; various contribs to legal pubns. *Recreation:* foreign travel. *Address:* Royal Courts of Justice, WC2. *Club:* Garrick.

BICKNELL, Mrs Christine Betty, MA (Oxon); Chairman: Civil Service Selection Boards, since 1970; Victoria Health Authority, since 1981; Member: Newspaper Panel, Monopolies and Mergers Commission, since 1973; Industrial Tribunals, since 1977; *b* 23 Dec. 1919; *er d* of Walter Edward and Olive Isabelle Reynolds; *m* 1960, Claud Bicknell, *qv* ; one step *s* two step *d* (one step *d* decd). *Educ:* St Martin-in-the-Fields High Sch. for Girls; Somerville Coll., Oxford (Exhibr). BA 1941. Board of Trade, 1941-60: Principal 1945; Sec., UK Trade Mission to Egypt, the Sudan and Ethiopia, 1954; Admin. Staff Coll., Henley, 1954; Asst Sec. 1958; Northern Regional Officer, Min. of Land and Natural Resources, 1965-67. Vice-Chm., Newcastle Family Planning Assoc., 1961-70; Chairman: Prudhoe and Monkton HMC, 1966-70 and Leavesden HMC, 1971-74; Kensington and Chelsea and Westminster AHA (T), 1973-77; Member: Newcastle RHB, 1961-70, and NW Metrop. RHB, 1971-74; Nat. Whitley Council for Nurses and Midwives, 1962-70; Northern Econ. Planning Bd, 1965-67; Nat. Exec., Family Planning Assoc., 1965-67; Bd of Governors, Royal Vic. Infirm., Newcastle upon Tyne, 1965-70 and St Bartholomew's Hosp., 1971-74; Platt Cttee on Med. Staffing (FPA), 1970; Mem., British Library Board, 1979-82; Pres., Hosp. Domestic Administrators' Assoc., 1970-74. *Recreations:* gardening, mountains, hill walking, sailing. *Address:* 20 Miller's Court, Chiswick Mall, W4 2PF. *Clubs:* Alpine, United Oxford & Cambridge University.

BICKNELL, Claud, OBE 1946; a Law Commissioner, 1970-75; a part-time Chairman of Industrial Tribunals, since 1975; *b* Rowlands Gill, near Newcastle upon Tyne, 15 June 1910; 2nd *s* of Raymond Bicknell and Phillis Bicknell (*née* Lovibond); *m* 1st, 1934, Esther Irene (*d* 1958), *e d* of Kenneth Bell; one *s* two *d* (one *d* decd); 2nd, 1960, Christine Betty Reynolds (*see* C. B. Bicknell). *Educ:* Corchester Prep. Sch., Corbridge on Tyne; Oundle Sch.; Queens' Coll., Cambridge (Scholar). MA 1935. Pres., Cambridge Univ. Mountaineering Club, 1930-31. Articled to A. L. Bird, Solicitor, Newcastle upon Tyne, 1931-34; admitted as a solicitor, 1934; Asst Solicitor, 1934-39, and partner, 1939-70, in firm of Stanton, Atkinson & Bird, Newcastle upon Tyne. Dir, Northern Corporation Ltd, 1939-53. Auxiliary Fire Service, Newcastle upon Tyne, 1939-41; Nat. Fire Service, 1941-45; Sen. Fire Staff Officer, Home Office, 1943-45. Mem. Planning Bd, Lake District Nat. Park, 1951-70 (Chm., Development Control Cttee, 1957-70); Mem. Lord Jellicoe's Cttee on water resources in the North-West, 1963; Newcastle upon Tyne Incorporated Law Society: Hon. Sec., 1966-70; Vice-Pres., 1967; Pres., 1969; Chm., Newcastle upon Tyne Housing Improvement Trust Ltd, 1966-70. *Recreation:* mountains. *Address:* 20 Miller's Court, Chiswick Mall, W4 2PF. *Clubs:* Garrick, Alpine; Achilles.

See also Sir J. R. Shelley, Bt.

BIDAULT, Georges; *b* Moulins, 5 Oct. 1899; *s* of Georges Bidault and Augustine Traverse; *m* 1945, Suzanne Borel. *Educ:* Collège des jésuites de Bollengo; Faculté des Lettres, Paris. Before war of 1939-45 was a professor of history and edited L'Aube, the journal of the Christian Democrats; served in the ranks, was taken prisoner but freed after 12 months; became chm. of the resistance council inside France, 1943; Minister for Foreign Affairs in Provisional Govts of 1944 and 1945; President of Provisional Govt, May 1945; Deputy from the Loire, 1945, re-elected 1946, 1951, 1956, 1958; Premier and Foreign Minister, France, 1946; Minister of Foreign Affairs, 1947-48; Pres. of the Council, 1950 and 1951, Vice-Pres., 1951-52 and 1952; Minister of National Defence, 1951-52; Minister of Foreign Affairs, Jan.-July 1954; Premier, April 1958; Pres., Provisional Bureau of Rassemblement pour L'Algérie française, Oct. 1959; charged with plot against security of the State, July 1962; in Brazil, March 1963-July 1967, Belgium 1967-68; returned to France, June 1968. Delegate to Council of Europe, 1949. Grand' Croix de la Légion d'honneur; Compagnon de la Libération. *Publications:* L'Algérie, l'oiseau aux ailes coupées, 1958; D'une Résistance à l'autre, 1965 (Resistance: the political autobiography of Georges Bidault, 1967); Le Point, 1968. *Address:* 21 rue du Colonel Moll, 75017 Paris, France.

BIDDULPH, family name of **Baron Biddulph.**

BIDDULPH, 4th Baron *cr* 1903; **Robert Michael Christian Biddulph;** *b* 6 Jan. 1931; *s* of 3rd Baron Biddulph and of Lady Amy Louise Agar, *d* of 4th Earl of Normanton; *S* father, 1972; *m* 1958, Lady Mary Maitland, *d* of

Viscount Maitland (killed in action, 1943) and *g d* of 15th Earl of Lauderdale; two *s* one *d. Educ:* Canford; RMA, Sandhurst. Lt 16/5 The Queen's Royal Lancers, retd. *Recreations:* shooting, fishing. *Heir: s* Hon. Anthony Nicholas Colin Maitland Biddulph, *b* 8 April 1959. *Address:* Makerstoun, Kelso, Roxburghshire, Scotland. *Clubs:* Cavalry and Guards; New (Edinburgh).

BIDDULPH, Constance; *see* Holt, C.

BIDDULPH, Sir Stuart (Royden), 10th Bt *cr* 1664; retired grazier; *b* 24 June 1908; *s* of Sir Francis Henry Biddulph, 9th Bt, and Janet (*d* 1956), *d* of Walter Bain Hannah, Brisbane; *S* father, 1980; *m* 1939, Muriel Margaret, 3rd *d* of Angus Harkness, Hamley Bridge, S Australia; one *s* two *d. Educ:* Brisbane Grammar School. *Recreation:* gliding. *Heir: s* Ian D'Olier Biddulph [*b* 28 Feb. 1940; *m* 1967, Margaret Eleanor, *o d* of late John Gablonski; one *s* two *d*]. *Address:* 119 Watson Street, Charleville, Queensland 4470, Australia.

BIDE, Sir Austin (Ernest), Kt 1980; Chairman, since 1973, Chief Executive, 1973-80, Glaxo Holdings Ltd; non-executive Chairman, BL Ltd, since 1982 (Director, since 1977; Deputy Chairman, 1980-82); *b* 11 Sept. 1915; *o s* of late Ernest Arthur Bide and Eliza Bide (*née* Young); *m* 1941, Irene (*née* Ward); three *d. Educ:* County Sch., Acton; Univ. of London. 1st cl. hons BSc Chemistry; FRIC. Govt Chemist's Dept, 1932-40; Research Chemist, Glaxo, 1940: i/c Chemical Develt and Industrial Property, 1944-54; Dep. Sec., 1954-59; Sec., 1959-65; Dir, 1963-71; Dep. Chm., 1971-73; Dir, J. Lyons & Co. Ltd, 1977-78. Member: CBI Council, 1974-; BIM Council, 1976-; Dir, BIM Foundn, 1977-79; Chairman: BIM Finance Cttee, 1976-79; CBI Res. and Technology Cttee, 1977-; Mem. Working Party on Biotechnology (under auspices of ACARD, ABRD and Royal Soc.) (Report 1980). CBIM (FBIM 1972). Chm., Visiting Cttee of the Open Univ., 1982-. Mem. Council, Imperial Soc. of Knights Bachelor, 1980-. *Publications:* papers in learned jls on organic chemical subjects. *Recreations:* fishing, handicrafts. *Address:* Clarges House, 6-12 Clarges Street, W1Y 8DH. *Club:* Hurlingham.

BIDGOOD, John Claude, MIEx; Chairman: Anglo-Dominion Finance Co. Ltd; Anglo-Dominion Construction Co. Ltd; Anglo-Dominion Trading Co. Ltd; *b* 12 May 1914; *s* of late Edward Charles Bidgood, Leeds; *m* 1945, Sheila Nancy Walker-Wood; one *s* two *d. Educ:* London Choir Sch.; Woodhouse Technical Sch. Served early part of War of 1939-45 as Pilot RAF. Mem. Leeds City Council, 1947-55 (late Chm. Works Cttee and City Architects Cttee); contested (C) N E Leeds, 1950, 1951; MP (C) Bury and Radcliffe, 1955-64; PPS to Joint Parly Secs, Min. of Pensions and Nat. Insurance, 1957-58; Mem. Parly Select Cttee on Estimates, 1958-64. Director: Bidgood Holdings Ltd; Edward Bidgood & Co. Ltd; Bidgood Larsson Ltd; Wright & Summerhill Ltd; R. Horsfield & Co. Ltd; Constructional Erection Ltd; Bidgood Larsson (Iraq) Ltd; Chm., Yorks Assoc. for the Disabled, 1950-58; Member: Inst. of Export; Leeds and Bradford Joint Aerodrome Cttee, 1951-55; W Riding Rating Valuation Court, 1955. Gen. Comr of Income Tax. Councillor, Chapeltown Corporation, 1976-. Governor, Bury Grammar Schs, 1955. Freeman, City of London; Liveryman and Mem., Worshipful Co. of Horners; Mem., Hon. Soc. of Knights of Round Table. *Recreations:* music, travel. *Address:* The Old Joinery, Walton, near Wetherby, W Yorks LS23 7DQ. *T:* Boston Spa 844028. *Clubs:* City Livery, Naval and Military; Leeds (Chm.) (Leeds).

BIDSTRUP, (Patricia) Lesley, MD, FRCP, FRACP; Member, Medical Appeals Tribunal, since 1970; Member, Industrial Injuries Advisory Council, since 1970; *b* 24 Oct. 1916; *d* of Clarence Leslie Bidstrup, Chemical Works Manager, South Australia, and Kathleen Helena Bidstrup (*née* O'Brien); *m* 1952, Ronald Frank Guymer, TD, MD, FRCP, FRCS, DPH, DIH; one step *s* one step *d. Educ:* Kadina High Sch. and Walford House, Adelaide, SA. MB, BS (Adel.) 1939; MD (Adel.) 1958; FRACP 1954; FRCP (Lond.) 1964. Resident Ho. Phys. and Registrar, Royal Adelaide Hosp., SA, 1939-41. Hon. Capt., AAMC, 1942-45. MO, UNRRA, Glyn-Hughes Hosp., Belsen, 1945-46. General practice: Acting Hon. Asst Phys., Royal Adelaide Hosp.; Tutor in Med., St Mark's Coll., Adelaide, and in Univ. of Adelaide Med. Sch.; Lectr in Med., Univ. of Adelaide Dental Faculty, 1942-45; Asst, Dept for Research in Industrial Medicine, MRC, 1947-58; Clinical Asst (Hon.), Chest Dept, St Thomas' Hosp., 1958-78. Private consulting concerned mainly with industrial medicine, 1958-. Mem., Scientific Sub-Cttee on Poisonous Substances used in Agriculture and Food Storage, 1956-58; Corr. Mem., Amer. Acad. of Occupational Medicine. Visiting Lectr, TUC Centenary Inst. of Occupational Health; Examiner for Diploma in Industrial Health: Conjoint Bd, 1965-71, 1980-; Society of Apothecaries, 1970-; External Examiner for Diploma in Industrial Health, Dundee, 1980-. Mayoress, Royal Borough of Kingston-upon-Thames, 1959, 1960. *Publications:* The Toxicity of Mercury and its Compounds, 1964; chapters in: Cancer Progress, 1960; The Prevention of Cancer, 1967; Clinical Aspects of Inhaled Particles 1972; contribs to Brit. Jl Indust. Med., Lancet, BMJ, Proc. Royal Soc. Med., ILO Encyclopaedia on Industrial Diseases. *Recreations:* people, theatre, music. *Address:* 11 Sloane Terrace Mansions, Sloane Terrace, SW1X 9DG. *T:* 01-730 8720.

BIDWELL, Sydney James; MP (Lab) Ealing-Southall, since 1974 (Southall, 1966-74); *b* Southall, 14 Jan. 1917; *s* of late Herbert Emmett Bidwell; *m* 1941; one *s* one *d. Educ:* Elementary sch., evening classes and trade union study. Railway worker; Tutor and Organiser, Nat. Council of Labour Colls. Mem., TGWU. TUC Reg. Educn Officer, London, 1963-66. Mem., Southall Bor. Council, 1951-55. Contested (Lab): E Herts, 1959; Herts SW, 1964. Former Mem., Parly Select Cttee on Race Relations and Immigration, 1968-79;

Mem., Select Cttee on Transport, 1979-. *Publications:* Red White and Black Book on Race-Relations, 1976; The Turban Victory, 1977; articles on TU and Labour history. *Recreations:* watching soccer, painting, cartooning. *Address:* House of Commons, SW1. *Club:* Southall Social and TU.

BIERBACH, Martin; Ambassador of the German Democratic Republic to the Court of St James's, since 1980; *b* 30 Nov. 1926; *m* 1953, Helene Lützel; one *s* one *d*. *Educ:* secondary school; studied foreign politics at university (Diploma in Political Sciences). Entered diplomatic service; leading functions in Min. of Foreign Affairs, German Democratic Republic, 1953-57; Counsellor, GDR Embassy, Peking, People's Republic of China, 1957-59; Consul General, GDR Embassy, Cairo, Arab Republic of Egypt, 1959-62; Head of Near and Middle East Dept. Min. of Foreign Affairs, 1962-66; Ambassador of GDR: Peking, 1966-68; Cairo, 1969-73; Head of South and South East Asia Dept, Min. of Foreign Affairs, 1973-80. Holder of several state awards. *Recreations:* sport, reading. *Address:* Brent Cross House, 124 The Broadway, NW9. *T:* 01-202 3847/9.

BIERER, Joshua, MD, DiplPsychol, DRerPol; FRCPsych; Medical Director, Institute of Social Psychiatry since 1946; Consultant Psychiatrist, Runwell Hospital, 1948-67; Founder, 1946, and Medical Director, Marlborough Day-Hospital, 1946-67; Founder, International Association of Social Psychiatry; Co-Founder, International Association of Group Psychotherapy; Editor-in-Chief, International Journal of Social Psychiatry; *b* 1 July 1901; *s* of Dr Josef Bierer, X-Ray specialist. *Educ:* Vienna Univ. Training in Individual Psychology by Prof. Alfred Adler and Dr A. Neuer (Vienna), 1926-28; Training-Analysis by Dr A. Neuer; private practice as Psychotherapist, 1927-; Lectr, Teaching Inst. of Individual Psychology, Berlin, 1928-29; Research: at Inst. of Physiology, Vienna Univ., 1933; in Psychotherapy and Psychiatry at Mental Hosp., Vienna Univ., 1934-36; at Runwell Hosp., Essex, 1938-40. Psychotherapist, Southend Gen. Hosp. and East Ham Memorial Hosp., 1939-43; Clinical Asst, Guy's Hosp., 1942-43; Visiting Psychotherapist, Runwell Mental Hosp., 1942-43 and 1946-48. Served as Specialist Psychiatrist, Major RAMC, 1944-46. Originated idea of Self-Governed Therapeutic Social Clubs, Day Hosps, Night and Week-end Hosps, Self governed Hostels, Therapeutic Communities, the Total Separation Treatment in Marriage Guidance and a new and revolutionary method in education. Co-Founder, Kibbutz Mishmar Haemek, Israel. *Publications:* (jt) Innovation in Social Psychiatry; The Day-Hospital, 1951; (ed) Therapeutic Social Clubs; pioneer research work in problems of social psychiatry, social psychotherapy, group psychotherapy, psychotherapy of psychotics in mental hosps and in out-patient depts by psychotherapy in Jl of Mental Science, Lancet, Brit. Med. Jl, Internat. Jl Soc. Psych., etc. *Recreations:* golf, swimming, tennis, table tennis, chess, bridge. *Address:* 140 Harley Street, W1 1AM. *T:* 01-935 1078. *Club:* Garrick.

BIFFEN, Rt. Hon. (William) John, PC 1979; MP (C) Oswestry Division of Salop since Nov. 1961; Lord President of the Council and Leader of the House of Commons, since 1982; *b* 3 Nov. 1930; *s* of Victor W. Biffen; *m* 1979, Mrs Sarah Wood (*née* Drew); one step *s* one step *d*. *Educ:* Dr Morgan's Grammar Sch., Bridgwater; Jesus Coll., Cambridge (BA). Worked in Tube Investments Ltd, 1953-60; Economist Intelligence Unit, 1960-61; Chief Sec. to the Treasury, 1979-81; Sec. of State for Trade, 1981-82. *Address:* Middle Farm, Kinton, Nesscliffe, Salop.

BIGG, Wilfred Joseph, CMG 1948; *b* 20 July 1897; 2nd *s* of late Joseph Henry Bigg; *m* 1925, Ivy Lillian Daniel (*d* 1973); three *d*. *Educ:* Bournemouth Sch. Entered GPO 1912. Served European War, 1914-19. Entered Colonial Office, 1919; Private Sec. to Permanent Under Sec., Dominions Office, 1930-31; returned to Colonial Office, June 1931; Asst Sec., 1943; retired 1957. Member: Commonwealth Shipping Cttee, 1952-57; Bd of Governors, Coll. of Aeronautics, 1955-58; Commonwealth Telecommunications Board, 1955-62. *Recreations:* gardening, motoring. *Address:* Headley, 35 Manwell Road, Swanage, Dorset. *T:* Swanage 2603.

BIGGAR, (Walter) Andrew, CBE 1980 (OBE 1967); MC 1945; FRAgS; farming since 1956; *b* 6 March 1915; *s* of Walter Biggar and Margaret Sproat; *m* 1945, Patricia Mary Irving Elliot; one *s* one *d*. *Educ:* Sedbergh Sch., Cumbria; Edinburgh Univ. (BScAgric). FRAgS 1969. Commnd Royal Signals, 1938; War Service, 51st Highland Div., 1939-46; POW, Germany, 1940-45. Rowett Res. Inst., 1935-54. Director and Trustee: Scottish Soc. for Research in Plant Breeding, 1958-; Animal Diseases Res. Assoc., 1966-. Member: Farm Animals Welfare Adv. Cttee, 1967-77; ARC, 1969-80; Scottish Agricultural Develt Council, 1971-82; Chm., Animals Bd, JCO, 1973-80 (Mem., JCO Consultative Bd, 1980-). Dir, Caledonian Produce (Holdings), 1969-. Governor: St Margaret's Sch., Edinburgh, 1960-81; Grassland Res. Inst., 1962-81; Scottish Crop Res. Inst., 1980-. *Recreations:* photography, committees. *Address:* Magdalenehall, St Boswells, Roxburghshire. *T:* St Boswells 3741. *Club:* Farmers'.

BIGGART, Thomas Norman, WS; Partner, Biggart Baillie & Gifford, WS, Solicitors, Glasgow and Edinburgh, since 1959; *b* 24 Jan. 1930; *o s* of Andrew Stevenson Biggart, JP and Marjorie Scott Biggart; *m* 1956, Eileen Jean Anne Gemmell; one *s* one *d*. *Educ:* Morrisons Acad., Crieff; Glasgow Univ. (MA 1951, LLB 1954). Served RN, 1954-56 (Sub-Lt RNVR). Law Society of Scotland: Mem. Council, 1977-; Vice-Pres., 1981-82; Pres., 1982-83. Pres., Business Archives Council, Scotland, 1977-. OStJ 1968. *Recreations:* golf, hill

walking. *Address:* Gailes, Kilmacolm, Renfrewshire PA13 4LZ. *T:* Kilmacolm 2645. *Clubs:* Royal Scottish Automobile, The Western (Glasgow).

BIGGS; see Ewart-Biggs.

BIGGS, Sir Lionel (William), Kt 1964; *b* 28 May 1906; *s* of William Henry Moore Biggs and Lilian (*née* Bush); *m* 1934, Doris Rose, *d* of late William Davies; one *s*. *Educ:* Manchester Gram. Sch. Served Royal Air Force, 1940-45 (despatches). Lord Mayor of Manchester, 1961-62. JP Manchester 1949. Chm., Aerodrome Owners' Assoc. of GB, 1955. *Recreations:* gardening, swimming. *Address:* Glen Corrig, 151 Richmond Park Road, Bournemouth, Dorset.

BIGGS, Brig. Michael Worthington, CBE 1962 (OBE 1944); MA; MICE; *b* 16 Sept. 1911; *s* of late Lt-Col Charles William Biggs, OBE, Cheltenham and late Winifred Jesse Bell Biggs (*née* Dickinson); *m* 1940, Katharine Mary, *d* of late Sir Walter Harragin, CMG, QC, Colonial Legal Service, and of Lady Harragin; two *d*. *Educ:* Cheltenham Coll.; RMA Woolwich; Pembroke Coll., Cambridge. MA (Cantab) 1946; MICE 1967. 2nd Lieut RE, 1931; served War of 1939-45, E Africa, Abyssinia (Bde Major), and Burma (GSO1 and CRE); Lt-Col 1942; Col 1954; Mil. Adviser to High Comr, Australia, 1954-57; Brig. 1960; Chief of Staff, E Africa Comd, 1960-62; Dir of Quartering (Army), MoD, 1963-66; retd, 1966. Group Building Exec., Forte's (Holdings) Ltd, 1966-67; Manager, Hatfield and Welwyn Garden City, Commn for New Towns, 1967-78. Member: Council, TCPA; Exec. Cttee, Hertfordshire Soc.; Chm., Herts Bldg Preservation Trust. Pres., KAR and EAF Officers' Dinner Club. *Recreations:* lawn tennis, golf, gardening (FRHS). *Address:* Strawyards, High Street, Kimpton, Herts. *T:* Kimpton 823498. *Club:* Army and Navy.

BIGGS, Sir Norman (Parris), Kt 1977; Deputy Chairman, Privatbanken Ltd, since 1980; Director, Banco de Bilbao, since 1981; *b* 23 Dec. 1907; *s* of John Gordon Biggs and Mary Sharpe Dickson; *m* 1936, Peggy Helena Stammwitz; two *s* one *d*. *Educ:* John Watson's Sch., Edinburgh. Bank of England, 1927-46; Dir, Kleinwort Sons & Co. Ltd, 1946-52; Esso Petroleum Company, Ltd: Dir, 1952-66, Chm., 1968-72; Chairman: Williams & Glyn's Bank Ltd, 1972-76; United International Bank Ltd, 1970-79; Dep. Chm., National and Commercial Banking Gp Ltd, 1974-76; Director: Royal Bank of Scotland, 1974-76; Gillett Bros Discount Co. Ltd, 1963-77. Mem., Bullock Cttee on Industrial Democracy, 1976. *Recreations:* sailing, travel. *Address:* Northbrooks, Danworth Lane, Hurstpierpoint, Sussex. *T:* Hurstpierpoint 832022.

BIGGS, Peter Martin, PhD, DSc; FRS 1976; Director, Houghton Poultry Research Station, since 1974; *b* 13 Aug. 1926; *s* of Ronald Biggs and Cécile Biggs (*née* Player); *m* 1950, Alison Janet Molteno; two *s* one *d*. *Educ:* Bedales Sch.; Cambridge Sch., USA; Queen's Univ., Belfast; Royal Veterinary Coll., Univ. of London (BSc 1953, DSc 1975); Univ. of Bristol (PhD 1958). FR.CVS, FRCPath. Served RAF, 1944-48; Research Asst, Univ. of Bristol, 1953-55, Lectr, 1955-59; Head of Leukosis Experimental Unit, Houghton Poultry Research Station, 1959-74 (Dep. Dir, 1971-74). Vis. Prof. of Veterinary Microbiology, RVC, Univ. of London, 1982. Hon. DVM Ludwig-Maximilians Univ., 1976; Tom Newman Meml Award, 1964; J. T. Edwards Meml Medal, 1969; Dalrymple-Champneys Cup and Medal, 1973; Bledisloe Veterinary Award, 1977; Joszef Marek Meml Medal, Vet. Univ. of Budapest, 1979. *Publications:* scientific papers on viruses and infectious disease. *Recreations:* music making, boating. *Address:* Willows, London Road, St Ives, Huntingdon, Cambridgeshire PE17 4ES. *T:* St Ives 63471.

BIGGS-DAVISON, Sir John (Alec), Kt 1981; MP (C) Epping Forest, since 1974 (Chigwell, 1955-74 (as Ind C 1957-58)); *b* 7 June 1918; *s* of late Major John Norman Biggs-Davison, RGA, retd; *m* 1948, Pamela Mary, 2nd *d* of late Ralph Hodder-Williams, MC; two *s* four *d*. *Educ:* Clifton (scholar); Magdalen Coll., Oxford (exhibitioner, MA). Royal Marines, 1939, Lieut 1940; served in RM Brigade and RM Division. Indian Civil Service: Asst Comr, 1942; Forward Liaison Officer, Cox's Bazar, 1943-44; Sub-Divisional Officer, Pindi Gheb, 1946; Political Asst and Comdt, Border Military Police, subsequently Dep. Comr, Dera Ghazi Khan, during and after transfer of Power to Dominion of Pakistan, 1947; retired from Pakistan Administrative Service, 1948. Conservative Research Dept, 1950-55; Sec., Brit. Conservative Delegn to Council of Europe, 1952, 1953. Contested (C) Coventry South, 1951. Co-founder Pakistan Soc., 1951. Indep. Observer of Malta Referendum, 1956. Mem. Parly Delegations: West Africa, 1960; Guernsey, 1961; Austria, 1964; France, 1965; Canada (Inter-Parly Union Conf.), 1965; Malawi, 1968; Tunisia, Gibraltar, 1969; Portugal, 1973. Vice-Pres., Franco-British Parly Relations Cttee; Chm., Cons. Parly NI Cttee; Vice-Chm., Cons. Parly Foreign and Commonwealth Affairs Cttee. An Opposition Front Bench spokesman on NI, 1976-78. Governor, Clifton Coll., 1972. Mem., Oxford Union Soc. *Publications:* George Wyndham, 1951; Tory Lives, 1952; The Uncertain Ally, 1957; The Walls of Europe, 1962; Portuguese Guinea: Nailing a Lie, 1970; Africa: Hope Deferred, 1972; The Hand is Red, 1974; Rock Firm for the Union, 1979; contribs to many periodicals. *Recreations:* reading, riding, tennis, walking (Gold Medal London-Brighton Pacesetters' Walk, 1963), took part in parliamentary parachute jump, 1980. *Address:* House of Commons, SW1. *Clubs:* Carlton, Special Forces, Oxford Union Society.

BIGHAM, family name of **Viscount Mersey** and of **Lady Nairne.**

BIGLAND, Ernest Frank, MBE (mil.) 1945; TD 1946; a Deputy Chairman, Guardian Royal Exchange Assurance Ltd, since 1978; *b* 7 Dec. 1913; *s* of

Robert Taylor Bigland and Helen Inglis Scott Bigland (*née* Hannay); *m* 1936, Mary Dalzell; two *s* one *d. Educ:* St Edward's Sch., Oxford. FCII. Joined Guardian Assurance Co. Ltd, 1930. Served Royal Artillery, 1939-45 (MBE, despatches); Lt-Col. Guardian Assurance Co. Ltd: Company Sec., 1950; Asst Gen. Manager, 1952; Dep. Gen. Manager, 1957; Gen. Man., 1960; Gp Gen. Man., 1964; Man. Dir, 1966-78; Vice-Chm., 1973-78. *Recreations:* shooting, fishing. *Address:* Lucas Green Manor, Lucas Green Road, West End, Woking, Surrey GU24 9LY. *T:* Brookwood 2234. *Clubs:* Naval and Military, Royal Automobile; Leander.

BIGNALL, John Reginald, FRCP; Physician, Brompton Hospital, 1957-79; *b* 14 Oct. 1913; *s* of Walter and Nellie Bignall; *m* 1939, Ruth Thirtle; one *s* three *d. Educ:* Nottingham High Sch.; St John's Coll. Cambridge; London Hospital. MA 1938; MD 1947; FRCP 1961. Served in RAMC, 1941-46, Middle East and Mediterranean (Major). *Address:* 8 Engliff Lane, Pyrford, Woking, Surrey GU22 8SU. *T:* Byfleet 42603.

BIKANER, Maharaja of; Dr Karni Singhji Bahadur, *b* 21 April 1924; *e s* of late Lt-Gen. HH Maharaja Sri Sadul Singhji Bahadur of Bikaner, GCSI, GCIE, CVO; *S* father as Maharaja of Bikaner, 1950; *m* 1944, Princess Sushila Kumari, *d* of Maharawal Shri Sir Lakshman Singh Bahadur of Dungapur, *qv*; one *s* two *d. Educ:* St Stephen's Coll., Delhi; St Xavier's Coll., Bombay. BA (Hons) (History and Politics); PhD (thesis) Bombay Univ., 1964. Visited Middle East War Front in Nov. 1941 with his grandfather, Maharaja Sri Ganga Singhji Bahadur. Insignia Grand Commander: Order of Vikram Star (Bikaner), Order of Sadul Star (Bikaner), Order of Star of Honour (Bikaner); Africa Star; War Medal; India Service Medal; Arjun Award for Shooting, 1961. Has travelled extensively in Europe, Egypt, USA, Mexico, Honolulu and Far East, etc. Elected to House of People (Parliament of India) as an Independent, 1952; re-elected for 2nd and 3rd terms; elected 4th time, 1967, with largest margin (193,816) in the country; elected 5th time, 1971; left Parliament, 1977; served on various consultative cttees of different ministries. Member: Asiatic Soc. of India; Bombay Natural History Soc. *Recreations:* tennis; shooting (National Champion in clay pigeon traps and skeet for many years; rep. India, clay pigeon shooting, Olympic Games: Rome, 1960, Pre-Olympics, Tokyo, 1963, Tokyo, 1964 (Captain), Mexico, 1968, Munich, 1972, Moscow, 1980; World Shooting Championships: Oslo, 1961; Cairo (Captain), 1962 (2nd in world after tie for 1st place); Wiesbaden, 1966 (Captain); Bologna, 1967; San Sebastian, Spain, 1969; Asian Shooting Championships: Tokyo, 1967; Seoul, 1971 (Captain, Gold Medal); Won Clay Pigeon Welsh Grand Prix, N Wales Cup and NW England Cup, 1981; Asian Games, Tehran, 1974 (Silver Medal); Kuala Lumpur 1975 (Silver Medal)); golf; flying (qualified for private pilot's licence); cricket; mechanics; photography; oil painting. *Address:* Lallgargh Palace, Bikaner, Rajasthan, India. *Clubs:* Royal Wimbledon Golf; Clay Pigeon Shooting Assoc., Essex (Hon. Life Vice-Pres.); Willingdon Sports, Cricket Club of India, Bombay Flying, Bombay Presidency Golf, Western India Automobile Association (Bombay); Delhi Golf (Delhi); National Sports Club of India (in all 4 cities).

BILBY, Prof. Bruce Alexander, BA, PhD; FRS 1977; Professor of the Theory of Materials, University of Sheffield, since 1966; *b* 3 Sept. 1922; *e s* of late George Alexander Bilby and Dorothy Jean (*née* Telfer); *m* 1st, 1946, Hazel Joyce (*née* Casken); two *s* one *d*; 2nd, 1966, Lorette Wendela (*née* Thomas); two *s. Educ:* Dover Grammar Sch.; Peterhouse, Cambridge (BA); Univ. of Birmingham (PhD). Admiralty, 1943-46. Research, Birmingham, 1946-51; Univ. of Sheffield: Royal Soc. Sorby Res. Fellow, 1951-57; J. H. Andrew Res. Fellow, 1957-58; Reader in Theoretical Metallurgy, 1958-62, Prof., 1962-66. Has made contributions to theory of dislocations and its application to the deformation, transformation and fracture of metallic crystals. Rosenhain Medal, 1963. *Publications:* contribs to learned jls. *Recreation:* sailing. *Address:* 32 Devonshire Road, Totley, Sheffield S17 3ND. *T:* Sheffield 361086; Department of the Theory of Materials, The University, Mappin Street, Sheffield S1 3JD. *T:* Sheffield 78555 (ext. 5244).

BILL, Commander Robert, DSO 1940; FRICS; FRGS; RN, retired 1955; Consultant, retired 1975; *b* 1 April 1910; *s* of late R. W. Bill, Penn, Staffs; *m* 1st, 1933, Peggy Shaw (marr. diss. 1952), *d* of late Comdr A. R. S. Warden, AM, RN (retd), Paignton, Devon; 2nd, 1952, Wendy Jean (*d* 1962), *d* of late C. P. Booth, Hampstead, NW2; one *s* one *d*; 3rd, 1965, Mrs Nancy Elizabeth Johnson (*d* 1973), *d* of late Major Arthur Edward Phillips, DSO, MFH, Mompesson House, Salisbury; 4th, 1975, Gillian Ruth, 2nd *d* of late Dr Geoffrey Clarke, and *g d* of late Sir William Clarke of Chatteris. *Educ:* RNC, Dartmouth and Greenwich. Specialised in Hydrographic Survey, 1931, and in Electronic Distance Measurement, 1956; Special Director, Vickers Instruments Ltd, 1956-65; Dir and Man. Dir, Tellurometer (UK) Ltd, 1960-66. *Address:* Sheiling Cottage, North Street, Petworth, West Sussex. *T:* Petworth 42357.

BILLAM, John Bertram Hardy, CB 1979; DFC 1944; Legal Adviser and Deputy Secretary, Department of Employment, since 1976; *b* 20 Oct. 1920; *s* of late John Wilfred Ambrose Billam and Bertha; *m* 1944, Mary (*née* Armitage); one *s* one *d. Educ:* Merchant Taylors'; King's Coll., London (LLB 1947). RAF, 1941-46 (Flt-Lt). Called to Bar, Gray's Inn, 1947; Legal Asst, Min. of Labour, 1948; Asst Solicitor, 1967. *Publication:* contrib. Halsbury's Laws of England, 3rd edn (Trade and Labour), 1962. *Address:* Caxton House, Tothill Street, SW1. *T:* 01-213 4369. *Clubs:* Athenæum, Royal Air Force.

BILLETT, Paul Rodney, CB 1981; *b* 19 Feb. 1921; *s* of late Arthur William and Grace Hilda Billett; *m* 1945, Muriel Gwendoline Marsh (*d* 1977); one *s. Educ:* Commonweal and College Grammar Schools, Swindon. Entered Exchequer and Audit Dept, 1939. Served RASC, 1941-46. Deputy Secretary, Exchequer and Audit Dept, 1975-81 (retired). *Address:* c/o Exchequer and Audit Department, Audit House, Victoria Embankment, EC4Y 0DS. *T:* 01-353 8901.

BILLING, Melvin George, CMG 1961; retired as Provincial Commissioner, Provincial Administration, Northern Rhodesia (1951-62); *b* 24 June 1906; *s* of Stuart Morrison Billing and Gertrude Roswell Billing; *m* 1934, Kathleen Jane, *d* of late A. N. Brand; no *c. Educ:* Dulwich Coll.; Worcester Coll., Oxford. Provincial Administration, Northern Rhodesia: Cadet, 1930; District Officer, 1932; Grade II, 1942; Grade I, 1946; Senior, 1950. *Recreations:* bowls, photography. *Address:* c/o Box 67033, Bryanston, Transvaal, S Africa. *Club:* Royal Commonwealth Society.

BILLINGHAM, Prof. Rupert Everett, FRS 1961; MA, DPhil, DSc Oxon; Professor and Chairman, Department of Cell Biology, Southwestern Medical School, University of Texas Health Center at Dallas, since 1971; *b* 15 Oct. 1921; *o s* of Albert Everett and Helen Louise Billingham, Oxford; *m* 1951, Jean Mary Morpeth; two *s* one *d. Educ:* City of Oxford High Sch.; Oriel Coll., Oxford. Served 1942-46, as Lieut RNVR. Asst Lectr, later Lectr in Zoology, University of Birmingham, 1947; Junior Research Fellow, British Empire Cancer Campaign, 1950; Intermediate Research Fellow, Brit. Emp. Cancer Campaign, 1953; Hon. Res. Asst, later Res. Associate, Dept of Zoology, University Coll., London, 1951; Wistar Prof. of Zoology, Univ. of Pennsylvania, USA, and Mem. of Wistar Institute of Anatomy and Biology, Philadelphia, 1957; Prof. and Chm., Dept of Medical Genetics, Univ. of Pennsylvania Med. Sch., Pa, 1965-71. Member: Allergy and Immunology Study Section, Nat. Insts of Health, US Public Health Service, 1958-62; Transplantation and Immunology Cttee, Nat. Insts of Health, 1968-70, 1971-73; Scientific Adv. Cttee, Massachusetts General Hospital, 1976-79; Nat. Allergy and Infectious Diseases Council, Nat. Insts of Health, 1980-83; Sigma Xi College of Nat. Lecturers, 1981-83; Pres., Transplantation Soc., 1974. Fellow, New York Acad. of Sciences, 1962; Fellow, Amer. Acad. of Arts and Sciences, 1965; Alvarenga Prize, Coll. Physicians, Philadelphia, 1963; Herman Beerman Lecture, Soc. for Investigative Dermatology, 1963; Hon. Award Medal, American Assoc. of Plastic Surgeons, 1964; AOA Honor Med. Soc., 1974; Lectures: 1 J. S. Ravdin, Amer. College of Surgeons, 1964; *Sigma Xi*, Yale, 1965; Nat. Insts of Health, 1965; J. W. Jenkinson Meml, Oxford, 1965-66; Harvey, NY, 1966; Kinyoun, Nat. Inst. of Allergy and Infectious Diseases, 1979; Dist. Guest, Soc. for Gyn. Investigation, 1982. Adair Award, Amer. Gynecological Soc., 1971. Hon. DSc, Trinity Coll., Hartford, Conn, USA. *Publications:* The Immunobiology of Transplantation (with W. K. Silvers), 1971; The Immunobiology of Mammalian Reproduction (with A. E. Beer) 1976; contribs to scien. jls on biology of skin, and immunology of tissue transplantation. *Recreations:* woodwork, gardening. *Address:* Department of Cell Biology, University of Texas, Health Science Center, 5323 Harry Hines Boulevard, Dallas, Texas 75235, USA; (home) 6181 Preston Haven Drive, Dallas, Texas 75230, USA. *T:* (214) 661-9895.

BILLINGTON, Kevin; film, theatre and television director; *b* 12 June 1934; *s* of Richard and Margaret Billington; *m* 1967, Lady Rachel Mary Pakenham (*see* Lady Rachel Billington); two *s* two *d. Educ:* Bryanston Sch.; Queens' Coll., Cambridge (BA). Film dir, BBC prog., Tonight, 1960-63; documentary film dir, BBC, 1963-67; films include: A Sort of Paradise; Many Mexicos; The Mexican Attitude; Twilight of Empire; Mary McCarthy's Paris; These Humble Shores; Matador; A Few Castles in Spain; The English Cardinal; A Socialist Childhood; Madison Avenue, USA; ATV documentary, All The Queen's Men. Feature Film Director: Interlude, 1967; The Rise and Rise of Michael Rimmer, 1969; The Light at the Edge of the World, 1970; Voices, 1974. Television Director: And No One Can Save Her, 1973; Once Upon a Time is Now (documentary), 1978; The Music Will Never Stop (documentary), 1979; The Jail Diary of Albie Sachs, 1980; The Good Soldier, 1981; Outside Edge, 1982. Theatre Director: Find Your Way Home, 1970; Me, 1973; The Birthday Party, 1974; The Caretaker, 1975; Bloody Neighbours, 1975; Emigres, 1976; The Homecoming, 1978. Screenwriters' Guild Award, 1966 and 1967; Guild of TV Producers and Directors Award, 1966 and 1967. *Address:* 30 Addison Avenue, W11 4QR. *T:* 01-603 4318. *Club:* Garrick.

BILLINGTON, Michael; Drama Critic of The Guardian, since 1971; *b* 16 Nov. 1939; *s* of Alfred Billington and Patricia (*née* Bradshaw); *m* 1978, Jeanine Bradlaugh. *Educ:* Warwick Sch.; St Catherine's Coll., Oxford (BA). Trained as journalist with Liverpool Daily Post and Echo, 1961-62; Public Liaison Officer and Director for Lincoln Theatre Co., 1962-64; reviewed plays, films and television for The Times, 1965-71. Film Critic: Birmingham Post, 1968-78; Illustrated London News, 1968-81. Contributor to numerous radio and television Arts programmes, incl. Kaleidoscope, Critics' Forum, The Book Programme, Arena. Presenter, The Distinction Interview and Theatre Call, BBC World Service. Prof. of Drama, Colorado Coll., 1981. IPC Critic of the Year, 1974. *Publications:* The Modern Actor, 1974; How Tickled I Am, 1977; (ed) The Performing Arts, 1980. *Recreations:* work, travel, cricket. *Address:* 15 Hearne Road, W4 3NJ. *T:* 01-995 0455. *Club:* Critics' Circle.

BILLINGTON, Lady Rachel (Mary); writer; *b* 11 May 1942; *d* of 7th Earl of Longford, *qv*, and Countess of Longford, *qv*; *m* 1967, Kevin Billington, *qv*; two *s* two *d. Educ:* London Univ. (BA English). Work includes: four BBC radio plays; two BBC TV plays, Don't be Silly, 1979, and Life After Death, 1981. *Publications:* All Things Nice, 1969; The Big Dipper, 1970; Lilacs out of the Dead Land, 1971; Cock Robin, 1973; Beautiful, 1974; A Painted Devil, 1975; A Woman's Age, 1979; Rosanna and the Wizard-Robot, 1981; Occasion of Sin, 1982. *Recreation:* children. *Address:* 30 Addison Avenue, W11 4QP. *T:* 01-603 4318. *Clubs:* Society of Authors, PEN.

BILLOT, Barbara Kathleen; Deputy Director (Under-Secretary), Department for National Savings, 1974–80; *b* 26 May 1920; *d* of Alfred Billot and Agnes Billot (*née* Hiner). *Educ:* Petersfield County High Sch. for Girls. Post Office Savings Bank: Clerical Officer 1938; Exec. Off. 1939; Higher Exec. Off. 1946; Sen. Exec. Off. 1953; Chief Exec. Off. 1957; Principal, Post Office Headquarters, 1960; Sen. Chief Exec. Off., PO Savings Dept, 1961; Principal Exec. Off. (Estabt Off.), 1969; Asst Sec., Dept for Nat. Savings, 1971. *Recreations:* reading, theatre-going. *Address:* 6 Springbank, Chichester, W Sussex PO19 4BX. *T:* Chichester 776295.

BILNEY, Air Vice-Marshal Christopher Neil Hope, CB 1949; CBE 1946 (OBE 1940); RAF, retired; *b* 26 Oct. 1898; *s* of late William A. and late Maud H. Bilney, Fir Grange, Weybridge, Surrey; *m* 1926, Nellie G. Perren; two *d. Educ:* Tonbridge Sch. Joined RNAS, 1917; commissioned 1917; served European War, 1914–18, N Sea and Middle East (despatches); Flt-Lieut RAF, 1926; India, 1925–30 (despatches); Sqdn Leader, 1935, serving at Air Ministry; Wing Comdr, 1939; served War of 1939–45: Boscombe Down, 1939; MAP, 1940–41; Group Capt, 1941; Air Cdre, Vice-Pres. Ordnance Board, 1942; HQ Bomber Comd as Comd Armament Officer, 1944 (despatches); AOC No. 25 Group, 1945 (CBE); Air Ministry, Dir Technical Training, 1947–49 (CB); Air Officer i/c Administration, HQ Maintenance Comd, 1949–51; Dir-Gen. of Technical Services (1), Air Ministry, 1951–52; Pres. Ordnance Board, Ministry of Supply, 1953–54; retd 1954. Took up scouting: District Comr, Andover, 1954; County Comr, Hampshire, 1960–67; awarded Silver Acorn for good service by Chief Scout. *Recreations:* shooting, gardening. *Address:* Old Parsonage Cottage, Hatchet Lane, Cranbourne, Windsor Forest, Berks.

BILTON, Percy; Chairman, Percy Bilton Ltd, London, W5, and other companies; *b* 28 Nov. 1896; *s* of Christopher G. Bilton, Ormskirk, Lancs, and Hannah Dunlop, Edinburgh; three *s* two *d.* Founder: Vigzol Oil Co. Ltd, 1919; Percy Bilton Ltd, 1927; and various other property companies. Past Master, Worshipful Co. of Fan Makers, 1959. *Recreations:* yachting, racing, golf, farming (pedigree Jerseys at 5000 acre farm, De Hoek, CP). *Address:* Bilton Towers, W1. *Clubs:* Royal Thames Yacht; Civil Service (Cape Town), etc.

bin YEOP, Tan Sri Abdul Aziz, Al-Haj; PSM (Malaysia); Hon. GCVO 1972; Member, Malaysian Parliament; Partner in legal firm, Aziz and Mazlan, Advocates and Solicitors, 1966-71, and since 1973; *b* 5 Oct. 1916; *m* 1942, Puan Sri Hamidah Aziz; six *s* three *d. Educ:* King Edward VII Sch., Perak, Malaysia. Malay Administrative Service, 1937; called to Bar, Lincoln's Inn, 1950; Malayan Civil Service, 1951; First Asst State Sec., Perak 1954; London Univ. (course in Community Development), 1955. Permanent Sec., Min. of Agriculture, 1958–62; Dep. Sec., Malaysian Affairs Div., Prime Minister's Dept, 1962–64; Permanent Sec., Min. of Education, 1964-66. Chm. and Dir of firms in Malaysia, 1966–71. High Comr for Malaysia in London, 1971–73. First Chm., Bd of Governors of BERNAMA (Malaysia's National News Agency), 1967–71; Chairman: Council, Universiti Teknologi, Malaysia, 1974- (Pro-chancellor, 1977-); Majlis Amanah Raayat, Malaysia, 1975-. *Recreations:* walking, reading, fishing. *Address:* c/o Aziz and Mazlan, 17 Jalan Klyne, Kuala Lumpur, Malaysia.

BINCHY, Daniel A.; Senior Professor, Dublin Institute for Advanced Studies, 1950-75; *b* 3 June 1900. *Educ:* Clongowes Wood Coll.; University Coll., Dublin; Munich, Berlin, Paris and The Hague. MA (NUI and Oxford); Dr Phil (Munich). Prof. of Jurisprudence and Legal History, University Coll., Dublin, 1925-45; Senior Research Fellow, Corpus Christi Coll., Oxford, 1945-50, Hon. Fellow, 1971. Envoy Extraordinary and Minister Plenipotentiary for the Irish Free State to Germany, 1929–32. Mem. Council, Royal Irish Academy, 1926, Vice-Pres., 1945. Rhys Lectr, British Academy, 1943; Lowell Lectr, Boston, 1954; Visiting Prof. of Celtic, Harvard Univ., 1962–63; Gregynog Lectr, Univ. of Wales, 1966; O'Donnell Lectr, Oxford, 1967–68. DLitt (*hc*): Dublin, 1956; Wales, 1963; Belfast, 1973; NUI, 1973; DèsL (*hc*) Rennes, 1971. Corresp. Mem., Norwegian Instituttet for Sammenlignende Kulturforsking, 1960; For. Mem., Amer. Acad. of Arts and Sciences, 1962; Corresp. Fellow, British Acad., 1976. *Publications:* Church and State in Fascist Italy, 1941, repr. 1970; Crith gablach, An Early Irish Legal Tract, 1940, repr. 1970; Celtic and Anglo-Saxon Kingship, 1970; Corpus Juris Hibernici, 6 vols., 1979; papers on Old Irish law; various articles in Irish, English, and German reviews. *Address:* Lisnagree, Castleknock, Co. Dublin. *Club:* United Service (Dublin).

BING, Sir Rudolf (Franz Joseph), KBE 1971 (CBE 1956); General Manager, Metropolitan Opera, New York, 1950-72; Distinguished Professor, Brooklyn College, City University of New York, 1972-75; Director Columbia Artists Management, since 1973; *b* Vienna, 9 Jan. 1902; *m* 1929, Nina (*née* Schelemskaja). *Educ:* Vienna. Hessian State Theatre, Darmstadt, 1928–30; Civic Opera, Berlin-Charlottenburg, 1930-33. Gen. Manager, Glyndebourne Opera, 1935-49; Artistic Director, Edinburgh Festival, 1947-49. Holds hon. doctorates in music and in letters, from the US. Légion d'Honneur, 1958;

Comdr's Cross of Order of Merit, Federal Republic of Germany, 1958; Grand Silver Medal of Honour, Republic of Austria, 1959; Comdr, Order of Merit, Republic of Italy, 1959, Grand Officer, 1970. *Publication:* 5000 Nights at the Opera, 1972. *Address:* Essex House, 160 Central Park South, New York, NY 10019, USA.

BINGHAM, family name of **Baron Clanmorris** and of **Earl of Lucan.**

BINGHAM, Lord; George Charles Bingham; *b* 21 Sept. 1967; *s* and *heir* of 7th Earl of Lucan, *qv.*

BINGHAM, Caroline Margery Conyers; professional writer; *b* 7 Feb. 1938; *o d* of Cedric and Muriel Worsdell; *m* 1958, Andrew Bingham (marr. diss. 1972); one *d. Educ:* Mount Sch., York; Convent de la Sagesse, Newcastle upon Tyne; Cheltenham Ladies' Coll.; Univ. of Bristol (BA Hons History). *Publications:* The Making of a King: the early years of James VI and I, 1968 (USA 1969); James V, King of Scots, 1971; (contrib.) The Scottish Nation: a history of the Scots from Independence to Union, 1972; The Life and Times of Edward II, 1973; The Stewart Kingdom of Scotland, 1371-1603, 1974 (USA 1974); The Kings and Queens of Scotland, 1976 (USA 1976); The Crowned Lions: the Early Plantagenet Kings, 1978; James VI of Scotland, 1979; The Voice of the Lion (verse anthology), 1980; James I of England, 1981; A Short History of Scotland, 1983. *Recreation:* taking pleasure in everything I do. *Address:* 199 Prince of Wales Road, NW5 3QB. *T:* 01-267 2931.

BINGHAM, Hon. Charlotte Mary Thérèse; playwright and novelist; *b* 29 June 1942; *d* of Baron Clanmorris, *qv*; *m* 1964, Terence Brady, *qv*; one *s* one *d. Educ:* The Priory, Haywards Heath; Sorbonne. TV series with Terence Brady: Boy Meets Girl; Take Three Girls; Upstairs Downstairs; Away From It All; Play for Today; No—Honestly; Yes-Honestly; Pig in the Middle; Thomas and Sarah; The Complete Lack of Charm of the Bourgeoisie; Nanny. *Publications:* Coronet among the Weeds, 1963; Lucinda, 1965; Coronet among the Grass, 1972; with Terence Brady: Victoria, 1972; Rose's Story, 1973; Victoria and Company, 1974; Yes—Honestly, 1977. *Recreations:* horse riding, gardening. *Address:* The Pink House, 111 East Sheen Avenue, SW14 8AX; c/o A. D. Peters, Literary Agent, 10 Buckingham Street, WC2N 6BU.

BINGHAM, James; Chairman, Greater Manchester County Council, 1980-81 (Member, 1974-81); *b* 29 June 1916; *s* of James and Beatrice Bingham; *m* 1940, Jessie Noden. *Educ:* Manchester Central Grammar Sch.; Alsager Teacher Trng Coll. Insurance agent, 1938-39. Served War: RA from 1940; commnd 1943; in Eighth Army in N Africa, Italy, Austria; attained rank of Captain. Teacher in local schools, 1946-52; Headmaster: Eccles Parish Sch., 1952-59; St Paul's C of E Sch., Walkden, 1959-78, retired. Worsley UDC: Mem., 1962, 1965-73; last Chm., 1973-74; Chm., Recreation and Arts Cttee, GMC, 1977-80, and mem. other cttees. Member: NW Arts; Royal Exchange Theatre Trust; Hallé Concerts Soc. Cttee; NW Tourist Bd. *Recreations:* geology, keen golfer, cutting and polishing stones, fell walking. *Address:* 30 Ryecroft Lane, Worsley, Manchester M28 4PN. *T:* 061-794 3885.

BINGHAM, John; *see* Clanmorris, 7th Baron.

BINGHAM, John, FRS 1977; Deputy Chief Scientific Officer at the Plant Breeding Institute, Cambridge, since 1981; *b* 19 June 1930. SPSO, Plant Breeding Inst., Cambridge, to 1981. Has researched in plant breeding, culminating in production of improved, highly successful winter wheat varieties for British agriculture. Mullard Medal of Royal Society, 1975. *Address:* 25 Stansgate Avenue, Cambridge CB2 2QZ. *T:* Cambridge 247737; Plant Breeding Institute, Maris Lane, Trumpington, Cambridge CB2 2LQ. *T:* Trumpington 2411.

BINGHAM, Richard Martin, TD 1949; QC 1958; **His Honour Judge Bingham;** a Circuit Judge, since 1972; *b* 26 Oct. 1915; *s* of late John and Dorothy Ann Bingham; *m* 1949, Elinor Stephenson; one *d. Educ:* Harrow; Clare Coll., Cambridge. Called to Bar, Inner Temple, 1940; Bencher, 1964; joined Northern Circuit, 1946; Recorder of Oldham, 1960-71; Judge of Appeal, IoM, 1965-72. Served with 59th Med. Regt, RA (TA), 1937-46 and 1947-49: Major from 1945; Campaigns, Dunkirk and NW Europe (despatches, 1944). Mem. of Liverpool City Council, 1946-49. MP (C) Garston Division of Liverpool, Dec. 1957-March 1966. Member: HO Departmental Cttee on Coroners, 1965; Royal Commn Assizes and Quarter Sessions, 1966. *Publications:* Cases on Negligence, 1st edn 1961, 3rd edn 1978; Cases and Statutes on Crime, 1980. *Address:* Hook End, Gayton, Merseyside L60 3SR. *Clubs:* Royal Automobile; Royal Liverpool Golf.

BINGHAM, Hon. Sir Thomas (Henry), Kt 1980; **Hon. Mr Justice Bingham;** a Judge of the High Court of Justice, Queen's Bench Division, since 1980; *b* 13 Oct. 1933; *o s* of late Dr T. H. Bingham and of Dr C. Bingham, Reigate; *m* 1963, Elizabeth, *o d* of late Peter Loxley; two *s* two *d. Educ:* Sedbergh; Balliol Coll., Oxford (MA). Royal Ulster Rifles, 1952-54 (2nd Lt); London Irish Rifles (TA) 1954-59. Univ. of Oxford: Gibbs Schol. in Mod. Hist., 1956; 1st cl. Hons, Mod. Hist., 1957. Eldon Law Schol., 1957; Arden Schol., Gray's Inn, 1959; Cert. of Honour, Bar Finals, 1959; called to Bar, Gray's Inn, 1959; Bencher, 1979. Standing Jun. Counsel to Dept of Employment, 1968-72; QC 1972; a Recorder of the Crown Court, 1975-80. Leader, Investigation into the supply of petroleum and petroleum products to

Rhodesia, 1977-78. Mem., Lord Chancellor's Law Reform Cttee. Governor, Sedbergh, 1978. *Publication:* Chitty on Contracts, (Asst Editor) 22nd edn, 1961. *Recreations:* walking, theatre. *Address:* Royal Courts of Justice, Strand, WC2.

BINNEY, H(arry) A(ugustus) Roy, CB 1950; UN Adviser on Standards to Government of Cyprus, 1974-77; Adviser, International, British Standards Institution, 1972-73 (Director and Secretary, later Director-General, BSI, 1951-70; Director-General, International, BSI, 1971-72); *b* 18 May 1907; *s* of Harry Augustus Binney, Churston, Devon; *m* 1944, Barbara Poole (*d* 1975); three *s* one *d* (and one *d* decd). *Educ:* Royal Dockyard Sch., Devonport; London Univ. BSc(Eng). Entered Board of Trade, 1929; Under-Sec. of the Board of Trade, 1947-51. Chm., Standardization Cttee, European Productivity Agency, 1953-58; first Chm., Exec. Cttee, ISO, 1967-69 (Mem. Council ISO, and Vice-Pres., 1964-69); Chm., Cttee for European Standardization (CEN), 1963-65; Chm., ISO/CERTICO, 1970-73. Mem. Council, Queen Elizabeth Coll., 1952-68, now Associate; Member: Gen. Bd, and Exec. Cttee, Nat. Physical Laboratory, 1957-63. Hon. Life Fellow, Standards Engineers Soc. of America; Hon. Life Mem., American Soc. for Testing and Materials. FRSA. *Recreation:* gardening. *Address:* Hambutts Orchard, Edge Lane, Painswick, Glos GL6 6UW.

BINNEY, Marcus Hugh Crofton; author; Chairman, Save Britain's Heritage; *s* of late Lt-Col Francis Crofton Simms, MC and of Sonia, *d* of Rear-Adm. Sir William Marcus Charles Beresford-Whyte, KCB, CMG (she *m* 2nd, Comdr Sir George Binney, DSO, RN); *m* 1st, 1966, Hon. Sara Anne Vanneck (marr. diss. 1976), *e d* of 6th Baron Huntingfield; 2nd, 1981, Anne, *d* of Dr T. H. Hills, Merstham, Surrey; one *c. Educ:* Magdalene Coll., Cambridge (BA 1966; MA 1977). Architectural Editor, Country Life. Sec., UK Cttee, Internat. Council on Monuments and Sites, 1972-81. *Publications:* (with Peter Burman): Change and Decay: the future of our churches, 1977; Chapels and Churches: who cares?, 1977; (ed jtly) Railway Architecture, 1979; (ed jtly) Our Past Before Us, 1981; many papers on architecture and preservation. *Address:* (office) 3 Park Square West, NW1; (home) 21 Cambridge Street, SW1.

BINNIE, Alfred Maurice, FRS 1960; Fellow of Trinity College (1944) and University Reader Emeritus in Engineering, Cambridge; *b* 6 Feb. 1901; *s* of late David Carr Binnie. *Educ:* Weymouth Coll.; Queens' Coll., Cambridge. Jun. Research Engineer, Bridge Stress Cttee, 1923-25; Demonstrator and Lectr, Engrg Lab., Oxford, 1925-44; Rhodes Travelling Fellow, 1932-33; Lectr, New Coll., Oxford, 1933-44; Univ. Lectr, Engrg Lab., Cambridge, 1944-54; Sen. Research Fellow, California Inst. of Technology, 1951-52; Scott Visiting Fellow, Ormond Coll., Univ. of Melbourne, 1966; Vis. Scholar, Univ. of California, Berkeley, 1967-68. FIMechE 1937; FICE 1947; Founder Fellow, Fellowship of Engineering, 1976. *Publications:* articles in scientific and engrg jls. *Recreation:* mountaineering. *Address:* Trinity College, Cambridge CB2 1TQ. *T:* 358201. *Club:* Alpine.

BINNIE, David Stark, OBE 1979; FCIT; FInstM; FBIM; railway and rapid transport consultant; *b* 2 June 1922; *s* of Walter Archibald Binnie and Helen (*née* Baxter), Bonkle, Lanarkshire; *m* 1947, Leslie Archibald; one *s* one *d. Educ:* Wishaw High School. British Railways: Gen. and Signalling Asst to Gen. Manager Scottish Region, 1955; Asst District Operating Supt 1961, District Operating Supt 1963, Glasgow North; Divisional Movements Manager, Glasgow Div., 1965; Movements Manager, Scottish Region, 1967; Divisional Manager, SE Div., Southern Region, 1969; Asst Gen. Manager, Southern Region, 1970, Gen. Manager, 1972; Exec. Dir, Freight, BR Board, 1974-76; Gen. Manager, BR, London Midland Region, 1977-80. Lt-Col Engineer and Railway Staff Corps, RE (T&AVR). OStJ. *Recreation:* Highland life. *Address:* Copse Cottage, Oak Hill Road, Sevenoaks, Kent. *T:* Sevenoaks 53425.

BINNIE, Geoffrey Morse, FRS 1975; Consultant to Binnie & Partners since 1973; *b* 13 Nov. 1908; *s* of William Eames Binnie and Ethel Morse; *m* 1st, 1932, Yanka Paryczko (*d* 1964); one *s* one *d* ; 2nd, 1964, Elspeth Maud Cicely Thompson. *Educ:* Charterhouse; Trinity Hall, Cambridge (MA); Zurich Univ. FICE, FIWE, FASCE, FGS. Served War of 1939-45, RE (Major). Asst Engr, Gorge Dam, Hong Kong, 1933-37; Chief Asst, Eye Brook Reservoir, Northants, 1937-39; Partner, Binnie & Partners, 1939, resumed practice, 1945; responsible for design and supervision of construction of several water supplies in UK; Sen. Partner 1956-72, resp. for design and supervision of constr. of major projects abroad incl. Dokan dam, Iraq, completed 1960 and Mangla project, W Pakistan, compl. 1970. Chm., Panel advising on design and constr. of 2500 MW Peace River Hydro-electric project, BC, 1962-68. Chief Technical Supervisor, Poechos Dam, Peru, 1972-76; Chm., Advisory Board for Mornos dam, Greece, 1975-76; Chm., Chadwick Trust; Mem., Severn Barrage Cttee, 1978-81; Pres., JInstE, 1955; Vice-Pres., ICE, 1970-72; Fellow Imperial Coll. 1972. Telford Gold Medal, 1968; (1st) Smeaton Gold Medal, 1974. Fellow, Fellowship of Engineering, 1976. *Publications:* Early Victorian Water Engineers, 1981; techn. articles on engrg subjects, papers for World Power Conf., Internat. Commn on Large Dams and ICE. *Recreation:* gardening. *Address:* St Michael's Lodge, Benenden, Cranbrook, Kent TN17 4EZ. *T:* Cranbrook 240498. *Club:* Athenæum.

BINNING, Lord; John George Baillie-Hamilton; *b* 21 Dec. 1941; *o s* of 12th Earl of Haddington, *qv* ; *m* 1975, Prudence Elizabeth (marr. diss. 1981), *d* of

A. Rutherford Hayles. *Educ:* Ampleforth. *Address:* Mellerstain, Gordon, Berwickshire; Tyninghame, Dunbar, East Lothian. *Club:* Turf.

BINNING, Kenneth George Henry, CMG 1976; Under-Secretary, Department of Industry, since 1976; *b* 5 Jan. 1928; *o s* of late Henry and Hilda Binning; *m* 1953, Pamela Dorothy, *o d* of A. E. and D. G. Pronger; three *s* one *d. Educ:* Bristol Grammar Sch.; Balliol Coll., Oxford. Joined Home Civil Service, 1950; Nat. Service, 1950-52; HM Treasury, 1952-58; Private Sec. to Financial Sec., 1956-57; AEA, 1958-65; seconded to Min. of Technology, 1965; rejoined Civil Service, 1968; Dir-Gen. Concorde, 1972-76 and Under-Sec., DTI later Dept of Industry, 1972-. Mem., BSC, 1980-. *Recreations:* music, gardening. *Address:* 12 Kemerton Road, Beckenham, Kent. *T:* 01-650 0273.

BINNS, David John; General Manager, Warrington and Runcorn Development Corporation, since 1981; *b* 12 April 1929; *s* of Henry Norman Binns, OBE and Ivy Mary Binns; *m* 1957, Jean Margaret Evans; one *s* (one *d* decd). *Educ:* Fleetwood Grammar Sch.; Rossall Sch.; Sheffield Univ. LLB 1951. Solicitor 1954. Articled Clerk, Sheffield City Council, 1949; Asst Solicitor, Warrington County Borough Council, 1954; Dep. Town Clerk, Warrington County Borough Council, 1958; Gen. Manager, Warrington Develt Corp., 1969-81. *Recreations:* walking, gardening, music. *Address:* 4 Cedarways, Appleton, Warrington, Cheshire WA4 5EW. *T:* Warrington 62169. *Club:* Warrington (Warrington).

BINNS, Edward Ussher Elliott E.; *see* Elliott-Binns.

BINNS, Geoffrey John; His Honour Judge Binns; a Circuit Judge, since 1980; *b* 12 Oct. 1930; *s* of Rev. Robert Arthur Geoffrey Binns and Elizabeth Marguerite Binns; *m* 1964, Elizabeth Anne Poole Askew. *Educ:* Perse Sch.; Jesus Coll., Cambridge (MA). Admitted solicitor, 1956; Partner, Fraser, Woodgate & Beall, Wisbech, 1958-80; a Recorder of the Crown Court, 1977-80. Chm., N Cambs Hosp. Management Cttee, 1970-74; Member: E Anglian Reg. Hosp. Bd, 1972-74; E Anglian RHA, 1974-76; Panel of Chairmen, Cambridge Univ. Ct of Discipline, 1976-80. Registrar, Archdeaconry of Wisbech, 1972-80. *Recreations:* golf, gardening. *Address:* Fairway, Barton Road, Wisbech, Cambs. *T:* Wisbech 3929. *Club:* Norfolk (Norwich).

BINNS, Surgeon Rear-Adm. George Augustus, CB 1975; ophthalmic medical practitioner; *b* 23 Jan. 1918; *s* of Dr Cuthbert C. H. Binns and Julia Binns (*née* Frommel); *m* 1949, Joan Whitaker; one *s* two *d. Educ:* Repton Sch.; St Bartholemew's Hosp. MRCS, LRCP, DO. Casualty House Surgeon, Luton and Dunstable Hosp., 1942. Served War of 1939-45: joined RNVR, Dec. 1942. Served as Specialist in Ophthalmology, 1952, and promoted to Sen. Specialist in Ophthalmology, 1962; subseq. Admiralty Medical Bd, HMS Excellent, and RN Hosp., Gibraltar; MO in Charge, RN Hosp., Plymouth, and Command MO, 1972-75. QHS 1972-75. FRSocMed; Member: BMA; Southern Ophthalmological Soc. CStJ 1972. *Recreations:* photography, house and garden maintenance, brewing, wine making, listening to music. *Address:* Netherseal, Hindhead Road, Haslemere, Surrey GU27 3PJ. *T:* Haslemere 4281. *Club:* Naval and Military.

BINNS, Professor Howard Reed, CMG 1958; OBE 1948; MA (Cantab), BSc (Edin), MRCVS; *b* 3 Aug. 1909; *s* of Cuthbert Evelyn Binns and Edith Mildred Edwards; *m* 1935, Katharine Vroom Lawson; one *s* one *d. Educ:* Bootham Sch., York; St John's Coll., Cambridge; Royal (Dick) Veterinary Coll.; Edinburgh Univ. Veterinary Officer, Nyasaland, 1935-39; Veterinary Research Officer, Palestine, 1940-41; Senior Veterinary Research Officer, Palestine, 1941-47; Dep. Dir of Veterinary Services, Palestine, 1947-48; Director, East African Veterinary Research Organization, 1950-67 (Principal Scientific Officer, EAVRO, 1948-50); Dir, Centre for Internat. Programs, and Prof. of Veterinary Microbiology, Univ. of Guelph, 1969-75; Vis. Prof., Univ. of Guelph, 1975-80; Vis. Lectr, Animal Path. Divn, Canada Dept of Agric., 1981, 1982; Consultant to Internat. Develt Res. Centre, Ottawa, 1976, 1978; Vis. Prof., Univ. of Saskatchewan, 1980; Vis. Lectr, US Univs, 1980. Scientific missions to: USA and Canada, 1939; Syria and the Lebanon, 1945; India, 1946; USA, 1947; South Africa, 1949; Australia, 1960; USA and Germany, 1966; West Indies and S America, 1970; West Africa, 1971; India, 1973; Kenya, 1975, 1976; Carnegie Corp. Grant, 1956; Rockefeller Foundn Grants, 1966, 1970; Commonwealth Foundn Grant, 1971. Consultant to US Nat. Acad. of Sciences, on animal science in tropical Africa, 1959. Mem. Scientific Council for Africa, 1961-65 (Assoc. Mem., 1955-61). Hon. Prof. of Vet. Science in Univ. of East Africa. *Publications:* contribs to scientific jls. *Recreations:* travel, reading, gardening. *Address:* San Diego, Estepona, Malaga, Spain.

BINNS, John; *b* June 1914; *m* ; one *s. Educ:* Holycroft Sec. Sch., Keighley. Mem., Keighley Borough Council, 1945; Alderman, 1954; Mayor, 1958-59. Joined Labour Party, 1944; MP (Lab) Keighley, 1964-70. Contested (Social Dem.) Keighley, Feb. 1974. Mem. Amalgamated Engineering Union; former Trades Union Officer.

BINNS, Kenneth Johnstone, CMG 1960; Under-Treasurer and Commissioner of State Taxes, Government of Tasmania, 1952-76; now Deputy Chairman, Tasmanian Government Insurance Office; Member, Retirement Benefits Fund Trust, since 1976; *b* New South Wales, Australia, 3 June 1912; *s* of late Kenneth Binns, CBE; *m* 1940, Nancy H. Mackenzie; no *c. Educ:* Melbourne

Church of England Grammar Sch.; Queen's Coll., Univ. of Melbourne (MA, BCom); Harvard Univ., USA. First Canberra Scholarship, 1930; Fellow, Commonwealth Fund of NY, 1950. Tasmanian Treasury, 1942-76. Mem., State Library Bd of Tasmania, 1942-78. Fiscal Review Comr to Federal Republic of Nigeria, 1964; with IMF as Adviser to Minister of Finance, Indonesia, 1969. Dir, Comalco Aluminium (Bell Bay) Ltd, 1960-80. Mem., State Grants Commn, 1976-80. *Publications:* Federal-State Financial Relations, Canada and Australia, 1948; Social Credit in Alberta, 1947; various government reports; articles in Economic Record. *Recreations:* fishing, reading. *Address:* 3 Ellington Road, Sandy Bay, Tasmania 7005, Australia. *T:* 25 1863. *Clubs:* Athenæum, Tasmanian, Hobart.

BINNS, Malcolm; concert pianist; *b* 29 Jan. 1936; *s* of Douglas and May Binns. *Educ:* Bradford Grammar Sch.; Royal Coll. of Music (ARCM, Chappell Gold Medal, Medal of Worshipful Co. of Musicians). London début, 1957; Henry Wood Proms début, 1960; Royal Festival Hall début, 1961; Festival Hall appearances in London Philharmonic Orchestra International series, 1969-; concerts at Aldeburgh Festival, Leeds Festival and Three Choirs Festival (1975); regular appearances at Promenade concerts. First complete recording of Beethoven piano sonatas on original instruments, 1980. *Recreation:* collecting antique gramophone records. *Address:* 233 Court Road, Orpington, Kent. *T:* Orpington 31056.

BINNY, John Anthony Francis; *b* 13 Dec. 1911. *Educ:* Wellington College. Supplementary Reserve of Officers, 15th/19th The King's Royal Hussars, 1936. Served War of 1939-45, France and Burma (despatches). A Governor of Wellington Coll., 1968. *Address:* Byways, Pound Lane, Burley, Ringwood, Hampshire. *Clubs:* Cavalry and Guards, White's, MCC.

BIOBAKU, Dr Saburi Oladeni, CMG 1961; MA, PhD; Research Professor and Director, Institute of African Studies, University of Ibadan, since 1976; *b* 16 June 1918; *s* of late Chief S. O. Biobaku, Aré of Iddo, Abeokuta; *m* 1949, Muhabat Folasade, *d* of Alhaji L. B. Agusto, barrister-at-law, Lagos; one *s. Educ:* Govt Coll., Ibadan; Higher Coll., Yaba; University Coll., Exeter; Trinity Coll., Cambridge. BA London, 1945; BA Cantab, 1947, MA 1951; PhD London, 1951. Education Officer, Nigeria, 1947-53; Registrar, University Coll., Ibadan, 1953-57; Dir, Yoruba Historical Research Scheme, 1956-; Sec. to Premier and Executive Council, Western Nigeria, 1957-61; Pro-Vice-Chancellor, Univ. of Ife, Nigeria, 1961-65; Vice-Chancellor, Univ. of Lagos, 1965-72; Chairman, Management Consultant Services Ltd, Lagos, 1972-76. Created: Aré of Iddo, Abeokuta, 1958; Agbakin of Igbore, 1972; Maye of Ife, 1980; Baapitan of Egbaland, 1980. *Publications:* The Origin of the Yoruba, 1955; The Egba and Their Neighbours, 1842-1872, 1957; contribs to Africa, jl of Nigerian Historical Soc., Ödu (Joint Ed.), etc. *Recreations:* soccer, tennis, badminton, swimming, walking. *Address:* PO Box 7741, Lagos, Nigeria. *T:* (home) 961430. *Clubs:* Metropolitan (Lagos); Dining (Ibadan).

BIRCH, Alexander Hope, CMG 1970; OBE 1961; HM Diplomatic Service, retired; *b* 19 Jan. 1913; *s* of Denys Goldney and Lucy Helen Booth Birch; *m* 1st, 1940, Honor Pengelley (marr. diss., 1948); 2nd, 1953, Joan Hastings-Hungerford (*d* 1982); no *c. Educ:* St Catherine's and St Mark's Colls, Alexandria, and privately. Appointed to: HM Embassy, Cairo, 1937; Addis Ababa, 1942; Moscow, 1946; Budapest, 1947; Tel-Aviv, 1949; Second Sec. (Inf.), Baghdad, 1950, First Sec. and Consul, Seoul, 1951, and Djakarta, 1954; First Sec. (Commercial), Khartoum, 1956, and Paris, 1961; Counsellor (Commercial), Paris, 1962, and Baghdad, 1965; Counsellor (Economic and Commercial), Accra, 1967-70; Dep. High Comr, Perth, WA, 1970-73; Administrative Adviser to Premier of Antigua, 1973-75. *Recreations:* international affairs, reading, walking. *Address:* Woodrow, Edgehill Road, Clevedon, Avon BS21 7BZ. *Club:* Oriental.

BIRCH, Prof. Anthony Harold, PhD; Professor of Political Science, University of Victoria, British Columbia, since 1977; *b* 17 Feb. 1924; *o s* of late Frederick Harold Birch and of Rosalind Dorothy Birch; *m* 1953, Dorothy Madeleine Overton, Bayport, New York; one *s* one *d. Educ:* The William Ellis Sch.; University Coll., Nottingham; London Sch. of Economics. BSc (Econ) London, with 1st cl. hons, 1945; PhD London, 1951. Asst Principal, Board of Trade, 1945-47; University of Manchester: Asst Lectr in Govt, 1947-51; Lectr, 1951-58; Senior Lectr in Government, 1958-61; Prof. of Political Studies, Univ. of Hull, 1961-70; Prof. of Political Sci., Exeter Univ., 1970-77. Commonwealth Fund Fellow at Harvard Univ. and University of Chicago, 1951-52. Consultant to Government of Western Region of Nigeria, 1956-58. Vis. Prof. Tufts Univ., 1968. Vice-Pres., Internat. Political Sci. Assoc., 1976-79; Life Vice-Pres., UK Political Studies Assoc., 1976- (Chm., 1972-75). *Publications:* Federalism, Finance and Social Legislation, 1955; Small-Town Politics, 1959; Representative and Responsible Government, 1964; The British System of Government, 1967, 5th edn 1982; Representation, 1971; Political Integration and Disintegration in the British Isles, 1977; articles in various journals. *Recreation:* sailing. *Address:* Department of Political Science, University of Victoria, Victoria, BC, Canada.

BIRCH, Prof. Arthur John, CMG 1979; DPhil (Oxon), MSc; FRS 1958; PAA, FRACI; Professor of Organic Chemistry, Australian National University, 1970-80, now Emeritus Professor; *b* 3 Aug. 1915; *s* of Arthur Spencer and Lily Birch; *m* 1948, Jessie Williams; three *s* two *d. Educ:* Sydney Technical High Sch.; Sydney Univ. Scholar of the Royal Commission for the Exhibition of 1851, Oxford, 1938-41; Research Fellow, 1941-45; ICI Research Fellow, Oxford, 1945-48; Smithson Fellow of the Royal Society,

Cambridge, 1949-52; Prof. of Organic Chemistry, University of Sydney 1952-55; Prof. of Organic Chemistry, Manchester Univ., 1955-67; Dean Research Sch. of Chemistry, ANU, Canberra, 1967-70, 1973-76; Newto Abraham Prof. of Organic Chemistry, Univ. of Oxford, 1980-81. Treas Australian Acad. Science, 1969-73, Pres., 1982-; Pres., RACI, 1978. Chairma Ind. Enquiry into CSIRO, 1976-; Aust. Marine Sciences and Technologie Adv. Cttee, 1978-81. Foreign Mem., USSR Acad. of Science, 1976. Hor FRCS 1980. Hon. DSc Sydney, 1977. Davy Medal, Royal Soc., 1972 *Publications:* How Chemistry Works, 1950; about 400 original scientifi communications, chiefly in jnl of Chemical Soc. and Australian Journa of Chemistry. *Address:* Department of Chemistry, Australian Nationa University, PO Box 4, Canberra, ACT 2600, Australia.

BIRCH, Dr Bryan John, FRS 1972; Reader in Mathematics, University o Oxford, and Fellow of Brasenose College, Oxford, since 1966; *b* 25 Sep 1931; *s* of Arthur Jack and Mary Edith Birch; *m* 1961, Gina Margaret Christie two *s* one *d. Educ:* Shrewsbury Sch.; Trinity Coll., Cambridge (MA, PhD) Harkness Fellow, Princeton, 1957-58; Fellow: Trinity Coll., Cambridge 1956-60; Churchill Coll., Cambridge, 1960-62; Sen. Lectr, later Reader, Univ of Manchester, 1962-65. *Publications:* articles in learned jls, mainly on numbe theory; various editorships. *Recreations:* gardening (theoretical), musi (passive). *Address:* Green Cottage, Boars Hill, Oxford OX1 5DQ. *T:* Oxfor 735367; Mathematical Institute, 25-29 St Giles, Oxford. *T:* Oxford 54295.

BIRCH, Dennis Arthur, CBE 1977; DL; Councillor, West Midlands County Council, 1974-77; *b* 11 Feb. 1925; *s* of George Howard and Leah Birch; *n* 1948, Mary Therese Lyons; one *d. Educ:* Wolverhampton Municipa Grammar Sch. Wolverhampton County Borough Council: elected, 1952 served, 1952-74; Alderman, 1970-73; Mayor, 1973-74; Leader, 1967-73 Elected (following Local Govt reorganisation) Chm. West Midlands CC 1974-76. DL West Midlands, 1979. MInstM. *Address:* 3 Tern Close Wolverhampton Road East, Wolverhampton WV4 6AU. *T:* Sedgley 3837.

BIRCH, John Allan; HM Diplomatic Service; Counsellor, British Embassy Budapest, since 1980; *b* 24 May 1935; *s* of C. Allan Birch, MD, FRCP; *n* 1960, Primula Haselden; three *s* one *d. Educ:* Leighton Park Sch.; Corpu Christi Coll., Cambridge (MA). Served HM Forces, Middlesex Regt, 1954- 56. Joined HM Foreign Service, 1959; served: Paris, 1960-63; Singapore 1963-64; Bucharest, 1965-68; Geneva, 1968-70; Kabul, 1973-76; Royal Coll of Defence Studies, 1977; Comprehensive Test Ban Treaty Negotiations Geneva, 1977-80. *Recreations:* tennis, skiing. *Address:* c/o Foreign anc Commonwealth Office, SW1; 30 Gloucester Circus, Greenwich, SE10. *T* 01-858 9056. *Club:* Athenæum.

BIRCH, John Anthony, MA; FRCM, FRCO(CHM), LRAM; University Organist since 1967, and Visiting Lecturer in Music, since 1971, University of Sussex; Organist and Director of the Choir, Temple Church, since 1982 Organist to the Royal Choral Society, since 1966; Professor, Royal College of Music, since 1959; Fellow, Corporation of SS Mary and Nicolas (Woodard Schools), since 1973; *b* 9 July 1929; *s* of late Charles Aylmer Birch, Leek Staffs; unmarried. *Educ:* Trent Coll.; Royal Coll. of Music (ARCM) Organist and Choirmaster, St Thomas's Church, Regent Street, London 1950-53; Accompanist to St Michael's Singers, 1952-58; Organist anc Choirmaster, All Saints Church, Margaret Street, London, 1953-58; Sub- Organist, HM Chapels Royal, 1957-58; Organist and Master of the Choristers Chichester Cathedral, 1958-80; Musical Advr, Chichester Festival Theatre 1962-80; Choirmaster, Bishop Otter Coll., Chichester, 1963-69. Regr, 1950- 66, and Man. Dir, 1966-73, C. A. Birch Ltd, Staffs. Accompanist, Roya Choral Soc., 1965-70; Examr to Associated Bd, Royal Schs of Music, 1958-77 Special Comr, Royal Sch. of Church Music; Mem. Council, Royal Coll. of Organists; Governor: Hurstpierpoint Coll., 1974-; St Catherine's, Bramley 1981-. Has made concert appearances in France, Belgium, Germany Switzerland, Netherlands, Spain, Scandinavia and Far East; recital tours Canada and US, 1966 and 1967, Australia and NZ, 1969, S Africa, 1978. Hon MA Sussex, 1971. *Address:* 14 Spencer Walk, Putney, SW15 1PL. *T:* 01-789 6022. *Club:* Garrick.

BIRCH, Reginald; Chairman, Communist Party of Britain (Marxist Leninist) since 1968; Member, General Council of the TUC, 1975-79; Member Executive Council, AUEW, 1966-79; *b* 7 June 1914; *s* of Charles and Anne Birch; *m* 1942, Dorothy; three *s. Educ:* St Augustine's Elementary Sch. Kilburn. Apprentice toolmaker, 1929; at trade (toolmaker), until 1960 Divisional Organiser, AEU, 1960-66. Mem., Energy Commn, 1977-79 *Recreations:* swimming, growing herbs. *Address:* 29 Langley Park, NW7. *T* 01-959 7058.

BIRCH, Robert Edward Thomas, CBE 1979; Solicitor to the Metropolitan Police, 1976-82; *b* 9 May 1917; *s* of late Robert Birch and Edith Birch; *n* 1946, Laura Pia Busini; two *d. Educ:* Dulwich Coll. Served RA, 1940-46 Africa, Italy, NW Europe; Major. Admitted solicitor, 1942; joined Solicitors Dept, New Scotland Yard, 1946; Dep. Solicitor, 1968. *Recreations* swimming, travel. *Address:* c/o New Scotland Yard, Broadway, SW1H 0BC *T:* 01-230 7224.

BIRCH, William, PhD; Director, Bristol Polytechnic, since 1975; *b* 24 Nov 1925; *s* of Frederick Arthur and Maude Olive Birch; *m* 1950, Mary Vine Stammers; one *s* one *d. Educ:* Ranelagh Sch.; Univ. of Reading. BA 1949

PhD 1957. Royal Navy, 1943–46, Sub-Lt RNVR. Lectr, Univ. of Bristol, 1950–60; Prof. of Geography, Grad. Sch. of Geog., Clark Univ., Worcester, Mass, USA, 1960–63; Prof., and Chm. of Dept of Geog., Univ. of Toronto, Canada, 1963–67; Prof., and Head of Dept of Geog., Univ. of Leeds, 1967–75. Pres., Inst. of British Geographers, 1976–77; Chm., Cttee of Directors of Polytechnics, 1982–84. *Publications:* The Isle of Man: a study in economic geography, 1964; contrib.: geography and planning, Trans Inst. Brit. Geographers, Geog. Jl, Economic Geog., Annals Assoc. Amer. Geographers, Jl Environmental Management, etc. *Recreations:* sailing, squash, travel, theatre, pottery. *Address:* 13 Richmond Park Road, Clifton, Bristol BS8 3AS. *T:* 39719.

BIRCHALL, Prof. James Derek, FRS 1982; FRSC; ICI Senior Research Associate, Mond Division, since 1975; *b* 7 Oct. 1930; *s* of David Birchall and Dora Mary Birchall; *m* 1952, Pauline Mary Jones; two *s.* Joined ICI, 1957; Research Leader, 1965; Research Associate, 1970. Visiting Professor, Univ. of Surrey, 1976–; Industrial Fellow, Wolfson Coll., Oxford, 1977–79. *Publications:* A Classification of Fire Hazards, 1952, 2nd edn 1961; contribs to various encyclopedias and to learned jls, *ie* Nature, on inorganic chemistry and materials science. *Recreations:* old books, new cars. *Address:* Braeside, Stable Lane, Mouldsworth, Chester CH3 8AN. *T:* Manley 320.

BIRCHENOUGH, (John) Michael, BSc, PhD; Chief Inspector, Inner London Education Authority, since 1973; *b* 17 Jan. 1923; *s* of John Buckley Birchenough and Elsie Birchenough; *m* 1945, Enid Humphries; two *s. Educ:* Ashford Grammar Sch., Kent; Chiswick County Sch.; London Univ. Chemist, May & Baker Ltd, 1943–45; teaching posts, 1946–60; HM Inspector of Schools, 1960; Staff Inspector, 1966; Chief Inspector, 1968–72. Pres., Educn Section, BAAS Annual Meeting, Stirling, 1974. *Publications:* contribs to Jl of Chem. Soc. and other scientific jls. *Address:* 43 Watford Road, Radlett, Herts. *T:* Radlett 5176.

BIRD, Rev. Dr Anthony Peter; General Medical Practitioner, since 1979; Principal of The Queen's College, Edgbaston, Birmingham, 1974–79; *b* 2 March 1931; *s* of Albert Harry Bird and Noel Whitehouse Bird; *m* 1962, Sabine Boehmig; two *s* one *d. Educ:* St John's Coll., Oxford (BA LitHum, BA Theol, MA); Birmingham Univ. (MB, ChB, 1970). Deacon, 1957; Priest, 1958; Curate of St Mary's, Stafford, 1957–60; Chaplain, then Vice-Principal of Cuddesdon Theological Coll., 1960–64. General Medical Practitioner, 1972–73. Member: Home Office Policy Adv. Cttee on Sexual Offences, 1976–80; Parole Board, 1977–80. *Publication:* The Search for Health: a response from the inner city, 1981. *Recreations:* water, Wolverhampton Wanderers FC, walking, music—J. S. Bach, innovation in primary health care. *Address:* 92 Bournbrook Road, Birmingham B29 7BU.

BIRD, Lt-Gen. Sir Clarence August, KCIE 1943; CB 1940; DSO 1917; late RE; *b* 5 Feb. 1885; *m* 1919, Dorothea Marian, MBE 1918, K-i-H 1932, *d* of late Major W. E. Nichols; one *s* (and one *s* died on active service). *Educ:* Cheltenham Coll. Joined Royal Engineers, 1904; served in India, 1907–13, 1917–25, 1930–33, 1939–44; with Indian Expeditionary Force in France, 1914–15; with BEF in France, 1916–17 (Bt Maj.); psc 1921; AHQ India, 1922–25; Army Course, London Sch. of Economics, 1925; Chief Instructor in Fortification, SME, Chatham, 1926–29; Commandant, KGVO Bengal Sappers and Miners, 1930–33; Bt Lieut-Col, 1926; Lieut-Col, 1929; Col, 1933; AQMG Aldershot Command, 1933–35; Chief Engineer, Aldershot Command, 1935–39; Maj.-Gen. 1939; Engineer-in-Chief, Army Headquarters, India, 1939–42; Lieut-Gen. 1941; Master Gen. of Ordnance, India, 1942–44; retd 1944. Col Comdt RE, 1942–52; Col Comdt Indian Electrical and Mechanical Engineers, 1944–48. Dept of Food, Govt of India: Regional Commissioner, NW Region, 1944–45; Special Commissioner, 1945–47; Min. of Food: Divisional Food Officer, North Midland Div., 1947–48; Chm., Rhodesia Railways, 1948–53. FRSA. *Address:* Polesden Lacey, Dorking, Surrey.

BIRD, Sir Cyril (Pangbourne), Kt 1968; Company Director, Perth, Western Australia, retired 1978; *b* 5 April 1906; *s* of late Walter Pangbourne Bird and late Alice Emma Bird; *m* 1st, 1934, Margery Isabel (*d* 1974); two *s* three *d*; 2nd, 1976, Agnes Jarvie. *Educ:* Perth, W Australia. FASA. *Recreations:* fishing, music. *Address:* 4 Riverside Drive, Mosman Park, WA 6012, Australia. *T:* 3846884. *Club:* Royal King's Park Tennis.

BIRD, Air Vice-Marshal Frank Ronald, CB 1971; DSO 1945; DFC 1944; AFC 1958; Treasurer, since 1973, Fellow, since 1978, Lady Margaret Hall, Oxford; *b* 18 Nov. 1918; *s* of Frank Bird and Minnie (*née* Robinson); *m* 1943, Joan Dodson, WAAF; two *s. Educ:* Chesterfield Sch., Halton; RAF Coll., Cranwell. Commnd RAF, 1939; Flying Instruction and Experimental Flying, 1940–43; 105 Sqdn Bomber Comd (Pathfinder Force), 1943–45; Empire Test Pilots Sch. and A & AEE, 1945–46; RAF Coll., Cranwell (Cadet Wing), 1946–48; Perm. Commng Bds, Air Min., 1948–50; RAF Staff Coll., Andover, 1950–51; Brit. Jt Services Mission, Washington, USA, 1951–54; A & AEE, Boscombe Down, 1954–57; HQ Bomber Comd (Plans), 1957; CO, RAF Gaydon, 1957–60; Bomber Ops Staff, Air Min., 1960–63; Canadian Nat. Def. Coll., Kingston, Ont., 1963–64; Comdt, A & AEE Boscombe Down, 1964–68; Director Gen. of Organisation (RAF), 1968–71; Asst Chief of Staff, Automatic Data Processing Division, SHAPE, 1971–73. *Recreations:* fell walking, golf, music, photography. *Address:* 36 North Street, Islip, Oxon. *T:* Kidlington 2808. *Club:* Royal Air Force.

BIRD, (George William) Terence; Director: Pilkington Brothers Ltd, since 1962 (Executive Vice-Chairman, 1971–77); Rockware Group Ltd, since 1976; *b* 27 July 1914; *er s* of George Webber Bird and Jane (*née* Hockin); *m* 1942, Hylda Owen Craven; one *d* (one *s* decd). *Educ:* Prescot Grammar Sch.; Imperial Coll. of Science and Technology (BSc, ARCS). FBIM 1972. Physicist, Pilkington Bros Ltd, 1935; Laboratory Manager, Triplex Northern Ltd, 1936; Pilkington Bros Ltd: Develt Physicist, 1939; Dir, 1962; Chm., Flat Glass Div., 1966. Member Council: Manchester Business Sch., 1971– (Chm., Finance and Gen. Purposes Cttee, 1978–); Parliament and Industry Trust, 1979–. *Recreations:* gardening, spectator sports. *Address:* 21 Grange Drive, Eccleston Hill, St Helens, Merseyside WA10 3BG. *Club:* Windermere Motor Boat Racing.

BIRD, James Gurth, MBE 1945; TD 1951; *b* 30 Jan. 1909; *s* of Charles Harold Bird and Alice Jane Bird (*née* Kirtland); *m* 1940, Phyllis Ellis Pownall; one *s* two *d. Educ:* King William's Coll., Isle of Man (Scholar); St Catharine's Coll., Cambridge (exhibnr). Classical Tripos Pts I and II, BA 1931, MA 1933. Asst Master, Rossall Sch., 1931–33; Asst Master and House Master, Denstone Coll., 1933–47 (interrupted by War Service); Head Master, William Hulme's Grammar Sch., Manchester, 1947–74. *Recreations:* sailing, gardening. *Address:* Ty Deryn, Ravenspoint Road, Trearddur Bay, Holyhead, Gwynedd LL65 2AX.

BIRD, John Louis; Joint Managing Director, Cable and Wireless plc, since 1982; *b* 18 Jan. 1929; *s* of Sydney Warner Bird and Florence Katherine Byford; *m* 1950, Mary Arnold; one *s* one *d. Educ:* Grammar School. National Cash Register Co., 1950–56; Addressograph-Multigraph Corp., 1956–68; Ultra Electronic Holdings Ltd, 1968–75; Cable & Wireless Ltd, 1975–: Man. Dir, Communications Systems and Services, 1977–81. *Recreations:* golf, caravanning. *Address:* 16 Parkside Drive, Watford, Herts.

BIRD, Michael Gwynne; Chairman, Massey-Ferguson Holdings Ltd, since 1980 (Managing Director, 1978–81); *b* 16 Aug. 1921; *s* of Edward Gwynne Bird, Chaplain, RN, and Brenda Bird (*née* Rumney); *m* 1944, Frances Yvonne Townley; one *s* two *d. Educ:* Harrow Sch.; St Catharine's Coll., Cambridge. Served war: commnd, Rifle Bde, 1941; demobilised (Major), 1946. Colonial Service (Administration), Malawi, 1948–54; called to the Bar, Inner Temple, 1955; joined Massey-Ferguson, 1955; Director, Legal Services, Massey-Ferguson Ltd, 1977; Chm., Perkins Engines Group, 1980; Vice-Pres., Massey-Ferguson Ltd, and Chm. European Corp., 1982. *Address:* Broad Oak, Clive Road, Esher, Surrey. *T:* Esher 66241. *Clubs:* Oriental, MCC.

BIRD, Sir Richard Dawnay Martin-; *see* Martin-Bird.

BIRD, Sir Richard (Geoffrey Chapman), 4th Bt *cr* 1922; *b* 3 Nov. 1935; *er surv. s* of Sir Donald Bird, 3rd Bt, and of Anne Rowena (*d* 1969), *d* of late Charles Chapman; *S* father, 1963; *m* 1st, 1957, Gillian Frances (*d* 1966), *d* of Bernard Haggett, Solihull; two *s* four *d* ; 2nd, 1968, Helen Patricia, *d* of Frank Beaumont, Pontefract; two *d. Educ:* Beaumont. *Heir: s* John Andrew Bird, *b* 19 Jan. 1964. *Address:* 39 Ashleigh Road, Solihull, W Midlands B91 1AF.

BIRD, Richard Herries; Deputy Secretary, Department of Education and Science, since 1980; *b* 8 June 1932; *s* of Edgar Bird and Armorel (*née* Dudley-Scott); *m* 1963, Valerie, *d* of Edward and Mary Sanderson; two *d. Educ:* Winchester Coll.; Clare Coll., Cambridge. Min. of Transport and Civil Aviation, 1955; Private Sec. to Permanent Sec., 1958–60; Principal, 1960, Asst Sec., 1966, Min. of Transport; Principal Private Sec. to Minister of Transport, 1966–67; CSD 1969; DoE 1971; DES 1973, Under Sec. 1975. *Address:* High Beech, 53 Kippington Road, Sevenoaks, Kent TN13 2LL. *T:* Sevenoaks 56777.

BIRD, Terence; *see* Bird, G. W. T.

BIRD, Veronica; Editor, Woman's Realm, 1971–77; *b* 16 Oct. 1932; *o d* of Reginald John Fearn; *m* 1st, 1954, Alec Xavier Snobel (marr. diss. 1974); one *s* one *d* ; 2nd, 1974, Michael Bird. *Educ:* Kingsley Sch., Leamington Spa. Editor, Parents magazine, 1963–64; Editor, Mother magazine, 1964–71. *Publication:* Pressing Problems, 1982. *Recreations:* theatre, cinema. *Address:* 5 Glentham Gardens, SW13 9JN. *T:* 01-748 6344.

BIRD-WILSON, Air Vice-Marshal Harold Arthur Cooper, CBE 1962; DSO 1945; DFC 1940 and Bar 1943; AFC 1946 and Bar 1955; *b* 20 Nov. 1919; *m* 1942, Audrey Wallace; one *s* one *d. Educ:* Liverpool Coll. Joined RAF, Nov. 1937; No 17 Fighter Sqdn, Kenley, 1938. Served War of 1939–45 (France, Dunkirk, Battle of Britain): Sqdn Comdr Nos 152 and 66, 1942 (despatches); Wing Leader, No 83 Gp, 1943; Comd and Gen. Staff Sch., Fort Leavenworth, Kansas, USA, 1944; Wing Leader, Harrowbeer, Spitfire Wing and then Bentwater Mustang Wing, 1944–45; CO, Jet Conversion Unit, 1945–46; CO, Air Fighting Development Sqdn, CFE, 1946–47; Op. Staff, HQ, MEAF, 1948; RAF Staff Coll., Bracknell, 1949; Personal Staff Officer to C-in-C, MEAF, 1949–50; RAF Flying Coll., Manby, 1951; OC Tactics, CFE, 1952–54; Staff, BJSM, Washington, USA, 1954–57; Staff, Air Sec. Dept, Air Min., 1957–59; CO, RAF Coltishall, 1959–61; Staff Intell., Air Min., 1961–63; AOC and Comdt, CFS, 1963–65; AOC Hong Kong, 1965–67; Dir of Flying (Research and Develt), Min. of Technology, 1967–70; AOC No 23 Gp, 1970–73; Comdr, S Maritime Air Region, RAF, 1973–74, retired. Now with

British Aerospace. Czechoslovak Medal of Merit 1st class, 1945; Dutch DFC, 1945.

BIRDSALL, Mrs Doris; Lord Mayor of Bradford Metropolitan District, 1975-76; *b* 20 July 1915; *d* of Fred and Violet Ratcliffe; *m* 1940, James Birdsall; one *s* one *d. Educ:* Hanson Girls' Grammar School. Mem. Bradford City Council, 1958, Chm. of Educn Cttee, 1972-74; Mem. Bradford Univ. Council, 1963-. Hon. MA Bradford, 1975; Hon. LHD Lesley Coll., Mass, 1976. *Address:* 24 Baildon Road, Baildon, Bradford, West Yorks. *T:* Bradford 596251.

BIRDWOOD, family name of **Baron Birdwood.**

BIRDWOOD, 3rd Baron, *cr* 1938, of Anzac and of Totnes; **Mark William Ogilvie Birdwood;** Bt 1919; *b* 23 Nov. 1938; *s* of 2nd Baron Birdwood, MVO, and of Vere Lady Birdwood, CVO; *S* father, 1962; *m* 1963, Judith Helen, *e d* of R. Seymour Roberts, Newton Aycliffe, Darlington, Co. Durham; one *d. Educ:* Radley Coll.; Trinity Coll., Cambridge. *Address:* 5 Holbein Mews, SW1; Russell House, Broadway, Worcs. *Club:* Brooks's.

BIRGI, Muharrem Nuri; Turkish diplomat, retired; *b* Istanbul, 4 Feb. 1908; *o s* of late Ziya Nuri Birgi Pasha, Prof., Faculty of Med., Univ. of Istanbul, later Mem. Grand Nat. Assembly, Turkey, and of Mme Husniye Birgi, *d* of Hassan Rami Pasha, Minister of Marine; *m* (marr. diss.). *Educ:* Lycée Galata Saray, Istanbul; Sch. of Pol. Sciences, Paris (Grad. 1929); Faculty of Law, Geneva (LLB 1931). Entered Turkish For. Min., 1932; 3rd, 2nd and then 1st Sec., Turkish Embassy, Warsaw, 1935-39; Min. for For. Affairs, 1939-41; 1st Sec., Turkish Embassy, Paris-Vichy, 1941; transferred to Madrid, 1942, later promoted Counsellor there. Min. for For. Affairs, Ankara: Co-Dir-Gen. 1st Political Dept, 1944; Dir-General: Dept of Internat. Affairs, 1945; Dept of Co-ordination, 1946; Dept of Consular Affairs, 1946; 2nd Political Dept, 1950; Dep. Sec.-Gen., 1951; Under-Sec. of State, 1952; Sec.-Gen., 1954-57; Turkish Ambassador to Court of St James's, 1957-60. Turkish Permanent Representative to NATO, 1960-72, retired 1972. Pres., Atlantic Treaty Assoc., 1979-82. *Recreation:* painting. *Address:* Toprakli Sokak 11, Salacak, Usküdar, Istanbul, Turkey. *T:* Istanbul 331591.

BIRK, family name of **Baroness Birk.**

BIRK, Baroness *cr* 1967 (Life Peer), of Regent's Park in Greater London; **Alma Birk,** JP; journalist; *d* of late Barnett and Alice Wilson; *m* Ellis Birk; one *s* one *d. Educ:* South Hampstead High Sch.; LSE. BSc Econ (Hons) London. Leader of Labour Group, Finchley Borough Council, 1950-53; contested (Lab): Ruislip-Northwood, 1950; Portsmouth West, 1951, 1955. Baroness in Waiting (Govt Whip), March-Oct. 1974; Parly Under-Sec. of State, DoE, 1974-79; Minister of State, Privy Council Office, 1979. Associate Editor, Nova, 1965-69. Dir, New Shakespeare Co. Ltd, 1979-. Formerly Lectr and Prison Visitor, Holloway Prison. Mem., Youth Service Develt Council, 1967-71; Chm., Health Educn Council, 1969-72; Vice-President: Council for Children's Welfare, 1968-75; H. G. Wells Soc., 1967-; Stamford Hill Associated Clubs, 1967-70; Redbridge Jewish Youth Centre, 1970-; Member: Fabian Soc., 1946- (Sec., Fabian Soc. Res. Cttee on Marriage and Divorce, 1951-52); Howard League for Penal Reform, 1948- (Mem. Council, 1979-); Hendon Group Hosp. Management Cttee, 1951-59; Panel, London Pregnancy Adv. Service, 1968-; RCOG working party on the unplanned pregnancy, 1969-72; Exec. Council of Christians and Jews, 1971-77; Hon. Cttee, Albany Trust; Ct of Governors, LSE, 1971-; Council, British Museum Soc., 1979-; Chm. Arts Sub-Cttee, Holocaust Meml Cttee, 1979-. Trustee, Yorkshire Sculpture Park, 1980-; Governor: BFI, 1981-; Mander Mitchenson Theatre Collection, 1981-. FRSA 1980. JP Highgate, 1952. *Publications:* pamphlets, articles. *Recreations:* travelling, theatre, reading, talking, especially to men. *Address:* 13 Hanover Terrace, NW1.

BIRKENHEAD, 3rd Earl of, *cr* 1922; **Frederick William Robin Smith;** Bt 1918; Baron Birkenhead 1919; Viscount Birkenhead 1921; Viscount Furneaux 1922; *b* 17 April 1936; *o s* of 2nd Earl of Birkenhead, TD, and of Hon. Sheila Berry, 2nd *d* of 1st Viscount Camrose; *S* father, 1975. *Educ:* Eton; Christ Church, Oxford. Mem. Council, RSL, 1975-. *Publications:* (as Robin Furneaux): The Amazon, 1969; William Wilberforce, 1974 (Heinemann Award, 1975). *Address:* 48 Arthur Road, Wimbledon, SW19. *T:* 01-947 3983; The Cottage, Charlton, Banbury, Oxon. *T:* Banbury 811224. *Clubs:* Buck's, White's, Portland, All England Lawn Tennis.

BIRKENHEAD, Bishop Suffragan of, since 1974; **Rt. Rev. Ronald Brown;** *b* 7 Aug. 1926; *s* of Fred and Ellen Brown; *m* 1951, Joyce Hymers; one *s* one *d. Educ:* Kirkham Grammar Sch.; Durham Univ. (BA, DipTh). Vicar of Whittle-le-Woods, 1956; Vicar of St Thomas, Halliwell, Bolton, 1961; Rector and Rural Dean of Ashton-under-Lyne, 1970. *Recreations:* antiques and golf. *Address:* Trafford House, Queen's Park, Chester CH4 7AX. *T:* Chester 675895. *Club:* National Liberal.

BIRKETT, family name of **Baron Birkett.**

BIRKETT, 2nd Baron *cr* 1958, of Ulverston; **Michael Birkett;** Director for Recreation and Arts, Greater London Council, since 1979; film producer since 1961; *b* 22 Oct. 1929; *s* of 1st Baron Birkett, PC and Ruth Birkett (*née* Nilsson, she *d* 1969); *S* father, 1962; *m* 1st, 1960, Junia Crawford (*d* 1973); 2nd, 1978, Gloria Taylor; one *s. Educ:* Stowe; Trinity Coll., Cambridge. Asst

Dir at Ealing Studios and Ealing Films, 1953-59; Asst Dir, 1959-61, on films including: The Mark; The Innocents; Billy Budd; Associate Producer: Som People, 1961-62; Modesty Blaise, 1965; Producer: The Caretaker, 1962 Marat/Sade, 1966; A Midsummer Night's Dream, 1967; King Lear, 1968-69 Director: The Launching and The Soldier's Tale, 1963; Overture an Beginners, the More Man Understands, 1964; Outward Bound, 1971. Dep Dir, National Theatre, 1975-77; Consultant to Nat. Theatre on films, TV an sponsorship, 1977-79. Master, Curriers' Co., 1975-76. *Recreations:* music printing, horticulture, ballet. *Heir: s* Hon. Thomas Birkett, *b* 25 July 1982 *Address:* House of Lords, SW1.

BIRKETT, George William Alfred, CBE 1960; CEng, FIEE, FIMechE Director of Weapons Production, Ministry of Defence (Naval), 1965-70 retired; *b* 16 June 1908; *m* 1939, Doris Lillian Prince; one *s. Educ:* Portsmouth Municipal College. Portsmouth Dockyard, 1929; Techn. Officer, HM Signa Sch., 1938; Prin. Scientific Officer, RNSS, 1946; Sen. Prin. Production Engr Admty Production Pool, 1953; Supt of Production Pool, Admty, 1956 *Recreation:* sailing. *Address:* 81 Ferndale, Inhurst Wood, Waterlooville Portsmouth, Hants. *T:* Waterlooville 52695.

BIRKIN, Sir Charles (Lloyd), 5th Bt *cr* 1905; *b* 24 Sept. 1907; *s* of late Co Charles Wilfrid Birkin, CMG (4th *s* of 1st Bt); *S* uncle, 1942; *m* 1940, Jane Johnson; one *s* two *d. Educ:* Eton. Served War of 1939-45, with 112th Regt 9th Sherwood Foresters. *Publications:* collections of short stories: The Kiss of Death, 1964; The Smell of Evil, 1965; Where Terror Stalks, 1966; My Name is Death, 1966; Dark Menace, 1968; So Cold . . . So Fair, 1970; Spawn of Satan 1971. *Heir: s* John Christian William Birkin, *b* 2 July 1953. *Address:* Wes Kella, Sulby, Isle of Man. *T:* Sulby 7544. *Club:* Carlton.

BIRKIN, Air Commodore James Michael, CB 1956; DSO 1944; OBE 1951 DFC 1944; AFC 1942; AE 1947; DL; Director, Birkin & Company Limited New Basford, Nottingham (Lace Manufacturers); *b* 23 April 1912; *s* of late Major H. L. Birkin, Lincoln House, The Park, Nottingham, and late Olive Isobel, *d* of late Rev. H. C. Russell, Wollaton, Notts; *m* 1st, 1956, Antonia Edith (marr. diss. 1977), *d* of late Lt-Col A. F. Stanley Clarke and late Mr Charles Graves; one *s* one *d* ; 2nd, 1980, Susan, *d* of late Edward Mitchell Ryde, IoW. *Educ:* Harrow; Trinity Coll., Cambridge (MA). London Stock Exchange until 1939; Birkin & Co. Ltd, 1945-. RAFVR, 1938-47; RAuxAF 1947-63 (Inspector, 1952-62); Hon. Air Commodore, 1956. ADC to the Queen, 1957-63. High Sheriff 1977, DL 1978, Isle of Wight. *Address:* c/o Birkin & Co. Ltd, New Basford, Nottingham. *T:* Nottingham 79351. *Clubs* MCC, Pathfinder; Royal Yacht Squadron, Cowes Corinthian Yacht.

BIRKINSHAW, Prof. John Howard, DSc; FRSC; retired as Professor of Biochemistry and Head of Department of Biochemistry, London School of Hygiene and Tropical Medicine, University of London (1956-62), now Emeritus; *b* 8 Oct. 1894; *s* of John Thomas and Madeline Birkinshaw Garforth, near Leeds; *m* 1929, Elizabeth Goodwin Guthrie, Ardrossan, Ayrshire; one *s* one *d. Educ:* Leeds Modern Sch.; Leeds Univ. War service, 1915, West Yorks Regt and Machine Gun Corps (POW); demobilised, 1919. BSc Hons 1920, MSc 1921, DSc 1929, Leeds. Research Biochemist to Nobel's Explosives Co. (later ICI), 1920-30; Research Asst to Prof. Raistrick, London Sch. of Hygiene and Tropical Medicine, 1931; Senior Lecturer, 1938; Reader 1945. *Publications:* about 60 scientific papers in Biochemical Journal, Philos. Trans. Royal Society, etc. *Recreation:* photography. *Address:* 87 Barrow Point Avenue, Pinner, Mddx. *T:* 01-866 4784.

BIRKMYRE, Sir Henry, 2nd Bt *cr* 1921, of Dalmunzie; *b* 24 March 1898; *er s* of Sir Archibald Birkmyre, 1st Bt and Anne, *e d* of Capt. James Black; *S* father, 1935; *m* 1922, Doris Gertrude, *er d* of late Col H. Austen Smith CIE; one *s* one *d. Educ:* Wellington. War Service in France with RFA, 1917. *Heir: s* Archibald Birkmyre [*b* 12 Feb. 1923; *m* 1953, Gillian Mary, *o d* of Eric Downes, OBE; one *s* two *d*.] *Recreation:* golf. *Address:* 11 Crittles Court, Wadhurst, E Sussex TN5 6BY. *T:* Wadhurst 3486.

BIRKS, Maj.-Gen. (retired) Horace Leslie, CB 1945; DSO 1941; *b* 7 May 1897; *m* 1920, Gladys Hester (*d* 1957), MBE, *d* of Lieut-Col Hugh Harry Haworth Aspinall, OBE; one *s. Educ:* University College Sch. Enlisted London Rifle Brigade, 1915; 2nd Lieut Machine Gun Corps Heavy Branch, 1917, later Tank Corps; served France, 1915-16 and again 1917 (twice wounded); Instructor RTC Schools, 1919-24; Staff Coll., Quetta, 1927, 1928; General Staff, Western Command and War Office, 1930-37; Instructor Staff Coll., Quetta, 1937-39; India, 1924-29 and 1937-39; GSO1, 7th Armoured Division, Army of the Nile, 1939-40; 2nd in Command 4th Armoured Bde., 1940-41 (DSO, despatches twice); Commander 11th Armoured Brigade, 1941, Commander 10th Armoured Division, 1942; MG, RAC, CMF, 1944 (CB); retired pay, 1946. Secretary, University College Hospital Medical Sch., 1946-63, retired. *Recreations:* travel, golf. *Address:* c/o Williams and Glyn's Bank, Kirkland House, Whitehall, SW1. *T:* 01-788 7307. *Clubs:* Army and Navy, Roehampton (President).

BIRKS, Dr Jack, CBE 1975; a Managing Director, British Petroleum, 1978-82, Chairman: Schroder Energy Inc., since 1981; Charterhouse Petroleum, since 1982; NMI Ltd, since 1982; Director: London American Energy, since 1981; George Wimpey, since 1982; Jebsens Drilling Ltd, since 1982; *b* 1 Jan. 1920; *s* of late Herbert Horace Birks and of Ann Birks; *m* 1948, Vere Elizabeth Burrell-Davis; two *s* two *d. Educ:* Ecclesfield Grammar Sch.; Univ. of Leeds (BSc, PhD). Served with REME, Europe and India, 1941-46 (despatches,

Captain). Exploration Research Div., Anglo Iranian Oil Co., 1948-57; Man., Petroleum Engrg Research, BP Research Centre, Sunbury, 1957-59; Vice-Pres. Exploration, BP North America, NY, 1959-62; various techn. and managerial appts, subseq. Dir and Gen. Man., Iranian Oil Exploration & Producing Co., Teheran and Masjid-i-Sulaiman, 1962-70; Gen. Man., Exploration and Production Dept, British Petroleum Co. Ltd, London, 1970-72; Technical Dir, BP Trading Ltd, and Dep. Chm., BP Trading Exec. Cttee, 1972-77; Chairman: BP Minerals Internat., 1981-82; BP Coal, 1981-82; Selection Trust, 1981-82. Member: SRC, 1976-80; Meteorological Cttee, 1977-; Adv. Council on R&D, Dept of Energy, 1978-; Offshore Energy Technology Bd, Dept of Energy, 1978-. President: Soc. for Underwater Technology, 1974; Pipeline Industries Guild, 1979-. *Publications:* contribs to technical internat. oil jls, sci. papers on oilfields develts and North Sea oil. *Recreations:* tennis, cricket, golf. *Address:* 1A Alwyne Road, Canonbury, N1 2HH. *T:* 01-226 4905; High Silver, High Street, Holt, Norfolk NR25 7NA. *T:* Holt 2847. *Clubs:* Athenæum; Mill Hill Golf, St George's Hill Golf.

BIRKS, Michael; Registrar, West London County Court, since 1966; a Recorder of the Crown Court, since 1979; *b* 21 May 1920; *s* of late Falconer Moffat Birks, CBE, and Monica Katherine Lushington (*née* Mellor); *m* 1947, Ann Ethne, *d* of Captain Henry Stafford Morgan; one *d. Educ:* Oundle; Trinity Coll., Cambridge. Commissioned 22nd Dragoons, 1941; attached Indian Army, 1942, invalided out, 1943. Admitted Solicitor, 1946; Assistant Registrar: Chancery Div., High Court, 1953-60; Newcastle upon Tyne group of County Courts, 1960-61; Registrar, Birkenhead gp of County Courts, 1961-66. Adv. Editor, Atkins Court Forms, 1966-; Jt Editor, County Court Practice, 1976-. Mem. County Court Rule Cttee, 1980-. *Publications:* Gentlemen of the Law, 1960; Small Claims in the County Court, 1973; Enforcing Money Judgments in the County Court, 1980; contributed titles: County Courts and Interpleader (part), 4th edn Halsbury's Laws of England; Judgments and Orders (part), References and Inquiries (part), Service (part), and Transfer (part), Atkins Court Forms; contribs to legal jls. *Recreations:* sailing, painting. *Address:* West London County Court, 43 North End Road, W14.

BIRKS, Prof. Peter Brian Herrenden; Professor of Civil Law, Edinburgh University, since 1981; *b* 3 Oct. 1941; *e s* of Dr Peter Herrenden Birks and Mary (*née* Morgan). *Educ:* Trinity Coll., Oxford (MA); University Coll., London (LLM). Lectr in Laws, UCL, 1966-71; Law Fellow, Brasenose Coll., Oxford, 1971-81. *Address:* 39 East Trinity Road, Trinity, Edinburgh EH5 3DL. *T:* 031-552 4632.

BIRLEY, Anthony Addison, CB 1979; Clerk of Public Bills, House of Commons, since 1973; *b* 28 Nov. 1920; *s* of Charles Fair Birley and Eileen Mia Rouse; *m* 1951, Jane Mary Ruggles-Brise; two *d. Educ:* Winchester (exhibnr); Christ Church, Oxford (MA). Served War in RA (Ayrshire Yeomanry), 1940-45, in North Africa and Italian campaigns (wounded). Asst Clerk, House of Commons, 1948; Clerk of Standing Cttees, 1970. *Recreations:* gardening, walking, racing. *Address:* Holtam House, Paxford, Chipping Campden, Glos. *T:* Paxford 318. *Club:* Army and Navy.

BIRLEY, Derek; Rector, Ulster Polytechnic, since 1970; *b* 31 May 1926; *s* of late Sydney John and late Margaret Birley; *m* 1948, Margery Duckworth; two *s. Educ:* Hemsworth Grammar Sch.; Queens' Coll., Cambridge; Manchester Univ. BA 1950, MA 1954, Cantab. Royal Artillery, 1944-48; Schoolmaster, Queen Elizabeth Grammar Sch., Wakefield, 1952-55; Admin. Asst, Leeds Educn Cttee, 1955-59; Asst Educn Officer: Dorset, 1959-61; Lancs, 1961-64; Dep. Dir of Educn, Liverpool, 1964-70. *Publications:* The Education Officer and his World, 1970; (with Anne Dufton) An Equal Chance, 1971; Planning and Education, 1972; The Willow Wand, 1979. *Recreations:* books, cricket, jazz. *Address:* Gaywood, 127 Circular Road, Newtownabbey, Co. Antrim BT37 0RE.

BIRLEY, Prof. Eric, MBE 1943; FSA 1931; FBA 1969; Professor of Roman-British History and Archæology, University of Durham, 1956-71, now Professor Emeritus; *b* 12 Jan. 1906; *y s* of J. Harold Birley; *m* 1934, Margaret Isabel, *d* of Rev. James Goodlet; two *s. Educ:* Clifton Coll.; Brasenose Coll., Oxford. Lecturer, University of Durham, 1931; Reader, 1943. War of 1939-45: Military Intelligence, Lt-Col, GSO1 Military Intelligence Research Section; Chief of German Military Document Section, War Dept. Vice-Master, Hatfield Coll., Durham, 1947-49, Master, 1949-56; first Dean of Faculty of Social Sciences, Univ. of Durham, 1968-70. President: Soc. of Antiquaries of Newcastle upon Tyne, 1957-59; Cumberland and Westmorland Antiquarian and Archaeological Soc., 1957-60; Architectural and Archæological Soc. of Durham and Northumberland, 1959-63; Member: German Archæological Inst.; Ancient Monuments Board for England, 1966-76; Hon. Member, Gesellschaft Pro Vindonissa (Switzerland); Hon. FSAScot, 1980; Chm., Vindolanda Trust, 1970-. Hon. Dr Phil Freiburg i Br, 1970; Hon. DLitt Leicester, 1971. Polonia Restituta, 1944; Legion of Merit, 1947. *Publications:* The Centenary Pilgrimage of Hadrian's Wall, 1949; Roman Britain and the Roman Army, 1953; (ed) The Congress of Roman Frontier Studies 1949, 1952; Research on Hadrian's Wall, 1961; (jt ed) Roman Frontier Studies 1969, 1974; Fifty-one Ballades, 1980; numerous papers on Roman Britain and on the Roman army, excavation reports, etc. *Recreation:* archæology. *Address:* Sele Cottage, Hexham, Northumberland NE46 3LN. *T:* Hexham 603873.

BIRLEY, James Leatham Tennant, FRCP, FRCPsych, DPM; Consultant Psychiatrist, Bethlem Royal and Maudsley Hospitals, since 1969; Dean, Royal College of Psychiatrists, since 1982; *b* 31 May 1928; *s* of late Dr James Leatham Birley and Margaret Edith (*née* Tennant); *m* 1954, Julia Davies; one *s* three *d. Educ:* Winchester Coll.; University Coll., Oxford; St Thomas' Hosp., London. Maudsley Hospital: Registrar, 1960; Sen. Registrar, 1963; Mem. Scientific Staff, MRC Social Psychiatry Research Unit, 1965; Dean, Inst. of Psychiatry, SE5, 1971-82. *Publications:* contribs to scientific jls. *Recreations:* music, gardening. *Address:* 133 Sydenham Hill, SE26 6LW.

BIRLEY, Michael Pellew, MA (Oxon); Housemaster at Marlborough College, 1970-80, Assistant Master, since 1980; *b* 7 Nov. 1920; *s* of late Norman Pellew Birley, DSO, MC, and of Eileen Alice Morgan; *m* 1949, Ann Grover (*née* Street); two *s* two *d. Educ:* Marlborough Coll.; Wadham Coll., Oxford. 1st class Classical Honour Moderations, 1940; 1st class *Litterae Humaniores,* 1947; MA 1946. Served War of 1939-45 with the Royal Fusiliers; joined up, Sept. 1940; commissioned, April 1941; abroad, 1942-45 (despatches); demobilised, Jan. 1946. Taught Classics: Shrewsbury Sch., 1948-50; Eton Coll., 1950-56; Headmaster, Eastbourne College, 1956-70. *Recreations:* sailing, gardening, wine-making. *Address:* Long Summers, Cross Lane, Marlborough, Wilts.

BIRMINGHAM, Archbishop of, (RC), since 1982; **Most Rev. Maurice Noël Léon Couve de Murville;** *b* 27 June 1929; *s* of Noël Couve de Murville and Marie, *d* of Sir Louis Souchon. *Educ:* Downside School; Trinity Coll., Cambridge (MA); STL (Institut Catholique, Paris); MPhil (Sch. of Oriental and African Studies, Univ. of London). Priest, 1957; Curate: St Anselm's, Dartford, 1957-60; Priest-in-Charge, St Francis, Moulsecoomb, 1961-64; Catholic Chaplain: Univ. of Sussex, 1961-77; Univ. of Cambridge, 1977-82. *Recreations:* walking, gardening, local history. *Address:* 57 Mearse Lane, Barnt Green, Birmingham B45 8HJ. *T:* 021-445 1467.

BIRMINGHAM, Bishop of, since 1978; **Rt. Rev. Hugh William Montefiore,** MA, BD; *b* 12 May 1920; *s* of late Charles Sebag-Montefiore, OBE, and Muriel Alice Ruth Sebag-Montefiore; *m* 1945, Elisabeth Mary Macdonald Paton, *d* of late Rev. William Paton, DD, and Mrs Grace Paton; three *d. Educ:* Rugby Sch.; St John's Coll., Oxford (Hon. Fellow, 1981). Served during war, 1940-45; Capt. RA (Royal Bucks Yeo). Deacon 1949, priest 1950. Curate, St George's, Jesmond, Newcastle, 1949-51; Chaplain and Tutor, Westcott House, Cambridge, 1951-53; Vice-Principal, 1953-54; Examining Chaplain: to Bishop of Newcastle, 1953-70; to Bishop of Worcester, 1957-60; to Bishop of Coventry, 1957-70; to Bishop of Blackburn, 1966-70; Fellow and Dean of Gonville and Caius Coll., 1954-63; Lectr in New Testament, Univ. of Cambridge, 1959-63; Vicar of Great Saint Mary's, Cambridge, 1963-70; Canon Theologian of Coventry, 1959-70; Hon. Canon of Ely, 1969-70; Bishop Suffragan of Kingston-upon-Thames, 1970-78. Mem., Archbishops' Commn on Christian Doctrine, 1967-76. Chm., Indep. Commn on Transport, 1973. Hon. DD Aberdeen, 1976. *Publications:* (contrib.) The Historic Episcopate and the Fullness of the Church, 1954; To Help You To Pray, 1957; (contrib.) Soundings, 1962; Josephus and the New Testament, 1962; (with H. E. W. Turner) Thomas and the Evangelists, 1962; Beyond Reasonable Doubt, 1963; (contrib.) God, Sex and War, 1963; Awkward Questions on Christian Love, 1964; A Commentary on the Epistle to the Hebrews, 1964; Truth to Tell, 1966; (ed) We Must Love One Another Or Die, 1966; (contrib.) The Responsible Church, 1966; Remarriage and Mixed Marriage, 1967; (contrib.) Journeys in Belief, 1968; (ed) Sermons From Great St Mary's, 1968; My Confirmation Notebook, 1968; The Question Mark, 1969; Can Man Survive, 1970; (ed) More Sermons From Great St Mary's, 1971; Doom or Deliverance?, 1972; (ed) Changing Directions, 1974; (ed) Man and Nature, 1976; Apocalypse, 1976; (ed) Nuclear Crisis, 1977; (ed) Yes to Women Priests, 1978; Taking our Past into our Future, 1978; Paul the Apostle, 1981; contribs to New Testament and Theological jls. *Address:* Bishop's Croft, Birmingham, W Midlands B17 0BG. *T:* 021-427 2062. *Club:* Royal Commonwealth Society.

See also Rev. Canon D. M. Paton, Ven. M. J. M. Paton, Prof. Sir W. D. M. Paton.

BIRMINGHAM, Auxiliary Bishops of, (RC); *see* Cleary, Rt Rev. Joseph, McCartie, Rt Rev. P. L.

BIRMINGHAM, Provost of; *see* Moss, Very Rev. B. S.

BIRMINGHAM, Archdeacon of; *see* Hollis, Ven. G.

BIRSAY, Hon. Lord; Harald Robert Leslie, KT 1973; CBE 1963 (MBE (mil.) 1945); TD 1944; MA 1927, LLB (Glas.) 1930; QC (Scot.), 1949; DL Orkney, 1965; Hon. LLD: Strathclyde, 1966; Glasgow, 1966; Hon. FEIS 1966; Chairman, Scottish Land Court, 1965-78; *b* 8 May 1905; *s* of Robert Leslie, Master Mariner, Stromness, Orkney, and Margaret Mowat Cochrane, Stromness; *m* 1945, Robina Margaret Marwick, MB, ChB (Edin.), *o d* of ex-Provost J. G. Marwick, FSA (Scot.), Stromness, Orkney; one *s* one *d. Educ:* Earlston Public Sch.; Berwickshire High Sch.; Glasgow High Sch.; Glasgow Univ. Served in Glasgow High Sch. (1918-23) and Glasgow Univ. (1923-30) OTCs. Extracted as Solicitor, 1930; called to Scottish Bar, 1937. War of 1939-45 (MBE; despatches); served in the Royal Scots and on HQs 15 (S) Div.; 8 Corps and 21 Army Group; released, 1945, to TARO, as (Hon.) Lieut-Col. Standing Counsel to Dept of Agriculture; Junior Assessor to City of Edinburgh Assessor and Dean of Guild and Burgh Courts, 1949; Senior

Assessor, 1960; Advocate-Depute, Scottish Bar, 1947-51; Sheriff of Roxburgh, Berwick and Selkirk, 1956-61; Sheriff of Caithness, Sutherland, Orkney and Zetland, 1961-65. Candidate (Lab) for Orkney and Shetland Constituency, 1950; Chairman: Scottish Advisory Council on the Treatment of Offenders, 1959; Scottish Cttee of British Council, 1963-70; Scottish Joint Council for Teachers' Salaries, 1964; Executive Edinburgh Council of Social Service, 1956-69; Cttee on Gen. Med. Services in the Highlands and Islands, 1964-67; Loaningdale Approved Sch.; Nat. Savings Cttee for Scotland, 1965-72, Pres., 1972-78; Board of Governors, St Hilary's Sch., Edinburgh, 1959-81; Salvation Army Adv. Bd, Edinburgh, 1967-77; Scottish Adv. Cttee on the Travelling People, 1971-77; St Columba's Hospice, Edinburgh, 1971-81, now Vice-Pres.; Hon. President: Glasgow, Orkney and Shetland Association also Edinburgh, Orkney and Zetland Association, 1962; Scottish Council for National Parks until 1965; Hon. Vice-President, Boys' Brigade, 1966- (Hon. Pres., Leith Bn, 1963-); Scottish Council of Boys' Clubs and Youth Clubs, 1962; Shipwrecked Fishermen and Mariners' Royal Benevolent Society (Scotland), 1966; Orkney Council of Social Service, 1966; Pres., Scottish Nat. Dictionary Assoc., 1968-. Lord High Commissioner to the General Assembly of the Church of Scotland, 1965 and 1966. Hon. Air Cdre, No 2 (City of Edinburgh) Maritime HQ Unit, RAuxAF, 1967-82. *Address:* 27 Queensferry Road, Edinburgh EH4 3HB. *T:* 031-332 3315; Queenafjold, Birsay, Orkney KW17 2LZ. *T:* (Orkney) Birsay 286. *Clubs:* Royal Scots, Caledonian, Arts (Edinburgh).

BIRT, John; Director of Programmes, London Weekend Television, since 1982; *b* 10 Dec. 1944; *s* of Leo Vincent Birt and Ida Birt; *m* 1965, Jane Frances (*née* Lake); one *s* one *d. Educ:* St Mary's Coll., Liverpool; St Catherine's Coll., Oxford (MA). Producer, Nice Time, 1968-69; Joint Editor, World in Action, 1969-70; Producer, The Frost Programme, 1971-72; Executive Producer, Weekend World, 1972-74; Head of Current Affairs, LWT, 1974-77; Co-Producer, The Nixon Interviews, 1977; Controller of Features and Current Affairs, LWT, 1977-81. *Recreation:* walking. *Address:* c/o London Weekend Television, SE1. *T:* 01-261 3434.

BIRT, Prof. (Lindsay) Michael, CBE 1980; Vice-Chancellor, University of New South Wales, since 1981; *b* 18 Jan. 1932; *s* of Robert Birt and Florence Elizabeth Chapman; *m* 1959, Avis Jennypher Tapfield; two *s. Educ:* Melbourne Boys' High Sch.; Univ. of Melbourne; Univ. of Oxford. BAgrSc, BSc and PhD (Melb), DPhil (Oxon). Univ. of Melbourne: Lectr in Biochemistry, 1960-63, Sen. Lectr in Biochem., 1964; Sen. Lectr in Biochem., Univ. of Sheffield, 1964-67; Foundn Prof. of Biochemistry, ANU, 1967-73; Vice-Chancellor designate, Wollongong Univ. Coll., Nov. 1973; Vice-Chancellor, Univ. of Wollongong, 1975-81; Emer. Prof., ANU, 1974. Hon. DLitt Wollongong, 1981. *Publication:* Biochemistry of the Tissues (with W. Bartley and P. Banks), 1968 (London), 1970 (Germany, as Biochemie), 1972 (Japan). *Recreations:* music, reading. *Address:* University of New South Wales, PO Box 1, Kensington, NSW 2033, Australia. *T:* 02-663 0351. *Clubs:* Union (Sydney); Wollongong; Melbourne Cricket.

BIRT, Rev. Canon William Raymond; Assistant Rector of West Woodhay; *b* 25 Aug. 1911; *s* of Rev. Douglas Birt, Rector of Leconfield with Scorborough, and Dorothy Birt; *m* 1936, Marie Louise Jeaffreson; one *s* two *d. Educ:* Christ's Hospital; Ely Theological Coll. Journalist until 1940. Major, 22nd Dragoons (RAC), 1941-46 (despatches). Publisher, 1946-55. Deacon, 1956; priest, 1957; Curate, Caversham, 1956-59; Vicar, St George, Newbury, 1959-71; Rector of West Woodhay, 1971-81; Rural Dean of Newbury, 1969-73; Archdeacon of Berkshire, 1973-77; Hon. Canon of Christ Church Cathedral, Oxford, 1980. *Recreations:* gardens and gardening. *Address:* West Woodhay Rectory, Newbury, Berkshire RG15 0BL. *T:* Inkpen 359.

BIRTWISTLE, Maj.-Gen. Archibald Cull, CBE 1976 (OBE 1971); Signal Officer in Chief (Army), since 1980; *b* 19 Aug. 1927; *s* of Walter Edwin Birtwistle and Eila Louise Cull; *m* 1956, Sylvia Elleray; two *s* one *d. Educ:* Sir John Deane's Grammar School, Northwich; St John's Coll., Cambridge (MA Mech. Sciences). CEng, MIEE. Commissioned, Royal Signals, 1949; served: Korea (despatches, 1952); UK; BAOR; CCR Sigs 1 (Br) Corps, 1973-75; Dep. Comdt, RMCS, 1975-79; Chief Signal Officer, BAOR, 1979-80. *Recreations:* all sports, especially Rugby (former Chairman, Army Rugby Union), soccer and cricket; gardening. *Address:* Manor House, The Green, Romanby, Northallerton, North Yorks. *T:* Northallerton 2685.

BIRTWISTLE, Harrison; composer; an Associate Director, National Theatre, since 1975; *b* 1934; *m* Sheila; three *s. Educ:* Royal Manchester Coll. of Music; RAM. Dir of Music, Cranborne Chase Sch., 1962-65. Vis. Fellow, Princeton Univ., 1966-68; Cornell Vis. Prof. of Music, Swarthmore Coll., 1973; Vis. Slee Prof., State Univ. of NY at Buffalo, 1974-75. *Publications:* Refrains and Choruses, 1957; Monody for Corpus Christi, 1959; Précis, 1959; The World is Discovered, 1960; Chorales, 1962, 1963; Entre'actes and Sappho Fragments, 1964; Three Movements with Fanfares, 1964; Tragoedia, 1965; Ring a Dumb Carillon, 1965; Carmen Paschale, 1965; The Mark of the Goat, 1965, 1966; The Visions of Francesco Petrarca, 1966; Verses, 1966; Punch and Judy, 1966-67; Three Lessons in a Frame, 1967; Linoii, 1968; Nomos, 1968; Verses for Ensembles, 1969; Down by the Greenwood Side, 1969; Hoquetus David (arr. of Machaut), 1969; Cantata, 1969; Ut Hermita Solvs, 1969; Medusa, 1969-70; Prologue, 1970; Nenia on the Death of Orpheus, 1970; An Imaginary Landscape, 1971; Meridian, 1971; The Fields of Sorrow, 1971; Chronometer, 1971; Epilogue—Full Fathom Five, 1972; Tombeau, 1972; The Triumph of Time, 1972; La Plage: eight arias of remembrance, 1972; Dinah and Nick's Love Song, 1972; Chanson de Geste, 1973; The World is Discovered, 1973;

Grimethorpe Aria, 1973; 5 Chorale Preludes from Bach, 1973; Chorales from a Toyshop, 1973; Interludes from a Tragedy, 1973; Orpheus; Melencolia I 1975; Pulse Field, Bow Down, Silbury Air, 1977; For O, for O, the Hobby-horse is forgot, 1977; Carmen Arcardiae Mechanicae Perpetuum, 1978 agm, 1979; On the Sheer Threshold of the Night, 1980; Quintet, 1981; Pulse Sampler, 1981. *Address:* c/o Allied Artists Agency, 42 Montpelier Square, SW7 1JZ.

BISCOE, Rear-Adm. Alec Julian; *see* Tyndale-Biscoe.

BISCOE, Prof. Timothy John; Jodrell Professor of Physiology, University College London, since 1979; *b* 28 April 1932; *s* of late Rev. W. H. Biscoe and Mrs A M. G. Biscoe; *m* 1955, Daphne Miriam (*née* Gurton); one *s* two *d. Educ:* Latymer Upper School; The London Hospital Medical College. BSc (Hons) Physiology, 1953; MB, BS 1957. London Hospital, 1957-58; RAMC Short Service Commission, 1958-62; Physiologist, CDEE, Porton Down 1959-62; ARC Inst. of Animal Physiology, Babraham, 1962-65; Res. Fellow in Physiology, John Curtin Sch. of Med. Res., Canberra, 1965-66; Associate Res. Physiologist, Cardiovascular Res. Inst., UC Medical Center, San Francisco, 1966-68; University of Bristol: Res. Associate, Dept of Physiology, 1968-70; 2nd Chair of Physiology, 1970-79; Head of Dept of Physiology, 1975-79. Hon. Sec., Physiological Soc., 1980- (Sec., 1977). *Publications:* papers on neurophysiology in Journal of Physiology, etc. *Recreations:* looking, listening, reading. *Address:* Department of Physiology, University College London, Gower Street, WC1E 6BT. *T:* 01-387 7050.

BISHOP, family name of **Baron Bishopston.**

BISHOP, Alan Henry; Assistant Under-Secretary of State, Scottish Office, since 1980; *b* 12 Sept. 1929; *s* of Robert Bishop and May Watson; *m* 1959, Marjorie Anne Conlan; one *s* one *d. Educ:* George Heriot's Sch., Edinburgh; Edinburgh Univ. (MA 1st Cl. Hons Econ. Science, 1951, 2nd Cl. Hons History, 1952). Served RAF Educn Br., 1952-54. Asst Principal, Dept of Agric. for Scotland, 1954; Private Sec. to Parly Under-Secs of State, 1958-59; Principal, 1959; First Sec., Food and Agric., Copenhagen and The Hague, 1963-66; Asst Sec., Scottish Develt Dept, 1968; Asst Sec., Commn on the Constitution, 1969-73. *Recreation:* contract bridge (Pres., Scottish Bridge Union, 1979-80). *Address:* 10 Wester Coates Avenue, Edinburgh EH12 5LS. *T:* 031-337 2163. *Clubs:* Royal Commonwealth Society; Melville (Edinburgh).

BISHOP, Maj.-Gen. Sir Alec, (Alexander); *see* Bishop, Maj.-Gen. Sir W. H. A.

BISHOP, Ann, FRS 1959; ScD; *b* 19 Dec. 1899; *o d* of late James Kimberly and Ellen Bishop. *Educ:* Manchester High Sch. for Girls; Manchester Univ.; Cambridge Univ. BSc 1921, DSc 1932, Manchester; PhD 1926, ScD 1941, Cambridge. Hon. Research Fellow, Manchester Univ., 1925-26; Research Asst, Medical Research Council, 1926-29; Beit Memorial Research Fellow, 1929-32; Yarrow Fellow of Girton Coll., Cambridge, 1932-37; Research Fellow of Girton Coll., Cambridge, 1937-66, Life Fellow, 1966; Mem., MRC Staff, 1937-42; Director, MRC Chemotherapy Research Unit at the Molteno Inst., Univ. of Cambridge, 1942-64. *Publications:* articles on the biology of Protozoa, and Chemotherapy, published in Scientific Journals. *Address:* 47 Sherlock Close, Cambridge CB3 0HP.

BISHOP, Dr Arthur Clive; Deputy Director, British Museum (Natural History), since 1982, and Keeper of Mineralogy since 1975; *b* 9 July 1930; *s* of late Charles Henry Bishop and Hilda (*née* Clowes); *m* 1962, Helen (*née* Bennison); one *d. Educ:* Wolstanton County Grammar Sch., Newcastle, Staffs; King's Coll., Univ. of London. BSc 1951, PhD 1954. Geologist, HM Geological Survey, 1954; Lectr in Geology, Queen Mary Coll., Univ. of London, 1958; Principal Sci. Officer, British Museum (Natural History), 1969, Deputy Keeper 1972. Geological Society: Daniel Pidgeon Fund, 1958; Murchison Fund, 1970; Vice-Pres., 1977-78; Mineralogical Society: Gen. Sec. 1965-72; Vice-Pres., 1973-74; Pres., Geologists' Assoc., 1978-80; Vice-Pres., Inst. of Science Technology, 1973-82. *Publications:* An Outline of Crystal Morphology, 1967; (with W. R. Hamilton and A. R. Woolley) Hamlyr Guide to Minerals, Rocks and Fossils, 1974; papers in various jls, mainly on geology of Channel Is and Brittany, and on dioritic rocks. *Recreations* drawing and painting. *Address:* British Museum (Natural History), Cromwell Road, SW7 5BD. *T:* 01-589 6323.

BISHOP, Rt. Rev. Clifford Leofric Purdy; *b* 1908; *s* of Rev. E. J. Bishop *m* 1949, Ivy Winifred Adams. *Educ:* St John's, Leatherhead; Christ's Coll. Cambridge (MA); Lincoln Theological Coll. Deacon 1932; Priest, 1933 Curacies, 1932-41; Vicar, St Geo., Camberwell, 1941-49; Rural Dean, 1943-49; Curate-in-charge, All Saints, Newington, 1944-47; Rector of: Blakeney 1949-53 (Rural Dean of Walsingham, 1951-53); Bishop Wearmouth, 1953-62 (Rural Dean of Wearmouth and Surrogate, 1953-62); Hon. Canon of Durham, 1958-62; Bishop Suffragan of Malmesbury, 1962-73; Canon of Bristol, 1962-73. *Address:* Rectory Cottage, Cley-next-Sea, Holt, Norfolk. *T.* Cley 740250.

BISHOP, Sir Frederick (Arthur), Kt 1975; CB 1960; CVO 1957; Director-General of the National Trust, 1971-75; *b* 4 Dec. 1915; *o s* of A. J. Bishop, Bristol; *m* 1940, Elizabeth Finlay Stevenson; two *s* one *d. Educ:* Colston's Hospital, Bristol. LLB (London). Inland Revenue, 1934. Served in RAF and

Air Transport Auxiliary, 1942–46. Ministry of Food, 1947, where Principal Private Secretary to Ministers, 1949–52; Asst Secretary, Cabinet Office, 1953–55; Principal Private Secretary to the Prime Minister, 1956–59; Deputy Secretary: of the Cabinet, 1959–61; Min. of Agriculture, Fisheries and Food, 1961–64; Perm. Sec., Min. of Lands and Natural Resources, 1964–65, resigned. Chm., Home Grown Timber Advisory Cttee, 1966–73; Member: BBC Gen. Adv. Council, 1971–75; Crafts Adv. Council, 1973–75. Director: S. Pearson & Son Ltd, 1970–75; Pearson Longman, 1970–77; English China Clays Ltd, 1975–; Devon and Cornwall Bd, Lloyds Bank Ltd, 1976–. Mem., Devon and Cornwall Reg. Cttee, Nat. Trust, 1976–. *Address:* Lombard Mill, Lanteglos-by-Fowey, Cornwall.

BISHOP, George Robert, DPhil; FRSE; FInstP; Director, Ispra Establishment, Joint Research Centre, European Commission, Ispra, Italy, since 1982; *b* 16 Jan. 1927; *s* of George William Bishop and Lilian Elizabeth Garrod; *m* 1952, Adriana Giuseppina, *d* of Luigi Caberlotto and Giselda Mazzariol; two *s* one *d*. *Educ:* Christ Church, Oxford (MA, DPhil). ICI Research Fellow, Univ. of Oxford, 1951; Research Fellow, St Antony's Coll., Oxford, 1952; Chercheur, Ecole Normale Supérieure, Paris, 1954; Ingénieur-Physicien, Laboratoire de l'Accelerateur Linéaire, ENS, Orsay, 1958; Prof., Faculté des Sciences, Univ. de Paris, 1962; Kelvin Prof. of Natural Philosophy, Univ. of Glasgow, 1964–76; Dir, Dept of Natural and Physical Sciences, JRC, Ispra, 1974–81. Hon. DSc, Strathclyde, 1979. *Publications:* Handbuch der Physik, Band XLII, 1957, β and X-Ray Spectroscopy, 1960; Nuclear Structure and Electromagnetic Interactions, 1965; numerous papers in learned jls on nuclear and high energy physics. *Recreations:* literature, music, swimming, tennis, gardening, travel. *Address:* via Santa Caterina 12, Leggiuno, Varese, Italy. *T:* (0332) 647 913.

BISHOP, Sir George (Sidney), Kt 1975; CB 1958; OBE 1947; Director, Booker McConnell Ltd, 1961–82 (Vice-Chairman, 1970–71, Chairman 1972–79); Director: Barclays Bank International, since 1972; Barclays Bank Ltd, since 1974; Ranks Hovis McDougall, since 1976; International Basic Economy Corporation, USA, since 1980; *b* 15 Oct. 1913; *o s* of late J. and M. Bishop; *m* 1940, Marjorie Woodruff (marr. diss. 1961); one *d*; *m* 1961, Una Padel. *Educ:* Ashton-in-Makerfield Grammar Sch.; London Sch. of Economics. Social service work in distressed areas, 1935–38; SW Durham Survey, 1939; Ministry of Food, 1940; Private Secretary to Minister of Food, 1945–49; Under-Secretary, Ministry of Agriculture, Fisheries and Food, 1949–59, Dep. Secretary, 1959–61. Chm. Bookers Agricultural Holdings Ltd, 1964–70; Director: Nigerian Sugar Co. Ltd, 1966–70; Agricultural Mortgage Corp. Ltd, 1973–79. Chairman: Internat. Sugar Council, 1957; West India Cttee, 1969–71 (Pres., 1977–); Industry Co-operative Programme, 1976–78; Council, Overseas Develt Inst., 1977–; Vice-Chm., Internat. Wheat Council, 1959; Member: Panel for Civil Service Manpower Review, 1968–70; Royal Commn on the Press, 1974–77; Council, CBI, 1973–80; Council, RGS, 1980– (Hon. Fellow, 1980; a Vice-Pres., 1981); Dir, Industry Council for Develt, USA (Chm., 1979); Governor, Nat. Inst. for Economic and Social Research, 1968–. Mem., Management Cttee, Mount Everest Foundn, 1980–. *Recreations:* mountaineering, motoring, photography. *Address:* Brenva, Eghams Wood Road, Beaconsfield, Bucks. *T:* Beaconsfield 3096. *Clubs:* Reform, Alpine, Royal Geographical Society, MCC; Club Alpin Français.

BISHOP, Sir Harold, Kt, *cr* 1955; CBE 1938; FCGI; BSc (Engineering) London; Hon. FIEE, FIMechE; FIEEE; *b* 29 Oct. 1900; 3rd *s* of Henry Thomas Bishop; *m* 1925, Madge Adeline, *d* of Frank Harry Vaus; two *d* (one *s* decd). *Educ:* Alleyn's Sch., Dulwich; City and Guilds Coll. Engineer, HM Office of Works, 1920–22; Engineer, Marconi's Wireless Telegraph Co. Ltd, 1922–23; Senior Supt BBC, 1923–29; Asst Chief Engineer, BBC, 1929–43; Chief Engineer, 1943–52; Dir of Engineering, 1952–63; Consultant, BICC Gp, 1963–68. Hon. FIEE (Pres. 1953–54, Vice-Pres. 1948–53); President: Electrical Industries Benevolent Assoc., 1955–56; Association of Supervising Electrical Engineers, 1956–58; Institution of Electrical and Electronic Techn. Engineers, 1965–69; Royal Television Soc., 1960–62; Fellow, Imperial Coll. of Science and Technology. *Address:* Little Carbis, Harborough Hill, Pulborough, W Sussex. *T:* West Chiltington 3325.

BISHOP, Rev. Hugh, (William Fletcher Bishop); Licensed to preach, Diocese of Wakefield; *b* 17 May 1907; *e s* of John and Mary Bishop, Haughton House, Shifnal, Shropshire. *Educ:* Malvern Coll.; Keble Coll., Oxford (MA). Cuddesdon Coll., Oxford, 1932–33; Deacon, 1933; Priest, 1934. Curate of St Michael's, Workington, 1933–35; Curate of Cuddesdon and Lectr, Cuddesdon, 1935–37. Mem., Community of the Resurrection, Mirfield, (taking name of Hugh), 1940–74; Chaplain to the Forces (EC), 1940–45 (POW, 1942–45); Warden, Hostel of the Resurrection, Leeds, 1946–49; Guardian of Novices, Mirfield, 1949–52; Principal of the College, 1956–65, Father Superior of the Community of the Resurrection, 1965–74, released from the Community of the Resurrection, 1974. *Publications:* The Passion Drama, 1955; The Easter Drama, 1958; Life is for Loving, 1961; (contrib. to) Mirfield Essays in Christian Belief, 1962; The Man for Us, 1968. *Address:* 19 St John's Terrace, Leeds LS3 1DY. *T:* Leeds 459180.

BISHOP, James Drew; Editor and Publisher of the Illustrated London News, since 1971; *b* 18 June 1929; *s* of late Sir Patrick Bishop, MBE, MP, and Eva Drew; *m* 1959, Brenda Pearson; two *s*. *Educ:* Haileybury; Corpus Christi Coll., Cambridge. Reporter, Northampton Chronicle & Echo, 1953; joined editorial staff of The Times, 1954; Foreign Correspondent, 1957–64; Foreign News Editor, 1964–66; Features Editor, 1966–70. Contributor of American

section of Annual Register, 1960–, Mem. Adv. Bd, 1970–. *Publications:* A Social History of Edwardian Britain, 1977; Social History of the First World War, 1982. *Recreations:* reading, walking, looking and listening. *Address:* (home) 11 Willow Road, NW3 1TJ. *T:* 01-435 4403; (office) 4 Bloomsbury Square, WC1. *T:* 01-404 4300. *Clubs:* United Oxford & Cambridge University, MCC.

BISHOP, Dr John Edward; Principal Lecturer, Tutor in Organ and Head of Admissions, Birmingham School of Music, since 1979; *b* 23 Feb. 1935; *s* of late Reginald John Bishop and of Eva Bishop (*née* Lucas). *Educ:* Cotham Sch., Bristol; St John's Coll., Cambridge (Exhibr); Reading and Edinburgh Univs. MA, MusB Cantab; DMus Edin.; FRCO (CHM); ADCM. John Stewart of Rannoch Schol. (Univ. prize) 1954. Organist and Asst Dir of Music, Worksop Coll., Notts, 1958–69; Dir of Music, Worksop Coll., 1969–73; Birmingham School of Music: Dir of Studies, 1973–74; Sen. Lectr, 1974–79. Hon. Dir of Music, Cotham Parish Church, Bristol, 1976–; Organ recitalist (incl. many broadcasts) and choral conductor, accompanist, examiner, adjudicator and reviewer, 1960–. Former Pres., Sheffield, Birmingham and Bristol Organists' Assocs. *Publications:* various articles on history and practice of church music and 19th century organ design. *Recreations:* walking, ecclesiology, savouring cities and towns, railways, architecture. *Address:* 93 High Kingsdown, Bristol BS2 8ER. *T:* Bristol 423373.

BISHOP, Dame (Margaret) Joyce, DBE 1963 (CBE 1953); MA Oxon; Head Mistress of The Godolphin and Latymer School, Hammersmith, W6, 1935–63, retired; *b* 28 July 1896; 2nd *d* of Charles Benjamin and Amy Bishop. *Educ:* Edgbaston High Sch., Birmingham; Lady Margaret Hall, Oxford. English Mistress, Hertfordshire and Essex High Sch., 1918–24; Head Mistress, Holly Lodge High Sch., Smethwick, Staffs, 1924–35. Member Working Party set up by Minister of Education to enquire into Recruitment of Women to Teaching Profession, 1947. President, Association of Head Mistresses, 1950–52. Member: Secondary School Examinations Council, 1950–62; University Grants Cttee, 1961–63; Council for Professions Supplementary to Medicine, 1961–70; TV Research Cttee set up by Home Secretary, 1963–69. Chairman, Joint Cttee of the Four Secondary Associations, 1956–58. FKC 1973. *Recreations:* reading, the theatre. *Address:* 22 Malbrook Road, Putney, SW15. *T:* 01-788 5862.

BISHOP, Michael David; Chairman and Managing Director, British Midland Holdings Ltd, since 1978; Chairman and Managing Director, British Midland Airways Ltd, its subsidiary and associated cos, since 1978; Board Member, East Midlands Electricity Board, since 1980; *b* 10 Feb. 1942; *s* of Clive Leonard Bishop and Lilian Bishop (*née* Frost). *Educ:* Mill Hill School. Joined Mercury Airlines, Manchester, 1963; British Midland Airways Ltd: Manager, North of England, 1964–69; General Manager and Director, 1969–72; Managing Director, 1972–. Dir, E Midlands Reg. Bd, Central Indep. Television, 1981–; Chm., Manx Airlines Ltd, 1982–. *Publications:* contribs to aviation publications. *Recreation:* music. *Address:* Staunton House, Staunton Harold, near Ashby-de-la-Zouch, Leicestershire LE6 5RW. *T:* Ashby-de-la-Zouch 414082. *Club:* St James's (Manchester).

BISHOP, Prof. Peter Orlebar, DSc; FRS 1977; FAA; Visiting Fellow, Department of Behavioural Biology, Research School of Biological Sciences, Australian National University, since 1983; *b* 14 June 1917; *s* of Ernest John Hunter Bishop and Mildred Alice Havelock Bishop (*née* Vidal); *m* 1942, Hilare Louise Holmes; one *s* two *d*. *Educ:* Barker Coll., Hornsby; Univ. of Sydney (MB, BS, DSc). Neurol Registrar, Royal Prince Alfred Hosp., Sydney, 1941–42; Surgeon Lieut, RANR, 1942–46; Fellow, Postgrad. Cttee in Medicine (Sydney Univ.) at Nat. Hosp., Queen Square, London, 1946–47 and Dept Anatomy, UCL, 1947–50; Sydney University: Res. Fellow, Dept Surgery, 1950–51; Sen. Lectr, 1951–54, Reader, 1954–55, Prof. and Head, Dept Physiology, 1955–67; Prof. and Head of Dept of Physiology, John Curtin School of Medical Res., ANU, 1967–82. Vis. Prof., Japan Soc. for Promotion of Science, 1974. FAA 1967; Fellow, Aust. Postgrad. Fedn in Medicine, 1969. Hon. Member: Neurosurgical Soc. of Aust., 1970; Ophthalmol Soc. of NZ, 1973; Aust. Assoc. of Neurologists, 1977. *Publications:* contribs on physiological optics and visual neurophysiology. *Recreation:* bushwalking. *Address:* Department of Behavioural Biology, Research School of Biological Sciences, Australian National University, Canberra, ACT 2600, Australia.

BISHOP, Prof. Richard Evelyn Donohue, CBE 1979; FRS 1980, FEng 1977, FIMechE, FRINA, MRAeS; Vice-Chancellor and Principal, Brunel University, since 1981; Fellow of University College London, since 1964; *b* London, 1 Jan. 1925; *s* of Rev. Dr N. R. Bishop; *m* 1949, Jean Paterson, London; one *s* one *d*. *Educ:* The Roan Sch., Greenwich. RNVR, 1943–46. University Coll., London, 1946–49 (DSc Eng); Commonwealth Fund Fellow in Stanford Univ., California, 1949–51 (MS, PhD). Sen. Scientific Officer, Ministry of Supply, 1951–52; Cambridge Univ.: Demonstrator, 1952; Fellow of Pembroke Coll., 1954; University Lecturer in Engineering, 1955 (MA, ScD); Kennedy Prof. of Mechanical Engrg, Univ. of London, 1957–82. Visiting Prof.: Massachusetts Institute of Technology, Summer, 1959; Visiting Lecturer, National Science Foundation, USA, Spring, 1961; Member of Council, Instn of Mechanical Engineers, 1961–64, 1969–70; President, British Acoustical Soc., 1966–68; Hon. Member Royal Corps of Naval Constructors, 1968; John Orr Meml Lectr, S Africa, 1971; Originator of Greenwich Forum, 1974; C. Gelderman Foundn Vis. Prof., Technical Univ., Delft, 1976. Mem. Senate, London Univ., 1980–81. George Stephenson Res. Prize, IMechE, 1959; Thomas Hawksley Gold Medal, IMechE, 1965; Silver Medal of Skoda Works, 1967; Křižík Gold Medal, Acad. Sci. CSSR, 1969; Rayleigh Gold Medal, Brit.

Acoustical Soc., 1972; Clayton Prize, IMechE, 1972; RINA Bronze Medals, 1975, 1977. *Publications:* (with D. C. Johnson) Vibration Analysis Tables, 1956; (with D. C. Johnson) The Mechanics of Vibration, 1960; (with G. M. L. Gladwell and S. Michaelson) The Matrix Analysis of Vibration, 1965; Vibration, 1965; (with W. G. Price) Probabilistic Theory of Ship Dynamics, 1974; (with W. G. Price) Hydroelasticity of Ships, 1979; many scientific papers. *Recreation:* sailing. *Address:* Brunel University, Uxbridge, Middlesex UB8 3PH. *Club:* Royal Naval and Royal Albert Yacht (Portsmouth) (Chm., 1979-82).

BISHOP, Ronald Eric, CBE 1946; FRAeS; Deputy Managing Director, de Havilland Aircraft Co. Ltd, 1958-64; Design Director, de Havilland Aircraft Co. Ltd, Hatfield, 1946-64; *b* 1903. Joined de Havilland Aircraft Co. Ltd, as an apprentice, 1921; entered Drawing Office; appointed in charge, 1936. Responsible for following designs: Flamingo, Mosquito, Hornet, Vampire, Dove, Venom, Heron, DH 108, DH 110, Comet Jet Airliner. Gold Medal, RAeS, 1964.

BISHOP, Stanley Victor, MC 1944; management consultant; Director, Britarge Ltd; *b* 11 May 1916; *s* of George Stanley Bishop, MA; *m* 1946, Dorothy Primrose Dodds, Berwick-upon-Tweed; two *s* one *d. Educ:* Leeds. Articled to Beevers & Adgie, Leeds; CA 1937. Served War of 1939-45: enlisted London Scottish (TA), 1938; commissioned, West Yorkshire Regt, 1940; served overseas, 1940-45, Middle East, India and Burma (MC) (Hon. Major). Joined Albert E. Reed and Co. Ltd, 1946; Brush Group, 1951; Massey Ferguson Ltd, 1959-79; Perkins Diesel Engine Group, 1963. Man. Dir, British Printing Corp., 1966-70; Chm. and Dir various cos, 1970-73; Dir, Massey-Ferguson Europe Ltd, 1973-79. Has lectured to British Institute of Management, Institute of Chartered Accountants, Oxford Business Summer School, etc. *Publication:* Business Planning and Control, 1966. *Recreations:* golf, swimming, pottering. *Address:* Halidon, Rogers Lane, Ettington, Stratford-upon-Avon, Warwicks CV37 7TA. *Club:* Army and Navy.

BISHOP, Stephen; *see* Bishop-Kovacevich.

BISHOP, Terence Alan Martyn, FBA 1971; *b* 1907; *s* of Cosby Martyn Bishop. *Educ:* Christ's Hospital; Keble Coll., Oxford. 2nd Mods, 1928; 2nd Hist. 1930; BA 1931, MA 1947. *Publications:* books and articles on palaeography, etc, incl.: Facsimiles of English Royal Writs to AD 1100 (with P. Chaplais), 1957; Scriptores Regis, 1961; (ed) Umbrae Codicum Occidentalium (Vol. 10), 1966 (Holland); English Caroline Minuscule, 1971. *Address:* The Annexe, Manor House, Hemingford Grey, Huntingdon, Cambs.

BISHOP, Instructor Rear-Adm. Sir William (Alfred), KBE 1955 (OBE 1941); CB 1950; MA; Director of Naval Education Service, 1948-56, retired; *b* 29 May 1899; *s* of late Alfred Bishop, Purley, Surrey; *m* 1929, Stella Margaret Macfarlane, MBE; no *c. Educ:* Whitgift Sch.; Corpus Christi, Cambridge. 2nd Lieut, RE Signals, 1918; Cambridge 1919. Entered RN as Instructor Lieut, 1922; Instructor Lieut-Comdr, 1928; Instructor Comdr, 1936; Instructor Captain, 1945; Instructor Rear-Adm., 1951. Chief Naval Meteorological Officer, South Atlantic Station, 1939; Asst Director of Naval Meteorological Service, 1944; Dep. Director of Education Dept, 1947. Naval ADC to the King, 1950. Retired Sept. 1956. *Address:* Myrtle Cottage, Burlawn, Wadebridge, Cornwall PL27 7LD. *T:* Wadebridge 2773.

BISHOP, Rev. William Fletcher; *see* Bishop, Rev. Hugh.

BISHOP, Maj.-Gen. Sir (William Henry) Alexander, (Alec), KCMG 1964 (CMG 1961); CB 1946; CVO 1961; OBE 1941; psc; psa; *b* 20 June 1897; *s* of Walter Edward and Elizabeth Bishop; *m* 1926, Mary Patricia *d* (1977), *d* of Henry Corbett, Physician, Plymouth; one *s. Educ:* Plymouth Coll.; RMC Sandhurst. Served European War, 1914-19, Mesopotamia and Palestine; with Dorset Regt; Bt Lt-Col 1938; Col 1941; Brig. 1941; Maj.-Gen. 1944. Served in India, 1919-25, War Office, 1933-35 and Colonial Office, 1937-39; served in East Africa, North Africa, and West Africa during War, 1939-44; Director of Quartering, War Office, 1944-45; Chief of Information Services and Public Relations, CCG, 1945-46; Deputy Chief of Staff, CCG, 1946-48; Regional Commissioner, Land North Rhine/Westphalia, 1948-50; Asst Sec., CRO, 1951; Principal Staff Officer to Secretary of State for Commonwealth Relations, 1953-57; British Dep. High Commissioner in Calcutta, 1957-62; Director of Information Services and Cultural Relations, CRO, 1962-64; British High Commissioner, Cyprus, 1964-65, retired. CStJ 1951. Ehren-Nadel, Johanniter Orden, 1951; Comdr, Verdienstkreuz (Germany), 1978. *Recreations:* reading, gardening. *Address:* Combe Lodge, Beckley, Sussex. *T:* Beckley 221. *Clubs:* Army and Navy; Dormy House (Rye); Bengal (Calcutta).

BISHOP-KOVACEVICH, Stephen; pianist; *b* 17 Oct. 1940. *Educ:* studied under Lev Shorr and Myra Hess. Solo and orchestral debut, San Francisco, USA 1951; London debut, Nov. 1961. Concert tours: in England, Europe and USA, with many of the world's leading orchestras, incl. New York Philharmonic, Los Angeles Philharmonic, Israel Philharmonic, Amsterdam Concertgebouw, London Symphony, London Philharmonic, and BBC Symphony. Has appeared at Edinburgh, Bath, Berlin and San Sebastian Festivals. Gave 1st performance of Richard Rodney Bennett's Piano Concerto, 1969 (this work is dedicated to and has been recorded by him, under Alexander Gibson). Performed all Mozart Piano concertos, 1969-71. Edison

Award for his recording of Bartok's 2nd Piano Concerto and Stravinsky Piano Concerto, with BBC Symphony Orchestra, under Colin Davis *Recreations:* chess, films, tennis. *Address:* c/o Harrison-Parrott Ltd, 1. Penzance Place, W11 4PA. *T:* 01-229 9166.

BISHOPSTON, Baron *cr* 1981 (Life Peer), of Newark in the County o Nottinghamshire; **Edward Stanley Bishop,** PC 1977; JP; AMRAeS, MIED *b* 3 Oct. 1920; *e s* of Frank Stanley Bishop and Constance Camilla Bishop *(née* Dawbney); *m* 1945, Winifred Mary Bryant, JP, *o c* of Frank and Elizabeth Bryant; four *d. Educ:* S Bristol Central Sch.; Merchant Venturers Technical Coll.; Bristol Univ. Former Aeronautical Design Engineer, (British Aircraft Corp.). Member Bristol City Council, 1946-59, 1963-66 (Dep Leader and Chm. Finance and General Purposes Cttee, 1956-59). JP, City anc County of Bristol, 1957-73, Notts 1973-; Visiting Magistrate, HM Bristo Prison, 1959-71. Contested (Lab): Bristol West, 1950; Exeter, 1951; S Gloucester, 1955; MP (Lab) Newark, Notts, 1964-79; Chm., SW Reg Council, Labour Party, 1953-54; Asst Govt Whip, 1966-67; Opposition Spokesman: on Agric., 1970; on Aviation, Trade and Industry, 1970-74; Parly Sec., MAFF, March-Sept. 1974; Minister of State, MAFF, 1974-79; UK Parly deleg. to N Atlantic Assembly, 1966-74, and Chm., Assembly's Economic Cttee, 1969-72. Promoted Matrimonial Property Bill, 1969-70. Vice-Presiden RDC Assoc., 1965-74; Member: Archbishop of Canterbury's Commn on Organisation of Church by Dioceses in London and SE England, 1965-67 Redundant Churches Fund, 1970-74; Council, Nat. Trust, 1980-. A Church Commissioner, 1968-; Second Church Estates Comr, 1974. TEng (CEI) FAMS. *Recreations:* archæology, genealogy; being with family. *Address:* 5 London Road, Newark-on-Trent, Nottinghamshire NG24 1RZ. *T:* Newark 702443.

BISS, Godfrey Charles D'Arcy; retired as Senior Partner, Ashurst, Morris Crisp & Co., Solicitors, 1977; *b* 2 Sept. 1909; *s* of Gerald Biss and Sarah Ann Coutts Allan; *m* 1946, Margaret Jean Ellis; two *s. Educ:* St Paul's Sch (Scholar); Worcester Coll., Oxford (Exhibitioner). 1st Class Jurisprudence 1932. Solicitor, 1935; Partner in Ashurst, Morris, Crisp & Co., 1947. Roya Artillery, 1940-46; Staff Capt. RA, 23rd Indian Div. Chairman: The Fairey Company Ltd, 1958-70; UKO International (formerly UK Optical & Industrial Holdings Ltd), 1958-78; Director: Siebe Gorman & Co. Ltd 1963-81; Trafalgar House Ltd, to 1981; International Press Centre Ltd *Recreations:* gardening, racing. *Address:* Swandon, Thornborough Buckingham MK18 2DJ. *T:* Buckingham 2157. *Club:* Oriental.

BISSELL, Claude Thomas, CC 1969; MA, PhD; FRSC 1957; Professor University of Toronto, since 1971 (President of the University, 1958-71); *b* 10 Feb. 1916; *m* 1945, Christina Flora Gray; one *d. Educ:* University o Toronto; Cornell Univ. BA 1936, MA 1937, Toronto; PhD Cornell, 1940 Instructor in English, Cornell, 1938-41; Lecturer in English, Cornell, 1938-41 Lecturer in English, Toronto, 1941-42. Canadian Army, 1942-46; demobilised as Capt. University of Toronto: Asst Prof. of English, 1947-51; Assoc. Prof of English, 1951-56; Prof. of English, 1962; Asst to Pres., 1948-52; Vice-Pres. 1952-56; Dean in Residence, University Coll., 1946-56; Pres., Carleton Univ. Ottawa, 1956-58; Chm., The Canada Council, 1960-62. President, Nat Conference of Canadian Universities and Colleges, 1962-; Chairman Canadian Universities Foundation, 1962-; President, World University Service of Canada, 1962-63. Visiting Prof. of Canadian Studies, Harvard 1967-68. Aggrey-Fraser-Guggisberg Meml Lectr, Ghana Univ., 1976. Hon DLitt: Manitoba, 1958; W Ontario, 1971; Lethbridge, 1972; Leeds, 1976 Toronto, 1977; Hon. LLD: McGill, 1958; Queen's, 1959; New Brunswick 1959; Carleton, 1960; Montreal, 1960; The St Lawrence, 1962; British Columbia, 1962; Michigan, 1963; Columbia, 1965; Laval, 1966; Prince o Wales Coll., 1967; Windsor, 1968; St Andrews, 1972. *Publications:* (ed University College, A Portrait, 1853-1953, 1953; (ed) Canada's Crisis in Higher Education, 1957; (ed) Our Living Tradition, 1957; (ed) Grea Canadian Writing, 1966; The Strength of the University, 1968; Halfway up Parnassus, 1974; The Humanities in the University, 1977; number of article on literary subjects in Canadian and American jls. *Address:* 229 Erskin Avenue, Toronto, Ontario, Canada. *Clubs:* Arts and Letters, York (Toronto) Cercle Universitaire (Ottawa).

BISZTYGA, Jan; Officer's Cross of the Order of Polonia Restituta 1970 Order of Merit 1973; Ambassador of Poland to the Court of St James's 1978-81; *b* 19 Jan. 1933; *s* of Kazimierz Bisztyga; *m* 1956, Otylia; one *s Educ:* Jagiellonian Univ. (MSc Biochemistry). Asst Professor, Jagiellonia Univ., Cracow, 1954-57; political youth movement, 1956-59; Min. fo Foreign Affairs, 1959-63; Attaché, New Delhi, 1963-64; Min. for Foreig Affairs, 1964-69; Head of Planning Dept, Min. for Foreign Affairs, 1969-71 Dep. Foreign Minister, 1972-75; Ambassador in Athens, 1975-78. *Recreations* game shooting, fishing, history. *Address:* c/o Foreign Office, Warsaw, Poland *Club:* Travellers'.

BJARNASON, Sigurdur; Commander with Star, Order of the Icelandic Falcon, 1950; Hon. Emblem, Foundation of the Icelandic Republic, 1944 Ambassador of Iceland (stationed in Reykjavik) to India, Thailand and othe West Asian countries, since 1982; *b* 18 Dec. 1915; *s* of Bjarni Sigurdsson and Björg Bjornsdóttir; *m* 1956, Olöf Pálsdóttir, sculptress; one *s* one *d. Educ* Univ. of Iceland (Law); Univ. of Cambridge (Internat. and Company Law) Editor of weekly newspaper, 1942-47; Political Editor, Morgunblaðid, 1947 56, Editor in Chief, 1956-70. Mem. Icelandic Parlt (Althing), 1942-70; Pres Lower House, 1949-56 and 1963-70; Chm. Cttee of Foreign Affairs, 1963-70

Mem. govt and municipal cttees, including Pres. Municipal Council of Isfajórdur, 1946-50; Mem. Council of State Radio of Iceland, 1947-70, Chm. 1959 and Vice-Chm. 1960-70. Pres. Icelandic Sect. of Soc. for Interscandinavian Understanding, 1965-70. Member Nordic Council, 1952-59 and 1963-70; Vice-Pres., 1952-56 and 1959; Pres., 1965 and 1970. Delegate of Iceland to UN Gen. Assembly, 1960, 1961 and 1962; Mem. Cultural Cttee of Nordic Countries, 1954-70. Mem. Icelandic Cttee on territorial rights, 1957-58. Ambassador to Denmark, 1970-76; to Turkey, 1970-76; to China, 1973-76. Commander of the Finnish Lion, 1958; Commander, Order of the Vasa (Sweden), 1958; Grand Cross: Order of Dannebrog (Denmark), 1970; Order of Orange-Nassau (Netherlands), 1982. *Publications:* articles for foreign periodicals, especially within the field of culture and Scandinavian co-operation. *Recreations:* fishing, bird watching. *Address:* Utsalir, Seltjarnarnes, Iceland.

BJELKE-PETERSEN, Hon. Johannes, MLA; Premier of Queensland, since 1968; *b* Dannevirke, NZ, 13 Jan. 1911; *s* of late C. G. Bjelke-Petersen, Denmark; *m* 1952, Florence Isabel (elected as Senator for Queensland in Commonwealth Parliament, 1981), *d* of J. P. Gilmour; one *s* three *d. Educ:* Taabinga Valley Sch.; corresp. courses, and privately. MLA National Party (formerly Country Party): for Nanango, 1947-50; for Barambah, 1950-. Minister for Works and Housing, Qld, 1963-68. *Address:* (office) Premier's Department, George Street, Brisbane, Queensland 4000, Australia; (home) Bethany, Kingaroy, Queensland 4610.

BJÖRNSSON, Henrik Sveinsson, KBE (Hon.) 1963; Icelandic diplomat; Ambassador to Belgium, Luxembourg and Greece, concurrently accredited to European Economic Community, and Permanent Icelandic Representative to NATO, since 1979; *b* 2 Sept. 1914; *s* of Sveinn Björnsson (late President of Iceland) and Georgia Hoff-Hansen; *m* 1941, Gróa Torfhildur Jónsdóttir; one *s* two *d. Educ:* Reykjavik Grammar Sch.; Univ. of Iceland. Graduated in Law, 1939. Entered Foreign Service, 1939; served in Copenhagen, Washington, DC, Oslo, Paris and Revkjavik; Secretary to President of Iceland, 1952-56; Secretary-General of Min. of Foreign Affairs, Iceland, 1956-61; Ambassador to: the Court of St James's, 1961-65, also to Royal Netherlands Court, and Minister to Spain and Portugal, 1961-65; Belgium and Permanent Representative to NATO, 1965-67, France, Luxembourg, Yugoslavia, 1965-76, UAR and Ethiopia, 1971-76, and concurrently Permanent Rep. to Council of Europe, 1968-70, and OECD and UNESCO, 1965-76; Permt Under Secretary, Ministry for Foreign Affairs, 1976-79. Kt Comdr of the Order of the Icelandic Falcon, 1963. Holds various foreign decorations. *Address:* Ministry for Foreign Affairs, Reykjavik, Iceland.

BLACHE-FRASER, Louis Nathaniel, HBM 1971; CMG 1959; Chairman, Insurance Brokers West Indies Ltd; Director, Furness Trinidad Ltd; George Wimpey (Caribbean) Ltd; Central Bank of Trinidad and Tobago; Trinidad Building and Loan Association; National Insurance Board; *b* 19 Feb. 1904; *s* of late Winford and Emma Blache-Fraser, Trinidad; *m* 1941, Gwenyth, *d* of George Kent, Grenada; two *s* one *d* (and one *d* decd). *Educ:* Queen's Royal Coll., Trinidad. Joined Trinidad and Tobago Government Service, 1924; Dep. Accountant-General, 1947; Accountant-General, 1948; Dep. Financial Secretary, 1952; Financial Secretary, 1953; Financial Secretary, The West Indies, 1956-60; Chairman, Public Service Commission of The West Indies, 1961-62. Asst Sec., Alstons Ltd, 1962-65, Sec., 1965-70. Past Pres., Trinidad Chamber of Commerce. *Address:* 14 Coblentz Gardens, St Ann's, Trinidad. *Clubs:* Queen's Park Cricket, Harvard Sports (Trinidad).

BLACK, family name of **Baron Black.**

BLACK, Baron *cr* 1968 (Life Peer), of Barrow in Furness; **William Rushton Black;** Kt 1958; *b* 12 Jan. 1893; *s* of J. W. and F. M. Black; *m* 1916, Patricia Margaret Dallas (*d* 1976); one *d* (one *s* decd). *Educ:* Barrow Secondary Sch.; Barrow Technical Coll. Apprenticed Vickers Ltd (Engineer), 1908; Works Manager, Vickers Crayford, 1924; General Manager, Weymanns Motor Bodies, 1928; Director and General Manager, Park Royal Vehicles Ltd, 1934, Man. Dir 1939, Chairman 1962-79; Director, Associated Commercial Vehicles Ltd, 1949, Chm. and Managing Dir 1957-78. Chairman: National Research Development Corporation, 1957-69; Leyland Motor Corporation, 1963-67. Pres., SMMT, 1953. *Recreations:* golf, gardening. *Address:* Rushtons, Longdown, Guildford, Surrey. *Club:* Royal Automobile.

BLACK, Archibald Niel; Professor of Engineering, University of Southampton, 1968-72, retired; *b* 10 June 1912; *s* of late Steuart Gladstone Black, Glenormiston, Victoria, Australia, and Isabella McCance (*née* Moat); *m* 1940, Cynthia Mary Stradling; one *s* two *d. Educ:* Farnborough Sch.; Eton Coll.; Trinity Coll., Cambridge. 1st cl. hons with distinction in Applied Mechanics in Mech. Sciences Tripos, Cambridge, 1934; MA 1938. Lectr and Demonstrator in Engrg Science, Oxford Univ., 1935; Donald Pollock Reader in Engrg Science, Oxford Univ., 1945-50; Prof. of Mech. Engrg, Southampton Univ., 1950-67. Dep. Chm., Universities Central Council on Admissions, 1964-72. Hon. DSc Southampton, 1975. *Publications:* (with K. Adlard Coles) North Biscay Pilot, 1970, revd edn 1977; papers in Proc. Royal Soc. and technical jls. *Recreation:* sailing. *Address:* Little Pensbury, Compton Street, Compton, Winchester, Hants SO21 2AS. *T:* Twyford 712360. *Club:* Royal Ocean Racing.

BLACK, Sir Cyril (Wilson), Kt 1959; JP; *b* 1902; *s* of Robert Wilson Black, JP, and Annie Louise Black (*née* North); *m* 1930, Dorothy Joyce, *d* of Thomas

Birkett, Wigston Hall, Leicester; one *s* two *d. Educ:* King's College Sch. Chartered Surveyor, FRICS; Consultant to Knight & Co., Arthur Road, SW19. Chairman: Temperance Permanent Building Soc., 1939-73; Beaumont Properties Ltd, 1933-80; London Shop Property Trust Ltd, 1951-79; M. F. North Ltd, 1948-81, and other companies. JP County of London, 1942; Member Wimbledon Borough Council, 1942-65; Mayor, 1945-46, 1946-47; Alderman, 1942-65; Member, London Borough of Merton Council, 1965-78; Mayor, 1965-66; Member Surrey County Council, 1943-65; County Alderman, 1952-65, and Chm., 1956-59; MP (C) Wimbledon, 1950-70. DL Surrey, 1957-66; DL Greater London, 1966-82. Governor of King's College Sch., Wimbledon Coll., Ursuline Convent Sch., Wimbledon, and other Schools. Freedom of City of London, 1943; Freedom of Wimbledon, 1957. Hon. Mem., Houses of Parliament Christian Fellowship; Patron, Wimbledon Youth Cttee; Chairman, Wimbledon Community Assoc.; Member: SW Metrop. Regional Hospital Board, 1959-62; Baptist Union Council (Pres., 1970-71); Free Church Federal Council; Vice-President: Girls' Bde, 1969- (Hon. Treasurer, 1939-69); Boys' Bde, 1970- (Hon. Treasurer, 1962-69). Pres., United Nations Association (London Region), 1964-65. *Recreations:* public work, music, reading. *Address:* Rosewall, Calonne Road, Wimbledon, SW19. *T:* 01-946 2588. *Clubs:* Carlton, City Livery, Inner London Justices'.

BLACK, Sir David; *see* Black, Sir R. D.

BLACK, Sir Douglas (Andrew Kilgour), Kt 1973; MD, PRCP; Professor of Medicine, Manchester University and Physician, Manchester Royal Infirmary, 1959-77, now Emeritus; Chief Scientist, Department of Health and Social Security, 1973-77 (on secondment); *b* 29 May 1913; *s* of late Rev. Walter Kilgour Black and Mary Jane Crichton; *m* 1948, Mollie Thorn; one *s* two *d. Educ:* Forfar Academy; St Andrews Univ. BSc 1933; MB, ChB 1936; MD 1940; MRCP 1939; FRCP 1952; FACP, FRACP, FRCPGlas, 1978; FRCPath, FRCPI, FRCPE, 1979; FRCPsych, 1982. MRC Research Fellow, 1938-40; Beit Memorial Research Fellow, 1940-42. Major RAMC, 1942-46. Lecturer, then Reader, in Medicine, Manchester Univ., 1946-58. Horder Travelling Fellow, 1967; Sir Arthur Sims Commonwealth Travelling Prof., 1971. Lectures: Goulstonian, RCP, 1953; Bradshaw, RCP, 1965; Lumleian, RCP, 1970; Harben, RIPH&H, 1973; Crookshank, RCR, 1976; Harveian Orator, RCP, 1977; Maurice Bloch, Glasgow, 1979; Linacre, St John's Coll., Cambridge, 1980; Lloyd Roberts, RSM, 1980. Secretary, Manchester Medical Soc., 1957-59. Member: Medical Research Council, 1966-70 and 1971-77 (Chm., Clinical Res. Bd, 1971-73); Assoc. of Physicians; Medical Research Soc.; Renal Assoc., etc. Pres., RCP, 1977-83; Pres. Section X, British Assoc., 1977. Trustee, 1968-77, Chm., 1977-, Smith Kline & French Foundn. Chm., Research Working Group on Inequalities in Health, 1977-80. Hon. DSc: St Andrews, 1972; Manchester, 1978; Leicester, 1980. *Publications:* Sodium Metabolism in Health and Disease, 1952; Essentials of Fluid Balance, 4th edn, 1967; The Logic of Medicine, 1968; (ed) Renal Disease, 4th edn, 1979; contributions to various medical journals. *Recreations:* reading and writing. *Address:* The Old Forge, Duchess Close, Whitchurch-on-Thames, near Reading, RG8 7EN. *T:* Pangbourne 4693. *Club:* Athenæum.

BLACK, Eugene R(obert); Banker, United States; Chairman: Blackwell Land Co. Inc.; Scandinavian Securities Corp.; Director, Warner Communications; *b* Atlanta, Ga, USA, 1 May 1898; *s* of Eugene R. Black and Gussie Grady; *m* 1st, 1918, Elizabeth Blalock (decd); one *s* one *d*; 2nd, 1930, Susette Heath; one *s. Educ:* Univ. of Georgia. Atlanta Office, Harris, Forbes & Co. (NY Investment Bankers), 1919; Manager, Atlanta Office, Chase-Harris, Forbes Corp., in charge of Atlanta, New Orleans, Houston and Dallas offices, 1933; Chase National Bank of the City of NY: 2nd Vice-Pres., 1933; Vice-Pres., 1937; Senior Vice-Pres., 1949, resigned. US Executive Director, Internat. Bank for Reconstruction and Development, 1947-49, President, 1949-53. Consultant and Dir, Chase Manhattan Bank, 1963-70; Consultant, American Express Co., 1970-78. Special Adviser to President Johnson on SE Asia development, 1965-69; Trustee, Corporate Property Investors, and other financial trusteeships. Medal of Freedom (US), 1969. Holds numerous hon. doctorates and has been decorated by many countries. *Publications:* The Diplomacy of Economic Development, 1963 (trans. other languages); Alternative in Southeast Asia, 1969. *Recreations:* golf, fishing; student of William Shakespeare. *Address:* (office) American Express Plaza, New York, NY 10004, USA. *T:* 212-480-3527; (home) 178 Columbia Heights, Brooklyn, New York 11201. *Clubs:* Athenæum (London, England); Lotos, River (New York); International (Washington, DC); National Golf Links of America (Southampton, NY), etc.

BLACK, George Joseph, DSO 1944; DFC 1942 and Bar 1944; **His Honour Judge Black;** a Circuit Judge, since 1977; *b* 24 Jan. 1918; *s* of Tom Walton Black and Nellie Black; *m* 1955; one *s* one *d. Educ:* Queens Coll., Taunton. LLB. Articled Clerk, C. James Hardwick & Co., Solicitors, Cardiff, 1935-39; joined RAF, Sept. 1939; Sgt Pilot 1940; commnd 1942; Sqdn Ldr 1944; fighter bombers, Middle East, Sicily, Italy, 1941-44; Sen. Personnel Staff Officer, 1944-45; released from service, 1946; admitted Solicitor, 1947; private practice, 1947-49; Legal Dept, New Scotland Yard, 1950-58; Partner, Adams & Black, Cardiff, 1958-77. A Recorder of the Crown Court, 1972-77. *Recreations:* sailing. *Address:* 11 Sealawns, Cold Knap, Barry, S Glamorgan.

BLACK, Prof. Gordon; Professor of Computation, Faculty of Technology, University of Manchester, since 1964; Director, University of Manchester Regional Computing Centre, since 1969; Member, National Electronics Council, since 1967; *b* 30 July 1923; *s* of Martin Black and Gladys (*née* Lee),

Whitehaven, Cumbria; *m* 1953, Brenda Janette, *y d* of H. Josiah Balsom, London; two *s* two *d. Educ:* Workington Grammar Sch.; Hatfield Coll., Durham Univ.; Imperial Coll., London Univ. BSc Durham, 1945; MSc Manchester, 1968; PhD, DIC London, 1954; FInstP 1952; FBCS 1968. Physicist, British Scientific Instrument Research Assoc., 1946-56. UKAEA, 1956-66; Principal Sci. Officer, 1956-58; Senior Principal Sci. Officer, 1958-60; Dep. Chief Sci. Officer, 1960-64. Dir, Nat. Computing Centre, 1965-69. Dir, Internat. Computers Ltd, 1976-. Chm., Computer Policy Cttee, Vickers Ltd, 1977-79. Governor, Huddersfield Polytechnic, 1974-80. FRSA. *Publications:* scientific papers in learned jls (physics and computers). *Recreations:* piano playing; listening to piano players; old clocks. *Address:* University of Manchester Institute of Science and Technology, Sackville Street, Manchester. *T:* 061-236 3311; Highlawn, Alan Drive, Hale, Greater Manchester. *T:* 061-980 4644. *Club:* Athenæum.

BLACK, Sir Hermann David, Kt 1974; Chancellor of the University of Sydney, New South Wales, Australia, since 1970; Fellow, University of Sydney, since 1949; Part-time Lecturer in Economics and Education; also a radio commentator on economics and international affairs, in Australia; *b* 1905. Former Economic Adviser to the Treasury, NSW; former Pres., Economic Soc. of Australia and NZ; Pres., Australian Instn of Internat. Affairs. Hon. DLitt Univ. of Newcastle, NSW. *Address:* University of Sydney, Sydney, New South Wales 2006, Australia; 99 Roseville Avenue, Roseville, NSW 2069, Australia.

BLACK, Iain James, QC 1971; a Recorder of the Crown Court, since 1972; Called to the Bar, Gray's Inn, 1947; Dep. Chm., Staffs QS, 1965-71. Mem., Criminal Injuries Compensation Bd, 1975-. *Address:* 3 Fountain Court, Steelhouse Lane, Birmingham B4 6DR. *T:* 021-236 5854; 3 Pump Court, Temple, EC4. *T:* 01-353 0711.

BLACK, Ian Hervey Stuart, TD 1980; Chairman, General Accident Fire and Life Assurance Corporation Ltd, 1972-79; *b* 8 June 1908; *s* of Archibald Arrol Stuart Black and Edith Mary Macmichael; *m* 1935, Margaret Helen, *d* of Maj.-Gen. Sir Cecil Pereira and Lady Pereira; two *s* two *d. Educ:* Winchester Coll.; Magdalen Coll., Oxford (3rd Cl. Hons PPE). Commnd Ayrshire Yeomanry, 1930; Captain 1940; served War: WO, 1941-43; Min. of War Transport, N and W Africa, 1943-44, and France, 1944-45. Joined Glasgow Steam Shipping Co. Ltd, 1930, Dir 1933; Dir, Donaldson Line Ltd, and Donaldson Bros & Black Ltd, 1938-68 (Dep. Chm., 1956-68). Gen. Accident Assurance Group: Dir, 1950; Dep. Chm., 1970; chm. or dir, subsid. and assoc. cos, 1950-79. Dir, Scottish United Investors Ltd, 1953-79. Chairman: Scottish Br., Inst. of Dirs, 1976-78; Glasgow Dock Labour Bd, 1946-49; Glasgow & Clyde Shipowners' Assoc., 1952; Glasgow Port Welfare Cttee, 1956-70; Scottish Council, King George's Fund for Sailors, 1950-62 and 1969-73; Glasgow Sea Cadet Corps, 1947-55; Scottish Central Cttee, Royal Life Saving Soc., 1969-72; former Chm., Glasgow Sailors' Home. Dep. Chairman: (former), Clyde Navigation Trust; (former), Clyde Pilotage Authority; Scotland's Garden Scheme, 1947-51. Former Dir, Merchants House, Glasgow. Member: (former), Council, Chamber of Shipping; Scottish Cttee, Council of Indust. Design, 1953-62. Hon. Sec., Lanarkshire and Renfrewshire Foxhounds, 1953-72. OStJ. Medal of Freedom, USA, 1945. *Recreations:* gardening, horses, wine. *Address:* Little Dunbarnie, Bridge of Earn, Perth PH2 9ED. *T:* Bridge of Earn 2205. *Clubs:* White's, Carlton; Western (Glasgow).

See also Sir David Lawrence, Bt.

BLACK, James Walter, QC 1979; a Recorder of the Crown Court, since 1976; *b* 8 Feb. 1941; *s* of Dr James Black and Mrs Clementine M. Black (*née* Robb); *m* 1964, Jane Marie Keyden; two *s* one *d. Educ:* Harecroft Hall, Gosforth, Cumbria; Trinity Coll., Glenalmond, Perthshire; St Catharine's Coll., Cambridge (MA). Called to the Bar, Middle Temple, 1964. *Recreations:* fishing, sailing, golf. *Address:* August Hill, West Hay, Wrington, Bristol BS18 7NW. *T:* Wrington 862435. *Club:* Constitutional (Bristol).

BLACK, Sir James (Whyte), Kt 1981; FRCP; FRS 1976; Director of Therapeutic Research, Wellcome Research Laboratories, since 1978; *b* 14 June 1924. *Educ:* Beath High Sch., Cowdenbeath; Univ. of St Andrews (MB, ChB). Asst Lectr in Physiology, Univ. of St Andrews, 1946; Lectr in Physiology, Univ. of Malaya, 1947-50; Sen. Lectr, Univ. of Glasgow Vet. Sch., 1950-58; ICI Pharmaceuticals Ltd, 1958-64; Head of Biological Res. and Dep. Res. Dir, Smith, Kline & French, Welwyn Garden City, 1964-73; Prof. and Head of Dept of Pharmacology, University College, London, 1973-77. Mem., British Pharmacological Soc., 1961-. Mullard Award, Royal Soc., 1978. *Address:* Wellcome Research Laboratories, Langley Court, South Eden Park Road, Beckenham, Kent BR3 3BS.

BLACK, John Newman, CEng, FICE, FIMarE; FRGS; Chief Executive, since 1982, and Board Member, since 1978, Port of London Authority; *b* 29 Sept. 1925; *s* of late John Black and late Janet Black (*née* Hamilton); *m* 1952, Euphemia Isabella Elizabeth Thomson; two *d. Educ:* Cumberland and Medway Technical Colls. Civil and marine engrg naval stations and dockyards, UK and abroad, incl. Singapore, Hong Kong, Colombo, Gibraltar and Orkney Isles, 1941-64; joined PLA as Civil Engr, 1964; Planning and Construction, Tilbury Docks, 1964-66; Planning Manager, 1967; seconded to Thames Estuary Develt Co. Ltd, for work on Maplin Airport/Seaport Scheme, 1969; Asst Dir Planning, PLA, 1970; Director: Maplin, 1972; Tilbury Docks, 1974; all London Docks, 1977; Man. Dir, 1978-81. Dep. Chm., PLA

(Met. Terminals) Ltd, 1974; Director: PLACON Ltd (PLA's cons. subsid. co.) 1972; Orsett Depot Ltd, 1974; Port Documentation Services Ltd (Chm.), 1978 Chm., Thames Riparian Housing Assoc., 1974. Member: Exec. Council, BPA 1982-; BNC, Permt Internat. Assoc. of Navigation Congresses, 1981-; Londo Maritime Assoc., 1975; PLA Representative: Internat. Assoc. of Ports an Harbours; Council, RGS. Co-Adviser to Indian Govt on port ops an potential, 1968; lectures for UN, Alexandria, 1975. FInstPet. Freeman: Cit of London, 1977; Watermen and Lightermen of River Thames, 197 *Publications:* numerous articles and papers in Geographical Jl, Civil Engr an other learned jls. *Recreations:* shooting, fishing. *Address:* Westdene Cottage Tanyard Hill, Shorne, near Gravesend, Kent DA12 3EN. *T:* Shorne 311.

BLACK, John Nicholson, MA, DPhil, DSc, FRSE; Director and Secretary The Wolfson Foundation, since 1981; *b* 28 June 1922; *e s* of Harold Black MD, FRCP, and Margaret Frances Black (*née* Nicholson); *m* 1st, 1952, Mar Denise Webb (*d* 1966); one *s* one *d* ; 2nd, 1967, Wendy Marjorie Waterston two *s. Educ:* Rugby Sch.; Exeter Coll., Oxford. MA 1952, DPhil 1952 Oxford; DSc 1965, Adelaide; FRSE 1965. Served War, RAF, 1942-4(Oxford Univ., 1946-49; BA Hons Cl. 1 (Agri.) 1949; Agricl Research Counc Studentship, 1949-52; Lectr, Sen. Lectr, Reader, Univ. of Adelaide (Wait Agricl Research Inst.), 1952-63; André Mayer Fellowship (FAO), 1958; Prov of Forestry and Natural Resources, Univ. of Edinburgh, 1963-71; Principa Bedford Coll., Univ. of London, 1971-81. Mem., Nat. Environment Research Council, 1968-74. *Publications:* The Dominion of Man, 1970; papers on ecological subjects in scientific jls; Italian opera libretti. *Recreation:* music *Address:* Westholm, Orchehill Avenue, Gerrards Cross, Bucks.

BLACK, Prof. Joseph, CBE 1980; PhD; FEng, FIMechE, FRAeS; Professo of Engineering, University of Bath, since 1960, Head of School o Engineering, 1960-70 and since 1973; *b* 25 Jan. 1921; *s* of Alexander Blacl and Hettie Black; *m* 1946, Margaret Susan Hewitt; three *s* one *d. Educ:* Roya Belfast Academical Instn; QUB (BScEng, MSc). PhD Bristol; FRAeS 196 FIMechE 1964, FEng 1981. Scientific Officer, RAE, 1941-44; Res. Fellow QUB, 1944-45; Aerodynamicist, de Havilland Aircraft, 1945-46; Lectr/Ser Lectr in Engrg, Univ. of Bristol, 1946-59. Gillette Fellow, USA, 196: Pro-Vice-Chancellor, Univ. of Bath, 1970-73. Member: Planning and Bld Cttees, Univ. of Bath, 1965-73; UGC, 1964-74 (Chm. Educl Technol Cttee); (founder) Council for Educnl Technol., 1974-; A/M Cttee, SRC 1975-79; Design Council, 1977- (Chm. Engrg Components Awards 1976 Engrg Products Awards 1977); Mech. Engrg and Machine Tool Requiremen Bd, DoI, 1979-81. Trustee, Holborne Mus., Bath. Silver Jubilee Medal, 197 *Publications:* Introduction to Aerodynamic Compressibility, 1950; contrib aeronaut., mech. engrg and printing jls (UK and Europe). *Recreations* photography, antiquarian books, fine art, music. *Address:* 20 Summerhi Road, Bath BA1 2UR. *T:* Bath 23970. *Club:* Shearwater Sailing (Wilts).

BLACK, Kenneth Oscar, MA, MD Cantab, FRCP, BChir, MRCS Consulting Physician, St Bartholomew's Hospital; *b* 10 Nov. 1910; *s* of lat George Barnard Black, Scarborough; *m* 1959, Virginia, *d* of Herbert Lee Petersham, Surrey; two *d. Educ:* Bootham Sch., York; King's Coll Cambridge (1st Class Nat. Science Tripos part 1, Senior Exhibitioner); S Bartholomew's Hospital, London. Demonstrator of Physiology and Medica Chief Asst, St Bartholomew's Hospital; Physician, St Bartholomew's Hospital 1946. MB, BChir 1937; MRCP 1937; MD 1942; FRCP 1946. War servic temp. Lt-Col RAMC; served W. Africa and India as Medical Specialist and OC Medical Div. Mem., Assoc. of Physicians; Fellow Royal Societ Medicine. Examiner in Medicine: University of London, 1953; Soc. o Apothecaries, 1957; for MRCP London, 1967. *Publications:* contributions t journals and textbooks on diabetes and other medical topics. *Recreatior* natural history. *Address:* 28 Palmeira Avenue, Hove, East Sussex BN 3GB.

BLACK, Margaret McLeod; Head Mistress, Bradford Girls' Grammar Schoo 1955-75; *b* 1 May 1912; *d* of James Black and Elizabeth Malcolm. *Educ:* Kels High Sch.; Edinburgh Univ. (MA). Classics Mistress, Lancaster Girl Grammar Sch., 1936-44, and Manchester High Sch. for Girls, 1944-50; Hea Mistress, Great Yarmouth Girls' High Sch., 1950-55. President: Leeds Branc of Classical Assoc., 1963-65; Joint Assoc. of Classical Teachers, 1967-69 Yorkshire Divl Union of Soroptimist Clubs, 1968-69. *Recreation:* music *Address:* 8 Gig Lane, Heath and Reach, Leighton Buzzard, Beds LU7 0BC *T:* Heath and Reach 363. *Club:* Royal Over-Seas League.

BLACK, Very Rev. Matthew, DD, DLitt, DTheol, LLD; FRSE; FBA 195 Professor of Divinity and Biblical Criticism, and Principal of St Mary College, University of St Andrews, 1954-78; now Emeritus Professor; Dea of the Faculty of Divinity, 1963-67; *b* 3 Sept. 1908; *s* of James and Hele Black, Kilmarnock, Ayrshire; *m* 1938, Ethel M., *d* of late Lt-Comdr A. H Hall, Royal Indian Navy; one *s* one *d. Educ:* Kilmarnock Academy; Glasgov Univ. Glasgow: 1st cl. hons MA Classics, 1930; 2nd cl. hons Menta Philosophy, 1931; BD with distinction in Old Testament, 1934; DLitt 194 Dr Phil Bonn, 1937. Hon. DTheol Münster; Hon. LLD St Andrews, 198C Hon. DD: Glasgow; 1954; Cambridge, 1965; Queen's, Ontario, 1967 Buchanan Prize, Moral Philosophy, 1929; Caird Scholar, Classics, 193C Crombie Scholar, Biblical Criticism, 1933 (St Andrews award); Brow Downie Fellow, 1934; Maxwell Forsyth Fellow and Kerr Travellin Scholarship, Trinity Coll., Glasgow, 1934. Asst to Prof. of Hebrew, Glasgow 1935-37; Warden of Church of Scotland Students' Residence, 1936-37; As: Lecturer in Semitic Languages and Literatures, University of Manchester

1937-39; Bruce Lectr, Trinity Coll., Glasgow, 1940; Lectr in Hebrew and Biblical Criticism, Univ. of Aberdeen, 1939-42; Minister of Dunbarney, Church of Scotland, 1942-47; Officiating CF, Bridge of Earn, 1943-47; Lecturer in New Testament Language and Literature, Leeds Univ., 1947-52; Prof. of Biblical Criticism and Biblical Antiquities, University of Edinburgh, 1952-54. Chm., Adv. Cttee of Peshitta Project of Univ. of Leiden, 1968-. Morse Lectr, 1956 and De Hoyt Lectr, 1963, Union Theological Seminary, NY; Thomas Burns Lectr, Otago, 1967. Pres., Soc. for Old Testament Study, 1968. FRSE 1977. Corresp. Mem., Göttingen Akademie der Wissenschaften, 1957; Mem., Royal Soc. of Scis, Uppsala, 1979; Hon. Member: Amer. Soc. of Biblical Exegesis, 1958; American Bible Soc., 1966. British Academy Burkitt Medal for Biblical Studies, 1962. *Publications:* Rituale Melchitarum (Stuttgart), 1938; An Aramaic Approach to the Gospels and Acts, 3rd edn, 1967; A Christian Palestinian Syriac Horologion, Texts and Studies, Contributions to Patristic Literature, New Series, Vol. I, 1954; The Scrolls and Christian Origins, 1961; General and New Testament Editor, Peake's Commentary on the Bible (revised edn, 1962); Bible Societies' edn of the Greek New Testament (Stuttgart), 1966; (Jt Editor) In Memoriam Paul Kahle (Berlin), 1968; (Editor and contributor) The Scrolls and Christianity, 1968; (with A. M. Denis) Apocalypsis Henochi Graece Fragmenta Pseudepigraphorum, 1970; Commentary on Romans, 1973; (ed with William A. Smalley) On Language, Religion and Culture, in honor Eugene A. Nida, 1974; (organising Editor) The History of the Jewish People in the Age of Jesus Christ, vol. I, ed by G. Vermes and F. Millar, 1973, vol. II, ed jtly with G. Vermes and F. Millar, 1979; Editor, New Testament Studies, to 1977; articles in learned journals. *Address:* St Michael's, 40 Buchanan Gardens, St Andrews, Fife. *Clubs:* Athenæum; Royal and Ancient (Hon. Chaplain).

BLACK, Prof. Paul Joseph, PhD; Professor of Science Education and Director, Centre for Science and Mathematics Education, Chelsea College, University of London, since 1976; *b* 10 Sept. 1930; *s* of Walter and Susie Black; *m* 1957, Mary Elaine Weston; four *s* one *d. Educ:* Rhyl Grammar Sch.; Univ. of Manchester (BSc); Univ. of Cambridge (PhD). Royal Society John Jaffé Studentship, 1953-56. Univ. of Birmingham: Lectr in Physics, 1956-66; Reader in Crystal Physics, 1966-74; Prof. of Physics (Science Education), 1974-76; Dean, Faculty of Educn, Univ. of London, 1978-82. Bragg Medal, Inst. of Physics, 1973. Kt of St Gregory, 1973. *Publications:* (jtly) Nuffield Advanced Physics Project, 1972; (contrib.) Higher Education Learning Project Books, 1977; papers in Crystallography, Physics and Science Education Jls. *Address:* 16 Wilton Crescent, SW19 3QZ. *T:* 01-542 4178.

BLACK, Peter Blair, JP; Senior Partner, P. Blair Black & Partners, since 1948; *b* 22 April 1917; *s* of Peter Blair Black and Cissie Crawford Samuel; *m* 1952, Mary Madeleine Hilly, Philadelphia; one *s* three *d. Educ:* Sir Walter St John's, Battersea; Bearsden Acad.; Sch. of Building. CC 1949, Alderman 1961, Middlesex; Mem., GLC, 1963-, Chm., 1970-71, Leader, Recreation and Community Services Policy Gp, 1977-81; motivator of Thames Barrier project; Chm., Cons. Group, GLC, 1982. Chm., Thames Water Authority, 1973-78; Pres., Pure Rivers Soc., 1976-. Frequent performer on TV and radio. Former Member: Thames Conservancy Bd; Metrop. Water Bd; Jager Cttee on Sewage Disposal; PLA; Council, Nat. Fedn of Housing Socs; Founder Chm., Omnium Housing Assoc., 1962; Chm., Abbeyfield, London Region. JP Thames Div., 1961. *Recreations:* small boats and fishing. *Address:* Members Lobby, County Hall, SE1; 101 Limmer Lane, Felpham, Sussex. *T:* Middleton-on-Sea 2054. *Clubs:* Middleton Sports; Sewers Synonymous.

BLACK, Prof. Robert; Professor of Scots Law, University of Edinburgh, since 1981; *b* 12 June 1947; *s* of James Little Black and Jeannie Findlay Lyon. *Educ:* Lockerbie Acad.; Dumfries Acad.; Edinburgh Univ. (LLB); McGill Univ., Montreal (LLM). Advocate, 1972. Vis. Lectr in Law, Univ. of the Witwatersrand, Johannesburg, 1971; Lectr in Scots Law, Univ. of Edinburgh, 1972-75; Sen. Legal Officer, Scottish Law Commn, 1975-78; in practice at Scottish Bar, 1978-81; Temp. Sheriff, 1981-. Dep. Gen. Editor, Stair Memorial Encyclopaedia of the Laws of Scotland, 1981-. *Publications:* An Introduction to Written Pleading, 1982; articles in UK and S African legal jls. *Recreation:* baiting sociologists. *Address:* 6/4 Glenogle Road, Edinburgh EH3 5HW. *T:* 031-557 3571. *Clubs:* Sloane; Scottish Arts (Edinburgh).

BLACK, Sir Robert (Brown), GCMG 1962 (KCMG 1955; CMG 1953); OBE 1949 (MBE 1948); *b* 3 June 1906; *s* of late Robert and Catherine Black, formerly of Blair Lodge, Polmont, Stirlingshire; *m* 1937, (Elsie) Anne Stevenson, CStJ; two *d. Educ:* George Watson's Coll.; Edinburgh Univ. Colonial Administrative Service, 1930; served in Malaya, Trinidad, N Borneo, Hong Kong. Served War of 1939-45, commissioned in Intelligence Corps, 1942; 43 Special Military Mission; POW Japan, 1942-45. Colonial Secretary, Hong Kong, 1952-55; Governor and C-in-C: Singapore, 1955-57; Hong Kong, 1958-64. Chancellor: Hong Kong Univ., 1958-64; Chinese University of Hong Kong, 1963-64. Mem., Commonwealth War Graves Commn. Chm., Clerical, Medical and General Life Assurance Soc., 1975-78. Chm., Internat. Social Service of GB, 1965-73, Pres., 1973-82. LLD (*hc*): Univ. of Hong Kong; Chinese Univ. of Hong Kong. KStJ. Grand Cross Order of Merit, Peru. *Recreations:* walking, fishing. *Address:* Mapletons House, Ashampstead Common, near Reading, Berks RG8 8QN. *Club:* East India, Devonshire, Sports and Public Schools.

BLACK, Sir (Robert) David, 3rd Bt *cr* 1922; *b* 29 March 1929; *s* of Sir Robert Andrew Stransham Black, 2nd Bt, ED, and Ivy (*d* 1980), *d* of late Brig.-Gen. Sir Samuel Wilson, GCMG, KCB, KBE; *S* father, 1979; *m* 1st,

1953, Rosemary Diana (marr. diss. 1972), *d* of Sir Rupert John Hardy, 4th Bt; three *d*; 2nd, 1973, Dorothy Maureen, *d* of Major Charles R. Eustace Radclyffe and *widow* of A. R. D. Pilkington. *Educ:* Eton. Lieut, Royal Horse Guards, 1949; Captain 1953; Major 1960; retired, 1961. Served with Berkshire and Westminster Dragoons, TA, 1964-67, and Berkshire Territorials, TAVR III, 1967-69. Joint Master, Garth and South Berks Foxhounds, 1965-73. *Recreations:* hunting, shooting, stalking and fishing. *Heir:* none. *Address:* Elvendon Priory, Goring, near Reading, Berks. *T:* Goring-on-Thames 872160. *Club:* Cavalry and Guards.

BLACK, Prof. Robert Denis Collison, FBA 1974; Professor of Economics, and Head of Department of Economics, Queen's University Belfast, since 1962; *b* 11 June 1922; *s* of William Robert Black and Rose Anna Mary (*née* Reid), Dublin; *m* 1953, Frances Mary, *o d* of William F. and Mary Weatherup, Belfast; one *s* one *d. Educ:* Sandford Park Sch. and Trinity Coll., Dublin. BA 1941, BComm 1941, PhD 1943, MA 1945. Dep. for Prof. of Polit. Economy, Trinity Coll., Dublin, 1943-45; Asst Lectr in Economics, Queen's Univ., Belfast, 1945-46, Lectr, 1946-58, Sen. Lectr, 1958-61, Reader, 1961-62. Rockefeller Post-doctoral Fellow, Princeton Univ., 1950-51; Visiting Prof. of Economics, Yale Univ., 1964-65; Dean of Faculty of Economics and Social Sciences, QUB, 1967-70; Pro-Vice-Chancellor, 1971-75. MRIA 1974. *Publications:* Centenary History of the Statistical Society of Ireland, 1947; Economic Thought and the Irish Question 1817-1870, 1960; Catalogue of Economic Pamphlets 1750-1900, 1969; Papers and Correspondence of William Stanley Jevons, Vol. I, 1972, Vol. II, 1973, Vols III-VI, 1977, Vol. VII, 1981; articles in Economic Jl, Economica, Oxford Econ. Papers, Econ. History Review, etc. *Recreations:* travel, music. *Address:* Department of Economics, Queen's University, Belfast, Northern Ireland BT7 1NN. *T:* Belfast 45133.

BLACK, Sheila (Psyche); Feature Writer; Director, Mills and Allen International, since 1976; *b* 6 May 1920; *d* of Clement Johnston Black, CA, and Mildred Beryl Black; *m* 1st, 1939, Geoffrey Davien, Sculptor (marr. diss. 1951); one *d* (one *s* decd); 2nd, 1951, L. A. Lee Howard (from whom she obtained a divorce, 1973). *Educ:* Dorset; Switzerland; RADA. Actress, until outbreak of War of 1939-45, she became Asst to production manager of an electrical engineering factory. Post-war, in advertising; then in journalism, from the mid-fifties; Woman's Editor, Financial Times, 1959-72; Dir, Debenhams Ltd, 1975-76, Consultant, 1976-77; Chm., Interflex Data Systems (UK) Ltd, 1975-. Features writer for The Director, Financial Weekly, Punch, Mediaworld, and many newspapers and magazines. Chm., Nat. Gas Consumers' Council, 1981-; Member: Furniture Develt Council, 1967-70; Liquor Licensing Laws Special Cttee, 1971-72; (part-time) Price Commn, 1973-77; Nat. Consumer Council, 1981-. Mem. Council, Inst of Directors, 1975-. *Publications:* The Black Book, 1976; Mirabelle: cuisine de qualité et tradition, 1979; The Reluctant Money Minder, 1980. *Recreations:* horticulture in London, grandchildren, football. *Address:* 12A Earls Court Gardens, SW5 0TD.

BLACK-HAWKINS, (Clive) David, MA (Cantab); Head Master, University College School, Hampstead, 1956-75; *b* 2 July 1915; *o c* of late Capt. C. C. R. Black-Hawkins, Hants Regt, and Stella Black-Hawkins (*née* Stein); *m* 1941, Ruth Eleanor (*d* 1977), 3rd *d* of late H. Crichton-Miller, MA, MD, FRCP; one *s* one *d. Educ:* Wellington Coll.; Corpus Christi Coll., Cambridge. Asst Master, University College Sch., 1938; Vice-Master, 1953. Intelligence Corps, Capt., 1940-46; GHQ Middle East, 1942-44. Governor: Westfield Coll., Univ. of London, 1977-; Royal Masonic Instn for Girls, 1975-. *Recreations:* travel, reading memoirs. *Address:* 14A Wedderburn Road, Hampstead, NW3 5QG.

BLACKBURN, Bishop of, since 1982; **Rt. Rev. David Stewart Cross;** *b* 4 April 1928; *s* of Charles Stewart and Constance Muriel Cross; *m* 1954, Mary Margaret Workman Colquhoun; one *s* two *d. Educ:* Trinity Coll., Dublin (MA 1956). Deacon 1954, priest 1955; Curate of Hexham, 1954-57; on staff of Cathedral and Abbey Church of St Alban, St Albans, Herts, 1957-63; Precentor, 1960-63; Curate of St Ambrose, Chorlton-on-Medlock and Asst Chaplain to Manchester Univ., 1963-67; BBC Producer in religious broadcasting, 1968-76 (Religious Broadcasting Assistant, BBC North, 1968-71, then Religious Broadcasting Organiser, Manchester Network Production Centre, 1971-76); Bishop Suffragan of Doncaster, 1976-82; Chairman: Local Radio Council, BBC Radio Sheffield, 1980-82; Churches Adv. Cttee on Local Broadcasting, 1980-; British Churches' Cttee for Channel Four, 1981-. *Recreations:* photography, making music and exchanging puns. *Address:* Bishop's House, Clayton-le-Dale, Blackburn, Lancs BB1 9EF.

BLACKBURN, Archdeacon of; *see* Carroll, Ven. C. W. D.

BLACKBURN, Provost of; *see* Jackson, Very Rev. Lawrence.

BLACKBURN, Anthony; *see* Blackburn, D. A. J.

BLACKBURN, Comdr (David) Anthony (James), MVO 1978; RN; Ministry of Defence (Navy), since 1981; *b* 18 Jan. 1945; *s* of late Lieut J. Blackburn, DSC, RN, and late Mrs M. J. G. Pickering-Pick; *m* 1973, Elizabeth Barstow; three *d. Educ:* Taunton Sch. RNC Dartmouth, 1963; HMS Kirkliston (in comd), 1972-73; Equerry-in-Waiting to the Duke of Edinburgh, 1976-78; Exec. Officer, HMS Antrim, 1978-81. *Address:* Rillet

Cottage, Selborne, Alton, Hants GU34 3LH. *T:* Selborne 385. *Club:* Royal Cruising.

BLACKBURN, Fred; *b* 29 July 1902; *s* of Richley and Mary Blackburn, Mellor; *m* 1930, Marion, *d* of Walter W. and Hannah Fildes, Manchester; two *s. Educ:* Queen Elizabeth's Grammar Sch., Blackburn; St John's Coll., Battersea; Manchester Univ. Teacher. MP (Lab) Stalybridge and Hyde Div. of Cheshire, 1951-70, retired 1970. *Publications:* The Regional Council; Local Government Reform; George Tomlinson. *Address:* 114 Knutsford Road, Wilmslow, Cheshire. *T:* Wilmslow 523142.

BLACKBURN, Guy, MBE 1944; MChir, FRCS; Consultant Surgeon Emeritus, Guy's Hospital; *b* 20 Nov. 1911; *s* of Dr A. E. Blackburn, Beckenham; *m* 1953, Joan, *d* of Arthur Bowen, Pontycymmer, Wales; one *d* (and one *s* by a previous marriage). *Educ:* Rugby; Clare Coll., Cambridge (MA). MRCS, LRCP 1935; MB, BChir 1935; FRCS 1937; MChir 1941. House appointments, St Bartholomew's Hospital, 1935-37; Brackenbury Scholar in Surgery, 1935; Demonstrator of Anatomy and Chief Asst in Surgery, 1938-39; Military Service, 1942-46; Lt-Col i/c Surgical Div., 1945-46; served in N Africa and Italy. Hunterian Prof., RCS, 1946; late Examiner in Surgery, Univs of Cambridge and London; Member Court of Examiners, RCS, 1962-68. Hon. Visiting Surgeon, Johns Hopkins Hospital, Baltimore, USA, 1957; President, Medical Society of London, 1964-65. Hon. Consulting Surgeon, British Army at Home, 1967-76. Pres., Assoc. of Surgeons of GB and Ireland, 1976-77. Senior Warden, Soc. of Apothecaries, 1979-80, Master, 1980-81. *Publications:* (co-ed) A Textbook of Surgery, 1958; (co-ed) Field Surgery Pocket Book, 1981; various publications in medical jls and books. *Address:* 4 Holly Lodge Gardens, N6 6AA. *T:* 01-340 9071. *Clubs:* Garrick, Royal Automobile.

BLACKBURN, John Graham, MP (C) Dudley West, since 1979; *b* 2 Sept. 1933; *s* of Charles Frederick Blackburn and Grace Blackburn; *m* 1958, Marjorie (*née* Thompson); one *s* one *d. Educ:* Liverpool Collegiate Sch.; Liverpool Univ. Staff/Sgt, Special Investigation Br., Royal Military Police, 1949-53; D/Sgt, Liverpool Police, 1953-65; National Sales Manager with an Internat. Public Engrg Gp, 1965-79; Sales Dir, Solway Engrg Co. Ltd, 1965-. Member, Wolverhampton Council, 1970-79. Member, Post Office Users National Council, 1972-. FInstM 1979; FISE 1975; FInstMSM 1976. *Recreation:* keen yachtsman. *Address:* 129 Canterbury Road, Penn, Wolverhampton WV4 4EQ. *T:* Wolverhampton 36222. *Clubs:* Wolverhampton and Bilston Athletic (Vice-President); Traeth Coch Yacht (Executive Member).

BLACKBURN, Michael Scott; a Recorder of the Crown Court, since 1981; *b* 16 Jan. 1936; *m* 1961, Vivienne (*née* Smith); one *s* one *d. Educ:* Dame Allen's Sch., Newcastle upon Tyne; William Hulme's Grammar Sch., Manchester; Keble Coll., Oxford (MA). President, Manchester Law Society, 1979-80; Member, No 7 (NW) Area Legal Aid Cttee, 1980; Chairman, Greater Manchester Legal Services Cttee, 1981. *Recreations:* squash rackets, hill walking, fishing. *Address:* 123 Deansgate, Manchester M3 2BU. *T:* 061-832 3000. *Club:* Northern Lawn Tennis (Manchester).

BLACKBURN, Ronald Henry Albert; a Planning Appeals Commissioner for Northern Ireland, since 1980; *b* 9 Feb. 1924; *s* of late Sidney James and Ellen Margaret Selina Blackburn; *m* 1950, Annabell Hunter; two *s. Educ:* Royal Belfast Academical Institution; Univ. of London (LLB (Hons)). Intelligence Service, 1943; Dept of the Foreign Office, 1944-46. Parly Reporting Staff (N Ire.), 1946-52; Second Clerk Asst, Parlt of N Ire., 1952-62; Clerk Asst, 1962-71; Clerk of the Parliaments, 1971-73; Clerk to NI Assembly, 1973-79; Clerk to NI Constitutional Convention, 1975-76. *Recreations:* golf, gardening. *Address:* Trelawn, Jordanstown Road, Newtownabbey, Co. Antrim, N Ireland. *T:* Whiteabbey 62035.

BLACKBURNE, Rt. Rev. Hugh Charles; *b* 4 June 1912; *s* of late Very Rev. Harry William Blackburne; *m* 1944, Doris Freda, *widow* of Pilot Officer H. L. N. Davis; two *s* one *d. Educ:* Marlborough; Clare Coll., Cambridge (MA); Westcott House, Cambridge. Deacon 1937; Priest, 1938; Curate of Almondbury, Yorks, 1937-39. Chaplain to the Forces, 1939-47; served with 1st Guards Bde, 11th Armoured Div., HQ Anti-Aircraft Comd, and as Chaplain, RMC, Sandhurst. Rector, Milton, Hants, 1947-53; Vicar, St Mary's, Harrow, 1953-61. Rector of the Hilborough Group, 1961-72; Vicar of Ranworth and Chaplain for the Norfolk Broads, 1972-77; Hon. Canon of Norwich, 1965-77; Chaplain to the Queen, 1962-77. Bishop Suffragan of Thetford, 1977-80. *Recreations:* sailing, bird-watching. *Address:* 39 Northgate, Beccles, Suffolk NR34 9AU.

BLACKER, Gen. Sir Cecil (Hugh), GCB 1975 (KCB 1969; CB 1967); OBE 1960; MC 1944; Adjutant-General, Ministry of Defence (Army), 1973-76, retired; ADC (General) to the Queen, 1974-76; *b* 4 June 1916; *s* of Col Norman Valentine Blacker and Olive Georgina (*née* Hope); *m* 1947, Felicity Mary, *widow* of Major J. Rew and *d* of Major I. Buxton, DSO; two *s. Educ:* Wellington Coll. Joined 5th Royal Inniskilling Dragoon Guards, 1936; Commanded 23rd Hussars, 1945; Instructor, Staff Coll., Camberley, 1951-54; Commanded 5th Royal Inniskilling Dragoon Guards, 1955-57; Military Asst to CIGS, 1958-60; Asst Commandant, RMA, Sandhurst, 1960-62; Commander, 39 Infantry Brigade Group, 1962-64; GOC 3rd Div., 1964-66; Dir, Army Staff Duties, MoD, 1966-69; GOC-in-C Northern Command, 1969-70; Vice-Chief of the General Staff, 1970-73. Colonel Commandant:

RMP, 1971-76; APTC, 1971-76; Col, 5th Royal Inniskilling Dragoor Guards, 1972-81. Mem., Jockey Club, 1954; President: BSJA, 1976-80; BEF 1980-. *Publications:* The Story of Workboy, 1960; Soldier in the Saddle, 196? *Recreations:* painting; amateur steeplechase rider, 1947-54; represented GB i World Modern Pentathlon Championships, 1951; represented GB i Showjumping, 1959-61. *Address:* Whitchurch House, Whitchurch Aylesbury, Bucks. *Club:* Cavalry and Guards.

BLACKER, Captain Derek Charles, RN; Director of Naval Oceanograph and Meteorology, Ministry of Defence, since 1981; *b* 19 May 1929; *s* o Charles Edward Blacker and Alexandra May Farrant; *m* 1952, Brenda Mar Getgood; one *s* one *d. Educ:* County Sch., Isleworth; King's Coll., Univ. o London (BSc Hons 1950). Entered RN, 1950; specialisations: navigation meteorology, oceanography; HMS Birmingham, HMS Albion, BRN(Dartmouth, HMS Hermes, 1956-69; Comdr 1965; NATO Command SACLANT, 1969; CINCHAN, 1972; SACEUR, 1974; Captain 1975; Dir o Public Relations (RN), 1977-79; Bd Pres., Admiralty Interview Bd, 1980; o staff of C-in-C, Naval Home Comd, 1980-81. *Recreations:* music, tenni fishing, shooting. *Club:* Army and Navy.

BLACKETT, Sir George (William), 10th Bt *cr* 1673; *b* 26 April 1906; *s* o Sir Hugh Douglas Blackett, 8th Bt, and Helen Katherine (*d* 1943), *d* of lat George Lowther; *S* brother, 1968; *m* 1st, 1933, Euphemia Cicely (*d* 1960), of late Major Nicholas Robinson; 2nd, 1964, Daphne Laing, *d* of late Majo Guy Laing Bradley, TD, Hexham, Northumberland. Served with Shropshir Yeomanry and CMP, 1939-45. *Recreations:* hunting, forestry, farming. *Hei b* Major Francis Hugh Blackett [*b* 16 Oct. 1907; *m* 1950, Elizabeth Eily Barri (*d* 1982), 2nd *d* of late Howard Dennison; two *s* two *d*.] *Address:* Colwyn Corbridge, Northumberland. *T:* Corbridge 2252. *Club:* English-Speakin Union.

BLACKETT-ORD, Andrew James; His Honour Vice-Chancello Blackett-Ord; a Circuit Judge since 1972; Vice-Chancellor, County Palatin of Lancaster, since 1973; Member, Council of Duchy of Lancaster, since 197∶ *b* 21 Aug. 1921; 2nd *s* of late John Reginald Blackett-Ord, Whitfield Northumberland; *m* 1945, Rosemary Bovill; three *s* one *d. Educ:* Eton; Nev Coll., Oxford (MA). Scots Guards, 1943-46; called to Bar, 1947; Count Court Judge, 1971. Chancellor, dio. of Newcastle-upon-Tyne, 1971- *Recreations:* reading, shooting. *Address:* Helbeck Hall, Brough, Kirkb Stephen, Cumbria. *T:* Brough 323. *Clubs:* Garrick, Lansdowne.

BLACKFORD, 4th Baron *cr* 1935; William Keith Mason; Bt 1918; *b* 2 March 1962; *s* of 3rd Baron Blackford, DFC, and of Sarah, *d* of Sir Shirle Worthington-Evans, 2nd Bt; *S* father, 1977. *Educ:* Harrow School. *Address* 135 Cranmer Court, SW1.

BLACKHAM, Rear-Adm. Joseph Leslie, CB 1965; DL; *b* 29 Feb. 1912; of Dr Walter Charles Blackham, Birmingham, and Margaret Eva Blackhar (*née* Bavin); *m* 1938, Coreen Shelford Skinner, *er d* of Paym. Captain W. ₷ Skinner, CBE, RN; one *s* one *d. Educ:* West House Sch., Edgbaston; RN(Dartmouth. Specialised in Navigation; served war of 1939-45; JSSC 195(Comdr, RNC Greenwich, 1953-54; Captain 1954; Admty, 1955-57; Ser Officer, Reserve Fleet at Plymouth, 1957-59; Admty Naval Staff, 1959-6₴ Cdre. Supt, HM Dockyard, Singapore, 1962-63; Rear-Adm. 1963; Admira Supt, HM Dockyard, Portsmouth, 1964-66; retired. Mem., IoW Hosp Management Cttee, 1968-74; Vice-Chm., IoW AHA 1974-82; Chm., Fami Practitioners Cttee, IoW, 1971-; Mem., Bd of Visitors, HM Prison, Parkhurs 1967- (Chm. 1974-77). CC Isle of Wight, 1967-77 (Chm., 1975-77); D Hants and IoW, 1970-; High Sheriff, IoW, 1975. Mentioned in despatches fo service in Korea, 1951. *Address:* Downedge, The Mall, Brading, Isle of Wigh PO36 0BS. *T:* Brading 218.

BLACKIE, John Ernest Haldane, CB 1959; retired as Chief Inspector of th Department of Education (1951-66); *b* 6 June 1904; *e s* of late Rt Rev. E M. Blackie, sometime Bishop of Grimsby and Dean of Rochester and lat Caroline, *d* of Rev. J. Haldane Stewart of Ardsheal; *m* 1st, 1933, Kathleer Mary (*d* 1941), *d* of F. S. Creswell; no *c*; 2nd, 1942, Pamela Althea Vernor *d* of A. J. Margetson, HMI; two *s* two *d. Educ:* Bradfield; Magdalene Coll Cambridge (MA). Asst Master: Lawrenceville Sch., NJ, USA, 1926-27 Bradfield, 1928-33; Asst Director, Public Schools Empire Tour to NZ 1932-33; HM Inspector of Schools, 1933; District Inspector, Mancheste₨ 1936-47; Divisional Inspector, Eastern Divn, 1947-51; Chief Inspector o Further Educn, 1951-58; Primary Educn, 1958-66; Secretary of State's Assesso on Central Advisory Council (Plowden), 1963-66. Lectr (part-time Homerton Coll. of Educn, Cambridge, 1966-70. Mem. Directorate, Anglo American Primary Project, 1969. Sen. Counsellor, Open Univ., 1970-73. 47t County of Lancaster Home Guard, 1940-44. FRES. *Publications:* Schoo Holidays Abroad (with Pamela Blackie), 1961; Good Enough for th Children?, 1963; Inside the Primary School, 1967; English Teaching fc Non-Specialists, 1969; Inspecting and the Inspectorate, 1970; Changing th Primary School, 1974; Bradfield 1850-1975, 1976; various books and article on education, travel and entomology. *Recreations:* travel, gardening, natura history. *Address:* The Bell House, Alconbury, Huntingdon, Cambs. ⅁ Huntingdon 890270. *Club:* Pitt (Cambridge).

BLACKLOCK, Captain Ronald William, CBE 1944; DSC 1917; RN (retired); *b* 21 June 1889; *s* of late J. H. Blacklock, JP, Overthorpe, Banbur₷ *m* 1920, Aline Frances Anstell (*d* 1975); one *s. Educ:* Preparatory Sch.; HM

Britannia. Midshipman, 1906. Specialised in Submarines in 1910. Served European War in Submarines (despatches twice, DSC); Captain 1931; retd owing to ill-health, 1938; War of 1939-45, Director of Welfare Services, Admiralty. *Address:* 3 Tipperlinn Road, Edinburgh EH10 5ET. *Clubs:* Naval and Military; Royal Yacht Squadron.

BLACKMAN, Gilbert Albert Waller, CBE 1978 (OBE 1973); FEng, FIMechE, FInstE; CBIM; Member, Central Electricity Generating Board, since 1977; *b* 28 July 1925; *s* of Ernest Albert Cecil Blackman and Amy Blackman; *m* 1948, Lilian Rosay. *Educ:* Wanstead County High Sch.; Wandsworth Tech. Coll. (CEng, FIMechE 1967). FInstF 1964. Trainee Engr, London Div., Brit. Electricity Authority, 1948-50; various appts in power stns, 1950-63; Central Electricity Generating Board: Stn Supt, Belvedere, 1963-64; Asst Reg. Dir, E Midlands Div., 1964-67; Asst Reg. Dir, Midlands Reg., 1967-70; Dir of Generation, Midlands Reg., 1970-75; Dir Gen., N Eastern Reg., 1975-77. *Recreations:* shooting, photography, walking. *Address:* Gryphon Lodge, 15 Norton Park, St Mary's Hill, Sunninghill, Berks. *T:* Ascot 24374.
See also L. C. F. Blackman.

BLACKMAN, Dr Lionel Cyril Francis; Director, British American Tobacco Co. Ltd, since 1980 (General Manager, Group Research and Development, 1978-80); *b* 12 Sept. 1930; *s* of Ernest Albert Cecil Blackman and Amy McBain; *m* 1955, Susan Hazel Peachey; one *s* one *d. Educ:* Wanstead High Sch.; Queen Mary Coll., London. BSc 1952; PhD 1955. Scientific Officer, then Senior Research Fellow, RN Scientific Service, 1954-57; ICI Research Fellow, then Lectr in Chemical Physics of Solids, Imperial Coll., London, 1957-60; Asst Dir (London), then Dir, Chemical Research Div., BR, 1961-64; Dir of Basic Research, then Dir Gen., British Coal Utilisation Research Assoc., 1964-71; Director: Fibreglass Ltd (subsid. of Pilkington Bros Ltd), 1971-78; Compocem Ltd, 1975-78; Cemfil Corp. (US), 1975-78; Vice-Pres., Cementos y Fibras SA (Spain), 1976-78. CEng; CChem; FRSC; DIC; SFInstE. *Publications:* (ed) Modern Aspects of Graphite Technology, 1970; papers in various scientific and technical jls on dropwise condensation of steam, ferrites, sintering of oxides, graphite and its crystal compounds, glass surface coatings, glass reinforced cement. *Recreations:* gardening, music, wine. *Address:* Griffin House, Knowl Hill, The Hockering, Woking, Surrey GU22 7HL. *T:* Woking 66328. *Club:* Athenæum.
See also G. A. W. Blackman.

BLACKMAN, Prof. Moses, FRS 1962; Professor of Physics, Imperial College of Science and Technology, London, 1959-76, now Professor Emeritus; Senior Research Fellow, Imperial College, since 1976; *b* 6 Dec. 1908; *e s* of late Rev. Joseph Blackman and Esther Oshry; *m* 1959, Anne Olivia, *d* of late Arthur L. Court, Sydney, Australia. *Educ:* Victoria Boys' High Sch., Grahamstown, SA; Rhodes University Coll., Grahamstown; Universities of Göttingen, London and Cambridge. MSc (SA) 1930; DPhil (Göttingen) 1933; PhD (London) 1936; PhD (Cantab) 1938. Queen Victoria Scholar (University of SA) 1931; Beit Scholar (Imperial Coll.) 1933; DSIR Sen. Res. Scholar, 1935; Member staff Physics Dept, Imperial Coll., 1937-. Mem. British Cttee on Atomic Energy, 1940-41; scientific work for Min. of Home Security, 1942-45. Member Internat. Commn on Electron Diffraction, 1957-66. Member Safety in Mines Research Advisory Board, Min. of Power, 1963-74. *Publications:* scientific papers on the physics of crystals. *Address:* 48 Garden Royal, Kersfield Road, SW15. *T:* 01-789 1706.

BLACKMAN, Raymond Victor Bernard, MBE 1970; CEng, FIMarE, FRINA; Editor of Jane's Fighting Ships, 1949-50 to 1972-73 editions; Author and Journalist; *b* 29 June 1910; *e s* of late Leo Albert Martin Blackman and late Laura Gertrude, *e d* of Albert Thomas; *m* 1935, Alma Theresa Joyce, *y d* of late Francis Richard Hannah; one *s* one *d. Educ:* Southern Grammar Sch., Portsmouth. Contrib. to general and technical press, and associated with Jane's Fighting Ships since 1930; Naval Correspondent, Hampshire Telegraph and Post, 1936-46, Sunday Times, 1946-56. Served Royal Navy, 1926-36 and War of 1939-45, HMS Vernon, Mine Design Dept, Admiralty. Member of The Press Gang. Broadcaster on naval topics. *Publications:* Modern World Book of Ships, 1951; The World's Warships, 1955, 1960, 1963, 1969; Ships of the Royal Navy, 1973; contrib. to The Statesman's Year Book, The Diplomatist, Encyclopædia Britannica Book of the Year, Warships and Navies 1973, The Motor Ship, The Engineer, Navy, Lloyd's List, etc. *Recreations:* seagoing, foreign travel, philately. *Address:* 72 The Brow, Widley, Portsmouth, Hants PO7 5DA. *T:* Cosham 376837. *Clubs:* Anchorites; Press; Royal Naval and Royal Albert Yacht (Portsmouth).

BLACKMUN, Harry A(ndrew); Associate Justice, United States Supreme Court, since 1970; *b* Nashville, Illinois, 12 Nov. 1908; *s* of late Corwin Manning Blackmun and of Theo Huegely (*née* Reuter); *m* 1941, Dorothy E. Clark; three *d. Educ:* Harvard Univ.; Harvard Law Sch. AB, LLB. Admitted to Minnesota Bar, 1932; private legal practice with Dorsey, Colman, Barker, Scott & Barber, Minneapolis, 1934-50: Associate, 1934-38; Jun. Partner, 1939-42; General Partner, 1943-50; Instructor: St Paul Coll. of Law, 1935-41; Univ. of Minnesota Law Sch., 1945-47; Resident Counsel, Mayo Clinic, Rochester, 1950-59; Judge, US Ct of Appeals, 8th Circuit, 1959-70. Member: American Bar Assoc.; Amer. Judicature Soc.; Minnesota State Bar Assoc.; 3rd Judicial Dist (Minn) Bar Assoc.; Olmsted Co. (Minn) Bar Assoc.; Judicial Conf. Adv. Cttee on Judicial Activities; Rep. of Judicial Br., Nat. Historical Pubns and Records Commn; Mem., Bd of Mems, Mayo Assoc. Rochester, 1953-60; Bd of Dirs and Exec. Cttee, Rochester Methodist Hosp., 1954-70;

Trustee: Hamline Univ., St Paul, 1964-70; William Mitchell Coll. of Law, St Paul, 1959-74. Chm. Faculty, Salzburg Seminar in Amer. Studies (Law), 1977; participant, Franco-Amer. Colloquium on Human Rights, Paris, 1979. Hon. LLD: De Pauw Univ., 1971; Hamline Univ., 1971; Ohio Wesleyan Univ., 1971; Morningside Coll., 1972; Wilson Coll., 1972; Dickinson Sch. of Law 1973; Drake Univ., 1975; Southern Illinois Univ., 1976; Pepperdine Univ., 1976; Emory Univ., 1976; Rensselaer Polytech. Inst., 1979; Hon. DPS, Ohio Northern Univ., 1973; Hon. DHL Oklahoma City, 1976. *Publications:* contrib. legal and medical jls. *Recreations:* gardening, reading, music. *Address:* Supreme Court Building, 1 First Street NE, Washington, DC 20543, USA. *Club:* Cosmos (Washington, DC).

BLACKSHAW, Alan, VRD 1970; business consultant and author; Consultant, National Coal Board, since 1979; Consultant Director, Strategy International Ltd, since 1980; *b* 7 April 1933; *s* of Frederick William and late Elsie Blackshaw; *m* 1956, Jane Elizabeth Turner (separated 1980); one *d. Educ:* elem. schs; Merchant Taylors' Sch., Crosby (Foundn Schol.); Wadham Coll., Oxford (Open Major Schol., MA). Royal Marines, 1954-56: commnd 1955; subseq. Royal Marines Reserve until 1974. Entered Home Civil Service, Min. of Power, 1956; 1st Sec., UK Delegn to OECD, Paris, 1965-66 (on loan to FO); Principal Private Sec. to Minister of Power, 1967-69; Iron and Steel Div., DTI, 1969; with Charterhouse Gp on loan, 1972-73; Dept of Energy: Under Sec., 1974; Offshore Supplies Office, 1974-78 (Dir-Gen., 1977-78); Coal Div., 1978-79. Member: Offshore Energy Technol. Bd, 1977-78; Ship and Marine Technol. Requirements Bd, 1977-78. Achieved substantial High Court damages for libel against Daily Mail and Daily Telegraph, 1981. Pres., Oxford Univ. Mountaineering Club, 1953-54; Alpine Club: Editor, Alpine Jl, 1968-70; Trustee, 1968-; Vice-Pres., 1979-81; Leader, British Alpine Ski Traverse, 1972; Ski Club of Great Britain: Mem. Council, 1973-76; Vice-Pres., 1977-80; Pery Medal, 1977; Pres., Eagle Ski Club, 1979-81; Chm., Ski Touring and Mountaineering Cttee, British Ski Fedn, 1980-; Mem. Cttee of Management, Mount Everest Foundn Trust, 1968-73; British Mountaineering Council: Pres., 1973-76; Patron, 1979-; Chm., Standing Adv. Cttee on Mountain Trng Policy, 1980-. Freeman, City of London. FRGS; FInstPet. *Publication:* Mountaineering, 1965, 3rd revision 1975. *Recreations:* mountaineering and ski-ing. *Address:* 4 St George's Square, SW1V 2HP. *T:* 01-821 8720. *Club:* Royal Scottish Automobile.

BLACKSHAW, James William, CMG 1951; MBE 1920; Assistant Secretary, Ministry of Supply, 1946-55, retired; *b* 8 June 1895; *s* of Arthur Joseph Blackshaw; *m* 1927, Edith Violet, *d* of George Hansford. *Educ:* Doncaster Grammar Sch. Civil Service from 1911. *Address:* 70 Victoria Avenue, Shanklin, Isle of Wight. *T:* Shanklin 2336.

BLACKSHAW, William Simon; Headmaster of Brighton College, since 1971; *b* 28 Oct. 1930; *s* of late C. B. Blackshaw, sometime Housemaster, Cranleigh School and Kathleen Mary (who *m* 1965, Sir Thomas McAlpine, Bt, *qv*); *m* 1956, Elizabeth Anne Evans; two *s* one *d. Educ:* Sherborne Sch.; Hertford Coll., Oxford. 2nd cl. hons Mod. Langs. Repton School: Asst Master, 1955-71; Head of Modern Languages Dept, 1961-66; Housemaster, 1966-71. *Publication:* Regardez! Racontez!, 1971. *Recreations:* philately, painting, cricket, golf. *Address:* Brighton College, Eastern Road, Brighton BN2 2AL. *T:* Brighton 605788.

BLACKSTONE, Prof. Tessa Ann Vosper, PhD; Professor of Educational Administration in the University of London at the Institute of Education, since 1978; *b* 27 Sept. 1942; *d* of Geoffrey Vaughan Blackstone and Joanna Blackstone; *m* 1963, Tom Evans (marr. diss.); one *s* one *d. Educ:* Ware Grammar Sch.; London School of Economics (BScSoc, PhD). Associate Lectr, Enfield Coll., 1965-66; Asst Lectr, then Lectr, Dept of Social Administration, LSE, 1966-75; Adviser, Central Policy Review Staff, Cabinet Office, 1975-78. Fellow, Centre for Studies in Social Policy, 1972-74. *Publications:* Students in Conflict (jtly), 1970; A Fair Start, 1971; Education and Day Care for Young Children in Need, 1973; The Academic Labour Market (jtly), 1974; Social Policy and Administration in Britain, 1975; Disadvantage and Education (jtly), 1982; Educational Policy and Educational Inequality (jtly), 1982. *Address:* 11 Grazebrook Road, N16 0HU. *T:* 01-802 1132.

BLACKWELL, Basil Davenport, MA, BSc(Eng), FEng; Vice-Chairman and Chief Executive, Westland Group of Companies, since 1974; Chairman: Westland Helicopters Ltd, since 1976; British Hovercraft Corpn., since 1979; Normalair-Garrett Ltd, since 1979; *b* Whitkirk, Yorks, 8 Feb. 1922; *s* of late Alfred Blackwell and late Mrs H. Lloyd; *m* 1948, Betty Meggs, *d* of late Engr Captain Meggs, RN; one *d. Educ:* Leeds Grammar Sch.; St John's Coll., Cambridge (MA; Hughes Prize); London Univ. (BScEng). FIMechE; FRAeS; CBIM. Sci. Officer, Admiralty, 1942; Rolls-Royce Ltd, 1945; Engine Div., Bristol Aeroplane Co. Ltd, 1949; Bristol Siddeley Engines Ltd: Dep. Chief Engr, 1959; Sales Dir, 1963; Man. Dir, Small Engine Div., 1965 (subseq. Small Engines Div. of Rolls-Royce Ltd). Commercial Dir, Westland Aircraft Ltd, 1970; Man. Dir, Westland Helicopters Ltd, 1972. Member Council: BIM; CBI; NDIC; SBAC (Vice-Pres., 1978; Pres., 1979 and 1980; Dep. Pres., 1980). *Publications:* contrib. professional jls. *Recreations:* gardens and gardening. *Address:* High Newland, Newland Garden, Sherborne, Dorset DT9 3AF. *T:* Sherborne 3516.

BLACKWELL, Sir Basil Henry, Kt 1956; JP; President of B. H. Blackwell Ltd (Chairman, 1924-69); Chairman, Basil Blackwell and Mott Ltd, 1922-69, and The Shakespeare Head Press, 1921-69; *b* 29 May 1889; *s* of late Benjamin

Henry and late Lydia Blackwell; *m* 1914, Marion Christine (*d* 1977), *d* of late John Soans; one *s* three *d* (and one *s* decd). *Educ:* Magdalen College Sch.; Merton Coll., Oxford. 2nd Class Lit. Hum; studied publishing at the Oxford Press, Amen Corner; joined father in Oxford, 1913; started publishing independently, 1919; formed the Shakespeare Head Press Ltd to carry on and develop the work of the late A. H. Bullen, 1921; formed Basil Blackwell and Mott Ltd (publishers), 1922; succeeded father (the founder of the firm) as Chairman of B. H. Blackwell Ltd (booksellers), 1924; President: International Association of Antiquarian Booksellers, 1925 and 1926; Associated Booksellers of Great Britain and Ireland, 1934 and 1935; The Classical Assoc., 1964–65; William Morris Soc., 1968–79; English Assoc., 1969–70. Hon. Mem., Company of Stationers, 1973. Hon. Freeman of Oxford City. Hon. Fellow, Merton Coll., Oxford; Hon. LLD Manchester Univ., 1965; Hon. DCL Oxford, 1979. Officier d'Académie, France. *Recreation:* reading. *Address:* Osse Field, Appleton, Abingdon, Oxon. *T:* Oxford 862436. *Clubs:* Athenæum; Leander.
See also Julian Blackwell.

BLACKWELL, Prof. Donald Eustace, MA, PhD; Savilian Professor of Astronomy, University of Oxford, and Fellow of New College, Oxford, since 1960; *b* 27 May 1921; *s* of John Blackwell and Ethel Bowe; *m* 1951, Nora Louise Carlton; two *s* two *d*. *Educ:* Merchant Taylors' Sch.; Sandy Lodge; Sidney Sussex Coll., Cambridge. Isaac Newton Student, University of Cambridge, 1947; Stokes Student, Pembroke Coll., Cambridge, 1948; Asst Director, Solar Physics Observatory, Cambridge, 1950–60. Various Astronomical Expeditions: Sudan, 1952; Fiji, 1955; Bolivia, 1958 and 1961; Canada, 1963; Manuae Island, 1965. Pres., RAS, 1973–75. *Publications:* papers in astronomical journals. *Address:* Department of Astrophysics, South Parks Road, Oxford.

BLACKWELL, John Kenneth, CBE 1965; HM Diplomatic Service, retired; *b* 8 May 1914; *s* of late J. W. Blackwell; *m* 1951, Joan Hilary, *d* of late D. W. Field; two *s* one *d*. *Educ:* Downing Coll., Cambridge (MA). HM Foreign Service, 1938; Vice-consular posts, in China and Mozambique, 1938–45; Second Secretary, British Embassy, Copenhagen, 1946; Consul, Canton, 1947; served in FO, 1950; Consul: Recife, 1952; Basle, 1956; First Secretary and Head of Chancery, British Embassy, Seoul, 1957; served in FO, 1959; First Secretary with UK Delegn to the European Communities in Brussels, 1961; Consul-General: Hanoi, 1962; Lille, 1965; Sen. Trade Comr, Hong Kong, 1969–72; Ambassador to Costa Rica, 1972–74. *Recreations:* linguistics and entomology; walking. *Address:* Oakley Hay, Vincent Road, Selsey, Sussex.

BLACKWELL, Julian, (Toby); Chairman, The Blackwell Group Ltd, since 1980; *b* 10 Jan. 1929; *s* of Sir Basil Henry Blackwell, *qv* ; *m* 1953, Jennifer Jocelyn Darley Wykeham; two *s* one *d*. *Educ:* Winchester; Trinity Coll., Oxford. Served 5th RTR, 1947–49; 21st SAS (TA), 1950–59. Dir and Chm., various Blackwell companies, 1956–. Chm. Council, ASLIB, 1966–68 (Vice-Pres., 1982); Mem., Library and Inf. Services Council, 1981–; Co-founder and Chm., Mail Users' Council, 1975–78; Pres., Booksellers' Assoc., 1980–82. *Recreations:* sawing firewood, sailing. *Address:* c/o 50 Broad Street, Oxford OX1 3BQ. *T:* Oxford 44944. *Clubs:* Athenæum; Leander (Henley); Royal Southern Yacht (Southampton).

BLACKWELL, Thomas Francis, MBE (mil.) 1944; DL; Chairman: Colne Valley Water Company, since 1963; Turf Newspapers Ltd, since 1955; *b* 31 July 1912; *s* of late Thomas Geoffrey Blackwell and Shirley Maud Lawson-Johnston; *m* 1948, Lisette Douglas Pilkington (marr. dis. 1959); one *s* one *d*. *Educ:* Harrow, Magdalene Coll., Cambridge (MA). Mem. London Stock Exchange, 1935–42. Served War, Coldstream Guards, 1940–45: Bde Major, 5th Gds Armd Bde, 1944–45. Member of Lloyds, 1946. Captain Royal and Ancient Golf Club, 1963; Senior Steward of the Jockey Club, 1965 (Dep. Sen. Steward, 1973–76); Mem., Horserace Betting Levy Board, 1976–78. Chm., St John Council for Suffolk, 1970–82; KStJ 1981. Governor, Harrow School, 1975–82. DL Suffolk, 1974. *Recreations:* racing, shooting, golf. *Address:* Langham Hall, Bury St Edmunds, Suffolk. *T:* Walsham-le-Willows 271. *Clubs:* White's, Pratt's; Jockey (Newmarket).

BLACKWOOD, HAMILTON-TEMPLE-; family name of **Marquess of Dufferin.**

BLACKWOOD, Sir Francis (George), 7th Bt *cr* 1814; Retired Chemical Engineer; now in private practice as a Consulting Engineer; *b* 20 May 1916; *s* of Captain Maurice Baldwin Raymond Blackwood, DSO, RN (*d* 1941) (3rd *s* of 4th Bt) and Dorothea (*d* 1967), *d* of Hon. G. Bertrand Edwards, Sydney, NSW; *S* cousin, 1979; *m* 1941, Margaret Alice, *d* of Hector Kirkpatrick, Lindfield, NSW; two *s* one *d*. *Educ:* Knox Grammar School; Sydney Technical Coll. (ASTC). ARACI, FIEAust. Worked in the chemical industry, mainly for Union Carbide, Australia Ltd (formerly Timbrol Ltd) as a design engineer, 1936–78. *Recreations:* community service and domestic. *Heir:* *s* John Francis Blackwood, architect [*b* 18 Oct. 1944; *m* 1971, Kay Greenhill]. *Address:* 408 Bobbin Head Road, North Turramurra, NSW 2074, Australia. *T:* 44 5189. *Clubs:* Royal Automobile of Australia, Rotary.

BLACKWOOD, Wing Comdr George Douglas; Chairman, William Blackwood & Sons Ltd, publishers and printers, since 1948; Editor of Blackwood's Magazine, and Managing Director of William Blackwood & Sons Ltd, 1948–76; *b* 11 Oct. 1909; *e s* of late James H. Blackwood and *g g*

g s of Wm Blackwood, founder of Blackwood's Magazine; *m* 1936, Phyllis Marion, *y d* of late Sir John Caulcutt, KCMG; one *s* one *d*. *Educ:* Eton; Clare Coll., Cambridge. Short Service Commission in RAF, 1932–38; re-joined 1939. Formed first Czech Fighter Squadron, 1940–41; Battle of Britain (despatches); commanded Czech Wing of Royal Air Force 2nd TAF, 1944 (despatches); retired 1945. Czech War Cross, 1940; Czech Military Medal 1st class, 1944. *Recreations:* countryside activities. *Address:* Airhouse, Oxton, Berwickshire; 32 Thistle Street, Edinburgh. *T:* 031-225 3411.

BLACKWOOD, Dame Margaret, DBE 1981 (MBE 1964); PhD; Senior Associate and Cytogeneticist, University of Melbourne, since 1974; *b* 26 April 1909; *d* of late Robert Leslie Blackwood and Muriel Pearl Henry. *Educ:* Melbourne CofE Girls' Grammar Sch.; Melbourne Univ. (BSc, MSc 1938); Newnham Coll., Cambridge (PhD 1954). Served War, 1941–46; Wing Officer, WAAAF. University of Melbourne: Lectr, Sen. Lectr, Reader in Botany and Genetics, 1946–74; Dean of Women, Mildura Br., 1946–48; Founder Fellow, First Chm. of Council, Janet Clarke Hall, 1961; Fellow, Trinity Coll., 1980; Mem. Council, 1976–; Dep. Chancellor, 1980, 1981, 1982. Res. Asst, Univ. of Wisconsin, 1958; Carnegie Travel Fellow, 1958; Hon. Res. Fellow, Birmingham Univ., 1959. Hon. Organising Sec., Melbourne Congress, ANZAAS, 1977; former Sec., Internat. Fedn of Univ. Women (Victoria); Aust.-NZ Chm., Soroptimist Internat., 1957–58; Hon. Mem., SI of SW Pacific. Member: Royal Soc. of Vic; Aust. Genetics Soc.; British Lichen Soc. FANZAAS 1979. Chapman Medal, Inst. of Engrs, 1975. *Publications:* contribs to scientific jls. *Recreations:* music, photography, lichenology. *Address:* 63 Morrah Street, Parkville, Vic 3052, Australia; Botany School, University of Melbourne, Grattan Street, Parkville, Vic 3052. *Club:* Lyceum (Melbourne).
See also Sir R. R. Blackwood.

BLACKWOOD, Sir Robert (Rutherford), Kt 1961; Chairman, Dunlop Australia Ltd, 1972–79 (General Manager, 1948–66); *b* Melbourne, 3 June 1906; *s* of Robert Leslie Blackwood and Muriel Pearl (*née* Henry); *m* 1932, Hazel Lavinia McLeod; one *s* one *d*. *Educ:* Melbourne C of E Grammar Sch.; Univ. of Melbourne. BEE 1929, MCE 1932, Melbourne. Senior Demonstrator and Res. Scholar, University of Melbourne, 1928–30; Lecturer in Agric. Engineering, 1931–33; Res. Engineer Dunlop Rubber, Australia, Ltd, 1933–35; Tech. Man., 1936–46; Prof. of Mech. Engineering, University of Melbourne, 1947. Chm. Interim Council, Monash Univ., 1958–61; Chancellor, Monash Univ., 1961–68. Member Cttee on Medical Education, Victoria, 1960. Trustee, National Museum of Victoria, 1964–78, Pres. Council, 1971–78; Pres., Royal Soc. of Victoria, 1973–74. FIE Aust, 1948; Hon. LLD Monash, 1971; Hon. DTech Asian Inst. of Technology, Bangkok, 1978. *Publications:* Monash University: the first ten years, 1968; Beautiful Bali, 1970; papers in engrg jls. *Recreation:* painting. *Address:* 8 Huntingfield Road, Melbourne, Victoria 3186, Australia. *T:* 592-5925. *Clubs:* Melbourne, Athenæum (Melbourne).
See also Dame M. Blackwood.

BLACKWOOD, Prof. William; Professor of Neuropathology, University of London, at the Institute of Neurology, The National Hospital, Queen Square, 1958–76, now Professor Emeritus; *b* 13 March 1911; *m* 1940, Cynthia Gledstone; one *s* one *d*. *Educ:* Cheltenham Coll.; Edinburgh Univ. MB, ChB Edinburgh 1934; FRCSEd 1938; FRCPEd 1961; FRCPath (FCPath 1963). Pathologist, Scottish Mental Hospitals Laboratory; Neuropathologist, Edinburgh Royal Infirmary, and Municipal Hospitals, 1939; Senior Lecturer in Neuropathology, University of Edinburgh, 1945; Asst Pathologist, 1947, Pathologist, 1949, The National Hospital, Queen Square, London. *Publications:* Atlas of Neuropathology, 1949; (ed jtly) Greenfield's Neuropathology, 3rd 3dn, 1976. *Address:* 71 Seal Hollow Road, Sevenoaks, Kent. *T:* Sevenoaks 454345.

BLADES, family name of **Baron Ebbisham.**

BLAGDEN, Sir John (Ramsay), Kt 1970; OBE 1944; TD 1943; Regional Chairman of Industrial Tribunals for East Anglia, 1969–80; *b* Davos, Switzerland, 25 July 1908; *s* of John William Blagden, PhD, MA, and Johanna Alberta (*née* Martin); *m* 1937, Pauline Catherine Robinson; three *d*. *Educ:* Hawtreys; Marlborough; Emmanuel Coll., Cambridge (MA). Joined 7th Bn The Essex Regt TA, 2nd Lieut, 1928; Capt. 1935; Major 1938; called to Bar, Lincoln's Inn, 1934; Practised at Bar, 1934–39; War Service, 1939–45; Lt-Col, CO 64th HAA Regt, RA, 1943; BNAF, 1943; CMF and Land Forces Adriatic, 1944–45; BLA, 1945 (OBE, despatches twice, TD two clasps). Col 1945, Perm. Pres., Mil. Govt Courts, BAOR, Nov. 1945; Judge of Control Commn Courts, Germany, 1947; Sen. Magistrate, Sarawak, 1950; Actg Puisne Judge and Sen. Magistrate, Sarawak, 1951–56; Co-Ed. Sarawak Gazette, 1955; Puisne Judge, Trinidad, 1956–60; Trinidad Ed., West Indian Reports, 1959–60; Puisne Judge, Northern Rhodesia, 1960–64; Justice of Appeal, Northern Rhodesia and Zambia, 1964–65; Chief Justice, Zambia, 1965–69. Grand Cordon of Order of Star of Honour of Ethiopia, 1965. *Recreations:* photography, ski-ing, riding, walking, tennis, alpinism; watching cricket and motor racing. *Address:* Jackdaws Ford, Chelsworth, Ipswich, Suffolk. *T:* Bildeston 740461. *Club:* Special Forces.

BLAIKLEY, Robert Marcel; HM Diplomatic Service, retired; *b* 1 Oct. 1916; *s* of late Alexander John Blaikley and late Adelaide Blaikley (*née* Miller); *m* 1942, Alice Mary Duncan; one *s* one *d*. *Educ:* Christ's Coll., Finchley; St John's Coll., Cambridge. Served HM Forces, 1940–46. Inland Revenue, 1946–48;

General Register Office, 1948-65, Asst Secretary, 1958; transferred to Diplomatic Service as Counsellor, 1965; on loan to Colonial Office, 1965-66; Head of Aviation and Telecommunications Dept, CO, 1966-68; Counsellor, Jamaica, 1968-71, Ghana, 1971-73. *Recreations:* walking, choral singing. *Address:* 17 Chestnut Grove, Upper Westwood, Bradford-on-Avon, Wilts.

BLAIR, Sir Alastair Campbell, KCVO 1969 (CVO 1953); TD 1950; WS; JP; *b* 16 Jan. 1908; 2nd *s* of late William Blair, WS, and late Amelia Mylne Campbell; *m* 1933, Catriona Hatchard, *o d* of late Dr William Basil Orr; four *s. Educ:* Cargilfield; Charterhouse; Clare Coll., Cambridge (BA); Edinburgh Univ. (LLB). Writer to the Signet, 1932; retired 1977 as Partner, Dundas & Wilson, CS. RA (TA) 1939; served 1939-45 (despatches); Secretary, Queen's Body Guard for Scotland, Royal Company of Archers, 1946-59; appointed Captain 1982. Purse Bearer to The Lord High Commissioner to the General Assembly of the Church of Scotland, 1961-69. JP Edinburgh, 1954. *Recreations:* archery, curling, golf, shooting. *Address:* 14 Ainslie Place, Edinburgh EH3 6AS. *T:* 031-225 3081. *Club:* New (Edinburgh).
    See also M. C. Blair.

BLAIR, Lt.-Gen. Sir Chandos, KCVO 1972; OBE 1962; MC 1941 and bar, 1944; GOC Scotland and Governor of Edinburgh Castle, 1972-76; *b* 25 Feb. 1919; *s* of Brig.-Gen. Arthur Blair and Elizabeth Mary (*née* Hoskyns); *m* 1947, Audrey Mary Travers; one *s* one *d. Educ:* Harrow; Sandhurst. Commnd into Seaforth Highlanders, 1939; comd 4 KAR, Uganda, 1959-61; comd 39 Bde, Radfan and N. Ireland. GOC 2nd Division, BAOR, 1968-70; Defence Services Secretary, MoD, 1970-72. Col Comdt, Scottish Div., 1972-76; Col, Queen's Own Highlanders, 1975-. *Recreations:* golf, tennis, fishing, shooting, hunting. *Address:* c/o Royal Bank of Scotland, 44 Brompton Road, SW3. *Club:* Naval and Military.

BLAIR, Charles Neil Molesworth, CMG 1962; OBE (mil.) 1948; Lt-Col; *b* 22 Oct. 1910; *o s* of late Col J. M. Blair, CMG, CBE, DSO, Glenfoot, Tillicoultry, Scotland; *m* 1938, Elizabeth Dorothea, *d* of late Lord Justice Luxmoore, PC; one *d* (one *s* decd). *Educ:* Stowe; RMC Sandhurst. 2nd Lieut The Black Watch, 1930. Served War of 1939-45 in Europe, North Africa and Sicily; Instructor, Army Staff Coll., 1941 and 1944; commanded 1st Black Watch, 1945. Retired from Army on account of war wounds, 1951. Attached FO, 1951-67. *Address:* Portbane, Kenmore, Perthshire. *T:* Kenmore 229. *Club:* Army and Navy.

BLAIR, Claude; FSA 1956; Keeper, Department of Metalwork, Victoria and Albert Museum, since 1972; *b* 30 Nov. 1922; *s* of late William Henry Murray Blair and Lilian Wearing; *m* 1952, Joan Mary Greville Drinkwater; one *s. Educ:* William Hulme's Grammar Sch., Manchester; Manchester Univ. (MA). Served War, Army (Captain RA), 1942-46. Manchester Univ., 1946-51; Asst, Tower of London Armouries, 1951-56; Asst Keeper of Metalwork, V&A, 1956-66; Dep. Keeper, 1966-72. Hon. Editor, Jl of the Arms and Armour Soc., 1953-77. Hon. President: Soc. for Study of Church Monuments; Meyrick Soc.; Hon. Vice-Pres., Monumental Brass Soc. Hon. Freeman, Cutlers' Co. Liveryman: Goldsmiths' Co.; Armourers and Brasiers' Co. Medal of Musée Militar, Barcelona, 1969. *Publications:* European Armour, 1958 (2nd edn, 1972); European and American Arms, 1962; The Silvered Armour of Henry VIII, 1965; Pistols of the World, 1968; Three Presentation Swords in the Victoria and Albert Museum, 1972; The James A. de Rothschild Collection: Arms, Armour and Miscellaneous Metalwork, 1974; numerous articles and reviews in Archaeological Jl, Jl of Arms and Armour Soc., Connoisseur, Waffen-und Kostümkunde, etc. *Recreations:* travel, looking at churches, listening to music. *Address:* 90 Links Road, Ashtead, Surrey KT21 2HW. *T:* Ashtead 75532. *Club:* Anglo-Polish.

BLAIR, David Arthur, MBE 1943; MC 1944; Chairman, Export Committee (Scotch Whisky), 1965-80, retired; *b* 25 Aug. 1917; *s* of Brig.-Gen. A. Blair, DSO; *m* 1947, Elizabeth Adela Morton; two *s* one *d* (and one *d* decd). *Educ:* Harrow; Sandhurst. Commnd Seaforth Highlanders, 1937; served War of 1939-45, Middle East and Europe; psc, India 1945; resigned commn and entered Distillers Co. Ltd, 1949, as export representative, Dir, 1964-79; Chm., United Glass Ltd, 1976-79. *Recreations:* golf, field sports. *Address:* Lilliesleaf House, Lilliesleaf, Roxburghshire. *Clubs:* White's; New (Edinburgh); Royal and Ancient St Andrews (Captain 1978-79).

BLAIR, G. W. S.; *see* Scott Blair.

BLAIR, Rev. Canon Harold Arthur, MA, BD; Canon Residentiary and Chancellor of Truro Cathedral, 1960-75, now Emeritus; *b* 22 Sept. 1902; *s* of Rev. A. A. Blair, SPG Mission, India, some time rector of Saxlingham, Holt, Norfolk; *m* 1933, Honor MacAdam, *d* of Col W. MacAdam, CB, RE; two *s* one *d. Educ:* Lancing Coll.; St Edmund Hall, Oxford. BA (2nd cl. Hons Theol.) 1925; MA 1937; BD (Oxon) 1945. Classical Tutor, Dorchester Missionary Coll., 1925-27; Gold Coast Administrative Service, 1927; Asst District Comr, 1928; District Comr, 1935, retd 1939. Ordained Deacon, 1939, Priest, 1940; Asst Curate, Sherborne, 1939-41; Vicar of: Horningsham, Wilts, 1941-45; Winterbourne Earls with Winterbourne Dauntsey and Winterbourne Gunner, 1945-54; St James, Southbroom, Devizes, 1954-60. Hon. Canon of Salisbury, 1953 (prebend of Alton Australis); Examining Chaplain: to Bishop of Salisbury, 1952-60; to Bishop of Truro, 1960-81. *Publications:* A Creed before the Creeds, 1954; The Ladder of Temptations, 1960; A Stranger in the House, 1963; essay in Agreed Syllabus of Religious Education (Cornwall), 1964; two essays in Teilhard Re-assessed (symposium),

1970; various articles in Church Quarterly Review. *Recreations:* gardening, cycling, story-telling. *Address:* Beech Cottage, 79 Acreman Street, Sherborne, Dorset DT9 3PH. *T:* Sherborne 2353.

BLAIR, Rt. Rev. James Douglas, CBE 1975; *b* 22 Jan. 1906; *s* of Rev. A. A. Blair; unmarried. *Educ:* Marlborough; Keble Coll., Oxford; Cuddesdon Coll. 2nd class Lit. Hum., 1928. Deacon, Penistone, Yorks, 1929; Priest, 1930; Oxford Mission Brotherhood of the Epiphany, Calcutta, 1932-; Asst Bishop of Calcutta, with charge of East Bengal, 1951; Bishop of East Bengal, 1956; title of diocese changed to Dacca, 1960; retired as Bishop of Dacca, 1975. *Recreation:* walking. *Address:* Oxford Mission, Barisha, Calcutta 700008, India.

BLAIR, Sir James H.; *see* Hunter Blair.

BLAIR, Michael Campbell; Circuit Administrator, Midland and Oxford Circuit, since 1982; *b* 26 Aug. 1941; *s* of Sir Alastair Blair, *qv* ; *m* 1966, Halldóra Isabel (*née* Tunnard); one *s. Educ:* Rugby Sch.; Clare Coll., Cambridge (MA, LLB); Yale Univ., USA (Mellon Fellow; MA). Called to the Bar, Middle Temple, 1965 (Harmsworth Law Scholar). Lord Chancellor's Dept, 1966-: Private Sec. to the Lord Chancellor, 1968-71; Sec., Law Reform Cttee, 1977-79; Under-Sec., 1982. *Publications:* Sale of Goods Act 1979, 1980; legal articles in Modern Law Rev., Lancet, New Law Jl, Civil Justice Qly. *Address:* Wootton House, 34 Brook Street, Warwick CV34 4BL. *T:* Warwick 491774; 3 Burbage Road, SE24 9HJ. *T:* 01-274 7614. *Club:* Athenæum.

BLAIR, Thomas Alexander, QC (NI) 1958; Chief Social Security (formerly National Insurance) Commissioner (Northern Ireland), since 1969; *b* 12 Dec. 1916; *s* of late John Blair and of Wilhelmina Whitla Blair (*née* Downey); *m* 1947, Ida Irvine Moore; two *s* one *d. Educ:* Royal Belfast Academical Instn; Queen's Univ. Belfast (BA, LLB). Served War, in Royal Navy, 1940-46 (commissioned, 1941). Called to Bar of N Ireland, 1946. Chairman: Wages Councils; War Pensions Appeal Tribunal. Sen. Crown Counsel for Co. Tyrone; Mem. Departmental Cttee on Legal Aid. Apptd Dep. Nat. Insurance Umpire, 1959; Pres., Industrial Tribunals (NI), 1967-69; Chief Nat. Insurance Commissioner (NI), 1969. *Recreation:* golf. *Address:* 10 Knockdene Park, Belfast BT5 7AD. *T:* 655182.

BLAIR-CUNYNGHAME, Sir James (Ogilvy), Kt 1976; OBE 1945 (MBE 1943); Chairman, The Royal Bank of Scotland Group plc, 1968-78, Director 1968-82; Director: Royal Bank of Scotland plc (Chairman, 1971-76); Williams & Glyn's Bank plc (Chairman, 1976-78); Provincial Insurance plc (Deputy Chairman, since 1979); Scottish Mortgage and Trust plc; *b* 28 Feb. 1913; 2nd *s* of late Edwin Blair-Cunynghame and Anne Tod, both of Edinburgh. *Educ:* Sedbergh Sch.; King's Coll., Cambridge (MA). Elected Fellow, St Catharine's Coll., 1939. Served War of 1939-45 (MBE, OBE); RA and Intelligence, Mediterranean and Europe, Lt-Col 1944. FO, 1946-47; Chief Personnel Officer, BOAC, 1947-55; Dir-Gen. of Staff, National Coal Board, 1955-57; Mem. for Staff of Nat. Coal Bd, 1957-59; part-time Mem., Pay Board, 1973-74. Member: Scottish Economic Council, 1965-74; Exec. Cttee Scottish Council Devel and Industry; Council of Industry for Management Educn; Ct of Governors London Sch. of Economics and Political Science; Council Industrial Soc.; Governor, Sedbergh Sch.; Trustee, Internat. Centre for Res. in Accountancy. FBIM; CIPM. Mem., Queen's Body Guard for Scotland. Hon. LLD St Andrews, 1965; Hon. DSc (Soc. Sci.) Edinburgh, 1969. Hon. FRCSE 1978; FIB 1977. *Publications:* various articles on aspects of personnel management and the economy. *Recreation:* fishing. *Address:* Broomfield, Moniaive, Thornhill, Dumfriesshire. *T:* Moniaive 217. *Clubs:* Savile, Flyfishers'; New, Scottish Arts (Edinburgh).

BLAIR-KERR, Sir William Alexander, (Sir Alastair Blair-Kerr), Kt 1973; President of the Court of Appeal for Bermuda, since 1979; President of the Court of Appeal for the Bahamas, since 1978; Member, Court of Appeal for Gibraltar, since 1982; *b* 1 Dec. 1911; *s* of William Alexander Milne Kerr and Annie Kerr (*née* Blair), Dunblane, Perthshire, Scotland; *m* 1942, Esther Margaret Fowler Wright; one *s* one *d. Educ:* McLaren High Sch., Callander; Edinburgh Univ. (MA, LLB). Solicitor in Scotland, 1939; Advocate (Scots Bar), 1951. Advocate and Solicitor, Singapore, 1939-41; Straits Settlements Volunteer Force, 1941-42; escaped from Singapore, 1942; Indian Army: Staff Capt. "A" Bombay Dist. HQ, 1942-43; DAAG 107 Line of Communication area HQ, Poona, 1943-44; British Army: GSO2, War Office, 1944-45; SO1 Judicial, BMA Malaya, 1945-46. Colonial Legal Service (HM Overseas Service): Hong Kong: Magistrate, 1946-48; Crown Counsel, 1949; Pres. Tenancy Tribunal, 1950; Crown Counsel, 1951-53; Sen. Crown Counsel, 1953-59; District Judge, 1959-61; Puisne Judge, Supreme Court, 1961-71; Sen. Puisne Judge, Supreme Court, 1971-73; sometime Actg Chief Justice of Hong Kong. Pres., various Commns of Inquiry. *Recreations:* golf, walking, music. *Address:* Gairn, Kinbuck, Dunblane, Perthshire FK15 0NQ. *T:* Dunblane 823377. *Club:* Royal Over-Seas League.

BLAIR-OLIPHANT, Air Vice-Marshal David Nigel Kington, CB 1966; OBE 1945; *b* 22 Dec. 1911; *y s* of Col P. L. K. Blair-Oliphant, DSO, Ardblair Castle, Blairgowrie, Perthshire, and Laura Geraldine Bodenham; *m* 1942, Helen Nathalie Donald, *yr d* of Sir John Donald, KCIE; one *s* (and one *s* and one *d* decd). *Educ:* Harrow; Trinity Hall, Cambridge (BA). Joined RAF, 1934; Middle East and European Campaigns, 1939-45; RAF Staff Coll., 1945-48; Group Capt. 1949; Air Cdre 1958; Director, Weapons Engineering, Air Ministry, 1958-60; British Defence Staffs, Washington, 1960-63; Acting

Air Vice-Marshal, 1963; Pres., Ordnance Board, 1965-66; Air Vice-Marshal, 1966. *Address:* 9 Northfield Road, Sherfield-on-Lodon, Basingstoke, Hants. *Clubs:* Royal Air Force.

BLAKE, family name of **Baron Blake.**

BLAKE, Baron *cr* 1971 (Life Peer), of Braydeston, Norfolk; **Robert Norman William Blake,** FBA 1967; JP; Provost of The Queen's College, Oxford, since 1968; Pro-Vice-Chancellor, Oxford University, since 1971; Editor, Dictionary of National Biography, since 1980; *b* 23 Dec. 1916; *er s* of William Joseph Blake and Norah Lindley Daynes, Brundall, Norfolk; *m* 1953, Patricia Mary, *e d* of Thomas Richard Waters, Great Plumstead, Norfolk; three *d. Educ:* King Edward VI Sch., Norwich; Magdalen Coll., Oxford (MA), 1st Cl. Final Honour Sch. of Modern Greats, 1938; Eldon Law Scholar, 1938. Served War of 1939-45; Royal Artillery; North African campaign, 1942; POW in Italy, 1942-44; escaped, 1944; despatches, 1944. Lectr in Politics, Christ Church, Oxford, 1946-47; Student and Tutor in Politics, Christ Church, 1947-68, Emeritus Student, 1969; Censor, 1950-55; Senior Proctor, 1959-60; Ford's Lectr in English History for 1967-68; Mem., Hebdomadal Council, 1959-. Member: Royal Commn on Historical Manuscripts, 1975-; Bd of Trustees, BM, 1978-. Chm., Hansard Soc. Commn on Electoral Reform, 1975-76. Mem. (Conservative) Oxford City Council, 1957-64. Governor of Norwich Sch., of Trent, Bradfield and Malvern Colls, and of St Edward's Sch., Oxford; Rhodes Trustee, 1971. Prime Warden, Dyers' Co., 1976-77. Hon. Student, Christ Church, Oxford, 1977. Hon. DLitt Glasgow, 1972. *Publications:* The Private Papers of Douglas Haig, 1952; The Unknown Prime Minister (Life of Andrew Bonar Law), 1955; Disraeli, 1966; The Conservative Party from Peel to Churchill, 1970; The Office of Prime Minister, 1975; (ed with John Patten) The Conservative Opportunity, 1976; A History of Rhodesia, 1977; Disraeli's Grand Tour, 1982. *Address:* The Queen's College, Oxford; Riverview House, Brundall, Norfolk. *Clubs:* Beefsteak, Brooks's, United Oxford & Cambridge University; Vincent's (Oxford); Norfolk County.

BLAKE, Sir Alfred (Lapthorn), KCVO 1979 (CVO 1975); MC 1945; Director, The Duke of Edinburgh's Award Scheme, 1967-78; Partner in Blake, Lapthorn, Rea & Williams, Solicitors, Portsmouth and area; *b* 6 Oct. 1915; *s* of late Leonard Nicholson Blake and Nora Woodfall Blake (*née* Lapthorn); *m* 1st, 1940, Beatrice Grace Nellthorp (*d* 1967); two *s*; 2nd, 1969, Mrs Alison Kelsey Dick, Boston, Mass, USA. *Educ:* Dauntsey's Sch. LLB (London), 1938. Qual. Solicitor and Notary Public, 1938. Royal Marines Officer, 1939-45: Bde Major 2 Commando Bde, 1944; Lieut-Col comdg 45 (RM) Commando and Holding Operational Commando, 1945 (despatches). Mem., Portsmouth CC, 1950-67 (Past Chm., Portsmouth Educn Cttee); Lord Mayor of Portsmouth, 1958-59. Mem., Youth Service Development Coun., 1960-66; Pres., Portsmouth Youth Activities Cttee. Lay Canon, Portsmouth Cathedral, 1962-72. Hon. Fellow, Portsmouth Polytechnic, 1981. *Recreation:* golf. *Address:* 1 A'Becket Court, St Thomas's Street, Portsmouth, PO1 2HQ. *T:* Portsmouth 823094. *Club:* Royal Naval and Royal Albert Yacht (Portsmouth).

BLAKE, Charles Henry, CB 1966; a Commissioner of Customs and Excise, 1968-72; European Adviser, British American Tobacco Co., 1972-76; *b* 29 Nov. 1912; *s* of Henry and Lily Blake, Westbury on Trym, Bristol; *m* 1938, M. Jayne McKinney (*d* 1974), *d* of James and Ellen McKinney, Castle Finn, Co. Donegal; three *d. Educ:* Cotham Grammar Sch.; Jesus Coll., Cambridge (Major Scholar). Administrative Class, Home Civil Service, 1936; HM Customs and Excise: Princ., 1941; Asst Sec., 1948; Comr and Sec., 1957-64; Asst Under-Sec. of State, Air Force Dept, MoD, 1964-68. *Recreation:* gardens. *Address:* 33 Grenville Court, Chorleywood, Herts. *T:* Chorleywood 3795. *Clubs:* United Oxford & Cambridge University; Moor Park.

BLAKE, Prof. Christopher, FRSE; Bonar Professor of Applied Economics, University of Dundee, since 1974; *b* 28 April 1926; *s* of George Blake and Eliza Blake; *m* 1951, Elizabeth McIntyre; two *s* two *d. Educ:* Dollar Academy; St Andrews Univ. MA St Andrews 1950, PhD St Andrews 1965. Served in Royal Navy, 1944-47. Teaching posts, Bowdoin Coll., Maine, and Princeton Univ., 1951-53; Asst. Edinburgh Univ., 1953-55; Stewarts & Lloyds Ltd, 1955-60; Lectr and Sen. Lectr, Univ. of St Andrews, 1960-67; Sen. Lectr and Prof. of Economics, Univ. of Dundee, 1967-74. Director: Alliance Trust Co. plc, 1974-; William Low & Co. plc, 1980-. Member: Council for Applied Science in Scotland, 1978-; Royal Commn on Envtl Pollution, 1980-; Dep. Chm., Clothing Industry Wages Council, 1981-. *Publications:* articles in economic and other jls. *Recreation:* golf. *Address:* 1 Osborne Place, Dundee DD2 1BE. *T:* Dundee 641060. *Clubs:* Royal Scottish Automobile (Glasgow), Royal and Ancient (St Andrews).

BLAKE, Dr Eugene Carson; General Secretary, World Council of Churches, 1966-72; *b* St Louis, Mo, USA, 7 Nov. 1906; *s* of Orville P. Blake and Lulu (*née* Carson); *m* 1st, 1929, Valina Gillespie; 2nd, 1974, Jean Ware Hoyt. *Educ:* Princeton Univ.; New Coll., Edinburgh; Princeton Theological Seminary. Taught at Forman Christian Coll., Lahore, 1928-29; Asst Pastor, St Nicholas, NYC, 1932-35; Pastor: First Presbyterian Church, Albany, 1935-40; Pasadena Presbyterian Church, 1940-51. Stated Clerk, Gen. Assembly: Presbyterian Church of USA, 1951-58; United Presbyterian Church in USA, 1958-66. National Council of Churches of Christ in USA: Pres., 1954-57; subseq. Mem., Gen. Board; Chm., Commn on Religion and Race. Member: Central Cttee, Exec. Cttee, World Council of Churches, 1954-66. Trustee: Princeton

Seminary; Occidental Coll.; San Francisco Theol Seminary. Visiting Lect Williams Coll., 1938-40. Has many hon. degrees. *Publications:* He is Lord c All, 1956; The Church in the Next Decade, 1966. *Recreation:* golf. *Addres* 204 Davenport Drive, Stamford, Conn 06902, USA.

BLAKE, Sir Francis Michael, 3rd Bt *cr* 1907; *b* 11 July 1943; *o s* of Sir ⊮ Edward C. Blake, 2nd Bt and Olive Mary (*d* 1946) *d* of Charles Lidde Simpson; *S* father, 1950; *m* 1968, Joan Ashbridge, *d* of F. C. A. Miller; tw *s. Educ:* Rugby. Heir: *s* Francis Julian Blake, *b* 17 Feb. 1971. *Address:* Th Dower House, Tillmouth Park, Cornhill-on-Tweed, Northumberland. *T* Coldstream 2443.

BLAKE, Henry E.; *see* Elliott-Blake.

BLAKE, (Henry) Vincent; marketing consultant; Secretary, Glassfibe Reinforced Cement Association, since 1977; *b* 7 Dec. 1912; *s* of Arthu Vincent Blake and Alice Mabel (*née* Kerr); *m* 1938, Marie Isobel Todd; on *s. Educ:* King Edward's High Sch., Birmingham. Pupil apprentice, Chanc Brothers, Lighthouse Engineers, Birmingham, 1931-34; subseq. Asst Salc Manager, 1937 and Sales Manager there, of Austinlite Ltd, 1945; Textil Marketing Manager, Fibreglass Ltd, 1951; Commercial Manager: Glass Yarn and Deeside Fabrics Ltd, 1960; BTR Industries Ltd, Glass and Resin Div 1962-63, Plastics Group, 1963-66; Gen. Manager, Indulex Engineering Cc Ltd, 1966-71. Mem. Council and Chm., Reinforced Plastics Gp, Britis Plastics Fedn, 1959. Mem. Council, Royal Yachting Assoc., 1980- (Vice Chm., Thames Valley Region, 1979-). *Publications:* articles in technical jls o reinforced plastics. *Recreations:* sailing, motoring, reading, and talking abou reinforced plastics. *Address:* Farthings End, Dukes Ride, Gerrards Cross Bucks. *T:* Gerrards Cross 82606. *Club:* Datchet Water Sailing (Hon. Lif Mem.), Cookham Reach Sailing (Hon. Life Mem.).

BLAKE, John Clifford, CB 1958; *b* 12 July 1901; *s* of late Alfred Harold an Ada Blake, Prestwich, Lancs; *m* 1928, Mary Lilian Rothwell; one *s* two c *Educ:* Manchester Grammar Sch.; Queen's Coll., Oxford (MA). Admitte solicitor, 1927. Ministry of Health Solicitor's Dept, 1929; Solicitor and Lega Adviser to Ministries of Health and Housing and Local Government, and t Registrar Gen., 1957-65; Mem., Treasurer and Jt Exec. Sec., Anglican Methodist Unity Commn, 1965-69; Vice-Pres., Methodist Conference, 1968 *Recreations:* music, especially organ and choral. *Address:* 3 Clifton Court, 29 Clifton Drive South, St Anne's on Sea, Lancs FY8 1HN. *T:* St Anne' 728365.

BLAKE, John William, CBE 1972; Professor of History, New University o Ulster, 1972-77, now Emeritus; *b* 7 Dec. 1911; *s* of Robert Gay Blake an Beatrice Mary Blake (*née* Tucket); *m* 1938, Eileen Florence Lord; two *s* on *d. Educ:* Kilburn Grammar Sch.; King's Coll., London (MA). Inglis Studen and Derby Scholar, 1933-34; QUB: Asst Lectr, 1934; Lectr, 1944; Sen. Lectr 1945; served War of 1939-45 in Civil Defence and as Offical War Historia to NI Govt; Prof. of History, Univ. of Keele (until 1962 University Coll. o N Staffs), 1950-64; Acting Principal of University Coll. of N Staffs, 1954-56 Vice-Chancellor, Univ. of Botswana, Lesotho and Swaziland (formerl Basutoland, Bechuanaland Protectorate and Swaziland), 1964-71. Vis. Prof. Univ. of North Carolina at Asheville, 1979. Mem. Staffs Co. Educn Cttee 1955-61; Mem. Inter-Univ. Council for Higher Educn Overseas, 1955-64 FRHistS. Hon. Fellow, Hist. Soc., Ghana. Hon. DLitt: Keele 1971; Botswana Lesotho and Swaziland, 1971. *Publications:* European Beginnings in Wes Africa, 1937; Europeans in West Africa, 2 vols 1942; Official War Histor of Northern Ireland, 1956; West Africa: Quest for God and Gold, 1977 contribs to historical jls. *Recreations:* gardening, philately. *Address:* Willow Cottage, Myroe, Limavady, Northern Ireland BT49 9EG.

BLAKE, Mary Netterville, MA; Headmistress, Manchester High School fo Girls, 1975-Sept. 1983; *b* 12 Sept. 1922; *d* of John Netterville Blake and Agne Barr Blake. *Educ:* Howell's Sch., Denbigh; St Anne's Coll., Oxford (MA Asst Mistress, The Mount Sch., York, 1945-48; Head of Geography Dept King's High Sch., Warwick, 1948-56; Associate Gen. Sec., Student Christia Movement in Schools, 1956-60; Head Mistress, Selby Grammar Sch., 1960-75 Pres., Assoc. of Headmistresses, 1976-77; first Pres., Secondary Heads Assoc 1978. *Address:* (to Sept. 1983) Manchester High School for Girls Grangethorpe Road, Manchester M14 6HS. *T:* 061-224 2456; (from Sep 1983) 2A Hartington Road, Bramhall, Stockport SK7 2DZ. *T:* 061-43 5165.

BLAKE, Peter Thomas, RA 1980 (ARA 1974); ARCA; painter; *b* 25 Jun 1932; *s* of Kenneth William Blake; *m* 1963, Jann Haworth (marr. diss. 1982) now lives with Chrissy Wilson; two *d. Educ:* Gravesend Tech. Coll Gravesend Sch. of Art; RCA. Works exhibited: ICA, 1958, 196C Guggenheim Competition, 1958; Cambridge, 1959; RA, 1960; Musée d'Ar Moderne, Paris, 1968; Waddington Galls, 1970, 1972 and 1979; Stedlijk Mus Amsterdam, 1973; Kunstverein, Hamburg, 1973; Gemeentemuseum, Arnhem 1974; Palais des Beaux-Arts, Brussels, 1974; Galleria Documenta, Turin, 1982 retrospective exhibn, Tate Gall., 1982; works in public collections: Trinity Coll., Cambridge; Carlisle City Gall.; Tate Gall.; Arts Council of GB; Mus of Modern Art, NY; V & A Mus.; Mus. Boymans-van Beuningen, Rotterdam Calouste Gulbenkian Foundn, London; RCA; Whitworth Art Gall., Univ. o Manchester; Baltimore Mus. of Art, Md; *Publications:* illustrations for Oxford Illustrated Old Testament, 1968; Roger McGough, Summer with Monica, 1978; cover illustration, Arden Shakespeare: Othello, 1980; Anthon and Cleopatra, 1980; Timon of Athens, 1980; contribs to: Times Educnl Supp.; Ark; Graphis 70; World of Art; Architectural Rev.; House and Garden; Painter and Sculptor. *Recreations:* sculpture, wining and dining, going to rock and roll concerts, boxing and wrestling matches; living well is the best revenge. *Address:* c/o Waddington Galleries Ltd, 2 Cork Street, W1X 1PA.

BLAKE, Quentin Saxby, RDI; freelance artist and illustrator, since 1957; Head of Department of Illustration, Royal College of Art, since 1978 (Tutor, 1965, Senior Tutor, 1977); *b* 16 Dec. 1932; *s* of William Blake and Evelyn Blake. *Educ:* Downing Coll., Cambridge (MA). FSIAD. Cartoonist and illustrator for Punch, Spectator and other magazines; illustrator and storyteller for children's television. Exhibns of watercolour drawings, Workshop Gallery: Invitation to the Dance, 1972; Runners and Riders, 1973; Creature Comforts, 1974; Water Music, 1976. *Publications:* (author and illustrator) for children: Patrick, 1968; Jack and Nancy, 1969; Angelo, 1970; Snuff, 1973; The Adventures of Lester, 1977; (ed and illus.) Custard and Company, by Ogden Nash, 1979; Mr Magnolia, 1980 (Fedn of Children's Bk Gps Award; Kate Greenaway Medal, 1981); (illustrator) for children: Russell Hoban, How Tom Beat Captain Najork and his Hired Sportsmen, 1974 (Whitbread Lit. Award, 1975; Hans Andersen Honour Book, 1975); Russell Hoban, A Near Thing for Captain Najork, 1976; Andrew Lloyd Webber and Tim Rice, Joseph and the Amazing Technicolour Dreamcoat, 1982; books by John Yeoman, Joan Aiken, Roald Dahl, Clement Freud, Sid Fleischman, Michael Rosen, Sylvia Plath, Margaret Mahy and Dr Seuss; (illustrator) for adults: Aristophanes, The Birds, 1971; Lewis Caroll, The Hunting of the Snark, 1976; Stella Gibbons, Cold Comfort Farm, 1977; Evelyn Waugh, Black Mischief, 1980, Scoop, 1981. *Address:* 30 Bramham Gardens, SW5 0HF. *T:* 01-373 7464.

BLAKE, Sir Richard; see Blake, Sir T. R. V.

BLAKE, Richard Frederick William; Editor, Whitaker's Almanack, since 1981; *b* 9 April 1948; *s* of late Frederick William Blake and of Doris Margaret Blake; *m* 1973, Christine Vaughan; one *d. Educ:* Archbishop Tenison's Grammar School. Joined J. Whitaker & Sons, Ltd (Whitaker's Almanack Dept), 1966; apptd Asst Editor of Whitaker's Almanack, 1974. *Recreations:* music, sport. *Address:* 23 Tenbury Close, Romford Road, E7.

BLAKE, Sir (Thomas) Richard (Valentine), 17th Bt *cr* 1622, of Menlough; *b* 7 Jan. 1942; *s* of Sir Ulick Temple Blake, 16th Bt, and late Elizabeth Gordon (she *m* 1965, Vice-Adm. E. Longley-Cook, *qv*); *S* father, 1963; *m* 1976, Mrs Jacqueline Hankey; *m* 1982, Bertice Reading. *Educ:* Bradfield Coll., Berks. Former Member, Standing Council of Baronets. *Recreations:* shooting; Royal Naval Reserve. *Heir:* kinsman Anthony Teilo Bruce Blake, *b* 5 May 1951. *Clubs:* West Sussex County (Chichester); Chequers (Bognor Regis).

BLAKE, Vincent; see Blake, H. V.

BLAKE, Mrs William J.; see Stead, Christina E.

BLAKELY, Colin George Edward; actor and director since 1957; *b* 23 Sept. 1930; *s* of Victor Charles and Dorothy Margaret Ashmore Blakely; *m* 1961, Margaret Elsa Whiting; three *s. Educ:* Sedbergh School. Manager, Athletic Stores Ltd, Belfast, 1948-57; 1st prof. acting job, Children's Touring Theatre (Gwent), 1957; Group Theatre, Belfast, 1957-59; Cock a Doodle Dandy, Royal Court, 1959; Moon for the Misbegotten, Arts, 1960; The Naming of Murderers Rock, Royal Court, 1960; entered TV and films (Saturday Night and Sunday Morning), 1960-61; Hastings, in Richard III, and Touchstone, in As You Like It, Royal Shakespeare Co., Stratford, 1961; subseq. various films, TV, etc; Nat. Theatre, 1963-68: Pizarro, in Royal Hunt of the Sun; Captain Boyle, in Juno and the Paycock; Proctor, in Crucible; Philoctetes, in Philoctetes; Kite, in Recruiting Officer; Volpone, in Volpone; Hobson, in Hobson's Choice; Captain Shot-over, in Heartbreak House; Astrov, in Uncle Vanya, and Schmidt, in Fire Raisers, Royal Court; Torvald, in A Doll's House, Criterion, 1973; Vukhow, in Judgement, Royal Court, 1976; Dysart, in Equus, Albery, 1976; Dennis, in Just Between Ourselves, Queen's, 1977; Filumena, Lyric, 1977; Enjoy, Vaudeville, 1980; All My Sons, Wyndham's, 1981. Principal films include: This Sporting Life; Decline and Fall; Watson, in The Private Life of Sherlock Holmes; The National Health; It Shouldn't Happen to a Vet; The Pink Panther Strikes Again; Equus; Dogs of War; Evil under the Sun; TV appearances incl. Christ, in Son of Man, Peer Gynt, in Peer Gynt and Antony in Antony and Cleopatra. *Recreations:* piano, painting, sketching, golf. *Address:* c/o Leading Artists, 60 St James's Street, SW1. *T:* 01-491 4400.

BLAKEMORE, Alan, CBE 1976; Town Clerk and Chief Executive (formerly Town Clerk), Croydon, 1963-82; *b* 17 May 1919; *s* of late John William and Mary Blakemore, Salford; *m* 1956, José Margaret Cavill; two *s. Educ:* North Manchester School. Solicitor, 1943. Articled to Town Clerk, Salford, 1936; RASC (TA), 1939; Army service to 1946; released with hon. rank Lt-Col. Asst Solicitor, Salford, 1946-48; Deputy Town Clerk: Wigan, 1948-52; Bolton, 1952-57; Town Clerk, Stockport, 1957-63. Hon. Clerk, General Purposes Cttee, London Boroughs Assoc., 1971-82. *Address:* Chaseley, 4 Waterfield Drive, Warlingham, Surrey CR3 9HP. *Club:* Royal Over-Seas League.

BLAKEMORE, Prof. Colin Brian; Waynflete Professor of Physiology, Oxford University, since 1979; Fellow of Magdalen College, since 1979; *b* 1

June 1944; *s* of Cedric Norman Blakemore and Beryl Ann Smith; *m* 1965, Andrée Elizabeth Washbourne; three *d. Educ:* King Henry VIII Sch., Coventry; Corpus Christi Coll., Cambridge (Smyth Scholar; BA 1965, MA 1969); Univ. of Calif, Berkeley (PhD 1968). Harkness Fellow, Neurosensory Lab., Univ. of Calif, Berkeley, 1965-68; Cambridge University: Fellow and Dir of Medical Studies, Downing Coll., 1971-79; Univ. Demonstr in Physiol., 1968-72; Univ. Lectr in Physiol., 1972-79; Leverhulme Fellow, 1974-75. Royal Soc. Locke Res. Fellow, 1976-79. Chm., Neurobiology and Mental Health Bd Grants Cttee, MRC, 1977-79. Vis. Professor: NY Univ., 1970; MIT, 1971; Royal Soc. Study Visit, Keio Univ., Tokyo, 1974; Lethaby Prof., RCA, 1978; Storer Vis. Lectr, Univ. of Calif, Davis, 1980. Member: Central Council, Internat. Brain Res. Org., 1973-; BBC Science Consultative Group, 1975-. BBC Reith Lectr, 1976; Lectures: Aubrey Lewis, Inst. of Psych., 1979; Lord Charnwood, Amer. Acad. of Optometry, 1980; Vickers, Neonatal Soc., 1981; Kershman, Eastern Assoc. of Electroencephalographers, NY, 1981; Harveian, Harveian Soc. of London, 1982; Christmas, Royal Instn, 1982; Earl Grey Meml, Newcastle Univ., 1982. Robert Bing Prize for res. in neurol. and neurophysiol., Swiss Acad. of Med. Sciences, 1975; Richardson Cross Medal, S Western Opthalmol Soc., 1978; Copeman Medal for med. res., Corpus Christi Coll., Cambridge, 1976; Man of the Year, Royal Assoc. for Disability and Rehabilitation, 1978; Phi Beta Kappa Award in Sci., 1978. *Publications:* Handbook of Psychobiology (with M. S. Gazzaniga), 1975; Mechanics of the Mind, 1977; res. reports in Jl of Physiol., Brit. Med. Bull., Nature, etc. *Recreation:* wasting time. *Address:* University Laboratory of Physiology, Parks Road, Oxford OX1 3PT.

BLAKEMORE, Michael Howell; freelance director; *b* Sydney, NSW, 18 June 1928; *s* of Conrad Blakemore and late Una Mary Blakemore (*née* Litchfield); *m* 1960, Shirley (*née* Bush); one *s* ; lives with Tanya McCallin; one *d. Educ:* The King's Sch., NSW; Sydney Univ.; Royal Academy of Dramatic Art. Actor with Birmingham Rep. Theatre, Shakespeare Memorial Theatre, etc, 1952-66; Co-dir, Glasgow Citizens Theatre (1st prod., The Investigation), 1966-68; Associate Artistic Dir, Nat. Theatre, 1971-76. Dir, Players, NY, 1978. Resident Dir, Lyric Theatre, Hammersmith, 1980. Best Dir, London Critics, 1972. Vis. Fellow in Theatre Studies, Surrey Univ., 1977. *Productions include:* A Day in the Death of Joe Egg, 1967; Arturo Ui, 1969; Forget-me-not Lane, 1971; Design for Living, 1973; Knuckle, 1974; Separate Tables, 1976; Privates on Parade, 1977; Candida, 1977; All My Sons, 1981; *National Theatre productions:* The National Health, 1969; Long Day's Journey Into Night, 1971; The Front Page, Macbeth, 1972, The Cherry Orchard, 1973; Plunder, 1976. *Lyric Theatre, Hammersmith:* Make and Break, 1980 (his opening production); Travelling North, 1980; The Wild Duck, 1980; Noises Off (transf. to Savoy), 1982. *Film:* A Personal History of the Australian Surf, 1981. *Publication:* Next Season, 1969 (novel). *Recreation:* surfing. *Address:* 11a St Martin's Almshouses, Bayham Street, NW1. *T:* 01-267 3952.

BLAKENEY, Hon. Allan Emrys; PC (Canada) 1982; Leader of the Opposition, Saskatchewan, since 1982; Member of Legislative Assembly, Saskatchewan, since 1960; *b* Bridgewater, NS, 7 Sept. 1925; *m* 1st, 1950, Mary Elizabeth (Molly) Schwartz (*d* 1957), Halifax, NS; one *s* one *d* ; 2nd, 1959, Anne Gorham, Halifax; one *s* one *d. Educ:* Dalhousie Univ. (BA, LLB); Queen's Coll., Oxford (MA). Univ. Medal for Achievement in Coll. of Law, Dalhousie; Rhodes Schol. Sec. and Legal Adviser, Saskatchewan Crown Corps, 1950; Chm., Saskatchewan Securities Commn, 1955-58; private law practice, 1958-60 and 1964-70. Formerly Minister of Educn, Provincial Treas. and Health Minister; Chm., Wascana Centre Authority, 1962-64; Opposition Financial Critic, 1964-70; Dep. Leader, 1967-70; Federal New Democratic Party President, 1969-71; Saskatchewan NDP Leader and Leader of Opposition, 1970; Premier, 1971-82. Formerly Dir and Vice-Pres., Sherwood Co-op. and Sherwood Credit Union. Hon. DCL Mount Allison, 1980; Hon. LLD Dalhousie, 1981. *Recreations:* reading, swimming, formerly hockey and badminton. *Address:* Office of the Leader of the Opposition, Legislative Building, Regina, Saskatchewan S4S 0B3, Canada.

BLAKENEY, Frederick Joseph, CBE 1968; Australian diplomat, retired 1978; *b* Sydney, NSW, 2 July 1913; *s* of Frederick Joseph Blakeney, Sydney; *m* 1943, Marjorie, *d* of John Martin, NSW; one *d. Educ:* Marist Darlinghurst and Mittagong; Univ. of Sydney. AMF, 1940-41; RAAF Flt Lieut (Navigator), 1942-45. Teaching Fellow, Univ. of Sydney, 1946; Dept of External Affairs, Canberra, 1946; 2nd Sec. and 1st Sec., Austr. Embassy, Paris, 1947; 1st Sec., then Chargé d'Affaires, Austr. Embassy, Moscow, 1949-51; Dept of Ext. Affairs, Canberra, 1952-53; Counsellor, Austr. Embassy, Washington, 1953-56; Minister to Vietnam and Laos, 1957-59, and to Cambodia, 1957; Asst Sec. (S and SE Asia), Dept of Ext. Affairs, Canberra, 1959-62; Australian Ambassador to Federal Republic of Germany, 1962-68; Australian Ambassador to USSR, 1968-71; First Asst Sec. (Defence), Dept of Foreign Affairs, Canberra, 1972-74; Australian Ambassador to the Netherlands, 1974-77; Australian Ambassador and Perm. Rep. to the UN, Geneva, 1977-78. *Address:* 19 Grey Street, Deakin, Canberra, ACT, Australia.

BLAKENHAM, 2nd Viscount *cr* 1963, of Little Blakenham; **Michael John Hare;** Chief Executive, S. Pearson & Son, since 1978; *b* 25 Jan. 1938; *s* of 1st Viscount Blakenham, PC, OBE, VMH, and of Hon. Beryl Nancy Pearson, *d* of 2nd Viscount Cowdray; *S* father, 1982; *m* 1965, Marcia Persephone, *d* of Hon. Alan Hare, *qv* ; one *s* two *d. Educ:* Eton College; Harvard Univ. (AB Econ.). Life Guards, 1956-57; English Electric, 1958; Harvard, 1959-61;

Lazard Brothers, 1961-63; Standard Industrial Group, 1963-71; Royal Doulton, 1972-77; S. Pearson, 1977-; Chairman: Pearson Longman; Doulton; Madame Tussaud's; Royal Soc. for the Protection of Birds. *Heir: s* Hon. Caspar John Hare, *b* 8 April 1972. *Address:* 17th Floor, Millbank Tower, SW1. *T:* 01-828 9020.

BLAKER, George Blaker, CMG 1963; Under-Secretary, HM Treasury, 1955-63, and Department of Education and Science, 1963-71 retired; *b* Simla, India, 30 Sept. 1912; *m* 1938, Richenda Dorothy Buxton; one *d. Educ:* Eton; Trinity Coll., Cambridge. Private Sec. to Ministers of State in the Middle East, 1941-43; Cabinet Office, 1943; Private Sec. to Sec. of War Cabinet, 1944; Principal Private Sec. to Minister of Production and Presidents of the Board of Trade, 1945-47; accompanied Cabinet Mission to India, 1946; Sec. of UK Trade Mission to China, 1946; HM Treasury, 1947; UK Treasury Representative in India, Ceylon and Burma, 1957-63. Pres., Surrey Trust for Nature Conservation, 1969-80. Jt Hon. Sec., Scientific and Medical Network, 1973-. Gold Medal, Royal Soc. for the Protection of Birds, 1934. *Address:* Lake House, Ockley, Surrey RH5 5NS.

BLAKER, Sir John, 3rd Bt *cr* 1919; *b* 22 March 1935; *s* of Sir Reginald Blaker, 2nd Bt, TD, and of Sheila Kellas, *d* of Dr Alexander Cran; *S* father, 1975; *m* 1st, 1960, Catherine Ann (marr. diss. 1965), *d* of late F. J. Thorold; 2nd, 1968, Elizabeth Katherine, *d* of late Col John Tinsley Russell, DSO. *Address:* Barton Hill Farm, Barton-on-the-Heath, Moreton-in-Marsh, Glos.

BLAKER, Nathaniel Robert, QC 1972; **His Honour Judge Blaker;** a Circuit Judge, since 1976; *b* 31 Jan. 1921; *s* of Major Herbert Harry Blaker and Annie Muriel Blaker (*née* Atkinson); *m* 1951, Celia Margaret, *o d* of W. Hedley, DSO, KC, and Mrs Hedley; two *d. Educ:* Winchester; University College, Oxford (MA). Royal Signals, 1940-47. Called to the Bar, Inner Temple, 1948; Bencher, 1971. Dep. Chm., Dorset QS, 1970; a Recorder of the Crown Court, 1972-76. Wine Treasurer, Western Circuit, 1964-76. *Address:* 16 Embankment Gardens, SW3 4LW. *T:* 01-352 0792; 2 Culver Road, Winchester, Hants.

BLAKER, Peter Allan Renshaw, MA; MP (C) Blackpool South, since 1964; Minister of State for the Armed Forces, Ministry of Defence, since 1981; *b* Hong Kong, 4 Oct. 1922; *s* of late Cedric Blaker, CBE, MC; *m* 1953, Jennifer, *d* of late Sir Pierson Dixon, GCMG, CB; one *s* two *d. Educ:* Shrewsbury; Trinity Coll., Toronto (BA, 1st class, Classics); New Coll., Oxford (MA). Served 1942-46: Argyll and Sutherland Highlanders of Canada (Capt., wounded). Admitted a Solicitor, 1948. New Coll., Oxford, 1949-52; 1st Class, Jurisprudence, Pass degree in PPE. Pres. Oxford Union. Called to Bar, Lincoln's Inn, 1952. Admitted to HM Foreign Service, 1953; HM Embassy, Phnom Penh, 1955-57; UK High Commn, Ottawa, 1957-60; FO, 1960-62; Private Sec. to Minister of State for Foreign Affairs, 1962-64. Attended Disarmament Conf., Geneva; UN Gen. Assembly, 1962 and 1963; signing of Nuclear Test Ban Treaty, Moscow, 1963. An Opposition Whip, 1966-67; PPS to Chancellor of Exchequer, 1970-72; Parliamentary Under-Secretary of State: (Army), MoD, 1972-74; FCO, 1974; Minister of State, FCO, 1979-81. Joint Secretary: Conservative Party Foreign Affairs Cttee, 1965-66; Trade Cttee, 1967-70; Exec. Cttee of 1922 Cttee, 1967-70; Vice-Chairman: Cons. For. and Commonwealth Affairs Cttee, 1974-79; All-Party Tourism Cttee, 1974-79; Mem., Select Cttee on Conduct of Members, 1976-77; Chm., Hong Kong Parly Gp, 1970-72; Mem. Exec. Cttee, British-American Parly Gp, 1975-79; Hon. Sec., Franco-British Parly Relations Cttee, 1975-79. Chm., Bd, Royal Ordnance Factories, 1972-74; Chm. Governors, Welbeck Coll., 1972-74; Mem. Council: GB-USSR Assoc., 1974-79; Chatham House, 1977-79; Governor, Atlantic Inst., 1978-79. *Address:* c/o House of Commons, SW1A 0AA.

BLAKEWAY, John Denys; HM Diplomatic Service, retired; *b* 27 May 1918; *s* of late Sir Denys Blakeway, CIE; *m* 1946, Jasmine Iremonger; one *s* two *d. Educ:* Rugby (Schol.); Magdalen Coll., Oxford (Schol., MA). British and Indian Army, 1939-46 (wounded). Joined Foreign (subseq. Diplomatic) Service, 1946; served Sofia, Lyons, Athens (twice), Tripoli, FO (twice), Bologna, Rome, Ibadan, The Hague; Consul-Gen., Istanbul, 1975-78. *Recreation:* angelology. *Address:* Row Farm, Zeals, Warminster, Wilts. *T:* Bourton (Dorset) 840209. *Club:* Royal Commonwealth Society.

BLAKISTON, Sir Ferguson Arthur James, 9th Bt *cr* 1763; *b* 19 Feb. 1963; *er s* of Sir Arthur Norman Hunter Blakiston, 8th Bt, and of Mary Ferguson, *d* of late Alfred Ernest Gillingham, Cave, S Canterbury, NZ; *S* father, 1977. *Heir: b* Norman John Balfour Blakiston, *b* 7 April 1964. *Address:* 28 McKenzie Street, Geraldine, S Canterbury, New Zealand.

BLAKSTAD, Michael Björn; Director of Programmes, Television South, since 1980; Chairman, Blackrod Ltd, since 1981; *b* 18 April 1940; *s* of Clifford and Alice Blakstad; *m* 1965, Patricia Marilyn Wotherspoon; one *s* twin *d. Educ:* Ampleforth Coll.; Oriel Coll., Oxford (MA Lit. Hum.). General trainee, BBC, 1962-68; Producer, Yorkshire Television, 1968-71; freelance tv producer, 1971-74; Programme Editor, BBC, 1974-80. Founder and Managing Director, Blackrod, 1980. Awards include: Radio Industries Club, 1975, 1977, 1979; RTS, 1976; BAFTA/Shell Prize, 1976; BIM/John Player, 1976; Nyon, 1978. FRSA; MRI. *Publications:* The Risk Business, 1979; Tomorrow's World looks to the Eighties, 1979; regular contributor to Design Magazine. *Recreations:* squash raquets, writing. *Address:* The Tudor House,

Workhouse Lane, East Meon, Hants. *Clubs:* Reform, British Academy of Film and Television Arts.

BLAMEY, Norman Charles, RA 1975 (ARA 1970); Senior Lecturer, Chelsea School of Art, London, 1963-79; *b* 16 Dec. 1914; *s* of Charles H. Blamey and Ada Blamey (*née* Beacham); *m* 1948, Margaret (*née* Kelly); one *s. Educ:* Holloway Sch., London; Sch. of Art, The Polytechnic, Regent Street, London; ROI 1952; Hon. ROI 1974. Exhibited at: RA, RHA, ROI, RBA, NEAC and provincial galleries; *mural decorations in:* Anglican Church of St Luke, Leagrave, Beds, 1956; Lutheran Church of St Andrew, Ruislip Manor, Middx, 1964; *works in permanent collections:* Municipal Gall., Port Elizabeth, S Africa; Beaverbrook Gall., Fredericton, NB; Beecroft Art Gall., Southend-on-Sea; Towner Art Gall., Eastbourne; Preston Art Gall.; Pennsylvania State Univ. Mus of Art; La Salle Coll., Pa; V & A Museum; Chantry Bequest purchase, 1972; *portraits include:* Mrs Alison Munro, Dr Harry Pitt, Rev Dennis Nineham. Works in private collections in UK and USA. *Recreation:* walking. *Address:* 39 Lyncroft Gardens, NW6. *T:* 01-435 9250.

BLAMIRE, Roger Victor; Director of Veterinary Field Services, Ministry of Agriculture, Fisheries and Food, since 1979; *b* 9 July 1923; *s* of Thomas Victor Blamire and Anetta Elizabeth (*née* Lawson); *m* 1947, Catherine Maisie Ellis Davidson; two *d. Educ:* Kendal Sch.; Royal (Dick) Veterinary Coll. Edinburgh. MRCVS, DVSM. RAVC, 1945-48 (Captain); served India, Burma and Malaya. MAF, 1949; Asst Vet. Officer, City of London, 1949; Dep. Chief Advr on Meat Inspection, MOF, 1952; Dep. Dir, Vet. Field Services, MAFF, 1968. *Recreations:* walking, gardening, listening to music. *Address:* 4 Mandeville Drive, Surbiton, Surrey KT6 5OT. *T:* 01-398 4773.

BLAMIRE-BROWN, John, DL; County Clerk and Chief Executive, Staffordshire County Council, 1973-78; *b* 16 April 1915; *s* of Rev. F. J. Blamire Brown, MA; *m* 1945, Joyce Olivia Pearson; two *s. Educ:* Cheam Sch.; St Edmund's Sch., Canterbury. Solicitor 1937. Served War of 1939-45, Royal Marines (Captain). Asst Solicitor, Wednesbury, 1937; West Bromwich, 1946; Staffs CC, 1948; Deputy Clerk of County Council and of Peace, 1962; Clerk, Staffs CC, 1972; Clerk to Lieutenancy, 1972-78; Sec., Staffs Probation and After Care Cttee; Hon. Sec., W Mids Planning Authorities Conf., 1972-78. Dep. Chm., Manpower Services Commn Area Board, Staffs, Salop, W Midlands (North), 1978-. Mem. Council, Beth Johnson Foundn, 1978-; Governor, Newcastle-under-Lyme Endowed Schools, 1978-; Chm., St Giles Home Ltd, 1979-. DL Staffs, 1974. *Recreations:* beagling, gardening. *Address:* The Mount, Codsall Wood, Wolverhampton, West Midlands. *T:* Codsall 2044.

BLANCH, Mrs Lesley, (Madame Gary); FRSL; author; *b* 1907; *m* 2nd, 1945, Romain Gary Kacew (Romain Gary) (marr. diss. 1962; he *d* 1980). *Educ:* by reading, and listening to conversation of elders and betters. FRSL 1969. *Publications:* The Wilder Shores of Love (biog.), 1954; Round the World in Eighty Dishes (cookery), 1956; The Game of Hearts (biog.), 1956; The Sabres of Paradise (biog.), 1960; Under a Lilac Bleeding Star (travels), 1963; The Nine Tiger Man (fict.), 1965; Journey into the Mind's Eye (autobiog.), 1968; Pavilions of the Heart (biog.), 1974. *Recreations:* travel, opera, acquiring useless objects, animal welfare, gardening. *Address:* Roquebrune Village, 06190 Roquebrune-Cap-Martin, France. *Club:* Taharir (formerly Mahommed Ali) (Cairo).

BLANCH, Most Rev. and Rt. Hon. Stuart Yarworth; *see* York, Archbishop of.

BLANCHARD, Francis; Director-General, International Labour Office, Geneva, since 1974; *b* Paris, 21 July 1916; *m* 1940, Marie-Claire Boué; two *s. Educ:* Univ. of Paris. French Home Office; Internat. Organisation for Refugees, Geneva, 1947-51; Internat. Labour Office, Geneva, 1951-, Asst Dir-Gen., 1956-68, Dep. Dir-Gen., 1968-74. *Recreations:* ski-ing, hunting, riding. *Address* (office) International Labour Office, 4 chemin des Morillons, Geneva, Switzerland. *T:* 99.61.11; (home) Prébailly, 01170 Gex, France. *T:* 41-51-70 Gex.

BLANCO WHITE, Thomas Anthony, QC 1969; *b* 19 Jan. 1915; *s* of late G. R. Blanco White, QC, and Amber Blanco White, OBE; *m* 1950, Anne Katherine Ironside-Smith; two *s* one *d. Educ:* Gresham's Sch.; Trinity Coll., Cambridge. Called to Bar, Lincoln's Inn, 1937, Bencher 1977. Served RAFVR, 1940-46. *Publications:* Patents for Inventions, 1950, 1955, 1962, 1974, etc. *Recreations:* gardening, photography. *Address:* Francis Taylor Building, EC4.

BLAND, (Francis) Christopher (Buchan); Chairman, Sir Joseph Causton & Sons, since 1977; Director: National Provident Institution, since 1978; LWT (Holdings), since 1982; *b* 29 May 1938; *e s* of James Franklin MacMahon Bland and Jess Buchan Bland (*née* Brodie); *m* 1981, Jennifer Mary, Viscountess Enfield, *er d* of late Rt Hon. W. M. May, PC, FCA, MP, and of Mrs May, Merton Hall, Holywood, Co. Down. *Educ:* Sedbergh; The Queen's Coll. Oxford (Hastings Exhibnr). 2nd Lieut, 5th Royal Inniskilling Dragoon Guards, 1956-58; Lieut, North Irish Horse (TA), 1958-69. Dir, NI Finance Corp., 1972-76; Dep. Chm., IBA, 1972-80. Mem. GLC, for Lewisham, 1967-70; Chm., ILEA Schs Sub-Cttee, 1970; Mem. Burnham Cttee, 1970; Chm., Bow Group, 1969-70; Editor, Crossbow, 1971-72; Chairman: NHS Rev. Gp on Nat. Trng Council and Nat. Staff Cttees, 1982; Hammersmith Special Health Authority, 1982-. Governor, Prendergast Girls Grammar Sch.

and Woolwich Polytechnic, 1968-70; Mem. Council, RPMS, 1982-. *Publications:* Bow Group pamphlet on Commonwealth Immigration. *Recreations:* fishing, skiing; formerly: Captain, OU Fencing Team, 1961; Captain, OU Modern Pentathlon Team, 1959-60; Mem. Irish Olympic Fencing Team, 1960. *Address:* Abbots Worthy House, Abbots Worthy, Winchester, Hants. *T:* Winchester 881333; 10 Catherine Place, SW1E 6HF. *T:* 01-834 0021. *Club:* Beefsteak.

BLAND, Sir Henry (Armand), Kt 1965; CBE 1957; FRSA; *b* 28 Dec. 1909; *s* of Emeritus Prof. F. A. Bland, CMG, and Elizabeth Bates Jacobs; *m* 1933, Rosamund, *d* of John Nickal; two *d* (and one *d* decd). *Educ:* Sydney High Sch.; Univ. of Sydney. LLB (Hons) 1932. Admitted Solicitor Supreme Court of NSW, 1935. Entered NSW Public Service, 1927; Alderman, Ryde (NSW) Municipal Council, 1937-39; Acting Agent-Gen. for NSW in London, 1940-41; Adviser on Civil Defence to NSW and Commonwealth Govts, 1941; Princ. Asst to Dir-Gen. of Manpower, 1941-45; Asst Sec., First Asst Sec., 1946-51, Sec. 1952-67, Dept of Labour and National Service; Sec., Dept of Defence, Australia, 1967-70. Leader, Austr. Govt Delegns to Confs: 1948, 1953, 1957, 1960, 1962, 1963, 1964, 1966; Austr. Govt Rep. on the Governing Body of ILO, 1963-67; Adviser on industrial relations to Singapore Govt, 1958. Bd of Inquiry into Victorian Land Transport System, 1971; Chairman: Cttee on Administrative Discretions, 1972-73; Bd of Inquiry into Victorian Public Service, 1973-75; Commonwealth Admin. Rev. Cttee, 1976; ABC, 1976; Arbitrator between Aust. Nat. Railways and Tasmanian Govt, 1978. Chm. and Dir of numerous cos, 1970-. *Address:* Yarrunga, Yean Street, Burradoo, NSW 2576, Australia. *T:* (048) 613320. *Clubs:* Athenæum (Melbourne); Bowral Golf.

BLAND, Lt-Col Sir Simon Claud Michael, KCVO 1982 (CVO 1973; MVO 1967); Comptroller, Private Secretary and Equerry to Princess Alice Duchess of Gloucester and the Duke and Duchess of Gloucester, since 1972; *b* 4 Dec. 1923; *s* of late Sir Nevile Bland, KCMG, KCVO; *m* 1954, Olivia, *d* of Major William Blackett; one *s* three *d*. *Educ:* Eton College. Served War of 1939-45, Scots Guards, in Italy; BJSM, Washington, 1948-49; 2nd Bn, Scots Guards, Malaya, 1949-51; Asst Mil. Adviser at UK High Commn, Karachi, 1959-60; Comptroller and Asst Private Sec. to late Duke of Gloucester, 1961-74 and Private Sec. to late Prince William, 1968-72. Dir, West End Bd, Commercial Union. CStJ 1978. *Recreation:* shooting. *Address:* Tower Flat, Kensington Palace, W8 4PY. *T:* 01-937 6374; Gabriels Manor, Edenbridge, Kent. *T:* Edenbridge 862340. *Club:* Buck's.

BLANDFORD, Marquess of; Charles James Spencer-Churchill; at Cirencester Agricultural College; *b* 24 Nov. 1955; *e s* and *heir* of 11th Duke of Marlborough, *qv. Educ:* Pinewood; Harrow. *Address:* Blenheim Palace, Woodstock, Oxon; 70 Warwick Square, SW1. *Clubs:* Turf; Annabel's; Racquet and Tennis (New York).

BLANDFORD, Eric George, CBE 1967; formerly a Judge of the Supreme Court of Aden; *b* 10 March 1916; *s* of George and Eva Blanche Blandford; *m* 1940, Marjorie Georgina Crane; one *s. Educ:* Bristol Grammar Sch. Admitted Solicitor Supreme Court, England, 1939; LLB (London) 1939. War Service, 1939-46 (despatches): India, Burma, Malaya; rank on release Temp. Major RA. Solicitor in London, 1946-51; Asst Comr of Lands, Gold Coast, 1951; Dist Magistrate, Gold Coast, 1952; called to the Bar, Inner Temple, 1955; Chief Registrar, Supreme Court, Gold Coast, 1956; Registrar of High Court of Northern Rhodesia, 1958; Judge, Supreme Court of Aden, 1961-68; Dep. Asst Registrar of Criminal Appeals, 1968-78; Asst Registrar of Criminal Appeals, Royal Courts of Justice, 1978-81. Chm. Aden Municipality Inquiry Commn, 1962. *Publication:* Civil Procedure Rules of Court, Aden, 1967. *Recreations:* country pursuits. *Address:* Boot Lane, Dinton, Bucks HP17 8UJ. *Club:* Royal Commonwealth Society.

BLANDFORD, Heinz Hermann, CBE 1981; Member Governing Body, British Postgraduate Medical Federation, since 1969 (Chairman, 1977-79, Deputy Chairman, since 1980, Honorary Treasurer, since 1964); Member of Council, Royal Postgraduate Medical School, Hammersmith Hospital, since 1962 (Fellow, 1973, Honorary Treasurer, since 1964); Member of Council, School of Pharmacy, London University, since 1975 (Vice Chairman, since 1979, Honorary Treasurer, since 1975); Member of Management Committee, Institute of Opthalmology (Moorfields Eye Hospital), since 1974; *b* Berlin, Germany, 28 Aug. 1908; *s* of late Judge Richard Blumenfeld and Hedwig Kersten; *m* 1933, Hilde Kleczewer; one *s* one *d. Educ:* Augusta Gymnasium; (classical scholar) Univs of Berlin and Hamburg. Controller of continental cos in ceramic, pharmaceutical, iron and steel industries, 1933-39. Chm., Ulvir Ltd and various cos, 1936-76. Pioneered synthesis, manufacture and use of Liquid Fertilisers in the UK, 1945-60. Founded (Mem. Bd of Trustees), Blandford Trust for advancement of health and prevention and relief of sickness by med. research and teaching. Governor, London House for Overseas Graduates, 1977-80. Member: Org. Cttee, 6th World Congress of Cardiology, London, 1971; Board of Governors: Hammersmith and St Mark's Hospitals, 1972-74; LSHTM, 1982-. *Publications:* various essays and papers in chemical and horticultural jls. *Recreations:* farming, gardening. *Address:* Holtsmere End, Redbourn, Herts. *T:* Redbourn 2206. *Club:* Farmers'.

BLANDY, Prof. John Peter, MA, DM, MCh, FRCS, FACS; Consultant Surgeon: The London Hospital, since 1964; St Peter's Hospital for the Stone, since 1969; Professor of Urology, University of London, since 1969; *b* 11 Sept. 1927; *s* of late Sir E. Nicolas Blandy, KCIE, CSI, ICS and Dorothy Kathleen

(*née* Marshall); *m* 1953, Anne, *d* of Hugh Mathias, FRCS, Tenby; four *d. Educ:* Clifton Coll.; Balliol Coll., Oxford; London Hosp. Med. Coll. BM, BCh 1951; MA 1953; FRCS 1956; DM 1963; MCh 1963; FACS 1980. House Phys. and House Surg., London Hosp., 1952; RAMC, 1953-55; Surgical Registrar and Lectr in Surgery, London Hosp., 1956-60; exchange Fellow, Presbyterian St Luke's Hosp., Chicago, 1960-61; Sen. Lectr, London Hosp., 1961; Resident Surgical Officer, St Paul's Hosp., 1963-64. Member: BMA; RSM; Internat. Soc. Pædiatric Urol. Surg.; Internat. Soc. of Urological Surgeons; British Assoc. Urological Surgeons; Fellow, Assoc. of Surgeons. Hon. Fellow: Urological Soc. of Australasia, 1973; Mexican Coll. of Urology, 1974. Hunterian Prof., Royal College of Surgeons, 1964. Maurice Davidson Award, Fellowship of Postgrad. Med., 1980. *Publications:* (with A. D. Dayan and H. F. Hope-Stone) Tumours of the Testicle, 1970; Transurethral Resection, 1971; (ed) Urology, 1976; Lecture Notes on Urology, 1976; Operative Urology, 1978; papers in surgical and urological jls. *Recreation:* painting. *Address:* The London Hospital, Whitechapel, E1. *T:* 01-247 5454.

BLANKENHORN, Herbert, GCVO (Hon.) 1965; Special Consultant to Director-General, UNESCO, since 1976 (Member and Vice-President, Executive Board, 1970-76); *b* 15 Dec. 1904; *s* of Erich Blankenhorn; *m* 1944, Gisela Krug; two *s* two *d. Educ:* Gymnasiums in Strasbourg, Berlin, and Karlsruhe; Universities of Munich, London, Heidelberg and Paris. Entered Foreign Service, 1929; served in: Athens, 1932-35; Washington, 1935-39; Helsinki, 1940; Berne, 1940-43; Foreign Office, Berlin (Protocol Section), 1943-45; Dep. Sec.-Gen., Zonal Advisory Council, Hamburg, 1946-48; Sec.-Gen. Christian Democratic Party (British Zone), 1948; Private Sec. to President of Parliamentary Council, Bonn (Dr Adenauer), 1948-49; Political Dir, Foreign Office, 1950-55; German Ambassador: to NATO, 1955-58; to France, 1958-63; to Italy, 1963-65; to London, 1965-70. *Publication:* (political memoirs) Verständnis und Verständigung, 1980. *Address:* 7847 Badenweiler, Hintere Au 2, Germany.

BLANKS, Howard John; Under-Secretary, Department of Trade, since 1980; *b* 16 June 1932; *s* of Lionel and Hilda Blanks; *m* 1958, Judith Ann (*née* Hughes). *Educ:* Barking Abbey Sch.; Keble Coll., Oxford (BA 1st Cl. Hons Music). National Service, RAF (Pilot), 1956-58. Air Traffic Control Officer, Min. of Aviation, 1958-64; Principal, Min. of Aviation (later Min. of Technology and Aviation Supply), 1964-71; Private Sec. to Chief Executive, Min. of Defence (Procurement Executive), 1972; Assistant Secretary: MoD, 1972-75; Cabinet Office, 1975-77; Dept of Trade, 1977-79; Under-Secretary, Head of Civil Aviation Policy Div., Dept of Trade, 1980-. *Recreations:* music, travel. *Address:* 11 Tudor Close, Cobham, Surrey KT11 2PH. *T:* Cobham 5209.

BLANTYRE, Archbishop of, (RC), since 1968; **Most Rev. James Chiona;** *b* 1924. *Educ:* Nankhunda Minor Seminary, Malaŵi; Kachebere Major Seminary, Malaŵi. Priest, 1954; Asst Parish Priest, 1954-57; Prof., Nankhunda Minor Seminary, 1957-60; study of Pastoral Sociology, Rome, 1961-62; Asst Parish Priest, 1962-65; Auxiliary Bishop of Blantyre and Titular Bishop of Bacanaria, 1965; Vicar Capitular of Archdiocese of Blantyre, 1967. *Recreation:* music. *Address:* Archbishop's House, PO Box 385, Blantyre, Malaŵi. *T:* (10)633516.

BLASCHKO, Hermann Karl Felix, MD, FRS 1962; Emeritus Reader in Biochemical Pharmacology, Oxford University, and Emeritus Fellow, Linacre College, Oxford, since 1967; *b* Berlin, 4 Jan. 1900; *o s* of late Prof. Alfred Blaschko, MD and late Johanna Littmann; *m* 1944, Mary Douglas Black, *d* of late John Robert Black, Yelverton, S Devon; no *c. Educ:* Universities of Berlin, Freiburg im Breisgau and Göttingen. MD Freiburg; PhD Cambridge; MA Oxon. Research Asst to late Prof. O. Meyerhof at Berlin-Dahlem and Heidelberg at various periods, 1925-32; University Asst in Physiology, Univ. of Jena, 1928-29; worked at UCL, 1929-30 and 1933-34; Physiological Lab., Cambridge Univ., 1934-44; came to Oxford, 1944. Visiting Professor: Yale Univ., 1967-68; Upstate Medical Center, Syracuse, NY, 1968; RCS, 1968-73; Univ. of Pennsylvania, 1969; Univ. of Bergen, Norway, 1969-70. Hon. Prof., Faculty of Medicine, Heidelberg, 1966. Member of Editorial Board of: Pharmacological Reviews, 1957-64; British Journal of Pharmacology and Chemotherapy, 1959-65; Journal of Physiology, 1965-72; Neuropharmacology, 1962-72; Naunyn-Schmiedebergs Arch. Exp. Pharmak., 1966; Molecular Pharmacol., 1966-77. Mem. Neuropharmacology Panel, International Brain Research Organisation (IBRO). Hon. FR.SocMed, 1978; Hon. Member: British Pharmacological Soc., 1979; Hungarian Pharm. Soc., 1979; Physiological Soc., 1980; Berliner Medizinische Ges., 1980; Corresp. Mem., German Pharmacolog. Soc. Schmiedeberg Plakette, 1972. First Thudichum Lectr and Medallist, London, 1974; Aschoff Lectr, Freiburg, 1974. Hon. MD Berlin (Free Univ.), 1966. *Publications:* numerous papers in scientific publications. *Address:* Department of Pharmacology, South Parks Road, Oxford OX1 3QT; 24 Park Town, Oxford OX2 6SH.

BLASHFORD-SNELL, Col John Nicholas, MBE 1969; in command, The Fort George Volunteers, since 1982; Chairman (Hon.) Scientific Exploration Society, since 1969; *b* 22 Oct. 1936; *s* of late Rev. Prebendary Leland John Blashford Snell and Gwendolen Ives Sadler; *m* 1960, Judith Frances (*née* Sherman); two *d. Educ:* Victoria Coll., Jersey, CI; RMA, Sandhurst. Commissioned Royal Engineers, 1957; 33 Indep. Fd Sqdn RE Cyprus, 1958-61; comd Operation Aphrodite (Expedition) Cyprus, 1959-61; Instructor: Junior Leaders Regt RE, 1962-63; RMA Sandhurst, 1963-66; Adjt

3rd Div. Engineers, 1966-67; comd Great Abbai Expedn (Blue Nile), 1968; sc RMCS Shrivenham and Camberley, 1968-69; comd Dahlak Quest Expedn, 1969-70; GSO2 MoD, 1970-72; comd British Trans-Americas Expedn, 1971-72; OC 48 Fd Sqdn RE, service in Belize, Oman, Ulster, 1972-74; comd Zaire River Expedn, 1974-75; CO Junior Leaders Regt RE, 1976-78; Dir of Operations, Operation Drake, 1977-81; on staff (GSO1), MoD, 1978-82. Darien Medal (Colombia), 1972. *Publications:* Weapons and Tactics (with Tom Wintringham), 1970; (with Richard Snailham) The Expedition Organiser's Guide, 1970, 2nd edn 1976; Where the Trails Run Out, 1974; In the Steps of Stanley, 1975, 2nd edn 1975; (with A. Ballantine) Expeditions the Experts' Way, 1977, 2nd edn 1978; A Taste for Adventure, 1978; Operation Drake, 1981. *Recreations:* motoring, shooting, underwater diving, stamp collecting. *Address:* c/o Lloyds Bank Ltd, 9 Broad Street, St Helier, Jersey, CI. *Clubs:* Royal Automobile, Little Ship; Explorers' (New York).

BLAXTER, Sir Kenneth (Lyon), Kt 1977; FRS 1967; FRSE 1965; Director, Rowett Research Institute, Bucksburn, Aberdeen, and Consultant Director, Commonwealth Bureau of Nutrition (formerly Animal Nutrition), 1965-82; Honorary Research Associate, Rowett Research Institute, since 1982; *b* 19 June 1919; *s* of Gaspard Culling Blaxter and Charlotte Ellen Blaxter; *m* 1957, Mildred Lillington Hall; two *s* one *d. Educ:* City of Norwich Sch.; University of Reading; University of Illinois. BSc(Agric.), PhD, DSc, NDA (Hons). Scientific Officer, Nat. Inst. for Research in Dairying, 1939-40 and 1941-44. Served RA, 1940-41. Research Officer, Ministry of Agriculture Veterinary Laboratory, 1944-46; Commonwealth Fellow, University of Ill, 1946-47; Head of Dept of Nutrition, Hannah Inst., Ayr, Scotland, 1948-65. President: British Soc. of Animal Production, 1970-71; Nutrition Soc., 1974; RSE, 1979-82. For. Mem., Lenin Acad. of Agric. Sciences, 1970. Hon. DSc: QUB, 1974; Leeds, 1977; Hon. LLD Aberdeen, 1981; Hon. DAgric Agricl Univ., Norway, 1975; Hon. MRCVS, 1978. Thomas Baxter Prize and Gold Medal, 1960; Gold Medal, RASE, 1964; Wooldridge Gold Medal, British Vet. Assoc., 1973; De Laval medal, Royal Swedish Acad. Engrg Scis, 1976; Messel Medal, Soc. of Chem. Industry, 1976; Keith Medal and Prize, RSE, 1977; Massey-Ferguson Award, 1977; Wolf Foundn Internat. Prize, 1979. *Publications:* Energy Metabolism of Ruminants, 1962; Energy Metabolism, 1965. Scientific papers in Jl Endocrinology, Jl Agricultural Science, British Jl Nutrition, Research in Veterinary Science, etc. *Recreation:* painting. *Address:* Stradbroke Hall, Stradbroke, near Eye, Suffolk.

BLAYNEY, Elizabeth Carmel, (Eily Blayney); Head of Library and Records Department and Departmental Record Officer, Foreign and Commonwealth Office, since 1977; *b* 19 July 1925; *d* of William Blayney, MRCS, LRCP, Medical Practitioner of Harrold, Beds, and Mary Henrietta (*née* Beveridge). *Educ:* St Mary's Convent, Shaftesbury; The Triangle, S Molton Street. Chartered Librarian. Served War, WTS(FANY) in UK, India and Ceylon (Force 136), 1944-46. Library Asst, Hampstead Borough Libraries, 1947-50; Assistant Librarian: RSA, 1950-52; CO/CRO Jt Library, CRO, 1953; Head of Printed Library, FO, 1959-68; Librarian i/c, ODM, 1968-69; Librarian, FCO, 1969-77. *Address:* c/o Foreign and Commonwealth Office, SW1A 2AH. *Club:* Royal Commonwealth Society.

BLEACKLEY, David, CMG 1979; DPhil; Head, Overseas Division, and Assistant Director, Institute of Geological Sciences, 1975-80; *b* 1 Feb. 1919; *s* of Alfred Mason and Hilda Gertrude Bleackley; *m* 1st, 1945, Peggy Florence Chill (*d* 1966); one *s* one *d* ; 2nd, 1973, Patricia Clavell Strakosch (*née* Hore); two step *s* one step *d. Educ:* City of Oxford Sch.; The Queen's Coll., Oxford (BA 1939, MA 1942, DPhil 1960). Served War, Royal Engineers, 1939-45. Geologist: Shell Oil Co., 1946-50; Geological Survey, British Guiana, 1954-57, Dep. Dir, 1957-60; Overseas Geological Surveys, 1960-65; Dep. Head, Overseas Div., Inst. of Geological Sciences, 1965-75. FIMM 1969; FGS 1943. *Publications:* papers in various jls. *Recreations:* walking, shooting. *Address:* Well Farm, Dagnall, near Berkhamsted, Herts HP4 1QU. *T:* Little Gaddesden 3232.

BLEAKLEY, Rt. Hon. David Wylie, PC (NI) 1971; Chief Executive, Irish Council of Churches, since 1980; *b* 11 Jan. 1925; *s* of John Wesley Bleakley and Sarah Bleakley (*née* Wylie); *m* 1949, Winifred Wason; three *s. Educ:* Ruskin Coll., Oxford; Queen's Univ., Belfast. MA, DipEconPolSci (Oxon). Belfast Shipyard, 1940-46; Oxford and Queen's Univ., 1946-51; Tutor in Social Studies, 1951-55; Principal, Belfast Further Educn Centre, 1955-58; Lectr in Industrial Relations, Kivukoni Coll., Dar-es-Salaam, 1967-69; Head of Dept of Economics and Political Studies, Methodist Coll., Belfast, 1969-79. MP (Lab) Victoria, Belfast, Parliament of N Ireland, 1958-65; contested: (Lab) East Belfast, General Elections, 1970, Feb. and Oct. 1974. Minister of Community Relations, Govt of NI, March-Sept. 1971; Member (NILP), E Belfast: NI Assembly, 1973-75; NI Constitutional Convention, 1975-76. Mem., Cttee of Inquiry on Police, 1978. Chm., Standing Adv. Commn on Human Rights, 1980-. Irish Deleg. to Anglican Consultative Council, 1976; Deleg. to World Council of Churches; Pres., Church Missionary Soc., 1983-; WEA and Open Univ. tutor; Vis. Sen. Lectr in Peace Studies, Univ. of Bradford, 1974-. Hon. MA Open, 1975. *Publications:* Ulster since 1800: regional history symposium, 1958; Young Ulster and Religion in the Sixties, 1964; Peace in Ulster, 1972; Faulkner: a biography, 1974; Saidie Patterson, Irish Peacemaker, 1980; In Place of Work, 1981; regular contribs to BBC and to press on community relations and industrial studies. *Address:* 8 Thornhill, Bangor, Co. Down, Northern Ireland BT19 1RD. *T:* Bangor 54898.

BLEANEY, Prof. Brebis, CBE 1965; FRS 1950; MA, DPhil; Warren Research Fellow, Royal Society, 1977-80, Leverhulme Emeritus Fellow, 1980-82; Senior Research Fellow, Wadham College, Oxford, since 1977 (Fellow, 1957-77); Dr Lee's Professor of Experimental Philosophy, University of Oxford, 1957-77, now Emeritus Professor; *b* 6 June 1915; *m* 1949, Betty Isabelle Plumpton; one *s* one *d. Educ:* Westminster City Sch.; St John's Coll., Oxford. Lecturer in Physics at Balliol Coll., Oxford, 1947-50. Research Fellow, Harvard Univ. and Mass Institute of Technology, 1949. University Demonstrator and Lectr in Physics, Univ. of Oxford, 1945-57; Fellow and Lectr in Physics, St John's Coll., Oxford, 1947-57; Tutor, 1950-57; Hon. Fellow, 1968. Visiting Prof. in Physics in Columbia Univ., 1956-57; Harkins Lectr, Chicago Univ., 1957; Kelvin Lectr, Instn Electrical Engineers, 1962; Morris Loeb Lectr, Harvard Univ., 1981; Cherwell Simon Meml Lectr, Oxford Univ., 1981-82; Visiting Professor: Univ. of California, Berkeley, 1961; Univ. of Pittsburgh, 1962-63; Manitoba, 1968; La Plata, Argentina, 1971; Amer. Univ. in Cairo, 1978; Univ. of NSW, 1981. Mem. Council for Scientific and Industrial Res., 1960-62. FRSA 1971. Corr. Mem. Acad. of Sciences, Inst. of France, 1974, Associé Etranger, 1978; For. Hon. Mem., Amer. Acad. of Arts and Scis, 1978. Charles Vernon Boys Prize, Physical Soc., 1952; Hughes Medal, Royal Society, 1962. *Publications:* (with B. I. Bleaney) Electricity and Magnetism, 1957, 3rd edn, 1976; (with A. Abragam) Electron Paramagnetic Resonance, 1970; various papers in Proceedings of the Royal Society and Proceedings of the Physical Society, etc. *Recreations:* music and tennis. *Address:* Clarendon Laboratory, Oxford.

BLEASDALE, Raymond John, CBE 1982; RIBA; Director, Estates and Environment, Scottish Development Agency, since 1976; *b* 3 Sept. 1924; *s* of John William Bleasdale and Rose Bleasdale; *m* 1951, Patricia Feather; two *s* one *d. Educ:* Bradford Grammar Sch.; Leeds Sch. of Architecture. Dipl.Arch 1949; RIBA 1950; FRIAS 1967; AICArb 1967. Served RAF, USA and SE Asia, 1943-47. Development Dept, English Electric Co., 1949-60; Chief Architect, English Electric Gp, 1960-65; Building Dir, Scottish Industrial Estates Corp., 1965-75; joined Scottish Develt Agency, 1975. *Publications:* articles in sundry technical jls. *Recreations:* sailing, walking, painting in oils. *Address:* 9 Kersland Drive, Milngavie, Glasgow G62 8DG. *T:* 041-956 1528. *Club:* Royal Scottish Automobile (Glasgow).

BLEASE, family name of **Baron Blease.**

BLEASE, Baron *cr* 1978 (Life Peer), of Cromac in the City of Belfast; **William John Blease,** JP; Industrial Relations Consultant; Labour Party Spokesman in House of Lords on Northern Ireland, since 1979; *b* 28 May 1914; *e s* of late William and Sarah Blease; *m* 1939, Sarah Evelyn Caldwell; three *s* one *d. Educ:* elementary and technical schs; Nat. Council of Labour Colls; WEA. Retail Provision Trade (apprentice), 1929; Retail Grocery Asst (Branch Manager), 1938-40; Clerk, Belfast Shipyard, 1940-45; Branch Manager, Co-operative Soc., Belfast, 1945-59; Divl Councillor, Union of Shop Distributive Workers, 1948-59; NI Officer, 1959-75, Exec. Consultant, 1975-76, Irish Congress of Trade Unions; Divl Chm. and Nat. Exec. Mem., Nat. Council of Labour Colls, 1948-61; Exec. Mem., NI Labour Party (Dep. Chm., 1957-58); Trade Union Side Sec., NI CS Industrial Jt Council, 1975-77. Member: NI Economic Council, 1964-75; Review Body on Local Govt, NI, 1970-71; Review Body on Ind. Relations, NI, 1970-73; Working Party on Discrimination in Employment, NI, 1972-73; NI Trng Res. Cttee, 1966-80; NI Regional Adv. Bd, BIM, 1971-80; NUU Vocational Guidance Council, 1974-; Ind. Appeals Tribunals, 1974-76; Local Govt Appeals Tribunal, 1974-; Govt Cttee, Presbyterian Church in Ireland, 1974-80, General Bd, 1974-80; Working Party, Irish Council of Churches, 1974-; IBA, 1974-79; Standing Adv. Commn on Human Rights, NI, 1977-79; Police Complaints Bd, 1977-80; Conciliation Panel, Ind. Relations Agency, 1978-; Security Appeal Bd, NI SC Commn, 1979-. Chm., Public Service Order Cttee, 1979-80; Rapporteur, EEC Cross Border Communications Study on Londonderry/Donegal, 1978; Vice-Pres., NI Assoc., NACRO, 1970-. Pres., NI Hospice, 1981-. Ford Foundn Travel Award, USA, 1959. Hon. Res. Fellow, New Univ. of Ulster, 1976-; Jt Hon. Res. Fellow, TCD, 1976-79. Hon. FBIM 1981 (MBIM 1960). JP Belfast, 1976. Hon. DLitt New Univ. of Ulster, 1972; Hon. LLD QUB, 1982. *Recreation:* reading. *Address:* 27 Ferguson Drive, Belfast BT4 2AZ. *Club:* Sloane.

BLECH, Harry, OBE 1962; Hon. RAM, 1963; Musical Director, Haydn-Mozart Society, and Founder, and Conductor, London Mozart Players, since 1949; *b* 2 March 1910; British; *m* 1935, Enid Marion Lessing (*d* 1977); one *s* two *d* ; *m* 1957, Marion Manley, pianist; one *s* three *d. Educ:* Central London Foundation; Trinity Coll. of Music (Fellow); Manchester Coll. of Music (Fellow). Violin soloist, 1928-30; joined BBC Symphony Orchestra, 1930-36. Responsible for formation of: Blech Quartet, 1933-50; London Wind Players, 1942 (conductor); London Mozart Players, 1949; Haydn-Mozart Soc., 1949; London Mozart Choir, 1952. Dir of Chamber Orchestra, RAM, 1961-65. FRSA. *Address:* The Owls, 70 Leopold Road, Wimbledon, SW19 7JQ.

BLEDISLOE, 3rd Viscount *cr* 1935; **Christopher Hiley Ludlow Bathurst,** QC 1978; *b* 24 June 1934; *s* of 2nd Viscount Bledisloe, QC, and of Joan Isobel Krishaber; *S* father, 1979; *m* 1962, Elizabeth Mary, 2nd *d* of Sir Edward Thompson, *qv* ; two *s* one *d. Educ:* Eton; Trinity Coll., Oxford. Called to the Bar, Gray's Inn, 1959. *Heir: s* Hon. Rupert Edward Ludlow Bathurst, *b* 13 March 1964. *Address:* Lydney Park, Glos GL15 6BT. *T:* Dean 42566; Fountain Court, Temple, EC4Y 9DH. *T:* 01-353 7356.

BLEEHEN, Prof. Norman Montague; Cancer Research Campaign Professor of Clinical Oncology and Hon. Director of MRC Unit of Clinical Oncology and Radiotherapeutics, University of Cambridge, since 1975; Fellow of St John's College, Cambridge, since 1976; *b* 24 Feb. 1930; *s* of Solomon and Lena Bleehen; *m* 1969, Tirza, *d* of Alex and Jenny Loeb. *Educ:* Manchester Grammar Sch.; Haberdashers' Aske's Sch.; Exeter Coll., Oxford (Francis Gotch medal, 1953); Middlesex Hosp. Med. School. BA 1951, BSc 1953, MA 1954, BM, BCh 1955, Oxon; MRCP 1957, FRCP 1973; FRCR 1964; DMRT 1962. MRC Res. Student, Biochem. Dept, Oxford, 1951; house appts: Middlesex Hosp., 1955-56; Hammersmith Hosp., 1957; Asst Med. Specialist Army, Hanover, 1957; Med. Specialist Army, Berlin, 1959 (Captain); Jun. Lectr in Medicine, Dept of Regius Prof. of Medicine, Oxford, 1959-60; Registrar and Sen. Registrar in Radiotherapy, Middlesex Hosp. Med. Sch., 1961-66; Lilly Res. Fellow, Stanford Univ., 1966-67; Locum Consultant, Middlesex Hosp., 1967-69; Prof. of Radiotherapy, Middlesex Hosp. Med. Sch., 1969-75. Member: Jt MRC/CRC Cttee for jtly supported insts, 1971-74; Coordinating Cttee for Cancer Res., 1973-79; Council, Imperial Cancer Res. Fund, 1973-; Council, Brit. Inst. of Radiology, 1974-77; Sci. Cttee, Cancer Res. Campaign, 1976-; Vice President: Bd of Dirs, Internat. Assoc. for Study of Lung Cancer; Internat. Soc. of Radiation Oncology, 1971-; Chairman: British Assoc. for Cancer Res., 1976-79; MRC Cancer Therapy Cttee. *Publications:* (Scientific Editor) British Medical Bulletin 24/1, The Scientific Basis of Radiotherapy; various on medicine, biochemistry cancer and radiotherapy. *Recreations:* gardening, ski-ing, television. *Address:* 21 Bentley Road, Cambridge CB2 2AW. *T:* Cambridge 354320. *Club:* Athenæum.

BLELLOCH, John Niall Henderson; Deputy Under-Secretary of State, Ministry of Defence, since 1982; *b* 24 Oct. 1930; *s* of late Ian William Blelloch, CMG and Leila Mary Henderson; *m* 1958, Pamela, *d* of late James B. Blair and E. M. Blair; one *s* (and one *s* decd). *Educ:* Fettes Coll.; Gonville and Caius Coll., Cambridge (BA). Nat. Service, RA, 1949-51 (commnd 1950). Asst Principal, War Office, 1954; Private Sec. to successive Parly Under Secs of State, 1956-58; Principal, 1958; MoD, 1964-80; London Business Sch. (EDP 3), 1967; Asst Sec., 1968; RCDS, 1974; Asst Under-Sec. of State (Air), Procurement Exec., 1976; Asst Under-Sec. of State, Defence Staff, 1979; Dep. Sec., NI Office, 1980-82. *Recreations:* golf, squash, skiing, learning the piano. *Address:* c/o Bank of Scotland, 57/60 Haymarket, SW1. *Clubs:* Roehampton; Royal Mid-Surrey Golf.

BLENKINSOP, Dorothy; Regional Nursing Officer, Northern Regional Health Authority, since 1973; *b* 15 Nov. 1931; *d* of late Joseph Henry Blenkinsop, BEM, and Thelma Irene (*née* Bishop). *Educ:* South Shields Grammar Sch. for Girls. MA Dunelm 1978. SRN 1953; SCM 1954; Health Visitors Cert. 1962. Ward Sister, Royal Victoria Infirm., Newcastle upon Tyne, 1955-61; Health Visitor, South Shields, 1962-64; Dep. Matron, Gen. Hosp., South Shields, 1964-67; Durham Hosp. Management Cttee: Principal Nurse, Durham City Hosps, 1967-69; Principal Nursing Officer (Top), 1969-71; Chief Nursing Officer, 1971-73. Mem. Methodist Church (Circuit Steward, 1968-82; Sunday School Teacher). *Publications:* (with E. G. Nelson): Changing the System, 1972; Managing the System, 1976; articles in nursing press. *Recreation:* gardening. *Address:* 98 Stanhope Road, South Shields, Tyne and Wear. *T:* South Shields 561429.

BLENNERHASSETT, Francis Alfred, QC 1965; **His Honour Judge Blennerhassett;** a Circuit Judge, since 1978; *b* 7 July 1916; 2nd *s* of John and Annie Elizabeth Blennerhassett; *m* 1948, Betty Muriel Bray; two *d. Educ:* Solihull Sch. Served War of 1939-45 RA and Royal Warwicks Regt, Britain and East Africa (Captain). Called to Bar, Middle Temple, 1946; Bencher, 1971; Oxford Circuit. Dep. Chm., Staffordshire QS, 1963-71; Recorder of New Windsor, 1965-71; a Recorder of the Crown Court, 1972-78; Hon. Recorder of New Windsor, 1972-76; Hon. Recorder of Windsor and Maidenhead, 1976-. Legal Assessor to GMC and Dental Council, 1971-78; Chm., Govt Cttee on Drinking and Driving, 1975-76; Mem., Parole Bd, 1981-. *Recreation:* golf. *Address:* Manor Cottage, Hampton in Arden, Warwickshire. *T:* Hampton in Arden 2660. *Clubs:* Union (Birmingham); Copt Heath Golf.

BLENNERHASSETT, Sir (Marmaduke) Adrian (Francis William), 7th Bt, *cr* 1809; *b* 25 May 1940; *s* of Lieut Sir Marmaduke Blennerhassett, 6th Bt, RNVR (killed in action, 1940), and Gwenfra (*d* 1956), *d* of Judge Harrington-Morgan, Churchtown, Co. Kerry, and of Mrs Douglas Campbell; *S* father 1940; *m* 1972, Carolyn Margaret, *yr d* of late Gilbert Brown; one *s* one *d. Educ:* Michael Hall, Forest Row; McGill Univ.; Imperial Coll., Univ. of London (MSc); Cranfield Business Sch. (MBA). *Recreations:* flying (private pilot's licence), ocean racing (sailing), ski-ing. *Heir: s* Charles Henry Marmaduke Blennerhassett, *b* 18 July 1975. *Address:* 41 Park Road, Chiswick, W4. *Club:* Royal Ocean Racing.

BLESSLEY, Kenneth Harry, CBE 1974 (MBE 1945); ED; Valuer and Estates Surveyor, Greater London Council, 1964-77; *b* 28 Feb. 1914; *s* of Victor Henry le Blond Blessley and Ellen Mary Blessley; *m* 1946, Gwendeline MacRae; two *s. Educ:* Haberdashers' Aske's Hampstead Sch.; St Catharine's Coll., Cambridge (MA); Coll. of Estate Management. FRICS. Private practice, West End and London suburbs. Served War of 1939-45, TA Royal Engrs, Persia, Middle East, Sicily, Italy (despatches 1942 and 1944). Sen. Property Adviser, Public Trustee, 1946-50; Dep. County Valuer, Mddx CC, 1950-53; County Valuer, Mddx CC, 1953-65. Mem. Urban Motorways Cttee,

1970-72; Chm., Covent Garden Officers' Steering Gp, 1970-77; Chm., Thamesmead Officers' Steering Gp, 1971-76; Pres., Assoc. of Local Authority Valuers and Estate Surveyors, 1962 and 1972; Mem. Gen. Council, RICS, 1972-78, Pres., Gen. Practice Div., 1976-77. Pres., Old Haberdashers' Assoc., 1963 (Pres. RFC, 1966-68). *Publications:* numerous articles and papers on compensation, property valuation and development. *Recreations:* music, drama, sport, motoring. *Address:* 99 Maplehurst Road, Summersdale, Chichester, West Sussex. *T:* Chichester 528188. *Club:* MCC.

BLEWITT, Major Shane Gabriel Basil, MVO 1981; Assistant Keeper of the Privy Purse, since 1975; *b* 25 March 1935; *s* of late Col Basil Blewitt; *m* 1969, Julia Morrogh-Bernard, *widow* of Major John Morrogh-Bernard, Irish Guards, and *d* of Mr Robert Calvert; one *s* one *d* (and one step *s* one step *d*). *Educ:* Ampleforth Coll.; Christ Church, Oxford (MA Hons Mod. Languages). Served Irish Guards, 1956-74; Antony Gibbs and Sons, 1974. *Recreations:* gardening, shooting. *Address:* South Corner House, Duncton, near Petworth, West Sussex. *T:* Petworth 42143. *Club:* Army and Navy.

BLIGH, family name of **Earl of Darnley.**

BLIN-STOYLE, Prof. Roger John, FRS 1976; Professor of Theoretical Physics, University of Sussex, since 1962; *b* 24 Dec. 1924; *s* of Cuthbert Basil St John Blin-Stoyle and Ada Mary (*née* Nash); *m* 1949, Audrey Elizabeth Balmford; one *s* one *d. Educ:* Alderman Newton's Boys' Sch., Leicester; Wadham Coll., Oxford (Scholar). MA, DPhil Oxon; FInstP; ARCM. Pressed Steel Co. Res. Fellow, Oxford Univ., 1951-53; Lectr in Math. Physics, Birmingham Univ., 1953-54; Sen. Res. Officer in Theoret. Physics, Oxford Univ., 1952-62; Fellow and Lectr in Physics, Wadham Coll., Oxford, 1956-62; Vis. Associate Prof. of Physics, MIT, 1959-60; Vis. Prof. of Physics, Univ. of Calif, La Jolla, 1960; Sussex University: Dean, Sch. of Math. and Phys. Sciences, 1962-68; Pro-Vice-Chancellor, 1965-67; Dep. Vice-Chancellor, 1970-72; Pro-Vice-Chancellor (Science), 1977-79. Member: Royal Greenwich Observatory Cttee, 1966-70; Nuclear Physics Bd, SRC, 1967-70. Rutherford Medal and Prize, IPPS, 1976. *Publications:* Theories of Nuclear Moments, 1957; Fundamental Interactions and the Nucleus, 1973; papers on nuclear and elementary particle physics in scientific jls. *Recreation:* making music. *Address:* 14 Hill Road, Lewes, E Sussex BN7 1DB. *T:* Lewes 3640.

BLISHEN, Anthony Owen, OBE 1968; HM Diplomatic Service; Counsellor, Foreign and Commonwealth Office, since 1981; *b* 16 April 1932; *s* of Henry Charles Adolphus Blishen and Joan Cecile Blishen (*née* Blakeney); *m* 1963, Sarah Anne Joscelyne; three *s* one *d. Educ:* Clayesmore Sch., Dorset; SOAS, London Univ. Commnd Royal Hampshire Regt, 1951; Lt 1st Bn: BAOR, 1953; Malaya, 1953-55; Captain, GSO3 HQ 18 Inf. Bde, Malaya, 1955-56; attached HQ Land Forces, Hong Kong (language trng), 1957-59; GSO3 HQ Far East Land Forces, Singapore, 1960-62; FO, 1963-65; First Sec. and Consul, Peking, 1965-67; First Sec., FCO, 1968-70; Chargé d'Affaires (ad interim), Ulan Bator, 1970; Trade Comr (China trade), Hong Kong, 1971-73; First Sec., FCO, 1973-77; First Sec., 1977-78, Counsellor, 1978-81, Tokyo. *Recreations:* Renaissance music, oriental languages. *Address:* c/o Foreign and Commonwealth Office, SW1A 2AH.

BLISHEN, Edward; author; *b* 29 April 1920; *s* of William George Blishen and Elizabeth Anne (*née* Pye); *m* 1948, Nancy Smith; two *s. Educ:* Queen Elizabeth's Grammar Sch., Barnet. Weekly Newspaper reporter, 1937-40; agricultural worker, 1941-46. Teaching: Prep. Schoolmaster, 1946-49; Secondary Modern School Teacher, 1950-59. Soc. of Authors Travelling Scholarship, 1979. *Publications:* Roaring Boys, 1955; This Right Soft Lot, 1969; (with Leon Garfield) The God Beneath the Sea, 1970; (with Leon Garfield) The Golden Shadow, 1972; A Cackhanded War, 1972; Uncommon Entrance, 1974; Sorry, Dad, 1978; A Nest of Teachers, 1980; Shaky Relations, 1981 (J. R. Ackerley Prize); Lizzie Pye, 1982; edited: Junior Pears Encyclopaedia, 1961-; Oxford Miscellanies, 1964-69; Blond Encyclopaedia of Education, 1969; The School that I'd Like, 1969; The Thorny Paradise, 1975; compiled: Oxford Book of Poetry for Children, 1964; Come Reading, 1967. *Recreations:* walking, photography, listening to music. *Address:* 12 Bartrams Lane, Hadley Wood, Barnet EN4 0EH. *T:* 01-449 3252.

BLISS, Christopher John Emile, PhD; Nuffield Reader in International Economics, Oxford University, and Fellow of Nuffield College, since 1977; *b* 17 Feb. 1940; *s* of John Llewllyn Bliss and Patricia Paula (*née* Dubern); *m* 1964, Heather (*née* Midmer) (separated 1977); one *s* two *d. Educ:* Finchley Catholic Grammar Sch.; King's Coll., Cambridge (BA 1962, MA 1964, PhD 1966). Fellow of Christ's Coll., Cambridge, 1965-71; Asst Lectr, 1965-67, and Lectr, 1967-71, Cambridge Univ.; Prof. of Econs, Univ. of Essex, 1971-77. Fellow, Econometric Soc., 1978. Editor or Asst Editor, Rev. of Econ. Studies, 1967-71. Dir, General Funds Investment Trust Ltd, 1980-. *Publications:* Capital Theory and the Distribution of Income, 1975; (with N. H. Stern) Palanpur: the economy of an Indian village, 1982; papers and reviews in learned jls. *Recreation:* gratification of the higher appetites. *Address:* Nuffield College, Oxford OX1 1NF. *T:* Oxford 48014.

BLISS, John Cordeux, QPM; retired as Deputy Assistant Commissioner, Metropolitan Police, 1971 (seconded as National Co-ordinator of Regional Crime Squads of England and Wales from inception, 1964-71); *b* 16 March 1914; *s* of late Herbert Francis Bliss and Ida Muriel (*née* Hays); *m* 1947, Elizabeth Mary, *d* of Charles Gordon Howard; one *s* two *d. Educ:* Haileybury

Coll. Metropolitan Police Coll., Hendon, 1936-37. Served in RAF, 1941-45, Flt Lt, 227 Sqdn, MEF. Various ranks of Criminal Investigation Dept of Metropolitan Police, 1946-62; seconded as Dir of Criminal Law at Police Coll., Bramshill, 1962-63; Dep. Comdr, 1963-64. Barrister, Middle Temple, 1954. Mem., Parole Bd, 1973-76 and 1978-81. Liveryman, Merchant Taylors' Company. Churchill Memorial Trust Fellowship, 1967; Queen's Police Medal, 1969. *Recreations:* squash rackets, hillwalking; but mostly gardening; formerly: Rugby football, tennis. *Address:* Foxhanger Down, Hurtmore, Godalming, Surrey. *T:* Godalming 22487. *Club:* Royal Air Force.

BLISS, Kathleen Mary, (Mrs Rupert Bliss), MA Cantab 1934; Lecturer in Religious Studies, University of Sussex, 1967-72; *b* 5 July 1908; *née* Moore; *m* 1932, Rev. Rupert Bliss; three *d. Educ:* Girton Coll., Cambridge. Educational work in India, 1932-39; Editor, the Christian Newsletter, 1945-49; organized Christian-humanist debate, BBC, 1951-55; Studies of education in industry, 1956-57; General Sec., Church of England Board of Education, 1958-66. Member of Public Schools Commn, 1967-70. Hon. DD (Aberdeen), 1949. Select Preacher before the Univ. of Cambridge, 1967. *Publications:* The Service and Status of Women in the Churches, 1951; We the People, 1963; The Future of Religion, 1969. *Address:* 26B Ellerdale Road, Hampstead, NW3 6BB.

BLISS, Mrs Rupert; *see* Bliss, K. M.

BLISSETT, Alfreda Rose; *see* Hodgson, A. R.

BLIX, Hans, PhD, LLD; Director General, International Atomic Energy Agency, since 1981; *b* 28 June 1928; *s* of Gunnar Blix and Hertha Blix (*née* Wiberg); *m* 1962, Eva Margareta Kettis; two *s. Educ:* Univ. of Uppsala; Columbia Univ.; Univ. of Cambridge (PhD); Stockholm Univ. (LLD). Associate Prof. in International Law, 1960; Ministry of Foreign Affairs, Stockholm: Legal Adviser, 1963-76; Under-Secretary of State, in charge of internat. development co-operation, 1976; Minister for Foreign Affairs, 1978; Under-Secretary of State, in charge of internat. development co-operation, 1979. Member: Sweden's delegn to UN General Assembly, 1961-81; Swedish delegn to Conference on Disarmament in Geneva, 1962-78. *Publications:* Treaty Making Power, 1959; Statsmyndigheternas Internationella Förbindelser, 1964; Sovereignty, Aggression and Neutrality, 1970; The Treaty-Maker's Handbook, 1974. *Recreations:* skiing, hiking. *Address:* International Atomic Energy Agency, POB 100, A-1400 Vienna, Austria. *T:* 2360, ext. 1111.

BLOCH, Prof. Felix, PhD; Professor of Physics, Stanford University, USA, 1934-71, Professor Emeritus, since 1971; *b* 23 Oct. 1905; *s* of Gustav Bloch and Agnes Mayer; *m* 1940, Lore Misch; three *s* one *d. Educ:* Zurich, Switzerland. PhD Leipzig, 1928. Asst Zurich, 1928-29; Lorentz Fellow, Holland, 1929-30; Asst Leipzig, 1930-31; Oersted Fellow, Copenhagen, 1931-32; Lecturer, Leipzig, 1932-33; Rockefeller Fellow, Rome, 1933-34; Director-General European Council for Nuclear Research, Geneva, 1954-55. Hon. DSc: Grenoble, 1959; Oxon, 1960; Jerusalem, 1962; Brandeis, 1976; Pavia, 1977; Hon. DPhil Zurich, 1966. Fellow American Phys. Society (Pres., 1965-66); Member: Nat. Academy of Sciences, 1948; RSE; Royal Dutch Acad. of Sciences; Hon. Mem., French Physical Soc.; Hon. Fellow, Weizmann Inst., 1958. (jointly) Nobel Prize for Physics, 1952. Pour le Mérite Order, 1979. *Publications:* about 80 articles on atomic and nuclear physics in various European and American scientific journals. *Recreations:* ski-ing, mountaineering, piano. *Address:* 1551 Emerson Street, Palo Alto, Calif 94301, USA. *T:* 327-8156.

BLOCH, Prof. Konrad E.; Higgins Professor of Biochemistry, Harvard University, since 1954; *b* 21 Jan. 1912; *s* of Frederick D. Bloch and Hedwig (*née* Striemer); *m* 1941, Lore Teutsch; one *s* one *d. Educ:* Technische Hochschule, Munich; Columbia Univ., New York. Instructor and Research Associate, Columbia Univ., 1939-46; Univ. of Chicago: Asst Prof., 1946-48; Associate Prof., 1948-50; Prof., 1950-54. Nobel Prize for Medicine (jointly), 1964. *Publications:* Lipide Metabolism, 1961; numerous papers in biochemical journals. *Address:* 16 Moon Hill Road, Lexington, Mass 02173, USA. *T:* Volunteer 2-9076; Department of Chemistry, Harvard University, 12 Oxford Street, Cambridge, Mass 02138, USA.

BLOCH, Mrs Sidney; *see* Park, Merle F.

BLOCK, Maj.-Gen. Adam Johnstone Cheyne, CB 1962; CBE 1959 (OBE 1951); DSO 1945; *b* 13 June 1908; *s* of late Col Arthur Hugh Block, RA; *m* 1945, Pauline Bingham, *d* of late Col Norman Kennedy, CBE, DSO, TD, DL, Doonholm, Ayr; two *d* (and one *d* decd). *Educ:* Blundell's; RMA Woolwich. 2nd Lieut RA 1928; served War of 1939-45 (France, UK, N Africa and Italy); CO 24th Field Regt, RA, 1943-45. GSO1, RA and AMS, GHQ, 1945-47; AQMG and GSO1 Trg AA Comd, 1947-50; Lieut-Col, 1950; Senior Directing Staff (Army). Joint Services Staff College, 1950-53; Col, 1953; CRA 6 Armd Div., 1953; Comdt, School of Artillery, Larkhill, 1956; Maj.-Gen. 1959; GOC Troops, Malta, 1959-62; retd. Chief Information Officer to General Synod (formerly Church Assembly), 1965-72. Mem. Basingstoke DC, 1973-75. Col Comdt, Royal Regt of Artillery, 1965-73. *Recreations:* all country pursuits. *Address:* St Cross House, Whitchurch, Hants. *T:* Whitchurch 2344. *Club:* Army and Navy.

BLOCK, Brig. David Arthur Kennedy William, CBE 1961; DSO 1945; MC 1943; retired; *b* 13 June 1908; *s* of late Col Arthur Hugh Block; *m* 1949; Elizabeth Grace (*d* 1975), *e d* of Lieut-Col E. G. Troyte-Bullock, Zeals House, Wiltshire, and *widow* of Major G. E. Sebag-Montefiore, D'Anvers House, Culworth, near Banbury; no *c. Educ:* Blundell's; RMA, Woolwich. Served War of 1939-45 (despatches, MC, DSO); CO 152nd (Ayrshire Yeomanry) Field Regt, RA, 1943-45. CO 2nd Regt RHA, 1950-53; CRA, 7th Armoured Div., 1954-57; Comd 18th Trg Bde, RA, 1958-61; retired, 1961. ADC to the Queen, 1959. *Recreations:* hunting, shooting, golf. *Address:* Benville Manor, Lodge, Corscombe, Dorchester, Dorset DT2 0NW. *T:* Corscombe 205. *Club:* Army and Navy.

BLOEMBERGEN, Prof. Nicolaas; Gerhard Gade University Professor, Harvard University, since 1980; *b* 11 March 1920; *m* 1950, Huberta Deliana Brink; one *s* two *d. Educ:* Univ. of Utrecht (BA, MA); Univ. of Leiden (PhD). Research Associate, Leiden, 1947-48; Harvard University: Associate Prof., 1951; Gordon McKay Prof. of Applied Physics, 1957; Rumford Prof of Physics, 1974. (Jtly) Nobel Prize in Physics, 1981. *Publications:* Nuclear Magnetic Relaxation, 1948 (New York 1961); Nonlinear Optics, 1965, 4th printing, 1982; over 250 papers in scientific jls. *Address:* Pierce Hall, Harvard University, Cambridge, Mass 02138, USA. *T:* (617) 495-3336.

BLOEMFONTEIN, Bishop of, since 1982; **Rt. Rev. Thomas Shaun Stanage;** *b* 6 April 1932; *s* of Robert and Edith Clarice Stanage. *Educ:* King James I Grammar Sch., Bishop Auckland; Univ. of Oxford (MA, Hons Theology, 1956). Curate, St Faith, Great Crosby, 1958-61; Minister of Conventional District of St Andrews, Oxford, 1961-63; Vicar, St Andrew Oxford, 1963-70; Rector, All Saints, Somerset West, 1970-75; Dean of Kimberley, 1975-78; Bishop Suffragan of Johannesburg, 1978-82. Liaison Chaplain to Missions to Seamen, Southern Africa. *Recreations:* flying (private pilot); music (organ, violin and piano). *Address:* Bishop's House, 16 York Road, Bloemfontein, S Africa. *T:* (051) 314351. *Club:* Bloemfontein.

BLOFELD, John Christopher Calthorpe, QC 1975; a Recorder of the Crown Court, since 1975; *b* 11 July 1932; *s* of T. R. C. Blofeld, CBE; *m* 1961, Judith Anne, *er d* of Alan Mohun and Mrs James Mitchell; two *s* one *d. Educ:* Eton; King's Coll., Cambridge. Called to Bar, Lincoln's Inn, 1956. Chancellor, Dio. St Edmundsbury and Ipswich, 1973. *Recreations:* cricket, gardening. *Address:* Harlequin House, Ickleton, Saffron Walden, Essex. *Club:* Boodle's.

BLOIS, Sir Charles (Nicholas Gervase), 11th Bt, *cr* 1686; farming since 1965; *b* 25 Dec. 1939; *s* of Sir Gervase Ralph Edmund Blois, 10th Bt and Mrs Audrey Winifred Blois (*née* Johnson); *S* father, 1968; *m* 1967, Celia Helen Mary Pritchett; one *s* one *d. Educ:* Harrow; Trinity Coll., Dublin; Royal Agricultural Coll., Cirencester. Australia, 1963-65. *Recreations:* yachting, shooting. *Heir: s* Andrew Charles David Blois, *b* 7 Feb. 1971. *Address:* Red House, Westleton, Saxmundham, Suffolk. *T:* Westleton 200. *Clubs:* Cruising Association; Ocean Cruising.

BLOKH, Alexandre, PhD, (pen-name **Jean Blot**); writer, since 1956; International Secretary, PEN Club, since 1982; *b* Moscow, 31 March 1923; *s* of Arnold Blokh, man of letters, and Anne (*née* Berlinrote); *m* 1956, Nadia Ermolaiev; one *d. Educ:* Bromsgrove Public Sch., Worcester; Univ. of Paris (PhD Law, PhD Letters). International Civil Servant, United Nations, 1947-62: New York, until 1956; Geneva, 1958-62; Director, Arts and Letters, UNESCO, Paris, 1962-81. Critic, arts and letters, in reviews: Arche, Preuves, NRF. Prix des Critiques, 1972; Prix Valéry Larbaud, 1977. *Publications: novels:* Le Soleil de Cavouri, 1956; Les Enfants de New York, 1959; Obscur Ennemi, 1961; Les Illusions Nocturnes, 1964; La Jeune Géante, 1969; La Difficulté d'aimer, 1971; Les Cosmopolites, 1976; Gris du Ciel, 1981; *essays.* Marguerite Yourcenar; Ossip Mandelstan; Là où tu iras; Sporade; Ivan Goutchorov. *Address:* 34 Square Montsouris, 75014 Paris. *T:* 589 34 16; 38 King Street, WC2. *T:* 01-379 7939.

BLOM-COOPER, Louis Jacques, QC 1970; Joint Director of Legal Research Unit, Dept of Sociology, Bedford College, University of London, since 1967; *b* 27 March 1926; *s* of Alfred Blom-Cooper and Ella Flesseman, Rotterdam; *m* 1952 (marr. diss. 1970); two *s* one *d* ; *m* 1970, Jane Elizabeth, *e d* of Maurice and Helen Smither, Woodbridge, Suffolk; one *s* two *d. Educ:* Port Regis Prep. Sch.; Seaford Coll.; King's Coll., London; Municipal Univ. of Amsterdam; Fitzwilliam Coll., Cambridge. LLB London, 1952; Dr Juris Amsterdam, 1954. HM Army, 1944-47: Capt., E Yorks Regt. Called to Bar, Middle Temple, 1952; Bencher, 1978. Mem., Home Secretary's Adv. Council on the Penal System, 1966-78. Chm., Howard League for Penal Reform, 1973-. Chm., BBC London Local Radio Adv. Council, 1970-73. Joint Editor, Common Market Law Reports. JP Inner London, 1966-79 (transf. City of London, 1969). *Publications:* Bankruptcy in Private International Law, 1954; The Law as Literature, 1962; The A6 Murder (A Semblance of Truth), 1963; (with T. P. Morris) A Calendar of Murder, 1964; Language of the Law, 1965; (with O. R. McGregor and Colin Gibson) Separated Spouses, 1970; (with G. Drewry) Final Appeal: a study of the House of Lords in its judicial capacity, 1972; (ed) Progress in Penal Reform, 1975; (ed with G. Drewry) Law and Morality, 1976; contrib. to Modern Law Review, Brit. Jl of Criminology, Brit. Jl of Sociology. *Recreations:* watching and reporting on Association football, reading, music, writing, broadcasting. *Address:* 25 Richmond Crescent, N1 0LY. *T:* 01-607 8045; Howards End, Old Gaol House,

Montgomery, Powys. *T*: Montgomery 458; Goldsmith Building, EC4Y 7BL. *T*: 01-353 6802. *Club*: MCC.

BLOMEFIELD, Peregrine Maitland; His Honour Judge Blomefield; a Circuit Judge (formerly County Court Judge), since 1969; *b* 25 Oct. 1917; 2nd *s* of Lt-Col Wilmot Blomefield, OBE; *m* 1941, Angela Catherine, *d* of Major Geoffrey Hugh Shenley Crofton, Heytesbury, Wilts; one *s*. *Educ*: Repton Sch.; Trinity Coll., Oxford (MA). Royal Signals, 1940-46 (Captain). Called to the Bar, Middle Temple, 1947, Bencher, 1967; Oxford Circuit; Recorder of Burton-on-Trent, 1969; Dep. Chm., Berkshire QS, 1967-71. *Address*: The Coach House, Frilsham, Newbury, Berks. *T*: Hermitage 201421.

BLOMEFIELD, Sir Thomas Edward Peregrine, 5th Bt, *cr* 1807; *b* 31 May 1907; *s* of late Commander T. C. A. Blomefield, *e s* of 4th Bt and Margaret, *e d* of E. P. Landon; *S* grandfather, 1928; *m* 1947, Ginette Massart, Paris; one *s*. *Educ*: Wellington; Trinity Coll. Oxford. Temp. Lieut-Comdt RNVR, 1939-46. *Heir*: *s* Thomas Charles Peregrine Blomefield [*b* 24 July 1948; *m* 1975, Georgina, *d* of Commander Charles Over]. *Address*: 1 Great Lane, Shaftesbury, Dorset. *T*: Shaftesbury 3788.

BLOMFIELD, Brig. John Reginald, OBE 1957; MC 1944; *b* 10 Jan. 1916; *s* of late Douglas John Blomfield, CIE, and Coralie, *d* of F. H. Tucker, Indian Police; *m* 1939, Patricia Mary McKim; two *d*. *Educ*: Clifton Coll.; RMA, Woolwich; Peterhouse, Cambridge (MA). Commissioned Royal Engineers, 1936; Lt-Col 1955; Col 1961; Brig. 1965. Retired as Dep. Director, Military Engineering Experimental Establishment, 1969. New Towns Commn Manager, Hemel Hempstead, 1969-78. MBIM 1966. *Recreations*: cruising, ocean racing. *Address*: 9 Armstrong Close, Brockenhurst, Hants. *Clubs*: Royal Ocean Racing; Royal Lymington Yacht.

BLONDEL, Prof. Jean Fernand Pierre; Professor of Government, University of Essex, since 1964; *b* Toulon, France, 26 Oct. 1929; *s* of Fernand Blondel and Marie Blondel (*née* Santelli); *m* 1954, Michèle (*née* Hadet) (marr. diss. 1979); two *d*; *m* 1982, Mrs Theresa Martineau. *Educ*: Collège Saint Louis de Gonzague and Lycée Henri IV, Paris; Institut d'Etudes Politiques and Faculté de Droit, Paris; St Antony's Coll., Oxford. Asst Lectr, then Lectr in Govt, Univ. of Keele, 1958-63; Visiting ACLS Fellow, Yale Univ., 1963-64. Dean, Sch. of Comparative Studies, Univ. of Essex, 1967-69; Visiting Prof., Carleton Univ., Canada, 1969-70; Exec. Dir, European Consortium for Political Res., 1970-79. *Publications*: Voters, Parties and Leaders, 1963; (jtly) Constituency Politics, 1964; (jtly) Public Administration in France, 1965; An Introduction to Comparative Government, 1969; (jtly) Workbook for Comparative Government, 1972; Comparing Political Systems, 1972; Comparative Legislatures, 1973; The Government of France, 1974; Thinking Politically, 1976; Political Parties, 1978; World Leaders, 1980; The Discipline of Politics, 1981; articles in: Political Studies, Parliamentary Affairs, Public Administration, Revue Française de Science Politique, etc. *Recreation*: holidays in Provence. *Address*: Little Braxted Mill, Witham, Essex. *T*: Witham 513384; 11 rue Général de Partouneaux, Mourillon, Toulon, France.

BLOOD, (Peter) Bindon; Director-General, Institute of Marketing, since 1972; *b* 24 Sept. 1920; *o s* of Brig. William Edmunds Robarts Blood, CBE, MC, Croix de Guerre, and Eva Gwendoline (*née* Harrison); *m* 1953, Elizabeth Ann, *d* of Harold Drummond Hillier, MC; one *s* one *d*. *Educ*: Imperial Service Coll., Windsor. Family public works and civil engineering business, 1938-41; served Royal Engineers, 1941-46 (despatches 1944); Engineering Div., Forestry Commn, 1946-48; Regular commn, RE, 1948; Second i/c, RE Officer Training Unit, 1948-51; Staff Coll., Camberley, 1951; Sec., Army Bd, NATO Mil. Agency for Standardisation, 1952-53; invalided from service, 1953. Intelligence Co-ordination Staff, FO, 1953-58; Founder and formerly Managing Director: Isora Integrated Ceilings Ltd; Clean Room Construction Ltd; Mitchel and King (Sales) Ltd; Dep. Chm. and Group Marketing Dir, King Group; Dir of Marketing Services, Inst. of Marketing, 1971. Chm. of Governors, Berks Coll. of Art and Design, 1981-. FRSA, FInstM. *Recreations*: photography, travel, music, local community activities. *Address*: Westward House, Berries Road, Cookham, Berks SL6 9SD. *T*: Bourne End 20064.

BLOOM, André Borisovich; *see* Anthony, Metropolitan.

BLOOM, Claire; *b* London, 15 Feb. 1931; *d* of late Edward Bloom and of Elizabeth Bloom; *m* 1st, 1959, Rod Steiger (marr. diss. 1969); one *d*; 2nd, 1969. *Educ*: Badminton, Bristol; America and privately. First work in England, BBC, 1946. Stratford: Ophelia, Lady Blanche (King John), Perdita, 1948; The Damask Cheek, Lyric, Hammersmith, 1949; The Lady's Not For Burning, Globe, 1949; Ring Round the Moon, Globe, 1949-50. Old Vic: 1952-53: Romeo and Juliet; 1953: Merchant of Venice; 1954: Hamlet, All's Well, Coriolanus, Twelfth Night, Tempest; 1956: Romeo and Juliet (London, and N American tour). Cordelia, in Stratford Festival Company, 1955 (London, provinces and continental tour); Duel of Angels, Apollo, 1958; Rashomon, NY, 1959; Altona, Royal Court, 1961; The Trojan Women, Spoleto Festival, 1963; Ivanov, Phoenix, 1965; A Doll's House, NY, 1971; Hedda Gabler, 1971; Vivat! Vivat Regina!, NY, 1971; A Doll's House, Criterion, 1973 (filmed 1973); A Streetcar Named Desire, Piccadilly, 1974; Rosmersholm, Haymarket, 1977; The Cherry Orchard, Chichester Fest., 1981; These are Women, a portrait of Shakespeare's heroines, US tour, 1981-82. First film, Blind Goddess, 1947; *films include*: Limelight; The Man Between;

Richard III; Alexander the Great; The Brothers Karamazov; The Buccaneers; Look Back in Anger; Three Moves to Freedom; The Brothers Grimm; The Chapman Report; The Haunting; 80,000 Suspects; Alta Infedelta; Il Maestro di Vigevano; The Outrage; The Spy Who Came in From The Cold; Charly; Three into Two won't go; A Severed Head; Red Sky at Morning; Islands In The Stream; The Clash of the Titans, 1979. First appearance on television programmes, 1952, since when she has had frequent successes on TV in the US; In Praise of Love, 1975; *Television*: BBC series: A Legacy, 1975; Katharine in Henry VIII, 1979; Gertrude in Hamlet, 1980; ITV series: Brideshead Revisited, 1980. *Publication*: Limelight and After (autobiog.), 1982. *Recreations*: ballet, reading. *Address*: c/o Michael Linnitt, Globe Theatre, W1.

BLOOM, G(eorge) Cromarty, CBE 1974; Director: Selkirk Communications Ltd; Independent Radio Sales Ltd; Cablevision (Wellingborough) Ltd; *b* 8 June 1910; *s* of late George Highfield Bloom and Jessie Bloom (*née* Cromarty); *m* 1st, 1940, Patricia Suzanne Ramplin (*d* 1957); two *s*; 2nd, 1961, Sheila Louise Curran; one *s*. *Educ*: Australia and China, privately; Keble Coll., Oxford. With Reuters, 1933-60. Gen. Manager and Chief Exec., The Press Assoc. Ltd, 1961-75. Vice-Chm., Internat. Press Telecommunications Council, 1971-75; Vice-Pres., Alliance Européenne des Agences de Presse, 1971-75; Chm., CPU Telecommunications Cttee, 1973-77. *Address*: 1 Tivoli Court, Tivoli Road, Cheltenham GL50 2TD. *T*: Cheltenham 39413.

BLOOM, Ronald; HM Diplomatic Service, retired; free-lance political/commercial consultant; Director, Philadelphia Services Group Inc.; *b* 21 Jan. 1926; *s* of John I. Bloom and Marjorie Bloom (*née* Barker); *m* 1956, Shirley Evelyn Edge; one *s* two *d*. *Educ*: inadequately. HM Forces, DLI, E Yorks Regt, 1943-57. Joined HM Diplomatic Service, 1958; Hong Kong, 1958-61; Singapore, 1961-63; FO, 1963-65; Zomba, 1965-67; FO, 1967-69; Kuala Lumpur, 1969-71; Singapore, 1971-74; Counsellor, FO, 1974-81. *Publications*: reviews in Man (Royal Anthropol Inst.), occasional articles on uniforms and model soldiers. *Address*: The Old House, Deep Street, Prestbury, Glos. *T*: Cheltenham 44141; Trefoil Associates, 85/87 Jermyn Street, SW1Y 6JD. *T*: 01-930 0138. *Club*: Brooks's.

BLOOM, Ursula, (Mrs Gower Robinson); authoress; *b* Chelmsford, Essex; *o d* of late Rev. J. Harvey Bloom, MA; *m* 1st, 1916, Capt. Arthur Brownlow Denham-Cookes, 24th London Regt (Queen's) (*d* 1918); one *s*; 2nd, 1925, Paymaster Comdr Charles Gower Robinson (*d* 1979), RN (retired). *Educ*: privately. First book, Tiger, published privately when seven years old. Writing under the names of Ursula Bloom, Lozania Prole, Sheila Burnes, Mary Essex and Rachel Harvey has published some 500 books. *Publications include*: The Great Beginning, 1924; Vagabond Harvest, 1925; The Driving of Destiny, 1925; Our Lady of Marble, 1926; The Judge of Jerusalem, 1926; Candleshades, 1927; Spilled Salt, 1927; Base Metal, 1928; An April After, 1928; Tarnish, 1929; To-morrow for Apricots, 1929; The Passionate Heart, 1930; The Secret Lover, 1930; Lamp in the Darkness: a volume of Religious Essays, 1930; Fruit on the Bough, 1931; Packmule, 1931; The Pilgrim Soul, 1932; The Cypresses Grow Dark, 1932; The Log of an NO's Wife, 1932; Wonder Cruise, 1933; Mistress of None, 1933; Rose Sweetman, 1933; Pastoral, 1934; Holiday Mood, 1934; The Questing Trout, 1934; The Gypsy Vans Come Through, 1935; Harvest of a House, 1935; The Laughing Lady, 1936; Laughter on Cheyne Walk, 1936; Three Cedars, 1937; Leaves Before the Storm, 1937; The Golden Venture, 1938; Without Makeup, 1938; The ABC of Authorship, 1938; A Cad's Guide to Cruising, 1938; Lily of the Valley, 1938; Beloved Creditor, 1939; These Roots Go Deep, 1939; The Woman Who Was To-morrow, 1940; Log of No Lady, 1940; The Flying Swans, 1940; Dinah's Husband, 1941; The Virgin Thorn, 1941; Lovely Shadow, 1942; Time, Tide and I, 1942; Age Cannot Wither, 1942; No Lady Buys a Cot, 1943; Robin in a Cage, 1943; The Fourth Cedar, 1943; The Faithless Dove, 1944; No Lady in Bed, 1944; The Painted Lady, 1945; The Changed Village, 1945; Rude Forefathers, 1945; No Lady With a Pen, 1946; Four Sons, 1946; Adam's Daughter, 1947; Three Sisters, 1948; Façade, 1948; No Lady Meets No Gentleman, 1948; Next Tuesday, 1949; Elinor Jowitt, Antiques; No Lady in the Cart; Song of Philomel, 1950; The King's Wife, 1950; Mum's Girl was no Lady, 1950; Pavilion, 1951; Nine Lives, 1951; How Dark, My Lady!, 1951; The Sentimental Family, 1951; As Bends the Bough, 1952; Twilight of a Tudor, 1952; Sea Fret, 1952; The Gracious Lady, 1953; The First Elizabeth, 1953; Hitler's Eva, 1954; Trilogy, 1954; Curtain Call for the Guvnor, 1954; Matthew, Mark, Luke and John, 1954; Daughters of the Rectory, 1955; The Silver Ring, 1955; The Tides of Spring Flow Fast, 1955; Victorian Vinaigrette, 1956; No Lady Has a Dog's Day, 1956; Brief Springtime, 1957; The Elegant Edwardian, 1957; Monkey Tree in a Flower Pot, 1957; He Lit the Lamp, 1958; The Abiding City, 1958; Down to the Sea in Ships, 1958; The Inspired Needle, 1959; Youth at the Gate, 1959; Undarkening Green, 1959; Sixty Years of Home, 1960; The Thieving Magpie, 1960; Prelude to Yesterday, 1961; The Cactus has Courage, 1961; War Isn't Wonderful, 1961; Ship in a Bottle, 1962; Harvest Home Come Sunday, 1962; Parson Extraordinary. 1963; The Gated Road, 1963; Mrs Bunthorpe's Respects, 1963; The House That Died Alone, 1964; The Rose of Norfolk, 1964; The Ring Tree, 1964; The Ugly Head, 1965; The Quiet Village, 1965; Rosemary for Stratford-on-Avon, 1965; Price Above Rubies, 1965; The Dandelion Clock, 1966; The Mightier Sword, 1966; The Old Adam, 1967; A Roof and Four Walls, 1967; Two Pools in a Field, 1967; The Dragon Fly, 1968; Yesterday is To-morrow, 1968; Flight of the Peregrine, 1969; The House of Kent, 1969; The Hunter's Moon, 1970; Rosemary for Frinton, 1970; The Tune of Time,

1970; The Great Tomorrow, 1971; Perchance to Dream, 1971; Rosemary for Chelsea (autobiog.), 1971; The Caravan of Chance, 1972; The Cheval Glass, 1972; The Duke of Windsor, 1972; The Old Rectory, 1973; Princesses in Love, 1973; Requesting the Pleasure, 1973; The Old Elm Tree, 1974; Miracle on the Horizon, 1974; Royal Baby, 1975; Twisted Road, 1975; Turn of Life's Tide, 1976; Life is no Fairy Tale (autobiog.), 1976; The Great Queen Consort, 1976. *Address:* c/o Newtown House, Walls Drive, Ravenglass, Cumbria.

BLOOMER, Rt. Rev. Thomas, DD 1946 (TCD); *b* 14 July 1894; *s* of Thomas and Mary Bloomer; *m* 1935, Marjorie Grace (*d* 1969), *d* of late Rev. David Hutchison; one *s* two *d* ; *m* 1973, Marjorie, widow of I. M. Orr. *Educ:* Royal Sch., Dungannon, N Ireland; Trinity Coll., Dublin. Ordained to curacy of Carrickfergus, N Ireland, 1918; Curate of: Castleton, Lancs, 1922; Cheltenham, Glos, 1923; Vicar of St Mark's, Bath, 1928; Vicar of Barking, 1935–46; Rural Dean of Barking and Canon of Chelmsford Cathedral, 1943–46; Bishop of Carlisle, 1946–66. Chaplain to: the King, 1944–47; House of Lords, 1953–66. Proctor in Convocation of Canterbury, 1945. Freedom of City of Carlisle, 1966. *Publications:* A Fact and a Faith, 1943; A Fact and an Experience, 1944. *Recreations:* golf, gardening. *Address:* 33 Greengate, Levens, Kendal, Cumbria. *T:* Sedgwick 60771.

BLOOMFIELD, Barry Cambray, MA, FLA; Director, India Office Library and Records, British Library (formerly Foreign and Commonwealth Office), since 1978; *b* 1 June 1931; *s* of Clifford Wilson Bloomfield and Eileen Elizabeth (*née* Cambray); *m* 1958, Valerie Jean Philpot. *Educ:* East Ham Grammar Sch.; University College of the South-West, Exeter; University Coll. London; Birkbeck Coll., London. Served in Intelligence Corps, Malaya, 1952–54. Assistant, National Central Library, 1955; Librarian, College of S Mark and S John, Chelsea, 1956–61; Asst Librarian, London Sch. of Economics, 1961–63; Dep. Librarian, 1963–72, Librarian, 1972–78, School of Oriental and African Studies. Chm., SCONUL Group of Orientalist Libraries, 1975–80; Vice-Pres., Bibliographical Soc., 1979–; Member: Council, Royal Asiatic Soc., 1980–; British Assoc. for Cemeteries in S Asia, 1980–; Exec. Cttee, Friends of the Nat. Libraries, 1981–. Vis. Professor, Univ. of Florida, 1963; Vis. Fellow, Univ. of Hawaii, 1977. *Publications:* New Verse in the '30s, 1960; W. H. Auden: a bibliography, 1964, 2nd edn 1972; ed, Autobiography of Sir J. P. Kay Shuttleworth, 1964; ed, (with V. J. Bloomfield, J. D. Pearson) Theses on Africa, 1964; ed, Theses on Asia, 1967; ed, The Acquisition and Provision of Foreign Books by National and University Libraries in the UK, 1972; An Author Index to Selected British 'Little' Magazines, 1976; Philip Larkin: a bibliography 1933–1976, 1979; (ed) Middle East Studies and Libraries, 1980; numerous articles in library and bibliog. jls. *Recreations:* reading, music. *Address:* 99 Morden Hill, SE13 7NP. *T:* 01-692 7214. *Club:* Royal Commonwealth Society.

BLOOMFIELD, Hon. Sir John (Stoughton), Kt 1967; QC (Victoria) 1965; LLB; Member for Malvern, Legislative Assembly, Victoria, 1953–70, retired; *b* 9 Oct. 1901; *s* of Arthur Stoughton Bloomfield, Chartered Accountant, Melbourne, and Ada Victoria Bloomfield; *m* 1931, Beatrice Madge, *d* of W. H. Taylor, Overnewton, Sydenham, Victoria; one *s* one *d*. *Educ:* Geelong Grammar Sch.; Trinity Coll., Melbourne Univ. Served AIF, 1940–45; Lieut-Col retired. Solicitor, 1927–45; called to Victorian Bar, 1945. Government of Victoria: Minister of Labour and Industry and of Electrical Undertakings, 1955–56; Minister of Education, 1956–67. Mem. Council, University of Melbourne, 1956–70. *Publications:* Company Law Amendments, 1939; Screens and Gowns: Some Aspects of University Education Overseas, 1963; articles in professional journals. *Recreation:* painting. *Address:* 25 Mercer Road, Armadale, Victoria 3143, Australia. *T:* 20-2947. *Clubs:* Melbourne, Naval and Military (Melbourne).

BLOOMFIELD, Kenneth Percy, CB 1982; Permanent Secretary, Department of Commerce, Northern Ireland, since 1981; *b* 15 April 1931; *o c* of Harry Percy Bloomfield and Doris Bloomfield, Belfast; *m* 1960, Mary Elizabeth Ramsey; one *s* one *d*. *Educ:* Royal Belfast Academical Instn; St Peter's Coll., Oxford (MA). Min. of Finance, N Ireland, 1952–56; Private Sec. to Ministers of Finance, 1956–60; Dep. Dir, British Industrial Develt Office, NY, 1960–63; Asst and later Dep. Sec. to Cabinet, NI, 1963–72; Under-Sec., Northern Ireland Office, 1972–73; Sec. to Northern Ireland Executive, Jan.–May 1974; Permanent Secretary: Office of the Executive, NI, 1974–75; Dept of Housing, Local Govt and Planning, NI, 1975–76; Dept of the Environment, NI, 1976–81. *Recreations:* reading history and biography, swimming. *Address:* Department of Commerce, Belfast. *T:* Belfast 34488.

BLOSSE, Sir Richard Hely L.; see Lynch-Blosse.

BLOT, Jean; see Blokh, A.

BLOUGH, Roger M.; former Partner, White & Case; former Chairman of the Board of Directors, United States Steel Corporation; *b* 19 Jan. 1904; *s* of Christian E. Blough and Viola (*née* Hoffman); *m* 1928, Helen Martha Decker; twin *d*. *Educ:* Susquehanna Univ. (AB); Yale Law Sch. (LLB). General practice of law with White & Case, New York City, 1931–42; General Solicitor, US Steel Corp. of Delaware, 1942–51; Exec. Vice-President law and Secretary, US Steel Corp., 1951; Vice-Chairman, Director and Member Finance Cttee, US Steel Corp., 1952; General Counsel, 1953–55; Chairman, Chief Exec. Officer and Member Exec. Cttee, 1955–69; Dir and Mem. Finance and Exec. Cttees, 1969–. Holds numerous hon. degrees. *Publication:* Free Man and the Corporation, 1959. *Address:* (business) 300 Keystone Street, Hawley,

Pa 18428, USA; (home) Blooming Grove, Hawley, Pennsylvania 18428, USA. *Clubs:* Blooming Grove Hunting and Fishing (Pa); Board Room, Recess, Links (NYC); Pine Valley Golf; and numerous others.

BLOUNT, Bertie Kennedy, CB 1957; DrPhilNat; CChem, FRSC; *b* 1 April 1907; *s* of late Col G. P. C. Blount, DSO, and late Bridget Constance, *d* of Maj.-Gen. J. F. Bally, CVO; unmarried. *Educ:* Malvern Coll.; Trinity Coll., Oxford (MA 1932, BSc 1929); Univ. of Frankfurt (DrPhilNat 1931). Ramsay Memorial Fellow, 1931; 1851 Senior Student, 1933; Dean of St Peter's Hall, Oxford, 1933–37; Messrs Glaxo Laboratories Ltd: Head of Chemical Research Laboratory, 1937; Principal Technical Executive, 1938–40. Served Army (Intelligence Corps), War of 1939–45; Capt. 1940; Major 1942; Col 1945. Asst Director of Research, The Wellcome Foundation, 1947; Director of Research Branch, Control Commission for Germany, 1948, and subsequently also Chief of Research Div. of Military Security Board; Director of Scientific Intelligence, Min. of Defence, 1950–52; Dep. Secretary, DSIR, 1952; Min. of Technology, 1964; retired 1966. Chairman Steering Cttees: Torry Res. Station and Forest Products Res. Lab., 1958–66; Lab. of the Govt Chemist, 1962–66; Building Res. Station, Joint Fire Res. Organisation, Hydraulics Res. Stat., Water Pollution Res. Lab., Warren Spring Lab., 1965–66. Member Exec. Cttee, British Council, 1957–66. Royal Society of Arts: Armstrong Lecturer, 1955; Cantor Lecturer, 1963. Member Parry Cttee to review Latin American Studies in British Universities, 1962; Pres., Exec. Cttee, Internat. Inst. of Refrigeration, 1963–71, Hon. Pres. 1971; Hon. Mem., (British) Inst. of Refrigeration, 1971. *Publications:* papers in scientific and other journals. *Recreations:* travel, walking, gardening. *Address:* Tarrant Rushton House, Blandford, Dorset. *T:* Blandford 52256. *Club:* Athenæum.

BLOUNT, Sir Walter (Edward Alpin), 12th Bt *cr* 1642; DSC 1943 and two Bars 1945; consultant solicitor; farmer; *b* 31 Oct. 1917; *s* of Sir Edward Robert Blount, 11th Bt, and Violet Ellen (*d* 1969), *d* of Alpin Grant Fowler; *S* father, 1978; *m* 1954, Eileen Audrey, *d* of late Hugh B. Carritt; one *d*. *Educ:* Beaumont College; Sidney Sussex Coll., Cambridge (MA). Served RN, 1939–47. Qualified as Solicitor, 1950; practised Gold Coast, West Africa, 1950–52; London and Cambridge, 1952–76; Consultant, London, 1976. Farmer, Tilkhurst, East Grinstead, Sussex, 1978–. Lloyds Underwriter. *Recreation:* sailing. *Heir:* none. *Address:* 19 St Anns Terrace, St John's Wood, NW8. *T:* 01-722 0802; Regent House, Seaview, IoW. *Clubs:* Bembridge Sailing, Seaview Yacht, Cambridge Cruising, RNVR Sailing, Law Society Yacht, Island Sailing.

BLOW, Prof. David Mervyn, FRS 1972; Professor of Biophysics, since 1977, and Dean of the Royal College of Science, since 1981, at Imperial College, University of London; *b* 27 June 1931; *s* of Rev. Edward Mervyn and Dorothy Laura Blow; *m* 1955, Mavis Sears; one *s* one *d*. *Educ:* Kingswood Sch.; Corpus Christi Coll., Cambridge (MA, PhD). FInstP. Fulbright Scholar, Nat. Inst. of Health, Bethesda, Md, and MIT, 1957–59; MRC Unit for Study of Molecular Biological Systems, Cambridge, 1959–62; MRC Lab. of Molecular Biology, Cambridge, 1962–77; College Lectr and Fellow, Trinity Coll., Cambridge, 1968–77. Biochem. Soc. CIBA Medal, 1967; Charles Léopold Meyer Prize, 1979. *Publications:* papers and reviews in scientific jls. *Recreations:* hill walking, sailing. *Address:* Blackett Laboratory, Imperial College of Science and Technology, SW7 2BZ.

BLOW, Joyce, (Mrs Anthony Darlington), FIPR; Under Secretary (Establishment Management Services and Manpower Division), Departments of Industry and Trade Common Services, since 1980; *b* 4 May 1929; *d* of late Walter Blow and Phyllis (*née* Grainger); *m* 1974, Lt-Col J. A. B. Darlington, RE retd. *Educ:* Bell Baxter Sch., Cupar, Fife; Edinburgh Univ. (MA Hons). FIPR 1964. John Lewis Partnership, 1951–52; FBI, 1952–53; Press Officer, Council of Indust. Design, 1953–63; Publicity and Advertising Manager, Heal & Son Ltd, 1963–65; entered Civil Service on first regular recruitment of direct entry Principals from business and industry: BoT, 1965–67; Monopolies Commn (gen. enquiry into restrictive practices in supply of prof. services), 1967–70; DTI, 1970, Asst Sec. 1972; Dept of Prices and Consumer Protection, 1974–77; Dir of Consumer Affairs, Office of Fair Trading, 1977–80. Founder Mem. and Past Pres. Assoc. of Women in Public Relations. FBIM. *Recreations:* music, particularly opera; travel. *Address:* 17 Fentiman Road, SW8 1LD. *T:* 01-735 4023; 9 Crouchfield Close, Seaford, E Sussex. *Club:* Arts.

BLOW, Sandra, RA 1978 (ARA 1971); *b* 14 Sept. 1925; *d* of Jack and Lily Blow. *Educ:* St Martin's School of Art; Royal Academy Sch.; Accademia di Belle Arti, Rome. Tutor, Painting School, Royal Coll. of Art, 1960–75. *One-man Exhibitions:* Gimpel Fils, 1952, 1954, 1960, 1962; Saidenburg Gallery, NY, 1957; New Art Centre, London, 1966, 1968, 1971, 1973. Represented in group exhibitions in Britain (including British Painting 74, Hayward Gall.), USA, Italy, Denmark, France. Won British Section of Internat. Guggenheim Award, 1960; 2nd prize, John Moore's Liverpool Exhibition, 1961; Arts Council Purchase Award, 1965–66. *Official Purchases:* Peter Stuyvesant Foundation; Nuffield Foundation; Arts Council of Great Britain; Arts Council of N Ireland; Walker Art Gallery, Liverpool; Allbright Knox Art Gallery, Buffalo, NY; Museum of Modern Art, NY; Tate Gallery; Gulbenkian Foundation; Min. of Public Building and Works; Contemp. Art Society; silk screen prints: Victoria and Albert Museum; Fitzwilliam Museum, Cambridge; City of Leeds Art Gall.; Graves Art Gall., Sheffield; painting purchased for liner Queen Elizabeth II. *Address:* 12 Sydney Close, SW3. *T:* 01-589 8610.

BLOY, Rt. Rev. Francis Eric Irving, DD, STD; *b* Birchington, Isle of Thanet, Kent, England, 17 Dec. 1904; *s* of Rev. Francis Joseph Field Bloy and Alice Mary (*née* Poynter); *m* 1929, Frances Forbes Cox, Alexandria, Va; no *c. Educ:* University of Missouri (BA); Georgetown Univ. of Foreign Service; Virginia Theological Seminary (BD). Rector, All Saints Ch., Reisterstown, Maryland, 1929-33; Assoc. Rector, St James-by-the-Sea, La Jolla, Calif, 1933-35, Rector, 1935-37; Dean, St Paul's Cathedral, Los Angeles, Calif, 1937-48; Bishop of Los Angeles, 1948-73. DD: Ch. Divinity Sch. of the Pacific, Berkeley, Calif, 1942; Occidental Coll., Los Angeles, 1953; Va Theol Sem., 1953; STD: Ch. Divinity Sch. of the Pacific, 1948; Univ. of S Calif, 1955. Pres., Church Federation of Los Angeles, 1946-47; Pres., Univ. Religious Conf., 1956; Hon. Chm. Bd of Trustees, Good Samaritan Hosp.; Trustee, Occidental Coll.; Mem. Town Hall. *Address:* 3919 Starland Drive, Flintridge, Calif 91011, USA. *Clubs:* California; Jonathan (Los Angeles).

BLUCKE, Air Vice-Marshal Robert Stewart, CB 1946; CBE 1945; DSO 1943; AFC 1936, Bar 1941; RAF, retired; *b* 22 June 1897; *s* of late Rev. R. S. K. Blucke, Monxton Rectory, Andover, Hants; *m* 1926, Nancy, *d* of late Frank Wilson, Auckland, NZ; one *d* (one *s* decd). *Educ:* Malvern Coll. Dorset Regt and RFC, 1915-18; Mesopotamia, 1916-18; Royal Air Force, 1922; India, 1927-32; Test Pilot Royal Aircraft Establishment, Farnborough, 1933-37; Air Ministry, 1938-42; served in Bomber Comd, 1942-46; AOC No 1 Group RAF, 1945; SASO, AHQ, India, 1947; AOA, Technical Trg Comd, 1947-49; AOA, Far East Air Force, 1949-50; AOC Malaya, 1951; AOC-in-C Transport Comd, 1952; retired 1952. General Manager, National Assoc. for Employment of Regular Sailors, Soldiers and Airmen, 1952-65. *Address:* Flat 3, Melrose House, South View Road, Crowborough, East Sussex. *T:* Crowborough 61638. *Club:* RAF.

BLUGLASS, Prof. Robert Saul, MD, FRCPsych; Professor of Forensic Psychiatry, University of Birmingham, since 1979 (Regional Postgraduate Clinical Tutor in Forensic Psychiatry, since 1967); *b* 22 Sept. 1930; *s* of Henry Bluglass and Fay (*née* Griew); *m* 1962, Jean Margaret Kerry (*née* Montgomery); one *s* one *d. Educ:* Warwick Sch., Warwick; Univ. of St Andrews (MB, ChB 1957, MD 1967). DPM 1962; FRCPsych 1976 (MRCPsych 1971). Formerly, Sen. Registrar in Psych., Royal Dundee Liff Hosp. and Maryfield Hosp., Dundee; Consultant in For. Psych., W Midlands RHA, Birmingham AHA(T), and the Home Office, 1967-; Consultant i/c Midland Centre for For. Psych., All Saints Hosp., Birmingham, 1967-; Hon. Lectr in For. Psych., Univ. of Birmingham, 1968-75, Sen. Clin. Lectr in For. Psych., 1975-79; Jt Dir, Midland Inst. of For. Medicine, 1975-. Advisor on For. Psych., DHSS, 1980-; Member: Adv. Cttee on Alcoholism, DHSS, 1975-80; Adv. Council on Probation, Home Office, 1974-77. Royal College of Psychiatrists: Mem., Ct of Electors, 1976-79; Mem. Council, 1973-76, 1976-78, 1980-; Chm., For. Psych. Specialist Section, 1978-. FR.SocMed 1975; Past Pres., Sect. of Psych., Birmingham Med. Inst.; Mem., Brit. Acad. of For. Sciences. *Publications:* Psychiatry, The Law and The Offender, 1980; articles in Brit. Jl of Hosp. Med., BMJ, and Med., Science and the Law. *Recreations:* water-colour painting, cooking, gardening, swimming. *Address:* 1 White House Way, Solihull, West Midlands B91 1SR.

BLUMBERG, Prof. Baruch Samuel, MD, PhD; Associate Director for Clinical Research, The Institute for Cancer Research, since 1964; University Professor of Medicine and Anthropology, University of Pennsylvania, since 1970; *b* 28 July 1925; *s* of Meyer Blumberg and Ida Blumberg; *m* 1954, Jean Liebesman Blumberg; two *s* two *d. Educ:* Union Coll. (BS Physics, 1946); Columbia University Coll. of Physicians and Surgeons (MD 1951); Balliol Coll., Oxford Univ. (PhD Biol Sciences, 1957). US Navy, 1943-46 (Lieut JG). US Public Health Service (rank of med. dir, col), and Chief, Geographic Medicine and Genetics Sect., Nat. Insts. of Health, Bethesda, Md, 1957-64. George Eastman Vis. Prof., Oxford Univ., 1983-84. Mem. Nat. Acad. of Sciences, Washington, DC. Hon. Fellow, Balliol Coll., Oxford, 1977. Hon. DSc: Univ. of Pittsburgh, 1977; Union Coll., Schenectady, NY, 1977; Med. Coll. of Pa, 1977; Dickinson Coll., Carlisle, Pa, 1977; Hahnemann Med. Coll., Philadelphia, Pa, 1977; Dr *hc* Univ. of Paris VII, 1978. (Jt) Nobel Prize in Physiology or Medicine, 1976. *Publications: chapters in:* McGraw-Hill Encyclopedia of Science and Technology Yearbook, 1962; The Genetics of Migrant and Isolate Populations, ed E. Goldschmidt, 1963; Hemoglobin: its precursors and metabolites, ed F. W. Sunderman and F. W. Sunderman, Jr, 1964; McGraw-Hill Yearbook of Science and Technology, 1970; (also co-author chapter) Viral Hepatitis and Blood Transfusion, ed G. N. Vyas and others, 1972; Hematology, ed W. J. Williams and others, 1972; Progress in Liver Disease, Vol. IV, ed H. Popper and F. Schaffner, 1972; Australia Antigen, ed J. E. Prier and H. Friedman, 1973; Drugs and the Liver, ed. W. Gerok and K. Sickinger, 1975 (Germany); *(jtly) chapters in:* Progress in Medical Genetics, ed A. G. Steinberg and A. G. Bearn, 1965 (also London); Viruses Affecting Man and Animals, ed M. Sanders and M. Schaeffer, 1971; Perspectives in Virology, 1971; Transmissable Disease and Blood Transfusion, ed T. J. Greenwalt and G. A. Jamieson, 1975; Physiological Anthropology, ed A. Damon, 1975; Hepatite a Virus B et Hemodialyse, 1975 (Paris); Onco-Developmental Gene Expression, 1976; (ed) Genetic Polymorphisms and Geographic Variations in Disease, 1961; (ed jtly) Medical Clinics of North America: new developments in medicine, 1970; contrib. symposia; over 260 articles in scientific jls. *Recreations:* squash, canoeing, middle distance running, cattle raising. *Address:* The Institute for Cancer Research, 7701 Burholme Avenue, Philadelphia, Pa 19111, USA. *T:* 215-728-2203. *Clubs:* Explorers (NY); Provincetown Yacht (Provincetown, Mass); Chesapeake and Ohio Canal Association.

BLUMENTHAL, W(erner) Michael, PhD; Chairman and Chief Executive Officer, Burroughs Corporation, 1981; *b* Germany, 3 Jan. 1926; *s* of Ewald Blumenthal and Rose Valerie (*née* Markt) (father escaped to Shanghai from Buchenwald Concentration Camp where he was sent by the Nazis in 1938; family interned by Japanese, 1943); *m* 1951, Margaret Eileen Polley; three *d. Educ:* Univ. of California at Berkeley; Princeton Univ. Went to USA, 1947; naturalised, 1952; worked as waiter, doorman, etc, to finance univ. studies; Research Associate, Princeton Univ., 1954-57; Labor Arbitrator, State of New Jersey, 1955-57; Vice-Pres., Dir, Crown Cork Internat. Corp., 1957-61. Dep. Asst Sec. of State for Econ. Affairs, Dept of State, 1961-63; also USA Rep. to UN Commn on Internat. Commodity Trade; Mem. US Delegn to Punta del Este Conf. (Alliance for Progress), 1961; Dep. Special Rep. of the President (with rank Ambassador) for Trade Negotiations, 1963-67. Chm., US Delegn to Kennedy Round Tariff talks, Geneva, 1963-67. Pres., Bendix Internat., 1967-70; Dir, Bendix Corp., 1967-77; Vice-Chm., June-Dec. 1970; Pres. and Chief Operating Officer, 1971-72; Chm. and Chief Exec. Officer, 1972-77; US Secretary of the Treasury, 1977-79; Vice Chm., Burroughs Corp., 1980. Director: Burroughs Corp.; Chemical NY Corp.; Chemical Bank (Chm., Internat. Adv. Bd); Pillsbury Co.; Equitable Life Assurance Soc. of US. Trustee: Rockefeller Foundation; Council on Foreign Relns; The Asia Soc., Inc. *Recreations:* tennis, skiing. *Address:* Burroughs Corporation, Burroughs Place, Detroit, Michigan 48232, USA.

BLUMFIELD, Clifford William, OBE 1976; Director, Dounreay Nuclear Power Development Establishment, since 1975; *b* 18 May 1923. *Educ:* Ipswich Boys' Central Sch. CEng, FIMechE. With Reavell & Co. Ltd, 1938-44; served REME, 1944-47 (Major); Min. of Supply, Harwell, 1947-54; UKAEA, Harwell, 1954-58; Atomic Energy Estabt, Winfrith, 1958-68 (Group Leader, Design Gp, and Head of Gen. Ops and Tech. Div.); Asst Dir, Ops and Engineering, later Dep. Dir, Dounreay, 1968-75. *Address:* UKAEA, Dounreay Nuclear Power Development Establishment, Thurso, Caithness KW14 7TZ.

BLUMGART, Prof. Leslie Harold, MD; FRCS, FRCSE, FRCSGlas; Professor of Surgery, Royal Postgraduate School of London, since 1979; Director of Surgery, Hammersmith Hospital, since 1979; *b* 7 Dec. 1931, of S African parentage; *m* 1955, Pearl Marie Navias (decd); *m* 1968, Sarah Raybould Bowen; two *s* two *d. Educ:* Jeppe High Sch., Johannesburg, SA; Univ. of Witwatersrand (BDS); Univ. of Sheffield (MB, ChB Hons; MD 1969). Prize Medal, Clin. Med. and Surg.; Ashby-de-la-Zouche Prize, Surg., Med., Obst. and Gynaecol. FRCS 1966, FRCSGlas 1973, FR.CSE 1976. General dental practice, Durban, SA, 1954-59; Sen. Surgical Registrar, Nottingham Gen. Hosp. and Sheffield Royal Infirmary, 1966-70; Sen. Lectr and Dep. Dir, Dept of Surgery, Welsh Nat. Sch. of Med., also Hon. Cons. Surg., Cardiff Royal Inf., 1970-72; St Mungo Prof. of Surgery, Univ. of Glasgow, and Hon. Cons. Surg., Glasgow Royal Inf., 1972-79. Moynihan Fellow, Assoc. of Surgs of Gt Brit. and Ire., 1972; Mayne Vis. Prof., Univ. of Queensland, Brisbane, 1976; Vis. Prof., Univ. of Lund, Sweden, 1977; Nimmo Vis. Prof., Adelaide Univ., 1982; Purvis Oration, 1974; President's Oration, Soc. for Surgery of Aliment. Tract, Toronto, 1977; Honyman Gillespie Lecture, Univ. of Edinburgh, 1978. Examiner in Surgery: Univs of: Cambridge, 1976-; Hong Kong, 1978-; Edinburgh, 1978-. Member: BMA, 1963-; Assoc. of Surgs of Gt Brit. and Ire., 1971-; Surgical Research Soc., 1971-; Brit. Assoc. of Surgical Oncology, 1976-; Brit. Soc. of Gastroenterology, 1972-; Editorial Cttee, Brit. Jl of Surgery, 1973-; Hon. Mem., Soc. for Surgery of Aliment. Tract, USA, 1977. *Publications:* Integrated Textbook of Human Diseases for Dental Students (with A. C. Kennedy), 1977; chapters in: Recent Advances in Surgery, 1973; Abdominal Operations, 1974; Advances in Surgery, 1975; Textbook of Surgical Physiology, 1977; Hepatotrophic Factors, 1978; Clinics in Gastroenterology, 1978; papers, mainly on liver, biliary and pancreatic surgery and hepatic pathophysiology, in med. and surgical jls. *Recreations:* water colour painting, wood carving. *Address:* 12 Glebe Road, Barnes, SW13 0EA. *T:* 01-878 3752.

BLUNDELL, Commandant Daphne Mary, CB 1972; Director, WRNS, 1970-73; *b* 19 Aug. 1916. *Educ:* St Helen's Sch., Northwood; Bedford Coll., London. Worked for LCC as Child Care Organiser. Joined WRNS, Nov. 1942; commnd 1943; served in Orkneys, Ceylon, E Africa; Malta, 1954-56; Staff of Flag Officer Naval Air Comd, 1964-67; Staff of C-in-C Portsmouth, 1967-69; Supt WRNS Training and Drafting, 1969-70. Supt 1967; Comdt 1970, retd 1973; Hon. ADC to the Queen, 1970-73. Governor, St Helen's Sch., Northwood. *Address:* 22 Marsham Court, Marsham Street, SW1P 4JY.

BLUNDELL, Sir (Edward) Denis, GCMG 1972; GCVO 1974; KBE 1967 (OBE (mil.) 1944); QSO 1977; Governor-General of New Zealand, 1972-77; *b* 29 May 1907; British; *m* 1945, June Daphne (QSO 1977), *d* of Jack Halligan; one *s* one *d. Educ:* Waitaki High Sch. (NZ); Trinity Hall, Cambridge Univ. Called to Bar, Gray's Inn, 1929; admitted as Barrister and Solicitor of the Supreme Court of New Zealand at end of 1929. Served War, 1939-44 with 2nd NZ Div. in Greece, Crete, ME and Italy. Formerly Sen. Partner, Bell, Gully & Co., Barristers and Solicitors, Wellington, NZ. President of the New Zealand Law Society, 1962-68. High Comr for NZ in London, 1968-72. Principal Companion of the Queen's Service Order, 1975-77. Pres., NZ Cricket Council, 1957-60. KStJ 1972. *Recreations:* cricket (cricket Blue Cambridge, 1928, 1929; rep. NZ, 1936-37), golf, swimming, tennis. *Address:* 655 Riddell Road, Glendowie, Auckland, New Zealand. *Clubs:* Wellington; Wellesley, Northern (New Zealand).

BLUNDELL, Sir Michael, KBE 1962 (MBE 1943); *b* 7 April 1907; *s* of Alfred Herbert Blundell and Amelia Woodward Blundell (*née* Richardson); *m* 1946, Geraldine Lötte Robarts; one *d. Educ:* Wellington Coll. Settled in Kenya as farmer, 1925. 2nd Lieut, RE, 1940; Major, 1940; Lieut-Col, 1941; Col, 1944; served Abyssinian campaign and SEAC. Commissioner, European Settlement, 1946–47; MLC, Rift Valley Constituency, Kenya, 1948–62; Leader European Members, 1952–54; Minister on Emergency War Council, Kenya, 1954–55; Minister of Agriculture, Kenya, 1955–59 and April 1961–June 1962; Leader of New Kenya Group, 1959–63. Chairman: Pyrethrum Board of Kenya, 1949–54; Egerton Agricultural Coll., 1962–72; EA Breweries Ltd, 1964–77; Uganda Breweries Ltd, 1965–76; Dir, Barclays Bank of Kenya Ltd, 1968–82. Chm., Kenya Soc. for the Blind, 1977–81. Freeman, Goldsmiths' Co., 1950; Hon. Col, 3rd KAR, 1955–61; Judge, Guernsey cattle, RASE, 1977. *Publication:* So Rough a Wind, 1964; The Wild Flowers of Kenya, 1982. *Recreations:* gardening, music, 18th century English porcelain. *Address:* Box 30181, Nairobi, Kenya. *T:* Nairobi 512278. *Clubs:* Brooks's; Muthaiga (Nairobi).

BLUNDEN, George; Executive Director, Bank of England, since 1976; *b* 31 Dec. 1922; *s* of late George Blunden and Florence Holder; *m* 1949, Anne, *d* of late G. J. E. Bulford; two *s* one *d. Educ:* City of London Sch.; University Coll., Oxford (MA). Royal Sussex Regt, 1941–45; Bank of England, 1947–55; IMF, 1955–58; Bank of England: rejoined 1958; Dep. Chief Cashier, 1968–73; Chief of Management Services, 1973–74; Head of Banking Supervision, 1974–76. On staff of Monopolies Commn, 1968; Chm., Group of Ten Cttee on Banking Regulations and Supervisory Practices at Bank for Internat. Settlements, Basle, 1974–77. Hon. Treasurer: Inst. of Urology, 1975–78; Dovedale Almshouses Trust, 1973–79; UK Friends of Insead, 1979–. Chm. Governors, St Peter's Gp of Hosps, 1978–82; Mem. Council, Imperial Cancer Res. Fund, 1981–; Inst. of Urology, 1982–; Trustee: St Peter's Trust for Kidney Res., 1971–; Samuel Lewis Housing Trust, 1980–; Mem. Court, Mermaid Theatre Trust, 1979–. *Address:* Bank of England, Threadneedle Street, EC2R 8AH. *T:* 01-601 4444.

BLUNDEN, Sir William, 6th Bt, *cr* 1766; RN, retired; *b* 26 April 1919; *s* of 5th Bt and Phyllis, *d* of P. C. Creaghe; *S* father, 1923; *m* 1945, Pamela Mary Purser, 2nd Officer WRNS, *d* of John Purser, Prof. of Civil Engineering, TCD; six *d. Educ:* Repton. Lieut-Comdr, RN, 1949; retired 1958. *Heir: b* Philip Overington Blunden [*b* 27 Jan. 1922; *m* 1945, Jeanette Francesca (WRNS), *e d* of Captain D. Macdonald, RNR, Portree, Isle of Skye; two *s* one *d*]. *Address:* Castle Blunden, Kilkenny. *T:* Kilkenny 21128.

BLUNT, Prof. Anthony (Frederick); Professor of the History of Art, University of London, and Director of the Courtauld Institute of Art, 1947–Sept. 1974; Surveyor of the Queen's Pictures, 1952–72 (of the Pictures of King George VI, 1945–52); Adviser for the Queen's Pictures and Drawings, 1972–78; *b* 26 Sept. 1907; *y s* of late Rev. A. S. V. Blunt, Vicar of St John's, Paddington. *Educ:* Marlborough Coll.; Trinity Coll., Cambridge. Served War of 1939–45: France, 1939–40; WO, 1940–45. Fellow, Trinity Coll., Cambridge, 1932–36; on staff of Warburg Inst., London, 1937–39; Reader in History of Art, London Univ., and Dep. Dir, Courtauld Inst. of Art, 1939–47. Slade Prof. of Fine Art: Oxford, 1962–63; Cambridge, 1965–66. Hon. Fellow, Trinity Coll., Cambridge, 1967–79. FSA 1960–79; Hon. FRIBA, 1973–79. Hon. DLitt: Bristol, 1961; Durham, 1963; Oxon, 1971; DèsL *hc* Paris, 1966. Commander: Order of Orange Nassau (Holland), 1948; Legion of Honour (France), 1958. *Publications:* (with Walter Friedlaender), The Drawings of Nicolas Poussin, 1939–75; Artistic Theory in Italy, 1940; François Mansart, 1941; French Drawings at Windsor Castle, 1945; (with Margaret Whinney) The Nation's Pictures, 1951; Rouault's Miserere, 1951; Poussin's Golden Calf, 1951; Art and Architecture in France, 1500–1700, 1953, rev. edn 1981; The Drawings of G. B. Castiglione and Stefano della Bella at Windsor Castle, 1954; Venetian Drawings at Windsor Castle, 1957; Philibert de l'Orme, 1958; The Art of William Blake, 1960; (with H. L. Cooke) The Roman Drawings at Windsor Castle, 1960; (with Phoebe Pool) Picasso: The Formative Years, 1962; Nicolas Poussin: Catalogue raisonné, 1966; Nicolas Poussin (2 vols), 1967; Sicilian Baroque, 1968; Picasso's Guernica, 1969; Supplement to Italian and French Drawings at Windsor, 1971; Neapolitan Baroque and Rococo Architecture, 1975; (with A. Laing *et al*) Baroque and Rococo Architecture and Decoration, 1978; Borromini, 1979; The Drawings of Nicolas Poussin, 1979; articles in Burlington Magazine, Jl of Warburg and Courtauld Insts, Spectator, etc. *Address:* 45 Portsea Hall, Portsea Place, W2.

BLUNT, Christopher Evelyn, OBE 1945; FBA 1965; retired; *b* 16 July 1904; 2nd *s* of Rev. A. S. V. Blunt and Hilda Violet Blunt; *m* 1930, Elisabeth Rachel Bazley (*d* 1980); one *s* two *d. Educ:* Marlborough (Foundation Scholar). Entered merchant banking firm of Higginson & Co., 1924; partner, 1947; executive director of successor companies, 1950–64. Served War, 1939–46; 52 AA (TA) Regt; GHQ (Gen. Staff), BEF (despatches), Home Forces; 21 Army Group; SHAEF; retired 1946 (Col). FSA 1936; President British Numismatic Soc., 1946–50; Royal Numismatic Soc., 1956–61; Wilts Arch. Soc., 1970–74; Soc. of Medieval Archaeol., 1978–80. Medals of Royal, British and Amer. Numismatic Socs. Officer Legion of Merit (USA), 1945. *Publications:* The Coinage of Athelstan, 1974; contributions to Numismatic Chronicle, British Numismatic Journal, Archæologia, etc. *Recreation:* numismatics. *Address:* Ramsbury Hill, Ramsbury, Marlborough, Wilts. *T:* Marlborough 20358. *Club:* Travellers'.

BLUNT, Sir David Richard Reginald Harvey, 12th Bt *cr* 1720; *b* 8 Nov. 1938; *s* of Sir Richard David Harvey Blunt, 11th Bt and Elisabeth Malvine

Ernestine, *d* of Comdr F. M. Fransen Van de Putte, Royal Netherlands Navy (retd); *S* father, 1975; *m* 1969, Sonia Tudor Rosemary (*née* Day); one *d. Heir: kinsman:* Robin Anthony Blunt, CEng, MIMechE [*b* 23 Nov. 1926; *m* 1st, 1949, Sheila Stuart (marr. diss. 1962), *d* of C. Stuart Brindley; one *s* ; 2nd, 1962, June Elizabeth, *d* of Charles Wigginton; one *s*].

BLUNT, Maj.-Gen. Peter, CB 1978; MBE 1955; GM 1959; Managing Director, ANGEX Ltd, since 1980; Joint Managing Director, Angex-Watson, since 1980; *b* 18 Aug. 1923; *s* of A. G. Blunt and M. Blunt; *m* 1949, Adrienne, *o d* of Gen. T. W. Richardson; three *s.* Joined Army aged 14 yrs, 1937; commnd Royal Fusiliers; served Duke of Cornwall's LI and Royal Scots Fusiliers, until 1946; foreign service, 1946–49; Staff Coll., 1957; Jt Services Staff Coll., 1963; RCDS, 1972; comd 26 Regt, Bridging, 1965; GSO 1 Def. Plans, FARELF, 1968; Comdr RCT 1 Corps, 1970; Dep. Transport Officer-in-Chief (Army), later Transp. Off.-in-Chief, 1973; Asst Chief of Personnel and Logistics (Army), MoD, 1977–78; Asst Chief of Defence Staff (Personnel and Logistics), MoD, 1978–79. Man. Dir, Earls Court Ltd, 1979–80; Exec. Vice-Chm., Brompton and Kensington Special Catering Co. Ltd, 1979–80. Col Comdt, RCT, 1974–. Liveryman, Co. of Carmen, 1973. *Recreation:* fishing. *Address:* Greenbank, Bracknell Lane, Hartley Wintney, Hants. *T:* Hartley Wintney 2313. *Club:* Army and Navy.

BLUNT, Wilfrid Jasper Walter; Curator of the Watts Gallery, Compton, since 1959; *b* 19 July 1901; *s* of late Rev. Arthur Stanley Vaughan Blunt and Hilda Violet Master. *Educ:* Marlborough Coll.; Worcester Coll., Oxford; Royal College of Art. Art Master, Haileybury Coll., 1923–38; Drawing Master, Eton Coll., 1938–59. ARCA (London) 1923. Introduced into the Public Schs the craft of pottery (Haileybury, 1927) and Italic handwriting (Eton, 1940). FLS 1969. *Publications:* The Haileybury Buildings, 1936; Desert Hawk, 1947; The Art of Botanical Illustration, 1950; Tulipomania, 1950; Black Sunrise, 1951; Sweet Roman Hand, 1952; Japanese Colour Prints, 1952; Georg Dionysius Ehret, 1953; Pietro's Pilgrimage, 1953; Sebastiano, 1956; Great Flower Books (with Sacheverell Sitwell and Patrick Synge), 1956; A Persian Spring, 1957; Lady Muriel, 1962; Of Flowers and a Village, 1963; Cockerell, 1964; Omar, 1966; Isfahan, 1966; John Christie of Glyndebourne, 1968; The Dream King, 1970; The Compleat Naturalist, 1971; The Golden Road to Samarkand, 1973; On Wings of Song, 1974; 'England's Michelangelo', 1975; The Ark in the Park, 1976; Splendours of Islam, 1976; In for a Penny: a prospect of Kew Gardens, 1978; (with Sandra Raphael) The Illustrated Herbal, 1979. *Recreations:* writing, formerly singing and travel. *Address:* The Watts Gallery, Compton, near Guildford, Surrey. *T:* Guildford 810235.

BLYDE, Sir Henry (Ernest), KBE 1969 (CBE 1952); former Chairman, Taranaki Harbours Board; Director, Lepperton Dairy Co., for 37 years, and Chairman for 25 years; *b* 25 Oct. 1896; *s* of James Blyde; *m* 1929, Mary, *d* of W. J. McCormick; two *s* two *d. Educ:* St Paul's School, St Leonards-on-Sea, Sussex. Formerly Chairman, Taranaki Hospital Bd. JP. *Recreations:* bowling, billiards. *Address:* 233 Carrington Street, New Plymouth, New Zealand. *T:* 88928 New Plymouth.

BLYE, Douglas William Alfred, CMG 1979; OBE 1973; Secretary for Monetary Affairs, Hong Kong, since 1977; *b* 15 Dec. 1924; *s* of William Blye and Ethel Attwood; *m* 1955, Juanita Buckley. *Educ:* King's Road Sch., Herne Bay; Maidstone Polytechnic. ACMA. Served War, RAF, 1941–46. Various commercial and industrial appts in UK, 1947–55; Govt of Fedn of Malaya, 1955–58; Hong Kong Govt, 1958–. *Recreations:* squash, tennis. *Address:* 4 Gough Hill Path, The Peak, Hong Kong. *T:* Hong Kong 97728.

BLYTH, family name of **Baron Blyth.**

BLYTH, 4th Baron *cr* 1907; **Anthony Audley Rupert Blyth;** Bt 1895; *b* 3 June 1931; *er s* of 3rd Baron Blyth and Edna Myrtle (*d* 1952), *d* of Ernest Lewis, Wellington, NZ; *S* father, 1977; *m* 1st, 1954, Elizabeth Dorothea (marr. diss., 1962), *d* of R. T. Sparrow, Vancouver, BC; one *s* two *d* ; 2nd, 1963, Oonagh Elizabeth Ann, *yr d* of late William Henry Conway, Dublin; one *s* one *d. Educ:* St Columba's College, Dublin. *Heir: s* Hon. Riley Audley John Blyth, *b* 4 March 1955. *Address:* Blythwood Estate, Athenry, Co. Galway.

BLYTH, Charles, (Chay Blyth), CBE 1972; BEM; Director, Sailing Ventures (Hampshire) Ltd, since 1969; *b* 14 May 1940; *s* of Robert and Jessie Blyth; *m* 1962, Maureen Margaret Morris; one *d. Educ:* Hawick High School. HM Forces, Para. Regt, 1958–67. Cadbury Schweppes, 1968–69. Rowed North Atlantic with Captain John Ridgway, June–Sept. 1966; circumnavigated the world westwards solo in yacht British Steel, 1970–71; circumnavigated the world eastwards with crew in yacht Great Britain II, 1973–74; Atlantic sailing record, Cape Verde to Antigua, 1977; won Round Britain Race in yacht Great Britain IV, 1978 (crew Robert James); won The Observer/Europe 1 doublehanded transatlantic race in record time, 1981 (crew Robert James). *Publications:* A Fighting Chance, 1966; Innocent Aboard, 1968; The Impossible Voyage, 1971; Theirs is the Glory, 1974. *Recreations:* sailing, horse-riding, hunting. *Address:* Penquite Farm, Rosecraddoc, Liskeard, Cornwall. *Clubs:* Royal Southern Yacht, Royal Western Yacht.

BLYTH, Charles Henry, OBE 1977; Chairman, National Dock Labour Board, since 1977; *b* 16 Feb. 1916; *s* of Edward Henry Blyth and Emma (*née*

Elsey); *m* 1941, Winifred Irene, *d* of Charles and Gertrude Green, Southampton; two *d. Educ:* elem. sch., Grimsby, Lincs; Dept of Navigation, University Coll., Southampton. Merchant Navy, 1932-49; Officer, National Union of Seamen, 1949-65. Internat. Transportworkers Federation: Hong Kong Rep., 1965-66; Section Sec., 1966-67; Asst Gen. Sec., 1967-68; elected Gen. Sec. at Wiesbaden Congress, 1968; re-elected at Vienna Congress, 1971, and at Stockholm Congress, 1974; retd, 1977. Pres., Internat. Trade Secretariat's Gen. Conf., 1974-77. Mem., Nat. Ports Council, 1979-81. Mem., Exec. Cttee and Management Cttee, Merchant Seamen's War Meml Soc. *Recreations:* simple cooking, making wooden toys. *Address:* 118 Chiltern Drive, Surbiton, Surrey. *T:* 01-399 7762.

BLYTH, James; Head of Defence Sales, Ministry of Defence, since 1981; *b* 8 May 1940; *s* of Daniel Blyth and Jane Power Carlton; *m* 1967, Pamela Anne Campbell Dixon; one *d* (one *s* decd). *Educ:* Spiers Sch.; Glasgow Univ. (MA Hons). Mobil Oil Co., 1963-69; General Foods Ltd, 1969-71; Mars Ltd, 1971-74; Director and General Manager: Lucas Batteries Ltd, 1974-77; Lucas Aerospace Ltd, 1977-81; Dir, Joseph Lucas Ltd, 1977-81. Mem. Council, SBAC, 1977-81. Liveryman, Coachmakers' and Coach Harness Makers' Co. *Recreations:* ski-ing, tennis, paintings, theatre. *Club:* East India.

BLYTH, John Douglas Morrison, CMG 1981; HM Diplomatic Service; Counsellor, Foreign and Commonwealth Office, since 1977; *b* 23 July 1924; *s* of late William Naismith Blyth and Jean (*née* Morrison); *m* 1st, 1949, Gabrielle Elodie (*née* Belloc) (*d* 1971); three *s* two *d* ; 2nd, 1973, Lucy Anne (*née* Alcock); one *s* one *d. Educ:* Christ's Coll.; Lincoln Coll., Oxford (MA); Downing Coll., Cambridge (MA). Served War, RNVR, 1942-46. Editor, The Polar Record (publd by Scott Polar Res. Inst., Cambridge), 1949-54; joined FO, 1954; served: Geneva, 1955; Athens, 1959; Leopoldville, 1963; Accra, 1964; FO, 1966; Athens, 1968; FCO, 1972; Vienna, 1974. *Publications:* articles in The Polar Record. *Recreations:* gardening, military history, enjoying wine. *Address:* c/o Foreign and Commonwealth Office, SW1; Crownland Hall, Walsham-le-Willows, Suffolk IP31 3BU. *T:* Walsham-le-Willows 369. *Club:* Naval and Military.

BLYTHE, James Forbes, TD 1946; **His Honour Judge Blythe;** a Circuit Judge, since 1978; Solicitor; *b* Coventry, 11 July 1917; *s* of J. F. Blythe; *m* 1949, Margaret, *d* of P. D. Kinsey; two *d. Educ:* Wrekin Coll.; Birmingham Univ. (LLB). Commissioned TA, Royal Warwickshire Regt, 1936-53 (Major); served War of 1939-45 with BEF in France (Dunkirk), 1939-40; Central Mediterranean Force (Tunisia, Sicily, Corsica, S France and Austria), 1942-45; Air Liaison Officer GSO II (Ops) with RAF (Despatches). Admitted solicitor, 1947; private practitioner in partnership in Coventry and Leamington Spa, 1948. HM Deputy Coroner for City of Coventry and Northern Dist of Warwickshire, 1954-64; HM Coroner for City of Coventry, 1964-78; a Recorder of the Crown Court, 1972-78. Pres., Warwicks Law Soc., 1978-79. *Recreations:* shooting, sailing; past player and Sec. Coventry Football Club (RU). *Address:* Hazlewood, Upper Ladyes' Hill, Kenilworth, Warwickshire. *T:* Kenilworth 54168. *Clubs:* Army and Navy; Drapers (Coventry); Tennis Court (Leamington Spa).

BLYTHE, Rex Arnold; Under-Secretary, Board of Inland Revenue, since 1981; *b* 11 Nov. 1928; *s* of late Sydney Arnold Blythe and Florence Blythe (*née* Jones); *m* 1953, Rachel Ann Best; one *s* two *d. Educ:* Bradford Grammar Sch.; Trinity Coll., Cambridge (BA Classics). Entered Inland Revenue as Inspector of Taxes, 1953; Sen. Inspector, 1962; Principal Inspector, 1968; Asst Sec., 1974. *Recreation:* golf. *Address:* 32 Townsend Lane, Harpenden, Herts AL5 2QS. *T:* Harpenden 5833. *Club:* MCC.

BLYTON, family name of **Baron Blyton.**

BLYTON, Baron, *cr* 1964 (Life Peer); **William Reid Blyton;** *b* 2 May 1899; *s* of late Charles H. Blyton, retired labourer, and Hannah A. Blyton; *m* 1919, Jane B. Ord; three *d. Educ:* Elementary Education Holy Trinity Sch. and Dean Road Sch., South Shields. Served in HM Submarines in European War, 1914-18. Chm., Harton Miners' Lodge, Durham Miners' Assoc., 1928-41, Sec., 1941-45; Mem., Durham Miners' Exec. Cttee, 1930-32, 1942-43. Chm. South Shields Labour Party, 1928-29, 1931-32; Councillor, S Shields Borough Council, 1936-45; Chm. of South Shields Education Cttee, 1943, and of South Shields Electrical Cttee, 1937-40; MP (Lab) Houghton-le-Spring Div. of County Durham, 1945-64; late PPS to Ministry of Civil Aviation; resigned, 1949. Chm. High Sch. Governors and Chm. Secondary and Technical Cttee of South Shields. *Address:* 139 Brockley Avenue, South Shields, Tyne and Wear; Dylan Hotel, 14 Devonshire Terrace, W2.

BOAG, Prof. John Wilson; Professor of Physics as Applied to Medicine, University of London, Institute of Cancer Research, 1965-76, retired; *b* Elgin, Scotland, 20 June 1911; *s* of John and Margaret A. Boag; *m* 1938, Isabel Petrie; no *c. Educ:* Universities of Glasgow, Cambridge and Braunschweig. Engineer, British Thomson Houston Co., Rugby, 1936-41; Physicist, Medical Research Council, 1941-52; Visiting Scientist, National Bureau of Standards, Washington, DC, 1953-54; Physicist, British Empire Cancer Campaign, Mount Vernon Hospital, 1954-64; Royal Society (Leverhulme) Visiting Prof. to Poland, 1964. President: Hosp. Physicists' Assoc., 1959; Assoc. for Radiation Res. (UK), 1972-74; Internat. Assoc. for Radiation Res., 1970-74; British Inst. of Radiology, 1975-76. L. H. Gray Medal, ICRU, 1973; Barclay Medal, BIR, 1975. *Publications:* papers on radiation dosimetry, statistics, radiation

chemistry, radiodiagnosis. *Address:* Flat 1, 40 Overton Road, Sutton, Surrey.

BOAM, Maj.-Gen. Thomas Anthony, CBE 1978 (OBE 1973); Head, British Defence Staff Washington, Defence and Military Attaché, since 1981; *b* 14 Feb. 1932; *s* of late Lt-Col T. S. Boam, OBE, and of Mrs Boam; *m* 1961, Penelope Christine Mary Roberts; one *s* two *d. Educ:* Bradfield Coll.; RMA Sandhurst. Commissioned Scots Guards, 1952; Canal Zone, Egypt (with 1SG), 1952-54; GSO3, MO4 War Office, 1959-61; psc 1962; Kenya (with 2SG), 1963-64; DAA&QMG 4GDS Bde, 1964-65; Malaysia (with 1SG), 1966-67; BM 4GDS Bde, 1967-69; GSO1 (DS) Staff Coll., Camberley, 1970-71; CO 2SG, 1972-74; RCDS 1974-75; Comd BAAT Nigeria, 1976-78; BGS (Trg) HQ UKLF, 1978; Dep. Comdr and COS Hong Kong, 1979-81. *Recreations:* shooting, fishing, gardening, sport. *Address:* c/o Barclays Bank Ltd, 23 Euston Road, NW1 2SB. *Club:* MCC.

BOARDMAN, family name of **Baron Boardman.**

BOARDMAN, Baron *cr* 1980 (Life Peer), of Welford in the County of Northamptonshire; **Thomas Gray Boardman,** MC 1944; TD 1952; DL; Chairman, The Steetley Co. Ltd, since 1978 (Director, since 1981); Director: National Westminster Bank, since 1979 (Chairman, Eastern Region); MEPC Ltd, since 1980; *b* 12 Jan. 1919; *s* of John Clayton Boardman, late of Daventry, and Janet Boardman, formerly Houston; *m* 1948, Norah Mary Deirdre, widow of John Henry Chaworth-Musters, Annesley Park, Nottingham, and *d* of Hubert Vincent Gough; two *s* one *d. Educ:* Bromsgrove. Served Northants Yeomanry, 1939-45 and subsequently; Commanding Northants Yeomanry, 1956. Qualified as a Solicitor, 1947. MP (C) Leicester SW, Nov. 1967-74, Leicester South Feb.-Sept. 1974; Minister for Industry, DTI, 1972-74; Chief Sec. to Treasury, 1974. Jt Hon. Treas., Cons. Party, 1981-82. Chm. Chamberlain Phipps Ltd, 1958-72; Dir, Allied Breweries Ltd, 1968-72 and 1974-77 (Vice-Chm., 1975-76). Pres., Assoc. of British Chambers of Commerce, 1977-80. DL Northants, 1977-, High Sheriff, Northants, 1979. *Recreation:* riding. *Address:* 29 Tufton Court, Tufton Street, SW1. *T:* 01-222 6793; The Manor House, Welford, Northampton. *T:* Welford 235. *Club:* Cavalry and Guards.

See also Baron Ellenborough.

BOARDMAN, Harold; *b* 12 June 1907; *m* 1936, Winifred May, *d* of Jesse Thorlby, Derbys; one *d. Educ:* Bolton and Derby. Formerly Trade Union Official. Joined Labour party, 1924; formerly Chm., Derby Labour Party; for 3 yrs Mem. Derby Town Council. MP (Lab) Leigh, 1945-79; PPS to Ministry of Labour, 1947-51. ILO Confs in Geneva, 1947, 1949, 1950, and San Francisco, 1948; Delegate to Council of Europe, 1960, 1961. Former Exec. Mem., NW Industrial Develt Assoc., from 1946. *Address:* 18 Norris Road, Brooklands, Sale, Manchester.

BOARDMAN, Prof. John, FSA 1957, FBA 1969; Lincoln Professor of Classical Archaeology and Art, and Fellow of Lincoln College, University of Oxford, since 1978; *b* 20 Aug. 1927; *s* of Frederick Archibald Boardman; *m* 1952, Sheila Joan Lyndon Stanford; one *s* one *d. Educ:* Chigwell Sch.; Magdalene Coll., Cambridge. BA 1948, MA 1951, Walston Student, 1948-50; Cromer Greek Prize, 1959. 2nd Lt, Intell. Corps, 1950-52. Asst Dir, British Sch. at Athens, 1952-55; Asst Keeper, Ashmolean Museum, Oxford, 1955-59; Reader in Classical Archaeology, Univ. of Oxford, 1959-78; Fellow of Merton Coll., Oxford, 1963-78, Hon. Fellow, 1978. Geddes-Harrower Prof., Aberdeen Univ., 1974. Editor, Journal of Hellenic Studies, 1958-65. Conducted excavations on Chios, 1953-55, and at Tocra, in Libya, 1964-65. Delegate, OUP, 1979; Corr. Fellow, Bavarian Acad. of Scis, 1969; For. Mem., Royal Danish Acad., 1979. *Publications:* Cretan Collection in Oxford, 1961; Date of the Knossos Tablets, 1963; Island Gems, 1963; Greek Overseas, 1964, rev. edn 1980; Greek Art, 1964, rev. edn 1973; Excavations at Tocra, vol. I 1966, vol. II 1973; Pre-Classical, 1967, repr. 1978; Greek Emporio, 1967; Engraved Gems, 1968; Archaic Greek Gems, 1968; Greek Gems and Finger Rings, 1970; (with D. Kurtz) Greek Burial Customs, 1971; Athenian Black Figure Vases, 1974; Athenian Red Figure Vases, 1975; Intaglios and Rings, 1975; Corpus Vasorum, Oxford, vol. 3, 1975; Greek Sculpture, Archaic Period, 1978; (with M. Robertson) Corpus Vasorum, Castle Ashby, 1978; (with M. L. Vollenweider) Catalogue of Engraved Gems, Ashmolean Museum, 1978; (with D. Scarisbrick) Harari Collection of Finger Rings, 1978; (with E. La Rocca) Eros in Greece, 1978; articles in jls. *Address:* 11 Park Street, Woodstock, Oxford. *T:* Woodstock 811259.

BOARDMAN, Sir Kenneth (Ormrod), Kt 1981; Founder Chairman, Planned Giving Ltd, since 1959; chairman of other charitable bodies; *b* 18 May 1914; *s* of Edgar Nicholas Boardman and Emily Boardman; *m* 1939, Lucy Stafford; one *s* two *d. Educ:* St Peter's Sch., Swinton, Lancs. Trooper, Duke of Lancaster's Own Yeomanry, 1932-33; served War, 1939-45, Major RA. Chm., K. O. Boardman Internat. Ltd, 1954-78. Hon. Treasurer, NW Area of Conservative Party, 1977-; holds many other offices in Cons. Party. Liveryman, Farriers Co., 1965-. *Recreations:* gardening, racing and breeding horses. *Address:* Clarendon House, Carrwood Road, Bramhall, Cheshire SK7 3LR. *Clubs:* St James's, The Manchester (Manchester); Royal Anglesey Yacht (Beaumaris).

BOARDMAN, Norman Keith, PhD, ScD; FRS 1978; FAA; Member of Executive, Commonwealth Scientific and Industrial Research Organization, since 1977; *b* 16 Aug. 1926; *s* of William Robert Boardman and Margaret

Boardman; *m* 1952, Mary Clayton Shepherd; two *s* five *d. Educ:* Melbourne Univ. (BSc 1946, MSc 1949); St John's Coll., Cambridge (PhD 1954, ScD 1974). FAA 1972. ICI Fellow, Cambridge, 1953-55; Fulbright Scholar, Univ. of Calif, LA, 1964-66. Res. Officer, Wool Res. Section, CSIRO, 1949-51; CSIRO Div. of Plant Industry: Sen. Res. Scientist, 1956; Principal Res. Scientist, 1961; Sen. Prin. Res. Scientist, 1966; Chief Res. Scientist, 1968. Member: Aust. Res. Grants Cttee, 1971-75; Council, ANU, 1979-. Corresp. Mem., Amer. Soc. of Plant Physiologists. David Syme Res. Prize, Melbourne Univ., 1967; Lemberg Medal, Aust. Biochem. Soc., 1969. *Publications:* scientific papers on plant biochemistry, partic. photosynthesis and structure, function and biogenesis of chloroplasts. *Recreations:* reading, listening to music. *Address:* 6 Somers Crescent, Forrest, ACT 2603, Australia. *T:* (062) 95-1746. *Club:* Commonwealth (Canberra).

BOAS, Leslie, OBE 1961; HM Diplomatic Service, retired; *b* Buenos Aires, Argentine, 25 Feb. 1912; *s* of late Gustavus Thomas Boas and late Flora Shield McDonald; *m* 1st, 1944, Margaret Ann Jackson (marr. diss. 1951); one *s* ; 2nd, 1951, Patricia Faye Fenning (*d* 1972); 3rd, 1972, Natalie K. Prado (*née* Kitchen). *Educ:* Spain; Gibraltar; Granada University. In business, 1933-39. Joined Coldstream Guards, 1940; commissioned in Royal Ulster Rifles, 1940; invalided out of Army as result of injuries, 1944. Joined Latin American Section of BBC, 1944. Apptd Temp. Press Attaché, Panama, 1946; Temp. First Sec. (Inf.), Bogotá, 1948; Temp. First Sec. (Inf.), Caracas, 1952; estab. as a Permanent First Sec., 1959; Regional Inf. Counsellor, Caracas, 1962-69; Chargé d'Affaires, Panama, April-May 1964; Ambassador to Santo Domingo, 1969-72. Dir, Secretariat of British Bicentennial Liaison Cttee of FCO, 1973-75. *Recreations:* golf, chess, Latin American studies. *Address:* c/o The Royal Bank of Scotland Ltd, 97 New Bond Street, W1Y 0EU. *Clubs:* Bucks; Jockey (Bogotá, Colombia).

BOASE, Alan Martin, MA, PhD; Officier de la Légion d'Honneur; *b* 1902; *s* of late W. Norman Boase, CBE, St Andrews; *m* 1931, Elizabeth Grizelle (*d* 1977), *e d* of late Prof. E. S. Forster; four *s. Educ:* Eton Coll.; New College, Oxford; Trinity Coll., Cambridge; Univ. of Paris. Lectr in French, Univ. of Sheffield, 1929-36; Prof. of French, University Coll., Southampton, 1936-37; Marshall Prof. of French, Univ. of Glasgow, 1937-65. Ex-Chm. of Assoc. of Heads of French Depts. Visiting Professor: Univ. of Calif (Berkeley), 1962; Monash Univ., Australia, 1969; Collège de France, 1974. Chm., Consultative Cttee, Inst. Français d'Ecosse. Grand Prix du Rayonnement Français de l'Académie Française, 1979. *Publications:* Montaigne, Selected Essays (with Arthur Tilley), 1934; The Fortunes of Montaigne, 1935, repr. (NY) 1970; Contemporary French Literature (in France: A Companion to French Studies, ed R. L. G. Ritchie), 1937; Les Poèmes de Jean de Sponde, 1950; The Poetry of France, Part III, 1952, Part I, 1964, Part IV, 1969, Part II, 1973; Les Méditations de Jean de Sponde, 1954; La Vie de Jean de Sponde, 1977; Jean de Sponde, œuvres littéraires (ed Corti), 1978; articles and reviews in periodicals. *Recreation:* gardening. *Address:* 39 Inverleith Place, Edinburgh. *T:* 031-552 3005.

BOASE, Arthur Joseph, CMG 1968; OBE 1951; Warden, Ophthalmic Hospital of the Order of St John, Jerusalem, 1956, retired; *b* 23 June 1901; 2nd *s* of William George Boase, medical practitioner; *m* 1929, Alice Mary, *d* of Sir Charles Griffin, QC; four *s* five *d* (and one *s* decd). *Educ:* Mount St Mary's Coll., Derbyshire; St Thomas' Hosp., London. MRCS, LRCP 1923; DOMS 1933; FRCS 1952. Uganda Med. Service, 1924; Sen. Med. Off., 1937; Specialist (Ophthalmologist), 1945; Sen. Specialist, 1954; retd from Uganda, 1956. Past Pres., E African Assoc. of Surgs. Coronation Medal, 1953. Kt, Order of St Gregory (Papal), 1951; KStJ 1961; Kt, Order of Holy Sepulchre (Greek Orthodox), 1965; Kt, Order of Holy Sepulchre (Armenian), 1969. Istiqlal (Independence) Order, 2nd cl. (Jordan), 1967. *Recreation:* woodworking. *Address:* Linden Cottage, Uckfield, East Sussex TN22 2EH.
See also Sir J. B. Griffin.

BOATENG, Prof. Ernest Amano, GM 1968; Executive Chairman, Environmental Protection Council, Ghana, 1973-81, now retired; *b* 30 Nov. 1920; 2nd *s* of Rev. Christian Robert Boateng and Adelaide Akonobea, Aburi, Ghana; *m* 1955, Evelyn Kensema Danso, *e d* of late Rev. Robert Opong Danso, and of Victoria Danso, Aburi; four *d. Educ:* Achimota Coll.; St Peter's Hall, Oxford (Gold Coast Govt Schol.). Henry Oliver Beckit Meml Prize, 1949; BA (Geog.) 1949, MA 1953, BLitt 1954. UC Ghana: Lectr in Geography, 1950-57; Sen. Lectr, 1958-61; Prof. of Geography, 1961-73; Dean, Faculty of Social Studies, 1962-69; Principal, 1969-71, Vice-Chancellor, 1971-73, Univ. of Cape Coast, Ghana. Vis. Asst Prof., Univ. of Pittsburgh and UCLA, 1960-61. Pres., Ghana Geographical Assoc., 1959-69; Foundn Fellow, Ghana Acad. of Arts and Sciences (Sec. 1959-62, Pres., 1973-76); Mem., Unesco Internat. Adv. Cttee on Humid Tropics Research, 1961-63; Mem., Scientific Council for Africa, 1963-; Mem., Nat. Planning Commn of Ghana, 1961-64; Smuts Vis. Fellow, Univ. of Cambridge, 1965-66; Vis. Prof., Univ. of Pittsburgh, 1966; Deleg., UN Conf. on geographical names, Geneva, 1967; Mem., Council for Scientific and Industrial Research, Ghana, 1967-75; Dir, Ghana Nat. Atlas Project, 1965-77; Chm., Geographical Cttee, Ghana 1970 population census; Member: Nat. Economic Planning Council of Ghana, 1974-78; Chm., Land Use Planning Cttee of Ghana, 1978-79; Pres., Governing Council of UNEP, 1979; Mem. Presidential Task Force on Investments, Ghana, 1980; Nat. Council for Higher Educn, 1975-; Chm., W African Exams Council, 1977-. Pres., Ghana Wildlife Soc., 1974-. Alternate Leader, Ghana Delegn to UN Conf., Vancouver, 1976. FRSA 1973. Hon. DLitt Ghana, 1979.

Nat. Book Award, Ghana, 1978. *Publications:* A Geography of Ghana, 1959 (contrib.) Developing Countries of the World, 1968; (contrib.) Population Growth and Economic Development in Africa, 1972; Independence and Nation Building in Africa, 1973; A Political Geography of Africa, 1978. African Unity: the dream and the reality (J. B. Danquah Memorial Lectures 1978), 1979; various pamphlets, Britannica and other encyclopaedia articles and articles in geographical and other jls and reference works. *Recreations:* photography, gardening. *Address:* PO Box 84, Trade Fair Site, Accra, Ghana. *T:* Accra 77875.

BOATENG, Paul Yaw; Solicitor; Member for Walthamstow, since 1981, and Chairman, Police Committee, since 1981, Greater London Council; *b* 14 June 1951; *s* of Eleanor and Kwaku Boateng; *m* 1980, Janet Alleyne; one *d. Educ:* Ghana Internat. Sch.; Accra Acad.; Apsley Grammar Sch.; Bristol Univ. (LLB Hons); Coll. of Law. Admitted Solicitor, 1976; Solicitor, Paddington Law Centre, 1976-79; Solicitor and Partner, B. M. Birnberg and Co., 1979-. Legal Advr, Scrap Sus Campaign, 1977-81. Vice-Chm., Ethnic Minorities Cttee, GLC, 1981-. Chairman: Afro-Caribbean Educn Resource Project, 1978-; Westminster CRC, 1979-81; Vice-Pres., Waltham Forest CRC, 1981-. Mem. Exec., NCCL, 1980-. Chm. Governors, Priory Park Sch., 1978-; Governor Police Staff Coll., Bramshill, 1981-. *Recreations:* escapist. *Address:* 21 Wingmore Road, Brixton, SE24 0AS. *T:* 01-733 6957. *Clubs:* Mangrove Black and White Café (Bristol).

BOCK, Prof. Claus Victor, MA, DrPhil; Professor of German Language and Literature, Westfield College, University of London, since 1969; *b* Hamburg, 7 May 1926; *o s* of Frederick Bock, merchant and manufacturer, and Margot (*née* Meyerhof). *Educ:* Quaker Sch., Eerde, Holland; Univs of Amsterdam, Manchester, Basle. DrPhil (insigni cum laude) Basle 1955. Asst Lectr in German, Univ. of Manchester, 1956-58; University of London: Lectr, Queen Mary Coll., 1958-69; Reader in German Lang. and Lit., 1964; Chm., Bd of Studies in Germanic Langs and Lit., 1970-73; Hon. Dir, Inst. of Germanic Studies, 1973-81; Dean, Fac. of Arts, 1980-; Mem., Senate, 1981-; Mem., Acad. Council, 1981-; Mem., Central Research Fund (A), 1981-. Member Council: English Goethe Soc., 1965-; Stichting Castum Peregrini, 1971-. Hon. Pres., Assoc. of Teachers of German, 1973-75. Mem., Maatschappij der Nederlandse Letteren, 1977. Mem. Editl Bd, Bithell Series of Dissertations, 1978-. *Publications:* Deutsche erfahren Holland 1725-1925, 1956; Q. Kuhlmann als Dichter, 1957; ed (with Margot Ruben) K. Wolfskehl Ges. Werke, 1960; ed (with G. F. Senior) Goethe the Critic, 1960; Pente Pigadia und die Tagebücher des Clement Harris, 1962; ed (with L. Helbing) Fr. Gundolf Briefwechsel mit H. Steiner und E. R. Curtius, 1963; Wort-Konkordanz zur Dichtung Stefan Georges, 1964; ed (with L. Helbing) Fr. Gundolf Briefe Neue Folge, 1965; A Tower of Ivory?, 1970; (with L. Helbing and K. Kluncker) Stefan George: Dokumente seiner Wirkung, 1974; (ed) London German Studies, 1980; (with K. Kluncker) Wolfgang Cordan: Jahre der Freundschaft, 1982; articles in English and foreign jls and collections. *Recreation:* foreign travel. *Address:* Westfield College, Kidderpore Avenue, NW3 7ST. *T:* 01-435 7141; 4/8 Heath Drive, NW3 7SN. *T:* 01-435 8598.

BOCKETT, Herbert Leslie, CMG 1961; Member, Shipping Industry Tribunal, since 1972; Professional Accountant, and Member New Zealand Society of Accountants; *b* 29 June 1905; *s* of C. F. Bockett and L. M. Bockett (*née* Bridger); *m* 1932, Constance Olive Ramsay; two *d. Educ:* Dilworth Sch.; Seddon Memorial Technical Coll. Joined NZ Public Service, 1921; Accountant, Unemployment Board, 1934; Asst Director: Social Security Dept, 1939; National Service Dept, 1940; Controller of Man-power, 1942; Dir of National Service, 1944; Sec. of Labour, New Zealand, 1947-64; retd Dec. 1964. Chm., Workers' Compensation Bd, NZ, 1960-75. *Recreation:* bowls. *Address:* 189 The Parade, Island Bay, Wellington, NZ. *T:* 838-549.

BODDIE, Donald Raikes; Consultant in Public Affairs, since 1975; *b* 27 June 1917; *o s* of William Henry and Violet May Boddie; *m* 1941, Barbara Stuart Strong; one *s. Educ:* Colston's Sch., Bristol. Joined: London Star, 1942-47; Natal Mercury, Durban, 1947-52; London Evening News, 1953 (held various exec. posts, to Dep. Editor, 1966 and Editor, 1972-74); Dir, Harmsworth Publications Ltd, 1973-74; Vice-Chm., Evening News Ltd, 1974. *Recreations:* travel, theatre, cinematography. *Address:* 87 Regent Street, W1. *T:* 01-439 6992. *Club:* London Press.

BODDIE, George Frederick, BSc Edinburgh; FRCVS; FRSE; William Dick Chair of Veterinary Medicine, Edinburgh University (in the Royal Dick School of Veterinary Studies), 1953-70; *b* 23 Jan. 1900; *m* 1st, 1926 (she *d* 1968); one *s* two *d* ; 2nd, 1971. *Educ:* Merchiston Castle Sch.; Edinburgh Univ.; Royal (Dick) Veterinary College, Edinburgh. Clinical Asst Royal (Dick) Veterinary College, 1924; gen. veterinary practice, 1924-30; veterinary inspector local authority; Prof. of Medicine and Pharmacology Royal (Dick) Veterinary College, Edinburgh, 1930. Pres., RCVS, 1964-65, Vice-Pres., 1959-60, 1963-64 and 1965-66. Director: Hill Farm Research Organisation, 1957-66; Scottish Soc. for Prevention of Cruelty to Animals; former Chm. of Cttee, Edinburgh Dog and Cat Home; formerly Hon. Advisory Officer, Highlands and Islands Veterinary Services Scheme. Member: Medicine Commn, 1969-71; Poisons Bd, 1964-76. *Publications:* Diagnostic Methods in Veterinary Medicine, 1944, sixth edn, 1969; An Introduction to Veterinary Therapeutics, 1952; Editor Hoare's Veterinary Materia Medica and Therapeutics (6th edn), 1942 (jointly); many articles in veterinary and scientific jls. *Address:* 8/2 Myreside Court, Edinburgh EN10 5LX.

BODDINGTON, Lewis, CBE 1956; *b* 13 Nov. 1907; *s* of James and Anne Boddington; *m* 1936, Morfydd, *d* of William Murray; no *c*. *Educ:* Lewis' Sch., Pengam; City of Cardiff Technical Coll.; University Coll. of S Wales and Monmouthshire. Pupil Engineer, Fraser & Chalmers Engineering Works, Erith, 1928-31; Asst to Major H. N. Wylie, 1931-36; Royal Aircraft Establishment, 1936; Head of Catapult Section, 1938; Supt of Design Offices, 1942-45; Head of Naval Aircraft Dept, 1945-51; Asst Dir (R&D) Naval, Min. of Supply, 1951-53; Dir Aircraft R&D (RN), 1953-59; Dir-Gen., Aircraft R&D, 1959-60; Dir and Consultant, Westland Aircraft, 1961-72. Medal of Freedom of USA (Bronze Palm), 1958. *Address:* Flat 5 Bermuda Court, 20 Winn Road, Southampton SO2 1WT.

BODDY, Jack Richard, MBE 1973; JP; Group Secretary, Agricultural and Allied Workers Trade Group, Transport and General Workers Union, since 1982 (General Secretary, National Union of Agricultural and Allied Workers, 1978-82); Member, TUC General Council, since 1978; *b* 23 Aug. 1922; *s* of Percy James Boddy and Lucy May Boddy; JP; *m* 1943, Muriel Lilian (*née* Webb); three *s* one *d*. *Educ:* City of Norwich Sch. Agricultural worker, 1939; farm foreman, 1943. District Organiser: Lincolnshire NUAAW, 1953; Norfolk NUAAW, 1960. Leader, Workers' side, Agricl Wages Bd. Freeman, City of Norwich. JP Swaffham, 1947. *Recreation:* caravanning. *Address:* (home) 36 Station Street, Swaffham, Norfolk. *T:* Swaffham 22916; (office) 308 Gray's Inn Road, WC1X 8DS. *T:* 01-278 7801.

BODEN, Edward Arthur; retired; Agent-General for Saskatchewan, Canada, 1973-77; *b* 13 Nov. 1911; *s* of English and Welsh parents; *m* 1939, Helen Harriet Saunders; one *s* one *d*. *Educ:* Cutknife, Saskatchewan, Canada. Born and raised on a Saskatchewan farm and actively farmed until 1949, retaining interest in farm until 1973. Royal Canadian Mounted Police, 1932-39. Saskatchewan Wheat Pool and Canadian Fedn of Agriculture, 1939-73; held several active positions in these organisations and retired, as 1st Vice-Pres., 1973; in this field acted on various provincial and national govtl bds and cttees; Advr to Saskatchewan Dept of Industry and Commerce, 1977-78; policy Advr, Dept of Agriculture, and Co-ordinator of Sask's 75th Anniv. Celebration for Agricl features 1980, 1979-81; with others, rep. Canada at internat. agricultural confs in different parts of the world. Sen. Counsellor, Provincial Sen. Citizens' Council, 1982-. *Recreations:* boxing, hunting. *Address:* Box 988, Battleford, Saskatchewan S0M 0E0, Canada.

BODEN, Leonard, RP; FRSA; portrait painter; *b* Greenock, Scotland, 1911; *s* of John Boden; *m* Margaret Tulloch (portrait painter, as Margaret Boden, PS, FRSA); one *d*. *Educ:* Sedbergh; Sch. of Art, Glasgow; Heatherley Sch. of Art, London. Has exhibited at: The Royal Scottish Academy, Royal Society of Portrait Painters, etc. *Official portraits* include: HM Queen Elizabeth II; HRH The Prince Philip, Duke of Edinburgh; HM Queen Elizabeth the Queen Mother; HRH The Prince of Wales; The Princess Royal; HH Pope Pius XII; Field Marshals Lord Milne and Lord Slim, Margaret Thatcher, and many others. Vice-President: Artists' Gen. Benevolent Instn; St Ives Soc. of Artists; Governor, Christ's Hospital; Liveryman, Painter-Stainers Co. *Work reproduced in:* The Connoisseur, The Artist, Fine Art Prints. *Address:* 27 Warwick Gardens, Kensington, W14. *Clubs:* Savage, Chelsea Arts.

BODEN, Thomas Bennion, OBE 1978; JP; Deputy President, National Farmers' Union of England and Wales, 1979; *b* 23 Oct. 1915; *s* of late Harry Bertram Boden and Florence Nellie Mosley; *m* 1939, Dorothy Eileen Ball; one *s* two *d*. *Educ:* Alleynes Grammar Sch., Uttoxeter; Nottingham Univ. BSc course up to final year, when moved into farming on death of father, 1937; became involved in agricultural politics through NFU, 1948; office holder of NFU, 1977. JP Staffs 1957. *Publications:* articles on agricultural taxation. *Recreations:* cricket, tennis, swimming, hockey. *Address:* Denstone Hall, Denstone, Uttoxeter, Staffs. *T:* Rocester 590243. *Clubs:* Farmers', NFU.

BODGER; *see* Steele-Bodger.

BODILLY, Sir Jocelyn, Kt 1969; VRD; Chairman, Industrial Tribunals for London, since 1976; Chief Justice of the Western Pacific, 1965-75; *b* 1913. *Educ:* Munro Coll., Jamaica; Schloss Schule, Baden; Wadham Coll., Oxford. Called to Bar, Inner Temple, 1937; engaged in private practice until War; Royal Navy until 1946; RNVR, 1937-56 (Lt-Comdr (S)). High Court Judge, Sudan, 1946-55; Crown Counsel, Hong Kong, 1955, Principal Crown Counsel, 1961-65. *Address:* 10 Equarius, Eel Pie Island, Twickenham, Middlesex TW1 3DY. *Club:* Royal Ocean Racing.

BODMER, Dr Walter Fred, FRS 1974; Director of Research, Imperial Cancer Research Fund, since 1979; *b* 10 Jan. 1936; *s* of Dr Ernest Julius and Sylvia Emily Bodmer; *m* 1956, Julia Gwynaeth Pilkington; two *s* one *d*. *Educ:* Manchester Grammar Sch.; Clare Coll., Cambridge. BA 1956, MA, PhD 1959, Cambridge. Research Fellow 1958-61, Official Fellow 1961, Clare Coll., Cambridge; Demonstrator in Genetics, Univ. of Cambridge, 1960-62; Asst Prof. 1962-66, Assoc. Prof. 1966-68, Prof. 1968-70, Dept of Genetics, Stanford Univ.; Prof. of Genetics, Univ. of Oxford, 1970-79. Mem., BBC Gen. Adv. Council, 1981-; Chm., BBC Sci. Consultative Gp, 1981-. Vice-Pres., Royal Instn, 1981-82. For. Associate, US Nat. Acad. of Scis, 1981; For. Hon. Mem., Amer. Acad. Arts and Scis, 1972. Hon. Fellow, Keble Coll., Oxford, 1982. *Publications:* The Genetics of Human Populations (with L. L. Cavalli-Sforza), 1971; (with A. Jones) Our Future Inheritance: choice or chance?, 1974; (with L. L. Cavalli-Sforza) Genetics, Evolution and Man, 1976; research papers in

genetical, statistical and mathematical jls, etc. *Recreations:* playing the piano, riding, swimming. *Address:* Imperial Cancer Research Fund, Lincoln's Inn Fields, WC2. *T:* 01-242 0200. *Club:* Athenæum.

BODMIN, Archdeacon of; *see* Temple, Ven. G. F.

BODY, Richard Bernard; MP (C) Holland with Boston, since 1966; *b* 18 May 1927; *s* of Lieut-Col Bernard Richard Body, formerly of Hyde End, Shinfield, Berks; *m* 1959, Marion, *d* of late Major H. Graham, OBE; one *s* one *d*. Called to the Bar, Middle Temple, 1949. Underwriting Mem. of Lloyd's. Contested (C) Rotherham, 1950; Abertillery bye-election, 1950; Leek, 1951; MP (C) Billericay Div., Essex, 1955-Sept. 1959. Member: Jt Select Cttee on Consolidation of Law, 1975; Commons Select Cttee on Agric., 1979. Chm., Open Seas Forum, 1971; President: Free Trade League, 1981; Cobden Club, 1981. Jt Chm., Council, Get Britain Out referendum campaign, 1975. *Publications:* The Architect and the Law, 1954; (contrib.) Destiny or Delusion, 1971; (ed jtly) Freedom and Stability in the World Economy, 1976; The Triumph and the Shame, 1982. *Address:* Jewell's Farm, Stanford Dingley, near Reading, Berks. *T:* Reading 744295. *Clubs:* Carlton, Reform.

BOEGNER, Jean-Marc; Officier Légion d'Honneur; Commandeur, Ordre National du Mérite; Ambassadeur de France, 1973; *b* 3 July 1913; *s* of Marc and Jeanne Boegner; *m* 1945, Odilie de Moustier; three *d*. *Educ:* Lycée Janson-de-Sailly; Ecole Libre des Sciences Politiques; Paris University (LesL). Joined French diplomatic service, 1939; Attaché: Berlin, 1939; Ankara, 1940; Beirut, 1941; Counsellor: Stockholm, 1945; The Hague, 1947; Ministry of Foreign Affairs, Paris, 1952-55; Minister to Pres. of Council, 1955-58; Counsellor to Charles de Gaulle, 1958-59; Ambassador to Tunisia, 1959-61; Permanent Representative of France: to EEC, 1961-72; to OECD, 1975-78. *Publication:* Le Marché commun de Six à Neuf, 1974. *Recreations:* music, golf. *Address:* 19 rue de Lille, 75007 Paris, France.

BOERMA, Addeke Hendrik; Director-General, Food and Agriculture Organisation of the United Nations, 1968-75; *b* 3 April 1912; *m* 1953, Dinah Johnston; five *d*. *Educ:* Agricultural Univ., Wageningen. Netherlands Farmers' Organisation, 1935-38; Ministry of Agriculture of the Netherlands, 1938-45; Commissioner for Foreign Agricultural Relations, 1946; FAO positions: Regional Representative for Europe, 1948-51; Dir, Economics Div., 1951-58; Head of Programme and Budgetary Service, 1958-62; Asst Dir-Gen., 1960; Exec. Dir, World Food Programme, 1962-67. Holds Hon. Degrees from Univs in USA, Netherlands, Belgium, Hungary, Canada, Italy and Greece. Wateler Peace Prize, Carnegie Foundn, The Hague, 1976. Comdr, Netherlands Order of Lion; Commander, Order of Leopold II, Belgium; Officer, Ordre Mérite Agricole, France; Cavaliere di Gran Croce (Italy). *Address:* Prinz Eugenstrasse 44/10, 1040 Vienna, Austria.

BOEVEY, Sir Thomas (Michael Blake) C.; *see* Crawley-Boevey.

BOGARDE, Dirk; *see* Van den Bogaerde, D. N.

BOGDANOV, Michael; an Associate Director of the National Theatre of Great Britain, since 1980; *b* 15 Dec. 1938; *s* of Francis Benzion Bogdin and Rhoda Rees Bogdin; *m* 1966, Patsy Ann Warwick; two *s* one *d*. *Educ:* Lower School of John Lyon, Harrow; Univ. of Dublin Trinity Coll. (MA); Univs of the Sorbonne, and Munich. Writer, with Terence Brady, ATV series, Broad and Narrow, 1965; Producer/Director with Telefis Eireann, 1966-68; opening production of Theatre Upstairs, Royal Court, A Comedy of the Changing Years, 1969; The Bourgeois Gentilhomme, Oxford Playhouse, 1969; Asst Dir, Royal Shakespeare Theatre Co., 1970-71; Associate Dir, Peter Brook's A Midsummer Night's Dream, Stratford 1970, New York 1971, World Tour 1972; Dir, Two Gentlemen of Verona, São Paulo, Brazil, 1971; Associate to Jean Louis Barrault, Rabelais, 1971; Associate Director: Tyneside Th. Co., 1971-73; Haymarket Th., Leicester; Director: Phoenix Th., Leicester, 1973-77; Young Vic Th., London, 1978-80; Directed: The Taming of the Shrew, RSC, Stratford 1978, London 1979 (SWET Dir of the Year award, 1979); The Seagull, Toho Th. Co., Tokyo, 1980; Shadow of a Gunman, RSC, 1980; The Knight of the Burning Pestle, RSC, 1981; National Theatre productions: Sir Gawain and the Green Knight, The Hunchback of Notre Dame, 1977-78; The Romans in Britain, Hiawatha, 1980; One Woman Plays, The Mayor of Zalamea, The Hypochondriac, 1981; Uncle Vanya, The Spanish Tragedy, 1982. Co-author, plays, adaptations and children's theatre pieces. *Recreations:* cricket, football, music, farmhouse in Wales. *Address:* c/o The National Theatre, SE1.

BOGDANOVICH, Peter; director, producer, writer, actor; President: Saticoy Productions; Copa de Oro Productions; Moon Pictures; *b* Kingston, NY, 30 July; *s* of Borislav Bogdanovich and Herma Robinson; *m* Polly Platt (marr. diss.); two *d*. *Educ:* Collegiate Sch., New York; Stella Adler Theatre Studio. *Theatre:* Actor, NY Shakespeare Fest., Amer. Shakespeare Fest., and others; also television, 1955-58; Dir-Prod., The Big Knife, off-Broadway revival, 1959; Artistic Dir, Phoenicia Playhouse, NY, and dir revivals of Camino Real, Ten Little Indians, Rocket to the Moon, etc., 1961; Dir-co-prod., Once in a Lifetime, off-Broadway revival, 1964. *Films, TV, etc:* Second unit director-writer, The Wild Angels, 1966; filmed TV interview, The Great Professional: Howard Hawks Talks with Peter Bogdanovich, BBC-TV, 1967; Dir-prod.-writer-actor, Targets, 1968; Dir-writer, The Last Picture Show, 1971 (jtly, Best Screenplay, NY Film Critics' Award, British Acad. Award); Dir-writer, Directed by John Ford, documentary with film clips from Ford's movies, interviews with John Wayne, James Stewart, Henry Fonda, John Ford, 1971; Dir-prod., What's Up, Doc?, 1972 (jtly, Best Screenplay, Writers' Guild of America Award); Paper Moon, 1973 (Best Picture, Conchaca de Plata); Daisy Miller, 1974 (Best Dir, Brussels Award); Dir-prod.-writer, At Long Last Love, 1975; Dir-writer, Nickelodeon, 1976; co-writer, Dir, actor, Saint Jack, 1979 (winner, Premio Pasinetti, Venice Film Festival Award, 1979); Dir-prod.-writer, They All Laughed, 1981. Moving picture critic and feature writer, 1958-68. *Publications:* John Ford, 1968; Fritz Lang in America, 1969; Allan Dwan: the last pioneer, 1971; Pieces of Time, 1973 (Picture Shows, Eng., 1975); monographs on Cinema of: Orson Welles, 1961; Howard Hawks, 1962; Alfred Hitchcock, 1963; articles in Esquire, NY Times, Variety, Village Voice, Movie, Cahiers du Cinéma, New York, Film Culture, Film Qly, Vogue, Saturday Evening Post, etc. *Address:* (office) 212 Copa de Oro Road, Los Angeles, Calif 90077, USA.

BOGGIS-ROLFE, Hume, CB 1971; CBE 1962; farmer; *b* 20 Oct. 1911; *s* of Douglass Horace Boggis-Rolfe and Maria Maud (*née* Bailey); *m* 1941, Anne Dorothea, *e d* of Capt. Eric Noble, Henley-on-Thames; two *s* one *d. Educ:* Westminster Sch.; Freiburg Univ.; Trinity Coll., Cambridge. Called to Bar, Middle Temple, 1935. Army, Intelligence Corps, 1939-46 (Lieut-Col). Private Sec. to Lord Chancellor, 1949-50; Asst Solicitor in Lord Chancellor's Office, 1951-65; Sec. to Law Commn, 1965-68; Deputy Clerk of the Crown in Chancery, and Asst Perm. Sec. to Lord Chancellor, 1968-75, and Deputy Secretary, Lord Chancellor's Office, 1970-75. Master, Merchant Taylors' Co., 1971-72. Chm., Friends of the Elderly and Gentlefolks' Help, 1977-. *Recreations:* gardening, travelling. *Address:* 22 Victoria Square, SW1W 0RB. *T:* 01-834 2676; The Grange, Wormingford, Colchester, Essex. *T:* Bures 227303. *Club:* Athenæum.

BOGGON, Roland Hodgson, MS, MB London; FRCS, LRCP; *b* 11 Aug. 1903; *s* of late Richard Octavius Boggon, OBE, Civil Servant; *m* 1932, Mollie Daphne, *d* of T. H. Newall; one *s* one *d. Educ:* St Paul's Sch. Retired as Consulting Surg. to St Thomas' Hospital, London. Mem. Court of Examiners of the Royal College of Surgeons; Examiner in Surgery, Univ. of London. *Publications:* numerous medical. *Address:* Gittisham Hill House, Honiton, Devon EX14 8TY.

BOGLE, David Blyth, CBE 1967; formerly Senior Partner, Lindsays, WS, Edinburgh; Member of Council on Tribunals, 1958-70, and Chairman of Scottish Committee, 1962-70; *b* 22 Jan. 1903; *s* of late Very Rev. Andrew Nisbet Bogle, DD and Helen Milne Bogle; *m* 1955, Ruth Agnes Thorley. *Educ:* George Watson's Coll., Edinburgh; Edinburgh Univ. (LLB). Writer to the Signet, 1927. Commissioned in the Queen's Own Cameron Highlanders, 1940, and served in UK and Middle East, 1942-45; demobilised, with rank of Major, 1945. *Recreation:* curling. *Address:* Hartwood House, West Calder, Midlothian. *T:* West Calder 871248. *Club:* New (Edinburgh).

BOHAN, William Joseph; Assistant Under Secretary of State, Criminal Policy Department, Home Office, since 1979; *b* 10 April 1929; *s* of John and Josephine Bohan; *m* 1955, Brenda Skevington; two *c. Educ:* Finchley Catholic Grammar Sch.; Cardinal Vaughan Sch., Kensington; King's Coll., Cambridge (Chancellor's Classical Medallist, 1952). Home Office: Asst Principal, 1952; Principal, 1958; Sec., Cttee on Immigration Appeals, 1966-67; Asst Sec., 1967. *Recreations:* languages and literature, walking. *Address:* c/o Home Office, SW1. *T:* 01-213 4083.

BOHEMAN, Erik, Order of the Seraphim; Grand Cross, Order of Vasa; KBE (hon.) 1948; Swedish diplomat; Director of companies; *b* 19 Jan. 1895; *s* of Carl Boheman and Ellen Abramson; *m* 1932, Margaret Mattsson; two *s* two *d. Educ:* Stockholm Univ. Lieut 4th Hussars, 1915; entered Foreign Service, 1918, served at legations in Paris and London, 1918-19: Sec., Councillor and Director. Political Dept, Foreign Office, Stockholm, 1919-31; Minister to Ankara and Athens, 1931-34, to Warsaw, 1934-37; Sec. Gen., Foreign Office, 1938-45; Minister to Paris, 1945-47, to London, 1947; Ambassador to London, 1947-48; Ambassador to Washington, 1948-58. Attended council meetings and assemblies, League of Nations, as Sec. and Deleg., 1920-32. Conducted negotiations for commercial treaties with several countries. Headed Swedish Delegation for War Trade Agreements with Gt Britain during War of 1939-45; Deleg. to Gen. Assembly of UN, 1949-50, 1960-62. Mem of Swedish Parliament (First Chamber) for City of Gothenburg, 1959-70; Speaker of First Chamber, 1965-70. Grand Cross: Order of Danish Dannebrog; Finnish White Rose; Grand Officer, Legion of Honour (France). *Publications:* På Vakt (memoires), 3 vols, 1963-68. *Recreations:* travelling, farming, golf. *Address:* Anneberg, Gränna, Sweden.

BOHM, Prof. David (Joseph), PhD; Professor of Theoretical Physics, Birkbeck College, University of London, since 1961; *b* 20 Dec. 1917; *s* of Samuel and Freda Bohm; *m* 1956, Sarah Woolfson; no *c. Educ:* Pennsylvania State Coll. (BS); University of Calif (PhD). Research Physicist, University of Calif, Radiation Laboratory, 1943-47; Asst Prof., Princeton Univ., 1947-51; Prof., University de São Paulo, Brazil, 1951-55; Prof., Technion, Haifa, Israel, 1955-57; Research Fellow, Bristol Univ., 1957-61. *Publications:* Quantum Theory, 1951; Causality and Chance in Modern Physics, 1957; Special Theory of Relativity, 1965; Fragmentation and Wholeness, 1976; Wholeness and Order: cosmos and consciousness, 1979; Wholeness and the Implicate Order, 1980; various papers in Physical Review, Nuovo Cimento, Progress of Theoretical Physics, British Jl for Philosophy of Science, etc, inc. papers on

Implicate Order and A New Mode of Description in Physics. *Recreations:* walking, conversation, music (listener), art (viewer). *Address:* Physic Department, Birkbeck College, Malet Street, WC1.

BOHR, Prof. Aage Niels, DSc, DrPhil; physicist, Denmark; Professor o Physics, University of Copenhagen, since 1956; *b* Copenhagen, 19 June 1922 *s* of Prof. Niels Bohr and Margrethe Nørlund; *m* 1st, Marietta Bettina (*née* Soffer) (*d* 1978); two *s* one *d* ; 2nd, 1981, Bente, *d* of late Chief Physician Johannes Meyer and Lone (*née* Rubow) and widow of Morten Scharff. *Educ* Univ. of Copenhagen. Jun. Scientific Officer, Dept of Scientific and Industria Research, London, 1943-45; Research Asst, Inst. for Theoretical Physics, Univ of Copenhagen, 1946; Dir, Niels Bohr Inst. (formerly Inst. for Theoretica Physics), 1963-70. Bd Mem., Nordita, 1958-74, Dir, 1975-81. Member: Roya Danish Acad. of Science, 1955-; Royal Physiolog. Soc., Sweden, 1959-; Roya Norwegian Acad. of Sciences, 1962-; Acad. of Tech. Sciences, Copenhagen 1963-; Amer. Phil. Soc., 1965-; Amer. Acad. of Arts and Sciences, 1965-; Nat Acad. of Sciences, USA, 1971-; Royal Swedish Acad. of Sciences, 1974- Yugoslavia Acad. of Sciences, 1976-; Pontificia Academia Scientiarum, 1978- Norwegian Acad. of Sciences, 1979-; Polish Acad. of Sciences, 1980-; Finska Vetenskups-Societeten, 1980-; Deutsche Akademie der Naturforscher Leopoldina, 1981-. Awards: Dannie Heineman Prize, 1960; Pius XI Medal 1963; Atoms for Peace Award, 1969; H. C. Ørsted Medal, 1970; Rutherford Medal, 1972; John Price Wetherill Medal, 1974; (jointly) Nobel Prize for Physics, 1975; Ole Rømer Medal, 1976. Dr *hc* : Manchester, 1961; Oslo, 1969 Heidelberg, 1971; Trondheim, 1972; Uppsala, 1975. *Publications:* Rotationa States of Atomic Nuclei, 1954; (with Ben R. Mottelson) Nuclear Structure vol. I, 1969, vol. II 1975. *Address:* Granhøjen 10, 2900 Hellerup, Copenhagen Denmark. *T:* 650346.

BOHUSZ-SZYSZKO, Dame Cicely (Mary Strode); *see* Saunders, Dame C. M. S.

BOILEAU, Sir Guy (Francis), 8th Bt *cr* 1838; Company Director; *b* 23 Feb. 1935; *s* of Sir Edmond Charles Boileau, 7th Bt, and of Marjorie Lyle, *d* of Claude Monteath D'Arcy; *S* father, 1980; *m* 1962, Judith Frances, *d* of George Conrad Hannan; two *s* three *d. Educ:* Xavier College, Melbourne; Royal Military Coll., Duntroon, Australia. Lieut. Aust. Staff Corps, 1956; Platoon Comdr, 3rd Bn, Royal Aust. Regt, Malaysia, 1957-58; Observer, UN Mil Observer Gp in India and Pakistan, 1959-60; Instructor, Aust. Army Training Team, Vietnam, 1963-64; attached US Dept of Defence, Washington, DC, 1966-68; Security Adviser, Dept of the Administrator, Territory of Papua-New Guinea, 1970-71; CO, Army Intelligence Centre, 1972-74; Directing Staff (Instructor), Aust. Staff Coll., 1975-76; SO1 Personnel, HQ Third Mil. Dist, 1979. *Recreations:* tennis, boating, fishing. *Heir:* *s* Nicolas Edmond George Boileau, *b* 17 Nov. 1964. *Address:* 14 Faircroft Avenue, Glen Iris, Victoria 3146, Australia. *T:* (03) 20 8273. *Club:* The Heroes (Toorak, Victoria).

BOJAXHIU, Agnes Gonxha; *see* Teresa, Mother.

BOK, Derek Curtis; President, Harvard University, since 1971, Professor of Law, since 1961; *b* 22 March 1930, Bryn Mawr, Pa; *s* of late Curtis and of Margaret Plummer Bok (now Mrs William S. Kiskadden); *m* 1955, Sissela Ann Myrdal, *d* of Karl Gunnar and Alva Myrdal, *qqv* ; one *s* two *d. Educ:* Stanford Univ., BA; Harvard Univ., JD; Inst. of Political Science, Univ. of Paris (Fulbright Scholar); George Washington Univ., MA in Economics. Served AUS, 1956-58. Asst Prof. of Law, Harvard Univ., 1958-61, Dean of Law Sch., 1968-71. *Publications:* The First Three Years of the Schuman Plan, 1955; (ed with Archibald Cox) Cases and Materials on Labor Law, 5th edn 1962, 6th edn 1965, 7th edn 1969, 8th edn 1977; (with John Dunlop) Labor and the American Community, 1970; Beyond the Ivory Tower, 1982. *Recreations:* gardening, tennis, skiing. *Address:* Office of the President, Harvard University, Cambridge, Mass 02138, USA.

BOKSENBERG, Prof. Alexander, PhD; FRS 1978; Director, Royal Greenwich Observatory, since 1981; *b* 18 March 1936; *s* of Julius Boksenberg and Ernestina Steinberg; *m* 1960, Adella Coren; one *s* one *d. Educ:* Stationers Co.'s Sch.; Univ. of London (BSc, PhD). Dept of Physics and Astronomy, University Coll. London: SRC Res. Asst, 1960-65; Lectr in Physics, 1965-75; Head of Optical and Ultraviolet Astronomy Res. Group, 1969-81; Reader in Physics, 1975-78; SRC Sen. Fellow, 1976-81; Prof. of Physics, 1978-81; Visiting Professor: Dept of Physics and Astronomy, UCL, 1981-; Astronomy Centre, Univ. of Sussex, 1981-. *Publications:* contrib. learned jls. *Address:* Herstmonceux Castle, Hailsham, East Sussex BN27 1RP. *T:* Herstmonceux 3171.

BOLAM, James; actor; *b* Sunderland, 16 June 1938; *s* of Robert Alfred Bolam and Marion Alice Bolam (*née* Drury). *Educ:* Bede Grammar Sch., Sunderland; Bemrose Sch., Derby. First stage appearance, The Kitchen, Royal Court, 1959; later plays include: Events While Guarding the Bofors Gun, Hampstead, 1966; In Celebration, Royal Court, 1969; Veterans, Royal Court, 1972; Treats, Royal Court, 1976; Who Killed 'Agatha' Christie?, Ambassadors, 1978; King Lear (title rôle), Young Vic, 1981. *Films:* Straight on till Morning, Crucible of Terror, Otley, A Kind of Loving, Half a Sixpence, Murder Most Foul, The Likely Lads, In Celebration, Whatever Happened to the Likely Lads?, The Great Question. *Television series:* The Likely Lads; Whatever Happened to the Likely Lads? When the Boat Comes In; The Limbo Connection (Armchair Thriller Series); Only When I Laugh; also As You Like It, in BBC

Shakespeare. *Address:* c/o Barry Burnett Organisation Ltd, Suite 42-43, Grafton House, 2-3 Golden Square, W1.

BOLAND, Bridget; author; *b* 13 March 1913; *d* of late John Boland. *Educ:* Sacred Heart Convent, Roehampton; Oxford Univ. (BA 1935). Screenwriter 1937-; numerous films. Served War, 1941-46, in ATS; Senior Comdr. Stage plays: Abca Play Unit productions, 1946; Cockpit, 1948; The Damascus Blade, 1950; Temple Folly, 1952; The Return, 1953; The Prisoner, 1954 (adapted film version, 1955); Gordon, 1961; The Zodiac in the Establishment, 1963; Time out of Mind, 1970. *Publications: novels:* The Wild Geese, 1938; Portrait of a Lady in Love, 1942; Caterina, 1975; *non-fiction:* (with M. Boland) Old Wives' Lore for Gardeners, 1976; Gardener's Magic and Other Old Wives' Lore, 1977; At My Mother's Knee, 1978. *Address:* Bolands, Hewshott Lane, Liphook, Hants.

BOLAND, Frederick Henry; Irish diplomat, retired; Chancellor, Dublin University; *b* 1904; 2nd *s* of Henry Patrick Boland and Charlotte (*née* Nolan), Dublin; *m* 1935, Frances Kelly, Drogheda; one *s* four *d*. *Educ:* Clongowes Wood Coll.; Trinity Coll., Dublin; King's Inns, Dublin. BA; LLB 1925; LLD (jure dignitatis), 1950. University Studentship in Classics, TCD, 1925; Rockefeller Research Fellowship in Social Sciences (Harvard and University of Chicago), 1926-28; 3rd Sec., Dept of External Affairs, 1929; 1st Sec., Paris, 1932; Principal Officer Dept of Industry and Commerce, 1936; Dept of External Affairs: Asst Sec., 1938; Permanent Sec., 1946; Irish rep., Cttee on European Economic Co-operation, Paris, 1947; Irish Ambassador to the Court of St James's, 1950-56; Permanent Representative of Eire at UN, 1956-63 (Pres., 1960); Irish Representative UN Security Council, 1962-63. Dir, Arthur Guinness Son & Co., to 1979. Member: Cttee on Seasonal Migration, 1936; Cttee on Design in Industry, 1938; Royal Irish Acad. Pres., Coll. Historical Soc., TCD. Knight Comdr, Order of St Gregory the Great, 1948; Grand Cross, Order of the North Star of Sweden, 1950. *Recreations:* reading, piano, fishing. *Address:* 60 Ailesbury Road, Dublin, Eire. *T:* Dublin 693599. *Clubs:* Stephens Green; Royal Irish Yacht.

BOLAND, John Anthony; Public Trustee, since 1980; *b* 23 Jan. 1931; *s* of late Daniel Boland, MBE, and Hannah Boland (*née* Barton), Dublin; *m* 1972, Ann, *d* of James C. Doyle and Maureen Doyle, Fermoy, Co. Cork. *Educ:* Castleknock Coll.; Christian Brothers, Synge Street; Trinity Coll., Dublin (MA, LLB). Called to the Bar, Middle Temple, 1956; called to Irish Bar, 1967. Joined Public Trustee Office, 1956; Chief Administrative Officer, 1974-79; Asst Public Trustee, 1979-80. Hon. Member, College Historical Soc., TCD; Trustee of Trinity College Dublin (Univ. of Dublin) Trust; Mem. London Cttee, Irish Sch. of Econs. *Recreations:* travel, reading, walking. *Address:* Stewart House, Kingsway, WC2B 6JX. *T:* 01-405 4300. *Clubs:* Kildare Street and University (Dublin); Thames Sailing.

BOLES, Sir Jeremy John Fortescue, 3rd Bt, *cr* 1922; *b* 9 Jan. 1932; *s* of Sir Gerald Fortescue Boles, 2nd Bt, and Violet Blanche (*d* 1974), *er d* of late Major Hall Parlby, Manadon, Crown Hill, S Devon; *S* father 1945; *m* 1st, 1955, Dorothy Jane (marr. diss. 1970), *yr d* of James Alexander Worswick; two *s* one *d* ; 2nd, 1970, Elisabeth Gildroy, *yr d* of Edward Phillip Shaw; one *d* ; 3rd, 1982, Marigold Aspey (*née* Seckington). *Heir: s* Richard Fortescue Boles, *b* 12 Dec. 1958.

BOLES, John Dennis, MBE 1960; Director General of the National Trust, since 1975; *b* 25 June 1925; *s* of late Comdr Geoffrey Coleridge Boles and Hilda Frances (*née* Crofton); *m* 1st, 1953, Benita (*née* Wormald) (*d* 1969); two *s* three *d* ; 2nd, 1971, Lady Anne Hermione, *d* of 12th Earl Waldegrave, *qv. Educ:* Winchester Coll. Rifle Brigade, 1943-46. Colonial Administrative Service (later Overseas Civil Service), North Borneo (now Sabah), 1948-64; Asst Sec., National Trust, 1965, Sec., 1968. *Address:* The Old Rectory, Englefield, near Reading, Berks. *T:* Reading 302497. *Club:* Travellers'.

BOLINGBROKE, 7th Viscount *cr* 1712, **AND ST JOHN,** 8th Viscount *cr* 1716; **Kenneth Oliver Musgrove St John;** Bt 1611; Baron St John of Lydiard Tregoze, 1712; Baron St John of Battersea, 1716; *b* 22 March 1927; *s* of Geoffrey Robert St John, MC (*d* 1972) and Katherine Mary (*d* 1958), *d* of late A. S. J. Musgrave; *S* cousin, 1974; *m* 1st, 1953, Patricia Mary McKenna (marr. diss. 1972); one *s* ; 2nd, 1972, Jainey Anne McRae; two *s*. *Educ:* Eton; Geneva Univ. Chairman, A&P Sp of Cos, 1958-75; Director: Shaw Savill Holidays Pty Ltd; Bolingbroke and Partners Ltd; Wata Investment Inc., Panama. Pres., Travel Agents Assoc. of NZ, 1966-68; Dir, World Assoc. of Travel Agencies, 1966-75; Chm., Aust. Council of Tour Wholesalers, 1972-75. Fellow, Aust. Inst. of Travel; Mem., NZ Inst. of Travel. *Recreations:* golf, cricket, tennis, history. *Heir: s* Hon. Henry Fitzroy St John, *b* 18 May 1957. *Address:* PO Box 211, Christchurch, New Zealand; Andover Street, Christchurch, New Zealand. *Club:* Christchurch (Christchurch, NZ).

BOLITHO, Major Simon Edward, MC 1945; JP; Director: Barclays Bank, 1959; English China Clays; Vice-Lord-Lieutenant of Cornwall, since 1970; *b* 13 March 1916; *s* of late Lieut-Col Sir Edward Bolitho, KBE, CB, DSO; *m* 1953, Elizabeth Margaret, *d* of late Rear-Adm. G. H. Creswell, CB, DSO, DSC; two *s* two *d. Educ:* Royal Naval Coll., Dartmouth; RMC Sandhurst. Grenadier Guards, 1936-49; Lt-Col, DCLI, 1957-60. DL Cornwall, 1964; High Sheriff of Cornwall, 1956-57; JP 1959; CC 1953-67. *Recreations:* shooting, fishing, hunting, sailing, gardening. *Address:* Trengwainton,

Penzance, Cornwall. *T:* Penzance 3106. *Clubs:* Pratt's, MCC, Royal Yacht Squadron.

BÖLL, Heinrich Theodor; author; *b* Cologne, 21 Dec. 1917; *s* of Victor Böll and Maria Hermanns; *m* 1942, Annemarie Cech; three *s. Educ:* Gymnasium, Cologne; Univ. of Cologne. Member: German Acad. for Language and Poetry; Bavarian Acad. Fine Arts; Hon. Mem., Union of German Translators. Pres., Internat. PEN, 1971-74; a Founder, World Producers Union, 1970; Mem., Gruppe 47, 1950-. Hon. DSc Aston, 1973; Hon. DTech Brunel, 1973; Hon. LittD TCD, 1973. Winner of numerous prizes and awards, incl. Nobel Prize for Literature, 1972. *Publications:* Auch Kinder sind Zivilisten, 1948 (Children are Civilians Too, 1973); Der Zug war pünktlich, 1949 (The Train was on Time, UK, 1967); Wanderer, kommst du nach Spa . . ., 1950 (Traveller, if you come to Spa, 1956); Wo warst du, Adam?, 1951 (And Where Were You, Adam?, 1973); Die schwarzen Schafe, 1951; Nicht nur zur Weihnachtszeit, 1952; Und sagte kein einziges Wort, 1953 (Acquainted with the Night, UK, 1954; reprinted as And Never Said a Word, 1978); Haus ohne Hüter, 1954 (The Unguarded House, UK, 1957); Die Waage der Baleks, 1954; Dr Murkes gesammeltes Schweigen und andere Satiren, 1955; Das Brot der frühen Jahre, 1955 (The Bread of those Early Years, 1977); So ward Abend und Morgen, 1955; Unberechenbare Gäste; Erzählungen, 1956; Im Tal der donnernden Hufe, 1957; Irisches Tagebuch, 1957 (Irish Journal); Der Bahnhof von Zimpren, 1958; Abenteuer eines Brotbeutels, und andere Geschichten, 1958; Brief an einen jungen Katholiken, 1958; Billard um Halbzehn, 1959 (Billiards at Half Past Nine, UK, 1965); Als der Krieg ausbrach, 1961; Als der Krieg zu Ende war, 1962; Anekdote zur Senkung der Arbeitsmoral, 1963; Erzählungen, Hörspiele, Aufsätze, 1961; Ein Schluck Erde (play), 1962; Ansichten eines Clowns, 1963 (The Clown, UK, 1965); Entfernung von der Truppe, 1964 (Absent Without Leave, UK, 1967); Frankfurter Vorlesungen, 1966; Ende einer Dienstfahrt, 1966 (End of a Mission, UK, 1968); Aufsätze, Kritiken, Reden, 1967; Veränderung in Staech, 1969; Hausfriedensbruch, 1970; Aussatz (play), 1970; Gruppenbild mit Dame, 1971 (Group Portrait with a Lady, UK, 1973); Erzählungen 1950-1970, 1972; Gedichte, 1972; Neue politische und literarische Schriften, 1973; Die verlorene Ehre der Katharina Blum, 1974 (The Lost Honour of Katharina Blum, UK, 1975); Berichte zur Gesinnungslage der Nation, 1975; Einmischung erwünscht, 1977; Werke, vols 1-5, 1977, vols 6-10, 1978; Missing Persons and other essays, 1978; Fürsorgliche Belagerung, 1979 (The Safety Net, 1982); Gesammelte Erzählungen 1947-1980, 1981; Was soll aus dem Jungen bloss werden?, 1981; Vermintes Gelände, 1982; (jtly) Ein Artikel und seine Folgen, 1982; radio plays, translations, etc. *Address:* 5 Köln 1, 5165 Hürtgenwald-Grosshau, an der Nülheck 19, Federal Republic of Germany.

BOLLAND, Sir Edwin, KCMG 1981 (CMG 1971); HM Diplomatic Service, retired; Ambassador to Yugoslavia, 1980-82; *b* 20 Oct. 1922; *m* 1948, Winifred Mellor; one *s* three *d* (and one *s* decd). *Educ:* Morley Grammar Sch.; University Coll., Oxford. Served in Armed Forces, 1942-45. Foreign Office, 1947; Head of Far Eastern Dept, FO, 1965-67; Counsellor, Washington, 1967-71; St Antony's Coll., Oxford, 1971-72; Ambassador to Bulgaria, 1973-76; Head of British delegn to Negotiations on MBFR, 1976-80. *Recreations:* walking, gardening. *Address:* Lord's Spring Cottage, Godden Green, Sevenoaks, Kent. *T:* Sevenoaks 61105.

BOLLAND, Group Captain Guy Alfred, CBE 1943; Chief Intelligence Officer, BJSM (AFS), Washington, USA, 1956-59, retired; *b* 5 Nov. 1909; 3rd *s* of late Capt. L. W. Bolland; *m* 1935, Sylvia Marguerite, 2nd *d* of late Oswald Duke, Cambridge; one *s* three *d. Educ:* Gilbert Hannam Sch., Sussex. Commissioned RAF, 1930. Served in Iraq and Home Squadrons. Served War of 1939-45: commanded 217 Squadron during attacks on French ports, 1940; North African Operations, 1943 (despatches, CBE). *Recreation:* golf. *Address:* The Oaks, Shaftesbury Road, Woking, Surrey. *T:* Woking 60548.

BOLLAND, John; His Honour Judge Bolland; a Circuit Judge since 1974; *b* 30 March 1920; *s* of late Dominic Gerald Bolland and Gladys Bolland; *m* 1947, Audrey Jean Toyne (*née* Pearson); one *s* one step *s* one step *d. Educ:* Malvern Coll.; Trinity Hall, Cambridge (BA). Commnd Royal Warwicks Regt, 1939; 2nd Bn 6th Gurkha Rifles, 1941-46. Called to Bar, Middle Temple, 1948. *Recreations:* cricket, Rugby, golf, theatre. *Address:* 11 Firle Road, North Lancing, Sussex BN15 0NY. *T:* Lancing 5337.

BOLLERS, Hon. Sir Harold (Brodie Smith), Kt 1969; Chief Justice of Guyana, 1966-81; *b* 5 Feb. 1915; *s* of late John Bollers; *m* 1st, 1951, Irene Mahadeo (*d* 1965); two *s* one *d* ; 2nd, 1968, Eileen Hanoman; one *s. Educ:* Queen's Coll., Guyana; King's Coll., London; Middle Temple. Called to the Bar, Feb. 1938; Magistrate, Guyana, 1946, Senior Magistrate, 1959; Puisne Judge, Guyana, 1960. *Recreations:* reading, walking. *Address:* c/o Chief Justice's Residence, 245 Vlissengen Road, Georgetown, Guyana. *T:* 5204. *Club:* Royal Commonwealth Society.

BOLS, Hon. Maj.-Gen. Eric Louis, CB 1945; DSO 1944, and bar 1945; *b* 8 June 1904; *s* of Lt-Gen. Sir Louis Bols, KCB, KCMG, DSO; *m* 1st, 1930, Rosa Vaux (marr. diss., 1947); one *s* ; 2nd, 1948, Marion du Plessis (marr. diss., 1965); 3rd, 1967, Barbara Beardshaw (*née* Brown). *Educ:* Wellington Coll.; Royal Military Coll., Sandhurst. 2nd Lieut Devonshire Regt 1924; Capt The King's Regt 1935; Major, 1940; Temp. Lieut-Col 1941; Temp Col 1944; Temp. Brig. 1944; Temp. Maj.-Gen. and War Subs. Col 1945; Comdr 6th Airborne Div., 1945; retd pay, 1948. War Service in Ceylon, UK, and NW Europe. *Address:* Stone Cottage, Peppering Eye, near Battle, East Sussex.

BOLSOVER, George Henry, CBE 1970 (OBE 1947); Director, School of Slavonic and East European Studies, University of London, 1947–76; *b* 18 Nov. 1910; *yr s* of Ernest and Mary Bolsover; *m* 1939, Stephanie Kállai; one *d. Educ:* Leigh Grammar Sch.; Univ. of Liverpool; Univ. of London. BA 1931, MA (Liverpool), 1932, PhD (London), 1933. Univ. of Birmingham, Resident Tutor in Adult Education in Worcs, 1937–38; Asst Lectr in Modern European History, Univ. of Manchester, 1938–43; Attaché and First Sec., HM Embassy, Moscow, 1943–47; Mem. of Editorial Board, Slavonic and East European Review, 1947–63, and Chm., 1958–63; Member: UGC Sub-Cttee on Oriental, African, Slavonic and East European Studies, 1961–71; Treasury Cttee for Studentships in Foreign Languages and Cultures, 1948–58; Inst. of Historical Res. Cttee, 1948–75; Adv. Cttee on Educn of Poles in Gt Britain, 1948–67; Ct of Govs of London Sch. of Economics and Political Science, 1955–77; Council and Exec. Cttee of St Bartholomew's Med. Coll., 1962–76; Council of Royal Dental Hosp. London Sch. of Dental Surgery, 1966–77; Min. of Educn Cttee on Teaching of Russian, 1960–62; Senior Treasurer of University of London Union, 1958–77; Chm., Tutorial Classes Cttee of Council for Extra-Mural Studies of Univ. of London, 1965–76; Chm., Council for Extra-Mural Studies, 1968–76; Mem., 1951–, Treas., 1966–72, British Nat. Historical Cttee; Mem. Governing Body, GB/East Europe Centre, 1967–78; Governor, Northwood Coll. for Girls, 1963–. *Publications:* essays in: Essays presented to Sir Lewis Namier, 1956, Transactions of Royal Historical Society, 1957; articles in English Historical Review, Journal of Modern History, Slavonic and East European Review, International Affairs, etc. *Recreations:* music, travel. *Address:* 7 Devonshire Road, Hatch End, Mddx. *T:* 01-428 4282.

BOLT, Rear-Adm. Arthur Seymour, CB 1958; DSO 1951; DSC 1940 and bar 1941; *b* 26 Nov. 1907; *s* of Charles W. Bolt, Alverstoke, Hants; *m* 1933, Evelyn Mary June, *d* of Robert Ellis, Wakefield, Yorks; four *d. Educ:* Nautical Coll., Pangbourne; RN Coll., Dartmouth. Joined RN, 1923. Served War of 1939–45; HMS Glorious and Warspite (DSC and Bar), and at Admiralty. Capt. HMS Theseus (Korea), 1949–51; Dir Naval Air Warfare, Admty, 1951–53; Chief of Staff to Flag Officer Air (Home), 1954–56; Dep. Controller of Military Aircraft, Min. of Supply, 1957–60; retd. Capt. 1947; Rear-Adm. 1956. *Recreations:* tennis, squash, sailing. *Address:* 12 Mount Boone Way, Dartmouth, Devon. *T:* Dartmouth 3448. *Clubs:* Royal Naval and Royal Albert Yacht (Portsmouth); Royal Naval Sailing Association; Royal Dart Yacht.

BOLT, Air Marshal Sir Richard (Bruce), KBE 1979 (CBE 1973); CB 1977; DFC 1945; AFC 1959; Chief of Defence Staff, New Zealand, 1976–80; *b* 16 July 1923; *s* of George Bruce Bolt and Mary (*née* Best); *m* 1946, June Catherine South; one *s* one *d. Educ:* Nelson Coll., NZ. Began service with RNZAF in mid 1942; served during 2nd World War in RAF Bomber Command (Pathfinder Force); Chief of Air Staff, NZ, 1974–76. *Recreations:* fly fishing, golf. *Address:* 12 Monaghan Avenue, Karori, Wellington, NZ. *Club:* Wellington (Wellington, NZ).

BOLT, Robert Oxton, CBE 1972; playwright; *b* 15 Aug. 1924; *s* of Ralph Bolt and Leah Binnion; *m* 1st, 1949, Celia Ann Roberts (marr. diss., 1967); one *s* two *d*; 2nd, 1967, Sarah Miles (marr. diss. 1976); one *s*; 3rd, 1980, Ann Zane. *Educ:* Manchester Grammar Sch. Left sch., 1941; Sun Life Assurance Office, Manchester, 1942; Manchester Univ., 1943; RAF and Army, 1943–46; Manchester Univ., 1946–49; Exeter Univ., 1949–50; teaching, 1950–58; English teacher, Millfield Sch., 1952–58. Hon. LLD Exeter, 1977. *Plays:* The Critic and the Heart, Oxford Playhouse, 1957; Flowering Cherry, Haymarket, 1958; A Man for All Seasons, Globe, 1960 (filmed 1967); The Tiger and The Horse, Queen's, 1960; Gentle Jack, Queen's, 1963; The Thwarting of Baron Bolligrew, 1966; Vivat! Vivat Regina!, Piccadilly, 1970; State of Revolution, Nat. Theatre, 1977; *screenplays:* Lawrence of Arabia, 1962; Dr Zhivago, 1965 (Academy Award); Man for all Seasons, 1967 (Academy Award); Ryan's Daughter, 1970; Lady Caroline Lamb, 1972 (also dir.); TV and radio plays. *Address:* c/o Margaret Ramsay Ltd, 14a Goodwins Court, St Martin's Lane, WC2. *Club:* The Spares (Somerset) (Hon. Life Mem.).

BOLTE, Dame Edith (Lilian), (Lady Bolte), DBE 1973 (CBE 1959); *d* of D. F. M. Elder; *m* 1934, Hon. Sir Henry E. Bolte, *qv.* Member State Council: Girl Guide Movement, Victoria; Red Cross, Victoria. *Recreations:* tennis, golf. *Address:* Kialla, Meredith, Vic 3333, Australia. *Clubs:* Alexandra, Liberal Women's, Victoria League.

BOLTE, Hon. Sir Henry (Edward), GCMG 1972 (KCMG 1966); MLA; Premier and Treasurer of the State of Victoria, Australia, 1955–72; *b* Skipton, Victoria, 20 May 1908; *s* of J. H. Bolte; *m* 1934, Edith Lilian (*see* Dame Edith Bolte). *Educ:* Skipton State Sch.; Ballarat C of E Grammar Sch. Grazier, with sheep property near Meredith in western district of Victoria. Entered Parliament as MLA for Hampden, 1947; Minister of: Water Supply and Mines, 1948–50; Soil Conservation, 1949–50; Water Supply and Soil Conservation, 1950; Leader of Liberal Party (formerly Liberal and Country Party), 1953–72 (Dep. Leader, Nov. 1950–53). Freedom, City of Melbourne, 1975. Hon. LLD: Melbourne Univ., 1965; Monash Univ., 1967. *Recreations:* golf, shooting, turf. *Address:* Kialla, Meredith, Victoria 3333, Australia. *Clubs:* Australian, Athenæum (Melbourne); Geelong (Geelong).

BOLTON, 7th Baron, *cr* 1797; **Richard William Algar Orde-Powlett;** *b* 11 July 1929; *s* of 6th Baron Bolton; *S* father, 1963; *m* 1st, 1951, Hon. Christine Helena Weld Forester (marr. diss.), *e d* of 7th Baron Forester, and

of Marie Louise Priscilla, CStJ, *d* of Sir Herbert Perrott, 6th Bt, CH, CB; twe *s* one *d* ; 2nd, 1981, Masha Anne, *d* of Major F. E. Hudson, Winterfield House Hornby, Bedale, Yorks. *Educ:* Eton; Trinity Coll., Cambridge (BA) Chairman, Richmond Div., Conservative Assoc., 1957–60; Chairmar Yorkshire Div., Royal Forestry Soc., 1962–64; Member Council, Timbe. Growers' Organization. Chm., Waterers Group; Director, Yorkshire Genera Life Co. JP, North Riding of Yorkshire, 1957. FRICS. *Recreations:* shooting fishing. *Heir: s* Hon. Harry Algar Nigel Orde-Powlett [*b* 14 Feb. 1954; *n* 1977, Philippa, *d* of Major P. L. Tapply; two *s*]. *Address:* Bolton Hall Leyburn, North Yorkshire. *T:* Wensleydale 22303. *Clubs:* White's; Centra African Deep Sea Fishing.

BOLTON, Archdeacon of; *see* Hoyle, Ven. F. J.

BOLTON, Group Captain David; Director, Royal United Services Institute for Defence Studies, since 1981; *b* 15 April 1932; *o s* of late George Edward Bolton and Florence May (*née* Standing); *m* 1955, Betty Patricia Simmonds three *d. Educ:* Bede Collegiate Sch., Sunderland. Entered RAF as Nationa Serviceman; commnd RAF Regt, 1953; subsequent service in Egypt, Jordan Singapore, Aden, Cyprus, Malta and Germany; RAF Staff Coll., 1969 National Def. Coll., 1972; Central Planning Staff, MoD, 1973–75; OC 33 Wing RAF Regt, 1975–77; Comdt RAF Regt Depot, Catterick, 1977–80 retd 1980; Dep. Dir and Dir of Studies, RUSI, 1980–81. Member: RUSI Council, 1973–79; IISS, 1964–; RIIA, 1975–; Council, British Atlantic Cttee 1981–. Hon. Steward, Westminster Abbey, 1981. Trench Gascoigne Essay Prize, RUSI, 1972. *Publications:* contrib. learned jls. *Recreations:* formerly athletics, hockey, Rugby; now music, theatre, jogging. *Address:* Royal United Services Institute for Defence Studies, Whitehall, SW1A 2ET. *T:* 01-930 5854. *Club:* Royal Air Force.

BOLTON, Eric James; Chief Inspector of Schools, Department of Education and Science, since 1981; *b* 11 Jan. 1935; *s* of late James and Lilian Bolton; *m* 1960, Ann Gregory; one *s* twin *d. Educ:* Wigan Grammar Sch.; Chester Coll.; Lancaster Univ. MA. English teacher at secondary schs, 1957–68; Lectr Chorley Teacher Training Coll., 1968–70; Inspector of Schs, Croydon, 1970–73; HM Inspector of Schs, 1973–79; Staff Inspector (Educn Disadvantage), 1979–81. *Publications:* Verse Writing in Schools, 1964; various articles in educnl jls. *Recreations:* reading, music and opera, fly fishing, photography. *Address:* 50 Addington Road, Sanderstead, South Croydon, Surrey. *T:* 01-657 6368.

BOLTON, Sir Frederic (Bernard), Kt 1976; MC; FIMarE; Chairman, The Bolton Group, since 1953; Chairman or Director of other companies (subsidiaries); Chairman, Dover Harbour Board, since 1983 (Member, 1957–62 and since 1980); *b* 9 March 1921; *s* of late Louis Hamilton Bolton and late Beryl Dyer; *m* 1st, 1950, Valerie Margaret Barwick (*d* 1970); two *s* ; 2nd, 1971, Vanessa Mary Anne Robarts; two *s* two *d. Educ:* Rugby. Served War, with Welsh Guards, 1940–46 (MC 1945, Italy); Northants Yeomanry, 1952–56. Member: Lloyd's, 1945–; Baltic Exchange, 1946–. Chm., Atlantic Steam Nav. Co. & Subs, 1960–71; Dir, B.P. Tanker Co., 1968–; Mem., Brit. Rail Shipping & Int. Services Bd, 1970–82 (now Sealink UK Ltd). Pres., Chamber of Shipping of UK, 1966; Mem., Lloyd's Register of Shipping Gen. Cttee. 1961–; Chairman: Ship & Marine Technol. Requirements Bd, 1977–81; PLA, 1964–71; Nat. Ports Council, 1967–74; President: Inst. of Marine Engineers, 1968–69 and 1969–70; British Shipping Fedn, 1972–75; Internat. Shipping Fedn, 1973–; Gen. Council of British Shipping, 1975–76. Grafton Hunt: J: Master, 1956–67, Chm., 1967–72. *Recreations:* country sports. *Address.* Pudlicote, near Charlbury, Oxon OX7 3HX. *Club:* City of London.

BOLTON, Prof. Geoffrey Curgenven, DPhil; Professor of Australian Studies, University of London, since 1982; *b* 5 Nov. 1931; *s* of Frank and Winifred Bolton, Perth, W Australia; *m* 1958, (Ann) Carol Grattan; two *s. Educ:* North Perth State Sch.; Wesley Coll., Perth; Univ. of Western Australia; Balliol Coll., Oxford, (DPhil). FRHistS 1967; FAHA 1974; FASSA 1976. Res. Fellow, ANU, 1957–62; Sen. Lectr, Monash Univ., 1962–65; Prof. of Modern Hist., Univ. of Western Australia, 1966–73; Prof. of Hist., 1973–82, Pro-Vice-Chancellor, 1973–76, Murdoch Univ. *Publications:* Alexander Forrest, 1958; A Thousand Miles Away, 1963; The Passing of the Irish Act of Union, 1966; Dick Boyer, 1967; A Fine Country to Starve In, 1972; Spoils and Spoilers: Australians Make Their Environment, 1981; articles in learned jls. *Recreation:* sleep. *Address:* Centre for Australian Studies, 28 Russell Square, WC1B 5DS; 6 Melvista Avenue, Claremont, WA 6010, Australia. *Club:* Royal Commonwealth Society.

BOLTON, Col Geoffrey George Hargreaves, CBE 1960 (MBE 1946); MC 1916; DL; Chairman, North Western Division, National Coal Board, 1951–60 (Marketing Director, 1946–49, Deputy Chairman, 1950–51); *b* 5 Aug. 1894; 4th and *o surv. s* of late Henry Hargreaves Bolton, MBE, Newchurch-in-Rossendale, Lancs; *m* 1st, 1919, Ethel (*d* 1942), 2nd *d* of late Rev. James Robinson, Broughton, Preston; one *s* one *d* (and one *s* decd); 2nd, 1943, Margaret, *y d* of late Rev. James Robinson. *Educ:* Clifton Coll., Bristol. Served European War, 1914–18, East Lancs Regt (Gallipoli, Sinai, France); Comd East Lancs Regt TA, 1920–28 (retired 1928). Associated with Coal Industry, 1912–; Dir, Hargreaves Collieries Ltd, 1932–46; Exec. Officer, Lancashire Associated Collieries, 1935–46. DL 1935, JP 1935, Lancaster; High Sheriff, Lancashire, 1962–63. KStJ 1969. *Address:* Fairfield House, Chatburn, Clitheroe, Lancs BB7 4BB. *T:* Clitheroe 41335.

BOLTON, John; Chief Works Officer and Director General of Works, Department of Health and Social Security, since 1977; *b* 30 Dec. 1925; *s* of John and Elizabeth Ann Bolton, Great Harwood, Lancs; *m* 1950, Nell Hartley Mount, *d* of John and Kathleen Mount; three *d. Educ:* Blackburn Coll. of Technology and Art. LLB (Hons) London; CEng, FICE, FIMechE, FInstE, FCIArb. Mech. Engrg Apprentice, Bristol Aeroplane Co. Ltd; Civil Engrg Pupil, Courtaulds Ltd; subseq. with English Electric Co. Ltd and NW Gas Board. Entered Health Service as Group Engr, W Manchester HMC, 1954; subseq. Chief Engr to Board of Govs of United Liverpool Hosps, Dep. Regional Engr to Leeds Regional Hosp. Board and Regional Engr to E Anglian Regional Hosp. Board; Chief Engr, DHSS, 1969–77. Part-time lectr in building and engrg subjects, 1948–55; Principal, 1955–59, Irlam Evening Inst., Manchester. Liveryman, Fanmakers' Co. Vice Pres., CIBS, 1981–; Hon. FCIBS, Hon. FIPHE, Hon. FIHospE. *Publications:* contribs to: British Hosps Export Council Yearbooks, 1973, 1974, 1975; The Efficient Use of Energy, 1975; papers to internat. confs and to British learned Societies; technical articles in various jls. *Recreations:* theatre, music, reading, gardening, swimming. *Address:* Allsprings House, High Street, Little Shelford, Cambs. *T:* Cambridge 842591.

BOLTON, John Eveleigh, CBE 1972; DSC 1945; DL; Chairman and Managing Director, Growth Capital Ltd, since 1968; Chairman: Hall Bolton Estates Ltd; Atesmo Ltd; Crosshold Ltd; Riverview Investments Ltd; Development Capital Ltd; Development Capital (Finance) Ltd; Development Capital (Second Finance) Ltd; Development Capital Investments Ltd; Development Capital (NCDC) Ltd; Director: NCR Co. Ltd; Black & Decker; Black & Decker (Leasing) Ltd; Black & Decker Group Inc.; Black & Decker Holdings Inc.; Black & Decker Investment Co.; Black & Decker Manufacturing Co. Inc.; Plasmec Ltd; Dawson International Ltd; Johnson Wax Ltd; Redland Ltd; Guildford anc Counties Broadcasting Co. Ltd; *b* 17 Oct. 1920; *s* of late Ernest and Edith Mary Bolton; *m* 1948, Gabrielle Healey Hall, *d* of late Joseph and Minnie Hall; one *s* one *d. Educ:* Ilkley Sch.; Wolverhampton Sch.; Trinity Coll., Cambridge; Harvard, USA. Articled pupil to Chartered Acct, 1937–40; intermed. exam. of Inst. of Chartered Accts, 1940. Served War of 1939–45 (DSC). Destroyers, Lt RNVR, 1940–46. Cambridge, Hons Economics, MA; Cassel Travelling Schol., 1948; Harvard Business Sch., 1948–50; Baker Scholar, 1949; Master in Business Admin. (with Dist.), 1950. Research for Harvard in British Industry, 1950–51; Finance Dir, Solartron Laboratory Instruments Ltd, Kingston-upon-Thames, 1951–53 (Chm., 1953); Chm. and Man. Dir: Solartron Engineering Ltd, 1952; The Solartron Electronic Group Ltd, Thames Ditton and subseq. Farnborough, Hants, 1954–63 (Dep. Chm., 1963–65). British Institute of Management: Chm. Council, 1964–66; Bowie Medal 1969; CBIM; Life Vice-Pres.; Pres., Engrg Industries Assoc., 1981–; Chm. and Founder Subscriber: Advanced Management Programmes Internat. Trust; Foundn for Management Educn; Business Grads Assoc.; Dir, Management Publications Ltd, 1966–73 (Chm., 1969); Mem. Exec. Cttee, AA; Hon. Treasurer, Surrey Univ., 1975–82 (Past Chm.); Member: Sub-Cttee on Business Management Studies, UGC; Council of Industry for Management Educn; Harvard Business Sch. Vis. Cttee, 1962–75. Mem. Org. Cttee, World Research Hospital. Member: UK Automation Council, 1964–65; Adv. Cttee for Management Efficiency in NHS, 1964–65; Cttee for Exports to New Zealand, 1965–68; Adv. Cttee, Queen's Award to Industry, 1972–; Chm., Economic Develt Cttee for the Rubber Industry, 1965–68; Vice-Chm., Royal Commn on Local Govt in England, 1966–69; Chm., Committee of Inquiry on Small Firms, 1969–71. DL Surrey, 1974; High Sheriff of Surrey, 1980–81. DUniv Surrey, 1982. *Publications:* articles in: Scope; Control; The Listener; Christian Science Monitor; various radio and TV broadcasts on industrial topics. *Recreations:* shooting, swimming, tennis, gardening, opera, antiques. *Address:* Brook Place, Chobham, Woking, Surrey. *T:* Chobham 8157. *Clubs:* Harvard Business School Club of London, Harvard Club of London; Philippics (Surrey).

BOMBAY, Archbishop of, (RC), since 1978; **Most Rev. Simon Ignatius Pimenta;** *b* 1 March 1920; *s* of late Joseph Anthony Pimenta and Rosie E. Pimenta. *Educ:* St Xavier's Coll., Bombay (BA with Maths); Propaganda Univ., Rome (Degree in Canon Law). Secretary at Archbishop's House, Bombay, 1954; also Vice-Chancellor and Defensor Vinculi; Vice Rector of Cathedral, 1960; Visiting Prof. of Liturgy, Bombay Seminary, 1960–65; Rector of Cathedral and Episcopal Vicar for Liturgy and Pastoral Formation of Junior Clergy, 1967; Rector of Seminary, 1971; Auxiliary Bishop, 1971; Coadjutor Archbishop with right of succession, 1977. *Publications:* (edited) The Catholic Directory of Bombay, 1960 and 1964 edns; Circulars and Officials of the Archdiocese of Bombay, 3 vols; booklet on the Cathedral of the Holy Name. *Address:* Archbishop's House, 21 N.P. Marg, Bombay 400039, India. *T:* 231093, 231193, 231293.

BOMFORD, Nicholas Raymond, MA; Headmaster of Uppingham School, since 1982; *b* 27 Jan. 1939; *s* of late Ernest Raymond Bomford and of Patricia Clive Bomford (*née* Brooke), JP; *m* 1966, Gillian Mary Reynolds; two *d. Educ:* Kelly Coll.; Trinity Coll., Oxford (MA, Mod. History). Teaching appts, 1960–64; Lectr in History and Contemp. Affairs, BRNC, Dartmouth, 1964–66, Sen. Lectr, 1966–68; Wellington Coll., 1968–76 (Housemaster, 1973–76); Headmaster, Monmouth Sch., 1977–82. Mem. Navy Records Soc. (Councillor, 1967–70, 1973–76). *Publications:* Documents in World History, 1914–70, 1973; (contrib.) Dictionary of World History, 1973. *Recreations:* shooting (Captain OURC, 1959–60; England VIII (Élcho match), 1960), fishing, gardening, music, enjoying Welsh border country. *Address:* Uppingham School, Rutland LE15 9QE.

BOMPAS, Donald George, CMG 1966; Deputy Secretary, United Medical Schools of Guy's and St Thomas's Hospitals, since 1982; *b* 20 Nov. 1920; *yr s* of Rev. E. Anstie Bompas; *m* 1946, Freda Vice, *y d* of F. M. Smithyman, Malawi; one *s* one *d. Educ:* Merchant Taylors' Sch., Northwood; Oriel Coll., Oxford. MA Oxon, 1947. Overseas Audit Service, 1942–66, retired; Nyasaland, 1942–47; Singapore, 1947–48; Malaya (now Malaysia), 1948–66; Deputy Auditor-General, 1957–60; Auditor-General, Malaysia (formerly Malaya), 1960–66. Dep. Sec., Guy's Hosp. Med. and Dental Schools, 1966–69, Sec., 1969–82. Chm., Univ. of London Purchasing Gp, 1976–82. Mem. Exec., Federated Pension Schemes, 1979–. Liveryman, Merchant Taylors' Co., 1951. JMN (Hon.) Malaya, 1961. *Address:* 8 Birchwood Road, Petts Wood, Kent. *T:* Orpington 21661. *Club:* Royal Commonwealth Society.

BONALLACK, Michael Francis, OBE 1971; Managing Director, Miller Buckley Golf Services Ltd, since 1974; Chairman, Miller Buckley Leisure, since 1982; Director, Buckley Investments Ltd, since 1976; *b* 31 Dec. 1934; *s* of Sir Richard (Frank) Bonallack, *qv* ; *m* 1958, Angela Ward; one *s* three *d. Educ:* Chigwell; Haileybury ISC. National Service, 1953–55 (1st Lieut, RASC). Joined family business, 1955; Director, 1962–74. Chairman: Golf Foundn, 1977–; Professional Golfers' Assoc., 1976–82; Pres., English Golf Union, 1982. *Recreation:* golf (British Amateur Champion, 1961, 1965, 1968, 1969, 1970; English Amateur Champion, 1962–63, 1965–67 and 1968; Captain, British Walker Cup Team, 1971; Bobby Jones Award for distinguished sportsmanship in golf, 1972). *Address:* The Old Rectory, North Fambridge, Chelmsford, Essex. *T:* Maldon 740907. *Clubs:* Golfers'; Royal and Ancient (St Andrews); Chantilly (France); Pine Valley (USA).

BONALLACK, Sir Richard (Frank), Kt 1963; CBE 1955 (OBE 1944); MIMechE; President, Freight Bonallack, since 1974 (Chairman, 1971–74, formerly of Bonallack & Sons, Ltd, 1953–71); Director, Alcan Transport Products Ltd; *b* 2 June 1904; *s* of Francis and Ada Bonallack; *m* 1930, Winifred Evelyn Mary Esplen; two *s* one *d. Educ:* Haileybury. War service in TA; transferred to TA Reserve, 1946, with rank of Colonel. Chm., Freight Container Section, SMMT. Member, Basildon Development Corporation, 1962–77. *Recreation:* golf. *Address:* 4 The Willows, Thorpe Bay, Essex. *T:* Southend 588180.
See also M. F. Bonallack.

BONAR, Sir Herbert (Vernon), Kt 1967; CBE 1946; Chairman, 1949–74, and Managing Director, 1938–73, The Low & Bonar Group Ltd; retired 1974; *b* 26 Feb. 1907; *s* of George Bonar and Julia (*née* Seehusen); *m* 1935, Marjory (*née* East); two *s. Educ:* Fettes Coll.; Brasenose Coll., Oxford (BA). Joined Low & Bonar Ltd, 1929; Director, 1934; Managing Director, 1938; Chairman and Managing Director, 1949. Jute Control, 1939–46; Jute Controller, 1942–46. Trustee, WWF, UK, 1974–80 (Vice Pres. 1981). Hon. LLD: St Andrews, 1955; Birmingham, 1974. Comdr, Order of the Golden Ark, Netherlands, 1974. *Recreations:* golf, fishing, photography, wild life preservation. *Address:* St Kitts, Albany Road, Broughty Ferry, Dundee, Angus. *T:* Dundee 79947. *Clubs:* Blairgowrie Golf; Panmure Golf.

BOND, Arthur, CBE 1972; Chairman, Yorkshire Electricity Board, 1962–71; *b* 19 July 1907; *s* of Rev. A. and Mrs Anne Bond, Darwen, Lancs; *m* 1935, Nora Wadsworth; one *s* one *d. Educ:* Darwen Grammar Sch. Solicitor for Cleethorpes Corporation, 1930; Dep. Town Clerk, Luton, 1935; Town Clerk: Macclesfield, 1938; Stockport, 1944; Secretary, Eastern Electricity Board, 1948; Dep. Chairman, Yorkshire Electricity Board, 1952. Solicitor, Legal Member, TPI; Comp. IEE; CBIM. *Address:* 5 Linton Road, Wetherby, West Yorks. *T:* Wetherby 62847.

BOND, Rt. Rev. (Charles) Derek; see Bradwell, Bishop Suffragan of.

BOND, Edward; playwright and director; *b* 18 July 1934; *m* 1971, Elisabeth Pablé. Northern Arts Literary Fellow, 1977–79. Hon. DLitt Yale, 1977. George Devine Award, 1968; John Whiting Award, 1968. Opera Libretti: We Come to the River (music by Hans Werner Henze), 1976; The English Cat (music by Hans Werner Henze), 1982; ballet libretto: Orpheus; translations: Chekhov, The Three Sisters, 1967; Wedekind, Spring Awakening, 1974. *Publications:* (plays): Saved, 1965; Narrow Road to the Deep North, 1968; Early Morning, 1968; The Pope's Wedding, 1971; Passion, 1971; Black Mass, 1971; Lear, 1972; The Sea, 1973; Bingo, 1974; The Fool, 1976; A-A-merica! (Grandma Faust, and The Swing), 1976; Stone, 1976; The Woman, 1978; The Bundle, 1978; Theatre Poems and Songs, 1978; The Worlds and The Activist Papers, 1980; Restoration, 1981; Summer: a play for Europe, 1982. *Recreation:* the study of physics, because in physics the problems of human motives do not have to be considered. *Address:* c/o Margaret Ramsay, 14A Goodwins Court, St Martin's Lane, WC2N 4LL.

BOND, Prof. George, FRS 1972; Hooker Professor of Botany, University of Glasgow, 1973–76, now Emeritus Professor (Titular Professor, 1965–73); *b* 21 Feb. 1906; *m* 1st, 1931, Gwendolyne Kirkbride (*d* 1960); one *s* one *d* (and one *s* decd); 2nd, 1961, Mary Catherine McCormick; two *s. Educ:* The Brunts Sch., Mansfield; UC Nottingham. BSc, PhD, DSc, FIBiol. Asst Lectr, Dept of Botany, Univ. of Glasgow, 1927; subseq. Lectr, then Reader. Technical Officer, Min. of Food, Dehydration Div., 1942–45. *Publications:* articles in various learned jls on symbiotic fixation of nitrogen. *Recreation:* gardening. *Address:* 23 Westland Drive, Glasgow G14 9NY. *T:* 041-959 4201.

BOND, Maj.-Gen. George Alexander, CB 1956; CBE 1953 (OBE 1942); late RASC; *b* 31 Dec. 1901; *s* of late Alexander Maxwell Bond, Dover; *m* 1929, Dora Margaret, *d* of late H. A. Gray; two *s. Educ:* Dover Grammar Sch.; RMC. Served War of 1939-45 (despatches, OBE); Brig. 1948; Director of Supplies and Transport, BAOR, 1950-53; DDST, Southern Command, 1953-54; Maj.-Gen. 1955; Inspector RASC, War Office, 1954-57; Dir, Supplies and Transport, 1957, retd. Col Comdt, RASC, 1960-65; Col Comdt, Royal Corps of Transport, 1965-66. *Address:* Coldharbour Hall, Rake, Liss, Hants GU33 7JQ.

BOND, Maj.-Gen. Henry Mark Garneys, JP; DL; *b* 1 June 1922; *s* of W. R. G. Bond, Tyneham, Dorset; unmarried. *Educ:* Eton. Enlisted as Rifleman, 1940; commnd in Rifle Bde, 1941; served Middle East and Italy; seconded to Parachute Regt, 1947-50; ADC to Field Marshal Viscount Montgomery of Alamein, 1950-52; psc 1953; served in Kenya, Malaya, Cyprus and Borneo; Comd Rifle Bde in Cyprus and Borneo, 1964-66; Comd 12th Inf. Bde, 1967-68; idc 1969; Dir of Defence Operational Plans and Asst Chief of Defence Staff (Ops), 1970-72; retd 1972. Pres., Dorset Natural History and Archaeological Soc., 1972-75; Chairman: Dorset Br., CPRE, 1975-78; Dorset Community Council, 1978-81. Mem., Dorset CC, 1973- (Vice-Chm., 1981-). Chm., Dorset Police Authority, 1980-; JP Dorset, 1972, High Sheriff of Dorset, 1977, DL Dorset, 1977. *Recreations:* forestry, reading. *Address:* Moigne Combe, Dorchester, Dorset. *T:* Warmwell 852265. *Club:* Boodle's.

BOND, Sir Kenneth (Raymond Boyden), Kt 1977; Deputy Managing Director, General Electric Company plc, since 1966 (Financial Director 1962-66); *b* 1 Feb. 1920; *s* of late James Edwin and Gertrude Deplidge Bond; *m* 1958, Jennifer Margaret, *d* of late Sir Cecil and Lady Crabbe; three *s* three *d. Educ:* Selhurst Grammar School. Served TA, Europe and Middle East, 1939-46. FCA 1960 (Mem. 1949). Partner, Cooper & Cooper, Chartered Accountants, 1954-57; Dir, Radio & Allied Industries Ltd, 1957-62. Mem., Industrial Develt Adv. Bd, 1972-77; Mem., Cttee to Review the Functioning of Financial Instns, 1977-80. *Recreation:* golf. *Address:* White Gables, Austenwood Common, Gerrards Cross, Bucks. *T:* Gerrards Cross 83513. *Club:* Addington Golf.

BOND, Maurice Francis, CB 1978; MVO 1976; OBE 1955; Clerk of the Records, 1946-81, and Principal Clerk, Information Services, 1974-81, House of Lords; *b* 29 Oct. 1916; *s* of William Francis Bond and Ada Louise Bond (*née* Lightfoot), Windsor; *m* 1954, Shelagh Mary (*d* 1973), *d* of Hulbert Lionel and Katharine Lewis, Northampton. *Educ:* Windsor Boys Sch.; Selwyn Coll., Cambridge (Exhibnr 1933, BA 1936, Cert. of Educn 1937, MA 1941). Head of dept of History and Geography, Beaumont Coll., 1937-46. Clerk, House of Lords, 1946-81. Mem., Royal Commn on Historical MSS, 1981-. Hon. Custodian of the Muniments, St George's Chapel, Windsor Castle, 1947-75; Mem. Council, British Records Assoc., 1948-66 (Chm. Records Preservation section, 1961-66); Mem. Cttee, Windsor and Eton Soc., 1948-63; Hon. Archivist, Borough of Windsor, 1950-80; Mem. Tech. Cttee, Soc. of Archivists, 1956-74; Governor, Windsor Boys' Sch., 1957-; Hon. Gen. Editor: St George's Chapel Monographs, 1960-; Windsor Records Publications, 1966-80; Dir, Simon de Montfort Exhibn, Houses of Parliament, 1965; Mem. Cttee of Management, Inst. of Historical Research, 1968-77; Vice-Pres., Berkshire Archaeological Soc., 1973-; Hon. Consultant, Berks Record Office, 1981-; Dir, Chapel of Kings Exhibn, Windsor Castle, 1975. FSA 1947, FRHistS 1971. Hon. Associate, Royal Holloway Coll., London Univ., 1975-. *Publications:* (ed) The Inventories of St George's Chapel, 1947; The Romance of St George's Chapel, 1947, 12th edn 1980; (ed jtly) The Dictionary of English Church History, 1948; (ed) The Manuscripts of the House of Lords 1710-1714, 2 vols, 1949, 1953, and Addenda, 1514-1714, 1962; (jtly) The Manuscripts of St George's Chapel, 1957; The Seventh Centenary of Simon de Montfort's Parliament, 1965; Pictorial History of the Houses of Parliament, 1967; Guide to the Records of Parliament, 1971; St George's Chapel, Quincentenary Souvenir Book, 1975; The Diaries and Papers of Sir Edward Dering, 1644-1684, 1976; (with David Beamish) Black Rod, 1976; (with David Beamish) The Lord Chancellor, 1977; (ed) Works of Art in the House of Lords, 1980; contributions to: Eng. Hist. Review; Bulletin of Inst. of Hist. Research; Jl of Eccles. Hist.; The Table; Jl of Soc. of Archivists; Archives. *Recreations:* travel, music. *Address:* 19 Bolton Crescent, Windsor, Berks. *T:* Windsor 65132. *Club:* National Liberal.

BOND, Michael; author; *b* 13 Jan. 1926; *s* of Norman Robert and Frances Mary Bond; *m* 1950, Brenda Mary Johnson (marr. diss. 1981); one *s* one *d*; *m* 1981, Susan Marfrey Rogers. *Educ:* Presentation College, Reading. RAF and Army, 1943-47; BBC Cameraman, 1947-66; full-time author from 1966. Paddington TV series, 1976. *Publications:* A Bear Called Paddington, 1958; More About Paddington, 1959; Paddington Helps Out, 1960; Paddington Abroad, 1961; Paddington at Large, 1962; Paddington Marches On, 1964; Paddington at Work, 1966; Here Comes Thursday, 1966; Thursday Rides Again, 1968; Paddington Goes to Town, 1968; Thursday Ahoy, 1969; Parsley's Tail, 1969; Parsley's Good Deed, 1969; Parsley's Problem Present, 1970; Parsley's Last Stand, 1970; Paddington Takes the Air, 1970; Thursday in Paris, 1970; Michael Bond's Book of Bears, 1971; Michael Bond's Book of Mice, 1972; The Day the Animals Went on Strike, 1972; Paddington Bear, 1972; Paddington's Garden, 1972; Parsley the Lion, 1972; Parsley Parade, 1972; The Tales of Olga da Polga, 1972; Olga Meets her Match, 1973; Paddington's Blue Peter Story Book, 1973; Paddington at the Circus, 1973; Paddington Goes Shopping, 1973; Paddington at the Sea-side, 1974; Paddington at the Tower,

1974; Paddington on Top, 1974; Windmill, 1975; How to make Flying Things, 1975; Eight Olga Readers, 1975; Paddington's Loose End Book, 1976; Paddington's Party Book, 1976; Olga Carries On, 1976; Paddington's Pop-up Book, 1977; Paddington Takes the Test, 1979; Paddington's Cartoon Book 1979; J. D. Polson and the Liberty-Head Dime, 1980; J. D. Polson and the Dillogate Affair, 1981; Paddington on Screen, 1981; Olga Takes Charge, 1982 *Recreations:* photography, travel, cars, wine. *Address:* 22 Maida Avenue, W. 1SR. *T:* 01-262 4280. *Club:* Wig and Pen.

BOND, Ralph Norman, CMG 1953; OBE 1950; *b* 31 Aug. 1900; *s* of Ralph Bond, Morecambe, Lancs; *m* 1929, Dorothy Ward; three *d. Educ:* Roya Grammar Sch., Lancaster; St John's Coll., Cambridge. BA Classical Tripos 1922; MA 1929. Eastern Cadetship in Colonial Service, Dec. 1923; arrived in Ceylon, Jan. 1924; Revenue and judicial posts, 1924-36; Customs (Landing Surveyor and Deputy Collector), 1936-39; Import, Export and Exchange Control, 1939-42; Assistant Chief Secretary, 1942-45; Secretary to C-in-C Ceylon, 1945-46; Permanent Secretary to Ministry of Posts and Broadcasting Ceylon, 1947-55; retired, 1955. *Recreations:* formerly Rugby, soccer, hockey cricket, tennis and swimming; now gardening. *Address:* 48 Stuart Avenue Morecambe, Lancs. *T:* Morecambe 418799.

BOND-WILLIAMS, Noel Ignace, CBE 1979; Director, National Exhibition Centre Ltd, since 1970; Vice-Chairman, Lucas (Industries) Ltd, since 1979 (Director, since 1972); Chairman, Remploy Ltd, since 1979 (Vice-Chairman 1978-79); *b* 7 Nov. 1914; *s* of late W. H. Williams, Birmingham; *m* 1939 Mary Gwendoline Tomey; one *s* two *d. Educ:* Oundle Sch.; Birmingham Univ. (BSc). FIM, FBIM. Pres. Guild of Undergrads 1936-37, Pres. Guild of Grads 1947, Birmingham Univ. Various appts in metal industry; Director Enfield Rolling Mills Ltd, 1957-65 Delta Metal Co. Ltd, 1967-77; Industrial Adviser, DEA, 1965-67. Pres., Birmingham Chamber of Commerce, 1969 Member: Commn on Industrial Relations, 1971-74; Price Commn, 1977-79 Mem. Council, Industrial Soc., 1947-78; Pres., Brit. Non-ferrous Metals Fedn 1974-75. Feoffee of Lapworth Charity. Pro-Chancellor, Univ. of Aston in Birmingham, 1970-81. Hon. DSc Aston, 1975. *Publications:* papers and article on relationships between people in industry. *Recreation:* sailing. *Address*. Kiftsgate, Weston Subedge, Chipping Campden GL55 6QH. *T:* Evesham 840088. *Clubs:* Metallics; Royal Ocean Racing, Royal Cruising, Royal Lymington Yacht.

BONDI, Prof. Sir Hermann, KCB 1973; FRS 1959; FRAS; Chairman, Natural Environment Research Council, since 1980; Master of Churchill College, Cambridge, from August 1983; Professor of Mathematics, King's College, London, since 1954 (on leave of absence 1967-71); *b* Vienna, 1 Nov. 1919; *s* of late Samuel and Helene Bondi, New York; *m* 1947, Christine M Stockman, *d* of late H. W. Stockman, CBE; two *s* three *d. Educ:* Realgymnasium, Vienna; Trinity Coll., Cambridge (MA). Temporary Experimental Officer, Admiralty, 1942-45; Fellow Trinity Coll., Cambridge, 1943-49, and 1952-54; Asst Lecturer, Mathematics, Cambridge, 1945-48; University Lecturer, Mathematics, Cambridge, 1948-54. Dir-Gen., ESRO, 1967-71; Chief Scientific Advr, MoD, 1971-77; Chief Scientist, Dept of Energy, 1977-80. Research Associate, Cornell Univ., 1951; Lecturer, Harvard Coll. Observatory, 1953; Lowell Lecturer, Boston, Mass, 1953; Visiting Prof. Cornell Univ., 1960; Halley Lecturer, Oxford, 1962; Tarner Lectr, Cambridge, 1965; Lees-Knowles Lectr, Cambridge, 1974. Chairman: Space Cttee, MoD, 1964-65; Nat. Cttee for Astronomy, 1963-67; Adv. Council or Energy Conservation, 1980-82; Secretary, Royal Astronomical Soc., 1956-64 Mem., SRC, 1973-80. President: Inst. of Mathematics and its Applications, 1974-75; British Humanist Assoc.; Assoc. of British Science Writers, 1981-; Soc. for Res. into Higher Educn, 1981-; Assoc. for Science Educn, 1982. Member: Rationalist Press Assoc. Ltd; Science Policy Foundn; Hon. Vice-President Advisory Centre for Education (ACE); Mem., Ct, London Univ., 1963-67. Fellow, King's Coll., London, 1968. Hon. DSc: Sussex 1974; Bath 1974; Surrey 1974; York 1980; Southampton 1981; Salford, 1982. Hon. FIEE 1979. *Publications:* Cosmology, 1952 (2nd edn, 1960); The Universe at Large, 1961; Relativity and Commonsense, 1964; Assumption and Myth in Physical Theory, 1968; papers on astrophysics, etc, in Proc. Royal Society, Monthly Notices, Royal Astronomical Society, Proc. Cam. Phil. Society, etc. *Recreation:* travelling. *Address:* East House, Buckland Corner, Reigate Heath, Surrey. *T:* Reigate 45945.

BONE, Charles, PRI, ARCA, FRSA; President, Royal Institute of Painters in Water Colours, since 1979; Governor, 1976-81, Director, since 1981 Federation of British Artists; *b* 15 Sept. 1926; *s* of William Stanley and Elizabeth Bone; *m* Sheila Mitchell, FRBS, ARCA, Pres. of Soc. of Portrait Sculptors; two *s. Educ:* Farnham Coll. of Art; Royal Coll. of Art (ARCA). FBI Award for Design. Consultant, COSIRA, 1952-70; Craft Adviser, Malta Inds Assoc., Malta, 1952-78, still advising unofficially; Lecturer, Brighton Coll. of Art, 1950-; Director, RI Galleries, Piccadilly, 1965-70. Many mural paintings completed, including those in Eaton Square and Meretea, Italy; oils and water colours in exhibns of RA, London Group, NEAC and RBA, 1950- twenty one-man exhibns, 1950-; works in private collections in France, Italy Malta, America, Canada, Japan, Australia, Norway, Sweden, Germany Designer of Stourhead Ball, 1959-69; produced Ceramic Mural on the History of Aerial Photography. Critic for Arts Review. Mem. Council, RI, 1964- (Vice-Pres. 1974). *Address:* Winters Farm, Puttenham, Guildford, Surrey. *T:* Guildford 810226.

BONE, Ven. John Frank Ewan; Archdeacon of Buckingham, since 1978; *b* 28 Aug. 1930; *s* of Jack and Herberta Blanche Bone; *m* 1954, Ruth Margaret Crudgington; two *s* two *d. Educ:* Monkton Combe School, Bath; St Peter's Coll., Oxford (MA); Ely Theological Coll.; Whitelands Coll. of Education (Grad. Cert. in Education). Ordained, 1956; Assistant Curate: St Gabriel's, Warwick Square, 1956-60; St Mary's, Henley on Thames, 1960-63; Vicar of Datchet, 1963-76; Rector of Slough, 1976-78; Rural Dean of Burnham, 1974-77. *Recreations:* collecting maps and prints, brass rubbing, classical music, do-it-yourself, gardening. *Address:* 60 Wendover Road, Aylesbury, Bucks HP21 7LW. *T:* Aylesbury 23269.

BONE, Mrs Stephen; *see* Adshead, Mary.

BONE, Dr Thomas Renfrew; Principal, Jordanhill College of Education, since 1972; *b* 1935; *s* of James Renfrew Bone and Mary Williams; *m* 1959, Elizabeth Stewart; one *s* one *d. Educ:* Greenock High Sch.; Glasgow Univ. MA 1st cl. English 1956, MEd 1st cl. 1962, PhD 1967. Teacher, Paisley Grammar Sch., 1957-62; Lecturer: Jordanhill Coll., 1962-63; Glasgow Univ., 1963-67; Hd of Educn Dept, Jordanhill Coll., 1967-71. Chairman: Scottish Council for Educnl Technology, 1981-; Standing Conf. on Studies in Educn, 1983- (Vice-Chm., 1980-83); Vice-Chm., Scottish (formerly SCE) Exam. Bd, 1977-; Convener, Supply Cttee of Gen. Teaching Council for Scotland, 1976-; Member: CNAA Cttee for Scotland, 1979-; Exec., Commonwealth Council for Educn Admin, 1974-; IBA Educn Adv. Council, 1977-; Exec., British Educn Admin Soc., 1978-; Editorial Bd, Jl of Educn Admin, 1973-. *Publications:* Studies in History of Scottish Education, 1967; School Inspection in Scotland, 1968; chapters in: Whither Scotland, 1971; Education Administration in Australia and Abroad, 1975; Administering Education: international challenge, 1975; European Perspectives in Teacher Education, 1976; Education for Development, 1977; Practice of Teaching, 1978; World Yearbook of Education, 1980; various articles in professional jls. *Recreation:* golf. *Address:* Jordanhill College of Education, Southbrae Drive, Glasgow G13 1PP. *T:* 041-959 1232. *Clubs:* Royal Commonwealth Society; Western Gailes Golf; Paisley Burns; Paisley Bohemians.

BONHAM, Major Sir Antony Lionel Thomas, 4th Bt, *cr* 1852; late Royal Scots Greys; *b* 21 Oct. 1916; *o s* of Maj. Sir Eric H. Bonham, 3rd Bt, and Ethel (*d* 1962), *y d* of Col Leopold Seymour; *S* father 1937; *m* 1944, Felicity, *o d* of late Col. Frank L. Pardoe, DSO, Bartonbury, Cirencester; three *s. Educ:* Eton; RMC. Served Royal Scots Greys, 1937-49; retired with rank of Major, 1949. *Heir: s* (George) Martin (Antony) Bonham [*b* 18 Feb. 1945; *m* 1979, Nenon Baillieu, *e d* of R. R. Wilson and Hon. Mrs Wilson, Durford Knoll, Upper Durford Wood, Petersfield, Hants; one *s* one *d*]. *Address:* Ash House, Ampney Crucis, Cirencester, Glos. *T:* Poulton 391.

BONHAM-CARTER, Sir (Arthur) Desmond, Kt 1969; TD 1942; Director, Unilever Ltd, 1953-68, retired; *b* 15 Feb. 1908; 2nd *s* of Gen. Sir Charles Bonham-Carter, GCB, CMG, DSO, and Beryl, *née* Codrington; *m* 1st, 1933, Ann Parker Hazelwood (*d* 1972); one *s* ; 2nd, 1973, Diane Anastasia, *e d* of Mervyn Madden. *Educ:* Magdalene Coll., Cambridge. Served with Royal Tank Regt, 1938-45 (Lt-Col). With Unilever, 1929-68, Dir, 1953-68. Member: Royal Commission to consider Pay of Doctors and Dentists, 1957-60; Advisory Cttee, Recruitment for the Forces, 1958; Plowden Cttee on Representational Services Overseas, 1962-64; Central Health Services Council, 1965-74. Trustee, Nightingale Fund, 1961-; Chairman: Board of Governors, University College Hospital, 1963-74; S-W Metropolitan Regional Hospital Board, 1968-74; UK Rep., Internat. Hosp. Fedn, 1969-73; Mem., Camden and Islington AHA, 1974-78. *Address:* 15 Ashfield Close, Midhurst, Sussex. *T:* Midhurst 2109.

See also V. Bonham-Carter.

BONHAM-CARTER, John Arkwright, CVO 1975; DSO 1942; OBE 1967; ERD 1952; Chairman and General Manager, British Railways London Midland Region, 1971-75; *b* 27 March 1915; *s* of late Capt. Guy Bonham-Carter, 19th Hussars, and Kathleen Rebecca (*née* Arkwright); *m* 1939, Anne Louisa Charteris; two *s. Educ:* Winchester Coll.; King's Coll., Cambridge (Exhibitioner). 1st class hons Mech. Scis, Cantab, 1936; MA 1970. Joined LNER Co. as Traffic Apprentice, 1936; served in Royal Tank Regt, 1939-46 (despatches, 1940 and 1942); subsequently rejoined LNER; held various appointments; Asst General Manager, BR London Midland Region, 1963-65; Chief Operating Officer, BR Board, 1966-68; Chm. and Gen. Manager, BR Western Region, 1968-71. Lieut-Col, Engr and Rly Staff Corps RE (TA), 1966-71, Col 1971-. FCIT. CStJ 1979; Comr, St John Ambulance Brigade, Dorset, 1976-. *Recreations:* theatre, foreign travel, cabinet making and carpentry. *Address:* Redbridge House, Crossways, Dorchester, Dorset DT2 8DY. *T:* Warmwell 852669. *Club:* Army and Navy.

BONHAM CARTER, Hon. Mark Raymond; Director: William Collins Publishers, since 1981; National Video Corporation Ltd, since 1982; Chairman, Covent Garden Video Productions Ltd, since 1981; a Director, Royal Opera House, Covent Garden, since 1958; Governor, The Royal Ballet; *b* 11 Feb. 1922; *e s* of late Sir Maurice Bonham Carter, KCB, KCVO, and Violet, *d* of 1st Earl of Oxford and Asquith, KG, PC (Baroness Asquith of Yarnbury, DBE); *m* 1955, Leslie, *d* of Condé Nast, NY; three *d. Educ:* Winchester; Balliol Coll., Oxford (Scholar); University of Chicago (Commonwealth Fund Fellowship). Served Grenadier Guards, 1941-45; 8th Army (Africa) and 21st Army Group (NW Europe); captured, 1943; escaped; (despatches). Contested (L) Barnstaple, 1945; MP (L), Torrington Div. of

Devonshire, March 1958-59; Mem., UK Delegn to the Council of Europe, 1958-59; contested (L) Torrington, 1964. Director, Wm Collins & Co. Ltd, 1955-58. First Chm., Race Relations Bd, 1966-70; Chm., Community Relations Commn, 1971-77; Vice-President: Consumers' Assoc., 1972- (Mem. Council, 1966-71); Educnl Interchange Council, 1972-76; Mem. Council, Inst. of Race Relations, 1966-72. Chm., Writers and Scholars Educnl Trust, 1977-. Vice Chm. and a Governor, BBC, 1975-81. Chm., Outer Circle Policy Unit, 1976-80. Mem. Court of Governors, LSE, 1970-81. Hon. Fellow, Manchester Polytechnic. Hon. LLD Dundee, 1978. *Publications:* (ed) The Autobiography of Margot Asquith, 1962; contributor to: Radical Alternative (essays), 1962; articles, reviews in various jls. *Address:* 49 Victoria Road, W8. *T:* 01-937 4142. *Clubs:* Brooks's, MCC.

See also Hon. R. H. Bonham Carter.

BONHAM CARTER, Hon. Raymond Henry; Executive Director, S. G. Warburg & Co. Ltd, 1967-77; *b* 19 June 1929; *s* of Sir Maurice Bonham Carter, KCB, KCVO, and Lady Violet Bonham Carter, DBE (later Baroness Asquith of Yarnbury); *m* 1958, Elena Propper de Callejon; two *s* one *d. Educ:* Winchester Coll.; Magdalen Coll., Oxford (BA 1952); Harvard Business Sch. (MBA 1954). Irish Guards, 1947-49. With J. Henry Schröder & Co., 1954-58; acting Advr, Bank of England, 1958-63; Alternate Exec. Dir for UK, IMF, and Mem., UK Treasury and Supply Delegn, Washington, 1961-63; S. G. Warburg & Co. Ltd, 1964-; Director: Transport Development Group Ltd, 1969-77; Banque de Paris et des Pays Bas NV, 1973-77; Mercury Securities Ltd, 1974-77; seconded as Dir, Industrial Develt Unit, DoI, 1977-79. Mem. Council, Internat. Inst. for Strategic Studies, 1974-, and Hon. Treasurer. *Recreation:* skiing. *Address:* 7 West Heath Avenue, NW11 7QS. *T:* 01-455 8434.

See also Hon. M. R. Bonham Carter.

BONHAM-CARTER, Richard Erskine; Physician to the Hospital for Sick Children, Great Ormond Street, 1947-75, to University College Hospital, 1948-66; *b* 27 Aug. 1910; *s* of late Capt. A. E. Bonham-Carter and late M. E. Bonham-Carter (*née* Malcolm); *m* 1946, Margaret (*née* Stace); three *d. Educ:* Clifton Coll.; Peterhouse, Cambridge; St Thomas' Hospital. Resident Asst Physician, Hospital for Sick Children, Great Ormond Street, 1938. Served War of 1939-45 in RAMC; DADMS 1 Airborne Div., 1942-45; despatches, 1944. *Publications:* contributions to Text-Books of Pædiatrics and to medical journals. *Recreations:* gardening, fishing. *Address:* 18 Doughty Mews, WC1N 2PF. *T:* 01-405 3062; Castle Sweyn Cottage, Achnamara, Argyll.

BONHAM-CARTER, Victor; Joint Secretary, Society of Authors, 1971-78, Consultant, 1978-82; Secretary, Royal Literary Fund, 1966-82; *b* 13 Dec. 1913; *s* of Gen. Sir Charles Bonham-Carter, GCB, CMG, DSO, and Gabrielle Madge Jeanette (*née* Fisher); *m* 1st, 1938, Audrey Edith Stogdon (marr. diss. 1979); two *s* ; 2nd, 1979, Cynthia Claire Sanford. *Educ:* Winchester Coll.; Magdalene Coll., Cambridge (MA); Hamburg and Paris. Worked on The Countryman, 1936-37; Dir, School Prints Ltd, 1937-39, 1945-60; Army, R Berks Regt and Intell. Corps, 1939-45; farmed in W Somerset, 1947-59; historian of Dartington Hall Estate, Devon, 1951-66; joined staff of Soc. of Authors, 1963; active in Exmoor National Park affairs, 1955-; Pres., Exmoor Soc., 1975-; Partner, Exmoor Press, 1969-. *Publications:* The English Village, 1952; (with W. B. Curry) Dartington Hall, 1958; Exploring Parish Churches, 1959; Farming the Land, 1959; In a Liberal Tradition, 1960; Soldier True, 1965; Surgeon in the Crimea, 1969; The Survival of the English Countryside, 1971; Authors by Profession, vol. I, 1978; many contribs to jls, radio, etc on country life and work; also on authorship matters, esp. Public Lending Right. *Recreations:* music, bathing in warm climates, conversation. *Address:* The Mount, Milverton, Taunton TA4 1QZ. *Club:* Authors'.

See also Sir A. D. Bonham-Carter.

BONINGTON, Christian John Storey, CBE 1976; mountaineer, writer and photographer; *b* 6 Aug. 1934; *s* of Charles Bonington, journalist, and Helen Anne Bonington (*née* Storey); *m* 1962, Muriel Wendy Marchant; two *s* (and one *s* decd). *Educ:* University Coll. Sch., London. RMA Sandhurst, 1955-56; commnd Royal Tank Regt, 1956-61. Unilever Management Trainee, 1961-62; writer and photographer, 1962-. Climbs: Annapurna II, 26,041 ft (1st ascent) 1960; Central Pillar Freney, Mont Blanc (1st ascent), 1961; Nuptse, 25,850 ft (1st ascent), 1961; North Wall of Eiger (1st British ascent), 1962; Central Tower of Paine, Patagonia (1st ascent), 1963; Mem. of team, first descent of Blue Nile, 1968; Leader: successful Annapurna South Face Expedition, 1970; British Everest Expedition, 1972; (1st ascent) Brammah, Himalayas, 1973; (1st ascent) Changabang, Himalayas (co-leader), 1974; British Everest Expedition (1st ascent SW face), 1975; first ascent Ogre, 1977; first ascent Kongur, NW China (jt leader), 1981. Vice-Pres., British Mountaineering Council, 1976-79. FRGS (Founders' Medal, 1974). Hon. Fellow, UMIST, 1976. Hon. MA Salford, 1973; Hon. DSc Sheffield, 1976. *Publications:* I Chose to Climb (autobiog.), 1966; Annapurna South Face, 1971; The Next Horizon (autobiog.), 1973; Everest, South West Face, 1973; Everest the Hard Way, 1976; Quest for Adventure, 1981; Kongur: the elusive summit, 1982. *Recreation:* mountaineering. *Address:* Badger Hill, Nether Row, Hesket Newmarket, Wigton, Cumbria. *T:* Caldbeck 286. *Clubs:* Alpine, Alpine Ski, Army and Navy, Climbers (Vice-Pres.).

BONNER, Frederick Ernest, CBE 1974; Deputy Chairman, Central Electricity Generating Board, since 1975; Member (part-time), UKAEA, since 1977; *b* 16 Sept. 1923; *s* of George Frederick Bonner and late Mrs Bonner, Hammersmith; *m* 1st, 1957, Phyllis (*d* 1976), *d* of late Mr and Mrs H. Holder;

2nd, 1977, Mary, widow of Ellis Walter Aries, AFC, ARICS. *Educ:* St Clement Danes Holborn Estate Grammar Sch. BSc(Econ) London; DPA, JDipMA. Local Govt (Fulham and Ealing Borough Councils), 1940-49. Central Electricity Authority: Sen. Accountant, 1949-50; Asst Finance Officer, 1950-58; Central Electricity Generating Board: Asst Chief Financial Officer, 1958-61; Dep. Chief Financial Officer, 1961-65; Chief Financial Officer, 1965-69; Member, 1969-75. FCA, IPFA, CBIM. *Recreations:* music, gardening, reading. *Address:* c/o Central Electricity Generating Board, Sudbury House, 15 Newgate Street, EC1A 7AU.

BONNER, Paul Max; Channel Controller, Channel Four Television Co. Ltd, since 1980; *b* 30 Nov. 1934; *s* of Jill and Frank Bonner; *m* 1956, Jenifer Hubbard; two *s* one *d. Educ:* Essex. National Service commission, 1953-55. Local journalism, 1955; Radio production, BBC Bristol, 1955-57; Television production, BBC Bristol, 1957-59, BBC Lime Grove, 1959-62; Television Documentary prodn and direction, BBC Lime Grove and Kensington House, 1962-74; Editor, Community Programmes for BBC, 1974-77; Head of Science and Features Programmes for BBC, 1977-80. A Manager, Royal Instn. *Publications: documentaries include:* Strange Excellency, 1964; Climb up to Hell, 1967; Lost: Four H Bombs, 1967; Search for the Real Che Guevara, 1971; Who Sank the Lusitania?, 1972. *Recreations:* photography, the theatre, sailing, walking, listening to good conversation. *Address:* North View, Wimbledon Common, SW19 4UJ. *Club:* BAFTA.

BONNET, C. M.; *see* Melchior-Bonnet.

BONNEY, George Louis William, MS, FRCS; Senior Consultant Orthopædic Surgeon to St Mary's Hospital, London; Consulting Orthopædic Surgeon to the Dispensaire Français; *b* 10 Jan. 1920; *s* of late Dr Ernest Bonney and Gertrude Mary Williams; *m* 1950, Margaret Morgan; two *d. Educ:* Eton (Scholar); St Mary's Hospital Medical Sch. MB, BS, MRCS, LRCP 1943; FRCS 1945; MS (London) 1947. Formerly: Surg.-Lieut RNVR; Research Assistant and Senior Registrar, Royal National Orthopædic Hospital; Consultant Orthopædic Surgeon, Southend Group of Hospitals. Travelling Fellowship of British Postgraduate Med. Fedn, Univ. of London, 1950. Watson-Jones Lectr, RCS, 1976. Mem. Council, Medical Defence Union; Mem., SICOT. *Publications:* Chapters in Operative Surgery, 1957; papers in medical journals on visceral pain, circulatory mechanisms, nerve injuries and on various aspects of orthopædic surgery. *Recreations:* fishing, shooting, photography, music. *Address:* 71 Porchester Terrace, W2 3TT. *T:* 01-262 4236; Wyeside Cottages, Much Fawley, Hereford HR1 4SP. *Club:* Leander.

BONSALL, Sir Arthur (Wilfred), KCMG 1977; CBE 1957; *b* 25 June 1917; *s* of late Wilfred Bonsall and Sarah Bonsall; *m* 1941, Joan Isabel Wingfield; four *s* three *d. Educ:* Bishop's Stortford Coll.; St Catharine's Coll., Cambridge. 2nd Cl. Hons Mod. Langs. Joined Air Ministry, 1940; transf. to FO 1942; IDC, 1962; Dir, Govt Communications HQ, 1973-78. *Recreation:* coarse gardening. *Address:* 176 Slad Road, Stroud, Glos GL5 1RJ.
See also F. F. Bonsall.

BONSALL, Prof. Frank Featherstone, FRS 1970; Professor of Mathematics, University of Edinburgh, since 1965; *b* 1920; *s* of late Wilfred Bonsall and Sarah Bonsall; *m* 1947, Gillian Patrick. *Educ:* Bishop's Stortford Coll.; Merton Coll., Oxford. *Publications* (all with J. Duncan): Numerical Ranges of Operators on Normed Spaces and of Elements of Normed Algebras, 1971; Numerical Ranges II, 1973; Complete Normed Algebras, 1973. *Recreation:* walking. *Address:* Department of Mathematics, James Clerk Maxwell Building, Mayfield Road, Edinburgh EH9 3JZ.
See also Sir A. W. Bonsall.

BONSER, Ven. David; Archdeacon of Rochdale, since 1982; Vicar of St Chad's, and Team Rector of the Benefice of Rochdale, since 1982; *b* 1 Feb. 1934; *s* of George Frederick and Alice Bonser; *m* 1960, Shirley Wilkinson; one *s* two *d. Educ:* Hillhouse Secondary Sch., Huddersfield; King's Coll., London Univ. (AKC); Manchester Univ. (MA). Curate: St James's, Heckmondwike, 1962-65; St George's, Sheffield, 1965-68; Rector of St Clement's, Chorlton-cum-Hardy, 1968-82; Hon. Canon of Manchester Cathedral, 1980-82; Area Dean of Hulme, 1981-82. *Recreations:* theatre, reading, walking, skiing, music. *Address:* The Vicarage, Sparrow Hill, Rochdale, Lancs OL16 1QT. *T:* Rochdale 45014. *Club:* Royal Commonwealth Society.

BONSER, Air Vice-Marshal Stanley Haslam, CB 1969; MBE 1942; CEng, FRAeS; Director, Easams Ltd, 1972-81; *b* 17 May 1916; *s* of late Sam Bonser and late Phoebe Ellen Bonser; *m* 1941, Margaret Betty Howard; two *s. Educ:* Sheffield University. BSc 1938; DipEd 1939. Armament Officer, Appts, 1939-44; British Air Commn, Washington, DC, 1944-46; Coll. of Aeronautics, 1946-47; RAE, Guided Weapons, 1947-51; Chief Instr (Armament Wing) RAF Techn. Coll., 1951-52; Staff Coll., Bracknell, 1953, psa 1953; Project Officer, Blue Streak, Min. of Technology, 1954-57; Asst Dir, GW Engineering, 1957-60; Senior RAF Officer, Skybolt Development Team, USA, 1960-62; Dir, Aircraft Mechanical Engineering, 1963-64; Dir, RAF Aircraft Development (mainly Nimrod), 1964-69; Dep. Controller: of Equipment, Min. of Technology and MoD, 1969-71; Aircraft C, MoD, 1971-72. *Recreations:* scout movement, gardening. *Address:* Chalfont, Waverley Avenue, Fleet, Aldershot, Hants. *T:* Fleet 5835. *Club:* Royal Air Force.

BONSOR, Sir Nicholas (Cosmo), 4th Bt *cr* 1925; MP (C) Nantwich, since 1979; *b* 9 Dec. 1942; *s* of Sir Bryan Cosmo Bonsor, 3rd Bt, MC, TD, and of Elizabeth, *d* of late Captain Angus Valdimar Hambro; *S* father, 1977; *m* 1969, Hon. Nadine Marisa Lampson, *d* of 2nd Baron Killearn, *qv*; one *s* one *d. Educ:* Eton; Keble College, Oxford (MA). Barrister-at-law, Inner Temple. Served Royal Buckinghamshire Yeomanry, 1964-69. Practised at the Bar, 1967-75. CLA Legal and Parly Sub-Cttee, 1978-; Sec., Cons. Africa Sub-Cttee, 1979-80; Vice-Chm., Cons. Foreign Affairs Cttee, 1981-. FRSA 1970. *Publications:* political pamphlets on law and trades unions and defence. *Recreations:* sailing, shooting, military history. *Heir: s* Alexander Cosmo Walrond Bonsor, *b* 8 Sept. 1976. *Address:* Liscombe Park, Leighton Buzzard, Beds; Calveley House, Bunbury, Cheshire. *Clubs:* White's; Royal Yacht Squadron; Potters' (Stoke-on-Trent).

BONY, Prof. Jean V., MA; Professor of the History of Art, University of California at Berkeley, 1962-80, now Emeritus; *b* Le Mans, France, 1 Nov. 1908; *s* of Henri Bony and Marie Normand; *m* 1st, 1936, Clotilde Roure (*d* 1942); one *d*; 2nd, 1953, Mary England. *Educ:* Lycée Louis-le-Grand, Paris; Sorbonne. Agrégé d'Histoire Paris; MA Cantab; Hon. FSA; Corres. Fellow, British Academy. Bulteau-Lavisse Research Scholarship, 1935-37; Asst Master, Eton Coll., 1937-39 and 1945-46. Served War of 1939-45; 1st Lieut, French Infantry, 1939-44; POW, Germany, June 1940-Dec. 1943. Research Scholar, Centre Nat. de la Recherche Scientifique, 1944-45; Lecturer in History of Art at the French Inst. in London, 1946-61. Focillon Fellow and Vis. Lectr, Yale Univ., 1949; Slade Prof. of Fine Art, University of Cambridge, and Fellow of St John's Coll., Cambridge, 1958-61; Vis. Prof. and Mathews Lectr, Columbia Univ., 1961; Lecturer in History of Art at the University of Lille, France, 1961-62; Wrightsman Lectr, New York Univ., 1969; Vis. Fellow, Humanities Res. Centre, ANU, 1978; John Simon Guggenheim Meml Fellow, 1981; Kress Prof., Nat. Gall. of Art, Washington, 1982. *Publications:* Notre-Dame de Mantes, 1946; French Cathedrals (with M. Hürlimann and P. Meyer), 1951 (revised edn, 1967); (ed) H. Focillon: The Art of the West in the Middle Ages, English edn 1963, new edn 1969; The English Decorated Style, 1979; French Gothic Architecture of the 12th and 13th centuries, 1982; articles in Bulletin Monumental, Congrès Archéologiques de France, Journal of Warburg and Courtauld Institutes, Journal of British Archæological Assoc., etc. *Address:* Department of History of Art, University of California, Berkeley, California 94720, USA.

BONYNGE, Dame Joan; *see* Sutherland, Dame Joan.

BONYNGE, Richard, CBE 1977; Musical Director, Australian Opera Company, since 1976; *b* Sydney, 29 Sept. 1930; *s* of C. A. Bonynge, Epping, NSW; *m* 1954, Dame Joan Sutherland, *qv*; one *s. Educ:* Sydney Conservatorium (pianist). Official debut, as Conductor, with Santa Cecilia Orch. in Rome, 1962; conducted Faust (1st opera, stage), in Vancouver, 1963; Covent Garden debut, 1964. Has since made numerous concert and operatic appearances. Artistic Dir, Principal Conductor, Sutherland/Williamson Internat. Grand Opera Co., Aust., 1965; Artistic Dir, Vancouver Opera Assoc., 1974-78. Has conducted in major opera houses in Australia, America, Europe, etc. Florence, 1968: Semiramide, etc; Hamburg and New York, 1969-71: Giulio Cesare, Lucia; New York, 1970: Norma, Orfeo; 1973: Tales of Hoffman, also Sydney Opera House, 1974. Records: opera, orchestral works, ballet. *Recreations:* collector of antiques (espec. Staffordshire china), also autographed letters. *Address:* c/o Australian Opera, PO Box R233, Royal Exchange, Sydney, NSW 2000, Australia.

BOOKER, Christopher John Penrice; journalist and author; *b* 7 Oct. 1937; *s* of John and Margaret Booker, Shillingstone, Dorset; *m* 1979, Valerie, *d* of Dr M. S. Patrick, OBE; two *s. Educ:* Dragon Sch., Oxford; Shrewsbury Sch.; Corpus Christi Coll., Cambridge (History). Liberal News, 1960; jazz critic, Sunday Telegraph, 1961; Editor, Private Eye, 1961-63, and regular contributor, 1965-; resident scriptwriter, That Was The Week That Was, 1962-63, and Not So Much A Programme, 1963-64; contributor to Spectator, 1962-, Daily Telegraph, 1972-, and to many other newspapers and jls; book reviewer, Sunday Telegraph, 1979-. Wrote extensively on property develt, planning and housing, 1972-77 (with Bennie Gray, Campaigning Journalist of the Year, 1973); City of Towers—the Rise and Fall of a Twentieth Century Dream (TV prog.), 1979. *Publications:* The Neophiliacs: a study of the revolution in English life in the 50s and 60s, 1969; (with Candida Lycett-Green) Goodbye London, 1973; The Booker Quiz, 1976; The Seventies, 1980; The Games War: a Moscow journal, 1981; contrib. Private Eye anthologies. *Recreations:* Jungian psychology, music, following Somerset cricket team. *Address:* The Old Shop, Lamyatt, near Shepton Mallet, Somerset BA4 6NP. *T:* Bruton 2401.

BOOKER-MILBURN, Donald; Sheriff of Lothian and Borders, since 1980; *b* Dornoch, 20 May 1940; *s* of late Captain Booker Milburn, DSO, MC, Coldstream Guards, and late Betty Calthrop Calthrop; *m* 1963, Marjorie Lilian Elizabeth Burns; one *s* one *d. Educ:* Trinity College, Glenalmond; Grenoble Univ.; Jesus Coll., Cambridge (BA); Edinburgh Univ. (LLB). Admitted to Faculty of Advocates, 1968; Standing Junior Counsel to RAF, 1977-80. *Recreations:* golf, skiing. *Address:* 1 Essex Road, Edinburgh EH4 6LF. *T:* 031-339 6444. *Clubs:* New (Edinburgh); Royal Dornoch Golf.

BOOLELL, Sir Satcam, Kt 1977; Minister of Agriculture and Natural Resources, Mauritius, 1959-82; *b* New Grove, Mauritius, 11 Sept. 1920; *m* 1948, Inderjeet Kissoodaye; two *s* one *d. Educ:* primary and secondary schs in New Grove, Mare d'Albert, Rose Belle, and Port-Louis; LSE (LLB Hons 1951). Called to the Bar, Lincoln's Inn, 1952. Civil servant, Mauritius, 1944-48. Mem. Central Exec., Mauritius Labour Party, 1955-. Rep. Mauritius, internat. confs. Founder, French daily newspaper, The Nation. *Recreations:* reading travel books, gardening, walking in the countryside. *Address:* 4bis Bancilhon Street, Port-Louis. *T:* 2-0079.

BOON, George Counsell, FSA; FRHistS; FRNS; Keeper of Archaeology and Numismatics, National Museum of Wales, since 1976; *b* 20 Sept. 1927; *s* of Ronald Hudson Boon and Eveline Counsell; *m* 1956, Diana Margaret Martyn; two *s* one *d*. *Educ:* Bristol Univ. BA Hons (Latin). FRNS 1954; FSA 1955; FRHistS 1978. Archaeological Assistant, Reading Museum and Art Gallery, 1950-56; Asst Keeper, Dept of Archaeology, 1957-76. Member: Ancient Monuments Bd for Wales, 1979-; Royal Commn on Ancient and Historical Monuments (Wales), 1979-. Vice-President: Soc. for Promotion of Roman Studies, 1977-; Soc. of Antiquaries, 1979-83. Corresp. Mem., German Archaeological Inst., 1968. *Publications:* Roman Silchester, 1957, 2nd edn 1974; Isca, the Roman Legionary Fortress at Caerleon, Mon., 1972; Welsh Tokens of the Seventeenth Century, 1973; Cardiganshire Silver and the Aberystwyth Mint in Peace and War, 1981; contribs to learned journals. *Recreations:* none worth mention. *Address:* 43 Westbourne Road, Penarth, South Glam CF6 2HA. *T:* Penarth 709588. *Clubs:* unclubbable.

BOON, John Trevor, CBE 1968; Chairman, Mills & Boon Ltd, since 1972; *b* 21 Dec. 1916; 3rd *s* of Charles Boon and Mary Boon (*née* Cowpe); *m* 1943, Felicity Ann, *d* of Stewart and Clemence Logan; four *s*. *Educ:* Felsted Sch.; Trinity Hall, Cambridge (scholar). 1st Cl. Pts I and II History Tripos. Served War, 1939-45: with Royal Norfolk Regt and S Wales Borderers (despatches). Historical Section of War Cabinet, 1945-46. Joined Mills & Boon Ltd, 1938, Man. Dir, 1963, Chm., 1972-. Dir, Wood Bros Glass Works Ltd, 1968, Chm., 1973-75, Dep. Chm., 1975-78. Vice Chm., Harlequin Enterprises Ltd, Toronto, 1972-. Chairman: Harlequin Overseas, 1978-; Marshall Editions, 1977-; Director: Harmex, 1978-82; Harlequin France, 1980-82 (Chm., 1978-80); Torstar Corp., Toronto, 1981-. President: Soc. of Bookmen, 1981; Internat. Publishers Assoc., 1972-76 (Hon. Mem., 1982); Chairman: Publishers Adv. Panel of British Council, 1977-81; Book Trade Res. Cttee, 1978-82; Director: Book Tokens Ltd, 1964-; Book Trade Improvements Ltd, 1966-; Publishers Association: Mem. Council, 1953, Treas., 1959-61, Pres., 1961-63, Vice-Pres., 1963-65. Over-seas missions: for British Council, to SE Asia, USSR (twice), Czechoslovakia; for Book Development Council, to Malaysia, Singapore, and New Zealand. Mem. Management Cttee, Wine Soc., 1971-77. *Recreations:* walking, swimming, wine, books, friends. *Address:* c/o Williams and Glyn's Bank Ltd (Holt's Branch), Kirkland House, Whitehall, SW1. *Clubs:* Beefsteak, Garrick, Royal Automobile, Savile; Hawks (Cambridge).

BOON, Sir Peter Coleman, Kt 1979; Director, Hoover Ltd; *b* 2 Sept. 1916; *s* of Frank Boon and Evelyn Boon; *m* 1940, Pamela; one *s* one *d*. *Educ:* Felsted. Stock Exchange, 1933-34; Lloyds & National Provincial Foreign Bank, 1934-35; Dennison Mfg Co., USA, 1936-39; Armed Services, War of 1939-45, 1939-46; Dennison Mfg, 1946; graduate trainee, Hoover Ltd, 1946, Managing Dir (Australia), 1955-65; Managing Dir, Hoover Ltd, 1965-75, Chm., 1975-78. Chm., Highclere Investment Trust, 1979-. FBIM; FRSA 1980. Hon. LLD Strathclyde, 1978. Chevalier de l'Ordre de la Couronne, Belgium. *Recreations:* horses, swimming, golf, theatre, economics, National Trust for Scotland, boys clubs, education. *Clubs:* Hurlingham, Royal Wimbledon Golf; Burkes, Western Racing, Australian, Imperial Services, Killara Golf, American National, Royal Sydney Yacht Squadron, Australian Jockey, Sydney Turf (Australia); St Anne, Cercle des Nations (Belgium).

BOON, Dr William Robert, FRS 1974; retired; *b* 20 March 1911; *s* of Walter and Ellen Boon; *m* 1938, Marjorie Betty Oury; one *s* two *d*. *Educ:* St Dunstan's Coll., Catford; King's Coll., London. BSc, PhD, FRSC, FKC 1976. Research, Chemotherapy and Crop Protection, ICI, 1936-69; Dir, Jealott's Hill Res. Station, 1964-69; Man. Dir, Plant Protection Ltd, 1969-73. Vis. Prof., Reading Univ., 1968. Member: Adv. Bd for the Research Councils, 1972-76; NERC, 1976-79. Hon. DSc Cranfield, 1981. Mullard Medal of Royal Society, 1972. *Publications:* papers in Jl Chem. Soc., Jl Soc. Chem. Ind., etc. *Recreations:* gardening, photography, woodwork. *Address:* The Gables, Sid Road, Sidmouth, Devon EX10 9AQ. *T:* Sidmouth 4069. *Club:* Farmers'.

BOORD, Sir Nicolas (John Charles), 4th Bt *cr* 1896; scientific translator; English training specialist; *b* 10 June 1936; *s* of Sir Richard William Boord, 3rd Bt, and of Yvonne, Lady Boord, *d* of late J. A. Hubert Bird; *S* father, 1975; *m* 1965, Françoise Renée Louise Mouret. *Educ:* Eton (Harmsworth Lit. Prize, 1952); Sorbonne, France; Societa Dante Alighieri, Italy; Univ. of Santander, Spain. *Publications:* (trans. jtly) The History of Physics and the Philosophy of Science—Selected Essays (Armin Teske), 1972; numerous translations of scientific papers for English and American scientific and technical jls. *Recreations:* English and French literature and linguistics. *Heir:* *b* Antony Andrew Boord [*b* 21 May 1938; *m* 1960, Anna Christina von Krogh; one *s* one *d*]. *Address:* Résidence Les Aloadès, Bâtiment L, 94 Traverse Prat, 13008 Marseille, France. *T:* 73.13.95.

BOORMAN, Maj.-Gen. Derek, CB 1982; Commander, British Forces Hong Kong, and Major-General, Brigade of Gurkhas, since 1982; *b* 13 Sept. 1930; *s* of late N. R. Boorman, MBE, and of Mrs A. L. Boorman (*née* Patman);

m 1956, Jennifer Jane Skinner; one *s* two *d*. *Educ:* Wolstanton; RMA Sandhurst. Commnd N Staffords, 1950; Adjt 1 Staffords, 1958-59; Staff Coll., 1961; HQ 48 Gurkha Inf. Bde, 1962-64; Jt Services Staff Coll., 1968; CO 1 Staffords, 1969-71; Instr, Staff Coll., 1972-73; Comdr 51 Inf. Bde, 1975-76; RCDS, 1977; Dir, Public Relations (Army), 1978-79; Director of Military Operations, 1980-82. *Recreations:* shooting, gardening, music. *Address:* c/o Lloyds Bank Ltd (Cox's & King's Branch), Pall Mall, SW1. *Club:* Naval and Military.

BOORMAN, Edwin Roy Pratt; Managing Director, Kent Messenger Group, since 1965; Managing Director, Messenger Print Ltd; *b* 7 Nov. 1935; *s* of H. R. P. Boorman, *qv; m* Merrilyn Ruth Pettit (marr. diss. 1982); four *d*. *Educ:* Rydal; Queen's Coll., Cambridge (MA Econ. History). National Service, 1954-56. Cambridge Univ., 1956-59; Kent Messenger, 1959; Editor: South Eastern Gazette, 1960-62; Kent Messenger, 1962-65. Summer sch., S Illinois Univ., Carbondale, St Louis, 1962; Kentucky Colonel 1962. Councillor, Newspaper Soc.; Chm., Kent Section, London Chamber of Commerce (Mem., Econ. Affairs Cttee); Member: Freedom Assoc. (W Kent Chm.); Kent Co. Show Exec. Cttee; Kent Co. Playing Fields Exec. Cttee; Livery Cttee, Worshipful Co. of Stationers and Newspapermakers; President: Dickens Area Newsagents' Benevolent Assoc.; Maidstone Surgical Aid; Vice-Pres., Kent Br. Royal British Legion; Finance Dir, Royal British Legion Industries; Chairman: Publicity Cttee, Medway Regatta; St John Ambulance Appeals Cttee; Governor: Sutton Valence Sch.; Cornwallis Sch. Trustee, Playhouse Theatre Project, Ashford. Vice-Pres., Age Concern, Kent. Tax Comr, Maidstone District 2. *Recreation:* sailing. *Address:* 136 High Street, Tenterden, Kent. *Clubs:* Press, Veteran Car, Locomotive of GB; Kent CCC; Royal Yachting Association, Medway Yacht, Ocean Cruising.

BOORMAN, Henry Roy Pratt, CBE 1966 (MBE 1945); Chairman, Kent Messenger Group, since 1970; *b* 21 Sept. 1900; *s* of Barham Pratt Boorman and Elizabeth Rogers Boorman; *m* 1st, 1933, Enid Starke; one *s*; 2nd, 1947, Evelyn Clinch; one *d*. *Educ:* Leys Sch., Cambridge; Queens' Coll., Cambridge (MA). FJI 1936. Entered journalism, 1922; Proprietor and Editor, Kent Messenger, 1928; Chairman, South Eastern Gazette, 1929. Chairman, Kent Newspaper Proprietors' Assoc., 1931, 1932 and 1951; Mem. Council, Newspaper Soc., 1958, President, 1960. War Service: Regional Information Officer, SE Region, Tunbridge Wells, 1939; Dep. Welfare Officer for Kent, 1941; Major 1944; War Correspondent in Europe, 1939-40 and 1944, Berlin, 1949. Association of Men of Kent and Kentish Men: Editor, Journal Kent, 1931-62 (Chm. Council, 1949-51); Association's Sir Edward Hardy Gold Medal, 1964; in 1981, tenor bell in renewed peal in Canterbury Cathedral presented in his name by Kent Messenger staff. Maidstone Town Council: Councillor, 1934-46 and 1961-70; Mayor of Maidstone, 1962, Alderman, 1964. Liveryman, Worshipful Co. of Stationers and Newspaper Makers, 1933 (Mem. Ct of Assts, 1966-72). JP Maidstone Div. of Kent 1962; DL Kent, 1968-82. SBStJ 1946 (Mem. Council, StJ, 1960-66). *Publications:* Merry America (Royal Tour of Canada and United States), 1939; Hell's Corner, 1940; Kent—Our Glorious Heritage, 1951; Kentish Pride, 1952; Kent and the Cinque Ports, 1958; Kent Messenger Centenary, 1959; Kent—a Royal County, 1966; Spirit of Kent—Lord Cornwallis, 1968; Kent Our County, 1979. *Recreation:* world travel. *Address:* St Augustine's Priory, Bilsington, Ashford, Kent TN25 7AU. *T:* Aldington 252. *Clubs:* City Livery, Royal Commonwealth Society, Press, United Wards.

See also E. R. P. Boorman.

BOORSTIN, Dr Daniel J.; FRHistS; (12th) Librarian of Congress, since Nov. 1975; *b* 1 Oct. 1914; *s* of Samuel Boorstin and Dora (*née* Olsan); *m* 1941, Ruth Carolyn Frankel; three *s*. *Educ:* schs in Tulsa, Okla; Harvard Univ. (AB, summa cum Laude); Balliol Coll., Oxford (Rhodes Schol., BA Juris. 1st Cl. Hons, BCL 1st Cl. Hons); Yale Univ. Law Sch. (Sterling Fellow, JSD). Called to Bar, Inner Temple, 1937; admitted Mass Bar, 1942. Instr, tutor in history and lit., Harvard Univ. and Radcliffe Coll., 1938-42; Lectr, legal history, Law Sch., Harvard, 1939-42; Sen. Attorney, Office of Lend Lease Admin, Washington, DC, 1942-43; Office of Asst SG, USA, 1942-43; Asst Prof. of History, Swarthmore Coll., 1942-44; Univ. of Chicago, 1944-69: Asst Prof., 1944-49; Associate Prof., Preston and Sterling Morton Distinguished Prof. of Amer. History, 1956-69. During his 25 years tenure at Chicago, Visiting Lectr at Rome and Kyoto Univs, Sorbonne and Cambridge (Fellow, Trinity Coll., and Pitt Prof. of Amer. History and Instns; LittD 1968). Smithsonian Institution: Dir, Nat. Museum History and Techn., 1969-73; Sen. Historian, 1973-75. Many public service membership assignments, trusteeships, and active concern with a number of Amer. Assocs, esp. those relating to Amer. history, educn and cultural affairs. Past Pres., American Studies Assoc. Hon. LittD Sheffield, 1979; Hon. DLitt Univ. of East Anglia, 1980; numerous other Hon. degrees. *Publications: include:* The Mysterious Science of the Law, 1941; The Lost World of Thomas Jefferson, 1948; The Genius of American Politics, 1953; The Americans: The Colonial Experience, 1958 (Bancroft Prize); America and the Image of Europe, 1960; The Image, 1962; The Americans: The National Experience, 1965 (Parkman Prize); The Decline of Radicalism, 1969; The Sociology of the Absurd, 1970; The Americans: The Democratic Experience, 1973 (Pulitzer Prize for History and Dexter Prize, 1974); Democracy and Its Discontents, 1974; The Exploring Spirit (BBC 1975 Reith Lectures), 1976; The Republic of Technology, 1978; (with Brooks M. Kelley) A History of the United States, 1980; (for young readers) Landmark History of the American People, vol. I, From Plymouth to Appomattox, 1968; vol. II, From Appomattox to the Moon, 1970; (ed) Delaware Cases 1792-1830, 1943; (ed) An American Primer, 1966; (ed) American Civilization, 1971; (ed)

The Chicago History of American Civilization (30 vols). *Address:* (home) 3541 Ordway Street, NW, Washington, DC 20016, USA; (office) Library of Congress, Washington, DC 20540. *T:* Library of Congress 287-5000. *Clubs:* Cosmos, National Press (Washington); Elizabethan (Yale); International House (Japan).

BOOT, Dr Henry Albert Howard; Senior Principal Scientific Officer, Royal Naval Scientific Service, 1954-77 (Principal Scientific Officer, 1948-54); *b* 29 July 1917; *s* of late Henry James and late Ruby May Boot; *m* 1948, Penelope May Herrington; two *s. Educ:* King Edward's High Sch., Birmingham (Scholar); Univ. of Birmingham. BSc 1938; PhD 1941. Invention of the cavity magnetron (with Prof. J. T, Randall, FRS), 1939; research on the cavity magnetron at Univ. of Birmingham, 1939-45; Nuffield Research Fellow in Physics at Univ. of Birmingham, 1945-48. Royal Society of Arts Thomas Gray Memorial Prize (with J. T. Randall), 1943; Award by Royal Commission on Awards to Inventors, 1949; John Price Wetherill Medal of the Franklin Institute, 1958; John Scott Award, 1959 (with Prof. J. Randall). *Publications:* various papers on the production of high power ultra high frequency oscillation and controlled thermonuclear fusion, also optical masers. *Recreation:* sailing. *Address:* The Old Mill Cottage, Rushden, near Buntingford, Herts. *T:* Broadfield 231.

BOOTE, Col Charles Geoffrey Michael, MBE 1945; TD 1943; DL; Vice Lord-Lieutenant of Staffordshire, 1969-76; *b* 29 Sept. 1909; *s* of Lt-Col Charles Edmund Boote, TD, The North Staffordshire Regt (killed in action, 1916); *m* 1937, Elizabeth Gertrude (*d* 1980), *er d* of Evan Richard Davies, Market Drayton, Salop; three *s. Educ:* Bedford Sch. 2nd Lt 5th Bn North Staffordshire Regt, 1927. Served 1939-45, UK and NW Europe; despatches, 1945; Lt-Col, 1947. Director, H. Clarkson (Midlands) Ltd, 1969-75. Dir, Brit. Pottery Manufacturers' Fedn (Trustee) Ltd, 1955, retd Dec. 1969; Pres., Brit. Pottery Manufacturers' Fedn, 1957-58; Vice-Chm., Glazed and Floor Tile Manufacturers' Assoc., 1953-57. Hon. Col 5/6 Bn North Staffordshire Regt, 1963-67; Mem. Staffs TAVR Cttee, retd 1976. JP, Stoke-on-Trent, 1955-65; DL, 1958, JP 1959, High Sheriff, 1967-68, Staffordshire. Chm., Eccleshall PSD, 1971-76; Mem. Court of Governors, Keele Univ., 1957. *Recreations:* salmon fishing; British Racing Drivers' Club (Life Mem.); North Staffordshire Hunt (Hon. Sec. 1948-59). *Address:* Morile Mhor, Tomatin, Inverness-shire. *T:* Tomatin 319. *Club:* Army and Navy.

BOOTE, Robert Edward, CVO 1971; first Director General, Nature Conservancy Council, 1973-80; *b* 6 Feb. 1920; *s* of Ernest Haydn Boote and Helen Rose Boote; *m* 1948, Vera (*née* Badian); one *s* one *d. Educ:* London Univ. (BSc Econ). DPA, FCIS. War service, 1939-46, Actg Lt-Col, Hon. Major. Admin. Officer, City of Stoke-on-Trent, 1946-48; Chief Admin. Officer, Staffs County Planning and Develt Dept, 1948-54; Principal, 1954-64, Dep. Dir, 1964-73, Nature Conservancy. Sec. 1965-71, formerly Dep. Sec., Countryside in 1970 Confs, 1963, 1965, 1970 and numerous study groups; UK Deleg. to Council of Europe Cttee for Conservation of Nature and Natural Resources, 1963-71; various posts in UN, UNESCO, EEC and OECD, 1968-; Chm. Preparatory Gp for Conservation Year 1970; Chm. Organising Cttee for European Conservation Conf. 1970 (Conf. Vice-Pres.); Chm. European Cttee, 1969-71; Consultant for European Architectural Heritage Year 1975. Mem., Governing Council and Bureau, IUCN, 1975-81, a Vice-Pres., 1978-81 (Treasurer, 1975-78). FRSA 1971; Council Member: FFPS; BTCV (Vice-Pres.); RSNC (Vice-Pres.); WWF; Ecological Parks Trust; Patron: CSV; FPA internat. campaign; Chm., Inst. of Environmental Sciences, 1981-; Hon. Associate, Landscape Inst., 1971; Hon. MRTPI, 1978. Greek Distinguished Service Medal, 1946; van Tienhoven Prize, 1980. Member Editorial Boards: Town Planning Review; Internat. Jl of Environmental Studies; Internat. Jl Environmental Educn and Information. *Publications:* (as Robert Arvill) Man and Environment, 1967 (5th edn 1982); numerous papers, articles, addresses, TV and radio broadcasts, over 2 decades in UK and internat. professional confs in 16 countries. *Recreations:* walking, music. *Address:* 3 Leeward Gardens, SW19 7QR. *T:* 01-946 1551. *Club:* Athenæum.

BOOTH; *see* Gore-Booth.

BOOTH; *see* Sclater-Booth, family name of Baron Basing.

BOOTH, Alan Shore, QC 1975; **His Honour Judge Alan Booth;** a Circuit Judge, since 1976; *b* Aug. 1922; 4th *s* of Parkin Stanley Booth and Ethel Mary Shore; *m* 1954, Mary Gwendoline Hilton; one *s* one *d. Educ:* Shrewsbury Sch.; Liverpool Univ. (LLB). Served War of 1939-45, RNVR, Fleet Air Arm (despatches 1944): Sub-Lt 1942; HMS Illustrious, 1943-45; Lieut 1944. Called to Bar, Gray's Inn, 1949. A Recorder of the Crown Court, 1972-76. Governor, Shrewsbury Sch., 1969. *Recreations:* golf, reading. *Address:* 18 Abbey Road, West Kirby, Wirral L48 7EW. *T:* 051-625 5796. *Clubs:* Royal Liverpool Golf; Royal and Ancient (St Andrews).

BOOTH, Rt. Hon. Albert Edward, PC 1976; MP (Lab), Barrow-in-Furness since 1966; *b* 28 May 1928; *e s* of Albert Henry Booth and Janet Mathieson; *m* 1957, Joan Amis; three *s. Educ:* St Thomas's Sch., Winchester; S Shields Marine Sch.; Rutherford Coll. of Technology. Engineering Draughtsman. Election Agent, 1951 and 1955. County Borough Councillor, 1962-65. Contested (Lab) Tynemouth, 1964. Minister of State, Dept of Employment, 1974-76; Sec. of State for Employment, 1976-79; Opposition spokesman on

transport, 1980-. Chm., Select Cttee on Statutory Instruments, 1970-74. *Address:* House of Commons, SW1.

BOOTH, Catherine B.; *see* Bramwell-Booth.

BOOTH, Charles Leonard, CMG 1979; MVO 1961; HM Diplomatic Service; High Commissioner in Malta, since 1982; *b* 7 March 1925; *s* of Charles Leonard and Marion Booth; *m* 1958, Mary Gillian Emms, two *s* two *d. Educ:* Pembroke Coll., Oxford Univ., 1942-43 and 1947-50. Served RA (Capt.), 1943-47. Joined HM Foreign Service, 1950; Foreign Office, 1950-51; Third and Second Secretary, Rangoon, 1951-55; FO, 1955-60 (Private Sec. to Parly Under-Sec. of State, 1958-60); First Sec., Rome, 1960-63; Head of Chancery, Rangoon, 1963-64, and Bangkok, 1964-67; FO, 1967-69. Counsellor, 1968; Deputy High Comr, Kampala, 1969-71; Consul-General and Counsellor (Administration), Washington, 1971-73; Counsellor, Belgrade, 1973-77; Ambassador to Burma, 1978-82. Officer of Order of Merit of Italian Republic, 1961. *Recreations:* Italian opera, gardening, walking. *Address:* c/o Foreign and Commonwealth Office, SW1. *Club:* Travellers'.

BOOTH, Dr Christopher Charles; Director, Clinical Research Centre, Medical Research Council, since 1978; *b* 22 June 1924; *s* of Lionel Barton Booth and Phyllis Petley Duncan; *m* 1st, 1959, Lavinia Loughridge, Belfast; one *s* one *d* ; 2nd, 1970, Soad Tabaqchali; one *d. Educ:* Sedbergh Sch., Yorks; University of St Andrews; MB 1951, MD 1958 (Rutherford Gold Medal). Junior appointments at Dundee Royal Infirmary, Hammersmith Hosp. and Addenbrooke's Hosp., Cambridge; successively Medical Tutor, Lecturer in Medicine and Senior Lecturer, Postgraduate Medical School of London; Prof. and Dir of Dept of Medicine, RPMS, London Univ., 1966-77. Mem., MRC, 1981-. FRCP 1964; FRCPEd 1967; Hon. FACP 1973. For. Mem., Amer. Philosophical Soc., 1981. Docteur (*hc*): Paris, 1975; Poitiers, 1981; Hon. LLD Dundee, 1982. Dickie Gold Medal, Dutch Soc. of Gastroenterology, 1973. Chevalier de l'Ordre National du Mérite (France), 1977. *Publications:* (with Betsy C. Corner) Chain of Friendship: Letters of Dr John Fothergill of London, 1735-1780; papers in med. jls on relationship of nutritional disorders to disease of the alimentary tract, and on medical history. *Recreations:* fishing, history. *Address:* 33 Dukes Avenue, W4. *T:* 01-994 4914. *Club:* Athenæum.

BOOTH, Rev. Canon David Herbert, MBE 1944; Provost, Shoreham Grammar School, Sussex, since 1977 (Headmaster, 1972-77); Chaplain to the Queen, 1957-77; *b* 26 Jan. 1907; *s* of Robert and Clara Booth; *m* 1942, Diana Mary Chard; two *s* one *d. Educ:* Bedford Sch.; Pembroke Coll., Cambridge; Ely Theological Coll. BA (3rd cl. Hist. Trip. part II), 1931; MA 1936; deacon, 1932; priest, 1933; Curate, All Saints', Hampton, 1932-34; Chaplain, Tonbridge Sch., 1935-40; Chaplain, RNVR, 1940-45; Rector of Stepney, 1945-53; Vicar of Brighton, 1953-59; Prebendary of Waltham in Chichester Cathedral, 1953-59; Archdeacon of Lewes, 1959-71; Prebendary of Bury in Chichester Cathedral, 1972-76; Canon Emeritus of Chichester, 1976. Select Preacher, University of Cambridge, 1947. Mem. of Archbishop's Commission on South East, 1965. *Recreations:* horses, gardening and family life. *Address:* Hurst Mill Cottage, Ram Lane, Hothfield, Ashford, Kent. *T:* Pluckley 549.

BOOTH, Sir Douglas Allen, 3rd Bt, *cr* 1916; writer, mainly for television; *b* 2 Dec. 1949; *s* of Sir Philip Booth, 2nd Bt, and Ethel, *d* of Joseph Greenfield, NY, USA; *S* father 1960. *Educ:* Beverly Hills High Sch.; Harvard Univ. (Harvard Nat. Scholarship, Nat. Merit Scholarship, 1967); BA (magna cum laude) 1975. *Recreations:* music, back-packing. *Heir: b* Derek Blake Booth, *b* 7 April 1953. *Address:* 438 South Cochran, Apt 108, Los Angeles, Calif 90036, USA.

BOOTH, Eric Stuart, CBE 1971; FRS 1967; Chairman, Yorkshire Electricity Board, 1972-79; Member Central Electricity Generating Board, 1959-71; *b* 14 Oct. 1914; *s* of Henry and Annie Booth; *m* 1945, Mary Elizabeth Melton; two *d. Educ:* Batley Grammar Sch.; Liverpool Univ. Apprentice, Metropolitan Vickers Electrical Co. Ltd, 1936-38; Technical Engineer, Yorks Electric Power Co., 1938-46; Dep., later City Electrical Engineer and Manager, Salford Corporation, 1946-48; various posts associated with construction of Power Stations with British, later Central, Electricity Authority, 1948-57, Dep. Chief Engineer (Generation Design and Construction), 1957; Chief Design and Construction Engineer, Central Electricity Generating Bd, 1958-59. Part-time Mem., UKAEA, 1965-72; Pres., IEE, 1976-77. Consultant to Electricity Council, 1979-; Dir, British Electricity International, 1979-. *Address:* Pinecroft, Upper Dunsforth, York YO5 9RU. *T:* Boroughbridge 2821.

BOOTH, Sir Gordon, KCMG 1980 (CMG 1969); CVO 1976; HM Diplomatic Service, retired; adviser on international trade and investment; Director: Hanson Trust plc, since 1980; Trident Casinos, since 1980; Chairman, Simplification of International Trade Procedures Board, since 1980; *b* 22 Nov. 1921; *s* of Walter and Grace Booth, Bolton, Lancs; *m* 1944, Jeanne Mary Kirkham; one *s* one *d. Educ:* Canon Slade Sch.; London Univ. (BCom). Served War of 1939-45: Capt. RAC and 13/18th Royal Hussars, 1941-46. Min. of Labour and Bd of Trade, 1946-55; Trade Comr, Canada and West Indies, 1955-65; Mem. HM Diplomatic Service, 1965-80; Counsellor (Commercial), British Embassy in Copenhagen, 1966-69; Dir, Coordination of Export Services, DTI, 1969-71; Consul-General, Sydney, 1971-74; HBM Consul-Gen., NY, and Dir-Gen. of Trade Devel't in USA, 1975-80. Mem.

BOTB, 1981-. Advr to Port Authority of NY and NJ, 1982-. *Recreations:* golf, bridge. *Address:* Pilgrims Corner, Ebbisham Lane, Walton on the Hill, Surrey KT20 5BT. *T:* Tadworth 3788. *Clubs:* Brooks's; Walton Heath Golf.

BOOTH, James; His Honour Judge Booth; a Circuit Judge (formerly a County Court Judge), since 1969; *b* 3 May 1914; *s* of James and Agnes Booth; *m* 1954, Joyce Doreen Mather; two *s* one *d. Educ:* Bolton Sch.; Manchester Univ. Called to Bar, Gray's Inn, 1936 (Arden Scholar, Gray's Inn). Town Clerk, Ossett, Yorks, 1939-41. RAFVR, 1941-46 (Flt-Lieut). Contested (L): West Leeds, 1945; Darwen, 1950. Recorder of Barrow-in-Furness, 1967-69. *Recreation:* fell walking. *Address:* Spinney End, Worsley, Lancs M28 4QN. *T:* 061-790 2003. *Club:* Manchester (Manchester).

BOOTH, John Antony W.; *see* Ward-Booth.

BOOTH, John Dick L.; *see* Livingston Booth.

BOOTH, John Wells; *b* 19 May 1903; *s* of late Charles and Grace Wells Booth, Liverpool; *m* 1929, Margaret, *d* of late Mr and Mrs S. J. Lawry; two *s* one *d. Educ:* Royal Naval Colls Osborne and Dartmouth. Royal Navy, 1917-25 (Lieut Comdr). Booth Steamship Co. Ltd., 1926-45 (Chm., 1939-45); Dir, Alfred Booth & Co. Ltd, 1935-79 (Chm., 1952-74). Civil Aviation, 1945-50. Chm., British South American Airways Corporation, 1946-49; Dep. Chm., BOAC, 1949-50; Bd Mem., BOAC, 1950-65; Dir, Phoenix Assurance Co. Ltd, 1945-73. Former Chairman: Liverpool Seamens' Welfare Cttee (Mem. Seamens' Welfare Bd); Liverpool Steamship Owners' Assoc.; former JP for Co. of Cheshire. *Address:* Hill Cottage, Tripp Hill, Fittleworth, West Sussex. *Club:* Flyfishers'.

BOOTH, Hon. Dame Margaret (Myfanwy Wood), DBE 1979; **Hon. Mrs Justice Booth;** a Judge of the High Court, Family Division, since 1979; *b* 1933; *d* of late Alec Wood Booth and of Lilian May Booth. *Educ:* Northwood Coll.; University Coll., London (LLM; Fellow, 1982). Called to the Bar, Middle Temple, 1956; Bencher, 1979. QC 1976. Chm., Family Law Bar Assoc., 1976-78. Governor, Northwood Coll., 1975-; Mem. Council, Univ. Coll. London, 1980-. *Publications:* (co-ed) Rayden on Divorce, 10th-13th edns; (co-ed) Clarke Hall and Morrison on Children, 9th edn 1977. *Address:* c/o Royal Courts of Justice, Strand, WC2A 2LL.

BOOTH, Michael Addison John W.; *see* Wheeler-Booth.

BOOTH, Sir Michael Savile G.; *see* Gore-Booth.

BOOTH, Richard George William Pitt; Chairman, Richard Booth (Booksellers) Ltd, since 1961; *b* 12 Sept. 1938; *m* (marr. diss.). *Educ:* Rugby; Univ. of Oxford. Established Richard Booth (Booksellers) Ltd, 1961. *Publications:* Country Life Book of Book Collecting, 1976; Independence for Hay, 1977; Bureaucracy in Brecon and Radnor, 1982. *Recreations:* creating a monarchy in Hay (began home rule movement, 1 April 1977); gardening. *Address:* Hay Castle, Hay-on-Wye, via Hereford.

BOOTH, Sir Robert (Camm), Kt 1977; CBE 1967; TD; Chairman, National Exhibition Centre Ltd, 1975-82 (Founder Director, 1970-82; Chief Executive, 1977-78); *b* 9 May 1916; *s* of late Robert Wainhouse Booth; *m* 1939, Veronica Courtenay, *d* of late F. C. Lamb; one *s* three *d. Educ:* Altrincham Grammar Sch.; Manchester Univ. (LLB). Called to Bar, Gray's Inn. War Service 8th (A) Bn Manchester Regt, France, Malta, Middle East, Italy, 1939-46. Sec., Birmingham Chamber of Industry and Commerce, 1958-65, Dir, 1965-78, Pres., 1978-79. Local non-exec. dir, Barclays Bank, 1977-; Member: W Midlands Econ. Planning Council, 1974-77; BOTB Adv. Council, 1975-82; Midlands Adv. Bd, Legal and General Assurance Soc., 1979-; Midlands and NW Bd, BR, 1979-; Bd, Inst. of Occupational Health, 1980-. Trustee, Nuffield Trust for the Forces of the Crown, 1977-. Life Mem., Court of Governors, 1969, Birmingham Univ. (Mem. Council, 1973-78); Governor, Sixth Form Coll., Solihull, 1974-77; Hon. Mem., British Exhbns Promotions Council, 1982. Overseas travel with 20 trade missions and author of marketing and economic publications. Hon. DSc Aston, 1975; Hon. FInstM; FRSA 1975. Midland Man of the Year Press Radio and TV Award, 1970. Officer, Légion d'Honneur, 1982. *Address:* White House, 7 Sandal Rise, Solihull B9 3ET. *T:* 021-705 5311. *Club:* Naval and Military.

BOOTH, Rev. William James; Chaplain, Westminster School, London, since 1974; *b* 3 Feb. 1939; *s* of William James Booth and Elizabeth Ethel Booth (*née* Leckey). *Educ:* Ballymena Acad., Co. Antrim; TCD (MA). Curate, St Luke's Parish, Belfast, 1962-64; Chaplain, Cranleigh Sch., Surrey, 1965-74. Priest-in-Ordinary to The Queen, 1976-. *Recreations:* music, hi-fi, cooking. *Address:* 14 Barton Street, SW1P 3NE. *T:* 01-222 3707.

BOOTH-CLIBBORN, Rt. Rev. Stanley Eric Francis; *see* Manchester, Bishop of.

BOOTHBY, family name of Baron Boothby.

BOOTHBY, Baron *cr* 1958, of Buchan and Rattray Head (Life Peer); **Robert John Graham Boothby,** KBE 1953; President, Anglo-Israel Association, 1962-75; *b* 1900; *o s* of late Sir Robert Tuite Boothby, KBE, Beechwood, Edinburgh, and Mabel, *d* of late H. H. Lancaster; *m* 1st, 1935, Diana (marr.

diss. 1937), *d* of late Lord Richard Cavendish, PC, CB, CMG; 2nd, 1967, Wanda, *d* of Giuseppe Sanna, Sardinia. *Educ:* Eton; Magdalen Coll., Oxford. BA 1921, MA 1959. Contested Orkney and Shetland, 1923; MP (U) East Aberdeenshire, 1924-58; Parliamentary Private Sec. to the Chancellor of the Exchequer (Rt Hon. Winston S. Churchill, MP), 1926-29; Parliamentary Sec., Ministry of Food, 1940-41; a British delegate to the Consultative Assembly of the Council of Europe, 1949-57; Vice-Chm. Cttee on Economic Affairs, 1952-56; Hon. Pres., Scottish Chamber of Agriculture, 1934. Rector, University of St Andrews, 1958-61; Chm., Royal Philharmonic Orchestra, 1961-63, Hon. Life Mem., 1976; Vice-Pres., Delius Soc. Radner Lectr, Columbia Univ., NY, 1960. Hon. LLD St Andrews, 1959. Hon. Burgess of the Burghs of Peterhead, Fraserburgh, Turriff and Rosehearty. Officer of the Legion of Honour, 1950. *Publications:* The New Economy, 1943; I Fight to Live, 1947; My Yesterday, Your Tomorrow, 1962; Boothby: recollections of a rebel, 1978. *Address:* 1 Eaton Square, SW1. *Club:* Royal and Ancient (St Andrews).

BOOTHBY, Basil; *see* Boothby, E. B.

BOOTHBY, (Evelyn) Basil, CMG 1958; HM Diplomatic Service, retired; Tutor, London University Extra-Mural Studies, since 1970; *b* 9 Sept. 1910; *s* of Basil T. B. Boothby and Katherine Knox; *m* 1946, Susan Asquith; two *s* one *d* (and one *s* decd). *Educ:* Winchester; CCC, Cambridge. Student Interpreter, China Consular Service, 1933; appointed a Vice-Consul in China, 1936; served at Shanghai and Hankow (periods Acting Consul); Vice-Consul, Boston, 1940; employed at New York, Dec. 1941-June 1942, when reappointed a Vice-Consul in China and transf. to Chungking; seconded to Govt of India for service in Chinese Relations Office, Calcutta, Oct. 1943-July 1944; Actg Consul Kweilin and Kunming, also Athens, successively, 1944-45; promoted Consul, Sept. 1945; apptd Foreign Service Officer, Grade 7, in Foreign Office, Nov. 1946; promoted Counsellor, Foreign Service Officer, Grade 6, and became Head of UN (Economic and Social) Dept, Sept. 1949; seconded to Commonwealth Relations Office for service in Ontario and attached to Canadian National Defence Coll., Sept. 1950; apptd Counsellor, Rangoon, Nov. 1951 (Chargé d'Affaires, 1952); Counsellor, British Embassy, Brussels, 1954; Head of African Dept, Foreign Office, 1959; British Ambassador to Iceland, 1962-65; Permanent British Rep. to Council of Europe, 1965-69. Lectr, Morley Coll., 1969-70. *Address:* 23 Holland Park Avenue, W11.

See also P. P. Read.

BOOTHBY, Sir Hugo (Robert Brooke), 15th Bt, *cr* 1660; JP; Lieutenant, South Glamorgan, 1974-81 (Vice-Lieutenant of Glamorgan, 1957-74); *b* 10 Aug. 1907; *s* of Sir Seymour William Brooke Boothby, 14th Bt, and Clara Margaret (*d* 1969), *d* of late Robert Valpy; *S* father 1951; *m* 1938, Evelyn Ann, *o d* of H. C. R. Homfray; one *s* two *d. Educ:* Lancing; Hertford Coll., Oxford. Served War of 1939-45, Capt. RA 53 (Welsh) Div., 1942-44. Capt. RA (TA). Dir, Wales Tourist Bd, 1965-70; S Wales Regional Dir, Lloyds Bank, 1963-78; Dir, Divisional Bd for Wales, Nationwide Building Soc., 1971-; Member: Cardiff Rural Dist Council, 1936-58 (Chm. 1948-49 and 1949-50); Representative Body, Church in Wales, 1955-65; National Broadcasting Council for Wales, 1953-56; Glamorgan County Agricultural Executive Cttee, 1953-62; Court and Council, Nat. Museum of Wales, 1955. Chm., Historic Houses Assoc. in Wales. Fellow, Woodard Corporation, 1961-. JP 1950, DL 1953, Glamorgan; High Sheriff, Glamorgan, 1953. *Recreation:* shooting. Heir: *s* Brooke Charles Boothby [*b* 6 April 1949; *m* 1976, Georgiana Alexandra, *d* of Sir John (Wriothesley) Russell, *qv*; one *d*]. *Address:* Fonmon Castle, Barry, South Glamorgan CF6 9ZN. *T:* Rhoose 710206. *Clubs:* Brooks's; Cardiff and County (Cardiff).

BOOTHE, Clare; *see* Luce, Mrs Henry R.

BOOTHROYD, Basil; *see* Boothroyd, J. B.

BOOTHROYD, Betty; MP (Lab) West Bromwich West, since 1974 (West Bromwich, May 1973-1974); *b* Yorkshire, 8 Oct. 1929; *d* of Archibald and Mary Boothroyd. *Educ:* Dewsbury Coll. of Commerce and Art. Personal/Political Asst to Labour Ministers. Accompanied Parly delegns to: European Confs, 1955-60; Soviet Union, China and Vietnam, 1957; delegate to N Atlantic Assembly, 1974. An Asst Govt Whip, Oct. 1974-Nov. 1975; Mem., Select Cttee on Foreign Affairs, 1979-81; Mem., Speaker's Panel of Chairmen, 1979-. Mem., European Parlt, 1975-77. Mem., Labour Party NEC, 1981-. Worked with late President Kennedy's election campaign, 1960; Legislative Asst to US Congressman, 1960-62. Councillor, Hammersmith Borough Council, 1965-68. Contested (Lab): SE Leicester (by-elec.), 1957; Peterborough (gen. elec.), 1959; Nelson and Colne (by-elec.), 1968; Rossendale (gen. elec.), 1970. *Recreations:* dominoes, scrabble. *Address:* House of Commons, SW1A 0AA.

BOOTHROYD, (Edith) Hester, (Mrs Francis Boothroyd); *b* 11 Jan. 1915; *d* of late Stanley John Benham; *m* 1940, Francis Boothroyd; one *d* (and one *d* decd). *Educ:* St Felix Sch., Southwold; Newnham Coll., Cambridge (MA). Min. of Economic Warfare, 1939-44; BoT, 1945-49; Statistician and Prin., Treasury, 1949-64; Asst Sec., DEA, 1965-67, Asst Under-Sec. of State, DEA, 1967-69; Under-Sec., Treasury, 1969-75; Mem., Bd of Crown Agents, 1975-77. Hon. Treasurer, Aldeburgh Festival/Snape Maltings Foundn, 1976-81. Associate Fellow of Newnham Coll., Cambridge, 1981- (Associate, since

1975); *Recreations:* gardening, music, travel. *Address:* Ranworth House, Nayland, near Colchester CO6 4CJ. *T:* Nayland 262331.

BOOTHROYD, (John) Basil; writer and broadcaster; *b* 4 March 1910; *m* 1st, 1939, Phyllis Barbara Youngman (*d* 1980); one *s* ; 2nd, 1981, June Elizabeth Leonhardt Mortimer. *Educ:* Lincoln Cathedral Choir Sch.; Lincoln Sch. Bank Clerk, 1927. Served with RAF Police, 1941-45; Personal Asst to Provost-Marshal from 1943. Punch contributor continuously from 1938, an Asst Editor, 1952-70, Mem. Punch Table, 1955. Much broadcasting and miscellaneous frivolous journalism; some lecturing and public speaking. Imperial Tobacco Radio Award, best comedy script, 1976. *Television includes:* adaptation of: The Diary of a Nobody, BBC series, 1979; A. J. Wentworth, BA, ITV series, 1982. *Publications:* Home Guard Goings-On, 1941; Adastral Bodies, 1942; Are Sergeants Human? 1945; Are Officers Necessary?, 1946; Lost, A Double-Fronted Shop, 1947; The House About a Man, 1959; Motor If You Must, 1960; To My Embarrassment, 1961; The Whole Thing's Laughable, 1964; You Can't be Serious, 1966; Let's Stay Married, 1967 (and US, 1967); Stay Married Abroad, 1968; Boothroyd at Bay (radio talks), 1970; Philip (an approved biography of HRH the Duke of Edinburgh), 1971 (and US, 1971); Accustomed As I Am, 1975; Let's Move House, 1977; In My State of Health, 1981. *Recreations:* playing the piano, working. *Address:* Peelers, Church Street, Cuckfield, Sussex. *T:* Haywards Heath 454340/412173. *Club:* Savage.

BOOTLE-WILBRAHAM, family name of **Baron Skelmersdale.**

BOR, Walter George, CBE 1975; FRIBA, DistTP; FRTPI; Consultant, Llewelyn-Davies Weeks, since 1976; Partner, Llewelyn-Davies Weeks Forestier-Walker & Bor, London, 1966-76; *b* 1916, Czech parentage; father chemical engineer; two *s* one *d. Educ:* Prague Univ. (degree of Arch.); Bartlett Sch. of Architecture and Sch. of Planning and Regional Research, London (Dip.). Private architectural practice, London, 1946-47; London County Council, 1947-62 (in charge of planning of London's East End, 1958; Dep. Planning Officer with special responsibility for civic design, 1960-62); Liverpool City Planning Officer, 1962-66. Mem. Minister's Planning Advisory Gp, 1964-65. In private practice as architect and planning consultant, 1966-. Pres., Town Planning Inst., 1970-71; Vice-Pres., Housing Centre Trust, 1971-. Visiting Professor: Princeton Univ., 1977-79; Rice Univ., Houston, 1980-81. Mem., Severn Barrage Cttee, 1978-81. *Publications:* Liverpool Interim Planning Policy, 1965; Liverpool City Centre Plan (jt), 1966; Two New Cities in Venezuela (jt), 1967-69; The Milton Keynes Plan (jt), 1970; Airport City (Third London Airport urbanisation studies) (jt), 1970; The Making of Cities, 1972; Urban Motorways Studies for DOE (jt), 1972; SE London and the Fleet Line for LTE (jt), 1973; Bogota Urban Development for UNDP (jt), 1974; Concept Plan for Tehran new city centre, 1974; Shetland Draft Structure Plan, 1975; (jtly) Birmingham Inner Area Study, 1977; articles for jls of RTPI, RIBA, TCPA, ICE, RICS, Amer. Inst. of Planners, Princeton Univ.; L'Architecture d'aujourd'hui, Urbanistica, Habitat Internat.; Ekistics. *Recreations:* music, theatre, skiing, tennis, swimming, sketching, sculpting. *Address:* 99 Swains Lane, Highgate, N6 6PJ. *T:* 01-340 6540. *Club:* Reform.

BORDEN, Henry, OC 1969; CMG 1943; QC 1938; Canadian Lawyer; Hon. Director, Canada Trustco Mortgage Co.; *b* Halifax, NS, 25 Sept. 1901; *s* of Henry Clifford and Mabel (Ashmere) Barnstead Borden, both of Halifax, NS; *m* 1929, Jean Creelman, *d* of late Dr D. A. MacRae, Toronto, Ont; three *s* two *d. Educ:* King's Coll. Sch., Windsor, NS; McGill Univ.; Dalhousie Law Sch.; Exeter Coll., Oxford (Rhodes Schol.). BA Political Science and Economics, McGill, 1921; BA Oxon, 1926. With Royal Bank of Canada, 1921-22. Called to Bar, Lincoln's Inn, 1927; to Bar of Nova Scotia, 1927; to Bar of Ont, 1927. Senior Mem., Borden, Elliot, Kelley, Palmer, 1936-46; Gen. Counsel, Dept of Munitions and Supply, Ottawa, 1939-42; Chairman: Wartime Industries Control Bd, Ottawa, and Co-ordinator of Controls, Dept of Munitions and Supply, Sept. 1942-43; Royal Commission on Energy, 1957-59. Pres., Brazilian Traction, Light & Power Co., 1946-63, Chm., 1963-65; Chm. and Pres., Brinco Ltd (formerly British Newfoundland Corporation Ltd), 1965-69; Dir Emeritus, Canadian Imperial Bank of Commerce; Dir, Mem. Exec. Cttee and Past Pres., Royal Agric. Winter Fair. Formerly Lectr, Corp. Law, Osgoode Hall Law Sch.; Past Pres. Canadian Club of Toronto. Past Chm., Bd of Governors, Univ. of Toronto. Hon. LLD: St Francis Xavier, 1960; Dalhousie, 1968; Toronto, 1972; Hon. DCL Acadia, 1960. Is an Anglican. Grand Officer, Nat. Order of the Southern Cross (Brazil), 1962; Canada Centennial Medal, 1967. *Publications:* (jtly) Fraser & Borden, Hand Book of Canadian Companies, 1931; ed, Robert Laird Borden: His Memoirs, 1938; ed, Letters to Limbo, by Rt Hon. Sir Robert L. Borden, 1971. *Recreations:* farming, fishing. *Address:* Vinegar Hill, RR No 2, King, Ont. L0G 1K0, Canada. *Club:* York (Toronto).

BOREEL, Sir Francis (David), 13th Bt, *cr* 1645; Counsellor, Netherlands Foreign Service, since 1966 (Attaché, 1956); *b* 14 June 1926; *s* of Sir Alfred Boreel, 12th Bt and Countess Reiniera Adriana (*d* 1957), *d* of Count Francis David Schimmelpenninck; *S* father 1964; *m* 1964, Suzanne Campagne; three *d. Educ:* Utrecht Univ. *Recreations:* tennis, sailing. *Heir:* kinsman Stephen Gerard Boreel [*b* 9 Feb. 1945; *m* Francien P. Kooyman; one *s*]. *Address:* Netherlands Embassy, Strässchensweg 10, 5300 Bonn 1, Germany.

BOREHAM, Sir (Arthur) John, KCB 1980 (CB 1974); Director, Central Statistical Office, and Head of the Government Statistical Service, since 1978;

b 30 July 1925; 3rd *s* of late Ven. Frederick Boreham, Archdeacon of Cornwall and Chaplain to the Queen, and late Caroline Mildred Boreham; *m* 1948, Heather, *o d* of Harold Edwin Horth, FRIBA, and Muriel Horth; three *s* one *d. Educ:* Marlborough; Trinity Coll., Oxford. Agricultural Economic Research Inst., Oxford, 1950; Min. of Food, 1951; Min. of Agric., 1952; Gen. Register Office, 1955; Central Statistical Office, 1958; Chief Statistician, Gen. Register Office, 1963; Dir of Economics and Statistics, Min. of Technology 1967-71; Central Statistical Office: Asst Dir, 1971-72; Dep. Dir, 1972-78. Vis. Fellow, Nuffield Coll., Oxford, 1981-. *Recreations:* music, golf. *Address:* Piperscroft, Brittain's Lane, Sevenoaks, Kent. *T:* Sevenoaks 54678.

BOREHAM, Hon. Sir Leslie Kenneth Edward, Kt 1972; **Hon. Mr Justice Boreham;** a Judge of the High Court, Queen's Bench Division, since 1972 Presiding Judge, North Eastern Circuit, 1974-79; Deputy Chairman Agricultural Lands Tribunal; *m* ; one *s* one *d.* Served War of 1939-45, RAF Called to the Bar at Lincoln's Inn, Nov. 1947; Bencher 1972. QC 1965 Recorder of Margate, 1968-71. Joined South-Eastern Circuit. Dep. Chm 1962-65, Chm. 1965-71, East Suffolk QS. *Recreations:* gardening, golf *Address:* 1 Paper Buildings, Temple, EC4.

BORG, Alan Charles Nelson, PhD; FSA; Director, Imperial War Museum since 1982; *b* 21 Jan. 1942; *s* of Charles John Nelson Borg and Frances Mary Olive Hughes; *m* 1st, 1964, Anne (marr. diss.), *d* of late Dr William Blackmore; one *s* one *d* ; 2nd, 1976, Caroline, *d* of late Captain Lord (Arthur) Francis (Henry) Hill; two *d. Educ:* Westminster Sch.; Brasenose Coll., Oxford (MA); Courtauld Inst. of Art (PhD). Lecteur d'anglais, Université d'Aix-Marseille, 1964-65; Lectr, History of Art, Indiana Univ., 1967-69; Asst Prof of History of Art, Princeton Univ., 1969-70; Asst Keeper of the Armouries HM Tower of London, 1970-78; Keeper, Sainsbury Centre for Visual Arts Univ. of E Anglia, 1978-82. *Publications:* Architectural Sculpture in Romanesque Provence, 1972; European Swords and Daggers in the Tower o London, 1974; Torture and Punishment, 1975; Heads and Horses, 1976; Arms and Armour in Britain, 1979; (ed with A. R. Martindale) The Vanishing Past studies presented to Christopher Hohler; articles in learned jls. *Recreations* music, travel. *Address:* Imperial War Museum, Lambeth Road, SE1 6HZ. *T* 01-735 8922.

See also J. Cooper.

BORG, Björn Rune; tennis player; *b* 6 June 1956; *s* of Rune and Margaretha Borg; *m* 1980, Mariana Simionescu. *Educ:* Blombacka Sch., Södertälje. Started to play tennis at age of 9; won Wimbledon junior title, 1972; became professional player in 1972. Mem., Swedish Davis Cup team, annually 1972-80 (youngest player ever in a winning Davis Cup team, 1975). Championship titles: Italian, 1974, 1978; French, 1974, 1975, 1978, 1979, 1980, 1981 Wimbledon, record of 5 consecutive singles titles, 1976-80; World Champion 1979, 1980; Masters, 1980, 1981. *Publication:* (with Eugene Scott) Björn Borg my life and game, 1980. *Address:* c/o International Management Group, 58 Queen Anne Street, W1.

BORG COSTANZI, Prof. Edwin J.; Visiting Fellow, Faculty of Mathematical Studies, University of Southampton, since 1980; *b* 8 Sept. 1925 2nd *s* of late Michael Borg Costanzi and M. Stella (*née* Camilleri); *m* 1948 Lucy Valentino; two *s* one *d. Educ:* Lyceum, Malta; Royal University on Malta (BSc, BE&A); Balliol College, Oxford (BA 1946, MA 1952); Malta Rhodes Scholar, 1945. Professor of Mathematics, Royal University of Malta 1950-64; Rector, Old Univ., Malta (formerly Univ. of Malta), 1964-80 Chm., 1976-77, Mem., 1965-66, 1968-69, 1972-74, 1977-78, Council of ACU *Recreations:* fishing, photography. *Address:* Computer Studies Group University of Southampton, Highfield, Southampton SO9 5NH. *Club* Casino (Valletta, Malta).

BORGES, Jorge Luis; poet; Director, National Library of Argentina, 1955-73 *b* Buenos Aires, 24 Aug. 1899; *s* of late Jorge Borges and Leonor Acevedo de Borges. *Educ:* Collège de Géneve; Univ. of Cambridge. Prof. of English and N American Literature, Univ. of Buenos Aires, 1955-70. Member Argentine Nat. Acad., 1955; Uruguayan Acad. of Letters; Goethe Acad. of São Paulo, Brazil; Pres., Argentine Writers' Assoc., 1950-53 (grand prize 1945) Hon. Pres., Argentine branch, Dickens Fellowship of London; Vice-Pres. Amigos de la Literatura Inglesa. Hon. DLitt Oxford 1970; Hon. Dr Jerusalem 1971. Premio de Honor, Prix Formentor (with Samuel Beckett), 1961; Fondo de las Artes, 1963. Hon. KBE. *Publications: poems:* Fervor de Buenos Aires 1923; Luna de Enfrente, 1925; Cuaderno San Martín, 1929; Elogio de la Sombra, 1969 (trans. as In Praise of Darkness, 1975); Selected Poems 1923-1967, 1972; *essays:* Inquisiciones, 1925; El Idioma de los Argentinos, 1928 Evaristo Carriego, 1930; Discusión, 1932; Historia de la Eternidad, 1936 Antología Clásica de la Literatura Argentina, 1942; Nueva Refutación de Tiempo, 1947; Otras Inquisiciones, 1937-52, 1952 (trans. as Other Inquisitions 1964); *stories:* Historia Universal de la Infamia, 1935; Tlön, Uqbar, Orbi Tertius, 1938; El Jardín de Senderos que se bifurcan, 1941; Ficciones, 1945 (trans. 1962); El Aleph, 1949 (trans. 1973); La Muerte y la Brújula, 1951; (with Adolfo Bioy-Casares) Cronicas de Bustos Domecq, 1967 (trans. as Chronicle of Bustos Domecq, 1982); El Informe de Brodie, 1971 (trans. as Dr Brodie's Report, 1974); El libro de arena, 1975; Obras completas, 1975; (with Adolfo Bioy-Casares) Six Problems for Don Isidro Parodi, 1981; *collections:* E Hacedor, 1960 (trans. as Dreamtigers, 1964); Antología Personal, 1961 (trans as A Personal Anthology, 1962); Labyrinthe, 1960 (trans. as Labyrinths, 1962) El Libra de los Seres Imaginarios (with Margarita Guerrero), 1967 (trans. a The Book of Imaginary Beings, 1969); Prólogos, 1975; The Book of Sand

1979. *Recreations:* study of Old English and of Old Norse. *Address:* Maipú 994, Buenos Aires, Argentina.

BORGES, Thomas William Alfred; Managing Director, Thomas Borges & Partners Ltd, since 1949; Chairman, Smith Whitworth Ltd, since 1974; *b* 1 April 1923; *s* of Arthur Borges, Prague, and Paula Borges; *m* 1st (marr. diss.); 2nd, 1966, Serena Katherine Stewart (*née* Jamieson); two *s*. *Educ:* Dunstable Grammar Sch.; Luton Technical Coll. Served War, 1941-45. Trained in banking, shipping and industry, 1945-49; Dir, Borges Law & Co., Sydney and Melbourne, 1951. Governor, Royal National Orth. Hosp., 1968- (Dep. Chm., 1978-80, Chm., 1980-82); Dir, Inst. of Orths, Univ. of London, 1968- (Dep. Chm., 1978-80, Chm., 1980-82); Member: Grants Cttee, King Edward VII Hosp. Fund, 1975-80; Council, Professions Supp. to Medicine, 1980- (Dep. Chm., 1982); Treasurer, Riding for Disabled Assoc., 1977-. *Publication:* Two Expeditions of Discovery in North West and Western Australia by George Grey, 1969. *Recreations:* travel, collecting Australiana, restoring old buildings, swimming, gardening. *Address:* 10 Regent's Park Terrace, NW1 7EE. *T:* 01-485 4855. *Clubs:* Athenæum, Garrick.

BORINGDON, Viscount; Mark Lionel Parker; *b* 22 Aug. 1956; *s* and *heir* of 6th Earl of Morley, *qv*. *Educ:* Eton. Commissioned, Royal Green Jackets, 1976. *Address:* Pound House, Yelverton, Devon.

BORLAND, David Morton; former Chairman, Cadbury Ltd; Director, Cadbury Schweppes Ltd; *b* 17 Jan. 1911; *s* of David and Annie J. Borland; *m* 1947, Nessa Claire Helwig; one *s* one *d*. *Educ:* Glasgow Academy; Brasenose Coll., Oxford (BA). Management Trainee, etc., Cadbury Bros Ltd, Bournville, Birmingham, 1933. War service, Royal Marines (Lieut-Col), 1940-46. Sales Manager, J. S. Fry & Sons Ltd, Somerdale, Bristol, 1946; Sales Dir and a Man. Dir, J. S. Fry & Sons Ltd, 1948; a Man. Dir, British Cocoa & Chocolate Co. Ltd, 1959, and of Cadbury Bros Ltd, 1963. Mem. Council of Bristol Univ. and of Univ. Appts Bd, 1962; Mem. Govt Cttee of Inquiry into Fatstock and Meat Marketing and Distribution, 1962. Hon. LLD Bristol, 1980. *Recreations:* golf, sailing. *Address:* Garden Cottage, 3 Hollymead Lane, Stoke Bishop, Bristol BS9 1LN. *T:* Bristol 683978. *Clubs:* Achilles; Vincent's (Oxford).

BORLAUG, Norman Ernest, PhD; Director of Wheat Improvement Program, International Center for Maize and Wheat Improvement; *b* 25 March 1914; *s* of Henry O. and Clara Vaala Borlaug; *m* 1937, Margaret Gibson; one *s* one *d*. *Educ:* Univ. of Minnesota; BS 1937; MS 1940; PhD 1942. US Forest Service (USDA), 1935-1937-1938; Biologist, Dupont de Nemours & Co, 1942-44; Plant Pathologist and Genetist, Wheat Improvement, employed by Rockefeller Foundn (Associate Dir of Agricultural Sciences) and Dir of Wheat Program, International Center for Maize and Wheat Improvement (CIMMYT), 1944-. Dir, Population Crisis Cttee, 1971; Asesor Especial, Fundación para Estudios de la Población (Mexico), 1971-; Member: Adv. Council, Renewable Natural Resources Foundn, 1973-; Citizens' Commn on Science, Law and Food Supply, 1973-; Council for Agricl Science and Tech., 1973-; Commn on Critical Choices for Americans 1973-. Outstanding Achievement Award, Univ. of Minnesota, 1959; Mem., Nat. Acad. of Sciences (USA), 1968; Sitara-Imtiaz (Star of Distinction) (Pakistan), 1968, Hilal-I-Imtiaz 1978. Nobel Peace Prize, 1970. Holds numerous hon. doctorates in Science, both from USA and abroad; and more than 30 Service Awards by govts and organizations, including US Medal of Freedom, 1977. *Publications:* more than 70 scientific and semi-popular articles. *Recreations:* hunting, fishing, baseball, wrestling, football, golf. *Address:* c/o International Center for Maize and Wheat Improvement (CIMMYT), Apartado Postal 6-641, Londres 40, Mexico 6 DF, Mexico. *T:* 585-43-55.

BORLEY, Lester; Chief Executive, English Tourist Board, since 1975; *b* 7 April 1931; *er s* of Edwin Richard Borley and Mary Dorena Davies; *m* Mary Alison, *e d* of Edward John Pearce and Kathleen Florence Barratt; three *d*. *Educ:* Dover Grammar Sch.; Queen Mary Coll. and Birkbeck Coll., London Univ. Pres. of Union, QMC, 1953; Dep. Pres., Univ. of London Union, 1954; ESU debating team tour of USA, 1955. Joined British Travel Assoc., 1955; Asst to Gen. Man., USA, 1957-61; Manager: Chicago Office, 1961-64; Australia, 1964-67; West Germany, 1967-69; Chief Executive, Scottish Tourist Bd, 1970-75. Member: Exec. Cttee, Scotland's Garden Scheme, 1970-75; Council, Nat. Gardens Scheme, 1975-; Park and Gardens Cttee, Zool Soc. of London, 1979-. Founder Fellow, Tourism Soc., 1978. Hon. Kentucky Col, 1963. *Recreations:* listening to music, looking at pictures, gardening. *Address:* 27 Blandy Road, Henley-on-Thames, Oxon. *T:* Henley-on-Thames 6613. *Club:* Caledonian.

BORN, Gustav Victor Rudolf, FRCP 1976; FRS 1972; Professor of Pharmacology, King's College, University of London, since 1978; *b* 29 July 1921; *s* of late Prof. Max Born, FRS; *m* 1st, 1950, Wilfrida Ann Plowden-Wardlaw (marr. diss., 1961); two *s* one *d*; 2nd, 1962, Dr Faith Elizabeth Maurice-Williams; one *s* one *d*. *Educ:* Oberrealschule, Göttingen; Perse Sch., Cambridge; Edinburgh Academy; University of Edinburgh. Vans Dunlop Scholar; MB, ChB, 1943; DPhil (Oxford), 1951, MA 1956. Med. Officer, RAMC, 1943-47; Mem. Scientific Staff, MRC, 1952-53; Research Officer, Nuffield Inst. for Med. Research, 1953-60 and Deptl Demonstrator in Pharmacology, 1956-60, University of Oxford; Vandervell Prof. of Pharmacology, RCS and Univ. of London, 1960-73; Sheild Prof. of Pharmacology, Univ. of Cambridge, and Fellow, Gonville and Caius Coll., Cambridge, 1973-78. Vis. Prof. in Chem., NW Univ., Illinois, 1970-; William

S. Creasy Vis. Prof. in Clin. Pharmacol., Brown Univ., 1977. Hon. Dir, MRC Thrombosis Res. Gp, 1964-73. Pres., Internat. Soc. on Thrombosis and Haemostasis, 1977-79; Trustee, Heineman Med. Res. Center, Charlotte, NC; Scientific Adviser, Vandervell Foundn. Member: Ed. Board, Heffters' Handbook of Experimental Pharmacology; Cttee of Enquiry into Relationship of Pharmaceut. Industry with Nat. Health Service (Sainsbury Cttee), 1965-67; Sci. Council, Fondation Cardiologique Princesse Liliane Coronary Sclerosis Commn, Fritz-Thyssen Foundn, Cologne; Hon. Life Mem., New York Acad. of Scis. Lectures: Beyer, Wisconsin Univ., 1969; Sharpey-Schäfer, Edinburgh Univ., 1973; Cross, RCS, 1974; Wander, Bern Univ., 1974; Johnson Meml, Paris, 1975; Lo Yuk Tong Foundn, Hong Kong Univ., and Heineman Meml, Charlotte, NC, 1978; Carlo Erba Foundn, Milan, 1979; Sir Henry Dale, RCS, 1981. Chevalier de l'Ordre National de Mérite, France, 1980. Mem., Akad. Leopoldina; Corresp. Mem., German Pharmacological Soc. Hon. Fellow, St Peter's Coll., Oxford, 1972; Dr *hc:* Bordeaux, 1978; Münster, 1980; Leuven, 1981; Edinburgh, 1982. Albrecht von Haller Medal, Göttingen Univ., 1979; Ratschow Medal, Internat. Kur. of Angiology, 1980. *Publications:* articles in scientific jls and books. *Recreations:* music, walking. *Address:* King's College, Strand, WC2R 2LS; 10 Woodland Gardens, N10. *T:* 01-444 7911. *Club:* Garrick.

BORNEMAN, Roy Ernest, QC 1952; *b* 1904; *s* of Ernest Borneman, London; *m* 1st, 1932, Winifred Dixon, *d* of Dr William Hunter, Aberdeen; two *s*; 2nd, 1973, Sarah Anderson, *d* of Thomas Paterson, North Berwick. *Educ:* University Coll., Reading; University Coll., London. BA 1924. Called to the Bar, Gray's Inn, 1929; Bencher, 1956; Treasurer, 1972; Vice-Treasurer, 1973. Chm., Board of Referees and Finance Act 1960 Tribunal, 1960-77. Served War of 1939-45, Wing Comdr, Royal Air Force. *Recreations:* golf, music, travel. *Address:* 11 New Square, Lincoln's Inn, WC2; Spindles, Hotley Bottom Lane, Prestwood, Great Missenden, Bucks. *T:* Great Missenden 4858.

BORODALE, Viscount; Sean David Beatty; *b* 12 June 1973; *s* and *heir* of 3rd Earl Beatty, *qv*.

BORODIN, George; see Sava, George.

BORRADAILE, Maj.-Gen. Hugh Alastair, CB 1959; DSO 1946; Vice Adjutant-General, War Office, 1960-63, retired; *b* 22 June 1907; *s* of late Lt-Col B. Borradaile, RE, Walnut Cottage, Wylye, Wilts; *m* 1936, Elizabeth Barbara, *d* of late R. Powell-Williams, Woodcroft, Yelverton, Devon; one *s* one *d*. *Educ:* Wellington Coll.; RMC Sandhurst. Commissioned Devon Regt, 1926; King's African Rifles, 1931-37; Staff Coll., Camberley, 1939; GSO1, GHQ West Africa, 1942-43; CO 5, E Lancs Regt, 1944; CO 7 Somerset LI, 1944-45; GSO1, 30 Corps, 1945; Asst Chief of Staff (Exec.), CCG, 1945-46; CO 1 Devon, 1946-48; Dep. Chief Intelligence Div., CCG, 1948-50; National Defence Coll., Canada, 1950-51; Brig. A/Q AA Command, 1951-53; Comd 24 Inf. Bde, 1953-55; Dept Military Sec. (A), War Office, 1955-57; Gen. Officer Commanding South-West District and 43rd (Wessex) Infantry Div., TA, 1957-60. Col, Devon and Dorset Regt, 1962-67. Master, Worshipful Co. of Drapers', 1971-72 (Liveryman 1956-). *Recreations:* golf, shooting, fishing. *Address:* Almora, 33 Park Avenue, Camberley, Surrey. *T:* Camberley 21827. *Club:* Army and Navy.

BORRETT, Ven. Charles Walter; Archdeacon of Stoke-upon-Trent and Hon. Canon of Lichfield Cathedral, 1971-82, now Archdeacon Emeritus; Priest-in-charge of Sandon, Diocese of Lichfield, 1975-82; a Chaplain to the Queen, since 1980; *b* 15 Sept. 1916; *s* of Walter George Borrett, farmer, and Alice Frances (*née* Mecrow); *m* 1941, Jean Constable, *d* of Charles Henry and Lilian Constable Pinson, Wolverhampton; one *s* two *d*. *Educ:* Framlingham Coll., Suffolk; Emmanuel Coll., Cambridge (MA); Ridley Hall, Cambridge. Deacon, 1941; Priest, 1943; Curate: of All Saints, Newmarket, 1941-45; of St Paul, Wolverhampton, 1945-48; of Tettenhall Regis, 1948-49; Vicar of Tettenhall Regis, 1949-71; Rural Dean of Trysull, 1958-71; Prebendary of Flixton in Lichfield Cathedral, 1964-71. Chm., C of E Council for Deaf, 1976-. Fellow, Woodard Schs. *Recreations:* golf, riding. *Address:* 34 Queensway, Mildenhall, Bury St Edmunds IP28 7JL. *T:* Mildenhall 712718. *Club:* Hawks (Cambridge).

BORRETT, Louis Albert Frank; barrister-at-law; a Recorder of the Crown Court, since 1980; *b* 8 Aug. 1924; *e s* of late Albert B. Borrett and Louise Alfreda Eudoxie Forestier; *m* 1946, Barbara Betty, *er d* of late Frederick Charles Bamsey and of Lily Gertrude Thompson. *Educ:* France and England; Folkestone Teachers' Trng Coll.; King's Coll., Univ. of London (LLB 1954). Called to the Bar, Gray's Inn, 1955. Served War, Army: volunteered, 1940; RASC, London Dist and South Eastern Comd; commnd Royal Sussex Regt, 1944; served India and Burma Border; Intell. Officer, 9th Royal Sussex, during invasion of Malaya, 1945; GSO III (Ops), ALFSEA, 1946 (Burma Star, Defence Medal, Victory Medal); demob., 1946 (Captain). Schoolmaster, 1947-53; barrister, in practice on South-Eastern circuit, 1955-; Asst Comr, Boundary Commn, 1964-67. *Recreations:* hunting, horse riding, music, the French language. *Address:* Queen Elizabeth Building, Temple, EC4Y 9BS. *T:* 01-353 0832; 54 Farm Close, East Grinstead, West Sussex RH19 3QG. *T:* East Grinstead 312350; Chantry Cottage, Tunstall, Woodbridge, Suffolk IP12 2JW.

BORRIE, Sir Gordon Johnson, Kt 1982; Director General of Fair Trading, since 1976; *b* 13 March 1931; *s* of Stanley Borrie, Solicitor; *m* 1960, Dorene, *d* of Herbert Toland, Toronto, Canada; no *c. Educ:* John Bright Grammar Sch., Llandudno; Univ. of Manchester (LLB, LLM). Barrister-at-Law and Harmsworth Scholar of the Middle Temple; called to Bar, Middle Temple, 1952; Bencher, 1980. Nat. Service: Army Legal Services, HQ Brit. Commonwealth Forces in Korea, 1952-54. Practice as a barrister, London, 1954-57. Lectr and later Sen. Lectr, Coll. of Law, 1957-64; Sen. Lectr in Law, Univ. of Birmingham, 1965-68; Prof. of English Law and Dir, Inst. of Judicial Admin, Birmingham Univ., 1969-76, and Dean of Faculty of Law, 1974-76. Member: Law Commn Adv. Panel on Contract Law, 1966-; Parole Bd for England and Wales, 1971-74; CNAA Legal Studies Bd, 1971-76; Circuit Adv. Cttee, Birmingham Gp of Courts, 1972-74; Council, Consumers' Assoc., 1972-75; Consumer Protection Adv. Cttee, 1973-76; Equal Opportunities Commn, 1975-76. Sen. Treasurer, Nat. Union of Students, 1955-58. Contested (Lab): Croydon, NE, 1955; Ilford, S, 1959. Gov., Birmingham Coll. of Commerce, 1966-70. *Publications:* Public Law (2nd edn), 1970; The Consumer, Society and the Law (with Prof. A. L. Diamond) (3rd edn), 1973, 4th edn 1981; Law of Contempt (with N. V. Lowe), 1973; Stevens and Borrie's Mercantile Law (16th edn), 1973; Commercial Law (5th edn), 1980. *Recreations:* gardening, gastronomy, piano playing, travel. *Address:* Manor Farm, Abbots Morton, Worcestershire. *T:* Inkberrow 792330; 33 Sloane Gardens, SW1. *T:* 01-730 5443. *Club:* Reform.

BORRIE, Peter Forbes, MD, FRCP; retired; Physician in charge of the Skin Department, St Bartholomew's Hospital, 1968-78; Consultant Dermatologist to Moorfields, Westminster and Central Eye Hospitals, 1950-78, and to Barnet General Hospital, 1954-78; *b* 26 March 1918; *s* of late Dr David Forbes Borrie and Martha Ruth Downing; *m* 1942, Helen Patricia, *e d* of Major H. G. Chesney; two *s* two *d. Educ:* Rugby Sch.; Clare Coll., Cambridge; St Bartholomew's Hospital. BA (Nat. Sci. Tripos) 1939; MB, BChir Cantab 1942; MRCP 1948; FRCP 1960; MA Cantab 1950; MD Cantab 1951. House Physician, St Bartholomew's Hospital, 1942; Senior Registrar, Skin Dept, St Mary's Hospital, Paddington, 1948; Chief Asst, Skin Dept, St Bartholomew's Hospital, 1950. Fellow Royal Society of Medicine; Mem. British Association of Dermatology; Lecturer at the Institute of Dermatology. *Publications:* Editor, Roxburgh's Common Skin Diseases, 11th-14th edns, 1959-75; Modern Trends in Dermatology, Series iv, 1971; many articles in medical journals. *Address:* Daymer Dunes, Trebetherick, Wadebridge, Cornwall PL27 6SF. *T:* Trebetherick 2315.

BORTHWICK, Jason; *see* Borthwick, W. J. M.

BORTHWICK OF BORTHWICK, Major John Henry Stuart, TD 1943; DL, JP; The Borthwick of Borthwick; 24th Lord Borthwick; Baron of Heriotmuir, Borthwick and Locherwart; Chairman: Heriotmuir Properties Ltd, since 1965; Heriotmuir Exporters Ltd, since 1972; Director, Ronald Morrison & Co. Ltd, since 1972; *b* 13 Sept. 1905; *s* of Henry, 23rd Lord Borthwick (*d* 1937); *m* 1938, Margaret Frances (*d* 1976), *d* of Alexander Campbell Cormack, Edinburgh; twin *s. Educ:* Fettes Coll., Edinburgh; King's Coll. Newcastle (DipAgric 1926). Formerly RATA, re-employed 1939; served NW Europe, Allied Mil. Govt Staff (Junior Staff Coll., SO 2), 1944; CCG (CO 1, Lt-Col), 1946. Dept of Agriculture for Scotland, 1948-50; farming own farms, 1950-71; Partner in Crookston Farms, 1971-79. National Farmers Union of Scotland: Mid and West Lothian Area Cttee, 1967-73 (Pres. 1970-72); Mem. Council, 1968-72; Member: Lothians Area Cttee, NFU Mutual Insurance Soc., 1969; Scottish Southern Regional Cttee, Wool Marketing Bd, 1966. Mem., Scottish Landowners' Fedn, 1937- (Mem., Land Use Cttee, 1972; Mem., Scottish Livestock Export Gp, 1972). Chm., Area Cttee, South of Scotland Electricity Bd Consultative Council, 1972-76. Chm., Monitoring Cttee for Scottish Tartans, 1976. County Councillor, Midlothian, 1937-48; JP 1938; DL Midlothian (now Lothian Region), 1965; Member: Local Appeal Tribunal (Edinburgh and the Lothians), 1963-75; Midlothian Valuation Appeal Cttee, 1966-78. Member: Standing Council of Scottish Chiefs; The Committee of the Baronage of Scotland (International Delegate); Mem. Corresp., Istituto Italiano di Genealogia e Araldica, Rome and Madrid, 1964; Hon. Mem., Council of Scottish Clans Assoc., USA, 1975. Hon. Mem., Royal Military Inst. of Canada, 1976. KLJ, GCLJ 1975; Comdr, Rose of Lippe, 1971. *Recreations:* shooting, travel, history. *Heir: er twin s* John Hugh, Master of Borthwick [*b* 14 Nov. 1940; *m* 1974, Adelaide, *d* of A. Birkmyre; one *d*]. *Address:* Crookston, Heriot, Midlothian EH38 5YS. *Clubs:* New, Puffins (Edinburgh).

BORTHWICK, Sir John Thomas, 3rd Bt *cr* 1908; MBE 1945; *b* 5 Dec. 1917; *s* of Hon. James Alexander Borthwick (*d* 1961), and Irene, *d* of late George Wise, Sydney, Australia; *S* to Btcy of uncle (1st and last Baron Whitburgh), 1967; *m* 1st, 1939, Irene (marr. diss. 1961), *o c* of Joseph Heller; three *s*; 2nd, 1962, Irene, *d* of Leo Fink; two *s. Educ:* Eton; Trinity Coll., Oxford. Formerly Major, Rifle Brigade, TA. Served War of 1939-45 (MBE). *Heir: s* Antony Thomas Borthwick [*b* 12 Feb. 1941; *m* 1966, Gillian Deirdre Broke, *d* of late Lieut Nigel Vere Broke Thurston, RN; one *s* two *d*]. *Address:* Fox Hills Dower House, Long Cross, Surrey; 28 Lennox Gardens, SW1.

BORTHWICK, Kenneth W., CBE 1980; JP; DL; Rt Hon. Lord Provost of the City of Edinburgh, 1977-80; Lord Lieutenant of the City and County of Edinburgh, 1977-80; *b* 4 Nov. 1915; *s* of Andrew Graham Borthwick; *m* 1942, Irene Margaret Wilson, *d* of John Graham Wilson, Aberdeen; two *s* one *d. Educ:* George Heriot Sch., Edinburgh. Served War of 1939-45: Flying Officer, RAF. Elected Edinburgh Town Council, 1963; Lothian Regional Council, 1974-77; Edinburgh District Council, 1976. Judge of Police, 1972-

75. Member: Lothians River Bd, 1969-73; Organising Cttee, Commonwealth Games, Edinburgh, 1970; Edinburgh and Lothian Theatre Trust, 1975-76 Lothian and Borders Police Bd, 1975-77; British Airports Authorities Consultative Cttee, 1977-80; Convention of Scottish Local Authorities, 1977 Scottish Council Develt and Industry, 1977; Chairman: Edinburgh Dist Licensing Court, 1975-77; Edinburgh Internat. Festival Soc., 1977-80 Edinburgh Military Tattoo Policy Cttee, 1977-80; Queen's Silver Jubilee Edinburgh Appeal Fund, 1977. Curator of Patronage, Univ. of Edinburgh 1977-80. Governor, George Heriot Sch., 1965-73. Vice-President (ex officio) RZS of Scotland, 1977-80; Lowland TA&VRA, 1977-80. DL City of Edinburgh, 1980. Hon. Consul for Malaŵi, 1982. OStJ. *Recreations:* golf gardening. *Address:* 7 Duddingston Crescent, Edinburgh EH15 3AS. *Club* Caledonian (Hon. Mem.).

BORTHWICK, (William) Jason (Maxwell), DSC 1942; *b* 1 Nov. 1910; *er s* of late Hon. William Borthwick and Ruth (*née* Rigby); *m* 1937, Elizabeth Elworthy (*d* 1978), Timaru, NZ; one *s* three *d. Educ:* Winchester; Trinity Coll., Cambridge (BA). Called to Bar, Inner Temple, 1933. Commnd RNVR, 1940, Comdr (QO) 1945. Joined Thomas Borthwick & Sons Ltd 1934, Dir 1946-76; Dir, International Commodities Clearing House Ltd and subsids, 1954; Dir, Commonwealth Develt Corp., 1972-78; Mem., Central Council of Physical Recreation, 1955-; Chm., Nat. Sailing Centre, 1965-79. *Recreations:* yachting, shooting. *Address:* Brancaster Staithe, King's Lynn Norfolk. *T:* Brancaster 475. *Clubs:* United Oxford & Cambridge University, Royal Thames Yacht.

BORWICK, family name of **Baron Borwick.**

BORWICK, 4th Baron, *cr* 1922; **James Hugh Myles Borwick;** Bt *cr* 1916; MC 1945; Major HLI retired; *b* 12 Dec. 1917; *s* of 3rd Baron and Irene Phyllis *d* of late Thomas Main Paterson, Littlebourne, Canterbury; *S* father 1961; *m* 1954, Hyllarie Adalia Mary, *y d* of late Lieut-Col William Hamilton Hall Johnston, DSO, MC, DL, Bryn-y-Groes, Bala, N Wales; four *d. Educ:* Eton. RMC, Sandhurst. Commissioned as 2nd Lieut HLI, 1937; Capt. 1939; Major 1941; retired, 1947. *Recreations:* field sports, sailing and ocean racing. *Heir: half b* Hon. George Sandbach Borwick [*b* 18 Oct. 1922; *m* 1981, Esther, Lady Ellerman]. *Address:* Knap Farm, Owermoigne, Dorchester, Dorset. *T:* Warmwell 852365. *Club:* Royal Ocean Racing.

BORWICK, Lt-Col Michael George; farmer; Director, Blair Trust Co.; Vice-Lieutenant for Ayr and Arran, since 1974; *b* 27 March 1916; *s* of late Col Malcolm Borwick; *m* 1946, Veronica, *d* of late Lt-Col J. F. Harrison and Hon. Mrs Harrison; two *s* decd. *Educ:* Harrow; in France. Joined Leicestershire Yeomanry, 1935; joined Royal Scots Greys, 1937; joined Middle East Commandos, 1940, fought in Dodecanese Islands and in Crete, 1941 (POW); rejoined Greys, 1945; comd 1954-57. Chm., Royal Scots Greys Assoc., 1963. Joint Master, Eglinton Foxhounds, 1960-63 and 1972-75. Mem., Royal Company of Archers, Queen's Body Guard for Scotland. Mem. Ayrshire CC 1958-66, resigned; DL Ayrshire, 1960. *Recreations:* hunting, shooting. *Address:* Blair, Dalry, Ayrshire KA24 4ER. *Club:* Cavalry and Guards.

BOSANQUET, Charles Ion Carr, MA; DL; Vice-Chancellor of University of Newcastle upon Tyne, 1963-68 (Rector of King's College, Newcastle upon Tyne, 1952-63); *b* 19 April 1903; *s* of Robert Carr Bosanquet and Ellen S. Bosanquet; *m* 1931, Barbara, *d* of William Jay Schieffelin, New York; one *s* three *d. Educ:* Winchester; Trinity Coll., Cambridge (Scholar). Asst Gen. Manager, Friends Provident and Century Life Office, 1933-39; Principal Asst Sec., Ministry of Agriculture and Fisheries, 1941-45; Treasurer of Christ Church, Oxford, 1945-52. Fellow of Winchester Coll., 1951-73; Chm., Reorganisation Commission for Pigs and Bacon, 1955-56; Development Comr, 1956-70; Chm. Min. of Agric. Cttee of Enquiry into Demand for Agricultural Graduates. Hon DCL Durham; Hon LLD Cincinnati; Hon. DLitt Sierra Leone; Hon. DSc City. High Sheriff, 1948-49, DL 1971, Northumberland. Comdr, Order of St Olav. *Address:* Rock Moor, Alnwick, Northumberland. *T:* Charlton Mires 224. *Clubs:* Farmers'; Northern Counties (Newcastle).

BOSCAWEN, family name of **Viscount Falmouth.**

BOSCAWEN, Hon. Robert Thomas, MC 1944; MP (C) Wells since 1970; a Lord Commissioner of HM Treasury (Government Whip), since 1981 (Assistant Government Whip, 1979-81); *b* 17 March 1923; 4th *s* of 8th Viscount Falmouth and of Dowager Viscountess Falmouth, CBE; *m* 1949 Mary Alice, JP London 1961, *e d* of Col Sir Geoffrey Ronald Codrington, KCVO, CB, CMG, DSO, OBE, TD; one *s* two *d. Educ:* Eton; Trinity College, Cambridge. Served Coldstream Guards, 1941-50; NW Europe 1944-45. Mem., London Exec. Council, Nat. Health Service, 1954-65; Underwriting Mem. of Lloyds, 1952-. Contested Falmouth and Camborne (C), 1964, 1966. Mem., Select Cttee on Expenditure, 1974; Vice-Chm. Conservative Parly Health and Social Security Cttee, 1974. Mem. Parly Delegns, USSR 1977, Nepal 1981. *Recreation:* sailing. *Address:* House of Commons, SW1A 0AA. *Clubs:* Pratt's; Royal Yacht Squadron.

BOSCH, Baron Jean van den, Hon. GCVO 1966; Belgian Ambassador to the Court of St James's and Belgian Permanent Representative to the Council of Western European Union, 1966-72; Director, Lloyds Bank International, 1972-78; *b* 27 Jan. 1910; *s* of Baron Firmin van den Bosch and Anne de Volder; *m* 1944, Hélène Cloquet; two *d. Educ:* Ecole Abbatiale, Maredsous; Notre-

Dame de la Paix, Namur; Université Catholique de Louvain. Docteur en droit; licencié en sciences historiques; licencié en sciences politiques et diplomatiques. Entered Belgian Diplomatic Service, 1934; Attaché, London and Paris, 1934; Sec., Pekin, 1937; 1st Sec., Ottawa, 1940; Chargé d'Affaires to Luxembourg Govt in London, 1943; Counsellor, Prince Regent's Household, 1944; Counsellor and Chargé d'Affaires, Cairo, 1948; Counsellor, 1949, Minister, 1953, Paris; Minister, Consul-Gen., Hong Kong, Singapore and Saigon, 1954; Ambassador, Cairo, 1955; accredited Minister, Libya, 1956; Sec.-Gen. of Min. of For. Aff. and For. Trade, 1959–June 1960, and again, Sept. 1960–1965; Ambassador, Congo, July–Aug. 1960. Dir, Lloyds Bank International (Belgium) SA, 1972–78 (Chm., 1973–78). Grand Officier, Ordres Léopold, Couronne, Léopold II. Médaille Civique (1st cl.). Holds foreign decorations. *Address:* 114 avenue Winston Churchill, B1, 1180 Brussels, Belgium. *T:* 347.29.09. *Clubs:* Beefsteak, White's, Anglo-Belgian.

BOSE, Vivian; *b* Ahmedabad, India, 9 June 1891; *s* of late Lalit Mohun Bose and *g s* of late Sir Bipin Krishna Bose; *m* 1930, Irene, *d* of late Dr John R. Mott (winner of Nobel Prize, 1946); one *s* one *d. Educ:* Dulwich Coll.; Pembroke Coll., Cambridge. (BA, LLB). Called to Bar, Middle Temple, 1913; practised at the Nagpur Bar; Principal, University Coll. of Law, Nagpur, 1924–30; Govt Advocate and Standing Counsel to the Govt of the Central Provinces and Berar, 1930–36; Additional Judicial Commissioner, Nagpur, for short periods, 1931–34; Puisne Judge, Nagpur High Court, 1936–49; Chief Justice, High Court of Judicature, Nagpur, 1949–51; Puisne Judge, Supreme Court of India, New Delhi, 1951–56, retd; recalled as *ad hoc* Judge, Supreme Court, Sept. 1958–Aug. 1959; Chm., two Government Commissions of Inquiry, 1958–62. Member International Commission of Jurists, 1958–; Pres., 1959–66 (Actg Sec.-Gen. March–Oct. 1963); Hon. Pres. 1966 (toured, on Commission's behalf: Europe, Asia Minor, Australia, Indonesia, Malaya, Burma, East and West Africa, UK, Ireland, Eire, USA, Brazil, 1961 and 1962–63). Hon. Provincial Sec., Boy Scouts Assoc. Central Provinces and Berar, 1921–34; Provincial Commissioner, 1934–37; Chief Commissioner for India, 1948; National Commissioner, 1959–62; Silver Wolf, 1942; Capt. the Nagpur Regt, Indian Auxiliary Force. Volunteer Long Service Medal, 1929; King's Silver Jubilee Medal, 1935; Kaisar-i-Hind Silver Medal, 1936. *Recreations:* photography, wireless, motoring (from and to India, etc), travel; amateur magic, mainly stage illusions. *Address:* Vishranti Farm, Doddakallasandra Post, Bangalore 560 062, India. *T:* 40419.

BOSSOM, Hon. Sir Clive, 2nd Bt, *cr* 1953; *b* 4 Feb. 1918; *s* of late Baron Bossom (Life Peer); *S* to father's Baronetcy, 1965; *m* 1951, Lady Barbara North, *sister* of 9th Earl of Guilford, *qv*; three *s* one *d. Educ:* Eton. Regular Army, The Buffs, 1939–48; served Europe and Far East. Kent County Council, 1949–52; Chm. Council Order of St John for Kent, 1951–56; Mem. Chapter General, Order of St John (Mem., Jt Cttee, 1961–; Chm., Ex-Services War Disabled Help and Homes Dept, 1973–). Contested (C) Faversham Div., 1951 and 1955. MP (C) Leominster Div., Herefordshire, 1959–Feb. 1974; Parliamentary Private Secretary: to Jt Parly Secs, Min. of Pensions and Nat. Insce, 1960–62; to Sec. of State for Air, 1962–64; to Minister of Defence for RAF, 1964; to Home Secretary, 1970–72. Chm., Europ Assistance Ltd; Dir, Vosper Ltd. President: Anglo-Belgian Union, 1970–73 (Chm., 1967–70; Vice-Pres., 1974–); Anglo-Netherlands Soc., 1978–; Vice-President: Industrial Fire Protection Assoc., 1981–; Fédération Internationale de L'Automobile, 1975–81 (Hon. Pres., 1982–); Chairman: RAC, 1975–78; RAC Motor Sports Council, 1975–81; RAC Motor Sports Assoc. Ltd, 1979–; Iran Soc. 1973–76 (Vice-Pres., 1977); Mem. Council, RGS, 1982–. Liveryman of Worshipful Companies of Grocers (Master, 1979), Needlemakers. FRSA. KStJ 1961. Comdr, Order of Leopold II; Order of Homayoun III (Iran), 1977; Comdr, Order of the Crown (Belgium), 1977; Kt Comdr, Order of Orange Nassau (Netherlands), 1980. *Recreation:* travel. Heir: *s* Bruce Charles Bossom, *b* 22 Aug. 1952. *Address:* Parsons Orchard, Eastnor, near Ledbury, Herefordshire. *T:* Ledbury 2318; 3 Eaton Mansions, Cliveden Place, SW1. *T:* 01-730 1108. *Clubs:* Royal Automobile, Carlton, MCC.

BOSSY, Rev. Michael Joseph Frederick, SJ; Headmaster, Stonyhurst College, since 1972; *b* 22 Nov. 1929; *s* of F. J. Bossy and K. Bossy (née White). *Educ:* St Ignatius Coll., Stamford Hill; Heythrop Coll., Oxon (STL); Oxford Univ. (MA). Taught at: St Ignatius Coll., Stamford Hill, 1956–59; St Francis Xavier's Coll., Liverpool, 1963–64; Stonyhurst Coll., 1965–. *Recreation:* watching games. *Address:* Stonyhurst College, via Blackburn, Lancashire BB6 9PZ. *T:* Stonyhurst 247.

BOSTOCK, James Edward, RE 1961 (ARE 1947); ARCA London; painter and engraver; *b* Hanley, Staffs, 11 June 1917; *s* of William George Bostock, pottery and glass-worker, and Amy (née Titley); *m* 1939, Gwladys Irene (née Griffiths); three *s. Educ:* Borden Grammar Sch., Sittingbourne; Medway Sch. of Art, Rochester; Royal College of Art. War Service as Sgt in Durham LI and Royal Corps of Signals. Full-time Teacher, 1946–78; Vice-Principal, West of England Coll. of Art, 1965–70; Academic Develt Officer, Bristol Polytechnic, 1970–78. Elected Mem. of Soc. of Wood Engravers, 1950. Mem. Council. Soc. of Staffs Artists, 1963. Mem., E Kent Art Soc., 1980. Exhibited water-colours, etchings, wood engravings and drawings at RA, NEAC, RBA, and other group exhibitions and in travelling exhibitions to Poland, Czechoslovakia, South Africa, Far East, New Zealand, USA, and the provinces. One-man shows: Mignon Gall., Bath; Univ. of Bristol; Bristol Polytechnic; Margate Library Gall.; Deal Lib. Gall.; Broadstairs Lib. Gall. Works bought by V & A Museum, British Museum, British Council, Hull, Swindon, Stoke-on-Trent and Bristol Education Cttees, Hunt Botanical

Library, Pittsburgh, Hereford Mus., and private collectors. Commissioned work for: ICI Ltd, British Museum (Nat. Hist.), Odhams Press, and other firms and public authorities. *Publications:* Roman Lettering for Students, 1959; articles in: Times, Guardian, Staffordshire Sentinel, Studio, Artist; reproductions in Garrett, History of British Wood Engraving, 1978. *Address:* White Lodge, 80 Lindenthorpe Road, Broadstairs, Kent CT10 1DB. *T:* Thanet 69782.

BOSTOCK, Rev. Canon Peter Geoffrey, MA; Clergy Appointments Adviser, 1973–76; Deputy Secretary, Board for Mission and Unity, General Synod of Church of England, 1971–73; Canon Emeritus, Diocese of Mombasa, 1958; *b* 24 Dec. 1911; *s* of Geoffrey Bostock; *m* 1937, Elizabeth Rose; two *s* two *d. Educ:* Charterhouse; The Queen's Coll., Oxon; Wycliffe Hall, Oxon. Deacon, 1935; Priest, 1937; CMS Kenya, 1935–58; became Canon of Diocese of Mombasa, 1952; Archdeacon, 1953–58; Vicar-Gen., 1955–58. Examining Chaplain to Bishop of Mombasa, 1950–58; Chm., Christian Council of Kenya, 1957–58; Archdeacon of Doncaster and Vicar, High Melton, 1959–67; Asst Sec., Missionary and Ecumenical Council of Church Assembly, 1967–71. *Recreations:* home and gardening. *Address:* 6 Moreton Road, Oxford OX2 7AX. *T:* Oxford 55460. *Club:* Royal Commonwealth Society.

BOSTON, family name of Baron Boston of Faversham.

BOSTON, 10th Baron *cr* 1761; Timothy George Frank Boteler Irby; Bt 1704; *b* 27 March 1939; *s* of 9th Baron Boston, MBE, and of Erica N., *d* of T. H. Hill; *S* father, 1978; *m* 1967, Rhonda Anne, *d* of R. A. Bate; two *s* one *d. Educ:* Clayesmore School, Dorset; Southampton Univ. (BSc Econ.). *Heir: s* Hon. George William Eustace Boteler Irby, *b* 1 Aug. 1971. *Address:* 33 Cloncurry Street, Fulham, SW6. *T:* 01-731 1936.

BOSTON OF FAVERSHAM, Baron *cr* 1976 (Life Peer), of Faversham, Kent; Terence George Boston; QC 1981; barrister; Opposition Front Bench Spokesman on Home Office affairs, since 1979; Chairman, Television South plc (TVS), since 1980; *b* 21 March 1930; *yr surv. s* of George T. Boston and Kate (née Bellati); *m* 1962, Margaret Joyce (Member: SE Metropolitan Regional Hospital Board, 1970–74; Mental Health Review Appeals Tribunal (SE Metropolitan area); market research consultant, *er d* of late R. H. J. Head and of Mrs H. F. Winters, and step *d* of late H. F. Winters, Melbourne, Australia. *Educ:* Woolwich Polytechnic Sch.; King's Coll., University of London. Dep. President, University of London Union, 1955–56. Commnd in RAF during Nat. Service, 1950–52; later trained as pilot with University of London Air Sqdn. Called to the Bar: Inner Temple, 1960; Gray's Inn, 1973; BBC News Sub-Editor, External Services, 1957–60; Senior BBC Producer (Current Affairs), 1960–64; also Producer of Law in Action series (Third Programme), 1962–64. Joined Labour Party, 1946; contested (Lab) Wokingham, 1955 and 1959; MP (Lab) Faversham, Kent, June 1964–70; PPS to: Minister of Public Building and Works, 1964–66; Minister of Power, 1966–68; Minister of Transport, 1968–69; Asst Govt Whip, 1969–70; Minister of State, Home Office, 1979. UK Deleg. to UN Gen. Assembly., XXXIst, XXXIInd and XXXIIIrd Sessions, 1976–78. Member: Executive Cttee, International Union of Socialist Youth, 1950; Select Cttee on Broadcasting Proceedings of Parliament, 1966; Speaker's Conference on Electoral Law, 1965–68. Trustee, Parly Lab. Party Benevolent Fund, 1967–74. Founder Vice-Chm., Great Britain—East Europe Centre, 1967–69; Chm., The Sheppey Gp, 1967–. *Recreations:* opera (going, not singing), fell-walking. *Address:* 27 Capstan Square, Isle of Dogs, E14 9EU; 1 Gray's Inn Square, Gray's Inn, WC1R 5AA.

BOSTON, David Merrick, OBE 1976; MA; Director (formerly Curator), Horniman Museum and Library, London, since 1965; *b* 15 May 1931; *s* of late Dr H. M. Boston, Salisbury; *m* 1961, Catharine, *d* of Rev. Prof. E. G. S. Parrinder, *qv*; one *s* two *d. Educ:* Rondebosch, Cape Town; Bishop Wordsworth's, Salisbury; Selwyn Coll., Cambridge; Univ. of Cape Town. BA History Cantab 1954; MA 1958. RAF, 1950–51; Adjt, Marine Craft Trng School. Field survey, S African Inst. of Race Relations, 1955; Keeper of Ethnology, Liverpool Museums, 1956–62; Asst Keeper, British Museum, New World archaeology and ethnography, 1962–65. Chm., British Nat. Cttee of Internat. Council of Museums, 1976–80; Mem. Council: Museums Assoc., 1969; Royal Anthropological Inst., 1969 (Vice-Pres., 1972–75, 1977–80). Vis. Scientist, National Museum of Man, Ottawa, 1970. FMA; FRAS; FRGS. Ordenom Jugoslavenske Zastave sa zlatnom zvezdom na ogrlici (Yugoslavia), 1981. *Publications:* Pre-Columbian Pottery of the Americas, 1980; contribs to learned jls and encyclopaedias and on Pre-European America, in World Ceramics (ed R. J. Charleston). *Address:* 10 Oakleigh Park Avenue, Chislehurst, Kent. *T:* 01-467 1049.

BOSTON, Richard; Editor, Quarto, since 1979; *b* 29 Dec. 1938. *Educ:* King's Coll., Cambridge (MA). Editor, The Vole, 1977–80. *Publications:* The Press We Deserve (ed), 1969; An Anatomy of Laughter, 1974; The Admirable Urquhart, 1975; Beer and Skittles, 1976; Baldness Be My Friend, 1977; The Little Green Book, 1979; C. O. Jones's Compendium of Practical Jokes, 1982. *Address:* The Old School, Aldworth, Reading, Berks. *T:* Compton 587. *Club:* Goring Social.

BOSVILLE MACDONALD OF SLEAT, Sir Ian Godfrey, 17th Bt, *cr* 1625; ARICS, MRSH; 25th Chief of Sleat; *b* 18 July 1947; *er s* of Sir (Alexander) Somerled Angus Bosville Macdonald of Sleat, 16th Bt, MC, 24th Chief of

Sleat and of Mary, Lady Bosville Macdonald of Sleat; S father 1958; m 1970, Juliet Fleury, o d of Maj.-Gen. J. M. D. Ward-Harrison, qv ; one s one d. Educ: Pinewood Sch.; Eton Coll.; Royal Agricultural Coll. ARICS 1972. Member (for Bridlington South), Humberside CC, 1981-. MRSH 1972; Mem., Econ. Res. Council, 1979-. Heir: s Somerled Alexander Bosville Macdonald, younger of Sleat, b 30 Jan. 1976. Recreation: ornithology. Address: Thorpe Hall, Rudston, Driffield, North Humberside. T: Kilham 239; Upper Duntulm, By Portree, Isle of Skye. T: Duntulm 206. Clubs: Lansdowne, Brooks's; Puffin's (Edinburgh).

BOSWALL, Sir (Thomas) Alford H.; see Houstoun-Boswall.

BOSWELL, Lt-Gen. Sir Alexander Crawford Simpson, KCB 1982; CBE 1974 (OBE 1971; MBE 1962); GOC Scotland and Governor of Edinburgh Castle, since 1982; b 3 Aug. 1928; s of Alexander Boswell Simpson Boswell and Elizabeth Burns Simpson Boswell (née Park); m 1956, Jocelyn Leslie Blundstone Pomfret, d of Surg. Rear-Adm. A. A. Pomfret, qv ; five s. Educ: Merchiston Castle Sch.; RMA, Sandhurst. Enlisted in Army, 1947; Commnd, Argyll and Sutherland Highlanders, Dec. 1948; regimental appts, Hong Kong, Korea, UK, Suez, Guyana, 1949-58; sc Camberley, 1959; Mil. Asst (GSO2) to GOC Berlin, 1960-62; Co. Comdr, then Second in Comd, 1 A and SH, Malaya and Borneo, 1963-65 (despatches 1965); Directing Staff, Staff Coll., Camberley, 1965-68; CO, 1 A and SH, 1968-71; Col GS Trng Army Strategic Comd, 1971; Brig. Comdg 39 Inf. Bde, 1972-74; COS, 1st British Corps, 1974-76; NDC (Canada), 1976-77; GOC 2nd Armd Div., 1978-80; Dir, TA and Cadets, 1980-82. Col, Argyll and Sutherland Highlanders, 1972-82; Hon. Col, Tayforth Univs OTC, 1982-; Col Comdt, Scottish Div., 1982-. Captain of Tarbert, 1974-82. Address: c/o Bank of Scotland, Palmerston Place Branch, 32 West Maitland Street, Edinburgh EH12 5DZ. Clubs: Army and Navy; New (Edinburgh).

BOSWORTH, George Simms, CBE 1968; CEng, FIEE; Director of Newcastle upon Tyne Polytechnic, 1969-77; b 12 Aug. 1916; s of George Bosworth and Mabel Anne Simms; m 1940, Helen Cowan Rusack; two s two d. Educ: Herbert Strutt Grammar Sch.; Gonville and Caius Coll., Cambridge. MA (Mechanical Sci. Tripos). Served RAF, Engineer Officer; Sqdn Ldr, 1940-46. English Electric Co., London, 1946-69: Chief of Technical Personnel Administration; Director of Group Personnel Services; Director of Personnel. Hon. DTech Bradford, 1968; Hon. DCL Newcastle upon Tyne, 1978. Address: 111 Park Place, Park Parade, Harrogate HG1 5NS. Club: Royal Air Force.

BOSWORTH, (John) Michael (Worthington), CBE 1972; FCA; Deputy Chairman, British Railways Board, since 1972 (Vice-Chairman, 1968-72); b 22 June 1921; s of Humphrey Worthington Bosworth and Vera Hope Bosworth; m 1955, Patricia Mary Edith Wheelock; one s one d. Educ: Bishop's Stortford Coll. Served Royal Artillery, 1939-46. Peat, Marwick, Mitchell & Co., 1949-68, Partner, 1960. Chairman: British Rail Engineering Ltd, 1969-71; British Rail Property Bd, 1971-72; British Rail Shipping and International Services Ltd, now Sealink UK Ltd, 1976-; BR Hovercraft Ltd, 1976-81; British Transport Hotels, 1978-; British Rail Investments Ltd, 1981-; Dir, Hoverspeed (UK) Ltd, 1981-. Vice Pres., Société Belgo-Anglaise des Ferry-Boats, 1979-. Recreations: ski-ing, vintage cars. Address: Ivy House, 11 King Street, Emsworth, Hants. Club: Royal Automobile.

BOSWORTH, Neville Bruce Alfred, CBE 1982; Senior Partner, Bosworth, Bailey Cox & Co., Solicitors, Birmingham; b 18 April 1918; s of W. C. N. Bosworth; m 1945, Charlotte Marian Davis; one s two d. Educ: King Edward's Sch., Birmingham; Birmingham Univ. LLB. Admitted Solicitor, 1941. Birmingham City Council, 1950-; County Bor. Councillor (Erdington Ward), 1950-61; Alderman, 1961-74; Dist Councillor (Edgbaston Ward), 1973-; Lord Mayor of Birmingham, 1969-70; Dep. Mayor, 1970-71; Leader of Birmingham City Council, 1976-80; Leader of Opposition, 1972-76 and 1980-; Cons. Gp Leader, 1972- (Dep. Gp Leader, 1971-72); Chairman: Gen. Purposes Cttee, 1966-69; Finance and Priorities Cttee, 1976-80; National Exhibn Centre Cttee, 1976-80. County Councillor (Edgbaston Ward), W Midlands CC, 1973-; Chm., Legal and Property Cttee, 1977-79; Vice-Chm., Finance Cttee, 1980-81. Chm., Sutton Coldfield Cons. Assoc., 1963-66; Vice-Chm., Birmingham Cons. Assoc., 1972-; Mem., Local Govt Adv. Cttee, National Union of Cons. and Unionist Assocs, 1973-. Vice Chm., Assoc. of Metropolitan Authorities, 1978-80, and Mem. Policy Cttee, 1976-80; Vice-Pres., Birmingham and Dist Property Owners Assoc.; Dir, Nat. Exhibn Centre Ltd, 1970-72, 1974-; Mem., W Midlands Econ. Council, 1978-79. Trustee, several charitable trusts; Mem. Council, Birmingham Univ.; Governor, King Edward VI Schs, Birmingham (Dep. Bailiff, 1979-80). Recreations: politics, politics, football (Dir, Birmingham City Football Club Ltd). Address: Hollington, Luttrell Road, Four Oaks, Sutton Coldfield, Birmingham B74 2SR. T: 021-308 0647; 54 Newhall Street, Birmingham B3 3QG. T: 021-236 8091. Club: Birmingham (Birmingham).

BOTHA, Matthys (Izak); South African Ambassador to the Court of St James's, 1977-78; b 31 Oct. 1913; s of Johan Hendrik Jacobus Botha and Anna Botha (née Joubert); m 1940, Hester le Roux (née Bosman); two s. Educ: Selborne Coll.; Pretoria Univ. BA, LLB. Called to the Transvaal Bar. Dept of Finance, Pretoria, 1931-44; S African Embassy, Washington, 1944-51; S African Permanent Mission to UN, NY, 1951-54; Head, Political Div., Dept Foreign Affairs, Pretoria, 1955-59; Envoy Extraordinary and Minister Plenipotentiary, Switzerland, 1959-60; Minister, London, 1960-62;

Ambassador and Permanent Rep., UN, NY, 1962-70; Ambassador to: Canada 1970-73; Italy, 1973-77. Member: Simon Vanderstel Foundn; South African Foundn. Knight of Grand Cross, Order of Merit (Italy), 1977. Recreations swimming, skiing, cycling. Address: 7 de Jongh Street, The Strand, Cape Province, 7140, South Africa.

BOTHA, Hon. Pieter Willem, DMS; MP for George, Parliament of South Africa, since 1948; Prime Minister, and Minister of National Intelligence Service, Republic of South Africa, since Sept. 1978; b 12 Jan. 1916; s of Pieter Willem and Hendriena Christina Botha; m 1943, Anna Elizabeth Rossouw two s three d. Educ: Paul Roux; Bethlehem, Orange Free State; Univ. of Orange Free State, Bloemfontein. Deputy Minister of the Interior, 1958 Minister of Community Development and of Coloured Affairs, 1961 Minister of Public Works, 1964; Minister of Defence, 1966-80. Leader of th National Party in the Cape Province, 1966. Hon. Doctorate in: War History 1976; Philosophy, 1981. Recreations: horseriding, walking, reading. Address Private Bag X193, Cape Town 8000, South Africa; Room 1813, H. F Verwoerd Building, Cape Town.

BOTHA, Roelof Frederik, (Pik Botha), DMS 1981; Minister of Foreign Affairs, South Africa, since 1977; Minister of Information, since 1978; MP (National Party) for Westdene, since 1977; b 27 April 1932. Educ: Volkskool Potchefstroom; Univ. of Pretoria. Dept of Foreign Affairs, 1953: diplomatic missions, Europe, 1956-62; Mem. team from S Africa, in SW Africa case Internat. Court of Justice, The Hague, 1963-66, 1970-71; Agent for S African Govt, Internat. Court of Justice, 1965-66; Legal Adviser, Dept of Foreign Affairs, 1966-68; Under-Sec. and Head of SW Africa and UN Sections 1968-70. National Party, MP for Wonderboom, 1970-74. Mem., SA Delegr to UN Gen. Assembly, 1967-69, 1971, 1973-74. Served on select Party Cttees 1970-74. South African Permanent Representative to the UN, NY, 1974-77 South African Ambassador to the USA, 1975-77. Grand Cross, Order of Good Hope, 1980; Order of the Brilliant Star with Grand Cordon, 1980. Address House of Assembly, Cape Town, South Africa; c/o Department of Foreign Affairs, Pretoria, South Africa.

BOTT, Ian Bernard; Director General, Guided Weapons and Electronics Ministry of Defence, since 1981; b 1 April 1932; s of late Edwin Bernard and of Agnes Bott; m 1955, Kathleen Mary (née Broadbent); one s one d. Educ Nottingham High Sch.; Southwell Minster Grammar Sch.; Stafford Technica Coll.; Manchester Univ. BSc Hon. Physics; FIEE, FInstP. Nottingham Lace Industry, 1949-53. Royal Air Force, 1953-55. English Electric, Stafford 1955-57; Royal Radar Établt, 1960-75 (Head of Electronics Group, 1973-75) Counsellor, Defence Research and Development, at British Embassy Washington DC, 1975-77; Ministry of Defence: Dep. Dir Underwater Weapons Projects (S/M), 1977-79; Asst Chief Scientific Advr (Projects) 1979-81. Publications: papers on physics and electronics subjects in jls o learned socs. Recreations: building, horology, music. Address: 7 Eaton Mew North, SW1. Club: Royal Automobile.

BOTT, Prof. Martin Harold Phillips, FRS 1977; Professor of Geophysics University of Durham, since 1966; b 12 July 1926; s of Harold Bott and Dorothy (née Phillips); m 1961, Joyce Cynthia Hughes; two s one d. Educ Claysmore Sch. Dorset; Magdalene Coll., Cambridge (Scholar). MA, PhD Nat. Service, 1945-48 (Lieut, Royal Signals). Durham University: Turner and Newall Fellow, 1954-56; Lectr, 1956-63; Reader, 1963-66. Anglican Lay Reader. Mem. Council, Royal Soc., 1982-. Murchison Medallist, Geologica Soc. of London, 1977; Clough Medal, Geol Soc. of Edinburgh, 1979; Sorby Medal, Yorkshire Geol Soc., 1981. Publications: The Interior of the Earth 1971; papers in learned jls. Recreations: walking, mountains. Address: 11 S Mary's Close, Shincliffe, Durham. T: Durham 64021.

BOTTINI, Reginald Norman, CBE 1974; General-Secretary, National Union of Agricultural and Allied Workers, 1970-78; Member, General Council of TUC, 1970-78; b 14 Oct. 1916; s of Reginald and Helena Teresa Bottini; m 1946, Doris Mary Balcomb; no c. Educ: Bec Grammar School Apptd Asst in Legal Dept of Nat. Union of Agricultural Workers, 1945; Hea of Negotiating Dept, 1954; elected Gen.-Sec., Dec. 1969. Member Agricultural Wages Bd, 1963-78; Agricultural Economic Development Cttee 1970-78; (part-time) SE Electricity Bd, 1974-; Food Hygiene Adv. Council 1973-; BBC Agric. Adv. Cttee, 1973-78; Econ. and Soc. Cttee, EEC, 1975-78 Clean Air Council, 1975-80; Adv. Cttee on Toxic Substances, 1977-80; Mea and Livestock Commn, 1977- (and Chm. of its Consumers Cttee); Pane Mem., Central Arbitration Cttee, 1977-; Commn on Energy and th Environment, 1978-81; Waste Management Adv. Council, 1978-81 Formerly: Secretary: Trade Union Side, Forestry Commn Ind. and Trade Council; Trade Union Side, British Sugar Beet Nat. Negotiating Cttee; Chm Trade Union Side, Nat. Jt Ind. Council for River Authorities; formerly Member: Central Council for Agric. and Hort. Co-operation; Nat. Jt Ind Council for County Roadmen. Recreations: gardening, driving. Address: 4 Knights End Road, Great Bowden, Market Harborough, Leics LE16 7EY. T Market Harborough 64229. Club: Farmers'.

BOTTOMLEY, Rt. Hon. Arthur George, PC 1951; OBE 1941; MP (Lab) Teesside, Middlesbrough, since 1974 (Middlesbrough East, 1962-74); b 7 Feb 1907; s of late George Howard Bottomley and Alice Bottomley; m 1936 Bessie Ellen Wiles (see Dame Bessie Bottomley); no c. Educ: Gamuel Roac Council Sch.; Extension Classes at Toynbee Hall. London Organiser or National Union of Public Employees, 1935-45, 1959-62. Walthamstow

Borough Council, 1929-49; Mayor of Walthamstow, 1945-46; Chairman of Emergency Cttee and ARP Controller, 1939-41. Dep. Regional Commissioner for S-E England, 1941-45. MP (Lab) Chatham Division of Rochester, 1945-50, Rochester and Chatham 1950-59. Parliamentary Under-Secretary of State for Dominions, 1946-47; Sec. for Overseas Trade, Board of Trade, 1947-51; Sec. of State for Commonwealth Affairs, 1964-66; Minister of Overseas Develt, 1966-67. Land Tax Comr, Becontree Div. of Essex; Special Govt Mission to Burma, 1947; Deleg. to UN, New York, 1946, 1947 and 1949; Leader: UK delegation to World Trade and Employment Conference, Havana, 1947; UK Delegn to Commonwealth Conference, Delhi, 1949; Trade Mission to Pakistan, 1950; Special Mission to West Indies, 1951; Member: Consultative Assembly, Council of Europe, 1952, 1953 and 1954; Leader: Parliamentary Labour Party Mission to Burma, 1962, to Malaysia, 1963; UK Delegation to CPA Conferences, Australia, Canada, Malawi, Malaysia, Mauritius; Member, Parliamentary Missions to: India, 1946; Kenya, 1954; Ghana, 1959; Cyprus, 1963; Hong Kong, 1964. Chairman: Commonwealth Relations and Colonies Group, Parly Labour Party, 1963; Select Parly Cttee on Race Relations and Immigration, 1969; Select Cttee on Cyprus, 1975; Special Parly Cttee on Admin and Orgn of House of Commons Services, 1976; House of Commons Commn, 1980-; Treasurer, Commonwealth Parly Assoc., 1974- (Vice-Chm., UK Branch, 1968 and 1974-77). Chm., Attlee Foundn, 1978-; President: Britain-India Forum; Britain-Burma Soc. Hon. Freeman of Chatham, 1959; Freeman of Middlesbrough, 1976. Awarded title of Aung San Tagun, Burma, 1981. *Publications:* Why Britain should Join the Common Market, 1959; Two Roads to Colonialism, 1960; The Use and Abuse of Trade Unions, 1961. *Recreations:* walking and theatre-going. *Address:* 19 Lichfield Road, Woodford Green, Essex.

BOTTOMLEY, Dame Bessie (Ellen), DBE 1970; *b* 28 Nov. 1906; *d* of Edward Charles Wiles and Ellen (*née* Estall); *m* 1936, Rt Hon. Arthur George Bottomley, *qv*; no *c. Educ:* Maynard Road Girls' Sch.; North Walthamstow Central Sch. On staff of NUT, 1925-36. Member: Walthamstow Borough Council, 1945-48; Essex CC, 1962-65; Chm., Labour Party Women's Section, E Walthamstow, 1946-71, Chingford, 1973-. Mem., Forest Group Hosp. Man. Cttee, 1949-73; Mem., W Roding Community Health Council, 1973-76. Chm., Walthamstow Nat. Savings Cttee, 1949-65; Vice-Pres., Waltham Forest Nat. Savings Cttee, 1965- (Chm., 1975-). Mayoress of Walthamstow, 1945-46. Mem., WVS Regional Staff (SE England), 1941-45. Past Mem., Home Office Adv. Cttee on Child Care. Chm. of Govs of two Secondary Modern Schools, 1948-68, also group of Primary and Infant Schools; Chm. of Governors of High Schools. Mem., Whitefield Trust. JP 1955-76 and on Juvenile Bench, 1955-71; Dep. Chm., Waltham Forest Bench. *Recreations:* theatre, gardening. *Address:* 19 Lichfield Road, Woodford Green, Essex.

BOTTOMLEY, Sir James (Reginald Alfred), KCMG 1973 (CMG 1965); HM Diplomatic Service, retired; Director, Johnson, Matthey & Co. Ltd, since 1979; *b* 12 Jan. 1920; *s* of Sir (William) Cecil Bottomley, KCMG, and Alice Thistle Bottomley (*née* Robinson), JP; *m* 1941, Barbara Evelyn (Vardon); two *s* two *d* (and one *s* decd). *Educ:* King's College Sch., Wimbledon; Trinity Coll., Cambridge. Served with Inns of Court Regt, RAC, 1940-46. Dominions Office, 1946; Pretoria, 1948-50; Karachi, 1953-55; Washington, 1955-59; UK Mission to United Nations, 1959; Dep. High Commissioner, Kuala Lumpur 1963-67; Asst Under-Sec. of State, Commonwealth Office (later FCO), 1967-70; Dep. Under-Sec. of State, FCO, 1970-72; Ambassador to South Africa, 1973-76; Perm. UK Rep. to UN and other Internat. Organisations at Geneva, 1976-78. Mem., British Overseas Trade Bd, 1972. *Recreation:* golf. *Address:* Chiltern Rise, Aldbury, Tring, Herts HP23 5SA. *T:* Aldbury Common 304.

See also P. J. Bottomley.

BOTTOMLEY, Peter James; MP (C) for Greenwich, Woolwich West, since June 1975; *b* 30 July 1944; *er s* of Sir James Bottomley, *qv*; *m* Virginia Garnett, JP, *er d* of W. John Garnett, *qv*; one *s* two *d. Educ:* comprehensive sch.; Westminster Sch.; Trinity Coll., Cambridge (BA Econ, MA). Driving, industrial sales, industrial relations, industrial economics. Contested (C) GLC elect., Vauxhall, 1973; (C) Woolwich West, Gen. Elecs, 1974. Secretary: Cons. Parly Social Services Cttee, 1977-79; Cons. Parly For. and Commonwealth Cttee, 1979-81. Mem., Transport House Br., T&GWU, 1971-; Pres., Cons. Trade Unionists, 1978-80; Vice-Pres., Fedn of Cons. Students, 1980-. Chairman: British Union of Family Orgns 1977-80; Family Forum, 1980-. Mem. Council, MIND, 1981-; Trustee, Christian Aid, 1978-. Parly Swimming Champion, 1980 and 1981. *Recreation:* children. *Address:* St Barnabas Villas, SW8 2EH. *T:* 01-720 4282.

BOTTRALL, (Francis James) Ronald, OBE 1949; MA; FRSL; *b* Camborne, Cornwall, 2 Sept. 1906; *o s* of Francis John and Clara Jane Bottrall; *m* 1st, 1934, Margaret Florence (marr. diss., 1954), *o d* of Rev. H. Saumarez Smith; one *s*; 2nd, 1954, Margot Pamela Samuel. *Educ:* Redruth County Sch.; Pembroke Coll., Cambridge. Foundress' Scholar; First Class English Tripos, Parts I and II (with distinction); Charles Oldham Shakespeare Scholarship, 1927. Lector in English, Univ. of Helsingfors, Finland, 1929-31; Commonwealth Fund Fellowship, Princeton Univ., USA, 1931-33; Johore Prof. of English Language and Literature, Raffles Coll., Singapore, 1933-37; Asst Dir, British Inst., Florence, 1937-38; Sec., SOAS, London Univ., 1939-45; Air Ministry: Temp. Admin. Officer, 1940; Priority Officer, 1941; British Council Representative: in Sweden, 1941; in Italy, 1945; in Brazil, 1954; in Greece, 1957; in Japan (and Cultural Counsellor, HM Embassy, Tokyo), 1959;

Controller of Educ. 1950-54. Chief, Fellowships and Training Br., Food and Agriculture Org. of UN, 1963-65. Syracuse Internat. Poetry Prize, 1954. FRSL 1955. Grande Ufficiale dell'Ordine al Merito della Repubblica Italiana, 1973. KStJ 1972. Coronation Medal, 1953. *Publications:* The Loosening and other Poems, 1931; Festivals of Fire, 1934; The Turning Path, 1939; (with Gunnar Ekelöf) T. S. Eliot: Dikter i Urval, 1942; Farewell and Welcome, 1945; (with Margaret Bottrall) The Zephyr Book of English Verse, 1945; Selected Poems, 1946; The Palisades of Fear, 1949; Adam Unparadised, 1954; Collected Poems, 1961; Rome (Art Centres of the World), 1968; Day and Night, 1974; Poems 1955-73, 1974; Reflections on the Nile, 1980. *Recreations:* music, travel. *Address:* 10 Lampard House, 8 Maida Avenue, W2 1SS. *Club:* Athenæum.

BOTVINNIK, Mikhail Moisseyevich; Order of Lenin, 1957; Order of the Badge of Honour, 1936 and 1945; Order of the Red Banner of Labour, 1961; Order of the October Revolution, 1981; Senior Scientist, USSR Research Institute for Electro-energetics, since 1955; *b* Petersburg, 17 Aug. 1911; *s* of a dental technician; *m* 1935, Gayane Ananova; one *d. Educ:* Leningrad Polytechnical Institute (Grad.). Thesis for degree of: Candidate of Technical Sciences, 1937; Doctor of Technical Sciences, 1952; Professor, 1972. Chess master title, 1927; Chess grandmaster title, 1935. Won Soviet chess championship in 1931, 1933, 1939, 1941, 1944, 1945, 1952; World chess title, 1948-57, 1958 and 1961. Honoured Master of Sport of the USSR, 1945. *Publications:* Flohr-Botvinnik Match, 1934; Alekhin-Euwe Return Match, 1938; Selected Games, 1937, 1945, 1960; Tournament Match for the Absolute Champion Title, 1945; Botvinnik-Smyslov Match, 1955; Eleventh Soviet Chess Championship, 1939; Smyslov-Botvinnik Return Match, 1960; Regulation of Excitation and Static Stability of Synchronous Machines, 1950; Asynchronized Synchronous Machines, 1960; Algorithm Play of Chess, 1968; Controlled AC Machines (with Y. Shakarian), 1969; Computers, Chess and Long-Range Planning, 1971; Botvinnik's Best Games 1947-70, 1972; Three matches of Anatoly Karpov, 1975; On Cybernetic Goal of Game, 1975; A Half Century in Chess, 1979; On Solving of Inexact Search, 1979; Fifteen Games and their History, 1981; Selected Games 1967-70, 1981; Achieving the Aim, 1981. *Address:* 3 Frunsenskaja 7 (flat 154), Moscow, USSR. *T:* 242.15,86.

BOUCHIER, Prof. Ian Arthur Dennis; Professor of Medicine, University of Dundee, since 1973; Dean, Faculty of Medicine and Dentistry, since 1982; *b* 7 Sept. 1932; *s* of E. A. and M. Bouchier; *m* 1959, Patricia Norma Henshilwood; two *s. Educ:* Rondebosch Boys' High Sch., Cape Town; Univ. of Cape Town. MB, ChB, MD, FRCP, FRCPE. Groote Schuur Hospital: House Officer, 1955-58; Registrar, 1958-61; Asst Lectr, Royal Free Hosp., 1962-63; Instructor in Medicine, Boston Univ. Sch. of Medicine, 1964-65; Sen. Lectr 1965-70, Reader in Medicine 1970-73, Univ. of London. *Publications:* Clinical Investigation of Gastrointestinal Function, 1969, 2nd edn 1981; Gastroenterology, 1973, 3rd edn 1982; Clinical Skills, 1976, 2nd edn 1981. *Recreations:* music, history of whaling. *Address:* Department of Medicine, Ninewells Hospital, Dundee DD1 9SY. *T:* Dundee 60111.

BOUGH, Francis Joseph; broadcaster; *b* 15 Jan. 1933; *m*; three *s. Educ:* Oswestry; Merton College, Oxford (MA). With ICI, 1957-62; joined BBC, 1962; presenter of Sportsview, 1964-67, of Grandstand, 1967-82, of Nationwide, 1972-83, of breakfast television, 1983-. Former Oxford soccer blue, Shropshire sprint champion. *Publication:* Cue Frank! (autobiog.), 1980. *Address:* c/o BBC Television, Lime Grove Studios, Shepherds Bush, W12.

BOUGHEY, John Fenton C.; see Coplestone-Boughey.

BOUGHEY, Sir John (George Fletcher), 11th Bt *cr* 1798; *b* 12 Aug. 1959; *s* of Sir Richard James Boughey, 10th Bt, and of Davina Julia (now Hon. Mrs Spencer Loch), *d* of FitzHerbert Wright; *S* father, 1978. *Heir:* *b* James Richard Boughey, *b* 29 Aug. 1960. *Address:* 11 Rutland Gate, SW7.

BOULET, Gilles; President, University of Quebec, since 1978; *b* 5 June 1926; *s* of Georges-A. Boulet and Yvonne Hamel; *m* 1971, Florence Lemire; one *s* one *d. Educ:* Coll. St Gabriel de St Tite; Séminaire St Joseph de Trois-Rivières; Laval Univ. (LTh 1951); Université Catholique de Paris (LPh, MA 1953). Prof. of Literature and History, Séminaire Ste Marie, Shawinigan, 1953-61; Centre d'Etudes Universitaires de Trois-Rivières: Founder, 1960; Dir, 1960-69; Prof. of Lit. and Hist., 1961-66; Laval University: Prof. of French, Faculty of Lit., 1955-62; Aggregate Prof., Fac. of Arts, 1969; Rector, Univ. du Québec à Trois-Rivières, 1969-78. Duvernay Award, Soc. St-Jean-Baptiste de Trois-Rivières (literature award), 1978. *Publications:* Nationalisme ou Séparatisme, Nationalisme et Séparatisme, 1961; (with Lucien Gagné) Le Français Parlé au Cours Secondaire, vols I and II, 1962, vols III and IV, 1963; Textes et Préceptes Littéraires, vol. I, 2nd edn, 1967, vol. II, 1964; (with others) Le Boréal Express, Album no 1, 1965, Album no 2, 1967. *Recreations:* reading, skiing, skating. *Address:* 3021 de la Promenade, Ste Foy, Quebec G1W 2J5, Canada. *T:* (418) 659-2599. *Clubs:* Quebec Garrison, Cercle Universitaire (Québec).

BOULEZ, Pierre; composer; Director, Institut de Recherche et de Coordination Acoustique/Musique, since 1976; *b* Montbrison, Loire, France, 26 March 1925. *Educ:* Saint-Etienne and Lyon (music and higher mathematics); Paris Conservatoire. Studied with Messiaen and René Leibowitz. Theatre conductor, Jean-Louis Barrault Company, Paris, 1948; visited USA with French Ballet Company, 1952. Has conducted major orchestras in his own and standard classical works in Great Britain, Europe and USA, including Edinburgh Festival, 1965; also conducted Wozzeck in Paris and Frankfurt; Parsifal at Bayreuth, 1966; Chief Conductor, BBC Symphony Orchestra, 1971-75; Chief Conductor and Music Dir, NY Philharmonic, 1971-77; Dir, Bayreuth Festival, 1976-80. Hon. DMus Cantab, 1980. Interested in poetry and aesthetics of Baudelaire, Mallarmé and René Char. *Compositions include:* Trois Psalmodies (Piano solo), 1945; Sonata No 1 (piano), 1946; Sonatine for flute and piano, 1946; Sonata No 2 (piano), 1948; Polyphonie X for 18 solo instruments, 1951; Visage nuptial (2nd version), 1951; Structures for 2 pianos, 1952; Le Marteau sans Maître (voice and 6 instruments), 1954; Sonata No 3 (piano), 1956; Deux Improvisations sur Mallarmé for voice and 9 instruments, 1957; Doubles for orchestra, 1958; Poésie pour Pouvoir (text by René Char) for chorus and orchestra, 1958; Soleil des Eaux (text by René Char) for chorus and orchestra, 1958; Pli selon Pli: Hommage à Mallarmé, for voices and orchestra, 1958; Domaines for solo clarinet, 1968; Cummings ist der Dichter (16 solo voices and instruments), 1970; Eclat/Multiples, 1970; Explosante Fixe (8 solo instruments), 1972; Rituel, for orchestra, 1975; Messagesquisses (7 celli), 1977; Notations, for orch., 1980; Répons, for orch. and live electronics, 1981-82. *Publications:* Penser la musique d'aujourd'hui, 1966 (Boulez on Music Today, 1971); Relevés d'apprenti, 1967; Par volonté et par hasard, 1976. *Address:* IRCAM, 31 rue St Merri, 75004 Paris, France. *T:* 277 1233.

BOULIND, Mrs (Olive) Joan, CBE 1975; Fellow, 1973-79, and Tutor, 1974-79, Hughes Hall, Cambridge; *b* 24 Sept. 1912; *e d* of Douglas Siddall and Olive Raby; *m* 1936, Henry F. Boulind, MA, PhD; *two s one d. Educ:* Wallasey High Sch., Cheshire; Univ. of Liverpool (BA 1st class Hons History, Medieval and Modern; DipEd); MA Cantab 1974. Teacher: Wirral Co. Sch. for Girls, 1934-36; Cambridgeshire High Sch. for Girls, 1963. Mem., Domestic Consumers' Cttee, Min. of Power, 1948-52; Founder Chm., Eastern Regional Cttee, Women's Adv. Council on Solid Fuel, 1962-66; Nat. Pres., Nat. Council of Women, 1966-68 (Sen. Vice-Pres., 1964-66); Co-Chm., Women's Consultative Council, 1966-68; Leader, British delegn to conf. of Internat. Council of Women, Bangkok, 1970; Co-Chm., Women's Nat. Commn, 1973-75; Co-Chm., UK Co-ordinating Cttee for Internat. Women's Year, 1975; Chm., Westminster College Management Cttee, 1980-. Member: Commn on the Church in the Seventies, Congregational Church in England and Wales, 1970-72 (Vice-Chm., 1971-72); Ministerial Trng Cttee, United Reformed Church, 1972-79 and 1982- (Chm., 1982); East Adv. Council, BBC, 1976- (Chm. 1981-). Deacon, Emmanuel Congregational Ch., Cambridge, 1958-66. Trustee, Homerton Coll. of Educn, 1955-. *Recreations:* reading, travel, music. *Address:* 28 Rathmore Road, Cambridge CB1 4AD. *Club:* University Women's.

BOULT, Sir Adrian (Cedric), CH 1969; Kt 1937; MA; DMus Oxon; Hon. DMus RCM; Vice-President, Council of Royal College of Music, since 1963; *b* Chester, 8 April 1889; *o s* of late Cedric R. Boult, JP, formerly of Liverpool, and Katharine Florence Barman; *m* 1933, Ann, *yr d* of late Capt. F. A. Bowles, RN, JP, Dully, Sittingbourne, Kent. *Educ:* Westminster Sch.; Christ Church, Oxford; Leipzig Conservatorium (now Hochschule). President, Oxford Univ. Musical Club, 1910. Musical Staff, Royal Opera, 1914; Asst Director of Music, 1926. During 1914-18 War, served in War Office and Commission Internationale de Ravitaillement. Teaching staff of Royal College of Music, 1919-30 and 1962-66; Conductor of Patron's Fund, 1919-29; Conductor: Bach Choir, 1928-33; Birmingham Fest. Choral Soc., 1923-30; Musical Director, Birmingham City Orchestra, 1924-30 and 1959-60; Vice-President, City of Birmingham Symphony Orchestra, 1960-; Director of Music, BBC, 1930-42; first Conductor, BBC Symphony Orchestra, 1931-50; assisted Sir Henry Wood and Basil Cameron as conductors of Promenade Concerts in 1942, and took part in nearly every season until 1977; Conductor, London Philharmonic Orchestra, 1950-57, President, 1966-. Since 1922, has conducted in many European countries as well as USA and Canada, introducing British Music wherever possible. Has also directed a number of classes for conductors, especially for BBC and Schools' Music Assoc., and has taken charge of many festivals, notably Petersfield, 1920-39. Assisted at Coronation Services, 1937, 1953, and took part in concerts and services during Westminster Abbey 900th Anniversary Year, 1966. President: Incorp. Society of Musicians, 1928-29; Nat. Youth Orchestra, 1947-57; Schools' Music Assoc., 1947-; Leith Hill Musical Festival, 1955-78; Royal Scottish Academy of Music, 1959-. Hon. Pres., BBC Symphony Club, 1980-. Hon. LLD: Birmingham; Liverpool; Reading; Hon. MusDoc: Edinburgh; Cambridge; Hon. DLitt Oxford, 1979; Hon. RAM; Hon. DMus RCM 1982; Hon. Student, Christ Church, Oxon; FRCM (Vice-Pres.); Hon. Fellow, Manchester Coll., Oxford; Hon. Member Royal Academy of Music, Sweden; Hon. GSM; Hon. TCL (Vice-Pres.); Gold Medal, Royal Philharmonic Soc., 1944; Harvard Medal, with Dr Vaughan Williams, 1956. OStJ. *Publications:* A Handbook on The Technique of Conducting, 1920, rev. edn 1968; (joint) Bach's Matthew Passion, 1949; Thoughts on Conducting, 1963; My Own Trumpet (autobiog.), 1973; (with J. N. Moore) Music and Friends, 1979; contribs on musical subjects to various journals. *Address:* Fox Yard Cottage, West Street, Farnham, Surrey GU9 7EX. *T:* Farnham 715881. *Clubs:* Athenæum (Life Mem.), Royal Commonwealth Society; Leander (Henley).

BOULTER, Eric Thomas, CBE 1978; Director-General, Royal National Institute for the Blind, 1972-80; *b* 7 July 1917; *s* of Albert and Ethel Boulter; *m* 1946, Martha Mary McClure; *one s one d. Educ:* St Marylebone Grammar School. World Council for Welfare of Blind: Sec.-General, 1951-59; Vice-Pres., 1959-64; Pres., 1964-69; Hon. Life Mem., 1969. Chm., Council of World Organisations for Handicapped, 1958-61; Mem. Exec., Internat.

Council of Educators of Blind Youth, 1962-70; Assoc. Dir, American Foundn for Overseas Blind, 1956-70; Dep. Dir-Gen., RNIB, 1971-72; Sec., British Nat. Cttee for Prevention of Blindness, 1976-. Order of the Andes (Bolivia), 1960; Silver Medal for service to mankind, City of Paris, 1975; Helen Keller Internat. Award, 1978; Louis Braille Gold Medal, 1978. *Publication:* (with John H. Dogree) Blindness and Visual Handicap—the facts, 1982. *Address:* 40 Snaresbrook Drive, Stanmore, Mddx. *T:* 01-958 8681.

BOULTING, John Edward; Producer-Director: Charter Film Productions Ltd (Joint Managing Director), since 1973; BLC Films Ltd; *b* 21 Nov. 1913; *s* of Arthur Boulting and Rose Bennett. *Educ:* Reading Sch. Office boy in Wardour Street, 1933. Spent eighteen months selling bad films to reluctant exhibitors; joined independent producer as general factotum on production, 1935; served hard but educative apprenticeship, in small studios. Went to Spain, served in International Brigade, front line ambulance driver, 1937; returned to England. Nov. 1937 formed independent film production company with twin brother Roy. Served War of 1939-45; joined RAF as AC2, 1940; retired Flt-Lieut, 1946. Continued film production; since War has produced Fame is the Spur, The Guinea Pig, Seagulls over Sorrento, Josephine and Men, Brothers in Law; has directed Brighton Rock, Seven Days to Noon, The Magic Box, Lucky Jim (Edinburgh Festival 1957); directed, and co-author of, screen-play Private's Progress, 1955; produced Carlton-Browne of the FO, 1958; directed and co-author screenplay, I'm All Right Jack, 1959; produced The Risk and The French Mistress, 1960; co-author novel and screen-play and director, Heavens Above!, 1962; produced films: The Family Way, 1966; There's a Girl in my Soup, 1970; Soft Beds, Hard Battles, 1974. Dir, 1958-72. Man. Dir, 1966-72, Consultant, 1972, British Lion Films Ltd. Former Chm., Local Radio Assoc. *Recreations:* cricket, tennis, reading, film making, horse riding and irritating the conservative minded in all stratas. *Address:* Charter Film Productions, 8a Glebe Place, Chelsea, SW3 5LB.

BOULTING, Roy; Producer and Joint Managing Director, Charter Film Productions Ltd, since 1973; *b* 21 Nov. 1913; *s* of Arthur Boulting and Rose Bennett. *Educ:* HMS Worcester; Reading Sch. Formed independent film production company with twin brother John, 1937. Served War of 1939-45, RAC, finishing as Capt.; films for Army included Desert Victory and Burma Victory. Producer: Brighton Rock, 1947; Seven Days to Noon, 1950; Private's Progress, 1955; Lucky Jim (Edinburgh Festival), 1957; I'm All Right Jack, 1959; Heavens Above!, 1962. Director: Pastor Hall, 1939; Thunder Rock, 1942; Fame is the Spur, 1947; The Guinea Pig, 1948; High Treason, 1951; Singlehanded, 1952; Seagulls over Sorrento, Crest of the Wave, 1953; Josephine and Men, 1955; Run for the Sun, 1955; Brothers in Law, 1956; Happy is the Bride, 1958; Carlton-Browne of the FO, 1958-59; I'm All Right Jack, 1959; The Risk, 1960; The French Mistress, 1960; Suspect, 1960; The Family Way, 1966; Twisted Nerve, 1968; There's a Girl in my Soup, 1970; Soft Beds, Hard Battles, 1974; Danny Travis, 1978; The Last Word, 1979. *Play:* (with Leo Marks) Favourites, 1977. Dir, British Lion Films Ltd, 1958-72. *Address:* Charter Film Productions Ltd, 8a Glebe Place, Chelsea, SW3. *Club:* Lord's Taverners.

BOULTING, S. A.; *see* Cotes, Peter.

BOULTON, Sir Christian; *see* Boulton, Sir H. H. C.

BOULTON, Clifford John; Principal Clerk, Table Office, House of Commons, since 1979; *b* 25 July 1930; *s* of Stanley Boulton and Evelyn (*née* Hey), Cocknage, Staffs; *m* 1955, Anne, *d* of Rev. E. E. Raven, Cambridge; one adopted *s* one adopted *d. Educ:* Newcastle-under-Lyme High School; St John's Coll., Oxford (exhibnr). MA (Modern History). National Service, RAC, 1949-50; Lt Staffs Yeomanry (TA). A Clerk in the House of Commons, 1953-: Clerk of Select Cttees on Procedure, 1964-68 and 1976-77; Public Accounts, 1968-70; Parliamentary Questions, 1971-72; Privileges, 1972-77; Clerk of the Overseas Office, 1977-79. A school Governor and subsequently board mem., Church Schools Company, 1965-79. *Publications:* contribs to Erskine May's Parliamentary Practice, 17th-19th edns, Halsbury's Laws of England, 4th edn, and Parliamentary journals. *Address:* 35 Westminster Gardens, Marsham Street, SW1P 4JD. *T:* 01-834 2170.

BOULTON, Sir (Harold Hugh) Christian, 4th Bt *cr* 1905; *b* 29 Oct. 1918; *s* of Sir (Denis Duncan) Harold (Owen) Boulton, 3rd Bt, and Louise McGowan (*d* 1978), USA; *S* father, 1968. *Educ:* Ampleforth College, Yorks. Late Captain, Irish Guards (Supplementary Reserve). *Address:* c/o Bank of Montreal, City View Branch, 1481 Merivale Road, Ottawa 5, Ontario, Canada.

BOULTON, Prof. James Thompson; Professor of English Studies and Head of Department of English Language and Literature, since 1975, Dean of the Faculty of Arts, since 1981, University of Birmingham; *b* 17 Feb. 1924; *e s* of Harry and Annie M. P. Boulton; *m* 1949, Margaret Helen Leary; one *s* one *d. Educ:* University College, Univ. of Durham; Lincoln Coll. Oxford. BA Dunelm 1948; BLitt Oxon 1952; PhD Nottingham 1960. FRSL 1968. Served in RAF, 1943-46 (Flt-Lt). Lectr, subseq. Sen. Lectr and Reader in English, Univ. of Nottingham, 1951-64; John Cranford Adams Prof. of English, Hofstra Univ., NY, 1967; Prof. of English Lit., Univ. of Nottingham, 1964-75, Dean, Faculty of Arts, 1970-73. Editorial Adviser, Studies in Burke and his Time, 1960-77; Mem. Exec. Cttee, Anglo-American Associates (NY), 1968-75. Editor, Renaissance and Modern Studies, 1969-75. General Editor: The Letters of D. H. Lawrence, 1973-; The Works of D. H. Lawrence, 1975-

Publications: (ed) Edmund Burke: A Philosophical Enquiry into . . . the Sublime and Beautiful, 1958; (ed) C. F. G. Masterman: The Condition of England, 1960; The Language of Politics in the Age of Wilkes and Burke, 1963, 2nd edn 1975; (ed) Dryden: Of Dramatick Poesy etc, 1964; (ed) Defoe: Prose and Verse, 1965, 2nd edn 1975; (with James Kinsley) English Satiric Poetry: Dryden to Byron, 1966; (ed) Lawrence in Love: Letters from D. H. Lawrence to Louie Burrows, 1968; (ed) Samuel Johnson: The Critical Heritage, 1971; (with S. T. Bindoff) Research in Progress in English and Historical Studies in the Universities of the British Isles, vol. 1, 1971, vol. 2, 1976; (ed) Defoe: Memoirs of a Cavalier, 1972; (ed) The Letters of D. H. Lawrence, vol. 1, 1979, vol. 2, 1982; (contrib.) Renaissance and Modern Essays (ed G. R. Hibbard), 1966; (contrib.) The Familiar Letter in the 18th Century (ed H. Anderson), 1966; papers in Durham Univ. Jl, Essays in Criticism, Renaissance and Modern Studies, Modern Drama, etc. *Recreations:* tennis, gardening. *Address:* Department of English Language and Literature, University of Birmingham, PO Box 363, Birmingham B15 2TT.

BOULTON, Prof. Norman Savage, DSc, FICE; Emeritus Professor of Civil Engineering, University of Sheffield, since 1964 (Professor, 1955–64); *b* 8 May 1899; *s* of late Professor William Savage Boulton; *m* 1929, Constance (*d* 1968), *d* of late H. Deakin; one *d*. *Educ:* King Edward's Sch., Birmingham; University of Birmingham. RGA, 1918; BSc (Birmingham), First Class Hons and Bowen Research Schol., 1922; MSc and Dudley Docker Res. Schol., 1923; DSc (Civil Engineering), 1966. Engineering Asst, Public Works Dept, City of Birmingham, 1924–29; University Lecturer in Civil Engineering, King's Coll., Newcastle upon Tyne, 1929–36; Sen. Lecturer in charge of Dept of Civil Engineering, University of Sheffield, 1936–55. Chairman, Yorkshire Assoc. Inst. Civil Engineers, 1947–48 and 1961–62. AMICE, 1927; MICE, 1950. *Publications:* various technical papers in Proc. Instns Civil and Mechanical Engineers, Philosophical Magazine, Jl of Hydrology, Water Resources Research, etc. *Recreations:* music, swimming. *Address:* 68 Endcliffe Vale Road, Sheffield S10 3EW. *T:* Sheffield 661049.

BOULTON, Very Rev. Walter, MA Oxon; *s* of Walter and Clara Elizabeth Boulton, Smallthorne, Staffs.; *m* 1932, Kathleen Lorna York Batley; one *s* four *d*. *Educ:* Balliol Coll., Oxford. Exhibitioner of Balliol, 2nd Class Modern History, 1922, BA 1923, MA 1930. Cuddesdon Coll., 1923. Deacon, 1924; Priest, 1925; Curate of St Mark, Woodhouse, Leeds, 1924–27; Asst Chaplain of the Cathedral Church, Calcutta, 1927–34; Chaplain of Lebong, 1934–35. Furlough, 1937. Chaplain, Shillong, 1935–39; St Paul's Cathedral, Calcutta, 1939–45; Canon of Calcutta, 1940–48. Furlough, 1945. Chaplain, Shillong, 1945–47; Vicar of Fleet, Hampshire, 1948–52; Provost of Guildford and Rector of Holy Trinity with St Mary, Guildford, 1952–61; Rector of Market Overton with Thistleton, 1961–72. *Address:* Milton House, Lindfield, Haywards Heath, W Sussex.

BOULTON, Sir William (Whytehead), 3rd Bt *cr* 1944; Kt 1975; CBE 1958; TD 1949; Secretary, Senate of the Inns of Court and the Bar, 1974–75; *b* 21 June 1912; *s* of Sir William Boulton, 1st Bt, and Rosalind Mary (*d* 1969), *d* of Sir John Davison Milburn, 1st Bt, of Guyzance, Northumberland; *S* brother, 1982; *m* 1944, Margaret Elizabeth, *o d* of late Brig. H. N. A. Hunter, DSO; one *s* two *d*. *Educ:* Eton; Trinity Coll., Cambridge. Called to Bar, Inner Temple, 1936; practised at the Bar, 1937–39. Secretary, General Council of the Bar, 1950–74. Served War of 1939–45: with 104th Regt RHA (Essex Yeo.) and 14th Regt RHA, in the Middle East, 1940–44; Staff Coll., Camberley, 1944. Control Commission for Germany (Legal Div.), 1945–50. Gazetted 2nd Lieut TA (Essex Yeo.), 1934; retired with rank of Hon. Lieut-Col. *Publications:* A Guide to Conduct and Etiquette at the Bar of England and Wales, 1st edn 1953, 6th edn, 1975. *Heir:* *s* John Gibson Boulton, *b* 18 Dec. 1946. *Address:* The Quarters House, Alresford, near Colchester, Essex. *T:* Wivenhoe 2450; 53 Montpelier Walk, SW7. *T:* 01-589 1663.

BOURASSA, Robert; Prime Minister of Québec, 1970–76; Member of Québec National Assembly for Mercier, 1966–76; *b* 14 July 1933; *s* of Aubert Bourassa and Adrienne Courville; *m* 1958, Andrée Simard; one *s* one *d*. *Educ:* Jean-de-Brébeuf Coll.; Univs of Montreal, Oxford and Harvard. Gov.-Gen.'s Medal Montreal 1956. MA Oxford 1959. Admitted Quebec Bar 1957. Fiscal Adviser to Dept of Nat. Revenue and Prof. in Econs and Public Finance, Ottawa Univ., 1960–63; Sec. and Dir of Research of Bélanger Commn on Public Finance, 1963–65; Special Adviser to Fed. Dept of Finance on fiscal and econ. matters, 1965–66; financial critic for Quebec Liberal Party, Pres. Polit. Commn and Mem. Liberal Party's Strategy Cttee; Leader, Quebec Liberal Party, 1970–77; Minister of Finance, May–Nov. 1970; Minister of Inter-govtl Affairs, 1971–72. Lectures: Institut d'Etudes Européennes, Brussels, 1977–78; Center of Advanced Studies, Johns Hopkins Univ., 1978. *Address:* 190 Maplewood Street, Ontremont, Québec H2V 2M7, Canada.

BOURDEAUX, Rev. Michael Alan; International Director, Keston College, Keston, Kent, since 1982; *b* 19 March 1934; *s* of Richard Edward and Lilian Myra Bourdeaux; *m* 1st, 1960, Gillian Mary Davies (*d* 1978); one *s* one *d*; 2nd, 1979, Lorna Elizabeth Waterton. *Educ:* Truro Sch.; St Edmund Hall, Oxford (MA Hons Mod. Langs); Wycliffe Hall, Oxford (Hons Theology). Moscow State Univ., 1959–60; Deacon, 1960; Asst Curate, Enfield Parish Church, Mddx, 1960–64; researching at Chislehurst, Kent, on the Church in the Soviet Union, with grant from Centre de Recherches, Geneva, 1965–68; Vis. Prof., St Bernard's Seminary, Rochester, NY, 1969; Vis. Fellow, LSE, 1969–71; Research Fellow, RIIA, Chatham House, 1971–73; Dawson Lectr on Church and State, Baylor Univ., Waco, Texas, 1972; Chavasse Meml Lectr,

Oxford Univ., 1976; Kathryn W. Davis Prof. in Slavic Studies, Wellesley Coll., Wellesley, Mass, 1981. Founded Keston College, a research centre on religion in the Communist countries, 1969: (first) Director, 1969–81. Founder of journal, Religion in Communist Lands, 1973–. *Publications:* Opium of the People, 1965, 2nd edn 1977; Religious Ferment in Russia, 1968; Patriarch and Prophets, 1970, 2nd edn 1975; Faith on Trial in Russia, 1971; Land of Crosses, 1979. *Recreations:* singing in the Philharmonia Chorus; officiating, as Member British Tennis Umpires Assoc., at Wimbledon and abroad. *Address:* 34 Lubbock Road, Chislehurst, Kent BR7 5JJ. *T:* 01-467 3550. *Club:* Athenæum.

BOURDILLON, Henry Townsend, CMG 1952; Assistant Under-Secretary of State, Department of Education and Science, 1964–73; *b* 19 Aug. 1913; 2nd *s* of late Sir Bernard Henry Bourdillon, GCMG, KBE, and Lady (Violet Grace) Bourdillon; *m* 1942, Margareta d'Almaine (*née* Tham); one *s* two *d*. *Educ:* Rugby Sch.; Corpus Christi Coll., Oxford. Asst Principal, Colonial Office, 1937; Acting Principal, Colonial Office, 1940; lent to: Foreign Office, 1942; Cabinet Office, 1943; Ministry of Production, 1944; returned to Colonial Office, 1944; Asst Secretary, 1947–54; Asst Under-Secretary of State, Colonial Office, 1954–59; Deputy UK Commissioner for Singapore, 1959–61; returned to Colonial Office, 1961; Under-Secretary, Ministry of Education, 1962–64. *Recreations:* gardening, music. *Address:* Orchard House, Horsenden Lane, Princes Risborough, Bucks. *T:* Princes Risborough 5416.

BOURDILLON, Mervyn Leigh, JP; Vice Lord-Lieutenant, Powys, since 1978; *b* 9 Aug. 1924; *s* of late Prebendary G. L. Bourdillon; *m* 1961, Penelope, *d* of late P. W. Kemp-Welch, OBE; one *s* three *d*. *Educ:* Haileybury. Served RNVR, 1943–46. Forestry Comr, 1973–76. Mem. Brecon County Council, 1962–73; DL 1962, JP 1970, High Sheriff 1970, Brecon. *Address:* Llwyn Madoc, Beulah, Llanwrtyd Wells, Powys LD5 4TU.

BOURDON, Derek Conway, FIA; Director since 1981, and General Manager since 1979, Prudential Assurance Co. Ltd; *b* 3 Nov. 1932; *s* of Walter Alphonse Bourdon and late Winifred Gladys Vera Bourdon; *m* 1st, Camilla Rose Bourdon (marr. diss.); one *s* one *d*; 2nd, Jean Elizabeth Bourdon. *Educ:* Bancroft's School. FIA 1957. RAF Operations Research (Pilot Officer), 1956–58. Joined Prudential, 1950; South Africa, 1962–65; Dep. General Manager, 1976–79. Chairman, Vanbrugh Life, 1974–79. Member, Policyholders Protection Board, 1980–; Chm., Industrial Life Offices Assoc., 1982– (Vice-Chm., 1980–82). *Recreations:* golf, squash rackets. *Address:* 6 Loggetts, Alleyn Park, Dulwich SE21 8AT. *T:* 01-761 3189.

BOURKE, family name of **Earl of Mayo.**

BOURKE, Christopher John; Metropolitan Stipendiary Magistrate, since 1974; *b* 31 March 1926; *e s* of late John Francis Bourke of the Oxford Circuit and late Eileen Winifred Bourke (*née* Beddoes); *m* 1956, Maureen, *y d* of late G. A. Barron-Boshell; two *s* one *d*. *Educ:* Stonyhurst; Oriel Coll., Oxford. Called to Bar, Gray's Inn, 1953; Oxford Circuit, 1954–55; Dir of Public Prosecutions Dept, 1955–74. *Recreations:* history of art, music. *Address:* 27 Beverley Road, Barnes, SW13. *T:* 01-876 9939.

BOURKE, Sir Paget John, Kt 1957; Judge of the Courts of Appeal, Bahamas and Bermuda, since 1965, British Honduras, since 1968 (President of Courts, 1970–75), Gibraltar, 1970–79; *b* 1906; *s* of H. C. Bourke, Amana, Ballina, Co. Mayo, Ireland; *m* 1936, Susan Dorothy (*née* Killeen); three *s* one *d*. *Educ:* Mount St Mary's Coll., Chesterfield; Trinity Coll., Dublin (Mod. BA, LLB). Barrister-at-law, King's Inn, 1928, Gray's Inn, 1957. Legal Adviser and Crown Prosecutor, Seychelles, 1933; MEC and MLC; Chief Magistrate, Palestine, 1936; Relieving President, District Court, 1941; President, 1945; Judge of Supreme Court of Kenya, 1946; Chief Justice, Sierra Leone, 1955–57; Cyprus, 1957–60. Senior Counsel, Irish Bar, 1961. Acting Chief Justice, Gibraltar, Oct.–Dec., 1965. *Publication:* (ed) Digest of Cases, Seychelles, 1870–1933. *Address:* 9 Barnacoille Park, Dalkey, Co. Dublin. *Club:* Royal St George Yacht (Dun Laoghaire).

BOURN, James; HM Diplomatic Service, retired; *b* 30 Aug. 1917; *s* of James and Sarah Gertrude Bourn; *m* 1st, 1944, Isobel Mackenzie (*d* 1977); one *s*; 2nd, 1981, Moya Livesey. *Educ:* Queen Elizabeth's Grammar Sch., Darlington; Univ. of Edinburgh (MA Hons 1979). Executive Officer, Ministry of Health, 1936. War of 1939–45; served (Royal Signals), in India, North Africa and Italy; POW; Captain. Higher Exec. Officer, Ministry of National Insurance, 1947; Asst Principal, Colonial Office, 1947; Principal, 1949; Secretary to the Salaries Commission, Bahamas, 1948–49; Private Sec. to Perm. Under-Sec., 1949; seconded to Tanganyika, 1953–55; UK Liaison Officer to Commn for Technical Co-operation in Africa (CCTA), 1955–57; Commonwealth Relations Office, 1961; seconded to Central African Office, 1962; Dar es Salaam, 1963; Deputy High Commissioner in Zanzibar, Tanzania, 1964–65; Counsellor and Dep. High Comr, Malawi, 1966–70; Ambassador to Somalia, 1970–73; Consul-General, Istanbul, 1973–75. *Address:* c/o Lloyds Bank Ltd, Butler Place, Victoria Street, SW1.

BOURN, John Bryant; Assistant Under-Secretary of State, Ministry of Defence, since 1977; *b* 21 Feb. 1934; *s* of Henry Thomas Bryant Bourn and late Beatrice Grace Bourn; *m* 1959, Ardita Ann Fleming; one *s* one *d*. *Educ:* Southgate County Grammar Sch.; LSE. 1st cl. hons BScEcon 1954, PhD 1958. Air Min. 1956–63; HM Treasury, 1963–64; Private Sec. to Perm. Under-Sec., MoD, 1964–69; Asst Sec. and Dir of Programmes, Civil Service Coll.,

1969-72; Asst Sec., MoD, 1972-74; Under-Sec., Northern Ireland Office, 1974-77. *Publications:* articles and reviews in professional jls. *Recreations:* swimming, squash rackets. *Address:* Ministry of Defence, Main Building, Whitehall, SW1A 2HB.

BOURNE, Lt-Col Geoffrey (H.), FRSM, FZS; DPhil, DSc; Vice Chancellor, and Professor of Nutrition, St George's University School of Medicine, Grenada, since 1978; *b* West Perth, Western Australia, 17 Nov. 1909; *s* of Walter Howard Bourne and Mary Ann Mellon; *m* 1935, Gwenllian Myfanwy Jones, BA; two *s* ; *m* 1965, Maria Nelly Golarz, PhD. *Educ:* Perth Modern Sch., W Australia; University of Western Australia (BSc 1930, BSc Hons 1931; MSc 1932, DSc 1935); University of Melbourne. DPhil (Oxford), 1943; Hackett Research Student, University of W Australia, 1931-33; Biologist and in charge of Experimental Work, Australian Institute of Anatomy, Canberra, 1933-35; Biochemist Commonwealth of Austr. Advisory Council on Nutrition, 1935-37; Beit Memorial Fellow for Medical Research, Oxford, 1938-41; Mackenzie-Mackinnon Research Fellow of Royal College of Physicians of London and Royal College of Surgeons of England, 1941-44; Demonstrator in Physiology, Oxford, 1941-44, 1946, 1947; in charge of research and development (rations and physiological matters) for Special Forces in South-East Asia, 1944-45; Nutritional Adviser to British Military Administration, Malaya, 1945-46; Reader in Histology, University of London, at the London Hospital Medical Coll., 1947-57; Prof. and Chm. of Anatomy, Emory Univ., Atlanta, Ga, USA, 1957-63; Dir, Yerkes Regional Primate Research Center of Emory Univ., 1962-78. Member: Soc. Experimental Biology; Nutrition Soc. (foundation Mem.); Anatomical Soc. of Gt Brit. and N Ireland, Internat. Soc. for Cell Biology; Aerospace Med. Soc., etc. *Publications:* Nutrition and the War, 1940; Wartime Food for Mother and Child, 1942; Cytology and Cell Physiology (ed and part author), 1942, 2nd edn 1951; Starvation in Europe, 1943; How Your Body Works, 1949; The Mammalion Adrenal Gland, 1949; Aids to Histology, 1950; (ed jtly) International Review of Cytology, 1952; (ed jtly) Biochemistry and Physiology of Nutrition, Vols 1, 2; Introduction to Functional Histology; Biochemistry and Physiology of Bone; (ed jtly) The Biology of Ageing; Structure and function of Muscle; The Division of Labour in Cells; (ed jtly) Muscular Dystrophy in Man and Animals; World Review of Nutrition and Dietetics, 1962; Atherosclerosis and its origins; Structure and Function of Nervous Tissue, 1969; The Ape People, 1971; Primate Odyssey, 1974; The Gentle Giants, 1975; (with HSH Prince Rainier III of Monaco) Primate Conservation; Hearts and Heart-like Organs, 1981; contributor on Famine to Encyclopædia Britannica; contributions to scientific and medical journals. *Recreations:* water ski-ing, tennis, ballet and running (State Mile Championship and Record Holder, Australia). *Address:* St George's University School of Medicine, PO Box 7, St George's, Grenada, West Indies.

BOURNE, Gordon Lionel, FRCS, FRCOG; Consultant, since 1961, and Head of Department, since 1975, Department of Obstetrics and Gynæcology, St Bartholomew's Hospital, London; Consultant Gynæcologist to Royal Masonic Hospital since 1973; *b* 3 June 1921; *s* of Thomas Holland Bourne and Lily Anne (*née* Clewlow); *m* 1948, Barbara Eileen Anderson; three *s* one d. *Educ:* Queen Elizabeth Grammar Sch., Ashbourne; St Bartholomew's Hosp.; Harvard Univ. MRCS, LRCP 1945, FRCS 1954; MRCOG 1956, FRCOG 1962; FRSocMed. Highlands Hosp., 1948; Derbs Royal Infirm., 1949; City of London Mat. Hosp., 1952; Hosp. for Women, Soho, 1954; Gynæcol Registrar, Middlesex Hosp., 1956; Sen. Registrar, Obsts and Gynae., St Bartholomew's Hosp., 1958; Nuffield Trav. Fellow, 1959; Res. Fellow, Harvard, 1959; Cons. Gynæcol., St Luke's Hosp., 1963. Arris and Gale Lectr, RCS, 1964; Mem. Bd of Professions Suppl. to Medicine, 1964; Regional Assessor in Maternal Deaths, 1974; Examr in Obsts and Gynae., Univs of London, Oxford and Riyadh, Jt Conjt Bd and RCOG, Central Midwives Bd; Mem. Ct of Assts, Haberdashers' Co., 1968, Junior Warden, 1975; Mem. Bd of Governors, 1971-, Chm., 1980-, Haberdashers' Aske's Schs, Hatcham. *Publications:* The Human Amnion and Chorion, 1962; Shaw's Textbook of Gynæcology, 9th edn, 1970; Recent Advances in Obstetrics and Gynæcology, 11th edn, 1966—13th edn, 1979; Modern Gynæcology with Obstetrics for Nurses, 4th edn, 1969 and 5th edn, 1973; Pregnancy, 1972, 2nd edn 1975; numerous articles in sci. and professional jls. *Recreations:* ski-ing, water-ski-ing, shooting, swimming, writing, golf. *Address:* 147 Harley Street, W1N 1DL. *T:* 01-935 4444; Oldways, Bishop's Avenue, N2 0BN. *T:* 01-458 4788. *Club:* Carlton.

BOURNE, James Gerald, MA, MD (Cantab), FFARCS; Consulting Anæsthetist: St Thomas' Hospital, London; Salisbury Hospital Group; *b* 6 March 1906; *y s* of late W. W. Bourne, Garston Manor, Herts and of late Clara (*née* Hollingsworth); *m* 1957, Jenny Liddell (*d* 1967); one *s* ; *m* 1968, Susan Clarke; two *s*. *Educ:* Rugby; Corpus Christi Coll., Cambridge; St Thomas' Hospital. 1st class Geographical Tripos Part I, 1925; 1st class Geographical Tripos Part II, 1926; Exhibition and Prizes; MRCS, LRCP 1937; MB, BChir Cantab 1939; DA England 1945; FFARCS 1953; MD (Cantab), 1960. Major RAMC, 1939-45. *Publications:* Nitrous Oxide in Dentistry: Its Danger and Alternatives, 1960; Studies in Anæsthetics, 1967; contributions to medical literature. *Recreations:* ski-ing, riding, fishing. *Address:* Melstock, Nunton, Salisbury, Wilts. *T:* Salisbury 29734.

BOURNE, Sir (John) Wilfrid, KCB 1979 (CB 1975); QC 1981; Clerk of the Crown in Chancery, and Permanent Secretary, Lord Chancellor's Office, 1977-82; Barrister-at-Law; *b* 27 Jan. 1922; *s* of late Capt Rt Hon. R. C.

Bourne, MP, and of Lady Hester Bourne; *m* 1958, Elizabeth Juliet, *d* of late G. R. Fox, of Trewardreva, Constantine, Cornwall; two *s. Educ:* Eton; New Coll., Oxford (MA). Served War, Rifle Brigade, 1941-45. Called to Bar, Middle Temple, 1948, Bencher 1977; practised at Bar, 1949-56; Lord Chancellor's Office, 1956-82, Principal Assistant Solicitor, 1970-72, Deputy Sec., 1972-77. *Recreations:* gardening, sailing. *Address:* Povey's Farm, Ramsdell, Basingstoke, Hants. *Clubs:* Army and Navy; Leander (Henley-on-Thames).

BOURNE, (Rowland) Richard; journalist and author; *s* of Arthur Brittan and Edith Mary Bourne; *m* 1966, Juliet Mary, *d* of John Attenborough, CBE; two *s* one d. *Educ:* Uppingham Sch., Rutland; Brasenose Coll., Oxford (BA Mod. Hist.). Journalist, The Guardian, 1962-72 (Education correspondent, 1968-72); Asst Editor, New Society, 1972-77; Evening Standard: Dep. Editor, 1977-78; London Columnist, 1978-79; Founder Editor, Learn Magazine, 1979. Consultant, Internat. Broadcasting Trust, 1980-81. *Publications:* Political Leaders of Latin America, 1969; (with Brian MacArthur) The Struggle for Education, 1970; Getulio Vargas of Brazil, 1974; Assault on the Amazon, 1978; Londoners, 1981. *Recreations:* theatre, fishing, supporting Charlton Athletic. *Address:* 65 Lee Road, SE3 9EN. *T:* 01-852 9645. *Club:* Royal Automobile.

BOURNE, Stafford, MA Cantab; Chairman, 1938-72, President, 1972-79, Bourne & Hollingsworth Ltd (relinquished all connection, on retirement after 57 years service); *b* 20 Feb. 1900; *e s* of late Walter William and Clara Louisa Bourne (*née* Hollingsworth), Garston Manor, Herts; *m* 1940, Magdalene Jane, *d* of Frederick and Anne Leeson; one *s* one *d* (and one *s* decd). *Educ:* Rugby; Corpus Christi, Cambridge; and in France. War of 1939-45, Admiralty Ferry Crews. Co-Founder and First Pres., Oxford Street Assoc., 1958-68. Is actively interested in interchange of young people between UK and W Europe for business and cultural purposes. *Recreations:* yachting, painting, chess. *Address:* Drokes, Beaulieu, Brockenhurst, Hants SO4 7XE. *T:* Bucklers Hard 252. *Clubs:* United Oxford & Cambridge University, Royal Cruising; Royal Lymington Yacht.

BOURNE, Sir Wilfrid; *see* Bourne, Sir J. W.

BOURNE-ARTON, Major Anthony Temple, MBE 1944; *b* 1 March 1913; 2nd *s* of W. R. Temple Bourne, Walker Hall, Winston, Co. Durham, and Evelyn Rose, 3rd *d* of Sir Frank Wills, Bristol; assumed surname of Bourne-Arton, 1950; *m* 1938, Margaret Elaine, er *d* of W. Denby Arton, Sleningford Park, Ripon, Yorks; two *s* two *d. Educ:* Clifton. Served Royal Artillery, 1933-48; active service, 1936, Palestine; 1939-45: France, N Africa, Sicily and Italy (despatches, MBE); Malaya, 1947-48. Gen. Commissioner Income Tax, 1952-80; has served on Bedale RDC, and N Riding County Agric. Cttee; County Councillor, N Riding of Yorks, 1949-61; CC, W Riding of Yorks, 1967-70; Chm., Yorkshire Regional Land Drainage Cttee, 1973-80. MP (C) Darlington, 1959-64; PPS to the Home Sec., 1962-64. JP N Riding of Yorks, 1950-80. *Recreations:* fishing and shooting. *Address:* The Old Rectory, West Tanfield, Ripon, N Yorks. *T:* Bedale 70333.

BOURNS, Prof. Arthur Newcombe; President and Vice-Chancellor, 1972-80, Professor of Chemistry since 1953, McMaster University; *b* 8 Dec. 1919; *s* of Evans Clement Bourns and Kathleen Jones; *m* 1943, Marion Harriet Blakney; two *s* two *d. Educ:* schs in Petitcodiac, NB; Acadia Univ. (BSc); McGill Univ. (PhD). Research Chemist, Dominion Rubber Co., 1944-45; Lectr, Acadia Univ., 1945-46; Asst Prof. of Chemistry, Saskatchewan Univ., 1946-47; McMaster Univ.: Asst Prof., 1947-49; Associate Prof., 1949-53; Dean, Faculty of Grad. Studies, 1957-61; Chm., Chemistry Dept, 1965-67; Vice-Pres., Science and Engrg Div., 1967-72; Actg Pres., 1970. Nuffield Trav. Fellow in Science, University Coll., London, 1955-56. Chm., Gordon Res. Conf. on Chem. and Physics of Isotopes (Vice-Chm. 1959-60; Chm., 1961-62); Nat. Res. Council of Canada: Mem. Grant Selection Cttee in Chem., 1966-69 (Chm. 1968-69); Mem. Council, 1969-75; Mem. Exec. Cttee, 1969-75; Mem. or Chm. various other cttees; Natural Scis and Engrg Res. Council: Member: Council, 1978-; Exec. Cttee, 1978-; Allocations Cttee, 1978-; Cttee on Strategic Grants, 1978-; Chm., Grants and Scholarships Cttee, 1978-; Mem., Adv. Cttee on University/Industry Interface, 1979-. Member: Ancaster Public Sch. Bd, 1963-64; Bd, Royal Botanic Gdns, 1972-80 (Vice-Chm.); Scientific Adv. Council of Canadian Bd, Weizman Inst. of Sci., 1974-; Cttee on Univ. Affairs, Prov. Ontario (Chm. Sub-cttee on Grad. Studies and Res., 1964-69; Mem. Capital Studies Cttee, 1967-71); Canadian Cttee for Financing Univ. Res., 1978-; Council of Ontario Univs, 1972-80 (Exec. Cttee, 1974-79; Vice-Chm., 1976-78; Chm., Cttee on Nominations, 1976-78); Bd of Dirs and Exec. Cttee, Assoc. of Univs and Colleges of Canada, 1974-77; Mohawk Coll. Bd of Dirs, 1975-; Pres. and Chm. Exec. Cttee, Canadian Bureau for Internat. Educn, 1973-76. McMaster Univ. Med. Centre: Member: Bd of Trustees, 1972-80; Exec. Cttee, 1972-80; Mem., Interim Jt Bd of Trustees, Chedoke McMaster Hosp., 1978, Exec. Cttee and Bd of Trustees, 1979-80. Director: Nuclear Activation Services, 1978-80; Slater Steel Industries Ltd, 1975-. British Council Lectr, 1963. Assoc. Editor, Canadian Jl Chemistry, 1966-69; Mem. Editorial Bd, Science Forum, 1967-73. FCIC 1954 (Chm. Hamilton Section, 1952-53; Mem. Educn Cttee, 1953-59; Mem. Council, 1966-69; Montreal Medal, 1976); FRSC 1964; FCS 1968. Hon. DSc: Acadia, 1968; McGill, 1977. *Address:* President's Office, McMaster University, Hamilton, Ontario, Canada, L8S 4L8. *T:* 525-9140.

BOURTON, Cyril Leonard, CB 1977; Deputy Secretary (Finance), and Accountant General, Department of Health and Social Security, 1974-76; *b* 28 Dec. 1916; *s* of late Leonard Victor Bourton; *m* 1940, Elizabeth Iris Savage; two *s* one *d. Educ:* St Dunstan's Coll., Catford. Nat. Debt Office, 1933-37; Min. of Health, later DHSS: Dep. Accountant-Gen., 1958; Asst Sec., Exec. Councils Div., 1964; Under-Sec. for Finance and Accountant Gen., 1967. *Recreations:* fishing, photography, genealogy. *Address:* 58 Manor Way, Beckenham, Kent BR3 3LJ. *T:* 01-658 6121.

BOUVERIE; *see* Pleydell-Bouverie, family name of Earl of Radnor.

BOVELL, Hon. Sir (William) Stewart, Kt 1976; JP; Agent-General for Western Australia, in London, 1971-74; *b* 19 Dec. 1906; *s* of A. R. Bovell and Ethel (*née* Williams), Busselton, Western Australia. *Educ:* Busselton, WA. Banking, 1923-40. Served War, RAAF, 1941-45, Flt Lt. MLA: for Sussex, WA, 1947-50; for Vasse, WA, 1950-71. Minister: for Labour, WA, 1961-62; for Lands, Forests and Immigration, WA, 1959-71. Govt Whip, WA, 1950-53; Opposition Whip, WA, 1953-57. Rep., Australian States Gen. Council, at British Commonwealth Parly Assoc., in Nairobi, Kenya, and Victoria Falls, S Rhodesia, 1954. Mem. Bd of Governors, Bunbury CofE Cathedral Grammar Sch., 1974 (Vice-Chm.). Hon. Lay Canon, St Boniface CofE Cathedral, Bunbury, WA, 1975. JP 1949, WA. Patron: Polocrosse Assoc. of WA; Geographe Bay Yacht Club. *Recreations:* swimming, tennis, walking. *Address:* 24 West Street, Busselton, WA 6280, Australia.

BOVENIZER, Vernon Gordon Fitzell, CMG 1948; Assistant Under-Secretary of State, Ministry of Defence, 1964-68, retired; *b* 22 July 1908; *s* of Rev. Michael Fitzell Bovenizer and Mary Gordon; *m* 1937, Lillian Cherry (*d* 1970), *d* of John Henry Rowe, Cork; two *s* two *d. Educ:* Liverpool Coll.; Sidney Sussex Coll., Cambridge (Scholar). War Office, 1931-45; Control Commission for Germany, 1945, until return to War Office, 1948; Asst Private Sec. to Secretaries of State for War, 1936, and 1940-42; Resident Clerk, 1934-37; Asst Sec., 1942, civilian liaison with US Armies in the UK; Establishment Officer and Dir of Organisation, CCG, 1945; Asst Sec. and Dep. Comptroller of Claims, War Office, 1948-58; Counsellor, UK Delegation to NATO, 1958-60; Asst Under-Sec. of State, War Office, 1960-64. US Medal of Freedom, 1945. *Recreations:* tennis and squash. *Address:* 6 Cambanks, Union Lane, Cambridge; 9 The Square, Annalong, Co. Down. *Club:* Reform.

BOVET, Prof. Daniel; Nobel Prize for Physiology and Medicine, 1957; Professor f.r., University of Rome, Italy; *b* Neuchatel, Switzerland, 23 March 1907; *s* of Pierre Bovet and Amy Babut; *m* Filomena Nitti; three *s.* Institut Pasteur, Paris, 1929-47 (first as an asst and afterwards Chief of the Laboratory of Therapeutic Chemistry); Chief of the Laboratory of Therapeutic Chemistry, Instituto Superiore di Sanità, Rome, 1947-64; Prof. of Pharmacology, Fac. of Medicine, Univ. of Sassari, Italy, 1964-71; Prof. of Psychobiol., Faculty of Sci., Rome Univ., 1971-77. Mem. of the Accademia Nazionale dei XL, 1969; Mem. of Accademia naz. dei Lincei, 1958; Foreign Mem., Royal Soc., 1962. Grande Ufficiale dell' Ordine della Repubblica Italiana, 1959; Comdr, Légion d'Honneur, 1980. *Publications:* (in collaboration with F. Bovet-Nitti) Structure chimique et activité pharmacodynamique du système nerveux végétatif, 1948 (Bale, Switzerland); (in collaboration with F. Bovet-Nitti and G. B. Marini-Bettolo) Curare and Curare-like Agents, 1957 (Amsterdam, Holland); (in collaboration with R. Blum and others) Controlling Drugs, 1974 (San Francisco). *Recreation:* wandering in Amazonia. *Address:* 33 Piazza S Apollinare, 00186 Rome, Italy. *T:* 6565297; Istituto di Fisiologia generale, Citta Universitaria, 00185 Roma, Italy.

BOVEY, Dr Leonard; Head of Technological Requirements Branch, Department of Industry, since 1977; *b* 9 May 1924; *s* of late Alfred and Gladys Bovey; *m* 1943, Constance Hudson; one *s* one *d. Educ:* Heles Sch., Exeter; Emmanuel Coll., Cambridge (BA, PhD). FInstP. Dunlop Rubber, 1943-46; Post-doctoral Fellow, Nat. Res. Council, Ottawa, 1950-52; AERE Harwell, 1952-65; Head W Mids Regional Office, Birmingham, Min. of Technology, 1966-70; Regional Dir, Yorks and Humberside, DTI, 1970-73; Counsellor (Scientific and Technological Affairs), High Commn, Ottawa, 1974-77. *Publications:* Spectroscopy in the Metallurgical Industry, 1963; papers on spectroscopy in Jl Optical Soc. Amer., Spectrochimica Acta, Jl Phys. Soc. London. *Recreations:* repairing neglected household equipment, work, reading (particularly crime novels), walking, theatre, music. *Address:* 32 Radnor Walk, Chelsea SW3 4BN. *T:* 01-352 4142. *Club:* Civil Service.

BOWMAN, Sir J(ohn) Vansittart, 4th Bt *cr* 1914; *b* 6 April 1918; *s* of Captain Victor Spencer Bowater (*d* 1967) (3rd *s* of 1st Bt) and Hilda Mary (*d* 1918), *d* of W. Henry Potter; *S* uncle, Sir Thomas Dudley Blennerhassett Bowater, 3rd Bt, 1972; *m* 1943, Joan Kathleen, *d* of late Wilfrid Scullard; one *s* one *d. Educ:* Branksome School, Godalming, Surrey. Served Royal Artillery, 1939-46. *Heir: s* Michael Patrick Bowater [*b* 18 July 1949; *m* 1968, Alison, *d* of Edward Wall; four *d*]. *Address:* 214 Runnymede Avenue, Bournemouth, Dorset BH11 9SP. *T:* Northbourne 71782.

BOWATER, Sir Noël Vansittart, 2nd Bt, *cr* 1939; GBE 1954; MC 1917; *b* 25 Dec. 1892; *s* of Sir Frank H. Bowater, 1st Bt and Ethel Anita (*d* 1943), *d* of late Mark Fryar, Burmah; *S* father 1947; *m* 1921, Constance Heiton Bett; one *s* two *d. Educ:* Rugby. Commnd Territorial Force RA, 1913; served in France, 1915-19 (MC). Sheriff of City of London, 1948, Lord Mayor,

1953-54; Master, Company of Vintners, 1954-55. KStJ; Kt Comdr Royal Order of the North Star; Kt Comdr Order of Menelik the Second. *Heir: s* Euan David Vansittart Bowater, BA Cantab [*b* 9 Sept. 1935; *m* 1964, Susan Mary Humphrey, *d* of A. R. O. Slater, FCA, and Mrs N. M. Slater; two *s* two *d*]. *Address:* Conifers, St George's Hill, Weybridge, Surrey. *T:* Weybridge 42744; Riscombe, Exford, Somerset. *T:* Exford 280. *Clubs:* City Livery, United Wards, Guildhall.

BOWDELL, Wilfred, CBE 1973; Management Consultant since 1974; *b* 28 Nov. 1913; *s* of Harry Bowdell and Sarah Alice Bowdell (*née* Roscoe); *m* 1939, Alice Lord. *Educ:* Bury High Sch.; Univ. of London (BScEcon); Inst. of Public Finance and Accountancy (Pres., 1972-73). Finance Asst, Bury County Borough Council, 1930-36; Chief Accountancy Asst, Swinton and Pendlebury Borough Council, 1936-39; Chief Accountant, York City Council, 1939-46; Dep. Treas., Enfield Urban District Council, 1946-48; Dep. Treas. 1948-62, Borough Treas. 1962-65, St Marylebone Borough Council; City Treas., Westminster City Council, 1965-74. Member: Public Works Loan Bd, 1975- (Dep. Chm., 1980-); London Housing Staff Commn, 1979-. *Recreations:* music, photography, gardening. *Address:* 72 Highfield Way, Rickmansworth, Herts. *T:* Rickmansworth 73459.

BOWDEN, family name of **Baron Aylestone** and **Baron Bowden.**

BOWDEN, Baron, *cr* 1963, of Chesterfield (Life Peer); **Bertram Vivian Bowden,** MA, PhD, FIEE, FIEEE, MScTech; Principal, The University of Manchester Institute of Science and Technology (called Manchester College of Science and Technology until May 1966), 1964-76, retired; *b* 18 Jan. 1910; *s* of B. C. Bowden, Chesterfield; *m* 1939, Marjorie Browne (marr. diss., 1954; she *d* 1957); one *s* two *d* ; *m* 1967, Mary Maltby (*d* 1971); *m* 1974, Mrs Phyllis James (*see* Lady Bowden). *Educ:* Chesterfield Grammar Sch.; Emmanuel Coll., Cambridge. Worked with late Lord Rutherford, 1931-34; PhD 1934; University of Amsterdam, 1934-35. Physics Master, Liverpool Collegiate Sch., 1935-37; Chief Physics Master, Oundle Sch., 1937-40; Radar Research in England, 1940-43; Radar Research in USA, 1943-46; Sir Robert Watson Watt and Partners, 1947-50; Ferranti Ltd, Manchester (Digital Computers), 1950-53; Dean of the Faculty of Technology, Manchester Univ., and Principal, Manchester Coll. of Science and Technology, 1953-64. Chm. Electronics Research Council of Ministry of Aviation, 1960-64; Minister of State, Dept of Education and Science, 1964-65 (on leave of absence as Principal of Manchester Coll. of Science and Technology). Pres. The Science Masters Assoc., 1962. Pres., Nat. Television Rental Assoc., 1975-82. Hon. FICE 1975; Hon. DS Rensellaer Polytechnic, USA, 1974; Hon. LLD Manchester, 1976; Hon. DSc Kumasi, Ghana, 1977. Pioneer Award, IEEE Aerospace & Electronic Systems Gp, 1973. *Publications:* Faster Than Thought, 1953; The Development of Manchester College of Science and Technology; numerous papers on education. *Recreation:* listening to music. *Address:* Pine Croft, Stanhope Road, Bowdon, Altrincham, Cheshire WA14 3LB. *T:* 061-928 4005. *Club:* Athenæum.

BOWDEN, Lady; Phyllis Bertha Mabel Bowden; President, Lucy Cavendish College, Cambridge, since 1979; *b* 10 June 1918; *d* of Stanley Ernest and Bertha Myson; *m* 1st, 1941, John Henry Lewis James (*d* 1962); one *d* ; 2nd, 1974, Baron Bowden, *qv. Educ:* Wimbledon High Sch; Newnham Coll., Cambridge (MA). Commonwealth (now Harkness) Fellow, 1957-58. BoT, 1941; Principal 1947; Asst Sec., 1960; DEA, 1964-69; Min. of Technology, 1969-70; Dept of Trade and Industry, 1970-75; Asst Under-Sec. of State 1972; Regional Dir, NW Region, DTI, subseq. DoI, 1972-75. Member: Monopolies and Mergers Commn, 1975-78; Local Govt Boundary Commn for England, 1977-81; W Midlands Cttee, National Trust, 1976-81. Chm., Manchester Marriage Guidance Council, 1976-79. Member: Court, Manchester Univ., 1976-; Court and Council, UMIST, 1978-80. *Publications:* The Concept of Growth Centres, 1968; Gardens through the Ages, 1971; Regional Policy in Action, 1980; contrib. Public Administration, Encycl. Britannica. *Recreations:* landscape architecture, collecting art nouveau. *Address:* 18 Trafalgar Road, Cambridge CB4 1EU. *Club:* University Women's.

BOWDEN, Andrew, MBE 1961; MP (C) Kemp Town Division of Brighton since 1970; *b* 8 April 1930; *s* of William Victor Bowden, Solicitor, and Francesca Wilson; *m* Benita Napier; one *s* one *d. Educ:* Ardingly College. Paint industry, 1955-68; Man. Dir, Personnel Assessments Ltd, 1969-71; Man. Dir, Haymarket Personnel Selection Ltd, 1970-71; Director: Sales Education & Leadership Ltd, 1970-71; Jenkin and Purser (Holdings) Ltd, 1973-77. Jt Chm., All Party Old Age Pensioners Parly Gp, 1972-; Chm., All Party BLESMA Gp; Mem. Select Cttee on Expenditure, 1973-74, on Abortion, 1975, on Employment, 1979-. Contested (C): North Hammersmith, 1955; North Kensington, 1964; Kemp Town, Brighton, 1966. Nat. Chm., Young Conservatives, 1960-61; Mem., Wandsworth Borough Council, 1956-62. Vice-Pres., 1975-, Public Affairs Consultant, 1977-, Council for Internat. Contact. *Recreations:* fishing, chess, golf. *Address:* House of Commons, SW1. *T:* 01-219 5047. *Club:* Carlton.

BOWDEN, Major Aubrey Henry, DSO 1918; Chairman, Bowden Bros Ltd; *e s* of Henry White Bowden, MICE, Great Missenden; *m* 1st, 1918, Helen (*d* 1939), *o d* of late R. G. Modera, Wilbury Lodge, Hove; one *s* one *d* ; 2nd, 1941, Andrée Marguerite July; one *s* two *d. Educ:* Oundle. Electrical Engineer. Training: Brompton and Kensington Electricity Supply Co.; London Underground Railway; Metropolitan Railway; Oerlikon Co.; from here commissioned: to 11th Service Batt. Royal Warwicks Regt, to Capt. and Brigade Machine Gun Officer, to Machine Gun Corps. *Address:* 28 Berkeley Court, Baker Street, NW1.

BOWDEN, Sir Frank Houston, 3rd Bt *cr* 1915; MA Oxon; industrialist and landowner; *b* 10 Aug. 1909; *o s* of Sir Harold Bowden, 2nd Bt, GBE, and of Vera, *d* of Joseph Whitaker, JP, FZS; *S* father 1960; *m* 1st, 1935; one *s* ; 2nd, 1937, Lydia Eveline (*d* 1981), *d* of Jean Manolovici, Bucharest; three *s*. *Educ:* Rugby; Merton Coll., Oxford. Served with RNVR, 1939–44. President: University Hall, Buckland, 1967–71; British Kendo Association, 1969. Hon. Vice-Pres., 3rd World Kendo Championships, 1976. *Recreation:* collecting weapons and armour, particularly Japanese (Vice-Chm. Japan Soc. of London, 1970–75, 1979–82; Mem., Soc. for Preservation of Art Swords of Japan, Tokyo). *Heir:* s Nicholas Richard Bowden, *b* 13 Aug. 1935. *Address:* Thame Park, Oxon. *Clubs:* White's, Royal Thames Yacht.

BOWDEN, Prof. Kenneth Frank, DSc, FInstP; Professor of Oceanography in the University of Liverpool, since 1962, now Emeritus; *b* 23 Dec. 1916; *s* of Frank and Margaret N. Bowden; *m* 1946, Lilias T. M. Nicol; one *d. Educ:* Itchen Secondary Sch.; University Coll., Southampton. Scientific Officer, Anti-Submarine Experimental Establishment (Admiralty), 1939–45; Lecturer in Oceanography, University of Liverpool, 1945–52; Principal Scientific Officer, Nat. Inst. of Oceanography, 1952–54; Dean, Faculty of Science, 1959–62, Pro-Vice-Chancellor, 1968–71, Univ. of Liverpool. *Publications:* papers on physical oceanography in various scientific journals. *Address:* 19 Forest Close, Meols, Wirral, Merseyside. *T:* 051-632 4083.

BOWDEN, Logan S.; *see* Scott Bowden.

BOWDEN, Dr Richard Charles, OBE 1941; PhD, MSc, FRSC, FCS; Consultant, Ministry of Aviation (formerly Ministry of Supply), 1952–60; *b* 31 Aug. 1887; *s* of Richard Charles Bowden, Bristol, and Minnie Clara Thatcher; *m* 1913, Nina Adeline, *er d* of Thomas Fisher, Bristol; no *c. Educ:* Merchant Venturers Sch., Bristol; Merchant Venturers Technical Coll., Bristol; Bristol Univ. (Hons, Physical Chemistry). Asst Chemist, Research Dept, Royal Arsenal, Woolwich, 1911; Chemist, Royal Gunpowder Factory, 1912; Chemist 2nd Class, 1915; Chemist in Charge, 1923; Technical Asst (temp.) under Dir of Ordnance Factories, War Office, 1930; Technical Asst, 1932; Chemical Engineer, 1934; Superintendent, Royal Ordnance Factories, 1934–41; Asst Dir of Ordnance Factories (X); Dep Dir of Ordnance Factories (X), 1941; Dir, of Ordnance Factories (X), 1942–52. Patentee or Joint Patentee of various patents relating to chemical processes and chemical plant. Medals: Silver Jubilee, 1935; Coronation, 1937 and 1953. *Publications:* Author or Joint Author of publications in Journal of Chemical Society, 1911, 1912, 1923. *Address:* Villa Maria, 66–68 Croham Road, South Croydon, Surrey CR2 7BB.

BOWDEN, Prof. Ruth Elizabeth Mary, OBE 1980; DSc London, MB, BS, FRCS; Professor of Anatomy, Royal Free Hospital School of Medicine, University of London, 1951–80, now Emeritus; Hon. Research Fellow, Institute of Neurology, since 1980; part-time Lecturer, Department of Anatomy, St Thomas's Hospital Medical School, since 1980; *b* 21 Feb. 1915; *o c* of late Frank Harold and Louise Ellen Bowden. *Educ:* Westlands Sch.; St Paul's Girls' Sch.; London (Royal Free Hospital) Sch. of Medicine for Women, University of London. House Surg. and later House Physician, Elizabeth Garrett Anderson Hosp. (Oster House branch), 1940–42; House Surg., Royal Cancer Hosp., 1942; Grad. Asst in Nuffield Dept of Orthopædic Surgery, Peripheral Nerve Injury Unit, Oxford, 1942–45; Asst Lecturer in Anatomy, Royal Free Hospital Sch. of Medicine, 1945; later Lecturer, then University Reader in Human Anatomy, 1949; Rockefeller Travelling Fellowship, 1949–50; Hunterian Prof., RCS, 1950. WHO Consultant in anatomy, Khartoum Univ., 1972, 1974, 1977. President: Anat. Soc. of Gt Brit. and Ireland, 1970; Medical Women's Fedn, 1981. FRSM; Fellow: Brit. Orthopædic Assoc.; Linnaean Soc. Vice-President: Council of Chartered Soc. of Physiotherapy (Chm., 1960–70); Inst. of Science Technology (Pres., 1960–65); Riding for the Disabled Assoc. DLJ 1978, CMLJ 1980. Jubilee Medal, 1977. *Publications:* contribs to Peripheral Nerve Injuries Report of Medical Research Council; Peripheral Nerve Injuries; contribs to medical and scientific jls. *Recreations:* reading, music, painting, walking, gardening, carpentry. *Address:* 6 Hartham Close, Hartham Road, N7. *T:* 01-607 3464.

BOWEN, Edward George, CBE 1962; PhD; FRS 1975; FAA; Counsellor (Scientific) at the Australian Embassy in Washington, DC, USA, 1973–76; *b* 14 Jan. 1911; *s* of G. Bowen, Swansea. *Educ:* Univ. of Wales (MSc); London Univ. (PhD); DSc Sydney. Mem., Radar Develt Team, 1935; Air Ministry Research Station, Bawdsey, 1936–40; British Air Commn Washington, 1940–42; Radiation Lab., MIT, 1943; Chief, Div. of Radiophysics, CSIRO, 1946–71. Chm., Anglo-Australian Telescope Board, 1967–73. Vice-Pres., Aust. Acad. of Science, 1962–63; Foreign Member: Amer. Acad. of Arts and Scis; US Nat. Acad. of Engrg. Fellow, King's Coll., 1981. Thurlow Award, Amer. Inst. of Navigation, 1950. *Address:* 1/39 Clarke Street, Narrabeen, NSW 2101, Australia. *Club:* Athenæum.

BOWEN, Maj.-Gen. Esmond John, CB 1982; Director, Army Dental Service, 1978–82; *b* 6 Dec. 1922; *s* of Major Leslie Arthur George Bowen, MC, and Edna Grace Bowen; *m* 1948, Elsie (*née* Midgley); two *s* two *d* (and one *d* decd). *Educ:* Clayesmore Sch.; Univ. of Birmingham. LDS Birmingham

1946. Commd Lieut, RADC, 1947; Captain 1948; Major 1955; Lt-Col 1962, Chief Instructor, Depot and Training Establishment RADC, 1966–69: CC Nos 2 and 3 Dental Groups, 1969–74; Asst Dir, Army Dental Service, 1974–76, Comdt, HQ and Training Centre, RADC, 1976–77; Brig. 1977; Dep. Dir, Dental Service, HQ BAOR, 1977–78. QHDS, 1977–82. Col Comdt, RADC 1982–. FBIM. OStJ 1975. *Recreations:* target rifle and muzzle loading shooting. *Address:* 72 Winchester Road, Andover, Hants. *T:* Andover 3252 *Club:* Lansdowne.

BOWEN, (Evan) Roderic, QC 1952; MA, LLD; Master Emeritus of the Middle Temple; Social Security (formerly National Insurance) Commissioner, since 1967; *b* 6 Aug. 1913; 2nd *s* of late Evan Bowen, JP, and late Margaret Ellen Twiss, The Elms, Cardigan. *Educ:* Cardigan Schs; University Coll., Aberystwyth; St John's Coll., Cambridge. Practised at the bar with chambers in Cardiff until 1940; served in HM Forces, 1940–45, in the ranks and subsequently as an officer on staff of Judge Advocate-Gen. MP (L), County of Cardigan, 1945–66; Dep. Chm. of Ways and Means, House of Commons, 1965–66. Recorder of: Carmarthen, 1950; Merthyr Tydfil, 1953–60; Swansea 1960–64; Cardiff, 1964–67; Chm., Montgomeryshire QS, 1959–71. Chm. Welsh Parliamentary Party, 1955. Pres., St David's UC, Lampeter, 1977– Hon. LLD Wales, 1972. *Address:* 3 Maynard Court, Fairwater Road, Llandaff, Cardiff. *T:* Cardiff 563207. *Clubs:* National Liberal; County (Cardiff).

BOWEN, Sir Geoffrey Fraser, Kt 1977; Managing Director, Commercial Banking Company of Sydney Ltd, Australia, 1973–76, retired (General Manager, 1970–73); *m* 1st, Ruth (decd), *d* of H. E. Horsburgh; two *s* one *d* ; 2nd, Isabel, *d* of H. T. Underwood. *Address:* Cavendish, 16/562 Pacific Highway, Killara, NSW 2071, Australia. *Clubs:* Union (Sydney); Warrawee Bowling; Killara Golf.

BOWEN, Gordon, CB 1962; CMG 1956; Director, Metrication Board, 1969–74; *b* 17 June 1910; *e s* of late Arthur Thomas Bowen and late Dora Drinkwater; *m* 1938, Elsa Catriona, *y d* of late Rev. Dr Alexander Grieve, MA, PhD; one *s* (and one *s* decd). *Educ:* Birkenhead Institute Sch.; University of Liverpool. Asst Lecturer in Geography, University of Glasgow, 1933–36; Commonwealth Fund Fellow, University of Calif., 1936–38; Lecturer in Geography, University of Glasgow, 1938–41; Principal, Board of Trade, 1941–44; Asst Sec., Board of Trade, 1944–53; United Kingdom Senior Trade Commissioner in Canada, 1953–58; Under Secretary: Board of Trade, 1958–66 Min. of Technology, 1966–69. *Address:* 5 Knowehead Gardens, Albert Drive, Pollokshields, Glasgow G41 5RE.

BOWEN, Ian; *see* Bowen, Ivor I.

BOWEN, Ivor, CMG 1954; MSc, FRAeS, MIEE; Consultant in Aeronautical Engineering; *b* 21 Feb. 1902; *o s* of James and Barbara Bowen, Oxton, Ches; *m* 1941, Hilda, *o d* of Arthur and Florence Mary Fakes, Cambridge; one *s* one *d. Educ:* Birkenhead Institute; University of Liverpool; Trinity Coll. Cambridge. Oliver Lodge Fellow, University of Liverpool, 1923–24 Research Asst to Sir J. J. Thomson, OM, FRS, 1924–26; Demonstrator in Physics, Cavendish Laboratory, Cambridge, 1925–26; Founder Mem. of Cambridge Univ. Air Squadron, 1925. Lecturer in Air Navigation and Aircraft Instruments, Imperial Coll. of Science, 1938–40; Hon. Sec. Instn of Professional Civil Servants, 1938–40; Dep. Dir of Armament Research, Min of Aircraft Production, 1940; Dir of Instrument Research and Development, Min. of Supply, 1941–47; Chm. Air Photography Research Cttee, 1945–47 Mem. of Council, British Scientific Instrument Research Assoc., 1945–47 Chief Superintendent, Aeroplane and Armament Experimental Establishment, Boscombe Down, 1947–50; Scientific Adviser to UK High Comr to Australia, and Head of UK Min. of Supply Staff, Australia, 1951–53; Principal Dir of Aircraft Equipment Research and Development, Ministry of Supply, 1953–54; Chm. Air Navigation Cttee of Aeronautical Research Council, 1958–61: Mem. Council, Air League of the British Empire; Mem. Air Traffic Control and Navigation Cttee of Electronics Research Council, 1961–68. Mem., Ct of Common Council, City of London, Ward of Broad Street, 1970– Liveryman of Worshipful Company of Carpenters, 1959 (Freeman 1954), and of Worshipful Company of Scientific Instrument Makers. Freeman of City of London, 1955. *Publications:* numerous scientific papers on Physics and Aeronautics. *Recreations:* archæology, arboriculture, shooting. *Address* Stancote, Kippington Road, Sevenoaks, Kent. *T:* Sevenoaks 52495. *Clubs* Athenæum, City Livery, Royal Air Force.

BOWEN, Prof. (Ivor) Ian, MA Oxon; *b* Cardiff, 3 Dec. 1908; *s* of Ivor Bowen, KC, later County Court Judge, and Edith May (*née* Dummett); *m* 1st, 1935, Erica Baillie (marr. diss., 1950); one *s* one *d* ; 2nd, 1951, Isobel Margaret Lindsay Smith; one *s* one *d. Educ:* Westminster Sch.; Christ Church, Oxford. Fellow, All Souls Coll., 1930–37, and 1968; Lecturer, Brasenose Coll. 1931–40; Chief Statistical Officer, Ministry of Works, 1940–45; Lectr, Hertford Coll., 1946–47; Prof. of Economics and Commerce, Hull Univ., 1947–58; Prof. of Economics, Univ. of WA, 1958–73; Editor, Finance and Development (IMF and World Bank Group), 1974–77. *Publications:* Cobden (Great Lives Series), 1934; Britain's Industrial Survival, 1947; Population (Cambridge Economic Handbooks), 1954; Acceptable Inequalities, 1970 Economics and Demography, 1976. *Recreation:* golf. *Address:* Xalet Verena La Massana, Andorra. *T:* Andorra 35-2-21. *Club:* Reform.

BOWEN, John Griffith; playwright and novelist; freelance drama producer for television; *b* 5 Nov. 1924; *s* of Hugh Griffith Bowen and Ethel May Cook unmarried. *Educ:* Queen Elizabeth's Grammar Sch., Crediton; Pembroke Coll., Oxford; St Antony's Coll., Oxford. Frere Exhibition for Indian Studies, Oxford, 1951-52 and 1952-53. Asst Editor, The Sketch, 1954-57; Advertising Copywriter and Copy Chief, 1957-60; Consultant on TV Drama, Associated TV, 1960-67; productions for Thames TV, LWT, Yorkshire TV, 1978-. *Publications:* The Truth Will Not Help Us, 1956; After the Rain, 1958; The Centre of the Green, 1959; Storyboard, 1960; The Birdcage, 1962; A World Elsewhere, 1965; The Essay Prize, 1965; *plays:* I Love You, Mrs Patterson, 1964; After the Rain, 1967; Fall and Redemption, 1967; Little Boxes, 1968; The Disorderly Women, 1968; The Corsican Brothers, 1970; The Waiting Room, 1970; Robin Redbreast, 1972; Heil Caesar, 1973; Florence Nightingale, 1975; Which Way Are You Facing?, 1976; Singles, 1977; Bondage, 1978; The Inconstant Couple (adaptation of Marivaux, L'Heureux Stratageme), 1978; Uncle Jeremy, 1981. *Recreations:* science fiction, cooking. *Address:* Old Lodge Farm, Sugarswell Lane, Edgehill, Banbury, Oxon. *T:* Tysoe 401.

BOWEN, Very Rev. Lawrence; Dean of St Davids Cathedral since 1972; *b* 9 Sept. 1914; *s* of William and Elizabeth Ann Bowen; *m* 1941, Hilary Myrtle Bowen; two *d. Educ:* Llanelli Gram. Sch.; Univ. Coll. of Wales, Aberystwyth (BA 1st Cl.); St Michael's Coll., Llandaff (Crossley Exhibnr and Sen. Student). Ordained in St Davids Cathedral, 1938; Curate of Pembrey, 1938-40; Minor Canon, St Davids Cathedral, 1940-46; Vicar of St Clears with Llanginning, 1946-64; Rector of Tenby, 1964-72; Rector of Rectorial Benefice of Tenby with Gumfreston and Penally, 1970-72; Canon of St Davids Cathedral (Mathry), 1972. Surrogate. *Recreations:* golf, cricket, writing Welsh poetry. *Address:* The Deanery, St Davids, Dyfed. *T:* St Davids 202.

BOWEN, Most Rev. Michael George; see Southwark, Archbishop and Metropolitan of, (RC).

BOWEN, Hon. Sir Nigel (Hubert), KBE 1976; Chief Judge, Federal Court of Australia, since 1976; *b* Summerland, BC, Canada, 26 May 1911; *s* of late O. P. Bowen, Ludlow, England; *m* 1947, Eileen C., *d* of F. J. Mullens; three *d. Educ:* King's Sch., Sydney; St Paul's Coll., Sydney Univ. (BA, LLB). Served 2nd AIF, 1942-46 (Captain). Admitted NSW Bar 1936, Victorian Bar 1954; QC (Austr.) 1953; Vice-Pres., Law Council of Australia, 1957-60; Pres., NSW Bar Council, 1959-61. Lectr in Company Law and Taxation, Sydney Univ., 1957-58; Editor, Australian Law Jl, 1946-58. MHR (L) Australia for Parramatta, NSW, 1964-73, retired; Attorney-General, Australia, 1966-69 and March-Aug. 1971; Minister for Educn and Science, 1969-71; Minister for Foreign Affairs, Aug. 1971-Dec. 1972. Judge of Court of Appeal of NSW, 1973-76; Chief Judge in Equity, 1974-76. Head of Austr. Delegn and Vice-Pres. of UN Internat. Conf. on Human Rights, 1968; Leader of Austr. Delegations: to Unesco Inter-Govtl Conf. of Ministers on Cultural Policies, 1970; to UN, 1971 and 1972. *Publications (Reports):* Conflict between Public Duty and Private Interest, 1979; Legal Education in New South Wales, 1979. *Recreations:* swimming, music. *Address:* 43 Grosvenor Street, Wahroonga, NSW 2076, Australia. *Club:* Union (Sydney).

BOWEN, Roderic; see Bowen, (Evan) Roderic.

BOWEN, Stanley, CBE 1972; Hon. Sheriff, Lothian and Borders, since 1975; *b* Carnoustie, Angus, 4 Aug. 1910; *s* of late Edward Bowen and Ellen Esther Bowen, (*née* Powles), Birmingham; *m* 1943, Mary Shepherd Greig, *d* of late Alexander Greig and Mary Shand Greig (*née* Shepherd), Carnoustie; two *s* one *d. Educ:* Barry Sch., Angus; Grove Academy, Dundee; University Coll., Dundee. Enrolled Solicitor, in Scotland, 1932; entered Procurator Fiscal Service, in Scotland, 1933; Procurator Fiscal Depute at Hamilton, Lanarkshire, 1937; Interim Procurator Fiscal at Airdrie, Lanarkshire, 1938; Crown Office, Edinburgh: Legal Asst, 1941; Principal Asst, 1945; Crown Agent for Scotland, 1967-74. Chm., Sec. of State for Scotland's working party on forensic pathology services, 1975; Member: Sec. of State for the Environment's working party on drinking and driving offences, 1975; Sub-Cttee for legislation on transplantation of human tissues, Council of Europe, 1975-76; Police Adv. Bd for Scotland, sub-cttee on police discipline, 1976, and working party on Cadet entry, 1979; Sec. of State for Scotland's working group on identification evidence in criminal cases, 1977; Council, Scottish Assoc. for Care and Resettlement of Offenders, 1978; Council, Corstorphine Trust, 1978 (Vice-Chm., 1981). *Recreations:* golf, gardening. *Address:* Achray, 20 Dovecot Road, Corstorphine, Edinburgh EH12 7LE. *T:* 031-334 4096. *Clubs:* New, Press (Edinburgh); Carnoustie Golf.

BOWEN, Thomas Edward Ifor L.; see Lewis-Bowen.

BOWEN, Sir Thomas Frederic Charles, 4th Bt *cr* 1921; *b* 11 Oct. 1921; *s* of 2nd Bt and May Isobel (*d* 1972), *d* of John Frederick Roberts; *S* brother, 1939; *m* 1947, Jill, *d* of Lloyd Evans, Gold Coast; one *s* two *d. Heir: s* Mark Edward Mortimer Bowen, *b* 17 Oct. 1958. *Address:* 1 Barford Close, Fleet, Hants GU13 9HJ.

BOWEN, Prof. William G(ordon), PhD; President, Princeton University, since 1972; Professor of Economics, Princeton University, since 1958; *b* 6 Oct. 1933; *s* of Albert A. and Bernice C. Bowen; *m* 1956, Mary Ellen Maxwell; one *s* one *d. Educ:* Denison Univ. (AB); Princeton Univ. (PhD). Princeton Univ.: Asst Prof. of Economics, Associate Prof. of Economics; Provost, 1967-72. Hon. LLD: Denison, Rutgers, Pennsylvania and Yale, 1972; Harvard,

1973; Jewish Theol Seminary, 1974; Seton Hall Univ., 1975. *Publications:* Economic Aspects of Education, 1964; (with W. J. Baumol) Performing Arts: the Economic Dilemma, 1966; (with T. A. Finegan) Economics of Labor Force Participation, 1969, etc; contribs to Amer. Econ. Review, Economica, Quarterly Jl of Economics, etc. *Address:* 1 Nassau Hall, Princeton University, Princeton, NJ, USA. *T:* 609-452-6100.

BOWER, Air Marshal Sir Leslie William Clement, KCB 1962 (CB 1954); DSO 1945; DFC 1944; *b* 11 July 1909; *s* of William Clarke Bower, Co. Cork, Eire; *m* 1963, Clare (*d* 1971), *widow* of Commander Jasper Abbott, RN, Uppaton, Yelverton, S Devon, and *d* of H. W. Etkins, OBE, Curlews, Constantine Bay, N Cornwall; *m* 1979, Patricia Fearon, *widow* of Wing Comdr D. N. Fearon. *Educ:* Harvey Grammar Sch., Folkestone; Cranwell. Royal Air Force 1929; served War of 1939-45 (despatches twice, DFC, DSO), in Europe and Canada; OC 217 (TB) Sqdn, 1941-42; Dir Op. Trg, HQ, RCAF, Ottawa, 1942-43; OC 138 Wing 2nd TAF, 1943-45; AOC 81 (Fighter) Group, 1952-54; Senior Air Staff Officer, HQ Fighter Command, 1954-57; Senior Air Staff Officer, MEAF, 1957-58; Dep. Commander-in-Chief, Middle East Air Force, 1958-59; Air Officer Commanding No 19 Group, RAF Coastal Command, 1959-61; UK Representative in Ankara on Permanent Military Deputies Group of Central Treaty Organisation (Cento), 1962-65; retired. Air Marshal, 1962. *Address:* c/o Lloyds Bank Ltd, Cox's & King's Branch, 6 Pall Mall, SW1. *Club:* Royal Air Force.

BOWER, Michael Douglas; Organiser, Sheffield Co-operative Development Group, since 1981; *b* 25 Aug. 1942; *s* of Stanley Bower and Rachael Farmer; *m* 1966, Susan Millington; two *d. Educ:* Colwyn Bay Grammar Sch.; Royal Coll. of Advanced Technol., Salford. Civil engr, 1961-64; journalist, 1965-77; with The Star, Sheffield, 1968-77; Regional Organiser, NUJ, 1977-81. Mem., Press Council, 1976-77. Mem., Sheffield Metropolitan DC, 1976-. Parly Cand. (Lab), Hallam Div. of Sheffield, 1979. *Recreations:* walking, golf. *Address:* 8 St Quentin Drive, Bradway, Sheffield S17 4PP. *T:* Sheffield 362737. *Club:* Carlton Working Men's (Gleadless, Sheffield).

BOWER, Norman; *b* 18 May 1907. *Educ:* Rugby; Wadham Coll., Oxford. Called to Bar, Inner Temple, 1935; contested West Bermondsey, 1931, North Hammersmith, 1935; MP (C) Harrow West, 1941-51; Member Westminster City Council, 1937-45. *Recreations:* golf, cricket, theatre. *Club:* Carlton.

BOWER, Lt-Gen. Sir Roger (Herbert), KCB 1959 (CB 1950); KBE 1957 (CBE 1944); *b* 13 Feb. 1903; *s* of Herbert Morris Bower and Eileen Francis Fitzgerald Bower, Ripon; *m* 1939, Hon. Catherine Muriel Hotham, *d* of late Capt. H. E. Hotham, and *y sister* of 7th Baron Hotham, CBE; (one adopted *s*) one *d* (and one *s* decd). *Educ:* Repton; RMC, Sandhurst. Served in India with KOYLI, 1923-30; Staff Coll., Camberley, 1935-36; Bde Major, Hong Kong, 1937-38. Served War of 1939-45; NW Europe with HQ Airborne Corps, 1944; Norway, 1945; Comd 1 and 6 Air Landing Bdes; Palestine, 1945-46 (despatches); Comd Hamburg District, 1948-49, with rank of Maj.-Gen.; Director Land/Air Warfare, War Office, 1950-51; Director of Military Training and Director of Land/Air Warfare, 1951-52; Commander East Anglian District, 1952-55; Chief of Staff, Allied Forces, Northern Europe, 1955-56; GOC and Director of Operations, Malaya, 1956-57; Commander-in-Chief, Middle East Land Forces, 1958-60, retired. Col The KOYLI, 1960-66. Treasurer to HRH Princess Margaret, Nov. 1960-Feb. 1962; Lieut HM Tower of London, 1960-63. US Bronze Star, 1944; King Haakon VII Liberty Cross, 1945. *Recreations:* sailing, shooting, fishing. *Address:* Ash House, St Mary Bourne, Andover, Hants. *T:* St Mary Bourne 263. *Clubs:* Army and Navy, Royal Cruising.

BOWER, Stephen Ernest D.; see Dykes Bower.

BOWERMAN, David Alexander; *b* 19 April 1903; *s* of Frederick and Millicent Bowerman; *m* 1925, Constance Lilian Hosegood (*d* 1959); four *s* one *d* ; *m* 1962, June Patricia Ruth Day. *Educ:* Queen's Coll., Taunton. Farmer, 1923-36; Wholesale Fruit and Potato Merchant (Director), 1936-60. Chairman, Horticultural Marketing Council, 1960-63. Director, 1963-75: Jamaica Producers Marketing Co. Ltd; JP Fruit Distributors Ltd; Horticultural Exports (GB) Ltd. *Recreations:* sailing, golf, gardens. *Address:* The Spinney, Brenchley, Kent. *T:* Brenchley 2149. *Clubs:* Lamberhurst Golf; Isle of Purbeck Golf.

BOWERMAN, Brig. John Francis, CBE 1946; Indian Army (retired); *b* 28 Nov. 1893; *s* of John Bowerman, Cullompton, Devon; *m* 1931, Mary Monica Faed Macmillan; one *d. Educ:* Queen Elizabeth's Sch., Crediton. Commissioned West Yorks Regt, 1915; served European War, 1914-18, Mesopotamia, Marri Field Force, 1914-18 (wounded); transferred 129th Duke of Connaught's Own Baluchis, Nov. 1918; active service Afghanistan, 1919, Zhob, 1919-21, Waziristan, 1921-23 and NW Frontier, 1930; Burma Rebellion, 1931-32. Served War of 1939-45, Burma; Chief Liaison Officer, 6th Chinese Army, 1942; Brigadier 1942, as Inspector General Burma Frontier Force; with Chinese-American Forces, Burma, 1943-45; despatches, 1946; retired 1946. King's Police Medal, 1928; American Bronze Star, 1945. *Publications:* Report on exploration, China, Burma, Tibet Border (MacGregor Memorial Medal of United Services Institution, India, 1928); paper on Frontier Areas of Burma (Silver Medal of RSA, 1947). *Recreations:* golf, fishing. *Address:* Tanglewood, Abberton Field, Hassocks Road, Hurstpierpoint, Sussex.

BOWERS, Prof. Fredson Thayer; Linden Kent Professor of English, University of Virginia, USA, 1968-75, now Emeritus; *b* 25 April 1905; *s* of Fredson Eugene Bowers and Hattie May Quigley; *m* 1st, 1924, Hyacinth Sutphen; three *s* one *d* ; 2nd, 1942, Nancy Hale. *Educ:* Brown Univ. (PhB); Harvard Univ. (PhD). Instructor in English: Harvard Univ., 1926-36; Princeton Univ., 1936-38; Asst Prof., Univ. of Virginia, 1938-46. USNR, Comdr, 1942-46. Associate Prof., Univ. of Virginia, 1946-48, Prof., 1948-75, Alumni Prof., 1959-68 (Dean of the Faculty, 1968-69). Fulbright Fellow for Research in UK, 1953; Guggenheim Fellow, 1959, 1972; Sandars Reader in Bibliography, Cambridge, 1958; Lyell Reader in Bibliography, Oxford, 1959; Vis. Fellow, All Souls Coll., Oxford, 1972, 1974; Fellow Commoner, Churchill Coll., Cambridge, 1975; Exec. Council, Mod. Lang. Assoc. of Amer., 1964-68 (Pres., S Atlantic MLA, 1969); Corresp. FBA, 1968; Fellow: Amer. Acad. Arts and Scis, 1972; Amer. Antiquarian Soc., 1973. Gold Medal, Bibliographical Soc., 1969; Thomas Jefferson Award, 1971. Editor, Studies in Bibliography, 1948-. Hon. DLitt: Brown, 1970; Clark, 1970; Hon. MA Oxon, 1972; Hon. LHD Chicago, 1973. *Publications:* Elizabethan Revenge Tragedy, 1940; Randolph's Fairy Knight (ed), 1942; Principles of Bibliographical Description, 1949; George Sandys: A Bibliographical Catalogue, 1950; Dramatic Works of Thomas Dekker (ed, 4 vols), 1953-61; On Editing Shakespeare and the Elizabethan Dramatists, 1955; Whitman's Manuscripts, 1955; Textual and Literary Criticism, 1959; Bibliography and Textual Criticism, 1964; Dramatic Works in the Beaumont and Fletcher Canon (general ed), 1966-; Works of Stephen Crane (ed), 1969-75; Works of Christopher Marlowe (ed, 2 vols), 1973, rev. edn 1982; (ed) Tom Jones, 1975; Works of William James (text editor), 1975-; Essays in Bibliography, Text and Editing, 1975; (ed) Lectures in Literature by V. Nabokov, 1980; (ed, with introduction) Lectures in Russian Literature by V. Nabokov, 1981. *Recreations:* philately, music. *Address:* Woodburn, Box 7, Route 11, Charlottesville, Virginia 22901, USA. *T:* 804-973-3629.

BOWES, Sir (Harold) Leslie, KCMG 1968; CBE 1943; Chairman, The Pacific Steam Navigation Company, 1960-65, Managing Director, 1952-65 (Deputy Chairman 1959-60); Chairman, Royal Mail Lines Ltd, 1960-65, Managing Director, 1958-65 (Deputy Chairman 1959-60); *b* 18 Nov. 1893; *m* 1st, 1921; two *s* one *d* ; 2nd 1950; one *d.* Served European War, RFC and RAF. The Pacific Steam Navigation Company: Manager for Chile, 1921-48; Director and General Manager, 1949-51. Director: Rea Bros Ltd; Ocean Wilsons (Holdings) Ltd; Member: General Purposes Cttee of Shipping Federation, 1958-61; Central Transport Consultative Cttee, 1959-61; Chairman Liverpool Steam Ship Owners' Assoc., 1954; Chairman General Council of British Shipping, 1954; Chairman Liverpool Port Welfare Cttee, 1955-58; Chairman Liverpool Marine Engineers' and Naval Architects Guild, 1955-56; Chairman Govt Cttee of Inquiry into Canals and Inland Waterways, 1956-58; Member General Cttee of Lloyd's Register of Shipping, 1956-65; Director, "Indefatigable" and Nat. Sea Training Sch. for Boys, 1954-58; Chairman Liverpool Chamber of Commerce, 1957-58; Governor, City of Liverpool College of Commerce, 1958-60; President: Institute of Shipping and Forwarding Agents, 1957-58; Vice-President: British Ship Adoption Society, 1968- (Chm. 1958-68); Institute of Transport, 1958-59 (Mem. Council, 1959-; Chairman Shipping Advisory Cttee, 1959-65); Member: Mersey Docks and Harbour Board, 1956-58; Shipping Advisory Council of BTC, 1960-62; Shipping and International Services Cttee of British Railways Board, 1963; Chairman, BNEC Cttee for Exports to Latin America, 1966-67 (Dep. Chm. 1964-66). Member Exec. Cttee: Anglo-Chilean Society, 1960-70 (Vice-Pres., 1970); Anglo-Peruvian Society (Vice-Pres. 1970); Hispanic and Luso-Brazilian Councils, 1960-69 (Vice-Pres. 1969-; Chm. 1963-64 and 1965-66); Anglo-Brazilian Soc.; Member: Cttee of Management, Canning Club; Exec. Cttee, Anglo-Portuguese Society; Vice-Pres., British Mexican Soc., 1974. Liveryman Worshipful Company of Shipwrights (Past Prime Warden). Hon. Citizen of Valparaiso, Chile, 1982. Comdr of Chilean Order of Merit, 1942, Grand Officer, 1952; Comdr, Ecuadorian Order of Merit, 1956; Comdr, Peruvian Order of Merit, 1957, Grand Cross, 1959; Order of Vasco Nuñez de Balboa, 1963; Grand Officer, Orden de Mayo, Argentina, 1964; Grand Cross, Order of San Carlos (Colombia), 1966; Comdr, Cruziero do Sul, Brazil, 1975. *Address:* 7 Chester Row, SW1W 9JF. *T:* 01-730 1523. *Clubs:* Canning, City Livery, Naval and Military.

BOWES LYON, family name of **Earl of Strathmore.**

BOWETT, Prof. Derek William, LLD; QC 1978; Whewell Professor of International Law, Cambridge University, since 1981; a Professorial Fellow of Queens' College, Cambridge; *b* 20 April 1927; *s* of Arnold William Bowett and Marion Wood; *m* 1953, Betty Northall; two *s* one *d.* *Educ:* William Hulme's Sch., Manchester; Downing Coll., Cambridge. MA, LLB, LLD (Cantab), PhD (Manchester). Called to the Bar, Middle Temple, 1953, Hon. Bencher, 1975. Lectr, Law Faculty, Manchester Univ. 1951-59; Legal Officer, United Nations, New York, 1957-59; Lectr, Law Faculty, Cambridge Univ., 1960-76, Reader, 1976-81; Fellow of Queens' Coll., 1960-69, President 1969-82. Gen. Counsel, UNRWA, Beirut, 1966-68. Mem., Royal Commn on Environmental Pollution, 1973-77. *Publications:* Self-defence in International Law, 1958; Law of International Institutions, 1964; United Nations Forces, 1964; Law of the Sea, 1967; Search for Peace, 1972; Legal Régime of Islands in International Law, 1978. *Recreations:* music, cricket, tennis. *Address:* Queens' College, Cambridge. *T:* Cambridge 65511.

BOWEY, Prof. Angela Marilyn, PhD; Professor of Business Administration, Strathclyde Business School, University of Strathclyde, Glasgow, since 1981;

b 20 Oct. 1940; *d* of Jack Nicholas Peterson and Kathleen (*née* Griffin); *m* 1st, 1960, Miklos Papp; two *s* one *d* ; 2nd, 1965, Gregory Bowey (marr. diss. 1980); one *s* one *d.* *Educ:* Withington Girls Sch., Manchester; Univ. of Manchester (BA Econ, PhD). Technical Asst, Nuclear Power Gp, 1961-62; Asst Lectr, Elizabeth Gaskell Coll. of Educn, 1967-68; Manchester Business School: Res. Associate, 1968-69; Res. Fellow, 1969-72; Lectr, 1972-76; Prof. of Industrial Relations, Strathclyde Business Sch., 1976-81. Vis. Professor: Admin. Staff Coll. of India, 1975; Western Australian Inst. of Technology, 1976; Univ. of WA, 1977; Prahran Coll. of Advanced Educn, Australia, 1978; Massey Univ., NZ, 1978. ACAS Arbitrator, 1977-; Dir, Pay and Rewards Res. Centre, 1978-; Comr, Equal Opportunities Commn, 1980-; Mem., Scottish Econ. Council, 1980-. Editor, Management Decision, 1979-82. *Publications:* Job and Pay Comparisons (with Tom Lupton), 1973, 2nd edn 1974; A Guide to Manpower Planning, 1974, 2nd edn 1977; (with Tom Lupton) Wages and Salaries, 1974, 2nd edn 1982; Handbook of Salary and Wage Systems, 1975, 2nd edn 1982; The Sociology of Organisations, 1976; articles in Brit. Jl of Indust. Relations, Jl of Management Studies, and Management Decision. *Address:* Market Park, Gartmore, Perthshire FK8 3RR. *T:* Aberfoyle 369.

BOWEY, Olwyn, RA 1975 (ARA 1970); practising artist (painter); *b* 10 Feb. 1936; *o d* of James and Olive Bowey. *Educ:* William Newton Sch., Stockton; West Hartlepool Sch. of Art; Royal Coll. of Art. One-man shows: Zwemmer Gall., 1961; New Grafton Gall., 1969; also exhibited at Leicester Gall., Royal Academy; work purchased through Chantrey Bequest for Tate Gall., Royal Academy, Min. of Works, etc. *Recreations:* natural history, music. *Address:* Folley Cottage, Barlavington, Petworth, West Sussex GU28 0LG. *T:* Petworth 7231.

BOWICK, David Marshall, CBE 1977; Member, British Railways Board, since 1976; *b* 30 June 1923; *s* of George Bowick, Corstorphine, Edinburgh; *m* Gladys May (*née* Jeffries); one *d.* *Educ:* Boroughmuir Sch., Edinburgh; Heriot-Watt Coll., Edinburgh. Served with Fleet Air Arm, 1942-46. Movements Supt, Kings Cross, 1962; Planning Officer, British Railways Board Headquarters, 1963; Asst Gen. Man., London Midland Region, BR, 1965; Exec. Dir, Personnel, BRB Headquarters, 1969; Gen. Manager, London Midland Region, BR, 1971; Chief Exec. (Railways), BR, 1971-78; Vice-Chm. (Rail), BRB, 1978-80. Pres., Group of Nine EEC Railways, 1978-80. Mem. Council, Manchester Business Sch. Col RE, T&AVR. FInstM; FREconS; FCIT; FBIM; FRSA. *Recreations:* sailing, swimming, golf, travel, theatre. *Address:* Villa Tuffolina, Shipwreck Promenade, Xemxija, St Paul's Bay, Malta. *Clubs:* Caledonian; Union (Sliema, Malta).

BOWIE, Rev. Alexander Glen (QHC 1980; Principal Chaplain (Church of Scotland and Free Churches), Royal Air Force, since 1980; *b* 10 May 1928; *s* of Alexander Bowie and Annie (*née* McGhie); *m* 1953, Mary McKillop; two *d.* *Educ:* Stevenson High Sch.; Irvine Royal Acad.; Glasgow Univ. (BSc); BA Open Univ., 1977. Assistant, Beith High Church, 1952-54; ordained, 1954; entered RAF Chaplains' Br., 1955; Asst Principal Chaplain, 1975. *Recreations:* oil painting, collecting antiques, travel. *Address:* 16 Weir Road, Hemingford Grey, Huntingdon, Cambs PE18 9EH. *T:* Huntingdon 63269. *Club:* Royal Air Force.

BOWIE, David; international recording artist and performer; film and stage actor; video and film producer; graphic designer; *b* 8 Jan. 1947; *s* of Hayward Stenton Jones and Margaret Mary Burns; *m* (marr. diss.); one *s.* *Educ:* Stansfield Road Sch., Brixton. Artiste from age of 16; many major recordings, 1970-, and video productions, 1979-; numerous live musical stage performances; guest appearances on television shows. Actor: films: The Man who Fell to Earth, 1976; Just a Gigolo, 1978; The Hunger, 1982; stage: The Elephant Man, New York 1980; television: Baal, 1982. Recipient of internat. music and entertainment awards. *Recreations:* painting, skiing. *Address:* Suite 2411, 250 West 57th Street, New York, NY 10107, USA.

BOWIE, Stanley Hay Umphray, DSc; FRS 1975; FEng 1976; FRSE, FIMM; Consultant Geologist; Assistant Director, Chief Geochemist, Institute of Geological Sciences, 1968-77; *b* 24 March 1917; *s* of Dr James Cameron and Mary Bowie; *m* 1948, Helen Elizabeth, *d* of Dr Roy Woodhouse and Florence Elizabeth Pocock; two *s.* *Educ:* Grammar Sch. and Univ. of Aberdeen (BSc, DSc). Meteorological Office, 1942; commissioned RAF, 1943; HM Geological Survey of Gt Britain: Geologist, Sen. Geologist and Principal Geologist, 1946-55; Chief Geologist, Atomic Energy Div., 1955-67; Chief Consultant Geologist to UKAEA, 1955-77. Visiting Prof. of Applied Geology, Univ. of Strathclyde, 1968-; Chairman: Internat. Mineralogical Assoc., Commn on Ore Microscopy, 1970-78; Royal Soc. Working Party on Envtl Geochem. and Health, 1979-; Mem., Radioactive Waste Management Adv. Cttee, 1978-. Vice-Pres., Geological Soc., 1972-74. FGS 1959; FMSA 1963; FRSE 1970; FIMM 1972 (Pres. 1976-77). Silver Medal, RSA, 1959. *Publications:* contributions to Nuclear Geology, 1954; Physical Methods in Determinative Mineralogy, 1967, 2nd edn 1977; (ed jtly) Uranium Prospecting Handbook, 1972; Uranium Exploration Methods, 1973; numerous papers in scientific and technical jls on uranium geology and economics, mineralogy, geophysics and geochemistry. *Recreations:* fishing, shooting, farming, gardening, photography. *Address:* Tanyard Farm, Clapton, Crewkerne, Somerset. *T:* Crewkerne 72093. *Club:* Geological Society's.

BOWKER, Alfred Johnstone, (John), MC 1944; Regional Chairman of Industrial Tribunals, Southampton, since 1978; *b* 9 April 1922; *s* of Alfred

Bowker and Isabel Florence (*née* Brett); *m* 1947, Ann, *er d* of late John Christopher Fairweather and Gunhild Fairweather; one *s* one *d*. *Educ:* Winchester Coll.; Christ Church, Oxford (MA). Served War, Coldstream Guards, 1941-47: Italian Campaign; Captain. Solicitor in private practice, Winchester, 1949-57; Resident Magistrate, Northern Rhodesia, 1957-65; solicitor in private practice, Salisbury, Wilts, 1965-71; Chm. of Indust. Tribunals, Newcastle upon Tyne, 1972-75. Winchester City Councillor, 1954-57. Liveryman, Skinners Co., 1943. Master, Meon Valley Beagles, 1954-56; Jt Master, Hursley Foxhounds, 1968-69 and 1970-71. *Recreations:* hunting, reading history. *Address:* c/o National Westminster Bank Ltd, 105 High Street, Winchester, Hants SO23 9AW.

BOWKER, Sir (Reginald) James, GBE 1961; KCMG 1952 (CMG 1945); *b* 2 July 1901; *yr s* of Lieut-Col F. J. Bowker, Hampshire Regt, and Edith Sophie Mary Elliott; *m* 1947, Elsa, *d* of Michel Gued and Mme Gued Vidal. *Educ:* Charterhouse; Oriel Coll., Oxford. 3rd Secretary, Foreign Office and Diplomatic Service, 1925. Served in Paris, Berlin, Ankara, Oslo and Madrid. British Minister in Cairo, 1945-47; High Commissioner in Burma, 1947-48; Ambassador to Burma, 1948-50; an Asst Under-Secretary of State, FO, 1950-53; Ambassador to Turkey, 1954-58; Ambassador to Austria, 1958-61; retired from Foreign Service, 1961. *Address:* 3 West Eaton Place, SW1X 8LU. *T:* 01-235 3852. *Club:* Brooks's.

BOWLBY, Sir Anthony Hugh Mostyn, 2nd Bt, *cr* 1923; *b* 13 Jan. 1906; *e s* of Sir Anthony Bowlby, 1st Bt and Maria Bridget (*d* 1957), *d* of Rev. Canon Hon. Hugh W. Mostyn; *S* father, 1929; *m* 1930, Dora Evelyn, *d* of John Charles Allen; two *d*. *Educ:* Wellington Coll.; New Coll., Oxford. *Heir: b* Edward John Mostyn Bowlby, *qv*. *Address:* The Old Rectory, Ozleworth, near Wotton-under-Edge, Glos.

See also Sir E. H. P. Brown, J. Dromgoole.

BOWLBY, (Edward) John (Mostyn), CBE 1972; MD; FRCP, FRCPsych, FBPsS; Hon. Consultant Psychiatrist, Tavistock Clinic, London, since 1972; *b* 26 Feb. 1907; 2nd *s* of late Sir Anthony A. Bowlby, 1st Bt (Pres. Roy. Coll. of Surgeons, 1920-23), and late Maria Bridget, *d* of Rev. Canon Hon. Hugh W. Mostyn; *heir-pres.* to *b* Sir Anthony Hugh Mostyn Bowlby, 2nd Bt, *qv* ; *m* 1938, Ursula, 3rd *d* of late Dr T. G. Longstaff (Pres. Alpine Club, 1947-49) and Mrs D. H. Longstaff, JP; two *s* two *d*. *Educ:* RNC Dartmouth; Trinity Coll., Cambridge (MA Nat. Scis); UCH (MD). FRCP 1964; FRCPsych (Foundation Fellow) 1971, Hon. Fellow 1980; FBPsS 1945; Mem., Brit. PsychoAnalyt. Soc. Staff Psych., London Child Guidance Clinic, 1937-40; Consultant Psychiatrist: RAMC, 1940-45 (Temp. Lt-Col, 1944-45); Tavistock Clinic, 1946-72 (Chm., Dept for Children and Parents, 1946-68); pt-time Mem., ext. scientific staff, MRC, 1963-72. Consultant: in mental health, WHO, 1950-; Nat. Inst. of Mental Health, Bethesda, Md, 1958-63. Fellow, Center for Advanced Studies in Behavioral Sciences, Stanford, Calif, 1957-58; Vis. Prof. in Psych., Stanford Univ., Calif, 1968; H. B. Williams Trav. Prof., Aust. and NZ Coll. of Psychiatrists, 1973; Frend Meml Vis. Prof., UCL, 1980. Pres., Internat. Assoc. for Child Psych. and Allied Professions, 1962-66; Foreign Hon. Mem., Amer. Acad. of Arts and Sciences, 1981-. Hon. DLitt Leicester, 1971; Hon. ScD Cambridge, 1977. Sir James Spence Medal, Brit. Paediatric Assoc., 1974; G. Stanley Hall Medal, Amer. Psychol Assoc., 1974; Distinguished Scientific Contrib. Award, Soc. for Res. in Child Develt. 1981. *Publications:* Personal Aggressiveness and War (with E. F. M. Durbin), 1938; Forty-four Juvenile Thieves, 1946; Maternal Care and Mental Health, 1951 (12 trans); Child Care and the Growth of Love, 1953 (2nd edn 1963); Attachment and Loss (6 trans): Vol. 1, Attachment, 1969; Vol. 2, Separation: anxiety and anger, 1973; Vol. 3, Loss: sadness and depression, 1980; The Making and Breaking of Affectional Bonds, 1979; papers in Brit. and US jls of psych., psychol. and psychoanalysis. *Recreations:* natural history and outdoor activities. *Address:* Wyldes Close Corner, Hampstead Way, NW11 7JB.

BOWLBY, Hon. Mrs Geoffrey, CVO 1937; Extra Woman of the Bedchamber to Queen Elizabeth, the Queen Mother; 4th *d* of 11th Viscount Valentia, Bletchington Park, Oxford; *m* 1911, Capt. Geoffrey Vaux Salvin Bowlby, Royal Horse Guards (killed in action, 1915); one *s* one *d*. Commandant of Auxiliary Hospital, 1916-19 (despatches twice); a Lady-in-Waiting to Duchess of York, 1932; Woman of the Bedchamber to the Queen, 1937-45. *Address:* Flat 10, Ritchie Court, 380 Banbury Road, Oxford. *T:* Oxford 50414.

See also Earl of Meath.

BOWLBY, John; see Bowlby, E. J. M.

BOWLBY, Rt. Rev. Ronald Oliver; see Southwark, Bishop of.

BOWLE, John Edward; historian; *b* 19 Dec. 1905; *o s* of Edward Francis Bowle, Salisbury, and Edith Beatrice, *y d* of late Silas Taunton, Fugglestone, Wilton, Wilts. *Educ:* The Old Malthouse, Langton Matravers; Marlborough Coll. (Council and Keith Rae Exhibitioner); Balliol Coll., Oxford (Brackenbury Scholar, 1924; BA 1927; MA 1932). Senior History Master, Westminster Sch., 1932-40; History Master, Eton, 1940-41. Air Ministry and Foreign Office, 1941-45. Lecturer in Modern History, Wadham Coll., Oxford, 1947-49; Leverhulme Research Fellow, 1949-50; Visiting Prof., Columbia Univ., NY, 1949; Dir, Preparatory Session, College of Europe, Bruges, 1949; Prof. of Political Theory, Bruges, 1950-67. Visiting Professor: Grinnell Coll., Iowa, 1961; Occidental Coll., Los Angeles, 1965; Indiana

Univ., 1966; Lecturer, Smith Coll., Northampton, Mass, 1967. Editor, The World To-day, for RIIA, 1949-51. *Publications:* Western Political Thought, 1947 (Arts Council Prize, 1966); The Unity of European History, 1948, rev. edn, 1970; Hobbes and his Critics, 1951; Politics and Opinion in the Nineteenth Century, 1954; Viscount Samuel, a biography, 1957; (ed) The Concise Encyclopædia of World History, 1958; A New Outline of World History, 1963; Henry VIII, a biography, 1964, repr. 1973; England, a portrait, 1966; The English Experience, 1971; The Imperial Achievement, 1974; Napoleon, 1974; Charles I, a biography, 1975; Man Through the Ages, 1977; A History of Europe, 1980; John Evelyn and his World, 1981; contrib. to various periodicals; writes for radio and broadcasts. *Recreations:* travel, painting. *Address:* 24 Woodstock Close, Oxford. *T:* 58379. *Club:* Travellers'.

BOWLER, Geoffrey, FCIS; Chief General Manager, Sun Alliance & London Insurance Group, since 1977; *b* 11 July 1924; *s* of James Henry Bowler and Hilda May Bowler. *Educ:* Sloane Sch., Chelsea. FCIS 1952. Chm., British Insurance Assoc., 1979-80 (Dep. Chm., 1977); Chm., British Aviation Insurance Co., 1977-. *Address:* 13 Green Lane, Purley, Surrey. *T:* 01-660 0756.

BOWLER, Ian John, CBE 1971 (OBE 1957); President, Iranian Management & Engineering Group Ltd, since 1965; Chairman: International Management & Engineering Group Ltd, since 1973; Wilmeg, Tehran, since 1979; *b* 1920; *s* of Major John Arthur Bowler; *m* 1963, Hamideh, *d* of Prince Yadollah Azodi, GCMG; two *d*, and one step *s* one step *d*. *Educ:* King's Sch., Worcester; privately; Oxford Univ. Director of Constructors, John Brown, 1961-64; Man. Dir, Internat. Management & Eng. Group Ltd, 1964-68. MInstPet. *Publication:* Predator Birds of Iran, 1973. *Recreations:* ornithology, yachting. *Address:* 4 Kucheh, Bagh Bank, Golhak, Tehran, Iran; 28 Mallord Street, SW3. *T:* 01-352 9795. *Clubs:* Travellers', Royal Thames Yacht, Goat; S.R.R. (La Rochelle, France).

BOWLES, Dame Ann P.; see Parker Bowles.

BOWLES, Chester; United States Ambassador to India, 1963-69; *b* Springfield, Mass, 5 April 1901; *s* of Allen Bowles and Nellie Harris; *g s* of Samuel Bowles, Founder of the Springfield Republican; *m* 1934, Dorothy Stebbins Bowles; two *s* three *d*. *Educ:* Choate Sch., Wallingford, Conn.; Yale Univ., New Haven, Conn. Founded advertising and marketing research agency in NY City with William Benton, 1929; Chm. Board of this agency (Benton & Bowles, Inc.), 1936-41, when sold out interests. Administrator of Office of Price Administration, 1943-46, appointed by President Roosevelt; Mem. of War Production Bd, 1943-46; appointed Dir of Economic Stabilization by President Truman, 1946, and resigned from that post, 1946; Special Asst to UN Sec.-Gen., 1946-48; Governor of Connecticut, 1949-51; American Ambassador to India, and first American Ambassador to Nepal, 1951-53; Mem., 86th Congress, House of Representatives, 1959-60 (2nd Dist. Conn); Under-Sec. of State, USA, Jan.-Nov. 1961; President's Special Representative and Adviser on African, Asian and Latin American Affairs with rank of Ambassador, Nov. 1961-May 1963; Mem. of Congress, US (2nd Dist Conn). Member: Democratic Advisory Council on Foreign Policy; Institute of International Education; American African Soc.; American National Commission for United Nations Economic, Scientific and Cultural Organizations Conference in Paris, 1946; (Internat. Chm.) UN Appeal for Children, 1947; Board of Advisers, Fletcher Sch. of Law and Diplomacy, Medford, Mass; Delivered The Anna Howard Shaw Memorial Lectures at Bryn Mawr Coll., 1953-54; Godkin Lectr, Harvard Univ., 1956; Berkeley Lectr, University of Calif, 1956; Chubb Lectr, Yale Univ., 1957; Rosenfeld Lectr, Grinnell Coll., 1959. Conn Delegate to Democratic Nat. Convention, 1940, 1944, 1948, 1956, 1960; Chm., Platform Cttee, Democratic National Convention, July 1960. Franklin Delano Roosevelt Award for fight against racial discrimination, 1950; Roosevelt Coll. Award for outstanding public service, 1953. Associate Fellow Silliman Coll., Yale Univ.; Hon. DSc The New Sch. for Social Research, New York; Hon. Dr of Laws, Howard Univ., Washington, DC, Hon. Dr of Law: Oberlin Coll., 1957; Bard Coll., 1957; Hon. LLD: American Univ., Washington, DC; Univ. of Rhode Island, 1958; Yale, 1968; Davidson Coll., 1972. *Publications:* Tomorrow Without Fear, 1946; Ambassador's Report, 1954; The New Dimensions of Peace, 1955; American Politics in a Revolutionary World, 1956; Africa's Challenge to America, 1956; Ideas, People and Peace, 1958; The Coming Political Breakthrough, 1959; Conscience of a Liberal, 1962; Makings of a Just Society, 1963; A View from New Delhi, 1969; Promises to Keep: my years in public life, 1941-1969, 1971; and many articles on economic problems and foreign policy. *Recreation:* sailing. *Address:* Hayden's Point, Essex, Conn 06426, USA. *TA:* Essex, Conn. *Clubs:* Essex Yachting (Essex, Conn); Cruising Club of America, Yale (New York).

BOWLES, Rt. Rev. Cyril William Johnston; see Derby, Bishop of.

BOWLEY, Martin Richard; QC 1981; a Recorder of the Crown Court, since 1979; *b* 29 Dec. 1936; *s* of late Charles Colin Stuart Bowley and Mary Evelyn Bowley. *Educ:* Magdalen Coll. Sch., Oxford; Queen's Coll., Oxford (Styring Exhibnr, 1955; MA; BCL 1961). National Service, 1955-57: commnd Pilot Officer as a Fighter Controller; served 2nd Tactical Air Force, 1956-57. Called to the Bar, Inner Temple, 1962; Midland and Oxford Circuit. Chm., Questors Theatre, 1972- (Sec., 1963-72); Mem. Standing Cttee, Little Theatre Guild of GB, 1974- (Vice-Chm., 1979-81, Chm., 1981-). *Recreations:* playing at theatre, watching cricket, island hopping. *Address:* Flat E, 23/24 Great James Street, WC1N 3EL. *T:* 01-405 0834; 1 King's Bench Walk, Temple, EC4Y 7DB. *T:* 01-353 8436. *Clubs:* MCC, Questors.

BOWMAN; *see* Kellett-Bowman.

BOWMAN, (Edwin) Geoffrey; Deputy Parliamentary Counsel, since 1981; *b* 27 Jan. 1946; *er s* of John Edwin Bowman and Lillian Joan Bowman (*née* Nield); *m* 1969, Carol Margaret, *er d* of late Alexander Ogilvie and of Ethel Ogilvie; two *s* one *d. Educ:* Roundhay Sch., Leeds; Trinity Coll., Cambridge (Senior Scholar; MA, LLB). Called to Bar, Lincoln's Inn (Cassel Scholar), 1968; in practice, Chancery Bar, 1969–71; joined Parliamentary Counsel Office, 1971 (with Law Commission, 1977–79). *Publication:* The Elements of Conveyancing (with E. L. G. Tyler), 1972. *Recreations:* music (bassoon), English medieval history. *Address:* 16 Woodberry Avenue, North Harrow, Mddx. *T:* 01-427 4499. *Clubs:* Les Amis du Basson Français (Paris); International Double Reed Society.

BOWMAN, Sir George, 2nd Bt *cr* 1961, of Killingworth, Northumberland; *b* 2 July 1923; *s* of Sir James Bowman, 1st Bt, KBE, and of Jean, *d* of Henry Brook, Ashington, Northumberland; *S* father, 1978; *m* 1960, Olive (*née* Case); three *d.* Heir: none. *Address:* Parkside, Killingworth Drive, Newcastle upon Tyne NE12 0ES.

BOWMAN, James Thomas; counter-tenor; *b* Oxford, 6 Nov. 1941; *s* of Benjamin and Cecilia Bowman. *Educ:* Ely Cathedral Choir Sch.; King's Sch., Ely; New Coll., Oxford. MA (History) 1967; DipEd 1964. Schoolmaster, 1965–67. Many concert performances with: English Opera Gp, 1967–; Early Music Consort, 1967–76; operatic performances with: Sadler's Wells Opera, 1970–; Glyndebourne Festival Opera, 1970–; Sydney Opera, Australia, 1978; Opéra Comique, Paris, 1979; in USA at Santa Fe and Wolf Trap Festivals, Dallas and San Francisco Operas; at Aix-en-Provence Fest., 1979; operatic roles include: Oberon, in A Midsummer Night's Dream; Endymion, in La Calisto; the Priest, in Taverner; Polinesso, in Ariodante; Apollo, in Death in Venice; Astron, in Ice Break; Ruggiero in Alcina; title rôles: Gulio Cesare; Tamerlano; Xerxes; Scipione. Has made recordings of oratorio and Medieval and Renaissance vocal music. Lay Vicar, Westminster Abbey, 1969. *Recreations:* ecclesiastical architecture; collecting records. *Address:* 19a Wetherby Gardens, SW5 0JP.

BOWMAN, Dr John Christopher, PhD; FIBiol; Secretary, Natural Environment Research Council, since 1981; *b* 13 Aug. 1933; *s* of M. C. Bowman and C. V. Simister; *m* 1961, S. J. Lorimer; three *d. Educ:* Manchester Grammar Sch.; Univ. of Reading (BSc); Univ. of Edinburgh (PhD). Geneticist, later Chief Geneticist, Thornbers, Mytholmroyd, Yorks, 1958–66. Post-doctoral Fellow, North Carolina State Univ., Raleigh, NC, USA, 1964–65; University of Reading: Prof. of Animal Production, 1966–81; Head of Dept of Agric., 1967–71; Dir, Univ. Farms, 1967–78; Dir, Centre for Agricl Strategy, 1975–81. *Publications:* An Introduction to Animal Breeding, 1974; Animals for Man, 1977; papers published in: Heredity; British Poultry Science; Animal Production; Animal Breeding Abstracts; Genetical Research. *Recreations:* golf, tennis, gardening. *Address:* Farm House, Sonning, Reading, Berks RG4 0TH. *T:* (office) Swindon 40101.

BOWMAN, Sir John Paget, 4th Bt, *cr* 1884; *b* 12 Feb. 1904; *s* of Rev. Sir Paget Mervyn Bowman, 3rd Bt, and Rachel Katherine (*d* 1936), *d* of late James Hanning, Kilcrone, Co. Cork; *S* father 1955; *m* 1st, 1931, Countess Cajetana Hoyos (*d* 1948), *d* of Count Edgar Hoyos, Schloss Stoss, Lower Austria; one *s* one *d*; 2nd, 1948, Frances Edith Marian, *d* of Sir Beethom Whitehead, KCMG (*d* 1928), Efford Park, Lymington. *Educ:* Eton. Formerly 2nd Lieut 98th (Surrey and Sussex Yeomanry) Field Brigade RA. Heir: *s* David Anthony Paget Bowman [*b* 16 Oct. 1935; *m* 1968, Valerie Winifred, *o d* of R. C. Tatham, N Ferriby, Yorks]. *Address:* Bishops Green House, Newbury, Berks.

BOWMAN, (Thomas) Patrick; Chairman: PA Management Consultants Ltd, 1966–75; PA International Management Consultants, 1971–75; Governor, Sundridge Park Management Centre, 1961–75; *b* 25 Sept. 1915; *s* of late Thomas Marshall Bowman and Louisa Hetherington Macfarlane; *m* 1950, Norma Elizabeth Deravin; one *s. Educ:* Oundle Sch.; Hertford Coll., Oxford. Joined Industrial Engineering Div. of Thomas Hedley & Co. (now Proctor & Gamble Ltd), 1937; P A Management Consultants Ltd, 1945 (Dir, 1955; Managing Dir, 1961). Member: Monopolies Commn, 1969–72; Council, CBI, 1970–74. Chairman, UK Management Consultants Assoc., 1966, 1974; Founder Member and Fellow of Inst. of Management Consultants; Pres., European Fedn of Management Consultants, 1967–69. Chm., Wimbledon and Putney Conservators Bd, 1976–. FBIM 1959. *Address:* 9 Clement Road, Wimbledon, SW19 7RJ. *T:* 01-946 3828. *Club:* Royal Thames Yacht.

BOWMAN-SHAW, (George) Neville; Chairman: Lancer Boss Rentals Ltd, since 1971; Lancer Boss France SA, since 1967; Lancer Boss Fördergeräte Vertriebsgesellschaft, mbH (Austria), since 1966; Lancer Boss Ireland Ltd, since 1966; Lancer Boss Group Ltd, since 1966; Lancer Boss Ltd, since 1967; Boss Trucks & Equipment, since 1959; Lancer Boss International SA Lausanne (formerly BS Exports SA Geneva), since 1962; Boss Engineers Ltd, since 1961; Potters Ltd, since 1972; *b* 4 Oct. 1930; *s* of George Bowman-Shaw and Hazel Bowman-Shaw (*née* Smyth); *m* 1962, Georgina Mary Blundell; three *s* one *d. Educ:* Caldicott Preparatory Sch.; then private tutor. Farming Trainee,

1947; Management Trainee in Engineering Co., 1948. Commissioned in 5th Royal Inniskilling Dragoon Guards, 1950. Sales Manager: Matling Ltd, Wolverhampton, 1953; Materials Handling Equipment (GB) Ltd, London, and Matbro Ltd, London, 1955. Member: Development Commn, 1970–77; Design Council, 1979–; BOTB, 1982–. Pres., Bedfordshire Rural Community Council. Governor, Hawtreys School. *Recreations:* shooting, wildfowl collection. *Address:* Toddington Manor, Toddington, Bedfordshire. *T:* Toddington 2576. *Clubs:* Constitutional, Cavalry and Guards, Hurlingham.

BOWMONT, Marquis of; Charles Robert George Innes-Ker; *b* 18 Feb. 1981; *s* and *heir* of Duke of Roxburghe, *qv.*

BOWN, Jane Hope, (Mrs M. G. Moss); Photographer for The Observer, since 1950; *b* 13 March 1925; *d* of Charles Wentworth Bell and Daisy Bown; *m* 1954, Martin Grenville Moss; two *s* one *d. Educ:* William Gibbs Sch., Faversham. Chart corrector, WRNS, 1944–46; student photographer, Guildford School of Art, 1946–50. *Publication:* The Gentle Eye: a book of photographs, 1980. *Recreations:* restoring old houses; chickens. *Address:* Lasham House, near Alton, Hants. *T:* Herriard 216.

BOWNESS, Alan, CBE 1976; Director of the Tate Gallery, since 1980; *b* 11 Jan. 1928; *er s* of George Bowness and Kathleen (*née* Benton); *m* 1957, Sarah Hepworth-Nicholson, *d* of Ben Nicholson, OM, and Dame Barbara Hepworth, DBE, (one *s* one *d. Educ:* University Coll. Sch.; Downing Coll., Cambridge (Hon. Fellow 1980); Courtauld Inst. of Art, Univ. of London. Worked with Friends' Ambulance Unit and Friends' Service Council, 1946–50; Reg. Art Officer, Arts Council of GB, 1955–57; Courtauld Inst., 1957–79, Dep. Dir, 1978–79; Reader, 1967–78, Prof. of Hist. of Art, 1978–79, Univ. of London. Vis. Prof., Humanities Seminar, Johns Hopkins Univ., Baltimore, 1969. Mem. Internat. Juries: Premio Di Tella, Buenos Aires, 1965; São Paulo Bienal, 1967; Lehmbruck Prize, Duisburg, 1970; Rembrandt Prize, 1979. Arts Council: Mem., 1973–75 and 1978–80; Mem., Art Panel, 1960–80 (Vice-Chm., 1973–75, Chm., 1978–80); Mem., Arts Film Cttee, 1968–77 (Chm., 1972–75). Member: Fine Arts Cttee, Brit. Council, 1960–69 and 1970– (Chm., 1981–); Exec. Cttee, Contemp. Art Soc., 1961–69 and 1970–; Cultural Adv. Cttee, UK National Commn for UNESCO, 1973–82. Governor, Chelsea Sch. of Art, 1965–; Hon. Sec., Assoc. of Art Historians, 1973–76; Dir, Barbara Hepworth Museum, St Ives, Cornwall, 1976–. Mem. Council, RCA, 1978–. Hon. Fellow, Bristol Polytechnic, 1980. Exhibitions arranged and catalogued include: 54:64 Painting and Sculpture of a Decade (with L. Gowing), 1964; Dubuffet, 1966; Sculpture in Battersea Park, 1966; Van Gogh, 1968; Rodin, 1970; William Scott, 1972; French Symbolist Painters (with G. Lacambre), 1972; Ceri Richards, 1975; Courbet (with M. Laclotte), 1977. Chevalier, l'Ordre des Arts et des Lettres, France, 1973. *Publications:* William Scott Paintings, 1964; Impressionists and Post Impressionists, 1965; Henry Moore: complete sculpture 1955–64, 1965; Modern Sculpture, 1965; Barbara Hepworth Drawings, 1966; Alan Davie, 1967; Recent British Painting, 1968; Gauguin, 1971; Barbara Hepworth: complete sculpture 1960–70, 1971; Modern European Art, 1972; Ivon Hitchens, 1973; (contrib.) Picasso 1881–1973, ed R. Penrose, 1973; (contrib.) The Genius of British Painting, ed D. Piper, 1975; Henry Moore: complete sculpture 1964–73, 1977; Henry Moore: complete sculpture 1973–81, 1982; articles in Burlington Magazine, TLS, Observer, and Annual Register. *Recreations:* listening to music; reading, especially poetry and 19th century fiction. *Address:* 91 Castelnau, SW13 9EL. *T:* 01-748 9696; 16 Piazza, St Ives, Cornwall. *T:* St Ives 5444. *Club:* Athenæum.

BOWNESS, Peter Spencer, CBE 1981; DL; Partner, Horsley, Weightman, Richardson and Sadler, Solicitors, Purley, since 1970; Leader of Croydon Council, since 1976; *b* 19 May 1943; *s* of Hubert Spencer Bowness and Doreen (Peggy) Bowness; *m* 1969, Marianne Hall; one *d. Educ:* Whitgift Sch., Croydon. Admitted Solicitor, 1966. Elected (C) Croydon Council, 1968; Mayor of Croydon, 1979–80; Chm., London Boroughs Assoc., 1978–; Dep. Chm., Assoc. of Metropolitan Authorities, 1978–80. DL Greater London, 1981. *Recreations:* travel, theatre. *Address:* Dutch Lodge, 107 Purley Downs Road, Sanderstead, South Croydon CR2 0RH. *T:* 01-657 1192. *Clubs:* Carlton; Conservative (Croydon).

BOWRING, Edgar Rennie Harvey, MC 1945; Director, Marsh & McLennan Cos Inc., New York, since 1980; Chairman, C. T. Bowring & Co. Ltd, 1973–78; *b* 5 Nov. 1915; *y s* of Arthur Bowring; *m* 1940, Margaret Grace (*née* Brook); two *s* one *d. Educ:* Eastbourne Coll.; Clare Coll., Cambridge (MA); Berkeley Coll., Yale, USA (Mellon Fellow). War of 1939–45: commissioned Kent Yeomanry, RA, 1939; served in Iceland, France and Germany (despatches, 1944); demobilised, 1946. Solicitor, 1949; Partner in Cripps Harries Hall & Co., 1950–55. Member of Lloyd's, 1962. Joined C. T. Bowring & Co. (Insurance) Ltd, 1956 (Dir, 1960); Dep. Chm., 1966, Chief Exec., 1970, Chm., 1973–77, C. T. Bowring (Insurance) Holdings Ltd. Chairman: English & American Insurance Co. Ltd, 1965–71; Crusader Insurance Co. Ltd, 1973–77; Bowmaker Ltd, 1973–77. Pres., Insurance Inst. of London, 1971–72 (Dep. Pres., 1970–71); Vice-Pres., Corporation of Insurance Brokers, 1970–77; Mem., Insurance Brokers Registration Council, 1979–81. Chm., City Cttee for Electoral Reform, 1978–82. Comdt, West Kent Special Constab., 1965–71. CBIM. *Recreations:* gardening, golf. *Address:* Leopards Mill, Horam, Sussex. *T:* Horam Road 2687; 18 Denbigh House, Hans Place, SW1X 0EX. *T:* 01-584 0781. *Clubs:* City University; Rye (Rye); Piltdown Golf.

BOWRING, Maj.-Gen. John Humphrey Stephen, CB 1968; OBE 1958; MC 1941; FICE; Director, Consolidated Gold Fields, since 1969; *b* 13 Feb. 1913; *s* of late Major Francis Stephen Bowring and late Mrs Maurice Stonor; *m* 1956, Iona Margaret (*née* Murray); two *s* two *d*. *Educ:* Downside; RMA Woolwich; Trinity Coll., Cambridge. MA 1936. Commissioned, 1933; Palestine, 1936; India, 1937-40; Middle East, 1940-42; India and Burma, 1942-46; British Military Mission to Greece, 1947-50; UK, 1951-55; CRE, 17 Gurkha Div., Malaya, 1955-58; Col GS, War Office, 1958-61; Brig., Chief Engineer, Far East, 1961-64; Brig. GS, Ministry of Defence, 1964-65; Engineer-in-Chief, 1965-68. Col, The Gurkha Engineers, 1966-71; Col Comdt, RE, 1968-73. *Recreation:* riding. *Address:* Lower Swillbrook Farm, Minety, Malmesbury, Wilts. *T:* Minety 439. *Clubs:* Army and Navy, Royal Ocean Racing.

BOWRING, Air Vice-Marshal John Ivan Roy, CB 1977; CBE 1971; CEng, FRAeS; FBIM; Head of Technical Training and Maintenance, British Aircraft Corporation, Riyadh, Saudi Arabia, since 1978; *b* 28 March 1923; *s* of Hugh Passmore Bowring and Ethel Grace Bowring; *m* 1945, Irene Mary Rance; two *d*. *Educ:* Great Yarmouth Grammar Sch., Norfolk; Aircraft Apprentice, RAF Halton-Cosford, 1938-40; Leicester Tech. Coll.; commissioned, RAF, 1944; NW Europe, 1944-47; RAF, Horsham St Faith's, Engrg duties, 1947-48; RAF South Cerney, Pilot trng, 1949; Engr Officer: RAF Finningly, 1950-51; RAF Kai-Tak, 1951-53; Staff Officer, AHQ Hong Kong, ADC to Governor, Hong Kong, 1953-54; Sen. Engr Officer, RAF Coltishall, 1954-56; exchange duties with US Air Force, Research and Develt, Wright Patterson Air Force Base, Ohio, 1956-60; RAF Staff Coll., Bracknell, 1960; Air Min. Opl Requirements, 1961-64; OC Engrg Wing, RAF St Mawgaw, 1964-67; Head of F111 Procurement Team, USA, 1967-68; OC RAF Aldergrove, NI, 1968-70; RCDS, 1971; Dir of Engrg Policy, MoD, 1972-73; AO Engrg, RAF Germany, 1973-74; SASO, RAF Support Comd, 1974-77; AO Maintenance, 1977. FBIM. *Recreations:* sailing, golf. *Address:* 2 Burdock Close, Goodworth, Clatford, Andover, Hants. *T:* Andover 66229. *Club:* Royal Air Force.

BOWRING, Peter; Chairman, C. T. Bowring & Co. Ltd, 1978-82; Director, Marsh & McLennan Cos Inc., New York, since 1980; *b* 22 April 1923; *e s* of Frederick Clive Bowring and Agnes Walker (*née* Cairns); *m* 1946, Barbara Ekaterina Brewis (marr. diss.); one *s* one *d* ; *m* 1979, Carol Gillian Hutchings. *Educ:* Shrewsbury Sch. Served War, 1939-45: commnd Rifle Bde, 1942; served in Egypt, N Africa, Italy, Austria (mentioned in despatches, 1945); demobilised 1946. Joined Bowring Group of Cos, 1947: Dir, C. T. Bowring & Co. Ltd, 1956, Dep. Chm. 1973; Chairman: C. T. Bowring Trading (Holdings) Ltd, 1967; Bowmaker (Plant) Ltd, 1972-; Bowring Steamship Co. Ltd, 1974-82; Bowmaker Ltd, 1978-82; C. T. Bowring (UK) Ltd, 1980-. Mem. of Lloyd's, 1968-. Chm., Help the Aged Ltd, 1977-. Mem., Action Resource Centre Adv. Council; Vice-Pres., Aldeburgh Festival-Snape Maltings Foundn Ltd. Chm. Bd of Governors, St Dunstan's Educnl Foundn; Mem. Bd of Governors, Shrewsbury Sch. Mem., Guild of Freemen of City of London. FRSA. *Recreations:* sailing, motoring, listening to music, cooking. *Address:* 69 Onslow Square, SW7 3LS. *T:* 01-584 8946. *Clubs:* Boodle's, Royal Thames Yacht.

BOWRON, John Lewis; solicitor; Secretary-General, The Law Society, since 1974; *b* 1 Feb. 1924; *e s* of John Henry and Lavinia Bowron; *m* 1950, Patricia, *d* of Arthur Cobby; two *d*. *Educ:* Grangefield Grammar Sch., Stockton-on-Tees; King's Coll., London (LLB, FKC 1976). Principal in Malcolm Wilson & Cobby, Solicitors, Worthing, 1952-74. Member of the Council of the Law Society, 1969-74. *Recreations:* golf, music. *Address:* Wellington Cottage, Albourne, Hassocks, W Sussex. *T:* Hurstpierpoint 833345.

BOWSER of Argaty and the King's Lundies, David Stewart, JP; a Forestry Commissioner since 1974; landowner since 1947; *b* 11 March 1926; *s* of late David Charles Bowser, CBE and Maysie Murray Bowser (*née* Henderson); *m* 1951, Judith Crabbe; one *s* four *d*. *Educ:* Harrow; Trinity Coll., Cambridge (BA Agric). Captain, Scots Guards, 1944-47. Member: Nat. Bd of Timber Growers Scotland Ltd (formerly Scottish Woodland Owners' Assoc.), 1960- (Chm. 1972-74); Regional Adv. Cttee, West Scotland Conservancy, Forestry Commn, 1964-74 (Chm. 1970-74). Pres., Highland Cattle Soc., 1970-72; Vice-Pres., Blackface Sheep Breeders' Assoc., 1981-. Mem. Perth CC, 1954-61; JP Co. Perth, 1956. *Recreations:* shooting, fishing, stalking. *Address:* Auchlyne, Killin, Perthshire. *Club:* Army and Navy.

BOWSHER, Peter Charles, QC 1978; *b* 9 Feb. 1935; *m* 1960, Deborah, *d* of Frederick Wilkins, Vancouver; two *s*. *Educ:* Ardingly; Oriel Coll., Oxford (MA). Commnd Royal Artillery, 1954; Territorial Army XX Rifle Team, 1957. Called to the Bar, Middle Temple, 1959. Harmsworth Scholar; Blackstone Entrance Scholar; Blackstone Pupillage Prize. Medico-Legal correspondent to British Medical Journal, 1960-70. A Legal Assessor to GMC and GDC, 1979-. *Recreations:* photography, music. *Address:* 10 South Square, Gray's Inn, WC1R 5EU. *T:* 01-242-2902. *Clubs:* Brooks's, United Oxford & Cambridge University, Royal Automobile.

BOWTELL, Ann Elizabeth; Under Secretary, Department of Health and Social Security, since 1980; *b* 25 April 1938; *d* of John Albert and Olive Rose Kewell; *m* 1961, Michael John Bowtell; two *s* two *d*. *Educ:* Kendrick Girls' Sch., Reading; Girton Coll., Cambridge (BA). Asst Principal, Nat. Assistance Board, 1960; Principal: Nat. Assistance Board, 1964; Min. of Social Security, 1966; DHSS, 1968; Asst Sec.; DHSS, 1973. *Recreations:* children, cooking,

walking. *Address:* 26 Sidney Road, Walton-on-Thames, Surrey KT12 2NA. *T:* Walton-on-Thames 29260.

BOWYER, family name of **Baron Denham.**

BOWYER, Gordon Arthur, OBE 1970; RIBA; FSIAD; Partner, Gordon Bowyer & Partners, Chartered Architects, since 1948; *b* 21 March 1923; *s* of Arthur Bowyer and Kathleen Mary Bowyer; *m* 1950, Ursula Meyer; one *s* one *d*. *Educ:* Dauntsey's Sch.; Regent Street Polytechnic Sch. of Architecture. Architect in private practice, in partnership with Ursula Bowyer and Iain Langlands, 1948-. Design work includes: Sports Section, South Bank Exhibn, Fest. of Britain, 1951; Inventions Section, British Pavilion, Brussels World Exhibn 1958; BoT exhibit, British Exhibn, NY, 1960; The British Scene, British Govt Pavilion, Osaka, 1970; design consultancy: D. H. Evans, 1956-59; offices, showrooms and shops for Max Factor Ltd, 1955, Dollond & Aitchison, 1956-60, Vidal Sassoon in England, USA and Germany, 1963-76; British Travel and Holiday Assoc. in London and Toronto, 1962-64; Asprey & Co., 1977; Interiors for Royal Lancaster Hotel, 1967, Treasury at Gloucester Cathedral, 1976; Hosps for Sick Children, 1977-79; numerous office conversions for IBM (UK) Ltd, 1970-79. Architectural work includes, 1952-: several private houses; offices for Sogenique (Services) Ltd, 1958; schs and hostel for handicapped children in Peckham, Bermondsey and Dulwich, 1966-75; housing for Southwark, GLC, Family Housing Assoc., London & Quadrant Housing Assoc. and Greenwich Housing Soc., 1969-79; Peckham Methodist Church, 1975; offices for Pharmax Ltd at Bexley, 1976, Rank City Wall at Brighton, 1975 and Folkestone 1976. Vanbrugh Castle restoration, 1977. Hon. Sec., SIAD, 1957-58; Mem., Cttee for Art and Design, CNAA, 1980-; Governor, Bath Academy of Art, 1971-; Trustee, Nat. Maritime Museum, 1977-. *Address:* 111 Maze Hill, SE10 8XQ. *T:* (office) 01-636 8101.

BOWYER, William, RA 1981 (ARA 1974); RP, RBA, RWS; Head of Fine Art, Maidstone College of Art, since 1971; *b* 25 May 1926; *m* 1951, Vera Mary Small; two *s* one *d*. *Educ:* Burslem School of Art; Royal College of Art (ARCA). Hon. Sec., New English Art Club. *Recreations:* cricket (Chiswick and Old Meadonians Cricket Clubs), snooker. *Address:* 12 Cleveland Avenue, Chiswick, W4 1SN. *T:* 01-994 0346. *Club:* Chelsea Arts.

BOWYER-SMYTH, Sir T. W.; *see* Smyth.

BOX, Betty Evelyn, (Mrs P. E. Rogers), OBE 1958; Film Producer; *b* 25 Sept.; *m* 1949, Peter Edward Rogers; no *c*. *Educ:* home. Director: Welbeck Film Distributors Ltd, 1958-; Ulster Television, 1955-. *Films include:* Dear Murderer; When the Bough Breaks; Miranda; Blind Goddess; Huggett Family series; It's Not Cricket; Marry Me; Don't Ever Leave Me; So Long at the Fair; Appointment with Venus; Venetian Bird; A Day to Remember; The Clouded Yellow; Doctor in the House; Mad About Men; Doctor at Sea; The Iron Petticoat; Checkpoint; Doctor at Large; Campbell's Kingdom; A Tale of Two Cities; The Wind Cannot Read; The 39 Steps; Upstairs and Downstairs; Conspiracy of Hearts; Doctor in Love; No Love for Johnnie; No, My Darling Daughter; A Pair of Briefs; The Wild and the Willing; Doctor in Distress; Hot Enough for June; The High Bright Sun; Doctor in Clover; Deadlier than the Male; Nobody Runs Forever; Some Girls Do; Doctor in Trouble; Percy; The Love Ban; Percy's Progress. *Address:* Pinewood Studios, Iver, Bucks.

BOX, Donald Stewart; Member, The Stock Exchange and Senior Partner, Lyddon & Co., Stockbrokers; *b* 22 Nov. 1917; *s* of late Stanley Carter Box and Elizabeth Mary Stewart Box; *m* 1st, 1940, Margaret Kennington Bates (marr. diss. 1947); 2nd, 1948, Peggy Farr, *née* Gooding (marr. diss. 1973); 3rd, 1973, Margaret Rose Davies; one *d*. *Educ:* Llandaff Cathedral Sch.; St John's Sch., Pinner; County Sch., Harrow. RAF ranks, 1939, commissioned, 1941; overseas service Egypt, Palestine, Transjordan, 1941-44; demobbed with rank of Flt-Lieut, 1945. MP (C) Cardiff North, 1959-66. *Recreations:* indifferent tennis, studying race form, doodling and doggerel. *Address:* Laburnum Cottage, Sully Road, Penarth, S Glam. *T:* Penarth 707966; 27A Smith Street, SW3. *T:* 01-351 2834. *Clubs:* City of London; Cardiff and County (Cardiff).

BOX, Sydney; author and film producer; *b* 29 April 1907; *m* 1st, 1929, Katherine Knight (marr. diss. 1934); 2nd, 1935, Muriel Baker (marr. diss. 1969); one *d* ; 3rd, 1969, Sylvia Knowles. In 1939 founded Verity Films Ltd, which produced more than 100 documentary and training films for War Office, Ministry of Information, etc; Producer, Two Cities Films, Denham Studios, 1941-42; Producer, Riverside Studios, 1943-45; Man. Dir and Executive Producer, Gainsborough Pictures, 1946-50. Films include: The Seventh Veil (Academy award for best original screen play, 1946); Quartet; Trio; Holiday Camp; Portrait from Life; The Years Between; The Man Within; The Passionate Stranger, and The Truth About Women (both with Muriel Box). Author (often in collaboration with Muriel Box) of more than 50 one-act plays, including Not This Man, winner of British Drama League National Festival at Old Vic, 1937. In charge of production London Independent Producers, 1951. Dir, Tyne Tees Television (ITA), 1958-65; Chairman: London Independent Television Producers Ltd, 1963; National Film Corp. Ltd, 1965; Triton Publishing Co. Ltd. Mem., W Australia Arts Council, 1974-77. *Publications:* Diary of a Drop Out, 1969; The Golden Girls, 1971; Alibi in the Rough, 1977; The Lion That Lost Its Way, 1978; Second Only to Murder, 1978. *Address:* 21/71 Mount Street, Perth, WA 6000, Australia.

BOXALL, Bernard, CBE 1963; Deputy Chairman, Lancer Boss Group Ltd; Director, Erma Ltd; b 17 Aug. 1906; s of late Arthur Boxall and of Mrs Maud Mary Boxall (née Mills); m 1931, Marjorie Lilian, d of late William George Emery and Mrs Emery; one s one d. Educ: King's Coll. Sch., Wimbledon; Imperial Coll., London Univ. (BSc (Hons), FCGI), Fellow 1971. James Howden & Co. Ltd, 1928-33; J. A. King & Co. Ltd, 1934-42; Production-Engineering Ltd, 1942-59; Management Consultant, 1959-. Chm., British United Trawlers Ltd, 1969-71. Dir, Lindustries Ltd, and Chm. of its engineering cos, 1960-71. Member: Highland Trnspt Bd, 1963-66; IRC, 1966-71; Scottish Economic Planning Council, 1967-71; Monopolies Commn, 1969-74. Mem., Company of Coachmakers and Coach Harness Makers (Master, 1977-78). FIMechE, FIProdE, Assoc. CIT. Recreations: golf, sailing. Address: Gilridge, Sandy Lane, Kingswood, Surrey KT20 6NQ. T: Mogador 832125. Club: Walton Heath Golf.

BOXALL, Mrs Lewis; see Buss, Barbara Ann.

BOXER, Air Vice-Marshal Sir Alan (Hunter Cachemaille), KCVO 1970; CB 1968; DSO 1944; DFC 1943; b 1 Dec. 1916; s of late Dr E. A. Boxer, CMG, Hastings, Hawkes Bay, NZ; m 1941, Pamela Sword; two s one d. Educ: Nelson Coll., New Zealand. Commissioned in RAF, 1939. Served War of 1939-45; Trng Comd until 1942; flying and staff appts, Bomber Comd, 1942-45. RAF Staff Coll., 1945; Jt Staff, Cabinet Offices, 1946-47; Staff Coll., Camberley, 1948; Strategic Air Comd, USAF and Korea, 1949-51; Central Fighter Estabt, 1952-53; Mem. Directing Staff, RAF Staff Coll., 1954-56; CO No 7 Sqdn, RAF, 1957; Group Capt. and CO, RAF Wittering, 1958-59; Plans, HQ Bomber Comd, 1960-61; Air Cdre, idc, 1962; SASO: HQ No 1 Gp, RAF, 1963-65; HQ Bomber Comd, 1965-67; Defence Services Sec., MoD, 1967-70. Virtuti Militari (Polish), Bronze Star (US), Air Medal (US). Address: Lisle Farmhouse, Lymington, Hampshire SO4 8SH. Club: Royal Air Force.

BOXER, Charles Ian; writer; b 11 Feb. 1926; s of Rev. William Neville Gordon Boxer and Margaret Boxer; m 1968, Hilary Fabienne Boxer. Educ: Glasgow High Sch.; Edinburgh Univ. (BL). Church of England ministry, 1950-54; apprentice to solicitors, 1954-58; Mem., Dominican Order (RC), 1958-67; Sen. Community Relations Officer for Wandsworth, 1967-77; Dir, Community Affairs and Liaison Div., Commn for Racial Equality, 1977-81. Recreation: music. Address: 56 Alder Row, West Woodlands, Frome, Somerset. T: Frome 61510.

BOXER, (Charles) Mark (Edward), ('Marc'); cartoonist and publisher; b 19 May 1931; s of Lt-Col Harold Stephen Boxer and Isobel Victoria Hughlings Jackson; m 1st, 1956, Lady Arabella Stuart, 3rd d of 18th Earl of Moray, MC (marr. diss. 1982); one s one d; 2nd, 1982, Anna Ford; one d. Educ: Berkhamsted Sch.; King's Coll., Cambridge. Editor, Granta, 1952-53; Art Director, Queen, 1957-61; 1st Editor, Sunday Times magazine, 1962-65; Director, Sunday Times, 1964-66; Editorial Dir, London Life, 1965; Times cartoonist, 1969-; Asst Editor, Sunday Times, 1966-79; caricaturist for New Statesman, 1970-78, London Review of Books, 1981, etc. Director, Weidenfeld & Nicolson, 1980-. Cartoonist of the Year, 1972. Publications: Trendy Ape, 1968; The Times We Live In, 1978; illus. publications by Clive James: Felicity Fark, 1975, Britannia Bright, 1976, and Charles Charming, 1981. Recreations: bridge, chess. Address: c/o Weidenfeld & Nicolson, 91 Clapham High Street, SW4. T: 01-622 9933.

BOXER, Prof. Charles Ralph, FBA 1957; Emeritus Professor of Portuguese, University of London, since 1968; Fellow, King's Coll., 1967; b 8 March 1904; s of Col Hugh Boxer and Jane Boxer (née Patterson); m 1945, Emily Hahn; two d. Educ: Wellington Coll.; Royal Military Coll., Sandhurst. Commissioned Lincs Regt, 1923. Served War of 1939-45 (wounded, POW in Japanese hands, 1941-45). Retired with rank of Major, 1947. Camoens Prof. of Portuguese, London Univ., 1947-51; Prof. of the History of the Far East, London Univ., 1951-53; resigned latter post and re-apptd Camoens Prof., 1953-67; Prof. of History of Expansion of Europe Overseas, Yale, 1969-72. Visiting Research Prof., Indiana Univ., 1967-79; Emeritus Prof. of History, Yale, 1972-. Hon. Fellow, SOAS, 1974. A Trustee of National Maritime Museum, 1961-68. For. Mem., Royal Netherlands Acad. of Scis, 1976. Dr hc Universities of Utrecht (1950), Lisbon (1952), Bahia (1959), Liverpool (1966), Hong Kong (1971), Peradeniya (1980); Order of Santiago da Espada (Portugal); Grand Cross of the Order of the Infante Dom Henrique (Portugal); Kt Order of St Gregory the Great, 1969. Publications: The Commentaries of Ruy Freyre de Andrade, 1929; The Journal of M. H. Tromp, Anno 1639, 1930; Jan Compagnie in Japan, 1600-1817, 1936 (2nd edn 1950); Fidalgos in the Far East, 1550-1770, 1948; The Christian Century in Japan, 1549-1640, 1951, 2nd edn 1967; Salvador de Sá and the Struggle for Brazil and Angola, 1952; South China in the 16th Century, 1953; The Dutch in Brazil, 1624-1654, 1957; The Tragic History of the Sea, 1589-1622, 1959; The Great Ship from Amacon, 1959; Fort Jesus and the Portuguese in Mombasa, 1960; The Golden Age of Brazil, 1695-1750, 1962; Race Relations in the Portuguese Colonial Empire, 1415-1825, 1963; The Dutch Seaborne Empire, 1600-1800, 1965; Portuguese Society in the Tropics, 1966; Further Selections from the Tragic History of the Sea, 1969; The Portuguese Seaborne Empire, 1415-1825, 1969; Anglo-Dutch Wars of the 17th Century, 1974; Mary and Misogyny, 1975; João de Barros: Portuguese humanist and historian of Asia, 1981; numerous articles in learned periodicals. Address: Ringshall End, Little Gaddesden, Herts HP4 1NF. Clubs: Athenæum; Yale (New York).

BOXER, Air Cdre Henry Everard Crichton, CB 1965; OBE 1948; idc, ndc, psc; b 28 July 1914; s of late Rear-Adm. Henry P. Boxer; m 1938, Enid Anne Louise, d of late Dr John Moore Collyns; two s two d. Educ: Shrewsbury Sch. RAF Coll., Cranwell. Commissioned RAF, 1935; No 1 Fighter Squadron, 1935-37; No 1 Flying Training Sch., 1937-39; Specialist Navigator, 1939. Served War of 1939-45, in UK, S Africa and Europe. BJSM, Washington, DC, 1945-48; directing Staff, RAF Staff Coll., 1949-50; Coastal Command, 1951-52; Nat. Defence Coll., Canada, 1952-53; Air Ministry, 1953-56; OC RAF Thorney Island, 1956-58. ADC to the Queen, 1957-59; IDC, 1959; Sen Air Liaison Officer and Air Adviser to British High Comr in Canada, 1960-62; AO i/c Admin, HQ Coastal Comd, 1962-65; Dir of Personnel (Air), MoD (RAF), 1965-67; retd, 1967. Counsellor (Defence Equipment), British High Commn, Ottawa, 1967-74; retd, 1975. Address: Orchard House, Fairfield Close, Lymington, Hants. Club: Royal Air Force.

BOXER, Mark; see Boxer, Charles M. E.

BOYCE, Air Vice-Marshal Clayton Descou Clement, CB 1946; CBE 1944; Assistant Controller of Aircraft, Ministry of Supply, 1957-59, retired; b 19 Sept. 1907; er s of Col C. J. Boyce, CBE, late IA; m 1928, Winifred (d 1981), d of late J. E. Mead, Castletown, Isle of Man; one s. Educ: Bedford Sch.; Cranwell. Sec.-Gen., Allied Air Forces, Central Europe, 1953; AOC, Cyprus and Levant, 1954-56. Address: c/o Lloyds Bank, Cox's and King's Branch, 6 Pall Mall, SW1.

BOYCE, Guy Gilbert L.; see Leighton-Boyce.

BOYCE, Joseph Frederick, JP; FRICS; General Manager, Telford Development Corporation, since 1980; b 10 Aug. 1926; m 1953, Nina Margaret, o d of A. F. Tebb, Leeds; two s. Educ: Roundhay Sch., Leeds; Leeds Coll. of Technology. Pupil and Asst Quantity Surveyor, Rex Procter & Miller, Chartered Quantity Surveyors, 1942-53; Sen. Quantity Surveyor, Bedford Corp., 1953-55; Group Quantity Surveyor, Somerset CC, 1955-60; Principal Asst Quantity Surveyor, Salop CC, 1960-64; Telford Development Corporation: Chief Quantity Surveyor, 1964-71; Technical Co-ordinator, 1971-76; Dep. Gen. Manager, 1976-80. JP Shrewsbury, 1975. Publications: technical articles and publications on new towns, in learned journals. Recreations: reading, travel, hill walking, sport. Address: The Uplands, 5 Port Hill Gardens, Shrewsbury, Shropshire SY3 8SH. T: (office) Telford 613131.

BOYCE, Sir Robert (Charles) Leslie, 3rd Bt cr 1952; b 2 May 1962; s of Sir Richard (Leslie) Boyce, 2nd Bt, and of Jacqueline Anne (who m 2nd, 1974, Christopher Boyce-Dennis), o d of Roland A. Hill; S father, 1968. Educ: Cheltenham Coll. Heir: uncle John Leslie Boyce [b 16 Nov. 1934; m 1957, Finola Mary, d of late James Patrick Maxwell; one s three d]. Address: The Barn House, Ascott Earl, Ascott under Wychwood, Oxon OX7 6AG.

BOYCE, Walter Edwin, OBE 1970; Director of Social Services, Essex County Council, 1970-78; b 30 July 1918; s of Rev. Joseph Edwin Boyce and Alice Elizabeth Boyce; m 1942, Edna Lane (née Gargett); two d. Educ: High Sch. for Boys, Trowbridge, Wilts. Admin. Officer, Warwickshire CC, 1938-49. Served war, commnd RA; Gunnery sc, 1943; demob. rank Major, 1946. Dep. County Welfare Officer: Shropshire, 1949-52; Cheshire, 1952-57; Co. Welfare Officer, Essex, 1957-70. Adviser to Assoc. of County Councils, 1965-78; Mem., Sec. of State's Adv. Personal Social Services Council, 1973 until disbanded, 1980 (Chm., People with handicaps Gp); Mem., nat. working parties on: Health Service collaboration, 1972-74; residential accommodation for elderly and mentally handicapped, 1974-78; boarding houses, 1981. Pres., County Welfare Officers Soc., 1967-68. Governor, Queen Elizabeth's Foundn for the Disabled, 1980-. Recreations: sailing, in sports, particularly Rugby and athletics, voluntary services, travel. Address: Highlanders Barn, Newmans Green, Long Melford, Suffolk CO10 0AD.

BOYCOTT, Prof. Brian Blundell, FRS 1971; Director, Medical Research Council Cell Biophysics Unit, since 1980; Professor of Biology by title, since 1971; b 10 Dec. 1924; s of Percy Blundell Boycott and Doris Eyton Lewis; m 1950, Marjorie Mabel Burchell; one s (and one s decd). Educ: Royal Masonic Sch. Technician, Nat. Inst. Medical Research, and undergraduate (BSc), Birkbeck Coll., London, 1942-46; University Coll., London: Asst Lectr, Zoology, 1946-47; Hon. Res. Asst, Anatomy, 1947-52; Lectr, Zoology, 1952-62; Reader in Zoology, Univ. of London, 1962, Prof. of Zoology, 1968-70. Vis. Lectr, Harvard Univ., 1963. Member: Adv. Council, British Library Board, 1976-80; Council, Open Univ., 1975-; Council, Royal Soc., 1976-78; Univ. of London Cttee on Academic Organization, 1980-82; Comr, 1851 Exhibition, 1974-. Scientific medal, Zoological Soc. London, 1965. Publications: various articles in learned jls on structure and function of nervous systems. Recreations: nothing of special notability. Address: c/o Department of Biophysics, King's College, 26-29 Drury Lane, WC2. T: 01-836 8851.

BOYCOTT, Geoffrey; cricketer; b 21 Oct. 1940; s of late Thomas William Boycott and Jane Boycott. Educ: Kinsley Modern Sch.; Hemsworth Grammar Sch. Joined Yorkshire Cricket Club, 1962, received County Cap, 1963, Captain of Yorkshire, 1970-78. Played for England, 1964-74, 1977-82; scored 100th hundred, England v Australia, 1977; passed former world record no of runs scored in Test Matches, Delhi, Dec. 1981. Publications: Geoff Boycott's Book for Young Cricketers, 1976; Put to the Test: England in Australia 1978-79, 1979; Geoff Boycott's Cricket Quiz, 1979; On Batting, 1980;

Opening Up, 1980; In the Fast Lane, 1981; Master Class, 1982. *Recreations:* golf, tennis. *Address:* c/o Yorkshire County Cricket Club, Headingley Cricket Ground, Leeds, Yorks LS6 3BY.

BOYD; *see* Lennox-Boyd.

BOYD, family name of **Baron Kilmarnock.**

BOYD OF MERTON, 1st Viscount *cr* 1960; **Alan Tindal Lennox-Boyd,** PC 1951; CH 1960; DL; Joint Vice-Chairman of Arthur Guinness, Son & Co. Ltd, 1967-79 (Managing Director, 1960-67); *b* 18 Nov. 1904; 2nd *s* of Alan Walter Lennox-Boyd, and Florence, *d* of James Warburton Begbie; *m* 1938, Lady Patricia Guinness, 2nd *d* of 2nd Earl of Iveagh, KG, CB, CMG, FRS; three *s. Educ:* Sherborne; Christ Church, Oxford (Scholar; MA; Beit Prizeman; Hon. Student, 1968). Pres. of the Oxford Union, 1926. Served with RNVR, 1940-43. Contested Gower Div. of Glamorgan, 1929; MP (C) Mid-Beds, 1931-60; Parliamentary Sec., Ministry of Labour, 1938-39; Parliamentary Sec., Ministry of Home Security, 1939; Parliamentary Sec., Ministry of Food, 1939-40; Called to the Bar, Inner Temple, 1941; Parliamentary Sec., Ministry of Aircraft Production, 1943-45; Minister of State for Colonial Affairs, 1951-52; Minister of Transport and Civil Aviation, 1952-54; Sec. of State for the Colonies, 1954-Oct. 1959. Director: Royal Exchange, 1962-70; Tate & Lyle, 1966-74; ICI, 1967-75. President: British Leprosy Relief Assoc., 1960-; Overseas Service Resettlement Bureau, 1962-79; Royal Commonwealth Soc., 1965- (Chm., 1961-64); Overseas Service Pensioners Assoc., 1972-; RNVR Officers' Assoc., 1964-72; Chairman: Voluntary Service Overseas, 1962-64; Brewers Soc., 1965; Maritime Trust, 1976-78; Trustee, BM, 1962-78; Trustee, Natural History Museum, 1963-76; Governor, Sherborne Sch., 1962-, Chm. of Governors, 1968; Mem. Council, Institute of Directors, 1962-. Prime Warden, Goldsmiths' Co., 1964-65. Hon. Fellow, London Sch. of Hygiene and Tropical Medicine, 1977. Hon. LLD Exeter, 1980. Messel Medal, Soc. of Chemical Industry, 1966. DL Beds, 1954-61, Cornwall 1965. DK Brunei, 1971. *Heir: s* Hon. Simon Donald Rupert Neville Lennox-Boyd, *qv. Address:* Ince Castle, Saltash, Cornwall. *T:* Saltash 2274. *Clubs:* Carlton, Pratt's, Buck's, Naval, Royal Automobile, Royal Commonwealth Society; Royal Yacht Squadron, Royal Western Yacht.

See also Hon. Mark Lennox-Boyd.

BOYD, Sir Alexander Walter, 3rd Bt, *cr* 1916; *b* 16 June 1934; *s* of late Cecil Anderson Boyd, MC, MD, and Marjorie Catharine, *e d* of late Francis Kinloch, JP, Shipka Lodge, North Berwick; *S* uncle, 1948; *m* 1958, Molly Madeline, *d* of late Ernest Arthur Rendell; two *s* three *d. Heir: s* Ian Walter Rendell Boyd, *b* 14 March 1964. *Address:* RR 3, Vernon, British Columbia, Canada.

BOYD, Arthur Merric Bloomfield, AO 1979; OBE 1970; painter; *b* 24 July 1920; *s* of William Merric Boyd and Doris Lucy Eleanor Gough; *m* 1945, Yvonne Hartland Lennie; one *s* two *d. Educ:* State Sch., Murrumbeena, Vic., Australia. Was taught painting and sculpture by parents and grandfather, Arthur Merric Boyd; first exhibited painting in Melbourne, 1937; served in Australian Army, 1940-43; painted and exhibited, 1944-59, exhibited ceramic sculpture, 1953-56, in Australia; first visited Europe, 1959; first one-man exhibn painting, London, 1960; designed for Ballet at Edinburgh Festival and Sadler's Wells Theatre, 1961, and at Covent Garden Royal Opera House, 1963; retrospective exhibn of painting at Whitechapel Gallery, 1962; retrospective exhbn, Nat. Gallery of S Australia, Adelaide, 1964. *Relevant publication:* Arthur Boyd, by Franz Philipp, 1967. *Address:* c/o Bank of New South Wales, 34 Piccadilly, W1.

BOYD, Atarah, (Mrs Douglas Boyd); *see* Ben-Tovim, A.

BOYD, Christopher; *see* Boyd, T. C.

BOYD, David John; QC 1982; Secretary and Chief Legal Officer, Inco Europe, since 1972; *b* 11 Feb. 1935; *s* of David Boyd and Ellen Jane Boyd (*née* Gruer); *m* 1960, Raija Sinikka Lindholm, Finland; one *s* one *d. Educ:* Eastbourne Coll.; St George's Sch., Newport, USA (British-Amer. schoolboy schol.); Gonville and Caius Coll., Cambridge (MA). FCIArb 1979. Various secretarial posts, ICI, 1957-62; Legal Asst, Pfizer, 1962-66; called to the Bar, Gray's Inn, 1963; Sec. and Legal Officer, Henry Wiggin & Co., 1966; Asst Sec. and Sen. Legal Officer (UK), Internat. Nickel, 1968; Dir, Impala Platinum, 1972-78. Gen. Comr of Income Tax, 1978-. Chm., Bar Assoc. for Commerce, Finance and Industry, 1980-81; Mem., Senate of Inns of Court and Bar, 1978-81. *Recreations:* theatre-going, holidaying in France. *Address:* 123A Ashley Gardens, Thirleby Road, SW1. *T:* 01-834 1160; Beeches, Upton Bishop, Ross-on-Wye, Herefordshire. *T:* Upton Bishop 214. *Club:* Naval.

BOYD, Dennis Galt; Chief Conciliation Officer, Advisory, Conciliation and Arbitration Service, since 1980; *b* 3 Feb. 1931; *s* of late Thomas Ayre Boyd and Minnie (*née* Galt); *m* 1953, Pamela Mary McLean; one *s* one *d. Educ:* South Shields High School for Boys. National Service, 1949-51; Executive Officer, Civil Service: Min. of Supply/Min. of Defence, 1951-66; Board of Trade, 1966-69; Personnel Officer, Forestry Commission, 1969-75; Director of Corporate Services Health and Safety Executive, Dept of Employment, 1975-79; Director of Conciliation (ACAS), 1979-80. *Recreations:* golf, compulsory gardening. *Address:* Dunelm, Silchester Road, Little London, near Basingstoke. *Club:* Civil Service.

BOYD, Sir Francis; *see* Boyd, Sir J. F.

BOYD, Gavin, CBE 1977; Consultant, Boyds, solicitors, since 1978; Chairman, Scottish Opera Theatre Royal Ltd, since 1973; *b* 4 Aug. 1928; *s* of Gavin and Margaret Boyd; *m* 1954, Kathleen Elizabeth Skinner; one *s. Educ:* Glasgow Acad.; Univ. of Glasgow. MA (Hons); LLB. Partner, Boyds, solicitors, Glasgow, 1955-77. Director: Stenhouse Holdings Ltd, 1970-79 (Chm., 1971-78); Scottish Opera, 1970-; North Sea Assets plc, 1972- (Dep. Chm., 1981-); Paterson Jenks plc, 1972-81; Scottish Television plc, 1973-; Ferranti plc, 1975-; British Carpets plc, 1977-81. Trustee, Scottish Hosps Endowment Res. Trust, 1978. Member: Court, Univ. of Strathclyde (Convener, Finance Cttee, 1979-); Law Soc. of Scotland. Hon. LLD Strathclyde, 1982. *Recreations:* music and the performing arts, particularly opera; yacht racing and cruising. *Address:* 4A Prince Albert Road, Glasgow G12 9JX. *Club:* Glasgow Art.

BOYD, Ian Robertson; HM Stipendiary Magistrate, West Yorkshire, since 1982; *b* 18 Oct. 1922; *s* of Arthur Robertson Boyd, Edinburgh, and Florence May Boyd (*née* Kinghorn), Leeds; *m* 1952, Joyce Mary Boyd (*née* Crabtree); one *s* one *d. Educ:* Roundhay Sch.; Leeds Univ. LLB (Hons)). Served Army, 1942-47: Captain Green Howards; Royal Lincolnshire Regt in India, Burma, Malaya, Dutch East Indies. Leeds Univ., 1947; called to Bar, Middle Temple, 1952; practised North Eastern Circuit, 1952-72; HM Stipendiary Magistrate, sitting at Hull, 1972-82. Sometime Asst/Dep. Recorder of Doncaster, Newcastle, Hull and York. *Recreation:* gardener *manqué. Address:* The Town Hall, Leeds 1.

BOYD, James Edward, CA; Director and Financial Adviser: Denholm group of companies, since 1968; Lithgows (Holdings) Ltd, since 1962; *b* 14 Sept. 1928; *s* of Robert Edward Boyd and Elizabeth Reid Sinclair; *m* 1956, Judy Ann Christey Scott; two *s* two *d. Educ:* Kelvinside Academy; The Leys Sch., Cambridge. CA Scot. (dist.) 1951. Director: Ayrshire Metal Products plc, 1965-; Invergordon Distillers (Holdings) plc, 1966-; GB Papers plc, 1977-; Carlton Industries plc, 1978-; English & Caledonian Investment plc, 1981-. Partner, McClelland Ker & Co. CA (subseq. McClelland Moores & Co.), 1953-61; Finance Director: Lithgows Ltd, 1962-69; Scott Lithgow Ltd, 1970-78; Chm., Fairfield Shipbuilding & Engrg Co. Ltd, 1964-65; Man. Dir, Invergordon Distillers (Holdings) Ltd, 1966-67; Dir, Nairn & Williamson (Holdings) Ltd, 1968-75. Member: Clyde Port Authority, 1974-80; Working Party on Scope and Aims of Financial Accounts (the Corporate Report), 1974-75; Exec. Cttee, Accountants Jt Disciplinary Scheme, 1979-81; Mem. Council, Inst. of Chartered Accountants of Scotland, 1977- (Vice-Pres., 1980-82, Pres., 1982-). *Recreations:* tennis, golf, gardening. *Address:* Dunard, Station Road, Rhu, Dunbartonshire, Scotland G84 8LW. *T:* Rhu 820441.

BOYD, James Fleming, CB 1980; Director General (Management), Board of Inland Revenue, 1978-81; *b* 28 April 1920; *s* of late Walter and late Mary Boyd; *m* 1949, Daphne Steer, Hendon; one *s* one *d. Educ:* Whitehill Sch., Glasgow. Tax Officer, Inland Revenue, 1937; served with HM Forces, RAF, 1940-46; Inspector of Taxes, 1950; Principal Inspector, 1964; Senior Principal Inspector, 1970; Dep. Chief Inspector of Taxes, 1973; Dir of Operations, Inland Revenue, 1975-77. *Recreations:* history, gardening. *Address:* 2A The Avenue, Potters Bar, Herts EN6 1EB. *T:* Potters Bar 55905.

BOYD, John Dixon Iklé; HM Diplomatic Service; Counsellor (Economic and Social Affairs), United Kingdom Mission to the United Nations, since 1981; *b* 17 Jan. 1936; *s* of Prof. James Dixon Boyd and Amélie Lowenthal; *m* 1st, 1968, Gunilla Kristina Ingegerd Rönngren; one *s* one *d*; 2nd, 1977, Julia Daphne Raynsford; three *d. Educ:* Westminster Sch.; Clare Coll., Cambridge (BA); Yale Univ. (MA). Joined HM Foreign Service, 1962: Hong Kong, 1962-64; Peking, 1965-67; Foreign Office, 1967-69; Washington, 1969-73; 1st Sec., Peking, 1973-75; secondment to HM Treasury, 1976; Counsellor (Economic), Bonn, 1977-81. *Recreations:* music, fly fishing. *Address:* c/o Foreign and Commonwealth Office, SW1; 22 Dovercourt Road, SE22. *T:* 01-693 4585.

BOYD, Sir (John) Francis, Kt 1976; a Vice-President, Commons Preservation Society; *b* 11 July 1910; *s* of John Crichton Dick Boyd and Kate Boyd, Ilkley, Yorks; *m* 1946, Margaret, *d* of George Dobson and Agnes Dobson, Scarborough, Yorks; one *s* two *d. Educ:* Ilkley Grammar Sch.; Silcoates Sch., near Wakefield, Yorks. Reporter: Leeds Mercury, 1928-34; Manchester Guardian, 1934-37; Parly Correspondent, Manchester Guardian, 1937-39. Aux. Fire Service, London, 1939; Monitoring Unit, BBC, 1940; Army, 1940-45. Political Correspondent, Manchester Guardian and Guardian, 1945-72; Political Editor, 1972-75. Chm., Lobby Journalists, 1949-50. Hon. LLD Leeds, 1973. *Publications:* Richard Austen Butler, 1956; (ed) The Glory of Parliament, by Harry Boardman, 1960; British Politics in Transition, 1964. *Recreations:* reading, walking, gardening. *Address:* 62 Gainsborough Road, N12 8AH. *T:* 01-445 0607.

BOYD, Sir John (McFarlane), Kt 1979; CBE 1974; General Secretary, Amalgamated Union of Engineering Workers, 1975-82; *b* 8 Oct. 1917; *s* of James and Mary Boyd; *m* 1940, Elizabeth McIntyre; two *d. Educ:* Hamilton St Elem. Sch.; Glencairn Secondary Sch. Engrg apprentice, 1932-37; Engr, 1937-46. AUEW: Asst Div. Organiser, 1946-50; Div. Organiser, 1950-53; Mem. Executive, 1953-75. Pres., Conf. of Shipbuilding and Engineering Unions, 1964; Member: TUC Gen. Council, 1967-75 and 1978-82; Council, ACAS, 1978-82; Director: BSC; UKAEA (Mem., 1980). Chm., Labour Party,

1967. *Recreations:* brass banding, gardening. *Address:* 24 Pearl Court, Cornfield Terrace, Eastbourne, Sussex. *Club:* Caledonian.

BOYD, Dr John Morton, FRSE; Director, Scotland, Nature Conservancy Council, since 1971; *b* Darvel, Ayrshire, 31 Jan. 1925; *s* of Thomas Pollock Boyd and Jeanie Reid Morton; *m* 1954, Winifred Isobel Rome; four *s. Educ:* Kilmarnock Acad.; Glasgow Univ. (BSc, PhD, DSc). FRSE 1968. Served War, 1943-47: Flt Lieut RAF. Nature Conservancy Council: Reg. Officer, 1957-68; Asst Dir, 1969-70. Nuffield Trav. Fellow, ME and E Africa, 1964-65; Leader, British Jordan Expedn, 1966; Mem., Royal Soc. Aldabra Expedn, 1967. Member: Council, Royal Scottish Zool Soc., 1963-69, 1980-; Council, Azraq Internat. Biol Stn, Jordan, 1967-69; Council, National Trust for Scotland, 1971-; Seals Adv. Cttee, NERC, 1973-79; BBC Scottish Agr. Adv. Cttee, 1973-76; Exec. Bd, Internat. Waterfowl Res. Bureau, 1976-78; Council, Royal Soc. of Edinburgh, 1978-81; Consultative Panel on Conservation of the Line and Phoenix Islands (Central Pacific), 1981-. Internat. Union for Conservation of Nature and Natural Resources: British Rep., Kinshasa, 1975, Geneva, 1977, Ashkhabad, 1978, and Christchurch, 1981; Mem. Commn on Ecology, 1976-; Consultancies, Senegal/Gambia and Switzerland, 1980, Holland, 1981 and Catalonia, 1982. Co-Chm., Area VI Anglo-Soviet Environmental Protection Agreement, 1977-; Chm., UK Internat. Conservation Cttee, 1980. Lectures: Keith Entwistle Meml, Cambridge, 1968; British Council, Amman, Nicosia and Ankara, 1972; Meml in Agr. Zool., W of Scotland Agr. Coll., 1976; Sir William Weipers Meml, Glasgow Univ. Vet. Sch., 1980; Nat. Trust for Scotland Jubilee, 1981. *Publications:* (with K. Williamson) St Kilda Summer, 1960; (with K. Williamson) Mosaic of Islands, 1963; (with F. F. Darling) The Highlands and Islands, 1964; Travels in the Middle East and East Africa, 1966; (with P. A. Jewell and C. Milner) Island Survivors, 1974; (ed) The Natural Environment of the Outer Hebrides, 1979; scientific papers on nature conservation and animal ecology. *Recreations:* travel, painting, photography. *Address:* 57 Hailes Gardens, Edinburgh EH13 0JH. *T:* 031-441 3220. *Club:* New (Edinburgh).

BOYD, Leslie Balfour, CBE 1977; Courts Administrator, Central Criminal Court, 1972-77; *b* 25 Nov. 1914; *e s* of late Henry Leslie Boyd, Mem. of Lloyds, of Crowborough, Sussex, and Beatrix Boyd, *d* of Henry Chapman, for many years British Consul at Dieppe; *m* 1936, Wendy Marie, *d* of George and Nancy Blake, Oswestry, Salop; one *s* one *d. Educ:* Evelyn's; Royal Naval College, Dartmouth. Invalided out of Royal Navy, 1931. Called to the Bar, Gray's Inn, 1939; joined staff of Central Criminal Court, 1941; Dep. Clerk of Court, 1948; Clerk of the Court, 1955-71; Dep. Clerk of Peace, 1949-55, Clerk of the Peace, 1955-71, City of London and Town and Borough of Southwark. Master, Worshipful Company of Gold and Silver Wyre Drawers, 1969. *Publications:* contributor to Criminal Law and Juries titles, 3rd edn, Juries title, 4th edn, of Halsbury's Laws of England. *Recreations:* gardening and travel. *Address:* 12 Burgh Street, Islington, N1. *Club:* Bar Yacht.

BOYD, Prof. Robert Lewis Fullarton, CBE 1972; DSc; FRS 1969; Professor of Physics in the University of London since 1962; Director, Mullard Space Science Laboratory of Department of Physics and Astronomy of University College, London, since 1965; *b* 1922; *s* of late William John Boyd, PhD, BSc; *m* 1949, Mary, *d* of late John Hingley; two *s* one *d. Educ:* Whitgift Sch.; Imperial Coll., London (BSc (Eng) 1943); University Coll., London (PhD 1949). FIEE 1967; FInstP 1972. Exp. Officer at Admty Mining Estabt, 1943-46; DSIR Res. Asst, 1946-49; ICI Res. Fellow, 1949-50, Maths Dept, UCL; ICI Res. Fellow, Physics Dept, UCL, 1950-52; Lectr in Physics, UCL, 1952-58, Reader in Physics, UCL, 1959-62. Prof. of Astronomy (part-time), Royal Institution, 1961-67; IEE Appleton Lectr, 1976; Bakerian Lectr, Royal Soc., 1978; Halley Lectr, Univ. of Oxford, 1981. Chairman: Meteorol Res. Cttee, MoD, 1972-75; Astronautics Cttee, MoD, 1972-77; Member: BBC Science Cons. Gp, 1970-79; SRC, 1977-81 (Chm., Astronomy, Space and Radio Bd, 1977-80); Council, Physical Soc., 1958-60; Council, RAS, 1962-66 (Vice-Pres., 1964-66); British Nat. Cttee on Space Res., 1976-. Pres., Victoria Inst., 1965-76. Governor, Croydon Coll., 1966-80. Hon. DSc Heriot-Watt, 1979. *Publications:* The Upper Atmosphere (with H. S. W. Massey), 1958; Space Research by Rocket and Satellite, 1960; Space Physics, 1975; papers in sci. jls on space sci. and other topics. *Recreation:* elderly Rolls Royce motor cars. *Address:* Ariel House, Holmbury St Mary, Dorking, Surrey; Roseneath, 41 Church Street, Littlehampton, West Sussex.

BOYD, Robert Stanley, CB 1982; Solicitor of Inland Revenue, since 1979; *b* 6 March 1927; *s* of Robert Reginald Boyd (formerly Indian Police) and Agnes Maria Dorothea, *d* of Lt-Col Charles H. Harrison; *m* 1965, Ann, *d* of Daniel Hopkin. *Educ:* Wellington; Trinity Coll., Dublin (BA, LLB). Served RN, 1945-48. Called to Bar, Inner Temple, 1954. Joined Inland Revenue, 1959; Prin. Asst Solicitor, 1971-79. *Address:* 28 Canonbury Grove, N1 2HR.

BOYD, Stewart Craufurd, QC 1981; *b* 25 Oct. 1943; *s* of Leslie Balfour Boyd and Wendy Marie Boyd; *m* 1970, Catherine Jay; one *s* two *d. Educ:* Winchester Coll.; Trinity Coll., Cambridge (MA). Called to the Bar, Middle Temple, 1967. *Publication:* (ed) Scrutton, Charterparties, 18th edn 1972. *Recreations:* boats, pianos, gardens. *Address:* 1 Gayton Crescent, NW3 1TT. *T:* 01-431 1581.

BOYD, (Thomas) Christopher; farmer; *b* 1916; *m* ; one *s* two *d.* Army, 1940-44; civil servant, 1939 and 1944-48; MP (Lab) Bristol NW, 1955-59;

Chelsea Borough Councillor, 1953-59. *Address:* Middlegill, Moffat, Dumfriesshire. *T:* Beattock 415.

BOYD, William, CC (Canada) 1968; FRSC; *b* 21 June 1885; *s* of Dugald Cameron and Eliza M. Boyd; *m* Enid G. Christie. *Educ:* Trent Coll., Derbyshire; Edinburgh Univ. MB, ChB 1908; MD Edinburgh (Gold Medal), 1911; Diploma in Psychiatry, Edinburgh, 1912; MRCPE 1912; FRCP 1932; LLD Saskatchewan, 1937; MD Oslo, 1945; DSc Manitoba, 1948; FRCS Canada, 1949; FRCPE 1955; FRCSEd 1966; LLD Queen's, 1956. MO, Derby Borough Asylum, Derby, England, 1909-12; Pathologist, Winwick Asylum, Warrington, England, 1912-13; Pathologist, Royal Wolverhampton Hosp., Wolverhampton, 1913-14; Prof. of Pathology, University of Manitoba, Winnipeg, 1915-37; Prof. of Pathology and Bacteriology, University of Toronto, 1937-51, Prof. of Pathology, University of British Columbia, 1951-53. Capt. 3rd Field Ambulance, 46th Div. Imperial Forces, France, 1914-15. *Publications:* With a Field Ambulance at Ypres, 1917; The Physiology and Pathology of the Cerebrospinal Fluid, 1920; Pathology for the Surgeon, 8th edn, 1967; Pathology for the Physician, 7th edn, 1965; Text-Book of Pathology, 8th edn, 1970; Introduction to the Study of Disease, 6th edn, 1971; The Spontaneous Regression of Cancer, 1966. *Recreations:* mountaineering, golf, gardening. *Address:* 40 Arjay Crescent, Toronto, Ont, Canada.

BOYD-CARPENTER, family name of **Baron Boyd-Carpenter.**

BOYD-CARPENTER, Baron *cr* 1972 (Life Peer), of Crux Easton in the County of Southampton; **John Archibald Boyd-Carpenter,** PC 1954; DL; Chairman, Rugby Portland Cement, since 1976, Director, 1970-76); *b* 2 June 1908; *s* of late Sir Archibald Boyd-Carpenter, MP; *m* 1937, Margaret, *e d* of Lieut-Col G. L. Hall, OBE; one *s* two *d. Educ:* Stowe; Balliol Coll., Oxford. Pres. Oxford Union, 1930; BA (History, 1930); Diploma Economics, 1931; toured USA with Oxford Univ. Debating Team, 1931; Harmsworth Law Scholar, Middle Temple, 1933; Council of Legal Education's Prize for Constitutional Law, 1934; called to Bar, Middle Temple, 1934, and practised in London and SE Circuit. Contested (MR) Limehouse for LCC, 1934. Joined Scots Guards, 1940; held various staff appointments and served with AMG in Italy, retired with rank of Major. MP (C) for Kingston-upon-Thames, 1945-72; Financial Sec., to the Treasury, 1951-54; Minister of Transport and Civil Aviation, 1954-Dec. 1955; Minister of Pensions and National Insurance, Dec. 1955-July 1962; Chief Sec. to the Treasury and Paymaster-Gen., 1962-64; Opposition Front Bench Spokesman on Housing, Local Government and Land, 1964-66; Chm., Public Accounts Cttee, 1964-70. Chairman: Greater London Area Local Govt Cttee, Conservative Party, 1968; London Members Cttee, 1966-; Pres. Wessex Area, Nat. Union of Conservative and Unionist Assocs, 1977-. Chm., CAA, 1972-77. Chairman: Orion Insurance Co., 1969-72; CLRP Investment Trust, 1970-72; Dir of other cos; Mem. Council, Trust Houses Forte Ltd, 1977-. Governor, Stowe School; Chairman: Carlton Club, 1979-; Assoc. of Indep. Unionist Peers, 1979- (Dep. Chm. 1977-79). High Steward, Royal Borough of Kingston-upon-Thames, 1973. DL Greater London, 1973. *Publications:* Way of Life, 1980; newspaper articles. *Recreations:* tennis and swimming. *Address:* 12 Eaton Terrace, SW1. *T:* 01-730 7765; Crux Easton House, Crux Easton, near Highclere, Hants. *T:* Highclere 253037. *Club:* Carlton.
See also D. M. Hogg.

BOYD-ROCHFORT, Sir Cecil (Charles), KCVO 1968 (CVO 1952); Trainer of Racehorses, Newmarket, retired 1968; *b* 16 April 1887; 3rd *s* of late Major R. H. Boyd-Rochfort, 15th Hussars, Middleton Park, Westmeath; *m* 1944, Hon. Mrs Henry Cecil, *d* of Sir James Burnett, of Leys, 13th Bt, CB, CMG, DSO; one *s. Educ:* Eton. Late Capt. Scots Guards (SR); served European War, 1914-18 (wounded, Croix de Guerre). *Relevant publication:* The Captain, by B. Curling, 1970. *Address:* Kilnahard Castle, Ballyheelan, Co. Cavan, Eire. *T:* Ballyheelan 112. *Clubs:* Turf; Kildare Street and University (Dublin).

BOYDE, Prof. Patrick, PhD; Serena Professor of Italian, since 1981, and Fellow of St John's College, since 1965, University of Cambridge; *b* 30 Nov. 1934; *s* of Harry Caine Boyde and Florence Colonna Boyde; *m* 1956, Catherine Mavis Taylor; four *s. Educ:* Braintree County High Sch.; Wanstead County High Sch.; St John's Coll., Cambridge. BA 1956, MA 1960, PhD 1963. Nat. service, commnd RA, 1956-58. Research, St John's Coll., Cambridge, 1958-61; Asst Lectr in Italian, Univ. of Leeds, 1961-62; Asst Lectr, later Lectr, Univ. of Cambridge, 1962-81. *Publications:* Dante's Lyric Poetry (with K. Foster), 1967; Dante's Style in his Lyric Poetry, 1971; Dante Philomythes and Philosopher: Man in the Cosmos, 1981. *Recreations:* walking, backpacking, music. *Address:* 23 Hartington Grove, Cambridge CB1 4UA. *T:* Cambridge 247482.

BOYDELL, (The Worshipful Chancellor) Peter Thomas Sherrington, QC 1965; Chairman, Planning and Local Government Committee of the Bar, since 1973; Leader, Parliamentary Bar, since 1975; Chancellor of Diocese of Truro since 1957, Oxford since 1958 and Worcester since 1959; *b* 20 Sept. 1920; *s* of late Frank Richard Boydell, JP, and late Frances Barton Boydell, Blenheim Lodge, Whitegate Drive, Blackpool; unmarried. *Educ:* Arnold Sch., Blackpool; Manchester Univ. LLB Manchester 1940. Served War of 1939-45; Adjt, 17th Field Regt, RA, 1943; Bde Major, RA, 1st Armoured Div., 1944; Bde Major, RA, 10th Indian Div., 1945. Qualified as Solicitor, 1947. Called to Bar, Middle Temple, 1948, Bencher, 1970. Mem., Legal Board of Church

Assembly, 1958-71. Contested (C) Carlisle, 1964. ARICS (by invitation and election), 1982. *Recreations:* mountaineering, music, travel. *Address:* 45 Wilton Crescent, SW1. *T:* 01-235 5505; 2 Harcourt Buildings, Temple, EC4. *T:* 01-353 8415. *Clubs:* Garrick, Royal Automobile; Climbers.

BOYDEN, (Harold) James; *b* 19 Oct. 1910; *s* of late Claude James and late Frances Mary Boyden; *m* 1935, Emily Pemberton. *Educ:* Elementary Sch., Tiffin Boys, Kingston; King's Coll., London. BA (History), 1932; BSc (Econ), London External, 1943; Barrister-at-law, Lincoln's Inn, 1947. Pres., King's Coll. Union Soc., 1931-32. Master: Henry Mellish Grammar Sch., 1933-35; Tiffin Boys Sch., 1935-40; Lectr, Extra-Mural Depts of London, Nottingham and Southampton Univs, 1934-47. RAF, 1940-45; Sqdn-Ldr, 1944-45; Chief Training Officer, Admiralty, 1945-47; Dir Extra-Mural Studies, Durham Univ., 1947-59. Durham City and County Magistrate, 1951-; CC for Durham City, 1952-59; Chm. Durham County Education Cttee, 1959 (Vice-Chm. 1957-59); Chm., Exec. Cttee Nat. Inst. for Adult Education, 1958-61; Mem. Newcastle Regional Hospital Board, 1958-64; Fabian Soc. Executive, 1961-65. MP (Lab) Bishop Auckland, 1959-79; Jt Parly Under-Sec. of State, Dept of Education and Science, 1964-65; Parliamentary Sec., Ministry of Public Building and Works, 1965-67; Parly Under-Sec. (Army), MoD, 1967-69. Chm., Select Cttee of Expenditure, 1974-79; Sec., Anglo-French Parly Cttee, 1974-79. Overseas Lecture Tours: for Foreign Office, Germany, 1955 and 1957; for British Council, Ghana, Sierra Leone, 1956; Sierra Leone, 1961; for Admiralty, Malta, 1959. Member: WEA; Fabian Soc.; Nat. Union of General and Municipal Workers; National Trust; Council of Europe, 1970-73, WEU, 1970-73. FKC 1969. *Recreations:* walking, gardening, foreign travel, swimming, local government. *Address:* Winterbourne, Higher Fortescue, Sidmouth, Devon EX10 9QE. *Clubs:* South Church Workman's, Eldon Lane Workman's (Bishop Auckland); Southerne (Newton Aycliffe).

BOYER, John Leslie, OBE 1982; Chairman, Antony Gibbs Holdings Ltd, since 1981; *b* 13 Nov. 1926; *s* of Albert and Gladys Boyer; *m* 1953, Joyce Enid Thomasson; one *s* two *d*. *Educ:* Acton Grammar Sch. Served Army, 1944-48: commnd into South Lancashire Regt, 1946, and attached to Baluch Regt, then Indian Army. Joined Hongkong and Shanghai Banking Corp., 1948: served Hong Kong, Burma, Japan, India, Malaysia, Singapore; General Manager, Hong Kong, 1973; Director, March 1977; Dep. Chm., Sept. 1977-81. *Recreations:* walking, swimming, bridge, reading. *Address:* Friars Lawn, Norwood Green Road, Norwood Green, Mddx UB2 4LA. *T:* 01-574 8489. *Clubs:* Oriental, Institute of Directors; Hongkong, Shek O (Hong Kong); Tanglin (Singapore).

BOYES, Sir Brian Gerald B.; *see* Barratt-Boyes.

BOYES, James Ashley; Headmaster of City of London School since 1965; *b* 27 Aug. 1924; *s* of late Alfred Simeon Boyes and of Edith May Boyes; *m* 1st, 1949, Diana Fay (*née* Rothera), MA Cantab; two *d*; 2nd, 1973, April Tanner (*née* Rothery). *Educ:* Rugby Sch.; Clare Coll., Cambridge. Lieut RNVR; N Russian convoys and Brit. Pacific Fleet, 1942-46. Cambridge Univ., 1942, 1946-48; 1st class Hons Mod. Hist., 1948; Mellon Fellowship, Yale Univ., 1948-50; MA Yale, 1950. Asst Master, Rugby Sch., 1950-55; Headmaster, Kendal Grammar Sch., Westmorland, 1955-60; Dir of Studies, Royal Air Force Coll., Cranwell, 1960-65. *Recreations:* squash racquets, sailing. *Address:* City of London School, EC4Y 0DL; 12 Linver Road, SW6. *Clubs:* Royal Automobile, Hurlingham; Harlequins RUFC (Hon. Mem.); Hawks (Cambridge); Royal Windermere Yacht.

BOYES, Prof. John, FRCSE, FDS England, FDS Edinburgh; Professor of Dental Surgery, Edinburgh, 1958-77; Hon. Dental Surgeon, Royal Victoria Infirmary, Newcastle; *b* 23 June 1912; *s* of John and Helen Boyes; *m* 1946, Jean Wood; one *s*. *Educ:* George Watson's Coll., Edinburgh; Dental Sch. and Sch. of Medicine of the Royal Colleges, Edinburgh. House Surg. and Clinical Asst, Edinburgh Dental Hosp.; House Surg., Mddx Hosp.; Res. Surgical Officer and Dental Surg., Plastic and Jaw Unit, Bangour EMS Hosp.; Br. Corresp. of Amer. Dental Assoc.; Mem. of Dental Advisory Cttee of RCSE; Nuffield Prof. of Oral Medicine, University of Durham; Sub-Dean of King's Coll., at Dental Sch.; Dir Newcastle upon Tyne Dental Hospital. *Publications:* Dental Analgesia in A Textbook of Anaesthetics, by Minnitt & Gillies. *Recreations:* book and picture collecting; hill walking. *Address:* 12 Kingsburgh Road, Edinburgh EH12 6DZ. *Clubs:* Oral Surgery; Scottish Arts (Edinburgh); Cairngorm (Aberdeen).

BOYES, Kate Emily Tyrrell, (Mrs C. W. Sanders); Chairman, Civil Service Selection Boards, since 1978; *b* 22 April 1918; *e d* of S. F. Boyes, Sandiacre, Derbyshire; *m* 1944, Cyril Woods Sanders, *qv*; one *s* three *d*. *Educ:* Long Eaton Grammar Sch.; (Scholar) Newnham Coll., Cambridge. Economics Tripos, 1939; MA (Cantab). Administrative Class, Home Civil Service, 1939; Private Sec. to Parly Sec., 1942-45; Principal, 1945; Sec. to Council on Prices, Productivity and Incomes, 1958-60; Asst Sec., 1961; Speechwriter to President of Bd of Trade, 1963-64; Under-Sec., Europe, Industry and Technology Div., DTI, later Dept of Trade, 1972-78. Member: Council, National Trust, 1967-79; Exec., Keep Britain Tidy Gp, 1980-. *Recreations:* climbing, sailing, ski-ing, archæology. *Address:* 41 Smith Street, SW3 1NQ. *T:* 01-352 8053; Giles Point, Winchelsea, Sussex. *T:* Winchelsea 431; Canower, Cashel, Connemara, Ireland. *Clubs:* Ski Club of Gt Britain; Island Cruising (Salcombe).

BOYES, Roland; Member (Lab) Durham, European Parliament, since 1979; Member G&MWU. *Address:* (home) 12 Spire Hollin, Peterlee, Co. Durham. *T:* Peterlee 863917; (office) Room 4/74, County Hall, Durham. *T:* Durham 49371. *Clubs:* Peterlee Labour, Chester le Street Labour, Sherburn Village Working Men's; Peterlee Cricket.

BOYLAND, Prof. Eric, PhD London, DSc Manchester; Professor of Biochemistry, University of London, at Chester Beatty Research Institute, Institute of Cancer Research, Royal Marsden Hospital, 1948-70, now Emeritus Professor; Visiting Professor in Environmental Toxicology, London School of Hygiene and Tropical Medicine, 1970-76; *b* Manchester, 24 Feb. 1905; *s* of Alfred E. and Helen Boyland; *m* 1931, Margaret Esther, *d* of late Maj.-Gen. Sir Frederick Maurice, KCMG, CB; two *s* one *d*. *Educ:* Manchester Central High Sch.; Manchester Univ. BSc Tech. 1926; MSc 1928; DSc 1936. Research Asst in Physiology, Manchester Univ., 1926-28; Grocers' Company Scholar and Beit Memorial Fellow for Med. Research at Lister Institute for Preventive Medicine, 1928-30, and Kaiser Wilhelm Institut für Medizinische Forschung, Heidelberg, 1930-31; Physiological Chemist to Royal Cancer Hosp., London, 1931; Reader in Biochemistry, University of London, 1935-47. Research Officer in Ministry of Supply, 1941-44; Ministry of Agriculture, 1944-45. Consultant to Internat. Agency for Research on Cancer, Lyon, 1970-72; Member WHO Panel on Food Additives. Hon. FFOM, RCP, 1982. Judd Award for Cancer Research, New York, 1948. *Publications:* The Biochemistry of Bladder Cancer, 1963; Modern Trends in Toxicology, vol. I, 1962, vol. II, 1974; scientific papers in biochemistry and pharmacology. *Recreations:* walking, looking at paintings. *Address:* London School of Hygiene and Tropical Medicine, WC1; 42 Bramerton Street, SW3. *T:* 01-352 2601; Maltmayes, Warnham, Horsham, Sussex. *T:* Oakwood Hill 428. *Clubs:* Athenæum; Rucksack (Manchester).

BOYLE, family name of Earls of Cork, Glasgow, and Shannon.

BOYLE, Viscount; Richard Henry John Boyle; in catering trade; *b* 19 Jan. 1960; *s* and *heir* of 9th Earl of Shannon, *qv*. *Educ:* Northease Manor School, Lewes. *Recreations:* motocross and trials.

BOYLE, Andrew Philip More; author, journalist, broadcaster; *b* Dundee, 27 May 1919; *er s* of Andrew Boyle and Rose McCann; *m* 1943, Christina, *y d* of Jack Galvin; one *s* one *d*. *Educ:* Blairs, Aberdeen; Paris Univ. Escaped from France as student, June 1940. RAFVR, 1941-43; Military Intelligence, Far East, 1944-45; also Military Corresp., Far East (Major), 1945-46. Joined BBC as scriptwriter/producer, Radio Newsreel, 1947; Asst Editor, 1954; Founding Editor, World At One, 1965, World This Weekend, PM etc, 1967-75; Head of News and Current Affairs (Radio and TV), BBC Scotland, 1976. Successfully resisted Inland Revenue's attempt to tax literary prizes in 1978 Test Case. Work published, 1979, led to exposure of the Blunt affair. *Publications:* No Passing Glory, Biography of Group Captain Cheshire, VC, 1955; Trenchard, Man of Vision, 1962; Montagu Norman: A Biography, 1967; Only the Wind will Listen: Reith of the BBC, 1972; Poor, Dear Brendan: The Quest for Brendan Bracken, 1974 (Whitbread Award for Biography, 1974); The Riddle of Erskine Childers, 1976; The Climate of Treason, 1979, rev. edn 1980; co-author of four other books; occasional contribs to Observer, Sunday Times, Times, Spectator, Listener, Washington Post, and formerly to Catholic Herald, Tablet, etc. *Recreations:* walking, swimming, conversation, music, watching bad football matches from public terraces, especially at Fulham. *Address:* 16 Deodar Road, Putney, SW15. *T:* 01-788 2678.

BOYLE, Archibald Cabbourn, MD; FRCP; DPhysMed; Director, Department of Rheumatology, Middlesex Hospital; Honorary Consultant Rheumatologist, King Edward VII Hospital for Officers; Hon. Clinical Adviser, Department of Rheumatological Research, Middlesex Hospital Medical School; *b* 14 March 1918; *s* of late Arthur Hislop Boyle and of Flora Ellen Boyle; *m* 1st, Patricia Evelyn Tallack (*d* 1944); one *d*; 2nd, Dorothy Evelyn, widow of Lieut G. B. Jones; one *s*. *Educ:* Dulwich Coll.; St Bartholomew's Hospital. House Physician, St Bartholomew's Hosp., 1941-42. Served War of 1939-45 in Far East, and later as Command Specialist in Physical Medicine. Registrar and Sen. Asst, 1946-49, and Asst Physician, 1949-54, Mddx Hosp.; Consultant in Physical Medicine, Bromley Gp of Hosps, 1950-54; Physician, Arthur Stanley Inst. for Rheumatic Diseases, 1950-65. Member: Bd of Governors, Mddx Hosp.; Bd of Governors, Charterhouse Rheumatism Clinic; Bd of Studies in Medicine, Univ. of London; Council, British Assoc. for Rheumatology and Rehabilitation (Pres., 1973-74); British League against Rheumatism (Vice-Pres., 1972-77; Pres., 1977-81); Council, Section of Physical Medicine, RSM, 1950- (Pres., 1956-58; Vice-Pres., 1970-); Heberden Soc.; Cttee on Rheumatology and Rehabilitation, RCP. Ernest Fletcher Meml Lectr, RSM, 1971. Formerly: Examnr in Physical Medicine, RCP; Examnr to Chartered Soc. of Physiotherapy; Editor, Annals of Physical Medicine, 1956-63; Sec., Internat. Fedn of Physical Medicine, 1960-64; Chm., Physical Medicine Gp, BMA, 1956-58; Pres., London Br., Chartered Soc. of Physiotherapy. Former Member: Council, British Assoc. of Physical Medicine and Rheumatology, 1949-72 (Vice-Pres., 1965-68; Pres., 1970-72); Cttee on Chronic Rheumatic Diseases, RCP; Regional Scientific and Educn, Sub-Cttees, Arthritis and Rheumatism Council; Physiotherapists Bd, Council for Professions Supplementary to Medicine; Central Consultants and Specialists Cttee, BMA; Med. Adv. Cttee, British Rheumatism and Arthritis Assoc. *Publications:* A Colour Atlas of Rheumatology, 1974; contribs to medical jls, mainly on rheumatic disease. *Recreation:* gardening. *Address:* Iping Barn, Iping, near Midhurst, West Sussex GU29 0PE. *T:* Midhurst 6467. *Club:* Sesame.

BOYLE, Marshal of the Royal Air Force Sir Dermot (Alexander), GCB 1957 (CB 1946); KCVO 1953; KBE 1953 (CBE 1945); AFC 1939; Vice-Chairman, British Aircraft Corporation, 1962-71; *b* 2 Oct. 1904; 2nd and *e* surv. *s* of A. F. Boyle, Belmont House, Queen's Co., Ire.; *m* 1931, Una Carey; two *s* one *d* (and one *s* decd). *Educ:* St Columba's Coll., Ireland; RAF (Cadet) Coll., Cranwell. Commissioned RAF 1924; Air ADC to the King, 1943; Air Commodore, 1944; Air Vice-Marshal, 1949; Air Marshal, 1954; Air Chief Marshal, 1956; Marshal of the Royal Air Force, 1958; Dir-Gen. of Personnel, Air Ministry, 1948-49; Dir-Gen. of Manning, Air Ministry, 1949-51; AOC No. 1 Group Bomber Command, 1951-53; AOC-in-C, Fighter Command, 1953-55; Chief of Air Staff, 1956-59. Master, Guild of Air Pilots and Air Navigators, 1965-66. Chairman: Bd of Trustees, RAF Museum, 1965-74; Ct of Governors, Mill Hill Sch., 1969-76; Dep. Chm., RAF Benevolent Fund, 1971-80. J. P. Robertson Meml Trophy, Air Public Relations Assoc., 1973. *Address:* Fair Gallop, Brighton Road, Sway, Hants. *Club:* Royal Air Force.

BOYLE, Kay, (Baroness Joseph von Franckenstein); writer; Professor in English Department, San Francisco State University, 1963-80, now Emeritus; *b* St Paul, Minn, USA, 19 Feb. 1902; *d* of Howard Peterson Boyle; *m* 1921, 1931 and 1943; one *s* five *d*. Member: National Institute of Arts and Letters, 1958; Amer. Acad. and Inst. of Arts and Letters, 1978. O. Henry Memorial Prize for best short story of the year, 1936, 1941; Guggenheim Fellowship, 1934, 1961; Center for Advanced Studies Wesleyan Univ. Fellowship, 1963; Radcliffe Inst. for Independent Study, 1964, 1965. Writer-in-residence, Hollins Coll., Virginia, 1970-71. Hon. DLitt, Columbia Coll., Chicago, 1971; Hon. DHL Skidmore Coll., 1977; Hon. Dr of Letters, 1982. *Publications: novels:* Plagued by the Nightingale; Year Before Last; Gentlemen, I Address You Privately; My Next Bride; Death of a Man; Monday Night; Primer for Combat; Avalanche; A Frenchman Must Die; "1939"; His Human Majesty; The Seagull on the Step, 1955; Three Short Novels, 1958; Generation Without Farewell, 1959; The Underground Woman, 1975; *volumes of short stories:* Wedding Day; The First Lover; The White Horses of Vienna; The Crazy Hunter; Thirty Stories; The Smoking Mountain; Nothing Ever Breaks Except the Heart, 1966; Fifty Stories, 1980; Breaking the Silence (essay), 1962; The Long Walk at San Francisco State and other essays, 1970; *memoirs:* The Autobiography of Emanuel Carnevali, 1967; Being Geniuses Together, 1968; *poetry:* A Glad Day; American Citizen; Collected Poems, 1962; Testament for my Students and other poems, 1970. *For Children:* The Youngest Camel; Pinky, the Cat Who Liked to Sleep, 1966; Pinky in Persia, 1968. *Recreations:* ski-ing, mountain climbing. *Address:* c/o Ann Watkins Inc., 150 East 35th Street, New York, NY 10016, USA.

BOYLE, Sir Lawrence, Kt 1979; JP; Director: Short Loan and Mortgage Co. Ltd, since 1980; Scottish Mutual Assurance Society, since 1980; Pension Fund Property Unit Trust, since 1980; Partner, Sir Lawrence Boyle Associates, Financial and Management Consultants, Glasgow, since 1980; *b* 31 Jan. 1920; *s* of Hugh Boyle and Kate (*née* Callaghan); *m* 1952, Mary McWilliam; one *s* three *d*. *Educ:* Holy Cross Acad., Leith, Edinburgh; Edinburgh Univ. BCom, PhD. Depute County Treasurer, Midlothian CC, 1958-62; Depute City Chamberlain, Glasgow, 1962-70; City Chamberlain, Glasgow, 1970-74; Chief Exec., Strathclyde Regional Council, 1974-80. Vis. Prof., Strathclyde Univ. Business Sch., 1979-. Mem., Public Works Loan Bd, 1972-74. Vice-Pres., Soc. of Local Authority Chief Execs, 1977-78 (Hon. Pres., Scottish Br.). Chm., Scottish Nat. Orch. Soc. Ltd, 1980-. Member: Council, Scottish Business Sch., 1974-79; Strathclyde Univ. Court, 1980-; Steering Bd, Strathclyde Univ. Business Sch., 1974-. IPFA (Mem. Council, and Chm. Scottish Br., 1973-74); CBIM (Mem. Adv. Bd for Scotland, 1973-82). JP Glasgow, 1971. *Publications:* Equalisation and the Future of Local Government Finance, 1966; numerous articles and papers in economic jls, etc. *Recreation:* music. *Address:* 24 Broomburn Drive, Newton Mearns, Glasgow. *T:* 041-639 3776.

BOYLE, Leonard Butler, CBE 1977; Director and General Manager, Principality Building Society, Cardiff, 1956-78; *b* 13 Jan. 1913; *s* of Harold and Edith Boyle; *m* 1938, Alice Baldwin Yarborough; two *s. Educ:* Roundhay Sch., Leeds. FCBSI. Chief of Investment Dept, Leeds Permanent Building Soc., 1937; Asst Man., Isle of Thanet Bldg Soc., 1949; Jt Asst Gen. Man., Hastings and Thanet Bldg Soc., 1951, Sec. 1954. Building Socs Assoc.: Mem. Council, 1956-78 (Chm. Gen. Purposes Cttee, 1958-60; Chm. Develt Cttee, 1967-71); Chm. of Council, 1973-75 (Dep. Chm. 1971-73; Vice-Pres., 1978); Vice-Pres., CBSI. Consultant, Manchester Exchange Trust; Dir, Greenwood Homes. *Recreations:* gardening, walking, golf. *Address:* Northwick Cottage, Marlpit Lane, Seaton, Devon EX12 2HH. *T:* Seaton 22194.

BOYLE, Sir Richard (Gurney), 4th Bt *cr* 1904; *b* 14 May 1930; *s* of Sir Edward Boyle, 2nd Bt, and Beatrice (*d* 1961), *er d* of Henry Greig, Belvedere House, Kent; *S* to baronetcy of brother, Baron Boyle of Handsworth, 1981; *m* 1961, Elizabeth Anne (marr. diss. 1974), *yr d* of Norman Dennes; three *s. Heir: s* Stephen Gurney Boyle, *b* 15 Jan. 1962. *Address:* Paris Hall Cottage, Hastingwood, Harlow, Essex.

BOYLES, Edgar William; Under Secretary, Inland Revenue, 1975-81; *b* 24 March 1921; *s* of William John Boyles and Jessie Louisa Boyles; *m* 1950, Heather Iris Hobart, SRN; three *s* one *d. Educ:* Bedford Modern Sch. RAF,

1940-46. Tax Officer, Inland Revenue, 1939; Principal Inspector of Taxes 1962; Sen. Principal Inspector, 1967. *Recreations:* chess, gardening, watching cricket. *Address:* The Keeley, 155 Bedford Road, Wootton, Bedford MK4: 9BA. *T:* Bedford 851875.

BOYNE, 10th Viscount *cr* 1717; **Gustavus Michael George Hamilton-Russell,** DL; JP; Baron Hamilton, 1715; Baron Brancepeth, 1866; Deputy Chairman, Telford Development Corporation, since 1975 (Member, since 1963); a Lord in Waiting, since 1981; *b* 10 Dec. 1931; *s* of late Hon. Gustavu. Lascelles Hamilton-Russell and *g s* of 9th Viscount; *S* grandfather, 1942; *m* 1956, Rosemary Anne, 2nd *d* of Major Sir Dennis Stucley, Bt, *qv*; one *s* three *d. Educ:* Eton; Sandhurst; Royal Agricl Coll., Cirencester. Commissioned Grenadier Guards, 1952. JP 1961, DL 1965, Salop. Dir, Nat. Westminster Bank, 1976- (Chm., W Midlands and Wales Regional Bd). Governor Wrekin Coll., Telford. CStJ. *Heir: s* Hon. Gustavus Michael Stucley Hamilton-Russell, *b* 27 May 1965. *Address:* Burwarton House, Bridgnorth, Salop. *T:* Burwarton 203. *Clubs:* Turf, Royal Over-Seas League.
See also Lord Forbes.

BOYNE, Donald Arthur Colin Aydon, CBE 1977; Editorial Director, The Architectural Review and The Architects' Journal, since 1974; *b* 15 Feb. 1921 2nd *s* of late Lytton Leonard Boyne and Millicent (*née* Nisbet); *m* 1947, Rosemary Pater; two *s* one *d. Educ:* Tonbridge Sch.; Architectural Assoc. School of Architecture, 1943-47. Indian Army, 8/13 FF Rifles, 1940-43. Editor, Architects' Jl, 1953-70; Chm., Editorial Bd, Architectural Review and Architects' Jl, 1971-74. Hon. FRIBA 1969. *Address:* Kentlands, Hildenborough, Kent TN11 8NR. *T:* Hildenborough 833539.

BOYNE, Sir Henry Brian, (Sir Harry Boyne), Kt 1976; CBE 1969; Political Correspondent, The Daily Telegraph, London, 1956-76; *b* 29 July 1910; 2nd *s* of late Lockhart Alexander Boyne, Journalist, Inverness, and late Elizabeth Jane Mactavish; *m* 1935, Margaret Little Templeton, Dundee; one *d. Educ:* High Sch. and Royal Academy, Inverness. Reporter, Inverness Courier, 1927; Dundee Courier and Advertiser, 1929. On active service, 1939-45, retiring with rank of Major, The Black Watch (RHR). Staff Correspondent, Glasgow Herald, at Dundee, 1945, and Edinburgh, 1949; Political Correspondent, Glasgow Herald, 1950. Dir of Communications, Conservative Central Office, 1980-82. Chairman: Parly Lobby Journalists, 1958-59 (Hon. Sec., 1968-71); Parly Press Gallery, 1961-62. Political Writer of Year, 1972. Mem., Police Complaints Bd, 1977-80; Chm., Bd of Visitors, HM Prison, Pentonville, 1980. *Publication:* The Houses of Parliament, 1981. *Recreations:* reading, playgoing, cycling. *Address:* 122 Harefield Road, Uxbridge UB8 1PN. *T:* Uxbridge 55211. *Clubs:* Press, Victory; Western (Dundee).

BOYNE, Maj.-Gen. John, MBE 1965; CEng, FIMechE; FBIM; Vice Adjutant General and Director of Manning (Army), since 1982; *b* 7 Nov. 1932; *s* of John Grant Boyne and Agnes Crawford (*née* Forrester); *m* 1956, Norma Beech; two *s. Educ:* King's Sch., Chester; Royal Military Coll. of Science, Shrivenham (BScEng 1st Cl. Hons). CEng, FIMechE 1975; FBIM 1975; psc 1963, jssc 1968, rcds 1979. Served in Egypt, Cyprus, Libya and UK, 1951-62; Staff Coll., Camberley, 1963; DAQMG(Ops) HQ MEC, Aden, 1964-66; OC 11 Infantry Workshop, REME, BAOR, 1966-67; Jt Services Staff Coll., 1968; GSO2 MoD, 1968-70; GSO1 (DS), Staff Coll., 1970-72; Comdr REME, 2nd Div., BAOR, 1972-73; AAG MoD, 1973-75; CSO (Personnel) to CPL, MoD, 1975-76; Dep. Dir Elec. and Mech. Engrg, 1st British Corps, 1976-78; RCDS, 1979; Dep. Dir Personal Services (Army), MoD, 1980-82. *Recreations:* choral singing, football. *Address:* c/o Midland Bank, Runcorn, Cheshire.

BOYNTON, Sir John (Keyworth), Kt 1979; MC 1944; LLB; MRTPI; DL; Chief Executive, Cheshire County Council, 1974-79; Solicitor; *b* 14 Feb. 1918; *s* of late Ernest Boynton, Hull; *m* 1st, 1947, Gabrielle Stanglmaier, Munich (*d* 1978); two *d* ; 2nd, 1979, Edith Laane, The Hague. *Educ:* Dulwich Coll. Served War, 15th Scottish Reconnaissance Regt, 1940-46 (despatches, MC). Dep. Clerk, Berks CC, 1951-64; Clerk, Cheshire CC, 1964-74. Member: Planning Law Cttee of Law Soc., 1964-; Economic Planning Council for NW, 1965; Exec. Council of Royal Inst. of Public Admin., 1970; Council of Industrial Soc., 1974-; Council, PSI, 1978-. Pres., RTPI, 1976. Election Commissioner, Southern Rhodesia, 1979-80. DL Cheshire 1975. *Publications:* A Practical Guide to Compulsory Purchase and Compensation, 1964 (4th edn 1977). *Recreation:* golf. *Address:* Flat 2, 1 Redington Gardens, NW3 7RY. *T:* 01-435 0012. *Club:* Army and Navy.

BOYS-SMITH, Captain Humphry Gilbert, DSO 1940; DSC 1943; RD; RNR, retired; *b* 20 Dec. 1904; *s* of late Rev. Edward Percy Boys Smith, MA, Rural Dean of Lyndhurst, Hants, and Charlotte Cecilia, *d* of late Thomas Backhouse Sandwith, CB, HM Consular Service; *m* 1935, Marjorie Helen (*d* 1981), *d* of Capt. Matthew John Miles Vicars-Miles; no *c. Educ:* Pangbourne Nautical Coll. Joined Royal Naval Reserve, 1921; Merchant Navy, 1922-35; Extra Master's Certificate, 1930; HM Colonial Service, 1935-40 (Palestine) and 1946-50 (Western Pacific High Commission as Marine Supt); Addnl Mem. RNR Advisory Cttee, 1949-51; War Course, Royal Naval Coll., Greenwich, 1950-51. Courtaulds Ltd, Central Staff Dept, 1951-68. Placed on Retired List of RNR, 1952; Younger Brother of Trinity House, 1944; Mem. of Hon Company of Master Mariners, 1946; Assoc. Instn Naval Architects, 1948; served War of 1939-45 (DSO and Bar, DSC, despatches and American despatches). *Address:* Dibben's, Semley, Shaftesbury, Dorset SP7 9BW. *T:* East Knoyle 358.

BOYS SMITH, Rev. John Sandwith, MA; Master of St John's College, Cambridge, 1959-69 (Fellow, 1927-59 and since 1969; Senior Bursar, 1944-59); Vice-Chancellor, University of Cambridge, 1963-65; Canon Emeritus of Ely Cathedral since 1948; *b* 8 Jan. 1901; *e s* of late Rev. E. P. Boys Smith, formerly Vicar of Hordle, Hants, and Charlotte Cecilia, *e d* of late T. B. Sandwith, CB; *m* 1942, Gwendolen Sara, *o d* of late W. J. Wynn; two *s*. *Educ:* Sherborne Sch.; St John's Coll., Cambridge. Economics Tripos Part I, Class II, division 2, 1921; BA, Theological Tripos, Part I, Sec. B, Class I, 1922; Scholar and Naden Student in Divinity, St John's Coll., 1922; Theological Tripos Part II, Sec. V, Class 1, 1924; Burney Student, 1924; Marburg University, 1924-25; Deacon, 1926; Curate of Sutton Coldfield, Birmingham, 1926-27; Priest, 1927; Chaplain of St John's Coll., Cambridge, 1927-34, and Director of Theological Studies, 1927-40, and 1944-52; Assistant Tutor, 1931-34; Tutor, 1934-39; Junior Bursar, 1939-40; University Lecturer in Divinity, Cambridge, 1931-40; Stanton Lecturer in the Philosophy of Religion, Cambridge Univ., 1934-37; Ely Professor of Divinity in the University of Cambridge and Canon of Ely Cathedral, 1940-43. Hon. Fellow: Trinity Coll., Dublin, 1968; Darwin Coll., Cambridge, 1969. Hon. LLD, Cambridge, 1970. *Publication:* (with late J. M. Creed) Religious Thought in the Eighteenth Century, 1934. *Address:* Trinity House, 2 Castle Street, Saffron Walden, Essex CB10 1BP. *T:* Saffron Walden 23692; St John's College, Cambridge.

BOYSE, Edward Arthur, MD; FRS 1977; Member, Sloan-Kettering Institute for Cancer Research, New York, since 1967; *b* 11 Aug. 1923; *s* of late Arthur Boyse, FRCO, and Dorothy Vera Boyse (*née* Mellersh); *m* 1951, Jeanette (*née* Grimwood); two *s* one *d*. *Educ:* St Bartholomew's Hosp. Med. Sch., Univ. of London. MB BS 1952; MD 1957. Aircrew, RAF, 1941-46, commnd 1943. Various hospital appts, 1952-57; research at Guy's Hosp., 1957-60; research appts at NY Univ. and Sloan-Kettering Inst., 1960-. Prof. of Biology, Cornell, 1969. Mem., Amer. Acad. of Arts and Scis, 1977. Cancer Research Institute Award in Tumor Immunology, 1975; Isaac Adler Award, Rockefeller and Harvard Univs, 1976. *Publications:* papers relating genetics and immunology to development and cancer. *Address:* 245 East 68th Street, New York, NY 10021, USA. *T:* (212) 861-2373.

BOYSON, Dr Rhodes; MP (C) Brent North, since Feb. 1974; Parliamentary Under-Secretary of State, Department of Education and Science, since 1979; *b* 11 May 1925; *s* of Alderman William Boyson, MBE, JP and Mrs Bertha Boyson, Haslingden, Rossendale, Lancs; *m* 1st, 1946, Violet Burletson (marr. diss.); two *d*; 2nd. 1971, Florette MacFarlane. *Educ:* Haslingden Grammar Sch.; UC Cardiff; Manchester Univ.; LSE; Corpus Christi Coll., Cambridge. BA, MA, PhD. Served with Royal Navy. Headmaster: Lea Bank Secondary Modern Sch., Rossendale, 1955-61; Robert Montefiore Secondary Sch., Stepney, 1961-66; Highbury Grammar Sch., 1966-67; Highbury Grove Sch., 1967-74. Chm., Nat. Council for Educnl Standards, 1974-79; Councillor: Haslingden, 1957-61; Waltham Forest, 1968-74 (Chm. Establishment Cttee, 1968-71); Chm., London Boroughs Management Services Unit, 1968-70. Formerly Youth Warden, Lancs Youth Clubs. Contested (C) Eccles, 1970. Vice-Chm., Cons Parly Educn Cttee, 1975-76; Hon. Sec. Cons. Adv. Cttee on Educn, 1975-78; Opposition spokesman on educn, 1976-79. Educnl columnist, Spectator, 1969. *Publications:* The North-East Lancashire Poor Law 1838-1871, 1965; The Ashworth Cotton Enterprise, 1970; (ed) Right Turn, 1970; (ed) Down with the Poor, 1971; (ed) Goodbye to Nationalisation, 1972; (ed) Education: Threatened Standards, 1972; (ed) The Accountability of Schools, 1973; Oversubscribed: the story of Highbury Grove, 1974; Crisis in Education, 1975; (jt ed) Black Papers on Education; (ed) 1985: An Escape from Orwell's 1984, 1975; Centre Forward, 1978. *Recreations:* reading, writing, talk, hard work, meeting friends, routing the millenialistic Left in education and politics. *Address:* Laneham, 71 Paines Lane, Pinner, Harrow, Mddx. *T:* 01-866 2071; House of Commons, SW1. *Clubs:* Carlton, St Stephen's; Wembley Conservative, Churchill (N Wembley).

BOZZOLI, Guerino Renzo, DSc(Eng); Chairman of Council, Mangosuthu Technikon, Kwa Zulu, since 1978; Vice-Chancellor and Principal, University of the Witwatersrand, Johannesburg, 1969-77; *b* Pretoria, 24 April 1911; *s* of late B. Bozzoli; *m* 1936, Cora Collins, *d* of late L. N. B. Collins; one *s* three *d*. *Educ:* Sunnyside and Boys' High Sch., Pretoria; Witwatersrand Univ. BSc(Eng) 1933, DSc(Eng) 1948; PrEng. Major, SA Corps of Signals, 1940-45 (commendation 1944). Asst Engr, African Broadcasting Co., 1934-36; Jun. Lectr, Dept of Electrical Engrg, Witwatersrand Univ., Lectr, 1939, Sen. Lectr, 1942; apptd Prof. and Head of Dept of Electrical Engineering, 1948. Dean, Univ. Residence, Cottesloe, 1948-56; Dean, Faculty of Engrg, 1954-57 and 1962-65; Senate Mem., Council of the Univ., 1957-68; Deputy Vice-Chancellor, 1965-68. Member: Straszacker Commn of Enquiry into Univ. Educn of Engineers, 1957-68; de Vries Commn of Enquiry into SA Univs, 1968-75; Nat. Educn Council, 1975-. President: SAIEE, 1955; AS&TS of SA, 1969-70; SA Assoc. for Advancement of Science, 1972. Hon. FSAIEE; Hon. FRSSAf 1976. Hon. LLD: Univ. of Cape Town, 1977; Univ. of Witwatersrand, 1978. *Publications:* numerous articles and papers on engineering education. *Recreations:* swimming, woodwork, electronics. *Address:* 121 Dundalk Avenue, Parkview, Johannesburg, 2193, South Africa. *T:* Johannesburg 41-1015. *Clubs:* Johannesburg, Scientific and Technical (all in Johannesburg).

BRAADLAND, Erik; diplomat, retired; *b* 21 Nov. 1910; *m* 1940, Aase Rydtun; one *s* two *d*. *Educ:* Oslo Univ. (Degree in Economics). Served in Hamburg, Marseille, Stockholm, Berlin; various periods Ministry of Foreign Affairs, Oslo; Acting Head of Military Mission in Berlin, 1949; Chargé d'Affaires at Bonn, 1951; Minister in Belgrade, 1952; Ambassador in Moscow, 1954-58, in London, 1959-61, for Norway; Mem. of Storting, 1961-69. Knight Commander, Order of St Olav; Order of the Yugoslav Flag, 1st Class. *Address:* Oer, 1750 Halden, Norway. *Clubs:* Norwegian, London; Norske Selskab (Oslo).

BRABAZON, family name of **Earl of Meath.**

BRABAZON OF TARA, 3rd Baron *cr* 1942; **Ivon Anthony Moore-Brabazon;** Member of the Stock Exchange, since 1972; *b* 20 Dec. 1946; *s* of 2nd Baron Brabazon of Tara, CBE, and of Henriette Mary, *d* of late Sir Rowland Clegg; *S* father, 1974; *m* 1979, Harriet Frances, *o d* of Mervyn P. de Courcy Hamilton, Salisbury, Zimbabwe. *Educ:* Harrow. *Recreations:* sailing, Cresta Run. *Heir:* none. *Address:* 35 Cloncurry Street, SW6 6DR. *T:* 01-736 3705. *Clubs:* White's; Royal Yacht Squadron; Bembridge Sailing, St Moritz Tobogganing.

BRABHAM, Sir John Arthur, (Sir Jack Brabham), Kt 1979; OBE 1966; retired, 1970, as Professional Racing Driver; Managing Director: Jack Brabham (Motors) Ltd; Jack Brabham (Worcester Park) Ltd; Brabham Racing Organisation Ltd; Engine Developments Ltd; *b* Sydney, Australia, 2 April 1926; *m* 1951, Betty Evelyn; three *s*. *Educ:* Hurstville Technical Coll., Sydney. Served in RAAF, 1944-46. Started own engineering business, 1946; Midget Speedway racing, 1946-52; several championships (Australian, NSW, South Australian); numerous wins driving a Cooper-Bristol, Australia, 1953-54; to Europe, 1955; Australian Grand Prix, 1955 and 1963 (debut of Repco Brabham); World Champion Formula II, 1958, also many firsts including Casablanca, Goodwood, Brands Hatch, NZ Grand Prix, Belgian Grand Prix; Formula II Champion of France, 1964. World Champion Driver: (after first full Formula I Season with 2½-litre car), 1959-60, 1960-61, 1966. First in Monaco and British Grandes Epreuves, 1959; won Grand Prix of: Holland, Belgium, France, Britain, Portugal, Denmark, 1960; Belgium, 1961. Elected Driver of the Year by Guild of Motoring Writers, 1959, 1966 and 1970, Sportsman of the Year by Australian Broadcasting Co., 1959; left Cooper to take up building own Grand Prix cars, 1961; debut, 1962; first ever constructor/driver to score world championship points, 1963; cars finished first: French GP; Mexican GP, 1964; Formula II and Formula III cars world-wide success, 1963; awarded Ferodo Trophy, 1964 and again, 1966; won French Grand Prix and British Grand Prix, 1966; won French Grand Prix, 1967. RAC Gold Medal, 1966; BARC Gold Medal, 1959, 1966, 1967; Formula I Manufacturers' Championship, 1966, 1967. *Publications:* Jack Brabham's Book of Motor Racing, 1960; When the Flag Drops, 1971; contribs to British journals. *Recreations:* photography, water ski-ing, underwater swimming, flying. *Address:* c/o 248 Hook Road, Chessington, Surrey. *T:* 01-397 4343. *Clubs:* Royal Automobile, British Racing and Sports Car, British Racing Drivers'; Australian Racing Drivers'.

BRABOURNE, 7th Baron, *cr* 1880; **John Ulick Knatchbull,** 16th Bt, *cr* 1641; film and television producer; *b* 9 Nov. 1924; *s* of 5th Baron and Lady Doreen Geraldine Browne (Order of the Crown of India; DStJ) (*d* 1979), *y d* of 6th Marquess of Sligo; *S* brother, 1943; *m* 1946, Lady Patricia Edwina Victoria Mountbatten (*see* Countess Mountbatten of Burma); four *s* two *d* (and one *s* decd). *Educ:* Eton; Oxford. Films Produced: Harry Black, 1958; Sink the Bismarck!, 1959; HMS Defiant, 1961; Othello, 1965; The Mikado, 1966; Romeo and Juliet; Up the Junction, 1967; Dance of Death, 1968; Tales of Beatrix Potter, 1971; Murder on the Orient Express, 1974; Death on the Nile, 1978; Stories from a Flying Trunk, 1979; The Mirror Crack'd, 1980; Evil Under the Sun, 1982. TV Series: National Gallery, 1974; A Much-Maligned Monarch, 1976. Director: Thames Television, 1978-; Thorn EMI, 1981-. Governor: BFI, 1979-; National Film Sch.; Member Cinematograph Films Council; Interim Action Cttee on Future of Film Business; Trustee, British Acad. of Film and TV Arts. Pres., Kent Trust for Nature Conservation; Chairman: Council, Caldecott Community; Governors, Norton Knatchbull Sch.; Governor: Wye Coll.; Gordonstoun Sch.; United World Colleges; Mem. Council, Univ. of Kent. *Heir:* s Lord Romsey, *qv*. *Address:* Newhouse, Mersham, Ashford, Kent TN25 6NQ. *T:* Ashford 23466; Mersham Productions Ltd, 41 Montpelier Walk, SW7 1JH. *T:* 01-589 8829.

BRABY, Frederick Cyrus, CBE 1962; MC 1918; DL; CEng, FIMechE; Hon. Major; retired, from Frederick Braby and Co. Ltd, etc.; *b* 1 May 1897; *e s* of late Cyrus and Mabel Braby (*née* Weddell), of Sutton, Surrey, and High Hurstwood, Sussex; *m* 1931, Margaret Isabel (*d* 1975), *e d* of late F. H. Marshall, Sutton and Hove; no *c*. *Educ:* Charterhouse; Manchester Univ. (BSc (Eng.)). Served 1915-19 with Lancashire Fusiliers (wounded twice, despatches, MC), and 1921-23 in TA. Apprenticeship with Metropolitan-Vickers Electrical Co. Ltd, Manchester, 1922-24; joined Frederick Braby & Co. Ltd (estab. 1839), 1925, and held various appointments; Director, 1929; Chairman, 1942-65. President: Engineering and Allied Employers' London & District Assoc., 1941-43; Nat. Council, Building Material Producers, 1960-65; Chairman: Industrial Coal Consumers' Council, 1958-65; British Non-Ferrous Metals Res. Assoc., 1958-64. Member of UK Employer/Trade Union Mission to USA, 1941; Vice-President, Engineering and Allied Employers' National Federation, 1952-56; President, 1956-58. County Commissioner (Kent), Boy Scouts Assoc., 1952-67; Member, Sevenoaks RDC, 1963-70; a Governor, Star and Garter Home for Disabled Sailors, Soldiers and Airmen, 1963-73, Vice-Pres., 1974-; Master, Carpenters' Company, 1968-69 (Warden, 1965-68). DL (Kent), 1955. *Recreations:* fishing, photography. *Address:* Three Chimneys, Cooden Beach, East Sussex.

BRACEGIRDLE, Dr Brian, FSA, FRPS, FIBiol; Keeper, Wellcome Museum of the History of Medicine, Science Museum, London, since 1977; *b* 31 May 1933; *o c* of Alfred Bracegirdle; *m* 1st, 1958, Margaret Lucy Merrett (marr. diss. 1974); one *d*; 2nd, 1975, Patricia Helen Miles; no *c. Educ:* King's Sch., Macclesfield; Univ. of London (BSc, PhD). DipRMS. FRPS 1969; FIBiol 1976; FSA 1981. Technician in industry, 1950-57; Biology Master, Erith Grammar Sch., 1958-61; Sen. Lectr in Biol., S Katharine's Coll., London, 1961-64; Head, Depts of Nat. Science and Learning Resources, Coll. of All Saints, London, 1964-77. Chief Examr in Zool., London, 1970-76; Hon. Lectr in History of Medicine, University Coll. London. Hon. Treasurer, ICOM, UK. *Publications:* Photography for Books and Reports, 1970; The Archaeology of the Industrial Revolution, 1973; The Evolution of Microtechnique, 1978; (with W. H. Freeman): An Atlas of Embryology, 1963; An Atlas of Histology, 1966; An Atlas of Invertebrate Structure, 1971; An Advanced Atlas of Histology, 1976; (with P. H. Miles): An Atlas of Plant Structure, vol. I, 1971; An Atlas of Plant Structure, Vol. II, 1973; Thomas Telford, 1973; The Darbys and the Ironbridge Gorge, 1974; An Atlas of Chordate Structure, 1977; papers on photography for life sciences, on scientific topics, and on history of science/medicine. *Recreations:* walking, music, travel. *Address:* 67 Limerston Street, Chelsea, SW10 0BL. *T:* 01-351 0548. *Club:* Athenæum.

BRACEWELL, Joyanne Winifred, (Mrs Roy Copeland); QC 1978; a Recorder of the Crown Court, since Nov. 1975; barrister-at-law; *b* 5 July 1934; *d* of Jack and Lilian Bracewell; *m* 1963, Roy Copeland; one *s* one *d. Educ:* Manchester Univ. (LLB, LLM). Called to Bar, Gray's Inn, 1955; pupillage at the Bar, 1955-56; in practice, Northern Circuit, 1956-. *Recreations:* antiques, cooking, reading, walking, bridge. *Address:* (home) Springfield, Macclesfield Road, Alderley Edge, Cheshire SK9 7BW. *T:* Alderley 582000; (chambers) 28 St John Street, Manchester M3 4DJ. *T:* 061-834 8418.

BRACEWELL-SMITH, Sir Guy, 3rd Bt *cr* 1947; *b* 12 Dec. 1952; *er s* of Sir George Bracewell Smith, 2nd Bt, MBE, and Helene Marie (*d* 1975), *d* of late John Frederick Hydock, Philadelphia, USA; *S* father, 1976. *Educ:* Harrow. *Heir: b* Charles Bracewell-Smith, *b* 13 Oct. 1955.

BRADBROOK, Prof. Muriel Clara, MA, PhD, 1933; LittD Cantab 1955; *b* 27 April 1909; *d* of Samuel Bradbrook, Supt HM Waterguard at Liverpool and Glasgow. *Educ:* Hutcheson's Sch., Glasgow; Oldershaw Sch., Wallasey; Girton Coll., Cambridge. English Tripos, Class I, 1929, 1930; Harness Prize, 1931, Allen Scholar, 1935-36; in residence, Somerville Coll., Oxford, 1935-36. Cambridge University: Univ. Lecturer, 1945-62; Reader, 1962-65; Professor of English, 1965-76; Mistress of Girton College, 1968-76 (Vice-Mistress, 1962-66; Fellow, 1932-35, 1936-68, and 1976-). Board of Trade, Industries and Manufactures Depts 2 and 3, 1941-45; in residence at Folger Library, Washington, and Huntington Library, California, 1958-59; Fellow, Nat. Humanities Center, N Carolina, 1979. Tour of the Far East for Shakespeare's Fourth Centenary, 1964; Trustee, Shakespeare's Birthplace, 1967-82. Freedom of the City of Hiroshima. Visiting Professor: Santa Cruz, California, 1966; Kuwait, 1969; Tokyo, 1975; Kenyon Coll., USA, 1977; Rhodes Univ., SA, 1979; Clark Lecturer, Trinity Coll., Cambridge, 1968. FRSL 1947. Hon. LittD: Liverpool, 1964; Sussex, 1972; London, 1973; Hon. LLD Smith Coll., USA, 1965; Hon. PhD, Gothenburg, 1975; Hon. LHD Kenyon Coll., USA, 1977. Foreign Member Norwegian Acad. of Arts and Sciences, 1966; Hon. Mem., Mod. Lang. Assoc. of America, 1974. *Publications:* Elizabethan Stage Conditions, 1932; Themes and Conventions of Elizabethan Tragedy, 1934; The School of Night, 1936; Andrew Marvell (with M. G. Lloyd Thomas), 1940; Joseph Conrad, 1941; Ibsen the Norwegian, 1947; T. S. Eliot, 1950; Shakespeare and Elizabethan Poetry, 1951; The Queen's Garland, 1953; The Growth and Structure of Elizabethan Comedy, 1955; Sir Thomas Malory, 1957; The Rise of the Common Player, 1962; English Dramatic Form, 1965; That Infidel Place, 1969; Shakespeare the Craftsman, 1969; Literature in Action, 1972; Malcolm Lowry: his art and early life, 1974; The Living Monument, 1976; Shakespeare: the poet in his world, 1978; John Webster, Citizen and Dramatist, 1980; Collected Papers, 1982; numerous articles and reviews. *Recreations:* travel, theatre. *Address:* 91 Chesterton Road, Cambridge CB4 3AP. *T:* Cambridge 352765. *Clubs:* University Women's; ADC (Cambridge).

BRADBURN, John; Registrar in Bankruptcy and of the Companies Court, High Court of Justice, Clerk of the Restrictive Practices Court, and Lord Chancellor's Legal Visitor, Court of Protection, since 1980; *b* 4 April 1915; *s* of Harold and Fanny Louise Bradburn; *m* 1948, Irène Elizabeth Norman, *yr d* of Denham Grindley and Bertha Norman; two *s. Educ:* Repton; Trinity Coll., Oxford (MA). Served War, 1939-46; Oxfordshire and Bucks LI; Major. Called to the Bar, Inner Temple, 1939; practised at Chancery Bar, Lincoln's Inn, 1946-79; Mem., Gen. Council of the Bar, 1962-66; Bencher, Lincoln's Inn, 1972-; a Conveyancing Counsel of the Supreme Court, 1977-80. *Address:* Greenlanes, 7 Green Lane, Burnham, Bucks SL1 8DR. *T:* Burnham 5071. *Club:* MCC.

BRADBURY, family name of **Baron Bradbury.**

BRADBURY, 2nd Baron, *cr* 1925, of Winsford; **John Bradbury;** *b* 7 Jan. 1914; *s* of 1st Baron Bradbury, GCB, and Hilda (*d* 1949), 2nd *d* of W. A. Kirby; *S* father 1950; *m* 1st, 1939, Joan, *o d* of W. D. Knight, Darley, Addlestone, Surrey; one *s* one *d*; 2nd, 1946, Gwerfyl, *d* of late E. S. Roberts, Gellifor, Ruthin; one *d. Educ:* Westminster; Brasenose Coll., Oxford. *Heir: s* Hon. John Bradbury [*b* 17 March 1940; *m* 1968, Susan, *d* of late W. Liddiard, East Shefford, Berks; two *s*]. *Address:* Wingham, Summerhays, Leigh Hill Road, Cobham, Surrey. *T:* Cobham 7757.

BRADBURY, Edgar; Managing Director, Skelmersdale Development Corporation, since 1976; *b* 5 June 1927; *s* of Edgar Furniss Bradbury and Mary Bradbury; *m* 1954, Janet Mary Bouchier Lisle; two *s* one *d. Educ:* Grove Park Sch., Wrexham; The High Sch., Newcastle, Staffs; King's Coll., Durham Univ. LLB (Hons). Solicitor. Asst Solicitor: Scarborough BC, 1952-54; St Helens CBC, 1954-57; Dep. Town Clerk, Loughborough, 1957-59; Town Clerk and Clerk of the Peace, Deal, 1960-63; Legal Dir, Skelmersdale Develt Corp., 1963-76. *Recreations:* tennis, bridge. *Address:* Overdale, Granville Park, Aughton, Ormskirk. *T:* Aughton Green 422308.

BRADBURY, (Elizabeth) Joyce, CBE 1970; retired Headmistress; *b* Newcastle upon Tyne, 12 Dec. 1918; *o c* of Thomas Edwin and Anne Bradbury. *Educ:* private sch.; Queen Elizabeth's Grammar Sch., Middleton, near Manchester; Univ. of Leeds. BA (Hons Hist.); Dip. in Educn. Various teaching appts, 1941-57; Dep. Headmistress, Stand Grammar Sch. for Girls, Whitefield, near Manchester, 1957-59; Headmistress: Bede Grammar Sch. for Girls, Sunderland, 1959-67; Pennywell Sch. (co-educnl comprehensive), 1967-72; Thornhill Sch. (co-educnl comprehensive), 1972-78. President, Association of Headmistresses, 1974-76. *Recreations:* travel at home and abroad, walking, pursuing historical interests, music and the theatre, domestic 'arts'. *Address:* 6 Cliffe Court, Roker, Sunderland SR6 9NT. *T:* Sunderland 77135. *Clubs:* Soroptimist, British Federation of University Women.

BRADBURY, Surgeon Vice-Adm. Sir Eric (Blackburn), KBE 1971; CB 1968; FRCS 1972; Medical Director-General of the Navy, 1969-72; Chairman, Tunbridge Wells District Health Authority, since 1981; *b* 2 March 1911; *s* of late A. B. Bradbury, Maze, Co. Antrim; *m* 1939, Elizabeth Constance Austin; three *d. Educ:* Royal Belfast Academical Instn; Queen's Univ., Belfast; MB, BCh 1934; DMRD (London) 1949; Hon. LLD 1973. Joined RN (Medical Service), 1934; served at sea in HMS Barham, HMS Endeavour, HMS Cumberland, 1935-38 and in HMS Charybdis and HMHS Oxfordshire, 1941-45; served in RN Hospitals: Haslar, Chatham, Plymouth and Malta; Med. Officer-in-Charge, RN Hosp., Haslar, and Comd MO, Portsmouth, 1966-69. QHP 1966-72. *Address:* The Gate House, Nevill Park, Tunbridge Wells, Kent TN4 8NN. *T:* 27661.

BRADBURY, Joyce; *see* Bradbury, E. J.

BRADBURY, Prof. Malcolm Stanley; FRSL; Professor of American Studies, University of East Anglia, since 1970; *b* 7 Sept. 1932; *s* of Arthur Bradbury and Doris Ethel (*née* Marshall); *m* 1959, Elizabeth Salt; two *s. Educ:* University Coll. of Leicester (BA); Queen Mary Coll., Univ. of London (MA); Univ. of Manchester (PhD). Staff Tutor in Literature and Drama, Dept of Adult Education, Univ. of Hull, 1959-61; Lectr in English Language and Literature, Dept of English, Univ. of Birmingham, 1961-65; Lectr (later Sen. Lectr and Reader) in English and American Literature, Sch. of English and American Studies, Univ. of East Anglia, 1965-70. Visiting Prof., Univ. of Zürich, 1972. Editor: Arnold Stratford-upon-Avon Studies series; Methuen Contemporary Writers series. *Publications:* Eating People is Wrong (novel), 1959; Evelyn Waugh, 1962; E. M. Forster: a collection of critical essays (ed), 1965; Stepping Westward (novel), 1965; What is a Novel?, 1969; A Passage to India: a casebook, 1970; (ed) Penguin Companion to Literature, vol. 3: American (with E. Mottram), 1971; The Social Context of Modern English Literature, 1972; Possibilities: essays on the state of the novel, 1973; The History Man (novel), 1975; (with J. W. McFarlane) Modernism, 1976; Who Do You Think You Are? (short stories), 1976; (ed) The Novel Today, 1977; (ed) An Introduction to American Studies (with H. Temperley), 1981; The After Dinner Game (television plays), 1982; Saul Bellow, 1982; All Dressed Up And Nowhere To Go (humour), 1982. *Recreations:* none. *Address:* School of English and American Studies, University of East Anglia, Norwich NR4 7TJ. *T:* Norwich 56161.

BRADBURY, Ray Douglas; author; *b* Waukegan, Ill, USA, 22 Aug. 1920; *s* of Leonard S. Bradbury and Esther Moberg; *m* 1947, Marguerite Susan McClure; four *d. Educ:* Los Angeles High Sch. First Science-Fiction stories, 1941-44; stories sold to Harpers', Mademoiselle, The New Yorker, etc., 1945-56. Stories selected for: Best American Short Stories, 1946, 1948, 1952, 1958; O. Henry Prize Stories, 1947, 1948; and for inclusion in numerous anthologies. *Screenplays:* Moby Dick, 1954; Icarus Montgolfier Wright, 1961; The Martian Chronicles, 1964; The Picasso Summer, 1968; The Halloween Tree, 1968; The Dreamers; And The Rock Cried Out. Benjamin Franklin Award for Best Story Published in an Amer. Magazine of General Circulation, 1954; 1000 dollar Grant from Inst. of Arts and Letters, 1954. *Publications: novels:* Dark Carnival, 1947; Fahrenheit 451, 1953 (filmed); (for children) Switch on the Night, 1955; Dandelion Wine, 1957; Something Wicked This Way Comes, 1962; The Small Assassin, 1973; Mars and the Minds of Man, 1973; The Mummies of Guanajuato, 1978; The Ghosts of Forever, 1981; *short stories:* The Martian Chronicles, 1950 (English edn, The Silver Locusts, 1957); The Illustrated Man, 1951 (filmed with The Day It Rained Forever); The

Golden Apples of the Sun, 1953; The October Country, 1955; A Medicine for Melancholy (English edn, The Day It Rained Forever), 1959; (for children) R Is For Rocket, 1962; (for children) S Is For Space, 1962; The Machineries of Joy, 1964; The Autumn People, 1965; The Vintage Bradbury, 1965; Tomorrow Midnight, 1966; Twice Twenty-Two, 1966; I Sing the Body Electric!, 1969; Long After Midnight, 1976; *general:* Zen and the Art of Writing, 1973; *poems:* When Elephants Last in the Dooryard Bloomed, 1973; Where Robot Mice and Robot Men Run Round in Robot Towns, 1977; This Attic where the Meadow Greens, 1980; The Haunted Computer and the Android Pope, 1981; *plays:* The Meadow, 1947; The Anthem Sprinters (one-act), 1963; The World of Ray Bradbury (one-act), 1964; The Wonderful Ice Cream Suit and Other Plays (one-act), 1965; Any Friend of Nicholas Nickleby's is a Friend of Mine, 1968; Pillar of Fire, 1975. *Recreations:* oil painting, ceramics, collecting native masks. *Address:* 10265 Cheviot Drive, Los Angeles, Calif 90064, USA.

BRADBURY, Rear-Adm. Thomas Henry, CB 1979; Group Personnel Director, Inchcape Group of Cos, since 1979; *b* 4 Dec. 1922; *s* of Thomas Henry Bradbury and Violet Buckingham; *m* 1st, 1945, Beryl Doreen Evans (marr. diss. 1979); one *s* one *d* ; 2nd, 1979, Sarah Catherine, *d* of Harley Hillier and Mrs Susan Hillier. *Educ:* Christ's Hosp. CO HMS Jufair, 1960-62; Supply Officer, HMS Hermes, 1965-67; Sec. to Controller of Navy, MoD, 1967-70; CO HMS Terror, 1970-71; RCDS, 1972; Dir, Naval Admin. Planning, MoD, 1974-76; Flag Officer, Admiralty Interview Bd, 1977-79. *Recreations:* sailing, gardening. *Address:* Churches Green, Dallington, Heathfield, Sussex. *T:* Rushlake Green 830657.

BRADBY, Edward Lawrence; Principal, St Paul's College, Cheltenham, 1949-72; *b* 15 March 1907; *y s* of late H. C. Bradby, Ringshall End, near Berkhamsted, Herts; *m* 1939, Bertha Woodall, *y d* of late Henry Woodall, Yotes Court, Mereworth, Maidstone; three *s* one *d.* *Educ:* Rugby Sch.; New College, Oxford (MA). Asst Master, Merchant Taylors' Sch., 1930-34; International Student Service, 1934-39; Secretary to Cttee for England and Wales, 1934-36; Asst General Secretary, Geneva, 1936-37; General Secretary, Geneva, 1937-39; Principal, Royal Coll., Colombo, Ceylon, 1939-46; Principal, Eastbourne Emergency Training Coll., 1946-49. Hon. MEd Bristol, 1972. *Publications:* Editor, The University Outside Europe, a collection of essays on university institutions in 14 countries, 1939; Seend, a Wiltshire Village Past and Present, 1981. *Address:* Beech House, Seend, Melksham, Wilts. *T:* Seend 456. *Club:* Royal Commonwealth Society.

BRADDON, Russell Reading; author; *b* 25 Jan. 1921; *s* of Henry Russell Braddon and Thelma Doris Braddon (*née* Reading). *Educ:* Sydney Church of England Grammar Sch.; Sydney Univ. (BA). Failed Law finals; began writing, by chance, 1949; been writing ever since. *Publications:* The Piddingtons, 1950; The Naked Island, 1951; Those in Peril, 1954; Cheshire, VC, 1954; Out of the Storm, 1956; Nancy Wake, 1956; End of a Hate, 1958; Gabriel Comes to 24, 1958; Proud American Boy, 1960; Joan Sutherland, 1962; The Year of the Angry Rabbit, 1964; Roy Thomson of Fleet Street, 1965; Committal Chamber, 1966; When the Enemy is Tired, 1968; The Inseparables, 1968; Will You Walk a Little Faster, 1969; The Siege, 1969; Prelude and Fugue for Lovers, 1971; The Progress of Private Lilyworth, 1971; End Play, 1972; Suez: splitting of a nation, 1973; The Hundred Days of Darien, 1974; All the Queen's Men, 1977; The Finalists, 1977; The Shepherd's Bush Case, 1978; The Predator, 1980; A Clock Striking, 1982. *Recreations:* reading, bridge, squash, not writing. *Address:* c/o John Farquharson Ltd, Bell House, 8 Bell Yard, WC1.

BRADEN, Bernard; free-lance actor and dabbler; television performer; *b* 16 May 1916; *s* of Rev. Dr Edwin Donald Braden and Mary Evelyn Chastey; *m* 1942, Barbara Kelly; one *s* two *d.* *Educ:* Maple Grove Public Sch., Point Grey Junior High Sch., Magee High Sch., Vancouver, Canada. Radio engineer, announcer, singer, actor in Vancouver, Canada, 1937-40; wrote and performed in plays for Canadian Broadcasting Corporation, 1940-43; went to Toronto, 1943; wrote and produced plays for Canadian Broadcasting Corporation, 1943-49; came to England, 1949. London plays include: Street-Car Named Desire; Biggest Thief in Town; The Man; No News From Father; Anniversary Waltz; The Gimmick; Period of Adjustment; Spoon River Anthology. Also performs for radio, television and films. Hon. Chancellor, London School of Economics, 1955. *Publication:* These English (Canada), 1948. *Recreations:* family, tennis, swimming.

BRADEN, Hugh Reginald, CMG 1980; Director, A. B. Jay Ltd; *b* 1923; *s* of late Reginald Henry Braden and Mabel Braden (*née* Selby); *m* 1946, Phyllis Grace Barnes; one *d.* *Educ:* Worthing High School for Boys; Brighton College of Technology. Joined War Office, 1939; served War, Royal Navy, 1942-45; Far East Land Forces, 1946-50; British Army of the Rhine, 1953-56; War Office and Min. of Defence, 1956-66; jssc 1967; British Embassy, Washington, 1968-70; Min. of Defence, 1971-80 (Asst Under Sec. of State, 1978-80). *Recreations:* gardening, golf. *Address:* Field House, Honeysuckle Lane, High Salvington, Worthing, West Sussex. *T:* Worthing 60203.

BRADFORD, 7th Earl of, *cr* 1815; **Richard Thomas Orlando Bridgeman;** Bt 1600; Baron Bradford, 1794; Viscount Newport, 1815; *b* 3 Oct. 1947; *s* of 6th Earl of Bradford, TD, and of Mary Willoughby, *er d* of Lt-Col T. H. Montgomery, DSO; *S* father, 1981; *m* 1979, Joanne Elizabeth, *d* of B. Miller; two *s.* *Educ:* Harrow; Trinity College, Cambridge. Owner of Porters Restaurant of Covent Garden, and Bones Restaurant, Chelsea Cloisters; Dir,

Ringingham Ltd. *Heir: s* Viscount Newport, *qv. Address:* Weston Park, Shifnal, Salop. *T:* Weston-under-Lizard 218.

BRADFORD, Bishop of, since 1981; **Rt. Rev. Geoffrey John Paul;** *b* 4 March 1921; *s* of Robert John Paul and Ethel Mary (*née* Arthur); *m* 1951, Pamela Maisie Watts; five *d.* *Educ:* Rutlish School, Merton; Queens' Coll., Cambridge (MA); King's Coll., London (MTh, AKC). Deacon 1948; Curate of Little Ilford, E12; priest 1949; Church of S India, from Oct. 1950. Chaplain, St John's Coll., Palayamkotta, 1950-52; Kerala United Theological Seminary, 1952-65 (Principal, 1962-65); Church Missionary Society, 1965-66; Residentiary Canon, Bristol Cathedral, (Director of Ordination Training, Examining Chaplain), 1966-71; Hon. Canon of Bristol, 1971-77; Warden, Lee Abbey, 1971-77; Bishop Suffragan of Hull, 1977-81. *Publications:* The Gospel according to St Mark, 1957, and St John's Gospel, 1965, both published by Christian Students' Library in India. *Address:* Bishopscroft, Ashwell Road, Bradford, W Yorks BD9 4AU.

BRADFORD, Provost of; see Jackson, Very Rev. B. D.

BRADFORD, Archdeacon of; see Sargeant, Ven. F. P.

BRADFORD, (Sir) Edward Alexander Slade, 5th Bt, *cr* 1902 (but does not use the title); *b* 18 June 1952; *s* of Major Sir Edward Montagu Andrew Bradford, 3rd Bt and his 2nd wife, Marjorie Edith (*née* Bere); *S* half-brother, Sir John Ridley Evelyn Bradford, 4th Bt, 1954. *Heir:* uncle Donald Clifton Bradford [*b* 22 May 1914; *m* 1949, Constance Mary Morgan; three *d*]. *Address:* Faith Cottage, Pett, near Hastings, E Sussex.

BRADFORD, Prof. Eric Watts, MDS (Sheffield), DDSc (St Andrews); Professor of Dental Surgery, University of Bristol, since 1959; Dean of the Faculty of Medicine, 1975-79; *b* 4 Nov. 1919; *e s* of E. J. G. and C. M. Bradford; *m* 1946, Norah Mary Longmuir; two *s* three *d. Educ:* King Edward VII Sch., Sheffield; High Storrs Grammar Sch., Sheffield; Univ. of Sheffield (Robert Styring Scholar). LDS, Sheffield, 1943; BDS, Sheffield, 1944; MDS, Sheffield, 1950; DDSc St Andrews, 1954. Lieut, Army Dental Corps, Nov. 1944; Capt. Nov. 1945. Lectr, Univ. of Sheffield, 1947-52; Senior Lectr, Univ. of St Andrews, 1952-59. Mem., Gen. Dental Council, 1979-. *Publications:* many papers on dental anatomy in British and other journals. *Address:* 11 Grove Road, Coombe Dingle, Bristol BS9 2RQ. *T:* 681849.

BRADFORD, Ernle; independent free-lance writer, principally on historical subjects; *b* 11 Jan. 1922; *s* of Jocelyn Ernle Bradford and Ada Louisa (*née* Dusgate); *m* 1957, Marie Blanche Thompson; one *s. Educ:* Uppingham Sch. RNVR, 1940-46 (despatches 1943). Founder Editor, Antique Dealer and Collectors' Guide, 1947. *Publications:* Contemporary Jewellery and Silver Design, 1950; Four Centuries of European Jewellery, 1953 (new edn 1968); The Journeying Moon, 1958; The Mighty 'Hood', 1959 (paperback 1974, new edn 1975); English Victorian Jewellery, 1959 (new edn 1968); The Wind off the Island, 1960; Southward the Caravels: the story of Henry the Navigator, 1961; The Great Siege, 1961 (paperback 1964); The Touchstone, 1962; Antique Collecting, 1963; Companion Guide to the Greek Islands, 1963 (3rd edn 1975); Dictionary of Antiques, 1963; Ulysses Found, 1963; Three Centuries of Sailing, 1964; The America's Cup, 1964; Drake, 1965; Wall of England, 1966; The Great Betrayal: Constantinople, 1204, 1967 (new edn 1975); The Sultan's Admiral: the life of Barbarossa, 1969; Antique Furniture, 1970; Cleopatra, 1971 (paperback 1974); Gibraltar: the history of a fortress, 1971; Mediterranean: portrait of a sea, 1971; The Shield and the Sword: the Knights of St John, 1973 (paperback 1974); Christopher Columbus, 1973; The Sword and the Scimitar: the saga of the crusades, 1974; Paul the Traveller, 1975; Nelson, 1977; The Year of Thermopylae, 1980; Hannibal, 1982; The Story of the Mary Rose, 1982. *Recreations:* swimming, sailing, idling. *Address:* c/o A. M. Heath & Co., 40-42 William IV Street, WC2N 4DD. *Club:* Casino Maltese (Malta).

BRADFORD, Rt. Hon. Roy Hamilton, PC (NI) 1969; Member (U) for East Belfast, Northern Ireland Assembly, 1973-75; Minister for the Environment, Northern Ireland Executive, 1973-74; *b* 7 July 1921; *s* of Joseph Hamilton Bradford, Rockcorry, Co. Monaghan, and Isabel Mary (*née* McNamee), Donemana, Co. Tyrone; *m* 1946, Hazel Elizabeth, *d* of Capt. W. Lindsay, Belfast; two *s. Educ:* Royal Belfast Academical Institution; Trinity Coll., Dublin. Foundation Schol. 1940; First Class Hons (BA) German and French (with Gold Medal) 1942 (TCD). Army Intelligence, 1943-47 (France, Belgium, Germany). BBC and ITV Producer and Writer, 1950-. Dir, Geoffrey Sharp Ltd, 1962-. MP (U) for Victoria, Parlt of NI, 1965-73; Asst Whip (Unionist Party), 1966; Parly Sec., Min. of Educn, 1967; Chief Whip, Sept. 1968-April 1969; Minister of Commerce, NI, 1969-71; Minister of Develt, NI, 1971-72. Contested (Off U) North Down, 1974. *Publications:* Excelsior (novel), 1960; The Last Ditch (novel), 1981. *Recreations:* golf, architecture. *Address:* Ardkeen, Carnalea, Bangor, Co. Down, N Ireland. *T:* Bangor 65012. *Club:* Ulster (Belfast).

BRADFORD HILL, Sir Austin; see Hill.

BRADING, Keith, CB 1974; MBE 1944; Chief Registrar of Friendly Societies and Industrial Assurance Commissioner, 1972-81; *b* 23 Aug. 1917; *s* of late Frederick C. Brading and late Lilian P. Brading (*née* Courtney); *m* 1949, Mary Blanche Robinson. *Educ:* Portsmouth Grammar Sch. Called to Bar, Gray's Inn, 1950. Entered Inland Revenue (Estate Duty Office), 1936. Served

War, Royal Navy, 1941–46 (Lieut RNVR); Solicitor's Office, Inland Revenue, 1950; Asst Solicitor, 1962; Asst Registrar of Friendly Societies and Dep. Industrial Assurance Commissioner, 1969. Vice-Pres., Bldg Socs Assoc., 1982–. *Publications:* contrib. Halsbury's Laws of England and Atkins Court Forms and Precedents. *Address:* 35 Chiswick Staithe, W4. *T:* 01-995 0517. *Club:* Saville.

BRADING, Brig. Norman Baldwin, CMG 1958; CBE 1945; retired; *b* 25 May 1896; *s* of late Rev. F. C. Brading, Ditton, Kent; *m* Helen Margaret, *d* of G. Gatey, Windermere; one *s* one *d*. *Educ:* Whitgift; Royal Military College, Sandhurst. 2nd Lieut East Surrey Regt, 1915; served European War, 1914–19 (wounded); War of 1939–45; France, Holland, Germany; despatches, 1945; Lieut-Col 1940, Col 1943, Brig. 1944. Lent to UNO as Dep. Dir for Ops in Brit. Zone of Germany; National Health Services, 1949; lent to Nigerian Govt as House Governor, University Coll. Hospital, Ibadan, Nigeria, 1952. FHA. Knight Comdr Order of Orange Nassau, with swords (Netherlands), 1945. *Recreations:* polo, swimming. *Address:* Woodstock House, Woodstock, Oxford OX7 1UG. *Club:* Royal Over-Seas League.

BRADLAW, Prof. Sir Robert (Vivian), Kt 1965; CBE 1950; Hon. Professor of Oral Pathology, Royal College of Surgeons of England, since 1948; Emeritus Professor of Oral Medicine, University of London; Emeritus Consultant, Royal Navy; *b* 14 April 1905; *s* of Philip Archibald Bradlaw, Blackrock, Co. Dublin; unmarried. *Educ:* Cranleigh; Guy's Hosp.; University of London. Hilton Prize, Guy's Hosp.; Hon. Degrees, Univs of Belfast, Birmingham, Boston, Durham, Leeds, Malta, Melbourne, Meshed, Montreal and Newcastle upon Tyne; Fellow, Royal Colleges of Surgeons of England, Edinburgh, Glasgow, Ireland, etc; Hon. Fellow, RSM, 1975. Tomes Prize for Research, RCS 1939–41; Howard Mummery Prize for Research, BDA, 1948–53; Colyer Gold Medal, RCS; Hunterian Prof., RCS 1955; Hon. Gold Medal, RCS, 1972; Chevalier de la Santé Publique (France), 1950; Knight, Order of St Olaf, Norway; Commander, Order of Homayoun, Iran. *Recreations:* fishing, golf, orchids, oriental ceramics. *Address:* The Manse, Stoke Goldington, Newport Pagnell, Bucks. *Club:* Athenæum.

BRADLEY, Clive; Chief Executive and Secretary, Publishers Association, since 1976; *b* 25 July 1934; *s* of Alfred and Kathleen Bradley. *Educ:* Felsted Sch., Essex; Clare Coll., Cambridge (MA); Yale Univ. (Mellon Fellow). Barrister-at-Law. Broadcasting Officer, Labour Party, 1963–64; Political Editor, Statist, 1965–67; Gp Labour Adviser, Internat. Publishing Corp. Ltd, 1967–69; Newspaper Exec. (IPC and Observer), 1969–75. Broadcaster on current affairs. Dep. Chm., Central London Valuation Panel. Governor, Felsted Sch. *Publications:* various books, articles and pamphlets on politics, economics, the press, television, industrial relations. *Recreations:* reading, travel. *Address:* 39 Bolton Gardens, SW5. *T:* 01-370 6494.

BRADLEY, Prof. Daniel Joseph, PhD; FRS 1976; Professor of Optical Electronics, Trinity College Dublin, since 1980; Emeritus Professor of Optics, London University, 1980; *b* 18 Jan. 1928; *s* of John Columba Bradley and Margaret Mary Bradley; *m* 1958, Winefride Marie Therese O'Connor; four *s* one *d*. *Educ:* St Columb's Coll., Londonderry; St Mary's Trng Coll., Belfast; Birkbeck and Royal Holloway Colls, London (BSc Maths, BSc Physics, PhD). Primary Sch. Teacher, Londonderry, 1947–53; Secondary Sch. Teacher, London area, 1953–57; Asst Lectr, Royal Holloway Coll., 1957–60; Lectr, Imperial Coll. of Science and Technol., 1960–64; Reader, Royal Holloway Coll., 1964–66; Prof. and Head of Dept of Pure and Applied Physics, QUB, 1966–73; Prof. of Optics, 1973–80, and Head of Physics Dept, 1976–80, Imperial Coll., London. Vis. Scientist, MIT, 1965; Consultant, Harvard Observatory, 1966. Lectures: Scott, Cambridge, 1977; Tolansky Meml, RSA, 1977. Chairman: Laser Facility Cttee, SRC, 1976–79; British Nat. Cttee for Physics, 1979–80; Quantum Electronics Comm, IUPAP, 1982; Member: Rutherford Lab. Estab. Cttee, SRC, 1977–79; Science Bd, SRC, 1977–80; Council, Royal Soc., 1979–80. MRIA 1969; Fellow, Optical Soc. of America, 1975. Thomas Young Medal, Inst. of Physics, 1975. *Publications:* papers on optics, lasers, spectroscopy, chronoscopy and astronomy in Proc. Roy. Soc., Phil. Mag., Phys. Rev., J. Opt. Soc. Amer., Proc. IEEE, Chem. Phys. Letts, Optics Communications. *Recreations:* television, walking, manual labour. *Address:* Trinity College, Dublin 2, Ireland. *Club:* Athenæum.

BRADLEY, Prof. Donald Charlton, CChem, FRSC; FRS 1980; Professor of Inorganic Chemistry since 1965, and Head of Chemistry Department, 1978–82, Queen Mary College, University of London; *b* 7 Nov. 1924; *m* 1948, Constance Joy Hazeldean; one *s*. *Educ:* Hove County School for Boys; Birkbeck Coll., Univ. of London (BSc 1st Cl. Hons Chemistry, PhD, DSc). Research Asst, British Electrical and Allied Industries Research Assoc., 1941–47; Asst Lectr in Chemistry, 1949–52, Lectr in Chemistry, 1952–59, Birkbeck Coll.; Prof. of Chemistry, Univ. of Western Ontario, Canada, 1959–64. Univ. of London: Chm., Bd of Studies in Chemistry and Chemical Industries, 1977–79; Mem. Senate. Mem., Soc. of Chem. Industry; MRI. *Publications:* (jtly) Metal Alkoxides, 1978; numerous pubns on synthesis and structure of metallo-organic compounds, co-ordination chemistry and inorganic polymers, mainly in Jl of Chemical Soc. *Recreations:* travelling, gardening, listening to music; amateur interest in archaeology. *Address:* Department of Chemistry, Queen Mary College, Mile End Road, E1 4NS. *T:* 01-980 4811.

BRADLEY, Edgar Leonard, OBE 1979; Metropolitan Stipendiary Magistrate, since 1967; *b* 17 Nov. 1917; 2nd *s* of Ernest Henry and Letitia

Bradley, W. Felton, Oswestry; *m* 1942, Elsa, *o d* of Colin and Elizabeth Matheson, Edinburgh; two *s* three *d*. *Educ:* Malvern Coll.; Trinity Hall, Cambridge. BA 1939; MA 1944. Called to Bar, Middle Temple, 1940. Served 1940–46, RA; Capt. and Adjt, 1943–45; Major, GSO2, Mil. Govt of Germany, 1946. Practised at Bar, 1946–51, SE Circuit, Central Criminal Ct, S London and Surrey Sessions. Legal Dept of Home Office, 1951-54. Sec., Departmental Cttee on Magistrates' Courts Bill, 1952; Sec. of Magistrates' Courts Rule Cttee, 1952-54; Clerk to Justices: Wrexham and Bromfield, 1954-57; Poole, 1957-67. Justices' Clerks Society: Mem. Council, 1957–67; Hon. Sec., 1963–67 Mem., Nat. Adv. Council on Trng of Magistrates, 1965-67; Magistrates Association: Mem. Council, 1968–; Chm. Legal Cttee, 1973–. Adv. tour of Magistrates' Courts in Ghana, 1970. *Publications:* (with J. J. Senior) Bail in Magistrates' Courts, 1977; articles in legal jls. *Recreations:* gardening, golf. *Address:* Camberwell Green Magistrates' Court, SE5. *T:* 01–703 0909.

BRADLEY, Harry, CBE 1951; (First) Director, British Boot, Shoe and Allied Trades Research Association (SATRA), 1922–63, retired; Emeritus President, British Boot and Shoe Institution; *b* 1897; *s* of late George Craven Bradley, Silsden, Yorks; *m* 1921, Bertha Ceridwen, *d* of late Rev. T. Henry Jones, USA and North Wales; one *s* two *d*. *Educ:* Keighley Grammar Sch.; Royal College of Science; Imperial Coll. of Science and Technology. Served European War, 1914–18, RFC and RNVR Anti-submarine Div. On demobilisation completed ARCS (hons), BSc (1st cl. hons); 1 yr research for Admiralty; 1 yr Lectr/Demonstrator, 3rd yr Physics, Royal College of Science. John Arthur Wilson Memorial Lectures, Amer. Leather Chemists' Assoc., 1966. Mem., Royal Institution. *Publications:* many research reports, scientific papers and articles in various jls. *Recreations:* music, gardening, reading; fond of dogs and horses. *Address:* Volta, 38 Piper's Hill Road, Kettering, Northants. *T:* Kettering 513210.

BRADLEY, Maj.-Gen. Peter Edward Moore, CB 1968; CBE 1964 (OBE 1955); DSO 1946; Trustee, Vindolanda Trust, since 1982 (Secretary, 1975-82); *b* 12 Dec. 1914; *s* of late Col Edward de Winton Herbert Bradley, CBE, DSO, MC, DL; *m* Margaret, *d* of Norman Wardhaugh of Haydon Bridge, Northumberland; three *s*. *Educ:* Marlborough; Royal Military Academy, Woolwich. 2nd Lieut, Royal Signals, 1934. Served War of 1939–45; India, Middle East, Italy and North West Europe (DSO 6th Airborne Div.). Lieut-Col 1954; Col 1957; Brig. 1962; Maj.-Gen. 1965; Signal Officer in Chief (Army), Ministry of Defence, 1965–67; Chief of Staff to C-in-C Allied Forces Northern Europe, Oslo, 1968–70, retired. Dunlop Ltd, 1970-75. Col Comdt, Royal Signals, 1967–82, Master of Signals, 1970–82; Col. Gurkha Signals, 1967–74. CEng, FIEE, 1966; FBIM, 1970. *Address:* Hill House, Haydon Bridge, near Hexham, Northumberland. *T:* Haydon Bridge 234. *Club:* Army and Navy.

BRADLEY, Richard Alan; Headmaster, Rivers Country Day School, Massachusetts, USA, since 1981; *b* 6 Oct. 1925; *s* of late Reginald Livingstone Bradley, CBE, MC, and of Phyllis Mary Richardson; *m* 1971, Mary Ann Vicary; one *s* two *d* by previous marriage. *Educ:* Marlborough Coll.; Trinity Coll., Oxford (Scholar). 2nd cl. hons Mod. History. Royal Marines, 1944–46; Oxford, 1946–48; Club Manager, Oxford and Bermondsey Club, 1949. Asst Master: Dulwich Coll., 1949–50; Tonbridge Sch., 1950–66 (Head of History Dept, 1957-66; Housemaster of Ferox Hall, 1961-66); Warden of St Edward's Sch., Oxford, 1966–71; Headmaster, Ridley Coll., Canada, 1971–81. *Recreations:* games, dramatics, mountains. *Address:* Rivers Country Day School, on Nonesuch Pond, 333 Winter Street, Weston, Mass 02193, USA. *Club:* Vincent's (Oxford).

BRADLEY, Thomas George; MP Leicester East, since 1974 (Leicester NE, July 1962-1974) (Lab, 1962-1981, SDP, since 1981); *b* 13 April 1926; *s* of George Henry Bradley, Kettering; *m* 1953, Joy, *d* of George Starmer, Kettering; two *s*. *Educ:* Kettering Central Sch., Northants. Elected to Northants County Council, 1952, County Alderman, 1961; Mem., Kettering Borough Council, 1957-61. Transport Salaried Staffs' Association: Branch Officer, 1946-58; Mem. Exec. Cttee, 1958–; Treasurer, 1961–64; Pres., 1964-77. Contested (Lab) Rutland and Stamford, 1950, 1951 and 1955, Preston South, 1959. PPS: to Minister of Aviation, 1964-65; to Home Secretary, 1966-67; to Chancellor of the Exchequer, 1967-70; Chm., Select Cttee on Transport, 1979-. Vice-Chm., Labour Party, 1974-75, Chm., 1975-76; Mem., Labour Party NEC, 1966-81. Chm., Kettering Town Football Club. *Address:* The Orchard, 111 London Road, Kettering, Northants. *T:* Kettering 3019. *Club:* Savile.

BRADLEY, William Ewart; Special Commissioner of Income Tax 1950-75; *b* 5 Sept. 1910; *s* of W. E. Bradley, Durham City; *m* 1949, Mary Campbell Tyre; two *s*. *Educ:* Johnston Sch., Durham; LSE, London Univ. Inland Revenue, 1929-50. *Address:* 3 Bourne Lane, Tonbridge, Kent. *T:* Tonbridge 352880.

BRADLEY GOODMAN, Michael; *see* Goodman, M. B.

BRADMAN, Sir Donald (George), Kt 1949; President of South Australian Cricket Association, 1965–73; Chairman, Australian Cricket Board, 1960-63 and 1969-72; *b* Cootamundra, NSW, 27 Aug. 1908; *s* of George and Emily Bradman; *m* 1932, Jessie, *d* of James Menzies, Mittagong, NSW; one *s* one *d*. *Educ:* Bowral Intermediate High Sch. Played for NSW 1927-34; for S Australia, 1935-49; for Australia 1928-48, Capt. 1936-48; records include: highest aggregate and greatest number of centuries in England *v* Australia test matches; highest score for Australia *v* England in test matches (334 at Leeds, 1930). Formerly stock and share broker and Mem. Stock Exchange of Adelaide Ltd. *Publications:* Don Bradman's Book, 1930; How to Play Cricket, 1935; My Cricketing Life, 1938; Farewell to Cricket, 1950; The Art of Cricket, 1958. *Relevant publication:* Irving Rosenwater, Sir Donald Bradman, 1978. *Recreations:* cricket, golf, tennis, billiards, squash. *Address:* 118 King William Street, Adelaide, South Australia. *Clubs:* MCC (Hon. Life Mem.); Commerce (Adelaide).

RADSHAW, Prof. Anthony David, PhD; FRS 1982; Holbrook Gaskell Professor of Botany, University of Liverpool, since 1968; *b* 17 Jan. 1926; *m* Betty Margaret Bradshaw; three *d. Educ:* St Paul's Sch., Hammersmith; Jesus Coll., Cambridge (BA 1947; MA 1951); PhD Wales 1959. Lectr, 1952-63, Sen. Lectr, 1963-64, Reader in Agricl Botany, 1964-68, UCNW, Bangor. Member: Nature Conservancy Council, 1969-78; Natural Environment Res. Council, 1969-74; Bd of Management, Sports Turf Res. Inst., 1976-. Pres., British Ecological Soc., 1981-. *Publications:* (ed jtly) Teaching Genetics, 1963; (with M. J. Chadwick) The Reclamation of Land, 1980; (with others) Quarry Reclamation, 1982; (with others) Mine Wastes Reclamation, 1982; (with R. A. Dutton) Land Reclamation in Cities, 1982; contribs to symposia and learned jls. *Recreations:* dinghy sailing, gardening, appreciating land. *Address:* Botany Department, The University, Liverpool L69 3BX.

RADSHAW, Kenneth Anthony, CB 1982; Clerk Assistant of the House of Commons, since 1979; *b* 1 Sept. 1922; *s* of late Herbert and Gladys Bradshaw. *Educ:* Ampleforth Coll.; St Catharine's Coll., Cambridge (1st Cl. Hons History); MA 1947. War Service, 1942-45; served with Royal Ulster Rifles (2nd Bn), NW Europe (despatches). Temp. Asst Principal, Min. of Supply, Oct.-Dec. 1946; Asst Clerk, House of Commons, 1947; seconded as Clerk of the Saskatchewan Legislature, 1966 session; Clerk of Overseas Office, 1972-76; Principal Clerk, Table Office, House of Commons, 1976-79. Jt Sec., Assoc. of Secs Gen. of Parlts, 1955-71. *Publication:* (with David Pring) Parliament and Congress, 1972. *Address:* 8 Cornwall Mansions, SW10 0PE. *Club:* Garrick.

RADSHAW, Maurice Bernard, OBE 1978; Secretary-General, 1958-79, Governor, 1979-81, a Director, since 1981, Federation of British Artists; *b* 7 Feb. 1903; 7th *s* of John Bradshaw; *m* 1927, Gladys, 2nd *d* of Henry Harvey Frost; one *d. Educ:* Christ's Coll., Finchley. Jun. Clerk, Furness Withy & Co., 1918. Dir, Art Exhibns Bureau, 1926-; Asst Sec., British Artists Exhibns, 1927-35; Organising Sec., Floating Art Gall. aboard Berengaria, 1928; Sec., Empire Art Loan Exhibn Soc., 1932-; Sec., Modern Architectural Res. Gp, 1938. Commissioned RAFVR, 1941-45. Sec. following art socs: Royal Inst. Oil Painters, 1966-74, Royal Inst. Painters in Watercolours, 1969-79, Royal Soc. British Artists, 1958-74, Royal Soc. Marine Artists, 1938-72, Royal Soc. Portrait Painters, 1955-, Royal Soc. Miniature Painters, Sculptors and Gravers, 1959-72, Royal British Colonial Soc. of Artists (temp. known as Commonwealth Soc. of Artists), 1930-, Artists of Chelsea, 1949-72, National Soc., 1968-74, New English Art Club, 1955-74, Pastel Soc., 1968-77, Soc. Aviation Artists, 1954-, Soc. Graphic Artists, 1968-75, Soc. Mural Painters, 1968-, Soc. Portrait Sculptors, 1969-, Soc. Wildlife Artists, 1963-80, Soc. Women Artists, 1968-74, Senefelder Gp, 1968-. *Recreation:* woodwork. *Address:* Flat Two, 110 Elm Park Gardens, Chelsea, SW10 9PF. *T:* 01-352 7242. *Clubs:* Army and Navy, Chelsea Arts, Eccentric.

RADSHAW, Prof. Peter, FRS 1981; Professor of Experimental Aerodynamics, Aero Department, Imperial College of Science and Technology, University of London, since 1978; *b* 26 Dec. 1935; *s* of Joseph W. N. Bradshaw and Frances W. G. Bradshaw; *m* 1968, Sheila Dorothy (*née* Brown). *Educ:* Torquay Grammar Sch.; St John's Coll., Cambridge (BA). Scientific Officer, Aerodynamics Div., National Physical Lab., 1957-69; Sen. Lectr, Dept of Aeronautics, Imp. Coll. of Science and Technol., 1969-71, Reader, 1971-78. *Publications:* Experimental Fluid Mechanics, 1964, 2nd edn 1971; An Introduction to Turbulence and its Measurement, 1971, 2nd edn 1975; (with T. Cebeci) Momentum Transfer in Boundary Layers, 1977; (ed) Topics in Applied Physics: Turbulence, 1978; (with T. Cebeci and J. H. Whitelaw) Engineering Calculation Methods for Turbulent Flow, 1981; (with T. Cebeci) Heat Transfer in Boundary Layers, 1984; author or co-author of over 100 papers in Jl of Fluid Mechanics, AIAA Jl, etc. *Recreations:* ancient history, walking. *Address:* 67a Blandford Road, Teddington, Mddx TW11 0LG. *T:* (office) 01-589 5111, ext. 1833.

RADSHAW, Lt-Gen. Sir Richard (Phillip), KBE 1977; Director General, Army Medical Services, 1977-81; *b* 1 Aug. 1920; *s* of late John Henderson Bradshaw and late May Bradshaw (*née* Phillips); *m* 1946, Estelle, *d* of late Emile Meyer; one *d. Educ:* Newport High Sch.; London Univ.; Westminster Hosp. MRCS, LRCP 1945; FRCPath 1967; FFCM 1977; DTM&H 1953; FRSocMed, FRSTM&H, Mem. BMA. House appts Westminster and Kent and Canterbury Hosps. Commnd RAMC, 1946; appts as Hosp. Pathologist, Mil. Hosps in UK and Ceylon; Staff appts in Path., WO, 1950-52; Comd Cons. Pathologist, E Africa, 1954-57; Exch. Officer, Armed Forces Inst. of Path., Washington, 1958-59; Demonstr in Path., Royal Army Med. Coll., Millbank, 1961-63; Asst Dir of Path., BAOR, 1966-69; Prof. of Path., Royal Army Med. Coll., Millbank, 1969-71; CO, Cambridge Mil. Hosp., Aldershot, 1971-73; Comdt RAMC Trng Centre, 1973-75; DMS, BAOR, 1975-77. QHP 1975-81. CStJ 1977. *Publications:* articles and reports in professional jls. *Recreations:* sailing, bird-watching, gardening, joinery. *Address:* c/o Lloyds Bank Ltd, 19 Horseferry Road, SW1P 2AD.

BRADSHAW, Thornton Frederick; Chairman and Chief Executive Officer, RCA, New York, since 1981; *b* 4 Aug. 1917; *s* of Frederick and Julia Bradshaw; *m* 1st, 1940, Sally Davis (marr. diss. 1974); one *s* two *d* ; 2nd, 1974, Patricia Salter West; four step *s. Educ:* Phillips Exeter Acad.; Harvard Coll. (BA); Harvard Grad. Sch. of Business (MBA, Dr of Commercial Science). Associate Prof., Sch. of Bus. Admin, Harvard (with time out for Navy service, seven battle stars), 1942-52; Cresap, McCormick & Paget, 1952-56; Atlantic Richfield Co., 1956-81: Vice Pres. and Gen. Man., Finance and Accounting Dept, Jan. 1958; Mem., Bd of Dirs, Feb. 1958; Exec. Vice Pres., 1962; Pres., and Mem. Exec. Cttee of Bd of Dirs, 1964-81; Chm. Exec. Cttee, Jan.-June 1981. Hon. LLD Pepperdine Univ., 1974; Hon. DSSc Villanova Univ., 1975. Many awards, including: Freedom and Justice Award, NAACP, 1976; Amer. Jewish Cttee Human Relations Award, 1976; Business Statesman Award, Harvard Bus. Sch., 1977; Earl Warren Award for 1980, Amer. Soc. for Public Admin, 1981. *Publications:* Corporations and their Critics, 1980; articles and pubns. *Recreations:* boating, tennis, swimming; also a prolific reader, fond of history and biography. *Address:* 635 Park Avenue, New York, NY 10021, USA; (office) 30 Rockefeller Plaza, New York, NY 10020. *T:* (212) 621-6000. *Clubs:* Mark's; Economic, Harvard, Knickerbocker, River, University (New York); California (LA); Valley Hunt (Pasadena, Calif).

BRADSHAW-ISHERWOOD, Christopher William; see Isherwood, Christopher.

BRADWELL, Bishop Suffragan of, since 1976; **Rt Rev. (Charles) Derek Bond;** *b* 4 July 1927; *s* of Charles Norman Bond and Doris Bond; *m* 1951, Joan Valerie Meikle; two *s* two *d. Educ:* Bournemouth Sch.; King's Coll., London. AKC (2nd hons). Curate of Friern Barnet, 1952; Midlands Area Sec. of SCM in Schools and Public Preacher, dio. Birmingham, 1956; Vicar: of Harringay, 1958; of Harrow Weald, 1962; Archdeacon of Colchester, 1972-76. *Recreation:* travel. *Address:* 188 New London Road, Chelmsford CM2 0AR. *T:* Chelmsford 84235.

BRADY, Very Rev. Ernest William; Priest-in-Charge, Priory Church of St Mary of Mount Carmel, South Queensferry, 1974-82 and Dean of Edinburgh, 1976-82; *b* 10 Nov. 1917; *s* of Ernest and Malinda Elizabeth Brady; *m* 1948, Violet Jeanne Louise Aldworth; one *s* one *d. Educ:* Harris Academy, Dundee (Dux and Classics Medallist, 1936); Univ. of St Andrews; Edinburgh Theological Coll. (Luscombe Schol. 1942). LTh (Dunelm) 1942. Deacon 1942, Priest 1943; Asst Curate, Christ Church, Glasgow, 1942; Asst Curate, St Alphage, Hendon, 1946; Rector, All Saints, Buckie, 1949; Rector, All Saints, Edinburgh, 1957; Chaplain, Royal Infirmary of Edinburgh, 1959-74; Canon of St Mary's Cathedral, Edinburgh, 1967; Synod Clerk, Diocese of Edinburgh, 1969. *Recreations:* Holy Land pilgrimage; choral music; ecclesiastical vestments and embroidery. *Address:* 44 Glendevon Place, Edinburgh EH12 5UJ. *T:* 031-337 9528.

BRADY, Terence Joseph; playwright, novelist and actor, since 1962; *b* 13 March 1939; *s* of Frederick Arthur Noel and Elizabeth Mary Brady; *m* Charlotte Mary Thérèse Bingham, *qv* ; one *s* one *d. Educ:* Merchant Taylors', Northwood; TCD (BA Moderatorship, History and Polit. Science). Actor: Would Anyone who saw the Accident?, The Dumb Waiter, Room at the Top, 1962; Beyond the Fringe, 1962-64; Present from the Corporation, In the Picture, 1967; Quick One 'Ere, 1968; films include: Baby Love; Foreign Exchange; TV appearances include plays, comedy series and shows, incl. Nanny, 1981, and Pig in the Middle, 1981 and 1982. Writer for TV: Broad and Narrow; TWTWTW; radio: Lines from my Grandfather's Forehead (BBC Radio Writers' Guild Award, Best Radio Entertainment, 1972); TV series with Charlotte Bingham: Boy Meets Girl; Take Three Girls; Upstairs Downstairs; Away From It All; Play for Today; Plays of Marriage; No—Honestly; Yes—Honestly; Thomas and Sarah; Pig in the Middle; The Complete Lack of Charm of the Bourgeoisie; Nanny. *Publications:* Rehearsal, 1972; The Fight Against Slavery, 1976; with Charlotte Bingham: Victoria, 1972; Rose's Story, 1973; Victoria and Company, 1974; Yes—Honestly, 1977. *Recreations:* painting, music, horse-riding, gardening, avoiding dinner parties. *Address:* The Pink House, 111 East Sheen Avenue, SW14 8AX; c/o A.D. Peters, Literary Agent, 10 Buckingham Street, WC2. *Clubs:* Roehampton; Stage Golfing.

BRAGG, Melvyn; writer; Presenter and Editor, The South Bank Show, for ITV, since 1978; *b* 6 Oct. 1939; *s* of Stanley Bragg and Mary Ethel (*née* Parks); *m* 1st, 1961, Marie-Elisabeth Roche (decd); one *d* ; 2nd, 1973, Catherine Mary Haste; one *s* one *d. Educ:* Nelson-Thomlinson Grammar Sch., Wigton; Wadham Coll., Oxford (MA). BBC Radio and TV Producer, 1961-67; writer and broadcaster, 1967-. Novelist, 1964-. FRSL. Mem. ACTT. Presenter, BBC TV series: 2nd House, 1973-77; Read all About It (also editor), 1976-77. Mem. Arts Council, and Chm. Literature Panel of Arts Council, 1977-80. *Plays:* Mardi Gras, 1976 (musical); Orion (TV), 1977; *screenplays:* Isadora; Jesus Christ Superstar; (with Ken Russell) Clouds of Glory. *Publications:* For Want of a Nail, 1965; The Second Inheritance, 1966; Without a City Wall, 1968; The Hired Man, 1969; A Place in England, 1970; The Nerve, 1971; Josh Lawton, 1972; The Silken Net, 1974; Speak for England, 1976; A Christmas Child, 1976; Autumn Manoeuvres, 1978; Kingdom Come, 1980; weekly column (Arts Counsel) in Punch; articles for various English jls. *Recreations:* walking, books. *Address:* 12 Hampstead Hill Gardens, NW3. *T:* 01-435 7215. *Clubs:* Garrick, PEN.

BRAGG, Stephen Lawrence, MA, SM; FEng; FIMechE; FRAeS; engineering consultant, since 1981; *b* 17 Nov. 1923; *e s* of late Sir Lawrence Bragg, CH, MC, FRS; *m* 1951, Maureen Ann (*née* Roberts); three *s. Educ:* Rugby Sch.; Cambridge Univ.; Massachusetts Inst. of Technology. BA 1945, MA 1949 (Cambridge); SM 1949 (MIT). FEng 1981. Rolls-Royce Ltd, 1944–48; Commonwealth Fund Fellow, 1948–49; Wm Jessop Ltd, Steelmakers, 1949–51; Rolls-Royce Ltd, 1951–71: Chief Scientist, 1960–63; Chief Research Engineer, 1964–68; Dir, Aero Div., 1969–71. Vice-Chancellor, Brunel Univ., 1971–81. Eastern Region Broker, SERC, 1981–. Chm., Cambridge DHA, 1982–. Member: Univ. Grants Cttee, 1966–71; Aeronautical Research Council, 1970–73; Court of ASC, Henley, 1972–81; SRC Engineering Bd, 1976–79; Airworthiness Requirements Bd, 1979–81; Chm., Adv. Cttee on Falsework, 1973–75. Hon. DEng (Sheffield), 1969. Corres. Mem. Venezuelan Acad. Sci., 1975. *Publications:* Rocket Engines, 1962; articles on Jet Engines, Research Management, University/Industry Collaboration, etc. *Recreation:* railway history. *Address:* 22 Brookside, Cambridge CB2 1JQ. *T:* Cambridge 62208. *Club:* Athenæum.

BRAHAM, Allan John Witney, PhD; Keeper and Deputy Director, the National Gallery, since 1978; *b* 19 Aug. 1937; *s* of Dudley Braham and Florence Mears; *m* 1963, Helen Clare Butterworth; two *d. Educ:* Dulwich Coll.; Courtauld Inst. of Art, Univ. of London (BA 1960, PhD 1967). Asst Keeper, National Gall., 1962, Dep. Keeper, 1973. Arts Council Exhibn (with Peter Smith), François Mansart, 1970–71; National Gall. Exhibitions: (co-ordinator and editor) The Working of the National Gallery, 1974; Velázquez, The Rokeby Venus, 1976; Giovanni Battista Moroni, 1978; Italian Renaissance Portraits, 1979; El Greco to Goya, 1980. *Publications:* Dürer, 1965; Murillo (The Masters), 1966; The National Gallery in London: Italian Painting of the High Renaissance, 1971; (with Peter Smith) François Mansart, 1973; Funeral Decorations in Early Eighteenth Century Rome, 1975; (with Hellmut Hager) Carlo Fontana: The Drawings at Windsor Castle, 1977; The Architecture of the French Enlightenment, 1980 (Hitchcock medal, Banister Fletcher Prize); National Gall. catalogues: The Spanish School (revised edn), 1970, and booklets: Velázquez, 1972; Rubens, 1972; Architecture, 1976; contrib. prof. jls, etc. *Recreation:* history of architecture. *Address:* 15A Acol Road, NW6 3AA.

BRAHAM, Harold, CBE 1960; HM Diplomatic Service, retired; *b* Constantinople, 11 Oct. 1907; *er s* of late D. D. Braham, of The Times; *m* 1941, Cicely Edith Norton Webber; one *s* one *d. Educ:* St Peter's Coll., Adelaide; New College, Oxford. Entered HM Consular Service, China, 1931. Retired as HM Consul-Gen., Paris, 1966. *Recreations:* contemporary Spanish history, carpentry. *Address:* Caserio Torret 19, San Luis, Prov. Baleares, Spain.

BRAHIMI, Lakhdar; Member, Central Committee, National Liberation Front, Algeria, since 1979; *b* 1934; *m* 1964; two *s* one *d. Educ:* Faculté de Droit and Institut des Sciences Politiques, Algiers; then Paris. Permanent Rep. of FLN and later of Provisional Govt of Algeria, in SE Asia, 1956–61; Gen. Secretariat, Min. of External Affairs, 1961–63; Ambassador to UAR and Sudan, and Permanent Rep. to Arab League, 1963–70; Ambassador to Court of St James's, 1971–79. *Address:* Immeuble Dulon, Chemin du Parc Gatliff, Algiers, Algeria.

BRAHMS, Caryl; critic and novelist; journalist specialising in criticism of the theatre arts; ballet critic; writer of film, broadcast and television scripts; *b* Surrey. *Educ:* privately and at Royal Academy of Music. Wrote stage versions of: Cindy-Ella, 1962; Sing a Rude Song (stage biography of Marie Lloyd), 1970; Television: The Great Inimitable Mr Dickens, 1970; Ooh! La! La!, adapted series of Feydeau farces, 1973; A Rather Reassuring Programme, 1977; (with Ned Sherrin): Beecham, 1980; The Mitford Girls, 1981. Mem., Nat. Theatre Bd, 1980–. Ivor Novello Award (with Ned Sherrin), 1966. *Publications:* The Moon on my Left, 1930; Footnotes To The Ballet, 1936; Robert Helpmann, Choreographer, 1943; Seat at the Ballet, 1951; Away went Polly, 1952; No Castanets, 1963; The Rest of the Evening's My Own (theatre criticism), 1964; (with S. J. Simon): A Bullet in the Ballet, 1937; Casino for Sale, 1938; The Elephant is White, 1939; Envoy on Excursion, 1940; Don't, Mr Disraeli, 1940 (Evening Standard Book of the Year); No Bed for Bacon, 1941; No Nightingales, 1944 (filmed); Titania Has a Mother, 1944; Six Curtains for Stroganova, 1945; Trottie True, 1946 (filmed); To Hell with Hedda, 1947; You Were There, 1950; (with Ned Sherrin): Cindy-Ella or I gotta Shoe, 1962; Rappel 1910, 1964; Benbow was his Name, 1966; film script: Girl/stroke/Boy, 1971; Paying the Piper (play; adapted from Feydeau), 1972; After You Mr Feydeau, 1975; Gilbert and Sullivan: Lost Chords and Discords, 1975; Nickleby and Me, 1975; Reflections in a Lake, 1976; Enter a Dragon, Stage Centre, 1979. *Recreations:* collecting Edwardian postcards and glass walking-sticks. *Address:* 3 Cambridge Gate, Regent's Park, NW1. *T:* 01-935 6439.

BRAILSFORD, Prof. Frederick, PhD; FIEE; Professor of Electrical Engineering, University College, London, 1951–70, now Emeritus Professor; *b* 22 Sept. 1903; *s* of John James and Frances Ann Brailsford; *m* 1934, Sarah Remington Smyth, Knock, County Down; one *d. Educ:* University Coll., Swansea. Whitworth Scholar, 1923; BSc(Eng) London (1st Class Hons), 1927; PhD, London, 1939. Apprentice in HM Dockyard, Pembroke, 1919–23; Electrical Engineer with Metropolitan-Vickers Electrical Co., Manchester, 1926–50. *Publications:* Magnetic Materials, 1960; Physical Principles of Magnetism, 1966; Introduction to the Magnetic Properties of Materials, 1968;

various papers to Institution of Electrical Engineers and elsewhere. *Addres* Locks Green, 244 Brooklands Road, Weybridge, Surrey. *T:* Weybrid 47548.

BRAILSFORD, John William; Keeper, Department of Prehistoric ar Romano-British Antiquities, British Museum, 1969–73; *b* 14 July 1918; *o* of Alfred and Dorothy H. M. Brailsford; *m* 1945, Mary Freeman Boaden; on *s* one *d. Educ:* Bedales; Emmanuel College, Cambridge. Sen. Exhibnr ar Scholar, BA, MA 1943. Royal Artillery (Survey), 1939–45; Intell. (Air Pho Interpretation), 1945–46. Asst Keeper, Dept of British and Mediev Antiquities, Brit. Mus., 1946; Dep. Keeper, 1963. FMA; FSA 1949; Fellov German Archaeolog. Inst., 1967. *Publications:* Museum Handbooks Mildenhall Treasure, 1947; Antiquities of Roman Britain, 1951; Late Prehistoric Antiquities of the British Isles, 1953; Antiquities from Hod Hi in the Durden Collection, 1962; (ed) Hod Hill: Excavations, 1951–58; 196 Early Celtic Masterpieces from Britain in the British Museum, 1975; pape in learned jls. *Recreations:* various. *Address:* Sunnyside, Brook En Chadlington, Oxon. *T:* Chadlington 378.

BRAIN, family name of **Baron Brain.**

BRAIN, 2nd Baron *cr* 1962, of Eynsham; **Christopher Langdon Brain;)** 1954; *b* 30 Aug. 1926; *s* of 1st Baron Brain, MA, DM, FRS, FRCP and Stell *er d* of late Reginald L. Langdon-Down; *S* father 1966; *m* 1953, Susan Mar *d* of George P. and Ethelbertha Morris; three *d. Educ:* Leighton Park Sch Reading; New College, Oxford. MA 1956. Royal Navy, 1946–4 Liveryman, 1955, Upper Warden, 1974–75, Asst, 1980–, Worshipful Co. c Weavers. Chm., Rhone-Alps Regional Council, British Chamber c Commerce, France, 1967. *Recreations:* bird watching, sailing, ski-ing. *Hei b* Hon. Michael Cottrell Brain, MA, DM, FRCP, FRCP Canada, Prof. c Medicine, McMaster Univ. [*b* 6 Aug. 1928; *m* 1960, Dr The Hon. Elizabe Ann Herbert, *e d* of Baron Tangley, KBE; one *s* two *d.*] *Address:* Woodland 52 Bove Town, Glastonbury, Somerset BA6 8JE. *Clubs:* Royal Harwic Yacht; Oxford and Cambridge Sailing Society.

BRAIN, Albert Edward Arnold; Regional Director (East Midlands Department of the Environment, and Chairman of Regional Economi Planning Board, 1972–77; *b* 31 Dec. 1917; *s* of Walter Henry and Henriet Mabel Brain; *m* 1947, Patricia Grace Gallop; two *s* one *d. Educ:* Rendcon Coll., Cirencester; Loughborough College. BSc (Eng) London, external; DL hons Loughborough; CEng, MICE, MIMunE. Royal Engineers, 1940–4 Bristol City Corp., 1946–48; Min. of Transport: Asst Engr, London, 1948–5 Civil Engr, Wales, 1954–63; Sen. Engr, HQ, 1963–67; Asst Chief Engr, H(1967–69; Divl Road Engr, W Mids, now Regional Controller (Roads an Transportation), 1969–72. *Recreations:* gardening, campanology. *Addres* Withyholt Lodge, Moorend Road, Charlton Kings, Cheltenham GL53 9BW *T:* Cheltenham 76264.

BRAIN, Sir (Henry) Norman, KBE 1963 (OBE 1947); CMG 1953; *b* 19 Jul 1907; *s* of late B. Brain, Rushall, Staffs; *m* 1939, Nuala Mary, *d* of late Cap A. W. Butterworth; one *s* (and one *s* decd). *Educ:* King Edward's Sch Birmingham; The Queen's Coll., Oxford (MA). Entered the Consula Service, 1930, and served at Tokyo, Kobe, Osaka, Tamsui, Manila, Mukdei Shanghai and Dairen; interned by Japanese, 1941–42; repatriated and served i Foreign Office, 1943; appointed to Staff of Supreme Allied Comdr, South East Asia, 1944–46; Political Adviser to Saigon Control Commission, 194 served with Special Commissioner in South-East Asia, at Singapore, 1946–4 Counsellor in Foreign Office, 1949; Inspector of HM Foreign Service Establ 1950–53; Minister, Tokyo, 1953–55; Ambassador to Cambodia, 1956–58; Asi Under-Sec. of State, FO, 1958–61; Ambassador to Uruguay, 1961–66, retire 1966. Chairman: Royal Central Asian Soc., 1970–74; Japan Soc. of Londoi 1970–73; Pres., British Uruguayan Soc., 1974–. *Recreations:* music, gol *Address:* St Andrews, Abney Court, Bourne End, Bucks. *Club:* Canning.

BRAIN, Ronald, CB 1967; Chairman, London and Quadrant Housing Trus 1977–79; *b* 1 March 1914; *s* of T. T. G. Brain, RN, and E. C. Brain (*née* Fruin *m* 1943, Lilian Rose (*née* Ravenhill); one *s* one *d. Educ:* Trowbridge Hig Sch. Audit Asst, Min. of Health, 1932; Principal, Min. of Health, 1946; As Sec., Min. of Housing and Local Govt, 1952; Under-Sec., 1959; Dep. Sec Dept of Environment (formerly Min. of Housing and Local Govt), 1966–7 *Recreations:* music, chess. *Address:* Flat 4, Badminton, Galsworthy Roa Kingston-upon-Thames, Surrey.

BRAINE, Sir Bernard (Richard), Kt 1972; DL; MP (C) South-East Divisio of Essex since 1955 (Billericay Division of Essex, 1950–55); *b* Ealing, Midd: 24 June 1914; *s* of Arthur Ernest Braine; *m* 1935, Kathleen Mary Faun; thre *s. Educ:* Hendon County Grammar Sch. Served North Staffs Regt in Wa of 1939–45: West Africa, SE Asia, NW Europe; Staff Coll., Camberley, 194 (sc); Lt-Col. Chm., British Commonwealth Producers' Organisation, 1958–6 Parly Sec., Min. of Pensions and National Insurance, 1960–61; Parly Under Sec. of State for Commonwealth Relations, 1961–62; Parly Sec., Min. c Health, 1962–64; Conservative front bench spokesman on Commonwealt Affairs and Overseas Aid, 1967–70; Chm., Select Cttees on Overseas Aic 1970–71, on Overseas Develt, 1973–74; Treasurer, UK Branch o Commonwealth Parly Assoc., 1974–77 (Dep. Chm., 1964 and 1970–74 Vice-Pres., Commonwealth Youth Exchange Council, 1979–; Chairmar British-German Parly Group, 1970–; British-Greek Parly Group, 1979–; Na Council on Alcoholism, 1973–82; UK Chapter, Soc. of Internat. Develt, 1976–

UK Section, Confedn des Anciens Combattants, 1980-; Dep. Chm., UK Standing Conf. on Refugees. President: Soc. for Defence of Unjustly Prosecuted, 1980-; River Thames Soc., 1981-. Associate Mem., Inst. of Develt Studies, Univ. of Sussex, 1971-; a Governor, Commonwealth Inst., 1968-81, Trustee, 1981-. FRSA 1971. DL Essex, 1978. CStJ. Grand Cross, German Order of Merit, 1974; European Peace Cross, 1979. *Address:* King's Wood, Rayleigh, Essex. *Clubs:* Carlton, Beefsteak.

BRAINE, John (Gerard); Author; *b* 13 April 1922; *s* of Fred and Katherine Braine; *m* 1955, Helen Patricia Wood; one *s* three *d. Educ:* St Bede's Grammar Sch., Bradford. Furniture-shop asst, bookshop asst, laboratory asst, progress chaser, in rapid succession, 1938-40; Asst, Bingley Public Library, 1940-49; HM Navy, 1942-43; Chief Asst, Bingley Public Library, 1949-51; free-lance writer, London and Yorks, with interval in hospital, 1951-54; Branch Librarian, Northumberland County Library, 1954-56; Branch Librarian, West Riding of Yorks County Library, 1956-57. Writer in Residence, Purdue Univ., 1978. ALA 1950. *Publications:* Room at the Top, 1957 (filmed 1958); The Vodi, 1959; Life at the Top, 1962 (filmed 1965); The Jealous God, 1964; The Crying Game, 1968; Stay with Me till Morning, 1970 (adapted for TV, 1980); The Queen of a Distant Country, 1972 (adapted for TV, 1978); Writing a Novel, 1974; The Pious Agent, 1975; Waiting for Sheila, 1976 (adapted for TV, 1977); Finger of Fire, 1977; J. B. Priestley, 1979; One and Last Love, 1981. *TV Series:* Man at the Top, 1970, 1972. *Recreations:* walking, talking, Victoriana, and dieting. *Address:* Lavender Cottage, 3 Lower Manor Road, Farncombe, Godalming, Surrey. *Club:* PEN.

BRAINE, Rear-Adm. Richard Allix, CB 1956; Retired; *b* 18 Nov. 1900; *m* 1922; one *s. Educ:* Dean Close Memorial Sch., Cheltenham. Joined RN as asst clerk, 1918; Comdr (S), Dec. 1938; Capt. (S), Dec. 1948; Rear-Adm. 1954. Command Supply Officer, Staff of Flag Officer Air (Home), 1954-56, Portsmouth, 1956-57. *Address:* The Old Cottage, Littlewick Green, near Maidenhead, Berks. *T:* Littlewick Green 4484.

BRAININ, Norbert, OBE 1960; Leader of Amadeus String Quartet; Professor of Chamber Music, Hochschule für Musik, Cologne, since 1979; *b* Vienna, 12 March 1923; *s* of Adolph and Sophie Brainin; *m* 1948, Kathe Kottow; one *d. Educ:* High Sch., Vienna. Commenced musical training in Vienna at age of seven and continued studies there until 1938; emigrated to London in 1938 and studied with Carl Flesch and Max Rostal; won Carl Flesch prize for solo violinists at the Guildhall Sch. of Music, London, 1946. Formed Amadeus String Quartet, 1947. DUniv York, 1968. Grand Cross of Merit, 1st cl. Fed. Republic of Germany, 1972; Cross of Honour for Arts and Science (Austria), 1972. *Address:* 19 Prowse Avenue, Bushey Heath, Herts. *T:* 01-950 7379.

BRAITHWAITE, Bernard Richard; His Honour Judge Braithwaite; a Circuit Judge (formerly County Court Judge), since 1971; *b* 20 Aug. 1917; *s* of Bernard Leigh Braithwaite and Emily Dora Ballard Braithwaite (*née* Thomas); unmarried. *Educ:* Clifton; Peterhouse, Cambridge. BA (Hons), Law. Served War: 7th Bn Somerset LI, 1939-43; Parachute Regt, 1943-46; Captain, Temp. Major. Called to Bar, Inner Temple, 1946. *Recreations:* hunting, sailing. *Address:* Summerfield House, Uley, Gloucestershire. *Club:* Boodle's.

BRAITHWAITE, Eustace Edward Adolph Ricardo; writer; Ambassador of Guyana to Venezuela, 1968-69; *b* 27 June 1922. *Educ:* New York Univ.; Cambridge Univ. Served War of 1939-45, RAF. Schoolteacher, London, 1950-57; Welfare Officer, LCC, 1958-60; Human Rights Officer, World Veterans Foundation, Paris, 1960-63; Lecturer and Education Consultant, Unesco, Paris, 1963-66; Permanent Rep. of Guyana to UN, 1967-68. Ainsfield-Wolff Literary Award, 1961; Franklin Prize. *Publications:* To Sir With Love, 1959; Paid Servant, 1962; A Kind of Homecoming, 1962; Choice of Straws, 1965; Reluctant Neighbours, 1972; Honorary White, 1976. *Recreations:* dancing and tennis.

BRAITHWAITE, Sir (Joseph) Franklin (Madders), Kt 1980; CBIM; Chairman: Baker Perkins Holdings plc, since 1980; Peterborough Independent Hospital plc; *b* 6 April 1917; *s* of late Sir John Braithwaite and Martha Janette (*née* Baker); *m* 1939, Charlotte Isabel, *d* of late Robert Elmer Baker, New York; one *s* one *d. Educ:* Bootham Sch.; King's Coll., Cambridge, 1936-39 (BA 1939, MA 1955). Served Army, 1940-46 (Captain). Joined Baker Perkins Ltd, 1946, Director 1950, Vice-Chm. 1956; Chairman, Baker Perkins Exports Ltd, 1966; Man. Dir, Baker Perkins Holdings Ltd, 1971. Director, Lloyds Bank Ltd, Eastern Counties Regional Board, 1979. Member: Mech. Engrg Industry Economic Development Cttee, 1974-; Management Board, 1978-82, Commercial and Econ. Cttee, 1977-, Engrg Employers' Fedn; Board of Fellows, 1974-79, Economic and Social Affairs Cttee, 1979-, BIM; Peterborough Develt Corp. President, Process Plant Assoc., 1977-79, Hon. life Vice-Pres., 1981. *Recreations:* music, golf. *Address:* 21 Westwood Park Road, Peterborough PE3 6JL. *T:* Peterborough 54238.

BRAITHWAITE, Prof. Richard Bevan, FBA 1957; Emeritus Knightbridge Professor of Moral Philosophy in the University of Cambridge; *b* 15 Jan. 1900; *s* of William Charles Braithwaite, Banbury; *m* 1st, 1925, Dorothea Cotter (*d* 1928), *d* of Sir Theodore Morison; 2nd, 1932, Margaret Mary, *d* of Rt Hon. C. F. G. Masterman; one *s* one *d. Educ:* Sidcot Sch., Somerset; Bootham Sch., York; King's Coll., Cambridge (Scholar, Prizeman, Research Student). MA Camb. 1926; Fellow of King's Coll., Camb. 1924-; University Lectr in Moral Science, 1928-34; Sidgwick Lectr in Moral Science, 1934-53; Knightbridge

Prof. of Moral Philosophy, 1953-67; Tarner Lectr at Trinity Coll., Camb., 1945-46; Pres. Mind Assoc., 1946; Pres. Aristotelian Soc., 1946-47; Annual Philosophical Lectr to British Academy, 1950; Pres. Brit. Soc. for the Philosophy of Science, 1961-63; Deems Lectr, New York Univ., 1962; Forwood Lectr, Liverpool Univ., 1968; Visiting Prof. of Philosophy: Johns Hopkins Univ., 1968; Univ. of Western Ontario, 1969; City Univ. of New York, 1970. Syndic Cambridge Univ. Press, 1943-62; Mem. Gen. Bd of Faculties, 1945-48; Mem. Council Senate, 1959-64. Hon. DLitt Bristol, 1963. *Publications:* Moral Principles and Inductive Policies (British Acad. Lecture, 1950); Scientific Explanation, 1953; Theory of Games as a tool for the Moral Philosopher (Inaugural Lecture), 1955; An Empiricist's view of the nature of Religious Belief (Eddington Lecture), 1955; Introd. to trans. of Gödel, 1962. Articles in Mind, Proc. Aristotelian Soc., etc. *Recreation:* reading novels. *Address:* King's College, Cambridge. *T:* Cambridge 350411; 11 Millington Road, Cambridge. *T:* Cambridge 350822.

BRAITHWAITE, Rodric Quentin, CMG 1981; HM Diplomatic Service; Minister Commercial, Washington, since 1982; *b* 17 May 1932; *s* of Henry Warwick Braithwaite and Lorna Constance Davies; *m* 1961, Gillian Mary Robinson; three *s* one *d* (and one *s* decd). *Educ:* Bedales Sch.; Christ's Coll., Cambridge. 1st cl. Mod. Langs, Pts I and II. Mil. Service, 1950-52. Joined Foreign (subseq. Diplomatic) Service, 1955; 3rd Sec., Djakarta, 1957-58; 2nd Sec., Warsaw, 1959-61; FO, 1961-63; 1st Sec. (Commercial), Moscow, 1963-66; 1st Sec., Rome, 1966-69; FCO, 1969-72; Vis. Fellow, All Souls Coll., Oxford, 1972-73; Head of European Integration Dept (External), FCO, 1973-75; Head of Chancery, Office of Permanent Rep. to EEC, Brussels, 1975-78; Head of Planning Staff, FCO, 1979-80; Asst Under Sec. of State, FCO, 1981. *Recreations:* chamber music (viola); sailing; Russia. *Address:* c/o Foreign and Commonwealth Office, SW1A 2AL.

BRAMALL, Sir Ashley; *see* Bramall, Sir E. A.

BRAMALL, Field Marshal Sir Edwin (Noel Westby), GCB 1979 (KCB 1974); OBE 1965; MC 1945; Chief of the Defence Staff, since 1982; *b* 18 Dec. 1923; *s* of Major Edmund Haselden Bramall and Mrs Katherine Bridget Bramall (*née* Westby); *m* 1949, Dorothy Avril Wentworth Vernon; one *s* one *d. Educ:* Eton College. Commnd into KRRC, 1943; served in NW Europe, 1944-45; occupation of Japan, 1946-47; Instructor, Sch. of Infantry, 1949-51; psc 1952; Middle East, 1953-58; Instructor, Army Staff Coll., 1958-61; on staff of Lord Mountbatten with special responsibility for reorganisation of MoD, 1963-64; CO, 2 Green Jackets, KRRC, Malaysia during Indonesian confrontation, 1965-66; comd 5th Airportable Bde, 1967-69; idc 1970; GOC 1st Div. BAOR, 1972-73; Lt-Gen., 1973; Comdr, British Forces, Hong Kong, 1973-76; Gen., 1976; C-in-C, UK Land Forces, 1976-78; Vice-Chief of Defence Staff (Personnel and Logistics), 1978-79; Chief of the General Staff, 1979-82. ADC (Gen.), 1979-82. Col Comdt, 3rd Bn Royal Green Jackets, 1973-; Col, 2nd Goorkhas, 1976-. *Recreations:* cricket, painting, tennis, travel. *Address:* Office of Chief of the Defence Staff, Ministry of Defence, Whitehall, SW1. *Clubs:* Travellers', Pratt's, MCC, I Zingari, Free Foresters, Butterflies.
See also Sir E. A. Bramall.

BRAMALL, Sir (Ernest) Ashley, Kt 1975; DL; Member (Lab), Greater London Council, Bethnal Green and Bow, since 1973 (Tower Hamlets, 1964-73); Chairman of the GLC, 1982-83; *b* 6 Jan. 1916; *er s* of Major E. H. Bramall and Mrs K. B. Bramall (*née* Westby); *m* ; three *s. Educ:* Westminster and Canford Schs; Magdalen Coll., Oxford. Served in Army, 1940-46; Major; psc 1945. Contested Fareham Div. of Hants, 1945; MP (Lab) for Bexley, 1946-50; contested Bexley, 1950, 1951, 1959; Watford, 1955. Barrister, Inner Temple. Member: LCC (Lab) Bethnal Green, 1961; Westminster City Council, 1959-68; Chm., 1965-67, Leader, 1970-81, ILEA; Chm., Council of LEAs, 1975-76, 1977-78, Vice-Chm., 1976-77; Leader, Management Panel, Burnham Cttee (Primary and Secondary), 1973-78; Chm., Nat. Council for Drama Trng, 1981. DL Greater London, 1981. *Address:* 2 Egerton House, 59 Belgrave Road, SW1. *T:* 01-828 0973.
See also Field Marshal Sir E. N. W. Bramall.

BRAMALL, Margaret Elaine, OBE 1969; MA; JP; Director, National Council for One Parent Families (formerly National Council for the Unmarried Mother and her Child), 1962-79; Lecturer, Applied Social Studies Course, University of Surrey, since 1979; *b* 1 Oct. 1916; *d* of Raymond Taylor, MA and Nettie Kate Taylor, BA; *m* 1939, Sir Ashley Bramall (marr. diss.); two *s. Educ:* St Paul's Girls' Sch., Hammersmith; Somerville Coll., Oxford (BA 1939, MA 1942); LSE (Social Science Hon. Certif. 1950); Inst. of Almoners (Certif. 1951). JP Richmond 1965. Dep. Chm., Juvenile Court Panel; Member: Probation Case Cttee; Co. After-Care Cttee. *Publications:* contrib., One Parent Families, ed Dulan Barber, 1975; contrib. social work jls. *Recreations:* gardening, family. *Address:* 5 Trafalgar Road, Twickenham, TW2 5EJ. *T:* 01-894 3998.

BRAMBLE, Courtenay Parker, CIE 1946; *b* 10 June 1900; *s* of Frank Bramble and Violet, *d* of Col M. G. Totterdell, VD; *m* 1st, 1928, Margaret Louise Lawrence, MBE, 1943, *d* of late Sir Henry Lawrence, KCSI; two *s* one *d* : 2nd, 1958, Doreen, *d* of C. E. Cornish, Lytham St Annes, Lancs. *Educ:* St Paul's Cathedral Choir Sch. (Coronation Medal, 1911); Cranleigh Sch.; King's Coll., Cambridge (MA, LLB). Barrister-at-law, Middle Temple; with The Bombay Co. Ltd, India, 1922-33; Senior partner Drennan & Co., Bombay, 1933-52; Silver Jubilee Medal, 1935; Coronation Medal, 1937. Man. Dir, Abercrombie, Bramble & Co. Ltd, 1954-73. Dir, East India Cotton

Assoc., Bombay, 1925-33; Mem., Indian Central Cotton Cttee, 1935-50. Mem. of Legislature, Bombay, 1935-50 (Leader, Progress Party); JP and Hon. Magistrate, Bombay; Chm., Children's Aid Soc., Bombay, 1931-39; Pres. Bombay Chamber of Commerce, 1940, 1945-46; Dep. Pres. Associated Chambers of Commerce, India, 1945; Chm. European Assoc., Bombay Branch, 1942-44; Mem., Bombay Presidency War Cttee, 1941-45; Trustee of Port of Bombay, 1949. Music critic, Times of India, 1925-41. Chairman: All India Quadrangular Cricket Cttee, 1935-39; UK Citizens Assoc. (Bombay), 1948-50; National Service Advisory Cttee, 1940-45; Bombay European Hospital Trust, 1943-50; Hon. Lieut, RINVR, 1940-45. Dir (Pres. 1962), Liverpool Cotton Association; Member Council: Cotton Research Corp., 1960-; Liverpool Sch. of Tropical Medicine, 1974-. *Address:* Lyndhurst, Childer Thornton, Cheshire. *T:* 051-339 3545. *Clubs:* United Oxford & Cambridge University; Royal Yacht (Bombay).

BRAMMA, Harry Wakefield, FRCO; Organist, Southwark Cathedral, since 1976; *b* 11 Nov. 1936; *s* of Fred and Christine Bramma. *Educ:* Bradford Grammar Sch.; Pembroke Coll., Oxford (MA). FRCO 1958. Dir of Music, King Edward VI Grammar Sch., Retford, Notts, 1961; Asst Organist, Worcester Cathedral, 1963; Dir of Music, The King's Sch., Worcester, 1965. Conductor, Kidderminster Choral Soc., 1972-79. Examnr, Associated Bd of Royal Schs of Music, 1978. Mem. Council, RCO, 1979. *Recreations:* travel, walking. *Address:* 52 Bankside, Southwark, SE1. *T:* 01-261 1291.

BRAMMER, Leonard Griffith, RE 1956 (ARE 1932); painter and etcher; Supervisor of Art and Crafts, Stoke-on-Trent Education Authority, 1952-69; *b* 4 July 1906; *s* of Frederick William Brammer and Minnie Griffith; *m* 1934, Florence May, *d* of William and Mary Barnett, Hanley; one *d. Educ:* Burslem Sch. of Art; Royal College of Art (Diploma Associate); awarded Travelling Scholarship, School of Engraving, Royal College of Art, 1930; represented in Tate Gallery, Victoria & Albert Museum, Ashmolean, Oxford, City of Stoke-on-Trent Art Gallery, City of Carlisle Art Gallery, Wedgwood Museum, Barlaston, Keele Univ., Gladstone Pottery Museum, Collection of Contemporary Art Soc., The Collections of The British Council, etc.; exhibitor at Royal Academy and all leading English and American exhibitions. *Recreation:* golf. *Address:* Swn-y-Wylan, Beach Road, Morfa Bychan, Porthmadog, Gwynedd.

BRAMWELL-BOOTH, Catherine, CBE 1971; a Commissioner of the Salvation Army; *b* London, 20 July 1883; *e c* of late General Bramwell Booth. Entered Salvation Army as an Officer, 1903; engaged in training Cadets at International Training Coll., 1907-17; International Sec. for Salvation Army in Europe, 1917; command of Women's Social Work in Great Britain and Ireland, 1926; International Sec. for Europe, 1946-48; retired 1948. Best Speaker award, Guild of Professional Toastmasters, 1978. *Publications:* Messages to the Messengers; A Few Lines; Bramwell Booth, 1933; (compiler) Bramwell Booth Speaks, 1947; Verse, 1947; Catherine Booth, the story of her loves, 1970. *Address:* North Court, Finchampstead, Berks.

BRANCH, Sir William Allan Patrick, Kt 1977; Managing Director and Grenada Representative on the Windward Islands Banana Association (Mirabeau, Capitol, Hope Development and Dougaldston Estates); *b* 17 Feb. 1915; *m* Thelma (*née* Rapier); one *s. Educ:* Grenada Boys' Secondary Sch. Dep. Manager, Mt Horne Agricl Estate, 1936; Manager Mt Horne, Boulogne, Colombier, Industry and Grand Bras Agricl Estates, 1941. Chairman, Eastern Dist Agricl Rehabilitation Cttee; Dep. Chm. Bd of Dirs, Grenada Banana Co-op Soc.; Director: Grenada Cocoa Industry; Parochial and Island Anglican Church Council; Managing Cttee: Grenada Boy Scouts Assoc.; St Andrew's Anglican Secondary Sch; Member, Central Agricl Rehabilitation Cttee. Knighthood awarded for services to agriculture, Grenada, Windward Islands. *Address:* Dougaldston, Gouyave, St John's, Grenada.

BRANCKER, Sir (John Eustace) Theodore, Kt 1969; President of the Senate, Barbados, 1971-76; *b* 9 Feb. 1909; *s* of Jabel Eustace and Myra Enid Vivienne Brancker; *m* 1967, Esme Gwendolyn Walcott. *Educ:* Harrison Coll., Barbados; Grad., Inst. of Political Secretaries; LSE (Certificate in Colonial Admin, 1933). Called to Bar, Middle Temple, 1933; in private practice; QC (Barbados) 1961. Mem., House of Assembly, Barbados, 1937-71 (Leader of Opposition, 1956-61; Speaker, 1961-71). Mem., Medico-Legal Soc. Mem., CPA. Life Fellow, Royal Commonwealth Soc.; Life Mem., Barbados Mus. and Historical Soc. Chm., 1973, Hon. Awards Liaison Officer, 1978, Duke of Edinburgh Award Scheme. Charter Pres., Rotary Club, Barbados. Mem. Adv. Bd, St Joseph Hosp. of Sisters of the Sorrowful Mother. Hon. LLD, Soochow Univ., 1973. FZS; FRSA (Life Fellow). Queen's Coronation Medal, 1953; Silver Jubilee Medal, 1977. *Recreations:* classical music, chess, drama. *Address:* Valencia, Holetown, St James's, Barbados. *T:* 20775. *Clubs:* Royal Over-Seas League (Life Mem.), Challoner (London); Empire, Bridgetown, Sunset Crest (Barbados); Rotary International.

BRAND, family name of **Viscount Hampden.**

BRAND, Hon. Lord; David William Robert Brand; a Senator of the College of Justice in Scotland, since 1972; *b* 21 Oct. 1923; *s* of late James Gordon Brand, Huntingdon, Dumfries, and Frances (*née* Bull); *m* 1st, 1948, Rose Josephine Devlin (*d* 1968); four *d*; 2nd, Bridget Veronica Lynch (*née* Russell), widow of Thomas Patrick Lynch, Beechmount, Mallow, Co. Cork. *Educ:* Stonyhurst Coll.; Edinburgh Univ. Served War of 1939-45; Commissioned Argyll and Sutherland Highlanders, 1942; Capt. 1945.

Admitted to Faculty of Advocates, 1948; Standing Junior Counsel to Dept of Education for Scotland, 1951; Advocate-Depute for Sheriff Court, 1953; Extra Advocate-Depute for Glasgow Circuit, 1955; Advocate-Depute, 1957-59; QC Scot. 1959; Senior Advocate-Depute, 1964; Sheriff of Dumfries and Galloway, 1968; Sheriff of Roxburgh, Berwick and Selkirk, 1970; Solicitor-General for Scotland, 1970-72. Kt, SMO Malta. *Publications:* Joint Editor, Scottish Edn of Current Law, 1948-61; Scottish Editor, Encyclopedia of Road Traffic Law and Practice, 1960-64; contributor to Scots Law Times. *Recreation:* golf. *Address:* Gospatric House, Dalmeny, W Lothian EH30 9TT. *T:* 031-331 1224. *Clubs:* New (Edinburgh); Honourable Company of Edinburgh Golfers.

BRAND, Alexander George, MBE 1945; Deputy Chairman of Traffic Commissioners (Scottish Area), since 1979; *b* 23 March 1918; *s* of David Wilson Brand and Janet Ramsay Brand (*née* Paton); *m* 1947, Helen Constance Campbell; one *s* one *d. Educ:* Ayr Academy; Univ. of Glasgow. MA 1940, LLB 1948. Admitted Solicitor, 1948. Served in Royal Air Force, 1940-46 (Flt Lt). Legal Asst: Dumbarton CC, 1948; in Office of Solicitor to the Secretary of State for Scotland, 1949; Sen. Legal Asst, 1955; Asst Solicitor, 1964; Dep. Solicitor, 1972-79. Sec. of Scottish Law Commn, 1965-72. *Recreations:* golf, theatre, music, reading. *Address:* 16 Queen's Avenue, Edinburgh EH4 2DF. *T:* 031-332 4472. *Club:* Bruntsfield Links Golfing Society (Edinburgh).

BRAND, Prof. Charles Peter; Professor of Italian, University of Edinburgh, since 1966; *b* 7 Feb. 1923; *er s* of Charles Frank Brand and Dorothy (*née* Tapping); *m* 1948, Gunvor, *yr d* of Col I. Hellgren, Stockholm; one *s* three *d. Educ:* Cambridge High Sch.; Trinity Hall, Cambridge. War Service, Intelligence Corps, 1943-46. Open Maj. Scholar, Trinity Hall, 1940; 1st Class Hons. Mod. Languages, Cantab., 1948; PhD, Cantab., 1951. Asst Lecturer, Edinburgh Univ., 1952; Asst Lecturer, subsequently Lecturer, Cambridge Univ., 1952-66. Cavaliere Ufficiale, al Merito della Repubblica Italiana, 1975. General Editor, Modern Language Review, 1971-77; Editor, Italian Studies, 1977-. *Publications:* Italy and the English Romantics, 1957; Torquato Tasso, 1965; Ariosto: a preface to the Orlando Furioso, 1974; contributions to learned journals. *Recreations:* sport, travel, gardening. *Address:* 21 Succoth Park, Edinburgh EH12 6BX. *T:* 031-337 1980.

BRAND, David William Robert; *see* Brand, Hon. Lord.

BRAND, Geoffrey Arthur; Under-Secretary, Department of Employment; *b* 13 June 1930; *s* of Arthur William Charles Brand and Muriel Ada Brand; *m* 1954, Joy Trotman; two *d. Educ:* Andover Grammar Sch.; University Coll., London. Entered Min. of Labour, 1953; Private Sec. to Parly Sec., 1956-57; Colonial Office, 1957-58; Private Sec. to Minister of Labour, 1965-66; Asst. Sec., Industrial Relations and Research and Planning Divisions 1966-72; Under-Sec., 1972-. *Address:* Cedarwood, Seer Green, Beaconsfield, Bucks. *T:* Beaconsfield 6637.

BRANDES, Lawrence Henry, CB 1982; Under Secretary, Office of Arts and Libraries, Department of Education and Science, 1978-82; *b* 16 Dec. 1924; *m* 1950, Dorothea Stanyon; one *s* one *d. Educ:* Beltane Sch.; London Sch. of Economics. Min. of Health, 1950; Principal Private Sec. to Minister, 1959; Nat. Bd for Prices and Incomes, 1966; Dept of Employment and Productivity, 1969; Under-Sec., DHSS, 1970; HM Treasury, 1975-78. *Address:* 4 Hogarth Hill, NW11.

BRANDO, Marlon; American actor, stage and screen; *b* Omaha, Nebraska, 3 April 1924; *s* of Marlon Brando; *m* 1957, Anna Kashfi (marr. diss., 1959); one *s. Educ:* Libertyville High Sch., Illinois; Shattuck Military Academy, Minnesota. Entered Dramatic Workshop of New School for Social Research, New York, 1943; has studied with Elia Kazan and Stella Adler. *Plays include:* I Remember Mama, Broadway, 1944; Truckline Café, 1946; Candida, 1946; A Flag is Born, 1946; The Eagle Has Two Heads, 1946; A Streetcar Named Desire, 1947. *Films include:* The Men, 1950; A Streetcar Named Desire, 1951; Viva Zapata!, 1952; Julius Cæsar, 1953; The Wild Ones, 1953; Désirée, 1954; On the Waterfront, 1954; Guys and Dolls, 1955; Tea House of the August Moon, 1956; Sayonara, 1957; The Young Lions, 1958; The Fugitive Kind, 1960; Mutiny on the Bounty, 1962; The Ugly American, 1963; Bedtime Story, 1964; The Satoteur, Code Name-Morituri, 1965; The Chase, 1966; Appaloosa, 1966; Southwest to Sonora, 1966; A Countess from Hong Kong, 1967; Reflections in a Golden Eye, 1967; Candy, 1968; The Night of the Following Day, 1969; Quiemad!, 1970; The Nightcomers, 1971; The Godfather, 1972; Last Tango in Paris, 1972; The Missouri Breaks, 1975; Apocalypse Now, 1977; Superman, 1978; The Formula, 1981. Directed, produced and appeared in One-Eyed Jacks, 1959. Academy Award, best actor of year, 1954, 1972. *Address:* Box 809, Beverly Hills, Calif, USA.

BRANDON, family name of **Baron Brandon of Oakbrook.**

BRANDON of OAKBROOK, Baron *cr* 1981 (Life Peer), of Hammersmith in Greater London; **Henry Vivian Brandon;** Kt 1966; MC 1942; PC 1978; a Lord of Appeal in Ordinary, since 1981; *b* 3 June 1920; *y s* of late Captain V. R. Brandon, CBE, RN, and late Joan Elizabeth Maud Simpson; *m* 1955, Jeanette Rosemary, *e d* of J. V. B. Janvrin; three *s* one *d. Educ:* Winchester Coll. (Scholar); King's Coll., Cambridge (Scholar 1938, Stewart of Rannoch Scholar 1939). Commnd 2nd Lieut RA 1939; Major 1944; served Madagascar, 1942, India and Burma, 1942-45. BA 1946. Barrister, Inner Temple, 1946 (Entrance and Yarborough Anderson Scholar); Member Bar Council, 1951-

53; QC 1961; Judge of the High Court of Justice, Probate, Divorce and Admiralty Division, 1966-71, Family Division, 1971-78; Judge of the Admiralty Court, 1971-78; Judge of the Commercial Court, 1977-78; a Lord Justice of Appeal, 1978-81. Member panel of Lloyd's arbitrators in salvage cases, 1961-66; Member panel from which Wreck Commissioners chosen, 1963-66. *Recreation:* cricket. *Address:* 6 Thackeray Close, SW19. *T:* 01-947 6344; House of Lords, SW1. *Club:* MCC.

BRANDON, (Oscar) Henry; Associate Editor and Chief American correspondent of the Sunday Times; *b* 9 March 1916; *m* 1970, Mabel Hobart Wentworth; one *d. Educ:* Univ. of Prague and Lausanne. Joined Sunday Times, 1939; War Correspondent, N Africa and W Europe, 1943-45; Paris Correspondent, 1945-46; Roving Diplomatic Correspondent, 1947-49; Washington Correspondent, 1950-; Syndicated Columnist for Washington Star, 1979-81. Hon. LittD Williams Coll., 1979. Foreign corresp. award, Univ. of California, Los Angeles, 1957; award, Lincoln Univ. Jefferson City, Missouri, 1962; Hannen Swaffer award, 1964. *Publications:* As We Are, 1961; In The Red, 1966; Conversations with Henry Brandon, 1966; The Anatomy of Error, 1970; The Retreat of American Power, 1973. *Recreations:* ski-ing, tennis, swimming, photography. *Address:* 531 National Press Building, Washington, DC 20045, USA. *T:* 628-4310. *Clubs:* National Press, Overseas Writers (Washington, DC).

BRANDON, Prof. Percy Samuel, (Prof. Peter Brandon); Professor of Electrical Engineering, since 1971, Head of Electrical Division, since 1981, University of Cambridge; *b* 9 Nov. 1916; *s* of P. S. Brandon, OBE; *m* 1942, Joan Edith Marriage, GRSM (London), LRAM; two *s. Educ:* Chigwell Sch.; Jesus Coll., Cambridge (MA). Joined The Marconi Company, 1939; Research Div., 1940-71. Frequency Measurement, 1940-44: Aerial Section, 1944-45. FM Radar, 1945-53; Chief of Guidance Systems, 1953-57; Chief of Mathematics and Systems Analysis Gp, 1957-65; Manager of Theoretical Sciences Laboratory, 1965-68; Asst Dir of Research, 1965-68; Manager of Research Div. of GEC-Marconi Electronics, 1968-71. Part-time lecturing at Mid-Essex Technical Coll., and others, 1945-66. FInstP, FIEE. *Publications:* contribs to Marconi Review, IEE Proc., Agardograph, Electronic Engineering, etc. *Recreation:* colour photography. *Address:* University Engineering Laboratory, Trumpington Street, Cambridge CB2 1PZ. *T:* Cambridge 66466; New Courts, 8 Bridge Lane, Little Shelford, Cambs CB2 5HE. *T:* Cambridge 842541.

BRANDRETH, Gyles Daubeney; author, broadcaster, journalist, theatrical producer; Chairman, Victorama Ltd, since 1974; *b* 8 March 1948; *s* of late Charles Brandreth and of Alice Addison; *m* 1973, Michèle Brown; one *s* two *d. Educ:* Lycée Français de Londres; Betteshanger Sch., Kent; Bedales Sch., Hants; New Coll., Oxford (Scholar). Pres. Oxford Union, Editor of Isis. Chm., Archway Productions Ltd, 1971-74; Dir, Colin Smythe Ltd, 1971-73. Freelance journalist, 1968-: contrib. Observer, Guardian, Daily Mail, Daily Mirror, Evening Standard, Spectator, Punch, Homes & Gardens, She, Woman's Own; Columnist: Honey, 1968-69; Manchester Evening News, 1971-72; Woman, 1972-73; Press Assoc. weekly syndicated column in USA, 1981-. Broadcaster, 1969-: over 1000 appearances on radio and TV; series for ITV incl.: Child of the Sixties, 1969; Puzzle Party, 1977; Chatterbox, 1977-78; Memories, 1982. Theatrical producer, 1971-: Through the Looking-Glass, 1972; Oxford Theatre Fest., 1974, 1976; The Dame of Sark, Wyndham's, 1974; The Little Hut, Duke of York's, 1974; Dear Daddy, Ambassador's, 1976; also Son et Lumière. Founder, British Pantomime Assoc., 1971. Dir, Europ. Movement's People for Europe campaign, 1975. Founder, National Scrabble Championships, 1971; Europ. Monopoly Champion, 1974; three times holder, world record for longest-ever after-dinner speech (4 hrs 19 mins, 1976; 11 hrs, 1978; 12 hrs 30 mins, 1982). *Publications: general:* Created in Captivity, 1972; Discovering Pantomime, 1973; Brandreth's Bedroom Book, 1973; I Scream for Ice Cream, 1974; A Royal Scrapbook, 1976; Yarooh!, 1976; The Funniest Man on Earth, 1977; The Magic of Houdini, 1978; The Complete Husband, 1978; Pears Book of Words, 1979; The Last Word, 1979; The Joy of Lex, 1980; More Joy of Lex, 1982; Theatrical Disasters, 1982; *family entertainment:* Brandreth's Party Games, 1972; Complete Book of Home Entertainment, 1974; Games for Trains, Planes & Wet Days, 1974; Brandreth's Christmas Book, 1975; Brandreth's Book of Waiting Games, 1975; (with Cyril Fletcher) Generation Quiz Book, 1975; Knight Book of Scrabble, 1975; Pears Family Quiz Book, 1976; (with David Farris) Scrambled Exits, 1976; Pears All the Year Round Quiz Book, 1977; Teach Yourself Indoor Games, 1977; Pears Round the World Quiz Book, 1978; The Little Red Darts Book, 1978; Everyman's Indoor Games, 1981; The Puzzle Mountain, 1981; *for children:* over fifty books of stories, jokes, riddles, games, puzzles, magic and fun. *Address:* Victorama Ltd, 14-16 Regent Street, SW1Y 4PS. *T:* 01-727 4290.

BRANDRICK, David Guy, CBE 1981; Secretary, National Coal Board, since 1972; *b* 17 April 1932; *s* of Harry and Minnie Brandrick; *m* 1956, Eunice Fisher; one *s* one *d. Educ:* Newcastle-under-Lyme High Sch.; St John's Coll., Oxford (MA). Joined National Coal Board, 1955; Chairman's Office, 1957; Principal Private Secretary to Chairman, 1961; Departmental Sec., Production Dept, 1963; Dep. Sec. to the Board, 1967. *Recreation:* walking. *Address:* c/o Hobart House, Grosvenor Place, SW1.

BRANDT, Peter Augustus; Chairman, Atkins Fulford Ltd, since 1977; *b* 2 July 1931; *s* of late Walter Augustus Brandt and late Dorothy Gray Brandt (*née* Crane); *m* 1962, Elisabeth Margaret (*née* ten Bos); two *s* one *d. Educ:*

Eton Coll.; Trinity Coll., Cambridge (MA). Joined Wm Brandt's Sons & Co. Ltd, Merchant Bankers, 1954; Mem. Bd, 1960; Chief Executive, 1966; resigned, 1972. Director: London Life Assoc., 1962; Corp. of Argentine Meat Producers (CAP) Ltd and affiliates, 1970; Edward Bates (Holdings) Ltd, 1972-77; Edward Bates & Sons Ltd, 1972-77 (Chm., 1974-77). *Recreations:* sailing, rowing, steam engines, wild fowl. *Address:* Spout Farm, Boxford, Colchester, Essex. *Clubs:* Carlton; Leander (Henley-on-Thames); Royal Harwich Yacht (Ipswich).

BRANDT, William, (Bill Brandt), RDI 1978; photographer; *b* 1904; parents of Russian descent; British by birth. *Educ:* studied under Man Ray, Paris, in 1930s. Spent much of early youth in Germany and Switzerland; worked in Paris for many years. At age of 25 became a photo-journalist; settled in London, 1931; towards the end of War of 1939-45 he began to photograph nudes and did portraits and landscapes. Exhibition at Museum of Modern Art, New York, Oct.-Nov. 1969; the Arts Council put on this exhibition at the Hayward Gallery, London, Apr.-May 1970 (Prof. Aaron Scharf wrote introd. to catalogue, Herbert Spencer designed catalogue and poster); subseq. the exhibits were shown at 12 centres outside London and then returned to New York; exhibn of portraits, Nat. Portrait Gall., 1982. Selected The Land exhibition, V and A, 1975-76, Edinburgh, Belfast and Cardiff, 1976. Hon. FRPS 1980. Hon. Dr RCA, 1977. Médaille de la Ville de Paris, 1980. *Publications:* Perspective of Nudes, 1961; Shadow of Light, 1966, rev. edn 1977; (ed) The Land: twentieth century landscape photographs, 1975; Nudes 1945-1980, 1980; contrib. to magazines in Europe, USA, etc.

BRANDT, Willy; Chairman, Social Democratic Party (SPD), Federal Republic of Germany, since 1964; Member, German Federal Parliament, 1949-57, and since 1969; Member, European Parliament, since 1979; *b* 18 Dec. 1913; *m* 1948, Rut Hansen; three *s* one *d. Educ:* Johanneum, Lübeck; University of Oslo. Fled from Lübeck to Norway, 1933. Chief Editor, Berliner Stadtblatt, 1950-51. Mem., Social Democratic Party (SPD), 1931-; Rep. Federal Board of SPD (German Social Democratic Party) in Berlin, 1948-49, Deputy Chairman of SPD, 1962-63. President Berlin House of Representatives, 1955-57; Governing Mayor of W Berlin, 1957-66; President German Conference of Mayors, 1958-63; President German Federal Council, 1957-58; Vice-Chancellor and Foreign Minister, 1966-69, Chancellor 1969-74, Federal Republic of Germany. Pres., Socialist International, 1976. Chm., Commn on Develt Issues, 1977-80. Dr (*hc*): Pennsylvania Univ., 1959; Maryland Univ., 1960; Harvard Univ., 1963; Hon. DCL, Oxford Univ., 1969. Nobel Prize for Peace, 1971. Grosskreuz des Verdienstordens der Bundesrepublik Deutschland, 1959. *Publications:* Efter segern, 1944; Forbrytere og andre Tyskere, 1946; (with Richard Löwenthal) Ernst Reuter: Ein Leben für die Freiheit, 1957; Von Bonn nach Berlin, 1957; Mein Weg nach Berlin (recorded by Leo Lania), 1960; Plädoyer für die Zukunft, 1961; The Ordeal of Co-existence, 1963; Begegnungen mit Kennedy, 1964; (with Günter Struve) Draussen, 1966 (UK, as In Exile, 1971); Friedenspolitik in Europa, 1968; Essays, Reflections and Letters 1933-47, 1971; Der Wille zum Frieden, 1971; Uber den Tag hinaus, 1974; Begegnungen und Einsichten, 1976 (UK as People and Politics, 1978); Frauen heute, 1978; many publications on topical questions in Sweden and Norway; articles in home and foreign journals. *Address:* (office) Erich-Ollenhauer-Strasse 1, 5300 Bonn 1, Germany. *T:* 5321.

BRANIGAN, Sir Patrick (Francis), Kt 1954; QC; Chairman, Pensions Appeal Tribunal, 1955-81; *b* 30 Aug. 1906; *e s* of late D. Branigan and Teresa, *d* of Thomas Clinton, Annagassan, Co. Louth; *m* 1935, Prudence, *yr d* of late Dr A. Avent, Seaton, Devon; one *s* one *d. Educ:* Newbridge Coll., Co. Kildare; Trinity Coll., Dublin. BA 1st Class Hons in Law and Political Science and gold medallist, 1928; called to Irish Bar, Certificate of Honour, 1928 (1st Victoria Prize, 1927); called to Bar, Gray's Inn, 1935. Practised at Irish Bar, 1928-30; Downing Coll., Cambridge, 1930-31; Colonial Administrative Service, Kenya, 1931; Crown Counsel, Tanganyika, 1934; Solicitor-General, N. Rhodesia, 1938; Chairman NR Man-power Cttee, 1939-41; Chairman Conciliation Board, Copperbelt Strike, 1940; Member NR. Nat. Arbitration Tribunal, 1940-46; Member Strauss Arbitration Tribunal, Bulawayo, 1944; Chairman, Road Transport Services Board and Electricity Board of N. Rhodesia, 1939-46; Legal Secretary to Govt of Malta and Chairman Malta War Damage Commission, 1946-48; periodically acting Lieut-Governor of Malta, 1947-48. Minister of Justice and Attorney-General, Gold Coast, 1948-54; QC Gold Coast, 1949; retired, 1955. Chairman of Commission of inquiry into Copperbelt industrial unrest, 1956; Member Industrial Disputes Tribunal, 1955-59. Dep. Chm. Devon QS, 1958-71; a Recorder of the Crown Court, 1972-75. Chairman: Agricultural Land Tribunal for SW Area of England, 1955-79; Nat. Insurance Med. Appeal Tribunal, SW Reg., 1960-78; Mental Health Review Tribunal, SW England, 1960-78. Knight Commander of Order of St Gregory, 1956. *Recreations:* golf, fishing. *Address:* Willhayne, Colyton, Devon. *T:* Colyton 52435.

BRANN, Col William Norman, OBE 1967; ERD; Lord Lieutenant for County Down, since 1980; *b* 16 Aug. 1915; *s* of Rev. William Brann, BA, LLB, and Francesca Brann; *m* 1950, Anne Elizabeth Hughes; one *s* two *d. Educ:* Campbell Coll., Belfast. With Beck & Scott Ltd, Food Importers, Belfast, 1934-80. Served War of 1939-45, Army; TA, 1947-53. High Sheriff, County Down, 1982. *Recreations:* farming, gardening, hunting. *Address:* Drumavaddy, Craigantlet, Newtownards, Co. Down, N Ireland. *T:* Holywood 2224. *Club:* Ulster (Belfast).

BRANNAN, Charles Franklin; lawyer; *b* 23 Aug. 1903; *s* of John Brannan and Ella Louise Street; *m* 1932, Eda Seltzer; no *c. Educ:* Regis Coll., and University of Denver Law Sch., Denver, Colorado, USA. Private law practice, Denver, Colorado, 1929-35; Asst Regional Attorney: Resettlement Administration, Denver, 1935-37; Regional Attorney, Office of the Solicitor, US Dept of Agriculture, Denver, 1937-41; Regional Director of Farm Security Administration, US Dept of Agriculture, Denver, 1941-44; Asst Administrator, Farm Security Administration, US Dept of Agriculture, Washington, DC, April-June 1944; Asst Secretary of Agriculture, Washington, DC, June 1944-48; Secretary of Agriculture, USA, 1948-Jan. 1953. Pres., Bd of Water Commissioners, Denver, 1976. Hon. Degrees: Doctor of Laws from the University of Denver and Doctor of Science from the Colorado Agricultural and Mechanical Coll. *Address:* (home) 3131 East Alameda, Denver, Colorado 80209, USA; (office) 12025 E 45th Avenue, Denver, Colo 80239. *Club:* Denver Athletic (Denver, Colorado).

BRANSON, Rear Adm. Cecil Robert Peter Charles, CBE 1975; Managing Director, UK Trawlers Mutual Insurance Co. Ltd (Hull), since 1977; *b* 30 March 1924; *s* of Cecil Branson and Marcelle Branson; *m* 1946, Sonia Moss; one *d. Educ:* RNC, Dartmouth. Served, HMS Dragon, W Africa, S Atlantic, Indian Ocean and Far East (present during time of fall of Singapore and Java), 1941-42; Sub-Lieut's Courses, 1942-43; qual. as submarine specialist, served in HM S/M Sea Rover, Far East, 1944-45; various appts in S/Ms, 1945-53; First Lieut, HMS Defender, 1953-55; jssc; CO, HMS Roebuck, Dartmouth Trng Sqdn, 1957; Staff, Flag Officer Flotillas Mediterranean, 1959-60; Jt Planning Staff, MoD, 1960-62; Exec. Officer, HMS Victorious, Far East, 1962-64; CO, HMS Rooke, Gibraltar, 1965; NATO Def. Coll., 1965; Defence Planning Staff, MoD, 1966-68; CO, HMS Phoebe, and Captain (D) Londonderry Sqdn, 1968-70; Naval Attaché, Paris, 1970-73; CO, HMS Hermes, 1973-74 (Hermes headed RN task force evacuating Brit. and foreign subjects from Cyprus beaches after Turkish invasion, 1973); Asst Chief of Naval Staff (Ops), MoD, 1975-77; retired. Comdr 1957, Captain 1965, Rear Adm. 1975. *Address:* The Old Parsonage, West End, Swanland, North Humberside. *Club:* Army and Navy.

BRANSON, Edward James, MA; a Metropolitan Stipendiary Magistrate, since 1971; barrister-at-law; *b* 10 March 1918; *s* of late Rt Hon. Sir George Branson, PC, sometime Judge of High Court, and late Lady (Mona) Branson; *m* 1949, Evette Huntley, *e d* of late Rupert Huntley Flindt; one *s* two *d. Educ:* Bootham Sch., York; Trinity Coll., Cambridge. Served War, 1939-46, Staffordshire Yeomanry: Palestine, Egypt, and Western Desert 1941-42; GSO 3 (Ops) attd 2 NZ Div. for Alamein, 1942; GS02 (Ops), attd 6 (US) Corps for Salerno and Anzio landings, 1943-44; subseq. GSO2 (Ops) 53 (W) Div. in Germany. Called to the Bar, Inner Temple, 1950; practised London and SE Circuit. *Recreations:* shooting, riding, fishing, archaeology. *Address:* Tanyard Farm, Shamley Green, near Guildford, Surrey. *T:* Guildford 893133.

BRANSON, William Rainforth, CBE 1969; retired; *b* 2 Jan. 1905; *s* of late A. W. Branson, JP; *m* 1932, Dorothy Iris Green (*d* 1982); no *c. Educ:* Rydal Sch.; University of Leeds. BSc, 1st Class Hons (Fuel and Gas Engrg), 1927; MSc 1930. Asst Engineer, Gas Light & Coke Co., London, 1927-37; Asst Engineer, later Dep. Engineer, Cardiff Gas Light & Coke Co., 1937-45; Dep. Controller, later Controller, Public Utilities Br., Control Commn for Germany, 1945-49; Planning Engineer, Wales Gas Board, 1949-51; Technical Officer, E. Midlands Gas Board, 1952-54; Dep. Chairman, W. Midlands Gas Board, 1954-65; Chm., Scottish Gas Bd, 1965-68; Dir, Woodall-Duckham Group Ltd, 1969-73. President, Instn of Gas Engineers, 1964-65. *Recreation:* music. *Address:* 3 Meldon Court, East Budleigh Road, Budleigh Salterton EX9 6HE.

BRANT, Colin Trevor, CMG 1981; CVO 1979; HM Diplomatic Service; Consul General and Director of Trade Promotion, Johannesburg, since 1982; *b* 2 June 1929; *m* 1954, Jean Faith Walker; one *s* two *d. Educ:* Christ's Hospital, Horsham; Sidney Sussex Coll., Cambridge (MA). Served Army, 4th Hussars (now Queen's Royal Irish Hussars), active service, Malaya, 1948-49; Pilot, Cambridge Univ. Air Squadron, 1951-52. Joined Sen. Br., Foreign Office, 1952; MECAS, Lebanon, 1953-54; Bahrain, 1954; Amman, 1954-56; FO, 1956-59; Stockholm, 1959-61; Cairo, 1961-64; Joint Services Staff Coll., Latimer, Bucks, 1964-65 (jssc); FO, 1965-67; Head of Chancery and Consul, Tunis, 1967-68; Asst Head, Oil Dept, FCO, 1969-71; Counsellor (Commercial), Caracas, 1971-73; Counsellor (Energy), Washington, 1973-78; Ambassador to Qatar, 1978-81; FCO Fellow, St Antony's Coll., Oxford, 1981-82. Donation Governor, Christ's Hosp., 1980. *Recreations:* music, painting, history. *Address:* c/o Foreign and Commonwealth Office, SW1; Wethersfield Manor, Braintree, Essex. *Clubs:* Travellers', Royal Commonwealth Society.

BRASH, Rev. Alan Anderson, OBE 1962; Moderator, Presbyterian Church of New Zealand, 1978-79; *b* 5 June 1913; *s* of Thomas C. Brash, CBE, New Zealand, and Margaret Brash (*née* Allan); *m* 1938, Eljean Ivory Hill; one *s* one *d. Educ:* Dunedin Univ., NZ (MA); Edinburgh Univ. (BD). Parish Minister in NZ, 1938-46 and 1952-56; Gen. Sec., NZ Nat. Council of Churches, 1947-52 and 1957-64, East Asia Christian Conf., 1958-68; Dir, Christian Aid, London, 1968-70; Dir, Commn on Inter-Church Aid, Refuge and World Service, WCC, 1970-73; Dep. Gen. Sec., WCC, 1974-78. Hon. DD Toronto, 1971. *Address:* 13 Knightsbridge Drive, Forrest Hill, Auckland 10, New Zealand.

BRASH, Robert, CMG 1980; HM Diplomatic Service; Ambassador t(Indonesia, since 1981; *b* 30 May 1924; *s* of Frank and Ida Brash; *m* 1954 Barbara Enid Clarke; three *s* one *d. Educ:* Trinity Coll., Cambridge (Exhbnr) War Service, 1943-46. Entered Foreign Service, 1949; Djakarta, 1951-55; FO 1955-58; First Sec., 1956; Jerusalem, 1958-61; Bonn, 1961-64; Bucharest 1964-66; FCO, 1966-70; Counsellor, 1968; Canadian Nat. Defence Coll. 1970-71; Counsellor and Consul-Gen., Saigon, 1971-73; Counsellor, Vienna 1974-78; Consul-Gen., Düsseldorf, 1978-81. *Recreations:* walking, gardening golf. *Address:* c/o Foreign and Commonwealth Office, SW1. *Club:* Roya Automobile.

BRASHER, Christopher William; Columnist and Olympic Correspondent The Observer, since 1961; Race Director, London Marathon since 1980 Chairman, Fleetfoot Ltd, since 1979; Director: New Balance Athletic Shoe: (UK) Ltd, since 1982; Brasher Leisure Ltd, since 1977; *b* 21 Aug. 1928; *s* of William Kenneth Brasher and Katie Howe Brasher; *m* 1959, Shirley Bloomer one *s* two *d. Educ:* Rugby Sch.; St John's Coll., Cambridge. MA. Pres. Mountaineering Club and Athletic Club, Cambridge Univ. Managemen Trainee and Jun. Executive, Mobil Oil Co., 1951-57; Sports Editor, The Observer, 1957-61; BBC Television: Reporter, Tonight, 1961-65; Editor Time Out, and Man Alive, 1964-65; Head of Gen. Features, 1969-72 reporter/producer, 1972-. Rep. GB, Olympic Games, 1952 and 1956; Golc Medal for 3,000 metres Steeplechase, 1956. National Medal of Honour Finland, 1975. *Publications:* The Red Snows (with Sir John Hunt), 1960 Sportsmen of our Time, 1962; Tokyo 1964: a diary of the XVIIIth Olympiad 1964; Mexico 1968: a diary of the XIXth Olympics, 1968; Munich 72, 1972 *Recreations:* mountains, orienteering, social running. *Address:* The Navigator's House, River Lane, Richmond, Surrey. *T:* 01-940 8822. *Clubs* Alpine, Hurlingham; Ranelagh Harriers (Petersham).

BRASNETT, Rev. Dr Bertrand Rippington, DD Oxon, 1935; *b* 22 Jan 1893; *e s* of Stanley Brasnett, The Manor House, Marham, Norfolk, *gs* of Edward Rowing Brasnett, West Bilney House, Norfolk; unmarried. *Educ* Oxford High Sch.; private tutor; Keble Coll., Oxford; Cuddesdor Theological Coll. Squire Scholar of the University of Oxford, 1911-15, 2nc class Classical Moderations, 2nd class Literæ Humaniores, BA, MA, Diploma in Theology with Distinction, BD; Deacon, 1916; Priest, 1918; Chaplain and Asst Master, Bradfield Coll., Berks, 1916-18; Priest-in-charge, Coleshill Bucks, 1918-22; Chaplain and Lecturer, Bishops' Coll., Cheshunt, 1922-25 Vice-Principal, 1925-29, Principal and Pantonian Prof., 1930-42, of the Theological Coll. of the Scottish Episcopal Church, Edinburgh; Hon Chaplain of St Mary's Cathedral, Edinburgh, 1926-29; Canon, 1930-42, and Chancellor, 1940-42, of St Mary's Cathedral, Edinburgh; Examining Chaplair to the Bishop of Edinburgh, 1930-42; Select Preacher, University of Oxford 1941-43. *Publications:* The Suffering of the Impassible God, 1928; The Infinity of God, 1933; God the Worshipful, 1935. *Address:* Pleasant View, 15 Jack Straw's Lane, Headington, Oxford OX3 0DL.

BRASNETT, John; HM Diplomatic Service; Counsellor (Economic anc Commercial), Ottawa, since 1980; *b* 30 Oct. 1929; *s* of late Norman Vincen(Brasnett and of Frances May Brasnett (*née* Hewlett); *m* 1956, Jennifer Anr Reid; one *s* one *d. Educ:* Blundells Sch.; Selwyn Coll., Cambridge (BA) Served Royal Artillery, 1948-49. Colonial Administrative Service, Uganda 1953-65; retired from HM Overseas CS as Dep. Administrator, Karamoja District, 1965; entered HM Diplomatic Service, 1965; 1st Sec., OECD Delegn 1968; Dep. High Comr, Freetown, 1970; FCO, 1973; Olympic Attaché Montreal, 1975-76; Dep. High Comr, Accra, 1977-80. *Recreations:* reading photography. *Address:* c/o Foreign and Commonwealth Office, SW1A 2AH *Club:* Royal Commonwealth Society.

BRASS, John, CBE 1968; BSc, FEng, FIMinE, MICE; FRSA; Member National Coal Board, 1971-73; Chairman, Amalgamated Constructior Company, Barnsley, since 1977; *b* 22 Oct. 1908; 2nd *s* of late John Brass Mining Engineer, and late Mary Brass (*née* Swainston); *m* 1934, Jocelyn Constance Cape, Stroud, Glos; three *s* one *d. Educ:* Oundle Sch.; Birmingham Univ. (BSc Hons). Various appointments, all in mining; Chm., W idlands Division, NCB, 1961-67; Regional Chm., Yorks and NW Areas, NCB 1967-71. *Address:* 2 Fledborough Road, Wetherby, W Yorks.

BRASS, Prof. William, CBE 1981; FBA 1979; Professor of Medical Demography since 1972, Director of Centre for Population Studies since 1978 and Head of Department of Medical Statistics and Epidemiology since 1977 London School of Hygiene and Tropical Medicine; *b* 5 Sept. 1921; *s* of Johr Brass and Margaret Tait (*née* Haigh); *m* 1948, Betty Ellen Agnes Topp; two *d. Educ:* Royal High Sch., Edinburgh; Edinburgh Univ. (MA Hons Math and Nat. Phil., 1943). Scientific Officer, Royal Naval Scientific Service 1943-46; E African Statistical Dept, Colonial Service, 1948-55; Lectr ir Statistics, 1955-64, Sen. Lectr 1964, Aberdeen Univ.; London Sch. of Hygiene and Trop. Medicine: Reader in Med. Demography, 1965-72; Dir, Centre for Overseas Population Studies, 1974-78; Vice-Pres. and Pres.-elect, Internat Union for the Scientific Study of Population, 1981-. Mindel Sheps Award for distinguished contribn to demography, Population Assoc. of America, 1978 *Publications:* The Demography of Tropical Africa, 1968; Metodos para estimar la fecundidad y la mortalidad en poblaciones con datos Limitados selección de trabajos, 1974; Methods of Estimating Fertility and Mortality from Limited and Defective Data, 1975; about 100 papers in learned jls *Recreations:* travel, observing art and archaeology. *Address:* 3 Holt Close N10 3HW. *T:* 01-883 1195.

BRASSEY, family name of **Baron Brassey of Apethorpe.**

BRASSEY OF APETHORPE, 3rd Baron, *cr* 1938, of Apethorpe; **David Henry Brassey**; Bt 1922; JP; DL; *b* 16 Sept. 1932; *er s* of 2nd Baron Brassey of Apethorpe, MC, TD, and late Lady Brassey of Apethorpe; *S* father, 1967; *m* 1st, 1958, Myrna Elizabeth (*d* 1974), *o d* of Lt-Col John Baskervyle-Glegg; one *s*; 2nd, 1978, Caroline, *y d* of late Lt-Col G. A. Evill; two *d*. Commissioned, Grenadier Guards, 1951; Major, 1966, retired, 1967. JP 1970, DL 1972, Northants. *Heir: s* Hon. Edward Brassey, *b* 9 March 1964. *Address:* The Manor House, Apethorpe, Peterborough. *T:* Kingscliffe 231. *Club:* White's.

BRASSEY, Brevet-Col Hugh Trefusis, OBE 1959; MC 1944; Lord Lieutenant of Wiltshire, since 1981; *b* 5 Oct. 1915; *s* of Lieut-Col Edgar Hugh Brassey, MVO, and Margaret Harriet (*née* Trefusis); *m* 1939, Joyce Patricia, *d* of Captain Maurice Kingscote; two *s* two *d* (an *d* one *d* decd). *Educ:* Eton; Sandhurst. Regular Commission, The Royal Scots Greys, 1935-46; served Palestine, Africa, Italy and NW Europe, Lieut-Col Comdg Royal Wilts Yeomanry, 1955-58. ADC (TA) to the Queen, 1964-69; Exon, Queen's Bodyguard, Yeoman of the Guard, 1964-70, Ensign, 1970-79, Lieutenant, 1979-, Adjutant and Clerk of the Cheque, 1971. Col, The Royal Scots Dragoon Guards, 1974-79. Regional Dir (Salisbury), Lloyds Bank. Chairman, Chippenham Conservative Assoc., 1951-53, 1966-68 (Pres. 1968). Pres., Wilts Assoc. of Boys Clubs, 1968. JP 1951, DL 1955, High Sheriff 1959, Vice Lord-Lieutenant, 1968-81, Wilts. Croix de Guerre (France), 1944. *Recreation:* country. *Address:* Manor Farm, Little Somerford, Chippenham, Wilts. *T:* Malmesbury 2255. *Club:* Cavalry and Guards.

BRASSEY, Lt-Col Hon. Peter (Esmé); DL; Lord-Lieutenant of Cambridgeshire, 1975-81; *b* 5 Dec. 1907; *o surv. s* of 1st Baron Brassey of Apethorpe; *m* 1944, Lady Romayne Cecil, 2nd *d* of 5th Marquess of Exeter, KG, CMG; two *s* one *d*. *Educ:* Eton; Magdalene Coll., Cambridge. Barrister-at-Law, Inner Temple, Midland Circuit, 1931. Northamptonshire Yeomanry, Lieut-Col, 1945; served NW Europe (wounded). Dir, The Essex Water Co. Ltd, 1970- (Chm., 1981-). DL 1961, High Sheriff, 1966, and Vice-Lieutenant, 1966-74, County of Huntingdon and Peterborough; DL County of Cambridge, 1974. KStJ 1976. *Recreations:* shooting, fishing. *Address:* The Close House, Barnack, Stamford, Lincs PE9 3DY. *T:* Stamford 740 238. *Club:* Carlton.

BRATBY, Jean Esme Oregon; *see* Cooke, J. E. O.

BRATBY, John Randall, RA 1971 (ARA 1959); ARCA; FIAL; RBA; Painter and Writer; Member of London Group; Editorial Adviser for Art Quarterly; *b* 19 July 1928; *s* of George Alfred Bratby and Lily Beryl Randall; *m* 1953, Jean Esme Oregon Cooke, RA (*see* Jean E. Cooke) (marr. diss. 1977); three *s* one *d*; *m* 1977, Patti Prime. *Educ:* Tiffin Boys' Sch.; Kingston School of Art; Royal College of Art. Teacher: Carlisle College of Art, 1956; Royal College of Art, 1957-58. Gained prizes and scholarships, 1954-57. Numerous one-man exhibitions at Beaux Arts Gallery from 1954; Zwemmer Gallery from 1959; Thackeray Gallery; Furneaux Gallery; Nat. Theatre, 1978; also in galleries abroad. Exhibited: Royal Academy (yearly) from 1955; has also shown pictures in various international exhibitions and festivals; Venice Biennale, 1956. Guggenheim Award for Great Britain, 1956 and 1958; won junior section of John Moores Liverpool Exhibn, 1957; Paintings for film The Horse's Mouth, 1958. Works in public collections: Tate Gallery; Arts Council of Great Britain; British Council; Contemporary Arts Society. National Galleries: Canada; New Zealand; NSW and Victoria; galleries in many cities and towns of Great Britain; Victoria and Albert Museum; Ashmolean Museum; Museum of Modern Art, New York; also in many other public and private art collections, in Great Britain, the Commonwealth and USA. Has made television appearances and sound broadcasts. FRSA; FZS. *Recreation:* philosophy. *Publications:* fiction: Breakdown, 1960; Breakfast and Elevenses, 1961; Break-Pedal Down, 1962 (also TV play); Break 50 Kill, 1963; non-fiction: studio publication of colour reproductions of own work, 1961; contrib., illustrations, Oxford Illustrated Old Testament, 1968; Stanley Spencer, 1969. *Address:* The Cupola, Belmont Road, Hastings, Sussex. *T:* Hastings 434037.

BRATT, Guy Maurice, CMG 1977; MBE 1945; HM Diplomatic Service, retired; Counsellor, Foreign and Commonwealth Office, since 1977 (re-employed); *b* 4 April 1920; *s* of late Ernst Lars Gustaf Bratt and late Alice Maud Mary Bratt (*née* Raper); *m* 1945, Françoise Nelly Roberte Girardet; two *s* one *d*. *Educ:* Merchant Taylors' Sch.; London Univ. (BA). Served Army, 1939-46 (MBE): Major, Royal Signals. Solicitor 1947. Asst Sec., Colonial Develt Corp.; joined HM Foreign (subseq. Diplomatic) Service, 1952; served FO, 1952-54; Berlin, 1954-56; Brussels, 1956-58; FO, 1958-62; Vienna, 1962-66; FCO, 1966-70; Geneva, 1970-72; FCO, 1972-74; Washington, 1974-77. *Recreations:* music, railways, mountaineering. *Address:* 2 Orchehill Rise, Gerrards Cross, Bucks SL9 8PR. *T:* Gerrards Cross 83106. *Club:* Travellers'.

BRATTAIN, Dr Walter H(ouser); Research Physicist, Bell Telephone Laboratories, Inc., 1929-67; Overseer Emeritus, Whitman College; engaged with others in research investigating the properties of lipid membranes in salt solutions; *b* Amoy, China, 10 Feb. 1902; *s* of Ross R. Brattain and Ottilie Brattain (*née* Houser); *m* 1st, 1935, Keren Gilmore (*d* 1957); one *s*; 2nd, 1958, Emma Jane Miller (*née* Kirsch). *Educ:* Whitman Coll., Walla Walla,

Washington; University of Oregon, Eugene, Oregon; University of Minnesota, Minneapolis, Minn. BS 1924, Whitman Coll.; MA 1926, University of Oregon; PhD 1929, University of Minnesota. Asst Physicist, Bureau of Standards, 1928-29; Technical Staff, Bell Telephone Labs, Inc., 1929-67. Division of War Research, Columbia Univ., 1942-44. Visiting Lecturer, Harvard Univ., 1952-53; Visiting Prof. of Physics (part-time) Whitman Coll., 1963-72. Fellow, Explorers' Club, 1977. Hon. Dr of Science: Portland Univ., 1952; Union Coll., 1955; Whitman Coll., 1955; University of Minnesota, 1957; Gustavus Adolphus Coll., 1963; Hon. LHD Hartwick Coll., 1964. Stuart Ballantine Medal, Franklin Institute, 1952; John Scott Medal, City of Philadelphia, 1955; Nobel Prize for Physics (with J. Bardeen and W. Shockley), 1956. Fellow: American Academy of Arts and Sciences, 1956; National Academy of Sciences, 1959; Hon. MIEEE 1981. *Publications:* many scientific papers on Thermionics and Semiconductors in various physics journals. *Recreation:* golf. *Address:* Whitman College, Walla Walla, Washington 99362, USA. *T:* (509) 527-5223.

BRAY, Denis Campbell, CMG 1977; CVO 1975; Secretary for Home Affairs, Hong Kong, 1973-77 and since 1980; *b* 24 Jan. 1926; *s* of Rev. Arthur Henry Bray and Edith Muriel Bray; *m* 1952, Marjorie Elizabeth Bottomley; four *d* (one *s* decd). *Educ:* Kingswood Sch.; Jesus Coll., Cambridge (MA). BScEcon London. RN, 1947-49. Colonial Service Devonshire Course, 1949-50; Admin. Officer, Hong Kong, 1950; Dist Comr, New Territories, 1971; Hong Kong Comr in London, 1977-80. *Recreations:* ocean racing and cruising. *Address:* Government Secretariat, Hong Kong. *Clubs:* Travellers', London Rowing, Royal Ocean Racing; Leander (Henley-on-Thames); Hong Kong, Royal Hong Kong Jockey, Royal Hong Kong Yacht; Tai Po Boat.
See also J. W. Bray.

BRAY, Jeremy William; MP (Lab) Motherwell and Wishaw, since Oct. 1974; *b* 29 June 1930; *s* of Rev. Arthur Henry Bray and Mrs Edith Muriel Bray; *m* 1953, Elizabeth (*née* Trowell); four *d. Educ:* Aberystwyth Grammar Sch.; Kingswood Sch.; Jesus Coll., Cambridge. Researched in pure mathematics at Cambridge, 1953-55; Choate Fellow, Harvard Univ., USA, 1955-56; Technical Officer, Wilton Works of ICI. Contested (Lab) Thirsk and Malton, General Election, 1959; MP (Lab) Middlesbrough West, 1962-70; Member: Select Cttee on Nationalised Industries, 1962-64; Select Cttee on Treasury and Civil Service, 1979- (Chm., Sub-cttee, 1981-82); Chairman: Labour, Science and Technology Group, 1964-66; Economic Affairs Estimates Sub-Cttee, 1964-66; Parly Sec., Min. of Power, 1966-67; Jt Parly Sec., Min. of Technology, 1967-69. Dir, Mullard Ltd, 1970-73; Consultant, Battelle Res. Centre, Geneva, 1973; Sen. Res. Fellow, 1974, Vis. Prof., 1975-79, Univ. of Strathclyde. Dep. Chm., Christian Aid, 1972-; Co-Dir, Programme of Res. into Econometric Methods, Imperial Coll., 1971-74. Chm., Fabian Soc., 1971-72. *Publications:* Decision in Government, 1970; Production Purpose and Structure, 1982; Fabian pamphlets and articles in jls. *Recreation:* sailing. *Address:* 29a Colquhoun Street, Helensburgh, Dunbartonshire G84 8UX.
See also D. C. Bray.

BRAY, Hon. Dr John Jefferson; AC 1979; Chancellor of the University of Adelaide, since 1968; *b* 16 Sept. 1912; *s* of Harry Midwinter Bray and Gertrude Eleonore Bray (*née* Stow). *Educ:* St Peter's Coll., Adelaide; Univ. of Adelaide. LLB 1932, LLB Hons 1933, LLD 1937. Admitted to South Australian Bar, 1933; QC 1957. Univ. of Adelaide: Actg Lectr in Jurisprudence, 1941, 1943, 1945, 1951; Actg Lectr in Legal History, 1957-58; Lectr in Roman Law, 1959-66; Chief Justice of Supreme Court of SA, 1967-78. *Publications:* Poems, 1962; Poems 1961-1971, 1972; Poems 1972-1979, 1979; contrib. Australian Law Jl. *Address:* 39 Hurtle Square, Adelaide, South Australia 5000. *Club:* University of Adelaide.

BRAY, Gen. Sir Robert (Napier Hubert Campbell), GBE 1966 (CBE 1952); KCB 1962 (CB 1957); DSO 1944, and Bar 1945; retired; late Duke of Wellington's Regiment (Colonel of the Regiment, 1965-75); *b* 1908; *s* of late Brig.-Gen. Robert Napier Bray, CMG, DSO; *m* 1936, Nora, *d* of G. C. G. Gee, Rothley, Leics.; three *s. Educ:* Gresham's Sch., Holt; Royal Military Coll. 2nd Lieut, Duke of Wellington's Regt, 1928. Served War of 1939-45 Norway, Middle East and North Western Europe (despatches, DSO and Bar); Lieut-Col 1941; Brig., 1945; Brig. General Staff British Army of the Rhine, 1950-52; Korea, 1954; Director of Land-Air Warfare, and Director of North Atlantic Treaty Organisation Standardisation, War Office, 1954-57; Maj.-Gen., 1954; General Officer Commanding 56 Infantry Div. (TA), 1957-59; Commander, Land Forces, Arabian Peninsula, 1959; GOC, MELF, 1961; Lieut-Gen. 1961; General Officer Commanding-in-Chief, Southern Command, 1961-63; Commander-in-Chief, Allied Forces, Northern Europe, 1963-67; Dep. Supreme Comdr Allied Powers Europe, 1967-70; General 1965; ADC General to the Queen, 1965-68. *Recreations:* sailing, shooting. *Address:* c/o Lloyds Bank, 6 Pall Mall, SW1Y 5NH. *Clubs:* Army and Navy, Royal Cruising.

BRAY, Ronald William Thomas; mechanical engineer; farmer; Underwriting Member of Lloyd's; *b* 5 Jan. 1922; *s* of William Ernest Bray, mech. engr and co. dir, Earls Court, and Ada Bray, Killington, Westmorland; *m* 1944, Margaret Florence, *d* of James B. Parker, St Margarets-on-Thames; no *c. Educ:* Latymer Upper School. Joined family business, 1938; Man. Dir 1946; pioneered develt of British construction equipment incl. heavy earthmoving equipment, four-wheel-drive tractor shovels; travelled extensively, Europe, N and S Africa, America, Canada, Caribbean and Middle East, developing exports; served on numerous professional and British

Standards cttees; resigned 1959. Mem., Woking UDC, 1959-62; Chm./Vice-Chm. of various cttees; Mem., N Yorks CC, 1977-. Contested (C) Stockton-on-Tees, 1964; MP (C) Rossendale, 1970-Sept. 1974; Mem. Parly delegns to India, Malaŵi, Sri Lanka, Sweden. Vice-Chm., Assoc. of Cons. Clubs, 1972-75; Vice-Pres., Lancashire Fedn of Cons. Clubs. FFB. *Recreations:* swimming, riding, walking. *Address:* Hallbeck, Beckermonds, Buckden, Skipton, N Yorks. *T:* Kettlewell 832. *Clubs:* Royal Automobile; Royal Automobile Country (Epsom).

BRAY, Sir Theodor (Charles), Kt 1975; CBE 1964; Chancellor, Griffith University, Brisbane, since 1975; *b* 11 Feb. 1905; *s* of Horace and Maude Bray; *m* 1931, Rosalie, *d* of Rev. A. M. Trengove; three *s* two *d* (and one *s* one *d* decd). *Educ:* state schs; Adelaide Univ. Apprentice Printer, Reporter, Register, Adelaide; Sub-editor, Chief Sub-editor, The Argus, Melbourne; Editor (26 yrs), Editor-in-Chief, Jt Man. Dir, Queensland Newspapers Pty Ltd, 1936-70, Dir, 1956-80; Chm., Australian Associated Press, 1968-70; Mem., Austr. Council for the Arts, 1969-73; Austr. Chm., Internat. Press Inst., 1962-70; Chm., Griffith Univ. Council, 1970-75. *Recreations:* bowls, travel. *Address:* 10/64 Macquarie Street, St Lucia, Qld 4067, Australia. *T:* 3707442. *Clubs:* Queensland, Johnsonian, Twelfth Night Theatre (Brisbane).

BRAY, William John, CBE 1975; Director of Research, Post Office, 1966-75 (Dep. Director, 1965); *b* 10 Sept. 1911; British; *m* 1936, Margaret Earp; one *d* (and one *d* decd). *Educ:* Imperial Coll., London Univ. Electrical engineering apprenticeship, Portsmouth Naval Dockyard, 1928-32; Royal and Kitchener Scholarships, Imperial Coll., 1932-34; entered PO Engineering Dept as Asst Engineer, 1934; Commonwealth Fund Fellowship (Harkness Foundation) for study in USA, 1956-57; Staff Engineer, Inland Radio Br., PO Engineering Dept, 1958. Vis. Prof., UCL, 1974-78. External Examr, MSc (Communications), Imperial Coll., London, 1976-80. Participation in work of International Radio Consultative Cttee of International Telecommunication Union and European Postal and Telecommunication Conferences; Consultant to UK Council for Educnl Technology, 1976-78. MSc(Eng), FCGI, DIC, FEng, FIEE; DUniv. Essex, 1976. J. J. Thomson Medal, IEE, 1978. *Publications:* papers in Proc. IEE (IEE Ambrose Fleming Radio Sect. and Electronics Div. Premium Awards). *Recreations:* sailing, travel. *Address:* The Pump House, Bredfield, Woodbridge, Suffolk IP13 6AH. *T:* Woodbridge 5838.

BRAY, Winston, CBE 1970; Deputy Chairman and Deputy Chief Executive, BOAC, 1972-74; Member Board, BOAC, 1971-74; Member Board, BAAC Ltd (formerly BOAC (AC Ltd), 1969-74; *b* 29 April 1910; *s* of late Edward Bray and Alice Walker; *m* 1937, Betty Atterton Miller; one *s* two *d*. *Educ:* Highgate Sch.; London Univ. (BCom). Missouri Pacific Railroad, USA, 1932; Asst to Traffic Manager, British Airways, 1938; Traffic Dept, BOAC, 1940; Sales Promotion Supt, 1946; Sales Manager, 1950; Sales Planning Manager, 1954; Dir of Planning, 1964; Planning Dir, 1969; Dep. Managing Dir, 1972. FCIT. *Recreations:* sailing, gardening. *Address:* Greenacres, Frith Hill, Great Missenden, Bucks. *Club:* Royal Automobile.

BRAYBROOK, Edward John, CB 1972; *b* 25 Oct. 1911; *s* of late Prior Wormsley Braybrook and Kate Braybrook; *m* 1937, Eva Rosalin Thomas; one *s* two *d*. *Educ:* Edmonton Latymer Secondary Sch. Asst Naval Store Officer, Admty, Chatham, Malta and Devonport, 1930-37; Deputy Naval Store Officer, Admty, 1938-39; Naval Store Officer, Admty and Haslemere, 1940-43; Suptg Naval Store Officer, Levant, 1943; Comdr/Captain (SP) RNVR Suptg Naval Store Officer, Ceylon and Southern India, 1944-46; Supt, Perth, Scotland, 1946-47; Asst Director of Stores, Admty, 1947-53; Suptg Naval Store Officer, Chatham, 1953-55; Deputy Director of Stores, Admty, 1955-64; Director of Stores (Naval), MoD, 1964-70; Dir-Gen. Supplies and Transport (Naval), MoD, 1970-73. *Recreations:* gardening, photography, painting, handicrafts. *Address:* 22 Church Drive, North Harrow, Middlesex. *T:* 01-427 0838.

BRAYBROOKE, 9th Baron *cr* 1788; **Henry Seymour Neville;** JP; DL; Hon. MA Camb. 1948; Hereditary Visitor of Magdalene College, Cambridge; Patron of four livings; *b* 5 Feb. 1897; *er s* of late Rev. Hon. Grey Neville (2nd *s* of 6th Baron) and late Mary Peele, *e d* of late Canon Francis Slater; *S* cousin, 1943; *m* 1st, 1930, Muriel Evelyn (*d* 1962), *d* of late William C. Manning and *widow* of E. C. Cartwright; one *s* ; 2nd, 1963, Angela Mary, *d* of late William H. Hollis and *widow* of John Ree. *Educ:* Shrewsbury Sch. (Scholar); Magdalene Coll., Cambridge. Served European War, 1914-18, in RNA Service and RAF; later held various appointments with Anglo-Iranian and Shell Groups of oil companies. Chm., Diocesan Bd of Finance, Chelmsford, 1950-68. JP Saffron Walden, 1953; DL, 1950-. *Heir:* s Hon. Robin Henry Charles Neville [*b* 29 Jan. 1932; *m* 1st, 1955, Robin Helen (marr. diss. 1974), *d* of late T. A. Brockhoff, Sydney, Australia; four *d* (and one *d* decd); 2nd, 1974, Linda Norman; two *d*]. *Address:* Bruncketts, Wendens Ambo, Saffron Walden, Essex CB11 4JL. *T:* Saffron Walden 40200.

BRAYBROOKE, Neville Patrick Bellairs; writer; *b* 30 May 1925; *s* of Patrick Philip William Braybrooke and Lettice Marjorie Bellairs; *m* 1953, June Guesdon Jolliffe; one step *d*. *Educ:* Ampleforth. *Publications:* This is London, 1953; London Green: The Story of Kensington Gardens, Hyde Park, Green Park and St James's Park, 1959; London, 1961; The Idler: novel, 1961; The Delicate Investigation (play for BBC), 1969; *edited:* The Wind and the Rain: quarterly, 1941-1951; T. S. Eliot: a symposium for his 70th birthday,

1958, 3rd edn 1970; A Partridge in a Pear Tree: a celebration for Christmas 1960; Pilgrim of the Future: a Teilhard de Chardin symposium, 1966, 2nd edn 1968; The Letters of J. R. Ackerley, 1975; contrib. Guardian, Saturday Review, Times, Times Lit. Suppl., Sunday Telegraph, Tablet. *Recreations:* cats, walking, reading little reviews. *Address:* Grove House, Castle Road Cowes, IoW PO31 7QZ. *T:* Cowes 293950; 10 Gardnor Road, NW3 1HA. *T:* 01-435 1851. *Club:* Island Sailing.

BRAYE, 7th Baron *cr* 1529; **Thomas Adrian Verney-Cave;** JP; DL; Major late 13/18th Royal Hussars; *b* 26 July 1902; *er s* of 6th Baron Braye and Ethel Mary (*d* 1955), *d* of Capt. Edward Bouverie Pusey, RN; *S* father, 1952; *m* 1934, Dorothea, *yr d* of late Daniel C. Donoghue, Philadelphia; one *d*. *Educ:* Eton. Major, 13/18th Royal Hussars; formerly Flying Officer, RAF, 1939-46; served on personal staff of The Prince of the Netherlands, 1945-46 (Order of Orange Nassau). Former Dir, George Spencer Ltd. CC Northants, 1952-64; JP Leicestershire, 1953, DL, 1954. *Heir:* d Hon. Penelope Mary [*b* 28 Sept. 1941; *m* 1981, Edward Henry Lancelot Aubrey-Fletcher]. *Address:* Stanford Hall, Lutterworth, Leics LE17 6DH. *T:* Rugby 860250. *Club:* Cavalry and Guards.

BRAYNE, Richard Bolding, MBE 1957; Clerk of the Worshipful Company of Ironmongers, since 1973; *b* 28 Oct. 1924; 3rd *s* of late Brig. Frank Lugard Brayne, MC, CSI, CIE, ICS, and late Iris Goodeve Brayne, K-i-H; *m* 1947, Anne Stoddart Forrest; one *s* two *d*. *Educ:* Sherborne Sch.; Pembroke Coll. Cambridge. Indian Army, 3rd (Peshawar) Indian Mountain Battery, India Burma and Far East, 1942-46. Entered Colonial Service as DO, Tanganyika 1948; Staff Officer to HRH The Princess Margaret's tour of Tanganyika 1956; Dist Comr, 1957; Principal, Admin. Trng Centre and Local Govt Trng Centre, 1960. Prin. Asst Sec., Min. of Educn, 1963; Mem., E African UGC and Makerere Univ. College Council, 1963; retd from Colonial Service, 1964 Sec., Brit. Paper and Board Makers' Assoc., 1964; Trng Adviser and Devel Manager, Construction Industry Trng Bd, 1966. Asst Clerk of Worshipful Co. of Ironmongers, 1971. Member: Exec. Cttee, Nat. Assoc. of Almshouses 1972- (Chm., 1981); Cttee, Royal Surgical Aid Soc., 1972- (Chm., 1982). *Recreations:* shooting, golf, D-I-Y. *Address:* Ironmongers' Hall, Barbican EC2Y 8AA. *T:* 01-606 2725.

BRAYNE-BAKER, John, CMG 1957; Colonial Administrative Service, Nigeria (retired); *b* 13 Aug. 1905; *s* of Francis Brayne-Baker and Dorothea Mary Brayne-Baker (*née* Porcher); *m* 1947, Ruth Hancock; no *c*. *Educ:* Marlborough Coll.; Worcester Coll., Oxford. Nigeria: Asst District Officer, 1928; District Officer, 1938; Senior District Officer, 1948; Resident, 1953. Senior Resident and Deputy Commissioner of the Cameroons, 1954-56; retired 1956. Member, Tiverton RDC, 1959-74, Tiverton DC, 1973-76 *Recreations:* gardening and golf. *Address:* East Grantlands, Uffculme, Cullompton, Devon. *T:* Craddock 40236. *Club:* Tiverton Golf (Tiverton).

BRAYNE-NICHOLLS, Rear-Adm. Francis Brian Price, CB 1965; DSC 1942; General Secretary, Officers Pensions Society, 1966-79; *b* 1 Dec. 1914; *s* of late Dr G. E. E. Brayne-Nicholls and *o s* of Sir Francis W. T. Brain; *m* 1939, Wendy (*née* Donnelly); one *d*. *Educ:* RNC, Dartmouth. Sub-Lieut and Lieut, HMS Bee on Yangtse River, 1936-39; specialised in Navigation, 1939; Navigating Officer of: HM Ships Nelson, Rodney, Cardiff, 1939-41, Manxman (during many mining ops, Malta convoys and Madagascar op.) 1941-42; Combined Ops, taking part in Sicily (despatches), Salerno, and Normandy landings. Navigating Officer: HMS Glory, 1944-46; HMS Vanguard, 1948; Comdr 1948; Comdg Officer: HMS Gravelines, 1952-53; HMS St Kitts, 1953-54; Capt 1954; Naval Asst to First Sea Lord, 1954-55; Comdg Officer, HMS Apollo, 1955-57; NATO Standing Group, Washington, 1957-59; Captain of Navigation Direction Sch., HMS Dryad, 1959-61; Admiralty, 1961-63; Rear-Adm. 1963; Chief of Staff to Commander, Far East Fleet, 1963-65. Younger Brother, Trinity House. Mem., Nautical Inst. *Recreation:* golf. *Address:* 3 Tedworth Square, SW3 4DU. *T:* 01-352 1681. *Club:* Naval and Military.

BRAYNEN, Sir Alvin (Rudolph), Kt 1975; JP; Consultant to Shell, Bahamas, 1969-82; High Commissioner for the Commonwealth of the Bahamas in London, 1973-77; *b* 6 Dec. 1904; *s* of William Rudolph Braynen and Lulu Isabelle Braynen (*née* Griffin); *m* 1969, Ena Estelle (*née* Elden); (one *s* one *d* by a previous marriage). *Educ:* Public Sch., The Current, Eleuthera, Bahamas; Boys' Central Sch., Nassau, Bahamas (teacher trng). Public Sch. Headmaster, 1923-25. Entered commercial world, 1925, as clerk; founded his own petroleum commn firm, 1930, disposing of it in 1965. MP for Cat Island, 1935-42 and constituency for what is now known as St John, 1942-72; Dep. Speaker of House of Assembly, 1949-53, and 1963-66; MEC, 1953-58; Speaker of House of Assembly, 1967-72. During years 1952-58 he was Chairman of several Boards, incl. those responsible for Educn, Public Works, Prisons and Traffic; past Member: Bds of Agriculture, Health, Tourism, Out Island Develt and Educn; Mem., both Constitutional Confs from the Bahamas to London in 1963 and 1968; Chm., Exec. Cttee of Conf. of Commonwealth Caribbean Parliamentary Heads and Clerks; also served as either Chm. or Dep. Chm. of important Nat. Festivities for many years, such as Coronation of the Queen, visit of Princess Margaret, First Constitutional Day, 1964, and supervised arrangements for Conf. of Delegates of Commonwealth Parliamentary Conf. held at Nassau, 1968. Organised Bahamas Chamber of Commerce (first Exec. Sec.); Founder and first Pres., Nassau Mutual Aid Assoc.; first Pres., Kiwanis Club (Montague Branch). JP Bahamas 1952. *Recreations:* swimming; collects books on the Bahamas; collects coins and stamps. *Address:* PO Box N42, Nassau, Bahamas.

BRAYSHAW, (Alfred) Joseph, CBE 1975 (OBE 1964); JP; Secretary, The Magistrates' Association, 1965-77; *b* Manchester, 20 Dec. 1912; *er s* of late Shipley Neave Brayshaw and late Ruth Cotterell (*née* Holmes), JP; *m* 1st, Joan Hawkes (*d* 1940); 2nd, 1943, Marion Spencer, *y d* of late Spencer Johnson, Bury St Edmunds; three *s. Educ:* Sidcot Sch., Somerset; engineering factories; Dalton Hall, Univ. of Manchester. Brayshaw Furnaces & Tools Ltd, 1934-40; CBCO, 1941-46; Asst Sec., then Gen. Sec., Friends' Relief Service, 1946-48; Gen. Sec., Nat. Marriage Guidance Council, 1949-64 (a Vice-Pres., 1964-); Vice-Pres., Guildford and District Marriage Guidance Council, 1974-. JP Surrey, 1958; Chm., Farnham Bench, 1979-; Chm., Surrey Magistrates' Soc., 1979-; Mem. Council, Magistrates' Assoc., 1979-. *Publication:* Public Policy and Family Life, 1980. *Recreations:* gardening, walking. *Address:* Apple Trees, Beech Road, Haslemere, Surrey GU27 2BX. *T:* Haslemere 2677.

BRAZENDALE, George William, CMG 1958; FCA; *b* 1909; *s* of late Percy Ridout Brazendale, and late Edith Mary Brazendale (*née* Maystre); *m* 1938, Madeleine, *o d* of Thomas and Betty Wroe; two *d. Educ:* Arnold Sch., Blackpool, Lancs. Chief Accountant, Colclough China Ltd, Stoke-on-Trent, 1936-41; Asst Area Officer, MAP, 1941-42; Chief Progress Officer, ROF Swynnerton, 1942-43; Secretary, Midland Regional Board, 1943-45; Regional Controller Board of Trade; Northern Region, 1945-46; North-Western Region, 1946-50; Asst Secretary, Board of Trade, 1946; Trade Commissioner for the UK in charge Calcutta, 1950-60. Principal British Trade Commissioner: in the Federation of Rhodesia and Nyasaland, 1961-63; also Economic Adviser to British High Commissioner in Rhodesia, 1964-65; Economic Adviser to Special British Representative in East and Central Africa, 1966-67; retired from HM Diplomatic Service, 1967. ACA 1931. *Recreations:* fishing, gardening. *Address:* 23 Heathlands Avenue, West Parley, Wimborne, Dorset BH22 8RW. *Club:* Oriental.

BRAZIER, Rt. Rev. Percy James; *b* 3 Aug. 1903; *m* 1933, Joan Cooper, MB, BS; one *s* four *d. Educ:* Weymouth Coll., Dorset; Emmanuel Coll., Cambridge. 2nd class Hist. Trip., Part I, 1924, 2nd class, Part II, and BA, 1925; MA 1939. Ridley Hall, Cambridge, 1925-27, Deacon, 1927; Priest, 1928; Curate of St John the Evangelist, Blackheath, 1927-29; CMS (Ruanda Mission), 1930; Kabale, 1930-34; Kigeme, Diocese of Uganda, 1934-50; Archdeacon of Ruanda-Urundi, 1946-51; Asst Bishop of Uganda for Ruanda-Urundi, 1951-60; Bishop of Rwanda and Burundi, 1960-64 (name of diocese changed when Ruanda-Urundi was granted independence, 1962); retired 1964. Rector of Padworth and Vicar of Mortimer West End, Diocese of Oxford, 1964-70. Chevalier de l'Ordre Royal du Lion (Belgium), 1955. *Recreations:* photography, gardening, ornithology. *Address:* Lark Rise, Peasemore, Newbury, Berks. *T:* Chieveley 548.

See also D. C. Clarke.

BRAZIER-CREAGH, Maj.-Gen. Sir (Kilner) Rupert, KBE 1962 (CBE 1947); CB 1954; DSO 1944; Secretary of the Horse Race Betting Levy Board, 1961-65; Director of Staff Duties, War Office, 1959-61, retired; *b* 12 Dec. 1909; 2nd *s* of late Lt-Col K. C. Brazier-Creagh; *m* 1st, 1938, Elizabeth Mary (*d* 1967), *d* of late E. M. Magor; one *s* two *d*; 2nd, 1968, Mrs Marie Nelson. *Educ:* Rugby; RMA, Woolwich. 2nd Lieut, 1929; served War of 1939-45 (despatches, DSO); Bde Major, 9th Armoured Div., 1941; GSO1 12th Corps, 1943; Commanded 25th Field Regt, 1944; BGS 21st Army Group and BAOR, 1945-48 (CBE); idc 1949; DDRA, War Office, 1950; CRA 11th Armoured Div., 1951-52; Chief of Staff Malaya Command, 1952-55 (despatches, CB); Asst Comdt, Staff Coll., 1955-57; Chief of Staff, Eastern Command, 1957-59. Officer, American Legion of Merit, 1945. *Recreation:* racing. *Address:* Travis Corners Road, Garrison, New York, USA.

BREADALBANE AND HOLLAND, 10th Earl of, *cr* 1677; **John Romer Boreland Campbell;** Mac Chailein Mhic Dhonnachaidh (celtic designation); Viscount of Tay and Paintland; Lord Glenorchy, Benederaloch, Ormelie and Weik, 1677; Bt of Glenorchy; Bt of Nova Scotia, 1625; *b* 28 April 1919; *o s* of 9th Earl of Breadalbane and Holland, MC; *S* father, 1959; *m* 1949, Coralie (marr. diss.), *o d* of Charles Archer. *Educ:* Eton; RMC, Sandhurst; Basil Patterson Tutors; Edinburgh Univ. Served Black Watch (Royal Highlanders), 1939; served France, 1939-41 (despatches); invalided, 1942. *Recreations:* piobaireachd, Scottish highland culture. *Heir:* none. *Address:* House of Lords, SW1; 29 Mackeson Road, Hampstead, NW3.

BREAM, Julian, OBE 1964; guitarist and lutenist; *b* 15 July 1933; *e s* of Henry G. Bream; *m* 1st, Margaret Williamson; one adopted *s*; 2nd, 1980, Isobel Sanchez. *Educ:* Royal College of Music (Junior Exhibition Award, 1945 and Scholarship, 1948). Began professional career at Cheltenham, 1947; London début, Wigmore Hall, 1950; subsequently has appeared in leading world festivals in Europe, USA, Australia and Far East. A leader in revival of interest in Elizabethan Lute music, on which he has done much research; has encouraged contemporary English compositions for the guitar. Formed Julian Bream Consort, 1960; inaugurated Semley Festival of Music and Poetry, 1971. DUniv Surrey, 1968. *Recreations:* playing the guitar; cricket, table tennis, gardening, backgammon. *Address:* c/o Harold Holt Ltd, 134 Wigmore Street, W1.

BREARE, William Robert Ackrill; Chairman and Managing Director: R. Ackrill Ltd, 1955-81; Lawrence & Hall Ltd, 1963-81; *b* 5 July 1916; *s* of late

Robert Ackrill Breare and late Emily Breare (*née* Waddington); *m* 1942, Sybella Jessie Macduff Roddick, *d* of late John Roddick, Annan; one *s* two *d. Educ:* Old College, Windermere; Charterhouse; Wadham Coll., Oxford (MA). BCL Oxon 1938. Sub-Lt RNVSR, 1935-39; Comdr RNVR, 1942-44. Dir, R. Ackrill Ltd, newspaper publishers, 1938. Pres., Yorks Newspaper Soc., 1953 and 1972; Mem. Council, Newspaper Soc., 1967-81; Mem. Press Council, 1972-81. Contested (C) Rother Valley, 1950. *Recreations:* music, sailing. *Address:* Harrison Hill House, Starbeck, Harrogate, N Yorks. *T:* Harrogate 883302.

BREARLEY, Christopher John Scott; Director of Scottish Services, Property Services Agency, Department of the Environment, since 1981; *b* 25 May 1943; *s* of Geoffrey Brearley and Winifred (*née* Scott); *m* 1971, Rosemary Stockbridge; two *s. Educ:* King Edward VII Sch., Sheffield; Trinity Coll., Oxford. MA 1964, BPhil 1966. Entered Ministry of Transport, 1966; Private Sec. to Perm. Sec., 1969-70; Principal, DoE, 1970; Sec. to Review of Develt Control Procedures (Dobry), DoE, 1973-74; Private Sec. to the Secretary of the Cabinet, Cabinet Office, 1974-76; Department of the Environment: Asst Sec., 1977; Under Sec., 1981. *Recreations:* crosswords, walking. *Address:* 4 Hatton Place, Edinburgh EH9 1UD. *T:* 031-667 6205. *Club:* Royal Commonwealth Society.

BREARLEY, (John) Michael, OBE 1978; Captain, Middlesex County Cricket Club, 1971-82; *b* 28 April 1942; *s* of Horace and Midge Brearley. *Educ:* City of London Sch.; St John's Coll., Cambridge (MA). Lectr in Philosophy, Univ. of Newcastle-upon-Tyne, 1968-71. Middlesex County Cricketer, intermittently, 1961-82; capped, 1964; played first Test Match, 1976; Captain of England XI, 1977-80, 1981. *Publications:* (with Dudley Doust) The Return of the Ashes, 1978; (with Dudley Doust) The Ashes Retained, 1979; Phoenix: the series that rose from the ashes, 1982; articles for the Sunday Times. *Club:* MCC.

BREARLEY, Sir Norman, Kt 1971; CBE 1965; DSO 1916; MC; AFC; FRAeS; Company Director, Western Australia, retired 1977; *b* Geelong, Vic., 22 Dec. 1890; *s* of late Robert Hillard Brearley, Perth, WA; *m* 1917, Violet, *d* of late Hon. Sydney Stubbs, CMG, MLA, Perth; one *s* one *d. Educ:* state and private schs, Geelong; Technical Coll., Perth, WA. Enlisted, after engineering training. Served War, RFC and RAF, also Major in Liverpool Regt, France and England, 1914-1919 (wounded, despatches, AFC, MC, DSO); War of 1939-45; Gp Capt., RAAF. Founder (1921) of West Australian Airways; was the first airmail contractor to Australian Govt. Pioneer of Australian Air Services. *Publication:* Australian Aviator, 1971. *Recreations:* tennis, golf. *Address:* 6 Esplanade, Peppermint Grove, Cottesloe, WA 6011, Australia. *T:* 312293. *Club:* Weld (Perth, WA).

BRECHIN, Bishop of, since 1975; **Rt. Rev. Lawrence Edward Luscombe;** *b* 10 Nov. 1924; *s* of Reginald John and Winifred Luscombe; *m* 1946, Doris Carswell Morgan, BSc, MB, ChB; one *d. Educ:* Torquay Grammar Sch.; Kelham Theological Coll.; King's Coll., London. CA 1952, ASAA 1957. FSAScot 1980. Served Indian Army, 1942-47. Partner, Galbraith, Dunlop & Co, Chartered Accountants, Glasgow, 1952-63. Ordained deacon, 1963; priest, 1964; Curate, St Margaret's, Glasgow, 1963-66; Rector, St Barnabas', Paisley, 1966-71; Provost of St Paul's Cathedral, Dundee, 1971-75. Hon. DLitt Geneva Theological Coll., 1972. *Recreations:* reading, Indian affairs. *Address:* 7 Shaftesbury Road, Dundee DD2 1HF.

BRECKNOCK, Earl of; David George Edward Henry Pratt; *b* 13 Aug. 1930; *o s* of 5th Marquess Camden, *qv*, and Marjorie, Countess of Brecknock, *qv*; *m* 1961, Virginia Ann, *o d* of late F. H. H. Finlaison, Arklow Cottage, Windsor, Berks; one *s* one *d* (and one *s* decd). Late Lieutenant, Scots Guards. *Educ:* Eton. Dir, Clive Discount Co. Ltd, 1958-69. *Heir:* s Viscount Bayham, *qv. Address:* Cowdown Farm House, Andover, Hants. *T:* Andover 52085.

BRECKNOCK, Marjorie Countess of, DBE 1967; Superintendent-in-Chief, St John Ambulance Brigade, 1960-70, retired, Chief President, 1972; *b* 28 Mar. 1900; *o c* of late Col A. E. Jenkins and of late Mrs Anna Jenkins, Wherwell Priory, Andover, Hants; *m* 1920, Earl of Brecknock (now Marquess Camden; from whom she obtained a divorce, 1941); one *s* one *d. Educ:* at home and Heathfield, Ascot. A Lady-in-waiting to Princess Marina, Duchess of Kent, 1937-39. War of 1939-45: Company Asst, ATS, 1940; Junior Commander, 1941; Senior Commander, 1942 (Senior ATS Officer SHAEF, 1944-45); despatches 1945; Bronze Star (USA), 1945. Commanded 310 (Southern Command) Bn WRAC (TA), 1948-54. Joined St John Ambulance Brigade HQ, 1947; appointed Controller Overseas Dept, 1950. GCStJ 1971 (DStJ 1958). Mem. Order of Mercy. *Publication:* Edwina Mountbatten—her life in pictures, 1961. *Recreations:* gardening, shooting, travelling, fishing. *Address:* 2 Kinnerton Street, SW1. *T:* 01-235 9362; Wherwell Priory, Andover, Hampshire. *T:* Chilbolton 388.

BREDIN, George Richard Frederick, CBE 1947; MA; Sudan Political Service (retired); Hon. Fellow of Pembroke College, Oxford; *b* 8 June 1899; *s* of late Dr Richard Bredin, Valparaiso, Chile; *m* 1932, Dorothy Wall, *d* of late T. R. Ellison, West Kirby, Cheshire; one *s* one *d. Educ:* Clifton College; Oriel College, Oxford. MA (Oxon) 1925; served European War, 1914-18, Lieut RE (64th Field Company) (despatches). Oriel College, Oxford, 1919-21; Hons Degree in Lit. Hum. (Distinction), 1921. Asst District Comr, Sudan Political Service, 1921; District Comr, 1930; Dep. Governor, 1935; Dep. Civil Sec., 1939; Governor Blue Nile Province, Sudan, 1941-48; Mem.,

Governor-General's Council, 1945-48; Chm., Governing Body of Gordon Meml University Coll., Khartoum, 1945-48; retired, 1948. Asst Registrar, Univ. of Liverpool, 1948-49; Fellow and Bursar, Pembroke Coll., Oxford, 1950-66; a Church Comr, 1951-; Chm., Oxford Diocesan Board of Finance, 1956-58; Chm., Oxford Diocesan Trusts Corp., 1965-70; a Curator of the Oxford Univ. Chest, 1957-69. Chm. of Governors of Abingdon Sch., 1966-72; Vice-Chm., Dorset House Sch. of Occupational Therapy, Oxford; Mem. Exec. Cttee, Gordon Boys School, Woking; Oxford City Councillor, 1965-67. Order of the Nile (3rd Cl.), 1937. *Address:* Rough Lea, Boar's Hill, Oxford. *T:* Oxford 735375.

BREDIN, Maj.-Gen. Humphrey Edgar Nicholson, CB 1969; DSO 1944 (and bars, 1945 and 1957); MC 1938 (and bar, 1939); Appeals Secretary, Cancer Research Campaign, Essex and Suffolk, since 1971; *b* 28 March 1916; *s* of Lieut-Colonel A. Bredin, late Indian Army, and Ethel Bredin (*née* Homan); *m* 1st, 1947, Jacqueline Geare (marr. diss., 1961); one *d*; 2nd, 1965, Anne Hardie; two *d*. *Educ:* King's School, Canterbury; RMC, Sandhurst. Commissioned Royal Ulster Rifles, 1936; Commanded: 6th Royal Inniskilling Fusiliers, 1944; 2nd London Irish Rifles, 1945; Eastern Arab Corps, Sudan Defence Force, 1949-53; 2nd Parachute Regt, 1956-57; 99th Gurkha Infty Bde Group, 1959-62. Campaigns: Dunkirk, 1940; N Africa, 1943; Italy, 1943-45; Palestine, 1937-39 and 1946-47; Suez, 1956; Cyprus, 1956-57; Singapore-Malaya Internal Security, 1959-62; Chief of British Commander-in-Chief's Mission to Soviet Forces in Germany, 1963-65; Commanded 42nd Div. (TA), 1965-68. Brig. 1964; Maj.-Gen. 1965; Dir, Volunteers, Territorials and Cadets, 1968-71; retired 1971. Col Comdt, The King's Division, 1968-71; Col of the Regt, Royal Irish Rangers, 1979-; Hon. Col D (London Irish Rifles) Co., 4th (V) Bn, The Royal Irish Rangers, 1980-. *Recreations:* shooting, fishing, gardening. *Address:* Bovills Hall, Ardleigh, Essex. *T:* Colchester 230217. *Club:* Army and Navy.

BREDIN, James John; Managing Director, Border Television Ltd, since 1964; *b* 18 Feb. 1924; *s* of John Francis and late Margaret Bredin; *m* 1958, Virginia Meddowes, *d* of John Meddowes and Mrs K. Thomas; one *s* two *d*. *Educ:* Finchley Catholic Grammar Sch.; London University. Served Fleet Air Arm, RNVR, S/Lieut, 1943-46. Scriptwriter, This Modern Age Film Unit, 1946-50; Producer, current affairs programmes, BBC TV, 1950-55; Sen. Producer, Independent Television News, 1955-59; Smith-Mundt Fellowship, USA, 1957; Producer of Documentaries, Associated Television, 1959-64. Chm., Guild of Television Producers and Directors, 1961-64. Director: Independent Television News Ltd, 1970-72; Independent Television Publications Ltd. *Address:* The Old Vicarage, Crosby-on-Eden, Carlisle CA6 4QZ. *T:* Crosby-on-Eden 672. *Clubs:* Beefsteak, Reform; County and Border (Carlisle).

BREEN, Dame Marie (Freda), DBE 1979 (OBE 1958); JP 1948; *b* 3 Nov. 1902; *d* of Frederick and Jeanne Chamberlin; *m* 1928, Robert Tweeddale Breen (*d* 1968); three *d*. *Educ:* St Michael's C of E Girls' Grammar Sch. Senator for Victoria, 1962-68, retired. Hon. Internat. Sec., Nat. Council of Women of Victoria, 1948-52, Pres., 1954-58, now Hon. Member; Vice-Pres., Australian/Asian Assoc. of Victoria, 1956-74; Chm., UNICEF Victorian Cttee, 1969-73; President: Victorian Family Council, 1958-78 (now Hon. Life Member); Victorian Assoc. of Citizens' Advice Bureaux, 1970-78; Australian Assoc. of Citizens' Advice Bureaux, 1973-75, 1977-79; Victorian Family Planning Assoc., 1970-71; Executive Mem. and Vice-Pres., Queen Elizabeth Hosp. for Mothers and Babies, 1943-78; Chm., Victorian Consultative Cttee on Social Develt, 1980-82. Mayoress of Brighton, Vic., 1941-42. *Recreations:* music, reading. *Address:* 51 Carpenter Street, Brighton, Victoria 3186, Australia. *T:* 592 2314. *Club:* Lyceum (Melbourne).

BREHONY, Dr John Albert Noel; HM Diplomatic Service; Counsellor, Cairo, since 1981; *b* 11 Dec. 1936; *s* of Patrick Paul Brehony and Agnes Maher; *m* 1961, Jennifer Ann (*née* Cox); one *s* one *d*. *Educ:* London Oratory Sch.; Univ. of Durham (BA, PhD). Tutor, Durham Univ., 1960; Economist Intell. Unit, 1961; Res. Fellow, Jerusalem (Jordan), 1962; Lectr, Univ. of Libya, 1965-66; FO, 1966; Kuwait, 1967-69; Aden, 1970-71; Amman, 1973-77. *Recreations:* Middle Eastern history, tennis, squash. *Address:* c/o Foreign and Commonwealth Office, King Charles Street, SW1A 2AH. *Clubs:* Athenæum; Gezira (Cairo).

BREMRIDGE, John Henry, OBE 1976; Financial Secretary, Hong Kong, since 1981; *b* 12 July 1925; *m* 1956, Jacqueline Everard; two *s* two *d*. *Educ:* Dragon Sch.; Cheltenham Coll.; St John's Coll., Oxford (MA). Army service: The Rifle Brigade, 1943-47. Joined John Swire & Sons, 1949; retired as Chm., John Swire & Sons (HK) Ltd, 1980. Hon. DSSc Chinese Univ., 1980; Hon. LLD Hong Kong Univ., 1982. *Recreation:* bad golf. *Address:* 45 Shouson Hill, Hong Kong. *T:* 530455. *Clubs:* Hong Kong, Shek O (Hong Kong).

BRENAN, (Edward Fitz-) Gerald, CBE 1982; MC 1918; Author; *b* 7 April 1894; English; *m* 1931, Elisabeth Gamel Woolsey (*d* 1968); one *d*. *Educ:* self-educated. Served War: Croix de Guerre, 1918. *Publications:* The Spanish Labyrinth, 1943; The Face of Spain, 1950; The Literature of the Spanish People, 1953; South from Granada, 1957; A Holiday by the Sea, 1961; À Life of One's Own (autobiog.), 1962; The Lighthouse Always Says Yes, 1966; St John of the Cross: his life and poetry, 1971; Personal Record (autobiog.), 1974; Thoughts in a Dry Season, 1978. *Recreations:* walking and talking. *Address:* c/o Jonathan Cape, 30 Bedford Square, WC1B 3EL.

BRENAN, Gerald; *see* Brenan, Edward Fitz-Gerald.

BRENAN, John Patrick Micklethwait, MA, BSc Oxon; FLS; FIBiol; Director, Royal Botanic Gardens, Kew, 1976-81; *b* 19 June 1917; *s* of Alexander Richard Micklethwait Brenan, MD, and Jill Fraser Brenan (*née* Parker); *m* 1950, Jean Helen Edwardes; one *s* two *d*. *Educ:* Tonbridge; Brasenose Coll., Oxford. At Imperial Forestry Inst., Oxford, 1940-48; Mem. Cambridge Botanical Expedn to Nigeria and Cameroons, 1948; apptd Sen. Scientific Officer in the Herbarium, Royal Botanic Gardens, Kew, 1948; Principal Sci. Off., 1954; i/c of Tropical African Section, 1959-65; Keeper of the Herbarium, and Dep. Dir, Royal Botanic Gardens 1965-76. Vis. Prof., Univ. of Reading, 1977. Hon. Botanical Adviser, Commonwealth War Graves Commn, 1978-. Pres., Assoc. for Tropical Biology, 1970-71; Vice Pres., Botanical Soc. of the British Isles, 1978; Botanical Sec., Linnean Soc. of London, 1965-72; Mem. Council, RHS, 1979-. Hon. Mem., Sociedade Broteriana, 1978. FRSA 1978. VMH 1979; Special Medal, South African Assoc. of Botanists, 1982. *Publications:* Check List of the Forest Trees and Shrubs of Tanganyika Territory, 1949 (with Dr P. J. Greenway); contrib. various accounts to Flora of Tropical East Africa, etc.; numerous papers on flowering plants of Europe and Africa in scientific jls. *Recreations:* reading, fishing, natural history, walking. *Address:* 24 Taylor Avenue, Kew Gardens, Richmond, Surrey. *T:* 01-876 6062. *Club:* Athenæum.

BRENCHLEY, Thomas Frank, CMG 1964; MA Oxon; HM Diplomatic Service, retired; Deputy Secretary General and Chief Executive, Arab-British Chamber of Commerce, since 1976; *b* 9 April 1918; *m* 1946, Edith Helen Helfand (*d* 1980); three *d*. Served with Royal Corps of Signals, 1939-46; Major on Staff of Military Attaché, Ankara, 1943-45; Director, Telecommunications Liaison Directorate, Syria and Lebanon, 1945-46. Civil Servant, 1947; transferred to Foreign Office, 1949; First Secretary: Singapore, 1950-53; Cairo, 1953-56; FO, 1956-58; MECAS, 1958-60; Counsellor, Khartoum, 1960-63; Chargé d'Affaires, Jedda, 1963; Head of Arabian Department, Foreign Office, 1963-67; Assistant Under-Secretary of State, Foreign Office, 1967-68; Ambassador to: Norway, 1968-72; Poland, 1972-74; Dep. Sec., Cabinet Office, 1975-76. *Publications:* New Dimensions of European Security (ed); Norway and her Soviet Neighbour: NATO's Arctic Frontier. *Recreations:* collecting (and sometimes reading) books, studying at the Open University. *Address:* 19 Ennismore Gardens, SW7. *Club:* Travellers'.

BRENDEL, Alfred; concert pianist since 1948; *b* 5 Jan. 1931; *s* of Albert Brendel and Ida Brendel (*née* Wieltschnig); *m* 1960, Iris Heymann-Gonzala (marr. diss. 1972); one *d*; *m* 1975, Irene Semler; one *s* two *d*. Studied piano with: S. Deželić, 1937-43; L. V. Kaan, 1943-47; also under Edwin Fischer, P. Baumgartner and E. Steuermann; composition with Artur Michl. Vienna State Diploma, 1947; Premio Bolzano Concorso Busoni, 1949. Hon. RAM; Hon. DMus London, 1978. Concerts: most European countries, North and Latin America, Australia and New Zealand, also N and S Africa and Near and Far East. Many appearances Vienna and Salzburg Festivals, 1960-. Other Festivals: Athens, Granada, Bregenz, Würzburg, Aldeburgh, York, Cheltenham, Edinburgh, Bath, Puerto Rico, Barcelona, Prague, Lucerne, Dubrovnik, etc. Many long playing records (Bach to Schoenberg) incl. first complete recording of Beethoven's piano works (Grand Prix du Disque, 1965). Cycle of Beethoven Sonatas: London, 1962, 1977; Copenhagen, 1964; Vienna, 1965; Puerto Rico, 1968; BBC and Rome, 1970; London, Munich and Stuttgart, 1977. *Publications:* Musical Thoughts and Afterthoughts (Essays), 1976; essays on music, in: HiFi Stereophonie, Music and Musicians, Phono, Fono Forum, Osterreichische Musikzeitschrift, etc. *Recreations:* literature, art galleries, architecture, unintentional humour, "kitsch". *Address:* Ingpen & Williams, 14 Kensington Court, W8.

BRENIKOV, Prof. Paul, FRTPI; Professor and Head of Department of Town and Country Planning, University of Newcastle upon Tyne, since 1964; *b* 13 July 1921; *o s* of Pavel Brenikov and Joyce Mildred Jackson, Liverpool; *m* 1943, Margaret, *e d* of Albert McLevy, Burnley, Lancs; two *s* one *d*. *Educ:* St Peter's Sch., York; Liverpool Coll.; Univ. of Liverpool (BA (Hons Geog.), MA, DipCD). War service with RNAS, 1941-46. Sen. Planning Officer, Lancs CC, 1950-55; Lectr, Dept of Civic Design, Univ. of Liverpool, 1955-64; Planning Corresp., Architect's Jl, 1957-63; Environmental Planning Consultant: in UK, for Bootle CB, 1957-64; Govt of Ireland, 1963-67; overseas, for UN; Chile, 1960-61; E Africa, 1964; OECD; Turkey, 1968. Royal Town Planning Institute: Mem. Council, 1967-78; Chm., Northern Br., 1973-74. Mem., Subject Cttee of UGC, 1975-. *Publications:* contrib. Social Aspects of a Town Development Plan, 1951; contrib. Land Use in an Urban Environment, 1961; (jtly) The Dublin Region: preliminary and final reports, 1965 and 1967; other technical pubns in architectural, geographical, planning and sociological jls. *Recreations:* listening to music, walking, reading. *Address:* Department of Town and Country Planning, The University, Newcastle upon Tyne NE1 7RU. *T:* Newcastle upon Tyne 328511.

BRENNAN, Anthony John Edward, CB 1981; Deputy Secretary, Northern Ireland Office, since 1982; *b* 24 Jan. 1927; 2nd *s* of late Edward Joseph Brennan and Mabel Brennan (*née* West); *m* 1958, Pauline Margery, *d* of late Percy Clegg Lees; two *s* one *d*. *Educ:* St Joseph's; London Sch. of Economics (Leverhulme Schol.). BSc Econ 1946. Served Army, RA, RAEC, 1946-49; Asst Principal, Home Office, 1949; Private Sec. to Parly Under-Sec. of State, 1953-54; Principal, 1954; Principal Private Sec. to Home Sec., 1963; Asst Sec.,

1963; Asst Under Sec. of State, Criminal Dept, 1971-75, Immigration Dept, 1975-77; Dep. Under-Sec. of State, Home Office, 1977-82. Sec., Royal Commn on Penal System, 1964-66; Mem., UN Cttee on Crime Prevention and Control, 1979. *Recreations:* bridge, theatre, athletics. *Address:* c/o Northern Ireland Office, Great George Street, SW1P 3AJ.

BRENNAN, Archibald Orr, (Archie Brennan), OBE 1981; Director, Edinburgh Tapestry Co., since 1962; Visiting Artist, Papua New Guinea, since 1978; *s* of James and Jessie Brennan; *m* 1956, Elizabeth Hewitt Carmichael; three *d. Educ:* Boroughmuir Sch., Edinburgh; Edinburgh College of Art (DA). Training as tapestry weaver/student, 1947-62; Lectr, Edinburgh College of Art, 1962-78. Pres., Society of Scottish Artists, 1977-78; Chm., British Craft Centre, 1977-78; travelling lectr, UK, USA, Canada, Australia, Papua New Guinea, 1962-78. Fellow, ANU, 1974-75. *Publications:* articles in various jls. *Address:* 8 Bridge Place, Edinburgh EH3 5JJ. *T:* 031-332 2897.

BRENNAN, Brian John, MC 1944; Deputy Chairman, Lloyd's, since 1981 (Underwriting Member, since 1950); Non-Executive Director, Sedgwick Group Ltd, since 1981; *b* 17 May 1918; *s* of Alfred Eric Brennan and Jean (*née* Wallace); *m* 1950, Mary Patricia Newbould; one *s* two *d. Educ:* Dulwich College. Joined E. W. Payne, Lloyd's Brokers, 1936. Member, HAC, 1938; commnd Cameronians (Scottish Rifles), 1939; India, 1/Cameronians, 1940-45; Burma, 1942; Burma, 1944; commanded 26 Column 1/Cameronians 111 Bde Special Force; Lt-Col 1/Cameronians, 1944-45. Director, E. W. Payne, 1947, Chm., 1966-74; Director, Montagu Trust, 1967-74; Dep. Chm., Bland Payne Holdings, 1974-78; Chm., Bland Payne Reinsurance Brokers, 1974-78; Dir, Sedgwick Forbes Bland Payne Holdings, 1979; Chm., Sedgwick Payne, 1979; Dir, Sedgwick Gp Ltd, 1980. Mem., Cttee of Lloyd's, 1975-80, 1981-. *Recreations:* Rugby (played for Old Alleynians, Kent, London, Barbarians); sailing, tennis, gardening. *Address:* Weybank House, Meadrow, Godalming, Surrey GU7 3BZ. *Clubs:* MCC, City of London, Royal London Yacht, Lloyd's Yacht, British Sportsman's.

BRENNAN, Hon. Sir (Francis) Gerard, KBE 1981; Hon. Mr Justice Brennan; Justice of the High Court of Australia, since 1981; *b* 22 May 1928; *s* of Hon. Mr Justice (Frank Tenison) Brennan and Mrs Gertrude Brennan; *m* 1953, Patricia (*née* O'Hara); three *s* four *d. Educ:* Christian Brothers Coll., Rockhampton, Qld; Downlands Coll., Toowoomba, Qld; Univ. of Qld (BA, LLB). Called to the Queensland Bar, 1951; QC (Australia) 1965. Judge, Aust. Indust. Court, and Additional Judge of Supreme Court of ACT, 1976-81; Judge, Fed. Court of Australia, 1977-81. President: Admin. Appeals Tribunal, 1976-79; Admin. Review Council, 1976-79; Bar Assoc. of Qld, 1974-76; Aust. Bar Assoc., 1975-76; National Union of Aust. Univ. Students, 1949. Member: Exec. Law Council of Australia, 1974-76; Aust. Law Reform Commn, 1975-77. *Recreation:* gardening. *Address:* 10 Kurundi Place, Hawker, ACT 2614, Australia. *T:* (062) 546794. *Clubs:* Commonwealth, Canberra (Canberra).

BRENNAN, Lt-Gen. Michael; retired as Chief Superintendent of Divisions, Office of Public Works, Dublin. Chief of Staff, Irish Army, 1931-40. *Address:* South Hill, Killiney, Co. Dublin.

BRENNAN, William Joseph, Jr; Legion of Merit, 1945; Associate Justice, Supreme Court of the US, since 1956; *b* 25 April 1906; *s* of William J. Brennan and Agnes McDermott; *m* 1928, Marjorie Leonard; two *s* one *d. Educ:* University of Pennsylvania; Harvard. BS Univ. of Pennsylvania, 1928; LLB Harvard, 1931. Admitted to New Jersey Bar, 1931; practised in Newark, New Jersey, 1931-49, Member Pitney, Hardin, Ward & Brennan; Superior Court Judge, 1949-50; Appellate Division Judge, 1950-52; Supreme Court of New Jersey Justice, 1952-56; served War of 1939-45 as Colonel, General Staff Corps, United States Army. Hon. LLD: Pennsylvania, 1957; Wesleyan, 1957; St John's, 1957; Rutgers, 1958; Notre Dame, 1968; Harvard, 1968; Hon. DCL: New York Univ., 1957; Colgate, 1957; Hon. SJD Suffolk Univ., 1956. *Address:* 3037 Dumbarton Avenue, Washington, DC 20007, USA. *Club:* University (Washington, DC).

BRENNER, Sydney, DPhil, FRCP, FRS 1965; Director, Laboratory of Molecular Biology, Cambridge, since 1979 (Member of Scientific Staff, since 1957); Fellow of King's College, Cambridge, since 1959; *b* Germiston, South Africa, 13 Jan. 1927; *s* of Morris Brenner and Lena (*née* Blacher); *m* 1952, May Woolf Balkind; one *s* two *d* (and one step *s*). *Educ:* Germiston High School; University of the Witwatersrand, S Africa; Oxford University. MSc 1947, MB, BCh 1951, Univ. of the Witwatersrand; DPhil Oxon., 1954; FRCP 1979. Member: MRC, 1978-; Science Council, Celltech 1980-81. Carter-Wallace Lectr, Princeton, 1966, 1971; Gifford Lectr, Glasgow, 1978-79. Foreign Hon. Member, American Academy of Arts and Sciences, 1965; Foreign Associate, Nat. Acad. of Sciences, USA, 1977; Mem., Deutsche Akademie der Naturforscher, Leopoldina, 1976 (Gregor Mendel Medal, 1970); For. Mem., Amer. Philosophical Soc., 1979. Hon. FRSE, 1979; Hon. DSc: Dublin, 1967; Witwatersrand, 1972; Chicago, 1976; Hon. LLD Glasgow, 1981. Warren Triennial Prize, 1968; William Bate Hardy Prize, Cambridge Philosophical Soc., 1969; (jtly) Lasker Award for Basic Medical Research, 1971; Royal Medal, Royal Soc., 1974; (jtly) Prix Charles Leopold Mayer, French Acad. of Science, 1975; Gairdner Foundn Annual Award, 1978; Krebs Medal, FEBS, 1980; CIBA Medal, Biochem. Soc., 1981. *Publications:* papers in scientific journals. *Recreations:* conversation, scheming. *Address:* MRC Laboratory of Molecular Biology, University Postgraduate Medical School, Hills Road, Cambridge. *T:* Cambridge 248011.

BRENT, Prof. Leslie, FIBiol; Professor of Immunology, St Mary's Hospital Medical School, London, since 1969; *b* 5 July 1925; *s* of Charlotte and Arthur Baruch; *m* 1954, Joanne Elisabeth Manley; one *s* two *d. Educ:* Bunce Court Sch., Kent; Birmingham Central Technical Coll.; Univ. of Birmingham; UCL. BSc Birmingham, PhD London; FIBiol 1964. Laboratory technician, 1941-43; Army service, 1943-47; Lectr, Dept of Zoology, UCL, 1954-62; Rockefeller Res. Fellow, Calif Inst. of Technology, 1956-57; Res. scientist, Nat. Inst. for Med. Res., 1962-65; Prof. of Zoology, Univ. of Southampton, 1965-69. European Editor, Transplantation, 1963-68; Gen. Sec., British Transplantation Soc., 1971-75, Pres., The Transplantation Society, 1976-78; Chm. Organising Cttee, 9th Internat. Congress of The Transplantation Soc., 1978-82. Pres., Guild of Undergrads, Birmingham Univ., 1950-51. Chairman: Haringey Community Relations Council, 1979-80; Haringey SDP, 1981-. Vice-Chancellor's Prize, Birmingham Univ., 1951; Scientific Medal, Zool Soc., 1963. Played hockey for UAU and Staffs, 1949-51. *Publications:* articles in scientific and med. jls on immunology of tissue transplantation and immunological tolerance. *Recreations:* music, walking/climbing, chess, squash, community relations, politics. *Address:* 8 Wood Vale, N10.

BRENTFORD, 3rd Viscount, *cr* 1929; Bt, *cr* 1919 and 1956; **Lancelot William Joynson-Hicks;** DL; solicitor; formerly Senior Partner of Joynson-Hicks & Co.; elected Member, Church Assembly, 1934-70; *b* 10 April 1902; 2nd *s* of 1st Viscount Brentford, PC, DL, and Grace Lynn (*d* 1952), *o c* of Richard Hampson Joynson, JP, Bowdon, Cheshire; *S* brother, 1958; *m* 1931, Phyllis (*d* 1979), *o d* of late Major Herbert Allfrey, Newnton House, Tetbury, Gloucestershire; one *s. Educ:* Winchester College; Trinity College, Oxford (MA). Admitted a Solicitor, 1926. Served War of 1939-45 as acting Lt-Comdr, RNVR. MP (C) Chichester Division of West Sussex, 1942-58; Parliamentary Secretary, Ministry of Fuel and Power, Nov. 1951-Dec. 1955. Chairman, Automobile Association, 1956-74. Pres., Southern Regional Assoc. for the Blind, 1972-. DL East Sussex, 1977. *Heir:* *s* Hon. Crispin William Joynson-Hicks [*b* 7 April 1933; *m* 1964, Gillian Evelyn, *er d* of G. E. Schluter, OBE, Valehyrst, Sevenoaks; one *s* three *d. Educ:* Eton; New College, Oxford]. *Address:* Newick Park, East Sussex.

BRENTON, Howard; playwright; *b* 13 Dec. 1942; *s* of Donald Henry Brenton and Rose Lilian (*née* Lewis); *m* 1970, Jane Fry; two *s. Educ:* Chichester High Sch. for Boys; St Catharine's Coll., Cambridge (BA Hons English). *Full-length stage plays:* Revenge, 1969; Hitler Dances, and Measure for Measure (after Shakespeare), 1972; Magnificence, 1973; The Churchill Play, 1974; Government Property, 1975; Weapons of Happiness, 1976; Epsom Downs, 1977; Sore Throats, 1979; The Romans in Britain, 1980; Thirteenth Night, 1981; *one-act stage plays:* Gum and Goo, Heads, The Education of Skinny Spew, and Christie in Love, 1969; Wesley, 1970; Scott of the Antarctic, and A Sky-blue Life, 1971; How Beautiful with Badges, 1972; Mug, 1973; The Thing (for children), 1982; *collaborations:* (with six others) Lay-By, 1970; (with six others) England's Ireland, 1971; (with David Hare) Brassneck, 1973; (with Trevor Griffiths, David Hare and Ken Campbell), Deeds, 1978; (with Tony Howard) A Short Sharp Shock, 1980; *television plays:* Lushly, 1971; Brassneck (adaptation of stage play), 1974; The Saliva Milkshake, 1975 (also perf. theatre); The Paradise Run, 1976; *translations:* Bertolt Brecht, The Life of Galileo, 1980; Georg Buchner, Danton's Death, 1982. *Publications:* many plays published. *Recreation:* painting. *Address:* c/o Margaret Ramsay Ltd, 14A Goodwin's Court, St Martin's Lane, WC2N 4LL. *T:* 01-240 0691.

BRENTWOOD, Bishop of, (RC), since 1980; **Rt. Rev. Thomas McMahon;** *b* 17 June 1936. *Address:* Bishop's House, Stock, Ingatestone, Essex CM4 9B4. *T:* Stock 840268.

BRESSON, Robert; film producer since 1934; *b* 25 Sept. 1907; *s* of Léon Bresson and Marie-Elisabeth Clausels; *m* 1926, Leidia Van der Zee. *Educ:* Lycée Lakanal, Sceaux. Started as painter; then producer of short films, Affaires Publiques. Full-length films produced include: Les Anges du Péché, 1943; Les Dames du Bois de Boulogne, 1948; Journal d'un Curé de Campagne, 1951 (Internat. Grand Prix, Venice); Un Condamné à Mort s'est Echappé, 1956; Pickpocket, 1960; Le Procès de Jeanne d'Arc, 1962 (Jury's special prize, Cannes); Au Hasard Balthazar, 1966; Mouchette, 1967; Une Femme Douce, 1969; Quatre nuits d'un rêveur, 1971; Lancelot du Lac, 1974; Le diable, probablement, 1977. *Publication:* Notes sur le cinématographe, 1976. *Address:* 49 quai de Bourbon, 75004 Paris, France.

BRETHERTON, Russell Frederick, CB 1951; Under-Secretary, the Treasury, 1961-68; *b* 3 Feb. 1906; *s* of F. H. Bretherton, Solicitor, Gloucester; *m* 1930, Jocelyn Nina Mathews; three *s* one *d. Educ:* Clifton College; Wadham College, Oxford. Fellow of Wadham College, 1928-45, Lecturer and Tutor in Economics and Modern History; University Research Lecturer, 1936-39. Temporary Civil Servant, Ministry of Supply and Board of Trade, 1939-45; Under-Secretary, Raw Materials Dept, Board of Trade, 1946-48; Cabinet Office (Economic Section), 1949-51; Under-Secretary: Min. of Materials, 1951-54; Board of Trade, 1954-61; Treasury, 1961-68. *Publications:* (with R. L. Lennard and others) Englishmen at Rest and Play (17th Century Studies), 1932; (with Burchardt and Rutherford) Public Investment and the Trade Cycle, 1941; articles in Social Survey of Oxford, Economic Journal, Econometrica, and in various entomological journals, etc. *Recreations:* walking, mountaineering, entomology. *Address:* Folly Hill, Birtley Green, Bramley, Guildford, Surrey GU5 0LE. *T:* Guildford 893377.

BRETT, family name of **Viscount Esher.**

BRETT, Charles Edward Bainbridge, CBE 1981; Partner, L'Estrange & Brett, Solicitors, Belfast, since 1954; Chairman, Northern Ireland Housing Executive, since 1979; *b* 30 Oct. 1928; *s* of Charles Anthony Brett and Elizabeth Joyce (*née* Carter); *m* 1953, Joyce Patricia Worley; three *s*. *Educ:* Rugby Sch.; New Coll., Oxford (Schol.; MA History). Solicitor, 1953. Journalist, Radiodiffusion Française and Continental Daily Mail, 1949-50. Member: Child Welfare Council of Northern Ireland, 1958-61; Northern Ireland Cttee, National Trust, 1956- (Mem. Council, 1975-); Arts Council of N Ireland, 1970-76; Chairman: N Ireland Labour Party, 1962; Ulster Architectural Heritage Soc., 1968-78 (Pres., 1979-); HEARTH Housing Assoc., 1978. Hon. Mem., Royal Society of Ulster Architects, 1973. *Publications:* Buildings of Belfast 1700-1914, 1967; Court Houses and Market Houses of Ulster, 1973; Long Shadows Cast Before, 1978; lists and surveys for Ulster Architectural Heritage Soc., National Trusts of Guernsey and Jersey, and Alderney Soc. *Address:* 9 Chichester Street, Belfast. *Club:* United Oxford & Cambridge University.

BRETT, George P., jun.; retired from The Macmillan Company, New York, 1961; *b* Darien, Conn., 9 Dec. 1893; *s* of George Platt and Marie Louise (Tostevan) Brett; *m* 1917, Isabel Yeomans; two *s*. *Educ:* Collegiate School, New York City; Salisbury School, Salisbury, Conn. Joined staff of The Macmillan Company, Sept. 1913; six months training with competing publishing house, Doubleday, 1915. Served European War, 1914-18, with US Army, private 1916, 2nd Lieut 1917, 1st Lieut Jan. 1918, Capt. July 1918, 16 months service in France, 1918-19; Maj. Reserve Corps until 1940; Lieut-Col, Asst Chief of Staff, NY Guard, 1940-43; Adviser to War Production Board, State Dept, 1943-45. Returned to Macmillan, 1919; Dir and Sales Manager, 1920; Treas., 1920-31; General Manager, 1928-34; Pres., 1931-58; Chairman of the Board, 1959-61. Trustee: Union Square Savings Bank, New York City, 1926-61; Southport (Connecticut) Savings Bank, 1954-58. President: Sasquanaug Assoc. for Southport Improvement, 1954-56; Pequot Library, Southport, Connecticut, 1955-56. *Publications:* occasional contributor to trade journals. *Recreations:* walking, sailing, fishing. *Address:* (home) 240 Main Street, Southport, Connecticut 06490, USA. *Clubs:* Century, Players, Cruising of America (New York); Pequot Yacht (Cdre, 1951-53); Fairfield County Hunt (Conn); Lake Placid (NY); Key Largo Anglers' (Fla).

BRETT, Jeremy, (Peter Jeremy William Huggins); actor; *b* 3 Nov. 1935; *s* of Lt-Col H. W. Huggins, DSO, MC, DL, and late Elizabeth Huggins; *m* 1958 (marr. diss.); one *s*; *m* 1978; one *s*. *Educ:* Eton; Central Sch. of Drama. National Theatre, 1967-70: Orlando, in As You Like It; Berowne, in Love's Labour's Lost; Tesman, in Hedda Gabler; Bassanio, in The Merchant of Venice; Che Guevara, in Macrune's Guevara; The Son, in Voyage round my Father, Haymarket, 1972; Otto, in Design for Living, Phoenix, 1973-74; The Way of the World, Stratford, Ont, 1976; Prospero, in The Tempest, Toronto, 1982. Films include: Nicholas, in War and Peace, 1955; Freddie, in My Fair Lady, 1965; also TV appearances, including: Max de Winter in Rebecca, 1978; George, Duke of Bristol, in On Approval, 1980; Edward Ashburnham in The Good Soldier, 1981; title rôle in Macbeth The Last Visitor, 1982; title rôle in William Pitt the Younger, 1982. *Recreation:* archery. *Address:* 5860 Carolus Drive, Los Angeles, Calif 90068, USA. *Club:* Woodmen of Arden (Meriden).

BRETT, John Alfred, MA; Headmaster, Durham School, Durham, 1958-67; retired; *b* 26 Oct. 1915; *s* of Alfred Brett, Harrogate, Yorks; *m* 1939, Margaret Coode; one *s* three *d*. *Educ:* Durham School; St Edmund Hall, Oxford. MA (Hons Modern History). Temp. teacher, Stowe School, 1938; Teacher, Diocesan College, Rondebosch, South Africa, 1939; restarted Silver Tree Youth Club for non-Europeans, Cape Town. Army: Gunner to Major, RA, 1940-44; Instructor 123 OCTU Catterick; invasion of Normandy, 1944 (lost right eye); Military testing officer, WOSBs, finally Senior Military Testing Officer, War Office Selection Centre. Returned to post at Diocesan College, Rondebosch, 1946; Housemaster, 1948; Temp. teacher, Canford School, Wimborne, Dorset, 1954; Headmaster, Shaftesbury Grammar School, 1954. Diocesan Lay Reader. Member Council: Brathay Hall Centre; McAlpine Educnl Endowments Ltd. Governor, Bernard Gilpin Society. *Recreations:* sport (Captain Oxford University Rugby Football Club, 1937, and Member British Touring XV to Argentina, 1936); travel; reading. *Address:* Flat 2, 1 Lancaster Road, Harrogate.

BRETT, Lionel; see Esher, 4th Viscount.

BRETT, Sir Lionel, Kt 1961; *b* 19 Aug. 1911; 3rd *s* of late Very Rev. H. R. Brett, Dean of Belfast, and Constance Brett (*née* White). *Educ:* Marlborough; Magdalen College, Oxford. BA 1934; MA 1946. Called to Bar, Inner Temple, 1937. War service, 1939-46, released as Major. Joined Colonial Legal Service as Crown Counsel, Nigeria, 1946; Justice, Supreme Court of Nigeria, 1958-68. *Recreations:* reading, walking. *Address:* The Cottage, Puckington, near Ilminster, Somerset. *Club:* United Oxford & Cambridge University.

BRETT, Michael John Lee; Editor, Investors Chronicle, 1977-82; Director: Throgmorton Publications; Financial Times Business Publishing Division; *b* 23 May 1939; *s* of John Brett and Margaret Brett (*née* Lee). *Educ:* King's Coll. Sch., Wimbledon; Wadham Coll., Oxford (BA Modern Langs). Investors Review, 1962-64; Fire Protection Assoc., 1964-68; Investors Chronicle,

1968-82, Dep. Editor, 1973-77. *Recreations:* travelling, reading. *Address:* 134 Offord Road, N1. *T:* 01-609 2362.

BRETT, Prof. Raymond Laurence; G. F. Grant Professor of English, University of Hull, since 1952; *b* 10 January 1917; *s* of late Leonard and Ellen Brett, Clevedon, Avon; *m* 1947, Kathleen Tegwen, *d* of late Rev. C. D. Cranmer; two *s*. *Educ:* Bristol Cathedral School; University of Bristol; University College, Oxford (Plumptre Exhibitioner). 1st Class Hons BA, English and Philosophy, Bristol, 1937; Taylor Prizeman, Hannam-Clark Prizeman, Haldane of Cloan Post-Grad. Studentship; BLitt, Oxf., 1940. Service in Admiralty, 1940-46; on Staff of First Lord; Lectr in English, Univ. of Bristol, 1946-52; Dean, Faculty of Arts, Hull Univ., 1960-62. Visiting Professor: Univ. of Rochester, USA, 1958-59; Kiel Univ., Osnabrück Univ. 1977; Baroda Univ., Jadavpur Univ., 1978. *Publications:* The Third Earl of Shaftesbury: A Study in 18th Century Literary Theory, 1951; Coleridge's Theory of Imagination (English Essays), 1949; George Crabbe, 1956; Reason and Imagination, 1961; (with A. R. Jones) a critical edition of Lyrical Ballads by Wordsworth and Coleridge, 1963; Thomas Hobbes (The English Mind), 1964; (ed) Poems of Faith and Doubt, 1965; An Introduction to English Studies, 1965; Fancy and Imagination, 1969; (ed) S. T. Coleridge, 1971; William Hazlitt, 1978; (ed) Barclay Fox's Journal, 1979; (ed) Andrew Marvell, 1979; Coleridge (Writers and their Work), 1981; articles in: The Times, Time and Tide, Essays and Studies, Review of English Studies, Modern Language Review, Philosophy, English, South Atlantic Qly, Critical Qly, etc. *Address:* The Gables, Station Walk, Cottingham, North Humberside. *T:* Hull 847115.

BRETT-JAMES, (Eliot) Antony; author (Military History); Head of War Studies and International Affairs Department, Royal Military Academy Sandhurst, 1970-80 (Deputy Head, 1968-69); *b* 4 April 1920; *er surv. s* of late Norman George Brett-James, MA, BLitt, FSA, Mill Hill, and Gladys Brett-James. *Educ:* Mill Hill Sch.; Paris; Sidney Sussex Coll., Cambridge. 2nd cl. Mod. Langs Tripos, 1947; MA. Served War of 1939-45: Royal Signals, 2nd Lt, 1941; 2nd Air Formation Signals; Lebanon, Syria; 5th Indian Divl Signals, in Alamein Line, 1942; Iraq, India; Capt., 1943; commanded 9th Indian Inf. Bde Signals, Arakan, Imphal, Burma (despatches), 1944; Burma, 1945. Entered publishing: George G. Harrap (mod. langs editor), 1947-52; Chatto & Windus (reader and publicity manager), 1952-58; Cassell, 1958-61 (educl manager, 1960-61). Lectr, then Sen. Lectr, in Mil. Hist., RMA Sandhurst, 1961-67. Helped Field Marshal Montgomery write A History of Warfare, 1964-68; Mil. Advr, BBC TV for Tolstoy's War and Peace, 1971-72. Question setter for Mastermind, BBC TV, 1974-. Mem., RUSI; FRHistS 1970. *Publications:* Report My Signals, 1948; Ball of Fire: the 5th Indian Division in the Second World War, 1951; The Triple Stream, 1953; General Graham, Lord Lynedoch, 1959; Wellington at War, 1794-1815, 1961; (with Lt-Gen. Sir G. Evans) Imphal, 1962; The Hundred Days, 1964; 1812, 1966; The British Soldier 1793-1815, 1970; Europe against Napoleon, 1970; Daily Life in Wellington's Army, 1972; (ed) Escape from the French: Captain Hewson's Narrative, 1981; articles in: Dictionary of National Biography, History Today, Purnell's History of the Second World War; reviews in TLS. *Recreations:* meeting people, watching cricket, browsing in antiquarian bookshops, gardening, music. *Address:* Vine Cottage, Steep, Petersfield, Hants. *T:* Petersfield 4927.

BRETTEN, George Rex, QC 1980; barrister-at-law; *b* 21 Feb. 1942; *s* of Horace Victor Bretten and Kathleen Edna Betty Bretten; *m* 1965, Maureen Gillian Crowhurst; one *d*. *Educ:* King Edward VII Sch., King's Lynn; Sidney Sussex Coll., Cambridge (MA, LLB). Lectr, Nottingham Univ., 1964-68; Asst Director, Inst. of Law Research and Reform, Alberta, Canada, 1968-70; called to the Bar, Lincoln's Inn; in practice, 1971-. *Publication:* Special Reasons, 1977. *Recreations:* hobby farming, tennis, riding. *Address:* Church Farm, Great Eversden, Cambridgeshire CB3 7HN. *T:* Comberton 3538.

BREW, Richard Maddock, CBE 1982; Member of Greater London Council; Leader of the Opposition, since 1982; *b* 13 Dec. 1930; *s* of late Leslie Maddock Brew and Phyllis Evelyn Huntsman; *m* 1953, Judith Anne Thompson Hancock; two *s* two *d*. *Educ:* Rugby Sch.; Magdalene Coll., Cambridge (BA). Called to the Bar, Inner Temple, 1955. After practising for short time at the Bar, joined family business, Brew Brothers Ltd, SW7, 1955, and remained until takeover, 1972. Chm., Budget Lifts Ltd. Farms in Essex. Member: Royal Borough of Kensington Council, 1959-65; Royal Borough of Kensington and Chelsea Council, 1964-70; Greater London Council: Alderman, 1968-73; Vice-Chm., Strategic Planning Cttee, 1969-71; Chm., Covent Garden Jt Development Cttee, 1970-71 and Environmental Planning Cttee, 1971-73; Mem. for Chingford, 1973-; Dep. Leader of Council and Leader, Policy and Resources Cttee, 1977-81; Dep. Leader, Cons. Party and Opposition Spokesman on Finance, 1981-82. *Recreations:* Pony Club, hunting, tennis. *Address:* The Abbey, Coggeshall, Essex. *T:* Coggeshall 61246. *Clubs:* Carlton, Farmers'.

BREWER, Dr Derek Stanley, LittD; FSA; Master of Emmanuel College, Cambridge, since 1977, and Reader in Medieval English, University of Cambridge, since 1976; *b* 13 July 1923; *s* of Stanley Leonard Brewer and Winifred Helen Forbes; *m* 1951, Lucie Elisabeth Hoole; three *s* two *d*. *Educ:* elementary school; The Crypt Grammar Sch.; Magdalen Coll., Oxford (Matthew Arnold Essay Prize, 1948; BA, MA 1948); Birmingham Univ. (PhD 1956). LittD Cantab 1980. Commnd 2nd Lieut, Worcestershire Regt, 1942; Captain and Adjt, 1st Bn Royal Fusiliers, 1944-45. Asst Lectr and Lectr in

English, Univ. of Birmingham, 1949-56; Prof. of English, Internat. Christian Univ., Tokyo, 1956-58; Lectr and Sen. Lectr, Univ. of Birmingham, 1958-64; Lectr in English, Univ. of Cambridge, 1965-76; Fellow of Emmanuel Coll., Cambridge, 1965-77 (Seatonian Prize, 1969, 1972, and jtly, 1979, 1980). Founder, D. S. Brewer Ltd, for the publication of academic books, 1972. Sir Israel Gollancz Meml Lectr, British Academy, 1974; first William Matthews Lectr, Univ. of London, 1982. Pres., The English Assoc., 1982-83. FSA 1977. Hon. Mem., Japan Acad., 1981. Hon. LLD Keio Univ., Tokyo, 1982. *Publications:* Chaucer, 1953, 3rd edn 1973; Proteus, 1958 (Tokyo); (ed) The Parlement of Foulys, 1960; Chaucer in his Time, 1963; (ed and contrib.) Chaucer and Chaucerians, 1966; (ed) Malory's Morte Darthur: Parts Seven and Eight, 1968; (ed and contrib.) Writers and their Backgrounds: Chaucer, 1974; (ed) Chaucer: the Critical Heritage, 1978; Chaucer and his World, 1978; Symbolic Stories, 1980; (ed jtly) Aspects of Malory, 1981; English Gothic Literature, 1982; Tradition and Innovation in Chaucer, 1982; Chaucer: the Poet as Storyteller, 1983; numerous articles in learned jls, reviews, etc. *Recreations:* reading, book-collecting, walking, opera, looking at paintings and antiquities, travelling, publishing other people's books. *Address:* The Master's Lodge, Emmanuel College, Cambridge CB2 3AP. *T:* Cambridge 350484.

BREWER, Frank, CMG 1960; OBE 1953; Foreign and Commonwealth Office (formerly Foreign Office), 1960-76; *b* 1915; *s* of late Lewis Arthur Brewer; *m* 1950, Eileen Marian, *d* of A. J. Shepherd. *Educ:* Swindon Commonweal School; Pembroke College, Oxford (MA). Malayan Civil Service, 1937-59; War Service, 1941-45, Special Forces (POW Sumatra) Chinese Secretariat, Labour Dept; Secretary for Chinese Affairs and Dep. Chief Sec., Fed. of Malaya, 1955-57; Sec. for Defence, 1957-59. *Address:* 18 Forest Way, Tunbridge Wells, Kent. *T:* Tunbridge Wells 24850. *Clubs:* Royal Commonwealth Society, Special Forces.

BREWER, Rear-Adm. George Maxted Kenneth, CB 1982; Flag Officer Medway and Port Admiral Chatham, 1980-82; *b* Dover, 4 March 1930; *s* of George Maxted Brewer and Cecilia Victoria (*née* Clark). *Educ:* Pangbourne College. In Command: HMS Carysfort, Far East and Mediterranean, 1964-65; HMS Agincourt, Home, 1967; HMS Grenville, Far East and Mediterranean, 1968-69; HMS Juno, and Captain Fourth Frigate Sqdn, Home and Mediterranean, 1974; rcds 1975; In Command: HMS Tiger, and Flag Captain to Flag Officer Second Flotilla, Far East, 1978; HMS Bulwark, NATO area, 1979-80. *Recreation:* watercolour painting. *Address:* c/o National Westminster Bank Ltd, High Street, Chatham, Kent. *Clubs:* Royal Navy Club of 1765 and 1785, Royal United Services Institute for Defence Studies.

BREWER, Rt. Rev. John; Titular Bishop of Britonia and Auxiliary Bishop of Shrewsbury, (RC), since 1971; *b* 24 Nov. 1929; *s* of Eric W. Brewer and Laura H. Brewer (*née* Webster). *Educ:* Ushaw College, Durham; Ven. English College, Rome, and Gregorian Univ. PhL, STL, JCL. Ordained priest, 1956; Parish Assistant, 1959-64; Vice-Rector, Ven. English Coll., Rome, 1964-71; Parish Priest of St Mary's, Middlewich, 1971-78. Officiating Chaplain, Royal Navy, 1966-71; Representative of RC Bishops of England and Wales in Rome, 1964-71. Chaplain to HH Pope Paul VI, 1965. *Recreations:* walking, golf. *Address:* The Council House, Shrewsbury. *T:* Shrewsbury 3513.

BREWIS, Henry John; Lord-Lieutenant of Wigtown, since 1981; Director, Border Television Ltd, since 1977; Managing Director, Ardwell Estates, Stranraer; farming; *b* 8 April 1920; *s* of Lt-Col F. B. Brewis, Norton Grove, Malton, Yorks; *m* 1949, Faith A. D. MacTaggart Stewart, Ardwell, Wigtownshire; three *s* one *d. Educ:* Eton; New College, Oxford. Served Royal Artillery, 1940-46 (despatches twice); on active service, North Africa and Italy; demobilized with rank of Major. Barrister-at-law, 1946. Wigtownshire County Council, 1955; Convener, Finance Cttee, 1958. MP (C) Galloway, April 1959-Sept. 1974; PPS to The Lord Advocate, 1960-61; Speaker's Panel of Chairmen, 1965; Chm., Select Cttee on Scottish Affairs, 1970; Member British Delegn: to Council of Europe, 1966-69; to European Parlt, Strasbourg, 1973-75; Vice-Chm., Cons. Agric. Cttee, 1971; Chm., Scottish Cons. Gp for Europe, 1973-76. Dist Chm., Queen's Jubilee Appeal, 1976-78. Reg. Chm., Scottish Landowners' Fedn, 1977-80; Chm., Scottish Woodlands Owners' Assoc., 1980; Vice-Chm., Forestry Cttee for GB; Mem., Comité Central Propriété Forestière, Brussels, 1979, and other forestry cttees. DL Wigtownshire, 1966. *Recreations:* golf, tennis, shooting. *Address:* Ardwell House, Stranraer. *T:* Ardwell 227; Norton Grove, Malton, N Yorks. *Clubs:* Caledonian; New (Edinburgh).

BREWIS, John Fenwick, CMG 1962; CVO 1957; HM Diplomatic Service (retired); *b* 26 April 1910; *s* of late Arthur and Mary Brewis; *m* 1948, Rachel Mary, *d* of late Hilary G. Gardner; one *s* one *d. Educ:* Repton; CCC, Camb. Entered China Consular Service in 1933 and served in China till 1944; First Secretary, Baghdad, 1946-49; Consul, Bordeaux, 1950-52; Foreign Office, 1945-46, 1954-55 and 1959-65; Counsellor, Lisbon, 1955-59; Consul-General, Lyons, 1965-67. Tourist and Publicity Officer for Winchester, 1968-75. *Recreations:* gardening, historical reading. *Address:* 49 St Cross Road, Winchester. *T:* Winchester 4187.

BREWSTER, George, CVO 1969; MD; practitioner of medicine, retired 1977; formerly Surgeon Apothecary to HM Household at Holyrood Palace, Edinburgh, resigned 1970; formerly Medical Officer to French Consulate-General in Scotland; *b* 27 Sept. 1899; *m* 1930; two *s. Educ:* High School, Stirling; Edinburgh Univ. MB, ChB, Edin., 1921; DPH Edin., 1924; MD (with distinction) Edin., 1926. House Surgeon, Edin. Royal Infirmary. Chevalier de la Légion d'Honneur (France), 1957. *Address:* 17 The Limes, Napier Road, Edinburgh EH10 5DL. *T:* 031-447 6183.

BREWSTER, Kingman; Lawyer; Counsel to Winthrop, Stimson, Putnam and Roberts, NYC, since 1981; *b* Longmeadow, Massachusetts, 17 June 1919; *s* of Kingman Brewster and Florence Besse; *m* 1942, Mary Louise Phillips; three *s* two *d. Educ:* Yale University; Harvard University. AB Yale, 1941; LLB Harvard, 1948. Military Service: Lieut (Aviation) USNR, 1942-46. Special Asst Coordinator Inter-American Affairs, 1941; Research Assoc., Dept Economics, Massachusetts Inst. of Technology, 1949-50; Asst. General Counsel, Office US Special Representative in Europe, 1948-49; Cons., Pres. Materials Policy Commission, 1951, Mut. Security Agency, 1952; Asst Prof. of Law, Harvard, 1950-58; Prof. of Law, Harvard, 1953-60; Provost, Yale, 1961-63; Pres., Yale Univ., 1963-77; Ambassador to Court of St James's, 1977-81. Member: President's Commn on Law Enforcement and Administration of Justice, 1965-67; President's Commn on Selective Service, 1966-68; Bd of Dirs, Carnegie Endowment Fund for Internat. Peace, 1975-; Member: Council on Foreign Relations; American Philosophical Soc. Holds many Hon. Degrees. Officer, Legion of Honour, 1977. *Publications:* Antitrust and American Business Abroad, 1959; (with M. Katz) Law of International Transactions and Relations, 1960. *Recreation:* sailing. *Address:* 38 Lincoln Street, New Haven, Conn 06511, USA. *Clubs:* Athenæum; Metropolitan (Washington); Yale, Century Association (New York); Tavern (Boston, Mass).

BREZHNEV, Leonid Ilyich; Order of Victory; Hero of the Soviet Union (two awards); five Orders of Lenin; two Orders of the Red Banner; Order of Bogdan Khmelnitsky (2nd cl.); Order of the Patriotic War (1st cl.); two Orders of the October Revolution; Order of the Red Star; Hero of Socialist Labour; President of the Presidium, Supreme Soviet of USSR, since 1977; General Secretary of Central Cttee, CPSU, since 1966; Member, Presidium of Supreme Soviet (President, 1960-64); *b* Kamenskoye (now Dnieprodzerzhinsk), Ukraine, 19 Dec. 1906. *Educ:* Institute of Metallurgy, Dnieprodzerzhinsk (graduate). Began career as engineer and was active in social work. Joined Communist Party, 1931; 1st Secretary, Central Cttee, Communist Party of Moldavia, 1950. Elected to Supreme Soviet of USSR, 1950, 1954, 1958, 1962. Member, Central Cttee, CPSU, 1952-; Alternate Member Presidium of Central Cttee, CPSU, 1952-57; Secretary, Central Cttee, Communist Party, Kazakhstan, 1954-56; Member Presidium of Central Cttee, CPSU, 1957-; Member Party Secretariat, Central Cttee, 1952-53, 1956-57, 1963-, First Secretary, 1964-66. Maj.-Gen. 1943; Lieut-Gen. 1953. Lenin Peace Prize, 1972; Lenin Prize for Literature, 1979. Karl Marx Gold Medal, USSR Acad. of Scis, 1977. Gold Star, Vietnam, 1980. *Publications:* Little Land, 1978; Rebirth, 1978; Virgin Lands, 1978; Socialism, Democracy and Human Rights, 1981. *Address:* Central Committee, CPSU, Kremlin, Moscow, USSR.

BRIANCE, John Albert, CMG 1960; HM Diplomatic Service, retired; *b* 19 Oct. 1915; *s* of late Albert Perceval and Louise Florence Briance; *m* 1950, Prunella Mary, *d* of Col. E. Haldane Chapman; one *s* one *d. Educ:* King Edward VII School. Colonial Police, Palestine, 1936-48; Foreign Office, 1949; British Embassy, Tehran, 1950-52; British Middle East Office, 1953; Foreign Office, 1954-57; Counsellor, British Embassy, Washington, 1958-60; Counsellor, Office of UK Commissioner for SE Asia Singapore, 1961-63; FCO (formerly FO), 1964-70; retired 1970. *Address:* 14 Pitt Street, W8. *Clubs:* Naval & Military, Hurlingham.

BRIANT, Bernard Christian, CVO 1977 (MVO 1974); MBE 1945; FRICS; Consultant, Messrs Daniel Smith, Chartered Surveyors, since 1982; Church Commissioner, since 1981; *b* 11 April 1917; *s* of Bernard Briant and Cecily (*née* Christian); *m* 1942, Margaret Emslie, *d* of A. S. Rawle; one *s* two *d. Educ:* Stowe Sch.; Trinity Coll., Oxford (MA). FRICS 1948. Served War, 1939-45: Tunisia, Italy and Austria; Major, Intell. Corps. Joined Briant & Son, Chartered Surveyors, 1938, Partner 1948; Partner, Daniel Smith, 1970, Sen. Partner, 1976-82. Mem. various cttees, RICS, 1948-70 (Mem. Council, 1962-70); Clerk, Co. of Chartered Surveyors, 1980-. Director: C of E Bldg Soc., 1953-67; S of England Building Soc., 1967-80; London and S of England Bldg Soc., 1980-; Mem., Cttee of Management, Lambeth and Southwark Housing Soc., 1971-. Land Steward, Manor of Kennington of Duchy of Cornwall, 1963-76; Agent, All Souls Coll., Oxford, 1966-79. Governor, Polytechnic of South Bank, 1980-. *Recreations:* golf, walking, reading. *Address:* 32 St James's Street, SW1A 1HT. *Clubs:* United Oxford & Cambridge University; Aldeburgh Golf, Rye Golf.

BRIAULT, Dr Eric William Henry, CBE 1976; Education Officer, Inner London Education Authority, 1971-76; Visiting Professor of Education, University of Sussex, 1977-81; *b* 24 Dec. 1911; *s* of H. G. Briault; *m* 1935, Marie Alice (*née* Knight); two *s* one *d. Educ:* Brighton, Hove and Sussex Grammar Sch.; Peterhouse, Cambridge (Robert Slade Schol.). 1st cl. hons Geography, 1933; MA Cantab 1937; PhD London 1939. School teaching, 1933-47; Inspector of Schools, LCC, 1948-56; Dep. Educn Officer, ILEA, 1956-71. Dir, res. project on falling rolls in secondary schs, 1978-80. Hon. Sec., RGS, 1953-63. Hon. DLitt Sussex, 1975. *Publications:* Sussex, East and West (Land Utilisation Survey report), 1942; (jtly) Introduction to Advanced Geography, 1957; (jtly) Geography In and Out of School, 1960; (jtly) Falling Rolls in Secondary Schools, Parts I and II, 1980. *Recreations:* travel, gardening, music, theatre and ballet; formerly athletics (Cambridge blue) and cross-country running (Cambridge half-blue). *Address:* Woodedge, Hampers Lane, Storrington, W Sussex. *T:* Storrington 3919. *Club:* Athenæum.

BRICE, Air Cdre Eric John, CBE 1971 (OBE 1957); CEng; AFRAeS; MBIM; RAF retd; stockbroker; *b* 12 Feb. 1917; *s* of Courtenay Percy Please Brice and Lilie Alice Louise Brice (*née* Grey); *m* 1942, Janet Parks, Roundhay, Leeds, Yorks; two *s* one *d. Educ:* Loughborough Coll. (DLC). Joined RAF, 1939; served War, MEAF, 1943–46 (Sqdn Ldr). Air Ministry, 1946–50; Parachute Trg Sch., 1950–52; Wing Comdr, 1952; RAE, Farnborough, 1952–58; Comd, Parachute Trg Sch., 1958–60; RAF Coll., Cranwell, 1960–61; Gp Capt., 1961; RAF Halton, 1961–64; Comd, RAF Innsworth, Glos, 1964–66; Dir, Physical Educn, RAF, MoD, 1966–68; Air Cdre, 1968; Dep. AOA, RAF Headqrs, Maintenance Comd, 1968–71; April 1971, retd prematurely. *Recreations:* athletics (Combined Services and RAF athletic blues); Rugby football (RAF trialist and Blackheath Rugby Club); captained Loughborough Coll. in three sports. *Address:* Durns, Boldre, Hampshire. *T:* Lymington 72196. *Clubs:* Royal Air Force; Royal Lymington Yacht.

BRICE, Geoffrey James Barrington Groves, QC 1979; barrister; a Recorder of the Crown Court, since 1980; *b* 21 April 1938; *s* of late Lt-Cdr John Edgar Leonard Brice, MBE and Winifred Ivy Brice; *m* 1963, Ann Nuala Brice, LLM (*née* Connor); one *s. Educ:* Magdalen Coll. Sch., Brackley; University Coll., London (LLB). Called to the Bar, Middle Temple, 1960; Harmsworth Scholar and Robert Garraway Rice Prize, 1960. Lloyd's Arbitrator, 1978–; Wreck Commissioner, 1979–. *Recreations:* music, opera. *Address:* Yew Tree House, Spring Coppice, Newmer Common, Lane End, Bucks. *T:* High Wycombe 881810; Queen Elizabeth Building, Temple, EC4Y 9BS. *T:* 01-353 5728. *Club:* Athenæum.

BRICKER, John William, LLB; Lawyer, USA; Republican; *b* 6 Sept. 1893; *s* of Lemuel Spencer Bricker and Laura (*née* King) *m* 1920, Harriet Day; one *s. Educ:* State Univ., Ohio. AB 1916; admitted to Bar, Ohio, 1917; LLB 1920. Solicitor, Grandview Heights, 1920–28; Assistant Attorney-General of Ohio, 1923–27; Attorney-General, 1933–37. Governor of Ohio, 1939–41, 1941–43, 1943–45. Candidate (Republican) for US Vice-Presidency, 1944; Senator from Ohio, 1947–58. Member firm of Bricker & Eckler. Member Public Utilities Commission, Ohio, 1929–32. LLD Ohio State University, 1940. Served European War, 1917–18, 1st Lieut. Holds various trusteeships. *Address:* 100 East Broad Street, Columbus, Ohio 43215, USA; 2407 Tremont Road, Columbus, Ohio 43221, USA.

BRICKHILL, Paul Chester Jerome; author; *b* 20 Dec. 1916; 3rd *s* of G. R. Brickhill, Sydney, Aust.; *m* 1950, Margaret Olive Slater, Sydney (marr. diss., 1964); one *s* one *d. Educ:* North Sydney High School; Sydney University. Journalist in Sydney, 1935–40; joined RAAF 1940; service in United Kingdom and Middle East as fighter pilot; three times wounded; shot down in Tunisia, 1943; POW Germany; Flight Lieut; Foreign Correspondent in Europe and USA, 1945–47; left journalism to concentrate on books, 1949. *Publications:* Escape to Danger (with Conrad Norton), 1946; The Great Escape, 1951; The Dam Busters, 1951; Escape or Die, 1952; Reach for the Sky, 1954; The Deadline, 1962. *Recreations:* reading, swimming. *Address:* c/o David Higham Associates Ltd, 5–8 Lower John Street, Golden Square, W1R 4HA. *Club:* Royal Air Force.

BRICKWOOD, Sir Basil (Greame), 3rd Bt *cr* 1927; *b* 21 May 1923; *s* of Sir John Brickwood, 1st Bt and Isabella Janet Gibson (*d* 1967), *d* of James Gordon; *S* half-brother, 1974; *m* 1956, Shirley Anne Brown; two *d. Educ:* King Edward's Grammar Sch., Stratford-upon-Avon; Clifton College. *Club:* Royal Air Force.

BRIDGE, family name of **Baron Bridge of Harwich.**

BRIDGE OF HARWICH, Baron *cr* 1980 (Life Peer), of Harwich in the County of Essex; **Nigel Cyprian Bridge;** Kt 1968; PC 1975; a Lord of Appeal in Ordinary, since 1980; *b* 26 Feb. 1917; *s* of late Comdr C. D. C. Bridge, RN; *m* 1944, Margaret Swinbank; one *s* two *d. Educ:* Marlborough College. Army Service, 1940–46; commnd into KRRC, 1941. Called to the Bar, Inner Temple, 1947; Junior Counsel to Treasury (Common Law), 1964–68; a Judge of High Court, Queen's Bench Div., 1968–75; Presiding Judge, Western Circuit, 1972–74; a Lord Justice of Appeal, 1975–80. Mem., Security Commn, 1977– (Chm. 1982–). *Address:* House of Lords, SW1.
See also Very Rev. A. C. Bridge.

BRIDGE, Very Rev. Antony Cyprian; Dean of Guildford since 1968; *b* 5 Sept. 1914; *s* of late Comdr C. D. C. Bridge, RN; *m* 1937, Brenda Lois Streatfeild; one *s* two *d. Educ:* Marlborough College. Scholarship to Royal Academy School of Art, 1932. Professional painter thereafter. War of 1939–45: joined Army, Sept. 1939; commissioned Buffs, 1940; demobilised as Major, 1945. Ordained, 1955; Curate, Hythe Parish Church till 1958; Vicar of Christ Church, Lancaster Gate, London, 1958–68. Mem., Adv. Council V&A Museum, 1976–79. *Publications:* Images of God, 1960; Theodora: portrait in a Byzantine landscape, 1978; The Crusades, 1980. *Recreations:* bird-watching, reading. *Address:* The Deanery, 1 Cathedral Close, Guildford, Surrey GU2 5TL. *T:* Guildford 60328.
See also Baron Bridge of Harwich.

BRIDGE, John, GC 1944; GM 1940 and Bar 1941; Director of Education for Sunderland Borough Council (formerly Sunderland County Borough

Council), 1963–76, retired; *b* 5 Feb. 1915; *s* of late Joseph Edward Bridge Culcheth, Warrington; *m* 1945, F. J. Patterson; three *d. Educ:* London Univ. BSc Gen. Hons, 1936 and BSc Special Hons (Physics), 1937; Teacher's Dip. 1938. Schoolmaster: Lancs CC, Sept.–Dec. 1938; Leighton Park, Reading, Jan.–Aug. 1939; Firth Park Grammar Sch., Sheffield, Sept. 1939–Aug. 1946 (interrupted by war service). Served War: RNVR June 1940–Feb. 1946, engaged on bomb and mine disposal; demobilised as Lt Comdr RNVR. *Recreations:* gardening, travel, fell walking, photography, fishing. *Address:* 37 Park Avenue, Roker, Sunderland, Tyne and Wear SR6 9NJ. *T:* Sunderland 486356.

BRIDGE, Keith James; Chief Executive, Humberside County Council, since 1978; *b* 21 Aug. 1929; *s* of late James Henry Bridge and Lilian Elizabeth (*née* Nichols); *m* 1960, Thelma Ruby (*née* Hubble); three *d* (and one *s* decd). *Educ:* Sir George Monoux Grammar Sch.; Corpus Christi Coll., Oxford (MA). CIPFA 1959. Local govt service, 1953; Dep. City Treasurer, York, 1965; Borough Treas., Bolton, 1967; City Treas., Manchester, 1971; County Treasurer, Greater Manchester Council, 1973. Financial Adviser to Assoc. of Metrop. Authorities, 1971–78; Mem. Council, 1972, Pres., 1982–83, Chartered Inst. of Public Finance and Accountancy. CBIM. *Publications:* papers in profess. jls. *Recreations:* gardening, literature, music. *Address:* County Hall, Beverley, N Humberside HU17 9BA.

BRIDGE, Ronald George Blacker; Director of Immigration, Hong Kong, since 1978; *b* 7 Sept. 1932; *s* of Blacker Bridge and Aileen Georgina Edith (*née* Shaw); *m* 1956, Olive Tyrrell Brown; two *s* two *d. Educ:* Charterhouse; Lincoln Coll., Oxford (MA). National Service, 1954–56. Colonial Office Devonshire Course, 1956–57; Hong Kong Admin. Service, 1957–: Dep. Sec. for Civil Service, 1973; Dep. Sec. for Security, 1976; Sec. for CS, 1977. *Recreations:* hockey, tennis, walking, reading. *Address:* 68 Mount Nicholson, Hong Kong. *T:* Hong Kong 5-734377. *Club:* Football (Hong Kong).

BRIDGEMAN, family name of **Earl of Bradford** and **Viscount Bridgeman.**

BRIDGEMAN, 2nd Viscount, *cr* 1929, of Leigh; **Robert Clive Bridgeman,** KBE 1954; CB 1944; DSO 1940; MC; psc; JP; HM Lieutenant of County of Salop, 1951–Dec. 1969; *b* April 1896; *e s* of 1st Viscount and Caroline Beatrix, DBE (*d* 1961), *er d* of Hon. Cecil Parker; *S* father, 1935; *m* 1930, Mary Kathleen (*d* 1981), 2nd *d* of Baron Bingley, PC; three *d. Educ:* Eton College. 2nd Lieut. The Rifle Bde, 1914; Lieut, 1916; Captain, 1921; Bt Major, 1932; Bt. Lieut-Col, 1935, acting Maj.-Gen., 1941; Col and Temp. Maj.-Gen., 1942; served European War (France), 1915–18; Private Secretary to his father when Parliamentary Secretary to Minister of Labour, 1918; Brigade Major, 7th Infantry Brigade, 1932–34; GSO2 War Office, 1935–37; retired pay, 1937; served War of 1939–45 (DSO); Deputy Director, Home Guard, 1941; Director-General, Home Guard and Territorial Army, 1941–44; Deputy Adjt-General, 1944–45. Pres., West Midland TA&VRA, 1968–69. Vice-Chm., Trust Houses Forte Council, 1971–. Alderman, Salop CC, 1951–74. JP Salop, 1951. *Heir: nephew* Robin John Orlando Bridgeman [*b* 5 Dec. 1930; *m* 1966, Harriet Lucy Turton; three *s*]. *Address:* Leigh Manor, Minsterley, Salop SY5 0EX. *T:* Worthen 210. *Club:* Naval and Military.
See also Rev. N. D. Stacey.

BRIDGEMAN, John Michael; Chief Registrar of Friendly Societies and Industrial Assurance Commissioner, since 1982; *b* 26 April 1931; *s* of John Wilfred Bridgeman, *qv* ; *m* 1958, June Bridgeman, *qv* ; one *s* four *d. Educ:* Marlborough Coll.; Trinity Coll., Cambridge. Asst Principal, BoT, 1954; HM Treasury, 1956–81, Under Sec., 1975–81. *Address:* Bridge House, Culverden Park Road, Tunbridge Wells, Kent.

BRIDGEMAN, John Wilfred, CBE 1960; BSc London, AKC; retired as Principal, Loughborough Training College, 1950–63; Principal, Loughborough Summer School, 1931–63; *b* 25 Jan. 1895; *s* of late John Edward Bridgeman and Alice Bridgeman, Bournemouth; *m* 1st, 1928, Mary Jane Wallace (*d* 1961); one *s* ; 2nd, 1963, Helen Ida Mary Wallace. *Educ:* King's College, University of London; London Day Training College. Industry, 1910–15; taught at technical colleges, Bournemouth, Bath and Weymouth, 1915–20; Asst Master, Lyme Regis Grammar School, 1923; Senior Maths Master, Wolverhampton Secondary Gram. Sch., 1926; Head of Dept for Training of Teachers, Loughborough Coll., 1930. Chm., Assoc. of Teachers in Colls and Depts of Education, 1952; Leader of Staff Panel, Pelham Cttee, 1955–63. Hon. MA Nottingham, 1961; Hon. DLitt Loughborough, 1978. *Recreations:* chess, reading. *Address:* Flat 3, Laleham Court, Woking, Surrey GU21 4AX. *T:* Woking 21523.
See also J. M. Bridgeman.

BRIDGEMAN, Mrs June; Under-Secretary, Department of Transport, since 1979; *b* 26 June 1932; *d* of Gordon and Elsie Forbes; *m* 1958, John Michael Bridgeman, *qv* ; one *s* four *d. Educ:* variously, England and Scotland; Westfield Coll., London Univ. (BA). Asst Principal, BoT, 1954; subseq. served in DEA, NBPI, Min. of Housing and Local Govt, DoE; Under Secretary: DoE 1974–76; Central Policy Review Staff, Cabinet Office, 1976–79. *Address:* Bridge House, Culverden Park Road, Tunbridge Wells, Kent TN4 9QX.

BRIDGER, Pearl, MBE 1947; Director, Central Personnel, Post Office, 1968–72, retired; *b* 9 Dec. 1912; *d* of Samuel and Lottie Bridger. *Educ:*

Godolphin and Latymer Girls' Sch., London, W6. BA (Hons) Open Univ., 1978. Entered Post Office as Executive Officer, 1931; Asst Telecommunications Controller, 1938; Principal, 1947; Asst Sec., 1954; Director, 1968. *Address:* 95 Deanhill Court, SW14. *T:* 01-876 8877. *Clubs:* Civil Service, Soroptimist.

BRIDGES, family name of **Baron Bridges.**

BRIDGES, 2nd Baron *cr* 1957; **Thomas Edward Bridges,** CMG 1975; HM Diplomatic Service; Deputy Under Secretary of State, Foreign and Commonwealth Office, since 1979; *b* 27 Nov. 1927; *s* of 1st Baron Bridges, KG, PC, GCB, GCVO, MC, FRS, and Hon. Katharine Dianthe, *d* of 2nd Baron Farrer; *S* father, 1969; *m* 1953, Rachel Mary, *y d* of late Sir Henry Bunbury, KCB; two *s* one *d. Educ:* Eton; New Coll., Oxford. Entered Foreign Service, 1951; served in Bonn, Berlin, Rio de Janeiro and at FO (Asst Private Sec. to Foreign Secretary, 1963-66); Head of Chancery, Athens, 1966-68; Counsellor, Moscow, 1969-71; Private Sec. (Overseas Affairs) to Prime Minister, 1972-74; RCDS 1975; Minister (Commercial), Washington, 1976-79. *Heir: s* Hon. Mark Thomas Bridges [*b* 25 July 1954; *m* 1978, Angela Margaret, *er d* of J. L. Collinson, Mansfield, Notts; one *d*]. *Address:* c/o Foreign and Commonwealth Office, SW1.

BRIDGES, John Gourlay, OBE 1954 (MBE 1944); Consultant: Tourism Promotion, Travel and Capital Development; Supervisor, Press, Publicity and Information to Church of Scotland, 1967-72; Director-General, British Travel and Holidays Association, 1945-63, retd; *b* 5 Dec. 1901; *e s* of late David McKay Bridges and late Margaret Gourlay Bridges, Glasgow; *m* 1931, Marion, *d* of late Andrew Bell, MBE, JP, Glasgow; one *s* one *d. Educ:* elementary and secondary schools, Glasgow; Glasgow and West of Scotland Commercial College and School of Accountancy. Secretary, and latterly Director-Secretary, of private Ltd. Co., Glasgow and London, 1922-24; Accountant, Straits Trading Co. Ltd., Singapore and FM States, 1924-30; Sec. at Edinburgh, and later Gen. Sec. for Scotland, of The Overseas League, 1931-35; then Development Sec. of the movement; Development Sec., Overseas League and Gen. Sec., Overseas League in Canada, 1935-38; Gen. Tours Manager, Donaldson Atlantic Line, Great Britain, Canada and USA, 1939. Served in RAF as Embarkation Officer (Personnel) Liverpool, 1940-45; demobilized with rank of Squadron Leader, 1945. Pres. 1960, and Mem., Council of Honour, International Union of Official Travel Organizations (with consultative status UN). Director of Studies and Professor of Tourism, Hawaii Univ., 1964-65. FRGS; Associate Institute of Transport. Member: Association of Scientific Tourism Experts; Exec. Cttee, Scottish Council for Development and Industry; Scottish Tourist Cons. Council. *Publications:* numerous articles on Travel and allied subjects. *Recreations:* motoring, fishing, gardening. *Address:* 35A Cluny Drive, Edinburgh EH10 6DT. *T:* 031-447 4966. *Club:* Royal Over-Seas League.

BRIDGES, Dame Mary (Patricia), DBE 1981; *b* 6 June 1930; *d* of Austin Edward and Lena Mabel Fawkes; *m* 1951, Bertram Marsdin Bridges; one step *s.* First active in politics at age of 15, helping Cons. candidate contest Bassetlaw; Chm., Honiton Div. Cons. Assoc., 1968-71; Chm., Western Area, covering 29 constituencies from Cornwall to Glos, 1976-79; past Chm., Cons. Western Area Women's Adv. Cttee and CPC Cttee; Mem. Cttee, Littleham Urban Ward, Exmouth (Pres., 1981). Chm., Devon County Women's Section of Royal British Legion, 1979-; (Pres., Exmouth Branch, 1965-); former Mem., Exe Vale HMC; Founder Chm., Exmouth Council of Voluntary Service. Chm., Exmouth Campaign Cttee, Cancer Research, 1975-; Mem. Exec., Resthaven, Exmouth, 1970- (Chm., League of Friends, 1971-); Pres., Exmouth and Budleigh Salterton Br., CRUSE, 1980-; Mem., SW Electricity Consultative Council, 1982; Mem., Exmouth Cttee, LEPRA, 1962- (Hon. Sec., 1964-); Co-optative Trustee, Exmouth Welfare Trust, 1979-; Governor, Rolle Coll., Exmouth, 1982; Mem. Exmouth Team, medical supplies, BRC, 1960-; Hon. Life Mem., Retford Cricket Club, 1951; Hon. Vice-Pres., Exmouth Cricket Club, 1981. *Recreations:* cricket, reading. *Address:* Walton House, Fairfield Close, Exmouth, Devon EX8 2BN. *T:* Exmouth 5317.

BRIDGES, Ven. Peter Sydney Godfrey; Archdeacon of Coventry since 1977; Canon-Theologian of Coventry Cathedral, since 1977; *b* 30 Jan. 1925; *s* of Sidney Clifford Bridges and Winifred (*née* Livette); *m* 1952, Joan Penlerick (*née* Madge); two *s. Educ:* Raynes Park Grammar Sch.; Kingston upon Thames Sch. of Architecture; Lincoln Theol College. ARIBA 1950, Dip. Liturgy and Architecture 1967. Gen. and ecclesiastical practice, 1950-54; Lectr, Nottingham Sch. of Architecture, 1954-56. Deacon, 1958; Priest, 1959. Asst Curate, Hemel Hempstead, 1958-64; Res. Fellow, Inst. for Study of Worship and Religious Architecture, Univ. of Birmingham, 1964-67 (Hon. Fellow, 1967-72 and 1978); Warden, Anglican Chaplaincy and Chaplain to Univ. of Birmingham, 1965-68; Lectr, Birmingham Sch. of Arch., 1967-72; eccles. architect and planning consultant, 1968-75; Chm., New Town Ministers Assoc., 1968-72; Co-Dir, Mids Socio-Religious Res. Gp, 1968-75; Dir, Chelmsford Diocesan R&D Unit, 1972-77; Archdeacon of Southend, 1972-77. Mem., Cathedrals Advisory Commn for England, 1981-. *Publications:* Socio-Religious Institutes, Lay Academies, etc, 1967; contrib. Church Building, res. bulletins (Inst. for Study of Worship and Relig. Arch.), Clergy Review, Prism, Christian Ministry in New Towns, Cathedral and Mission, Church Architecture and Social Responsibility. *Recreations:* architecture, singing. *Address:* Archdeacon's House, Baginton, Coventry, Warwicks CV8 3AR. *T:* Coventry 302508. *Club:* Royal Commonwealth Society.

BRIDGES, Hon. Sir Phillip (Rodney), Kt 1973; CMG 1967; **Hon. Mr Justice Bridges;** Chief Justice of The Gambia, since 1968; *b* 9 July 1922; *e s* of late Captain Sir Ernest Bridges and Lady Bridges; *m* 1st, 1951, Rosemary Ann Streeten (marr. diss. 1961); two *s* one *d* ; 2nd, 1962, Angela Mary (*née* Dearden), widow of James Huyton. *Educ:* Bedford School. Military Service (Capt., RA) with Royal W African Frontier Force in W. Africa, India and Burma, 1941-47. Admitted Solicitor (England), 1951; Colonial Legal Service, 1954; Barrister and Solicitor, Supreme Court of The Gambia, 1954; Solicitor-General of The Gambia, 1963; QC (Gambia) 1964; Attorney-General of The Gambia, 1964-68. *Address:* Weavers, Coney Weston, Bury St Edmunds, Suffolk; Supreme Court, Banjul, The Gambia. *Club:* Travellers'.

BRIDGES-ADAMS, John Nicholas William; a Recorder of the Crown Court, since 1972; *b* 16 Sept. 1930; *s* of late William Bridges-Adams, CBE; *m* 1962, Jenifer Celia Emily, *d* of David Sandell, FRCS. *Educ:* Stowe; Oriel Coll., Oxford (Scholar; MA, DipEd). Commnd Royal Artillery, 1949, transf. to RAFVR 1951 and served with Oxford and London Univ. Air Sqdn; Flying Officer, 2623 Sqdn RAuxAF Regt, 1980. Called to Bar, Lincoln's Inn, 1958 (Gray's Inn *ad eundem* 1979); Head of Chambers, 1979; Mem., Young Barristers Cttee, Bar Council, 1960-61; Actg Junior, Mddx Sessions Bar Mess, 1965-67. Mem., Exec. Cttee, Soc. of Cons. Lawyers, 1967-69 (Chm., Rates of Exchange sub-cttee); Chm., panel from which representations Cttees under Dumping at Sea Act 1974 are drawn, 1976-. Contested (C) West Bromwich West, Oct. 1974. Governor, St Benedict's Upper Sch., 1980-. Member: RIIA; IISS; FCIArb. *Publication:* contrib. on collisions at sea, 3rd edn of Halsbury's Laws of England, Vol. 35. *Recreations:* sailing, shooting, cooking. *Address:* 4 Verulam Buildings, Gray's Inn, WC1R 5LW. *T:* 01-405 6114; Fornham Cottage, Fornham St Martin, Bury St Edmunds, Suffolk. *T:* Bury St Edmunds 5307. *Clubs:* Savile, Garrick; Tiger (Redhill Aerodrome).

BRIDGEWATER, Bentley Powell Conyers; Secretary of the British Museum, 1948-73; *b* 6 Sept. 1911; *s* of Conyers Bridgewater, OBE, Clerk to Commissioners of Taxes for City of London, and Violet Irene, *d* of Dr I. W. Powell, Victoria, BC. *Educ:* Westminster School (King's Schol.); Christ Church, Oxford (Westminster Schol., BA 1933, MA 1965). Asst Keeper, British Museum, 1937; Asst Sec., 1940. Seconded to Dominions Office, 1941-42, and to Foreign Office, 1942-45; returned to British Museum, 1946; Deputy Keeper, 1950; Keeper, 1961; retired, 1973. *Recreation:* music. *Address:* 4 Doughty Street, WC1N 2PH. *Club:* Athenæum.

BRIDGLAND, Milton Deane, FRACI, FAIM; Executive Director since 1971, Managing Director since 1978 and Chairman since 1980, ICI Australia Ltd; *b* 8 July 1922; *s* of late Frederick H. and Muriel E. Bridgland, Adelaide; *m* 1945, Christine L. Cowell; three *d. Educ:* St Peter's Coll., Adelaide; Adelaide Univ. (BSc). FRACI 1960; FAIM 1974. Joined ICI Australia Ltd, 1945; Technical Manager, Plastics Gp, 1955-62; Dulux Australia Ltd: Ops Dir, 1962-67; Man. Dir, 1967-71; Chm., 1978-. Director: Nylex Corp., 1978-; Aust. Inst. of Petroleum, 1980-; Pres., Aust. Chemical Industry Council, 1977; Vice-Pres., Aust. Industry Develt Assoc., 1981-; Member: National Energy Adv. Cttee, 1977-80; Australia Japan Business Co-operation Cttee; Pacific Econ. Basin Council; Cook Soc.; Aust. Round Table. *Recreations:* tennis, golf. *Address:* 178 Barkers Road, Hawthorn, Vic 3122, Australia. *T:* (03) 819 3939. *Clubs:* Athenæum, Australian, Peninsula Country (Melbourne).

BRIDLE, Rear-Adm. Gordon Walter, CB 1977; MBE 1952; maritime consultant; *b* 14 May 1923; *s* of Percy Gordon Bridle and Dorothy Agnes Bridle; *m* 1944, Phyllis Audrey Page; three *s. Educ:* King Edward's Grammar Sch., Aston, Birmingham; Northern Grammar Sch., Portsmouth; Royal Dockyard Sch., Portsmouth (Whitworth Scholar); Imperial Coll., London (ACGI). CEng, FIEE. Loan Service Pakistan, 1950-52; Naval Electrical Dept, Bath; jssc; subseq. HMS Newfoundland, Min. of Aviation, HMS Devonshire; Project Man. Sea Dart, Min. of Technology; comd HMS Collingwood, 1969-71; Dir, Surface Weapons/Electronic Projects, Portsmouth, 1972-74; Asst Controller of the Navy, 1974-77. Governor, Royal Naval Scholarship Fund, 1976. Mem. Council, C of E Soldiers', Sailors' and Airmens' Clubs, 1982. *Recreations:* sailing, walking. *Address:* 25 Heatherwood, Midhurst, Sussex GU29 9LH. *T:* Midhurst 2838.

BRIDLE, Ronald Jarman; Controller of Research and Development, Department of Transport, since 1980; Director, Transport and Road Research Laboratory, since 1980; *b* 27 Jan. 1930; *s* of Raymond Bridle and Dorothy (*née* Jarman); *m* Beryl Eunice (*née* Doe); two *d. Educ:* West Monmouth Grammar Sch.; Bristol Univ. (BSc). FEng, FICE, FIHE. Graduate Asst, Monmouthshire CC, 1953-55; Exec. Engr, Gold Coast Govt, 1955-57; Sen. Engr, Cwmbran Develt Corp., 1957-60; Principal Designer, Cardiff City, 1960-62; Project Engr, Sheffield-Leeds Motorway, West Riding CC, 1962-65; Dep. County Surveyor II, Cheshire CC, 1965-67; Dir, Midland RCU, DoE, 1967-71; Dep. Chief Highway Engr, 1971-73, Under-Sec., Highways 1, 1973-75, Chief Highway Engr, 1975-76, DoE; Chief Highway Engr, Dept of Transport, 1976-80. FRSA. Mem. Council, ICE; Mem., EDC for Civil Engrg; Pres., IHE; Chm., Building and Civil Engineering Council BSI. *Publications:* papers in jls of ICE, IHE and internat. confs. *Recreations:* golf, painting. *Address:* L'Escalier, 204 Thames Side, off Blacksmith Lane, Laleham, near Staines, Mddx. *T:* Staines 61017. *Club:* Royal Automobile.

BRIDPORT, 4th Viscount, *cr* 1868; **Alexander Nelson Hood;** Baron Bridport, 1794; 7th Duke of Bronte in Sicily (*cr* 1799); *b* 17 March 1948; *s* of 3rd Viscount Bridport and Sheila Jeanne Agatha, *d* of Johann van Meurs;

S father, 1969; *m* 1st, 1972, Linda Jacqueline Paravicini (marr. diss.), *d* of Lt-Col and Mrs V. R. Paravicini, Nutley Manor, Basingstoke, Hants; one *s*; 2nd, 1979, Mrs Nina Rindt-Martyn. *Educ:* Eton; Sorbonne. *Heir: s* Hon. Peregrine Alexander Nelson Hood, *b* 30 Aug. 1974. *Address:* Villa Jonin, 1261 Le Muids, Vaud, Switzerland. *T:* 022-661705. *Club:* Brooks's.

BRIEGEL, Geoffrey Michael Olver; Deputy Master of the Court of Protection, since 1977; *b* 13 July 1923; *s* of late Roy C. Briegel, TD, and Veria Lindsey Briegel; *m* 1947, Barbara Mary Richardson; three *s* one *d*. *Educ:* Highgate Sch. Served War, RAF, 1942-46 (514 Sqdn Bomber Command). Called to Bar, Lincoln's Inn, 1950; Public Trustee Office, 1954; Clerk of the Lists, Queen's Bench Div., and Legal Sec. to Lord Chief Justice of England, 1963; Dep. Circuit Administrator, South Eastern Circuit, 1971. *Recreations:* target rifle and pistol shooting, most other sports and games (now non-actively), particularly cricket and rugby. *Address:* Staffordshire House, 25 Store Street, WC1. *T:* 01-636 6877. *Club:* Royal Air Force.

BRIEN, Alan; Film Critic, Sunday Times, since 1976; Columnist, Punch, since 1972; *b* 12 March 1925; *s* of late Ernest Brien and Isabella (*née* Patterson); *m* 1st, 1947, Pamela Mary Jones; three *d*; 2nd, 1961, Nancy Newbold Ryan; one *s* one *d*; 3rd, 1973, Jill Sheila Tweedie, *qv*. *Educ:* Bede Grammar Sch., Sunderland; Jesus Coll., Oxford. BA (Eng Lit). Served war RAF (air-gunner), 1943-46. Associate Editor: Mini-Cinema, 1950-52; Courier, 1952-53; Film Critic and Columnist, Truth, 1953-54; TV Critic, Observer, 1954-55; Film Critic, 1954-56, New York Correspondent, 1956-58, Evening Standard; Drama Critic and Features Editor, Spectator, 1958-61; Columnist, Daily Mail, 1958-62; Columnist, Sunday Dispatch, 1962-63; Political Columnist, Sunday Pictorial, 1963-64; Drama Critic, Sunday Telegraph, 1961-67; Columnist, Spectator, 1963-65; Columnist, New Statesman, 1966-72; Diarist, Sunday Times, 1967-75; Contributor various American publications: Saturday Evening Post, Holiday, Vogue, Mademoiselle, Theatre Arts. Regular broadcaster on radio, 1952-, and television, 1955-. Hannen Swaffer Critic of Year, 1966, 1967. *Publications:* Domes of Fortune, 1979; contrib. novel by several hands, I Knew Daisy Smuten, 1970; various collections of Spectator and Punch pieces. *Recreations:* eating, drinking, walking, talking, and sleeping in libraries. *Address:* 14 Falkland Road, NW5. *T:* 01-485 9074. *Club:* Garrick.

BRIERLEY, John David, CB 1978; retired Civil Servant; *b* 16 March 1918; *s* of late Walter George Brierley and late Doris Brierley (*née* Paterson); *m* 1956, Frances Elizabeth Davis; one (adopted) *s* one (adopted) *d*. *Educ:* elementary schools, London and Croydon; Whitgift Sch., Croydon; Lincoln Coll., Oxford. *Lit. Hum.,* BA Hons, 1940. Served War: Army, RASC, 1940-46. Ministry of Education: Asst Principal, 1946; Principal, 1949; Dept of Education and Science: Asst Sec., 1960; Under-Sec., 1969; Principal Finance Officer, 1969-75; Under Sec., DES, 1969-77. Dean of Studies, Working Mens' Coll., NW1, 1978-81, Mem. Corp., 1980-; Governor, Croydon High Sch. (GPDST), 1980-. *Recreations:* fell-walking, cycling, photography, music. *Address:* Little Trees, Winterbourne, near Newbury, Berks.

BRIERLEY, Zachry, CBE 1978 (MBE 1969); Chairman: Z. Brierley Ltd, since 1957 (Chairman and Managing Director, 1957-73); Z. Brierley (Australia) Pty Ltd, since 1973; President, Z. Brierley (USA) Inc., since 1972; *b* 16 April 1920; *s* of late Zachry Brierley and of Nellie (*née* Ashworth); *m* 1946, Iris Macara; one *d*. *Educ:* Rydal Sch., Colwyn Bay. Served War: commnd RAF, 1941. Joined family business, Z. Brierley Ltd, 1938: Dir, 1952; Chm. and Man. Dir, 1957. Dir, Develt Corp. for Wales, 1974-. Mem., CBI Central Council, 1970- (also mem. cttees); Chm., Wales Reg. Council, CBI, 1976-77. Chairman: Small and Medium Firms Commn, Union des Industries de la Communauté Européenne, Brussels, 1975-77; Wales Adv. Cttee, Design Council, 1977- (Mem. Design Council, 1976-). Member: Welsh Indust. Develt Bd, Welsh Office, 1972-; Welsh Develt Agency, 1975-; Bd, Civic Trust for Wales, 1976-; Cttee to Review Functioning of Financial Instns, 1977-80; Council, Machine Tool Trade Assoc., 1977-; Bd of Governors, Llandrillo Tech. Coll., 1975-; Bd of Governors, Penrhos Coll., 1980-. Chairman: Conservative Polit. Centre (Wales), 1975-79; Conway Cons. and Unionist Assoc., 1980- (also past Chm. and Vice Pres.). Vice Chm., North Wales Medical Centre, 1979-. Liveryman, Basketmakers' Co., 1978-; Freeman, City of London, 1977. *Recreations:* philately, travel, reading, sketching. *Address:* West Point, Gloddaeth Avenue, Llandudno, Gwynedd, N Wales LL30 2AN. *T:* Llandudno 76970. *Club:* Carlton.

BRIERS, Richard; actor since 1955; *b* 14 Jan. 1934; *s* of Joseph Briers and Morna Richardson; *m* 1957, Ann Davies; two *d*. *Educ:* Rokeby Prep. Sch., Wimbledon; private tuition. RADA, 1954-56 (silver medal). First appearance in London in Gilt and Gingerbread, Duke of York's, 1959. *Plays:* (major parts in): Arsenic and Old Lace, 1965; Relatively Speaking, 1966; The Real Inspector Hound, 1968; Cat Among the Pigeons, 1969; The Two of Us, 1970; Butley, 1972; Absurd Person Singular, 1973; Absent Friends, 1975; Middle Age Spread, 1979; The Wild Duck, 1980; Arms and the Man, 1981. *Television series:* Brothers-in-Law; Marriage Lines; The Good Life; OneUpManShip; The Other One; Norman Conquests; Goodbye Mr Kent. *Publication:* Natter Natter, 1981. *Recreations:* reading, gardening. *Address:* c/o ICM Ltd, 388-396 Oxford Street, W1N 9HE.

BRIGDEN, Wallace, MA, MD, FRCP; Physician: London Hospital, and Cardiac Department, London Hospital, since 1949; National Heart Hospital, since 1949; Consulting Cardiologist to the Royal Navy, since 1962; *b* 8 June 1916; *s* of Wallis Brigden and Louise Brigden (*née* Clarke). *Educ:* Latymer School; University of Cambridge; King's College Hospital; Yale University. Senior Scholar, King's College, Cambridge; First Class Natural Sciences Tripos, Parts I and II, 1936, 1937; Henry Fund Fellowship, Yale University, USA, 1937-38; Burney Yeo Schol., King's College Hospital, 1938. RAMC, 1943-47, Med. Specialist and O/C Medical Division. Lecturer in Medicine, Post-Grad. Med. School of London; Physician, Hammersmith Hospital, 1948-49; Asst Physician, London Hospital and Asst Physician, Cardiac Dept, 1949; Asst Physician, National Heart Hospital, 1949; Cons. Cardiologist, Special Unit for Juvenile Rheumatism, Taplow, 1955-59; Director Inst. of Cardiology, 1962-66. Cons. Physician to Munich Re-Insurance Co., 1974-. St Cyres Lectr, 1956; R. T. Hall Lectr, Australia and New Zealand, 1961; Hugh Morgan Vis. Prof., Vanderbilt Univ., 1963. Late Assistant Editor, British Heart Journal. Mem. British Cardiac Society and Assoc. of Physicians. *Publications:* Section on Cardio-vascular disease in Price's Textbook of Medicine; Myocardial Disease, Cecil-Loeb Textbook of Medicine; contributor to the Lancet, British Heart Jl, British Medical Jl. *Recreation:* painting. *Address:* 45 Wimpole Street, W1. *T:* 01-935 1201; Willow House, Totteridge Common, N20 8NE. *T:* 01-959 6616.

BRIGGS, family name of **Baron Briggs.**

BRIGGS, Baron *cr* 1976 (Life Peer), of Lewes, E Sussex; **Asa Briggs,** MA, BSc (Econ); FBA 1980; Provost, Worcester College, Oxford, since 1976; Chancellor, Open University, since 1978; *b* 7 May 1921; *o s* of William Walker Briggs and Jane Briggs, Keighley, Yorks; *m* 1955, Susan Anne Banwell, *o d* of late Donald I. Banwell, Keevil, Wiltshire; two *s* two *d*. *Educ:* Keighley Grammar School; Sidney Sussex College, Cambridge (1st cl. History Tripos, Pts I and II, 1940, 1941; 1st cl. BSc (Econ.), Lond., 1941). Gerstenberg studentship in Economics, London, 1941. Served in Intelligence Corps, 1942-45. Fellow of Worcester College, Oxford, 1945-55; Reader in Recent Social and Economic History, Oxford, 1950-55; Member, Institute for Advanced Study, Princeton, USA, 1953-54; Faculty Fellow of Nuffield College, Oxford, 1953-55; Professor of Modern History, Leeds Univ., 1955-61; University of Sussex: Professor of History, 1961-76; Dean, School of Social Studies, 1961-65; Pro Vice-Chancellor, 1961-67; Vice-Chancellor, 1967-76. Chm. Bd of Governors, Inst. of Develt Studies, 1967-76. Mem., 1976-. Visiting Professor: ANU, 1960; Chicago Univ., 1966, 1972. Dep. Pres., WEA, 1954-58, Pres., 1958-67. Member: UGC, 1959-67; Hong Kong UPGC, 1977-; Chm., Cttee on Nursing, 1970-72 (Cmnd 5115, 1972). Trustee: Glyndebourne Arts Trust, 1966-; Internat. Broadcasting Inst., 1968-; (Chm.) Heritage Educn Gp, 1976-; Civic Trust, 1976-; Chairman: Standing Conf. for Study of Local History, 1969-76; Council, European Inst. of Education, 1975-; Vice-Chm. of Council, UN Univ., 1974-80; Governor, British Film Institute, 1970-77; Pres., Social History Soc., 1976-. Mem., Ct of Governors, Administrative Staff Coll., 1971-. Mem., Amer. Acad. of Arts and Sciences, 1970. Hon. Fellow: Sidney Sussex Coll., Cambridge, 1968; Worcester Coll., Oxford, 1969; St Catharine's Coll., Cambridge, 1977. Hon. DLitt: East Anglia, 1966; Strathclyde, 1973; Leeds, 1974; Cincinnati, 1977; Liverpool, 1977; Open Univ., 1979; Hon. DSc Florida Presbyterian, 1966; Hon. LLD: York, Canada, 1968; New England, 1972; Sussex, 1976; Bradford, 1978; Rochester, NY, 1980. Marconi Medal for Communications History, 1975. *Publications:* Patterns of Peace-making (with D. Thomson and E. Meyer), 1945; History of Birmingham (1865-1938), 1952; Victorian People, 1954; Friends of the People, 1956; The Age of Improvement, 1959; (ed) Chartist Studies, 1959; (ed with John Saville) Essays in Labour History, Vol. I, 1960, Vol. II, 1971, Vol. III, 1977; (ed) They Saw it Happen, 1897-1940, 1961; A Study of the Work of Seebohm Rowntree, 1871-1954, 1961; History of Broadcasting in the United Kingdom: vol. I. The Birth of Broadcasting, 1961; vol. II, The Golden Age of Wireless, 1965; vol. III, The War of Words, 1970; Vol. IV, Sound and Vision, 1979; Victorian Cities, 1963; William Cobbett, 1967; How They Lived, 1700-1815, 1969; (ed) The Nineteenth Century, 1970; (ed with Susan Briggs) Cap and Bell: Punch's Chronicle of English History in the Making 1841-1861, 1973; (ed) Essays in the History of Publishing, 1974; Iron Bridge to Crystal Palace: impact and images of the Industrial Revolution, 1979; Governing the BBC, 1979; The Power of Steam, 1982. *Recreation:* travelling. *Address:* The Provost's Lodgings, Worcester College, Oxford; (private) The Caprons, Keere Street, Lewes, Sussex. *Club:* Beefsteak.

BRIGGS, Hon. Sir Francis Arthur, Kt 1961; a Federal Justice of Supreme Court, Federation of Rhodesia and Nyasaland, 1958-63, retired; *b* 9 July 1902; *yr s* of late William Francis Briggs, Preston, Lancs, and late Jane Greig, *yr d* of late Thomas Macmillan, Glasgow; *m* 1953, Edna Dorothy, *d* of late William Thomas Keylock; no *c*. *Educ:* Charterhouse (Schol.); Trinity College, Oxford (Open Classical Schol.). Called to Bar, Inner Temple (Cert. of Honour and Jardine Studentship), 1927. Advocate and Solicitor, FMS, SS and Johore, 1928-40. Served in RAFVR, 1940-46 (despatches), Wing Commander. Colonial Legal Service, 1947; Registrar, Supreme Court, Federation of Malaya, 1948; Puisne Judge, Malaya, 1949; Justice of Appeal, E African Court of Appeal, 1953, Vice-President, 1957. *Address:* Shillingford, La Brecque, Alderney, Channel Islands. *T:* 2019.

BRIGGS, Sir Geoffrey (Gould), Kt 1974; President: Pensions Appeal Tribunals for England and Wales, since 1980; Brunei Court of Appeal, since 1979; *b* 6 May 1914; 2nd *s* of late Reverend C. E. and Mrs Briggs, Amersham, Buckinghamshire; unmarried. *Educ:* Sherborne; Christ Church, Oxford (BA, BCL). Called to Bar (Gray's Inn), 1938; served War of 1939-45, County of London Yeomanry (Major). Attorney-General, E Region, Nigeria, 1954-58;

QC (Nigeria), 1955; Puisne Judge, Sarawak, N Borneo and Brunei, 1958-62; Chief Justice of the Western Pacific, 1962-65; a Puisne Judge, Hong Kong, 1965-73; Chief Justice: Hong Kong, 1973-79; Brunei, 1973-79. DSNB 1974. *Address:* 1 Farley Court, Melbury Road, Kensington, W14 8LJ. *Club:* Athenæum.

BRIGGS, Rt. Rev. George Cardell, CMG 1980; *b* Latchford, Warrington, Cheshire, 6 Sept. 1910; *s* of George Cecil and Mary Theodora Briggs; unmarried. *Educ:* Worksop Coll., Notts; Sidney Sussex Coll., Cambridge (MA); Cuddesdon Theological Coll. Deacon 1934; priest 1935; Curate of St Alban's, Stockport, 1934-37; Missionary priest, Diocese of Masasi, Tanzania, 1937; Archdeacon of Newala and Canon of Masasi, 1955-64; Rector of St Alban's, Dar-es-Salaam, 1964-69; Warden of St Cyprian's Theological Coll., Masasi, 1969-73; Bishop of Seychelles, 1973-79; Asst Bishop, Diocese of Derby, and Assistant Priest, parish of St Giles, Matlock, 1979-80. *Recreations:* walking, reading, music. *Address:* c/o The Archbishop, Bishop's House, Phoenix, Mauritius. *Club:* Royal Commonwealth Society.

BRIGGS, Prof. George Edward, MA; FRS 1935; Fellow of St John's College, Cambridge (President, 1952-63); Professor Emeritus of Botany, Cambridge University; Professor of Botany, 1948-60; Professor of Plant Physiology, 1946-48, Cambridge University; *b* 25 June 1893; *m* 1920, Nora Burman; one *s* one *d. Educ:* Wintringham Grammar School; St John's College, Cambridge. *Publications:* Electrolytes and Plant Cells (with A. B. Hope and R. N. Robertson), 1961; Movement of Water in Plants, 1967. *Address:* 1 Margery Lane, Tewin, Welwyn, Herts AL6 0JP. *T:* Tewin 7419.

BRIGGS, John; *see* Briggs, Peter J.

BRIGGS, (Peter) John; a Recorder of the Crown Court, since 1978; *b* 15 May 1928; *s* of late Percy Briggs and of Annie M. Folker; *m* 1956, Sheila Phyllis Walton; one *s* three *d. Educ:* King's Sch., Peterborough; Balliol Coll., Oxford. MA, BCL. Called to the Bar, Inner Temple, 1953. Legal Member, Mersey Mental Health Review Tribunal, 1969 (Dep. Chm., 1971, Chm., 1981). *Recreations:* badminton, music. *Address:* Park Lodge, 107 Tarbock Road, Huyton, Merseyside L36 5TD. *T:* 051-489 2664.

BRIGGS, Maj.-Gen. Raymond, CB 1943; DSO 1942; psc†; President, Metropolitan Area, Royal British Legion; *b* 19 Jan. 1895; *yr s* of late James Burnett Briggs, Claughton, Cheshire; *m* 1927, Helen Wainwright, *d* of Charles Edward Kenworthy, Liverpool and New Orleans; one *d*. Served European War, 1914-18, France, Belgium, and Mesopotamia, Liverpool Scottish, King's Own Regt, and MGC, 2nd Lieut, 1915 (wounded twice); Royal Tank Corps, 1920; Bt Major, 1933; Bt Lt-Col, 1938; Colonel, 1941; Acting Brig., 1940; Major-General, 1944. Served War of 1939-45, France and Belgium, 1940 (GSO 1), Middle East and North Africa, 1941-43 (Comd 2 Armd Bde, GOC 1 Armd Division); Director, Royal Armoured Corps, War Office, 1943-47. Member Tank Board, 1943-46 (wounded, despatches twice, DSO, CB, Commander Legion of Merit, USA); retired, 1947. *Address:* 1 Linden Gardens, W2 4HA. *T:* 01-229 3711. *Club:* Army and Navy.

BRIGGS, Raymond Redvers, DFA; freelance illustrator, since 1957; author, since 1961; *b* 18 Jan. 1934; *s* of Ernest Redvers Briggs and Ethel Bowyer; *m* 1963, Jean Taprell Clark (*d* 1973). *Educ:* Rutlish Sch., Merton; Wimbledon School of Art; Slade School of Fine Art. NDD; DFA London. Part-time Lecturer in Illustration, Faculty of Art, Brighton Polytechnic, 1961-. *Publications:* The Strange House, 1961; Midnight Adventure, 1961; Ring-A-Ring O'Roses, 1962; Sledges to the Rescue, 1963; The White Land, 1963; Fee Fi Fo Fum, 1964; The Mother Goose Treasury, 1966 (Kate Greenaway Medal, 1966); Jim and the Beanstalk, 1970; The Fairy Tale Treasury, 1972; Father Christmas, 1973 (Kate Greenaway Medal, 1973); Father Christmas Goes On Holiday, 1975; Fungus The Bogeyman, 1977; The Snowman, 1978; Gentleman Jim, 1980; When the Wind Blows, 1982; Fungus the Bogeyman Plop-Up Book, 1982. *Recreations:* gardening, reading, walking, second-hand bookshops. *Address:* Weston, Underhill Lane, Westmeston, Hassocks, Sussex BN6 8XG. *T:* Hassocks 2638.

BRIGGS, Rear-Admiral Thomas Vallack, CB 1958; OBE (mil.) 1945; DL; a Vice-Patron, Royal Naval Association (President, 1971-76); *b* 6 April 1906; *e s* of late Admiral Sir Charles John Briggs, and Lady Briggs (*née* Wilson); *m* 1947, Estelle Burland Willing, Boston, USA; one step *s. Educ:* The Grange, Stevenage, Herts; Imperial Service College, Windsor. Joined Royal Navy 1924; Rear-Admiral 1956. Advanced Gunnery Specialist. Served War of 1939-45: HMS Ark Royal, 1939-40; AA Comdr HMS Excellent, 1941-42; HMS Newcastle, 1943-44; staff of Flag Officer 2nd in Command, Eastern Fleet, 1944-45 (despatches twice). US Naval War Coll., Newport, RI, 1946-47; commanded 5th Destroyer Flotilla, HMS Solebay, 1949-50, and HMS Cumberland, 1954-55; IDC, 1951; Chief of Staff: Plymouth, 1952-53, Home Fleet and Eastern Atlantic, 1956-57; Asst Controller of the Navy, 1958, retired. Director: Hugh Stevenson & Sons Ltd, 1958-69; Hugh Stevenson & Sons (North East) Ltd, 1966; Bowater-Stevenson Containers Ltd, 1969-71; Free-Stay Holidays Ltd, 1971; Internat. Consumer Incentives Ltd, 1974; Meru Group Ltd, 1978. Vice-Chm., City of Westminster Soc. for Mentally Handicapped Children, 1969; Mem., Management Cttee, Haileybury and ISC Junior Sch., Windsor, 1959-80 (Chm., 1978-80); Life Governor, Haileybury and Imperial Service Coll., 1959 (Mem. Council, 1959-80); Pres., Haileybury Soc., 1973-74. Fellow, Inst. of Marketing, 1970. Chm., Aldeburgh Festival Club, 1979-80. DL Greater London, 1970-82 (Representative DL, Kingston

upon Thames, 1970-79). *Recreations:* golf, shooting. *Address:* King's Legend, Aldeburgh, Suffolk IP15 5QB. *Clubs:* White's, English-Speaking Union; Aldeburgh Festival; RN Golfing Society, Aldeburgh Golf (Captain, 1981-82); RN Sailing Association; RN Ski.

BRIGHT, Hon. Sir Charles (Hart), KBE 1980; Chancellor, Flinders University, since 1971; *b* 25 Nov. 1912; *s* of Rev. Charles Bright and Annie Florence Bright; *m* 1940, Elizabeth Holden, *d* of H. B. Flaxman; two *s* one *d. Educ:* Scotch Coll.; Univ. of Adelaide (BA, LLB). Called to the Bar of SA, 1934; QC 1960; Judge, Supreme Court of SA, 1963-78, retd. Pres., Law Soc. of SA, 1960-61; Vice-Pres., Law Council of Aust., 1960-61; Chm., SA Health Cttee, 1979-80; Mem., various Royal Commns and Enquiries. *Publications:* contrib. learned jls. *Recreations:* reading, travelling. *Address:* 1A/97 MacKinnon Parade, North Adelaide, SA 5006, Australia. *T:* 267.3081; Turner House, 36 Chalcot Square, NW1 8YP. *T:* 01-586 3338. *Club:* Adelaide (Adelaide).

BRIGHT, Graham Frank James; MP (C) Luton East, since 1979; *b* 2 April 1942; *s* of Robert Frank Bright and Agnes Mary (*née* Graham); *m* 1972, Valerie Woolliams. *Educ:* Hassenbrook County Sch.; Thurrock Technical Coll. Marketing Exec., Pauls & White Ltd, 1958-70; Man. Dir, 1970-, and Chm., 1977-, Dietary Foods (Bletchley) Ltd. Vice Chm., Cons. Backbench Smaller Businesses Cttee, 1980- (Sec., 1979); Secretary: Cons. Backbench Aviation Cttee, 1980-; Cons. Backbench Food and Drinks Sub-Cttee. Member: Thurrock Bor. Council, 1965-79; Essex CC, 1967-70. Contested: Thurrock, 1970 and Feb. 1974; Dartford, Oct. 1974; Chm., Eastern Area CPC, 1977-80; Mem., Nat. CPC, 1980-; Vice Chm., YC Org., 1970-72; Pres., Eastern Area YCs, 1981-. Vice Chm., Smaller Businesses Bureau, 1980-. *Recreations:* foreign travel, motoring, conservation, photography. *Address:* House of Commons, SW1A 0AA. *Club:* Carlton.

BRIGHT, Keith, PhD, CChem, FRSC; Chairman and Chief Executive, London Transport Executive, since 1982; *b* 30 Aug. 1931; *s* of Ernest William Bright and Lilian Mary Bright; *m* 1959, Patricia Anne (separated); one *s* one *d. Educ:* University of London (BSc, PhD). Chief of Research, Passfield Research Laboratories; Supervisor and examiner for higher degrees in Univs of Lancaster, Surrey, City and London, 1961-67; Man. Dir, Formica International Ltd, 1967-73; Group Chief Exec., Sime Darby (Holdings) Ltd, 1974-77; Group Chief Exec., Associated Biscuit Manufacturers Ltd, 1977-82. Mem., British Airports Authy, 1982-; Director: Extel Group, 1979-; London & Continental Advertising, 1979-. *Publications:* numerous papers in technical and scientific jls. *Recreations:* music, golf. *Address:* c/o London Transport Executive, 55 Broadway, SW1H 0BD.

BRIGHTLING, Peter Henry Miller; Assistant Under Secretary of State, Ministry of Defence, 1973-81; *b* 12 Sept. 1921; *o s* of late Henry Miller Brightling and Eva Emily Brightling (*née* Fry); *m* 1951, Pamela Cheeseright; two *s* two *d. Educ:* City of London Sch.; BSc(Econ), London. War of 1939-45: Air Ministry, 1939-40; MAP, 1940-41; served in RAF, 1941-46. Ministry of: Supply, 1946-59; Aviation, 1959-67; Technology, 1967-70; Aviation Supply, 1970-71; MoD (Procurement Executive), 1971. *Address:* 5 Selwyn Road, New Malden, Surrey KT3 5AU. *T:* 01-942 8014.

BRIGHTMAN, family name of **Baron Brightman.**

BRIGHTMAN, Baron *cr* 1982 (Life Peer), of Ibthorpe in the County of Hampshire; **John Anson Brightman;** Kt 1970; PC 1979; a Lord of Appeal in Ordinary, since 1982; *b* 20 June 1911; 2nd *s* of William Henry Brightman, St Albans, Herts; *m* 1945, Roxane Ambatielo; one *s. Educ:* Marlborough College; St John's College, Cambridge. Called to the Bar, Lincoln's Inn, 1932; Bencher 1966. QC 1961. Able Seaman, 1939-40; RNVR (Lieut-Commander), 1940-46; Assistant Naval Attaché, Ankara, 1944. Attorney-General of the Duchy of Lancaster, and Attorney and Serjeant within the County Palatine of Lancaster, 1969-70; Judge of the High Court of Justice, Chancery Div., 1970-79; a Lord Justice of Appeal, 1979-82; Judge, Nat. Industrial Relns Court, 1971-74. Member, General Council of the Bar, 1956-60, 1966-70. *Recreations:* sailing, ski-ing, topiary. *Address:* House of Lords, SW1.

BRIGINSHAW, family name of **Baron Briginshaw.**

BRIGINSHAW, Baron *cr* 1974 (Life Peer), of Southwark; **Richard William Briginshaw;** General Secretary, National Society of Operative Printers, Graphical and Media Personnel, 1951-75; Member, Council, Advisory, Conciliation and Arbitration Service, 1974-76; *b* Lambeth; married. *Educ:* Stuart School, London. Later studied economics, trade union and industrial law, and physical anthropology (UCL diploma course). Elected Asst Secretary, London Machine Branch of Union, 1938. Joined Services, 1940; subseq. in Army, saw service overseas in India, Iraq, Persia, Palestine, Egypt, France, etc; left Army, 1946. Returned to printing trade; re-elected to full-time trade union position, 1949. Vice-Pres. 1961-72, Mem. Exec. Council 1951-72, Printing and Kindred Trades Fedn; TUC: Mem. Gen. Council, 1965-75; Member of Finance and General Purposes, Economic, Organisation, and International Cttees; Member: BOTB, 1975-77; British Nat. Oil Corp., 1976-79. Pres. of two London Confs on World Trade Development, 1963. Member: Joint Committee on Manpower, 1965-70; Bd of Govs, Dulwich Coll., 1967-72; Court, Cranfield Inst. of Technology. Hon. LLD New Brunswick, 1968. *Publications:* (four booklets): Britain's World Rating, 1962; Britain and the World Trade Conference, 1963; Britain's World Rating, 1964;

Britain's Oil, the Big Sell Out?, 1979. *Recreations:* swimming, painting, music. *Address:* House of Lords, SW1.

BRIGSTOCKE, Mrs Heather Renwick; High Mistress of St Paul's Girls' School since 1974; *b* 2 Sept. 1929; *d* of late Sqdn-Ldr J. R. Brown, DFC and Mrs M. J. C. Brown, MA; *m* 1952, Geoffrey Brigstocke (*d* 1974); three *s* one *d. Educ:* Abbey Sch., Reading; Girton Coll., Cambridge (MA). Univ. Winchester Reading Prize, 1950. Classics Mistress, Francis Holland Sch., London, SW1, 1951-53; part-time Classics Mistress, Godolphin and Latymer Sch., 1954-60; part-time Latin Teacher, National Cathedral Sch., Washington, DC, 1962-64; Headmistress, Francis Holland Sch., London, NW1, 1965-74. Non-exec. Dir, LWT, 1982-. Trustee: Nat. Gall., 1974-82; Kennedy Meml Trust, 1980-; Member: Council, London House for Overseas Graduates, 1965- (Vice-Chm., 1975-80); Council, Middlesex Hosp. Med. Sch., 1971-80; Council, Royal Holloway Coll., 1977-; Council, The City Univ., 1978-; Cttee, AA, 1975-. Governor: Wellington Coll., 1975-; The Royal Ballet Sch., 1977-; United World Coll. of the Atlantic, 1980-; President: Bishop Creighton House Settlement, Fulham, 1977-; Girls' Schools Assoc., 1980-81. *Address:* St Paul's Girls' School, Brook Green, W6 7BS.

BRILLIANT, Fredda, (Mrs Herbert Marshall); sculptor; *b* 7 April 1908; *d* of Mordechai and Raeisell Brilliant; *m* 1935, Herbert P. J. Marshall, *qv. Educ:* The Gymnasium (High Sch.), Lodz, Poland; Chelsea Art Sch. (drawing). Sculptor, 1932-; actress and singer, USA, 1930-33; actress and script writer in England, 1937-50. Sculptures include: Nehru, Krishna Menon, Paul Robeson, Herbert Marshall, Mahatma Gandhi, Buckminster Fuller, Carl Albert, Sir Maurice Bowra, Lord Elwyn-Jones. Exhibns in London include: Royal Academy, Leicester Galls, Royal Watercolour Soc., Whitechapel Gall., St Paul's Cathedral; other exhibns in Melbourne, Moscow, Bombay and Washington. Work in permanent collections: Nat. Art Gall., New Delhi; Mayakovsky Mus. and Shevchenko Mus., USSR; Southern Illinois Univ. FRSA; FIAL. Mem. Soc. of Portrait Sculptors. *Publication:* Biographies in Bronze (The Sculpture of Fredda Brilliant), 1982. *Recreations:* writing lyrics, composing songs and singing, attending classical concerts. *Address:* 1204 Chautaugua Street, Carbondale, Illinois 62901, USA.

BRIMACOMBE, Prof. John Stuart, FRSE, FRIC; Roscoe Professor of Chemistry, University of Dundee, since 1969; *b* Falmouth, Cornwall, 18 Aug. 1935; *s* of Stanley Poole Brimacombe and Lillian May Kathleen Brimacombe (*née* Candy); *m* 1959, Eileen (*née* Gibson); four *d. Educ:* Falmouth Grammar Sch.; Birmingham Univ. (DSc). DSc Dundee Univ. Lectr in Chemistry, Birmingham Univ., 1967-69. Meldola Medallist, 1964. *Publications:* (co-author) Mucopolysaccharides, 1964; numerous papers, reviews, etc, in: Jl Chem. Soc., Carbohydrate Research, etc. *Recreations:* sport, swimming. *Address:* 29 Dalhousie Road, Barnhill, Dundee. *T:* Dundee 79214.

BRIMELOW, family name of **Baron Brimelow.**

BRIMELOW, Baron *cr* 1976 (Life Peer), of Tyldesley, Lancs; **Thomas Brimelow,** GCMG 1975 (KCMG 1968; CMG 1959); OBE 1954; Chairman, Occupational Pensions Board, 1978-82; *b* 25 Oct. 1915; *s* of late William Brimelow and Hannah Smith; *m* 1945, Jean E. Cull; two *d. Educ:* New Mills Grammar School; Oriel College, Oxford; Hon. Fellow, 1973. Laming Travelling Fellow of the Queen's College, Oxford, 1937, Hon. Fellow, 1974. Probationer Vice-Consul, Danzig, 1938; served in Consulate, Riga, 1939 and Consulate-Gen., New York, 1940; in charge of Consular Section of Embassy, Moscow, 1942-45; Foreign Office, 1945; Foreign Service Officer, Grade 7, 1946; First Sec. (Commercial), and Consul, Havana, 1948; trans. to Moscow, 1951; Counsellor (Commercial), Ankara, 1954; Head of Northern Department of the Foreign Office, 1956; Counsellor, Washington, 1960-63; Minister, British Embassy, Moscow, 1963-66; Ambassador to Poland, 1966-69; Dep. Under-Sec. of State, FCO, 1969-73; Permanent Under-Sec. of State, FCO, and Head of the Diplomatic Service, 1973-75. Mem., European Parlt, 1977-78. *Address:* 12 West Hill Court, Millfield Lane, N6 6JJ. *Club:* Athenæum.

BRINCKMAN, Colonel Sir Roderick (Napoleon); 5th Bt, *cr* 1831; DSO 1940; MC 1941; *b* 27 Dec. 1902; 2nd *s* of Colonel Sir Theodore Brinckman, 3rd Bt, CB; *S* brother 1954; *m* 1st, 1931, Margaret Southam, Ottawa, Canada; two *s*; 2nd, 1942, Rosemary Marguerite Gilbey, *yr d* of late Lt-Col J. C. Hope Vere, Blackwood, Lanarkshire; one *d. Educ:* Osborne; Dartmouth. Served in Royal Navy two years (HMS Temeraire, Barham); joined Grenadier Guards in 1922; ADC to Lord Somers (Governor of Victoria), 1926-27; ADC to Lord Willingdon (Governor-General of Canada), 1930-31; served in Egypt, 1931-32, and France, 1940 (DSO, MC, despatches); commanded 2nd (Armoured) Bn Grenadier Guards, 1943; Chief of Staff Military Mission in Moscow, 1944-45; head of British Military Mission to the Netherlands Government in London, 1945-46. *Heir: s* Theodore George Roderick Brinckman [*b* 20 March 1932; *m* 1958, Helen Mary Anne, *d* of A. E. Cook, Toronto; two *s* one *d*]. *Address:* 7 Mallord Street, Chelsea, SW3 6DT. *T:* 01-352 9935; Crosskeys, Sandwich, Kent; St Helena, Barbados, BWI. *Club:* White's.

BRIND, (Arthur) Henry, CMG 1973; HM Diplomatic Service; *b* 4 July 1927; *o s* of late T. H. Brind and late N. W. B. Brind; *m* 1954, Barbara Harrison; one *s* one *d. Educ:* Barry; St John's Coll., Cambridge. HM Forces, 1947-49. Colonial Administrative Service: Gold Coast/Ghana, 1950-60; Regional Sec., Trans-Volta Togoland, 1959. HM Diplomatic Service, 1960-: Acting High Comr, Uganda, 1972-73; High Comr, Mauritius, 1974-77; Ambassador to Somali Democratic Republic, 1977-80. *Recreations:* walking, swimming,

books. *Address:* c/o Foreign and Commonwealth Office, SW1; 20 Grove Terrace, NW5 1PH. *Club:* Reform.
See also B. E. Capstick.

BRIND, George Walter Richard; Secretary-General, The Stock Exchange, 1971-75; *b* 13 Oct. 1911; *er s* of late Walter Charles and late Mary Josephine Brind; *m* 1942, Joyce, *er d* of late Matthew and Mary Graham; two *d. Educ:* Chiswick. Joined staff of Council of Stock Exchange, London, 1928, and has had no other employment than that with the Exchange. *Recreation:* bowls. *Address:* 7 Amberley Close, Send, Woking, Surrey. *T:* Guildford 223762.

BRIND, Henry; *see* Brind, A. H.

BRIND, Maj.-Gen. Peter Holmes Walter; CBE 1962 (OBE 1948); DSO 1945; DL; Deputy President, Surrey Branch, British Red Cross Society, since 1977; *b* 16 Feb. 1912; *yr s* of late General Sir John Brind, KCB, KBE, CMG, DSO; *m* 1942, Patricia Stewart Walker, *er d* of late Comdr S. M. Walker, DSC, RN, Horsalls, Harrietsham, Kent; three *s. Educ:* Wellington College; RMC, Sandhurst. Commissioned Dorset Regt, 1932. ADC to Governor of Bengal, 1936-39; Adjt, NW Europe, 1940; GSO 3 War Office, 1940-41; DAAG, HQ 12 Corps and Canadian Corps, 1941-42; Bde Major 1942; GSO 2 (MO) War Office, 1942; Comdt, Battle School, 1944, Comdg 2 Devons, NW Europe, 1944-45, GSO 1 (MT) War Office, 1946; GSO 1 (Ops), Palestine, 1948; GSO 1 (Plans), Egypt, 1949; GSO 1 (SD), War Office, 1950-54; Bt Lt-Col, 1952; Comdg 5th KAR (Kenya), 1954; Lt-Col, 1954; Col, 1955; Comdg 5 Inf. Bde Gp (BAOR), 1956; IDC 1959; Brig., 1960; Brig., AQ Middle East, 1960; BGS Eastern Comd, 1962; ADC to the Queen, 1964; Maj.-Gen., 1965; COS, Northern Comd, 1965-67. Dir, BRCS (Surrey Branch), 1968-77. Governor, St Catherine's School, 1968. DL Surrey, 1970. *Recreations:* gardening, music. *Address:* Pine Ridge, Hill Road, Haslemere, Surrey.

BRINDLEY, Prof. Giles Skey, MA, MD; FRS 1965; FRCP; Professor of Physiology in the University of London at the Institute of Psychiatry, since 1968; Hon. Director, Medical Research Council Neurological Prostheses Unit, since 1968; *b* 30 April 1926; *s* of Arthur James Benet Skey and late Dr Margaret Beatrice Marion Skey (*née* Dewhurst), later Brindley; *m* 1st, 1959, Lucy Dunk Bennell (marr. diss.); 2nd, 1964, Dr Hilary Richards; one *s* one *d. Educ:* Leyton County High School; Downing College, Cambridge (Hon. Fellow, 1969); London Hospital Medical College. Various jun. clin. and res. posts, 1950-54; Russian lang. abstractor, British Abstracts of Medical Sciences, 1953-56; successively Demonstrator, Lectr and Reader in physiology, Univ. of Cambridge, 1954-68; Fellow: King's Coll., Cambridge, 1959-62; Trinity Coll., Cambridge, 1963-68. Chm. of Editorial Board, Journal of Physiology, 1964-66 (Member 1959-64). Visiting Prof., Univ. of California, Berkeley, 1968. Liebrecht-Franceschetti Prize, German Ophthalmological Soc., 1971; Feldberg Prize, Feldberg Foundn, 1974. *Publications:* Physiology of the Retina and Visual Pathway, 1960, 2nd edn 1970; papers in scientific, musicological and medical journals. *Recreations:* ski-ing, orienteering, cross-country and track running, designing, making and playing various musical instruments (inventor of the logical bassoon). *Address:* 102 Ferndene Road, SE24. *T:* 01-274 2598. *Club:* Thames Hare and Hounds.

BRINK, Prof. Charles Oscar, LittD Cambridge; PhD Berlin; FBA; Kennedy Professor of Latin in the University of Cambridge, 1954-74, and Fellow of Gonville and Caius College, since 1955; *b* 13 March 1907; *m* 1942, Daphne Hope Harvey; three *s. Educ:* School and University, Berlin; Travelling Scholarship, Oxford. Member of editorial staff, Thesaurus linguæ Latinæ, 1933-38; Member of editorial staff, Oxford Latin Dictionary, 1938-41; Acting Classical Tutor, Magdalen College, Oxford, 1941-45; Member of Faculty of Literæ Humaniores, Oxford, 1941-48; MA Oxford (decree), 1944); Senior Classics Master, Magdalen College School, Oxford, 1943-48; Senior Lecturer in Humanity, University of St Andrews, 1948-51; Professor of Latin, University of Liverpool, 1951-54; MA Cambridge (BIII 6), 1954. Member Inst. for Advanced Study, Princeton, US, 1960-61, 1966. De Carle Lecturer, University of Otago, NZ, 1965; Vis. Prof., Univ. of Bonn, 1970; Professore Ospite Linceo, Scuola Normale Superiore, Pisa, 1977; James C. Loeb Lectr, Harvard Univ., 1978. Hon. Member, Jt Assoc. of Classical Teachers (Pres. 1969-71). Chm., Classics Committee, Schools Council, 1965-69; Trustee, Robinson Coll., Cambridge, 1973- (Chm., 1975-). Vice Pres., Internat. Cttee, Thesaurus Linguæ Latinæ, 1971-. Corresp. Mem., Bayerische Akad. der Wissenschaften, Munich, 1972-. Founding Jt Editor, Cambridge Classical Texts and Commentaries, 1963-. *Publications:* Imagination and Imitation (Inaug. Lect., Liverpool, 1952), 1953; Latin Studies and the Humanities (Inaug. Lect., Cambridge, 1956), 1957; On reading a Horatian Satire, 1965; Horace on Poetry: vol. I, Prolegomena, 1963; vol. II, The Ars Poetica, 1971; Studi classici e critica testuale in Inghilterra (Pisa), 1978; Epistles Book II, 1982; papers on Latin and Greek subjects. *Address:* Gonville and Caius College, Cambridge.

BRINK, David Maurice, DPhil; FRS 1981; Fellow and Tutor, Balliol College, Oxford, since 1958; University Lecturer, Oxford, since 1958; *b* 20 July 1930; *s* of Maurice Ossian Brink and Victoria May Finlayson; *m* 1958, Verena Wehrli; one *s* two *d. Educ:* Friends' Sch., Hobart; Univ. of Tasmania (BSc); Univ. of Oxford (DPhil). Rhodes Scholar, 1951-54: Rutherford Scholar, 1954-58; Lecturer, Balliol Coll., Oxford, 1954-58. Instructor, MIT, 1956-57. Rutherford Medal and Prize, Inst. of Physics, 1982. *Publications:* Angular Momentum, 1962, 2nd edn 1968; Nuclear Forces, 1965. *Recreations:*

birdwatching, mountaineering. *Address:* 21 Northmoor Road, Oxford OX2 6UW. *T:* Oxford 513613.

BRINKWORTH, George Harold, CBE 1960; Legal Adviser and Solicitor to Pay Board, 1973-74; *b* 16 Nov. 1906; *yr s* of George Alban Brinkworth and Hana Mary Brinkworth; *m* 1935, Dorothy Betty Suffield; one *s* one *d. Educ:* Wimbledon College; University College, London. LLB (Lond.) 1927. Admitted Solicitor, 1931. Entered Solicitor's Dept, Ministry of Labour, 1935; transf. to Ministry of Nat. Insce, 1945; Asst Solicitor, Min. of Pensions and Nat. Insce, 1948; Principal Asst Sol., DHSS (formerly Min. of Social Security), 1965-71. *Address:* 22 Stevens Parade, Black Rock, Victoria 3193, Australia. *T:* Melbourne 598-6556.

BRINTON, Denis Hubert, DM Oxon; FRCP; retired; *b* 9 Dec. 1902; *er s* of Hubert Brinton, Eton College; *m* 1st, 1928, Joan Violet (*d* 1971), *d* of James A. Hood; one *s* (and one *s* decd); 2nd, 1972, Rosemary Cockerill. *Educ:* Eton; New College, Oxford University; St Mary's Hospital, London University. MRCS, LRCP 1927; BM, BCh, 1928; MRCP 1929; DM Oxon 1937; FRCP 1938. Served War of 1939-45 (despatches), Air Commodore, RAF, Consultant in Neuropsychiatry. Member Internat. Neurological Congress, London, 1935; Physician-in-charge, Department of Nervous Diseases, St Mary's Hospital, 1935-63; Dean, St Mary's Hospital Medical School, 1946-51; Physician, National Hospital for Nervous Diseases, 1935-65; Council RCP, 1956-59. Member Assoc. British Neurologists; Member Assoc. Physicians Great Britain; Ed. Quart. Jl Med., 1954-68. *Publications:* Cerebrospinal Fever, 1941; articles in medical jls. *Address:* Bromfields, Burley, near Ringwood, Hants BH24 4HH. *T:* Burley 2319.
See also T. D. Brinton.

BRINTON, Major Sir (Esme) Tatton (Cecil), Kt 1964; President, Brintons Ltd, Kidderminster, since 1981 (Joint Managing Director, 1952-81, Chairman, 1968-81); *b* 4 Jan. 1916; *o s* of Colonel Cecil Charles Brinton, JP, and Cathleen Cecil Brinton (*née* Maude); *m* 1st, 1938, Mary Elizabeth Fahnestock (*d* 1960); four *s* one *d*; 2nd, 1961, Mrs Irene Sophie Borthwick (*d* 1978); 3rd, 1979, Mrs Mary Ellen Cappel. *Educ:* Eton; Caius College, Cambridge; and in Vienna and Paris. Served with XIIth R. Lancers, France, Desert, Italy, 1939-45. Technical Intelligence, Germany, 1945-46. Contested (C) Dudley, 1945; MP (C) Kidderminster, 1964-Feb. 74; Mayor of Kidderminster, 1953-54; High Sheriff of Worcestershire, 1961-62; President: Kidderminster Conservative Assoc., 1981- (Chm., 1955-56 and 1958-61); W Midlands Cons. Union, 1972-75 (Treasurer, 1958-61; Chm., 1962-64); Jt Treasurer of Conservative Party, 1966-74. Pres., Fedn of British Carpet Manufrs, 1974-76 (Chm., Home Exec. Cttee, 1960-64); Pres., British Carpet Manufrs Assoc., 1976; Chm British Carpets Promotion Council, 1960-66. High Steward of Kidderminster, 1978-. DL Worcs, 1968-81. OStJ 1962. *Address:* 35D Queens Gate, SW7. *Club:* Carlton.

BRINTON, Timothy Denis; MP (C) Gravesend, since 1979; broadcasting consultant; *b* 24 Dec. 1929; *s* of Dr Denis Hubert Brinton, *qv*; *m* 1st, 1954, Jane Mari Coningham; one *s* three *d*; 2nd, 1965, Jeanne Frances Wedge; two *d. Educ:* Summer Fields, Oxford; Eton Coll., Windsor; Geneva Univ.; Central Sch. of Speech and Drama. BBC staff, 1951-59; ITN, 1959-62; freelance, 1962-. Mem., Kent CC, 1974-81. *Address:* c/o House of Commons, SW1A 0AA. *T:* 01-219 5038. *Club:* Carlton.

BRISBANE, Archbishop of, and Metropolitan of the Province of Queensland, since 1980; also **Primate of Australia,** since 1982; **Most Rev. John Basil Rowland Grindrod;** *b* 14 Dec. 1919; *s* of Edward Basil and Dorothy Gladys Grindrod; *m* 1949, Ailsa W., *d* of G. Newman; two *d. Educ:* Repton School; Queen's College, Oxford; Lincoln Theological College. BA 1949; MA 1953. Deacon, 1951; Priest, 1952, Manchester. Curate: St Michael's, Hulme, 1951-54; Bundaberg, Qld, 1954-56; Rector: All Souls, Ancoats, Manchester, 1956-60; Emerald, Qld, 1960-61; St Barnabas, N Rockhampton, Qld, 1961-65; Archdeacon of Rockhampton, Qld, 1960-65; Vicar, Christ Church, S Yarra, Vic, 1965-66; Bishop of Riverina, NSW, 1966-71; Bishop of Rockhampton, 1971-80. *Address:* Bishopsbourne, 39 Eldernell Avenue, Hamilton, Qld 4007, Australia.

BRISBANE, Archbishop of, (RC), since 1973; **Most Rev. Francis Roberts Rush,** DD; *b* 11 Sept. 1916; *s* of T. J. Rush. *Educ:* Christian Brothers' Coll., Townsville; Mt Carmel, Charters Towers; St Columba's Coll., Springwood; Coll. de Propaganda Fide, Rome. Assistant Priest, Townsville, Mundingburra and Ingham; Parish Priest, Abergowrie and Ingham; Bishop of Rockhampton, 1960-73. *Address:* Wynberg, 790 Brunswick Street, New Farm, Queensland 4005, Australia.

BRISBANE, Assistant Bishop of; *see* Wicks, Rt Rev. R. E.

BRISCO, Sir Donald Gilfrid, 8th Bt *cr* 1782; JP; *b* 15 Sept. 1920; *s* of Sir Hylton (Musgrave Campbell) Brisco, 7th Bt and Kathleen, *d* of W. Fenwick McAllum, New Zealand; *S* father, 1968; *m* 1945, Irene, *o d* of Henry John Gage, Ermine Park, Brockworth, Gloucestershire; three *d.* Served War of 1939-45 with Royal New Zealand Air Force and Royal Air Force (prisoner of war in Germany and Italy). Retired Farmer. JP Hawke's Bay, 1967. *Heir:* uncle Oriel Arthur Brisco [*b* 6 June 1892; *m* 1921, Lilian Frederica, *d* of E. E. D. Saunderson, Christchurch, NZ; *m* 1960, Sarah Louise, RRC (*d* 1971), *d* of R. O. Clark, Auckland, NZ]. *Address:* Longworth, PO Box 165, Havelock North, Hawke's Bay, New Zealand.

BRISCOE, Captain Henry Villiers, CIE 1945; OBE 1943; RN (retd); *b* 9 Nov. 1896; *s* of late Maj. A. V. Briscoe, late RA, and G. M. Briscoe; *m* 1925, Lily Miller, *widow* (*decd*); one *s*; *m* 1948, Adaline Mary, *d* of Adam McIntosh, South Bantaskine, Falkirk, Stirling. *Educ:* Yarlet Hall, Staffs; RN Colleges, Osborne and Dartmouth. Royal Navy, 1909-22: Commercial Employment, 1922-31. Colonial Civil Servant, 1931-51; recalled to RN 1941-45; retd from Colonial Service, 1951. *Address:* 1 Thanet House, 4 Vernon Square, Ryde, IoW PO33 2JG.

BRISCOE, Sir John (Leigh Charlton), 4th Bt *cr* 1910; DFC 1945; *b* 3 Dec. 1911; *er s* of Sir Charlton Briscoe, 3rd Bt, MD, FRCP, and Grace Maud (*d* 1973) *d* of late Rev. W. S. Stagg; *S* father 1960; *m* 1948, Teresa Mary Violet, OBE 1972, *d* of late Brig.-Gen. Sir Archibald Home, KCVO, CB, CMG, DSO; two *s* one *d. Educ:* Harrow; Magdalen College, Oxford, BA 1933; ACA 1937; MA 1949. Served War of 1939-45 (DFC); RAFVR, 1942-46; Director of Aerodromes, Ministry of Aviation, 1961-66; Dir of Operations, British Airports Authy, 1966-72. *Recreations:* old cars, castles, and carpets. *Heir:* s John James Briscoe, *b* 15 July 1951. *Address:* Little Acres, Grays Park Road, Stoke Poges, Bucks. *T:* Farnham Common 2394. *Club:* Royal Air Force.

BRISE; *see* Ruggles-Brise.

BRISTER, William Arthur Francis; Deputy Director General of Prison Service, since 1982; *b* 10 Feb. 1925; *s* of Arthur John Brister and Velda Mirandoli; *m* 1949, Mary Speakman; one *s* one *d* (and one *s* decd). *Educ:* Douai Sch.; Brasenose Coll., Oxford (MA 1949). Asst Governor Cl. II, HM Borstal, Lowdham Grange, 1949-52; Asst Principal, Imperial Trng Sch., Wakefield, 1952-55; Asst Governor II, HM Prison, Parkhurst, 1955-57; Dep. Governor, HM Prison: Camp Hill, 1957-60; Manchester, 1960-62; Governor, HM Borstal: Morton Hall, 1962-67; Dover, 1967-69; Governor II, Prison Dept HQ, 1969-71; Governor, HM Remand Centre, Ashford, 1971-73; Governor I, Prison Dept HQ, 1973-75, Asst Controller, 1975-79; Chief Inspector of the Prison Service, 1979-81; Dep. Chief Inspector of Prisons, 1981-82. Nuffield Travelling Fellow, Canada and Mexico, 1966-67. *Recreations:* shooting, music, Venetian history. *Address:* Prison Department, Home Office, 89 Eccleston Square, SW1. *T:* 01-828 9848. *Clubs:* United Oxford & Cambridge University, English-Speaking Union.

BRISTOL, 6th Marquess of, *cr* 1826; **Victor Frederick Cochrane Hervey;** Baron Hervey, 1703; Earl of Bristol, 1714; Earl Jermyn, 1826; *b* 6 Oct. 1915; *s* of 5th Marquess of Bristol; *S* father 1960; *m* 1st, 1949, Pauline Mary (marr. diss., 1959), *d* of late Herbert Coxon Bolton; one *s*; 2nd, 1960, Lady Anne Juliet Wentworth Fitzwilliam (marr. diss. 1972), *o c* of 8th Earl Fitzwilliam, DSC, and of Olive Countess Fitzwilliam, Co. Wicklow; one *s*; 3rd, 1974, Yvonne Marie, *d* of Anthony Sutton; one *s* two *d. Educ:* Eton; Royal Military College. The Hereditary High Steward of the Liberty of St Edmund; Grand Master, High Stewards' Assoc.; Lord High Interrogator; Patron of 30 Livings; had estates in W, N and E Suffolk, Lincs, Essex, Dominica. Former owner of Ickworth Stud. Founder and first Pres., Nat. Yacht Harbour Assoc.; Vice Pres., Income Tax Payers' Union; Member: West India Cttee; Monday Club; Council, Bristol Soc. (Pres.); European Atlantic Group; Chancellor and Ambassador-at-Large, Grand Council, Monarchist League. Chairman: Radio Marina; British International Airways Ltd; Bristol Powersport Co.; Dominica Paradise Ltd; Marquis of Bristol & Co.; VLC Associated Ltd; Atlantis Project, Cyprus; Director of 30 other companies. Formerly: an expert on Central American Affairs and adviser to Govts; Chm. Jersey & Co. (Finland) Ltd; Mil. Advr to Finnish Govt (1960). GCLJ. Grand Officer, Royal Order of St Alexander (1292 AD) with Cordon. *Recreations:* yachting, shooting, antiques, beautiful women. *Heir: s* Earl Jermyn, *qv. Address:* Le Formentor, Avenue Princesse Grace, Monte Carlo, Monaco; (seat) Ickworth, Bury St Edmunds, Suffolk. *Clubs:* Hurlingham, Eccentric, Marks, House of Lords Motoring; Guards Polo; Royal Worlington Golf; House of Lords Yacht; East Hill (Nassau); Monte Carlo Yacht, Monte Carlo Country (Monaco).

BRISTOL, Bishop of, since 1976; **Rt. Rev. Ernest John Tinsley;** Special Lecturer in Theology, University of Bristol, since 1976; *b* 22 March 1919; *s* of Ernest William and Esther Tinsley; *m* 1947, Marjorie Dixon (*d* 1977); two *d. Educ:* St John's Coll., Univ. of Durham (BA, MA, BD); Westcott House, Cambridge. Priest, 1942; Curate: S Mary-le-Bow, Durham, 1942-44; South Westoe, 1944-46. Lectr in Theology, University Coll. of Hull, 1946-61; Sen. Lectr and Head of Dept of Theology, Univ. of Hull, 1961-62; Lectr of St Mary, Lowgate, Hull, 1955-62; Prof. of Theology, 1962-75, and Dean of Faculty of Arts, 1965-67, Univ. of Leeds. Hulsean Preacher, Cambridge Univ., 1982; Bishop John Prideaux Lectr, Exeter Univ., 1982. Examining Chaplain: to Archbp of York, 1957-63; to Bp of Sheffield, 1963-75. Hon. Canon of Ripon Cath., 1966-75. Jt Chm., Gen. Synod's Bd of Educn and Nat. Soc. for Promoting Religious Educn, 1979-; Member: Doctrinal Commn, 1967-69; Home Office Cttee on obscenity and film censorship, 1977-79. *Publications:* The Imitation of God in Christ, 1960; The Gospel according to Luke, 1965; (ed) Modern Theology, 1979; contributor to: The Church and the Arts, 1960; Vindications, 1966; A Dictionary of Christian Ethics, 1967; A Dictionary of Christian Theology, 1969; Art and Religion as Communication, 1974. *Recreations:* France, Romanesque art, gardening. *Address:* Bishop's House, Clifton Hill, Bristol BS8 1BW. *T:* Bristol 30222.

BRISTOL, Dean of; *see* Dammers, Very Rev. A. H.

BRISTOL, Archdeacon of; *see* Balmforth, Ven. A. J.

BRISTOW, Alan Edgar, OBE 1966; Chairman, Bristow Helicopter Group Ltd, since 1967; *b* 3 Sept. 1923; *m* 1945; one *s* one *d*. *Educ:* Portsmouth Grammar School. Cadet, British India Steam Navigation Co., 1939-43; Pilot, Fleet Air Arm, 1943-46; Test Pilot, Westland Aircraft Ltd, 1946-49; Helicopair, Paris/Indo-China, 1949-51; Man. Dir, Air Whaling Ltd (Antarctic Whaling Expedns), 1951-54; Man. Dir, Bristow Helicopters Ltd, 1954-68; Dir, British United Airways Ltd, 1960-70, Man. Dir 1967-70. Cierva Memorial Lectr, RAeS, 1967. FRAeS 1967. Croix de Guerre (France), 1950. *Publications:* papers to RAeS. *Recreations:* flying, shooting, sailing, farming, four-in-hand driving. *Address:* Baynards Park Estate, Cranleigh, Surrey. *T:* Cranleigh 4674.

BRISTOW, Hon. Sir Peter (Henry Rowley), Kt 1970; **Hon. Mr Justice Bristow;** a Judge of the High Court, Queen's Bench Division, since 1970; *b* 1 June 1913; *s* of Walter Rowley Bristow, FRCS and Florence (*née* White); *m* 1st, 1940, Josephine Noel Leney (*d* 1969); one *s* one *d*; 2nd, 1975, Elsa, *widow* of H. B. Leney. *Educ:* Eton; Trinity College, Cambridge. Pilot, RAFVR, 1936-45. Called to the Bar, Middle Temple, 1936, Bencher 1961, Treasurer 1977; QC 1964; Mem., Inns of Court Senate, 1966-70 (Hon. Treas., 1967-70); Judge, Court of Appeal, Guernsey, and Court of Appeal, Jersey, 1965-70; Dep. Chm., Hants QS, 1964-71; Judge of the Commercial Court and Employment Appeals Tribunal, 1976-78; Vice-Chm., Parole Bd, 1977-78 (Mem. 1976); Presiding Judge, Western Circuit, 1979-82. *Recreations:* sailing, fishing, shooting, gardening. *Address:* Royal Courts of Justice, Strand, WC2; 36 Eaton Place, SW1; The Folly, Membury, Axminster, Devon. *Club:* Royal Ocean Racing.

BRITISH COLUMBIA, Metropolitan of Ecclesiastical Province of; *see* New Westminster, Archbishop of.

BRITISH COLUMBIA, Bishop of, since 1980; **Rt. Rev. Hywel James Jones;** *b* 4 March 1918; *s* of Ifor James and Ann Jones; *m* 1946, Dorothy Margaret Wilcox; one *s* one *d*. *Educ:* Emmanuel Coll., Univ. of Saskatchewan (LTh). Deacon, then priest, 1942; Curate, Tofield, 1942; travelling priest, 1942-44; Incumbent of Parksville-Qualicum Beach, 1944-47; Colwood-Langford, 1947-56; Rector, St Mary the Virgin, Oak Bay, 1956-80. Hon. Canon of BC, 1959-68; Archdeacon of Quatsino, 1968-71, of Victoria, 1971-77; Archdeacon Emeritus, 1977-80. *Recreations:* reading, music, gardening. *Address:* 2028 Frederick Norris Road, Victoria, BC V8P 2B2, Canada. *T:* 604-592-7658. *Club:* Union (Victoria, BC).

BRITTAN, Rt. Hon. Leon, PC 1981; QC 1978; MP (C) Cleveland and Whitby since Feb. 1974; Chief Secretary to the Treasury, since 1981; *b* 25 Sept. 1939; *s* of late Dr Joseph Brittan and Mrs Rebecca Brittan; *m* 1980, Diana Peterson. *Educ:* Haberdashers' Aske's Sch.; Trinity Coll., Cambridge (MA); Yale Univ. (Henry Fellow). Chm., Cambridge Univ. Conservative Assoc., 1960; Pres., Cambridge Union, 1960; debating tour of USA for Cambridge Union, 1961. Called to Bar, Inner Temple, 1962. Chm., Bow Group, 1964-65; contested (C) North Kensington, 1966 and 1970. Editor, Crossbow, 1966-68; Mem. Political Cttee, Carlton Club; Vice-Chm. of Governors, Isaac Newton Sch., 1968-71; Mem. European North American Cttee, 1970-78; Vice-Chm., Nat. Assoc. of School Governors and Managers, 1970-78; Vice-Chm., Parly Cons. Party Employment Cttee, 1974-76; opposition front bench spokesman on Devolution, 1976-79, on employment, 1978-79; Minister of State, Home Office, 1979-81. *Publications:* (contrib.) The Conservative Opportunity; (jtly) Millstones for the Sixties, Rough Justice, Infancy and the Law, How to Save Your Schools (pamphlets). *Recreations:* opera, art, cricket, walking, travel. *Address:* 14 Ponsonby Terrace, SW1P 4QA. *T:* 01-821 7290; Lease Rigg Farm, Grosmont, Whitby, N Yorks. *T:* Grosmont 280. *Clubs:* Carlton, MCC.

See also Samuel Brittan.

BRITTAN, Samuel; Principal Economic Commentator, since 1966, and Assistant Editor, since 1977, Financial Times; *b* 29 Dec. 1933; *s* of late Joseph Brittan, MD, and of Rebecca Brittan (*née* Lipetz). *Educ:* Kilburn Grammar Sch.; Jesus Coll., Cambridge. 1st Class in Economics, 1955; MA Cantab. Various posts in Financial Times, 1955-61; Economics Editor, Observer, 1961-64; Adviser, DEA, 1965. Fellow, Nuffield Coll., Oxford, 1973-74, Vis. Fellow, 1974-; Vis. Prof. of Economics, Chicago Law Sch., 1978. Financial Journalist of the Year Award 1971; George Orwell Prize (for political journalism), 1980. *Publications:* The Treasury under the Tories, 1964, rev. edn, Steering the Economy, 1969, 1971; Left or Right: The Bogus Dilemma, 1968; The Price of Economic Freedom, 1970; Capitalism and the Permissive Society, 1973; Is There an Economic Consensus?, 1973; Second Thoughts on Full Employment Policy, 1975; (with P. Lilley) The Delusion of Incomes Policy, 1977; The Economic Consequences of Democracy, 1977; How to End the Monetarist Controversy, 1981; articles in various jls. *Address:* Flat 10, The Lodge, Kensington Park Gardens, W11.

See also Rt Hon. Leon Brittan.

BRITTEN, Brig. Charles Richard, OBE 1966; MC 1916; DL, JP; Extra Gentleman Usher to the Queen, since 1955; *b* 25 June 1894; 2nd *s* of late Rear-Admiral R. F. Britten and Hon. Blanche Cecile Colville, *o d* of 11th Baron Colville of Culross; *m* 1st, 1915, Dorothy (*d* 1970), *d* of late Hon. P. Allsopp; one *s*; 2nd, 1971, Pamela, *yr d* of E. G. Attenborough. *Educ:* Eton; RMC Sandhurst. Served European War, 1914-19 (served France, wounded Sept. 1916 and Nov. 1917); and War of 1939-45; Grenadier Guards, 1914; Capt. 1917; Lieut-Col 1935; Bt. Col 1937; Col 1938; Brig. 1939; Comdg

Grenadier Guards, 1937-39, and 1st (London) Infantry Bde, 1937-41; attached RAF Regiment, 1942; retired, 1946. Pres., Worcs and Hereford Branch, Gren. Guards Assoc. Mem., Worcs CC, 1946-74 (CA 1963); Mem., Martley RDC, 1948-74. DL 1947, JP 1946, High Sheriff 1952, Worcs. *Recreations:* shooting, hunting (former Chm., Wyre Forest Beagles) and fishing. *Address:* Kenswick Manor, Worcester. *T:* Worcester 640210. *Clubs:* Cavalry and Guards; Union and County (Worcester).

BRITTEN, Brig. George Vallette, CBE 1947 (OBE 1942, MBE 1940); HM Diplomatic Service, retired; *b* 19 March 1909; *s* of John Britten, Bozeat Manor, Northamptonshire, and Elizabeth Franziska Britten (*née* Vallette); *m* 1937, Shirley Jean Stewart Wink; three *s*. *Educ:* Wellingborough; RMC Sandhurst. Regtl duty in UK, 1929-38; Staff Coll., Camberley, 1938-39. Served War: HQ 2 Corps, France and Belgium, 1939-40; Staff appts in UK, 1940-41; with 1st Airborne Div. in UK, N Africa and Sicily, 1942-43; DCS, 5(US) Army, N Africa and Italy, 1943-44; HQ, 21st Army Gp, NW Europe, 1944-45. DCS, Brit. Military Govt, Germany, 1945-47. Regtl Duty, Berlin and Austria, 1947-49; WO, 1949-51; Comdt. Sch. of Infty, Hythe, 1952-54; Instr, US Army Staff Coll., Kansas, 1954-56; Planning Staff, NATO, Fontainebleau, 1956-58; Mil. Attaché, Brit. Embassy, Bonn, 1958-61; retired from Army, 1961; Ghana Desk, Commonwealth Office, 1961-62; with British High Commissions, Enugu, Kaduna, and Bathurst, 1962-66; Head of Chancery, British Embassy, Berne, 1967-71. American Legion of Merit, 1946; W German Grosses Verdienst Kreuz, 1959. *Recreation:* gardening. *Address:* 67 Bradbourne Park Road, Sevenoaks, Kent.

BRITTEN, Rae Gordon, CMG 1972; HM Diplomatic Service, retired; *b* 27 Sept. 1920; *s* of Leonard Arthur Britten and Elizabeth Percival Taylor; *m* 1952, Valentine Alms (marr. diss. 1974); one *s* three *d*; *m* 1977, Mrs Joan Dorothy Bull. *Educ:* Liverpool Institute High School; Magdalen College, Oxford. Served War 1941-45 (artillery and infantry). Research Assistant with Common Ground Ltd, 1947; apptd Commonwealth Relations Office, 1948; 2nd Sec., Brit. High Commn in India (Calcutta, 1948-49, Delhi, 1949-50): 1st Sec. Brit. High Commn., Bombay, 1955-58, Karachi, 1961-62; Deputy High Commissioner: Peshawar, March 1962; Lahore, June 1962-July 1964; Kingston, Jamaica, 1964-68; Head of Trade Policy Dept, FCO, 1968-71; Dep. High Comr, Dacca, 1971-72; Counsellor and Head of Chancery, Oslo, 1973-76; Head of SW Pacific Dept, FCO, 1976-78; Counsellor on Special Duties, FCO, 1978-80. *Address:* 4 Albany Crescent, Claygate, Esher, Surrey. *Club:* Royal Commonwealth Society.

BRITTEN, Maj.-Gen. Robert Wallace Tudor, CB 1977; MC; *b* 28 Feb. 1922; *s* of Lt-Col Wallace Ernest Britten, OBE; *m* 1947, Elizabeth Mary, *d* of Edward H. Davies, Pentre, Rhondda; one *s* one *d*. *Educ:* Wellington Coll.; Trinity Coll., Cambridge. CBIM. 2nd Lieut RE, 1941; served War of 1939-45, Madras Sappers and Miners, 19th Indian Div., India and Burma; Comdr 21 Fd Pk Sqn and 5 Fd Sqn RE, 1947-50; on staff WO, 1951-53; British Liaison Officer to US Corps of Engrs, 1953-56; comd 50 Fd Sqn RE, 1956-58; on staff WO, 1958-61; on staff of 1 (BR) Corps BAOR, 1961-64; Lt-Col in comd 1 Trg Regt RE, 1964-65; GSO1 (DS), Jt Services Staff Coll., 1965-67; Comd 30 Engr Bde (V) and Chief Engr Western Comd, 1967; idc 1969; Dir of Equipment Management, MoD (Army), 1970-71; DQMG, 1971-73; GOC West Midland Dist, 1973-76, retired. Brig. 1967; Maj.-Gen. 1971. Col Comdt, RE, 1977-. Chm., RE Assoc., 1978-. Hon. Col, Birmingham Univ. OTC, 1978-. *Recreations:* sailing, fishing, dowsing (Mem. Council, Brit. Soc. Dowsers). *Address:* Birch Trees, Fernden Lane, Haslemere, Surrey. *T:* Haslemere 2261. *Club:* Army and Navy.

BRITTENDEN, (Charles) Arthur; Director of Corporate Relations, News International, since 1981; General Manager (Editorial), Times Newspapers, since 1982; *b* 23 Oct. 1924; *o s* of late Tom Edwin Brittenden and Caroline (*née* Scrivener); *m* 1st, 1953, Sylvia Penelope Cadman (marr. diss., 1960); 2nd, 1966, Ann Patricia Kenny (marr. diss. 1972); 3rd, 1975, Valerie Arnison. *Educ:* Leeds Grammar School. Served in Reconnaissance Corps, 1943-46. Yorkshire Post, 1940-43, 1946-49; News Chronicle, 1949-55; joined Sunday Express, 1955: Foreign Editor, 1959-62; Northern Editor, Daily Express, 1962-63; Dep. Editor, Sunday Express, 1963-64; Exec. Editor, 1964-66, Editor, 1966-71, Daily Mail; Dep. Editor, The Sun, 1972-81. Dir, Harmsworth Publications Ltd, 1967-71. Man. Dir, Wigmore Cassettes, 1971-72. Mem., Press Council, 1982-. *Address:* 6 Strathearn Place, W2 2NG; 42 Oxford Street, Woodstock, Oxon.

BRITTON, Andrew James Christie; Director, National Institute of Economic and Social Research, since 1982; *b* 1 Dec. 1940; *s* of Prof. Karl William Britton, *qv* ; *m* 1963, Pamela Anne, *d* of Judge Edward Sutcliffe, *qv* ; three *d*. *Educ:* Royal Grammar Sch., Newcastle upon Tyne; Oriel Coll., Oxford (BA); LSE (MSc). Joined HM Treasury as Cadet Economist, 1966; Econ. Asst, 1968; Econ. Adviser, 1970; Sen. Econ. Adviser: DHSS, 1973; HM Treasury, 1975; London Business Sch., 1978-79; Under Sec., HM Treasury, 1980-82. *Address:* 15 Hawthorn Road, Wallington, Surrey SM6 0SY.

BRITTON, Prof. Denis King, CBE 1978; Professor of Agricultural Economics at Wye College, since 1970; *b* 25 March 1920; *s* of Rev. George Charles Britton and Harriet Rosa (*née* Swinstead); *m* 1942, Margaret Alice Smith; one *s* two *d*. *Educ:* Caterham School; London School of Economics, London University (BSc (Econ.)). Asst Statistician, Ministry of Agriculture and Fisheries, 1943-47; Lecturing and Research at University of Oxford, Agricultural Economics Res. Inst., 1947-52; MA Oxon 1948 (by decree);

Economist, United Nations Food and Agriculture Organisation, Geneva, 1952-59; Gen. Manager, Marketing and Economic Res., Massey-Ferguson (UK) Ltd, 1959-61; Prof. of Agricultural Economics, Univ. of Nottingham, 1961-70; Dean, Faculty of Agriculture and Horticulture, Univ. of Nottingham, 1967-70. Member: EDC for Agriculture, 1966-; Home Grown Cereals Authy, 1969-; Adv. Council for Agriculture and Horticulture, 1973-80; Chairman: Council, Centre for European Agricl Studies, Wye Coll., 1974-79; Adv. Cttee, Nuffield Centre for Agric. Strategy, 1975-80. President: Internat. Assoc. of Agric. Economists, 1976-79; British Agric. Economics Soc., 1977-78; Special Adviser, House of Commons Select Cttee on Agric., 1980-. Vis. Prof., Uppsala, 1973; Winegarten Lecture, NFU, 1981. Farmers' Club Cup, 1966. FSS 1943; FRAgS 1970; Hon. FRASE 1980. Hon. DAgric, Univ. of Bonn, 1975. *Publications:* Cereals in the United Kingdom, 1969; (with Berkeley Hill) Size and Efficiency in Farming, 1975; articles in Jl of Royal Statistical Society, Jl of Agricultural Economics, Jl of RSA, Farm Economist, etc. *Recreations:* music, golf. *Address:* 29 Chequers Park, Wye, Ashford, Kent. *Club:* Farmers'.

BRITTON, Sir Edward (Louis), Kt 1975; CBE 1967; Senior Research Fellow, Education Division, Sheffield University, 1975-79; retired; *b* 4 Dec. 1909; *s* of George Edwin and Ellen Alice Britton; *m* 1936, Nora Arnald; no *c. Educ:* Bromley Grammar School, Kent; Trinity College, Cambridge. Teacher in various Surrey schools until 1951; Headmaster, Warlingham County Secondary School, Surrey, 1951-60; General Secretary, Association of Teachers in Technical Institutions, 1960-68. National Union of Teachers: President, 1956-57; General Secretary, 1970-75. Member: TUC General Council, 1970-74; Beloe Cttee on Secondary Schs Exams, 1960; Schools Council, 1964-75; Adv. Cttee for Supply and Trng of Teachers, 1973-75; Burnham Primary and Secondary Cttee, 1956-75 (Jt Sec. and Leader of Teachers' Panel, 1970-75); Burnham Further Educn Cttee, 1959-69 (Jt Sec. and Leader of Teachers' Panel, 1961-69); Officers' Panel, Soulbury Cttee (and Leader), 1970-75; Staff Panel, Jt Negotiating Cttee Youth Leaders (and Leader), 1970-75; Warnock Cttee on Special Educn, 1974-78; Council and Exec., CGLI, 1974-77; Central Arbitration Cttee, 1977-; Vice-Pres., NFER, 1979. Fellow College of Preceptors, 1967; Hon. FEIS, 1974. Hon. DEd CNAA, 1969. *Publications:* many articles in educational journals. *Address:* 40 Nightingale Road, Guildford, Surrey.

BRITTON, Prof. Karl William; Professor of Philosophy, University of Newcastle upon Tyne, 1951-75; *b* Scarborough, Yorks, 12 Oct. 1909; *s* of Rev. J. Nimmo Britton and Elsie Clare Britton (*née* Slater); *m* 1936, Sheila Margaret Christie; one *s* two *d* (and one *s* one *d* decd). *Educ:* Southend High School; Clare College, Cambridge. Pres. Cambridge Union Society, 1931. Choate Fellow at Harvard University, USA, 1932-34; Lecturer in Philosophy: University College of Wales, 1934-37; University College of Swansea, 1937-51. War of 1939-45, Regional Commissioner's Office, Reading, 1941-45. Public Orator, Durham University, 1959-62; Dean of the Faculty of Arts, Newcastle upon Tyne, 1961-63 and 1966-69. Examiner, Moral Sciences Tripos: 1949, 1954, 1955, 1964, 1966. Mill Centenary Lectr, Toronto Univ., 1973. Sec., Mind Assoc., 1948-60, Pres. 1963. Hon. DLitt Durham, 1976. *Publications:* Communication: A Philosophical Study of Language, 1939, repr. 1971; John Stuart Mill, 1953, repr. 1969; Philosophy and the Meaning of Life, 1969; Communication and Understanding, 1978; A Memoir of C. D. Broad, 1978; contrib. to: The Times, Proc. Aristotelian Society, Mind, Philosophy, Analysis, Jl of Philosophy, Cambridge Review, etc. *Address:* Harthope, Millfield Road, Riding Mill, Northumberland. *T:* Riding Mill 354.

See also A. J. C. Britton.

BRITZ, Jack; General Secretary, Clearing Bank Union, since 1980; *b* 6 Nov. 1930; *s* of Alfred and Hetty Britz; *m* 1955, Thelma Salaver; one *s* two *d*. *Educ:* Luton Grammar School. Entered electrical contracting industry, 1944; various posts in industry; Director, Rolfe Electrical Ltd, 1964-65. National Recruitment Officer, EETPU, 1969-74; short period with Commission on Industrial Relations as sen. industrial relations officer, 1974; Personnel Manager, Courage Eastern Ltd, 1974-77; Gp Personnel Director, Bowthorpe Group Ltd, 1977-80. *Recreations:* walking, history, wargaming, etc. *Address:* (business) 14 St Clement's Street, Winchester SO23 9HH. *T:* Winchester 64351.

BROACKES, Nigel; Chairman, Trafalgar House Ltd; Chairman, London Docklands Development Corporation, since 1981; *b* Wakefield, 21 July 1934; *s* of late Donald Broackes and Nan Alford; *m* 1956, Joyce Edith Horne; two *s* one *d. Educ:* Stowe. Nat. Service, commnd 3rd Hussars, 1953-54. Stewart & Hughman Ltd, Lloyds Underwriting agents, 1952-55; various property developments, etc, 1955-57; Trafalgar House Investments Ltd: Man. Dir 1958; Dep. Chm. and Jt Man. Dir 1968; Chm. 1969. Ship and Marine Technology Requirements Bd, 1972-77; Dep. Chm., Offshore Energy Technology Bd, 1975-77. Hon. Treas., Kensington Housing Trust, 1963-69; Vice-Chairman: Mulberry Housing Trust, 1965-69; London Housing Trust, 1967-70; Mem. Council, Nat. Assoc. of Property Owners, 1967-73. Governor, Stowe Sch., 1974-81. Trustee, Royal Opera House Trust; Mem. Advisory Council, Victoria and Albert Museum, 1980-. Dir, Horserace Totalisator Bd, 1976-81. Guardian Young Businessman of the Year, 1978. *Publication:* A Growing Concern, 1979. *Recreation:* silversmith. *Address:* 41 Chelsea Square, SW3; Checkendon Court, Checkendon, Oxon.

BROADBENT, Donald Eric, CBE 1974; MA, ScD; FRS 1968; on External Staff, Medical Research Council, since 1974; *b* 6 May 1926; *m* 1st, 1949,

Margaret Elizabeth Wright; two *d*; 2nd, 1972, Margaret Hope Pattison Gregory. *Educ:* Winchester College; Pembroke College, Cambridge. RAF Engrg short course, 1st cl., 1944; Moral Science Tripos (Psychology), 1st cl., 1949. Scientific Staff, Applied Psychology Res. Unit, 1949-58 (Dir, 1958-74). Fellow, Pembroke College, Cambridge, 1965-74. Pres., British Psychol. Society, 1965; Pres., Sect. J. Brit. Assoc. for Advancement of Science, 1967; Vis. Fellow, All Souls College, Oxford, 1967-68; Fellow, Wolfson Coll., Oxford, 1974. Member: Biol. Res. Bd, MRC, 1966-70; Psychology Cttee, SSRC, 1969-75; SSRC, 1973-75; Fellow, Acoustical Soc. of Amer.; past or present Council Member: Royal Soc.; British Acoustical Soc.; British Psychol Soc.; Ergonomics Res. Soc.; Experimental Psychology Soc.; Fellow, Human Factors Soc.; Governor, Technical Change Centre, 1980-. Lectures: Lister, Brit. Assoc.; Gregynog, Aberystwyth; Pillsbury, Cornell; Fitts, Michigan; William James, Harvard; Fairey, Southampton; Fletcher-Stevens, Utah; Bartlett, Experimental Psychology Soc. For. Associate, US Nat. Acad. Sci., 1971. Hon. DSc: Southampton, 1974; York, 1979. APA Dist. Scientist Award, 1975. *Publications:* Perception and Communication, 1958; Behaviour, 1961; Decision and Stress, 1971; In Defence of Empirical Psychology, 1973; many papers in jls of above societies and of Amer. Psychol Assoc. *Recreations:* reading, camping, photography. *Address:* Department of Experimental Psychology, 1 South Parks Road, Oxford OX1 3UD.

BROADBENT, Dr Edward Granville, FRS 1977; FEng, FRAeS, FIMA; Deputy Chief Scientific Officer (IM), Aerodynamics Department, Royal Aircraft Establishment, since 1969; *b* 27 June 1923; *s* of Joseph Charles Fletcher Broadbent and Lucetta (*née* Riley); *m* 1949, Elizabeth Barbara (*née* Puttick). *Educ:* Huddersfield Coll.; St Catharine's Coll., Cambridge (State Scholarship, 1941; Eng Scholar; MA, ScD). FRAeS 1959; FIMA 1965. Joined RAE (Structures Dept), 1943; worked on aero-elasticity (Wakefield Gold Medal, RAeS, 1960); transf. to Aerodynamics Dept, 1960; worked on various aspects of fluid mechanics and acoustics. *Publication:* The Elementary Theory of Aero-elasticity, 1954. *Recreations:* duplicate bridge, chess, music, theatre. *Address:* 11 Three Stiles Road, Farnham, Surrey GU9 7DE. *T:* Farnham 714621.

BROADBENT, Ewen, CB 1973; CMG 1965; Second Permanent Under Secretary of State, Ministry of Defence, since 1982; *b* 9 Aug. 1924; *s* of late Rev. W. Broadbent and of Mrs Mary Broadbent; *m* 1951, Squadron Officer Barbara David, *d* of F. A. David, Weston-super-Mare; one *s. Educ:* King Edward VI School, Nuneaton; St John's College, Cambridge. Served with Gordon Highlanders, 1943-47 (Captain); Cambridge, 1942-43 and 1947-49; Air Ministry, 1949; Private Sec. to Secretary of State for Air, 1955-59; Asst Secretary, 1959; Dep. Chief Officer, Sovereign Base Areas, Cyprus, 1961, Chief Officer, 1964; MoD 1965-; Private Sec. to Sec. of State for Defence, 1967-68; Asst Under-Sec. of State, 1969-72; Dep. Under-Sec. of State (Air), 1972-75; Dep. Under-Sec. of State (Civilian Management), 1975-82. *Recreation:* golf. *Address:* 18 Park Hill, Ealing, W5. *T:* 01-997 1978. *Club:* Royal Commonwealth Society.

BROADBENT, Sir William Francis, 3rd Bt, *cr* 1898; *b* 29 Nov. 1904; *s* of Sir John Francis Harpin Broadbent, MD, FRCP, Bt and Margaret Elizabeth Field (*d* 1958); *S* father 1946; *m* 1935, Veronica Pearl Eustace (*d* 1951); no *c. Educ:* Winchester College; Trinity College, Oxford (MA). Solicitor, 1933-72, retired. *Heir: cousin* George Walter Broadbent [*b* 23 April 1935; *m* 1962, Valerie Anne, *o d* of C. F. Ward; one *s* one *d*]. *Address:* Flat 43, Ritchie Court, 380 Banbury Road, Oxford. *Club:* United Oxford & Cambridge University.

BROADBRIDGE, family name of **Baron Broadbridge.**

BROADBRIDGE, 3rd Baron *cr* 1945, of Brighton; **Peter Hewett Broadbridge;** Bt 1937; Directorships within the Ravendale Securities Group, since 1980; *b* 19 Aug. 1938; *s* of 2nd Baron Broadbridge and Mabel Daisy (*d* 1966), *o d* of Arthur Edward Clarke; *S* father, 1972; *m* 1967, Mary, *o d* of W. O. Busch; two *d. Educ:* Hurstpierpoint Coll., Sussex; St Catherine's Coll., Oxford (MA, BSc). Unilever Ltd, 1963-65; Colgate Palmolive Ltd, 1966; Gallaher Ltd, 1967-70; Peat, Marwick Mitchell & Co., EC2, 1970-77; Management Consultant, Coopers and Lybrand and Associates Ltd, 1977-80. Pres., Nat. Assoc. of Leisure Gardeners; Freeman, City of London, 1980; Worshipful Co. of Goldsmiths, 1980. *Recreations:* tennis, squash, antiques, silversmithing, bee-keeping. *Heir: uncle* Hon. Ralph George Cameron Broadbridge [*b* 20 Nov. 1901; *m* 1925, Emma Rose Hancock (*d* 1965), *d* of Harry Van der Weyden; three *d*]. *Address:* House of Lords, SW1A 0PW.

BROADHURST, Air Chief Marshal (retd) Sir Harry, GCB 1960 (KCB 1955; CB 1944); KBE 1945; DSO and Bar, 1941; DFC 1940, and Bar, 1942; AFC 1937; Managing Director, A. V. Roe & Co. Ltd, 1961-66; Director, 1961-76, Deputy Managing Director 1965-76, Hawker Siddeley Aviation Ltd; Director, Hawker Siddeley Group Ltd, 1968-76; *b* 1905; *m* 1st, 1929, Doris Kathleen French; one *d*; 2nd, 1946, Jean Elizabeth Townley; one *d*. SASO to AOC Western Desert, 1942; AOC Allied Air Forces, W. Desert, 1943; 83 Group Commander Allied Expeditionary Air Force, 1944-45; AO i/c Admin. Fighter Command, 1945-46; AOC 61 Group, 1947-48; idc 1949; SASO, BAFO (now 2nd TAF), Germany, 1950-51; ACAS (Ops), 1952-53; C-in-C 2nd Tactical Air Force, Germany, 1954-56; Air Officer Commanding-in-Chief, Bomber Command, Jan. 1956-May 1959; Cmdr Allied Air Forces, Central Europe, 1959-61. Vice-Pres., 1973-74, Pres., 1974-75, Dep. Pres., 1975-76, SBAC. Kt Grand Cross of Order of Orange Nassau, 1948; Legion of Merit (US). *Address:* Lock's End House, Birdham, Chichester, W Sussex. *T:* Birdham 512717. *Club:* Royal Air Force.

BROADLEY, Sir Herbert, KBE 1947 (CBE 1943); Representative in Britain of United Nations Children's Fund, 1958-68; *b* 23 Nov. 1892; *s* of late Stephenson S. Broadley, Louth, Lincs; *m* 1927, Kathleen May, *d* of late Alfred J. Moore, Camden Square, London; no *c. Educ:* King Edward VI Grammar Sch., Louth; Birkbeck Coll., Univ. of London. Pres. Students' Union; Editor, Coll. Magazine Lodestone, 1922-23. Civil Service, 1912; served in India Office (Military Dept), 1912-1920; served in BoT, 1920-26; Sec., Imperial Customs Conf., 1921, German (Reparations) Act Cttee, 1921, and Imperial Economic Cttee, 1925-26; Asst Sec., Anglo-Soviet Commercial Treaty, 1924; Sec., Anglo-German Commercial Treaty, 1925; Asst Sec., Imperial Econ. Conf., 1926; resigned from Civil Service, 1926, and joined firm of W. S. Crawford Ltd (Advertising Agents), 1927; Dir, W. S. Crawford Ltd and Man. Dir of their Berlin Branch, 1927-32; i/c Distribution and Res. Dept, W. S. Crawford Ltd, London, 1932-39; Fellow and Mem. Council, Inst. of Incorp. Practitioners in Advertising and Chm., Res. Cttee, 1936-39; joined Ministry of Food at outbreak of War, 1939; Asst Sec., Nov. 1939; Principal Asst Sec., 1940; Dep. Sec., 1941; Second Sec., 1945-48; Leader, UK Delegn to Internat. Wheat Confs, 1947 and 1948; UK repr. at UNFAO Confs: Quebec, 1945; Copenhagen, 1946; Dep. Dir-Gen., UNFAO, 1948-58 (Acting Dir-Gen., 1955-56), retd. Trustee, UK Nat. Freedom from Hunger (Mem. Cttee, 1960-). Hon. Freeman of Louth (Lincs) 1961. Hon. Fellow, Birkbeck Coll., Univ. of London, 1963; a Governor, Birkbeck Coll., 1965-. Haldane Meml Lecture on Food and People, Univ. of London, 1964. Commander of the Order of the Crown of Belgium, 1948. *Publication:* The People's Food (with Sir William Crawford), 1938. *Address:* Hollingsworth, Redlands Lane, Ewshot, Farnham, Surrey GU10 5AS. *T:* Aldershot 850437. *Club:* Naval and Military.

BROADLEY, John Kenneth Elliott; HM Diplomatic Service; Head of Security Department, Foreign and Commonwealth Office, since 1981; *b* 10 June 1936; *s* of late Kenneth Broadley and of Rosamund Venn (*née* Elliott); *m* 1961, Jane Alice Rachel (*née* Gee); one *s* two *d. Educ:* Winchester Coll.; Balliol Coll., Oxford (Exhibnr, MA). Served Army, 1st RHA, 1954-56. Entered HM Diplomatic Service, 1960; Washington, 1963-65; La Paz, 1965-68; FCO, 1968-73; UK Mission to UN, Geneva, 1973-76; Counsellor, Amman, 1976-79; Head of Personnel Policy Dept, FCO, 1979-81. *Recreations:* climbing, squash, tennis, family. *Address:* c/o Foreign and Commonwealth Office, SW1; 5 Pound Lane, Sevenoaks, Kent. *Club:* Royal Commonwealth Society.

BROATCH, James, CBE 1961; Deputy Chairman of the Cotton Board, 1963; Deputy Chairman, Textile Council, 1967-68; *b* 13 May 1900; *s* of Alfred and Mary Broatch; *m* 1927, Mary Booth. *Educ:* Manchester Grammar School; University College, Oxford. Editor, Manchester Guardian Commercial, 1930-39; Assistant Secretary, The Cotton Board, 1939-43; Secretary 1943-53; Director-General, 1953-62. *Address:* 5 Lynton Drive, Hillside, Southport, Merseyside. *T:* Southport 67976.

BROCAS, Viscount; Patrick John Bernard Jellicoe; *b* 29 Aug. 1950; *s* and *heir* of 2nd Earl Jellicoe, *qv*; *m* 1971, separated 1971, marr. diss. 1980; two *s* (*b* 1970, 1977). *Educ:* Eton. Profession, engineer.

BROCK, Arthur Guy C.; *see* Clutton-Brock.

BROCK, Michael George, CBE 1981; Warden of Nuffield College, Oxford, since 1978; Pro-Vice-Chancellor, Oxford University, since 1980; *b* 9 March 1920; *s* of late Sir Laurence George Brock and Ellen Margery Brock (*née* Williams); *m* 1949, Eleanor Hope Morrison; three *s. Educ:* Wellington Coll. (Schol.); Corpus Christi Coll., Oxford (Open Schol.; First Cl. Hons Mod. Hist. 1948; MA 1948). FRHistS 1965. War service (Middlesex Regt) 1940-45. Corpus Christi Coll., Oxford: Jun. Res. Fellow, 1948-50; Fellow and Tutor in Modern History and Politics, 1950-66, Fellow Emeritus, 1977; Hon. Fellow, 1982; Oxford University: Jun. Proctor, 1956-57; Univ. Lectr, 1951-70; Mem., Hebdomadal Council, 1965-76, 1978-; Vice Pres. and Bursar, Wolfson Coll., Oxford, 1966-76; Prof. of Educn and Dir. of Educn, Exeter Univ., 1977-78. Hon. Fellow, Wolfson Coll., Oxford, 1977; Hon. DLitt Exeter, 1982. *Publications:* The Great Reform Act, 1973; many articles on historical topics and on higher education. *Address:* Nuffield College, Oxford; 186 Woodstock Road, Oxford OX2 7NQ. *Clubs:* Athenæum; Oxford Union.

BROCK, Rear-Admiral Patrick Willet, CB 1956; DSO 1951; RN retd; Chairman, The Naval Review, 1967-78; *b* 30 Dec. 1902; *e s* of R. W. and M. B. Brock, Kingston, Ontario; *m* 1st, 1931, M. D. Collinson (*d* 1974); 2nd, 1976, Mrs Rosemary Harrison Stanton. *Educ:* Royal Royal Naval College of Canada. Transferred from Royal Canadian Navy to RN, 1921; Commander 1938; Exec. Officer, HMS Mauritius, 1942-44 (despatches); Captain 1944; Senior Naval Officer, Schleswig-Holstein, 1946; commanded HMS Kenya, Far East, 1949-51 (despatches, DSO); Director Operations Div., 1951-53; Rear-Admiral, 1954; Flag Officer, Middle East, 1954-56; Admiralty Material Requirements Committee, 1956-58, retired. Chm., Kipling Soc., 1973-76. Trustee, National Maritime Museum, 1960-74; a Vice-Pres., Soc. for Nautical Research, 1970-. Croix de Guerre (France), 1945; Bronze Star Medal (US), 1951. *Publications:* RUSI Eardley-Wilmot Gold Medal Essay, 1935; (with Basil Greenhill) Steam and Sail in Great Britain and North America,

1973. *Recreations:* gardening, naval history. *Address:* Kiln Cottage, Critchmere, Haslemere, Surrey. *T:* Haslemere 2542.

BROCK, Dr Sebastian Paul, FBA 1977; University Lecturer in Aramaic and Syriac, University of Oxford, since 1974; *b* 1938; *m* 1966, Helen M. C. (*née* Hughes). *Educ:* Eton College; Univ. of Cambridge (BA 1962, MA 1965); MA and DPhil Oxon 1966. Asst Lectr, 1964-66, Lectr, 1966-67, Dept of Theology, Univ. of Birmingham; Lectr, Hebrew and Aramaic, Univ. of Cambridge, 1967-74. Fellow of Wolfson Coll., Oxford, 1974-. *Publications:* Pseudepigrapha Veteris Testamenti Graece II; Testamentum Iobi, 1967; The Syriac Version of the Pseudo-Nonnos Mythological Scholia, 1971; (with C. T. Fritsch and S. Jellicoe) A Classified Bibliography of the Septuagint, 1973; The Harp of the Spirit: Twelve Poems of St Ephrem, 1975; The Holy Spirit in Syrian Baptismal Tradition, 1979; contrib. JSS, JTS, Le Muséon, Oriens Christianus, Orientalia Christiana Periodica, Parole de l'Orient, Revue des études arméniennes. *Address:* Wolfson College, Oxford; Oriental Institute, Pusey Lane, Oxford.

BROCK, Prof. William Ranulf; Fellow of Selwyn College, Cambridge, since 1947; Professor of Modern History, University of Glasgow, 1967-81, now Emeritus; *b* 16 May 1916; *s* of Stewart Ernst Brock and Katherine Helen (*née* Temple Roberts); *m* 1950, Constance Helen (*née* Brown); one *s* one *d. Educ:* Christ's Hosp.; Trinity Coll., Cambridge (MA, PhD). Prize Fellow 1940 (in absentia). Military service (Army), 1939-45; Asst Master, Eton Coll., 1946-47. Commonwealth Fund Fellow, Berkeley, Calif, Yale and Johns Hopkins, 1952-53, 1958; Vis. Professor: Michigan Univ., 1968; Washington Univ., 1970; Maryland Univ., 1980; Charles Warren Fellow, Harvard Univ., 1976; Leverhulme Emeritus Fellow, 1981. *Publications:* Lord Liverpool and Liberal Toryism, 1941; The Character of American History, 1960; An American Crisis, 1963; The Evolution of American Democracy, 1970; Conflict and Transformation 1844-1877, 1973; The Sources of History: the United States 1790-1890, 1975; Parties and Political Conscience, 1979; Scotus Americanus, 1982; contrib. New Cambridge Mod. History, Vols VII and XI; articles and reviews in Eng. Hist. Review, History, Jl Amer. Studies, etc. *Recreation:* antiques. *Address:* 49 Barton Road, Cambridge CB3 9LG. *T:* Cambridge 313606.

BROCKBANK, (James) Tyrrell, DL; solicitor; *b* 14 Dec. 1920; *y s* of late James Lindow Brockbank; *m* 1950, Pamela, *yr d* of late Lt-Col J. Oxley Parker, TD, and Mary Monica (*née* Hills); four *s. Educ:* St Peter's Sch., York; St John's Coll., Cambridge (MA). Served War of 1939-45 with Sherwood Foresters and Inns of Court Regt. Asst Solicitor, Wolverhampton, 1949-51; Asst Clerk, Hertfordshire, 1951-54; Dep. Clerk, Nottinghamshire, 1954-61; Clerk of the Peace, Durham, 1961-71; Clerk of Durham CC, 1961-74; Clerk to the Lieutenancy, 1964-; DL Durham 1970. Member, Local Govt Boundary Commn for England, 1976-. *Recreations:* fishing, shooting, golf. *Address:* The Orange Tree, Shincliffe, Durham DH1 2NN. *T:* Durham 65569. *Clubs:* Travellers'; Durham County (Durham).

BROCKBANK, Maj.-Gen. John Myles, CBE 1972; MC 1943; Director, British Field Sports Society, since 1976; *b* 19 Sept. 1921; *s* of Col J. G. Brockbank, CBE, DSO, and Eireine Marguerite Robinson; *m* 1953, Gillian Findlay, three *s* one *d. Educ:* Eton Coll.; Oxford Univ. Commissioned into 12 Royal Lancers, 1941. Served War, North Africa, Italy, 1941-45. Served Germany: 1955-58, 1964-68 and 1970-72; Cyprus, 1959; USA, 1961-64; Staff Coll., 1950; IDC 1969; CO, 9/12 Royal Lancers; Comdr, RAC, HQ 1 Corps; Chief of Staff, 1 Corps; Dir, RAC, 1972-74; Vice-Adjutant General, MoD, 1974-76. Col, 9/12 Lancers, 1982-. *Recreations:* field sports, gardening, bird watching. *Address:* Manor House, Steeple Langford, Salisbury, Wilts. *T:* Stapleford 353. *Club:* Cavalry and Guards.

BROCKBANK, Prof. John Philip, PhD; Director of the Shakespeare Institute and Professor of English, University of Birmingham, since 1979; *b* 4 Jan. 1922; *s* of John Brockbank and Sarah Cooper; *m* 1947, Doreen Winterbottom; two *s. Educ:* Oldershaw Grammar Sch., Wallasey; Trinity Coll., Cambridge (MA, PhD). Served RAF, Navigator, 1940-46. Professor of English, Saarbrücken, 1953-54; Asst Lectr, Cambridge, and College Lectr, Jesus Coll., 1954-58; Sen. Lectr, Reading, 1958-62; Prof. of English, York, 1962-79. General Editor, New Cambridge Shakespeare, 1978-. *Publications:* Marlowe's Dr Faustus, 1961, repr. 1979; ed, Pope, Selected Poems, 1962, repr. 1974; ed, Ben Jonson, Volpone, 1967, repr. 1980; ed, Shakespeare, Coriolanus, 1976; contribs to books on Shakespeare, Milton, Pope, Marvell, and to Shakespeare Survey, TLS, etc. *Recreations:* theatre, water-colours. *Address:* 14 Scholars Lane, Stratford-upon-Avon CV37 6HE. *T:* Stratford-upon-Avon 295058.

BROCKBANK, Tyrrell; *see* Brockbank, J. T.

BROCKBANK, William, TD 1946; MA, MD Cambridge; FRCP; Consulting Physician, Royal Infirmary, Manchester, since 1965; Hon. Medical Archivist Manchester University, 1965-75, Hon. Archivist and Keeper, John Rylands University of Manchester Library, since 1975; Hon. Archivist, Manchester Royal Infirmary, 1965-77, Hon. Consultant Archivist, since 1978; *b* Manchester, 28 Jan. 1900; *s* of Edward Mansfield and Mary Ellwood Brockbank; unmarried. *Educ:* Bootham School, York; Caius College, Cambridge; Manchester University. Medical Officer, Manchester Grammar School, 1929-46; Physician, Manchester Royal Infirmary, 1932-65. Lecturer in Medicine, Manchester University, 1933-65; Dean of Clinical Studies,

Manchester University, 1939-65. RAMC, Major, 1939-41; Lieut-Colonel, 1941-46. Director, Asthma Clinic, Manchester Royal Infirmary, 1946-65. Fitzpatrick Lecturer, Royal College of Physicians, 1950-51; Chairman Manchester University Medical Library Cttee, 1951-54; Member Council, Royal College of Physicians, 1955-58; President Manchester Medical Society, 1955-56; Vicary Lecturer, Royal College of Surgeons, 1956; Member Hinchliffe Cttee (Cost of Prescribing), 1957-59; Gideon de Laune Lectr, Soc. of Apothecaries, 1963. Dist Comr (now Hon.) Boy Scouts Assoc.; awarded Silver Acorn, 1950. Vice-President, Lancashire CC Club, 1967-. Hon. MSc Manchester, 1972. Special Correspondent for Life for the Manchester Literary and Philosophical Soc. *Publications:* Portrait of a Hospital, 1952; Ancient Therapeutic Arts, 1954; The Honorary Medical Staff of the Manchester Royal Infirmary 1830-1948, 1965; The Diary of Richard Kay, 1716-51, 1968; The History of Nursing at the Manchester Royal Infirmary, 1752-1929, 1970; numerous papers to the Lancet, mostly on asthma, and to Medical History. *Recreations:* Medical History, archaeology; collecting cricket literature and water colours. *Address:* 51 Palatine Road, Manchester M20 9LJ. *T:* 061-445 3259. *Club:* National Liberal.

BROCKET, 3rd Baron, *cr* 1933; **Charles Ronald George Nall-Cain**, Bt 1921; *b* 12 Feb. 1952; *s* of Hon. Ronald Charles Manus Nall-Cain (*d* 1961), and of Elizabeth Mary (who *m* 2nd, 1964, Colin John Richard Trotter), *d* of R. J. Stallard; *S* grandfather, 1967; *m* 1982, Isabell Maria Lorenzo, *o d* of Gustavo Lorenzo, Whaleneck Drive, Merrick, Long Island, NY. *Educ:* Eton. 2nd Lieut, 14/20 Hussars, 1971; Lieut, 1974. *Heir:* b Hon. Richard Philip Christopher Nall-Cain [*b* 5 April 1953; *m* 1978, Juliet, *d* of J. E. V. Forester, St Brelade, Jersey]. *Address:* Brocket Hall, Welwyn, Herts.

BROCKHOFF, Sir Jack (Stuart), Kt 1979; company director; *b* 1908; *s* of Mr and Mrs Frederick Douglas Brockhoff. *Educ:* Wesley Coll., Vic. Chairman and Managing Director: Brockhoff's Biscuits Pty Ltd; Arnott-Brockhoff-Guest Pty Ltd; Dir, Arnotts Ltd; Chm. of Dirs, Jack Brockhoff Foundn. *Recreations:* golf, bowls, fishing. *Address:* 113 Beach Road, Sandringham, Vic 3191, Australia. *T:* 598 9227. *Clubs:* Woodlands Golf, Victoria Golf, Sandringham, Sandringham Yacht, Royal Automobile of Victoria, Victoria Racing, Victoria Amateur Turf.

BROCKHOLES, Michael John F.; *see* Fitzherbert-Brockholes.

BROCKHOUSE, Dr Bertram Neville, FRS 1965; Professor of Physics, McMaster University, Canada, since 1962; *b* 15 July 1918; *s* of Israel Bertram Brockhouse and Mable Emily Brockhouse (*née* Neville); *m* 1948, Doris Isobel Mary (*née* Miller); four *s* two *d*. *Educ:* University of British Columbia (BA); University of Toronto (PhD). Served War of 1939-45 with Royal Canadian Navy. Lectr, University of Toronto, 1949-50; Research Officer, Atomic Energy of Canada Ltd, 1950-59; Branch Head, Neutron Physics Br., 1960-62. Hon. DSc Waterloo, 1969. *Publications:* some 75 papers in learned journals. *Address:* Department of Physics, McMaster University, Hamilton, Ontario, Canada L8S 4M1. *T:* (416) 648-6329.

BROCKINGTON, Prof. Colin Fraser; Professor of Social and Preventive Medicine, Manchester University, 1951-64, Emeritus, 1964; *b* 8 Jan. 1903; *s* of late Sir William Brockington; *m* 1933, Dr Joyce Margaret Furze; three *s* one *d*. *Educ:* Oakham Sch.; Gonville and Caius Coll., Cambridge; Guy's Hosp., London. MD, MA, DPH, BChir Cantab, MSc Manchester, MRCS, MRCP; barrister-at-law, Middle Temple. Medical Superintendent, Brighton Infectious Diseases Hosp. and Sanatorium, 1929; Asst County Medical Officer, Worcs CC, 1930-33; general medical practice, Kingsbridge, Devon, 1933-36; Medical Officer of Health, Horsham and Petworth, 1936-38; Dep. County Medical Officer of Health, Warwickshire CC, 1938-42; County Medical Officer of Health: Warwickshire CC, 1942-46; West Riding CC, 1946-51. Member: Central Adv. Council for Educn (Eng.), 1945-56; Central Training Council in Child Care (Home Office), 1947-53; Adv. Council for Welfare of Handicapped (Min. of Health), 1949-54; Nursing Cttee of Central Health Services Council (Min. of Health), 1949-51; Council of Soc. of Med. Officers of Health, 1944-66; Public Health Cttee of County Councils Assoc., 1945-49. Chairman: WHO Expert Cttee on School Health, 1950; Symposium on "Mental Health-Public Health Partnership," 5th Internat. Congress on Mental Health, Toronto, 1954; WHO Research Study Group on Juvenile Epilepsy, 1955; UK Cttee of WHO, 1958-61. Took part as Expert in Technical Discussions on Rural Health at World Health Assembly, 1954; Far Eastern Lecture Tour for British Council, 1956-57; visited India, 1959, 1962, S America 1960, Jordan 1966-67, Spain 1967, Arabia 1968, Turkey 1955, 1969, 1970, 1972, Greece 1970, for WHO. Lecture Tour: S Africa and Middle East, 1964. *Publications:* Principles of Nutrition, 1952; The People's Health, 1955; A Short History of Public Health, 1956 (2nd edn 1966); World Health, 1958 (3rd edn 1975); The Health of the Community, 1955, 1960, 1965; Public Health in the Nineteenth Century, 1965; The Social Needs of the Over-Eighties, 1966; wide range of contribs to learned jls. *Recreations:* bookbinding, travel. *Address:* Werneth, Silverburn, Ballasalla, Isle of Man. *T:* Castletown (Isle of Man) 3465.

BROCKLEBANK, Sir Aubrey (Thomas), 6th Bt *cr* 1885; ACA; Director; Augill Castle Antiques Ltd; *b* 29 Jan. 1952; *s* of Sir John Montague Brocklebank, 5th Bt, TD, and of Pamela Sue, *d* of late William Harold Pierce, OBE; *S* father, 1974; *m* 1979, Dr Anna-Marie Dunnet; one *s*. *Educ:* Eton; University Coll., Durham (BSc Psychology). *Recreations:* shooting, motor

racing. *Heir: s* Aubrey William Thomas Brocklebank, *b* 15 Dec. 1980. *Address:* 37 Kyrle Road, SW11.

BROCKLEBANK-FOWLER, Christopher, MP Norfolk North West, since 1974 (King's Lynn, 1970-74) (C, 1970-81, SDP, since 1981); Chairman, Overseas Trade and Development Agency Ltd, since 1979; *b* 13 Jan. 1934; 2nd *s* of Sidney Straton Brocklebank Fowler, MA, LLB; *m* 1st, 1957, Joan Nowland (marr. diss. 1975); two *s*; 2nd, 1975, Mrs Mary Berry. *Educ:* Perse Sch., Cambridge. Farm pupil on farms in Suffolk, Cambridgeshire and Norfolk, 1950-55. National service (submarines), Sub-Lt, RNVR, 1952-54. Farm Manager, Kenya, 1955-57; Lever Bros Ltd (Unilever Cos Management Trainee), 1957-59; advertising and marketing consultant, 1959-79. Mem. Bow Group, 1961-81 (Chm., 1968-69; Dir, Bow Publications, 1968-71). Mem. London Conciliation Cttee, 1966-67; Vice-Chm. Information Panel, Nat. Cttee for Commonwealth Immigrants, 1966-67; Mem. Exec. Cttee, Africa Bureau, 1970-74; Chm., SOS Childrens Villages, 1978-. Chm., Conservative Parly Sub-Cttee on Horticulture, 1972-74; Vice-Chairman: Cons. Parly Cttee on Agriculture, 1974-75; Cons. Parly Foreign and Commonwealth Affairs Cttee, 1979 (Jt Sec., 1974-75, 1976-77); Cons. Parly Trade Cttee, 1979-80; SDP Agriculture Policy Cttee, 1982-; Chairman: UN Parly Gp, 1979- (Jt Sec., 1971-78); Cons. Parly Overseas Develt Sub-Cttee, 1979-81; SDP Third World Policy Cttee, 1981-; Member: Select Cttee for Overseas Develt, 1973-79; Select Cttee on Foreign Affairs, 1979-81; SDP Nat. Steering Cttee, 1981-; SDP Parly spokesman on Agriculture and Overseas Develt, 1981-. Contested (C) West Ham (North), Gen. Elec., 1964. Vice Chm., Centre for World Develt of Educn, 1980-81; Governor, Inst. of Develt Studies, 1978-81. FRGS; MInstM; M CAM; FInstD; Hon. Fellow IDS. *Publications:* pamphlets and articles on race relations, African affairs, overseas development. *Recreations:* painting, fishing, shooting, swimming. *Address:* The Long Cottage, Flitcham, near King's Lynn, Norfolk. *T:* Hillington 255.

BROCKLEHURST, Major-General Arthur Evers, CB 1956; DSO 1945; late RA; *b* 20 July 1905; *m* 1940, Joan Beryl Parry-Crooke; twin *d*. *Educ:* King's School, Canterbury; RMA Woolwich. 2nd Lieut, RA, 1925; CRA 6th Armoured Div., 1951; IDC 1954; DDPS (B) 1955; Chief of Staff, Malaya Comd, 1956-57; GOC, Rhine Dist, BAOR, 1958-59; Dep. Comdr BAOR, 1959-61; retired 1961. Chm., Devizes Constituency Cons. Assoc., 1963-65. *Recreations:* fishing, gardening. *Address:* Woodborough Manor, Pewsey, Wilts. *Club:* Army and Navy.

BROCKLEHURST, Prof. John Charles, FRCPE, FRCPGlas; Professor of Geriatric Medicine, University of Manchester, since 1970; *b* 31 May 1924; *s* of late Harold John Brocklehurst and of Dorothy Brocklehurst; *m* 1956, Susan Engle; two *s* one *d*. *Educ:* Glasgow High Sch.; Ayr Academy; Univ. of Glasgow (MB ChB 1947; MD Hons 1950). MRCPE 1961, FRCPE 1970; FRCPGlas 1972. Christine Hansen Research Fellow, Glasgow Univ., 1948-49; RAMC (to rank of Major), 1949-51; MO, Grenfell Mission, Northern Newfoundland and Labrador, 1955-57; Medical Registrar, Stobhill Hosp., and Asst Lectr, Dept of Materia Medica and Therapeutics, Glasgow Univ., 1959-60; Asst Physician (SHMO) in Geriatrics to Bournemouth and E Dorset Hosp. Gp, 1960-61; Cons. Geriatrician, Bromley Hosp. Gp and Cray Valley and Sevenoaks Hosp. Gp, 1961-69; Cons. in Geriatric and Gen. Med., Guy's Hosp., London, 1969-70. Dir, Geigy Unit for Research in Aging, Univ. of Manchester, 1974-; Chm., Age Concern England, 1973-77, Hon. Vice-Pres., 1980-; Governor, British Foundn for Age Research, 1980-; Pres., Soc. of Chiropodists, 1977-. Vis. Professor of Geriatric Med. and Chm., Div. of Geriatric Med., Univ. of Saskatchewan, Canada, 1978-79. Hon. MSc Manchester 1974. Bellahouston Gold Medal, Univ. of Glasgow, 1950; Willard Thomson Gold Medal, Amer. Geriatrics Soc., 1978. *Publications:* Incontinence in Old People, 1951; The Geriatric Day Hospital, 1971; ed and part author, Textbook of Geriatric Medicine and Gerontology, 1973, 2nd edn 1978; ed and part author, Geriatric Care in Advanced Societies, 1975; (jtly) Geriatric Medicine for Students, 1976, 2nd edn, 1981; (jtly) Progress in Geriatric Day Care, 1980. *Recreations:* violin playing, water colour painting. *Address:* 59 Stanneylands Road, Wilmslow, Cheshire SK9 4EX. *T:* Wilmslow 526795. *Clubs:* East India and Devonshire, Royal Society of Medicine.

BROCKLEHURST, Mrs Mary D.; *see* Dent-Brocklehurst.

BROCKLEHURST, Robert James, DM; Emeritus Professor of Physiology, University of Bristol, since 1965; *b* Liverpool, 16 Sept. 1899; *e s* of George and Sarah Huger Brocklehurst, Liverpool; *m* 1st, 1928, Sybille (*d* 1968), *y d* of Captain R. H. L. Risk, CBE, RN; two *s* one *d*; 2nd, 1970, Dora Millicent, *y d* of late Alexander Watts. *Educ:* Harrow Sch.; University College, Oxford (Scholar; 1st Class Honours in Physiology); St Bartholomew's Hospital. BA 1921; MA, BM, BCh, 1924; DM, 1928; MRCS, LRCP, 1925; Demonstrator of Physiology, St Bartholomew's Hosp. Medical Coll., 1925-26; Radcliffe Travelling Fellow, 1926-28; Lecturer, 1928-29, and Senior Lecturer, 1929-30, in Dept of Physiology and Biochemistry, Univ. Coll., London; Prof. of Physiology, 1930-65, and Dean of Med. Fac., 1934-47, Univ. of Bristol, and Univ. Rep. on GMC, 1935-65 (Jt Treas., 1962-65); Long Fox Meml Lectr, 1952; Mem. Inter-departmental Cttee on Dentistry, 1943; Mem. Dental Bd of UK, 1945-56; Additional Mem., GDC, 1956-65; Pres., Bath, Bristol and Somerset Branch, BMA 1959-60; Fellow BMA, 1967; Pres. Bristol Medico-Chirurgical Society, 1960-61; Member Council, 1958-63, and President Sect. I (Physiology), 1950, British Association; Mem., S-W Regional Hosp. Bd, and Bd of Govs of United Bristol Hosps, 1947-66; Chm, Moorhaven Hosp. Management Cttee, 1966-71; a representative of Diocese of Bristol in the

Church Assembly, 1945-65; Member, Central Board of Finance, 1957-65; Chm., Bristol Diocesan Bd of Finance, 1951-65. Mem., Council Westonbirt School, 1955-75 (Chm., 1956-68); Member Council, Christ Church College, Canterbury, 1961-73; Churchwarden, Stoke Bishop, 1939-60; a Vice-President Gloucester and Bristol Diocesan Association of Church Bell Ringers. Chm., Glos, Somerset and N Devon Regional Group, YHA, 1934-45. Served in Tank Corps, 1918-19. *Publications:* Papers on physiological, biochemical and educational subjects in medical and scientific jls. *Recreation:* gardening. *Address:* Cleeve, Court Road, Newton Ferrers, Plymouth, Devon PL8 1DE. *T:* Plymouth 872397. *Clubs:* Alpine, Royal Commonwealth Society, Royal Over-Seas League.

BROCKMAN, John St Leger; Under Secretary and Principal Assistant Solicitor, Department of Health and Social Security, since 1978; *b* 24 March 1928; *s* of late Prof. Ralph St Leger Brockman and Estelle Wilson; *m* 1954, Sheila Elizabeth Jordan; one *s* two *d* (and one *d* decd). *Educ:* Ampleforth; Gonville and Caius Coll., Cambridge. BA, LLB. Called to the Bar, Gray's Inn, 1952. Legal Asst, Min. of National Insurance, 1953; Sen. Legal Asst, Min. of Pensions and National Insurance, 1964; Asst Solicitor, DHSS, 1973. *Publications:* compiled and edited: The Law relating to Family Allowances and National Insurance, 1961; The Law relating to National Insurance (Industrial Injuries), 1961. *Recreations:* St Vincent de Paul Society, pottery, a little walking. *Address:* 304 The Greenway, Epsom, Surrey KT18 7JF. *T:* Epsom 20242.

BROCKMAN, Vice-Admiral Sir Ronald, KCB 1965; CSI 1947; CIE 1946; CVO 1979; CBE 1943; Extra Gentleman Usher to the Queen, since 1979 (Gentleman Usher, 1967-79); *b* 8 March 1909; *er s* of late Rear-Adm. H. S. Brockman, CB; *m* 1932, Marjorie Jean Butt; one *s* three *d. Educ:* Weymouth Coll., Dorset. Entered Navy, 1927; Assistant Secretary to First Sea Lord, Admiral of the Fleet Sir Roger Backhouse, 1938-39; Lieut-Commander 1939; Admiral's Secretary to First Sea Lord, Admiral of the Fleet Sir Dudley Pound, 1939-43; Commander 1943; Admiral's Secretary to Admiral of the Fleet Lord Mountbatten in all appointments, 1943-59; Private Secretary to Governor-General of India, 1947-48. Principal Staff Officer to the Chief of Defence Staff, Min. of Defence, 1959-65. Captain, 1953; Rear-Admiral, 1959; Vice-Admiral, 1963; retired list, 1965. Mem., Rugby Football Union Cttee, 1956-; County Pres., St John Ambulance, Devon; Mem., Devon and Exeter Steeplechases Exec.; Pres., Devon County Agric. Assoc., 1980; Vice Pres. and Governor, Royal Western Sch. for Deaf, Exeter. DL Devon. CStJ. Special Rosette of Cloud and Banner (China), 1946; Chevalier Legion of Honour and Croix de Guerre, 1946; Bronze Star Medal (USA), 1947. *Address:* 3 Court House, Basil Street, SW3. *T:* 01-584 1023. *Clubs:* White's; MCC; Royal Western Yacht Club of England; Coastal Forces Sailing (Commodore).

BROCKMAN, Hon. Sir Thomas Charles D.; *see* Drake-Brockman.

BROCKWAY, family name of **Baron Brockway.**

BROCKWAY, Baron *cr* 1964 (Life Peer); **Archibald Fenner Brockway;** *b* Calcutta, 1888; *s* of Rev. W. G. Brockway and Frances Elizabeth Abbey; *m* 1914, Lilla, *d* of Rev. W. Harvey-Smith; four *d* ; *m* 1946, Edith Violet, *d* of Archibald Herbert King; one *s. Educ:* Sch. for the Sons of Missionaries (now Eltham Coll.). Joined staff Examiner, 1907; sub-editor Christian Commonwealth, 1909; Labour Leader, 1911; editor, 1912-17; secretary No Conscription Fellowship, 1917; sentenced to one month's imprisonment under DORA Aug. 1916, and to three months, six months, and two years hard labour under Military Service Act, Dec. 1916, Feb. 1917, and July 1917; Joint Secretary British Committee of Indian National Congress and editor India, 1919; Joint Secretary Prison System Enquiry Cttee, 1920: Organising Secretary ILP 1922; General Secretary ILP, 1928 and 1933-39; Editor of New Leader, 1926-29, and 1931-46; Labour candidate Lancaster, 1922; Chairman No More War Movement and War Resister's International, 1923-28; Labour candidate Westminster 1924; Exec. Labour and Socialist International, 1926-31; Fraternal Delegate Indian Trade Union Congress and Indian National Congress, 1927; MP (Lab) East Leyton, 1929-31; Chairman ILP, 1931-33; took part in last public Socialist campaign against Hitler in Germany, 1932; Political Secretary ILP, 1939-46; Chairman British Centre for Colonial Freedom, 1942-47; ILP candidate, Upton Division of West Ham, 1934, Norwich, 1935, Lancaster, 1941, and Cardiff East, 1942; ILP Fraternal Delegate Hamburg Trade Union May Day Demonstrations and German Social Democratic Party Conference, Hanover, 1946. Resigned from ILP, 1946, and rejoined Labour Party; MP (Lab) Eton and Slough, 1950-64. Member Internat. Cttee of Socialist Movement for United Europe, 1947-52; first Chairman of Congress of Peoples against Imperialism, 1948-; Fraternal Delegate, Tunisian Trade Union Conf., 1951; Mem. unofficial Fact-finding mission, Kenya, 1952; Chairman: Liberation (formerly Movement for Colonial Freedom), 1954-67 (President, 1967-); British Asian and Overseas Socialist Fellowship, 1959-66; Peace in Nigeria Cttee, 1967-70; Peace Mission to Biafra and Nigeria, 1968; Brit. Council for Peace in Vietnam, 1965-69; Pres., British Campaign for Peace in Vietnam, 1970-; Co-Chm. (with Lord Noel-Baker), World Disarmament Campaign, 1979-. *Publications:* Labour and Liberalism, 1913; The Devil's Business, 1915 (proscribed during the war); Socialism and Pacifism, 1917; The Recruit, 1919; Non-Co-operation, 1919; The Government of India, 1920; English Prisons To-day (with Stephen Hobhouse), 1921; A Week in India, 1928; A New Way with Crime, 1928; The Indian Crisis, 1930; Hungry England, 1932; The Bloody Traffic, 1933; Will Roosevelt Succeed?, 1934; Purple Plague (a novel), 1935; Workers'

Front, 1938; Inside the Left: a Political Autobiography, 1942; Death pays a Dividend (with Frederic Mullally), 1944; German Diary, 1946; Socialism Over Sixty Years; The Life of Jowett of Bradford, 1946; Bermondsey Story: Life of Alfred Salter, 1949; Why Mau Mau?, 1953; African Journeys, 1955; 1960-Africa's Year of Destiny, 1960; Red Liner (novel in dialogue), 1961; Outside the Right, 1963; African Socialism, 1964; Commonwealth Immigrants: What is the Answer? (with Norman Pannell), 1965; Woman Against the Desert (with Miss Campbell-Purdie) 1967; This Shrinking Explosive World, 1968; The Next Step to Peace, 1970; The Colonial Revolution, 1973; Towards Tomorrow (autobiog.), 1977; Britain's First Socialists, 1980; numerous ILP and Movement for Colonial Freedom pamphlets. *Address:* 67 Southway, N20 8DE. *T:* 01-445 3054.

BRODIE, Sir Benjamin David Ross, 5th Bt *cr* 1834; *b* 29 May 1925; *s* of Sir Benjamin Collins Brodie, 4th Bt, MC, and Mary Charlotte (*d* 1940), *e d* of R. E. Palmer, Ballyheigue, Co. Kerry; *S* father, 1971; *m* ; one *s* one *d. Educ:* Eton. Formerly Royal Corps of Signals. *Heir: s* Alan Brodie.

BRODIE, Colin Alexander, QC 1980; *b* 19 April 1929; *s* of Sir Benjamin Collins Brodie, 4th Bt, MC, and late Mary Charlotte, *e d* of R. E. Palmer, Ballyheigue, Co. Kerry; *m* 1955, Julia Anne Irene, *yr d* of Norman Edward Wates; two *s. Educ:* Eton; Magdalen Coll., Oxford. 2/Lieut 8th KRI Hussars, 1949-50. Called to the Bar, Middle Temple, 1954. *Recreations:* polo, hunting. *Address:* 24 Old Buildings, Lincoln's Inn, WC2. *T:* 01-405 1124.

BRODIE OF BRODIE, (Montagu) Ninian (Alexander), DL; JP; Chief of Clan Brodie; landowner since 1953; *b* 12 June 1912; *s* of late I. A. M. Brodie of Brodie (*d* 1943) and late C. V. M. Brodie of Brodie (*née* Hope); *m* 1939, Helena Penelope Mills Budgen; one *s* one *d. Educ:* Eton. Stage, films, TV, 1933-40 and 1945-49. Served Royal Artillery, 1940-45. JP Morayshire, 1958; Hon. Sheriff-Substitute, 1958; DL Nairn, 1970. *Recreations:* shooting, collecting pictures. *Heir: s* Alastair Ian Ninian Brodie, Younger of Brodie [*b* 7 Sept. 1943; *m* 1968, Mary Louise Johnson; two *s* one *d*]. *Address:* Brodie Castle, Forres, Moray IV36 0TE, Scotland. *T:* Brodie 202.

BRODIE, Peter Ewen, OBE 1954; QPM 1963; an Assistant Commissioner, Metropolitan Police, 1966-72; *b* 6 May 1914; 2nd *s* of late Captain E. J. Brodie, Lethen, Nairn; *m* 1st, 1940, Betty Eve Middlebrook Horsfall (*d* 1975); one *s* ; 2nd, 1976, Millicent Joyce Mellor. *Educ:* Harrow School. Metropolitan Police, 1934-49 (Seconded to Ceylon Police, 1943-47); Chief Constable, Stirling and Clackmannan Police force, 1949-58; Chief Constable, Warwicks Constabulary, 1958-64; HM Inspector of Constabulary for England and Wales, 1964-66. Member: Adv. Cttee on Drug Dependence, 1967-70; Exec. Cttee, Internat. Criminal Police Organisation-Interpol, 1967-70. Chm. Council, Order of St John for Warwicks, 1977-. CStJ 1978. *Address:* The Old Vicarage, Lower Shuckburgh, Daventry, Northants NN11 6DX. *T:* Daventry 71590.

BRODIE, Very Rev. Peter Philip, DD; Minister of St Mungo's, Alloa, since 1947; Moderator of General Assembly of Church of Scotland, May 1978-1979; *b* 22 Oct. 1916; *s* of Robert Brodie and Margaret Jack; *m* 1949, Constance Lindsay Hope; three *s* one *d. Educ:* Airdrie Acad.; Glasgow Univ. (MA, BD, LLB, DD); Trinity Coll., Glasgow. Minister, St Mary's, Kirkintilloch, 1942. Church of Scotland: Vice Chm., Gen. Trustees, 1965-; Convener, Gen. Admin Cttee, 1976. Hon. DD Glasgow, 1975. *Publications:* Four Ways Sunday School Plan, 1964; contrib. jls. *Recreations:* fishing, gardening. *Address:* Manse of St Mungo's, Alloa, Clackmannanshire. *T:* Alloa 213872. *Clubs:* New, Caledonian (Edinburgh).

BRODIE, Stanley Eric, QC 1975; a Recorder of the Crown Court, since 1975; *b* 2 July 1930; *s* of Abraham Brodie, MB, BS and Cissie Rachel Brodie; *m* 1956, Gillian Rosemary Joseph; two *d* ; *m* 1973, Elizabeth Gloster; one *s* one *d. Educ:* Bradford Grammar Sch.; Balliol Coll., Oxford (MA). Pres., Oxford Univ. Law Soc., 1952. Called to Bar, Inner Temple, 1954; Mem. NE Circuit, 1954; Lectr in Law, Univ. of Southampton, 1954-55. *Recreations:* opera, boating, winter sports, fishing. *Address:* 21 Campden Hill Square, W8 7JY. *T:* 01-727 3241. *Club:* United Oxford & Cambridge University.

BRODIE, Maj.-Gen. Thomas, CB 1954; CBE 1949; DSO 1951; late The Cheshire Regt; *b* 20 Oct. 1903; *s* of Thomas Brodie, Bellingham, Northumberland; *m* 1938, Jane Margaret Chapman-Walker; three *s* one *d.* Commanded: 2 Manchester Regt, 1942-43; 14th Infantry Brigade in Wingate Expedition, 1944; 1 Cheshire Regt, 1946-47; Palestine, 1947-48 (CBE and despatches); commanded 29 Inf. Bde, Korea, 1951 (DSO, US Silver Star Medal, US Legion of Merit); GOC 1 Infantry Div., MELF, 1952-55; Colonel The Cheshire Regiment 1955-61; retired 1957. *Address:* Chapmore End House, Chapmore End, Ware, Herts. *Club:* Army and Navy.

BRODRICK, family name of **Viscount Midleton.**

BRODRICK, Norman John Lee, QC 1960; JP; MA; **His Honour Judge Brodrick;** a Circuit Judge (formerly a Judge of the Central Criminal Court), since 1967; *b* 4 Feb. 1912; 4th *s* of late William John Henry Brodrick, OBE; *m* 1940, Ruth Severn, *d* of late Sir Stanley Unwin, KCMG; three *s* one *d. Educ:* Charterhouse; Merton College, Oxford. Called to Bar, Lincoln's Inn, 1935, Bencher, 1965; Mem. Senate of Four Inns of Court, 1970-71. Western Circuit, 1935. Temporary civil servant (Ministry of Economic Warfare and Admiralty), 1939-45. Bar Council, 1950-54 and 1962-66. Recorder: of

Penzance, 1957-59; of Bridgwater, 1959-62; of Plymouth, 1962-64. Chairman, Mental Health Review Tribunal, Wessex Region, 1960-63; Deputy Chairman, Middlesex Quarter Sessions, 1961-65; Recorder of Portsmouth, 1964-67; Chm., IoW QS, 1964-67, Dep. Chm. 1967-71. Chm., Deptl Cttee on Death Certification and Coroners, 1965-71. JP Hants, 1967. *Recreations:* gardening, model railways. *Address:* Slade Lane Cottage, Rogate, near Petersfield, Hants GU31 5BL. *T:* Rogate 605. *Club:* Hampshire (Winchester).

BROGAN, Lt.-Gen. Sir Mervyn (Francis), KBE 1972 (CBE 1964; OBE 1944); CB 1970; Chief of the General Staff, Australia, 1971-73, retired; *b* 10 Jan. 1915; *s* of Bernard Brogan, Dubbo, NSW; *m* 1941, Sheila, *d* of David S. Jones, Canberra; two *s*. *Educ:* RMC Duntroon; Wesley Coll., Univ. of Sydney. Commnd 1935; BEng Sydney, 1938. Served War of 1939-45: New Guinea, 1942-45 (despatches 1943); trng UK and BAOR, 1946-47; Chief Instructor, Sch. of Mil. Engrg, 1947-49; trng UK and USA, 1950-52; jssc 1952; Chief Engr, Southern Comd, 1953-54; Dir of Mil. Trng, 1954-55; BGS: Army HQ, 1956; FAR.ELF, 1956-58; idc 1959; Comdt Australian Staff Coll., 1960-62; GOC Northern Comd, 1962-64; Dir Jt Service Plans, Dept of Defence, 1965-66; QMG 1966-68; GOC Eastern Comd, 1968-71. Director: Simon Engineering (Aust.) Pty Ltd; Reef Oil NL; Basin Oil NL; Consultant, J. B. Meling and Co. (Australasia) Pty Ltd. Hon. FIEAust; FAIM. JP. *Recreations:* surfing, tennis. *Address:* 71/53 Ocean Avenue, Double Bay, NSW 2028, Australia. *T:* 32-9509. *Clubs:* Imperial Service, Union, Australian Jockey, Tattersall's, Royal Sydney Golf, Rugby (Sydney).

BROINOWSKI, John Herbert, CMG 1969; FCA; Chairman: Sims Consolidated Ltd, since 1962; Aquila Steel Ltd, 1973-81; Clive Hall Ltd, since 1978; Utilux Ltd, since 1977; Hin Kong Ltd (in Hong Kong), since 1977; Judson Steel Ltd (in USA), since 1979; Peko Wallsend Ltd, since 1962; Deputy Chairman, Castlemaine Tooheys Ltd, since 1977; *b* 19 May 1911; *s* of late Dr G. H. Broinowski and late Mrs Ethel Broinowski (*née* Hungerford); *m* 1939, Jean Gaerloch Broinowski (*née* Kater); one *s* one step *s*. *Educ:* Sydney Church of England Grammar Sch. Served Australian Imperial Forces (Captain), 1940-44, New Guinea. J. H. Broinowski and Storey, Chartered Accountants, 1944-54; Founder and Managing Dir, Consolidated Metal Products Ltd, 1954-62; Chief Exec. and Dep. Chm., Schroder Darling and Co. Ltd, 1963-73. President: Aust. Council for Rehabilitation of the Disabled, 1964-68; NSW Soc. for Crippled Children, 1970-77; Vice-Pres., Internat. Soc. for Rehabilitation of the Disabled, 1966-72. *Recreation:* cattle breeding. *Address:* 1c Wentworth Place, Point Piper, Sydney, NSW 2027, Australia. *T:* 02/3287534. *Clubs:* Union, Australian, Royal Sydney Golf (all in Sydney).

BROKE; *see* Willoughby de Broke.

BROKE, Major George Robin Straton, MVO 1977; RA; Equerry-in-Waiting to the Queen, 1974-77; *b* 31 March 1946; *s* of Maj.-Gen. R. S. Broke, *qv*; *m* 1978, Patricia Thornhill Shann, *d* of Thomas Thornhill Shann. *Educ:* Eton. Commissioned into Royal Artillery, 1965. *Recreation:* country sports. *Address:* Holme Hale Hall, Thetford, Norfolk. *T:* Holme Hale 440225. *Club:* Lansdowne.

BROKE, Maj.-Gen. Robert Straton, CB 1967; OBE 1946; MC 1940; Director, Wellman Engineering Corporation, since 1968, and Chairman of eight companies within the Corporation; *b* 15 March 1913; *s* of Rev. Horatio George Broke and Mary Campbell Broke (*née* Adlington); *m* 1939, Ernine Susan Margaret Bonsey; two *s*. *Educ:* Eton College (KS); Magdalene College, Cambridge (BA). Commissioned Royal Artillery, 1933. Commander Royal Artillery: 5th Division, 1959; 1st Division, 1960; 1st (British) Corps 1961; Northern Army Group, 1964-66, retired. Col Comdt, RA, 1968-78; Representative Col Comdt, 1974-75. Chm., Iron and Steel Plant Contractors Assoc., 1972, 1977. Pres., Metallurgical Plantmakers' Fedn, 1977-79. *Recreations:* country sports. *Address:* Holme Hale Hall, Thetford, Norfolk. *T:* Holme Hale 440225. *Clubs:* Army and Navy, MCC.
  See also G. R. S. Broke.

BROME, Vincent; author; *s* of Nathaniel Gregory and Emily Brome. *Educ:* Streatham Grammar School; Elleston School; privately. Formerly: Feature Writer, Daily Chronicle; Editor, Menu Magazines; Min. of Information; Asst Editor, Medical World. Since then author biographies, novels, plays and essays; broadcaster. Mem., British Library Adv. Cttee, 1975-. *Plays:* The Sleepless One (prod. Edin), 1962; BBC plays. *Publications:* Anthology, 1936; Clement Attlee, 1947; H. G. Wells, 1951; Aneurin Bevan, 1953; The Last Surrender, 1954; The Way Back, 1956; Six Studies in Quarrelling, 1958; Sometimes at Night, 1959; Frank Harris, 1959; Acquaintance With Grief, 1961; We Have Come a Long Way, 1962; The Problem of Progress, 1963; Love in Our Time, 1964; Four Realist Novelists, 1964; The International Brigades, 1965; The World of Luke Jympson, 1966; Freud and His Early Circle, 1967; The Surgeon, 1967; Diary of A Revolution, 1968; The Revolution, 1969; The Imaginary Crime, 1969; Confessions of a Writer, 1970; The Brain Operators, 1970; Private Prosecutions, 1971; Reverse Your Verdict, 1971; London Consequences, 1972; The Embassy, 1972; The Day of Destruction, 1975; The Happy Hostage, 1976; Jung—Man and Myth, 1978; Havelock Ellis—philosopher of sex, 1978; Ernest Jones: Freud's alter ego, 1982; contrib. The Times, Sunday Times, Observer, Manchester Guardian, New Statesman, New Society, Encounter, Spectator, TLS etc. *Recreations:*

writing plays and talking. *Address:* 45 Great Ormond Street, WC1. *T:* 01-405 0550. *Club:* Savile.

BROMET, Air Vice-Marshal Sir Geoffrey R., KBE 1945 (CBE 1941; OBE 1919); CB 1943; DSO 1917; DL; *b* 28 Aug. 1891; *e s* of late G. A. Bromet, Tadcaster; *m* 1917, Margaret (*d* 1961), *e d* of late Maj. Ratliffe, Hardingstone, Northampton; (one *d* decd); *m* 1965, Air Comdt Dame Jean Conan Doyle, *qv*. *Educ:* Bradfield; Royal Naval Colls, Osborne and Dartmouth. Royal Navy, 1904-14; RNAS, 1914-18; RAF, 1918-38; retired list, 1938; re-employed Sept. 1939; SASO HQ Coastal Command, 1940-41; AOC 19 Group Plymouth, 1941-43; Senior British Officer Azores Force, 1943-45; reverted to retired list, Oct. 1945; Lieutenant-Governor, Isle of Man, 1945-52; a Life Vice-President: Royal Air Force Association; RNLI. DL Kent, 1958. *Address:* Home Green, Littlestone-on-Sea, Kent; 72 Cadogan Square, SW1. *Club:* Royal Air Force.

BROMET, Air Comdt Dame Jean (Lena Annette), (Lady Bromet); *see* Conan Doyle, Air Comdt Dame J. L. A.

BROMHEAD, Sir John Desmond Gonville, 6th Bt *cr* 1806; *b* 21 Dec. 1943; *s* of Sir Benjamin Denis Gonville Bromhead, 5th Bt, OBE, and of Nancy Mary, *d* of late T. S. Lough, Buenos Aires; *S* father, 1981. *Educ:* Wellington. *Heir: cousin* John Edmund de Gonville Bromhead [*b* 10 Oct. 1939; *m* 1965, Janet Frances, *e d* of Harry Vernon Brotherton, Moreton-in-Marsh, Glos; one *s* one *d*]. *Address:* Thurlby Hall, Aubourn, Lincoln.

BROMLEY, Archdeacon of; *see* Francis, Ven. E. R.

BROMLEY, Lance Lee, MA; MChir; FRCS; Honorary Consultant Cardiothoracic Surgeon, St Mary's Hospital, W2; *b* 16 Feb. 1920; *s* of late Lancelot Bromley, MChir FRCS, of London and Seaford, Sussex, and Dora Ridgway Bromley, Dewsbury, Yorks; *m* 1952, Rosemary Anne Holbrook; three *d*. *Educ:* St Paul's School; Caius Coll., Cambridge. Late Capt. RAMC. Late Travelling Fell. Amer. Assoc. for Thoracic Surgery. Vis. Thoracic Surgeon, St Bernard's Hosp., Gibraltar. *Publications:* various contributions to medical journals. *Recreations:* sailing, golf. *Address:* 26 Molyneux Street, W1. *T:* 01-262 7175. *Club:* Royal Ocean Racing.
  See also Sir Charles Knowles, Bt.

BROMLEY, Leonard John, QC 1971; a Recorder of the Crown Court, since 1980; Barrister-at-Law; *b* 21 Feb. 1929; 2nd *s* of George Ernest and Winifred Dora Bromley; *m* 1962, Anne (*née* Bacon); three *d*. *Educ:* City of Leicester Boys' Sch.; Selwyn Coll., Cambridge (exhibnr). MA, LLB (Cantab). National Service: 2nd Lt, RA, Hong Kong, 1947-49. Selwyn Coll., Cambridge, 1949-53; called to Bar, Lincoln's Inn, 1954; Bencher, 1978; Greenland Scholar, Lincoln's Inn. In practice, Chancery Bar, 1954-. Gen. Council of the Bar: Mem., 1970-74; Chm., Law Reform Cttee, 1972-74; Mem., Exec. Cttee, 1972-74. Chm., Performing Right Tribunal, 1980-. A Legal Assessor to: GMC, 1977-; GDC, 1977-. Governor, Latymer Sch., Edmonton, 1978-. Vice Cdre, Bar Yacht Club, 1971-75. *Recreations:* sailing, walking. *Address:* (home) 106 Queen Elizabeth's Drive, Southgate, N14 6RE. *T:* 01-886 6113; (professional) 7 Stone Buildings, Lincoln's Inn, WC2A 3SZ. *T:* 01-405 3886.

BROMLEY, Prof. Peter Mann; Professor of Law since 1965, Dean of Faculty of Law, 1966-68, 1972-74 and since 1981, University of Manchester (Pro-Vice-Chancellor, 1977-81); *b* 20 Nov. 1922; *s* of Frank Bromley and Marion Maud (*née* Moy); *m* 1943, Beatrice Mary, *d* of Eric Charles Cassels Hunter and Amy Madeleine (*née* Renold). *Educ:* Ealing Grammar Sch.; The Queen's College, Oxford (MA 1948). Called to the Bar, Middle Temple, 1951. Served War, Royal Artillery, 1942-45. Asst Lectr 1947-50, Lectr 1950-61, Sen. Lectr 1961-65, Univ. of Manchester; Principal, Dalton Hall, Univ. of Manchester, 1958-65. Member: Adv. Cttee on Legal Educn, 1972-75; University Grants Cttee, 1978- (Chm., Social Studies Sub-cttee, 1979-). *Publications:* Family Law, 1957, 6th edn 1981; articles in various legal jls. *Recreation:* walking. *Address:* Paddock Brow, Faulkners Lane, Mobberley, Cheshire WA16 7AL. *T:* Mobberley 2183. *Club:* United Oxford & Cambridge University.

BROMLEY, Sir Rupert Charles, 10th Bt, *cr* 1757; *b* 2 April 1936; *s* of Major Sir Rupert Howe Bromley, MC, 9th Bt, and Dorothy Vera (*d* 1982), *d* of late Sir Walford Selby, KCMG, CB, CVO; *S* father, 1966; *m* 1962, Priscilla Hazel, *d* of late Maj. Howard Bourne, HAC; three *s*. *Educ:* Michaelhouse, Natal; Rhodes Univ.; Christ Church, Oxford. *Recreations:* equestrian. *Heir: s* Charles Howard Bromley, *b* 31 July 1963. *Address:* Brendon House, Selwyn Road, Kenilworth, CP, South Africa.

BROMLEY, Sir Thomas Eardley, KCMG 1964 (CMG 1955); HM Diplomatic Service, retired; Secretary, Churches Main Committee, Dec. 1970-72; *b* 14 Dec. 1911; *s* of late Thomas Edward Bromley, ICS; *m* 1944, Diana Marion, *d* of Sir John Pratt, KBE, CMG; *m* 1966, Mrs Alison Toulmin. *Educ:* Rugby; Magdalen College, Oxford. Entered Consular Service, 1935; Vice-Consul, Japan, 1938; Asst Private Sec. to the Permanent Under-Secretary of State, 1943, and Private Secretary, 1945; Grade 7, 1945; served in Washington, 1946; Bagdad, 1949; Counsellor, 1953; Head of African Department, Foreign Office, March 1954-Jan. 1956; Imperial Defence College, 1956; Foreign Office Inspectorate, 1957; seconded to Cabinet Office, Oct. 1957; Consul-General at Mogadishu, 1960; Ambassador: to Somali Republic, 1960-61; to Syrian Arab Republic, 1962-64; to Algeria, 1964-65;

FO, 1966; Ambassador to Ethiopia, 1966-69. *Address:* 11 Belbroughton Road, Oxford OX2 6UZ.

BROMLEY-DAVENPORT, Lt-Col Sir Walter Henry, Kt 1961; TD; DL; *b* 1903; *s* of late Walter A. Bromley-Davenport, Capesthorne, Macclesfield, Cheshire, and late Lilian Emily Isabel Jane, DBE 1954, JP, *d* of Lt-Col J. H. B. Lane; *m* 1933, Lenette F., *d* of Joseph Y. Jeanes, Philadelphia, USA; one *s* one *d. Educ:* Malvern. Joined Grenadier Guards, 1922; raised and comd 5 Bn Cheshire Regt, Lt-Col 1939. MP (C) Knutsford Div. 1945-70; Conservative Whip, 1948-51. DL Cheshire, 1949. British Boxing Board of Control, 1953. *Address:* 39 Westminster Gardens, Marsham Street, SW1. *T:* 01-834 2929; Capesthorne Hall, Macclesfield, Cheshire. *T:* Chelford 861221; Fiva, Aandalsnes, Norway. *Clubs:* White's, Cavalry and Guards, Carlton, Pratt's.

BROMMELLE, Norman Spencer; Director, Hamilton Kerr Institute, Fitzwilliam Museum, Cambridge, since 1978; *b* 9 June 1915; *s* of James Valentine Brommelle and Ada Louisa Brommelle (*née* Bastin); *m* 1959, Rosa Joyce Plesters. *Educ:* High Pavement School, Nottingham; University College, Oxford. Scientific research in industry on Metallography and Spectroscopy, 1937-48; Picture Conservation, National Gallery, 1949-60; Keeper, Dept of Conservation, V&A Mus., 1960-77. Secretary-General, International Institute for Conservation of Historic and Artistic Works, 1957-64, 1966- (Vice-President, 1964-66). Governor, Central Sch. of Art and Design, 1971-77. *Publications:* contributions to: Journal of the Institute of Metals; Studies in Conservation; Museums Journal. *Recreation:* gardening. *Address:* 5 Lyndhurst Square, SE15. *T:* 01-701 0607; Hamilton Kerr Institute, University of Cambridge, Whittlesford, Cambridge CB2 4NE. *T:* Cambridge 832040.

BRON, Eleanor; actress and writer; *d* of Sydney and Fagah Bron. *Educ:* North London Collegiate Sch., Canons, Edgware; Newnham Coll., Cambridge (BA Hons Mod. Langs). De La Rue Co., 1961. Appearances include: revue, Establishment Nightclub, Soho, 1962, and New York, 1963; Not so much a Programme, More a Way of Life, BBC TV, 1964; several TV series written with John Fortune, and TV series, Making Faces, written by Michael Frayn, 1976; Nina, Play for Today, 1978; My Dear Palestrina, 1980. *Stage roles include:* Jennifer Dubedat, The Doctor's Dilemma, 1966; Jean Brodie, The Prime of Miss Jean Brodie, 1967; title role, Hedda Gabler, 1969; Portia, The Merchant of Venice, 1975; Amanda, Private Lives, 1976; Elena, Uncle Vanya, 1977; Charlotte, The Cherry Orchard, 1978; Margaret, A Family, 1978; On Her Own, 1980; Goody Biddy Bean; The Amusing Spectacle of Cinderella and her Naughty, Naughty Sisters, Lyric, Hammersmith, 1980; Betrayal, 1981; Heartbreak House, 1981; Duet for One, 1982. *Films include:* Help!; Alfie; Two for the Road; Bedazzled; Women in Love; The Day that Christ Died, 1980. Author: song-cycle with John Dankworth, 1973; verses for Saint-Saens' Carnival of the Animals, 1975 (recorded). *Publications:* Is Your Marriage Really Necessary (with John Fortune), 1972; (contrib). My Cambridge, 1976; (contrib.) More Words, 1977; Life and Other Punctures, 1978. *Address:* c/o Fraser & Dunlop Ltd, 91 Regent Street, W1. *Club:* Zoological Society.

BRONFMAN, Edgar Miles; Chairman and Chief Executive Officer: The Seagram Company Ltd, since 1977; Joseph E. Seagram & Sons Inc.; *b* 20 June 1929; *s* of Samuel Bronfman and Saidye Rosner. *Educ:* Trinity College Sch., Port Hope, Ont., Canada; Williams Coll., Williamstown, Mass, US; McGill Univ., Montreal (BA 1951). President: Joseph E. Seagram & Sons, Inc, 1957; The Seagram Company Ltd, 1971; Chairman: Clevepak Corp.; Gulfstream Land and Development Corp.; Dir, E. I. duPont de Nemours & Co. Pres., World Jewish Congress, 1980-. Hon. LHD Pace Univ., NY, 1982. *Address:* 375 Park Avenue, New York, NY 10152, USA. *T:* (212) 572-7000.

BROOK, Caspar; Director, David Owen Centre for Population Growth Studies, University College Cardiff, since 1974; *b* 24 Aug. 1920; one *s* one *d. Educ:* UCW, Cardiff. Royal Tank Regt, Glider Pilot Regt, 1940-46. British Export Trade Research Organisation, 1947; machine tool and electrical engrs, 1947-53; Publications Editor, Economist Intelligence Unit Ltd, 1953-58; Dir, Consumers' Assoc., 1958-64; Man. Dir, Equipment Comparison Ltd, 1964-67; Dir, Industrial Training and Publishing Div., Pergamon Press, 1966-67; Dir, Family Planning Assoc., 1968-74. Mem., Welsh Consumer Council, 1975-79. Social Develt Advr (Sudan), Ministry of Overseas Develt, 1976-; Consultant: UN Fund for Population Activities, 1978-; Internat. Planned Parenthood Fedn, 1981-. *Recreations:* talking, sailing. *Address:* 58 Neville Street, Cardiff CF1 8LS. *T:* Cardiff 44950. *Club:* Reform.

BROOK, Prof. George Leslie, MA, PhD; Professor of English Language 1945-77, and of Medieval English Literature, 1951-77, University of Manchester, now Professor Emeritus; Dean of the Faculty of Arts, 1956-57; Pro-Vice-Chancellor, 1962-65; Presenter of Honorary Graduands, 1964-65; *b* 6 March 1910; 3rd *s* of late Willie Brook, Shepley, Huddersfield; *m* 1949, Stella, *d* of Thomas Maguire, Salford. *Educ:* University of Leeds; Ripon English Literature Prize, 1931. Visiting Professor, University of California, Los Angeles, 1951. *Publications:* An English Phonetic Reader, 1935; English Sound-Changes, 1935; Glossary to the Works of Sir Thomas Malory, 1947; An Introduction to Old English, 1955; A History of the English Language, 1958; English Dialects, 1963; The Modern University, 1965; The Language of Dickens, 1970; Varieties of English, 1973; The Language of Shakespeare, 1976; Books and Book Collecting, 1980; Words in Everyday Life, 1981; edited: The Harley Lyrics, 1948; The Journal of the Lancashire Dialect Society,

1951-54; (with R. F. Leslie) Layamon's Brut, Vol. I, 1963, Vol. II, 1978; (with C. S. Lewis) Selections from Layamon's Brut, 1963. *Address:* 33 Priory Lane, Kents Bank, Grange-Over-Sands, Cumbria LA11 7BH. *T:* Grange-Over-Sands 3732.

BROOK, (Gerald) Robert, CBE 1981; Chief Executive, since 1977, and Deputy Chairman, since 1978, National Bus Company; *b* 19 Dec. 1928; *s* of Charles Pollard Brook and Doris Brook (*née* Senior); *m* 1957, Joan Marjorie Oldfield; two *s* one *d. Educ:* King James Grammar Sch., Knaresborough. FCIS, FCIT, CBIM. Served Duke of Wellington's Regt, 1947-49. Appointments in bus companies, from 1950; Company Secretary: Cumberland Motor Services Ltd, 1960; Thames Valley Traction Co. Ltd, 1963; General Manager: North Western Road Car Co. Ltd, 1968; Midland Red Omnibus Co. Ltd, 1972; Regional Director, National Bus Company, 1974. *Publications:* papers for professional instns and learned socs. *Recreation:* reading military history. *Address:* 25 New Street Square, EC4A 3AP. *T:* 01-583 9177. *Club:* Army and Navy.

BROOK, Helen, (Lady Brook); Founder, 1963, and President, Brook Advisory Centre for Young People (Chairman, 1964-74); *b* 12 Oct. 1907; *d* of John and Helen Knewstub; *m* 1937, Sir Robin Brook, *qv* ; two *d* (and one *d* of previous marriage). *Educ:* Convent of Holy Child Jesus, Mark Cross, Sussex. Voluntary Worker, Family Planning Association, 1949-. *Recreations:* painting, gardening. *Address:* 31 Acacia Road, NW8 6AS. *T:* 01-722 5844; Claydene Garden Cottage, Cowden, Kent.

BROOK, Leopold, BScEng, FICE, FIMechE; Chairman: Associated Nuclear Services Ltd, since 1977; Chamberlain Group Ltd, since 1979; Brown & Sharpe Group Ltd, since 1979; *b* 2 Jan. 1912; *s* of Albert and Kate Brook, Hampstead; *m* 1st, 1940, Susan (*d* 1970), *d* of David Rose, Hampstead; two *s* ; 2nd, 1974, Mrs Elly Rhodes; two step *s* one step *d. Educ:* Central Foundation School, London; University College, London. L. G. Mouchel & Partners, Cons. Engineers, 1935-44; Simon Engineering Ltd, 1944-77 (Chief Exec., 1967-70; Chm., 1970-77). Fellow, UCL, 1970-. CBIM; FRSA 1973. *Recreations:* music, theatre, golf. *Address:* 55 Kingston House North, Prince's Gate, SW7 1LW. *T:* 01-584 2041. *Clubs:* Athenæum, Hurlingham.

BROOK, Peter Stephen Paul, CBE 1965; Producer; Co-Director, The Royal Shakespeare Theatre; *b* 21 March 1925; 2nd *s* of Simon Brook; *m* 1951, Natasha Parry, stage and film star; one *s* one *d. Educ:* Westminster, Greshams and Magdalen College, Oxford. Productions include: The Tragedy of Dr Faustus, 1942; The Infernal Machine, 1945; Birmingham Repertory Theatre: Man and Superman, King John, The Lady from the Sea, 1945-46; Stratford: Romeo and Juliet, Love's Labour's Lost, 1947; London: Vicious Circle, Men Without Shadows, Respectable Prostitute, The Brothers Karamazov, 1946; Director of Productions, Royal Opera House, Covent Garden, 1947-50: Boris Godunov, La Bohème, 1948; Marriage of Figaro, The Olympians, Salome, 1949. Dark of the Moon, 1949; Ring Round the Moon, 1950; Measure for Measure, Stratford, 1950, Paris, 1978; The Little Hut, 1950; The Winter's Tale, 1951; Venice Preserved, 1953; The Little Hut, New York, Faust, Metropolitan Opera House, 1953; The Dark is Light Enough; Both Ends Meet, 1954; House of Flowers, New York, 1954; The Lark, 1955; Titus Andronicus, Stratford, 1955; Hamlet, 1955; The Power and the Glory, 1956; Family Reunion, 1956; The Tempest, Stratford, 1957; Cat on a Hot Tin Roof, Paris, 1957; View from the Bridge, Paris, 1958; Irma la Douce, London, 1958; The Fighting Cock, New York, 1959; Le Balcon, Paris, 1960; The Visit, Royalty, 1960; King Lear, Stratford and Aldwych, 1962; The Physicists, Aldwych, 1963; Sergeant Musgrave's Dance, Paris, 1963; The Persecution and Assassination of Marat..., Aldwych, 1964 (New York, 1966); The Investigation, Aldwych, 1965; US, Aldwych, 1966; Oedipus, National Theatre, 1968; A Midsummer Night's Dream, Stratford, 1970, NY, 1971; Timon of Athens, Paris, 1974 (Grand Prix Dominique, 1975; Brigadier Prize, 1975); The Ik, Paris, 1975, London, 1976; Ubu Roi, Paris, 1977; Antony and Cleopatra, Stratford, 1978, Aldwych, 1979; Ubu, Young Vic, 1978; Conference of the Birds, France, Australia, NY, 1980; The Cherry Orchard, Paris, 1981; La tragédie de Carmen, Paris, 1981; work with Internat. Centre of Theatre Research, Paris, Iran, W Africa, and USA, 1971, Sahara, Niger and Nigeria, 1972-73. *Directed films:* The Beggar's Opera, 1952; Moderato Cantabile, 1960; Lord of the Flies, 1962; The Marat/Sade, 1967; Tell Me Lies, 1968; King Lear, 1969; Meetings with Remarkable Men, 1979. Hon. DLitt Birmingham. Officier de l'Ordre des Arts et des Lettres; Freiherr von Stein Foundn Shakespeare Award, 1973. *Publication:* The Empty Space, 1968. *Recreations:* painting, piano playing and travelling by air. *Address:* c/o CIRT, 9 rue du Cirque, Paris 8, France.

BROOK, Sir Ralph Ellis; see Brook, Sir Robin.

BROOK, Robert; see Brook, G. R.

BROOK, Sir Robin, Kt 1974; CMG 1954; OBE 1945; Chairman, Leda Investment Trust Ltd; Director, United City Merchants; Member: City and E London Area Health Authority, 1974-82 (Vice Chairman, 1974-79); City and Hackney District Health Authority, 1982; *b* 19 June 1908; *s* of Francis Brook, FRCS, Harley Street, and Mrs E. I. Brook; *m* 1937, Helen (see Helen Brook), *e d* of John Knewstub; two *d. Educ:* Eton; King's College, Cambridge. Served 1941-46; Brig., 1945 (OBE, despatches, Legion of Merit (Commander), Legion of Honour, Croix de Guerre and Bar, Order of Leopold (Officer), Belgian Croix de Guerre). Director, Bank of England, 1946-49. Chm., 1966-68, Pres., 1968-72, London Chamber of Commerce and

Industry; Pres., Assoc. of British Chambers of Commerce, 1972-74; Pres., Assoc. of Chambers of Commerce of EEC, 1974-76; Leader of Trade Missions: for HM Govt to Libya and Romania; for London or British Chambers of Commerce to France, Iran, China, Greece, Finland and Hungary; HM Govt Dir, BP Co., 1970-73; Deputy Chairman: British Tourist and Holidays Board, 1946-50; Colonial Development Corp., 1949-53. Sports Council: Mem., 1971-78; Vice-Chm., 1974; Chm., 1975-78; Chm., Sports Develt Cttee, 1971-74. Mem., Cttee on Invisible Exports, 1969-74; Mem. Council, Finance and Hon. Degrees Cttees, City Univ.; Hon. Treasurer: CCPR, 1961-77; Family Planning Association, 1966-75. High Sheriff of County of London, 1950; Mem. Council, Festival of Britain. Mem. Council and Exec. Cttee, King Edward's Fund; St Bartholomew's Hospital: Governor, 1962-74; Treasurer and Chm., 1969-74; Chm., Special Trustees, 1974-; Pres., St Bartholomew's Med. Coll., 1969-; Governor, Royal Free Hosp., 1962-74. Past Master, Wine Warden, Haberdashers' Co. *Recreation:* British Sabre Champion, 1936; Olympic Games, 1936, 1948; Capt. British Team, 1933 (3rd in European Championship), etc. *Address:* 31 Acacia Road, NW8 6NS.

BROOK, William Edward; British Council Officer, retired; *b* 18 Jan. 1922; *s* of William Stafford Brook and Dorothy Mary (*née* Thompson); *m* 1950, Rene Dorothy Drew; two *s* one *d. Educ:* Highgate Sch.; St Edmund Hall, Oxford (BA Mod. Langs, 1949; MA 1953). Served RAF, 1940-46: Africa, ME and Italy. Apptd to British Council, 1949; Lectr, Salonika, 1949-51; Asst Dir, Northern Provinces, Nigeria, 1951-56; Lecturer: Kuwait, 1956-59; Tripoli, Libya, 1959-62; Regional Director: Moshi, Tanganyika, 1962-67; Frankfurt, W Germany, 1967-72; Rep., Bahrain (with Qatar, UAE and Oman), 1972-76; Dir, Overseas Educnl Appts Dept, 1976; Controller, Appts Div., 1977-79; Representative, Canada, and Counsellor (Cultural), Ottawa, 1979; retd 1982. *Recreations:* music, gardening, bird-watching. *Address:* 1 Fearnley Road, Welwyn Garden City, Herts AL8 6HW. *T:* Welwyn Garden 21655.

BROOK-PARTRIDGE, Bernard; Member, Greater London Council for Havering, 1967-73, and for Havering (Romford), since 1973; Chairman of the Greater London Council, 1980-81; Partner, Carsons, Brook-Partridge & Co. (Planning Consultants), since 1972; *b* Croydon, 1927; *o s* of late Leslie Brook-Partridge and Gladys Vere Burchell (*née* Brooks), Sanderstead; *m* 1st, 1951, Enid Elizabeth (marr. diss. 1965), 2nd *d* of late Frederick Edmund Hatfield and late Enid Hatfield (*née* Lucas), Sanderstead; two *d*; 2nd, 1967, Carol Devonald, *o d* of Arnold Devonald Francis Lewis and Patricia (*née* Thomas), Gower, S Wales; two *s. Educ:* Selsdon County Grammar Sch.; Cambridgeshire Tech. Coll.; Cambridge Univ.; London Univ.; Gray's Inn. Military Service, 1945-48. Studies, 1948-50. Cashier/Accountant, Dominion Rubber Co. Ltd, 1950-51; Asst Export Manager, British & General Tube Co. Ltd, 1951-52; Asst Sec., Assoc. of Internat. Accountants, 1952-59; Sec.-Gen., Institute of Linguists, 1959-62; various teaching posts, Federal Republic of Germany, 1962-66; Special Asst to Man. Dir, M. G. Scott Ltd, 1966-68. Business consultancy work on own account, incl. various dirships with several client cos, 1968-72; Dir and Sec., Roban Engineering Ltd and predecessor company, 1971-. Contested (C) St Pancras North, LCC, 1958; Mem. (C) St Pancras Metropolitan Borough Council, 1959-62. Prospective Party Cand. (C), Shoreditch and Finsbury, 1960-62; contested (C) Nottingham Central, 1970. Chairman: GLC Planning and Transportation (NE) Area Bd, 1967-71; Town Planning Cttee, 1971-73; Arts Cttee, 1977-78; Public Services and Safety Cttee, 1978-79; Opposition spokesman for Arts and Recreation, 1973-77; Member: Exec. Cttee, Greater London Arts Assoc., 1973-78; Exec. Council, Area Museums Service for SE England, 1977-78; Council and Exec., Greater London and SE Council for Sport and Recreation, 1977-78; GLC Leaders' Cttee with special responsibility for Law and Order and Police Liaison matters, 1977-79; Dep. Leader, Recreation and Community Services Policy Cttee, 1977-79. Member: Exec. Cttee, Exmoor Soc., 1974-79; BBC Radio London Adv. Council, 1974-79; Gen. Council, Poetry Soc., 1977-; Board Member: Peterborough Develt Corp., 1972- (Chm., Queensgate Management Services); London Festival Ballet (and Trustee), 1977-79; Young Vic Theatre Ltd, 1977-; London Orchestral Concert Bd Ltd, 1977-78; ENO, 1977-78; London Contemp. Dance Trust, 1979-; Governor and Trustee: SPCK, 1976-; Sadler's Wells Foundn, 1977-79; Chairman: London Music Hall Protection Soc. Ltd (Wilton's Music Hall), 1978-; London Symphony Chorus Develt Cttee, 1981-; Pres., British Sch. of Osteopathy Appeal Fund, 1980-. President: Witan (GLC Staff) Rifle Club, 1979-; City of London Rifle League, 1980-; Gtr London Horse Show, 1982-. FCIS (Mem. Council, 1981-); MBIM. Hon. FIE. Hon. PhD California Pacific, 1982. Order of Gorkha Dakshina Bahu (2nd cl.), Nepal, 1981. *Publications:* Europe—Power and Responsibility: Direct Elections to the European Parliament (with David Baker), 1972; contribs to learned jls and periodicals on linguistics and translation, the use of language, political science and contemporary politics. *Recreations:* hunting, conversation, opera, ballet, classical music and being difficult. *Address:* 51 Redcliffe Square, SW10. *T:* 01-373 1223. *Club:* Romford Conservative and Constitutional.

BROOKE, family name of Viscount Alanbrooke, of Baron Brooke of Cumnor, of Baroness Brooke of Ystradfellte and of Viscount Brookeborough.

BROOKE, Lord; David Robin Francis Guy Greville; *b* 15 May 1934; *s* and heir of 7th Earl of Warwick, *qv*; *m* 1956, Sarah Anne (marr. diss. 1967), *d* of Alfred Chester Beatty and Mrs Pamela Neilson; one *s* one *d. Educ:* Eton. Life Guards, 1952; Warwicks Yeo. (TA), 1954. *Heir:* *s* Hon. Guy David Greville [*b* 30 Jan. 1957; *m* 1981, Mrs Susan Cobbold]. *Address:* Leeward

Marina, Providenciales, Turks & Caicos Islands, BW1. *Clubs:* White's; The Brook (NY); Travellers' (Paris); Eagle Ski (Gstaad).

BROOKE OF CUMNOR, Baron (Life Peer), *cr* 1966; **Henry Brooke,** PC 1955; CH 1964; *b* 9 April 1903; *y s* of L. Leslie Brooke and Sybil Diana, *d* of Rev. Stopford Brooke; *m* 1933, Barbara (*see* Baroness Brooke of Ystradfellte), *y d* of Canon A. A. Mathews; two *s* two *d. Educ:* Marlborough; Balliol College, Oxford. MP (C) West Lewisham, 1938-45, Hampstead, 1950-66. Deputy Chairman, Southern Railway Company, 1946-48. Member of Central Housing Advisory Committee, 1944-54; Member of London County Council, 1945-55, and of Hampstead Borough Council, 1936-57. Financial Secretary to the Treasury, 1954-57; Minister of Housing and Local Government and Minister for Welsh Affairs, 1957-61; Chief Secretary to the Treasury and Paymaster-General, 1961-62; Home Secretary, 1962-64. Chm., Jt Select Cttee on Delegated Legislation, 1971-73. *Address:* The Glebe House, Mildenhall, Marlborough, Wilts SN8 2LX.
See also H. Brooke, Hon. P. L. Brooke.

BROOKE OF YSTRADFELLTE, Baroness *cr* 1964 (Life Peer); **Barbara Brooke,** DBE 1960; *b* 14 Jan. 1908; *y d* of late Canon A. A. Mathews; *m* 1933, Henry Brooke (*see* Baron Brooke of Cumnor); two *s* two *d. Educ:* Queen Anne's School, Caversham. Joint Vice-Chm., Conservative Party Organisation, 1954-64. Member: Hampstead Borough Council, 1948-65; North-West Metropolitan Regional Hospital Board, 1954-66; Management Cttee, King Edward's Hospital Fund for London, 1966-71; Chairman: Exec. Cttee Queen's Institute of District Nursing, 1961-71; Governing Body of Godolphin and Latymer School, Hammersmith, 1960-78. Hon. Fellow, Westfield College. *Address:* The Glebe House, Mildenhall, Marlborough, Wilts.
See also H. Brooke, Hon. P. L. Brooke, Rev. A. K. Mathews.

BROOKE, Arthur Caffin, CB 1972; Chairman, Arts Council of Northern Ireland, since 1982 (Member, since 1979); *b* 11 March 1919; *s* of late Rev. James M. Wilmot Brooke and Constance Brooke; *m* 1942, Margaret Florence Thompson; two *s. Educ:* Abbotsholme Sch.; Peterhouse, Cambridge (MA). Served War, Royal Corps of Signals, 1939-46 (Lt-Col 1945). Northern Ireland Civil Service, 1946-79; Ministry of Commerce, 1946-73: Principal, 1952; Asst Sec., Head of Industrial Development Div., 1955; Sen. Asst Sec., Industrial Development, 1963; Second Sec., 1968; Permanent Sec., 1969; Permanent Sec., Dept of Educn, 1973-79. Mem., EFTA Working Party on Growth Centres, 1966-68; Chairman: Jt Working Party on Community and Recreational Provision by District Councils in NI, 1974-75; Working Party on Social Entertainment in Belfast City Centre, 1978-79. *Address:* 53 Osborne Park, Belfast, Northern Ireland. *T:* 669192.

BROOKE, Vice-Admiral (Retd) Basil Charles Barrington, CB 1949; CBE 1947; *b* 6 April 1895; *s* of John C. E. H. Brooke and Hon. Violet M. Barrington; *m* 1925, Nora Evelyn Toppin (*d* 1981); two *s* two *d. Educ:* Malvern College. Royal Navy, 1913; Captain, 1938; Rear-Admiral, 1947; retired, 1949. Vice-Admiral (Retd), 1950. *Address:* Highfield, Mandeville Road, Saffron Walden, Essex CB11 4AQ.

BROOKE, Prof. Bryan Nicholas, MD, MChir, FRCS; Consultant Editor, World Medicine, 1980-82; Emeritus Professor (Professor of Surgery, University of London, at St George's Hospital 1963-80); lately consultant surgeon, St George's Hospital; *b* 21 Feb. 1915; *s* of George Cyril Brooke, LittD, FSA (numismatist) and Margaret Florence Brooke; *m* 1940, Naomi Winefride Mills; three *d. Educ:* Bradfield College, Berkshire; Corpus Christi College, Cambridge; St Bartholomew's Hospital, London. FRCSEng 1942; MChir (Cantab.) 1944; MD (Birm.) with hons 1954. Lieut-Colonel, RAMC, 1945-46. Lecturer in Surgery, Aberdeen Univ., 1946-47; Reader in Surgery, Birmingham Univ., 1947-63; Hunterian Prof. RCS, 1951. Examiner in Surgery, Universities of: Birmingham, 1951-63; Cambridge, 1958-; Bristol, 1961-; London, 1962-; Glasgow, 1969; Oxford, 1970; Hong Kong, 1972; Nigeria, 1975; RCS, 1973; Chm., Ct of Examnrs, RCS, 1978. Member, Medical Appeals Tribunal, 1948-. Pres., Ileostomy Assoc. of GB, 1957-82. Chm., Malvern Girls' Coll., 1972-82. Copeman Medal for Scientific Research, 1960; Graham Award (Amer. Proctologic Soc.), 1961; Award of NY Soc., Colon and Rectal Surgeons, 1967. Hon. FRACS, 1977; Hon. Mem., British Soc. of Gastroenterology, 1979. *Publications:* Ulcerative Colitis and its Surgical Treatment, 1954; You and Your Operation, 1957; United Birmingham Cancer Reports, 1953, 1954, 1957; (co-editor) Recent Advances in Gastroenterology, 1965; (co-author) Metabolic Derangements in Gastrointestinal Surgery, 1966; Understanding Cancer, 1971; Crohn's Disease, 1977; Editor, Jl Clinics in Gastroenterology; contrib. to various surgical works. Numerous articles on large bowel disorder, medical education, steroid therapy. *Recreations:* painting, pottery. *Address:* 112 Balham Park Road, SW12 8EA.

BROOKE, Prof. Christopher Nugent Lawrence, MA; FSA; FRHistS; FBA 1970; Dixie Professor of Ecclesiastical History, and Fellow, Gonville and Caius College, University of Cambridge, since 1977; *b* 1927; *y s* of late Professor Zachary Nugent Brooke and Rosa Grace Brooke; *m* 1951, Rosalind Beckford, *d* of Dr and Mrs L. H. S. Clark; three *s. Educ:* Winchester College (Scholar); Gonville and Caius College, Cambridge (Major Scholar). BA 1948; MA 1952; LittD 1973. Army service in RAEC, Temp. Captain 1949. Cambridge University: Fellow of Gonville and Caius College, 1949-56; College Lecturer in History, 1953-56; Praelector Rhetoricus, 1955-56; Asst

Lectr in History, 1953-54; Lectr, 1954-56; Prof. of Mediæval History, University of Liverpool, 1956-67; Prof. of History, Westfield Coll., Univ. of London, 1967-77. Member: Royal Commn on Historical Monuments (England), 1977-; Reviewing Cttee on Export of Works of Art, 1979-82. Vice-Pres., Soc. of Antiquaries, 1975-79, Pres., 1981-. Corresp. Fellow, Medieval Acad. of America, 1981. Lord Mayor's Midsummer Prize, City of London, 1981. *Publications:* The Dullness of the Past, 1957; From Alfred to Henry III, 1961; The Saxon and Norman Kings, 1963; Europe in the Central Middle Ages, 1964; Time the Archsatirist, 1968; The Twelfth Century Renaissance, 1970; Structure of Medieval Society, 1971; Medieval Church and Society (sel. papers), 1971; (with W. Swaan) The Monastic World, 1974; (with G. Keir) London, 800-1216, 1975; Marriage in Christian History, 1977; part Editor: The Book of William Morton, 1954; The Letters of John of Salisbury, vol. I, 1955, vol. II, 1979; Carte Nativorum, 1960; (with A. Morey) Gilbert Foliot and his letters, 1965 and (ed jtly) The Letters and Charters of Gilbert Foliot, 1967; (with D. Knowles and V. London) Heads of Religious Houses, England and Wales 940-1216, 1972; (with D. Whitelock and M. Brett) Councils and Synods, vol. I, 1981; contributed to A History of St Paul's Cathedral, 1957; Studies in the Early British Church, 1958; Celt and Saxon, 1963; Studies in Church History, Vol. I, 1964, Vol. VI, 1970; A History of York Minster, 1977; general editor: Oxford (formerly Nelson's) Medieval Texts, Nelson's History of England; articles and reviews in English Historical Review, Cambridge Historical Journal, Bulletin of Inst. of Historical Research, Downside Review, Traditio, Bulletin of John Rylands Library, Jl of Soc. of Archivists, etc. *Address:* Faculty of History, West Road, Cambridge CB3 9EF.

BROOKE, Sir George (Cecil Francis), 3rd Bt, *cr* 1903; MBE 1949; Major, 17/21 Lancers, retired; *b* 1903; MBE 1949; Major, 17/21 Lancers, retired; *b* 30 March 1916; *s* of Sir Francis Brooke, 2nd Bt, and Mabel (*d* 1982), *d* of Sir John Arnott, 1st Bt; *S* father 1954; *m* 1959, Lady Melissa Wyndham-Quin, *er d* of 6th Earl of Dunraven, CB, CBE, MC; one *s* one *d. Educ:* Stowe. Served War of 1939-45 (wounded, despatches twice), in North Africa and Italy. *Heir: s* Francis George Windham Brooke, *b* 15 Oct. 1963. *Address:* Glenbevan, Croom, Co. Limerick. *Clubs:* Cavalry and Guards, Pratt's, White's; Kildare Street and University (Dublin).

BROOKE, Henry, QC 1981; *b* 19 July 1936; *s* of Lord Brooke of Cumnor, *qv* and Lady Brooke of Ystradfellte, *qv*; *m* 1966, Bridget Mary Kalaugher; three *s* one *d. Educ:* Marlborough College; Balliol Coll., Oxford. MA (1st Cl. Classical Hon. Mods, 1st Cl. Lit. Hum.). Called to the Bar, Inner Temple, 1963; Junior Counsel to the Crown, Common Law, 1978-81. *Publication:* (contrib.) Halsbury's Laws of England, 4th edn. *Address:* Fountain Court, Temple, EC4 9DH. *T:* 01-353 7356; 1 Dynevor Road, Richmond, Surrey. *T:* 01-940 4418.

BROOKE, Humphrey; *see* Brooke, T. H.

BROOKE, John; Chairman, Brooke Bond Liebig Ltd, retired 1971; *b* 7 March 1912; *m* 1936, Bridget (*née* May); two *s* one *d. Educ:* Bedales, Petersfield, Hants. Joined Brooke Bond & Co. Ltd, Oct. 1930, as Trainee Salesman. *Address:* 10 Parsonage Lane, Market Lavington, near Devizes, Wilts. *T:* Lavington 2204.

BROOKE, Major Sir John Weston, 3rd Bt, *cr* 1919; TD; DL; JP; Lovat Scouts; *b* 26 Sept. 1911; *s* of Major Sir Robert Weston Brooke, 2nd Bt, DSO, MC, DL, and Margery Jean, MBE (*d* 1975), *d* of Alex. Geddes of Blairmore, Aberdeenshire; *S* father, 1942; *m* 1st, 1945, Rosemary (marr. diss. 1963; she *d* 1979), *d* of late Percy Nevill, Birling House, West Malling, Kent; two *s*; 2nd, 1966, Lady Macdonald (*née* Phoebe Napier Harvey) (*d* 1977), MB, FFARCS, DA, *widow* of Sir Peter Macdonald, Newport, IoW. *Educ:* Repton; Trinity College, Cambridge. Apprenticed in engineering trade with Crompton Parkinsons, Electrical Engineers, Chelmsford; employed previous to hostilities as Constructional Engineer with Associated Portland Cement Manufacturers. DL, Ross and Cromarty, 1964; JP Ross-shire, 1960. *Recreations:* shooting, sailing, ski-ing, farming. *Heir: s* Alistair Weston Brooke, *b* 12 Sept. 1947. *Address:* Midfearn, Ardgay, Ross-shire. *T:* Ardgay 250. *Club:* Royal Ocean Racing.

BROOKE, Sir (Norman) Richard (Rowley), Kt 1964; CBE 1958; FCA; *b* 23 June 1910; *s* of William Brooke, JP, Scunthorpe, Lincs; *m* 1st, 1948, Julia Dean (marr. diss. 1957); one *s* one *d*; 2nd, 1958, Nina Mari Dolan. *Educ:* Charterhouse School. Joined Guest, Keen & Nettlefolds Ltd, 1935; Dir, Guest, Keen & Nettlefolds Ltd, 1961-67; Dir and/or Chm. of several GKN subsidiary cos until retirement in 1967; Director: Eagle Star Insurance Co. (Wales Bd), 1955-80; L. Ryan Hldgs Ltd, 1972-78; a Founder Dir, Develt Corp. for Wales, until 1967, now Hon. Vice-Pres. Founder Mem. and Dep. Chm., British Independent Steel Producers Assoc., 1967. Hon. Life Vice-President, Wales Conservative and Unionist Council, 1966; President, Cardiff Chamber of Commerce, 1960-61; Member Exec. Cttee and Council, British Iron and Steel Federation, to 1967 (Joint Vice-Pres., 1966-67); Vice-Pres., University College, Cardiff, 1965-81, Mem. Council, 1982-. JP Glamorgan, 1952-64, 1970-74. OStJ 1953. *Recreations:* bridge, music, reading. *Address:* New Sarum, Pwllmelin Lane, Llandaff, Cardiff. *T:* Cardiff 563692. *Clubs:* Sloane; Cardiff and County (Cardiff); Royal Porthcawl Golf.

BROOKE, Hon. Peter Leonard; MP (C) City of London and Westminster South, since Feb. 1977; a Lord Commissioner of HM Treasury, since 1981; *b* 3 March 1934; *s* of Lord Brooke of Cumnor, *qv*, and Lady Brooke of

Ystradfellte, *qv*; *m* 1964, Joan Margaret Smith; three *s* (and one *s* decd). *Educ:* Marlborough; Balliol College, Oxford (MA); Harvard Business School (MBA). Vice-Pres., Nat. Union of Students, 1955-56; Chm., Nat. Conf. Student Christian Movement, 1956; Pres., Oxford Union, 1957; Harkness Fellow, 1957-59. Research Assistant, IMEDE, Lausanne, 1960-61. Spencer Stuart & Associates, Management Consultants, 1961-79 (Director of parent company, 1965-79, Chairman 1974-79); lived in NY and Brussels, 1969-73. Director, Ecole St Georges, Switzerland, 1964-79. Mem., Camden Borough Council, 1968-69. Chm., St Pancras N Cons. Assoc., 1976-77. Contested (C) Bedwellty, Oct. 1974; an Asst Govt Whip, 1979-81. Pres., London Council on Alcoholism, 1981-; Member: Adv. Council, Business Graduates Assoc., 1979-; Foundn for Management Educn, 1979-; Pres., Incorp. Assoc. of Prep Schs, 1980-; Governor, Marlborough Coll., 1977-; Trustee: Dove Cottage 1976-; Cusichaca Project, 1978-; Rantavan Foundn, 1969-. Lay Adviser, St Paul's Cathedral, 1980-. *Recreations:* churches, conservation, cricket, planting things. *Address:* 110A Ashley Gardens, SW1. *T:* 01-834 1563. *Clubs:* Brook's, City Livery, MCC, I Zingari, St George's (Hanover Square); Conservative.

BROOKE, Sir Richard; *see* Brooke, Sir N. R. R.

BROOKE, Sir Richard (Neville), 10th Bt *cr* 1662; *b* 1 May 1915; *s* of Sir Richard Christopher Brooke, 9th Bt, and Marian Dorothea (*d* 1965), *d* of late Arthur Charles Innes, MP, of Dromantine, Co. Down; *S* father, 1981; *m* 1st, 1937, Lady Mabel Kathleen Jocelyn (marr. diss. 1959), *d* of 8th Earl of Roden; two *s*; 2nd, 1960, Jean Evison, *d* of late Lt-Col A. C. Corfe, DSO. *Educ:* Eton. Served as Lieutenant, Scots Guards, 1939-46; prisoner of war (escaped). Chartered Accountant (FCA), 1946; Senior Partner, Price Waterhouse & Co., European Firms, 1969-75; retired, 1975. *Recreations:* racing, fishing. *Heir: s* Richard David Christopher Brooke [*b* 23 Oct. 1938; *m* 1st, 1963, Carola Marion (marr. diss. 1978), *d* of Sir Robert Erskine-Hill, 2nd Bt; two *s*; 2nd, 1979, Lucinda Barlow, *o d* of late J. F. Voelcker and of Jean Constance Voelcker, Lidgetton, Natal]. *Address:* 44 Castellaras-le-Vieux, 06370 Mouans-Sartoux, France. *T:* (93) 752460. *Clubs:* Boodle's; Travellers' (Paris).

BROOKE, Rodney George; Chief Executive and Clerk, West Yorkshire Metropolitan County Council, since 1981 (Director of Administration, 1973-81); *b* 22 Oct. 1939; *s* of George Sidney Brooke and Amy Brooke; *m* 1967, Dr Clare Margaret Cox; one *s* one *d. Educ:* Queen Elizabeth's Grammar Sch., Wakefield. Admitted solicitor, 1962. Asst Solicitor: Rochdale County Bor. Council, 1962-63; Leicester CC, 1963-65; Stockport County Bor. Council: Sen. Asst Solicitor, 1965-67; Asst Town Clerk, 1967-69; Dep. Town Clerk, 1969-71; Dir of Admin, 1971-73. *Publications:* articles on local govt. *Recreations:* skiing, opera, Byzantium. *Address:* Stubham Lodge, Clifford Road, Middleton, Ilkley, West Yorks LS29 0AX. *T:* Ilkley 601869.

BROOKE, (Thomas) Humphrey, CVO 1969 (MVO 1958); Secretary, Royal Academy of Arts, Piccadilly, W1, 1952-68; *b* 31 Jan. 1914; *y s* of late Major Thomas Brooke, Grimston Manor, York, and late B. Gundreda, *d* of Sir Hildred Carlile, 1st and last Bt; *m* 1946, Countess Nathalie Benckendorff, *o d* of Count Benckendorff, DSO; one *d* (one *s* one *d* decd). *Educ:* Wellington Coll; Magdalen Coll., Oxford. 1st Cl. Hons Mod. History Oxon, 1935; BLitt 1937. Asst Keeper, Public Record Office, 1937. Served War of 1939-45, commissioned KRRC, 1943. Dir of Archives, Sub-Commn for Monuments, Fine Arts and Archives, Allied Control Commn, Italy, 1944-45; Controller, Monuments and Fine Arts Branch, Allied Commission for Austria, 1946; Dep. Director, Tate Gallery, 1948; Ministry of Town and Country Planning, 1949; Resigned from Civil Service on appointment to Royal Acad., 1951. Member Order of Santiago (Portugal), 1955; Commander Ordine al Merito della Republica Italiana, 1956; Officier de l'Ordre de l'Etoile Noire (France), 1958. *Recreations:* shooting, fishing, gardening. *Address:* 8 Pelham Crescent, SW7. *T:* 01-589 5690; Lime Kiln, Claydon, Suffolk. *T:* Ipswich 830334. *Club:* Chelsea Arts.

BROOKE-LITTLE, John Philip Brooke, MVO 1969; Norroy and Ulster King of Arms, since 1980; Librarian, since 1974, and Treasurer, since 1978, College of Arms; *b* 6 April 1927; *s* of late Raymond Brooke-Little, Unicorns House, Swalcliffe; *m* 1960, Mary Lee, *o c* of late John Raymond Pierce and Mrs E. G. Pierce, Colehill, Wimborne Minster; three *s* one *d. Educ:* Clayesmore Sch; New Coll., Oxford (MA). Earl Marshal's staff, 1952-53; Gold Staff Officer, Coronation, 1953; Bluemantle Pursuivant of Arms, 1956-67; Richmond Herald, 1967-80; Registrar, Coll. of Arms, 1974-82. Founder of Heraldry Soc. and Chm., 1947; Hon. Editor-in-Chief, The Coat of Arms, 1950; Governor, Clayesmore Sch. (Chm. 1971-); Fellow, Soc. of Genealogists, 1969. Hon. Fellow, Inst. of Heraldic and Genealogical Studies, 1979. Freeman and Liveryman, Scriveners' Co. of London. FSA 1961. KStJ 1975; Knight of Malta, 1955 (Chancellor, 1973-77); Comdr Cross of Merit of Order of Malta, 1966; Cruz Distinguida (1st cl.) de San Raimundo de Peñafort, 1955. *Publications:* Royal London, 1953; Pictorial History of Oxford, 1954; Boutell's Heraldry, 1970, 1973 and 1978 (1963 and 1966 edns with C. W. Scott-Giles); Knights of the Middle Ages, 1966; Prince of Wales, 1969; Fox-Davies' Complete Guide to Heraldry, annotated edn, 1969; (with Don Pottinger and Anne Tauté) Kings and Queens of Great Britain, 1970; An Heraldic Alphabet, 1973; (with Marie Angell) Beasts in Heraldry, 1974; The British Monarchy in Colour, 1976; Royal Arms, Beasts and Badges, 1977; Royal Ceremonies of State, 1979; genealogical and heraldic articles. *Recreations:* cooking, painting. *Address:* Heyford House, Lower Heyford, near Oxford. *T:* Steeple Aston 40337; College of Arms, EC4. *T:* 01-248 1310. *Clubs:* City Livery, Chelsea Arts (Hon. Member).

BROOKE-ROSE, Prof. Christine; novelist and critic; Professor of English Language and Literature, University of Paris, since 1975 (Lecturer, 1969-75). *Educ:* Oxford and London Univs. MA Oxon 1953, PhD London 1954. Research and criticism, 1957-. Reviewer for: The Times Literary Supplement, The Times, The Observer, The Sunday Times, The Listener, The Spectator, and The London Magazine, 1956-68; took up post at Univ. of Paris VIII, Vincennes, 1969. Has broadcast in book programmes on BBC, and on 'The Critics', and ABC Television. Travelling Prize of Society of Authors, 1964; James Tait Black Memorial Prize, 1966; Arts Council Translation Prize, 1969. *Publications:* novels: The Languages of Love, 1957; The Sycamore Tree, 1958; The Dear Deceit, 1960; The Middlemen, 1961; Out, 1964; Such, 1965; Between, 1968; Thru, 1975; *criticism:* A Grammar of Metaphor, 1958; A ZBC of Ezra Pound, 1971; A Rhetoric of the Unreal, 1981; *short stories:* Go when you see the Green Man Walking, 1969; short stories and essays in various magazines, etc. *Recreations:* people, travel. *Address:* c/o Cambridge University Press, PO Box 110, Cambridge CB2 3RL.

BROOKE TURNER, Alan, CMG 1980; HM Diplomatic Service; Minister, Moscow, since 1979; *b* 4 Jan. 1926; *s* of late Arthur Brooke Turner, MC; *m* 1954, Hazel Alexandra Rowan Henderson; two *s* two *d. Educ:* Marlborough; Balliol Coll., Oxford (Sen. Schol.). 1st cl Hon. Mods 1949; 1st cl. Lit. Hum. 1951. Served in RAF, 1944-48. Entered HM Foreign (subseq. Diplomatic) Service, 1951; FO, 1951; Warsaw, 1953; 3rd, later 2nd Sec. (Commercial), Jedda, 1954; Lisbon, 1957; 1st Sec., FO, 1959 (UK Delegn to Nuclear Tests Conf., Geneva, 1962); Cultural Attaché, Moscow, 1962; FO, 1965; Fellow, Center for Internat. Affairs, Harvard Univ., 1968; Counsellor, Rio de Janeiro, 1969-71; Head of Southern European Dept, FCO, 1972-73; Counsellor and Head of Chancery, British Embassy, Rome, 1973-76; Civil Dep. Comdt and Dir of Studies, NATO Defense Coll., Rome, 1976-78; Internat. Inst. for Strategic Studies, 1978-79. *Address:* c/o Foreign and Commonwealth Office, SW1; 11 Marsham Court, Marsham Street, SW1. *T:* 01-834 8863; Poultons, Dormansland, Lingfield, Surrey. *T:* Lingfield 832079. *Club:* Travellers'.

BROOKEBOROUGH, 2nd Viscount *cr* 1952, of Colebrooke; **John Warden Brooke,** PC (NI) 1971; DL; Bt 1822; Member (UPNI) for North Down, Northern Ireland Constitutional Convention, 1975-76; *b* 9 Nov. 1922; *s* of 1st Viscount Brookeborough, KG, PC, CBE, MC, and Cynthia Mary, DBE 1959 (*d* 1970), *d* of late Captain Charles Warden Sergison; *S* father, 1973; *m* 1949, Rosemary Hilda Chichester; two *s* three *d. Educ:* Eton. Joined Army, 1941; Captain 10th Royal Hussars; wounded, Italy, 1942; subseq. ADC to Field Marshal Alexander in Italy and to Gen. Sir Brian Robertson in Germany; ADC to Viceroy of India, Field Marshal Lord Wavell, 1946; invalided, 1947. Fermanagh County Councillor, 1947-73, Chairman, 1961-73; pioneered streamlining of local govt by voluntary amalgamation of all councils in the county, 1967. MP (U) Lisnaskea Div., Parlt of NI, 1968-73; Mem. (U), N Down, NI Assembly, 1973-75; Parly Sec. to Min. of Commerce with special responsibilities for tourism, Apr. 1969; Parly Sec. to Dept of the Prime Minister (still retaining Commerce office), with responsibility for general oversight of Government's publicity and information services, Jan. 1970; Minister of State, Min. of Finance and Govt Chief Whip, 1971-72. DL Co. Fermanagh, 1967. *Recreations:* shooting, fishing, riding. *Heir:* s Hon. Alan Henry Brooke [*b* 30 June 1952; *m* 1980, Janet, *o d* of John Cooke, Doagh, Co. Antrim. Commissioned 17/21 Lancers, 1972; Captain, UDR, 1977]. *Address:* Ashbrooke, Brookeborough, Enniskillen, Co. Fermanagh. *T:* Brookeborough 242.

BROOKER, William, ARA 1980; painter; Principal, Wimbledon School of Art, 1969-81; *b* 26 June 1918; *s* of Charles Frederick Brooker and Winifred Victoria Colverson; *m* 1975, Katina Montesinos Belón; two *d* by a previous marriage. *Educ:* Royal Masonic Sch.; Croydon Sch. of Art; Chelsea Sch. of Art. Served War, 1940-46: Captain, RA and Staff Officer III; served in NW Europe campaign from Normandy until end of war in 86th Anti-Tank Regt, RA (5th Btn Devonshire Regt). Sen. Asst, Bath Acad. of Art, 1949-53; Senior Lecturer in Painting: Willesden and Harrow Sch. of Art, 1953-60; Ealing Sch. of Art, 1960-65; Central Sch. of Art and Design, 1965-69. One-man exhibitions: Arthur Tooth & Sons, 1955, 1962, 1964, 1967, 1968, 1971, 1975; Arts Centre, Lusaka, Zambia, 1968; Villiers, NSW, 1971; Thos Agnew & Sons Ltd, 1979; group exhibitions: numerous, incl. London Gp, John Moore's Biennial (Liverpool), Edinburgh Open 100, British Council, Royal Academy, Royal Soc. of British Artists, Leicester Galls and Thos Agnew & Sons Ltd; works in public collections: Tate Gall.; National Gallery of: Canada; NZ; S Australia; Castle Museum, Nottingham; Aberdeen Art Gall.; Manchester City Art Gall.; Glynn Vivian Museum, Swansea; Southampton Art Gall.; contemporary Art Soc.; Museum of Modern Art, Belo Horizonte, Brazil; City Art Gall., Rotherham; Laing Art Gall., Newcastle; Oldham Art Gall.; Arts Centre, Lusaka, Zambia; works in numerous private collections incl. in USA, Far East and Australasia. *Recreations:* listening to music, reading poetry, playing Russian Roulette without a revolver. *Address:* 5 Bankside Close, Carshalton Beeches, Surrey. *T:* 01-669 5168. *Club:* Muriel's.

BROOKES, family name of **Baron Brookes.**

BROOKES, Baron *cr* 1975 (Life Peer), of West Bromwich; **Raymond Percival Brookes,** Kt 1971; Life President, Guest, Keen & Nettlefolds Ltd (Group Chairman and Chief Executive, 1965-74); *b* 10 April 1909; *s* of

William and Ursula Brookes; *m* 1937, Florence Edna Sharman; one *s.* Part-time Mem., BSC, 1967-68. First Pres., British Mechanical Engrg Confedn, 1968-70; a Vice-Pres., Engrg Employers' Fedn, 1967-75. Member: Council, UK S Africa Trade Assoc. Ltd, 1967-74; Council, CBI, 1968-75; BNEC, 1969-71; Wilberforce Ct of Inquiry into electricity supply industry dispute, Jan. 1971; Industrial Develt Adv. Bd, 1972-75. Member: Exec. Cttee, 1970-, Council, 1969-, Pres., 1974-75, Soc. of Motor Manufacturers & Traders Ltd; Court of Governors, Univ. of Birmingham, 1966-75; Council, Univ. of Birmingham, 1968-75. Pres., Motor Ind. Res. Assoc., 1973-75. Chm., Rea Brothers (Isle of Man) Ltd; Director: Plessey Co. Ltd; Mannin Industries Ltd. *Recreations:* golf, fly-fishing. *Address:* Guest, Keen & Nettlefolds Ltd, Group Head Office, Smethwick, Warley, Worcs; (private) Mallards, Santon, Isle of Man.

BROOKES, Beata; Member (C) North Wales, European Parliament, since 1979; *b* 1931. *Educ:* Lowther College, Abergele; Univ. of Wales, Bangor; studied politics in USA (US State Dept Scholarship). Former social worker, Denbighshire CC; company secretary and farmer. Contested (C) Widnes, 1955, Warrington, 1963, Manchester Exchange, 1964. Member: Clwyd AHA, 1973-80 (Mem., Welsh Hosp. Bd, 1963-74); Clwyd Family Practitioner Cttee; Clwyd CC Social Services Cttee, 1973-81; Flintshire Soc. for Mentally Handicapped; N Wales Council for Mentally Handicapped; Council for Professions Supplementary to Medicine; Exec. Cttee, N Wales Cons. Group; European Parlt Educn Cttee, and Agricultural Cttee. Pres., N Wales Assoc. for the Disabled. *Address:* The Cottage, Wayside Acres, Bodelwyddan, near Rhyl, North Wales.

BROOKES, Air Vice-Marshal Hugh Hamilton, CB 1954; CBE 1951; DFC 1944; RAF retd; *b* 14 Oct. 1904; *s* of late W. H. Brookes and of Evelyn, *d* of J. Forster Hamilton (she married 2nd Sir John Simpson, KBE, CIE); *m* 1932, Elsie Viola Henry; one *d. Educ:* Bedford School; Cranwell. Bomber Command, 1924; 84 Sqdn Iraq, 1929; Staff College, 1933; Sqdn Bomber Command, 1937; Iraq, 1938; Western Desert, 1939; Aden, 1941; Station Bomber Command, 1943; Iraq, 1946; Director of Flying Training, 1949; AOC Rhodesia, 1951; AOC Iraq, 1954; AOC No 25 Group, Flying Training Command, 1956-58, retd. *Club:* Royal Air Force.

BROOKES, Peter C.; *see* Cannon-Brookes, P.

BROOKES, Sir Wilfred (Deakin), Kt 1979; CBE 1972; DSO 1944; AEA 1945; Chairman and director of companies; *b* 17 April 1906; *s* of Herbert Robinson Brookes and Ivy Deakin; *m* 1928, Betty (*d* 1968), *d* of A. H. Heal; one *s. Educ:* Melbourne Grammar Sch.; Melbourne Univ. Exec., later Alternate Dir, Aust. Paper Manufacturers Ltd, 1924-38; Exec. Dir, Box and Container Syndicate, 1938-39. War Service, 1939-45, as Sqdn Officer, RAAF, 1939-42 (despatches), Comdr, 78th Fighter Wing, New Guinea Offensive, 1943-45, Dir of Postings, RAAF HQ, rank of Gp Captain, 1945. Chm., Apsonor Pty Ltd (Dir, 1960-); Director: BH South Group, 1956-; Alcoa of Australia, 1961-; North Broken Hill, 1970-; Collins Wales Pty Ltd, 1974- (formerly Chm.). Chairman: Associated Pulp and Paper Mills, 1952-78 (Dir, 1945-78); Colonial Mutual Life Soc., 1965-78 (Dir 1955-78); Electrolytic Refining & Smelting Co. of Australia Ltd, 1956-80. Past Pres., Inst. of Public Affairs; Chm., Edward Wilson Charitable Trust (Trustee, 1960-); Associate Trustee, Deakin Foundn; Dep. Chm., Corps of Commissionaires, 1979- (Governor, 1975-). *Recreations:* swimming, walking. *Address:* 20 Heyington Place, Toorak, Victoria 3142, Australia. *T:* 20 4553. *Clubs:* Melbourne, Australian (Melbourne).

BROOKNER, Prof. Anita; Reader, Courtauld Institute of Art, since 1977; *b* 16 July 1938; *o c* of Newson and Maude Brookner. *Educ:* James Allen's Girls' Sch.; King's Coll., Univ. of London; Courtauld Inst.; Paris. Vis. Lectr, Univ. of Reading, 1959-64; Slade Professor, Univ. of Cambridge, 1967-68; Lectr, Courtauld Inst. of Art, 1964. Fellow, New Hall, Cambridge. *Publications:* Watteau, 1968; The Genius of the Future, 1971; Greuze: the rise and fall of an Eighteenth Century Phenomenon, 1972; Jacques-Louis David, 1980; A Start in Life (novel), 1981; Providence (novel), 1982; articles in Burlington Magazine, etc. *Address:* 68 Elm Park Gardens, SW10. *T:* 01-352 6894.

BROOKS, family name of **Barons Brooks of Tremorfa** and **Crawshaw.**

BROOKS OF TREMORFA, Baron *cr* 1979 (Life Peer), of Tremorfa in the County of South Glamorgan; **John Edward Brooks;** *b* 12 April 1927; *s* of Edward George Brooks and Rachel Brooks (*née* White); *m* 1948 (marr. diss. 1956); one *s* one *d; m* 1958, Margaret Pringle; two *s. Educ:* elementary schools; Coleg Harlech. Secretary, Cardiff South East Labour Party, 1966-; Member, South Glamorgan CC, 1973- (Leader, 1973-77; Chm., 1981-). Contested (Lab) Barry, Feb. and Oct. 1974; Parliamentary Agent to Rt Hon. James Callaghan, MP, Gen. Elections, 1970, 1979. Chm., Labour Party, Wales, 1978-79. Opposition defence spokesman, 1980-. *Recreations:* reading, most sports. *Address:* 57 Janet Street, Splott, Cardiff. *T:* Cardiff 40709.

BROOKS, Prof. Cleanth; Gray Professor of Rhetoric, Yale University, USA, 1947-75, now Emeritus Professor; *b* 16 Oct. 1906; *s* of Rev. Cleanth and Bessie Lee Witherspoon Brooks; *m* 1934, Edith Amy Blanchard; no *c. Educ:* The McTyeire School; Vanderbilt, Tulane and Oxford Universities. Rhodes Scholar, Louisiana and Exeter, 1929; Lecturer, later Prof., Louisiana State Univ., 1932-47; Prof. of English, later Gray Prof. of Rhetoric, Yale Univ.,

1947-75. Visiting Professor: Univ. of Texas; Univ. of Michigan; Univ. of Chicago; Univ. of Southern California; Bread Loaf School of English; Univ. of South Carolina, 1975; Tulane Univ., 1976; Univ. of North Carolina, 1977; Univ. of Tennessee, 1978. Cultural Attaché at the American Embassy, London, 1964-66. Managing Editor and Editor (with Robert Penn Warren), The Southern Review, 1935-42. Fellow, Library of Congress, 1953-63; Guggenheim Fellow, 1953 and 1960; Sen. Fellow, Nat. Endowment for the Humanities, 1975. Member: Amer. Acad. of Arts and Scis; Amer. Acad. Inst. of Arts and Letters; Amer. Philos. Soc.; RSL. Hon. DLitt: Upsala Coll., 1963; Kentucky, 1963; Exeter, 1966; Washington and Lee, 1968; Tulane, 1969; Univ. of the South, 1974; Newberry Coll., 1979; Hon. LHD: St Louis, 1968; Centenary Coll., 1972; Oglethorpe Univ., 1976; St Peter's Coll., 1978. *Publications:* Modern Poetry and the Tradition, 1939; The Well Wrought Urn, 1947; (with R. P. Warren) Understanding Poetry, 1938; (with R. P. Warren) Modern Rhetoric, 1950; (with W. K. Wimsatt, Jr) Literary Criticism: A Short History, 1957; The Hidden God, 1963; William Faulkner: The Yoknapatawpha Country, 1963; A Shaping Joy, 1971; (with R. W. B. Lewis and R. P. Warren) American Literature: the Makers and the Making, 1973; William Faulkner: Toward Yoknapatawpha and Beyond, 1978; (Gen. Editor, with David N. Smith and A. F. Falconer) The Percy Letters; contrib. articles, reviews to literary magazines, journals. *Address:* Forest Road, Northford, Conn 06472, USA. *Club:* Athenæum.

BROOKS, Douglas; Director, Walker Brooks and Partners Ltd, since 1980; *b* 3 Sept. 1928; *s* of Oliver Brooks and Olive Brooks; *m* 1952, June Anne (*née* Branch); one *s* one *d. Educ:* Newbridge Grammar Sch.; University Coll., Cardiff (Dip. Soc. Sc.). CIPM; APMI. Girling Ltd: factory operative, 1951-53; Employment Officer, 1953-56; Hoover Ltd: Personnel Off., 1956-60; Sen. Personnel Off., 1960-63; Dep. Personnel Man., 1963-66; Indust. Relations Advr, 1966-69; Gp Personnel Man., 1969-73; Personnel Dir, 1973-78; Group Personnel Manager, Tarmac Ltd, 1979-80. Mem. Council, SSRC, 1976-. Mem., BBC Consultative Gp on social effects of television, 1978-80. Vice-Pres., IPM, 1972-74. Chm., Wooburn Fest. Soc. Ltd, 1978-. *Publications:* various articles in professional jls. *Recreations:* talking, music, reading, gardening, cooking. *Address:* Bull Farm House, Park Lane, Beaconsfield, Bucks. *T:* Beaconsfield 5253. *Club:* Reform.

BROOKS, Edwin, PhD; Dean of Commerce and Director, Albury-Wodonga Campus, Riverina College of Advanced Education, Wagga Wagga, New South Wales, since 1982 (Dean of Business and Liberal Studies, 1977-82); *b* Barry, Glamorgan, 1 Dec. 1929; *s* of Edwin Brooks and Agnes Elizabeth (*née* Campbell); *m* 1956, Winifred Hazel Soundie; four *s* one *d. Educ:* Barry Grammar Sch.; St John's Coll., Cambridge. PhD (Camb) 1958. National Service, Singapore, 1948-49. MP (Lab) Bebington, 1966-70. Univ. of Liverpool: Lectr, Dept of Geography, 1954-66 and 1970-72; Sen. Lectr, 1972-77; Dean, College Studies, 1975-77. Councillor, Birkenhead, 1958-67. Mem., Courses Cttee, Higher Educn Bd of NSW, 1978-82. *Publications:* This Crowded Kingdom, 1973; (ed) Tribes of the Amazon Basin in Brazil, 1973. *Recreations:* gardening, do-it-yourself. *Address:* Riverina College of Advanced Education, PO Box 588, Wagga Wagga, NSW 2650, Australia. *T:* 069-23-24-84.

BROOKS, Eric Arthur Swatton, MA; Head of Claims Department, Foreign Office, 1960 until retirement, 1967; *b* 9 Oct. 1907; *yr s* of late A. E. Brooks, MA, Maidenhead; *m* 1947, Daphne Joyce, *yr d* of late George McMullan, MD, FRCSE, Wallingford; one *s* one *d. Educ:* Reading Sch.; New Coll., Oxford (MA). 2nd cl. hons Jurisprudence, 1929. Solicitor, 1932; practised in London, 1932-39. Mem. Law Soc., 1934- (Mem. Overseas Relations Cttee, 1949-). Served War of 1939-45 in Admty and Min. of Aircraft Production, and in Operational Research as Hon. Ft-Lieut RAFVR until 1944; Disposal of Govt Factories of Min. of Aircraft Production, 1944-Dec. 1945. Foreign Office, 1946-. Served on Brit. Delegns in negotiations with: Polish and Hungarian Governments, 1953, 1954; Bulgarian Government, 1955; Rumanian Government, 1955, 1956, 1960; USSR, 1964, 1965, 1966, 1967. British Representative on Anglo-Italian Conciliation Commn, until 1967. Councillor: Borough of Maidenhead, 1972-74; Royal Borough of Windsor and Maidenhead, 1973-. *Publications:* articles, on Compensation in International Law, and Distribution of Compensation, in legal jls, and on local history and amenities. *Recreations:* golf (Oxford Univ. team *v* Cambridge Univ., 1929; various later Amateur European Championships); ski-ing; skating; gardening. *Address:* Kitoha, 116b Grenfell Road, Maidenhead, Berks. *T:* Maidenhead 21621.

BROOKS, Most Rev. Francis Gerard; *see* Dromore, Bishop of, (RC).

BROOKS, Leslie James, CEng, FRINA; RCNC; Deputy Director of Engineering (Constructive), Ship Department, Ministry of Defence (Procurement Executive), 1973-76, retired; *b* 3 Aug. 1916; *yr s* of late C. J. D. Brooks and Lucy A. Brooks, Milton Regis, Sittingbourne, Kent; *m* 1941, Ruth Elizabeth Olver, Saltash, Cornwall; two *s. Educ:* Borden Grammar Sch., Sittingbourne, Kent; HM Dockyard Schs, Sheerness and Chatham; Royal Naval Engrg Coll., Keyham; RNC, Greenwich. War of 1939-45: Asst Constructor, Naval Construction Dept, Admty, Bath, 1941-44; Constr Lt-Comdr on Staff of Allied Naval Comdr, Exped. Force, and Flag Officer, Brit. Assault Area, 1944. Constr in charge Welding, Naval Constrn Dept, Admty, Bath, 1945-47; Constr Comdr, Staff of Comdr-in-Chief, Brit. Pacific Fleet, 1947-49; Constr in charge, No 2 Ship Tank, Admty Experiment Works, Haslar, Gosport, 1949-54. Naval Constrn Dept, Admty, Bath: Constr

Merchant Shipping Liaison, 1954-56; Chief Constr in charge of Conversion of First Commando Ships, and of Operating Aircraft Carriers, 1956-62; Dep. Supt, Admty Exper. Works, Haslar, 1962-65; Ship Dept, Bath: Asst Dir of Naval Constrn, Naval Constrn Div., MoD(N), 1965-68; Asst Dir of Engrg (Ships), MoD(PE), 1968-73; Dep. Dir of Engrg/Constr., MoD(PE), 1973. Mem., Royal Corps of Naval Constructors. *Recreations:* walking, photography, natural history. *Address:* Merrymeet, Perrymead, Bath BA2 5AY. *T:* Bath 832856.

BROOKS, Mel; writer, director, actor; *b* Brooklyn, 1926; *m* Florence Baum; two *s* one *d* ; *m* 1964, Anne Bancroft; one *s*. TV script writer for series: Your Show of Shows, 1950-54; Caesar's Hour, 1954-57; Get Smart, 1965-70. Films: (cartoon) The Critic (Academy Award), 1963; The Producers (Academy Award), 1968; The Twelve Chairs, 1970; Blazing Saddles, 1973; Young Frankenstein, 1974; Silent Movie, 1976; High Anxiety, 1977; Elephant Man, 1980; History of the World Part 1, 1981. Several album recordings. *Address:* c/o Twentieth Century-Fox Film Corporation, Box 900, Beverly Hills, Calif 90213, USA.

BROOKS, Oliver; Managing Director, Peninsular and Oriental Steam Navigation Co., 1979-June 1983; *b* 22 Jan. 1920; *s* of late Percy Albert Victor Brooks and of Winifred Brooks; *m* 1944, Lillian Reeve; one *d. Educ:* St John's Primary Sch., Fulham; Wandsworth Commercial Sch. ACIS. Various appts, 1937-47; Gray Dawes & Co. Ltd, 1947-70; Financial Director: Inchcape & Co. Ltd, 1970-73; The Peninsular and Oriental Steam Navigation Co., 1973-79. Dir, Burmah Oil Co. Ltd, 1975-. *Recreations:* family life, work. *Address:* Tanglewood, 98 Sandy Lane, Cheam, Surrey SM2 7EP. *T:* 01-642 9915.

BROOKS, William Donald Wykeham, CBE 1956; MA, DM (Oxon); FRCP; Consulting Physician: St Mary's Hospital; Brompton Hospital; to the Royal Navy; to the King Edward VII Convalescent Home for Officers, Osborne; Chief Medical Officer, Eagle Star Insurance Co.; *b* 3 Aug. 1905; *er s* of A. E. Brooks, MA (Oxon), Maidenhead, Berks; *m* 1934, Phyllis Kathleen, *e d* of late F. A. Juler, CVO; two *s* two *d. Educ:* Reading School; St John's College, Oxford (White Scholar); St Mary's Hospital, London (University Scholar); Strong Memorial Hospital, Rochester, New York. First Class Honours, Final Honour School of Physiology, 1928; Cheadle Gold Medallist, 1931; Fereday Fellow St John's College, Oxford, 1931-34; Rockefeller Travelling Fellow, 1932-33; Goulstonian Lecturer, 1940; Marc Daniels Lecturer, RCP, 1957. Asst Registrar, 1946-50, RCP; Censor, RCP, 1961- (Council, 1959-61, Senior Vice-President and Senior Censor, 1965); Member Association of Physicians of Great Britain and Ireland. Served War 1940-45 as Surgeon Captain, RNVR. Editor, Quarterly Jl of Medicine, 1946-67. *Publications:* numerous articles on general medical topics and on chest diseases in various medical journals; Sections on Chest Wounds, Respiratory Diseases and Tuberculosis, Conybeare's Textbook of Medicine; Respiratory Diseases section in the Official Naval Medical History of the War. *Recreations:* golf, shooting, gardening, bridge. *Address:* Two Acres, Fryern Road, Storrington, Sussex. *T:* Storrington 2159.

BROOKS GRUNDY, Rupert Francis; *see* Grundy, R. F. B.

BROOKSBANK, Col Sir (Edward) William, 2nd Bt, *cr* 1919; TD 1953; DL; Yorkshire Hussars; *b* 15 June 1915; *e s* of late Col Edward York Brooksbank and Hazel, *d* of late H. F. Brockholes Thomas; *S* grandfather, 1943; *m* 1943, Ann, 2nd *d* of Col T. Clitherow; one *s. Educ:* Eton. Colonel, Comdg Queen's Own Yorkshire Yeomanry, 1957. Hon. Col, Queen's Own Yorkshire Yeomanry (TA), 1963-69, T&AVR, 1969-71, 1972-75. DL East Riding of Yorks, and City and County of Kingston upon Hull, 1959. *Heir:* s Edward Nicholas Brooksbank, late Captain, Blues and Royals [*b* 4 Oct. 1944; *m* 1970, Emma, *o d* of Baron Holderness, *qv* ; one *s*]. *Address:* Menethorpe Hall, Malton, North Yorks. *Clubs:* Turf; Yorkshire.

BROOKSBANK, Kenneth, DSC and Bar, 1944; Chief Education Officer, Birmingham, 1968-77; *b* 27 July 1915; *s* of Ambrose and Ethel Brooksbank; *m* 1939, Violet Anne Woodrow; two *d. Educ:* High Storrs Gram. Sch., Sheffield; St Edmund Hall, Oxford; Manchester University. Asst Master, Hulme Gram. Sch., Oldham, 1937-41; Royal Navy, 1941-46; Dep. Educn Off., York, 1946-49; Sen. Admin. Asst, Birmingham, 1949-52; Asst Sec. for Educn, NR Yorks CC, 1952-56; Dep. Educn Off., Birmingham, 1956-68. Leader, Unesco Educn Planning Mission to Bechuanaland, Basutoland and Swaziland, 1964. Chairman: Management Cttee, Adult Literacy Unit, Nat. Inst. of Adult Educn, 1978-80, Adult Literacy and Basic Skills Unit, 1980-; Council for Environmental Educn, 1978-; Community Educn Centre, 1981-; Member: Engineering Ind. Trng Bd, 1970-79; Ind. Trng Service Bd, 1974-77. President: Educnl Equipment Assoc., 1970-71; Soc. of Educn Officers, 1971-72. Mem. Council, Aston Univ., 1968-. Hon. Fellow, Birmingham Univ., 1981. *Publications:* (ed) Educational Administration, 1980; (ed) School Governors, 1981. *Address:* 29 Wycome Road, Hall Green, Birmingham B28 9EN. *T:* 021-777 4407.

BROOKSBANK, Sir William; *see* Brooksbank, Sir E. W.

BROOKSBY, John Burns, CBE 1973; FRS 1980; Director, Animal Virus Research Institute, Pirbright, 1964-79; *b* 25 Dec. 1914; *s* of George B. Brooksby, Glasgow; *m* 1940, Muriel Weir; one *s* one *d. Educ:* Hyndland Sch., Glasgow; Glasgow Veterinary Coll.; London University. MRCVS 1935; FRCVS 1978; BSc (VetSc) 1936; PhD 1947; DSc 1957; FRSE 1968; Hon. DSc

Edinburgh, 1981. Research Officer, Pirbright, 1939; Dep. Dir, 1957; Dir, 1964. *Publications:* papers on virus diseases of animals in scientific jls. *Address:* Heatherdale House, Compton Way, Farnham, Surrey. *T:* Runfold 2164.

BROOM, Air Marshal Sir Ivor (Gordon), KCB 1975 (CB 1972); CBE 1969; DSO 1945; DFC 1942 (Bar to DFC 1944, 2nd Bar 1945); AFC 1956; international aerospace consultant; Director, Plessey Airports Ltd; *b* Cardiff, 2 June 1920; *s* of Alfred Godfrey Broom and Janet Broom; *m* 1942, Jess Irene Broom (*née* Cooper); two *s* one *d*. *Educ:* West Monmouth Grammar Sch.; Pontypridd County Sch., Glam. Joined RAF, 1940; commissioned, 1941; 114 Sqdn, 107 Sqdn, 1941; CFS Course, 1942; Instr on: 1655 Mosquito Trg Unit; 571 Sqdn, 128 Sqdn, and 163 Sqdn, 1943-45; HQ, ACSEA, 1945-46. Commanded 28 (FR) Sqdn, 1946-48; RAF Staff Coll. Course, Bracknell, 1949; Sqdn Comdr, No 1 ITS, 1950-52; No 3 Flying Coll. Course, Manby, 1952-53; commanded 57 Sqdn, 1953-54; Syndicate Leader, Flying Coll., Manby, 1954-56; commanded Bomber Development Unit, Wittering, 1956-59; Air Secretary's Dept, 1959-62; commanded RAF Bruggen, 1962-64; IDC, 1965-66; Dir of Organisation (Establishments), 1966-68; Commandant, Central Flying School, 1968-70; AOC No 11 (Fighter) Gp, Strike Comd, 1970-72. Dep. Controller, 1972-74, Controller, 1974-77, Nat. Air Traffic Services; Mem., CAA, 1974-77. *Recreations:* golf, skiing. *Address:* Cherry Lawn, Bridle Lane, Loudwater, Rickmansworth, Herts WD3 4JB. *Club:* Royal Air Force.

BROOME, David, OBE 1970; farmer; British professional show jumper; *b* Cardiff, 1 March 1940; *s* of Fred and Amelia Broome, Chepstow, Gwent; *m* 1976, Elizabeth, *d* of K. W. Fletcher, Thirsk, N Yorkshire; one *s*. *Educ:* Monmouth Grammar Sch. for Boys. European Show Jumping Champion (3 times); World Show Jumping Champion, La Baule, 1970; Olympic Medallist (Bronze) twice, 1960, 1968; King George V Gold Cup 5 times (a record, in 1981). Mounts include: Sunsalve, Aachen, 1961; Mr Softee, Rotterdam, 1967, and Hickstead, 1969; Beethoven, La Baule, France, 1970, as (1st British) World Champion; Sportsman and Philco, Cardiff, 1974; Professional Champion of the World. *Publication:* Jump-Off, 1971. *Recreations:* hunting (MFH), shooting, golf. *Address:* Mount Ballan Manor, Crick, Chepstow, Gwent, Wales. *T:* Caldicot 42077.

BROOMFIELD, Nigel Hugh Robert Allen; Head of Eastern European and Soviet Department, Foreign and Commonwealth Office, since 1981; *b* 19 March 1937; *s* of Arthur Allen Broomfield and Ruth Sheilagh Broomfield; *m* 1963, Valerie Fenton; two *s*. *Educ:* Haileybury Coll.; Trinity Coll., Cambridge (BA (Hons) English Lit.). Commnd 17/21 Lancers, 1959, retired as Major, 1968. Joined FCO as First Sec., 1969; First Secretary: British Embassy, Bonn, 1970-72; British Embassy, Moscow, 1972-74; European Communities Dept, London, 1975-77; RCDS, 1978; Political Advr and Head of Chancery, British Mil. Govt, Berlin, 1979-81. Captain, Cambridge Squash Rackets and Real Tennis, 1957-58; British Amateur Squash Champion, 1958-59 (played for England, 1957-60). *Recreations:* tennis, squash, cricket, gardening, reading, music. *Address:* c/o Foreign and Commonwealth Office, SW1A 2AH. *Clubs:* Royal Automobile, MCC; Hawks (Cambridge).

BROOMHALL, Maj.-Gen. William Maurice, CB 1950; DSO 1945; OBE 1932; *b* 16 July 1897; *o s* of late Alfred Edward Broomhall, London. *Educ:* St Paul's School; Royal Military Academy, Woolwich. Commissioned Royal Engineers, 1915; France and Belgium, 1914-21 (wounded twice); Waziristan, 1921-24 (medal and clasp); NW Frontier of India, 1929-31 (despatches, clasp, OBE); Staff College, Camberley, 1932-33. Served North-West Europe, 1939-45 (Despatches, DSO); Chief Engineer, Allied Forces, Italy, 1946; Chief Engineer, British Army of the Rhine, 1947-48; Chief Engineer, Middle East Land Forces, 1948-51; retired, 1951. *Address:* The Cottage, Park Lane, Beaconsfield, Bucks HP9 2HR. *Club:* Army and Navy.

BROPHY, Brigid (Antonia), (Lady Levey), FRSL; author and playwright; *b* 12 June 1929; *o c* of late John Brophy; *m* 1954, Sir Michael Levey, *qv*; one *d*. *Educ:* St Paul's Girls' Sch.; St Hugh's Coll., Oxford. Awarded Jubilee Scholarship at St Hugh's Coll., Oxford, 1947 and read classics. Exec. Councillor, Writers' Guild of GB, 1975-78; a Vice-Chm., British Copyright Council, 1976-80. A Vice-Pres., Nat. Anti-Vivisection Soc., 1974-. Awarded Cheltenham Literary Festival First Prize for a first novel, 1954; London Magazine Prize for Prose, 1962. *Publications:* Hackenfeller's Ape, 1953; The King of a Rainy Country, 1956; Black Ship to Hell, 1962; Flesh, 1962; The Finishing Touch, 1963; The Snow Ball, 1964; Mozart the Dramatist, 1964; Don't Never Forget, 1966; (in collaboration with Michael Levey and Charles Osborne) Fifty Works of English Literature We Could Do Without, 1967; Black and White: a portrait of Aubrey Beardsley, 1968; In Transit, 1969; Prancing Novelist, 1973; The Adventures of God in his Search for the Black Girl, and other fables, 1973; Pussy Owl, 1976; Beardsley and his World, 1976; Palace Without Chairs, 1978. *Plays:* The Burglar, Vaudeville, 1967 (published with preface, 1968); The Waste Disposal Unit, Radio (published 1968). *Visual Art:* (with Maureen Duffy, *qv*) Prop Art, exhibn, London, 1969. *Address:* Flat 3, 185 Old Brompton Road, SW5 0AN. *T:* 01-373 9335.

BROSAN, Dr George Stephen, CBE 1982; TD 1960; Director, North East London polytechnic, 1970-82; *b* 8 Aug. 1921; *o s* of Rudolph and Margaret Brosan; *m* 1952, Maureen Dorothy Foscoe; three *d*. *Educ:* Kilburn Grammar Sch.; Faraday House; The Polytechnic; Birkbeck Coll., London. Faraday Scholar, 1939. BSc (Eng) 1944, BSc 1947; PhD 1951; DFH hons 1957; Hon. FIProdE 1980; FIEE 1964; FIMA 1966; FIMechE 1971; CBIM (formerly

FBIM) 1975. Dir, British Diamix Ltd, 1945-49; teaching staff: Woolwich Polytechnic, 1949-50; Regent Street Polytechnic, 1950-58; Head of Dept, Willesden Coll. of Technology, 1958-60; Further Educn Officer, Middlesex CC, 1960-62; Principal, Enfield Coll. of Technology, 1962-70. Pres., Tensor Club of GB, 1973-; Pres., IProdE, 1975-77; Mem. Council, BIM, 1975-79; Chairman: CEI Educn Cttee, 1978-79; Accountancy Educn Consultative Bd, 1979-82. Life Mem., ASME, 1977. Hon. MIED 1968. *Publications:* (jtly) Advanced Electrical Power and Machines, 1966; (jtly) Patterns and Policies in Higher Education, 1971; numerous articles and papers in academic and professional press. *Recreation:* yachting. *Address:* Winton Priors, Compton, Surrey GU3 1DT. *Club:* Reform.

BROTHERHOOD, Air Cdre William Rowland, CBE 1952; retired as Director, Guided Weapons (Trials), Ministry of Aviation (formerly Supply), 1959-61; *b* 22 Jan. 1912; *s* of late James Brotherhood, Tintern, Mon.; *m* 1939, Margaret (*d* 1981), *d* of late Ernest Sutcliffe, Louth, Lincs; one *s* one *d*. *Educ:* Monmouth School; RAF College, Cranwell. Joined RAF, 1930; Group Captain, 1943; Air Commodore, 1955; Director, Operational Requirements, Air Ministry, 1955-58. *Address:* Inglewood, Llandogo, Monmouth, Gwent. *T:* Dean 530333.

BROTHERS, Air Cdre Peter Malam, CBE 1964; DSO 1944; DFC 1940, and Bar, 1943; Managing Director, Peter Brothers Consultants Ltd, since 1973; *b* 30 Sept. 1917; *s* of late John Malam Brothers; *m* 1939, Annette, *d* of late James Wilson; three *d*. *Educ:* N. Manchester Sch. (Br. of Manchester Grammar). Joined RAF, 1936; Flt-Lieut 1939; RAF Biggin Hill, Battle of Britain, 1940; Sqdn-Ldr 1941; Wing Comdr 1942; Tangmere Fighter Wing Ldr, 1942-43; Staff HQ No. 10 Gp, 1943; Exeter Wing Ldr, 1944; US Comd and Gen. Staff Sch., 1944-45; Central Fighter Estab., 1945-46; Colonial Service, Kenya, 1947-49; RAF Bomber Sqdn, 1949-52; HQ No. 3 Gp, 1952-54; RAF Staff Coll., 1954; HQ Fighter Comd, 1955-57; Bomber Stn, 1957-59; Gp Capt., and Staff Officer, SHAPE, 1959-62; Dir of Ops (Overseas), 1962-65; Air Cdre, and AOC Mil. Air Traffic Ops, 1965-68; Dir of Public Relations (RAF), MoD (Air), 1968-73; retired 1973. Freeman, Guild Air Pilots and Air Navigators, 1966 (Liveryman, 1968; Warden, 1971; Master, 1974-75); Freeman, City of London, 1967. Editorial Adviser, Defence and Foreign Affairs publications. Patron, Spitfire Assoc., Australia; Chm., Devon Emergency Volunteers. MBIM; MIPR. *Recreations:* golf, sailing, fishing, swimming, flying. *Address:* c/o National Westminster Bank, Topsham, Devon. *Clubs:* Royal Air Force; RAF Yacht; Honiton Golf.

BROTHERSTON, Sir John (Howie Flint), Kt 1972; Professor of Community Medicine, University of Edinburgh, 1977-80, Emeritus Professor, since 1981; President, Faculty of Community Medicine, 1978-81; Hon. Physician to the Queen, 1965-68; *b* Edinburgh, 9 March 1915; *s* of late William Brotherston, WS, Edinburgh, and Dr Margaret M. Brotherston, MBE, Edinburgh; *m* 1939, Elizabeth Irene Low; two *s* two *d*. *Educ:* George Watson's College, Edinburgh; University of Edinburgh. Graduated: MA 1935, MB, ChB 1940, MD 1950, Edinburgh Univ.; FRCPE 1958; FRCPGlas 1964; FFCM 1973; FRCP 1978; DrPH Johns Hopkins University 1952. DPH London University, 1947. Served War of 1939-45 with RAMC, 1941-46. Rockefeller Fellow in Preventive Medicine, 1946-48; Lecturer in Social and Preventive Medicine at Guy's Hospital Medical School and London School of Hygiene and Tropical Medicine, 1948-51; Senior Lecturer, subsequently Reader, Public Health, London School of Hygiene and Tropical Medicine, 1951-55; Prof. of Public Health and Social Medicine, University of Edinburgh, 1955-64; Dean of the Faculty of Medicine, University of Edinburgh, 1958-63; Chief MO, Scottish Home and Health Dept, 1964-77. Mem. MRC, 1974-77. Hon. FRSH 1967. Hon. LLD Aberdeen, 1971; Hon. MD Bristol, 1981. Bronfman Prize, 1971. *Publications:* Observations on the early Public Health Movement in Scotland, 1952; various contribs to medical and other jls on social medicine and medical education. *Address:* 26 Mortonhall Road, Edinburgh EH9 2HN. *T:* 031-667 2849.

BROTHERTON, Michael Lewis; MP (C) Louth since Oct. 1974; *b* 26 May 1931; *s* of late John Basil Brotherton and Maud Brotherton; *m* 1968, Julia, *d* of Austin Gerald Comyn King and Katherine Elizabeth King, Bath; three *s* one *d*. *Educ:* Prior Park; RNC Dartmouth. Served RN, 1949-64: qual. Observer 1955; Cyprus, 1957 (despatches); Lt-Comdr 1964, retd. Times Newspapers, 1967-74. Chm., Beckenham Conservative Political Cttee, 1967-68; contested (C) Deptford, 1970; Pres., Hyde Park Tories, 1975. Mem., Select Cttee on violence in the family, 1975-76. *Recreations:* cricket, cooking. *Address:* The Old Vicarage, Wrangle, Boston, Lincs. *T:* Old Leake 688. *Clubs:* Carlton; MCC; Conservative Working Men's (Louth).

BROTHWOOD, John, MB, DPM; MRCP, FFCM, FRCPsych; Chief Medical Officer, Esso Petroleum (UK), and Esso Chemicals, since 1979; *b* 23 Feb. 1931; *s* of Wilfred Cyril Vernon Brothwood and late Emma Bailey; *m* 1957, Dr Margaret Stirling Meyer; one *s* one *d*. *Educ:* Marlborough Coll.; Peterhouse, Cambridge (Schol.); Middlesex Hosp. MB BChir (Cantab) 1955; MRCP 1960, DPM (London) 1964, FFCM 1972, FRCPsych 1976. Various posts in clinical medicine (incl. Registrar, Maudsley Hosp. and military service as Captain RAMC), 1955-64; joined DHSS (then Min. of Health) as MO, 1964; posts held in mental health, regional liaison, chronic disease policy and medical manpower and educn; SPMO and Under Secretary, DHSS, 1975-78. *Publications:* various, on NHS matters, especially mental health policy and related topics. *Recreations:* diverse. *Address:* 13 Great Spilmans, SE22. *T:* 01-693 8273. *Club:* United Oxford & Cambridge University.

BROUGH, Dr Colin, MRCPE; FFCM; Chief Administrative Medical Officer, Lothian Health Board, since 1980; *b* 4 Jan. 1932; *s* of Peter Brough and Elizabeth C. C. Chalmers; *m* 1957, Maureen Jennings; four *s* one *d. Educ:* Bell Baxter Sch., Cupar; Univ. of Edinburgh (MB ChB). DPH 1965; DIH 1965; FFCM 1978; MRCPE 1981. House Officer, Leicester General Hosp. and Royal Infirmary of Edinburgh, 1956-57; Surg.-Lieut, Royal Navy, 1957-60; General Practitioner, Leith and Fife, 1960-64; Dep. Medical Supt, Royal Inf. of Edinburgh, 1965-67; ASMO, PASMO, Dep. SAMO, South-Eastern Regional Hosp. Board, Scotland, 1967-74; Community Medicine Specialist, Lothian Health Board, 1974-80. *Recreations:* golf, shooting, fishing, first aid. *Address:* The Saughs, Gullane, East Lothian EH31 2AL. *T:* Gullane 842179.

BROUGH, Edward; Chairman, Volker Stevin (UK) Ltd, 1980-82; *b* 28 May 1918; *s* of late Hugh and Jane Brough; *m* 1941, Peggy Jennings; two *s. Educ:* Berwick Grammar School; Edinburgh University (MA). Joined Unilever Ltd, 1938. War service, KOSB, 1939-46 (Captain). Rejoined Unilever, 1946; Commercial Dir, 1951, Man. Dir, 1954, Lever's Cattle Foods Ltd; Chairman, Crosfields (CWG) Ltd, 1957; Lever Bros & Associates Ltd: Development Dir, 1960; Marketing Dir, 1962; Chm., 1965; Hd of Unilever's Marketing Div., 1968-71; Dir of Unilever Ltd and Unilever NV, 1968-74, and Chm. of UK Cttee, 1971-74. Chm., Adriaan Volker (UK) Ltd, 1974-80. Mem., NBPI, 1967-70. FBIM 1967. *Recreations:* flyfishing, golf. *Address:* Far End, The Great Quarry, Guildford, Surrey. *T:* Guildford 504064; St John's, Chagford, Devon. *Club:* Farmers'.

BROUGH, Prof. John, MA, DLitt; FBA 1961; Professor of Sanskrit, University of Cambridge, since 1967; Fellow of St John's College; *b* 1917; *er s* of Charles and Elizabeth Brough, Maryfield, Dundee; *m* 1939, Marjorie Allan, *d* of Dr W. A. Robertson; one *d. Educ:* High School, Dundee; University of Edinburgh; St John's College, Cambridge. First Class Hons in Classics, Edinburgh, 1939; First Class in Classical Tripos, Part II, 1940; First Class in Oriental Langs Tripos, Parts I and II, 1941 and 1942; Fellow St John's College, Cambridge, 1945-48. DLitt Edinburgh, 1945. Worked in agriculture, 1940-43, and as asst in agricultural research, 1943-44. Asst Keeper, Dept of Oriental Printed Books and MSS, British Museum, 1944-46; Lecturer in Sanskrit, SOAS, Univ. of London, 1946-48; Prof. of Sanskrit in the University of London, 1948-67. *Publications:* Selections from Classical Sanskrit Literature, 1951; The Early Brahmanical System of Gotra and Pravara, 1953; The Gāndhārī Dharmapada, 1962; Poems from the Sanskrit, 1968; articles in Chambers's Encyclopædia and Encyclopædia Britannica; and in specialist journals. *Recreations:* music, gardening. *Address:* 5 Thorn Grove, Bishop's Stortford, Herts CM23 5LB. *T:* Bishop's Stortford 51407.

BROUGHAM, family name of **Baron Brougham and Vaux.**

BROUGHAM AND VAUX, 5th Baron *cr* 1860; **Michael John Brougham;** *b* 2 Aug. 1938; *s* of 4th Baron and Jean, *d* of late Brig.-Gen. G. B. S. Follett, DSO, MVO; *S* father, 1967; *m* 1st, 1963, Olivia Susan (marr. diss. 1968), *d* of Rear-Admiral Gordon Thomas Seccombe Gray; one *d*; 2nd, 1969, Catherine Gulliver (marr. diss. 1981), *d* of W. Gulliver; one *s. Educ:* Lycée Jaccard, Lausanne; Millfield School. *Heir: s* Hon. Charles William Brougham, *b* 9 Nov. 1971. *Address:* 45 Overstrand Mansions, Prince of Wales Drive, SW11.

BROUGHSHANE, 2nd Baron (UK), *cr* 1945; **Patrick Owen Alexander Davison;** *b* 18 June 1903; *er s* of 1st Baron and Beatrice Mary, *d* of Sir Owen Roberts; *S* father 1953; *m* 1929, Bettine, *d* of Sir Arthur Russell, 6th Bt; one *s. Educ:* Winchester; Magdalen College, Oxford. Barrister, Inner Temple, 1926. Served War of 1939-45: with Irish Guards, 1939-41; Assistant Secretary (Military), War Cabinet, 1942-45. Has US Legion of Merit. *Heir: s* Hon. Alexander Davison, *b* 1936. *Address:* 21 Eaton Square, SW1; 28 Fisher Street, Sandwich, Kent. *Clubs:* White's, Garrick.

BROUGHTON, family name of **Baron Fairhaven.**

BROUGHTON, Air Marshal Sir Charles, KBE 1965 (CBE 1952); CB 1961; RAF retired; Air Member for Supply and Organization, Ministry of Defence, 1966-68; *b* 27 April 1911; *s* of Charles and Florence Gertrude Broughton; *m* 1939, Sylvia Dorothy Mary Bunbury; one *d* (and one *d* decd). *Educ:* New Zealand; RAF College, Cranwell. Commissioned, 1932; India, 1933-37; Flying Instructor, 1937-40. Served War of 1939-45 in Coastal Command and Middle East (despatches four times). Flying Training Command, 1947-49; Air Ministry, 1949-51; Imperial Defence College, 1952; NATO, Washington DC, 1953-55; Far East, 1955-58; Transport Command, 1958-61; Dir-General of Organization, Air Min. (subseq. Min. of Defence), 1961-64; UK Representative in Ankara on Permanent Military Deputies Group of Central Treaty Organization (Cento), 1965-66. *Address:* c/o 52 Shrewsbury House, Cheyne Walk, SW3. *Club:* Royal Air Force.

BROUGHTON, Major Sir Evelyn Delves, 12th Bt, *cr* 1660; *b* 2 Oct. 1915; *s* of Major Sir Henry Delves Broughton, 11th Bt, and Vera Edyth Boscawen (*d* 1968); *S* father, 1942; *m* 1st, 1947, Hon. Elizabeth Florence Marion Cholmondeley (marr. diss., 1953), *er d* of 4th Baron Delamere; 2nd, 1955, Helen Mary (marr. diss. 1974), *d* of J. Shore, Wilmslow, Cheshire; three *d* (one *s* decd); 3rd, 1974, Mrs Rona Crammond. *Educ:* Eton; Trinity Coll., Cambridge. Formerly 2nd Lieut Irish Guards and Major RASC. *Heir presumptive: kinsman* David Delves Broughton, *b* 7 May 1942. *Address:* 37

Kensington Square, W8. *T:* 01-937 8883; Doddington, Nantwich, Cheshire. *Clubs:* Brooks's; Tarporley Hunt.
See also Baron Lovat.

BROUGHTON, Leonard, DL; Member, Lancashire County Council, since 1974 (Chairman and Leader, 1974-81); *b* 21 March 1924; *s* of Charles Cecil Broughton and Florence (*née* Sunman); *m* 1949, Kathleen Gibson; one *d. Educ:* Kingston-upon-Hull. Served RASC, 1942-47. Estates Manager, Bedford Borough Council, 1957; business man. Member: Blackpool County Borough Council, 1961-74 (Leader, 1968-73); Blackpool Bor. Council, 1974-79; NW Co. Boroughs' Assoc., 1968-74; NW Economic Planning Council, 1970-72; Assoc. of Co. Councils, 1973-77; Board, Central Lancs Develt Corp., 1976-. Mem. Courts, Lancaster and Salford Univs, 1974-81; Lay Mem., Greater Manch. and Lancs Rent Assessment Panel, 1971-; Vice-President: Lancs Youth Clubs Assoc., 1974-81; NW Arts Assoc., 1974-81; Blackpool Social Service Council, 1974-; Chm., Blackpool and Fylde Civilian Disabled Soc. 1964-. Freeman, Co. Borough of Blackpool, 1973. DL Lancs, 1975. *Recreations:* gardening, overseas travel. *Address:* Kingsmede, 157 Whitegate Drive, Blackpool, Lancs FY3 9ER. *Club:* Royal Over-Seas League.

BROUMAS, Nikolaos; retired General; Hon. Deputy Chief, Hellenic Armed Forces; Ambassador of Greece to the Court of St James's, 1972-74; *b* 22 Aug. 1916; *s* of Taxiarches and Kostia Broumas; *m* 1945, Claire Pendelis; two *d. Educ:* Greek Military Academy. US Infantry Coll., 1947-48; Greek Staff Coll., 1952; Greek Nat. Defence Coll., 1954. Co. Comdr, Greece, 1940-41, Western Desert, 1942-43 and Italy, 1944; Co. and Bn Comdr, Greek Guerrilla War, 1946-49; Liaison Officer, Allied Comd Far East, Korean War, 1951; Dep. Nat. Rep. to NATO Mil. Cttee, 1959-61; Dep. Chief of Greek Armed Forces, 1969-72. Kt Comdr, Orders of George I and of the Phoenix. (Greek) Gold Medal for Valour (4 times); Military Cross (twice); Medal for Distinguished Services (twice); Medal of Greek Italian War; Medal of Middle East War; UN Medal of Korean War, 1951; US Bronze Star Medal with oak leaf cluster, 1951. *Recreation:* hunting. *Address:* 5 Argyrokastrou Street, Papagos, Athens, Greece.

BROUN, Sir Lionel John Law, 12th Bt, *cr* 1686; *b* 25 April 1927; *s* of 11th Bt and Georgie, *y d* of late Henry Law, Sydney, NSW; *S* father 1962. *Heir: c* William Windsor Broun [*b* 1917; *m* 1952, D'Hrie King, NSW; two *d*]. *Address:* 89 Penshurst Street, Willoughby, NSW 2068, Australia.

BROWALDH, Tore; Grand Cross, Order of Star of the North, 1974; Kt Comdr's Cross, Order of Vasa, 1963; Vice Chairman, Svenska Handelsbanken, since 1978; Deputy Chairman, Nobel Foundation; *b* 23 Aug. 1917; *s* of Knut Ernfrid Browaldh and Ingrid Gezelius; *m* 1942, Gunnel Eva Ericson; three *s* one *d. Educ:* Stockholm Univ. (MA Politics, Economics and Law, 1941). Financial Attaché, Washington, 1943; Asst Sec., Royal Cttee of Post-War Econ. Planning, and Admin. Sec., Industrial Inst. for Econ. and Social Res., 1944-45; Sec. to Bd of Management, Svenska Handelsbanken, 1946-49; Dir of Econ., Social, Cultural and Refugee Dept, Secretariat Gen., Council of Europe, Strasbourg, 1949-51; Exec. Vice Pres., Confedn of Swedish Employers, 1951-54; Chief Gen. Man., Svenska Handelsbanken, 1955-66, Chm., 1966-78. Chairman: Svenska Cellulosa AB, 1965-; Swedish IBM, 1978-; Swedish Unilever AB, 1977-; Industrivärden, 1976-; Deputy Chairman: Beijerinvest AB, 1975-; AB Volvo, 1977-; Director: Volvo Internat. Adv. Bd, 1980-; IBM World Trade Corp., Europe/ME/Africa, New York, 1979-; Unilever Adv. Bd, Rotterdam and London, 1976-. Member: Swedish Govt's Econ. Planning Commn, 1962-73 and Res. Adv. Bd, 1966-70; Consultative Cttee, Internat. Fedn of Insts for Advanced Study, 1972-; UN Gp of Eminent Persons on Multinational Corps, 1973-74; Royal Swedish Acad. of Scis; Hudson Inst., USA; Soc. of Scientists and Members of Parlt, Sweden; Royal Swedish Acad. of Engrg Scis; Royal Acad. of Arts and Scis, Uppsala. Dr of Technol. *hc* Royal Inst. of Technol., 1967; Dr of Econs *hc* Gothenburg, 1980. St Erik's Medal, Sweden, 1961; Gold Medal for public service, Sweden, 1981. *Publications:* Management and Society, 1961; (autobiography): vol. I, The Pilgrimage of a Journeyman, 1976; vol. II, The Long Road, 1980. *Recreations:* jazz, piano, golf, chess. *Address:* (office) Svenska Handelsbanken, Kungsträdgårdsgatan 2, 103 28 Stockholm, Sweden. *T:* 46-08-22 92 20; (home) Skeppargatan 66, 114 59 Stockholm. *T:* 46-08-61 96 43. *Club:* Sällskapet (Stockholm).

BROWN; *see* Clifton-Brown.

BROWN; *see* George-Brown.

BROWN, Baron *cr* 1964 (Life Peer); **Wilfred Banks Duncan Brown,** PC 1970; MBE 1944; lately Chairman, The Glacier Metal Co. Ltd (1939-65), and Director, Associated Engineering Ltd; *b* 29 Nov. 1908; British; *m* 1939, Marjorie Hershell Skinner; three *s. Educ:* Rossall Sch. Joined The Glacier Metal Co. Ltd, 1931; Sales Manager, 1935; Director, 1936; Joint Managing Director, 1937; Managing Director and Chairman, 1939-65. A Minister of State, Board of Trade, 1965-70. Mem., Industrial Develt Adv. Bd, 1975-; Chm., Machine Tool Adv. Cttee, 1975-. Pro-Chancellor, Brunel University, 1966-80. Hon. Degrees: DTech Brunel, 1966; Doctor of Laws Illinois, 1967; DSc Cranfield, 1972. *Publications:* (with Mrs W. Raphael) Managers, Men and Morale, 1947; Exploration in Management, 1960; Piecework Abandoned, 1962; (with Elliott Jaques) Product Analysis Pricing, 1964; (with Elliott Jaques) Glacier Project Papers, 1965; Organization, 1971; The Earnings Conflict, 1973. *Recreation:* golf. *Address:* 9 Blenheim Road, NW8 0LU. *T:* 01-624 1446. *Club:* Reform.

BROWN, Alan James; HM Diplomatic Service, retired; Deputy Commissioner-General, UN Relief and Works Agency for Palestine Refugees, since 1977; *b* 28 Aug. 1921; *s* of W. Y. Brown and Mrs E. I. Brown; *m* 1966, Joy Aileen Key Stone (*née* McIntyre); one *s*, and two step *d. Educ:* Magdalene College, Cambridge (MA). Served with HM Forces, 1941-47; CRO 1948; 2nd Sec., Calcutta, 1948-50; CRO, 1951; Private Sec. to Parly Under-Secretary of State, 1951-52; 1st Secretary, Dacca, Karachi, 1952-55; CRO, 1955-57; Kuala Lumpur, 1957-62; CRO, 1962-63; Head of Information Policy Dept, 1963-64; Dep. High Comr, Nicosia, 1964; Head of Far East and Pacific Dept, CRO, 1964-66; Dep. High Comr, Malta, 1966-70; Dep High Comr, later Consul-Gen., Karachi, 1971-72; Ambassador to Togo and Benin, 1973-75; Head of Nationality and Treaty Dept, FCO, 1975-77. *Recreation:* sailing. *Address:* UNRWA HQ, Vienna International Centre, PO Box 800, Vienna 1400, Austria. *Club:* United Oxford & Cambridge University.

BROWN, Alan Thomas, CBE 1978; DL; Chief Executive, Oxfordshire County Council, since 1973; *b* 18 April 1928; *s* of Thomas Henry Brown and Lucy Lilian (*née* Betts); *m* 1962, Marie Christine East; two *d. Educ:* Wyggeston Grammar Sch., Leicester; Sidney Sussex Coll., Cambridge (Wrangler, Maths Tripos 1950, MA 1953). Fellow CIPFA, 1961. Asst, Bor. Treasurer's Dept, Wolverhampton, 1950-56; Asst Sec., IMTA, 1956-58; Dep. Co. Treas., Berks CC, 1958-61; Co. Treas., Cumberland CC, 1961-66; Town Clerk and Chief Exec., Oxford City Council, 1966-73. Mem., SE Econ. Planning Council, 1975-79. DL Oxon 1978. *Recreations:* chess, horticulture, music, reading. *Address:* 7 Field House Drive, Oxford OX2 7NT. *T:* Oxford 55809.

BROWN, Alan Winthrop; Chief Executive, Training Services Division, Manpower Services Commission, since 1979; *b* 14 March 1934; *s* of James Brown and Evelyn V. Brown (*née* Winthrop); *m* 1959, Rut Berit (*née* Ohlson); two *s* one *d. Educ:* Bedford Sch.; Pembroke Coll., Cambridge (BA Hons); Cornell Univ., NY (MSc). Joined Min. of Labour, 1959; Private Sec. to Minister, 1961-62; Principal, 1963; Asst Sec., 1969. Dir of Planning, Employment Service Agency, 1973-74; Under-Sec. and Head of Incomes Div., DoE, 1975; Chief Exec., Employment Service Div., Manpower Services Commn, 1976-79. *Publications:* papers on occupational psychology and industrial training. *Recreations:* orienteering, tennis, squash, gardening. *Address:* Groton, Ballfield Road, Godalming, Surrey GU7 2HE.

BROWN, (Albert) Peter (Graeme); Consultant in Press and Public Relations to the Imperial Cancer Research Fund, since 1978; Press Officer to Royal Commission on National Health Service, 1979; *b* 5 April 1913; *s* of William Edward Graeme Brown, accountant, and Amy Powell Brown; unmarried. *Educ:* Queen Elizabeth's Sch., Darlington. Reporter, Sub-Editor, Dep.-Chief Sub-Editor, Westminster Press, 1932-40. Served War of 1939-45: Royal Navy, Officer, Western Approaches; Normandy; Far East; destroyers and assault ships. Information Divs, Ministries of Health, Local Govt and Planning, also Housing and Local Govt, 1946; Chief Press and Inf. Officer, Min. of Housing and Local Govt, 1958; Dir of Information, DHSS, and Advr to Sec. of State for Social Services, 1968-77. *Recreations:* cricket, opera (Mem. Friends of Covent Garden), classical music. *Address:* 107 Hamilton Terrace, St John's Wood, NW8. *T:* 01-286 9192. *Club:* MCC.

BROWN, Alexander Cosens Lindsay, CB 1980; Chief Veterinary Officer, Ministry of Agriculture, Fisheries and Food, 1973-80; *b* Glasgow, 30 Jan. 1920; *s* of William Tait Brown and Margaret Rae; *m* 1945, Mary McDougal Hutchison; two *s. Educ:* Hutchesons' Grammar Sch., Glasgow; Glasgow Veterinary Coll. Diploma of RCVS; FRCVS 1980. Ministry of Agriculture, Fisheries and Food: appointed Vet. Officer to Dorset, 1943; Divisional Vet. Officer, HQ Tolworth, 1955; Divisional Vet. Officer, Essex, 1958-62; Dep. Regional Vet. Officer, W Midland Region, Wolverhampton, 1962-63; Regional Vet. Officer, Eastern Region, Cambridge, 1963; HQ Tolworth, 1967; Dep. Dir, Veterinary Field Services, 1969-70, Dir, 1970-73. Mem. ARC, 1975-80. *Publications:* contribs to Jl of Royal Soc. of Medicine, Veterinary Record, State Veterinary Jl. *Recreations:* gardening, swimming, reading. *Address:* 8 Keswick Road, Bookham, Leatherhead, Surrey KT22 9HH. *T:* Bookham 57997.

BROWN, Alexander Douglas G.; *see* Gordon-Brown.

BROWN, Sir Allen (Stanley), Kt 1956; CBE 1953; MA; LLM; Australian Commissioner for British Phosphate Commissioners and Christmas Island Phosphate Commission, 1970-76; *b* 3 July 1911; *m* 1936, Hilda May Wilke; one *s* two *d.* Dir-Gen. of Post-War Reconstruction, 1948. Sec., PM's Dept and Sec. to Cabinet, Commonwealth Govt, 1949-58; Deputy Australian High Commissioner to UK, 1959-65; Australian Ambassador to Japan, 1965-70. *Address:* 3 Devorgilla Avenue, Toorak, Victoria 3142, Australia. *Club:* Melbourne (Melbourne).

BROWN, Gen. Arnold, OC 1982; International Leader, and General, Salvation Army, 1977-81; *b* 13 Dec. 1913; *s* of Arnold Rees Brown and Annie Brown; *m* 1939, Jean Catherine Barclay; two *d. Educ:* Belleville Collegiate, Canada. Commnd Salvation Army Officer, 1935; Editor, Canadian War Cry, 1937-47; Nat. Publicity Officer, Canada, 1947-62; Nat. Youth Officer, Canada, 1962-64; Head of Internat. Public Relations, Internat. HQ, London, 1964-69; Chief of Staff, 1969-74; Territorial Comdr, Canada and Bermuda, 1974-77. Freeman, City of London, 1978. Hon. LHD Asbury Coll., USA,

1972; Hon. DD Olivet Coll., USA, 1981. *Publication:* What Hath God Wrought?, 1952. *Recreations:* reading, writing, music. *Address:* 117 Bannatyne Drive, Willowdale, Ontario M2L 2P5, Canada. *Club:* Rotary of London and Toronto.

BROWN, Rt. Rev. Arthur Durrant; a Suffragan Bishop of Toronto, since 1981; *b* 7 March 1926; *s* of Edward S. Brown and Laura A. Durrant; *m* 1949, Norma Inez Rafuse; three *d. Educ:* Univ. of Western Ontario (BA); Huron College (LTh). Ordained deacon, 1949; priest, 1950, Huron. Rector: of Paisley with Cargill and Pinkerton, 1949-51; of St Stephen, London, Ont., 1951-55, with Glanworth, 1951-53; of St John, Sandwich, Windsor, Ont., 1955-64; of St Michael and All Angels, Toronto, 1964-81; Canon of Toronto, 1972-74; Archdeacon of York, Toronto, 1974-81. Member: Judicial Council of Ontario, 1978-; Multi-Cultural Council of Ontario, 1979-81. Columnist, Toronto Sun. City of Toronto Citizens Award, 1981. Hon. DD: Huron Coll., 1979; Wycliffe Coll., 1981. *Address:* Bishop's Room, Aurora Conference Centre, RR2, Aurora, Ontario L4G 3G8, Canada. *T:* (416) 773-6036.

BROWN, Arthur Godfrey Kilner, MA; Headmaster, Worcester Royal Grammar School, 1950-78; *b* 21 Feb. 1915; *s* of Rev. Arthur E. Brown, CIE, MA, BSc, and Mrs E. G. Brown, MA, formerly of Bankura, India; *m* 1939, Mary Denholm Armstrong; one *s* three *d. Educ:* Warwick Sch.; Peterhouse, Cambridge. BA Cantab 1938; MA 1950. Assistant Master, Bedford School, 1938-39; King's School, Rochester, 1939-43; Cheltenham College, 1943-50. Elected to Headmasters' Conference, 1950. Chm. Council, Evendine Court, Malvern, 1968-; Chm. of Directors, Swan Theatre, Worcester, 1978-; Pres., Worcester Br., Historical Assoc., 1951-. *Recreations:* athletics (Gold and Silver Medallist, Olympic Games, 1936); music, gardening, house restoration, drama. *Address:* Hopecroft, 34 The Village, Clifton-upon-Teme, Worcester. *Clubs:* Achilles; Hawks (Cambridge); Probus (Worcester West).

See also Hon. Sir R. K. Brown.

BROWN, A(rthur) I(vor) Parry, FFARCS; Anæsthetist: London Hospital, 1936-73; London Chest Hospital, 1946-73; Harefield Hospital, 1940-73; Royal Masonic Hospital, 1950-73; retired; *b* 23 July 1908; *s* of A. T. J. Brown; *m* Joyce Marion Bash. *Educ:* Tollington Sch., London; London Hospital. MRCS, LRCP, 1931; MB, BS London, 1933; DA, 1935; FFARCS, 1951. Member of the Board of the Faculty of Anæsthetists, RCS; Pres., Sect. of Anæsthetics, RSM, 1972-73; Fellow, Assoc. of Anæsthetists; Member, Thoracic Soc. *Publications:* chapter in Diseases of the Chest, 1952; contributions to: Thorax, Anæsthesia. *Address:* Long Thatch, Church Lane, Balsham, Cambridge. *T:* Cambridge 893012.

BROWN, Sir (Arthur James) Stephen, KBE 1967; CEng, MIMechE; Chairman, Molins Ltd, 1971-78; Director, Porvair Ltd, since 1971; Chairman, Stone-Platt Industries Ltd, 1968-73 (Deputy Chairman, 1965-67); Deputy Chairman, Chloride Group, 1965-73; *b* 15 Feb. 1906; *s* of Arthur Mogg Brown, and Ada Kelk (*née* Upton); *m* 1935, Margaret Alexandra McArthur; one *s* one *d. Educ:* Taunton School; Bristol University (BSc(Eng.)). Apprenticed British Thomson-Houston Co. Ltd, 1928-32; joined J. Stone & Co. Ltd, 1932, Dir, 1945; Man. Dir J. Stone & Co. (Deptford) Ltd (on formation), 1951; Divisional Dir, Stone-Platt Industries Ltd (on formation), 1958; Dir, Fairey Co., 1971-76. Pres., Engineering Employers' Fedn, 1964-65; Pres., Confedn of British Industry, 1966-68, Vice-Pres., 1969-; Founder Mem., Export Council for Europe, 1960 (Dep. Chm. 1962-63); Mem., NEDC, 1966-71. Hon. DSc, Aston Univ., 1967. *Recreations:* shooting, fishing, golf. *Address:* Cut Hedges, Bolney, Sussex. *T:* Bolney 225.

BROWN, Prof. Arthur Joseph, CBE 1974; FBA 1972; Professor of Economics, University of Leeds, 1947-79, now Emeritus; Pro-Vice-Chancellor, Leeds University, 1975-77; *b* 8 Aug. 1914; *s* of J. Brown, Alderley Edge, Cheshire; *m* 1938, Joan H. M., *d* of Rev. Canon B. E. Taylor, Holy Trinity, Walton Breck, Liverpool; two *s* (and one *s* decd). *Educ:* Bradford Grammar School; Queen's College, Oxford. First Class Hons in Philosophy, Politics and Economics, 1936. Fellow of All Souls College, Oxford, 1937-46; Lectr in Economics, Hertford College, Oxford, 1937-40; on staff of: Foreign Research and Press Service, 1940-43; Foreign Office Research Dept, 1943-45; Economic Section, Offices of the Cabinet, 1945-47. Head of Dept of Economics and Commerce, University of Leeds, 1947-65. Visiting Professor of Economics, Columbia University, City of New York, Jan.-June 1950. President Section F, British Assoc. for the Advancement of Science, 1958; Member: East African Economic and Fiscal Commn, 1960; UN Consultative Group on Economic and Social Consequences of Disarmament, 1961-62; First Secretary of State's Advisory Group on Central Africa, 1962; Hunt Cttee on Intermediate Areas, 1967-69; UGC, 1969-78 (Vice-Chm., 1977-78). Pres., Royal Economic Soc., 1976-78, Vice-Pres., 1978-. Chairman, Adv. Panel on Student Maintenance Grants, 1967-68. Vis. Prof. ANU, 1963; directing Regional Economics project, National Institute of Economic and Social Research, 1966-72. Hon. DLitt: Bradford, 1975; Kent, 1979; Hon. LLD Aberdeen, 1978; Hon. LittD Sheffield, 1979. *Publications:* Industrialisation and Trade, 1943; Applied Economics-Aspects of the World Economy in War and Peace, 1948; The Great Inflation, 1939-51, 1955; Introduction to the World Economy, 1959; The Framework of Regional Economics in the United Kingdom, 1972; (with E. M. Burrows) Regional Economic Problems, 1977; articles in various journals. *Recreations:* gardening and walking. *Address:* 24 Moor Drive, Leeds LS6 4BY. *T:* Leeds 755799. *Club:* Athenæum.

BROWN, Brig. Athol Earle McDonald, CMG 1964; OBE 1956; *b* 2 Jan. 1905; *s* of W. J. C. G. and Alice Catherine Brown, Armidale, NSW; *m* 1929, Millicent Alice Heesh, Sydney; two *s* one *d. Educ:* The Armidale Sch., NSW; Royal Australian Naval Coll.; Sydney Univ. Served War of 1939-45: Royal Australian Artillery, AIF, Middle East and New Guinea; Director, War Graves Services, AIF, 1944-46; Lt-Col, 1944; Brigadier, 1946. Secretary-General: Imperial War Graves Commn, 1946-60; Commonwealth-Japanese Jt Cttee, 1956-69; Dir and Sec.-Gen., Commonwealth War Graves Commn, Pacific Region, 1960-69. *Recreations:* golf, bowls, motoring. *Address:* 351 Belmore Road, North Balwyn, Victoria 3104, Australia. *T:* 857 7544. *Club:* Royal Automobile of Victoria, Masonic (Melbourne).

BROWN, Dame Beryl P.; *see* Paston Brown.

BROWN, Bruce Macdonald; Deputy High Commissioner for New Zealand, in London, since 1981; *b* 1930; *s* of John Albert Brown and Caroline Dorothea Brown (*née* Jorgenson); *m* 1953, Edith Irene (*née* Raynor); two *s* one *d. Educ:* Victoria University of Wellington (MA Hons). Private Secretary to Prime Minister, 1957-59; Second Sec., Kuala Lumpur, 1960-62; First Sec. (later Counsellor), New Zealand Mission to UN, New York, 1963-67; Head of Administration, Min. of Foreign Affairs, Wellington, 1967-68; Director, NZ Inst. of International Affairs, 1969-71; NZ Dep. High Commissioner, Canberra, 1972-75; Ambassador to Iran, 1975-78, and Pakistan, 1976-78; Asst Sec., Min. of Foreign Affairs, 1978-81. *Publications:* The Rise of New Zealand Labour, 1962; ed, Asia and the Pacific in the 1970s, 1971. *Recreations:* reading, golf. *Address:* c/o New Zealand High Commission, Haymarket, SW1. *T:* 01-930 8422. *Club:* Reform.

BROWN, Carter; *see* Brown, John C.

BROWN, Lt-Col Sir Charles Frederick Richmond, 4th Bt, *cr* 1863; TD; DL; *b* 6 Dec. 1902; *er s* of Frederick Richmond Brown (*d* 1933; 2nd *s* of 2nd Bt); *S* uncle, 1944; *m* 1st, 1933, Audrey (marr. diss., 1948), 2nd *d* of late Col Hon. Everard Baring, CVO, CBE, and late Lady Ulrica Baring; one *s* two *d* ; 2nd, 1951, Hon. Gwendolen Carlis Meysey-Thomson (marr. diss. 1969), *y d* of 1st (and last) Baron Knaresborough; 3rd, 1969, Pauline, widow of Edward Hildyard, Middleton Hall, Pickering, Yorks. *Educ:* Eton. Joined Welsh Guards, 1921; Captain 1932; retired with a gratuity, 1936; joined 5th Bn Green Howards, Territorial Army, as a Major, March 1939; Lieut-Colonel comdg 7th Bn Green Howards, July 1939, and proceeded to France with 7th Bn, April 1940. DL, North Riding of County of York, 1962. *Heir:* s George Francis Richmond Brown, *b* 3 Feb. 1938. *Address:* Stonely Woods, Fadmoor, York. *T:* Kirby Moorside 31293. *Clubs:* Cavalry and Guards, Pratt's; Yorkshire (York).

BROWN, Sir (Charles) James Officer, Kt 1969; Consultant Thoracic Surgeon: Alfred Hosp.; St Vincent's Hosp.; Queen Victoria Memorial Hosp.; Austin Hosp. (all in Melbourne); *b* 24 Sept. 1897; *s* of David Brown; *m* 1932, Esme Mai Frankenberg; two *d. Educ:* Scotch Coll., Melbourne; Melbourne Univ. MB BS 1920, MD 1922, FRCS 1924, FRACS 1928. Surgeon, Alfred Hosp., 1929-57; Surgeon, Austin Hosp., 1926-67. Mem. Council, Royal Australian Coll. of Surgeons, 1956-68; Pres., National Heart Foundation (Victorian Division), 1966-72. *Publications:* papers in surgical journals. *Recreation:* golf. *Address:* 2/1 Monaro Road, Kooyong, Victoria 3144, Australia. *T:* (03) 2097944. *Clubs:* Melbourne, Royal Melbourne Golf (Melbourne); Victoria Racing.

BROWN, Admiral Charles Randall, Bronze Star 1943; Legion of Merit 1944; Presidential Unit Citation, 1945; DSM 1960; United States Navy, retired, 1962; *b* Tuscaloosa, Alabama, USA, 13 Dec. 1899; *s* of Robison Brown and Stella Seed Brown; *m* 1921, Eleanor Green, Annapolis, Maryland; two *s. Educ:* US Naval Academy; US Air University; US Naval War College. Graduated from US Naval Academy, 1921. During War served on original US Joint Chiefs of Staff and US-British Combined Chiefs of Staff organisations; later, Captain of USS Kalinin Bay and USS Hornet and Chief of Staff of a Fast Carrier Task Force. Commander, US Sixth Fleet, Mediterranean, 1956; C-in-C, Allied Forces Southern Europe, 1959-61. Vice-President for European Affairs, McDonnell Aircraft Corp. of St Louis, Mo, 1962-65. *Recreation:* gardening. *Address:* 4000 Massachusetts Avenue NW, Apartment 1428, Washington, DC 20016, USA. *Clubs:* Army and Navy, Army and Navy Country (Washington, DC); The Brook, New York Yacht (NY).

BROWN, Rev. Cyril James, OBE 1956; Rector of Warbleton, 1970-77; Chaplain to the Queen, 1956-74; *b* 12 Jan. 1904; *s* of late James Brown, Clifton, Bristol; *m* 1931, Myrtle Aufrère, *d* of late Mark Montague Ford, London; no *c. Educ:* Westminster Abbey Choir School; Clifton College; Keble College, Oxford; St Stephen's House, Oxford. Curate of St Gabriel's, Warwick Square, 1927-31; Chaplain, Missions to Seamen, Singapore, 1931-34, Hong Kong, 1934-41; Chaplain, Hong Kong RNVR, 1941-46; Youth Secretary, Missions to Seamen, 1946-47, Superintendent, 1947-51, General Superintendent, 1951-59, General Secretary, 1959-69; Prebendary of St Paul's, 1958-69. *Publications:* contributions to East and West Review, World Dominion, etc. *Recreation:* choral music. *Address:* 16 Merlynn, Devonshire Place, Eastbourne, Sussex. *Club:* Devonshire (Eastbourne).

BROWN, Sir (Cyril) Maxwell Palmer, (Sir Max), KCB 1969 (CB 1965); CMG 1957; Director: Ransome Hoffmann Pollard Ltd; ERA Technology

Ltd; *b* 30 June 1914; *s* of late Cyril Palmer Brown; *m* 1940, Margaret May Gillhespy; three *s* one *d. Educ:* Wanganui College; Victoria University College, NZ; Clare College, Cambridge. Princ. Private Secretary to Pres. Board of Trade, 1946-49; Monopolies Commn, 1951-55; Counsellor (Commercial) Washington, 1955-57; returned to Board of Trade Second Permanent Sec., 1968-70; Sec. (Trade), DTI, 1970-74; Permanent Sec., Dept of Trade, March-June 1974. Mem., 1975-81, Dep. Chm., 1976-81, Monopolies and Mergers Commn. Dir, John Brown & Co., 1975-82. *Address:* 20 Cottenham Park Road, Wimbledon, SW20. *T:* 01-946 7237.

BROWN, Dr Daniel McGillivray, BSc, PhD, ScD; FRS 1982; FRSC; Reader in Organic Chemistry, Cambridge University, since 1967; Fellow of King's College, Cambridge, since 1953; *b* 3 Feb. 1923; *s* of David Cunninghame Brown and Catherine Stewart (*née* McGillivray); *m* 1953, Margaret Joyce Herbert; one *s* three *d. Educ:* Glasgow Acad.; Glasgow Univ. (BSc); London Univ. (PhD); Cambridge Univ. (PhD, ScD). Res. Chemist, Chester Beatty Res. Inst., 1945-53; Asst Dir of Res., 1953-58, Lectr, 1959-67, Cambridge Univ.; Vice-Provost, King's Coll., Cambridge, 1974-81. Vis. Professor: Univ. of Calif, LA, 1959-60; Brandeis Univ., 1966-67. *Publications:* scientific papers, mainly in chemical jls. *Recreations:* modern art, gardening, spasmodic fly-fishing. *Address:* 226 Hills Road, Cambridge CB2 2QE. *T:* Cambridge 245304.

BROWN, Sir David, Kt 1968; Chairman, David Brown Holdings Ltd, and Vosper Ltd, until going to live abroad in 1978; *b* 10 May 1904; *s* of Francis Edwin (Frank) and Caroline Brown; *m* 1st, 1926, Daisie Muriel Firth (marr. diss. 1955); one *s* one *d* ; 2nd, 1955, Marjorie Deans (marr. diss. 1980); 3rd, 1980, Paula Benton Stone. *Educ:* Rossall School; Private Tutor in Engineering; Huddersfield Technical Coll.; FIMechE; AFRAeS. David Brown and Sons (Hudd.), Ltd, 1921; Dir, 1929; Man. Dir, 1932. Founded David Brown Tractors Ltd (first company to manufacture an all-British tractor in England), 1935; formed, 1951, The David Brown Corp. Ltd (Chm.), embracing gears, machine tools, castings, etc. Pres., Vosper Ltd, and Chm., Vosper Private Ltd, Singapore, 1978–; Director: David Brown Corp. of Australia Ltd, 1965–; David Brown Gear Industries Pty Ltd (Australia), 1963–; David Brown Gear Industries (Pty) Ltd (South Africa), 1969–. Underwriting Member of Lloyd's; Past Member: Board of Governors of Huddersfield Royal Infirmary; Council of Huddersfield Chamber of Commerce. First Englishman to open Canadian Farm and Industrial Equipment Trade Show, Toronto, 1959; inaugurated Chief Flying Sun of Iroquois Tribe of Mohawk Nation, Toronto, 1959. Hon. Dato SPMJ (Johore), 1979. *Address:* L'Estoril, 31 Avenue Princesse Grace, Monte Carlo, Monaco.

BROWN, Prof. David Anthony, PhD; Wellcome Professor of Pharmacology, School of Pharmacy, University of London, since 1979; *b* 10 Feb. 1936; *s* of Alfred William and Florence Brown; two *s* one *d. Educ:* Univ. of London (BSc, BSc, PhD). Asst Lectr 1961-65, Lectr 1965-73, Dept of Pharmacology, St Bart's Hosp. Med. Coll.; Dept of Pharmacology, School of Pharmacy, Univ. of London: Sen. Lectr, 1973-74; Reader, 1974-77; Professor, 1977-79. Visiting Professor: Univ. of Chicago, 1970; Univ. of Iowa, 1971, 1973; Univ. of Texas, 1979, 1980; Vis. Scientist, Armed Forces Radiobiology Res. Inst., Bethesda, Md, 1976. Member: Physiological Soc., 1970; British Pharmacological Soc., 1965–; Biochemical Soc., 1969–. *Publications:* contribs to Jl of Physiology, British Jl of Pharmacology. *Recreation:* relaxing. *Address:* 39 Grand Avenue, N10 3BS.

BROWN, David John Bowes, CBE 1982; FSIAD; Managing Director, DJB Engineering Ltd and Archer Components Ltd, since 1973; *b* 2 Aug. 1925; *s* of Matthew and Helene Brown; *m* 1954, Patricia Robson; two *s* two *d. Educ:* King James Grammar Sch., Knaresborough; Leeds College of Technology. Logging Contractor, UK and W Africa, 1946-60; joined Hunslet Engine Co. as Designer/Draftsman, 1960-62; designed and patented transmission and exhaust gas conditioning systems for underground mines tractors; joined Chaseside as Chief Designer, 1962-65; designed and patented 4 wheel drive loading shovels; became Director and Chief Executive of company; joined Muir-Hill Ltd as Man. Dir, 1965-73; designed and patented 4 wheel drive tractors, cranes, steering systems, transmissions, axles; started DJB Engineering Ltd, 1973; designed, manufactured and sold a range of articulated dump trucks in Peterlee, Co. Durham. The company has gained 3 Queen's Awards and 1 Design Council Award. *Address:* (home) The Abbey, Abbey Road, Knaresborough, North Yorks. *T:* Harrogate 863148; DJB Engineering Ltd, Peterlee, Co Durham SR8 2HX. *T:* Peterlee 863333.

BROWN, Vice-Adm. David Worthington; Flag Officer Plymouth, Port Admiral Devonport, Commander Central Sub Area Eastern Atlantic, Commander Plymouth Sub Area Channel, since 1982; *b* 28 Nov. 1927; *s* of Captain and Mrs J. R. S. Brown; *m* 1958, Etienne Hester Boileau; three *d. Educ:* HMS Conway. Joined RN, 1945; commanded HM Ships MGB 5036, MTB 5020, Dalswinton, Chailey, Cavendish, Falmouth, Hermione, Bristol; Dir, Naval Ops and Trade, 1971-72; Dir of Officers Appointments (Exec.), 1976-78; Asst Chief of Defence Staff (Ops), 1980-82. Younger Brother of Trinity House. *Recreations:* sailing, fishing. *Address:* c/o Barclays Bank, 107 Commercial Road, Portsmouth, Hants. *Club:* Army and Navy.

BROWN, Denise Lebreton, (Mrs Frank Waters), RE 1959 (ARE 1941); ARWA 1980; artist; *d* of Jeanne Lebreton and Frederick Peter Brown; *m* 1938, Frank William Eric Waters; one *s. Educ:* Lyzeum Nonnenwerth im Rhein; Royal College of Art. British Instn Schol. in Engraving, 1932; ARCA 1935;

prox. acc. 1936; Rome Scholarship in Engraving; Royal College of Art Travelling Schol., 1936. Has exhibited at: Royal Academy regularly, 1937-78; Royal Society of Painter-Etchers and Engravers; also in Canada, USA and S Africa. Work represented in British, V&A, and Ashmolean Museums. *Publications:* books illustrated include: several on gardening; children's books, etc. *Recreations:* music, gardening. *Address:* 21 Wolds End, Chipping Campden, Glos.

BROWN, Denys Downing, CMG 1966; MM 1945; HM Diplomatic Service, retired; *b* 16 Dec. 1918; *s* of A. W. Brown, Belfast, and Marjorie Downing; *m* 1954, Patricia Marjorie, *e d* of Sir Charles Bartley; one *s* one *d. Educ:* Hereford Cathedral School; Brasenose College, Oxford (Scholar). Oxf. and Bucks LI, 1939-45 (prisoner-of-war, 1940; escaped, 1945). Entered Foreign Service, 1946; served in Poland, Germany, Egypt, Yugoslavia, Sweden, and FO; Minister (Economic), Bonn, retired 1971; Dir, P&O Steam Navigation Co., 1971-80. *Recreations:* reading, travel. *Address:* Beechcroft, Priorsfield Road, Godalming, Surrey. *T:* Godalming 6635.

BROWN, Sir Derrick H.; *see* Holden-Brown.

BROWN, Douglas Dunlop, QC 1976; **His Honour Judge Brown;** a Circuit Judge, since 1980; *b* 22 Dec. 1931; *s* of late Robert Dunlop Brown, MICE, and of Anne Cameron Brown; *m* 1960, June Margaret Elizabeth McNamara; one *s.* Ryleys Sch., Alderley Edge; Manchester Grammar Sch.; Manchester Univ. (LLB). Served in RN, 1953-55; Lieut, RNR. Called to Bar, Gray's Inn, 1953; practised Northern Circuit from 1955; Mem. General Council of Bar, 1967-71; Asst Recorder, Salford City QS, 1971; a Recorder of the Crown Court, 1972-80. *Recreations:* cricket, golf, music. *Address:* Byeways, Moss Road, Alderley Edge, Cheshire. *T:* Alderley Edge 582027. *Club:* Wilmslow Golf.

BROWN, Douglas James, MBE 1959; HM Diplomatic Service, retired; Secretary to the Medical College, St Bartholomew's Hospital; *b* 6 May 1925; *s* of James Stephen Brown and Hilda May (*née* Hinch); unmarried. *Educ:* Edinburgh Univ. (MA). HMOCS, Nigeria, 1951-62 (Private Sec. to Governor-General, 1955-58); joined Diplomatic Service, 1962; Private Sec. to Comr-Gen. for SE Asia, 1962-63; FO, 1963-66; Asst to Special Representative in Africa, 1966-67; British High Commn, Nairobi, 1967-68; British Embassy, Djakarta, 1968-71; Inspector, FCO, 1971-73; Counsellor and Consul-Gen., Algiers, 1974-77; Consul-Gen., St Louis, 1977-80, retired. *Address:* 9 Amherst Avenue, Ealing, W13 8NQ. *T:* 01-997 7125; Via Privata Oliveta 41/18, 16035 Rapallo, Italy. *Club:* Royal Over-Seas League.

BROWN, Edmund Gerald, Jr, (Jerry Brown); lawyer and politician; Governor of California, 1975-83; Democratic Candidate for US Senator from California, 1982;*b* 7 April 1938; *s* of Edmund Gerald Brown and Bernice (*née* Layne). *Educ:* Univ. of California at Berkeley (BA 1961); Yale Law School (JD 1964). Admitted to Californian Bar, 1965; Research Attorney, Calif. Supreme Court, 1964-65; with Tuttle & Taylor, LA, 1966-69; Sec. of State, Calif., 1971-74. *Address:* c/o Governor's Office, State Capital, Sacramento, Calif 95814, USA.

BROWN, Sir Edward (Joseph), Kt 1961; MBE 1958; JP; Laboratory Technician (non-ferrous metals); company director; *b* 15 April 1913; *s* of Edward Brown; *m* 1940, Rosa, *d* of Samuel Feldman; one *s* one *d. Educ:* Greencoat Elementary; Morley College (Day Continuation). Leading Aircraftsman, RAF, 1942-46. Formerly Mem. Assoc. Supervisory Staffs Executives and Technicians (Chm., Enfield Branch, 1953-63); Dist Councillor for Union. Member Tottenham Borough Council, 1956-64. Chm., National Union of Conservative and Unionist Associations, 1959, 1960; Chm. Conservative Party Conference, 1960; former Vice-Chm., Assoc. of Conservative Clubs. Contested Stalybridge and Hyde (C), 1959; MP (C) Bath, 1964-79. JP (Middlesex) 1963. *Recreation:* campanology. *Address:* 71 Holly Walk, Enfield, Middlesex. *T:* 01-363 3450. *Clubs:* Tottenham Conservative; Harringay-West Green Constitutional.

BROWN, Edwin Percy, CBE 1981; Director of Social Services, North Yorkshire County Council, 1974-82; *b* 20 May 1917; *s* of late James Percy Brown and of Hetty Brown; *m* 1958, Margaret (*née* Askey); one *s* one *d. Educ:* Mundella Grammar Sch., Nottingham; Nottingham Univ. (Certif. in Social Studies). Social worker, Nottinghamshire CC, 1951-54; Sen. social worker, Lancashire CC, 1954-59; Children's Officer: Southampton CC, 1959-65; Wiltshire CC, 1965-71; Dir of Social Services, N Riding CC, 1971-74. Mem., Supplementary Benefits Commn, 1976-80. Adviser to Assoc. of County Councils, 1974-81; Pres., Assoc. of Directors of Social Services, 1977-78. *Recreations:* boating, gardening, cricket. *Address:* 21 The Green, Romanby, Northallerton, N Yorkshire.

BROWN, Prof. Eric Herbert, PhD; Professor of Geography, University College London, since 1966; *b* 8 Dec. 1922; *s* of Samuel Brown and Ada Brown, Melton Mowbray, Leics; *m* 1945, Eileen (*née* Reynolds), Llanhowell, Dyfed; two *d. Educ:* King Edward VII Grammar Sch., Melton Mowbray; King's Coll., London (BSc 1st Cl. Hons). MSc Wales, PhD London. Served War: RAF Pilot, Coastal Comd, 1941-45. Asst Lectr, then Lectr in Geography, University Coll. of Wales, Aberystwyth, 1947-49; Lectr, then Reader in Geog., UCL, 1950-66; Dean of Students, 1972-75. Vis. Lectr, Indiana Univ., USA, 1953-54; Vis. Prof., Monash Univ., Melbourne, 1971. Mem., NERC, 1981-. Geographical Adviser, Govt of Argentina, 1965-68;

Hon. Mem., Geograph. Soc. of Argentina, 1968. Chm., British Geomorphol Res. Group, 1971-72; Hon. Sec., RGS, 1977- (Back Grant, 1961); Pres., Inst. of British Geographers, 1978. *Publications:* The Relief and Drainage of Wales, 1961; (with W. R. Mead) The USA and Canada, 1962; (ed) Geography Yesterday and Tomorrow, 1980; contrib. Geog. Jl, Phil. Trans Royal Soc., Proc. Geologists' Assoc., Trans Inst. of British Geographers, and Geography. *Recreations:* Rugby football, wine. *Address:* Monterey, Castle Hill, Berkhamsted, Herts HP4 1HE. *T:* Berkhamsted 4077. *Clubs:* Athenæum, Geographical.

BROWN, Captain Eric Melrose, CBE 1970 (OBE 1945; MBE 1944); DSC 1942; AFC 1947; RN; Chief Executive, British Helicopter Advisory Board, since 1970; *b* 21 Jan. 1919; *s* of Robert John Brown and Euphemia (*née* Melrose); *m* 1942, Evelyn Jean Margaret Macrory; one *s. Educ:* Royal High Sch., Edinburgh; Edinburgh University. MA 1947. Joined Fleet Air Arm as Pilot, 1939; Chief Naval Test Pilot, 1944-49; Resident British Test Pilot at USN Air Test Center, Patuxent River, 1951-52; CO No 804 Sqdn, 1953-54; Comdr (Air), RN Air Stn, Brawdy, 1954-56; Head of British Naval Air Mission to Germany, 1958-60; Dep. Dir (Air), Gunnery Div., Admty, 1961; Dep. Dir, Naval Air Warfare and Adviser on Aircraft Accidents, Admty, 1962-64; Naval Attaché, Bonn, 1965-67; CO, RN Air Stn, Lossiemouth, 1967-70. FRAeS 1964 (Pres., 1982-83; Chm., RAeS Rotocraft Sect., 1973-76). Liveryman, GAPAN, 1978. British Silver Medal for Practical Achievement in Aeronautics, 1949. *Publications:* Wings on My Sleeve, 1961; (jtly) Aircraft Carriers, 1969; Wings of the Luftwaffe, 1977; Wings of the Navy, 1980; The Helicopter in Civil Operations, 1981; Wings of the Weird and the Wonderful, 1982. *Recreations:* golf, ski-ing, bridge. *Address:* Carousel, New Domewood, Copthorne, Sussex. *T:* Copthorne 712610. *Clubs:* Naval and Military; Explorers' (NY).

BROWN, Sir (Ernest) Henry Phelps, Kt 1976; MBE 1945; FBA 1960; Professor of Economics of Labour, University of London, 1947-68, now Emeritus Professor; *b* 10 Feb. 1906; *s* of E. W. Brown, Calne, Wiltshire; *m* 1932, Dorothy Evelyn Mostyn, *d* of Sir Anthony Bowlby, 1st Bt, KCB; two *s* one *d. Educ:* Taunton School; Wadham College, Oxford (Scholar). Secretary of Oxford Union, 1928; 1st Class Hons Modern History, 1927; Philosophy, Politics and Economics, 1929. Fellow of New College, Oxford, 1930-47; Hon. Fellow, Wadham College, Oxford, 1969-; Rockefeller Travelling Fellow in USA, 1930-31. Served War of 1939-45, with Royal Artillery; BEF; ADGB; First Army; Eighth Army (MBE). Member: Council on Prices, Productivity and Incomes, 1959; Nat. Economic Development Council, 1962; Royal Commn on Distribn of Income and Wealth, 1974-78. Chairman, Tavistock Inst. of Human Relations, 1966-68. Pres., Royal Economic Soc., 1970-72. Hon. DLitt Heriot-Watt, 1972; Hon. DCL Durham, 1981. *Publications:* The Framework of the Pricing System, 1936; A Course in Applied Economics, 1951; The Balloon (novel), 1953; The Growth of British Industrial Relations, 1959; The Economics of Labor, 1963; A Century of Pay, 1968; The Inequality of Pay, 1977. *Recreations:* walking; represented Oxford *v* Cambridge cross-country running, 1926. *Address:* 16 Bradmore Road, Oxford. *T:* Oxford 56320. *Club:* Athenæum.

BROWN, Dr Fred, FRS 1981; Deputy Director, since 1980, and Head of Biochemistry Department, since 1955, Animal Virus Research Institute, Pirbright, Surrey; *b* 31 Jan. 1925; *m* 1948, Audrey Alice Doherty; two *s. Educ:* Burnley Grammar Sch.; Manchester Univ. BSc 1944, MSc 1946, PhD 1948. Asst Lectr, Manchester Univ., 1946-48; Lectr, Bristol Univ. Food Preservation Res. Station, 1948-50; Senior Scientific Officer: Hannah Dairy Res. Inst., Ayr, 1950-53; Christie Hosp. and Holt Radium Inst., Manchester, 1953-55. *Publications:* papers on viruses causing animal diseases, in scientific journals. *Recreations:* cricket, Association football, listening to classical music, fell walking. *Address:* Syndal, Glaziers Lane, Normandy, Surrey GU3 2DF. *T:* Guildford 811107.

BROWN, Sir (Frederick Herbert) Stanley, Kt 1967; CBE 1959; BSc; CEng, FIMechE, FIEE; retired; Chairman, Central Electricity Generating Board, 1965-72 (Deputy-Chairman, 1959-64); *b* 9 Dec. 1910; *s* of Clement and Annie S. Brown; *m* 1937, Marjorie Nancy Brown; two *d. Educ:* King Edward's School, Birmingham; Birmingham University. Corp. of Birmingham Electric Supply Dept, 1932-46; West Midlands Joint Electricity Authority, 1946-47; Liverpool Corporation Electricity Supply Department, 1947-48; Merseyside and N. Wales Division of British Electricity Authority; Generation Engineer (Construction), 1948-49; Chief Generation Engineer (Construction), 1949-51; Deputy Generation Design Engineer of British Electricity Authority, 1951-54; Generation Design Engineer, 1954-57, Chief Engineer, 1957, of Central Electricity Authority; Member for Engineering, Central Elec. Generating Board, 1957-59. President: Instn. of Electrical Engineers, 1967-68; EEIBA, 1969-70. Member: Council, City and Guilds of London Inst., 1969-; Court of Govs, Univ. of Birmingham, 1969-. Hon. DSc: Aston, 1971; Salford, 1972. *Publications:* various papers to technical institutions. *Recreations:* gardening, motoring. *Address:* Cobbler's Hill, Compton Abdale, Glos. *T:* Withington 233.

BROWN, Hon. Geoffrey E.; *see* Ellman-Brown.

BROWN, Hon. George Arthur, CMG; Deputy Administrator, United Nations Development Programme, since 1978; *b* 25 July 1922; *s* of Samuel Austin Brown and Gertrude Brown; *m* 1964, Leila Leonie Gill; two *d* (and one *s* one *d* by previous marriage). *Educ:* St Simon's College, Jamaica; London

School of Economics. Jamaica Civil Service: Income Tax Dept, 1941; Colonial Secretary's Office. 1951; Asst Secretary, Min. of Finance, 1954; Director, General Planning Unit, 1957; Financial Secretary, 1962; Governor, Bank of Jamaica, 1967-78. *Publications:* contrib. Social and Economic Studies (University College of the West Indies). *Recreations:* hiking, boating, fishing. *Address:* c/o United Nations Development Programme, United Nations, New York, NY 10017, USA. *Clubs:* Jamaica, Kingston Cricket (Jamaica).

BROWN, George Frederick William, CMG 1974; Member, Melbourne Underground Railway Loop Authority, since 1971; *b* 12 April 1908; *s* of late G. Brown; *m* 1933, Catherine Mills; one *d* (and one *d* decd). *Educ:* Christian Brothers' Coll., Essendon; Phahran Techn. Coll.; Royal Melbourne Inst. Technology. FIE (Aust.), AMIME (Aust.), FCIT. Victorian Railways, 1923; Asst Engr 1929; Country Roads Bd, 1934; Plant Engr Newport Workshops, 1939-43; Supt Loco. Maintenance, 1943-53; Chief Mech. Engr, 1953-58; Comr, 1958-61; Dep. Chm., 1961-67; Chm., 1967-73; Mem., Victorian Railway Bd, 1973-77. Mem. Council, Royal Melb. Inst. Technology, 1958-74, Pres. 1970. *Publications:* articles in techn. jls on rail transport. *Recreation:* golf. *Address:* Unit 1, 10 Lucas Street, East Brighton, Victoria 3187, Australia. *Clubs:* Kelvin Victoria, Victoria Golf, MCC (Victoria).

BROWN, George Mackay, OBE 1974; FRSL 1977; author; *b* 17 Oct. 1921; *s* of John Brown and Mary Jane Mackay. *Educ:* Stromness Acad.; Newbattle Abbey Coll.; Edinburgh Univ. (MA). Hon. MA Open Univ., 1976; Hon. LLD Dundee, 1977. *Publications: fiction:* A Calendar of Love, 1967; A Time to Keep, 1969; Greenvoe, 1972; Magnus, 1973; Hawkfall, 1974; The Two Fiddlers, 1975; The Sun's Net, 1976; Pictures in the Cave, 1977; Six Lives of Frankle the Cat, 1980; *play:* A Spell for Green Corn, 1970; *poetry:* Fishermen with Ploughs, 1971; Winterfold, 1976; Selected Poems, 1977; *essays, etc:* An Orkney Tapestry, 1969; Letters from Hamnavoe, 1975; Under Brinkie's Brae, 1979; Portrait of Orkney, 1981. *Recreations:* ale tasting, watching television. *Address:* 3 Mayburn Court, Stromness, Orkney KW16 3DH.

BROWN, Prof. (George) Malcolm, FRS 1975; FRSE 1967; Director: Institute of Geological Sciences, since 1979; Geological Museum, since 1979; Geological Survey of Northern Ireland, since 1979; Geological Adviser to Minister of Overseas Development, since 1979; *b* 5 Oct. 1925; *s* of late George Arthur Brown and Anne Brown (*née* Fellows); *m* 1963, Valerie Jane Gale (marr. diss. 1977). *Educ:* Coatham Sch., Redcar; Durham Univ. (BSc, DSc); Oxford Univ. (MA, DPhil). RAF, 1944-47. FGS. Commonwealth Fund (Harkness) Fellow, Princeton Univ., 1954-55; Lectr in Petrology, Oxford Univ., 1955-66; Fellow, St Cross Coll., Oxford, 1965-67; Carnegie Instn Res. Fellow, Geophysical Lab., Washington DC, 1966-67; Prof. of Geology, 1967-79 (now Emeritus), Dean of Faculty of Science, 1978-79, and Pro-Vice-Chancellor, 1979, Durham Univ. NASA Principal Investigator, Apollo Moon Programme, 1967-75. Member: Natural Environment Res. Council, 1972-75; Council, Royal Soc., 1980-81. Vis. Prof., Univ. of Berne, 1977-78; UK Editor, Physics and Chemistry of the Earth, 1977-79. Daniel Pidgeon Fund Award, 1952, Wollaston Fund Award, 1963, Murchison Medal, 1981, Geol Soc. of London. *Publications:* (with L. R. Wager) Layered Igneous Rocks, 1968; (contrib.) Methods in Geochemistry, 1960; (contrib.) Basalts, 1967; (contrib.) Planet Earth, 1977; (contrib.) Origin of the Solar System, 1978; papers in several sci. jls. *Address:* Flat 5, 35 Emperor's Gate, SW7 4JA. *T:* 01-373 3615. *Club:* Athenæum.

BROWN, Dame Gillian (Gerda), DCVO 1981; CMG 1971; HM Diplomatic Service; Ambassador to Norway, since 1981; *b* 10 Aug. 1923; *er d* of late Walter Brown and late Gerda Brown (*née* Grenside). *Educ:* The Spinney, Gt Bookham; Stoatley Hall, Haslemere; Somerville Coll., Oxford (Hon. Fellow 1981). FO, 1944-52; 2nd Sec., Budapest, 1952-54; FO, 1954-59; 1st Sec., Washington, 1959-62; 1st Sec., UK Delegn to OECD, Paris, 1962-65; FO, 1965-66; Counsellor and Head of Gen. Dept, FO, subseq. Head of Aviation, Marine and Telecommunications Dept, later Marine and Transport Dept, FCO, 1967-70; Counsellor, Berne, 1970-74; Under Sec., Dept of Energy, 1975-78; Asst Under Sec. of State, FCO, 1978-80. Hon. LLD Bath, 1981. Grand Cross, Order of St Olav, 1981. *Address:* c/o Foreign and Commonwealth Office, SW1.

BROWN, Prof. Godfrey Norman; Professor of Education, University of Keele, 1967-80, now Emeritus; Director, Betley Court Gallery, since 1980; *b* 13 July 1926; *s* of Percy Charles and Margaret Elizabeth Brown; *m* 1960, Dr Freda Bowyer; three *s. Educ:* Whitgift Sch.; School of Oriental and African Studies, London; Merton Coll., Oxford (MA, DPhil). Army service, RAC and Intelligence Corps, 1944—48. Social Affairs Officer, UN Headquarters, NY, 1953-54; Sen. History Master, Barking Abbey Sch., Essex, 1954-57; Lectr in Educn, University Coll. of Ghana, 1958-61; Sen. Lectr, 1961, Prof., 1963, Univ. of Ibadan, Nigeria; Dir, Univ. of Keele Inst. of Educn, 1967-80. Visiting Prof., Univ. of Rhodesia and Nyasaland, 1963; Chm., Assoc. for Recurrent Educn, 1976-77; Mem., Exec. Cttee and Bd of Dirs, World Council for Curriculum and Instruction, 1974-77. OECD Consultant on teacher education, Portugal, 1980; Collector of the Year Award, Art and Antiques, 1981. *Publications:* An Active History of Ghana, 2 vols, 1961 and 1964; Living History, 1967; Apartheid, a Teacher's Guide, 1981; ed (with J. C. Anene) Africa in the Nineteenth and Twentieth Centuries, 1966; ed, Towards a Learning Community, 1971; ed (with M. Hiskett) Conflict and Harmony in Education in Tropical Africa, 1975; contrib. educnl jls. *Recreations:* family life; art history, conservation. *Address:* Betley Court, Betley, near Crewe, Cheshire. *T:* Crewe 820652.

BROWN, Harold, PhD; Distinguished Visiting Professor of National Security Affairs, School of Advanced International Studies, The Johns Hopkins Foreign Policy Institute, since 1981; *b* 19 Sept. 1927; *s* of A. H. Brown and Gertrude Cohen Brown; *m* 1953, Colene McDowell; two *d. Educ:* Columbia Univ. (AB 1945, AM 1946, PhD in Physics 1949). Res. Scientist, Columbia Univ., 1945-50, Lectr in Physics, 1947-48; Lectr in Physics, Stevens Inst. of Technol., 1949-50; Res. Scientist, Radiation Lab., Univ. of Calif, Berkeley, 1951-52; Gp Leader, Radiation Lab., Livermore, 1952-61; Dir, Def. Res. and Engrg, Dept of Def., 1961-65; Sec. of Air Force, 1965-69; Pres., Calif Inst. of Technol., Pasadena, 1969-77; Sec. of Defense, USA, 1977-81. Sen. Sci. Adviser, Conf. on Discontinuance of Nuclear Tests, 1958-59; Delegate, Strategic Arms Limitations Talks, Helsinki, Vienna and Geneva, 1969-77. Member: Polaris Steering Cttee, 1956-58; Air Force Sci. Adv. Bd, 1956-61; (also Consultant) President's Sci. Adv. Cttee, 1958-61. Hon. DEng Stevens Inst. of Technol., 1964; Hon. LLD: Long Island Univ., 1966; Gettysburg Coll., 1967; Occidental Coll., 1969; Univ. of Calif, 1969; Hon. ScD: Univ. of Rochester, 1975; Brown Univ., 1977; Univ. of the Pacific, 1978; Univ. of S Carolina, 1979. Member: Amer. Phys. Soc., 1946; Nat. Acad. of Engrg, 1967; Amer. Acad. of Arts and Scis, 1969; Nat. Acad. of Scis, 1977. One of Ten Outstanding Young Men of Year, US Jun. Chamber of Commerce, 1961; Columbia Univ. Medal of Excellence, 1963; Air Force Exceptl Civil. Service Award, 1969; Dept of Def. Award for Exceptionally Meritorious Service, 1969; Joseph C. Wilson Award, 1976; Presidential Medal of Freedom, 1981. Grand Cross, First Class, Order of Merit of Federal Republic of Germany, 1980. *Address:* School of Advanced International Studies, The Johns Hopkins Foreign Policy Institute, 1740 Massachusetts Avenue, NW, Washington, DC 20036, USA. *Clubs:* Bohemian (San Francisco); California (Los Angeles); City Tavern (Washington, DC).

BROWN, Harold Arthur Neville, CMG 1963; CVO 1961; HM Diplomatic Service, retired; *b* 13 Dec. 1914; *s* of Stanley Raymond and Gladys Maud Brown; *m* 1939, Mary McBeath Urquhart; one *s* one *d. Educ:* Cardiff High School; University College, Cardiff. Entered Ministry of Labour as 3rd Class Officer, 1939; Asst Principal, 1943; Private Sec. to Permanent Sec. of Min. of Labour and Nat. Service, 1944-46; Principal, 1946; Labour Attaché, Mexico City (and other countries in Central America and the Caribbean), 1950-54; transferred to Foreign Office, 1955; Head of Chancery, Rangoon, 1958 and 1959; British Ambassador in Liberia, 1960-63; Corps of Inspectors, Foreign Office, 1963-66; Ambassador to Cambodia, 1966-70; Consul-General, Johannesburg, 1970-73; Minister, Pretoria, Cape Town, 1973-74. Knight Great Band of the Humane Order of African Redemption, 1962. *Address:* 14 Embassy Court, King's Road, Brighton BN1 2PX.

BROWN, Harold James, AM 1980; BSc, ME; Hon. DSc; FIE(Australia); FIREE; management consultant, Adelaide, South Australia, since 1976; Technical Director, Philips Industries Holdings Ltd, Sydney, 1961-76; *b* 10 July 1911; *s* of Allison James and Hilda Emmy Brown; *m* 1936, Hazel Merlyn Dahl Helm; two *s* two *d. Educ:* Fort Street Boys' High Sch.; Univ. of Sydney, NSW, Australia. BSc 1933; BE (Univ. Medal) 1935; ME (Univ. Medal) 1945; Hon. DSc 1976. Research Engineer, Amalgamated Wireless Australasia Ltd, 1935-37; Electrical Engineer, Hydro-electric Commission of Tasmania, 1937-39; Research Officer and Principal Research Officer, Council for Scientific and Industrial Research, 1939-45; Chief Communications Engineer, Australian Nat. Airways Pty Ltd, 1945-47; Prof. of Electrical Engineering, Dean of Faculty of Engineering and Asst Director, NSW Univ. of Technology, 1947-52; Controller R&D, Dept of Supply, Melbourne, 1952-54; Controller, Weapons Research Establishment, Department of Supply, Commonwealth Government of Australia, 1955-58; Technical Director, Rola Co. Pty Ltd, Melbourne, 1958-61. Awarded Queen's Silver Jubilee Medal, 1977. *Publications:* numerous technical articles in scientific journals. *Recreations:* gardening, bowling. *Address:* 20 Woodbridge, Island Drive, Delfin Island, South Australia 5021.

BROWN, Sir Henry Phelps; *see* Brown, Sir E. H. P.

BROWN, Henry Thomas C.; *see* Cadbury-Brown.

BROWN, Prof. Herbert Charles, PhD; R. B. Wetherill Research Professor Emeritus, Purdue University, 1978 (Professor, 1947-60, R. B. Wetherill Research Professor, 1960-78); *b* 22 May 1912; *s* of Charles Brown and Pearl (*née* Gorinstein); *m* 1937, Sarah Baylen; one *s. Educ:* Wright Jun. Coll., Chicago (Assoc. Sci. 1935); Univ. of Chicago (BS 1936; PhD 1938). Univ. of Chicago: Eli Lilly Postdoctoral Res. Fellow, 1938-39; Instr, 1939-43; Wayne University: Asst Prof., 1943-46; Associate Prof., 1946-47. Member: Nat. Acad. of Sciences, USA, 1957-; Amer. Acad. of Arts and Sciences, 1966-; Hon. Mem., Phi Lambda Upsilon, 1961-; Hon. Fellow, Chem. Soc., London, 1978- (Centenary Lectr, 1955; C. K. Ingold Medal, 1978); Foreign Fellow, Indian Nat. Science Acad., 1978-. Hon. Dr of Science: Univ. of Chicago, 1968; Wayne State Univ., 1980; Hebrew Univ. Jerusalem, 1980; Pontifica Univ. Catolica de Chile, 1980; Wales, 1982; Purdue, 1982, etc. (Jtly) Nobel Prize in Chemistry, 1979. Amer. Chemical Society: Harrison Howe Award, 1953; Nichols Medal, 1959; Linus Pauling Medal, Oregon and Puget Sound Sects, 1968; Roger Adams Medal, Organic Div., 1971; Priestley Medal, 1981. Award for Creative Res. in Org. Chem., Soc. of Organic Chem. Mfg Assoc., 1960; Herbert Newby McCoy Award, Purdue Univ., 1965 (1st co-recipient); Nat. Medal of Science, US Govt, 1969; Madison Marshall Award, 1975; Allied Chemical Award for Grad. Trng and Innovative Chem., 1978 (1st recipient); Perkin Medal, Amer. Sect., Soc. of Chemical Industry, 1982. *Publications:*

Hydroboration, 1962; Boranes in Organic Chemistry, 1972; Organic Syntheses via Boranes, 1975; The Non-classical Ion Problem, 1977; over 780 scientific articles in Jl Amer. Chem. Soc., Jl Org. Chem., Jl Organometal. Chem., and Synthesis. *Recreations:* travel, photography. *Address:* Department of Chemistry, Purdue University, West Lafayette, Ind 47907, USA. *T:* (317) 494-8765.

BROWN, Herbert Macauley Sandes; a Judge of the High Court of Nigeria, 1945-58, retd; *b* Dublin, Feb. 1897; *o s* of late William Herbert Brown, KC, sometime County Court Judge, of Glenfern, Blackrock, Co. Dublin, and Elizabeth Rose (*née* Sandes); *m* 1928, Catherine Mary (*née* Hutchinson) (*d* 1971); one *d. Educ:* The Abbey Tipperary; Trinity College, Dublin. Served War of 1914-18 in Royal Marines. Called to the Irish Bar, 1921. Entered Administrative Service, Nigeria, 1924; Magistrate, 1934; Assistant Judge, 1943; Puisne Judge, 1945. *Address:* 9 Astra House, King's Road, Brighton BN1 2HJ.

BROWN, Prof. H(oward) Mayer; Ferdinand Schevill Distinguished Service Professor of Music, University of Chicago, since 1976; *b* 13 April 1930; *s* of Alfred R. and Florence Mayer Brown; unmarried. *Educ:* Harvard Univ. AB 1951, AM 1954, PhD 1959. Walter Naumburg Trav. Fellow, Harvard, 1951-53; Instructor in Music, Wellesley Coll., Mass, 1958-60; Univ. of Chicago: Asst Prof., 1960-63; Assoc. Prof., 1963-66; Prof., 1967-72; Chm., 1970-72; Dir of Collegium Musicum, 1960-; King Edward Prof. of Music, KCL, 1972-74. Guggenheim Fellow, Florence, 1963-64; Villa I Tatti Fellow, Florence, 1969-70; Andrew D. White Prof.-at-large, Cornell Univ., 1972-76; Prof. of Music, Univ. of Chicago, 1974-. Pres., Amer. Musicological Soc., 1978-80. *Publications:* Music in the French Secular Theater, 1963; Theatrical Chansons, 1963; Instrumental Music Printed Before 1600, 1965; (with Joan Lascelle) Musical Iconography, 1972; Sixteenth-Century Instrumentation, 1972; Music in the Renaissance, 1976; Embellishing Sixteenth-Century Music, 1976; contrib. Jl Amer. Musicological Soc., Acta musicologica, Musical Quarterly, etc. *Address:* 1415 E 54th Street, Chicago, Ill 60615, USA. *Club:* Reform.

BROWN, Hugh Dunbar; MP (Lab) Provan Division of Glasgow since 1964; *b* 18 May 1919; *s* of Neil Brown and Grace (*née* Hargrave); *m* 1947, Mary Glen Carmichael; one *d. Educ:* Allan Glen's School and Whitehill Secondary School, Glasgow. Formerly Civil Servant, Ministry of Pensions and National Insurance. Member of Glasgow Corporation, 1954; Magistrate, Glasgow, 1961. Parly Under-Sec. of State, Scottish Office, 1974-79. *Recreation:* golf. *Address:* 29 Blackwood Road, Milngavie, Glasgow.

BROWN, Jack, JP; General Secretary, Amalgamated Textile Workers Union, since 1976; *b* 10 Nov. 1929; *s* of Marjorie Brown and Edith (*née* Horrocks); *m* 1952, Alice (*née* Brown); one *s. Educ:* Pennington CofE Primary Sch., Leigh, Lancs; Leigh CofE Secondary Sch., Leigh. Commenced employment in cotton industry as operative, Dec. 1943; Royal Artillery, 1949-51; full time Trade Union Official (Organiser), 1954; District Sec., 1961-72; Asst Gen. Sec., 1972-76. JP Greater Manchester, 1967. *Recreations:* reading, Rugby League football. *Address:* 11 Thomas Street, Atherton, Manchester M29 9DP. *T:* Atherton 870218. *Clubs:* Soldiers and Sailors, Labour (both Atherton).

BROWN, Lt-Col James, RNZAC (retd); Official Secretary to the Governor-General of New Zealand, since 1977; *b* 15 Aug. 1925; *y s* of late John Brown and Eveline Bertha (*née* Cooper) Russells Flat, North Canterbury, NZ; *m* 1952, Patricia Sutton; two *d. Educ:* Christchurch Boys' High Sch., NZ; Royal Military Coll., Duntroon, Australia (grad 1947). NZ Regular Army, 1947-71: active service, Korea, 1951-52; Reg. Comr of Civil Defence, Dept of Internal Affairs, NZ, 1971-77. Col Comdt, RNZAC, 1982-. *Recreations:* fishing, shooting. *Address:* Government House, Wellington, New Zealand. *T:* Wellington 898-055. *Club:* United Services Officers (Wellington).

BROWN, Maj.-Gen. James, CB 1982; Director General Ordnance Services, since 1980; *b* 12 Nov. 1928. Commissioned, RAOC, 1948; served War Office and Baor, 1956-65; HQ Gurkha Inf. Bde, 1965-66 (despatches); MoD, 1966-67; Comdr RAOC, 4 Div., 1967-70; AAQMG (Ops/Plans), HQ 1 (BR) Corps, 1970-72; Central Ordnance Depot, Donnington, 1972; RAOC Bicester, 1973-75; Dep. Dir, Ordnance Services, MoD, 1975-77; Dep. Dir, Personal Services, MoD, 1977-80. *Address:* Director General Ordnance Services, Ministry of Defence (Army), Portway, Monxton Road, Andover, Hants SP11 8HT.

BROWN, Prof. James Alan Calvert, MA; Professor of Applied Economics, Oxford University, and Fellow of Merton College, since 1970; *b* Bury, Lancs, 8 July 1922; *s* of Harry and Mary Brown. *Educ:* Bury Grammar Sch.; Emmanuel Coll., Cambridge (BA 1946, MA 1951); MA Oxon 1970. War Service, 1942-46. Min. of Agriculture, Fisheries and Food, 1947-52; Research Officer, Dept of Applied Economics, Cambridge Univ., 1952-65, Fellow of Queens' Coll., 1961-65; Prof. of Econometrics, Bristol Univ., 1965-70. Mem., SW Electricity Bd, 1966-72. *Publications:* monographs: (with J. Aitchison) Lognormal Distribution, 1957; (with R. Stone) Computable Model of Economic Growth, 1962; Exploring, 1970; contribs to econ. and statistical lit. *Recreation:* travel. *Address:* Institute of Economics and Statistics, Manor Road, Oxford OX1 3UL. *T:* Oxford 49631.

BROWN, James Alexander, TD 1948; QC 1956; **His Honour Judge Brown;** Recorder of Belfast, 1978-82; *b* 13 June 1914; *s* of Rt Hon. Mr Justice

(Thomas Watters) Brown and Mary Elizabeth Brown; *m* 1950, Shirley Wallace Sproule; one *s* two *d. Educ:* Campbell College, Belfast; Balliol College, Oxford (BA; Pres., Oxford Union Soc., 1936). Served 1/Royal Ulster Rifles, 1939-45 (wounded; Captain). Called to Bar of NI, 1946; called English Bar (GI), 1950. County Court Judge, Co. Down, 1967-78.

BROWN, Dr James Barry Conway, OBE 1978; British Council Representative, and Cultural Counsellor, Mexico, since 1981; *b* 3 July 1937; *s* of Frederick Clarence and Alys Brown; *m* 1963, Anne Rosemary Clough; two *s* one *d. Educ:* Cambridge Univ. (BA Nat. Sci 1959; MA 1963); Birmingham Univ. (MSc 1960; PhD 1963). Research Officer, CEGB, Berkeley Nuclear Labs, 1963-67; British Council: Sen. Sci. Officer, Sci. Dept, 1967-69; Sci. Officer, Madrid, 1969-72, Paris, 1972-78; Head, Sci. and Technology Group, 1978-81. *Recreations:* music, travel in (and study of) countries of posting, singing, reading. *Address:* c/o Foreign and Commonwealth Office, King Charles Street, SW1A 2AH; 74 Westward Road, Cainscross, Stroud, Glos GL5 4JA. *T:* Stroud 5664. *Club:* University (Mexico City).

BROWN, Sir James Officer; *see* Brown, Sir (Charles) James Officer.

BROWN, Jerry; *see* Brown, E. G.

BROWN, Joe, MBE 1975; Freelance Guide and Climber; *b* 26 Sept. 1930; *s* of J. Brown, Longsight, Manchester; *m* 1957, Valerie Gray; two *d. Educ:* Stanley Grove, Manchester. Started climbing while working as plumber in Manchester; pioneered new climbs in Wales in early 1950's; gained internat. reputation after climbing West Face of Petit Dru, 1954; climbed Kanchenjunga, 1955; Mustagh Tower, 1956; Mt Communism, USSR, 1962; Climbing Instructor, Whitehall, Derbs, 1961-65; opened climbing equipment shops, Llanberis, 1965, Capel Curig, 1970; Leader of United Newspapers Andean Expedn, 1970; Roraima Expedn, 1973. Hon. Fellow, Manchester Polytechnic, 1970. *Publication:* (autobiog.) The Hard Years, 1967. *Recreations:* mountaineering, ski-ing, fishing, canoeing. *Address:* Menai Hall, Llanberis, Gwynedd. *T:* Llanberis 327. *Club:* Climbers'.

BROWN, John, CBE 1982; FIEE; Technical Director, Marconi Electronic Devices Ltd, since 1981; *b* 17 July 1923; *s* of George Brown and Margaret Ditchburn Brown; *m* 1947, Maureen Dorothy Moore; one *d. Educ:* Edinburgh University. Radar Research and Development Estab., 1944-51; Lectr, Imperial Coll., 1951-54; University Coll., London: Lectr, 1954-56; Reader, 1956-64; Prof., 1964-67; seconded to Indian Inst. of Technology as Prof. of Electrical Engrg, 1962-65; Prof. of Elect. Engineering, Imperial Coll. of Science and Technology, 1967-81 (Head of Dept, 1967-79). Mem., SRC, 1977-81 (Chm., Engrg Bd, 1977-81); Pres., IEE, 1979-80 (Vice-Pres., 1975-78; Dep. Pres., 1978-79). *Publications:* Microwave Lenses, 1953; (with H. M. Barlow) Radio Surface Waves, 1962; Telecommunications, 1964; (with R. H. Clarke) Diffraction Theory and Antennas, 1980; papers in Proc. IEE, etc. *Recreation:* gardening. *Address:* Marconi Electronic Devices Ltd, Doddington Road, Lincoln; Old House, Crab Lane, North Muskham, Newark, Notts. *Club:* Athenæum.

BROWN, John; HM Diplomatic Service; Counsellor and Head of Communications Operations Department, Foreign and Commonwealth Office, since 1981; *b* 13 July 1931; *s* of John Coultas Scofield Brown and Sarah Ellen Brown (*née* Brown); *m* 1955, Christine Ann Batchelor; one *d. Educ:* South Shields High School. Export Credits Guarantee Dept, 1949; Grenadier Guards, 1949-51; Board of Trade, 1967; seconded to HM Diplomatic Service, 1969; Diplomatic Service, 1975; First Secretary and Head of Chancery, Accra, 1977; FCO, 1979-. *Recreations:* reading, golf, walking. *Address:* c/o Foreign and Commonwealth Office, SW1A 2AH. *Club:* Royal Over-Seas League.

BROWN, John B.; *see* Blamire-Brown.

BROWN, (John) Carter; Director, National Gallery of Art, Washington, DC, since 1969; Chairman, Commission of Fine Arts, since 1971; *b* 8 Oct. 1934; *s* of John Nicholas Brown and Anne Kinsolving Brown; *m* 1976, Pamela Braga Drexel; one *s. Educ:* Harvard (AB *summa cum laude* 1956; MBA 1958); Inst. of Fine Arts, NY Univ. (Museum Trng Prog., Metropol. Museum of Art; MA 1962). Studied: with Bernard Berenson, Florence, 1958; Ecole du Louvre, Paris, 1958-59; Rijksbureau voor Kunsthistorische Documentatie, The Hague, 1961. National Gallery of Art: Asst to Dir, 1961-63; Asst Dir, 1964-68; Dep. Dir, 1968-69. Hon. Mem., Amer. Inst. of Architects, 1975. Hon. LLD Brown Univ., RI, 1970; Hon. LHD: Mount St Mary's Coll., Md, 1974; Georgetown Univ., Washington, DC, 1975; George Washington Univ., Washington, DC, 1978; Hon. DFA Roger Williams Coll., Bristol, RI, 1978; Hon. DPS Bowling Green Univ., Ohio, 1979. Gold Medal of Honour, National Arts Soc., 1972. Commandeur, l'Ordre des Arts et des Lettres, France, 1975; Chevalier de la Légion d'Honneur, France, 1976; Knight, Order of St Olav, Norway, 1979; Comdr, Order of the Republic, Egypt, 1979. Phi Beta Kappa, 1956. Author/Dir, (film), The American Vision, 1966. *Publications:* contrib. professional jls and exhibn catalogues. *Recreations:* sailing, riding, photography. *Address:* 3035 Dumbarton Avenue NW, Washington, DC 20007, USA. *T:* (office) (202) 737-4215. *Clubs:* Knickerbocker, Century Association, New York Yacht, Cruising Club of America (New York); Cosmos, 1925 F Street (Washington).

BROWN, John Cecil, CBE 1977; Chairman, Yorkshire Water Authority, 1973-78; *b* 21 Jan. 1911; *s* of John Smith Brown and Ady Mary (*née* Little); *m* 1938, Winifred Metcalfe; two *s. Educ:* Univ. of Durham, 1931-34 (BSc 1st Cl. Hons). Richardsons Westgarth (Marine Engrs), Hartlepool, 1926-31; Imperial Chemical Industries Ltd, 1934-73: Division Dir of Engrg, 1952, Techn. Man. Dir, 1959; Chm., Mond Div., 1967; Dir, Main Bd, 1970; retd 1973. *Publications:* various, in techn. and water industry jls. *Recreations:* horticulture, sea cruising. *Address:* Wayside, Firs Lane, Appleton, Warrington WA4 5LD. *T:* Warrington 63275. *Club:* Cruising Association.

BROWN, Sir John (Douglas Keith), Kt 1960; Chairman, McLeod Russel plc, London, 1972-79 (Director since 1963); Director of other companies; *b* 8 Sept. 1913; *s* of late Ralph Douglas Brown and Rhoda Miller Keith; *m* 1940, Margaret Eleanor, *d* of late William Alexander Burnet; two *s. Educ:* Glasgow Acad. CA 1937. Joined Messrs. Lovelock & Lewes, Chartered Accountants, Calcutta, October 1937 (Partnership, 1946; retired 1948); joined Jardine Henderson Ltd as a Managing Director, 1949; Chairman, 1957-63. Pres. Bengal Chamber of Commerce and Industry and Associated Chambers of Commerce of India, 1958-60; Pres. UK Citizens' Assoc. (India), 1961. Mem. Eastern Area Local Bd, Reserve Bank of India, 1959-63; Mem. Advisory Cttee on Capital Issues, 1958-63; Mem. Technical Advisory Cttee on Company Law, 1958-63; Mem. Companies Act Amendment Cttee, 1957; Mem. Central Excise Reorganisation Cttee, 1960. *Recreations:* gardening, walking. *Address:* Windover, Whitmore Vale Road, Hindhead, Surrey. *T:* Hindhead 4173. *Clubs:* Oriental, City of London; Bengal (Calcutta).

BROWN, Ven. John Edward; Archdeacon of Berkshire, since 1978; *b* 13 July 1930; *s* of Edward and Muriel Brown; *m* 1956, Rosemary (*née* Wood); one *s. Educ:* Wintringham Grammar Sch., Grimsby; Kelham Theological Coll., Notts. BD London. Deacon 1955, priest 1956; Master, St George's School, Jerusalem; Curate, St George's Cathedral, Jerusalem; Chaplain of Amman, Jordan, 1954-57; Curate-in-Charge, All Saints, Reading, 1957-60; Missionary and Chaplain, All Saints Cathedral, Khartoum, Sudan, 1960-64; Vicar: Stewkley, Buckingham, 1964-69; St Luke's, Maidenhead, 1969-73; Bracknell, Berkshire, 1973-77; Rural Dean of Sonning, 1974-77. Commissary for Archbishop of the Sudan and of Bishop of Omdurman. Warden, Soc. of Holy Trinity, Ascot Priory, 1980-. *Recreations:* walking; Middle East and African studies. *Address:* Beech Hill Vicarage, Reading, Berks. *T:* Reading 882569.

BROWN, Sir John (Gilbert Newton), Kt 1974; CBE 1966; MA; Chairman, B. H. Blackwell Ltd, and Director, Blackwell Group Ltd, since 1980; *b* 7 July 1916; *s* of John and Molly Brown, Chilham, Kent; *m* 1946, Virginia, *d* of late Darcy Braddell and Dorothy Braddell; one *s* two *d. Educ:* Lancing Coll.; Hertford Coll., Oxford (MA Zoology). Bombay Branch Oxford University Press, 1937-40; commissioned Royal Artillery, 1941; served with 5th Field Regiment, 1941-46; captured by the Japanese at Fall of Singapore, 1942; prisoner of war, Malaya, Formosa and Japan, 1942-45; returned Oxford University Press, 1946; Sales Manager, 1949; Publisher, 1956-80; Chm., University Bookshops (Oxford) Ltd; Director: Book Tokens Ltd; Willshaw Booksellers Ltd, Manchester. President, Publishers' Association, 1963-65. Member: Nat. Libraries Cttee; EDC for Newspapers, Printing and Publishing Industry, 1967-70; Adv. Cttee on Scientific and Technical Information, 1969-73; Communication Adv. Cttee for UK Nat. Cttee for UNESCO; Royal Literary Fund (Asst Treasurer); Bd of British Library, 1973-79; Royal Soc. Cttee on Scientific Information; formerly Mem. Bd, British Council. Professorial Fellow, Hertford Coll., Oxford, 1974-80. FRSA 1964. *Address:* Milton Lodge, Great Milton, Oxon. *T:* Great Milton 217 and 01-727 5487. *Club:* Garrick.

BROWN, (John) Michael; HM Diplomatic Service; Ambassador to Costa Rica since April 1979, also to Nicaragua since Nov. 1979; *m* 1955, Elizabeth Fitton; one *s* one *d. Served at:* Cairo, 1954-55; Doha, 1956-57; FO, 1957-60; Havana, 1960-62; FO, 1962-64; Jedda, 1965-66; Maseru, 1966-67; Bogotá, 1967-69; FCO, 1969-71; Ankara, 1971-73; Tripoli, 1973-75; FCO, 1976-79. *Address:* c/o Foreign and Commonwealth Office, SW1.

BROWN, Prof. John Russell; Professor of English, Sussex University, since 1971; Associate Director, The National Theatre, since 1973; *b* 15 Sept. 1923; *yr s* of Russell Alan and Olive Helen Brown, Coombe Wood, Somerset; *m* 1961, Hilary Sue Baker; one *s* two *d. Educ:* Monkton Combe Sch.; Keble Coll., Oxford. Sub-Lieut (AE) RNVR, 1944-46. Fellow, Shakespeare Inst., Stratford-upon-Avon, 1951-55; Lectr and Sen. Lectr, Dept of English, Birmingham Univ., 1955-63; Hd of Dept of Drama and Theatre Arts, Univ. of Birmingham, 1964-71; Reynolds Lectr, Colorado Univ., 1957; Vis. Prof. Graduate Sch., New York Univ., 1959; Mellon Prof. of Drama, Carnegie Inst., Pittsburgh, 1964; Vis. Prof., Zürich Univ., 1969-70; Univ. Lectr in Drama, Univ. of Toronto, 1970. Robb Lectr, Univ. of Auckland, 1976. Dir, Orbit Theatre Co. Member: Adv. Council of Victoria and Albert Museum; Adv. Council of Theatre Museum (Chm.); Arts Council of GB, 1980-, and Chm. Drama Panel, 1980- (formerly Dep. Chm.). *Theatre productions include:* Twelfth Night, Playhouse, Pittsburgh, 1964; Macbeth, Everyman, Liverpool, 1965; The White Devil, Everyman, 1969; Crossing Niagara, Nat. Theatre at the ICA, 1975; They Are Dying Out, Young Vic, 1976; Old Times, British Council tour of Poland, 1976; Judgement, Nat. Theatre, 1977; Hamlet (tour), 1978; Macbeth, Nat. Theatre (co-director), 1978; The Vienna Notes and The Nest, Crucible, Sheffield, 1979; Company, Nat. Theatre, 1980. Gen. Editor: Stratford-upon-Avon Studies, 1960-67; Stratford-upon-Avon Library, 1964-;

Theatre Production Studies, 1981-. *Publications:* (ed) The Merchant of Venice, 1955; Shakespeare and his Comedies, 1957; (ed) The White Devil, 1960; Shakespeare: The Tragedy of Macbeth, 1963; (ed) The Duchess of Malfi, 1965; (ed) Henry V, 1965; Shakespeare's Plays in Performance, 1966; Effective Theatre, 1969; Shakespeare's The Tempest, 1969; Shakespeare's Dramatic Style, 1970; Theatre Language, 1972; Free Shakespeare, 1974; Discovering Shakespeare, 1981; Shakespeare and his Theatre, 1982; articles in Shakespeare Survey, Critical Quarterly, Tulane Drama Review, Studies in Bibliography, etc. *Recreations:* gardening, travel. *Address:* c/o The National Theatre, SE1 8AE.

BROWN, Joseph Lawler, CBE 1978; TD 1953; FInstM; CBIM; DL; Chairman and Managing Director, The Birmingham Post & Mail Ltd, 1973-77; *b* 22 March 1921; *s* of late Neil Brown; *m* 1950, Mabel Smith, SRN, SCM; one *s* one *d. Educ:* Peebles; Heriot-Watt Coll., Edinburgh. FInstM 1976; CBIM (formerly FBIM) 1978. Served War, The Royal Scots, 1939-46 (Major). The Scotsman Publications Ltd, 1947-60; Coventry Newspapers Ltd: Gen. Man., 1960; Jt Man. Dir, 1961; Man. Dir, 1964-69; The Birmingham Post & Mail Ltd: Dep. Man. Dir, 1970; Man. Dir, 1971. Director: Cambridge Newspapers Ltd, 1965-69; Press Assoc., 1968-75 (Chm. 1972); Reuters Ltd, 1972-75; BPM (Holdings) Ltd, 1973-81. Pres., Birmingham Chamber of Industry and Commerce, 1979-80. Exec. Chm., Birmingham Venture, 1981-. Mem., Bromsgrove and Redditch DHA, 1982-. DL County of W Midlands, 1976. Commendatore, Order Al Merito Della Repubblica Italiana, 1973. *Recreations:* gardening, fishing, Japanese woodcuts. *Address:* Westerly, 37 Mearse Lane, Barnt Green, Birmingham B45 8HH. *T:* 021-445 1234.

BROWN, Kenneth Vincent, CMG 1954; Senior Judge, Supreme Court, Trinidad, 1943-52, retired; *b* 1 Nov. 1890; *m* 1942, Vere Alice Edghill (*d* 1944); one *s. Educ:* St George's Coll., Weybridge, Surrey. Barrister, Gray's Inn, 1915; Magistrate, Trinidad, 1925; Puisne Judge, 1936. Coronation Medals, 1937, 1953. *Recreations:* cricket, racing. *Address:* 1 Taylor Street, Woodbrook, Port-of-Spain, Trinidad. *Clubs:* Union, Trinidad Turf, Queen's Park Cricket (Port-of-Spain).

BROWN, Rt. Rev. Laurence Ambrose, MA; Priest-in-Charge of Odstock with Nunton and Bodenham, Diocese of Salisbury, since 1978; *b* 1 Nov. 1907; 2nd *s* of Frederick James Brown; *m* 1935, Florence Blanche, *d* of late William Gordon Marshall; three *d. Educ:* Luton Grammar School; Queens' College, Cambridge (MA); Cuddesdon Theological College, Oxford. Asst Curate, St John-the-Divine, Kennington, 1932-35; Curate-in-Charge, St Peter, Luton, Beds, 1935-40; Vicar, Hatfield Hyde, Welwyn Garden City, 1940-46; Sec. Southwark Dio. Reorganisation Cttee, 1946-60; Sec. S London Church Fund and Southwark Dio. Bd of Finance, 1952-60; Canon Residentiary, Southwark, 1950-60; Archdeacon of Lewisham and Vice-Provost of Southwark, 1955-60; Suffragan Bishop of Warrington, 1960-69; Bishop of Birmingham, 1969-77. Mem. Church Assembly, later General Synod, and Proctor in Convocation, 1954-77; Chairman: Advisory Council for Church's Ministry, 1966-71; Industrial Christian Fellowship, 1971-77; Mem., Religious Adv. Bd, Scout Assoc., 1953-. Mem., House of Lords, 1973-77. *Publications:* pamphlets on church building in post-war period. *Address:* 7 St Nicholas Road, Salisbury, Wilts. *T:* Salisbury 3138.

BROWN, Lawrence Michael, PhD; FRS 1982; Lecturer in Physics, University of Cambridge, since 1970; Director of Studies, Robinson College, Cambridge, since 1977 (Founding Fellow, 1977); *b* 18 March 1936; *s* of Bertson Waterworth Brown and Edith Waghorne; *m* 1965, Susan Drucker; one *s* two *d. Educ:* Univ. of Toronto (BASc); Univ. of Birmingham (PhD). Athlone Fellow, 1957; W. M. Tapp Research Fellowship to Gonville and Caius Coll., 1963; University Demonstrator, Cavendish Laboratory, 1965. *Publications:* many papers on structure and properties of materials and electron microscopy in Acta Metallurgica and Philosophical Magazine. *Address:* 74 Alpha Road, Cambridge CB4 3DG. *T:* Cambridge 62987.

BROWN, Leslie; Deputy Chairman, Prudential Assurance Co. Ltd, 1970-74 (a Director, 1965-77); *b* 29 Oct. 1902; *s* of late W. H. Brown and late Eliza J. Fiveash; *m* 1930, Frances V., *d* of T. B. Lever; two *s* one *d. Educ:* Selhurst Grammar School. Joined Prudential Assurance Co. Ltd, 1919; Secretary and Chief Investment Manager, Prudential Assurance Co. Ltd, 1955-64 (Joint Secretary 1942); Chairman: Prudential Unit Trust Managers Ltd, 1968-75; Prudential Pensions Ltd, 1970-75. Member, Jenkins Committee on Company Law Amendment, 1960. Deputy-Chairman, Insurance Export Finance Co. Ltd, 1962-65. Inst. of Actuaries: FIA 1929; Vice-Pres., 1949-51. *Recreation:* bowls. *Address:* 12 Park View, Christchurch Road, Purley, Surrey CR2 2NL.

BROWN, Leslie F.; see Farrer-Brown.

BROWN, Rt. Rev. Leslie Wilfrid, CBE 1965; *b* 10 June 1912; *s* of Harry and Maud Brown; *m* 1939, Annie Winifred, *d* of Hon. R. D. Megaw, Belfast; one *d. Educ:* Enfield Gram. School; London College of Divinity (London Univ.). BD 1936, MTh 1944, DD 1957. MA Cantab. hon. causa, 1953. Deacon, Curate St James' Milton, Portsmouth, 1935; priest, 1936. Missionary CMS, 1938 to Cambridge Nicholson Instn, Kottayam, Travancore, S India. Fellow Commoner and Chaplain, Downing College, Cambridge, 1943; Kerala United Theological Seminary, Trivandrum: tutor, 1945, Principal, 1946, and from 1951. Chaplain, Jesus Coll., Cambridge and Select Preacher before Univ. of Cambridge, 1950, 1967, 1979, Oxford, 1967. Archbishop of

Uganda, Rwanda and Burundi, 1961-65; Bishop of Namirembe, 1960-65 (of Uganda, 1953-60; name of diocese changed); Bishop of St Edmundsbury and Ipswich, 1966-78. Chm., ACCM, 1972-76. Hon. Fellow, Downing Coll., Cambridge, 1966. DD (*hc*) Trinity Coll., Toronto, 1963. Chaplain and Sub-Prelate, Order of St John, 1968. *Publications:* The Indian Christians of St Thomas, 1956, 2nd edn 1982; The Christian Family, 1959; God as Christians see Him, 1961; Relevant Liturgy, 1965; Three Worlds, One Word, 1981. *Address:* 47 New Square, Cambridge CB1 1EZ. *Club:* Royal Commonwealth Society.

BROWN, Prof. Lionel Neville; Professor of Comparative Law, University of Birmingham, since 1966; *b* 29 July 1923; *s* of Reginald P. N. Brown and Fanny Brown (*née* Carver); *m* 1957, Mary Patricia Vowles; three *s* one *d*. *Educ:* Wolverhampton Grammar Sch.; Pembroke Coll., Cambridge (Scholar; MA, LLB); Lyons Univ. (Dr en Droit). RAF, 1942-45; Cambridge, 1945-48; articled to Wolverhampton solicitor, 1948-50; Rotary Foundn Fellow, Lyons Univ., 1951-52; Lectr in Law, Sheffield Univ., 1953-55; Lectr in Comparative Law, Birmingham Univ., 1956, Sen. Lectr, 1957; Sen. Res. Fellow, Univ. of Michigan, 1960. Chm., Birmingham Nat. Insurance Local Tribunal, 1977. Visiting Professor: Univ. of Tulane, New Orleans, 1968; Univ. of Nairobi, 1974; Laval, 1975, 1979. Commonwealth Foundn Lectr (Caribbean), 1975-76. *Publications:* (with F. H. Lawson and A. E. Anton) Amos and Walton's Introduction to French Law, 2nd edn 1963 and 3rd edn 1967; (with J. F. Garner) French Administrative Law, 1967, 2nd edn 1973; (with F. G. Jacobs) Court of Justice of the European Communities, 1977. *Recreations:* landscape gardening, country walking, music. *Address:* Willow Rise, Waterdale, Compton, Wolverhampton, West Midlands. *T:* Wolverhampton 26666.

BROWN, Maj.-Gen. Llewellyn; *see* Brown, Maj.-Gen. R. L.

BROWN, Malcolm; *see* Brown, G. M.

BROWN, (Marion) Patricia; Under-Secretary (Economics), Treasury, since 1972; *b* 2 Feb. 1927; *d* of late Henry Oswald Brown and Elsie Elizabeth (*née* Thompson). *Educ:* Norwich High Sch. for Girls; Newnham Coll., Cambridge. Central Economic Planning Staff, Cabinet Office, 1947; Treasury, 1948-54; United States Embassy, London, 1956-59; Treasury, 1959-. Governor, Bedford Coll., Univ. of London. Godmother of Lucy Harland and Benjamin Watts. *Recreations:* bird watching, gardening, walking. *Address:* 28 The Plantation, SE3 0AB. *T:* 01-852 9011.

BROWN, Sir Max; *see* Brown, Sir C. M. P.

BROWN, Sir Mervyn, KCMG 1981 (CMG 1975); OBE 1963; HM Diplomatic Service; High Commissioner in Nigeria, since 1979, and concurrently Ambassador to Benin; *b* 24 Sept. 1923; *m* 1949, Elizabeth Gittings. *Educ:* Ryhope Gram. Sch., Sunderland; St John's Coll., Oxford. Served in RA, 1942-45. Entered HM Foreign Service, 1949; Third Secretary, Buenos Aires, 1950; Second Secretary, UK Mission to UN, New York, 1953; First Secretary, Foreign Office, 1956; Singapore, 1959; Vientiane, 1960; again in Foreign Office, 1963-67; Ambassador to Madagascar, 1967-70; Inspector, FCO, 1970-73; Head of Communications Operations Dept, FCO, 1973-74; Asst Under-Sec. of State (Dir of Communications), 1974; High Commissioner in Tanzania, 1975-78, and concurrently Ambassador to Madagascar; Minister and Dep. Perm. Representative to UN, 1978. *Publications:* Madagascar Rediscovered, 1978; articles and reviews on the history of Madagascar in Jl of African History, Tanzania Notes and Records, and Bulletin de l'Académie Malgache. *Recreations:* music, tennis, history. *Address:* c/o Foreign and Commonwealth Office, SW1. *Clubs:* Royal Commonwealth Society, Hurlingham.

BROWN, Michael; *see* Brown, J. M.

BROWN, Ven. Michael René Warneford; Archdeacon of Nottingham, 1960-77, now Archdeacon Emeritus; *b* 7 June 1915; *s* of late George and Irene Brown; *m* 1978, Marie Joyce Chaloner, *d* of late Walter Dawson, and of Sarah Dawson, Burbage, Leics; three step *s*. *Educ:* King's School, Rochester; St Peter's College, Oxford; St Stephen's House, Oxford (MA). Deacon 1941; priest, 1942; Asst Master, Christ's Hospital, 1939-43; Curate of West Grinstead, 1941-43. Chap. RNVR, 1943-46; chaplain and Dean of St Peter's College and Curate of St Mary the Virgin, Oxford, 1946; Lecturer, RN College, Greenwich, 1946-47; Librarian, 1948-50 and Fellow, 1948-52, of St Augustine's Coll., Canterbury; Priest-in-charge of Bekesbourne, 1948-50; Asst Secretary, CACTM, 1950-60. Examining Chaplain: to Bishop of Southwell, 1954-77; to Archbishop of Canterbury, 1959-60; Commissary to Bishop of Waikato, 1958-70. Mem., Church of England Pensions Board, 1966- (Commissioners' nominee, 1978-); Mem., Church Commissioners' Redundant Churches Cttee, 1978-; Chm., Redundant Churches' Uses Cttee in Canterbury Dio., 1980-; Vice-Chm., Diocesan Adv. Cttee for the Care of Churches, 1980-; Church Commissioner, 1968-78. *Recreations:* antiquarian and aesthetic, especially English paintings and silver. *Address:* Faygate, Liverpool Road, Walmer, Deal, Kent. *T:* Deal 61326. *Club:* Athenæum.

BROWN, Michael Russell; MP (C) Brigg and Scunthorpe, since 1979; *b* 3 July 1951; *s* of Frederick Alfred Brown and Greta Mary Brown (*née* Russell). *Educ:* Andrew Cairns County Secondary Modern School for Boys, Littlehampton; Univ. of York (BA (Hons) Economics and Politics). Graduate Management Trainee, Barclays Bank Ltd, 1972-74; Lecturer and Tutor,

Swinton Conservative Coll., 1974-75; part-time Asst to Michael Marshall, MP, 1975-76; Law Student, Middle Temple, 1976-77; Personal Asst to Nicholas Winterton, MP, 1976-79. *Recreations:* cricket, walking. *Address:* House of Commons, SW1. *Clubs:* Reform; Scunthorpe Conservative.

BROWN, Ormond John; retired Government Servant; *b* 30 Jan. 1922; *s* of Herbert John Brown and Janie Lee; *m* 1949, Margaret Eileen Beard; two *d*. *Educ:* Gourock High Sch.; Greenock High Sch. Served War, 1941-45: Outer Hebrides, N Africa, Italy, Greece, Austria. Sheriff Clerk Service, Scotland, 1939; Trng Organiser, Scottish Ct Service, 1957; Sheriff Clerk of Perthshire, 1970; Clerk of Justiciary, 1971; Principal Clerk of Session and Justiciary, Scotland, 1975-82. *Recreations:* music, golf, gardening. *Address:* 29 Atholl Place, Dunblane, Perthshire. *T:* Dunblane 822186. *Club:* Dunblane New Golf (Dunblane).

BROWN, Patricia; *see* Brown, M. P.

BROWN, Peter; *see* Brown, A. P. G.

BROWN, Prof. Peter Robert Lamont, FBA 1971; FRHistS; Professor of History and Classics, University of California at Berkeley, since 1978; *b* 26 July 1935; *s* of James Lamont and Sheila Brown, Dublin; *m* 1st, 1959, Friedl Esther (*née* Löw-Beer); two *d*; 2nd, 1980, Patricia Ann Meyer (*née* Fortini). *Educ:* Aravon Sch., Bray, Co. Wicklow, Ireland; Shrewsbury Sch.; New Coll., Oxford (MA). Harmsworth Senior Scholar, Merton Coll., Oxford and Prize Fellow, All Souls Coll., Oxford, 1956; Junior Research Fellow, 1963, Sen. Res. Fellow, 1970-73, All Souls Coll.; Fellow, All Souls Coll., 1956-75; Lectr in Medieval History, Merton Coll. Oxford, 1970-75; Special Lectr in late Roman and early Byzantine History, 1970-73, Reader, 1973-75, Univ. of Oxford; Prof. of History, Royal Holloway Coll., London Univ., 1975-78. Fellow, Amer. Acad. of Arts and Scis, 1978. Hon. DTheol Fribourg, 1975; Hon. DHL Chicago, 1978. *Publications:* Augustine of Hippo: a biography, 1967; The World of Late Antiquity, 1971; Religion and Society in the Age of St Augustine, 1971; The Making of Late Antiquity, 1978; The Cult of the Saints: its rise and function in Latin Christianity, 1980; Society and the Holy in Late Antiquity, 1982. *Address:* Department of Classics, Dwinelle Hall, University of California, Berkeley, Calif 94720, USA; 1411 Josephine Street, Berkeley, Calif 94703, USA.

BROWN, Philip Anthony Russell, CB 1977; Deputy Secretary, Department of Trade, since 1974; *b* 18 May 1924; *e s* of late Sir William Brown, KCB, KCMG, CBE, and of Elizabeth Mabel (*née* Scott); *m* 1954, Eileen (*d* 1976), *d* of late J. Brennan; *m* 1976, Sarah, *d* of late Sir Maurice Dean, KCB, KCMG. *Educ:* Malvern; King's Coll., Cambridge. Entered Home Civil Service, Board of Trade, 1947; Private Sec. to Perm. Sec., 1949; Principal, 1952; Private Sec. to Minister of State, 1953; Observer, Civil Service Selection Board, 1957; returned to BoT, 1959; Asst Sec., 1963; Head of Overseas Information Co-ordination Office, 1963; BoT, 1964; Under-Sec., 1969; Head of Establishments Div. 1, BoT, later DTI, 1969; Head of Cos Div., DTI, 1971. *Publication:* contrib. to Multinational Approaches: corporate insiders, 1976; articles in various jls. *Recreations:* reading, gardening, music. *Address:* 32 Cumberland Street, SW1. *T:* 01-821 9342. *Club:* United Oxford & Cambridge University.

BROWN, Ralph, RA 1972 (ARA 1968); ARCA 1955; sculptor; *b* 24 April 1928; *m* 1st, 1952, M. E. Taylor (marr. diss. 1963); one *s* one *d*; 2nd, 1964, Caroline Ann Clifton-Trigg; one *s*. *Educ:* Leeds Grammar School. Studied Royal College of Art, 1948-56; in Paris with Zadkine, 1954; travel scholarships to Greece 1955, Italy 1957. Tutor, RCA, 1958-64. Sculpture Prof., Salzburg Festival, Summer 1972. Work exhibited: John Moores, Liverpool (prizewinner 1957), Tate Gallery, Religious Theme 1958, British Sculpture in the Sixties 1965; Arnhem Internat. Open Air Sculpture, 1958; Middelheim Open Air Sculpture, 1959; Battersea Park Open Air Sculpture, 1960, 1963, 1966, 1977; Tokyo Biennale, 1963; British Sculptors '72, RA, 1972; Holland Park Open Air, 1975; Salisbury Festival Exhibn, 1981. One man Shows: Leicester Galls, 1961, 1963; Archer Gall., 1972; Salzburg, 1972; Munich 1973; Montpellier 1974; Marseilles 1975; Oxford 1975; Taranman Gall., 1976; Browse & Darby Gall., 1979. Work in Collections: Tate Gallery, Arts Council, Contemp. Art Society, Kröller-Müller, Gallery of NSW, Stuyvesant Foundation, City of Salzburg, Nat. Gallery of Wales and at Leeds, Bristol, Norwich, Aberdeen, etc. Public Sculpture: at Hatfield, Harlow, LCC Tulse Hill, Loughborough Univ., Newnham Coll., etc. *Address:* Seynckley House, Amberley, Stroud, Glos.

BROWN, Rt. Rev. Mgr Ralph; Vicar General, Diocese of Westminster, since 1976; *b* 30 June 1931; *s* of John William and Elizabeth Josephine Brown. *Educ:* Highgate Sch.; St Edmund's Coll., Old Hall Green, Herts; Pontifical Gregorian Univ., Rome. Licence in Canon Law, 1961, Doctorate, 1963. Commnd Middlesex Regt, 1949; Korea, 1950. Ordained priest, Westminster Cathedral, 1959; Vice-Chancellor, Vice Officialis, dio. of Westminster, 1964-69; Officialis, Westminster, 1969-76; Chancellor, Military Vicariate, 1968-. Pres., Canon Law Soc. of GB and Ireland, 1980-. *Publications:* Marriage Annulment, 1969, rev. edn 1977; articles in Heythrop Jl, Studia Canonica, Theological Digest, The Jurist. *Address:* 42 Francis Street, SW1P 1QW. *T:* (office) 01-834 3144, 01-828 5380. *Club:* Anglo-Belgian.

BROWN, Hon. Sir Ralph Kilner, Kt 1970; OBE 1945; TD 1952; DL; Hon. Mr Justice Kilner Brown; a Judge of the High Court, Queen's Bench

Division, since 1970; a Judge of Employment Appeal Tribunal, since 1976; b 28 Aug. 1909; s of Rev. A. E. Brown, CIE, MA, BSc; m 1943, Cynthia Rosemary Breffit; one s two d. Educ: Kingswood School; Trinity Hall, Cambridge (Squire Law Scholar). Barrister, Middle Temple; Midland Circuit, 1934 (Harmsworth Scholar). TA 1938; War Service, 1939-46; DAQMG NW Europe Plans; DAAG HQ53 (Welsh) Div.; AQMG (Planning), COSSAC; Col Q (Ops) and Brig. Q Staff HQ 21 Army Group (despatches, OBE). QC 1958; Recorder of Lincoln, 1960-64; Recorder of Birmingham, 1964-65. Master of the Bench, Middle Temple, 1964; Chairman, Warwicks QS, 1964-67 (Dep. Chm., 1954-64); a Judge of the Central Criminal Court, 1965-67; Recorder of Liverpool, and Judge of the Crown Court at Liverpool, 1967-69; Presiding Judge, N Circuit, 1970-75. Chairman, Mental Health Review Tribunal, Birmingham RHB Area, 1962-65. Contested (L) Oldbury and Halesowen, 1945 and 1950; South Bucks, 1959 and 1964; Pres., Birmingham Liberal Organisation, 1946-56; Pres., and Chm., W Midland Liberal Fedn, 1950-56; Mem., Liberal Party Exec., 1950-56. Pres., Birmingham Bn, Boys Bde, 1946-56; Mem., Exec., Boys Bde, 1950-55. DL Warwickshire, 1956. Guild of Freemen, City of London. Recreations: watching athletics (represented Cambridge University and Great Britain; British AAA Champion 440 yds hurdles, 1934); cricket, Rugby football. Address: Victoria Cottage, Best Beech Hill, Wadhurst, Sussex. Clubs: Naval and Military; Hawks (Cambridge).
See also A. G. K. Brown.

BROWN, Mrs Ray; see Vaughan, Elizabeth.

BROWN, Rev. Raymond; Principal, Spurgeon's College, London, since 1973; b 3 March 1928; s of Frank Stevenson Brown and Florence Mansfield; m 1966, Christine Mary Smallman; one s one d. Educ: Spurgeon's Coll., London (BD, MTh); Fitzwilliam Coll., Cambridge (MA, BD, PhD). Minister: Zion Baptist Church, Cambridge, 1956-62; Upton Vale Baptist Church, Torquay, 1964-71; Tutor in Church History, Spurgeon's Coll., 1971-73. Pres., Evangelical Alliance, 1975-76; Trustee, Dr Daniel Williams's Charity, 1980-. Publications: Their Problems and Ours, 1969; Let's Read the Old Testament, 1971; Skilful Hands, 1972; Christ Above All: the message of Hebrews, 1982. Recreations: music, fell walking. Address: Spurgeon's College, South Norwood Hill, SE25 6DJ. T: 01-653 1235.

BROWN, Sir Raymond (Frederick), Kt 1969; OBE; CompIEE; FIERE; Chairman, Muirhead plc, since 1972 (Chief Executive and Managing Director, 1970-82); Chairman, Racecourse Technical Services Ltd; Director, National Westminster Bank Ltd, Outer London Region, since 1978; b 19 July 1920; s of Frederick and Susan Evelyn Brown; m 1942, Evelyn Jennings (marr. diss. 1949); one d; m 1953, Carol Jacquelin Elizabeth, d of H. R. Sprinks, Paris; two s one d. Educ: Morden Terrace LCC School; SE London Technical College; Morley College. DSc. Joined Redifon as engineering apprentice, 1934; Sales Man., Communications Div., Plessey Ltd, 1949-50; formerly Chm., Man. Dir and Pres., Racal Electronics Ltd (Joint Founder, 1950), and subsidiary companies. Head of Defence Sales, MoD, 1966-69; Consultant Adviser on commercial policy and exports to DHSS, 1969-72. Mem., Brit. Overseas Trade Bd Working Gp on Innovation and Exports, 1972-74; Adviser to NEDO, to promote export of equipment purchased by nationalised industries, 1976-. Mem., Soc. of Pilgrims. Pres. Electronic Engrg Assoc., 1975; Pres. Egham and Thorpe Royal Agric. and Hort. Assoc., 1977-79. Liveryman: Scriveners' Co.; Scientific Instrument Makers' Co. Governor, SE London Coll., 1980-81. Hon. DSc Bath, 1980. Recreations: golf, farming, shooting, polo. Address: c/o Muirhead plc, 34 Croydon Road, Beckenham, Kent BR3 4BE. Clubs: City Livery, Travellers', Canada, Australia; Ends of the Earth; Sunningdale Golf; Guards Polo (life mem.); Swinley Forest Golf.

BROWN, Prof. Reginald Francis, PhD; (First) Cowdray Professor of Spanish Language and Literature in the University of Leeds, 1953-75, retired; b 23 April 1910; m 1939, Rica Eleanor Jones; one s one d. Educ: Lancaster Royal Grammar School; Liverpool University. BA First Class Hons. Spanish, 1932; PhD, 1939; University Fellowship, Liverpool, 1934. On Staff of Spanish Departments in Universities of Liverpool, Columbia, and New York, NYC, and Dartmouth College, NH, USA, 1939-43. War of 1939-45: service in RAF Intelligence (FO). Head of Dept of Spanish, University of Leeds, 1945-53. Vis. Prof. of Spanish, Princeton Univ., 1958-59. Pres., Modern Language Assoc., 1970. Leverhulme Emeritus Fellow, 1980-81. Diamond Jubilee Gold Medal, Inst. of Linguists, 1972. Encomienda of Order of Alfonso el Sabio, 1977. Publications: Bibliografía de la Novela Española, 1700-1850, (Madrid) 1953; Spanish-English, English-Spanish Pocket Dictionary, (Glasgow) 1954, 2nd edn, 1956; Spain, A Companion to Spanish Studies (ed. E. Allison Peers), 5th edn revised and enlarged, 1956; D. F. Sarmiento, Facundo, ed. Boston, 1960. Articles in Bulletin of Hispanic Studies, Hispania, Hispanic Review, Modern Languages, Year's Work in Modern Language Studies. Address: Rivington House, Clarence Road, Horsforth, near Leeds. T: Leeds 582443.

BROWN, Maj.-Gen. (Reginald) Llewellyn, CB 1950; CBE 1941; MA; FRICS (Council 1950-53); late RE; Hon. Colonel 135 Survey Engineer Regt TA, 1954-60; Consultant Surveyor; b 23 July 1895; m 1928, Nancy Katharine Coleridge, one s. Educ: Wellington College; Royal Military Acad. European War, pow, 1914-18. Served in Middle East, North Africa, Italy, 1939-45. Director of Military Survey, War Office, 1946; Director-General, Ordnance Survey, 1949-53. MA Oxon by decree, 1954 (Member of New College). Senior Lecturer in Surveying, 1954-55. FRGS (Hon. Vice-President, 1969). Consultant to: the Times Atlas, 1955-59; Spartan Air Services of Ottawa,

1956-71. Chm. Meridian Airmaps Ltd. President Photogrammetric Society 1957-59; President International Society for Photogrammetry, 1956-60 (Vice-President, 1960-64). Founder's Medal, RGS, 1978. Legion of Honour (USA) 1945. FRPSL 1975. Recreations: golf, philately. Address: Cricket Hill Cottage, Cricket Hill Lane, Yateley, Camberley, Surrey GU17 7BA. T. Yateley 872130. Club: Naval and Military.

BROWN, Prof. Robert, DSc London; FRS 1956; Regius Professor of Botany, Edinburgh University, 1958-77, now Emeritus Professor; b 29 July 1908; s of Thomas William and Ethel Minnie Brown; m 1940, Morna Doris Mactaggart. Educ: English School, Cairo; University of London. Assistant Lecturer in Botany, Manchester University, 1940-44; Lecturer in Botany, Bedford College, London, 1944-46; Reader in Plant Physiology, Leeds University, 1946-52; Professor of Botany, Cornell University, 1952-53; Director, Agricultural Research Council Unit of Plant Cell Physiology 1953-58. Publications: various papers on plant physiology in the Annals of Botany, Proceedings of Royal Society and Journal of Experimental Botany. Recreation: gardening. Address: 5 Treble House Terrace, Blewbury, Didcot Oxfordshire. T: Blewbury 850415.

BROWN, Sir Robert C.; see Crichton-Brown.

BROWN, Robert Crofton; MP (Lab) Newcastle upon Tyne West since 1966; b 16 May 1921; m 1945, Marjorie Hogg, Slaithwaite, Yorks; one s one d. Educ: Denton Road Elementary School; Atkinson Road Technical School. Rutherford Coll. Apprenticed plumber and gasfitter, Newcastle & Gateshead Gas Co., 1937. War Service, 1942-46. Plumber from 1946; Inspector, 1949; in service of Northern Gas Board until 1966. Secretary of Constituency Labour Party and Agent to MP for 16 years. Parly Sec., Ministry of Transport, 1968-70; Parly Under-Sec., Social Security, March-Sept. 1974; Parly Under-Sec. of State for Defence for the Army, 1974-79. Vice-Chm., Parly Lab Party Transport Gp, 1970-. Member Newcastle Co. Borough Council (Chief Whip, Lab. Gp), retd 1968. Recreations: walking, reading, gardening. Address: 82 Beckside Gardens, Newcastle upon Tyne NE5 1BQ. T: Newcastle upon Tyne 672199.

BROWN, Prof. Robert Hanbury, FRS 1960; Professor of Physics (Astronomy), in the University of Sydney, 1964-81, now Emeritus Professor b 31 Aug. 1916; s of Colonel Basil Hanbury Brown and Joyce Blaker; m 1952, Hilda Heather Chesterman; two s one d. Educ: Tonbridge School; Brighton Technical College; City and Guilds College, London. Air Ministry, Bawdsey Research Station, working on radar, 1936-42; British Air Commission, Washington, DC, 1942-45; Principal Scientific Officer, Ministry of Supply 1945-47; ICI Research Fellow of Manchester University, 1949; Professor of Radio-Astronomy in the University of Manchester, 1960-63. Holweck Prize, 1959; Eddington Medal, 1968; Lyle Medal, 1971; Britannica Australia Award, 1971; Hughes Medal, 1971. FAA 1967; Hon. FNA 1975; Hon. FASc 1975. Publications: The Exploration of Space by Radio, 1957; The Intensity Interferometer, 1974; Man and the Stars, 1978; publications in Physical and Astronomical Journals. Address: School of Physics, Sydney University Sydney, NSW 2006, Australia.

BROWN, Robert Ross Buchanan, CBE 1968; Chairman, Southern Electricity Board, 1954-74; b 15 July 1909; 2nd s of Robert and Rhoda Brown, Sydney, Australia; m 1940, Ruth Sarah Aird; one s two d. Educ: The King's School, Sydney; Sydney University; Cambridge University. BA (Cantab.), BSc. Deputy Gen. Manager, Wessex Electricity Co., 1938. Captain 4th County of London Yeomanry, 1940-45. Gen. Manager, Wessex Electricity Co., 1945; Deputy Chairman, Southern Electricity Board, 1948. Recreations: gardening, golf. Address: Mumbery Lodge, School Hill, Wargrave, Reading, Berks.

BROWN, Ven. Robert Saville; Archdeacon of Bedford, 1974-79, Archdeacon Emeritus since 1979; b 12 Sept. 1914; s of John Harold Brown and Frances May Brown; m 1947, Charlotte (née Furber); one s. Educ: Bedford Modern Sch.; Selwyn Coll., Cambridge (MA). Curate: G. Berkhamsted, 1940-44; St Mary's, Hitchin, 1944-47; Vicar, Wonersh, 1947-53. Rector, Gt Berkhamsted, 1953-69; Canon of St Albans Cath., 1965; Vicar of St Paul's, Bedford, 1969-74; Priest-in-Charge of Old Warden, 1974-79. Recreations: reading, travel, chess. Address: 9 Treachers Close, Chesham, Bucks HP5 2HD.

BROWN, Roland George MacCormack; Legal Adviser, Technical Assistance Group, Commonwealth Secretariat, since 1975; b 27 Dec. 1924; 2nd s of late Oliver and of Mona Brown; m 1964, Irene Constance, d of Rev Claude Coltman; two s one d. Educ: Ampleforth College; Trinity College Cambridge. Called to the Bar, Gray's Inn, Nov. 1949. Practised at the Bar Nov. 1949-May 1961; Attorney-Gen., Tanganyika, later Tanzania, 1961-65 Legal Consultant to Govt of Tanzania, 1965-72; Fellow, Inst. of Develt Studies, Sussex Univ., 1973-75; on secondment as Special Adviser to Sec. of State for Trade, 1974. Publication: (with Richard O'Sullivan, QC) The Law of Defamation. Recreation: swimming. Address: c/o Commonwealth Secretariat, Marlborough House, Pall Mall, SW1.

BROWN, Rt. Rev. Ronald; see Birkenhead, Bishop Suffragan of.

BROWN, Ronald, (Ron); MP (Lab) Edinburgh Leith, since 1979; b Edinburgh, 1940; s of James Brown and Margaret McLaren; m 1963, May

Smart; two s. *Educ:* Pennywell Primary Sch., Edinburgh; Ainslie Park High Sch., Edinburgh; Bristo Technical Inst., Edinburgh. National Service, Royal Signals. Five yrs engrg apprenticeship with Bruce Peebles and Co. Ltd, East Pilton, Edinburgh. Chm., Pilton Br., AUEW; formerly: Chm. Works Cttee, Edinburgh Dist of SSEB; Convenor of Shop Stewards, Parsons Peebles Ltd, Edinburgh. Formerly Councillor for Central Leith, Edinburgh Town Council; Regional Councillor for Royston/Granton, Lothian Reg. Council, 1974-79. Member: Lothian and Borders Fire Bd, 1974-79; Central Scotland Water Develt Bd, 1974-79. *Address:* c/o House of Commons, SW1A 0AA.

BROWN, Ronald William; JP; MP Hackney South and Shoreditch, since 1974 (Shoreditch and Finsbury, 1964-74) (Lab 1964-81, SDP since 1981); *b* 7 Sept. 1921; *s* of George Brown; *m* 1944, Mary Munn; one *s* two *d*. *Educ:* Elementary School, South London; Borough Polytechnic. Sen. Lectr in Electrical Engineering, Principal of Industrial Training Sch. Member: Council of Europe Assembly and WEU, 1965-68; European Parlt, 1977-79. Chm., Energy Commn, Rapporteur on Science, Technology and Aerospace questions; Parly Advr to Furniture, Timber and Allied Trades Union, 1967-81. Leader, Camberwell Borough Council, 1956; Alderman and Leader, London Bor. of Southwark, 1964. Asst Govt Whip, 1966-67. Member: Council of Europe, 1979-; WEU, 1979. FBIM. Assoc. Mem., Inst. of Engineering Designers. JP Co. London, 1961. *Address:* House of Commons, SW1; 91 Gore Road, Hackney, E9.
See also Baron George-Brown.

BROWN, Ronald William; Deputy Legal Adviser and Solicitor to Ministry of Agriculture, Fisheries and Food, to Forestry Commission and to (EEC) Intervention Board for Agricultural Produce, 1974-82; *b* 21 April 1917; *o s* of late William Nicol Brown and Eleanor Brown (*née* Dobson); *m* 1958, Elsie Joyce, *er d* of late Sir Norman Guttery, KBE, CB; two *s*. *Educ:* Dover Coll.; Corpus Christi Coll., Cambridge (MA). War service, 1939-45, King's Own Royal Regt (Lancaster), France, W Desert, Burma (Chindits) (Major). Called to Bar, Gray's Inn, 1946. Entered Legal Dept, Min. of Agric. and Fisheries, 1948; Asst Solicitor, MAFF, 1970. *Address:* 5 Gomshall Road, Cheam, Surrey SM2 7JZ. *T:* 01-393 4061.

BROWN, Roy Dudley; Director, Association of West European Shipbuilders, since 1977; *b* 5 Aug. 1916; *y s* of late Alexander and Jessie Brown; *m* 1941, Maria Margaret Barry McGhee; one *s* one *d*. *Educ:* Robert Gordon's Coll., Aberdeen; Aberdeen Univ. (MA 1935, LLB 1937). In private law practice, Glasgow, 1937-38; joined Shipbldg Conf., London, 1938; War Service, RN; Jt Sec. on amalgamation of Shipbldg Conf., Shipbldg Employers Fedn, and Dry Dock Owners and Repairers Central Council into Shipbuilders and Repairers National Assoc., 1967; Dep. Dir, 1973, until dissolution of Assoc. on nationalization, 1977. Sec., Shipbldg Corp. Ltd, 1943-77. Mem. Council, Royal Instn of Naval Architects. Liveryman, Worshipful Co. of Shipwrights. *Recreations:* golf, wine, gardening. *Address:* 1 Shirley Church Road, Croydon, Surrey. *T:* 01-654 2089. *Clubs:* Caledonian, Den Norske.

BROWN, Rear-Adm. Roy S. F.; *see* Foster-Brown.

BROWN, Rt. Rev. Russel Featherstone; *b* Newcastle upon Tyne, 7 Jan. 1900; *s* of Henry John George Brown and Lucy Jane Ferguson; *m* 1940, Priscilla Marian Oldacres (*d* 1948); three *s*. *Educ:* Bishop's Univ., Lennoxville, PQ, Canada. BA (Theo.) 1933. RAF, 1918-19; business, 1919-29; University, 1929-33; Deacon, 1933; Priest, 1934; Curate, Christ Church Cathedral, Montreal, 1933-36; Priest-in-Charge, Fort St John, BC, 1936-40; Rector of Sherbrooke, PQ, 1940-54; Canon, Holy Trinity Cathedral, Quebec, 1948; Rector, St Matthew's, Quebec, PQ, 1954-60; Archdeacon of Quebec, 1954-60; Bishop of Quebec, 1960-71; subsequently teaching in Papua New Guinea. Assistant Bishop of Montreal, 1976. Hon. DCL Bishop's Univ., Lennoxville, 1961; Hon. DD, Montreal Diocesan Theological College, 1968. *Address:* Montreal Diocesan Theological College, 3473 University Street, Montreal, Que H3A 2A8, Canada.

BROWN, Russell; *see* Brown, J. R.

BROWN, Simon Denis; First Junior Treasury Counsel, Common Law, since 1979; a Recorder of the Crown Court, since 1979; *b* 9 April 1937; *s* of late Denis Baer Brown and of Edna Elizabeth (*née* Abrahams); *m* 1963, Jennifer Buddicom; two *s* one *d*. *Educ:* Stowe Sch.; Worcester Coll., Oxford (law degree). Commnd 2nd Lt RA, 1955-57. Called to the Bar, Middle Temple, 1961; Master of the Bench, Hon. Soc. of Middle Temple, 1980-. *Recreations:* golf, skiing, theatre. *Address:* 2 Garden Court, Temple, EC4. *T:* 01-353 4741. *Club:* Denham Golf.

BROWN, Sir Stanley; *see* Brown, Sir F. H. S.

BROWN, Sir Stephen; *see* Brown, Sir A. J. S.

BROWN, Hon. Sir Stephen, Kt 1975; Hon. Mr Justice Stephen Brown; a Judge of the High Court, Queen's Bench Division, since 1977 (Family Division, 1975-77); *b* 3 Oct. 1924; *s* of Wilfrid Brown and Nora Elizabeth Brown, Longdon Green, Staffordshire; *m* 1951, Patricia Ann, *d* of Richard Good, Tenbury Wells, Worcs; two *s* (twins) three *d*. *Educ:* Malvern College; Queens' College, Cambridge. Served RNVR (Lieut), 1943-46. Barrister, Inner Temple, 1949; Bencher, 1974. Dep. Chairman, Staffs QS, 1963-71;

Recorder of West Bromwich, 1965-71; QC 1966; a Recorder, and Honorary Recorder of West Bromwich, 1972-75; Presiding Judge, Midland and Oxford Circuit, 1977-81. Member: Parole Board, England and Wales, 1967-71; Butler Cttee on mentally abnormal offenders, 1972-75; Adv. Council on Penal System, 1977-; Chairman: Adv. Cttee on Conscientious Objectors, 1971-75; Council of Malvern Coll., 1976-. *Recreation:* sailing. *Address:* 78 Hamilton Avenue, Harborne, Birmingham B17 8AR. *T:* 021-427 1313; Royal Courts of Justice, Strand, WC2. *Clubs:* Garrick, Naval; Birmingham (Birmingham).

BROWN, Sir Thomas, Kt 1974; Chairman, Eastern Health and Social Services Board, Northern Ireland (formerly NI Hospitals Authority), since 1967; *b* 11 Oct. 1915; *s* of Ephraim Hugh and Elizabeth Brown. *Educ:* Royal Belfast Academical Institution. Admitted Solicitor, 1938. Mem., Royal Commn on NHS, 1976-79. *Recreations:* boating, chairmanship. *Address:* Westgate, Portaferry, Co. Down, Northern Ireland. *T:* Portaferry 309.

BROWN, Prof. Thomas Julian, MA; FSA; FBA 1982; Professor of Palæography, University of London, since 1961; *b* 24 Feb. 1923; *s* of Tom Brown, land agent, Penrith, Cumberland, and Helen Wright Brown, MBE; *m* 1st, 1959, Alison Macmillan Dyson (marr. diss. 1979); two *d*; 2nd, 1980, Sanchia Mary David (*née* Blair-Leighton). *Educ:* Westminster School (KS); Christ Church, Oxford. 2nd class, Class. Hon. Mods, 1942, and Lit.Hum, 1948. The Border Regt, 1942-45, mostly attached Inf. Heavy Weapons School, Netheravon. Asst Keeper Dept of MSS, British Museum, 1950-60. FSA 1956. Member, Inst. for Advanced Study, Princeton, NJ, 1966-67. Lyell Reader in Bibliography, Univ. of Oxford, 1976-77; Vis. Fellow, All Souls Coll., Oxford, 1976-77. FKC, 1975. *Publications:* (with R. L. S. Bruce-Mitford, A. S..C. Ross, E. G. Stanley and others) Codex Lindisfarnensis, vol. ii, 1960; Latin Palæography since Traube (inaugural lecture), Trans. Camb. Bibliographical Society, 1963; The Stonyhurst Gospel (Roxburghe Club), 1969; The Durham Ritual, 1969; Northumbria and the Book of Kells (Jarrow Lect.), 1972; (with C. D. Verey and E. Coatsworth) The Durham Gospels, 1980. *Address:* King's College, Strand, WC2R 2LS. *T:* 01-836 5454; 1A Edenbridge Road, E9 7DR. *T:* 01-986 0692.

BROWN, Thomas Walter Falconer, CBE 1958; Consultant in Marine Engineering; *b* 10 May 1901; *s* of Walter Falconer Brown, MB, ChB, DPH, and Catherine Edith (*née* McGhie); *m* 1947, Lucy Mason (*née* Dickie); one *s* one *d*. *Educ:* Ayr Academy; Glasgow University; Harvard University. BSc (special dist. in Nat. Philos.), 1921; DSc (Glas.), 1927; SM (Harvard), 1928; Assoc. of Royal Technical College, Glasgow, 1922. Asst General Manager, Alex Stephen & Sons Ltd, Linthouse, 1928-35; Technical Manager, R. & W. Hawthorn Leslie & Co. Ltd, Newcastle upon Tyne, 1935-44; Director of Parsons and Marine Engineering Turbine Research and Development Assoc., Wallsend, 1944-62; Director of Marine Engineering Research (BSRA), Wallsend Research Station, 1962-66. Liveryman, Worshipful Co. of Shipwrights, Freedom City of London, 1946. Eng Lieut, and Eng Lt-Comdr RNVR, Clyde Div., 1924-36. De Laval Gold Medal, Sweden, 1957. *Publications:* various technical papers in Trans Instn Mech. Engineers, Inst. Marine Engineers, NE Coast Instn of Engineers & Shipbuilders, etc. *Recreations:* model-making and gardening. *Address:* Dumbreck, Wylam, Northumberland NE41 8JB. *T:* Wylam 2228.

BROWN, Air Cdre Sir Vernon, Kt 1952; CB 1944; OBE 1937; MA; CEng; FRAeS; *b* 10 Jan. 1889; *s* of Ernest J. Brown and H. M. Messent, Blackheath; *m* 1st, 1914, Constance Mary (*d* 1967), *d* of late F. E. Duckham (Port of London Authority) and Maud McDougall, Blackheath; one *d*; 2nd, 1971, Sheila Rigby, *d* of late T. M. Rigby and Agnes Carter. *Educ:* Eastbourne College; Jesus College, Cambridge (MA). Gas Engineering prior to 1915, then RFC (French Croix de Guerre). Served in UK, France, and after war in Iraq and Egypt. Retired 1937 and became Chief Inspector of Accidents, Air Ministry and later Ministry of Civil Aviation; retired as Permanent Civil Servant, 1952. Hon. FSLAET. *Recreation:* music. *Address:* Eastholme, Station Road, Yarmouth, Isle of Wight PO41 0QT. *T:* Yarmouth (IoW) 760189. *Clubs:* Naval and Military; Royal Solent Yacht.

BROWN, Walter Graham S.; *see* Scott-Brown.

BROWN, William, CBE 1971; Deputy Chairman since 1974, and Managing Director, since 1966, Scottish Television Ltd; *b* 24 June 1929; *s* of Robert C. Brown, Ayr; *m* 1955, Nancy Jennifer, 3rd *d* of Prof. George Hunter, Edmonton, Alta; one *s* three *d*. *Educ:* Ayr Academy; Edinburgh University. Lieut, RA, 1950-52. Scottish Television Ltd: London Sales Manager, 1958; Sales Dir, 1961; Dep. Man. Dir, 1963. Director: Independent Television Publications Ltd, 1968-; Scottish and Global Television Enterprises Ltd, 1970-; ITN, 1972-77; Radio Clyde Ltd, 1973-; Channel Four Co. Ltd, 1980-; Scottish Amicable Life Assurance Soc., 1981-. Director: Scottish Opera Theatre Royal Ltd, 1974-; Scottish Opera Theatre Trust Ltd, 1974-. Mem., Royal Commn on Legal Services in Scotland, 1976-80. Chm., Council, Independent Television Cos Assoc., 1978-80. *Recreations:* gardening, golf, music. *Address:* Ardencraig, 90 Drymen Road, Bearsden, Glasgow. *T:* 041-942 0115. *Club:* Caledonian.

BROWN, Sir William B. P.; *see* Pigott-Brown.

BROWN, Dr William Christopher, OBE 1966; RDI 1977; FICE, FIStructE, FASCE; Partner, Freeman, Fox & Partners, since 1970; *b* 16 Sept.

1928; s of William Edward Brown and Margaret Eliza Brown; m 1964, Celia Hermione Emmett. *Educ:* Monmouth Sch.; University Coll., Southampton (BScEng); Imperial Coll. of Science and Technol., London (DIC, PhD). FICE 1970; FIStructE 1978; FASCE 1978. Principal designer for major bridges, incl.: Volta River, 1956; Forth Road, 1964; Severn and Wye, 1966; Auckland Harbour, 1969; Erskine, 1971; Bosporus, 1973; Avonmouth, 1975; Humber. Holds patents on new concepts for long-span bridges. Designer for radio telescopes in Australia and Canada, and for other special structures. Hon. FRIBA 1978. McRobert Award, 1970; UK and European steel design awards, 1968, 1971, 1976. *Publications:* technical papers for engrg instns in UK and abroad. *Recreations:* archaeology, photography, motoring. *Address:* 1 Allen Mansions, Allen Street, W8 6UY. *T:* 01-937 6550. *Clubs:* Royal Automobile, Royal Over-Seas League.

BROWN, Maj.-Gen. William Douglas Elmes, CB 1967; CBE 1962 (OBE 1945; MBE 1941); DSO 1945; Secretary, The Dulverton Trust, since 1969; b 8 Dec. 1913; s of late Joseph William Brown, Manor House, Knaresborough, Yorks; m 1947, Nancy Ursula (d 1980), d of Colonel W. F. Basset, Netherton, nr Andover. *Educ:* Sherborne; RMA, Woolwich. 2nd Lieut, RA, 1934. Served War of 1939-45, E Africa, and N Africa (50 (Northumbrian) Div.) (despatches). Seconded to Royal Iraqi Army, 1947-50; Chief of Staff, Northern Ireland, 1961-62; Commandant, School of Artillery, 1962-64; ADC to the Queen, 1963-64; Director of Army Equipment Policy, 1964-66; Dep. Master-Gen. of the Ordnance, 1966-69. Lt-Col 1955; Brigadier, 1961; Major-General, 1964. Col Comdt, RA, 1970-78. *Recreations:* shooting, fishing, golf. *Address:* Gunner's Cottage, Littlewick Green, Maidenhead, Berks. *T:* Littlewick Green 2083. *Clubs:* Army and Navy; Hon. Co. of Edinburgh Golfers.

BROWN, William Eden T.; see Tatton Brown.

BROWN, W(illiam) Glanville, TD; Barrister-at-Law; b 19 July 1907; s of late Cecil George Brown, formerly Town Clerk of Cardiff, and late Edith Tyndale Brown; m 1st, 1935, Theresa Margaret Mary Harrison (decd); one s; 2nd, 1948, Margaret Isabel Dilks, JP, o d of late Thomas Bruce Dilks, Bridgwater. *Educ:* Llandaff Cathedral School; Magdalen College School and Magdalen College, Oxford; in France, Germany and Italy. Called to Bar, Middle Temple, 1932. Contested (L) Cardiff Central, 1935, St Albans, 1964. Served War of 1939-45, in Army (TA), Aug. 1939-Dec. 1945; attached to Intelligence Corps; served overseas 3½ years in E Africa Command, Middle East and North-West Europe. Junior Prosecutor for UK Internat. Military Tribunal for the Far East, Tokyo, 1946-48; Member: the National Arbitration Tribunal, 1949-51; Industrial Disputes Tribunal, 1959; Deputy-Chairman of various Wages Councils, 1950-64; Joint Legal Editor of English Translation of Common Market Documents for Foreign Office, 1962-63; Lectr in Germany on behalf of HM Embassy, Bonn, 1965-73. Mem., Mental Health Review Tribunal for NE Metropolitan RHB Area, 1960-79. Life Mem., RIIA. Fellow, Inst. of Linguists. *Publication:* Translation of Brunschweig's French Colonialism, 1871-1914, Myths and Realities. *Recreations:* walking, reading, watching cricket, travel. *Address:* 66 Brim Hill, N2 0HQ. *T:* 01-455 7260. *Club:* National Liberal.

BROWN, Rev. William Martyn; Priest-in-Charge, Field Dalling and Saxlingham, since 1977; b 12 July 1914; s of Edward Brown, artist; m 1939, Elizabeth Lucy Hill; one adopted s. *Educ:* Bedford School; Pembroke College, Cambridge (Scholar). 1st Class Honours in Modern Languages, 1936, MA 1947. Assistant Master, Wellington College, 1936-47; Housemaster 1943-47; Headmaster: The King's School, Ely, 1947-55; Bedford School, 1955-75. Commissioner of the Peace, 1954. Ordained 1976. *Recreation:* watercolour painting. *Address:* Lodge Cottage, Field Dalling, Holt, Norfolk. *T:* Binham 403.

BROWNE, family name of **Baron Craigton, Baron Kilmaine, Baron Oranmore, Marquess of Sligo.**

BROWNE, Major Alexander Simon Cadogan; JP; DL; b 22 July 1895; e s of late Major Alexander Browne of Callaly Castle, Northumberland; m 1918, Dorothy Mary (d 1979), d of late Major F. J. C. Howard, 8th Hussars of Moorefield, Newbridge, Co. Kildare and Baytown, Co. Meath; one d. *Educ:* Eton; RMC Sandhurst. Major 12th Royal Lancers; served European War, 1914-18; retired, 1925; re-employed, 1939-45; served HQ 23rd (Northumbrian) Div., BEF, 1940 (despatches) and with BLA 1945. Secretary to the Duke of Beaufort's Fox Hounds, 1928-38; Joint Master, Percy Fox Hounds, 1938-46. Pres., Berwick-upon-Tweed Conservative Assoc., 1970-73. Chairman, Rothbury RDC, 1950-55; CC, 1950-67, CA, 1967-74, Hon. Alderman, 1974, Northumberland; High Sheriff of Northumberland, 1958-59; JP 1946, DL 1961, Northumberland. *Address:* Callaly Castle, Alnwick, Northumberland NE66 4TA. *T:* Whittingham (Northumberland) 663. *Clubs:* Cavalry and Guards; Northern Counties (Newcastle upon Tyne).

BROWNE, Anthony Arthur Duncan M.; see Montague Browne.

BROWNE, Bernard Peter Francis K.; see Kenworthy-Browne.

BROWNE, Air Cdre Charles Duncan Alfred, CB 1971; DFC 1944; FBIM; RAF, retired; b 8 July 1922; s of Alfred Browne and Catherine (née MacKinnon); m 1946, Una Felicité Leader; one s. *Educ:* City of Oxford School. War of 1939-45: served Western Desert, Italy, Corsica and S France

in Hurricane and Spitfire Sqdns; post war service in Home, Flying Training, Bomber and Strike Commands; MoD; CO, RAF Brüggen, Germany, 1966-68; Comdt, Aeroplane and Armament Expr. Estab., 1968-71; Air Officer i/c Central Tactics and Trials Orgn, 1971-72. *Address:* c/o Midland Bank, Summertown, Oxford. *Club:* Royal Air Force.

BROWNE, Coral (Edith), (Mrs Vincent Price); actress; b Melbourne, Australia, 23 July 1913; d of Leslie Clarence Brown and Victoria Elizabeth (née Bennett); m 1950, Philip Westrope Pearman (d 1964); m 1974, Vincent Price. *Educ:* Claremont Ladies' Coll., Melb. Studied painting in Melbourne. First stage appearance, in Loyalties, Comedy Theatre, Melb., 1931; acted in 28 plays in Australia, 1931-34. First London appearance in Lover's Leap, Vaudeville, 1934, and then continued for some years playing in the West End. From 1940, successes include: The Man Who Came to Dinner, 1941; My Sister Eileen, 1943; The Last of Mrs Cheyney, 1944; Lady Frederick, 1946; Canaries Sometimes Sing, 1947; Jonathan, 1948; Castle in the Air, 1949; Othello, 1951; King Lear, 1952; Affairs of State, 1952; Simon and Laura, 1954; Nina, 1955; Macbeth, 1956; Troilus and Cressida, 1956; (Old Vic season) Hamlet, A Midsummer Night's Dream and King Lear, 1957-58; The Pleasure of His Company, 1959; Toys in the Attic, 1960; Bonne Soupe, 1961-62; The Rehearsal, 1963; The Right Honourable Gentleman, 1964-66; Lady Windermere's Fan, 1966; What the Butler Saw, 1969; My Darling Daisy, 1970; Mrs Warren's Profession, 1970; The Sea, 1973; The Waltz of the Toreadors, 1974; Ardèle, 1975; Charley's Aunt, 1976; The Importance of Being Ernest, 1977; Travesties, 1977. Has also appeared in United States and Moscow. *Films:* Auntie Mame; The Roman Spring of Mrs Stone; Dr Crippen; The Night of the Generals; The Legend of Lylah Clare; The Killing of Sister George, 1969; The Ruling Class, 1972; Theatre of Blood, 1973; The Drowning Pool, 1975; *TV series:* Time Express, 1979; Elenor, First Lady of the World, 1982. *Recreation:* needlepoint. *Address:* 16 Eaton Place, SW1.

BROWNE, Sir (Edward) Humphrey, Kt 1964; CBE 1952; FEng; Chairman, British Transport Docks Board, 1971-82; Deputy Chairman, Haden Carrier Ltd, since 1973; b 7 April 1911; m 1934, Barbara Stone (d 1970); two s. *Educ:* Repton; Magdalene College, Cambridge (BA 1931, MA 1943); Birmingham University (Joint Mining Degree). Manager, Chanters Colliery; Director and Chief Mining Engineer, Manchester Collieries Ltd, 1943-46; Production Director, North-Western Divisional Coal Board, 1947-48; Director-General of Production, National Coal Board, 1947-55; Chm., Midlands Div., NCB, 1955-60; Dep. Chm., NCB, 1960-67; Chairman: John Thompson Group, 1967-70; Woodall Duckham Gp, 1971-73 (Dep. Chm., 1967-71); Bestobell Ltd, 1973-79 (Dir, 1969). Mem., Commonwealth Develt Corp., 1969-72. President: The British Coal Utilisation Research Assoc., 1963-68; Inst. of Freight Forwarders, 1976-77. Director, National Industrial Fuel Efficiency Service, 1960-69; Pres., Institution of Mining Engineers, 1957. Pro-Chancellor, Univ. of Keele, 1971-75. *Address:* Beckbury Hall, near Shifnal, Salop. *T:* Ryton 207. *Club:* Brooks's.

BROWNE, (Edward) Michael (Andrew); QC 1970; b 29 Nov. 1910; yr s of Edward Granville Browne, Fellow of Pembroke Coll., Cambridge, and Alice Caroline Browne (née Blackburne Daniell); m 1937, Anna Florence Augusta, d of James Little Luddington; two d. *Educ:* Eton; Pembroke Coll., Cambridge (Scholar). 1st class History Tripos, 1932; MA. Barrister, Inner Temple, 1934, ad eundem Lincoln's Inn. Bencher, Inner Temple, 1964. Served War of 1939-45: RA (anti aircraft) and GS, War Office (finally GSO3, Capt.). *Address:* 19 Wallgrave Road, SW5. *T:* 01-373 3055; Wiveton Cottage, Wiveton, near Holt, Norfolk. *T:* Cley 740203. *Club:* Athenæum.

BROWNE, Hablot Robert Edgar, CMG 1955; OBE 1942; HM Diplomatic Service, retired; employed in Commonwealth Office (formerly CRO), 1959-67; b 11 Aug. 1905; s of Dr Hablot J. M. Browne, Hoylake, Cheshire; m 1933, Petra Elsie, d of Peter Tainsh, OBE; one d. *Educ:* St George's, Harpenden; Christ's College, Cambridge. Colonial Administrative Service, Nigeria, 1928; Assistant Colonial Secretary, Barbados, 1939; Asst. Secretary, Jamaica, 1943; Deputy Colonial Secretary, Jamaica, 1945; acted as Colonial Secretary on various occasions, 1945-49; Admin. Officer, Class I, Nigeria, 1950; Civil Secretary, Northern Region, Nigeria, 1951-55; Actg Lieut Governor, Northern Region, Nigeria, Sept. 1954; Actg Governor, Northern Region, Nigeria, Oct. 1954; retired from Colonial Administrative Service, 1955. Assistant Adviser to the Government of Qatar, Persian Gulf, 1956-57. *Recreation:* watching cricket. *Address:* 85 Bishop's Mansions, Bishop's Park Road, SW6. *T:* 01-731 3209. *Clubs:* Travellers', MCC.

BROWNE, Sir Humphrey; see Browne, Sir E. H.

BROWNE, John Ernest Douglas Delavalette; MP (C) Winchester, since 1979; Adviser to Barclays Bank Ltd, since 1978; Managing Director, Falcon Finance Management Ltd, since 1978; Director: Churchill Private Clinic, since 1980; Worms Investments Ltd, since 1981; b Hampshire, 17 Oct. 1938; s of Col Ernest Coigny Delavalette Browne, OBE, and late Victoria Mary Eugene (née Douglas); m 1965, Elizabeth Jeannette Marguerite Garthwaite. *Educ:* Malvern; RMA Sandhurst (Gwynn-Jones Schol.); Cranfield Inst. of Technology (MSc); Harvard Business Sch. (MBA). Served Grenadier Guards, British Guiana (Battalion Pilot), Cyprus, BAOR, 1959-67; Captain 1963; TA, Grenadier Guards (Volunteers), 1981-. Associate, Morgan Stanley & Co., New York, 1969-72; City of London, 1972-: with Pember & Boyle, 1972-74; Dir, Middle East Operations, European Banking Co., 1974-78; Adviser, Trustees Household Div., 1979-. Mem., Treasury Select Cttee, 1982-. Member: NFU,

1979-; Westminster CC, 1974-78; Royal United Services Inst. for Defence Studies, 1972-. Trustee, Winnall Community Assoc., 1981. Mem. Court, Univ. of Southampton, 1979-; Governor, Markham Coll., 1981-. Liveryman, Goldsmiths' Co., 1982-; Freeman of the City of London, 1979; OStJ. Interests include: economics, gold and internat. monetary affairs. *Publications*: various articles on finance, gold (A New European Currency—The Karl, ₭, 1972), defence, Middle East. *Recreations*: riding, skiing, sailing, shooting, squash. *Address*: House of Commons, SW1. *Clubs*: Boodle's, Turf.

BROWNE, Rev. Laurence Edward, DD (Cantab); MA (Manchester); Emeritus Professor, University of Leeds, since 1952; Vicar of Highbrook, Sussex, 1957-64; *b* 17 April 1887; *s* of late E. Montague Browne, Solicitor, Northampton; *m* 1st, 1920, Gladys May Dearden; one *s* two *d*; 2nd, 1938, Margaret Theresa Wingate Carpenter (*d* 1982); two *d*. *Educ*: Magdalen College School, Brackley; Sidney Sussex College, Cambridge. Lecturer and Fellow of St Augustine's College, Canterbury, 1913-20; Lecturer at Bishops' College, Calcutta, 1921-25; studying Islam in Cairo, Constantinople and Cambridge, 1926-29; Lecturer at the Henry Martyn School of Islamic Studies, Lahore, 1930-34; Rector of Gayton, Northants, 1935-46; Prof. of Comparative Religion at the University of Manchester, 1941-46; Professor of Theology, University of Leeds, 1946-52; Vicar of Shadwell, near Leeds, 1952-57. Examining Chaplain to Bp of Peterborough, 1937-50, to Bp of Ripon, 1946-57. Hulsean Lecturer, Cambridge, 1954; Godfrey Day Lectr, Trin. Coll., Dublin, 1956. *Publications*: Parables of the Gospel, 1913; Early Judaism, 1920 and 1929; Acts, in Indian Church Commentaries, 1925; From Babylon to Bethlehem, 1926, 1936 and 1951 (Telugu translation, 1932, Chinese translation 1935); The Eclipse of Christianity in Asia, 1933, New York, 1967; Christianity and the Malays, 1936; Prospects of Islam, 1944; Where Science and Religion Meet, 1951; The Quickening Word (Hulsean Lectures), 1955; Contrib. to New Peake's Commentary, 1962. *Address*: Ashton House, Bolnore Road, Haywards Heath, Sussex.

BROWNE, Mervyn Ernest, CBE 1976; ERD 1954; HM Diplomatic Service, retired 1976; *b* 3 June 1916; *s* of late Ernest Edmond Browne and of Florence Mary Browne; *m* 1942, Constance (*née* Jarvis); three *s*. *Educ*: Stockport Sec. Sch.; St Luke's Coll., Exeter; University Coll., Exeter. BScEcon London; BA Exeter. RA, 1940-46; TA, 1947-53; AER, RASC, 1953-60. Distribution of industry res., BoT, 1948-56; HM Trade Comr Service: Trade Comr, Wellington, NZ, 1957-61 and Adelaide, 1961-64; Principal Trade Comr, Kingston, Jamaica, 1964-68; HM Diplomatic Service: Counsellor (Commercial), Canberra, 1968-70; Dir, Brit. Trade in S Africa, Johannesburg, 1970-73; Consul-Gen., 1974-76 and Chargé d'Affaires, 1974 and 1976, Brit. Embassy, Manila. *Recreations*: militaria, lepidoptery, squash rackets. *Address*: 21 Dartmouth Hill, Greenwich, SE10 8AJ. *T*: 01-691 2993.

BROWNE, Michael; *see* Browne, E. M. A.

BROWNE, Lady Moyra (Blanche Madeleine), DBE 1977 (OBE 1962); Superintendent-in-Chief, St John Ambulance Brigade, since 1970; *b* 2 March 1918; *d* of 9th Earl of Bessborough, PC, GCMG; *m* 1945, Sir Denis John Browne, KCVO, FRCS (*d* 1967); one *s* one *d*. *Educ*: privately. State Enrolled Nurse, 1946. Dep. Supt-in-Chief, St John Ambulance Bde, 1964; Vice-Chm. Central Council, Victoria League, 1961-65; Vice-Pres., Royal Coll. of Nursing, 1970. DStJ 1970. *Recreations*: music, shooting, fishing, travel. *Address*: 16 Wilton Street, SW1. *T*: 01-235 1419.

BROWNE, Rt. Hon. Sir Patrick (Reginald Evelyn), PC 1974; Kt 1965; OBE (mil.) 1945; TD 1945; a Lord Justice of Appeal, 1974-80, retired; *b* 28 May 1907; *er s* of Edward Granville Browne, Sir Thomas Adams's Prof. of Arabic, Fellow of Pembroke Coll., Cambridge, and Alice Caroline (*née* Blackburne-Daniell); *m* 1st, 1931, Evelyn Sophie Alexandra (*d* 1966), *o d* of Sir Charles and Lady Walston; two *d*; 2nd, 1977, Lena, *y d* of late Mr and Mrs James Atkinson. *Educ*: Eton; Pembroke Coll., Cambridge (Hon. Fellow, 1975). Barrister-at-law, Inner Temple, 1931; QC 1960; Bencher, 1962. Deputy Chairman of Quarter Sessions, Essex, Co. Cambridge and Isle of Ely, 1963-65; a Judge of the High Court of Justice, Queen's Bench Div., 1965-74. A Controller, Royal Opera House Development Land Trust, 1981-. Served Army, 1939-45. *Address*: Thriplow Bury, Thriplow, Cambs. *T*: Fowlmere 234. *Clubs*: Garrick; Cambridge County.

BROWNE, Percy Basil; Director, Western Counties Building Society, since 1965; *b* 2 May 1923; *s* of late Lt-Col W. P. Browne, MC; *m* 1953, Jenefer Mary, *d* of late Major George Gerald Petherick and the late Lady Jeane Petherick (*née* Pleydell-Bouverie). *Educ*: The Downs, Colwall; Eton College. Served War of 1939-45 (commnd in Royal Dragoons): in Sicily, Italy and NW Europe. Farmer. Rode in Grand National, 1953. MP (C) Torrington Division of Devon, 1959-64. Dir, Appledore Shipbuilders Ltd, 1965-72 (former Chm.). N Devon District Councillor, 1973-79 (Vice-Chm., 1978-79). Mem., SW Reg. Hosp. Bd, 1967-70; Vice-Chm., N Devon HMC, 1967-74. High Sheriff, Devon, 1978. *Address*: Wheatley House, Dunsford, Exeter. *T*: Christow 52037.

BROWNE, Peter K.; *see* Kenworthy-Browne.

BROWNE, Sheila Jeanne, CB 1977; Senior Chief Inspector, Department of Education and Science, since 1974; *b* 25 Dec. 1924; *d* of Edward Elliott Browne. *Educ*: Lady Margaret Hall, Oxford (MA; Hon. Fellow 1978); Ecole des Chartes, Paris. Asst Lectr, Royal Holloway Coll., Univ. of London,

1947-51; Tutor and Fellow of St Hilda's Coll., Oxford and Univ. Lectr in French, Oxford, 1951-61, Hon. Fellow, St Hilda's Coll., 1978; HM Inspector of Schools, 1961-70; Staff Inspector, Secondary Educn, 1970-72; Chief Inspector, Secondary Educn, 1972; Dep. Sen. Chief Inspector, DES, 1972-74. Hon. DLitt Warwick, 1981. *Recreations*: medieval France, language, mountains. *Address*: 9 Rossmore Court, Park Road, NW1 6XX. *T*: 01-402 9931.

BROWNE, Stanley George, CMG 1976; OBE 1965; MD, FRCP, FRCS, DTM, FKC; Director, Leprosy Study Centre, London, 1966-80; Consultant Adviser in Leprosy, Department of Health and Social Security and Hon. Consultant in Leprosy, UCH, 1966-79; Secretary-Treasurer, International Leprosy Association; Medical Consultant, Leprosy Mission, 1966-78; Consultant Leprologist to: St Giles' Homes; Order of Charity; Association of European Leprosy Associations; All-Africa Leprosy Training and Rehabilitation Centre, Addis Ababa, 1966-81; President, Baptist Union, 1980-81; *b* 8 Dec. 1907; *s* of Arthur Browne and Edith Lillywhite; *m* 1940, Ethel Marion Williamson, MA (Oxon); three *s*. *Educ*: King's Coll. and KCH, London Univ. (Fellow, KCH Med. Sch., 1977); Inst. de Méd. Tropicale Prince Léopold, Antwerp. MRCS, LRCP, MB, BS (London) (Hons, Dist. in Surg., Forensic Med., Hygiene), AKC, 1933, FKC 1976; MRCP 1934 (Murchison Schol. RCP); FRCS 1935; DTM (Antwerp), 1936; MD (London), 1954; FRCP 1961. Leverhulme Res. Grant for investigating trng of African med. auxiliaries, 1954; Consultant, WHO Expert Cttee on Trng of Med. Auxiliaries; WHO Travel Grant to visit Leprosy Res. Instns, 1963. Med. Missionary, Baptist Miss. Soc., Yakusu, Belg. Congo, 1936-59; Médecin Directeur, Ecole agréée d'Infirmiers, Yakusu, 1936-59; Léproserie de Yalisombo, 1950-59; Mem. several Govt Commns concerned with health in Belgian Congo; Sen. Specialist Leprologist and Dir of Leprosy Res. Unit, Uzuakoli, E Nigeria, 1959-66; Associate Lectr in Leprosy, Ibadan Univ., 1960-65, 1968-; Vis. Lectr in leprosy in univs and med. schs in many countries. Med. Sec., British Leprosy Relief Assoc., 1968-73; Sec.-Gen., Internat. Leprosy Congress, London, 1968, Bergen, 1973, Mexico City, 1978. Associate Editor and Dir, Internat. Jl of Leprosy of Internat. Leprosy Assoc., Inc. FRSocMed; Mem. Council, 1967-71, and Fellow, Royal Soc. Trop. Med. Hygiene (Vice-Pres., 1971-73; Pres., 1977-79); Fellow, Hunterian Soc., 1974. President: Christian Med. Fellowship, 1969-71; Ludhiana British Fellowship, 1974-; Internat. Assoc. of Physicians for the Overseas Services, 1978-; Med. Missionary Assoc., 1982-; Co-founder and first Chm., Christian Med. Fellowship of Nigeria; Chairman: Internat. Congress of Christian Physicians, 1972-75 (Vice-Pres., 1975-); Editorial Board of Leprosy Review, 1968-73 (Consulting Editor, 1973-); Founder Member: Internat. Filariasis Assoc.; Internat. Soc. of Tropical Dermatology (and Mem., Bd of Dirs, 1976-79). Member: Leprosy Expert Cttee, WHO (Chm., 1976); Assoc. de Léprologues de langue française (Conseiller technique); Sections Dermatology, Med. Educn, RSM; Medical Policy Cttee, Methodist Missionary Soc.; Medical Adv. Cttee, Baptist Missionary Soc.; British Council, Dr Schweitzer's Hosp. Fund; Comité de Directeurs, Assoc. Internat. du Dr Schweitzer; Medical Commn, European Co-ordinating Cttee of Anti-Leprosy Assocs, 1966- (Chm. 1971-74); Med. Cttee, Hosp. for Tropical Diseases, London, 1966-79; Editorial Bd, Tropical Doctor; Soc. for Health Educn; Acid-Fast Club. Hon. Member: Associão Brasileira de Leprologia; Sociedad Argentina de Leprologia; Korean Leprosy Assoc.; Sociedad Mexicana de Dermatologia, 1975; Sociedad Mexicana de Leprologia, 1976; Dermatol. Soc. of S Africa; Hon. Life Mem., Nigeria Soc. of Health; Hon. Foreign Mem., Belgian Royal Acad. of Med., 1980. Lectures: A. B. Mitchell Meml, QUB, 1967; Godfrey Day Meml, Dublin, 1974; Kellersberger Meml, Addis Ababa, 1978; Rendle Short Meml, Christian Medical Fellowship, 1978; Gandhi Meml, New Delhi, 1978. Sir Charlton Briscoe Prize for Research, 1934; Medal, Royal African Soc., 1970 (Life Mem.); Stewart Prize for Epidemiology, BMA, 1975; Ambuj Nath Bose Prize in Tropical Medicine, RCPE, 1977; Damien-Dutton Award, USA, 1979; Special Appreciation prize, Nihon Kensho-kai, 1979; Silver Medal of St Lazarus of Jerusalem, 1981. J. N. Chowdury Gold Medallist and Orator, Calcutta, 1978. Holds foreign orders incl.: Chevalier de l'Ordre Royal du Lion, 1948; Officier de l'Ordre de Léopold II, 1958; Comdr, Order of Malta, 1973; Commandeur, Ordre de Léopold, 1980. *Publications*: As the Doctor sees it — in Congo, 1950; Leprosy: new hope and continuing challenge, 1967; numerous articles on trop. diseases, esp. leprosy and onchocerciasis, and on med. educn in learned jls; booklets on med. missionary work, med. ethics, etc. *Relevant publications*: Bonganga: the story of a missionary doctor, by Sylvia and Peter Duncan, 1958; Mister Leprosy, by Phyllis Thompson, 1980. *Recreations*: photography, reading, writing. *Address*: 16 Bridgefield Road, Sutton, Surrey SM1 2DG. *T*: 01-642 1656.

BROWNE, Sir Thomas Anthony G.; *see* Gore Browne.

BROWNE-CAVE, Sir Robert C.; *see* Cave-Browne-Cave.

BROWNE-WILKINSON, Hon. Sir Nicolas Christopher Henry, Kt 1977; Hon. Mr Justice Browne-Wilkinson; a Judge of the High Court, Chancery Division, since 1977; *b* 30 March 1930; *s* of late Canon A. R. Browne-Wilkinson and Molly Browne-Wilkinson; *m* 1955, Ursula de Lacy Bacon; three *s* two *d*. *Educ*: Lancing; Magdalen Coll., Oxford (BA). Called to Bar, 1953, Bencher, Lincoln's Inn, 1977; QC 1972. Junior Counsel: to Registrar of Restrictive Trading Agreements, 1964-66; to Attorney-General in Charity Matters, 1966-72; in bankruptcy, to Dept of Trade and Industry, 1966-72; a Judge of the Courts of Appeal of Jersey and Guernsey, 1976-77. Pres., Employment Appeal Tribunal, 1981-. *Publication*: (ed) chapter on Charities in Halsbury's Laws of England, 4th edn. *Recreations:* tennis, squash, gardening. *Address:* 4 St James's Square, SW1.

BROWNING, Dame Daphne, (Lady Browning); *see* du Maurier, Dame Daphne.

BROWNING, (David) Peter (James); Chief Education Officer of Bedfordshire, since 1973; *b* 29 May 1927; *s* of late Frank Browning and of Lucie A. (*née* Hiscock); *m* 1953, Eleanor Berry, *d* of late J. H. Forshaw, CB, FRIBA; three *s*. *Educ:* Christ's Coll., Cambridge (MA (Engl. and Mod. Langs Tripos)); Sorbonne; Univs of Strasbourg and Perugia. Personal Asst to Vice-Chancellor, Liverpool Univ., 1952-56; Asst Teacher, Willenhall Comprehensive Sch., 1956-59; Sen. Admin. Asst, Somerset LEA, 1959-62; Asst Dir of Educn, Cumberland LEA, 1962-66; Dep. Chief Educn Officer, Southampton LEA, 1966-69; Chief Educn Officer of Southampton, 1969-73. Member: Schools Council Governing Council and 5-13 Steering Cttee, 1969-75; Council, Univ. of Southampton, 1970-73; CofE Bd of Educn Schools Cttee, 1970-75; Council, Nat. Youth Orch., 1972-77; Merchant Navy Trng Bd, 1973-77; British Educnl Administration Soc. (Chm., 1974-78); UGC, 1974-79; Taylor Cttee of Enquiry into Management and Govt of Schs, 1975-77; Governing Body, Centre for Inf. on Language Teaching and Research, 1975-80; European Forum for Educational Admin (Chm., 1977); Library Adv. Council (England), 1978-81; Consultant, Ministry of Education: Sudan, 1976; Cyprus, 1977; Italy, 1981. *Publications:* Editor: Julius Caesar for German Students, 1957; Macbeth for German Students, 1959; contrib. London Educn Rev., Educnl Administration Jl, and other educnl jls. *Recreations:* gardening, music, travel. *Address:* 70 Putnoe Lane, Bedford MK41 9AF. *T:* Bedford 62117; Park Fell Cottage, Skelwith, near Ambleside, Cumbria.

BROWNING, Rt. Rev. Edmond Lee; Bishop of Diocese of Hawaii, since 1976; *b* 11 March 1929; *s* of Edmond Lucian Browning and Cora Mae Lee; *m* 1953, Patricia A. Sparks; four *s* one *d*. *Educ:* Univ. of the South (BA 1952); School of Theology, Sewanee, Tenn (BD 1954). Curate, Good Shepherd, Corpus Christi, Texas, 1954-56; Rector, Redeemer, Eagle Pass, Texas, 1956-59; Rector, All Souls, Okinawa, 1959-63; Japanese Lang. School, Kobe, Japan, 1963-65; Rector, St Matthews, Okinawa, 1965-67; Archdeacon of Episcopal Church, Okinawa, 1965-67; first Bishop of Okinawa, 1967-71; Bishop of American Convocation, 1971-73; Executive for National and World Mission, on Presiding Bishop's Staff, United States Episcopal Church, 1974-76. Hon. DD, Univ. of the South, Sewanee, Tenn, 1970. *Publication:* Essay on World Mission, 1977. *Address:* Queen Emma Square, Honolulu, Hawaii 96813, USA. *T:* 808/536-7776; (home) 2120 Mauna Place, Honolulu, Hawaii 96822. *T:* 808/537-6443.

BROWNING, Dr Keith Anthony, FRS 1978; in charge of Meteorological Office Radar Research Laboratory, Royal Signals and Radar Establishment, Malvern, Worcs, since 1966; *b* 31 July 1938; *s* of late Sqdn Ldr James Anthony Browning and Amy Hilda (*née* Greenwood); *m* 1962, Ann Muriel (*née* Baish), BSc, MSc; one *s* two *d*. *Educ:* Commonwealth Grammar Sch., Swindon, Wilts; Imperial Coll. of Science and Technology, Univ. of London. BSc, ARCS, PhD, DIC. Research atmospheric physicist, Air Force Cambridge Research Laboratories, Mass, USA, 1962-66; Meteorological Office: Principal Research Fellow, 1966-69; Principal Scientific Officer, 1969-72; Sen. Principal Scientific Officer, 1972-79; Dep. Chief Scientific Officer, 1979-; Ch. Scientist, Nat. Hail Res. Experiment, USA, 1974-75. Member: Council, Royal Met. Soc., 1971-74 (Vice-Pres., 1979-81); Editing Cttee, Qly Jl RMetS, 1975-78; Inter-Union Commn on Radio Meteorology, 1975-78; Internat. Commn on Cloud Physics, 1976-; British Nat. Cttee for Physics, 1979-; Vice-Chm., Met. and Atmos. Phys. Sub-Cttee, British Nat. Cttee for Geodesy and Geophysics, 1979-. L. F. Richardson Prize, 1968, Buchan Prize, 1972, RMetS; L. G. Groves Meml Prize for Meteorology, Met. Office, 1969; Meisinger Award, Amer. Met. Soc., 1974, Fellow of the Society, 1975; Charles Chree Medal and Prize, Inst. of Physics, 1981. *Publications:* meteorological papers in learned jls, mainly in Britain and USA. *Recreations:* home and garden. *Address:* Oak Lawn, 71 Albert Road South, Malvern, Worcs WR14 3AH. *T:* Malvern 61701.

BROWNING, Peter; *see* Browning, D. P. J.

BROWNING, Rex Alan; Deputy Secretary, Overseas Development Administration, since 1981; *b* 22 July 1930; *s* of Gilbert H. W. Browning and Gladys (*née* Smith); *m* 1961, Paula McKain; three *d*. *Educ:* Bristol Grammar Sch.; Merton Coll., Oxford (Postmaster) (MA). HM Inspector of Taxes, 1952; Asst Principal, Colonial Office, 1957; Private Sec. to Parly Under-Sec. for the Colonies, 1960; Principal, Dept of Techn. Co-operation, 1961; transf. ODM, 1964; seconded to Diplomatic Service as First Sec. (Aid), British High Commn, Singapore, 1969; Asst Sec., 1971; Counsellor, Overseas Develt, Washington, and Alternate UK Exec. Dir, IBRD, 1973-76; Under-Secretary: ODM, 1976-78; Dept of Trade, 1978-80; ODA, 1980-81. *Address:* 10 Fieldway, Orpington, Kent. *T:* Orpington 23675.

BROWNING, Prof. Robert, MA; FBA 1978; Professor Emeritus, University of London; *b* 15 Jan. 1914; *s* of Alexander M. Browning and Jean M. Browning (*née* Miller); *m* 1st, 1946, Galina Chichekova; two *d*; 2nd, 1972, Ruth Gresh. *Educ:* Kelvinside Academy, Glasgow; Glasgow Univ. (MA); Balliol Coll., Oxford. Served Army, Middle East, Italy, Balkans, 1939-46. Harmsworth Sen. Scholar, Merton Coll., Oxford, 1946; Lectr, University Coll. London, 1947, Reader, 1955; Prof. of Classics and Ancient History,

Birkbeck Coll., Univ. of London, 1965-81. Fellow, Dumbarton Oaks, Washington, DC, 1982. President, Soc. for Promotion of Hellenic Studies, 1974-77. Corresponding Mem., Athens Acad., 1981. Hon. DLitt Birmingham 1980. *Publications:* Medieval and Modern Greek, 1969; Justinian an? Theodora, 1971; Byzantium and Bulgaria, 1975; The Emperor Julian, 197? Studies in Byzantine History, Literature and Education, 1977; The Byzantine Empire, 1980; articles in learned jls of many countries. *Address:* 17 Belsiz? Park Gardens, NW3.

BROWNING, Rev. Canon Wilfrid Robert Francis; Canon Residentiary o? Christ Church Cathedral, Oxford, since 1965; *b* 29 May 1918; *s* of Charle? Robert and Mabel Elizabeth Browning; *m* 1948, Elizabeth Beeston; two *s* twe? *d*. *Educ:* Westminster School; Christ Church, Oxford; Cuddesdon Coll? Oxford. MA, BD Oxon. Deacon 1941, priest 1942, dio. of Peterborough; o? staff of St Deiniol's Library, Hawarden, 1946-48; Vicar of St Richard's, Hove? 1948-51; Rector of Great Haseley, 1951-59; Lectr, Cuddesdon Coll., Oxford? 1951-59 and 1965-70; Canon Residentiary of Blackburn Cath. and Warde? of Whalley Abbey, Lancs, 1959-65; Director of Ordinands and Post? Ordination Trng (Oxford dio.), 1965-; Dir of Trng for Non-Stipendiar? Ordinands and Clergy, 1972-; Examining Chaplain: Blackburn, 1960-7? Manchester, 1970-78; Oxford, 1965-. Member of General Synod, 1973-; Selec? Preacher, Oxford Univ., 1972, 1981. *Publications:* Commentary on St Luke'? Gospel, 1960, 5th edn 1979; Meet the New Testament, 1964; ed, The Anglica? Synthesis, 1965. *Address:* 70 Yarnells Hill, Oxford OX2 9BG. *T:* Oxfor? 721330.

BROWNLEE, Prof. George; Professor of Pharmacology, King's College? University of London, 1958-78, retired; now Emeritus Professor; *b* 1911; *s* o? late George R. Brownlee and of Mary C. C. Gow, Edinburgh; *m* 194?? Margaret P. M. Cochrane (*d* 1970), 2nd *d* of Thomas W. P. Cochrane an? Margaret P. M. S. Milne, Bo'ness, Scotland; three *s*; 2nd, 1977, Betty Jea? Gaydon (marr. diss. 1981), *o d* of Stanley H. Clutterham and Margaret M? Fox, Sidney, Australia. *Educ:* Tynecastle Sch.; Heriot Watt Coll., Edinburgh? BSc 1936, DSc 1950, Glasgow; PhD 1939, London. Rammell Schol? Biological Standardization Labs of Pharmaceutical Soc., London; subseq. Hea? of Chemotherapeutic Div., Wellcome Res. Labs, Beckenham; Reader i? Pharmacology, King's Coll., Univ. of London, 1949. Editor, Jl of Pharmac? and Pharmacology, 1955-. FKC, 1971. *Publications:* (with Prof. J. P? Quilliam) Experimental Pharmacology, 1952; papers on: chemotherapy o? tuberculosis and leprosy; structure and pharmacology of the polymyxins? endocrinology; toxicity of drugs; neurohumoral transmitters in smoot? muscle, etc., in: Brit. Jl Pharmacology; Jl Physiology; Biochem. Jl; Nature? Lancet; Annals NY Acad. of Science; Pharmacological Reviews, etc? *Recreations:* collecting books, making things. *Address:* 602 Gilbert House? Barbican, EC2. *T:* 01-638 9543. *Club:* Athenæum.
See also G. G. Brownlee.

BROWNLEE, Prof. George Gow, PhD; E. P. Abraham Professor o? Chemical Pathology, Sir William Dunn School of Pathology, University o? Oxford, since 1980; Fellow of Lincoln College, Oxford, since 1980; *b* 13 Jan? 1942; *s* of Prof. George Brownlee, *qv*; *m* 1966, Margaret Susan Kemp; on? *s* one *d*. *Educ:* Dulwich College; Emmanuel Coll., Cambridge (MA, PhD?) Scientific staff of MRC at Laboratory of Molecular Biology, Cambridge? 1966-80. Fellow, Emmanuel Coll., Cambridge, 1967-71. Colworth Medal? Biochemical Soc., 1977. *Publications:* Determination of Sequences in RNA? (Vol. 3, Part I of Laboratory Techniques in Biochemistry and Molecula? Biology), 1972; scientific papers in Jl of Molecular Biology, Nature, Cel? Nucleic Acids Research, etc. *Recreations:* gardening, cricket. *Address:* Si? William Dunn School of Pathology, South Parks Road, Oxford. *T:* Oxfor? 57321.

BROWNLIE, Albert Dempster; Vice-Chancellor, University of Canterbury? Christchurch, New Zealand, since 1977; *b* 3 Sept. 1932; *s* of Albert Newma? and Netia Brownlie; *m* 1955, Noelene Eunice (*née* Meyer); two *d*. *Educ?* Univ. of Auckland, NZ (MCom). Economist, NZ Treasury, 1954-5? Lecturer, Sen. Lectr, Associate Prof. in economics, Univ. of Auckland? 1956-64; Prof. and Head of Dept of Economics, Univ. of Canterbury? Christchurch, 1965-77. Chairman: Monetary and Economic Council, 1972-7? Australia-NZ Foundn, 1979-; UGC Cttee to Review NZ Univ. Educn, 1980-? Member: Commonwealth Experts Group on New Internat. Economic Orde? 1975-77; Commonwealth Experts Gp on Econ. Growth, 1980-; Wag? Hearing Tribunal, 1976. Silver Jubilee Medal, 1977. *Publications:* articles i? learned jls. *Address:* University of Canterbury, Christchurch, New Zealand? *T:* 488-489.

BROWNLIE, Prof. Ian, QC; DCL; FBA; FRGS; Chichele Professor o? Public International Law, and Fellow of All Souls College, University o? Oxford, since 1980; *b* 19 Sept. 1932; *s* of John Nason Brownlie and Am? Isabella (*née* Atherton); *m* 1st, 1957, Jocelyn Gale; one *s* two *d*; 2nd, 197? Christine Apperley. *Educ:* Alsop High Sch., Liverpool; Hertford Coll? Oxford (Gibbs Scholar, 1952; BA 1953); King's Coll., Cambridg? (Humanitarian Trust Student, 1955). DPhil Oxford, 1961; DCL Oxfor? 1976. Called to the Bar, Gray's Inn, 1958; QC 1979. Lectr, Nottingham Univ? 1957-63; Fellow and Tutor in Law, Wadham Coll., Oxford, 1963-76 an? Lectr, Oxford Univ., 1964-76; Prof. of Internat. Law, LSE, Univ. of London? 1976-80. Reader in Public Internat. Law, Inns of Ct Sch. of Law, 1973-7? Dir of Studies, Internat. Law Assoc., 1982-. Vis. Professor: Univ. of E Afric? 1968-69; Ghana, 1971; Florence, 1977. Lectr, Hague Acad. of Internat. Law?

1979. Counsel before Ct of Arbitration, Beagle Channel Case, 1974-76. Editor, British Year Book of International Law, 1974-. Assoc. Mem., Inst. of Internat. Law, 1977. FBA 1979; FRGS 1981. Japan Foundn Award, 1978. *Publications:* International Law and the Use of Force by States, 1963; Principles of Public International Law, 1966 (3rd edn 1979; Russian edn, ed G. I. Tunkin, 1977; Certif. of Merit, Amer. Soc. of Internat. Law, 1976); Basic Documents in International Law, 1967 (2nd edn 1972); The Law Relating to Public Order, 1968; Basic Documents on Human Rights, 1971 (2nd edn 1981); Basic Documents on African Affairs, 1971; African Boundaries, a legal and diplomatic encyclopaedia, 1979. *Recreations:* travel, philately. *Address:* 2 Crown Office Row, Temple, EC4Y 7HJ. *T:* 01-583 2681; All Souls College, Oxford OX1 4AL. *T:* Oxford 722251; 43 Fairfax Road, Chiswick, W4 1EN. *T:* 01-995 3647.

BROWNLOW, family name of **Baron Lurgan.**

BROWNLOW, 7th Baron *cr* 1776; **Edward John Peregrine Cust;** Bt 1677; Managing Director of Harris & Dixon (Underwriting Agencies) Ltd, since 1976; *b* 25 March 1936; *o s* of 6th Baron Brownlow and Katherine Hariot (*d* 1952), 2nd *d* of Sir David Alexander Kinloch, 11th Bt, CB, MVO; *S* father, 1978; *m* 1964, Shirlie Edith, 2nd *d* of late John Yeomans, The Manor Farm, Hill Croome, Upton-on-Severn, Worcs; one *s*. *Educ:* Eton. Member of Lloyd's, 1961-; Director, Hand-in-Hand Fire and Life Insurance Soc. (branch office of Commercial Union Assurance Co. Ltd), 1962-. High Sheriff of Lincolnshire, 1978-79. *Heir: s* Hon. Peregrine Edward Quintin Cust, *b* 9 July 1974. *Address:* The Mill, Manthorpe, Grantham, Lincolnshire NG31 8NH. *T:* Grantham 5244. *Club:* White's.

BROWNLOW, Air Vice-Marshal Bertrand, CB 1982; OBE 1967; AFC 1962; Director General, Training, Royal Air Force, since 1982; *b* 13 Jan. 1929; *s* of Robert John Brownlow and Helen Louise Brownlow; *m* 1958, Kathleen Shannon; two *s* one *d*. *Educ:* Beaufort Lodge Sch. Joined RAF, 1947; 12 and 101 Sqdns, ADC to AOC 1 Gp, 103 Sqdn, 213 Sqdn, Empire Test Pilots' Sch., OC Structures and Mech. Eng Flt RAE Farnborough, RAF Staff Coll., Air Min. Op. Requirements, 1949-64; Wing Comdr Ops, RAF Lyneham, 1964-66; Jt Services Staff Coll., 1966-67; DS RAF Staff Coll., 1967-68; Def. and Air Attaché, Stockholm, 1969-71; CO Experimental Flying, RAE Farnborough, 1971-73; Asst Comdt, Office and Flying Trng, RAF Coll., Cranwell, 1973-74; Dir of Flying (R&D), MoD, 1974-77; Comdt, A&AEE, 1977-80; Comdt, RAF Coll., Cranwell, 1980-82. *Recreations:* squash, tennis, golf, gliding (Gold C with one diamond). *Address:* (home) The Baulk House, 66 Bromham Road, Biddenham, Beds MK40 4AQ. *T:* Bedford 65595. *Club:* Royal Air Force.

BROWNLOW, James Hilton, QPM 1978; Chief Constable, South Yorkshire Police, since 1979; *b* 19 Oct. 1925; *s* of late Ernest Cuthbert Brownlow and of Beatrice Annie Elizabeth Brownlow; *m* 1947, Joyce Key; two *d*. *Educ:* Worksop Central School. Solicitor's Clerk, 1941-43; served war, RAF, Flt/Sgt (Air Gunner), 1943-47. Police Constable, Leicester City Police, 1947; Police Constable to Det. Chief Supt, Kent County Constabulary, 1947-69; Asst Chief Constable, Hertfordshire Constabulary, 1969-75; Asst to HM Chief Inspector of Constabulary, Home Office, 1975-76; Dep. Chief Constable, Greater Manchester Police, 1976-79. Queen's Commendation for Brave Conduct, 1972. Officer Brother OStJ 1981. *Recreations:* golf, gardening. *Club:* Royal Over-Seas League.

BROWNLOW, Kevin; author; film director; *b* 2 June 1938; *s* of Thomas and Niña Brownlow; *m* 1969, Virginia Keane. *Educ:* University College School. Entered documentaries, 1955; became film editor, 1958, and edited many documentaries; with Andrew Mollo dir. feature films: It happened Here, 1964; Winstanley, 1975; dir. Charm of Dynamite, 1967, about Abel Gance, and restored his classic film Napoleon (first shown London, Nov. 1980, NY, Jan. 1981). With David Gill prod and dir. Hollywood, TV series, 1980. *Publications:* The Parade's Gone By . . ., 1968; How it Happened Here, 1968; The War, the West and the Wilderness, 1978; Hollywood: the pioneers, 1979; many articles on film history. *Recreation:* motion pictures. *Address:* c/o Thames TV, Teddington Studios, Mddx.

BROWNRIGG, Sir Nicholas (Gawen), 5th Bt, *cr* 1816; *b* 22 Dec. 1932; *s* of late Gawen Egremont Brownrigg and Baroness Lucia von Borosini, *o d* of Baron Victor von Borosini, California; *S* grandfather, 1939; *m* 1959, Linda Louise Lovelace (marr. diss. 1965), Beverly Hills, California; one *s* one *d*; *m* 1971, Valerie Ann, *d* of Julian A. Arden, Livonia, Michigan, USA. *Educ:* Midland Sch.; Stanford Univ. *Heir: s* Michael Gawen Brownrigg, *b* Oct. 1961. *Address:* PO Box 548, Ukiah, Calif 95482, USA.

BROWNRIGG, Philip Henry Akerman, CMG 1964; DSO 1945; OBE 1953; TD 1945; *b* 3 June 1911; *s* of late Charles E. Brownrigg, Headmaster of Magdalen Coll. Sch., Oxford; *m* 1936, Marguerite Doreen Ottley; three *d*. *Educ:* Eton; Magdalen Coll., Oxford (BA). Journalist, 1934-52; Editor, Sunday Graphic, 1952. Joined Anglo American Corp. of S Africa, 1953: London Agent, 1956; Dir in Rhodesia, 1961-63; Dir in Zambia, 1964-65; retd, 1969. Director (apptd by Govt of Zambia): Nchanga Consolidated Copper Mines Ltd, 1969-80; Roan Consolidated Mines Ltd, 1969-80. Joined TA, 1938; served War of 1939-45 with 6 R Berks, and 61st Reconnaissance Regt (RAC); Lieut-Col 1944; CO 4/6 R Berks (TA) 1949-52. Insignia of Honour, Zambia, 1981. *Recreations:* golf, sport on TV. *Address:* Wheeler's, Checkendon, near Reading, Berks. *T:* Checkendon 680328.

BRUBECK, David Warren; musician, USA; composer; *b* Concord, Calif, 6 Dec. 1920; *s* of Howard Brubeck and Elizabeth Ivey; *m* 1942, Iola Whitlock; five *s* one *d*. *Educ:* Pacific Univ. (BA); Mills Coll. (postgrad.). Hon. PhD: Univ. of Pacific; Fairfield Univ. Pianist with dance bands and jazz trio, 1946-49; own trio, touring USA, 1950; formed Dave Brubeck Quartet, 1951; tours to festivals and colls, incl. tour of Europe and Middle East (for US State Dept); Europe and Australia, 1960; Europe, Australia, Canada, S America, with 3 sons, as Two Generations of Brubeck; Quartet at Festival Hall, London, 1961, and 1970-. Fellow, Internat. Inst. of Arts and Sciences; Duke Ellington Fellow, Yale Univ. Exponent of progressive Jazz; many awards from trade magazines; numerous recordings. Has composed: over 250 songs; Points on Jazz (ballet); Elementals (orch.); The Light in the Wilderness (oratorio; perf. Cincinnati Symph. Orch. and mixed chorus of 100 voices, 1968); Gates of Justice (Cantata); Truth (Cantata); They All Sang Yankee Doodle, variations for orch., 1975; La Fiesta de la Posada, 1975; Glances (ballet), 1976; Beloved Son (oratorio), 1978; To Hope (mass), 1980. *Address:* c/o Sutton Artists Corporation, 119 West 57th Street, Suite 818, NY, NY 10019, USA.

BRUCE, family name of **Barons Aberdare,** and **Bruce of Donington,** of **Lord Balfour of Burleigh,** and of **Earl of Elgin.**

BRUCE; *see* Cumming-Bruce and Hovell-Thurlow-Cumming-Bruce.

BRUCE, Lord; Charles Edward Bruce; *b* 19 Oct. 1961; *s* and *heir* of 11th Earl of Elgin, *qv. Educ:* Eton College. A Page of Honour to HM the Queen Mother, 1975-77. *Address:* Broomhall, Dunfermline KY11 3DU. *T:* Dunfermline 872222.

BRUCE OF DONINGTON, Baron *cr* 1974 (Life Peer), of Rickmansworth; **Donald William Trevor Bruce;** economist; Chartered Accountant, Halpern & Wolf, 24/27 Thayer Street, W1; writer; Member of European Parliament, 1975-79; *b* 3 Oct. 1912; *s* of late W. T. Bruce, Norbury, Surrey; *m* 1939, Joan Letitia Butcher (marr. diss.); one *s* two *d* (and one *d* decd). *Educ:* Grammar School, Donington, Lincs; FCA 1947. Re-joined Territorial Army, March 1939; commissioned, Nov. 1939; Major, 1942; served at home and in France until May 1945 (despatches). MP (Lab) for North Portsmouth, 1945-50; Parliamentary Private Sec. to Minister of Health, 1945-50; Member Min. of Health delegn to Sweden and Denmark, 1946, and of House of Commons Select Cttee on Public Accounts, 1948-50. *Publications:* miscellaneous contributions on political science and economics to newspapers and periodicals. *Address:* 24/27 Thayer Street, W1. *T:* 01-486 7188.

BRUCE, Alastair Henry, CBE 1951; DL; Chairman and Managing Director, The Inveresk Paper Company Ltd, 1964-68; Member, Monopolies Commission, 1964-68; Chairman, Paper and Paper Products Industry Training Board, 1968-71; *b* 14 April 1900; *s* of Patrick Chalmers Bruce and Lucy Walmsley Hodgson; *m* 1921, Jean Newton Callender (*d* 1981); one *s. Educ:* Cargilfield, Midlothian; Uppingham. President British Paper and Board Makers Association, 1938-42 and 1948-51; President British Paper and Board Research Association, 1948-51. DL Midlothian, 1943-. *Recreations:* shooting, and fishing. *Address:* Torduff, Juniper Green, Midlothian. *T:* 031-441 2274.

BRUCE, Alexander Robson, CMG 1961; OBE 1948; Assistant Secretary, Board of Trade, 1963-67, retired; *b* 17 April 1907; *m* 1936, Isobel Mary Goldie; four *d. Educ:* Rutherford Coll., Newcastle upon Tyne; Durham Univ. Asst Trade Comr, 1933-42, Trade Commissioner, 1942-43, Montreal; Commercial Sec., British Embassy, Madrid, 1943-46; Trade Comr, Ottawa, 1946-50; Asst Sec., Bd of Trade, 1950-54 and 1963-; Principal British Trade Commissioner in NSW, 1955-63. *Recreation:* golf. *Address:* 37 North Road, Highgate, N6. *Club:* Highgate Golf.

BRUCE, Sir Arthur Atkinson, KBE 1943; MC 1917; Director: Wallace Brothers & Co. Ltd, 1947-65; Chartered Bank of India, 1949-70; *b* 26 March 1895; *s* of late John Davidson Bruce, Jarrow-on-Tyne; *m* 1928, Kathleen Frances (*d* 1952), *d* of John Emeris Houldey, ICS (retd), Penn, Bucks; three *d. Educ:* Cambridge. Director Reserve Bank of India, 1935-46; Chairman Burma Chamber of Commerce, 1936, 1942, 1946. Member of Council, London Chamber of Commerce, 1960-65. *Address:* Silverthorne, 5 Grenfell Road, Beaconsfield, Bucks. *Club:* Oriental.

BRUCE, Christopher; dancer, choreographer, opera producer; Associate Choreographer, Ballet Rambert, since 1979 (Associate Director, 1975-79); *b* Leicester, 3 Oct. 1945. *Educ:* Ballet Rambert Sch. Joined Ballet Rambert Company, 1963; leading dancer with co. when re-formed as modern dance co., 1966; leading roles include: Pierrot Lunaire, The Tempest ((Tetley), L'Apres-Midi d'un Faune (Nijinsky); Cruel Garden (also choreographed with Lindsay Kemp); choreographed: for Ballet Rambert: George Frideric (1st work), 1969; Wings, 1970; Black Angels, 1976; Weekend, 1974; Ancient Voices of Children, 1975; Night with Waning Moon, 1977; Dancing Day, 1981; Ghost Dances, 1981; Berlin Requiem, 1982; for Tanz Forum, Cologne: Cantata, 1981; for Nederlands Dans Theater: Village Songs, 1981; works for Royal Ballet, Batsheva Dance Co., Munich Opera Ballet, Gulbenkian Ballet Co., Australian Dance Theatre, Royal Danish Ballet. Kent Opera: choreographed and produced Monteverdi's Il Ballo delle Ingrate, and Combattimento di Tancredi e Clorinda, 1980; chor. John Blow's Venus and Adonis, 1980; co-prod Handel's Agrippina, 1982. TV productions: Ancient Voices of Children, BBC, 1977; Cruel Garden, BBC, 1981-82; Ghost Dances,

Channel 4, 1982; Requiem, Danish-German co-production, 1982. Evening Standard's inaugural Dance Award, 1974. *Address:* c/o Ballet Rambert, 94 Chiswick High Road, W4 1SH.

BRUCE, David, CA; Partner, Deloitte Haskins & Sells, since 1974; *b* 21 Jan. 1927; *s* of David Bruce and Margaret (*née* Gregson); *m* 1955, Joy Robertson McAslan; four *d. Educ:* High School of Glasgow. Commissioned, Royal Corps of Signals, 1947-49. Qualified as Chartered Accountant, 1955; Partner, Kerr McLeod & Co., Chartered Accountants, 1961 (merged with Deloitte Haskins & Sells, 1974). Vice-Pres., Inst. of Chartered Accountants of Scotland, 1978-79 and 1979-80, Pres. 1980-81. *Recreations:* angling, curling, cooking. *Address:* 87 Speirs Road, Bearsden, Glasgow G61 2NU. *T:* 041-942 1264. *Club:* Caledonian.

BRUCE, Sir (Francis) Michael Ian; *see* Bruce, Sir Michael Ian.

BRUCE, Prof. Frederick Fyvie, MA Aberdeen, Cantab, Manchester, DD Aberdeen; FBA 1973; Rylands Professor of Biblical Criticism and Exegesis, University of Manchester, 1959-78, now Emeritus; *b* 12 Oct. 1910; *e s* of late P. F. Bruce, Elgin, Morayshire; *m* 1936, Betty, *er d* of late A. B. Davidson, Aberdeen; one *s* and *d. Educ:* Elgin Acad.; Univs of Aberdeen, Cambridge, Vienna. Gold Medallist in Greek and Latin; Fullerton Schol. in Classics, 1932; Croom Robertson Fellow, 1933; Aberdeen Univ.; Scholar of Gonville and Caius Coll., Camb., 1932; Sandys Student. Camb., 1934; Ferguson Schol. in Classics, 1933, and Crombie Scholar in Biblical Criticism, 1939, Scottish Univs; Diploma in Hebrew, Leeds Univ., 1943. Asst in Greek, Edinburgh Univ., 1935-38; Lectr in Greek, Leeds Univ., 1938-47: Professor of Biblical History and Literature, University of Sheffield, 1955-59 (Head of Dept, 1947-59). Lectures: John A. McElwain, Gordon Divinity School, Beverly Farms, Massachusetts, 1958; Calvin Foundation, Calvin Coll. and Seminary, Grand Rapids, Michigan, 1958; Payton, Fuller Theolog. Seminary, Pasadena, Calif, 1968; Norton, Southern Baptist Theolog. Seminary, Louisville, Kentucky, 1968; Smyth, Columbia Theological Seminary, Decatur, Ga, 1970; Earle, Nazarene Theological Seminary, Kansas City, Mo, 1970; N. W. Lund, N Park Theological Seminary, Chicago, 1970; Thomas F. Staley, Ontario Bible Coll., Toronto, 1973; Moore Coll., Sydney, 1977; Griffith Thomas, Wycliffe Hall, Oxford, 1982. Examr in Biblical Studies: Leeds University, 1943-47, 1957-60, 1967-69; Edinburgh University, 1949-52, 1958-60; Bristol University, 1958-60; Aberdeen University, 1959-61; London University, 1959-60; St Andrews University, 1961-64; Cambridge University, 1961-62; University of Wales, 1965-68; Sheffield University, 1968-70; Newcastle University, 1969-71; Keele Univ., 1971-73; Dublin Univ., 1972-75; Dean of Faculty of Theology, University of Manchester, 1963-64; President: Yorkshire Soc. for Celtic Studies, 1948-50; Sheffield Branch of Classical Association, 1955-58; Victoria Inst., 1958-65; Manchester Egyptian and Oriental Society, 1963-65; Soc. for Old Testament Study, 1965; Soc. for New Testament Studies, 1975. Burkitt Medal, British Acad., 1979. Editor: Yorkshire Celtic Studies, 1945-57; The Evangelical Quarterly, 1949-80; Palestine Exploration Quarterly, 1957-71. *Publications:* The NT Documents, 1943; The Hittites and the OT, 1948; The Books and the Parchments, 1950; The Acts of the Apostles, Greek Text with Commentary, 1951; The Book of the Acts, Commentary on English Text, 1954; Second Thoughts on the Dead Sea Scrolls, 1956; The Teacher of Righteousness in the Qumran Texts, 1957; Biblical Exegesis in the Qumran Texts, 1959; The Spreading Flame, 1958; Commentary on the Epistle to the Colossians, 1958; The Epistle to the Ephesians, 1961; Paul and his Converts, 1962; The Epistle of Paul to the Romans, 1963; Israel and the Nations, 1963; Commentary on the Epistle to the Hebrews, 1964; Expanded Paraphrase of the Epistles of Paul, 1965; New Testament History, 1969; This is That, 1969; Tradition Old and New, 1970; St Matthew, 1970; The Epistles of John, 1970; First and Second Corinthians (Century Bible), 1971; The Message of the New Testament, 1972; Jesus and Christian Origins outside the New Testament, 1974; Paul and Jesus, 1974; First-Century Faith, 1977; Paul: Apostle of the Free Spirit, 1977; The Time is Fulfilled, 1978; History of the Bible in English, 1979; The Work of Jesus, 1979; Men and Movements in the Primitive Church, 1980; In Retrospect, 1980; The Epistle to the Galatians, 1982; First and Second Thessalonians, 1982; contribs to classical and theological journals. *Recreation:* walking. *Address:* The Crossways, Temple Road, Buxton, Derbyshire. *T:* Buxton 3250.

BRUCE, George John Done, RP 1959; painter of portraits, landscapes, still life, flowers; *b* 28 March 1930; *s* of 11th Lord Balfour of Burleigh, Brucefield, Clackmannan, Scotland and Violet Dorothy, *d* of Richard Henry Done, Tarporley, Cheshire; *b* of 12th Lord Balfour of Burleigh, *qv. Educ:* Westminster Sch.; Byam Shaw Sch. of Drawing and Painting. Hon. Sec., Royal Soc. of Portrait Painters, 1970-. *Recreations:* hang-gliding, ski-ing. *Address:* 6 Pembroke Walk, W8. *T:* 01-937 1493. *Club:* Athenæum.

BRUCE, Sir Hervey (James Hugh), 7th Bt *cr* 1804; Major, The Grenadier Guards; *b* 3 Sept. 1952; *s* of Sir Hervey John William Bruce, 6th Bt, and of Crista, *y d* of late Lt-Col Chandos De Paravicini, OBE; *S* father, 1971; *m* 1979, Charlotte, *e d* of Jack Gore, Midhurst, Sussex. *Educ:* Eton; Officer Cadet School, Mons. *Heir:* uncle Ronald Cecil Juckes Bruce [*b* 22 Aug. 1921; *m* 1960, Jean, *d* of L. J. W. Murfitt; one *s*]. *Address :* 3 Halford Road, SW6.

BRUCE, Sir Michael (Ian), 12th Bt, *cr* 1629; partner, Gossard-Bruce Co., from 1953; *b* 3 April 1926; *s* of Sir Michael William Selby Bruce, 11th Bt and Doreen Dalziel, *d* of late W. F. Greenwell; *S* father 1957; is an American

citizen; has discontinued first forename, Francis; *m* 1st, 1947, Barbara Stevens (marr. diss., 1957), *d* of Frank J. Lynch; two *s* ; 2nd, 1961, Frances Keegar (marr. diss., 1963); 3rd, 1966, Marilyn Ann (marr. diss., 1975), *d* of Carte Mulally. *Educ:* Forman School, Litchfield, Conn; Pomfret, Conn. Served United States Marine Corps, 1943-46 (Letter of Commendation); S Pacific area two years, Bismarck Archipelago, Bougainville, Philippines. Owner Latitude 57° Marine Shipping Co., 1966; Master Mariner's Ticket, 1968 President: Newport Sailing Club, Inc., 1978; Newport Academy of Sail, Inc 1979; Owner, American Maritime Co., 1980; Chm. of Bd and Pres., MBH International Schools, 1981. *Recreations:* sailing, spear-fishing. *Heir:* s Michae Ian Richard Bruce, *b* 10 Dec. 1950. *Address:* 106 Via Antibes, Lido Isle Newport Beach, Calif 92663, USA. *T:* 714-673-8132. *Clubs:* Rockaway Hunt; Lawrence Beach; Balboa Bay (Newport Beach); Viking of Scandia (Los Angeles).

BRUCE, Michael Stewart Rae, QC (Scot.) 1975; *b* 26 July 1938; *s* of late Alexander Eric Bruce, Advocate in Aberdeen, and late Mary Gordon Bruce (*née* Walker); *m* 1963, Alison Mary Monfries Stewart; two *d. Educ:* Loretto Sch.; Aberdeen Univ. (MA, LLB). Admitted Faculty of Advocates, 1963 Standing Counsel: to Dept of Agriculture and Fisheries for Scotland, 1973 to Highlands and Islands Develt Bd, 1973. *Recreations:* fishing, golf. *Address:* 17 Wester Coates Terrace, Edinburgh EH12 5LR. *T:* 031-337 5883. *Clubs:* New (Edinburgh); Honourable Company of Edinburgh Golfers.

BRUCE of Sumburgh, Robert Hunter Wingate, CBE 1967; Lord-Lieutenant for Shetland (formerly for the County of Zetland), 1963-82; *b* 11 Oct. 1907; *s* of John Bruce of Sumburgh and Isobel Abel; *m* 1935, Valma Muriel, *d* of Charles Frederick Chamberlain and Lillian Muriel Smith; no *c Educ:* Rugby School; Balliol College, Oxford. LMS Railway, 1930-46; or loan to Min. of Economic Warfare, 1941-43; Manager, Northern Counties Rly, Belfast, 1943-46. Retired from LMS to manage Shetland property, 1946 Rep. Rio Tinto Co. in N and S Rhodesia and S Africa, Africa, 1952-57 Member Zetland CC, 1948-52, 1958-61. Member: Advisory Panel on Highlands and Islands, 1948-52, 1957-65; Crofters Commn, 1960-78 Chairman, Highland Transport Board, 1963-66. Medal of Freedom with Silver Palm, USA, 1948. *Recreations:* farming, reading history, golf, convivia argument. *Address:* Sand Lodge, Sandwick, Shetland ZE2 9HP. *T:* Sandwick 209. *Clubs:* New (Edinburgh); Hon. Co. of Edinburgh Golfers (Gullane).

BRUCE, Robert Nigel (Beresford Dalrymple), CBE 1972 (OBE (mil.) 1946); TD; CEng, Hon. FIGasE; *b* 21 May 1907; *s* of Major R. N. D. Bruce late of Hampstead; *m* 1945, Elizabeth Brogden, *d* of J. G. Moore; twin *s* two *d. Educ:* Harrow School (Entrance and Leaving Scholar); Magdalen College Oxford (Exhibitioner). BA (Hons Chem.) and BSc. Joined Territorial Army Rangers (KRRC), 1931; Major, 1939; served Greece, Egypt, Western Desert 1940-42; Lt-Col Comdg Regt, 1942; GHQ, MEF, Middle East Supply Centre, 1943-45; Col, Dir. of Materials, 1944. Joined Gas, Light and Coke Co. as Research Chemist, 1929; Asst to Gen. Manager, 1937, Controller o Industrial Relations, 1946; Staff Controller, 1949, Dep. Chm., 1956, North Thames Gas Bd; Chm., S Eastern Gas Bd, 1960-72. President: British Road Tar Assoc., 1964 and 1965; Coal Tar Research Assoc., 1966; Institution of Gas Engineers, 1968; Mem. Bd, CEI, 1968-80. Chm. Governing Body Westminster Coll., 1958-76. Sec., Tennis and Rackets Assoc., 1974-81 *Publications:* Chronicles of the 1st Battalion the Rangers (KRRC), 1939-45 contribs to Proc. Royal Society, Jl Soc. Chemical Industry, Jl Chemica Society. *Recreations:* travel, golf. *Address:* Fairway, 57 Woodland Grove Weybridge, Surrey KT13 9EQ. *T:* Weybridge 52372.

BRUCE, Hon. Mrs Victor, (Mildred Mary), FRGS; *b* 1895; *d* of Lawrence Joseph Petre, Coptfold Hall, Essex; *m* 1926, Hon. Victor Bruce (marr. diss. 1941), *y s* of 2nd Baron Aberdare. *Educ:* Convent of Sion. Travelled furthest north into Lapland by motor car; holds record for Double Channel Crossing Dover to Calais, by motor boat; holder of 17 World Records, motoring, and of 24-hour record; single-handed drive, covered longest distance for man or woman, 2164 miles, in 24 hours; Coupe des Dames, Monte Carlo Rally, 1927 Flying records: first solo flight from England to Japan, 1930; longest solo flight, 1930; record solo flight, India to French Indo-China, 1930; British Air refuelling endurance flight, 1933. Holds 24 hour record by motor boat covering 674 nautical miles, single handed, 1929; first crossing of Yellow Sea Show Jumping, 1st Royal Windsor Horse Show, 1939. Order of the Million Elephants and White Umbrella (French Indo-China). Fellow, Ancien Monuments Society. *Publications:* The Peregrinations of Penelope; 9000 Miles in Eight Weeks; The Woman Owner Driver; The Bluebird's Flight; Nine Lives Plus. *Address:* Priory Steps, Bradford-on-Avon, Wiltshire. *T:* Bradford-on-Avon 2230. *Clubs:* Royal Motor Yacht, British Racing Drivers, Roll Royce Enthusiasts'.

BRUCE-CHWATT, Prof. Leonard Jan, CMG 1976; OBE 1953; FRCP FIBiol; Professor of Tropical Hygiene and Director of Ross Institute, London School of Hygiene and Tropical Medicine, University of London, 1969-74 now Emeritus Professor; Editor, Tropical Doctor (Royal Society o Medicine), since 1975; *b* 9 June 1907; *s* of Dr Michael Chwatt and Anne Marquitant; *m* 1948, Joan Margaret Bruce; two *s. Educ:* Univ. of Warsaw (MD); Paris (Dipl. Méd. Col.); Univ. of London (DTM&H); Harvard (MPH). Wartime service Polish Army Med. Corps and RAMC, 1939-45 Colonial Medical Service (Senior Malariologist, Nigeria), 1946-58; Chief Research and Technical Intelligence, Div. of Malaria Eradication, WHO Geneva, 1958-68. Mem. Expert Cttee on Malaria, WHO, Geneva, 1956-

Vice-Pres., Royal Soc. Tropical Med. and Hygiene; Associate, Wellcome Mus. of Med. Science, 1975. Duncan Medal, 1942; North Persian Forces Memorial Medal, 1952; Darling Medal and Prize, 1971; Macdonald Meml Medal, 1978. KStJ 1975. *Publications:* Terminology of Malaria, 1963; chapter on malaria in Cecil and Loeb Textbook of Medicine, 1967 and 1970; Dynamics of Tropical Disease, 1973; The Rise and Fall of Malaria in Europe, 1980; Essential Malariology, 1980; Chemotherapy of Malaria, 1981; numerous papers in medical jls. *Recreations:* travel, music, walking. *Address:* 21 Marchmont Road, Richmond, Surrey. *T:* 01-940 5540.

BRUCE-GARDNER, Sir Douglas (Bruce), 2nd Bt, *cr* 1945; Director, Guest, Keen & Nettlefolds Ltd, 1960-82; Deputy Chairman, Guest, Keen & Nettlefolds (UK) Ltd; *b* 27 Jan. 1917; *s* of Sir Charles Bruce-Gardner, 1st Bt; *S* father, 1960; *m* 1st, 1940, Monica Flumerfelt (marr. diss. 1964), *d* of late Sir Geoffrey Jefferson, CBE, FRS; one *s* two *d* ; 2nd, 1964, Sheila Jane, *d* of Roger and late Barbara Stilliard, Seer Green, Bucks; one *s* one *d. Educ:* Uppingham; Trinity College, Cambridge. Lancashire Steel, 1938-51; Control Commn, Germany, 1945-46; joined GKN, 1951. Dir, GKN Ltd, 1960, Dep. Chm., 1974-77; Dep. Chm., GKN Steel Co. Ltd, 1962, Gen. Man. Dir, 1963-65, Chm., 1965-67; Chairman: GKN Rolled & Bright Steel Ltd, 1968-72; GKN (South Wales) Ltd, 1968-72; Exors of James Mills Ltd, 1968-72; Parson Ltd, 1968-72; Brymbo Steel Works Ltd, 1974-77; Miles Druce & Co. Ltd, 1974-77; Exec. Vice-Chm., UK Ops, Gen. Products, GKN Ltd, 1972-74. Director: Henry Gardner & Co. Ltd, 1952-68; Firth Cleveland Ltd, 1972-75; BHP-GKN Holdings Ltd, 1977-78; Iron Trades Employers Insurance Assoc. Ltd, 1977-. President: Iron and Steel Inst., 1966-67; British Indep. Steel Producers' Assoc., 1972; Pres., Iron and Steel Employers' Assoc., 1963-64. *Recreations:* fishing, photography. *Heir:* *s* Robert Henry Bruce-Gardner [*b* 10 June 1943; *m* 1979, Veronica Ann Hand-Oxborrow, *d* of late Rev. W. E. Hand and of Mrs R. G. Oxborrow, Caterham; one *s*]. *Address:* Bishopswood Grange, near Ross-on-Wye, Herefordshire. *T:* Dean 444. *Club:* Flyfishers'.

BRUCE-GARDYNE, John, (Jock); MP (C) Knutsford, since March 1979; Economic Secretary to HM Treasury, since 1981; *b* 12 April 1930; 2nd *s* of late Capt. E. Bruce-Gardyne, DSO, RN, Middleton, by Arbroath, Angus and Joan (*née* McLaren); *m* 1959, Sarah Louisa Mary, *o d* of Comdr Sir John Maitland and Bridget Denny; two *s* one *d. Educ:* Winchester; Magdalen College, Oxford. HM Foreign Service, 1953-56; served in London and Sofia; Paris correspondent, Financial Times, 1956-60; Foreign Editor, Statist, 1961-64. MP (C) South Angus, 1964-Oct. 1974; PPS to Secretary of State for Scotland, 1970-72; Minister of State, HM Treasury, 1981. Vice-Chm., Cons. Parly Finance Cttee, 1972-74, 1979-80. Columnist, Sunday Telegraph, 1979-81; editorial writer, Daily Telegraph, 1977-81. Consultant, Northern Engineering Industries, 1979-81. *Publications:* Whatever happened to the Quiet Revolution?, 1974; Scotland in 1980, 1975; (with Nigel Lawson) The Power Game, 1976. *Address:* 13 Kelso Place, W8; Illidge Green Farm, Brereton, Cheshire.

BRUCE LOCKHART, John Macgregor, CB 1966; CMG 1951; OBE 1944; *b* 9 May 1914; *e s* of late John Harold Bruce Lockhart and Mona Brougham; *m* 1939, Margaret Evelyn, *d* of late Rt Rev. C. R. Hone; two *s* one *d. Educ:* Rugby School; St Andrews University (Harkness Scholar). MA 2nd Class Hons Modern Languages, 1937. Asst Master, Rugby School, 1937-39; TA Commission, Seaforth Highlanders, 1938; served War of 1939-45, in UK, Middle East, North Africa, Italy (Lt-Col); Asst Military Attaché, British Embassy, Paris, 1945-47; Control Commission Germany, 1948-51; First Secretary, British Embassy, Washington, 1951-53; served Foreign Office, London, until resignation from the Diplomatic Service, 1965; in charge of planning and development, Univ. of Warwick, 1965-67; Head of Central Staff Dept, Courtaulds Ltd, 1967-71. Advisor on Post Experience Programme, City Univ. Business Sch., 1971-80 (Hon. Fellow, City Univ., 1980); Chm., Business Educn Council, 1974-80; Member: Schools Council, 1975-80; Naval Educn Adv. Cttee, 1973-80; London and Home Counties Regional Management Council, 1973-80 (Founder Mem.). Vis. Scholar, St Andrews Univ., 1981-82. *Publications:* articles and lectures on strategic studies at RCDS, RUSI, Kennedy Inst. of Politics, Harvard and Georgetown Univ., Washington, DC. *Recreations:* music, real tennis, golf, pictures. *Address:* 37 Fair Meadow, Rye, Sussex. *Clubs:* Reform, Boodle's; Rye Dormy.

BRUCE LOCKHART, Logie, MA; Headmaster of Gresham's School, Holt, 1955-82; *b* 12 Oct. 1921; *s* of late John Harold Bruce Lockhart; *m* 1944, Josephine Agnew; two *s* two *d* (and one *d* decd). *Educ:* Sedbergh School; St John's College, Cambridge (Schol. and Choral Studentship). RMC Sandhurst, 1941; served War of 1939-45; 9th Sherwood Foresters, 1942; 2nd Household Cavalry (Life Guards), 1944-45. Larmor Award, 1947; Asst Master, Tonbridge School, 1947-55. Sponsor, Nat. Council for Educnl Standards. *Publication:* The Pleasures of Fishing, 1981. *Recreations:* fishing, writing, music, natural history, games; Blue for Rugby football, 1945, 1946, Scottish International, 1948, 1950, 1953; squash for Cambridge, 1946. *Address:* Church Farm House, Holt, Norfolk. *T:* Holt 2137. *Club:* East India, Devonshire, Sports and Public Schools.

BRUCE LOCKHART, Rab Brougham, MA Cantab; Headmaster, Loretto School, Musselburgh, Edinburgh, 1960-76; *b* 1 Dec. 1916; *s* of late J. H. Bruce Lockhart; *m* 1941, Helen Priscilla Lawrence Crump; one *s* one *d* (and one *s* decd). *Educ:* Edinburgh Academy; Corpus Christi College, Cambridge. BA (Mod. Lang.) 1939; MA 1946. Assistant Master, Harrow, 1939. Served War

of 1939-45: Commissioned RA, 1940; Middle East, 1942-44; Major RA 1944; Intelligence, Italy and Austria, 1945. Assistant Master, Harrow, 1946-50; Housemaster, Appleby College, Oakville, Ont, Canada, 1950-54; Headmaster, Wanganui Collegiate School, Wanganui, New Zealand, 1954-60. *Recreations:* squash, golf and photography; formerly: a Scotland cricket XI, 1935; Scotland XV, 1937, 1939; Rugby "Blue" 1937, 1938. *Address:* Saul Hill, Burneside, near Kendal, Cumbria. *T:* Selside 646.

BRUCE-MITFORD, Rupert Leo Scott, FBA 1976; Research Keeper in the British Museum, 1975-77 (Keeper of British and Mediæval Antiquities, 1954-69, of Mediæval and Later Antiquities, 1969-75); *b* 14 June 1914; 4th *s* of C. E. Bruce-Mitford, Madras, and Beatrice (Allison), *e d* of John Fall, British Columbia; *m* 1st, 1941, Kathleen Dent (marr. diss. 1972); one *s* two *d* ; 2nd, 1975, Marilyn Roberta, *o d* of Robert J. Luscombe, Walton on the Hill, Staffs. *Educ:* Christ's Hospital; Hertford College, Oxford (Baring Scholar). Temp. Asst Keeper, Ashmolean Museum, 1937; Asst Keeper, Dept of British and Mediæval Antiquities, British Museum, 1938; Royal Signals, 1939-45; Deputy Keeper, British Museum, 1954. FSA 1947 (Sec., Soc. of Antiquaries, 1950-54, Vice-Pres., 1972-76); FSA Scot. Slade Professor of Fine Art, Univ. of Cambridge, 1978-79. Vis. Fellow, All Souls Coll., Oxford, and Emmanuel Coll., Cambridge, 1978-79; Faculty Visitor, Dept of English, ANU, Canberra, 1981. Excavations: Seacourt, Berks, 1938-39; Mawgan Porth, Cornwall, 1949-54; Sutton Hoo, Suffolk, 1965-68. Member: German Archæological Inst.; Italian Inst. of Prehistory and Protohistory; Corres. Member, Jutland Archæological Society; Hon. Mem., Suffolk Inst. of Archaeology; Member of Ancient Monuments Board, England, 1954-79; Member, Permanent Council, Internat. Congress of Prehistoric and Protohistoric Sciences, 1957-79; President, Society for Mediæval Archæology, 1957-59. Lectures: Dalrymple, Glasgow, 1961; Thomas Davis Radio, Dublin, 1964; Jarrow, 1967; O'Donnell, Wales, 1971; Garmonsway, York, 1973; Crake, Mount Allison Univ., NB, 1980. Liveryman, Worshipful Co. of Clockmakers. Hon. LittD Dublin 1966. *Publications:* The Society of Antiquaries of London; Notes on its History and Possessions (with others), 1952; Editor and contributor, Recent Archæological Excavations in Britain, 1956; (with T. J. Brown, A. S. C. Ross and others), Codex Lindisfarnensis (Swiss facsimile edn), 1957-61; (trans. from Danish) The Bog People, by P. V. Glob, 1969; The Sutton Hoo Ship-burial, a handbook, 1972, revd edn 1979; Aspects of Anglo-Saxon Archaeology, 1974; The Sutton Hoo Ship-burial, Vol. I, 1975, Vol. II, 1978; Vol. III in press; (ed) Recent Excavations in Europe, 1975; papers and reviews in learned journals. *Recreations:* reading, watching sport, travel. *Address:* 20 Kingsfield Road, Harrow on the Hill, Mddx. *T:* 01-422 0967. *Clubs:* Athenæum, Garrick, MCC.

BRÜCK, Prof. Hermann Alexander, CBE 1966; DPhil (Munich); PhD (Cantab); Astronomer Royal for Scotland and Regius Professor of Astronomy in the University of Edinburgh, 1957-75; now Professor Emeritus; Dean of the Faculty of Science, 1968-70; *b* 15 Aug. 1905; *s* of late H. H. Brück; *m* 1st, 1936, Irma Waitzfelder (*d* 1950); one *s* one *d* ; 2nd, 1951, Dr Mary T. Conway; one *s* two *d. Educ:* Augusta Gymnasium, Charlottenburg; Universities of Bonn, Kiel, Munich, and Cambridge. Astronomer, Potsdam Astrophysical Observatory, 1928; Lectr, Berlin University, 1935; Research Associate, Vatican Observatory, Castel Gandolfo, 1936; Asst Observer, Solar Physics Observatory, Cambridge, 1937; John Couch Adams Astronomer, Cambridge University, 1943; Asst Director, Cambridge Observatory, 1946; Director, Dunsink Observatory and Professor of Astronomy, Dublin Institute for Advanced Studies, 1947-57. Mem., Bd of Governors, Armagh Observatory, NI, 1971-82. MRIA, 1948; FRSE, 1958; Member Pontif. Academy of Sciences, Rome, 1955, Mem. Council, 1964-; Corr. Member Academy of Sciences, Mainz, 1955. Hon. DSc: NUI, 1972; St Andrews, 1973. *Publications:* scientific papers in journals and observatory publications. *Recreation:* music. *Address:* Craigower, Penicuik, Midlothian EH26 9LA. *T:* Penicuik 75918. *Club:* New (Edinburgh).

BRUDENELL-BRUCE, family name of **Marquess of Ailesbury.**

BRUFORD, Walter Horace, MA; FBA 1963; *b* Manchester, 1894; *s* of Francis J. and Annie Bruford; *m* 1925, Gerda (*d* 1976), *d* of late Professor James Hendrick; one *s* two *d. Educ:* Manchester Grammar School; St John's College, Cambridge; University of Zürich. BA Cambridge, 1915 (1st Class Hons. Med. and Mod. Langs). Bendall Sanskrit Exhibitioner; Master Manchester Grammar School; served Intelligence Division, Admiralty, with rank of Lieut RNVR. On demobilisation, research in University of Zürich; Lecturer in German, University of Aberdeen, 1920, Reader, 1923; Professor of German, University of Edinburgh, 1929-51. Seconded to Foreign Office, 1939-43. Schröder Professor of German, University of Cambridge, 1951-61. Corresponding member Deutsche Akademie für Sprache und Dichtung, 1957; Goethe-Medal in Gold, of Goethe-Institut, Munich, 1958; President: Mod. Lang. Assoc., 1959; Mod. Humanities Research Assoc., 1965; English Goethe Soc., 1965-75; Corresponding Member, Sächsische Akademie der Wissenschaften, Leipzig, 1965. Hon. LLD Aberdeen, 1958; Hon. DLitt: Newcastle, 1969; Edinburgh, 1974. *Publications:* Sound and Symbol (with Professor J. J. Findlay); Germany in the eighteenth century; Die gesellschaftlichen Grundlagen der Goethezeit; Chekhov and His Russia; two chapters in Essays on Goethe (ed. by W. Rose); Theatre, Drama and Audience in Goethe's Germany; Literary Interpretation in Germany; Goethe's Faust (introd., revised and annotated, Everyman's Library); Chekhov (Studies in Modern European Literature and Thought); The Organisation and Rise of Prussia and German Constitutional and Social Development, 1795-1830 (in Cambridge Modern History, New Series, Vols

VII and IX); Culture and Society in Classical Weimar; Deutsche Kultur der Goethezeit; Annotated edition and interpretation of Goethe's Faust, Part I; The German Tradition of Self-Cultivation: *Bildung* from Humboldt to Thomas Mann; articles and reviews in modern language periodicals. *Address:* 15 Strathfillan Road, Edinburgh EH9 2AG.

See also H. St J. B. Armitage.

BRUHN, Erik Belton Evers; Danish Ballet Dancer; Resident Producer, National Ballet of Canada, since 1973; *b* Copenhagen, Denmark, 3 Oct. 1928; *s* of Ernst Emil Bruhn, CE, and Ellen (*née* Evers); unmarried. *Educ:* Royal Danish Theatre, Copenhagen. Started at Royal Danish Ballet School, 1937; dancer with Danish Ballet, 1946-61, Amer. Nat. Ballet Theatre, 1949-58; Dir, Stockholm Opera Ballet, 1967-73; guest appearances with many major companies. Principal rôles include those in: Giselle, Swan Lake, Carmen, La Sylphide, Les Sylphides, The Sleeping Beauty, Miss Julie, Night Shadow, Spectre de la Rose, A Folk Tale; also classical pas de deux and various abstract ballets. *Publication:* Bournonville and Ballet Tecnic. *Address:* National Ballet of Canada, 157 King Street East, Toronto, Ontario M5C 1G9, Canada.

BRULLER, Jean; *see* Vercors.

BRUNA, Dick; graphic designer; writer and illustrator of children's books; *b* 23 Aug. 1927; *s* of A. W. Bruna and J. C. C. Erdbrink; *m* 1953, Irene de Jongh; two *s* one *d. Educ:* Primary Sch. and Gymnasium, Utrecht, Holland; autodidact. Designer of book jackets, 1945-, and of posters, 1947- (many prizes); writer and illustrator of children's books, 1953- (1st book, The Apple); also designer of postage stamps, murals, greeting cards and picture postcards. Exhibn based on Miffy (best-known character in children's books), Gemeentemuseum, Arnhem, 1977. Member: Netherlands Graphic Designers; Authors League of America Inc.; PEN Internat.; Alliance Graphique Internat. *Publications:* 43 titles published and 40 million copies printed by 1980; children's books translated into 21 languages. *Address:* (home) 10 Gabriellaan, Utrecht, Holland. *T:* 030-510769; (studio) 3 Jeruzalemstraat, Utrecht. *T:* 030-316042. *Club:* Art Directors (Netherlands).

BRUNEI, HH Sultan of; Hassanal Bolkiah Mu'izzaddin Waddaulah, DK, PSSUB, DPKG, DPKT, PSPNB, PSNB, PSLJ, SPMB, PANB; Hon. GCMG; DK (Kelantan), DK (Johor); Ruler of Brunei since 1967; *b* 15 July 1946; *s* of Sultan Sir Muda Omar 'Ali Saifuddin Sa'adul Khairi Waddin, DK, GCVO, KCMG, PSSUB, PHBS. *Educ:* Victoria Inst., Kuala Lumpur; RMA Sandhurst (Hon. Captain, Coldstream Guards, 1968). *Address:* Istana Darul Hana, Brunei.

BRUNER, Jerome Seymour, MA, PhD; Watts Professor of Psychology, University of Oxford, 1972-80; G. H. Mead University Professor, New School for Social Research, New York; Fellow, New York Institute for the Humanities; *b* New York, 1 Oct. 1915; *s* of Herman and Rose Bruner; *m* 1st, 1940, Katherine Frost (marr. diss. 1956); one *s* one *d* ; 2nd, 1960, Blanche Marshall McLane. *Educ:* Duke Univ. (AB 1937); Harvard Univ. (AM 1939, PhD 1941). US Intelligence, 1941; Assoc. Dir, Office Public Opinion Research, Princeton, 1942-44; govt public opinion surveys on war problems, 1942-43; political intelligence, France, 1943; Harvard University: research, 1945-72; Prof. of Psychology, 1952-72; Dir, Centre for Cognitive Studies, 1961-72. Lectr, Salzburg Seminar, 1952; Bacon Prof., Univ. of Aix-en-Provence, 1965. Editor, Public Opinion Quarterly, 1943-44; Syndic, Harvard Univ. Press, 1962-63. Member: Inst. Advanced Study, 1951; White House Panel on Educnl Research and Develt. Guggenheim Fellow, Cambridge Univ., 1955; Fellow: Amer. Psychol Assoc. (Pres., 1964-65; Distinguished Scientific Contrib. award, 1962); Amer. Acad. Arts and Sciences; Swiss Psychol Soc. (hon.); Soc. Psychol Study Social Issues (past Pres.); Amer. Assoc. Univ. Profs; Puerto Rican Acad. Arts and Sciences (hon.). Hon. DHL Lesley Coll., 1964; Hon. DSc: Northwestern Univ., 1965; Sheffield, 1970; Bristol, 1975; Hon. MA, Oxford, 1972; Hon. DSocSci, Yale, 1975; Hon. LLD: Temple Univ., 1965; Univ. of Cincinnati, 1966; Univ. of New Brunswick, 1969; Hon. DLitt: North Michigan Univ., 1969; Duke Univ., 1969; Dr *hc* : Sorbonne, 1974; Leuven, 1976; Ghent, 1977. *Publications:* Mandate from the People, 1944; (with Krech) Perception and Personality: A Symposium, 1950; (with Goodnow and Austin) A Study of Thinking, 1956; (with Smith and White) Opinions and Personality, 1956; (with Bresson, Morf and Piaget) Logique et Perception, 1958; The Process of Education, 1960; On Knowing: Essays for the Left Hand, 1962; (ed) Learning about Learning: A conference report, 1966; (with Olver, Greenfield, and others) Studies in Cognitive Growth; Toward a Theory of Instruction, 1966; Processes of Cognitive Growth: Infancy, Vol III, 1968; The Relevance of Education, 1971; (ed Anglin) Beyond the Information Given: selected papers of Jerome S. Bruner, 1973; (with Connolly) The Growth of Competence, 1974; (with Jolly and Sylva) Play: its role in evolution and development, 1976; Under Five in Britain, 1980; Communication as Language, 1982; contribs technical and professional jls. *Recreation:* sailing. *Address:* 2 Washington Square Village, New York, NY 10012, USA. *Clubs:* Royal Cruising, Cruising Club of America.

BRUNNER, Sir Felix (John Morgan), 3rd Bt, *cr* 1895; Director of various Companies, retired; *b* 13 Oct. 1897; *o s* of Sir John Brunner, 2nd Bt, and Lucy Marianne Vaughan (*d* 1941), *d* of late Octavius Vaughan Morgan, MP; *S* father 1929; *m* 1926, Dorothea Elizabeth, OBE 1965, JP, *d* of late Henry Brodribb Irving and late Dorothea Baird; three *s* (and two *s* decd). *Educ:* Cheltenham; Trinity College, Oxford (MA). Served European War, 1916-18, as Lieut RFA; contested (L) Hulme Division Manchester, 1924, Chippenham,

Wilts, 1929, and Northwich, Cheshire, 1945. Chairman, Henley Rural District Council, 1954-57. Chairman, Commons, Open Spaces and Footpaths Preservation Society, 1958-70. President, Liberal Party Organisation, 1962-63. *Heir: s* John Henry Kilian Brunner [*b* 1 June 1927; *m* 1955, Jasmine Cecily, *d* of late John Wardrop-Moore; two *s* one *d*]. *Address:* Greys Court, Henley-on-Thames, Oxon. *T:* Rotherfield Greys 296. *Club:* Reform.

See also Laurence Irving.

BRUNNER, Dr Guido; Grand Cross, Order of Federal Republic of Germany; German diplomat and politician; Ambassador of the Federal Republic of Germany in Madrid, since 1982; *b* Madrid, 27 May 1930; *m* 1958, Christa (*née* Speidel). *Educ:* Bergzabern, Munich; German Sch., Madrid; Univs of Munich, Heidelberg and Madrid (law and econs). LLD Munich; Licentiate of Law Madrid. Diplomatic service, 1955-74, 1981-; Private Office of the Foreign Minister, 1956; Office, Sec. of State for For. Affairs, 1958-60; German Observer Mission to the UN, New York, 1960-68; Min. for Foreign Affairs: Dept of scientific and technol relns, 1968-70; Spokesman, 1970-72; Head of Planning Staff, Ambassador and Head of Delegn of Fed. Rep. of Germany, Conf. for Security and Coop. in Europe, Helsinki/Geneva, 1972-74; Mem., Commn of the European Communities, (responsible for Energy, Research, Science and Educn), 1974-80; Mem., Bundestag, 1980-81; Mayor of Berlin and Minister of Economics and Transport, Jan.-May 1981; Ambassador, Min. of Foreign Affairs, Bonn, 1981-82. Hon. DLitt Heriot-Watt, 1977; Dr *hc* ; Technical Faculty, Patras Univ., Greece: City Univ., London, 1980. Melchett Medal, Inst. of Energy, 1978. Grand Cross: Order of Civil Merit, Spain; Order of Leopold, Belgium. *Publications:* Bipolarität und Sicherheit, 1965; Friedenssicherungsaktionen der Vereinten Nationen, 1968; Stolz wie Don Rodrigo, 1982; contrib. Vierteljahreshefte für Zeitgeschichte, Aussenpolitik, Europa-Archiv. *Address:* Embajada de la República Federal de Alemania C/Fortuny 8, Madrid-4, Spain.

BRUNSKILL, Brig. George Stephen, CBE 1941; MC 1914; *b* 26 Aug. 1891; *s* of late Major Arthur Stephen Brunskill, The King's Own Regt and West India Regt, of Buckland Tout Saints, S Devon, and Annie Louisa Churchward; *m* Moira Wallace (*née* Wares); one *s* one *d. Educ:* Eastbourne College; Royal Military College, Sandhurst; Staff College, Camberley (psc). Commissioned into Indian Army, 1911, and joined 47th Sikhs; served European War, 1914-18, in France, where twice severely wounded, and Italy as DÁAG (MC, Corona d'Italia and Order of St Maurice and Lazarus, Brevet Major); transferred to King's Shropshire Light Infantry, 1918; commanded First Battalion, 1934; Colonel 1937, and served on the staff as Temp. Brigadier in Palestine (CBE), in the Greece and Crete campaigns of 1941 (despatches twice, Greek MC, 1939-43 Star, N. African Star, Defence Medal, Czecho Slovak Order of White Lion, 3rd class); and on the Congo-Cairo War Supply Route, 1942-43; retired, 1945. Agent, Slingsby Estate, 1948-66. Councillor, Nidderdale RDC, 1950-66. *Address:* Cob Cottage, Woolstone, Faringdon, Oxon. *T:* Uffington 283.

BRUNT, Peter Astbury, FBA 1969; Camden Professor of Ancient History, Oxford University, and Fellow of Brasenose College, 1970-82; *b* 23 June 1917; *s* of Rev. Samuel Brunt, Methodist Minister, and Gladys Eileen Brunt. *Educ:* Ipswich Sch.; Oriel Coll., Oxford. Open Schol. in History, Oriel Coll., Oxford, 1935; first classes in Class. Mods, 1937, and Lit. Hum., 1939; Craven Fellowship, 1939. Temp. Asst Principal and (later) Temp. Principal, Min. of Shipping (later War Transport), 1940-45. Sen. Demy, Magdalen Coll., Oxford, 1946; Lectr in Ancient History, St Andrews Univ., 1947-51; Fellow and Tutor of Oriel Coll., Oxford, 1951-67, Dean, 1959-64, Hon. Fellow, 1973; Fellow and Sen. Bursar, Gonville and Caius Coll., Cambridge, 1968-70. Editor of Oxford Magazine, 1963-64; Chm., Cttee on Ashmolean Museum, 1967; Deleg., Clarendon Press, 1971-79; Mem. Council, British Sch. at Rome, 1972-; Pres., Soc. for Promotion of Roman Studies, 1980-. *Publications:* Thucydides (selections in trans. with introd.), 1963; Res Gestae Divi Augusti (with Dr J. M. Moore), 1967; Social Conflicts in the Roman Republic, 1971; Italian Manpower 225 BC-AD 14, 1971; ed, Arrian's Anabasis (Loeb Classical Library), vol. I, 1976, vol. II, 1983; articles in classical and historical jls. *Address:* 34 Manor Road, South Hinksey, Oxford. *T:* Oxford 739923.

BRUNTISFIELD, 1st Baron, *cr* 1942, of Boroughmuir; **Victor Alexander George Anthony Warrender,** MC 1918; 8th Bt of Lochend, East Lothian, *cr* 1715; late Grenadier Guards; *b* 23 June 1899; *s* of 7th Bt and Lady Maud Warrender (*d* 1945), *y d* of 8th Earl of Shaftesbury; *S* father's Baronetcy, 1917; *m* 1920, Dorothy (marr. diss., 1945), *y d* of late Colonel R. H. Rawson, MP, and Lady Beatrice Rawson; three *s* ; *m* 1948, Tania, *yr d* of Dr Kolin, St Jacob, Dubrovnik, Jugoslavia; one *s* one *d. Educ:* Eton. Served European War, 1917-18 (MC, Russian Order of St Stanislas, Star of Roumania, St Ann of Russia with sword); MP (U) Grantham Division of Kesteven and Rutland, 1923-42; an assistant Whip, 1928-31; Junior Lord of the Treasury, 1931-32; Vice-Chamberlain of HM Household, 1932-35; Comptroller of HM Household, 1935; Parliamentary and Financial Secretary to Admiralty, 1935; Financial Secretary, War Office, 1935-40; Parliamentary and Financial Secretary, Admiralty, 1940-42; Parliamentary Secretary, Admiralty, 1942-45. *Heir: s* Col Hon. John Robert Warrender, qv. *Address:* Chalet les Pommiers, 3780 Gstaad, OB, Switzerland. *T:* 030 42384. *Club:* Turf.

See also Lord Reay, Hon. R. H. Warrender.

BRUNTON, Sir (Edward Francis) Lauder, 3rd Bt, *cr* 1908; Physician; *b* 10 Nov. 1916; *s* of Sir Stopford Brunton, 2nd Bt, and Elizabeth, *o d* of late Professor J. Bonsall Porter; *S* father 1943; *m* 1946, Marjorie, *o d* of David

Sclater Lewis, MSc, MD, CM, FRCP (C); one s one d. *Educ:* Trinity College School, Port Hope; Bryanston School; McGill Univ. BSc 1940; MD, CM 1942; served as Captain, R.CAMC. Hon. attending Physician, Royal Victoria Hosp., Montreal. Fellow: American Coll. of Physicians; Internat. Soc. of Hematology; Member American Society of Hematology; Life Mem., Montreal Mus. of Fine Arts. *Heir: s* James Lauder Brunton [*b* 24 Sept. 1947; *m* 1967, Susan, *o d* of Charles Hons; one *s* one *d*]. *Address:* PO Box 140, Guysborough, Nova Scotia, Canada. *Club:* Royal Nova Scotia Yacht Squadron.

BRUNTON, Gordon Charles; President, International Thomson Organisation Ltd; Managing Director and Chief Executive, International Thomson Organisation plc, and The Thomson Organisation Ltd, since 1968; *b* 27 Dec. 1921; *s* of late Charles Arthur Brunton and late Hylda Pritchard; *m* 1st, 1946, Nadine Lucile Paula Sohr (marr. diss. 1965); one *s* two *d* (and one *s* decd); 2nd, 1966, Gillian Agnes Kirk; one *s* one *d. Educ:* Cranleigh Sch.; London Sch. of Economics. Commnd into RA, 1942; served Indian Army, Far East; Mil. Govt, Germany, 1946. Joined Tothill Press, 1947; Exec. Dir, Tothill, 1956; Man. Dir, Tower Press Gp of Cos, 1958; Exec. Dir, Odhams Press, 1961; joined Thomson Organisation, 1961; Man. Dir, Thomson Publications, 1961; Dir, Thomson Organisation, 1963; Chm., Thomson Travel, 1965-68; Director: Times Newspapers Ltd, 1967; Bemrose Corp., 1974 (Chm., 1978-); Sotheby Parke Bernet & Co., 1978- (Chm., 1982-). Dir of other printing and publishing cos. President: Periodical Publishers Assoc., 1972-74, 1981-; Nat. Advertising Benevolent Soc., 1973-75; History of Advertising Trust, 1981; Chm., EDC for Civil Engrg, 1978; Member: Printing and Publishing Ind. Trng Bd, 1974-78; Supervisory Bd, CBI Special Programmes Unit, 1980; Business in the Community Council, 1981; Chm., Appeals Cttee, Independent Adoption Soc. Governor: LSE (Fellow, 1978); Ashridge Management Coll., 1981; Mem. Council, Oxford Centre for Management Studies. *Recreations:* books, breeding horses. *Address:* North Munstead, Godalming, Surrey. *T:* Godalming 6313. *Club:* Garrick.

BRUNTON, Sir Lauder; *see* Brunton, Sir E. F. L.

BRUSH, Lt-Col Edward James Augustus Howard, CB 1966; DSO 1945; OBE 1946; *b* 5 March 1901; *s* of Major George Howard Brush, Drumnabreeze, Co. Down; *m* 1937, Susan Mary, *d* of Major F. H. E. Torbett, Britford, Salisbury; one *d. Educ:* Clifton Coll.; RMC. Commnd Rifle Brigade, 1920. Served War of 1939-45 (France; wounded; prisoner of war); retired 1946. Chairman, T&AFA, Co. Down, 1954-65. Mem., NI Convention, 1975-76. JP, DL Co. Down, 1953-74; Vice-Lieutenant, 1951-64; High Sheriff, 1953. Member, Irish Nat. Hunt Steeplechase Cttee. *Publication:* The Hunter Chaser, 1947. *Address:* Drumnabreeze, Magheralin, Craigavon, N Ireland. *T:* Moira 611284.

BRUTON, John (Gerard), Teachta Dala (TD) (Fine Gael), Meath, Dáil Eireann (Parliament of Ireland), since 1969; *b* 18 May 1947; *s* of Matthew Joseph Bruton and Doris Bruton (*née* Delany); *m* 1981, Finola Gill. *Educ:* Clongowes Wood Coll., Co. Kildare; University Coll., Dublin (BA, BL); King's Inns, Dublin. National Secretary, Fine Gael Youth Group, 1966-69. Mem., Dáil Committee of Procedure and Privileges, 1969-73; Fine Gael Spokesman on Agriculture, 1972-73; Parliamentary Secretary: to Minister for Education, 1973-75; to Minister for Industry and Commerce, 1975-77; Fine Gael Spokesman: on Agriculture, 1977-81; on Finance, Jan.-June 1981; Minister for Finance, 1981-82. Hon. Citizen of Sioux City, Iowa, USA, 1970. *Recreation:* reading history. *Address:* Government Buildings, Upper Merrion Street, Dublin 2, Ireland. *T:* 255573; Cornelstown, Dunboyne, Co. Meath.

BRYAN, Sir Andrew (Meikle), Kt 1950; DSc; Hon. LLD (Glasgow); CEng, FIMinE, FICE, FRSE; Consulting Mining Engineer; Member of National Coal Board, 1951-57; *b* 1 March 1893; 2nd *s* of John Bryan, Burnbank, Hamilton, Lanarkshire; *m* 1st, 1922, Henrietta Paterson (*d* 1977), *y d* of George S. Begg, Allanshaw, Hamilton; one *s*; 2nd, 1980, Mrs Winifred Henderson Ruttledge, widow. *Educ:* Greenfield Public School; Hamilton Acad.; Glasgow University, graduated 1919 with Special Distinction. Served in University OTC and HM Forces, 1915-18. Obtained practical mining experience in the Lanarkshire Coalfield; HM Junior Inspector of Mines in the Northern Division, 1920; Senior rank, 1926; Dixon Professor of Mining, University of Glasgow, Professor of Mining, Royal College of Science and Technology, Glasgow, 1932-40; Gen. Manager, 1940, Dir, 1942, Managing Director, 1944, Shotts Iron Co. Ltd; also Director Associated Lothian Coal Owners Ltd; Deputy-Director of Mining Supplies, Mines Department, 1939-40; Chief Inspector of Mines, 1947-51. Mem. Council, IMinE (Hon. Treas.; Hon. Mem., 1957; Pres., 1950 and 1951; Inst. Medal, 1954); Mem., Mining Qualifications Bd, 1947-62, Chm., 1962-72; former Mem. Council, Inst. Mining and Metallurgy, 1951; Hon. Member: Nat. Assoc. of Colliery Managers, 1957 (Futers Gold Medal, 1937; former Mem. Council; Past Pres.); Geol Soc. of Edinburgh; former Mem. Council and Past Pres., Mining Inst. of Scotland; John Buddle Medal, N England Inst. of Mining and Mech. Engrs, 1967. Fellow, Imperial College of Science and Technology. *Publications:* St George's Coalfield, Newfoundland, 1937; The Evolution of Health and Safety in Mines, 1976; contribs to technical journals. *Address:* 3 Hounslow Gardens, Hounslow, Mddx TW3 2DU.

BRYAN, Sir Arthur, Kt 1976; Chairman, Wedgwood Ltd, Barlaston, Staffs, since 1968, and Managing Director since 1963; Lord-Lieutenant of Staffordshire, since 1968; *b* 4 March 1923; *s* of William Woodall Bryan and Isobel Alan (*née* Tweedie); *m* 1947, Betty Ratford; one *s* one *d. Educ:* Longton High Sch., Stoke-on-Trent. Trainee, Barclays Bank. Served with RAFVR, 1941-45. Josiah Wedgwood & Sons Ltd, 1947-49; London Man., 1953-57; General Sales Man., 1959-60; Director and President, Josiah Wedgwood & Sons Inc. of America, 1960-62; Director: Josiah Wedgwood & Sons Ltd, Barlaston, 1962; Josiah Wedgwood & Sons (Canada) Ltd; Josiah Wedgwood & Sons (Australia) Pty Ltd; Phoenix Assurance Co., 1976-. Mem., BOTB, 1978-82 (Chm., N American Adv. Gp, 1973-82). Pres., British Ceramic Manufacturers' Fedn, 1970-71; Mem., Design Council, 1977-. Mem. Ct, Univ. of Keele. FRSA 1964 (Mem. Council, 1980-); Fellow, Inst. of Marketing (grad. 1950); CBIM (FBIM 1968); Comp. Inst. Ceramics. KStJ 1972. Hon. MUniv. Keele, 1978. *Recreations:* walking, tennis, swimming and reading. *Address:* Parkfields Cottage, Tittensor, Stoke-on-Trent, Staffs. *T:* Barlaston 2686.

BRYAN, Denzil Arnold, CMG 1960; OBE 1947; HM Diplomatic Service, retired; *b* 15 Oct. 1909; *s* of James Edward Bryan; *m* 1965, Hope Ross (*née* Meyer) (*d* 1981). *Educ:* in India; Selwyn Coll., Cambridge. Appointed to Indian Civil Service in 1933 and posted to Punjab. Dep. Commissioner, Hissar, 1938; Registrar, Lahore High Court, 1939-41; Dep. Comr, Dera Ghazi Khan, 1941-44; Sec. to Prime Minister, Punjab, 1944-47; and to Governor of Punjab, 1947; retired from ICS, 1947. Appointed to UK Civil Service, Bd of Trade, as Principal, 1947; Asst Sec., 1950; Under Secretary, 1961; served as a Trade Comr in India, 1947-55; UK Senior Trade Comr: in New Zealand, 1955-58; in Pakistan, 1958-61; in South Africa, 1961; Minister (Commercial, later Economic), S Africa, 1962-69. *Address:* 29 Wildcroft Manor, Wildcroft Road, SW15; c/o Lloyds Bank Ltd, 6 Pall Mall, SW1.

BRYAN, Dora, (Mrs William Lawton); actress; *b* 7 Feb. 1924; *d* of Albert Broadbent and Georgina (*née* Hill); *m* 1954, William Lawton; one *s* (and one *s* one *d* adopted). *Educ:* Hathershaw Council Sch., Lancs. Pantomimes: London Hippodrome, 1936; Manchester Palace, 1937; Alhambra, Glasgow, 1938; Oldham Repertory, 1939-44; followed by Peterborough, Colchester, Westcliff-on-Sea. ENSA, Italy, during War of 1939-45. Came to London, 1945, and appeared in West End Theatres: Peace in our Time; Travellers' Joy; Accolade; Lyric Revue; Globe Revue; Simon and Laura; The Water Gypsies; Gentlemen Prefer Blondes; Six of One; Too True to be Good; Hello, Dolly!; They Don't Grow on Trees; Rookery Nook, Her Majesty's, 1979. Chichester Festival seasons, 1971-74; London Palladium season, 1971; London Palladium Pantomime season, 1973-74. Has also taken parts in farces televised from Whitehall Theatre. *Films include:* The Fallen Idol, 1949; A Taste of Honey, 1961 (British Acad. Award); Two a Penny, 1968. *TV series:* appearances on A to Z; Sunday Night at the London Palladium; According to Dora, 1968; Both Ends Meet, 1972. Cabaret in Canada, Hong Kong and Britain. Has made recordings. *Recreations:* reading, patchwork quilts, helping husband and family who run hotel. *Address:* Clarges Hotel, Marine Parade, Brighton, East Sussex. *T:* Brighton 606551.

BRYAN, Gerald Jackson, CMG 1964; CVO 1966; OBE 1960; MC 1941; General Manager, Bracknell Development Corporation, 1973-82; *b* 2 April 1921; *yr s* of late George Bryan, OBE, LLD, and Ruby Evelyn (*née* Jackson), Belfast; *m* 1947, Georgiana Wendy Cockburn, OStJ, *d* of late William Barraud and Winnifred Hull; one *s* two *d. Educ:* Wrekin Coll.; RMA, Woolwich; New Coll., Oxford. Regular Commn, RE, 1940; served Middle East with No 11 (Scottish) Commando, 1941; retd 1944, Capt. (temp. Maj.). Apptd Colonial Service, 1944; Asst District Comr, Swaziland, 1944; Asst Colonial Sec., Barbados, 1950; Estabt Sec., Mauritius, 1954; Administrator, Brit. Virgin Is, 1959; Administrator of St Lucia, 1962-67, retired; Govt Sec. and Head of Isle of Man Civil Service, 1967-69; Gen. Man., Londonderry Develt Commn, NI, 1969-73. FBIM. CStJ. *Recreation:* riding. *Address:* Whitehouse, Murrell Hill, Binfield, Berks; 30 Queen Street, Castletown, Isle of Man. *Club:* Naval and Military.

BRYAN, Sir Paul (Elmore Oliver), Kt 1972; DSO 1943; MC 1943; MP (C) Howden Division of Yorkshire (East Riding), since 1955; *b* 3 Aug. 1913; *s* of Reverend Dr J. I. Bryan, PhD; *m* 1st, 1939, Betty Mary (*née* Hoyle) (*d* 1968); three *d*; 2nd, 1971, Cynthia Duncan (*née* Ashley Cooper), *d* of late Sir Patrick Ashley Cooper and of Lady Ashley Cooper, Hexton Manor, Herts. *Educ:* St John's School, Leatherhead (Scholar); Caius College, Cambridge (MA). War of 1939-45: 6th Royal West Kent Regt; enlisted, 1939; commissioned, 1940; Lieut-Col, 1943; served in France, N Africa, Sicily, Italy; Comdt 164th Inf. OCTU (Eaton Hall), 1944. Sowerby Bridge UDC, 1947; contested Sowerby, By-Election, 1948, and General Elections, 1950 and 1951. Member Parliamentary Delegation: to Peru, 1955, to Algeria, 1956, to Germany, 1960, to USA and Canada, 1961, to India, 1966, to Uganda and Kenya, 1967, to Hong Kong, 1969, to Japan and Indonesia, 1969, to China, 1972, to Mexico, 1981. Assistant Government Whip, 1956-58; Parliamentary Private Secretary to Minister of Defence, 1956; a Lord Commissioner of the Treasury, 1958-61; Vice-Chairman, Conservative Party Organisation, 1961-65; Conservative Front Bench Spokesman on Post Office and broadcasting, 1965; Minister of State, Dept of Employment, 1970-72. Chm., All Party Hong Kong Parly Gp, 1974-; Vice-Chm., Conservative 1922 Cttee, 1977-. Director: Granada TV Rental Ltd, 1966-70; Granada Television, 1972-; Granada Theatres, 1973-; Greater Manchester Independent Radio Ltd, 1972-; Scottish Lion Insurance Co. Ltd, 1981-. *Address:* Park Farm, Sawdon, near Scarborough, North Yorks. *T:* Scarborough 85370; Westminster Gardens, Marsham Street, SW1. *T:* 01-834 2050.

BRYAN, Robert Patrick, OBE 1980; Police Adviser to Foreign and Commonwealth Office, and Inspector General of Dependent Territories Police, since 1980; *b* 29 June 1926; *s* of Maurice Bryan and Elizabeth (*née* Waite); *m* 1948, Hazel Audrey (*née* Braine); three *s*. *Educ:* Plaistow Secondary Sch.; Wanstead County High Sch. Indian Army (Mahratta LI), 1944–47. Bank of Nova Scotia, 1948–49; Metropolitan Police: Constable, 1950; Dep. Asst Commissioner, 1977, retired 1980. National Police College: Intermediate Comd Course, 1965; Sen. Comd Course, 1969; occasional lecturer. RCDS 1974. *Publications:* contribs to police and related pubns, particularly on community relations and juvenile delinquency. *Recreations:* people, gardening, music, squash, swimming, reading. *Address:* c/o Foreign and Commonwealth Office, SW1. *T:* 01-273 4723. *Clubs:* Royal Commonwealth Society, Roehampton.

BRYAN, Willoughby Guy, TD 1945; Director: Barclays Bank, 1957–81 (Vice-Chairman, 1964–70, Deputy Chairman, 1970–74); Barclays Bank Trust Company Ltd, 1970–81 (Chairman, 1970–74); Barclays Unicorn Group Ltd, 1977–81; *b* 16 Jan. 1911; *e s* of late C. R. W. Bryan; *m* 1936, Esther Victoria Loveday, *d* of late Major T. L. Ingram, DSO, MC; one *d*. *Educ:* Winchester; Hertford College, Oxford. Barclays Bank Ltd, 1932; various appointments including: Local Director, Oxford, 1946; Local Director, Reading, 1947; Local Director, Birmingham, 1955; Chm. Local Bd, Birmingham, 1957–64. Served War of 1939–45, Queen's Own Oxfordshire Hussars. *Recreation:* golf. *Address:* 28 Crooked Billet, Wimbledon Common, SW19 4RQ. *T:* 01-946 5645. *Clubs:* Army and Navy; Rye Golf, Royal Wimbledon Golf.

BRYANS, Dame Anne (Margaret), DBE 1957 (CBE 1945); DStJ; Chairman, Order of St John of Jerusalem and BRCS Service Hospitals Welfare and VAD Committee, since 1960; Vice-Chairman, Joint Committee, Order of St John and BRCS, 1976–81; *b* 29 Oct. 1909; *e d* of late Col Rt Hon. Sir John Gilmour, 2nd Bt, GCVO, DSO, MP of Montrave and late Mary Louise Lambert; *m* 1932, Lieut-Comdr J. R. Bryans, RN, retired; one *s*. *Educ:* privately. Joined HQ Staff British Red Cross Society, 1938; Deputy Commissioner British Red Cross and St John War Organisation, Middle East Commission, 1943; Commissioner Jan.–June 1945. Dep. Chm., 1953–64, Vice-Chm., 1964–76, Exec. Cttee, BRCS; Lay Mem., Council for Professions Supplementary to Med., to 1979; Member: Ethical practices Sub-Cttee, Royal Free Hosp., 1974–; Royal Free Hosp. Sch. Council, 1968–; Bd of Governors, Eastman Dental Hosp., 1973–79; Camden and Islington AHA, 1974–79; Vice-Pres., Open Sect., RSocMed, 1975, Pres. 1980–82; former Member: ITA, later IBA; Govt Anglo-Egyptian Resettlement Bd; BBC/ITA Appeals Cttee; Med. Sch. St George's Hosp.; Special Trustee and former Chm., Royal Free Hosp. and Friends of Royal Free Hosp.; former Chairman: Bd of Governors, Royal Free Hosp.; Council, Florence Nightingale Hosp.; Trustee, Florence Nightingale Aid in Sickness Trust, 1979–; Vice-Pres., Royal Coll. of Nursing; former Governor, Westminster Hosp. FRSM 1976. *Address:* 57 Elm Park House, Elm Park Gardens, SW10. *Clubs:* VAD Ladies; Royal Lymington Yacht.

BRYANS, Tom, MBE 1975; Chief General Manager, Trustee Savings Bank Central Board (formerly TSB Association Ltd), since 1975; *b* 16 Sept. 1920; *s* of Thomas and Martha Bryans; *m* 1947, Peggy Irene Snelling; two *s*. *Educ:* Royal Belfast Academical Instn. AIB 1950; FSBI 1972. Served War, 1939-46. Joined Belfast Savings Bank, 1938; Asst Gen. Man., 1969; Gen. Man., 1971. *Recreations:* sailing, golfing, gardening and music. *Address:* 3 Copthall Avenue, EC2P 2AB.

BRYANT, Sir Arthur, Kt 1954; CH 1967; CBE 1949; Hon. LLD: Edinburgh; St Andrews; New Brunswick; MA (Oxon); FRHistS; FRSL; Council, Society of Authors; Royal Literary Fund; Trustee: Historic Churches Preservation Trust; English Folk Music Fund; Member, Architectural Advisory Panel, Westminster Abbey; President, Friends of the Vale of Aylesbury; *b* 18 Feb. 1899; *e s* of late Sir Francis Bryant, CB, CVO, CBE, ISO, JP, The Pavilion, Hampton Court; *m* 1st, 1924, Sylvia Mary (marr. diss. 1939; she *m* 2nd, F. D. Chew, and *d* 1950), *d* of Sir Walter Shakerley, Bt, Somerford Park, Cheshire; 2nd, 1941, Anne Elaine (marr. diss. 1976), *y d* of Bertram Brooke (HH Tuan Muda of Sarawak). *Educ:* Harrow; BEF France; Queen's Coll., Oxford. Barrister-at-law, Inner Temple. Principal, Cambridge School of Arts, Crafts and Technology, 1923–25; Lectr in History to Oxford Univ. Delegacy for Extra-Mural Studies, 1925–36; Watson Chair in American History, London Univ., 1935; Corres. Member of La Real Academia de la Historia of Madrid; succeeded G. K. Chesterton as writer of Our Note Book, Illustrated London News, 1936–. Chairman: Ashridge Council, 1946–49; Soc. of Authors, 1949–53; St John and Red Cross Library Dept, 1945–74. President: English Association, 1946; Common Market Safeguards Campaign. Chesney Gold Medal, RUSI; Gold Medal, RICS. Hon. Freedom and Livery, Leathersellers' Company; Hon. Member: Southampton Chamber of Commerce; Rifle Brigade Club; Light Infantry Club. KGStJ. *Publications:* King Charles II, 1931; Macaulay, 1932; Samuel Pepys, the Man in the Making, 1933; The National Character, 1934; The England of Charles II, 1934; The Letters and Speeches of Charles II, 1935; Samuel Pepys, the Years of Peril, 1935; George V, 1936; The American Ideal, 1936; Postman's Horn, 1936; Stanley Baldwin, 1937; Humanity in Politics, 1938; Samuel Pepys, the Saviour of the Navy, 1938; Unfinished Victory, 1940; English Saga, 1940; The Years of Endurance, 1942; Dunkirk, 1943; Years of Victory, 1944; Historian's Holiday, 1947; The Age of Elegance, 1950 (Sunday Times Gold Medal and Award for Literature); The Turn of the Tide, 1957; Triumph in the West, 1959; Jimmy, 1960; The Story of England: Makers of the Realm, 1953; The Age of Chivalry, 1963;

The Fire and the Rose, 1965; The Medieval Foundation, 1966; Protestant Island, 1967; The Lion and the Unicorn, 1969; Nelson, 1970; The Great Duke, 1971; Jackets of Green, 1973; Thousand Years of British Monarchy, 1975; Pepys and the Revolution, 1979; The Elizabethan Deliverance, 1980; Spirit of England, 1982; prologue and epilogue to David Fraser's Alanbrooke, 1982. *Relevant Publication:* Arthur Bryant: portrait of a historian, by Pamela Street, 1979. *Address:* Myles Place, The Close, Salisbury, Wilts. *Clubs:* Athenæum, Beefsteak, Grillion's, Pratt's, Saintsbury, MCC.

BRYANT, Rear-Adm. Benjamin, CB 1956; DSO 1942 (two bars, 1943); DSC 1940; *b* 16 Sept. 1905; *s* of J. F. Bryant, MA, FRGS, ICS (retd); *m* 1929, Marjorie Dagmar Mynors (*née* Symonds) (*d* 1965); one *s* one *d* ; *m* 1966, Heather Elizabeth Williams (*née* Hance). *Educ:* Oundle; RN Colls Osborne and Dartmouth. Entered submarine branch of RN, 1927; Commanded: HMS/M Sea Lion, 1939–41; HMS/M Safari, 1941–43; comd 7th and 3rd Submarine Flotillas, 1943–44; comd 4th s/m Flotilla, British Pacific Fleet, 1945–47; comd HMS Dolphin Submarine School, and 5th Submarine Flotilla, 1947–49; Commodore (submarines), 1948; idc 1950; Commodore, RN Barracks, Devonport, 1951–53; Flag Captain to C-in-C Mediterranean, 1953–54; Rear-Admiral, 1954. Deputy Chief of Naval Personnel (Training and Manning), 1954-57; retired, 1957. Staff Personnel Manager, Rolls Royce Scottish Factories, 1957–68. *Recreations:* fishing, golf, shooting. *Address:* Pines, Symington, Biggar, Lanarkshire.

BRYANT, David John, CBE 1980 (MBE 1969); Director, Drakelite Ltd (International Bowls Consultants), since 1978; international bowler; *b* 27 Oct. 1931; *s* of Reginald Samuel Harold Bryant and Evelyn Claire (*née* Weaver); *m* 1960, Ruth Georgina (*née* Roberts); two *d*. *Educ:* Weston Grammar Sch.; St Paul's Coll., Cheltenham; Redland Coll., Bristol (teacher training colls). National Service, RAF, 1950-52; teacher trng, 1953-55; schoolmaster, 1955-71; company director, sports business, 1971–78. World Singles Champion, 1966 and 1980; World Indoor Singles Champion, 1979, 1980 and 1981; World Triples Champion, 1980; Commonwealth Games Gold Medalist: Singles: 1962, 1970, 1974 and 1978; Fours: 1962. Numerous national and British Isles titles, both indoor and outdoor. *Publication:* Bryant on Bowls, 1966. *Recreations:* angling, gardening, table tennis. *Address:* 47 Esmond Grove, Clevedon, Avon BS21 7HP. *T:* Clevedon 877551. *Clubs:* Clevedon Bowling, Clevedon Conservative.

BRYANT, Rt. Rev. Denis William, DFC 1942; Rector of Dalkeith, W Australia, since 1975; *b* 31 Jan. 1918; *s* of Thomas and Beatrice Maud Bryant; *m* 1940, Dorothy Linda (*née* Lewis); one *d*. *Educ:* Clark's Coll., Ealing; Cardiff Techn. Coll. Joined RAF; Wireless Operator/Air Gunner, 1936; Navigator, 1939; France, 1940 (despatches); Pilot, 1941; commn in Secretarial Br., 1950; Adjt, RAF Hereford, 1950; Sqdn-Ldr i/c Overseas Postings Record Office, Gloucester, 1951; Sqdn-Ldr DP7, Air Min., 1953. Ordinand, Queen's Coll., Birmingham, 1956; Deacon, 1958; Priest, 1959. Bishop of Kalgoorlie, 1967 until 1973 when Kalgoorlie became part of Diocese of Perth; Asst Bishop of Perth, and Archdeacon and Rector of Northam, 1973-75. *Recreations:* squash, tennis, oil painting. *Address:* St Lawrence Church, The Rectory, 42 Alexander Road, Dalkeith, WA 6009, Australia.

BRYANT, Michael; actor; National Theatre player, since 1977; *b* 5 April 1928; *s* of William and Ann Bryant; *m* 1958, Josephine Martin (marr. diss. 1980); two *s* two *d*. *Educ:* Battersea Grammar Sch. Merchant Navy, 1945; Army, 1946–49; drama sch., 1949–51; theatre and television, 1957–77; RSC, 1964–65. Best Actor: SWET awards, 1977; British Theatrical Assoc., 1981. Governor, RADA, 1982. *Recreations:* none. *Address:* 38 Killyon Road, SW8.

BRYANT, Prof. Peter Elwood; Watts Professor of Psychology, Oxford University, since 1980; Fellow of St John's College, Oxford, since 1967. *Educ:* Clare College, Cambridge (BA 1963, MA 1967). University Lecturer in Human Experimental Psychology, 1967-80. *Address:* St John's College, Oxford.

BRYANT, Peter George Francis; Under Secretary, Chemicals and Textiles Division, Department of Industry, since 1981; *b* 10 May 1932; *s* of late George Bryant, CBE and Margaret Bryant; *m* 1961, Jean (*née* Morris); one *s* one *d*. *Educ:* Sutton Valence Sch.; Birkbeck Coll., London Univ. (BA). Joined Civil Service as Exec. Officer, Min. of Supply, 1953; Higher Exec. Officer, BoT, 1960; Principal, 1967; 1st Sec. (Commercial), Vienna (on secondment to HM Diplomatic Service), 1970; Dir of British Trade Drive in S Germany, 1973; Asst Sec., Dept of Trade, 1974 (Head, Overseas Projs Gp); Civil Aviation Internat. Relations Div., 1978. *Address:* Greenacre, 77 Lane End Drive, Knaphill, Woking, Surrey GU21 2QG. *T:* Brookwood 2350.

BRYANT, Richard Charles, CB 1960; Under-Secretary, Board of Trade, 1955–68; *b* 20 Aug. 1908; *s* of Charles James and Constance Byron Bryant, The Bounds, Faversham, Kent; *m* 1938, Elisabeth Ellington, *d* of Dr. A. E. Stansfeld, FRCP; two *s* two *d*. *Educ:* Rugby; Oriel College, Oxford. Entered Board of Trade, 1932; Ministry of Supply, 1939-44. *Address:* Marsh Farm House, Brancaster, Norfolk. *T:* Brancaster 206. *Club:* Travellers'.

BRYARS, Donald Leonard; Commissioner of Customs and Excise, since 1978 and Director, Personnel, since 1979; *b* 31 March 1929; *s* of late Leonard and Marie Bryars; *m* 1953, Joan (*née* Yealand); one *d*. *Educ:* Goole Grammar Sch.; Leeds Univ. Joined Customs and Excise as Executive Officer, 1953, Principal, 1964, Asst Sec., 1971; on loan to Cabinet Office, 1976–78; Director,

General Customs, 1978-79. *Address:* 15 Ellwood Rise, Chalfont St Giles, Bucks HP8 4SU. *T:* Chalfont St Giles 5466. *Club:* Civil Service.

BRYARS, John Desmond, CB 1982; Deputy Under Secretary of State, Finance and Budget, Ministry of Defence, since 1979; *b* 31 Oct. 1928; *s* of William Bryars, MD and Sarah (*née* McMeekin); *m* 1964, Faith, *d* of Frederick Momber, ARCM and Anne Momber. *Educ:* St Edward's Sch., Oxford; Trinity Coll., Oxford (schol.; MA). Army, 1946-48. Entered Civil Service, Air Ministry, 1952; HM Treasury, 1960-62; Private Sec. to Sec. of State for Air, 1963-64, to Minister of Defence, RAF, 1964-65; Asst Sec., MoD, 1965-73; RCDS 1973; Asst Under-Sec. of State, MoD, 1973-75 and 1977-79; Under Sec., Cabinet Office, 1975-77. *Address:* 42 Osterley Road, Osterley, Isleworth, Middlesex. *Club:* Royal Commonwealth Society.

BRYCE, Gabe Robb, OBE 1959; Sales Manager (Operations) British Aircraft Corporation, 1965-75; now occupied in breeding dogs and boarding cats; *b* 27 April 1921; *m* 1943, Agnes Lindsay; one *s* now *d. Educ:* Glasgow High School. Served in RAF, 1939-46. Vickers-Armstrongs (Aircraft) Ltd, 1946-60 (Chief Test Pilot, 1951-60). Participated as First or Second Pilot, in Maiden Flights of following British Aircraft: Varsity; Nene Viking; Viscount 630, 700 and 800; Tay Viscount; Valiant; Pathfinder; Vanguard; VC-10; BAC 1-11; Chief Test Pilot, British Aircraft Corporation, 1960-64. Fellow Soc. of Experimental Test Pilots (USA), 1967. Sir Barnes Wallis Meml Medal, GAPAN, 1980. *Recreations:* squash, tennis. *Address:* Meadows, Elm Corner, Ockham, Ripley, Surrey. *T:* Ripley 3916.

BRYCE, Sir Gordon; see Bryce, Sir W. G.

BRYCE, Ian James G.; see Graham-Bryce.

BRYCE, Dame Isabel G.; see Graham Bryce.

BRYCE, Rt. Rev. Jabez Leslie; see Polynesia, Bishop in.

BRYCE, Sir (William) Gordon, Kt 1971; CBE 1963; Chief Justice of the Bahamas, 1970-73; *b* 2 Feb. 1913; *s* of James Chisholm Bryce and Emily Susan (*née* Lees); *m* 1940, Molly Mary, *d* of Arthur Cranch Drake; two *d. Educ:* Bromsgrove Sch.; Hertford Coll., Oxford (MA). Called to Bar, Middle Temple. War Service, 1940-46 (Major). Colonial Service: Crown Counsel, Fiji, 1949; Solicitor General, Fiji, 1953; Attorney General: Gibraltar, 1956; Aden, 1959; Legal Adviser, S Arabian High Commn, 1963; Attorney General, Bahamas, 1966. Comr, revised edn of Laws: of Gilbert and Ellice Islands, 1952; of Fiji, 1955; Comr, Bahamas Law Reform and Revision Commn, 1976. *Recreations:* riding, gardening. *Address:* Broom Croft, Lydeard St Lawrence, Taunton, Somerset.

BRYDEN, William Campbell Rough, (Bill Bryden); Associate Director, The National Theatre, since 1975; *b* 12 April 1942; *s* of late George Bryden and of Catherine Bryden; *m* 1971, Hon. Deborah Morris, *d* of Baron Killanin, *qv* ; one *s* one *d. Educ:* Hillend Public Sch.; Greenock High Sch. Documentary writer, Scottish Television, 1963-64; Assistant Director: Belgrade Theatre, Coventry, 1965-67; Royal Court Th., London, 1967-69; Associate Dir, Royal Lyceum Th., Edinburgh, 1971-74; Dir, Cottesloe Theatre (Nat. Theatre), 1978-80. Member Board, Scottish Television, 1979-. *Publications:* plays: Willie Rough, 1972; Benny Lynch, 1974; Old Movies, 1977; *screenplay:* The Long Riders, 1980. *Recreation:* music. *Address:* The National Theatre, South Bank, SE1 9PX. *T:* 01-928 2033.

BRYDEN, Sir William (James), Kt 1978; CBE 1970; QC (Scot.) 1973; Sheriff Principal of the Lothians and Borders, 1975-78, Hon. Sheriff since 1978; Sheriff of Chancery in Scotland, 1973-78; *b* 2 Oct. 1909; *y s* of late James George Bryden, JP and late Elizabeth Brown Tyrie; *m* 1937, Christina Mary, *e d* of late Thomas Bannatyne Marshall, CBE, JP; two *s* one *d. Educ:* Perth Academy; Brasenose College, Oxford; Edinburgh University. Barrister-at-Law, Inner Temple, 1933; Advocate of the Scottish Bar, 1935; External Examiner in English Law, Edinburgh University, 1937-40; served in RNVR, 1940-45; Hon. Sheriff-Substitute of Dumfries and Galloway, 1946; Sheriff-Substitute of Lanarkshire at Hamilton, 1946-53; Sheriff-Substitute, later Sheriff, of Lanarkshire at Glasgow, 1953-73; Sheriff Principal, Lothians and Peeblesshire, 1973-75. Member: Law Reform Cttee for Scotland, 1957-61; Scottish Adv. Council on the Treatment of Offenders, 1959-63; Deptl Cttee on Adoption of Children, 1969-72; Grieve Cttee on Admin of Sheriffdoms, 1981-82; Chm., Working Gp on Identification Procedure under Scottish Criminal Law, 1976-78. *Address:* Whinneyknowe, Peebles EH45 9JF. *Club:* New (Edinburgh).

BRYHER, (Annie) Winifred; Author; *d* of Sir John Reeves Ellerman, 1st Bt, CH, and late Hannah Ellerman (*née* Glover); *m* 1st, 1921, Robert McAlmon (marr. diss., 1926); 2nd, 1927, Kenneth Macpherson (marr. diss., 1947); no *c. Educ:* Queenwood, Eastbourne. *Publications:* Development, 1920, etc; The Fourteenth of October, 1952; The Player's Boy, 1953; Roman Wall, 1954; Beowulf, 1956; Gate to the Sea, 1958; Ruan, 1960; The Heart to Artemis, 1963; The Coin of Carthage, 1964; Visa for Avalon, 1965; This January Tale, 1966; The Colors of Vaud, 1970; The Days of Mars, 1972. *Recreations:* travel, the sea, archæology. *Address:* Kenwin, Burier, Vaud, Switzerland.

BRYMER, Jack, OBE 1960; Hon. RAM; Principal Clarinettist, London Symphony Orchestra, since 1972; *b* 27 Jan. 1915; *s* of J. and Mrs M. Brymer, South Shields, Co. Durham; *m* 1939, Joan Richardson, Lancaster; one *s. Educ:* Goldsmiths' College, London University. Schoolmaster, Croydon, general subjects, 1935-40. RAF, 1940-45. Principal Clarinettist: Royal Philharmonic Orchestra, 1946-63; BBC Symphony Orchestra, 1963-72; Prof., Royal Acad. of Music, 1950-58; Prof., Royal Military Sch. of Music, Kneller Hall, 1969-; Member of Wigmore, Prometheus and London Baroque ensembles; Director of London Wind Soloists. Has directed recordings of the complete wind chamber music of Mozart, Beethoven, Haydn and J. C. Bach. Presenter of several BBC music series, inc. At Home (nightly). Hon. RAM 1955; Hon. MA Newcastle upon Tyne, 1973. *Publications:* The Clarinet (Menuhin Guides), 1976; From Where I Sit (autobiog.), 1979. *Recreations:* golf, tennis, swimming, carpentry, gardening, music. *Address:* Underwood, Ballards Farm Road, South Croydon, Surrey. *T:* 01-657 1698. *Club:* Croham Hurst Golf.

BRYSON, Col (James) Graeme, OBE 1954; TD 1949; JP; Deputy Circuit Judge, Northern Circuit, since 1978; Vice-Lord-Lieutenant of Merseyside, since 1979; *b* 4 Feb. 1913; 3rd *s* of John Conway Bryson and Oletta Bryson; *m* Jean (*d* 1981), *d* of Walter Glendinning; two *s* four *d* (and one *s* decd). *Educ:* St Edward's Coll.; Liverpool Univ. (LLM). Admitted solicitor, 1935. Commnd 89th Field Bde RA (TA), 1936; served War, RA, 1939-45 (Lt-Col 1944); comd 470 (3W/Lancs) HAA Regt, 1947-52, and 626 HAA Regt, 1952-55; Bt-Col 1955; Hon. Col 33 Signal Regt (V), 1975-81. Sen. Jt Dist Registrar and Liverpool Admiralty Registrar, High Court of Justice, Liverpool, and Registrar of Liverpool County Court, 1947-78. President: Assoc. of County Court Registrars, 1969; Liverpool Law Soc., 1969; NW Area, Royal British Legion, 1979. Chm., Med. Appeal Tribunal, 1978-; Member: Lord Chancellor's Cttee for enforcement of debts (Payne), 1965-69; IOM Commn to reform enforcement laws, 1972-74; Council, Nat. Assoc. for Employment of Regular Sailors, Soldiers and Airmen, 1952-. JP Liverpool, 1956; DL Lancs, 1965, later Merseyside. The Queen's Commendation for Brave Conduct, 1961. KHS 1974. *Publication:* (jtly) Execution, in Halsbury's Laws of England, 3rd edn 1976. *Recreations:* local history, boating. *Address:* Sunwards, Thirlmere Road, Hightown, Liverpool L38 3RQ. *T:* 051-929 2652. *Club:* Athenæum (Liverpool; Pres., 1969).

BRYSON, Vice-Adm. Sir Lindsay (Sutherland), KCB 1981; FEng; Controller of the Navy, since 1981; *b* 22 Jan. 1925; *s* of James McAuslan Bryson and Margaret Bryson (*née* Whyte); *m* 1951, Averil Curtis-Willson; one *s* two *d. Educ:* Allan Glen's Sch., Glasgow; London Univ. (External) (BSc (Eng)); FIEE, FRaeS. Engrg Cadet, 1942; Electrical Mechanic, RN, 1944; Midshipman 1946; Lieut 1948; Comdr 1960; Captain 1967; comd HMS Daedalus, RNAS Lee-on-Solent, 1970-71; RCDS 1972; Dir, Naval Guided Weapons, 1973; Dir, Surface Weapons Project (Navy), 1974-77; Dir-Gen. Weapons (Naval), 1977-81, and Chief Naval Engr Officer, 1979-81. Faraday Lectr, IEE, 1976-77. Liveryman, Worshipful Co. of Cooks, 1964, Assistant, 1980. *Publications:* contrib. Jl RAeS, Seaford Papers, Control Engineering. *Recreations:* fair weather sailing, gardening, badminton. *Address:* 74 Dyke Road Avenue, Brighton BN1 5LE. *T:* Brighton 553638. *Clubs:* Naval and Military; Hove (Hove).

BUCCLEUCH, 9th Duke of, *cr* 1663, **AND QUEENSBERRY,** 11th Duke of, *cr* 1684; **Walter Francis John Montagu Douglas Scott,** KT 1978; VRD; JP; Baron Scott of Buccleuch, 1606; Earl of Buccleuch, Baron Scott of Whitchester and Eskdaill, 1619; Earl of Doncaster and Baron Tynedale (Eng.), 1662; Earl of Dalkeith, 1663; Marquis of Dumfriesshire, Earl of Drumlanrig and Sanquhar, Viscount of Nith, Torthorwold, and Ross, Baron Douglas, 1684; Lieutenant-Commander RNR; Captain, the Queen's Body Guard for Scotland, Royal Company of Archers; Lord-Lieutenant of Roxburgh, since 1974, of Ettrick and Lauderdale, since 1975; *b* 28 Sept. 1923; *o s* of 8th Duke of Buccleuch, KT, PC, GCVO, and of Vreda Esther Mary, *er d* of late Major W. F. Lascelles and Lady Sybil Lascelles, *d* of 10th Duke of St Albans; *S* father, 1973; *m* 1953, Jane, *d* of John McNeill, QC, Appin, Argyll, and Hongkong; three *s* one *d. Educ:* Eton; Christ Church, Oxford. Served War of 1939-45, RNVR. MP (C) Edinburgh North, 1960-73; PPS to the Lord Advocate, 1961-62 and to the Sec. of State for Scotland, 1962-64; Chm., Cons. Party Forestry Cttee, 1967-73. Chm., Royal Assoc. for Disability and Rehabilitation; President: Royal Highland & Agricultural Soc. of Scotland, 1969; St. Andrew's Ambulance Assoc.; Royal Scottish Agricultural Benevolent Inst.; Scottish Nat. Inst. for War Blinded; Royal Blind Asylum & School; Galloway Cattle Soc.; East of England Agricultural Soc., 1976; Commonwealth Forestry Assoc.; Vice-Pres., RSSPCC; Hon. President: Animal Diseases Research Assoc.; Scottish Agricultural Organisation Soc. DL, Selkirk 1955, Midlothian 1960, Roxburgh 1962, Dumfries 1974; JP Roxburgh 1975. *Heir: s* Earl of Dalkeith, *qv. Address:* Bowhill, Selkirk. *T:* Selkirk 20732.

BUCHAN, family name of **Baron Tweedsmuir.**

BUCHAN, 16th Earl of, *cr* 1469; **Donald Cardross Flower Erskine;** Lord Auchterhouse, 1469; Lord Cardross, 1606; Baron Erskine, 1806; *b* 3 June 1899; *s* of 6th Baron Erskine and Florence (*d* 1936), *y d* of Edgar Flower; *S* father, 1957 (as Baron Erskine); and kinsman, 1960 (as Earl of Buchan); *m* 1927, Christina, adopted *d* of Lloyd Baxendale, Greenham Lodge, Newbury; one *s* two *d. Educ:* Charterhouse; Royal Military College, Sandhurst. Lieut 9th Lancers, 1918; Captain, 1928; retired, 1930; re-employed, 1939; Lieut-Colonel

1943. *Heir: s* Lord Cardross, *qv. Address:* Little Orchard, Moreton-in-Marsh, Gloucestershire. *T:* Moreton-in-Marsh 50274.

BUCHAN OF AUCHMACOY, Captain David William Sinclair, JP; Chief of the Name of Buchan; *b* 18 Sept. 1929; *o s* of late Captain S. L. Trevor, late of Lathbury Park, Bucks, and late Lady Olivia Trevor, *e d* of 18th Earl of Caithness; *m* 1961, Susan Blanche Fionodbhar Scott-Ellis, *d* of 9th Baron Howard de Walden, *qv*; four *s* one *d. Educ:* Eton; RMA Sandhurst. Commissioned 1949 into Gordon Highlanders; served Berlin, BAOR and Malaya; ADC to GOC, Singapore, 1951-53; retired 1955. Member of London Stock Exchange. Sen. Partner, Messrs Gow and Parsons, 1963-72. Changed name from Trevor through Court of Lord Lyon King of Arms, 1949, succeeding 18th Earl of Caithness as Chief of Buchan Clan. Member: Queen's Body Guard for Scotland; The Pilgrims; Friends of Malta GC; Worshipful Company of Broderers. JP London, 1972-. OStJ 1981. *Recreations:* cricket, tennis, squash. *Address:* 28 The Little Boltons, SW10. *T:* 01-373 0654; Auchmacoy House, Ellon, Aberdeenshire. *T:* Ellon 20229. *Clubs:* White's, Royal Automobile, Turf, MCC, City of London, Pitt; Puffin's (Edinburgh).

BUCHAN, Ven. Eric Ancrum; Archdeacon of Coventry, 1965-77, Archdeacon Emeritus, since 1977; *b* 6 Nov. 1907; *s* of late Frederick Samuel and Florence Buchan. *Educ:* Bristol Grammar School; St Chad's College, University of Durham (BA). Curate of Holy Nativity, Knowle, Bristol, 1933-40. Chaplain RAFVR, 1940-45. Vicar of St Mark's with St Barnabas, Coventry, 1945-59; Hon. Canon of Coventry Cathedral, 1953; Chaplain Coventry and Warwickshire Hospital, 1945-59; Sec. Laymen's Appeal, Dio. of Coventry, 1951-53; Rural Dean of Coventry, 1954-63; Rector of Baginton, 1963-70. Member Central Board of Finance, 1953-80 (Chm., Develt and Stewardship Cttee, 1976-80; Mem., Church Commrs and CBF Joint Liaison Cttee, 1976-80); Mem. Schools Council, 1958-65; Chm. Dio. Board of Finance, 1958-77; Organiser of Bishop's Appeal, 1958-61; Dio. Director of Christian Stewardship, 1959-65; Domestic Chaplain to Bishop of Coventry, 1961-65; Church Commissioner, 1964-78; Member, Governing Body, St Chad's College, Durham University, 1966-. Awarded Silver Acorn for outstanding services to the Scout Movement, 1974. *Address:* 6B Millers Green, The Cathedral, Gloucester GL1 2BN. *T:* Gloucester 415944.

BUCHAN, Janey, (Jane O'Neil Buchan); Member (Lab) Glasgow, European Parliament, since 1979; Regional Councillor, Strathclyde Regional Council, since 1974; *b* 30 April 1926; *d* of Joseph and Christina Kent; *m* 1945, Norman Findlay Buchan, *qv*; one *s. Educ:* secondary sch.; commercial coll. Housewife; Socialist; Councillor; occasional scriptwriting and journalism. Vice-Chm., Educn Cttee, Strathclyde Reg. Council; Chm., local consumer gp; formerly Chm., Scottish Gas Consumers' Council. *Recreations:* books, music, theatre, television. *Address:* 72 Peel Street, Glasgow G11 5LR. *T:* 041-339 2583.

BUCHAN, Sir John, (Sir Thomas Johnston Buchan), Kt 1971; CMG 1961; Chairman and Chief Executive, Buchan, Laird and Buchan, Architects and Engineers; *b* 3 June 1912; *s* of Thomas Johnston Buchan; *m* 1948, Virginia, *d* of William Ashley Anderson, Penn., USA; one *s* two *d. Educ:* Geelong Grammar School. Served Royal Aust. Engineers (AIF), 1940-44 (Capt.). Member Melbourne City Council, 1954-60. Member Federal Exec., Liberal Party, 1959-62; President, Liberal Party, Victorian Division, Australia, 1959-62, Treasurer, 1963-67; Pres., Australian American Assoc., Victoria, 1964-68, Federal Pres., Australian American Assoc., 1968-70, Vice-Pres., 1971-. Member: Council, Latrobe University, 1964-72; Cttee of Management, Royal Melbourne Hosp., 1968-78. Co-Founder Apex Association of Australia. *Recreations:* golf, reading. *Address:* 11 Fairlie Court, South Yarra, Vic 3141, Australia. *Club:* Melbourne (Melbourne).

BUCHAN, Norman Findlay; MP (Lab) Renfrewshire West since 1964; *b* Helmsdale, Sutherlandshire, 27 Oct. 1922; *s* of John Buchan, Fraserburgh, Aberdeenshire; *m* 1945, Janey Kent (*see* Janey Buchan); one *s. Educ:* Kirkwall Grammar School; Glasgow University. Royal Tank Regt (N Africa, Sicily and Italy, 1942-45). Teacher (English and History). Parly Under-Sec., Scottish Office, 1967-70. Opposition Spokesman on Agriculture, Fisheries and Food, 1970-74; Minister of State, MAFF, March-Oct. 1974 (resigned); Opposition Spokesman on: social security, 1980-81; food, agriculture and fisheries, 1981-. *Publications:* (ed) 101 Scottish Songs; The Scottish Folksinger, 1973; The MacDunciad, 1977; contributions to New Statesman, Tribune and other journals. *Address:* 72 Peel Street, Glasgow G11 5LR. *T:* 041-339 2583.

BUCHAN, Dr Stevenson, CBE 1971; Chief Scientific Officer, Deputy Director, Institute of Geological Sciences, 1968-71; *b* 4 March 1907; *s* of late James Buchan and Christian Ewen Buchan (*née* Stevenson), Peterhead; *m* 1937, Barbara, *yr d* of late Reginald Hadfield, Droylsden, Lancs; one *s* one *d. Educ:* Peterhead Acad.; Aberdeen Univ. BSc 1st cl. hons Geology, James H. Hunter Meml. Prize, Senior Kilgour Scholar, PhD; FRSE, FGS, FIWES, Hon. FIPHE. Geological Survey of Great Britain: Geologist, 1931; Head of Water Dept, 1946; Asst Dir responsible for specialist depts in GB and NI, 1960; Chief Geologist, Inst. of Geological Sciences, 1967. Mem. various hydrological cttees; Founder Mem., Internat. Assoc. of Hydrogeologists, Pres., 1972-77; Pres., Internat. Ground-Water Commn of Internat. Assoc. of Hydrological Sciences, 1963-67; British Deleg. to Internat. Hydrological Decade; Scientific Editor, Hydrogeological Map of Europe; Vis. Internat. Scientist, Amer. Geol Inst.; Pres. Section C (Geology), Brit. Assoc., Dundee, 1968. Awarded Geol Soc.'s Lyell Fund, and J. B. Tyrrell Fund for travel in

Canada. *Publications:* Water Supply of County of London from Underground Sources; papers on hydrogeology and hydrochemistry. *Recreations:* travel, photography, gardening, philately. *Address:* Far End, 14 Monks Road, Banstead, Surrey SM7 2EP. *T:* Burgh Heath 54227.

BUCHAN, Sir Thomas Johnston; *see* Buchan, Sir John.

BUCHAN-HEPBURN, Sir Ninian (Buchan Archibald John), 6th Bt, *cr* 1815, of Smeaton-Hepburn; is a painter; Member, Queen's Body Guard for Scotland, Royal Company of Archers; *b* 8 Oct. 1922; *s* of Sir John Buchan-Hepburn, 5th Bt; *S* father 1961; *m* 1958, Bridget (*d* 1976), *er d* of late Sir Louis Greig, KBE, CVO. *Educ:* St Aubyn's, Rottingdean, Sussex; Canford School, Wimborne, Dorset. Served QO Cameron Hldrs, India and Burma, 1939-45. Studied painting, Byam Shaw School of Art. Exhibited at: Royal Academy, Royal Scottish Academy, London galleries. Work in many private collections. *Recreations:* music, gardening, shooting. *Heir: kinsman* John Alistair Trant Kidd Buchan-Hepburn [*b* 27 June 1931; *m* 1957, Georgina Elizabeth Turner; one *s* three *d*]. *Address:* Logan, Port Logan, Wigtownshire. *T:* Ardwell 239. *Clubs:* New, Puffin's (Edinburgh).

BUCHANAN, Most Rev. Alan Alexander; Archbishop of Dublin and Primate of Ireland, 1969-77; *m* 1935, Audrey Kathryn, *d* of W. A. Crone, Knock, Belfast; two *d. Educ:* Trinity College, Dublin. Exhibitioner, Moderator, 1928, TCD Deacon, 1930; Priest, 1931. Assistant Missioner, Church of Ireland Mission, Belfast, 1930-33, Head Missioner, 1933-37; Incumbent of Inver, Larne, 1937-45; Incumbent of St Mary, Belfast, 1945-55; Rural Dean of Mid-Belfast, 1951-55; Rector of Bangor, Co. Down, 1955-58; Canon of St Patrick's Cathedral, Dublin, 1957-58; Bishop of Clogher, 1958-69. Chaplain to the Forces, Emergency Commission, 1942-45. *Address:* Kilbride, Castleknock, Co. Dublin.

BUCHANAN, Andrew George; farmer; chartered surveyor in private practice; *b* 21 July 1937; *s* and *heir* of Major Sir Charles Buchanan, Bt, *qv*; *m* 1966, Belinda Jane Virginia (*née* Maclean), *widow* of Gresham Neilus Vaughan; one *s* one *d*, and one step *s* one step *d. Educ:* Eton; Trinity Coll., Cambridge; Wye Coll., Univ. of London. Nat. Service, 2nd Lieut, Coldstream Guards, 1956-58. Chartered Surveyor with Smith-Woolley & Co, 1965-70. Vice-Chm., Bd of Visitors, HM Prison Ranby, 1982-. Commanded A Squadron (SRY), 3rd Bn Worcs and Sherwood Foresters (TA), 1971-74. High Sheriff, Notts, 1976-77. *Recreations:* skiing, stalking, gardening (under protest). *Address:* Hodsock Priory, Blyth, Worksop, Notts S81 0TY. *T:* Blyth (Notts) 204. *Club:* Strafford (Cambridge).

BUCHANAN, Sir Charles Alexander James L.; *see* Leith-Buchanan.

BUCHANAN, Major Sir Charles James, 4th Bt, *cr* 1878; HLI; retired; *b* 16 April 1899; *s* of 3rd Bt and Constance (*d* 1914), *d* of late Commander Tennant, RN; *S* father, 1928; *m* 1932, Barbara Helen, *o d* of late Lieut-Colonel Rt Hon. Sir George Stanley, PC, GCSI, GCIE; two *s* two *d. Educ:* Harrow; Sandhurst. Served in North Russian Relief Force, 1919; with BEF France, 1939-40 and with AMG in Italy, 1943-44; retired 1945. ADC to Governor of Madras, 1928-32. A member of the Queen's Body Guard for Scotland (Royal Company of Archers); County Commissioner Nottinghamshire, Boy Scouts Association, 1949-62. JP 1952; DL 1954, Notts; High Sheriff of Nottinghamshire, 1962. *Recreations:* fishing and gardening. *Heir: s* Andrew George Buchanan, *qv. Address:* St Anne's Manor, Sutton Bonington, Loughborough. *Club:* Lansdowne.

BUCHANAN, Prof. Sir Colin (Douglas), Kt 1972; CBE 1964; Lieut-Colonel; consultant with Colin Buchanan & Partners, 47 Princes Gate, London; *b* 22 Aug. 1907; *s* of William Ernest and Laura Kate Buchanan; *m* 1933, Elsie Alice Mitchell; two *s* one *d. Educ:* Berkhamsted School; Imperial College, London. Sudan Govt Public Works Dept, 1930-32; Regional planning studies with F. Longstreth Thompson, 1932-35; Ministry of Transport, 1935-39. War Service in Royal Engineers, 1939-46 (despatches). Ministry of Town and Country Planning (later Ministry of Housing and Local Govt), 1946-61; Urban Planning Adviser, Ministry of Transport, 1961-63; Prof. of Transport, Imperial Coll., London, 1963-72; Prof. of Urban Studies and Dir, Sch. for Advanced Urban Studies, Bristol Univ., 1973-75. Vis. Prof., Imperial Coll., London, 1975-78. Member: Commn on Third London Airport, 1968-70; Royal Fine Art Commn, 1972-74. Pres., CPRE, 1980-. Hon. DCL Oxon, 1972; Hon. DSc: Leeds, 1972; City, 1972. *Publications:* Mixed Blessing, The Motor in Britain, 1958; Traffic in Towns (Ministry of Transport report), 1963, (paperback edn), 1964; The State of Britain, 1972; No Way to the Airport, 1981; numerous papers on town planning and allied subjects. *Recreations:* photography, carpentry, caravan touring. *Address:* Tunnel House, Box, near Minchinhampton, Glos GL6 9HB. *T:* Nailsworth 2951.

BUCHANAN, Rev. Colin Ogilvie; Principal, St John's College, Bramcote, Nottingham, since 1979; Hon. Canon of Southwell Minster, since 1982; *b* 9 Aug. 1934; *s* of late Prof. Robert Ogilvie Buchanan and of Kathleen Mary (*née* Parnell); *m* 1963, Diana Stephenie Gregory; two *d. Educ:* Whitgift Sch., S Croydon; Lincoln Coll., Oxford (BA, 2nd Cl. Lit. Hum., MA). Theological training at Tyndale Hall, Bristol, 1959-61; deacon, 1961; Curate, Cheadle, Cheshire, 1961-64; joined staff of London Coll. of Divinity (now St John's Coll., Nottingham), 1964; posts held: Librarian, 1964-69; Registrar, 1969-74; Director of Studies, 1974-75; Vice-Principal, 1975-78. Member: Church of

England Liturgical Commn, 1964–; General Synod of C of E, 1970–; Assembly of British Council of Churches, 1971–80. *Publications:* (ed) Modern Anglican Liturgies 1958-1968, 1968; (ed) Further Anglican Liturgies 1968-1975, 1975; (jtly) Growing into Union, 1970; (ed jtly) Anglican Worship Today, 1980; editor: Grove Booklets on Ministry and Worship, 1972–; Grove Liturgical Studies, 1975– (regular author in these series); News of Liturgy, 1975–; contrib. learned jls. *Recreations:* interested in electoral reform, sport, etc. *Address:* St John's College, Bramcote, Nottingham NG9 3DS. *T:* (office) Nottingham 251114.

BUCHANAN, George (Henry Perrott); poet; *b* 9 Jan. 1904; 2nd *s* of Rev. C. H. L. Buchanan, Kilwaughter, Co. Antrim, and Florence Moore; *m* 1st, 1938, Winifred Mary Corn (marr. diss. 1945; she *d* 1971); 2nd, 1949, Noel Pulleyne Ritter (*d* 1951); 3rd, 1952, Janet Margesson (*d* 1968), *e d* of 1st Viscount Margesson; two *d*; 4th, 1974, Sandra Gail McCloy, Vancouver. *Educ:* Campbell College; Queen's University, Belfast. On editorial staff of The Times, 1930-35; reviewer, TLS, 1928-40; columnist, drama critic, News Chronicle, 1935-38; Operations Officer, RAF Coastal Command, 1940-45; Chm. Town and Country Development Cttee, N Ireland, 1949-53; Member, Exec. Council, European Soc. of Culture, 1954–. *Publications:* Passage through the Present, 1932; A London Story, 1935; Words for To-Night, 1936; Entanglement, 1938; The Soldier and the Girl, 1940; Rose Forbes, 1950; A Place to Live, 1952; Bodily Responses (poetry), 1958; Green Seacoast, 1959; Conversation with Strangers (poetry), 1961; Morning Papers, 1965; Annotations, 1970; Naked Reason, 1971; Minute-book of a City (poetry), 1972; Inside Traffic (poetry), 1976; The Politics of Culture, 1977; Possible Being (poetry), 1980; *plays:* A Trip to the Castle, 1960; Tresper Revolution, 1961; War Song, 1965. *Address:* 27 Ashley Gardens, Westminster, SW1. *T:* 01-834 5722. *Club:* Savile.

BUCHANAN, Isobel Wilson, (Mrs Jonathan King); soprano; *b* 15 March 1954; *d* of Stewart and Mary Buchanan; *m* 1980, Jonathan Stephen Geoffrey King (otherwise Jonathan Hyde, actor, RSC); one *d*. *Educ:* Cumbernauld High Sch.; Royal Scottish Academy of Music and Drama (DRSAMD 1974). Australian Opera principal singer, 1975-78; freelance singer, 1978–; British debut, Glyndebourne, 1978; Vienna Staatsoper debut, 1978; American debut: Santa Fé, 1979; Chicago, 1979; New York, 1979; German debut: Cologne, 1979; French debut, Aix-en-Provence, 1981. Performances also with Scottish Opera, Covent Garden, Munich Radio, Belgium, Norway, etc. Various operatic recordings. *Recreations:* reading, gardening, cooking, dressmaking, knitting, tennis. *Address:* c/o Harrison/Parrott, 12 Penzance Place, W11.

BUCHANAN, John David, MBE 1944; DL; Headmaster of Oakham School, Rutland, 1958-77; *b* 26 Oct. 1916; *e s* of late John Nevile Buchanan and Nancy Isabel (*née* Bevan); *m* 1946, Janet Marjorie, *d* of late Brig. J. A. C. Pennycuick, DSO; three *s* four *d* (and one *s* decd). *Educ:* Stowe; Trinity College, Cambridge. Served with Grenadier Guards, 1939-46; Adjutant, 3rd Bn Grenadier Guards, 1941-43; Brigade Major, 1st Guards Bde, 1944-45; Private Secretary to Sir Alexander Cadogan, Security Council for the UN, 1946. Assistant Master, Westminster Under School, 1948; Assistant Master, Sherborne School, 1948-57. Administrator, Inchcape Educational Scholarship Scheme, 1978–; Educnl Consultant to Jerwood Foundn, 1978–. DL Leics, 1980. *Recreation:* golf. *Address:* Rose Cottage, Owston, Leics.

BUCHANAN, Vice-Adm. Sir Peter (William), KBE 1980; Chief Executive, London World Trade Centre Association, since 1982; *b* 14 May 1925; *s* of Lt-Col Francis Henry Theodore Buchanan and Gwendolen May Isobel (*née* Hunt); *m* 1953, Audrey Rowena Mary (*née* Edmondson); three *s* one *d*. *Educ:* Malvern Coll. Royal Navy, 1943-82: Rear-Adm. 1976; Naval Sec., 1976-78; Vice-Adm., 1979; Chief of Staff, Allied Naval Forces Southern Europe, 1979-82. Younger Brother of Trinity House. Mem. Council, Malvern Coll. FNI; MRIN; FBIM. *Recreations:* sailing, walking. *Address:* Whitewalls, 30 The Square, Titchfield, Fareham, Hants. *T:* Titchfield 42146. *Clubs:* Caledonian; Royal Naval Sailing Association.

BUCHANAN, Richard, JP; *b* 3 May 1912; *s* of late Richard Buchanan and late Helen Henderson; *m* 1st, 1938, Margaret McManus (*d* 1963); six *s* two *d*; 2nd, 1971, Helen Duggan, MA, DipEd. *Educ:* St Mungo's Boys' School; St Mungo's Academy; Royal Technical Coll. Councillor, City of Glasgow, 1949-64 (Past Chm. Libraries, Schools and Standing Orders Cttees); Hon. City Treasurer, 1960-63. MP (Lab) Springburn, Glasgow, 1964-79; PPS to Treasury Ministers, 1967-70; Mem. Select Cttees: Public Accounts; Services. Chm., West Day School Management, 1958-64; Governor, Notre Dame College of Education, 1959-64, etc. Chm., Belvidere Hospital; Member Board of Managers, Glasgow Royal Infirmary; Hon. Pres., Scottish Library Assoc. (Pres., 1963); Chairman: Scottish Central Library; Adv. Cttee, Nat. Library of Scotland; Cttee on Burrell Collection; H of C Library Cttee; Director, Glasgow Citizens Theatre. JP Glasgow, 1954. *Recreations:* theatre, walking, reading. *Address:* 18 Gargrave Avenue, Garrowhill, Glasgow. *T:* 041-771 7234. *Club:* St Mungo's Centenary (Glasgow).

BUCHANAN-DUNLOP, Commodore David Kennedy, DSC 1945; RN retired; *b* 30 June 1911; *s* of Colonel Archibald Buchanan-Dunlop, OBE and Mary (*née* Kennedy); *m* 1945, Marguerite, *d* of William Macfarlane; no *c*. *Educ:* Loretto; RNC, Dartmouth. Served as young officer in submarines in Mediterranean and Far East, then Specialist in Fleet Air Arm. Served War of 1939-45 (despatches) in aircraft-carriers world-wide. Asst Naval Attaché,

Paris, 1949-52; Dep. Director Nav. Air Org. Naval Staff, 1954-56; Staff of NATO Defence College, Paris, 1957-59; Naval and Military Attaché, Santiago, Lima, Quito, Bogotá and Panama, 1960-62; Captain, Royal Naval College, Greenwich, 1962-64, President, 1964. *Recreation:* fishing. *Address:* Les Nereides, 20110-Propriano, Corsica. *Club:* Flyfishers'.

BUCHANAN-DUNLOP, Richard, QC 1966; *b* 19 April 1919; *s* of late Canon W. R. Buchanan-Dunlop and Mrs R. E. Buchanan-Dunlop (*née* Mead); *m* 1948, Helen Murray Dunlop; three *d*. *Educ:* Marlborough College; Magdalene College, Cambridge. Served in Royal Corps of Signals, 1939-46 (Hon. Major). BA (Hons.) Law, Cambridge, 1949; Harmsworth Scholar, 1950. Called to the Bar, 1951. *Recreations:* painting, writing. *Address:* Skiathos, Greece.

BUCHANAN-JARDINE, Sir A. R. J.; see Jardine.

BUCHANAN-SMITH, family name of **Baron Balerno**.

BUCHANAN-SMITH, Rt. Hon. Alick (Laidlaw); PC 1981; MP (U) North Angus and Mearns since 1964; Minister of State, Ministry of Agriculture, Fisheries and Food, since 1979; *b* 8 April 1932; 2nd *s* of Baron Balerno, *qv* and late Mrs Buchanan-Smith; *m* 1956, Janet, *d* of late Thomas Lawrie, CBE; one *s* three *d*. *Educ:* Edinburgh Academy; Trinity College, Glenalmond; Pembroke College, Cambridge; Edinburgh University. Commissioned Gordon Highlanders, National Service, 1951; subseq. Captain, TA (5th/6th Gordon Highlanders). Parly Under-Sec. of State, Scottish Office, 1970-74. *Address:* House of Cockburn, Balerno, Midlothian. *T:* 031-449 4242; Castleton, Fettercairn, Laurencekirk, Kincardineshire. *T:* Fettercairn 273. *Club:* New (Edinburgh).

BUCHTHAL, Hugo, FBA 1959; PhD; Ailsa Mellon Bruce Professor, 1970-75, Professor of Fine Arts, 1965-70, New York University Institute of Fine Arts; now Emeritus Professor; *b* Berlin, 11 Aug. 1909; *m* 1939, Amalia Serkin; one *d*. *Educ:* Universities of Berlin, Heidelberg, Paris and Hamburg. PhD, Hamburg, 1933; Resident in London from 1934; Lord Plumer Fellowship, Hebrew University, 1938; Librarian, Warburg Institute, 1941; Lecturer in History of Art, University of London, 1944; Reader in the History of Art, with special reference to the Near East, 1949; Professor of the History of Byzantine Art in the University of London, 1960. Visiting Scholarship, Dumbarton Oaks, Harvard University, 1950-51, 1965, 1974, 1978; Temp. Member Inst. for Advanced Study, Princeton, NJ, 1959-60, 1968, 1975-76; Visiting Professor Columbia University, New York, 1963. Prix Schlumberger, Académie des Inscriptions et Belles Lettres, 1958, 1981; Guggenheim Fellow, 1971-72; Corres. Mem., Oesterreichische Akad. der Wissenschaften, 1975; Hon. Fellow, Warburg Inst., 1975. *Publications:* The Miniatures of the Paris Psalter, 1938; (with Otto Kurz) A Handlist of illuminated Oriental Christian Manuscripts, 1942; The Western Aspects of Gandhara Sculpture, 1944; Miniature Painting in the Latin Kingdom of Jerusalem, 1957; Historia Trojana, studies in the history of mediaeval secular illustration, 1971; (jtly) The Place of Book Illumination in Byzantine Art, 1976; (with Hans Belting) Patronage in Thirteenth Century Constantinople: an atelier of late Byzantine illumination and calligraphy, 1978; The Musterbuch of Wolfenbüttel and its position in the art of the thirteenth century, 1979; numerous articles in learned journals. *Address:* 22 Priory Gardens, N6. *T:* 01-348 1664.

BUCHWALD, Art, (Arthur); American journalist, author, lecturer and columnist; *b* Mount Vernon, New York, 20 Oct. 1925; *s* of Joseph Buchwald and Helen (*née* Kleinberger); *m* 1952, Ann McGarry, Warren, Pa; one *s* two *d*. *Educ:* University of Southern California. Sergeant, US Marine Corps, 1942-45. Columnist, New York Herald Tribune: in Paris, 1949-62; in Washington, 1962–. Syndicated columnist whose articles appear in 550 newspapers throughout the world. *Publications:* (mostly published later in England) Paris After Dark, 1950; Art Buchwald's Paris, 1954; The Brave Coward, 1957; I Chose Caviar, 1957; More Caviar, 1958; A Gift from the Boys, 1958; Don't Forget to Write, 1960; Art Buchwald's Secret List to Paris, 1961; How Much is That in Dollars?, 1961; Is it Safe to Drink the Water?, 1962; I Chose Capitol Punishment, 1963; . . . and Then I told the President, 1965; Son of the Great Society, 1966; Have I Ever Lied to You?, 1968; The Establishment is Alive and Well in Washington, 1969; Sheep on the Runway (Play), 1970; Oh, to be a Swinger, 1970; Getting High in Government Circles, 1971; I Never Danced at the White House, 1973; I Am not a Crook, 1974; Bollo Caper, 1974; Irving's Delight, 1975; Washington is Leaking, 1976; Down the Seine and up the Potomac, 1977; The Buchwald Stops Here, 1978. *Recreations:* tennis, chess, marathon running. *Address:* 1750 Pennsylvania Avenue NW, Washington, DC 20006, USA. *T:* Washington 393-6680. *Club:* Overseas Press (NY).

BUCK, Albert Charles; business consultant; *b* 1 March 1910; *y s* of William and Mary Buck; *m* 1st, 1937, Margaret Court Hartley; one *d*; 2nd, 1951, Joan McIntyre; one *d*; 3rd, 1970, Mrs Aileen Ogilvy. *Educ:* Alderman Newton's Sch., Leicester; Selwyn Coll., Cambridge (MA). Joined J. J. Colman Ltd, as management trainee, 1931; Export Manager, 1939; Director: Reckitt & Sons Ltd, 1941; Joseph Farrow & Co. Ltd, 1947-69; Thomas Green & Son, 1950-60; Reckitt & Colman (Household) Div.; Industrial Adviser to HM Govt, 1969-73. Member: Incorporated Soc. of British Advertisers (Pres., 1961-63); Internat. Union of Advertiser Societies (Pres. 1963-65); Advertising Standards Authority, 1962-71; Internat. Foundation for Research in Advertising (Pres.,

1965-71). Mackintosh medal for personal and public services to Advertising, 1965. *Publications:* sundry articles to jls and newspapers. *Recreations:* winter sports, shooting, fishing. *Address:* Mill Farm, Burton Pidsea, East Yorkshire. *T:* Patrington 70328.

BUCK, Antony; see Buck, P. A. F.

BUCK, Leslie William; Director, British Aerospace (plc), 1981-82 (Member, British Aerospace, 1977-80; Member Organising Committee, 1976-77); *b* 30 May 1915; *s* of Walter Buck and Florence Greenland; *m* 1941, Dorothea Jeanne Bieri; two *s. Educ:* Willesden County Grammar Sch. Apprentice panel beater; shop steward; Nat. Union of Sheet Metal Workers and Braziers: District Officer, 1957-60; Dist Sec., 1960-62; Gen. Sec., Nat. Union of Sheet Metal Workers, Coppersmiths, Heating and Domestic Engineers, 1962-77. Member: Confedn of Shipbuilding and Engineering Unions Executive, 1964-77, Pres., 1975-76; Engrg Industry Trng Bd, 1964-79; General Council, TUC, 1971-77. *Recreations:* music, gardening, reading. *Address:* 178 Meadvale Road, Ealing, W5. *T:* 01-998 3943.

BUCK, (Philip) Antony (Fyson), QC 1974; MP (C) Colchester since 1961; Barrister-at-Law; *b* 19 Dec. 1928; *yr s* of late A. F. Buck, Ely, Cambs; *m* 1955, Judy Elaine, *o d* of late Dr C. A. Grant, Cottesloe, Perth, W Australia, and late Mrs Grant; one *d. Educ:* King's School, Ely; Trinity Hall, Cambridge. BA History and Law, 1951, MA 1954. Chm. Cambridge Univ. Cons. Assoc. and Chm. Fedn of Univ. Conservative and Unionist Associations, 1951-52. Called to the Bar, Inner Temple, 1954; Legal Adviser, Nat. Association of Parish Councils, 1957-59, Vice-Pres., 1970-74; sponsored and piloted through the Limitation Act, 1963. PPS to Attorney-General, 1963-64; Parly Under-Sec. of State for Defence (Navy), MoD, 1972-74. Sec., Conservative Party Home Affairs Cttee, 1964-70, Vice-Chm., 1970-72, Chm. Oct./Nov. 1972; Chm., Cons. Parly Defence Cttee, 1979-; Mem. Exec., 1922 Cttee, Oct./Nov. 1972, 1977-; Chm., Select Cttee on Parly Comr for Administration (Ombudsman), 1977-. *Recreations:* most sports, reading. *Address:* Pete Hall, Abberton, near Colchester, Essex. *T:* Peldon 230; 4 Paper Buildings, Temple, EC4. *T:* 01-353 8408/0196. *Club:* United Oxford & Cambridge University.

BUCKEE, His Honour Henry Thomas, DSO 1942; a Circuit Judge (formerly Judge of County Courts), 1961-79; *b* 14 June 1913; *s* of Henry Buckee; *m* 1939, Margaret Frances Chapman; two *d. Educ:* King Edward VI School, Chelmsford. Called to Bar, Middle Temple, 1939. Served RNVR, 1940-46; Lieut-Comdr 1944. *Address:* Rough Hill House, East Hanningfield, Chelmsford, Essex. *T:* Chelmsford 400226.

BUCKHURST, Lord; William Herbrand Sackville; stockbroker, with Mullens & Co.; *b* 10 April 1948; *s* and *heir* of 10th Earl De La Warr, *qv* ; *m* 1978, Anne, Countess of Hopetoun, *e d* of Arthur Leveson; two *s. Educ:* Eton. *Heir:* s Hon. William Herbrand Thomas Sackville, *b* 13 June 1979. *Address:* 49 Smith Street, SW3. *T:* 01-352 1317. *Clubs:* White's, Turf.

BUCKINGHAM, Bishop Suffragan of, since 1974; **Rt. Rev. Simon Hedley Burrows;** *b* 8 Nov. 1928; *s* of Very Rev. H. R. Burrows, *qv* ; *m* 1960, Janet Woodd; two *s* three *d. Educ:* Eton; King's Coll., Cambridge (MA); Westcott House, Cambridge. Curate of St John's Wood, 1954-57; Chaplain of Jesus Coll., Cambridge, 1957-60; Vicar of Wyken, Coventry, 1960-67; Vicar of Holy Trinity, Fareham, 1967-74, and Rector of Team Ministry, 1971-74. *Address:* Sheridan, Grimms Hill, Great Missenden, Bucks. *T:* Great Missenden 2173.

BUCKINGHAM, Archdeacon of; see Bone, Ven. J. F. E.

BUCKINGHAM, Amyand David, FRS 1975; Professor of Chemistry, University of Cambridge, since 1969, Fellow of Pembroke College, since 1970; *b* 28 Jan. 1930; 2nd *s* of late Reginald Joslin Buckingham and late Florence Grace Buckingham (formerly Elliot); *m* 1965, Jillian Bowles; one *s* two *d. Educ:* Barker Coll., Hornsby, NSW; Univ. of Sydney; Corpus Christi Coll., Cambridge (Shell Postgraduate Schol.), Univ. Medal 1952, MSc 1953, Sydney; PhD Cantab 1956. 1851 Exhibn Sen. Studentship, 1955-57; Lectr and subseq. Student, Tutor, and Censor of Christ Church, Oxford, 1955-65; Univ. Lectr in Inorganic Chem. Lab., Oxford, 1958-65; Prof. of Theoretical Chem., Univ. of Bristol, 1965-69. Vis. Lectr, Harvard, 1961; Visiting Professor: Princeton, 1965; Univ. of California (Los Angeles), 1975; Univ. of Illinois, 1976; Univ. of Wisconsin, 1978; Vis. Fellow, ANU, 1979. FRACI 1961 (Masson Meml Schol. 1952; Rennie Meml Medal, 1958); FRSC (formerly FCS) (Harrison Meml Prize, 1959; Tilden Lectr 1964; Theoretical Chemistry and Spectroscopy Prize, 1970; Member Faraday Div. (Council, 1965-67, 1975-)); FInstP; Fellow, Optical Soc. of America; Mem., Amer. Chem. Soc. Associate Editor, Jl of Chem. Physics, 1964-66; Editor: Molecular Physics, 1968-72; Chemical Physics Letters, 1978-. Member: Chemistry Cttee, SRC, 1967-70; Adv. Council, Royal Mil. Coll. of Science, Shrivenham, 1973-. Senior Treasurer: Oxford Univ. Cricket Club, 1959-64; Cambridge Univ. Cricket Club, 1976-. Hon. Dr, Univ. de Nancy I, 1979. *Publications:* The Laws and Applications of Thermodynamics, 1964; Organic Liquids, 1978; papers in scientific jls. *Recreations:* walking, woodwork, cricket, tennis, travel. *Address:* 37 Millington Road, Cambridge CB3 9HW.

BUCKINGHAM, George Somerset; retired; *b* 11 May 1903; *s* of Horace Clifford Buckingham, Norwich; *m* 1927, Marjorie Lanaway Bateson (*d* 1981);

one *s* (one *d* decd). *Educ:* Norwich Sch.; Faraday House Electrical Engrg Coll. (Gold Medallist; Dipl.). BSc (Eng); CEng; FIEE; CBIM. Asst Engr, Yorks Electric Power Co., Leeds, 1924-26; District Engr and Br. Man., Birmingham, for Pirelli-General Cable Works Ltd of Southampton, 1928-48; Midlands Electricity Board: Chief Purchasing Officer, 1948-57; Chief Engr, 1957-62; Dep. Chm., 1962-64; Chm., 1964-69. Member: Electricity Council, 1964-69; Electricity Supply Industry Trng Bd, 1965-69; W Midlands Sports Council, 1966-71; Mem. Council, Univ. of Aston in Birmingham; Mem. Council, Electrical Research Assoc., 1967-72; various sci. and profl Instns and Cttees; Pres. Birmingham Branch, Institute of Marketing, 1967-68. Chairman: South Midland Centre, IEE, 1966-67; Midland Centre, Council of Engineering Instns, 1968-70; Past President, Council of Birmingham Electric Club, 1965; Past President, Faraday House Old Students' Assoc., 1962; Vice-President, Outward Bound Schs Assoc. (Birm. and Dist), 1964-72. *Publications:* papers, articles and reviews in scientific and electrical engrg jls and works of professional engrg bodies. *Recreations:* walking, bridge. *Address:* Parklands, Blossomfield Road, Solihull, West Midlands. *T:* 021-705 2066.

BUCKINGHAM, John, CB 1953; Director of Research Programmes and Planning, Admiralty, 1946-Dec. 1959, retired; *b* 23 Dec. 1894; *e s* of late John Mortimer Buckingham, South Molton, N Devon; unmarried. *Educ:* Berkhamsted Sch.; St John's Coll., Cambridge (MA). Joined Admiralty scientific staff for anti-submarine duties under Lord Fisher, 1917, and was, until 1959, engaged continuously upon scientific work for the Admiralty; Deputy Director of Scientific Research, 1932; Apptd Chief Scientific Officer in RN Scientific Service on its formation in 1946. *Publications:* Matter and Radiation, 1930. Various publications in scientific journals. *Address:* 71 Pall Mall, SW1. *T:* 01-930 4152. *Clubs:* Travellers', United Oxford & Cambridge University.

BUCKINGHAM, Prof. Richard Arthur; Professor of Computer Education, Birkbeck College, University of London, 1974-78, now Professor Emeritus; *b* 17 July 1911; *s* of George Herbert Buckingham and Alice Mary Watson (*née* King); *m* 1939 Christina O'Brien; one *s* two *d. Educ:* Gresham's Sch., Holt; St John's Coll., Cambridge. Asst Lecturer in Mathematical Physics, Queen's University, Belfast, 1935-38; Senior 1851 Exhibitioner, University College, London and MIT, 1938-40. At Admiralty Research Laboratory, Teddington, and Mine Design Dept, Havant, 1940-45. University Coll., London: Lecturer in Mathematics, 1945-50; Lecturer in Physics, 1950-51; Reader in Physics, 1951-57; Dir, Univ. of London Computer Unit, later Inst. of Computer Science, 1957-73, and Prof. of Computing Science, 1963-74. FBCS; FRSA. *Publications:* Numerical Methods, 1957; papers in Proc. Royal Soc., Proc. Phys. Soc., London, Jl Chem. Physics, Trans. Faraday Soc., Computer Journal, etc. *Recreation:* travel. *Address:* Challens, Heather Way, Sullington, West Sussex.

BUCKINGHAMSHIRE, 9th Earl of, *cr* 1746; **Vere Frederick Cecil Hobart-Hampden;** Bt 1611; Baron Hobart of Blickling, 1728; *b* 17 May 1901; *s* of Arthur Ernest and Henrietta Louisa Hobart-Hampden; *S* cousin, 1963; *m* 1972, Margot Macrae, *widow* of F. C. Bruce Hittmann, FRACS, Sydney, Australia. *Educ:* St Lawrence College, Ramsgate; Switzerland. Left England for Australia via Canada, 1919; sheep farming and wool business. Served in Royal Australian Air Force, 1942-46; returned to England, 1949. Company Director. *Heir: cousin* (George) Miles Hobart-Hampden [*b* 15 Dec. 1944; *m* 1975, Alison Wightman (*née* Forrest); two step *s. Educ:* Univ. of Exeter (BA Hons History); Birkbeck Coll. and Inst. of Commonwealth Studies, Univ. of London (MA Area Studies)]. *Address:* House of Lords, SW1.

BUCKLAND, Maj.-Gen. Ronald John Denys Eden, CB 1974; MBE 1956; Chief Executive Adur District Council, since 1975; *b* 27 July 1920; *s* of late Geoffrey Ronald Aubert Buckland, CB and Lelgarde Edith Eleanor (*née* Eden); *m* 1968, Judith Margaret Coxhead; two *d. Educ:* Winchester; New College, Oxford (MA). Commissioned into Coldstream Gds, Dec. 1940. Served War of 1939-45: NW Europe, with 4th Coldstream Gds, 1944-45 (wounded twice). GSO3, Gds Div., BAOR, 1946; Adjt, 1st Bn Coldstream Gds, Palestine and Libya, 1948; DAA&QMG, 2nd Gds Bde, Malaya, 1950; DAAG, 3rd Div., Egypt, 1954; Bde Major, 1st Gds Bde, Cyprus, 1958; commanded 1st Bn, Coldstream Gds, 1961, British Guiana, 1962; GSO1, 4th Div., BAOR, 1963; Comdr, 133 Inf. Bde (TA), 1966; ACOS, Joint Exercises Div., HQ AFCENT, Holland, 1967; idc 1968; DA&QMG, 1st British Corps, BAOR, 1969; Chief of Staff, HQ Strategic Command, 1970; Maj.-Gen. i/c Admin, UKLF, 1972-75. *Recreations:* cricket, travel, philately. *Address:* c/o Lloyds Bank Ltd, 6 Pall Mall, SW1. *Clubs:* Pratt's, Leander.

BUCKLE, (Christopher) Richard (Sandford), CBE 1979; writer; critic; exhibition designer; Member, Advisory Council, Theatre Museum; *b* 6 Aug. 1916; *s* of late Lieut-Col C. G. Buckle, DSO, MC, Northamptonshire Regt, and of Mrs R. E. Buckle (*née* Sandford). *Educ:* Marlborough; Balliol. Founded "Ballet", 1939. Served Scots Guards, 1940-46; in action in Italy (despatches, 1944). Started "Ballet" again, 1946; it continued for seven years. Ballet critic of the Observer, 1948-55: ballet critic of the Sunday Times, 1959-75; advised Canada Council on state of ballet in Canada, 1962; advised Sotheby & Co. on their sales of Diaghilev Ballet material, 1967-69. First play, Gossip Column, prod Q Theatre, 1953; Family Tree (comedy), prod Connaught Theatre, Worthing, 1956. *Organised:* Diaghilev Exhibition, Edinburgh Festival, 1954, and Forbes House, London, 1954-55; The Observer Film Exhibition, London, 1956; Telford Bicentenary Exhibition, 1957; Epstein Memorial Exhibition, Edinburgh Festival, 1961; Shakespeare

Exhibition, Stratford-upon-Avon, 1964–65; a smaller version of Shakespeare Exhibition, Edinburgh, 1964; Treasures from the Shakespeare Exhibition, National Portrait Gallery, London, 1964–65; The Communities on the March area in the Man in the Community theme pavilion, Universal and Internat. Exhibition of 1967, Montreal; Exhibition of Beaton Portraits, 1928–68, National Portrait Gallery, 1968; Gala of ballet, Coliseum, 1971; exhibn of Ursula Tyrwhitt, Ashmolean Mus., Oxford, 1974; exhibn Omaggio ai Disegnatori di Diaghilev, Palazzo Grassi, Venice, 1975; exhibn of ballet, opera and theatre costumes, Salisbury Fest., 1975; exhibn Happy and Glorious, 130 years of Royal photographs, Nat. Portrait Gallery, 1977; presented Kama Dev in recital of Indian dancing, St Paul's Church, Covent Garden, 1970; *designed:* (temporary) Haldane Library for Imperial College, South Kensington; new Exhibition Rooms, Harewood House, Yorks, 1959; redesigned interior of Dundee Repertory Theatre, 1963 (burnt down 3 months later). *Publications:* John Innocent at Oxford (novel), 1939; The Adventures of a Ballet Critic, 1953; In Search of Diaghilev, 1955; Modern Ballet Design, 1955; The Prettiest Girl in England, 1958; Harewood (a guide-book), 1959 and (re-written and re-designed), 1966; Dancing for Diaghilev (the memoirs of Lydia Sokolova), 1960; Epstein Drawings (introd. only), 1962; Epstein: An Autobiography (introd. to new edn only), 1963; Jacob Epstein: Sculptor, 1963; Monsters at Midnight: the French Romantic Movement as a background to the ballet Giselle (limited edn), 1966; The Message, a Gothick Tale of the A1 (limited edn), 1969; Nijinsky, 1971; Nijinsky on Stage: commentary on drawings of Valentine Gross, 1971; (ed) U and Non-U revisited, 1978; Diaghilev, 1979; (ed) Self Portrait with Friends, selected diaries of Cecil Beaton, 1979; Buckle at the Ballet, 1980; (with Roy Strong and others) Designing for the Dancer, 1981; *autobiography:* 1, The Most Upsetting Woman, 1981; 2, In the Wake of Diaghilev, 1982. *Recreations:* caricature, light verse. *Address:* Roman Road, Gutch Common, Semley, Shaftesbury, Dorset.

BUCKLE, Maj.-Gen. (Retd) Denys Herbert Vintcent, CB 1955; CBE 1948 (OBE 1945); Legion of Merit (USA) 1944; FCIT; Trustee, South Africa Foundation, since 1969; Director, Prince Vintcent & Co. (Pty) Ltd, Mossel Bay; *b* Cape Town, South Africa, 16 July 1902; *s* of Major H. S. Buckle, RMLI and ASC and of Agnes Buckle (*née* Vintcent), Cape Town; *m* 1928, Frances Margaret Butterworth; one *d. Educ:* Boxgrove School, Guildford; Charterhouse, Godalming; RMC Sandhurst. 2nd Lieut, E Surrey Regt, 1923; transf. to RASC, 1926; Shanghai Def. Force, 1927–28; Asst Adjt, RASC Trg Centre, 1929–32; Adjt 44th (Home Counties) Divnl RASC, TA, 1932–36; Student Staff Coll., Camberley, 1936–37; Adjt Ceylon ASC, 1938; Bde Maj., Malaya Inf Bde, 1938–40; GSO 2, Trg Directorate, WO, 1940; AA & QMG, 8th Armd Div., 1940–41; GSO 1, Staff Coll., Camberley, 1941–42; Brig. Admin. Plans, GHQ Home Forces, "Cossac" and SHAEF, 1942–44; Brig. Q Ops, WO, 1944; DDST and Brig. Q, 21 Army Gp and BAOR, 1945–46; DQMG, FARELF, 1946–48; DDST, S Comd, 1948–49; Spec. Appts (Brig.), USA, 1949–50; Dir of Equipment, WO, 1950–51, and special appt, Paris, 1951; Comdt RASC Trg Centre, 1952–53; DST, MELF, 1953–56; Brig. Admin. i/c Admin, GHQ, MELF, 1956–58; despatches, 1956 (Suez); retd 1958; ADC to King George VI 1951, to the Queen, 1952–54. FCIT 1971. Bursar, Church of England Training Colleges, Cheltenham, 1958–59. Divisional Manager SE Division, British Waterways, 1961–63; Director of Reorganisation, British Waterways, 1963–65. Dir, UK–S Africa Trade Assoc., 1965–68; Administrative Mem., Southern Africa Cttee, BNEC, 1967–68. Col Comdt RASC, 1959–64; Representative Col Comdt, RASC, 1961; Hon. Col 44th (Home Counties), RASC, 1962–65, Regt, RCT, 1965–67. Legion of Merit (USA), 1944. *Publication:* History of 44th Division, RASC, TA, 1932. *Recreations:* reading, broadcasting, writing, walking, swimming, travel. *Address:* 2 Chelsea Cloisters, Durban Road, Wynberg, Cape 7800, South Africa. *Clubs:* Army and Navy; Western Province Sports (Cape Town).

BUCKLE, Rt. Rev. Edward Gilbert; Bishop in the Northern Region, Diocese of Auckland, New Zealand, since 1981; *b* 20 July 1926; *s* of Douglas Gordon Buckle and Claire Ettie Wellman; *m* 1949, Mona Ann Cain; one *s* three *d. Educ:* Hurstville Central Coll.; Moore Theological Coll., Univ. of Sydney (LTh); St Augustine's College, Canterbury, Eng. (DipCC). Rector of Koorawatha, 1950–51; Chaplain, Snowy Mountains Hydro-Electric Authority, 1952–54; Rector, All Saints, Canberra, 1955–62; Canon, St Saviour's Cathedral, Goulburn, 1959; Dir of Adult Education for Gen. Bd of Religious Education, Melbourne, 1962–65. New Zealand: Vicar, St Matthews-in-the-City, Auckland, 1966–67; Bishop's Executive Officer, 1967–70; Diocesan and Ecumenical Develt Officer, 1970–81; Archdeacon of Auckland, 1970–81. *Publications:* The Disturber: The Episcopacy of Ernest Henry Burgmann, Bishop of Canberra and Goulburn, 1957; A Station of the Cross, 1959; Cost of Living, study material on MRI; Family Affair, 1966; Urban Development, 1968; Interview 69, 1969; The Churches and East Coast Bays, 1970; The Isthmus and Redevelopment, 1973; Inner City Churches, 1973; Otara and the Churches, 1974; The Churches East of the Tamaki, 1974; Paroikia—The House Alongside, 1978. *Recreations:* reading, sailing, squash. *Address:* 20 Tainui Street, Torbay, Auckland 10, New Zealand. *T:* Auckland 404-6372. *Club:* Wellesley (Wellington, NZ).

BUCKLE, Richard; see Buckle, C. R. S.

BUCKLEY, family name of **Baron Wrenbury.**

BUCKLEY, Anthony James Henthorne; consultant; *b* 22 May 1934; *s* of late William Buckley, FRCS; *m* 1964, Celia Rosamund Sanderson, *d* of late C. R. Sanderson; one *s* two *d. Educ:* Haileybury and ISC; St John's Coll.,

Cambridge. MA, LLB, FCA. Peat Marwick Mitchell & Co., 1959–62; Rank Organisation Ltd, 1962–66; Slater Walker Securities Ltd, 1966–75, Man. Dir, 1972–75. *Address:* 2 St Mary's Grove, SW13.

BUCKLEY, Rt. Hon. Sir Denys (Burton), PC 1970; Kt 1960; MBE 1945; a Lord Justice of Appeal, 1970–81; *b* 6 Feb. 1906; 4th *s* of 1st Baron Wrenbury; *m* 1932, Gwendolen Jane, *yr d* of late Sir Robert Armstrong-Jones, CBE, FRCS, FRCP; three *d. Educ:* Eton; Trinity College, Oxford. Called to the Bar, Lincoln's Inn, 1928, Bencher, 1949, Pro-Treasurer, 1967, Treasurer, 1969, Pres., Senate of the Inns of Court, 1970–72. Served War of 1939–45, in RAOC, 1940–45; Temporary Major; GSO II (Sigs Directorate), War Office. Treasury Junior Counsel (Chancery), 1949–60; Judge of High Court of Justice, Chancery Div., 1960–70. Member, Restrictive Practices Ct, 1962–70, President, 1968–70; Member: Law Reform Cttee, 1963–73; Cttee on Departmental Records, 1952–54; Advisory Council on Public Records, 1958–79. Hon. Fellow: Trinity Coll., Oxford, 1969; Amer. Coll. of Trial Lawyers, 1970. Master, Merchant Taylors' Co., 1972. CStJ 1966. Medal of Freedom (USA), 1945. *Address:* Flat 6, 105 Onslow Square, SW7. *T:* 01-584 4735; Stream Farm, Dallington, Sussex. *T:* Rushlake Green 830223. *Clubs:* Brooks's, Beefsteak.

BUCKLEY, Eric Joseph, MA; FIOP; Printer to the University of Oxford, since 1978; Fellow of Linacre College, Oxford, since 1979; *b* 26 June 1920; *s* of Joseph William Buckley and Lillian Elizabeth Major (*née* Drake); *m* 1st, 1945, Joan Alice Kirby (*d* 1973); one *s* one *d* ; 2nd, 1978, Harriett, *d* of Mr and Mrs Robert Williams Hawkins, Caruthersville, Mo, USA. *Educ:* St Bartholomew's, Dover. MA Oxon 1979 (by special resolution; Linacre College). Served War, RAOC and REME, ME and UK, 1939–45. Apprentice, Amalgamated Press, London, 1935; Dir, Pergamon Press Ltd, 1956–74; joined Oxford Univ. Press as Dir, UK Publishing Services, 1974. Liveryman, Stationers and Newspaper Makers Co., 1981; Freeman, City of London, 1980. *Recreations:* reading, theatre, cats. *Address:* 43 Sandfield Road, Oxford OX3 7RN. *T:* Oxford 60588.

BUCKLEY, George Eric; Counsellor, Atomic Energy, British Embassy, Tokyo, 1976–81; *b* 4 Feb. 1916; *s* of John and Florence Buckley; *m* 1941, Mary Theresa Terry; one *s* one *d. Educ:* Oldham High Sch.; Manchester Univ. BSc (Hons) Physics; MInstP. Lectr in Physics, Rugby Coll. of Technol., 1938. War service, Sqdn Ldr, RAF, 1940–46. Manager, Health Physics and Safety, Windscale Works, 1949; Works Manager, Capenhurst Works, 1952; Chief Ops Physicist, Risley, 1956; Chief Tech. Manager, Windscale and Calder Works, 1959; Superintendent: Calder Hall and Windscale Advanced Gas Cooled Reactors, 1964; Reactors, and Head of Management Services, 1974. *Recreations:* travel, good food, golf. *Address:* 12 Wast Water Rise, Seascale, Cumbria CA20 1LB. *T:* Seascale 28405.

BUCKLEY, James Arthur, CBE 1975; Member, British Gas Corporation, 1973–76 (Gas Council, 1968–72); *b* 3 April 1917; *s* of late James Buckley and of Elizabeth Buckley; *m* 1939, Irene May Hicks; two *s. Educ:* Christ's Hosp., Horsham, Sussex; Westminster Technical Coll.; Bradford Technical Coll. RAFVR, 1940–46. Gas Light & Coke Co.; Gas Supply Pupil, 1934; Actg Service Supervisor, 1939; Service Supervisor, 1946; North Thames Gas Board: Divisional Man., 1954; Commercial Man., 1962; Commercial Man. and Bd Mem., 1964; East Midlands Gas Board: Dep. Chm., 1966–67; Chm., 1967–68.

BUCKLEY, Sir John (William), Kt 1977; FRSA 1978; Hon. FIChemE; FIProdE; Chairman, Davy Corporation (formerly Davy International Ltd), 1973–82; *b* 9 Jan. 1913; *s* of John William and Florence Buckley; *m* 1st, 1935, Bertha Bagnall (marr. diss. 1967); two *s* ; 2nd, 1967, Molly Neville-Clarke; one step *s* (and one step *s* decd). *Educ:* techn. coll. (Dipl. Engrg). George Kent Ltd, 1934–50 (Gen. Man. 1945–50); Man. Dir, Emmco Pty Ltd, 1950–55; Man. Dir, British Motor Corp. Pty Ltd, 1956–60; Vice Chm. and Dep. Chm., Winget, Gloucester Ltd, 1961–68; Man. Dir and Dep. Chm., Davy International Ltd, 1968–73; Chm., Alfred Herbert Ltd, 1975–79; Chm., Engelhard Industries, 1979–; Dir, Fuerst Day Lawson, 1981–. Dir, British Overseas Trade Bd, 1973–76. Chm., EDC for Process Plant Industry, 1977–79; Pres., British-Soviet Chamber of Commerce, 1977–. Mem., BSC, 1978–81. Hon. FIChemE 1975. Order of the Southern Cross (Brazil), 1977. *Recreations:* gardening, music, photography, fishing, painting. *Address:* 21 Mulberry Walk, SW3. *T:* 01-352 1861. *Clubs:* Boodle's; Union (Sydney).

BUCKLEY, Rear-Adm. Sir Kenneth (Robertson), KBE 1961; FIEE, MBritIRE; *b* 24 May 1904; 2nd *s* of late L. E. Buckley, CSI, TD; *m* 1937, Bettie Helen Radclyffe Dugmore; one *s* two *d. Educ:* RN Colleges Osborne and Dartmouth. Joined Navy Jan. 1918. Served War of 1939–45 (despatches). Comdr 1942; Capt. 1949; Rear-Adm. 1958. ADC to the Queen, 1956–58. Director of Engineering and Electrical Training of the Navy, and Senior Naval Electrical Officer, 1959–62. *Recreations:* golf, gardening. *Address:* Meadow Cottage, Cherque Lane, Lee-on-Solent, Hants. *T:* Lee 550646.

BUCKLEY, Rear-Adm. Peter Noel, CB 1964; DSO 1945; retd; Head of Naval Historical Branch, Ministry of Defence, 1968–75; *b* 26 Dec. 1909; *s* of late Frank and Constance Buckley, Hooton, Cheshire; *m* 1945, Norah Elizabeth Astley St Clair-Ford, *widow* of Lt-Comdr Drummond St Clair-Ford; one *d* (and two step *s* one step *d*). *Educ:* Holmwood School, Formby, Lancs; RNC, Dartmouth. Midshipman, HMS Tiger, 1927, HMS Cornwall, 1928–30; Lieut: qual. 1931. Submarine Service, 1931–38, in submarines;

Lieut-Comdr, CO of HMS Shark, 1938. War of 1939-45 (despatches): POW Germany, 1940-45. Comdr 1945; HMS: Rajah and Formidable, 1946; Siskin, 1947; Glory, 1949; RN Barracks, Portsmouth, 1951; Capt. 1952; Capt. D, Plymouth, 1953; Capt. of Dockyard, Rosyth, 1954; Chief Staff Officer to Flag Officer Comdg Reserve Fleet, 1957; Capt of Fleet, Med. Fleet, 1959; Rear-Adm. 1962; Dir-Gen., Manpower, 1962-64; retd 1965. *Address:* Forest Cottage, Sway, Lymington, Hants. *T:* Lymington 682442.

BUCKLEY, Lt-Comdr Sir (Peter) Richard, KCVO 1982 (CVO 1973; MVO 1968); Private Secretary to the Duke and Duchess of Kent since 1961; *b* 31 Jan. 1928; 2nd *s* of late Alfred Buckley and of Mrs E. G. Buckley, Crowthorne, Berks; *m* 1958, Theresa Mary Neve; two *s* one *d. Educ:* Wellington Coll. Cadet, RN, 1945. Served in HM Ships: Mauritius, Ulster, Contest, Defender, and BRNC, Dartmouth. Specialised in TA/S. Invalided from RN (Lt-Comdr), 1961. *Recreations:* fishing, sailing. *Address:* Coppins Cottages, Iver, Bucks SL0 0AT. *T:* Iver 653004. *Clubs:* Army and Navy, Royal Automobile; Royal Dart Yacht.

BUCKLEY, Roger John, QC 1979; *b* 26 April 1939; *s* of Harold and Marjorie Buckley; *m* 1965, Margaret Gillian, *d* of Robert and Joan Cowan; one *s* one *d. Educ:* Mill Hill Sch.; Manchester Univ. (LLB (Hons)). Called to the Bar, Middle Temple, 1962 (Harmsworth Schol.). *Recreations:* squash, theatre, bloodstock. *Address:* 1 Brick Court, Temple, EC4Y 9BY. *Club:* Old Mill Hillians.

BUCKLEY, Hon. Dame Ruth (Burton), DBE 1959; JP; *b* 12 July 1898; 4th *d* of 1st Baron Wrenbury, PC. *Educ:* Cheltenham Ladies' College. Called to Bar, Lincoln's Inn, 1926. E Sussex County Council: Member of Council, 1936-74; Alderman, 1946-74; Vice-Chm. 1949-52; Chm. 1952-55. Member of South Eastern Metropolitan Regional Hospital Board, 1948-69; Part-time member of Local Govt Boundary Commn for England, 1958-66. JP Sussex, 1935-. Hon. LLD Sussex, 1977. *Address:* Toll Wood Cottage, Netherfield, Battle, East Sussex TN33 9QA. *T:* Brightling 222.

BUCKLEY, Major William Kemmis, MBE 1959; DL; Chairman, Buckley's Brewery Ltd, since 1972 (Director, 1960, Vice-Chairman, 1963-72); *b* 18 Oct. 1921; *o s* of late Lt-Col William Howell Buckley, DL, and Karolie Kathleen Kemmis. *Educ:* Radley Coll.; New Coll., Oxford (MA). Commnd into Welsh Guards, 1941; served N Africa, Italy (despatches, 1945); ADC, 1946-47, Mil. Sec., 1948, to Governor of Madras; Staff Coll., Camberley, 1950; GSO2, HQ London Dist, 1952-53; OC Guards Indep. Para. Co., 1954-57; Cyprus, 1956; Suez, 1956; War Office, 1957; Mil. Asst to Vice-Chief of Imp. Gen. Staff, 1958-59; US Armed Forces Staff Coll., Norfolk, Va., 1959-60. Director: Rhymney Breweries Ltd, 1962; Whitbread (Wales) Ltd, 1969; Felinfoel Brewery Co., 1975; Guardian Assurance Co. (S Wales), 1966 (Dep. Chm., 1967-). Mem. Council, Brewers' Soc., 1967; Chm., S Wales Brewers' Assoc., 1971-74; Dep. Chm. and Treas., Nat. Trade Develt Assoc., 1966 (Chm., S Wales Panel, 1965); Lay Mem., Press Council, 1967-73. Chm., Council of St John of Jerusalem for Carms, 1966; Pres., Carms Antiquarian Soc., 1971- (Chm., 1968); Mem., Nat. Trust Cttee for Wales, 1962-70; Mem., T&AFA (Carms), 1962 and T&AFA (S Wales and Mon.), 1967; Jt Master and Hon. Sec., Pembrokeshire and Carms Otter Hounds, 1962. High Sheriff of Carms, 1967-68, DL Dyfed (formerly Carms) 1969. CStJ 1966. *Publications:* contributions in local history journals. *Recreations:* gardening, bee-keeping (Pres. Carmarthenshire Bee-Keepers Assoc., 1972-), tapestry work. *Address:* Briar Cottage, Ferryside, Dyfed, S Wales. *T:* Ferryside 359. *Clubs:* Brooks's; Cardiff and County (Cardiff).

BUCKMASTER, family name of Viscount Buckmaster.

BUCKMASTER, 3rd Viscount *cr* 1933, of Cheddington; **Martin Stanley Buckmaster,** OBE 1979; Baron 1915; HM Diplomatic Service, retired; *b* 11 April 1921; *s* of 2nd Viscount Buckmaster and Joan, Viscountess Buckmaster (*d* 1976), *d* of Dr Garry Simpson; *S* father, 1974. *Educ:* Stowe. Joined TA, 1939; served Royal Sussex Regt (Captain) in UK and Middle East, 1940-46. Foreign Office, 1946; Middle East Centre for Arab Studies, Lebanon, 1950-51; qualified in Arabic (Higher Standard); served in Trucial States, Sharjah (1951-53) and Abu Dhabi (Political Officer, 1955-58) and subsequently in Libya, Bahrain, FO, Uganda, Lebanon and Saudi Arabia, 1958-73; First Sec., FCO, 1973-77; Head of Chancery and Chargé d'Affaires, Yemen Arab Republic, 1977-81. FRGS 1954. *Recreations:* walking, music, railways; Arab and African studies. *Heir: b* Hon. Colin John Buckmaster [*b* 17 April 1923; *m* 1946, May, *o d* of late Charles Henry Gibbon; three *s* two *d*]. *Address:* 8 Redcliffe Square, SW10 9JZ. *T:* 01-370 2247. *Club:* Travellers'.

BUCKMASTER, Rev. Cuthbert Harold Septimus; *b* 15 July 1903; *s* of Charles John and Evelyn Jean Buckmaster; *m* 1942, Katharine Mary Zoë (*d* 1974), 3rd *d* of Rev. Canon T. N. R. Prentice, Stratford-on-Avon; two *d. Educ:* RN Colls, Osborne and Dartmouth. Asst Curate St John's, Middlesbrough, 1927-30; Curate of Wigan, 1930-33; Chaplain of Denstone Coll., 1933-35; Warden of St Michael's Coll., Tenbury, Worcs, 1935-46; Rector of: Ashprington, with Cornworthy, 1957-59; Chagford, 1959-71. Chaplain RNVR, 1940; RN 1947. *Address:* 21 Marquis Street, Ashburton, Vic 3147, Australia.

BUCKMASTER, Colonel Maurice James, OBE 1943; Independent Public Relations Consultant, since 1960; *b* 11 Jan. 1902; *s* of Henry James Buckmaster and Eva Matilda (*née* Nason); *m* 1st, 1927, May Dorothy (*née* Steed); one

s two *d* ; 2nd, 1941, Anna Cecilia (*née* Reinstein). *Educ:* Eton College. J. Henry Schroder & Co., Merchant Bankers, 1923-29; Asst to Chairman, Ford Motor Co. Ltd, 1929-32; Manager, Ford Motor Co. (France), 1932-36; Head of European Dept, Ford Motor Co. Ltd, 1936-39 and 1945-50; Dir of Public Relations, 1950-60. Served War of 1939-45: 50th Div., G3I, Intelligence, 1939-40 (despatches); Intelligence Officer (Captain), Dakar expedition; Special Operations Executive, Head of French Section, 1941-45. Chevalier de la Légion d'Honneur, 1945, Officier 1978 (France); Croix de Guerre with Palms, Médaille de la Résistance (France), 1945; Legion of Merit (US), 1945. *Publications:* Specially Employed, 1961; They Fought Alone, 1964. *Recreation:* family life. *Address:* Hathaway, Ashdown Road, Forest Row, East Sussex. *T:* Forest Row 2379. *Clubs:* Special Forces, Institute of Directors.

BUCKNILL, Peter Thomas, QC 1961; *b* 4 Nov. 1910; *o s* of late Rt Hon. Sir Alfred Bucknill, PC, OBE; *m* 1935, Elizabeth Mary Stark; three *s* two *d* (and one *d* decd). *Educ:* Gresham's Sch., Holt; Trinity Coll., Oxford (MA). Called to the Bar, Inner Temple, 1935 (Bencher, 1967). Ordinand, Chichester Theol. Coll., 1939; Deacon, 1941; Priest, 1942; received into RC Church, 1943; resumed Bar practice. Appointed Junior Counsel to the Treasury (Admiralty), 1958; resigned on becoming QC. On rota for Lloyd's Salvage Arbitrators, Wreck Commissioner, 1962-78, retired from practice, 1978. *Publications:* contributed to Halsbury's Laws of England, shipping vol., 2nd and 3rd edns. *Recreation:* gardening. *Address:* High Corner, The Warren, Ashtead, Surrey KT21 2SL.

BUCKSEY, Verity Ann, (Mrs C. M. Bucksey); *see* Lambert, V. A.

BUCKTON, Raymond William; General Secretary, Associated Society of Locomotive Engineers and Firemen, since 1970; *b* 20 Oct. 1922; *s* of W. E. and H. Buckton; *m* 1954, Barbara Langfield; two *s. Educ:* Appleton Roebuck School. MCIT, FCIT 1982. Employed in Motive Power Department, British Railways, 1940-60. Elected Irish Officer of ASLEF, 1960 (Dublin); District Organiser, York, Jan. 1963; Assistant General Secretary, July 1963; General Secretary, 1970. Member: Gen. Council, TUC, 1973-; IBA Gen. Adv. Council, 1976-; Occupational Pensions Bd, 1976-82; Health Services Bd, 1977-80; Health and Safety Commn, 1982-. Member: CIT Council, 1970-; Industrial Soc., 1973-; Standing Adv. Cttee, TUC Centenary Inst. of Occupational Health, 1974-; Nat. Adv. Council on Employment of Disabled People, 1975-; Industrial Injuries Adv. Council, 1976-; Dangerous Substances Adv. Cttee, 1976-; Adv. Cttee on Alcoholism, 1977-; Railway Industry Adv. Cttee, 1977-82; TUC Internat. Cttee, 1978-; EEC Economic and Social Cttee, 1978-82; Exec., ETUC, 1982-; Commonwealth TUC, 1982-. Councillor, York City Council, 1952-55, Alderman, 1955-57. *Address:* 9 Arkwright Road, Hampstead, NW3. *T:* 01-435 6300.

BUDAY, George, RE 1953 (ARE 1939); wood engraver; author on graphic arts subjects; *b* Kolozsvar, Transylvania, 7 April 1907; *s* of late Prof. Arpad Buday, Roman archaeologist, and Margaret Buday. *Educ:* Presbyterian Coll., Kolozsvar; Royal Hungarian Francis Joseph Univ., Szeged (Dr). Apptd Lectr in Graphic Arts, Royal Hungarian F. J. Univ., 1933-41; Rome Scholar, 1936-37; won travelling schol. to England (and has stayed permanently) 1937. Broadcaster, BBC European Service, 1940-42; in a Dept of Foreign Office, 1942-45. Dir, Hungarian Cultural Inst., London, 1947-49, resigned. Illustrated numerous folk-tale and folk-ballad collections, vols of classics and modern authors, publ. in many countries. Since 1938 exhib. Royal Acad., Royal Soc. of Painter-Etchers and Engravers, Soc. of Wood Engravers, and in many countries abroad. Works represented in: Depts of Prints and Drawings, Brit. Mus.; Victoria and Albert Mus.; Glasgow Univ.; New York Public Library; Florence Univ.; Museums of Fine Arts, Budapest, Prague, Warsaw; Phillips Memorial Gall., Washington, DC; etc. Grand Prix, Paris World Exhibn, 1937 (for engravings); subsequently other art and bibliophile prizes. Officer's Cross, Order of Merit (Hungary), 1947. *Publications:* Book of Ballads, 1934; The Story of the Christmas Card, 1951; The History of the Christmas Card, 1954 (1964); (wrote and illustr.): The Dances of Hungary, 1950; George Buday's Little Books, I-XII, incl. The Language of Flowers, 1951; The Cries of London, Ancient and Modern, 1954; Proverbial Cats and Kittens, 1956 (1968); The Artist's Recollections, for a volume of his 82 Selected Engravings, 1970; Multiple Portraiture: Illustrating a Poetical Anthology, 1981; contrib. articles to periodicals. *Relevant publication:* George Buday by Curt Visel, in Illustration 63, 1971. *Recreations:* bibliophile hand-printing on his 1857 Albion hand-press and collecting old Christmas cards (probably most representative collection of Victorian cards extant). *Address:* Downs House, Netherne, PO Box 150, Coulsdon, Surrey CR3 1YE.

BUDD, Bernard Wilfred, MA; QC 1969; *b* 18 Dec. 1912; *s* of late Rev. W. R. A. Budd; *m* 1944, Margaret Alison, *d* of late Rt Hon. E. Leslie Burgin, PC, LLD, MP; two *s. Educ:* Cardiff High Sch.; W Leeds High Sch.; Pembroke Coll., Cambridge (schol. in natural sciences). Joined ICS, 1935; various Dist appts incl. Dep. Comr, Upper Sind Frontier, 1942-43; Collector and Dist Magistrate, Karachi, 1945-46; cont. in Pakistan Admin. Service, 1947; Dep. Sec., Min. of Commerce and Works, Govt of Pakistan, 1947; Anti-corruption Officer and Inspector-Gen. of Prisons, Govt of Sind, 1949. Called to Bar, Gray's Inn, 1952. Contested (L), Dover, 1964 and 1966, Folkestone and Hythe, Feb. and Oct. 1974 and 1979. Chm., Assoc. of Liberal Lawyers, 1978-82. *Recreations:* tennis, birds, hill walking. *Address:* Highlands, Elham, Canterbury, Kent. *T:* Elham 350; 3 Pump Court, Temple, EC4. *T:* 01-353

4122. *Clubs:* United Oxford & Cambridge University, National Liberal; Sind (Karachi).

BUDD, Stanley Alec; Scottish Representative, Commission of the European Communities, since 1975; *b* 22 May 1931; *s* of Henry Stanley Budd and Ann Mitchell; *m* 1955, Wilma McQueen Cuthbert; three *s* one *d. Educ:* George Heriot's Sch., Edinburgh. Newspaper reporter, feature writer and sub-editor, D. C. Thomson & Co, Dundee, 1947-57 (National Service, 1949-51). Research writer, Foreign Office, 1957-60; 2nd Secretary, Beirut, Lebanon, 1960-63; 1st Sec., Kuala Lumpur, Malaysia, 1963-69; FO, 1969-71; Dep. Head of Information, Scottish Office, 1971-72; Press Secretary to Chancellor of Duchy of Lancaster, 1972-74; Chief Information Officer, Cabinet Office, 1974-75. *Recreations:* music, painting, oriental antiques, bridge. *Address:* 2 Bellevue Crescent, Edinburgh EH3 6ND; 7 Alva Street, Edinburgh EH2 4PH. *T:* 031-225 2058.

BUDDEN, Kenneth George, FRS 1966; MA, PhD; Reader in Physics, University of Cambridge, 1965-82, now Emeritus; Fellow of St John's College, Cambridge, since 1947; *b* 23 June 1915; *s* of late George Easthope Budden and Gertrude Homer Rea; *m* 1947, Nicolette Ann Lydia de Longesdon Longsdon; no *c. Educ:* Portsmouth Grammar Sch.; St John's College, Cambridge (MA, PhD). Telecommunications Research Establishment, 1939-41; British Air Commn., Washington, DC, 1941-44; Air Command, SE Asia, 1945. Research at Cambridge, 1936-39 and from 1947. *Publications:* Radio Waves in the Ionosphere, 1961; The Wave-Guide Mode Theory of Wave Propagation, 1961; Lectures on Magnetoionic Theory, 1964; numerous papers in scientific jls, on the propagation of radio waves. *Recreation:* gardening. *Address:* 15 Adams Road, Cambridge. *T:* Cambridge 354752.

BUDGEN, Nicholas William; MP (C) Wolverhampton South-West, since Feb. 1974; *b* 3 Nov. 1937; *s* of Captain G. N. Budgen; *m* 1964, Madeleine E. Kittoe; one *s* one *d. Educ:* St Edward's Sch., Oxford; Corpus Christi Coll., Cambridge. Called to Bar, Gray's Inn, 1962; practised Midland and Oxford Circuit. An Asst Govt Whip, 1981-82. *Recreations:* hunting, racing. *Address:* Malt House Farm, Colton, near Rugeley, Staffs. *T:* Rugeley 77059.

BUFFET, Bernard; Chevalier de la Légion d'Honneur; artist, painter; *b* Paris, 10 July 1928; *m* 1958, Annabel May Schwob de Lure; one *s* two *d.* Début at Salon des Moins de Trente Ans, 1944. From 1948 has had one-man shows, annually, at Drouant-David and Visconti Galleries, from 1956 at Galerie Maurice Garnier. Grand Prix de la Critique, 1948. Solo retrospective exhibition of his works was held at Charpentier Gallery, Paris, 1958. He has exhibited, oils, water colours and drawings and is a lithographer, mural painter and illustrator of books. Work represented in permanent collections: Musée du Petit Palais and Musée National d'Art Moderne, in Paris; Buffet Museum founded in Japan, 1973; large room of his mystic works in Vatican Museum; work shown at Venice Biennale, 1956; exhibitions: Lefevre Gallery, London, 1961, 1963, 1965. Stage designs: Le Rendez-vous manqué (ballet), 1959; Patron (musical comedy), 1959; ballets at L'Opéra, Paris, 1969. Mem. Salon d'Automne and Salon des Indépendants. Officier des Arts et des Lettres; Membre de l'Institut, 1974. *Address:* c/o Galerie Maurice Garnier, 6 avenue Matignon, 75008 Paris, France.

BUFFEY, Brig. William, DSO 1940; TD 1940; DL; *b* 24 Sept. 1899; *s* of late William Buffey, Bromley, Kent; *m* 1926, Dorothy Wensley, *d* of late William Rogers, Nelson, New Zealand; two *d. Educ:* St Dunstan's College, Catford. Served War of 1939-45, Cmd 91st Fd Regt RA, France, Belgium (DSO), India, Persia, 1939-43; CRA 5 Div. Middle East, Italy, BLA, 1943-45 (despatches thrice); Hon. Col 291st Airborne Fd Regt RA (TA), 1946-55. Governor, St Dunstan's College, 1954-79. DL Co. London, subseq. Greater London, 1954-82. *Recreation:* gardening. *Address:* 7 Broad Oak, Groombridge, Tunbridge Wells, Kent. *T:* Groombridge 309.

BUFTON, Air Vice-Marshal Sydney Osborne, CB 1945; DFC 1940; *b* 12 Jan. 1908; *2nd s* of late J. O. Bufton, JP, Llandrindod Wells, Radnor; *m* 1943, Susan Maureen, *d* of Colonel E. M. Browne, DSO, Chelsea; two *d. Educ:* Dean Close School, Cheltenham. Commissioned RAF 1927; psa, 1939; idc, 1946. Served War of 1939-45, Bomber Comd, Nos 10 and 76 Sqdns, RAF Station, Pocklington, 1940-41; Dep. Dir Bomber Ops, 1941-43; Dir of Bomber Ops, Air Min., 1943-45; AOC Egypt, 1945-46; Central Bomber Establishment, RAF, Marham, Norfolk, 1947-48; Dep. Chief of Staff (Ops/Plans), Air Forces Western Europe, 1948-51; Dir of Weapons, Air Min., 1951-52; AOA Bomber Command, 1952-53; AOC Brit. Forces, Aden, 1953-55; Senior Air Staff Officer, Bomber Comd, 1955-58; Assistant Chief of Air Staff (Intelligence), 1958-61; retired Oct. 1961. Temp. Gp Capt. 1941; Temp. Air Cdre 1943; Subst. Gp Capt. 1946; Air Cdre 1948; Actg Air Vice-Marshal, 1952; Air Vice-Marshal, 1953. FRAeS 1970. High Sheriff of Radnorshire, 1967. Comdr Legion of Merit (US); Comdr Order of Orange Nassau (with swords), Netherlands. *Recreations:* hockey (Welsh International 1931-37, Combined Services, RAF), golf, squash. *Address:* 1 Castle Keep, London Road, Reigate. *T:* Reigate 43707. *Club:* Royal Air Force.

BUGOTU, Francis, CBE 1979; Secretary-General, South Pacific Commission, since 1982; *b* 27 June 1937; *s* of Tione Kalapalua Bugotu and Rachael Samoa; *m* 1962, Ella Vehe; one *s* one *d. Educ:* NZ, Australia, Scotland, England and Solomon Is. Teacher and Inspector of Mission Schs for Ch. of Melanesia (Anglican), 1959-60; Mem., 1st Legislative Council, 1960-62; Lectr, Solomon Is Teachers Coll., 1964-68; Chief Educn Officer and Perm. Sec., Min. of Educn, 1968-75; Perm. Sec. to Chief Minister and Council of Ministers, and titular Head of Civil Service, 1976-78; Sec. for For. Affairs and Roving Ambassador/High Comr of Solomon Is, 1978-82. Chairman: Review Cttee on Educn, 1974-75; Solomon Is Tourist Authority, 1970-73; Solomon Is Scholarship Cttee, 1969-75. Consultant, esp. for S Pacific Commn; Founder Mem. and Chief Adviser, Kakamora Youth Club, 1968-75; Chief Comr of Scouts for Solomon Is, 1970-77; Lay Canon of Ch. of Melanesia, 1970-. *Publications:* (with A. V. Hughes) This Man (play), 1970 (also award winning film); papers on: impact of Western culture on Solomon Is; politics, economics and social aspects in Solomons; recolonising and decolonising; Solomon Is Pidgin. *Recreation:* interested in most ball games (soccer, cricket, basketball, Rugby, tennis, table-tennis, softball, snooker), swimming, music, dancing. *Address:* South Pacific Commission, Post Box D 5, Noumea CEDEX, New Caledonia.

BUHLER, Robert, RA 1956 (ARA 1947); painter; Hon. Fellow, Royal College of Art; tutor, RCA, 1948-75; *b* London, 23 Nov. 1916; *s* of Robert Buhler, journalist; *m* Evelyn Rowell (marr. diss. 1951); one *s*; *m* 1962, Prudence Brochocka (*née* Beaumont) (marr. diss. 1972); two *s. Educ:* Switzerland; Bolt Court; St Martin's School of Art; Royal College of Art. Trustee, Royal Academy, 1975-. Exhibited at: Royal Academy, New English Art Club, London Group, London galleries. Work in permanent collections: Chantrey Bequest; Stott Fund; provincial art galleries; galleries in USA, Canada, Australia, NZ. *Address:* 33 Alderney Street, SW1V 4ES. *T:* 01-828 2825; (studio) 3 Avenue Studios, Sydney Close, SW3.

BUIST, John Latto Farquharson; Under Secretary, International Division, Foreign and Commonwealth Office (Overseas Development Administration), since 1976; *b* 30 May 1930; *s* of Lt-Col Thomas Powrie Buist, RAMC, and Christian Mary (*née* Robertson). *Educ:* Dalhousie Castle Sch.; Winchester Coll.; New Coll., Oxford (MA). Asst Principal, CO, 1952-54; Sec., Kenya Police Commn, 1953; seconded Kenya Govt, 1954-56; Principal, CO, 1956-61; Dept of Tech. Cooperation, 1961-62; Brit. High Commn, Dar-es-Salaam, 1962-64; Consultant on Admin, E African Common Services Org./Community, 1964-69; Sec., Commn on E African Cooperation and related bodies, 1966-69; Asst Sec., Min. of Overseas Develt, 1966-76. Co-founder and several times Pres., Classical Assoc. of Kenya; Member: Campaign for Homosexual Equality; John Bate Choir; United Reformed Church. *Recreations:* singing and other music-making, walking. *Address:* 9 Manor Gate, St John's Avenue, SW15. *T:* 01-789 4490.

BUITER, Prof. Willem Hendrik, PhD; Cassel Professor of Economics, London School of Economics and Political Science, University of London, since 1982; *b* 26 Sept. 1949; *s* of Harm Geert Buiter and Hendrien Buiter, *née* van Schooten; *m* 1973, Jean Archer. *Educ:* Cambridge Univ. (BA 1971); Yale Univ. (PhD 1975). Asst Prof., Princeton Univ., 1975-76; Lectr, LSE, 1976-77; Asst Prof., Princeton Univ., 1977-79; Prof. of Economics, Univ. of Bristol, 1980-82. Consultant, IMF, 1979-80; Specialist Adviser, House of Commons Select Cttee on the Treasury and CS, 1980-. Associate Editor, Econ. Jl, 1980-. *Publications:* Temporary and Long Run Equilibrium, 1979; articles in learned jls. *Recreations:* tennis, bridge, music. *Address:* 26 Hearne Road, W4.

BÜLBRING, Edith, MA Oxon; MD Bonn; FRS 1958; Professor of Pharmacology, Oxford University, 1967-71, now Emeritus (University Reader, 1960-67) and Honorary Fellow, Lady Margaret Hall, 1971; *b* 27 Dec. 1903; *d* of Karl Daniel Bülbring, Professor of English, Bonn University, and Hortense Leonore Bülbring (*née* Kann). *Educ:* Bonn, Munich and Freiburg Universities. Postgraduate work in Pharmacology Department of Berlin University, 1929-31; Pediatrics, University of Jena, 1932; Virchow Krankenhaus University of Berlin, 1933; Pharmacological Laboratory of Pharmaceutical Society of Great Britain, University of London, 1933-38; Pharmacological Dept, University of Oxford, 1938-71. Research work on: autonomic transmitters, suprarenals, smooth muscle, peristalsis. Schmiedeberg-Plakette der Deutschen Pharmakologischen Gesellschaft, 1974. Honorary Member: Pharmaceutical Soc., Torino, Italy, 1957; British Pharmacological Soc., 1975; Deutsche Physiolgische Gesellschaft, 1976; Physiol Soc., 1981. Hon. Dr med: Univ. of Groningen, Netherlands, 1979; Leuven, 1981. *Publications:* mainly in Jl of Physiology, Brit. Jl of Pharmacology and Proc. Royal Soc. of London, Series B. *Recreation:* music. *Address:* 15 Northmoor Road, Oxford. *T:* Oxford 57270; Lady Margaret Hall, Oxford.

BULGER, Anthony Clare, BA, BCL; **His Honour Judge Bulger;** a Circuit Judge (formerly County Court Judge), since 1963; *b* 1912; *s* of Daniel Bulger; *m* Una Patricia Banks; one *s* one *d. Educ:* Rugby; Oriel Coll., Oxford. Called to the Bar, Inner Temple, 1936. Oxford Circuit; Dep Chm., 1958-70, Chm. 1970-71, Glos QS; Dep. Chm. Worcs QS, 1962-71. Recorder of Abingdon, 1962-63. *Address:* Forthampton, Glos.

BULKELEY, Sir Richard H. D. W.; *see* Williams-Bulkeley.

BULL, Anthony, CBE 1968 (OBE 1944); Transport Consultant: Kennedy and Donkin, since 1971; Freeman Fox and Partners, since 1971; *b* 18 July 1908; 3rd *s* of Rt Hon. Sir William Bull, 1st Bt, PC, MP, JP, FSA (*d* 1931), and late Lilian, 2nd *d* of G. S. Brandon, Oakbrook, Ravenscourt Park; *m* 1946, Barbara (*d* 1947), *er d* of late Peter Donovan, Yonder, Rye, Sussex; one *d. Educ:* Gresham's Sch., Holt; Magdalene Coll., Cambridge (Exhibitioner; MA). Joined Underground Group of Cos, 1929; served in Staff, Publicity and

Public Relations Depts and Chairman's Office. Sec. to Vice-Chm. London Passenger Transport Board, 1936-39. Served War, 1939-45; RE; Transportation Br., War Office, 1939-42; GHQ, Middle East, 1943; Staff of Supreme Allied Comdr, SE Asia (end of 1943); Col 1944; Transp. Div., CCG, 1945-46. Returned to London Transport as Chief Staff and Welfare Officer, 1946; Member: LTE, 1955-62; LTB, 1962-65; Vice-Chm., LTE (formerly LTB), 1965-71. Advr to House of Commons Transport Cttee, 1981-82. Inst. of Transport: served on Council, 1956-59; Vice-Pres., 1964-66; Hon. Librarian, 1966-69; Pres., 1969-70. Mem. Regional Advisory Council for Technological Educn, 1958-62 (Transp. Adv. Cttee, 1950-62; Chm. Cttee, 1953-62); Mem., King's Lynn Area Hosps Management Cttee, 1972-74. CStJ 1969. Bronze Star (USA), 1946. *Publications:* contrib. to transport journals. *Recreation:* travel. *Address:* 35 Clareville Grove, SW7 5AU. *T:* 01-373 5647; Trowland Cottage, Burnham Norton, Norfolk. *T:* Burnham Market 297. *Club:* United Oxford & Cambridge University.
See also Sir George Bull, Bt, Sir Robin Chichester-Clark.

BULL, Sir George, 3rd Bt *cr* 1922, of Hammersmith; Senior Partner of Bull & Bull, Solicitors, 11 Stone Buildings, Lincoln's Inn, and 4 Castle Street, Canterbury; *b* 19 June 1906; 2nd *s* of Rt Hon. Sir William Bull, 1st Bt, and late Lilian, 2nd *d* of G. S. Brandon, Oakbrook, Ravenscourt Park, and Heene, Worthing, Sussex; *S* brother 1942; *m* 1933, Gabrielle, 2nd *d* of late Bramwell Jackson, MC, Bury St Edmunds; one *s* one *d. Educ:* RN Colleges, Osborne and Dartmouth; Paris; Vienna. Admitted Solicitor, 1929. Served War of 1939-45 in RNVR; Comdr, 1942. Chm., London Rent Assessment Cttees, 1966-78. Vice-Chm. Governors, Godolphin and Latymer Sch.; Governor, Latymer Foundation; Trustee Hammersmith United Charities; Member, Hammersmith Borough Council, 1968-71. Chm., Standing Council of the Baronetage, 1977-80. Liveryman Fishmongers' Company; Freeman of City of London; Hon. Solicitor, Royal Society of St George. Pres., London Corinthian Sailing Club. *Recreations:* sailing, travelling. *Heir: s* Simeon George Bull [*b* 1 Aug. 1934; *m* 1961, Annick, *y d* of late Louis Bresson and of Mme Bresson, Chandai, France; one *s* two *d*]. *Address:* 3 Hammersmith Terrace, W6. *T:* 01-748 2400; 11 Stone Buildings, Lincoln's Inn. *T:* 01-405 7474. *Clubs:* 1900, MCC, Arts.
See also A. Bull.

BULL, George Anthony; Editor-in-Chief, The Director, since 1974; *b* 23 Aug. 1929; *s* of George Thomas Bull and Bridget Philomena (*née* Nugent); *m* 1957, Pido Marjorie Griffin; two *s* two *d. Educ:* Wimbledon Coll.; Brasenose Coll., Oxford (MA). National Service, Royal Fusiliers, 1947-49. Reporter, Financial Times, 1952-56, Foreign News Editor, 1956-59; News Editor, London Bureau, McGraw-Hill World News, 1959-60; The Director, 1960-: successively Dep. Editor, Editor, Editor-in-Chief. Dir 1971-, and Trustee 1976-, The Tablet; Trustee, The Universe, 1970-. Director: Anvil Prodns (Oxford Playhouse) Ltd, 1980-; Editorial Design Consultants Ltd, 1981-. Chm., Commn for Internat. Justice and Peace, Episcopal Conf. of England and Wales, 1971-74; Hon. Treasurer, Soc. for Renaissance Studies, 1967-; a Governor, St Mary's Coll., Strawberry Hill, 1976-. *Publications:* (with A. Vice) Bid for Power, 1958, 2nd edn 1960; Vatican Politics, 1966; The Renaissance, 1968, new edn 1973; (ed) The Director's Handbook, 1969, 2nd edn 1978; (with E. D. Foster) The Director, his Money and his Job, 1970; (with Peter Hobday and John Hamway) Industrial Relations: the boardroom viewpoint, 1972; Venice: the most triumphant city, 1980 (Folio Society); Inside the Vatican, 1982; (trans.) Artists of the Renaissance, 1979-; translations for Penguin Classics: Life of Cellini, 1956 (1980); Machiavelli, The Prince, 1961 (1981); Vasari, Lives of the Artists, 1965 (1980); Castiglione, The Book of the Courtier, 1967 (1979); Aretino, Selected Letters, 1976. *Recreations:* book collecting, travelling. *Address:* 16 Worcester Road, Sutton, Surrey. *T:* 01-642 2470. *Clubs:* Garrick, Savile.

BULL, Sir Graham (MacGregor), Kt 1976; retired; *b* 30 Jan. 1918; *s* of Dr A. B. Bull; *m* 1947, Megan Patricia Jones (*see* M. P. Bull); three *s* one *d. Educ:* Diocesan Coll., Cape Town; Univ. of Cape Town (MD). FRCP. Tutor in Medicine and Asst, Dept of Medicine, Univ. of Cape Town, 1940-46; Lecturer in Medicine, Postgraduate Medical Sch. of London, 1947-52; Professor of Medicine, The Queen's Univ., Belfast, 1952-66; Mem., MRC, 1962-66; Dir, MRC Clinical Research Centre, 1966-78. Research Fellow, SA Council for Scientific and Industrial Research, 1947; Chairman: CIBA Foundn Exec. Cttee, 1977-; Appropriate Health Resources & Technologies Action Gp Ltd, 1978-80; 2nd Vice-Pres., RCP, 1978-79. *Publications:* contrib. to medical journals. *Address:* 29 Heath Drive, NW3 7SB. *T:* 01-435 1624.

BULL, Prof. Hedley Norman, MA, BPhil (Oxon); BA (Sydney); Montague Burton Professor of International Relations, University of Oxford, and Fellow of Balliol College, Oxford, since 1977; *b* Sydney, 10 June 1932; *s* of J. N. Bull, Sydney; *m* 1954, Frances M., *d* of F. A. E. Lawes; one *s* two *d. Educ:* Fort Street High Sch.; Univ. of Sydney; University Coll., Oxford. Asst Lectr, Internat. Relations, London Sch. of Economics, 1955-57, Lectr 1959; also Rockefeller Fellow, Harvard Univ., 1957-58; Research Associate, Princeton Univ., 1963; Reader in Internat. Relations, London Sch. of Economics, 1963; Dir, Arms Control and Disarmament Research Unit, Foreign Office, London, 1965-67; Prof. of Internat. Relns, Aust. Nat. Univ., 1967-77. Member Council: Inst. for Strategic Studies, London, 1968-77, 1981-; RIIA, 1980-. Res. Dir, Aust. Inst. of Internat. Affairs, 1968-73. Visiting Professor: Polit. Sci., Columbia Univ., 1970-71; Jawaharlal Nehru Univ., New Delhi, 1974-75; Vis. Fellow, All Souls Coll., Oxford, 1975-76. FASSA 1968. *Publications:* The Control of the Arms Race, 1961; The Anarchical

Society, 1977. *Recreation:* walking. *Address:* Balliol College, Oxford OX1 3BJ. *Club:* Travellers'.

BULL, James William Douglas, CBE 1976; MA, MD, FRCP, FRCS, FRCR; Honorary Consultant Radiologist (diagnostic): National Hospital for Nervous Diseases, Queen Square; Maida Vale Hospital for Nervous Diseases; St Andrew's Hospital, Northampton; St George's Hospital; University Hospital, West Indies; Teacher, Institute of Neurology (University of London); Consultant Adviser in Diagnostic Radiology, Department of Health and Social Security, until 1975; Consultant Neuroradiologist to Royal Navy, until 1975; *b* 23 March 1911; *o s* of late D. W. A. Bull, MD, JP, Stony Stratford, Bucks; *m* 1941, Edith (*d* 1978), *e d* of late Charles Burch, Henley-on-Thames; one *s* one *d. Educ:* Repton; Gonville and Caius Coll., Cambridge; St George's Hospital. Entrance schol., 1932. Usual house appts; Asst Curator of Museum, Med. registrar, St George's Hospital, Rockefeller Travelling Schol. (Stockholm), 1938-39. Served War, 1940-46, Temp. Major RAMC (POW Singapore). Dean, Inst. of Neurology, Univ. of London, 1962-68. President: 4th Internat. Symposium Neuroradiologicum, London, 1955; British Inst. of Radiology, 1960; Section of Radiology, 1968-69, Section of Neurology, 1974-75, RSM; Pres., Faculty of Radiologists, 1969-72 (Vice-Pres., 1963). Member: Assoc. of British Neurologists; Brit. Soc. of Neuroradiologists; Pres., European Soc. of Neuroradiology, 1972-75. Examiner in Diagnostic Radiology: Conjoint Board, 1957; Univ. of Liverpool, 1959; for Fellowship, Faculty of Radiologists, London, 1965. Watson Smith Lectr, RCP, 1962; Skinner Lectr, Faculty of Radiologists, 1965; Dyke Meml Lectr, Columbia Univ., New York, 1969; Mackenzie Davidson Meml Lectr, Brit. Inst. Radiol., 1972; Langdon Brown Lectr, RCP, 1974. Member: Council, RCP London, 1964-67; Council, RCS, 1968-73. FRSM; Hon. Fellow: American Coll. of Radiologists; Italian Neuroradiological Soc.; Brazilian Radiological Soc.; Royal Australian Coll. of Radiology; Fac. Radiol. RCSI; Radiological Soc. of N America. Hon. Member: Canadian Neurological Soc.; American Neurological Assoc.; French Radiological Soc.; Amer. Soc. of Neuroradiology. *Publications:* Atlas of Positive Contrast Myelography (jointly), 1962. Contrib. to A. Feiling's Modern Trends in Neurology; various papers in medical journals, mostly connected with neuroradiology. *Recreations:* golf, travel. *Address:* Wellington Hospital, NW8. *T:* 01-586 5959; Springalls, Park Corner, Nettlebed, Henley-on-Thames, Oxon RG9 6DR. *T:* Nettlebed 641365. *Club:* United Oxford & Cambridge University.

BULL, Dr John Prince, CBE 1973; Director of MRC Industrial Injuries and Burns Unit, since 1952; *b* 4 Jan. 1917; *s* of Robert James Bull and Ida Mary Bull; *m* 1939, Irmgard Bross; four *d. Educ:* Burton-on-Trent Grammar Sch.; Cambridge Univ.; Guy's Hospital. MA, MD, BCh Cantab; MRCS, FRCP; MFOM. Casualty Res. Officer, Min. of Home Security, 1941; RAMC, 1942-46; Mem. Research Staff 1947, Asst Dir 1948, MRC Unit, Birmingham Accident Hosp.; Hon. Reader in Traumatology, Univ. of Birmingham. Mem., MRC, 1971-75; Chairman: Regional Res. Cttee, West Midlands RHA, 1966-; Inst. of Accident Surgery, 1980-. Mem., Med. Res. Soc. FRSocMed. *Publications:* contrib. scientific and med. jls. *Recreations:* bricolage, gardening. *Address:* MRC Unit, Accident Hospital, Bath Row, Birmingham B15 1NA. *T:* 021-643 7041.

BULL, Megan Patricia, (Lady Bull), OBE 1982; Governor, Holloway Prison, 1973-82; *b* Naaupoort, S Africa, 17 March 1922; *d* of Dr Thomas and Letitia Jones; *m* 1947, Sir Graham MacGregor Bull, *qv* ; three *s* one *d. Educ:* Good Hope Seminary, Cape Town; Univ. of Cape Town. MB, ChB Cape Town 1944, DCH London 1947, MSc QUB 1961, DPM London 1970, MRCP 1974. Lectr in Physiology, Belfast Coll. of Technology, 1954-61; Med. Officer Student Health Dept, QUB, 1961-66; Prison Med. Officer, Holloway Prison, 1967-73. *Publications:* papers in various medical jls. *Address:* 29 Heath Drive, NW3 7SB.

BULL, Oliver Richard Silvester; Headmaster, Oakham School, Rutland, since 1977; *b* 30 June 1930; *s* of Walter Haverson Bull and Margaret Bridget Bull; *m* 1956, Anne Hay Fife; one *s* four *d. Educ:* Rugby Sch.; Brasenose Coll. Oxford (MA). Mil. Service (1st Beds and Herts), 1949-51. Asst Master, Eton Coll., 1955-77 (Housemaster, 1968-77). *Recreations:* music, walking, reading, ball games. *Address:* Headmaster's House, Oakham School, Rutland. *T:* Oakham 2179.

BULL, Richard; see Bull, O. R. S.

BULL, Sir Walter (Edward Avenon), KCVO 1977 (CVO 1964); FRICS; Consultant, Vigers, chartered surveyors, since 1974; *b* 17 March 1902; *s* of Walter Bull, FRICS, and Florence Bull; *m* 1933, Moira Christian, *d* of William John Irwin and Margaret Irwin, Dungannon, N Ireland; one *s. Educ:* Gresham's Sch.; Aldenham. Sen. Partner, Vigers, 1942-74. Dir, City of London Building Soc., 1957-74. Mem. Council, Duchy of Lancaster, 1957-74. Pres., RICS, 1956. Dep. Comr, War Damage Commn, 1952-75. Liveryman, Merchant Taylors' Co. Silver Jubilee Medal, 1977. *Publications:* papers to RICS on Landlord and Tenant Acts. *Recreations:* music, golf, bowls. *Address:* The Garden House, 1 Park Crescent, Brighton BN2 3HA. *T:* Brighton 681196. *Clubs:* Naval and Military, Gresham.

BULLARD, Denys Gradwell; Member, Anglian Water Authority and Chairman, Broads Committee, since 1974; *b* 15 Aug. 1912; *s* of John Henry Bullard; *m* 1970, Diana Patricia Cox; one *s* one *d. Educ:* Wisbech Grammar

Sch.; Cambridge Univ. Farmer. Broadcaster on agricultural matters both at home and overseas. MP (C) SW Div. of Norfolk, 1951-55; MP (C) King's Lynn, 1959-64. PPS: to Financial Sec., Treasury, 1955: to Min. of Housing and Local Govt, 1959-64. *Address:* Elm House, Elm, Wisbech, Cambs. *T:* Wisbech 3021. *Club:* Farmers'.

BULLARD, Giles Lionel, CMG 1981; HM Diplomatic Service; Ambassador to Bulgaria, since 1980; *b* 24 Aug. 1926; 2nd *s* of late Sir Reader Bullard and late Miriam (*née* Smith); *m* 1952, Hilary Chadwick Brooks (*d* 1978); two *s* two *d. Educ:* Blundell's Sch.; Balliol Coll., Oxford. Army service, 1944-48; Oxford Univ., 1948-51 (Capt. OURFC); H. Clarkson & Co. Ltd, 1952-55; HM Foreign (later Diplomatic) Service, 1955; 3rd Sec., Bucharest, 1957; 2nd Sec., Brussels, 1958; 1st Sec., Panama City, 1960; FO, 1964; DSAO, 1965; Head of Chancery, Bangkok, 1967; Counsellor and Head of Chancery, Islamabad, 1969; FCO Fellow, Centre of South Asian Studies, Cambridge, 1973; Inspectorate, FCO, 1974; Consul-Gen., Boston, 1977. *Address: c/o* Foreign and Commonwealth Office, SW1; Manor House, West Hendred, Wantage, Oxon. *T:* East Hendred 373.
    See also Sir J. L. Bullard.

BULLARD, Sir Julian Leonard, KCMG 1982 (CMG 1975); HM Diplomatic Service; Deputy Under-Secretary of State, since 1979, and Deputy to the Permanent Under Secretary of State and Political Director, since 1982, Foreign and Commonwealth Office; *b* 8 March 1928; *s* of late Sir Reader Bullard, KCB, KCMG, CIE, and late Miriam, *d* of late A. L. Smith, Master of Balliol Coll., Oxford; *m* 1954, Margaret Stephens; two *s* two *d. Educ:* Rugby; Magdalen Coll., Oxford. Fellow of All Souls Coll., Oxford, 1950-57; Army, 1950-52; HM Diplomatic Service, 1953-: served at: FO, 1953-54; Vienna, 1954-56; Amman, 1956-59; FO, 1960-63; Bonn, 1963-66; Moscow, 1966-68; Dubai, 1968-70; Head of E European and Soviet Dept, FCO, 1971-75; Minister, Bonn, 1975-79. *Address:* 8 Lowndes Close, SW1X 8BZ. *T:* 01-235 4811.
    See also G. L. Bullard.

BULLEN, Air Vice-Marshal Reginald, CB 1975; GM 1945; MA; Senior Bursar and Fellow, Gonville and Caius College, Cambridge, since 1976; *b* 19 Oct. 1920; *s* of Henry Arthur Bullen and Alice May Bullen; *m* 1953, Christiane (*née* Phillips); one *s* one *d. Educ:* Grocers' Company School. 39 Sqdn RAF, 458 Sqdn RAAF, 1942-44; Air Min., 1945-50; RAF Coll. Cranwell, 1952-54; psa 1955; Exchange USAF, Washington, DC, 1956-58; RAF Staff Coll., Bracknell, 1959-61; Admin. Staff Coll., Henley, 1962; PSO to Chief of Air Staff, 1962-64; NATO Defence Coll., 1965; HQ Allied Forces Central Europe, 1965-68; Dir of Personnel, MoD, 1968-69; idc 1970; Dep. AO i/c Admin, HQ Maintenance Comd, 1971; AOA Training Comd, 1972-75. Chm., Huntingdon DHA, 1981-. MA Cantab, 1975. FBIM 1979 (MBIM 1971). *Publications:* various articles. *Address:* Gonville and Caius College, Cambridge; *c/o* Lloyds Bank Ltd, Cox's & King's Branch, 6 Pall Mall, SW1Y 5NH. *Clubs:* Athenæum, Royal Air Force.

BULLEN, Dr William Alexander; *s* of Francis Lisle Bullen and Amelia Morgan; *m* 1943, Phyllis (marr. diss. 1955), *d* of George Leeson; three *d. Educ:* Merchant Taylors' Sch., Crosby; London Hosp. Med. Coll. MRCS, LRCP, MRCGP. Royal Tank Regt, UK and Middle East, 1939-45 (Hon. Major). Med. Dir, Boehringer Pfizer, 1957, Sales Man. 1958; Pres., Pfizer Canada, 1962; Gen. Man., Pfizer Consumer Opns UK, 1964-66; Chm., Coty (England), 1965; Man. Dir, Scribbans Kemp, 1966; Man. Dir, 1967-77, Dep. Chm., 1974, Chm., 1975-81, Thomas Borthwick & Sons Ltd; Chm., Whitburgh Investments, 1976-80. Président-Directeur Général, Boucheries Bernard, 1977-81. FBIM 1975. Liveryman, Butchers' Co.; Freeman, City of London. *Publication:* paper on acute heart failure in London Hosp. Gazette. *Recreations:* sailing, reading, music. *Address:* Church House, Diptford, near Totnes, Devon. *Club:* Royal Thames Yacht.

BULLER; *see* Manningham-Buller, family name of Viscount Dilhorne.

BULLER; *see* Yarde-Buller, family name of Baron Churston.

BULLER, Prof. Arthur John, ERD 1969; FRCP; Research Development Director, Muscular Dystrophy Group of GB, since 1982; Emeritus Professor of Physiology, University of Bristol; Research Development Director, Muscular Dystrophy Group of Great Britain and Northern Ireland, since 1982; Honorary Consultant in Clinical Physiology, Bristol District Hospital (T); *b* 16 Oct. 1923; *s* of Thomas Alfred Buller, MBE, and Edith May Buller (*née* Wager); *m* 1946, Helena Joan (*née* Pearson); one *s* one *d* (and one *d* decd). *Educ:* Duke of York's Royal Military Sch., Dover; St Thomas's Hosp. Med. Sch. (MB, BS); BSc; FRCP 1976; FIBiol 1978; FRSA 1979. Kitchener Scholar, 1941-45; Lectr in Physiology, St Thomas' Hosp., 1946-49. Major, RAMC (Specialist in Physiology; Jt Sec., Military Personnel Research Cttee), 1949-53. Lectr in Medicine, St Thomas' Hosp., 1953-57. Royal Society Commonwealth Fellow, Canberra, Aust., 1958-59. Reader in Physiology, King's Coll., London, 1961-65; Gresham Prof. of Physic 1963-65; Prof. of Physiology, Univ. of Bristol, 1965-82, Dean, Fac. of Medicine, 1976-78, on secondment as Chief Scientist, DHSS, 1978-81. Visiting Prof., Monash Univ., Aust., 1972; Long Fox Meml Lectr, Bristol, 1978. Member: Bd of Governors, Bristol Royal Infirmary, 1968-74; Avon Health Authority (T), 1974-78; MRC, 1975-81; Chm., Neurosciences and Mental Health Bd, MRC, 1975-77. External Scientific Advisor, Rayne Inst., St Thomas' Hosp., 1979-. Milroy Lectr, RCP, 1983. *Publications:* contribs to books and various jls on normal

and abnormal physiology. *Recreations:* clarets and conversation. *Address:* Flat 8, Seawalls, Seawalls Road, Bristol BS9 1PG. *T:* Bristol 683225. *Club:* Athenæum.

BULLERS, Ronald Alfred, QFSM 1974; FIFireE; Chief Officer, London Fire Brigade, since 1981; *b* 17 March 1931; *m* 1954, Mary M. Bullers. *Educ:* Queen Mary's Grammar Sch., Walsall. Deputy Asst Chief Officer, Lancashire Fire Brigade, 1971; Dep. Chief Officer, Greater Manchester Fire Brigade, 1974, Chief Officer, 1977. Adviser: Nat. Jt Council for Local Authority Fire Brigades, 1977-; Assoc. of Metropolitan Authorities, 1977-. *Recreations:* gardening, travel. *Address:* London Fire Brigade Headquarters, 8 Albert Embankment, SE1 7SD. *T:* 01-582 3811.

BULLEY, Rt. Rev. Sydney Cyril; *b* 12 June 1907; 2nd *s* of late Jethro Bulley, Newton Abbot, Devon; unmarried. *Educ:* Newton Abbot Grammar Sch.; Univ. of Durham. BA 1932; MA 1936; DipTh 1933; Van Mildert Scholar, Univ. of Durham, 1932; Hon. DD Dunelm 1972. Deacon, 1933; priest, 1934; Curate of Newark Parish Church, 1933-42; Director of Religious Education, Diocese of Southwell, 1936-42; Vicar of St Anne's, Worksop, 1942-46; Chaplain to High Sheriff of Notts, 1943; Hon. Canon of Southwell Minster, 1945; Vicar and Rural Dean of Mansfield, 1946-51; Proctor in Convocation of York, 1945-51; Vicar of Ambleside with Rydal, 1951-59; Archdeacon of Westmorland and Dir Religious Education, Diocese Carlisle, 1951-58; Archdeacon of Westmorland and Furness, 1959-65; Suffragan Bishop of Penrith, 1959-66; Hon. Canon of Carlisle Cathedral, 1951-66; Examining Chaplain to the Bishop of Carlisle, 1952-66; Bishop of Carlisle, 1966-72; Chaplain and Tutor, All Saints' Coll., Bathurst, NSW, 1973-74; Hon. Asst Bishop, Dio. Oxford, 1974. Chaplain to the Queen, 1955-59. Chairman: Southwell Diocese Education Cttee, 1942-51; Worksop Youth Cttee, 1943-45; Mansfield Youth Cttee, 1947-48; Member: Southwell Diocese Board of Finance, 1942-51; Central Council of the Church for Education, 1951-54; Westmorland Education Cttee, 1951-64. Gov. Derby Training Coll., 1938-51, Ripon Training Coll., 1953-58, Lancaster Coll. of Education, 1963-69; Chairman of Governing Body: Casterton Sch., 1962-72; St Chad's Coll., Durham Univ., 1969; St Mary's Sch., Wantage, 1979. *Publication:* The Glass of Time (autobiog.), 1981. *Address:* The Manor, Longcot, Faringdon, Oxon.

BULLMORE, (John) Jeremy David; Chairman, J. Walter Thompson Co. Ltd, since 1976; *b* 21 Nov. 1929; *s* of Francis Edward Bullmore and Adeline Gabrielle Bullmore (*née* Roscow); *m* 1958, Pamela Audrey Green; two *s* one *d. Educ:* Harrow; Christ Church, Oxford. Military service, 1949-50. Joined J. Walter Thompson Co. Ltd, 1954: Dir, 1964; Dep. Chm., 1975; Dir, J. Walter Thompson Co. (USA), 1980-. Member: Nat. Cttee for Electoral Reform, 1978-; Bd, Royal Hosp. and Home for Incurables, Putney, 1977-; Chm., Advertising Assoc., 1981-. *Address:* 20 Embankment Gardens, SW3. *T:* 01-351 2197. *Club:* Arts.

BULLOCK, family name of **Baron Bullock.**

BULLOCK, Baron *cr* 1976 (Life Peer), of Leafield, Oxon; **Alan Louis Charles Bullock,** Kt 1972; FBA 1967; Founding Master of St Catherine's College, Oxford, 1960-80, Fellow, since 1980; Vice-Chancellor, Oxford University, 1969-73; *b* 13 Dec. 1914; *s* of Frank Allen Bullock; *m* 1940, Hilda Yates, *d* of Edwin Handy, Bradford; three *s* one *d* (and one *d* decd). *Educ:* Bradford Grammar Sch.; Wadham Coll., Oxford (Scholar). MA; 1st Class Lit Hum, 1936; 1st Class, Modern Hist., 1938. DLitt Oxon, 1969. Fellow, Dean and Tutor in Modern Hist., New Coll., 1945-52; Censor of St Catherine's Soc., Oxford, 1952-62; Chairman: Research Cttee of RIIA, 1954-78; Nat. Advisory Council on the Training and Supply of Teachers, 1963-65; Schools Council, 1966-69; Cttee on Reading and Other Uses of English Language, 1972-74 (Report, A Language for Life, published 1975); Trustees, Tate Gallery, 1973-80; Friends of Ashmolean Museum; Cttee of Enquiry on Industrial Democracy, 1976 (Report publ. 1977); Member: Arts Council of Great Britain, 1961-64; SSRC, 1966; Adv. Council on Public Records, 1965-77; Organising Cttee for the British Library, 1971-72. Joined Social Democratic Party, 1981. Trustee: Aspen Inst.; The Observer, 1957-69. Dir, The Observer, 1977-81. Raleigh Lectr, British Acad., 1967; Stevenson Meml Lectr, LSE, 1970; Leslie Stephen Lectr, Cambridge, 1976. Hon. Fellow: Merton Coll.; Wadham Coll.; Linacre Coll.; Wolfson Coll. For. Mem., Amer. Acad. Arts and Sciences, 1972. Hon. Dr Univ. Aix-Marseilles; Hon. DLitt: Bradford; Reading; Open; Newfoundland. Hon. FRIBA. Chevalier Légion d'Honneur, 1970. *Publications:* Hitler, A Study in Tyranny, 1952 (rev. edn 1964); The Liberal Tradition, 1956; The Life and Times of Ernest Bevin, Vol. I, 1960, Vol. II, 1967; (ed) The Twentieth Century, 1971; (ed with Oliver Stallybrass) Dictionary of Modern Thought, 1977; (ed) The Faces of Europe, 1980. Gen. Editor (with Sir William Deakin) of The Oxford History of Modern Europe. *Address:* 45 Granville Court, Cheney Lane, Oxford. *T:* Oxford 44336; The Old Manse, Leafield, Oxon.

BULLOCK, Edward Anthony Watson; HM Diplomatic Service; HM Consul-General, Marseilles, since 1978; *b* 27 Aug. 1926; *yr s* of the late Sir Christopher Bullock, KCB, CBE, and late Lady Bullock (*née* Barbara May Lupton); *m* 1953, Jenifer Myrtle, *e d* of late Sir Richmond Palmer, KCMG, and late Lady Palmer (*née* Margaret Isabel Abel Smith); two *s* one *d. Educ:* Rugby Sch. (Scholar); Trinity Coll., Cambridge (Exhibitioner). HM Forces, 1944-47; Joined Foreign Service, 1950; served: FO, 1950-52; Bucharest, 1952-54; Brussels, 1955-58; FO, 1958-61; La Paz, 1961-65; ODM, 1965-67;

FCO, 1967-69; Havana, 1969-72; HM Treasury, 1972-74; Head of Pacific Dependent Territories Dept, FCO, 1974-77. *Address:* c/o National Westminster Bank Ltd, 36 St James's Street, SW1. *Clubs:* United Oxford & Cambridge University; Union (Cambridge).
See also R. H. W. Bullock.

BULLOCK, Hugh, Hon. GBE 1976 (Hon. KBE 1957; Hon. OBE 1946); FRSA 1958; Chairman and Chief Executive Officer, Calvin Bullock Ltd; *b* 2 June 1898; *s* of Calvin Bullock and Alice Katherine (*née* Mallory); *m* 1933, Marie Leontine' Graves; two *d. Educ:* Hotchkiss Sch.; Williams Coll. (BA). Investment banker since 1921; President and Director: Calvin Bullock, Ltd, 1944-66; Bullock Fund, Ltd; Canadian Fund, Inc.; Canadian Investment Fund, Ltd; Dividend Shares, Inc.; Chairman and Director: Carriers & General Corp.; Nation-Wide Securities Co.; US Electric Light & Power Shares, Inc.; High Income Shares Inc.; Money Shares Inc. Civilian Aide to Sec. of the Army, for First Army Area, United States, 1952-53 (US Army Certificate of Appreciation). Trustee: Roosevelt Hospital; Estate and Property of Diocesan Convention of New York; Williams Coll., 1960-68. President: Pilgrims of US; Calvin Bullock Forum. Member Exec. Cttee, Marshall Scholarship Regional Cttee, 1955-58. Member: Amer. Legion; Academy of Political Science; Amer. Museum of Nat. History; Acad. of Amer. Poets (Dir.); Assoc. Ex-mems Squadron A (Gov. 1945-50); Council on Foreign Relations; Ends of the Earth; English-Speaking Union; Foreign Policy Assoc.; Investment Bankers Assoc. of Amer. (Gov. 1953-55); New England Soc.; Nat. Inst. of Social Sciences (Pres. 1950-53); Newcomen Soc.; St George's Soc. Hon. LLD; Hamilton Coll., 1954; Williams Coll., 1957. 2nd Lieut Infantry, European War, 1914-18; Lieut-Col, War of 1939-45 (US Army Commendation Ribbon). Distinguished Citizens' Award, Denver, 1958; Exceptional Service Award, Dept of Air Force, 1961; US Navy Distinguished Public Service Award, 1972. Assoc. KStJ 1961, and Vice-Pres. Amer. Society. Knight Comdr, Royal Order of George I (Greece), 1964. Is an Episcopalian. *Publication:* The Story of Investment Companies, 1959. *Address:* (office) 33rd Floor, 1 Wall Street, New York, New York, NY 10005. *T:* Bowling Green 9-8800; (home) 1030 Fifth Avenue, New York, NY 10028. *T:* Trafalgar 9-5858. *Clubs:* White's (London); Bond, Century, Racquet and Tennis, Recess, River, Union, Williams, Church, New York Yacht (New York); Denver County (Denver, Colo.); Chevy Chase, Metropolitan (Washington); Edgartown Yacht (Cdre) (Mass); West Side Tennis (Forest Hills, NY); Mount Royal (Montreal).

BULLOCK, Prof. Kenneth, PhD, MSc, CChem, FRSC, MChemA, FPS; Professor of Pharmacy, Manchester University, 1955-70, Emeritus 1970; *b* 27 Dec. 1901; *s* of late James William Bullock, Wigan, Lancashire; *m* 1926, Winifred Mary, *d* of late Rev. F. Ives Cater. *Educ:* Wigan Grammar Sch.; Manchester Univ. Research and Technical Chemist, 1925-32; joined teaching staff of Pharmacy Dept, Manchester Univ., 1932; Lecturer, 1937; Senior Lecturer, 1946; Reader, 1950. Chairman, British Pharmaceutical Conf., 1956. Formerly Examiner for Univs of Dublin, London, Nottingham, and Manchester and for Pharmaceutical Socs of Great Britain and Ireland. *Publications:* original contributions to science, mainly in Journal of Pharmacy and Pharmacology. *Recreations:* gardening and biology. *Address:* 39 Knutsford Road, Wilmslow, Cheshire SK9 6JB. *T:* Wilmslow 522892.

BULLOCK, Richard Henry Watson, CB 1971; Consultant, Faulkbourn Consultancy Services, and Company Director; retired Civil Servant; Consultant Director: Electronic Components Industry Federation; Berkeley Seventh Round Ltd; Grosvenor Place Amalgamations Ltd; Director, Rugby School Development Campaign; *b* 12 Nov. 1920; *er s* of late Sir Christopher Bullock, KCB, CBE and late Lady Bullock (*née* Barbara May Lupton); *m* 1946, Beryl Haddan, *o d* of late Haddan J. Markes, formerly Malay Civil Service; one *s* one *d. Educ:* Rugby Sch. (Scholar); Trinity Coll., Cambridge (Scholar). Joined 102 OCTU (Westminster Dragoons), Nov. 1940; Commnd Westminster Dragoons, (2nd County of London Yeo.), 1941; served in England, NW Europe (D-day), Italy, Germany, 1941-45; Instructor, Armoured Corps Officers' Training Sch., India, 1945-46; demobilized 1947, rank of Major. Established in Home Civil Service by Reconstruction Competition; joined Min. of Supply as Asst Principal, 1947; Principal, 1949; Asst Sec., 1956; on loan to War Office, 1960-61; Ministry of Aviation, 1961-64; Under-Sec., 1963; Min. of Technology, 1964-70. Head of Space Div., 1969-70, Dep. Sec., 1970; DTI, 1970-74; Dept of Industry, 1974-80; retired Nov. 1980. Mem., BOTB, 1975-78. Vice-Pres. (and Chm. 1978-82), Westminster Dragoons Assoc.; Vice-Pres., Old Rugbeian Soc., 1982. *Recreations:* fly-fishing, hockey (playing and administering) (President: Dulwich Hockey Club, 1962-; Rugby Alternatives HC, 1976-; Civil Service Hockey Cttee/Assoc., 1978-), lawn tennis, watching cricket. *Address:* 17 Deodar Road, SW15 2NP. *T:* 01-788 5378. *Clubs:* Army and Navy, MCC, Hurlingham; Union (Cambridge).
See also E. A. W. Bullock.

BULLOUGH, Prof. Donald Auberon, FSA, FRHistS; Professor of Mediaeval History, University of St Andrews, since 1973; *b* 13 June 1928; *s* of late William Bullough and of Edith Shirley (*née* Norman); *m* 1963, Belinda Jane Turland; two *d. Educ:* Newcastle-under-Lyme High Sch.; St John's Coll., Oxford (BA 1950, MA 1952). FRHistS 1958; FSA 1968. National Service, 1946-48: commnd RA (attached RHA). Harmsworth Scholar, Merton Coll., Oxford, 1951; Medieval Scholar, British Sch. at Rome, 1951; Fereday Fellow, St John's Coll., Oxford, 1952-55; Lectr, Univ. of Edinburgh, 1955-66; Prof. of Med. History, Univ. of Nottingham, 1966-73. Vis. Prof., Southern Methodist Univ., Dallas, Tex, 1965-66; British Acad.

Overseas Vis. Fellow, Max-Planck-Inst. für Gesch., 1972-73; Ford's Lectr in English Hist., Univ. of Oxford, 1979-80; Scott-Hawkins Lectr, Southern Methodist Univ., Dallas, 1980; Andrew Mellon Lectr, Catholic Univ. Washington, 1980; Lilly Endowment Fellow, Pennsylvania Univ., 1980-81. Mem. Council, Exec., Finance Cttee, British School at Rome, 1975- (Chm. Faculty of Hist., Archeol., and Letters, 1975-79). Senate Mem., Nottingham Univ. Council, 1970-73; Mem., Nottingham Univ. Hosp. Management Cttee, 1971-74; Senatus Assessor, St Andrews Univ. Ct, 1977-81. Dir, Paul Elek Ltd, 1968-79. Major RA (TA); seconded OTC, 1957-67. *Publications:* The Age of Charlemagne, 1965 (2nd edn 1974; also foreign trans); (ed with R. L. Storey) The Study of Medieval Records, 1971; contrib. XIX, XX, XXI, Settimana di Studi del Centro ital. di St. sull'Alto Medioevo; contrib. TLS, British and continental hist. jls, philatelic jls. *Recreations:* talk, looking at buildings, postal history. *Address:* 23 South Street, St Andrews, Fife. *T:* St Andrews 72932. *Clubs:* Athenæum, Savage; Scottish Arts (Edinburgh).

BULLOUGH, Prof. William Sydney, PhD, DSc Leeds; Professor of Zoology, Birkbeck College, University of London, 1952-81, now Emeritus; *b* 6 April 1914; *o s* of Rev. Frederick Sydney Bullough and Letitia Anne Cooper, both of Leeds; *m* 1942, Dr Helena F. Gibbs (*d* 1975), Wellington, NZ; one *s* one *d. Educ:* William Hulme Grammar Sch., Manchester; Grammar Sch., Leeds; Univ. of Leeds. Lecturer in Zoology, Univ. of Leeds, 1937-44, McGill Univ., Montreal, 1944-46; Sorby Fellow of Royal Society of London, 1946-51; Research Fellow of British Empire Cancer Campaign, 1951-52; Hon. Fellow, Soc. for Investigative Dermatology (US). *Publications:* Practical Invertebrate Anatomy, 1950; Vertebrate Sexual Cycles, 1951; (for children) Introducing Animals, 1953; Introducing Animals-with-Backbones, 1954; Introducing Man, 1958; The Evolution of Differentiation, 1967; scientific papers on vertebrate reproductive cycles, hormones, and chalones published in a variety of journals. *Recreation:* gardening. *Address:* Oktober, 5 Uplands Road, Kenley, Surrey. *T:* 01-660 9764.

BULLUS, Wing Comdr Sir Eric (Edward), Kt 1964; journalist; *b* 20 Nov. 1906; 2nd *s* of Thomas Bullus, Leeds; *m* 1949, Joan Evelyn, *er d* of H. M. Denny; two *d. Educ:* Leeds Modern Sch.; Univ. of Leeds. Commnd RAFVR Aug. 1940; served War of 1939-45; Air Min. War Room, 1940-43; joined Lord Louis Mountbatten's staff in SE Asia, 1943; Wing Comdr, 1944; served India, Burma and Ceylon; demobilized, 1945. Journalist Yorkshire Post, Leeds and London, 1923-46. Mem. Leeds City Council, 1930-40; Sec., London Municipal Soc., 1947-50; Mem., Harrow UDC, 1947-50; Vice-Pres. Assoc. of Municipal Corps, 1953. MP (C) Wembley N, 1950-Feb. 1974; PPS to Secretary for Overseas Trade, and to Minister of State, 1953-56, to Minister of Aviation, 1960-62, to Secretary of State for Defence, 1962-64. FRGS, 1947; Fellow Royal Statistical Society, 1949. Foundation Mem. of Brotherton Collection Cttee of Univ. of Leeds, 1935; Member: Archdeaconry Council of Delhi, 1944; Management Board, Cambridge Mission to Delhi, 1954; House of Laity, Church Assembly, 1960. Ripon Diocesan Reader, 1929; London Diocesan Reader, 1947; St Alban's Diocesan Reader, 1960; Canterbury Diocesan Reader, 1967; Central Readers' Board, 1960; London Readers' Board, 1954; Council Westfield Coll., Univ. of London. Pres., Soc. of Yorkshiremen in London, 1969-70. *Publications:* History of Leeds Modern School, 1931; History of Church in Delhi, 1944; History of Lords and Commons Cricket, 1959. *Recreations:* played Headingley RU Football Club 15 years and Yorkshire Amateurs Assoc. Football Club; cricket and swimming (bronze and silver medallions). *Address:* Westway, Herne Bay, Kent. *Clubs:* St Stephen's Constitutional, MCC.

BULMER, Esmond; see Bulmer, J. E.

BULMER, Dr Gerald; Rector of Liverpool Polytechnic, since April 1970; *b* 17 Nov. 1920; *s* of Edward and Alice Bulmer; *m* 1943, Greta Lucy Parkes, MA; two *d. Educ:* Nunthorpe Sch., York; Selwyn Coll., Cambridge. BA 1941; PhD 1944; MA 1945; CChem, FRSC. Asst Master, King's Sch., Canterbury, 1945-49; Sen. Lecturer, Woolwich Polytechnic, 1949-53; Head of Dept of Science and Metallurgy, Constantine Technical Coll., Middlesbrough, 1954-57; Vice-Principal, Bolton Technical Coll., 1958-59; Principal, West Ham Coll. of Technology, 1959-64; Dir, Robert Gordon's Inst. of Technology, Aberdeen, 1965-70. Mem. Council CNAA, 1967-78. Freeman City of York, 1952. *Publications:* papers on organic sulphur compounds in Jl Chem. Soc. and Nature. *Address:* Liverpool Polytechnic, Liverpool; 11 Capilano Park, Winifred Lane, Aughton, Ormskirk, Lancs.

BULMER, (James) Esmond; MP (C) Kidderminster, since Feb. 1974; *b* 19 May 1935; *e s* of late Edward Bulmer and Margaret Rye; *m* 1959, Morella Kearton; three *s* one *d. Educ:* Rugby; King's Coll., Cambridge (BA); and abroad. Commissioned Scots Guards, 1954. Dir, H. P. Bulmer Holdings Ltd, 1962- (Dep. Chm., 1980, Chm., 1982-); Mem. Exec. Cttee, Nat. Trust. *Recreations:* gardening, fishing. *Address:* The Old Rectory, Pudleston, Leominster, Herefordshire HR6 0RA. *T:* Steensbridge 234. *Club:* Boodle's.

BULMER-THOMAS, Ivor, FSA 1970; writer; Chairman, Ancient Monuments Society; Chairman, Faith Press; Hon. Director, Friends of Friendless Churches; Vice-President, Church Union; *b* 30 Nov. 1905; *s* of late A. E. Thomas, Cwmbran, Newport, Mon.; *m* 1st, 1932, Dilys (*d* 1938), *d* of late Dr W. Llewelyn Jones, Merthyr Tydfil; one *s* ; 2nd, 1940, Margaret Joan, *d* of late E. F. Bulmer, Adam's Hill, Hereford; one *s* two *d.* Assumed additional surname Bulmer by deed poll, 1952. *Educ:* West Monmouth Sch.,

Pontypool; Scholar of St John's and Senior Demy of Magdalen Coll., Oxford. 1st Class Math. Mods, 1925; 1st Class Lit. Hum., 1928; Liddon Student, 1928; Ellerton Essayist, 1929; Junior Denyer and Johnson Scholar, 1930; MA 1937; represented Oxford against Cambridge at Cross-country Running, 1925–27, and Athletics, 1926–28, winning Three Miles in 1927; Welsh International Cross-country Runner, 1926; Gladstone Research Student at St Deiniol's Library, Hawarden, 1929–30; on editorial staff of Times, 1930–37; chief leader writer to News Chronicle, 1937–39; acting deputy editor, Daily Telegraph, 1953–54. Served War of 1939–45 with Royal Fusiliers (Fusilier), 1939–40, and Royal Norfolk Regt (Captain, 1941), 1940–42, 1945. Contested (Lab) Spen Valley div., 1935; MP Keighley, 1942–50 (Lab 1942–48; C 1949–50); contested Newport, Mon (C), 1950. Parliamentary Secretary, Ministry of Civil Aviation, 1945–46; Parliamentary Under-Sec. of State for the Colonies, 1946–47. Delegate to Gen. Assembly, UN, 1946; first UK Mem., Trusteeship Council, 1947. Mem. of the House of Laity of the Church Assembly, 1950–70, of General Synod, 1970–. Lately Chm., Executive Cttee, Historic Churches Preservation Trust; Chm., Redundant Churches Fund, 1969–76. Hon. DSc Warwick, 1979. Stella della Solidarietà Italiana, 1948. *Publications:* Coal in the New Era, 1934; Gladstone of Hawarden, 1936; Top Sawyer, a biography of David Davies of Llandinam, 1938; Greek Mathematics (Loeb Library), 1939–42; Warfare by Words, 1942; The Problem of Italy, 1946; The Socialist Tragedy, 1949;(ed) E. J. Webb, The Names of the Stars, 1952; The Party System in Great Britain, 1953; The Growth of the British Party System, 1965; (ed) St Paul, Teacher and Traveller, 1975; East Shefford Church, 1978; contrib. to Dictionary of Scientific Biography, Classical Review. *Address:* 12 Edwardes Square, W8 6HG. *T:* 01-602 6267; Old School House, Farnborough, Berks; Ty'n Mynydd, Rhoscolyn, Anglesey. *Clubs:* Athenæum; Vincent's (Oxford).

BULPITT, Cecil Arthur Charles, (Philip Bulpitt); Director, BIM Foundation Ltd, since 1977 (Chairman, 1979–82); Vice-Chairman, BIM, since 1979; *b* 6 Feb. 1919; *s* of A. E. Bulpitt; *m* 1943, Joyce Mary Bloomfield; one *s* one *d. Educ:* Spring Grove Sch., London; Regent Street Polytechnic. Territorial Army, to rank of Staff Capt., RA, 1937–45. Carreras Ltd: joined firm, 1935; Gen. Manager, 1960; Asst Managing Dir, 1962; Dep. Chm. and Chief Exec., 1968; Chm. 1969–70. Dir, Thomas Tilling, 1973–81; Chairman: Tilling Construction Services Ltd, 1978–81; InterMed Ltd, 1978–81; Graham Building Services Ltd, 1979–81; Newey & Eyre Gp Ltd, 1979–81. MIPM, 1955; FBIM, 1963. *Recreations:* fishing, climbing, reading, travelling. *Address:* 3 Potters Cross, Iver Heath, Bucks. *T:* Iver Heath 4571. *Clubs:* Travellers', Lansdowne; Stoke Poges Golf.

BULTEEL, Christopher Harris, MC 1943; Headmaster, Ardingly College, 1962–80; *b* 29 July 1921; *er s* of late Major Walter Bulteel and Constance (*née* Gaunt), Charlestown, Cornwall; *m* 1958, Jennifer Anne, *d* of late Col K. E. Previté, OBE and of Frances (*née* Capper), Hindgaston, Marnhull, Dorset; one *s* two *d. Educ:* Wellington Coll.; Merton Coll., Oxford. Served War with Coldstream Guards, 1940–46 (MC). Assistant Master at Wellington Coll., 1949–61; Head of history dept, 1959–61. Hon. Sec., Wellington Coll. Mission, 1959–61. *Recreations:* natural history, sailing. *Address:* Point Cottage, Helford, Helston, Cornwall. *T:* Manaccan 598.

BUMBRY, Grace; opera singer and concert singer; *b* St Louis, Mo, 4 Jan. 1937. *Educ:* Boston Univ.; Northwestern Univ.; Music Academy of the West (under Lotte Lehmann). Debut: Paris Opera, 1960; Vienna State Opera, 1963; Salzburg Festival, 1964; Metropolitan Opera, 1965; La Scala, 1966. Appearances also include: Bayreuth Festival, 1961–; Royal Opera Covent Garden, London, 1963–, and in opera houses in Europe, S America and USA. Film, Carmen, 1968. Richard Wagner Medal, 1963. Hon. Dr of Humanities, St Louis Univ., 1968; Hon. doctorates: Rust Coll., Holly Spring, Miss; Rockhurst Coll., Kansas City; Univ. of Missouri at St Louis. Has made numerous recordings. *Recreations:* tennis, sewing, flying, body building, psychology, entertaining. *Address:* c/o Columbia Artists Management, attention R. Douglas Sheldon, 165 West 57th Street, New York, NY 10019, USA.

BUMSTEAD, Kenneth, CVO 1958; CBE 1952; *b* 28 April 1908; *s* of Ernest and Nellie Bumstead; *m* 1940, Diana, *e d* of Archibald Smollett Campbell; three *s. Educ:* Wallasey Grammar Sch.; Emmanuel Coll., Cambridge. Entered China Consular Service, 1931; served Peking, Tsingtao, Canton, Chungking, Shanghai, 1932–42 (Consul 1939); Madagascar, 1943; London, 1944; Chicago, 1945–48; Shanghai, 1949–52 (Consul-General, 1950); Seattle, 1953–56; Consul-General, Rotterdam, 1957–61; FO Res. Dept, 1963–72, retired. Commander, Order of Oranje Nassau. *Address:* 4 Perry Way, Hilland, Headley, Hants GU35 8NE.

BUNBURY; *see* McClintock-Bunbury, family name of Baron Rathdonnell.

BUNBURY, Bishop of, since 1977; **Rt. Rev. Arthur Stanley Goldsworthy;** *b* 18 Feb. 1926; *s* of Arthur and Doris Irene Goldsworthy; *m* 1952, Gwen Elizabeth Reeves; one *s* one *d. Educ:* Dandenong High School, Vic; St Columb's Theological Coll., Wangaratta. Deacon 1951, priest 1952; Curate of Wodonga, in charge of Bethanga, 1951–52; Priest of Chiltern, 1952; Kensington, Melbourne, 1955; Yarrawonga, Wangaratta, 1959; Shepparton (and Archdeacon), 1972; Parish Priest of Wodonga, and Archdeacon of Diocese of Wangaratta, 1977. Chaplain to Community of the Sisters of the Church, 1956–77. *Recreations:* music, bush walking. *Address:* Bishopscourt, Bunbury, WA 6230, Australia. *T:* 097.21-2163.

BUNBURY, Brig. Francis Ramsay St Pierre, CBE 1958; DSO 1945, Bar 1953; *b* 16 June 1910; *s* of late Lt-Col Gerald Bruce St Pierre Bunbury, Indian Army, and Frances Mary Olivia (*née* Dixon); *m* 1933, Elizabeth Pamela Somers (*née* Liscombe) (*d* 1969); one *s* one *d. Educ:* Rugby and Sandhurst. Commissioned into The Duke of Wellington's Regiment, 1930; Staff Coll., 1941; commanded 1st Bn, The King's Own Royal Regt, Italian Campaign, 1944–45 (despatches, DSO); commanded 1st Bn The Duke of Wellington's Regt, 1951–54, Germany, Korea (Bar to DSO), Gibraltar; AAG, War Office, 1954–56; commanded 50 Independent Infantry Brigade, Cyprus, 1956–59 (despatches, CBE). Dep. Adjt-Gen., Rhine Army, 1959–61; retired 1962.

BUNBURY, Sir (John) William Napier, 12th Bt, *cr* 1681; *b* 3 July 1915; *s* of Sir Charles H. N. Bunbury, 11th Bt, and Katherine (*d* 1965), *d* of H. E. Reid; *S* father, 1963; *m* 1940, Pamela, *er d* of late T. Sutton, Westlecott Manor, Swindon; three *s* (and one *s* decd). *Educ:* Eton; Jesus Coll., Cambridge. 2nd Lieut (TA), 1936. Commissioned, KRRC, 1940; Capt. 1942. High Sheriff of Suffolk 1972. *Recreations:* golf, fishing. *Heir: e* surv. *s* Michael William Bunbury, [*b* 29 Dec. 1946; *m* 1976, Caroline, *d* of Col A. D. S. Mangnall; one *s* one *d*]. *Address:* Hollesley House, Hollesley, Woodbridge, Suffolk. *T:* Shottisham 411250. *Club:* Army and Navy.

BUNBURY, Sir Michael; *see* Bunbury, Sir R. D. M. R.

BUNBURY, Lt-Comdr Sir (Richard David) Michael (Richardson-), 5th Bt, *cr* 1787; RN; *b* 27 Oct. 1927; *er s* of Richard Richardson-Bunbury (*d* 1951) and Florence Margaret Gordon, *d* of late Col Roger Gordon Thomson, CMG, DSO, late RA; *S* kinsman 1953; *m* 1961, Jane Louise, *d* of late Col Alfred William Pulverman, IA; two *s. Educ:* Royal Naval College, Dartmouth. Midshipman (S), 1945; Sub-Lieut (S), 1947; Lieut (S), 1948; Lieut-Comdr, 1956; retd 1967. *Heir: s* Roger Michael Richardson-Bunbury, *b* 2 Nov. 1962. *Address:* Woodlands, Mays Hill, Worplesdon, Guildford, Surrey. *T:* Guildford 232034.

BUNBURY, Sir William; *see* Bunbury, Sir J. W. N.

BUNCH, Austin Wyeth, CBE 1978 (MBE 1974); Chairman, Electricity Council, 1981–83; Chairman, British Electricity International Ltd, since 1977; *b* 1918; *s* of Horace William and Winifred Ada Bunch; *m* 1944, Joan Mary Peryer; four *d. Educ:* Christ's Hospital. FCA, CompIEE. Deloitte, Plender, Griffiths, 1935–48; Southern Electricity Board, 1949–76; Area Man., Newbury, 1962; Area Man., Portsmouth, 1966; Dep. Chm., 1967; Chm., 1974. Dep. Chm., Electricity Council, 1976–81. *Recreation:* sports for the disabled. *Address:* Sumner, School Lane, Cookham, Berks.

BUNDY, McGeorge; Professor of History, New York University, since 1979; *b* 30 March 1919; *s* of Harvey Hollister Bundy and Katharine Lawrence Bundy (*née* Putnam); *m* 1950, Mary Buckminster Lothrop; four *s. Educ:* Yale Univ. AB 1940. Political analyst, Council on Foreign Relations, 1948–49. Harvard University: Vis. Lectr, 1949–51; Associate Prof. of Government, 1951–54; Prof., 1954–61; Dean, Faculty of Arts and Sciences, 1953–61. Special Asst to the Pres. for National Security Affairs, 1961–66; President of the Ford Foundation, 1966–79. Mem., American Political Science Assoc. *Publications:* (with H. L. Stimson) On Active Service in Peace and War, 1948; The Strength of Government, 1968; (ed) Pattern of Responsibility, 1952. *Address:* Department of History, New York University, Room 501, 19 University Place, New York, NY 10003, USA.

BUNFORD, John Farrant, MA, FIA; Hon.FFA; Director, National Provident Institution for Mutual Life Assurance, since 1964 (Manager and Actuary 1946–64); *b* 4 June 1901; *s* of late John Henry Bunford and Ethel Farrant Bunford; *m* 1929, Florence Louise, *d* of late John and Annie Pearson, Mayfield, Cork; two *s* one *d. Educ:* Christ's Hosp.; St Catharine's Coll., Cambridge. (MA). Scottish Amicable Life Assurance Soc., 1923–29. Royal Exchange Assurance, 1929–32; National Provident Institution: Dep. Asst Actuary, 1932; Asst Sec., 1933; Asst Manager, 1937. Institute of Actuaries: Fellow, 1930; Hon. Sec., 1944–45; Vice-Pres., 1948–50; Treas., 1952–53; Pres., 1954–56. Hon. Fellow the Faculty of Actuaries, 1956. *Recreation:* gardening. *Address:* 14 Shepherds Way, Liphook, Hants. *T:* Liphook 722594.

BUNKER, Albert Rowland, CB 1966; Chairman: Civil Service Pensioners Joint Consultative Committee; Executive Committee, First Division Pensioners Group; Member: Public Service Pensioners Council; Official Side Panel of Civil Service Appeal Board; *b* 5 Nov. 1913; *er* and *o* surv. *s* of late Alfred Francis Bunker and late Ethel Trudgian, Lanjeth, St Austell, Cornwall; *m* 1939, Irene Ruth Ella, 2nd *d* of late Walter and late Ella Lacey, Ealing; two *s. Educ:* Ealing Gram. Sch. Served in Royal Air Force, 1943–45. Service in Cabinet Office, HM Treasury, Ministry of Home Security and Home Office; Dep. Under Sec. of State, Home Office, 1972–75. *Recreation:* golf. *Address:* 35 Park Avenue, Ruislip. *T:* Ruislip 35331. *Clubs:* Royal Air Force; Denham Golf.

BUNN, Dr Charles William, FRS 1967; Dewar Research Fellow of the Royal Institution of Great Britain, 1963–72; *b* 15 Jan. 1905; *s* of Charles John Bunn and Mary Grace Bunn (*née* Murray); *m* 1931, Elizabeth Mary Mold; one *s* one *d. Educ:* Wilson's Grammar Sch., London, SE; Exeter Coll.,

Oxford. BA, BSc, (Oxon.), 1927; DSc (Oxon.), 1953; FInstP, 1944. Mem. Research Staff, Imperial Chemical Industries, Winnington, Northwich, Cheshire (now Mond Div.), 1927-46; transf. to ICI Plastics Div., 1946 (Div. Leader of Molecular Structure Div. of Research Dept, and later of Physics Div.); retd 1963. Chm., X-Ray Analysis Group of The Inst. of Physics and The Physical Soc., 1959-62. Amer. Physical Soc. Award in High Polymer Physics (Ford Prize), 1969. *Publications:* Chemical Crystallography, 1945 (2nd edn 1961); Crystals, Their Role in Nature and in Science, 1964; papers in: Proc. Royal Society; Trans. Faraday Soc.; Acta Crystallographica. *Recreations:* music and horticulture. *Address:* 6 Pentley Park, Welwyn Garden City, Herts. *T:* Welwyn Garden 23581.

BUNN, Douglas Henry David; Chairman: All England Jumping Course, Hickstead; White Horse Caravan Co. Ltd; *b* 1 March 1928; *s* of late G. H. C. Bunn and A. A. Bunn; *m* 1st, 1952, Rosemary Pares Wilson; three *d* ; 2nd, 1960, Susan Dennis-Smith; two *s* one *d* ; 3rd, 1979, Lorna Kirk; one *d*. *Educ:* Chichester High Sch.; Trinity Coll., Cambridge (MA). Called to Bar, Lincoln's Inn; practised at Bar, 1953-59; founded Hickstead, 1960; British Show Jumping Team, 1957-68; Vice-Chm., British Show Jumping Assoc. (Chm. 1969); Mem. British Equestrian Fedn; founded White Horse Caravan Co. Ltd, 1958; Chm., Southern Aero Club, 1968-72. *Recreations:* horses, flying, books, wine. *Address:* Hickstead Place, Sussex. *T:* Bolney 268. *Clubs:* Buck's, Saints and Sinners.

BUNSTER, Don Alvaro; Fellow, Institute of Development Studies, University of Sussex, since 1977; *b* 25 May 1920; *m* 1965, Raquel de Bunster (*née* Parot); three *s*. *Educ:* National Institute, Santiago; School of Law, Univ. of Chile; Faculty of Law, Central Univ. of Brazil, Rio de Janeiro; Faculty of Jurisprudence, Univ. of Rome, Italy. Judge Advocate of the Army, Chile, 1950-57; Prof. of Penal Law, Univ. of Chile, 1953-73; Gen. Sec., Univ. of Chile, 1957-69. Vis. Prof., Univ. of Calif., Berkeley, 1966-67. Vice-Pres., Inst. of Penal Sciences, 1969-70; Dir, Enciclopedia Chilena, 1970; Chilean Ambassador to Court of St James's, 1971-73; lecturing at Univs of Oxford and Liverpool, 1973-74; Senior Vis. Fellow, Centre of Latin-American Studies, Univ. of Cambridge, 1974-77. *Publications:* La malversación de caudales públicos, 1948; La voluntad del acto delictivo, 1950; articles, descriptive commentaries, etc, in various nat. and foreign magazines. *Recreations:* music, theatre. *Address:* 194 Surrenden Road, Brighton BN1 6NN.

BUNTING, Prof. Arthur Hugh, CMG 1971; Professor of Agricultural Development Overseas, Reading University, 1974-82; *b* 7 Sept. 1917; *e s* of S. P. and R. Bunting; *m* 1941, Elsie Muriel Reynard; three *s*. *Educ:* Athlone High Sch., Johannesburg, S Africa; Univ. of the Witwatersrand, Johannesburg; Oriel Coll., University of Oxford. BSc 1937. BSc (Hons Botany), MSc 1938, Witwatersrand; Rhodes Scholar for the Transvaal, 1938; DPhil Oxford, 1941; FIBiol. Asst Chemist, Rothamsted Experimental Station, 1941-45; Member Human Nutrition Research Unit, Medical Research Council, 1945-47; Chief Scientific Officer, Overseas Food Corporation, 1947-51; Senior Research Officer, Sudan Min. of Agriculture, 1951-56; Prof. of Agricultural Botany, 1956-73, Dean, Faculty of Agriculture, 1965-71, Univ. of Reading. Pres., Assoc. of Applied Biologists, 1963-64, Hon. Mem., 1979-; Jt Editor, Journal of Applied Ecology, 1964-68. Foundn Mem., 1968-72, and Mem., 1974-80, Vice-Chm. 1975-77, and Chm. 1977-80, Board of Trustees, Internat. Inst. of Tropical Agriculture, Ibadan, Nigeria; Member: UK Council for Scientific Policy, 1970-72; UN Adv. Cttee on the Applications of Science and Technology to Develt (ACAST), 1972-75; Governing Bodies, Grassland Res. Inst., Hurley, 1959-77, Plant Breeding Inst., Cambridge, 1960-76; Consultant and then Mem., Scientific Cttee, Cotton Res. Corp., 1958-76 (Chm., 1972-76); Member: Panel of Scientific Advisers, CDC, 1957-; Meteorological Cttee, MoD(Air), 1973-; IUC, later IUPC, 1958-68, 1974-; CICHE, 1981-; Foundn Mem., Internat. Bd for Plant Genetic Resources, 1974-78. LLD *hc* Ahmadu Bello Univ., 1968. *Publications:* (ed) Change in Agriculture, 1970; (ed jtly) Policy and Practice in Rural Development, 1976; (ed jtly) Advances in Legume Science, 1980; numerous papers in scientific and agricultural journals. *Recreation:* music. *Address:* 27 The Mount, Caversham, Reading, Berks. *T:* Reading 472487.

BUNTING, Basil; poet; *b* 1 March 1900; *s* of T. L. Bunting, MD, and Annie Bunting (*née* Cheesman); *m* 1st, 1930, Marian Culver; two *d* (one *s* decd); 2nd, 1948, Sima Alladadian; one *s* one *d*. *Educ:* Ackworth Sch.; Leighton Park Sch.; Wormwood Scrubbs; London Sch. of Economics. Has had a varied undistinguished career. President: The Poetry Soc., 1972-76; Northern Arts, 1973-76. Hon. Life Vis. Prof., Univ. of Newcastle upon Tyne. Hon. DLitt Newcastle upon Tyne, 1971. *Publications:* Redimiculum Matellarum, 1930; Poems, 1950; The Spoils, 1965; Loquitur, 1965; First Book of Odes, 1965; Briggflatts, 1966; Collected Poems, 1968. *Address:* The Cottage, Greystead, Tarset, Hexham NE48 1LE.

BUNTING, Sir (Edward) John, AC 1982; KBE 1977 (CBE 1960); Kt 1964; BA; Australian civil servant (retired); Chairman, Roche-Maag Ltd, since 1978; National Co-ordinator, Sir Robert Menzies Memorial Trust; *b* Ballarat, Vic, 13 Aug. 1918; *s* of late G. B. Bunting; *m* 1942, (Pauline) Peggy, *d* of late D. C. MacGruer; three *s*. *Educ:* Trinity Grammar School, Melbourne; Trinity Coll., Univ. of Melbourne (BA Hons). Asst Sec., Prime Minister's Dept, Canberra, 1949-53; Official Sec., Office of the High Commissioner for Australia, London, 1953-55; Deputy Sec., Prime Minister's Dept, Canberra, 1955-58; Secretary: Australian Cabinet, 1959-75; Prime Minister's Dept,

1959-68; Dept of the Cabinet Office, 1968-71; Dept of the Prime Minister and Cabinet, 1971-75; High Comr for Australia in UK, 1975-77. Mem. Australia Council, 1978-82. *Recreations:* cricket, golf, music, reading. *Address:* 8 Arnhem Place, Red Hill, ACT 2603, Australia. *Clubs:* Commonwealth (Canberra); Athenæum (Melbourne); Melbourne Cricket; Royal Canberra Golf.

BUNTING, John Reginald, CBE 1965; author and educational consultant; *b* 12 Nov. 1916; *s* of John Henry and Jane Bunting, Mansfield; *m* 1940, May Hope Sturdy, Malvern, Jamaica; no *c*. *Educ:* Queen Elizabeth's Grammar Sch., Mansfield; Queen's Coll., Oxford (MA, DipEd). Sen. English Master and Housemaster, Munro Coll., Jamaica, 1939-42; Headmaster, Wolmer's Sch., Jamaica, 1943-49; Principal, King's Coll., Lagos, 1949-54; Actg Dir of Broadcasting, Nigeria, June-Oct. 1952; Actg Inspector of Educn, Western Region, Nigeria, April-Oct. 1954; Dep. Chief Federal Adviser on Educn, Nigeria, 1954-58; Chief Federal Adviser on Educn, Nigeria, 1958-61; Educn Adviser, W Africa, Brit. Council, 1961 and Head, Graduate VSO Unit, 1962; Asst Controller, Educn Div., 1964; Evans Bros Ltd: Editorial Consultant, 1965-68; Dir, Overseas Sales and Publications, 1969; Dir-Gen., Centre for Educnl Develt Overseas, 1970-74; Adviser on Educn to British Council, 1974-76. Hon. Jt Editor, W African Jl of Educn, 1956-61. *Publications:* Civics for Self-Government, 1956; New African English Course (Book 5), 1960; (jtly) Caribbean Civics, 1960; (jtly) Civics for East Africa, 1961; Primary English Course (Book 6): for Ghana, 1962, for Sierra Leone, 1969, for West Cameroon, 1971; Civics: a course in citizenship and character training, 1973; To Light a Candle, 1976. *Recreations:* cricket, tennis, golf, fishing, painting, bowls. *Address:* 8 Springhill Gardens, Lyme Regis, Dorset. *T:* Lyme Regis 3726. *Clubs:* MCC, Royal Commonwealth Society; Lyme Regis Golf.

BUNTON, George Louis, MChir (Cantab), FRCS; Consultant Surgeon to University College Hospital, London, since 1955, to Metropolitan Hospital, 1957-70, and to Northwood Hospital since 1958; *b* 23 April 1920; *s* of late Surg. Capt. C. L. W. Bunton, RN, and Marjorie Denman; *m* 1948, Margaret Betty Edwards; one *d*. *Educ:* Epsom; Selwyn Coll., Cambridge; UCH. MB, BChir Cantab 1951; MRCS, LRCP 1944; FRCS 1951; MChir Cantab 1955. Served in RNVR 1944-47. Mem., Court of Examiners, RCS. Fellow, Assoc. of Surgeons; Fellow, British Assoc. of Pædiatric Surgeons. *Publications:* contribs. to journals and books on surgical subjects. *Recreations:* gardening, music. *Address:* Hither Dennets, Hawridge Common, Chesham, Bucks. *T:* Cholesbury 565.

BUÑUEL, Luis; film director; *b* Calanda, Spain, 22 Feb. 1900; *s* of Leonardo and Maria Buñuel; *m* Jeanne Rucar; two *s*. *Educ:* Univ. of Madrid; Académie du Cinéma, Paris. *Films include:* Un Chien Andalou, 1929; L'Age d'Or, 1930; Las Hurdes (Land Without Bread), 1936; España, 1936; Gran Casino, 1947; El Gran Calavera, 1949; Los Olivados (The Young and the Damned), 1950 (Best Dir Award, Cannes Film Festival, 1951); Subida al Cielo (Mexican Bus Ride), 1952 (best avant-garde film, Cannes, 1952); El (This Strange Passion), 1952; Abismos de Pasión, 1952; The Adventures of Robinson Crusoe, 1953; Ensayo de un Crimen (The Criminal Life of Archibald de la Cruz), 1955; Cela S'Appelle l'Aurore, 1955; La Mort en ce Jardin, 1956; Nazarin, 1958 (Special Internat. Jury Prize, Cannes, 1959); La Jeune Fille, 1959; La Fièvre Monte à El Pau, 1960; The Young One, 1960; The Republic of Sin, 1960; Viridiana, 1961 (jtly, Golden Palm Award, Cannes, 1961); Island of Shame, 1961; El Angel Exterminador, 1962 (Best film, Cannes, 1962); Le Journal d'une Femme de Chambre, 1964; Simon of the Desert, 1965; Belle de Jour, 1966 (Golden Lion of St Mark Award, Venice Film Festival, 1967); La Voie Lactée, 1969; Tristana, 1970; The Discreet Charm of the Bourgeoisie, 1972; Le Fantôme de la liberté, 1974; Cet Obscur Objet du Désir, 1978. *Address:* c/o Greenwich Film Production, 72 avenue des Champs-Elysées, 75008 Paris, France.

BUNYARD, Robert Sidney, QPM 1980; Chief Constable, Essex Police, since 1978; *b* 20 May 1930; *s* of Albert Percy Bunyard and Nellie Maria Bunyard; *m* 1948, Ruth Martin; two *d*. *Educ:* Queen Elizabeth Grammar Sch., Faversham; Regent Street Polytechnic Management Sch. (Dip. in Man. Studies). MIPM. Metropolitan Police, 1952; Asst Chief Constable, Leics, 1972; Dep. Chief Constable, Essex, 1977. *Publications:* Police: organization and command, 1978; Police Management Handbook, 1979; contrib. police jls. *Recreations:* music, opera, painting. *Address:* Police Headquarters, Springfield, Chelmsford, Essex CM2 6DA. *T:* Chelmsford 67267.

BURBIDGE, (Eleanor) Margaret, (Mrs Geoffrey Burbidge), FRS 1964; Professor of Astronomy, since 1964, Director, Center for Astrophysics and Space Sciences, since 1979, University of California at San Diego; *d* of late Stanley John Peachey, Lectr in Chemistry and Research Chemist, and of Marjorie Peachey; *m* 1948, Geoffrey Burbidge, *qv* ; one *d*. *Educ:* Francis Holland Sch., London; University Coll., London (BSc); Univ. of London Observatory (PhD). Asst Director, 1948-50, Actg Director, 1950-51, Univ. of London Observatory; fellowship from Internat. Astron. Union, held at Yerkes Observatory, Univ. of Chicago, 1951-53; Research Fellow, California Inst. of Technology, 1955-57; Shirley Farr Fellow, later Associate Prof., Yerkes Observatory, Univ. of Chicago, 1957-62; Research Astronomer, Univ. of California at San Diego, 1962-64; Dir, Royal Greenwich Observatory, 1972-73. Abby Rockefeller Mauzé Vis. Prof., MIT, 1968. Member: American Acad. of Arts and Scis, 1969; US Nat. Acad. of Scis, 1978; Nat. Acad. of Scis Cttee on Science and Public Policy, 1979-81; President: Amer. Astronomical Soc., 1976-78; Amer. Assoc. for Advancement of Science, 1982. Hon. DSc: Smith Coll., Massachusetts, USA, 1963; Sussex, 1970; Bristol, 1972; Leicester,

1972; City, 1974; Michigan, 1978; Massachusetts, 1978; Williams Coll., 1979. Fellow University Coll., London, 1967; Hon. Fellow, Lucy Cavendish Collegiate Soc., 1971. Catherine Wolfe Bruce Medal, Astr. Soc. of the Pacific, 1982. *Publications:* Quasi-Stellar Objects (with Geoffrey Burbidge), 1967 (also USA, 1967); contribs to learned jls (mostly USA), Handbuch der Physik, etc. *Address:* Center for Astrophysics and Space Sciences, C-011, University of California at San Diego, La Jolla, California 92093, USA. *T:* (714) 452-4477. *Club:* University Woemn's.

BURBIDGE, Geoffrey, FRS 1968; Director, Kitt Peak National Observatory, Arizona, since 1978; *b* 24 Sept. 1925; *s* of Leslie and Eveline Burbidge, Chipping Norton, Oxon; *m* 1948, Margaret Peachey (*see* E. M. Burbidge); one *d. Educ:* Chipping Norton Grammar Sch.; Bristol University; Univ. Coll., London. BSc (Special Hons Physics) Bristol, 1946; PhD London, 1951. Asst Lectr, UCL, 1950-51; Agassiz Fellow, Harvard Univ., 1951-52; Research Fellow, Univ. of Chicago, 1952-53; Research Fellow, Cavendish Lab., Cambridge, 1953-55; Carnegie Fellow, Mount Wilson and Palomar Observatories, Caltech, 1955-57; Asst Prof., Dept of Astronomy, Univ. of Chicago, 1957-58; Assoc. Prof., 1958-62; Assoc. Prof., Univ. of California, San Diego, 1962-63, Prof. of Physics, 1963-78. Phillips Vis. Prof., Harvard Univ., 1968. Elected Fellow, UCL, 1970. Pres., Astronomical Soc. of the Pacific, 1974-76; Trustee, Assoc. Universities Inc., 1973-; Editor, Annual Review Astronomy and Astrophysics, 1973-. *Publications:* (with Margaret Burbidge) Quasi-Stellar Objects, 1967; scientific papers in Astrophysical Jl, Nature, Rev. Mod. Phys, Handbuch der Physik, etc. *Address:* Kitt Peak National Observatory, PO Box 26732, Tucson, Arizona 85726, USA.

BURBIDGE, Mrs Geoffrey; *see* Burbidge, E. M.

BURBIDGE, Sir Herbert (Dudley), 5th Bt *cr* 1916; *b* 13 Nov. 1904; *s* of Herbert Edward Burbidge (*d* 1945) 2nd *s* of 1st Bt, and Harriet Georgina (*d* 1952), *d* of Henry Stuart Hamilton, Londonderry; *S* cousin, 1974; *m* 1933, Ruby Bly, *d* of Charles Ethelbert Taylor; one *s. Educ:* University Sch., Victoria, BC, Canada. Harrods Ltd, Knightsbridge, 1923-28; R. P. Clarke (Stock Brokers), Vancouver, BC, 1929-31; Merchandising Manager, Silverwood Industries of Vancouver, BC, 1931-70; retired 1970. President: Vancouver Executive Club, 1942; Vancouver Sales Executive Club, 1948. Mem. Bd of Referees, Workmen's Compensation Bd, 1943-61. *Recreation:* landscape gardening. *Heir: s* Peter Dudley Burbidge [*b* 20 June 1942; *m* 1967, Peggy Marilyn, *d* of Kenneth Anderson, Ladner, BC; one *s* one *d*]. *Address:* 12549/27th Avenue, Surrey, British Columbia V4A 2M6, Canada. *Club:* Vancouver Executive.

BURBIDGE, Mrs Margaret; *see* Burbidge, E. M.

BURBIDGE, Prof. Percy William, CBE 1957; MSc NZ; BARes Cambridge; Professor Emeritus of Physics, University of Auckland; *b* 3 Jan. 1891; *s* of R. W. Burbidge and Agnes Mary Edwards; *m* 1923, Kathleen Black, Wellington; one *s* three *d. Educ:* Wellington Boys' Coll.; Victoria Univ. Coll., Wellington; Trinity Coll., Cambridge. Took 1st class honours in Physics (NZ); gained 1851 Exhibition Research Scholarship, 1913; volunteered NZEF, 1917; took BA Research at Cavendish Laboratory, 1920; Carnegie Corporation Travel Grants, 1933, 1951; Mem. NZ Defence Scientific Advisory Cttee, 1940-47. *Publications:* papers on Fluctuations of Gamma Rays, Absorption of X-Rays, Humidity, Frictional Electricity, Photoconduction in Rock Salt. *Address:* University, Auckland, NZ.

BURBIDGE, Ven. (John) Paul, MA Oxon and Cantab; Archdeacon of Richmond and Canon Residentiary of Ripon Cathedral, since 1976; *b* 21 May 1932; *e s* of late John Henry Gray Burbidge and Dorothy Vera Burbidge; *m* 1956, Olive Denise Grenfell; four *d. Educ:* King's Sch., Canterbury; King's Coll., Cambridge; New Coll., Oxford; Wells Theolog. Coll. Nat. Service Commn in RA, 1957. Jun. Curate, 1959, Sen. Curate, 1961, Eastbourne Parish Church; Vicar Choral of York Minster, 1962-66; Chamberlain, 1962-76; Canon Residentiary, 1966-76; Succentor Canonicorum, 1966; Precentor, 1969-76. *Recreation:* model engineering. *Address:* The Old Vicarage, Sharow, Ripon. *T:* Ripon 5771.
See also S. N. Burbidge.

BURBIDGE, Stephen Nigel, MA; Under Secretary, Department of Trade (Exports), since 1980; *b* 18 July 1934; *s* of late John Henry Gray Burbidge and late Dorothy Vera (*née* Pratt). *Educ:* King's Sch., Canterbury; Christ Church, Oxford (Open History Schol. MA). National Service, 2 Lieut, RA, 1953-55. Asst Principal, Bd of Trade, 1958-62; Trade Commissioner, Karachi, 1963-65; 1st Secretary (Economic), Rawalpindi, 1965-67; Principal, BoT (marine), 1967-71; CS Selection Bd, 1971; Assistant Secretary: Dept of Trade (finance, research, marine), 1971-78; Dept of Industry (industrial policy), 1978-80. *Recreations:* active sports, reading, collecting. *Address:* Department of Trade, 1 Victoria Street, SW1. *T:* 01-215 5343. *Clubs:* Royal Commonwealth Society; Rye Golf; West Sussex Golf.
See also J. P. Burbidge.

BURBURY, Hon. Sir Stanley Charles, KCMG 1981; KCVO 1977; KBE 1958; Governor of Tasmania, 1973-82; *b* 2 Dec. 1909; *s* of Daniel Charles Burbury and Mary Burbury (*née* Cunningham); *m* 1934, Pearl Christine Barren; no *c. Educ:* Hutchins Sch., Hobart; The Univ. of Tasmania. LLB 1933; Hon. LLD 1970. Admitted to Bar, 1934; QC 1950; Solicitor-Gen. for Tasmania, 1952; Chief Justice, Supreme Court of Tasmania, 1956-73. Pres.,

Nat. Heart Foundn of Australia, 1967-73; Nat. Pres., Winston Churchill Memorial Trust. KStJ 1974. Hon. Col, Royal Tasmanian Regt, 1974-82. *Recreations:* music and lawn bowls. *Address:* 3 Mona Street, Kingston, Tasmania 7150, Australia. *Clubs:* Tasmanian, Athenæum, Royal Hobart Bowls (Hobart).

BURCH, Cecil Reginald, CBE 1958; FRS 1944; BA; DSc; Research Associate, 1936-44 and Fellow, since 1944, of H. H. Wills Physics Laboratory, Bristol University; Warren Research Fellow in Physics, 1948-66; *b* 12 May 1901; *s* of late George James Burch, MA, DSc, FRS, and of Constance Emily Jeffries, sometime Principal of Norham Hall, Oxford; *m* 1937, Enid Grace (*d* 1981), *o d* of Owen Henry Morice, Ipswich; one *d. Educ:* Oxford Preparatory School; Oundle Sch.; Gonville and Caius Coll., Cambridge. Physicist, Research Dept, Metropolitan Vickers Co., Trafford Park, Manchester, 1923-33; Leverhulme Fellow (in Optics), Imperial Coll. of Science and Technology, 1933-35. Rumford Medal, Royal Society, 1954. *Publications:* A Contribution to the Theory of Eddy Current Heating (with N. Ryland Davis); scientific papers on various subjects in physics and technology in Phil. Mag., Proc. Royal Society, etc. *Recreation:* walking. *Address:* 2 Holmes Grove, Henleaze, Clifton, Bristol BS9 4EE. *T:* Bristol 621650.

BURCH, Maj.-Gen. Geoffrey, CB 1977; Director of Management Development, Courtaulds Group, since 1977; *b* 29 April 1923; *s* of late Henry James Burch, LDS, RCS (Eng); *m* 1948, Jean Lowrie Fyfe; one *s. Educ:* Felsted Sch. Served War: commissioned 2/Lt RA, 1943; served in Italy, 1943-45. India, 1946-47; ptsc 1951; psc 1953; British Defence Liaison Staff, Ottawa, 1962-65; Comd Flintshire and Denbighshire Yeomanry, 1965-66. Programme Director UK/Germany/Italy 155mm project, 1968-71; Dep. Commandant, Royal Military Coll. of Science, 1971-73; Dir-Gen. Weapons (Army), 1973-75; Dep. Master-General of the Ordnance, 1975-77. Col Comdt, RA, 1978-. FInstD, FBIM. *Recreations:* cricket, golf, squash, tennis, bridge. *Address:* c/o Lloyds Bank Ltd, Cox's & King's Branch, 6 Pall Mall, SW1Y 5NH. *Clubs:* Royal Automobile, MCC.

BURCH, Rt. Rev. William Gerald, DD; *m* 1942, Carroll Borrowman; four *d. Educ:* University of Toronto (BA); Wycliffe Coll., Toronto. Deacon, 1936; Priest, 1938. Curate, Christ Church, Toronto, 1936-40; Incumbent, Scarborough Junction with Sandown Park, 1940-42; Rector: St Luke, Winnipeg, 1942-52; All Saints, Windsor, 1952-56; Exam. Chaplain to Bishop of Huron, 1955-56; Canon of Huron, 1956; Dean and Rector, All Saints Cathedral, Edmonton, 1956-60; Suffragan Bishop of Edmonton, 1960-61; Bishop of Edmonton, 1961-76. *Address:* 901 Richmond Avenue, Victoria, BC V8S 3Z4, Canada. *T:* (604) 598 4369.

BURCHAM, Prof. William Ernest, CBE 1980; FRS 1957; Emeritus Professor of Physics, Birmingham University, since 1981; *b* 1 Aug. 1913; *er s* of Ernest Barnard and Edith Ellen Burcham; *m* 1942, Isabella Mary (*d* 1981), *d* of George Richard Todd and of Alice Louisa Todd; two *d. Educ:* City of Norwich Sch.; Trinity Hall, Cambridge. Stokes Student, Pembroke Coll., Cambridge, 1937; Scientific Officer, Ministry of Aircraft Production, 1940, and Directorate of Atomic Energy, 1944; Fellow of Selwyn Coll., Cambridge, 1944; Univ. Demonstrator in Physics, Cambridge, 1945; Univ. Lecturer in Physics, Cambridge, 1946; Oliver Lodge Prof. of Physics, Univ. of Birmingham, 1951-80. Member: SRC, 1974-78; Council, Royal Soc., 1977-79. *Publications:* Nuclear Physics: an Introduction, 1963; Elements of Nuclear Physics, 1979; papers in Nuclear Physics A, Phys. Letters B, Phys. Rev. Letters. *Address:* 95 Witherford Way, Birmingham B29 4AN. *T:* 021-472 1226.

BURCHFIELD, Dr Robert William, CBE 1975; Editor, A Supplement to the Oxford English Dictionary, since 1957; Chief Editor, The Oxford English Dictionaries, since 1971; Senior Research Fellow, St Peter's College, Oxford, since 1979 (Tutorial Fellow, 1963-79); *b* Wanganui, NZ, 27 Jan. 1923; *s* of Frederick Burchfield and Mary Burchfield (*née* Blair); *m* 1949, Ethel May Yates (marr. diss. 1976); one *s* two *d; m* 1976, Elizabeth Austen Knight. *Educ:* Wanganui Technical Coll.; New Zealand, 1934-39; Victoria University Coll., Wellington, NZ, 1940-41, 1946-48; MA (NZ) 1948; Magdalen Coll., Oxford, 1949-53; BA (Oxon) 1951, MA 1955. Served War, Royal NZ Artillery, NZ and Italy, 1941-46. NZ Rhodes Scholar, 1949. Junior Lectr in English Lang., Magdalen Coll., Oxford, 1952-53; Lectr in English Lang., Christ Church, Oxford, 1953-57; Lectr, St Peter's Coll., Oxford, 1955-63. Hon. Sec., Early English Text Society, 1955-68 (Mem. Council, 1968-80); Editor, Notes and Queries, 1959-62; Pres., English Assoc., 1978-79. Hon. For. Mem., American Acad. of Arts and Scis, 1977-. Hon. DLitt, Liverpool, 1978. *Publications:* (with C. T. Onions and G. W. S. Friedrichsen) The Oxford Dictionary of English Etymology, 1966; A Supplement of Australian and New Zealand Words, in the Pocket Oxford Dictionary (5th edn), 1969; A Supplement to the Oxford English Dictionary, vol. I (A-G), 1972, vol. II (H-N), 1976, vol. III (O-Scz), 1982; (with D. Donoghue and A. Timothy) The Quality of Spoken English on BBC Radio, 1979; The Spoken Language as an Art Form, 1981; The Spoken Word, 1981; contribs to: Medium Ævum, Notes and Queries, Times Lit. Supp., Trans Philological Soc., Encounter, etc. *Recreations:* adapting to village life, investigating spoken English, travelling. *Address:* The Barn, 14 The Green, Sutton Courtenay, Oxon. *T:* Sutton Courtenay 645.

BURCHMORE, Air Cdre Eric, CBE 1972 (OBE 1963; MBE 1945); JP; Technicare International Ltd, Newbury, since 1981; *b* 18 June 1920; *s* of Percy William Burchmore and Olive Eva Ingledew; *m* 1941, Margaret Ovendale;

one *d. Educ:* Robert Atkinson Sch., Thornaby; RAF Halton; Heriot-Watt Coll., Edinburgh. CEng, MRAeS. Royal Air Force: Aircraft Apprentice, 1936-39; Fitter 2, 1939-41; Engr Officer, 1941: served in Fighter Comd; Air Comd SE Asia, 1943-45; Air Min. and various home postings; Far East, 1952-55; London and Staff Coll.; Near East, 1960-62; comd RAF Sealand, 1963-66; Far East, 1967-68; Dir RAF Project (subseq. Dir Harrier Projects), MoD(PE), 1969-75; retired 1975. Dep. Dir of Housing, London Borough of Camden, 1975-80. JP Godstone, Surrey, 1979. *Address:* 3 Broad Walk, Caterham, Surrey CR3 5EP. *T:* Caterham 44391. *Club:* Royal Air Force.

BURDEN, family name of **Baron Burden.**

BURDEN, 2nd Baron *cr* 1950, of Hazlebarrow, Derby; **Philip William Burden;** *b* 21 June 1916; *s* of 1st Baron Burden, CBE, and of Augusta, *d* of David Sime, Aberdeen; *S* father, 1970; *m* 1951, Audrey Elsworth, *d* of Major W. E. Sykes; three *s* three *d. Educ:* Raines Foundation School. *Heir: s* Hon. Andrew Philip Burden, *b* 20 July 1959. *Address:* Northdown House Farm, Churchinford, near Taunton, Somerset.

BURDEN, Derrick Frank; HM Diplomatic Service, retired; Counsellor and Head of Claims Department, Foreign and Commonwealth Office, 1973-78; *b* 4 June 1918; *s* of late Alfred Burden and Louisa Burden (*née* Dean); *m* 1942, Marjorie Adeline Beckley; two *d. Educ:* Bec Sch., London. Crown Agents, 1936. Served War, King's Royal Rifle Corps, 1939-41. Joined Foreign Office, 1945; Comr-Gen.'s Office, Singapore, 1950-53; 2nd Sec., Moscow, 1954-56; 2nd Sec., Tokyo, 1957-59; HM Consul, Lourenço Marques, 1959-61; FO, 1962-67 (Asst Head of Protocol Dept, 1965); HM Consul, Khorramshahr (Iran), 1967-69; 1st Sec., Nairobi, 1969-71; HM Consul, Luanda (Angola), 1972-73. *Recreations:* golf, gardening. *Address:* 12 Strathmore Drive, Charvil, Reading, Berks RG10 9QT. *T:* Twyford (Berks) 340564. *Clubs:* Travellers'; Nairobi (Nairobi); Badgemore Park Golf, Phyllis Court (Henley-on-Thames).

BURDEN, Sqn Ldr Sir Frederick Frank Arthur, Kt 1980; MP (C) Gillingham, Kent, since 1950; *b* 27 Dec. 1905; *s* of A. F. Burden, Bracknell, Berks; *m* Marjorie Greenwood; one *d. Educ:* Sloane Sch., Chelsea. Company Director. Served War of 1939-45, RAF: first with a Polish unit, later with SE Asia Command, and on the staff of Lord Louis Mountbatten. Pres., Textile Distributors Assoc., 1981-. Freeman of Gillingham, 1971. *Recreation:* fishing. *Address:* 291 Latymer Court, W6. *T:* 01-748 1916; The Knapp, Portesham, Dorset. *T:* Abbotsbury 366.

BURDEN, Major Geoffrey Noel, CMG 1952; MBE 1938; *b* 9 Dec. 1898; *s* of late A. G. Burden, Exmouth, Devon; *m* 1927, Yolande Nancy, *d* of late G. H. B. Shaddick, Kenilworth, Cape Town; one *s* one *d. Educ:* Exeter Sch.; Royal Military College, Sandhurst. Served European War, 1914-18, Devon Regt, 1915-18; Indian Army, 1918-23. Joined Colonial Administrative Service, Nyasaland, 1925; Director of Publicity, 1936; Nyasaland Labour Officer to S Rhodesia, 1937-38; Nyasaland/N Rhodesian Labour Officer in the Union of South Africa, 1939; Chief Recruiting Officer, Nyasaland, 1940. War of 1939-45: military service in Somaliland, Abyssinia, and N Rhodesia, King's African Rifles, 1941-43. Asst Chief Sec., Nyasaland, 1945-46; Commissioner of Labour, Gold Coast, 1946-50; Chief Commissioner, Northern Territories, Gold Coast, 1950-53. Nyasaland Govt Representative in S Rhodesia, 1954-63. *Address:* The Croft, Hillside Road, Frensham, Surrey. *T:* Frensham 2584.

BURDER, Sir John Henry, Kt 1944; ED; *b* 30 Nov. 1900; *s* of late H. C. Burder; *m* 1928, Constance Aileen Bailey; two *d. Educ:* Eton College. Joined Jardine Skinner & Co., 1920; Chm., Jardine Henderson Ltd, 1939-47. Chm., Indian Tea Market Expansion Bd, 1939; President: Local Board, Imperial Bank of India, 1943-44; Bengal Chamber of Commerce, 1943-44; Associated Chambers of Commerce of India, 1943-44; Royal Agricultural and Horticultural Soc. of India, 1938-41; Calcutta Soc. for the Prevention of Cruelty to Animals, 1939-41; Lt-Col Commanding Calcutta Light Horse, 1944; Member of Council of State, 1943-44. *Address:* Pytts Piece, Burford, Oxon. *T:* Burford 2287. *Club:* Oriental.

BURDETT, Sir Savile (Aylmer), 11th Bt, *cr* 1665; Managing Director: Rapaway Ltd; Rydraulic Compressors Ltd; *b* 24 Sept. 1931; *s* of Sir Aylmer Burdett, 10th Bt; *S* father, 1943; *m* 1962, June E. C. Rutherford; one *s* one *d. Educ:* Wellington Coll.; Imperial Coll., London. *Heir: s* Crispin Peter Burdett, *b* 8 Feb. 1967. *Address:* Farthings, 35 Park Avenue, Solihull, West Midlands B91 3EJ. *T:* 021-705 3360.

BURDUS, (Julia) Ann; Director of Strategic Planning and Development, Interpublic, since 1981; *b* 4 Sept. 1933; *d* of Gladstone Beaty and Julia W. C. Booth. *Educ:* Durham Univ. (BA Psychology). Clinical psychologist, 1956-60; Res. Exec., Ogilvy, Benson & Mather, 1961-67; Res. Dir, McCann Erickson, 1971-75, Vice Chm., 1975-77; Senior Vice-Pres., McCann Internat., 1977-79; Chm., McCann & Co., 1979-81. Chm., Advertising Assoc., 1980-81. *Recreations:* horse racing, work. *Address:* The Interpublic Group of Companies, 1271 Avenue of the Americas, New York, NY 10020, USA.

BURFORD, Earl of; Murray de Vere Beauclerk; Partner: Burfords, chartered accountants; Burford & Co.; *b* 19 Jan. 1939; *s* and *heir* of 13th Duke of St Albans, *qv* and 1st wife (now Mrs Nathalie C. Eldrid); *m* 1st, 1963, Rosemary Frances Scoones (marr. diss. 1974); one *s* one *d* ; 2nd, 1974, Cynthia

(Lady Hooper), *d* of late Lt-Col W. J. H. Howard, DSO. *Educ:* Tonbridge. Chartered Accountant, 1962. *Heir: s* Lord Vere of Hanworth, *qv. Address:* 3 St George's Court, Gloucester Road, SW7. *T:* 01-589 1771. *Club:* Hurlingham.

BURFORD, Eleanor; *see* Hibbert, Eleanor.

BURGE, James, QC 1965; a Recorder, 1972-75; *b* 8 Oct. 1906; *s* of George Burge, Masterton, New Zealand; *m* 1938, Elizabeth, *d* of Comdr Scott Williams, RN, Dorset; two *s* one *d. Educ:* Cheltenham Coll.; Christ's Coll., Cambridge. Barrister, 1932, Master of the Bench, 1971, Inner Temple; Yarborough Anderson Scholar, Profumo Prizeman, Paul Methuen Prizeman. Pilot Officer RAFVR, 1940; Sqdn Ldr; Dep. Judge Advocate, 1941-44. Formerly Prosecuting Counsel, GPO, at CCC; Deputy Chairman, West Sussex Quarter Sessions, 1963-71. *Address:* Casa Burge, Denia, Spain.

BURGE, Stuart, CBE 1974; freelance director and actor; *b* 15 Jan. 1918; *s* of late H. O. Burge and K. M. Haig; *m* 1949, Josephine Parker; three *s* two *d. Educ:* Eagle House, Sandhurst; Felsted Sch., Essex. Served War of 1939-45, Intell. Corps. Actor; trained Old Vic, 1936-37; Oxford Rep., 1937-38; Old Vic and West End, 1938-39; Bristol Old Vic, Young Vic, Commercial Theatre, 1946-49; 1st Dir, Hornchurch, 1951-53; productions for theatre and TV, 1953-; Dir., Nottingham Playhouse, 1968-74; Artistic Dir., Royal Court Theatre, 1977-80. *Theatre:* Measure for Measure, The Devil is an Ass, Edinburgh Fest. and Nat. Theatre, 1977; Another Country, Greenwich 1981 and Queen's 1982; (actor) The Seagull, Royal Court, 1981. *Television:* Bill Brand, Sons and Lovers, The Old Men at the Zoo, etc. Hon. Prof. of Drama, Nottingham Univ. *Publication:* (ed) King John (Folio Society), 1973. *Address:* c/o Barclay's Bank Ltd, 75 King Street, Hammersmith, W6.

BURGEN, Sir Arnold (Stanley Vincent), Kt 1976; FRS 1964; Master of Darwin College, Cambridge, since 1982; *b* 20 March 1922; *s* of late Peter Burgen and Elizabeth Wolfers; *m* 1946, Judith Browne; two *s* one *d. Educ:* Christ's Coll., Finchley. Student, Middlesex Hospital Med. Sch., 1939-45; Ho. Phys., Middlesex Hospital, 1945; Demonstrator, 1945-48, Asst Lectr, 1948-49, in Pharmacology, Middlesex Hospital Med. Sch. Prof. of Physiology, McGill Univ., Montreal, 1949-62; Dep. Dir, Univ. Clinic, Montreal Gen. Hospital, 1957-62; Sheild Prof. of Pharmacology, Univ. of Cambridge, 1962-71; Fellow of Downing Coll., Cambridge, 1962-71, Hon. Fellow 1972; Dir, Nat. Inst. for Med. Res., 1971-82. Hon. Dir, MRC Molecular Pharmacology Unit, 1967-72. Member: MRC, 1969-71, 1973-77 (Chm., Tropical Medicine Res. Bd, 1977-81); Council, Royal Soc., 1972-73, 1980- (Vice Pres., 1980- Foreign Sec., 1981-); Pres., Internat. Union of Pharmacology, 1972-75; Member: Nat. Biol. Standards Bd, 1975-; Med. Cttee, British Council, 1973-77. Hon. DSc: Leeds, 1973; McGill, 1973. Hon. FRCP Canada. *Publications:* Physiology of Salivary Glands, 1961; papers in Journals of Physiology and Pharmacology. *Recreation:* sculpture. *Address:* Darwin College, Cambridge CB3 9EU; Penshurst, Hill Crescent, Totteridge, N20.

BURGER, Warren Earl; Chief Justice of the United States since 1969; *b* St Paul, Minn, 17 Sept. 1907; *s* of Charles Joseph Burger and Katharine Schnittger; *m* 1933, Elvera Stromberg; one *s* one *d. Educ:* Univ. of Minnesota; St Paul Coll. of Law, later Mitchell Coll. of Law (LLB *magna cum laude*, LLD). Admitted to Bar of Minnesota, 1931; Mem. Faculty, Mitchell Coll. of Law, 1931-46. Partner in Faricy, Burger, Moore & Costello until 1953. Asst Attorney-Gen. of US, 1953-56; Judge, US Court of Appeals, Washington, DC, 1956-69. Chm., ABA Proj. Standards for Criminal Justice. Past Lectr, Law Schools in US and Europe. Hon. Master of the Bench of the Middle Temple, 1969. Pres. Bentham Club, UCL, 1972-73. Chancellor and Regent, Smithsonian Instn, Washington, DC; Hon. Chm., Inst. of Judicial Admin; Trustee: Nat. Gall. of Art, Washington, DC; Nat. Geographic Soc.; Trustee Emeritus: Mitchell Coll. of Law, St Paul, Minn; Macalester Coll., St Paul, Minn; Mayo Foundn, Rochester, Minn. *Publications:* articles in legal and professional jls. *Address:* Supreme Court, Washington, DC 20543, USA.

BURGES, Alan; *see* Burges, N. A.

BURGES, Mrs (Margaret) Betty (Pierpoint), MBE 1937; Headmistress, Staines Preparatory School, since 1973; Chairman, Surrey County Council Conservative Group, since 1980; *d* of Frederick Eales Hanson and Margaret Pierpoint Hanson (*née* Hurst); *m* 1937, Cyril Travers Burges, MA (*d* 1975). *Educ:* Edgbaston High Sch., Birmingham. Civil Service, 1929-37 and 1940-45. Councillor, Surrey County Council, 1967-; Chairman, General Purposes Cttee, 1974-. *Recreations:* walking, travel. *Address:* 1 Gresham Road, Staines, Mddx TW18 2BT. *T:* Staines 52916 and 52852.

BURGES, (Norman) Alan, CBE 1980; MSc, PhD; FIBiol; FLS; Vice-Chancellor, New University of Ulster, Coleraine, Northern Ireland, 1966-Sept. 1976; *b* 5 Aug. 1911; *s* of late Lieut J. C. Burges, East Maitland, NSW; *m* 1940, Florence Evelyn (*née* Moulton); three *d. Educ:* Sydney Univ., Australia; Emmanuel Coll., Cambridge. Graduated, Sydney, BSc Hons., 1931; MSc, 1932; PhD Cambridge, 1937. Senior 1851 Scholar, 1937. Research Fellow, Emmanuel Coll., 1938; Prof. of Botany, Sydney Univ., 1947-52; Dean of Faculty of Science and Fellow of Senate, 1949-52; Holbrook Gaskell Prof. of Botany, Univ. of Liverpool, 1952-66, Acting Vice-Chancellor, 1964-65; Pro-Vice-Chancellor, 1965-66. Hon. Gen. Sec., ANZAAS, 1947-52; President: British Ecological Soc., 1958, 1959; British Mycological Soc., 1962; Mem. Cttee, Nature Conservancy, England, 1959-66; Mem., Waste

Management Adv. Council; Joint Editor, Flora Europæa Project, 1956-. Chm., NI Adv. Council for Education, 1966-75; Chairman: Ulster American Folk Park, 1975-; NI American Bicentennial Cttee, 1975-77; Chm., Nat. Trust NI Cttee, 1978-81. Served War of 1939-45, RAF Bomber Command (despatches). Hon. LLD QUB, 1973; Hon. DTech Loughborough, 1975; Hon. DSc Ulster, 1977. *Publications*: Micro-organisms in the Soil, 1958; (with F. Raw) Soil Biology, 1967; various in scientific journals on plant diseases and fungi. *Recreation*: sailing. *Address*: Beechcroft, Glenkeen Road, Aghadowey, Coleraine, Co. Londonderry. *T*: Aghadowey 224.

BURGES, Maj.-Gen. Rodney Lyon Travers, CBE 1963; DSO 1946; *b* 19 March 1914; *s* of Richard Burges and Hilda Christine Burges (*née* Lyon); *m* 1946, Sheila Marion Lyster Goldby, *d* of H. L. Goldby; one *s* one *d. Educ*: Wellington; RMA, Woolwich. 2nd Lieut RA, 1934; war service in Burma, 1942 and 1944-45; CO The Berkshire Yeomanry (145 Fd Regt, RA), 1945; Comdr, E Battery, RHA, 1949-51; Bt Lt-Col 1953; Dir in comd, 1 RHA, 1954-55; CO 3 RHA, 1955-57; CRA 3 Div., 1958-59; IDC, 1960; Brig. Q (Ops) WO, 1961-63; CCRA, 1 Corps, BAOR, 1963-64; Maj.-Gen. 1964; GOC, Cyprus District, 1964-66; VQMG, MoD, 1966-67. Joined Grieveson, Grant & Co., 1968, Partner 1971, retd 1978; Consultant to Pat Simon Wines Ltd, 1978. Freeman and Liveryman, Fishmongers' Co., 1974. *Recreations*: racing, drinking wine in the sun. *Address*: Freemantle, Over Wallop, Hants. *Club*: Buck's.

BURGES WATSON, Richard Eagleson Gordon; *see* Watson, R. E. G. B.

BURGESS, Anthony, BA, DLitt; FRSL; novelist and critic; *b* 25 Feb. 1917; *s* of Joseph Wilson and Elizabeth Burgess; *m* 1942, Llewela Isherwood Jones, BA (*d* 1968); *m* 1968, Liliana Macellari, *d* of Contessa Maria Lucrezia Pasi della Pergola; one *s. Educ*: Xaverian Coll., Manchester; Manchester Univ. Served Army, 1940-46. Lecturer: Birmingham Univ. Extra-Mural Dept., 1946-48; Ministry of Education, 1948-50; English Master, Banbury Grammar Sch., 1950-54; Education Officer, Malaya and Brunei, 1954-59. Vis. Fellow, Princeton Univ., 1970-71; Distinguished Prof., City Coll., NY, 1972-73. Hon. DLitt Manchester, 1982. *Publications*: Time for a Tiger, 1956; The Enemy in the Blanket, 1958; Beds in the East, 1959 (these three, as The Malayan Trilogy, 1972, and as The Long Day Wanes, 1982); The Right to an Answer, 1960; The Doctor is Sick, 1960; The Worm and the Ring, 1961; Devil of a State, 1961; A Clockwork Orange, 1962 (filmed, 1971); The Wanting Seed, 1962; Honey for the Bears, 1963; The Novel Today, 1963; Language Made Plain, 1964; Nothing like the Sun, 1964; The Eve of Saint Venus, 1964; A Vision of Battlements, 1965; Here Comes Everybody-an introduction to James Joyce, 1965; Tremor of Intent, 1966; A Shorter Finnegans Wake, 1966; The Novel Now, 1967; Enderby Outside, 1968; Urgent Copy, 1968; Shakespeare, 1970; MF, 1971; Joysprick, 1973; Napoleon Symphony, 1974; The Clockwork Testament, 1974; Moses, 1976; A Long Trip to Teatime, 1976; Beard's Roman Women, 1976; ABBA ABBA, 1977; New York, 1977; L'Homme de Nazareth, 1977; Ernest Hemingway and His World, 1978; 1985, 1978; Man of Nazareth, 1979; They Wrote in English (trans.) 1979; The Land Where the Ice Cream Grows, 1979; Earthly Powers, 1980; On Going to Bed, 1982; This Man and Music, 1982; Scripts of TV Series Moses the Lawgiver and Jesus of Nazareth, 1977; trans. Rostand, Cyrano de Bergerac, 1971; trans. Sophocles: Oedipus the King, 1973; as *Joseph Kell*: One Hand Clapping, 1961; Inside Mr Enderby, 1963; as *John Burgess Wilson*: English Literature: A Survey for Students, 1958; contributor to Observer, Spectator, Listener, Encounter, Queen, Times Literary Supplement, Hudson Review, Holiday, Playboy, American Scholar, Corriere della Sera, Le Monde, etc. *Recreations*: music composition, piano-playing, cooking, language-learning, travel. *Address*: 44 rue Grimaldi, Monaco; 1 and 2 Piazza Padella, Bracciano, Italy; 168 Triq Il-Kbira, Lija, Malta.

BURGESS, Claude Bramall, CMG 1958; OBE 1954; Minister for Hong Kong Commercial Relations with the European Communities and the Member States, since 1974; *b* 25 Feb. 1910; *s* of late George Herbert Burgess, Weaverham, Cheshire, and Martha Elizabeth Burgess; *m* 1952, Margaret Joan Webb (marr. diss. 1965); one *s*; *m* 1969, Linda Nettleton, *e d* of William Grothier Beilby, New York. *Educ*: Epworth Coll.; Christ Church, Oxford. Eastern Cadetship in HM Colonial Administrative Service, 1932. Commissioned in RA, 1940; POW, 1941-45; demobilized with rank of Lieut-Col, RA, 1946. Colonial Office, 1946-48. Attended Imperial Defence Coll., London, 1951. Various Government posts in Hong Kong; Colonial Secretary (and Actg Governor on various occasions), Hong Kong, 1958-63, retd; Head of Co-ordination and Develt Dept, EFTA, 1964-73. *Recreations*: tennis, golf. *Address*: British Embassy, Hong Kong Government Office, Avenue Louise 228, 1050 Brussels, Belgium. *T*: 648.38.33; 56 rue Jules Lejeune, 1060 Brussels, Belgium. *T*: 343.32.20. *Club*: Carlton.

BURGESS, Rev. Canon David John; Canon of St George's Chapel, Windsor, since 1978; *b* 4 Aug. 1939; *e s* of Albert Burgess and Mary Burgess (*née* Kelsey); *m* 1976, Dr Kathleen Louise, *d* of Philip Lindsay Costeloe; one *s* one *d. Educ*: King's School, Peterborough; Trinity Hall, Cambridge; Cuddesdon Theological Coll. Orthodox Studentship, Halki, Istanbul, 1963-64. Curate, All Saints, Maidstone, 1965; Assistant Chaplain, University Coll., Oxford, 1966; Fellow, 1969; Chaplain, 1970; Domestic Bursar, 1971. Hon. Fellow, Inst. of Clerks of Works, 1978. *Publications*: articles and reviews. *Recreations*: alpine walking, opera, art, cooking. *Address*: 6 The Cloisters, Windsor Castle, Berks. *T*: Windsor 66313.

BURGESS, Lt.-Gen. Sir Edward Arthur, KCB 1982; OBE 1972; Commander, UK Field Army, since 1982; *b* 30 Sept. 1927; *s* of Edward Burgess and Alice Burgess; *m* 1954, Jean Angelique Leslie Henderson; one *s* one *d. Educ*: All Saints Sch., Bloxham; Lincoln Coll., Oxford; RMA, Sandhurst. Commnd RA 1948; served Germany and ME, 1949-59; psc 1960; GSO 2 WO, 1961-63; served Germany and Far East, 1963-65; jssc 1966; Mil. Asst to C-in-C BAOR, 1966-67; GSO I (DS) Staff Coll., 1968-70; CO 25 Light Regt, RA, 1970-72; CRA 4th Div., 1972-74; Dir of Army Recruiting, 1975-77; Dir, Combat Development (Army), 1977-79; GOC Artillery Div., 1979-82. Col Comdt, RA, 1982-. *Publications*: articles in military jls. *Recreations*: sailing, fishing, music, reading, gardening. *Address*: c/o Lloyds Bank, Winton, Bournemouth, Dorset. *Club*: Army and Navy.

BURGESS, Geoffrey Harold Orchard; Chief Scientist (Agriculture and Horticulture), Ministry of Agriculture, Fisheries and Food, since 1982; *b* 28 March 1926; *s* of Harold Frank and Eva M. F. Burgess, Reading; *m* 1952, Barbara Vernon, *y d* of late Rev. Gilbert Vernon Yonge; two *s. Educ*: Reading Grammar Sch.; Univ. of Reading; UC Hull. BSc Reading, 1951 (Colin Morley Prizewinner 1950); PhD London, 1955. FRSE 1971. Special research appt, Univ. of Hull, 1951; Sen. Scientific Officer, DSIR, Humber Lab., Hull, 1954; PSO, Torry Res. Stn, Aberdeen, 1960; Officer i/c, Humber Lab., Hull, 1962; Director, Torry Res. Station, 1969-79; Head of Biology Div., Agrictl Science Service, and Officer i/c Slough Lab., MAFF, 1979-82. Hon. Res. Lectr in Fish Technology, Univ. of Aberdeen, 1969-79; Buckland Lectr, 1964; Hon. Lectr in Fish Technology, Univ. of Leeds, 1966-69; Mem. Adv. Cttee on Food Science, Univ. of Leeds, 1970-; Mem., Panel of Fish Technology Experts, FAO, 1962-. *Publications*: Developments in the Handling and Processing of Fish, 1965; (with Lovern, Waterman and Cutting) Fish Handling and Processing, 1965; The Curious World of Frank Buckland, 1967; scientific and technical papers, reviews, reports etc concerning handling, processing, transport and preservation for food, of fish, from catching to consumption. *Recreations*: music, book collecting, walking. *Address*: 14 Main Road, Naphill, High Wycombe, Bucks.

BURGESS, Ven. John Edward; Archdeacon of Bath, since 1975; *b* 9 Dec. 1930; *s* of Herbert and Dorothy May Burgess; *m* 1958, Jonquil Marion Bailey; one *s* one *d. Educ*: Surbiton County Gram. Sch.; London Univ. (St John's Hall). BD (2nd Cl.), ALCD (1st Cl.). Shell Chemicals Ltd, 1947-53. Asst Curate, St Mary Magdalen, Bermondsey, 1957-60; Asst Curate, St Mary, Southampton, 1960-62; Vicar of Dunston with Coppenhall, Staffs, 1962-67; Chaplain, Staffordshire Coll. of Technology, 1963-67; Vicar of Keynsham with Queen Charlton and Burnett, Somerset, 1967-75; Rural Dean of Keynsham, 1971-74. *Recreation*: history of railways. *Address*: The Archdeaconry, Corston, Bath, Avon BA2 9AP. *T*: Saltford 3609.

BURGESS, Sir John (Lawie), Kt 1972; OBE 1944; TD 1945; DL; Chairman, Cumbrian Newspapers Group Ltd, since 1945; Vice-Chairman, Border Television Ltd, since 1981 (Chairman, 1960-81); *b* 17 Nov. 1912; *s* of late R. N. Burgess, Carlisle and Jean Hope Lawie, Carlisle; *m* 1948, Alice Elizabeth, *d* of late F. E. Gillieron, Elgin; two *s* one *d. Educ*: Trinity Coll., Glenalmond. Served War of 1939-45, Border Regt, France, Middle East, Tobruk, Syria, India and Burma; comd 4th Bn, Chindit Campaign, Burma, 1944 (despatches, OBE); Hon. Col 4th Bn The Border Regt, 1955-68. Chm., Reuters Ltd, 1959-68; Dir, Press Assoc. Ltd, 1950-57 (Chm. 1955); Mem. Council, Newspaper Soc., 1947-82. Mem. Council, Commonwealth Press Union. DL Cumberland, 1955; High Sheriff of Cumberland, 1969; JP City of Carlisle, 1952-82. *Recreations*: dowsing; anything to do with Cumbria. *Address*: The Limes, Cavendish Terrace, Carlisle, Cumbria. *T*: Carlisle 37450. *Clubs*: Garrick, Army and Navy.

BURGH, 7th Baron, *cr* 1529 (title called out of abeyance, 1916; by some reckonings he is 9th Baron (from a *cr* 1487) and his father was 8th and grandfather 7th); **Alexander Peter Willoughby Leith;** *b* 20 March 1935; *s* of 6th (or 8th) Baron Burgh; *S* father 1959; *m* 1957, Anita Lorna Eldridge; two *s* one *d. Educ*: Harrow; Magdalene Coll., Cambridge (BA). *Heir*: *s* Hon. Alexander Gregory Disney Leith, *b* 16 March 1958.

BURGH, Sir John (Charles), KCMG 1982; CB 1975; Director-General of the British Council, since 1980; *b* 9 Dec. 1925; *m* 1957, Ann Sturge; two *d. Educ*: Friends' Sch., Sibford; London Sch. of Economics (BSc Econ.). Leverhulme post-intermediate Schol.; Pres. of Union, 1949. Asst Principal, BoT, 1950; Private Sec. to successive Ministers of State, BoT, 1954-57; Colonial Office, 1959-62; Mem., UK Delegation to UN Conf. on Trade Develt, 1964; Asst Sec., DEA, 1964; Principal Private Sec. to successive First Secretaries of State and Secretaries of State for Econ. Affairs, 1965-68; Under-Sec., Dept of Employment, 1968-71; Dep.-Chm., Community Relations Commn, 1971-72; Deputy Secretary: Cabinet Office (Central Policy Rev. Staff), 1972-74; Dept of Prices and Consumer Protection, 1974-79; Dept of Trade, 1979-80. Member: Executive, PEP, 1972-78; Council, Policy Studies Inst., 1978-; Council, RSA, 1982-; Council, VSO, 1980-; Sec., Nat. Opera Co-ordinating Cttee, 1972-; Asst Sec., Bd of Dirs, Royal Opera House, Covent Gdn, 1972-80. Governor, LSE, 1980-. *Recreations*: friends, music, the arts generally. *Address*: The British Council, 10 Spring Gardens, SW1A 2BN. *Club*: Arts.

BURGHERSH, Lord; Anthony David Francis Henry Fane; *b* 1 Aug. 1951; *s* and *heir* of 15th Earl of Westmorland, *qv. Educ*: Eton. *Address*: Kingsmead, Didmarton, Badminton, Avon.

BURGHLEY, Lord; William Michael Anthony Cecil; *b* 1 Sept. 1935; *s* and heir of 7th Marquess of Exeter, *qv* ; *m* 1967, Nancy Rose, *d* of Lloyd Arthur Meeker; one *s* one *d*. *Educ*: Eton. Rancher and businessman in 100 Mile House, 1954–. *Publication*: (jtly) Spirit of Sunrise, 1979. *Heir: s* Hon. Anthony John Cecil, *b* 9 Aug. 1970. *Address*: Box 8, 100 Mile House, BC VOK 2E0, Canada. *T*: 604-395-2767; 4 Bank House, 1A Kensington High Street, W8. *T*: 01-937 7763.

BURGNER, Thomas Ulric; Under Secretary, HM Treasury, since 1980; *b* 6 March 1932; *s* of John Henry Burgner and Clara Doerte Burgner (*née* Wolff); *m* 1958, Marion (*née* Chasik); two *s*. *Educ*: Haberdashers' Aske's, Hampstead; St Catharine's Coll., Cambridge (BA (Hons), MA); Dip. Personnel Management. Flying Officer, RAF, 1954-55. National Coal Board, 1955-61; Assoc. of Chemical and Allied Employers, 1961-65; Principal, Dept of Economic Affairs, 1965-69; HM Treasury: Principal, 1969-72; Asst Secretary, 1972-76; Head of Exchange Control Div., 1972-74; Head of General Aid Div., 1974-76; Under Secretary, 1976; on secondment as Sec., NEDC, 1976-80. Mem., BSC, 1980–. *Address*: 12 Kingsley Place, Highgate, N6 5EA. *T*: 01-340 9759.

BURGON, Geoffrey; composer; *b* 15 July 1941; *s* of Alan Wybert and Ada Vera Burgon; *m* 1963, Janice Elizabeth Garwood (marr. diss.); one *s* one *d*. *Educ*: Pewley Sch., Guildford; Guildhall School of Music and Drama (GGSM). Composer and freelance trumpeter, 1964-71: engagements included Royal Opera House (stage band), Philomusica, Jacques, London Mozart Players, Northern Sinfonia and Capriol Orchestras, also session work, theatres and jazz bands. Full time composer, 1971–; commissions from many Festivals, incl. Bath, Edinburgh, Three Choirs, and Camden; also many works for Dance, incl. Ballet Rambert and London Contemporary Dance Theatre; work performed internationally. *Major works*: Gending, Requiem, Canciones del Alma, The Fire of Heaven, Joan of Arc, Running Figures, Songs, Lamentations and Praises, Mirandola (opera) and Orpheus (one act opera); also very many scores for film, television and radio, incl. Life of Brian (film), Tinker, Tailor, Soldier, Spy, and Brideshead Revisited (TV). Prince Pierre of Monaco Award, 1969; Silver Disc for Brideshead record, 1982. *Publications*: over thirty scores of works in most musical genres. *Recreations*: playing jazz, cricket, wasting money on old cars, particularly Bristols. *Address*: c/o J. & W. Chester Ltd, Eagle Court, EC1M 5QD. *T*: 01-253 6947.

BURGOYNE, Rear-Adm. Robert Michael, CB 1982; Senior Naval Member, Directing Staff, Royal College of Defence Studies, 1980-82; *b* 20 March 1927; *s* of Robert and Elizabeth Burgoyne; *m* 1951, Margaret (Hilda) McCook; one *s* one *d*. *Educ*: Bradfield College; Magdalene College, Cambridge. Joined RN 1945; CO HMS Cleopatra, 1967-68; Captain 2nd Frigate Sqdn and CO HMS Undaunted, 1972-73; Dir, Maritime Tactical Sch., 1974-75; CO HMS Antrim, 1975-77; Comdr, British Navy Staff, Washington and UK Rep. to SACLANT, 1977-80. FBIM (MBIM 1969); MNI 1973. *Address*: c/o Midland Bank, Gerrards Cross, Bucks.

BURKE, Adm. Arleigh Albert; Navy Cross; DSM (3 Gold Stars); Legion of Merit (with 2 Gold Stars and Army Oak Leaf Cluster). Silver Star Medal, Purple Heart, Presidential Unit Citation Ribbon (with 3 stars), Navy Unit Commendation Ribbon; retired as Chief of Naval Operations, US Navy and Member of Joint Chiefs of Staff (1955-61); Member of Board of Directors: United Services Life Insurance Corporation; Freedoms Foundation, at Valley Forge; *b* 19 Oct. 1901; *s* of Oscar A. and Claire Burke; *m* 1923, Roberta Gorsuch; no *c*. *Educ*: United States Naval Academy; Univ. of Michigan (MSE). Commnd ensign, USN, 1923, advancing through grades to Admiral, 1955. USS Arizona, 1923-28; Gunnery Dept, US Base Force, 1928; Post-graduate course (explosives), 1929-31; USS Chester, 1932; Battle Force Camera Party, 1933-35; Bureau of Ordnance, 1935-37; USS Craven, 1937-39; USS Mugford, Captain, 1939-40; Naval Gun Factory, 1940-43; Destroyer Divs 43 and 44, Squadron 12 Comdg, 1943; Destroyer Squadron 23 Comdg, 1943-44; Chief of Staff to Commander Task Force 58 (Carriers), 1944-45; Head of Research and Development Bureau of Ordnance, 1945-46; Chief of Staff, Comdr Eighth Fleet and Atlantic Fleet, 1947-48; USS Huntington, Captain, 1949; Asst Chief of Naval Ops, 1949-50; Cruiser Div. 5, Comdr, 1951; Dep. Chief of Staff, Commander Naval Forces, Far East, 1951; Director Strategic Plans Div., Office of the Chief of Naval Operations, 1952-53; Cruiser Division 6, Commanding, 1954; Commander Destroyer Force, Atlantic, 1955. Member: American Legion; American Soc. of Naval Engineers and numerous other naval assocs, etc.; National Geographic Society; also foreign societies, etc. Holds several hon. degrees. UI Chi Medal (Korea), 1954; Korean Presidential Unit Citation, 1954. *Recreations*: reading, gardening. *Address*: 8624 Fenway Drive, Bethesda, Maryland 20034, USA. *Clubs*: Army-Navy Town, Metropolitan, Chevy Chase, Alfalfa, Circus Saints and Sinners, Ends of the Earth, etc (Washington, DC; Quindecum (Newport, US); The Brook, Lotos, Salmagundi, Inner Wheel, Seawanhaka Corinthian Yacht (New York); Bohemian (San Francisco).

BURKE, Sir Aubrey (Francis), Kt 1959; OBE 1941; Vice-Chairman retired from Executive Duties, 1969; *b* 21 April 1904; *m* 1936, Rosalind Laura, *d* of Rt Hon. Sir Henry Norman, 1st Bt, PC, OBE, and Hon. Lady Norman, CBE, JP; one *s* three *d* (and one *d* decd). Pres., SBAC, 1958-1959-1960. FCIT; FRSA. High Sheriff of Hertfordshire, 1966-67. *Recreations*: shooting, fishing, sailing. *Address*: Rent Street Barns, Bovingdon, Hertfordshire; Clos de la Garoupe, 06600 Antibes, France. *Club*: Royal Automobile.

BURKE, Desmond Peter Meredyth, MA Oxon; Headmaster, Clayesmore School, 1945-66; *b* 10 May 1912; *yr s* of late Maj. Arthur Meredyth Burke. *Educ*: Cheltenham Coll.; Queen's Coll., Oxford. Honours, Modern Greats, 1933. Housemaster and Senior Modern Language Master, Clayesmore School, 1936-40; served in Army Intelligence Corps at home, Belgium and Germany, 1940-45. *Recreations*: the theatre, travel, tennis, bridge. *Address*: The Old Lodge, 92 Alumhurst Road, Bournemouth West. *T*: Westbourne 762329.

BURKE, Rt. Rev. Geoffrey; Titular Bishop of Vagrauta and Auxiliary Bishop of Salford (RC), since 1967; *b* 31 July 1913; *s* of Dr Peter Joseph Burke and Margaret Mary (*née* Coman). *Educ*: St Bede's Coll., Manchester; Stonyhurst Coll.; Oscott Coll., Birmingham; Downing Coll., Cambridge (MA). Taught History, St Bede's Coll., 1940-66; Prefect of Studies, 1950; Rector, 1966. Consecrated Bishop 29 June 1967. *Address*: St John's Cathedral, 250 Chapel Street, Salford, Lancashire M3 5LL. *T*: 061-834 0333.

BURKE, John Barclay; Deputy Chairman, Royal Bank of Scotland plc, since 1982; Director, Royal Bank of Scotland Group; Chairman, Loganair Ltd; Vice-Chairman, Lloyds and Scottish Ltd; *b* 12 Feb. 1924; *m* 1953, Evelyn Petrie; one *s* one *d*. *Educ*: Hutchesons' Boys' Grammar Sch., Glasgow. Joined former National Bank of Scotland Ltd, 1941. Served Royal Navy, 1942-46. Gen. Manager, Nat. Commercial & Schroders Limited, 1965-66; Gen. Manager and Dir: Nat. Commercial Bank of Scotland Ltd, 1968-69; Royal Bank of Scotland Ltd, 1969-70; Managing Director: Royal Bank of Scotland, 1970-82; Royal Bank of Scotland Gp, 1976-82; Director: Williams & Glyn's Bank Ltd; Scottish Agricultural Securities Corp. Ltd. Chm., Cttee of Scottish Clearing Bankers, 1970-73, 1977-79; Pres., The Inst. of Bankers in Scotland, 1973-75. Jt Hon. Treasurer: The Earl Haig Fund (Scotland); Officers' Assoc. (Scottish Branch); Chm. Exec. Cttee, Scottish Council of Social Service. OStJ. FIB(Scot.); FBIM. *Recreations*: golf, hill walking, flying. *Address*: 3 Cammo Gardens, Edinburgh EH4 8EJ. *T*: 031-339 2872. *Clubs*: Caledonian; New (Edinburgh); Royal and Ancient (St Andrews).

BURKE, John Kenneth; a Recorder of the Crown Court, since 1980; *b* 4 Aug. 1939; *s* of Kenneth Burke and Madeline Burke; *m* 1962, Margaret Anne (*née* Scattergood); three *d*. *Educ*: Stockport Grammar Sch. Served Cheshire Regt, 1958-60; TA Parachute Regt, 1962-67. Called to the Bar, Middle Temple, 1965. *Recreations*: painting and drawing, walking. *Address*: Yeardsley Hall Farm, Furness Vale, High Peak SK12 7PZ. *T*: New Mills 42680; (chambers) 18 St John Street, Manchester M3 4EA. *T*: 061 834 9843.

BURKE, Sir Joseph (Terence Anthony), KBE 1980 (CBE 1973; OBE 1946); MA; Professor of Fine Arts, University of Melbourne, 1946-78, now Emeritus Professor; Fellow, Trinity College Melbourne, since 1973; Consultant in Art, National Bank of Australia, since 1979; *b* 14 July 1913; *s* of late R. M. J. Burke; *m* 1940, Agnes, *d* of late Rev. James Middleton, New Brunswick, Canada; one *s*. *Educ*: Ealing Priory Sch.; King's Coll., Univ. of London; Courtauld Institute of Art; Yale Univ., USA. Entered Victoria and Albert Museum, 1938; lent to Home Office and Min. of Home Security, Sept. 1939; private sec. to successive Lord Presidents of the Council (Rt Hon. Sir John Anderson, Rt Hon. C. R. Attlee, Rt Hon. Lord Woolton), 1942-45; and to the Prime Minister (Rt Hon. C. R. Attlee), 1945-46; Trustee of Felton Bequest; Fellow, Australian Acad. of the Humanities, Pres., 1971-73. Hon. DLitt Monash, 1977. *Publications*: Hogarth and Reynolds: A Contrast in English Art Theory, 1943; ed William Hogarth's Analysis of Beauty and Autobiographical Notes, 1955; (with Colin Caldwell) Hogarth: The Complete Engravings, 1968; vol. IX, Oxford History of English Art, 1714-1800, 1976; articles in Burlington Magazine, Warburg Journal and elsewhere. *Recreations*: golf, swimming. *Address*: Dormers, Falls Road, Mount Dandenong, Victoria 3767, Australia. *Clubs*: Athenæum; Melbourne (Melbourne).

BURKE, Prof. Philip George, PhD; FRS 1978; MRIA 1974; Professor of Mathematical Physics, Queen's University of Belfast, since 1967; *b* 18 Oct. 1932; *s* of Henry Burke and Frances Mary Sprague; *m* 1959, Valerie Mona Martin; four *d*. *Educ*: Wanstead County High Sch.; Univ. of Exeter (BSc 1953); University Coll. London (PhD 1956). Res. Fellow, UCL, 1956-57; Asst Lectr, Univ. of London Inst. for Computer Science, 1957-59; Res. Fellow, Lawrence Berkeley Lab., Calif, 1959-62; Res. Fellow, then Principal Scientific Officer, later Sen. Prin. Sci. Officer, Atomic Energy Res. Authority, Harwell, 1962-67. Hd, Dir. of Theory and Computational Sci., SRC (later SERC) Daresbury Lab., 1977-82. Hon. DSc Exeter, 1981. *Publications*: many papers in learned journals. *Recreations*: walking, reading. *Address*: 13 Rugby Road, Belfast BT7 1PT; Brook House, Norley Lane, Crowton, near Northwich, Cheshire. *T*: Kingsley 88301.

BURKE, Richard; Member, Commission of the European Communities, 1977-81 and since 1982; *b* 29 March 1932; *s* of David Burke and Elisabeth Burke; *m* 1961, Mary Freeley; two *s* three *d*. *Educ*: University Coll., Dublin (MA). Called to the Bar, King's Inns. Mem., Dublin Co. Council, 1967-73 (Chm., 1972-73); Mem. Dail Eireann, for South County Dublin, 1969-77, for Dublin West, 1981; Fine Gael Chief Whip and spokesman on Posts and Telegraphs, 1969-73; Minister for Education, 1973-76. Mem., Commn of EC, with special responsibility for Transport, Taxation, Consumer Protection, Relations with European Parlt, Research, Educ. and Sci., 1977-81. *Recreations*: music, golf, walking. *Address*: Commission of the European Communities, 200 rue de la Loi, 1049 Brussels, Belgium.

BURKE, Sir Thomas (Stanley), 8th Bt, *cr* 1797; *b* 20 July 1916; *s* of Sir Gerald Howe Burke, 7th Bt and Elizabeth Mary (*d* 1918), *d* of late Patrick Mathews, Mount Hanover, Drogheda; *S* father 1954; *m* 1955, Susanne Margaretha, *er d* of Otto Salvisberg, Thun, Switzerland; one *s* one *d*. *Educ:* Harrow; Trinity Coll., Cambridge. *Heir: s* James Stanley Gilbert Burke, *b* 1 July 1956. *Address:* 18 Elmcroft Avenue, NW11 0RR. *T:* 01-455 9407.

BURKE, Tom; Press Officer, European Environment Bureau, since 1979; *b* 5 Jan. 1947; *s* of J. V. Burke, DSM, and Mary (*née* Bradley). *Educ:* St Boniface's, Plymouth; Liverpool Univ. (BA (Hons) Philosophy). Great George's Community Arts Project, 1969-70; Lecturer: West Cheshire Coll., 1970-71; Old Swan Technical Coll., 1971-73; Co-ordinator, Merseyside Friends of the Earth, 1971-73; Friends of the Earth: Local Groups Co-ordinator, 1973-75; Executive Director, 1975-79; Dir of Special Projects, 1979-80; Vice-Chm., 1980-81. Member: Bd of Dirs, Earth Resources Research, 1975-; Waste Management Adv. Council, 1981; Packaging Council, 1978-. Royal Humane Society Testimonials: on Vellum, 1966; on Parchment, 1968. *Publications:* Europe: environment, 1981; (jtly) Pressure Groups in the Global System, 1982. *Recreations:* photography, military modelling. *Address:* 111 Palace Road, SW2. *T:* 01-671 2753. *Club:* Explorers' (New York).

BURKE-GAFFNEY, Michael Anthony Bowes, QC 1977; *b* Dar-es-Salaam, Tanzania, 1 Aug. 1928; *s* of Henry Joseph O'Donnell Burke-Gaffney and Constance May (*née* Bishop); *m* 1961, Constance Caroline (*née* Murdoch); two *s* one *d*. *Educ:* Douai Sch.; RMA, Sandhurst. Commissioned Royal Irish Fusiliers, 1948; served with 1st Bn, Suez Canal Zone, Akaba, Gibraltar, BAOR and Berlin; served with Royal Ulster Rifles, Korean War, 1951, and in Hong Kong; qual. as interpreter in Turkish (studied at London Univ. and in Istanbul), 1955; Staff Captain, HQ 44 Div., 1956-58, when resigned commn and read for the Bar; joined Gray's Inn, 1956 (Lord Justice Holker Sen. Scholar); called to the Bar, 1959. Jun. Counsel to HM Treasury in certain planning matters, 1974-77. Author, Three Lakes Inquiry Report, 1976. *Recreations:* family, cricket, wildlife, viniculture, plant breeding. *Address:* Lamb Building, Temple, EC4. *T:* 01-353 6701.

BURKETT, Mary Elizabeth, OBE 1978; FRGS; FMA; Director of Abbot Hall Art Gallery, and Museum of Lakeland Life and Industry, since 1967, and Borough Museum, Kendal, since 1977; *d* of Ridley Burkett and Mary Alice Gaussen. *Educ:* Univ. of Durham (BA, Teachers' Cert.). FRGS 1978; FMA 1980. Taught art, craft, maths, etc, at Wroxall Abbey, 1948-54; Art and Craft Lectr, Charlotte Mason Coll., Ambleside, 1954-62; seven months in Turkey and Iran, 1962; Asst Dir, Abbot Hall, 1963-66. Formerly part-time Teacher of Art, Bela River Prison. Member: numerous cttees including National Trust (NW Region), 1979-; Carlisle Diocesan Adv. Cttee, 1980-. *Publications:* The Art of the Felt Maker, 1979; Kurt Schwitters (in the Lake District), 1979; contrib. art and archaeol jls, and gall. and museum catalogues. *Recreations:* travel, bird watching, photography, picking up stones. *Address:* Demavend, Bowness-on-Windermere, Cumbria. *T:* Windermere 3767.

BURKILL, John Charles, FRS 1953; ScD; Honorary Fellow, Peterhouse, Cambridge; Emeritus Reader in Mathematical Analysis; *b* 1 Feb. 1900; *m* 1928, Margareta, *d* of Dr A. Braun; one *s* one *d* (and one *d* decd). *Educ:* St Paul's; Trinity Coll., Cambridge (Fellow 1922-28). Smith's Prize, 1923; Professor of Pure Mathematics in the University of Liverpool, 1924-29; Fellow of Peterhouse, 1929-67; Master of Peterhouse, 1968-73. Adams Prize, 1949. *Address:* 2 Archway Court, Barton Road, Cambridge CB3 9LW.

BURKITT, Denis Parsons, CMG 1974; MD, FRCSE; FRS 1972; Medical Research Council External Scientific Staff, 1964-76; Hon. Senior Research Fellow, St Thomas's Hospital Medical School, since 1976; *b* Enniskillen, NI, 28 Feb. 1911; *s* of James Parsons Burkitt and Gwendoline (*née* Hill); *m* 1943, Olive Mary (*née* Rogers); three *d*. *Educ:* Dean Close Sch., Cheltenham; Dublin Univ. BA 1933; MB, BCh, BAO 1935; FRCSE 1938; MD 1946. Surgeon, RAMC, 1941-46. Joined HM Colonial Service: Govt Surgeon, in Uganda, 1946-64, and Lectr in Surgery, Makerere University Coll. Med. Sch.; final appt: Sen. consultant surgeon to Min. of Health, Uganda, 1961. First described a form of cancer common in children in Africa, now named Burkitt's Lymphoma. Foundn and Hon. Fellow, E Africa Assoc. of Surgeons; Hon. Fellow, Sudan Assoc. of Surgeons; former Pres., Christian Medical Fellowship; a Vice-Pres., CMS. Hon. FRCSI, 1973; Hon. FR.CPI, 1977. Hon. DSc East Africa, 1970. Harrison Prize, ENT Section of RSM, 1966; Stuart Prize, 1966, Gold Medal, 1978, BMA. Arnott Gold Medal, Irish Hosps and Med. Schs Assoc., 1968; Katharine Berkan Judd Award, Sloan-Kettering Inst., New York, 1969; Robert de Villiers Award, Amer. Leukaemia Soc., 1970; Walker Prize for 1966-70, RCS, 1971; Paul Ehrlich-Ludwig Darmstaedter Prize, Paul Ehrlich Foundn, Frankfurt, 1972; Soc. of Apothecaries' Medal, 1972; Albert Lasker Clinical Chemotherapy Award, 1972; Gairdner Foundn Award, 1973; (jtly) Bristol-Myers Award for Cancer Research, 1982. Hon. FTCD; Hon. MD Bristol, 1979; Hon. DSc Leeds, 1982. *Publications:* Co-editor: Treatment of Burkitt's Lymphoma (UICC Monograph 8), 1967; Burkitt's Lymphoma, 1970; Refined Carbohydrate Foods and Disease, 1975; Don't Forget the Fibre in your Diet, 1979; Western Diseases, their emergence and prevention, 1981; over 250 contribs to scientific jls. *Recreations:* photography, carpentry. *Address:* The Old House, Bussage, near Stroud, Glos GL6 8AX. *T:* Brimscombe 882248.

BURLAND, Prof. John Boscawen, FEng; Professor of Soil Mechanics in the University of London, since 1980, and Head of the Department of Civil Engineering at Imperial College of Science and Technology, since 1982; *b* 4 March 1936; *s* of John Whitmore Burland and Margaret Irene Burland (*née* Boscawen); *m* 1963, Gillian Margaret, *d* of J. K. Miller; two *s* one *d*. *Educ:* Parktown Boys' High Sch., Johannesburg; Univ. of the Witwatersrand (BSc Eng, MSc Eng); Univ. of Cambridge (PhD). MSAICE; MICE; MIStructE; FEng 1981. Res. Asst, Univ. of the Witwatersrand, 1960; Engineer, Ove Arup and Partners, London, 1961-63; Res. Student, Cambridge Univ., 1963-66; Building Research Station: SSO and PSO, 1966-72; Head of Geotechnics Div., 1972-79; Asst Dir and Head of Materials and Structures Dept, 1979-80. Visiting Prof., Dept of Civil Engineering, Univ. of Strathclyde, 1973-82. Instn of Structural Engineers: Mem. of Council, 1979-82; Murray Buxton Silver Medal; Oscar Faber Bronze Medal; named in Special Award to DoE for Underground Car Park at Palace of Westminster. Telford Premium of Instn of Civil Engrs; Brit. Geotechnical Soc. Prize on three occasions. *Publications:* numerous papers on soil mechanics and civil engineering. *Recreations:* sailing, golf, painting, classical guitar. *Address:* 13 Barton Road, Wheathampstead, St Albans, Herts AL4 8QG. *T:* Wheathampstead 2366.

BURLEIGH, (George) Hall; HM Diplomatic Service; Counsellor, Foreign and Commonwealth Office, since 1981; *b* 24 June 1928; *s* of William Burleigh and Hannah (*née* Hall); *m* 1957, Barbara Patricia Rigby; two *d*. *Educ:* Friends Sch., Lisburn; Trinity Coll., Dublin (MA); Trinity Coll., Cambridge. HM Colonial Service (later HMOCS), 1951-62: Asst Dist Comr, Gambaja, Northern Territories, Gold Coast, 1951; Dist Comr, Naurongo, 1952; Govt Agent, Salaga, 1953-54, Tamale, 1955, Zuarungu, 1955-56, Lawra, 1957 and Gambaga, 1958; Sen. (later Principal) Asst Sec., Min. of Communications and Works, 1959-62; FO, 1962-64; Aden, 1965; FO, 1965-68; First Sec., Dubai, 1968-70 and Bahrain, 1970; FCO, 1971; First Sec., Jakarta, 1972-75 and Stockholm, 1976-81. *Recreations:* books, cricket, travel. *Address: c/o* Foreign and Commonwealth Office, SW1; Lawra, Roedean Road, Tunbridge Wells, Kent TN2 5JX. *T:* Tunbridge Wells 22359. *Club:* Travellers'.

BURLEIGH, Very Rev. John H. S., DD, BLitt; Professor of Ecclesiastical History, Edinburgh University, 1931-64, Emeritus, since 1964; Dean of the Faculty of Divinity, 1956-64; Moderator of the General Assembly of the Church of Scotland, May 1960-May 1961; *b* Ednam, Kelso, 19 May 1894; *s* of Rev. J. Burleigh; *m* 1926, Mary, *d* of Rev. C. Giles; one *s* one *d*. *Educ:* Kelso High Sch., George Watson's Coll. and Univ., Edinburgh; Strasbourg; Oxford. Parish Minister of Fyvie, Aberdeenshire, and St Enoch's, Dundee. Principal, New Coll., Edinburgh, 1956-64. *Publications:* Christianity in the New Testament Epistles; City of God: a Study of St Augustine's Philosophy; St Augustine: Earlier Writings; A Church History of Scotland. *Address:* 21 Kingsmuir Drive, Peebles EH45 9AA. *T:* Peebles 20224.

BURLEIGH, Thomas Haydon, CBE 1977; Director, John Brown & Co. Ltd, 1965-77; *b* 23 April 1911; *s* of late J. H. W. Burleigh, Great Chesterford; *m* 1933, Kathleen Mary Lenthall, *d* of late Dr Gurth Eager, Hertford; two *s*. *Educ:* Saffron Walden Sch. RAF, short service commission, No 19 (F) Sqdn, 1930-35; Westland Aircraft Ltd, 1936-45; Thos. Firth & John Brown Ltd, 1945-48; Firth Brown Tools Ltd, 1948-77. Pres., Sheffield Chamber of Commerce, 1963-64; Pres. Nat. Fedn of Engineers' Tool Manufacturers, 1968-70; Master of Company of Cutlers in Hallamshire in the County of York, 1970-71. *Recreations:* golf, gardening. *Address:* Kirkgate, Holme next Sea, Hunstanton, Norfolk. *T:* Holme 387. *Clubs:* Royal Air Force; Royal and Ancient Golf (St Andrews).

BURLEY, Sir Victor (George), Kt 1980; CBE 1969; FIE(Aust); FIMechE, FIProdE; Chairman, Advisory Council of Commonwealth Scientific and Research Organization (CSIRO), 1979-81; *b* 4 Dec. 1914; *s* of G. H. Burley and M. A. Luby; *m* 1941, Alpha Loyal Lord; one *s* three *d*. *Educ:* High Sch., Tasmania; Univ. of Tasmania (BE). MIEE, FIFST; FInstD, FAIM. Cadbury-Fry-Pascall Pty Ltd, Australia, 1938-71: Chief Engr, Director and Vice-Chm.; Director, Cadbury Schweppes Aust Ltd, 1971-78; Cons. Dir, Cadbury Fry Hudson NZ; Technical Cons., Cadbury Schweppes UK, 1978-. Member, Adv. Council, CSIRO, 1961-78; Chm., State Cttee, Tas. CSIRO, 1964-78; Foundn Mem., Commonwealth Adv. Cttee on Advanced Educn, 1965-71; Foundn Chm., Council of Advanced Educn, Tasmania, 1968-76; Mem., Sci. and Industry Forum, Aust. Acad. of Science, 1967-81. University of Tasmania: Warden of Convocation, 1964-74; Mem., Faculty of Engrg, 1968-; Mem. Council, 1982-. *Recreations:* music, reading. *Address:* Montaigne, Sandy Bay Road, Hobart, Tasmania 7005. *T:* Hobart (002) 252-583. *Clubs:* Melbourne (Melbourne); Tasmanian (Hobart).

BURLINGTON, Earl of; William Cavendish; *b* 6 June 1969; *s* and *heir* of Marquess of Hartington, *qv*.

BURMAN, Sir (John) Charles, Kt 1961; DL; JP; *b* 30 Aug. 1908; *o s* of Sir John Burman, JP; *m* 1936, Ursula Hesketh-Wright, JP; two *s* two *d*. *Educ:* Rugby Sch. City Council, 1934-66 (Lord Mayor of Birmingham, 1947-49); General Commissioner of Income Tax, 1941-73; Indep. Chm., Licensing Planning Cttee, Birmingham Conservative and Unionist Assoc., 1963-72; County Pres. St John Ambulance Brigade, 1950-63; Member, Govt Cttee on Administrative Tribunals, 1955; Member Royal Commission on the Police, 1960. Director: Tarmac Ltd, 1955-71 (Chm., 1961-71); S Staffs Waterworks Co., 1949-82 (Chm. 1959-79). Life Governor and Chm. Trustees, Barber Institute, at University of Birmingham. JP 1942; High Sheriff,

Warwickshire, 1958, DL 1967. KStJ, 1961. *Address:* Little Bickerscourt, Danzey Green, Tanworth-in-Arden, Warwickshire B94 5BL. *T:* Tanworth-in-Arden 2711. *Club:* Birmingham (Birmingham).

BURMAN, Sir Stephen (France), Kt 1973; CBE 1954 (MBE 1943); MA; Chairman, Serck Ltd, Birmingham, 1962-70; Director: Averys, Ltd, 1951-73; Imperial Chemical Industries Ltd, 1953-75; Imperial Metal Industries Ltd, 1962-75; J. Lucas Industries Ltd, 1952-75, and of other industrial companies; *b* 27 Dec. 1904; *s* of Henry Burman; *m* 1931, Joan Margaret Rogers; one *s* (and one *s* decd). *Educ:* Oundle. Pres. Birmingham Chamber of Commerce, 1950-51 (Vice-Pres. 1949); Chm. United Birmingham Hosps., 1948-53; Dep. Chm. 1953-56. Dir, Midland Bank Ltd, 1959-76. Governor Birmingham Children's Hosp., 1944-48; Dep. Chm. Teaching Hosps. Assoc., 1949-53; Member, Midlands Electricity Board, 1948-65; Chm. Birmingham and District Advisory Cttee for Industry, 1947-49; Member Midland Regional Board for Industry, 1949-65, Vice-Chm. 1951-65; Member of Council and Governor, Univ. of Birmingham, 1949-76, Pro-Chancellor, 1955-66; General Commissioner for Income Tax, 1950-68. Member Royal Commission on Civil Service, 1953-56. Hon. LLD Birmingham, 1972. *Recreation:* shooting. *Address:* 12 Cherry Hill Road, Barnt Green, Birmingham B45 8LJ. *T:* 021-445 1529.

BURN, Andrew Robert, DLitt; FSA 1979; historian; *b* 25 Sept. 1902; *s* of Rev. A. E. Burn and Celia Mary, *d* of Edward Richardson; *m* 1938, Mary, *d* of Wynn Thomas, OBE, Ministry of Agriculture. *Educ:* Uppingham Sch.; Christ Church, Oxford. DLitt Oxon, 1982. Sen. Classical Master, Uppingham Sch., 1927-40; British Council Rep. in Greece, 1940-41; Intelligence Corps, Middle East, 1941-44; 2nd Sec., British Embassy, Athens, 1944-46; Sen. Lectr and sole Mem. Dept of Ancient History, Univ. of Glasgow, 1946; Reader, 1965; resigned, 1969; Vis. Prof. at "A College Year in Athens", Athens, Greece, 1969-72. Pres. Glasgow Archæological Soc., 1966-69. Silver Cross of Order of Phoenix (Greece). *Publications:* Minoans, Philistines and Greeks, 1930; The Romans in Britain, 1932; The World of Hesiod, 1936; This Scepter'd Isle: an Anthology, 1940 (Athens); The Modern Greeks, 1942 (Alexandria); Alexander and the Hellenistic World, 1947; Pericles and Athens, 1948; Agricola and Roman Britain, 1953; The Lyric Age of Greece, 1960; Persia and the Greeks, 1962; The Pelican History of Greece, 1966; The Warring States of Greece (illustrated), 1968; Greece and Rome (Hist. of Civilisation Vol. II), 1970 (Chicago); (with Mary W. Burn) The Living Past of Greece, 1980; contributions to encyclopædias and historical journals. *Recreation:* travel. *Address:* 23 Ritchie Court, 380 Banbury Road, Oxford OX2 7PW. *T:* Oxford 50423.

BURN, Angus Maitland P.; *see* Pelham Burn.

BURN, Duncan (Lyall); economist, historian; *b* 10 Aug. 1902; *s* of Archibald William and Margaret Anne Burn; *m* 1930, Mollie White; two *d*. *Educ:* Holloway County Sch.; Christ's Coll. (Scholar), Cambridge. Hist. Tripos, Pts I and II, Cl. I, Wrenbury Schol. 1924, Bachelor Research Schol. 1924, Christ's Coll., Cambridge. Lecturer in Economic History: Univ. of Liverpool, 1925; Univ. of Cambridge, 1927. Min. of Supply (Iron and Steel Control), 1939; Member US-UK Metallurgical Mission, New York and Washington, 1943; leader writer and Industrial Correspondent of the Times, 1946-62. Director of the Economic Development Office set up by AEI, English Electric, GEC, and Parsons, 1962-65. Visiting Professor of Economics: Manchester Univ., 1967-69; Bombay Univ., 1971. Member: Advisory Cttee on Census of Production, 1955-65; Exec. Cttee, Nat. Inst. of Econ. and Social Research, 1957-69; Econ. Cttee, DSIR, 1963-65; Specialist Adviser, House of Commons Select Cttee on Energy, 1980-. *Publications:* Economic History of Steelmaking, 1867-1939, 1940; The Steel Industry, 1939-59, 1961; The Political Economy of Nuclear Energy, 1967; Chemicals under Free Trade, 1971, repr. in Realities of Free Trade: Two Industry Studies (with B. Epstein), 1972; Nuclear Power and the Energy Crisis: politics and the atomic industry, 1978; ed and contrib. The Structure of British Industry, 2 vols, 1958; also contrib. to Journals, Bank Reviews, etc. *Recreations:* walking, gardening. *Address:* 5 Hampstead Hill Gardens, NW3 2PH. *T:* 01-435 5344. *Club:* United Oxford & Cambridge University.

BURN, Michael Clive, MC 1945; writer; *b* 11 Dec. 1912; *s* of late Sir Clive Burn; *m* 1947, Mary Booker (*née* Walter); no *c*. *Educ:* Winchester; New Coll., Oxford (open scholar); Hons Degree in Soc. Scis, Oxford, 1945, with distinction in all subjects (awarded whilst POW at Colditz). Journalist, The Times, 1936-39; Lieut 1st Bn Queens Westminsters, KRRC, 1939-40; Officer in Independent Companies, Norwegian Campaign, 1940, subseq. Captain No. 2 Commando; taken prisoner in raid on St Nazaire, 1942; prisoner in Germany, 1942-45. Foreign Correspondent for The Times in Vienna, Jugoslavia and Hungary, 1946-49. Keats Poetry First Prize, 1973. *Plays:* The Modern Everyman (prod. Birmingham Rep., 1947); Beyond the Storm (Midlands Arts Co., and Vienna, 1947); The Night of the Ball (prod. New Theatre, 1956). *Publications:* novels: Yes, Farewell, 1946, repr. 1975; Childhood at Oriol, 1951; The Midnight Diary, 1952; The Trouble with Jake, 1967; sociological: Mr Lyward's Answer, 1956; The Debatable Land, 1970; poems: Poems to Mary, 1953; The Flying Castle, 1954; Out On A Limb, 1973; Open Day and Night, 1978; play: The Modern Everyman, 1948.

BURN, Rodney Joseph, RA 1962 (ARA 1954); Artist; *b* Palmers Green, Middlesex, 11 July 1899; *s* of Sir Joseph Burn, KBE, and Emily Harriet Smith; *m* 1923, Dorothy Margaret, *d* of late Edward Sharwood-Smith; one *s* two *d*.

Educ: Harrow Sch. Studied art at Slade Sch.; Asst Teacher at Royal Coll. of Art, South Kensington, 1929-31 and since 1946; Director of School of the Museum of Fine Arts, Boston, Mass., USA, 1931; returned to England, 1934; Asst Master, City & Guilds of London Art Sch.; Tutor, Royal Coll. of Art, 1947-65. Hon. Secretary New English Art Club until 1963; Member Royal West of England Academy, 1963; Hon. Fellow Royal Coll. of Art, 1964; Fellow University Coll. London, 1966; Hon. Mem., Soc. of Marine Artists, 1975. *Address:* 1 The Moorings, Strand on the Green, Chiswick, W4. *T:* 01-994 4190.

BURNELL, (Susan) Jocelyn (Bell), PhD; FRAS; astronomer; part-time research, Mullard Space Science Laboratory, University College London, since 1974; *b* 15 July 1943; *d* of G. Philip and M. Allison Bell; *m* 1968, Martin Burnell; one *s*. *Educ:* The Mount Sch., York; Glasgow Univ. (BSc); New Hall, Cambridge (PhD). FRAS 1969. Res. Fellowships, Univ. of Southampton, 1968-73. An Editor, The Observatory, 1973-76. Mem., IAU, 1979-. Michelson Medal, Franklin Inst., Philadelphia (jtly with Prof. A. Hewish), 1973; J. Robert Oppenheimer Meml Prize, Univ. of Miami, 1978; Rennie Taylor Award, Amer. Tentative Soc., NY, 1978. *Publications:* papers in Nature, Astronomy and Astrophysics, Jl of Geophys. Res., Monthly Notices of RAS. *Recreations:* Quaker interests, walking. *Address:* Mullard Space Science Laboratory, Holmbury St Mary, near Dorking, Surrey RH5 6NT. *T:* Forest Green 292.

BURNES, Sheila; *see* Bloom, Ursula.

BURNET, Alastair; *see* Burnet, J. W. A.

BURNET, Sir (Frank) Macfarlane, OM 1958; AK 1978; KBE 1969; Kt 1951; FRS 1942; MD, ScD (Hon.) Cambridge, 1946; DSc (Hon.) Oxford, 1968; FRCP 1953; Past Director, Walter and Eliza Hall Institute for Medical Research, Melbourne, and Professor of Experimental Medicine, Melbourne University, 1944-1965 (Assistant Director, 1928-31 and 1934-44); Emeritus Professor, Melbourne University, 1965; Chairman, Commonwealth Foundation, 1966-69; *b* 3 Sept. 1899; *s* of Frank Burnet, Traralgon, Victoria; *m* 1st, 1928, Edith Linda (*d* 1973), *d* of F. H. Druce; one *s* two *d*; 2nd, 1976, Hazel Jenkin (*née* Foletta). *Educ:* Geelong Coll., Melbourne Univ. (MD). Resident Pathologist, Melbourne Hosp., 1923-24; Beit Fellow for Medical Research at Lister Institute, London, 1926-27; Visiting worker at National Institute for Medical Research, Hampstead, 1932-33; Dunham Lecturer Harvard Medical Sch., Jan. 1944; Croonian Lecturer, 1950 (Royal Society); Herter Lecturer, 1950 (Johns Hopkins Univ.); Abraham Flexner Lecturer (Vanderbilt Univ.), 1958. Pres., Australian Acad. of Science, 1965-69. Hon. FRCS 1969. Royal Medal of Royal Society, 1947; Galen Medal in Therapeutics, Society of Apothecaries, 1958; Copley Medal, Royal Society, 1959; Nobel Prize for Medicine, 1960. *Publications:* Biological Aspects of Infectious Disease, 1940 (4th edn (with D. O. White) Natural History of Infectious Disease, 1972); Virus as Organism, 1945; Viruses and Man (Penguin), 1953; Principles of Animal Virology, 1955; Enzyme Antigen and Virus, 1956; Clonal Selection Theory of Acquired Immunity, 1959; Integrity of the Body, 1962; (with I. R. Mackay) Autoimmune Diseases, 1962; Changing Patterns (autobiography), 1968; Cellular Immunology, 1969; Dominant Mammal, 1970; Immunological Surveillance, 1970; Genes, Dreams and Realities, 1971; Walter and Eliza Hall Institute 1915-65, 1971; Auto-immunity and Auto-immune Disease, 1972; Intrinsic Mutagenesis, 1974; Immunology, 1976; Immunity, Aging and Cancer, 1976; Endurance of Life, 1978; Credo and Comment, 1979; technical papers. *Address:* 48 Monomeath Avenue, Canterbury, Victoria 3126, Australia.

BURNET, James William Alexander, (Alastair Burnet); broadcaster with Independent Television News, since 1976; Associate Editor, News at Ten, since 1982; *b* 12 July 1928; *s* of late Alexander and Schonaid Burnet, Edinburgh; *m* 1958, Maureen Campbell Sinclair. *Educ:* The Leys Sch., Cambridge; Worcester Coll., Oxford. Sub-editor and leader writer, Glasgow Herald, 1951-58; Commonwealth Fund Fellow, 1956-57; Leader writer, The Economist, 1958-62; Political editor, Independent Television News, 1963-64; Editor, The Economist, 1965-74; Editor, Daily Express, 1974-76. Ind. Dir, Times Newspapers Hldgs Ltd, 1982-. Has appeared regularly on TV progs, News at Ten, Panorama, This Week. Member: Cttee of Award, Commonwealth Fund, 1969-76; Cttee on Reading and Other Uses of English Language, 1972-75; Monopolies Commn specialist panel on newspaper mergers, 1973-. Richard Dimbleby Award, BAFTA, 1966, 1970, 1979; Judges' Award, RTS, 1981. *Address:* 43 Hornton Court, Campden Hill Road, W8. *T:* 01-937 7563; 33 Westbourne Gardens, Glasgow. *T:* 041-339 8073. *Club:* Reform.

BURNET, Mrs Pauline Ruth, CBE 1970; JP; Chairman, Cambridgeshire Area Health Authority (Teaching), 1973-82; *b* 23 Aug. 1920; *d* of Rev. Edmund Willis and Constance Marjorie Willis (*née* Bostock); *m* 1940, John Forbes Burnet, Fellow of Magdalene Coll., Cambridge; one *s* one *d* (and one *s* decd). *Educ:* St Stephen's Coll., Folkestone (now at Broadstairs), Kent. Member: Windsor and Eton Hosp. Management Cttee, 1948-50; Fulbourn and Ida Darwin HMC, 1951-74 (Chm., 1969-74). Member: E Anglian Regional Hosp. Bd, 1968-74; Bd of Governors of United Cambridge Hosps, 1966-74; Mem. Council, Assoc. of Hosp. Management Cttees until 1974 (Chm., 1966-68). Pres., Cambridgeshire Mental Welfare Assoc., 1977- (Chm. 1964-76). Mem., Farleigh Hosp. Cttee of Inquiry, 1970. JP City of Cambridge, 1957-; Chm., Cambs Magistrates' Courts Cttee, 1978-80.

Recreations: walking, swimming. *Address:* 28 Selwyn Gardens, Cambridge CB3 9AZ. *T:* Cambridge 350726.

BURNETT, of Leys, Baronetcy of (unclaimed); *see under* Ramsay, Sir Alexander William Burnett, 7th Bt.

BURNETT, Most Rev. Bill Bendyshe, MA; LTh; *b* 31 May 1917; *s* of Richard Evelyn Burnett and Louisa Dobinson; *m* 1945, Sheila Fulton Trollip; two *s* one *d. Educ:* Bishop's College (Rondebosch); Michaelhouse (Natal); Rhodes University College; St Paul's Theological College, Grahamstown and Queen's College, Birmingham. Schoolmaster, St John's College, Umtata, 1940; Army, 1940-45; Deacon, St Thomas', Durban, 1946; Priest, 1947; Assistant priest, St Thomas', Durban, 1946-50; Chaplain, Michaelhouse, 1950-54; Vicar of Ladysmith, 1954-57; Bishop of Bloemfontein, 1957-67; Gen. Secretary, S African Council of Churches, 1967-69; Asst Bishop of Johannesburg, 1967-69; Bishop of Grahamstown, 1969-74; Archbishop of Cape Town and Metropolitan of S Africa, 1974-81. ChStJ 1975. Hon. DD Rhodes, 1980. *Publications:* Anglicans in Natal, 1953; (contrib.) Bishop's Move, 1978. *Recreation:* painting. *Address:* c/o St Alban's Rectory, 5 Durham Road, Vincent, East London, 5247, South Africa.

BURNETT, Air Chief Marshal Sir Brian (Kenyon), GCB 1970 (KCB 1965; CB 1961); DFC 1942; AFC 1939; RAF, retired; Chairman, All England Lawn Tennis Club, Wimbledon, since 1974; *b* 10 March 1913; *s* of late Kenneth Burnett and Anita Catherine Burnett (*née* Evans); *m* 1944, Valerie Mary (*née* St Ludger); two *s. Educ:* Charterhouse; Wadham Coll., Oxford (Hon. Fellow, 1974); Joined RAFO 1932; RAF 1934; Long Distance Record Flight of 7,158 miles from Egypt to Australia, Nov. 1938. Served War of 1939-45, in Bomber and Flying Training Commands; RAF Staff Coll. Course, 1944; Directing Staff, RAF Staff Coll., 1945-47; UN Military Staff Cttee, New York, 1947-49; Joint Planning Staff, 1949-50; SASO HQ No. 3 (Bomber) Group, 1951-53; CORAF Gaydon, 1954-55; ADC to the Queen, 1953-57; Director of Bomber and Reconnaissance Ops, Air Ministry, 1956-57; Imperial Defence Coll., 1958; Air Officer Administration, HQ Bomber Command, 1959-61; AOC No 3 Gp, Bomber Command, 1961-64; Vice-Chief of the Air Staff, 1964-67; Air Secretary, MoD, 1967-70; C-in-C, Far East Command, Singapore, 1970-71; retired 1972. Air ADC to the Queen, 1969-72. Pres., Squash Rackets Assoc., 1972-75. *Recreations:* tennis, squash rackets, golf, ski-ing. *Address:* Heather Hill, Littleworth Cross, Seale, Farnham, Surrey. *Clubs:* Royal Air Force; Vincent's (Oxford); All England Lawn Tennis; Ski Club of Great Britain; Jesters Squash; International Lawn Tennis Club of Great Britain; Hankley Common Golf.

BURNETT, Sir David Humphery, 3rd Bt *cr* 1913; MBE 1945; TD; Director, Guardian Royal Exchange Assurance and other companies; one of HM Lieutenants of the City of London; *b* 27 Jan. 1918; *s* of Sir Leslie Trew Burnett, 2nd Bt, CBE, TD, DL, and Joan, *d* of late Sir John Humphery; *S* father 1955; *m* 1948, Geraldine Elizabeth Mortimer, *d* of Sir Godfrey Arthur Fisher, KCMG; two *s* (and one *s* decd). *Educ:* Harrow; St John's Coll., Cambridge, MA. Served War of 1939-45 (despatches, MBE), in France, N Africa, Sicily and Italy; Temp. Lt-Col GSO1, 1945. Dir, Proprietors of Hay's Wharf Ltd, 1950-80 (Chm., 1965-80). Chairman: South London Botanical Institute, 1976-81; London Assoc. of Public Wharfingers, 1964-71. Mem. PLA, 1962-75. Mem. Council, Brighton Coll. Master: Company of Watermen and Lightermen of the River Thames, 1964; Girdlers Company, 1970. FRICS 1970 (ARICS 1948); FBIM 1968; FLS 1979. *Heir: s* Charles David Burnett, *b* 18 May 1951. *Address:* Tandridge Hall, near Oxted, Surrey RH8 9NJ; Tillmouth Park, Cornhill-on-Tweed, Northumberland TD12 4UT. *Club:* Turf.

BURNETT, Dr John Harrison; Principal and Vice-Chancellor, University of Edinburgh, since 1979; *b* 21 Jan. 1922; *s* of Rev. T. Harrison Burnett, Paisley; *m* 1945, E. Margaret, *er d* of Rev. Dr E. W. Bishop; two *s. Educ:* Kingswood Sch., Bath; Merton Coll., Oxford. BA, MA 1947; DPhil 1953; Christopher Welch Scholar, 1946. FR.SE 1957; FIBiol 1969. Lecturer, Lincoln Coll., 1948-49; Fellow (by Exam.) Magdalen Coll., 1949-53; Univ. Lecturer and Demonstrator, Oxford, 1949-53; Lecturer, Liverpool Univ., 1954-55; Prof. of Botany: Univ. of St Andrews, 1955-60; King's Coll., Newcastle, Univ. of Durham, 1961-63, Univ. of Newcastle, 1963-68; Dean of Faculty of Science, St Andrews 1958-60, Newcastle, 1966-68; Public Orator, Newcastle, 1966-68; Regius Prof. of Botany, Univ. of Glasgow, 1968-70; Oxford University: Sibthorpian Prof. of Rural Economy and Fellow, St John's Coll., 1970-79; Member: Gen. Bd of Faculties, 1972-77 (Vice-Chm, 1974-76); Hebdomadal Council, 1974-79. Chm. Scottish Horticultural Research Inst., 1959-74; Mem., Nature Conservancy (Scottish Cttee), 1961-66; Trustee, Nuffield Foundn Biol. Project, 1962-68 (Chm., 1965-68); Trustee, The New Phytologist, 1962-; Mem. Academic Adv. Council, Univs of St Andrews and Dundee, 1964-66. Mem., Newcastle Reg. Hosp. Bd, 1964-68. Served 1942-46 as Lieut RNVR (despatches). *Publications:* The Vegetation of Scotland, ed and contrib., 1964; Fundamentals of Mycology, 1968, 2nd edn 1976; Mycogenetics, 1975; Fungal Walls and Hyphal Growth, ed and contrib., 1979; papers in various scientific journals. *Recreations:* walking, writing, gardens. *Address:* Old College, University of Edinburgh, South Bridge, Edinburgh EH8 9YL. *Clubs:* Caledonian, New (Edinburgh).

BURNETT, Lt-Col Maurice John Brownless, DSO 1944; JP; DL; *b* 24 Sept. 1904; *o s* of late Ernest Joseph Burnett, MBE, JP, The Red House, Saltburn-by-the-Sea, Yorks, and late Emily Maud Margaret, 2nd *d* of John Brownless, Whorlton Grange, Barnard Castle and Dunsa Manor, Dalton; *m* 1930, Crystal, *d* of late Col H. D. Chamier, The Connaught Rangers; one *s. Educ:* Aysgarth Sch.; Rugby Sch.; RMA, Woolwich; Staff Coll., Camberley. 2nd Lieut RA 1924; psc 1937; Lt-Col 1942; served 1939-45; comd 127th (Highland) Field Regt in 51st Highland Division, Normandy to the Rhine; retd 1948. JP, 1957, DL, 1958, N Yorks. Member: N Riding Yorks Education Cttee, 1956-69; NR Yorks Standing Joint Cttee, and York and NE Yorks Police Cttee, 1958-74; Richmond, Yorks, RDC 1958-74 (Chm., 1967-69); N Riding CC, 1962-74 (Chm., Civil Protection Cttee, 1969-74); N Yorks CC, 1974- (Vice Chm., 1981-); Church Assembly, 1955-70, General Synod, 1970-80; Ripon Diocesan Bd of Finance, 1953 (Vice-Chm. 1956-79); Exec. Cttee, N Riding Yorks Assoc. of Youth Clubs, 1950-71 (Chm. 1952 and 1965, Pres. 1971-). Governor, Barnard Castle Sch., 1959-63, 1973-; Chm. of Governors, Richmond Sch., 1970-; District Comr, Scouts Assoc., (formerly Boy Scouts Assoc.), NR Yorks, 1950, County-Comr, 1961-69. Sec., N Riding Yorks Territorial and Auxiliary Forces Assoc., 1950-68. *Recreations:* country sports and pursuits, interest in local government and youth work. *Address:* Dunsa Manor, Dalton, Richmond, N Yorks DL11 7HE. *T:* Darlington 718251. *Club:* Army and Navy.

BURNETT, Rev. Canon Philip Stephen; Church of England Board of Education, 1970-80; *b* 8 Jan. 1914; *s* of late Philip Burnett and Mrs Burnett, Salton, York; *m* 1954, Joan Hardy, *e d* of C. F. Hardy, Sheffield; one *s* one *d. Educ:* Scarborough Coll.; Balliol Coll., Oxford; Westcott House, Cambridge. Admitted Solicitor, 1936; Lay Missionary, Dio. Saskatchewan, Canada, 1939-41. Intelligence Corps, 1942-44; Staff Capt., GHQ, New Delhi, 1944-45, Deacon, 1947, Priest, 1948; Curate of St Andrew's, Chesterton, Cambridge, and Staff Sec., Student Christian Movement, 1947-49; Asst Gen. Sec., SCM, 1949-52; Vicar of St Mary, Bramall Lane, Sheffield, 1952-61; Rural Dean of Ecclesall, 1959-65; Canon Residentiary of Sheffield Cathedral, and Educn Secretary, Diocese of Sheffield, 1961-70, Canon Emeritus 1970-. Hon. Sec., Fellowship of the Maple Leaf, 1965-. *Address:* 91 Chelverton Road, Putney, SW15 1RW. *T:* 01-789 9934.

BURNETT, Rear-Adm. Philip Whitworth, CB 1957; DSO 1945; DSC 1943, and Bar, 1944; *b* 10 Sept. 1908; *s* of Henry Ridley Burnett; *m* 1947, Molly, *widow* of Brig. H. C. Partridge, DSO, and *d* of H. M. Trouncer; one *s* two *d. Educ:* Preparatory Sch., Seascale; Royal Naval Coll., Dartmouth. Served War of 1939-45; HMS Kelly, 1939-41; HMS Osprey, 1941-43; Western Approaches Escort Groups, 1943-45. Chief of Staff to Comdr-in-Chief, Portsmouth, 1955-57; retd list 1958. Lieut 1930; Comdr 1940; Capt. 1945; Rear-Adm. 1955. Sec. of the Royal Institution of Chartered Surveyors, 1959-65.

BURNEY, Sir Anthony (George Bernard), Kt 1971; OBE 1945; MA, FCA; Chairman, Brent Walker, since 1980; *b* 3 June 1909; *o s* of Theodore and Gertrude Burney; *m* 1947, Dorothy Mary Vere, *d* of Col Clements Parr; no *c. Educ:* Rugby; Corpus Christi Coll., Cambridge (Hon. Fellow 1979). MA; FCA. Served War of 1939-45, Army: RE and RASC, Europe (Lt-Col). Partner, Binder, Hamlyn & Co., Chartered Accountants, 1938-71. Chm., Debenhams Ltd, 1971-80 (Dir, 1970-80). Dir, Commercial Union, to 1980; Dir of Reorganisation, The Cotton Bd, 1959-60; Mem. Shipbuilding Inquiry Cttee, 1965-66; Chm., Freight Integration Council, 1968-75; Mem. National Ports Council, 1971; Pres., Charities Aid Foundn. *Publication:* Illustrations of Management Accounting in Practice, 1959. *Recreations:* gardening, photography. *Address:* 6 Greville Place, NW6. *T:* 01-624 4439. *Clubs:* Buck's, Garrick.

BURNEY, Sir Cecil (Denniston), 3rd Bt *cr* 1921; Chairman, Hampton Trust Ltd; *b* 8 Jan. 1923; *s* of Sir Charles Dennistoun Burney, 2nd Bt, CMG, and Gladys (*d* 1982), *d* of George Henry High; *S* father, 1968; *m* 1957, Hazel Marguerite de Hamel, *yr d* of late Thurman Coleman; two *s. Educ:* Eton; Trinity Coll., Cambridge. Man. Dir, 1951-68, Chm., 1968-78, Northern Motors Ltd; Dir, Security Building Soc., 1959-71. Member of Legislative Council, N Rhodesia, 1959-64; MP Zambia, 1964-68; Chairman, Public Accounts Cttee, Zambia, 1963-67. *Recreations:* tennis, skiing. *Heir: s* Nigel Dennistoun Burney, *b* 6 Sept. 1959. *Address:* PO Box 32037, Lusaka, Zambia; 5 Lyall Street, SW1. *T:* 01-235 4014. *Clubs:* Carlton, Turf, Buck's; Leander; Salisbury, Bulawayo (Zimbabwe); Ndola (Zambia).

BURNHAM, 5th Baron, *cr* 1903; **William Edward Harry Lawson,** Bt 1892; JP; DL; Lieutenant-Colonel; Scots Guards, retired 1968; *b* 22 Oct. 1920; *er s* of 4th Baron Burnham, CB, DSO, MC, TD, and (Marie) Enid, Lady Burnham, CBE (*d* 1979), *d* of Hugh Scott Robson, Buenos Aires; *S* father, 1963; *m* 1942, Anne, *yr d* of late Major Gerald Petherick, The Mill House, St Cross, Winchester; three *d* (one *s* decd). *Educ:* Eton. Royal Bucks Yeomanry, 1939-41; Scots Guards, 1941-68; commanded 1st Bn, 1959-62. Chm., Sail Training Assoc.; Vice-Chm. (Bucks), East Wessex TAVRA. Chm., Masonic Housing Assoc. JP Bucks 1970, DL Bucks 1977. *Recreations:* sailing, shooting, ski-ing. *Heir: b* Hon. Hugh John Frederick Lawson [*b* 15 Aug. 1931; *m* 1955, Hilary Mary, *d* of Alan Hunter; one *s* two *d*]. *Address:* Hall Barn, Beaconsfield, Bucks. *T:* Beaconsfield 3315. *Clubs:* Garrick, Turf; Royal Yacht Squadron.

BURNHAM, Forbes; *see* Burnham, L. F. S.

BURNHAM, James; Writer; an Editor, National Review, since 1955; *b* 22 Nov. 1905; *s* of Claude George Burnham and Mary May Gillis; *m* 1934,

Marcia Lightner; two s one d. *Educ:* Princeton Univ.; Balliol Coll., Oxford Univ. Prof. of Philosophy, New York Univ., 1932-54. *Publications:* (jtly) A Critical Introduction to Philosophy, 1932; The Managerial Revolution, 1941, rev. edn 1972; The Machiavellians, 1943; The Struggle for the World, 1947; (jtly) The Case for De Gaulle, 1948; The Coming Defeat of Communism, 1950; Containment or Liberation, 1953; The Web of Subversion, 1954; Congress and the American Tradition, 1959; Suicide of the West, 1964; The War We Are In, 1967. *Address:* Fuller Mountain Road, Kent, Conn. 06757, USA. *T:* Kent, Conn., 203-927-3117.

BURNHAM, (Linden) Forbes (Sampson), OE (Guyana) 1973; SC (Guyana); first Executive President of Co-operative Republic of Guyana, since 1980; Leader, People's National Congress, since 1957; *b* 20 Feb. 1923; *s* of J. E. Burnham, Headteacher of Kitty Methodist Sch., and Rachel A. Burnham (*née* Sampson); *m* 1st, 1951, Sheila Bernice Lataste; three *d* ; 2nd, 1967, Viola Victorine Harper; two *d. Educ:* Kitty Methodist Sch., Central High Sch., Queen's Coll.; London Univ. British Guiana Scholarship, 1942; BA (London) 1944; Best Speaker's Cup at Univ. of London, 1947; Pres. W Indian Students Union (Brit.), 1947-48; Delegate, Internat. Union of Students, Paris and Prague, 1947, 1948; LLB (Hons) 1947. Called to the Bar, 1948; QC (British Guiana), 1960, SC 1966. Entered local politics, 1949; Co-founder and Chm., People's Progressive Party, 1949; Minister of Education, 1953; re-elected to Legislature, 1957 and 1961; Founder and Leader, People's Nat. Congress, 1957; Leader of Opposition, 1957-64; Prime Minister of British Guiana, 1964-66, of Guyana, 1966-70, of Co-operative Republic of Guyana, 1970-80. Pres. Kitty Brotherhood, 1947-48, 1949-50; Town Councillor, 1952; Mayor of Georgetown, 1959, 1964; Pres. Bar Association, 1959; Pres. Guyana Labour Union, 1953-56, 1963-65 (Pres. on leave, 1965-). Patron: Guyana Lawn Tennis Assoc.; Soc. for the Blind; Red Cross Soc. Hon. LLD Dalhousie Univ., Nova Scotia, 1977. *Publication:* A Destiny to Mould, 1970. *Recreations:* horse-riding, swimming, fishing, hunting, chess (Pres., Guyana Chess Assoc.); special interest, farming. *Address:* Presidential Secretariat, Vlissengen Road, Georgetown, Guyana. *Clubs:* Demerara Cricket, Malteenoes Sports, Guyana Sports, Cosmos Sports, Georgetown Cricket, Non Pareil, Park Tennis, Guyana Motor Racing (Patron) (all in Guyana).

BURNINGHAM, John Mackintosh; free-lance author-designer; *b* 27 April 1936; *s* of Charles Burningham and Jessie Mackintosh; *m* 1964, Helen Gillian Oxenbury; one *s* two *d. Educ:* Summerhill School, Leiston, Suffolk; Central School of Art, Holborn, 1956-59 (Diploma). Now free-lance: illustration, poster design, exhibition, animated film puppets, and writing for children. *Publications:* Borka, 1963 (Kate Greenaway Medal, 1963); Trubloff, 1964; Humbert, 1965; Cannonball Simp, 1966; Harquin, 1967; Seasons, 1969; Mr Gumpy's Outing, 1970 (Kate Greenaway Award, 1971); Around the World in Eighty Days, 1972; Mr Gumpy's Motor Car, 1973; "Little Books" series: The Baby, The Rabbit, The School, The Snow, 1974; The Blanket, The Cupboard, The Dog, The Friend, 1975; The Adventures of Humbert, Simp and Harquin, 1976; Come Away from the Water, Shirley, 1977; Time to Get Out of the Bath, Shirley, 1978; Would You Rather, 1978; The Shopping Basket, 1980. *Address:* c/o Jonathan Cape Ltd, 30 Bedford Square, WC1.

BURNISTON, George Garrett, CMG 1972; OBE 1968; Chairman and Director, Division of Rehabilitation Medicine, Department of Medicine, Prince Henry, Prince of Wales and Eastern Suburbs Hospitals, NSW, 1963-79; *b* Sydney, NSW, 23 Nov. 1914; *s* of George Benjamin Burniston, Melbourne, Vic.; unmarried. *Educ:* Sydney High Sch.; Sydney Univ. (MB, BS). Served in RAAF Medical Service, 1940-47 (RAF Orthopaedic Service, UK, 1941-43); Gp Captain, RAAF Med. Reserve (retired). Dep. Co-ordinator of Rehabilitation, Min. of Post-War Reconstruction (Aust.), 1946-48. SMO, Dept of Social Services, 1948-53; Fulbright Fellow, USA and UK, 1953-54; PMO, Dept of Social Services, 1954-62; Sen. Lectr, 1963-77, Associate Prof., 1977-79, Sch. of Medicine, Univ. of NSW. Member: WHO Expert Advisory Panel on Medical Rehabilitation, 1958-; Council, Cumberland Coll. of Allied Health Sciences, NSW, 1978- (Chm., 1980-); Nat. Adv. Council for the Handicapped, Aust., 1977-; Advanced Educn Council, Tertiary Educn Commn, 1979-; Vice-Pres., Internat. Rehabilitation Med. Assoc., 1978-; Pres., Aust. Coll. of Rehabilitation Med., 1980-. Foundation Fellow, Aust. Coll. of Med. Administrators, 1968; Foundn Diplomate, Physical and Rehabilitation Medicine, 1971; FRSH 1973; FRACP 1976. *Recreations:* golf, swimming, painting, reading. *Address:* 701 Tradewinds, Boorima Place, Cronulla, NSW 2230, Australia. *T:* 523-8383; Suite 703, 135 Macquarie Street, Sydney 2000, Australia. *Club:* University (Sydney).

BURNLEY, Suffragan Bishop of, since 1970; **Rt. Rev. Richard Charles Challinor Watson;** Hon. Canon of Blackburn Cathedral since 1970; *b* 16 Feb. 1923; *o s* of Col Francis W. Watson, CB, MC, DL, The Glebe House, Dinton, Aylesbury, Bucks; *m* 1955, Anna, *er d* of Rt Rev. C. M. Chavasse, OBE, MC, MA, DD, then Bishop of Rochester; one *s* one *d. Educ:* Rugby; New Coll., Oxford; Westcott House, Cambridge. Served Indian Artillery, Lt and Capt. RA, 1942-45. Oxford Hon. Sch. Eng. Lang. and Lit., 1948, Theology 1949; Westcott House, Cambridge, 1950-51. Curate of Stratford, London E, 1952-53; Tutor and Chaplain, Wycliffe Hall, Oxford, 1954-57; Chaplain of Wadham Coll. and Chaplain of Oxford Pastorate, 1957-61; Vicar of Hornchurch, 1962-70; Examining Chaplain to Bishop of Rochester, 1956-61, to Bishop of Chelmsford, 1962-70; Asst Rural Dean of Havering, 1967-70; Rector of Burnley, 1970-77. *Recreations:* reading, gardening. *Address:* Palace House, Burnley, Lancashire. *T:* Burnley 23564. *Club:* Lansdowne.

BURNLEY, Christopher John; Financial Director, British Airports Authority, since 1975; *b* 1 May 1936; *s* of John Fox Burnley and Helena Burnley; *m* 1960, Joan Quirk; two *d. Educ:* King William's College, Isle of Man. Chartered Accountant. Articled Clerk, 1953-59; Military service, 1959-62; Computer Systems Analyst, IBM, 1962-66; Management Consultant, Peat Marwick, 1966-67; Systems Planning Manager, Castrol, 1967-68; Sen. Planner, IBM, 1969-72; Financial Dir, Foseco FS, 1972-74; Group Treasurer, Foseco Minsep, 1974-75. *Recreation:* railway enthusiast. *Address:* Thirlmere, 173 Worcester Road, West Hagley, West Midlands DY9 0PB. *T:* Hagley 3592. *Club:* Royal Automobile.

BURNS, Mrs Anne, (Mrs D. O. Burns); British Gliding Champion, 1966; Principal Scientific Officer, Royal Aircraft Establishment, Farnborough, Hants, 1953-77; *b* 23 Nov. 1915; *d* of late Major Fleetwood Hugo Pellew, W Yorks Regt, and of late Violet Pellew (*née* Du Pré); *m* 1947, Denis Owen Burns; no *c. Educ:* The Abbey Sch., Reading; St Hugh's Coll., Oxford (BA). Joined Min. of Supply, 1940. Engaged in aircraft research at RAE, Farnborough, Hants, under various ministries, 1940-. Feminine International Records: 4 gliding records in S Africa, 1961; records, S Africa, 1963, 1965; Colorado USA, 1967. Queen's Commendation for Valuable Services in the Air, 1955 and 1963. Lilienthal Medal, Fédération Aéronautique Internationale, 1966. *Publications:* contrib. scientific jls. *Recreations:* gliding, fishing. *Address:* Clumps End, Lower Bourne, Farnham, Surrey. *T:* Frensham 3343.

BURNS, Arthur F.; economist; Ambassador of the United States of America to the Federal Republic of Germany, since 1981; *b* Stanislau, Austria, 27 April 1904; *s* of Nathan Burns and Sarah Juran; *m* 1930, Helen Bernstein; two *s. Educ:* Columbia Univ. AB and AM 1925, PhD 1934. Rutgers Univ.: Instructor in Economics, 1927-30; Asst Prof., 1930-33; Associate Prof., 1933-43; Prof., 1943-44; Columbia Univ.: Vis. Prof., 1941-44; Prof., 1944-59; John Bates Clark Prof., 1959-69, now Prof. Emeritus. Nat. Bureau of Econ. Research: Res. Associate, 1930-31; Mem. Res. Staff, 1933; Dir of Res., 1945-53; Pres., 1957-67; Chm. of Bureau, 1967-69; Counsellor to the President of the US, 1969-70; Chm., Bd of Governors of Fed. Reserve System in the US, 1970-78; Alternate Governor, IMF, 1973-78; Distinguished Professorial Lectr, Georgetown Univ., 1978-81; Distinguished Scholar in Residence, Amer. Enterprise Inst., 1978-81; Consultant, Lazard Frères, 1978-81; Mem., Trilateral Commn, 1978-81. Dir and Trustee of various orgs; Member (or Past Mem. or Consultant) of govt and other advisory bds. Chm., President's Coun. of Economic Advisors, 1953-56; Mem., President's Adv. Cttee on Labor-Management Policy, 1961-66, etc. Fellow: Amer. Statistical Assoc.; Econometric Soc.; Philos. Soc.; Amer. Acad. of Arts and Sciences; Amer. Econ. Assoc. (Pres. 1959); Acad. of Polit. Sci. (Pres., 1962-68); Phi Beta Kappa. Many hon. doctorates, 1952-. Alexander Hamilton Medal, Columbia Univ.; Dist. Public Service Award, Tax Foundn. Mugungwha Decoration, S Korea. Commander, French Legion of Honour; Decoration (1st class), Order of the Rising Sun, Japan. *Publications:* Production Trends in the United States since 1870, 1934; Economic Research and the Keynesian Thinking of our Times, 1946; (jtly) Measuring Business Cycles, 1946; Frontiers of Economic Knowledge, 1954; Prosperity Without Inflation, 1957; The Management of Prosperity, 1966; The Business Cycle in a Changing World, 1969; Reflections of an Economic Policy Maker, 1978. *Address:* Embassy of the USA, Deichmanns Aue, 5300 Bonn 2, Federal Republic of Germany. *Clubs:* Century Association (New York); Cosmos, City Tavern (Washington).

BURNS, Dr B(enedict) Delisle, FRS 1968; Visiting Professor, Department of Anatomy, University of Newcastle upon Tyne, since 1980; *b* 22 Feb. 1915; *s* of C. Delisle Burns and Margaret Hannay; *m* 1st, 1938, Angela Ricardo; four *s* ; 2nd, 1954, Monika Kasputis; one *d. Educ:* University Coll. Sch.; Tübingen Univ.; King's Coll., Cambridge; University Coll. Hospital. MRCS, LRCP 1939. Univ. extension lecturing for WEA, 1936-38; operational research, 1939-45; Research Asst, Nat. Inst. for Med. Research, 1945-49; Assoc. Prof of Physiology, McGill Univ., Canada, 1950-58; Scientific Advisor to Dept of Veterans' Affairs, 1950-67; Prof. of Physiology, 1958-67, Chm., Dept of Physiology, 1965-67, McGill Univ., Canada; Head, Div. of Physiology and Pharmacology, Nat. Inst. of Medical Research, 1967-76; MRC External Staff, Anatomy Dept, 1976-80, Hon. Prof. of Neurobiology, 1977-80, Univ. of Bristol. *Publications:* The Mammalian Cerebral Cortex, 1958; The Uncertain Nervous System, 1968; about 60 articles on neurophysiology in scientific jls. *Recreations:* tennis, ski-ing, painting, interior decoration. *Address:* Department of Anatomy, University of Newcastle upon Tyne, NE1 7RU. *T:* Newcastle upon Tyne 328511 ext. 2973.

BURNS, Bryan Hartop; Hon. Consulting Orthopaedic Surgeon: St George's Hospital; St Peter's Hospital, Chertsey; Heatherwood Hospital, Ascot; *b* 14 Dec. 1896; *s* of Hartop Burns, Grendon, Northampton; *m* 1938, Hon. Dorothy Garthwaite, *d* of late Lord Duveen. *Educ:* Wellingborough Sch.; Clare Coll., Cambridge; St George's Hospital Medical Sch. Allingham Scholarship in surgery, St George's Hospital, 1924; joined Northants Regt 1915, Captain 1917. Orthopaedic Surgeon, Royal Masonic Hospital, 1945-61. Ex-Pres. Orthopaedic Section, Royal Society Med.; Mem. of Court of Examiners, Royal College of Surgeons, 1943-46; Emer. Fellow, British Orthopaedic Association; Member Société Internationale de Chirurgie Orthopédique. *Publications:* Recent Advances in Orthopaedic Surgery, 1937 (jointly); articles on orthopaedic subjects. *Address:* 6 Chesterfield Hill, W1. *T:* 01-493 3435. *Clubs:* Boodle's, Brooks's.

BURNS, Sir Charles (Ritchie), KBE 1958 (OBE 1947); MD, FRCP; FRACP; Consulting Physician and Consulting Cardiologist, Wellington Hospital, since 1958; Director, Clinical Services, National Society on Alcoholism (Inc.), NZ, since 1970; Consultant Physician, National Society on Alcoholism and Drug Dependence, since 1975; *b* Blenheim, Marlborough, NZ, 27 May 1898; *s* of Archibald Douglas Burns, Lands and Survey Dept, NZ; *m* 1st, 1935, Margaret Muriel (decd 1949), *d* of John Laffey, Dunedin, NZ; one *s* one *d* ; 2nd, 1963, Doris Ogilvy, *d* of Keith Ramsay (sen.), Dunedin, New Zealand. *Educ:* St Mary's Sch., Blenheim, NZ; Marlborough and Nelson Colls, NZ. MB, ChB (NZ) 1922 (with distinction and Med. Travelling Scholarship; Batchelor Memorial Medal); MRCP 1925; MD (NZ) 1925; Foundation Fellow RACP 1937; FRCP (Lond.) 1943; FMANZ. Med. Registrar Dunedin Hospital, and Medical Tutor Otago Univ., 1925–27; Asst Phys., Dunedin Hospital, 1927–37; Senior Phys. and Cardiologist, Wellington Hospital, NZ, 1940–58; Phys., Home of Compassion, Island Bay, NZ, 1940–68; Mem. Med. Council, NZ, 1943–55; Examr in Medicine, Univ. of NZ, 1947–53, 1959, 1963. Mem. NZ Bd of Censors for RACP, 1954–61; Corresp. Mem. Brit. Cardiac Soc., 1952–71; Life Mem. Cardiac Soc. of Australia and NZ, 1972 (Mem., 1952–72; Mem. Council, 1956–58; Chm. 1964–65); Member: Council and NZ Vice-Pres., RACP, 1956–58; NZ Lepers' Trust Bd, 1958–; Advisory Cttee, The Nat. Soc. on Alcoholism (NZ); Council, Wellington Med. Research Foundn; President: NZ Nutrition Soc., 1967–70; NZ Med. Soc. on Alcohol and Alcoholism, 1978–80; Chm., Industry Cttee, Alcohol Liquor Adv. Council, 1977–80; Patron: NZ Asthma Soc.; NZ Diabetic Soc. (Wellington Br.); Deaf Children's Parents Soc. (Wellington Br.); Soc. for Promotion of Community Standards. Sixth Leonard Ball Oration, Melbourne, 1973. Mem., Guild of Sts Luke Cosmos and Damian, 1954– (Pres., 1966–69). Served War, 1944–47, Military Hospitals, 2nd NZEF, Italy and Japan (OBE). Hon. DSc Otago, 1975. KSG 1977. *Publications:* contrib. medical journals and jls of anciliary medical services. *Recreations:* walking and medical writing. *Address:* Flat One, Clifton Towers, 202 Oriental Parade, Wellington, New Zealand. *T:* Wellington 849-249.

BURNS, David Allan; HM Diplomatic Service; Counsellor and Consul General, Bangkok, since 1979; *b* 20 Sept. 1937; *s* of Allan Robert Desmond Burns, GM, and Gladys Frances Dine; *m* 1971, Inger Ellen Kristiansson; one *s* one *d*. *Educ:* Sir Anthony Browne's Sch., Brentwood, Essex. Served HM Forces, 1956–58. Language student and Third Secretary, British Embassy, Belgrade, 1962–65; Second Secretary, Bangkok, 1966–68; First Secretary, Washington, 1969–72; Head of Chancery, Belgrade, 1973–76; Asst Head of Arms Control Dept, FCO, 1976–79. *Recreation:* walking. *Address:* c/o Foreign and Commonwealth Office, SW1. *Club:* Royal Bangkok Sports.

BURNS, Mrs Denis Owen; *see* Burns, Mrs Anne.

BURNS, Lt-Gen. Eedson Louis Millard, CC (Canada) 1967; DSO 1944; OBE 1935; MC; idc; *b* 17 June 1897; *m* 1927, Eleanor Phelan; one *d*. *Educ:* Royal Military Coll., Kingston, Canada; Staff Coll., Quetta. Served European War, 1916–18 (France, Belgium) with Royal Canadian Engineers, Signals, Staff; Can. Perm. Force, 1918–39. War of 1939–45; GOC 2nd Can. Div., 1943 (Maj.-Gen.); 5th Can. Div., 1944; 1st Can. Corps, 1944. Dir-Gen. of Rehabilitation, Dept Veteran Affairs, 1945–46, Asst Dep. Minister, 1946–50, Dep. Minister, 1950–54. Chief of Staff, UN Truce Supervision Organisation, Palestine, 1954–56; Comdr UN Emergency Force, 1956–59; Adviser to Govt of Canada on Disarmament, 1960–69, retd; Leader of Canadian Delegation to 18-Nation Disarmament Conference, Geneva, 1962–68. Res. Fellow, Carleton Univ., 1970–71, Prof. of Strategic Studies, 1971–73. Nat. Pres. UNA, Canada, 1952–53 (Altern. Deleg. to UN, 1949). Officier Légion d'Honneur. *Publications:* Manpower in the Canadian Army, 1939–45, 1955; Between Arab and Israeli, 1962; Megamurder, 1966; General Mud, 1970; A Seat at the Table, 1972; Defence in the Nuclear Age, 1976. *Address:* RR 1, Box 132, Manotick, Ont. K0A 2N0, Canada.

BURNS, Maj.-Gen. Sir George; *see* Burns, Maj.-Gen. Sir W. A. G.

BURNS, Ian Morgan; Under Secretary, Northern Ireland Office, since 1979; *b* 3 June 1939; *s* of Donald George Burns and late Margaret Brenda Burns; *m* 1965, Susan Rebecca (*née* Wheeler); two *d*. *Educ:* Bootham, York. LLB, LLM London. Examiner, Estate Duty Office, 1960; Asst Principal, 1965, Principal, 1969, Home Office; Principal, 1972, Asst Sec., 1974, Northern Ireland Office; Asst Sec., Home Office, 1977. *Recreations:* listening to music, DIY. *Address:* c/o Northern Ireland Office, Great George Street, SW1.

BURNS, James, CBE 1967; GM 1941; Chairman, Southern Gas Board, 1967–69, retired; *b* 27 Feb. 1902; *s* of William Wilson Burns and Isobella MacDonald; *m* 1934, Kathleen Ida Holt (*d* 1976); one *d* (one *s* decd). *Educ:* Inverness Royal Academy; Aberdeen Univ.; Cambridge Univ. BSc 1st cl. Hons 1925, PhD 1928, Aberdeen. Entered Research Dept, Gas Light & Coke Co., 1929; worked as Chem. Engr with Chemical Reactions Ltd, in Germany, 1930–32; Production Engr, Gas Light & Coke Co., 1941, dep. Chief Engr, 1945; Chief Engr, North Thames Gas Board, 1949, Dep-Chm. 1960–62; Chm. Northern Gas Board, 1962–67. President: Instn Gas Engrs, 1957–58; Inst. Fuel, 1961–62, etc. *Publications:* contrib. Jls Instn Gas Engrs, Inst. Fuel, etc. *Recreations:* golf, shooting, country pursuits. *Address:* 4 Corfu, Chaddesley Glen, Canford Cliffs, Dorset. *T:* Canford Cliffs 707370.

BURNS, Prof. James Henderson; Professor of the History of Political Thought, University College London, since 1966; *b* 10 Nov. 1921; *yr s* of late William Burns and Helen Craig Tait Henderson; *m* 1947, Yvonne Mary Zéla Birnie, *er d* of late Arthur Birnie, MA, and of Yvonne Marie Aline Louis; two *s* (and one *d* decd). *Educ:* George Watson's Boys' Coll., Edinburgh; Univ. of Edinburgh; Balliol Coll., Oxford. MA (Edinburgh and Oxon), PhD (Aberdeen). Sub-Editor, Home News Dept, BBC, 1944–45; Lectr in Polit. Theory, Univ. of Aberdeen, 1947–60; Head of Dept of Politics, 1952–60; Reader in the History of Political Thought, University Coll. London, 1961–66; Head of History Dept, UCL, 1970–75. Gen. Editor, The Collected Works of Jeremy Bentham, 1961–79; Hon. Sec., Royal Historical Soc., 1965–70; Sec., Bentham Cttee, 1966–78. FRHistS 1962. *Publications:* Scottish University (with D. Sutherland Graeme), 1944; Scottish Churchmen and the Council of Basle, 1962; contributor to: (with S. Rose) The British General Election of 1951, by D. E. Butler, 1952; Essays on the Scottish Reformation, ed D. McRoberts, 1962; Mill: a collection of critical essays, ed J. B. Schneewind, 1968; Bentham on Legal Theory, ed M. H. James, 1973; Jeremy Bentham: ten critical essays, ed B. Parekh, 1974; edited (with H. L. A. Hart): Jeremy Bentham, An Introduction in the Principles of Morals and Legislation, 1970; Jeremy Bentham, A Comment on the Commentaries and A Fragment on Government, 1977; articles and reviews in: English Historical Review, Scottish Historical Review, Innes Review, Political Studies, History, Trans of RHistSoc, etc. *Address:* 39 Amherst Road, Ealing, W13. *T:* 01-997 7538.

BURNS, Sir John (Crawford), Kt 1957; Director, James Finlay & Co. Ltd, 1957–74; *b* 29 Aug. 1903; *s* of William Barr Burns and Elizabeth Crawford; *m* 1941, Eleanor Margaret Haughton James; one *s* three *d*. *Educ:* Glasgow High Sch. Commissioned 2/16th Punjab Regt (Indian Army), 1940–46 (despatches). *Recreations:* golf, fishing. *Address:* Glenorchard, Dunblane, Perthshire. *Club:* Oriental.

BURNS, Sir Malcolm (McRae), KBE 1972 (CBE 1959); Principal, Lincoln Agricultural College, New Zealand, 1952–74; *b* 19 March 1910; *s* of J. E. Burns and Emily (*née* Jeffrey); *m* 1936, Ruth, *d* of J. D. Waugh, St Louis, USA; one *s* two *d*. *Educ:* Rangiora High Sch.; Univs of Canterbury (NZ), Aberdeen and Cornell. Plant Physiologist, DSIR, NZ, 1936; Sen. Lectr, Lincoln Agric. Coll., 1937–48; Dir, NZ Fert. Manuf. Res. Assoc., 1948–52. Chairman: Physical Environment Commn, 1968–70; Fact-finding Gp on Nuclear Power, 1976–77; Member: Nat. Develt Council, 1969–74; Nat. Museum Council, 1974–; Beech Forests Council, 1972–78; Trustee, Norman Kirk Meml, etc. FNZIC; FNZIAS; FRSNZ; FAAAS. Chm., DSIR Research Council, 1959–62. NZ Representative, Harkness Fellowships, 1961–76. Hon. DSc Canterbury, 1974. *Publications:* articles in scientific jls. *Recreations:* bowls, fishing, gardening. *Address:* 7 Royds Street, Christchurch 1, New Zealand.

BURNS, Terence; Chief Economic Adviser to the Treasury and Head of the Government Economic Service, since 1980; *b* 13 March 1944; *s* of Patrick Owen and Doris Burns; *m* 1969, Anne Elizabeth Powell; one *s* two *d*. *Educ:* Houghton-Le-Spring Grammar Sch.; Univ. of Manchester (BAEcon Hons). London Business School: Research posts, 1965–70; Lecturer in Economics, 1970–74; Sen. Lectr in Economics, 1974–79; Prof. of Economics, 1979; Director, LBS Centre for Economic Forecasting, 1976–79. Member, HM Treasury Academic Panel, 1976–79. *Publications:* various articles in economic jls. *Recreations:* soccer spectator, music, fishing, walking. *Address:* c/o HM Treasury, Parliament Street, SW1P 3AG. *T:* 01-233 4508. *Club:* Reform.

BURNS, Thomas Ferrier; Editor of The Tablet, 1967–82; Chairman of Burns & Oates Ltd, 1948–67; Director, The Tablet Publishing Company, since 1936; *b* 21 April 1906; *s* of late David Burns and late Clara (*née* Swinburne); *m* 1944, Mabel Marañon; three *s* one *d*. *Educ:* Stonyhurst. Press Attaché, British Embassy, Madrid, 1940–45. *Recreations:* painting and gardening. *Address:* 14 Ashley Gardens, SW1. *T:* 01-834 1385. *Clubs:* Garrick, Pratt's.

BURNS, Prof. Tom, FBA 1982; Professor of Sociology, University of Edinburgh, 1965–81; *b* 16 Jan. 1913; *s* of John and Hannah Burns; *m* 1944, Mary Elizabeth Nora Clark; one *s* four *d*. *Educ:* Hague Street LCC Elementary Sch.; Parmiters Foundation Sch.; Univ. of Bristol (BA). Teaching in private schools in Tunbridge Wells and Norwich, 1935–39. Friends Ambulance Unit, 1939–45 (PoW, Germany, 1941–43). Research Asst, W Midland Gp on Post-war Reconstruction and Planning, 1945–49; Lectr, Sen. Lectr and Reader, Univ. of Edinburgh, 1949–65. Vis. Prof., Harvard, 1973–74. Mem., SSRC, 1969–70. *Publications:* Local Government and Central Control, 1954; The Management of Innovation (with G. M. Stalker), 1961; (ed) Industrial Man, 1969; (ed with E. Burns) Sociology of Literature and Drama, 1973; The BBC: Public Institution and Private World, 1977; articles in a number of jls in Britain, USA, France, etc. *Recreations:* music, walking. *Address:* 47 Great King Street, Edinburgh EH3 6RP.

BURNS, Maj.-Gen. Sir (Walter Arthur) George, KCVO 1962; CB 1961; DSO 1944; OBE 1953; MC 1940; retired; Lord-Lieutenant of Hertfordshire since Dec. 1961; *b* 29 Jan. 1911; *s* of late Walter Spencer Morgan and Evelyn Ruth Burns. *Educ:* Eton; Trinity Coll., Cambridge. BA Hons History. Commissioned Coldstream Guards 1932; ADC to Viceroy of India, 1938–40; Adjt 1st Bn, 1940–41 (MC); Brigade Major: 9 Inf. Bde, 1941–42; Sp. Gp Gds Armd Div., 1942; 32 Gds Bde, 1942–43; CO 3rd Bn Coldstream Gds, Italy, 1943–44 (DSO); Staff Coll., Camberley, 1945. Brigade Major, Household Bde, 1945–47; CO 3rd Bn Coldstream Gds, Palestine, 1947–50; AAG, HQ London Dist, 1951, 1952; Regimental Lt-Col Coldstream Gds, 1952–55;

Comdg 4th Gds Bde, 1955-59. GOC London District and The Household Brigade, 1959-62; Col, Coldstream Guards, 1966-. Steward, The Jockey Club, 1964-. KStJ 1972. *Recreations:* shooting and racing. *Address:* Home Farm, North Mymms Park, Hatfield, Hertfordshire. *T:* Potters Bar 45117. *Clubs:* Jockey, Pratt's, Buck's.

BURNS, Sir Wilfred, Kt 1980; CB 1972; CBE 1967; MEng, PPRTPI, MICE; Member, Local Government Boundary Commission for England, since 1982; *b* 11 April 1923; *m* 1945, Edna Price; one *s* one *d*. *Educ:* Ulverston Grammar Sch.; Liverpool Univ. Admty, 1944-45; Leeds Corp., 1946-49; Prin. Planning Officer, Coventry Corp., 1949-58; Dep. Planning Officer, Surrey CC, 1958-60; City Planning Officer, Newcastle upon Tyne, 1960-68; Chief Planner, 1968-82, and Dep. Sec., 1971-82, DoE (formerly Min. of Housing and Local Govt). Hon. DSc, Univ. of Newcastle upon Tyne, 1966. *Publications:* British Shopping Centres, 1959; New Towns for Old, 1963; Newcastle upon Tyne: A Study in Planning, 1967. *Address:* 29a Sydenham Hill, SE26. *T:* 01-670 3525.

BURNS, Prof. William, CBE 1966; Emeritus Professor of Physiology, University of London; Professor of Physiology, Charing Cross Hospital Medical School, 1947-77; Hon. Consultant Otologist, Charing Cross Group of Hospitals; *b* 15 Oct. 1909; *e s* of late Charles Burns, MB, ChB, JP and Mary Sillars, lately of Stonehaven, Scotland; *m* 1936, Margaret, *o d* of late W. A. Morgan, Glasgow; one *s* one *d*. *Educ:* Mackie Acad., Stonehaven; Aberdeen Univ. BSc 1933, MB ChB 1935, DSc 1943 Aberdeen. FRCP 1973. Asst in Physiology, Aberdeen, 1935; Lectr in Physiology, Aberdeen, 1936; War-time duty with Admiralty, 1942; established in RN Scientific Service, 1946; Supt RN Physiological Laboratory, 1947; Consultant in Acoustic Science to RAF; Chm., Flying Personnel Res. Cttee, RAF, 1978-80; Hon. Civil Consultant to RN in Audiology; pt-time activity for MRC, 1977-. Member: Physiological Soc.; Council, British Association for the Advancement of Science, 1956-61; Noise Adv. Council, 1977-81; BMA; British Inst. of Acoustics; British Soc. Audiology. *Publications:* Noise and Man, 1968, 2nd edn 1973; (with D. W. Robinson) Hearing and Noise in Industry, 1970; articles on various aspects of hearing, in Journal of the Acoustical Soc. of America, Annals of Occupational Hygiene, Proc. Assoc. of Industrial Med. Officers, etc. *Recreations:* working in wood and metal; interested in engineering in general. *Address:* Cairns Cottage, Blacksmith's Lane, Laleham-on-Thames, Mddx TW18 1UB. *T:* Staines 53066.

BURNSIDE, Dame Edith, DBE 1976 (OBE 1957); *m* W. K. Burnside. Awarded DBE for services to hospitals and the community, Toorak, Victoria. *Address:* Flat 6-1, 9 Struan Street, Toorak, Victoria 3142, Australia.

BURNSTOCK, Prof. Geoffrey, FAA; Professor of Anatomy, University of London, and Head of Department of Anatomy and Embryology, University College London, since 1975; *b* 10 May 1929; *s* of James Burnstock and Nancy Green; *m* 1957, Nomi Hirschfeld; three *d*. *Educ:* King's Coll., London; Melbourne Univ. BSc 1953, PhD 1957 London; DSc Melbourne 1971. National Inst. for Medical Res., Mill Hill, 1956-57; Dept of Pharmacology, Oxford Univ., 1957-59; Rockefeller Travelling Fellowship, Univ. of Ill, 1959; Dept of Zoology, Univ. of Melbourne: Sen. Lectr, 1959-62; Reader, 1962-64; Prof. of Zoology and Chm. of Dept, 1964-75; Associate Dean (Biological Sciences), 1969-72. Vis. Prof., Dept of Pharmacology, Univ. of Calif, LA, 1970. Hon. MSc Melbourne 1962; FAA 1971. Silver Medal, Royal Soc. of Victoria, 1970. *Publications:* (with M. Costa) Adrenergic Neurons: their organisation, function and development in the peripheral nervous system, 1975; (with Y. Uehara and G. R. Campbell) An Atlas of the fine structure of Muscle and its innervation, 1976; papers on smooth muscle and autonomic nervous system, incl. purinergic nerves, in sci. jls. *Recreations:* tennis, wood sculpture. *Address:* Department of Anatomy and Embryology, University College London, Gower Street, WC1E 6BT. *T:* 01-387 7050.

BURNTON, Stanley Jeffrey; QC 1982; *b* 25 Oct. 1942; *s* of Harry and Fay Burnton; *m* 1971, Gwenyth Frances Castle; one *s* two *d*. *Educ:* Hackney Downs Grammar Sch.; St Edmund Hall, Oxford. MA. Called to the Bar, Middle Temple, 1965. *Recreations:* music, wine. *Address:* 1 Essex Court, Temple, EC4Y 9AR. *T:* 01-353 5362.

BURRELL, Derek William; Headmaster, Truro School, since 1959; *b* 4 Nov. 1925; *s* of late Thomas Richard Burrell and of Flora Frances Burrell (*née* Nash). *Educ:* Tottenham Grammar Sch.; Queens' Coll., Cambridge. Assistant Master at Solihull Sch. (English, History, Religious Instruction, Music Appreciation), 1948-52. Senior English Master, Dollar Academy, 1952-59. *Recreations:* music of any kind, theatre, wandering about London. *Address:* Truro School, Cornwall. *T:* Truro 2763. *Club:* East India, Devonshire, Sports and Public Schools.

BURRELL, Vice-Adm. Sir Henry Mackay, KBE 1960 (CBE 1955); CB 1959; RAN retired, now a grazier, Illogan Park, Braidwood, NSW; *b* 13 Aug. 1904; British (father *b* Dorset; mother *b* Australia, of Scottish parents); *m* 1944, Ada Theresa Weller (*d* 1981); one *s* two *d*. *Educ:* Royal Australian Naval Coll., Jervis Bay, Australia. Cadet-Midshipman, 1918; specialist in navigation, psc Greenwich, 1938; Commands: HMAS Norman, 1941-42 (despatches); Bataan, 1945; Dep. Chief of Naval Staff, Navy Office, Melbourne, 1947-48; HMAS Australia, 1949; idc 1950; HMAS Vengeance, 1953-54; Second Naval Mem., Australian Commonwealth Naval Board, 1956-57; Flag Officer Commanding HM Australian Fleet, 1955 and 1958;

Chief of the Australian Naval Staff, 1959-62. *Recreations:* tennis and lawn tennis. *Address:* 49 National Circuit, Forrest, Canberra, ACT 2603, Australia. *Club:* Commonwealth (Canberra, ACT).

BURRELL, His Honour John Glyn, QC 1961; a Circuit Judge (formerly County Court Judge), 1964-80; *b* 10 Oct. 1912; *o s* of Lewis Morgan Burrell and Amy Isabel Burrell; *m* 1941, Dorothy, 2nd *d* of Prof. T. Stanley Roberts, MA Cantab, Aberystwyth; two *d*. *Educ:* Friars Sch., Bangor; Univ. Coll. of Wales. Called to Bar, Inner Temple, 1936. Practised Northern Circuit (Liverpool); Recorder of Wigan, 1962-64; Chm., Radnorshire QS, 1964-71. Army service, 1940-45. *Address:* Longhedge, Spittal, Haverfordwest, Dyfed.

BURRELL, Joseph Frederick, CVO 1976; Partner, Farrer & Co., Lincoln's Inn Fields, 1938-76; Solicitor to the Duchy of Cornwall, 1972-76; *b* 27 July 1909; *s* of Arthur J. T. Burrell and Marie Birt; *m* 1940, Diana Margaret Beachcroft, *d* of Cyril Beachcroft and Vivien Hughes. *Educ:* Eton; Trinity College, Cambridge. Sapper, TA, 1938-40; Gunner, 1940-45. Governor and Mem. Bd of Management, Royal Hosp. and Home for Incurables, 1978-; Mem. Council, DGAA, 1978-; Trustee, Grants Cttee of Florence Nightingale Fund for Aid in Sickness, 1978-. *Address:* 54 Murray Road, Wimbledon, SW19. *Club:* Travellers'.

BURRELL, Peter, CBE 1957; Director, The National Stud, 1937-71; *b* 9 May 1905; *s* of Sir Merrik R. Burrell, 7th Bt; *m* 1st, 1929, Pamela Pollen (marr. diss., 1940); two *s*; 2nd, 1971, Mrs Constance P. Mellon (*d* 1980). *Educ:* Eton; Royal Agricultural Coll., Cirencester. *Recreations:* shooting, stalking, hunting. *Address:* Pineland Plantation, PO Box 4, Newton, Ga 31770, USA.

BURRELL, Robert John, QC 1973; *b* London, 28 Nov. 1923; *s* of late Robert Burrell, QC; *m* 1948, Thelma Louise Mawdesley Harris; no *c*. *Educ:* Rugby; Trinity Hall, Cambridge (MA). Served War, Royal Navy, 1942-46: Fleet Minesweepers and Motor Torpedo Boats, English Channel and Adriatic; participated in D Day landings, 1944; demobilised, 1946, Lieut RNVR. Called to Bar, Inner Temple, 1948; Bencher, Inner Temple, 1980. Mem., Paddington Borough Council, 1949-56 (Chm. Housing Cttee, 1953-56); Chairman: Plant Varieties and Seeds Tribunal, 1974-; Pres., Ligue Internationale contre la Concurrence Déloyale (Paris), 1980-82 (Vice-Pres., 1978-80); Mem., EEC Working Cttee, EEC Trade Mark Law, 1975-77. *Recreations:* music (piano), mountain walking. *Address:* 1 Essex Court, Temple, EC4Y 9AR. *T:* 01-353 8507.

BURRELL, Sir Walter (Raymond), 8th Bt, *cr* 1774; CBE 1956 (MBE 1945); TD; DL; Trustee Royal Agricultural Society of England, since 1948, President 1964, Chairman of Council, 1967-72; *b* 11 Dec. 1903; *er s* of Sir Merrik Burrell, 7th Bt, CBE; *S* father 1957; *m* 1931, Hon. Anne Judith Denman, OBE, *o d* of 3rd Baron Denman, PC, GCMG, KCVO; two *s* two *d*. *Educ:* Eton. Major 98th Field Regt (Surrey and Sussex Yeo.), Royal Artillery (TA), 1938; Lt-Col (Chief Instructor) 123 OCTU, 1942; Lt-Col BAS (Washington), 1943; Comd 3 Super Heavy Regt, RA 1945 (MBE). Pres. Country Landowners' Assoc., 1952-53; Pres., South of England Agricultural Soc., 1974-. DL Sussex, 1937, West Sussex 1974; County Alderman, 1950; Vice-Chm. West Sussex County Council, 1953. *Heir:* *s* John Raymond Burrell [*b* 20 Feb. 1934; *m* 1st, 1959, Rowena Pearce (marr. diss. 1971); one *s* one *d*; 2nd, 1971, Margot Lucy, *d* of F. E. Thatcher, Sydney, NSW; one *s* one *d*. *Educ:* Eton]. *Address:* Knepp Castle, West Grinstead, Horsham, West Sussex. *T:* Coolham 247. *Club:* Boodle's.
See also Peter Burrell, J. F. E. Smith.

BURRENCHOBAY, Sir Dayendranath, KBE 1978; CMG 1977; CVO 1972; Governor-General of Mauritius, since 1978; *b* 24 March 1919; *s* of Mohabeer Burrenchobay, MBE, and Anant Kumari Burrenchobay; *m* 1957, Oomawatee Ramphul; one *s* two *d*. *Educ:* Royal Coll., Curepipe, Mauritius; Imperial Coll., London (BScEng Hons); Inst. of Education, London (Postgrad. CertEd). Education Officer, Govt of Mauritius, 1951-60, Sen. Educn Officer, 1960-64; Chief Educn Officer, 1964; Permanent Secretary: Min. of Education and Cultural Affairs, 1964-68; Min. of External Affairs, Tourism and Emigration, also Prime Minister's Office, 1968-76; Secretary to Cabinet and Head of Civil Service, 1976-78. Attended various confs and seminars as Govt rep.; Chm., Central Electricity Bd, 1968-79. Hon. DCL, Univ. of Mauritius, 1978. Chevalier, Légion d'Honneur, 1975; Grand Cross, 1st Cl., Order of Merit, Fed. Republic of Germany, 1978. *Recreations:* swimming, walking. *Address:* Government House, Le Réduit, Mauritius; S. Ramphul Street, Curepipe Road, Mauritius.

BURRETT, (Frederick) Gordon, CB 1974; Deputy Secretary, Civil Service Department, 1972-81; Chairman, Redundant Churches Fund, since 1982; *b* 31 Oct. 1921; *s* of Frederick Burrett and Marion Knowles; *m* 1943, Margaret Joan Giddins; one *s* two *d*. *Educ:* Emanuel Sch.; St Catharine's Coll., Cambridge. Served in Royal Engrs, N Africa, Italy, Yugoslavia, Greece, 1942-45 (despatches). HM Foreign, subseq. Diplomatic, Service, 1946; 3rd Sec., Budapest, 1946-49; FO, 1949-51; Vice-Consul, New York, 1951-54; FO, 1954-57; 1st Sec., Rome, 1957-60; transf. to HM Treasury, 1960; Private Sec. to Chief Sec., Treasury, 1963-64; Asst Secretary: HM Treasury, 1964; Cabinet Office, 1967-68; Secretary: Kindersley Review Body on Doctors' and Dentists' Remuneration; Plowden Cttee on Pay of Higher Civil Service, 1967-68; Civil Service Dept, 1968, Under-Sec. 1969. Mem., Civil Service Pay

Res. Unit Bd, 1978-81; conducted govt scrutiny of V&A and Sci. Museums, 1982. *Publication*: article on the watercolours of John Massey Wright (1777-1866) in vol. 54 of the Old Water-Colour Society's Club Annual. *Recreations*: music, books, walking, cruising on inland waterways. *Address*: Trinity Cottage, Church Road, Claygate, Surrey. *T*: Esher 62783.

BURRIDGE, Alan; Certification Officer for Trade Unions and Employers' Associations, since 1981; *b* 15 Feb. 1921; *m* 1961, Joan Edith Neale; one *s*. *Educ*: William Ellis Sch.; Bristol Univ. (BA 1st Cl. Hons 1950). Served War, Army, 1939-46. Northern Assurance Co., 1936-39; Bristol Univ., 1947-50; Swinton Coll., 1950-53; London Municipal Soc., 1953-56; General Electric Co., 1956-67; Dept of Employment, 1967-81. *Address*: 1 Castle Hill Avenue, Berkhamsted, Herts HP4 1HJ. *T*: Berkhamsted 5276.

BURROUGH, Alan, CBE 1970; Director, James Burrough Ltd, since 1946 (Chairman, 1968-82); *b* 22 Feb. 1917; *s* of Ernest James Burrough and Sophie (*née* Burston); *m* 1939, Rosemary June Bruce; two *s* one *d*. *Educ*: St Paul's Sch., London; Jesus Coll., Cambridge Univ. (MA). Joined James Burrough Ltd, 1935. War of 1939-45: 91st Field Regt, RA, and 5th RHA (Captain). Rejoined James Burrough Ltd, 1945: Director, 1946; Deputy Chairman, 1967; Chairman, 1968; Dir, Corby Distilleries Ltd, Montreal, 1980-82. Dep. Pres., Oxon Br., British Red Cross. *Address*: Manor Garden, Henley-on-Thames, Oxon. *Clubs*: Naval and Military; Leander (Henley-on-Thames); Royal Channel Islands Yacht.

BURROUGH, John Outhit Harold, CB 1975; CBE 1963; *b* 31 Jan. 1916; *s* of Adm. Sir Harold M. Burrough, GCB, KBE, DSO, and late Nellie Wills Outhit; *m* 1944, Suzanne Cecile Jourdan; one *s* one *d*. *Educ*: Manor House, Horsham; RNC Dartmouth. Midshipman, 1934; Sub-Lt 1936; Lieut 1938; Lt-Comdr 1944; retd 1947. Foreign Office (GCHQ), 1946-65; IDC 1964; British Embassy, Washington, 1965-67; Under-Sec., Cabinet Office, 1967-69; an Under Sec., FCO (Govt Communications HQ), 1969-76. Director: Racal Communications Systems Ltd, 1976-82; Racal Communications Ltd, 1979-82. *Address*: The Little Warrens, Stanton, Broadway, Worcs. *T*: Stanton 260. *Club*: Naval and Military (Chm., 1969-72).

BURROUGH, Rt. Rev. John Paul, MBE 1946; MA Oxon; Rector of Empingham, and an Hon. Assistant Bishop, Diocese of Peterborough, since 1981; *b* 5 May 1916; *s* of Canon E. G. Burrough; *m* 1962, Elizabeth (Bess), widow of Stephen John White; one step-*d*. *Educ*: St Edward's Sch.; St Edmund Hall, Oxford; Ely Theol. College. Coach, Tigre Boat Club, Buenos Aires, 1938-39. Captain, Royal Signals, Malaya Campaign (POW), 1940-45. Asst, Aldershot Parish Church, 1946-51; Mission Priest, Dio. of Korea, 1951-59; Anglican Chaplain to Overseas Peoples in Birmingham, 1959-68; Canon Residentiary of Birmingham, 1967-68; Bishop of Mashonaland, 1968-81. Chaplain and Sub-Prelate, Order of St John of Jerusalem, 1969-. *Publication*: Lodeleigh, 1946. *Recreation*: rowing (Oxford crews, 1937 and 1938). *Address*: The Rectory, 5 Nook Lane, Empingham, Oakham, Leics LE15 8PT. *Clubs*: Leander (Henley); Vincent's (Oxford); Salisbury (Salisbury).

BURROW, Prof. Harold, MRCVS, DVSM; Professor of Veterinary Medicine, Royal Veterinary College, University of London, 1944-63; Professor Emeritus since 1963; *b* 24 Aug. 1903; *s* of Henry Wilson and Elizabeth Jane Burrow, Hest Bank Lodge, near Lancaster; *m* 1933, Frances Olivia, *d* of Orlando Atkinson Ducksbury, MRCVS, and Mrs Frances Mary Ducksbury, Lancaster; one *d*. *Educ*: Lancaster Royal Grammar Sch.; Royal (Dick) Veterinary Coll., Edinburgh. Asst Veterinary Officer, City of Birmingham, 1927-30; Chief Veterinary Officer: Birkenhead, 1930-35; Derbyshire CC, 1935-38; Divisional Veterinary Officer, Min. of Agriculture, 1938-42; Private Veterinary Practice, 1942-44. Examiner: to Royal Coll. of Veterinary Surgeons, 1937-44; to Univs. of Liverpool, London, Reading, Edinburgh, Bristol and Ceylon (various dates). Pres. Old Lancastrian Club, 1953; Member of Council, Royal Society Health, 1950-64 (Chairman, 1956-57, Vice-Pres. 1958-65, Life Vice-Pres., 1965). *Publications*: numerous contributions to veterinary scientific press. *Recreation*: gardening. *Address*: Primrose Cottage, Donnington, Moreton-in-Marsh, Glos.

BURROW, Prof. Thomas, MA, PhD; FBA 1970; Boden Professor of Sanskrit in the University of Oxford, and Fellow of Balliol College, 1944-76; Emeritus Fellow of Balliol, 1976; *b* 29 June 1909; *e s* of Joshua and Frances Eleanor Burrow; *m* 1941, Inez Mary (*d* 1976), *d* of Herbert John Haley. *Educ*: Queen Elizabeth's Sch., Kirkby Lonsdale; Christ's Coll., Cambridge. Research Fellow of Christ's Coll., Cambridge, 1935-37; Asst Keeper in Dept of Oriental Printed Books and Manuscripts, British Museum, 1937-44. Leverhulme Research Fellow, 1967-68. Fellow, Sch. of Oriental and African Studies, 1974. *Publications*: The Language of the Kharosthi Documents from Chinese Turkestan, 1937; A Translation of the Kharosthi Documents from Chinese Turkestan, 1940; (with S. Bhattacharya) The Parji Language, 1953; The Sanskrit Language, 1955; (with M. B. Emeneau) A Dravidian Etymological Dictionary, 1961; Supplement, 1968; (with S. Bhattacharya) The Pengo Language, 1970; The Problem of Shwa in Sanskrit, 1979. *Address*: 1 Woodlands, Kidlington, Oxford OX5 2ER. *T*: Kidlington 5283.

BURROWES, Edmund Stanley Spencer, CMG 1959; Financial Secretary, Barbados, 1951-66; *b* 16 Dec. 1906; *m* 1st, 1934, Mildred B. Jackson (decd); one *s* three *d*; 2nd, 1965, Gwen Searson. *Educ*: Queen's Coll., British Guiana. British Guiana Colonial Secretariat, 1924; Inspector of Labour, 1940; Deputy

Commissioner, 1945; Labour Commissioner, Barbados, 1947. *Publication*: Occupational Terms on Sugar Estates in British Guiana, 1945. *Recreations*: diving, gardening. *Address*: 66 Meadow Mount, Churchtown, Dublin.

BURROWES, Norma Elizabeth; opera and concert singer; *d* of Henry and Caroline Burrowes; *m* 1969, Steuart Bedford, *qv* (marr. diss.). *Educ*: Sullivan Upper Sch., Holywood, Co. Down; Queen's Univ., Belfast (BA); Royal Academy of Music (ARAM). Operas include: Zerlina in Don Giovanni, Glyndebourne Touring Opera (début); Blöndchen in Die Entführung aus dem Serail, Salzburg Festival, and again Blöndchen, Paris Opera, 1976 (début); Fiakermili, Royal Opera House (début), also Oscar, Despina, Nanetta, Woodbird; Entführung aus dem Serail, Ballo in Maschera, Der Rosenkavalier, Metropolitan, NY; Daughter of the Regiment, Midsummer Night's Dream, Elisir d'Amore, Canada; Cosi Fan Tutte, Romeo and Juliet, France; Marriage of Figaro, Germany; Gianni Schicchi, Switzerland; Marriage of Figaro, La Scala. Television operas include: Nanetta in Falstaff; Susanna in Marriage of Figaro and Lauretta in Gianni Schicchi. Sings regularly with major opera companies, gives concerts and recitals, GB and abroad; many recordings. Hon. DMus Queen's Univ. Belfast. *Recreations*: swimming, gardening, needlework. *Address*: 56 Rochester Road, NW1 9JG. *T*: 01-485 7322.

BURROWS, Sir Bernard (Alexander Brocas), GCMG 1970 (KCMG 1955; CMG 1950); Consultant, Federal Trust for Education and Research (Director-General, 1973-76); *b* 3 July 1910; *s* of Edward Henry Burrows and Ione, *d* of Alexander Macdonald; *m* 1944, Ines, *d* of late John Walter; one *s* one *d*. *Educ*: Eton; Trinity Coll., Oxford. Entered HM Foreign Service (later Diplomatic Service), 1934; served at HM Embassy, Cairo, 1938-45; Foreign Office, 1945-50; Counsellor HM Embassy, Washington, 1950-53; Political Resident in the Persian Gulf, 1953-58; Ambassador to Turkey, 1958-62; Dep. Under-Secretary of State, FO, 1963-66; Permanent British Representative to N Atlantic Council, 1966-70, retired 1970. Chm. Council, British Inst. of Archaeology, Ankara. *Publications*: (with C. Irwin) Security of Western Europe, 1972; Devolution or Federalism, 1980; (with G. Edwards) The Defence of Western Europe, 1982; contributed to: A Nation Writ Large, 1973; Federal Solutions to European Issues, 1978; The Third World War 1985, 1978; The Third World War: the untold story, 1982; articles and reviews in New Europe, etc. *Address*: Steep Farm, Petersfield, Hants. *T*: Petersfield 2287. *Club*: Travellers'.

BURROWS, Fred, CMG 1981; Legal Counsellor, Foreign and Commonwealth Office, since 1980; *b* 10 Aug. 1925; *s* of late Charles Burrows; *m* 1955, Jennifer Winsome Munt; two *s*. *Educ*: Altrincham Grammar Sch.; Trinity Hall, Cambridge (MA). Served in RAF, 1944-47. Called to Bar, Gray's Inn, 1950; Asst Legal Adviser, Foreign Office, 1956-65; Legal Adviser, British Embassy, Bonn, 1965-67; returned to FO, 1967; Legal Counsellor, FCO, 1968-77; Counsellor (Legal Adviser), Office of UK Perm. Rep. to European Communities, 1977-80. *Recreations*: sailing, carpentry. *Address*: c/o Foreign and Commonwealth Office, SW1.

BURROWS, Very Rev. Hedley Robert; Dean Emeritus of Hereford; Dean of Hereford, 1947-61, resigned in Oct. 1961; *b* 15 Oct. 1887; *s* of late Rt Rev. L. H. Burrows; *m* 1921, Joan Lumsden (*d* 1964), *d* of late Rt Rev. E. N. Lovett, CBE; one *s* (*er s* died on active service, 1945), two *d*. *Educ*: Charterhouse; New Coll., Oxford; Wells Theological Coll. Deacon, 1911; Priest, 1912; Curate of Petersfield, Hants, 1911-14; Temp. CF European War, 1914-16, invalided; Hon. CF; Priest in charge St Columba's, Poltalloch, Argyll, 1917-18; Domestic Chaplain to Dr Lang, when Archbishop of York, 1918-19; Curate in charge Dock Street Mission, Southampton, 1919-21; Rector of Stoke Abbott, Dorset, 1921-25; Vicar of St Stephen's, Portsea, 1925-28; Hon. Chaplain to 1st Bishop of Portsmouth, 1927-28. Vicar of Grimsby and Rural Dean of Grimsby and Cleethorpes, 1928-36; Vicar of St Peter's, Bournemouth, 1936-43; Rural Dean of Bournemouth, 1940-43; Prebendary and Canon of Sutton-in-Marisco, Lincoln Cathedral, 1933-43; Archdeacon of Winchester, and Residentiary Canon of the Cathedral, 1943-47. Chm., Midland Region Religious Cttee of the BBC, 1952-57 (*ex-officio*: Member Midland Council of BBC and Member Headquarters Council of BBC Central Religious Cttee, London). Elected a Church Commissioner for England, and Member Board of Governors, 1952-58. OStJ, 1947. *Publication*: Hereford Cathedral, 1958. *Address*: Brendon House, Park Road, Winchester, Hants SO23 7BQ. *Club*: Athenæum.
See also Bishop of Buckingham.

BURROWS, Sir John; see Burrows, Sir R. J. F.

BURROWS, Lionel John, CBE 1974; Chief Inspector of Schools, Department of Education and Science, 1966-73; Educational Adviser, Methodist Residential Schools, since 1974; *b* 9 March 1912; *s* of H. L. Burrows, HM Inspector of Schools, and Mrs C. J. Burrows; *m* 1939, Enid Patricia Carter; one *s* one *d*. *Educ*: King Edward VI Sch., Southampton; Gonville and Caius Coll., Cambridge. BA Cantab (1st cl. hons Mod. Langs Tripos) 1933. West Buckland Sch., Devon, Tiffin Sch., Kingston-upon-Thames and primary schools in London and Surrey, 1934-41; HM Forces (RASC and Intell. Corps), 1941-46; Commendation from US Army Chief of Staff, 1945; HM Inspector of Schools, 1946; Divisional Inspector, Metropolitan Div., 1960. Vice-Pres., Nat. Assoc. for Gifted Children, 1975-. *Publication*: The Middle School: high road or dead end?, 1978. *Recreations*: natural history, fell-walking. *Address*: 34 Groby Road, Ratby, Leicester LE6 0LJ. *Club*: English-Speaking Union.

BURROWS, Reginald Arthur, CMG 1964; HM Diplomatic Service, retired; *b* 31 Aug. 1918; *s* of late Arthur Richard Burrows; *m* 1952, Jenny Louisa Henriette Campiche; one *s* one *d. Educ:* Mill Hill Sch.; St Catharine's Coll., Cambridge. Served with Royal Air Force during War; comd No. 13 (bomber) Sqdn, 1945. Entered the Foreign Service (now the Diplomatic Service), 1947; served in: Paris; Karachi; Tehran; Saigon; The Hague; Istanbul; Foreign Office; Minister, Islamabad, 1970-72; Univ. of Leeds, 1972-73; on secondment as Under-Sec., Civil Service Selection Bd, 1974-75; Asst Under-Sec. of State, 1975-78. *Recreations:* ski-ing, tennis. *Address:* 10 Elvaston Place, SW7. *Club:* Hurlingham.

BURROWS, Sir (Robert) John (Formby), Kt 1965; MA, LLB; Solicitor; *b* 29 May 1901; *s* of Rev. Canon Francis Henry and Margaret Nelson Burrows; *m* 1926, Mary Hewlett, *y d* of Rev. R. C. Salmon; one *s* one *d. Educ:* Eton Coll. (Scholar); Trinity Coll., Cambridge (Scholar); Harvard Law Sch. Pres. of The Law Soc., 1964-65. *Recreation:* forestry. *Address:* Ridlands Cottage, Limpsfield Chart, Surrey. *T:* Limpsfield Chart 3288. *Club:* Buck's.
See also W. Hamilton.

BURROWS, Rt. Rev. Simon Hedley; *see* Buckingham, Bishop Suffragan of.

BURSTALL, Prof. Aubrey Frederic; Professor of Mechanical Engineering, University of Newcastle upon Tyne (formerly King's College, University of Durham), 1946-67, now Emeritus; Dean of Faculty of Applied Science, 1955-57; *b* 15 Jan. 1902; *s* of Prof. Frederic William Burstall of Univ. of Birmingham and Lilian Maud Burstall (*née* Adley); *m* 1923, Nora Elizabeth (*née* Boycott); two *s* one *d. Educ:* King Edward VI Grammar Sch., Birmingham, Univ. of Birmingham; St John's Coll., Cambridge. BScEng Birmingham, 1922, First Class Hons; MScEng Birmingham, 1923; PhD Cantab 1925; DSc Melbourne; Hon. DSc (NUI), 1959. Research student, St John's Coll., Cambridge, 1923-25. Employed on the staff of Synthetic Ammonia and Nitrates Ltd (later merged into ICI Ltd) as research engineer, asst chief engineer and works engineer at Billingham Factory, 1925-34; Aluminium Plant and Vessel Co., London, as Technical Adviser to the Board responsible for design of chemical plant, 1934-37; Prof. of Engineering and Dean of Faculty of Engineering, Univ. of Melbourne, Australia, 1937-45. Developed mechanical respirators for infantile paralysis epidemic, 1937-38; gas producers for motor vehicles, and built new workshops at the Univ.; part-time Comr of State Electricity Commn of Victoria, 1941-43; leave of absence to work for British Min. of Supply in Armaments Design Dept, Fort Halstead, Kent, 1943-44. Member of Nat. Advisory Cttee on Technical Educ., 1948; Chm. North Eastern Branch IMechE, 1956; Member Board of Governors, United Newcastle upon Tyne Hospitals, 1964-67; Member Council of Univ. of Durham, 1964-67; Fellow, NEC Inst. Engineers and Shipbuilders; FIMechE. *Publications:* A History of Mechanical Engineering, 1963; Simple Working Models of Historic Machines, 1968; numerous in engineering journals in Britain and Australia. *Address:* The Firs, Kilmington, Axminster, Devon EX13 7SS. *T:* Axminster 32385.

BURSTEIN, Hon. Dame Rose; *see* Heilbron, Hon. Dame R.

BURSTON, Sir Samuel (Gerald Wood), Kt 1977; OBE 1966; Grazier at Noss Estate, Casterton, Victoria, since 1945; President, Australian Woolgrowers and Graziers Council, 1976-79; *b* 24 April 1915; *s* of Maj.-Gen. Sir Samuel Burston, KBE, CB, DSO, VD, late RAAMC, and late Lady Burston; *m* 1940, Verna Helen Peebles (*d* 1980); one *s* one *d. Educ:* St Peter's Coll., Adelaide. Major, AIF, 1939-45 (despatches). Chm., Country Fire Authority, Vic, 1964-65; Pres., Graziers Assoc. of Vic, 1973-76; Councillor, Nat. Farmers Fedn, 1979-; Vice-Pres., Confedn of Aust. Industry, 1978-; Member: Nat. Employers Policy Cttee, 1970-78; Australian Wool Industry Policy Cttee, 1976-78; Aust. Sci. and Technol. Council, 1976-; Aust. Stats Adv. Council, 1976-80; Aust. Govt Econ. Consultative Gp, 1976-; Nat. Labour Consultative Council, 1977-; Reserve Bank Bd, 1977-; Aust. Trade Develt Council, 1979-; Trade Practices Cons. Council, 1979-; Aust. Manufacturing Council, 1979-; Chm., Perpetual Executors & Trustee Co. of Australia. Mem., Victorian Selection Cttee, Winston Churchill Meml Trust, 1967-81. *Recreations:* golf, swimming. *Address:* Noss Estate, Casterton, Vic 3311, Australia. *T:* 055 811147. *Clubs:* Melbourne (Melbourne); Adelaide, Naval, Military and Air Force of South Australia (Adelaide); Royal Adelaide Golf.

BURT, Hon. Sir Francis (Theodore Page), KCMG 1977; Lieutenant-Governor of Western Australia, since 1977; Chief Justice of Western Australia, since 1977 (a Judge of the Supreme Court since 1969); *b* Perth, WA, 14 June 1918; *s* of A. F. G. Burt; *m* 1943, Margaret, *d* of Brig. J. E. Lloyd; two *s* two *d. Educ:* Guildford Grammar Sch.; Univ. of Western Australia (LLB, LLM); Hackett Schol., 1941; admitted to Bar of WA, 1941. Served War, RAN and RAAF, 1940-45. QC 1960; Pres., Law Soc. of WA, 1960-62. Visiting Lectr in Law, Univ. of WA, 1945-65. Chairman: Inst. of Radiotherapy, WA, 1960-62; Bd of Management, Sir Charles Gairdner Hosp., Hollywood, WA, 1962-72; Queen Elizabeth II Medical Centre Trust, 1966-; Mem., Senate of Univ. of WA, 1968-76. *Recreations:* tennis, fishing. *Address:* 64 Leake Street, Cottesloe, WA 6011, Australia. *Club:* Weld (Perth).

BURT, Gerald Raymond, BEM 1947; FCIT; Chief Secretary, British Railways Board, since 1976; *b* 15 Feb. 1926; *s* of Reginald George Burt and Lilian May Burt; *m* 1948, Edna Ivy Elizabeth Sizeland; two *s. Educ:* Latyme Upper Sch. FCIT 1971. Joined GWR as Booking Clerk, 1942: RF (Movement Control), 1944-47; BR Management Trainee, 1951-54; Gen Staff, British Transport Commn, 1956-59; Divl Planning Officer, Bristol 1959-62; Planning Officer, LMR, 1962-64; Divl Man., St Pancras, 1965 Traffic Man., Freightliners, 1967-70; Principal Corporate Planning Officer British Railways Bd, 1970-76. Mem. Council, Chartered Inst. of Transport 1967-70, 1981-; Governor, British Transport Staff Coll., 1976-82. Scoutin Medal of Merit, 1978. *Recreations:* gardening, the countryside. *Address* Sizelands, Mill Lane, Wingrave, Aylesbury, Bucks HP22 4PL. *T:* Aston Abbotts 458.

BURT, Leonard James, CVO 1954; CBE 1957; Commander of Specia Branch, New Scotland Yard, 1946-58, retired; *b* 20 April 1892; *s* of Charle Richard Burt; *m* 1918, Grace Airey; one *s. Educ:* Totton High Sch., Hants CID, 1919-40; Chief Superintendent, CID, 1940; Intelligence Corps (Lieut Col) 1940-46. Officer Legion of Honour, 1950; Officer Order of Orang Nassau, 1951; Chevalier Order of Danebrog, 1951. *Publication:* Commande Burt of Scotland Yard, 1959. *Address:* Flat 1, Hedley Court, 67/69 Putne Hill, SW15. *T:* 01-788 4598.

BURT, Maurice Edward, FRAeS; Deputy Director, Building Research Establishment, 1975-81, retired; *b* 17 Nov. 1921; *s* of Reginald Edward Bur and Bertha Winifred Burt; *m* 1947, Monica Evelyn Amy; one *s* three *d. Educ* Victoria Coll., Jersey; Taunton's Sch., Southampton; BA Hons London, 1948 CEng, MICE; FRAeS 1965. Aircraft industry, 1938-48; RAE, 1948-66 (Sup Airworthiness, 1961-66); Head of Structures Dept, Transport and Road Res Lab., 1966-73; Head of Res. Management, Dept of Environment, 1973-75 *Publications:* technical reports and articles. *Recreations:* golf, walking gardening. *Address:* Roselle, Rue de Haut, St Lawrence, Jersey, CI. *T:* Jerse 35933.

BURT-ANDREWS, Air Commodore Charles Beresford Eaton, CB 1962 CBE 1959; RAF retired; *b* 21 March 1913; *s* of late Major C. Burt-Andrews RE; *m* 1st, 1941, Elizabeth Alsina Helen, *d* of late Sir Maurice Linford Gwyer GCIE, KCB, KCSI; one *s* one *d* ; 2nd, 1977, Joan Tresor (*née* Cayzer-Evans) *Educ:* Lindisfarne Coll.; Collège des Frères Chrétiens Sophia. Commnd RAF 1935; served NWF India, 1937-42; S Waziristan ops, 1937; Burma, 1942 comd Army Co-op. Sqdn RAF, 1943; special ops, 1943-44; Air Attaché British Embassy, Warsaw, 1945-47; Staff Coll., 1948; Sec. Gen. Allied Air Forces Central Europe, Fontainebleau, 1950-52; directing Staff RAF Staf Coll., 1953-55; Head of Far East Defence Secretariat, Singapore, 1955-58; Firs Comdt, Pakistan Air Force Staff Coll., 1959-61; UK Nat. Mil. Rep., SHAPE Paris, 1962-65; Asst Comdt, RAF Staff Coll., Bracknell, 1965-68; retd 1968 *Recreation:* painting. *Address:* c/o Savvides & Savvides, Kanika Court Makarios Avenue, Limassol, Cyprus.
See also S. G. Burt-Andrews.

BURT-ANDREWS, Stanley George, CMG 1968; MBE 1948; retired; *b* Feb. 1908; *s* of Major Charles and Menie Celina Burt-Andrews; *m* 1937, Ver Boyadjieva; one *d. Educ:* Lindisfarne Coll., Westcliff-on-Sea; St Andrew Coll., Bloemfontein, S Africa. Vice-Consul, 1946-47, Consul, 2nd Secretary Sofia, 1948; Consul, Barranquilla, 1949-52; Commercial Secretary, British Embassy, Buenos Aires, 1952-53; Consul: Baltimore, 1953-59; Bilbao, 1959 62; Venice, 1962-64; Consul-General, St Louis, Mo., 1965-67. *Recreations* golf, fishing. *Address:* Villa Verial, 1 Aldwick Place, Fish Lane, Aldwick Bognor Regis, W Sussex. *Club:* Bognor Regis Golf.
See also Air Cdre C. B. E. Burt-Andrews.

BURTON, family name of **Baroness Burton of Coventry.**

BURTON, 3rd Baron, *cr* 1897; **Michael Evan Victor Baillie;** *b* 27 June 1924 *er s* of Brig. Hon. George Evan Michael Baillie, MC, TD (*d* 1941) and *g* of Baroness Burton (2nd in line); *S* grandmother, 1962; *m* 1st, 1948, Elizabet Ursula Forster (marr. diss. 1977), *er d* of late Capt. A. F. Wise; two *s* fou *d* ; 2nd, 1978, Coralie Denise, 2nd *d* of late Claud R. Cliffe. *Educ:* Eton. Lieut Scots Guards, 1944. Mem., CC, 1948-75, JP 1961-75, DL 1963-65, Inverness shire. *Heir: s* Hon. Evan Michael Ronald Baillie [*b* 19 March 1949; *m* 1970 Lucinda, *e d* of Robert Law, Newmarket; two *s* one *d*]. *Address:* Dochfour Inverness. *T:* Dochgarroch 252. *Clubs:* Cavalry and Guards, Brooks's; New (Edinburgh).

BURTON OF COVENTRY, Baroness, *cr* 1962, of Coventry (Life Peer **Elaine Frances Burton;** Chairman, Mail Order Publishers' Authority, an President, Association of Mail Order Publishers, since 1970; President Institute of Travel Managers in Industry and Commerce; *b* Scarborough, March 1904; *d* of Leslie and Frances Burton. *Educ:* Leeds Girls' Modern Sch City of Leeds Training Coll. Leeds elementary schools and evening institutes 1924-35; South Wales Council of Social Service and educational settlements 1935-37; National Fitness Council, 1938-39; John Lewis Partnership, 1940-45 Writer, lecturer, broadcaster, public relations consultant, 1945-50. MP (Lab Coventry South, 1950-59. Member of parliamentary delegation t Netherlands, 1952 and to Soviet Union, 1954; Siam, 1956; South America 1958; deleg. to Council of Europe; first woman Chm., Select Cttee o Estimates (sub-Cttee); Mem., Select Cttee on Practice and Procedure (Hous of Lords). Chairman: Domestic Coal Consumers' Council, 1962-65; Counci on Tribunals, 1967-73; Member: Council Industrial Design, 1963-68; ITA 1964-69; Sports Council, 1965-71. Founder Mem., Social Democratic Party

1981-. Consultant to: John Waddington Ltd, 1959-61; The Reader's Digest, 1969-70; Courtaulds Ltd, 1960-73; Hon. Consultant, Air Transport Users Cttee, 1979- (Mem., 1973-79); Director: Consultancy Ltd, 1949-73; Imperial Domestic Appliances Ltd, 1963-66. *Publications:* What of the Women, 1941; And Your Verdict?, 1943; articles for press, magazines and political journals. *Recreations:* reading, ballet, opera; World's Sprint Champion, 1920; Yorkshire 1st XI (hockey), 1924-32. *Address:* 47 Molyneux Street, W1. *T:* 01-262 0864.

BURTON, Sir Carlisle (Archibald), Kt 1979; OBE 1968; Chairman, Public Service Commission, Barbados, since 1981; *b* 29 July 1921; *m* 1946, Hyacinth Marjorie Adelle Barker. *Educ:* Harrison Coll., Barbados, WI; Univ. of London (BA); School of Librarianship, Leeds (ALA); Univ. of Pittsburgh (MS). Assistant Master, Harrison Coll., Barbados, 1943-50; Sen. Asst Master, Bishop's High Sch., Tobago, 1950-51; Public Librarian, Barbados, 1953-58; Permanent Secretary: Min. of Educn, 1958-63; Min. of Health, 1963-71; Perm. Sec., Prime Minister's Office, and Head of Civil Service, 1972-81. Director: Barbados National Bank, 1978-; Insurance Corp. of Barbados, 1978- (Chm., 1981-). FRSA 1953. *Recreations:* (active) table tennis, swimming, bridge, reading; (spectator) cricket (Life Member, Barbados Cricket Assoc.), athletics (Life Member, Barbados Amateur Athletic Assoc.), soccer. *Address:* Caradelle, Mountjoy Avenue, Pine Gardens, St Michael, Barbados, West Indies. *T:* 93724.

BURTON, Sir George (Vernon Kennedy), Kt 1977; CBE 1972 (MBE (mil.) 1945); DL; Chairman, Fisons plc, since 1973 (Chief Executive, 1966-76, Senior Vice-Chairman, 1966-71, Deputy Chairman, 1971-72); Director: Thomas Tilling, since 1976; Rolls-Royce Ltd, since 1976; *b* 21 April 1916; *s* of late George Ethelbert Earnshaw and Francesca Burton; *g s* of Sir Bunnell Burton, Ipswich; *m* 1st, 1945, Sarah Katherine Tcherniavsky (marr. diss.); two *s*; 2nd, 1975, Priscilla Margaret Gore, *d* of Cecil H. King, *qv. Educ:* Charterhouse; Germany. Served RA, 1939-45, N Africa, Sicily, Italy, Austria. Dir, Barclays Bank Internat. plc, 1976-82; Member: Export Council for Europe, 1965-71 (Dep. Chm., 1967-71); Council, CBI, 1970- (Chm., CBI Overseas Cttee, 1975-81); BOTB, 1972-73 (BOTB European Trade Cttee, 1972-; British Overseas Trade Adv. Council, 1975-79); Investment Insce Adv. Cttee, ECGD, 1971-76; Council on Internat. Develt of ODM, 1977-79; Council, BIM, 1968-70 (FBIM); NEDC, 1975-79; Whitford Cttee to Consider Law on Copyright and Designs, 1974-77; Ipswich County Borough Council, 1947-51; Ipswich Gp HMC; Assoc. for Business Sponsorship of the Arts, 1978-; Governing Body, British National Cttee of Internat. Chamber of Commerce, 1979-; Governor, Sutton's Hosp. in Charterhouse, 1979-; Chm., Ipswich Conservative Assoc., 1982-. FRSA 1978. DL Suffolk, 1980. Commander: Order of Ouissam Alaouite, Morocco, 1968; Order of Léopold II, Belgium, 1974. *Recreation:* music. *Address:* Aldham Mill, Hadleigh, Suffolk.

BURTON, Graham Stuart; HM Diplomatic Service; Counsellor, Tripoli, since 1981; *b* 8 April 1941; *s* of late Cyril Stanley Richard Burton and of Jessie Blythe Burton; *m* 1965, Julia Margaret Lappin; one *s* one *d. Educ:* Sir William Borlase's Sch., Marlow. Foreign Office, 1961; Abu Dhabi, 1964; Middle East Centre for Arabic Studies, 1967; Kuwait, 1969; FCO, 1972; Tunis, 1975; UK Mission to United Nations, 1978. *Recreations:* golf, watching all sport, opera. *Address:* c/o Foreign and Commonwealth Office, SW1.

BURTON, Air Marshal Sir Harry, KCB 1971 (CB 1970); CBE 1963 (MBE 1943); DSO 1941; Air Officer Commanding-in-Chief, Air Support Command, 1970-73, retired; Managing Director, Toynbee Goodwood Gardens Ltd; *b* 2 May 1919; *s* of Robert Reid Burton, Rutherglen; *m* 1945, Jean, *d* of Tom Dobie; one *s* one *d. Educ:* Glasgow High Sch. Joined RAF 1937; served War of 1939-45, Europe, India, and Pacific (POW, 1940, escaped 1941; despatches); CO, RAF Scampton, 1960-62; SASO 3 (Bomber) Group, RAF, 1963-65; Air Executive to Deputy for Nuclear Affairs, SHAPE, 1965-67; AOC 23 Group, RAF, 1967-70. Group Captain 1958; Air Cdre 1963; Air Vice-Marshal 1965; Air Marshal 1971. *Address:* Mayfield, West Drive, Middleton-on-Sea, Sussex. *Club:* Royal Air Force.

BURTON, Humphrey McGuire; Executive Producer, Performing Arts, BBC Television, since 1981; *b* 25 March 1931; *s* of Harry (Philip) and Kathleen Burton; *m* 1st, 1957, Gretel (*née* Davis); one *s* one *d*; 2nd, 1970, Christina (*née* Hellstedt); one *s* one *d. Educ:* Long Dene Sch., Chiddingstone; Judd Sch., Tonbridge; Fitzwilliam House, Cambridge (BA). BBC Radio, 1955-58; BBC TV, 1958-67: Editor, Monitor, 1962; Exec. Producer Music Programmes, 1963; Head of Music and Arts Programmes, 1965, productions inc. Workshop, Master Class, In Rehearsal, Britten at 50, Conversations with Glenn Gould. Head of Music and Arts, BBC TV, 1975-81; since 1975, Exec. Producer opera relays from Covent Garden and Glyndebourne (Capriccio, Cosi fan Tutte); Producer, Omnibus at Santa Fe Opera; Host of BBC series: Omnibus, 1976-78; Young Musician of the Year, 1978, 1980, 1982; Wagner's Ring, 1982; In Performance, 1978-; Opera Month, 1979; other arts and music programmes; *London Weekend TV:* Head of Drama, Arts and Music, 1967; Editor/Introducer, Aquarius, 1970-75, programmes incl. Mahler Festival, Verdi Requiem, Trouble in Tahiti, The Great Gondola Race, Anatomy of a Record, etc; *other ITV programmes:* 5 Glyndebourne operas, adapted and produced, Southern, 1972-74; The Beach at Falesa, World Premiere, Harlech, 1974; UN Day Concert with Pablo Casals, 1971; *French TV:* Berlioz' Requiem at Les Invalides, 1975; many free-lance prodns in Austria, Germany and USA, inc. Mahler and Beethoven Cycles with Bernstein and Vienna

Philharmonic, concerts with von Karajan and Berlin Philharmonic, Giulini with LA Philharmonic, and Solti and Chicago SO. Chm., EBU Music Experts Gp, 1976-82. Desmond Davis Award, SFTA, 1966; Royal TV Soc. Silver Medal, 1971; Emmy, 1971 for 'Beethoven's Birthday' (CBS TV); Peabody Award, 1972; SFTA Best Specialised Series, 1974; Christopher Award, 1979. *Publications:* contrib. RSA Jl and Listener. *Recreations:* music-making, tennis, swimming, travel. *Address:* c/o BBC Television, Kensington House, Richmond Way, W14. *Club:* Garrick.

BURTON, Iris Grace; Editor, Woman's Own, since 1980; *d* of Arthur Burton and late Alice Burton; *m*; one *s* one *d. Educ:* Roan Girls' Grammar Sch., Greenwich; City of London Coll. Local newspaper, SE London Mercury, until 1966; Writer, then Features Editor, Woman's Own, 1966-78; Asst Editor, TV Times, 1978-80. *Address:* King's Reach, Stamford Street, SE1; (home) Anerley, SE20.

BURTON, Rev. John Harold Stanley, MA Oxon; General Secretary, Church Lads' Brigade, 1954-64 and 1973-Jan. 1977; Member, Church of England Youth Council, 1954-64; *b* 6 Feb. 1913; *o s* of late John Stanley Burton, Grenadier Guards (killed in action 1916), and Lilian Bostock; *m* 1st, 1943, Susan Lella (*d* 1960), *o d* of Sir John Crisp, 3rd Bt; two *d*; 2nd, 1960, Jacqueline Mary Margaret, *o d* of P. L. Forte, Clifton, Bristol; one *d. Educ:* Marlborough; University Coll., Oxford; Westcott House, Cambridge. BA 2nd Class Hons. in Theology, Oxford, 1935; MA 1937; Deacon, 1936; Priest, 1938; Curate of Christ Church, Woburn Square, WC1, 1936-39; Cranleigh, Surrey, 1939-40; Head of Cambridge Univ. Settlement, Camberwell, 1940-43; Chaplain RAFVR, 1943; Fighter Command, 1943-44; 2nd Tactical Air Force, 1944; Bomber Command, 1945; Ordination Secretary, Air Command, SE Asia, and Chaplain 9 RAF General Hospital, Calcutta, 1945-46; demobilised Aug. 1946. Chaplain of Middlesex Hospital, W1, 1946-50; Chaplain of the Royal Free Hospital, 1950-54; Chairman of Hospital Chaplains Fellowship, 1953-54. *Publications:* (contrib.) A Priest's Work in Hospital, 1955; (contrib.) Trends in Youth Work, 1967. *Recreations:* Beagling, fishing, shooting, most games. *Address:* 45 Westbourne Terrace, W2. *T:* 01-262 5780. *Club:* Royal Air Force.

BURTON, Prof. Kenneth, FRS 1974; Professor of Biochemistry, University of Newcastle-upon-Tyne, since 1966; *b* 26 June 1926; *s* of Arthur Burton and Gladys (*née* Buxton); *m* 1955, Hilda Marsden; one *s* one *d. Educ:* High Pavement Sch., Nottingham; Wath-upon-Dearne Grammar Sch.; King's Coll., Cambridge (MA, PhD). Asst Lectr in Biochem., Univ. of Sheffield, 1949, Lectr 1952; Res. Associate, Univ. of Chicago, 1952-54; MRC Unit for Research in Cell Metabolism, Oxford, 1954-66. Vis. Lectr in Medicine, Harvard, 1964; William Evans Vis. Prof., Univ. of Otago, 1977-78; Mem. Biological Research Bd, MRC, 1967-71. *Publications:* (ed) Nucleic Acids, 1974; papers in Biochemical Jl, etc. *Recreations:* music, hill-walking. *Address:* 42 Cade Hill Road, Stocksfield, Northumberland NE43 7PU. *T:* Stocksfield 2289.

BURTON, Maurice, DSc; retired 1958; now free-lance author and journalist; *b* 28 March 1898; *s* of William Francis and Jane Burton; *m* 1929, Margaret Rosalie Maclean; two *s* one *d. Educ:* Holloway County Sch.; London Univ. Biology Master, Latymer Foundation, Hammersmith, 1924-27; Zoology Dept, British Museum (Natural History), SW7, 1927-58. Science Editor, Illustrated London News, 1946-64; Nature Correspondent, Daily Telegraph, 1949-. FZS. Kt of Mark Twain, 1980. *Publications:* The Story of Animal Life, 1949; Animal Courtship, 1953; Living Fossils, 1954; Phœnix Re-born, 1959; Systematic Dictionary of Mammals, 1962; (jtly) Purnell's Encyclopedia of Animal Life, 1968-70; Encyclopaedia of Animals, 1972; Introduction to Nature (for children), 1972; Prehistoric Animals, 1974; Deserts, 1974; How Mammals Live, 1975; Just Like an Animal, 1978; A Zoo at Home, 1979, numerous publications on Sponges in a variety of scientific journals. *Recreation:* gardening. *Address:* Weston House, Albury, Guildford, Surrey GU5 9AE. *T:* Shere 2369.

BURTON, Michael St Edmund, CVO 1979; HM Diplomatic Service; Head of South Asian Department, Foreign and Commonwealth Office, since 1981; *b* 18 Oct. 1937; *s* of late Brig. G. W. S. Burton, DSO, and of Barbara Burton (*née* Kemmis Betty); *m* 1967, Jindra Hones; one *s* one *d* (and one *d* decd). *Educ:* Bedford Sch.; Magdalen Coll., Oxford. MA. 2nd Lt, Rifle Brigade, 1955-57. Foreign Office, 1960; Asst Political Agent, Dubai, Trucial States, 1962-64; Private Sec. to Minister of State, FO, 1964-67; Second (later First) Sec. (Information), Khartoum, 1967-69; First Sec. (Inf.), Paris, 1969-72; Asst, Science and Technology Dept, FCO, 1972-75; First Sec. and Head of Chancery, Amman, 1975-77; Counsellor, Kuwait, 1977-79; Head of Maritime, Aviation and Environment Dept, FCO, 1979-81. *Recreations:* tennis, golf, travel. *Address:* c/o Foreign and Commonwealth Office, SW1. *Clubs:* United Oxford & Cambridge University, Hurlingham.

BURTON, Neil Edward David; Secretary, Monopolies and Mergers Commission, since 1981; *b* 12 May 1930; *s* of late Edward William Burton and Doris Burton; *m* 1954, Jane-Anne Crossley Perry; three *s. Educ:* Welwyn Garden City Grammar Sch.; City of London Sch.; Trinity Coll., Oxford (MA). Asst Principal, Min. of Supply; Asst Sec., MAFF, 1966, subseq. CSD and Price Commn; Asst Dir, Office of Fair Trading, 1976; Dir, Restrictive Trade Practices, 1976; Dir of Competition Policy, 1977-81. *Recreations:* reading, walking, travel. *Address:* 29 Brittains Lane, Sevenoaks, Kent. *T:* Sevenoaks 455608.

BURTON, Richard, CBE 1970; stage and film actor; *b* Pontrhydfen, South Wales, 10 Nov. 1925; *m* 1st, 1949, Sybil Williams (marr. diss., 1963; she *m* 1965, Jordan Christopher); two *d*; 2nd, 1964, Elizabeth Taylor (marr. diss., 1974, remarried 1975, marr. diss., 1976), *qv*; 4th, 1976, Susan Hunt (marr. diss. 1982). *Educ:* Port Talbot Secondary Sch.; Exeter Coll., Oxford. Hon. Fellow, St Peter's Coll., Oxford, 1972. First appeared on stage as Glan in Druid's Rest, Royal Court Theatre, Liverpool, 1943; played same rôle, St Martin's, London, 1944. Served with Royal Air Force, 1944–47. Returned to stage in Castle Anna, Lyric, Hammersmith, 1948; subsequent stage appearances include: Richard in the Lady's Not For Burning, Globe, 1949, New York, 1950; Cuthman in The Boy With a Cart, Lyric, Hammersmith, 1950. Played Hamlet with Old Vic Company, Edinburgh Festival, 1953, and subsequently; has also appeared with Old Vic Company in King John, The Tempest, Twelfth Night, Coriolanus, etc. Old Vic Season, 1955-56: Othello, Iago, Henry V; Time Remembered, New York, 1957-58; Camelot, New York, 1960, throughout US, 1980-81; Hamlet, New York, 1964; Equus, NY, 1976. *Films include:* The Last Days of Dolwyn; My Cousin Rachel; The Desert Rats; The Robe; The Prince of Players; Alexander the Great; The Rains of Ranchipur; Sea Wyf and Biscuit; Bitter Victory; Look Back in Anger; Bramblebush; Ice Palace; Cleopatra; The VIP's; Becket; Hamlet (from Broadway prod.); The Night of the Iguana; The Sandpiper; The Spy Who Came in from the Cold; Who's Afraid of Virginia Woolf; The Taming of the Shrew; Dr Faustus; The Comedians; Boom; Where Eagles Dare; Candy; Staircase; Anne of the Thousand Days; Villain; Hammersmith is Out; Raid on Rommel; Under Milk Wood; The Assassination of Trotsky; Bluebeard; The Kinsman; Massacre in Rome; Exorcist II: The Heretic; Equus; The Medusa Touch; The Wild Geese; Wagner. *Relevant publication:* Richard Burton, by J. Cottrell and F. Cashin, 1971. *Address:* c/o Major Donald Neville-Willing, 85 Kinnerton Street, SW1. *T:* 01-235 4640.

BURTON, Sydney Harold, JP; FCBSI; Director, Gateway Building Society, since 1981 (Managing Director, 1975-81); *b* 6 April 1916; *s* of Sydney Collard Burton and Maud Burton; *m* 1941, Jean Cowling; one *d*. *Educ:* Belle Vue High Sch., Bradford. Various appts with Bradford Equitable Building Soc. (excl. war years), 1932-63; joined Temperance Permanent Building Soc., 1963; Jt Gen. Manager, 1965; Gen. Man. and Sec., 1972; following merger of Temperance Permanent and Bedfordshire Bldg Socs became Chief Gen. Man. and Sec. of Gateway Bldg Soc., 1974. Pres., Building Societies Inst., 1976-77; Mem. Council, Building Societies Assoc., 1971-81. JP Worthing, 1974. *Recreations:* music and theatre, social and religious work. *Address:* Gull's Croft, 34 Oval Waye, Ferring, Sussex BN12 5RA. *T:* Worthing 46207.

BURTON-CHADWICK, Sir Robert, 2nd Bt, *cr* 1935; (Sir Peter); *b* 22 June 1911; *s* of Sir Robert Burton-Chadwick, 1st Bt and Catherine Barbara (*d* 1935), *d* of late Thomas Williams; *S* father 1951; *m* 1st, 1937, Rosalind Mary (marr. diss., 1949), *d* of Harry John Stott; two *d*; 2nd, 1950, Beryl Joan, *d* of Stanley Frederick J. Brailsford; one *s* one *d*. *Educ:* St George's Sch., Harpenden, Herts. Served War of 1939-45, with NZMF, N Africa, Italy, 1942-45. *Heir: s* Joshua Kenneth Burton-Chadwick, *b* 1 Feb. 1954. *Address:* 102 Meadowbank Road, Remuera, Auckland 5, New Zealand.

BURTON-TAYLOR, Sir Alvin, Kt 1972; FCA (Aust.); FAIM; Chairman: P&O Australia Ltd; Bishopsgate Insurance Australia Ltd; Country Television Services Ltd; Slumberland (Aust.) Pty Ltd; Mannesman Demag Pty Ltd; Director: Email Finance Ltd; Email Ltd; Formica Plastics Pty Ltd; International Combustion Australia Ltd; NSW Division, National Heart Foundation of Australia; O'Connell Street Associates Pty Ltd; *b* 17 Aug. 1912; *s* of A. A. W. Taylor, Adelaide, and Ruby Ella Burton, Adelaide; *m* 1949, Joan L. Toole; two *s* two *d*. *Educ:* Sydney Church of England Grammar Sch. Cooper Bros Way & Hardie, 1930-37; Asst Gen. Manager, then Gen. Manager, Rheem Aust. Ltd, 1937-57; Man. Dir, Email Ltd (Group), 1957-74. *Recreations:* sailing, golf, fishing. *Address:* Unit 6 Gainsborough, 50-58 Upper Pitt Street, Kirribilli, NSW 2061, Australia. *Clubs:* Union, Royal Sydney Yacht Squadron, Elanora Country (all in NSW).

BURY, John, OBE 1979; Associate Director (Head of Design), National Theatre, since 1973; free-lance designer for theatre, opera and film; *b* 27 Jan. 1925; *s* of C. R. Bury; *m* 1st, 1947, Margaret Leila Greenwood (marr. diss.); one *s*; 2nd, 1966, Elizabeth Rebecca Blackborrow Duffield; two *s* one *d*. *Educ:* Cathedral Sch., Hereford; University Coll., London. Served with Fleet Air Arm (RN), 1942-46. Theatre Workshop, Stratford, E15, 1946-63; Assoc. Designer, Royal Shakespeare Theatre, 1963-73, Head of Design, 1965-68. Arts Council: Designers' Working Gp, 1962-78; Mem., Drama Panel, 1960-68 and 1975-77; Chm., Soc. of British Theatre Designers, 1975–. FRSA 1970. Co-winner, Gold Medal for Scene Design, Prague Quadrienale, 1975; Antoinette Perry Awards (Best Set Design and Best Lighting), for Broadway prodn of Amadeus, 1981. *Address:* 14 Woodlands Road, Barnes, SW13.

BURY, Hon. Leslie Harry Ernest, CMG 1979; MHR (Lib) for Wentworth, NSW, 1956-74; *b* London, 25 Feb. 1913; *s* of late Rev. E. Bury, Bournemouth, England; *m* 1940, Anne Helen, *d* of late C. E. Weigall; four *s*. *Educ:* Queens' Coll., Cambridge (MA). Bank of NSW, 1935-45. Served War of 1939-45, AIF, 12th Aust. Radar Det. Commonwealth Dept of External Affairs, i/c Economic Relations, 1945-47; Treasury, 1948-51; Alternate Dir, IBRD, IMF, 1951-53, Exec. Dir, 1953-56. Minister: for Air, 1961-62; for Housing, 1963-66; for Labour and Nat. Service, 1966-69; Treasurer, 1969-71; Minister for Foreign Affairs, March-Aug. 1971, resigned. Aust. Rep., Commonwealth Finance Ministers' internat. meetings, etc.

Recreations: carpentry, gardening, home repairs. *Address:* 85 Vaucluse Road, Vaucluse, NSW 2030, Australia. *Clubs:* Union, Royal Sydney Golf (Sydney).

BURY, Michael Oswell, OBE 1968; Director, Corporate Affairs, Confederation of British Industry; *b* 20 Dec. 1922; *o s* of Lt-Col Thomas Oswell Bury, TD, and Constance Evelyn Bury; *m* 1954, Jean Threlkeld Wood, *d* of late William Threlkeld Wood; two *s* one *d*. *Educ:* Charterhouse; London Sch. of Economics. Served War of 1939-45: The Rifle Brigade (ranks of Rifleman to Captain), 1941-47. Steel Company of Wales, 1947-49; British Iron and Steel Fedn, 1949-64 (Dep. Dir, Labour and Trng, 1962-64); Dir, Iron and Steel Industry Trng Bd, 1964-70. Mem., Manpower Services Commn, 1974-81. *Recreations:* gardening, fishing, travel. *Address:* Hull Bush, Mountnessing, Brentwood, Essex CM13 1UH. *T:* Ingatestone 3958. *Club:* Reform.

BURY, Air Cdre Thomas Malcolm Grahame, CB 1972; OBE 1962; Head of Technical Training and Maintenance, British Aircraft Corporation, Saudi Arabia, since 1973; *b* 11 Sept. 1918; *s* of late Ernest Bury, OBE; *m* 1951, Dillys Elaine Jenkins, MBE, *d* of Dr Aneurin Jenkins, Swansea; two *s* one *d*. *Educ:* Forest Sch., E17. Served War, 1939-45, NW Europe, Arabia. Joined RAF, 1935; STSO, HQ, 1 Gp, 1961-64; DDME, MoD, 1965-66; Senior Engr Officer, Air Forces Gulf, 1967-68; Command Mech. Engr, HQ Strike Command, 1968-73; retired 1973. *Address:* c/o Lloyds Bank, 6 Pall Mall, SW1. *Club:* Royal Air Force.

BUSBY, Sir Matthew, Kt 1968; CBE 1958; President, Manchester United Football Club, since 1980; *b* 26 May 1909; *m* 1931, Jean Busby; one *s* one *d* (and four *s* decd). *Educ:* St Brides, Bothwell. Footballer: Manchester City, 1929-36; Liverpool, 1936-39. Served Army, 1939-45. Manchester United Football Club: Manager, 1945-69; Gen. Manager, 1969-71; Dir, 1971-82. Mem., Football League Management Cttee, 1981-82. Freeman of Manchester, 1967. KCSG. *Publication:* My Story, 1957. *Recreations:* golf, theatre. *Address:* 210 Kings Road, Manchester M21 1XQ.

BUSCH, Rolf Trygve; Comdr, Order of St Olav; Norwegian Ambassador to the Court of St James's and to Ireland, since 1982; *b* 15 Nov. 1920; *s* of Aksel Busch and Alette (*née* Tunby); *m* 1950, Solveig Helle; one *s*. *Educ:* Oslo Univ. (degree in Law); National Defence Coll. Dep. Judge, 1946-47; entered Norwegian Foreign Service, 1947; Min. of For. Affairs, 1947-50; Sec., Cairo, 1950-52; Vice-Consul, New York, 1952-54; Min. of For. Affairs, 1954-56; National Def. Coll., 1956-57; First Sec., Norwegian Delegn to NATO, Paris, 1957-60; Min. of For. Affairs, 1960-65; Counsellor and Dep. Perm. Rep., Norwegian Delegn to NATO, Paris and Brussels, 1965-70; Dir-Gen., Min. of For. Affairs, 1970-71; Perm. Rep. to N Atlantic Council, 1971-77; Ambassador to Fed. Republic of Germany, 1977-82. Officer, Order of the Nile, Egypt; Comdr with Star, Order of the Falcon, Iceland; Grand Cross, Order of Merit, Fed. Republic of Germany. *Address:* 10 Palace Green, W8. *T:* 01-937 2247.

BUSH, Alan, Composer; Conductor; Pianist; Professor of Composition, Royal Academy of Music, 1925-78; *b* 22 Dec. 1900; *s* of Alfred Walter Bush and Alice Maud (*née* Brinsley); *m* 1931, Nancy Rachel Head; two *d* (and one *d* decd). *Educ:* Highgate Sch.; Royal Academy of Music; Univ. of Berlin. ARAM 1922; Carnegie Award 1924; FRAM 1938; BMus London, 1940; DMus London, 1968. Arts Council Opera Award, 1951; Händel Prize, City Council of Halle (Saale), 1962; Corresp. Member, Deutsche Akademie der Künste, 1955. FRSA 1966. Hon. DMus Dunelm, 1970. Appeared as piano-recitalist, London, Berlin, etc., 1927-33; played solo part in own Piano Concerto, BBC, 1938, with Sir Adrian Boult conducting. Toured Ceylon, India, Australia as Examiner for Assoc. Board of Royal Schools of Music, London, 1932-33; concert tours as orchestral conductor, introducing British Music and own compositions, to USSR, 1938, 1939, 1963, Czechoslovakia, Yugoslavia, Poland, Bulgaria, 1947, Czechoslovakia and Bulgaria again, 1949, Holland, 1950, Vienna, 1951, Berlin (German Democratic Republic) and Hungary, 1952, and Berlin again, 1958; Première of opera "Wat Tyler" at the Leipzig Opera House, 1953; Première of opera "Men of Blackmoor" at the German National Theatre, Weimar, 1956; Première of opera "The Sugar Reapers" at the Leipzig Opera House, 1966; Première of opera "Joe Hill (The Man Who Never Died)", German State Opera, Berlin, 1970. Musical Adviser, London Labour Choral Union, 1929-40; Chairman Workers' Music Assoc., 1936-41 (President 1941-). Chairman Composers' Guild of Great Britain, 1947-48. *Publications:* In My Eighth Decade and Other Essays, 1980; *operas:* Wat Tyler; Men of Blackmoor; The Sugar Reapers; Joe Hill (The Man Who Never Died); and children's operettas; *choral works:* The Winter Journey, Op. 29; Song of Friendship, Op. 34; The Ballad of Freedom's Soldier, Op. 44 (mixed voices); The Dream of Llewelyn ap Gruffydd, Op. 35 (male voices); The Alps and Andes of the Living World, Op. 66 (mixed chorus); Song for Angela Davis; Africa is my Name, Op. 85; Folksong arrangements; *song cycles:* Voices of the Prophets, for tenor and piano, Op. 41; Seafarers' Songs for baritone and piano, Op. 57; The Freight of Harvest, for tenor and piano, Op. 69; Life's Span, for mezzo-soprano and piano, Op. 77; Three Songs for baritone and piano, Op. 86; Woman's Life, for soprano and piano, Op. 87; Two Shakespeare Sonnets, Op. 91; *orchestral works:* Dance Overture, Op. 12; Piano Concerto, Op. 18; Symphony No 1 in C, Op. 21; Overture "Resolution", Op. 25; English Suite for strings, Op. 28; Piers Plowman's Day Suite, Op. 30; Violin Concerto, Op. 32; Symphony No 2 "The Nottingham", op. 33; Concert Suite for 'cello and orchestra, Op. 37; Dorian Passacaglia and

Fugue, Op. 52; Symphony No 3 "The Byron Symphony", op. 53; Variations, Nocturne and Finale on an English Sea Song for piano and orchestra, Op. 60; Partita Concertante, Op. 63; Time Remembered for Chamber Orchestra, Op. 67; Scherzo for Wind Orchestra with Percussion, Op. 68; Africa: Symphonic Movement for piano and orchestra, Op. 73; Concert Overture for an Occasion, Op. 74; The Liverpool Overture, Op. 76; *chamber music:* String Quartet, Op. 4; Piano Quartet, Op. 5; Five Pieces for Violin, Viola, Cello, Clarinet and Horn, Op. 6; Dialectic for string quartet, Op. 15; Three Concert Studies for piano trio, Op. 31; Suite for Two Pianos, Op. 65; Serenade for String Quartet, Op. 70; Suite of six for String Quartet, Op. 81; Compass Points, Suite for Pipes, Op. 83; Trio for clarinet, cello and piano, Op. 91; Concertino for two violins and piano, Op. 94; *instrumental solos and duos:* Prelude and Fugue for piano, Op. 9; Relinquishment for piano, Op. 11; Concert Piece for 'cello and piano, Op. 17; Meditation on a German song of 1848 for violin and String Orchestra or piano, Op. 22; Lyric Interlude for violin and piano, Op. 26; Le Quatorze Juillet for piano, Op. 38; Trent's Broad Reaches for horn and piano, Op. 36; Three English Song Preludes for organ, Op. 40; Northumbrian Impressions for oboe and piano, Op. 42a; Autumn Poem for horn and piano, Op. 45; Two Ballads of the Sea for piano, Op. 50; Two Melodies for viola with piano accompaniment, Op. 47; Suite for harpsichord or piano, Op. 54; Three African Sketches for flute with piano accompaniment, Op. 55; Two Occasional Pieces for organ, Op. 56; Prelude, Air and Dance for violin with accompaniment for string quartet and percussion, Op. 61; Two Dances for Cimbalom, Op. 64; Pianoforte Sonata in A flat, Op. 71; Corentyne Kwe-Kwe for piano, Op. 75; Sonatina for recorders and piano, Op. 82; Twenty-four Preludes for Piano, Op. 84; Sonatina for viola and piano, Op. 88; Rhapsody for cello and piano, Op. 92; Meditation and Scherzo for double-bass and piano, Op. 93; *Textbook:* Strict Counterpoint in Palestrina Style; *essays:* In My Eighth Decade and other essays, 1980. *Recreations:* walking, foreign travel. *Address:* 25 Christchurch Crescent, Radlett, Herts. *T:* Radlett 6422.

BUSH, Hon. Sir Brian Drex, Kt 1976; **Hon. Mr Justice Bush; a** Judge of the High Court, Family Division, since 1976; Presiding Judge, Midland and Oxford Circuit, since 1982; *b* 5 Sept. 1925; *s* of William Harry Bush; *m* 1954, Beatrice Marian Lukeman; one *s* one *d. Educ:* King Edward's Sch., Birmingham; Birmingham Univ. (LLB). Served, RNVR, 1943-46. Called to the Bar, Gray's Inn, 1947, Bencher, 1976. Dep. Chm., Derbyshire Quarter Sessions, 1966-71; a Circuit Judge, 1969-76. Chm., Industrial Tribunal, 1967-69; Member: Parole Bd, 1971-74; W Midlands Probation and After Care Cttee, 1975-77. *Recreations:* sailing, golf. *Address:* Royal Courts of Justice, Strand, WC2. *Clubs:* Royal Naval Sailing Association, Bar Yacht.

BUSH, Bryan; barrister-at-law practising on North Eastern Circuit, since 1961; a Recorder of the Crown Court, since 1978; *b* 28 Nov. 1936; *s* of Maurice and Hetty Bush; *m* 1963, Jacqueline (née Rayman); two *s* one *d. Educ:* Leeds Grammar Sch.; Keble Coll., Oxford (MA). Called to the Bar, Gray's Inn, 1961. *Recreations:* theatre, tennis, squash. *Address:* 40 Primley Park Crescent, Leeds LS17 7HZ. *T:* Leeds 684472.

BUSH, Douglas; *see* Bush, J. N. D.

BUSH, Captain Eric Wheler, DSO 1940 (and Bars 1942 and 1944); DSC 1915; RN; psc; *b* 12 Aug. 1899; *s* of late Rev. H. W. Bush, Chaplain to the Forces, and Edith Cornelia (née Cardew); *m* 1938, Mollie Noël, *d* of Col B. Watts, DSO; two *s. Educ:* Stoke House, Stoke Poges; Royal Naval Colleges, Osborne and Dartmouth. Midshipman in HMS Bacchante, 1914; present at Battle of Heligoland Bight, 28 Aug. 1914; took part in defence of Suez Canal Jan.-March 1915; present at original landing at Anzac, Gallipoli, 25 April 1915, and subsequent operations, also original landing at Suvla Bay 1915 (despatches twice, DSC); Midshipman HMS Revenge 1916 and present at Battle of Jutland, 31 May 1916; Sub-Lieut 1917; Lieut 1920; Qualified Interpreter in Hindustani, 1924; Lt-Comdr 1927; Qualified RN Staff Coll., 1931; Commander, 1933; Captain, 1939; Chief of Staff and afterwards Captain Auxiliary Patrol, Dover Command, 1939-40 (DSO); HMS Euryalus in Command, Mediterranean, 1941-43 (Bar to DSO); Senior Officer Assault Group S3, invasion of Normandy, 1944 (2nd Bar to DSO), afterwards in Command of HMS Malaya; Chief of Staff, Naval Force 'W', SEAC, 1945 (despatches twice); in Command HMS Ganges, Boys' Training Establishment, Shotley, Suffolk, 1946-48; Sec. Sea Cadet Council, 1948-59. Gen. Manager, Red Ensign Club, Stepney, 1959-64. School Liaison British-India Steam Navigation Co. Ltd, 1965-71. Retired list, 1948. *Publications:* How to Become a Naval Officer (Special Entry); Bless our Ship; The Flowers of the Sea; How to Become a Naval Officer (Cadet Entry); Salute the Soldier; Gallipoli. *Address:* Flat 2, Bishops Croft, Camden Park, Tunbridge Wells, Kent. *T:* Tunbridge Wells 21768.

BUSH, George Herbert Walker; Vice-President of the United States of America, since 1981; *b* Milton, Mass, 12 June 1924; *s* of Prescott Sheldon Bush and Dorothy (née Walker); *m* 1945, Barbara, *d* of Marvin Pierce, NY; four *s* one *d. Educ:* Phillips Acad., Andover, Mass; Yale Univ. (BA Econs 1948). Served War, USNR, Lieut, pilot (DFC, three Air Medals). Co-founder and Dir, Zapata Petroleum Corp., 1953-59; Founder, Zapata Offshore Co., Houston, 1954, Pres., 1956-64, Chm. Bd, 1964-66. Chm., Republican Party, Harris Co., Texas, 1963-64; Delegate, Republican Nat. Convention, 1964, 1968; Republican cand. US Senator from Texas, 1964, 1970; Mem., 90th and 91st Congresses, 7th District of Texas, 1967-70; US Perm. Rep. to UN, 1971-73; Chm., Republican Party Nat. Cttee, 1973-74; Chief, US Liaison

Office, Peking, 1974-75; Dir, US Central Intelligence Agency, 1976-77. Cand. for Republican Presidential nomination, 1980. State Chm., Heart Fund. Hon. degrees from Beaver Coll., Adelphi Univ., Austin Coll., N Michigan Univ. *Recreation:* tennis. *Address:* The Vice-President's House, Washington, DC 20501, USA.

BUSH, Prof. Ian (Elcock), MA; PhD; MB, BChir; Research Professor of Psychiatry and Physiology, Dartmouth Medical School, USA, since 1977 (Senior Research Associate, 1974-77); Associate Chief of Staff, Research and Development, Veterans' Administration Hospital, White River Junction, Vermont, since 1977; *b* 25 May 1928; *s* of late Dr Gilbert B. Bush and of Jean Margaret Bush; *m* 1st, 1951, Alison Mary Pickard (marr. diss., 1966); one *s* two *d* ; 2nd, 1967, Joan Morthland (marr. diss. 1972); one *s* one *d. Educ:* Bryanston Sch.; Pembroke Coll., Cambridge BA 1949. Natural Sciences Tripos, 1st class I and II; MA, PhD 1953; MB, BChir. 1957. Medical Research Council Scholar (Physiology Lab. Cambridge; National Institute for Medical Research), 1949-52; Commonwealth Fellow 1952 (University of Utah; Mass. General Hospital); Part-time Research Asst, Med. Unit, St Mary's Hosp. London and med. student, 1953-56; Grad. Asst, Dept Regius Prof. of Med., Oxford, 1956-59; Mem. ext. Scientific Staff, Med. Research Council (Oxford), 1959-61. Hon. Dir Med. Research Council Unit for research in chem. pathology of mental disorders, 1960; Bowman Prof. of Physiology and Dir of Dept of Physiology, Univ. of Birmingham, 1960-64; Senior Scientist, The Worcester Foundation for Experimental Biology, 1964-67; Chm. of Dept and Prof. of Physiology, Medical Coll. of Virginia, 1967-70; Pres. and Dir of Laboratories, Cybertek Inc., New York, 1970-72, and Prof. of Physiology, New York Univ. Med. Sch., 1970-77. Fellow, Amer. Acad. of Arts and Sciences, 1966. *Publications:* Chromatography of Steroids, 1961. Contributions to: Jl Physiol.; Biochem. Jl; Jl Endocrinol.; Nature; The Analyst; Jl Biolog. Chem.; Brit. Med. Bulletin; Acta Endocrinologica; Experientia; Biochem. Soc. Symposia, etc. *Recreations:* music, chess, sailing, fishing, philosophy. *Address:* c/o Dartmouth Medical School, Hanover, NH 03755, USA.

BUSH, Adm. Sir John (Fitzroy Duyland), GCB 1970 (KCB 1965; CB 1963); DSC 1941, and Bars, 1941, 1944; Vice-Admiral of the United Kingdom and Lieutenant of the Admiralty, since 1979; *b* 1 Nov. 1914; *s* of late Fitzroy Bush, Beach, Glos; *m* 1938, Ruth Kennedy Horsey; three *s* two *d. Educ:* Clifton Coll. Entered Navy, 1933; served in Destroyers throughout War. Commanded HM Ships: Belvoir, 1942-44; Zephyr, 1944; Chevron, 1945-46. Comdr Dec. 1946; Plans Div., Admiralty, 1946-48; graduated Armed Forces Staff Coll., USA, 1949; Comd, HMS Cadiz, 1950-51; Capt. June 1952; Dep. Sec. Chiefs of Staff Cttee, 1953-55; Capt. (F) Sixth Frigate Sqdn, 1955-56; Cdre, RN Barracks, Chatham, 1957-59; Dir. of Plans, Admiralty, 1959-60; Rear-Adm. 1961; Flag Officer Flotillas (Mediterranean), 1961-62; Vice-Adm. 1963; Comdr, British Naval Staff and Naval Attaché, Washington, 1963-65; Vice-Chief of the Naval Staff, Ministry of Defence, 1965-67; C-in-C Western Fleet, C-in-C Eastern Atlantic, and C-in-C Channel (NATO), 1967-70; Admiral 1968; retd, 1970. Rear-Admiral of the UK, 1976-79. Dir, Gordon A. Friesen International Inc., Washington, DC, 1970-73. Adm., Texas (USA) Navy. Governor, Clifton Coll., 1973- (Chm. Council, 1978-81; Pres., 1982-). Pres., Old Cliftonians Soc., 1967-69. Mem., E Hants District Council, 1974-76. *Recreations:* fishing, gardening. *Address:* Becksteddle House, Colemore, near Alton, Hants. *T:* Tisted 367.

BUSH, (John Nash) Douglas; Professor of English, Harvard University, 1936-66, Gurney Professor, 1957-66; *b* Morrisburg, Ontario, Canada, 21 March 1896; *s* of Dexter C. and Mary E. Bush; *m* 1927, Hazel Cleaver; one *s. Educ:* Univ. of Toronto, Canada; Harvard Univ., USA. Sheldon Fellow in England, 1923-24; Instructor in English, Harvard, 1924-27; Department of English, Univ. of Minnesota, 1927-36; Guggenheim Fellow, in England, 1934-35; Member American Philosophical Society; Pres. Modern Humanities Research Association, 1955; Corr. Fellow, British Academy, 1960. Hon. LittD: Tufts Coll., 1952; Princeton Univ., 1958; Toronto Univ., 1958; Oberlin Coll., 1959; Harvard Univ., 1959; Swarthmore Coll., 1960; Boston Coll., 1965; Michigan State Univ., 1968; Merrimack Coll., 1969; LHD Southern Illinois Univ., 1962; LHD, Marlboro Coll., 1966. *Publications:* Mythology and the Renaissance Tradition in English Poetry, 1932 (revised edition, 1963); Mythology and the Romantic Tradition in English Poetry, 1937; The Renaissance and English Humanism, 1939; Paradise Lost in Our Time, 1945; English Literature in the Earlier Seventeenth Century, 1600-1660 (Oxford History of English Literature), 1945 (revised edition 1962); Science and English Poetry, 1950; Classical Influences in Renaissance Literature, 1952; English Poetry: The Main Currents, 1952; John Milton, 1964; Prefaces to Renaissance Literature, 1965; John Keats, 1966; Engaged and Disengaged, 1966; Pagan Myth and Christian Tradition in English Poetry, 1968; Matthew Arnold, 1971; Jane Austen, 1975; Editor: The Portable Milton, 1949; Tennyson: Selected Poetry, 1951; John Keats: Selected Poems and Letters, 1959; (with A. Harbage), Shakespeare's Sonnets, 1961; Complete Poetical Works of John Milton, 1965; Variorum Commentary on Milton, vol. 1, Latin and Greek Poems, 1970, vol. 2 (with A. S. P. Woodhouse and E. Weismiller), Minor English Poems, 1972. *Address:* 3 Clement Circle, Cambridge, Mass 02138, USA.

BUSH, Maj.-Gen. Peter John, OBE 1968; Controller, Army Benevolent Fund, since 1980; *b* 31 May 1924; *s* of Clement Charles Victor Bush and Kathleen Mabel Peirce; *m* 1948, Jean Mary Hamilton; two *s* one *d. Educ:* Maidenhead County Sch. Commnd Somerset LI, 1944; comd LI Volunteers,

1966; GSO 1 HQ 14 Div./Malaya Dist, 1968; Comdr 3 Inf. Bde, 1971 (mentioned in despatches, 1973); Asst Comdt RMA Sandhurst, 1974; Chief of Staff and Head of UK Delegn to Live Oak, SHAPE, 1977-79, retd. Col, The Light Infantry, 1977-82. *Recreations:* natural history, golf, tennis, walking, reading. *Address:* c/o Barclays Bank, High Street, Maidenhead, Berks.

BUSH, Ronald Paul, CMG 1954; OBE 1946; Colonial Administrative Service, retired; *b* 22 Aug. 1902; *s* of late Admiral Sir Paul Bush; *m* 1938, Anthea Mary Fetherstonhaugh; two *s* one *d. Educ:* Marlborough Coll. Appointed to Colonial Administrative Service, 1925; service in Northern Rhodesia: confirmed as District Officer, 1927; promoted Provincial Commissioner, 1947, Sec. for Native Affairs, 1949; retired, 1954; on Commission to enquire into Local Government in Basutoland, 1954. *Address:* Sandbrow, Churt, near Farnham, Surrey. *T:* Frensham 2832. *Club:* Royal Commonwealth Society.

BUSHBY, Frederick Henry; Director of Services, Meteorological Office, since 1978; *b* 10 Jan. 1924; *s* of Mr and Mrs Frederick George Bushby; *m* 1945, Joan Janet (*née* Gates); one *s. Educ:* Portsmouth Southern Secondary Sch.; Imperial Coll. of Science and Technol. (BSc 1st Cl. Hons Special Maths). ARCS. Meteorol Br., RAF, 1944-48; Meteorol Office, 1948-; Asst Dir (Forecasting Res.), 1965-74; Dep. Dir (Dynamical Res.), 1974-77, (Forecasting), 1977—78. *Recreation:* bridge. *Address:* 25 Holmes Crescent, Wokingham, Berks RG11 2SE. *T:* Wokingham 784930, (office) Bracknell 20242.

BUSHELL, John Christopher Wyndowe, CMG 1971; HM Diplomatic Service, retired; Ambassador to Pakistan, 1976-79; *b* 27 Sept. 1919; *s* of late Colonel C. W. Bushell, RE, and Mrs Bushell, Netherbury, Dorset; *m* 1964, Mrs Theodora Todd, *d* of late Mr and Mrs Senior; one *s* (and one step *s* one step *d*). *Educ:* Winchester; Clare Coll., Cambridge. Served War of 1939-45, RAF. Entered FO, 1945; served in Moscow, Rome, FO; 1st Sec., 1950; NATO Defence Coll., Paris, 1953-54; Deputy Sec.-Gen., CENTO, 1957-59; Counsellor, 1961; Political Adviser to the Commander-in-Chief, Middle East, 1961-64; UK Delegn to NATO, Brussels, 1964-68; seconded to Cabinet Office, 1968-70; Minister and Deputy Commandant, British Mil. Govt, Berlin, 1970-74; Ambassador to Saigon, 1974-75; FCO 1975-76. *Recreations:* varied. *Address:* 19 Bradbourne Street, SW6. *Club:* Travellers'.

BUSHNELL, Alexander Lynn, CBE 1962; County Clerk and Treasurer, Perth County Council, 1946-75, retired; *b* 13 Aug. 1911; *s* of William and Margaret Bushnell; *m* 1939, Janet Braithwaite Porteous; two *d. Educ:* Dalziel High Sch., Motherwell; Glasgow University. *Recreation:* golf. *Address:* 18 Fairies Road, Perth, Scotland. *T:* Perth 22675. *Club:* Royal Perth Golfing Society.

BUSK, Sir Douglas Laird, KCMG 1959 (CMG 1948); *b* 15 July 1906; *s* of late John Laird Busk, Westerham, Kent, and late Eleanor Joy; *m* 1937, Bridget Anne Moyra, *d* of late Brig.-Gen. W. G. Hemsley Thompson, CMG, DSO, Warminster, Wilts; two *d. Educ:* Eton; New Coll., Oxford; Princeton Univ., USA (Davison Scholar). Joined Diplomatic Service, 1929; served in Foreign Office and Tehran, Budapest, Union of S Africa (seconded to United Kingdom High Commission), Tokyo, Ankara, Baghdad; Ambassador to Ethiopia, 1952-56; to Finland, 1958-60; to Venezuela, 1961-64. *Publications:* The Delectable Mountains, 1946; The Fountain of the Sun, 1957; The Curse of Tongues, 1965; The Craft of Diplomacy, 1967; Portrait d'un guide, 1975. *Recreations:* mountaineering and ski-ing. *Address:* Broxton House, Chilbolton, near Stockbridge, Hants. *T:* Chilbolton 272. *Clubs:* Alpine, Travellers', United Oxford & Cambridge University, Lansdowne.

BUSS, Barbara Ann, (Mrs Lewis Boxall) freelance journalist, since 1976; Editor-in-Chief, Woman magazine, 1974-75; Consultant, IPC Magazines Ltd, 1975-76; *b* 14 Aug. 1932; *d* of late Cecil Edward Buss and Victoria Lilian (*née* Vickers); *m* 1966, Lewis Albert Boxall; no *c. Educ:* Lady Margaret Sch., London. Sec., Conservative Central Office, 1949-52; Sec./journalist, Good Taste magazine, 1952-56; Journalist: Woman and Beauty, 1956-57; Woman, 1957-59; Asst Editor, Woman's Illustrated, 1959-60; Editor, Woman's Illustrated, 1960-61; Journalist, Daily Herald, 1961; Associate Editor, Woman's Realm, 1961-62; Editor: Woman's Realm, 1962-64; Woman, 1964-74. *Recreations:* reading, theatre, cinema. *Address:* 1 Arlington Avenue, N1. *T:* 01-226 3265.

BUSVINE, Prof. James Ronald; Professor of Entomology as applied to Hygiene in the University of London, 1964-76, Emeritus Professor 1977; *b* 15 April 1912; *s* of William Robert and Pleasance Dorothy Busvine; *m* 1960, Joan Arnfield; one *s* one *d. Educ:* Eastbourne Coll.; Imperial Coll. of Science and Technology, London Univ. BSc Special (1st Class Hons) 1933; PhD 1938; DSc 1948, London. Imperial Chemical Industries, 1936-39; MRC Grants, 1940-42; Entomological Adviser, Min. of Health, 1943-45; London Sch. of Hygiene and Tropical Medicine: Lecturer 1946; Reader 1954; Professor 1964. Member: WHO Panel of Experts on Insecticides, 1956- (Cttee Chm. 1959 and 1968); FAO Panel of Experts on Pest Resistance, 1967- (Cttee Rapporteur). Has travelled professionally in Malaya, Ceylon, Africa, USA, India, etc. *Publications:* Insects and Hygiene, 1951 (3rd edn 1980); A Critical Review of the Techniques for Testing Insecticides, 1957, 2nd edn 1971; Anthropod Vectors of Disease, 1975; Insects, Hygiene and History, 1976; numerous

scientific articles. *Recreations:* painting, golf. *Address:* Musca, 26 Braywick Road, Maidenhead, Berks. *T:* Maidenhead 22888.

BUTCHER, Anthony John, QC 1977; *b* 6 April 1934; *s* of F. W. Butcher and O. M. Butcher (*née* Ansell); *m* 1959, Maureen Workman (*d* 1982); one *s* two *d. Educ:* Cranleigh Sch.; Sidney Sussex Coll., Cambridge (MA, LLB). Called to the Bar, Gray's Inn, 1957; in practice at English Bar, 1957-. *Recreations:* enjoying the Arts and acquiring useless information. *Address:* Anthony Cottage, Polecat Valley, Hindhead, Surrey. *T:* Hindhead 4155; 22 Old Buildings, Lincoln's Inn, WC2A 3UJ. *T:* 01-405 2072. *Club:* Garrick.

BUTCHER, Willard Carlisle; Chairman and Chief Executive, Chase Manhattan Bank (formerly Chase National Bank), New York City, since 1981; *b* Bronxville, NY, 25 Oct. 1926; *s* of Willard F. Butcher and Helen Calhoun; *m* 1st, 1949, Sarah C. Payne (*d* 1955); two *d*; 2nd, 1956, Elizabeth Allen (*d* 1978); one *s* one *d*; 3rd, 1979, Carole E. McMahon; one *s. Educ:* Scarsdale High School, New York; Middlebury Coll., Vermont; Brown Univ., Rhode Island (BA). Served with USNR, 1944-45. Joined Chase National Bank, 1947; Asst Vice-Pres., 1956; Vice-Pres., 1958; Sen. Vice-Pres., 1961; assigned Internat. Dept, 1968; Exec. Vice-Pres. in charge of Dept, 1969; Vice-Chm. 1972; Pres. 1972; Chief Exec. Officer, 1979. *Address:* 1 Chase Manhattan Plaza, New York City, NY 10081, USA.

BUTE, 6th Marquess of, *cr* 1796; **John Crichton-Stuart,** JP; Viscount Ayr, 1622; Bt 1627; Earl of Dumfries, Lord Crichton of Sanquhar and Cumnock, 1633; Earl of Bute, Viscount Kingarth, Lord Mountstuart, Cumrae, and Inchmarnock, 1703; Baron Mountstuart, 1761; Baron Cardiff, 1776; Earl of Windsor; Viscount Mountjoy, 1796; Hereditary Sheriff of Bute; Hereditary Keeper of Rothesay Castle; Lieutenant (RARO) Scots Guards, 1953; *b* 27 Feb. 1933; *er s* (twin) of 5th Marquess of Bute and of Eileen, Marchioness of Bute, *yr d* of 8th Earl of Granard; *S* father, 1956; *m* 1st, 1955, Nicola (marr. diss. 1977), *o d* of late Lt-Comdr W. B. C. Weld-Forester, CBE; two *s* two *d*; 2nd, 1978, Mrs Jennifer Percy. *Educ:* Ampleforth Coll.; Trinity Coll., Cambridge. Pres., Scottish Standing Cttee for Voluntary Internat. Aid, 1968-75 (Chm., 1964-68); Chairman: Council and Exec. Cttee, National Trust for Scotland, 1969-; Scottish Cttee, National Fund for Res. into Crippling Diseases, 1966-; Member: Countryside Commission for Scotland, 1970-78; Design Council, Scottish Cttee, 1972-76; Development Commission, 1973-78; Oil Develt Council for Scotland, 1973-78. Trustee, Nat. Galleries of Scotland, 1980-. Hon. Sheriff-Substitute, County of Bute, 1976. Fellow, Inst. of Marketing, 1967; Hon. FIStructE, 1976. Pres., Scottish Veterans' Garden City Assoc. (Inc.), 1971-. Buteshire CC, 1956-75; Convener, 1967-70; DL Bute, 1961, Lord Lieutenant, 1967-75; JP Bute 1967. Hon. LLD Glasgow, 1970. *Heir:* *s* Earl of Dumfries, *qv. Address:* Mount Stuart, Rothesay, Isle of Bute. *T:* Rothesay 2730. *Clubs:* Turf, White's; New, Puffin's (Edinburgh); Cardiff and County (Cardiff).

BUTEMENT, William Alan Stewart, CBE 1959 (OBE 1945); DSc (Adel.); Chief Scientist Department of Supply, Australia (in exec. charge Australian Defence Scientific Research and Development which includes the Rocket Range at Woomera), 1949-67; a Director of Plessey Pacific, 1967-81; *b* Masterton, NZ, 18 Aug. 1904; *s* of William Butement, Physician and Surgeon, Otago, and Amy Louise Stewart; *m* 1933, Ursula Florence Alberta Parish; two *d. Educ:* Scots Coll., Sydney; University Coll. Sch., Hampstead, London; University Coll., London Univ. (BSc). Scientific Officer at Signals Exptl Estabt, War Office Outstation, Woolwich (now SRDE, Christchurch, Hants), 1928-38; Senior Scientific Officer Bawdsey Research Stn, War Office Outstation; later, under Min. of Supply, Radar Research, 1938-39 (Station moved to Christchurch, Hants, 1939; now RRE, Malvern); Prin. Scientific Officer, Sen. Prin. Scientific Officer, Asst Dir of Scientific Research, Min. of Supply, HQ London, 1940-46; Dep. Chief Scientific Officer of party to Australia under Lt-Gen. Sir John Evetts to set up Rocket Range, 1947; First Chief Supt of Long Range Weapons Estabt (now Weapons Research Establishment), of which Woomera Range is a part, 1947-49. FIEE, CEng, FInstP, FAIP, FIREE (Aust.), FTS. *Publications:* Precision Radar, Journal IEE, and other papers in scientific journals. *Address:* 5a Barry Street, Kew, Victoria 3101, Australia. *T:* 861 8375.

BUTENANDT, Prof. Adolf; Dr phil.; Dr med. hc; Dr med. vet. hc; Dr rer. nat. hc; Dr phil. hc; Dr sci. hc; Dr ing. eh; President, Max Planck Society, 1960-72, Hon. President since 1972; Director, Max Planck Institute for Biochemistry, München (formerly Kaiser Wilhelm Institute for Biochemistry, Berlin-Dahlem), 1936-72; Professor Ord. of Physiological Chemistry, München, 1956-71; Nobel Prize for Chemistry, 1939; *b* Bremerhaven-Lehe, 24 March 1903; *m* 1931, Erika von Ziegner; two *s* five *d. Educ:* Universities of Marburg and Göttingen. Privatdozent, Univ. of Göttingen, 1931; Prof. Ord. of Organic Chemistry, Technische Hochschule, Danzig, 1933; Honorarprofessor, Univ. Berlin, 1938; Prof. Ord. of Physiological Chemistry, Tübingen, 1945. Foreign Member: Royal Society, 1968; Académie des Sciences, Paris, 1974. *Publications:* numerous contribs to Hoppe-Seyler, Liebigs Annalen, Berichte der deutschen chemischen Gesellschaft, Zeitschrift für Naturforschung, etc. *Address:* München 60, Marsop Str. 5, Germany. *T:* (089) 885490.

BUTLAND, Sir Jack (Richard), KBE 1966; Founder and Chairman: J. R. Butland Pty Ltd, 1922; NZ Cheese Ltd, 1926-80; Butland Tobacco Co. Ltd, 1936-82; Butland Industries Ltd, 1949-81; Chairman: Greenacres (Morrinsville) Ltd; Blandford Lodge Ltd; Rothmans (NZ) Ltd, 1956; *s* of late

Henry Butland, Westport, NZ; *m* Gretta May Taylor (*d* 1962); two *s* one *d*; *m* Joan Melville Bull. *Educ:* Hokitika High Sch. Chairman: NZ Honey Control Board, 1933-38; NZ Packing Corp., 1953-60. Pres., Food Bank of NZ, 1970; Dir, Rothmans Industries, 1971. Hon. LLD Auckland, 1967. *Address:* (home) 542 Remuera Road, Remuera, Auckland, NZ; (office) J. R. Butland Pty Ltd, Queen Street, Auckland, NZ. *Club:* Northern (Auckland).

BUTLER, family name of **Earl of Carrick,** of **Baron Dunboyne,** of **Earl of Lanesborough,** of **Viscount Mountgarret,** and of **Marquess of Ormonde.**

BUTLER, Hon. Adam Courtauld, MP (C) Bosworth since 1970; Minister of State, Northern Ireland Office, since 1981; *b* 11 Oct. 1931; *s* of late Baron Butler of Saffron Walden, KG, CH, PC and late Sydney, *o c* of late Samuel Courtauld; *m* 1955, Felicity Molesworth-St Aubyn; two *s* one *d. Educ:* Eton; Pembroke College, Cambridge. National Service, 2nd Lieut KRRC, 1949-51. Cambridge (BA History/Economics), 1951-54. ADC to Governor-General of Canada, 1954-55; Courtaulds Ltd, 1955-73; Director: Aristoc Ltd, 1966-73; Kayser Bondor Ltd, 1971-73; Capital and Counties Property Co., 1973-79. PPS to: Minister of State for Foreign Affairs, 1971-72; Minister of Agriculture, Fisheries and Food, 1972-74; PPS to Leader of the Opposition, 1975-79; an Asst Govt Whip, 1974; an Opposition Whip, 1974-75; Min. of State, DoI, 1979-81. Mem. NFU. Liveryman of Goldsmiths' Co. *Recreations:* field sports, music, pictures. *Address:* The Old Rectory, Lighthorne, near Warwick. *T:* Moreton Morrell 214.
See also Hon. Sir R. C. Butler.

BUTLER, Rt. Rev. Arthur Hamilton, MBE 1944; DD; MA; *b* 8 March 1912; *s* of George Booker and Anne Maude Butler; *m* 1938, Betty (*d* 1976), *d* of Seton Pringle, FRCSI; one *s*; *m* 1979, Dr Elizabeth Mayne. *Educ:* Friars School, Bangor; Trinity Coll., Dublin. Curate: Monkstown, Dublin, 1935-37; Christ Church, Crouch End, N8, 1937; Holy Trinity, Brompton, SW3, 1938-39. Army, 1939-45: Chaplain, 2nd DCLI, 1939-43; Senior Chaplain, 1st Div., 1943-45. Incumbent of Monkstown, 1945-58; Bishop of Tuam, Killala and Achonry, 1958-69; Bishop of Connor, 1969-81. *Recreation:* golf. *Address:* 1 Spa Grange, Ballynahinch, Co. Down BT24 8PD. *T:* Ballynahinch 562966. *Club:* Ulster (Belfast).

BUTLER, Mrs Audrey Maude Beman, MA; Headmistress, Queenswood, Hatfield, Herts, since 1981; *b* 31 May 1936; *d* of Robert Beman Minchin and Vivien Florence Fraser Scott; *m* 1959, Anthony Michael Butler (marr. diss. 1981); two *d. Educ:* Queenswood, Hatfield; St Andrews Univ., Scotland (1st Cl. MA Hons, Geography and Polit. Economy; Scottish Univs Medal, RSGS, 1957-58). Asst Geography Teacher, Queenswood, 1958-59; part-time teacher, Raines Foundn Sch. for Girls, Stepney, 1959-61; Head of Geography, S Michael's, Burton Park, 1970-73 and 1976-78; first House Mistress of Manor House, Lancing Coll., 1978-81. Hon. Vice-Pres., Sussex County Ladies Golf Assoc., 1981-. FRGS; Mem. Geographical Assoc. *Recreations:* tennis and hockey (Blues, St Andrews Univ., 1956-57); golf (Sussex County Colours, 1970). *Address:* Queenswood, Shepherd's Way, Brookmans Park, Hatfield, Herts AL9 6NS. *T:* Potters Bar 52262.

BUTLER, Rt. Rev. (Basil) Christopher, OSB, MA; Auxiliary Bishop to the Cardinal Archbishop of Westminster since Dec. 1966; President, St Edmund's College, Ware, since 1968, and Chairman of the Board of Governors, since 1969; Titular Bishop of Nova Barbara; Hon. Fellow, St John's College, Oxford; *b* 1902; 2nd *s* of late W. E. Butler, Reading. *Educ:* Reading Sch.; St John's Coll., Oxford (White Schol.; Craven Schol.; Gaisford Greek Prose Prize; prox. acc. Hertford Schol.; 1st Class Classical Mods Greats and Theology). Tutor of Keble Coll., Oxford; Classical Master, Brighton Coll., 1927; Downside Sch., 1928; received into Catholic Church, 1928; entered the noviciate at Downside, 1929; Priest, 1933; Headmaster of Downside Sch., 1940-46; Abbot of Downside, 1946-66. Abbot-President of English Benedictine Congregation, 1961-66. Chm., Editorial Bd, Clergy Review, 1966-80; Mem., Editorial Bd, New English Bible, 1972-. Member: Anglican/Roman Catholic Preparatory Commn, 1967-69; Anglican-Roman Catholic Internat. Commn, 1970-81. President, Social Morality Council, 1968-. Consultor, Congregation for Catholic Education, 1968-73; Member, Congregation for the Doctrine of the Faith, 1968-73. Assistant to the Pontifical Throne, 1980-. Hon. LLD: Notre Dame Univ.; Catholic Univ. of America. *Publications:* St Luke's Debt to St Matthew (Harvard Theological Review, 1939); The Originality of St Matthew, 1951; The Church and Infallibility, 1954; Why Christ?, 1960; The Church and the Bible, 1960; Prayer: an adventure in living, 1961; The Idea of the Church, 1962; The Theology of Vatican II, 1967, 2nd enlarged edn, 1981; In the Light of the Council, 1969; A Time to Speak, 1972; Searchings, 1974; The Church and Unity, 1979; An Approach to Christianity, 1981; articles in Dublin Review, Downside Review, Journal of Theological Studies, Clergy Review. *Address:* St Edmund's College, Old Hall Green, Ware, Herts SG11 1DS. *Club:* Athenæum.

BUTLER, Dr Clifford Charles, FRS 1961; BSc, PhD; Vice-Chancellor of Loughborough University of Technology, since 1975; *b* 20 May 1922; *s* of C. H. J. and O. Butler, Earley, Reading; *m* 1947, Kathleen Betty Collins; two *d. Educ:* Reading Sch.; Reading Univ. BSc 1942, PhD 1946, Reading. Demonstrator in Physics, Reading Univ., 1942-45; Asst Lecturer in Physics, 1945-47, Lecturer in Physics, 1947-53, Manchester Univ.; Reader in Physics,

1953-57, Professor of Physics, 1957-63, Asst Dir, Physics Dept, 1955-62; Prof. of Physics and Head of Physics Dept, 1963-70, Imperial College; Dean, Royal Coll. of Science, 1966-69; Dir, Nuffield Foundn, 1970-75. Charles Vernon Boys Prizeman, London Physical Soc., 1956. Member: Academic Planning Board, Univ. of Kent, 1963-71; Schools Council, 1965-; Nuclear Physics Board of SRC, 1965-68; University Grants Cttee, 1966-71; Council, Charing Cross Hosp. Med. Sch., 1970-73; Council, Open Univ., 1971-; Science Adv. Cttee, British Council, 1980-; Chm., Standing Education Cttee, Royal Society, 1970-80; Chm., Council for the Educn and Training of Health Visitors, 1977-; Chm., Adv. Council for Supply and Educn of Teachers, 1980-. First Vice-Pres., Internat. Union of Pure and Applied Physics, 1972-75, Pres., 1975-78 (Sec.-Gen., 1963-72). Hon. DSc Reading, 1976. *Publications:* scientific papers on electron diffraction, cosmic rays and elementary particle physics in Proc. Royal Society and Physical Society, Philosophical Magazine, Nature, and Journal of Scientific Instruments, etc. *Address:* University of Technology, Loughborough, Leics LE11 3TU. *T:* Loughborough 63171; Low Woods Farm House, Low Woods Lane, Belton, near Loughborough, Leics. *Club:* Athenæum.

BUTLER, Dr Colin Gasking, OBE 1970; FRS 1970; retired as Head of Entomology Department, Rothamsted Experimental Station, Harpenden, 1972-76 (Head of Bee Department, 1943-72); *b* 26 Oct. 1913; *s* of Rev. Walter Gasking Butler and Phyllis Pearce; *m* 1937, Jean March Innes; one *s* one *d. Educ:* Monkton Combe Sch., Bath; Queens' Coll., Cambridge. MA 1937, PhD 1938, Cantab. Min. of Agric. and Fisheries Research Schol., Cambridge, 1935-37; Supt Cambridge Univ. Entomological Field Stn, 1937-39; Asst Entomologist, Rothamsted Exper. Stn, 1939-43. Hon. Treas., Royal Entomological Soc., 1961-69, Pres., 1971-72; Pres., Internat. Union for Study of Social Insects, 1969-73. FRPS 1957; FIBiol. Silver Medal, RSA, 1945. *Publications:* The Honeybee: an introduction to her sense physiology and behaviour, 1949; The World of the Honeybee, 1954; (with J. B. Free) Bumblebees, 1959; scientific papers. *Recreations:* nature photography, fishing, sailing. *Address:* Silver Birches, Porthpean, St Austell, Cornwall PL26 6AU. *T:* St Austell 2480.

BUTLER, David Edgeworth; Fellow of Nuffield College, Oxford, since 1954; *b* 1924; *yr s* of late Professor Harold Edgeworth Butler and Margaret, *d* of Prof. A. F. Pollard; *m* 1962, Marilyn, *d* of Sir Trevor Evans, CBE; three *s. Educ:* St Paul's; New Coll., Oxford (MA, DPhil). J. E. Procter Visiting Fellow, Princeton Univ., 1947-48; Student, Nuffield Coll., 1949-51; Research Fellow, 1951-54; Dean and Senior Tutor, 1956-64. Served as Personal Assistant to HM Ambassador in Washington, 1955-56. Hon. DUniv Paris, 1978. *Publications:* The British General Election of 1951, 1952; The Electoral System in Britain 1918-51, 1953; The British General Election of 1955, 1955; The Study of Political Behaviour, 1958; (ed) Elections Abroad, 1959; (with R. Rose) The British General Election of 1959, 1960; (with J. Freeman) British Political Facts, 1900-1960, 1963; (with A. King) The British General Election of 1964, 1965; The British General Election of 1966, 1966; (with D. Stokes) Political Change in Britain, 1969; (with M. Pinto-Duschinsky) The British General Election of 1970, 1971; The Canberra Model, 1973; (with D. Kavanagh) The British General Election of February 1974, 1974; (with D. Kavanagh) The British General Election of October 1974, 1975; (with U. Kitzinger) The 1975 Referendum, 1976; (ed) Coalitions in British Politics, 1978; (ed with A. H. Halsey) Policy and Politics, 1978; (with A. Ranney), Referendums, 1978; (with A. Sloman) British Political Facts 1900-79, 1980; (with D. Kavanagh) The British General Election of 1979, 1980; (with D. Marquand) European Elections and British Politics, 1981; (with A. Ranney) Democracy at the Polls, 1981; (co-ed) Electoral Studies, vol. 1, 1982. *Address:* Nuffield College, Oxford. *T:* Oxford 48014. *Club:* United Oxford & Cambridge University.

BUTLER, Denis William Langford; Comptroller and City Solicitor to the City of London, since 1981; *b* 26 Oct. 1926; *s* of late William H. Butler, Shrewsbury and Kitty Butler; *m* 1953, Marna (*née* Taylor); three *d. Educ:* Repton. Admitted Solicitor, 1951. Assistant Solicitor: Norfolk CC, 1953-54; Shropshire CC, 1954-57; Sen. Asst Solicitor, Lindsey (Lincs) CC, 1957-60; Dep. Clerk, 1960-74, County Solicitor and Clerk, 1974-81, Wilts CC. Chm., County Secs Soc., 1974-76. *Recreations:* travel, cinephotography, gardening. *Address:* 5 Stone House, 9 Weymouth Street, W1. *T:* 01-580 2707.

BUTLER, Edward Clive Barber, FRCS; Surgeon: The London Hospital, E1, 1937-69; Haroldwood Hospital, Essex, 1946-69; retired; *b* 8 April 1904; *s* of Dr Butler, Hereford; *m* 1939, Nancy Hamilton Harrison, Minneapolis, USA; two *s* one *d. Educ:* Shrewsbury Sch.; London Hospital. MRCS, LRCP 1928; MB, BS London, 1929; FRCS 1931. Resident posts London Hosp., 1928-32; Surgical Registrar, London Hosp., 1933-36; Surgeon, RMS Queen Mary, Cunard White Star Line, 1936. Hunterian Prof., RCS, 1939; examinerships at various times to London Univ. and Coll. of Surgeons. Pres. section of Proctology, Royal Soc. of Medicine, 1951-52; Member: Medical Soc. London; Royal Soc. Medicine. *Publications:* chapter on bacteraemia, in British Surgical Practice, 1948; on hand infections, in Penicillin (by Fleming), 1950; (jointly) on combined excision of rectum, in Treatment of Cancer and Allied Diseases (New York), 1952; articles on various surgical subjects in Lancet, BMJ, Proc. Royal Soc. Med., British Journal Surgery. *Recreations:* golf, gardening and yachting. *Address:* Flat 304, Enterprise House, Chingford, E4. *Club:* United Hospitals Sailing.

BUTLER, Air Vice-Marshal Eric Scott, CB 1957; OBE 1941; RAF; AOA HQ Fighter Command, 1957-61; *b* 4 Nov. 1907; *s* of Archibald Butler, Maze Hill, St Leonards-on-Sea, Sussex; *m* 1936, Alice Evelyn Tempest Meates; three *s* one *d. Educ:* Belfast Academy. Commissioned RAF 1933; Bomber Command European War, 1939-45; idc 1952; Director of Organisation, Air Ministry, 1953-56. *Address:* Camden Cottage, High Street, Pevensey, Sussex BN24 5JP. *T:* Westham 353. *Club:* Royal Air Force.

BUTLER, Esmond Unwin, CVO 1972; Secretary to the Governor-General of Canada, since 1959; Secretary-General, Order of Canada, since 1967 and Order of Military Merit, since 1972; *b* 13 July 1922; *s* of Rev. T. B. Butler and Alice Lorna Thompson; *m* 1960, Georgiana Mary North; one *s* one *d. Educ:* Weston Collegiate; Univs of Toronto and Geneva; Inst. Internat. Studies, Geneva. BA, Licence ès Sciences politiques. Journalist, United Press, Geneva, 1950-51; Asst Sec.-Gen., Internat. Union of Official Travel Organizations, Geneva, 1951-52; Information Officer, Dept of Trade and Commerce, Dept of Nat. Health and Welfare, 1953-54; Asst Sec. to Governor-Gen., 1955-58; Asst Press Sec. to Queen, London, 1958-59 and Royal Tour of Canada, 1959. CStJ 1967. *Recreations:* fishing, shooting, collecting Canadiana, ski-ing. *Address:* Rideau Cottage, Government House, Ottawa, Ont K1A OA1. *T:* (office) 749-5933. *Clubs:* Zeta Psi Fraternity (Toronto); White Pine Fishing.

BUTLER, Frank Chatterton, CBE 1961; MA 1934; retd from HM Diplomatic Service, 1967, and re-employed in Foreign Office Library until 1977; *b* 23 June 1907; *s* of late Leonard Butler and late Ada Chatterton Rutter; *m* 1945, Iris, *d* of late Ernest Strater and of Ida Mary Vinall; two *s. Educ:* Central Secondary Sch., Sheffield; Gonville and Caius Coll., Cambridge (Scholar); University of Grenoble. 1st Class Hons, Modern and Medieval Langs Tripos; Exhibitioner of the Worshipful Company of Goldsmiths, 1927, German Prize Essayist, 1928 and 1929. Consular Service, 1930 (head of list); Vice-Consul: Paris, 1931; New York, 1932; Mexico City, 1933-36; Panama, 1936-39; Naples, 1939-40; Barcelona, 1940-43; Consul, Barcelona, 1943-45; First Secretary (Commercial), Bogota, 1945-47; Consul General, Düsseldorf, 1948-52; Consul, Bordeaux, 1952-54; Consul General, Dakar, 1955, and Frankfurt, 1956-60; Counsellor at Shanghai, 1960-62; Consul-General at Cape Town, 1962-67. Fellow, Royal Commonwealth Soc. *Recreations:* golf, riding, motoring. *Address:* Wedgwood, Knowl Hill, Woking, Surrey.

BUTLER, (Frederick Edward) Robin; Principal Private Secretary to the Prime Minister, since 1982; *b* 3 Jan. 1938; *s* of Bernard Butler and Nora Butler; *m* 1962, Gillian Lois Galley; one *s* two *d. Educ:* Harrow Sch.; University Coll., Oxford (BA Lit. Hum., 1961). Joined HM Treasury, 1961; Private Sec. to Financial Sec. to Treasury, 1964-65; Sec., Budget Cttee, 1965-69; seconded to Cabinet Office as Mem., Central Policy Rev. Staff, 1971-72; Private Secretary: to Rt Hon. Edward Heath, 1972-74; to Rt Hon. Harold Wilson, 1974-75; returned to HM Treasury as Asst Sec. i/c Gen. Expenditure Intell. Div., 1975; Under Sec., Gen. Expenditure Policy Gp, 1977-80; Prin. Establishments Officer, 1980-82. Governor, Harrow Sch., 1975-. *Recreation:* competitive games. *Address:* 28 Half Moon Lane, SE24 9HU. *T:* 01-737 3169. *Club:* Anglo-Belgian.

BUTLER, George, RWS 1958; RBA; NEAC; painter, principally in watercolour, in England and Provence; *b* 17 Oct. 1904; *s* of John George Butler; *m* 1933, Kcenia Kotliarevskaya; one *s* one *d. Educ:* King Edward VII School, Sheffield; Central School of Art. Director and Head of Art Dept, J. Walter Thompson Co. Ltd, 1933-60. Hon. Treas., Artists General Benevolent Institution, 1957-77. Mem., Société des Artistes Indépendants Aixois. *Address:* Riversdale, Castle Street, Bakewell, Derbyshire. *T:* Bakewell 3133. *Club:* Arts.

BUTLER, George William P.; *see* Payne-Butler.

BUTLER, Gerald Norman, QC 1975; **His Honour Judge Butler;** a Circuit Judge, since 1982; *b* 15 Sept. 1930; *s* of Joshua Butler and Esther Butler (*née* Lampel); *m* 1959, Stella, *d* of Harris Isaacs; one *s* two *d. Educ:* Ilford County High Sch.; London Sch. of Economics; Magdalen Coll., Oxford. LLB London 1952, BCL Oxon 1954. 2nd Lieut, RASC, 1956-57. Called to Bar, Middle Temple, 1955. A Recorder of the Crown Court, 1977-82. *Recreations:* Rugby, bridge, Japanese pottery, Victorian paintings. *Address:* 28 St John's Road, Loughton, Essex. *T:* 01-508 7439. *Club:* MCC.

BUTLER, Maj.-Gen. Hew Dacres George, CB 1975; DL; Secretary, Beit Trust, since 1978; *b* 12 March 1922; *s* of late Maj.-Gen. S. S. Butler, CB, CMG, DSO; *m* 1954, Joanna, *d* of late G. M. Puckridge, CMG, ED; two *s* one *d. Educ:* Winchester. Commnd Rifle Bde, 1941; Western Desert, 1942-43; POW, 1943-45; psc 1951; BM 7th Armd Bde, 1951-53; Kenya, 1954-55; Instructor, Staff Coll., 1957-60; CO 1 RB, 1962-64; Cyprus (despatches, 1965); comd 24 Inf. Bde, Aden, 1966-67; idc 1969; ACOS G3 Northag, 1970-72; GOC Near East Land Forces, 1972-74. Chief of Staff (Contingencies Planning), SHAPE, 1975-76; retired 1977. Underwriting Mem. of Lloyds. DL Hants, 1980. *Recreations:* shooting, golf, horticulture. *Address:* Bury Lodge, Hambledon, Hants. *Clubs:* Boodle's, MCC.

BUTLER, James; *see* Butler, P. J.

BUTLER, James Walter, RA 1972 (ARA 1964); RWA; FRBS; *b* 25 July 1931; *m* (marr. diss.); one *d*; *m* 1975, Angela, *d* of Col Roger Berry,

Johannesburg, South Africa; three *d. Educ:* Maidstone Grammar Sch.; Maidstone Coll. of Art; St Martin's Art Sch.; Royal Coll. of Art. National Diploma in Sculpture, 1950. Worked as Architectural Carver, 1950-53, 1955-60. Tutor, Sculpture and Drawing, City and Guilds of London Art School, 1960-75, now Visitor. Major commissions include: Portrait statue of Pres. Kenyatta, Nairobi, 1973; Monument to Freedom Fighters of Zambia, Lusaka, 1974; Statue, The Burton Cooper, Burton-on-Trent, 1977; Memorial Statue, Richard III, Leicester, 1980. *Address:* Old School House, Greenfield, Beds. *T:* Flitwick 2028.

BUTLER, John Manton, MSc; *b* 9 Oct. 1909; *m* 1940, Marjorie Smith, Melbourne; one *s* one *d. Educ:* Southland, NZ; Univ. of Otago (Sen. Schol., NZ, Physics; BSc 1929; Smeaton Schol. Chemistry, 1930, John Edmond Fellow, 1930; MSc 1st class Hons). Pres., Students' Union; Graduate Rep. Univ. Council. Joined Shell, NZ, 1934; served various Shell cos in UK, Australia and S Africa until 1957; Man. Dir, Lewis Berger (GB) Ltd, 1957; Dir, Berger, Jenson & Nicholson Ltd, 1969-74. Chm., BNEC Cttee for Exports to NZ, 1967 (Dep. Chm., 1965). Pres., NZ Soc., 1971. Member: Cttee, Spastics Soc.; St David's Cttee, Conservative Assoc., 1979-80; Aust. Inst. of Internat. Affairs, 1981-. Consultant. *Recreations:* travel, golf, photography. *Address:* 2 Whitton Court, Black Rock, Victoria 3193, Australia. *T:* 598 7073. *Clubs:* Royal Wimbledon Golf; Australian (Melbourne); Royal Melbourne Golf.

BUTLER, Mrs Joyce Shore; Chairman, Hornsey Housing Trust; *m* ; one *s* one *d. Educ:* King Edward's High Sch., Birmingham. Member: Wood Green Council, 1947-64 (Leader, 1954-55; Deputy Mayor, 1962-63); First Chm., London Borough of Haringey, 1964-65; First Mayoress, 1965-66. MP (Lab & Co-op) Wood Green, 1955-74, Haringey, Wood Green, 1974-79; Vice-Chm., Labour Parly Housing and Local Govt Gp, 1959-64; Member: Estimates Cttee, 1959-60; Chairman's Panel, House of Commons, 1964-79; Jt Chm., Parly Cttee on Pollution, 1970-79; PPS to Minister for Land and Natural Resources, 1965. A Vice-Chm., Parly Labour Party, 1968-70. Exec. Mem., Housing and Town Planning Council; Founder and First Pres., Women's Nat. Cancer Control Campaign; Pres., London Passenger Action Confedn. *Address:* 8 Blenheim Close, N21.

BUTLER, Keith Stephenson, CMG 1977; HM Diplomatic Service, retired; Appeal Director for various charities, since 1978; *b* 3 Sept. 1917; *s* of late Raymond R. Butler and Gertrude Stephenson; *m* 1st, 1952, Geraldine Marjorie Clark (*d* 1979); 2nd, 1979, Mrs Priscilla Wittels; no *c. Educ:* King Edward's Sch., Birmingham; Liverpool Coll.; St Peter's Coll., Oxford (MA). HM Forces, 1939-47 (despatches): served, RA, in Egypt, Greece and Crete; POW, Germany, 1941-45. Foreign Correspondent for Sunday Times and Kemsley Newspapers, 1947-50. Joined HM Foreign Service, 1950; served: First Sec., Ankara and Caracas; Canadian Nat. Defence Coll.; Paris; Montreal. HM Consul-General: Seville, 1968; Bordeaux, 1969; Naples, 1974-77. *Publications:* contrib. historical and political reviews. *Recreation:* historical research. *Address:* Easter Cottage, Westbrook, Boxford, near Newbury, Berks. *T:* Boxford 557.

BUTLER, Sir Michael; *see* Butler, Sir R. M. T.

BUTLER, Sir Michael (Dacres), KCMG 1980 (CMG 1975); HM Diplomatic Service; Ambassador and Permanent UK Representative to the European Communities, Brussels, since 1979; *b* 27 Feb. 1927; *s* of T. D. Butler, Almer, Blandford, and Beryl May (*née* Lambert); *m* 1951, Ann, *d* of Rt Hon. Lord Clyde; two *s* two *d. Educ:* Winchester; Trinity Coll., Oxford. Joined HM Foreign Service, 1950; served in: UK Mission to UN, New York, 1952-56; Baghdad, 1956-58; FO, 1958-61 and 1965-68; Paris, 1961-65; Counsellor, UK Mission in Geneva, 1968-70; Fellow, Center for Internat. Affairs, Harvard, 1970-71; Counsellor, Washington, 1971-72; Head of European Integration Dept, FCO, 1972-74; Asst Under-Sec. in charge of European Community Affairs, FCO, 1974-76; Dep. Under-Sec. of State, FCO, 1976-79. Mem. Council, Oriental Ceramic Soc., 1977-80. *Recreations:* collecting Chinese porcelain, ski-ing, tennis. *Address:* c/o Foreign and Commonwealth Office, SW1.

BUTLER, (Percy) James, CBE 1981; FCA; Partner in charge of London Region, Peat, Marwick, Mitchell & Co., since 1981; farmer, since 1974; *b* 15 March 1929; *s* of Percy Ernest Butler and Phyllis Mary Butler (*née* Bartholomew); *m* 1954, Margaret Prudence Copland; one *s* two *d. Educ:* Marlborough Coll.; Clare Coll., Cambridge (MA). Joined Peat, Marwick, Mitchell & Co., 1952; qualified, 1955; Partner, 1965; Gen. Partner, 1971. Mem. of Lloyd's. Dir, Mersey Docks and Harbour Co., 1972-; Business Advr to Treasury and CS Cttee, 1980-; Mem., Cttee on review of Railway Finance, 1982. Treasurer, Pilgrims Soc., 1982-. Liveryman: Worshipful Co. of Curlers; Worshipful Co. of Chartered Accountants in England and Wales. *Recreations:* bridge, tennis. *Address:* East Lymden, Ticehurst, East Sussex TN5 7JB. *T:* Ticehurst 200397; 28 Eaton Mews North, SW1X 8AS. *T:* 01-235 1120. *Clubs:* Carlton, Pilgrims.

BUTLER, Sir (Reginald) Michael (Thomas), 3rd Bt *cr* 1922; QC (Canada); Barrister and Solicitor; Partner of Butler, Angus, Victoria, BC; Director: Teck Corporation; Elco Mining Ltd; *b* 22 April 1928; *s* of Sir Reginald Thomas, 2nd Bt, and Marjorie Brown Butler; S father, 1959; *m* Marja McLean (marr. diss.); three *s* ; one *s* adopted. *Educ:* Brentwood Coll., Victoria, BC; Univ. of British Columbia (BA). Called to Bar (Hons) from Osgoode Hall Sch. of

Law, Toronto, Canada, 1954. Chm., Brentwood Coll. Assoc. *Heir: s* (Reginald) Richard Michael Butler, *b* 3 Oct. 1953. *Address:* 634 Avalon Street, Victoria, BC, Canada. *Clubs:* Vancouver (Vancouver); Union (Victoria).

BUTLER, Hon. Sir Richard (Clive), Kt 1981; DL; President, National Farmers' Union, since 1979; farmer since 1953; *b* 12 Jan. 1929; *e s* of late Baron Butler of Saffron Walden, KG, CH, PC and late Sydney, *o c* of late Samuel Courtauld; *m* 1952, Susan Anne Maud Walker; twin *s* one *d. Educ:* Eton Coll.; Pembroke Coll., Cambridge (MA). 2nd Lieut, Royal Horse Guards, 1947–49. Mem. Council, NFU, 1962-, Vice-Pres. 1970-71, Dep. Pres., 1971–79. Member: Agricultural Adv. Council, 1968-72; Central Council for Agricultural and Horticultural Co-operation, 1970-79. Chm., Essex Peas Ltd. DL Essex, 1972. *Recreations:* hunting, shooting, tennis. *Address:* Penny Pot, Halstead, Essex. *T:* Halstead 472828. *Club:* Farmers'.
See also Hon. A. C. Butler.

BUTLER, Robin; *see* Butler, F. E. R.

BUTLER, Dr Rohan D'Olier, CMG; MA; DLitt; FRHistS; Fellow of All Souls since 1938 (a Senior Research Fellow since 1956; Sub-Warden, 1961-63; representative at 12th International Historical Congress at Vienna, 1965, at 11th Anglo-American Conference of Historians, 1982); Member: Court, University of Essex, since 1971; Lord Chancellor's Advisory Council on Public Records, since 1982; *b* St John's Wood, 21 Jan. 1917; surv. *s* of late Sir Harold Butler, KCMG, CB, MA, and Lady Butler, *y c* of late Asst Inspector-General S. A. W. Waters, RIC; *m* Lucy Rosemary, FRHS (Lady of the Manor of White Notley, Essex), *y c* of late Eric Byron, Lord of the Manor. *Educ:* Eton; abroad and privately; Balliol Coll., Oxford (Hall Prizeman, 1938). BA (1st Class Hons in History), 1938; on International Propaganda and Broadcasting Enquiry, 1939; on staff of MOI, 1939-41 and 1942-44, of Special Operations Executive, 1941; served with RAPC, 1941-42, with HG, 1942-44 (Defence Medal, War Medal); on staff of FO, 1944-45; Editor of Documents on British Foreign Policy (1919-39), 1945-65 (with late Sir Llewellyn Woodward, FBA, 1945-54; Senior Editor, 1955-65); Leverhulme Research Fellow, 1955-57. Governor, Felsted Sch., 1959-77, representative on GBA, 1964-77; Trustee, Felsted Almshouses, 1961-77; Noel Buxton Trustee, 1961-67. Historical Adviser to Sec. of State for Foreign Affairs, 1963-68, for Foreign and Commonwealth Affairs, 1968-82 (from 14th Earl of Home to 6th Baron Carrington). On management of Inst. of Hist. Research, Univ. of London, 1967-77. Laureate, Inst. de France. *Publications:* The Roots of National Socialism, 1941; Documents on British Foreign Policy, 1st series, vols i-ix, 2nd series, vol. ix, 1947-65; The Peace Settlement of Versailles (in New Cambridge Modern History), 1960; Paradiplomacy (in Studies in Diplomatic History in honour of Dr G. P. Gooch, OM, CH, FBA), 1961; Introduction to Anglo-Soviet historical exhibition of 1967; Choiseul, 1980 (Prix Jean Debrousse, Acad. des Scis Morales et Politiques). *Recreation:* idling. *Address:* All Souls College, Oxford; White Notley Hall, near Witham, Essex. *Clubs:* Beefsteak, Bertorelli Luncheon; Alastair Buchan (Oxford).

BUTLER, Ven. Dr Thomas Frederick; Archdeacon of Northolt, since 1980; *b* 1940; *s* of Thomas John Butler and Elsie Butler (*née* Bainbridge); *m* 1964, Barbara Joan Clark; one *s* one *d. Educ:* Univ. of Leeds (BSc 1st Cl. Hons, MSc, PhD). CEng; MIEE. College of the Resurrection, Mirfield, 1962-64; Curate: St Augustine's, Wisbech, 1964-66; St Saviour's, Folkestone, 1966-68; Lecturer and Chaplain, Univ. of Zambia, 1968-73; Acting Dean of Holy Cross Cathedral, Lusaka, Zambia, 1972; Chaplain to Univ. of Kent at Canterbury, 1973-80. Six Preacher, Canterbury Cathedral, 1979-. *Recreations:* reading, mountain walking. *Address:* Gayton Lodge, 71 Gayton Road, Harrow, Mddx. *T:* 01-863 1530.

BUTLER, Col Sir Thomas Pierce, 12th Bt *cr* 1628; CVO 1970; DSO 1944; OBE 1954; Resident Governor and Major, HM Tower of London, 1961-71, Keeper of the Jewel House, 1968-71; *b* 18 Sept. 1910; *o s* of Sir Richard Pierce Butler, 11th Bt, OBE, DL, and Alice Dudley (*d* 1965), *d* of Very Rev. Hon. James Wentworth Leigh, DD; *S* father, 1955; *m* 1937, Rosemary Liège Woodgate Davidson-Houston, *d* of late Major J. H. Davidson-Houston, Pembury Hall, Kent; one *s* two *d. Educ:* Harrow; Trinity Coll., Cambridge. BA (Hons) Cantab, 1933. Grenadier Guards, 1933; served War of 1939-45 (wounded, POW, escaped); BEF France; 6th Bn, Egypt, Syria, Tripoli, N Africa; Staff Coll., 1944 (psc); Comd Guards Composite Bn, Norway, 1945-46; Comd 2nd Bn Grenadier Guards, BAOR, 1949-52; AQMG, London District, 1952-55; Col, Lt-Col Comdg the Grenadier Guards, 1955-58; Military Adviser to UK High Comr in New Zealand, 1959-61. Pres., London (Prince of Wales's) District, St John Ambulance Brigade. JP Co. of London 1961-71. CStJ. *Recreations:* fishing, travelling. *Heir: s* Richard Pierce Butler [*b* 22 July 1940; *m* 1965, Diana, *yr d* of Col S. J. Borg; three *s* one *d*]. *Address:* 6 Thurloe Square, SW7. *T:* 01-584 6361; Ballin Temple, Co. Carlow. *Club:* Cavalry and Guards.

BUTLER, Vincent, RSA 1977; sculptor; *b* 1933. *Educ:* Edinburgh Coll. of Art (DA 1955); Accademia di Belle Arti, Milan. One man exhibitions: London, 1969; Manchester, 1973, 1977; Bradford, 1974; Bury, 1977; Torquay, 1976; Haddington, 1978; Wolfsburg, 1979; Edinburgh, 1980. *Address:* 17 Deanpark Crescent, Edinburgh EH4 1PH. *T:* 031-332 5884.

BUTLER-SLOSS, Hon. Dame (Ann) Elizabeth (Oldfield), DBE 1979; Hon. Mrs Justice Butler-Sloss; a Judge of the High Court of Justice, Family

Division, since 1979; *b* 10 Aug. 1933; *d* of late Sir Cecil Havers, QC, and late Enid Snelling; *m* 1958, Joseph William Alexander Butler-Sloss, *qv* ; two *s* one *d. Educ:* Wycombe Abbey Sch. Called to Bar, Inner Temple, Feb. 1955, Bencher, 1979; practice at Bar, 1955-70; Registrar, Principal Registry of Probate, later Family, Division, 1970-79. Contested (C), Lambeth, Vauxhall, 1959. A Vice Pres., Medico-Legal Soc. *Publications:* Joint Editor: Phipson on Evidence (10th edn); Corpe on Road Haulage (2nd edn); a former Editor, Supreme Court Practice, 1976 and 1979. *Address:* 10 King's Bench Walk, Temple, EC4. *T:* 01-583 4649; Higher Marsh Farm, Marsh Green, Rockbeare, Exeter, Devon EX5 2EX. *T:* Whimple 822663.
See also Rt. Hon. Sir R. M. O. Havers.

BUTLER-SLOSS, Joseph William Alexander; a Recorder of the Crown Court, since 1972; *b* 16 Nov. 1926; 2nd and *o* surv. *s* of late Francis Alexander Sloss and Alice Mary Frances Violet Sloss (*née* Patchell); *m* 1958, Ann Elizabeth Oldfield Havers (*see* Hon. Dame (Ann) Elizabeth (Oldfield) Butler-Sloss); two *s* one *d. Educ:* Bangor Grammar Sch., Co. Down; Hertford Coll., Oxford. Ordinary Seaman, RN, 1944; Midshipman 1945, Sub-Lieut 1946, RNVR. MA (Jurisprudence) Hertford Coll., Oxford, 1951. Called to Bar, Gray's Inn, 1952; joined Western Circuit, 1954; joined Inner Temple. Joint Master, East Devon Foxhounds, 1970-76. *Recreations:* hunting; the violin. *Address:* 10 King's Bench Walk, Temple, EC4Y 7EB. *T:* 01-583 4649; Higher Marsh Farm, Marsh Green, Rockbeare, Exeter, Devon. *T:* Whimple 822663. *Club:* Carlton.

BUTLIN, Martin Richard Fletcher; Keeper of Historic British Collection, Tate Gallery, since 1967; *b* 7 June 1929; *s* of Kenneth Rupert Butlin and Helen Mary (*née* Fletcher); *m* 1969, Frances Caroline Chodzko. *Educ:* Rendcomb Coll.; Trinity Coll., Cambridge (MA); Courtauld Inst. of Art, London Univ. (BA). Asst Keeper, Tate Gall., 1955-67. *Publications:* A Catalogue of the Works of William Blake in the Tate Gallery, 1957, 2nd edn 1971; Samuel Palmer's Sketchbook of 1824, 1962; Turner Watercolours, 1962; (with Sir John Rothenstein) Turner, 1964; (with Mary Chamot and Dennis Farr) Tate Gallery Catalogues: The Modern British Paintings, Drawings and Sculpture, 1964; The Later Works of J. M. W. Turner, 1965; William Blake, 1966; The Blake-Varley Sketchbook of 1819, 1969; (with E. Joll) The Paintings of J. M. W. Turner, 1977 (jtly, Mitchell Prize for the History of Art, 1978); The Paintings and Drawings of William Blake, 1981 (George Wittenborn Meml Award, 1981); selected paintings and prepared catalogues for following exhibitions: (with Andrew Wilton and John Gage) Turner 1775-1851, 1974; William Blake, 1978; articles and reviews in Burlington Mag., Connoisseur, Master Drawings, Blake Newsletter, Blake Studies. *Recreations:* music, travel. *Address:* Tate Gallery, Millbank, SW1P 4RG. *T:* 01-821 1313.

BUTT, Sir (Alfred) Kenneth (Dudley), 2nd Bt *cr* 1929; Underwriting Member of Lloyd's, 1931-74; farmer and bloodstock breeder; *b* 7 July 1908; *o s* of Sir Alfred Butt, 1st Bt and Lady Georgina Mary Butt (*née* Say); *S* father, 1962; *m* 1st, 1938, Kathleen Farmar (marr. diss., 1948); 2nd, 1948, Mrs Ivor Birts (*née* Bain), widow of Lt-Col Ivor Birts, RA (killed on active service). *Educ:* Rugby; Brasenose Coll., Oxford. Lloyd's, 1929-39. Royal Artillery, 1939-45, Major RA. Chairman, Parker Wakeling & Co. Ltd, 1946-54; Managing Director, Brook Stud Co., 1962-81. Pres., Aberdeen-Angus Cattle Soc., 1968-69; Chm., Thoroughbred Breeders Assoc., 1973. *Recreations:* shooting, horse-racing, travelling, paintings. *Address:* Wheat Hill, Sandon, Buntingford, Herts. *T:* Kelshall 203; Flat 29, 1 Hyde Park Square, W2. *T:* 01-262 3988. *Clubs:* Carlton, etc.

BUTT, Sir Kenneth; *see* Butt, Sir A. K. D.

BUTT, Richard Bevan; on secondment as Counsellor, UK Permanent Representation to European Economic Community, Brussels, since 1981; *b* 27 Feb. 1943; *s* of Roger William Bevan and Jean Mary (*née* Carter); *m* 1975, Amanda Jane Finlay; one *s. Educ:* Magdalen Coll., Oxford (BA Hist.); Lancaster Univ. (MA Regional Econs). Asst Principal, Min. of Housing, 1965-68; Res. Associate, Birmingham Univ., 1969-72; Consultant, 1972; HM Treasury: Principal, 1972-78; Asst Sec., 1978-80. *Recreations:* pottery, architecture, travel, gardening. *Address:* 23 Sotheby Road, N5.

BUTTER, Major David Henry, MC 1941; JP; landowner and farmer; company director; HM Lord-Lieutenant of Perth and Kinross, since 1975; *b* 18 March 1920; *s* of late Col Charles Butter, OBE, DL, JP, Pitlochry, and Agnes Marguerite (Madge), *d* of late William Clark, Newark, NJ, USA; *m* 1946, Myra Alice, *d* of Hon. Maj.-Gen. Sir Harold Wernher, 3rd Bt, GCVO, TD; one *s* four *d. Educ:* Eton; Oxford. Served War of 1939-45: 2nd Lieut Scots Guards, 1940, Western Desert and North Africa, Sicily (Staff), 1941-43; Italy (ADC to GOC 8th Army, Gen. Sir Oliver Leese, 1944); Temp. Major, 1946; retd Army, 1948. Brig., Queen's Body Guard for Scotland (Royal Company of Archers); Pres., Highland T&AVR, 1979. County Councillor, Perth, 1955-74; DL Perthshire, 1956, Vice-Lieutenant of Perth, 1960-71; HM Lieutenant of County of Perth, 1971-75, and County of Kinross, 1974-75. Governor of Gordonstoun School. *Recreations:* shooting, golf, ski-ing, travel. *Address:* Cluniemore, Pitlochry, Scotland. *T:* Pitlochry 2006; 64 Rutland Gate, SW7. *T:* 01-589 6731. *Clubs:* Turf; Royal and Ancient (St Andrews).
See also Lord Ramsay.

BUTTER, John Henry, CMG 1962; MBE 1946; Financial Director to Government of Abu Dhabi, 1970-82; *b* 20 April 1916; *s* of late Captain A.

E. Butter, CMG, and late Mrs Baird; *m* 1950, Joyce Platt; three *s. Educ:* Charterhouse; Christ Church, Oxford. Indian Civil Service, 1939-47; Pakistan Admin. Service, 1947-50 (served in Punjab, except for period 1942-46 when was Asst to Political Agent, Imphal, Manipur State). HM Overseas Civil Service, Kenya, 1950-65 (Perm. Sec. to the Treasury, 1959-65); Financial Adviser, Kenya Treasury, 1965-69. *Recreations:* golf, bridge. *Address:* PO Box 30181, Nairobi, Kenya; Whitehill, Gordon, Berwickshire. *Club:* East India, Devonshire, Sports, and Public Schools.
See also Prof. P. H. Butter.

BUTTER, Neil (McLaren), QC 1976; **His Honour Judge Butter;** a Circuit Judge, since 1982; *b* 10 May 1933; *y s* of late Andrew Butter, MA, MD and late Ena Butter, MB, ChB; *m* 1974, Claire Marianne Miskin. *Educ:* The Leys Sch.; Queens' Coll., Cambridge (MA). Called to Bar, Inner Temple, 1955. An Asst and Dep. Recorder of Bournemouth, 1971; Recorder of the Crown Court, 1972-82. Mem., Senate of the Inns of Court and the Bar, 1976-79. Inspector, for Dept of Trade, Ozalid Gp Hldgs Ltd, 1977-79. A Legal Assessor to GMC and GDC, 1979-82. Trustee, Kingdon-Ward Speech Therapy Trust, 1980-. *Recreations:* motoring, holidays, browsing through Who's Who. *Address:* Carpmael Building, Temple, EC4Y 7AT. *T:* 01-353 5537. *Clubs:* United Oxford & Cambridge University; Hampshire (Winchester).

BUTTER, Prof. Peter Herbert; Regius Professor of English, Glasgow University, since 1965; *b* 7 April 1921; *s* of Archibald Butter, CMG, and Helen Cicely (*née* Kerr); *m* 1958, Bridget Younger; one *s* two *d. Educ:* Charterhouse; Balliol Coll., Oxford. Served in RA, 1941-46. Assistant, 1948, Lecturer, 1951, in English, Univ. of Edinburgh; Professor of English, Queen's Univ., Belfast, 1958-65. *Publications:* Shelley's Idols of the Cave, 1954; Francis Thompson, 1961; Edwin Muir, 1962; Edwin Muir: Man and Poet, 1966; (ed) Shelley's Alastor and Other Poems, 1971; (ed) Selected Letters of Edwin Muir, 1974; (ed) Selected Poems of William Blake, 1982; articles in periodicals. *Address:* Ashfield, Bridge of Weir, Renfrewshire. *T:* Bridge of Weir 613139. *Club:* New (Edinburgh).
See also J. H. Butter.

BUTTERFIELD, Charles Harris, QC (Singapore) 1952; HMOCS, retired; *b* 28 June 1911; 2nd *s* of William Arthur Butterfield, OBE, and Rebecca Butterfield; *m* 1st, 1938, Monica, *d* of Austin Harrison, London; one *d* ; 2nd, by special permission of Mrs Butterfield, Ellen, *d* of Ernest John Bennett, Singapore and *widow* of J. E. King, Kuala Lumpur, Singapore and Hooe. *Educ:* Downside; Trinity Coll., Cambridge. Barrister-at-law, Middle Temple, 1934. Entered Colonial Legal Service, 1938; Crown Counsel, Straits Settlements, 1938. Served Singapore RA (Volunteer) and RA, 1941-46; POW, 1942-45. Solicitor-General, Singapore, 1948-55, Attorney-General, 1955-57; Legal Adviser's Dept CRO and FCO, 1959-69; DoE and Sec. of State's Panel of Inspectors (Planning), 1969-74. *Address:* 18 Kewhurst Avenue, Cooden, Bexhill on Sea, E Sussex. *Club:* Pevensey Marsh Beagles.

BUTTERFIELD, John Michael; Chief Executive, National Association of Youth Clubs, since 1975; *b* 2 July 1926; *s* of late John Leslie Butterfield and Hilda Mary Butterfield (*née* Judson); *m* 1955, Mary Maureen, *d* of John Martin; one *s* twin *d* (and one *s* decd). *Educ:* Leeds Modern Sch.; Leeds Univ. John Butterfield & Son, Leeds, 1949-60; John Atkinson & Sons (Sowerby Bridge) Ltd, 1960-61. Youth Officer, Coventry Cathedral, 1961-68; Liverpool Council of Social Service: Head of Youth and Community Dept, 1968-72; Operations Dir, 1972-75. Member: British Council of Churches, 1954-73; British Council of Churches Youth Dept, 1952-68 (Chm. Exec. Cttee, 1962-67). *Recreations:* music, reading, walking, railways. *Address:* 4 Church Farm Court, Aston Flamville, near Hinckley, Leics LE10 3AW. *T:* Hinckley 611027.

BUTTERFIELD, Prof. Sir (William) John (Hughes), Kt 1978; OBE 1953; DM; FRCP; Regius Professor of Physic, University of Cambridge, since 1976; Master of Downing College, Cambridge, since 1978; *b* 28 March 1920; *s* of late William Hughes Butterfield and of Mrs Doris North; *m* 1st, 1946, Ann Sanders (decd); one *s* ; 2nd, 1950, Isabel-Ann Foster Kennedy; two *s* one *d. Educ:* Solihull Sch.; Exeter Coll., Oxford (Hon. Fellow, 1978); Johns Hopkins Univ. MA, MD Cantab 1975. Repr. Oxford Univ.: Rugby football, *v* Cambridge, 1940-41; hockey, 1940-42 (Captain); cricket, 1942 (Captain). Member, Scientific Staff, Medical Research Council, 1946-58: Major RAMC, Army Operational Research Group, 1947-50; Research Fellow, Medical Coll. of Virginia, Richmond, Va, USA, 1950-52; seconded to Min. of Supply, 1952; seconded to AEA, 1956; Prof. of Experimental Medicine, Guy's Hospital, 1958-63; Prof. of Medicine, Guy's Hosp. Med. Sch., and Additional Physician, Guy's Hosp., 1963-71; Vice-Chancellor, Nottingham Univ. 1971-75; Professorial Fellow, Downing Coll., Cambridge, 1975-78. Chairman: Bedford Diabetic Survey, 1962; Woolwich/Erith New Town Medical Liaison Cttee, 1965-71; SE Met. Reg. Hospital Board's Clinical Research Cttee, 1960-71; Scientific Advisory Panel, Army Personnel Research Cttee, 1970-; Council for the Education and Training of Health Visitors, 1971-76; East Midlands Economic Planning Council, 1974-75; Medicines Commn, 1976-81; Member: UGC Medical Sub-Cttee, 1966-71; Council, British Diabetic Assoc., 1963-74 (Chm. 1967-74, Vice-Pres. 1974-); DHSS Cttee on Medical Aspects of Food Policy, 1964-; DHSS Panel on Medical Research, 1974-76; MRC Cttee on General Epidemiology, 1965-74; MRC Clinical Res. Grants Bd, 1969-71; MRC, 1976-80; Anglo-Soviet Consultative Cttee; Minister of Health's Long Term Study Group; Health Educn Council, DHSS, 1973-77; Trent RHA, 1973-75; IUC Council and Exec. Cttee, 1973-; British Council Med. Adv.

Cttee, 1971-; Northwick Park Adv. Cttee, 1971-76; Council, European Assoc. for Study of Diabetes, 1968-71 (Vice-Pres.); Hong Kong Univ. and Polytechnic Grants Cttee, 1975-. Chm., Jardine Educnl Trust; Trustee, Croucher Foundn, Hong Kong, 1979-. Consultant, WHO Expert Cttee on Diabetes, 1964-80; Visitor, King Edward's Hospital Fund, 1964-71; Examiner in Medicine: Oxford Univ., 1960-66; Univ. of E Africa, 1966; Cambridge Univ., 1967-75; Pfizer Vis. Professor, NZ and Australia, 1965; Vis. Professor, Yale, 1966. Oliver-Sharpey Lectr, 1967; Linacre Lectr, 1979; Rock Carling Fellow, 1968; Banting Lectr, 1970. Dir, Prudential Assurance Co., 1981-. Member: Editorial Board, Diabetaloga, 1964-69; Jl Chronic Diseases, 1968-. Hon. Fellow, NY Acad. Science, 1962; Corres. FACP, 1973. Patron, Richmond Soc., 1968-71. FRSA 1971. Hon. LLD Nottingham, 1977. *Publications:* (jointly) On Burns, 1953; Tolbutamide after 10 years, 1967; Priorities in Medicine, 1968; Health and Sickness: the choice of treatment, 1971; over 100 contribs to med. and allied literature incl. books, chapters, official reports and articles on diabetes, health care and educnl topics. *Recreations:* tennis (not lawn), cricket (village) and talking (too much). *Address:* The Master's Lodge, Downing College, Cambridge. *T:* Cambridge 59491. *Clubs:* Athenæum, MCC, Queen's.

BUTTERWORTH, Sir (George) Neville, Kt 1973; DL; Chairman, Tootal Ltd (formerly English Calico Ltd), 1968-74; Member, Royal Commission on Distribution of Income and Wealth, 1974-79; *b* 27 Dec. 1911; *s* of Richard Butterworth and Hannah (*née* Wright); *m* 1947, Barbara Mary Briggs; two *s. Educ:* Malvern; St John's Coll., Cambridge. Served with Royal Artillery, at home and overseas, 1939-45. Joined English Sewing Cotton Co. Ltd, 1933; Man. Dir, 1966; Dep. Chm., 1967; Chm., 1968, on merger with The Calico Printers' Assoc. Ltd. Dir, National Westminster Bank (North Regional Board), 1969-82. Chm., NW Regional Council of CBI, 1968-70; Former Mem., Grand Council of CBI; Trustee, Civic Trust for the North-West, 1967; Mem., Textile Council, 1970; CompTI 1973. Member: Court of Governors, Manchester Univ., 1973-; Council, UMIST, 1973-79. FBIM 1968. High Sheriff 1974, DL 1974, Greater Manchester. *Recreation:* farming. *Address:* Oak Farm, Ollerton, Knutsford, Cheshire. *T:* 061-567 3150. *Club:* St James's (Manchester).

BUTTERWORTH, Henry, CEng, MIMechE; Director General, Royal Ordnance Factories (Ammunition), since 1979; *b* 21 Jan. 1926; *s* of late Henry and Wilhemena Butterworth; *m* 1948, Ann Smith; two *s. Educ:* St Mary's, Leyland, Lancs. DipProd Birmingham. Apprenticeship, 1940-47; Draughtsman, 1947-52; Technical Asst, 1952-53; progressively, Shop Manager, Asst Manager, Manager, 1953-71; Director ROF: Cardiff, Burghfield, Glascoed, 1971-79. *Recreation:* coarse fishing. *Address:* 9 Crowsley Road, Lower Shiplake, Henley-on-Thames, Oxon. *T:* Wargrave 2067.

BUTTERWORTH, Prof. Ian, FRS 1981; Professor of Physics, since 1971, and Head of the Department of Physics, since 1980, Imperial College of Science and Technology; *b* 3 Dec. 1930; *s* of Harry and Beatrice Butterworth; *m* 1964, Mary Therese (*née* Gough); one *d. Educ:* Bolton County Grammar Sch.; Univ. of Manchester. BSc 1951; PhD 1954. Sen. Scientific Officer, UK Atomic Energy Authority, 1954-58; Lectr, Imperial Coll., 1958-64; Vis. Physicist, Lawrence Radiation Laboratory, Univ. of California, 1964-65; Sen. Lectr, Imperial Coll., 1965-68; Group Leader, Bubble Chamber Research Gp, Rutherford High Energy Laboratory, 1968-71; Science and Engineering Research Council (formerly Science Research Council): Mem., 1979- (Mem., Nuclear Physics Bd, 1972-75 and 1978-, Chm., 1979-; Mem., Particle Physics Cttee, 1978-79; Chm., Film Analysis Grants Cttee, 1972-75); UK deleg. on Council, European Organisation for Nuclear Research, 1979- (Mem., Research Bd, 1976-; Chm., Super Proton Synchroton Cttee, 1976-79). *Publications:* numerous papers in learned jls (on Hadron Spectroscopy and Application of Bubble Chamber to Strong and Weak Interaction Physics): Annual Review of Nuclear Science; Physical Review; Nuovo Cimento; Nuclear Physics; Physical Review Letters; Physics Letters, etc. *Recreation:* history of art. *Address:* c/o Physics Department, Blackett Laboratory, Imperial College, Prince Consort Road, SW7 2BZ. *T:* 01-589 5111.

BUTTERWORTH, John Blackstock, CBE 1982; JP; DL; Vice-Chancellor, University of Warwick, since 1963; *b* 13 March 1918; *o s* of John William and Florence Butterworth; *m* 1948, Doris Crawford Elder; one *s* two *d. Educ:* Queen Elizabeth's Grammar Sch., Mansfield; The Queen's Coll., Oxford. Served in Royal Artillery, 1939-46. MA 1946. Called to Bar, Lincoln's Inn, 1947. New Coll., Oxford: Fellow, 1946-63; Dean, 1952-56; Bursar and Fellow, 1956-63; Sub Warden, 1957-58. Junior Proctor, 1950-51; Faculty Fellow of Nuffield Coll., 1953-58; Member of Hebdomadal Council, Oxford Univ., 1953-63. Managing Trustee, Nuffield Foundation, 1964-. Chairman: Inter-Univ. Council for Higher Educn Overseas, 1968-77; Universities Cttee for Non-teaching Staffs, 1970-; Inquiry into work of Probation Officers and Social Workers in Local Authorities and Nat. Service, 1971-73; Midland Community Radio Ltd, 1978-; Standing Cttee on Internat. Co-operation in Higher Educn, 1981-; Inter-Univ. and Polytechnic Council, 1981-. Member: Royal Commn on the Working of the Tribunals of Inquiry (Act), 1921, 1966; Intergovernmental Cttee on Law of Contempt in relation to Tribunals of Inquiry, 1968; Noise Advisory Council, 1974-81; Bd, British Council, 1981-; British delegn to Commonwealth Educn Conferences in Lagos, 1968, Canberra, 1971, Kingston, 1974, Accra, 1977, Colombo, 1980. Governor, Royal Shakespeare Theatre, 1964-; Trustee, Shakespeare Birthplace Trust, 1966-. DL Warwickshire, 1967-74, DL West Midlands 1974-; JP City of

Oxford, 1962, Coventry, 1963-. Hon DCL, Univ. of Sierra Leone, 1976. *Address:* The University of Warwick, Coventry CV4 7AL. *T:* Coventry 24011. *Club:* Athenæum.

BUTTERWORTH, Sir Neville; *see* Butterworth, Sir G. N.

BUTTFIELD, Archie Montague Carey, CMG 1959; formerly Chairman, Advisory Board, NSW, National Bank of Australasia Ltd; Director: Mauri Bros & Thomson Ltd; Mount Isa Mines Ltd; Dellingham Corporation of Australia; Member, Principal Board, National Bank of Australasia Ltd; *b* Wagin, WA, 27 Aug. 1898; *s* of late F. Montgomery Buttfield, Wagin; *m* 1930, Ella, *d* of E. Warner; one *s* two *d. Educ:* Perth Modern Sch. Joined Australian Mutual Provident Society, 1914; General Manager, 1948-60. Past Chairman, Life Offices' Assoc. for Australasia; Past Member Council, Aust. Administrative Staff Coll. AAII 1926. *Recreations:* trout fishing, golf, tennis, bowls. *Address:* 146 Middle Harbour Road, Lindfield, NSW 2070, Australia. *Clubs:* Union (Sydney); Elanora Country.

BUTTFIELD, Dame Nancy (Eileen), DBE 1972; formerly Senator for South Australia; *b* 12 Nov. 1912; *d* of Sir Edward Wheewall Holden and Hilda May Lavis; *m* 1936, Frank Charles Buttfield; two *s. Educ:* Woodlands Church of England Girls' Grammar Sch., Adelaide; Composenea; Paris; Univ. of Adelaide, SA. Senator for South Australia, Oct. 1955-June 1965, re-elected July 1968-74. Exec. Mem., Commonwealth Immigration Adv. Council, 1955-; Vice-President: Good Neighbour Council of SA, 1956-62; Phoenix Soc. for the Physically Handicapped, 1959-. Dir, Co-operative Building Soc. of SA, 1959-. Mem. Council, Bedford Industries, 1965-. Mem., Nat. Council of Women of SA. *Recreations:* farming, dress-making, gourmet cooking, music. *Address:* 52 Strangeways Terrace, North Adelaide, SA 5006, Australia. *Clubs:* Queen Adelaide, Lyceum, Royal Adelaide Golf (all SA).

BUTTIGIEG, Dr Anton; President of the Republic of Malta, 1976-82; *b* Gozo, 19 Feb. 1912; *s* of Saviour Buttigieg and Concetta (*née* Falzon); *m* 1st, 1944, Carmen Bezzina (decd); two *s* one *d* ; 2nd, 1953, Connie Scicluna (decd); 3rd, 1975, Margery Patterson. *Educ:* Royal Univ. of Malta (BA, LLD). Notary Public 1939; Advocate 1941. Police Inspector during Second World War; Law Reporter and Leader Writer, Times of Malta, 1944-48; Actg Magistrate 1955; Editor, The Voice of Malta, 1959-70. MP, 1955-76; Pres., Malta Labour Party, 1959-61, Dep. Leader, 1962-76; Dep. Prime Minister, 1971-76; Minister of Justice and Parly Affairs, 1971-76. Deleg., Malta Constitutional Confs, London, 1958 and 1964; Rep. to Consult. Assembly, Council of Europe, 1966-71, Vice-Pres., 1967-68. Mem., Acad. of Maltese Language. 1st Prize for poetry, Govt of Malta, 1971; Guze Muscat Azzopardi Prize for poetry, 1972; Silver Plaque for poetry, Circolo Culturale Rhegium Julii, Reggio, Calabria, 1975; Internat. Prize for Poetry, Centro di Cultura Mediterranea, Palermo, 1977; First Prize and Special Diploma for Poetry, Centro Culturale Artistico Letterario, Brindisi, 1979; Malta Literary Award (First Prize), 1979; Medal for Poetry, Accad. Pontiana, Naples, 1980. *Publications: lyrical poetry:* Mill-Gallerija ta' Zghoziti (From the balcony of my youth), 1945; Fanali bil-lejl (Lamps in the night), 1949; Qasba mar-Rih (A reed in the wind), 1968; Fl-Arena (In the Arena), 1970; *humorous poetry:* Ejjew Nidhku Ftit (Let us laugh a little), 1963; Ejjew nidhku ftit iehor (Let us laugh a little more), 1966; *Haikus and Tankas:* Il-Muza bil-Kimono (The Muse in Kimono), 1968 (English and Japanese trans); Ballati Maltin (Maltese Ballads), 1973; Il Mare di Malta, 1974, new edn 1980; Il-Ghanja tas-Sittin (The song of the sixty year old), 1975; The Lamplighter, 1977; Poeziji Migbura-L-Ewwel Volum (Collected Poems, vol. 1), 1978; Qabas el Misbah, 1978; Der Laternenanzünder, 1979; *autobiog.:* Toni, the Seaman's Son, vol. 1, 1978; L-Ghazla tat-Trieq (The Choice of the Way), vol. 2, 1980. *Recreations:* horse racing, gardening. *Address:* The White Lodge, Kappara, Malta.

BUTTLE, Prof. Gladwin Albert Hurst, OBE (mil.) 1942; MA, MB Cantab; FRCP; Wellcome Professor of Pharmacology, School of Pharmacy, London University 1946-66, and Professor, St Bartholomew's Hospital Medical School, 1948-60, now Emeritus Professor; *b* 11 April 1899; *s* of William and Mary Buttle; *m* 1936, Eva Korella; one *s. Educ:* Whitgift Sch.; St John's Coll., Cambridge; MRCS, LRCP, 1924; MA 1927; BCh 1967; FRCP 1970; MD Louvain, 1945. Qualified University Coll. Hospital, 1924; Pharmacologist Wellcome Physiological Research Laboratories for 14 years. RMA Woolwich, 1917; Lieut RE, 1918. Served War of 1939-45, RAMC (Lt-Col); adviser in Blood Transfusion, MEF and BLA, 1940-45. Expert, FAO, Mexico City, 1967-69; Professor of Pharmacology: Addis Ababa, 1972-74; Riyadh Univ., 1974-78. FRSocMed (JP Section of Therapeutics and Past Mem.); Past Member: British Pharmacopoeia Codex Action and Uses Cttee; MRC Drug Safety Cttee; Colonial Office Leprosy Cttee; Min. of Agric. Food Additives Cttee; Med. cons to MoD. Co-founder and Dep. Chm., Buttle Trust for Children. *Publications:* contribs on chemotherapy and pharmacology to medical jls. *Recreations:* gardening, tennis. *Address:* 12 Ewhurst, Kersfield Road, SW15. *T:* 01-789 8030; 300 Vauxhall Bridge Road, SW1. *T:* 01-828 7311.

BUTTON, Air Vice-Marshal Arthur Daniel, CB 1976; OBE 1959; CEng; Director, Association of Recognised English Language Schools Examinations Trust, since 1976; Director of RAF Education Branch, 1972-76; *b* 26 May 1916; *o s* of late Leonard Daniel Button and of Agnes Ann (*née* Derbyshire); *m* 1944, Eira Guelph Waterhouse, *o d* of late Reginald Waterhouse Jones; one *s* decd. *Educ:* County High Sch., Ilford; University Coll., Southampton (BSc(Hons), (Lond)). Joined RAF Educnl Service, 1938; Gen. Duties Br.,

RAF, 1941-46; (Queen's Commendation for Valuable Service in the Air, 1946); returned to RAF Educn Br., 1946. *Recreations:* music, do-it-myself. *Address:* Dragons, 23 Upper Icknield Way, Aston Clinton, Aylesbury, Bucks HP22 5NF. *Club:* Royal Air Force.

BUTTON, Henry George; author; *b* 11 Aug. 1913; *e s* of late Rev. Frank S. and Bertha B. Button; *m* 1938, Edith Margaret Heslop (*d* 1972); two *d. Educ:* Manchester Grammar Sch.; Christ's Coll., Cambridge (Scholar). Mod. and Medieval Langs Tripos, Part II, 1st Class (with dist.) 1934; MLitt 1977; Tiarks German Scholar (research at Univ. of Bonn), 1934-35; Sen. Studentship of Goldsmiths' Company, 1935-36. Entered Civil Service, 1937; Board of Trade, 1937-57 (served in Min. of Production, 1942; Counsellor, UK Delegn to OEEC, Paris, 1952-55; on staff of Monopolies Commn, 1955-56); transf. Min. of Agriculture, Fisheries and Food, 1957; Under-Sec., Min. of Agriculture, Fisheries and Food, 1960-73 (Principal Finance Officer, 1965-73). Res. Student, Christ's Coll., Cambridge, 1974-76 (MLitt). Mem. Agricultural Research Council, 1960-62. Leader of various UK Delegns to FAO in Rome. BBC Brain of Britain for 1962; rep. Great Britain in radio quiz in Johannesburg, 1966; Bob Dyer's TV show, Sydney, 1967. *Publications:* The Guinness Book of the Business World (with A. Lampert), 1976; contribs to various jls both learned and unlearned, and to newspapers. *Recreations:* reading, writing, studying old businesses (hon. review ed., Business Archives Council, 1966-75; Hon. Sec., Tercentenarians' Club), showing visitors round the colleges. *Address:* 7 Amhurst Court, Grange Road, Cambridge CB3 9BH. *T:* 355698. *Club:* Civil Service.

BUTTROSE, Murray; a Deputy Circuit Judge, 1975-77; *b* 31 July 1903; *s* of William Robert and Frances Buttrose, both British; *m* 1935, Jean Marie Bowering; one *s. Educ:* St Peter's Coll. and Adelaide Univ., South Australia. Admitted and enrolled as a barrister and solicitor of the Supreme Court of S Australia, 1927; apptd to HM Colonial Legal Service, 1946; Crown Counsel, Singapore, 1946, Senior Crown Counsel, 1949, and Solicitor-General, Singapore, 1955; Puisne Judge, Singapore, 1956-68, retired. Admitted and enrolled as a solicitor of the Supreme Court of Judicature in England, 1955; a Recorder of the Crown Court, 1972-74. Formerly Temp. Dep. Chm. (part time), London QS. Served with Royal Air Force (RAFVR), 1940-45. *Recreations:* reading, tennis, and golf. *Address:* 6 Norfolk Court, Norfolk Square, Bognor Regis, West Sussex PO21 2JA. *T:* Bognor Regis 863965. *Clubs:* Singapore (Singapore); Royal Singapore Golf.

BUXTON, family name of **Barons Buxton of Alsa** and **Noel-Buxton.**

BUXTON OF ALSA, Baron *cr* 1978 (Life Peer), of Stiffkey in the County of Norfolk; **Aubrey Leland Oakes Buxton,** MC 1943; DL; Director: Anglia Television, since 1958; Survival Anglia Ltd; Chairman: Independent Television News Ltd, since 1981; UPITN Inc., USA, since 1981; *b* 15 July 1918; *s* of Leland Wilberforce Buxton and Mary, *d* of Rev. Thomas Henry Oakes; *m* 1946, Pamela Mary, *d* of Sir Henry Birkin, 3rd Bt; two *s* four *d. Educ:* Ampleforth; Trinity Coll., Cambridge. Served 1939-45, RA; combined ops in Arakan, 1942-45 (despatches, 1944). Extra Equerry to Duke of Edinburgh, 1964. A Trustee of the British Museum (Natural History), 1971-73. Member: Countryside Commn, 1968-72; Royal Commission on Environmental Pollution, 1970-74; British Vice-Pres., World Wildlife Fund; Trustee, Wildfowl Trust; Treasurer, London Zoological Soc.; Former Pres., Royal Television Soc.; Chm., Independent Television Cos Assoc., 1972-75. Wildlife Film Producer, Anglia TV; has made more than 250 TV films. Golden Awards, Internat. TV Festival, 1963 and 1968; Silver Medal, Zoological Society of London, 1967; Silver Medal, Royal TV Society, 1968; Queen's Award to Industry, 1974; Gold Medal, Royal TV Soc., 1977. High Sheriff of Essex 1972; DL Essex, 1975. *Publications:* (with Sir Philip Christison) The Birds of Arakan, 1946; The King in his Country, 1955; numerous articles and papers on wildlife and exploration. *Recreations:* travel, natural history, painting, sport. *Address:* Stiffkey, Wells-next-sea, Norfolk. *T:* Binham 347. *Club:* White's.

BUXTON, Adrian Clarence, CMG 1978; HM Diplomatic Service; Ambassador to Ecuador, since 1981; *b* 12 June 1925; *s* of Clarence Buxton and Dorothy (*née* Lintott); *m* 1958, Leonora Mary Cherkas; three *s. Educ:* Christ's Hosp., Horsham; Trinity Coll., Cambridge. RNVR, 1944-46; FO, 1947; 3rd Sec., Bangkok, 1948-52; FO, 1952-53; 2nd Sec., Khartoum, 1953-55; 2nd later 1st Sec., Bonn, 1955-58; 1st Sec. (Commercial) and Consul, Bogota, 1958-62; FO, 1962-64; 1st Sec., Saigon, 1964-67; 1st Sec. (Commercial), Havana, 1967-69; UK Dep. Permanent Rep. to UN and other internat. organisations at Geneva, 1969-73; Univ. of Surrey, 1973-74; Head of Training Dept and Dir Language Centre, FCO, 1974-75; Head of Maritime and Gen. Dept, FCO, 1975-77; Ambassador to Bolivia, 1977-81. *Address:* c/o Foreign and Commonwealth Office, SW1. *Club:* Travellers'.

BUXTON, Major Desmond Gurney, DL; 60th Rifles, retired; retired as Local Director (Norwich) Barclays Bank, 1958; Member Norfolk County Council, 1958-74; *b* 4 Jan. 1898; *e s* of late Edward G. Buxton, Catton Hall, Norwich, and of late Mrs Buxton, The Beeches, Old Catton, Norwich; *m* 1930, Rachel Mary, *yr d* of late Colonel A. F. Morse, Coltishall Mead, Norwich; two *s* three *d* (and one *d* decd). *Educ:* Eton; RMC Sandhurst. 60th Rifles, 1917-29; France and Belgium, 1917-18; NW Europe, 1945. Sheriff of Norwich, 1936-37; Lieut-Colonel Royal Norfolk Regt (TA), 1939-40. High Sheriff, Norfolk, 1960; DL Norfolk, 1961. CStJ 1972. *Recreations:* forestry, chess, bridge. *Address:* Hoveton Hall, Wroxham, Norwich NR12 8RJ.

BUXTON, Paul William Jex; Under Secretary, Northern Ireland Office, since 1981; *b* 20 Sept. 1925; *s* of late Denis Buxton and Emily Buxton (*née* Hollins); *m* 1st, 1950, Katharine Hull (marr. diss. 1971, she *d* 1977); two *s* one *d* ; 2nd, 1971, Hon. Margaret Aston (*née* Bridges); two *d*. *Educ:* Rugby Sch.; Balliol Coll., Oxford. Coldstream Guards, 1944-47. HM Foreign, later Diplomatic, Service, 1950-71; served Delhi, UN, Guatemala and Washington, latterly as Counsellor. Investment banking, 1972-74. NI Office, 1974-. *Address:* Castle House, Chipping Ongar, Essex. *T:* Ongar 362642. *Club:* Brooks's.

BUXTON, Raymond Naylor, OBE 1975; BEM 1957; QPM 1971; *b* 16 Sept. 1915; *s* of late Tom Bird Buxton and Ethel Buxton, Rushall, Walsall; *m* 1939, Agatha, *d* of late Enoch and Elizabeth Price, Essington, Wolverhampton; three *s*. *Educ:* King Edward VI Grammar Sch., Stafford. Constable to Chief Supt in Staffordshire Co. Police. Served War, RAF, Navigator, 1943-45 (FO). Police Coll. Staff, 1958-61; Asst Chief Constable, then Dep. Chief Constable of Herts, 1963-69, Chief Constable, 1969-77; HM Inspector of Constabulary, 1977-79. *Address:* Mannicotts, Radford Rise, Weeping Cross, Stafford. *Club:* Special Forces.

BUXTON, Dame Rita (Mary), DBE 1969 (CBE 1955; OBE 1944); *b* 1900; *d* of Charles James Neunhoffer and Alice Neunhoffer (*née* O'Connor), Melbourne, Australia; *m* 1922, Leonard R. Buxton; three *d*. *Educ:* Sacré-Coeur Convent. Interested in philanthropic work. Member of the Victoria League. *Recreations:* golf, tennis, bridge. *Address:* 48 Hampden Road, Armadale, Victoria, Australia. *T:* 50-3333; Mount Martha, Victoria, Australia. *T:* Mount Martha 741-216. *Clubs:* English-Speaking Union; Alexandra (Melbourne); Metropolitan Golf, Peninsula County Golf, Frankston Golf.

BUXTON, Ronald Carlile; MA Cantab; *b* 20 Aug. 1923; *s* of Murray Barclay Buxton and Janet Mary Muriel Carlile; *m* 1959, Phyllida Dorothy Roden Buxton; two *s* two *d*. *Educ:* Eton; Trinity Coll., Cambridge. Chartered Structural Engineer (AMIStructE). Director of H. Young & Co., London and associated companies. MP (C) Leyton, 1965-66. *Recreations:* travel, music, riding. *Address:* Kimberley Hall, Wymondham, Norfolk; 67 Ashley Gardens, SW1. *Club:* Carlton.

BUXTON, Sir Thomas Fowell Victor, 6th Bt *cr* 1840; *b* 18 Aug. 1925; *s* of Sir Thomas Fowell Buxton, 5th Bt, and Hon. Dorothy Cochrane (*d* 1927), *yr d* of 1st Baron Cochrane of Cults; *S* father, 1945; *m* 1955, Mrs D. M. Chisenhale-Marsh (*d* 1965). *Educ:* Eton; Trinity Coll., Cambridge. *Heir:* cousin Jocelyn Charles Roden Buxton [*b* 8 Aug. 1924; *m* 1960, Ann Frances, *d* of Frank Smitherman, *qv* ; three *d*].

BUZZARD, Sir Anthony (Farquhar), 3rd Bt *cr* 1929; educational consultant and tutor; Teacher of modern languages, The American School in London, since 1974; *b* 28 June 1935; *s* of Rear-Admiral Sir Anthony Wass Buzzard, 2nd Bt, CB, DSO, OBE, and of Margaret Elfreda, *d* of Sir Arthur Knapp, KCIE, CSI, CBE; *S* father, 1972; *m* 1970, Barbara Jean Arnold, Mendon, Michigan, USA; two *d*. *Educ:* Charterhouse; Christ Church, Oxford (MA); Ambassador Coll., Pasadena, USA (BA). ARCM. Lecturer in French, Ambassador Coll., Pasadena, 1962-65; Peripatetic Music Teacher for Surrey County Council, 1966-68; Lectr in French and Hebrew, Ambassador Coll., Bricket Wood, Herts, 1969-74. *Publications:* articles on eschatology in Words of Life magazine (organ of Conditional Immortality Mission), 1981. *Recreations:* tennis, squash, music. *Heir:* *b* Timothy Macdonnell Buzzard [*b* 28 Jan. 1939; *m* 1970, Jennifer Mary, *d* of late Peter Patching; one *s* one *d*]. *Address:* Robin Hill, Amersham Road, Chalfont St Giles, Bucks. *T:* Chalfont St Giles 2136.

BUZZARD, John Huxley; His Honour Judge Buzzard; a Circuit Judge at the Central Criminal Court, since 1974; *b* 12 Aug. 1912; *s* of late Brig.-Gen. Frank Anstie Buzzard, DSO, and Joan, *d* of late Hon. John Collier; *m* 1946, Hilary Ann Courtney Buzzard (*née* Antrobus); two *s* one *d*. *Educ:* Wellington Coll.; New Coll., Oxford. Open Classical Scholar, New Coll., 1931; commissioned 4th Queen's Own Royal West Kent Regt, TA, 1931; transferred to TA Reserve of Officers, 1935. Called to Bar, 1937 (Master of the Bench, Inner Temple, 1965). Served with RAFVR, in UK, Iceland, and SE Asia, 1940-45 (despatches). Recorder: Great Yarmouth, 1958-68; Dover, 1968-71; Crown Court, 1971-74; Second Sen. Prosecuting Counsel to the Crown, 1964-71, First Sen. Prosecuting Counsel, 1971-74. Consultant Editor, Archbold's Criminal Pleading; Jt Editor, Phipson on Evidence. *Recreations:* mountaineering, ski-ing, sailing. *Address:* Central Criminal Court, Old Bailey, EC4. *Clubs:* Alpine, Lansdowne, Climbers', Cruising Association.

BYAM SHAW, Glencairn Alexander, CBE 1954; a Director, Sadler's Wells, since 1966; *b* 13 Dec. 1904; *s* of Byam Shaw, artist, and Evelyn Pyke-Nott; *m* 1929, Angela Baddeley, CBE (*d* 1976); one *s* one *d*. *Educ:* Westminster Sch. First stage appearance, Pavilion Theatre, Torquay, 1923; Mem. J. B. Fagan's Company at Oxford Repertory Theatre; played Trophimof, in The Cherry Orchard, New York; Konstantin Treplev, in The Seagull and Baron Tusenbach, in The Three Sisters, London. Was in Max Reinhardt's production of The Miracle. Went to S Africa with Angela Baddeley in repertory of plays. Played Darnley in Queen of Scots and Laertes in John Gielgud's production of Hamlet; was mem. of company for Gielgud's season at Queen's Theatre. Produced plays in London, New York and Stratford-upon-Avon. A Director of Old Vic Theatre Centre; a Governor, Royal Shakespeare Theatre, 1960-;

Mem. Directorate, English Nat. Opera, 1974-. Co-Dir, with Anthony Quayle, of Shakespeare Memorial Theatre, Stratford-upon-Avon, 1952-56; Director, 1956-59; directed: Ross, Haymarket, 1960; The Lady From the Sea, Queen's, 1961; The Complaisant Lover and Ross, New York, 1961; The Rake's Progress and Idomeneo, Sadler's Wells, 1962; The Tulip Tree, Haymarket, 1962; Cosi fan Tutte, Der Freischütz, Hansel and Gretel, Sadler's Wells, 1963; Where Angels Fear to Tread, St Martin's, 1963; The Right Honourable Gentleman, Her Majesty's, 1964; Faust, Sadler's Wells, 1964; A Masked Ball, Sadler's Wells, 1964; You Never Can Tell, Haymarket, 1966; Die Fledermaus, Sadler's Wells, 1966, Coliseum, 1980; The Rivals, Haymarket, 1966; The Dance of Death, National Theatre, 1967; Orpheus and Eurydice, Sadler's Wells, 1967; The Merchant of Venice, Haymarket, 1967; The Wild Duck, Criterion, 1970; Duke Bluebeard's Castle, 1972; with John Blatchley: The Mastersingers of Nuremberg, 1968; The Valkyrie, 1970; Twilight of the Gods, 1971; The Rhinegold, 1972; Siegfried, 1973; The Ring Cycle, 1973; Tristan und Isolde, 1981. In the Royal Scots during War of 1939-45. Hon. DLitt Birmingham, 1959. *Address:* Barn Acre, Loddon Drive, Wargrave, Berks. *Club:* Reform.
See also J. J. Byam Shaw.

BYAM SHAW, (John) James, CBE 1972; *b* 12 Jan. 1903; *er* surv. *s* of John Byam Shaw and Evelyn Pyke-Nott; *m* 1st, 1929, Eveline (marr. diss., 1938), *d* of Capt. Arthur Dodgson, RN; 2nd, 1945, Margaret (*d* 1965), *d* of Arthur Saunders, MRCVS; one *s* ; 3rd, 1967, Christina, *d* of Francis Ogilvy and widow of W. P. Gibson. *Educ:* Westminster; Christ Church, Oxford. Scholar of Westminster and Christ Church; MA 1925; Hon. DLitt Oxford 1977. Worked independently in principal museums of Europe, 1925-33; Lecturer and Assistant to the Director, Courtauld Institute of Art, Univ. of London, 1933-34; joined P. & D. Colnaghi & Co., 1934; Director, 1937-68. Served in Royal Scots, UK, India and Burma, 1940-46 (wounded); Major, 1944. Lectr, Christ Church, Oxford, 1964-73; Associate Curator of pictures, Christ Church, Oxford, 1973-74; Hon. Student of Christ Church, 1976. Member: Council of the Byam Shaw Sch. of Art, 1957-77; Exec. Cttee, Nat. Art Collections Fund; Council, British Museum Soc., 1969-74; Gulbenkian Cttee on conservation of paintings and drawings, 1970-72; Conservation Cttee, Council for Places of Worship, 1970-77; Adv. Cttee, London Diocesan Council for Care of Churches, 1974-76. Trustee, Watts Gall. FSA; FRSA. Hon. Fellow: Pierpont Morgan Library, NY; Ateneo Veneto. *Publications:* The Drawings of Francesco Guardi, 1951; The Drawings of Domenico Tiepolo, 1962; Catalogue of Paintings by Old Masters at Christ Church Oxford, 1967; Catalogue of Drawings by Old Masters at Christ Church, Oxford, 1976; Catalogue of exhibition, Disegni Veneti della Collexione Lugt, Venice, 1981; Catalogue of Italian Drawings at the Fondation Custodia (Lugt Collection), Institut Néerlandais, Paris, 1982; publications in Old Master Drawings (1926-39), Print Collectors' Quarterly, Burlington Magazine, Apollo, Master Drawings (New York), Art Quarterly (Detroit), Arte Veneta, etc. *Address:* 4 Abingdon Villas, Kensington, W8. *T:* 01-937 6128. *Club:* Athenæum.
See also G. A. Byam Shaw.

BYAM SHAW, Nicholas Glencairn; Managing Director, Macmillan Publishers Ltd (formerly Macmillan and Co.), since 1969; *b* 28 March 1934; *s* of David Byam Shaw and Clarita Pamela Clarke; *m* 1st, 1956, Joan Elliott; two *s* one *d* ; 2nd, 1974, Suzanne Filer (*née* Rastello). *Educ:* Royal Naval Coll., Dartmouth. Commnd RN, 1955 (Lieut). Joined William Collins Sons & Co. Ltd, Glasgow, as salesman, 1956; Sales Manager, 1960; Macmillan and Co.: Sales Manager, 1964; Sales Dir, 1965; Dep. Man. Dir, 1967. *Recreations:* gardening, travel. *Address:* 9 Kensington Park Gardens, W11 3HB. *T:* 01-221 4547.

BYATT, Antonia Susan, (Mrs P. J. Duffy); writer; Senior Lecturer in English, University College, London, since 1981; *b* 24 Aug. 1936; *d* of John Frederick Drabble, *qv* ; *m* 1st, 1959, Ian Charles Rayner Byatt, *qv* (marr. diss. 1969); one *d* (one *s* decd); 2nd, 1969, Peter John Duffy; two *d*. *Educ:* Sheffield High Sch.; The Mount Sch., York; Newnham Coll., Cambridge (BA Hons); Bryn Mawr Coll., Pa, USA; Somerville Coll., Oxford. Extra-Mural Lectr, Univ. of London, 1962-71; Lectr in Literature, Central Sch. of Art and Design, 1965-69; Lectr in English, UCL, 1972-81. Associate of Newnham Coll., Cambridge, 1977-. Member: Social Effects of Television Adv. Gp, BBC, 1974-77; Bd of Communications and Cultural Studies, CNAA, 1978-. Broadcaster, reviewer; judge of literary prizes (Hawthornden, Booker, David Higham). *Publications:* Shadow of a Sun, 1964; Degrees of Freedom, 1965; The Game, 1967; Wordsworth and Coleridge in their Time, 1970; Iris Murdoch, 1976; The Virgin in the Garden, 1978; (ed) George Eliot, The Mill on the Floss, 1979. *Address:* 37 Rusholme Road, SW15. *T:* 01-789 3109, (office) 01-387 7050.

BYATT, Hugh Campbell, CMG 1979; HM Diplomatic Service; Ambassador to Portugal, since 1981; *b* 27 Aug. 1927; *e s* of late Sir Horace Byatt, GCMG, and late Olga Margaret Campbell, MBE; *m* 1954, Fiona, *d* of Ian P. Coats; two *s* one *d*. *Educ:* Gordonstoun; New College, Oxford. Served in Royal Navy, 1945-48; HMOCS Nigeria, 1952-57; Commonwealth Relations Office, 1958; Bombay, 1961-63; CRO, 1964-65; seconded to Cabinet Office, 1965-67; Head of Chancery, Lisbon, 1967-70; Asst, South Asian Dept, FCO, 1970-71; Consul-General, Lourenço Marques, 1971-73; Inspector, HM Diplomatic Service, 1973-75; RCDS, 1976; Dep. High Comr, Nairobi, 1977-78; Ambassador to Angola, 1978-81, to São Tomé, 1980-81. *Recreations:* sailing, fishing, gardening. *Address:* c/o Foreign and Commonwealth Office,

SW1. *Clubs:* Travellers', Royal Ocean Racing; Leander; Grémio Literário (Lisbon).
See also R. A. C. Byatt.

BYATT, Ian Charles Rayner; Deputy Chief Economic Adviser, HM Treasury, since 1978; *b* 11 March 1932; *s* of Charles Rayner Byatt and Enid Marjorie Annie Byatt (*née* Howat); *m* 1959 (marr. diss. 1969); one *s* one *d. Educ:* Kirkham Grammar Sch.; Oxford University. Commonwealth Fund Fellow, Harvard, 1957-58; Lectr in Economics, Durham Univ., 1958-62; Economic Consultant, HM Treasury, 1962-64; Lectr in Economics, LSE, 1964-67; Sen. Economic Adviser, Dept of Educn and Science, 1967-69; Dir of Econs and Stats, Min. of Housing and Local Govt, 1969-70; Dir Economics, DoE, 1970-72; Under Sec., HM Treasury, 1972-78. *Publications:* The British Electrical Industry 1875-1914, 1979; articles on economics in learned jls. *Address:* 17 Thanet Street, WC1. *T:* 01-388 3888.

BYATT, Ronald Archer Campbell, CMG 1980; HM Diplomatic Service; High Commissioner in Harare, since 1980; *b* 14 Nov. 1930; *s* of late Sir Horace Byatt, GCMG and late Olga Margaret Campbell, MBE; *m* 1954, Ann Brereton Sharpe, *d* of C. B. Sharpe; one *s* one *d. Educ:* Gordonstoun; New Coll., Oxford; King's Coll., Cambridge. Served in RNVR, 1949-50. Colonial Admin. Service, Nyasaland, 1955-58; joined HM Foreign (now Diplomatic) Service, 1959; FO, 1959; Havana, 1961; FO, 1963; UK Mission to UN, NY, 1966; Kampala, 1970; Head of Rhodesia Dept, FCO, 1972-75; Vis. Fellow, Glasgow Univ., 1975-76; Counsellor and Head of Chancery, UK Mission to UN, NY, 1977-79; Asst Under Sec. of State, FCO, 1979-80. *Recreations:* sailing, boating (OUBC 1953), bird-watching, gardening. *Address:* c/o Foreign and Commonwealth Office, SW1; Drim-na-Vullin, Lochgilphead, Argyll. *T:* Lochgilphead 2615. *Clubs:* United Oxford & Cambridge University; Leander (Henley-on-Thames).
See also H. C. Byatt.

BYERS, family name of **Baron Byers.**

BYERS, Baron *cr* 1964 (Life Peer); **Charles Frank Byers,** PC 1972; OBE 1944; DL; Liberal Leader, House of Lords, since 1967; Chairman of the Liberal Party, 1950-52, 1965-67 (Vice-President, 1954-65); Liberal Chief Whip, 1946-50; MP (L) North Dorset, 1945-50; *b* 24 July 1915; *e s* of late C. C. Byers, Lancing, Sussex; *m* 1939, Joan Elizabeth Oliver; one *s* three *d. Educ:* Westminster; Christ Church, Oxford (MA Hons); Exchange Scholar at Milton Acad., Mass, USA. Blue for Athletics, Oxford, 1937, 220 yds Hurdles; Pres. OU Liberal Club, 1937. Enlisted Sept. 1939, RA; commissioned March 1940; served MEF, CMF, 1940-44; GSO1 Eighth Army, Lt-Col, 1943; served NW Europe, 1944-45, GSO1 HQ, 21 Army Group (despatches thrice); Chevalier Legion of Honour, Croix de Guerre (palmes). Chm., Company Pensions Information Centre, 1973-. FBIM 1965. DL Surrey, 1974. *Address:* Hunters Hill, Blindley Heath, Lingfield, Surrey.

BYERS, Sir Maurice (Hearne), Kt 1982; CBE 1978; QC 1960; Solicitor-General of Australia, since 1973; *b* 10 Nov. 1917; *s* of Arthur Tolhurst Byers and Mabel Florence Byers (*née* Hearne); *m* 1949, Patricia Therese Davis; two *s* one *d. Educ:* St Aloysius Coll., Milson's Point, Sydney; Sydney Univ. LLB. Called to the Bar, 1944. Mem., Exec. Council, Law Council of Australia, 1966-68; Vice-Pres., NSW Bar Assoc., 1964-65, Pres., 1965-67. Leader, Australian delegations to: UN Commn on Internat. Trade Law, 1974, 1976-81; Diplomatic Conf. on Sea Carriage of Goods, Hamburg, 1979. Mem. Council, ANU, 1975-78. *Address:* 14 Morella Road, Clifton Gardens, NSW 2088, Australia. *T:* 969 8257; (office) 17th level, Law Courts Building, Queens Square, Sydney, NSW 2000. *T:* 231 3666. *Club:* Commonwealth (Canberra).

BYERS, Dr Paul Duncan; Head of Department of Morbid Anatomy, Institute of Orthopaedics, University of London, since 1980 (Dean of Institute, 1971-79); *b* Montreal, 1922; *s* of A. F. Byers and Marion Taber; *m* 1959, Valery Garden. *Educ:* Bishops College Sch., PQ, Canada; McGill Univ. (BSc, MD, CM); Univ. of London (DCP, PhD). FRCPath. Alan Blair Memorial Fellow, Canadian Cancer Soc., 1955-57. Asst Morbid Anatomist, Inst. of Orthopaedics, 1960; Reader in Morbid Anatomy, Univ. of London, 1974. Hon. Consultant, Royal National Orthopaedic Hosp., 1965; Hon. Senior Lectr, Royal Postgrad. Med. Sch., 1969. Mem., Management Cttee, Courtauld Inst. of Art, Univ. of London, 1979-82. *Publications:* articles in medical press on arthritis, metabolic bone disease, bone tumours, medical education. *Recreation:* arts. *Address:* 18 Wimpole Street, W1M 7AD. *T:* 01-580 5206.

BYFORD, Lawrence, CBE 1979; QPM 1973; HM Inspector of Constabulary for North Eastern Region, since 1978; *b* 10 Aug. 1925; *s* of George Byford and Monica Irene Byford; *m* 1950, Muriel Campbell Massey; two *s* one *d. Educ:* Univ. of Leeds (LLB Hons). Barrister-at-Law. Joined W Riding Police, 1947; served on Directing Staff of Wakefield Detective Sch., 1959-62, and National Police Coll., Bramshill, 1964-66; Divl Comdr, Huddersfield, 1966-68; Asst Chief Constable of Lincs, 1968, Dep. Chief Constable 1970, Chief Constable, 1973-77; HM Inspector of Constabulary for SE Region, 1977-78. Lecture tour of univs, USA and Canada, 1976; Head of British Police Mission to Turkey, 1978-79; Vis. Lectr to National Police Coll., Scottish Police Coll., and Army Staff Coll., Camberley. *Publications:* articles in Forensic Science Jl, police magazines and newspapers. *Recreations:* gardening, walking. *Address:*

Dalefield, Grange Lane, Riseholme, Lincoln. *T:* Lincoln 22641. *Clubs:* Royal Over-Seas League, MCC.

BYGRAVES, Max Walter; entertainer; *b* 16 Oct. 1922; *s* of Henry and Lilian Bygraves, Rotherhithe, SE16; *m* 1942, Gladys Blossom Murray; one *s* two *d. Educ:* St Joseph's, Rotherhithe. Began in advertising agency, carrying copy to Fleet Street, 1936. Volunteered for RAF, 1940; served 5 years as fitter. Performed many shows for troops; became professional, 1946; has appeared in venues all over English-speaking world, incl. 18 Royal Command Performances; best selling record artist. *Publications:* I Wanna Tell You a Story (autobiog.), 1976; The Milkman's on his Way (novel), 1977. *Recreations:* golf, painting, reading, writing. *Address:* Roebuck House, Victoria, SW1E 5BE. *T:* 01-828 4595. *Club:* 21.

BYNG, family name of **Earl of Strafford,** and of **Viscount Torrington.**

BYNOE, Dame Hilda Louisa, DBE 1969; in General Medical Practice, Port of Spain, Trinidad, since 1975; *b* Grenada, 18 Nov. 1921; *d* of late Thomas Joseph Gibbs, CBE, JP, Estate Proprietor, and Louisa Gibbs (*née* La Touche); *m* 1947, Peter Cecil Alexander Bynoe, ARIBA, Dip. Arch., former RAF Flying Officer; two *s. Educ:* St Joseph's Convent, St George's, Grenada; Royal Free Hospital Medical Sch., Univ. of London. MB, BS (London), 1951, MRCS, LRCP, 1951. Teacher, St Joseph's Convents, Trinidad and Grenada, 1939-44; hospital and private practice, London, 1951-53; public service with Govt of Trinidad and Tobago, 1954-55, with Govt of Guyana (then British Guiana), 1955-58, with Govt of Trinidad and Tobago, 1958-65; private practice, Trinidad, 1961-68; Governor of Associated State of Grenada, WI, 1968-74. Chm., Nat. Foundn for Arts and Culture, Trinidad and Tobago, 1980-. Patron, Caribbean Women's Assoc., 1970-. *Recreations:* swimming, music, reading, poetry-writing. *Address:* 5A Barcant Avenue, Maraval, Trinidad.

BYRNE, Sir Clarence (Askew), Kt 1969; OBE 1964; DSC 1945; Company Director, Mining, Insurance and Construction, Queensland; *b* 17 Jan. 1903; *s* of George Patrick Byrne, Brisbane, Qld, and Elizabeth Emma Askew, Dalby, Qld; *m* 1928, Nellie Ann Millicent Jones; one *s* one *d. Educ:* Brisbane Technical Coll. Mining Develt and Exploration, 1925-30; Oil Exploration, Roma, Qld, 1930-40. Served War, 1940-46 (DSC, Amer. Bronze Star Medal): Lt-Comdr; CO, HMAS Warrego, 1944-45. Pres., Qld Chamber of Mines, 1961-70; Exec. Dir, Conzinc Riotinto of Australia Ltd (Resident, Qld, 1957-68); Chm., Qld Alumina Ltd; Director: Thiess Holdings Ltd; Walkers Ltd. Mem. Aust. Mining Industries Council, Canberra. *Recreations:* fishing, ocean cruising. *Address:* Culverston, Dingle Avenue, Caloundra, Qld 4551, Australia. *T:* Caloundra 91-1228. *Clubs:* United Service, Queensland (Brisbane).

BYRNE, Douglas Norman; Head of Marine Division, Department of Trade, since 1980; *b* 30 Jan. 1924; *s* of Leonard William Byrne and Clarice Evelyn Byrne; *m* 1949, Noreen Thurlby Giles; one *s* one *d. Educ:* Portsmouth Grammar Sch.; St John's Coll., Cambridge (MA). RAF, 1942-46. Asst Principal, Min. of Supply, 1949; BoT, 1956; Cabinet Office, 1961-64; Asst Sec., 1964; on staff of Monopolies Commn, 1966-68; Under-Sec., Dept of Industry, 1974-77; Hd of Fair Trading Div., Dept of Prices and Consumer Protection, 1977-79; Under-Sec., Dept of Trade, 1979-. *Recreations:* hill walking, natural history. *Address:* Sunley House, 90-93 High Holborn, WC1V 6LP. *T:* 01-405 6911.

BYRNE, John Keyes; *see* Leonard, Hugh.

BYRNE, Muriel St Clare, OBE 1955; writer and lecturer; Editor of The Lisle Letters (1533-40); *b* 31 May 1895; *o c* of Harry St Clare Byrne, Hoylake, Ches, and Artemisia Desdemona Burtner, Iowa, USA. *Educ:* Belvedere, Liverpool (GPDST); Somerville Coll., Oxford (Hon. Fellow, 1978). English Hons, 1916, BA and MA 1920. Teaching: Liverpool Coll., 1916-17; S Hampstead High Sch., 1917-18; English Lectr in Rouen, Army Educn (YMCA), 1918-19; Temp. Asst English Tutor, Somerville, 1919, and English coaching for Final Hons at Oxford, 1920-25; Oxford and London Univ. Extension Lectr, 1920-37; Lectr, Royal Academy of Dramatic Art, London, 1923-55; Eng. Lectr, Bedford Coll., 1941-45; Leverhulme Res. Grant, 1945; Bedford Coll. Research Fellowship, 1955; Brit. Acad. Pilgrim Trust Res. Grants, 1958 and 1959; Phoenix Trust Res. Grant, 1970; Twenty Seven Foundn Res. Grant, 1971; Brit. Acad. Research in the Humanities Grant, 1964, 1965, 1966; Leverhulme Research Fellowship, 1968. Examr, London Univ. Dipl. in Dramatic Art, 1951-60. Hon. Sec., Malone Soc., 1926-37; Mem. Council, Bibliographical Soc., 1932-39; Mem. Bd, 1952-, Exec., 1959-, Friends of Girls' Public Day Sch. Trust; Mem., Cttee of Soc. for Theatre Research; History Selection Cttee, Nat. Film Archive, 1968; Mem. Council, RADA, 1973. Governor: Royal Shakespeare Theatre, 1960; Bedford Coll., 1968. Mem., Literary Advisory Panel, Shakespeare Exhibn 1564-1964. FSA 1963. *Publications:* History of Somerville College (with C. H. Godfrey), 1921; Elizabethan Life in Town and Country, 1925 (8th revised edn 1961, American edn 1962, Polish edn 1971); The Elizabethan Home, 1925 (3rd rev. edn 1949); The Elizabethan Zoo, 1926; Letters of King Henry VIII, 1936, 2nd edn 1968, US edn 1968; Common or Garden Child, 1942; (ed) The Lisle Letters 1533-40, 6 vols, 1981; (ed) Selected Lisle Letters, 1982; contributed: Shakespeare's Audience, to Shakespeare in the Theatre, 1927; The Social Background, to A Companion to Shakespeare Studies, 1934; Queen Mary I, to Great Tudors, 1935; History of Stage Lighting and History of Make-Up, to Oxford

Companion to the Theatre, 1951; The Foundations of Elizabethan Language, to Shakespeare in his own Age, 1964; Elizabethan Life in the Plays, to The Reader's Encyclopedia of Shakespeare, 1966; Dramatic Intention and Theatrical Realization, to The Triple Bond; essays in honor of Arthur Colby Sprague, 1975; edited: Anthony Munday's John a Kent (Malone Society), 1923; Massinger's New Way to Pay Old Debts, 1949; The French Litleton of Claudius Holyband, 1953; Essays and Studies, Vol. 13 (Eng. Assoc.), 1960; 4-vol. paper-back illustr. edn of Granville Barker's Prefaces to Shakespeare, with Introd. and Notes, 1963; plays produced: England's Elizabeth, 1928 and 1953; "Well, Gentlemen . . ." (with Gwladys Wheeler), 1933; Busman's Honeymoon (with Dorothy L. Sayers), 1936 (American edn, 1981); No Spring Till Now (Bedford Coll. Centenary Play), 1949; Gen. Ed. Pubns for Soc. for Theatre Research, 1949-59; Eng. edit. rep. of and contrib. to Enciclopedia dello Spettacolo, 1955-58; prep. Arts Council's exhibn and Catalogue, A History of Shakespearian Production in England, 1947 (repr. USA 1970); contributor to: The Times, TLS and Times Educ. Suppt; The Library; Review of Eng. Studies; Mod. Lang. Review; Shakespeare Survey; Shakespeare Quarterly; Drama; Theatre Notebook; Sunday Times; Theatre Research; Essays and Studies Vol. 18 (Eng. Assoc.), etc. *Recreations:* playgoing and all theatrical activities. *Address:* 28 St John's Wood Terrace, NW8. *T:* 01-722 0967.

BYRNE, Rev. Father Paul Laurence, OMI; OBE 1976; Secretary General, Conference of Major Religions Superiors of Ireland, since 1980; Vicar Provincial, Oblates of Mary Immaculate, since 1976; *b* 8 Aug. 1932; *s* of late John Byrne and Lavinia Byrne. *Educ:* Synge Street Christian Brothers' Sch. and Belcamp Coll., Dublin; University Coll., Dublin (BA,Hons Phil.); Oblate Coll., Piltown. Teacher, Belcamp Coll., 1959-65; Dean of Belcamp Coll., 1961-65; Dir, Irish Centre, Birmingham, 1965-68; Dir, Catholic Housing Aid Soc. (Birmingham) and Family Housing Assoc., Birmingham, 1965-69; Nat. Dir, Catholic Housing Aid Soc., and Dir, Family Housing Assoc., London, 1969-70; Dir SHAC (a housing aid centre) 1969-76. Board Member: Threshold Centre; Servite Houses; SHAC; Housing Corp., 1974-77; Irish Sch. of Ecumenics. Associate, Inst. of Housing, 1972. *Recreations:* golf, squash, theatre-going. *Address:* 170 Merrion Road, Ballsbridge Road, Dublin 4. *T:* 0001-693658. *Clubs:* Foxrock Golf; Connemara Golf.

BYRON, 11th Baron *cr* 1643; **Rupert Frederick George Byron;** farmer and grazier since 1921; *b* 13 Aug. 1903; *er s* of late Col Wilfrid Byron, Perth, WA, and of Sylvia Mary Byron, 12 College Street, Winchester, England, *o d* of late Rev. C. T. Moore; *S* kinsman, 1949; *m* 1931, Pauline Augusta, *d* of T. J. Cornwall, Wagin, W Australia; one *d. Educ:* Gresham's Sch., Holt. Served War of 1939-45, Lieut RANVR, 1941-46. *Heir:* kinsman, Richard Geoffrey Gordon Byron, DSO [*b* 3 Nov. 1899; *m* 1st, 1926, Margaret Mary Steuart (marr. diss. 1946); 2nd, 1946, Dorigen, *o c* of P. Kennedy Esdaile; two *s. Educ:* Eton]. *Address:* 16 Barnsley Road, Mount Claremont, WA 6010, Australia. *Club:* Naval and Military (Perth, WA).

BYRT, (Henry) John, QC 1976; a Recorder of the Crown Court, since 1976; *b* 5 March 1929; *s* of Dorothy Muriel Byrt and Albert Henry Byrt, CBE; *m* 1957, Eve Hermione Bartlett; one *s* two *d. Educ:* Charterhouse; Merton Coll., Oxford (BA, MA). Called to the Bar, Middle Temple, 1953; called within the Bar, 1976. Vice-Principal, Working Mens' Coll., London, 1978-; Mem. Council, Queen's Coll., London, 1982-. *Recreations:* building, gardening, sailing, music. *Address:* 65 Gloucester Crescent, NW1. *T:* 01-485 0341; 4 Paper Buildings, Temple, EC4Y 7EX. *Club:* Leander.

BYWATERS, Eric George Lapthorne, CBE 1975; MB (London); FRCP; Emeritus Professor of Rheumatology, Royal Postgraduate Medical School, University of London; Senior Medical Research Council Research Fellow, Bone and Joint Unit, London Hospital, since 1977; Hon. Consultant Physician, Hammersmith Hospital and Canadian Red Cross Memorial Hospital, Taplow, Bucks; *b* 1 June 1910; *s* of George Ernest Bywaters and Ethel Penney; *m* 1935, Betty Euan-Thomas; three *d. Educ:* Sutton Valence Sch., Kent; Middx Hosp. (Sen. Broderip Schol., Lyell Gold Medallist). McKenzie McKinnon Fellow, RCP, 1935; Asst Clin. Pathologist, Bland Sutton Inst., 1936; Rockefeller Travelling Fellow and Harvard Univ. Research Fellow in Med., 1937-39; Beit Memorial Fellow, 1939; Actg Dir, MRC Clin. Res. Unit (Shock), 1943; Lectr in Med., Postgrad. Med. Sch., 1945; late Dir, MRC Rheumatism Res. Unit, Taplow. Pres., European League against Rheumatism, 1977. Hon. FACP, 1973; Hon. FRCP&S (Canada), 1977. Hon. MD Liège, 1973. Gairdner Foundation Medical Award, 1963; Heberden Orator and Medallist, 1966; Bunim Lectr and Medallist, 1973; Ewart Angus Lectr, Toronto, 1974. Hon. Mem. Dutch, French, Amer., German, Czech, Spanish, Portuguese, Aust., Indian, Canadian, Chilean, Peruvian, Jugoslav and Argentine Rheumatism Assocs. *Address:* Long Acre, 53 Burkes Road, Beaconsfield, Bucks.

C

CABALLÉ, Montserrat; Cross of Lazo de Dama of Order of Isabel the Catholic, Spain; opera and concert singer; *b* Barcelona, 12 April 1933; *d* of Carlos and Ana Caballé; *m* 1964, Bernabé Marti, tenor; one *s* one *d. Educ:* Conservatorio del Liceo, Barcelona. Continued to study singing under Mme Eugenia Kemeny. Carnegie Hall début as Lucrezia Borgia, 1965. London début in this role, with the London Opera Society, at the Royal Festival Hall, 1968. Has sung at Covent Garden, Glyndebourne, Metropolitan Opera, La Scala, Mexico City, and other main opera venues. Major roles include Maria Stuarda, Luisa Miller, Queen Elizabeth in Roberto Devereux, Imogene in Il Pirata, Violetta in La Traviata, Marguerite in Faust, Desdemona in Otello, Norma and also those of contemporary opera. Has made many recordings. *Address:* c/o Columbia Artists Management Inc., 165 W 57th Street, New York, NY 10019, USA.

CABLE, Sir James (Eric), KCVO 1976; CMG 1967; HM Diplomatic Service, retired; writer; *b* 15 Nov. 1920; *s* of late Eric Grant Cable, CMG; *m* 1954, Viveca Hollmerus; one *s. Educ:* Stowe; CCC, Cambridge. PhD 1973. Served Royal Signals, 1941-46, Major. Entered Foreign (now Diplomatic) Service, 1947; 2nd Sec., 1948; Vice-Consul, Batavia, 1949; 2nd Sec., Djakarta, 1949; acted as Chargé d'Affaires, 1951 and 1952; Helsinki, 1952; FO, 1953; 1st Sec., 1953; Mem. of British Delegn to Geneva Conf. on Indo-China, 1954; 1st Sec. (Commercial), Budapest, 1956; Head of Chancery and Consul, Quito, 1959; acted as Chargé d'Affaires, 1959 and 1960; FO, 1961 and Head of SE Asia Dept, Dec. 1963; Counsellor, Beirut, 1966; acted as Chargé d'Affaires at Beirut, 1967, 1968 and 1969; Research Associate, Institute for Strategic Studies, 1969-70; Head of Western Organisations Dept, FCO, 1970-71; Counsellor, Contingency Studies, FCO, 1971; Head of Planning Staff, 1971-75, and Asst Under-Sec. of State, 1972-75, FCO; Ambassador to Finland, 1975-80; Leverhulme Res. Fellow, 1981-82. *Publications:* Britain in Tomorrow's World, 1969 (as Grant Hugo); Appearance and Reality in International Relations, 1970 (as Grant Hugo); Gunboat Diplomacy, 1971, rev. edn 1981; The Royal Navy and the Siege of Bilbao, 1979; Britain's Naval Future, 1983; articles in various jls. *Address:* c/o Lloyds Bank, 16 St James's Street, SW1. *Club:* Athenæum.

CABLE-ALEXANDER, Sir Desmond William Lionel, 7th Bt (1809); *b* 1910; *S* 1956; *m* 1st, Mary Jane (who obtained a divorce), *d* of James O'Brien, JP, Enniskillen; one *s*; 2nd, Margaret Wood, *d* of late John Burnett, Dublin; two *d. Educ:* Harrow; Oxford. Assumed addtl name of Cable before that of Alexander, by deed poll, 1931. *Heir:* *s* Patrick Desmond William Cable-Alexander, Lt-Col Royal Scots Dragoon Guards [*b* 19 April 1936; *m* 1961, Diana Frances Rogers (marr. diss. 1976); two *d* ; *m* 1976, Jane Mary, *d* of Dr Anthony Arthur Gough Lewis, MD, FRCP, of York; one *s*]. *Address:* c/o Barclays Bank Ltd, 16 Whitehall, SW1.

CABORN, Richard George; Member (Lab) Sheffield, European Parliament, since 1979; *b* 6 Oct. 1943; *s* of George and Mary Caborn; *m* 1966, Margaret Caborn; one *s* one *d. Educ:* Hurlfield Comprehensive Sch.; Granville Coll. of Further Educn; Sheffield Polytechnic. Engrg apprentice, 1959-64; Convenor of Shop Stewards, Firth Brown Ltd, 1967-79. Prospective Parly Cand. (Lab) Sheffield Park, 1982-. *Recreation:* amateur football. *Address:* 29 Quarry Vale Road, Sheffield S12 3EB. *T:* Sheffield 393802. *Club:* Carlton Working Men's (Sheffield).

CACCIA, family name of Baron Caccia.

CACCIA, Baron *cr* 1965 (Life Peer), of Abernant; **Harold Anthony Caccia,** GCMG 1959 (KCMG 1950; CMG 1945); GCVO 1961 (KCVO 1957); Provost of Eton, 1965-77; *b* 21 Dec. 1905; *s* of late Anthony Caccia, CB, MVO; *m* 1932, Anne Catherine, *d* of late Sir George Barstow, KCB; one *s* two *d. Educ:* Eton; Trinity Coll., Oxford. Laming Travelling Fellowship, Queen's Coll., Oxford, 1928, Hon. Fellow, 1974. Entered HM Foreign Service as 3rd Sec., FO, 1929; transferred to HM Legation, Peking, 1932; 2nd Sec., 1934; FO 1935; Asst Private Sec. to Sec. of State, 1936; HM Legation, Athens, 1939; 1st Sec. 1940; FO 1941; seconded for service with Resident Minister, North Africa, 1943, and appointed Vice-Pres., Political Section, Allied Control Commission, Italy; Political Adviser, GOC-in-C Land Forces, Greece, 1944; Minister local rank, HM Embassy, Athens, 1945; Asst Under-Sec. of State, 1946, Dep. Under-Sec. of State, 1949, Foreign Office; British Ambassador in Austria, 1951-54, and also British High Comr in Austria, 1950-54; Dep. Under-Sec. of State, FO, 1954-56; British Ambassador at Washington, 1956-61; Permanent Under-Sec. of State, FO, 1962-65; Head of HM Diplomatic Service, 1964-65, retired. Hon. Fellow, Trinity Coll., Oxford, 1963. Chairman: Standard Telephones & Cables, 1968-79; ITT (UK) Ltd, 1979-81; Director: F. & C. Eurotrust Ltd; Orion Bank (Chm., 1973-74). Chm., Gabbitas-Thring Educational Trust, 1967-73. Mem., Advisory Council on Public Records, 1968-73. Pres., MCC, 1973-74. Lord Prior of the Order of St John of Jerusalem, 1969-80; GCStJ. *Address:* Abernant, Builth-Wells, Powys LD2 3YR. *T:* Erwood 233.

CACOYANNIS, Michael; director, stage and screen, since 1954; *b* 11 June 1922; *s* of late Sir Panayotis Cacoyannis and Angeliki, *d* of George M. Efthyvoulos and Zoe Constantinides, Limassol, Cyprus. *Educ:* Greek Gymnasium; Gray's Inn and Old Vic Sch., London. Radio Producer, BBC Greek Service, 1941-50. Actor on English stage, 1946-51; parts included:

Herod, in Salome, 1946; Caligula, in Caligula, 1949, etc. Directed films: Windfall in Athens, 1953; Stella, 1954; Girl in Black, 1956; A Matter of Dignity, 1958; Our Last Spring, 1960; The Wastrel, 1961; Electra, 1962; Zorba the Greek, 1964; The Day the Fish Came Out, 1967; The Trojan Women, 1971; Attila '74, 1975; Iphigenia, 1977. Directed plays: produced several of these in Athens for Ellie Lambetti's Company, 1955-61; The Trojan Women, New York, 1963-65, Paris, 1965; Things That Go Bump in the Night, and The Devils, New York, 1965; Mourning Becomes Electra, Metropolitan Opera, NY, 1967; Iphigenia in Aulis, New York, 1968; La Bohème, Juillard, NY, 1972; King Oedipus, Abbey Theatre, Dublin, 1973; Miss Margarita, Athens, 1975; The Bacchae, Comédie Française, 1977, New York, 1980; The Glass Menagerie, Nat. Theatre, Athens, 1978; Antony and Cleopatra, Athens, 1979. Hon. DH Columbia Coll., Chicago, 1981. Order of the Phœnix (Greece), 1965; Officier des Arts et des Lettres, 1979. *Recreations:* walking, swimming. *Address:* 15 Mouson Street, Athens 401, Greece.

CADBURY, Sir (George) Adrian (Hayhurst), Kt 1977; Chairman, Cadbury Schweppes Ltd, since 1975; a Director of the Bank of England, since 1970; *b* 15 April 1929; *s* of Laurence John Cadbury, *qv*; *m* 1956, Gillian Mary, *d* of late E. D. Skepper, Neuilly-sur-Seine; two *s* one *d. Educ:* Eton Coll.; King's Coll., Cambridge (MA Economics). Coldstream Guards, 1948-49; Cambridge, 1949-52. Man. Dir, Cadbury Schweppes Ltd, 1969-73; Director: Cadbury Group Ltd, 1962; Cadbury Bros Ltd, 1958; J. S. Fry & Sons, 1964; James Pascall, 1964; IBM UK Ltd, 1975-. Chancellor, Univ. of Aston in Birmingham, 1979-. Chairman: West Midlands Economic Planning Council, 1967-70; Food & Drink Industries Council, 1981-. Mem., Covent Garden Market Authority, 1974-. Mem. Council: CBI; Industry for Management Educn; Industrial Soc. Hon. DSc Aston, 1973. *Address:* Cadbury Schweppes Ltd, Bournville, Birmingham B30 2LU. *T:* 021-458 2000. *Clubs:* Boodle's; Hawks (Cambridge); Leander (Henley).

CADBURY, George Woodall; Chairman Emeritus, Governing Body of International Planned Parenthood Federation, since 1975 (Chairman, 1969-75, Vice-Chairman, and Chairman of the Executive, 1963-69, and Special Representative, since 1960); President, Conservation Council of Ontario, since 1978 (Chairman, 1972-74 and 1976-78); *b* 19 Jan. 1907; *s* of George Cadbury and Edith Caroline Cadbury (*née* Woodall); *m* 1935, Mary Barbara Pearce; two *d. Educ:* Leighton Park Sch., Reading; King's Coll., Cambridge; MA (Economics Tripos); Wharton Sch. of Finance and Commerce, Univ. of Pennsylvania. Man. Dir, British Canners Ltd, 1929-35; Marketing Controller and Man. Dir, Alfred Bird & Sons Ltd, 1935-45; Auxiliary, later Nat., Fire Service, 1939-41; Dep. Dir Material Production, Min. of Aircraft Production and British Air Commn (USA), 1941-45; Chm. Economic Advisory and Planning Bd, and Chief Industrial Executive, Prov. of Saskatchewan, 1945-51; Dir, Technical Assistance Administration, UN, 1951-60 (Dir of Ops, 1951-54; Adviser to Govts of Ceylon, Burma, Indonesia, Jamaica and Barbados, 1954-60). New Democratic Party of Canada: Pres., Ont, 1961-66; Fed. Treasurer, 1965-69; Mem., Fed. Council, 1961-71; Life Mem., 1980. Trustee: Bournville Village Trust, 1928-; Youth Hostels Trust, 1931-; Sponsor and Council Mem., Minority Rights Group, 1967-; Member: TGWU (Life Mem., 1973); League for Industrial Democracy, NY, 1928, Bd Mem., 1951-. Mem. Meetings Cttee, RIIA, 1931-35; Sec., W Midland Group for Post-War Reconstruction and Planning, 1939-41; Resident, Toynbee Hall, 1929-35, 1941-43. *Publications:* (jointly) When We Build Again, 1940; English County, 1942; Conurbation, 1942; Essays on the Left, 1971; A Population Policy for Canada, 1973. *Recreation:* railway practice and history. *Address:* 35 Brentwood Road, Oakville, Ont L6J 4B7, Canada. *T:* 416-845 3171.

CADBURY, Kenneth Hotham, CBE 1974; MC 1944; *b* 25 Feb. 1919; *s* of J. Hotham Cadbury, manufacturer, Birmingham; *m* 1st, Margaret R. King (marr. diss.); one *s* one *d*; 2nd, Marjorie I. Lilley; three *d. Educ:* Bootham Sch., York; Univ. of Birmingham. Served in Royal Artillery in Middle East and Italy, 1939-46 (despatches, MC; Major). Joined Foreign Service, 1946. Transferred to GPO, 1947; served in Personnel Dept and Inland Telecommunications Dept; Cabinet Office, 1952-55; PPS to PMG, 1956-57; Dep. Director, 1960, Director, 1962, Wales and Border Counties GPO; Director: Clerical Mechanisation and Buildings, GPO, 1964-65; Inland Telecommunications, GPO, 1965-67; Purchasing and Supply, GPO, 1967-69; Sen. Dir, Planning and Purchasing, PO, 1969-75; Asst Man. Dir, Telecommunications, PO, 1975-77; Dep. Man. Dir, Telecommns, PO, 1978-79. Trustee, PO Staff Superannuation Fund, 1969-75. *Recreation:* gardening. *Address:* Lower Graddon Farm, Highampton, Beaworthy, Devon EX21 5JX.

CADBURY, Laurence John, OBE 1919; *b* 1889; *s* of late George Cadbury; *m* 1925, Joyce, *d* of Lewis O. Mathews, Birmingham; two *s* one *d* (and two *s* one *d* decd). *Educ:* Leighton Park Sch.; Trinity Coll., Cambridge (MA). Economics Tripos. Man. Dir, Cadbury Bros Ltd and associated cos, 1919-59; Chm., Cadbury Bros Ltd, 1944-49 and of J. S. Fry & Sons Ltd, 1952-59; Dir, Bank of England, 1936-61. Director: British Cocoa & Chocolate Co. Ltd, 1920-59; Nation Proprietory Co. Ltd, Tyne Tees Television Ltd, 1958-67; Daily News Ltd; News Chronicle, 1930-60 and Star, 1930-60; Cocoa Investments Ltd, 1937-64; EMB Co. Ltd; Chm., Bournville Village Trust, 1954-78; Treasurer, Population Investigation Cttee, 1936-76. Trustee, Historic Churches Preservation Trust (Exec. Cttee); Head, Economic Section, Mission to Moscow, 1941. High Sheriff of County of London, 1947-48 and 1959-60. Hon. LLD Birmingham, 1970. Mons Medal; 1914 Star; Croix de Guerre. *Publications:* This Question of Population; numerous contribs to the press and

periodicals on economics and demographic subjects. *Address:* The Davids, Northfield, Birmingham. *T:* 021-475 1441. *Clubs:* United Oxford & Cambridge University; Leander (Henley); Hawks (Cambridge).
See also Sir G. A. H. Cadbury.

CADBURY, Paul Strangman, CBE 1948; Chairman, Cadbury Bros Ltd, 1959-65; *b* 3 Nov. 1895; *s* of late Barrow Cadbury; *m* 1919, Rachel E. Wilson; two *s* two *d. Educ:* Leighton Park Sch., Reading. Friends' Ambulance Unit, 1915-19; Chm. Friends Ambulance Unit, 1939-48; Bournville Village Trust. Hon. DSc Aston, 1971. *Publication:* Birmingham-Fifty Years On, 1952. *Address:* Low Wood, 32 St Mary's Road, Harborne, Birmingham B17 0HA. *T:* 021-427 1636. *Clubs:* Reform; Birmingham (Birmingham).

CADBURY, Peter (Egbert); Chairman: Westward Travel Ltd, since 1982; Educational Video Index Ltd, since 1981; *b* Great Yarmouth, Norfolk, 6 Feb. 1918; *s* of late Sir Egbert Cadbury, DSC, DFC; *m* 1st, 1947, Eugenie Benedicta (marr. diss. 1968), *d* of late Major Ewen Bruce, DSO, MC and of Mrs Bruce; one *s* one *d*; 2nd, 1970, Mrs Jennifer Morgan-Jones (marr. diss. 1976), *d* of Major Michael Hammond Maude, Ramsden, Oxon; one *s*; 3rd, 1976, Mrs Jane Mead; two *s. Educ:* Leighton Park Sch.; Trinity Coll., Cambridge (BA, MA 1939). Called to Bar, Inner Temple, 1946; practised at Bar, 1946-54. Served Fleet Air Arm, 1940, until released to Ministry of Aircraft Production, 1942, as Prodn, Research and Experimental Test Pilot. Contested (L) Stroud (Glos), 1945. Member, London Tourist Cttee, 1958-60; Chm. and Man. Dir, Keith Prowse Group, 1954-71; Chairman: Alfred Hays Ltd, 1955-71; Ashton & Mitchell Ltd and Ashton & Mitchell Travel Co. Ltd, 1959-71; Air Westward Ltd, 1977-79; Air West Ltd, 1977-79; Exec. Chm., Westward Television Ltd, 1960-80; Director: Independent Television News Ltd, 1972-79; Willett Investments Ltd, 1955-. Chm., George Cadbury Trust, 1979-. Freeman of City of London, 1948. *Recreations:* theatre, racing, flying, golf, tennis, sailing. *Address:* Armsworth Hill, Alresford, Hants SO24 9RJ. *T:* Alresford 4656; c/o Educational Video Index Ltd, 25 Thurloe Street, SW7. *T:* 01-581 8733. *Clubs:* MCC; Royal Motor Yacht, RAF Yacht.

CADBURY-BROWN, Henry Thomas, OBE 1967; TD; RA 1975 (ARA 1971); FRIBA; Professor of Architecture, Royal Academy, since 1975; Hon. Fellow RCA; architect; *b* 20 May 1913; *s* of Henry William Cadbury-Brown and Marion Ethel Sewell; *m* 1953, Elizabeth Romeyn, *d* of Prof. A. Elwyn, Croton on Hudson, NY. *Educ:* Westminster Sch.; AA Sch. of Architecture (Hons Diploma). Architect in private practice since winning competition for British Railways Branch Offices, 1937. Work includes pavilions for "The Origins of the People", main concourse and fountain display at Festival of Britain; schools, housing, display and interiors. Architect for new civic centre at Gravesend and halls for residence for Birmingham Univ. and, with Sir Hugh Casson and Prof. Robert Goodden, for new premises for Royal College of Art; awarded London Architecture Bronze Medal, 1963; lecture halls for Univ. of Essex; in group partnership with Eric Lyons, Cunningham Partnership for W Chelsea redevelopment for RBK&C. Taught at Architectural Association Sch., 1946-49; Tutor at Royal Coll. of Art, 1952-61. Invited as Visiting Critic to Sch. of Architecture, Harvard Univ., 1956. Member: RIBA Council, 1951-53; British Cttee Internat. Union of Architects, 1951-54; MARS (Modern Architectural Research) group. Pres. Architectural Assoc., 1959-60. TA and military service, 1939-45; Major RA (TD). *Recreations:* numerous, including work. *Address:* 32 Neal Street, WC2. *T:* 01-240 3353; Church Walk, Aldeburgh, Suffolk. *T:* Aldeburgh 2591.

CADELL, Colin Simson, CBE 1944; Air Cdre RAF, retired; Vice Lieutenant for West Lothian since 1972; *b* 7 Aug. 1905; *s* of late Lt-Col J. M. Cadell, DL, Foxhall, Kirkliston, W Lothian; *m* 1939, Rosemary Elizabeth, *d* of Thomas Edward Pooley; two *s* one *d. Educ:* Merchiston; Edinburgh Univ.; Ecole Supérieur d'électricité, Paris. MA; AMIEE; Ingénieur ESE. Commnd RAF, 1926; Dir of Signals, Air Min., 1944; retd 1947. Man. Dir, International Aeradio, 1947-58; Director: Carron Company, 1958-71; Royal Bank of Scotland, 1963-69. Mem., Edinburgh Airport Consultative Cttee, 1972- (Chm., 1972-82). Mem. Queen's Body Guard for Scotland (Royal Company of Archers). DL: Linlithgowshire, 1963-72. Officer, US Legion of Merit, 1945. *Recreations:* shooting, gardening. *Address:* 2 Upper Coltbridge Terrace, Edinburgh EH12 6AD. *Club:* New (Edinburgh).

CADELL, Vice-Adm. John Frederick; Chief of Staff to Commander Allied Forces Southern Europe, since 1982; *b* 6 Dec. 1929; *s* of Henry Dunlop Mallock Cadell and Violet Elizabeth (*née* Van Dyke); *m* 1958, Jaquetta Bridget Nolan; one *s* two *d. Educ:* Britannia Royal Naval Coll., Dartmouth. Served in HMS Frobisher, 1946, then Mediterranean, Persian Gulf, North and Baltic Seas; 2 years with RNZN, to 1960; served in HMS Ashton, Dartmouth, HMS Leopard, 9th Minesweeping Sqdn, SACLANT, HMS Bulwark, 1960-70; Naval Asst to First Sea Lord, 1970-72; HMS Diomede, 1972-74; RCDS 1974-75; RN Presentation Team, 1975-76; Comd, Sch. of Maritime Ops, 1976-79; Dir Gen. Naval Personal Services, 1979-81. *Recreations:* tennis, skiing, wind surfing. *Address:* COS Allied Forces Southern Europe, BFPO 8.

CADIEUX, Hon. Léo, PC 1965; OC 1975; Ambassador of Canada to France, 1970-75; *b* 28 May 1908; *s* of Joseph E. Cadieux and Rosa Paquette, both French Canadian; *m* 1962, Monique, *d* of Placide Plante; one *s. Educ:* Commercial Coll. of St Jerome and Seminary of Ste Thérèse de Blainville, Quebec. Editorial staff of La Presse, Montreal, Quebec, 1930-41; Associate Dir of Public Relations, Can. Army, 1941-44; War Corresp. for La Presse,

Montreal, 1944; Mayor of St Antoine des Laurentides, Que., 1948. First elected to House of Commons, gen. elec., 1962; re-elected gen. elec., 1963, 1965, 1968; apptd Associate Minister of Nat. Defence, 1965; Minister of National Defence, Canada, 1967-70. *Address:* 20 Driveway, Appt 1106, Ottawa, Canada.

CADMAN, family name of **Baron Cadman.**

CADMAN, 3rd Baron *cr* 1937, of Silverdale; **John Anthony Cadman;** farmer since 1964; *b* 3 July 1938; *s* of 2nd Baron Cadman and Marjorie Elizabeth Bunnis; *S* father, 1966; *m* 1975, Janet Hayes; two *s. Educ:* Harrow; Selwyn Coll., Cambridge; Royal Agricultural Coll., Cirencester. *Heir: s* Hon. Nicholas Anthony James Cadman, *b* 18 Nov. 1977. *Address:* Eakley Manor Farm, Stoke Goldington, Newport Pagnell, Bucks. *T:* Stoke Goldington 249.

CADMAN, Surg. Rear-Adm. (D) Albert Edward; CB 1977; Director of Naval Dental Services, 1974-77; *b* 14 Oct. 1918; *m* 1st, 1946, Margaret Henrietta Tomkins-Russell (*d* 1974); one *s* one *d*; 2nd, 1975, Mary Croil Macdonald, Superintendent, WRNS. *Educ:* Dover Grammar Sch.; Guy's Hosp. Dental Sch. LDS RCS 1941. Surg. Lieut (D) RNVR, 1942; transf. to RN, 1947; served as Asst to Dir, Naval Dental Services, 1967-70; Comd Dental Surgeon on staff of Flag Officer, Naval Air Comd, 1970-74. QHDS 1974-77. *Recreations:* music, gardening, golf. *Address:* Solent House, 2 Solent Way, Alverstoke, Hants. *T:* Gosport 86648. *Club:* Royal Naval and Royal Albert Yacht.

CADOGAN, family name of **Earl Cadogan.**

CADOGAN, 7th Earl, *cr* 1800; **William Gerald Charles Cadogan,** MC 1943; DL; Baron Cadogan, 1718; Viscount Chelsea, 1800; Baron Oakley, 1831; Lieut-Colonel Royal Wiltshire Yeomanry, RAC; Captain Coldstream Guards R of O until 1964 (retaining hon. rank of Lieut-Colonel); *b* 13 Feb. 1914; *s* of 6th Earl and Lilian Eleanora Marie (who *m* 2nd, 1941, Lt-Col H. E. Hambro, CBE; she *d* 1973), *d* of George Coxon, Craigleith, Cheltenham; *S* father, 1933; *m* 1st, 1936, Hon. Primrose Lillian Yarde-Buller (from whom he obtained a divorce, 1959), *y d* of 3rd Baron Churston; one *s* three *d*; 2nd, 1961, Cecilia, *y d* of Lt-Col H. K. Hamilton-Wedderburn, OBE. *Educ:* Eton; RMC Sandhurst. Served war of 1939-45 (MC); Hereditary Trustee of the British Museum, 1935-63; Mem. Chelsea Borough Council, 1953-59; Mayor of Chelsea, 1964. DL County of London, 1958. *Heir: s* Viscount Chelsea, *qv. Address:* 28 Cadogan Square, SW1. *T:* 01-584 2335; Snaigow, Dunkeld, Perthshire. *T:* Caputh 223. *Club:* White's.
See also Baron Lurgan, Baron Rockley.

CADOGAN, Prof. John Ivan George, PhD, DSc London; FRS 1976; FRSE, CChem, FRSC; Research Director, British Petroleum Group, since 1981; Visiting Professor of Chemistry, Imperial College of Science and Technology, since 1979; Professorial Fellow, University College of Swansea, University of Wales, since 1979; *b* Pembrey, Carmarthenshire, 1930; *er s* of Alfred and Dilys Cadogan; *m* 1955, Margaret Jeanne, *d* of late William Evans, iron founder, Swansea; one *s* one *d. Educ:* Grammar Sch., Swansea; King's Coll., London (1st cl. Hons Chem. 1951). Research at KCL, 1951-54. Civil Service Research Fellow, 1954-56; Lectr in Chemistry, King's Coll., London, 1956-63; Purdie Prof. of Chemistry and Head of Dept, St Salvator's Coll., Univ. of St Andrews, 1963-69; Forbes Prof. of Organic Chemistry, Edinburgh Univ., 1969-79; Chief Scientist, BP Res. Centre, 1979-81. Member: Chemistry Cttee, SRC, 1967-71 (Chm. 1972-75); Council, SERC, 1981- (Chm., Science Bd, 1981-; Mem., Science Bd, SRC, 1972-75); Council, Chem. Soc., 1966-69, 1973-76; Council, RIC, 1979-80; Chem. Soc.-RIC Unification Cttee, 1975-80; First Council, RSC, 1980- (Pres. RSC, 1982-); Council of Management, Macaulay Inst. for Soil Res., Aberdeen, 1969-79; Council, St George's Sch. for Girls, 1974-79; Council, RSE, 1975-80 (Vice-Pres., 1978-80); Bd of Trustees, Royal Observatory Trust, Edinburgh, 1979-. Pres., Chem. Sect., British Assoc. for Advancement of Science, 1981. Fellow, KCL, 1976 (Mem. Council, 1980-). Tilden Lectr, Chem. Soc., 1971; David Martin Royal Soc. BAYS Lectr, 1981; Humphry Davy Lectr, Royal Instn, 1982. Samuel Smiles Prize, KCL, 1950; Millar Thomson Medallist, KCL, 1951; Meldola Medallist, Soc. of Maccabaeans and Royal Inst. of Chemistry, 1959; Corday-Morgan Medallist, 1965, Chem. Soc. *Publications:* Organophosphorus Reagents in Organic Synthesis; about 190 scientific papers, mainly in Jl Chem. Soc. *Address:* British Petroleum Company plc, Britannic House, Moor Lane, EC2Y 9BU. *T:* 01-920 6457; *Telex* 888811. *Club:* Athenæum.

CADOGAN, Peter William; lecturer and writer; Secretary, East-West Peace People; *b* 26 Jan. 1921; *s* of Archibald Douglas Cadogan and Audrey Cadogan (*née* Wannop); *m* 1949, Joyce, *d* of William Stones, MP (marr. diss. 1969); one *d. Educ:* Tynemouth Sch., Tynemouth; Univ. of Newcastle, 1946-51 (BA (Hons) History, DipEd; Joseph Cowen Meml Prize, 1951). Served War, Air Sea Rescue Service, RAF, 1941-46. Teaching, Kettering and Cambridge, 1951-65. Committed politically to the Far Left, 1945-60; broke with Marxism, 1960. Founding Secretary, East Anglian Committee of 100: exploring theory and practice of non-violent direct action, 1961; Sec., Internat. Sub-Cttee of Cttee of 100: rediscovering internationalism, 1962; Sec. (full-time), National Cttee of 100, 1965-68. Mem., Nat. Council of CND, mix-sixties; Founding Sec., Save Biafra Campaign, 1968-70; Gen. Sec., South Place Ethical Soc., 1970-81; Co-Founder, Turning Point, 1975. *Publications:* Extra-Parliamentary Democracy, 1968; Direct Democracy, 1974, rev. 1975; Early

Radical Newcastle, 1975; Six Ballads for the Seventies, 1976; many articles in learned jls, periodicals and elsewhere. *Recreations:* scholarship, conviviality, walking. *Address:* Studio House, 1 Hampstead Hill Gardens, NW3 2PH. *T:* 01-794 5590.

CADWALLADER, Air Vice-Marshal Howard George, CB 1974; RAF retd; Director of Purchasing, Post Office, 1978-79; *b* 16 March 1919; British; *m* 1950, Betty Ethel Samuels; no *c. Educ:* Hampton Sch., Mddx. Sen. Equipment Staff Officer: HQ Transport Comd, 1963-65; HQ FEAF Singapore, 1965-68; Dep. Dir of Equipment 14 MoD (Air), 1968-69; Comdt of RAF Supply Control Centre, Hendon, 1969-72; Dir of Movts (RAF), MoD (Air), 1972-73; SASO HQ Support Comd, RAF, 1973-74. Controller of Contracts, PO, 1974-78. *Recreations:* golf, sailing. *Address:* Spain.

CADWALLADER, Sir John, Kt 1967; Chairman and Managing Director of Allied Mills Ltd since 1949; President, Bank of New South Wales, 1959-78; *b* 25 Aug. 1902; *m* 1935, Helen Sheila Moxham; two *s* one *d. Educ:* Sydney Church of England Grammar Sch., NSW. *Recreations:* reading, golf. *Address:* 27 Marian Street, Killara, NSW 2071, Australia. *T:* 498 1974. *Clubs:* Commonwealth (Canberra, ACT); Australian, Union, Royal Sydney Golf (all Sydney, NSW); Elanora Country (NSW).

CÆSAR, Rev. Canon Anthony Douglass; Sub-Dean of Her Majesty's Chapels Royal, Deputy Clerk of the Closet, Sub-Almoner and Domestic Chaplain to the Queen, since 1979; *b* 3 April 1924; *s* of Harold Douglass and Winifred Kathleen Cæsar. *Educ:* Cranleigh School; Magdalene Coll., Cambridge; St Stephen's House, Oxford. MA, MusB, FRCO. Served War with RAF, 1943-46. Assistant Music Master, Eton Coll., 1948-51; Precentor, Radley Coll., 1952-59; Asst Curate, St Mary Abbots, Kensington, 1961-65; Asst Sec., ACCM, 1965-70; Chaplain, Royal School of Church Music, 1965-70; Deputy Priest-in-Ordinary to the Queen, 1967-68, Priest-in-Ordinary, 1968-70; Resident Priest, St Stephen's Church, Bournemouth, 1970-73; Precentor and Sacrist, Winchester Cathedral, 1974-79; Hon. Canon of Winchester Cathedral, 1975-76 and 1979-, Residentiary Canon, 1976-79. *Publications:* 2 Part Songs, 1948, 1949. *Recreation:* other people. *Address:* Marlborough Gate, St James's Palace, SW1. *T:* 01-930 6609.

CÆSAR, Irving; author-lyrist; Past President of Songwriters' Protective Association; Member Board of Directors, American Society of Composers, Authors and Publishers; *b* New York, 4 July 1895; *s* of Rumanian Jews. *Educ:* public school; Chappaqua Quaker Inst.; City Coll. of New York. Protégé of Ella Wheeler Wilcox, who, when he was a boy of nine, became interested in bits of verse he wrote and published at the time; at twenty became attached to the Henry Ford Peace Expedition, and spent nine months travelling through neutral Europe (during the War) as one of the secretaries of the Ford Peace Conference; returned to America, and became interested in writing for the musical comedy stage. *Publications:* most important work up to present time, No, No, Nanette; has written hundreds of songs and collaborated in many other musical comedies; writer and publisher of Sing a Song of Safety, a vol. of children's songs in use throughout the public and parochial schools of USA; also Sing a Song of Friendship, a series of songs based on human rights; in England: The Bamboula, Swanee, Tea for Two, I Want to be Happy, I Was So Young; author of "Peace by Wireless" proposal for freedom of international exchange of radio privilege between governments. *Recreations:* reading, theatre, swimming. *Address:* 850 Seventh Avenue, New York, NY10019, USA. *Clubs:* Friars, Green Room, City (New York).

CAFFERTY, Michael Angelo; HM Diplomatic Service; Ambassador and Consul-General to Santo Domingo, since 1979; *b* 3 March 1927; *m* 1950, Eileen E. Geer; two *s* three *d. Educ:* Univ. of London. BoT, 1951; Asst Trade Comr, Johannesburg, 1955, Pretoria, 1957; seconded to FO, Buenos Aires, 1958; Trade Comr, Singapore, 1964; FCO, 1968; Consul (Commercial), Milan, 1974; First Sec. and Head of Chancery, Rome (Holy See), 1977. *Address:* c/o Foreign and Commonwealth Office, SW1.

CAFFIN, Albert Edward, CIE 1947; OBE 1946; Indian Police (retired); *b* 16 June 1902; *s* of Claud Carter and Lilian Edith Caffin, Southsea; *m* 1929, Hilda Elizabeth Wheeler, Bournemouth; no *c. Educ:* Portsmouth. Joined Indian Police as Asst Supt, Bombay Province, 1922; Asst Inspector General, Poona, 1939; Dep. Comr, Bombay, 1944, Comr of Police, Bombay, 1947. *Recreation:* bowls. *Address:* C22 San Remo Towers, Sea Road, Boscombe, Bournemouth, Dorset. *Club:* Royal Bombay Yacht.

CAFFIN, A(rthur) Crawford; a Recorder of the Crown Court since 1972; solicitor since 1932; *b* 10 June 1910; *s* of Charles Crawford Caffin and Annie Rosila Caffin; *m* 1933, Mala Pocock; one *d. Educ:* King's Sch., Rochester. Asst Solicitor: to Norfolk CC, 1933-37; to Bristol Corporation, 1937-46. Partner in firm of R. L. Frank & Caffin, Solicitors, Truro, 1946-72; Consultant with that firm, 1972-. Pres., Cornwall Law Soc., 1960; Mem. Council, the Law Society, 1966-76; Dep. Chm., Traffic Commissioners for Western Traffic Area, 1964-. *Recreation:* swimming. *Address:* Cotna House, Gorran, St Austell, Cornwall. *Club:* Farmers' (Truro).

CAFFYN, Brig. Sir Edward (Roy), KBE 1963 (CBE 1945; OBE 1942); CB 1955; TD 1950; DL; Chairman, County of Sussex Territorial and Auxiliary Forces Association, 1947-67; Vice-Chairman, Council of Territorial and Auxiliary Forces Associations, 1961-66; *b* 27 May 1904; *s* of Percy Thomas Caffyn, Eastbourne; *m* 1st, 1929, Elsa Muriel, *d* of William Henry Nurse,

Eastbourne; two s; 2nd, 1946, Delphine Angelique, d of Major William Chilton-Riggs. *Educ:* Eastbourne and Loughborough Colleges. Commissioned RE (TA), 1930. Raised and commanded an Army Field Workshop, 1939; served with 51st Highland Division in France, 1940; Brigadier, 1941; a Deputy Director, War Office, on formation of REME, 1942; served on Field Marshal Montgomery's staff as Director of Mechanical Engineering (despatches twice), 1943–45. JP Eastbourne, 1948, transferred East Sussex, 1960; Chairman, Hailsham Bench, 1962–74; DL Sussex, 1956; Chairman, Sussex Agricultural Wages Board, 1951–74. CC for East Sussex, 1958–69, Alderman, 1964, Vice-Chairman 1967; Chm., Sussex Police Authy, 1971–74. *Recreations:* shooting, fishing. *Address:* Norman Norris, Vines Cross, Heathfield, East Sussex. *T:* Horam Road 2674. *Club:* Royal Automobile.

CAGE, Edward Edwin Henry; General Manager, Craigavon Development Commission, 1966–73; *b* 15 May 1912; *s* of Edward H. Cage and A. M. Windiate; *m* 1938, Hilda W. M. Barber; no *c. Educ:* Cannock House Sch., Eltham; King's Coll., London. Articles, Chartered Accts, 1929–34; Kent CC, 1935–41; Borough Councils: Dagenham, 1941–42; Willesden, 1942–44; Treas., Eton RDC, and Clerk, Jt Hosp Bd, 1944–47; Local Govt BC, 1947–48; Crawley Development Corp.: Chief Finance Officer, 1948–58, Gen. Manager, 1958–61; Chief Finance and Development Officer, Commn for New Towns, 1961–66. *Publications:* contrib. professional, etc., jls and newspapers. *Recreations:* golf, gardening. *Address:* Charters, Pitney Lortie, Langport, Somerset. *Club:* Sherborne Golf.

CAGIATI, Dr Andrea; Grand Cross, Italian Order of Merit; Hon. GCVO; Italian Ambassador to the Court of St James's, since 1980; *b* Rome, 11 July 1922; *m* 1968, Sigrid von Morgen; one *s* one *d. Educ:* University of Siena (Dr of Law). Entered Foreign Service, 1948. Served: Secretary, Paris, 1950; Principal Private Sec. to Minister of State, 1951; Vice-Consul-General, New York, 1953; Prin. Private Sec. to Minister of State and subsequently Dept of Political Affairs, 1955; Counsellor, Athens, 1957; Counsellor, Mexico City, 1960; Delegate, Disarmament Cttee, Geneva, March–Dec. 1962; Italian Delegation, UN, June 1962; Head, NATO Dept, Dec. 1962; Minister-Counsellor, Madrid, 1966; Ambassador, Bogotá, 1968; Inst for Diplomatic Studies, 1971; Diplomatic Adviser to Prime Minister, 1972; Ambassador, Vienna, 1973. Hon. GCVO during State Visit to Italy of HM The Queen, Oct. 1980. *Recreations:* sculpture, golf. *Address:* 4 Grosvenor Square, W1Y 2EH. *T:* 01-629 8200. *Clubs:* White's; Swinley Forest Golf.

CAHAL, Dr Dennis Abraham; Senior Principal Medical Officer, Department of Health and Social Security (formerly Ministry of Health), 1963–81; *b* 1 Oct. 1921; *s* of Henry Cahal and Helen Wright; *m* 1948, Joan, *d* of Allan and Laura Grover; one *s. Educ:* Bradford Grammar Sch.; Univ. of Leeds. MB, ChB (Hons) Leeds, 1953; MD (Dist.) Leeds, 1959; MRCP 1968. RA, Indian Artillery and Special Allied Airborne Reconnaissance Force, 1939–46. Hospital appointments and general practice, 1953–55; Lecturer in Pharmacology, Univ. of Leeds, 1955–59; industrial research into drugs, 1959–62. Vis. Prof. of Pharmacology and Therapeutics, St Mary's Hosp. Med. Sch., London, 1967–69. Med. Assessor, Cttee on Safety of Drugs, 1963–70. *Publications:* various articles on drugs in scientific jls. *Recreations:* reading, cricket, rugby football, horses. *Address:* 207 Merryhill Road, Bushey, Herts. *Club:* MCC.

CAHILL, Patrick Richard, CBE 1970 (OBE 1944); *b* 21 Feb. 1912; *er s* of late Patrick Francis and Nora Christina Cahill; *m* 1st, 1949, Gladys Lilian May Kemp (*d* 1969); one *s*; 2nd, 1969, Mary Frances Pottinger. *Educ:* Hitchin Grammar Sch. Joined Legal & General Assurance Soc. Ltd, 1929; Pensions Manager, 1948; Agency Manager, 1952; Asst Manager, 1954; Asst General Manager, 1957; Gen. Manager, 1958; Chief Exec., 1969–71; Mem. Board, 1969–77. Served War with RASC, 1940–45 (despatches, OBE); N Africa, Italy, and N Europe, 1st, 7th and 11th Armd Divs; rank of Lt-Col. Managing Dir, Gresham Life Assurance Soc. Ltd and Dir, Gresham Fire and Accident Insurance Soc. Ltd, 1958–72. A Vice-Pres., Chartered Insurance Inst., 1961–63, Pres., 1969; Pres., Insurance Charities, 1965–66; Chm., London Salvage Corps, 1964–65; Chm., British Insurance Assoc., 1967–69. *Address:* Flat G, 47 Beaumont Street, W1. *T:* 01-935 2608; Thorndene, Pluckley, Kent. *T:* Pluckley 306.

CAHN, Sir Albert Jonas, 2nd Bt, *cr* 1934; company director; marriage guidance counsellor; marital and sexual therapist; *b* 27 June 1924; *s* of Sir Julien Cahn, 1st Bt, and Phyllis Muriel, *d* of A. Wolfe, Bournemouth; *S* father, 1944; *m* 1948, Malka, *d* of late R. Bluestone; two *s* two *d. Educ:* Headmaster's House, Harrow. *Recreations:* cricket, horse riding, photography. *Heir: s* Julien Michael Cahn, *b* 15 Jan. 1951. *Address:* 10 Edgecoombe Close, Warren Road, Kingston upon Thames, Surrey. *T:* 01-942 6956.

CAHN, Charles Montague, CBE 1956; *b* 27 Dec. 1900; *yr s* of Gottfried Cahn and Lilian Juliet Cahn (*née* Montague); *m* 1939, Kathleen Rose (*d* 1981), *d* of Auguste and Kathleen Thoumine; two *d. Educ:* Westminster Sch.; Christ Church, Oxford. BA 1923; MA 1968. Called to the Bar, Inner Temple, 1924. Served War of 1939-45 in Army (France and Middle East). Deputy Judge Advocate, 1945; Asst Judge Advocate-General, 1946; Deputy Judge Advocate-General, BAOR and RAF Germany (2 TAF), 1957–60; Vice Judge Advocate-General, 1963–67, retired 1967. Legal Chairman, Pensions Appeal Tribunals, 1967–77. *Recreation:* walking up and down hills. *Address:* 8 Crundwell Court, East Street, Farnham, Surrey GU9 7TB. *T:* Farnham 724558.

CAILLARD, Air Vice-Marshal Hugh Anthony, CB 1981; Deputy Chief of Staff for Operations and Intelligence, HQ Allied Air Forces Central Europe, 1979–82; *b* 16 April 1927; *s* of late Col F. Caillard, MC, and of Mrs M. Y. Caillard; *m* 1957, Margaret-Ann Crawford, Holbrook, NSW, Australia; four *s. Educ:* Downside; Oriel Coll., Oxford. Cranwell, 1947–49; served, 1949–65: 13 Sqdn, Egypt; ADC to C-in-C MEAF, and to AOC-in-C Malta; Trng Comd; 101 Sqdn, Binbrook; RAAF No 2 Sqdn; 49 Sqn (Sqdn Ldr) and 90 Sqdn; RN Staff Coll.; HQ Bomber Comd (Wg Cdr); OC 39 Sqdn, Malta, 1965–67; Jt Services Staff Coll., 1967; Planning Staffs, MoD, 1967–70; Asst Air Attaché, Washington (Gp Captain), 1970–73; OC Marham, 1974–75; Def. Intell. Staff (Air Cdre), 1975–79. *Recreations:* outdoor; music, model steam engines. *Address:* c/o Barclay's Bank Ltd, 75 High Street, Wimbledon, SW19. *Club:* Royal Air Force.

CAILLAT, Claude; Swiss Ambassador to the Court of St James's, since 1980; *b* 24 Sept. 1918; *s* of Aymon Caillat and Isabelle Caillat (*née* Bordier); *m* 1948, Béatrice de Blonay; two *s* one *d. Educ:* Univ. of Geneva (law degree). Div. of Foreign Interests, Swiss Federal Political Dept, Berne, then served successively in London, Berne, Athens and (as Counsellor) Washington, 1942–60; Federal Office of Foreign Trade, Berne, 1960; Ambassador's Deputy, Swiss Embassy, Paris, 1962; Swiss Federal Council's Rep. at OECD, Paris, with rank of Ambassador, 1967; Swiss Ambassador to the Netherlands, 1969; Head of Swiss Mission to European Communities, Brussels, 1974. *Recreation:* golf. *Address:* (office) 16-18 Montagu Place, W1H 2BQ; 21 Bryanston Square, W1H 7FG. *T:* 01-723 0701. *Clubs:* White's, Travellers'.

CAIN; see Nall-Cain.

CAIN, Sir Edward (Thomas), Kt 1972; CBE 1966; Commissioner of Taxation, Australia, 1964–76; retired; *b* Maryborough, Qld, Australia, 7 Dec. 1916; *s* of Edward Victor and Kathleen Teresa Cain; *m* 1942, Marcia Yvonne Cain (*née* Parbery); one *s* one *d. Educ:* Nudgee Coll., Queensland; Univ. of Queensland (BA, LLB). Commonwealth Taxation Office: in Brisbane, Sydney, Perth and Canberra, 1936–. Served War, 2/9th Bn, AIF, 1939–43. *Recreations:* golf, fishing. *Address:* 99 Buxton Street, Deakin, Canberra, Australia. *T:* 811462. *Clubs:* Commonwealth, Royal Canberra Golf (Canberra); Royal Automobile (Melbourne).

CAIN, Maj.-Gen. George Robert T.; see Turner Cain.

CAIN, Thomas William; HM Attorney General for Isle of Man, since 1980; *b* 1 June 1935; *s* of late James Arthur Cain and Mary Edith Cunningham (*née* Lamb); *m* 1961, Felicity Jane, *d* of Rev. Arthur Stephen Gregory; two *s* one *d. Educ:* King's College Choir Sch., Cambridge; Marlborough Coll.; Worcester Coll., Oxford (BA 1958, MA 1961). National Service, 2nd Lieut RAC, 1953–55. Called to the Bar, Gray's Inn, 1959; Advocate, Manx Bar, 1961. *Recreations:* sailing; Chairman, Manx Nature Conservation Trust. *Address:* Ivie Cottage, Kirk Michael, Isle of Man. *T:* Kirk Michael 266.

CAINE, Michael; actor; *b* Old Kent Road, London, 14 March 1933 (Maurice Joseph Micklewhite); *s* of late Maurice and of Ellen Frances Marie Micklewhite; *m* 1st, 1955, Patricia Haines (marr. diss.); one *d*; 2nd, 1973, Shakira Baksh; one *d. Educ:* Wilson's Grammar Sch., Peckham. Began acting in youth club drama gp. Served in Army, Berlin and Korea, 1951–53. Asst Stage Manager, Westminster Rep., Horsham, Sx, 1953; actor, Lowestoft Rep., 1953–55; Theatre Workshop, London, 1955; numerous TV appearances (over 100 plays), 1957–63; *play:* Next Time I'll Sing for You, Arts, 1963; *films:* A Hill in Korea, 1956; How to Murder a Rich Uncle, 1958; Zulu, 1964; The Ipcress File, 1965; Alfie, 1966; The Wrong Box, 1966; Gambit, 1966; Hurry Sundown, 1967; Woman Times Seven, 1967; Deadfall, 1967; The Magus, 1968; Battle of Britain, 1968; Play Dirty, 1968; The Italian Job, 1969; Too Late the Hero, 1970; The Last Valley, 1971; Get Carter, 1971; Zee & Co., 1972; Kidnapped, 1972; Pulp, 1972; Sleuth, 1973; The Black Windmill, Marseilles Contract, The Wilby Conspiracy, 1974; Fat Chance, The Romantic Englishwoman, The Man who would be King, Harry and Walter Go to New York, 1975; The Eagle has Landed, A Bridge too Far, Silver Bears, 1976; The Swarm, 1977; California Suite, 1978; Ashanti, 1979; Beyond the Poseidon Adventure, 1979; The Island, 1979; Dressed to Kill, 1979; Escape to Victory, 1980; Death Trap, 1981; Jigsaw Man, 1982. *Recreations:* cinema, theatre, travel, gardening. *Address:* c/o Jerry Pam, 120 El Camino Drive, Beverly Hills, Calif 90212, USA.

CAINE, Michael Harris; Chairman, since 1979, Vice-Chairman, 1973–79, Chief Executive, since 1975, Director, since 1964, Booker McConnell plc; *b* 17 June 1927; *s* of Sir Sydney Caine, *qv*; *m* 1952, Janice Denise (*née* Mercer); one *s* one *d. Educ:* Bedales; Lincoln Coll., Oxford; George Washington Univ., USA. Joined Booker McConnell Ltd, 1952; Chm., Bookers Shopkeeping Holdings Ltd, 1963; Director, IBEC Inc., NY, 1980-. Chm., Council for Technical Educn and Training for Overseas Countries, 1973-75. Member: Council, Inst. of Race Relations, 1969–72; Council, Bedford Coll., London, 1966–; Governing Body, Inst. of Develt Studies, Sussex Univ., 1975–; Chm., UK Council for Overseas Student Affairs, 1980–. *Address:* Wilton House, 33 High Street, Hungerford, Berks. *T:* Hungerford 2861. *Club:* Reform.

CAINE, Sir Sydney, KCMG 1947 (CMG 1945); Director of the London School of Economics and Political Science, 1957–67; *b* 27 June 1902; *s* of Harry Edward Caine; *m* 1st, 1925, Muriel Anne (*d* 1962), *d* of A. H. Harris, MA; one *s*; 2nd, 1965, Doris Winifred Folkard (*d* 1973); 3rd, 1975, Elizabeth, *d* of late J. Crane Nicholls and *widow* of Sir Eric Bowyer, KCB, KBE. *Educ:* Harrow County Sch.; London Sch. of Economics. BSc (Econ.) 1st Class Hons 1922. Asst Inspector of Taxes, 1923-26; entered Colonial Office, 1926; Sec., West Indian Sugar Commn, 1929; Sec., UK Sugar Industry Inquiry Cttee, 1934; Fin. Sec., Hong Kong, 1937; Asst Sec., Colonial Office, 1940; Member Anglo-American Caribbean Commission, 1942; Financial Adviser to Sec. of State for the Colonies, 1942; Assistant Under-Secretary of State, Colonial Office, 1944; Deputy Under-Secretary of State, Colonial Office, 1947-48; Third Secretary, Treasury, 1948; Head of UK Treasury and Supply Delegn, Washington, 1949-51; Chief, World Bank Mission to Ceylon, 1951; Vice-Chancellor, Univ. of Malaya, 1952-56. Chairman: British Caribbean Federation Fiscal Commission, 1955; Grassland Utilisation Cttee, 1957-58; Internat. Inst. of Educational Planning, 1963-70; Governor (new bd), Reserve Bank of Rhodesia, 1965-67; Planning Bd of Independent Univ., 1969-73; Council, University Coll. of Buckingham, 1973-. Mem., ITA, 1960-67 (Dep. Chm., 1964-67). Coordinator, Indonesian Sugar Study, 1971-72. Hon. LLD Univ. of Malaya, 1956. Grand Officer, Orange Nassau (Netherlands), 1947; Comdr, Order of Dannebrog (Denmark), 1965. *Publications:* The Foundation of the London School of Economics, 1963; British Universities: Purpose and Prospects, 1969. *Recreations:* reading, walking. *Address:* Buckland House, Tarn Road, Hindhead, Surrey. *Club:* Reform.

See also M. H. Caine.

CAINES, Eric; Director, Regional Organisation, Department of Health and Social Security, since 1981; *b* 27 Feb. 1936; *s* of Ernest and Doris Caines; *m* 1958; three *s. Educ:* Rothwell Grammar School, Wakefield; Leeds Univ. (LLB Hons). Short Service Commission, RAEC, 1958-61. NCB, 1961-65; BBC, 1965-66; as Principal, Min. of Health, Management Side Sec., General Whitley Council, 1966-70; Sec., NHS Reorganisation Management Arrangements Study, 1970-73; Assistant Sec., DHSS, 1973-77; IMF/World Bank, Washington, 1977-79; Under Sec., DHSS, 1979-. *Recreation:* travelling on foot with a book. *Address:* Mill Farm, Church Road, Brasted, near Westerham, Kent. *T:* Westerham 64478.

CAINES, John; Deputy Secretary, Department of Trade, and Chief Executive, British Overseas Trade Board, since 1980; *b* 13 Jan. 1933; *s* of John Swinburne Caines and Ethel May Stenlake; *m* 1963, Mary Lange; one *s* two *d. Educ:* Westminster Sch.; Christ Church, Oxford (MA). Asst Principal, Min. of Supply, 1957; Asst Private Sec., Min. of Aviation, 1960-61; Principal, Min. of Aviation, 1961-64; Civil Air Attaché in Middle East, 1964-66; Manchester Business Sch., 1967; Asst Sec., BoT, 1968; Sec., Commn on Third London Airport, 1968-71; Asst Sec., DTI, 1971-72; Principal Private Sec. to Sec. of State for Trade and Industry, 1972-74; Under-Sec., Dept of Trade, 1974-77; Sec., 1977-80, Mem. and Dep. Chief Exec., 1979-80, NEB. *Recreations:* travel, music, gardening, theatre. *Address:* 19 College Road, Dulwich, SE21 7BG. *T:* 01-693 5537.

CAIRD, Most Rev. Donald Arthur Richard; *see* Meath and Kildare, Bishop of.

CAIRD, Rev. George Bradford, MA(Cantab), DPhil, DD(Oxon); FBA 1973; Dean Ireland's Professor of Exegesis of Holy Scripture, Oxford, since 1977; *b* 19 July 1917; *s* of George Caird and Esther Love Caird (*née* Bradford), both of Dundee; *m* 1945, Viola Mary Newport; three *s* one *d. Educ:* King Edward's Sch., Birmingham; Peterhouse, Cambridge; Mansfield Coll., Oxford. Minister of Highgate Congregational Church, London, 1943-46; Prof. of OT Lang. and Lit., St Stephen's Coll., Edmonton, Alberta, 1946-50; Prof. of NT Lang. and Lit., McGill Univ., Montreal, 1950-59; Principal, United Theological Coll., Montreal, 1955-59; Sen. Tutor, 1959-70, Principal, 1970-77, Mansfield Coll., Oxford; Reader in Biblical Studies, Oxford Univ., 1969-77. Grinfield Lecturer on the Septuagint, Oxford Univ., 1961-65. Moderator of General Assembly of URC, 1975-76. Hon. Fellow, Mansfield Coll., 1977. Hon. DD: St Stephen's Coll., Edmonton, 1959; Diocesan Coll., Montreal, 1959; Aberdeen Univ., 1966. Burkitt Medal, British Acad., 1981. *Publications:* The Truth of the Gospel, 1950; The Apostolic Age, 1955; Principalities and Powers, 1956; The Gospel according to St Luke, 1963; The Revelation of St John the Divine, 1966; Our Dialogue with Rome, 1967; Paul's Letters from Prison, 1976; The Language and Imagery of the Bible, 1980 (Collins Bi-Ennial Religious Award, 1982); contribs to: Interpreter's Dictionary of the Bible; Hastings Dictionary of the Bible; Jl of Theological Studies; New Testament Studies; Expository Times. *Recreations:* bird-watching, chess, music. *Address:* The Queen's College, Oxford.

CAIRD, William Douglas Sime; Registrar, Family Division of High Court (formerly Probate, Divorce and Admiralty Division), 1964-82; *b* 21 Aug. 1917; *er s* of William Sime Caird and Elsie Amy Caird; *m* 1946, Josephine Mary, *d* of Peter and Elizabeth Seeney, Stratford on Avon; no *c. Educ:* Rutlish Sch., Merton. Entered Principal Probate Registry, 1937; Estabt Officer, 1954; Sec., 1959; Mem., Matrimonial Causes Rule Cttee, 1968-79. *Publications:* Consulting Editor, Rayden on Divorce, 10th edn 1967, 11th edn 1971, 12th edn 1974, 13th edn 1979. *Address:* 107 Salisbury Road, Worcester Park, Surrey. *T:* 01-337 0456.

CAIRNCROSS, Sir Alexander Kirkland, (Sir Alec Cairncross), KCMG 1967 (CMG 1950); FBA 1961; Chancellor, University of Glasgow, since 1972; Supernumerary Fellow, St Antony's College, Oxford, since 1978; *b* 11 Feb. 1911; 3rd *s* of Alexander Kirkland and Elizabeth Andrew Cairncross, Lesmahagow, Scotland; *m* 1943, Mary Frances Glynn, *d* of Maj. E. F. Glynn,

TD, Ilkley; three *s* two *d. Educ:* Hamilton Academy; Glasgow and Cambridge Univs. Univ. Lectr, 1935-39; Civil Servant, 1940-45; Dir of Programmes, Min. of Aircraft Production, 1945; Economic Advisory Panel, Berlin, 1945-46; Mem. of Staff of The Economist, 1946. Mem. of Wool Working Party, 1946; Economic Adviser to: BoT, economics; Organisation for European Economic Co-operation, 1949-50; Prof. of Applied Economics, Univ. of Glasgow, 1951-61; Dir, Economic Development Inst., Washington DC, 1955-56; Economic Adviser to HM Govt, 1961-64; Head of Govt Economic Service, 1964-69. Master of St Peter's Coll., Oxford, 1969-78, Hon. Fellow, 1978. Chm., independent advrs on reassessment of Channel Tunnel Project, 1974-75; Adviser to Minister of Transport on Channel Tunnel Project, 1979-81; Chm., Local Development Cttee, 1951-52; Member: Crofting Commn, 1951-54; Phillips Cttee, 1953-54; Anthrax Cttee, 1957-59; Radcliffe Cttee, 1957-59; Cttee on N Ireland, 1971; Cttee on Police Pay, 1978; Council of Management, Nat. Inst. of Economic and Social Research; Court of Governors, LSE (Hon. Fellow, 1980); Council, Royal Economic Soc. (Pres., 1968-70). President: Scottish Economic Soc., 1969-71; British Assoc. for Advancement of Science, 1970-71 (Pres. Section F, 1969); GPDST, 1972-. Editor, Scottish Journal of Political Economy, 1954-61. For. Hon. Mem., Amer. Acad. of Arts and Scis, 1973. Hon. LLD: Mount Allison, 1962; Glasgow, 1966; Exeter, 1969; Hon. DLitt: Reading, 1968: Heriot-Watt, 1969; Hon. DSc(Econ.): Univ. of Wales, 1971; QUB, 1972; DUniv Stirling, 1973. *Publications:* Introduction to Economics, 1944; Home and Foreign Investment, 1870-1913, 1953; Monetary Policy in a Mixed Economy, 1960; Economic Development and the Atlantic Provinces, 1961; Factors in Economic Development, 1962; Essays in Economic Management, 1971; Control over Long-term International Capital Movements, 1973; Inflation, Growth and International Finance, 1975; Snatches (poems), 1981. *Recreations:* colour photography, travel. *Address:* 14 Staverton Road, Oxford. *T:* Oxford 52358. *Club:* United Oxford & Cambridge University.

CAIRNCROSS, Neil Francis, CB 1971; Deputy Under-Secretary of State, Home Office, 1972-80; *b* 29 July 1920; *s* of late James and Olive Hunter Cairncross; *m* 1947, Eleanor Elizabeth Leisten; two *s* one *d. Educ:* Charterhouse; Oriel Coll., Oxford. Royal Sussex Regt, 1940-45. Called to the Bar, 1948. Home Office, 1948; a Private Sec. to the Prime Minister, 1955-58; Sec., Royal Commn on the Press, 1961-62; Dep. Sec., Cabinet Office, 1970-72; Dep. Sec., NI Office, March-Nov. 1972. Member: Parole Bd, 1982-; Home Grown Timber Adv. Cttee, 1981-. *Recreations:* painting, gardening. *Address:* Little Grange, The Green, Olveston, Bristol BS12 3EJ. *T:* Almondsbury 613060. *Club:* United Oxford & Cambridge University.

CAIRNS, family name of Earl Cairns.

CAIRNS, 5th Earl, *cr* 1878; **David Charles Cairns,** GCVO 1972 (KCVO 1969); CB 1960; Rear-Admiral; DL; Baron Cairns, 1867; Viscount Garmoyle, 1878; Her Majesty's Marshal of the Diplomatic Corps, 1962-71; Extra Equerry to the Queen, since 1972; *b* 3 July 1909; *s* of 4th Earl and Olive (*d* 1952), *d* of late J. P. Cobbold, MP; *S* father, 1946; *m* 1936, Barbara Jeanne Harrisson, *y d* of Sydney H. Burgess, Heathfield, Altrincham, Cheshire; two *s* one *d. Educ:* RNC Dartmouth. Served War of 1939-45 (despatches); Dep. Dir, Signal Dept, Admiralty, 1950, comd 7th Frigate Sqdn, 1952; HMS Ganges, 1953-54; Student Imperial Defence Coll., 1955; comd HMS Superb, 1956-57; Baghdad Pact Plans and Training Div., Admiralty, 1958; Pres., RNC Greenwich, 1958-61; retired. Pres., Navy League, 1966-77. DL Suffolk, 1973. *Heir:* *s* Viscount Garmoyle, *qv. Address:* The Red House, Clopton, near Woodbridge, Suffolk. *T:* Grundisburgh 262. *Club:* Turf.

CAIRNS, Rt. Hon. Sir David (Arnold Scott), PC 1970; Kt 1955; a Lord Justice of Appeal, 1970-77; *b* 5 March 1902; *s* of late David Cairns, JP, Freeman of Sunderland, and late Sarah Scott Cairns; *m* 1932, Irene Cathery Phillips; one *s* two *d. Educ:* Bede Sch., Sunderland; Pembroke Coll., Cambridge (Scholar) (Hon. Fellow, 1973); Senior Optime. MA, LLB (Cantab); BSc (London); Certificate of Honour, Bar Final, 1925. Called to Bar, Middle Temple, 1926; Bencher 1958. KC 1947. Liberal Candidate at By-election, Epsom Div., 1947. Mem. of Leatherhead UDC, 1948-54; Chm., Liberal Party Commn on Trade Unions, 1948-49; Mem. of Liberal Party Cttee, 1951-53; Chm., Monopolies and Restrictive Practices Commn, 1954-56; Recorder of Sunderland, 1957-60; Comr of Assize, 1957 (Midland Circuit), May 1959 (Western Circuit), Nov. 1959 (Wales and Chester Circuit); Judge of the High Court, Probate, Divorce and Admiralty Div., 1960-70. Chairman: Statutory Cttee of Pharmaceutical Soc. of Great Britain, 1952-60; Executive of Justice (British Section of International Commn of Jurists), 1959-60; Minister of Aviation's Cttee on Accident Investigation and Licence Control, 1959-60; Govt Adv. Cttee on Rhodesian Travel Restrictions, 1968-70. *Recreations:* swimming, gardening. *Address:* Applecroft, Ashtead, Surrey. *T:* Ashtead 74132.

CAIRNS, Air Vice-Marshal Geoffrey Crerar, CBE 1970; AFC 1960; FRAeS 1979; FBIM; Chief Executive, Trago Mills, since 1981; *b* 1926; *s* of late Dr J. W. Cairns, MD, MCh, DPH and Marion Cairns; *m* 1948, Carol, *d* of H. I. F. Evernden, MBE; four *d. Educ:* Loretto School, Musselburgh; Cambridge Univ. Joined RAF, 1944; served: Sqdns 43 and 93, Italy; Sqdn 73, Malta, 1946-49; Sqdn 72, UK, 1949-51; Adjutant, Hong Kong Auxiliary Air Force; test pilot A&AEE, Boscombe Down, 1957-60; Jt Planning Staff, MoD, 1961; Chief Instructor, Helicopters, CFS, RAF Ternhill, 1963; JSSC 1966; Supt Flying A&AEE 1968; Dir, Defence Operational Requirements Staffs, MoD, 1970; Commandant, Boscombe Down, 1972-74; ACAS (Op-

Requirements), MoD, 1974-76; Comdr, Southern Maritime Air Region, 1976-78; Chief of Staff No 18 Group, Strike Command, 1978-80. Consultant, Marconi Avionics, 1980-81. *Recreations:* golf, railways. *Address:* c/o Lloyds Bank, Cox's and King's Branch, 6 Pall Mall, SW1. *Club:* Royal Air Force.

CAIRNS, Hugh John Forster; DM; FRS 1974; Professor of Microbiology, Harvard School of Public Health, since 1980; *b* 21 Nov. 1922. *Educ:* Oxford Univ. BA 1943; BM, BCh 1946; DM 1952. Surg. Registrar, Radcliffe Infirmary, Oxford, 1945; Med. Intern, Postgrad. Med. Sch., London, 1946; Paediatric Intern, Royal Victoria Infirmary, Newcastle, 1947; Chem. Pathologist, Radcliffe Infirmary, 1947-49; Virologist, Hall Inst., Melbourne, Aust., 1950-51; Virus Research Inst., Entebbe, Uganda, 1952-54; Research Fellow, then Reader, Aust. Nat. Univ., Canberra, 1955-63; Rockefeller Research Fellow, California Inst. of Technology, 1957; Nat. Insts of Health Fellow, Cold Spring Harbor, NY, 1960-61; Dir, Cold Spring Harbor Lab. of Quantitative Biology, 1963-68 (Staff Mem., 1968-); Prof of Biology (Hon.), State Univ. of New York, Stony Brook, 1968-73, Amer. Cancer Soc. Prof. 1968-73; Head of Imperial Cancer Research Fund Mill Hill Laboratories, 1973-80. *Address:* Department of Microbiology, Harvard School of Public Health, 677 Huntington Avenue, Boston, Massachusetts 02115, USA. *T:* (617) 732 1240.

CAIRNS, Dr James Ford; MHR (ALP) for Lalor, 1969-78 (for Yarra, 1955-69); *b* 4 Oct. 1914; *s* of James John Cairns and Letitia Cairns (*née* Ford); *m* 1939, Gwendolyn Olga Robb; two *s*. *Educ:* Melton/Sunbury State Sch.; Northcote High Sch.; Melbourne Univ. MComm and PhD (Melb.). Australian Estates Co. Ltd, 1932; Victoria Police Force, 1935. Served War, AIF, 1945. Melbourne Univ.: Sen. Tutor, Lectr, Sen. Lectr (Economic Hist.), 1946-55. Minister for Overseas Trade, 1972-74; Treasurer of Australia, 1974-75; Dep. Prime Minister, 1974-75; Minister for the Environment, Australia, 1975. *Publications:* Australia, 1951 (UK); Living with Asia, 1965; The Eagle and the Lotus, 1969; Tariffs or Planning, 1970; Silence Kills, 1970; The Quiet Revolution, 1972; Oil in Troubled Waters, 1976; Vietnam: Scorched Earth Reborn, 1976; numerous articles in jls and press, incl. title Australia: History in Enc. Brit. *Recreations:* sleeping, reading.

CAIRNS, James George Hamilton Dickson; Chief Architect and Director of Works, Home Office, 1976-80; *b* 17 Sept. 1920; *s* of Percival Cairns and Christina Elliot Cairns; *m* 1944, G. Elizabeth Goodman; one *d*. *Educ:* Hillhead High Sch., Glasgow; London Polytechnic. ARIBA. Served War, Royal Corps of Signals (Intell.), 1941-46. Architects' Dept, GLC, 1946-75. Divisional Architect, Thameshead New Town, awarded Sir Patrick Abercrombie Prize by Internat. Union of Architects, 1969. *Recreations:* golf, sailing. *Address:* 6 Broom Hall, Oxshott, Surrey. *T:* Oxshott 2904; Elmsleigh, 12 Elmstead Park Road, West Wittering, W Sussex. *T:* West Wittering 3316. *Clubs:* Goodwood Golf, West Wittering Sailing.

CAIRNS, Julia, (Mrs Paul Davidson); writer and lecturer; Vice-President: London and Overseas Flower Arrangement Society; Society of Women Writers and Journalists; *o c* of late H. W. Akers, Oxford; *m* 1st, 1915, Frank H. James, The Royal Scots; 2nd, 1925, Capt. Paul Davidson, late 12th Royal Lancers (*d* 1942). *Educ:* Oxford. Entered journalism as a free-lance; Woman Editor of The Ideal Home, 1924; House and Home Director of Woman's Journal, 1927; Editor-in-Chief Weldons Publications, 1929-55; Home Editor, The Queen, 1956-58. President Women's Press Club of London Ltd, 1947 and 1948. *Publications:* Home-Making, 1950; How I Became a Journalist, 1960. *Recreation:* gardening. *Club:* University Women's.

CAITHNESS, 20th Earl of, *cr* 1455; **Malcolm Ian Sinclair,** ARICS; Lord Berriedale, 1455; Bt 1631; *b* 3 Nov. 1948; *s* of 19th Earl of Caithness, CVO, CBE, DSO, DL, JP; *S* father, 1965; *m* 1975, Diana Caroline, *d* of Major Richard Coke, MC; one *s* one *d*. *Educ:* Marlborough; Royal Agric. Coll., Cirencester. *Heir: s* Lord Berriedale, *qv*. *Address:* Finstock Manor, Finstock, Oxford.

CAITHNESS, Archdeacon of; *see* Hadfield, Ven. J. C.

CAKOBAU, Ratu Sir George (Kadavulevu), GCMG 1973; GCVO 1977; OBE 1953; Governor-General of Fiji, since 1973; *b* 1911; *s* of Ratu Popi Epeli Seniloli Cakobau; *m* Lealea S. Balekiwai, *d* of Vilikesa Balekiwai. *Educ:* Queen Victoria Sch.; Newington Coll., Australia; Wanganui Technical Coll., NZ. Served War, 1939-45; Captain, Fiji Military Forces. Member: Council of Chiefs, Fiji, 1938-72; Legislative Council, Fiji, 1951-70; Minister for Fijian Affairs and Local Government, 1970-71; Minister without Portfolio, 1971-72. KStJ 1973. *Address:* Government House, Suva, Fiji.

CALCUTT, David Charles, QC 1972; in practice at the Bar, since 1957; a Judge of the Court of Appeal of Jersey and of the Court of Appeal of Guernsey, since 1978; a Recorder of the Crown Court, since 1972; Chancellor of the Diocese of Exeter, since 1971; Chancellor of the Diocese of Bristol, since 1971; Chairman of the Civil Service Arbitration Tribunal, since 1979; *b* 2 Nov. 1930; *s* of late Henry Calcutt; *m* 1969, Barbara, JP, *d* of late Vivian Walker. *Educ:* Christ Church, Oxford (Chorister); Cranleigh Sch. (Music Schol.); King's Coll., Cambridge (Choral Schol.). MA, LLB, MusB. Stewart of Rannoch Schol. 1952, Prizeman (Law and music), Cambridge. Called to Bar, Middle Temple, 1955; Harmsworth Law Schol. 1956. Dir, Edington Music Festival, 1956-64. Staff of The Times, 1957-66. Member: Council,

RSCM, 1967-; Gen. Council of Bar, 1968-72; Dep. Chm., Somerset QS, 1970-71; Mem., Crown Court Rules Cttee, 1971-77; Dept of Trade Inspector, Cornhill Consolidated Group Ltd, 1974-77; Mem., Criminal Injuries Compensation Bd, 1977-; Fellow, Internat. Acad. of Trial Lawyers (NY), 1978-; Deputy Judge, High Court of Justice, 1978-; Chm., Provincial Tribunal of Enquiry, 1979; Member: Senate of the Inns of Court and the Bar, 1979- (Chm., Internat. Relations Cttee, 1981-); UK Deleg., Consultative Cttee, Bars and Law Socs, EEC, 1980-; Member: Council, RCM, 1980-; Council on Tribunals, 1980- (Chm., Legal Cttee, 1982-). Fellow Commoner, Magdalene Coll., Cambridge, 1980-. Governor: Cranleigh Sch., 1963-; SPCK, 1980-; Blundell's Sch., 1981-. Bencher, Middle Temple, 1981-. *Recreation:* living on Exmoor. *Address:* Lamb Building, Temple, EC4. *Clubs:* Athenæum; New (Edinburgh).

CALCUTTA, Archbishop of, (RC), since 1969; **His Eminence Lawrence Trevor Cardinal Picachy,** SJ; *b* 7 Aug. 1916; Indian. *Educ:* St Joseph's College, Darjeeling and various Indian Seminaries. 1952-60: Headmaster of St Xavier's School, Principal of St Xavier's College, Rector of St Xavier's, Calcutta. Parish Priest of Basanti, large village of West Bengal, 1960-62; (first) Bishop of Jamshedpur, 1962-69, Apostolic Administrator of Jamshedpur, 1969-70. Cardinal, 1976. Pres., Catholic Bishops' Conf. of India, 1976- (Vice-Pres., 1972-75). *Address:* Archbishop's House, 32 Park Street, Calcutta 700016, India. *T:* Calcutta 44-4666.

CALCUTTA, Bishop of, since 1982; **Rt. Rev. Dinesh Chandra Gorai;** *b* 15 Jan. 1934. *Educ:* Calcutta Univ. (BA 1956); Serampore Theological Coll. (BD 1959). Ordained, 1962; Methodist Minister in Calcutta/Barrackpore, 1968-70; first Bishop, Church of N India Diocese of Barrackpore, 1970-82; Dep. Moderator, Church of N India, 1980-. *Address:* Bishop's House, 51 Chowringhee Road, Calcutta 700 071, India. *T:* 44-5259.

CALDECOTE, 2nd Viscount *cr* 1939, of Bristol; **Robert Andrew Inskip,** DSC 1941; Chairman: Delta Group plc (formerly Delta Metal Co.), 1972-82; Finance for Industry, since 1980; *b* 8 Oct. 1917; *o s* of Thomas Walker Hobart Inskip, 1st Viscount Caldecote, PC, CBE, and Lady Augusta Orr Ewing (*d* 1967), *widow* of Charles Orr Ewing, MP for Ayr Burghs and *e d* of 7th Earl of Glasgow; *S* father, 1947; *m* 1942, Jean Hamilla, *d* of late Rear-Adm. H. D. Hamilton; one *s* two *d*. *Educ:* Eton Coll.; King's Coll., Cambridge. BA Cantab 1939; MA 1944. RNVR, 1939-45; RNC Greenwich, 1946-47; an Asst Manager, Vickers-Armstrong Naval Yard, Walker-on-Tyne, 1947-48; Mem., Church Assembly, 1950-55; Fellow, King's Coll., and Lectr, Engineering Dept, Cambridge Univ., 1948-55; Man. Dir, English Electric Aviation, 1960-63; Dep. Man. Dir, British Aircraft Corp., 1961-67 (Dir, 1960-69); Dir, English Electric Co., 1953-69; Chm., Legal and General Gp, 1977-80. Chairman: EDC Movement of Exports, 1965-72; Export Council for Europe, 1970-71. President: Soc. of British Aerospace Cos, 1965-66; Internat. Assoc. of Aeronautical and Space Equipment Manufacturers, 1966-68; Parliamentary and Scientific Cttee, 1966-69; Fellowship of Engineering, 1981-. Director: Consolidated Gold Fields, 1969-78; Lloyds Bank, 1975-; Lloyds Bank International, 1979-; Equity Capital for Industry, 1980-. Member: Review Bd for Govt Contracts, 1969-76; Inflation Accounting Cttee, 1974-75; Engineering Industries council, 1975-; British Railways Bd, 1979-; Adv. Council for Applied R & D, 1981-; Engrg Council, 1982-. Chm., Design Council, 1972-80. Chm., BBC Gen. Adv. Council, 1982-. Pro-Chancellor, Cranfield Inst. of Technology, 1976-. Mem. UK Delegn to UN, 1952; Fellow, Eton Coll., 1953-72; Pres., Dean Close Sch.; Vice-Pres., St Lawrence Coll. FEng, FIEE; MRINA; Hon. FIMechE 1982; Hon. FSIAD 1976. Hon. DSc: Cranfield, 1976; Aston, 1979; Hon. LLD London, 1981. *Recreations:* sailing, shooting, golf. *Heir: s* Hon. Piers James Hampden Inskip [*b* 20 May 1947; *m* 1970, Susan Bridget, *d* of late W. P. Mellen]. *Address:* Orchard Cottage, South Harting, Petersfield, Hants. *T:* Harting 264. *Clubs:* Pratt's, Athenæum, Boodle's; Royal Ocean Racing, Royal Yacht Squadron.

CALDER, John Mackenzie; Managing Director, John Calder (Publishers) Ltd and Calder & Boyars Ltd, since 1950; *b* 25 Jan. 1927; *e s* of James Calder, Ardargie, Forgandenny, Perthshire, and Lucianne Wilson, Montreal, Canada; *m* 1st, 1949, Mary Ann Simmonds; one *d*; 2nd, 1960, Bettina Jonic (marr. diss. 1975); one *d*. *Educ:* Gilling Castle, Yorks; Bishops College Sch., Canada; McGill Univ.; Sir George Williams Coll.; Zürich Univ. Studied political economy; subseq. worked in Calders Ltd (timber co.), Director; founded John Calder (Publishers) Ltd, 1950. Organiser of literary confs for Edinburgh Festival, 1962 and 1963, and Harrogate Festival, 1969. Founded Ledlanet Nights, 1963, in Kinross-shire (music and opera festival, closed 1974). Acquired book-selling business of Better Books, London, 1969, expanded Edinburgh, 1971. Dir of other cos associated with opera, publishing, etc, inc. Operabout Ltd, Riverrun Press Inc., USA, Canadian International Library Ltd, Canada. Dir of other cos associated with opera, publishing, etc. Active in fields related to the arts and on many cttees; Co-founder, Defence of Literature and the Arts Society; Chm., Fedn of Scottish Theatres, 1972-74. Contested (L): Kinross and W Perthshire, 1970; Hamilton, Oct. 1974; (European Parlt) Mid Scotland and Fife, 1979. FRSA 1974. Chevalier des Arts et des Lettres, 1975. *Publications:* (ed) A Samuel Beckett Reader; (ed) Beckett at 60; (ed) The Nouveau Roman Reader; (ed) Gambit International Drama Review, etc; articles in many jls. *Recreations:* writing (several plays, stories; criticism, etc; translations); music, theatre, opera, reading, chess, lecturing, conversation; travelling, promoting good causes, fond of good food and wine.

Address: c/o John Calder (Publishers) Ltd, 18 Brewer Street, W1. *Clubs:* Caledonian; Scottish Arts, Scottish Liberal (Edinburgh).

CALDER, Nigel David Ritchie, MA; science writer; *b* 2 Dec. 1931; *e s of* Baron Ritchie-Calder, CBE; *m* 1954, Elisabeth Palmer; two *s* three *d. Educ:* Merchant Taylors' Sch.; Sidney Sussex Coll., Cambridge. Physicist, Mullard Research Laboratories, 1954-56; Editorial staff, New Scientist, 1956-66; Science Editor, 1960-62; Editor, 1962-66. Science Correspondent, New Statesman, 1959-62 and 1966-71; Chairman, Assoc. of British Science Writers, 1962-64. TV series, The Whole Universe Show, 1977. (Jtly) UNESCO Kalinga Prize for popularisation of science, 1972. *Publications:* Electricity Grows Up, 1958; Robots, 1958; Radio Astronomy, 1958; (ed) The World in 1984, 1965; The Environment Game, 1967; (ed) Unless Peace Comes, 1968; Technopolis: Social Control of the Uses of Science, 1969; Living Tomorrow, 1970; (ed) Nature in the Round: a Guide to Environmental Science, 1973; Timescale, 1982; *books of own TV programmes:* The Violent Universe, 1969; The Mind of Man, 1970; The Restless Earth, 1972; The Life Game, 1973; The Weather Machine, 1974; The Human Conspiracy, 1975-76; The Key to the Universe, 1977; Spaceships of the Mind (TV series), 1978; Einstein's Universe, 1979; Nuclear Nightmares, 1979; The Comet is Coming!, 1980. *Recreation:* sailing. *Address:* 8 The Chase, Furnace Green, Crawley, W Sussex RH10 6HW. *T:* Crawley 26693. *Clubs:* Athenæum; Cruising Association (Chairman, 1980-81).

CALDER-MARSHALL, Arthur; author; *b* 19 Aug. 1908; *s* of late Arthur Grotjan Calder-Marshall and Alice Poole; *m* 1934, Violet Nancy Sales; two *d. Educ:* St Paul's Sch.; Hertford Coll., Oxford. *Publications:* novels: Two of a Kind, 1933; About Levy, 1933; At Sea, 1934; Dead Centre, 1935; Pie in the Sky, 1937; The Way to Santiago, 1940; A Man Reprieved, 1949; Occasion of Glory, 1955; The Scarlet Boy, 1961, rev. edn 1962; *short stories:* Crime against Cania, 1934; A Pink Doll, 1935; A Date with a Duchess, 1937; *for children:* The Man from Devil's Island, 1958; Fair to Middling, 1959; Lone Wolf: the story of Jack London, 1961; *travel:* Glory Dead, 1939; The Watershed, 1947; *biography:* No Earthly Command, 1957; Havelock Ellis, 1959; The Enthusiast, 1962; The Innocent Eye, 1963; Lewd, Blasphemous and Obscene, 1972; The Two Duchesses, 1978; *autobiography:* The Magic of My Youth, 1951; *miscellaneous:* Challenge to Schools: public school education, 1935; The Changing Scene, 1937; The Book Front, ed J. Lindsay, 1947; Wish You Were Here: the art of Donald McGill, 1966; Prepare to Shed Them Now . . .: the biography and ballads of George R. Sims, 1968; The Grand Century of the Lady, 1976; *essays:* Sterne, in The English Novelists, ed D. Verschoyle, 1936; Films, in Mind in Chains, ed C. Day Lewis; *edited:* Tobias Smollett, Selected Writings, 1950; J. London, The Bodley Head Jack London, Vols 1-4, 1963-66; Charles Dickens, David Copperfield, 1967, Nicholas Nickleby, 1968, Oliver Twist, 1970; Bleak House, 1976; The Life of Benvenuto Cellini, 1968; Jack London, The Call of the Wild, and other stories, 1969; Jane Austen, Emma, 1970; Thomas Paine, Common Sense and the Rights of Man, 1970. *Address:* c/o Elaine Greene Ltd, 31 Newington Green, N16 9PW.

CALDERBANK, Emeritus Prof. Philip Hugh; Professor of Chemical Engineering, University of Edinburgh, 1960-80; *b* 6 March 1919; *s* of Leonard and Rhoda Elizabeth Calderbank; *m* 1941, Kathleen Mary (*née* Taylor); one *s* one *d. Educ:* Palmer's Sch., Gray's, Essex; King's Coll., London Univ. Research and Development Chemist: Ministry of Supply, 1941-44; Bakelite Ltd, 1944-47. Lecturer in Chemical Engineering Dept, University Coll., London University, 1947-53; Professor in Chem. Engineering Dept, University of Toronto, 1953-56; Senior Principal Scientific Officer, Dept of Scientific and Industrial Research, 1956-60. *Publications:* contributor: Chemical Engineering Progress; Transactions Instn of Chemical Engineers; Chemical Engineering Science. *Recreations:* various crafts. *Address:* 11 Park Road, Kenley, Surrey. *T:* 01-668 9707.

CALDERWOOD, Robert; Chief Executive, Strathclyde Regional Council, since 1980; *b* 1 March 1932; *s* of Robert Calderwood and Jessie Reid (*née* Marshall); *m* 1958, Meryl Anne (*née* Fleming); three *s* one *d. Educ:* William Hulme's Sch., Manchester; Manchester Univ. (LLB (Hons)). Admitted solicitor, 1956; Town Clerk: Salford, 1966-69; Bolton, 1969-73; Manchester, 1973-79. Member: Parole Bd for England and Wales, 1971-73; Soc. of Local Authority Chief Execs; Scottish Consultative Cttee, Commn for Racial Equality. CBIM (Mem., Adv. Bd for Scotland). *Recreations:* theatre, watching Rugby League. *Address:* Strathclyde Regional Council, Regional Headquarters, 20 India Street, Glasgow G2 4PF; 6 Mosspark Avenue, Milngavie, Glasgow G62 8NL. *Clubs:* Royal Scottish Automobile (Glasgow); University Union (Manchester).

CALDICOTT, Hon. Sir John Moore, KBE 1963; CMG 1955; *b* 1900; *m* 1945, Evelyn Macarthur; one *s* two step *d. Educ:* Shrewsbury School. Joined RAF 1918. Came to Southern Rhodesia, 1925; farmed in Umvukwes District until 1970. President: Rhodesia Tobacco Assoc., 1943-45; Rhodesia National Farmers' Union, 1946-48. MP for Mazoe, S Rhodesia Parliament, 1948; Minister of Agriculture and Lands, 1951, of Agriculture, Health and Public Service, 1953, of Economic Affairs, 1958-62, of The Common Market, 1962, and of Finance, until 1963, Federation of Rhodesia and Nyasaland. *Address:* 24 Court Road, Greendale, Salisbury, Zimbabwe. *Club:* Salisbury (Salisbury, Zimbabwe).

CALDWELL, Surg. Vice-Adm. Sir Dick; *see* Caldwell, Surg.-Adm. Sir E. D.

CALDWELL, Edward George; Parliamentary Counsel, since 1981; *b* 21 Aug. 1941; *s* of Arthur Francis Caldwell and Olive Caldwell (*née* Riddle); *m* 1965, Bronwen Anne, *d* of John Andrew Crockett and late Bronwen Crockett; two *d. Educ:* St Andrew's, Singapore; Clifton College; Worcester College, Oxford. Solicitor. Law Commission, 1967-69; joined Office of Parly Counsel, 1969. *Recreations:* swimming, motorcycling. *Address:* Parliamentary Counsel Office, 36 Whitehall, SW1A 2AY. *T:* 01-273 4553.

CALDWELL, Surg. Vice-Adm. Sir (Eric) Dick, KBE 1969; CB 1965; Medical Director-General of the Royal Navy, 1966-69; Executive Director, Medical Council on Alcoholism, 1970-79; *b* 6 July 1909; *s* of late Dr John Colin Caldwell; *m* 1942, Margery Lee Abbott. *Educ:* Edinburgh Acad.; Edinburgh Univ. MB, ChB Edinburgh 1933; LRCP, LRCSE, LRFPS(G) 1933; MD Edinburgh 1950; MRCP 1956; FRCPE 1962; FRCP 1967. Joined Royal Navy, 1934. Served War of 1939-45 in Atlantic, Mediterranean and Pacific; survivor from torpedoeing of HMS Royal Oak and HMS Prince of Wales. Medical Specialist, RN Hosp., Hong Kong, 1947; Sen. Med. Specialist at RN Hosp., Haslar, 1956-58; Surg. Captain 1957; MO i/c of RN Hosp., Plymouth, 1963-66. RN Consultant in Medicine, 1962; Surg. Rear-Adm. 1963; Surg. Vice-Adm. 1966. QHP 1963-69. Gilbert Blane Gold Medal, 1962; FRSocMed. CStJ. *Recreations:* reading, travelling, trying to write. *Address:* 9A Holland Park Road, Kensington, W14 8NA. *T:* 01-602 3326.

CALDWELL, Erskine; author; Editor of American Folkways, 1940-55; Member: Authors' League; American PEN; (Hon.) American Academy and Institute of Arts and Letters; *b* 17 Dec. 1903; *s* of Ira Sylvester Caldwell and Caroline Preston Bell; *m* 1st, 1925, Helen Lannigan; two *s* one *d* ; 2nd, 1939, Margaret Bourke-White; 3rd, 1942, June Johnson; one *s* ; 4th, 1957, Virginia Moffett Fletcher. *Educ:* Erskine Coll.; Univ. of Virginia. Newspaper reporter on Atlanta (Ga) Journal; motion picture screen writer in Hollywood; newspaper and radio correspondent in Russia. *Publications:* The Bastard, 1929; Poor Fool, 1930; American Earth, 1931; Tobacco Road, 1932; God's Little Acre, 1933; We Are the Living, 1933; Journeyman, 1935; Kneel to the Rising Sun, 1935; Some American People, 1935; You Have Seen Their Faces, 1937; Southways, 1938; North of The Danube, 1939; Trouble in July, 1940; Jackpot, 1940; Say! Is This the USA?, 1941; All-Out on the Road to Smolensk, 1942; Moscow Under Fire, 1942; All Night Long, 1942; Georgia Boy, 1943; Tragic Ground, 1944; Stories, 1945; A House in the Uplands, 1946; The Sure Hand of God, 1947; This Very Earth, 1948; Place Called Estherville, 1949; Episode in Palmetto, 1950; Call It Experience, 1951; The Courting of Susie Brown, 1952; A Lamp for Nightfall, 1952; The Complete Stories of Erskine Caldwell, 1953; Love and Money, 1954; Gretta, 1955; Gulf Coast Stories, 1956; Certain Women, 1957; Molly Cottontail, 1958 (juvenile); Claudelle Inglish, 1959; When You Think of Me, 1959; Jenny By Nature, 1961; Close to Home, 1962; The Last Night of Summer, 1963; Around About America, 1964; In Search of Bisco, 1965; The Deer at Our House (juvenile), 1966; In the Shadow of the Steeple, 1966; Miss Mamma Aimee, 1967; Writing In America, 1967; Deep South, 1968; Summertime Island, 1968; The Weather Shelter, 1969; The Earnshaw Neighborhood, 1971; Annette, 1973; Afternoons in Mid-America, 1976. *Address:* c/o McIntosh & Otis Inc., 475 Fifth Avenue, New York, NY 10017, USA. *T:* New York: MU 9-1050; (home) PO Box 4550, Hopi Station, Scottsdale, Arizona 85258, USA. *Clubs:* Phoenix Press (Phoenix, Arizona); San Francisco Press (San Francisco, Calif).

CALDWELL, Maj.-Gen. Frank Griffiths, OBE 1953 (MBE 1945); MC 1941 and Bar 1942; *b* 26 Feb. 1921; *s* of William Charles Francis and Violet Marjorie Kathleen Caldwell; *m* 1945, Betty, *d* of Captain Charles Palmer Buesden; one *s* one *d. Educ:* Elizabeth Coll., Guernsey. Commnd Royal Engrs, 1940; served Western Desert RE, 1940-43 (MC and Bar); Special Air Service NW Europe, 1944-45 (MBE); Malaya, 1951-53 (OBE); Commd RE, 2 Div. BAOR, 1961-63; Corps Comdr RE, 1 (BR) Corps, 1967-68; Dir Defence Operational Plans, MoD, 1970; Engineer in Chief (Army), 1970-72; Asst CGS (Operational Requirements), 1972-74. Col Comdt, RE, 1975-80. Belgian Croix de Guerre, 1940, and Croix Militaire, 1945. *Recreations:* ornithology, golf. *Address:* The Eighteenth, Pond Road, Hook Heath, Woking, Surrey. *Clubs:* Army and Navy, MCC.

CALDWELL, Godfrey David; Under-Secretary, Department of Health and Social Security, 1970-75; *b* 7 Jan. 1920; *er s* of Dr J. R. Caldwell, Milnthorpe, Westmorland; *m* 1959, Helen Elizabeth, *d* of J. A. G. Barnes; one *d. Educ:* Heversham Grammar Sch., Westmorland; St Andrews Univ. (MA). Home Office, 1942; transferred to Min. of Nat. Insurance, 1945; Dept of Health and Social Security, 1968-75. *Address:* Low Ludderburn, Cartmel Fell, Windermere, Cumbria. *T:* Crosthwaite 428. *Club:* National Liberal.

CALDWELL, Janet Miriam Taylor, (Mrs W. R. Prestie); *see* Caldwell, Taylor.

CALDWELL, Prof. John Bernard, OBE 1979; PhD; FRINA; Professor of Naval Architecture, and Head of Department of Naval Architecture, University of Newcastle upon Tyne, since 1966; *b* 26 Sept. 1926; *s* of John Revie Caldwell and Doris (*née* Bolland); *m* 1955, Jean Muriel Frances Duddridge; two *s. Educ:* Bootham Sch., York; Liverpool Univ. (BEng); Bristol Univ. (PhD). CEng, MIStructE; FEng 1976; FRINA 1963. Res. Fellow, Civil Engrg, Bristol Univ., 1953; Sen. Scientific Officer 1955, Principal Sci. Off. 1958, Royal Naval Scientific Service; Asst Prof. of Applied Mechanics, RNC Greenwich, 1960-66. Vis. Prof. of Naval Arch., MIT, 1962-63. Pres., N-E Coast Instn of Engrs and Shipbuilders, 1976-78; Vice-

Pres., RINA, 1977. *Publications:* numerous papers on research and educn in naval arch. in Trans RINA. *Address:* The White House, Cadehill Road, Stocksfield, Northumberland NE43 7PT. *T:* Stocksfield 3445. *Club:* National Liberal.

CALDWELL, Philip; Chief Executive Officer since 1979, and Chairman of the Board since 1980, Ford Motor Co.; *b* Bourneville, Ohio, 27 Jan. 1920; *s* of Robert Clyde Caldwell and Wilhelmina (*née* Hemphill); *m* 1945, Betsey Chinn Clark; one *s* two *d*. *Educ:* Muskingum Coll. (BA Econs 1940); Harvard Univ. Graduate Sch. of Business (MBA Indust. Management, 1942). Served to Lieut, USNR, 1942-46. With Navy Dept, 1946-53 (Dep. Dir, Procurement Policy Div., 1948-53); with Ford Motor Co., 1953-: Vice Pres. and Gen. Man. Truck Ops, 1968-70; Pres. and Dir, Philco-Ford Corp. (subsid. of Ford Motor Co.), 1970-71; Vice Pres. Manufg Gp, N Amer. Automotive Ops, 1971-72; Chm. and Chief Exec. Officer, Ford of Europe, Inc., 1972-73; Exec. Vice Pres., Internat. Automotive Ops, 1973-77; Vice Chm. of Bd, 1977-79; Dep. Chief Exec. Officer, 1978-79; Pres., 1978-80; Dir, Ford Motor Co., Ford of Europe, Ford Latin America, Ford Mid-East and Africa, Ford Asia-Pacific, Ford Motor Credit Co., and Ford of Canada. Director: Digital Equipment Corp.; Detroit Renaissance; (also Vice Chm.), Motor Vehicle Manufrs Assoc.; INSEAD; Harvard Univ. Associates of Grad. Sch. of Business Admin; Detroit Symphony Orch.; Vice Chm., Bd of Trustees, New Detroit, Inc.; Member: Internat. Adv. Cttee, Chase Manhattan Bank; Business Council; Business Roundtable; Conf. Bd; Trilateral Commn. Trustee, Cttee for Econ. Develt; Muskingum Coll. Hon. DH Muskingum, 1974; Hon. DBA Upper Iowa Univ., 1978; Hon. LLD: Boston Univ. and Eastern Mich Univ., 1979; Miami Univ., 1980; Davidson Coll., 1982. 1st William A. Jump Meml Award, 1950; Meritorious Civilian Service Award, US Navy, 1953. *Address:* Ford Motor Co., The American Road, Dearborn, Mich 48121, USA; Bloomfield Hills, Mich 48013, USA. *Clubs:* Detroit, Bloomfield Hills Country, Detroit Athletic, Renaissance.

CALDWELL, Taylor, (Janet Miriam Taylor Caldwell; Mrs W. R. Prestie), FIAL; writer; *b* Prestwich, Manchester, England, 7 Sept. 1900; Scots parentage; citizen of USA; *m* 1st, William Fairfax Combs (marr. diss.; he *d* 1972); one *d* ; 2nd, Marcus Reback (*d* 1970); one *d* ; 3rd, 1972, William E. Stancell (marr. diss. 1973); 4th, 1978, William Robert Prestie. *Educ:* Univ. of Buffalo, Buffalo, NY. Wrote many years before publication. Formerly Sec. of Board of Special Inquiry, US Dept of Immigration and Naturalization, Buffalo, NY. Dr in lit. hum., St Bonaventure, 1977. Many awards and citations, national and international, including National Award, Nat. League of American Penwomen (gold medal), 1948, Grande Prix, Prix Chatrain, Paris, 1956, Award of Merit, Daughters of the American Revolution, 1956; McElligott Medal, Marquette Univ., Milwaukee. *Publications:* Dynasty of Death, 1938, repr. 1973; The Eagles Gather, 1939; The Earth is the Lord's, 1940; The Strong City, 1941; The Arm and the Darkness, 1942; The Turnbulls, 1943; The Final Hour, 1944; The Wide House, 1945; This Side of Innocence, 1946; There Was a Time, 1947; Melissa, 1948; Let Love Come Last, 1949; The Balance Wheel, 1951; The Devil's Advocate, 1952; Never Victorious, Never Defeated, 1954; Tender Victory, 1956; The Sound of Thunder, 1957; Dear and Glorious Physician, 1959; The Listener, 1960, (Engl. edn) The Man Who Listens, 1961; A Prologue to Love, 1962; To See the Glory, 1963; The Late Clara Beame, 1964; A Pillar of Iron, 1965; Dialogues with the Devil, 1968; Testimony of Two Men, 1968; Great Lion of God, 1970; On Growing up Tough, 1971; Captains and the Kings, 1973; Glory and the Lightning, 1974; Ceremony of the Innocent, 1976; Bright Flows the River, 1978; Answer as a Man, 1981. *Recreations:* just work; occasionally gardening. *Address:* Ivanhoe Lane, Greenwich, Conn 06830, USA. *Clubs:* American Legion, National League of American Penwomen (Buffalo, NY); League of Women Voters (Amherst Township, Erie County, NY); PEN (New York, NY); Women's National Republican (Washington, DC).

CALDWELL-MOORE, Patrick; *see* Moore, P. C.

CALEDON, 7th Earl of, *cr* 1800; **Nicholas James Alexander;** Baron Caledon, 1790; Viscount Caledon, 1797; *b* 6 May 1955; *s* of 6th Earl of Caledon, and Baroness Anne (*d* 1963), *d* of late Baron Nicolai de Graevenitz; *S* father, 1980; *m* 1979, Wendy, *d* of Spiro Coumantaros and Mrs Suzanne Dayton. *Educ:* Sandroyd School, Gordonstoun School (Round-Square House). *Recreations:* ski-ing, tennis, swimming, photography, travel. *Heir: cousin* Earl Alexander of Tunis, *qv*. *Address:* 3-23 Lowndes Square, SW1. *T:* 01-235 5605, 01-352 8957; Caledon Castle, Caledon, Co. Tyrone, Northern Ireland. *T:* Caledon 232.

CALEDONIA, Bishop of, since 1981; **Rt. Rev. John Edward Hannen;** *b* 19 Nov. 1937; *s* of Charles Scott Hannen and Mary Bowman Hannen (*née* Lynds); *m* 1977, Alana Susan Long. *Educ:* McGill Univ. (BA); College of the Resurrection (GOE). Asst Curate, St Alphege's, Solihull, Warwicks, 1961-64; Priest in Charge, Mission to the Hart Highway, Diocese of Caledonia, BC, 1965-67; Priest, St Andrew's, Greenville, BC, 1967-68; Priest in Charge, Church of Christ the King, Port Edward, BC, 1969-71; Rector, Christ Church, Kincolith, BC, 1971-81; Regional Dean of Metlakatla, 1972-78. *Recreations:* music, Irish wolfhounds. *Address:* Bishop's Lodge, 208 Fourth Avenue West, Prince Rupert, BC V8J 1P3, Canada. *T:* 624-6013.

CALGARY, Bishop of, since 1968; **Rt. Rev. Morse Lamb Goodman;** *b* Rosedale, Ont, 27 May 1917; *s* of Frederick James Goodman and Mary Mathilda Arkwright; *m* 1943, Patricia May Cunningham; three *s* one *d*. *Educ:*

Trinity Coll., Univ. of Toronto. BA Trin., 1940; LTh Trin., 1942. Deacon, 1942, Priest, 1943, Diocese of Algoma; Asst Curate, St Paul's, Ft William, 1942-43; Incumbent, Murillo, Algoma, 1943-46; Rector, St Thomas, Ft William, 1946-53; Rector, St James, Winnipeg, 1953-60; Dean of Brandon, 1960-65; Rector, Christ Church, Edmonton, 1965-67. Conductor of Canadian Broadcasting Corporation Programme, Family Worship, 1954-68. Hon. DD: Trinity, 1961; Emmanuel and St Chad's, 1968. Companion, Order of Coventry Cross of Nails, 1974; GCKLJ. *Recreations:* fishing, walking, photography, enology. *Address:* Bishop's Court, 12 Varanger Place NW, Calgary, Alta, Canada. *T:* 286 5127. *Clubs:* Ranchman's, United Services (Calgary, Alta); PPCLI Officers' Mess.

CALLAGHAN, Sir Allan (Robert), Kt 1972; CMG 1945; agricultural consultant, since 1972; *b* 24 Nov. 1903; *s* of late Phillip George Callaghan and late Jane Peacock; *m* 1928, Zillah May Sampson (decd); two *s* one *d*. (and one *s* decd); *m* 1965, Doreen Rhys Draper. *Educ:* Bathurst High Sch., NSW; St Paul's Coll., Univ. of Sydney (BSc Agr. 1924); St John's Coll., Oxford (Rhodes Scholar, BSc 1926, DPhil 1928). Asst Plant Breeder, NSW, Dept of Agriculture, 1928-32; Principal, Roseworthy Agricultural Coll., South Australia, 1932-49; Asst Dir (Rural Industry) in Commonwealth Dept of War Organisation of Industry, 1943; Chm., Land Development Executive in South Australia, 1945-51; Dir of Agriculture, South Australia, 1949-59; Commercial Counsellor, Australian Embassy, Washington, DC, 1959-65; Chm., Australian Wheat Bd, 1965-71. Farrer Medal (for distinguished service to Australian Agriculture), 1954; FAIAS 1959. *Publications:* (with A. J. Millington) The Wheat Industry in Australia, 1956; numerous articles in scientific and agricultural jls on agricultural and animal husbandry matters. *Recreations:* swimming, riding, gardening. *Address:* Tralee, 22 Murray Street, Clapham, SA 5062, Australia. *T:* 276-6524.

CALLAGHAN, Sir Bede (Bertrand), Kt 1976; CBE 1968; Managing Director, Commonwealth Banking Corporation, 1965-76; Chancellor of the University of Newcastle, NSW, since 1977; *b* 16 March 1912; *s* of S. K. Callaghan and Amy M. Ryan; *m* 1940, Mary T. Brewer; three *d*. *Educ:* Newcastle High Sch. FBIA; FAIM. Commonwealth Bank, 1927. Mem. Board Executive Directors, IMF and World Bank, 1954-59; Gen. Man., Commonwealth Develt Bank of Australia, 1959-65; Chm., Aust. European Finance Corp. Ltd, 1971-76; Chm., Foreign Investment Review Bd, 1976-. Chm., Lewisham Hospital Adv. Bd, 1975-. Chairman: Aust. Admin. Staff Coll., 1969-76; Inst. of Industrial Economics, 1976-; Mem. Council, Univ. of Newcastle, NSW, 1966-, Dep. Chancellor, 1973-77. Hon. DSc Newcastle, 1973. *Recreation:* lawn bowls. *Address:* 69 Darnley Street, Gordon, NSW 2072, Australia. *T:* (Sydney) 498-7583. *Club:* Union (Sydney).

CALLAGHAN, Rear-Adm. Desmond Noble, CB 1970; FRSA; Director-General, National Supervisory Council for Intruder Alarms, 1971-77; *b* 24 Nov. 1915; *s* of Edmund Ford Callaghan and Kathleen Louise Callaghan (*née* Noble); *m* 1948, Patricia Munro Geddes; one *s* two *d*. *Educ:* RNC Dartmouth. HMS Frobisher, 1933; RNEC Keyhan, 1934; HM Ships: Royal Oak, 1937; Iron Duke, 1938; Warspite, 1939; Hereward, 1941; Prisoner of War, 1941; HMS Argonaut, 1945; HMS Glory, 1946; RNC Dartmouth, 1947; Admiralty, 1949; C-in-C Med. Staff, 1950; HMS Excellent, 1953; HMS Eagle, 1956; RN Tactical Sch., 1958; Admiralty, 1960; HMS Caledonia, 1962; Admiralty, 1965; Vice-Pres. and Pres., Ordnance Board, 1968-71, retired 1971. *Recreations:* Rugby, tennis, swimming. *Address:* Bridge End, Abbotsbrook, Bourne End, Bucks. *T:* Bourne End 20519.

CALLAGHAN, James; MP (Lab) Middleton and Prestwich, since Feb. 1974; *b* 28 Jan. 1927. Lectr, Manchester Coll., 1959-74. Metropolitan Borough Councillor, 1971-74. *Recreations:* sport and art. *Address:* 139 Hollin Lane, Middleton, Manchester M24 3LA.

CALLAGHAN, Rt. Hon. (Leonard) James, PC 1964; MP (Lab) South Cardiff, 1945-50, South-East Cardiff since 1950; *b* 27 March 1912; *s* of James Callaghan, Chief Petty Officer, RN; *m* 1938, Audrey Elizabeth Moulton; one *s* two *d*. *Educ:* Elementary and Portsmouth Northern Secondary Schs. Entered Civil Service as a Tax Officer, 1929; Asst Sec., Inland Revenue Staff Fed., 1936-47 (with an interval during the War of 1939-45, when served in Royal Navy). Joined Labour Party, 1931. Parly Sec., Min. of Transport, 1947-50; Chm. Cttee on Road Safety, 1948-50; Parliamentary and Financial Sec., Admiralty, 1950-51; Opposition Spokesman: Transport, 1951-53; Fuel and Power, 1953-55; Colonial Affairs, 1956-61; Shadow Chancellor, 1961-64; Chancellor of the Exchequer, 1964-67; Home Secretary, 1967-70; Shadow Home Sec., 1970-71; Opposition Spokesman on Employment, 1971-72; Shadow Foreign Sec., 1972-74; Sec. of State for Foreign and Commonwealth Affairs, 1974-76; Minister of Overseas Develt, 1975-76; Prime Minister and First Lord of the Treasury, 1976-79; Leader, Labour Party, 1976-80; Leader of the Opposition, 1979-80. Deleg. to Council of Europe, Strasburg, 1948-50 and 1954. Mem., Nat. Exec. Cttee, Labour Party, 1957-; Treasurer, Labour Party, 1967-76, Vice-Chm. 1973, Chm. 1974. Consultant to Police Fedn of England and Wales and to Scottish Police Fedn, 1955-64. Chm., Adv. Cttee on Oil Pollution of the Sea, 1952-63; Pres., United Kingdom Pilots Assoc., 1963-76; Hon. Pres., Internat. Maritime Pilots Assoc., 1971-76. Visiting Fellow, Nuffield Coll., Oxford, 1959-67, Hon. Life Fellow, 1967; Hon. Fellow: UC Cardiff, 1978; Portsmouth Polytechnic, 1981; Hon. LLD: University Coll. of Wales, 1976; Sardar Patel Univ., India, 1978; Univ. of Birmingham, 1981. Hon. Bencher, Inner Temple, 1976. Hon. Freeman: City of Cardiff, 1974; City of Sheffield, 1979. Hubert H. Humphrey Internat.

Award, 1978. Grand Cross, 1st class, Order of Merit of Federal Republic of Germany, 1979. *Publication:* A House Divided: the dilemma of Northern Ireland, 1973. *Address:* House of Commons, SW1.
See also Peter Jay.

CALLAGHAN, Morley (Edward); Canadian novelist; *b* Toronto, 1903; *s* of Thomas Callaghan and Mary (*née* Dewan); *m* 1929, Lorrete Florence, *d* of late Joseph Dee; two *s. Educ:* St Michael's Coll., Univ. of Toronto (BA); Osgoode Hall Law School. Holds Hon. Doctorates. Canadian Council Prize, 1970; $50,000 Royal Bank of Canada Award, 1970. *Publications:* Strange Fugitive, 1928; Native Argosy, 1929; It's Never Over, 1930; No Man's Meat, 1931; Broken Journey, 1932; Such Is My Beloved, 1934; They Shall Inherit the Earth, 1935; My Joy in Heaven, 1936; Now That April's Here, 1937; Just Ask for George (play), 1940; Jake Baldwin's Vow (for children), 1948; The Varsity Story, 1948; The Loved and the Lost, 1951; The Man with the Coat, 1955 (MacLean's Prize, 1955); A Many Coloured Coat, 1960 (UK 1963); A Passion in Rome, 1961 (UK 1964); That Summer in Paris, 1963; Morley Callaghan, vols 1 and 2, 1964; A Fine and Private Place, 1976; Close to the Sun Again, 1977; No Man's Meat and The Enchanted Pimp, 1978. *Recreation:* sports. *Address:* 20 Dale Avenue, Toronto, Ont., Canada.

CALLAN, Prof. Harold Garnet, FRS 1963; FRSE; MA, DSc; Professor of Natural History, St Salvator's College, St Andrews, since 1950; *b* 5 March 1917; *s* of Garnet George Callan and Winifred Edith Brazier; *m* 1944, Amarillis Maria Speranza, *d* of Dr R. Dohrn, Stazione Zoologica, Naples, Italy; one *s* two *d. Educ:* King's Coll. Sch., Wimbledon; St John's Coll., Oxford (Exhibitioner). Casberd Scholar, St John's Coll., 1937; Naples Biological Scholar, 1938, 1939. Served War of 1939-45, Telecommunications Research Establishment, 1940-45, Hon. Commission, RAFVR. Senior Scientific Officer, ARC, Inst. of Animal Genetics, Edinburgh, 1946-50. Member: Advisory Council on Scientific Policy, 1963-64; SRC, 1972-76; Council, Royal Soc., 1974-76. Trustee, British Museum (Natural History), 1963-66. Vis. Prof., Univ. of Indiana, Bloomington, USA, 1964-65; Master of United Coll. of St Salvator and St Leonard's, 1967-68. *Publications:* scientific papers, mostly on cytology and cell physiology. *Recreations:* shooting, carpentry. *Address:* 2 St Mary's Street, St Andrews, Fife. *T:* St Andrews 72311; The University, St Andrews, Fife.

CALLAN, Maj.-Gen. Michael, CB 1979; CBIM; Registrar of The Corporation of the Sons of the Clergy, since 1982; *b* 27 Nov. 1925; *s* of Major John Callan and Elsie Dorothy Callan (*née* Fordham); *m* 1948, Marie Evelyn Farthing; two *s. Educ:* Farnborough Grammar Sch., Hants. rcds, jssc, psc. Enlisted Hampshire Regt, 1943; commnd 1st (KGV's Own) Gurkha Rifles (The Malaun Regt), 1944; resigned commn, 1947; re-enlisted, 1948; re-commnd, RAOC, 1949; overseas service: India, Burma, French Indo China, Netherlands East Indies, 1944-47; Kenya, 1950-53; Malaya/Singapore, 1958-61; USA, 1966-68; Hong Kong, 1970-71; Comdr, Rhine Area, BAOR, 1975-76; Dir Gen., Ordnance Services, 1976-80; retired. Col Comdt, RAOC, 1981- (Rep. Col Comdt 1982). *Recreations:* golf, sailing, DIY, gardening. *Address:* c/o Williams & Glyn's Bank Ltd, Kirkland House, Whitehall, SW1A 2EB. *Club:* Army and Navy.

CALLARD, Sir Eric John, (Sir Jack Callard), Kt 1974; FEng; Chairman, British Home Stores Ltd, 1976-82 (Director 1975-82); *b* 15 March 1913; *s* of late F. Callard and Mrs A. Callard; *m* 1938, Pauline M. Pengelly; three *d. Educ:* Queen's Coll., Taunton; St John's Coll., Cambridge. 1st cl. Hons Mech. Sci. Tripos; BA 1935; MA 1973; Harvard Business Sch. (Adv. Management Programme, 1953). Joined ICI Ltd, 1935; seconded to Min. of Aircraft Prodn, 1942; ICI Paints Div., 1947 (Jt Man. Dir, 1955-59; Chm., 1959-64); Chairman: Deleg. Bd, ICI (Hyde) Ltd, 1959; ICI (Europa) Ltd, 1965-67; ICI Ltd, 1971-75 (Dir, 1964-75; Dep. Chm., 1967-71); Director: Pension Funds Securities Ltd, 1963-67; Imp. Metal Industries Ltd, 1964-67; Imp. Chemicals Insurance Ltd, 1966-70; Midland Bank Ltd, 1971-; Ferguson Industrial Holdings, 1975-; Commercial Union Assurance Co., 1976-; Equity Capital for Industry, 1976-. Member Council: BIM, 1964-69; Manchester Univ. Business Sch., 1964-71; Export Council for Europe, 1965-71; Member: CBI Steering Cttee on Europe, 1965-71; Cambridge Univ. Appointments Bd, 1968-71; CBI Overseas Cttee, 1969-71; Council of Industry for Management Educn, 1967-73; Appeal Cttee of British Sch. of Brussels, 1970-73; Royal Instn of GB, 1971-; Vice-President: Combustion Engnrg Assoc., 1968-75; Manchester Business Sch. Assoc., 1971- (Hon. Mem., 1966-; Pres., 1969-71); Pres., Industrial Participation Assoc., 1971-76 (Dep. Chm., 1967-; Chm., 1967-71). Member: Hansard Soc. Commn on Electoral Reform, 1975-76; Cttee of Inquiry into Industrial Democracy, 1976-77. Trustee, Civic Trust, 1972-75; Governor, London Business Sch., 1972-75. Mem. Court, British Shippers' Council, 1972-75. FRSA 1970; CBIM (FBIM 1966); Hon. FIMechE. Hon. DSc Cranfield Inst. of Technology, 1974. *Recreations:* games, fishing, fell walking. *Address:* Crookwath Cottage, High Row, Dockray, Penrith, Cumbria CA11 0LG. *Club:* Flyfishers'.

CALLAWAY, Sir Frank (Adams), Kt 1981; CMG 1975; OBE 1970; Professor and Head of Department of Music, University of Western Australia, since 1959; *b* 16 May 1919; *s* of Archibald Charles Callaway and Mabel Callaway (*née* Adams); *m* 1942, Kathleen Jessie, *d* of R. Allan; two *s* two *d. Educ:* West Christchurch High Sch.; Dunedin Teachers' Coll., NZ; Univ. of Otago, NZ (MusB); Royal Academy of Music. FRAM, ARCM, FTCL; FACE. Head, Dept of Music, King Edward Tech. Coll., Dunedin, NZ, 1942-53; Reader in Music, Univ. of WA, 1953-59. Mem., RNZAF Band,

1940-42. Conductor: King Edward Tech. Coll. Symphony Orchestra, 1945-53; Univ. of WA Orchestral Soc., 1953-64; Univ. of WA Choral Soc. 1953-79; Guest Conductor: WA Symphony Orchestra; S Australia Symphony Orchestra; Adelaide Philharmonic Choir; Orpheus Choir, Wellington, NZ. Member: Australian Music Examinations Bd, 1955- (Chm., 1964-66 and 1977-79); Australian Nat. Commn for UNESCO, 1968-; Adv. Bd, Commonwealth Assistance to Australian Composers, 1966-72; Music Bd, Australia Council, 1969-74; Founding Pres. and Life Mem., Australian Soc. for Music Educn, 1966-71; Mem., Bd of Dirs, Internat. Soc. for Music Educn, 1958- (Pres., 1968-72, Treasurer, 1972-); Mem. Exec. Bd, Internat. Music Council of UNESCO, 1976- (Pres., 1980-81). Founding Editor: Australian Jl of Music Educn, 1967-; Studies in Music, 1967-; also General Editor, Music Series and Music Monographs. W Australian Citizen of the Year, 1975. Hon. MusD W Australia, 1975. *Publications:* (General Editor) Challenges in Music Education, 1975; (ed with D. E. Tunley) Australian Composition in the Twentieth Century, 1978. *Recreations:* reading, gardening. *Address:* 32 Northmore Street, Daglish, WA 6008, Australia. *T:* 381.9813.

CALLENDER, Dr Maurice Henry; Ministry of Defence, 1977-80; retired, 1980; *b* 18 Dec. 1916; *s* of Harry and Lizbeth Callender; *m* 1941, Anne Kassel; two *s. Educ:* Univ. of Durham (MA, PhD). FSA. Commissioned: Royal Northumberland Fusiliers, 1939-41; RAF, 1941-45. Lectr, Huddersfield Technical Coll., 1945-47; Research, Univ. of Durham, 1947-49; Lectr, Bristol Univ. Extra-Mural Dept, 1949-53; MoD, 1953-62; Joint Services Staff Coll., 1959-60; Cabinet Office, 1962-64; MoD, 1964-70; Cabinet Office, 1970-73; Counsellor, Canberra, 1973-77. *Publications:* Roman Amphorae, 1965; various articles in archaeological jls. *Recreations:* oil painting, golf, bridge. *Address:* 24 Glanleam Road, Stanmore, Mddx. *T:* 01-954 1435. *Club:* Aldenham Golf and Country.

CALLEY, Sir Henry (Algernon), Kt 1964; DSO 1945; DFC 1943; DL; Owner and Manager of a stud, since 1948; *b* 9 Feb. 1914; *s* of Rev. A. C. M. Langton and Mrs Langton (*née* Calley); changed surname to Calley, 1974; unmarried. *Educ:* St John's Sch., Leatherhead. Taught at Corchester. Corbridge-on-Tyne, 1933-35; Bombay Burmah Trading Corp., 1935-36; teaching, 1936-38; Metropolitan Police Coll., and Police Force, 1938-41; Royal Air Force, 1941-48; Pilot in Bombers, Actg Wing Comdr, 1944. Mem. Wiltshire CC, 1955; Chm. Finance Cttee, 1959-68; Chm. of Council, 1968-73; Chm. Wessex Area Conservative Assoc., 1963-66. DL Wilts, 1968. *Recreation:* shooting.

CALLINAN, Sir Bernard (James), Kt 1977; CBE 1971; DSO 1945; MC 1943; Consultant, Gutteridge, Haskins & Davey Pty Ltd, since 1978 (Chairman and Managing Director, 1971-78); *b* 2 Feb. 1913; *s* of Michael Joseph Callinan and Mary Callinan (*née* Prendergast); *m* 1943, Naomi Marian Callinan (*née* Cullinan); five *s. Educ:* Univ. of Melbourne (BCE; Dip. Town and Regional Planning). Hon. FIE Aust (Pres., 1971-72; P. N. Russell Meml Medal, 1973); FICE; FTS. Lieut to Lt-Col, AIF, 1940-46. Asst Engr, A. Gordon Gutteridge, 1934; Associate, 1946, Sen. Partner, 1948-71, Gutteridge, Haskins & Davey. Director: West Gate Bridge Authority, 1965- (Dep. Chm., 1971, Chm., 1981-); British Petroleum Co. of Aust. Ltd, 1969-; CSR Ltd, 1978-. Commissioner: State Electricity Commn, 1963; Royal Commn of Inquiry, Aust. PO, 1973-74; Aust. Atomic Energy Commn, 1976-; Australian Broadcasting Commn, 1977-; Victorian Post Secondary Educn Commn, 1979-. Chm., New Parlt House Authority (Canberra), 1979-. Special Advr, Aust. Overseas Project Corpn, 1978-82. Mem., Pontifical Commn on Justice and Peace, Rome, 1977-. Councillor: La Trobe Univ., 1964-72; Melbourne Univ., 1976-81. Hon. Col, 4/19 Prince of Wales's Light Horse Regt, 1973-78. Kernot Meml Medal, 1982. *Publications:* Independent Company, 1953; John Monash, 1981; contribs to Jl Instn of Engrs, Aust., Jl Royal Soc. of Vic. *Address:* 111 Sackville Street, Kew, Vic 3101, Australia. *T:* 80.1230. *Clubs:* Melbourne, Australian, Naval and Military (Melbourne); Melbourne Cricket (Pres., 1979-).

CALLMAN, Clive Vernon; His Honour Judge Callman; a Circuit Judge, since 1973, assigned to South-Eastern Circuit; *b* 21 June 1927; *o s* of Felix Callman, DMD, LDS, RCS and Edith Callman, Walton-on-Thames, Surrey; *m* 1967, Judith Helen Hines, BA, DipSocStuds (Adelaide), *o d* of Gus Hines, OBE, JP, and Hilde Hines, Springfield, Adelaide, S Aust.; one *s* one *d. Educ:* Ottershaw Coll.; St George's Coll., Weybridge; LSE, Univ. of London. BSc(Econ), Commercial Law. Called to the Bar, Middle Temple, 1951; Blackstone Pupillage Prizeman, 1951; practised as Barrister, London and Norwich, 1952-73, South-Eastern Circuit; Hon. Mem., Central Criminal Court Bar Mess; Dep. Circuit Judge in Civil and Criminal Jurisdiction, 1971-73. Dir, Woburn Press, Publishers, 1971-73; dir of finance cos, 1961-73. University of London: Fac. Mem., Standing Cttee of Convocation, 1954-79; Senator, 1978-; Mem. Careers Adv. Bd, 1979-; Mem., Commerce Degree Bureau Cttee, 1980; Mem., Adv. Cttee for Magistrates' Courses, 1979-; Vice-Pres., Graduates' Soc. Mem. Exec. Cttee, Soc. of Labour Lawyers, 1958; Chm., St Marylebone Constituency Labour Party, 1960-62. Mem. Council, Anglo-Jewish Assoc., 1956-. Editor, Clare Market Review, 1947; Mem. Editl Bd, Media Law and Practice. *Recreations:* reading, travelling, the arts. *Address:* 11 Constable Close, NW11 6UA. *T:* 01-458 3010. *Club:* Bar Yacht.

CALLOW, Robert Kenneth, FRS 1958; MA, DPhil, BSc; Member of Staff, Rothamsted Experimental Station, 1966-72; Member of Scientific Staff, Medical Research Council, 1929-66; *b* 15 Feb. 1901; 2nd *s* of late Cecil

Burman Callow and Kate Peverell; *m* 1937, Nancy Helen, *d* of J. E. Newman; one *s* one *d*. *Educ*: City of London Sch.; Christ Church, Oxford. Exhibitioner, 1919, and Research Scholar, 1927, of Christ Church. Served in RAF, 1940-45; relief of Datta Khel, 1941 (despatches). Mem. of Editorial Board, Biochemical Journal, 1946-53 (Dep. Chm., 1951-53); Chm., Biological and Medical Abstracts Ltd, 1955-61; Mem. of Council, Bee Research Association, 1962-74 (Chm., 1963-68; Vice-Pres., 1974-); Visitor, Royal Instn of GB, 1970-73. *Publications*: papers (many jointly) in jls of learned societies. *Recreations*: gardening, stamp-collecting, natural history. *Address*: Marrinagh, Ballajora, Maughold, Isle of Man.

CALMAN, Mel; artist, writer; cartoonist for The Times, The Sunday Times, and others; *b* 19 May 1931; *s* of Clement and Anna Calman; *m* 1st, 1957, Pat McNeill (marr. diss.); two *d*; 2nd, Karen Usborne (marr. diss. 1982). *Educ*: Perse School, Cambridge; St Martin's School of Art, London (NDD); Goldsmiths' Coll., London (ATD). Cartoonist for Daily Express, 1957-63; BBC Tonight Programme, 1963-64; Sunday Telegraph, 1964-65; Observer, 1965-66; Sunday Times, 1969-; The Times, 1979-. Free lance cartoonist for various magazines and newspapers, 1957-; also designer of book-jackets, advertising campaigns, and illustrator of books; started The Workshop-gallery devoted to original cartoons, illustrations etc., 1970; produced animated cartoon, The Arrow; syndicated feature, Men & Women, USA, 1976-82. FRSA; FSIA; AGI. *Publications*: Through The Telephone Directory, 1962; Bed-Sit, 1963; Boxes, 1964; Calman & Women, 1967; The Penguin Calman, 1968; (contrib.) The Evacuees, ed B. S. Johnson, 1968; My God, 1970; Couples, 1972; This Pestered Isle, 1973; (contrib.) All Bull, ed B. S. Johnson, 1973; The New Penguin Calman, 1977; Dictionary of Psychoanalysis, 1979; "But It's My Turn to Leave You", 1980; "How About a Little Quarrel before Bed?", 1981; Help!, 1982. *Recreations*: brooding and worrying. *Address*: 83 Lambs Conduit Street, WC1. *T*: 01-242 5335. *Club*: Garrick.

CALNAN, Prof. Charles Dermod, MA, MB, BChir Cantab; FRCP; Director, Department of Occupational Dermatoses, St John's Hospital for Diseases of the Skin, since 1974; Consultant Dermatologist, Royal Free Hospital and St John's Hospital for Diseases of the Skin, London; *b* 14 Dec. 1917; *s* of James Calnan, Eastbourne, Sussex; *m* 1950, Josephine Gerard Keane, *d* of late Lt-Col Michael Keane, RAMC; three *s* one *d*. *Educ*: Stonyhurst Coll.; Corpus Christi Coll., Cambridge; London Hospital. 1st Cl. Hons Nat. Sci. Trip., Cambridge 1939. RAMC Specialist in Dermatology, Major, 1942-46; Marsden Prof., Royal Free Hosp., 1958; Visiting Research Associate, Univ. of Pennsylvania, 1959; Prof. of Dermatology, Inst. of Dermatology, 1960-74. WHO Cons. Adviser to Nat. Inst. of Dermatology of Thailand, 1971-. Editor: Transactions of the St John's Hosp. Dermatological Soc., 1958-75; Contact Dermatitis, 1975-. Mem. BMA; Mem. Brit. Assoc. of Dermatology. FRSocMed (Mem. Dermatological Section); Fellow Hunterian Soc. *Publications*: Atlas of Dermatology, 1974; various papers in med. and dermatological jls. *Recreations*: squash, books, theatre. *Address*: 109 Harley Street, W1.

CALNAN, Prof. James Stanislaus, FRCP; FRCS; Professor of Plastic and Reconstructive Surgery, University of London, at the Royal Postgraduate Medical School and Hammersmith Hospital, since 1970; *b* 12 March 1916; *e s* of James and Gertrude Calnan, Eastbourne, Sussex; *m* 1949, Joan (formerly County Councillor for Great Berkhamsted and Dacorum District Councillor, and Town Councillor, Berkhamsted), *e d* of George Frederick and Irene Maud Williams, Roath Park, Cardiff; one *d*. *Educ*: Stonyhurst Coll.; Univ. of London at London Hosp. Med. Sch. LDS RCS 1941; MRCS, LRCP 1943; DA 1944; DTM&H 1948; MRCP (London and Edinburgh) 1948; FRCS 1949. Served War of 1939-45, F/Lt RAF, UK, France, India. RMO, Hosp. for Tropical Diseases, 1948; Sen. Lectr, Nuffield Dept of Plastic Surgery, Oxford, 1954; Hammersmith Hospital and Royal Postgraduate Med. Sch.: Lectr in Surgery, 1960; Reader, 1965; Professor, 1970. Hunterian Prof. RCS, 1959. Vis. Prof. in Plastic Surgery, Univ. of Pennsylvania, 1959. Member: BMA; British Assoc. of Plastic Surgeons; Sen. Mem., Surgical Research Soc. Fellow, Royal Soc. of Medicine; FCST 1966. Clemson Award for Bioengineering, 1980. *Publications*: contribs to medical and scientific jls and chapters in books, on cleft palate, wound healing, lymphatic diseases, venous thrombosis, research methods and organisation. *Recreations*: gardening, carpentry, reading and writing. *Address*: White Haven, 23 Kings Road, Berkhamsted, Herts. *T*: Berkhamsted 2320; Royal Postgraduate Medical School, Ducane Road, W12 0HS. *T*: 01-743 2030.
See also Prof. C. D. Calnan.

CALNE, Prof. Roy Yorke, MA, MS; FRCS; FRS 1974; Professor of Surgery, University of Cambridge, since 1965; Fellow of Trinity Hall, Cambridge, since 1965; Hon. Consulting Surgeon, Addenbrooke's Hospital, Cambridge, since 1965; *b* 30 Dec. 1930; *s* of Joseph Robert and Eileen Calne; *m* 1956, Patricia Doreen Whelan; two *s* four *d*. *Educ*: Lancing Coll.; Guy's Hosp. Med. Sch. MB, BS London with Hons (Distinction in Medicine), 1953. House Appts, Guy's Hosp., 1953-54; RAMC, 1954-56 (RMO to KEO 2nd Gurkhas); Deptl Anatomy Demonstrator, Oxford Univ., 1957-58; SHO Nuffield Orthopædic Centre, Oxford, 1958; Surg. Registrar, Royal Free Hosp., 1958-60; Harkness Fellow in Surgery, Peter Bent Brigham Hosp., Harvard Med. Sch., 1960-61; Lectr in Surgery, St Mary's Hosp., London, 1961-62; Sen. Lectr and Cons. Surg., Westminster Hosp., 1962-65; Mem., Ct of Examiners, RCS, 1970-76. Royal Coll. of Surgeons: Hallet Prize, 1957; Jacksonian Prize, 1961; Hunterian Prof., 1962; Cecil Joll Prize, 1966; Mem. Council. Fellow Assoc. of Surgeons of Gt Brit.; Mem. Surgical Research Soc.;

Corresp. Fellow, Amer. Surgical Assoc., 1972, Hon. Fellow 1981. Prix de la Société Internationale de Chirurgie, 1969; Faltin Medal, Finnish Surgical Soc., 1977. *Publications*: Renal Transplantations, 1963, 2nd edn 1967; (with H. Ellis) Lecture Notes in Surgery, 1965, 5th edn 1970; A Gift of Life, 1970; (ed and contrib.) Clinical Organ Transplantation, 1971; (ed and contrib.) Immunological Aspects of Transplantation Surgery, 1973; papers on tissue transplantation and general surgery; sections in several surgical text-books. *Recreations*: tennis, squash. *Address*: 22 Barrow Road, Cambridge. *T*: Cambridge 59831.

CALNE AND CALSTONE, Viscount; Simon Henry George Petty-Fitzmaurice; *b* 24 Nov. 1970; *s* and *heir* of Earl of Shelburne, *qv*.

CALTHORPE; see Anstruther-Gough-Calthorpe, and Gough-Calthorpe.

CALTHORPE, 10th Baron *cr* 1796; **Peter Waldo Somerset Gough-Calthorpe;** Bt 1728; *b* 13 July 1927; *s* of late Hon. Frederick Somerset Gough-Calthorpe and Rose Mary Dorothy, *d* of late Leveson William Vernon-Harcourt; *S* brother, 1945; *m* 1st, 1956, Saranne (marr. diss. 1971), *o d* of James Harold Alexander, Ireland; 2nd, 1979, Elizabeth, *d* of James and Sibyl Young, Guildford, Surrey. *Heir*: none. *Address*: c/o Isle of Man Bank Ltd, 2 Athol Street, Douglas, Isle of Man.

CALVERLEY, 3rd Baron *cr* 1945; **Charles Rodney Muff;** Member of the West Yorkshire Metropolitan Police; *b* 2 Oct. 1946; *s* of 2nd Baron Calverley and of Mary, *d* of Arthur Farrar, Halifax; *S* father, 1971; *m* 1972, Barbara Ann, *d* of Jonathan Brown, Kelbrook, nr Colne; two *s*. *Educ*: Fulneck School for Boys. *Heir*: *s* Hon. Jonathan Edward Muff, *b* 16 April 1975. *Address*: 110 Buttershaw Lane, Wibsey, Bradford, W Yorks BD6 2DA.

CALVERT, Mrs Barbara Adamson, QC 1975; barrister-at-law; a Recorder of the Crown Court, since 1980; *b* 30 April 1926; *d* of late Albert Parker, CBE; *m* 1948, John Thornton Calvert, CBE; one *s* one *d*. *Educ*: St Helen's, Northwood; London Sch. of Economics (BScEcon). Called to Bar, Middle Temple, 1959, Bencher 1982; admitted Sen. Bar of NI, 1978. Admin. Officer, City and Guilds of London Inst., 1961; practice at Bar, 1962-. Part-time Chm., Industrial Tribunals, London, 1974-. *Recreations*: gardening, swimming, poetry. *Address*: (home) 158 Ashley Gardens, SW1P 1HW; (chambers) 4 Brick Court, Temple, EC4Y 7AN.

CALVERT, Florence Irene, (Mrs W. A. Prowse); Principal, St Mary's College, University of Durham, 1975-77; *b* 1 March 1912; *d* of Ernest William Calvert and Florence Alice (*née* Walton); *m* 1977, William Arthur Prowse (*d* 1981). *Educ*: Univ. of Sheffield (BA, 1st Cl. Hons French and Latin, MA). Asst Language Teacher, Accrington Grammar Sch., 1936-39; Head, Modern Langs Dept, Accrington Girls' High Sch., 1939-48; Univ. of Durham: Lectr in Educn, 1948; Sen. Lectr, 1964-75. *Publications*: French Plays for the Classroom, 1951; L'Homme aux Mains Rouges, 1954; Contes, 1957; French by Modern Methods in Primary and Secondary Schools, 1965. *Address*: 7 St Mary's Close, Shincliffe, Durham DH1 2ND. *T*: Durham 65502.

CALVERT, Henry Reginald, Dr Phil; Keeper of Department of Astronomy and Geophysics in Science Museum, South Kensington, 1949-67; Keeper Emeritus, 1967-69; *b* 25 Jan. 1904; *e s* of late H. T. Calvert, MBE, DSc, of Min. of Health; *m* 1938, Eileen Mary Frow; two *d*. *Educ*: Bridlington Sch., East Yorks; St John's Coll., Oxford (Scholar, MA); Univ. of Göttingen, Germany (Dr Phil). 1st Cl. Hons BSc (External) London, 1925; Goldsmiths' Company's Exhibitioner, 1925. Research Physicist, ICI, 1928-30; Research Physicist, Callender's Cable & Construction Co., 1932-34. Entered Science Museum, 1934; Dep. Keeper, 1946. Ballistics research for Min. of Supply, 1940-46. Hon. Treas., British Soc. for History of Science, 1952-63. Fellow Royal Astronomical Soc. *Publications*: Astronomy, Globes, Orreries and other Models, 1967; Scientific Trade Cards, 1971; papers in learned journals. *Recreations*: chess, bridge, croquet, gardening. *Address*: 17 Burnham Drive, Reigate, Surrey RH2 9HD. *T*: Reigate 46893.

CALVERT, Louis Victor Denis; Comptroller and Auditor General for Northern Ireland, since 1980; *b* 20 April 1924; *s* of Louis Victor Calvert, Belfast and Gertrude Cherry Hobson, Belfast; *m* 1949, Vivien Millicent Lawson; two *s* one *d*. *Educ*: Belfast Royal Academy; Queen's Univ., Belfast (BScEcon); Admin. Staff Coll., Henley-on-Thames. Served with RAF, 1943-47, navigator (F/O). Northern Ireland Civil Service, 1947-: Min. of Agriculture, 1947-56; Dep. Principal 1951; Principal, Min. of Finance, 1956-63; Min. of Health and Local Govt, 1963-65; Asst Sec. 1964; Min. of Development, 1965-73; Sen. Asst Sec. 1970; Dep. Sec. 1971; Min. of Housing, Local Govt and Planning, 1973-76; DoE for NI, 1976-80. *Recreations*: gardening, golf, reading. *Address*: Exchequer and Audit Department, Rosepark House, Upper Newtownards Road, Belfast BT4 2NS.

CALVERT, Norman Hilton; retired; Deputy Secretary, Departments of the Environment and of Transport, 1978-80; *b* 27 July 1925; *s* of Clifford and Doris Calvert; *m* 1st, 1949, May Yates (*d* 1968); one *s* one *d*; 2nd, 1971, Vera Baker. *Educ*: Leeds Modern Sch.; Leeds Univ.; King's Coll., Durham Univ. BA Hons 1st cl. Geography, 1950. Served Royal Signals, 1943-47: 81 (W African) Div., India, 1945-47. Min. of Housing and Local Govt: Asst Principal, 1950-55; Principal, 1956-64; Asst Sec., 1964-71; Sec., Water Resources Bd, 1964-68; Principal Regional Officer, Northern Region, 1969-71; Regional Dir, Northern Region, and Chm, Northern Econ. Planning Bd,

1971-73; Under Sec., DoE, 1971-78. *Recreations:* fell walking, listening to music, motoring. *Address:* Treetops, Roundhill Way, Cobham, Surrey. *T:* Oxshott 2738.

CALVERT, Phyllis; actress; *b* 18 Feb. 1917; *d* of Frederick and Annie Bickle; *m* 1941, Peter Murray Hill (*d* 1957); one *s* one *d. Educ:* Margaret Morris Sch.; Institut Français. Malvern Repertory Company, 1935; Coventry, 1937; York, 1938. First appeared in London in A Woman's Privilege, Kingsway Theatre, 1939; Punch Without Judy, Embassy, 1939; Flare Path, Apollo, 1942; Escapade, St James's, 1953; It's Never Too Late, Strand, 1954; River Breeze, Phoenix, 1956; The Complaisant Lover, Globe, 1959; The Rehearsal, Globe, 1961; Ménage à Trois, Lyric, 1963; Portrait of Murder, Savoy, Vaudeville, 1963; A Scent of Flowers, Duke of York's, 1964; Present Laughter, Queen's, 1965; A Woman of No Importance, Vaudeville, 1967; Blithe Spirit, Globe, 1970; Crown Matrimonial, Haymarket, 1973; Dear Daddy, Ambassadors, 1976; Mrs Warren's Profession, Worcester, 1977; She Stoops to Conquer, Old World, Exeter, 1978; Suite in Two Keys, tour, 1978; Before the Party, Queen's, 1980. *Films include:* Kipps, The Young Mr Pitt, Man in Grey, Fanny by Gaslight, Madonna of the Seven Moons, They were Sisters, Time out of Mind, Broken Journey, My Own True Love, The Golden Madonna, A Woman with No Name, Mr Denning Drives North, Mandy, The Net, It's Never Too Late, Child in the House, Indiscreet, The Young and The Guilty, Oscar Wilde, Twisted Nerve, Oh! What a Lovely War, The Walking Stick. TV series: Kate, 1970. *Recreations:* swimming, gardening, collecting costume books. *Address:* Argyll Lodge, Towersey, Thame, Oxon.

CALVIN, Prof. Melvin; University Professor of Chemistry, University of California, since 1971; Professor of Molecular Biology, since 1963; *b* 8 April 1911; *s* of Rose and Elias Calvin; *m* 1942, Marie Genevieve Jemtegaard; one *s* two *d. Educ:* Univ. of Minnesota, Minneapolis (PhD). Fellow, Univ. of Manchester, 1935-37. Univ. of California, Berkeley: Instr., 1937; Asst Prof., 1941-45; Assoc. Prof., 1945-47; Prof., 1947-71; Dir, Laboratory of Chemical Biodynamics, 1960-80; Associate Dir, Lawrence Berkeley Lab., 1967-80. Foreign Mem., Royal Society, 1959. Member: Nat. Acad. of Sciences (US); Royal Netherlands Acad. of Sciences and Letters; Amer. Philos. Society. Nobel Prize in Chemistry, 1961; Davy Medal, Royal Society, 1964; Virtanen Medal, 1975; Gibbs Medal, 1977; Priestley Medal, 1978; Amer. Inst. Chemists Gold Medal, 1979. Hon. Degrees: Michigan Coll. of Mining and Technology, 1955; Univ. of Nottingham, 1958; Oxford Univ., 1959; Northwestern Univ., 1961; Univ. of Notre Dame, 1965; Brooklyn Polytechnic Inst., 1969; Rijksuniversiteit-Gent, 1970; Columbia Univ., 1979. *Publications:* very numerous, including (6 books): Theory of Organic Chemistry (with Branch), 1941; Isotopic Carbon (with Heidelberger, Reid, Tolbert and Yankwich), 1949; Chemistry of Metal Chelate Compounds (with Martell), 1952; Path of Carbon in Photosynthesis (with Bassham), 1957; Chemical Evolution, 1961; Photosynthesis of Carbon Compounds (with Bassham), 1962; Chemical Evolution, 1969. *Address:* University of California, Berkeley, Calif 94720, USA; (home) 2683 Buena Vista Way, Berkeley, Calif 94708, USA. *T:* 848-4036.

CALVINO, Italo; Italian writer; *b* 15 Oct. 1923; *s* of Mario Calvino and Eva Mameli; *m* 1964, Chichita Singer; one *d.* Hon. Member, American Academy and Institute of Arts and Letters, 1975; Oesterreichisches Staatspreis für Europäische Literatur, 1976; Grande Aigle d'Or du Festival du Livre de Nice, 1982. *Publications:* Il sentiero dei nidi di ragno (The Path of the Spider's Nest), 1947; Il visconte dimezzato (The Cloven Viscount), 1951; Fiabe italiane (Italian Folktales), 1956; Il barone rampante (The Baron on the Trees), 1957; Il cavaliere inesistente (The Nonexistent Knight), 1959; Cosmicomiche (Cosmicomics), 1965; Il castello dei destini incrociati (The Castle of Crossed Destinies), 1969; Le città invisibli (Invisible Cities), 1972; Se una notte d'inverno un viaggiatore (If on a Winter's Night a Traveller), 1979. *Address:* c/o G. Einaudi Editore SpA, via Gregoriana 38, Rome, Italy.

CALVO, Roberto Q.; see Querejazu Calvo.

CALVOCORESSI, Peter (John Ambrose); author; Chairman, Open University Educational Enterprises Ltd, since 1979; *b* 17 Nov. 1912; *s* of Pandia Calvocoressi and Irene (Ralli); *m* 1938, Barbara Dorothy Eden, *d* of 6th Baron Henley; two *s. Educ:* Eton (King's Scholar); Balliol Coll. Oxford. Called to Bar, 1935. RAF Intelligence, 1940-45; Wing Comdr. Trial of Major War Criminals, Nuremberg, 1945-46. Contested (L) Nuneaton, 1945. Staff of Royal Institute of International Affairs, 1949-54; Mem. Council, Royal Inst. of Internat. Affairs, 1955-70; Reader (part time) in International Relations, Univ. of Sussex, 1965-71; Member: Council, Inst. for Strategic Studies, 1961-71; Council, Inst. of Race Relations, 1970-71; UN Sub-Commn on the Prevention of Discrimination and Protection of Minorities, 1962-71; Chm., The Africa Bureau, 1963-71; Mem., Internat. Exec., Amnesty International, 1969-71; Chm., The London Library, 1970-73; Dep. Chm., N Metropolitan Conciliation Cttee, 1967-71. Dir of Chatto & Windus Ltd and The Hogarth Press Ltd, 1954-65; Editorial Dir, 1972-76, Publisher and Chief Exec., 1973-76, Penguin Books. *Publications:* Nuremberg: The Facts, the Law and the Consequences, 1947; Surveys of International Affairs, vol. 1, 1947-48; 1950; vol. 2, 1949-50, 1951; vol. 3, 1951, 1952; vol. 4, 1952, 1953; vol. 5, 1953, 1954; Middle East Crisis (with Guy Wint), 1957; South Africa and World Opinion, 1961; World Order and New States, 1962; World Politics since 1945, 1968; (with Guy Wint) Total War, 1972; The British Experience 1945-75, 1978; Top Secret Ultra, 1980. *Recreation:* walking. *Address:* 1 Queen's Parade, Bath. *T:* Bath 333903. *Club:* Garrick.

CAMBELL, Rear-Adm. Dennis Royle Farquharson, CB 1960; DSC 1940; *b* 13 Nov. 1907; *s* of Dr Archibald Cambell and Edith Cambell, Southsea; *m* 1933, Dorothy Elinor Downes; two *d. Educ:* Westminster Sch. Joined RN, 1925, HMS Thunderer Cadet Training; trained as FAA pilot, 1931; 1st Capt. of HMS Ark Royal IV, 1955-56; retired, 1960. *Address:* The Old School House, Colemore, Alton, Hants.

CAMBRIDGE, Sydney John Guy, CMG 1979; CVO 1979; HM Diplomatic Service; Ambassador in Rabat, since 1982; *b* 5 Nov. 1928; *o s* of late Jack and of Mona Cambridge; unmarried. *Educ:* Marlborough; King's Coll., Cambridge (BA). Entered HM Diplomatic Service, Sept. 1952; Oriental Sec., British Embassy, Jedda, 1952-56; Foreign Office, 1956-60; First Sec., UK Delegn to United Nations, at New York, 1960-64; Head of Chancery, British Embassy, Djakarta, 1964-66; FO, 1966-70; Counsellor, British Embassy, Rome, 1970-73; Head of Financial Relations Dept, FCO, 1973-75; Counsellor, British High Commn, Nicosia, 1975-77; Ambassador to Kuwait, 1977-82. *Address:* c/o Foreign and Commonwealth Office, SW1.

CAMDEN, 5th Marquess *cr* 1812; **John Charles Henry Pratt;** Baron Camden, 1765; Earl Camden, Viscount Bayham, 1786; Earl of Brecknock, 1812; DL, JP; Major R of O; late Scots Guards; *b* 12 April 1899; *er s* of 4th Marquess Camden, GCVO and Lady Joan Marion Nevill, CBE 1920 (*d* 1952), *d* of 3rd Marquess of Abergavenny; *S* father, 1943; *m* 1st, 1920, Marjorie (who obtained a divorce, 1941) (*see* Marjorie, Countess of Brecknock, DBE); one *s* one *d*; 2nd, 1942, Averil (*d* 1977), *er d* of late Col Henry Sidney John Streatfeild, DSO; one *s*; 3rd, 1978, Rosemary, *yr d* of late Brig. Hanbury Pawle, CBE, DL. *Educ:* Ludgrove, New Barnet, Herts; Eton Coll.; RMC Sandhurst. ADC to Gen. Lord Jeffreys, GOC London Dist, 1920-24. Raised and formed 45th Battery 16th Light AA Regt RA, 1938, and commanded during early part of war of 1939-45, then rejoined Scots Guards; late Hon. Col 516th LAA Regt, RA; Gold Staff at Coronation of King George VI and Queen Elizabeth, 1937. DL, JP, Kent. Conservative Peer: Younger Brother of Trinity House. Dir, Darracq Motor Engineering Co., Bayard Cars Ltd and late Dir of many cos; Dir, Nat. Sporting Club, 1937-40; Director: RAC Buildings Co. Ltd; RAC Country Club Ltd; RAC Travel Service Ltd; President: Tonbridge Area League of Mercy; Tunbridge Wells Area of RSPCA; SE Counties Agricultural Soc., 1948 (and Mem. Council); Tunbridge Wells Amateur Dramatic and Operatic Soc.; Royal Agricultural Soc. of England; Joint Pres. Royal Tunbridge Wells Civic Assoc.; Chm. Bd of Trustees, Living of King Charles-the-Martyr, Tunbridge Wells; Pres. St Pancras Almshouses; a Vice-Pres. and Mem. Cttee of Management of Royal Nat. Life-Boat Inst.; Mem. Council of Boy Scouts Assoc. for County of Kent; Hon. Pres., RAC Motor Sport Council. Late President: Women's Lying-in Hosp., Vincent Sq., SW1; Kent and Sussex Hosp., Tunbridge Wells; late Vice-Pres. Royal Northern Hospital, N7; late Trustee Kent Playing Fields Association. FMI. *Recreations:* shooting, boxing, motor-car racing, yachting, motor-boat racing; interests: farming and forestry. *Heir: s* Earl of Brecknock, *qv. Address:* Bayham Manor, Lamberhurst, Kent. *T:* Lamberhurst 890 500; 42 Limerston Street, SW10. *T:* 01-352 7838. *Clubs:* Brooks's (Life Mem.), Cavalry and Guards, Pratt's, Turf, Royal Automobile (Senior Vice-Chm., 1952, Vice-Pres., 1978-), British Automobile Racing, MCC; Royal Yacht Squadron (Vice-Cdre 1954-65); House of Lords Yacht (Vice-Cdre); Royal Motor Yacht (Vice-Adm.); Marine Motoring Assoc. (Vice-Pres.); Royal Naval Sailing Assoc. (Hon. Mem.); Yachtsmen's Assoc. of America (Hon. Mem.), etc.

CAMDEN, John; Chairman since 1974 and Managing Director since 1966, Ready Mixed Concrete Ltd; *b* 18 Nov. 1925; *s* of late Joseph Reginald Richard John Camden and Lilian Kate McCann; *m* 1972, Diane Mae Friese; two *d* (and one *s* two *d* of former *m*). *Educ:* Worcester Royal Grammar Sch.; Birmingham Univ. (BSc). Royal Tank Corps and Intell. Corps, 1943-47. Joined Ready Mixed Concrete Group, 1952; Dir responsible for Group's ops in Europe, 1962. Grand Decoration of Honour in Silver (Austria), 1978. *Recreations:* golf, gardening. *Address:* Westbourn, Wentworth, Surrey.

CAME, William Gerald, CIE 1944; BSc (Bristol); retired civil engineer; *b* 8 Dec. 1889; *s* of late John Mathew and Elizabeth Bessie Came, Woodhuish Barton, Brixham, Devon; *m* 1st, 1916, Ada Coombs; one *s* one *d* ; 2nd, 1937, Gertrude Marie Farmer; one *s.* Chief Engineer and Sec. to Govt (Roads and Buildings Dept), Bihar, India, 1942-45; retired 1945; re-appointed as Chief Engineer and Secretary of the I and E Depts, 1945-48. Appointed to PWD (B and O) in 1913; previously with T. B. Cooper & Co., Civil Engineers, Bristol. Old Totnesian and an Associate of Univ. Coll., Bristol. *Address:* Somerley View, Ringwood, Hants. *T:* Ringwood 3733.

CAMERON, Hon. Lord; John Cameron, KT 1978; Kt 1954; DSC; LLD Aberdeen and Edinburgh; DLitt Heriot-Watt; FRSE; HRSA; FRSGS; DL; a Senator of The College of Justice in Scotland and Lord of Session since 1955; *b* 1900; *m* 1st, 1927, Eileen Dorothea (*d* 1943), *d* of late H. M. Burrell; one *s* two *d* ; 2nd, 1944, Iris, *widow* of Lambert C. Shepherd. *Educ:* Edinburgh Acad.; Edinburgh Univ. Served European War, 1918, with RNVR; Advocate, 1924; Advocate-Depute, 1929-36; QC (Scotland), 1936. Served with RNVR, Sept. 1939-44 (despatches, DSC); released to reserve, Dec. 1944. Sheriff of Inverness, Elgin and Nairn, 1945; Sheriff of Inverness, Moray, Nairn and Ross and Cromarty, 1946-48; Dean of Faculty of Advocates, 1948-55. Member: Cttee on Law of Contempt of Court, 1972-; Royal Commn on Civil Liability and Compensation for Personal Injury, 1973-78. DL Edinburgh, 1953. *Address:* 28 Moray Place, Edinburgh. *T:* 031-225 7585.

Clubs: New, Scottish Arts (Edinburgh); Royal Forth Yacht.
See also D. B. Weir.

CAMERON, Prof. Alan Douglas Edward, FBA 1975; Anthon Professor of Latin Language and Literature, Columbia University, New York, since 1977; *b* 13 March 1938; *er s* of A. D. Cameron, Egham; *m* 1962, Averil Sutton (marr. diss. 1980; *see* Averil Cameron); one *s* one *d. Educ:* St Paul's Sch. (Schol.); New Coll., Oxford (Schol.). Craven Scholar 1958; 1st cl. Hon. Mods 1959; De Paravicini Scholar 1960; Chancellor's Prize for Latin Prose 1960; 1st cl. Lit. Hum. 1961; N. H. Baynes Prize 1967; John Conington Prize 1968. Asst Master, Brunswick Sch., Haywards Heath, 1956-57; Asst Lectr, then Lectr, in Humanity, Glasgow Univ., 1961-64; Lectr in Latin, 1964-71, Reader, 1971-72, Bedford Coll., London; Prof. of Latin, King's Coll., London, 1972-77. Vis. Prof., Columbia Univ., NY, 1967-68. Fellow, Amer. Acad. of Arts and Sciences, 1979. *Publications:* Claudian: Poetry and Propaganda at the Court of Honorius, 1970; (contrib.) Prosopography of the Later Roman Empire, ed Jones, Morris and Martindale, i, 1971, ii, 1980; Porphyrius the Charioteer, 1973; Bread and Circuses, 1974; Circus Factions, 1976; The Greek Anthology, 1982; articles and reviews in learned jls. *Recreation:* the cinema. *Address:* 454 Riverside Drive, New York, NY 10027, USA. *T:* 662 9319; Columbia University, Morningside Heights, New York, NY 10027, USA.

CAMERON, Lt-Gen. Sir Alexander (Maurice), KBE 1952; CB 1945; MC; retired; *b* 30 May 1898; *s* of late Major Sir Maurice Alexander Cameron, KCMG; *m* 1922, Loveday (*d* 1965), *d* of Col W. D. Thomson, CMG. *Educ:* Wellington Coll. 2nd Lieut Royal Engineers, 1916. Served European War, France and Belgium (wounded, despatches, MC, 2 medals); S Persia (medal and clasp); Iraq and Kurdistan (two clasps); psc 1929. Brevet Lieut-Col, 1939; RAF Staff Coll., 1939; Brig., 1940; Maj.-Gen. 1943; SHAEF, 1944-45; Dep. QMG, 1945-48; Maj.-Gen. i/c Administration, MELF, 1948-51; GOC East African Comd, 1951-53; retired 1954; Director of Civil Defence South-Eastern Region (Tunbridge Wells), 1955-60. *Club:* Army and Navy.

CAMERON, Major Allan John, JP; Vice Lord-Lieutenant, Highland Region (Ross and Cromarty), since 1977; *b* 25 March 1917; *s* of Col Sir Donald Cameron of Lochiel, KT, CMG (*d* 1951), and Lady Hermione Cameron (*d* 1978), *d* of 5th Duke of Montrose; *m* 1945, Mary Elizabeth Vaughan-Lee, Dillington, Somerset; two *s* two *d* (and one *s* decd.). *Educ:* Harrow; RMC Sandhurst. Served QO Cameron Highlanders, 1936-48; Major, Retd (POW Middle East, 1942). County Councillor, Ross-shire, 1955-75 (Chm. Educn Cttee, 1962-75); former Member: Red Deer Commn; Countryside Commn for Scotland; Broadcasting Council for Scotland. *Recreations:* curling (Past Pres. Royal Caledonian Curling Club), gardening, golf. *Address:* Allangrange, Munlochy, Ross-shire. *T:* Munlochy 249. *Club:* Naval and Military.
See also Col Sir Donald Cameron of Lochiel.

CAMERON, Prof. Averil Millicent, MA, PhD; FBA 1981; FSA; Professor of Ancient History, University of London, at King's College, since 1978; *b* 8 Feb. 1940; *d* of T. R. Sutton, Leek, Staffs; *m* 1962, Alan Douglas Edward Cameron, *qv* (marr. diss. 1980); one *s* one *d. Educ:* Westwood Hall Girls' High Sch., Leek, Staffs; Somerville Coll., Oxford (Passmore Edwards Schol. 1960; Rosa Hovey Schol. 1962; MA); Univ. of Glasgow; University Coll. London (PhD). FSA 1982. King's College London: Asst Lectr, 1965; Lectr, 1968; Reader in Ancient History, 1970. Vis. Professor, Columbia Univ., 1967-68; Vis. Member, Inst. of Advanced Study, Princeton, 1977-78; Summer Fellow, Dumbarton Oaks Center for Byzantine Studies, 1981. *Publications:* Procopius, 1967; Agathias, 1970; Corippus: In laudem Iustini minoris, 1976; Change and Continuity in Sixth-Century Byzantium, 1981; (ed jtly) Images of Women in Antiquity, 1982; (ed) Constantinople in the Eighth Century: the Parastaseis Syntomai Chronikai, 1983; articles in Jl Hellenic Studies, Byzantion, Jl Theol Studies, Annali Scuola Normale di Pisa, Past and Present, Dumbarton Oaks Papers, and others. *Recreations:* reading, seeing friends. *Address:* 81 Harrow View, Harrow, Middx HA1 4TA. *T:* 01-427 7052.

CAMERON, Dr Clive Bremner; Dean, Institute of Cancer Research, London, 1978-82; *b* 28 Sept. 1921; *s* of Clive Rutherford and Aroha Margaret Cameron; *m* 1958, Rosalind Louise Paget; two *s* one *d. Educ:* King's Coll., Auckland, NZ; Otago Univ., NZ (MD). Consultant in Clinical Pathology, Royal Marsden Hospital, 1961-82; Chairman, SW Thames Regional Cancer Council, 1976-81. Chm., Governing Body, St Mary's Sch., Calne, 1981-. Mem. Bd of Governors, Royal Marsden Hosp., 1977-82. *Publications:* papers on steroid biochemistry, biochemical and other aspects of cancer. *Recreation:* country pursuits. *Address:* 1 St Leonard's Terrace, SW3; East Kennett Manor, Marlborough, Wilts. *T:* Lockeridge 239.

CAMERON OF LOCHIEL, Colonel Sir Donald (Hamish), KT 1973; CVO 1970; TD 1944; JP; 26th Chief of the Clan Cameron; Lord-Lieutenant of County of Inverness, since 1971 (Vice-Lieutenant, 1963-70); Chartered Accountant; Director since 1954, Deputy Chairman, 1965-69, a Vice-Chairman, 1969-80, Royal Bank of Scotland; Chairman, Scotbits Securities Ltd, since 1968; *b* 12 Sept. 1910; *s* of Col Sir Donald Walter Cameron of Lochiel, KT, CMG, 25th Chief of the Clan Cameron, and Lady Hermione Emily Graham (*d* 1978), 2nd *d* of 5th Duke of Montrose; *S* father, as 26th Chief, 1951; *m* 1939, Margaret, *o d* of Lieut-Col Hon. Nigel Gathorne-Hardy, DSO; two *s* two *d. Educ:* Harrow; Balliol Coll., Oxford. Joined Lovat Scouts, 1929; Major 1940; Lieut-Col 1945; Lieut-Col comdg 4/5th Bn (TA) QO Cameron Highlanders, 1955-57; Col 1957 (TARO). Hon. Colonel: 4/5th Bn

QO Cameron Highlanders, 1958-67; 3rd (Territorial) Bn Queen's Own Highlanders (Seaforth and Camerons), 1967-69; 2nd Bn, 51st Highland Volunteers, 1970-75. Member (part-time): British Railways Bd, 1962-64; Scottish Railways Bd, 1964-72 (Chm. Scottish Area Bd, BTC, 1959-64); Transport Holding Co., 1962-65; Director: Culter Guard Bridge Holdings Ltd, 1970-77 (Chm., 1970-76); Scottish Widows Life Assurance Soc., 1955-81 (Chm., 1964-67). Crown Estate Comr, 1957-69. President: Scottish Landowners Fedn, 1979-; Royal Highland and Agricultural Soc. of Scotland, 1971 and 1979. Governor, Harrow Sch., 1967-77. *Heir: s* Donald Angus Cameron, younger of Lochiel [*b* 2 Aug. 1946; *m* 1974, Lady Cecil Kerr, *d* of Marquess of Lothian, *qv* ; one *s* two *d*]. *Address:* Achnacarry, Spean Bridge, Inverness-shire. *T:* Gairlochy 208. *Clubs:* Boodle's, Pratt's; New (Edinburgh).
See also A. J. Cameron, J. A. McL. Stewart of Ardvorlich.

CAMERON, Ellen; *see* Malcolm, E.

CAMERON, Sir (Eustace) John, Kt 1977; CBE 1970; MA Cantab; Tasmanian pastoralist, since 1946; *b* 8 Oct. 1913; *s* of Eustace Noel Cameron and Alexina Maria Cameron; *m* 1934, Nancie Ailsa Sutherland; one *d. Educ:* Geelong Grammar Sch.; Trinity Coll., Cambridge. Served RANVR, 1942-46. ICI, 1938-41. State Pres., Liberal Party, 1948-52. Pres., Tasmanian Stockowners Assoc., 1965-68; Vice-Pres., Aust. Graziers, 1968-71. University of Tasmania: Mem. Council, 1956-82; Dep. Chancellor, 1964-72; Chancellor, 1973-82. Member: Selection Cttee, Winston Churchill Fellowship, 1965-74; CSIRO Adv. Cttee, 1959-77; Housing Loan Insurance Corp., 1970-73. Hon. LLD Tasmania. *Publications:* contrib. Australian Dictionary of Biography. *Recreations:* Australiana, gardening, pottering. *Address:* Lochiel, Ross, Tas 7209, Australia. *T:* Ross 815253. *Clubs:* Tasmanian (Hobart); Launceston (Launceston).

CAMERON, Rt. Rev. Ewen Donald; Assistant Bishop, Diocese of Sydney, since 1975; *b* 7 Nov. 1926; *s* of Ewen Cameron, Balranald, NSW, and Dulce M. Cameron, Sydney, NSW; *m* 1952, Joan R., *d* of T. Wilkins, Mosman, NSW; one *s* two *d. Educ:* Sydney C of E Grammar Sch., N Sydney; Moore Theological Coll., Sydney. ACA (Aust.); BD (London); ThSchol (Aust. Coll. of Theol.). Public Accountancy, 1945-57. Lectr, Moore Theological Coll., 1960-63; Rector, St Stephen's, Bellevue Hill, 1963-65; Federal Secretary, CMS of Aust., 1965-72; Archdeacon of Cumberland with Sydney, 1972-75. *Address:* 3 Mildura Street, Killara, NSW 2071, Australia. *T:* 02-498-5816. *Club:* Union (Sydney).

CAMERON, Francis (Ernest), MA, DipEth (Oxon); FRCO(CHM), ARAM; Senior Lecturer in Musical Studies, Oxford Polytechnic, since 1982; Organist, Church of St Mary the Virgin, Iffley, since 1980; *b* London, 5 Dec. 1927; *er s* of Ernest and Doris Cameron; *m* 1952, Barbara Minns; three *d. Educ:* Mercers' Sch.; Caerphilly Boys' Secondary Sch.; Royal Acad. of Music; University Coll. Oxford. Henry Richards Prizewinner, RAM, 1946. Organist, St Peter's, Fulham, 1943; Pianist, Canadian Legion, 1944; Organist, St Luke's, Holloway, 1945; Sub-organist, St Peter's, Eaton Square, 1945; Organist, St James-the-Less, Westminster, 1946; commissioned RASC, 1948; Organ Scholar, University Coll., Oxford, 1950; Organist: St Anne's, Highgate, 1952; St Barnabas', Pimlico, 1953; St Mark's, Marylebone Road, 1957-58; received into Roman Catholic Church, Holy Week, 1959; Choirmaster, St Aloysius, Somers Town, 1959; Master of Music, Westminster Cathedral, 1959; Visiting Organist, Church of St Thomas of Canterbury, Rainham, Kent, 1961; Organist and Choirmaster, Church of Our Lady of the Assumption and St Gregory, 1962-68. Travel for UNESCO, 1952-55; Dep. Dir of Music, LCC (subsequently GLC), 1954-68; Asst-Dir of Music, Emanuel Sch., 1954; Music Master, Central Foundation Boys' Grammar Sch., 1956; Prof. of Organ and Composition, RAM, 1959-68; *locum tenens* Dir of Music, St Felix Sch., Southwold, 1963 and 1964; Asst Dir, 1968, Chm. of Musicology, 1974-79, NSW State Conservatorium of Music. Inaugural Conductor, Witan Operatic Soc., 1957-58; Conductor: "I Cantici", 1961-65; Francis Cameron Chorale, 1965-68; Singers of David, 1973-76; British Adjudicator, Fedn of Canadian Music Festivals, 1965; Examr Associated Bd of Royal Schools of Music, 1965-68; Dep. Chm., NSW Adv. Bd, Aust. Music Exams Bd, 1969-74. Field Officer, Deep Creek Aboriginal Monuments res. and recording prog., 1973; Mem., Lancefield Archaeol Expedn, 1975. President: "Open Score", 1946-68; Musicol Soc. of Aust., 1971-75 (jt leader, ethnomusicol expedn to New Hebrides, 1971-72); Sydney Univ. Anthropol Soc., 1974-75; Phoenix Photographic Circle, 1977-79; Conservatorium Professional Staff Assoc., 1978-79; Vice-Pres., Aust. Chapter, Internat. Soc. for Contemporary Music, 1970-77. Beethoven Commemorative Medal, Fed. Repub. of Germany, 1970. *Publications:* editor (with John Steele) Musica Britannica vol. xiv (The Keyboard Music of John Bull, part I), 1960; Old Palace Yard, 1963; Eight dances from Benjamin Cosyn's Second Virginal Book, 1964; I Sing of a Maiden, 1966; John Bull, ausgewählte Werke, 1967; I Believe, 1969; incidental music for film The Voyage of the New Endeavour, 1970; songs and incidental music for Congreve's Love for Love, 1972; contributor to: Church Music; Composer; The Conductor; Liturgy; Musical Times; Australian Jl of Music Education; Studies in Music; Music in Tertiary Educn; Con Brio; Musicology IV; Aust. Nat. Hist.; Nation Review. *Address:* 12 Norreys Avenue, Oxford OX1 4SS. *T:* Oxford 40058.

CAMERON, George Edmund, CBE 1970; retired; *b* 2 July 1911; *s* of William Cameron and Margaret Cameron (*née* Craig); *m* 1939, Winifred Audrey Brown; two *s. Educ:* Ballymena Academy. Chartered Accountant,

1933; Partner, Wright Fitzsimons & Cameron, 1937-79. Pres., Inst. of Chartered Accountants in Ireland, 1960-61. *Recreations:* golf, gardening. *Address:* Ardavon, Glen Road, Craigavad, Co. Down. *T:* Holywood 2232. *Clubs:* Ulster (Belfast); Royal County Down Golf, Royal Belfast Golf.

CAMERON, Prof. Gordon Campbell; Professor and Head of the Department of Land Economy, and Fellow of Wolfson College, Cambridge University, since 1980; *b* 28 Nov. 1937; *s* of Archibald Arthur Cameron and Elizabeth Forsyth; *m* 1962, Brenda; one *s* one *d. Educ:* Quarry Bank High Sch., Liverpool; Hatfield Coll., Univ. of Durham (BA Hons). Res. Asst, Univ. of Durham, 1960-62; Univ. of Glasgow: Asst Lectr in Polit. Econ., 1962-63; Lectr in Applied Econs, 1963-68, Sen. Lectr 1968-71, Titular Prof. 1971-74; Prof. of Town and Regional Planning, 1974-79, Dean of Social Sciences, 1979. Res. Fellow, Resources for the Future, Washington, DC, and Vis. Associate Prof., Pittsburgh Univ., 1966-67; Vis. Prof., Univ. of Calif, Berkeley, 1974. Parly Boundary Comr for Scotland, 1976-. Chm., Inner City Res. Panel, SSRC, 1980-; Member: Cttee of Enquiry into Local Govt Finance (Layfield Cttee), 1974-76; Bd, Peterborough Develt Corp., 1981-. Consultant on Urban Policy, Scottish Develt Dept, 1975-79; Economic Consultant to Sec. of State for Scotland, 1977-80; Consultant on Urban Finance, OECD, 1977-80. Consultant, Coopers & Lybrand, 1977-. Governor, Centre for Environmental Studies, London, 1975-. Editor, Urban Studies Jl, 1968-74. FRSA 1978. *Publications:* Regional Economic Development—the federal role, 1971; (with L. Wingo) Cities, Regions and Public Policy, 1974; (ed) The Future of the British Conurbations, 1980. *Recreations:* tennis, musical concerts, theatre. *Address:* Department of Land Economy, 19 Silver Street, Cambridge.

CAMERON, Gordon Stewart, RSA 1971 (ARSA 1958); Senior Lecturer, School of Drawing and Painting, Duncan of Jordanstone College of Art, Dundee, 1952-81, retired; *b* Aberdeen, 27 April 1916; *s* of John Roderick Cameron; *m* 1962, Ellen Malcolm, *qv. Educ:* Robert Gordon's Coll., Aberdeen; Gray's Sch. of Art, Aberdeen. Part-time teaching, Gray's Sch. of Art, 1945-50; engaged on anatomical illustrations for Lockhart's Anatomy of the Human Body, 1945-48; apptd Lectr in Duncan of Jordanstone Coll. of Art, 1952. Awarded Davidson Gold Medal, 1939; Guthrie Award, 1944; Carnegie Travelling Schol., 1946. Work in Public Galleries: Aberdeen, Dundee, Perth, Edinburgh, Glasgow; also in private collections in Scotland, England, Ireland and America. *Recreation:* gardening. *Address:* 7 Auburn Terrace, Invergowrie, Perthshire. *T:* Invergowrie 318.

CAMERON, James; see Cameron, M. J. W.

CAMERON, Sir James Clark, Kt 1979; CBE 1969; TD 1947; Member of Council, British Medical Association (immediate past Chairman of Council, 1976-79); *b* 8 April 1905; *s* of Malcolm Clark Cameron, Rannoch, Perthshire; *m* 1933, Irene, *d* of Arthur Ferguson, Perth; one *s* two *d. Educ:* Perth Academy; St Andrews Univ. (MB, ChB). FRCGP. Served War of 1939-45, as Captain RAMC attached to 1st Bn, The Rifle Bde (despatches), Calais; POW, 1940. Past Chm., Gen. Med. Services Cttee, BMA, 1964-74, and Hon. Life Member; Chm., Management Cttee, Central Inf. Service for Gen. Medical Practice Foundn, RCGP; Member: 1t Cttee on Post Grad. Trng for Gen. Practice (former Chm. Adv. Cttee); Adv. Cttee on Med. Trng, Commn of the European Communities; Vice Pres., British Supporting Gp, World Medical Assoc. Hon. Mem. Council, Cameron Fund Ltd. Gold Medal for distinguished merit, BMA, 1974. *Recreation:* medico-politics. *Address:* 201 Croydon Road, Wallington, Surrey SM6 7LT. *T:* 01-647 6123.
See also G. C. Ryan.

CAMERON, Prof. J(ames) Malcolm, MD, PhD(Glas), FRCPath, DMJ; Professor of Forensic Medicine, University of London, at The London Hospital Medical College, since 1973, and Director, Department of Forensic Medicine; Ver Heyden De Lancey Readership in Forensic Medicine, Council of Legal Education, since 1978; Hon. Consultant: to The London Hospital, since 1967; to the Army at Home, in Forensic Medicine, since 1971; to the Royal Navy, in Forensic Medicine, since 1972; Secretary-General of the British Academy of Forensic Sciences and Editor of Medicine, Science and Law; *b* 29 April 1930; *s* of late James Cameron and Doris Mary Robertson; *m* 1956, Primrose Agnes Miller McKerrell, LCST; one *d. Educ:* The High Sch. of Glasgow; Univ. of Glasgow (MB, ChB, MD, PhD). Ho. Phys., Belvidere Hosp., Glasgow, 1954; Ho. Surg., Western Infirm., Glasgow, 1954-55 (Orthop. Ho. Surg., 1955); Sen. Ho. Officer in Pathology, Southern Gen. Hosp., Glasgow, 1955-56; McIntyre Clin. Res. Schol., Depts of Path. and Surgery, Glasgow Roy. Infirm., 1956-57; Registrar in Orthop. Surg., Western Infirm., Glasgow, and The Royal Hosp. for Sick Children, Glasgow, 1957-59; Registrar in Lab. Med., 1959-60, and Sen. Registrar in Path., 1960-62, Southern Gen. Hosp., Glasgow; Lectr in Path., Univ. of Glasgow, 1962. The London Hosp. Med. Coll.: Lectr in Forensic Med., 1963-65; Sen. Lectr in Forensic Med., 1965-70; Reader in Forensic Med., 1970-72. Lectr in Forensic Med. at St Bartholomew's Hosp. Med. Coll. and Univ. Coll. Hosp. Med. Sch.; Lectr to Metropolitan Police Detective Trng Sch., SW Detective Trng Sch., Bristol, and Special Investigation Br. of RMP; former Examiner in Forensic Med. to Univ. of Dublin; former Convenor for Exams of Dip. in Med. Jurisp. of Honourable Soc. of Apothecaries of London; former Mem. Council, Royal Coll. of Pathologists. Member: BMA; Council, Brit. Assoc. in Forensic Med., British Acad. of Forensic Sciences (Sec. Gen.; Pres., 1978-79); Medico-Legal Soc. (past Vice-Pres.); Assoc. of Police Surgeons of Gt Britain (Hon. Fellow); Forensic Science Soc.; Assoc. of Clinical

Pathologists; Pathological Soc. of Gt. Britain and Ire.; Research Defence Soc.; Fellow, Amer. Acad. of Forensic Sciences; Mem., Academic Internationalis Medicinae Legalis et Medicinae Socialis. *Publications:* scientific papers in numerous learned jls, both med. and forensic. *Recreations:* sports medicine and legal medicine. *Address:* c/o Department of Forensic Medicine, The London Hospital Medical College, Turner Street, E1 2AD. *T:* 01-247 5454, ext. 360. *Clubs:* Savage, Royal Naval Medical.

CAMERON, Prof. James Munro; University Professor, St Michaels College, University of Toronto, 1971-78, now Emeritus; *b* 14 Nov. 1910; *o s* of Alan and Jane Helen Cameron; *m* 1933, Vera Shaw; one *s* one *d. Educ:* Central Secondary Sch., Sheffield; Keighley Grammar Sch.; Balliol Coll., Oxford (Scholar). Tutor, Workers' Educational Assoc., 1931-32; Staff Tutor, Univ. Coll., Southampton, 1932-35; Staff Tutor, Vaughan Coll., Leicester (Dept of Adult Education, Univ. Coll., Leicester), 1935-43. Univ. of Leeds: Staff Tutor for Tutorial Classes, 1943-47; Lectr in Philosophy, 1947-60 (Sen. Lectr from 1952); Acting Head of Dept of Philosophy, 1954-55 and 1959-60; Prof. of Philosophy, 1960-67; Master of Rutherford Coll., and Prof. of Philosophy, Univ. of Kent at Canterbury, 1967-71. Vis. Prof., Univ. of Notre Dame, Indiana, 1957-58, 1965; Terry Lectr, Yale Univ., 1964-65. Newman Fellow, Univ. of Melbourne, 1968; Christian Culture Award, Univ. of Windsor, Ont, 1972. *Publications:* Scrutiny of Marxism, 1948; (trans. with Marianne Kuschnitzky) Max Picard, The Flight from God, 1951; John Henry Newman, 1956; The Night Battle, 1962; Images of Authority, 1966; (ed) Essay on Development (1845 edn), by J. H. Newman, 1974; On the Idea of a University, 1978; contribs to other books, and articles and papers in many periodicals. *Address:* 389 Dundas Street, N16-6, London, Ontario N6B 3L5, Canada.

CAMERON, Sir John; see Cameron, Hon. Lord.

CAMERON, Sir John; see Cameron, Sir E. J.

CAMERON, John Alastair, QC (Scot.) 1979; *b* 1 Feb. 1938; *s* of William Philip Legerwood Cameron and Kathleen Milthorpe (*née* Parker); *m* 1968, Elspeth Mary Dunlop Miller; three *s. Educ:* Trinity Coll., Glenalmond; Pembroke Coll., Oxford (MA). Called to the Bar, Inner Temple, 1963; admitted Mem., Faculty of Advocates, 1966. Advocate-Depute, 1972-75; Standing Jun. Counsel: to Dept of Energy, 1976-79; to Scottish Develt Dept, 1978-79. Legal Chm., Pensions Appeal Tribunal, 1979-. *Recreations:* travel, sport, Africana. *Address:* 4 Garscube Terrace, Edinburgh EH12 6BQ. *T:* 031-337 3460. *Club:* Edinburgh Sports (Edinburgh).

CAMERON, John Charles Finlay; Member, London Transport Executive, since 1975; *b* 8 Feb. 1928; *s* of Robert John and Nancy Angela Cameron; *m* 1955, Ruth Constance, *d* of A. D. Thompson, Sydney, NSW; two *s* two *d. Educ:* privately; University Coll., Southampton. CEng, MICE, FCIT, MBIM. Served in Royal Marines, 1946-48. Joined British Railways, Southern Region, as civil engineering draughtsman, 1948; work study assistant in British Transport Commn, 1957; Personnel and Admin. Manager of BR Workshops, 1962-68; Dir of Personnel, Rank Precision Industries, 1968; Manpower Resources Adviser to Rank Organisation, 1970; Gen. Manager, Taylor Hobson Optics, 1971; Dir and Gen. Manager, Rank Optics, 1973. *Publications:* papers on industrial engrg to ICE and others. *Recreations:* building, garden construction, music. *Address:* Tarrawonga, Carlton Road, South Godstone, Surrey RH9 8LE. *T:* South Godstone 3263.

CAMERON, Prof. John Robinson; Regius Professor of Logic, University of Aberdeen, since 1979; *b* 24 June 1936; *s* of Rev. George Gordon Cameron and Mary Levering (*née* Robinson); *m* 1959, Mary Elizabeth (*née* Ranson); one *s* two *d. Educ:* Dundee High Sch.; Univ. of St Andrews (MA 1st Cl. Hons Maths, BPhil Philosophy); Univ. of Calif, Berkeley; Cornell Univ. Harkness Fellow, Berkeley and Cornell, USA, 1959-61; University of Dundee (formerly Queen's College): Asst in Phil., 1962-63; Lectr in Phil., 1963-73; Sen. Lectr in Phil., 1973-78. *Publications:* articles in phil jls. *Recreation:* bricolage. *Address:* 70 Cornhill Road, Aberdeen AB2 5DH. *T:* Aberdeen 46700.

CAMERON, Brigadier John S.; see Sorel Cameron.

CAMERON, John Taylor, QC (Scot.) 1973; *b* 24 April 1934; *s* of late John Reid Cameron, MA, formerly Director of Education, Dundee; *m* 1964, Bridget Deirdre Sloan; no *c. Educ:* Fettes Coll.; Corpus Christi Coll., Oxford; Edinburgh Univ. BA (Oxon), LLB (Edinburgh). Admitted to Faculty of Advocates, 1960. Lecturer in Public Law, Edinburgh Univ., 1960-64. Keeper of the Advocates' Library, 1977-; an Advocate-Depute, 1977-79. *Publications:* articles in legal jls. *Address:* 17 Moray Place, Edinburgh EH3 6DT. *T:* 031-225 7695.

CAMERON, Sir John (Watson), Kt 1981; OBE 1960; President, J. W. Cameron & Co., since 1977; *b* 16 Nov. 1901; *s* of Captain Watson Cameron and Isabel Mann; *m* 1930, Lilian Florence Sanderson; one *s* two *d. Educ:* Lancing Coll. Commnd Durham RGA, 1920. Joined J. W. Cameron & Co., brewery co., 1922; Man. Dir, 1940; Chm., 1943-75. Mem., Northern Area, Economic League, 1950-80. Chm., 1964-69, Treasurer, 1967-72, Northern Area Cons. Party; Hartlepool Conservative Party: Chm., 1942-45; Pres., 1945-76; Patron, 1976-78; Pres. and Patron, 1978-. Chm., Hartlepools Hosp.

Trust, 1973-80. *Recreations:* gardening, shooting, fishing. *Address:* Cowesby Hall, near Thirsk, N Yorks YO7 2JJ.

CAMERON, Prof. Kenneth, FBA 1976; Professor of English Language, University of Nottingham, since 1963; *b* Burnley, Lancs, 21 May 1922; *s* of late Angus W. Cameron and of E. Alice Cameron, Habergham, Burnley; *m* 1947, Kathleen (*d* 1977), *d* of late F. E. Heap, Burnley; one *s* one *d*. *Educ:* Burnley Grammar Sch.; Univ. of Leeds (BA Hons, Sch. of English Language and Literature); PhD Sheffield. Served War, 1941-45; Pilot, RAF. Asst Lectr in English Language, Univ. of Sheffield, 1947-50; Nottingham University: Lectr in English Language, 1950-59; Sen. Lectr, 1959-62; Reader, 1962-63. Sir Israel Gollancz Meml Lecture, British Academy, 1976; O'Donnell Lectr, 1979. Pres., Viking Soc., 1972-74; Hon. Dir, 1966-, Hon. Sec., 1972-, English Place-Name Soc. Gen. Editor, English Place-Name Survey, 1966-; Editor, Jl of the English Place-Name Soc., 1972-. FRHistS 1970. Hon. FilDr, Uppsala, 1977. Sir Israel Gollancz Meml Prize, British Academy, 1969. *Publications:* The Place-Names of Derbyshire, 1959; English Place-Names, 1961; Scandinavian Settlement in the Territory of the Five Boroughs: the place-name evidence, 1965; The Meaning and Significance of OE *walh* in English Place-Names, 1980; contribs to: Nottingham Medieval Studies; Medium Ævum; Mediaeval Scandinavia; Festschrifts, etc. *Recreations:* sports (supporting), home, "The Commercial". *Address:* 292 Queens Road, Beeston, Nottingham. *T:* Nottingham 254503.

CAMERON, (Mark) James (Walter), CBE 1979; journalist and author; *b* 17 June 1911; *s* of William Ernest Cameron, MA, LLB, and Margaret Douglas Robertson; *m* 1st, 1938, Eleanor Mara Murray (decd); one *d*; 2nd, 1944, Elizabeth O'Conor (marr. diss.); one *s* (and one step *s*); 3rd, 1971, Moneesha Sarkar; one step *s* one step *d*. *Educ:* erratically, at variety of small schools, mostly in France. Began journalism, in Dundee, 1928; after leaving Scotland joined many staffs and wrote for many publications, travelling widely as Foreign Correspt in most parts of the world; finally with (late) News Chronicle. Subseq. prod. numerous TV films, on contemporary subjects. Initiated travel series, Cameron Country, on BBC 2. Hon. Governor, Mermaid Theatre. Hon. DLitt: Lancaster, 1970; Bradford, 1977; Essex, 1978; Hon. LLD Dundee, 1980. Granada Award, Journalist of the Year, 1965; Granada Foreign Correspt of the Decade, 1966; Hannen Swaffer Award for Journalism, 1966; Gerald Barry Award for distinguished services to journalism, 1980. *Publications:* Touch of the Sun, 1950; Mandarin Red, 1955; "1914", 1959; The African Revolution, 1961; "1916", 1962; Witness in Viet Nam, 1966; Point of Departure, 1967; What a Way to Run a Tribe, 1968; An Indian Summer, 1974; The Best of Cameron, 1982; *Play:* The Pump, 1973 (radio, 1973, TV, 1980; Prix Italia 1973). *Recreations:* private life, public houses. *Address:* 3 Eton College Road, NW3. *T:* 01-586 5340. *Club:* Savile.

CAMERON, Marshal of the Royal Air Force Sir Neil, GCB 1976 (KCB 1975; CB 1971); CBE 1967; DSO 1945; DFC 1944; AE 1968; Principal of King's College, London, since 1980, Fellow, since 1980; *b* 8 July 1920; *s* of Neil and Isabella Cameron, Perth, Scotland; *m* 1947, Patricia Louise, *d* of Major Edward Asprey; one *s* one *d*. *Educ:* Perth Academy. Fighter and Fighter Bomber Sqdns, 1940-45; Directing Staff, Sch. of Land/Air Warfare, Old Sarum, 1945-48; Student, RAF Staff Coll., 1949; DS, RAF Staff Coll., 1952-55; CO, Univ. of London Air Sqdn, 1955-56; Personal Staff Officer, Chief of Air Staff, 1956-59; CO, RAF Abingdon, 1959-62; Imperial Defence Coll., 1963; Principal Staff Officer, Dep. Supreme Comdr, SHAPE, Paris, 1964; Asst Comdt, RAF Coll., Cranwell, 1965; Programme Evaluation Gp, MoD, 1965-66; Assistant Chief of Defence Staff (Policy), 1968-70; SASO Air Support Comd, 1970-72; Dep. Comdr, RAF Germany, 1972-73; AOC 46 Gp, RAF, 1974; Air Member for Personnel, MoD, 1974-76; Chief of the Air Staff, 1976-77; Chief of the Defence Staff, 1977-79. Air ADC to the Queen, 1976-77. Chm., RAF Museum Trustees; President: Scottish Flying Club; Military Commentators' Circle; Soldiers and Airmens Scripture Readers' Assoc.; Vice-Pres., Officers' Christian Union; Chm. Trustees, Project Trident. Regional Dir, Greater London Regional Bd, Lloyds Bank, 1980-. Hon. Companion, RAeS, 1981. Hon. LLD Dundee, 1981. *Publications:* articles in defence jls. *Recreations:* reading, Rugby football, defence affairs. *Address:* King's College, Strand, WC2. *Clubs:* Athenæum, Royal Air Force (Pres.).

CAMERON, Roy James, CB 1982; PhD; Australian Statistician, since 1977; *b* 11 March 1923; *s* of Kenneth Cameron and Amy Jean (*née* Davidson); *m* 1951, Dorothy Olive Lober; two *s* one *d*. *Educ:* Univ. of Adelaide (BSc 1st Cl. Hons, MEc); PhD Harvard. Lecturer in Economics, Canberra University College, 1949-51; Economist, World Bank, 1954-56; Australian Treasury official, 1956-73; Australian Ambassador to OECD, Paris, 1973-77. *Recreation:* lawn bowls. *Address:* Australian Bureau of Statistics, PO Box 10, Belconnen, ACT 2616, Australia. *T:* 062 526705. *Club:* Commonwealth (Canberra).

CAMERON, Stuart Gordon, MC 1943; Chairman and Chief Executive, Gallaher Ltd, since 1980; Director, American Brands Inc., since 1980; *b* 8 Jan. 1924; *s* of James Cameron and Dora Sylvia (*née* Godsell); *m* 1946, Joyce Alice, *d* of Roland Ashley Wood; three *s* one *d*. *Educ:* Chigwell School, Essex. Served War, 2nd Gurkha Rifles, 1942-46 (MC). Managing Director, 1976-78, Dep. Chm., 1978-80, Gallaher Ltd. *Address:* 65 Kingsway, WC2B 6TG. *T:* 01-242 1290. *Club:* Royal Thames Yacht.

CAMERON-RAMSAY-FAIRFAX-LUCY; *see* Fairfax-Lucy.

CAMERON WATT, Prof. Donald; Stevenson Professor of International History in the University of London, since 1981; *b* 17 May 1928; *s* of Robert Cameron Watt, *qv*; *m* 1st, 1951, Marianne Ruth Grau (*d* 1962); one *s*; 2nd, 1962, Felicia Cobb Stanley; one step *d*. *Educ:* Rugby Sch.; Oriel Coll., Oxford. BA 1951, MA 1954; FRHistS. Asst Editor, Documents on German Foreign Policy, 1918-1945, in Foreign Office, 1951-54; Asst Lectr, Lectr, Sen. Lectr in Internat. History, LSE, 1954-66; Reader in Internat. History in Univ. of London, 1966; Titular Prof. of Internat. History, 1972-81. Editor, Survey of Internat. Affairs, Royal Inst. of Internat. Affairs, 1962-71; Rockefeller Research Fellow in Social Sciences, Inst of Advanced Internat. Studies, Washington, 1960-61; Sec., 1967, Chm., 1976-, Assoc. of Contemporary Historians; Chm., Greenwich Forum, 1974-. Member Editorial Board: Political Quarterly, 1969-; Marine Policy, 1978-. *Publications:* Britain and the Suez Canal, 1956; (ed) Documents on the Suez Crisis, 1957; Britain looks to Germany, 1965; Personalities and Policies, 1965; (ed) Survey of International Affairs 1961, 1966; (ed) Documents on International Affairs 1961, 1966; (ed, with K. Bourne) Studies in International History, 1967; A History of the World in the Twentieth Century, Pt I, 1967; (ed) Contemporary History of Europe, 1969; (ed) Hitler's Mein Kampf, 1969; (ed) Survey of International Affairs 1962, 1969; (ed, with James Mayall): Current British Foreign Policy 1970, 1971; Current British Foreign Policy 1972, 1973; Too Serious a Business, 1975; (ed) Survey of International Affairs 1963, 1977; America in Britain's Place, 1900-1975, 1982. *Recreations:* exploring London, cats. *Address:* c/o London School of Economics and Political Science, Houghton Street, WC2A 2AE. *Clubs:* Playboy, Players Theatre.

CAMILLERI, His Honour Sir Luigi A., Kt 1954; LLD; Chief Justice and President of the Court of Appeal, Malta, 1952-57, retired; *b* 7 Dec. 1892; *s* of late Notary Giuseppe amd Matilde (*née* Bonello); *m* 1914, Erminia, *d* of Professor G. Cali'; five *s* three *d*. *Educ:* Gozo Seminary; Royal Univ. of Malta (LLD). Called to the Bar, 1913. Consular Agent for France in Gozo, Malta, 1919-24; Malta Legislative Assembly, 1921-24; Magistrate, 1924-30; Visitor of Notarial Acts, Chairman Board of Prison Visitors, Chairman Licensing Board, Magistrate in charge of Electoral Register, 1927-30; Judicial Bench, 1930; Royal Univ. of Malta representative on General Council of the Univ., 1933-36; Chairman Emergency Compensation Board, 1940-41; Court of Appeal, 1940-57; President Medical Council, Malta, 1959-68; Member Judicial Service Commission, 1959-62. Examiner in Criminal, Roman and Civil Law, Royal Univ. of Malta, 1931-70. Silver Jubilee Medal, 1935; Coronation Medals, 1937 and 1953. Knight of Sovereign Military Order of Malta, 1952. *Recreation:* walking. *Address:* Victoria Avenue, Sliema, Malta. *T:* Sliema 513532. *Club:* Casino Maltese (Malta).

CAMM, John Sutcliffe; Chairman and Chief Executive, Dickinson Robinson Group Ltd, since 1978; *b* 18 Jan. 1925; *s* of late Thomas Howard Camm and of Mary Ethel Sutcliffe; *m* 1956, Barbara Kathleen Small; three *s* three *d*. *Educ:* Wycliffe Coll.; Bristol Univ. (BA). RAF pilot, 1943-47. Schoolmaster, Wycliffe Coll., 1950-53. Dir, E. S. & A. Robinson (Holdings), 1963; Dickinson Robinson Group Ltd: Dir, 1967; Jt Man. Dir, 1972; Man. Dir, 1974; Dep. Chm., 1977. Mem. Council, Bristol Univ.; Governor, Wycliffe Coll. *Recreations:* gardening, cricket, country pursuits. *Address:* Bushy Farm, Breadstone, Glos GL13 9HG. *T:* Dursley 811013. *Clubs:* Naval and Military, MCC.

CAMMELL, John Ernest; Director, National Maritime Institute, since 1981; *b* 14 Nov. 1932; *s* of Ernest Alfred Cammell and Gladys Clara (*née* Burroughes); *m* 1976, Janis Linda Moody. *Educ:* Highfield Coll., Leigh-on-Sea, Essex. Mil. Service, Royal Signals. Joined Victualling Dept, Admiralty, 1952; DSIR, 1963; Min. of Technology, 1964; DTI, 1967; Dept of Industry, 1973. *Recreations:* amateur theatre, golf, cricket, eating. *Address:* 56 Ravenscourt Road, W6 0UG. *Club:* Players Theatre.

CAMOYS, 7th Baron *cr* 1264 (called out of abeyance, 1839); **Ralph Thomas Campion George Sherman Stonor;** Managing Director, Barclays Merchant Bank Ltd, since 1978; *b* 16 April 1940; *s* of 6th Baron Camoys and of Mary Jeanne, *d* of late Captain Herbert Marmaduke Joseph Stourton, OBE; *S* father, 1976; *m* 1966, Elisabeth Mary Hyde, *d* of Sir William Stephen Hyde Parker, 11th Bt; one *s* three *d*. *Educ:* Eton Coll.; Balliol Coll., Oxford (BA). Gen. Manager and Director, National Provincial and Rothschild (London) Ltd, 1968; Man. Director, Rothschild Intercontinental Bank Ltd, 1969; Chief Exec. Officer and Man. Dir, 1975-77, Chm., 1977-78, Amex Bank Ltd; Director: Barclays Bank Internat. Ltd, 1980-; Mercantile Credit Co. Ltd, 1980-; National Provident Instn, 1982-. Pres., Mail Users' Assoc., 1977-; Member: House of Lords EEC Select Cttee, 1979-81; Court of Assistants, Fishmongers' Co., 1980-. Order of Gorkha Dakshina Bahu, 1st class (Nepal), 1981. *Recreations:* the arts, shooting. *Heir:* *s* Hon. (Ralph) William (Robert Thomas) Stonor, *b* 10 Sept. 1974. *Address:* Stonor Park, Henley-on-Thames, Oxon. *Clubs:* Boodle's; Leander (Henley-on-Thames).

CAMP, Jeffery Bruce, ARA 1974; artist; Lecturer, Slade School of Fine Art, since 1961; *b* Oulton Broad, Suffolk, 1923; *s* of George Camp and Caroline Denny; *m* 1963, Laetitia Yhap. *Educ:* Lowestoft and Ipswich Schools of Art; Edinburgh Coll. of Art (under William Gillies). DA (Edin.). Awarded Andrew Grant Travelling Scholarship, 1945. Painted altarpiece for St Albans Church, Norwich, 1955; Mem., London Group, 1960; Teacher, Chelsea Sch. of Art, 1960-61. One-man exhibitions include: Galerie de Seine, 1958; Beaux

Arts Gallery, 1959, 1961, 1963; New Art Centre, 1968; Serpentine Gall., 1978; Bradford City Art Gallery, 1979; other exhibitions include: South London Art Gall., 1973 (retrospective); British Painting, Arts Council, Hayward Gall., 1974; Arts Council, 1975– (Chantrey Bequest purchase, 1975); British Painting 1952-77, RA, 1977; works in many public collections and in travelling exhibitions. *Publication:* Draw, 1981. *Recreation:* walking by the sea. *Address:* 12 The Croft, Hastings, Sussex. *T:* Hastings 426222.

CAMP, William Newton Alexander; communications consultant and author; *b* 12 May 1926; *s* of I. N. Camp, OBE, Colonial Administrative Service, Palestine, and Freda Camp; *m* 1st, 1950, Patricia Cowan (marr. diss. 1973); two *s* one *d* ; 2nd, 1975, Juliet Schubart. *Educ:* Bradfield Coll.; Oriel Coll., Oxford (Classical Scholar, MA). Served in Army, 1944–47. Asst Res. Officer, British Travel and Holidays Assoc., 1950-54; Asst Sec., Consumer Adv. Council, 1954-59; Asst Sec., Gas Council, 1960-63; Public Relations Adviser, Gas Council, 1963-67; Dir of Information Services, British Steel Corp., 1967-71; Mem., British Nat. Oil Corp., 1976-78; Special Adviser: milling and baking industries, 1972–; British Leyland Motor Corp., 1975; railway trades unions, 1975-76; C. A. Parsons & Co. Ltd, 1976-77; Prudential Assurance Co., 1978–; Northern Engineering Industries plc, 1978–; pt-time advr, British Railways Bd, 1977–; Chm., Camden Consultants Ltd, 1975–. Chm., Oxford Univ. Labour Club, 1949; contested (Lab) Solihull, 1950; Mem., Southwark Borough Council, 1953-56; Press Adviser (unpaid) to Prime Minister, Gen. Election, 1970. Founder Mem., Public Enterprise Group. *Publications: novels:* Prospects of Love, 1957; Idle on Parade, 1958; The Ruling Passion, 1959; A Man's World, 1962; Two Schools of Thought, 1964; Flavour of Decay, 1967; The Father Figures, 1970; *biography:* The Glittering Prizes (F. E. Smith), 1960. *Address:* 61 Gloucester Crescent, NW1. *T:* 01-485 5110; Keeper's Cottage, Marshfield, near Chippenham, Wilts. *T:* Marshfield 211. *Club:* Garrick.

CAMPBELL, family name of **Duke of Argyll,** of **Earl of Breadalbane,** of **Earl Cawdor,** and of **Barons Campbell of Alloway, Campbell of Croy, Campbell of Eskan, Colgrain, Glenavy** and **Stratheden.**

CAMPBELL OF ALLOWAY, Baron *cr* 1981 (Life Peer), of Ayr in the District of Kyle and Carrick; **Alan Robertson Campbell,** QC 1965; a Recorder of the Crown Court, since 1976; *b* 24 May 1917; *s* of late J. K. Campbell; *m* 1957, Vivien, *y d* of late Comdr A. H. de Kantzow, DSO, RN. *Educ:* Aldenham; Ecole des Sciences Politiques, Paris; Trinity Hall, Cambridge. Called to Bar, Inner Temple, 1939, Bencher, 1972; Western Circuit. Commissioned RA (Suppl. Res.), 1939; served France and Belgium, 1939-40; POW, 1940-45. Consultant to sub-cttee of Legal Cttee of Council of Europe on Industrial Espionage, 1965-74; Chm., Legal Res. Cttee, Soc. of Conservative Lawyers, 1968-80. Member: Law Adv. Cttee, British Council, 1974-; Management Cttee, UK Assoc. for European Law, 1975–. *Publications:* (with Lord Wilberforce) Restrictive Trade Practices and Monopolies, 1956, 2nd edn, 1966, Supplements 1 and 2, 1973; Restrictive Trading Agreements in the Common Market, 1964, and 1965 Supplement; Common Market Law, vols 1 and 2, 1969, vol. 3, 1973 and 1975 Supplement; Industrial Relations Act, 1971; EC Competition Law, 1980; Trade Unions and the Individual, 1980. *Address:* 1 Harcourt Buildings, Temple, EC4. *T:* 01-353 2214. *Clubs:* Carlton, Pratt's, Beefsteak.

CAMPBELL OF CROY, Baron *cr* 1974 (Life Peer), of Croy in the County of Nairn; **Gordon Thomas Calthrop Campbell,** PC 1970; MC 1944, and Bar, 1945; *b* 8 June 1921; *s* of late Maj.-Gen. J. A. Campbell, DSO; *m* 1949, Nicola Elizabeth Gina Madan; two *s* one *d. Educ:* Wellington and Hospital. War of 1939-45: commissioned in Regular Army, 1939; RA, Major, 1942; commanded 320 Field Battery in 15 Scottish Div.; wounded and disabled, 1945. Entered HM Foreign Service, 1946; served, until 1957, in FO, UK Delegn to the UN (New York), Cabinet Office and Vienna. MP (C) Moray and Nairn, 1959-Feb. 1974; Asst Govt Whip, 1961-62; a Lord Comr of the Treasury and Scottish Whip, 1962-63; Joint Parly Under-Sec. of State, Scottish Office, 1963-64; Opposition Spokesman on Defence and Scottish Affairs, 1966-70; Sec. of State for Scotland, 1970-74; Mem., Lords' Select Cttee on the European Communities, 1978–. Oil industry consultant, 1975–; Partner in Holme Rose Farms and Estate, 1975–; Chairman: Scottish Bd, Alliance Building Soc., 1976–; Stoic Insurance Services, 1979–. Vice-Pres., Adv. Cttee on Pollution of the Sea. Chairman: Scottish Council of Independent Schs, 1978-82; Scottish Cttee, Internat. Year of Disabled, 1981; Trustee, Thomson Foundn, 1980–; First Fellow, Nuffield Provincial Hospitals Trust Queen Elizabeth The Queen Mother Fellowship, 1980. *Publication:* Disablement: Problems and Prospects in the UK, 1981. *Recreations:* music, birds. *Address:* Holme Rose, Cawdor, Nairnshire, Scotland. *T:* Croy 223.

CAMPBELL OF ESKAN, Baron *cr* 1966 (Life Peer), of Camis Eskan; **John (Jock) Middleton Campbell;** Kt 1957; Chairman: Milton Keynes Development Corporation, since 1967; Commonwealth Sugar Exporters' Association, since 1950; President, Town & Country Planning Association, since 1980; Trustee: Runnymede Trust; Chequers Trust; *b* 8 Aug. 1912; *e s* of late Colin Algernon Campbell, Colgrain, Dunbartonshire and Underriver House, Sevenoaks, Kent and of Mary Charlotte Gladys (Barrington); *m* 1st, 1938, Barbara Noel (marr. diss. 1948), *d* of late Leslie Arden Roffey; two *s* two *d* ; 2nd, 1949, Phyllis Jacqueline Gilmour Taylor, *d* of late Henry Boyd, CBE. *Educ:* Eton; Exeter Coll., Oxford (Hon. Fellow, 1973). Chairman: Booker McConnell Ltd, 1952-66 (Pres., 1967-79); Statesman and Nation Publishing Co. Ltd, 1964-77; Statesman Publishing Co. Ltd, 1964-81; New

Towns Assoc., 1975-77; Director: London Weekend TV Ltd, 1967-74 (Dep. Chm., 1969-73); Commonwealth Develt Corp., 1968-81; Pres., West India Cttee, 1957-77. Mem., Community Relations Commn, 1968-77 (a Dep. Chm., 1968-71). Chm., Governing Body, Imperial Coll. of Tropical Agriculture, 1950-60. First Freeman of Milton Keynes. DUniv Open, 1973. *Recreations:* reading, hitting balls, painting. *Address:* Lawers, Crocker End, Nettlebed, Oxfordshire. *T:* Nettlebed 641202; 15 Eaton Square, SW1. *T:* 01-235 5695. *Clubs:* Beefsteak, All England Lawn Tennis; Huntercombe Golf.

CAMPBELL, Sir Alan (Hugh), GCMG 1979 (KCMG 1976; CMG 1964); HM Diplomatic Service, retired; Chairman, Society of Pension Consultants, since 1982; Director: National Westminster Bank; Mercantile and General Reinsurance Co.; H. Clarkson (Holdings) plc; *b* 1 July 1919; *y s* of late Hugh Campbell and Ethel Campbell (*née* Warren); *m* 1947, Margaret Taylor; three *d. Educ:* Sherborne Sch.; Caius Coll., Cambridge. Served in Devonshire Regt, 1940-46. 3rd Sec., HM Foreign (now Diplomatic) Service, 1946; appointed to Lord Killearn's Special Mission to Singapore, 1946; served in Rome, 1952, Peking, 1955; UK Mission to UN, New York, 1961; Head of Western Dept, Foreign Office, 1965; Counsellor, Paris, 1967; Ambassador to Ethiopia, 1969-72; Asst Under-Sec. of State, FCO, 1972-74; Dep. Under-Sec. of State, FCO, 1974-76; Ambassador to Italy, 1976-79; Foreign Affairs adviser to Rolls Royce Ltd, 1979-81. Governor, Sherborne Sch., 1973– (Chm. of Governors, 1982-). *Recreation:* lawn tennis. *Address:* 45 Carlisle Mansions, Carlisle Place, SW1. *Club:* Brooks's.

CAMPBELL, Hon. Alexander Bradshaw, PC (Canada) 1967; QC (Can) 1966; MLA; Judge, Supreme Court of Prince Edward Island, since 1978; *b* 1 Dec. 1933; *s* of Dr Thane A. Campbell and late Cecilia B. Campbell; *m* 1961, Marilyn Gilmour; two *s* one *d. Educ:* Dalhousie Univ. (BA, LLB). Called to Bar of Prince Edward Island, 1959; practised law with Campbell & Campbell, Summerside, PEI, 1959-66. MLA, Prince Edward Island, 1965-79; Leader of Liberal Party, Dec. 1966-78; Premier, 1966-78; served (while Premier) as Attorney-Gen., 1966-69, Minister of Development, 1969-72, Minister of Agriculture, 1972-74, and Minister of Justice, 1974-78. Dir, Inst. of Man and Resources, 1976–. Elder of Trinity United Church, Summerside. Hon. LLD: McGill 1967; PEI, 1978. *Recreations:* curling, skiing, golf, boating. *Address:* 330 Beaver Street, Summerside, PEI, Canada. *T:* 436-2714. *Clubs:* Summerside Board of Trade, Y's Men's (Summerside).

CAMPBELL, Alexander Buchanan, ARSA; FRIBA; architect in private practice, since 1949; Senior Partner, A. Buchanan Campbell and Partners, Glasgow, since 1949; *b* 14 June 1914; *s* of Hugh Campbell and Elizabeth Flett; *m* 1939, Sheila Smith; one *s* one *d. Educ:* Royal Technical Coll., Glasgow; Glasgow School of Art; Univ. of Strathclyde (BArch). ARSA 1973; PPRIAS. Assistant: Prof. T. Harold Hughes, 1937; G. Grey Wornum, 1938; City Architect, Glasgow, 1939; served War, Royal Engineers, 1940-46; Inspector, CIEME, 1947; Chief Technical Officer, Scottish Building Centre, 1948, Dep. Dir, 1949. Principal works include: Dollan Swimming Baths and Key Youth Centre, East Kilbride; Flats, Great Western Road, Glasgow; St Christopher's Church, Glasgow; Priesthill Church, Glasgow; St James Primary Sch., Renfrew; Callendar Park Coll. and Craigie College of Education at Falkirk and Ayr (Civic Trust Awards); High Rise Flats, Drumchapel. President: Glasgow Inst. of Architects, 1974-76; Royal Incorporation of Architects in Scotland, 1977-79. *Recreations:* music, art, golf, exhibiting show dogs. *Address:* 62 Whittinghame Court, Glasgow G12 0BQ. *T:* 041-339 7846. *Club:* Glasgow Art (President, 1972-74).

CAMPBELL, Prof. (Alexander) Colin (Patton), FRCPath, FRCPE; Procter Professor of Pathology and Pathological Anatomy, University of Manchester, 1950-73, now Professor Emeritus (formerly Dean, Faculty of Medicine and Pro-Vice Chancellor); formerly Director of Studies, Royal College of Pathologists; *b* 21 Feb. 1908; *s* of late A. C. Campbell, Londonderry; *m* 1943, Hon. Elisabeth Joan Adderley, 2nd *d* of 6th Baron Norton; two *s* one *d. Educ:* Foyle Coll., Londonderry; Edinburgh Univ. MB, ChB (Hons) Edinburgh 1930; FRCPE 1939. Rockefeller Fellow and Research Fellow in Neuropathology, Harvard Univ., 1935-36; Lectr in Neuropathology, Edinburgh Univ., 1937-39; Lectr in Pathology, Edinburgh Univ., and Pathologist, Royal Infirmary, Edinburgh, 1939-50. War service, 1940-46, RAFVR (Wing-Comdr). Hon. MSc Manchester, 1954. *Publications:* papers on pathological subjects in various medical and scientific jls. *Recreations:* carpentry and cabinet-making. *Address:* The Priory House, Ascott-under-Wychwood, Oxford OX7 6AW.

CAMPBELL, Archibald, CMG 1966; Assistant Under-Secretary of State, Ministry of Defence, 1969-74 (Assistant Secretary, 1967-69); *b* 10 Dec. 1914; *s* of Archibald Campbell and Jessie Sanders Campbell (*née* Halsall); *m* 1939, Peggie Phyllis Hussey; two *s* one *d. Educ:* Berkhamsted Sch.; Hertford Coll., Oxford. BA Oxford 1935. Barrister at Law, Middle Temple. Administrative Service, Gold Coast, 1936-46; Colonial Office, 1946; Colonial Attaché, British Embassy, Washington, 1953-56; Asst Secretary, Colonial Office, 1956-59 and 1962-67; Chief Secretary, Malta, 1959-62. Mem., British observer team, Rhodesian Elections, 1980. *Recreations:* cricket (capped for Bucks in Minor County Competition, 1951); fishing, climbing, gardening. *Address:* Bransbury, Long Park, Chesham Bois, Bucks. *T:* Amersham 7727. *Club:* MCC.

CAMPBELL, Archibald Hunter, LLM, BCL, MA, of Lincoln's Inn, Barrister-at-Law; Regius Professor of Public Law, University of Edinburgh, 1945-72, and Dean of the Faculty of Law, 1958-64; *b* Edinburgh, 1902; *o c* of late Donald Campbell, MA. *Educ:* George Watson's Coll., Edinburgh (Dux); Univ. of Edinburgh (MA, Mackenzie Class. Schol., Ferguson Class. Schol.); University Coll., Oxford (Class. Exhibitioner). 1st Class in Hon. Mods, Lit. Hum., Jurisprudence and BCL; Sen. Demy of Magdalen Coll., 1927-28; Sen. Student of Oxford Univ., 1928; Fellow of All Souls, 1928-30 and 1936-; Stowell Civil Law Fellow, University Coll., Oxford, 1930-35; Barber Professor of Jurisprudence, Univ. of Birmingham, 1935-45. Vice-President Society of Public Teachers of Law, 1961-62, President 1962-63. President Classical Assoc. of Scotland, 1963-. Hon. LLD Aberdeen, 1963. *Address:* 8 Braid Hills Road, Edinburgh EH10 6EZ. *Club:* New (Edinburgh).

CAMPBELL of Achalader, Brig. Archibald Pennant, DSO 1945; OBE 1939; psc 1930; retired, 1947; Ninth Chief of Baronial House of Campbell of Achalader since 1963; *b* 26 Jan. 1896; *s* of Brig.-Gen. J. C. L. Campbell of Achalader (*d* 1930); *m* 1st, 1926, Phyllis (*d* 1953), *d* of late Sir Henry Bax-Ironside, KCMG; one *d*; 2nd, 1961, Elsie, widow of Dr Howard Clapham, and *d* of late J. Thompson. *Educ:* Malvern; RMA. 2nd Lieut, RFA, 1914. Served European War, 1914-18, with RA 22nd Div. (despatches). Silver Staff Officer at Jubilee of HM King George V, 1935. GSO 2, HQ (British Troops), Egypt, 1937; Bt Lt-Col, 1939; temp. Brig., 1941; Col, 1943. Served War, 1939-45 (Egypt, UK, and NW Europe) as BGS 8 Corps Dist, CRA 47 Div., CCRA 2 Corps Dist and Comdr 8 AGRA. Served in Palestine as Comdr North Palestine Dist, 1944-46; Comdr Suez Canal South, 1946-47. Dist Comr, Boy Scouts Assoc., 1955; British Consular Agent, Moji, Japan, 1957-58. *Recreations:* shooting (big and small game), fishing, hunting. *Address:* 6 Rockley Road, South Yarra, Victoria 3141, Australia. *T:* Melbourne 248300. *Club:* Naval and Military (London).

CAMPBELL, Maj.-Gen. Charles Peter, CBE 1977; Director, Power Engineering Associates Ltd; *b* 25 Aug. 1926; *s* of late Charles Alfred Campbell and of Blanche Campbell; *m* 1949, Lucy Kitching; two *s*. *Educ:* Gillingham Grammar Sch.; Emmanuel Coll., Cambridge. FBIM. Commnd RE, 1945; psc 1957; DAA&QMG Trng Bde, RE, 1958-60; OC 11 Indep. Field Sqdn, RE, 1960-62; Jt Services Staff Coll., 1963; DAAG WO, 1963-65; Co. Comd, RMA Sandhurst, 1965-67; CO 21 Engr Regt, 1967-70; GSOI MoD, 1970-71; CRE 3 Div., 1971; Comd 12 Engr Bde, 1972-73; RCDS, 1974; COS HQ NI, 1975-77; Engineer-in-Chief (Army), 1977-80. Col Comdt, RE, 1981-. *Recreations:* painting and collecting militaria. *Address:* c/o Lloyds Bank Ltd, Cox's & King's Branch, 6 Pall Mall, SW1Y 5NH. *Club:* Naval and Military.

CAMPBELL, Sir Clifford (Clarence), GCMG 1962; GCVO 1966; Governor-General of Jamaica, 1962-73; *b* 28 June 1892; *s* of late James Campbell, civil servant, and Blanche, *d* of John Ruddock, agriculturist; *m* 1920, Alice Esthephene, *d* of late William Jolly, planter; two *s* two *d*. *Educ:* Petersfield Sch.; Mico Training Coll., Jamaica. Headmaster: Fullersfield Govt Sch., 1916-18; Friendship Elementary Sch., 1918-28; Grange Hill Govt Sch., 1928-44. Member Jamaica House of Representatives (Jamaica Labour Party) for Westmoreland Western, 1944-49; Chm., House Cttee on Education, 1945-49; 1st Vice-President, Elected Members Assoc., 1945; re-elected 1949; Speaker of the House of Representatives, 1950; Senator and President of the Senate, 1962. KStJ. *Recreations:* agricultural pursuits, reading. *Address:* 8 Cherry Gardens Avenue, Kingston 8, Jamaica. *Clubs:* (Hon. Member) Caymanas Golf and Country, Ex-Services, Kingston Cricket, Liguanea, Rotary, St Andrew's, Trelawny (all in Jamaica).

CAMPBELL, Colin; see Campbell, A. C. P.

CAMPBELL, Sir Colin Moffat, 8th Bt *cr* 1667, of Aberuchill and Kilbryde, Dunblane, Perthshire; MC 1945; Chairman: James Finlay plc, since 1975, and associated companies; *b* 4 Aug. 1925; *e s* of Sir John Campbell, 7th Bt and Janet Moffat (*d* 1975); *S* father, 1960; *m* 1952, Mary Anne Chichester Bain, *er d* of Brigadier G. A. Bain, Sandy Lodge, Chagford, Devon; two *s* (one *d* decd). *Educ:* Stowe. Scots Guards, 1943-47, Captain. Employed with James Finlay & Co. Ltd, Calcutta, 1948-58, Nairobi, 1958-71, Dir, 1971-, Dep. Chm., 1973-75. President Federation of Kenya Employers, 1962-70; Chairman: Tea Board of Kenya, 1961-71; E African Tea Trade Assoc., 1960-61, 1962-63, 1966-67. Member: Scottish Council, CBI, 1979-; Council, CBI, 1981-; Commonwealth Develt Corp., 1981-. FRSA 1982. *Recreations:* gardening, racing, cards. *Heir: s* James Alexander Moffat Bain Campbell, *b* 23 Sept. 1956. *Address:* Kilbryde Castle, Dunblane, Perthshire. *T:* Dunblane 823104. *Clubs:* Boodle's; Western (Glasgow); Royal Calcutta Turf, Tollygunge (Calcutta); Nairobi, Muthaiga (E Africa).

CAMPBELL, David John G.; see Graham-Campbell.

CAMPBELL, Donald le Strange, MC; Director: Project Services Overseas Ltd; Hovair Systems Ltd; Beechdean Farms; *b* 16 June 1919; *s* of late Donald Fraser Campbell and of Caroline Campbell, Heacham, Norfolk; *m* 1952, Hon. Shona Catherine Greig Macpherson, *y d* of 1st Baron Macpherson of Drumochter; one *s* one *d*. *Educ:* Winchester Coll.; Clare Coll., Cambridge. Served War, 1939-45, Major RA (MC). EFCO Ltd, 1947-55; MEECO Ltd, 1955-61; Davy-Ashmore Ltd, 1961-67. Dep. Chairman, BNEC Latin America, 1967. *Recreations:* farming, sailing, field sports. *Address:* Bagnor

Manor, Newbury, Berks RG16 8AJ. *Clubs:* Buck's; Royal Yacht Squadron.

CAMPBELL, Dr Fergus William, FRS 1978; Reader in Neurosensory Physiology, Physiological Laboratory, University of Cambridge, since 1973; Fellow of St John's College, Cambridge, since 1955; *b* 30 Jan. 1924; *s* of William Campbell and Anne Fleming; *m* 1948, Helen Margaret Cunningham; one *s* two *d* (and one *d* decd). *Educ:* Univ. of Glasgow (MA, MD, PhD, DOMS). Casualty and Eye Resident Surg., Western Infirmary, Glasgow, 1946-47; Asst. Inst. of Physiol., Glasgow, 1947-49, Lectr, 1949-52; Res. Graduate, Nuffield Lab. of Ophthalmology, Oxford, 1952-53; Univ. Lectr, Physiol Lab., Cambridge, 1953-72. Hon. FBOA 1962. Tillyer Medal, Optical Soc. of America, 1980. *Publications:* papers on neurophysiology and psychophysics of vision in Jl Physiol, and Vision Res. *Recreations:* music, photography. *Address:* 96 Queen Ediths Way, Cambridge CB1 4PP. *T:* Cambridge 247578.

CAMPBELL, Graham Gordon; Under-Secretary, Department of Energy, since 1974; *b* 12 Dec. 1924; *s* of late Lt-Col and Mrs P. H. Campbell; *m* 1955, Margaret Rosamond Busby; one *d*. *Educ:* Cheltenham Coll.; Caius Coll., Cambridge (BA Hist.). Served War, Royal Artillery, 1943-46. Asst Principal, Min. of Fuel and Power, 1949; Private Sec. to Parly Sec., Min. of Fuel and Power, 1953-54; Principal, 1954; Asst Sec., Min. of Power, 1965; Under-Sec., DTI, 1973. *Recreations:* watching birds, music, hill-walking. *Address:* 3 Clovelly Avenue, Warlingham, Surrey CR3 9HZ. *T:* Upper Warlingham 4671.

CAMPBELL, Sir Guy (Theophilus Halswell), 5th Bt *cr* 1815; OBE 1954; MC 1941; Colonel, late 60th Rifles, El Kaimakam Bey, Camel Corps, Sudan Defence Force, and Kenya Regiment; *b* 18 Jan. 1910; *s* of Major Sir Guy Colin Campbell, 4th Bt, late 60th Rifles, and Mary Arabella Swinnerton Kemeys-Tynte, sister of 8th Lord Wharton; *S* father, 1960; *m* 1936, Lizbeth Webb, Bickenhall Mansions, W1; two *s*. *Educ:* St Aubyn's, Rottingdean; Eton Coll.; St Andrews Univ. War of 1939-45 (wounded); served in KOYLI, 1931-42; seconded to Camel Corps, Sudan Defence Force, 1939-47; Comd 2/7 and 7 Nuba Bns, 1943-47; Shifta Ops, Eritrea, 1946; Acting Brig., 1945, HQ SDF Group (N Africa); Palestine, 1948; Mil. Adviser to Count Folke Bernadotte and Dr Ralph Bunche of United Nations, 1948; attached British Embassy as Civil Affairs Officer, Cairo, 1948; British Mil. Mission to Ethiopia, in Ogaden Province, 1949-51; 2nd i/c 1/60th Rifles, BAOR, 1951; comd Kenya Regt (TF), 1952-56, Mau Mau ops; Head of British Mil. Mission to Libya, 1956-60; retired Aug. 1960. MoD, 1965-72. Col R of O, 60th Rifles. Provided historical research, costume, weapons etc for United Artists film Khartoum, 1964. C-in-C's (MELF) Commendation, 1945; Gold Medal of Emperor Haile Selassie (non-wearable). *Recreations:* painting, writing, watching cricket, Rugby football, golf. *Heir: s* Lachlan Philip Kemeys Campbell, The Royal Green Jackets, *b* 9 Oct. 1958. *Address:* The Hermitage, Padbury, Buckingham. *Clubs:* Army and Navy, Special Forces; Puffins (Edinburgh); MCC, I Zingari; Royal and Ancient (St Andrews).

CAMPBELL, Maj.-Gen. Sir Hamish Manus, KBE 1963 (CBE 1958); CB 1961; *b* 6 Jan. 1905; *s* of late Major A. C. J. Campbell, Middlesex Regt and Army Pay Dept, and of Alice, *d* of late Comdr Yelverton O'Keeffe, RN; *m* 1929, Marcelle, *d* of late Charles Ortlieb, Neuchâtel, Switzerland; one *s*. *Educ:* Downside School; New Coll., Oxford. Commissioned in Argyll and Sutherland Highlanders, 1927; transferred to Royal Army Pay Corps, 1937; Lieut-Colonel and Staff Paymaster (1st Class), temp. 1945, subs. 1951; Colonel and Chief Paymaster, temp. 1954, subs. 1955; Major-General, 1959. Command Paymaster: Sierra Leone, 1940-42; Burma, 1946-48; Malta, 1953. Deputy Chief, Budget and Finance Division, SHAPE, 1954-56; Commandant, RAPC Training Centre, 1956-59; Paymaster-in-Chief, War Office, 1959-63; retired, 1963. Col Comdt, RAPC, 1963-70. *Address:* 27 Honey Park Road, Budleigh Salterton, Devon EX9 6EG. *T:* Budleigh Salterton 3818. *Club:* Army and Navy.

CAMPBELL, Harold Edward; Director, Greater London Secondary Housing Association, since 1978; Chairman, Sutton (Hastoe) Housing Association, since 1981; *b* 28 Feb. 1915; *s* of Edward Inkerman Campbell and Florence Annie Campbell. *Educ:* Southbury Road Elementary Sch.; Enfield Central Sch. Asst Sec., 1946-64, Sec., 1964-67, Cooperative Party; Mem., 1967-73, Dep. Chm., 1969-73, Housing Corp. Gen. Manager, Newlon Housing Trust, 1970-76; Chairman: Cooperative Planning Ltd, 1964-74; Co-Ownership Develt Soc. Ltd, 1966-76; Sutton Housing Trust, 1973-80 (Trustee, 1967-); Dir, Co-op. Housing Centre, and S British Housing Assoc., 1976-78; Dep. Chm., Stevenage Develt Corp., 1968-80; Mem., Cooperative Develt Agency, 1978-81; Pres., Enfield Highway Cooperative Soc. Ltd, 1976- (Dir, 1965-); Dir, CWS Ltd, 1968-73. Chairman: DoE Working Party on Cooperative Housing, 1973-75; DoE Working Group on New Forms of Housing Tenure, 1976-77; Housing Assoc. Registration Adv. Cttee, 1974-79; Hearing Aid Council, 1970-71. Borough Councillor, Enfield, 1959-63. *Recreations:* music, theatre, cinema. *Address:* 67A Derby Road, Enfield, Mddx EN3 4AJ. *T:* 01-804 2392. *Club:* Sloane.

CAMPBELL, Hugh, PhD; Career Consultant in Paris and London, since 1974; *b* 24 Oct. 1916; *s* of Hugh Campbell and Annie C. Campbell (née Spence); *m* 1946, Sybil Marian Williams, MB, ChB, *y d* of Benjamin and Sarah Williams; two *s*. *Educ:* University College Sch., London; St John's Coll., Cambridge (MA, PhD). Research, Dept of Colloid Science, Cambridge,

1938-45; Head of Physical Chem., Research Gp, May and Baker Ltd, 1945-61; Lectr, West Ham Techn. Coll., 1949-54; Research Manager, Chloride Electrical Storage Co. Ltd, 1961-65; Managing Dir: Alkaline Batteries Ltd, 1965-67; Electric Power Storage Ltd, 1968-71; Dir, Chloride Electrical Storage Co. Ltd, 1968-71; Industrial Advr, DTI, 1971-74. *Publications:* papers on various subjects in scientific jls. *Recreations:* skiing, theatre, travelling. *Address:* 4 The Courtyard, Barnsbury Terrace, N1 1JZ. *T:* 01-607 3834.

CAMPBELL, Ian, CEng, MIMechE, JP; MP (Lab) Dunbartonshire (West) since 1970; *b* 26 April 1926; *s* of William Campbell and Helen Crockett; *m* 1950, Mary Millar; two *s* three *d. Educ:* Dumbarton Academy; Royal Technical Coll., Glasgow (now Strathclyde Univ.). Engineer with South of Scotland Electricity Board for 17 years. Councillor, Dumbarton, 1958-70; Provost of Dumbarton, 1962-70. PPS to Sec. of State for Scotland, 1976-79. *Address:* 20 McGregor Drive, Dumbarton. *T:* Dumbarton 63612.

CAMPBELL, Ian Burns; barrister; a Recorder of the Crown Court, since 1981; *b* 7 July 1938; *s* of late James Campbell and of Laura Woolnough Dransfield; *m* 1967, Mary Elisabeth Poole, BArch, MCD Liverpool; two *s* one *d. Educ:* Tiffin Boys' Sch.; Cambridge Univ. (MA, LLB, PhD). Called to the Bar, Middle Temple, 1966. French Govt Scholar, 1961-62; Asst Lectr in Law, Liverpool Univ., 1962-64, Lectr 1964-69. *Recreation:* cycling. *Address:* 1 Exchange Flags, Liverpool L2 3XN. *T:* 051-236 7747. *Club:* Athenæum (Liverpool).

CAMPBELL, Ian Dugald, QHP 1977; FRCPE, FFCM; Chief Administrative Medical Officer, Lothian Health Board, 1973-80; *b* Dornie, Kintail, 22 Feb. 1916; *s* of John Campbell and Margaret Campbell; *m* 1943, Joan Carnegie Osborn; one *s* two *d. Educ:* Dingwall Acad.; Edinburgh Univ. (MB, ChB 1939). FRCPE 1973, FFCM 1974. Served War, 1941-46: UK, BAOR, MEF, RAMC; final appt OC Field Amb. (Lt-Col). Med. Supt, St Luke's Hosp., Bradford, 1946-49; Asst SMO, Leeds Reg. Hosp. Bd, 1949-57; Dep. Sen. Admin. MO, S-Eastern Reg. Hosp. Bd, Scotland, 1957-72, Sen. Admin. MO, 1972-73. WHO assignments, SE Asia, 1969, 1971, 1975. Treas., RCPE, 1981-. *Publications:* various medical. *Recreations:* fishing, shooting, golf. *Address:* 5 Succoth Park, Edinburgh EH12 6BX. *T:* 031-337 5965. *Clubs:* New (Edinburgh); Hon. Company of Edinburgh Golfers (Muirfield); Royal Burgess Golfing Society (Barnton, Edinburgh).

CAMPBELL, Ian George Hallyburton, TD; QC 1957; Lord Chancellor's Legal Visitor, 1963-79; *b* 19 July 1909; *s* of late Hon. Kenneth Campbell and Mrs K. Campbell; *m* 1949, Betty Yolande, *d* of late Somerset Maclean and *widow* of Lt-Col Allan Bruno, MBE; one adopted *s* one adopted *d. Educ:* Charterhouse, Trinity Coll., Cambridge. Barrister, Inner Temple and Lincoln's Inn, 1932. Served Artists Rifles and Rifle Brigade, 1939-45; Col 1945. Appts include: GSO2, HQ 1st Army; Chief Judicial Officer, Allied Commission, Italy; Chief Legal Officer, Military Govt, Austria (British zone). *Address:* Flat 26, The Abbey, Amesbury, Wilts. *T:* Amesbury 22612.

CAMPBELL, Ian James; defence and marine technology consultant; *b* 9 June 1923; *s* of Allan and Elizabeth Campbell; *m* 1946, Stella Margaret Smith. *Educ:* George Heriot's Sch.; Edinburgh Univ. (MA). Op. Res. Sect., HQ Bomber Comd, 1943-46; Asst Lectr in Astronomy, St Andrews Univ., 1946-48; Royal Naval Scientific Service, 1948; Dept of Aeronaut. and Eng Res., Admiralty, 1948-49; Admiralty Res. Lab., 1949-59; Admiralty Underwater Weapons Estab., 1959-68; Chief Scientist, Naval Construction Res. Estab., 1969-73; Head of Weapons Dept, Admiralty Underwater Weapons Estab., 1973-76; Ministry of Defence: Dir of Res. (Ships), 1976-78; Scientific Advr to Ship Dept, 1976-81; Dir Gen. Res. Maritime, 1978-81. *Publications:* papers on fluid mechanics in scientific jls. *Address:* Claremont, North Street, Charminster, Dorchester, Dorset. *T:* Dorchester 64270.

CAMPBELL, Ian Macdonald, CVO 1977; BSc; FEng; FICE; FCIT; Vice-Chairman, British Railways Board, since 1980; Chairman, Transmark, since 1978; *b* 13 July 1922; *s* of late John Isdale Campbell; *m* 1946, Hilda Ann Williams; one *s* three *d. Educ:* University Coll., London. BSc(Eng). British Rail: Asst District Engr, Sheffield, 1953-57; District Engr, Kings Cross, 1957-63; Asst Civil Engr, Scottish Region, 1963-65; Chief Civil Engr, Scottish Region, Asst Gen. Man., LM Region, 1968-70; Gen. Manager, E Region, 1970-73; Exec. Dir, BR, 1973-76; Chief Exec. (Railways), BRB, 1978-80, Exec. Mem. for Engrg and Research, 1977-80. Chm., British Rail Engineering, 1977-79. Pres., ICE, 1981-82 (Vice-Pres., 1978-81). *Recreations:* golf, music. *Address:* Rail House, Euston Square, NW1 2DZ.

CAMPBELL, Prof. Ian McIntyre, MA; Professor of Humanity, University of Edinburgh, 1959-82; *b* 14 Jan. 1915; *s* of late John Campbell and Janet Donaldson; *m* 1945, Julia Margaret Mulgan; two *s* one *d. Educ:* Spier's Sch., Beith; Univ. of Glasgow; Balliol Coll., Oxford. First cl. Hons Classics, Glasgow Univ., 1936; First cl., Class. Mods, 1938. Served in Intelligence Corps, Captain, 1939-45; Hon. War Memorial Research Student, Balliol Coll., 1946; Lecturer in Humanity and Comparative Philology, Glasgow Univ., 1947-54; Prof. of Latin, Univ. Coll. of S Wales and Monmouthshire, 1954-59. *Publications:* articles and reviews in learned journals. Jt Editor of *Archivum Linguisticum,* 1949-. *Recreation:* music. *Address:* 70 Thirlestane Road, Edinburgh EH9 1AR. *T:* 031-447 8994.

CAMPBELL, Mrs Ian McIvor; *see* Corbet, Mrs Freda K.

CAMPBELL, Air Vice-Marshal Ian Robert, CB 1976; CBE 1964; AFC 1948; *b* 5 Oct. 1920; *s* of late Major and Hon. Mrs D. E. Campbell; *m* 1953, Beryl Evelyn Newbigging (*d* 1982); one *s. Educ:* Eton; RAF Coll., Cranwell. Anti-Shipping Ops, 1940-42; POW, Italy and Germany, 1942-45; 540 Sqdn, Benson, 1946; psa 1949; PSO to C-in-C Far East, 1950; 124 (F) Wing Oldenburg, 1953; OC, RAF Sandwich, 1956; pfc 1957; OC 213 Sqdn, Bruggen, 1958; ACOS Plans HQ 2ATAF, 1959; OC, RAF Marham, 1961; MoD (Air) DASB, 1964; SASO, HQ No 1 Group, 1965; Air Attaché, Bonn, 1968; Dir of Management and Support Intell., MoD, 1970-73; C of S, No 18 (M) Group, Strike Command, 1973-75, retired. *Recreations:* shooting, golf, travel. *Address:* Poulton House, Cirencester, Glos. *Clubs:* Boodle's, Royal Air Force.

CAMPBELL, Maj.-Gen. Ian Ross, CBE 1954; DSO and Bar, 1941; *b* 23 March 1900; *m* 1927, Patience Allison Russell (*d* 1961); one *d* ; *m* 1967, Irene Cardamatis. *Educ:* Wesley Coll., Melbourne; Scots Coll., Sydney; Royal Military College, Duntroon, Canberra (Sword of Honour, 1922). psc Camberley, 1936-37. Served War of 1939-45, Middle East Campaigns, Libya, Greece and Crete (DSO and bar, Cross of Kt Comdr, Greek Order of Phoenix, pow 1941-45); comd Aust. forces in Korean War, 1951-53 (CBE); Comdt, Australian Staff Coll., 1953-54; Comdt, Royal Mil. Coll. Duntroon, 1954-57; retired, 1957, Mem. Federal Exec., RSL, 1955-56. Chm., NSW Div., Aust. Red Cross Soc., 1967-74. Pres., Great Public Schs Athletic Assoc., NSW, 1966-69. Hon. Col, NSW Scottish Regt, 1957-60. *Recreation:* walking. *Address:* 15/17 Wylde Street, Potts Point, Sydney, NSW 2011, Australia. *Clubs:* Imperial Service, Royal Sydney Golf (Sydney).

CAMPBELL, Sir Ilay (Mark), 7th Bt *cr* 1808, of Succoth, Dunbartonshire; *b* 29 May 1927; *o s* of Sir George Ilay Campbell, 6th Bt; *S* father, 1967; *m* 1961, Margaret Minette Rohais, *o d* of J. Alasdair Anderson; two *d. Educ:* Eton; Christ Church, Oxford. BA 1952. Joint Scottish Agent for Messrs Christie, Manson & Woods; Chm., Christie's & Edmistons, Glasgow. Pres., Assoc. for Protection of Rural Scotland; Vice-Chm., Scotland's Gardens Scheme; Scottish Rep. Nat. Art-Collections Fund. *Recreations:* heraldry, horticulture. *Heir:* none. *Address:* Crarae Lodge, Inveraray, Argyll PA32 8YA. *T:* Minard 274; Swiss Cottage, Coldstream, Berwickshire. *T:* Coldstream 2254. *Clubs:* Turf; Puffins (Edinburgh); Arts (Glasgow).

CAMPBELL, James Grant, CMG 1970; Consultant to Atlantic Division, Alcan Aluminium Ltd; *b* Springville, NS, Canada, 8 June 1914; *s* of John Kay Campbell and Wilna Archibald Campbell (*née* Grant); *m* 1941, Alice Isobel Dougall; one *d. Educ:* Mount Allison Univ., Canada. BSc, 1st cl. hons (Chem.). Chemical Engineer, Aluminium Co. of Canada, Arvida, Que, 1937-41; Demerara Bauxite Co. Ltd, Guyana, Gen. Supt, 1941-50; Aluminium Laboratories Ltd, London, England, 1950 (Headqrs for team investigating hydro power, bauxite and aluminium smelting in Asia, Africa and Europe); on staff of Dir of Operations, Aluminium Ltd, Montreal (concerned with world supply of raw materials for Aluminium Ltd), 1951-55; Managing Dir and Chm., Demerara Bauxite Co., Guyana, 1955-71; Vice-Pres., Alcan Ore Ltd, 1971-77; Overseas Representative, Alcan International Ltd, Montreal, 1977-79. Mem. Bd of Regents, Mount Allison Univ., 1972. Hon. LLD Mount Allison Univ., 1966. *Recreations:* music, golf. *Address:* 45 Eaton Square, SW1. *Clubs:* Brooks's, Travellers', American; University (New York); University (Montreal).

CAMPBELL, Sir (James) Keith, Kt 1982; CBE 1972; FCA; Chief Executive since 1964, and Chairman since 1974, Hooker Corporation Ltd; Deputy Chairman, Network Finance Ltd, since 1972; *b* 4 March 1928; *s* of late Edward Colin and Amanda Maud Campbell; *m* 1951, Marjorie Elizabeth (*née* Burford); one *s* three *d. Educ:* Homebush High Sch.; Australian Accountancy Coll. Chartered Accountant, 1950-62. Chairman, CitiNational Holdings Ltd, 1971-80; Director: Australian Industries Development Corp., 1974-80; IBM (Australia) Ltd, 1969-80; Chm., Australian Financial System Inquiry, 1979-81 Governor, Science Foundn, Sydney Univ., 1971-; Mem. Council: Univ. of NSW, 1981-; Salvation Army, 1981-; Chm., Shepherd Centre (Deaf), 1972- *Publication:* Final Report of the Committee of Inquiry—Australian Financial System, 1981. *Recreations:* golf, surfing, music. *Address:* 8 Hopetoun Avenue Mosman, NSW 2088, Australia. *T:* 969.3316. *Clubs:* Union, Elanora Golf (Sydney).

CAMPBELL, Prof. James Reid, PhD, FRCVS; William Dick Professor of Veterinary Surgery, Royal (Dick) School of Veterinary Studies, University of Edinburgh, since 1978; *b* 19 Sept. 1930; *s* of Andrew and Margaret Campbell; *m* 1957, Marette (*née* Martin); two *s* two *d. Educ:* Bentinck Primary Sch., Kilmarnock; Kilmarnock Acad.; Glasgow Univ. (BVMS, PhD) FRCVS 1968. House Surg., Univ. of Glasgow Vet. Hosp., 1954-55; Asst in Practice, Fife, 1955-57; Lectr in Vet. Surgery, Univ. of Glasgow Vet. Hosp. 1957-67, Sen. Lectr, 1968-78; seconded to Univ. of Ont, 1958; Sen. Lectr Faculty of Vet. Science, University Coll., Nairobi, 1964-65. *Publications* contrib. vet. jls. *Recreations:* golf, music, reading. *Address:* Glamis Cottage Carberry, Musselburgh EH21 8RZ. *T:* 031-665 2036.

CAMPBELL, John Davies, CVO 1980; CBE 1981 (MBE 1957); MC 1945 and bar 1945; HM Diplomatic Service, retired; Consul-General, Naples 1977-81; *b* 11 Nov. 1921; *s* of late William Hastings Campbell and of late The Hon. Mrs Campbell (Eugene Anne Westenra, subsequently Harbord), of 14th Baron Louth; *m* 1959, Shirley Bouch; one *s* two *d. Educ:* Cheltenham Coll.; St Andrews Univ. Served War, HM Forces, 1940-46. HM Colonial

Service (subseq. HMOCS), 1949–61 (despatches, 1957); HM Foreign (subseq. HM Diplomatic) Service, 1961; First Secretary, 1961; Counsellor, 1972; Counsellor (Information) Ottawa, 1972–77. Commendatore dell'ordine al merito della Repubblica Italiana, 1980. *Recreations:* golf, tennis. *Address:* Ridgeway, The Ludlow Road, Leominster, Herefordshire HR6 0DH. *Clubs:* Special Forces; (Life Mem.) Muthaiga Country (Nairobi); Mombasa.

CAMPBELL, Sir John Johnston, Kt 1957; General Manager, Clydesdale Bank Ltd, 1946–58, retired (Director, 1958–75); *b* 11 Dec. 1897; *s* of William Campbell, Stewarton, Ayrshire; *m* 1927, Margaret Fullarton (*d* 1967), *d* of John Brown, Dalry, Ayrshire; one *s* one *d. Educ:* Stewarton Secondary Sch. Joined service of The Clydesdale Bank at Stewarton, Ayrshire, 1913. Served with Royal Scots Fusiliers in Palestine, France, and Germany, 1916–19. London Manager, Clydesdale Bank, 1944. Pres., Institute of Bankers in Scotland, 1953–55; Chm.: Development Securities Ltd, 1958–67; Cttee of Scottish Bank Gen Managers, 1955–57. *Address:* 22 Saffrons Court, Compton Place Road, Eastbourne, E Sussex. *T:* 29271.

CAMPBELL of Canna, John Lorne; tacksman of the Isle of Canna, Inner Hebrides, which he presented to National Trust for Scotland, 1981; owner of Heiskeir and Humla; folklorist, editor and author; *b* 1 Oct. 1906; *s* of late Col Duncan Campbell of Inverneill and Ethel Harriet, *e d* of late John I. Waterbury, Morristown, NJ; *m* 1935, Margaret Fay (author of Folksongs and Folklore of South Uist), *y d* of late Henry Clay Shaw, Glenshaw, Pennsylvania (US); no *c. Educ:* Cargilfield; Rugby; St John's Coll., Oxford (MA 1933, DLitt, 1965). Hon. LLD, St Francis Xavier Univ., Antigonish, NS, 1953. Hon. DLitt, Glasgow Univ., 1965. *Publications:* Highland Songs of the Forty-Five, 1933; The Book of Barra (with Compton Mackenzie and Carl Hj. Borgstrom), 1936; (Ed.) Orain Ghaidhlig le Seonaidh Caimbeul, 1936; Sia Sgialachdan, Six Gaelic Stories from South Uist and Barra, 1938; Act Now for the Highlands and Islands (with Sir Alexander MacEwen), 1939; Gaelic in Scottish Education and Life, 1945; Gaelic Folksongs from the Isle of Barra (with Annie Johnston and John MacLean), 1950; Fr. Allan McDonald of Eriskay, Priest, Poet and Folklorist, 1954; Gaelic Words from South Uist and Eriskay, collected by Fr. Allan McDonald, 1958; Tales from Barra, told by the Coddy, 1960; Stories from South Uist, 1961; The Furrow Behind Me, the Autobiography of a Hebridean Crofter (trans. from tape recordings), 1962; Edward Lhuyd in the Scottish Highlands (with Prof. Derick Thomson), 1963; A School in South Uist (memoirs of Frederick Rea), 1964; Bardachd Mhgr Ailein, the Gaelic Poems of Fr. Allan McDonald, 1965; Strange Things (with Trevor H. Hall), 1968; Hebridean Folksongs (with F. Collinson), vol. i, 1969, vol. ii, 1977, vol. iii, 1981; Macrolepidoptera Cannae, 1970; Saoghal an Treobhaiche, 1972; (ed) A Collection of Highland Rites and Customes, 1975; Notes on Carmina Gadelica, 1982; contribs to various periodicals, etc. *Recreations:* entomology, sea fishing, music. *Address:* Isle of Canna, Scotland.

CAMPBELL, (John) Quentin; Metropolitan Stipendiary Magistrate, since 1981; *b* 5 March 1939; *s* of late John McKnight Campbell, OBE, MC, and Katharine Margaret Campbell; *m* 1st, Penelope Jane Redman (marr. diss. 1976); three *s* one *d*; 2nd, 1977, Ann Rosemary Beeching; one *s* one *d. Educ:* Loretto Sch., Musselburgh, Scotland; Wadham Coll., Oxford (MA). Admitted as Solicitor, 1965; private practice, Linnell & Murphy, Oxford (Partner, 1968–80). Chairman, Bd of Governors, Bessels Leigh Sch., near Oxford, 1979–. *Recreations:* opera, gardening, golf. *Address:* 12 Park Town, Oxford OX2 6SH. *T:* Oxford 56269. *Clubs:* Chelsea Arts; Frewen (Oxford).

CAMPBELL, Dame Kate (Isabel), DBE 1971 (CBE 1954); Medical Practitioner; Specialist Pædiatrician, 1937–76; *b* April 1899; *d* of late Donald Campbell and late Janet Campbell (*née* Mill); unmarried. *Educ:* Hawthorn State Sch.; Methodist Ladies' Coll., Melbourne; Melbourne Univ. MB, BS, 1922; MD 1924; FRCOG 1961; Resident MO: Melbourne Hosp., 1922; Children's Hosp., 1923, Women's Hosp., 1924; Lecturer in Neo-Natal Pædiatrics, Melbourne Univ., 1927–65. Hon. Phys. to Children's Dept, Queen Victoria Hosp., Melbourne, 1926–60; Hon. Pædiatric Consultant in active practice, Queen Victoria Hospital, 1960–66; Hon. Pædiatric Consultant, 1966–; Hon. Neo-Natal Pædiatrician, Women's Hosp., Melbourne, 1945–59; First assistant in Pædiatrics, Professorial Unit, Dept of Obstetrics, Melbourne Univ., 1960–65; Gen. Med. Practice, 1927–37. Consultant to Dept of Infant Welfare, Victoria, 1961–76. Associate, Dept of Paediatrics, Monash Univ., 1971–; Hon. Consultant Paediatrician, Royal Women's Hosp., 1979–. Hon. LLD 1966. Hon. FRACO, 1978. *Publications:* (co-author with late Dr Vera Scantlebury Brown) Guide to the care of the young child, 1947 (last edn 1972); section on The Newborn, in Townsend's Obstetrics for Students, 1964; articles on medical subjects in Medical Journal of Australasia (incl. one on retrolental fibroplasia, 1951) and Lancet. *Recreation:* theatre. *Address:* 1293 Burke Road, Kew, Melbourne, Victoria 3101, Australia. *T:* 80 2536. *Club:* Lyceum (Melbourne).

CAMPBELL, Sir Keith; *see* Campbell, Sir J. K.

CAMPBELL, Keith Bruce, QC 1964; **His Honour Judge Campbell;** a Circuit Judge, since 1976; *b* NZ, 25 Oct. 1916; *yr s* of late Walter Henry Pearson Campbell and late Ethel Rose Campbell; *m* 1939, Betty Joan Muffett; two *s* four *d. Educ:* Christchurch Tech. High Sch. and Canterbury Univ. Coll., NZ (LLB); London Univ. (LLB). Served Army, 1939–46: in ranks of 15th/19th Hussars, BEF France, Belgium; evacuated from Dunkirk; commnd

into RASC, 1941; with 1st and 8th Armies, N Africa, Italy. Called to New Zealand Bar, and to English Bar by Inner Temple, 1947; Master of the Bench, Inner Temple, 1970; a Recorder of the Crown Court, 1972–76. Gen. Council of the Bar, 1956–60, 1965–70, 1973–74; Mem., Senate of Inns of Court and Bar, 1974–75. Contested (C) Gorton Div. of Manchester, 1955; Oldham West, 1966; MP (C) Oldham West, June 1968–70. *Recreations:* boating, riding. *Address:* 2 King's Bench Walk, Temple, EC4. *T:* 01-353 3400.

CAMPBELL, Laurence Jamieson; Headmaster, Kingswood School, Bath, since 1970; *b* 10 June 1927; *er s* of George S. Campbell and Mary P. Paterson; *m* 1954, Sheena E. Macdonald; two *s* one *d. Educ:* Hillhead High Sch., Glasgow; Aberdeen Univ., Edinburgh Univ. (MA). Lieut RA, 1945–48. Housemaster, Alliance High Sch., Kenya, 1952–56; Educn Sec., Christian Council of Kenya, 1957–62; Headmaster, Alliance High Sch., Kenya, 1963–70. Contested North Kenya Constituency, Kenya General Election, 1961. Mem. Council, Univ. of East Africa, 1963–69; Chm., Heads Assoc. of Kenya, 1965–69; Official of Kenya Commonwealth Games Team, 1970. Schoolmaster Fellow, Balliol Coll., Oxford, 1970. Chairman: Christians Abroad, 1977–81; Bloxham Project, 1981–. *Recreations:* golf, athletics, church. *Address:* Kingswood School, Bath, Avon BA1 5RG. *T:* Bath 311627. *Club:* Royal Commonwealth Society.

CAMPBELL, Leila; Chairman, Inner London Education Authority, 1977–78; *b* 10 Aug. 1911; *d* of Myer and Rebecca Jaffe; *m* 1940, Andrew Campbell (*d* 1968); one *d. Educ:* Belvedere Sch., Liverpool. Art Teacher's Dip. Dress designer, 1932–42; large-scale catering, 1942–46; Sch. Meals' Service, LCC, 1946–50. Elected (Lab), Hampstead Bor. Council, 1961–65; elected new London Bor. of Camden, 1964–78 (later Alderman): Vice-Chm., Health Cttee (until re-org.); Mem., Social Services Cttee; Chm., Libraries and Arts Cttee. Elected LCC for Holborn and S St Pancras, 1958–65: Mem., Children's Cttee; Vice-Chm., Health Cttee. Elected GLC for Camden, 1964–67: Chm., Schools Sub-cttee; apptd additional Mem., ILEA; Rep. Camden on ILEA, 1970–78: Vice-Chm., Schs Cttee; Chm., Adv. Cttee on Special Educn; Vice-Chm. of ILEA, 1967–77. Governor of schs and of further and higher educnl instns. *Recreations:* cooking, the theatre in all its forms, listening to music, opera, jazz. *Address:* 56 Belsize Park, NW3 4EH. *T:* 01-722 7038.

CAMPBELL of Airds, Brig. Lorne Maclaine, VC 1943; DSO 1940; OBE 1968; TD 1941; Argyll and Sutherland Highlanders (TA); *b* 22 July 1902; *s* of late Col Ian Maxwell Campbell, CBE; *m* 1935, Amy Muriel Jordan (*d* 1950), *d* of Alastair Magnus Campbell, Auchendarroch, Argyll; two *s. Educ:* Dulwich Coll.; Merton Coll., Oxford (Postmaster, MA). 8th Bn Argyll and Sutherland Highlanders, 1921–42, commanded 7th Bn, 1942–43, and 13th Inf. Brigade, 1943–44; BGS, British Army Staff, Washington, 1944–45; War of 1939–45: despatches four times, DSO and Bar, VC. Hon. Col 8th Bn Argyll and Sutherland Highlanders, 1954–67. Past Master of Vintners' Company (Hon. Vintner). Officer US Legion of Merit. *Address:* 95 Trinity Road, Edinburgh EH5 3JX. *T:* 031-552 6851. *Club:* New (Edinburgh).

CAMPBELL, Sir Matthew, KBE 1963; CB 1959; FRSE; Deputy Chairman, White Fish Authority, and Chairman, Authority's Committee for Scotland and Northern Ireland, 1968–78; *b* 23 May 1907; *s* of late Matthew Campbell, High Blantyre; *m* 1939, Isabella, *d* of late John Wilson, Rutherglen; two *s. Educ:* Hamilton Academy; Glasgow Univ. Entered CS, 1928, and after service in Inland Revenue Dept and Admiralty joined staff of Dept of Agriculture for Scotland, 1935; Principal, 1938; Assistant Sec., 1943; Under Sec., 1953; Sec., Dept of Agriculture and Fisheries for Scotland, 1958–68. *Address:* 10 Craigleith View, Edinburgh. *T:* 031-337 5168.

CAMPBELL, Mungo, CBE 1946; MA; retired shipowner; former director, Barclays Bank Ltd, Newcastle upon Tyne; *b* 5 June 1900; 2nd *s* of late James Campbell, The Manor House, Wormley, Herts; *m* 1st, 1944, Esther McCracken (*d* 1971); one *d decd*; 2nd, 1976, Betty Kirkpatrick. *Educ:* Loretto; Pembroke Coll., Cambridge. Ministry of War Transport, 1939–46 (Dir Ship Repair Div., 1942–46). Hon. DCL Newcastle, 1972. Comdr Order of Orange Nassau (Netherlands), 1947. *Address:* Rothley Lake House, Morpeth, Northumberland NE61 4JY. *Club:* Bath.

CAMPBELL, Sir Niall (Alexander Hamilton), 8th Bt *cr* 1831, of Barcaldine and Glenure; 15th Chieftain, Hereditary Keeper of Barcaldine Castle; Clerk to Justices of N Devon Divisions of Barnstaple, Bideford and Great Torrington and South Molton, since 1976; *b* 7 Jan. 1925; *o s* of Sir Ian Vincent Hamilton Campbell, 7th Bt, CB, and Madeline Lowe Reid (*d* 1929), *e d* of late Hugh Anglin Whitelocke, FRCS; *S* father, 1948; *m* 1st, 1949, Patricia Mary (marr. diss. on his petition, 1956), *d* of R. G. Turner; 2nd, 1957, Norma Joyce, *d* of W. N. Wiggin; two *s* two *d* (including twin *s* and *d*). *Educ:* Cheltenham College (Scholar); Corpus Christi Coll., Oxford. Called to the Bar, Inner Temple. Served War, 1943–46, Lieut Royal Marines; in Inf. bn, NW Europe campaign and on staff of Comdr RM training bde. Appts as Hosp. Administrator, 1953–70, inside and outside NHS, including St Mary's, Paddington, London Clinic, and Royal Hosp. and Home for Incurables, Putney (Chief Exec.); Dep. Chief Clerk, Inner London Magistrates' Courts, 1970–76, and Dep. Coroner, Inner London (South), Southwark. Mem. Exec. Cttee, N Devon Community Health Council; Governor, Grenville Coll., Bideford; Mem. Management Cttee, N Devon Cheshire Home. *Publication:* Making the Best Use of Bed Resources—monograph based on lecture sponsored by King Edward's Hospital Fund, 1965. *Recreations:* village life, vegetable gardening, birds. *Heir: er s* Roderick Duncan Hamilton Campbell, of Barcaldine, Younger, *b* 24 Feb. 1961. *Address:* The Old Mill, Milltown, Muddiford, Barnstaple, Devon. *T:* Shirwell 341; The Law Courts, Civic Centre, Barnstaple. *T:* Barnstaple 72511; (seat) Barcaldine Castle, Benderloch via Connel, Argyllshire.

CAMPBELL, Prof. Peter Nelson; Courtauld Professor of Biochemistry, and Director of the Courtauld Institute, Middlesex Hospital Medical School, London University, since 1976; *b* 5 Nov. 1921; *s* of late Alan A. Campbell and Nora Nelson; *m* 1946, Mollie (*née* Manklow); one *s* one *d. Educ:* Eastbourne Coll.; Univ. Coll., London (Fellow, 1981). BSc, PhD, DSc, London; FIBiol. Research and Production Chemist with Standard Telephones and Cables, Ltd, 1942-46; PhD Student, UCL; 1946-47; Asst Lectr UCL, 1947-49; staff of Nat. Inst. for Med. Research, Hampstead and Mill Hill, 1949-54; Asst, Courtauld Inst. of Biochem., Middx Hosp. Med. Sch., 1954-57; Sen. Lectr, Middx Hosp. Med. Sch., 1957-64; Reader in Biochem., Univ. of London, 1964-67; Prof. and Head of Dept of Biochem., Leeds Univ., 1967-75. Hon. Lectr, Dept of Biochem., UCL, 1954-67. Fellow UCL, 1981. Diplôme d'Honneur, Fedn of European Biochemical Socs. *Publications:* Structure and Function of Animal Cell Components, 1966; (ed with B. A. Kilby) Basic Biochemistry for Medical Students, 1975; (ed) Biology in Profile, 1981; (with A. D. Smith) Biochemistry Illustrated, 1982; ed, Essays in Biochemistry and other vols; many scientific papers in Biochem. Jl. *Recreations:* theatre, travelling, conversation. *Address:* Courtauld Institute of Biochemistry, The Middlesex Hospital Medical School, W1P 7PN. *T:* 01-636 8333, ext. 7483.

CAMPBELL, Prof. Peter (Walter); Professor of Politics, Reading University, since 1964; *b* 17 June 1926; *o s* of late W. C. H. Campbell and of L. M. Locke. *Educ:* Bournemouth Sch.; New Coll., Oxford. 2nd class PPE, 1947; MA 1951; Research Student, Nuffield Coll., Oxford, 1947-49. Asst Lecturer in Govt, Manchester Univ., 1949-52; Lectr, 1952-60; Vice-Warden Needham Hall, 1959-60; Visiting Lectr in Political Science, Victoria Univ. Coll., NZ, 1954; Prof. of Political Economy, 1960-64, Dean, Faculty of Letters, 1966-69, Chm., Graduate Sch. of Contemporary European Studies, 1971-73, Reading University. Hon. Sec. Political Studies Assoc., 1955-58; Chm., Inst. of Electoral Research, 1959-65; Mem. Council, Hansard Soc. for Parly Govt, 1962-77; Editor of Political Studies, 1963-69; Hon. Treas., Joint Univ. Council for Social and Public Administration, 1965-69; Vice-Chm., Reading and District Council of Social Service, 1966-71; Vice-Pres., Electoral Reform Soc., 1972-. Member: CNAA Bds and Panels, 1971-78; Social Studies Sub-Cttee, UGC, 1973-83. Co-Pres., Reading Univ. Cons. Assoc., 1961-. Mem. Council, Campaign for Homosexual Equality, 1978-79; Convenor, Reading CHE, 1979-80; Newsletter Editor, Conservative Gp for Homosexual Equality, 1980-. *Publications:* (with W. Theimer) Encyclopædia of World Politics, 1950; French Electoral Systems and Elections, 1789-1957, 1958; (with B. Chapman) The Constitution of the Fifth Republic, 1958. Articles in British, French and New Zealand Jls of Political Science. *Recreations:* ambling, idling, managing, meddling. *Address:* The University, Reading RG6 2AA. *T:* Reading 875123.

CAMPBELL, Quentin; *see* Campbell, J. Q.

CAMPBELL, Sir Ralph Abercromby, Kt 1961; Chief Justice of the Bahamas, 1960-70; *b* 16 March 1906; 2nd *s* of Major W. O. Campbell, MC; *m* 1st, 1936, Joan Childers Blake (marr. diss., 1968); one *s* one *d*; 2nd, 1968, Shelagh Moore. *Educ:* Winchester; University Coll., Oxford. Barrister-at-Law, Lincoln's Inn, 1928; Western Circuit; Avocat à la Cour, Egypt, 1929; Pres. Civil Courts, Baghdad, Iraq, 1931-44; British Military Administration, Eritrea, Pres. British Military Court and Italian Court of Appeal, 1945; Resident Magistrate, Kenya, 1946; Judge of the Supreme Court, Aden, 1952 (redesignated Chief Justice, 1956)-1960. *Publications:* (Ed.) Law Reports of Kenya and East African Court of Appeal, 1950; Aden Law Reports, 1954-55; Bahamas Law Reports, 1968. *Recreations:* polo, golf, fishing. *Address:* Lomans Hill, Hartley Wintney, Hants. *T:* Hartley Wintney 3283.

CAMPBELL, Robert, MSc; FICE; Management Consultant; Chairman, Rem Campbell International; *b* 18 May 1929; *s* of Robert Stewart Campbell and Isobella Frances Campbell; *m* 1950, Edna Maud Evans. *Educ:* Emmanuel IGS; Loughborough Univ. (DLC (Hons), MSc). MIWES. Member of Gray's Inn, 1960. Contracts Engineer, Wyatts, Contractors, 1954-56; Chief Asst Engr, Stirlingshire and Falkirk Water Board, 1956-59; Water Engr, Camborne, 1959-60; Chief Asst City Water Engr, Plymouth, 1960-65; Civil Engr, Colne Valley Water Co., 1965-69; Engrg Inspector, Min. of Housing and Local Govt/DoE, 1969-74; Asst Dir, Resources, Planning, Anglian Water Authority, 1974-77; Chief Executive, Epping Forest Dist Council, 1977-79; Sec., ICE, 1979-81, and Man. Dir, Thomas Telford Ltd, Dir, Watt Cttee on Energy, and Hon. Sec., ICE Benevolent Fund, 1979-81. Freeman of City of London, 1977; Liveryman of Horners' Co. 1977-. *Publication:* The Pricing of Water, 1973. *Recreations:* golf, music, caravanning, cricket. *Address:* 6 The Croft, Lodsworth, Petworth, West Sussex GU28 9BW. *Clubs:* Athenæum, MCC.

CAMPBELL, Sir Robin Auchinbreck, 15th Bt *cr* 1628 (NS); *b* 7 June 1922; *s* of Sir Louis Hamilton Campbell, 14th Bt and Margaret Elizabeth Patricia, *d* of late Patrick Campbell; *S* father, 1970; *m* 1st, 1948, Rosemary, (Sally) (*d* 1978), *d* of Ashley Dean, Christchurch, NZ; one *s* two *d*; 2nd, 1978, Mrs Elizabeth Gunston, *d* of Sir Arthur Colegate, Bembridge, IoW. Formerly

Lieut (A) RNVR. *Heir:* *s* Louis Auchinbreck Campbell, *b* 17 Jan. 1953. *Address:* Glen Dhu, Motunau, Scargill, North Canterbury, New Zealand.

CAMPBELL, Robin Francis, CBE 1978; DSO 1943; Director of Art, Arts Council of Great Britain, 1969-78; *b* 1912; *s* of Rt. Hon. Sir Ronald Hugh Campbell, GCMG and Helen, *d* of Richard Graham; *m* 1st, 1936, Hon. Mary Hermione Ormsby Gore (marr. diss. 1945); two *s*; 2nd, 1945, Lady Mary Sybil St Clair Erskine (marr. diss. 1959); 3rd, 1959, Susan Jennifer Benson; two *s. Educ:* Wellington Coll.; New Coll., Oxford. Reuters correspondent, Berlin, Warsaw, 1936-39. Served N Africa, No 8 Commando and GHQ, Cairo, 1940-41; POW, 1941-43. Arts Council of GB, 1960-78. Hon. Dr RCA, 1978. Officier de l'Ordre des Arts et des Lettres, France, 1979. *Address:* 6 Noel Road, N1 8HA. *T:* 01-226 1009.

CAMPBELL, Ronald Francis Boyd, MA; *b* 28 Aug. 1912; *o s* of Major Roy Neil Boyd Campbell, DSO, OBE and Effie Muriel, *y d* of Major Charles Pierce, IMS; *m* 1939, Pamela Muriel Désirée, *o d* of H. L. Wright, OBE, late Indian Forest Service; one *s* two *d. Educ:* Berkhamsted Sch.; Peterhouse, Cambridge. Asst Master, Berkhamsted Sch., 1934-39. War of 1939-45: Supplementary Reserve, The Duke of Cornwall's Light Infantry, Sept. 1939; served in England and Italy; DAQMG, HQ 3rd Div., 1943; demobilized with hon. rank of Lt-Col, 1945. Housemaster and OC Combined Cadet Force, Berkhamsted Sch., 1945-51; Headmaster, John Lyon Sch., Harrow, 1951-68. Dir, Public Sch. Appointments Bureau, later Independent Schs Careers Orgn, 1968-78. Walter Hines Page Travelling Scholarship to USA, 1960. 1939-45 Star, Italy Star, Defence and Victory Medals; ERD (2 clasps). *Recreations:* sailing, fishing. *Address:* 30 Marine Drive, Torpoint, Cornwall PL11 2EN. *T:* Plymouth 813671. *Clubs:* Royal Cruising; Royal Western.

CAMPBELL, Rt. Hon. Sir Ronald Ian, PC 1950; GCMG 1947 (KCMG 1941; CMG 1932); CB 1937; Director of Royal Bank of Scotland, 1950-65 (Extra-ordinary Director, 1965-68); *b* 7 June 1890; *s* of Lieut-Col Sir Guy Campbell, 3rd Bt, and Nina, *d* of late Frederick Lehmann, 15 Berkeley Square, W1. *Educ:* Eton Coll.; Magdalen Coll., Oxford. Entered Diplomatic Service, 1914; Third Sec., Washington, 1915-20; Second and First Sec., Paris, 1920-23; Foreign Office, 1923-27; First Sec., Acting Counsellor and Counsellor Washington, 1927-31; Counsellor, Cairo, 1931-34; Counsellor in Foreign Office, 1934-38; Minister Plenipotentiary, British Embassy, Paris, 1938-39; Minister at Belgrade, 1939-41; Minister in Washington, 1941-45; an Asst Under-Sec. of State in the Foreign Office, 1945-46; Dep. to Sec. of State for Foreign Affairs on Council of Foreign Ministers, 1945-46; British Ambassador to Egypt, 1946-50; retired, 1950. Grand Officer of Legion of Honour. *Address:* 20 Sidegate, Haddington, East Lothian. *Clubs:* Brooks's, MCC; New (Edinburgh).
See also Sir Guy Campbell.

CAMPBELL, Ross, DSC 1944; Chairman, Atomic Energy of Canada Ltd, 1976-79; President: Atomic Energy of Canada International, 1979; Canus Technical Services Corporation; *b* 4 Nov. 1918; *s* of late William Marshall Campbell and of Helen Isabel Harris; *m* 1945, Penelope Grantham-Hill; two *s. Educ:* Univ. of Toronto Schs; Trin. Coll., Univ. of Toronto. BA, Faculty of Law, 1940. Served RCN, 1940-45. Joined Dept. of Ext. Affairs, Canada 1945; Third Sec., Oslo, 1946-47; Second Sec., Copenhagen, 1947-50 European Div., Ottawa, 1950-52; First Sec., Ankara, 1952-56; Head of Middle East Div., Ottawa, 1957-59; Special Asst to Sec. of State for Ext. Aff. 1959-62; Asst Under-Sec. of State for Ext. Aff., 1962-64; Adviser to Canadiar Delegns to: UN Gen. Assemblies, 1958-63; North Atlantic Coun., 1959-64 Ambassador to Yugoslavia, 1964-67, concurrently accredited Ambassador to Algeria, 1965-67; Ambassador and Perm. Rep. to NATO, 1967-73 (Paris May 1967, Brussels Oct. 1967); Ambassador to Japan, 1973-75, and concurrently to Republic of Korea, 1973. *Recreations:* tennis, skiing, gardening. *Address* Rivermead House, 179 Aylmer Road, Aylmer, Que J9H 5T8, Canada (office) Suite 2200, 320 Queen Street, Ottawa, K1R 5A3, Canada.

CAMPBELL, Ross; Director, International Military Services Ltd, since 1979 *b* 4 May 1916; 2nd *s* of George Albert Campbell and Jean Glendinning Campbell (*née* Ross); *m* 1st, 1952, Dr Diana Stewart (*d* 1977); one *s* two (and one *d* decd); 2nd, 1979, Jean Margaret Turner (*née* Ballinger). *Educ* Farnborough Grammar Sch.; Reading Univ. CEng, FICE. Articled to Municipal Engr; Local Authority Engr, 1936-39; Air Min. (UK), 1939-44 Sqdn Ldr, RAF, Middle East, 1944-47; Air Min. (UK), 1947-52; Supt Engr Gibraltar, 1952-55; Air Min. (UK), 1955-59; Chief Engr, Far East Air Force 1959-62 and Bomber Comd, 1962-63; Personnel Management, MPBW 1963-66; Chief Resident Engr, Persian Gulf, 1966-68; Dir Staff Management MPBW, 1968-69; Dir of Works (Air), 1969-72; Under-Sec., and Dir o Defence Services II PSA, DoE, 1972-75. Dir, 1975-77, Dep. Chief Exec 1977-79, Internat. Military Services Ltd. *Publications:* papers on professiona civil engrg and trng in ICE Jl. *Recreations:* golf, tennis, music. *Address* Thatch Tower, Troutstream Way, Loudwater, Rickmansworth, Herts. *T* Rickmansworth 73744. *Club:* Royal Air Force.

CAMPBELL, Sir Thomas Cockburn-, 6th Bt, *cr* 1821; Retired; *b* 8 Dec 1918; *e s* of Sir Alexander Thomas Cockburn-Campbell, 5th Bt, and Maud Frances Lorenzo (*d* 1926), *o d* of Alfred Giles, Kent Town, Adelaide; *S* father 1935; *m* 1944, Josephine Zoi (marr. diss. 1981), *e d* of Harold Dougla Forward, Curjardine, WA; one *s*, *m* Janice Laraine, *y d* of William Joh Pascoe, Bundoora, Vic. *Educ:* Melbourne C of E Grammar Sch. *Heir:* Alexander Thomas Cockburn-Campbell [*b* 16 March 1945; *m* 1969, Kerr

Ann, *e d* of Sgt K. Johnson; one *s* one *d*]. *Address:* 14 Lincoln Street, York, WA 6302, Australia.

CAMPBELL, Maj.-Gen. Victor David Graham, CB 1956; DSO 1940; OBE 1946; JP; DL; *b* 9 March 1905; *s* of late Gen. Sir David G. M. Campbell, GCB; *m* 1947, Dulce Beatrix, *d* of late G. B. Collier, and *widow* of Lt-Col J. A. Goodwin. *Educ:* Rugby; RMC Sandhurst. 2nd Lieut The Queen's Own Cameron Highlanders, 1924; AQMG and DA&QMG HQ AFNEI, 1945-46; Lt-Col Comdg 1st Bn The Gordon Highlanders, 1949; Brig. Comdg 31 Lorried Infantry Brigade, 1951; Chief of Staff, HQ Scottish Command, 1954-57; psc 1938; idc 1953. DL and JP, 1962, High Sheriff, 1968, County of Devon; Chairman: Totnes RDC, 1971-72; Totnes Petty Sessional Div., 1972-75. *Address:* Beggars Bush, South Brent, South Devon.

CAMPBELL, Hon. Sir Walter (Benjamin), Kt 1979; **Hon. Mr Justice Campbell;** Chief Justice of Queensland, Australia, since 1982; *b* 4 March 1921; *s* of Archie Eric Gordon Campbell and Leila Mary Campbell; *m* 1942, Georgina Margaret Pearce; one *s* one *d* (and one *s* decd). *Educ:* Univ. of Queensland (MA, LLB; Hon. LLD 1980). Served War, RAAF, 1941-46 (pilot). Called to the Qld Bar, 1948; QC 1960; Judge, Supreme Court, Qld, 1967. Chairman: Law Reform Commn of Qld, 1969-73; Remuneration Tribunal (Commonwealth), 1974-82; sole Mem., Academic Salaries Tribunal (Commonwealth), 1974-78. President: Qld Bar Assoc., 1965-67; Australian Bar Assoc., 1966-67; Mem. Exec., Law Council of Aust., 1965-67. Dir, Winston Churchill Meml Trust, 1969-80; Chm., Utah Foundn, 1977-. Mem. Senate 1963-, and Chancellor 1977-, Univ. of Qld. *Recreations:* golf, fishing. *Address:* 71 Enderley Road, Clayfield, Brisbane, Qld 4011, Australia. *T:* 2623849. *Clubs:* Queensland, Royal Queensland Golf (Brisbane); Australasian Pioneers (Sydney).

CAMPBELL, Maj.-Gen. William Tait, CBE 1945 (OBE 1944); retired; *b* 8 Oct. 1912; *s* of late R. B. Campbell, MD, FRCPE, Edinburgh; *m* 1942, Rhoda Alice, *y d* of late Adm. Algernon Walker-Heneage-Vivian, CB, MVO, Swansea; two *d*. *Educ:* Cargilfield Sch.; Fettes Coll.; RMC Sandhurst. 2nd Lieut, The Royal Scots (The Royal Regt), 1933; served War of 1939-45: 1st Airborne Div. and 1st Allied Airborne Army (North Africa, Sicily, Italy and Europe). Lieut-Col Commanding 1st Bn The Royal Scots, in Egypt, Cyprus, UK and Suez Operation (despatches), 1954-57; Col, Royal Naval War Coll., Greenwich, 1958; Brig. i/c Admin. Malaya, 1962; Maj.-Gen., 1964; DQMG, MoD (Army Dept), 1964-67; Col, The Royal Scots (The Royal Regt), 1964-74. Dir, The Fairbridge Soc., 1969-78. US Bronze Star, 1945. *Recreations:* gardening, golf, shooting, fishing. *Address:* c/o Lloyds Bank Ltd (Cox's & King's Branch), 6 Pall Mall, SW1Y 5NH; Ashwood, Boarhills, St Andrews, Fife KY16 8PR. *T:* Boarhills 394.

CAMPBELL GOLDING, F.; *see* Golding, F. C.

CAMPBELL-GRAY, family name of **Lord Gray.**

CAMPBELL-JOHNSON, Alan, CIE 1947; OBE 1946; Officer of US Legion of Merit, 1947; MA Oxon; FRSA, MRI; Chairman, Campbell-Johnson Ltd, Public Relations Consultants; *b* 16 July 1913; *o c* of late Lieut-Col James Alexander Campbell-Johnson and late Gladys Susanne Campbell-Johnson; *m* 1938, Imogen Fay de la Tour Dunlap; one *d* (one *s* decd). *Educ:* Westminster; Christ Church, Oxford (scholar). BA 2nd Cl. Hons Mod. Hist., 1935. Political Sec. to Rt Hon. Sir Archibald Sinclair, Leader of Parl. Lib. Party, 1937-40; served War of 1939-45, RAF; COHQ, 1942-43; HQ SACSEA (Wing Comdr i/c Inter-Allied Records Section), 1943-46. Contested (L) Salisbury and South Wilts. Div., Gen. Elections, 1945 and 1950. Press Attaché to Viceroy and Gov.-Gen. of India (Earl Mountbatten of Burma), 1947-48. Fellow Inst. of Public Relations, Pres. 1956-57. *Publications:* Growing Opinions, 1935; Peace Offering, 1936; Anthony Eden: a biography, 1938, rev. edn 1955; Viscount Halifax: a biography, 1941; Mission with Mountbatten, 1951, repr, 1972. *Recreations:* cricket, mountaineering. *Address:* 21 Ashley Gardens, Ambrosden Avenue, SW1P 1QD. *T:* 01-834 1532. *Clubs:* Brooks's, National Liberal, MCC.

CAMPBELL ORDE, Alan Colin, CBE 1943; AFC 1919; FRAeS; *b* Lochgilphead, Argyll, NB, 4 Oct. 1898; *s* of Colin Ridley Campbell Orde; *m* 1951, Mrs Beatrice McClure, *e d* of late Rev. Eliott-Drake Briscoe. *Educ:* Sherborne. Served European War, 1916-18, Flight Sub-Lieut, Royal Navy, and Flying Officer, Royal Air Force; active service in Belgium, 1917; one of original commercial Pilots on London-Paris route with Aircraft Transport & Travel Ltd, 1919-20; Instructor and Adviser to Chinese Govt in Peking, 1921-23; Instructor and latterly Chief Test Pilot to Sir W. G. Armstrong-Whitworth Aircraft, Ltd, Coventry, 1924-36; Operational Manager, British Airways, Ltd, 1936-39; subseq. Operations Manager, Imperial Airways Ltd; was Ops Director BOAC, during first 4 years after its inception in 1939; thereafter responsible for technical development as Development Dir until resignation from BOAC Dec. 1957. *Recreation:* reading in bed. *Address:* Smugglers Mead, Stepleton, Blandford, Dorset. *T:* Child Okeford 860268. *Club:* Boodle's.

CAMPBELL-ORDE, Sir John A.; *see* Orde.

CAMPBELL-PRESTON of Ardchattan, Robert Modan Thorne, OBE 1955; MC 1943; Vice-Lieutenant, Argyll and Bute, since 1976; *b* 7 Jan. 1909; *s* of Col R. W. P. Campbell-Preston, DL, JP, of Ardchattan and Valleyfield,

Fife, and Mary Augusta Thorne, MBE; *m* 1950, Hon. Angela Murray (*d* 1981), 3rd *d* of 2nd Viscount Cowdray and *widow* of George Anthony Murray; one *d*. *Educ:* Eton; Christ Church, Oxford (MA). Lt Scottish Horse, 1930; Lt-Col 1945. Hon. Col, Fife-Forfar Yeo./Scottish Horse, 1962-67. Member Royal Company of Archers, Queen's Body Guard for Scotland. Joint Managing Director, Alginate Industries Ltd, 1949-74. DL 1951, JP 1950, Argyllshire. Silver Star (USA), 1945. *Recreations:* shooting, fishing. *Address:* Ardchattan Priory, Connel, Argyll. *T:* Bonawe 274; 31 Marlborough Hill, NW8. *T:* 01-586 2291. *Club:* Puffin's (Edinburgh).

CAMPBELL-PURDIE, Cora Gwendolyn Jean, (Wendy); founded Tree Crops as demonstration and research project, Greece, 1981; *b* 8 June 1925; *d* of Edmund Hamilton Campbell Purdie and Janie Theodora Williams. *Educ:* Woodford House, New Zealand. Worked with Red Cross Transport Corps in Auckland, 1943-46. English Asst at Lycées in France and Corsica, 1954-56; worked simultaneously and subseq. full-time with British timber firm in Corsica, 1954-58; FAO, Rome, on Mediterranean Reafforestation Project, Aug. 1958. Has been planting trees in N Africa, 1959 onwards; Co-founder with Rev. Austen Williams as Chm., Sahara Re-afforestation Cttee, 1965, registered with Charity Comrs as Bou Saada Trust, 1969 (Dir, 1969-78, when Trust wound up); now expects at least 75 per cent success; planted: 1000 trees (given by Moroccan Min. of Agric.) in Tiznit, 1960 and again in 1961; 10,000 trees (given by Algerian Min. of Agric.) planted by local agricl authorities at Bou Saada, 1964, by 1970 approx. 130,000 trees established on 260 acres; grain, fruit trees and vegetables now also grown, and bees and hens kept. Has planted many more thousands of trees (money given by: Men of the Trees; War on Want; St Martin-in-the-Fields; the Bishop of Southwark's Diocesan Fund; CORSO (New Zealand), etc). Film made of Bou Saada project, 1970; since then has travelled with film, discussing re-afforestation and forestry techniques, in Commonwealth, USA, Africa, Near and Middle East. Attended: World Food Conf., Rome, 1974; Sahel Drought Conf., Senegal, 1975; began planting Forest of Peace with help of 8th Army veterans, March, 1979; work carried on by Commonwealth War Graves Commn after breaking hip in Nov. *Publications:* (in collaboration with Fenner Brockway) Woman against the Desert, 1967; contrib. The Ecologist. *Recreation:* classical music.

CAMPBELL-SAVOURS, Dale Norman; MP (Lab) Workington, Cumbria, since 1979; *b* 23 Aug. 1943; *s* of John Lawrence and Cynthia Lorraine Campbell-Savours; *m* 1970, Gudrun Kristin Runolfsdottir; two *s*. *Educ:* Keswick Sch.; Sorbonne, Paris. Dir, clock manufacturing co., 1971-78. Member, Ramsbottom UDC, 1972-73. Mem., TGWU, 1970-. Contested (Lab): Darwen Division of Lancashire, gen. elections, Feb. 1974, Oct. 1974; Workington, by-election, 1976. *Address:* House of Commons, SW1.

CAMPDEN, Viscount; Anthony Baptist Noel; *b* 16 Jan. 1950; *s* and *heir* of 5th Earl of Gainsborough, *qv*; *m* 1972, Sarah Rose, *er d* of Col T. F. C. Winnington; one *s*. *Educ:* Ampleforth; Royal Agricultural Coll., Cirencester. *Heir: s* Hon. Henry Robert Anthony Noel, *b* 1 July 1977. *Address:* Top House, Exton, Rutland, Leics LE15 8AX. *T:* Oakham 812587; 105 Earls Court Road, W8. *T:* 01-370 5650. *Club:* Turf.
    See also Sir F. S. W. Winnington, Bt.

CAMPION, Sir Harry, KCB 1957; CB 1949; CBE 1945; MA; retired as Director of Central Statistical Office, Cabinet Office, 1967; *b* 20 May 1905; *o s* of John Henry Campion, Worsley, Lancs. *Educ:* Farnworth Grammar Sch.; Univ. of Manchester. Rockefeller Foundation Fellow, United States, 1932; Robert Ottley Reader in Statistics, Univ. of Manchester, 1933-39. Dir of Statistical Office, UN, 1946-47; Mem. of Statistical Commission, United Nations, 1947-67; Pres.: International Statistical Institute, 1963-67; Royal Statistical Society, 1957-59; Hon. LLD, Manchester, 1967. *Publications:* Distribution of National Capital; Public and Private Property in Great Britain; articles in economic and statistical journals. *Address:* Rima, Priory Close, Stanmore, Mddx. *T:* 01-954 3267. *Club:* Reform.

CAMPION, Peter James, DPhil; FInstP; Deputy Director, National Physical Laboratory, since 1976; *b* 7 April 1926; *s* of Frank Wallace Campion and Gertrude Alice (*née* Lambert); *m* 1950, Beryl Grace Stanton, *e d* of John and Grace Stanton; one *s* one *d* (and one *s* decd). *Educ:* Westcliff High Sch., Essex; Exeter Coll., Oxford (MA, DPhil). FInstP 1964. RN, 1943. Nuffield Res. Fellow, Oxford, 1954; Chalk River Proj., Atomic Energy of Canada Ltd, 1955; National Physical Lab., Teddington, 1960-: Supt, Div. of Radiation Science, 1964; Supt, Div. of Mech. and Optical Metrology, 1974. Mem., Comité Consultatif pour les Etalons de Mesure des Rayonnements Ionisante, 1963-79; Chm., Sect. II, reconstituted Comité Consultatif, Mesure des radionucléides, 1970-79. Editor, Internat. Jl of Applied Radiation and Isotopes, 1968-71. *Publications:* A Code of Practice for the Detailed Statement of Accuracy (with A. Williams and J. E. Burns), 1973; technical and rev. papers in learned jls on neutron capture gamma rays, measurement of radioactivity, and on metrology generally. *Recreation:* winemaking and wine drinking. *Address:* National Physical Laboratory, Teddington, Mddx.

CAMPLING, Ven. Christopher Russell; Archdeacon of Dudley and Director of Religious Education in the Diocese of Worcester, since 1976; *b* 4 July 1925; *s* of Canon William Charles Campling; *m* 1953, Juliet Marian Hughes; one *s* two *d*. *Educ:* Lancing Coll.; St Edmund Hall, Oxford (MA; Hons Theol. cl. 2); Cuddesdon Theol. Coll. RNVR, 1943-47. Deacon 1951, priest 1952; Curate of Basingstoke, 1951-55; Minor Canon of Ely Cathedral and Chaplain of King's School, Ely, 1955-60; Chaplain of Lancing Coll., 1960-67; Vicar of

Pershore with Pinvin and Wick and Birlingham, 1968-76; RD of Pershore, 1970-76. Mem., General Synod of Church of England, 1970-; Chm., House of Clergy, Diocese of Worcester, 1981-. *Publications:* The Way, The Truth and The Life: Vol. 1, The Love of God in Action, 1964; Vol. 2, The People of God in Action, 1964; Vol. 3, The Word of God in Action, 1965; Vol. 4, God's Plan in Action, 1965; also two teachers' volumes; Words for Worship, 1969; The Fourth Lesson, Vol. 1 1973, Vol. 2 1974. *Recreations:* music, drama, golf. *Address:* The Archdeacon's House, Dodderhill, Droitwich, Worcs WR9 8LW. *Club:* Naval.

CAMPOLI, Alfredo; violinist; *b* 20 Oct. 1906; *s* of Prof. Romeo Campoli, Prof. of Violin at Accademia di Santa Cecilia, Rome, and Elvira Campoli, dramatic soprano; *m* 1942, Joy Burbridge. Came to London, 1911; gave regular public recitals as a child; Gold Medal, London Musical Festival, 1919; toured British Isles with Melba and with Dame Clara Butt, and was engaged for series of International Celebrity Concerts at age of 15. Has played all over the world. First broadcast from Savoy Hill, 1930; has subsequently made frequent broadcasts and television appearances, and made many gramophone records. *Recreations:* bridge, cine-photography, table tennis, billiards, croquet. *Address:* 50 Eversley Park Road, Winchmore Hill, N21.

CAMPOS, Prof. Christophe Lucien; Director, British Institute in Paris, since 1978; *b* 27 April 1938; *s* of Lucien Antoine Campos and Margaret Lilian (*née* Dunn); *m* 1977, Lucy Elizabeth Mitchell; four *d. Educ:* Lycée Lamoricière, Oran; Lycée Français de Londres; Lycée Henri IV, Paris; Gonville and Caius Coll., Cambridge. LèsL (Paris), PhD (Cantab). Lector in French, Gonville and Caius Coll., 1959; Lecturer in French: Univ. of Maryland, 1963; Univ. of Sussex, 1964; Lectr in English, Univ. i Oslo, 1969; Prof. of French, University Coll., Dublin, 1974. *Publications:* The View of France, 1964; contribs to Th. Qly, TLS, Univs Qly. *Recreations:* bees, football, gardening, gastronomy, navigation. *Address:* 71 bis rue de Vaugirard, 75006 Paris; 53 Houndean Rise, Lewes, Sussex.

CAMPOS, Roberto de Oliveira, Hon. GCVO 1976; Brazilian Ambassador to the Court of St James's, since 1975; *b* Cuiabá, Mato Grosso, 17 April 1917. *Educ:* Catholic Seminaries: Guaxupé and Belo Horizonte, Brazil (grad. Philosophy and Theol.); George Washington Univ., Washington (MA Econs); Columbia Univ., NYC (Hon. Dr). Entered Brazilian Foreign Service, 1939; Economic Counsellor, Brazil-US EDC, 1951-53; Dir 1952, Gen. Man. 1955, Pres. 1959, Nat. Economic Develt Bank; Sec. Gen., Nat. Develt Council, 1956-59; Delegate to internat. confs, incl. ECOSOC and GATT, 1959-61; Roving Ambassador for financial negotiations in W Europe, 1961; Ambassador of Brazil to US, 1961-63; Minister of State for Planning and Co-ord., 1964-67. Profs., Sch. of Econs, Univ. of Brazil, 1956-61. Mem. or past Mem., Cttees and Bds on economic develt (particularly inter-Amer. econ. develt). *Publications:* Ensaios de História Econômica e Sociologia; Economia, Planejamento e Nacionalismo; A Moeda, o Govêrno e o Tempo; A Técnica e o Riso; Reflections on Latin American Development; Do outro lado da cerca; Temas e Sistemas; Ensaios contra a maré; Política Econômica e Mitos Políticos (jtly); Trends in International Trade (GATT report); Partners in Progress (report of Pearson Cttee of World Bank); A Nova Economia Brasileira; Formas Criativas do Desenvolvimento Brasileiro; Omundo que vejo e não desejo; techn. articles and reports on develt and internat. econs, in jls. *Address:* Brazilian Embassy, 32 Green Street, W1. *T:* 01-499 0877.

CAMPS, William Anthony; Master of Pembroke College, Cambridge, 1970-81; *b* 28 Dec. 1910; *s* of P. W. L. Camps, FRCS, and Alice, *d* of Joseph Redfern, Matlock; *m* 1953, Miriam Camp, Washington, DC, *d* of Prof. Burton Camp, Wesleyan Univ., Connecticut. *Educ:* Marlborough Coll.; Pembroke Coll., Cambridge (Schol.). Fellow, Pembroke Coll., 1933; Univ. Lectr in Classics, 1939; Temp. Civil Servant, 1940-45; Asst Tutor, Pembroke Coll., 1945; Senior Tutor, 1947-62; Tutor for Advanced Students, 1963-70; Pres., 1964-70. Mem., Inst. for Advanced Study, Princeton, 1956-57; Vis. Assoc. Prof., UC Toronto, 1966; Vis. Prof., Univ. of North Carolina at Chapel Hill, 1969. *Publications:* edns of Propertius I, 1961, IV, 1965, III, 1966, II, 1967; An Introduction to Virgil's Aeneid, 1969; An Introduction to Homer, 1980; sundry notes and reviews in classical periodicals. *Recreations:* unremarkable. *Address:* c/o Pembroke College, Cambridge. *T:* Cambridge 52241. *Club:* United Oxford & Cambridge University.

CAMROSE, 2nd Viscount, *cr* 1941, of Hackwood Park; **John Seymour Berry,** TD; Bt 1921; Baron 1929; Deputy Chairman (Past Chairman) of The Daily Telegraph Ltd; *b* 12 July 1909; *e s* of 1st Viscount Camrose and Mary Agnes (*d* 1962), *e d* of late Thomas Corns, 2 Bolton Street, W; *S* father, 1954. *Educ:* Eton; Christ Church, Oxford. Major, City of London Yeomanry. Served War of 1939-45, North African and Italian Campaigns, 1942-45 (despatches). MP (C) for Hitchin Division, Herts, 1941-45. Vice-Chm. Amalgamated Press Ltd, 1942-59. Younger Brother, Trinity House. *Heir: b* Baron Hartwell, *qv. Address:* Hackwood Park, Basingstoke, Hampshire. *T:* Basingstoke 64630. *Clubs:* Buck's, White's, Beefsteak, Marylebone Cricket (MCC); Royal Yacht Squadron (Trustee).

See also Earl of Birkenhead.

CANADA, Primate of All; *see* Scott, Most Rev. E. W.

CANADA, Metropolitan of the Ecclesiastical Province of; *see* Fredericton, Archbishop of.

CANAVAN, Dennis Andrew; MP (Lab) West Stirlingshire, since Oct. 1974; *b* 8 Aug. 1942; *s* of Thomas and Agnes Canavan; *m* 1964, Elnor Stewart; three *s* one *d. Educ:* St Columba's High Sch., Cowdenbeath; Edinburgh Univ. (BSc Hons, DipEd). Head of Maths Dept, St Modan's High Sch., Stirling, 1970-74; Asst Headmaster, Holy Rood High Sch., Edinburgh, 1974. Treasurer, Scottish Parly Lab. Gp, 1976-79, Vice-Chm., 1979-80, Chm., 1980-81; Convener, Scottish Parly Lab Gp Educn Sub-Cttee, 1976-. Parly spokesman for Scottish Cttee on mobility for the disabled, 1977-. Mem. Local Exec., Educnl Inst. of Scotland, 1972-74; Organising Sec., W Stirlingshire Constituency Labour Party, 1972-74; Labour Party Agent, Feb. 1974; District Councillor, 1973-74; Leader of Labour Gp, Stirling District Council, 1974; Member: Stirling Dist Educn Sub-cttee, 1973-74; Stirlingshire Youth Employment Adv. Cttee, 1972-74; Mem., H of C Select Cttee on Foreign Affairs, 1982-. *Publications:* contribs to various jls on educn and politics. *Recreations:* walking, running, swimming, reading, football (Scottish Univs football internationalist, 1966-67 and 1967-68; Hon. Pres., Milton Amateurs FC). *Address:* 15 Margaret Road, Bannockburn, Stirlingshire. *T:* Bannockburn 812581; House of Commons, SW1A 0AA. *T:* 01-219 3000. *Club:* Bannockburn Miners' Welfare (Bannockburn).

CANBERRA AND GOULBURN, Archbishop of, (RC), since 1979; **Most Rev. Edward Bede Clancy,** DD; *b* 13 Dec. 1923; *s* of John Bede Clancy and Ellen Lucy Clancy (*née* Edwards). *Educ:* Marist Brothers Coll., Parramatta, NSW; St Patrick's Coll., Manly, NSW; Biblical Inst., Rome (LSS); Propaganda Fide Univ., Rome (DD). Ordained to priesthood, 1949; parish ministry, 1950-51; studies in Rome, 1952-54; parish ministry, 1955-57; seminary staff, 1958-61; studies in Rome, 1962-64; seminary staff, Manly, 1966-73; Auxiliary Bishop, Sydney, 1974-78. *Publications:* The Bible—The Church's Book, 1974; contribs to Australian Catholic Record. *Recreation:* golf. *Address:* Archbishop's House, Commonwealth Avenue, Canberra, ACT 2600, Australia. *T:* 486411 (02). *Club:* Federal Golf (Canberra).

CANBERRA AND GOULBURN, Bishop of, since 1972; **Rt. Rev. Cecil Allan Warren;** *b* 25 Feb. 1924; *s* of Charles Henry and Eliza Warren; *m* 1947, Doreen Muriel Burrows. *Educ:* Sydney Univ. (BA 1950); Queen's Coll., Oxford (MA 1959). Deacon 1950, priest 1951, Dio. of Canberra and Goulburn; appointments in Diocese of Oxford, 1953-57; Canberra, 1957-63; Organising Sec. Church Society, and Director of Forward in Faith Movement, Dio. of Canberra and Goulburn, 1963-65; Asst Bishop of Canberra and Goulburn, 1965-72. *Address:* 51 Rosenthal Street, Campbell, ACT 2601, Australia. *T:* Canberra 480716. *Club:* Commonwealth (Canberra).

CANDAU, Marcolino Gomes, MD, DPH; Director-General Emeritus, World Health Organization, Geneva, since 1973; *b* Rio de Janeiro, 30 May 1911; *s* of Julio Candau and Augusta Gomes; *m* 1936; two *s; m* 1973, Sita Reelfs. *Educ:* Univ. of Brazil, Rio de Janeiro; Johns Hopkins Univ., USA. Various posts in Health Services of State of Rio de Janeiro, 1934-43; Asst Superintendent, Servico Especial de Saude Publia, Min. of Education and Health, 1944-47, Superintendent 1947-50; World Health Organization: Dir, Div. of Org. of Public Health Services, Geneva, 1950-51; Asst Dir-General, Dept of Advisory Services, Geneva, 1951-52; Asst Dir, Pan-American Sanitary Bureau, Dep. Reg. Dir for the Americas, Washington, 1952-53; Dir-Gen., Geneva, 1953-73. Hon. Dr of Laws: Univ. of Michigan; Johns Hopkins Univ.; Univ. of Edinburgh; The Queen's Univ. of Belfast; Seoul Univ., Korea; Royal Univ. of Malta; Hon. Dr of Medicine: Univ. of Geneva; Karolinska Inst., Stockholm; Hon. Dr: Univ. of Brazil; Univ. of Sao Paulo, Brazil; Univ. of Bordeaux; Charles Univ., Prague; Inst. of Medicine and Pharmacy, Bucharest; Univ. of Abidjan; Hon. Dr of Science: Bates Coll., Maine, USA; Univ. of Ibadan; Semmelweis Univ. of Medicine, Budapest; Univ. of Cambridge; FRCP, Hon. FRSocMed, and Hon. FRSH (all GB), and various other hon. fellowships in America and Europe; Mem., Royal Soc. of Tropical Medicine and Hygiene, GB; For. Member USSR Acad. of Med. Sciences; Foreign Associated Mem., Nat. Acad. of Medicine, Paris. Mary Kingsley Medal of Liverpool Sch. of Tropical Medicine; Gold Medal of RSH, London, 1966; Harben Gold Medal, RIPH&H, London, 1973; Léon Bernard Medal and Prize, World Health Assembly, 1974; also prizes and medals for services to public health. *Publications:* scientific papers. *Address:* Le Mas, Route du Jura, 1296 Coppet, Vaud, Switzerland.

CANDELA OUTERINO, Felix; engineer and architect; Professor, Escuela Nacional de Arquitectura, University of Mexico, since 1953 (on leave of absence); *b* Madrid, 27 Jan. 1910; *s* of Felix and Julia Candela; *m* 1940, Eladia Martin Galan (*d* 1964); four *d; m* 1967, Dorothy H. Davies. *Educ:* Univ. of Madrid, Spain. Architect, Escuela Superior de Arquitectura de Madrid, 1935 Captain of Engineers, Republican Army, Spanish Civil War, 1936-39. Emigrated to Mexico, 1939; Mexican Citizen, 1941. General practice in Mexico as Architect and Contractor. Founded (with brother Antonio) Cubiertas ALA, SA, firm specializing in design and construction of reinforced concrete shell structures. Work includes Sports Palace for Mexico Olympics, 1968. Hon. Member: Sociedad de Arquitectos Colombianos, 1956; Sociedad Venezolana de Arquitectos, 1961; International Assoc. for Shell Structures, 1962. Charles Elliot Norton Prof. of Poetry, Harvard Univ., for academic year, 1961-62; Jefferson Meml Prof., Univ. of Virginia, 1966; Andrew D. White Prof., Cornell Univ., 1969-71; Prof. Dept of Architecture, Univ. of Illinois at Chicago, 1971-78; Prof. Honorario: Escuela Tecnica Superior de Arquitectura de Madrid, 1969; Univ. Nacional Federico Villareal, Peru, 1977 William Hoffman Wood Prof., Leeds Univ., 1974-75. Gold Medal, Instr. Structural Engineers, England, 1961; Auguste Perret Prize of Internationa

Union of Architects, 1961; Alfred E. Lindau Award, Amer. Concrete Inst., 1965; Silver Medal, Acad. d'Architecture, Paris, 1980; Gold Medal, Consejo Superior de Arquitectos de España, 1981. Hon. Fellow American Inst. of Architects, 1963; Hon. Corr. Mem., RIBA, 1963; Plomada de Oro, Soc. de Arquitectos Mexicanos, 1963; Doctor in Fine Arts (*hc*): Univ. of New Mexico, 1964; Univ. of Illinois, 1979; Dr Ing *hc* Univ. de Santa Maria, Caracas, 1968. Order of Civil Merit, Spain, 1978. *Publications:* several articles in architectural and engineering magazines all around the world; *relevant publication:* Candela, the Shell Builder, by Colin Faber, 1963. *Address:* PO Box 356, Bronxville, NY 10708, USA. *T:* (914)9617944; Avenida America 14-7, Madrid 2, Spain. *T:* 246 0096.

CANDY, Air Vice-Marshal Charles Douglas; CB 1963; CBE 1957; Air Member for Personnel, RAAF, 1966-69, retired; *b* 17 Sept. 1912; *s* of late C. H. and late Mrs Candy; *m* 1938, Eileen Cathryn Mary (*née* Poole-Ricketts); one *d*. Served War of 1939-45; Command and Staff appointments in Australia, the United Kingdom, West Africa and South-West Pacific Area; AOC North-Eastern Area, RAAF, 1946; Joint Services Staff Coll., 1947; Dept of Defence, Commonwealth of Australia, 1948-50; Director of Organisation and Staff Duties, HQ, RAAF, 1950-52; Imperial Defence Coll., 1953; SASO No. 3 Group Bomber Command, RAF, 1954-56; Deputy Chief of the Air Staff, RAAF, 1956-58 (Air Vice-Marshal, 1957); AOC Home Command, RAAF, 1958-59; Sen. Air Staff Officer, Far East Air Force, Royal Air Force, 1959-62; AOC Support Command, RAAF, 1962-66. *Recreation:* golf. *Address:* PO Box 128, Kingston, ACT 2604, Australia. *Clubs:* Commonwealth, Royal Canberra Golf (Canberra); Royal Singapore Golf (Singapore).

CANE, Prof. Violet Rosina; Professor of Mathematical Statistics, University of Manchester, 1971-81, now Emeritus; *b* 31 Jan. 1916; *d* of Tubal George Cane and Annie Louisa Lansdell. *Educ:* Newnham Coll., Cambridge (MA, Dipl. in Math. Stats). BoT, 1940; Univ. of Aberdeen, 1941; FO, 1942; Min. of Town and Country Planning, 1946; Statistician to MRC Applied Psychol. Unit, 1948; Queen Mary Coll., London, 1955; Fellow, Newnham Coll., Cambridge, 1957; Lectr, Univ. of Cambridge, 1960. Hon. MSc Manchester, 1974. *Publications:* (contrib.) Current Problems in Animal Behaviour, 1961; (contrib.) Perspectives in Probability and Statistics, 1975; papers in Jl of Royal Stat. Soc., Animal Behaviour, and psychol jls. *Recreation:* supporting old houses. *Address:* 13/14 Little St Mary's Lane, Cambridge CB2 1RR. *T:* Cambridge 357277; Statistical Laboratory, University of Cambridge, 16 Mill Lane, Cambridge CB2 1SB.

CANET, Maj.-Gen. Lawrence George, CB 1964; CBE 1956; BE; Master General of the Ordnance, Australia, 1964-67, retired; *b* 1 Dec. 1910; *s* of late Albert Canet, Melbourne, Victoria; *m* 1940, Mary Elizabeth Clift, *d* of Cecil Clift Jones, Geelong, Victoria; one *s*. *Educ:* RMC Duntroon; Sydney Univ. (BE). Served War of 1939-45 with 7th Australian Div. (Middle East and Pacific). GOC Southern Command, 1960-64. Brigadier 1953; Maj.-Gen. 1957. *Address:* 37 The Corso, Isle of Capri, Surfers Paradise, Qld 4217, Australia.

CANFIELD, Cass; Senior Editor, Harper & Row, Publishers; *b* 26 April 1897; *s* of August Cass and Josephine Houghteling; *m* 1st, 1922, Katharine Emmet; two *s*; 2nd, 1938, Jane White Fuller. *Educ:* Groton Sch.; Harvard Univ. (AB); Oxford Univ. Harris, Forbes & Co. 1921-22; NY Evening Post, 1922-23; Foreign Affairs (a quarterly magazine), 1923-24; Manager, London (England) office, Harper & Bros, 1924-27; Harper & Bros, NY City, 1927; President, Harper & Bros, 1931-45; Chairman of the Board, 1945-55; Chairman Exec. Cttee, 1955-67. Served European War, 1917-18, commissioned. President National Assoc. of Book Publishers, 1932-34; Trustee, Woodrow Wilson National Fellowship Foundation; Mem. Exec. Cttee, John Fitzgerald Kennedy Library; Chairman, Governing Body, International Planned Parenthood Federation, 1966-69, now Chm. Emeritus. During War of 1939-45 with Board of Economic Warfare, Washington, DC; special advisor to American Ambassador, London, in charge of Economic Warfare Division, 1943; Director, Office of War Information, France, 1945. Albert D. Lasker Award, 1964. Hon. Phi Beta Kappa. *Publications:* The Publishing Experience, 1969; Up and Down and Around, 1972; The Incredible Pierpont Morgan, 1974; Samuel Adams' Revolution, 1976; The Iron Will of Jefferson Davis, 1978; Outrageous Fortunes, 1981. *Address:* 10 East 53 Street, New York, NY 10022, USA. *T:* 593-7200. *Clubs:* Century Association (New York); Porcellian (Cambridge, Mass).

CANHAM, Brian John; Metropolitan Stipendiary Magistrate, since 1975; *b* 27 Dec. 1930; *s* of Frederick Ernest and Nora Ruby Canham; *m* 1955, Rachel, *yr d* of late Joseph and Martha Woolley, Bank House, Longnor, Staffs; three *s* one *d*. *Educ:* City of Norwich Sch.; Queens' Coll., Cambridge. MA, LLB. Called to Bar, Gray's Inn, 1955. Army Legal Services, BAOR: Staff Captain, 1956, Major, 1958. Private practice as barrister on SE Circuit, 1963-. *Recreations:* gardening, sailing, swimming. *Address:* 4 Paper Buildings, Temple, EC4Y 7EX. *T:* 01-353 8408.

CANHAM, Bryan Frederick, (Peter), MC 1943; FCIS; Chairman, Eurofi UK Ltd, since 1981; *b* 11 April 1920; *s* of Frederick William Canham and Emma Louisa Martin; *m* 1944, Rita Gwendoline Huggett; one *s*. *Educ:* Trinity County Sch. FCIS 1968 (ACIS 1950). Served War, 1939-46: N Africa, Italy and NW Europe; Captain 1st Royal Tank Regt. Accounting and financial appts, Shell cos in Kenya, Tanzania and French W Africa, 1947-56; Controller, S Europe and N Africa, Shell Internat. Petroleum Co., 1956-60;

Finance Dir, Shell Philippines and Ass. Cos, 1960-63; Finance Dir, Shell Malaysia and Ass. Cos, 1963-68; Personnel Adviser, finance and computer staff, Shell Internat. Pet. Co., 1968-73; Div. Hd, Loans, Directorate Gen. XVIII, Commn of European Communities, 1973-76, Dir, Investment and Loans, 1976-80. *Recreations:* reading, chess, pottering. *Address:* 25 London Road, Newbury, Berkshire. *T:* Newbury 31900; The Old Laundry, Penshurst, Kent. *T:* Penshurst 870 239.

CANHAM, Peter; *see* Canham, B. F.

CANN, Charles Richard; Under Secretary, Management Services Group, Ministry of Agriculture, Fisheries and Food, since 1981; *b* 3 Feb. 1937; *s* of Charles Alfred Cann and Grace Elizabeth Cann; *m* 1979, Denise Ann Margaret Love; two *s*. *Educ:* Merchant Taylors' Sch., Northwood, Mddx; St John's Coll., Cambridge (MA). Asst Principal, MAFF, 1960, Principal 1965; Cabinet Office, 1969-71; Asst Sec., MAFF, 1971. *Address: c/o* Ministry of Agriculture, Fisheries and Food, Whitehall Place, SW1A 2HH. *T:* 01-233 5319.

CANN, Prof. Johnson Robin, PhD; J. B. Simpson Professor of Geology, University of Newcastle upon Tyne, since 1977; *b* 18 Oct. 1937; *er s* of Johnson Ralph Cann and (Ethel) Mary (*née* Northmore); *m* 1963, Janet, *d* of Prof. Charles John Hamson, *qv*; two *s*. *Educ:* St Alban's Sch.; St John's Coll., Cambridge (MA, PhD). Research fellow, St John's Coll., 1962-66; post-doctoral work in Depts of Mineralogy and Petrology, and Geodesy and Geophysics, Cambridge, 1962-66; Dept of Mineralogy, British Museum (Natural History), 1966-68; Lectr, then Reader, School of Environmental Sciences, Univ. of East Anglia, 1968-77; research in rocks of ocean floor, creation of oceanic crust, obsidian in archaeology. Member, then Chm., JOIDES ocean crust panel, 1975-78; UK representative on JOIDES planning cttee, 1978-; co-chief scientist on Glomar Challenger, 1976 and 1979; Mem., UGC physical sciences sub-cttee, 1982-. *Publications:* papers in jls of earth science and archaeology. *Recreations:* walking, gathering, history, music. *Address:* Silverlaw House, 138 Newgate Street, Morpeth, Northumberland NE61 1DD. *T:* Morpeth 512789.

CANN, Robert John, MS London, FRCS; Surgeon Emeritus, Ear, Nose and Throat Department, Guy's Hospital (Surgeon, 1938-66); formerly Consulting Ear, Nose and Throat Surgeon, Caterham District Hospital and East Surrey Hospital, Redhill; *b* Wimbledon, 2 Feb. 1901; *e s* of Frederick Robert Cann; *m* 1929, Gwendolen Chambers; one *s* two *d*. *Educ:* Merchant Taylors' Sch.; Guy's Hospital Med. Sch.; Bordeaux Univ. MRCS, LRCP 1924; MB, BS 1926; MS (Gold Medal, Lond.) 1930; FRCS 1949. Ear, Nose and Throat Dept, Guy's Hospital: Chief Clinical Asst and Registrar, 1926; Asst Surgeon, 1934; Mem., Medical Staff Cttee, 1934-66 (Chm., 1961-66). Out Patient and Statistical Registrar, Central London ENT Hosp., 1926-34; Otologist to LCC Fever Hospitals, 1934-39; formerly Consulting Surgeon ENT: Evelina Hosp. for Children; Wimbledon Hosp.; Bromley Hosp.; St Helier Hosp.; EMS. Late Examiner, ENT: Univ. of London; RCS; RCP. Member: Bd of Governors, Guy's Hosp., 1960-74; Council of Governors, Guy's Hosp. Med. Sch., 1961-80 (Chm., 1968-74). Mem., Visiting Assoc. of ENT Surgeons of GB, 1947-66 (Pres., 1962). FRSM (Pres. Laryngology Section, 1957). Liveryman, Worshipful Soc. of Apothecaries; Freeman, City of London. *Publications:* Endoscopic Methods; Heredity of Deafness; Report on Diphtheria Carriers, etc. *Recreations:* collecting English literature, producing colour in a garden. *Address:* Cairngorm, North Street, South Petherton, Somerset. *T:* South Petherton 40881. *Club:* Athenæum.

CANNAN, Denis; dramatist and script writer; *b* 14 May 1919; *s* of late Captain H. J. Pullein-Thompson, MC, and late Joanna Pullein-Thompson (*née* Cannan); *m* 1st, 1946, Joan Ross (marr. diss.); two *s* one *d*; 2nd, 1965, Rose Evansky; he changed name to Denis Cannan, by deed poll, 1964. *Educ:* Eton. A Repertory factotum, 1937-39. Served War of 1939-45, Queen's Royal Regt, Captain (despatches). Actor at Citizens' Theatre, Glasgow, 1946-48. *Publications:* plays: Max (prod. Malvern Festival), 1949; Captain Carvallo (Bristol Old Vic and St James's Theatres), 1950; Colombe (trans. from Anouilh), New Theatre, 1951; Misery Me!, Duchess, 1955; You and Your Wife, Bristol Old Vic, 1955; The Power and The Glory (adaptation from Graham Greene), Phoenix Theatre, 1956, and Phoenix Theatre, New York, 1958; Who's Your Father?, Cambridge Theatre, 1958; US (original text), Aldwych, 1966; adapted Ibsen's Ghosts, Aldwych, 1966; One at Night, Royal Court, 1971; The Ik (adaptation and collaboration), 1975 (produced Paris, Berlin, London, Venice, Belgrade; tour of American univs, 1976; orig. prod. rev. for Australia, NY, 1980); Dear Daddy, Oxford Festival and Ambassadors, 1976 (Play of the Year award, 1976); the screenplays of several films, incl. The Beggar's Opera, A High Wind in Jamaica; TV plays, One Day at a Time, Home Movies, By George!; adaptations for series, Tales of the Unexpected; three radio plays; contribs to Times Literary Supplement. *Recreation:* loitering. *Address:* 103 Clarence Gate Gardens, Glentworth Street, NW1 6QP.

See also D. L. A. Farr.

CANNAN, Rt. Rev. Edward Alexander Capparis; *see* St Helena, Bishop of.

CANNING, family name of **Baron Garvagh.**

CANNING, Victor; author; *b* 16 June 1911; *m* 1976, Mrs Adria Irving Bell. Major, RA, 1940-46. *Publications:* Mr Finchley Discovers His England, 1934;

The Chasm, 1947; Golden Salamander, 1948; Forest of Eyes, 1949; Venetian Bird, 1951; House of the Seven Flies, 1952; Man from the "Turkish Slave", 1953; Castle Minerva, 1954; His Bones are Coral, 1955; The Hidden Face, 1956; Manasco Road, 1957; The Dragon Tree, 1958; Young Man on a Bicycle and other short stories, 1959; The Burning Eye, 1960; A Delivery of Furies, 1961; Black Flamingo, 1962; The Limbo Line, 1963; The Scorpio Letters, 1964; The Whip Hand, 1965; Doubled in Diamonds, 1966; The Python Project, 1967; The Melting Man, 1968; Queen's Pawn, 1969; The Great Affair, 1970; Firecrest, 1971; The Runaways, 1972; The Rainbird Pattern, 1972; Flight of the Grey Goose, 1973; The Finger of Saturn, 1973; The Painted Tent, 1974; The Mask of Memory, 1974; The Kingsford Mark, 1975; The Crimson Chalice, 1976; The Doomsday Carrier, 1976; The Circle of the Gods, 1977; The Immortal Wound, 1978; Birdcage, 1978; The Satan Sampler, 1979; Fall from Grace, 1980; The Boy on Platform One, 1981; Vanishing Point, 1982. *Recreations:* fishing, golf. *Address:* The Bridge House, Pembridge, Leominster, Herefordshire. *T:* Pembridge 355. *Club:* Flyfishers'.

CANNON, John Francis Michael; Keeper of Botany, British Museum (Natural History), since 1977; *b* 22 April 1930; *s* of Francis Leslie Cannon and Aileen Flora Cannon; *m* 1954, Margaret Joy (*née* Herbert); two *s* one *d*. *Educ:* Whitgift Sch., South Croydon, Surrey; King's Coll., Newcastle upon Tyne, Univ. of Durham (BSc 1st Cl. Hons Botany). Dept of Botany, British Museum (Nat. History), 1952, Dep. Keeper 1972. *Publications:* papers in scientific periodicals and similar pubns. *Recreations:* travel, music, gardening. *Address:* 26 Purley Bury Avenue, Purley, Surrey CR2 9JD. *T:* 01-660 3223.

CANNON, Air Vice-Marshal Leslie William, CB 1952; CBE 1945; retired; *b* 9 April 1904; *s* of late Captain W. E. Cannon, Beds, and Herts Regiment, and of Cathleen Mary Jackson, Bedford; *m* 1930, Beryl (*née* Heyworth). *Educ:* Hertford Grammar Sch.; RAF Coll., Cranwell. RAF Apprentice, 1920-23; Officer Cadet, 1923-25; Pilot Officer, No 2 (AC) Squadron, 1925-27; Flying Officer: No 441 Flight Fleet Air Arm, China Station, 1927; No 2 (AC) Squadron, 1928; Flying Instructor RAF Coll., Cranwell, 1929; F/O and Flight-Lt: Officer Engr. Course, RAF Henlow, 1929-31; Flight-Lt: Engr. Officer RAFMT Depot, Shrewsbury, 1931-32 and RAF Coll., Cranwell, 1932-33; Engr. SO, Air HQ, India, 1933-35; Flight Comdr No 60 (B) Squdn, Kohat, India, 1935-37 (despatches); Sqdn Ldr: OC No 5 (AC) Sqdn, India, 1937; Personnel SO, HQ Training Command, 1938; Student RAF Staff Coll., Andover, 1939. Served War of 1939-45 (despatches thrice, CBE, American Silver Star): Staff Officer Directorate of Operations, Air Ministry, 1939-40; Wing Comdr: Engr. SO, HQ Bomber Command, 1940; Chief Technical Officer, No. 21 Operational Training Unit, 1941; Group Captain: Directing SO RAF Staff Coll., 1942; OC Bomber Stations in No 2 (B) Group, 1942-43. Part of 2nd TAF (England, France, Belgium, Germany); GC and Air Commodore: AO i/c Admin. HQ No 2 (B) Group, 1943-46; AOC No 85 Group, Hamburg, 1946; idc, 1947; Asst Comdt and Comdt, RAF Staff Coll., Andover, 1948-49; Director of Organisation (Establishments), 1949-51; Commander-in-Chief, Royal Pakistan Air Force, 1951-55; Director-General of Organisation, Dec. 1955-Nov. 1958, retired. At CRO, 1959. Rolls-Royce Senior Representative, India, 1960-65. *Recreations:* represented RAF at athletics, boxing, pistol shooting. *Address:* 6 Stockwells, Berry Hill, Taplow, Maidenhead, Berks SL6 0DB. *T:* Maidenhead 30684. *Clubs:* Royal Air Force, Victory Services; Phyllis Court (Henley-on-Thames).

CANNON, Richard Walter, CEng, FIEE, FIERE; Joint Managing Director, Cable and Wireless plc, since 1977 (Executive Director, 1973); *b* 7 Dec. 1923; *s* of Richard William Cannon and Lily Harriet Cannon (*née* Fewins); *m* 1949, Dorothy (formerly Jarvis); two *d*. *Educ:* Eltham Coll. Joined Cable and Wireless Ltd, 1941. *Publications:* telecommunications papers for IEE and IERE.

CANNON-BROOKES, Peter, JP; PhD; FMA, FIIC; Keeper of the Department of Art, National Museum of Wales, Cardiff, since 1978; *b* 23 Aug. 1938; *s* of Victor Montgomery Cannon Brookes and Nancy Margaret (*née* Markham Carter); *m* 1966, Caroline Aylmer, *d* of John Aylmer Christie-Miller; one *s* one *d*. *Educ:* Bryanston; Trinity Hall, Cambridge (MA); Courtauld Inst. of Art, Univ. of London (PhD). FMA 1975. Gooden and Fox Ltd, London, 1963-64; Keeper, Dept of Art, City Museums and Art Gall., Birmingham, 1965-78; Sessional Teacher in History of Art, Courtauld Inst. of Art, London, 1966-68. Internat. Council of Museums: Mem. Exec. Bd, UK Cttee, 1973-81; Pres., Internat. Art Exhibns Cttee, 1977-79 (Dir, 1974-80; Sec., 1975-77); Dir, Conservation Cttee, 1975-81 (Vice Pres., 1978-81). Member: Town Twinning Cttee, Birmingham Internat. Council, 1968-78; Birm. Diocesan Synod, 1970-78; Birm. Diocesan Adv. Cttee for Care of Churches, 1972-78; Edgbaston Deanery Synod, 1970-78 (Lay Jt Chm., 1975-78); Art and Design Adv. Panel, Welsh Jt Educn Cttee, 1978-; Welsh Arts Council, 1979- (Mem., Art Cttee, 1978-). President: Welsh Fedn of Museums and Art Galleries, 1980-82; S Wales Art Soc., 1980-. Editor, Internat. Jl of Museum Management and Curatorship, 1981-. Freeman 1969, Liveryman 1974, Worshipful Co. of Goldsmiths. FRSA. JP Birmingham, 1973-78, Cardiff, 1978-. *Publications:* (with H. D. Molesworth) European Sculpture, 1964; (with C. A. Cannon-Brookes) Baroque Churches, 1969; Lombard Paintings, 1974; After Gulbenkian, 1976; The Cornbury Park Bellini, 1977; Michael Ayrton, 1978; contrib. Apollo, Art Bull., Arte Veneta, Burlington Mag., Connoisseur, and Museums Jl. *Recreations:* travel, photography, growing

vegetables. *Address:* c/o National Museum of Wales, Cardiff CF1 3NP. *T:* Cardiff 397951. *Clubs:* Athenæum; Birmingham (Birmingham).

CANOVAN, Peter; Director, Industries and Farms, Prison Department, Home Office, since 1980; *b* 5 July 1934; *s* of Harry and Ellen Canovan; *m* 1960, Winifred Emily, *d* of Arthur and Frances Seaton; one *d*. *Educ:* Ushaw Coll., Durham; Downing Coll., Cambridge (MA, CertEd). Assistant Master, Ampleforth College, 1959-63; Lecturer in English Literature, Northern Counties College, Newcastle upon Tyne, 1963-66, Sen. Lectr, 1966; Principal, Home Office, 1971; General Dept, 1971-73; Prison Dept, 1973-78; Asst Secretary, Nationality Division, 1978-80. *Recreations:* reading, gardening. *Address:* 158 Bromley Road, Beckenham, Kent BR3 2PG. *T:* 01-650 0642.

CANSDALE, George Soper, BA, BSc, FLS, MIWES; *b* 29 Nov. 1909; *y s* of G. W. Cansdale, Paignton, Devon; *m* 1940, Margaret Sheila, *o d* of R. M. Williamson, Indian Forest Service; two *s*. *Educ:* Brentwood Sch.; St Edmund Hall, Oxford. Colonial Forest Service, Gold Coast, 1934-48. Superintendent to Zoological Society of London, Regent's Park, 1948-53. Inventor, SWS Filtration Unit, 1975. *Publications:* The Black Poplars, 1938; Animals of West Africa, 1946; Animals and Man, 1952; George Cansdale's Zoo Book, 1953; Belinda the Bushbaby, 1953; Reptiles of West Africa, 1955; West African Snakes, 1961; Behind the Scenes at a Zoo, 1965; Animals of Bible Lands, 1970; articles in the Field, Geographical Magazine, Zoo Life, Nigerian Field, Natural History, etc. *Recreations:* natural history, photography, sailing. *Address:* Dove Cottage, Great Chesterford, Essex CB10 1PL. *T:* Saffron Walden 30274. *Club:* Royal Commonwealth Society.

CANT, Rev. Harry William Macphail; Minister of St Magnus Cathedral, Kirkwall, Orkney, since 1968; Chaplain to the Queen in Scotland since 1972; *b* 3 April 1921; *s* of late J. M. Cant and late Margaret Cant; *m* 1951, Margaret Elizabeth Loudon; one *s* two *d*. *Educ:* Edinburgh Acad.; Edinburgh Univ. (MA, BD); Union Theological Seminary, NY (STM). Lieut, KOSB, 1941-43; Captain, King's African Rifles, 1944-46; TA Chaplain, 7th Argyll and Sutherland Highlanders, 1962-70. Asst Minister, Old Parish Church, Aberdeen, 1950-51; Minister of Fallin Parish Church, Stirling, 1951-56; Scottish Sec., Student Christian Movt, 1956-59; Minister of St Thomas' Parish Church, 1960-68. *Publication:* Preaching in a Scottish Parish Church: St Magnus and Other Sermons, 1970. *Recreations:* angling, golf. *Address:* Cathedral Manse, Kirkwall, Orkney. *T:* Kirkwall 3312.

CANT, Rev. Canon Reginald Edward; Canon and Chancellor of York Minster, 1957-81, now Canon Emeritus; *b* 1 May 1914; 2nd *s* of late Samuel Reginald Cant; unmarried. *Educ:* Sir Joseph Williamson's Sch., Rochester; CCC, Cambridge; Cuddesdon Theological Coll. Asst Curate, St Mary's, Portsea, 1938-41; Vice-Principal, Edinburgh Theological Coll., 1941-46; Lecturer, Univ. of Durham, 1946-52 (Vice-Principal, St Chad's Coll. from 1949); Vicar, St Mary's the Less, Cambridge, 1952-57. *Publications:* Christian Prayer, 1961; part-author, The Churchman's Companion, 1964; (ed jtly) A History of York Minster, 1977. *Address:* 7 Sykes Close, St Olave's Road, York YO3 6HZ. *T:* York 23328. *Clubs:* Royal Commonwealth Society; Yorkshire (York).

CANT, Robert (Bowen); MP (Lab) Stoke-on-Trent Central since 1966; *b* 24 July 1915; *s* of Robert and Catherine Cant; *m* 1940, Rebecca Harris Watt; one *s* two *d*. *Educ:* Middlesbrough High Sch. for Boys; London Sch. of Economics. BSc (Econ.) 1945. Lecturer in Economics, Univ. of Keele, 1962-66. Member: Stoke-on-Trent City Council, 1953-74; Staffs CC, 1973-. Contested (Lab.) Shrewsbury, 1950, 1951. *Publication:* American Journey. *Recreation:* bookbinding. *Address:* House of Commons, SW1; (home) 119 Chell Green Avenue, Stoke-on-Trent, Staffordshire. *Club:* Chell Working Men's.

CANTACUZINO, Sherban, FRIBA; Secretary, Royal Fine Art Commission, since 1979; *b* 6 Sept. 1928; *s* of Georges M. Cantacuzino and Sanda Stirbey; *m* 1954, Anne Mary Trafford; two *d* (one *s* decd). *Educ:* Winchester Coll.; Magdalene Coll., Cambridge (MA). Partner, Steane, Shipman & Cantacuzino, Chartered Architects, 1956-65; private practice, 1965-73; Asst Editor, Architectural Review, 1967-73, Exec. Editor, 1973-79. Sen. Lectr, Dept of Architecture, College of Art, Canterbury, 1967-70. Trustee: Thomas Cubitt Trust, 1978-; Conran Foundn, 1981-; Member: Master Jury, Aga Khan Award for Architecture, 1980; Steering Cttee, Aga Khan Award for Architecture, 1980-. Mem. Council, RSA, 1980-. *Publications:* Modern Houses of the World, 1964, 3rd edn 1966; Great Modern Architecture, 1966, 2nd edn 1968; European Domestic Architecture, 1969; New Uses for Old Buildings, 1975; ed, Architectural Conservation in Europe, 1975; Wells Coates, a monograph, 1978; (with Susan Brandt) Saving Old Buildings, 1980; The Architecture of Howell, Killick, Partridge and Amis, 1981; articles in Architectural Rev. *Recreations:* music, cooking. *Address:* 11 Pembroke Studios, W8 6HX. *T:* 01-602 1029. *Club:* Garrick.

CANTERBURY, Archbishop of, since 1980; **Most Rev. and Rt. Hon. Robert Alexander Kennedy Runcie,** MC 1945; PC 1980; *b* 2 Oct. 1921 *s* of Robert Dalziel Runcie and Anne Runcie; *m* 1957, Angela Rosalind, *d* of J. W. Cecil Turner; one *s* one *d*. *Educ:* Merchant Taylors', Crosby; Brasenose Coll., Oxford (Squire Minor Schol.), Hon. Fellow, 1979; Westcott House, Cambridge. BA (1st Cl. Hons, Lit. Hum.), MA Oxon, 1948; FKC 1981. Served Scots Guards, War of 1939-45 (MC). Deacon, 1950; Priest, 1951

Curate, All Saints, Gosforth, 1950-52; Chaplain, Westcott House, Cambridge, 1953-54; Vice-Principal, 1954-56; Fellow, Dean and Asst Tutor of Trinity Hall, Cambridge, 1956-60, Hon. Fellow 1975; Vicar of Cuddesdon and Principal of Cuddesdon Coll., 1960-69; Bishop of St Albans, 1970-80. Canon and Prebendary of Lincoln, 1969. Hon. Bencher, Gray's Inn, 1980. Chm., BBC and IBA Central Religious Adv. Cttee, 1973-79. Teape Lectr, St Stephen's Coll., Delhi, 1962. Select Preacher: Cambridge, 1957 and 1975, Oxford, 1959 and 1973. Anglican Chm., Anglican-Orthodox Jt Doctrinal Commn, 1973-80. Freeman: St Albans, 1979; City of London, 1981. Hon. DD: Oxon, 1980; Cantab, 1981; Univ. of the South, Sewanee, 1981; Hon. DLitt Keele, 1981. *Publication:* (ed) Cathedral and City: St Albans Ancient and Modern, 1978. *Recreations:* travel, reading novels, pig keeping. *Address:* Lambeth Palace, SE1 7JU. *T:* 01-928 8282; Old Palace, Canterbury. *Club:* Athenæum.

CANTERBURY, Dean of; *see* de Waal, Very Rev. V. A.

CANTERBURY, Archdeacon of; *see* Simpson, Ven. J. A.

CANTLAY, George Thomson, CBE 1973; Partner, Murray & Co., since 1979; Chairman: Parkfield Foundries (Tees-side) Ltd; United Capitals Investment Trust Ltd; Director: A. B. Electronic Components Ltd; Christie-Tyler Ltd; Welsh National Opera Ltd (since inception); *b* 2 Aug. 1907; *s* of G. and A. Cantlay; *m* 1934, Sibyl Gwendoline Alsop Stoker; one *s* one *d*. *Educ:* Glasgow High Sch. Member of Stock Exchange. Vice-Pres., Welsh Region, Inst. of Directors. OStJ; FRSA. *Recreations:* music (opera), gardening. *Address:* 9 Park Road, Penarth CF6 2BD. *Clubs:* Carlton; Cardiff and County (Cardiff).

CANTLEY, Hon. Sir Joseph (Donaldson), Kt 1965; OBE 1945; **Hon. Mr Justice Cantley;** Judge of the High Court of Justice, Queen's Bench Division, since 1965; *b* 8 Aug. 1910; *er s* of Dr Joseph Cantley, Crumpsall, Manchester, and Georgina Cantley (*née* Kean); *m* 1966, Lady (Hilda Goodwin) Gerrard, *widow* of Sir Denis Gerrard. *Educ:* Manchester Grammar Sch.; Manchester Univ. Studentship and Certificate of Honour, Council of Legal Education, 1933; Barrister, Middle Temple, 1933 (Bencher 1963; Treasurer 1981); QC 1954. Served throughout War of 1939-45: Royal Artillery and on Staff; 2nd Lieut Royal Artillery 1940; N Africa and Italy, 1942-45 (despatches twice); Lieut-Colonel and AAG, 1943-45. Recorder of Oldham, 1959-60; Judge of Salford Hundred Court of Record, 1960-65; Judge of Appeal, Isle of Man, 1962-65; Presiding Judge: Northern Circuit, 1970-74; South Eastern Circuit, 1980. Member, General Council of the Bar, 1957-61. Hon. Col, Manchester and Salford Univs OTC, 1971-77. Hon. LLD Manchester, 1968. *Address:* Royal Courts of Justice, Strand, WC2A 2LL. *Club:* Travellers'.

CAPE, Donald Paul Montagu Stewart, CMG 1977; HM Diplomatic Service, retired; Ambassador and UK Permanent Representative to the Council of Europe, Strasbourg, 1978-82; *b* 6 Jan. 1923; *s* of late John Scarvell and Olivia Millicent Cape; *m* 1948, Cathune Johnston; four *s* one *d*. *Educ:* Ampleforth Coll.; Brasenose Coll., Oxford. Scots Guards, 1942-45. Entered Foreign Service, 1946. Served: Belgrade, 1946-49; FO, 1949-51; Lisbon, 1951-55; Singapore, 1955-57; FO, 1957-60; Bogota, 1960-61; Holy See, 1962-67; Head of Information Administration Dept, FCO, 1968-70; Counsellor, Washington, 1970-73; Counsellor, Brasilia, 1973-76; Ambassador to Laos, 1976-78. *Recreations:* riding, tennis, walking, swimming, skiing. *Address:* Hilltop, Wonersh, Guildford, Surrey.

CAPE, Maj.-Gen. Timothy Frederick, CB 1972; CBE 1966; DSO; idc, jssc, psc; FAIM; *b* Sydney, 5 Aug. 1915; *s* of C. S. Cape, DSO, Edgecliff, NSW; *m* 1961, Elizabeth, *d* of Brig. R. L. R. Rabett; one *d*. *Educ:* Cranbrook Sch., Sydney; RMC Duntroon. Served with RAA, 1938-40; Bde Major Sparrow Force, Timor, 1942; GS01: (Air) New Guinea Force, 1942-43; (Ops) Melbourne, 1944; (Air) Morotai, 1945; (Ops) Japan, 1946-47; (Plans) Melbourne, 1948-49; Instructor, UK, 1950-52; Comdt, Portsea, 1954-56; Dep. Master-Gen. Ordnance, 1957-59; COS Northern Comd, Brisbane, 1961; Dir of Staff Duties, Army HQ, Canberra, 1962-63; Comdr, Adelaide, 1964; GOC Northern Comd, Brisbane, 1965-68; Master-General of the Ordnance, 1968-72; retd 1972. Nat. Chm., Royal United Services Inst. of Australia, 1980-; Chm., Nat. Disaster Relief Cttee and Mem., Nat. Council, Australian Red Cross Soc. 1975-. Bronze Star (US). *Address:* 10 Scarborough Street, Red Hill, ACT 2603, Australia. *Clubs:* Melbourne, Naval and Military (Melbourne); Commonwealth (Canberra); Union (Sydney); Royal Sydney Golf.

CAPE TOWN, Archbishop of, and Metropolitan of South Africa, since 1981; **Most Rev. Philip Welsford Richmond Russell;** *b* 21 Oct. 1919; *s* of Leslie Richmond Russell and Clarice Louisa Russell (*née* Welsford); *m* 1945, Violet Eirene, *d* of Ven. Dr. O. J. Hogarth, sometime Archdeacon of the Cape; one *s* three *d*. *Educ:* Durban High Sch.; Rhodes Univ. College (Univ. of South Africa), BA 1948; LTh 1950. Served War of 1939-45; MBE 1943. Deacon, 1950; Priest, 1951; Curate, St Peter's, Maritzburg, 1950-54; Vicar: Greytown, 1954-57; Ladysmith, 1957-61; Kloof, 1961-66; Archdeacon of Pinetown, 1961-66; Bishop Suffragan of Capetown, 1966-70; Bishop of Port Elizabeth, 1970-74; Bishop of Natal, 1974-81. *Recreations:* caravanning, fishing. *Address:* Bishopscourt, Claremont, CP, 7700, South Africa.

CAPE TOWN, Cardinal Archbishop of; His Eminence Cardinal Owen McCann, DD, PhD, BCom; Archbishop of Cape Town (RC), since 1951; Assistant at Pontifical Throne, 1960; Cardinal since 1965 (Titular Church, St Praxedes); *b* 26 June 1907. *Educ:* St Joseph's Coll., Rondebosch, CP; Univ.

of Cape Town; Collegium Urbanianum de Propaganda Fide, Rome. Priest, 1935. Editor, The Southern Cross, 1940-48; Administrator, St Mary's Cathedral, Cape Town, 1948-50. Hon. DLitt Univ. of Cape Town, 1968. *Address:* Oak Lodge, Fair Seat Lane, Wynberg, CP, South Africa; Chancery Office, Cathedral Place, 12 Bouquet Street, Cape Town. *Club:* City and Civil Service (Cape Town).

CAPE TOWN, Bishops Suffragan of; *see* Matolengwe, Rt Rev. P. M., Swartz, Rt Rev. G. A.

CAPE TOWN, Dean of; *see* King, Very Rev. E. L.

CAPEL CURE, (George) Nigel, TD; JP; *b* 28 Sept. 1908; *o s* of late Major George Edward Capel Cure, JP, Blake Hall, Ongar; *m* 1935, Nancy Elizabeth, *d* of late William James Barry, Great Witchingham Hall, Norwich; two *s* one *d*. *Educ:* Eton; Trinity Coll., Cambridge. DL and JP, 1947, High Sheriff, 1951, Essex; Vice-Lieutenant, later Vice Lord-Lieutenant, Essex, 1958-78. *Recreations:* shooting, cricket. *Address:* Ashlings, Moreton Road, Ongar, Essex. *T:* Ongar 362634. *Clubs:* MCC, City University.

CAPELL, family name of **Earl of Essex.**

CAPLAN, Daniel; Under-Secretary, Department of the Environment, 1970-71; *b* 29 July 1915; *y s* of Daniel and Miriam Caplan; *m* 1945, Olive Beatrice Porter; no *c*. *Educ:* Elem. and Secondary Schools, Blackpool; St Catharine's Coll., Cambridge. Asst Principal, Import Duties Adv. Cttee, 1938; Private Secretary to three Permanent Secretaries, Ministry of Supply, 1940; Principal, 1942; Ministry of Supply Representative and Economic Secretary to British Political Representative in Finland, 1944-45; Asst Secretary, Board of Trade, 1948; Adviser to Chancellor of Duchy of Lancaster, 1957-60; Under-Secretary, Scottish Development Dept, 1963-65; Under-Secretary, National Economic Development Office, 1966; Asst Under-Sec. of State, DEA, 1966-69; Under-Sec., Min. of Housing and Local Govt, 1969-70; Consultant to Minister for Housing for Leasehold Charges Study, 1972-73. Indep. Review of Royal Commn on Historical Manuscripts, for HM Govt, 1980. *Publications:* People and Homes (indep. report on Landlord and Tenant Relations in England for British Property Fedn), 1975; Border Country Branch Lines, 1981; indep. report on the Historical Manuscripts Commission for HM Govt, 1981; numerous papers on religious and economic history in learned journals. *Recreations:* railways, historical research, gardening. *Address:* The Old Cottage, Whitemans Green, Cuckfield, West Sussex. *T:* Haywards Heath 454301.

CAPLAN, Leonard, QC 1954; *b* 28 June 1909; *s* of late Henry Caplan, Liverpool; *m* 1st, 1942, Tania (*d* 1974); two *d*; 2nd, 1977, Mrs Korda Herskovits, NY. Called to the Bar, Gray's Inn, 1935; Master of the Bench, 1964; Vice-Treasurer, 1978; Treasurer, 1979; joined South Eastern Circuit; Middle Temple, 1949; served War of 1939-45, Royal Artillery (Anti-Tank): Staff Captain, 47th Div.; Staff Captain ("Q" Operations), Southern Command, engaged in D-Day Planning; passed Staff Coll., Camberley; Major, DAAG and Lt-Col, AAG, HQ Allied Land Forces, South East Asia. Conservative candidate, N Kensington, 1950-51. Chm., Coll. Hall (Univ. of London), 1958-67. Chm., Mental Health Review Tribunal, SE Region, 1960-63; Senate of Inns of Court and the Bar, 1975-. Pres., Medico-Legal Soc., 1979-81. *Publication:* (with late Marcus Samuel, MP) The Great Experiment: a critical study of Soviet Five Year Plans, 1935. *Recreation:* yachting. *Address:* 1 Pump Court, Temple, EC4. *T:* 01-353 9332; Skol, Marbella, S Spain. *Clubs:* Savage, Authors'; Hurlingham; Marbella Yacht, Bar Yacht.

CAPLAN, Philip Isaac, QC (Scot.) 1970; Sheriff, Lothian and Borders, since 1979; *b* 24 Feb. 1929; *s* of Hyman and Rosalena Caplan; *m* 1st, 1953; two *s* one *d*; 2nd, 1974, Joyce Ethel Stone; one *d*. *Educ:* Eastwood Sch., Renfrewshire; Glasgow Univ. (MA, LLB). Solicitor, 1952-56; called to Bar, 1957; Standing Junior Counsel to Accountant of Court, 1977-79. Chm., Plant Varieties and Seeds Tribunal, Scotland. *Recreations:* reading, photography, music. *Address:* The Green, The Causeway, Duddingston Village, Edinburgh. *T:* 031-661 4254; *Club:* University Staff (Edinburgh).

CAPLAT, Moran Victor Hingston, CBE 1968; Director, Glyndebourne Productions Ltd; Editor, Glyndebourne Festival Programme Book, etc; *b* 1 Oct. 1916; *s* of Roger Armand Charles Caplat and Norah Hingston; *m* 1943, Diana Murray Downton; one *s* two *d* (and one *s* decd). *Educ:* privately; Royal Acad. of Dramatic Art. Actor, etc., 1934-39. Royal Navy, 1939-45. Glyndebourne: Asst to Gen. Man., 1945; Gen. Man., later known as Gen. Administrator, 1949-81. *Recreations:* gardening, sailing, travel, music (non-vocal). *Address:* The Yew Tree House, Barcombe, near Lewes, East Sussex BN8 5EF. *T:* Barcombe 400202. *Clubs:* Garrick, Royal Ocean Racing; Royal Yacht Squadron (Cowes).

CAPOTE, Truman; author; *b* New Orleans, USA, 30 Sept. 1924; *s* of Joseph G. Capote and Nina (*née* Faulk). *Educ:* St John's Academy and Greenwich High School (New York). O. Henry Memorial Award for short story, 1946; Creative Writing Award, Nat. Inst. of Arts and Letters, 1959. *Publications:* Other Voices, Other Rooms (novel), 1948; Tree of Night (short stories), 1949; Observations, 1949; Local Color (travel essays), 1950; The Grass Harp (novel), 1951 (dramatised, 1953); The Muses are Heard (essay), 1956; Breakfast at Tiffany's (short stories), 1958; Selected Writings, 1964; In Cold Blood, 1966; A Christmas Memory, 1966; (with H. Arlen), House of Flowers, 1968; The

Thanksgiving Visitor, 1969; The Dogs Bark, 1973; Music for Chameleons, 1981; short stories and articles (both fiction and non-fiction) contributed to numerous magazines. *Address:* c/o Random House Inc., 201 East 50th Street, New York, NY 10022, USA.

CAPPER, Rt. Rev. Edmund Michael Hubert, OBE 1961; LTh (Dur.); Auxiliary Bishop in the Diocese of Gibraltar in Europe, since 1973; Assistant Bishop of Southwark, since 1981; *b* 12 March 1908; *e s* of Arthur Charles and Mabel Lavinia Capper; unmarried. *Educ:* St Joseph's Academy, Blackheath; St Augustine's College, Canterbury. Deacon, 1932, Priest, 1933. Royal Army Chaplains' Dept, 1942-46 (EA); Archdeacon of Lindi and Canon of Masasi Cathedral, 1947-54; Archdeacon of Dar es Salaam, 1954-58. Provost of the Collegiate Church of St Alban the Martyr, Dar es Salaam, Tanganyika, 1957-62; Canon of Zanzibar, 1954-62; Member, Universities' Mission to Central Africa, 1936-62; Chairman, Tanganyika British Legion Benevolent Fund, 1956-62; President, Tanganyika British Legion, 1960-62; Chaplain, Palma de Mallorca, 1962-67; Bishop of St Helena, 1967-73; Chaplain of St George's, Malaga, 1973-76. *Recreations:* swimming and walking. *Address:* c/o Barclay's Bank Ltd, 119 Waterloo Road, SE1 8UN. *Club:* Travellers'.

CAPRA, Frank, Legion of Merit, 1943; DSM 1945; Hon. OBE (mil.) 1946; Writer, Director and Producer of Motion Pictures; President of own producing company, Liberty Films Inc.; *b* 18 May 1897; Italian parents; *m* 1932, Lucille Rayburn; two *s* one *d. Educ:* California Institute of Technology. Col, Signal Corps, US Army; released from Army, spring of 1945. Produced and directed following pictures: Submarine, The Strong Man, Flight, Dirigible, Ladies of Leisure, Platinum Blonde, American Madness, Lady for a Day, It Happened One Night, Mr Deeds Goes to Town, Broadway Bill, Lost Horizon, You Can't Take It With You, Mr Smith Goes to Washington, Meet John Doe, Arsenic and Old Lace, It's a Wonderful Life, State of the Union, Here Comes the Groom, A Hole in the Head, Pocketful of Miracles. Member of Motion Picture Academy and of Directors' Guild. Hon. Dr Arts Temple Univ., 1971; Hon. Dr Fine Arts Carthage Coll., 1972. *Publication:* Frank Capra: the name above the title (autobiog.), 1971. *Recreations:* hunting, fishing, music. *Address:* PO Box 98, La Quinta, Calif 92253, USA.

CAPRON, (George) Christopher; Head of Current Affairs Programmes, BBC Television, since 1981 (Assistant Head, 1979-80); *b* 17 Dec. 1935; *s* of late Lt-Col George Capron and of Hon. Mrs Christian Capron (*née* Hepburne-Scott); *m* 1958, Edna Naomi Goldrei; one *s* one *d. Educ:* Wellington Coll.; Trinity Hall, Cambridge (BA Hons Mod. Langs). British Broadcasting Corporation: radio producer, 1963-67; television producer, 1967-76; Editor, Tonight, 1976-77; Editor, Panorama, 1977-79. *Recreations:* village cricket, tennis. *Address:* 32 Amerland Road, SW18 1PZ.

CAPSTICK, Brian Eric, QC 1973; a Recorder of the Crown Court, since 1980; *b* 12 Feb. 1927; *o s* of late Eric and Betty Capstick; *m* 1960, Margaret Harrison; one *s* one *d. Educ:* Sedbergh; Queen's Coll., Oxford (Scholar) (MA). Served HM Forces, 1945-48: 17/21st Lancers, Palestine, 1947-48. Tancred Scholar, and called to Bar, Lincoln's Inn, 1952; Bencher, 1980. Dep. Chm., Northern Agriculture Tribunal, 1976. Asst Boundary Comr, 1978. *Recreations:* shooting, reading, cooking. *Address:* (home) 71 South End Road, NW3. *T:* 01-435 3540; Blue Mill, Thropton, Northumberland; (professional) 2 Crown Office Row, Temple, EC4. *T:* 01-583 2681. *Club:* Garrick.

See also A. H. Brind.

CAPSTICK, Charles William, CMG 1972; Director of Economics and Statistics, Ministry of Agriculture, Fisheries and Food, since 1977; *b* 18 Dec. 1934; *s* of William Capstick and Janet Frankland; *m* 1962, Joyce Alma Dodsworth; two *s. Educ:* King's Coll., Univ. of Durham (BSc (Hons)); Univ. of Kentucky, USA (MS). MAFF: Asst Agricl Economist, 1961; Principal Agricl Economist, 1966; Senior Principal Agricl Economist, 1968; Sen. Econ. Advr and Head, Milk and Milk Products Div., 1976; Under Sec., 1977. *Recreations:* gardening, golf. *Address:* 7 Dellfield Close, Radlett, Herts. *T:* Radlett 7640.

CARADON, Baron (Life Peer) *cr* 1964; **Hugh Mackintosh Foot,** PC 1968; GCMG 1957 (KCMG 1951; CMG 1946); KCVO 1953; OBE 1939; *b* 8 Oct. 1907; *s* of late Rt Hon. Isaac Foot, PC; *m* 1936, Florence Sylvia Tod; three *s* one *d. Educ:* Leighton Park Sch., Reading; St John's Coll., Cambridge, Pres. Cambridge Union, 1929; Administrative Officer, Palestine Govt, 1929-37; attached to the Colonial Office, 1938-39; Asst British Resident, Trans-Jordan, 1939-42; British Mil. Administration, Cyrenaica, 1943; Colonial Secretary: Cyprus, 1943-45, Jamaica, 1945-47; Chief Sec., Nigeria, 1947-51. Acting Governor: Cyprus, 1944, Jamaica, Aug. 1945-Jan. 1946, Nigeria, 1949 and 1950. Capt.-Gen. and Gov.-in-Chief of Jamaica, 1951-57; Governor and Comdr-in-Chief, Cyprus, Dec. 1957-60; Ambassador and Adviser in the UK Mission to the UN and UK representative on Trusteeship Council, 1961-62, resigned; Minister of State for Foreign and Commonwealth Affairs and Perm. UK Rep. at the UN, 1964-70. Consultant, Special Fund of the United Nations, 1963-64. Mem., UN Expert Group on South Africa, 1964; Consultant to UN Develt Programme, 1971-75. Visiting Fellow: Princeton, Harvard and Georgetown Univs, 1979. KStJ 1952. Hon. Fellow, St John's Coll., Cambridge, 1960. *Publication:* A Start in Freedom, 1964. *Address:* House of Lords, SW1; 203 Drake House, Dolphin Square, SW1.

See also Baron Foot, Rt Hon. Michael Foot.

CARBERRY, Sir John (Edward Doston), Kt 1956; Chief Justice, Jamaica, 1954-58, retired; *b* Grenada, WI, 20 Aug. 1893; *e s* of D. A. and Ruth Carberry; *m* 1920, Georgiana, *y d* of Charles Jackson; one *s* one *d. Educ:* Wesley Hall, Grenada; McGill Univ., Montreal (LLB). Served European War in 1st Bn British West Indies Regt, 1915-19. Called to Bar, Middle Temple, 1925; in practice in Jamaica until 1927, when joined Government Service as Clerk of the Courts; Resident Magistrate, 1932; Puisne Judge, Supreme Court, 1946; Senior Puisne Judge, Jamaica, 1949. *Recreation:* philately. *Address:* 8 East King's House Road, Kingston 6, Jamaica.

CARBERY, 11th Baron *cr* 1715; **Peter Ralfe Harrington Evans-Freke;** Bt 1768; *b* 20 March 1920; *o s* of Major the Hon. Ralfe Evans-Freke, MBE (*yr s* of 9th Baron) (*d* 1969), and Vera, *d* of late C. Harrington Moore; *S* uncle, 1970; *m* 1941, Joyzelle Mary, *o d* of late Herbert Binnie; three *s* two *d. Educ:* Downside School. MICE. Served War of 1939-45, Captain RE, India, Burmah. Member of London Stock Exchange, 1955-68. *Recreations:* hunting, tennis, winter sports. *Heir: e s* Hon. Michael Peter Evans-Freke [*b* 11 Oct. 1942; *m* 1967, Claudia Janet Elizabeth, *o d* of Captain P. L. C. Gurney; one *s* three *d*]. *Address:* Baskings House, Selsfield, East Grinstead, West Sussex. *T:* Sharpthorne 810761. *Clubs:* Kennel; Kildare Street and University (Dublin).

CARBERY, Prof. Thomas Francis; Head of Department of Office Organisation, since 1975 and Professor, since 1979, University of Strathclyde; *b* 18 Jan. 1925; *o c* of Thomas Albert Carbery and Jane Morrison; *m* 1954, Ellen Donnelly; one *s* two *d. Educ:* St Aloysius Coll., Glasgow; Univ. of Glasgow and Scottish Coll. of Commerce. Cadet Navigator and Meteorologist, RAFVR, 1943-47; Civil Servant, Min. of Labour, 1947-61; Sen. Lectr in Govt and Econs, Scottish College of Commerce, Glasgow, 1961-64; Sen. Lectr in Govt-Business Relations, Strathclyde Univ., 1964-75. Member: IBA (formerly ITA), 1970-79 (Chm., Scottish Cttee, 1970-79); Royal Commn on Gambling, 1976-78; Central Transport Users' Consultative Cttee, 1976-80 (Chm., Scottish Transport Users' Consultative Cttee, 1976-80); European Adv. Council, Salzburg Seminar, 1980-; Broadcasting Complaints Commn, 1981-; Dep. Chm., Scottish Consumer Council, 1980- (Mem. 1977-80); Chm., Scottish Cttee, Information Technology, 1982. Special Adviser, H of C Select Cttee on Scottish Affairs, 1982. Mem. Court 1968-71 and 1980-, Mem. Senate 1964-71 and 1973-, Univ. of Strathclyde. *Publication:* Consumers in Politics, 1969. *Recreations:* golf, conversation, spectating at Association football, watching television. *Address:* 32 Crompton Avenue, Glasgow G44 5TH. *T:* 041-637 0514. *Clubs:* University of Strathclyde, Glasgow Art, Ross Priory (Glasgow).

CARBONELL, William Leycester Rouse, CMG 1956; Commissioner of Police, Federation of Malaya, 1953-58, retired; *b* 14 Aug. 1912; *m* 1937; two *s. Educ:* Shrewsbury Sch.; St Catharine's Coll., Cambridge. Probationary Assistant Commissioner of Police, 1935; (title changed to) Asst Superintendent, 1938; Superintendent, 1949; Asst Commissioner, 1952: Senior, 1952; Commissioner, 1953. King's Police Medal, 1950. Perlawan Mangku Negara (PMN), Malaya, 1958. *Address:* Amery End, Tanhouse Lane, Alton, Hants.

CARD, Wilfrid Ingram, MD, FRCP; Professor Emeritus, University of Glasgow; Diagnostic Methodology Research Unit, Southern General Hospital, Glasgow; *b* 13 April 1908; *e s* of Henry Charles Card; *m* 1934, Hilda Margaret Brigstocke Frere (*d* 1975); one *s* two *d. Educ:* Tonbridge Sch.; St Thomas's Hospital Medical Sch. MB, BS, 1931; MD Lond. 1933; MRCP 1934; FRCP 1944, FRCPE 1953, FRCPGlas 1967. Formerly: Beit Research Fellow; Physician to Out-Patients, St Thomas' Hospital, 1939-48. Physician in Charge, Gastro-intestinal Unit, Western General Hospital, Edinburgh; Reader in Medicine, Edinburgh Univ., 1948-66; Prof. of Medicine in relation to Mathematics and Computing, Univ. of Glasgow, 1966-74; Physician to HM the Queen in Scotland, 1965-75. Member: Association of Physicians of GB; Scottish Soc. of Experimental Medicine. *Publications:* Diseases of the Digestive System; (ed) Modern Trends in Gastro-Enterology, Vols 3 and 4; contrib. to: Principles and Practice of Medicine; articles on gastro-enterological subjects in Gut, Gastro-enterology, and articles relating mathematical methods to medicine in Mathematical Biosciences, Methods of Information in Medicine, etc. *Recreation:* sailing. *Address:* 10 Bowmont Gardens, Glasgow G12 9LW. *Club:* Savile.

CARDEN, Derrick Charles, CMG 1974; JP; HM Diplomatic Service, retired; HM Ambassador, Sudan, 1977-79; *b* 30 Oct. 1921; *s* of Canon Henry Craven Carden and Olive (*née* Gorton); *heir pres.* to Sir John Craven Carden, 7th Bt, *qv* ; *m* 1952, Elizabeth Anne Russell; two *s* two *d. Educ:* Marlborough; Christ Church, Oxford. Sudan Political Service, 1942-54. Entered HM Diplomatic Service, 1954; Foreign Office, 1954-55; Political Agent, Doha, 1955-58; 1st Sec., Libya, 1958-62; Foreign Office, 1962-65; Head of Chancery, Cairo, 1965; Consul-General, Muscat, 1965-69; Dir, ME Centre of Arab Studies, 1969-73; Ambassador, Yemen Arab Republic, 1973-76. Governor, IDS, Sussex Univ., 1981-. JP Fareham, 1980. *Recreation:* pleasures of the countryside. *Address:* Wistaria Cottage, 174 Castle Street, Portchester, Hants PO16 9QH. *Club:* Vincent's (Oxford).

CARDEN, Sir Henry (Christopher), 4th Bt *cr* 1887; OBE (mil.) 1945; Regular Army Officer (17th/21st Lancers), retired; *b* 16 Oct. 1908; *o s* of Sir Frederick H. W. Carden, 3rd Bt; *S* father, 1966; *m* 1st, 1943, Jane St C. Daniell (whom he divorced, 1960); one *s* one *d* ; 2nd, 1962, Gwyneth S. Emerson (*née*

Acland), *widow* of Flt-Lt R. Emerson, Argentina (killed in action, RAF, 1944). *Educ*: Eton; RMC Sandhurst. 2/Lieut, 17/21 Lancers, 1928; served Egypt and India, 1930-39. Staff Coll., 1941; comd, 2 Armoured Delivery Regt, in France, 1944-45. CO 17/21 Lancers, in Greece and Palestine, 1947-48; War Office, 1948-51; Military Attaché in Stockholm, 1951-55; retired 1956. Comdr of the Order of the Sword (Sweden), 1954. *Recreations*: most field sports and games. *Heir*: s Christopher Robert Carden, b 24 Nov. 1946. *Address*: Moongrove, East Woodhay, near Newbury, Berks. *T*: Highclere 253661. *Club*: Cavalry and Guards.

CARDEN, Sir John Craven, 7th Bt, *cr* 1787; *b* 11 March 1926; *s* of Capt. Sir John V. Carden, 6th Bt and Dorothy Mary, *d* of Charles Luckrart McKinnon; *S* father, 1935; *m* 1947, Isabel Georgette, *y d* of late Robert de Hart; one *d*. *Educ*: Eton. *Heir*: *cousin* Derrick Charles Carden, *qv*. *Address*: PO Box N4802, Nassau, Bahamas. *Club*: White's.

CARDEW, Michael Ambrose, CBE 1981 (MBE 1965); potter, since 1923; *b* 26 May 1901; *s* of Arthur Cardew and Alexandra Rhoda (*née* Kitchin); *m* 1933, Mary-Ellen Baron Russell; two *s* (and one *s* decd). *Educ*: King's College Sch., Wimbledon; Exeter Coll., Oxford (BA (Lit. Hum.) 1923). Apprentice at Leach Pottery, St Ives, Cornwall, 1923-26; founded: Winchcombe Pottery, Glos, 1926; Wenford Bridge Pottery, Cornwall, 1939; Ceramist, Achimota Coll., Ghana, W Africa, 1942; founded Volta Pottery, Vume, Ghana, 1945; Pottery Officer, Nigeria, 1950-65; Vis. Lectr, Univ. of New South Wales, 1968; Workshops and Lectures: New Zealand, 1968; USA and Canada, 1967, 1971, 1972, 1976, 1978, 1980, 1981; Lectures, Nigeria and Ghana, 1973; Film (with A. Hallum), 1973. Hon. Dr RCA, 1982. *Publications*: Pioneer Pottery, 1969, (New York 1971); contribs to Pottery Qly, Ceramic Rev., Studio Potter (USA), Ceramics Monthly (USA). *Recreation*: writing. *Address*: Wenford Bridge Pottery, St Breward, Bodmin, Cornwall. *T*: Bodmin 850 471.

CARDIFF, Archbishop of, (RC), since 1961; **Most Rev. John A. Murphy**, DD; *b* Birkenhead, 21 Dec. 1905; *s* of John and Elizabeth Murphy. *Educ*: The English Coll., Lisbon. Ordained 1931; consecrated as Bishop of Appia and Coadjutor Bishop of Shrewsbury, 1948; Bishop of Shrewsbury, 1949-61. ChStJ 1974. *Address*: Archbishop's House, Westbourne Crescent, Whitchurch, Cardiff CF4 2XN. *T*: Cardiff 66063.

CARDIFF, Auxiliary Bishop in, (RC); see Mullins, Rt Rev. D. J.

CARDIFF, Brig. Ereld Boteler Wingfield, CB 1963; CBE 1958 (OBE 1943); *b* 5 March 1909; *m* 1932, Margaret Evelyn, *d* of late Major M. E. W. Pope, Ashwicke Hall, Marshfield; two *d*. *Educ*: Eton, 2nd Lieut, Scots Guards, 1930. Served War of 1939-45: (despatches thrice); 2nd Bn Scots Guards, 201 Guards Bde; 7th Armoured Div., Western Desert. Served Italy, France, Germany, Far ELF, 1955-58; SHAPE, 1958-63. Brig. 1958; retired, Nov. 1963. Chevalier, Order of Leopold, and Croix de Guerre, 1944. *Recreations*: shooting, fishing. *Address*: Easton Court, Ludlow, Salop. *T*: Tenbury Wells 475. *Clubs*: Cavalry and Guards, White's, Pratt's.
See also R. E. B. Lloyd.

CARDIFF, Jack; film director and cameraman; *b* 18 Sept. 1914; *s* of John Joseph and Florence Cardiff; *m* 1940, Julia Lily (*née* Mickleboro); three *s*. *Educ*: various schools, incl. Medburn Sch., Herts. Started as child actor, 1918; switched to cameras, 1928. World travelogues, 1937-39. Photographed, MOI Crown Film Unit: Western Approaches, 1942; best known films include: A Matter of Life and Death, Black Narcissus, The Red Shoes, Scott of the Antarctic, Under Capricorn, Pandora and the Flying Dutchman, African Queen, War and Peace. Started as Director, 1958. *Films include*: Sons and Lovers, My Geisha, The Lion, The Long Ships, Young Cassidy, The Mercenaries, The Liquidator, Girl on a Motorcycle, The Mutation, photographed: Ride a Wild Pony, The Prince and the Pauper, Behind the Iron Mask, Death on the Nile, Avalanche Express, The Awakening, The Dogs of War, Ghost Story. Awards: Academy Award (Oscar) Photography, Black Narcissus, 1947; Golden Globe Award, 1947; Coup Ce Soir (France), 1951; Film Achievement Award, Look Magazine; BSC Award, War and Peace; New York Critics Award for best film direction, Golden Globe Award, outstanding directorial award (all for Sons and Lovers); six Academy Award nominations. Hon. Dr of Art, Rome, 1953; Hon. Mem., Assoc. Française de Cameramen, 1971. *Publication*: Autobiography, 1975. *Recreations*: tennis, cricket, painting. *Address*: 75 Woodland Rise, N10. *Club*: MCC.

CARDIGAN, Earl of; David Michael James Brudenell-Bruce; *b* 12 Nov. 1952; *s* and *heir* of 8th Marquess of Ailesbury, *qv*; *m* 1980, Rosamond Jane, *er d* of Captain W. R. M. Winkley, Gable House, Parbrook, near Glastonbury, and of Mrs Jane Winkley, Wicks Cottage, Wootton Rivers, Marlborough; one *s*. *Educ*: Eton; Royal Agricultural Coll., Cirencester. *Heir*: *s* Viscount Savernake, *qv*. *Address*: Savernake Lodge, Savernake Forest, Marlborough, Wilts.

CARDINALE, Most Rev. Hyginus Eugene, DD, JCD; Papal Nuncio to Belgium and Luxembourg, since 1969 and to the European Economic Community, since 1970; Titular Archbishop of Nepte, since 1963; *b* 14 Oct. 1916; *s* of late Gaetano Cardinale and Uliana Cimino Cardinale. *Educ*: St Agnes Academy, Coll. Point, USA; Pontifical Roman Seminary, Rome; St Louis Theological Faculty, Naples; Pontifical Ecclesiastical Academy, Rome. Sec. of Apostolic Delegation in Egypt, Palestine, Transjordan and Cyprus,

1946-49; Auditor of Apostolic Internunciature to Egypt, 1949-52; Counsellor of Nunciature, 1952-61; Chief of Protocol of the Secretariat of State, 1961-63; Apostolic Delegate to Great Britain, Gibraltar, Malta and Bermuda, 1963-69; Special Envoy of the Holy See to the Council of Europe (Strasbourg), 1970-74. Under-Sec. of Techn. Organiz. Commn of Ecumenical Vatican Council II; Ecumenical Council Expert. Doctor of Theology, Canon Law; Diplomatic Sciences; Doctor (*hc*) Belles Lettres and Philosophy. Holds Grand Cross and is Knight Comdr in many orders. *Publications*: Le Saint-Siège et la Diplomatie, 1962; Chiesa e Stato negli Stati Uniti, 1958; La Santa Sede e il Diritto Consolare, 1963; Religious Tolerance, Freedom and Inter-Group Relations, 1966; Signs of the Times and Ecumenical Aspirations, 1967; The Unity of the Church, 1968; The Holy See and the International Order, 1976; Orders of Knighthood, Awards and the Holy See, 1982; contrib. to The Vatican and World Peace, 1969. *Address*: Avenue des Franciscains 9, 1150 Brussels, Belgium.

CARDROSS, Lord; Malcolm Harry Erskine; JP; *b* 4 July 1930; *s* and *heir* of 16th Earl of Buchan, *qv*; *m* 1957, Hilary Diana Cecil, *d* of late Sir Ivan McLannahan Power, 2nd Bt; two *s* two *d*. *Educ*: Eton. JP Westminster. *Heir*: *s* Hon. Henry Thomas Alexander Erskine, *b* 31 May 1960. *Address*: Newnham House, Newnham, Basingstoke, Hants. *Club*: Carlton.

CAREW, 6th Baron (UK) *cr* 1838; William Francis Conolly-Carew, CBE 1966; Baron Carew (Ireland), 1834; Bt Major retired, Duke of Cornwall's Light Infantry; *b* 23 April 1905; *e s* of 5th Baron and Catherine (*d* 1947), *o d* of late Thomas Conolly, MP, of Castletown, Co. Kildare; *S* father, 1927; *m* 1937, Lady Sylvia Maitland, CStJ, *o d* of 15th Earl of Lauderdale; two *s* two *d*. *Educ*: Wellington; Sandhurst. Gazetted DCLI 1925; ADC to Governor and Comdr-in-Chief of Bermuda, 1931-36. Chm., British Legion, 1963-66; Pres., Irish Grassland Assn, 1949; Br. Govt Trustee, Irish Sailors' and Soldiers' Land Trust. CStJ. *Heir*: *s* Hon. Patrick Thomas Conolly-Carew, Captain Royal Horse Guards, retd [*b* 6 March 1938; *m* 1962, Celia, *d* of late Col Hon. (Charles) Guy Cubitt, CBE, DSO, TD; one *s* three *d*]. *Address*: Oakville, Donadea, Naas, Co. Kildare, Ireland. *T*: Naas 68196.

CAREW, Sir Rivers (Verain), 11th Bt *cr* 1661; journalist and stud farmer; *b* 17 Oct. 1935; *s* of Sir Thomas Palk Carew, 10th Bt, and Phyllis Evelyn (*d* 1976), *o c* of Neville Mayman; *S* father, 1976; *m* 1968, Susan Babington, *yr d* of late H. B. Hill, London; one *s* three *d* (and one *s* decd). *Educ*: St Columba's Coll., Rathfarnham, Co. Dublin; Trinity Coll., Dublin. MA, BAgr (Hort.). Asst Editor, Ireland of the Welcomes (Irish Tourist Bd magazine), 1964-67; Joint Editor, The Dublin Magazine, 1964-69; Irish Television, 1967-. *Publication*: (with Timothy Brownlow) Figures out of Mist (verse). *Recreations*: reading; music; reflection. *Heir*: *s* Gerald de Redvers Carew, *b* 24 May 1975. *Address*: Killyon Manor, Hill of Down, Co. Meath, Ireland. *T*: Castlerickard 115. *Club*: Kildare Street and University (Dublin).

CAREW, Major Robert John Henry, MC; JP, DL; *b* 7 June 1888; *s* of late Col R. T. Carew, DL, of Ballinamona Park, Waterford, and Constance, *d* of Maj.-Gen. William Creagh; *m* 1st 1915, Leila Vernon (*d* 1934), *d* of late Sir Arthur V. Macan; 2nd, 1936, Dorothea Petrie (*d* 1968), *d* of late Col G. R. Townshend, RA; one *d*. *Educ*: Marlborough Coll.; RMC Sandhurst. Joined Royal Dublin Fus, 1908; served European War as Staff Captain and DAQMG; retired, 1920. *Recreations*: mechanical work; was Hon. Sec. of the Waterford Hunt, 1926-33. *Address*: Ballinamona Park, Waterford. *T*: Waterford 74429. *Club*: Army and Navy.

CAREW, William James, CBE 1937; Retired as Clerk of the Executive Council and Deputy Minister of Provincial Affairs, Newfoundland; *b* 28 Dec. 1890; *s* of late James and Mary Carew; *m* 1920, Mary Florence Channing (decd); one *s* (Titular Archbishop of Telde; Apostolic Delegate to Jerusalem and Palestine, including Israel and Syria, and Pro-Nuncio to Cyprus) three *d*. *Educ*: St Patrick's Hall (Christian Brothers), St John's, Newfoundland. Newspaper work, 1908-09; staff of Prime Minister's Office, 1909; Sec., 1914-34; acted as Sec. to Newfoundland Delegate to Peace Conference, 1919; Sec. of Newfoundland Delegation to Imperial Conference, 1923, 1926, 1930; Deputy Min. for External Affairs, 1932; Sec. Newfoundland Delegation to Imperial Economic Conference, Ottawa, 1932; Sec. Cttee for Celebration in Newfoundland of Coronation of King George VI, 1937; Sec. Royal Visit Cttees on occasion of visit of King George VI and Queen Elizabeth to Newfoundland, 1939. Commemorative Medals of the Royal Jubilee, 1935, the Coronation, 1937 and the Coronation, 1953. Knight Commander, Order of St Sylvester, 1976. *Address*: 74 Cochrane Street, St John's, Newfoundland.

CAREW POLE, Col Sir John (Gawen), 12th Bt *cr* 1628; DSO 1944; TD; JP; Lord-Lieutenant of Cornwall, 1962-77; Member of the Prince of Wales's Council, 1952-68; Member, Jockey Club (incorporating National Hunt Committee), since 1969; Steward, National Hunt Committee, 1953-56; Member, Garden Society; *b* 4 March 1902; *e s* of late Lt-Gen. Sir Reginald Pole-Carew, KCB, of Antony, Cornwall, and Lady Beatrice Pole-Carew, *er d* of 3rd Marquess of Ormonde; *S* kinsman, 1926; *m* 1st, 1928, Cynthia Mary, OBE 1959 (*d* 1977), *o d* of Waltar Burns, North Mymms Park, Hatfield; one *s* two *d*; 2nd, 1979, Joan, *widow* of Lt-Col Anthony Fulford, Dunsford, Devon. *Educ*: Eton; RMC, Sandhurst. Coldstream Guards, 1923-39; ADC to Commander-in-Chief in India, 1924-25; Comptroller to Governor-General, Union of S. Africa, 1935-36; Palestine, 1936; commanded 5th Bn Duke of Cornwall's LI (TA), 1939-43; commanded 2nd Bn Devonshire Regt, 1944;

Colonel, Second Army, 1944-45; Normandy, France, Belgium, Holland, Germany, 1944-45 (despatches, immediate DSO); raised and commanded post-war TA Bn, 4/5 Bn, DCLI, 1946-47; Hon. Col, 4/5 Bn DCLI (TA), 1958-60; Hon. Col DCLI (TA) 1960-67. Director: Lloyd's Bank, 1956-72 (Chm., Devon and Cornwall Cttee, 1956-72); English China Clays Ltd, 1969-73; Keith Prowse, 1969; Vice-Chm., Westward Television Ltd, 1960-72. Member: Central Transport Consultative Cttee for Great Britain, 1948-54; SW Electricity Consultative Council, 1949-52 (Vice-Chairman, 1951-52); Western Area Board, British Transport Commission, 1955-61. JP 1939, DL 1947, CA 1954-66, Cornwall; High Sheriff, Cornwall, 1947-48; Vice-Lt, Cornwall, 1950-62; Chairman Cornwall County Council, 1952-63. A Gentleman of HM Bodyguard of the Honourable Corps of Gentlemen-at-Arms, 1950-72, Standard Bearer, 1968-72. Prime Warden Worshipful Company of Fishmongers, 1969-70. KStJ 1972. Hon. LLD Exeter, 1979. *Recreations:* gardening, shooting, travel. *Heir:* s (John) Richard (Walter Reginald) Carew Pole, qv. *Address:* Antony House, Torpoint, Cornwall PL11 2QA. *T:* Plymouth 812406. *Clubs:* Army and Navy, Pratt's, MCC.

See also D. C. T. Quilter.

CAREW POLE, (John) Richard (Walter Reginald); farmer and chartered surveyor; *b* 2 Dec. 1938; *s* and *heir* of Sir John Gawen Carew Pole, qv; *m* 1st, 1966, Hon. Victoria Marion Ann Lever (marr. diss. 1974), *d* of 3rd Viscount Leverhulme, qv; 2nd, 1974, Mary, *d* of Lt-Col Ronald Dawnay; two *s. Educ:* Eton Coll.; Royal Agricultural Coll., Cirencester. ARICS 1967. Lieut, Coldstream Guards, 1958-63. Asst Surveyor, Laws & Fiennes, Chartered Surveyors, 1967-72. Member: Devon and Cornwall Police Authority, 1973-; SW Area Electricity Bd, 1981-; NT Cttee for Devon and Cornwall, 1979-. Pres., Royal Cornwall Agricultural Show, 1981; Governor, Seale Hayne Agric. Coll., 1979-. County Councillor, Cornwall, 1973-; High Sheriff of Cornwall, 1979. Liveryman, Fishmongers' Co., 1960. *Recreations:* travelling, walking, gardening. *Address:* Antony House, Torpoint, Cornwall PL11 2QA. *T:* Plymouth 812406. *Clubs:* White's, Pratt's.

CAREY, Group Captain Alban M., CBE 1943; Chairman: Chirit Investment Co. Ltd; Maden Park Property Investment Co. Ltd; *b* 18 April 1906; *m* 1934, Enid Morten Bond; one *s. Educ:* Bloxham. Commissioned RAF 1929; served War of 1939-45 with RAF Coastal Command both overseas and in the UK; left RAF 1946 to become Chm., Shaw & Sons Ltd Gp of Law Publishing Companies. *Recreations:* farming, shooting, fishing, yachting. *Address:* Church Farm, Great Witchingham, Norfolk NR9 5PE. *T:* Great Witchingham 511. *Clubs:* Royal Air Force; Royal Air Force Yacht.

CAREY, Charles John; Under Secretary, HM Treasury, since 1978; *b* 11 Nov. 1933; *s* of Richard Mein Carey and Celia Herbert Amy (née Conway). *Educ:* Rugby; Balliol Coll., Oxford. HM Treasury: Asst Principal, 1957; Principal, 1962; Asst Sec., 1971; seconded to HM Diplomatic Service as Counsellor (Econs and Finance), Office of UK Perm. Rep. to EEC, Brussels, 1974-77; Chm., EEC Council Budget Cttee, during UK Presidency of EEC Council, Jan.-June 1977. *Recreations:* mountaineering, Bavarian baroque churches, Trollope novels. *Clubs:* United Oxford & Cambridge University; Austrian Alpine (UK Br.).

CAREY, D(avid) M(acbeth) M(oir), MA, DCL Oxon; Joint Registrar to Faculty Office of Archbishop of Canterbury, since 1982; Legal Secretary to the Archbishop of Canterbury and Principal Registrar to the Province of Canterbury, 1958-82; Legal Secretary to the Bishops of Ely, 1953-82 and Gloucester, 1957-82; Registrar to the Diocese of Canterbury, 1959-82; *b* 21 Jan. 1917; *s* of Godfrey Mohun Carey, Sherborne, Dorset, and Agnes Charlotte Carey (née Milligan); *m* 1949, Margaret Ruth (née Mills), Highfield Sch., Liphook, Hants; three *s* one *d. Educ:* Westminster Sch. (King's Scholar); St Edmund Hall, Oxford. Articled Clerk, Messrs Lee, Bolton & Lee, 1938-40. Lt-Cdr (S) RNVR, 1940-46. Qualified Solicitor, 1947; Partnership with Lee, Bolton & Lee, 1948-82, Consultant, 1982-. *Recreation:* fishing. *Address:* 1 The Sanctuary, SW1P 3JT. *T:* 01-222 5381; Mulberry House, Ash, Canterbury, Kent. *T:* Ash 812534. *Club:* St Stephen's Constitutional.

CAREY, Denis; producer and actor; *b* London, 3 Aug. 1909; *s* of William Denis Carey and May (née Wilkinson); *m* Yvonne Coulette. *Educ:* St Paul's Sch.; Trinity Coll., Dublin. First appearance as Micky in The Great Big World, Royal Court, 1921; subseq. appeared in Dublin, 1929-34, London and New York, 1935-39; Pilgrim Players, 1940-43; Glasgow Citizens' Theatre, 1943-45; Arts Council Theatre, Coventry, 1945-46; in Galway Handicap, Men without Shadows, Lyric Hammersmith, 1947. First production, Happy as Larry, Mercury, later Criterion, 1947; Georgia Story, The Playboy of the Western World, London, 1948; Assoc. Producer, Arts Theatre, Salisbury, 1948; Dir, Bristol Old Vic Company, 1949-54; London and other productions include: Two Gentlemen of Verona (from Bristol), An Italian Straw Hat, Old Vic, 1952; Henry V (from Bristol), Old Vic, 1953; The Merchant of Venice, Stratford-on-Avon, 1953; Twelfth Night, The Taming of the Shrew, Old Vic, 1954; Salad Days (from Bristol), Vaudeville, 1954; Twelfth Night, Théatre Nat. de Belgique, Brussels, 1954; A Kind of Folly, Duchess, 1955; Follow That Girl, Vaudeville, 1960; Twelfth Night, Regent's Park, 1962. First Director, American Shakespeare Theatre, Stratford, Conn., 1955; prod Julius Cæsar, The Tempest. Director: Bristol Old Vic tour (British Council), India, Pakistan, Ceylon, 1963; The Golden Rivet, Phœnix Theatre, Dublin, 1964; Armstrong's Last Good-Night, Citizen Theatre, Glasgow, 1964; The Saints Go Cycling, Dublin Festival, 1965; African tour for British Council, 1964-65; Juno and the Paycock, Gaiety Theatre, Dublin, 1966; Hamlet, Dubrovnik Festival,

Homecoming, Atelje 212, Belgrade, 1967-69; Hamlet, Kentner Theatre, Istanbul, 1968; Troilus and Cressida, Athens, USA 1969; Androcles and the Lion, Stanford, USA, 1969; Julius Caesar, Kano, Nigeria, 1974-75. Played: Teleyegin in Uncle Vanya, Royal Court, 1970; Egeus and Quince in RSC world tour of A Midsummer Night's Dream, 1972-73; Gunga Din in Chez Nous, Globe, 1974; Da in Da, Liverpool Playhouse, 1975. *Recreations:* walking and gardening. *Address:* c/o Vernon Conway, 19 London Street, Paddington, W2 1HL.

CAREY, Rev. Dr George Leonard; Principal, Trinity College, Stoke Hill, Bristol, since 1982; *b* 13 Nov. 1935; *s* of George and Ruby Carey; *m* 1960, Eileen Harmsworth Hood, Dagenham, Essex; two *s* two *d. Educ:* Bifrons Secondary Modern Sch., Barking; London College of Divinity; King's College, London. BD Hons, MTh; PhD London. National Service, RAF Wireless Operator, 1954-56. Deacon, 1962; Curate, St Mary's, Islington, 1962-66; Lecturer: Oakhill Coll., Southgate, 1966-70; St John's Coll., Nottingham, 1970-75; Vicar, St Nicholas' Church, Durham, 1975-82. *Publications:* I Believe in Man, 1975; God Incarnate, 1976; (jtly) The Great Acquittal, 1980; contributor to numerous jls. *Recreation:* jogging. *Address:* 16 Ormerod Road, Bristol BS9 1BB.

CAREY, Hugh Leo; Governor of New York State, 1975-83; *b* Brooklyn, NY, 11 April 1919; *s* of Denis Carey and Margaret (née Collins); *m* 1st, 1947, Helen Owen Twohy (*d* 1974); seven *s* four *d* one adopted *d* (and two *s* decd); 2nd, 1981, Evangeline Gouletas. *Educ:* St Augustine's Academy and High School, Brooklyn; St John's Coll.; St John's Law School. JD 1951. Served War of 1939-45 (Bronze Star, Croix de Guerre with Silver Star); with US Army in Europe, 1939-46, rank of Lt-Col. Joined family business (petrochemicals), 1947. Called to Bar, 1951. Member US House of Reps, rep. 12th District of Brooklyn, 1960-75; Deputy Whip. Democrat. *Address:* c/o State Capitol, Albany, NY 12224, USA.

CAREY, Prof. John; Merton Professor of English Literature, Oxford University, since 1976; *b* 5 April 1934; *s* of Charles William Carey and Winifred Ethel Carey (née Cook); *m* 1960, Gillian Mary Florence Booth; two *s. Educ:* Richmond and East Sheen County Grammar Sch.; St John's Coll., Oxford (MA, DPhil). 2nd Lieut, East Surrey Regt, 1953-54; Harmsworth Sen. Scholar, Merton Coll., Oxford, 1957-58; Lectr, Christ Church, Oxford, 1958-59; Andrew Bradley Jun. Research Fellow, Balliol, Oxford, 1959-60; Tutorial Fellow, Keble Coll., Oxford, 1960-64; St John's Coll., Oxford, 1964-75. *Publications:* The Poems of John Milton (ed with Alastair Fowler), 1968; Milton, 1969; The Violent Effigy: a study of Dickens' imagination, 1973; Thackeray: Prodigal Genius, 1977; John Donne: Life, Mind and Art, 1981; (ed) The Private Memoirs and Confessions of a Justified Sinner, by James Hogg, 1981; articles in Rev. of English Studies, Mod. Lang. Rev., etc. *Recreations:* swimming, gardening, bee-keeping. *Address:* Brasenose Cottage, Lyneham, Oxon; 57 Stapleton Road, Headington, Oxford. *T:* Oxford 64304.

CAREY, Lionel Mohun, TD, MA; JP; Headmaster of Bromsgrove School, 1953-71; *b* 27 Jan. 1911; 4th *s* of late G. M. Carey; *m* 1943, Mary Elizabeth Auld, MBE; two *s. Educ:* Sherborne Sch.; Corpus Christi Coll., Cambridge. Teaching Diploma Institute of Education, London, 1934. Assistant Master, Bolton Sch., Lancs., 1934-37; Christ's Hospital, 1937-53, Housemaster 1940-53. JP Sherborne. *Recreations:* walking, gardening, people, contemplation of eternity. *Address:* Westbury Cottage, Sherborne, Dorset.

CAREY, Very Rev. Michael Sausmarez; Dean of Ely, 1970-82; *b* 7 Dec. 1913; *s* of Rev. Christopher Sausmarez and Jane Robinson Carey; *m* 1945, Muriel Anne Gibbs; one *s* one *d. Educ:* Haileybury Coll.; Keble Coll., Oxford (MA 1941). Ordained, 1939, Curate St John's Waterloo Rd, SE1; Chaplain Cuddesdon Coll., 1941-43; Mission Priest, Gambia, 1943-44; Rector of Hunsdon, Herts, 1945-51; Rector of Botley, Hants, 1951-62; Archdeacon of Ely, 1962-70, and Rector of St Botolph's, Cambridge, 1965-70. Exam. Chap. to Bp of Portsmouth, 1953-59. Hon. Canon, Portsmouth, 1961-62. MA Cantab Incorp. 1967. *Publication:* The Giver of Life, 1979. *Recreations:* music, painting, golf. *Address:* 23 Kingsway, Blakeney, Norfolk NR25 7PL.

CAREY, Sir Peter (Willoughby), GCB 1982 (KCB 1976; CB 1972); Permanent Secretary, Department of Industry, since 1976; *b* 26 July 1923; *s* of Jack Delves Carey and Sophie Carey; *m* 1946, Thelma Young; three *d. Educ:* Portsmouth Grammar Sch.; Oriel Coll., Oxford; Sch. of Slavonic Studies. Served War of 1939-45: Capt., Gen. List, 1943-45. Information Officer, British Embassy, Belgrade, 1945-46; FO (German Section), 1948-51; Bd of Trade, 1953; Prin. Private Sec. to successive Presidents, 1960-64; IDC, 1965; Asst Sec., 1963-67, Under-Sec., 1967-69, Bd of Trade; Under-Sec., Min. of Technology, 1969-71; Dep. Sec., Cabinet Office, 1971-72; Dep. Sec., 1972-73, Second Permanent Sec., 1973-74, DTI; Second Permanent Sec., DoI, 1974-76. *Recreations:* music, theatre, travel. *Address:* 19 Leeward Gardens, Wimbledon, SW19. *T:* 01-947 5530. *Club:* United Oxford & Cambridge University.

CAREY EVANS, Lady Olwen (Elizabeth), DBE 1969; *b* 3 April 1892; *d* of 1st Earl Lloyd-George of Dwyfor, PC, OM, and Margaret, GBE, *d* of Richard Owen, Mynydd Ednyfed, Criccieth; *m* 1917, Sir Thomas John Carey Evans, MC, FRCS (*d* 1947); two *s* two *d. Address:* Eisteddfa, Criccieth, Gwynedd.

CAREY-FOSTER, George Arthur, CMG 1952; DFC 1944; AFC 1941; Counsellor, HM Diplomatic (formerly Foreign) Service, 1946–68; *b* 18 Nov. 1907; *s* of George Muir Foster, FRCS, MRCP, and Marie Thérèse Mutin; *m* 1936, Margaret Aloysius Barry Egan ; one *d. Educ:* Clifton Coll., Bristol. Royal Air Force, 1929–35; Reserve of Air Force Officers, 1935–39; served War of 1939–45: Royal Air Force, 1939–46 (despatches, AFC, DFC), Group Capt. Served at Foreign Office, as Consul General at Hanover, as Counsellor and Chargé d'Affaires at Rio de Janeiro, Warsaw and The Hague, 1946–68; retired, 1968. *Recreations:* wine, gardening. *Address:* Kilkeran, Castle Freke, Co. Cork. *Clubs:* Royal Air Force; Haagsche (The Hague).

CAREY JONES, Norman Stewart, CMG 1965; Director, Development Administration, Leeds University, 1965–77; *b* 11 Dec. 1911; *s* of Samuel Carey Jones and Jessie Isabella Stewart; *m* 1946, Stella Myles; two *s. Educ:* Monmouth Sch.; Merton Coll., Oxford. Colonial Audit Service: Gold Coast, 1935; Northern Rhodesia, 1939; British Honduras, 1946; Kenya, 1950; Asst Financial Sec., Treasury, Kenya, 1954; Dep. Sec., Min. of Agric., Kenya, 1956; Perm. Sec., Min. of Lands and Settlement, Kenya, 1962. *Publications:* The Pattern of a Dependent Economy, 1952; The Anatomy of Uhuru, 1966; Politics, Public Enterprise and The Industrial Development Agency, 1974; articles and reviews for: Journal of Rhodes-Livingstone Inst.; E African Economics Review; Africa Quarterly; Geog. Jl. *Address:* Mawingo, Welsh St Donats, near Cowbridge, S Glam CF7 7SS. *Club:* Royal Commonwealth Society.

CARIBOO, Bishop of, since 1974; **Rt. Rev. John Samuel Philip Snowden.** *Educ:* Anglican Theological Coll., Vancouver (LTh 1951); Univ. of British Columbia (BA 1956). Deacon 1951, priest 1952; Curate: Kaslo-Kokanee, 1951-53; Oak Bay, 1953-57; Nanaimo, 1957-60; Incumbent of St Timothy, Vancouver, 1960-64; Priest Pastoral, Christ Church Cathedral, Vancouver, 1964-66; Rector of St Timothy, Edmonton, 1966-71; Dean and Rector of St Paul's Cathedral, Kamloops, 1971-74. Domestic Chaplain to Bishop of Cariboo, 1971-73. *Address:* 360 Nicola Street, Kamloops, BC V2C 2P5, Canada.

CARINGTON, family name of **Baron Carrington.**

CARLESS, Hugh Michael, CMG 1976; HM Diplomatic Service; Ambassador to Venezuela, since 1982; *b* 22 April 1925; *s* of late Henry Alfred Carless, CIE, and of Gwendolen Pattullo; *m* 1956, Rosa Maria, *e d* of Martino and Ada Frontini, São Paulo; two *s. Educ:* Sherborne; Sch. of Oriental Studies, London; Trinity Hall, Cambridge. Served in Paiforce and BAOR, 1943–47; entered Foreign (subseq. Diplomatic) Service, 1950; 3rd Sec., Kabul, 1951; 2nd Sec., Rio de Janeiro, 1953; Tehran, 1956; 1st Sec., 1957; FO, 1958; Private Sec. to Minister of State, 1961; Budapest, 1963; Civil Service Fellow, Dept of Politics, Glasgow Univ., 1966; Counsellor and Consul-Gen., Luanda, 1967–70; Counsellor, Bonn, 1970–73; Head of Latin American Dept, FCO, 1973–77; Minister and Chargé d'Affaires, Buenos Aires, 1977–80; on secondment to Northern Engineering Industries International Ltd, 1980–82. *Recreations:* mountains, history. *Address:* c/o Foreign and Commonwealth Office, SW1; 15 Bryanston Square, W1.

CARLESS, Prof. John Edward, BPharm, MSc, PhD; FPS; Professor and Head of Department of Pharmaceutics, School of Pharmacy, London University, since 1977; *b* 23 Nov. 1922; *s* of Alfred Edward Carless and Frances Mary (*née* Smith); *m* 1950, Dorothy Litherland; one *d* and two step *d. Educ:* Leominster Grammar Sch.; Leicester Coll. of Science and Technol. (BPharm); FPS 1947; Univ. of Manchester (MSc, PhD). Asst Lectr in Pharmacy, Univ. of Manchester, 1947–54; Chelsea College: Sen. Lectr in Pharmaceutics, 1954–61; Reader, 1961–67; Prof. of Pharmaceutics, 1967–77. Member: Cttee on Safety of Medicines, 1976–78; Veterinary Products Cttee, 1978–; Cttee on Review of Medicine, 1980–; Chm., Pharmacy Bd, CNAA, 1978–. Harrison Meml Medal, 1980. *Publications:* (ed jtly) Advances in Pharmaceutical Sciences: Vol. 1, 1964-vol. 5, 1982; (contrib.) Bentley's Text Book of Pharmaceutics, 1977. *Recreations:* photography, motoring. *Address:* Manton, Colley Manor Drive, Reigate, Surrey. *T:* Reigate 43670.

CARLESTON, Hadden Hamilton, CIE 1947; OBE 1944; *b* Pretoria, SA, 25 July 1904; *m* 1946, Eirene Leslie, *d* of Rev. H. L. Stevens, Torquay, S Devon; two *s* one *d. Educ:* St Olave's Sch., Southwark; Trinity Hall, Cambridge (MA). Indian Civil Service, 1927–47; Dist Magistrate of Civil and Military Station, Bangalore, 1939–43, and of various districts in Madras Presidency, including Vizagapatam, 1944–46, and The Nilgiris, 1947. Civil Liaison Officer with 19th and 25th Indian Inf. Divs, 1944. Sec. of St Cuthbert's Soc., Univ. of Durham, 1948–52; Admin. Sec., Cambridge Univ. Sch. of Veterinary Medicine, 1952–71. *Address:* Selborne, Cae Mair, Beaumaris, Gwynedd. *T:* Beaumaris 810586.

CARLETON, Mrs John; *see* Adam Smith, J. B.

CARLETON-SMITH, Maj.-Gen. Michael Edward, CBE 1980 (MBE 1966); Defence Adviser and Head of British Defence Liaison Staff, Canberra, Australia, also Military Adviser, Canberra, and Wellington, NZ, and Defence Adviser, Papua New Guinea, since 1982; *b* 5 May 1931; *s* of Lt-Col D. L. G. Carleton-Smith; *m* 1963, Helga Katja Stoss; three *s. Educ:* Radley Coll.; RMA, Sandhurst. Graduate: Army Staff Coll.; JSSC; NDC; RCDS. Commissioned into The Rifle Brigade, 1951; Rifle Bde, Germany, 1951–53; active service: Kenya, 1954-55; Malaya, 1957; Exchange PPCLI, Canada,

1958-60; GSO2 General Staff, HQ1(BR) Corps, 1962-63; Rifle Brigade: Cyprus, Hong Kong, active service, Borneo, 1965-66; Sch. of Infantry Staff, 1967-68; Comd Rifle Depot, 1970-72; Directing Staff NDC, 1972-74; Col General Staff, HQ BAOR, 1974-77; Commander Gurkha Field Force, Hong Kong, 1977-79; Dep. Director Army Staff Duties, MoD, 1982. *Recreations:* riding, sailing, fishing, travel. *Address:* c/o Lloyds Bank plc, Market Harborough, Leicestershire.

CARLILE, Rev. Edward Wilson; Liaison Officer, East Africa Church Army Appeal, since 1981; *b* 11 June 1915; *s* of Victor Wilson and Elsie Carlile; *m* 1946, Elizabeth (*née* Bryant); two *s* one *d. Educ:* Epsom Coll.; King's Coll., London (BD). Chartered Accountant, 1939. Deacon, 1943; priest, 1944; Curate, All Saints, Queensbury, 1943-46; Hon. Asst Sec. of Church Army, 1946-49; Chief Sec. of Church Army, 1949-60; Vicar of St Peter's with St Hilda's, Leicester, 1960-73; Rector of Swithland, Leicester, 1973-76; Priest in Charge of St Michael and All Angels, Belgrave, Leicester, 1976-30 Apr. 81. *Recreations:* race relations, evangelism, walking, travel, photography. *Address:* Church Cottage, Chadwell, Melton Mowbray, Leics. *T:* Scalford 347.

CARLILE, Thomas, CBE 1975; Managing Director, since 1968, Deputy Chairman, since 1978, Babcock International Ltd; *b* 9 Feb. 1924; *s* of late James Love Carlile and Isobel Scott Carlile; *m* 1955, Jessie Davidson Clarkson; three *d. Educ:* Minchenden County Sch.; City & Guilds Coll., London. Joined Babcock & Wilcox Ltd, 1944. Chm., Shipbuilding Industry Training Board, 1967-70. Mem., Energy Commn, 1977-79. Pres., Engineering Employers' Fedn, 1972-74, a Vice-Pres., 1979-. FCGI 1978; FEng 1979. *Address:* 8 Aldenham Grove, Radlett, Herts. *T:* Radlett 6881. *Club:* Caledonian.

CARLILL, Rear Adm. John Hildred, OBE 1969; Admiral President, Royal Naval College, Greenwich, 1980-82; *b* 24 Oct. 1925; *o s* of late Dr H. B. Carlill, MD, FRCP, and Mrs M. C. Carlill; *m* 1955, (Elizabeth) Ann, *yr d* of late Lt Col and Mrs W. Southern; three *d. Educ:* RNC Dartmouth. psc 1961; jssc 1967. Served War 1939-45. Joined RN as Exec. Cadet 1939, transferred to Accountant Branch 1943; HMS Mauritius 1943-45. Comdr 1963, Captain 1972 (Sec. to FO Naval Air Comd, Dir Naval Manning and Training (S), Sec. to Second Sea Lord, Admty Interview Board, Cdre HMS Drake); Rear Admiral 1980. Freeman, City of London, 1980. *Recreations:* walking, skiing, water colour painting. *Address:* Crownpits Barn, Crownpits Lane, Godalming, Surrey GU7 1NY. *T:* Godalming 5022. *Club:* Army and Navy.

CARLILL, Vice-Admiral Sir Stephen Hope, KBE 1957; CB 1954; DSO 1942; *b* Orpington, Kent, 23 Dec. 1902; *s* of late Harold Flamank Carlill; *m* 1928, Julie Fredrike Elisabeth Hildegard, *o d* of late Rev. W. Rahlenbeck, Westphalia; two *s. Educ:* Royal Naval Colleges, Osborne and Dartmouth. Lieut RN, 1925; qualified as Gunnery Officer, 1929; Commander 1937; Commanded HM Destroyers Hambledon, 1940, and Farndale, 1941-42; Captain 1942; Captain (D), 4th Destoyer Flotilla, HMS Quilliam, 1942-44 (despatches); Admiralty, 1944-46; Chief of Staff to C-in-C British Pacific Fleet, 1946-48; Captain, HMS Excellent, 1949-50; Commanded HMS Illustrious, 1950-51; Rear-Admiral, 1952; Senior Naval Member, Imperial Defence Coll., 1952-54; Vice-Admiral, 1954; Flag Officer, Training Squadron, 1954-55; Chief of Naval Staff, Indian Navy, 1955-58, retired. Representative in Ghana of West Africa Cttee 1960-66; Adviser to W Africa Cttee, 1966-67. *Recreations:* walking and gardening. *Address:* 22 Hamilton Court, Milford-on-Sea, Lymington, Hants. *T:* Milford-on-Sea 2958. *Club:* Naval and Military.

CARLISLE, 12th Earl of, *cr* 1661; **Charles James Ruthven Howard,** MC 1945; Viscount Howard of Morpeth, Baron Dacre of Gillesland, 1661; Lord Ruthven of Freeland, 1651; *b* 21 Feb. 1923; *o s* of 11th Earl of Carlisle, and Lady Ruthven of Freeland (*d* 1982) (11th in line); *S* father, 1963; *m* 1945, Hon. Ela Beaumont, OStJ, *o d* of 2nd Viscount Allendale, KG, CB, CBE, MC; two *s* two *d. Educ:* Eton. Served War of 1939-45 (wounded twice, MC). Lieut late Rifle Brigade. FRICS (FLAS 1953). *Heir:* *s* Viscount Morpeth, *qv. Address:* Naworth Castle, Brampton, Cumbria. *T:* Brampton 2621.

CARLISLE, Bishop of, since 1972; **Rt. Rev. Henry David Halsey;** *b* 27 Jan. 1919; *s* of George Halsey, MBE and Gladys W. Halsey, DSc; *m* 1947, Rachel Margaret Neil Smith; four *d. Educ:* King's Coll. Sch., Wimbledon; King's Coll., London (BA); Wells Theol College. Curate, Petersfield, 1942-45; Chaplain, RNVR, 1946-47; Curate, St Andrew, Plymouth, 1947-50; Vicar of: Netheravon, 1950-53; St Stephen, Chatham, 1953-62; Bromley, and Chaplain, Bromley Hosp., 1962-68; Rural Dean of Bromley, 1965-66; Archdeacon of Bromley, 1966-68; Bishop Suffragan of Tonbridge, 1968-72. Entered House of Lords, 1976. *Recreations:* cricket, sailing, reading, gardening, walking. *Address:* Rose Castle, Dalston, Carlisle CA5 7BZ. *T:* Raughton Head 274. *Club:* Army and Navy.

CARLISLE, Dean of; *see* Churchill, Very Rev. J. H.

CARLISLE, Archdeacon of; *see* Ewbank, Ven. W. F.

CARLISLE, Brian Apcar, CBE 1974; DSC 1945; Chairman, Saxon Oil Ltd, since 1980; *b* 27 Dec. 1919; 2nd *s* of Captain F. M. M. Carlisle, MC; *m* 1953, Elizabeth Hazel Mary Binnie, 2nd *d* of Comdr J. A. Binnie, RN; one *s* three *d. Educ:* Harrow Sch.; Corpus Christi Coll., Cambridge. Royal Navy,

1940–46, served in N Atlantic, Channel and Mediterranean in HMS Hood and destroyers; Sudan Political Service, 1946–54, served in Kassala, Blue-Nile and Bahr-el-Ghazal Provinces; Royal Dutch/Shell Group, 1955–74: served in India with Burmah Shell, 1960–64; Regional Co-ordinator, Middle East, and Dir, Shell International Petroleum, 1970–74; participated in pricing negotiations with OPEC states, 1970–73; Dir, Home Oil Co. Ltd, 1977–80; Oil Consultant to Lloyds Bank International, 1975–81. *Recreations:* gardening, crosswords, golf. *Address:* Heath Cottage, Hartley Wintney, Hants RG27 8RE. *T:* Hartley Wintney 2224.

CARLISLE, Hugh Bernard Harwood, QC 1978; *b* 14 March 1937; *s* of late W. H. Carlisle, FRCS (Ed), FRCOG, and Joyce Carlisle; *m* 1964, Veronica Marjorie, *d* of G. A. Worth, *qv*; one *s* one *d. Educ:* Oundle Sch.; Downing Coll., Cambridge. Nat. Service, 2nd Lt, RA. Called to the Bar, Middle Temple, 1961. Jun. Treasury Counsel for Personal Injuries Cases, 1975–78. Inspector, Bryanston Finance Ltd, 1978–. *Address:* 18 Ranelagh Avenue, SW6 3PJ. *T:* 01-736 4238. *Club:* Hurlingham.

CARLISLE, John Michael, CEng, FIMechE, FIMarE; Chairman, Deisel Marine International Ltd, since 1981; Director, Torday & Carlisle plc, since 1981; Chairman, Trent Regional Health Authority, since 1982; *b* 16 Dec. 1929; *s* of John Hugh Carlisle and Lilian Amy (*née* Smith); *m* 1957, Mary Scott Young; one *s* one *d. Educ:* King Edward VII Sch., Sheffield; Sheffield Univ. (BEng). MBIM. Served Royal Navy (Lieut), 1952–54. Production Engr, Lockwood & Carlisle Ltd, 1954–57, Man. Dir, 1958–70, Chm. and Man. Dir, 1970–81; Dir of overseas subsid. cos in Norway, Holland, Singapore and Hong Kong; Dir, Eric Woodward (Electrical) Ltd. Chairman: Sheffield AHA(T), 1974–82; N Sheffield Univ. HMC, 1971–74; Mem., Bd of Governors, United Sheffield Hosps, 1972–74; Mem. Council: Sheffield Chamber of Commerce, 1967–78; Production Engrg Res. Assoc., 1968–73; Chm., Sheffield Productivity Assoc., 1970; Pres., Sheffield Jun. Chamber of Commerce, 1967–68; Governor: Sheffield City Polytechnic, 1979–82 (Hon. Fellow, 1977); Sheffield High Sch. for Girls, 1977–; Member: Sheffield Univ. Court, 1968–; Sheffield Univ. Careers Adv. Bd, 1974–. Freeman, Co. of Cutlers in Hallamshire. *Recreations:* golf, sea sailing (in warm climates), country walking. *Address:* 7 Rushley Avenue, Dore, Sheffield S17 3EP. *T:* Sheffield 365988. *Clubs:* Sheffield; Sickleholme Golf.

CARLISLE, John Russell; MP (C) Luton West, since 1979; *b* 28 Aug. 1942; *s* of Andrew and Edith Carlisle; *m* 1964, Anthea Jane Lindsay May; two *d. Educ:* Bedford Sch.; St Lawrence Coll. Sidney C. Banks Ltd, Sandy, 1964–78; Dir, Granfin Agriculture Ltd, Stoke Ferry, Norfolk, 1978–, York, 1979–; Mem., London Corn Exchange. Chm., Mid Beds Cons. Assoc., 1974–76. Chm., Cons Parly Select Cttee on Sport, 1981–; Treas., Anglo-Gibraltar Gp, 1981–. *Recreations:* sport, music. *Address:* House of Commons, SW1. *T:* 01-219 4571. *Clubs:* Farmers', MCC, Rugby.

CARLISLE, Kenneth Melville; MP (C) Lincoln, since 1979; *b* 21 March 1941; *s* of Kenneth Ralph Malcolm Carlisle, *qv. Educ:* Harrow; Magdalen Coll., Oxford (BA History). Called to Bar, Inner Temple, 1965. Brooke Bond Liebig, 1966–74; farming in Suffolk, 1974–. PPS to Minister of State for Energy, 1981–. *Recreations:* botany, gardening, walking, history. *Address:* Wyken Hall Farm, Stanton, Bury St Edmunds, Suffolk. *T:* Stanton 50240.

CARLISLE, Kenneth Ralph Malcolm, TD; Director, Tribune Investment Trust Ltd; *b* 28 March 1908; *s* of late Kenneth Methven Carlisle and Minnie Marie Donner; *m* 1938, Hon. Elizabeth Mary McLaren, *d* of 2nd Baron Aberconway; one *s* three *d. Educ:* Harrow; Magdalen Coll., Oxford (BA). Binder, Hamlyn & Co., Chartered Accountants, 1931–32; Liebig's Extract of Meat Co. Ltd, Argentina, Paraguay, Uruguay, 1933–34; Liebig's Companies on Continent of Europe, 1935–37. Major, Rifle Bde, 1939–45. Distinguished Service Medal (Greece); Chevalier de l'Ordre de Leopold (Belgium), 1960. *Recreations:* sports, especially shooting. *Address:* (private) Laurie House, 16 Airlie Gardens, W8 7AW. *T:* 01-229 1714; Wyken Hall, Stanton, Bury St Edmunds, Suffolk IP31 2DW. *Club:* Boodle's.
See also K. M. Carlisle.

CARLISLE, Rt. Hon. Mark, PC 1979; QC 1971; MP (C) Runcorn, since 1964; a Recorder of the Crown Court, 1976–79 and since 1981; *b* 7 July 1929; 2nd *s* of late Philip Edmund and of Mary Carlisle; *m* 1959, Sandra Joyce Des Voeux; one *d. Educ:* Radley Coll.; Manchester Univ. LLB (Hons) Manchester, 1952. Called to the Bar, Gray's Inn, 1953, Bencher 1980; Northern Circuit. Member Home Office Advisory Council on the Penal System, 1966–70; Joint Hon. Secretary, Conservative Home Affairs Cttee, 1965–69; Conservative Front Bench Spokesman on Home Affairs, 1969–70; Parly Under-Sec. of State, Home Office, 1970–72; Minister of State, Home Office, 1972–74; Sec. of State for Educn and Science, 1979–81. Mem., Adv. Council, BBC, 1975–79. *Recreation:* golf. *Address:* 3 King's Bench Walk, Temple, EC4. *T:* 01-583 5766; Newstead, Mobberley, Cheshire. *T:* Mobberley 2275. *Club:* Garrick.

CARLOW, Viscount; Charles George Yuill Seymour Dawson-Damer; *b* 6 Oct. 1965; *s* and *heir* of 7th Earl of Portarlington, *qv*. A Page of Honour to the Queen, 1979–80. *Address:* 19 Coolong Road, Vancluse, NSW 2030, Australia.

CARLYLE, Joan Hildred; Principal Lyric Soprano, Royal Opera House, Covent Garden, since 1955; *b* 6 April 1931; *d* of late Edgar James and Margaret Mary Carlyle; *m*; two *d. Educ:* Howell's Sch., Denbigh, N Wales. Oscar in Ballo in Maschera, 1957–58 season; Sophie in Rosenkavalier, 1958–59; Micaela in Carmen, 1958–59; Nedda in Pagliacci (new Zeffirelli production), Dec. 1959; Mimi in La Bohème, Dec. 1960; Titania in Gielgud Production of Britten's Midsummer Night's Dream, London première, Dec. 1961; Pamina in Klemperer production of The Magic Flute, 1962; Countess in Figaro, 1963; Zdenko in Hartman production of Arabella, 1964; Sœur Angelica (new production), 1965; Desdemona in Otello, 1965, 1967; Sophie in Rosenkavalier (new production), 1966; Pamina in Magic Flute (new production), 1966; Arabella in Arabella, 1967; Marschallin in Rosenkavalier, 1968; Jenifer, Midsummer Marriage (new prod.), 1969; Donna Anna, 1970; Reiza, Oberon, 1970; Adrianna Lecouvreur, 1970; Russalka, for BBC, 1969; Elizabeth in Don Carlos, 1975. Roles sung abroad include: Oscar, Nedda, Mimi, Pamina, Zdenko, Micaela, Desdemona, Donna Anna, Arabella, Elizabeth. Has sung in Buenos Aires, Belgium, Holland, France, Monaco, Naples, Milan, Berlin, Capetown, Munich. Has made numerous recordings; appeared BBC, TV (in film). *Recreations:* gardening, cooking, interior decorating, countryside preservation. *Address:* The Griffin, Ruthin, Clwyd, N Wales. *T:* Ruthin 2792.

CARMAN, Hon. George Alfred, QC 1971; a Recorder of the Crown Court, since 1972; *b* 6 Oct. 1929; *o s* of Alfred George Carman and late Evelyn Carman; *m* 1st, 1960, Cecilia Sparrow (marr. diss. 1976); one *s*; 2nd, 1976, Frances Elizabeth Venning. *Educ:* St Joseph's Coll., Blackpool; Balliol Coll., Oxford. First Class, Final Hons Sch. of Jurisprudence, 1952. Captain RAEC, 1948–49. Called to the Bar (King George V Coronation Schol.) Lincoln's Inn, 1953, Bencher 1978; practised on Northern Circuit. *Address:* New Court, Temple, EC4Y 9BE; 12 Old Square, Lincoln's Inn, WC2. *Club:* Garrick.

CARMICHAEL, Mrs Catherine McIntosh, (Kay); social worker; *b* 22 Nov. 1925; *d* of John D. and Mary Rankin; *m* 1948, Neil George Carmichael, *qv*; one *d. Educ:* Glasgow and Edinburgh. Social worker, 1955–57; psychiatric social work, 1957–60; Dep. Dir, Scottish Probation Training Course, 1960–62; Lectr, 1962, Sen. Lectr 1974–80, Dept of Social Administration and Social Work, Univ. of Glasgow. Mem., 1969–75, Dep. Chm., 1975–80, Supplementary Benefits Commn. *Recreation:* Alexander technique. *Address:* 12 Holyrood Crescent, Glasgow G20 6HJ. *T:* 041-339 0247.

CARMICHAEL, Sir David William G. C.; *see* Gibson-Craig-Carmichael.

CARMICHAEL, Ian (Gillett); *b* 18 June 1920; *s* of Arthur Denholm Carmichael, Cottingham, E Yorks, and Kate Gillett, Hessle, E Yorks; *m* 1943, Jean Pyman Maclean, Sleights, Yorks; two *d. Educ:* Scarborough Coll.; Bromsgrove Sch. Studied at RADA, 1938–39. Served War of 1939–45 (despatches). First professional appearance as a Robot in "RUR", by Karel and Josef Capek, The People's Palace, Stepney, 1939; stage appearances include: The Lyric Revue, Globe, 1951; The Globe Revue, Globe, 1952; High Spirits, Hippodrome, 1953; Going to Town, St Martin's, 1954; Simon and Laura, Apollo, 1954; The Tunnel of Love, Her Majesty's, 1958; The Gazebo, Savoy, 1960; Critic's Choice, Vaudeville, 1961; Devil May Care, Strand, 1963; Boeing-Boeing, Cort Theatre, New York, 1965; Say Who You Are, Her Majesty's, 1965; Getting Married, Strand, 1968; I Do! I Do!, Lyric, 1968; Birds on the Wing, O'Keefe Centre, Toronto, 1969; Darling I'm Home, S African tour, 1972; Out on a Limb, Vaudeville, 1976; Overheard, Haymarket, 1981. Films include: (from 1955) Simon and Laura; Private's Progress; Brothers in Law; Lucky Jim; Happy is the Bride; The Big Money; Left, Right and Centre; I'm All Right Jack; School for Scoundrels; Light Up The Sky; Double Bunk; The Amorous Prawn; Hide and Seek; Heavens Above!; Smashing Time; The Seven Deadly Sins; From Beyond the Grave; The Lady Vanishes. TV series include: The World of Wooster; Bachelor Father; Lord Peter Wimsey. *Publication:* Will the Real Ian Carmichael . . . (autobiog.), 1979. *Recreations:* cricket, gardening, photography and reading. *Address:* c/o London Management, 235/241 Regent Street, W1A 2JT. *Club:* MCC.

CARMICHAEL, Dr James Armstrong Gordon, CB 1978; Chief Medical Adviser (Social Security), Department of Health and Social Security, 1973–78; *b* 28 July 1913; 2nd *s* of Dr Donald Gordon Carmichael and Eileen Mona Carmichael; *m* 1936, Nina Betty Ashton (*née* Heape) (*d* 1981); two *s. Educ:* Epsom Coll.; Guy's Hospital. FRCP, MRCS. Commnd RAMC, 1935; Consultant Physician, MELF, 1953–55; Consultant Physician and Prof. of Tropical Medicine, Royal Army Medical Coll., 1957–58, retd; Hon. Colonel 1958. MO 1958, SMO 1965, Min. of Pensions and Nat. Insce; PMO, Min. of Social Security, 1967; Dep. Chief Medical Advr, DHSS, 1971–73. *Publications:* contrib. to BMJ, Jl of RAMC. *Recreation:* gardening. *Address:* Adcote, Branksomewood Road, Fleet, Hants GU13 8JS. *T:* Fleet 5434.

CARMICHAEL, Sir John, KBE 1955; Director: Abbey National Building Society, since 1968; Adobe Oil and Gas Corp., Texas, since 1973; *b* 22 April 1910; *s* of late Thomas Carmichael and Margaret Doig Coupar; *m* 1940, Cecilia Macdonald Edwards; one *s* three *d. Educ:* Madras Coll., St Andrews; Univ. of St Andrews; Univ. of Michigan (Commonwealth Fund Fellow). Guardian Assurance Co., Actuarial Dept, 1935–36; Sudan Govt Civil Service, 1936–59; Member Sudan Resources Board and War Supply Dept, 1939–45; Secretary Sudan Development Board, 1944–48; Asst Financial Secretary, 1946–48; Dep. Financial Secretary, 1948–53; Director, Sudan Gezira Board,

1950-54; Chm. Sudan Light and Power Co., 1952-54; Acting Financial Secretary, then Permanent Under Secretary to Ministry of Finance, 1953-55; Financial and Economic Adviser to Sudan Government, 1955-59. Member: UK delegation to General Assembly of UN, 1959; Scottish Gas Board, 1960-70; Scottish Industrial Develt Adv. Bd, 1972-79; Dep. Chm., ITA, 1960-64, Acting Chm. ITA, 1962-63; Chm., Herring Industry Bd, 1962-65; Director: Fisons Ltd, 1961-80 (Chief Executive, 1962-66, Dep. Chm. 1967-71); Grampian Television, 1965-72; Jute Industries Ltd, later Sidlaw Industries Ltd, 1966-80 (Dep. Chm., 1969; Chm., 1970-80); Royal Bank of Scotland, 1966-80; Mem., Social and Economic Cttee, EEC, 1973-74. *Recreations:* golf, gardening. *Address:* Hayston Park, Balmullo, Fife. *T:* Balmullo 268. *Clubs:* Honourable Company of Edinburgh Golfers; Royal and Ancient Golf (St Andrews) (Captain, 1974-75); Augusta National Golf, Pine Valley Golf.

CARMICHAEL, Kay; *see* Carmichael, C. M.

CARMICHAEL, Neil George; MP (Lab) Glasgow, Kelvingrove, since 1974 (Glasgow, Woodside, 1962-74); *b* Oct. 1921; *m* 1948, Catherine McIntosh Rankin (*see* C. M. Carmichael); one *d. Educ:* Estbank Acad.; Royal Coll. of Science and Technology, Glasgow. Employed by Gas Board in Planning Dept. Past Member Glasgow Corporation. PPS to Minister of Technology, 1966-67; Jt Parly Sec., Min. of Transport, 1967-69; Parly Sec., Min. of Technology, 1969-70; Parliamentary Under-Secretary of State: DoE, 1974-75; DoI, 1975-76; Mem., Select Cttee on Transport, 1980-; Hon. Sec., Scottish Labour Gp of MPs, 1979-. *Address:* House of Commons, SW1; 53 Partick Hill Road, Glasgow G11 5AB.

CARMICHAEL, Peter, CBE 1981; Director, Small Business and Electronics Scottish Development Agency, since 1982; *b* 26 March 1933; *s* of Robert and Elizabeth Carmichael; *m* 1st; two *s* four *d*; 2nd, 1980, June Carmichael (*née* Philip). *Educ:* Glasgow Univ. (BSc 1st Cl. Hons Physics). Design Engineer with Ferranti Ltd, Edinburgh, 1958-65; Hewlett-Packard: Project Leader, 1965-67 (Leader of Project Team which won Queen's Award to Industry for Technical Innovation, 1967); Production Engrg Manager, 1967-68; Quality Assurance Manager, 1968-73; Engrg Manager, 1973-75; Manufacturing Manager, 1975-76; Division Gen. Man., 1976-82, and Jt Managing Director, 1980-82. *Recreations:* fishing, antique clock restoration. *Address:* 86 Craiglea Drive, Edinburgh EH10 5PH. *T:* (business) 031-343 1911.

CARNAC, Rev. Canon Sir (Thomas) Nicholas R.; *see* Rivett-Carnac.

CARNARVON, 6th Earl of, *cr* 1793; **Henry George Alfred Marius Victor Francis Herbert;** Baron Porchester, 1780; Lieut-Colonel 7th Hussars; *b* 7 Nov. 1898; *o s* of 5th Earl and Almina (who *m* 2nd, 1923, Lieut-Colonel I. O. Dennistoun, MVO; she *d* 1969), *d* of late Frederick C. Wombwell; *S* father, 1923; *m* 1st, 1922, Catherine (who obtained a divorce, 1936, and *m* 2nd, 1938, Geoffrey Grenfell (decd), and *m* 3rd, 1950, D. Momand), *d* of late J. Wendell, New York, and Mrs Wendell, Sandridgebury, Sandridge, Herts; one *s* one *d*; 2nd, 1939, Ottilie (marr. diss.), *d* of Eugene Losch, Vienna. *Educ:* Eton. Owns about 4000 acres. *Publications:* No Regrets (memoirs), 1976; Ermine Tales, 1980. *Heir: s* Lord Porchester, *qv. Recreations:* racing, and shooting. *Address:* Highclere Castle, near Newbury, Berks. *TA:* Carnarvon Highclere. *T:* Highclere 253204. *Clubs:* White's, Portland.

CARNE, Colonel James Power, VC 1953; DSO 1951; DL; *b* 11 April 1906; *s* of late G. N. Carne, Garras, Falmouth; *m* 1946, Mrs Jean Gibson, *widow* of Lt-Col J. T. Gibson, DSO, The Welch Regt; one *step s. Educ:* Imperial Service Coll.; Royal Military Coll., Sandhurst. Commissioned Gloucestershire Regt, 1925; seconded King's African Rifles, 1930-36; Adjutant 1st Bn Gloucestershire Regt, 1937-40. Served War of 1939-45: with KAR and on Staff, Madagascar, 1942, Burma, 1944; CO 6th and 26th Bns KAR, 1943-46. CO 5th Bn (TA) 1947-50, 1st Bn Gloucestershire Regt, 1950-51. Served Korean War of 1950-53 (DSO, VC). Freedom of Gloucester, 1953; Freedom of Falmouth, 1954. DSC (US), 1953. DL County of Gloucester, 1960. *Recreation:* fishing.

CARNEGIE, family name of **Duke of Fife** and of **Earls of Northesk** and **Southesk.**

CARNEGIE, Lt-Gen. Sir Robin (Macdonald), KCB 1979; OBE 1968; Director General of Army Training, 1981-82; *b* 22 June 1926; *yr s* of late Sir Francis Carnegie, CBE; *m* 1955, Iona, *yr d* of late Maj.-Gen. Sir John Sinclair, KCMG, CB, OBE, and of Esme Beatrice Sopwith; one *s* two *d. Educ:* Rugby. Commnd 7th Queen's Own Hussars, 1946; comd The Queen's Own Hussars, 1967-69; Comdr 11th Armd Bde, 1971-72; Student, Royal Coll. of Defence Studies, 1973; GOC 3rd Div., 1974-76; Chief of Staff, BAOR, 1976-78; Military Secretary, 1978-80. Col, The Queen's Own Hussars, 1981-. *Address:* c/o Lloyds Bank Ltd, 6 Pall Mall, SW1. *Club:* Cavalry and Guards.

CARNEGIE, Sir Roderick (Howard), Kt 1978; Chairman, since 1974, and Managing Director, since 1971, Conzinc Riotinto of Australia Ltd; *b* 27 Nov. 1932; *s* of Douglas H. Carnegie and Margaret F. Carnegie; *m* 1959, Carmen, *d* of W. J. T. Clarke; three *s. Educ:* Geelong Church of England Grammar Sch.; Trinity Coll., Univ. of Melbourne; New Coll., Oxford Univ.; Harvard Business Sch., Boston. BSc; MA Oxon; MBA Harvard. McKinsey & Co., New York, 1954-70: Principal, 1964-68, Director, 1968-70. Former Dir, Comalco Ltd; Director: Aust. Mining Industry Council, 1974-; Myer Emporium Ltd, 1978-. Mem., General Motors Aust. Council, 1979-.

Chm., Geelong, CofE Grammar Sch. Council, 1979-. *Recreations:* surfing, tennis, reading. *Address:* 55 Collins Street, Melbourne, Victoria 3000, Australia. *Clubs:* Melbourne (Victoria, Aust.); Links (New York).

CARNEGY OF LOUR, Baroness *cr* 1982 (Life Peer), of Lour in the District of Angus; **Elizabeth Patricia Carnegy of Lour;** Chairman: Manpower Services Commission Committee for Scotland, since 1981; Scottish Council for Community Education, since 1981 (Member, since 1978); President for Angus since 1971, and for Scotland since 1979, Girl Guides Association; farmer; *b* 28 April 1925; *e d* of late Lt Col U. E. C. Carnegy, DSO, MC, DL, JP, 11th of Lour, and Violet Carnegy, MBE. *Educ:* Downham Sch., Essex. Served Cavendish Lab., Cambridge, 1943-46. With Girl Guides Assoc., 1947-: County Comr, Angus, 1956-63; Trng Adviser, Scotland, 1958-62; Trng Adviser, Commonwealth HQ, 1963-65. Co-opted to Educn Cttee, Angus CC, 1967-75; Tayside Regional Council: Councillor, 1974-82; Convener: Recreation and Tourism Cttee, 1974-76; Educn Cttee, 1977-81. Chm., Working Party on Prof. Trng for Community Education in Scotland, 1975-77; Member: MSC, 1979-82; Council for Tertiary Educn in Scotland, 1979-. Hon. Sheriff, 1969-. *Address:* Lour, by Forfar, Angus DD8 2LR. *T:* Inverarity 237. *Club:* Lansdowne.

CARNELL, Rev. Canon Geoffrey Gordon; Rector of Boughton, Northampton, since 1971; Chaplain to the Queen, since 1981; Non-Residentiary Canon of Peterborough, since 1965; *b* 5 July 1918; *m* 1945, Mary Elizabeth Boucher Smith; two *s. Educ:* City of Norwich Sch.; St John's Coll., Cambridge (Scholar, 1937; BA 1940; Lightfoot Scholar, 1940; MA 1944); Cuddesdon Coll., Oxford. Ordained deacon, Peterborough Cathedral, 1942; priest, 1943. Asst Curate, Abington, Northampton, 1942-49; Chaplain and Lectr in Divinity, St Gabriel's Coll., Camberwell, 1949-53; Rector of Isham with Great and Little Harrowden, Northants, 1953-71. Examining Chaplain to Bishop of Peterborough, 1962-; Dir, Post-Ordination Trng and Ordinands, 1962-. *Recreations:* walking, music, art history, local history. *Address:* Boughton Rectory, Northampton NN2 8SG. *T:* Northampton 842382.

CARNER, Dr Mosco; Music Critic of The Times, 1961-69; Member of the BBC Score Reading Panel, 1944-72; *b* 15 Nov. 1904; *m* 1962, Dr Elisabeth Bateman (*d* 1970); *m* 1976, Hazel, *d* of late Mr and Mrs John Sebag-Montefiore. *Educ:* Vienna Univ. and Vienna Music Conservatory. Conductor at Danzig State Theatre, 1929-33. Resident in London since Autumn 1933, where active as conductor, musical author, critic and broadcaster. Music Critic of Time and Tide, 1949-62; Music Critic of The Evening News, 1957-61. Hon. Mem., The Critics' Circle, 1977. Silver Medal of the Italian Government, 1964. *Publications:* A Study of 20th-Century Harmony, 1942; Of Men and Music, 1944; The History of the Waltz, 1948; Puccini, A Critical Biography, 1958, 2nd rev. edn, 1974 (Ital. edn, 1961, Japanese edn 1968); (ed) The Letters of Giacomo Puccini, 1974; Alban Berg: the man and his work, 1975, rev. French edn, 1979, rev. and enlarged edn, 1982; Madam Butterfly, 1979; Major and Minor, 1980; The Songs of Hugo Wolf, 1982; *contribs to:* New Oxford History of Music, 1979; 6th edn of Grove's Dictionary of Music and Musicians; *symposia on:* Schubert, 1946; Schumann, 1952; The Concerto, 1952; Chamber Music, 1957; Choral Music, 1963. *Recreations:* reading, motoring and swimming. *Address:* 14 Elsworthy Road, NW3. *T:* 01-586 1553.

CARNEY, Most Rev. James F.; *see* Vancouver, Archbishop of, (RC).

CARNEY, Admiral Robert Bostwick, Hon. CBE 1946; DSM (US), 1942 (and Gold Stars, 1944, 1946, 1955); and numerous other American and foreign decorations; United States Navy; retired; *b* Vallejo, California, 26 March 1895; *s* of Robert E. and Bertha Carney; *m* 1918, Grace Stone Craycroft, Maryland; one *s* one *d. Educ:* United States Naval Acad., Annapolis, Md (BS). Served European War, 1914-18; Gunnery and Torpedo Officer aboard USS Fanning in capture of Submarine U-58 off coast of Ireland; War of 1939-45; North Atlantic, 1941-42; Commanding Officer, USS Denver, serving in Pacific, 1942-43; Chief of Staff to Admiral William Halsey (Commander, S Pacific Force), 1943-45, participating in nine battle engagements. Deputy Chief of Naval Operations, 1946-50; President of US Naval Inst., 1950-51, 1954-56; Commander Second Fleet, 1950; Commander-in-Chief, United States Naval Forces, Eastern Atlantic and Mediterranean, 1950-52; Commander-in-Chief, Allied Forces, Southern Europe (North Atlantic Treaty Organisation), 1951-53; Chief of Naval Operations, 1953-55; retired 1955. Hon. LLD, Loras Coll., 1955. *Publications:* various professional. *Recreations:* field sports, music. *Address:* 2801 New Mexico Avenue (NW), Washington, DC 20007, USA. *Clubs:* Chevy Chase Country, Alibi (Washington, DC); The Brook (NY).

CARNLEY, Most Rev. Peter Frederick; *see* Perth (Australia), Archbishop of.

CARNOCK, 4th Baron *cr* 1916, of Carnock; **David Henry Arthur Nicolson;** Bt (NS) 1637; solicitor; *b* 10 July 1920; *s* of 3rd Baron Carnock, DSO, and Hon. Katharine (*d* 1968), *e d* of 1st Baron Roborough; *S* father, 1982. *Educ:* Winchester; Balliol Coll., Oxford (MA). Admitted Solicitor, 1949. Served War of 1939-45, Royal Devon Yeomanry and on Staff, Major. *Heir: cousin* Nigel Nicolson, *qv. Address:* 90 Whitehall Court, SW1; Ermewood House, Harford, Ivybridge, S Devon.

CARNWATH, Sir Andrew Hunter, KCVO 1975; DL; a Managing Director, Baring Brothers & Co. Ltd, 1955-74; Chairman, London Multinational Bank,

1971-74; *b* 26 Oct. 1909; *s* of late Dr Thomas Carnwath, DSO, Dep. CMO, Min. of Health, and Margaret Ethel (*née* McKee); *m* 1st, 1939, Kathleen Marianne Armstrong (*d* 1963); five *s* one *d*; 2nd, 1973, Joan Gertrude Wetherell-Pepper. *Educ:* Eton (King's Scholar; Hon. Fellow 1981). Served RAF (Coastal Comd Intelligence), 1939-45. Joined Baring Bros & Co. Ltd, 1928; rejoined as Head of New Issues Dept, 1945. Chm., Save and Prosper Group Ltd, 1961-80 (Dir, 1960-80); Director: Equity & Law Life Assurance Soc. Ltd, 1955-; Scottish Agricultural Industries Ltd, 1969-75; Great Portland Estates Ltd, 1977-. Member: London Cttee, Hongkong and Shanghai Banking Corp., 1967-74; Council, Inst. of Bankers, 1955- (Dep. Chm., 1969-70, Pres., 1970-72, Vice-Pres., 1972-); Cttee on Consumer Credit; Central Bd of Finance of Church of England (Chm., Investment Management Cttee), 1960-74; Chairman: Migration of Companies Adv. Panel, 1976-; Chelmsford Diocesan Bd of Finance, 1969-75 (Vice-Chm., 1967-68); Member: Council, King Edward's Hosp. Fund for London, 1962- (Treasurer, 1965-74; Governor, 1976-); Royal Commn for Exhibn of 1851, 1964-; Council, Friends of Tate Gall., 1962- (Treasurer, 1966-). Trustee: Imp. War Graves Endowment Fund, 1963-74, Chm., 1964-74; Thalidomide Children's Trust, 1980-. A Governor, Felsted Sch., 1965-81; Treasurer: Essex Univ., 1973-82; Victoria League, 1974-. Pres., Saffron Walden Conservative Assoc. until 1977. Musicians Company: Mem., Ct of Assts, 1973-; Junior Warden, 1979-80; Sen. Warden, 1980-81; Master, 1981-82. Mem., Essex CC 1973-77; High Sheriff, 1965, DL 1972, Essex. FIB; FRSA. *Publications:* lectures and reviews for Inst. of Bankers, etc. *Recreations:* music (playing piano, etc), pictures, travel. *Address:* Garden Flat, 39 Palace Gardens Terrace, W8 4SB. *T:* 01-727 9145. *Club:* Athenæum.

CARO, Anthony (Alfred), CBE 1969; Sculptor; *b* 8 March 1924; *s* of Alfred and Mary Caro; *m* 1949, Sheila May Girling; two *s. Educ:* Charterhouse; Christ's Coll., Cambridge (Hon. Fellow); Regent Street Polytechnic; Royal Acad. Schs, London. Asst to Henry Moore, 1951-53; taught part-time, St Martin's Sch. of Art, 1953-79; taught sculpture at Bennington Coll., Vermont, 1963, 1965. Trustee, Tate Gall., 1982-. One-man Exhibitions: Galleria del Naviglio, Milan, 1956; Gimpel Fils, London, 1957; Whitechapel Art Gallery, London, 1963; Andre Emmerich Gallery, NY, 1964, 1966, 1968, 1970, 1972, 1973, 1974, 1977, 1978, 1979, 1982; Washington Gallery of Modern Art, Washington, DC, 1965; Kasmin Ltd, London, 1965, 1967, 1971, 1972; David Mirvish Gallery, Toronto, 1966, 1971, 1974; Galerie Bischofberger, Zurich, 1966; Kroller-Muller Museum, Holland, 1967; Hayward Gallery, London, 1969; Kenwood House, Hampstead, 1974, 1981; Galleria dell'Ariete, Milan, 1974; Watson/de Nagy Gall., Houston, 1975; Richard Gray Gall., Chicago, 1975; Lefevre Gall., London, 1976; Everson, Syracuse, 1976; Tel Aviv Mus., 1977; Piltzer-Rheims, Paris, 1977; Waddington & Tooth, London, 1977; Emmerich Gall., Zürich, 1978; Harkus Krackow Gall., Boston, 1978, 1981; Knoedler, London, 1978; Wentzel, Hamburg, 1978; Ace, Venice, Calif, 1978; Kahsahara, Japan, 1979; Glasgow, 1980; Mus. of Fine Arts, Boston, 1980; Acquarella Galls, NY, 1980; Galerie Andre, Berlin, 1980. British Council touring exhibn, 1977-79: Tel Aviv, NZ, Australia and Germany. Exhibited: First Paris Biennale, 1959 (sculpture prize); Battersea Park Open Air Exhibitions, 1960, 1963, 1966; Gulbenkian Exhibition, London, 1964; Documenta III Kassel, 1965; Primary Structures, Jewish Museum, NY, 1966 (David Bright Prize); Venice Biennale, 1958 and 1966; Pittsburgh International, 1967 and 1968; Metropolitan Museum of Art, 1968; São Paulo, 1969 (sculpture prize); Univ. of Pennsylvania, 1969; Everson Mus., Syracuse; Retrospective Exhibitions: Museum of Modern Art, New York, 1975; Walker Art Gall., Minn; Mus. of Fine Arts, Houston; Mus. of Fine Arts, Boston. Sculpture commnd by Nat. Gall. of Art, Washington, 1978. Given key to City of NY, 1976. Hon. Mem., Amer. Acad. and Inst. of Arts and Letters, 1979. Hon. DLitt: East Anglia; York Univ., Toronto; Brandeis. *Relevant publications:* Anthony Caro, by R. Whelan *et al*, 1974; Anthony Caro, by W. S. Rubin, 1975; Anthony Caro, by D. Blume (catalogue raisonnée), 1979, rev. edn 1981; Anthony Caro, by D. Waldman, 1982. *Recreation:* listening to music. *Address:* 111 Frognal, Hampstead, NW3.

CARO, Prof. David Edmund, OBE 1977; MSc, PhD; FInstP, FAIP, FACE; Vice-Chancellor, University of Melbourne, since 1982; *b* 29 June 1922; *s* of George Alfred Caro and Alice Lillian Caro; *m* 1954, Fiona Macleod; one *s* one *d. Educ:* Geelong Grammar Sch.; Univ. of Melbourne (MSc); Univ. of Birmingham (PhD). FInstP 1960, FAIP 1963, FACE 1982. Served War, RAAF, 1941-45. Demonstrator, Univ. of Melbourne, 1947-49; 1851 Overseas Res. Scholar, Birmingham, 1949-51; University of Melbourne: Lectr, 1952; Sen. Lectr, 1954; Reader, 1958; Foundn Prof. of Exper. Physics, 1961; Dean, Faculty of Science, 1970; Dep. Vice-Chancellor, 1972-77; Vice-Chancellor, Univ. of Tasmania, 1978-82. Chairman: Antarctic Res. Policy Adv. Cttee, 1979-; Aust. Vice-Chancellors Cttee, 1982-83. Hon. LLD Melbourne, 1978. *Publication:* (jtly) Modern Physics, 1961 (3rd edn 1978). *Recreations:* skiing, golf. *Address:* University of Melbourne, Parkville, Melbourne, Vic 3052, Australia. *Clubs:* Melbourne (Melbourne); Peninsula Golf (Vic).

CAROË, Sir (Einar) Athelstan (Gordon), Kt 1972; CBE 1958; President, Trustee Savings Banks, since 1976; Hon. President, EEC Savings Bank Group, since 1979 (Vice-Chairman, 1973-76; President and Chairman, 1976-78); Director, London Board, Norwich Union Group, 1968-78; Grain Merchant and Broker, W. S. Williamson and Co., Liverpool, 1935-73; Consul for Denmark, in Liverpool, 1931-73, also for Iceland since 1947; *b* 6 Oct. 1903; *s* of Johan Frederik Caröe and Eleanor Jane Alexandra Caröe (*née* Gordon); *m* 1st, 1934, Frances Mary Lyon (*d* 1947); two *s*; 2nd, 1952, Doreen Evelyn Jane Sandland; one *s* one *d. Educ:* Eton Coll. (King's Scholar); Trinity Coll.,

Cambridge (Scholar, BA). Chairman: Liverpool Savings Bank, 1947-48; Trustee Savings Banks Assoc., 1966-76 (Dep. 1951-66); Vice-Pres., National Savings Cttee, 1971-78. President, Liverpool Consular Corps, 1952; Chairman, Liverpool Chamber of Commerce, 1950-51. Pres., Minton Ltd, Stoke-on-Trent, 1970- (Chm. 1956-70); Chairman: Maritime Insurance Co. Ltd, Liverpool, 1951-68; Liverpool Corn Trade Assoc., 1963-67; Richards-Campbell Tiles Ltd, 1967-68. Pro-Chancellor, Liverpool Univ., 1966-75 (Dep. Treas., 1948-57; Treas., 1957-66; Pres., 1966-72); President, Lancashire County Lawn Tennis Assoc., 1953; Member Lawn Tennis Assoc. Council, 1954-66; President: Nat. Federation of Corn Trade Assocs, 1957-60; Internat. Savings Banks Inst., 1960-69 (Hon. Pres., 1969-). Hon. LLD, Liverpool, 1976. Officer, 1st Class, Order of Dannebrog, 1957 (Officer, 1945); Kt Commander, Order of Icelandic Falcon, 1974 (Officer 1958); Comdr, Order of Crown of Belgium, 1966; Comdr, Order of Leopold (Belgium), 1978. King Christian X Liberty Medal, 1946; Spanish Medal, Al Merito del Ahorro, 1973. *Recreations:* lawn tennis (Lancashire doubles champion, 1933); philately (Fellow RPS(L) 1939; Roll of Distinguished Philatelists, 1972). *Address:* Pedder's Wood, Scorton, near Preston, Lancs PR3 1BE. *T:* Garstang 4698. *Clubs:* British Pottery Manufacturers (Stoke-on-Trent); Liverpool Racquet.

CARON, Leslie, (Leslie Claire Margaret, *née* Caron); film and stage actress; *b* 1 July 1931; *d* of Claude Caron and Margaret Caron (*née* Petit); *m* 1956, Peter Reginald Frederick Hall (marr. diss. 1965); one *s* one *d*; *m* 1969, Michael Laughlin (marr. diss.). *Educ:* Convent of the Assumption, Paris. With Ballet des Champs Elysées, 1947-50, Ballet de Paris, 1954. *Films include:* American in Paris, 1950; subsequently, Lili; The Glass Slipper; Daddy Long Legs; Gaby; Gigi; The Doctor's Dilemma; The Man Who Understood Women; The Subterraneans; Fanny; Guns of Darkness; The L-Shaped Room; Father Goose; A Very Special Favour; Promise Her Anything; Is Paris Burning?; Head of the Family; Madron; QB VII; Valentino; Sérail; L'homme qui aimait les femmes; The Contract. *Plays:* Orvet, Paris, 1955; Gigi, London, 1956; Ondine, London, 1961. *Publication:* Vengeance (short stories), 1982. *Recreation:* collecting antiques. *Address:* c/o Hugh J. Alexander, International Artistes Representation, 4th Floor, 235 Regent Street, W1. *T:* 01-439 8401.

CARPENTARIA, Bishop of, since 1974; **Rt. Rev. Hamish Thomas Umphelby Jamieson;** *b* 15 Feb. 1932; *s* of Robert Marshall Jamieson and Constance Marzetti Jamieson (*née* Umphelby); *m* 1962, Ellice Anne McPherson; one *s* two *d. Educ:* Sydney C of E Grammar Sch.; St Michael's House, Crafers (ThL); Univ. of New England (BA). Deacon 1955; Priest 1956. Mem. Bush Brotherhood of Good Shepherd, 1955-62. Parish of Gilgandra, 1957; Priest-in-Charge, Katherine, NT, 1957-62; Rector and Canon, Darwin, 1962-67; Royal Australian Navy Chaplain, 1967-74; HMAS Sydney, 1967-68; HMAS Albatross, 1969-71; Small Ships Chaplain, 1972; HMAS Cerberus, 1972-74. *Recreations:* reading, music, gardening. *Address:* The Bishop's House, Thursday Island, Qld 4875, Australia. *T:* Thursday Island 96.

CARPENTER; see Boyd-Carpenter.

CARPENTER, Very Rev. Edward Frederick; Dean of Westminster since 1974; Lector Theologiae of Westminster Abbey, 1958; *b* 27 Nov. 1910; *s* of Frederick James and Jessie Kate Carpenter; *m* Lilian Betsy Wright; three *s* one *d. Educ:* Strodes Sch., Egham; King's Coll., University of London. BA 1932, MA 1934, BD 1935, PhD 1943; AKC 1935; FKC 1951; Hon. DD London, 1976. Deacon, 1935; Priest, 1936; Curate, Holy Trinity, St Marylebone, 1935-41; St Mary, Harrow, 1941-45; Rector of Great Stanmore, 1945-51; Canon of Westminster, 1951; Treasurer, 1959-74; Archdeacon, 1963-74. Fellow of King's Coll., London University, 1954. (AKC 1935). Chairman Frances Mary Buss Foundation, 1956-; Chairman Governing Body of: North London Collegiate Sch.; Camden Sch. for Girls, 1956-; Chairman of St Anne's Soc., 1958-; Joint Chm., London Soc. of Jews and Christians, 1960-; Member, Central Religious Advisory Cttee serving BBC and ITA, 1962-67; Chairman: Recruitment Cttee, ACCM, 1967; Religious Adv. Cttee of UNA, 1969-; President: London Region of UNA, 1966-67; Modern Churchmen's Union, 1966; World Congress of Faiths, 1966. *Publications:* Thomas Sherlock, 1936; Thomas Tenison, His Life and Times, 1948; That Man Paul, 1953; The Protestant Bishop, 1956; (joint author) of Nineteenth Century Country Parson, 1954, and of History of St Paul's Cathedral, 1957; Common Sense about Christian Ethics, 1961; (jtly) From Uniformity to Unity, 1962; (jtly) The Church's Use of the Bible, 1963; The Service of a Parson, 1965; (jtly) The English Church, 1966; (jtly) A House of Kings, 1966; Cantuar: the Archbishops in their office, 1971; contrib. Man of Christian Action, ed Ian Henderson, 1976. *Recreations:* walking, conversation, Association football. *Address:* The Deanery, Westminster, SW1. *T:* 01-222 2953.

CARPENTER, Ven. Frederick Charles; Archdeacon of the Isle of Wight, since 1977; Priest-in-charge of the Holy Cross, Binstead, Isle of Wight, since 1977; *b* 24 Feb. 1920; *s* of Frank and Florence Carpenter; *m* 1952, Rachel Nancy, widow of Douglas H. Curtis. *Educ:* Sir George Monoux Grammar Sch., Walthamstow; Sidney Sussex Coll., Cambridge (BA 1947, MA 1949); Wycliffe Hall, Oxford. Served with Royal Signals, 1940-46; Italy, 1944 (despatches). Curate of Woodford, 1949-51; Assistant Master and Chaplain, Sherborne School, Dorset, 1951-62; Vicar of Moseley, Birmingham, 1962-68; Director of Religious Education, Diocese of Portsmouth, 1968-75; Canon Residentiary of Portsmouth, 1968-77. *Recreations:* music, gardening. *Address:*

The Rectory, Pitts Lane, Binstead, Ryde, Isle of Wight PO33 3SU. *T:* Isle of Wight 62890.

CARPENTER, George Frederick, ERD 1954; Assistant Under-Secretary of State, Ministry of Defence, 1971-77; *b* 18 May 1917; *s* of late Frederick and Ada Carpenter; *m* 1949, Alison Elizabeth (*d* 1978), *d* of late Colonel Sidney Smith, DSO, MC, TD and Elizabeth Smith, Longridge, Lancs; two step *d. Educ:* Bec Sch.; Trinity Coll., Cambridge (MA). Commnd Royal Artillery (Supplementary Reserve), July 1939; War Service, 1939-46, France, 1940 and AA Comd; joined War Office, 1946; Asst Sec., 1958; Comd Sec., Northern Comd, 1961-65; Inspector of Establishments (A), MoD, 1965-71. Silver Jubilee Medal, 1977. *Address:* 10 Park Meadow, Hatfield, Herts. *T:* Hatfield 65581. *Club:* Civil Service

CARPENTER, Rt. Rev. Harry James, Hon. DD Oxford; *b* 20 Oct. 1901; *s* of William and Elizabeth Carpenter; *m* 1940, Urith Monica Trevelyan; one *s. Educ:* Churcher's Coll., Petersfield; Queen's Coll., Oxford. Tutor of Keble Coll., Oxford, 1927; Fellow, 1930; Warden of Keble Coll., 1939-55, Hon. Fellow, 1955; Hon. Fellow, Queen's Coll., Oxford, 1955; Canon Theologian of Leicester Cathedral, 1941-55; Bishop of Oxford, 1955-70. *Publications:* (ed) Bicknell, Thirty Nine Articles, 1955; contrib. to: Oxford Dictionary of the Christian Church, ed Cross, 1957; A Theological Word Book of the Bible, ed Richardson, 1963; The Interpretation of the Bible, ed Dugmore, 1944; Jl of Theological Studies. *Address:* 1 Meadow View, Baunton, Cirencester, Glos. *T:* Cirencester 4647.

CARPENTER, John; *see* Carpenter, V. H. J.

CARPENTER, John McG. K. K.; *see* Kendall-Carpenter.

CARPENTER, Leslie Arthur; Chief Executive, Reed International plc, since 1982; *b* 26 June 1927; *s* of William and Rose Carpenter; *m* 1952, Stella Louise Bozza; one *d. Educ:* Hackney Techn. Coll. Director: Country Life, 1965; George Newnes, 1966; Odhams Press Ltd (Managing), 1968; International Publishing Corp., 1972; Reed International Ltd, 1974; IPC (America) Inc., 1975; Chairman: Reed Hldgs Inc. (formerly Reed Publishing Hldgs Inc.), 1977; Reed Publishing Hldgs Ltd, 1981; Chm. and Chief Exec., IPC Ltd, 1974; Chief Exec., Publishing and Printing, Reed International Ltd, 1979. *Recreations:* racing, gardening. *Address:* c/o Reed International PLC, Reed House, Piccadilly, W1A 1EJ. *Club:* Royal Automobile.

CARPENTER, Trevor Charles; Mail Consultant, British Caledonian Airways; *b* 23 March 1917; *s* of late Walter Edward Carpenter and Florence Jane Carpenter, Newport, Mon.; *m* 1940, Margaret Lilian, *d* of late Frederick James and May Ethel Day; one *s* five *d. Educ:* Alexandra Road Primary Sch., Newport; Newport High Sch. Exec. Officer, GPO, 1936; Higher Exec. Officer, 1947; Principal, 1951; Private Secretary to PMG, 1962; Dep. Director, Scotland, 1964; Director of Postal Personnel, GPO, 1967-70; Director of Posts, Scotland, 1970-72; Chm., Scottish Postal Bd, 1972-77. *Recreations:* golf, Gaelic singing, watching Rugby football. *Address:* 26 Learmonth Terrace, Edinburgh EH4 1NZ. *T:* 031-332 8000.

CARPENTER, Maj.-Gen. (Victor Harry) John, CB 1975; MBE 1945; FCIT; Chairman of Traffic Commissioners, Yorkshire Traffic Area, since 1975; *b* 21 June 1921; *s* of Harry and Amelia Carpenter; *m* 1946, Theresa McCulloch; one *s* one *d. Educ:* Army schools; Apprentice Artificer RA; RMC Sandhurst. Joined the Army, Royal Artillery, 1936; commissioned into Royal Army Service Corps as 2nd Lieut, 1939. Served War of 1939-45 (Dunkirk evacuation, Western Desert, D-Day landings). Post-war appts included service in Palestine, Korea, Aden, and Singapore; also commanded a company at Sandhurst. Staff College, 1951; JSSC, 1960; served WO, BAOR, FARELF, 1962-71; Transport Officer-in-Chief (Army), MoD, 1971-73; Dir of Movements (Army), MoD, 1973-75. Lt-Col, 1960; Brig., 1967; Maj.-Gen., 1971. Col Comdt, RCT, 1975-83. Nat. Chm., 1940 Dunkirk Veterans Assoc; President: Artificers Royal Artillery Assoc.; RASC/RCT Assoc. Chm., Yorkshire Section, CIT, 1980-81. *Recreation:* gardening. *Address:* Traffic Commissioners, Yorkshire Traffic Area, Hillcrest House, 386 Harehills Lane, Leeds LS9 6NF. *Club:* Royal Over-Seas League.

CARR, family name of **Baron Carr of Hadley.**

CARR OF HADLEY, Baron *cr* 1975 (Life Peer), of Monken Hadley; **(Leonard) Robert Carr,** PC 1963; *b* 11 Nov. 1916; *s* of late Ralph Edward and of Katie Elizabeth Carr; *m* 1943, Joan Kathleen, *d* of Dr E. W. Twining; two *d* (and one *s* decd). *Educ:* Westminster Sch.; Gonville and Caius Coll., Cambridge, BA Nat. Sci. Hons, 1938; MA 1942. FIM 1957. Joined John Dale Ltd, 1938 (Dir, 1948-55; Chm., 1958-63); Director: Metal Closures Group Ltd, 1964-70 (Dep. Chm., 1960-63 and Jt Man. Dir, 1960-63); Carr, Day & Martin Ltd, 1947-55; Isotope Developments Ltd, 1950-55; Metal Closures Ltd, 1959-63; Scottish Union & National Insurance Co. (London Bd), 1958-63; S. Hoffnung & Co., 1963, 1965-70, 1974-80; Securicor Ltd and Security Services Ltd, 1961-63, 1965-70, 1974-; SGB Gp Ltd, 1974-; Prudential Assurance Co., 1976- (Dep. Chm., 1979-80, Chm., 1980-); Prudential Corporation Ltd, 1978- (Dep. Chm., 1979-80, Chm., 1980-); Cadbury Schweppes Ltd, 1979-; Mem., London Adv. Bd, Norwich Union Insurance Gp, 1965-70, 1974-76. Mem. Council, CBI, 1976- (Chm., Educn and Trng Cttee, 1977-82). MP (C) Mitcham, 1950-74, Sutton, Carshalton, 1974-76; PPS to Sec. of State for Foreign Affairs, Nov. 1951-April 1955, to Prime Minister, April-Dec. 1955;

Parly Sec., Min. of Labour and Nat. Service, Dec. 1955-April 1958; Sec. for Technical Co-operation, 1963-64; Sec. of State for Employment, 1970-72; Lord President of the Council and Leader of the House of Commons, April-Nov. 1972; Home Secretary, 1972-74. Governor: St Mary's Hosp., Paddington, 1958-63; Imperial Coll. of Science and Technology, 1959-63 and 1976-; St Mary's Medical Sch. Council, 1958-63; Hon. Treas., Wright Fleming Inst. of Microbiology, 1960-63. Pres., Consultative Council of Professional Management Orgns, 1976-. Duke of Edinburgh Lectr, Inst. of Building, 1976. *Publications:* (Jt) One Nation, 1950; (Jt) Change is our Ally, 1954; (Jt) The Responsible Society, 1958; (Jt) One Europe, 1965; articles in technical jls. *Recreations:* lawn tennis, music, gardening. *Address:* 14 North Court, Great Peter Street, SW1. *Club:* Brooks's.

CARR, (Albert) Raymond (Maillard), FRSL; FRHistS; FBA 1978; Warden of St Antony's College, Oxford, since 1968 (Sub-Warden, 1966-68); Fellow since 1964; *b* 11 April 1919; *s* of Reginald and Marion Maillard Carr; *m* 1950, Sara Strickland; three *s* one *d. Educ:* Brockenhurst Sch.; Christ Church, Oxford. Gladstone Research Exhnr, Christ Church, 1941; Fellow of All Souls' Coll., 1946-53; Fellow of New Coll., 1953-64. Director, Latin American Centre, 1964-68. Chm. Soc. for Latin American Studies, 1966-68. Prof. of History of Latin America, Oxford, 1967-68. Distinguished Prof., Boston Univ., 1980. Mem., Nat. Theatre Bd, 1968-77. Corresp. Mem., Royal Acad. of History, Madrid. *Publications:* Spain 1808-1939, 1966; Latin America (St Antony's Papers), 1969; (ed) The Republic and the Civil War in Spain, 1971; The Spanish Civil War, 1971; English Fox Hunting, 1976; The Spanish Tragedy: the Civil War in Perspective, 1977; (jtly) Spain: Dictatorship to Democracy, 1979; Modern Spain, 1980; articles on Swedish, Spanish and Latin American history. *Recreation:* fox hunting. *Address:* St Antony's College, Oxford; 29 Charlbury Road, Oxford. *T:* 58136. *Club:* United Oxford & Cambridge University.

CARR, Prof. Denis John; Professor, Research School of Biological Sciences, Australian National University, Canberra, since 1968; *b* 15 Dec. 1915; *s* of James E. Carr and Elizabeth (*née* Brindley), Stoke-on-Trent, Staffs; *m* 1955, Stella G. M. Fawcett; no *c. Educ:* Hanley High Sch., Staffs; Manchester Univ. RAF, 1940-46. Manchester Univ.: undergraduate, 1946-49; Asst Lectr in Plant Ecology, 1949-53; Guest Research Worker at Max-Planck-Inst. (Melchers), Tübingen, 1952; Sen. Lectr in plant physiology, 1953, Reader, 1959, Melbourne; Prof. of Botany, Queen's Univ., Belfast, 1960-67. Hon. MSc Melbourne, 1958. *Publications:* Plant Growth Substances 1970, 1972; numerous papers in scientific jls. *Recreations:* research, music. *Address:* Research School of Biological Sciences, ANU Canberra, PO Box 475, ACT 2601, Australia.

CARR, Edward Hallett, CBE 1920; FBA 1956; *b* 28 June 1892. *Educ:* Merchant Taylors' Sch., London; Trinity Coll., Cambridge. Temporary Clerk Foreign Office, 1916; attached to the British Delegation to the Peace Conference, 1919; Temporary Sec. at British Embassy, Paris, for work with the Conference of Ambassadors, 1920-21; 3rd Sec. and transferred to Foreign Office, 1922; 2nd Sec. and transferred to HM Legation at Riga, 1925; transferred to Foreign Office, 1929; Asst Adviser on League of Nations Affairs, 1930-33; First Sec., 1933; resigned, 1936; Wilson Prof. of International Politics, University Coll. of Wales, Aberystwyth, 1936-47. Director of Foreign Publicity, Min. of Information, Oct. 1939-April 1940. Asst Ed. of The Times, 1941-46. Tutor in Politics, Balliol Coll., Oxford, 1953-55; Fellow, Trinity Coll., Cambridge, 1955-; Hon. Fellow, Balliol Coll., Oxford, 1966. Hon. LittD: University of Manchester, 1964; University of Cambridge, 1967; University of Sussex, 1970; Hon. Dr of Law, University of Groningen, 1964. *Publications:* Dostoevsky, 1931; The Romantic Exiles, 1933; Karl Marx: A Study in Fanaticism, 1934; International Relations since the Peace Treaties, 1937; Michael Bakunin, 1937; The Twenty Years' Crisis, 1919-39, 1939; Britain: A Study of Foreign Policy from Versailles to the Outbreak of War, 1939; Conditions of Peace, 1942; Nationalism and After, 1945; The Soviet Impact on the Western World, 1946; Studies in Revolution, 1950; A History of Soviet Russia: The Bolshevik Revolution, 1917-1923, Vol. I, 1950, Vol. II, 1952, Vol. III, 1953; The Interregnum, 1923-1924, 1954; Socialism in One Country, 1924-26, Vol. I, 1958; Vol. II, 1959, Vol. III (in 2 parts), 1964; Foundations of a Planned Economy, 1926-1929, Vol. I (in 2 parts, in collaboration with R. W. Davies), 1969, Vol. II, 1971, Vol. III, parts 1 and 2, 1976, part 3, 1978; German-Soviet Relations Between the Two World Wars, 1919-39, 1951; The New Society, 1951; What is History?, 1961; 1917: Before and After, 1968; The Russian Revolution: Lenin to Stalin, 1979; From Napoleon to Stalin, and other essays, 1980. *Address:* Trinity College, Cambridge; Dales Barn, Barton, Cambs.

CARR, Dr Eric Francis, FRCP, FRCPsych; Lord Chancellor's Medical Visitor, since 1979; *b* 23 Sept. 1919; *s* of Edward Francis Carr and Maude Mary Almond; *m* 1954, Janet Gilfillan; two *s* one *d. Educ:* Mill Hill Sch.; Emmanuel Coll., Cambridge. MA, MB BChir; FRCP, 1971, FRCPsych, 1972; DPM. Captain, RAMC, 1944-46. Consultant Psychiatrist: St Ebba's Hosp., 1954-60; Netherne Hosp., 1960-67; Epsom and West Park Hosps, 1967-76; Hon. Consultant Psychiatrist, KCH, 1960-76; SPMO, DHSS, 1976-79. Fellow, RSocMed. *Recreations:* reading, listening to music, cooking. *Address:* 116 Holly Lane East, Banstead, Surrey. *T:* Burgh Heath 53675.

CARR, Frank George Griffith, CB 1967; CBE 1954; MA, LLB; FSA; FRAS; Associate RINA; FRInstNav; Director of the National Maritime Museum, Greenwich, SE10, 1947-66; *b* 23 April 1903; *e s* of Frank Carr, MA, LLD, and Agnes Maud Todd, Cambridge; m 1932, Ruth, d of Harold Hamilton Burkitt, Ballycastle, Co. Antrim; no c. Educ: Perse and Trinity Hall, Cambridge. BA 1926; LLB 1928; MA 1939. Studied at LCC Sch. of Navigation and took Yacht Master's (Deep Sea) BoT Certificate, 1927; Cambridge Univ.: Squire Law Scholar, 1922; Capt. of Boats, Trinity Hall, 1926; Pres., Law Soc., 1924; Vice-Pres., Conservative Assoc., 1925; Pres., Nat. Union of Students, 1925; Ed., The Cambridge Gownsman, 1925. Asst Librarian, House of Lords, 1929-47. Served War of 1939-45, RNVR, Lt-Comdr. Chm., Cutty Sark Ship Management Cttee, 1952-72; Mem., HMS Victory Advisory Technical Cttee, 1948-76; Vice-President: Soc. for Nautical Research; Foudroyant Trust; Internat. Sailing Craft Assoc.; Mariners International, 1978; Chm., World Ship Trust, 1978-; Internat. Chm., Ship Trust Cttee, NY, 1978-; Pres., Thames Shiplovers and Ship Model Soc., 1982-. Governor, HMS Unicorn Preservation Soc. James Monroe Award, 1974. Publications: Sailing Barges, 1931; Vanishing Craft, 1934; A Yachtsman's Log, 1935; The Yachtsman's England, 1936; The Yacht Master's Guide, 1940; (jtly) The Medley of Mast and Sail, 1976; Leslie A. Wilcox, RI, RSMA, 1977; numerous articles in yachting periodicals, etc. Recreations: yacht cruising; nautical research. Address: Lime Tree House, 10 Park Gate, Blackheath, SE3. T: 01-852 5181. Clubs: Athenæum, Royal Cruising, Cruising Association; Cambridge University Cruising (Cambridge).

CARR, Glyn; see Styles, F. S.

CARR, Henry Lambton, CMG 1945; MVO 1957; retired 1961; b 28 Nov. 1899; e s of Archibald Lambton and Ella Carr, Archangel; m 1924, Luba (d 1975), d of John George Edmund Eveleigh, London; two s. Educ: Haileybury Coll. Served N Russian Exped. Force (2nd Lieut), 1919. Foreign Office, 1920. HBM Passport Control Officer for Finland, 1927-41; Attaché at British Legation, Stockholm, 1941-45; Foreign Office, 1945; First Sec., HM Embassy, Copenhagen, 1955; Foreign Office, 1958. Chevalier (First Grade) of Order of Dannebrog, Denmark, 1957. Recreation: walking. Address: The Links, Forest Row, East Sussex. T: Forest Row 2091; c/o Barclays Bank, East Grinstead, West Sussex. Club: Danish.

CARR, Herbert Reginald Culling, MA; Headmaster, The Grammar School, Harrogate, Yorks, 1934-60; retired; b 16 July 1896; s of late Reginald Childers Culling Carr, OBE (ICS), and Enid Agnes Kenney Herbert; m 1927, Evelyn Dorothy Ritchie; one d. Educ: St Paul's Sch.; Pembroke Coll., Oxford (Open Scholar). Hons Modern History (2nd Class); Diplomas in Educn and Econs. Asst Master, Alleyn's Sch., Dulwich, 1927-31; Headmaster, Penrith Grammar Sch., Cumberland, 1931-34. Sub-Lieut RNVR, 1915-19; Flt-Lieut RAFVR, 1940-44 (Africa Star). Publications: The Mountains of Snowdonia, 1925; The Irvine Diaries: the enigma of Everest 1924, 1979. Recreation: antiques. Address: 22 The Abbey House, Cirencester, Glos GL7 2QU. T: Cirencester 4442. Club: Alpine.

CARR, Sir James (Henry Brownlow), Kt 1982; Chairman: J. H. B. Carr Pty Ltd, since 1960; Australian Jockey Club, since 1974 (Vice-Chairman, 1969-74); b 17 April 1913; s of James Carr and Jessie Amelia Carr; m 1943, Audrey Mathews; one s three d. Educ: Beecroft Grammar School, Sydney, Australia. Served War, 1st Armoured Div., AIF, 1941-43. Director, New South Wales Local Board, Colonial Mutual Life Assurance Soc. Ltd, 1972-. Mem. Cttee, Australian Jockey Club, Sydney, 1955-; Australian Jockey Club Representative on Totalizator Agency Board, NSW, 1974-. Recreation: racing. Address: Cherryford, Binda, NSW 2583, Australia. T: Binda 9 (048-3551). Clubs: Union, Royal Sydney Golf (Sydney).

CARR, Air Marshal Sir John Darcy B.; see Baker-Carr.

CARR, Rear-Adm. Lawrence George, CB 1971; DSC 1954; Chief of Naval Staff, New Zealand, and Member of the Defence Council, 1969-72; management consultant; b 31 Jan. 1920; s of late George Henry Carr and late Susan Elizabeth Carr; unmarried. Educ: Wellington Technical Coll., NZ; Victoria Coll., Univ. of New Zealand. Served War: entered RNZNVR, 1941; commissioned, 1942; on loan to RN, in HM Destroyers in N Atlantic, Medit., W Af. Coast, Eng. Channel, 1941-44; HMNZS Achilles in Pacific Theatre and NZ, 1945-46; permanent Commn, RNZN, 1946. Qual. as communications specialist, 1947; served in: British Medit. Fleet, 1948; RNZN, 1949-; various appts.; in command HMNZS Kaniere, in Korea, 1953-54 (DSC); Comdr Dec. 1953; Exec. Officer, HMNZS Philomel, 1954-55; jssc, 1956; Deputy Chief of Naval Personnel, 1957-59; Qual. Sen. Officers War Coll., Greenwich, 1959-60; Captain June 1960; in command HMNZS: Philomel, 1960-62, Taranaki, 1962-64; ide 1965; Commodore, Auckland, 1966-68. Chief of Naval Personnel, Second Naval Mem., NZ Naval Bd, 1968-69. Nat. Parly Cand., Nov. 1972; Chm., Nat. Party, Pakuranga Electorate, 1976. Exec. Dir, Laura Fergusson Trust for Disabled Persons (Auckland). Mem., Spirit of Adventure Trust Bd; Patron, Coastguard (NZ); Vice-Patron, Co. of Master Mariners, NZ. Recreations: golf, fishing, shooting, sailing, tennis, chess. Address: c/o Bank of New Zealand (Te Aro), Wellington, New Zealand; (home) 57 Pigeon Mountain Road, Half Moon Bay, Auckland, New Zealand. T: Auckland 5349692. Clubs: Wellington, Royal New Zealand Yacht Squadron.

CARR, Peter Derek; Labour Counsellor, Washington, since 1978; b 12 July 1930; s of George William Carr and Marjorie (née Tailby); m 1958, Geraldine Pamela (née Ward); one s one d. Educ: Fircroft Coll., Birmingham; Ruskin Coll., Oxford. National Service, RAF, 1951-53. Carpenter and joiner,

construction industry, 1944-51 and 1953-56; college, 1956-60; Lectr, Percival Whitley Coll., Halifax, 1960-65; Sen. Lectr in Indust. Relations, Thurrock Coll., and part-time Adviser, NBPI, 1965-69; Director: Commn on Industrial Relations, 1969-74; ACAS, 1974-78. Publications: directed study for CIR on worker participation and collective bargaining in Europe, and study for ACAS on industrial relations in national newspaper industry. Recreations: photography and, under marital pressure, occasional woodwork. Address. 5220½ Klingle Street, NW, Washington, DC 20016, USA; 6 Heath Road, Chadwell St Mary, Grays, Essex RM16 4UP. Club: International (Washington, DC).

CARR, Philippa; see Hibbert, Eleanor.

CARR, Raymond; see Carr, A. R. M.

CARR, Dr Thomas Ernest Ashdown, CB 1977; part-time medical referee, Department of Health and Social Security, since 1979; b 21 June 1915; s of late Laurence H. A. Carr, MScTech, MIEE, ARPS, Stockport, and late Norah E. V. Carr (n ée Taylor); m 1940, Mary Sybil (née Dunkey); one s two d. Educ: County High Sch. for Boys, Altrincham; Victoria Univ. of Manchester (BSc). MB, ChB 1939; FRCGP 1968; FFCM 1972; DObstRCOG. Jun. hosp. posts, Manchester and Ipswich, 1939-41; RAMC, UK and NW Europe, 1941-46 (Hon. Major, 1946). GP, Highcliffe, Hants, 1947; Mem. Hants Local Med. Cttee, 1952-55; Min. of Health: Regional Med. Officer, Southampton, 1956; Sen. Med. Officer, 1963; Principal Med. Officer, 1966; SPMO in charge of GP and Regional Med. Service, DHSS, 1967-79. Founder Mem., 1953, Provost of SE England Faculty 1962-64, Mem. Council 1964-66, RCGP; Mem. Exec. Cttee, Lambeth and Southwark Div., BMA, 1975-79. FRSocMed (Mem. Council, Gen. Practice Section, 1977-79). Member: Camping Club of GB and Ireland; Southampton Gramophone Soc., 1956-63 (Chm., 1957-58); Guildford Philharmonic Soc., 1964-; Guildford Soc., 1968-; Consumers' Assoc., 1974-; Nat. Soc. of Non-Smokers, 1981- (Chm., 1982-). Publications: papers on NHS practice organisation in Medical World, Practitioner, Update, Health Trends, faculty jls of RCGP, Proc. of RSM. Recreations: playing and listening to music, skin diving, amateur cinematography, motor caravanning. Address: Tollgate House, 2 Pilgrims Way, Guildford, Surrey. T: Guildford 63012; 2 Downside, Old Lyme Road, Charmouth, Dorset. Clubs: Civil Service; Yvonne Arnaud Theatre (Guildford).

CARR, William Compton; b 10 July 1918; m ; two s one d. Educ: The Leys Sch., Cambridge. MP (C) Barons Court, 1959-64; PPS to Min. of State, Board of Trade, 1963; PPS to Financial Sec. to the Treasury, 1963-64. Recreations: reading, theatre-going, skin diving, eating, dieting.

CARR-ELLISON, Sir Ralph (Harry), Kt 1973; TD; DL; Chairman, Tyne Tees Television Ltd, since 1974 (Director since 1966); b 8 Dec. 1925; s of late Major John Campbell Carr-Ellison; m 1951, Mary Clare, d of late Major Arthur McMorrough Kavanagh, MC; three s one d. Educ: Eton. Served Royal Glos Hussars and 1st Royal Dragoons, 1944-49; Northumberland Hussars (TA), (Lt-Col Comdg), 1949-69; TAVR Col, Northumbrian Dist, 1969-72; Col, Dep. Comdr (TAVR), NE Dist, 1973; Chm., N of England TA&VRA, 1976-80. ADC (TAVR) to HM the Queen, 1970-75; Hon. Col, Northumbrian Univs OTC, 1982-. Co. Comr, Northumberland Scouts 1958-68; Mem. Cttee of Council, Scout Assoc., 1960-67. Chm., Berwick-on-Tweed Constituency Cons. Assoc., 1959-62, Pres., 1973-77; Northern Area Cons. Assocs: Treas., 1961-66, Chm., 1966-69; Pres., 1974-78; Vice Chm., Nat. Union of Cons. and Unionist Assocs, 1969-71. Director: Newcastle & Gateshead Water Co., 1964-73; Trident Television, 1972-81 (Dep. Chm., 1976-81); Chm., Northumbrian Water Authority, 1973-82. Mem. Council, The Wildfowl Trust, 1981. Chm., Newcastle Univ. Develt Trust, 1978-81, Mem. Ct, Newcastle Univ., 1979-; Governor, Swinton Conservative College, 1967-81. High Sheriff, 1972, JP 1953-75, DL 1981, Northumberland. Recreation: Jt Master, West Percy Foxhounds, 1950-. Address: Hedgeley Hall, Powburn, Alnwick, Northumberland NE66 4HZ. T: Powburn 273; (office) Powburn 272. Clubs: Cavalry and Guards, White's, Pratt's; Northern Counties (Newcastle upon Tyne).

CARR-GOMM, Richard Culling; Executive Adviser to the Carr-Gomm Society and Morpeth Society (charity societies); b 2 Jan. 1922; s of Mark Culling Carr-Gomm and Amicia Dorothy (née Heming); m 1957, Susan, d of Ralph and Dorothy Gibbs; two s three d. Educ: Stowe Sch., Bucks. Served War: commnd Coldstream Guards, 1941; served 6th Guards Tank Bde, NW Europe (twice wounded, mentioned in despatches); Palestine, 1945; ME, resigned commn, 1955. Founded: Abbeyfield Soc., 1956; Carr-Gomm Soc. 1965; Morpeth Soc., 1972. Croix de Guerre (Silver Star), France, 1944. KStJ. Publication: Push on the Door (autobiog.), 1979. Recreations: golf, backgammon, painting. Address: Rectory Stables, Mells, near Frome, Somerset BA11 3PT. T: Mells 812401. Club: MCC.

CARR LINFORD, Alan, RWS 1955 (ARWS 1949); ARE 1946; ARCA 1946; b 15 Jan. 1926; m 1948, Margaret Dorothea Parish; one s one d. Educ: Royal College of Art, and in Rome. Was awarded the Prix de Rome, 1947. Recreation: shooting. Address: Midfield, Lower Green, Wimbish, Saffron Walden, Essex CB10 2XH. T: Radwinter 287.

CARREL, Philip, CMG 1960; OBE 1954; b 23 Sept. 1915; s of late Louis Raymond Carrel and Lucy Mabel (née Cooper); m 1948, Eileen Mary Bullock (née Hainworth); one s one d. Educ: Blundell's; Balliol. Colonial

Admin. Service, 1938, Zanzibar Protectorate. EA Forces, 1940. Civil Affairs, 1941-47 (OETA); Civilian Employee Civil Affairs, GHQ MELF, 1947-49 (on secondment from Som. Prot.); Colonial Admin. Service (Somaliland Protectorate), 1947; Commissioner of Somali Affairs, 1953; Chief Sec. to the Government, Somaliland Protectorate, 1959-60. Cttee Sec., Overseas Relns, Inst. of Chartered Accountants in England and Wales, 1961-77; retired. *Address:* Lych Gates, Chiltley Lane, Liphook, Hants GU30 7HJ. *T:* 722150.

CARRERAS, Sir James, KCVO 1980; Kt 1970; MBE 1945; *b* 30 Jan. 1909; *s* of Henry and Dolores Carreras; *m* 1927, Vera St John; one *s. Educ:* privately. Chm. and Chief Exec., Hammer Film Prodns Ltd, 1946-73; Director: Studio Film Laboratories Ltd; National Screen Service; Services Sound and Vision Corp. Vice-Chm., Royal Naval Film Corporation, 1961; Chairman, Variety International Exec. Bd, 1965. Consultant, Duke of Edinburgh's Award Scheme; Trustee: Police Dependents Trust; Young Volunteer Force Foundn; Attlee Memorial Foundation; Bowles Rocks Trust Ltd. Mem. Council, Cinema and Television Benevolent Fund; President: The London Fedn of Boys' Clubs; Cinema Veterans, 1982. Knight Grand Band, Order of African Redemption (Liberia), 1968; Grand Order of Civil Merit (Spain), 1974. *Recreation:* cooking. *Address:* Queen Anne Cottage, Friday Street, Henley-on-Thames, Oxon.

CARRICK, 9th Earl of, *cr* 1748; **Brian Stuart Theobald Somerset Caher Butler;** Baron Butler (UK), 1912; Viscount Ikerrin, 1629; *b* 17 Aug. 1931; *o s* of 8th Earl of Carrick; *S* father, 1957; *m* 1951, (Mary) Belinda (marr. diss. 1976) *e d* of Major David Constable-Maxwell, TD, Bosworth Hall, near Rugby; one *s* one *d. Educ:* Downside. Dir., The Bowater Corp. Ltd; Chm. and Man. Dir, Ralli Brothers Ltd; Chairman: Ralli Brothers and Coney Ltd; Malcolm Maclaine and Co. Ltd; Duncan Fox and Co. Ltd; Director: Nauman Gepp and Co. Ltd; Ralli Hong Kong Ltd; Ralli Europe BV; Cargill Albion Ltd; Mercantile House Holdings plc. Member: Council, London Chamber of Commerce and Industry; Hispanic and Luzo-Brazilian Councils; Canning House Economic Affairs Council Ltd. *Heir: s* Viscount Ikerrin, *qv. Address:* 10 Netherton Grove, SW10. *T:* 01-352 6328. *Clubs:* Pratt's, White's.

CARRICK, Edward; *see* Craig, E. A.

CARRICK, Senator Hon. Sir John (Leslie), KCMG 1982; Senator, Commonwealth Parliament of Australia, since 1971 (Leader of the Government in the Senate, since 1978); Minister for National Development and Energy, since 1979 (Cabinet Minister, since 1975); Vice-President of the Executive Council, since 1978; *b* 4 Sept. 1918; *s* of late A. J. Carrick and of E. E. Carrick; *m* 1951, Diana Margaret Hunter; three *d. Educ:* Univ. of Sydney (BEc). Res. Officer, Liberal Party of Aust., NSW Div., 1946-48, Gen. Sec., 1948-71; Minister for Educn, 1975-79; Minister Assisting Prime Minister in Fed. Affairs, 1975-78. *Recreations:* swimming, reading. *Address:* 8 Montah Avenue, Killara, NSW 2071, Australia. *T:* 02 498 6326. *Clubs:* Australian, Royal Automobile, Tattersalls (Sydney); Commonwealth (Canberra).

CARRICK, Roger John, MVO 1972; HM Diplomatic Service; Head of Overseas Estate Department, Foreign and Commonwealth Office, since 1982; *b* 13 Oct. 1937; *s* of John H. and Florence M. Carrick; *m* 1962, Hilary Elizabeth Blinman; two *s. Educ:* Isleworth Grammar Sch.; Sch. of Slavonic and East European Studies, London Univ. Served RN, 1956-58. Joined HM Foreign (subseq. Diplomatic) Service, 1956; SSEES, 1961; Sofia, 1962; FO, 1965; Paris, 1967; Singapore, 1971; FCO, 1973; Counsellor and Dep. Head, Personnel Ops Dept, FCO, 1976; Vis. Fellow, Inst. of Internat. Studies, Univ. of Calif, Berkeley, 1977-78; Counsellor, Washington, 1978. *Publication:* East-West Technology Transfer in Perspective, 1978. *Recreations:* sailing, racquet games, music, reading, avoiding gardening. *Address:* c/o Foreign and Commonwealth Office, SW1A 2AH; 43 Dornden Drive, Langton Green, Tunbridge Wells, Kent TN3 0AE. *T:* Langton Green 2495. *Club:* Royal Commonwealth Society.

CARRICK, Maj-Gen. Thomas Welsh, OBE 1959; retired; Specialist in Community Medicine, Camden and Islington Area Health Authority (Teaching), 1975-78; *b* 19 Dec. 1914; *s* of late George Carrick and late Mary Welsh; *m* 1948, Nan Middleton Allison; one *s. Educ:* Glasgow Academy; Glasgow Univ.; London Sch. of Hygiene and Tropical Med. MB, ChB 1937, FFCM 1972, DPH 1951, DIH 1961. House appts in medicine, surgery and urological surgery at Glasgow Royal Infirmary, 1937-38; Dep. Supt, Glasgow Royal Infirmary, 1939-40. Commissioned, RAMC, 1940. Later service appts include: Asst Dir, Army Health, 17 Gurkha Div., Malaya, 1961-63; Asst Dir, Army Health, HQ Scotland, 1964-65; Dir Army Personnel Research Estabt, 1965-68; Dep. Dir, Army Health, Strategic Command, 1968-70; Prof. of Army Health, Royal Army Med. Coll., 1970; Dir of Army Health and Research, MoD, 1971-72; Comdt and Postgraduate Dean, Royal Army Medical Coll., Millbank, 1973-75, retd. Col Comdt, RAMC, 1975-79. Blackham Lectr, RIPH 1977. QHS 1973. OStJ 1946. *Publications:* articles in Jl of RAMC, Army Review, Community Health. *Recreations:* gardening, walking, theatre. *Address:* Little Chantry, Gillingham, Dorset SP8 4NA.

CARRINGTON, 6th Baron (Ireland) *cr* 1796, (Great Britain) *cr* 1797; **Peter Alexander Rupert Carington,** PC 1959; KCMG 1958; MC 1945; Chairman, General Electric Company, since 1983; Director, Kissinger Associates, since 1982; *b* 6 June 1919; *s* of 5th Baron and Hon. Sibyl Marion (*d* 1946), *d* of 2nd Viscount Colville; *S* father, 1938; *m* 1942, Iona, *yr d* of

late Sir Francis McClean; one *s* two *d. Educ:* Eton Coll.; RMC Sandhurst. Served NW Europe, Major Grenadier Guards. Parly Sec., Min. of Agriculture and Fisheries, 1951-54; Parly Sec., Min. of Defence, Oct. 1954-Nov. 1956; High Comr for the UK in Australia, Nov. 1956-Oct. 1959; First Lord of the Admiralty, 1959-63; Minister without Portfolio and Leader of the House of Lords, 1963-64; Leader of the Opposition, House of Lords, 1964-70 and 1974-79. Secretary of State: for Defence, 1970-74; for Energy, 1974; for For. and Commonwealth Affairs, 1979-82; Minister of Aviation Supply, 1971-74. Chm., Cons. Party Organisation, 1972-74. Chairman, Australia and New Zealand Bank Ltd, 1967-70; Director: Barclays Bank, 1967-70, 1974-79; Cadbury Schweppes Ltd, 1969-70, 1974-79; Rio Tinto Zinc Corp., 1974-79; Barclays Bank International, 1975-; British Metal Corp., 1965-68; Amalgamated Metal Corpn Ltd, 1969-70; Schweppes Ltd, 1968-69; Hambros Bank, 1967-70. JP 1948, DL Bucks. Fellow of Eton Coll., 1966-81; Hon. Fellow, St Antony's Coll., Oxford, 1982. Hon. LLD: Cambridge, 1981; Leeds, 1981; Hon. Dr Laws, Univ. of Philippines, 1982. *Heir: s* Hon. Rupert Francis John Carington, *b* 2 Dec. 1948. *Address:* 32a Ovington Square, SW3. *T:* 01-584 1476; The Manor House, Bledlow, near Aylesbury, Bucks. *T:* Princes Risborough 3499. *Clubs:* Turf, Pratt's, White's, Carlton.

See also Baron Ashcombe.

CARRINGTON, Prof. Alan, FRS 1971; Royal Society Research Professor, University of Southampton, since 1979; *b* 6 Jan. 1934; *o s* of Albert Carrington and Constance (*née* Nelson); *m* 1959, Noreen Hilary Taylor; one *s* two *d. Educ:* Colfe's Grammar Sch.; Univ. of Southampton. BSc, MA, PhD. Univ. of Cambridge: Asst in Research, 1960; Fellow of Downing Coll., 1960; Asst Dir of Res., 1963; Prof. of Chemistry, Univ. of Southampton, 1967. Tilden Lectr, Chem. Soc., 1972; Sen. Fellowship, SRC, 1976. Harrison Mem. Prize, Chem. Soc., 1962; Meldola Medal, Royal Inst. of Chemistry, 1963; Marlow Medal, Faraday Soc., 1966; Corday Morgan Medal, Chem. Soc., 1967; Chem. Soc. Award in Structural Chemistry, 1970. *Publications:* (with A. D. McLachlan) Introduction to Magnetic Resonance, 1967; Microwave Spectroscopy of Free Radicals, 1974; numerous papers on topics in chemical physics in various learned jls. *Recreations:* family, music, fishing, golf, sailing. *Address:* 46 Lakewood Road, Chandler's Ford, Hants. *T:* Chandler's Ford 65092.

CARRINGTON, Charles Edmund, MC; writer and lecturer; *b* West Bromwich, 21 April 1897; *s* of late Very Rev. C. W. Carrington; *m* 1st, 1932, Cecil Grace MacGregor (marr. diss., 1954); one *d* decd; 2nd, 1955, Maysie Cuthbert Robertson. *Educ:* Christ's Coll., New Zealand; Christ Church, Oxford. Enlisted, 1914; first commission, 1915; Capt. 5th Royal Warwickshire Regt, 1917; served in France and Italy (MC); Major TA, 1927. BA Oxford, 1921; MA 1929; MA Cambridge, 1929. Asst Master, Haileybury Coll., 1921-24 and 1926-29; Lectr, Pembroke Coll., Oxford, 1924-25; Educational Sec. to the Cambridge Univ. Press, 1929-54. Military service, 1939, France, 1940; Lt-Col Gen. Staff, 1941-45. Prof. of British Commonwealth Relations at Royal Inst. of Internat. Affairs, 1954-62; organised unofficial Commonwealth conferences, New Zealand, 1959, Nigeria, 1962; Visiting Prof., USA, 1964-65. Has served on: LCC Educn Cttee; Classical Assoc. Council; Publishers Assoc. Educational Group; Royal Commonwealth Soc. Council; Inter-Univ. Council; Overseas Migration Board, Islington Soc., etc; Chm. Shoreditch Housing Assoc., 1961-67. *Publications:* An Exposition of Empire, 1947; The British Overseas, 1950; Godley of Canterbury, 1951; Rudyard Kipling, 1955, rev. edn 1978; The Liquidation of the British Empire, 1961; Soldier from the Wars Returning, 1965; (ed) The Complete Barrack-Room Ballads of Rudyard Kipling, 1973; Kipling's Horace, 1978; A History of England (with J. Hampden Jackson), 1932; (under pen-name of Charles Edmonds) A Subaltern's War, 1929; T. E. Lawrence, 1935; contributor to: Camb. Hist. of the British Empire, 1959; An African Survey, 1957; Surveys of International Affairs, 1957-58 and 1959-60, etc. *Recreations:* historical studies, travel. *Address:* 31 Grange Road, N1 2NP. *T:* 01-354 2832. *Club:* Travellers'.

CARROL, Charles Gordon; Director, Commonwealth Institute, Scotland, since 1971; *b* 21 March 1935; *s* of Charles Muir Carrol and Catherine Gray Napier; *m* 1970, Frances Anne, *o d* of John A. and Flora McL. Sinclair; three *s. Educ:* Melville Coll., Edinburgh; Edinburgh Univ. (MA); Moray House Coll. (DipEd). Education Officer: Govt of Nigeria, 1959-65; Commonwealth Inst., Scotland, 1965-71. Lay Member, Press Council, 1978-. *Recreations:* walking, reading, cooking. *Address:* 11 Dukehaugh, Peebles, Scotland EH45 9DN. *T:* Peebles 21296.

CARROLL, Ven. Charles William Desmond; Archdeacon of Blackburn, since 1973; Vicar of Balderstone, since 1973; *b* 27 Jan. 1919; *s* of Rev. William and Mrs L. Mary Carroll; *m* 1945, Doreen Daisy Ruskell; three *s* one *d. Educ:* St Columba Coll.; Trinity Coll., Dublin. BA 1943; Dip. Ed. Hons 1945; MA 1946. Asst Master: Kingstown Grammar Sch., 1943-45; Rickerby House Sch., 1945-50; Vicar of Stanwix, Carlisle, 1950-59; Hon. Canon of Blackburn, 1959; Dir of Religious Education, 1959; Hon. Chaplain to Bishop of Blackburn, 1961; Canon Residentiary of Blackburn Cathedral, 1964. *Publication:* Management for Managers, 1968. *Address:* Balderstone Vicarage, Blackburn, Lancs BB2 7LL. *Clubs:* Royal Commonwealth Society; Rotary (Blackburn).

CARROLL, Maj-Gen. Derek Raymond, OBE 1958; Kent Hospital Car Service, since 1980; *b* 2 Jan. 1919; *er s* of late Raymond and Edith Lisle Carroll; *m* 1946, Bettina Mary, *d* of late Leslie Gould; one *s* two *d.* Enlisted

TA, 1939; commnd into Royal Engineers, 1943; served Western Desert, 1941-43, Italy, 1943-44; psc 1945; various appts, 1946-66, in Germany, Sudan Defence Force, Libya, Malaya, CRE 4 Div., 1962-64; comd 12 Engr Bde, 1966-67; idc 1968; Chief Engr, BAOR, 1970-73; RARO, 1973. Bus driver, East Kent Road Car Co., 1974; Immigration Officer, Ramsgate Hoverport, 1975; coach driver/operator, 1975-79. *Recreations:* sailing, railways, airways. *Address:* c/o Barclays Bank Ltd, Wimbledon Broadway, SW19 1PU. *Club:* Royal Cinque Ports Yacht.

CARROLL, Madeleine; screen, stage, and radio actress; *d* of John Carroll, Co. Limerick, and Hélène de Rosière Tuaillon, Paris; *m* 1st, 1931, Capt. Philip Astley, MC (from whom she obtd a divorce, 1940); 2nd, 1942, Lieut Sterling Hayden, USMC (from whom she obtd a divorce, 1946); 3rd, 1946, Henri Lavorel (marr. diss.); 4th, 1950, Andrew Heiskell (marr. diss.); one *d. Educ:* private sch.; Birmingham Univ. (BA Hons French). Started theatrical career in touring company, playing French maid in The Lash; subsequently toured with Seymour Hicks in Mr What's his Name; became leading lady in British films as result of first screen test for The Guns of Loos; subsequently made Young Woodley, The School for Scandal, I was a Spy, and The Thirty Nine Steps; came to America in 1936 and made: The Case against Mrs Ames; The General Died at Dawn; Lloyds of London; On the Avenue; The Prisoner of Zenda; Blockade; Café Society; North-West Mounted Police; Virginia; One Night in Lisbon; Bahama Passage; My Favourite Blonde; White Cradle Inn; An Innocent Affair; The Fan. Radio appearances include the leading parts in: Cavalcade; Beloved Enemy; Romance; There's always Juliet. From 1941 until end of War, engaged exclusively in war activities.

CARRUTHERS, Alwyn Guy; Director of Statistics, Department of Employment, since 1981 (Deputy Director, 1972-80); *b* 6 May 1925; *yr s* of late John Sendall and of Lily Eden Carruthers, Grimsby; *m* 1950, Edith Eileen, *o d* of late William and Edith Addison Lumb; no *c. Educ:* Wintringham Grammar Sch., Grimsby; King's Coll., London Univ. BA First Cl. Hons in Mathematics, Drew Gold Medal and Prize, 1945. RAE, Farnborough, 1945-46; Instructor Lieut, RN, 1946-49; Rothamsted Experimental Station, 1949. Postgraduate Diploma in Mathematical Statistics Christ's Coll., Cambridge, 1951. Bd of Trade and DTI Statistics Divisions, 1951-72. *Publications:* articles in official publications and learned jls. *Recreations:* gardening, music. *Address:* 24 Red House Lane, Bexleyheath, Kent. *T:* 01-303 4898.

CARRUTHERS, Colin Malcolm, CMG 1980; HM Diplomatic Service; Head of South Pacific Department, Foreign and Commonwealth Office, since 1980; *b* 23 Feb. 1931; *s* of Colin Carruthers and late Dorothy Beatrice Carruthers; *m* 1954, Annette Audrey Buckton; three *s* one *d. Educ:* Monkton Combe School; Selwyn College, Cambridge (MA). Royal Signals, 1950-51; joined HMOCS Kenya, 1955; District Officer, Kenya, 1955-63; Dep. Civil Sec., Rift Valley Region, Kenya, 1963-65 (retired on Africanisation of post); Field Dir, Oxfam, Maseru, Lesotho, 1965-67; joined HM Diplomatic Service, 1968; First Sec. (Economic), Islamabad, 1969-73; First Sec., Ottawa, 1973-77; Counsellor and Hd of Chancery, Addis Ababa, 1977-80. Asst Election Comr, Zimbabwe-Rhodesia elecns, 1980. *Recreations:* tennis, golf, family. *Address:* c/o Foreign and Commonwealth Office, SW1; Thornbury, Frant, near Tunbridge Wells, Kent. *T:* Frant 238. *Club:* Royal Commonwealth Society.

CARRUTHERS, George, OBE 1979; FCIT; Member of Board, 1979-82, Deputy Chief Executive, 1981-82, National Bus Company; *b* 15 Nov. 1917; *s* of James and Dinah Carruthers; *m* 1941, Gabriel Joan Heath; one *s* one *d. Educ:* Nelson Sch., Wigton, Cumbria; St Edmund Hall, Oxford (BA). FBIM. Served War, Border Regt and Cameronians (Major), 1939-46 (despatches). Various management posts, Bus Industry (all at subsid. cos or Headquarters NBC): Eastern Counties, Norwich, 1946-59; Wilts and Dorset Omnibus Co., 1959-63; Dep. Gen. Manager, Hants and Dorset Omnibus Co., 1963-66; Gen. Manager, United Welsh-Swansea, 1967-69; Vice-Chm., South Wales (NBC), 1969-72; Regional Exec., Western Region (NBC), 1972-73; Gp Exec., NBC Headquarters, 1973-74; Director of Manpower, NBC HQ, 1974-79; Mem. for Personnel Services, 1979-81. *Publications:* papers for Jl and meetings of CIT (Road Passenger award for a paper, 1978). *Recreation:* the countryside. *Address:* 2 Mallard Close, Lower Street, Harnham, Salisbury, Wilts SP2 8JB. *T:* Salisbury 23084.

CARRUTHERS, James Edwin; Director General, Royal Ordnance Factories (Finance and Procurement), since 1980; *b* 19 March 1928; *er s* of James and Dollie Carruthers; *m* 1955, Phyllis Williams; one *s. Educ:* George Heriot's Sch.; Edinburgh Univ. (MA; Medallist in Scottish Hist.). FSAScot. Lieut, The Queen's Own Cameron Highlanders, 1949-51, and TA, 1951-55. Air Ministry: Asst Principal, 1951; Private Sec. to DCAS, 1955; Asst Private Sec. to Sec. of State for Air, 1956; Principal, 1956; Min. of Aviation, 1960-62; Private Secretary: to Minister of Defence for RAF, 1965-67; to Parly Under Sec. of State for RAF, 1967; Asst Sec., 1967; Chief Officer, Sovereign Base Areas Admin, Cyprus, 1968-71; Dep. Chief of Public Relations, MoD, 1971-72; Private Sec. to Chancellor of Duchy of Lancaster, Cabinet Office, 1973-74; Sec., Organising Cttee for British Aerospace, DoI, 1975-77; Under-Sec., 1977; seconded as Asst to Chm., British Aeropace, 1977-79. Mem., Chorleywood UDC, 1964-65. *Recreations:* painting, gardening, travel. *Address:* 129 Valley Road, Chorleywood, Herts WD3 4BN. *T:* Rickmansworth 76020.

CARSBERG, Prof. Bryan Victor; Arthur Andersen Professor of Accounting, London School of Economics and Political Science, University of London, since 1981; Director of Research, Institute of Chartered Accountants in England and Wales, since 1981; *b* 3 Jan. 1939; *s* of Alfred Victor Carsberg and Maryllia (*née* Collins); *m* 1960, Margaret Linda Graham; two *d. Educ:* Berkhamsted Sch.; London Sch. of Econs and Polit. Science (MScEcon). Chartered Accountant, 1960. Sole practice, chartered accountant, 1962-64; Lectr in Accounting, LSE, 1964-68; Vis. Lectr, Grad. Sch. of Business, Univ. of Chicago, 1968-69; Prof. of Accounting, Univ. of Manchester, 1969-81 (Dean, Faculty of Econ. and Social Studies, 1977-78). Vis. Prof. of Business Admin, Univ. of Calif, Berkeley, 1974; Asst Dir of Res. and Technical Activities, Financial Accounting Standards Bd, USA, 1978-81. Mem. Council, ICA, 1975-79. Director: Economists Adv. Gp, 1976-; Economist Bookshop, 1981-; Philip Allan (Publishers), 1981-. Hon. MAEcon Manchester, 1973. *Publications:* An Introduction to Mathematical Programming for Accountants, 1969; (with H. C. Edey) Modern Financial Management, 1969; Analysis for Investment Decisions, 1974; (with E. V. Morgan and M. Parkin) Indexation and Inflation, 1975; Economics of Business Decisions, 1975; (with A. Hope) Investment Decisions under Inflation, 1976; (with A. Hope) Current Issues in Accountancy, 1977; (with J. Arnold and R. Scapens) Topics in Management Accounting, 1980. *Recreations:* road running, theatre, music. *Address:* Woodlands, 14 The Great Quarry, Guildford, Surrey GU1 3XN. *T:* Guildford 572672. *Clubs:* London Road Runners; New York Road Runners.

CARSE, William Mitchell, CBE 1953; *b* 23 Aug. 1899; *o s* of Robert Allison Carse, Hawkhead, Renfrewshire; *m* 1928, Helen Knox (*d* 1976), *yr d* of J. B. Beaton, Milliken Park, Renfrewshire; one *s. Educ:* Glasgow High Sch.; Glasgow Univ.; Wellington Military Coll., Madras; St John's Coll., Cambridge. Passed Examination for RMC Sandhurst, 1917; proceeded to Wellington Military Coll., Madras, 1918; gazetted to Indian Army, 1918; served in South Persia until 1920; resigned Commission; entered HM Consular Service, 1923; served in USA, Guatemala, Germany, Portuguese East Africa, Portugal and Portuguese West Africa; Consul-Gen., Loanda, Angola, 1937-39; Consul at Teneriffe, 1939; Consul-Gen. at Reykjavik, Iceland, 1943; attached to British Political Mission in Hungary, 1945-46; Consul-Gen. at Tabriz, Persia, 1946-47, and at Ahwaz Persia, 1948, Deputy High Comr for the UK in Peshawar, Pakistan, 1948-51; Consul-Gen., São Paulo, Brazil, 1951-56, retd. Appointed to Distillers Company Ltd. (Industrial Group), London, 1957. *Recreations:* yachting, riding, chess. *Address:* Little Dene, St Alban's Road, Reigate, Surrey.

CARSON, Hon. Edward; Lieutenant Life Guards; *b* 17 Feb. 1920; *yr s* of Baron Carson, a Lord of Appeal in Ordinary; *m* 1943, Heather, *d* of Lt-Col Frank Sclater, OBE, MC; one *s* one *d. Educ:* Eton; Trinity Hall, Cambridge. MP (C) Isle of Thanet Div. of Kent, 1945-53. *Address:* 5 Old Timbertop Cottages, Bethel Road, Sevenoaks, Kent. *T:* Sevenoaks 59147. *Clubs:* Wig and Pen, MCC.

CARSON, John, CBE 1981; Draper; *b* 1934. Member of the Orange Order; Member, Belfast District Council, (formerly Belfast Corporation), 1971-; Official Unionist Councillor for Duncairn; Lord Mayor of Belfast, 1980-81. MP (UU) Belfast North, Feb. 1974-1979. *Address:* 20 Cardy Road, Greyabbey, Co. Down, N Ireland.

CARSON, Robert Andrew Glendinning, FBA 1980; Keeper, Department of Coins and Medals, British Museum, 1978-April 1983; *b* 7 April 1918; *s* of Andrew and Mary Dempster Carson; *m* 1949, Meta Fransisca De Vries; one *s* one *d. Educ:* Kirkcudbright Acad.; Univ. of Glasgow (MA (1st Cl. Hons Classics) 1940; Foulis Schol. 1940). Served War, RA, 1940-46, NW Europe; 2nd Lieut 1941, Captain 1945. Asst Keeper, 1947, Dep. Keeper, 1965, Dept of Coins and Medals, British Museum. Pres., Internat. Numismatic Commn, 1979-. Editor, Numismatic Chronicle, 1966-73; Mem., Adv. Cttee on Historic Wreck Sites, 1973-80; Pres., Royal Numismatic Soc., 1974-79 (Medallist, 1972; Hon. Fellow, 1980); Hon. Mem., British Numismatic Soc., 1979. Medallist: Soc. française de Numismatique, 1970; Luxembourg Museum, 1971; Amer. Numismatic Soc., 1978; Corresponding Member: Amer. Num. Soc., 1967; Austrian Num. Soc., 1971; Hon. Mem., Romanian Num. Soc., 1977. FSA 1965. Queen's Jubilee medal, 1977. *Publications:* (with H. Mattingly and C. H. V. Sutherland) Roman Imperial Coinage, 1951-; ed, Essays in Roman Coinage presented to Harold Mattingly, 1956; (with P. V. Hill and J. P. C. Kent) Late Roman Bronze Coinage, 1960; Coins, ancient, mediæval and modern, 1962, 2nd edn 1972; Catalogue of Roman Imperial Coins in the British Museum, vol. VI, 1962; ed, Mints, Dies and Currency, 1971; Principal Coins of the Romans, vol. I, 1978, vol. II, 1980, vol. III, 1981; ed, Essays presented to Humphrey Sutherland, 1978; articles in Numismatic Chron., Rev. Numismatique, etc. *Address:* 23 Latchmoor Way, Gerrards Cross, Bucks SL9 8LS. *T:* Gerrards Cross 84374.

CARSON, Air Cdre Robert John, CBE 1974; AFC 1964; Queen's Commendation (Air), 1962; Director, Leicestershire Medical Research Foundation, University of Leicester, since 1980; *b* 3 Aug. 1924; *e s* of Robert George and Margaret Etta Helena Carson; *m* 1945, Jane, *yr d* of James and Jane Bailie; three *d. Educ:* Regent House Sch., Newtownards, NI; RAF. MRAeS; MBIM; MIAM. India, Burma, Malaya, 1945-48; Rhodesia, 1949-50; Queens Univ. Air Sqdn, 1951-52; RAF HC Examining Unit, 1952-53; AHQ Iraq, 1953-54; RAF Staff Coll., 1955; Plans, Air Min., 1956-59; 16 Sqdn, Laarbruch, Germany, 1959-62; Wing Comdr Flying, RAF Swinderby, 1962-

64; Air Warfare Coll., Manby, 1964; Chief Nuclear Ops, 2ATAF Germany, 1964–67; JSSC Latimer, 1967; Chief Air Planner, UK Delegn, Live Oak, SHAPE, 1968–71; Station Comdr, RAF Leeming, 1971–73; Overseas Coll. Defence Studies, Canada, 1973–74; Air Adviser, British High Commission, Ottawa, 1974–75; Defence Advr to British High Comr in Canada, 1975–78; Manager, Panavia Office, Ottawa, and Grumman Aerospace Corp., NY, 1978–80. *Recreations:* Rugby, tennis, golf, gardening. *Address:* 20 Meadow Drive, Scruton, near Northallerton, North Yorks. *T:* Northallerton 748656; c/o Lloyds Bank, 118 High Street, Northallerton, N Yorks. *Clubs:* Royal Air Force; Royal Ottawa (Ottawa).

CARSON, William Hunter Fisher; jockey; *b* 16 Nov. 1942; *s* of Thomas Whelan Carson and Mary Hay; *m* 1963, Carole Jane Sutton (marr. diss. 1979); three *s*; *m* 1982, Elaine Williams. *Educ:* Riverside, Stirling, Scotland. Apprenticed to Captain G. Armstrong, 1957; trans. to Fred Armstrong, 1963–66; First Jockey to Lord Derby, 1967; first classic win, High Top, 1972; Champion Jockey, 1972, 1973, 1978 and 1980; became First Jockey to W. R. Hern, 1977; also appointed Royal Jockey, riding Dunfermline to the Jubilee Oaks and St Leger wins in the colours of HM the Queen; won the 200th Derby on Troy, trained by W. R. Hern, 1979; the same combination won the 1980 Derby, with Henbit, and the 1980 Oaks, with Bireme; also won King George VI and Queen Elizabeth Stakes, on Ela-Mana-Mou, 1980. *Recreation:* hunting. *Address:* West Ilsley, near Newbury, Berks. *T:* West Ilsley 348.

CARSTAIRS, Charles Young, CB 1968; CMG 1950; *b* 30 Oct. 1910; *s* of late Rev. Dr G. Carstairs, DD; *m* 1939, Frances Mary (*d* 1981), *o d* of late Dr Claude Lionel Coode, Stroud, Glos; one *s* one *d. Educ:* George Watson's Boys' Coll., Edinburgh; Edinburgh Univ. Entered Home Civil Service, 1934, Dominions Office; transf. Colonial Office, 1935; Asst Private Sec. to Sec. of State for the Colonies, 1936; Private Sec. to Perm. Under-Sec. of State for the Colonies, 1937; Asst Sec., West India Royal Commn, 1938–39; West Indian, Prodn, Res. and Mediterranean Depts, 1939–47; Administrative Sec., Development and Welfare Organisation, British West Indies, 1947–50; Sec., British Caribbean Standing Closer Assoc. Cttee, 1948–49; Dir of Information Services, Colonial Office, 1951–53, Asst Under-Sec., 1953–62; Deputy Sec., Medical Research Council, 1962–65; Under-Secretary, MPBW: Directorate-Gen., R and D, 1965–67, Construction Economics, 1967–70; Special Advr, Expenditure Cttee, House of Commons, 1971–75; Clerk to Select Cttee on Commodity Prices, House of Lords, 1976–77. *Address:* St Kea, 9 Ridgegate Close, Reigate, Surrey RH2 0HT. *T:* Reigate 44896. *Club:* Athenæum.

CARSTAIRS, Dr George Morrison, MD; FRCPE, FRCPsych; Vice-Chancellor, University of York, 1973–78; *b* Mussoorie, India, 18 June 1916; *s* of late Rev. Dr George Carstairs, DD, K-i-H, and Elizabeth H. Carstairs; *m* 1950, Vera Hunt; two *s* one *d. Educ:* George Watson's Coll., Edinburgh; Edinburgh Univ. Asst Phys., Royal Edinburgh Hosp., 1942. MO, RAF, 1942–46. Commonwealth Fellow, USA, 1948–49; Rockefeller Research Fellow, 1950–51; Henderson Res. Schol., 1951–52; Sen. Registrar, Maudsley Hosp., 1953; Scientific Staff, MRC, 1954–60; Prof. of Psychiatry, Univ. of Edinburgh, 1961–73. Dir, MRC Unit for Research on Epidemiological Aspects of Psychiatry, 1960–71. Vis. Prof. of Psychiatry, Post Grad. Inst., Chandigarh, India, 1979–81; Fellow, Woodrow Wilson Center, Smithsonian Instn, Washington, 1981–82. Reith Lectr, 1962. Pres., World Federation for Mental Health, 1967–71. *Publications:* The Twice Born, 1957; This Island Now, 1963; (with R. L. Kapur) The Great Universe of Kota, 1976; chapters and articles in medical publications. *Recreations:* travel, theatre; formerly athletics (Scottish Champion 3 miler, 1937–39). *Address:* c/o Lloyds Bank, 2 Pavement, York. *Club:* Royal Air Force.

CARSTEN, Prof. Francis Ludwig, DPhil, DLitt Oxon; FBA 1971; Masaryk Professor of Central European History in the University of London, 1961–78; *b* 25 June 1911; *s* of Prof. Paul Carsten and Frida Carsten (*née* Born); *m* 1945, Ruth Carsten (*née* Moses); two *s* one *d. Educ:* Heidelberg, Berlin and Oxford Univs. Barnett scholar, Wadham Coll., Oxford, 1939; Senior Demy, Magdalen Coll., Oxford, 1942; Lectr in History, Westfield Coll., Univ. of London, 1947; Reader in Modern History, Univ. of London, 1960. Co-Editor, Slavonic and East European Review, 1966–. *Publications:* The Origins of Prussia, 1954; Princes and Parliaments in Germany from the 15th to the 18th Century, 1959; The Reichswehr and Politics, 1918–1933, 1966; The Rise of Fascism, 1967, rev. edn, 1980; Revolution in Central Europe, 1918–1919, 1972; Fascist Movements in Austria, 1977; War against War: British and German Radical Movements in the First World War, 1982; ed and contributor, The New Cambridge Modern History, vol. V: The Ascendancy of France, 1961; articles in English Historical Review, History, Survey, Historische Zeitschrift, etc. *Recreations:* gardening, climbing, swimming. *Address:* 11 Redington Road, NW3. *T:* 01-435 5522.

CARSTENS, Dr Karl; President of the Federal Republic of Germany, since 1979; *b* 14 Dec. 1914; *s* of Dr Karl Carstens, teacher, and Gertrud (née Clausen); *m* 1944, Dr Veronica Carstens(*née* Prior). *Educ:* Univs of Frankfurt, Dijon, München, Königsberg, Hamburg, Yale. Dr Laws Hamburg 1936, LLM Yale 1949. Served with Army, 1939–45; lawyer, Bremen, 1945–49; rep. of Bremen in Bonn, 1949–54; rep. of Fed. Republic of Germany to Council of Europe, Strasbourg, 1954–55; teaching at Cologne Univ., 1950–73; Prof. of Constitutional and Internat. Law, 1960–73; FO, Bonn, 1955–60 (State Sec., 1960–66); Dep. Defence Minister, 1966–67; Head of Chancellor's Office, Bonn, 1968–69; Dir Research Inst., German Foreign Policy Assoc., 1969–72; Mem. German Bundestag (CDU), 1972–79; Leader of the Opposition,

1973–76; Pres. of Bundestag, 1976–79. *Publications:* Grundgedanken der amerikanischen Verfassung und ihre Verwirklichung, 1954; Das Recht des Europarats, 1956; Politische Führung—Erfahrungen im Dienst der Bundesregierung, 1971; Bundestagsreden und Zeitdokumente, 1977; Reden und Interviews, 1981. *Address:* Haus des Bundespräsidenten, Bonn, West Germany.

CARSWELL, John Patrick, CB 1977; Secretary, British Academy, since 1978; *b* 30 May 1918; *s* of Donald Carswell, barrister and author, and Catherine Carswell, author; *m* 1944, Ianthe Elstob; two *d. Educ:* Merchant Taylors' Sch.; St John's Coll., Oxford (MA). Served in Army, 1940–46. Entered Civil Service, 1946. Joint Sec., Cttee on Economic and Financial Problems of Provision for Old Age (Phillips Cttee), 1953–54; Asst Sec., 1955; Principal Private Sec. to Minister of Pensions and Nat. Insurance, 1955–56; Treasury, 1961–64; Under-Sec., Office of Lord Pres. of the Council and Minister for Science, 1964, Under-Sec., DES and Ministry of Health, 1964–74; Sec., UGC, 1974–77. *Publications:* The Prospector, 1950; The Old Cause, 1954; The South Sea Bubble, 1960; The Diary and Political Papers of George Bubb Dodington, 1965; The Civil Servant and his World, 1966; The Descent on England, 1969; From Revolution to Revolution: English Society 1688–1776, 1973; Lives and Letters, 1978; contribs to Times Literary Supplement and other periodicals. *Address:* 5 Prince Arthur Road, NW3. *T:* 01-794 6527. *Clubs:* Athenæum, Garrick.

CARSWELL, Robert Douglas, QC (NI) 1971; Senior Crown Counsel in Northern Ireland, since 1979; *b* 28 June 1934; *er s* of late Alan E. Carswell and of Nance E. Carswell; *m* 1961, Romayne Winifred, *o d* of late James Ferris, JP, Greyabbey, Co. Down, and of Eileen Ferris, JP; two *d. Educ:* Royal Belfast Academical Instn; Pembroke Coll., Oxford (Schol.; 1st Cl. Honour Mods, 1st Cl. Jurisprudence, MA); Univ. of Chicago Law Sch. (JD). Called to Bar of N Ireland, 1957, and to English Bar, Gray's Inn, 1972; Counsel to Attorney-General for N Ireland, 1970–71; Bencher, Inn of Court of N Ireland, 1979. Governor, Royal Belfast Academical Instn, 1967–. *Publications:* Trustee Acts (Northern Ireland), 1964; articles in legal periodicals. *Recreation:* golf. *Address:* Royal Courts of Justice, Belfast BT1 3JY. *Club:* Ulster (Belfast).

CARTER; see Bonham-Carter and Bonham Carter.

CARTER, Bernard Thomas; Hon. RE 1975; artist (painter and etcher); Keeper, Pictures and Conservation, National Maritime Museum, 1974–77; *b* 6 April 1920; *s* of Cecil Carter and Ethel Carter (*née* Darby); *m* Eugenie Alexander, artist and writer; one *s. Educ:* Haberdashers' Aske's; Goldsmith's College of Art, London Univ. NDD, ATD. RAF, 1939–46. Art lectr, critic and book reviewer, 1952–68; Asst Keeper (prints and drawings), Nat. Maritime Museum, 1968; Dep. Keeper (Head of Picture Dept), Nat. Maritime Museum, 1970. One-man exhibns in London: Arthur Jeffress Gall., 1955; Portal Gall., 1963, 1965, 1967, 1969, 1974, 1978, 1979, 1981; mixed exhibns: Royal Academy, Arts Council, British Council and galleries in Europe and USA; works in public collections, galleries abroad and British educn authorities, etc. TV and radio include: Thames at Six, Pebble Mill at One, Kaleidoscope, London Radio, etc. *Publications:* Art for Young People (with Eugenie Alexander), 1958. *Recreations:* reading, listening to music, gardening, theatre. *Address:* 56 King George Street, Greenwich, SE10 8QD. *T:* 01-858 4281.

CARTER, Dr Brandon, FRS 1981; Maître de Recherche (Centre National de la Recherche Scientifique), Groupe d'Astro-physique Relativiste, Observatoire de Paris, since 1975; *b* Sydney, Australia, 26 May 1942; *s* of Harold Burnell Carter and Mary (*née* Brandon Jones); *m* 1969, Lucette Defrise; three *d. Educ:* George Watson's Coll., Edinburgh; Univ. of St Andrews; Pembroke Coll., Cambridge (MA, PhD 1968, DSc 1976). Res. Student, Dept of Applied Maths and Theoretical Physics, Cambridge, 1964–67; Res. Fellow, Pembroke Coll., Cambridge, 1967–68; Staff Mem., Inst. of Astronomy, Cambridge, 1968–73; Univ. Asst Lectr, 1973–74, Univ. Lectr, 1974–75, Dept of Applied Maths and Theoretical Physics, Cambridge. *Recreations:* mountains and wilderness. *Address:* 19 rue de la Borne au Diable, 92 Sèvres, France. *T:* (Paris) 534—46-77.

CARTER, Bruce; see Hough, R. A.

CARTER, Sir Charles (Frederick), Kt 1978; FBA 1970; Chairman, Research Committee, Policy Studies Institute, since 1978; Vice-Chancellor, University of Lancaster, 1963–79; *b* Rugby, 15 Aug. 1919; *y s* of late Frederick William Carter, FRS; *m* 1944, Janet Shea; one *s* two *d. Educ:* Rugby Sch.; St John's Coll., Cambridge. Friends' Relief Service, 1941–45; Lectr in Statistics, Univ. of Cambridge, 1945–51; Fellow of Emmanuel Coll., 1947–51 (Hon. Fellow, 1965–); Prof. of Applied Economics, The Queen's Univ., Belfast, 1952–59; Stanley Jevons Prof. of Political Economy and Cobden Lectr, Univ. of Manchester, 1959–63. Chairman: Science and Industry Cttee, RSA, British Assoc. and Nuffield Foundn, 1954–59; Schools' Broadcasting Council, 1964–71; Joint Cttee of the Univs and the Accountancy Profession, 1964–70; Adv. Bd of Accountancy Educn, 1970–76; North-West Economic Planning Council, 1965–68; Centre for Studies in Social Policy, 1972–78; PO Rev. Cttee, 1976–77; NI Economic Council, 1977–; Sec.-Gen., Royal Econ. Soc., 1971–75; Member: UN Expert Cttee on Commodity Trade, 1953; Capital Investment Advisory Cttee, Republic of Ireland, 1956; British Assoc. Cttee on Metric System, 1958; Council for Scientific and Industrial Research, 1959–63; Commn on Higher Education, Republic of Ireland, 1960–67;

Heyworth Cttee on Social Studies, 1963; Advisory Council on Technology, 1964-66; North Western Postal Bd, 1970-73. President: Manchester Statistical Soc., 1967-69; BAAS, 1981-82; Vice-Pres., Workers' Educational Assoc.; Dir, Friends' Provident Life Office. Joint Editor: Journal of Industrial Economics, 1955-61; Economic Journal, 1961-70. Hon. Member, Royal Irish Academy; Trustee: Joseph Rowntree Meml Trust, 1966- (Vice-Chm., 1981-); Sir Halley Stewart Trust, 1969-. Hon. DEconSc, NUI, 1968; Hon. DSc: NUU, 1979; Lancaster, 1979; QUB, 1980; Hon. LLD: TCD, 1980; Liverpool, 1982. CBIM. *Publications:* The Science of Wealth, 1960, 3rd edn 1973; (with W. B. Reddaway and J. R. N. Stone) The Measurement of Production Movements, 1948; (with G. L. S. Shackle and others) Uncertainty and Business Decisions, 1954; (with A. D. Roy) British Economic Statistics, 1954; (with B. R. Williams) Industry and Technical Progress, 1957; Investment in Innovation, 1958; Science in Industry, 1959; (with D. P. Barritt) The Northern Ireland Problem, 1962, 2nd edn 1972; Wealth, 1968; (with G. Brosan and others) Patterns and Policies in Higher Education, 1971; On Having a Sense of all Conditions, 1971; (with J. L. Ford and others) Uncertainty and Expectation in Economics, 1972; Higher Education for the Future, 1980; articles in Economic Journal, etc. *Recreation:* gardening. *Address:* Bank Head, The Banks, Seascale, Cumbria CA20 1QN. *T:* Seascale 28050. *Club:* National Liberal.

See also Prof. G. W. Carter.

CARTER, David; see Carter, R. D.

CARTER, Sir Derrick (Hunton), Kt 1975; TD 1952; Vice-Chairman, Remploy Ltd, 1976-78 (Chairman, 1972-76; Director, 1967-79); *b* 7 April 1906; *s* of Arthur Hunton Carter, MD and Winifred Carter, Sedbergh; *m* 1st, 1933, Phyllis, *d* of Denis Best, Worcester; one *s* one *d* ; 2nd, 1948, Madeline, *d* of Col D. M. O'Callaghan, CMG, DSO; one *d. Educ:* Haileybury Coll.; St John's Coll., Cambridge (MA). 2nd Lieut, 27th (LEE) Bn RE, TA, 1936, mobilised Aug. 1939; in AA until Dec. 1941; 1st War Advanced Class; Major RA, Dept Tank Design; comd Armament Wing of DTD, Lulworth, 1942-45 (Lt-Col). Civil Engr, Dominion Bridge Co., Montreal, 1927-28; Res. Engr, Billingham Div., ICI, 1928-33; Asst Sales Controller, ICI, London, 1933-38; Asst Sales Man., ICI, 1938-39 and 1945-47; Gen. Chemicals Div., ICI: Sales Control Man., 1947; Commercial Dir, 1951; Man. Dir, 1953; Chm., 1961; also Chm. Alkali Div., 1963; Chm. (of merged Divs as) Mond Div., 1964; retd from ICI, 1967. Chm., United Sulphuric Acid Corp. Ltd, 1967-71; Chm., Torrance & Sons Ltd, 1971-79; Director: Avon Rubber Co. Ltd, 1970-81; Stothert & Pitt Ltd, 1971-79; BICERI Ltd, 1967-. Mem. Exec. Cttee: Gloucester Council for Small Industries in Rural Areas; Assoc. Boys' Clubs; Mem. Council of Management, Nat. Star Centre for Disabled Youth, 1977-. *Recreations:* shooting, gardening. *Address:* Withington House, Withington, Cheltenham, Glos. *T:* Withington 286. *Club:* Army and Navy.

CARTER, Dorothy Ethel Fleming, (Jane); Under-Secretary, Head of Energy Conservation Division, Department of Energy, since 1979; *b* 29 Aug. 1928; *d* of late Charles Edward Starkey and of Councillor Doris Alma Starkey (*née* Fleming), Newcastle-upon-Tyne; *m* 1952, Frank Arthur (Nick) Carter; two *d. Educ:* Dame Allen's Girls' Sch.; Swansea High Sch.; LSE (BSc (Econ) 1951). Joined CS as Exec. Officer, BoT, 1947; Principal, 1966; Min. of Technology, 1969-70; DTI, 1970-73; Asst Sec., Pay Bd, 1973-74; Dept of Energy, 1974-79. Chm., UK Chapter, Internat. Assoc. of Energy Economists, 1978-; Vice-Pres., British Inst. of Energy Economics, 1980-. Mem. Court, Cranfield Inst. of Technol., 1981-. *Recreations:* travelling, reading. *Address:* 27 Gilkes Crescent, Dulwich Village, SE21. *T:* 01-693 1889.

CARTER, Douglas, CB 1969; Under-Secretary, Department of Trade and Industry, 1970-71; *b* 4 Dec. 1911; 3rd *s* of Albert and Mabel Carter, Bradford, Yorks; *m* 1935, Alice, *d* of Captain C. E. Le Mesurier, CB, RN; three *s* one *d. Educ:* Bradford Grammar Sch.; St John's Coll., Cambridge (Scholar). First Cl. Hons, Historical Tripos Part I and Economics Tripos Part II. Wrenbury Research Scholarship in Economics, Cambridge, 1933. Asst Principal, Board of Trade, 1934; Sec., Imperial Shipping Cttee, 1935-38; Princ. BoT, 1939; Asst Sec., BoT, 1943; Chm., Cttee of Experts in Enemy Property Custodianship, Inter-Allied Reparations Agency, Brussels, 1946; Controller, Import Licensing Dept, 1949; Distribution of Industry Div., BoT, 1954; Industries and Manufacturers Div., 1957; Commercial Relations and Exports Div., 1960; Under-Sec., 1963; Tariff Div., 1965. *Publications:* articles in Bridge Magazine. *Recreations:* reading, golf, bridge, travel. *Address:* 12 Garbrand Walk, Ewell Village, Epsom, Surrey. *T:* 01-394 1316. *Club:* Walton Heath Golf.

CARTER, Hon. Sir Douglas (Julian), KCMG 1977; High Commissioner for New Zealand in the United Kingdom, 1976-79; *b* 5 Aug. 1908; *s* of Walter Stephen Carter and Agnes Isobel; *m* Mavis Rose Miles. *Educ:* Palmerston North High Sch.; Waitaki Boys' High Sch. Formerly, Executive Member: Federated Farmers of NZ; Primary Production Council; Pig Production Council. MP (National Party) Raglan, 1957-75; Chm., Govt Transport Cttee, 1960-70; Under Sec., Agriculture, 1966-69; Minister of Agriculture, 1969-72. *Address:* 6 Edwin Street, St Andrews, Hamilton, New Zealand.

CARTER, Edward Robert Erskine; QC (Can) 1978; Counsel, Borden and Elliot, Barristers and Solicitors; *b* 20 Feb. 1923; *s* of Arthur Norwood Carter, QC, and Edith Ireland; *m* 1947, Verna Leman Andrews; two *s* two *d. Educ:* Univ. of New Brunswick; (after War) Osgoode Hall, Toronto, Ont; Univ. of New Brunswick; Univ. of New Brunswick Law Sch. (BCL 1947); Rhodes Scholar for New Brunswick, 1947; Oxford Univ. (BCL 1949). Served War

with Royal Canadian Artillery, 1942-44; on loan to 7th King's Own Scottish Borderers, First British Airborne Div., 1944; PoW, Sept. 1944-April 1945. Read Law with McMillan, Binch, Wilkinson, Berry & Wright, Toronto, Ont; called to Bar of New Brunswick, 1947; Ontario 1951; associated with A. N. Carter, QC in practise of law, St John, NB, 1949-53; Legal Officer, Abitibi Power & Paper Co. Ltd, Toronto, Ont, 1953-54; joined Fennell, McLean, Seed & Carter, 1954; Partner, 1955-58. President and Chief Executive Officer: Patino Mining Corp., later Patino NV, 1958-72; Hambro Canada Ltd, 1973-75. Chm. and Dir, Advocate Mines Ltd; Director: Bank of Montreal; Westroc Industries Ltd; Sun Alliance Insurance Co.; Global Natural Resources Ltd; Imperial General Properties Ltd; British Canadian Resources Ltd. Member, Law Soc. of Upper Canada. Hon. Consul of Norway, 1977-. *Address:* (office) c/o Borden and Elliot, 250 University Avenue, Toronto, Ontario M5H 3E9, Canada.

CARTER, Elliott (Cook), DrMus; composer; *b* New York City, 11 Dec. 1908; *m* 1939, Helen Frost-Jones; one *s. Educ:* Harvard Univ. (MA); Ecole Normale, Paris (DrMus). Professor of Greek and Maths, St John's Coll., Annapolis, 1940-42; Professor of Music: Columbia Univ., 1948-50; Yale Univ., 1960-61. *Compositions include:* First Symphony, 1942-43; Quartet for Four Saxophones, 1943; Holiday Overture, 1944; Ballet, The Minotaur, 1946-47; Woodwind Quintet, 1947; Sonata for Cello and Piano, 1948; First String Quartet, 1950-51; Sonata for Flute, Oboe, Cello and Harpsichord, 1952; Variations for Orchestra, 1953; Second String Quartet, 1960 (New York Critics' Circle Award; Pulitzer Prize; Unesco 1st Prize); Double Concerto for Harpsichord and Piano, 1961 (New York Critics' Circle Award); Piano Concerto, 1967; Concerto for Orchestra, 1970; Third String Quartet, 1971 (Pulitzer Prize); Duo for Violin and Piano, 1973-74; Brass Quintet, 1974; A Mirror on which to Dwell (song cycle), 1976; A Symphony of Three Orchestras, 1977; Night Fantasies (for piano), 1980. Member: Nat. Inst. of Arts and Letters, 1956 (Gold Medal for Music, 1971); Amer. Acad. of Arts and Sciences (Boston), 1962; Amer. Acad. of Arts and Letters, 1971; Akad. der Kunste, Berlin, 1971. Sibelius Medal (Harriet Cohen Foundation), London, 1961; Premio delle Muse, City of Florence, 1969; Handel Medallion, New York City, 1978; Mayor of Los Angeles declared Elliott Carter Day, 27 April 1979; Ernst Von Siemens Prize, Munich, 1981. Holds hon. degrees. *Publication:* The Writings of Elliott Carter, 1977. *Address:* Mead Street, Waccabuc, NY 10597, USA.

CARTER, Eric Bairstow, BSc(Eng); CEng, FIMechE, FRAeS, FIProdE; consultant; *b* 26 Aug. 1912; *s* of John Bolton Carter and Edith Carter (*née* Bairstow); *m* 1st, 1934, Lily (*d* 1981), *d* of John Charles and Ethel May Roome; one *d* ; 2nd, 1981, Olive Hicks Wright, *d* of William George and Olive Theresa Groombridge. *Educ:* Halifax Technical Coll. Staff appt, Halifax Tech. Coll., 1932; Supt and Lectr, Constantine Technical Coll., Middlesbrough, 1936; apptd to Air Min. (Engine Directorate), Sept. 1939; subseq. Air Min. appts to engine firms and at HQ. Asst Dir (Research and Devel't, Ramjets and Liquid Propellant Rockets), Dec. 1955; Dir (Engine Prod.), 1960; Dir (Engine R&D), 1963; Dir-Gen. (Engine R&D), Min. of Technology, later MoD (Aviation Supply), 1969-72; Consultant Engineer, and Special Advr to Man. Dir, Noel Penny Turbines Ltd, 1972-77. *Address:* 15 Colyford Road, Seaton, Devon EX12 2DP. *Clubs:* Civil Service; Halifax Cricket.

CARTER, Eric Stephen; Adviser, Farming and Wildlife Advisory Group, since 1981; *b* 23 June 1923; *s* of Albert Harry Carter, MBE and Doris Margaret (*née* Mann); *m* 1948, Audrey Windsor; one *s. Educ:* Grammar Sch., Lydney; Reading Univ. BSc (Agric) 1945. Techn. Officer, Gloucester AEC, 1945-46; Asst District Officer, Gloucester NAAS, 1946-49, Dist Off. 1949-57; Sen. Dist Off., Lindsey (Lincs) NAAS, 1957-63, County Agric. Off. 1963-69; Yorks and Lancs Region: Dep. Regional Dir, NAAS, 1969-71; Regional Agric. Off., ADAS, 1971-73; Regional Off. (ADAS), 1973-74; Chief Regional Off., MAFF, 1974-75; Dep. Dir-Gen., Agricl Develt and Advisory Service, 1975-81. FIBiol 1974. *Publications:* contrib. press, agric. and techn. jls. *Recreations:* gardening, reading, music, countryside. *Address:* 15 Farrs Lane, East Hyde, Luton, Beds LU2 9PY. *T:* Harpenden 60504. *Club:* Farmers'.

CARTER, Ernestine Marie, (Mrs John Waynflete Carter), OBE 1964; Associate Editor, The Sunday Times, 1968-72; *m* 1936, John Waynflete Carter, CBE (*d* 1975). *Educ:* Pape Sch., Savannah, Georgia; Wellesley Coll., Wellesley, Mass., USA (BA). Asst Curator of Architecture and Industrial Art, The Museum of Modern Art, New York, 1933-35, Curator, 1936-37; Specialist, Display and Exhibns Div., Min. of Information, 1939-41; US Office of War Information, London, 1941-44, in charge of exhibns and displays; Asst in Fashion Section, Britain Can Make It Exhibn, 1946; Fashion Editor, Harper's Bazaar, 1946-49; Contributor to The Observer, 1952-54; Women's Editor, The Sunday Times, 1955-68. Member: Council, Royal Coll. of Art, 1960-61; Nat. Council for Diploma in Art and Design, 1962-68; Selection Panel, Duke of Edinburgh's Award for Design, 1965-67; Council, RSA, 1976-78. Hon. Dr RCA, 1976. *Publications:* Grim Glory, 1941; Flash in the Pan, 1953 (re-issued 1963); With Tongue in Chic, 1974; 20th Century Fashion: a scrapbook from 1900 to today, 1975; The Changing World of Fashion, 1977; Magic Names of Fashion, 1980; contributor to: Vogue, Telegraph Magazine Cosmopolitan, Costume, etc. *Recreation:* sleep. *Address:* 113 Dovehouse Street, Chelsea, SW3. *T:* 01-352 4344.

CARTER, Francis Jackson, CMG 1954; CVO 1963; CBE 1946; Under-Secretary of State of Tasmania and Clerk of Executive Council, 1953-64; also permanent head of Premier's and Chief Secretary's Department; *b* Fremantle, W Australia, 9 Sept. 1899; *s* of late Francis Henry Carter, formerly of Bendigo, Victoria; *m* 1926, Margaret Flora, *d* of late William Thomas Walker, Launceston; two *s* one *d*. *Educ:* Hobart High Sch.; Univ. of Tasmania. Entered Tasmanian Public Service, 1916; transferred to Hydro-Electric Dept, 1925; Asst Secretary, Hydro-Electric Commn, 1934; Secretary to Premier, 1935-39; Dep. Under-Secretary of State, 1939-53; served War of 1939-45 as State Liaison Officer to Commonwealth Dept of Home Security; Official Secretary for Tasmania in London, 1949-50; State Director for Royal Visit, 1954, 1958, 1963, and Thai Royal Visit, 1962. Executive Member, State Economic Planning Authority, 1944-55; Chairman, Fire Brigades Commn of Tasmania, 1945-70. Grand Master GL of Tasmania, 1956-59. FASA; FCIS. JP 1939. *Recreations:* music, golf and lawn bowls. *Address:* 568 Churchill Avenue, Sandy Bay, Hobart, Tasmania 7005. *T:* Hobart 252 382. *Clubs:* Royal Automobile of Tasmania, Masonic (Hobart).

CARTER, Frank Ernest Lovell, CBE 1956 (OBE 1949); Director General of the Overseas Audit Service, 1963-71; *b* 6 Oct. 1909; *s* of Ernest and Florence Carter; *m* 1966, Gerda (*née* Gruen). *Educ:* Chigwell Sch.; Hertford Coll., Oxford. Served in Overseas Audit Service in: Nigeria, 1933-42; Sierra Leone, 1943; Palestine, 1944-45; Aden and Somaliland, 1946-47; Tanganyika, 1950-54; Hong Kong, 1955-59; Deputy Director in London, 1960-62. Part-time Adviser: FCO, 1972-76; ODM, 1977-81. *Address:* 8 The Leys, N2 0HE. *T:* 01-458 4684. *Club:* East India, Devonshire, Sports and Public Schools.

CARTER, Frederick Brian; QC 1980; a Recorder of the Crown Court, since 1978; *b* 11 May 1933; *s* of late Arthur and Minnie Carter; *m* 1960, Elizabeth Hughes, *d* of late W. B. Hughes and of Mrs B. M. Hughes; one *s* three *d* (and one *s* decd). *Educ:* Stretford Grammar Sch.; King's Coll., London (LLB). Called to Bar, Gray's Inn, 1955, Northern Circuit. Prosecuting Counsel for Inland Revenue, Northern Circuit, 1973-80. *Recreations:* tennis, golf. *Address:* 55 Ogden Road, Bramhall, Stockport, Cheshire SK7 1HL. *T:* 061-439 3637. *Clubs:* Big Four (Manchester); Chorlton-cum-Hardy Golf.

CARTER, Prof. Geoffrey William, MA; FIEE; FIEEE; Professor of Electrical Engineering, University of Leeds, 1946-74, now Emeritus; *b* 21 May 1909; *s* of late Frederick William Carter, FRS; *m* 1938, Freda Rose Lapwood; one *s* one *d*. *Educ:* Rugby Sch.; St John's Coll., Cambridge. MA 1937. Student Apprentice, British Thomson-Houston Co. Ltd, Rugby, 1932-35, Research Engineer, 1935-45; University Demonstrator in Engineering Science, Oxford, 1946. *Publications:* The Simple Calculation of Electrical Transients, 1944; The Electromagnetic Field in its Engineering Aspects, 1954 (rev. edn 1967); (with A. Richardson) Techniques of Circuit Analysis, 1972; papers in Proc. IEE and elsewhere. *Recreations:* study of medals, painting, winemaking. *Address:* 14 Church Farm Garth, Leeds LS17 8HD. *T:* Leeds 668399.
See also Sir C. F. Carter.

CARTER, His Eminence Cardinal G(erald) Emmett; see Toronto, Archbishop of, (RC).

CARTER, Godfrey James; Parliamentary Counsel, 1972-79; *b* 1 June 1919; *s* of Captain James Shuckburgh Carter, Grenadier Guards (killed in action, 1918), and Diana Violet Gladys Carter (*née* Cavendish); *m* 1946, Cynthia, *e d* of Eric Strickland Mason; three *s*. *Educ:* Eton (KS); Magdalene Coll., Cambridge. BA 1945, LLB 1946. War Service (Rifle Bde), Middle East, 1940-43 (twice wounded). Called to Bar, Inner Temple, 1946; Asst Parly Counsel, 1949-56; commercial dept, Bristol Aeroplane Co. Ltd, and Bristol Siddeley Engines Ltd, 1956-64; re-joined Parly Counsel Office, 1964; Dep. Counsel, 1970. *Address:* Old Bournstream House, Wotton-under-Edge, Glos. *T:* Wotton-under-Edge 3246. *Club:* Travellers'.

CARTER, James Earl, Jr; President of the United States of America, 1977-81; *b* Archery, Georgia, USA, 1 Oct. 1924; *s* of James Earl Carter and Lillian (*née* Gordy); *m* 1946, Rosalynn Smith; three *s* one *d*. *Educ:* Plains High Sch.; Georgia Southwestern Coll.; Georgia Inst. of Technology; US Naval Acad. (BS); Union Coll., Schenectady, NY (post grad.). Served in US Navy submarines and battleships, then 1946-53; Ensign (commissioned, 1947); Lieut 1950; retd from US Navy, 1953. Became farmer and warehouseman, 1953, farming peanuts at Plains, Georgia. Member: Sumter Co. (Ga) School Bd, 1955-62 (Chm. 1960-62); Americus and Sumter Co. Hosp. Authority, 1956-70; Sumter Co. (Ga) Library Bd, 1961; President: Plains Develt Corp., 1963; Georgia Planning Assoc., 1968; Chm., W Central Georgia Area Planning and Develt Commn, 1964; Dir, Georgia Crop Improvement Assoc., 1957-63 (Pres., 1961). State Chm., March of Dimes, 1968-70; Dist Governor, Lions Club, 1968-69. State Senator (Democrat), Georgia, 1963-67; Governor of Georgia, 1971-75. Chm., Congressional Campaign Cttee, Democratic Nat. Cttee, 1974; Democratic Candidate for the Presidency of the USA, 1976. Baptist. Hon. degrees from Morehouse Coll., 1972, Morris Brown Coll., 1972, Notre Dame, 1977, Georgia Inst. Tech., 1979, Emory, 1979, Weizmann Inst., 1980, Kwansei Gakuim Univ., Japan, 1981. *Publications:* Why Not the Best?, 1975; A Government as Good as its People, 1977; Keeping Faith, 1982. *Address:* (home) 1 Woodland Drive, Plains, Georgia 31780, USA; (office) 75 Spring Street, SW, Atlanta, Ga 30303, USA.

CARTER, Maj.-Gen. James Norman, CB 1958; CBE 1955 (OBE 1946). *Educ:* Charterhouse; RMC Sandhurst. Commissioned The Dorset Regt, 1926; Captain, The Royal Warwickshire Regt, 1936; Lieut-Colonel, 1948; Colonel,

1950; Brigadier, 1954; Maj.-General, 1957. Asst Chief of Staff, Organisation and Training Div., SHAPE, 1955-57; Commander British Army Staff, British Joint Services Mission, Washington, 1958-60; Military Attaché, Washington, Jan.-July 1960; General Secretary, The Officers' Assoc., 1961-63.

CARTER, Jane; *see* Carter, D. E. F.

CARTER, Sir John, Kt 1966; QC (Guyana) 1962; Ambassador of Guyana to China, since 1976, to Democratic People's Republic of Korea, since 1976, and to Japan, since 1979; *b* 27 Jan. 1919; *s* of Kemp R. Carter; *m* 1959, Sara Lou (formerly Harris); two *s*. *Educ:* University of London and Middle Temple, England. Called to English Bar, 1942; admitted to Guyana (late British Guiana) Bar, 1945; Member of Legislature of Guyana, 1948-53 and 1961-64; Pro-Chancellor, Univ. of Guyana, 1962-66; Ambassador of Guyana to US, 1966-70; High Comr for Guyana in UK, 1970-76. *Recreations:* cricket, swimming. *Address:* Embassy of Guyana, No 1 Hsui Hsueh Tung Chieh, Chien Kuo Men Wai, China. *Clubs:* MCC; Georgetown (Guyana).

CARTER, John Somers; *b* 26 Feb. 1901; *s* of R. Carter. *Educ:* Edinburgh Academy; Bedford Sch.; Balliol Coll., Oxford, 1st Class Hon. Mods., 3rd Class Lit. Hum. Asst Master, Cheltenham Coll., 1924-32; Headmaster: St John's Sch., Leatherhead, 1933-47; Blundell's Sch., 1948-59. *Address:* Danny, Hurstpierpoint, Sussex BN6 9BB.

CARTER, Air Cdre North, CB 1948; DFC 1935; RAF retired; *b* 26 Nov. 1902; *s* of Lieut-Colonel G. L. Carter, CIE, Indian Army; *m* 1931, Kathleen Graham Machattie; one *s* one *d*. *Educ:* Wellington Coll.; RAF Coll., Cranwell. Commissioned from RAF Coll., 1922; No 5 Sqdn, India, 1923-27; RAF Depot, Iraq, 1929-32; No 56 Sqdn., North Weald, 1932-34; No 60 Sqdn., India, 1934 and 1935; RAF Staff Coll., 1936; Sqdn. Ldr, 1936; Staff Appointments, 1937-40; Wing Comdr, 1938; Commanded RAF Stations Dalcross, South Cerney, Pocklington and Castel Benito, 1941-45; Group Captain, 1946; Air Commodore, 1948; AOC Halton, 1949-50; SASO 205 Group Middle East Air Force 15, 1951-53; Provost Marshal and Chief of Air Force Police, 1953-54, retired 1954; Temp. Administrative Officer, Northern Region, Nigeria, 1955-63. *Address:* Gould's Bay, Hawkesbury River, PMB Brooklyn, NSW 2253, Australia.

CARTER, Peers Lee, CMG 1965; HM Diplomatic Service, retired; free-lance conference interpreter; *b* 5 Dec. 1916; *s* of Peers Owen Carter; *m* 1940, Joan Eleanor Lovegrove; one *s*. *Educ:* Radley; Christ Church, Oxford. Entered HM Foreign Service, 1939. Joined the Army in 1940; served in Africa and Europe. HM Embassy, Baghdad, 1945; First Secretary, Commissioner-General's Office, Singapore, 1951; Counsellor HM Embassy, Washington, 1958; (Temp. duty) UK Delegation to UN, New York, 1961; Head of UK Permanent Mission, Geneva, 1961; Inspector of Foreign Service Establishments, 1963-66; Chief Inspector of HM Diplomatic Service, 1966-68; Ambassador to Afghanistan, 1968-72; Ministerial Interpreter and Asst Under-Sec. of State, FCO, 1973-76. Mem., Internat. Assoc. of Conference Interpreters. Sardar-e A'ala, Afghanistan, 1971. *Recreations:* mountain walking, skiing, photography. *Address:* Dean Land Shaw, by Jobes, Balcombe, Sussex RH17 6HZ. *Clubs:* Special Forces, Travellers'.

CARTER, Peter Anthony, CMG 1970; HM Diplomatic Service, retired; *b* 16 Jan. 1914; *s* of Thomas Birchall Carter; *m* 1946, Mary Hutchison Heard; one *s* one *d*. *Educ:* Charterhouse; Sidney Sussex Coll., Cambridge. Metropolitan Police Office, 1936-39; Royal Tank Regt (Major), 1939-44; Colonial Office, 1947-60; Nyasaland, 1951-53; CRO, 1960-61; First Secretary, Dar-es-Salaam, 1961-64; Counsellor, Dublin, 1965-68; Head of British High Commission Residual Staff, Rhodesia, 1968-69; British High Commissioner, Mauritius, 1970-73; Senior Clerk, H of C, 1974-76. *Recreations:* golf, bridge, music. *Address:* Forth House, Beech Drive, Kingswood, Surrey. *Club:* Kingswood Golf.

CARTER, Philip David, CBE 1982; Managing Director, Littlewoods Organisation, since 1976; *b* 8 May 1927; *s* of Percival Carter and Isobell (*née* Stirrup); *m* 1946, Harriet Rita (*née* Evans); one *s* two *d*. *Educ:* Waterloo Grammar Sch., Liverpool. Professional career in Littlewoods Organisation. Chairman: Everton Football Club, 1978-; Mail Order Traders Assoc. of GB, 1979-; Vice-Chm., Empire Theatre Trust, Liverpool, 1980-; Chm., Man Made Fibres Sector Wkg Party, 1980-; Member: Jt Textile Cttee, NEDO, 1979-; Distributive Trades EDC, 1980-; Merseyside Develt Corp., 1981-. Vice-Pres., European Mail Order Traders Assoc., 1980-. *Recreations:* football, squash, music, theatre. *Address:* Oak Cottage, Noctorum Road, Noctorum, Wirral, Merseyside L43 9UQ. *T:* 051-652 4053.

CARTER, Raymond John; Executive, Marathon Oil Co., since 1980; *b* 17 Sept. 1935; *s* of John Carter; *m* 1959, Jeanette Hills; one *s* two *d*. *Educ:* Mortlake Co. Secondary Sch.; Reading Technical Coll.; Staffordshire Coll. of Technology. National Service, Army, 1953-55. Sperry Gyroscope Co.: Technical Asst, Research and Development Computer Studies, 1956-65. Electrical Engineer, Central Electricity Generating Bd, 1965-70. Mem., CEGB Management, 1979-80. Mem., Gen. Adv. Council, BBC, 1974-76. Mem. Easthampstead RDC, 1963.68. Contested: Wokingham, Gen. Elec., 1966; Warwick and Leamington, Bye-elec., March 1968; MP (Lab) Birmingham, Northfield, 1970-79; Parly Under-Sec. of State, Northern Ireland Office, 1976-79. Member: Public Accounts Cttee, 1973-74; Parly Science and Technology Cttee, 1974-76. Delegate: Council of Europe,

1974-76; WEU, 1974-76. *Recreations:* running, reading, book collecting. *Address:* 1 Lynwood Chase, Warfield Road, Bracknell, Berkshire. *T:* Bracknell 20237.

CARTER, Air Commodore Robert Alfred Copsey, CB 1956; DSO 1942; DFC 1943; Royal Air Force, retired; *b* 15 Sept. 1910; *s* of S. H. Carter and S. Copsey; *m* 1947, Sally Ann Peters, Va, USA; two *s* one *d*. *Educ:* Portsmouth Grammar Sch.; RAF Coll., Cranwell. Cranwell Cadet, 1930-32; commissioned in RAF, 1932; served in India, 1933-36; grad. RAF School of Aeronautical Engineering, 1938; served in Bomber Command, 1940-45; commanded 103 and 150 Sqdns, RAF, Grimsby; grad. RAF Staff Coll., 1945; attended US Armed Forces Staff Coll., Norfolk, Va, USA, 1947; attached to RNZAF, 1950-53; comd. RAF Station, Upwood, 1953-55; SASO, RAF Transport Command, 1956-58; Director of Personal Services, Air Ministry, 1958-61; AO i/c Admin, HQ, RAF Germany, 1961-64; retired 1964. MRAeS 1960; CEng, 1966. *Address:* The Old Cottage, Castle Lane, Whaddon, Salisbury, Wilts. *Club:* Royal Air Force.

CARTER, Robert William Bernard, CMG 1964; HM Diplomatic Service, retired; *b* 1913; 3rd *s* of late William Joseph Carter and late Lucy (*née* How); *m* 1945, Joan Violet, *o d* of Theodore and Violet Magnus; one *s* two *d* (and one *d* decd). *Educ:* St Bees Sch., Cumberland; Trinity Coll., Oxford (Scholar). Asst Master, Glenalmond, Perthshire, 1936. Served with the Royal Navy, 1940-46; Lieut, RNVR. Administrative Assistant, Newcastle upon Tyne Education Cttee, 1946; Principal, Board of Trade, 1949; Trade Commissioner: Calcutta, 1952; Delhi, 1955; Accra, 1956; Principal Trade Commissioner, Colombo (Assistant Secretary), 1959; Senior British Trade Commissioner in Pakistan, 1961; Minister (Commercial), Pakistan, and Dep. High Comr, Karachi, 1967-68; Dep. High Comr, 1969-73 and Consul-Gen., 1973, Melbourne. *Recreations:* reading, travelling, collecting beer-mugs. *Address:* The Old Parsonage, Heywood, Westbury, Wilts. *T:* Westbury 822194. *Club:* Oriental.

CARTER, Roland; Regional Organiser, North East England, National Society for Cancer Relief, since 1980; *b* 29 Aug. 1924; *s* of Ralph Carter; *m* 1950, Elisabeth Mary Green; one *s* two *d*. *Educ:* Cockburn High Sch., Leeds; Leeds Univ. Served War of 1939-45: Queen's Royal Regt, 1944; 6th Gurkha Rifles, 1945; Frontier Corps (South Waziristan and Gilgit Scouts), 1946. Seconded to Indian Political Service, as Asst Political Agent, Chilas, Gilgit Agency, 1946-47; Lectr, Zurich Univ. and Finnish Sch. of Economics, 1950-53. Joined Foreign Service, 1953: FO, 1953-54; Third Sec., Moscow, 1955; Germany, 1956-58; Second Sec., Helsinki, 1959 (First Sec., 1962); FO, 1962-67; Kuala Lumpur, 1967-69; Ambassador to People's Republic of Mongolia, 1969-71; seconded to Cabinet Office, 1971-74; Counsellor: Pretoria, 1974-77; FCO, 1977-80, retired. *Publication:* Näin Puhutaan Englantia (in Finnish; with Erik Erämetsä), 1952. *Recreations:* music, linguistics, Indian studies. *Address:* Barclays Bank, Malton, N Yorks.

CARTER, (Ronald) David, CBE 1980; RDI 1975; Chairman, DCA Design Consultants Ltd; Member of the Design Council, since 1972, Deputy Chairman since 1975; *b* 30 Dec. 1927; *s* of H. Miles Carter and Margaret Carter; *m* 1953, Theo (Marjorie Elizabeth), *d* of Rev. L. T. Towers; two *s* two *d*. *Educ:* Wyggeston Sch., Leicester; Central Sch. of Art and Design, London. Served RN, 1946-48. Appts in industry, 1951-60; Principal, David Carter Associates, 1960-75. Visiting Lectr, Birmingham Coll. of Industrial Design, 1960-65. Examnr, RCA, 1976-79. Pres., Soc. of Industrial Artists and Designers, 1974-75; Mem., Art and Design Cttee, CNAA, 1975-77; Chm., Art and Design Cttee, TEC, 1978; Mem., Nat. Adv. Body, Higher Educn Art and Design Working Party, 1982. Chm., Design Council Report on Industrial Design Educn in UK, 1977. Design Awards, 1961 and 1969; Duke of Edinburgh Prize for Elegant Design, 1967. FSIA 1967; FRSA 1975. *Recreations:* making coarse soup, galloping, dry stone walling. *Address:* 43 Beauchamp Avenue, Leamington Spa, Warwickshire. *T:* Leamington Spa 24864. *Club:* Reform.

CARTER, Ronald Louis, DesRCA; RDI 1971; FSIAD 1961; private consultancy design practice, since 1974; *b* 3 June 1926; *s* of Harry Victor Carter and Ruth Allensen; *m* 1953, Marilyn Adel Clement; three *d*. *Educ:* Birmingham Central College of Art: studied Industrial and Interior Design (NDD; Louisa Anne Ryland Schol. for Silver Design), 1946-49; Royal College of Art: studied Furniture Design (1st Cl. Dip.; Silver Medal for work of special distinction; Travelling Schol. to USA), 1949-52; DesRCA; Fellow, RCA, 1966; Hon. Fellow, 1974. Staff Designer with Corning Glass, 5th Avenue, NY City, 1952-53; freelance design practice, Birmingham and London, 1954; Tutor, School of Furniture, RCA, 1956-74; Partner: Design Partners, 1960-68; Carter Freeman Associates, 1968-74. *Recreation:* fishing. *Address:* 35 Great Queen Street, WC2B 5AA. *T:* 01-242 2291.

CARTER, His Honour Sir Walker (Kelly), Kt 1965; QC 1951; an Official Referee of the Supreme Court of Judicature, 1954-71; Chairman, Criminal Injuries Compensation Board, 1964-75; *b* 7 July 1899; *s* of late Walter Carter, CBE, and Annie Elizabeth Carter; *m* 1925, Phyllis Irene, *d* of late Edward Ernest Clarke, Bank Bldgs, Simla, India; one *d*. *Educ:* Repton Sch.; Sidney Sussex Coll., Cambridge, RFA, 1918-19. Called to Bar, Inner Temple, 1924; Bencher, 1965. RA 1939-43. Chairman, Quarter Sessions for Parts of Lindsey, 1945-67, and for Parts of Kesteven, 1961-67. *Address:* 65 Bedford Gardens, W8. *T:* 01-727 9862. *Club:* Reform.
See also Hon. Sir John Vinelott.

CARTER, Air Vice-Marshal Wilfred, CB 1963; DFC 1943; AOA, HQ Bomber Command, 1965-67; *b* 5 Nov. 1912; *s* of late Samuel Carter; *m* 1950, Margaret Enid Bray; one *s* one *d*. *Educ:* Witney Grammar Sch. RAF, 1929. Served War of 1939-45 with Bomber Command in UK and Middle East. Graduate, Middle East Centre for Arab Studies, 1945-46. Air Adviser to Lebanon, 1950-53; with Cabinet Secretariat, 1954-55; OC, RAF, Ternhill, 1956-58; Sen. RAF Dir, and later Commandant, Jt Services Staff Coll.; Asst Chief of Staff, Cento, 1960-63; Asst Commandant, RAF Staff Coll., 1963-65. Gordon Shephard Memorial Prize (for Strategic Studies), 1955, 1956, 1957, 1961, 1965, 1967. Officer, Order of Cedar of Lebanon, 1953. *Recreation:* ski-ing. *Address:* Blue Range, Macedon, Vic. 3440, Australia.

CARTER, William Nicholas, (Will Carter); Senior Partner, Rampant Lions Press, since 1967; *b* 24 Sept. 1912; *s* of Thomas Buchanan Carter and Margaret Theresa Stone; *m* 1939, Barbara Ruth Digby; one *s* three *d*. *Educ:* Sunningdale Sch.; Radley. Served War, RN, 1941-46: S Atlantic, Coastal Forces Eastern Med.; commnd 1943. Gen. career in printing, advertising, typography and inscriptional letter-carving; founded Rampant Lions Press, 1949. Artist-in-Residence, Dartmouth Coll., NH, USA, 1969. Member: Royal Mint Adv. Cttee, 1971-; Arch. Adv. Panel, Westminster Abbey, 1979-. Hon. Fellow, Magdalene Coll., Cambridge, 1977. Frederick W. Goudy Award, Rochester Inst. of Technol., New York State, 1975; Silver Jubilee Medal, 1977. *Publication:* (with Wilfrid Blunt) Italic Handwriting, 1954. *Address:* 12 Chesterton Road, Cambridge. *T:* Cambridge 357553. *Club:* Double Crown (Pres., 1961).

CARTER, Sir William (Oscar), Kt 1972; Consultant: Hill and Perks, Solicitors, Norwich; Bird Hill Wieringa, Amsterdam; *b* 12 Jan. 1905; *s* of late Oscar Carter and Alice Carter; *m* 1934, Winifred Thompson. *Educ:* Swaffham Grammar Sch.; City of Norwich Sch. Admitted Solicitor of Supreme Court of Judicature, 1931. Served War, 1940-45, RAF (Wing Comdr), UK and Middle East. Mem. Council, The Law Society, 1954-75, Vice-Pres. 1970, Pres. 1971-72; President: East Anglian Law Soc., 1952-80; Norfolk and Norwich Incorporated Law Soc., 1959; Internat. Legal Aid Assoc., 1974-80; Life Mem. Council, Internat. Bar Assoc. (first Vice-Pres., 1976-78). Member: County Court Rules Cttee, 1956-60; Supreme Court Rules Cttee, 1960-75; Criminal Injuries Compensation Board (Dep. Chm.). Former Chm., Mental Health Review Tribunals for E Anglian and NE Thames RHA Areas. Liveryman, Worshipful Co. of Glaziers; Hon. Mem., The Fellows of American Bar Foundn. *Recreations:* swimming, walking, foreign travel. *Address:* 83 Newmarket Road, Norwich NR2 2HP. *T:* Norwich 53772. *Clubs:* Army and Navy; New (Edinburgh); Norfolk (Norwich).

CARTER, William Stovold, CMG 1970; CVO 1956; retired; Secretary, Council on Tribunals, 1970-76; *b* 10 Oct. 1915, *s* of late R. S. Carter, Bournemouth, Hants; *m* 1944, Barbara Alice Kathleen Dines; two *s* one *d*. *Educ:* Bec; Christ's Coll., Cambridge. Entered Colonial Administrative Service (Nigeria), 1939; retd as Administrative Officer, Class I (Resident), 1957. Entered Colonial Office, 1959; Asst Sec., 1965; joined Commonwealth Office, 1966; joined Foreign and Commonwealth Office, 1968; Head of Hong Kong Dept, 1965-70. *Recreation:* golf. *Address:* Broad Oak Farm, Chiddingly, near Lewes, East Sussex. *T:* Chiddingly 267.

CARTER-JONES, Lewis; MP (Lab) Eccles since 1964; industrial training adviser; *b* Gilfach Goch, S Wales, 17 Nov. 1920; *s* of Tom Jones, Kenfig Hill, Bridgend, Glam.; *m* 1945, Patricia Hylda, *d* of late Alfred Bastiman, Scarborough, Yorks; two *d*. *Educ:* Bridgend County Sch.; University Coll. of Wales, Aberystwyth; BA (Chm. Student Finance Cttee). Served War of 1939-45 (Flight Sergeant Navigator, RAF). Head of Business Studies Dept, Yale Grammar-Technical Sch., Wrexham, Denbighshire. Contested (Lab) Chester, by-election, 1956, and general election, 1959. Chairman: Anglo-Columbian Gp; Cttee for Research for Apparatus for Disabled; Parly Labour Party Disablement Gp; Possum Research Foundation; Vice-Chairman: Parly Labour Party Aviation Gp; Disabled Income Gp (DIG); Secretary: Indo-British Parly Gp; All-Party BLESMA Gp. Special interest, application of technology for aged and disabled; Mem., Brit. Assoc. for the Retarded; Chm., British Cttee, Rehabilitation International. Parly Adviser to RNIB; Hon Adviser: British Assoc. of Occupational Therapists; Soc. of Physiotherapists. *Address:* House of Commons, SW1; Cader Idris, 5 Cefn Road, Rhosnessney, Wrexham, N Wales.

CARTER-RUCK, Peter Frederick; Senior Partner, Peter Carter-Ruck and Partners, Solicitors, since 1981 (Senior Partner, Oswald Hickson, Collier & Co., 1945-81); *b* 26 Feb. 1914; *s* of Frederick Henry Carter-Ruck and Nell Mabel Carter-Ruck; *m* 1940, Pamela Ann (*née* Maxwell); one *d* (one *s* decd). *Educ:* St Edward's, Oxford; Law Society; Solicitor of the Supreme Court (Hons). Admitted Solicitor, 1937; served RA, 1939-44, Captain Instr in gunnery. Specialist Member, Council of Law Soc., 1971-; Chm. Law Soc. Law Reform Cttee, 1980-; past Pres., City of Westminster Law Soc. Governor, St Edward's Sch., Oxford, 1950-78; past Chm. and Founder Governor, Shiplake Coll., Henley; Mem. Livery, City of London Solicitors' Co., 1949-; Underwriting Mem. of Lloyd's. *Publications:* Libel and Slander, 1953, 2nd edn 1972; (with Ian Mackrill) The Cyclist and the Law, 1953; (with Edmund Skone James) Copyright: modern law and practice, 1965. *Address:* Essex House, Essex Street, WC2R 3AH. *T:* 01-379 3456; Latchmore Cottage, Great Hallingbury, Bishop's Stortford, Herts. *T:* Bishop' Stortford 54357; Eilagadale, N Ardnamurchan, Argyll. *T:* Kilchoan 267. *Clubs:* Carlton, Garrick, Press; Royal Yacht Squadron, Lloyd's Yacht, Law Society Yacht (past Commodore), Royal Ocean Racing, Ocean Cruising (past Commodore).

CARTIER, Rudolph; Drama Producer, Television, since 1953; also Producer Television Operas, since 1956; *b* Vienna, Austria, 17 April 1908; *s* of Joseph Cartier; *m* 1949, Margaret Pepper; two *d. Educ:* Vienna Academy of Music and Dramatic Art (Max Reinhardt's Master-class). Film director and Scenario writer in pre-war Berlin; came to Britain, 1935; joined BBC Television. Productions include: Arrow to the Heart, Dybbuk, Portrait of Peter Perowne, 1952; It is Midnight, Doctor Schweitzer, L'Aiglon, The Quatermass Experiment, Wuthering Heights, 1953; Such Men are Dangerous, That Lady, Captain Banner, Nineteen-Eightyfour, 1954; Moment of Truth, The Creature, Vale of Shadows, Quatermass II, The Devil's General, 1955; The White Falcon, The Mayerling Affair, The Public Prosecutor, The Fugitive, The Cold Light, The Saint of Bleecker Street, Dark Victory, Clive of India, The Queen and the Rebels, 1956; Salome, Ordeal by Fire, Counsellor-at-Law, 1957; Captain of Koepenick, The Winslow Boy, A Tale of Two Cities, Midsummer Night's Dream, 1958; Quatermass and the Pit, Philadelphia Story, Mother Courage and her Children, (Verdi's) Othello, 1959; The White Guard, Glorious Morning, Tobias and the Angel (Opera), 1960; Rashomon, Adventure Story, Anna Karenina, Cross of Iron, 1961; Doctor Korczuk and the Children, Sword of Vengeance, Carmen, 1962; Anna Christie, Night Express, Stalingrad, 1963; Lady of the Camelias, The Midnight Men, The July Plot, 1964; Wings of the Dove, Ironhand, The Joel Brand Story, 1965; Gordon of Khartoum, Lee Oswald, Assassin, 1966; Firebrand, The Burning Bush, 1967; The Fanatics, Triumph of Death, The Naked Sun, The Rebel, 1968; Conversation at Night, An Ideal Husband, 1969; Rembrandt, The Bear (Opera), The Year of the Crow, 1970; The Proposal, 1971; Lady Windermere's Fan, 1972; The Deep Blue Sea, 1973; Fall of Eagles (episodes Dress Rehearsal, End Game), 1974; Loyalties, 1976; Gaslight, 1977. Prod. Film, Corridor of Mirrors. Directed Film, Passionate Summer. Guild of Television Producers and Directors "Oscar" as best drama producer of 1957. *Recreations:* motoring, serious music, going to films or watching television, stamp-collecting. *Address:* 26 Lowther Road, Barnes, SW13.

CARTIER-BRESSON, Henri; photographer; *b* France, 22 Aug. 1908. Studied painting with André Lhote, 1927-28. Asst Dir to Jean Renoir, 1936-39; Co-founder, Magnum Photos, 1947. Photographs exhibited: Mexico; Japan; Mus. of Modern Art, NY, 1947, 1968; Villa Medicis, Rome; Louvre, 1955, 1967, Grand Palais, 1970, Paris; V&A, 1969; Manege, Moscow, 1972; Edinburgh Festival, 1978; Hayward Gall., London, 1978; drawings exhibited: Carlton Gall., NY, 1975; Bischofberger Gall., Zürich, 1976; Forcalquier Gall., France, 1976; Mus. of Modern Art, Paris, 1981; Mus. of Modern Art, Mexico, 1982; Collection of 390 photographs at DeMenil Foundn, Houston, USA, V&A, Univ. of Fine Arts, Osaka, Japan, Bibliothèque Nationale, Paris. Documentary films: on hosps, Spanish Republic, 1937; (with J. Lemare) Le Retour, 1945; (with J. Boffety) Impressions of California, 1969; (with W. Dombrow) Southern Exposures, 1970. Mem., Amer. Acad. of Arts and Scis, 1974. Hon. DLitt Oxon, 1975. Awards: US Camera, 1948; Overseas Press Club of America, 1949; Amer. Soc. of Magazine Photography, 1953; Photography Soc. of America, 1958; Overseas Press Club, 1954 (for Russia), 1960 (for China), 1964 (for Cuba); German Photographic Soc. *Publications:* (ed) Images à la Sauvette (The Decisive Moment), 1952; Verve, 1952; The Europeans; Moscow, 1955; From One China to the Other, 1956; Photographs by Cartier-Bresson; Flagrants Délits (The World of Henri Cartier-Bresson, 1968); (with F. Nourrissier) Vive la France, 1970; Cartier-Bresson's France, 1971; (jtly) L'Homme et la Machine, 1972 (Man and Machine, 1969) for IBM; Faces of Asia, 1972; A Propos de l'URSS, 1973 (About Russia, 1974); History of Photography: Henri Cartier-Bresson, 1976; Henri Cartier-Bresson, Photographe, 1979. *Address:* c/o Magnum Photos, 2 rue Christine, 75006 Paris, France; c/o Helen Wright, 135 East 74th Street, New York, NY 10021, USA; c/o John Hillelson, 145 Fleet Street, EC4A 2BU.

CARTLAND, Barbara (Hamilton); authoress and playwright; *d* of late Major Bertram Cartland, Worcestershire Regiment; *m* 1st, 1927, Alexander George McCorquodale (whom she divorced, 1933; he *d* 1964), of Cound Hall, Cressage, Salop; one *d*; 2nd, 1936, Hugh (*d* 1963), 2nd *s* of late Harold McCorquodale, Forest Hall, Ongar, Essex; two *s.* Published first novel at the age of twenty-one, which ran into five editions; designed and organised many pageants in aid of charity, including Britain and her Industries at British Legion Ball, Albert Hall, 1930; carried the first aeroplane-towed glider-mail in her glider, the Barbara Cartland, from Manston Aerodrome to Reading, June 1931; 2 lecture tours in Canada, 1940; Hon. Junior Commander, ATS and Lady Welfare Officer and Librarian to all Services in Bedfordshire, 1941-49; Certificate of Merit, Eastern Command 1946; County Cadet Officer for St John Ambulance Brigade in Beds, 1943-47, County Vice-Pres. Cadets, Beds, 1948-50; organised and produced the St John Ambulance Bde Exhibn, 1945-50; Chm St John Ambulance Bde Exhibn Cttee, 1944-51; County Vice-Pres.: Nursing Cadets, Herts, 1951; Nursing Div., Herts, 1966; CC Herts (Hatfield Div.), 1955-64; Chm., St John Council, Herts, 1972-; Dep. Pres., St John Amb. Bde, Herts, 1978-; Pres. Herts Br. of Royal Coll. of Midwives, 1957-. Founder, Barbara Cartland-Onslow Romany Gypsy Fund (with Earl of Onslow and Earl of Birkenhead) to Provide sites for Romany Gypsies, 1961 (first Romany Gypsy Camp at Hatfield); Dep. Pres., National Association of Health, 1965; Pres., 1966-. DStJ 1972 (Mem. Chapter Gen.). Bestselling author in the world (Guinness Book of Records). *Publications: novels:* Jigsaw, 1923; Sawdust; If the Tree is Saved; For What?; Sweet Punishment; A Virgin in Mayfair; Just off Piccadilly; Not Love Alone; A Beggar Wished; Passionate Attainment; First Class, Lady?; Dangerous Experiment; Desperate Defiance; The Forgotten City; Saga at Forty; But Never Free; Bitter Winds; Broken Barriers; The Gods Forget; The Black Panther; Stolen Halo; Now Rough-Now Smooth; Open Wings; The Leaping Flame; Yet She Follows; Escape from Passion; The Dark Stream; After the Night; Armour against Love; Out of Reach; The Hidden Heart; Against the Stream; Again this Rapture; The Dream Within; If We Will; No Heart is Free; Sleeping Swords; Love is Mine; The Passionate Pilgrim; Blue Heather; Wings on My Heart; The Kiss of Paris; Love Forbidden; Lights of Love; The Thief of Love; The Sweet Enchantress; The Kiss of Silk; The Price is Love; The Runaway Heart; A Light to the Heart; Love is Dangerous; Danger by the Nile; Love on the Run; A Hazard of Hearts; A Duel of Hearts; A Knave of Hearts; The Enchanted Moment; The Little Pretender; A Ghost in Monte Carlo; Love is an Eagle; Love is the Enemy; Cupid Rides Pillion; Love Me For Ever; Elizabethan Lover; Desire of the Heart; The Enchanted Waltz; The Kiss of the Devil; The Captive Heart; The Coin of Love; Stars in My Heart; Sweet Adventure; The Golden Gondola; Love in Hiding; The Smuggled Heart; Love under Fire; The Messenger of Love; The Wings of Love; The Hidden Evil; The Fire of Love; The Unpredictable Bride; Love Holds the Cards; A Virgin in Paris; Love to the Rescue; Love is Contraband; The Enchanting Evil; The Unknown Heart; The Secret Fear; The Reluctant Bride; The Pretty Horse-Breakers; The Audacious Adventures; Halo for the Devil; The Irresistible Buck; Lost Enchantment; The Odious Duke; The Wicked Marquis; The Complacent Wife; The Little Adventure; The Daring Deception; No Darkness for Love; Lessons in Love; The Ruthless Rake; Journey to Paradise; The Dangerous Dandy; The Bored Bridegroom; The Penniless Peer; The Cruel Count; The Castle of Fear; The Glittering Lights; Fire on the Snow; The Elusive Earl; Moon over Eden; The Golden Illusion; No Time for Love; The Husband Hunters; The Slaves of Love; Passions in the Sand; An Angel in Hell; The Wild Cry of Love; The Blue-Eyed Witch; The Incredible Honeymoon; A Dream from the Night; Conquered by Love; Never Laugh at Love; The Secret of the Glen; The Dream and the Glory; The Proud Princess; Hungry for Love; The Heart Triumphant; The Disgraceful Duke; The Taming of Lady Lorinda; Vote for Love; The Mysterious Maid-Servant; The Magic of Love; Kiss the Moonlight; Love Locked In; The Marquis who Hated Women; Rhapsody of Love; Look Listen and Love; Duel with Destiny; The Wild Unwilling Wife; Punishment of a Vixen; The Curse of the Clan; The Outrageous Lady; A Touch of Love; The Love Pirate; The Dragon and the Pearl; The Temptation of Torilla; The Passion and the Flower; Love, Lords and Ladybirds; Love and the Loathsome Leopard; The Naked Battle; The Hell-Cat and the King; No Escape From Love; A Sign of Love; The Castle Made for Love; The Saint and the Sinner; A Fugitive from Love; Love Leaves at Midnight; The Problems of Love; The Twists and Turns of Love; Magic or Mirage; The Ghost who Fell in Love; The Chieftain without a Heart; Lord Ravenscar's Revenge; A Runaway Star; A Princess in Distress; The Judgement of Love; Lovers in Paradise; The Race for Love; Flowers for the God of Love; The Irresistible Force; The Duke and the Preacher's Daughter; The Drums of Love; Alone in Paris; The Prince and the Pekinese; A Serpent of Satan, 1978; Love in the Clouds, 1978; The Treasure is Love, 1978; Imperial Splendour, 1978; Light of the Moon, 1978; The Prisoner of Love, 1978; Love in the Dark, 1978; The Duchess Disappeared, 1978; Love Climbs In, 1978; A Nightingale Sang, 1978; Terror in the Sun, 1978; Who can Deny Love, 1978; Bride to the King, 1978; Only Love, 1979; The Dawn of Love, 1979; Love Has His Way, 1979; The Explosion of Love, 1979; Women Have Hearts, 1979; A Gentleman in Love, 1979; A Heart is Stolen, 1979; The Power and the Prince, 1979; Free From Fear, 1979; A Song of Love, 1979; Love for Sale, 1979; Little White Doves of Love, 1979; The Perfection of Love, 1979; Lost Laughter, 1979; Punished with Love, 1979; Lucifer and the Angel, 1979; Ola and the Sea Wolf, 1979; The Prude and the Prodigal, 1979; The Goddess and the Gaiety Girl, 1979; Signpost to Love, 1979; Money, Magic and Marriage, 1979; From Hell to Heaven, 1980; Pride and The Poor Princess, 1980; The Lioness and The Lily, 1980; A Kiss of Life, 1980; Love At The Helm, 1980; The Waltz of Hearts, 1980; Afraid, 1980; The Horizons of Love, 1980; Love in the Moon, 1980; Dollars for the Duke, 1981; Dreams Do Come True, 1981; Night of Gaiety, 1981; Count the Stars, 1981; Winged Magic, 1981; River of Love, 1981; Gift of the Gods, 1981; The Heart of the Clan, 1981; An Innocent in Russia, 1981; A Shaft of Sunlight, 1981; Love Wins, 1981; Enchanted, 1981; Wings of Ecstasy, 1981; Pure and Untouched, 1981; In the Arms of Love, 1981; Touch a Star, 1981; For All Eternity, 1981; Secret Harbour, 1981; Looking for Love, 1981; The Vibration of Love, 1981; Lies for Love, 1981; Love Rules, 1981; Moments of Love, 1981; Lucky in Love, 1981; Poor Governess, 1981; Music from the Heart, 1981; Caught by Love, 1981; A King in Love, 1981; Winged Victory, 1981; The Call of the Highlands, 1981; Love and the Marquis, 1981; Kneel for Mercy, 1981; Riding to the Moon, 1981; Wish for Love, 1981; Mission to Monte Carlo, 1981; A Miracle in Music, 1981; From Hate to Love, 1982; Light of the Gods, 1982; Love on the Wind, 1982; The Duke Comes Home, 1982; *philosophy:* Touch the Stars; *sociology:* You in the Home; The Fascinating Forties; Marriage for Moderns; Be Vivid, Be Vital; Love, Life and Sex; Look Lovely, Be Lovely; Vitamins for Vitality; Husbands and Wives; Etiquette; The Many Facets of Love; Sex and the Teenager; Charm; Living Together; Woman the Enigma; The Youth Secret; The Magic of Honey; Health Food Cookery Book; Book of Beauty and Health; Men are Wonderful; The Magic of Honey Cookbook; Food for Love; Recipes for Lovers; *biography:* Ronald Cartland, 1942; Bewitching Women; The Outrageous Queen; Polly, My Wonderful Mother, 1956; The Scandalous Life of King Carol; The Private Life of Charles II; The Private Life of Elizabeth, Empress of Austria; Josephine, Empress of France; Diane de Poitiers; Metternich; The Passionate Diplomat; *autobiography;* The

Isthmus Years, 1943; The Years of Opportunity, 1947; I Search for Rainbows, 1967; We Danced All Night, 1919-1929, 1971; I Seek the Miraculous, 1978; *general*: Useless Information (foreword by Earl Mountbatten of Burma); Light of Love (prayers), 1978; Love and Lovers (pictures), 1978; Barbara Cartland's Book of Celebrities, 1979, 1982; Barbara Cartland's Scrapbook, 1980; Romantic Royal Marriages, 1981; Written with Love, 1981; *verse*: Lines on Love and Life; *plays*: Blood Money; French Dressing (with Bruce Woodhouse); *revue*: The Mayfair Revue; *radio play*: The Caged Bird; *television*: Portrait of Successful Woman, 1957; This is Your Life, 1958; Success Story, 1959; Midland Profile, 1961; No Looking Back-a Portrait of Barbara Cartland, 1967; The Frost Programme, 1968; *radio*: The World of Barbara Cartland, 1970, and many other radio and television appearances. Editor of the Common Problem, by Ronald Cartland, 1943. *Address*: Camfield Place, Hatfield, Herts. *T*: Potters Bar 42612, 42657.
See also Countess Spencer.

CARTLAND, Sir George (Barrington), Kt 1963; CMG 1956; BA; Vice-Chancellor of the University of Tasmania, 1968-77; Chairman, Australian National Accreditation Authority for Translators and Interpreters, since 1977; *b* 22 Sept. 1912; *s* of William Arthur and Margaret Cartland, West Didsbury; *m* 1937, Dorothy Rayton; two *s. Educ*: Manchester Central High Sch.; Manchester Univ.; Hertford Coll., Oxford. Entered Colonial Service, Gold Coast, 1935; served Colonial Office, 1944-49; Head of African Studies Br. and Ed. Jl of Afr. Adminis., 1945-49; Sec. London Afr. Conf., 1948; Admin. Sec., Uganda, 1949; Sec. for Social Services and Local Govt, Uganda, 1952; min. for Social Services, Uganda, 1955; Min. of Education and Labour, Uganda, 1958; Chief Sec., Uganda, 1960; Deputy Gov. of Uganda, 1961-62 (Acting Gov., various occasions, 1952-62); Registrar of Univ. of Birmingham, 1963-67. Part-time Mem., West Midlands Gas Bd, 1964-67. Dep. Chm., Australian Vice-Chancellors' Cttee, 1975 and 1977. Chairman: Adv. Cttee on National Park in SW Tasmania, 1976-78; Tasmanian Council of Australian Trade Union Trng Authority, 1979. Appointed to review: Library and Archives Legislation of Tasmania, 1978; Tasmanian Govt Admin, 1979. Mem., Australian Nat. Cttee of Hoover Awards for Marketing, 1968-82. Chm., St John Council, Uganda, 1958-59; Pres., St John Council, Tasmania, 1969-78. Member Council: Makerere Coll., 1952-60; Royal Tech. Coll., Nairobi, 1952-60; UC of Rhodesia, 1963-67; Univ. of S Pacific, 1972-76. FACE 1970. Hon. LLD Univ. of Tasmania, 1978. KStJ 1972; awarded Belgian medal recognising services in connection with evacuation of the Congo, 1960. *Publication*: (jtly) The Irish Cartlands and Cartland Genealogy, 1978. *Recreations*: mountaineering, fishing. *Address*: 5 Aotea Road, Sandy Bay, Hobart, Tasmania 7005. *Clubs*: Athenæum; Tasmanian, Athenæum, Royal Tasmanian Yacht (all Hobart).

CARTLEDGE, Bryan George, CMG 1980; HM Diplomatic Service; Ambassador to Hungary, since 1980; *b* 10 June 1931; *s* of Eric Montague George Cartledge and Phyllis (*née* Mason); *m* 1960, Ruth Hylton Gass, *d* of John Gass; one *s* one *d. Educ*: Hurstpierpoint; St John's Coll., Cambridge. Queen's Royal Regt, 1950-51. Commonwealth Fund Fellow, Stanford Univ., 1956-57; Research Fellow, St Antony's Coll., Oxford, 1958-59. Entered HM Foreign (subseq. Diplomatic) Service, 1960; served in FO, 1960-61; Stockholm, 1961-63; Moscow, 1963-66; DSAO, 1966-68; Tehran, 1968-70; Harvard Univ., 1971-72; Counsellor, Moscow, 1972-75; Head of E European and Soviet Dept, FCO, 1975-77; Private Sec. (Overseas Affairs) to Prime Minister, 1977-79. *Recreations*: music, fishing. *Address*: c/o Foreign and Commonwealth Office, SW1A 2AH.

CARTWRIGHT, Ven. David; *see* Cartwright, Ven. E. D.

CARTWRIGHT, Ven. (Edward) David; Archdeacon of Winchester, Hon. Canon of Winchester Cathedral and Vicar of Sparsholt with Lainston, Hampshire, since 1973; *b* 15 July 1920; *o c* of John Edward Cartwright and Gertrude Cartwright (*née* Lusby), North Somercotes and Grimsby, Lincs; *m* 1946, Elsie Irene, *o c* of Walter and Jane Elizabeth Rogers, Grimsby; one *s* two *d. Educ*: Grimsby Parish Church Choir Sch.; Lincoln Sch.; Selwyn Coll. and Westcott House, Cambridge. 2nd Cl. Hons Hist. Tripos Pt 1, 1940; 2nd Cl. Hons Theol Tripos Pt 1, 1942; Steel Univ. Stud. in Divinity, 1941; BA 1941, MA 1945; Pres., SCM in Cambridge, 1941-42. Deacon, 1943; Priest, 1944; Curate of Boston, 1943-48; Vicar: St Leonard's, Redfield, Bristol, 1948-52; Olveston with Aust, 1952-60; Bishopston, 1960-73; Secretary, Bristol Diocesan Synod, 1967-73; Hon. Canon of Bristol Cathedral, 1970-73. Dir of Studies, Bristol Lay Readers, 1956-72; Proctor in Convocation, Mem. of Church Assembly and General Synod, 1956-73, 1975-. Member: Bristol Diocesan Bd of Finance, 1959-73; Central Bd of Finance of C of E, 1970-73; C of E Pensions Bd, 1980-. Church Commissioner, 1973 (Mem. Board of Governors, 1978-); Member: Dilapidations Legislation Commn, 1958-64; Working Party on Housing of Retired Clergy, 1972-73; Differential Payment of Clergy, 1976-77. Secretary, Bristol Council of Christian Churches, 1950-61; Chm., Winchester Christian Council, 1976-77. Anglican-Presbyterian Conversations, 1962-66; Convocations Jt Cttees on Anglican-Methodist Union Scheme, 1965. *Recreations*: book-hunting and rose-growing. *Address*: Sparsholt Vicarage, Winchester, Hants SO21 2NS. *T*: Sparsholt 265.

CARTWRIGHT, Frederick; *see* Cartwright, W. F.

CARTWRIGHT, Harry, CBE 1979 (MBE 1946); MA, CEng, MIMechE, MIEE; Director, Atomic Energy Establishment, Winfrith, since 1973; *b* 16 Sept. 1919; *s* of Edwin Harry Cartwright and Agnes Alice Cartwright (*née*

Gillibrand); *m* 1950, Catharine Margaret Carson Bradbury; two *s. Educ*: William Hulme's Grammar Sch., Manchester; St John's Coll., Cambridge (Schol.). 1st cl. Mechanical Sciences Tripos, 1940. Served War, RAF, 1940-46: Flt Lt, service on ground radar in Europe, India and Burma. Decca Navigator Co., 1946-47; English Electric Co., 1947-49; joined Dept of Atomic Energy, Risley, as a Design and Project Engr, 1949; Chief Engr, 1955; Dir in charge of UKAEA consultancy services on nuclear reactors, 1960-64; Dir, Water Reactors, 1964-70, and as such responsible for design and construction of Winfrith 100 MW(e) SGHWR prototype power station; Dir, Fast Reactor Systems, 1970-73. Pres., British Nuclear Energy Soc., 1979-82; Vice-Pres., European Nuclear Soc., 1980-. *Publications*: various techn. papers. *Recreations*: walking, gardening. *Address*: Tabbit's Hill House, Corfe Castle, Wareham, Dorset BH20 5HZ. *T*: Corfe Castle 480 582. *Club*: United Oxford & Cambridge University.

CARTWRIGHT, John Cameron; MP Greenwich, Woolwich East since Oct. 1974 (Lab, 1974-81, SDP, since 1981); *b* 29 Nov. 1933; *s* of Aubrey John Randolph Cartwright and Ivy Adeline Billie Cartwright; *m* 1959, Iris June Tant; one *s* one *d. Educ*: Woking County Grammar School. Exec. Officer, Home Civil Service, 1952-55; Labour Party Agent, 1955-67; Political Sec., RACS Ltd, 1967-72; Director, RACS Ltd, 1972-74. Leader, Greenwich Borough Council, 1971-74. Mem., Lab Party Nat. Exec. Cttee, 1971-75 and 1976-78. PPS to Sec. of State for Education and Science, 1976-77; Chm., Parly Labour Party Defence Group, 1979-81; Mem., Select Cttee on Defence, 1979-82; SDP party spokesman on environment, 1981-. Vice-Pres., Assoc. of Metropolitan Authorities, 1974-. Trustee, Nat. Maritime Museum, 1976-. *Recreations*: do-it-yourself, reading, watching television. *Address*: 17 Commonwealth Way, SE2 0JZ. *T*: 01-311 4394.

CARTWRIGHT, Rt. Hon. John Robert, CC (Canada) 1970; PC (Can.) 1967; MC 1917; Chief Justice of Canada, 1967-70; Judge, Supreme Court of Canada, 1949-70; *b* Toronto, Canada, 23 March 1895; *s* of James Strachan Cartwright, KC, MA, and Jane Elizabeth (*née* Young), Weymouth, England; *m* 1st, Jessie Carnegie, *d* of Thomas Alexander Gibson, KC, Toronto; one *d* ; 2nd, Mabel Ethelwyn Tremaine, *widow* of late Brig. Arthur Victor Tremaine, CBE, CD, and *d* of George William Parmelee, LLD, DCL, of Quebec. *Educ*: Upper Canada Coll., Toronto; Osgoode Hall, Toronto. Served European War, 1914-18; enlisted Canadian Expeditionary Force, Aug. 1914; Lieut 1915; Capt. 1916; with 3rd Canadian Infantry Bn until Dec. 1915 (wounded twice); ADC to GOC 3rd Canadian Div., 1915, until demobilization in 1919; Called to bar, Ontario, 1920, with honours and Silver Medal. Appointed KC (Ont) 1933; Bencher of Law Society of Upper Canada, 1946 (Hon. Bencher, 1970); practised at Toronto with firm Smith, Rae, Greer & Cartwright. Hon. LLD: Toronto, 1959; Osgoode Hall, 1963; Queen's Univ., Kingston, Ont, 1967; York Univ., Toronto, 1969; Ottawa, 1973; Hon. DCL Bishop's Univ., Lennoxville, 1970. *Recreations*: chess and reading. *Address*: Leitchcroft Farm, c/o Thornhill PO, Ontario L3T 3M9, Canada. *Clubs*: Rideau, Le Cercle Universitaire d'Ottawa (Ottawa); Toronto, Royal Canadian Military Institute (Toronto).

CARTWRIGHT, Dame Mary Lucy, DBE 1969; FRS 1947; ScD Cambridge 1949; MA Oxford and Cambridge; DPhil Oxford; Hon. LLD (Edin.) 1953; Hon. DSc: Leeds, 1958; Hull, 1959; Wales, 1962; Oxford, 1966; Brown (Providence, RI), 1969; Fellow of Girton College, Cambridge, 1934-49, and since 1968; *b* 1900; *d* of late W. D. Cartwright, Rector of Aynhoe. *Educ*: Godolphin Sch., Salisbury, and St Hugh's Coll., Oxford. Asst Mistress Alice Ottley Sch., Worcester, 1923-24, Wycombe Abbey Sch., Bucks, 1924-27; read for DPhil, 1928-30; Yarrow Research Fellow of Girton Coll., 1930-34; Univ. Lectr in Mathematics, Cambridge, 1935-59; Mistress of Girton Coll., Cambridge, 1949-68; Reader in the Theory of Functions, Univ. of Cambridge, 1959-68, Emeritus Reader, 1968-; Visiting Professor: Brown Univ., Providence, RI, 1968-69; Claremont Graduate Sch., California, 1969-70; Case Western Reserve, 1970; Polish Acad. of Sciences, 1970; Univ. of Wales (Swansea and Cardiff), 1971; Case Western Reserve, 1971. Consultant on US Navy Mathematical Research Projects at Stanford and Princeton Universities, Jan.-May 1949. Comdt, British Red Cross Detachment, Cambs 112, 1940-44. Fellow of Cambridge Philosophical Soc.; President: London Math. Soc., 1961-63; Mathematical Assoc., 1951-52 (now Hon. Mem.). Hon. FIMA, 1972; Hon. FRSE. Sylvester Medal, Royal Soc., 1964; De Morgan Medal, London Mathematical Soc., 1968; Medal of Univ. of Jyväskylä, Finland, 1973. Commander, Order of the Dannebrog, 1961. *Publications*: Integral Functions (Cambridge Tracts in Mathematics and Mathematical Physics), 1956; math. papers in various journals. *Address*: 38 Sherlock Close, Cambridge CB3 0HP. *T*: Cambridge 352574.
See also W. F. Cartwright.

CARTWRIGHT, Rt. Rev. Richard Fox; Assistant Bishop, Diocese of Truro, since 1982; *b* 10 Nov. 1913; *s* of late Rev. George Frederick Cartwright, Vicar of Plumstead, and Constance Margaret Cartwright (*née* Clark); *m* 1947, Rosemary Magdalen, *d* of Francis Evelyn Bray, Woodham Grange, Surrey; one *s* three *d. Educ*: The King's School, Canterbury; Pembroke Coll., Cambridge (BA 1935, MA 1939); Cuddesdon Theological Coll. Deacon, 1936; Priest, 1937; Curate, St Anselm, Kennington Cross, 1936-40; Priest-in-Charge, Lower Kingswood, 1940-45; Vicar, St Andrew, Surbiton, 1945-52; Proctor in Convocation, 1950-52; Vicar of St Mary Redcliffe, Bristol (with Temple from 1956 and St John Bedminster from 1965), 1952-72; Hon. Canon of Bristol, 1960-72; Suffragan Bishop of Plymouth, 1972-81. Sub-Chaplain, Order of St John, 1957-; Dir, Ecclesiastical Insurance Office Ltd, 1964-. Hon.

DD Univ. of the South, Tennessee, 1969. *Recreations:* fly-fishing, gardening. *Address:* Long Hay, Treligga, Delabole, N Cornwall PL33 9EE. *T:* Camelford 212506; 2a Litfield Place, Clifton, Bristol BS8 3LT. *T:* Bristol 738555. *Clubs:* Army and Navy; Royal Western Yacht (Plymouth).

CARTWRIGHT, (William) Frederick, CBE 1977; DL, MIMechE; Director, BSC (International) Ltd; a Deputy Chairman, British Steel Corporation, 1970–72; Group Managing Director, S Wales Group, British Steel Corporation, 1967–70; Chairman, The Steel Co. of Wales Ltd, 1967 (Managing Director, 1962–67); *b* 13 Nov. 1906; *s* of William Digby Cartwright, Rector of Aynhoe; *m* 1937, Sally Chrystobel Ware; two *s* one *d. Educ:* Rugby Sch. Joined Guest, Keen and Nettlefold, Dowlais, 1929; gained experience at steelworks in Germany and Luxembourg, 1930; Asst Works Manager, 1931, Tech, Asst to Managing Director, 1935, Dir and Chief Engineer, 1940, Dir and General Manager, 1943, Guest, Keen and Baldwin, Port Talbot Works; Dir and General Manager, Steel Co. of Wales, 1947; Asst Man. Dir and General Manager of the Steel Div., The Steel Co. of Wales Ltd, 1954. Pres., Iron and Steel Inst., 1960. Dir, Lloyds Bank, 1968–77 (Chm., S Wales Regional Bd, 1968–77). Dir, Develt Corp for Wales. Freeman of Port Talbot, 1970. DL, County of Glamorgan; High Sheriff, Glamorgan, 1961. OStJ. Hon. LLD Wales, 1968. Bessemer Gold Medal, 1958; Frederico Giolitti Steel Medal, 1960. *Recreations:* riding and yachting. *Address:* Castle-upon-Alun, St Brides Major, near Bridgend, Mid Glam. *T:* Southern-down 298. *Clubs:* Royal Ocean Racing, Royal Cruising; Royal Yacht Squadron.
See also Dame Mary Cartwright.

CARTWRIGHT SHARP, Michael; *see* Sharp, J. M. C.

CARUS, Louis Revell, Hon. RAM, FRSAMD; Principal, Birmingham School of Music, since 1975; *b* Kasauli, India, 22 Oct. 1927; *s* of Lt-Col Martin and Enid Carus-Wilson; *m* 1951, Nancy Reade Noell; two *s* one *d. Educ:* Rugby Sch.; Brussels Conservatoire (Premier Prix); Peabody Conservatory, USA. LRAM. Scottish National Orchestra, 1950; solo violinist and chamber music specialist, 1951–; Head of Strings, Royal Scottish Academy of Music, 1956; Scottish Trio and Piano Quartet, New Music Group of Scotland, 1956–75; Northern Sinfonia, Monteverdi Orchestras, 1963–73; Orchestra Da Camera, 1975; Adjudicator, 1960–. FRSAMD 1976; Hon. RAM 1977. *Publications:* various musical journalism, eg, daily press, Strad Magazine, ISM Jl, Gulbenkian Report. *Recreations:* painting, gardening, travel. *Address:* 24 Barlows Road, Edgbaston, Birmingham B15 2PL. *T:* 021-454 3391. *Clubs:* Royal Society of Musicians, Incorporated Society of Musicians, European String Teachers Association; Rotary (Birmingham).

CARVER, family name of **Baron Carver.**

CARVER, Baron *cr* 1977 (Life Peer); **Field-Marshal (Richard) Michael (Power) Carver,** GCB 1970 (KCB 1966; CB 1957); CBE 1945; DSO 1943 and Bar 1943; MC 1941; designated British Resident Commissioner in Rhodesia, 1977–78; Chief of the Defence Staff, 1973–76; *b* 24 April 1915; 2nd *s* of late Harold Power Carver and late Winifred Anne Gabrielle Carver (*née* Wellesley); *m* 1947, Edith, *d* of Lt-Col Sir Henry Lowry-Corry, MC; two *s* two *d. Educ:* Winchester Coll.; Sandhurst. 2nd Lieut Royal Tank Corps, 1935; War of 1939–45 (despatches twice); GSO1, 7th Armoured Div., 1942; OC 1st Royal Tank Regt, 1943; Comdr 4th Armoured Brigade, 1944; Tech. Staff Officer (1), Min. of Supply, 1947; Joint Services Staff Coll., 1950; AQMG, Allied Land Forces, Central Europe, 1951; Col GS, SHAPE 1952; Dep. Chief of Staff, East Africa, 1954 (despatches); Chief of Staff, East Africa, 1955; idc 1957; Dir of Plans, War Office, 1958–59; Comdr 6th Infty Brigade, 1960–62; Maj.-Gen. 1962; OC, 3 Div., 1962–64, also Comdr Joint Truce Force, Cyprus, and Dep. Comdr United Nations' Force in Cyprus, 1964; Dir, Army Staff Duties, Min. of Defence, 1964–66; Lt-Gen. 1966; comd FE Land Forces, 1966–67 (des., 1967; C-in-C, Far East, 1967–69; GOC-in-C, Southern Command, 1969–71; Chief of the General Staff, 1971–73; Field-Marshal 1973. Col Commandant: REME 1966–76; Royal Tank Regt, 1968–72; RAC, 1974–77; ADC (Gen.) 1969–72. *Publications:* Second to None (History of Royal Scots Greys, 1919–45), 1954; El Alamein, 1962; Tobruk, 1964; (ed) The War Lords, 1976; Harding of Petherton, 1978; The Apostles of Mobility, 1979; War Since 1945, 1980; A Policy for Peace, 1982. *Address:* Wood End House, Wickham, Fareham, Hants PO17 6JZ. *T:* Wickham 832143. *Club:* Anglo-Belgian.

CARVER, James, CB 1978; CEng, FMinE; consulting mining engineer; *b* 29 Feb. 1916; *s* of late William and Ellen Carver; *m* 1944, Elsie Sharrock; one *s* two *d* (of whom one *s* one *d* are twins). *Educ:* Wigan Mining and Technical Coll. Certificated Mine Manager. Asst Mine Manager, Nos 5, 6 and 7 mines, Garswood Hall, Lancs, 1941–43; HM Jun. Inspector Mines and Quarries, W Midlands Coalfields, 1943; Dist Inspector, Mines and Quarries, N Staffordshire, 1951; Senior District Inspector: M&Q, London Headquarters, 1957; M&Q, Doncaster Dist (in charge), 1962; Principal Inspector, M&Q, London Headquarters, 1967; Dep. Chief, M&Q, 1973; Chief Inspector, M&Q, 1975–77; Member, (3 man) Health and Safety Exec., 1976–77. *Publications:* author or co-author, papers in Trans IMinE; several papers to internat. mining confs. *Recreation:* golf. *Address:* 196 Forest Road, Tunbridge Wells, Kent TN2 5JB. *T:* Tunbridge Wells 26748. *Club:* Nevill Golf (Tunbridge Wells).

CARY, family name of **Viscount Falkland.**

CARY, Sir Roger Hugh, 2nd Bt *cr* 1955; Special Assistant to Managing Director, BBC Television, since 1977; *b* 8 Jan. 1926; *o s* of Sir Robert (Archibald) Cary, 1st Bt, and of Hon. Rosamond Mary Curzon, *d* of late Col Hon. Alfred Nathaniel Curzon; *S* father, 1979; *m* 1st, 1948, Marilda (marr. diss. 1951), *d* of Major Pearson-Gregory, MC; one *d* ; 2nd, 1953, Ann Helen Katharine, *e d* of Hugh Blair Brenan, OBE (formerly Asst Sec., Royal Hosp., Chelsea); two *s* one *d. Educ:* Ludgrove; Eton; New Coll., Oxford (BA Mod. Hist. 1949). Enlisted Grenadier Guards, 1943; Lieut 1945; Staff Captain and Instr, Sch. of Signals, Catterick, 1946; Signals Officer, Guards Trng Bn, 1946–47; R of O 1947. Sub-editor and Leader-writer, The Times, 1949–50; Archivist, St Paul's Cathedral, 1950; joined BBC, 1950: attached Home Talks, 1951; Producer, Overseas Talks, 1951–56; Asst, European Talks, 1956–58; Dep. Editor, The Listener, 1958–61; Man. Trng Organiser, 1961–66; Asst, Secretariat, 1966–72, Sen. Asst, 1972–74; Sec., Central Music Adv. Cttee, 1966–77; Special Asst (Public Affairs), 1974–77; Research, Richard Cawston's documentary film, Royal Family, 1969; Secretary: Sims Cttee on portrayal of violence on TV, 1978–79; Wenham Cttee on Subscription Television, 1980–81; Cotton Cttee on Sponsorship and BBC TV, 1981. British Deleg., Internat. Art-Historical Conf., Amsterdam, 1952; Salzburg Scholar in Amer. Studies, 1956. Associate, RHistS. *Recreations:* looking at pictures, collecting books. *Heir:* s Nicolas Robert Hugh Cary, *b* 17 April 1955. *Address:* 23 Bath Road, W4 1LJ. *T:* 01-994 7293. *Club:* Pratt's.

CASALONE, Carlo D.; *see* Dionisotti-Casalone.

CASE, Air Vice-Marshal Albert Avion, CB 1964; CBE 1957 (OBE 1943); General Secretary, Hospital Saving Association, 1969–82; *b* Portsmouth, 5 April 1916; *s* of late Group Captain Albert Edward Case and Florence Stella Hosier Case, Amesbury, Wilts; *m* 1949, Brenda Margaret, *e d* of late A. G. Andrews, Enfield, Middx; one *s* one *d. Educ:* Imperial Service Coll. Commd RAF, 1934; Sqdn Ldr, 1940; Wing Comdr, Commanding No 202 Squadron, 1942; Group Capt., Maritime Ops HQ, ACSEA, 1945; OC, RAF, Koggala, Ceylon, 1945–46; JSSC, 1950–51; OC, RAF, Chivenor, 1953–55; OC, RAF, Nicosia, 1956–57; IDC, 1959; Air Cdre, 1959; Air Min., Dir, Operational Requirements, 1959–62; Air Vice-Marshal, 1962; AOC No 22 Group RAF, Tech. Trg Comd, 1962–66; SASO HQ Coastal Comd, 1966–68; retd. FBIM. *Recreations:* swimming (RAF blue 1946), sailing. *Address:* High Trees, Dean Lane, Winchester. *Clubs:* Royal Air Force; Royal Air Force Yacht, Cruising Association.

CASE, Humphrey John; Keeper, Department of Antiquities, Ashmolean Museum, 1973–82; *b* 26 May 1918; *s* of George Reginald Case and Margaret Helen (*née* Duckett); *m* 1st, 1949, Jean Alison (*née* Orr); two *s* ; 2nd, 1979, Jocelyn (*née* Herickx). *Educ:* Charterhouse; St John's Coll., Cambridge (MA); Inst. of Archaeology, London Univ. Served War, 1939–46. Ashmolean Museum: Asst Keeper, 1949–57; Sen. Asst Keeper, 1957–69; Dep. Keeper, Dept of Antiquities, 1969–73. Vice-Pres., Prehistoric Soc., 1969–73; has directed excavations in England, Ireland and France. FSA 1954. *Publications:* in learned jls (British and foreign): principally on neolithic in Western Europe, prehistoric metallurgy and regional archaeology. *Recreations:* reading, music, swimming. *Address:* 187 Thame Road, Warborough, Oxon OX9 8DH.

CASE, Captain Richard Vere Essex, DSO 1942; DSC 1940; RD; RNR retired; Royal Naval Reserve ADC to the Queen, 1958; Chief Marine Superintendent, Coast Lines Ltd and Associated Companies, 1953–69; *b* 13 April 1904; *s* of late Prof. R. H. Case; *m* 1940, Olive May, *d* of H. W. Griggs, Preston, near Canterbury, Kent; one *s* one *d. Educ:* Thames Nautical Training Coll., HMS Worcester. Joined RNR 1920; commenced service in Merchant Service, 1920; Master's Certificate of Competency, 1928; Captain RNR, 1953; served War of 1939–45 (DSO, DSC and Bar, RD and Clasp). *Recreation:* bowls. *Address:* 14 Aigburth Hall Road, Liverpool L19 9DQ. *T:* 051-427 1016. *Clubs:* Athenæum (Liverpool); Liverpool Cricket.

CASEY, Most Rev. Eamonn; *see* Galway and Kilmacduagh, Bishop of, (RC).

CASEY, Michael Bernard; Chairman and Managing Director, Mather & Platt, since 1980; *b* 1 Sept. 1928; *s* of Joseph Bernard Casey, OBE, and late Dorothy (*née* Love); *m* 1963, Sally Louise, *e d* of James Stuart Smith; two *s* two *d. Educ:* Colwyn Bay Grammar Sch.; LSE (Scholar in Laws, 1952; LLB 1954). RAF, 1947–49. Principal, MAFF, 1961; Office of the Minister for Science, 1963–64; Asst Sec., DEA, 1967; DTI (later Dept of Prices and Consumer Protection), 1970; Under Sec., DoI, 1975–77; a Dep. Chm. and Chief Exec., British Shipbuilders, 1977–80. *Recreations:* golf, chess, bridge. *Address:* 7 Sibella Road, SW4.

CASEY, Michael Vince, BSc(Eng), CEng, FIMechE; Director of Mechanical and Electrical Engineering, British Railways Board, since 1982; *b* 25 May 1927; *s* of Charles John Casey and May Louise Casey; *m* 1954, Elinor Jane (*née* Harris); two *s* two *d. Educ:* Glossop Grammar Sch.; The College, Swindon. BSc(Eng) Hons London. Premium Apprentice, GWR Locomotive Works, Swindon, 1944–49; Univ. of London External Degree Course, 1949–52; British Rail Western Region: Locomotive Testing and Experimental Office, Swindon, 1952–58; Supplies and Contracts Dept, Swindon, 1958–61; Chief Mechanical and Electrical Engr's Dept, Paddington, 1961–63; Area Maintenance Engr, Old Oak Common, 1963–66; Chief Mech. and Elec. Engr's Dept, Paddington, 1966–71; Chief Mech. and Elec. Engineer: Scottish Region, Glasgow, 1971–76; Eastern Region, York, 1976–78; Engrg Dir,

British Rail Engrg Ltd, 1978-82. *Recreations:* gardening, philately. *Address:* Four Winds, 43 Broadway, Duffield, Derby DE6 4BU. *T:* Derby 841279.

CASEY, Rt. Rev. Patrick Joseph; Former Bishop of Brentwood; Parish Priest, Our Most Holy Redeemer and St Thomas More, Chelsea, since 1980; *b* 20 Nov. 1913; *s* of Patrick Casey and Bridget Casey (*née* Norris). *Educ:* St Joseph's Parochial Sch., Kingsland; St Edmund's Coll., Ware. Ordained priest, 1939; Asst, St James's, Spanish Place, 1939-61; Parish Priest of Hendon, 1961-63; Vicar Gen. of Westminster, 1963; Domestic Prelate, and Canon of Westminster Cathedral, 1964; Provost of Westminster Cathedral Chapter, 1967; Auxiliary Bishop of Westminster and Titular Bishop of Sufar, 1966-69; Bishop of Brentwood, 1969-79, then Apostolic Administrator. *Address:* 7 Cheyne Row, SW3 5HS.

CASEY, Dr Raymond, FRS 1970; retired; Senior Principal Scientific Officer (Special Merit), Institute of Geological Sciences, London, 1974-79; *b* 10 Oct. 1917; *s* of Samuel Gardner Casey and Gladys Violet Helen Casey (*née* Garrett); *m* 1943, Norah Kathleen Pakeman (*d* 1974); two *s. Educ:* St Mary's, Folkestone; Univ. of Reading. PhD 1958; DSc 1963. Geological Survey and Museum: Asst 1939; Asst Exper. Officer 1946; Exper. Officer 1949; Sen. Geologist 1957; Principal Geologist 1960. *Publications:* A Monograph of the Ammonoidea of the Lower Greensand, 1960-80; (ed, with P. F. Rawson) The Boreal Lower Cretaceous, 1973; numerous articles on Mesozoic palaeontology and stratigraphy in scientific press. *Recreation:* research into early Russian postal and military history (Past Pres., British Soc. of Russian Philately). *Address:* 38 Reed Avenue, Orpington, Kent. *T:* Farnborough (Kent) 51728.

CASEY, Terence Anthony, CBE 1977; KCHS 1976; FCP 1982; General-Secretary, National Association of Schoolmasters/Union of Women Teachers, 1975-83 (National Association of Schoolmasters, 1963-75), now Honorary Life Member; *b* 5 Sept 1920; *s* of Daniel Casey and Ellen McCarthy; *m* 1945, Catherine Wills; two *s* three *d. Educ:* Holy Cross, near Ramsgate; Camden Coll. Teacher's Certificate; Diploma in Mod. Hist. Teaching Service, LCC, 1946-63; Headmaster, St Joseph's Sch., Maida Vale, W9, 1956-63. Pres., Nat. Assoc. of Schoolmasters, 1962-63. Member: Burnham Cttee, 1961-; Nat. Advisory Cttee on Supply and Training of Teachers; Teachers' Council Working Party; TUC Local Govt Cttee; Council, Open Univ., 1975-; Treasurer, European Teachers' Trade Union Cttee; Vice Pres., Internat. Fedn of Free Teachers' Unions. *Publications:* The Comprehensive School from Within, 1964; contribs to Times Educl Supplement. *Recreations:* music, opera, motoring. *Address:* 10 Chelsing Rise, Leverstock Green, Hemel Hempstead, Herts. *Club:* Pathfinders'.

CASH, Sir Gerald (Christopher), GCMG 1980; KCVO 1977; OBE 1964; JP; Governor-General, Commonwealth of the Bahamas, since 1979 (Acting Governor-General, 1976-79); *b* Nassau, Bahamas, 28 May 1917; *s* of late Wilfred Gladstone Cash and of Lillian Cash; *m* Dorothy Eileen (*née* Long); two *s* one *d. Educ:* Govt High Sch., Nassau. Called to the Bar, Middle Temple, 1948. Counsel and Attorney, Supreme Court of Bahamas, 1940. Member: House of Assembly, Bahamas, 1949-62; Exec. Council, 1958-62; Senate, 1969-73 (Vice-Pres., 1970-72; Pres., 1972-73). Chm., Labour Bd, 1950-52. Member: Bd of Educn, 1950-62; Police Service Commn, 1964-69; Immigration Cttee, 1958-62; Road Traffic Cttee, 1958-62. Rep. Bahamas, Independence Celebrations of Jamaica, Trinidad and Tobago, 1962. Chairman: Vis. Cttee, Boys Indust. Sch., 1952-62; Bd of Governors, Govt High Sch., 1949-63 and 1965-76; Bahamas National Cttee, United World Colls, 1977-. Formerly: Hon. Vice-Consul for Republic of Haiti; Vice-Chancellor, Anglican Dio.; Admin. Adviser, Rotary Clubs in Bahamas to Pres. of Rotary Internat.; Treasurer and Dir, YMCA; Treas., Bahamas Cricket Assoc.; Chm., Boy Scouts Exec. Council; Mem. Board: Dirs of Central Bank of Bahamas; Dirs of Bahamas Assoc. for Mentally Retarded. Formerly: President: Rotary Club of E Nassau; Gym Tennis Club; Florida Tennis Assoc.; Bahamas Lawn Tennis Assoc.; Bahamas Table Tennis Assoc.; Vice-President: Boy Scouts Assoc.; Olympic Assoc., Amateur Athletic Assoc., Swimming Assoc., Football Assoc., Bahamas. JP Bahamas, 1940. Coronation Medal, 1953; Silver Jubilee Medal, 1977. *Recreations:* golf, tennis, table tennis, swimming. *Address:* Government House, PO Box N 8301, Nassau, Bahamas. *T:* 809-21875. *Clubs:* Royal Commonwealth Society; Kingston Cricket (Jamaica); Lyford Cay, Paradise Island Golf, South Ocean Golf, Ambassador Golf, Gym Tennis (Nassau).

CASHEL AND EMLY, Archbishop of, (RC), since 1960; Most Rev. Thomas Morris, DD; *b* Killenaule, Co. Tipperary, 16 Oct. 1914; *s* of James Morris and Johanna (*née* Carrigan). *Educ:* Christian Brothers Schs, Thurles; Maynooth Coll. Ordained priest, Maynooth, 1939; studied, Dunboyne Institute, 1939-41. (DD). Professor of Theology, St Patrick's Coll., Thurles, 1942-Dec. 1959, Vice-Pres., 1957-60; appointed Archbishop, 1959; consecrated, 1960. Pres., Catholic Communications Inst. Office-holder in Muintir na Tíre (rural community movement). *Recreation:* reading. *Address:* Archbishop's House, Thurles, Co. Tipperary, Ireland. *T:* Thurles 21512.

CASHEL AND OSSORY, Bishop of, since 1980; **Rt. Rev. Noel Vincent Willoughby;** *b* 15 Dec. 1926; *s* of George and Mary Jane Willoughby; *m* 1959, Valerie Moore, Dungannon, Tyrone; two *s* one *d. Educ:* Tate School, Wexford; Trinity Coll., Dublin (Scholar, Moderator and Gold Medallist in Philosophy). Deacon 1950, priest 1951, Armagh Cathedral; Curate: St Catherine's, Dublin, 1953-55; Bray Parish, 1955-59; Rector: Delgany Parish,

1959-69; Glenageary Parish, 1969-80; Hon. Sec., General Synod, 1976-80; Treasurer, St Patrick's Cathedral, Dublin, 1976-80; Archdeacon of Dublin, 1979-80. *Recreations:* gardening, golf, tennis, fishing. *Address:* The Palace, Kilkenny, Ireland. *T:* Kilkenny 21560.

CASHMAN, John Prescott; Under-Secretary, Department of Health and Social Security, since 1973; *b* 19 May 1930; *s* of late John Patrick Cashman and late Mary Cashman (*née* Prescott). *Educ:* Balliol Coll., Oxford. MA (English Lang. and Lit.). Army (Intell. Corps), 1948-49. Entered Min. of Health, 1951; Principal 1957; Private Sec. to Minister, 1962-65; Asst Sec. 1965; Nuffield Foundn Trav. Fellow, 1968-69; Private Sec. to Sec. of State, 1969. *Address:* 120 Cheston Avenue, Croydon, Surrey CR0 8DD. *T:* 01-777 7255.

CASHMORE, Rt. Rev. Thomas Herbert; *b* 27 April 1892; *s* of Thomas James and Julia Cashmore; *m* 1919, Kate Marjorie Hutchinson; two *s* two *d* (and one *s* decd). *Educ:* Codrington Coll., Barbados, BWI (BA, Durham). Ordained, Barbados, for Chota Nagpur, India, 1917; SPG Missionary, Ranchi, Chota Nagpur, 1917-24; Principal St James's Coll., Calcutta, 1924-33; Vicar: St James's Parish, Calcutta, 1924-33; Holmfirth, Yorks, 1933-42; Brighouse, Yorks, 1942-46; Hon. Canon of Wakefield Cathedral, 1942-46; Canon Missioner, Diocese of Wakefield, 1946-54; Suffragan Bishop of Dunwich, 1955-67. Examining Chaplain to Bishop of St Edmundsbury and Ipswich, 1955-67. Awarded Kaisar-i-Hind (2nd Class), 1929; Defence Medal (2nd World War). *Recreation:* motoring. *Address:* Lynton, Graham Avenue, Withdean, Brighton BN1 8HA. *T:* Brighton 553005.

CASS, Edward Geoffrey, CB 1974; OBE 1951; Alternate Governor, Reserve Bank of Rhodesia, 1978-79; *b* 10 Sept. 1916; *s* of Edward Charles and Florence Mary Cass; *m* 1941, Ruth Mary Powley; four *d. Educ:* St Olave's; Univ. Coll., London (Scholar); The Queen's Coll., Oxford (Scholar). BSc (Econ.) London (1st Cl.) 1937; George Webb Medley Scholarship, 1938; BA Oxon. (1st Cl. PPE) 1939. Lecturer in Economics, New Coll., Oxford, 1939. From 1940 served in Min. of Supply, Treasury, Air Ministry, MoD; Private Sec. to the Prime Minister, 1949-52; Chief Statistician, Min. of Supply, 1952; Private Sec. to Min. of Supply, 1954; Imperial Defence Coll., 1958; Asst Under-Sec. of State (Programmes and Budget), MoD, 1965-72; Dep. Under-Sec. of State (Finance and Budget), MoD, 1972-76. Mem., Review Bd for Govt Contracts, 1977-; Chm., Verbatim Reporting Study Gp, 1977-79. *Address:* 60 Rotherwick Road, NW11. *T:* 01-455 1664.

CASS, Geoffrey Arthur, MA; CBIM, FIIM; Chief Executive, Cambridge University Press, since 1972; Secretary, Press Syndicate of the University of Cambridge, since 1974; University Printer, since 1982; Fellow of Clare Hall, Cambridge, since 1979; *b* 11 Aug. 1932; *o c* of late Arthur Cass and Jessie Cass (*née* Simpson), Darlington and Oxford; *m* 1957, Olwen Mary, *o c* of late William Leslie Richards and Edith Louisa Richards, Llanelli and Brecon; four *d. Educ:* Queen Elizabeth Grammar Sch., Darlington (Captain of Sch.); Jesus Coll., Oxford (State Scholar; BA PPE 1954, MA 1958). MA Cantab, 1972. AMIMC 1964; FInstD 1968; FIWM, FIIM 1979; CBIM 1980 (MBIM 1967, FBIM 1979). Sen. Res. Scholar, Dept of Social and Admin. Studies, Oxford Univ., 1956-57; Res. Student, automation, Nuffield Coll., Oxford, 1957-58. Commnd RAFVR, fighter control, 1954; served RAF, 1958-60: Air Min. Directorate of Work Study; Pilot Officer, 1958; Flying Officer, 1960; Editor, Automation, 1960-61; Consultant, PA Management Consultants Ltd, 1960-65; Private Management Consultant, British Communications Corp., and Controls and Communications Ltd, 1965; Dir, Controls and Communications Ltd, 1966-69; Dir, George Allen and Unwin Ltd, 1965-67, Man. Dir, 1967-71; Man. Dir, CUP (Publishing Div.), 1971-72; Dir, Weidenfeld (Publishers) Ltd, 1972-74; Dir, Chicago Univ. Press (UK), 1971-. Chm. Governors, Perse Sch. for Girls, Cambridge, 1978-; Member: Jesus Coll., Cambridge, 1972-; Univ. of Cambridge Cttee of Management of Fenner's (and Exec. Sub-Cttee), 1976-; Univ. of Cambridge Appts Bd, 1977- (Exec. Cttee, 1982-); Governing Syndicate, Fitzwilliam Mus., Cambridge, 1977-78; Associate Mem., Gonville and Caius Coll., 1976-; Dining Mem., St Catharine's Coll., 1976-, and Girton Coll., 1977-; Hon. Mem., Ind. Hosp. Gp, 1979-. Founder Mem., Council, Royal Shakespeare Theatre Trust, 1967- (Vice Chm., 1982-); Trustee and Guardian, Shakespeare Birthplace Trust, 1982-; Royal Shakespeare Theatre: Mem., Court of Governors, Council of Ct of Governors, and Finance and Gen. Purposes Cttee of Council, 1975-, Chm. 1982-. Chm. and Sen. Treasurer, Cambridge Univ. Lawn Tennis Club, 1976-; Cambs County LTA: Mem. Exec., 1974-; Chm., Finance and Gen. Purposes Cttee, 1982-; Captain 1974-78; Pres., 1980-82; Hon. Life Vice-Pres., 1982-; Vice-Pres., Durham and Cleveland LTA, 1977-; Member: Council, 1976-, Rules and Internat. Cttee, and Rules Sub-Cttee, 1980-81, Nat. Trng Cttee, 1982-, LTA of GB; Exec. Cttee, and Selection and Discipline Sub-Cttee, Lawn Tennis Assoc. E Region Tennis Develt, 1978-; Prentice Cup Cttee (Oxford and Cambridge *v* Harvard and Yale), 1979-. Durham Co. lawn tennis singles champion, 1951; rep. Oxford Univ. against Cambridge: lawn tennis, 1953, 1954, 1955 (Sec., 1955); badminton, 1951, 1952 (Captain, 1952); rep. Oxford and Cambridge against Harvard and Yale, lawn tennis, 1954; played in Wimbledon Championships, 1954, 1955, 1956, 1959; played in inter-county lawn tennis championships for Durham County, then for Cambridgeshire, 1952-82; rep. RAF in Inter-Service lawn tennis championships, 1958, 1959; Cambs Co. lawn tennis singles champion, 1975; Brit. Veterans (over 45) singles champion, Wimbledon, 1978; Mem., Brit. Veterans' Internat. Dubler Cup Team, Eur. Zone, Barcelona, 1978, Milano Marittima, 1979 (Captain). Awarded Hon. Cambridge Tennis 'Blue', 1980. *Publications:* contrib. scientific and technical jls and periodicals

(Britain, France, Italy) on econ. and social effects of automation; articles on publishing. *Recreations:* lawn tennis, theatre. *Address:* Middlefield, Huntingdon Road, Cambridge CB3 0LH. *T:* Cambridge 276234. *Clubs:* Hurlingham, Queen's, Royal Automobile, Institute of Directors, International Lawn Tennis of GB, The 45, Veterans' Lawn Tennis of GB; Cambridge University Lawn Tennis, Cambridge Lawn Tennis.

CASS, John, QPM 1979; National Co-ordinator of Regional Crime Squads, since 1981; *b* 24 June 1925; *m* 1948, Dilys Margaret Hughes, SRN; three *d.* *Educ:* Nelson Sch., Wigton, Cumbria. Served no 40 RM Commando, 1944-45. Comdt, Detective Training Sch., Hendon, 1974; Commander: CID, New Scotland Yard, 1975; Complaints Bureau, 1978; Serious Crime Squads, New Scotland Yard, 1980. UK Rep., Interpol Conf. on crime prediction, Paris, 1976. Mem., British Acad. of Forensic Scis, 1965. Freeman, City of London, 1979. *Recreations:* walking, wild life. *Address:* 22 Stradbroke Grove, Buckhurst Hill, Essex IG9 5PF. *T:* 01-504 0505. *Club:* Royal Commonwealth Society.

CASS, Sir John (Patrick), Kt 1978; OBE 1960; Director: Farmers and Graziers Co-operative Co., since 1962; The Land Newspaper Ltd, since 1964; Queensland Country Life Newspaper, since 1977; *b* 7 May 1909; *s* of Phillip and Florence Cass; *m* 1932, Velma Mostyn; two *s.* *Educ:* Christian Brothers College, Young, NSW. Gen. Pres., Farmers and Settlers Assoc. of NSW, 1954-59; Senior Vice-Pres., Aust. NFU, 1960-70; Chm., NSW Wheat Research Cttee, 1954-72; Mem., Aust. Wheat Board, 1952-77, Chm., 1972-77. Agricultural Man of the Year in Australia, 1977. *Address:* Stoney Ridge, Crowther, NSW 2692, Australia. *Clubs:* Royal Automobile of Australia, Royal Automobile of Victoria.

CASSEL, Sir Harold (Felix), 3rd Bt *cr* 1920; TD 1975; QC 1970; **His Honour Judge Sir Harold Cassel, Bt;** a Circuit Judge since 1976; *b* 8 Nov. 1916; 3rd *s* of Rt Hon. Sir Felix Cassel, 1st Bt, PC, QC (*d* 1953), and Lady Helen Cassel (*d* 1947); *S* brother, 1969; *m* 1st, 1940, Ione Jean Barclay (marr. diss. 1963); three *s* one *d* ; 2nd, 1963, Mrs Eileen Elfrida Smedley. *Educ:* Stowe; Corpus Christi Coll., Oxford. Served War of 1939-45, Captain, 1941, Royal Artillery. Called to Bar, Lincoln's Inn, 1946. Recorder of Great Yarmouth, 1968-71, Hon. Recorder, 1972-76. JP, Herts, 1959-62; Dep. Chm., Herts QS, 1959-62. *Recreations:* shooting, swimming, opera going. *Heir: s* Timothy Felix Harold Cassel [*b* 30 April 1942; *m* 1st, 1971, Mrs Jenifer Samuel (marr. diss. 1977), *d* of Kenneth Bridge Puckle; one *s* one *d* ; 2nd, 1979, Ann, *o d* of late Sir William Mallalieu; one *d*]. *Address:* 49 Lennox Gardens, SW1. *T:* 01-584 2721.

CASSELS, Field-Marshal Sir (Archibald) James (Halkett), GCB 1961 (CB 1950); KBE 1952 (CBE 1944); DSO 1944; Chief of the General Staff, Ministry of Defence, 1965-68; *b* 28 Feb. 1907; *s* of late General Sir Robert A. Cassels, GCB, GCSI, DSO; *m* 1st, 1935, Joyce (*d* 1978), *d* of late Brig.-Gen. Henry Kirk and Mrs G. A. McL. Sceales; one *s* ; 2nd, 1978, Joy (Mrs Kenneth Dickson). *Educ:* Rugby Sch.; RMC, Sandhurst. 2nd Lieut Seaforth Highlanders, 1926; Lieut 1929; Capt. 1938; Major, 1943; Col 1946; temp. Maj.-Gen. 1945; Maj.-Gen. Lieut. 1954; Gen. 1958. Served War of 1939-45 (despatches twice): BGS 1944; Bde Comd 1944; GOC 51st Highland Div., 1945; GOC 6th Airborne Div., Palestine, 1946 (despatches); idc, 1947; Dir Land/Air Warfare, War Office, 1948-49; Chief Liaison Officer, United Kingdom Services Liaison Staff, Australia, 1950-51; GOC 1st British Commonwealth Div. in Korea (US Legion of Merit), 1951-52; Comdr, 1st Corps, 1953-54; Dir-Gen. of Military Training, War Office, 1954-57; Dir of Emergency Operations Federation of Malaya, 1957-59; PMN (Panglima Mangku Negara), 1958; GOC-in-C, Eastern Command, 1959; C-in-C, British Army of the Rhine and Comdr NATO Northern Army Group, 1960-63; Adjutant-Gen. to the Forces, 1963-64; Field-Marshal, 1968. ADC Gen. to the Queen, 1960-63. Col Seaforth Highlanders, 1957-61; Col Queen's Own Highlanders, 1961-66; Colonel Commandant: Corps of Royal Military Police, 1957-68; Army Physical Training Corps, 1961-65. Pres., Company of Veteran Motorists, 1970-73. *Recreations:* follower of all forms of sport. *Address:* Hamble End, Barrow, Bury St Edmunds, Suffolk. *Club:* Cavalry and Guards (Hon. Mem.).

CASSELS, His Honour Francis Henry, TD 1945; Senior Circuit Judge, Inner London Crown Court, 1972-79 (Chairman, SW London Quarter Sessions, 1965-72); *b* 3 Sept. 1910; 2nd *s* of late Sir James Dale Cassels; *m* 1939, Evelyn Dorothy Richardson (*d* 1979); one *s* one *d.* *Educ:* Sedbergh; Corpus Christi Coll., Cambridge (MA). Called to the Bar, Middle Temple, 1932. Served Royal Artillery, 1939-45. Dep. Chm., County of London Sessions, 1954-65. *Address:* 14 Buckingham House, Courtlands, Richmond, Surrey. *T:* 01-940 4180. *Clubs:* Royal Wimbledon Golf; Constitutional (Putney).

CASSELS, Field-Marshal Sir James; *see* Cassels, Field-Marshal Sir A. J. H.

CASSELS, Prof. James Macdonald, FRS 1959; Lyon Jones Professor of Physics, University of Liverpool, 1960-82, now Emeritus Professor and Honorary Research Fellow, Department of Physics; *b* 9 Sept. 1924; *s* of Alastair Macdonald Cassels and Ada White Cassels (*née* Scott); *m* 1947, Jane Helen Thera Lawrence (*d* 1977); one *s* one *d.* *Educ:* Rochester House Sch., Edinburgh; St Lawrence Coll., Ramsgate; Trinity College, Cambridge. BA, MA, PhD (Cantab.). Harwell Fellow and Principal Scientific Officer, Atomic Energy Research Establishment, Harwell, 1949-53. Lecturer, 1953, subseq.

Senior Lecturer, University of Liverpool. Prof. of Experimental Physics, University of Liverpool, 1956-59; Visiting Prof., Cornell Univ., 1959-60. Mem. Council, Royal Soc., 1968-69. Rutherford Medal, Inst. of Physics, 1973. *Publications:* Basic Quantum Mechanics, 1970; contributions to: scientific journals on atomic, nuclear and elementary particle physics; govt reports on district heating and combined heat and power. *Recreations:* fishing, walking, talking. *Address:* 14 Dudlow Court, Dudlow Nook Road, Liverpool L18 2EU. *T:* 051-722 2594.

CASSELS, John Seton, CB 1978; Second Permanent Secretary, Management and Personnel Office, since 1981; *b* 10 Oct. 1928; *s* of Alastair Macdonald Cassels and Ada White Cassels (*née* Scott); *m* 1956, Mary Whittington; two *s* two *d.* *Educ:* Sedbergh Sch.; Trinity Coll., Cambridge. Rome Scholar, Classical Archaeology, 1952-54. Entered Ministry of Labour, 1954; Secretary of the Royal Commission on Trade Unions and Employers' Associations, 1965-68; Under-Sec., NBPI, 1968-71; Managing Directors' Office, Dunlop Holdings Ltd, 1971-72; Chief Exec., Training Services Agency, 1972-75; Dir, Manpower Services Commn, 1975-81. *Address:* 10 Beverley Road, Barnes, SW13 0LX. *T:* 01-876 6270.

CASSELS, Prof. John William Scott, FRS 1963; FRSE 1981; MA, PhD; Sadleirian Professor of Pure Mathematics, Cambridge University, since 1967; Head of Department of Pure Mathematics and Mathematical Statistics, since 1969; *b* 11 July 1922; *s* of late J. W. Cassels (latterly Dir of Agriculture in Co. Durham) and late Mrs M. S. Cassels (*née* Lobjoit); *m* 1949, Constance Mabel Merritt (*née* Senior); one *s* one *d.* *Educ:* Neville's Cross Council Sch., Durham; George Heriot's Sch., Edinburgh; Edinburgh and Cambridge Univs. MA Edinburgh, 1943; PhD Cantab, 1949. Fellow, Trinity, 1949-; Lecturer, Manchester Univ., 1949; Lecturer, Cambridge Univ., 1950; Reader in Arithmetic, 1963-67. Mem. Council, Royal Society, 1970, 1971 (Sylvester Medal, 1973); Vice Pres., 1974-78. Mem. Exec., 1978-82, Internat. Mathematical Union; Pres., London Mathematical Soc., 1976-78. Dr (*hc*) Lille Univ., 1965; Hon. ScD Edinburgh, 1977. *Publications:* An Introduction to Diophantine Approximation, 1957; An Introduction to the Geometry of Numbers, 1959; Rational Quadratic Forms, 1978; Economics for Mathematicians, 1981; papers in diverse mathematical journals on arithmetical topics. *Recreations:* arithmetic (higher only), gardening (especially common vegetables). *Address:* 3 Luard Close, Cambridge CB2 2PL. *T:* 246108.

CASSELS, Vice-Adm. Sir Simon (Alastair Cassillis), KCB 1982; CBE 1976; Second Sea Lord, Chief of Naval Personnel and Admiral President, Royal Naval College, Greenwich, since 1982; *b* 5 March 1928; *o s* of late Comdr A. G. Cassels, RN, and Clarissa Cassels (*née* Motion); *m* 1962, Jillian Francies Kannreuther; one *s* one *d.* *Educ:* RNC, Dartmouth. Midshipman 1945; Commanding Officer: HM Ships Vigilant, Roebuck, and Tenby, 1962-63; HMS Eskimo, 1966-67; HMS Fearless, 1972-73; Principal Staff Officer to CDS, 1973-76; CO HMS Tiger, 1976-78; Asst Chief of Naval Staff (Op. Requirements), 1978-80; Flag Officer, Plymouth, Port Adm. Devonport, Comdr Central Sub Area Eastern Atlantic and Comdr Plymouth Sub Area Channel, 1981-82. Younger Brother of Trinity House. FRGS. *Publication:* Peninsular Portrait 1811-1814, 1963. *Recreations:* family, water colours, historical research. *Address:* c/o Lloyds Bank, Broadway, Worcs. *Club:* Army and Navy.

CASSIDI, Adm. Sir (Arthur) Desmond, KCB 1978; Chief of Naval Personnel and Second Sea Lord, 1979-82; *b* 26 Jan. 1925; *s* of late Comdr Robert A. Cassidi, RN and late Clare F. (*née* Alexander); *m* 1950, Dorothy Sheelagh Marie (*née* Scott) (*d* 1974); one *s* two *d.* *Educ:* RNC Dartmouth. Qual. Pilot, 1945; CO, 820 Sqdn (Gannet aircraft), 1955; 1st Lieut HMS Protector, 1955-56; psc 1957; CO, HMS Whitby, 1959-61; Fleet Ops Officer Home Fleet, 1962-64; Asst Dir Naval Plans, 1964-67; Captain (D) Portland and CO HMS Undaunted, 1967-68; idc 1969; Dir of Naval Plans, 1970-72; CO, HMS Ark Royal, 1972-73; Flag Officer Carriers and Amphibious Ships, 1974-75; Dir-Gen., Naval Manpower and Training, 1975-77; Flag Officer, Naval Air Command, 1978-79. Mem. Adv. Council, Science Museum, 1979-. *Recreation:* country pursuits. *Address:* c/o Barclays Bank Ltd, 16 Whitehall, SW1.

CASSIE, W(illiam) Fisher, CBE 1966; consulting civil engineer; Partner, Waterhouse & Partners, 1970-74; Professor of Civil Engineering, University of Newcastle upon Tyne (formerly King's College, University of Durham), 1943-70, now Emeritus; *b* 29 June 1905; Scottish; *m* 1933, Mary Robertson Reid; no *c.* *Educ:* Grove Academy, Dundee; University of St Andrews. BSc (St Andrews), 1925. Asst Engineer, City Engineer and Harbour Engineer, Dundee; Research at University Coll., Dundee; PhD (St Andrews), 1930; first Senior Sir James Caird Scholarship in Engineering, 1930; Research and Study, University of Illinois (USA), 1930-31; MS (Ill.), 1931. Lectured at: QUB and University Coll., Cardiff, UCL, 1931-40; King's Coll., Durham Univ., later Univ. of Newcastle upon Tyne, 1940-70. Past Chm. Northern Counties Assoc. of Instn of Civil Engineers; Founder Chm. Northern Counties Branch Instn of Structural Engineers; Pres. Inst. Highways Engrs, 1967-68; FRSE; FICE; FIStructE; PPInstHE; Hon. LLD Dundee, 1972; Hon. DTech Asian Inst. of Technology, 1979; Mem. Sigma XI. Bronze Medallist, Instn of Struct. Engrs; Gold badge, English Folk Dance and Song Soc. *Publications:* Structural Analysis 1947; (with P. L. Capper), Mechanics of Engineering Soils, 1949; (with J. H. Napper) Structure in Building, 1952; (with P. L. Capper and J. D. Geddes) Problems in Engineering Soils, 1966; Fundamental Foundations, 1968; Statics, Structures and Stress, 1973; (with T. Constantine) Student's

Guide to Success, 1977; contrib. Jls of ICE, IStructE, and other tech. papers. *Recreations:* photography and traditional cultures of England. *Address:* Benachie, Lochinver, by Lairg, Sutherland. *T:* Lochinver 302.

CASSILLIS, Earl of; Archibald Angus Charles Kennedy; *b* 13 Sept. 1956; *s* and *heir* of 7th Marquess of Ailsa, *qv* ; *m* 1979, Dawn Leslie Anne Keen; two *d. Recreations:* shooting, ski-ing, cadets and youth-work. *Address:* Cassillis House, Maybole, Ayrshire. *T:* Dalrymple 310. *Club:* New (Edinburgh).

CASSILLY, Richard; operatic tenor; *b* Washington, DC, 14 Dec. 1927; *s* of Robert Rogers Cassilly and Vera F. Swart; *m* 1951, Helen Koliopoulos; four *s* three *d. Educ:* Peabody Conservatory of Music, Baltimore, Md. New York City Opera, 1955-66; Chicago Lyric 1959-; Deutsche Oper, Berlin, 1965-; Hamburgische Staatsoper, 1966-; San Francisco Opera, 1966-; Covent Garden, 1968-; Staatsoper, Vienna, 1969; La Scala, Milan, 1970; Staatsoper, Munich, 1970; Paris Opera, 1972; Metropolitan Opera, NY, 1973-; *Television:* Otello, Peter Grimes, Fidelio, Wozzeck, Die Meistersinger; numerous recordings. *Address:* c/o Robert Lombardo Associates, 30 West 60th Street, New York, NY 10023, USA.

CASSIRER, Mrs Reinhold; *see* Gordimer, Nadine.

CASSON, Sir Hugh (Maxwell), KCVO 1978; Kt 1952; RA 1970; RDI 1951; MA Cantab; RIBA, FSIA; President of the Royal Academy, since 1976; Professor of Environmental Design, 1953-75, Provost since 1980, Royal College of Art; Member: Royal Fine Art Commission, since 1960; Royal Mint Advisory Committee, since 1972; *b* 23 May 1910; *s* of late Randal Casson, ICS; *m* 1938, Margaret Macdonald Troup (*see* Margaret MacDonald Casson); three *d. Educ:* Eastbourne Coll.; St John's Coll., Cambridge. Craven Scholar, British Sch. at Athens, 1933; in private practice as architect since 1937 with late Christopher Nicholson; served War of 1939-45, Camouflage Officer in Air Ministry, 1940-44; Technical Officer Ministry of Town and Country Planning, 1944-46; private practice, Sen. Partner, Casson Conder & Partners, 1946-48; Dir. of Architecture, Festival of Britain, 1948-51. Master of Faculty, RDI, 1969-71. Trustee: British Museum (Nat. Hist.), 1976-; Nat. Portrait Gall., 1976-; Mem. Bd, British Council, 1977-81. Mem., Royal Danish Acad., 1954; Hon. Associate, Amer. Inst of Architects, 1968; Hon. Mem., Royal Canadian Acad. of Arts, 1980. Hon. Dr: RCA 1975; Southampton, 1977; Hon. LLD, Birmingham, 1977. Italian Order of Merit, 1980. Regular contributor as author and illustrator to technical and lay Press. *Publications:* New Sights of London (London Transport), 1937; Bombed Churches, 1946; Homes by the Million (Penguin), 1947; (with Anthony Chitty) Houses-Permanence and Prefabrication, 1947; Victorian Architecture, 1948; Inscape: the design of interiors, 1968; (with Joyce Grenfell) Nanny Says, 1972; Diary, 1981. *Recreation:* drawing. *Address:* (home) 60 Elgin Crescent, W11 2JJ; (office) 35 Thurloe Place, SW7. *T:* 01-584 4581.

CASSON, Margaret MacDonald, (Lady Casson); Architect, Designer; Senior Tutor, School of Environmental Design, Royal College of Art, retired 1974; *b* 26 Sept. 1913; 2nd *d* of James MacDonald Troup, MD, and Alberta Davis; *m* 1938, Hugh Maxwell Casson, *qv,* three *d. Educ:* Wychwood Sch., Oxford; Bartlett Sch. of Architecture, University Coll. London; Royal Inst. of British Architecture. Office of late Christopher Nicholson, 1937-38; private practice, S Africa, 1938-39; Designer for Cockade Ltd, 1946-51; Tutor, Royal Coll. of Art, 1952; private practice as Architect and Designer for private and public buildings and interiors; also of china, glass, carpets, furniture, etc; Design consultant to various cos; Member: Design Council Index Cttees; Duke of Edinburgh's panel for Award for Elegant Design, 1962-63; Council for Design Council, 1967-73 (Chm. Panel for Design Council Awards for Consumer Goods, 1972); Three-Dimensional Design Panel of NCDAD, 1962-72 (Ext. Assessor for NCDAD, 1962-); Council of RCA, 1970; Arts Council, 1972-75; Cttee of Enquiry into Drama Training, 1973-75; Adv. Council of V&A Museum, 1975; Gardens and Park Cttee, Zoological Soc. of London, 1975; Craft Adv. Cttee, 1976-; Council, Royal Soc. of Arts, 1977-; Stamp Adv. Cttee, PO, 1980-; Design Cttee, London Transport, 1980-. Mem. Bd of Governors: Wolverhampton Coll. of Art, 1964-66; West of England Coll. of Art, 1965-67; BFI, 1973-79 (Chm., Regional Cttee, 1976-79). FSIA. Sen. Fellow RCA 1980. *Address:* 60 Elgin Crescent, W11 2JJ. *T:* 01-727 2999.

CASTERET, Norbert; Commandeur de la Légion d'Honneur, 1975 (Officier 1947); Croix de Guerre, 1917; archæologist, geologist, speleologist; *b* 19 Aug. 1897; *m* 1924, Elisabeth Martin (*d* 1940); one *s* four *d. Educ:* Lycée de Toulouse, Haute-Garonne. Bachelier; lauréat de l'Académie Française, 1934, 1936, 1938; lauréat de l'Académie des Sciences, 1935; mainteneur de l'Académie des Jeux Floraux, 1937; Grande Médaille d'Or de l'Académie des Sports, 1923; Médaille d'Or de l'Education Physique, 1947; Commandeur du Mérite de la Recherche et de l'Invention, 1956; Commandeur du Mérite sportif, 1958; Commandeur des Palmes académiques, 1964; Commandeur du Mérite National; "Oscar" du Courage Français, 1973; Médaille de Sauvetage, 1975; Médaille d'Or de la Société d'Encouragement au Bien, 1977; Grande Médaille d'Or de la Société de Géographie de Paris, 1979. *Publications:* 30 works translated into 17 languages: Dix ans sous terre (English edn: Ten Years Under the Earth); Au fond des gouffres; Mes Cavernes (English edn: My Caves); En Rampant; Exploration (English edn: Cave Men New and Old); Darkness Under the Earth; Trente ans sous terre (English edn: The Descent of Pierre Saint-Martin), etc.; contributions to L'Illustration, Illustrated

London News, Geographical Magazine, etc. *Recreation:* exploring caves *Address:* Castel Mourlon, 31800 Saint-Gaudens, France. *T:* St Gaudens 61.89.15.13.

CASTLE, Rt. Hon. Barbara (Anne), PC 1964; BA; Member (Lab) Greater Manchester North, European Parliament, since 1979; Vice Chairman, Socialist Group, European Parliament, since 1979; *b* 6 Oct. 1910; *d* of Frank and Annie Rebecca Betts; *m* 1944, Edward Cyril Castle, (later Baron Castle (*d* 1979) she prefers to remain known as Mrs Castle); no *c. Educ:* Bradford Girls Grammar Sch.; St Hugh's Coll., Oxford. Elected to St Pancras Borough Council, 1937; Member Metropolitan Water Board, 1940-45; Asst Editor, Town and County Councillor, 1936-40; Administrative Officer, Ministry of Food, 1941-44; Housing Correspondent and Forces Adviser, Daily Mirror, 1944-45. MP (Lab) Blackburn, 1945-50, Blackburn East, 1950-55, Blackburn 1955—79. Member of National Executive Cttee of Labour Party, 1950-; Chairman Labour Party, 1958-59 (Vice-Chm. 1957-58). Minister of: Overseas Development, 1964-65; Transport, 1965-68; First Secretary of State and Sec. of State for Employment and Productivity, 1968-70; Sec. of State for Social Services, 1974-76. Co-Chm., Women's Nat. Commn, 1975-76. Hon. Fellow, St Hugh's Coll., Oxford, 1966. Hon. DTech: Bradford, 1968; Loughborough, 1969. *Publications:* part author of Social Security, edited by Dr Robson, 1943; The Castle Diaries 1974-76, 1980. *Recreations:* poetry and walking. *Address:* 2 Queen Anne's Gate, SW1.

CASTLE, Enid; Headmistress, The Red Maids' School, Bristol, since 1982; *b* 28 Jan. 1936; *d* of Bertram and Alice Castle. *Educ:* Hulme Grammar Sch. for Girls, Oldham; Royal Holloway Coll., Univ. of London. BA Hons History Colne Valley High Sch., Yorks, 1958-62; Kenya High Sch., Nairobi, 1962-65; Queen's Coll., Nassau, Bahamas, 1965-68; Dep. Head, Roundhill High Sch., Leicester, 1968-72; Headmistress, High Sch. for Girls, Gloucester, 1973-81. *Recreations:* tennis, squash, bridge, choral music. *Address:* 3 Gatton Way, Hucclecote, Gloucester. *T:* Gloucester 67524. *Club:* Soroptimist International.

CASTLE, Mrs G. L; *see* Sharp, Margery.

CASTLE, Norman Henry; Chairman: Wace Ltd, since 1978; Gee & Watson Ltd, since 1978; Paul Developments Ltd, since 1980; Underwriting Member of Lloyds, since 1976; *b* 1 Sept. 1913; *s* of Hubert William Castle, MBE, and Elizabeth May Castle; *m* 1939, Ivy Olive Watson; one *d. Educ:* Norfolk House; Ludlow Grammar Sch. Joined Hafnia Konserves, Copenhagen, 1931 London: C. & E. Morton Ltd, 1933; Vacuum Packed Produce Ltd, 1938 Vacuum Foods Ltd, 1939. Served War of 1939-45, RAF. General Manager: A. L. Maizel Ltd, 1945; Times Foods Ltd, 1947; Director, Vacuum Foods Ltd 1951; Managing Dir, Haigh Castle & Co. Ltd, 1956; Man. Dir, Hafnia Ham Co. Ltd, 1956; Chm. and Man. Dir, S. & W. Berisford Ltd, 1971-78 (Dir. 1967); Chm., Ashbourne Investments Ltd, 1976-; Director: Incentive Investments Ltd, 1976; E. S. Schwab & Co. Ltd, 1976-81; Acatos and Hutcheson Ltd, 1979-. *Recreations:* travel, sailing. *Address:* The Penthouse, 39 Courcels, Black Rock, Brighton, E Sussex. *Clubs:* Lloyd's Yacht, Brighton Marina Yacht (Brighton).

CASTLE-MILLER, Rudolph Valdemar Thor; a Recorder of the Crown Court, 1972-75; *b* Britain, 16 March 1905; *s* of late Rudolph Schleusz-Mühlheram, Randers, Denmark; changed name by deed poll, 1930; *m* 1939, Colleen Ruth, *d* of late Lt-Col N. R. Whitaker; one *s* one *d. Educ:* Harrow; Hertford Coll., Oxford (MA). Called to Bar, Middle Temple, 1929. Past Master, Loriners' Company, 1968. Flt Lt, Intell. Br., RAF, 1940-46. *Recreations:* motoring, travel. *Address:* 6 Wood Road, Ashill, Ilminster, Somerset TA19 9NP.

CASTLE-SMITH, Roger, MBE (mil.) 1971; CEng, MIEE; Major, retired; Chief Engineer, Communications Engineering Department, Foreign and Commonwealth Office, since 1981; *b* 14 June 1934; *s* of George Musgrave Castle-Smith and Esme Josephine Winch; *m* 1960, Pamela Anne Coombes; two *s. Educ:* Marlborough Coll.; Royal Military College of Science, Shrivenham. BScEng. Royal Corps of Signals, 1952-71. Communications Engineering Dept, FCO, 1971-. *Recreations:* sailing, model engineering, amateur radio. *Address:* Field House, The Green, Hanslope, Milton Keynes, Bucks MK19 7LS. *T:* Milton Keynes 510457. *Club:* Royal Signals Yacht.

CASTLE STEWART, 8th Earl, *cr* 1800 (Ireland); **Arthur Patrick Avondale Stuart;** Viscount Stuart, 1793; Baron, 1619; Bt 1628; *b* 18 Aug. 1928; 3rd but *e surv. s* of 7th Earl Castle Stewart, MC, and Eleanor May, *er d* of late S. R. Guggenheim, New York; *S* father, 1961; *m* 1952, Edna Fowler; one *s* one *d. Educ:* Brambletye; Eton; Trinity Coll., Cambridge (BA). Lieut Scots Guards, 1949. MBIM. *Heir: s* Viscount Stuart, *qv. Address:* Stone House Farm, East Pennard, Shepton Mallet, Somerset. *T:* Ditcheat 240; Stuart Hall, Stewartstown, Co. Tyrone. *T:* Stewartstown 208. *Club:* Carlton.

CASTLEMAINE, 8th Baron *cr* 1812; **Roland Thomas John Handcock;** Major, Army Air Corps; *b* 22 April 1943; *s* of 7th Baron Castlemaine and Rebecca Ellen (*d* 1978), *d* of William T. Soady, RN; *S* father, 1973; *m* 1969, Pauline Anne, *e d* of John Taylor Bainbridge. *Educ:* Campbell Coll., Belfast. *Heir: cousin* Clifford Frederick Handcock [*b* 3 Oct. 1896; *m* 1928, Margaret (decd), *d* of late Captain Philip Nicholls]. *Address:* c/o Lloyds Bank, Aldershot, Hants.

CASTLEMAN, Christopher Norman Anthony; Chief Executive, Hill Samuel Group Ltd, since 1980; *b* 23 June 1941; *s* of late S. Phillips and of Mrs Joan S. R. Pyper; *m* 1st, 1965, Sarah Victoria (*née* Stockdale) (*d* 1979); one *s* one *d*; 2nd, 1980, Caroline Clare (*née* Westcott); one *d*. *Educ:* Harrow; Clare Coll., Cambridge (MA Law). Joined M. Samuel & Co. Ltd, 1963; General Manager, Hill Samuel Australia Ltd, 1970–72; Director, Hill Samuel & Co. Ltd, 1972; Man. Dir, Hill Samuel Group (SA) Ltd and Hill Samuel (SA) Ltd, 1978–80. *Recreations:* tennis, squash, cricket, travel. *Address:* 39 Compton Road, N1 2UP. *T:* 01-226 0078.

CASTLEREAGH, Viscount; Frederick Aubrey Vane-Tempest-Stewart; *b* 6 Sept. 1972; *s* and *heir* of 9th Marquess of Londonderry, *qv*.

CASTON, Geoffrey Kemp; Secretary-General, Committee of Vice-Chancellors and Principals, since 1979; *b* 17 May 1926; *s* of late Reginald and Lilian Caston, West Wickham, Kent; *m*; two *s* one *d*. *Educ:* St Dunstans Coll.; (Major Open Scholar) Peterhouse, Cambridge (MA). First Cl. Pt 1 History; First Cl. Pt II Law (with distinction) and Geo. Long Prize for Jurisprudence, 1950; Harvard Univ. (Master of Public Admin. 1951; Frank Knox Fellow, 1950–51). Sub-Lt, RNVR, 1945–47. Colonial Office, 1951–58; UK Mission to UN, New York, 1958–61; Dept of Techn. Co-op., 1961–64; Asst Sec., Dept of Educn and Sci. (Univs and Sci. Branches), 1964–66; Jt Sec., Schools Council, 1966–70; Under-Secretary, UGC, 1970–72; Registrar of Oxford Univ. and Fellow of Merton Coll., Oxford, 1972–79. Sec., Assoc. of First Div. Civil Servants, 1956–58; Adv. to UK Delegn to seven sessions of UN Gen. Assembly, 1953–63; UK Rep. on UN Cttee on Non-Self-Governing Territories, 1958–60; UN Techn. Assistance Cttee, 1962–64; Mem., UN Visiting Mission to Trust Territory of Pacific Islands, 1961. Chm., SE Surrey Assoc. for Advancement of State Educn, 1962–64; UK Delegn to Commonwealth Educn Conf., Ottawa, 1964. Ford Foundn travel grants for visits to schools and univs in USA, 1964, 1967, 1970. Vis. Associate, Center for Studies in Higher Educn, Univ. of Calif, Berkeley, 1978–81. Chairman: Planning Cttee, 3rd and 4th Internat. Curriculum Confs, Oxford, 1967, New York, 1968; Ford Foundn Anglo-American Primary Educn Project, 1968–70; Library Adv. Council (England), 1973–78; Nat. Inst. for Careers Educn and Counselling, 1975–; DES/DHSS Working Gp on Under 5s Res., 1980–82; Member: Steering Gp, OECD Workshops on Educnl Innovation, Cambridge 1969, W Germany, 1970, Illinois 1971; Vice-Chm., Educnl Res. Bd, SSRC, 1973–77; Exec. Cttee, Inter-Univ. Council for Higher Educn Overseas, 1977–. Governor, Centre for Educnl Development Overseas, 1969–70. Hon. LLD Dundee, 1982. *Publications:* contribs to educl jls. *Address:* 29 Tavistock Square, WC1H 9EZ.

CATCHESIDE, David Guthrie, FRS 1951; DSc London; Research Associate, Waite Agricultural Research Institute, South Australia, since 1975; *b* 31 May 1907; *s* of late David Guthrie Catcheside and Florence Susanna (*née* Boxwell); *m* 1931, Kathleen Mary Whiteman; one *s* one *d*. *Educ:* Strand Sch.; King's Coll., University of London. Asst to Professor of Botany, Glasgow Univ., 1928–30; Asst Lecturer, 1931–33, and Lecturer in Botany, University of London (King's Coll.), 1933–36; International Fellow of Rockefeller Foundation, 1936–37; Lecturer in Botany, University of Cambridge, 1937–50; Lecturer and Fellow, Trinity Coll., Cambridge, 1944; Reader in Plant Cytogenetics, Cambridge Univ., 1950–51; Prof. of Genetics, Adelaide Univ., S. Australia, 1952–55; Prof. of Microbiology, Univ. of Birmingham, 1956–64; Prof. of Genetics, 1964–72, Dir, 1967–72, Vis. Fellow, 1973–75, Res. Sch. of Biol Scis, ANU. Research Associate, Carnegie Instn of Washington, 1958. Visiting Professor, California Inst. of Technology, 1961. Foreign Associate, Nat. Acad. of Sciences of USA, 1974. Foundation FAA, 1954; FKC 1959. *Publications:* Botanical Technique in Bolles Lee's Microtomists' Vade-Mecum, 1937–50; Genetics of Micro-organisms, 1951; Genetics of Recombination, 1977; Mosses of South Australia, 1980; papers on genetics and cytology. *Address:* 16 Rodger Avenue, Leabrook, SA 5068, Australia.

CATER, Antony John E., *see* Essex-Cater.

CATER, Douglass; writer and educator in USA, since 1968; President, Washington College, Chestertown, Maryland, since 1982; Founding Fellow, and Trustee since 1982, Aspen Institute; *b* Montgomery, Ala, 24 Aug. 1923; *s* of Silas D. Cater and Nancy Chesnutt; *m* 1950, Libby Anderson; two *s* two *d*. *Educ:* Philip Exeter Acad. (grad.); Harvard Univ. (AB, MA). Served War, 1943–45, with OSS. Washington Editor, The Reporter (Magazine), 1950–63; Nat. Affairs Editor, 1963–64; Special Assistant: to Sec. of Army, 1951; to the President of the United States, 1964–68. Vice-Chm., The Observer, 1976–81. Consultant to Dir, Mutual Security Agency, 1952. Visiting Professor, 1959–: Princeton Univ.; Weslyan Univ., Middletown, Conn; Stanford Univ., etc. Guggenheim Fellow, 1955; Eisenhower Exchange Fellow, 1957; George Polk Meml Award, 1961; NY Newspaper Guild, Page One Award, 1961. Mem., Delta Sigma Chi. *Publications:* (with Marquis Childs) Ethics in a Business Society, 1953; The Fourth Branch of Government, 1959; Power in Washington, 1963; The Irrelevant Man, 1970. *Address:* Office of the President, Washington College, Chestertown, Md 21620, USA.

CATER, Sir Jack, KBE 1979 (CBE 1973; MBE 1956); Hong Kong Commissioner in London, since 1982; *b* 21 Feb. 1922; *yr s* of Alfred Francis Cater and Pamela Elizabeth Dukes; *m* 1950, Peggy Gwenda Richards; one *s* two *d*. *Educ:* Sir George Monoux Grammar Sch., Walthamstow. Served War of 1939–45, Sqdn Ldr, RAFVR; British Military Administration, Hong Kong, 1945; joined Colonial Administrative Service, 1946, appointed Hong Kong;

attended 2nd Devonshire Course, Oxford (The Queen's Coll.), 1949–50; various appts, incl. Registrar of Co-operative Societies and Director of Marketing, Dir of Agriculture and Fisheries, Dep. Economic Sec.; IDC 1966; Defence Sec./Special Asst to Governor/Dep. Colonial Sec. (Special Duties), 1967; Executive Dir, HK Trade Development Council, 1968–70; Director, Commerce and Industry, 1970–72; Secretary for Information, 1972; for Home Affairs and Information, 1973; Commissioner, Independent Commn Against Corruption, 1974–78; Chief Secretary, Hong Kong, 1978–81; actg Governor and Dep. Governor on several occasions. Mem., Internat. Bd of Dirs, United World Colls, UK, 1981. Hon. DSSc Univ. of Hong Kong, 1982. *Recreations:* work, walking, squash, bridge, reading, watching television. *Address:* Hong Kong Government Office, 6 Grafton Street, W1X 3LB. *T:* 01-499 9821; (home) 19 Cowley Street, SW1P 3LZ. *Clubs:* Hong Kong, Royal Hong Kong Jockey.

CATER, John Robert; Chairman, Distillers Co. Ltd, since 1976, Deputy Chairman 1975–76, Director since 1967 (Member Management Committee); *b* 25 April 1919; *s* of Sir John Cater; *m* 1945, Isobel Calder Ritchie; one *d*. *Educ:* George Watson's Coll., Edinburgh; Cambridge Univ. (MA). Trainee, W. P. Lowrie & Co. Ltd, 1946; James Buchanan & Co. Ltd, 1949: Dir 1950; Prodn Dir 1959; Prodn Asst, Distillers Co. Ltd, Edinburgh, 1959; Man. Dir, John Haig & Co. Ltd, 1965–70; Non-Exec. Dir, United Glass, 1969, Chm. 1972. *Recreations:* music, theatre, fishing, golf (Walker Cup team, 1955; played for Scotland, 1952–56). *Address:* 20 St James's Square, SW1Y 4JF. *T:* 01-930 1040. *Clubs:* New (Edinburgh); Royal Scottish Automobile (Glasgow); Royal and Ancient (St Andrews).

CATFORD, John Robin; Secretary for Appointments to the Prime Minister and Ecclesiastical Secretary to the Lord Chancellor, since 1982; *b* 11 Jan. 1923; *er s* of late Adrian Leslie Catford and Ethel Augusta (*née* Rolfe); *m* 1948, Daphne Georgina, *o d* of late Col J. F. Darby, CBE, TD; three *s* one *d*. *Educ:* Hampton Grammar Sch.; Univ. of St Andrews (BSc); St John's Coll., Cambridge (DipAgric). Joined Sudan Civil Service, 1946; with Dept of Agriculture and Forests: Kordofan Province, 1946–48; Equatoria Province, 1948–52; Blue Nile Province (secondment to White Nile Schemes Bd), 1952–55; various posts in industry and commerce, mainly in UK; joined Home Civil Service, MAFF, as Principal, 1966; sec. to Cttee of Inquiry on Contract Farming, 1971; Assistant Secretary: Food and Drink Industries Div., 1972–77; Horticulture Div., 1977–79; Under-Secretary: Agricultural Resources Policy and Horticulture Group, 1979–82; Plant Health, Seeds and Labour, 1981–82. Member: Economic Development Cttee for Hotels and Catering, 1972–76; EDC for Agriculture, 1979–82. Mem. Chichester Dio. Synod, 1979–. *Recreations:* sailing, theatre, avoiding gardening. *Address:* 27 Blackthorns, Lindfield, Haywards Heath, West Sussex RH16 2AX. *T:* Haywards Heath 451896. *Clubs:* United Oxford & Cambridge University; Birdham Yacht (Chichester).

CATHCART, family name of Earl Cathcart.

CATHCART, 6th Earl *cr* 1814; **Alan Cathcart,** CB 1973; DSO 1945; MC 1944; Viscount Cathcart, 1807; Baron Greenock (United Kingdom) and 15th Baron Cathcart (Scotland), 1447; Major-General; *b* 22 Aug. 1919; *o s* of 5th Earl and Vera, *d* of late John Fraser, of Cape Town; *S* father, 1927; *m* 1946, Rosemary (*d* 1980), *yr d* of late Air Commodore Sir Percy Smyth-Osbourne, CMG, CBE; one *s* two *d*. *Educ:* Eton; Magdalene Coll., Cambridge. Served War of 1939–45 (despatches, MC, DSO). Adjt RMA Sandhurst, 1946–47; Regimental Adjt Scots Guards, 1951–53; Brigade Major, 4th Guards Brigade, 1954–56; Commanding Officer, 1st Battalion Scots Guards, 1957; Lt-Col comd Scots Guards, 1960; Colonel AQ Scottish Command, 1962–63; Imperial Defence Coll., 1964; Brigade Comdr, 152 Highland Brigade, 1965–66; Chief, SHAPEX and Exercise Branch SHAPE, 1967–68; GOC Yorkshire District, 1969–70; GOC and British Comdt, Berlin, 1970–73; retd. A Dep-Chm. of Cttees and Dep. Speaker, House of Lords. Brigadier, Queen's Body Guard for Scotland, Royal Company of Archers. Pres., ACFA, 1975–82; Dep. Grand Pres., British Commonwealth Ex-Services League, 1976–. Cdre, RYS, 1974–80. *Heir: s* Lord Greenock, *qv. Address:* 2 Pembroke Gardens Close, W8. *T:* 01-602 4535. *Clubs:* Brooks's; Royal Yacht Squadron (Cowes).

CATHERWOOD, Sir (Henry) Frederick (Ross), Kt 1971; Member (C) Cambridgeshire, European Parliament, since 1979; Chairman, Committee for External Economic Relations, European Parliament, since 1979; Chairman, Wittenborg Automat Ltd; Director: The Goodyear Tyre and Rubber Co. (GB) Ltd; *b* 30 Jan. 1925; *s* of late Stuart and of Jean Catherwood, Co., Londonderry; *m* 1954, Elizabeth, *er d* of late Rev. Dr D. M. Lloyd Jones, Westminster Chapel, London; two *s* one *d*. *Educ:* Shrewsbury; Clare Coll., Cambridge. Articled Price, Waterhouse & Co.; qualified as Chartered Accountant, 1951; Secretary, Laws Stores Ltd, Gateshead, 1952–54; Secretary and Controller, Richard Costain Ltd, 1954–55; Chief Executive, 1955–60; Asst Managing Director, British Aluminium Co. Ltd, 1960–62; Managing Director, 1962–64; Chief Industrial Adviser, DEA, 1964–66; Dir-Gen., NEDC, 1966–71; Managing Dir and Chief Executive, John Laing & Son Ltd, 1972–74. British Institute of Management: Mem. Council, 1961–66, 1969–79; Vice-Chm., 1972; Chm., 1974–76; Vice-Pres., 1976–. Member of Council: NI Development Council, 1963–64; RIIA, 1964–71; BNEC, 1965–71; NEDC, 1964–71; Chm., BOTB, 1975–79. Vice-Pres., 1976, Pres., 1977, Fellowship of Independent Evangelical Churches; Chm. of Council, Univs and Colls Christian Fellowship (formerly Inter-Varsity Fellowship), 1971–77; Mem., Central Religious Adv. Cttee to BBC and IBA, 1975–79. Hon. DSc Aston,

1972; Hon. DSc (Econ.) QUB, 1973; Hon. DUniv Surrey, 1979. *Publications:* The Christian in Industrial Society, 1964, rev. edn, 1980; The Christian Citizen, 1969; A Better Way, 1976; First Things First, 1979. *Recreations:* music, gardening, reading. *Address:* 25 Woodville Gardens, W5; Sutton Hall, Balsham, Cambridgeshire; (office) 7 Rose Crescent, Cambridge. *T:* Cambridge 311310. *Club:* United Oxford & Cambridge University.

CATHERWOOD, Herbert Sidney Elliott, CBE 1979; Chairman of Ulsterbus and Citybus; *b* 1929. *Educ:* Belfast Royal Academy, N Ireland. Chairman, Ulsterbus Ltd, from inception, 1967; Member, NI Transport Holding Co., 1968; became Director of Merger of Belfast Corporation Transport with Ulsterbus, 1972. Director: RMC Catherwood; Sea Ferry Parcels. Member: NE Area Board, Ulster Bank, 1976. *Address:* Ulsterbus Ltd, Milewater Road, Belfast BT3 9BG; Boulderstone House, 917 Antrim Road, Templepatrick, Co. Antrim.

CATHIE, Ian Aysgarth Bewley, MD, BS, MRCP, FRCPath; JP; DL; *b* London, 3 Jan, 1908; 2nd *s* of George Cathie, Ewell, Surrey, and Lilly Pickford Evans; *m* 1938, Josephine (*d* 1982), *o d* of Joseph Cunning, FRCS, Broome Park, Betchworth, Surrey; one *s* three *d.* *Educ:* Guy's Hospital; Zürich Univ. Asst path. to Ancoats Hospital, Manchester, 1932; demonstrator in path. in Manchester Univ. and registrar in path. to Manchester Royal Inf., 1934; path. and res. Fellow in path., Christie Hospital and Holt Radium Inst., also path. to Duchess of York Hospital for Babies, Manchester, 1936. Clinical Pathologist to The Hospital for Sick Children, Great Ormond Street, London, 1938-58, retired. Pathologist in EMS, 1939; war service in RAMC, 1940-46; captured in Tobruk, POW 1942-43. Hon. Member, British Pædiatric Association. Lord of the Manor of Barton-on-the-Heath, Warwickshire; CC Warwicks, 1965-77 (Vice-Chm., 1973-74, Chm., 1974-76). DL Warwicks, 1974. *Publications:* Chapters in Moncrieff's Nursing and Diseases of Sick Children and (in collaboration) Garrod, Batten and Thursfield's Diseases of Children; also papers on pathology and pædiatrics in medical journals. Editor, Archives of Disease in Childhood, 1951-63. *Recreation:* gardening. *Address:* Barton House, Moreton-in-Marsh, Glos. *T:* Barton-on-the-Heath 303. *Clubs:* Chelsea Arts, Saintsbury.

CATLEDGE, Turner; Director, The New York Times, 1968-73; *b* 17 March 1901; *s* of Lee Johnson Catledge and Willie Anna (*née* Turner); *m* 1st; two *d*; 2nd, 1958, Abby Izard. *Educ:* Philadelphia (Miss.) High Sch.; Miss. State College. BSc 1922. Neshoba (Miss.) Democrat, 1921; Resident Editor, Tunica (Miss.) Times, 1922; Man. Editor, Tupelo (Miss.) Journal, 1923; Reporter, Memphis (Tenn.) Commercial Appeal, 1923-27; Baltimore (Md) Sun, 1927-29; New York Times: City Staff, 1929; Correspondent, Washington Bureau, 1930-36; Chief Washington news Correspondent, 1936-41; Chicago Sun: Chief Correspondent, 1941-42; Editor-in-Chief, 1942-43; Nat. Correspondent, New York Times, 1943-44; Managing Editor, 1951-64; Executive Editor, 1964-68 Vice-Pres., 1968-70. Member: Pulitzer Prizes Advisory Cttee, 1955-69; AP Managing Editors Assoc., 1954-64; Advisory Board, American Press Inst.; American Soc. of Newspaper Editors (Dir., Pres. 1961); Sigma Delta Chi. Hon. DLitt Washington and Lee Univ.; Hon. Dr of Humane Letters Southwestern at Memphis; Hon. LLD: Univ. of Kentucky; Tulane Univ. *Publications:* The 168 Days (with Joseph W. Alsop, Jr), 1937; My Life and The Times, 1971. *Address:* (office) 229 West 43rd Street, New York, NY 10036, USA. *T:* 556-1234; (home) 2316 Prytania Street, New Orleans, La 70130, USA. *T:* 522-2429. *Clubs:* National Press, Gridiron (Washington); Century, Silurians (New York); Boston (New Orleans), New Orleans Country.

CATLING, Hector William, OBE 1980; MA, DPhil, FSA; Director of the British School at Athens since 1971; *b* 26 June 1924; *s* of late Arthur William Catling and Phyllis Norah Catling (*née* Vyvyan); *m* 1948, Elizabeth Anne (*née* Salter); two *s* one *d.* *Educ:* The Grammar Sch., Bristol; St John's Coll., Oxford. Casberd Exhbr, 1948, BA 1950, MA 1954, DPhil 1957. Served War, RNVR, 1942-46. At Univ.: undergrad. 1946-50, postgrad. 1950-54. Goldsmiths' Travelling School, 1951-53. Archaeological Survey Officer, Dept of Antiquities, Cyprus, 1955-59; Asst Keeper, Dept of Antiquities, Ashmolean Museum, Univ. of Oxford, 1959-64, Sen. Asst Keeper, 1964-71. Fellow of Linacre Coll., Oxford, 1967-71. Corresp. Mem., German Archaeological Inst., 1961; Hon. Mem., Greek Archaeological Soc., 1975. *Publications:* Cypriot Bronzework in the Mycenaean World, 1964; contribs to jls concerned with prehistoric and classical antiquity in Greek lands. *Recreation:* ornithology. *Address:* The British School at Athens, Odos Souedias 52, Athens 140, Greece; 381 Woodstock Road, Oxford.

CATLING, Sir Richard (Charles), Kt 1964; CMG 1956; OBE 1951; *b* 22 Aug. 1912; *y s* of late William Catling, Leiston, Suffolk; *m* 1951, Mary Joan Feyer (*née* Lewis) (*d* 1974). *Educ:* The Grammar School, Bungay, Suffolk. Palestine Police, 1935-48; Federation of Malaya Police, 1948-54; Commissioner of Police, Kenya, 1954-63; Inspector General of Police, Kenya, 1963-64. Colonial Police Medal, 1942; King's Police Medal, 1945. Officer Brother, OStJ, 1956. *Recreations:* fishing, sailing. *Address:* Hall Fen House, Irstead, Norfolk NR12 8XT. *Club:* East India, Devonshire, Sports and Public Schools.

CATO, Hon. Sir Arnott Samuel; PC (Barbados) 1976; Kt 1977; President of the Senate of Barbados, since 1976; *b* St Vincent, 24 Sept. 1912. *Educ:* St Vincent Grammar Sch. (St Vincent Scholar, 1930); Edinburgh Univ. (MB, ChB). Returned to St Vincent; Asst Resident Surgeon, Colonial Hosp.,

1936-37; Ho. Surg., Barbados Gen. Hosp., 1937-41; private practice from 1941; Vis. Surgeon, Barbados Gen. Hosp., later Queen Elizabeth Hosp., and Chm. Med. Staff Cttee 1965-70. Past Pres., Barbados Br. BMA. Chm. Barbados Public Service Commn, 1972-76; (Prime Minister's Nominee) Senate of Barbados, following Gen. Election of Sept. 1976; Actg Governor Gen., 16 and 17 Nov. 1976, and 8 June-13 Aug. 1980. Hon. LLD, Univ. of West Indies, 1978. *Address:* Senate House, Bridgetown, Barbados.

CATO, Brian Hudson; Full-time Chairman of Industrial Tribunals, since 1975; *b* 6 June 1928; *s* of Thomas and Edith Willis Cato; *m* 1963, Barbara Edith Myles; one *s.* *Educ:* LEA elem. and grammar schs; Trinity Coll., Oxford; RAF Padgate. MA Oxon, LLB London. RAF, 1952-54. Called to Bar, Gray's Inn, 1952; in practice NE Circuit, 1954-75; a Recorder of the Crown Court, 1974-75. Special Lectr (part-time) in Law of Town and Country Planning, King's Coll., now Univ. of Newcastle, 1956-75; Hon. Examnr, Inst. of Landscape Architects, 1960-75. Pres., N of England Medico-legal Soc., 1973-75. Freeman of City of Newcastle upon Tyne by patrimony; Mem. Plumbers', Hostmen's, Goldsmiths' and Colliers' Companies; Founder Mem., Scriveners' Co. Hon. AILA. *Recreations:* family and village life. *Address:* 46 Bemersyde Drive, Newcastle upon Tyne NE2 2HJ. *T:* Newcastle 814226; The Cottage, Front Street, Embleton, Alnwick, Northumberland NE66 3UH. *T:* Embleton 334.

CATO, Rt. Hon. Robert Milton, PC 1981; Barrister; Prime Minister of St Vincent and the Grenadines, since 1979; *b* 3 June 1915; *m* Lucy Claxton. *Educ:* St Vincent Grammar Sch. Called to the Bar, Middle Temple, 1948; in private practice. Served War of 1939-45, Canadian Army. Leader, St Vincent Labour Party; Premier of St Vincent, 1967-72, 1974-79; former Minister of Finance. Mem., Kingstown Town Bd, 1952-59 (Chm., 1952-53); former Mem., Public Service Commn. A Governor, Caribbean Reg. Develt Bank for St Vincent. Former Pres., St Vincent Cricket Assoc. *Address:* c/o Office of the Prime Minister, Kingstown, St Vincent and the Grenadines. *Club:* Kingstown.

CATON-THOMPSON, Gertrude, FBA 1944; Hon. LittD Cantab 1954; former Fellow of Newnham College, Cambridge, Hon. Fellow 1981; *o d* of late William Caton-Thompson and Mrs E. G. Moore. *Educ:* Miss Hawtrey's, Eastbourne; Paris. Employed Ministry of Shipping, 1915-19; Paris Peace Conference, 1919; student British School of Archæology in Egypt, 1921-26; excavated at Abydos and Oxyrhynchos, 1921-22; Malta, 1921 and 1924; Qau and Badari, 1923-25; on behalf of the British School in Egypt inaugurated the first archæological and geological survey of the Northern Fayum, 1924-26; continued work as Field Director for the Royal Anthropological Institute, 1927-28; appointed in 1928 by the British Assoc. to conduct excavations at Zimbabwe and other Rhodesian sites; Excavations in Kharga Oasis, 1930-33; South Arabia, 1937-38; Cuthbert Peek award of the Royal Geographical Society, 1932; Rivers Medallist of the Royal Anthropological Institute, 1934; Huxley medallist, 1946. Burton Medal of Royal Asiatic Society, 1954. Former Governor, Bedford Coll. for Women, and School of Oriental and African Studies, University of London; former Member: Council British Inst. of History and Archæology in East Africa. *Publications:* contributions to the Encyclopædia Britannica and various scientific journals; The Badarian Civilisation (part author), 1928; The Zimbabwe Culture, 1931 (repr. 1969); The Desert Fayum, 1935; The Tombs and Moon Temple of Hureidha, Hadramaut, 1944; Kharga Oasis in Prehistory, 1952. *Recreation:* idleness. *Address:* Court Farm, Broadway, Worcs.

CATTANACH, Brig. Helen, CB 1976; RRC 1963; Matron-in-Chief (Army) and Director of Army Nursing Services, Queen Alexandra's Royal Army Nursing Corps, 1973-77; *b* 21 June 1920; *d* of late Francis Cattanach and Marjory Cattanach (*née* Grant). *Educ:* Elgin Academy; trained Woodend Hospital, Aberdeen. Joined QAIMNS (R) 1945; service in India, Java, United Kingdom, Singapore, Hong Kong and Germany, 1945-52; MELF, Gibraltar and UK, 1953-57; Staff Officer, MoD, 1958-61; Inspector of Recruiting, QARANC, 1961-62; Hong Kong, 1963-64; Matron: BMH Munster, 1968; Cambridge Military Hosp., Aldershot, 1969-71; Dir of Studies, QARANC, 1971-72. QHNS 1973-77. Col Comdt QARANC, 1978-81. CStJ 1976 (OStJ 1971). *Recreations:* walking, race meetings, theatre. *Address:* 22 Southview Court, Hill View Road, Woking, Surrey. *Club:* United Nursing Services.

CATTELL, George Harold Bernard; Group Managing Director, FMC, since 1978; Chief Executive, NFU Holdings Ltd, since 1978; *b* 23 March 1920; *s* of H. W. K. Cattell; *m* 1951, Agnes Jean Hardy; three *s* one *d.* *Educ:* Royal Grammar Sch., Colchester. Served Regular Army, 1939-58; psc 1945; despatches, Malaya, 1957; retired as Major, RA. Asst Director, London Engineering Employers' Assoc., 1958-60; Group Industrial Relations Officer, H. Stevenson & Sons, 1960-61; Director, Personnel and Manufacturing, Rootes Motors Ltd, 1961-68; Managing Director, Humber Ltd, Chm., Hills Precision Diecasting Ltd, Chm., Thrupp & Maberly Ltd, 1965-68; Dir, Manpower and Productivity Services, Dept of Employment and Productivity, 1968-70; Dir-Gen., NFU, 1970-78. Member Council: Industrial Soc. 1965-; CBI, 1970-. FRSA; FBIM. AMN Federation of Malaya, 1958. *Recreations:* tennis, fishing. *Address:* Little Cheveney, Yalding, Kent. *T:* Hunton 365. *Clubs:* Naval and Military, Institute of Directors.

CATTERALL, Dr John Ashley, FIM, FInstP; Head, Energy Technology Division, Department of Energy, since 1981; *b* 26 May 1928; *s* of John William Catterall and Gladys Violet Catterall; *m* 1960, Jennifer Margaret Bradfield; two *s.* *Educ:* Imperial Coll. of Science and Technol., London (BSc,

PhD, DIC). ARSM; FIM 1964; FInstP 1968; CEng 1978. National Physical Lab., 1952-75; Dept of Industry, 1975-81. Inst. of Metals Rosenhain Medal for Physical Metallurgy, 1970. *Publications:* (with O. Kubaschewski) Thermochemical Data of Alloys, 1956; contrib. Philos. Mag., Jl Inst. of Physics, Jl Inst. of Metals. *Recreation:* sailing. *Address:* 65 Hamilton Avenue, Pyrford, Woking, Surrey. *T:* Byfleet 46707.

CATTERMOLE, Joan Eileen, (Mrs J. Cattermole); *see* Mitchell, Prof. J. E.

CATTERMOLE, Lancelot Harry Mosse, ROI 1938; painter and illustrator; *b* 19 July 1898; *s* of Sidney and Josephine Cattermole; *g s* of George Cattermole, painter in water-colours and oils; *m* 1937, Lydia Alice Winifred Coles, BA; no *c. Educ:* Holmsdale House Sch., Worthing, Sussex; Odiham Grammar Sch., Hants. Senior Art Scholarship to Slade Faculty of Fine Art, University of London, and Central School of Arts and Crafts, London, 1923-26. Exhibitor RA, ROI, RBA, RP, etc., and Provincial Art Galleries. Signs work Lance Cattermole. *Recreations:* acting, reading and bridge. *Address:* Horizon, 17 Palmers Way, High Salvington, Worthing, W Sussex. *T:* Worthing 60436.

CATTO, family name of **Baron Catto.**

CATTO, 2nd Baron, *cr* 1936, of Cairncatto; Bt *cr* 1921; **Stephen Gordon Catto;** Chairman: Morgan Grenfell Holdings Ltd, since 1980; Australian Mutual Provident Society (UK Branch), since 1972; Yule Catto & Co. plc, since 1971; Director: The General Electric Co. plc; News International plc; The News Corporation, since 1979 (Australia); Times Newspapers Holdings Ltd, since 1981, and other companies; *b* 14 Jan. 1923; *o s* of 1st Baron Catto and Gladys Forbes (*d* 1980), *d* of Stephen Gordon; *S* father 1959; *m* 1st, 1948, Josephine Innes (marr. diss. 1965), *er d* of G. H. Packer, Alexandria, Egypt; two *s* two *d*; 2nd, 1966, Margaret, *d* of J. S. Forrest, Dilston, Tasmania; one *s* one *d. Educ:* Eton; Cambridge Univ. Served with RAFVR, 1943-47. Dir, 1957, Chief Exec., 1973-74, and Chm., 1973-79, Morgan Grenfell & Co. Ltd. Member, Advisory Council, ECGD, 1959-65; part-time Mem., London Transport Bd, 1962-68; Mem., London Adv. Cttee, Hong Kong & Shanghai Banking Corp., 1966-80. Chm. Council, RAF Benevolent Fund; Trustee and Chm., Exec. Cttee, Westminster Abbey Trust. *Heir: s* Thos. Innes Gordon Catto, *b* 7 Aug. 1950. *Address:* Morgan Grenfell Holdings Ltd, 23 Great Winchester Street, EC2P 2AX; 41 William Mews, Lowndes Square, SW1X 9HQ. *Clubs:* Oriental; Melbourne (Australia).

CAUGHEY, Sir Thomas Harcourt Clarke, KBE 1972 (OBE 1966); JP; Managing Director, since 1962, Chairman, since 1975, Smith & Caughey Ltd; *b* Auckland, 4 July 1911; *s* of James Marsden Caughey; *m* 1939, Patricia Mary, *d* of Hon. Sir George Panton Finlay; one *s* two *d. Educ:* King's Coll., Auckland. Major, Fiji Military Forces (Pacific), 1942-44. Director: New Zealand S British Insurance Group (Dep. Chm., 1981-); Guardian Trust and Executors Co. of NZ. Member: Caughey Preston Trust Bd, 1950-79 (Chm., 1954-79); Eden Park Trustees; Auckland Hosps Bd, 1953-74 (Chm., 1959-74); Hosps Adv. Council, 1960-74; Vice-Pres., NZ Exec. Hosps Bds Assoc., 1960-74; Chairman: NZ MRC, 1966-71; Social Council of NZ, 1971-73; Pres., Auckland Med. Res. Foundn, 1978-. Trustee, Post Grad. Med. Cttee, Auckland Sch. of Medicine. CStJ. *Recreations:* gardening, swimming. *Address:* 7 Judges Bay Road, Auckland, NZ. *Club:* Northern (Auckland, NZ).

CAULCOTT, Thomas Holt; Chief Executive, Birmingham City Council, since 1982; *b* 7 June 1927; *s* of late L. W. Caulcott and Doris Caulcott; *m* 1954, C. Evelyn Lowden (separated 1981); one *d* (and one *s* decd). *Educ:* Solihull Sch.; Emmanuel Coll., Cambridge. Asst Principal, Central Land Bd and War Damage Commn, 1950-53; transferred to HM Treasury, 1953; Private Sec. to Economic Sec. to the Treasury, 1955; Principal, Treasury supply divs, 1956-60; Private Sec. to successive Chancellors of the Exchequer, Sept. 1961-Oct. 1964; Principal Private Sec. to First Sec. of State (DEA), 1964-65; Asst Sec., HM Treasury, 1965-66; Min. of Housing and Local Govt, 1967-69; Civil Service Dept, 1969-70; Under-Sec., Machinery of Govt Gp, 1970-73; Principal Finance Officer, Local Govt Finance Policy, DoE, 1973-76; Sec., AMA, 1976-82. Harkness Fellowship, Harvard and Brookings Instn, 1960-61. *Address:* 5 Crescent Place, Brighton, Sussex. *T:* Brighton 697514; 24 St Dennis House, Melville Road, Birmingham B16 9NE. *T:* 021-454 4949.

CAULFEILD, family name of **Viscount Charlemont.**

CAULFIELD, Hon. Sir Bernard, Kt 1968; **Hon. Mr Justice Caulfield;** Judge of the High Court of Justice, Queen's Bench Division, since 1968; Presiding Judge, Northern Circuit, 1976-80; *b* 24 April 1914; *y s* of late John Caulfield and late Catherine Quinn; *m* 1953, Sheila Mary, *o d* of Dr J. F. J. Herbert; three *s* one *d. Educ:* St Francis Xavier's Coll.; University of Liverpool. LLB 1938, LLM 1940, Hon. LLD 1980. Solicitor, 1940. Army Service, 1940-46; Home and MEF; Commnd, Dec. 1942, RAOC; released with Hon. rank of Major. Barrister-at-Law, Lincoln's Inn, 1947; joined Midland Circuit, 1949; QC 1961; Recorder of Coventry, 1963-68; Dep. Chairman QS, County of Lincoln (Parts of Lindsey), 1963-71; Leader, Midland Circuit, 1965-68; Member, General Council of Bar, 1965-68. Bencher, Lincoln's Inn, 1968. Hon. Mem., Northern Circuit Bar Mess, 1979. *Address:* Royal Courts of Justice, WC2A 2LL.

CAUSEY, Prof. Gilbert, FRCS; retired; Sir William Collins Professor of Anatomy, Royal College of Surgeons, Professor of Anatomy, University of London, and Conservator of Hunterian Museum, 1952-70; *b* 8 Oct. 1907; 2nd *s* of George and Ada Causey; *m* 1935, Elizabeth, *d* of late F. J. L. Hickinbotham, JP, and of Mrs Hickinbotham; two *s* three *d. Educ:* Wigan Grammar Sch.; University of Liverpool. MB, ChB (1st Hons.), 1930; MRCS, LRCP, 1930; FRCS 1933; DSc 1964; FDSRCS 1971. Gold Medallist in Anatomy, Surgery, Medicine, and Obstetrics and Gynæcology; Lyon Jones Scholar and various prizes. Member of Anatomical and Physiological Societies. Asst Surgeon, Walton Hospital, Liverpool, 1935; Lecturer in Anatomy, University College, London, 1948; Rockefeller Foundation Travelling Fellow, 1950. John Hunter Medal, 1964; Keith Medal, 1970. *Publications:* The Cell of Schwann, 1960; Electron Microscopy, 1962; contributions to various scientific texts and journals. *Recreation:* music. *Address:* Orchard Cottage, Bodinnick-by-Fowey, Cornwall. *T:* Polruan 433.

CAUSLEY, Charles Stanley; poet; broadcaster; *b* Launceston, Cornwall, 24 Aug. 1917; *o s* of Charles Causley and Laura Bartlett. *Educ:* Launceston National Sch.; Horwell Grammar Sch.; Launceston Coll.; Peterborough Training Coll. Served on lower-deck in Royal Navy (Communications Branch), 1940-46. Literary Editor, 1953-56, of BBC's West Region radio magazines Apollo in the West and Signature. Awarded Travelling Scholarships by Society of Authors, 1954 and 1966. Mem., Arts Council Poetry Panel, 1962-66. Hon. Vis. Fellow in Poetry, Univ. of Exeter, 1973. FRSL 1958. Hon. DLitt Exeter, 1977; Hon. MA Open, 1982. Awarded Queen's Gold Medal for Poetry, 1967; Cholmondeley Award, 1971. *Publications:* Hands to Dance, 1951; Farewell, Aggie Weston, 1951; Survivor's Leave, 1953; Union Street, 1957; Peninsula (ed), 1957; Johnny Alleluia, 1961; Dawn and Dusk (ed), 1962; Penguin Modern Poets 3 (with George Barker and Martin Bell), 1962; Rising Early (ed), 1964; Modern Folk Ballads (ed), 1966; Underneath the Water, 1968; Figure of 8, 1969; Figgie Hobbin, 1971; The Tail of the Trinosaur, 1973; (ed) The Puffin Book of Magic Verse, 1974; Collected Poems, 1975; The Hill of the Fairy Calf, 1976; (ed) The Puffin Book of Salt-Sea Verse, 1978; Three Heads made of Gold, 1978; The Gift of a Lamb, 1978; The Animals' Carol, 1978; The Last King of Cornwall, 1978; (ed) Batsford Book of Stories in Verse for Children, 1979; (trans.) 25 Poems by Hamdija Demirović, 1980; The Ballad of Aucassin and Nicolette (verse play), 1981; (ed) The Sun, Dancing, 1982; contrib. to many anthologies of verse in Great Britain and America. *Recreations:* the theatre; European travel; the re-discovery of his native town; playing the piano with expression. *Address:* 2 Cyprus Well, Launceston, Cornwall PL15 8BT. *T:* Launceston 2731.

CAUTE, (John) David, MA, DPhil; writer; *b* 16 Dec. 1936; *m* 1st, 1961, Catherine Shuckburgh (marr. diss. 1970); two *s*; 2nd, 1973, Martha Bates; two *d. Educ:* Edinburgh Academy; Wellington; Wadham Coll., Oxford. Scholar of St Antony's Coll., 1959. Spent a year in the Army in the Gold Coast, 1955-56, and a year at Harvard Univ. on a Henry Fellowship, 1960-61. Fellow of All Souls Coll., Oxford, 1959-65; Visiting Professor, New York Univ. and Columbia Univ., 1966-67; Reader in Social and Political Theory, Brunel Univ., 1967-70. Regents' Lectr, Univ. of Calif., 1974. Literary Editor, New Statesman, 1979-80. Exec. Council, Writers' Guild, 1976-82, Dep. Chm., 1979-81, Chm., 1981-82. Plays: Songs for an Autumn Rifle, staged by Oxford Theatre Group at Edinburgh, 1961; The Demonstration, Nottingham Playhouse, 1969; Fallout, BBC Radio, 1972; The Fourth World, Royal Court, 1973; Brecht and Company, BBC TV, 1979. *Publications:* At Fever Pitch (novel), 1959 (Authors' Club Award and John Llewelyn Rhys Prize, 1960); Comrade Jacob (novel), 1961; Communism and the French Intellectuals, 1914-1960, 1964; The Left in Europe Since 1789, 1966; The Decline of the West (novel), 1966; Essential Writings of Karl Marx (ed), 1967; Fanon, 1970; The Confrontation: a trilogy, 1971 (consisting of The Demonstration (play), 1970; The Occupation (novel), 1971; The Illusion, 1971); The Fellow-Travellers, 1973; Collisions, 1974; Cuba, Yes?, 1974; The Great Fear, 1978; Under the Skin: the death of white Rhodesia, 1982; *as John Salisbury: novels* The Baby-Sitters, 1978; Moscow Gold, 1980. *Address:* 41 Westcroft Square, W6 0TA.

CAUTHERY, Harold William, CB 1969; *b* 5 May 1914; *s* of Joseph Cauthery, Manchester; *m* 1938, Dorothy Constance, *d* of George E. Sawyer, Sutton Coldfield; one *s* one *d* (and one *d* decd). *Educ:* Bishop Vesey's Grammar Sch., Sutton Coldfield; Christ's College, Cambridge. Asst Inspector of Taxes, Inland Revenue, 1936; Asst Principal, Ministry of Health, 1937; Instructor-Lieut, RN, 1942-45; Principal, Ministry of Health, 1944; Asst Secretary: Ministry of Health, 1950; Ministry of Housing and Local Government, 1951; Under-Sec., Min. of Transport, 1960-66; Dep. Sec., Min. of Land and Natural Resources, 1966; Dir and Sec. and Mem., Land Commn, 1967-71; Dep. Under-Sec. of State (Air), MoD, 1971-72; Sec., Local Govt Staff Commn, 1972-74. *Publication:* Parish Councillor's Guide, 10th Edition, 1958. *Recreations:* music, gardening. *Address:* Eastcote, Petworth Road, Haslemere, Surrey. *T:* Haslemere 51448. *Club:* United Oxford & Cambridge University.

CAVALIERO, Roderick; Deputy Director General, British Council, since 1981 (Assistant Director General, 1977-81); *b* 21 March 1928; *s* of Eric Cavaliero and Valerie (*née* Logan); *m* 1957, Mary McDonnell; one *s* four *d. Educ:* Tonbridge School; Hertford Coll., Oxford. Teaching in Britain, 1950-52; teaching in Malta, 1952-58; British Council Officer, 1958- (service in India, Brazil, Italy). Chm., Educnl and Trng Export Cttee, 1979–; Dir, Open Univ. Educnl Enterprises, 1980–. *Publications:* Olympia and the Angel, 1958; The Last of the Crusaders, 1960. *Address:* 10 Lansdowne Road, Tunbridge Wells, Kent TN1 2NJ.

CAVALLERA, Rt. Rev. Charles; *b* Centallo, Cuneo, Italy, 1909. *Educ:* International Missionary College of the Consolata of Turin; Pontifical Univ. of Propaganda Fide of Rome (degree in Missionology). Sec. to Delegate Apostolic of British Africa, 1936–40; Vice-Rector, then Rector, of Urban Coll. of Propaganda Fide of Rome, 1941–47; formerly Titular Bishop of Sufes; Vicar-Apostolic of Nyeri (Kenya), 1947–53; Bishop of Nyeri, 1953–64; Bishop of Marsabit, 1964–81. *Address:* Missioni Consolata, Viale Mura Aurelie 12, 00165 Rome, Italy.

CAVAN, 12th Earl of, *cr* 1647; **Michael Edward Oliver Lambart, TD; DL;** Baron Cavan, 1618; Baron Lambart, 1618; Viscount Kilcoursie, 1647; Vice Lord-Lieutenant, Salop, since 1975; *b* 29 Oct. 1911; *o s* of 11th Earl of Cavan and Audrey Kathleen (*d* 1942), *o d* of late A. B. Loder; *S* father 1950; *m* 1947, Essex Lucy, *o d* of Henry Arthur Cholmondeley, Shotton Hall, Hadnall, Shropshire; one *d* (and two *d* decd). *Educ:* Radley College. Served War of 1939-45, Shropshire Yeomanry (despatches). Lt-Col comdg Shropshire Yeomanry, 1955-58. DL Salop, 1959. *Address:* The Glebe House, Stockton, Shifnal, Shropshire TF11 9EF. *T:* Norton 236.

CAVANAGH, John Bryan; Dress Designer; Chairman and Managing Director, John Cavanagh Ltd, retired 1974; *b* 28 Sept. 1914; *s* of Cyril Cavanagh and Anne (*née* Murphy). *Educ:* St Paul's School. Trained with Captain Edward Molyneux in London and Paris, 1932-40. Joined Intelligence Corps, 1940, Captain (GS, Camouflage), 1944. On demobilisation, 1946, travelled throughout USA studying fashion promotion. Personal Assistant to Pierre Balmain, Paris, 1947-51; opened own business, 1952; opened John Cavanagh Boutique, 1959. Elected to Incorporated Society of London Fashion Designers, 1952 (Vice-Chm., 1956-59). Took own complete Collection to Paris, 1953; designed clothes for late Princess Marina and wedding dresses for the Duchess of Kent and Princess Alexandra. Gold Medal, Munich, 1954. *Recreations:* the theatre, swimming, travelling. *Address:* 10 Birchlands Avenue, SW12.

CAVE; *see* Verney-Cave, family name of Baron Braye.

CAVE, Alexander James Edward, MD, DSc, FRCS, FLS; Emeritus Professor of Anatomy, University of London; *b* Manchester, 13 Sept. 1900; *e s* of late John Cave and Teresa Anne d'Hooghe; *m* 1st, 1926, Dorothy M. Dimbleby (*d* 1961); one *d* ; 2nd, 1970, Catherine Elizabeth FitzGerald. *Educ:* Manchester High Sch.; Victoria University of Manchester. MB, ChB (distinction Preventive Medicine) 1923; MD (commendation) 1937; DSc, 1944; FRCS, 1959; DSc London, 1967. Senior Demonstrator (later Lecturer) in Anatomy, University of Leeds, 1924-34; Senior Demonstrator of Anatomy and Curator of Anatomical Museum, University College, London, 1934-35; Asst Conservator of Museum (1935-46), Arnott Demonstrator (1936-46), Arris and Gale Lectr, 1932, 1941, Professor of Human and Comparative Anatomy (1941-46), and Wood Jones Medalist 1978, Royal College of Surgeons of England; Prof. of Anatomy, St Bartholomew's Hospital Medical Coll., University of London, 1946-67, now Member Board Governors. Hunterian Trustee; Stopford Lecturer, 1967; Morrison Watson Research Fellow, 1961-72. Late Examiner in Anatomy, University of London, Royal University of Malta, Universities of Cambridge and Ireland, Primary FRCS and English Conjoint Board; Fellow (formerly Council Mem. and Pres.), Linnean Society; Fellow and Hon. Res. Associate (late Vice-Pres. and Council Mem.) and Silver Medallist Zoological Society; Life-Member (late Council Mem., Hon. Secretary and Recorder, Vice-Pres.) Anatomical Soc.; Hon. Associate BM (Nat. Hist.); Mem., American Assoc. of Physical Anthropologists; *Publications:* various papers on human and comparative anatomy, physical anthropology and medical history. *Address:* 18 Orchard Avenue, Finchley, N3. *T:* 01-346 3340. *Club:* Athenæum.

CAVE, Sir Charles (Edward Coleridge), 4th Bt, *cr* 1896; JP; DL; *b* 28 Feb. 1927; *o s* of Sir Edward Charles Cave, 3rd Bt, and Betty (*d* 1979), *o d* of late Rennell Coleridge, Salston, Ottery St Mary; *S* father 1946; *m* 1957, Mary Elizabeth, *yr d* of John Francis Gore, *qv* ; four *s*. *Educ:* Eton. Lieut The Devonshire Regt, 1946-48. CC Devon, 1955-64; High Sheriff of Devonshire, 1969. JP Devon 1972, DL Devon 1977. FRICS. *Heir: s* John Charles Cave, *b* 8 Sept. 1958. *Address:* Sidbury Manor, Sidmouth, Devon. *T:* Sidbury 207.

CAVE, Sir (Charles) Philip H.; *see* Haddon-Cave.

CAVE, John Arthur, FIB; Chairman: Midland Bank Finance Corporation Ltd, 1975-79; Midland Montagu Leasing Ltd, 1975-79; Forward Trust Ltd, 1975-79; Director, Midland Bank Ltd, 1974-79; *b* 30 Jan. 1915; *s* of Ernest Cave and Eva Mary Cave; *m* 1937, Peggy Pauline, *y d* of Frederick Charles Matthews Browne; two *s* two *d*. *Educ:* Loughborough Grammar Sch. FIB 1962. Served War, Royal Tank Regt, 1940-46. Entered Midland Bank, Eye, Suffolk, 1933; Manager, Threadneedle Street Office, 1962-64; Jt Gen. Man., 1965-72; Asst Chief Gen. Man., 1972-74; Dep. Chief Gen. Man., 1974-75. Dir, Midland Bank Trust Co. Ltd, 1972-76. Mem. Council, Inst. of Bankers, 1967-75 (Dep. Chm., 1973-75). Hon. Captain and Founder, Midland Bank Sailing Club (Cdre, 1967-75). *Recreation:* sailing. *Address:* Dolphin House,

Centre Cliff, Southwold, Suffolk. *T:* Southwold 722232. *Club:* Royal Norfolk and Suffolk Yacht (Lowestoft).

CAVE, Sir Richard (Guy), Kt 1976; MC 1944; Chairman, THORN EMI plc (Chairman, Thorn Electrical Industries Ltd, 1976-79); Director: Tunnel Holdings Ltd; Tate & Lyle Ltd; Thames Television Ltd, since 1981; *b* 16 March 1920; *s* of William Thomas Cave and Gwendolyn Mary Nichols; *m* 1957, Dorothy Gillian Fry; two *s* two *d*. *Educ:* Tonbridge; Gonville and Caius Coll., Cambridge. Joined Smiths Industries Ltd, 1946; Man. Dir, Motor Accessory Div., 1963; Chief Exec. and Man. Dir, 1968-73; Chm., 1973-76. Chm., Industrial Soc. *Recreation:* sailing. *Address:* Thamescote, Chiswick Mall, W4. *T:* 01-994 8017.

CAVE, Sir Richard (Philip), KCVO 1977 (MVO 1969); CB 1975; DL; Fourth Clerk at the Table (Judicial), House of Lords, 1965-77 and Principal Clerk, Judicial Department, House of Lords, 1959-77; Taxing Officer of Judicial Costs, House of Lords, 1957-77; Crown Examiner in Peerage Cases 1953-77; Secretary, Association of Lieutenants of Counties and Custodes Rotulorum, 1946-59, and 1964-77; Founder and President, Multiple Sclerosis Society of Great Britain and Northern Ireland (Chairman, 1953-76); a Vice-President, International Federation of Multiple Sclerosis Societies, 1967, Emeritus since 1981; *b* 26 April 1912; 4th *s* of late Charles John Philip Cave and late Wilhelmina Mary Henrietta (*née* Kerr); *m* 1936, Margaret Mary (*d* 1981), *e d* of Francis Westby Perceval; one *s*. *Educ:* Ampleforth Coll.; Trinity Coll., Cambridge (MA); Herts Institute of Agriculture; College of Estate Management. A Gold Staff Officer, Coronation of HM King George VI, 1937. Agent for Earl of Craven's Hamstead Marshall Estate, 1938-39. Royal Wilts Yeomanry (L. Corp.), 1939-40; The Rifle Bde (Captain; Officer i/c Cols Comdt's Office, KRRC and Rifle Bde), 1940-45. Territorial Efficiency Medal, 1946. Vice-Chm., Society for Relief of Distress, 1972; a Governor, Queen Elizabeth's Foundn for the Disabled, 1970. A Confrater of Ampleforth Abbey, 1971. DL Greater London, 1973. Gold Medal, Royal English Forestry Society, 1939; Silver Medal, RASE, 1939. KSG 1966; KCSG 1972; Kt of Honour and Devotion, SMO Malta, 1972; Kt of Justice, Sacred Military Order of Constantine of St George, 1972. *Publications:* Elementary Map Reading, 1941; articles in Atkin's Encyclopedia of Court Forms in Civil Proceedings, 1968 and 1973; Halsbury's Laws of England, 1974. *Recreations:* hill-walking, photography, collecting map postcards. *Address:* Watergate, 34 Ham Common, Richmond, Surrey TW10 7JG. *T:* 01-940 8014. *Clubs:* Royal Commonwealth Society; University Pitt (Cambridge).

CAVE-BROWNE-CAVE, Sir Robert, 16th Bt, *cr* 1641; President of Cave & Co. Ltd, and of Seaboard Chemicals Ltd; *b* 8 June 1929; *s* of 15th Bt, and Dorothea Plewman, *d* of Robert Greene Dwen, Chicago, Ill; *S* father 1945; *m* 1954, Lois Shirley, *d* of John Chalmers Huggard, Winnipeg, Manitoba; one *s* one *d*. *Educ:* University of BC (BA 1951). *Heir: s* John Robert Charles Cave-Browne-Cave, *b* 22 June 1957. *Address:* 6562 Laurel, Vancouver, BC, Canada. *Club:* Capilano Golf and Country (BC).

CAVELL, Rt. Rev. John K; *see* Southampton, Bishop Suffragan of.

CAVENAGH, Prof. Winifred Elizabeth, OBE 1977; JP; PhD, BScEcon; Professor of Social Administration and Criminology, University of Birmingham, 1972-76, now Emeritus; Barrister-at-Law; *d* of Arthur Speakman and Ethel Speakman (*née* Butterworth); *m* 1938, Hugh Cavenagh, one step *s*. *Educ:* London Sch. of Economics, Univ. of London; Bonn. BSc Econ (London); PhD (Birm.). Called to the Bar, Gray's Inn, 1964. With Lewis's Ltd, 1931-38; Min. of Labour, 1941-45. Univ. of Birmingham, 1946-. Birmingham: City Educn Cttee (co-opted expert), 1946-66; City Magistrate, 1949- (Dep. Chm., 1970-78); Police Authority, 1970-78. Governor, Birmingham United Teaching Hosps (Ministerial appt, 1958-64); W Midlands Economic Planning Council, 1967-71; Indep. Mem. of Wages Councils; Home Office Standing Advisory Cttee on Probation, 1958-67; Lord Chancellor's Standing Adv. Cttee: on Legal Aid, 1960-71; on Training of Magistrates, 1965-73. Nat. Chm., Assoc. of Social Workers, 1955-57; Council, Magistrates Assoc. (co-opted expert), 1965-78; BBC Gen. Adv. Council, 1977-80; Vice-Pres., Internat. Assoc. of Juvenile and Family Courts, 1978-; Chm., Industrial Tribunal, 1974-77. Visiting Prof., Univ of Ghana, 1971- Eleanor Rathbone Meml Lectr, 1976; Moir Cullis Lectr Fellowship, USA, 1977, Canada, 1980. *Publications:* Four Decades of Students in Social Work, 1953; The Child and the Court, 1959; Juvenile Courts, the Child and the Law, 1967; contrib. articles to: Public Administration, Brit. Jl Criminology, Justice of the Peace, Social Work To-day, etc. *Recreations:* walking, theatre, music films. *Address:* 25 High Point, Richmond Hill Road, Edgbaston, Birmingham B15 3RU. *T:* 021-454 0109. *Club:* University Women's.

CAVENAGH-MAINWARING, Captain Maurice Kildare, DSO 1940; Royal Navy; joined Simpson (Piccadilly) Ltd, 1961; *b* 13 April 1908; *yr s* of Major James Gordon Cavenagh-Mainwaring, Whitmore Hall, Whitmore, Staffordshire; *m* Iris Mary, *d* of late Colonel Charles Denaro, OBE; one *s*. *Educ:* RN College, Dartmouth. Joint Services Staff College, 1951-52; HMS St Angelo and Flag Captain to Flag Officer, Malta, 1952-54; President, Second Admiralty Interview Board, 1955-56; Naval Attaché, Paris, 1957-60. ADC to the Queen, 1960. Retired from RN, 1960. Cross of Merit Sovereign Order, Knights of Malta, 1955; Comdr Légion d'Honneur, 1960. *Address:* 47 Cadogan Gardens, SW3. *T:* 01-584 7870; Apollo Court, St Julian's, Malta *Club:* Naval and Military.

CAVENDISH, family name of **Baron Chesham,** of **Duke of Devonshire,** and of **Baron Waterpark.**

CAVENDISH, Maj.-Gen. Peter Boucher, CB 1981; OBE 1969; Chairman, Military Agency for Standardisation and Director, Armaments Standardisation and Interoperability Division, International Military Staff, HQ NATO, 1978-81; *b* 26 Aug. 1925; *s* of late Brig. R. V. C. Cavendish, OBE, MC (killed in action, 1943) and Helen Cavendish (*née* Boucher); *m* 1952, Marion Loudon (*née* Constantine); three *s. Educ:* Abberley Hall, Worcester; Winchester Coll.; New Coll., Oxford. Enlisted 1943; commnd The Royal Dragoons, 1945; transf. 3rd The King's Own Hussars, 1946; Staff Coll., Camberley, 1955; served Palestine, BAOR, Canada and N Africa to 1966; CO 14th/20th King's Hussars, 1966-69; HQ 1st British Corps, 1969-71; Comdt RAC Centre, 1971-74; Canadian Defence Coll., 1975; Sec. to Mil. Cttee and Internat. Mil. Staff, HQ NATO, 1975-78. MBIM 1972. Colonel, 14th/20th King's Hussars, 1978-81; Hon. Col, The Queen's Own Mercian Yeomanry, TAVR, 1982-. *Recreations:* shooting, country pursuits, DIY. *Address:* The Rock Cottage, Middleton-by-Youlgrave, Bakewell, Derby DE4 1LS. *T:* Youlgrave 225. *Club:* Cavalry and Guards.

CAVENDISH-BENTINCK, family name of **Duke of Portland.**

CAWDOR, 6th Earl *cr* 1827; **Hugh John Vaughan Campbell,** FRICS; Baron Cawdor, 1796; Viscount Emlyn, 1827; *b* 6 Sept. 1932; *er s* of 5th Earl Cawdor, TD, FSA, and Wilma Mairi (*d* 1982), *e d* of late Vincent C. Vickers; *S* father, 1970; *m* 1st, 1957, Cathryn (marr. diss. 1979), 2nd *d* of Maj.-Gen. Sir Robert Hinde, KBE, CB, DSO; two *s* three *d*; 2nd, 1979, Countess Angelika Ilona Lazansky von Bukowa. *Educ:* Eton; Magdalen Coll., Oxford; Royal Agricultural Coll., Cirencester. High Sheriff of Carmarthenshire, 1964. *Heir: s* Viscount Emlyn, *qv. Address:* Cawdor Castle, Nairn. *Club:* Pratt's.

CAWLEY, family name of **Baron Cawley.**

CAWLEY, 3rd Baron, *cr* 1918; **Frederick Lee Cawley,** 3rd Bt, *cr* 1906; *b* 27 July 1913; *s* of 2nd Baron and Vivienne (*d* 1978), *d* of Harold Lee, Broughton Park, Manchester; *S* father 1954; *m* 1944, Rosemary Joan, *y d* of late R. E. Marsden; six *s* one *d. Educ:* Eton; New Coll., Oxford. BA Nat. Science (Zoology), 1935, MA 1942. Called to the Bar, Lincoln's Inn, 1938; practised 1946-73; farmer. Served War of 1939-45, Capt. RA Leicestershire Yeomanry (wounded). Mem. Woking UDC, 1949-57. Dep.-Chm. of Cttees, House of Lords, 1958-67; Mem., Jt Parly Cttees: Consolidation Bills, 1956-73; Delegated Legislation, 1972-73; Ecclesiastical, 1974. *Recreations:* gardening, shooting. *Heir: s* Hon. John Francis Cawley [*b* 28 Sept. 1946; *m* 1979, Regina Sarabia, *e d* of Marquess de Hazas, Madrid; one *s* one *d*]. *Address:* Bircher Hall, Leominster, Herefordshire HR6 0AX. *T:* Yarpole 218. *Club:* Farmers'.

CAWLEY, Sir Charles (Mills), Kt 1965; CBE; Chief Scientist, Ministry of Power, 1959-67; a Civil Service Commissioner, 1967-69; *b* 17 May 1907; *s* of John and Emily Cawley, Gillingham, Kent; *m* 1934, Florence Mary Ellaline, *d* of James Shepherd, York; one *d. Educ:* Sir Joseph Williamson's Mathematical Sch., Rochester; Imperial Coll. of Science and Technology (Royal College of Sci.). ARCS, BSc (First Cl. Hons in Chem.), DIC; MSc; PhD; FRSC; DSc(London); SFInstF; FRSA; Fellow, Imperial Coll. of Science and Technology. Fuel Research Station, DSIR, 1929-53. Imperial Defence Coll., 1949. A Dir, Headquarters, DSIR, 1953-59. Chm., Admiralty Fuels and Lubricants Advisory Cttee, 1957-64. Melchett Medal, Inst. of Fuel, 1968. *Publications:* Papers in various scientific and technical journals. *Address:* 8 Glen Gardens, Ferring-by-Sea, Worthing, West Sussex BN12 5HG.

CAWLEY, Prof. Robert Hugh, PhD; FRCP, FRCPsych; Professor of Psychological Medicine, King's College Hospital Medical School, and Institute of Psychiatry, since 1975; Consultant Psychiatrist: King's College Hospital, since 1975; Bethlem Royal and Maudsley Hospitals, since 1967; *b* 16 Aug. 1924; *yr s* of Robert Ernest Cawley and Alice Maud (*née* Taylor). *Educ:* Solihull Sch.; Univ. of Birmingham (BSc Hons Zool., PhD, MB, ChB); Univ. of London (DPM). FRCP 1975; FRCPsych 1971. Univ. of Birmingham: Res. Scholar, 1947; Res. Fellow, 1949; Halley Stewart Res. Fellow, 1954; House Phys. and Surg., Queen Elizabeth Hosp., Birmingham, 1956-57; Registrar, then Sen. Registrar, Bethlem Royal and Maudsley Hosps, 1957-60; Clin. Lectr, Inst. of Psych., 1960-62; Sen. Lectr and First Asst in Psych., Univ. of Birmingham, and Hon. Consultant, United Birm. Hosps and Birm. RHB, 1962-67; Phys., Bethlem Royal and Maudsley Hosps, 1967-75. Mem., MRC, 1979-; Chm., Neurosciences Bd, 1979-81. Chief Examnr, Royal Coll. of Psychiatrists, 1981-. *Publications:* contribns on biological, medical and psychiatric subjects in scientific books and jls. *Address:* 12 Rivermill, 151 Grosvenor Road, SW1V 3JN. *Club:* Athenæum.

CAWSON, Prof. Roderick Anthony, MD; FDS, RCS and RCPS Glasgow; FRCPath; Professor (Hon. Consultant) and Head of Department of Oral Medicine and Pathology, Guy's Hospital Medical School since 1966; *b* 23 April 1921; *s* of Capt. Leopold Donald Cawson and Ivy Clunies-Ross; *m* 1949, Diana Hall, SRN; no *c. Educ:* King's College Sch. Wimbledon; King's College Hosp. Med. Sch. MD (London); MB, BS, BDS (Hons) (London); FDS, RCS; FDS, RCPS Glasgow; MRCPath; LMSSA. Served RAF, 1944-48; Nuffield Foundn Fellow, 1953-55; Dept of Pathology, King's Coll. Hosp., Sen. Lectr in Oral Pathology, King's Coll. Hosp. Med. Sch., 1955-62; Sen. Lectr in Oral Pathology, Guy's Hosp. Med. Sch., 1962-66. Examinerships:

Pathology (BDS) London, 1965-69; Univ. of Wales, 1969-71; Dental Surgery (BDS), Glasgow, 1966-70; BChD Leeds, 1966-70; Newcastle, 1967-71; FDS, RCPS Glasgow, 1967-; BDS Lagos, 1975-. Chairman: Dental Formulary Sub-cttee (BMA); Dental and Surgical Materials Cttee, Medicines Division, 1976-80; recently First Chm., Univ. Teachers' Gp (BDA). *Publications:* Essentials of Dental Surgery and Pathology 1962, 3rd edn, 1978; Medicine for Dental Students (with R. H. Cutforth), 1960; (with R. G. Spector) Clinical Pharmacology in Dentistry, 1975, 2nd edn, 1978; numerous papers, etc., in med. and dental jls. *Recreations:* reading, music, gardening (reluctantly). *Address:* 40 Court Lane, Dulwich, SE21 7DR. *T:* 01-693 5781.

CAWSTON, (Edwin) Richard, CVO 1972; documentary film-maker; Documentary Consultant to BBC Television; Special Projects Director, Video Arts Ltd; *b* 31 May 1923; *s* of Edwin Cawston and Phyllis, *d* of Henry Charles Hawkins; *m* 1st, 1951, Elisabeth Anne (*d* 1977), *d* of Canon R. L. Rhys; two *s*; 2nd, 1978, Andrea, *e d* of Michael and Dora Phillips, Cyprus. *Educ:* Westminster Sch.; Oriel Coll., Oxford. Served Royal Signals, 1941-46; Captain 1945; Major and SO2 HQ Southern Comd, India, 1946. Joined BBC TV, 1947, as Film Editor, then Producer of original Television Newsreel, 1950-54; producer and director of major documentary films, 1955-79; Head of Documentary Programmes, BBC TV, 1965-79. Chm., British Acad. of Film and TV Arts, 1976-79 (Trustee, 1971-; Mem. Council of Management, 1959-). Awards include: British Film Acad. Award, 1959; Screenwriters Guild Award, 1961; Silver Medal, Royal TV Soc., 1961; Guild of TV Producers and Dirs Award, 1962; Italia Prize, 1962; Desmond Davis Award, 1969; Silver Satellite of AWRT, 1970. *Major documentary films include:* This is the BBC, 1959; The Lawyers, 1960; Television and the World, 1961; The Pilots, 1963; Born Chinese, 1965; Royal Family, 1969; Royal Heritage, 1977. *Recreation:* making things. *Address:* 25 Lower Addison Gardens, W14 8BG.

CAWTHRA, Rear-Adm. Arthur James, CB 1966; Admiral Superintendent, HM Dockyard, Devonport, 1964-66; *b* 30 Sept. 1911; *s* of James Herbert Cawthra, MIEE, and Margaret Anne Cawthra; *m* 1959, Adrien Eleanor Lakeman Tivy, *d* of Cecil B. Tivy, MCh, Plymouth; one *s* (and one *s* decd). *Educ:* abroad. Joined Royal Navy, 1930; Imperial Defence Course, 1956; HMS Fisgard, 1958-59; Dir Underwater Weapons, Admiralty, 1960-63. Capt. 1955; Rear-Adm. 1964. *Address:* Lower Island, Blackawton, Totnes, Devon.

CAYFORD, Dame Florence Evelyn, DBE 1965; JP; Mayor, London Borough of Camden, 1969; *b* 14 June 1897; *d* of George William and Mary S. A. Bunch; *m* 1923, John Cayford; two *s. Educ:* Carlton Road Sch.; St Pancras County Secondary Sch., Paddington Technical Institute. Alderman, LCC, 1946-52; Member: LCC for Shoreditch and Finsbury, 1952-64; GLC (for Islington) and ILEA, 1964-67. Chairman: Hospital and Medical Services Cttee LCC, 1948; (Health Cttee). Division 7, 1948-49, Division 2 in 1949; Health Cttee, 1953-60; Welfare Cttee, 1965, of LCC; Metropolitan Water Bd, 1966-67 (Vice-Chm., 1965-66). Mem. Hampstead Borough Council, 1937-65 (Leader of Labour Group, 1945-58), Councillor for Kilburn until 1945, Alderman, 1945-65; Chm., LCC, 1960-61; Chairman: (Hampstead), Maternity and Child Welfare Cttee, 1941-45, Juvenile Court Panel, 1950-62; Dep. Mayoress, Camden Borough Council, 1967-68. Probation Cttee, 1959-; Leavesden Hosp. Management Cttee, 1948-63; Harben Secondary Sch., 1946-61. Member: Co-operative Political Party (ex-Chm. and Sec.); Co-operative Soc.; Labour Party; National Institute for Social Work Training, 1962-65; Min. of Health Council for Training of Health Visitors, 1962-65; Min. of Health Council for Training in Social Work, 1962-65. Chm., YWCA Helen Graham Hse, 1972-. JP, Inner London, 1941-. Freeman, London Borough of Camden (formerly Borough of Hampstead), 1961. Noble Order, Crown of Thailand, 3rd Class, 1964. *Address:* 26 Hemstal Road, Hampstead, NW6. *T:* 01-624 6181.

CAYLEY, Sir Digby (William David), 11th Bt *cr* 1661; MA Cantab; Managing Director, C. P. Stockbridge Ltd, Histon, Cambs (Antiques and Fine Arts); *b* 3 June 1944; *s* of Lieut-Comdr W. A. S. Cayley, RN (*d* 1964) (*g g s* of 7th Bt), and of Natalie M. Cayley, BA; *S* kinsman, 1967; *m* 1969, Christine Mary Gaunt, BA, *o d* of late D. F. Gaunt and of Mrs A. T. Gaunt, Clitheroe, Lancs; two *d. Educ:* Malvern Coll.; Downing Coll., Cambridge. Asst Classics Master, Portsmouth Grammar Sch., 1968-73; Stonyhurst Coll., 1973-81. *Recreations:* antiques export business, .22 rifle shooting, bridge. *Heir: cousin* George Paul Cayley [*b* 23 May 1940; *m* 1967, Shirley Southwell, *d* of Frank Woodward Petford; two *s*]. *Address:* The Close, Needingworth Road, St Ives, Cambs.

CAYLEY, Henry Douglas, OBE 1946; *b* 20 Jan. 1904; *s* of late Cyril Henry Cayley, MD; *m* 1940, Nora Innes Paton, *d* of Nigel F. Paton; one *s* two *d. Educ:* Epsom Coll. Joined National Bank of India Ltd, London, 1922; Eastern Staff, 1926; Dep. Exchange Controller, Reserve Bank of India, 1939-48; rejoined National Bank of India, 1948; appointed to London Head Office, 1952; Asst Gen. Manager 1957, Dep. Gen. Manager 1960, Chief Gen. Manager 1964-69, Director 1966-72, National & Grindlays Bank Ltd; Dir, Grindlays Australia Ltd, 1974-78; Dir, William Brandt Sons & Co. Ltd, 1965-72. *Recreations:* gardening, walking. *Address:* Virginia Lodge, Boronia Street, Bowral, NSW 2576, Australia. *Club:* Lansdowne.

CAYZER, family name of **Barons Cayzer** and **Rotherwick.**

CAYZER, Baron cr 1982 (Life Peer), of St Mary Axe in the City of London; **William Nicholas Cayzer**; Bt 1921; Chairman of: British & Commonwealth Shipping Co. Ltd; Clan Line Steamers Ltd; Cayzer, Irvine & Co. Ltd; Caledonia Investments Ltd; Union-Castle Mail Steamship Co. Ltd and associated cos; Scottish Lion Insurance Co. Ltd; Air Holdings Ltd; Meldrum Investment Trust; Air UK; *b* 21 Jan. 1910; *s* of Sir August Cayzer, 1st Bt, and Ina Frances (*d* 1935), 2nd *d* of William Stancombe, Blounts Ct, Wilts; *S* to father's baronetcy, 1943; *m* 1935, Elizabeth Catherine, *d* of late Owain Williams and *g d* of Morgan Stuart Williams, Aberpergwm, Glamorgan; two *d*. *Educ*: Eton; Corpus Christi Coll., Cambridge. Chm. Liverpool Steamship Owners Association, 1944–45; Pres. Chamber of Shipping of the UK, 1959; Pres. Inst. of Marine Engineers, 1963. Chairman: Gen. Council of Brit. Shipping, 1959; Chamber of Shipping's British Liner Cttee, 1960–63; Mem., MoT Shipping Adv. Panel, 1962–64; sometime Mem. Mersey Dock and Harbour Board; sometime Mem. National Dock Labour Board. Prime Warden, Shipwrights Company, 1969. *Heir* (to baronetcy): none. *Address*: The Grove, Walsham-le-Willows, Suffolk. *T*: Walsham-le-Willows 263; 95j Eaton Square, SW1. *T*: 01-235 5551. *Club*: Brooks's.
See also M. K. B. Colvin.

CAYZER, Hon. Anthony; see Cayzer, Hon. M. A. R.

CAYZER, Sir James Arthur, 5th Bt, *cr* 1904; *b* 15 Nov. 1931; *s* of Sir Charles William Cayzer, 3rd Bt, MP (*d* 1940), and Beatrice Eileen (*d* 1981), *d* of late James Meakin and Emma Beatrice (later wife of 3rd Earl Sondes); *S* brother, 1943. *Educ*: Eton. *Heir: cousin*, Baron Cayzer, *qv*. *Address*: Kinpurnie Castle, Newtyle, Angus. *T*: Newtyle 207. *Club*: Carlton.

CAYZER, Hon. (Michael) Anthony (Rathborne); shipowner; *b* 28 May 1920; 2nd *s* of 1st Baron Rotherwick; *m* 1952, Hon. Patricia Browne (*d* 1981), *er d* of 4th Baron Oranmore and Browne, *qv*, and late Hon. Mrs Hew Dalrymple; three *d*; *m* 1982, Baroness Sybille de Selys Longchamps. *Educ*: Eton; Royal Military Coll., Sandhurst. Commissioned Royal Scots Greys: served 1939–44 (despatches). Dep. Chairman: British & Commonwealth Shipping Co. Ltd; Air UK Ltd; Airwork Services Ltd; Air Holdings Ltd; Chairman: Servisair Ltd; Britavia Ltd; Director: Cayzer, Irvine & Co. Ltd; Caledonia Investments Ltd; Overseas Containers (Holdings) Ltd; Sterling Industries Ltd; Bristow Helicopters Group Ltd. President: Inst. of Shipping and Forwarding Agents, 1963–65; Chamber of Shipping of the United Kingdom, 1967; Herts Agric. Soc., 1974; Past Vice-Pres., British Light Aviation Centre. Past Mem. Mersey Docks and Harbour Bd. Chm. Liverpool Steamship Owners Assoc., 1956–67. Trustee: Nat. Maritime Museum, 1968– (Chm., 1977–); Maritime Trust, 1975–. *Address*: Great Westwood, Kings Langley, Herts. *T*: Kings Langley 62296. *Clubs*: Boodle's, Royal Yacht Squadron.

CAZALET, Edward Stephen, QC 1980; *b* 26 April 1936; *s* of late Peter Victor Ferdinand Cazalet and Leonora Cazalet (*née* Rowley); *m* 1965, Camilla Jane (*née* Gage); two *s* one *d*. *Educ*: Eton Coll.; Christ Church, Oxford (2nd Cl. Hons Jurisprudence). Called to the Bar, Inner Temple, 1960. Chairman, Horserace Betting Levy Appeal Tribunal, 1977–. *Recreations*: riding, ball games, chess. *Address*: 58 Seymour Walk, SW10. *T*: 01-352 0401. *Clubs*: White's, Garrick, Wig and Pen.

CAZALET, Peter Grenville; a Managing Director, British Petroleum Co. plc, since 1981; *b* 26 Feb. 1929; *e s* of Vice-Adm. Sir Peter (Grenville Lyon) Cazalet, KBE, CB, DSO, DSC, and of Lady (Elise) Cazalet (*née* Winterbotham); *m* 1957, Jane Jennifer, *yr d* of Charles and Nancy Rew, Guernsey, CI; three *s*. *Educ*: Uppingham Sch., Uppingham, Rutland; Magdalene Coll., Cambridge (MA Hons). General Manager, BP Tanker Co. Ltd, 1968; Regional Co-ordinator, Australasia and Far East, 1970; President, BP North America Inc., 1972; Director: BP Trading Ltd, 1975; Peninsular & Oriental Steam Navigation Co., 1980–; Chairman, BP Oil International, 1981–. *Recreations*: theatre, fishing. *Address*: Britannic House, Moor Lane, EC2Y 9BU. *T*: 01-920 8000. *Clubs*: Brooks's, Royal Wimbledon Golf, MCC.

CAZALET-KEIR, Thelma, CBE 1952; *d* of late W. M. Cazalet; *m* 1939, David (*d* 1969), *s* of Rev. Thomas Keir. Member of London County Council for East Islington, 1925–31; Alderman of County of London, 1931; contested by-election, East Islington, 1931; MP (Nat. C) East Islington, 1931–45; Parliamentary Private Secretary to Parliamentary Secretary to Board of Education, 1937–40; Parliamentary Secretary to Ministry of Education, May 1945. Member of Committee of Enquiry into conditions in Women's Services, 1942; of Committee on Equal Compensation (Civil Injuries), 1943; Chairman London Area Women's Advisory Committee, Conservative and Unionist Associations, 1943–46. Chairman Equal Pay Campaign Committee; Member Cost of Living Committee; Member Arts Council of Great Britain, 1940–49; Member Executive Committee of Contemporary Art Society; Member Transport Users Consultative Committee for London, 1950-52. A Governor of the BBC, 1956-61. Member Committee Royal UK Beneficent Association, 1962. President Fawcett Society, 1964. *Publications*: From the Wings, 1967; (ed) Homage to P. G. Wodehouse, 1973. *Recreations*: music, lawn tennis. *Address*: Flat J, 90 Eaton Square, SW1. *T*: 01-235 7378.

CECIL, family name of **Baron Amherst of Hackney, Marquess of Exeter, Baron Rockley,** and **Marquess of Salisbury**.

CECIL, Lord David; see Cecil, Lord E. C. D. G.

CECIL, Lord (Edward Christian) David (Gascoyne); CH 1949; CLit 1972; Goldsmiths' Professor of English Literature, Oxford, 1948–69; Fellow of New College, Oxford, 1939–69, now Honorary Fellow; *b* 9 April 1902; *yr s* of 4th Marquess of Salisbury, KG, GCVO; *m* 1932, Rachel (*d* 1982), *o d* of late Sir Desmond MacCarthy; two *s* one *d*. *Educ*: Eton; Christ Church, Oxford (Hon. Student, 1981). Fellow of Wadham Coll., Oxford, 1924–30. Trustee of National Portrait Gallery, 1937-51. Pres., The Poetry Soc., 1947–48. Leslie Stephen Lectr, Cambridge Univ., 1935; Clark Lectr, Cambridge, 1941; Rede Lecturer, Cambridge Univ., 1955. Hon. LittD Leeds, 1950; Hon. DLit London, 1957; Hon. LLD: Liverpool, 1951; St Andrews, 1951; Hon. DLitt Glasgow, 1962. *Publications*: The Stricken Deer, 1929; Sir Walter Scott, 1933; Early Victorian Novelists, 1934; Jane Austen, 1935; The Young Melbourne, 1939; Hardy, the Novelist, 1943; Two Quiet Lives, 1948; Poets and Story-Tellers, 1949; Lord M., 1954; The Fine Art of Reading, 1957; Max, 1964; Visionary and Dreamer: Two Poetic Painters—Samuel Palmer and Edward Burne-Jones, 1969; (ed) The Bodley Head Max Beerbohm, 1970; (ed) A Choice of Tennyson's Verse, 1971; The Cecils of Hatfield House, 1973; Library Looking-glass, 1975; A Portrait of Jane Austen, 1978. *Address*: Red Lion House, Cranborne, Wimborne, Dorset. *T*: Cranborne 244.

CECIL, Henry Richard Amherst; Trainer of Racehorses; *b* 11 Jan. 1943; *s* of late Hon. Henry Kerr Auchmuty Cecil and of Elizabeth Rohays Mary (who *m* 2nd, Sir Cecil Boyd-Rochfort, *qv*), *d* of Sir James Burnett, 13th Bt, CB, CMG, DSO; *m* 1966, Julia, *d* of Sir Noel Murless, *qv*; one *s* one *d*. *Educ*: Canford School. Commenced training under flat race rules, 1969; previously Assistant to Sir Cecil Boyd-Rochfort. *Recreation*: gardening. *Address*: Warren Place, Newmarket, Suffolk CB8 8QQ. *T*: Newmarket 2387.

CECIL, Rear-Adm. Sir (Oswald) Nigel Amherst, KBE 1979; CB 1978; Lieutenant Governor of the Isle of Man, since 1980; *b* 11 Nov. 1925; *s* of Comdr the Hon. Henry M. A. Cecil, OBE, RN, and the Hon. Mrs Henry Cecil; *m* 1961, Annette (CStJ 1980), *d* of Robert Barclay, Bury Hill, near Dorking, Surrey; one *s*. *Educ*: Royal Naval Coll., Dartmouth. Joined Navy, 1939; served during War, 1939–45. Comdr, 1959; Chief Staff Officer, London Div. RNR, 1959–61; in comd: HMS Corunna, 1961–63; HMS Royal Arthur, 1963–66; Captain 1966; Staff of Dep. Chief of Defence Staff (Operational Requirements), 1966–69; Captain (D) Dartmouth Trng Sqdn and in comd HMS Tenby and HMS Scarborough, 1969–71; Senior British Naval Officer, S Africa, and Naval Attaché, Capetown, as Cdre, 1971–73; Dir, Naval Operational Requirements, 1973–75; Naval ADC to the Queen, 1975; NATO Comdr SE Mediterranean, 1975–77; Comdr British Forces Malta, and Flag Officer Malta, 1975–79. KStJ 1980. *Recreations*: racing, cricket, tennis. *Address*: Government House, Isle of Man. *Clubs*: White's, MCC.

CECIL, Robert, CMG 1959; author; HM Diplomatic Service, retired; Chairman, Institute for Cultural Research, since 1968; *b* 25 March 1913; *s* of late Charles Cecil; *m* 1938, Kathleen, *d* of late Col C. C. Marindin, CBE, DSO; one *s* two *d*. *Educ*: Wellington Coll.; Caius Coll., Cambridge. BA Cantab. 1935, MA 1961. Entered HM Foreign Service, 1936; served in Foreign Office, 1939–45; First Sec., HM Embassy, Washington, 1945–48; assigned to Foreign Office, 1948; Counsellor and Head of American Dept, 1951; Counsellor, HM Embassy, Copenhagen, 1953-55; HM Consul-Gen., Hanover, 1955–57; Counsellor, HM Embassy, Bonn, 1957-59; Dir-Gen., British Information Services, New York, 1959–61; Head of Cultural Relations Dept, FO, 1962-67. Reader in Contemp. German Hist., Reading Univ., 1968-78; Chm., Grad. Sch. of Contemp. European Studies, 1976-78. *Publications*: Levant and other Poems, 1940; Time and other Poems, 1955; Life in Edwardian England, 1969; The Myth of the Master Race: Alfred Rosenberg and Nazi ideology, 1972; Hitler's Decision to Invade Russia, 1941, 1976; (ed) The King's Son (anthology), 1980; contrib. to periodicals. *Recreations*: gardening, chess, etc. *Address*: Hambledon, Hants. *T*: Hambledon 669. *Club*: Royal Automobile.

CELIBIDACHE, Sergiu; Chief Conductor, Munich Philharmonic Orchestra since 1979; Composer and Guest Conductor to leading orchestras all over the world; *b* Rumania, 28 June 1912; *s* of Demosthene Celibidache; *m* Maria Celibidache. *Educ*: Jassy; Berlin. Doctorate in mathematics, musicology, philosophy and Buddhist religion. Conductor and Artistic Dir, Berlin Philharmonic Orchestra, 1946-51. Member: Royal Acad. of Music, Sweden; Acad. of Music, Bologna. German Critics' Prize, 1953; Berlin City Art Prize 1955; Grand Cross of Merit, Federal Republic of Germany, 1954. *Recreations*: skiing, water-skiing. *Address*: Munich Philharmonic Orchestra, 8 Munich 2, Rindermarkt 3-4/III, Federal Republic of Germany.

CENTRAL AFRICA, Archbishop of, since 1980; **Most Rev. Walter Paul Khotso Makhulu**; Bishop of Botswana, since 1979; *b* Johannesburg, 1935; *m* 1966, Rosemary Sansom; one *s* one *d*. *Educ*: St Peter's Theological Coll. Rosettenville; Selly Oak Colls, Birmingham. Deacon 1957, priest 1958, Johannesburg; Curate: Johannesburg, 1957-60; Botswana, 1961-63; St Carantoc's Mission, Francistown, Botswana, 1961-63; St Andrew's Coll., Selly Oak, Birmingham, 1963-64; Curate: All Saints, Poplar, 1964-66; St Silas, Pentonville, with St Clement's, Barnsbury, Hons, 1966-68; Vicar of St Philip's Battersea, 1968-75; Secretary for E Africa, WCC, 1975-79; Pres., All Africa Conf. of Churches, 1981-. Officier, Ordre des Palmes Académiques (France), 1981. *Address*: PO Box 769, Gaborone, Botswana.

CHABAN-DELMAS, Jacques Pierre Michel; Commander Légion d'Honneur; Compagnon de la Libération; Deputy, French National Assembly, Department of Gironde, since 1946; Mayor of Bordeaux, since 1947; *b* Paris, 7 March 1915; *s* of Pierre Delmas and Georgette Delmas (*née* Barrouin); *m* 1947 (2nd marr.), Mme Geoffray (*née* Marie Antoinette Iôn) (*d* 1970); two *s* two *d* ; *m* 1971, Mme Micheline Chavelet. *Educ:* Lycée Lakanal, Sceaux; Faculté de Droit, Paris; Ecole Libre des Sciences Politiques (Dip.). Licencié en droit. Journalist with l'Information, 1933. Served War of 1939-45: Army, 1939-40 (an Alpine Regt); joined the Resistance; *nom de guerre* of Chaban added (Compagnon de la Libération, Croix de Guerre); attached to Min. of Industrial Production, 1941; Inspector of Finance, 1943; Brig.-Gen., 1944; Nat. Mil. Deleg. (co-ord. mil. planning) Resistance, 1944; Inspector Gen. of Army, 1944; Sec.-Gen., Min. of Inf., 1945. Deputy for Gironde (Radical), 1946. Leader of Gaullist group (Républicains Sociaux) in Nat. Assembly, 1953-56; also Mem. Consultative Assembly of Council of Europe; Minister of State, 1956-57; Minister of Nat. Defence, 1957-58; Pres., Nat. Assembly, France, 1958-69 and 1978-81; Prime Minister, June 1969-July 1972. *Publication:* L'ardeur, 1976. *Address:* 36 rue Emile Fourcand, 33000 Bordeaux, France; Mairie de Bordeaux, 33000 Bordeaux, France.

CHACKSFIELD, Air Vice-Marshal Sir Bernard, KBE 1968 (OBE 1945); CB 1961; CEng, FRAeS 1968; *b* 13 April 1913; *s* of Edgar Chacksfield, Ilford, Essex; *m* 1937, Myrtle, *d* of Walter Matthews, Rickmansworth, Herts; two *s* two *d* (and one *s* decd). *Educ:* Co. High Sch., Ilford; RAF, Halton; RAF Coll., Cranwell. NW Frontier, 1934-37; UK, India, Burma, Singapore, 1939-45 (OBE); Air Min., 1945-48; Western Union (NATO), Fontainebleau, 1949-51; RAF Staff Coll., 1951-53; Fighter Command, 1954-55; Director, Guided Weapons (trials), Min. of Supply, 1956-58; IDC, 1959; SASO, Tech. Trg Comd, RAF, 1960; AOC No. 22 Group RAF Technical Training Command, 1960-62; Comdt-Gen., RAF Regiment and Inspector of Ground Defence, 1963-68; retired 1968. Chm., Burma Star Council, 1977- (Vice-Chm., 1974-76). Chairman of Governors: Bedstone College, 1978- (Governor, 1977); Deyncourt Sch., 1980-. Order of Cloud and Banner with special rosette (Chinese), 1941. *Recreations:* scouting (HQ Comr, Air Activities, 1959-72; Chief Comr for England, 1970-77), sailing, fencing (Pres. RAF Fencing Union, 1963-68), gliding, travel, model aircraft (Pres. Soc. Model Aircraft Engrs, GB, 1965-), modern Pentathlon (Pres., RAF Pentathlon Assoc., 1963-68), shooting (Chm. RAF Small Arms Assoc., 1963-68); swimming; youth work, amateur dramatics. *Address:* 8 Rowan House, Bourne End, Bucks. *T:* Bourne End 20829. *Club:* Royal Air Force.

CHADDOCK, Prof. Dennis Hilliar, CBE 1962; Professor of Engineering Design, University of Technology, Loughborough, 1966-73, retired; Professor Emeritus, 1974; Consultant Professor, Quorn Engineering, since 1974; *b* 28 July 1908; *m* 1937, Stella Edith Dorrington; one *s* one *d* (and one *s* decd). *Educ:* University Coll. Sch. Engineering Apprentice, Sa Adolph Saurer, Switzerland, 1927-30; Research Engineer, Morris Commercial Cars Ltd, Birmingham, 1930-32; Asst Road Motor Engineer, LMS Railway Co., Euston, 1932-41. BSc (Eng) Hons, London, 1933; MSc (Eng) London, 1938. HM Forces, 1941-46; Inspecting Officer, Chief Inspector of Armaments, 1941-43; Dep. Chief Inspecting Officer, 1943-45; Chief Design Officer, Armament Design Estabt, 1945-46; relinquished commission with rank of Lieut-Col, 1946. Superintendent, Carriage Design Branch of Armament Design Estabt, 1947-50; Imperial Defence Coll., 1951; Dep. Chief Engineer, 1952-55; Principal Superintendent, Weapons and Ammunition Div., Armament Research and Development Estabt, 1955-62; Dir of Artillery Research and Development, Ministry of Defence (Army) 1962-66. *Recreation:* model engineering. *Address:* 29 Paddock Close, Quorndon, Leics. *T:* Quorn 42607.

CHADWICK, Sir Albert (Edward), Kt 1974; CMG 1967; formerly Chairman, Gas and Fuel Corporation of Victoria; *b* 15 Nov. 1897; *s* of Andrew and Georgina Chadwick; *m* 1924, Thelma Marea Crawley; one *s* one *d. Educ:* Tungamah State Sch., Vic.; University High Sch., Vic. European War, 1914-18; served 1915-19 (MSM; despatches 1918); War of 1939-45: served RAAF, 1940-45 (Group Capt.). Engr, Robt Bryce & Co. Ltd, 1920-25; Lubricant Manager, Shell Co. of Aust. Ltd, 1925-35; Asst Gen. Man., Metropolitan Gas Co. Melbourne, 1935-51; Asst. Gen. Man., subseq. Gen. Man., Gas and Fuel Corp. of Vic., 1951-63. Chm., Overseas Telecommunications Commn (Australia), 1962-68. *Publications:* various technical and economic works. *Recreations:* golf, cricket, football, racing. *Address:* 723 Orrong Road, Toorak, Vic 3142, Australia. *T:* Melbourne 240 1163. *Clubs:* Athenæum, Victorian Amateur Turf (Melbourne); Riversdale Golf; (Pres. 1964-79) Melbourne Cricket (Life Mem.).

CHADWICK, Charles McKenzie; British Council Representative, Canada, since 1981; *b* 31 July 1932; *s* of late Trevor McKenzie Chadwick and of Marjorie Baron; *m* 1965, Evelyn Ingeborg Ihlenfeldt; one *s. Educ:* Charterhouse School; Trinity Coll., Toronto (BA). Army service, 1950-52; HMOCS Provincial Administration, Northern Rhodesia, 1958-64; Head, Administrative Training, Staff Trng Coll., Lusaka, 1964-67; British Council Officer, 1967-; service in Kenya, Nigeria, Brazil, London; British Electron Supervisor, Zimbabwe, 1980. *Recreations:* music, gardening, cricket. *Address:* c/o British Council, 10 Spring Gardens, SW1A 2BN.

CHADWICK, Gerald William St John, (John Chadwick), CMG 1961; HM Diplomatic Service, retired; Director, London Science Centre, 1981; *b*

28 May 1915; *s* of late John F. Chadwick, Solicitor; *m* 1938, Madeleine Renée Boucheron; two *s. Educ:* Lancing; St Catharine's Coll., Cambridge (open Exhibitioner). Asst Principal, Colonial Office, 1938; transf. Dominions Office, following demobilisation, 1940; Sec., Parl. Mission to Newfoundland, 1943; further missions to Newfoundland and Bermuda, 1946 and 1947; attended United Nations, 1949; Office of UK High Commission, Ottawa, 1949-52; Counsellor, British Embassy, Dublin, 1952-53; UK Delegn to NATO, Paris, 1954-56; Asst Sec., CRO, 1956; Asst Under-Sec. of State, CRO, 1960-66; first Dir, Commonwealth Foundn, 1966-80. Governor, Commonwealth Inst., 1967-80. *Publications:* The Shining Plain, 1937; Newfoundland: Island into Province, 1967; International Organisations, 1969; (ed jtly) Professional Organisations in the Commonwealth, 1976; The Unofficial Commonwealth, 1982; contrib. to A Decade of the Commonwealth 1955-64, 1966; numerous reviews and articles. *Recreation:* travel. *Clubs:* Athenæum, Royal Commonwealth Society.

CHADWICK, Rt. Rev. Graham Charles; *b* 3 Jan. 1923; *s* of William Henry and Sarah Ann Chadwick; *m* 1955, Jeanne Suzanne Tyrell; one *s. Educ:* Swansea Grammar School; Keble Coll., Oxford (MA); St Michael's Coll., Llandaff. RNVR, 1942-46. Deacon 1950, priest 1951; Curate, Oystermouth, Dio. Swansea and Brecon, 1950-53; Diocese of Lesotho, 1953-63; Chaplain, University Coll., Swansea, 1963-68; Senior Bursar, Queen's Coll., Birmingham, 1968-69; Diocesan Missioner, Lesotho, and Warden of Diocesan Training Centre, 1970-76; Bishop of Kimberley and Kuruman, 1976-82. *Address:* c/o USPG, 15 Tufton Street, Westminster, SW1P 3QQ.

CHADWICK, Rev. Prof. Henry, DD; FBA 1960; Regius Professor of Divinity, Cambridge University, and Professorial Fellow of Magdalene College, Cambridge, since 1979; Hon. Canon of Ely, since 1979; *b* 23 June 1920; 3rd *s* of late John Chadwick, Barrister, Bromley, Kent, and Edith (*née* Horrocks); *m* 1945, Margaret Elizabeth, *d* of late W. Pemell Brownrigg; three *d. Educ:* Eton (King's Scholar); Magdalene Coll., Cambridge (Music Schol.). John Stewart of Rannoch Scholar, 1939. MusB. Asst Master, Wellington Coll., 1945; University of Cambridge: Fellow of Queens' Coll., 1946-58; Hon. Fellow, 1958; Junior Proctor, 1948-49. Regius Professor of Divinity and Canon of Christ Church, Oxford, 1959-69; Dean of Christ Church, Oxford, 1969-79 (Hon. Student, 1979); Pro-Vice-Chancellor, Oxford Univ., 1974-75; Delegate, OUP, 1960-79. Hon. Fellow, Magdalene Coll., Cambridge, 1962; Fellow, Eton, 1976-79; Hon. Fellow, St Anne's Coll., Oxford, 1979. Hulsean Lecturer, 1956; Visiting Prof., Univ. of Chicago, 1957; Forwood Lectr, Univ. of Liverpool, 1961; Hewett Lectr, Union Theological Seminary, 1962; Gifford Lectr, St Andrews Univ., 1962-64; Birkbeck Lectr, Cambridge, 1965; Burns Lectr, Otago, 1971; Sarum Lectr, Oxford, 1982-83. Editor, Journal of Theological Studies, 1954-. Member, Anglican-Roman Catholic International Commn, 1969-81. Mem., Amer. Philosophical Soc.; For. Hon. Mem., Amer. Acad. Arts and Sciences; Correspondant de l'Académie des Inscriptions et des Belles Lettres, Institut de France; Mem., Société des Bollandistes, Brussels. Hon. DD, Glasgow, Yale, Leeds and Manchester; Hon. Teol Dr, Uppsala; D Humane Letters, Chicago. *Publications:* Origen, Contra Celsum, 1953; Alexandrian Christianity (with J. E. L. Oulton), 1954; Lessing's Theological Writings, 1956; The Sentences of Sextus, 1959; The Circle and the Ellipse, 1959; St Ambrose on the Sacraments, 1960; The Vindication of Christianity in Westcott's Thought, 1961; Early Christian Thought and the Classical Tradition, 1966; The Early Church (Pelican), 1967; The Treatise on the Apostolic Tradition of St Hippolytus of Rome, ed G. Dix (rev. edn), 1968; Priscillian of Avila, 1976; Boethius, 1981; History and Thought of the Early Church, 1982. *Recreation:* music. *Address:* Magdalene College, Cambridge; 32 Wilberforce Road, Cambridge CB3 0EQ. *T:* Cambridge 354378.
See also Sir John Chadwick, Prof. W. O. Chadwick, Vice-Adm. A. W. R. McNicoll.

CHADWICK, John; *see* Chadwick, G. W. St J.

CHADWICK, John, FBA 1967; MA; LittD; Perceval Maitland Laurence Reader in Classics, University of Cambridge, since 1969; Collins Fellow, Downing College, Cambridge, since 1960; *b* 21 May 1920; *yr s* of late Fred Chadwick; *m* 1947, Joan Isobel Hill; one *s. Educ:* St Paul's Sch.; Corpus Christi Coll., Cambridge. Editorial Asst, Oxford Latin Dictionary, Clarendon Press, 1946-52; Asst Lectr in Classics, 1952-54, Lectr in Classics, 1954-66, Reader in Greek Language, 1966-69, Univ. of Cambridge. Corresponding Member: Deutsches Archäologisches Inst., 1957; Austrian Acad. of Scis, 1974; Acad. des Inscriptions et Belles-Lettres, Institut de France, 1975. Hon. Fellow, Athens Archaeol Soc., 1974. Hon. Dr of Philosophical Sch., University of Athens, 1958; Hon. Dr, Université Libre de Bruxelles, 1969; Hon. DLitt, Trinity Coll., Dublin, 1971. Medal of J. E. Purkyně Univ., Brno, 1966. *Publications:* (jtly) The Medical Works of Hippocrates, 1950; (jtly) Documents in Mycenaean Greek, 1956, rev. edn 1973; The Decipherment of Linear B, 1958, 2nd edn 1968 (trans. into 12 languages); The Pre-history of the Greek Language (in Camb. Ancient History), 1963; The Mycenaean World, 1976 (trans. into 4 languages); edns of Linear B Tablets, articles in learned jls on Mycenaean Greek. *Recreation:* travel. *Address:* Downing College, Cambridge; 52 Gough Way, Cambridge. *T:* Cambridge 356864.

CHADWICK, Sir John (Edward), KCMG 1967 (CMG 1957); HM Diplomatic Service, retired; Special Adviser, Asian Development Bank, since 1973; *b* 17 Dec. 1911; *e s* of late John Chadwick; *m* 1945, Audrey Lenfestey; one *s* two *d. Educ:* Rugby; Corpus Christi Coll., Cambridge (MA). Dept of Overseas Trade, 1934; Asst Trade Comr, Calcutta, 1938; Eastern Group

Supply Council, Simla, 1941; Commercial Secretary, Washington, 1946-48; First Sec., Tel Aviv, 1950-53; Counsellor (Commercial) Tokyo, 1953-56; Minister (Economic), Buenos Aires, 1960-62, (Commercial), Washington, 1963-67; Ambassador to Romania, 1967-68; UK Representative to OECD, Paris, 1969-71. Consultant, Sterling Industrial Securities, 1973. *Address:* Larkfields, Woodstock Road, Charlbury, Oxford OX7 3ES. *Club:* Travellers'.
See also Rev. Prof. Henry Chadwick, Prof. W. O. Chadwick, Vice-Adm. Sir A. W. R. McNicoll.

CHADWICK, John Murray, ED; QC 1980; *b* 20 Jan. 1941; *s* of Hector George Chadwick and Margaret Corry Laing; *m* 1975, Diana Mary Blunt; two *d*. *Educ:* Rugby School; Magdalene Coll., Cambridge (MA). Called to the Bar, Inner Temple, 1966. *Recreation:* sailing. *Address:* Queen Elizabeth Building, Temple, EC4Y 9BS. *T:* 01-353 9076. *Clubs:* Cavalry and Guards; Royal Cornwall Yacht.

CHADWICK, Lynn Russell, CBE 1964; sculptor since 1948; *b* 24 Nov. 1914; *s* of late Verner Russell Chadwick and Marjorie Brown Lynn; *m* 1942, Charlotte Ann Secord; one *s* ; *m* 1959, Frances Mary Jamieson (*d* 1964); two *d* ; *m*, Eva Reiner; one *s*. *Educ:* Merchant Taylors' Sch. Architectural Draughtsman, 1933-39; Pilot, FAA, 1941-44. Exhibitions have been held in London, in various galleries, and by the Arts Council; his works have also been shown in numerous international exhibitions abroad, including Venice Biennale, 1956. *Works in public collections:* Great Britain: Tate Gallery, London; British Council, London; Arts Council of Great Britain; Victoria and Albert Museum; Pembroke Coll., Oxford; City Art Gallery, Bristol; Art Gallery, Brighton; Whitworth Art Gallery, University of Manchester; France: Musée National D'Art Moderne, Paris; Holland: Boymans van Beuningen Museum, Rotterdam; Germany: Municipality of Recklinghausen; Staatliche Graphische Sammlung, Munich; Staatliche Kunstmuseum, Duisburg; Sweden: Art Gallery, Gothenburg; Belgium: Musées Royaux des Beaux-Arts de Belgique, Brussels; Italy: Galleria D'Arte Moderna, Rome; Museo Civico, Turin; Australia: National Gallery of SA, Adelaide; Canada: National Gallery of Canada, Ottawa; Museum of Fine Arts, Montreal; USA: Museum of Modern Art, New York; Carnegie Institute, Pittsburgh; University of Michigan; Albright Art Gallery, Buffalo; Art Institute, Chicago; Chile: Inst. de Artes Contemporáneas, Lima. *Address:* Lypiatt Park, Stroud, Glos.

CHADWICK, Prof. Owen; *see* Chadwick, Prof. W. O.

CHADWICK, Prof. Peter, PhD, ScD; FRS 1977; Professor of Mathematics, University of East Anglia, since 1965; Dean of School of Mathematics and Physics, 1979-82; *b* 23 March 1931; *s* of Jack Chadwick and Marjorie Chadwick (*née* Castle); *m* 1956, Sheila Gladys Salter, *d* of late Clarence F. Salter; two *d*. *Educ:* Huddersfield Coll.; Univ. of Manchester (BSc 1952); Pembroke Coll., Cambridge (PhD 1957, ScD 1973). Scientific Officer, then Sen. Scientific Officer, Atomic Weapons Res. Estabt, Aldermaston, 1955-59; Lectr, then Sen. Lectr, in Applied Maths, Univ. of Sheffield, 1959-65. Vis. Prof., Univ. of Queensland, 1972. Jt Exec. Editor, Qly Jl of Mechanics and Applied Maths, 1965-72, Trustee, 1977-. *Publications:* Continuum Mechanics, 1976; numerous papers on theoretical solid mechanics and the mechanics of continua in various learned journals and books. *Address:* School of Mathematics and Physics, University of East Anglia, University Plain, Norwich NR4 7TJ. *T:* Norwich 56161; 8 Stratford Crescent, Cringleford, Norwich NR4 7SF. *T:* Norwich 51655.

CHADWICK, Sir R. Burton; *see* Burton-Chadwick.

CHADWICK, Rt. Rev. William Frank Percival; Bishop of Barking, 1959-75. *Educ:* Wadham College, Oxford; Harvard Univ., USA (Davison Scholar). Deacon, 1929, Priest, 1930, Diocese Liverpool; Curate, St Helens, 1929-34; Vicar: Widnes, 1934-38; Christ Church, Crouch End, N8, 1938-47; Barking, 1947-59. Proctor, Diocese of London, 1946, Diocese of Chelmsford, 1951; Examining Chaplain to Bishop of Chelmsford, 1951; Asst RD Barking, 1950-53, RD, Barking, 1953; Hon. Canon of Chelmsford, 1954; Pro-Prolocutor, Lower House of Canterbury, 1956; Exchange Preacher, USA, British Council of Churches, 1958; Chm., Church of England's Commn on Roman Catholic Relations, 1968-75; Mem., Dioceses Commn, 1978-80. *Publication:* The Inner Life. *Recreation:* golf. *Address:* Harvard House, Acton, Long Melford, Suffolk. *T:* Sudbury 77015. *Club:* Royal Commonwealth Society.

CHADWICK, Prof. (William) Owen, KBE 1982; FBA 1962; Master of Selwyn College, Cambridge, since 1956, and Regius Professor of Modern History, since 1968; President of the British Academy, since 1981; *b* 20 May 1916; 2nd *s* of late John Chadwick, Barrister, Bromley, Kent, and Edith (*née* Horrocks); *m* 1949, Ruth Romaine, *e d* of B. L. Hallward, *qv* ; two *s* two *d*. *Educ:* Tonbridge; St John's Coll., Cambridge. Chaplain at Wellington Coll., 1942-46; Fellow of Trinity Hall, Cambridge, 1947-56 (Dean, 1949-56); Hulsean Lecturer, 1949-50; Birkbeck Lecturer in Ecclesiastical History, 1956; Dixie Professor of Ecclesiastical History, 1958-68; Chm. Trustees, University Coll., later Wolfson Coll., Cambridge, 1965-77, Hon. Fellow 1977; Vice-Chancellor, Cambridge Univ., 1969-71. Gifford Lectr, Edinburgh Univ., 1973-74; Ford's Lectr in English History, Oxford Univ., 1980-81. Chm., Archbishops' Commn on Church and State, 1966-70. Trustee, Nat. Portrait Gall., 1978-. DD 1955. Hon. Fellow of Trinity Hall; Hon. Fellow of St John's Coll., Cambridge. Hon. Mem., American Acad. of Arts and Scis, 1977. Hon.

DD: St Andrews; Oxford; Hon. DLitt: Kent; Bristol; Hon. LittD UEA; Hon. Dr of Letters, Columbia. *Publications:* John Cassian, 1950; The Founding of Cuddesdon, 1954; From Bossuet to Newman, 1957; Western Asceticism, 1958; Creighton on Luther, 1959; Mackenzie's Grave, 1959; The Mind of the Oxford Movement, 1960; Victorian Miniature, 1960; The Reformation, 1964; The Victorian Church, part I, 1966, 3rd edn 1971; part II, 1970, 3rd edn 1979; Freedom and the Historian, 1969; The Secularization of the European Mind in the 19th Century, 1976; Acton and Gladstone, 1976; Catholicism and History, 1978; The Popes and European Revolution, 1981; The Making of the Benedictine Ideal, 1981; contrib. to Studies in Early British History, 1954; articles and reviews in learned journals. *Recreations:* walking, music; Cambridge XV versus Oxford, 1936-38. *Address:* Master's Lodge, Selwyn College, Cambridge.
See also Rev. Prof. Henry Chadwick, Sir John Chadwick, Vice-Adm. Sir A. W. R. McNicoll.

CHADWYCK-HEALEY, Sir Charles Arthur, 4th Bt *cr* 1919; OBE 1945; TD; *b* 27 May 1910; *s* of Sir Gerald Chadwyck-Healey, 2nd Bt, CBE, and Mary Verena (*d* 1957), *d* of George Arthur Watson; S brother 1979; *m* 1939, Viola, *d* of late Cecil Lubbock; three *s* two *d*. *Educ:* Eton; Trinity College, Oxford. BA 1932, MA 1936. Served War of 1939-45, N Africa, Sicily, Italy (despatches twice, OBE); Lt-Col RA (TA). Fellow, SPCK. *Heir:* s Charles Edward Chadwyck-Healey [*b* 13 May 1940; *m* 1967, Angela Mary, *e d* of John Metson, Bassingbourn, Herts; one *s* two *d*]. *Address:* The Red House, Clare, Sudbury, Suffolk.

CHAGALL, Marc, Grand Cross Legion of Honour, 1977 (Grand Officer 1971; Commander 1965); artist; *b* Vitebsk, Russia, 7 July 1887; *m* 1915, Bella Rosenfeld (decd); one *s* one *d* ; *m* 1952, Valentine Brodsky. *Educ:* Vitebsk, Russia. Left Russia, 1910, for Paris; returned to Russia, 1914; left again for Paris, 1922. Worked with Ambroise Vollard, famous art editor; left France for America, 1941; returned to France, 1948; has settled in the South of France. Has painted mural paintings besides easel pictures, ballet and theatre settings and costumes; at present working on ceramics; has done over 300 engravings. Retrospective exhibitions in the museums of London (Tate Gallery), Paris, Amsterdam, Chicago, New York, Venice, Jerusalem, and Tel Aviv, 1946-; International Prize for engraving, Biennale Venice, 1948; Erasmus Prize, 1960 (with A. Kokoschka). Salle Chagall founded in Paris Musée d'Art Moderne, 1950. *Publications:* Ma Vie, 1931; Illustrations for: Dead Souls, The Fables of La Fontaine, The Bible, The Arabian Nights, Stories from Boccaccio (verve), Burning Lights and the First Meeting, by Bella Chagall. *Address:* La Colline, Quartier Les Gardettes, 06570 Saint-Paul-de-Vence, AM, France.

CHAIR, Somerset de; *see* de Chair.

CHAKAIPA, Most Rev. Patrick; *see* Harare, Archbishop of, (RC).

CHALDECOTT, John Anthony; Keeper, Science Museum Library, South Kensington, 1961-76; *b* 16 Feb. 1916; *o s* of Wilfrid James and Mary Eleanor Chaldecott; *m* 1940, Kathleen Elizabeth Jones; one *d*. *Educ:* Latymer Upper Sch., Hammersmith; Brentwood Sch.; Borough Road Coll., Isleworth; University College, London. BSc 1938, MSc 1949, PhD 1972. Meteorological Branch, RAFVR, 1939-45 (despatches). Lecturer, Acton Technical Coll., 1945-48; entered Science Museum as Asst Keeper, Dept of Physics, 1949; Deputy Keeper and Secretary to Advisory Council, 1957. Pres., British Society for the History of Science, 1972-74. FInstP. *Publications:* Josiah Wedgwood: the arts and sciences united (with J. des Fontaines and J. Tindall), 1978; Science Museum handbooks; papers on the history of science. *Address:* 19 The Grove, Ratton, Eastbourne, E Sussex BN20 9DA.

CHALFONT, Baron, *cr* 1964 (Life Peer); **(Alun) Arthur Gwynne Jones,** PC 1964; OBE 1961; MC 1957; *b* 5 Dec. 1919; *s* of Arthur Gwynne Jones and Eliza Alice Hardman; *m* 1948, Dr Mona Mitchell; no *c*. *Educ:* West Monmouth Sch. Commissioned into South Wales Borderers (24th Foot), 1940; served in: Burma 1941-44; Malayan campaign 1955-57; Cyprus campaign 1958-59; various staff and intelligence appointments; psc (Camberley), 1950; JSSC 1958; qual. as Russian interpreter, 1951; resigned commission, 1961, on appt as Defence Correspondent, The Times; frequent television and sound broadcasts on defence and foreign affairs, and consultant on foreign affairs to BBC Television, 1961-64; Minister of State, Foreign and Commonwealth Office, 1964-70; UK Permanent Rep. to WEU, 1969. Chm., All Party Defence Gp, House of Lords. Foreign Editor, New Statesman, 1970-71. Dir, IBM UK Ltd and IBM UK (Holdings) Ltd, 1973, Mem. European Adv. Council, IBM, 1973-; Dir, W. S. Atkins International, 1979-; Chairman: UNA, 1972-73; St David's Theatre Trust, 1972-; Industrial Cleaning Papers, 1979-; President: Welsh Inst.; Hispanic and Luso Brazilian Councils, 1973-79; RNID, 1980-; Llangollen Internat. Music Festival; Freedom in Sport, 1982-; Vice-President: European Atlantic Cttee; UK Cttee for Unicef; Member: Exec. Cttee; European Movement; Population Countdown Campaign Cttee, 1971-; IISS; RIIA. Hon. Fellow UCW Aberystwyth, 1974. Liveryman, Worshipful Co. of Paviors. Freeman, City of London. *Publications:* The Sword and The Spirit, 1963; contrib. The Ulster Debate, 1972; The Great Commanders, 1973; Montgomery of Alamein, 1976; (ed) Waterloo, 1979; contribs to The Times, Jl RUSI and other professional journals. *Recreations:* formerly Rugby football, cricket, lawn tennis; now music and theatre. *Address:* House of Lords, SW1. *Clubs:* Garrick, MCC, City Livery; Cardiff and County.

CHALK, Hon. Sir Gordon (William Wesley), KBE 1971; Hon. LLD; company director and business consultant; MP (Queensland), 1947-76; Minister for Transport, Govt of Queensland, 1957-65, Deputy Premier and Treasurer, 1965-76; Leader, Liberal Party of Australia (Queensland Div.), 1965-76; voluntarily retired, 1976; *b* 1913; of British parentage; *m* 1937, Ellen Clare Grant; one *s* one *d. Educ:* Gatton Senior High Sch., Qld. Formerly: Queensland Sales Manager, Toowoomba Foundry Pty Ltd; Registered Taxation Agent. Mem. Senate, Griffith Univ., 1976-81. Hon. LLD Queensland Univ., 1974. *Address:* 277 Indooroopilly Road, Indooroopilly, Qld. 4068, Australia. *T:* Brisbane 3711598. *Clubs:* Tattersall's (Brisbane, Qld); Rotary International (Gatton, Qld); Southport Yacht.

CHALKER, Mrs Lynda; MP (C) Wallasey since Feb. 1974; Parliamentary Under-Secretary of State, Department of Transport, since 1982; *b* 29 April 1942; *d* of Sidney Henry James Bates and late Marjorie Kathleen Randell; *m* 1st, 1967, Eric Robert Chalker (marr. diss. 1973); no *c* ; 2nd, 1981, Clive Landa. *Educ:* Roedean Sch.; Heidelberg Univ.; Westfield Coll., London; Central London Polytechnic. Statistician with Research Bureau Ltd (Unilever), 1963-69; Dep. Market Research Man. with Shell Mex & BP Ltd, 1969-72; Chief Exec. of Internat. Div. of Louis Harris International, 1972-74. Mem., BBC Gen. Adv. Cttee, 1975-79. Opposition Spokesman on Social Services, 1976-79; Parly Under-Sec. of State, DHSS, 1979-82. Jt Sec., Cons. Health and Social Services Cttee, 1975-76; Chm., Greater London Young Conservatives, 1969-70; Nat. Vice-Chm., Young Conservatives, 1970-71. *Publications:* (jtly) Police in Retreat (pamphlet), 1967; (jtly) Unhappy Families (pamphlet), 1971; (jtly) We are Richer than We Think, 1978. *Recreations:* music, the disabled, cooking, theatre, driving. *Address:* House of Commons, SW1A 0AA. *T:* 01-219 5098.

CHALKLEY, David Walter; Member for Deptford, Greater London Council; Chairman, Inner London Education Authority, 1979-80; *b* 11 May 1915; *m* 1941, Hilda Davis; one *s* one *d. Educ:* Sellincourt Sch.; Battersea Polytechnic. Parliamentary Labour Candidate: NW Croydon, 1959; Brentford-Chiswick, 1964; Mayor of Mitcham, 1961; Mem., GLC, 1964-67. *Publication:* article on Labour organisation and class voting in constituencies. *Recreation:* travel. *Address:* 70 Devonshire Road, SW19. *Club:* Progressive (Tooting).

CHALLANS, Mary; *see* Renault, Mary.

CHALLEN, Rt. Rev. Michael Boyd; Assistant Bishop, Diocese of Perth, W Australia, since 1978; *b* 27 May 1932; *s* of late B. Challen; *m* 1961, Judith, *d* of A. Kelly; two *d. Educ:* Mordialloc High School; Frankston High School; Univ. of Melbourne (BSc 1955); Ridley College, Melbourne (ThL 1956). Deacon 1957, priest 1958; Curate of Christ Church, Essendon, 1957-59; Member, Melbourne Dio. Centre 1959-63; Director, 1963-69; Priest-in-charge, St Luke, Fitzroy, 1959-61; St Alban's, N Melbourne, 1961-65; Flemington, 1965-69; Dir, Anglican Inner-City Ministry, 1970; Dir, Home Mission Dept, Perth, 1971-78; Priest-in-charge, Lockridge with Eden Hill, 1973; Archdeacon, Home Missions, Perth, 1975-78; Exec. Dir, Anglican Health and Welfare Service, Perth, 1977-78. *Address:* Box W2067, Perth, W Australia 6001.

CHALLENGER, Frederick, BSc (London); PhD (Göttingen); DSc (Birmingham); CChem, FRSC; Professor of Organic Chemistry, the University, Leeds, 1930-53, Emeritus Professor, 1953; *b* Halifax, Yorks, 15 Dec. 1887; *s* of Rev. S. C. Challenger; *m* 1922, Esther Yates, MA (*d* 1969); two *d. Educ:* Ashville Coll., Harrogate; Derby Technical Coll.; University College, Nottingham; University of Göttingen. 1851 Exhibition Scholar, 1910-12; Asst Lecturer in Chemistry, University of Birmingham, 1912; Lecturer in Chemistry, 1915; Senior Lecturer in Organic Chemistry, University of Manchester 1920; Vice-President of Royal Institute of Chemistry, 1948-51. Sir Jesse Boot Foundn Lectr (mainly on Prof. F. S. Kipping), Univ. of Nottingham, 1980. Hon. Life Mem., Phytochemical Soc. of Europe, 1981. Hon. Governor, Ashville Coll. *Publications:* Aspects of the Organic Chemistry of Sulphur, 1959; chapter in Organometals and Organometalloids: Occurrence and Fate in the Environment, 1978 (dedicated to him); numerous publications, mostly in the Journal of the Chemical Society, Biochemical Journal and Journal of Institute of Petroleum, dealing with organo-metallic compounds (particularly of bismuth), organic thiocyanates and selenocyanates, aromatic substitution, sulphur compounds of shale oil, and other heterocyclic sulphur compounds, microbiological chemistry; mechanism of biological methylation (especially by moulds) as applied to arsenic, tellurium, selenium and sulphur compounds and checked by use of compounds containing isotopic carbon; sulphonium and other compounds of sulphur in plants and animals and in metabolic disturbances (homocystinuria); reviews on the methionine-cystine relationship in mental retardation and on biosynthesis of organometallic and organometalloidal compounds related to environmental pollution; chemical biography. *Address:* 19 Elm Avenue, Beeston, Nottingham. *T:* Nottingham 257686.

CHALLENS, Wallace John, CBE 1967 (OBE 1958); Director, Atomic Weapons Research Establishment, Aldermaston, 1976-78; *b* 14 May 1915; *s* of late Walter Lincoln Challens and Harriet Sybil Challens (née Collins); *m* 1st, 1938, Winifred Joan Stephenson (*d* 1971); two *s* ; 2nd, 1973, Norma Lane. *Educ:* Deacons Sch., Peterborough; University Coll., Nottingham; BSc (Hons) London. Research Dept, Woolwich, 1936; Projectile Develt Estabt, Aberporth, 1939. British Commonwealth Scientific Office, Washington,

1946; Armament Research Estabt, Fort Halstead, 1947; Atomic Weapons Research Estabt: Fort Halstead, 1954; Aldermaston, 1955-78. Scientific Dir of trials at Christmas Island, 1957. Appointed: Chief of Warhead Develt, 1959; Asst Dir, 1965; Dep. Dir, 1972. FInstP 1944. US Medal of Freedom (Bronze) 1946. *Recreation:* golf. *Address:* Far End, Crossborough Hill, Basingstoke, Hampshire RG21 2AG. *T:* Basingstoke 64986.

CHALLIS, Dr Anthony Arthur Leonard, CBE 1980; Chief Scientist, Department of Energy, since 1980; *b* 24 Dec. 1921; *s* of Leonard Hough Challis and Dorothy (née Busby); *m* 1947, L. Beryl Hedley; two *d. Educ:* Newcastle upon Tyne Royal Grammar Sch.; King's Coll., Univ. of Durham. 1st cl. hons BSc Chemistry; PhD. Imperial Chemical Industries: joined Billingham Div., 1946; Research Man., HOC Div., 1962; Research Dir, Mond Div., 1966; Head of Corporate Lab., 1967; Gen. Man. Planning, 1970; Sen. Vice-Pres., ICI Americas Inc., 1975-76; Dir, Polymer Engrg, SRC, 1976-80. Mem., SERC (formerly SRC), 1973-. Mem. Court, Univ. of Stirling, 1968-74. *Publications:* contrib. chem. and managerial jls. *Recreations:* music, walking, sailing. *Address:* c/o Department of Energy, Thames House South, Millbank, SW1P 4QJ.

CHALLIS, Margaret Joan, MA; Headmistress of Queen Anne's School, Caversham, 1958-77; *b* 14 April 1917; *d* of R. S. Challis and L. Challis (née Fairbairn). *Educ:* Girton Coll., Cambridge. BA Hons., English Tripos, 1939, MA, 1943, Cambridge. English Mistress: Christ's Hospital, Hertford, 1940-44; Dartford Grammar School for Girls, 1944-45; Cheltenham Ladies' Coll., 1945-57. Housemistress at Cheltenham Ladies' Coll., 1949-57. *Recreations:* gardening, music, old churches. *Address:* 16 Glencairn Court, Lansdown Road, Cheltenham, Glos.

CHALMERS, George Buchanan, CMG 1978; HM Diplomatic Service, retired; *b* 14 March 1929; *s* of late George and Anne Buchanan Chalmers; *m* 1954, Jeanette Donald Cant. *Educ:* Hutcheson's Grammar Sch.; Glasgow and Leiden Univs. RAF, 1950-52; FO, 1952-54; 3rd Sec., Bucharest, 1954-57; 2nd Sec., Djakarta, 1957-58; 1st Sec., Bangkok, 1958-61; FO, 1961-64; 1st Sec., Seoul, 1964-66; 1st Sec. and subseq. Commercial Counsellor, Tel Aviv, 1966-70; Dir, California Trade Drive Office, 1971; Head of Oil Dept, FCO, 1971-72; Head of S Asian Dept, FCO, 1973-75; Counsellor, Tehran, 1975-76; Minister, Tehran, 1976-79; Consul-General, Chicago, 1979-82. *Recreations:* ski-ing, bridge. *Address:* East Bank House, Bowden, Melrose, Roxburghshire TD6 0ST.

CHALMERS, John, CBE 1978; retired; General Secretary, Amalgamated Society of Boilermakers, Shipwrights, Blacksmiths and Structural Workers, 1966-80; Member of the General Council of the TUC, 1977-80; *b* 16 May 1915; *s* of John Aitken Chalmers and Alexandrina McLean; two *d* (one *s* decd). *Educ:* Clydebank Sen. Secondary Sch. Apprenticeship, Boilermaker-Plater. Trade Union Official, 1954-; Mem., Nat. Exec. Cttee, Labour Party, 1966-77 (Vice-Chm. 1975-76; Chm. 1976-77). Member: Central Arbitration Cttee, 1976-; Lay Mem., Press Council, 1978-81. *Recreations:* reading, gardening, golf. *Address:* 23 Killingworth Drive, West Moor, Newcastle upon Tyne NE12 0ER. *T:* Newcastle upon Tyne 683246.

CHALMERS, Thomas Wightman, CBE 1957; *b* 29 April 1913; *s* of Thomas Wightman Chalmers and Susan Florence Colman. *Educ:* Bradfield Coll.; King's Coll., London. Organ Scholar, King's Coll., London, 1934-36; BSc (Engineering), 1936. Joined BBC programme staff, 1936; successively announcer, Belfast and London; Overseas Presentation Director; Chief Assistant, Light Programme, 1945, Controller, 1948-50; Director, Nigerian Broadcasting Service, 1950-56, on secondment from BBC; Controller, North Region, BBC, 1956-58; Director of the Tanganyika Broadcasting Corporation, 1958-62; Deputy Regional Representative, UN Technical Assistance Board, East and Central Africa, 1962-64; Special Asst, Overseas and Foreign Relations, BBC, 1964-71; Chief Exec., Radio Services, United Newspapers Ltd, and Dir, Radio Fleet Productions Ltd, 1971-75. *Recreations:* travelling, reading and music. *Address:* 75 Ainsworth Street, Cambridge CB1 2PF.

CHALMERS, William Gordon, CB 1980; MC 1944; Crown Agent for Scotland, since 1974; *b* 4 June 1922; *s* of Robert Wilson Chalmers and Mary Robertson Chalmers (née Clark); *m* 1948, Margaret Helen McLeod; one *s* one *d. Educ:* Robert Gordon's Coll., Aberdeen; Aberdeen Univ. (BL). University, 1940-42 and 1947-48; served with Queen's Own Cameron Highlanders, 1942-47; Solicitor in Aberdeen, 1948-50; Procurator Fiscal Depute at Dunfermline, 1950-59; Senior Procurator Fiscal Depute at Edinburgh, 1959-63; Asst in Crown Office, 1963-67; Deputy Crown Agent, 1967-74. *Recreations:* golf, bridge. *Address:* 21 Tantallon Place, Edinburgh EH9 7NZ. *T:* 031-667 5664.

CHALMERS, William John, CB 1973; CVO 1979; CBE 1954; *b* 20 Oct. 1914; *s* of late William Chalmers and Catherine Florence (née Munro), Inverness; *m* 1942, Jessie Alexandra Roy, *y d* of late George Johnston McGregor and Erika Amalie (née Jensen), Edinburgh; one *s* one *d. Educ:* Inverness Royal Academy; Edinburgh University. BL 1937. Staff Commonwealth War Graves Commission, 1938; served Queen's Own Cameron Highlanders, 1939-45; Bde Major 214th Infantry Bde, 1942-43 and 1944-45 (despatches); Commonwealth War Graves Commission, 1945; Assistant Secretary, 1948-56, Sec. and Dir-Gen., 1956-75. Appeal Secretary, The Queen's Silver Jubilee Appeal, 1975-78; Mem. Admin. Council, The

Royal Jubilee Trusts, 1978-80. Croix de Guerre, France, 1944; Coronation Medal, 1953; Jubilee Medal, 1977. *Address:* Holy Well House, Luston, Leominster, Herefordshire HR6 0DN. *T:* Leominster 5767.

CHALONER, family name of Baron Gisborough.

CHALONER, Prof. William Gilbert, FRS 1976; Hildred Carlile Professor of Botany, and Head of Department of Botany, Bedford College, University of London, since 1979; *b* London, 22 Nov. 1928; *s* of late Ernest J. and L. Chaloner; *m* 1955, Judith Carroll; one *s* two *d. Educ:* Kingston Grammar Sch.; Reading Univ. (BSc, PhD). 2nd Lt RA, 1955-56. Lectr and Reader, University Coll., London, 1956-72. Visiting Prof., Pennsylvania State Univ., USA, 1961-62; Prof. of Botany, Univ. of Nigeria, 1965-66; Prof. of Botany, Birkbeck Coll., Univ. of London, 1972-79. Vis. Prof., Univ. of Mass, 1981. *Publications:* papers in Palaeontology and other scientific jls, dealing with fossil plants. *Recreations:* swimming, tennis, visiting USA. *Address:* 20 Parke Road, SW13 9NG. *T:* 01-748 3863.

CHAMBERLAIN, Rev. Elsie Dorothea; *see* Chamberlain-Garrington, Rev. E. D.

CHAMBERLAIN, George Digby, CMG 1950; Chief Secretary, Western Pacific High Commission, 1947-52; *b* 13 Feb. 1898; *s* of Digby Chamberlain, late Knockfin, Knaresborough; *m* 1931, Kirsteen Miller Holmes; one *d* (one *s* decd). *Educ:* St Catharine's Coll., Cambridge. War Service, 1917-19, with Rifle Brigade, Lieut RARO. Asst District Commissioner, Gold Coast, 1925; Asst Principal, Colonial Office, 1930-32; Asst Colonial Secretary, Gold Coast, 1932; Asst Chief Secretary, Northern Rhodesia, 1939; Colonial Secretary, Gambia, 1943-47; Acting Governor, Gambia, July-Nov. 1943, and June-Aug. 1944; Acting High Commissioner, Western Pacific, Jan.-April, and Sept. 1951-July 1952; retired 1952. *Recreations:* shooting, fishing. *Address:* 18 Douglas Crescent, Edinburgh EH12 5BA. *Club:* New (Edinburgh).

CHAMBERLAIN, Air Vice-Marshal George Philip, CB 1946; OBE 1941; RAF, retired; *b* 18 Aug. 1905; *s* of G. A. R. Chamberlain, MA, FLAS, FRICS, Enville, Staffordshire; *m* 1930, Alfreda Rosamond Kedward; one *s* one *d. Educ:* Denstone Coll.; Royal Air Force Coll., Cranwell. Commissioned RAF 1925. On loan to Min. of Civil Aviation, 1947-48; Imperial Defence Coll., 1949; AOA 205 Group, MEAF, 1950; AOC Transport Wing, MEAF, 1951-52; Commandant, RAF Staff Coll., Andover, 1953-54; AO i/c A, HQ Fighter Command, 1954-57; Dep. Controller of Electronics, Min. of Supply, 1957-59, Min. of Aviation, 1959-60; Managing Director, Collins Radio Co. of England, 1961-66, non-executive director, 1967-75. *Recreations:* sailing, tennis. *Address:* Little Orchard, Adelaide Close, Stanmore, Middlesex. *Club:* Royal Air Force.

CHAMBERLAIN, Kevin John; Legal Counsellor, HM Diplomatic Service, since 1979; *b* 31 Jan. 1942; *s* of Arthur James Chamberlain and Gladys Mary (née Harris); *m* 1967, Pia Rosita Frauenlob; one *d. Educ:* Wimbledon Coll.; King's Coll., London (LLB). Called to the Bar, Inner Temple, 1965. Asst Legal Adviser, FCO, 1965-74; Legal Adviser: British Mil. Govt, Berlin, 1974-76; British Embassy, Bonn, 1976-77; Asst Legal Adviser, FCO, 1977-79. *Recreations:* opera, gardening, swimming, tennis, skiing. *Address:* c/o Foreign and Commonwealth Office, SW1.

CHAMBERLAIN, Prof. Owen, AB, PhD; Professor of Physics, University of California, since 1958; *b* San Francisco, 10 July 1920; *s* of W. Edward Chamberlain and Genevieve Lucinda Owen; *m* 1943, Babette Copper (marr. diss. 1978); one *s* three *d. Educ:* Philadelphia; Dartmouth Coll., Hanover, NH (AB). Atomic research for Manhattan District, 1942, transferred to Los Alamos, 1943; worked in Argonne National Laboratory, Chicago, 1947-48, and studied at University of Chicago (PhD); Instructor in Physics, University of California, 1948; Asst Professor, 1950; Associate Professor, 1954. Guggenheim Fellowship, 1957; Loeb Lecturer in Physics, Harvard Univ., 1959. Nobel Prize (joint) for Physics, 1959. Fellow American Phys. Soc.; Mem., Nat. Acad. of Sciences, 1960. *Publications:* papers in Physical Review, Physical Review Letters, Nature, Nuovo Cimento. *Address:* Department of Physics, University of California, Berkeley, California, USA.

CHAMBERLAIN, Hon. Sir (Reginald) Roderic (St Clair), Kt 1970; Judge of the Supreme Court of South Australia, 1959-71; *b* 17 June 1901; *s* of late Henry Chamberlain; *m* 1929, Leila Macdonald Haining; one *d. Educ:* St Peter's Coll.; Adelaide Univ. Crown Prosecutor, 1928; KC 1945; Crown Solicitor, 1952-59; Chm., SA Parole Board, 1970-75. Chm., Anti-Cancer Foundn. *Publication:* The Stuart Affair, 1973. *Recreations:* golf, bridge. *Address:* 72 Moseley Street, Glenelg South, SA 5045, Australia. *T:* 95.2036. *Clubs:* Adelaide, Royal Adelaide Golf (Adelaide).

CHAMBERLAIN, Richard, TD 1949; Master of the Supreme Court, Chancery Division, since 1964; *b* 29 Jan. 1914; *o s* of late John Chamberlain and Hilda (née Poynting); *m* 1938, Joan, *d* of late George and Eileen Kay; two *s* one *d. Educ:* Radley Coll.; Trinity Coll., Cambridge (MA). Admitted Solicitor, 1938. Served War, 1939-45: Devon Regt, TJFF, Staff Coll., Haifa. Partner, Kingsford Dorman & Co., 1948-64. Asst, Worshipful Co. of Solicitors of the City of London, 1966, Warden, 1973-74, Master, 1975. *Publication:* Asst Editor, Supreme Court Practice, 1967. *Recreations:* gardening, photography, travel, grandparental duties. *Address:* 23 Drax Avenue, Wimbledon, SW20 0EG. *T:* 01-946 4219. *Club:* Garrick.

CHAMBERLAIN, Hon. Sir Roderick; *see* Chamberlain, Hon Sir (Reginald) R.

CHAMBERLAIN, Ronald; Lecturer and Housing Consultant; *b* 19 April 1901; *m* Joan Smith McNeill (*d* 1950), Edinburgh; one *s* one *d*; *m* 1951, Florence Lilian Illingworth, Cricklewood. *Educ:* Owens Sch., Islington; Gonville and Caius Coll., Cambridge (MA). Formerly Secretary to National Federation of Housing Societies and (later) Chief Exec. Officer to the Miners' Welfare Commission; later engaged on administrative work for the National Service Hostels Corporation. MP (Lab) Norwood Division of Lambeth, 1945-50; Member of Middlesex County Council, 1947-52. Governor, Middlesex Hosp., 1947-74. *Recreation:* tennis. *Address:* 18 Basing Hill, Golders Green, NW11. *T:* 01-455 1491.

CHAMBERLAIN-GARRINGTON, Rev. Elsie Dorothea, BD (London); Minister, North Street Congregational Church, Taunton, and Chulmleigh Congregational Church, since 1981; Chairman, Congregational Federation Council, since 1977 (President, 1973-75); *m* 1947, Rev. J. L. St C. Garrington (*d* 1978). *Educ:* Channing Sch.; King's Coll., London (BD). Asst Minister Berkeley Street, Liverpool, 1939-41; Minister: Christ Church, Friern Barnet, 1941-46; Vineyard Congreational Church, Richmond, 1947-54; BBC Religious Dept, 1950-67; Associate Minister, The City Temple, 1968-70; Minister, Hutton Free Church, Brentwood, 1971-80. 1st woman chaplain, HM Forces, 1946-47. Chm., Congregational Union of England and Wales, 1956-57. *Publications:* (ed) Lift Up Your Hearts, 1959; (ed) Calm Delight: devotional anthology, 1959; (ed) 12 Mini-Commentaries on the Jerusalem Bible, 1970. *Recreation:* music. *Address:* The Manse, 12 Ashley Road, Taunton, Somerset TA1 5HP. *T:* Taunton 71353; The Manse, East Street, Chulmleigh, Devon. *T:* Chulmleigh 80583.

CHAMBERS, Hon. George Michael; MP (People's National Movement), St Ann's, since 1966; Prime Minister and Minister of Finance and Planning, Trinidad and Tobago, since 1981; *b* 4 Oct. 1928; *m* 1956, Juliana; one *d. Educ:* Nelson Street Boys' RC Sch.; Burke's Coll.; Osmond High Sch.; Wolsey Hall, Oxford. Parly Sec., Min. of Finance, 1966; Minister of Public Utilities and Housing, 1969; Minister of State in Min. of National Security and Minister of State in Min. of Finance, Planning and Develt, 1970; Minister of National Security, Nov. 1970; Minister of Finance, Planning and Development, 1971-73; Minister of Finance, 1973-75; Minister of Educn and Culture, 1975-76; Minister of Industry and Commerce and Minister of Agriculture, Lands and Fisheries, 1976-81. Formerly, Asst Gen. Sec. and Mem. Central Exec., Gen. Council, and Res. and Disciplinary Cttees, People's National Movement. Chm. Bd of Governors, World Bank and IMF, 1973; Governor, Caribbean Develt Bank, 1981-. *Address:* Prime Minister's Residence, Port-of-Spain, Trinidad.

CHAMBERS, Prof. Robert Guy; Professor of Physics, University of Bristol, since 1964; *b* 8 Sept. 1924; *s* of Â. G. P. Chambers; *m* 1950, Joan Brislee; one *d. Educ:* King Edward VI Sch., Southampton; Peterhouse, Cambridge. Work on tank armament (Ministry of Supply), 1944-46; Electrical Research Association, 1946-47; research on metals at low temperatures, Royal Society Mond Laboratory, Cambridge, 1947-57; Stokes Student, Pembroke Coll., 1950-53; PhD 1952; ICI Fellow, 1953-54; NRC Post-doctoral Fellow, Ottawa, 1954-55; University Demonstrator, Cambridge, 1955-57; Bristol University: Sen. Lectr, 1958-61; Reader in Physics, 1961-64; Pro-Vice-Chancellor, 1978-81. *Publications:* various papers in learned journals on the behaviour of metals at low temperatures. *Recreation:* star-gazing. *Address:* 9 Apsley Road, Clifton, Bristol BS8 2SH. *T:* Bristol 39833.

CHAMBERS, Prof. William Walker, MBE 1945; William Jacks Professor of German, 1954-79, now Emeritus Professor, University of Glasgow (Vice-Principal, 1972-76); *b* 7 Dec. 1913; *s* of William and Agnes Chambers; *m* 1947, Mary Margaret Best; one *s* one *d. Educ:* Wishaw Public Sch.; Wishaw High Sch.; Universities of Glasgow, Paris and Munich. MA (Glasgow) 1936; L. ès L. (Paris) 1940; PhD (Munich) 1939. Served War of 1939-45 (despatches, MBE); 2nd Lieut, RA, 1941; Intelligence Staff, HQ 8th Army, North Africa, Sicily, Italy and Austria, 1942-46; Asst Lecturer in German, University of Leeds, 1946-47, Lecturer 1947-50; Prof. of Modern Languages, University College, N. Staffs, 1950-54. Chm., Conf. of Univ. Teachers of German in GB and Ireland, 1973-75; Pres., Assoc. of Univ. Teachers, 1962-63. Member: General Teaching Council for Scotland, 1973-77; Commonwealth Scholarship Commn in Britain, 1962-66. Vice-Chm., Governors, Jordanhill Coll. of Educn, 1962-67. FEIS, 1964. Verdienstkreuz Erste Klasse, 1967; Ehrensenator, Univ. of Freiburg, 1976. *Publications:* (ed) Paul Ernst, Selected Short Stories, 1953; (ed) Fouque, Undine, 1956; (ed) Paul Ernst, Erdachte Gespräche, 1958; (with J. R. Wilkie) A Short History of the German Language, 1970. *Recreations:* gardening, music. *Address:* 26A Monreith Road, Glasgow G43 2NY. *T:* 041-632 1000.

CHAMIER, Anthony Edward Deschamps; Director of Establishments and Organisation, Department of Education and Science, since 1980; *b* 16 Aug. 1935; *s* of Brig. George Chamier, OBE and Marion (née Gascoigne), Achandounie, Alness, Ross-shire; *m* 1962, Anne-Carole Tweeddale Dalling, *d* of William and Kathleen Dalling, Transvaal, S Africa; one *s* one *d. Educ:* Stowe, Buckingham; Trinity Hall, Cambridge; Yale Univ. (Henry Fellow). Military service, 1st Bn Seaforth Highlanders, 1953-55. HM Foreign (later Diplomatic) Service, 1960; Third Secretary, Foreign Office, 1960-62; Second Sec., Rome, 1962-64; Asst Political Adviser, HQ Middle East Comd, Aden,

1964-66; First Sec., FCO, 1966-71; Head of Chancery, Helsinki, 1971-72; seconded, later transf. to Dept of Educn and Science; Principal, 1972-73; Principal Private Sec. to Sec. of State for Educn and Science, 1973-74; Asst Sec., 1974-79. *Recreations:* walking, shooting, gardening. *Address:* 233 Hanworth Road, Hampton, Mddx TW12 3EP. *T:* 01-979 8475. *Club:* Army and Navy.

CHAMPERNOWNE, David Gawen, MA; FBA 1970; Professor of Economics and Statistics, Cambridge University, 1970-78, now Emeritus; Fellow of Trinity College, Cambridge, since 1959; *b* Oxford, 9 July 1912; *s* of late F. G. Champernowne, MA, Bursar of Keble Coll., Oxford; *m* 1948, Wilhelmina Dullaert; two *s*. *Educ:* The College, Winchester; King's Coll., Cambridge. 1st Class Maths, Pts 1 and 2; 1st Class Economics Pt 2. Asst Lecturer at London Sch. of Economics, 1936-38; Fellow of King's Coll., Cambridge, 1937-48; University Lecturer in Statistics at Cambridge, 1938-40; Asst in Prime Minister's statistical dept, 1940-41; Asst dir of Programmes, Ministry of Aircraft Production, 1941-45; Dir of Oxford Univ. Institute of Statistics, 1945-48; Fellow of Nuffield Coll., Oxford, 1945-59; Prof. of Statistics, Oxford Univ., 1948-59; Reader in Economics, Cambridge Univ., 1959-70. Editor, Economic Jl, 1971-76. *Publications:* Uncertainty and Estimation in Economics (3 vols), 1969; The Distribution of Income between Persons, 1973. *Address:* 25 Worts Causeway, Cambridge CB1 4RJ. *T:* Cambridge 247829; Trinity College, Cambridge.

CHAMPION, family name of **Baron Champion.**

CHAMPION, Baron, *cr* 1962, of Pontypridd (Life Peer); **Arthur Joseph Champion,** PC 1967; JP; Deputy Speaker and Deputy Chairman of Committees, House of Lords, 1967-81; *b* 26 July 1897; *s* of William and Clara Champion, Glastonbury, Somerset; *m* 1930, Mary E. Williams, Pontypridd; one *d*. *Educ:* St John's Sch., Glastonbury. Signalman; 1914-18 War, 2nd Lieut, Royal Welch Fusiliers. MP (Lab.) Southern Division of Derbyshire, 1945-50, South-East Derbyshire, 1950-Sept. 1959; Parliamentary Private Secretary to Minister of Food, 1949-50, to Secretary of War, 1950-51; Joint Parliamentary Secretary, Ministry of Agriculture and Fisheries, April-Oct. 1951; Minister without Portfolio and Dep. Leader of the House of Lords, 1964-67. Formerly British Delegate to Consultative Assembly at Strasbourg; Govt appointed Director of the British Sugar Corporation, 1960-64, 1967-68. Hon. ARCVS, 1967; Hon. Mem., BVA, 1976. *Address:* 22 Lanelay Terrace, Pontypridd, Mid Glam. *T:* Pontypridd 402349.

CHAMPION, John Stuart, CMG 1977; OBE 1963; HM Diplomatic Service, retired; Chairman, Herefordshire Health Authority, since 1982; *b* 17 May 1921; *er s* of Rev. Sir Reginald Champion, KCMG, OBE and of Margaret, *d* of late Very Rev. W. M. Macgregor, DD, LLD; *m* 1944, Olive Lawrencina, *o d* of late Lawrence Durning Holt, Liverpool; five *s* two *d*. *Educ:* Shrewsbury Sch.; Balliol Coll., Oxford (Schol., BA). Commnd 11 Hussars PAO, 1941-46. Colonial Service (later HMOCS), Uganda, 1946-63: District Officer; Secretariat, 1949-52; Private Sec. to Governor, 1952; Asst Financial Sec., 1956; Actg Perm. Sec., Min. of Health, 1959; Perm. Sec., Min. of Internal Affairs, 1960; retd 1963; Principal, CRO, 1963; 1st Sec., FCO, 1965; Head of Chancery, Tehran, 1968; Counsellor, Amman, 1971; FCO 1973; British Resident Comr, Anglo/French Condominium of the New Hebrides, 1975-78. Mem., West Midlands RHA, 1980-81. County Vice-Pres., St John Ambulance, Hereford and Worcester, 1981-. Governor, Royal National Coll. for the Blind, 1980-. *Recreations:* hill walking, golf, music. *Address:* Farmore, Callow, Hereford HR2 8DB. *T:* Hereford 27485. *Club:* Royal Commonwealth Society.

CHAMSON, André; Member of the French Academy; Grand Croix de la Légion d'Honneur; Grand Officier de l'Ordre du Mérite; Curator of the Petit Palais since 1945; Directeur Général des Archives de France, since 1959; International President of the Pen, 1956; *b* 6 June 1900; *s* of Jean Chamson and Madeleine Aldebert; *m* 1924, Lucie Mazauric; one *d*. *Educ:* Ecole des Chartes. Joint Curator, Palais de Versailles, 1933-39. Served War of 1939-45 (Croix de Guerre, Médaille de la Résistance); Captain, Staff of 5th Army, 1939-40; Chef de bataillon, Bde Alsace Lorraine, 1944-45. Près., Collège des Conservateurs du Musée et Domaine de Chantilly. Docteur *hc* Université Laval, Quebec. Grand Officier de l'Ordre de Léopold; Commandeur de la Couronne, Belgium; Officier de Saint Sava, Norway; Officier of Merit, Italy; Grand Officier de l'Ordre du Soleil du Pérou; Grand Officier de l'Etoile Polaire de Suède; Grand Officier de l'Ordre National de la Côte d'Ivoire. *Publications:* Roux le bandit, 1925; Les Hommes de la route, 1927; Le Crime des justes, 1928; Les Quatre Eléments, 1932; La Galère, 1938; Le Puits des miracles, 1945; Le Dernier Village, 1946; La Neige et la fleur, 1950; Le Chiffre de nos jours, 1954; Adeline Vénician, 1956; Nos Ancêtres les Gaulois, 1958; Le Rendez-vous des Espérances, 1961; Comme une Pierre qui Tombe, 1964; La Petite Odyssée, 1965; La Superbe, 1967; La Tour de Constance, 1970; Les Taillons, ou la terreur blanche, 1974; La Reconquête, 1944-45, 1975; Suite guerrière, 1976; Sans peur et les brigands aux visages noirs, 1977; Castanet, le Camisard de l'Aigoual, 1979; Catinat, 1982. *Address:* 35 rue Mirabeau, 75016 Paris, France. *Club:* Pen (Pres.).

CHAN, Rt. Hon. Sir Julius, KBE 1980 (CBE 1975); PC 1981; Prime Minister of Papua New Guinea, 1980-82; *b* 29 Aug. 1939; *s* of Chin Pak and Tingoris Chan; *m* 1966, Stella Ahmat; three *s* one *d*. *Educ:* Marist Brothers Coll., Ashgrove, Qld; Univ. of Queensland, Australia (Agricl Science). Co-operative Officer, Papua New Guinea Admin, 1960-62; private business,

coastal shipping and merchandise, 1963-70; Mem., Papua New Guinea House of Assembly, 1968. Parliamentary Leader, People's Progress Party, 1970-; Minister for Finance, 1972-77; Dep. Prime Minister and Minister for Primary Industry, 1977-78. Governor: World Bank/IMF, 1976; Asian Development Bank, 1977; Fellowship Member, International Banker Assoc. Incorporation (USA), 1976. Fellow, Internat. Bankers Assoc., 1976. From 1970 on attended meetings and conferences worldwide as rep. of PNG, latterly as leader of PNG delegn; made State and official visits to Australia, Rep. of Korea, China, Vanuatu, Indonesia, UK, France, Italy, NZ. Hon. DEc Dankook (Republic of Korea) 1978. *Recreations:* swimming, walking, boating. *Address:* PO Box 423, Rabawl, Papua New Guinea.

CHANCE, Sqdn Ldr Dudley Raymond, FRGS; a Recorder of the Crown Court, since 1980; *b* 9 July 1916; *s* of Captain Arthur Chance, Sherwood Foresters, and Byzie Chance; *m* 1958, Jessie Maidstone, widow, *d* of John and Alice Dewing. *Educ:* Nottingham High Sch.; London Univ. (BA Oriental Religions and Philosophies, LLB 1969); BA Hons Internat. Politics and For. Policy, Open Univ., 1980. Called to Bar, Middle Temple, 1955. Commissioned in Royal Air Force, 1936; served Egypt, Transjordan, 1936-37; Bomber Comd (4 Gp), 1938; served in Bomber Comd Nos 97 and 77 Sqdns; took part in first raids on Norway; crashed off Trondheim; picked up later from sea by HMS Basilisk, later sunk at Dunkirk; Air Ministry, Whitehall, 1941-42, later in 2 Group, Norfolk, 21 Sqdn; also served in SEAC, Bengal/Burma. Sqdn Ldr, RAFO, until March 1961; gazetted to retain rank of Sqdn Ldr from that date. Member: panel of Chairmen of Medical Appeal Tribunals (DHSS), 1978-; panel of Independent Inspectors for motorway and trunk road inquiries for DoE, 1978-. Parly candidate (C), Norwich North, 1959. FRGS 1979. *Recreations:* violin, painting. *Address:* Lamb Buildings, Temple, EC4; Fenners Chambers, 5 Gresham Road, Cambridge. *Clubs:* Goldfish (RAF aircrew rescued from sea); Norfolk (Norwich).

CHANCE, Major Geoffrey Henry Barrington, CBE 1962; *b* 16 Dec. 1893; *s* of Ernest Chance, Burghfield, Berks; *m* 1st, 1914, Hazel Mary Louise Cadell (decd); two *d*; 2nd, 1933, Daphne Corona Wallace; one *s* one *d*. *Educ:* Eton. Engineering, 1913-14. Army, 1914-19. Qualified Chartered Accountant, 1928, practised, 1930-40; HM Treasury, 1941-45. Company director. CC, Alderman (Wilts), 1955-67; Chairman Chippenham Conservative Assoc., 1955-62; High Sheriff of Wiltshire, 1965. *Recreations:* fishing, shooting. *Address:* Flat 2, Hatton's Lodge, Braydon, Swindon, Wilts.

CHANCE, Ivan Oswald, CBE 1971; Chairman, Christies International Ltd, 1973-76 (Chairman, Christie, Manson and Woods Ltd, 1958-74); Consultant, 1976-80; *b* 23 June 1910; *s* of Brig.-Gen. O. K. Chance, CMG, DSO, and Fanny Isabel, *d* of Sir George Agnew, 2nd Bt; *m* 1936, Pamela Violet (*d* 1982), of Everard Martin Smith. *Educ:* Eton. Joined Christie's, 1930; became a partner, 1935. Served War of 1939-45: 58 Middx AA Bn (TA), and Coldstream Guards (despatches, 1945). Mem. Council, Nat Trust, 1977-80 (Mem., Exec. Cttee, 1976-80; Chm., Properties Cttee, 1976-80); Chm., 1968-80, Pres. 1980-, Georgian Group. *Recreations:* travel, gardening. *Address:* 38 Belgravia Court, Ebury Street, SW1; Colby Lodge, Stepaside, Narberth, Dyfed SA67 8PP. *Clubs:* Beefsteak, Brooks's, White's; Brook (New York).

CHANCE, Sir Roger (James Ferguson), 3rd Bt, *cr* 1900; MC; *b* 26 Jan. 1893; *e s* of George Ferguson Chance (2nd *s* of 1st Bt) and Mary Kathleen, *d* of Rev. Henry Stobart; *S* uncle 1935; *m* 1921, Mary Georgina, *d* of Col William Rowney, and Kate, *d* of Maj.-Gen. Fendall Currie; one *s* two *d* (and one *s* decd). *Educ:* Eton; Trinity Coll., Cambridge (MA); London University (PhD). Served European War, Aug. 1914-April 1918; Capt. and Adjutant 4th (RI) Dragoon Guards, 1916-17; Capt. 1st Batt. The Rifle Brigade, 1918 (twice wounded, despatches twice, MC); Editor, Review of Reviews, 1932-33; Press Attaché, British Embassy, Berlin, 1938; Sqdn Leader RAFVR, 1940-41. *Publications:* Until Philosophers are Kings (political philosophy), 1928; Conservatism and Wealth (with Oliver Baldwin, politics), 1929; Winged Horses (fiction), 1932; Be Absolute for Death (fiction), 1964; The End of Man (theology), 1973; Apple and Eve (a Cambridge symposium). *Heir: s* (George) Jeremy (ffolliott) Chance [*b* 24 Feb. 1926; *m* 1950, Cecilia Mary Elizabeth, *d* of Sir (William) Hugh (Stobart) Chance, CBE; two *s* two *d*]. *Address:* c/o Williams & Glyn's Bank Ltd, Whitehall, SW1. *Club:* Athenæum.

See also Sir R. T. Armstrong.

CHANCELLOR, Alexander Surtees; Editor of The Spectator, since 1975; *b* 4 Jan. 1940; *s* of Sir Christopher Chancellor, *qv*; *m* 1964, Susanna Elisabeth Debenham; two *d*. *Educ:* Eton College; Trinity Hall, Cambridge. Reuters News Agency, 1964-74 (Chief Correspondent, Italy, 1968-73); ITN, 1974-75. *Recreation:* music. *Address:* The Spectator, 56 Doughty Street, WC1. *T:* 01-405 1706.

CHANCELLOR, Sir Christopher (John), Kt 1951; CMG 1948; MA; *b* 29 March 1904; *s* of late Sir John Robert Chancellor, GCMG, GCVO, GBE, DSO; *m* 1926, Sylvia Mary (OBE 1976), *e d* of Sir Richard Paget, 2nd Bt, and Lady Muriel Finch-Hatton, *d* of 12th Earl of Winchilsea and Nottingham; two *s* two *d*. *Educ:* Eton Coll.; Trinity College., Cambridge (1st class in History). Joined Reuters in 1930; Reuters' Gen. Manager and Chief Corresp in Far East with headquarters in Shanghai, 1931-39; Gen. Manager of Reuters, Ltd, 1944-59, Trustee, 1960-65; Chairman: Daily Herald, 1959-61; Odhams Press Ltd, 1960-61 (Vice-Chm., 1959-60); Chm. and Chief Executive, The

Bowater Paper Corporation Ltd and associated cos, 1962-69. Sometime Director: The Observer Ltd; Northern and Employers Assurance Co. Ltd; Bristol United Press Ltd. Chm., Madame Tussaud's, 1961-72. Mem. Court, London Univ., 1956-62; Chm. Exec. Cttee of The Pilgrims Soc. of Great Britain, 1958-67; Mem. Board of Regents, Memorial Univ. of Newfoundland, 1963-68; Vice-Pres., National Council of Social Service, 1959-71; Dep.-Chm., Council of St Paul's Cathedral Trust, 1954-62; Chm., Appeal and Publicity Cttee, King George VI National Memorial Fund, 1952-54; Dep.-Chm., Exec. Cttee, 1955-56; Chm., Bath Preservation Trust, 1969-76. King Haakon VII Liberty Cross, 1947; Officer Order of Orange Nassau, 1950; Comdr Royal Order of Danebrog, 1951; Officer, Legion of Honour, 1951; Comdr Order of Civil Merit (Spain), 1952; Cross of Comdr Order of Phœnix, 1953; Comdr Order of Vasa, 1953; Comdr Order of Merit (Italy), 1959. *Address:* The Priory, Ditcheat, Shepton Mallet, Somerset. *Clubs:* Garrick, Travellers'.
See also A. C. Chancellor.

CHANDLER, Edwin George, CBE 1979; FRIBA, FRTPI; City Architect, City of London, 1961-79; *b* 28 Aug. 1914; *e s* of Edwin and Honor Chandler; *m* 1938, Iris Dorothy, *o d* of Herbert William Grubb; one *d*. *Educ:* Selhurst Grammar Sch., Croydon. Asst Architect, Hants County Council and City of Portsmouth, 1936-39. Served in HMS Vernon, Mine Design Dept, 1940-45. Gained distinction in thesis, ARIBA, 1942, FRIBA 1961. Dep. Architect and Planning Officer, West Ham, 1945-47; City Architect and Planning Officer, City of Oxford, 1947-61. Member: RIBA Council, 1950-52; Univ. Social Survey Cttee, Oxford; City of London Archaeological Trust; Trustee, Silver Jubilee Walkway Trust; Governor: Alleyn's Estate, Dulwich; James Allen's Sch., Dulwich; Liveryman, Gardeners' Co. *Publications:* Housing for Old Age, 1939; City of Oxford Development Plan, 1950; articles contrib. to press and professional jls. *Recreations:* landscaping, travel, swimming. *Address:* 1 Perifield, Dulwich, SE21 8NG. *T:* 01-670 3251. *Club:* Dulwich.

CHANDLER, Geoffrey, CBE 1976; Director General, National Economic Development Office, and Council Member, since 1978; *b* 15 Nov. 1922; *s* of Frederick George Chandler, MD, FRCP, and Marjorie Chandler; *m* 1955, Lucy Bertha Buxton; four *d*. *Educ:* Sherborne; Trinity Coll., Cambridge (MA History). Military Service, 1942-46: Captain 60th Rifles; Political Warfare Exec., Cairo; Special Ops Exec., Greece. Cambridge Univ., 1947-49; Captain, Univ. Lawn Tennis, 1949. BBC Foreign News Service, 1949-51; Leader Writer and Features Editor, Financial Times, 1951-56; Commonwealth Fund Fellow, Columbia Univ., New York, 1953-54; Shell Internat. Petroleum Co.: Manager, Econs Div., 1957-61; Area Co-ordinator, W Africa, 1961-64; Chm. and Man. Dir, Shell Trinidad Ltd, 1964-69; Shell Internat. Petroleum Co.: Public Affairs Co-ordinator, 1969-78; Dir, 1971-78; Dir, Shell Petroleum Co.; and Shell Petroleum NV, 1976-78. Pres., Inst. of Petroleum, 1972-74. Member: Council and Exec. Cttee, Overseas Develt Inst., 1969-78; British Overseas Trade Adv. Council; Council and Exec. Cttee, VSO. Hon. Fellow, Sheffield City Polytechnic, 1981; Hon. FInstPet 1982. FRSA. *Publications:* The Divided Land: an Anglo-Greek Tragedy, 1959; The State of the Nation: Trinidad & Tobago in the later 1960s, 1969; articles on oil, energy, transnational corporations, and development; numerous speeches, urging employee participation, coherent British indust. policy and industrially constructive use of N Sea oil revenues. *Recreations:* gardening, playing the oboe. *Address:* 57 Blackheath Park, SE3 9SQ. *T:* 01-852 0032. *Clubs:* Athenæum; Hawks (Cambridge).

CHANDLER, George, MA, PhD, FLA, FRHistS; ALAA; International Adviser and Editor in Library and Information Science; *b* England, 2 July 1915; *s* of W. and F. W. Chandler; *m* 1937, Dorothy Lowe; one *s*. *Educ:* Central Grammar Sch., Birmingham; Leeds Coll. of Commerce; University of London. Birmingham Public Libraries, 1931-37; Leeds Public Libraries, 1937-46; WEA Tutor Organiser, 1946-47; Borough Librarian, Dudley, 1947-50; Dep. City Librarian, Liverpool, 1950-52, City Librarian, 1952-74; Dir-Gen., Nat. Library of Australia, 1974-80. Sec. Dudley Arts Club, 1948-50; Pres., Internat. Assoc. of Met. City Libraries, 1968-71; Pres. 1962-71 (Hon. Sec. 1957-62), Soc. of Municipal and County Chief Librarians; Dir, 1962-74 (Hon. Sec. 1955-62), Liverpool and District Scientific, Industrial and Research Library Advisory Council; Hon. Librarian, 1957-74 (Hon. Sec. 1950-57), Historic Soc. of Lancs and Ches; Chm., Exec. Cttee, 1965-70, President, 1971, Library Assoc.; Member: DES Library Adv. Council for England and Wales, 1965-72; British Library Organising Cttee, 1972-73; British Library Bd, 1973-74. Hon. Editor, Internat. Library Review, 1969-. Unesco expert in Tunisia, 1964. FRSA. *Publications:* Dudley, 1949; William Roscoe, 1953; Liverpool 1207-1957; Liverpool Shipping, 1960; Liverpool under James I, 1960; How to Find Out, 1963 (5th edn 1981); Four Centuries of Banking: Martins Bank, Vol. I, 1964, Vol. II, 1968; Liverpool under Charles I, 1965; Libraries in the Modern World, 1965; How to Find Out About Literature, 1968; Libraries in the East, 1971; Libraries, Bibliography and Documentation in the USSR, 1972; Victorian and Edwardian Liverpool and the North West, 1972; An Illustrated History of Liverpool, 1972; (ed) International Librarianship, 1972; Merchant Venturers, 1973; Victorian and Edwardian Manchester, 1974; Liverpool and Literature, 1974; Recent Developments in International and National Library and Information Services, 1982; (ed) International Series of Monographs on Library and Information Science; (ed) series, Recent Developments in Library and Information Services, 1981-; contributions to educl and library press. *Recreations:* writing, research;

walking; foreign travel. *Address:* 17 Malcolm Place, Kambah, Canberra, ACT, Australia.

CHANDLER, Tony John; *b* 7 Nov. 1928; *s* of Harold William and Florence Ellen Chandler; *m* 1954, Margaret Joyce Weston; one *s* one *d*. *Educ:* King's Coll., London. MSc. PhD, AKC, MA. Lectr, Birkbeck Coll., Univ. of London, 1952-56; University Coll. London: Lectr, 1956-65; Reader in Geography, 1965-69; Prof. of Geography, 1969-73; Prof. of Geography, Manchester Univ., 1973-77; Master of Birkbeck Coll., Univ. of London, 1977-79. Sec., Royal Meteorological Soc., 1969-73. Member: Council, NERC; Health and Safety Commn; Cttee of Experts on Major Hazards; Royal Soc. Study Gp on Pollution in the Atmosphere, 1974-77; Clean Air Council; Royal Commn on Environmental Pollution, 1973-77; Standing Commn on Energy and the Environment 1978-. *Publications:* The Climate of London, 1965; Modern Meteorology and Climatology, 1972, 1981; contribs to: Geographical Jl, Geography, Weather, Meteorological Magazine, Bulletin of Amer. Meteorological Soc., etc. *Recreations:* music, reading, travel. *Address:* 44 Knoll Rise, Orpington, Kent BR6 0EL. *T:* Orpington 32880.

CHANDOS, 3rd Viscount *cr* 1954, of Aldershot; **Thomas Orlando Lyttelton;** Banker, Kleinwort, Benson Ltd, since 1974; *b* 12 Feb. 1953; *s* of 2nd Viscount Chandos and of Caroline Mary, *d* of Rt Hon. Sir Alan Lascelles, GCB, GCVO, CMG, MC; *S* father, 1980. *Educ:* Eton; Worcester College, Oxford (BA). *Heir:* *b* Hon. Matthew Peregrine Antony Lyttelton, *b* 21 April 1956. *Address:* 149 Gloucester Avenue, NW1. *T:* 01-722 8329.

CHANDOS-POLE, Lt-Col John, CVO 1979; OBE 1951; JP; Lord-Lieutenant for Northamptonshire since 1967; *b* 20 July 1909; *s* of late Brig.-Gen. Harry Anthony Chandos-Pole, CBE, DL, JP and late Ada Ismay, Heverswood, Brasted, Kent; *m* 1952, Josephine Sylvia, *d* of late Brig.-Gen. Cyril Randell Crofton, CBE, Limerick House, Milborne Port, near Sherborne; two step-*d*. *Educ:* Eton; Magdalene Coll., Cambridge (MA). 2nd Lieut Coldstream Guards, 1933; ADC: to Governor of Bombay, May-Nov., 1937; to Governor of Bengal, Nov. 1937-June 1938, Oct. 1938-Feb. 1939, also to Viceroy of India, June-Oct., 1938. Served War of 1939-45: France and Belgium (wounded); Palestine, 1948 (wounded, despatches); commanded 1st Bn, Coldstream Guards, 1947-48; Guards Depot, 1948-50; 2nd Bn, Coldstream Guards, 1950-52. Lieut-Col 1949; retired, 1953. A Member of the Hon. Corps of Gentlemen-at-Arms, 1956-79 (Harbinger, 1966-79). DL 1965, JP 1957, Northants. KStJ 1975. *Recreations:* racing and travel. *Address:* Newnham Hall, Daventry, Northants. *T:* Daventry 2711. *Clubs:* Boodle's; Pratt's.

CHANDOS-POLE, Major John Walkelyne, DL, JP; *b* 4 Nov. 1913; *o s* of late Col Reginald Walkelyne Chandos-Pole, TD, JP, Radburne Hall; *m* 1947, Ilsa Jill, *er d* of Emil Ernst Barstz, Zürich; one *d* (one *s* decd). *Educ:* Eton; RMC, Sandhurst. Commissioned Grenadier Guards, 1933; ADC to Viceroy of India, 1938-39; retired, 1947. JP 1951, DL 1961, Derbys; High Sheriff of Derbys, 1959. *Recreation:* shooting. *Address:* Radburne Hall, Kirk Langley, Derby DE6 4LZ. *T:* Kirk Langley 246. *Clubs:* Army and Navy, Lansdowne; MCC; County (Derby).

CHANDRA, Ram; *see* Ram Chandra.

CHANDRACHUD, Hon. Yeshwant Vishnu; Chief Justice of India, since 1978; *b* Poona (Maharashtra), 12 July 1920; *s* of Vishnu Balkrishna Chandrachud and Indira; *m* Prabha; one *s* one *d*. *Educ:* Bombay Univ. (BA, LLB). Advocate of Bombay High Court, 1943, civil and criminal work; part-time Prof. of Law, Government Law Coll., Bombay, 1949-52; Asst Govt Pleader, 1952; Govt Pleader, 1958; Judge, Bombay High Court, 1961-72; one-man Pay Commn for Bombay Municipal Corporation officers, later Arbitrator in dispute between Electricity Supply and Transport Undertaking and its employees' union; one-man Commn to inquire into circumstances leading to death of Deen Dayal Upadhyaya; Judge, Supreme Court of India, 1972-78. President: Internat. Law Assoc. (India Branch), 1978-; Indian Law Inst., 1978-. *Address:* (official) Supreme Court of India, New Delhi, India. *T:* 387165; 5 Krishna Menon Marg, New Delhi 110011. *T:* 374053, 372922; (permanent) 131 Budhwar Peth, Balkrishna Niwas, Poona 411002.

CHANDRASEKHAR, Subrahmanyan, FRS 1944; Morton D. Hull Distinguished Service Professor of Theoretical Astrophysics, University of Chicago, USA, since 1937; *b* 19 Oct. 1910; *m* 1936, Lalitha Doraiswamy. *Educ:* Presidency Coll., Madras; Trinity Coll., Cambridge (Government of Madras Research Scholar, PhD 1933, ScD 1942). Fellow of Trinity Coll., Cambridge, 1933-37, Hon. Fellow 1981. Managing Editor Astrophysical Journal, 1952-71. Nehru Memorial Lecture, India, 1968. Member: Nat. Acad. of Sciences (Henry Draper Medal, 1971); Amer. Philosophical Soc.; Amer. Acad. of Arts and Sciences (Rumford Medal, 1957). Hon. DSc Oxon 1972. Bruce Gold Medal, Astr. Soc. Pacific, 1952; Gold Medal, Royal Astronomical Soc. London, 1953; Royal Medal, Royal Society, 1962; Nat. Medal of Science (USA), 1966; Heineman Prize, Amer. Phys. Soc., 1974. *Publications:* An Introduction to the Study of Stellar Structure, 1939; Principles of Stellar Dynamics, 1942; Radiative Transfer, 1950; Hydrodynamic and Hydromagnetic Stability, 1961; Ellipsoidal Figures of Equilibrium, 1969; various papers in current scientific periodicals. *Address:* Laboratory for Astrophysics and Space Research, University of Chicago, 933 East 56th Street, Chicago, Illinois, USA. *T:* (312) 962-7860. *Club:* Quadrangle (Chicago).

CHANEY, Hon. Sir Frederick (Charles), KBE 1982 (CBE 1969); AFC 1946; Lord Mayor of Perth, Australia, 1978-82; Chairman, Home Building Society, since 1974; *b* 12 Oct. 1914; *s* of Frederick Charles Chaney and Rose Templar Chaney; *m* 1938; four *s* three *d*. *Educ*: Aquinas Coll.; Claremont Coll. Served War, RAAF, 1940-45. Teacher, 1936-40 and 1946-55. MHR (L) Perth, 1955-69; Govt Whip, 1961-63; Minister for the Navy, 1963-66; Administrator, Northern Territory, 1970-73. *Recreation:* golf. *Address:* 9A Melville Street, Claremont, WA 6010, Australia. *T:* 384.0596. *Clubs:* West Australian Cricket Assoc., East Perth Football (Perth); Mount Lawley Golf (WA).

CHANNING-WILLIAMS, Maj.-Gen. John William, CB 1963; DSO 1944; OBE 1951; jssc; psc; *b* 14 Aug. 1908; *s* of late W. A. Williams, Inkpen, Berks; *m* 1936, Margaret Blachford, *d* of late A. J. Wood, Maidenhead, Berks; three *s*. *Educ*: Trent Coll.; RMC Sandhurst. Commissioned 2nd Lieut, N. Staffs Regt, 1929. Served War of 1939-45 (despatches, DSO): BEF, France, 1939-40; Instructor, Senior Officers' School, 1942-43; GSO1, Staff Coll., Camberley, 1943-44; CO 4th Bn Welch Regt, 1944; served in France, 1944-45, India and Burma, 1945-46. Asst Instructor, Imperial Defence Coll., 1946-48; AA and QMG, 40th Inf. Div., Hong Kong, 1949-50; Colonel General Staff, HQ Land Forces, Hong Kong, 1951-52; Colonel, 1954; BGS (Operations and Plans), GHQ, MELF, 1955-58; Director of Quartering, War Office, 1960-61; Director of Movements, War Office, 1961-63; retired; Brigadier, 1957; Maj.-Gen., 1960. *Recreations:* shooting, fishing. *Address:* Hayes Well, Inkpen, Newbury, Berks.

CHANNON, Rt. Hon. (Henry) Paul (Guinness); PC 1980; MP (C) for Southend West, since Jan. 1959; Minister for the Arts, since 1981; *b* 9 Oct. 1935; *o s* of late Sir Henry Channon, MP, and of late Lady Honor Svejdar (*née* Guinness), *e d* of 2nd Earl of Iveagh, KG; *m* 1963, Ingrid Olivia Georgia Guinness (*née* Wyndham); one *s* two *d*. *Educ*: Lockers Park, Hemel Hempstead; Eton Coll., Christ Church, Oxford. 2nd Lieut Royal Horse Guards (The Blues), 1955-56. Pres. of Oxford Univ. Conservative Association, 1958. Parly Private Sec. to: Minister of Power, 1959-60; Home Sec., 1960-62; First Sec. of State, 1962-63; PPS to the Foreign Sec., 1963-64; Opposition Spokesman on Arts and Amenities, 1967-70; Parly Sec., Min. of Housing and Local Govt, June-Oct. 1970; Parly Under-Sec. of State, DoE, 1970-72; Minister of State, Northern Ireland Office, March-Nov. 1972; Minister for Housing and Construction, DoE, 1972-74; Opposition Spokesman on: Prices and Consumer Protection, March-Sept. 1974; environmental affairs, Oct. 1974-Feb. 1975; Minister of State, CSD, 1979-81. Dep. Leader, Cons. Delegn to WEU and Council of Europe, 1976-79. Mem., Gen. Adv. Council to ITA, 1964-66. *Address:* 96 Cheyne Walk, SW10. *T:* 01-351 0293; Kelvedon Hall, Brentwood, Essex. *T:* Ongar 362180. *Clubs:* Buck's; White's.

CHANTLER, Philip, CMG 1963; Director of Economic Planning, Cyprus, 1969-70, Swaziland, 1970-71; *b* 16 May 1911; *s* of Tom and Minnie Chantler; *m* 1938, Elizabeth Margaret Pentney; one *d*. *Educ*: Manchester Central High Sch.; Manchester Univ.; Harvard Univ Commonwealth Fund Fellow, 1934-36; Asst Lectr in Public Admin., Manchester Univ., 1936-38; Tariffs Adviser, UK Gas Corp. Ltd, 1938-40. Served War of 1939-45: RA 1940-41; War Cabinet Secretariat, 1941-45; Economic Adviser, Cabinet Office, 1945-47; Economic Adviser, Ministry of Fuel and Power, 1947-60 (seconded as Economic Adviser, Government of Pakistan Planning Board, 1955-57); Under-Sec., Electricity Div., Min. of Power, 1961-65; Chm., North-West Economic Planning Bd, 1965-69. *Publication:* The British Gas Industry: An Economic Study, 1938. *Recreations:* gardening, cine-photography, Victorian architecture, industrial archæology, domestic odd-jobbing. *Address:* 1 Fingal Place, Edinburgh EH9 1JX; 2 The Mill, Rockcliffe, Galloway.

CHAPLAIS, Pierre Théophile Victorien Marie; Médaille de la Résistance, 1946; FBA 1973; Reader in Diplomatic in the University of Oxford, since 1957; Professorial Fellow, Wadham College, Oxford, since 1964; *b* Châteaubriant, Loire-Atlantique, France, 8 July 1920; *s* of late Théophile Chaplais and Victorine Chaplais (*née* Roussel); *m* 1948, Mary Doreen Middlemast; two *s*. *Educ*: Collège St-Sauveur, Redon, Ille-et-Vilaine; Univ. of Rennes, Ille-et-Vilaine (Licence en Droit, Licence ès-Lettres); Univ. of London (PhD). Editor, Public Record Office, London, 1948-55; Lectr in Diplomatic, Univ. of Oxford, 1955-57; Literary Dir, Royal Hist. Soc., 1958-64. Corresp. Fellow, Mediaeval Acad. of America, 1979. *Publications:* Some Documents regarding . . . the Treaty of Brétigny, 1952; The War of St Sardos, 1954; Treaty Rolls, vol. I, 1955; (with T. A. M. Bishop) Facsimiles of English Royal Writs to AD 1100 presented to V. H. Galbraith, 1957; Diplomatic Documents, vol. I, 1964; English Royal Documents, King John-Henry VI, 1971; English Medieval Diplomatic Practice, Part II, 1975, Part I, 1982; Essays in Medieval Diplomacy and Administration, 1981; articles in Bulletin of Inst. of Historical Research, English Hist. Review, Jl of Soc. of Archivists, etc. *Recreations:* gardening, fishing. *Address:* Lew Lodge, Lew, Oxford OX8 2BE. *T:* Bampton Castle 850613.

CHAPLIN, Arthur Hugh, CB 1970; Principal Keeper of Printed Books, British Museum, 1966-70; *b* 17 April 1905; *e r s* of late Rev. Herbert F. Chaplin and Florence B. Lusher; *m* 1938, Irene Marcousé. *Educ*: King's Lynn Grammar Sch.; Bedford Modern Sch.; University Coll., London. Asst Librarian: Reading Univ. 1927-28; Queen's Univ., Belfast, 1928-29; Asst Keeper, Dept of Printed Books, British Museum, 1930-52; Dep. Keeper, 1952-59; Keeper, 1959-66. Exec. Sec., Organizing Cttee of Internat. Conf. on Cataloguing

Principles, Paris, 1961; Mem. Council, Library Assoc. 1964-70; Pres., Microfilm Assoc. of GB, 1967-71. Fellow UCL, 1969. *Publications:* contributions to Jl Documentation, Library Assoc. Record, Library Quarterly, and to Cataloguing Principles and Practice (ed M. Piggott), 1954; Tradition and Principle in Library Cataloguing, 1966. *Recreations:* walking; motoring. *Address:* 44 Russell Square, WC1. *T:* 01-636 7217.

CHAPLING, Norman Charles, CBE 1954; Managing Director, Cable and Wireless Ltd, 1951-65, retd; *b* 11 Feb. 1903; *s* of late Charles Chapling; *m* 1933, Lenora, *d* of late Ernest Hedges; one *s*. Past Man. Dir: Cable & Wireless (Mid-East) Ltd; Cable & Wireless (West Indies) Ltd; Direct West India Cable Co. Ltd; Eastern Extension Australasia & China Telegraph Co. Ltd; Eastern Telegraph Co. Ltd; Eastern Telegraph Co. (France) Ltd; Halifax & Bermudas Cable Co. Ltd; Mercury House Ltd; West Coast of America Telegraph Co. Ltd; Western Telegraph Co. Ltd. Past Dir, SA Belge de Câbles Télégraphiques. *Address:* Treveal, Mawnan Smith, Falmouth, Cornwall.

CHAPMAN, family name of **Baron Northfield.**

CHAPMAN, (Anthony) Colin (Bruce), CBE 1970; RDI 1979; Chairman, Group Lotus Car Cos Ltd; Designer of sports and racing cars; *b* 19 May 1928; *s* of late S. F. Kennedy Chapman; *m* 1954, Hazel Patricia Williams; one *s* two *d*. *Educ*: Stationers' Company's Sch., Hornsey; London Univ. (BSc Eng). Served as Pilot, RAF, 1950. Structural Engineer, 1951; Civil Engineer, Development engineer, British Aluminium Co., 1952. Formed own Company, Lotus Cars, manufacturing motor cars, 1955; Holder of Don Ferodo Trophy in perpetuity after three wins (1956, 1965, 1978); Winner of Formula 1 World Constructors Championship (1963, 1965, 1968, 1970, 1972, 1978). FRSA 1968; Fellow, UCL, 1972; Hon. Dr RCA 1980. *Recreation:* flying. *Address:* Lotus Cars Ltd, Norwich, Norfolk NR14 8EZ. *Clubs:* British Racing Drivers, British Automobile Racing; British Racing and Sports Car.

CHAPMAN, Colin; see Chapman, A. C. B.

CHAPMAN, Cyril Donald, QC 1965; **His Honour Judge Chapman;** a Circuit Judge, since 1972; *b* 17 Sept. 1920; *s* of Cyril Henry Chapman and Frances Elizabeth Chapman (*née* Braithwaite); *m* 1st, 1950, Audrey Margaret Fraser (*née* Gough) (marr. diss., 1959); one *s*; 2nd, 1960, Muriel Falconer Bristow; one *s*. *Educ*: Roundhay Sch., Leeds; Brasenose Coll., Oxford (MA). Served RNVR, 1939-45. Called to Bar, 1947; Harmsworth Scholar, 1947; North Eastern Circuit, 1947; Recorder of Huddersfield, 1965-69, of Bradford, 1969-71. Contested (C) East Leeds 1955, Goole 1964, Brighouse and Spenborough, 1966. *Recreation:* yachting. *Address:* Hill Top, Collingham, Wetherby, W Yorks. *T:* Collingham Bridge 72813. *Club:* Leeds (Leeds).

CHAPMAN, Daniel Ahmling; see Chapman Nyaho.

CHAPMAN, (Francis) Ian; Chairman: William Collins & Sons (Holding) plc, since 1981; William Collins Publishers Ltd, since 1979; Radio Clyde Ltd, since 1973; Harvill Press Ltd, since 1976; Hatchards Ltd, since 1976; Deben Bookshop Ltd, since 1976; *b* 26 Oct. 1925; *s* of late Rev. Peter Chapman and Frances Burdett; *m* 1953, Marjory Stewart Swinton; one *s* one *d*. *Educ*: Shawlands Academy, Glasgow. Served RAF, 1943-44; worked in coal mines, 1945-47. Joined Wm Collins Sons & Co. Ltd, 1947 as gen. trainee; Sales Man., 1955; Sales Dir, 1960; Jt Man. Dir, 1968-76; Dep. Chm., 1976-81. Director: Pan Books Ltd; Collins Liturgical Publications Ltd; Book Tokens Ltd, 1981-; also numerous overseas companies of Collins. Mem. Council, Publishers' Assoc., 1963-76, 1977- (Vice Pres., 1978-79 and 1981-82); Pres., 1979-81); Mem. Bd, Book Develt Council, 1970-73. *Publications:* various articles on publishing in trade jls. *Recreations:* music, golf, reading, skiing. *Address:* Kenmore, 46 The Avenue, Cheam, Surrey. *T:* 01-642 1820. *Clubs:* Garrick, MCC; Royal Wimbledon Golf; Prestwick Golf.

CHAPMAN, Prof. Garth; Professor of Zoology, Queen Elizabeth College, University of London, since 1958 (Vice Principal, 1974-80; Acting Principal, Sept. 1977-March 1978); *b* 8 Oct. 1917; *o s* of E. J. Chapman and Edith Chapman (*née* Attwood); *m* 1941, Margaret Hilda Wigley; two *s* one *d*. *Educ*: Royal Grammar Sch., Worcester; Trinity Hall, Cambridge (Major Scholar); ScD Cantab 1971. Telecommunications Research Establishment, Ministry of Aircraft Production, 1941-45. Asst Lecturer in Zoology, Queen Mary Coll., University of London, 1945-46; Lecturer in Zoology, Queen Mary Coll., University of London, 1946-58. Dean, Faculty of Science, Univ. of London, 1974-78. Vis. Prof., Univ. of California, Berkeley, 1967, Los Angeles, 1970-71. FIBiol 1963. Member: Cttee for Commonwealth Univ. Interchange, British Council, 1978-80; Inter-Univ. Council for Higher Educn Overseas, 1973-; Council, Westfield Coll., Univ. of London, 1978-; Central Research Fund Cttee B, 1978-; Management Cttee of Univ. Marine Biological Station, Millport, 1975-. *Publications:* Zoology for Intermediate Students (with W. B. Barker), 1964; Body Fluids and their Functions, 1967; various on structure and physiology of marine invertebrates. *Recreations:* gardening; wood-engraving. *Address:* Nunns, Coxtie Green, Brentwood, Essex. *Club:* Athenæum.

CHAPMAN, Sir George (Alan), Kt 1982; FCA; FCIS; Senior Partner, Chapman Ross & Co., Chartered Accountants; Chairman: BNZ Finance Ltd, since 1979 (Director, since 1977); Landmark Properties Ltd, since 1982; Deputy Chairman, Bank of New Zealand, since 1976 (Director, since 1968);

b 13 April 1927; *s* of late Thomas George Chapman and of Winifred Jordan Chapman; *m* 1950, Jacqueline Sidney (*née* Irvine); two *s* five *d*. *Educ:* Trentham Sch.; Hutt Valley High Sch.; Victoria University. Joined Chapman Ross & Co., 1948. Director; Maui Developments Ltd, 1979-; Offshore Mining Co. Ltd, 1979-; Liquigas Ltd, 1981-; Norwich Winterthur (NZ) Ltd, 1982-; NZ Bd, Norwich Union Life Insurance Soc., 1982-; Skellerup Industries Ltd, 1982-. NZ National Party: Member, 1948-; Vice-Pres., 1966-73; Pres., 1973-82. Councillor, Upper Hutt Bor. Council, 1952-53, Deputy Mayor, Upper Hutt, 1953-55; Member: Hutt Valley Drainage Bd, 1953-55; Heretaunga Bd of Governors, 1953-55; Pres., Upper Hutt Chamber of Commerce, 1956-57. *Publication:* The Years of Lightning, 1980. *Recreations:* golf, reading, tennis. *Address:* 53 Barton Avenue, Heretaunga, Wellington, New Zealand. *T:* 283-512. *Clubs:* Wellington Golf, Wellington Racing.

CHAPMAN, Harold Thomas, CBE 1951; FRAeS; MIMechE; formerly Director, Hawker Siddeley Group, retired 1969; *b* 4 Aug. 1896; 3rd *s* of Henry James and Elizabeth Chapman, Mornington, Wylam-on-Tyne; *m* 1923, Mabel Annie Graham. *Educ:* Rutherford Coll., Newcastle on Tyne. Served European War in RFC and RAF, 1917-19. Joined Armstrong Siddeley Motors Ltd as a Designer, 1926; Works Manager, 1936; Gen. Manager, 1945; Dir, 1946. *Recreations:* fishing, shooting, golfing. *Address:* Ty-Melyn, Rhydspence, Whitney-on-Wye, Hereford. *T:* Clifford 313.

CHAPMAN, Ian; *see* Chapman, F. I.

CHAPMAN, John Henry Benjamin, CB 1957; *b* 28 Dec. 1899; *s* of Robert Henry Chapman and Edith Yeo Chapman (*née* Lillicrap); *m* 1929, Dorothy Rowlerson; one *s* one *d*. *Educ:* HM Dockyard Sch., Devonport; RNC Greenwich. Dir of Naval Construction, Admiralty, 1958-61. Dir, Fairfield S & E Co. Ltd, 1962-66; Consultant, Upper Clyde Shipbuilders, 1966-68. Mem. of Royal Corps of Naval Constructors, 1922-61; Hon. Vice-Pres., RINA; Mem., Technical Consultative Cttee, RNLI. *Address:* The Small House, Delling Lane, Old Bosham, Sussex. *T:* Bosham 573331. *Club:* Bosham Sailing.

CHAPMAN, Kathleen Violet, CBE 1956; RRC 1953 (ARRC 1945); QHNS 1953-56; Matron-in-Chief, Queen Alexandra's Royal Naval Nursing Service, 1953-56, retired; *b* 30 May 1903; *d* of late Major H. E. Chapman, CBE, DL Kent, Chief Constable of Kent, and Mrs C. H. J. Chapman. *Educ:* Queen Anne's, Caversham. Trained St Thomas's Hospital, 1928-32. *Address:* Holmfield, Compton Chamberlayne, Salisbury, Wilts.

CHAPMAN, Kenneth Herbert; Managing Director, Thomas Tilling Ltd, 1967-73; Director: British Steam Specialities Ltd; Société Générale (France) Bank Ltd; Ready Mixed Concrete Ltd; Goodliffe Garages Ltd; former Director, Royal Worcester Ltd; *b* 9 Sept. 1908; *s* of Herbert Chapman and Anne Bennett Chapman (*n ée* Poxon); *m* 1937, Jean Martha Mahring; one *s*. *Educ:* St Peter's Sch., York. Articled Clerk, 1926; qual. Solicitor, 1931; private practice, 1931-36; joined professional staff, HM Land Registry, 1936; transf. Min. of Aircraft Prodn, 1940, Private Sec. to Perm. Sec.; transf. Min. of Supply, 1946. Joined Thomas Tilling Ltd, as Group Legal Adviser, 1948; at various times Chm. or Dir of more than 20 companies in Tilling Group. High Sheriff of Greater London, 1974. *Recreations:* Rugby football (Past Pres. and Hon. Treas. of RFU, mem. cttee various clubs), cricket (mem. cttee various clubs), golf. *Address:* Cumberland House, Thakeham, near Pulborough, Sussex RH20 3ER. *T:* West Chiltington 2103. *Clubs:* East India, Devonshire, Sports and Public Schools; West Sussex Golf; Harlequin Football.

CHAPMAN, Leslie Charles; Founder and Chairman, Campaign to Stop Waste in Public Expenditure, since 1981; *b* 14 Sept. 1919; *e s* of Charles Richard Chapman and Lilian Elizabeth Chapman; *m* 1947, Beryl Edith England; one *s*. *Educ:* Bishopshalt Sch. Served War, Army, 1939-45. Civil Service, 1939 and 1945-74; Regional Dir, Southern Region, MPBW and PSA, 1967-74. Chm. and mem., various cttees; Mem. (pt-time), LTE, 1979-80. *Publications:* Your Disobedient Servant, 1978, 2nd revised edn 1979; Waste Away, 1982. *Recreations:* reading, music, gardening. *Address:* Cae Caradog, Ffarmers, Llanwrda, Dyfed SA19 8LZ. *T:* Pumpsaint 504.

CHAPMAN, Mark Fenger, CVO 1979; HM Diplomatic Service; Counsellor, The Hague, since 1982; *b* 12 Sept. 1934; *er s* of Geoffrey Walter Chapman and Esther Maria Fenger; *m* 1959, Patricia Mary Long; four *s*. *Educ:* Cranbrook Sch.; St Catharine's Coll., Cambridge. Entered HM Foreign Service, 1958; served in: Bangkok, 1959-63; FO, 1963-67; Head of Chancery, Maseru, 1967-71; Asst Head of Dept, FCO, 1971-74; Head of Chancery, Vienna, 1975-76; Dep. High Comr and Counsellor (Econ. and Comm.), Lusaka, 1976-79; Diplomatic Service Inspector, 1979-82. *Address:* Half Moon House, Briston, Melton Constable, Norfolk; c/o Foreign and Commonwealth Office, SW1. *Club:* Royal Commonwealth Society.

CHAPMAN, Prof. Norman Bellamy, MA, PhD; CChem, FRSC; G. F. Grant Professor of Chemistry, Hull University, 1956-82; Pro-Vice-Chancellor, 1973-76; *b* 19 April 1916; *s* of Frederick Taylor Chapman and Bertha Chapman; *m* 1949, Fonda Maureen Bungey; one *s* one *d*. *Educ:* Barnsley Holgate Grammar Sch.; Magdalene Coll., Cambridge (Entrance Scholar). 1st Cl. Parts I and II Nat. Sciences Tripos, 1937 and 1938; BA 1938, MA 1942, PhD 1941. Bye-Fellow, Magdalene Coll., 1939-42; Univ. Demonstrator in Chemistry, Cambridge, 1945; Southampton Univ.: Lectr,

1947; Senior Lectr, 1949; Reader in Chemistry, 1955. Chm., Technical Sub-Cttee, UCCA, 1974-79; Dep. Chm., UCCA, 1979. R. T. French Visiting Prof., Univ. of Rochester, NY, 1962-63; R. J. Reynolds Vis. Prof., Duke Univ., N Carolina, 1971; Cooch Behar Prof., Calcutta, 1982. *Publications:* (ed with J. Shorter) Advances in Free Energy Relationships, 1972; (ed) Organic Chemistry, Series One, vol. 2: Aliphatic Compounds (MTP Internat. Review of Science), 1973, Series Two, vol 2, 1976; Correlation Analysis in Chemistry: recent advances, 1978; contribs to Jl Chem. Soc., Analyst, Jl Medicinal Chem., Tetrahedron, Jl Organic Chemistry, Chemistry and Industry. *Recreations:* music, gardening, cricket, Rugby football. *Address:* 61 Newland Park, Hull HU5 2DR. *T:* 42946.

CHAPMAN, Sir Robin, (Robert Macgowan), 2nd Bt *cr* 1958; CBE 1961; TD and Bar, 1947; JP; Consultant with Spicer and Pegler, Chartered Accountants; Joint Secretary, Shields Commercial Building Society, since 1939; Chairman, Commercial Union Assurance Co. Ltd (Local Board); Director: North Eastern Investment Trust Ltd (Manager); Shields Commercial Building Society; Chairman: James Hogg & Sons (North Shields) Ltd; John W. Pratt Ltd; Vice Lord-Lieutenant, Tyne and Wear, since 1974; *b* Harton, Co. Durham, 12 Feb. 1911; *er s* of 1st Bt and Lady Hélène Paris Chapman, JP (*née* Macgowan); *S* father, 1963; *m* 1941, Barbara May, *d* of Hubert Tonks, Ceylon; two *s* one *d*. *Educ:* Marlborough; Corpus Christi Coll., Cambridge (Exhibitioner). 1st Cl. Hons Maths, BA 1933; MA 1937. Chartered Accountant, ACA 1938; FCA 1945. Partner: Henry Chapman Son and Co., 1939-69; Chapman, Hilton and Dunford, 1969-80. Chairman: Northern Counties Provincial Area Conservative Associations, 1954-57; Jarrow Conservative Association, 1957-60; Pres., Northern Area Conservative Council, 1982. Pres., Northern Soc. of Chartered Accountants, 1958-59, Mem. Cttee, 1949-60; Member: Police Authority, Co. Durham, 1955-59, 1961-65; Appeals Cttee, 1955-62; Durham Diocesan Conf., 1953-70; Durham Diocesan Synod, 1971-72; Durham Diocesan Bd of Finance, 1953-71 (Chm. 1966-70); Durham County TA, 1948-68; N England TA, 1968-74; Chm., Durham Co. Scout Council, 1972-82 (Scout Silver Acorn Award, 1973). Governor, United Newcastle Hospitals, 1957-64. TA Army officer, 1933-51; served War of 1939-45: RA Anti-Aircraft Command; GSO 2, 1940; CO 325 LAA regt, RA (TA), 1948-51; Hon. Col 1963; JP 1946, DL, 1952; High Sheriff of County Durham, 1960. *Recreation:* lawn tennis. *Heir: er s* David Robert Macgowan Chapman [*b* 16 Dec. 1941; *m* 1965, Maria Elizabeth de Gosztony-Zsolnay, *o d* of Dr N. de Mattyasovsky-Zsolnay, Montreal, Canada; one *s* one *d*]. *Address:* Pinfold House, 6 West Park Road, Cleadon, Sunderland SR6 7RR. *T:* Boldon 367451. *Clubs:* Carlton; County (Durham); Hawks (Cambridge).

CHAPMAN, Roy de Courcy; Headmaster of Malvern College, since Jan. 1983; *b* 1 Oct. 1936; *s* of Edward Frederic Gilbert Chapman and Aline de Courcy Ireland; *m* 1959, Valerie Rosemary Small; two *s* one *d*. *Educ:* Dollar Academy; St Andrews Univ. (Harkness Schol.: MA 1959); Moray House Coll. of Educn, Edinburgh. Asst Master, Trinity Coll., Glenalmond, 1960-64; Marlborough College: Asst Master, 1964-68; Head of Mod. Langs, 1968-75; OC CCF, 1969-75; Rector of Glasgow Acad., 1975-82. *Publications:* Le Français Contemporain, 1971; (with D. Whiting) Le Français Contemporain: Passages for translation and comprehension, 1975. *Recreations:* squash, France, brewing, wine-making. *Address:* Headmaster's House, Malvern College, Worcs. *T:* Malvern 4472.

CHAPMAN, Hon. Sir Stephen, Kt 1966; Judge of the High Court of Justice, Queen's Bench Division, 1966-81; *b* 5 June 1907; 2nd *s* of late Sir Sydney J. Chapman, KCB, CBE, and of late Lady Chapman, JP; *m* 1963, Mrs Pauline Frances Niewiarowski, *widow* of Dmitri de Lobel Niewiarowski and *d* of late Lt-Col H. Allcard and late Mrs A. B. M. Allcard. *Educ:* Westminster; Trinity Coll., Cambridge. King's Scholar and Capt. Westminster; Entrance Scholar and Major Scholar, Trinity Coll., Cambridge; Browne Univ. Gold Medallist, 1927 and 1928; John Stuart of Rannoch Univ. Scholar, 1928; 1st Cl. Classical Tripos, Pt I, 1927, and in Pt II, 1929. Entrance Scholar, Inner Temple, 1929; Jardine student, 1931; 1st Cl. and Certificate of Honour, Bar Final, 1931; called to Bar, Inner Temple, 1931; SE Circuit, Herts-Essex Sessions; Asst Legal Adviser, Min. of Pensions, 1939-46; Prosecuting Counsel for Post Office on SE Circuit, 1947-50 (Leader, Circuit, 1962); QC 1955; Comr of Assize, Winchester, Autumn, 1961. Recorder of Rochester, 1959-61, of Cambridge, 1961-63; Judge of the Crown Court and Recorder of Liverpool, 1963-66. Dep. Chm. Herts QS, 1963. Mem. Bar Council, 1956; Hon. Treas. 1958; Vice-Chm. 1959-60. *Publications:* Auctioneers and Brokers, in Atkin's Encyclopædia of Court Forms, vol. 3, 1938; Insurance (non-marine), in Halsbury's Laws of England, 3rd edn, vol. 22, 1958; Statutes on the Law of Torts, 1962. *Recreation:* gardening. *Address:* 72 Thomas More House, Barbican, EC2Y 8AB. *T:* 01-628 9251; The Manor House, Ware, Herts. *T:* Ware 2123. *Club:* United Oxford & Cambridge University.

CHAPMAN, Sydney Brookes, RIBA; FRTPI; MP (C) Chipping Barnet, since 1979; Chartered Architect and Chartered Town and Country Planner; private planning consultant and freelance writer; *b* 17 Oct. 1935; *m* 1976, Claire Lesley McNab (*née* Davies); two *s* one *d*. *Educ:* Rugby Sch.; Manchester University. DipArch 1958; ARIBA 1960; DipTP 1961; AMTPI 1962. Nat. Chm., Young Conservatives, 1964-66 (has been Chm. and Vice-Chm. at every level of Movt); Sen. Elected Vice-Chm., NW Area of Nat. Union of C and U Assocs, 1966-70. Contested (C) Stalybridge and Hyde, 1964; MP (C) Birmingham, Handsworth, 1970-Feb. 1974; PPS to Sec. of State for Transport, 1979-81, to Sec. of State for Social Services, 1981-; Chm., Parly

Gp for Consultancy, 1980-. Lectr in Arch. and Planning at techn. coll., 1964-70; Dir (Information), British Property Fedn, 1976-79; Dir (non-exec.), Capital and Counties plc, 1980-. Originator of nat. tree planting year, 1973; Vice-Pres., Arboricultural Assoc.; Chm., Queen's Silver Jubilee London Tree Group, 1977; Mem. Court, Tree Foundn. RIBA: Vice-Pres., 1974-75; Chm., Public Affairs Bd, 1974-75; Mem. Council, 1972-77. Hon. ALI; FRSA. *Publications:* Town and Countryside: future planning policies for Britain, 1978; regular contributor to bldg and property jls and to political booklets. *Recreation:* tree spotting. *Address:* House of Commons, SW1A 0AA.

CHAPMAN-MORTIMER, William Charles; author; *b* 15 May 1907; *s* of William George Chapman-Mortimer and Martha Jane McLelland; *m* 1934, Frances Statler; *m* 1956, Ursula Merits; one *d. Educ:* privately. *Publications:* A Stranger on the Stair, 1950; Father Goose, 1951 (awarded James Tait Black Memorial Prize, 1952); Young Men Waiting, 1952; Mediterraneo, 1954; Here in Spain, 1955; Madrigal, 1960; Amparo, 1971. *Address:* Gisebo, 56190 Huskvarna, Sweden. *T:* 036-50409.

CHAPMAN NYAHO, Daniel Ahmling, CBE 1961; Director: Pioneer Tobacco Co. Ltd, Ghana (Member of British-American Tobacco Group), since 1967; Standard Bank Ghana Ltd, 1970-75; *b* 5 July 1909; *s* of William Henry Chapman and Jane Atsiamesi (*née* Atriki); *m* 1941, Jane Abam (*née* Quashie); two *s* four *d* (and one *d* decd). *Educ:* Bremen Mission Schs, Gold Coast and Togoland; Achimota Coll., Ghana; St Peter's Hall, Oxford. Postgraduate courses at Columbia Univ. and New York Univ.; Teacher, Government Senior Boys' School, Accra, 1930; Master, Achimota Coll., 1930-33, 1937-46. Area Specialist, UN Secretariat, Lake Success and New York, 1946-54; Sec. to Prime Minister and Sec. of Cabinet, Gold Coast/Ghana, 1954-57; Ghana's Ambassador to USA and Permanent Representative at UN, 1957-59; Headmaster, Achimota Sch., Ghana, 1959-63; Dir, UN Div. of Narcotic Drugs, 1963-66; Ambassador (Special Duties), Min. of External Affairs, Ghana, 1967. Gen. Sec., All-Ewe Conf., 1944-46; Commonwealth Prime Ministers' Conf., 1957; Mem., Ghana delegn to the conf. of indep. African States, Accra, 1958. First Vice-Chm., Governing Council of UN Special Fund, 1959; Chairman: Mission of Indep. African States to Cuba, Dominican Republic, Haiti, Venezuela, Bolivia, Paraguay, Uruguay, Brazil, Argentina, Chile, 1958; Volta Union, 1968-69. Vice-Chairman: Commn on Univ. Educn in Ghana, 1960-61; Ghana Constituent Assembly, 1978-79. Member: Board of Management, UN Internat. Sch., New York, 1950-54, 1958-59; UN Middle East and N. Africa Technical Assistance Mission on Narcotics Control, 1963; Dir, UN Consultative Gp on Narcotics Control in Asia and Far East, Tokyo, 1964; Member: Political Cttee of Nat. Liberation Council, 1967; Board of Trustees of General Kotoka Trust Fund; Chairman: Arts Council of Ghana, 1968-69; Council of Univ. of Science and Technology, Kumasi, 1972; Bd. of Directors, Ghana Film Industry Corporation, 1979-; Ghana National Honours and Awards Cttee, 1979-. Danforth Vis. Lectr, Assoc. Amer. Colls, 1969, 1970. Hon. LLD Greenboro Agric. and Techn. Coll., USA, 1958. Fellow, Ghana Acad. of Arts and Sciences. *Publications:* Human Geography of Eweland, 1946; Our Homeland—Book I: South-East Gold Coast, 1945; (Ed.) The Ewe News-Letter, 1945-46. *Recreations:* music, gardening, walking. *Address:* (Office) Tobacco House, Liberty Avenue, PO Box 5211, Accra, Ghana. *T:* 21111; (Home) 7 Ninth Avenue, Tesano, Accra, Ghana. *T:* 27180. *Clubs:* Royal Commonwealth Society (London); Accra (Ghana).

CHAPPELL, (Edwin) Philip, CBE 1976; a Vice-Chairman, Morgan Grenfell Holdings, since 1975; Director: Fisons; Guest Keen & Nettlefolds; *b* 12 June 1929; *s* of late Rev. C. R. Chappell; *m* 1962, Julia Clavering House, *d* of H. W. House, DSO, MC; one *s* three *d. Educ:* Marlborough Coll.; Christ Church, Oxford (MA). Joined Morgan Grenfell, 1954; Dir, Morgan Grenfell & Co. Ltd, 1964-; Chm., ICL, 1980-81. Chairman: Nat. Ports Council, 1971-77; EDC for Food and Drink Manufacturing Industry, 1976-80. Member: Council, Institute of Bankers, 1971-; Business Educn Council, 1974-80; SITPRO Board, 1974-77. Governor of BBC, 1976-81. *Address:* 22 Frognal Lane, NW3 7DT. *T:* 01-435 8627. *Club:* Athenæum.

CHAPPELL, William; dancer, designer, producer; *b* Wolverhampton, 27 Sept. 1908; *s* of Archibald Chappell and Edith Eva Clara Blair-Staples. *Educ:* Chelsea School of Art. Studied dancing under Marie Rambert. First appearance on stage, 1929; toured Europe with Ida Rubinstein's company, working under Massine and Nijinska; danced in many ballets, London, 1929-34; joined Sadler's Wells Co., 1934, and appeared there every season; Army service, 1940-45; designed scenery and costumes at Sadler's Wells, 1934-, and Covent Garden, 1947-, including Les Rendezvous, Les Patineurs, Coppelia, Giselle, Handel's Samson, Frederick Ashton's Walk to the Paradise Garden, and Ashton's Rhapsody (costumes); for many revues and London plays. Produced Lyric Revue, 1951, Globe Revue, 1952, High Spirits, Hippodrome, 1953, At the Lyric, 1953, Going to Town, St Martin's, 1954 (also arranging dances for many of these); An Evening with Beatrice Lillie, Globe, 1954 (asst prod.); Time Remembered, New, 1955; Moby Dick, Duke of York's, 1955 (with Orson Welles); The Buccaneer, Lyric, Hammersmith, 1955; The Rivals, Saville; Beaux' Stratagem, Chichester; Violins of St Jacques (also wrote libretto), Sadler's Wells; English Eccentrics; Love and a Bottle; Passion Flower Hotel; Travelling Light; Espresso Bongo; Living for Pleasure; Where's Charley?; appeared in and assisted Orson Wells with film The Trial; The Chalk Garden, Haymarket, 1971; Offenbach's Robinson Crusoe (1st English perf.), Camden Festival, 1973; Cockie, Vaudeville, 1973; Oh, Kay!, Westminster, 1974; National Tour, In Praise of Love, 1974; Fallen Angels,

Gate Theatre, Dublin, 1975; Marriage of Figaro (designed and directed), Sadler's Wells, 1977; The Master's Voice, Dublin, 1977; Memoir, Ambassadors, 1978; Gianni Schicci, Sadler's Wells, 1978; Nijinsky (film), 1979; Same Time Next Year, Dublin, 1980; for Dublin Theatre Festival, 1980: Speak of the Devil (musical); designs for Giselle, inc. 2 prodns for Anton Dolin; Choreographed: Travesties, RSC Aldwych, 1974, NY, 1975; Bloomsbury, Phoenix, 1974; Directed, designed costumes and choreographed: Purcell's Fairy Queen, London Opera Centre, 1974; Donizetti's Torquato Tasso, Camden Festival, 1975; Lully's Alceste, London Opera Centre, 1975; A Moon for the Misbegotten, Dublin, 1976; The Rivals, Dublin, 1976; teacher and adviser for: Nureyev season, 1979; Joffrey Ballet, NY, 1979. TV shows. Illustrator of several books. *Publications:* Studies in Ballet; Fonteyn (ed and jt author) Edward Burra: a painter remembered by his friends, 1982. *Recreations:* reading, cinema, painting. *Address:* 25 Rosenau Road, Battersea, SW11.

CHAPPLE, Frank Joseph; General Secretary, Electrical, Electronic, Telecommunication and Plumbing Union, since 1966; Member, General Council, TUC, since 1971, Chairman, 1982-83; *b* Shoreditch, 1921; *m* ; two *s. Educ:* elementary school. Started as Apprentice Electrician; Member ETU, 1937-; Shop Steward and Branch Official; Member Exec. Council, 1958; Asst General Secretary, 1963-66. Member: National Exec. Cttee of Labour Party, 1965-71; Cttee of Inquiry into Shipping, 1967; Royal Commn on Environmental Pollution, 1973-77; Horserace Totalisator Bd, 1976-; Energy Commn, 1977-79; NEDC, 1979-; Nat. Nuclear Corp., 1980-. *Recreation:* racing pigeons. *Address:* c/o Electrical, Electronic, Telecommunications and Plumbing Union, Hayes Court, West Common Road, Bromley BR2 7AU.

CHAPPLE, Maj-Gen. John Lyon, CBE 1980; Director of Military Operations, since 1982; *b* 27 May 1931; *s* of C. H. Chapple; *m* 1959, Annabel Hill; one *s* three *d. Educ:* Haileybury; Trinity Coll., Cambridge (MA). Joined 2nd KEO Goorkhas, 1954; served Malaya, Hong Kong, Borneo; Staff Coll., 1962; jssc 1969; Commanded 1st Bn 2nd Goorkhas, 1970-72; Directing Staff, Staff Coll., 1972-73; Commanded 48 Gurkha Infantry Bde, 1976; Gurkha Field Force, 1977; Principal Staff Officer to Chief of Defence Staff, 1978-79; Comdr, British Forces Hong Kong, and Maj.-Gen., Brigade of Gurkhas, 1980-82. Services Fellow, Fitzwilliam Coll., Cambridge, 1973, FZS, FRGS. OStJ.

CHAPPLE, Stanley; Director of Symphony and Opera, University of Washington, now Emeritus; *b* 29 Oct. 1900; *s* of Stanley Clements Chapple and Bessie Norman; *m* 1927, Barbara, *d* of late Edward Hilliard; no *c. Educ:* Central Foundation Sch., London. Began his musical education at the London Academy of Music at the age of 8, being successively student, professor, Vice-Principal, Principal until 1936; as a Conductor made début at the Queen's Hall, 1927, and has since conducted Symphony Orchestras in Berlin, Vienna, The Hague, Warsaw and Boston, St Louis, Washington, DC, and other American and Canadian cities. Assistant to Serge Koussevitzky at Berkshire Music Centre, 1940, 1941, 1942 and 1946; former conductor St Louis Philharmonic Orchestra and Chorus and Grand Opera Association. Hon. MusDoc Colby Coll. 1947. *Address:* 18270 47th Place NE, Seattle, Washington 98155, USA.

CHAPUT DE SAINTONGE, Rev. Rolland Alfred Aimé, CMG 1953; Preacher of retreats; *b* Montreal, Canada, 7 Jan. 1912; *s* of Alfred Edward and Hélène Jeté Chaput de Saintonge; *m* 1940, Barbara Watts; one *s* two *d. Educ:* Canada; USA; Syracuse Univ., NY (BA, MA); Geneva Univ. (D ès Sc. Pol.). Extra-Mural Lecturer in International Affairs: University College of the South-West, Exeter, University of Bristol, University College of Southampton, 1935-40; Staff Speaker, Min. of Information, South-West Region, 1940; served Army, 1940-46; Lieut-Col (DCLI); Asst Secretary, Control Office for Germany and Austria, 1946-48; Head of Government Structure Branch, CCG and Liaison Officer to German Parliamentary Council, 1948-49; Head of German Information Dept, FO, 1949-58; UN High Commission for Refugees: Dep. Chief, Information and Public Relations Sect., 1960-64; Rep. in Senegal, 1964-66; Programme Support Officer, 1966-67; Chief, N and W Europe Section, 1967-68; Special Projects Officer, 1968-73. Ordained, Diocese of Quebec, 1975; admitted Community of Most Holy Sacrament, 1976. *Publications:* Disarmament in British Foreign Policy, 1935; British Foreign Policy Since the War, 1936; The Road to War and the Way Out, 1940; Public Administration in Germany, 1961. *Address:* 8 Minley Court, Somers Road, Reigate, Surrey.

CHARKHAM, Jonathan Philip; on secondment from Bank of England as Director, PRO NED (Promotion of Non-Executive Directors), since 1982; *b* 17 Oct. 1930; *s* of late Louis Charkham and Phoebe Beatrice Barquet (*née* Miller); *m* Moira Elizabeth Frances, *d* of late Barnett A. Salmon and of Molly Salmon; twin *s* one *d. Educ:* St Paul's Sch. (scholar); Jesus Coll., Cambridge (Exhibitioner). BA 1952. Called to Bar, Inner Temple, 1953. Morris Charkham Ltd, 1953-63 (Man. Dir, 1957-63); Div. Dir, Rest Assured Ltd, 1963-68. Civil Service Department: Principal, Management Services, later Pay, 1969-73; Asst Sec., 1973-78, Personnel Management, 1973-75; Dir, Public Appts Unit, 1975-82; Under Sec., 1978, Management and Organisation, 1980-82. Mem. Council, Royal Inst. of Public Admin., 1981-82. Chm., CU Labour Club, 1952. Master, Worshipful Co. of Upholders, 1979-80, 1980-81. FRSA; MBIM. *Recreations:* music, playing golf, watching cricket, antique furniture, wine. *Address:* 14 Douro Place, Victoria Road, Kensington, W8

5PH. *T:* 01-937 8635. *Clubs:* Athenæum, MCC, Roehampton, City Livery.

CHARLEMONT, 13th Viscount *cr* 1665 (Ireland); **Charles Wilberforce Caulfeild;** Baron Caulfeild of Charlemont, 1620 (Ireland); retired Civil Servant, Canada; *b* 10 March 1899; *s* of Charles Hans Caulfeild (*d* 1950) and Ethel Jessie (*d* 1973), *d* of D. G. R. Mann; *S* cousin, 1979; *m* 1930, Dorothy Jessie, *d* of late Albert A. Johnston. *Educ:* Public and High schools, Ottawa, Canada. *Recreations:* curling and lawn bowling. *Heir: nephew* John Day Caulfeild [*b* 19 March 1934; *m* 1st, 1964, Judith Ann (*d* 1971), *d* of James E. Dodd; one *s* one *d* ; 2nd, 1972, Janet Evelyn, *d* of Orville R. Nancekivell]. *Address:* RR2, Cumberland, Ontario K0A 1S0, Canada.

CHARLES, Anthony Harold, ERD; TD; MA Cantab; MB; FRCS; FRCOG; Consulting Obstetric and Gynæcological Surgeon, St George's Hospital; Consulting Surgeon, Samaritan Hospital for Women (St Mary's); Consulting Gynæcologist, Royal National Orthopædic Hospital; Hon. Gynæcologist, King Edward VII Hospital for Officers; Consulting Gynæcologist, Caterham and District Hospital; Consulting Surgeon, General Lying-in-Hospital; late Hon. Consultant in Obstetrics and Gynaecology Army; 2nd *s* of H. P. Charles; *m* 1962, Rosemary Christine Hubert; three *d. Educ:* Dulwich; Gonville and Caius Coll., Cambridge. Examiner in Midwifery and Gynæcology: Univ. of Cambridge; Soc. of Apothecaries; RCOG; Univs of London, Hong Kong and Cairo. Past Mem., Board of Governors, St Mary's Hospital. Past President: Chelsea Clinical Soc.; Sect. of Obstetrics and Gynæcology, RSM. Late Vice-Dean, St George's Hospital Medical Sch.; late Resident Asst Surgeon and Hon. Asst Anæsthetist, St George's Hospital. Colonel AMS; late Hon. Colonel and OC, 308 (Co. of London) General Hospital, T&AVR. Hon. Surgeon to the Queen, 1957-59. Served 1939-45, Aldershot, Malta and Middle-East as Surgical Specialist; Officer-in-Charge, Surgical Division, 15 Scottish General Hospital and Gynæc. Adviser MEF. Past Pres., Alleyn Club. *Publications:* Women in Sport, in Armstrong and Tucker's Injuries in Sport, 1964; contributions since 1940 to Jl Obst. and Gyn., Postgrad. Med. Jl, Proc. Royal Soc. Med., Operative Surgery, BMJ. *Recreations:* golf, boxing (Middle-Weight, Cambridge *v* Oxford, 1930); Past President Rosslyn Park Football Club. *Address:* 95 Harley Street, W1. *T:* 01-935 4196; Gaywood Farm, Gay Street, Pulborough, Sussex. *Clubs:* Army and Navy, Bath, MCC; Hawks (Cambridge).

CHARLES, Bernard Leopold, QC 1980; *b* 16 May 1929; *s* of Chaskiel Charles and Mary Harris; *m* 1958, Margaret Daphne Abel; one *s* two *d. Educ:* King's Coll., Taunton. Called to the Bar, Gray's Inn, 1955. Practised in London and on South Eastern Circuit, from 1956. *Recreations:* music, politics. *Address:* Lamb Building, Temple, EC4. *T:* 01-353 6701.

CHARLES, Hon. Eugenia; *see* Charles, Hon. M. E.

CHARLES, Rt. Rev. Harold John; Bishop of St Asaph, 1971-March 1982; *b* 26 June 1914; *s* of Rev. David Charles and Mary Charles, Carmarthenshire; *m* 1941, Margaret Noeline; one *d. Educ:* Welsh Univ. Aberystwyth; Keble Coll., Oxford. BA Wales 1935; BA Oxford 1938, MA 1943. Curate of Abergwili, Carms, 1938-40; Bishop's Messenger, Diocese of Swansea and Brecon, 1940-48; Warden of University Church Hostel, Bangor, and Lecturer at University College, Bangor, 1948-52; Vicar of St James, Bangor, 1952-54; Canon Residentiary of Bangor, 1953-54; Warden of St Michael's Coll., Llandaff, 1954-57; Canon of Llandaff, 1956-57; Dean of St Asaph, 1957-71. ChStJ 1973. *Address:* 53 The Avenue, Woodland Park, Prestatyn, Clwyd.

CHARLES, Jack; Director of Establishments, Greater London Council, 1972-77, retired; *b* 18 Jan. 1923; *o s* of late Frederick Walter Charles and of Alice Mary Charles; *m* 1959, Jean, *d* of late F. H. Braund, London; one *s* one *d. Educ:* County High Sch., Ilford. Air Min., 1939-42; RAF, 1942-46; Min. of Supply, 1947-59 (Private Sec. to Minister of Supply, 1952-54); War Office, 1959-60; UKAEA, 1960-68 (Authority Personnel Officer, 1965-68); Dep. Dir of Estabs, GLC, 1968-72. *Recreation:* gardening. *Address:* Kings Warren, Enborne Row, Wash Water, Newbury, Berks RG15 0LY. *T:* Newbury 30161.

CHARLES, Sir John (Pendrill), KCVO 1975; MC 1945; Partner, Allen & Overy, 1947-78; *b* 3 May 1914; *yr s* of late Dr Clifford Pendrill Charles and Gertrude Mary (*née* Young); *m* 1st, 1939, Mary Pamela Dudley (marr. diss.); 2nd, 1959, Winifred Marie Heath; two *d. Educ:* Tonbridge; Magdalene Coll., Cambridge (MA). Solicitor, 1938. Served War, 1939-45: 11th Regt (HAC) RHA; ME, Sicily and Italy. Steward, British Boxing Bd of Control, 1961-. *Recreations:* travel, fishing, sailing. *Address:* 42 Belgrave Mews South, SW1X 8BT. *T:* 01-235 5792. *Club:* White's.

CHARLES, Leslie Stanley Francis; Managing Director, British Aluminium Co. Ltd, 1979-82 (Deputy Managing Director, 1968-79); Director, Birmid Qualcast plc, since 1981; *b* 28 July 1917; *s* of Samuel Francis Charles and Lena Gwendolyn (*née* Reed); *m* 1941, Henrietta Elizabeth Calvin Thomas; one *s. Educ:* Cardiff High Sch.; University Coll. of S Wales and Mon, Univ. of Wales (BScEng London, 1st Cl. Hons). Grad. Engr, Metropolitan Vickers Ltd, 1936-39; Regular Officer, REME, 1939-54; Consultant, Urwick Orr & Partners Ltd, 1954-60; Chief Engr Ops, UKAEA, 1960-63; Dir of Factories, Raleigh Industries Ltd, 1963-66; Man. Dir, Aluminium Wire & Cable Co. Ltd, 1966-68. Chm., European Aluminium Assoc., 1981-. *Recreations:* golf,

bridge, music. *Address:* Crana, Claydon Lane, Chalfont St Peter, Bucks SL9 8JU. *T:* Gerrards Cross 84290. *Club:* Army and Navy.

CHARLES, Hon. (Mary) Eugenia; Prime Minister and Minister of Finance and Foreign Affairs, Commonwealth of Dominica, since 1980; MP (Dominica Freedom Party) Roseau, since 1975; *b* 15 May 1918; *d* of John Baptiste Charles and Josephine (*née* Delauney). *Educ:* Convent High Sch., Roseau, Dominica; St Joseph's Convent, St George's, Grenada; University Coll., Univ. of Toronto (BA); London Sch. of Econs and Pol. Science. Called to the Bar, Inner Temple, 1947; admitted to practice, Dominica, 1949. Entered Parlt, 1970; Leader of the Opposition, 1975-80. *Recreations:* reading, gardening, travelling. *Address:* Office of the Prime Minister, Roseau, Commonwealth of Dominica. *T:* 2401.

CHARLES, Rev. Canon Sebastian; Residentiary Canon, Westminster Abbey, since 1978; Steward since 1978, also Treasurer since 1982; *b* 31 May 1932; *s* of Gnanamuthu Pakianathan Charles and Kamala David; *m* 1967, Frances Rosemary Challen; two *s* two *d. Educ:* Madras Univ. (BCom 1953); Serampore Univ. (BD 1965); Lincoln Theological Coll. Curate, St Mary, Portsea, Dio. Portsmouth, 1956-59; Priest-in-charge, St John the Evangelist, Dio. Rangoon, 1959-65; St Augustine's Coll., Canterbury, 1965-66; St Thomas, Heaton Chapel, Dio. Manchester, attached to Industrial Mission Team, 1966-67; Vicar of St Barnabas', Pendleton, 1967-74; Chaplain, Univ. of Salford, 1967-74; Asst Gen. Secretary and Secretary, Div. of Community Affairs, British Council of Churches, 1974-78. *Recreations:* reading, tennis, martial arts. *Address:* 5 Little Cloister, Westminster Abbey, SW1W 3PL. *T:* 01-222 6939.

CHARLES, William Travers; Fellow, Faculty of Law, Monash University, since 1976 (Special Lecturer, 1966-75); Judge of the High Court, Zambia, 1963-66; *b* Victoria, Australia, 10 Dec. 1908; *s* of William James Charles and Elizabeth Esther Charles (*née* Payne); *m* 1940, Helen Gibson Vale; one *s* one *d. Educ:* St Thomas Grammar Sch., Essendon, Victoria; University of Melbourne. Called to bar, Victoria, 1932; practised at bar, 1932-39. Served Australian Army Legal Service including Middle East, 1940-42 (Lieut-Col), seconded AAG (Discipline), AHQ Melbourne, 1942-46. Chief Magistrate and Legal Adviser, British Solomon Islands Protectorate, 1946-51; Judicial Commn, British Solomon Islands, 1951-53; Magistrate, Hong Kong, 1954-56; District Judge, Hong Kong, 1956-58; Judge of the High Court, Western Nigeria, 1958-63. *Recreations:* cricket, football, music, history. *Address:* 2 Burroughs Road, Balwyn, Vic 3103, Australia.

CHARLES-EDWARDS, Rt. Rev. Lewis Mervyn, MA, DD; *b* 6 April 1902; *s* of Dr Lewis Charles-Edwards and Lillian Hill; *m* 1933, Florence Edith Louise Barsley; one *s* one *d. Educ:* Shrewsbury School; Keble College, Oxford; Lichfield Theological College. Curate, Christ Church, Tunstall, 1925-28; St Paul, Burton on Trent, 1928-31; Droitwich Spa, 1931-33; Vicar, Marchington, 1933-37; Market Drayton, 1937-44; Newark on Trent, 1944-48; Rural Dean of Hodnet, 1938-44, of Newark, 1945-48; Vicar of St Martin in the Fields, London, WC2, 1948-56; Commissary to Bishop of Honduras, 1945-56; Chaplain to King George VI, 1950-52, to the Queen, 1952-56; Bishop of Worcester, 1956-70. Religious Adviser to Independent Television Authority, 1955-56. Chairman, Midland Region Religious Advisory Committee BBC, 1958-65. Member of Commission on Church and State, 1951. Chaplain and Sub-Prelate Order of St John of Jerusalem, 1965. Select Preacher, University of Cambridge; 1949; Oxford, 1964. *Publication:* Saints Alive!, 1953. *Address:* Brackenwood Cottage, East Tuddenham, Dereham, Norfolk NR20 3NF. *Club:* Athenæum.

CHARLESTON, Robert Jesse; Keeper of the Department of Ceramics, Victoria and Albert Museum, 1963-76; *b* 3 April 1916; *s* of late Sidney James Charleston, Lektor, Stockholms Högskola; *m* 1941, Joan Randle; one *s* one *d. Educ:* Berkhamsted Sch., Herts; New College, Oxford. Army (Major, RAPC), 1940-46; Asst, Bristol Museum, 1947; Asst Keeper, Victoria and Albert Museum, 1948; Deputy Keeper, 1959. Mem., Reviewing Cttee on Export of Works of Art, 1979-. *Publications:* Roman Pottery, 1955; (ed) English Porcelain, 1745-1850, 1965; (ed) World Ceramics, 1968; (with Donald Towner) English Ceramics, 1580-1830, 1977; Islamic Pottery, 1979; Masterpieces of Glass, 1980; The James A. de Rothschild Collection: (with J. G. Ayers) Meissen and Oriental Porcelain, 1971; (with Michael Archer and M. Marcheix) Glass and Enamels, 1977; numerous articles and reviews in The Connoisseur, Jl of Glass Studies, Burlington Magazine, etc. *Recreations:* foreign travel, music. *Address:* 1 Denbigh Gardens, Richmond, Surrey. *T:* 01-940 3592.

CHARLESWORTH, Stanley, OBE 1980; National Secretary, National Council of YMCAs, 1975-80; *b* 20 March 1920; *s* of Ernest and Amy Charlesworth; *m* 1942, Vera Bridge; three *d. Educ:* Ashton under Lyne Grammar Sch.; Manchester Coll. of Commerce. YMCA: Area Sec., Community Services, 1943-52, Dep. Sec., 1952-57; Asst Regional Sec., NW Region, 1957-67, Regional Sec., 1967-75. *Recreations:* sailing, golf, walking, gardening. *Clubs:* Rotary (Walthamstow); YMCA (Manchester).

CHARLISH, Dennis Norman; Panel Chairman, Civil Service Selection Board, since 1978 (Resident Chairman, 1975-78); *b* 24 May 1918; *s* of Norman Charlish and Edith (*née* Cherriman); *m* 1941, Margaret Trevor, *o d* of William Trevor and Margaret Ann Williams, Manchester; one *d. Educ:* Brighton Grammar Sch.; London Sch. of Economics. Rosebery Schol., 1947;

BSc (Econ) 1st class hons., 1951. Joined Civil Service as Tax Officer, Inland Revenue, 1936; Exec. Officer, Dept of Overseas Trade, 1937; Dep. Armament Supply Officer, Admty, 1941; Principal, BoT, 1949; Asst Secretary, 1959; Imperial Defence Coll., 1963; Under-Sec., BoT, 1967-69; Min. of Technology, 1969-70; Head of Personnel, DTI, 1971-74, Dept of Industry, 1974-75. *Address:* 28 Multon Road, SW18.

CHARLTON, Bobby; see Charlton, Robert.

CHARLTON, (Frederick) Noel, CB 1961; CBE 1946; *b* 4 Dec. 1906; *s* of late Frederick William Charlton and Marian Charlton; *m* 1932, Maud Helen Rudgard; no *c. Educ:* Rugby School; Hertford Coll., Oxford Univ. (MA). Admitted a Solicitor, 1932; in private practice as Solicitor in London, 1932-39. War Service, 1939-46 (attained rank of Colonel, Gen. List). Joined Treasury Solicitor's Dept, 1946; Principal Asst Solicitor (Litigation), Treasury Solicitor's Dept, 1956-71; Sec., Lord Chancellor's Cttee on Defamation, 1971-74; with Dept of Energy (Treasury Solicitor's Branch), 1975-81, retired. Chairman, Coulsdon and Purley UDC, 1953-54 and 1964-65; Hon. Alderman, London Borough of Croydon. Bronze Star (USA), 1945. *Recreations:* golf, travel. *Address:* Windyridge, 11 Hillcroft Avenue, Purley, Surrey. *T:* 01-660 2802. *Club:* Army and Navy.
See also T. A. G. Charlton.

CHARLTON, Graham; see Charlton, T. A. G.

CHARLTON, Prof. Graham, MDS; FDSRCSE; Dean of Dental Studies and Professor of Conservative Dentistry, University of Edinburgh, since 1978; *b* 15 Oct. 1928; *s* of Simpson R. Charlton and Georgina (*née* Graham); *m* 1956, Stella Dobson; two *s* one *d. Educ:* Bedlington Grammar Sch., Northumberland; St John's Coll., York (Teaching Cert.); King's Coll., Univ. of Durham (BDS); Univ. of Bristol (MDS). Teacher, Northumberland, 1948-52; National Service, 1948-50; Dental School, 1952-58; General Dental Practice, Torquay, 1958-64; University of Bristol: Lecturer, 1964-72; Cons. Sen. Lectr, 1972-78; Dental Clinical Dean, 1975-78. *Address:* Carnethy, Bog Road, Penicuik, Midlothian EH26 9BT. *T:* Penicuik 73639.

CHARLTON, John, (Jack Charlton), OBE 1974; Manager, Sheffield Wednesday Football Club, since 1977; *b* 8 May 1935; *s* of Robert and Elizabeth Charlton; *m* 1958, Patricia; two *s* one *d. Educ:* Hirst Park Sch., Ashington. Professional footballer, Leeds United, 1952-73; Manager, Middlesbrough, 1973-77. Mem., Sports Council, 1977-. *Recreations:* shooting, fishing, gardening. *Address:* c/o Sheffield Wednesday Football Club, Hillsborough, Sheffield S6 1SW. *T:* Sheffield 343123.
See also Robert Charlton.

CHARLTON, Prof. Kenneth; Professor of History of Education and Head of Department of Education, King's College, University of London, since 1972; *b* 11 July 1925; 2nd *s* of late George and Lottie Charlton; *m* 1953, Maud Tulloch Brown, *d* of late P. R. Brown, MBE and M. B. Brown; one *s* one *d. Educ:* City Grammar Sch., Chester; Univ. of Glasgow. MA 1949, MEd 1953, Glasgow. RNVR, 1943-46. History Master, Dalziel High Sch., Motherwell, and Uddingston Grammar Sch., 1950-54; Lectr in Educn, UC N Staffs, 1954-64; Sen. Lectr in Educn, Keele Univ., 1964-66; Prof. of History and Philosophy of Educn, Birmingham Univ., 1966-72. *Publications:* Recent Historical Fiction for Children, 1960, 2nd edn 1969; Education in Renaissance England, 1965; contrib. Educnl Rev., Brit. Jl Educnl Psych., Year Bk of Educn, Jl Hist. of Ideas, Brit. Jl Educnl Studies, Internat. Rev. of Educn, Trans Hist. Soc. Lancs and Cheshire, Irish Hist. Studies, Northern Hist. *Recreations:* gardening, listening to music. *Address:* King's College, Strand, WC2R 2LS.

CHARLTON, Robert, (Bobby Charlton), CBE 1974 (OBE 1969); Director, Wigan Athletic FC; *b* 11 Oct. 1937; *s* of Robert and Elizabeth Charlton; *m* 1961, Norma; two *d. Educ:* Bedlington Grammar Sch., Northumberland. Professional Footballer with Manchester United, 1954-73, for whom he played 751 games and scored 245 goals; FA Cup Winners Medal, 1963; FA Championship Medals, 1956-57, 1964-65 and 1966-67; World Cup Winners Medal (International), 1966; European Cup Winners medal, 1968. 100th England cap, 21 April 1970; 106 appearances for England, 1957-73. Manager, Preston North End, 1973-75. *Publications:* My Soccer Life, 1965; Forward for England, 1967; This Game of Soccer, 1967; Book of European Football, Books 1-4, 1969-72. *Recreation:* golf. *Address:* Garthollerton, Chelford Road, Ollerton, near Knutsford, Cheshire.
See also John Charlton.

CHARLTON, (Thomas Alfred) Graham, CB 1970; Secretary, Trade Marks, Patents and Designs Federation, since 1973; *b* 29 Aug. 1913; 3rd *s* of late Frederick William and Marian Charlton; *m* 1940, Margaret Ethel, *yr d* of A. E. Furst; three *d. Educ:* Rugby School; Corpus Christi Coll., Cambridge. Asst Principal, War Office, 1936; Asst Private Secretary to Secretary of State for War, 1937-39; Principal, 1939; Cabinet Office, 1947-49; Asst Secretary, 1949; International Staff, NATO, 1950-52; War Office, later MoD, 1952-73; Asst Under-Sec. of State, 1960-73. Coronation Medal, 1953. *Recreations:* golf, gardening. *Address:* Victoria House, Elm Road, Penn, Bucks HP10 8LQ. *T:* Penn 3195.
See also Frederick Noel Charlton.

CHARLTON, Prof. Thomas Malcolm; historian of engineering science; Jackson Professor of Engineering, University of Aberdeen, 1970-79, now Emeritus; *b* 1 Sept. 1923; *s* of William Charlton and Emily May Charlton (*née* Wallbank); *m* 1950, Valerie, *d* of late Dr C. McCulloch, Hexham; two *s* (and one *s* decd). *Educ:* Doncaster Grammar Sch. BSc (Eng) London, MA Cantab. Junior Scientific Officer, Min. of Aircraft Prodn, TRE, Malvern, 1943-46; Asst Engr, Merz & McLellan, Newcastle upon Tyne, 1946-54; Univ. Lectr in Engrg, Cambridge, 1954-63; Fellow, Sidney Sussex Coll., 1959-63; Prof. of Civil Engrg, Queen's Univ., Belfast, 1963-70; Dean, Faculty of Applied Science, QUB, 1967-70. Mem., Adv. Council UDR, 1969-71. For. Mem., Finnish Acad. of Technical Sciences, 1967. FRSE 1973. *Publications:* Model Analysis of Structures, 1954, new edn 1966; Energy Principles in Applied Statics, 1959; Analysis of Statically-indeterminate Frameworks, 1961; Principles of Structural Analysis, 1969, new edn 1977; Energy Principles in Theory of Structures, 1973; (contrib.) The Works of I. K. Brunel, 1976; History of Theory of Structures in the Nineteenth Century, 1982; papers on energy principles, hist. of structures. *Recreations:* old films, gardening, golf. *Address:* 33 The Rise, Darras Hall, Ponteland, Northumberland NE20 9LH. *T:* Ponteland 22113. *Club:* New (Edinburgh).

CHARLTON, Sir William Arthur, Kt 1946; DSC; retired as General Marine Superintendent at New York, Furness Withy & Co. SS Lines, 1960; *b* 25 Feb. 1893; *s* of William and Augusta Pauline Charlton; *m* 1919, Eleanor Elcoat (*d* 1978); two *s. Educ:* Blyth; Newcastle on Tyne. Master Mariner. DSC for service in N Africa landings, 1943. Younger Brother, Trinity House; Liveryman Hon. Company of Master Mariners; Fellow Royal Commonwealth Society. *Address:* Apartment 419, 81 Linden Avenue, Rochester, NY 14610, USA.

CHARNLEY, Sir John; see Charnley, Sir W. J.

CHARNLEY, Sir (William) John, Kt 1981; CB 1973; MEng, FEng, FRAeS, FRInstNav; idc; Controller, R&D Establishments and Research, Ministry of Defence, 1977-82; *b* 4 Sept. 1922; *s* of George and Catherine Charnley; *m* 1945, Mary Paden; one *s* one *d. Educ:* Oulton High Sch., Liverpool; Liverpool Univ. MEng 1945. Aerodynamics Dept, RAE Farnborough, 1943-55; Supt. Blind Landing Experimental Unit, 1955-61; Imperial Defence Coll., 1962; Head of Instruments and Electrical Engineering Dept, 1963-65, Head of Weapons Dept, 1965-68, RAE Farnborough; Head of Research Planning, 1968-69, Dep. Controller, Guided Weapons, Min. of Technology, later MoD, 1969-72; Controller, Guided Weapons and Electronics, MoD (PE), 1972-73; Chief Scientist (RAF), 1973-77, and Dep. Controller, R&D Establishments and Res. C, MoD, 1975-77. Gold Medal, RAeS, 1980. *Publications:* papers on subjects in aerodynamics, aircraft all weather operation, aircraft navigation, defence R&D. *Address:* Kirkstones, Brackendale Close, Camberley, Surrey. *T:* Camberley 22547. *Club:* Royal Air Force.

CHARNOCK, Henry, FRS 1976; Professor of Physical Oceanography, University of Southampton, 1966-71 and since 1978; *b* 25 Dec. 1920; *s* of Henry Charnock and Mary Gray McLeod; *m* 1946, Eva Mary Dickinson; one *s* two *d. Educ:* Queen Elizabeth's Grammar Sch., Municipal Techn. Coll., Blackburn; Imperial Coll., London. Staff, Nat. Inst. of Oceanography, 1949-58 and 1959-66; Reader in Physical Oceanography, Imperial Coll., 1958-59; Dir, Inst. of Oceanographic Scis (formerly Nat. Inst. of Oceanography), 1971-78. Pres., Internat. Union of Geodesy and Geophysics, 1971-75; Sec., Scientific Cttee on Oceanic Res., 1978-80. *Publications:* papers in meteorological and oceanographic jls. *Address:* 5 Links View Way, Southampton SO1 7GR. *T:* Southampton 769629.

CHARTERIS, family name of **Baron Charteris of Amisfield** and of **Earl of Wemyss.**

CHARTERIS OF AMISFIELD, Baron *cr* 1978 (Life Peer), of Amisfield, E Lothian; **Martin Michael Charles Charteris,** GCB 1977 (KCB 1972; CB 1958); GCVO 1976 (KCVO 1962; MVO 1953); QSO 1978; OBE 1946; PC 1972; Hon. RA 1981; Provost of Eton, since 1978; Chairman of Trustees, National Heritage Memorial Fund, since 1980; *b* 7 Sept. 1913; 2nd *s* of Hugo Francis, Lord Elcho (killed in action, 1916); *g s* of 11th Earl of Wemyss; *m* 1944, Hon. Mary Gay Hobart Margesson, *yr d* of 1st Viscount Margesson, PC, MC; two *s* one *d. Educ:* Eton; RMC Sandhurst. Lieut KRRC, 1936; served War of 1939-45; Lieut-Colonel, 1944. Private Secretary to Princess Elizabeth, 1950-52; Asst Private Secretary to the Queen, 1952-72; Private Secretary to the Queen and Keeper of HM's Archives, 1972-77. A Permanent Lord in Waiting to the Queen, 1978-. Director: Claridge's Hotel, 1978-; Connaught Hotel, 1978-; De La Rue Co., 1978-; Rio Tinto Zinc Corp., 1979-. Trustee, BM, 1979-. Hon. DCL Oxon, 1978; Hon. LLD London, 1981. *Recreation:* sculpting. *Address:* Provost's Lodge, Eton College, Windsor, Berks. *T:* Windsor 66304; Wood Stanway House, Wood Stanway, Glos GL54 5PE. *T:* Stanton 480. *Club:* White's.

CHARTERIS, Leslie; FRSA; author; *b* 1907; *m* 1st, Pauline Schishkin (divorced, 1937); one *d* ; 2nd, Barbara Meyer (divorced, 1941); 3rd, Elizabeth Bryant Borst (divorced, 1951); 4th, Audrey Long. *Educ:* Rossall; Cambridge Univ. Many years of entertaining, but usually unprofitable, travel and adventure, and can still be had. After one or two false starts created character of "The Saint" (trans. into 15 languages besides those of films, radio, television, and the comic strip). *Publications:* Meet the Tiger, 1928; Enter the Saint; The Last Hero; Knight Templar; Featuring the Saint; Alias the Saint;

She was a Lady (filmed 1938 as The Saint Strikes Back); The Holy Terror (filmed 1939 as The Saint in London); Getaway; Once More the Saint; The Brighter Buccaneer; The Misfortunes of Mr Teal; Boodle; The Saint Goes On; The Saint in New York (filmed 1938); Saint Overboard, 1936; The Ace of Knaves, 1937; Thieves Picnic, 1937; (trans., with introd.) Juan Belmonte, Killer of Bulls: The Autobiography of a Matador, 1937; Prelude for War, 1938; Follow the Saint, 1938; The Happy Highwayman, 1939; The First Saint Omnibus, 1939; The Saint in Miami, 1941; The Saint Goes West, 1942; The Saint Steps In, 1944; The Saint on Guard, 1945; The Saint Sees it Through, 1946; Call for the Saint, 1948; Saint Errant, 1948; The Second Saint Omnibus, 1952; The Saint on the Spanish Main, 1955; The Saint around the World, 1957; Thanks to the Saint, 1958; Señor Saint, 1959; The Saint to the Rescue, 1961; Trust the Saint, 1962; The Saint in the Sun, 1964; Vendetta for the Saint, 1965 (filmed 1968); The Saint on TV, 1968; The Saint Returns, 1969; The Saint and the Fiction Makers, 1969; The Saint Abroad, 1970; The Saint in Pursuit, 1971; The Saint and the People Importers, 1971; Paleneo, 1972; Saints Alive, 1974; Catch the Saint, 1975; The Saint and the Hapsburg Necklace, 1976; Send for the Saint, 1977; The Saint in Trouble, 1978; The Saint and the Templar Treasure, 1979; Count on the Saint, 1980; Supervising Editor of the Saint Magazine, 1953–67; columnist, Gourmet Magazine, 1966–68; concurrently has worked as special correspondent and Hollywood scenarist; contributor to leading English and American magazines and newspapers. *Recreations:* eating, drinking, horseracing, sailing, fishing, and loafing. *Address:* 8 Southampton Row, WC1. *Clubs:* Savage; Mensa, Yacht Club de Cannes.

CHARVET, Richard Christopher Larkins, RD 1972; JP; Director, Vogt and Maguire Group of companies, since 1981; *b* 12 Dec. 1936; *s* of Patrice and Eleanor Charvet; *m* 1961, Elizabeth Joan Johnson; two *s* one *d. Educ:* Rugby. MITT, ACIS, ACIArb. National Service, Royal Navy, 1955–57; Mem., London Div., RNR, 1955–. Union Castle Line, 1957–58; Killick Martin & Co, Ltd, Shipbrokers, 1958–81; Vogt and Maguire Ltd, Shipbrokers, 1981–. Mem., Court of Common Council for Aldgate Ward, City of London, 1970–76; Alderman, Aldgate Ward, 1976–. 3rd Warden, Worshipful Co. of Shipwrights. JP 1976. *Publication:* Peter and Tom in the Lord Mayor's Show, 1982. Hon. JSM, Malaysia, 1974. *Recreations:* gardening, travel, sailing. *Address:* The Old Rectory, Gilston, near Harlow, Essex CM20 2RF. *Clubs:* City Livery, United Wards, Aldgate Ward.

CHASE, Anya Seton; *see* Seton, A.

CHASE, Stuart; author, social scientist; *b* Somersworth, New Hampshire, USA, 8 March 1888; *s* of Harvey Stuart and Aaronette Rowe Chase; *m* 1st, 1914, Margaret Hatfield (divorced, 1929); one *s* one *d*; 2nd, 1930, Marian Tyler. *Educ:* Massachusetts Inst. of Technology; Harvard Univ. SB cum laude, 1910; seven years in accounting work; CPA degree from Massachusetts, 1916; four years in Government Service, ending 1921; since 1921 has been chiefly engaged in economic research and writing books and articles; some public lecturing; consulting work for government agencies, business organizations, UNESCO, etc. Member National Inst. of Arts and Letters, Phi Beta Kappa; LittD American Univ., 1949; DHL Emerson Coll., Boston, 1970; DHL New Haven Univ., 1974. *Publications:* The Tragedy of Waste, 1925; Your Money's Worth (with F. J. Schlink), 1927; Men and Machines, 1929; Prosperity: Fact or Myth?, 1929; The Nemesis of American Business, 1931; Mexico, 1931; A New Deal, 1932; The Economy of Abundance, 1934; Government in Business, 1935; Rich Land, Poor Land, 1936; The Tyranny of Words, 1938; The New Western Front, 1939; Idle Money, Idle Men, 1940; A Primer of Economics, 1941; The Road We Are Travelling, 1942; Goals for America, 1942; Where's the Money Coming From?, 1943; Democracy under Pressure, 1945; Men at Work, 1945; Tomorrow's Trade, 1945; For This We Fought, 1946; The Proper Study of Mankind, 1948 (revised, 1956); Roads to Agreement, 1951; Power of Words, 1954; Guides to Straight Thinking, 1956; Some Things Worth Knowing, 1958; Live and Let Live, 1960; American Credos, 1962; Money to Grow On, 1964; The Most Probable World, 1968; Danger-Men Talking, 1969; and many magazine articles for Harpers, Atlantic, The Saturday Review, etc. *Recreations:* tennis, ski-ing, sketching. *Address:* Georgetown, Conn 06829, USA. *Club:* Harvard (New York).

CHATAWAY, Rt. Hon. Christopher John; PC 1970; Vice Chairman, Orion Royal Bank (formerly Orion Bank), since 1980 (Managing Director, 1974–80); *b* 31 Jan. 1931; *m* 1st, 1959, Anna Lett (marr. diss. 1975); two *s* one *d*; 2nd, 1976, Carola Walker; two *s. Educ:* Sherborne Sch.; Magdalen Coll., Oxford. Hons. Degree, PPE. President OUAC, 1952; rep. Great Britain, Olympic Games, 1952 and 1956; briefly held world 5,000 metres record in 1954. Junior Exec. Arthur Guinness Son & Co., 1953–55; Staff Reporter, Independent Television News, 1955–56; Current Affairs Commentator for BBC Television, 1956–59. Elected for N Lewisham to LCC, 1958–61. MP (C): Lewisham North, 1959–66; Chichester, May 1969–Sept. 1974; PPS to Minister of Power, 1961–62; Joint Parly Under-Secretary of State, Dept of Education and Science, 1962–64; Minister of Posts and Telecommunications, 1970–72; Minister for Industrial Develt, DTI, 1972–74. Director: British Electric Traction Co., 1974–; Internat. General Electric Co. of New York Ltd, 1979–; Chairman: British Telecommunications Systems, 1979–; United Medical Enterprises, 1980– (Dir, 1976–); London Broadcasting Co., 1981–; Dep. Chm., United City Merchants, 1981–. Treasurer, Nat. Cttee for Electoral Reform, 1976–; Treasurer, Action in Distress, 1976–. Alderman, GLC, 1967–70; Leader Educn Cttee, ILEA, 1967–69. Nansen Medal, 1960. *Publication:* (with Philip

Goodhart) War Without Weapons, 1968. *Address:* 40 Addison Road, W14.

CHATER, Dr Anthony Philip John; Editor, Morning Star, since 1974; *b* 21 Dec. 1929; parents both shoe factory workers; *m* 1954, Janice (*née* Smith); three *s. Educ:* Northampton Grammar Sch. for Boys; Queen Mary Coll., London. BSc (1st cl. hons Chem.) 1951, PhD (Phys.Chem.) 1954. Fellow in Biochem., Ottawa Exper. Farm, 1954–56; studied biochem. at Brussels Univ., 1956–57; Teacher, Northampton Techn. High Sch., 1957–59; Teacher, Blyth Grammar Sch., Norwich, 1959–60; Lectr, subseq. Sen. Lectr in Phys. Chem., Luton Coll. of Technology, 1960–69; Head of Press and Publicity of Communist Party, 1969–74; Nat. Chm. of Communist Party, 1967–69. Contested (Com) Luton, Nov. 1963, 1964, 1966, 1970. Mem. Presidential Cttee, World Peace Council, 1969–. *Publications:* Race Relations in Britain, 1966; numerous articles. *Recreations:* walking, swimming, music, camping. *Address:* 8 Katherine Drive, Dunstable, Beds. *T:* Dunstable 64835.

CHATER, Nancy, CBE 1974; Headmistress, Stanley Park Comprehensive School, Liverpool, 1964–75, retired; *b* 18 July 1915; *d* of William John and Ellen Chater. *Educ:* Northampton Sch. for Girls; Girton Coll., Cambridge (Math. Schol., Bell Exhibr, MA); Cambridge Trng Coll. for Women (CertifEd). Asst Mistress, Huddersfield College Grammar Sch. for Boys, 1940–42; Asst Mistress, Fairfield High Sch. for Girls, Manchester, 1942–45; Sen. Maths Mistress, Thistley Hough High Sch., Stoke-on-Trent, 1945–49; Sen. Lectr, Newland Park Trng Coll. for Teachers, 1949–55; Dep. Head, Whitley Abbey Comprehensive Sch., Coventry, 1955–63. *Publications:* contrib. Math. Gazette. *Address:* c/o Stanley Park Comprehensive School, Priory Road, Liverpool L4 2SL. *T:* 051-263 5665. *Clubs:* Soroptomist International, Business and Professional Women's.

CHATFIELD, family name of **Baron Chatfield.**

CHATFIELD, 2nd Baron *cr* 1937, of Ditchling; **Ernle David Lewis Chatfield;** *b* 2 Jan. 1917; *s* of 1st Baron Chatfield, PC, GCB, OM, KCMG, CVO (Admiral of the Fleet Lord Chatfield), and Lillian Emma St John Matthews (*d* 1977); *S* father, 1967; *m* 1969, (Felicia Mary) Elizabeth, *d* of late Dr John Roderick Bulman, Hereford. *Educ:* RNC Dartmouth; Trinity Coll., Cambridge. ADC to Governor-General of Canada, 1940–44. *Heir:* none. *Address:* RR2, Williamstown, Ontario, Canada.

CHATT, Prof. Joseph, CBE 1978; ScD; FRS 1961; Professor of Chemistry, University of Sussex, 1964–80; now Emeritus; Director, Research Unit of Nitrogen Fixation, ARC, 1963–80 (in Sussex, 1964–80); *b* 6 Nov. 1914; *e s* of Joseph and M. Elsie Chatt; *m* 1947, Ethel, *y d* of Hugh Williams, St Helens, Lancs; one *s* one *d. Educ:* Nelson Sch., Wigton, Cumberland; Emmanuel Coll., Cambridge. PhD 1940; ScD 1956. Research Chemist, Woolwich Arsenal, 1941–42; Dep. Chief Chemist, later Chief Chemist, Peter Spence & Sons Ltd, Widnes, 1942–46; ICI Research Fellow, Imperial Coll., London, 1946–47; Head of Inorganic Chemistry Dept, Butterwick, later Akers, Research Laboratories, ICI Ltd, 1947–60; Group Manager, Research Dept, Heavy Organic Chemicals Div., ICI Ltd, 1961–62; Prof. of Inorganic Chem., QMC, Univ. of London, 1964. Visiting Professor: Pennsylvania State Univ., 1960; Yale Univ., 1963; Royal Society Leverhulme, Univ. of Rajasthan, India, 1966–67; Univ. of S Carolina, 1968. Chemical Society: Mem. Council, 1952–55, 1974–76; Hon. Sec., 1956–62; Vice-Pres., 1962–65, 1972–74; Pres. Dalton Div., 1972–74; Organometallic Chem. Award, 1970; Pres., Section B, British Assoc. for Advancement of Science, 1974–75; Member: Chemical Council, 1958–60; Commn on Nomenclature of Inorganic Chemistry, Internat. Union of Pure and Applied Chemistry, 1959–81, Hon-Sec., 1959–63, Chm., 1976–81; ARC Adv. Cttee on Plants and Soils, 1964–67; Comité de Direction du Laboratoire de Chimie de Coordination, Toulouse, 1974–77; Council, Royal Soc., 1975–77; national and internat. cttees concerned with chemistry, incl. Parly and Scientific Cttee. Founder, Internat. Confs on Coordination Chemistry, 1950. Lectures: Tilden, 1961–62; Liversidge, 1971–72; Debye, Cornell, 1975; Nyholm, 1976–77; Arthur D. Little, MIT, 1977; Julius Steiglitz, Chicago, 1978; Columbia, 1978 (and Chandler Medal); Univ. of Western Ontario, 1978; John Stauffer, S California, 1979; Dwyer Meml Lectr and Medallist, Univ. of NSW, 1980; Sunner Meml Lectr, Univ. of Lund, 1982. Gordon Wigan Prize for Res. in Chem., Cambridge, 1939; Amer. Chem. Soc. Award for dist. service to Inorganic Chemistry, 1971; Chugaev Commem. Dipl. and Medal, Kurnakov Inst. of Gen. and Inorganic Chemistry, Soviet Acad. of Sciences, 1976; Davy Medal of Royal Soc., 1979; Wolf Prize for Chemistry, 1981. Hon. DSc: East Anglia, 1974; Sussex, 1982; Hon. Fellow, Emmanuel Coll., Cambridge, 1978. Sócio corresp., Academia das Ciências de Lisboa, 1978; Hon. Life Mem., NY Acad. of Sciences, 1978; For. Fellow, Indian Nat. Science Acad., 1980. *Publications:* scientific papers, mainly in Jl Chem. Soc. *Recreations:* numismatics, photography. *Address:* 28 Tongdean Avenue, Hove, East Sussex BN3 6TN. *T:* Brighton 554377.

CHATTEN, Harold Raymond Percy, CB 1975; RCNC; Chief Executive, Royal Dockyards, 1975–79, and Head of Royal Corps of Naval Constructors, Apr.–Sept. 1979, Ministry of Defence. Production Manager, HM Dockyard, Chatham, 1967–70; General Manager, HM Dockyard, Rosyth, Fife, 1970–75. MA Cambridge 1946. *Address:* c/o National Westminster Bank, 39 Milsom Street, Bath.

CHATTERJEE, Dr Satya Saran, OBE 1971; JP; FRCP, FRCPE; Consultant Chest Physician and Physician in Charge, Department of Respiratory

Physiology, Wythenshawe Hospital, Manchester, since 1959; Chairman, Overseas Doctors Association, 1975-81, President, since 1981; *b* 16 July 1922; *m* 1948, Enid May (*née* Adlington); one *s* two *d*. *Educ*: India, UK, Sweden and USA. MB, BS; FCCP (USA). Asst Lectr, Dept of Medicine, Albany Med. Coll. Hosp., NY, 1953-54; Med. Registrar, Sen. Registrar, Dept of Thoracic Medicine, Wythenshawe Hosp., Manchester, 1954-59. Mem., NW RHA, 1976-. Chm., NW Conciliation Cttee, Race Relations Board, 1972-77; Member: Standing Adv. Council on Race Relations, 1977-; GMC, 1979-; Vice-Pres., Manchester Council for Community Relations, 1974-. President: Rotary Club, Wythenshawe, 1975-76; Indian Assoc., Manchester, 1962-71. *Publications*: research papers in various projects related to cardio/pulmonary disorders. *Address*: March, 20 Macclesfield Road, Wilmslow, Cheshire. *T*: Wilmslow 522559.

CHATTERTON, Rev. Sir Percy, KBE 1981 (OBE 1972); CMG 1977; *b* 8 Oct. 1898; *s* of Henry Herbert Chatterton and Alice Macro; *m* 1924, Christian Ritchie Finlayson. *Educ*: City of London Sch.; Univ. of London. LCP. Teacher, Friends Sch., Penketh, 1921-23; London Missionary Society, Papua: Teacher, 1924-39; Minister, 1939-64; Member for Moresby, Papua New Guinea House of Assembly, 1964-72; retired. Hon. LLD Papua New Guinea, 1972. *Publication*: Day that I have Loved: Percy Chatterton's Papua, 1972. *Recreations*: hockey, chess. *Address*: PO Box 1808, Port Moresby, Papua New Guinea. *T*: Port Moresby 255945.

CHAU, Hon. Sir Sik-Nin, Kt 1960; CBE 1950; JP 1940; Hon. Chairman, Hong Kong Chinese Bank Ltd; Chairman or Director of numerous other companies; President, Firecrackers and Fireworks Co. Ltd (Taiwan); State Trading Corporation (Far East) Ltd; *b* 13 April 1903; *s* of late Cheuk-Fan Chau, Hong Kong; *m* 1927, Ida Hing-Kwai, *d* of late Lau Siu-Cheuk; two *s*. *Educ*: St Stephen's Coll., Hong Kong; Hong Kong Univ.; London Univ.; Vienna State Univ. MB, BS, Hong Kong, 1923; DLO, Eng., 1925; DOMS 1926. LLD (Hon.), Hong Kong 1961. Member Medical Board, Hong Kong, 1935-41; Mem. Urban Council, 1936-41; Chm. Po Leung Kuk, 1940-41; MLC, Hong Kong, 1946-59; MEC, 1947-62. Dep. Chm., Subsid. British Commonwealth Parliamentary Assoc., Hong Kong, 1953-59. Chief Delegate of Hong Kong to ECAFE Conference in India, 1948, in Australia, 1949; Chairman ECAFE Conference in Hong Kong, 1955; Leader, Hong Kong Govt Trade Mission to Common Market countries, 1963; Asian Fair, Bangkok, 1967; first Trade Mission to USA, 1970. Fellow, Internat. Academy of Management; Pres. Indo-Pacific Cttee, 1964-67; Chairman: Hong Kong Trade Develt Council, 1966-70; Hong Kong Management Assoc., 1961-69; Fedn of Hong Kong Inds, 1959-66; Cttee for Expo '70, 1969-70; United Coll., Chinese Univ. of Hong Kong, 1959-61; Hong Kong Productivity Council, 1970-73. President, Japan Soc. of Hong Kong; Mem., Textiles Adv. Bd, 1962-74; Foreign Corresp. Nat. Ind. Conf. Bd Inc.; Member: Advisory Board to Lingnan Inst. of Business Administration; British Universities Selection Cttee, 1945-64; Council and Court of University of Hong Kong, 1945-64; Senior Member Board of Education Hong Kong, 1946-60; Chairman Hong Kong Model Housing Society; Vice-President, Hong Kong Anti-Tuberculosis Assoc.; Hon. Steward Hong Kong Jockey Club, 1974 (Steward 1946-74). Hon. President or Vice-President of numerous Assocs; Hon. Adviser of Chinese General Chamber of Commerce; Permanent Dir Tung Wah Hospital Advisory Board. Coronation Medal, 1937; Defence Medal, 1945; Coronation Medal, 1953; Silver Jubilee Medal, 1977; Freedom of New Orleans, 1966; San Francisco Port Authority Maritime Medal, 1968; 3rd Class Order of Sacred Treasure, Japan, 1969; granted permanent title of Honourable by the Queen, 1962. *Address*: IL 3547 Hatton Road, Hong Kong. *T*: 433695.

CHAUNCY, Major Frederick Charles Leslie, CBE 1958 (OBE 1953); *b* 22 Dec. 1904; *o s* of late Col C. H. K. Chauncy, CB, CBE, Indian Army; *m* 1932, Barbara Enid Miller; one *s*. *Educ*: Radley; Sandhurst. Commissioned British Army, 1924; transf. IA (45th Rattray's Sikhs), 1928; transf. IPS, 1930; served Persian Gulf, NWF India, Indian States; retired 1947; re-employed under HM's Foreign Office, 1949, as Consul-General at Muscat; retired 1958; appointed by Sultan of Muscat and Oman as his Personal Adviser, 1961-70. *Recreations*: Rugby football (Sandhurst); athletics (Sandhurst, Army, England, also UK in Olympic Games). *Address*: 10 Egmont Drive, Avon Castle, Ringwood, Hants BH24 2BN. *Club*: Naval and Military.

CHAUVIRÉ, Yvette, Officier de la Légion d'Honneur, 1974; Commandeur des Arts et des Lettres, 1975; Commandeur, Ordre National du Mérite, 1981 (Officier, 1972); ballerina assoluta, since 1950; *b* Paris, 22 April 1917. *Educ*: École de la Danse de l'Opéra, Paris. Paris Opera Ballet, 1930; first major rôles in David Triomphant and Les Créatures de Prométhée; Danseuse étoile 1942; danced Istar, 1942; Monte Carlo Opera Ballet, 1946-47; returned to Paris Opera Ballet, 1947-49. Has appeared at Covent Garden, London; also danced in the USA, and in cities of Rome, Moscow, Leningrad, Berlin, Buenos Aires, Johannesburg, Milan, etc; official tours: USA 1948; USSR 1958, 1966, 1968; Canada 1967; Australia. Leading rôles in following ballets; Les Mirages, Lac des Cygnes, Sleeping Beauty, Giselle, Roméo et Juliette, Suite en Blanc, Le Cygne (St Saens), La Dame aux Camélias, etc. Choreographer: La Péri, Roméo et Juliette, Le Cygne; farewell performances: Paris Opera, Giselle, Nov. 1972, Petrouchka and The Swan, Dec. 1972; Berlin Opera, Giselle, 1973; Artistic and Tech. Adviser, Paris Opera, 1963-72, teacher of Danse for style and perfection, 1970-; Aristic Dir, Acad. Internat. de la Danse, Paris, 1972-76; Reine Léda, Amphitryon, Paris, 1976. *Films*: La Mort du Cygne, 1937 (Paris); Carrousel Napolitain, 1953 (Rome). *Publication*: Je suis Ballerine.

Recreations: painting and drawing, collections of swans. *Address*: 21 Place du Commerce, Paris 75015, France.

CHAVAN, Yeshwantrao Balvantrao; *b* 12 March 1913; *m* 1942, Venubai, *d* of late R. B. More, Phaltan, district Satara. *Educ*: Rajaram Coll., Kolhapur; Law Coll., Poona Univ. (BA, LLB). Took part in 1930, 1932 and 1942 Movements; elected MLA in 1946, 1952, 1957 and 1962; Parly Sec. to Home Minister of Bombay, 1946-52; Minister for Civil Supplies, Community Developments, Forests, Local Self Govt, 1952-Oct. 1956; Chief Minister: Bombay, Nov. 1956-April 1960; Maharashtra, May 1960-Nov. 1962; Defence Minister, Govt of India, 1962-66; Minister of Home Affairs, 1966-70; Minister of Finance, 1970-74; Minister of External Affairs, 1974-77; Leader, Congress Parly Party, 1977; Dep. Prime Minister and Home Minister, 1979. Elected Member: Rajya Sabha, 1963; Lok Sabha, 1964, 1967, 1971, 1977, 1980. Mem. Working Cttee of All India Congress Cttee. Pres., Inst. for Defence Studies and Analyses. Hon. Doctorate: Aligarh Univ.; Kanpur Univ., Marathwada Univ., Shivaji Univ. *Address*: 1 Racecourse Road, New Delhi 11, India. *T*: 376477.

CHAVASSE, Christopher Patrick Grant; Clerk to the Grocers' Company, since 1981; *b* 14 March 1928; *s* of late Grant Chavasse and of Maureen Shingler (*née* Whalley); *m* 1955, Audrey Mary Leonard; two *s* one *d*. *Educ*: Bedford Sch.; Clare Coll., Cambridge (MA). Commissioned The Rifle Brigade, 1947; served in Palestine: RAFVR 1949. Admitted Solicitor, 1955; Partner: Jacobs & Greenwood, 1960; Woodham Smith, 1970; President, Holborn Law Soc., 1977-78. Hon. Steward of Westminster Abbey, 1950-; Treasurer, St Mary-le-Bow Church, 1981-; Secretary: Governing Body of Oundle Sch., 1981-; Grocers' Trust Co. Ltd, 1981-. *Publications*: Conveyancing Costs, 1971; Non-Contentious Costs, 1975; The Discretionary Items in Contentious Costs, 1980; various articles in Law Society's Gazette, New Law Jl, Solicitors Jl, and others. *Recreations*: beagling, sailing. *Address*: Yeomans Hall, Blackstone, Henfield, Sussex BN5 9TB. *T*: Henfield 493421; Grocers' Hall, Princes Street, EC2R 8AQ. *T*: 01-606 3113. *Clubs*: Royal Air Force; Leander (Henley on Thames).

CHAVASSE, Michael Louis Maude, MA; QC 1968; His Honour Judge Chavasse; a Circuit Judge, since 1977; *b* 5 Jan. 1923; 2nd *s* of late Bishop C. M. Chavasse, OBE, MC, DD, MA and Beatrice Cropper Chavasse (*née* Willink); *m* 1951, Rose Ethel, 2nd *d* of late Vice-Adm. A. D. Read, CB and late Hon. Rosamond Vere Read; three *d*. *Educ*: Dragon Sch., Oxford; Shrewsbury Sch.; Trinity Coll., Oxford (Schol.). Enlisted in RAC, Oct. 1941; commnd in Buffs, 1942; served in Italy with Royal Norfolk Regt, 1943-45 (Lieut). 2nd cl. hons (Jurisprudence) Oxon, 1946. Called to Bar, Inner Temple, 1949. A Recorder of the Crown Court, 1972-77. *Publications*: (jtly) A Critical Annotation of the RIBA Standard Forms of Building Contract, 1964; (with Bryan Anstey) Rights of Light, 1959. *Recreations*: shooting, photography. *Address*: 2 Paper Buildings, Temple, EC4; Park House, Chevening, Sevenoaks, Kent. *T*: Knockholt 2271.

CHAYTOR, Sir George Reginald, 8th Bt *cr* 1831; *b* 28 Oct. 1912; *s* of William Richard Carter Chaytor (*d* 1973) (*g s* of 2nd Bt) and Anna Laura (*d* 1947), *d* of George Fawcett; *S* cousin, Sir William Henry Clervaux Chaytor, 7th Bt, 1976. *Heir*: uncle Herbert Archibald Chaytor [*b* 1884; *m* 1911, Effie Bell, *d* of William Smith; one *s* one *d*]. *Address*: 32 Bonnie Avenue, Chilliwack, BC, Canada.

CHEADLE, Sir Eric (Wallers), Kt 1978; CBE 1973; Deputy Managing Director, The Thomson Organisation Ltd, 1959-74; retired 1974 after 50 years service with the same company (Hultons/Allied Newspapers/Kemsley Newspapers/The Thomson Organization); Director: Thomson International Press Consultancy Ltd; Lancs and Cheshire County Newspapers Ltd; Macclesfield Press Ltd; Macclesfield Times and Courier Ltd; Stockport Express Ltd; Northwestern Newspaper Co. Ltd; Sporting Chronicle Publications Ltd; Thomson Withy Grove Ltd; *b* 14 May 1908; *s* of Edgar and Nellie Cheadle; *m* 1938, Pamela, *d* of Alfred and Charlotte Hulme; two *s*. *Educ*: Farnworth Grammar Sch. Editorial Staff, Evening Chronicle and Daily Dispatch, Manchester, 1924-30; Publicity Manager, Allied Newspapers Ltd, 1931-37; Publicity Manager-in-Chief, Allied Newspapers Group, 1938; Organiser, War Fund for the Services, 1939. Served War, RAFVR, Sqdn Ldr, 1941-46. Dir and Gen. Manager, Kemsley Newspapers Ltd, 1947-53. Mem. Council: Newspaper Publishers Assoc., 1947-74; Newspaper Soc., 1959-78 (Pres., 1970-71; Chm. Editorial Cttee, 1971-78); NEDC for Printing and Publishing Industry; Mem., Jt Bd for Nat. Newspaper Industry, 1965-67; Pres., Assoc. of Lancastrians in London, 1959 and 1973-74; Pres. (former Hon. Sec.), Manchester Publicity Assoc., 1972-74 (Gold Medal, 1973); Pres., Printers' Charitable Corp., 1973-74 (Life Vice-Pres., 1975-, Chm. of Council, 1975-81, Trustee, 1981-); Chm., Jt Cttee, Newspaper and Periodical Publishers and Distributors, 1979-; Member: Bd, FIEJ/INCA (Fédération Internationale des Editeurs de Journaux et Publications), 1972-76; London Adv. Bd, Burnley Building Soc.; UK Newsprint Users' Cttee (Founder Mem.); Caxton Quincentary Commem. Cttee, 1976; Science Mus. Adv. Cttee (Printing); Council, Imp. Soc. of Knights Bachelor; Council, Chest, Heart and Stroke Assoc., 1981-; Ver Valley Soc.; Mem. Management Group and Trustee, St Albans Cathedral Appeal; Dir, Herts Bldg Preservation Trust Ltd, 1981-; Hon. Chm., the PS Tattershall Castle (Victoria Embankment) Trust; Chm., Soc. of St Michaels; Hon. Life Mem., Independent Adoption Soc. *Publication*: (ed) The Roll of Knights Bachelor, 1981. *Recreations*: golf, and newspaper affairs. *Address*: The Old Church House, 172 Fishpool Street, St Albans, Herts AL3

4SB. *T:* St Albans 59639. *Clubs:* Wig and Pen, Press, Variety, MCC, Porters Park Golf (Captain, 1974-75).

CHECKETTS, Sqdn Ldr Sir David (John), KCVO 1979 (CVO 1969; MVO 1966); an Extra Equerry to the Prince of Wales, since 1979; *b* 23 Aug. 1930; 3rd *s* of late Reginald Ernest George Checketts and late Frances Mary Checketts; *m* 1958, Rachel Leila Warren Herrick; one *s* three *d.* Flying Training, Bulawayo, Rhodesia, 1948-50; 14 Sqdn, Germany, 1950-54; Instructor, Fighter Weapons Sch., 1954-57; Air ADC to C-in-C Malta, 1958-59; 3 Sqdn, Germany, 1960-61; Equerry to Duke of Edinburgh, 1961-66, to the Prince of Wales, 1967-70; Private Sec. to the Prince of Wales, 1970-79. Director PPP Medical Centre Ltd; Elec. & Indus. Investment Co. Ltd; ESI London Ltd; Rediffusion Simulation Ltd; Penselworth Ltd; Initial Services Ltd; Initial Servs Internat. Ltd; Lizard Island Ltd; Nat. Electric Construction Co. Ltd; Reclamation & Disposal Ltd; Seeatic Ltd; United Trans. Overseas Ltd; Birmingham & District Investment Trust. *Recreation:* ornithology. *Address:* Church Cottage, Winkfield, Windsor, Berks. *T:* Winkfield Row 2289. *Club:* Brooks's.

CHECKLAND, Michael; Director of Resources, Television, BBC, since 1982; *b* 13 March 1936; *s* of Leslie and Ivy Florence Checkland; *m* 1960, Shirley Frances, *d* of Terence Alexander and Marjorie Frances Corbett; two *s* one *d. Educ:* King Edward's Grammar Sch., Fiveways, Birmingham; Wadham Coll., Oxford (BA Modern History). ACMA. Accountant: Parkinson Cowan Ltd, 1959-62; Thorn Electronics Ltd, 1962-64; BBC: Senior Cost Accountant, 1964; Head of Central Finance Unit, 1967; Chief Accountant, Central Finance Services, 1969, Chief Accountant, Television, 1971; Controller, Finance, 1976; Controller, Planning and Resource Management, Television, 1977. *Recreations:* sport, music, travel. *Address:* Maple Cottage, 5 Springfield Crescent, Horsham, West Sussex RH12 2PP. *T:* Horsham 54845.

CHECKLAND, Prof. Sydney George, MA, MCom, PhD; FRSE 1980; FBA 1977; Professor of Economic History, University of Glasgow, since 1957; *b* 9 Oct. 1916; *s* of Sydney Tom and Fanny Selina Savory Checkland, Ottawa; *m* 1942, Edith Olive, *d* of Robert Fraser and Edith Philipson Anthony; two *s* three *d. Educ:* Lisgar Collegiate Inst., Ottawa; Birmingham Univ. Associate, Canadian Bankers' Assoc., 1937; BCom 1st Cl. 1941, MCom 1946, Birmingham; PhD Liverpool, 1953; MA Cambridge, 1953; Pres. Nat. Union of Students, 1941-42, Internat. Union of Students, 1942-43. Served in British and Canadian Armies; Lieut, Gov.-Gen.'s Foot Guards, Normandy (severely wounded), Parly cand. (Commonwealth Party), Eccleshall, 1945. Asst Lecturer, Lecturer and Senior Lecturer in Economic Science, University of Liverpool, 1946-53; Univ. Lecturer in History, Cambridge, 1953-57; Lector in History, Trinity Coll., 1955-57. A Senate Assessor, and Mem. Finance Cttee, etc, Univ. Court, Glasgow, 1970-73. Vis. Fellow, ANU, 1981; Vis. Prof., Monash Univ., 1981. Member: Inst. for Advanced Study, Princeton, 1960, 1964; East Kilbride Develt Corp.; Scottish Records Advisory Council; Nat. Register of Archives (Scotland) (Chm. 1971); Economic History Soc. Council, 1958- (Pres., 1977-, Hon. Vice Pres., 1980); SSRC, 1979- (Mem. Econ. Hist. Cttee, 1970-72, 1979-82; Chm., Industry and Employment Cttee, 1982). Chm., Bd. of Management, Urban Studies, 1970-74; Vice-Pres., Business Archives Council of Scotland. *Publications:* The Rise of Industrial Society in England, 1815-1885, 1964; The Mines of Tharsis, 1967; The Gladstones: a family biography, 1764-1851, 1971 (Scottish Arts Council Book Award); ed (with E. O. A. Checkland) The Poor Law Report of 1834, 1974; Scottish Banking, a history, 1695-1973, 1975 (Saltire Soc. Prize); The Upas Tree: Glasgow, 1875-1980, 1982; articles and reviews in economic and historical journals. *Recreations:* painting, gathering driftwood. *Address:* Number 5, The University, Glasgow G12 8QG. *T:* 041-339 1801.

CHEDLOW, Barry William, QC 1969; a Recorder of the Crown Court, since 1974; Member, Criminal Injuries Compensation Board, since 1976; *b* Macclesfield, 8 Oct. 1921; *m* Anne Sheldon, BA; one *s* one *d. Educ:* Burnage High Sch.; Manchester Univ. Served RAF, 1941-46: USAAF, Flying Instructor, 1942; Flt-Lt 1943. Called to Bar, Middle Temple, 1947, Bencher, 1976; Prizeman in Law of Evidence. Practises in London, Midland and Oxford Circuits. *Publications:* author and editor of various legal text-books. *Recreations:* flying (private pilot's licence), languages, sailing. *Address:* 12 King's Bench Walk, Temple, EC4. *T:* 01-583 0811; Little Kimblewick Farm, Finch Lane, Amersham, Bucks. *T:* Little Chalfont 2156.

CHEESEMAN, Eric Arthur, BSc (Econ), PhD (Med) (London); Professor of Medical Statistics, The Queen's University of Belfast, 1961-77, now Emeritus; *b* 22 Sept. 1912; 1st *s* of late Arthur Cheeseman and Frances Cheeseman, London; *m* 1943, Henriette Edwina Woollaston; one *s. Educ:* William Ellis Sch.; London Univ. Mem. staff of Statistical Cttee of MRC, 1929-39. Served War of 1939-45, RA (TA); GSO3 21 Army Group, 1945. Research Statistician on staff of Statistical Research Unit of MRC and part-time lectr in Med. Statistics, London Sch. of Hygiene and Tropical Medicine, 1946-48; Lectr, later Reader, and Vice-Pres. (Finance), The Queen's Univ. of Belfast, 1948-77; Prof., 1961; Dep. Dean, Faculty of Medicine, 1971-75. Statistical Adviser to Northern Ireland Hospitals Authority, 1948-73; Mem. of Joint Authority for Higher Technicological Studies, 1965-70. Consulting Statistician to Northern Ireland Tuberculosis Authority, 1950-59; Mem., Statistical Cttee of Medical Research Council, 1950-61. Fellow Royal Statistical Soc.; Mem., Soc. for Social Medicine (Chm. 1976, Hon. Mem., 1979); Hon. Associate Mem., Ulster Med. Soc. Silver Jubilee Medal, 1977. *Publications:* Epidemics in Schools, 1950; (with G. F. Adams) Old People in

Northern Ireland, 1951; various papers dealing with medical statistical subjects in scientific journals. *Recreation:* cricket. *Address:* 43 Beverley Gardens, Bangor, Co. Down, N Ireland. *T:* Bangor 2822.

CHEESEMAN, Prof. Ian Clifford, PhD; ARCS; CEng, FRAeS, FCIT; Professor of Helicopter Engineering since 1970, and Head of Department of Aeronautics and Astronautics since 1979, University of Southampton; *b* 12 June 1926; *s* of Richard Charles Cheeseman and Emily Ethel Clifford; *m* 1957, Margaret Edith Pither; one *s* two *d. Educ:* Andover Grammar Sch.; Imperial Coll. of Science and Technology. Vickers Supermarine Ltd, 1951-53; Aeroplane and Armament Estab., 1953-56; Atomic Weapons Res. Estab., 1956-58; Nat. Gas Turbine Estab., 1958-70. *Publications:* contribs to Jl RAeS, Jl CIT, Jl Sound and Vibration, Procs Phys. Soc. 'A'. *Recreations:* dog breeding, gardening, sailing, camping. *Address:* Hill Cottage, Mansbridge Road, West End, Southampton. *T:* West End 3387.

CHEESEMAN, John William; a Metropolitan Stipendiary Magistrate since 1972; *b* 2 Feb. 1913; *m* 1946, Lilian McKenzie; one *s.* Called to Bar, Gray's Inn, 1953. *Address:* 2 Dr Johnson's Buildings, Temple, EC4Y 7AY. *T:* 01-353 5371.

CHEETHAM, Francis William, OBE 1979; FMA; Director, Norfolk Museums Service, since 1974; *b* 5 Feb. 1928; *s* of Francis Cheetham and Doris Elizabeth Jones; *m* 1954, Monica Fairhurst; three *s* one *d. Educ:* King Edward VII Sch., Sheffield; Univ. of Sheffield (BA). Dep. Art Dir and Curator, Castle Museum, Nottingham, 1960-63; Dir, City of Norwich Museums, 1963-74. Winston Churchill Fellow, 1967. Member: Management Cttee, Norfolk and Norwich Triennial Fest., 1966-; Crafts Council, 1978-81; Exec. Cttee, Eastern Arts Assoc., 1978-79; Bd, Norwich Puppet Theatre, 1981-; Founder Mem., National Heritage, 1970; Chairman: Norfolk and Norwich Film Theatre, 1968-70; Norfolk Contemporary Crafts Soc., 1972-. Museums Association: AMA 1959; FMA 1966; Hon. Treasurer, 1970-73; Vice-Pres., 1977-78, 1979-80; Pres., 1978-79; Chm., Soc. of County Museum Dirs, 1974-77; Mem., Exec. Bd, ICOM (UK), 1981-. Museum Advr to ACC, 1976-. *Publications:* Medieval English Alabaster Carvings in the Castle Museum, Nottingham, 1962, revd edn 1973; contrib. Jl of Museums Assoc. *Recreations:* hill-walking, music. *Address:* 25 St Andrew's Avenue, Thorpe St Andrew, Norwich NR7 0RG. *T:* Norwich 34091. *Club:* Rotary (Norwich).

CHEETHAM, John Frederick Thomas, CB 1978; Secretary, Exchequer and Audit Department, 1975-79; *b* 27 March 1919; *s* of late James Oldham Cheetham, MA, BCom; *m* 1943, Yvonne Marie Smith; one *s* one *d. Educ:* Penarth Grammar Sch.; Univ. of Wales. Entered Exchequer and Audit Dept, 1938; War Service, Royal Artillery, 1939-46; Office of Parly Comr for Administration, 1966-69; Dep. Sec., Exchequer and Audit Dept, 1973-74. *Recreations:* tennis, food and wine. *Address:* 70 Chatsworth Road, Croydon, Surrey CR0 1HB. *T:* 01-688 3740. *Club:* MCC.

CHEETHAM, Juliet; Lecturer in Applied Social Studies, Oxford University, since 1965; Fellow, Green College, Oxford; *b* 12 Oct. 1939; *d* of Harold Neville Blair and Isabel (*née* Sanders); *m* 1965, Christopher Paul Cheetham; one *s* one *d. Educ:* St Andrews Univ. (MA); Oxford Univ. (Dip. in Social and Admin. Studies). Qual. social worker. Probation Officer, Inner London, 1960-65. Member: Cttee of Enquiry into Immigration and Youth Service, 1966-68; Cttee of Enquiry into Working of Abortion Act, 1971-74; NI Standing Adv. Commn on Human Rights, 1974-77; Central Council for Educn and Trng in Social Work, 1973-; Commn for Racial Equality, 1977-. *Publications:* Social Work with Immigrants, 1972; Unwanted Pregnancy and Counselling, 1977; Social Work and Ethnicity, 1982; contrib. collected papers and prof. jls. *Recreation:* canal boats. *Address:* 101 Woodstock Road, Oxford OX2 6HL. *T:* Oxford 55105.

CHEETHAM, Sir Nicolas (John Alexander), KCMG 1964 (CMG 1953); *b* 8 Oct. 1910; *s* of late Sir Milne Cheetham, KCMG, and late Mrs Nigel Law, CBE, DStJ; *m* 1st, 1937, Jean Evison Corfe (marr. diss. 1960); two *s* ; 2nd, 1960, Lady Mabel Brooke (*née* Jocelyn). *Educ:* Eton College; Christ Church, Oxford. Entered HM Diplomatic Service, 1934; served in Foreign Office and at Athens, Buenos Aires, Mexico City and Vienna; UK Deputy Permanent Representative on North Atlantic Council, 1954-59; HM Minister to Hungary, 1959-61; Assistant Under-Secretary, Foreign Office, 1961-64; Ambassador to Mexico, 1964-68. *Publications:* A History of Mexico, 1970; New Spain, 1974; Mediaeval Greece, 1981; Keepers of the Keys, 1982. *Address:* 50 Cadogan Square, SW1. *Club:* Travellers'.

CHEEVERS, William Harold; Director, Penwell Ltd, since 1971; *b* 20 June 1918; *m* 1944, Shirley Cheevers; one *s. Educ:* Christ's Coll., London. Engineer, BBC Television, 1938-39. War Service, Army, PoW, 1941-45. Sen. Engr, BBC Television, 1946-54; Planning Engr, Radio-Corp. of America, in USA and Canada, 1954-55; Head of Engineering, Associated Rediffusion, 1955-60; Gen. Manager, Westward Television, Jt Man. Dir, 1963-67, Man. Dir, 1967-70; Dir, ITN News, 1967-70, and of IT Publications; Dir of Engrg, Granada Television, 1970-72; also Director: Keith Prowse, 1963-70; Prowest, 1967-70; Direct Line Services, 1964-. Chm., British Regional Television Assoc., 1968-69. Fellow British Kinematograph Soc.; MInstD; MBIM; AssIEE. *Publications:* articles for most TV Jls, and Symposiums, at home and abroad. *Recreations:* boating, golf, reading. *Address:* Devon Arms Hotel, Northumberland Place, Teignmouth, Devon. *T:* Teignmouth 4400. *Club:* Royal Western Yacht Club of England (Plymouth).

CHEGWIDDEN, Sir Thomas (Sidney), Kt 1955; CB 1943; CVO 1939; MA Oxon; Chevalier Légion d'Honneur, 1956; *b* 7 Feb. 1895; *s* of late Thomas Chegwidden, 8 Wimborne Road, Bournemouth; *m* 1st, 1919, Kathleen Muriel, *d* of A. O. Breeds; 2nd, 1934, Beryl Sinclair (*d* 1980), *d* of A. H. Nicholson; one *d. Educ:* Plymouth Coll.; Maidstone Grammar Sch.; Worcester Coll., Oxford. RMA Woolwich, 1916; Lieut RE, 1917-18. Resigned Commission and entered Upper Div. Civil Service, 1919; Asst Private Sec. to Dr T. J. Macnamara, Sir Montague Barlow, Mr Tom Shaw and Sir Arthur Steel-Maitland; Principal Private Sec. to Mr Oliver Stanley and Mr Ernest Brown; Under-Sec., Min. of Production, 1942-46; Civilian Dir of Studies, Imperial Defence Coll., 1946-47; Chm. of Public Services Bd and of Police Advisory Bd, S Rhodesia, 1947-53; Chm., Interim Federal Public Service Commission, Federation of Rhodesias and Nyasaland, 1953-55; Pres., Assoc. of Rhodesian Industries, 1958-61; Mem. Council, Univ. of Rhodesia, 1970-76; Fellow, Rhodesian Inst. of Management. *Publication:* The Employment Exchange Service of Great Britain (with G. Myrddin-Evans), 1934. *Address:* Huntington House, Hindhead, Surrey. *T:* Hindhead 4600. *Club:* Athenæum.

CHEKE, Dudley John, CMG 1961; MA Cantab; HM Diplomatic Service, retired; *b* 14 June 1912; *s* of late Thomas William Cheke, FRIC; *m* 1944, Yvonne de Méric, *d* of late Rear-Adm. M. J. C. de Méric, MVO; two *s. Educ:* St Christopher's, Letchworth; Emmanuel Coll., Cambridge. Entered HM Consular Service, 1934; served in Japan, Manchuria, Korea, 1935-41; served 1942-43, in East Africa and Ceylon; Foreign Office, 1944-49 and 1958-61; UK delegation to OEEC, Paris, 1949-50; Commissioner-Gen.'s Office, Singapore, 1950-51; idc 1952; HM Consul-Gen., Frankfurt-am-Main, 1953-55, Osaka-Kobe, 1956-58; Mem. of Foreign Service Corps of Inspectors, 1961-63; Minister, Tokyo, 1963-67; Ambassador to the Ivory Coast, Niger and Upper Volta, 1967-70. Chm., Japan Soc., 1979-82. *Recreations:* theatre, birdwatching, gardening. *Address:* Honey Farm, Bramley, Basingstoke, Hants. *Clubs:* United Oxford & Cambridge University; Union Society (Cambridge).

CHELMER, Baron *cr* 1963 (Life Peer), of Margaretting; **Eric Cyril Boyd Edwards,** Kt 1954; MC 1944; TD; JP; DL; Chairman: Provident Financial Group, since 1977; Greycoat Estates Ltd; Director, NEM Group of Cos, since 1970; *b* 9 Oct. 1914; *s* of Col C. E. Edwards, DSO, MC, TD, DL, JP, and Mrs J. Edwards; *m* 1939, Enid, *d* of F. W. Harvey; one *s. Educ:* Felsted Sch. Solicitor, 1937; LLB (London) 1937. Served Essex Yeomanry, 1940-54 (MC), Lieut-Col Commanding, 1945-46. Chm., Nat. Union of Conservative Associations, 1956, Pres., 1967; Chm., Nat. Exec. Cttee of Conservative and Unionist Assoc., 1957-65; Jt Treasurer of Conservative Party, 1965-77; Chm., Conservative Party Review Cttee, 1970-73. Member: Political Cttee, Carlton Club, 1961; Cttee of Musicians' Benevolent Fund; Ralph Vaughan Williams Trust. JP Essex, 1950; DL Essex 1971. *Recreation:* "improving". *Address:* Peacocks, Margaretting, Essex; 5 John Street, WC1. *Clubs:* Carlton, Buck's, Royal Ocean Racing.

CHELMSFORD, 3rd Viscount *cr* 1921, of Chelmsford; **Frederic Jan Thesiger;** Baron Chelmsford, 1858; Lloyd's Insurance Broker; Director, Willis Faber plc; *b* 7 March 1931; *s* of 2nd Viscount Chelmsford and of Gilian (*d* 1978), *d* of late Arthur Nevile Lubbock; *S* father, 1970; *m* 1958, Clare Rendle, *d* of Dr G. R. Rolston, Haslemere; one *s* one *d.* Formerly Lieut, Inns of Court Regt. *Heir: s* Hon. Frederic Corin Piers Thesiger, *b* 6 March 1962. *Address:* 26 Ormonde Gate, SW3; Hazelbridge Court, Chiddingfold, Surrey.

CHELMSFORD, Bishop of, since 1971; **Rt. Rev. Albert John Trillo,** MTh; *b* 4 July 1915; *s* of late Albert Chowns and late Margaret Trillo; *m* 1942, Patricia Eva Williams; two *s* one *d. Educ:* The Quintin Sch.; King's Coll., University of London. Business career, 1931-36; University, 1936-38, BD (1st Class Hons) and AKC (1st Class Hons), 1938; MTh 1943. Asst Curate, Christ Church, Fulham, 1938-41; Asst Curate, St Gabriel's, Cricklewood (in charge of St Michael's), 1941-45; Secretary, SCM in Schools, 1945-50; Rector of Friern Barnet and Lecturer in New Testament Greek, King's Coll., London, 1950-55; Principal, Bishops' Coll., Cheshunt, 1955-63; Bishop Suffragan of Bedford, 1963-68; Bishop Suffragan of Hertford, 1968-71. Examining Chaplain to Bishop of St Edmundsbury and Ipswich, 1955-63, to Bishop of St Albans, 1963-71. Hon. Canon, Cathedral and Abbey Church at St Albans, 1958-63; Canon Residentiary, 1963-65. Fellow of King's Coll., London, 1959. Proctor in Convocation for Dean and Chapter of St Albans, 1963-64; Proctor-in-Convocation for the Clergy, 1965. Governor: Aldenham Sch., 1963-71; Harper Trust Schs, Bedford, 1963-68; Queenswood Sch., 1969-71; Forest Sch., 1976-. Chairman: Church of England Youth Council, 1970-74; Exec. Cttee, British Council of Churches, 1974-77 (Chm., Fund for Ireland, 1978-); Church of England's Commn on Roman Catholic Relations, 1975-. *Recreations:* reading and walking. *Address:* Bishopscourt, Margaretting, Ingatestone, Essex CM4 0HD. *T:* Ingatestone 2001. *Club:* Royal Commonwealth Society.

CHELMSFORD, Provost of; *see* Moses, Very Rev. J. H.

CHELSEA, Viscount; Charles Gerald John Cadogan; *b* 24 March 1937; *o s* of 7th Earl Cadogan, *qv*; *m* 1963, Lady Philippa Wallop, *d* of 9th Earl of Portsmouth, *qv*; two *s* one *d. Educ:* Eton. *Heir: s* Hon. Edward Charles Cadogan, *b* 10 May 1966. *Address:* 7 Smith Street, SW3. *T:* 01-730 2465;

Marndhill, Ardington, near Wantage, Oxon. *T:* East Hendred 273. *Clubs:* White's, Royal Automobile.

CHELTENHAM, Archdeacon of; *see* Evans, Ven. T. E.

CHELWOOD, Baron *cr* 1974 (Life Peer), of Lewes; **Tufton Victor Hamilton Beamish,** Kt 1961; MC 1940; DL; *b* 27 Jan. 1917; *o* surv. *s* of late Rear-Admiral T. P. H. Beamish, CB, DL; *m* 1950, Janet Stevenson (marr. diss. 1973); two *d* ; *m* 1975, Mrs Pia McHenry (*née* von Roretz). *Educ:* Stowe Sch.; RMC, Sandhurst. 2nd Lieut Royal Northumberland Fusiliers, 1937; Active Service, Palestine, 1938-39; War of 1939-45 (wounded twice, despatches, MC); served in France, Belgium, 1940; Malaya, 1942; India and Burma front, 1942-43; North Africa and Italy, 1943-44; Staff Coll., Camberley, 1945 (psc). Hon. Col 411 (Sussex) Coast Regt RA (TA), 1951-57. Mem. Church of England Council on Inter-Church Relations, 1950-60. MP (C) Lewes Div. of E Sussex, 1945-Feb. 1974. Delegate to Council of Europe and Chm. Assembly Cttee, 1951-54; Vice-Chairman: British Group Inter-Parly Union, 1952-54; Conservative and Unionist Members Cttee, 1958-74; Chm. Cons. For. Affairs Cttee, 1960-64; an Opposition defence spokesman, 1965-67; Chm., Cons. Gp for Europe, 1970-73; Jt Dep. Leader, British Delegn to European Parlt, 1973-74. Member: Monnet Action Cttee for United States of Europe, 1971-76; Council, RSPB, 1948-61 (Pres., 1967-70; Vice-Pres., 1976-); Vice Pres., Soc. for Promotion of Nature Conservation, 1976-; Nature Conservancy Council, 1978-; President: Sussex Trust for Nature Conservation, 1968-78; Soc. of Sussex Downsmen, 1975-81. Governor, Stowe Sch., 1966-79. Dir of companies. DL East Sussex, 1970-. Hon. Freeman, Borough of Lewes, 1970. Golden Cross of Merit, 1944; Polonia Restituta, Poland; Comdr, Order of the Phoenix, Greece, 1949; Order of the Cedar, Lebanon, 1969. Mem. of the Soc. of Authors. *Publications:* Must Night Fall?, an account of Soviet seizure of power in Eastern Europe, 1950; Battle Royal, a new account for the 700th Anniversary of Simon de Montfort's struggle against Henry III, 1965; Half Marx: a warning that democracy in Britain is threatened by a Marx-influenced Labour Party, 1971; (with Guy Hadley) The Kremlin's Dilemma: the struggle for human rights in Eastern Europe, 1979; contribs to newspapers and periodicals. *Recreations:* gardening, bird-watching, music. *Address:* Plovers' Meadow, Blackboys, Uckfield, Sussex. *Club:* White's.

CHENEY, Christopher Robert, FBA 1951; Professor of Medieval History, University of Cambridge, 1955-72; Fellow, Corpus Christi College, Cambridge, 1955; *b* 1906; 4th *s* of George Gardner and Christiana Stapleton Cheney; *m* 1940, Mary Gwendolen Hall; two *s* one *d. Educ:* Banbury County Sch.; Wadham Coll., Oxford (Hon. Fellow, 1968). 1st class Modern History Sch., 1928; Asst Lectr in History, University Coll., London, 1931-33; Bishop Fraser Lectr in Ecclesiastical History, University of Manchester, 1933-37; Fellow of Magdalen Coll., Oxford, 1938-45; Univ. Reader in Diplomatic, 1937-45; Joint Literary Dir of Royal Historical Society, 1938-45; Prof. of Medieval History, Univ. of Manchester, 1945-55. Hon. Fellow, Wadham Coll., Oxford. Corresp. Fellow, Mediaeval Acad. of America; Corresp. Mem., Monumenta Germaniae Historica. Hon. DLitt: Glasgow, 1970; Manchester, 1978. *Publications:* Episcopal Visitation of Monasteries in the 13th Century, 1931; English Synodalia of the 13th Century, 1941; Handbook of Dates, 1945; English Bishops' Chanceries, 1950; (with W. H. Semple) Selected Letters of Pope Innocent III, 1953; From Becket to Langton, 1956; (with F. M. Powicke) Councils and Synods of the English Church, Vol. II, 1964; Hubert Walter, 1967; (with M. G. Cheney) Letters of Pope Innocent III concerning England and Wales, 1967; Notaries Public in England in the XIII and XIV Centuries, 1972; Medieval Texts and Studies, 1973; Pope Innocent III and England, 1976; (with M. G. Cheney) Studies in the Collections of XII Century Decretals, ed from papers of W. Holtzmann, 1979; The Papacy and England, 12th-14th Centuries (Variorum Reprints), 1982; The English Church and its Laws, 12th-14th Centuries (Variorum Reprints), 1982; articles and reviews in Eng. Hist. Rev., etc. *Address:* 236 Hills Road, Cambridge. *T:* Cambridge 247765.

CHERENKOV, Prof. Pavel Alexeevich; Soviet physicist; Member of the Institute of Physics, Academy of Sciences of the USSR; *b* 27 July 1904. *Educ:* Voronezh State Univ., Voronezh, USSR. Discovered the Cherenkov Effect, 1934. Corresp. Mem., 1964-70, Academician, 1970-, USSR Acad. of Scis. Awarded Stalin Prize, 1946; Nobel Prize for Physics (joint), 1958. *Address:* Institute of Physics, Academy of Sciences of the USSR, B Kaluzhskaya 14, Moscow, USSR.

CHERKASSKY, Shura; pianist; *b* 7 Oct. 1911; *s* of late Isaac and Lydia Cherkassky; *m* 1946, Genia Ganz (marr. diss. 1948). *Educ:* Curtis Institute of Music, Pa, USA (diploma). Plays with the principal orchestras and conductors of the world and is a constant soloist at Salzburg, Vienna and Edinburgh Festivals; concerts in Asia, America, Australia and Europe. Has made numerous recordings. *Address:* c/o Ibbs & Tillett Ltd, 450-452 Edgware Road, W2 1EG.

CHERMAYEFF, Serge, FRIBA, FRSA; architect; author; abstract painter; *b* 8 Oct. 1900; *s* of Ivan and Rosalie Chermayeff; *m* 1928, Barbara Maitland May; two *s. Educ:* Harrow Sch. Journalist, 1918-22; studied architecture, 1922-25; principal work in England, studios for BBC; Modern Exhibitions; Gilbey's Offices; ICI Laboratories; in Partnership: Bexhill Pavilion. Professor, Brooklyn Coll., 1942-46; Pres. and Dir, Inst. of Design, Chicago, 1946-51; Prof., Harvard Univ., 1953-62; Prof., Yale Univ., 1962-71, now Emeritus.

Hon. Fellow, Assoc. of Columbian Architects. Hon. Dr of Fine Art, Washington Univ., 1964; Hon. Dr of Humanities, Ohio State Univ., 1980. Gold Medal, Royal Architectural Inst., Canada, 1974; AIA and Assoc. of Collegiate Schs 1980 Award for excellence in educn; Misha Black Meml Medal for significant contribn to design educn, SIAD, 1980; Gold Medal, NY State Univ. at Buffalo, 1982. *Publications:* Art and Architectural Criticism; ARP, 1939; Community and Privacy, 1963; Shape of Community, 1970; Design and the Public Good (Collected Works), 1982. *Address:* Box NN, Wellfleet, Mass 02667, USA.

CHERMONT, Jayme Sloan, KCVO (Hon.) 1968; Brazilian Ambassador to the Court of St James's, 1966-68, retired; *b* 5 April 1903; *s* of Ambassador E. L. Chermont and Mrs Helen Mary Chermont; *m* 1928, Zaíde Alvim de Mello Franco Chermont (decd); no *c. Educ:* Law Sch., Rio de Janeiro Univ. Entered Brazilian Foreign Office, 1928; served in Washington, 1930-32; Rio de Janeiro, 1932-37; London, 1937; transf. to Brazil, 1938; 1st Sec., 1941; Buenos Aires, 1943-45; transf. to Brazil, 1945; Counsellor, Brussels, 1948-50; Minister Counsellor, London (periodically Chargé d'Affaires), 1950-53; various appts, Brazilian FO, 1953-57; Consul-Gen., New York, 1957-60; Ambassador to Haiti, 1960-61; Head of Political and Cultural Depts, Brazil, 1961; Sec.-Gen., FO, 1962-63; Ambassador to Netherlands, 1963-66. Headed Brazilian Delegn to UN Gen. Assembly, 1962. Holds Orders from many foreign countries. *Recreations:* golf, chess, bridge, stamps, coins, books. *Address:* Rua Siqueira Campos no 7-7, Copacabana, Rio de Janeiro, Brasil. *Clubs:* Jockey, Country, Itanhangá Golf (Rio).

CHERRY, Prof. Gordon Emanuel; Professor of Urban and Regional Planning since 1976, and Dean of Faculty of Commerce and Social Science since 1981, University of Birmingham; *b* 6 Feb. 1931; *s* of Emanuel and Nora Cherry; *m* 1957, Margaret Mary Loudon Cox; one *s* two *d. Educ:* Holgate and District Grammar Sch., Barnsley; QMC, Univ. of London (BA(Hons) Geog. 1953). Variously employed in local authority planning depts, 1956-68; Research Officer, Newcastle upon Tyne City Planning Dept, 1963-68; Sen. Lectr and Dep. Dir, Centre for Urban and Regional Studies, Univ. of Birmingham, 1968-76. Mem., Local Govt Boundary Commn for England, 1979-; Trustee, Bournville Village Trust, 1979-. FRICS; Pres., RTPI, 1978-79. *Publications:* Town Planning in its Social Context, 1970, 2nd edn 1973; (with T. L. Burton) Social Research Techniques for Planners, 1970; Urban Change and Planning, 1972; The Evolution of British Town Planning, 1974; Environmental Planning, Vol. II: National Parks and Recreation in the Countryside, 1975; The Politics of Town Planning, 1982; Editor: Urban Planning Problems, 1974; Rural Planning Problems, 1976; Shaping an Urban World, 1980; Pioneers in British Planning, 1981. *Recreations:* work, professional activities, ecumenical church involvement, sport, reading, music, enjoyment of family life. *Address:* 20 Blackthorne Close, Solihull, West Midlands B91 1PF. *T:* 021-705 8459.

CHERRYMAN, John Richard, QC 1982; *b* 7 Dec. 1932; *s* of Albert James and Mabel Cherryman; *m* 1963, Anna Greenleaf Collis; three *s* one *d. Educ:* Farnham Grammar Sch.; London School of Economics (LLB Hons); Harvard Law Sch. Called to Bar, Gray's Inn, 1955. *Recreation:* splitting hairs. *Address:* 4 Stone Buildings, Lincoln's Inn, WC2.

CHESHAM, 5th Baron *cr* 1858; **John Charles Compton Cavendish,** PC 1964; *b* 18 June 1916; *s* of 4th Baron and Margot, *d* of late J. Layton Mills, Tansor Court, Oundle; *S* father, 1952; *m* 1937, Mary Edmunds, 4th *d* of late David G. Marshall, White Hill, Cambridge; two *s* two *d. Educ:* Eton; Zuoz Coll., Switzerland; Trinity Coll., Cambridge. Served War of 1939-45, Lieut Royal Bucks Yeomanry, 1939-42; Capt. RA (Air OP), 1942-45. JP Bucks 1946, retd. Delegate, Council of Europe, 1953-56. A Lord-in-Waiting to the Queen, 1955-59; Parly Sec., Min. of Transport, 1959-64. Chancellor, Primrose League, 1957-59. Executive Vice-Chm. Royal Automobile Club, 1966-70; Chairman: British Road Federation, 1966-72 (Vice-Pres., 1972); Internat. Road Fedn, Geneva, 1973-76; Pres., British Parking Assoc., 1972-75; Fellowship of Motor Industry, 1969-71; Hon. Sec., House of Lords Club, 1966-72; Hon. FInstHE, 1970; Hon FIRTE, 1974 (Pres., 1971-73). *Heir: s* Hon. Nicholas Charles Cavendish [*b* 7 Nov. 1941; *m* 1st, 1965, Susan Donne (marr. diss. 1969), *e d* of Dr Guy Beauchamp; 2nd, 1973, Suzanne, *er d* of late Alan Gray Byrne, Sydney, Australia; two *s*]. *Address:* Manor Farm, Preston Candover, near Basingstoke, Hants. *T:* Preston Candover 230. *Clubs:* Carlton, Pratt's.

CHESHIRE, Group Captain (Geoffrey) Leonard, VC 1944; OM 1981; DSO 1940 and two Bars 1941, 1942; DFC 1941; RAF retired; *b* 7 Sept. 1917; *s* of late Geoffrey Chevalier Cheshire, FBA, DCL, and late Primrose Barstow; *m* 2nd, 1959, Susan Ryder (*see* Baroness Ryder of Warsaw); one *s* one *d. Educ:* Stowe Sch.; Merton Coll., Oxford. 2nd Class Hon. Sch. of Jurisprudence, 1939; OU Air Sqdn, 1936; RAFVR, 1937; Perm. Commn RAF, 1939; trained Hullavington; served Bomber Comd, 1940-45: 102 Sqdn, 1940; 35 Sqdn, 1941; CO 76 Sqdn, 1942; RAF Station, Marston Moor, 1943; 617 Sqdn (Dambusters), 1943; attached Eastern Air Command, South-East Asia, 1944; British Joint Staff Mission, Washington, 1945; official British observer at dropping of Atomic Bomb on Nagasaki, 1945; retd Dec. 1945. Founder of Cheshire Foundation Homes (220 Homes for the disabled in 45 countries); Co-founder of Ryder Cheshire Mission for the Relief of Suffering. Member: Pathfinders Assoc.; Air Crew Assoc. Hon. LLD: Liverpool, 1973; Manchester Polytechnic, 1979; Nottingham, 1981. Variety Club Humanitarian Award (jtly with wife), 1975. *Publications:* Bomber Pilot,

1943; Pilgrimage to the Shroud, 1956; The Face of Victory, 1961; The Hidden World, 1981. *Relevant publications:* Cheshire, VC, by Russell Braddon, 1954; No Passing Glory, by Andrew Boyle, 1955; New Lives for Old, by W. W. Russell, 1963. *Recreation:* tennis. *Address:* Cavendish, Suffolk. *Clubs:* Royal Air Force, Queen's (Hon. Life Mem.), All England Lawn Tennis.

CHESSHYRE, David Hubert Boothby, FSA; Chester Herald of Arms, since 1978; *b* 22 June 1940; *e s* of late Col Hubert Layard Chesshyre and of Katharine Anne (*née* Boothby), Canterbury, Kent. *Educ:* King's Sch., Canterbury; Trinity Coll., Cambridge (MA); Christ Church, Oxford (DipEd 1967). FSA 1977. Taught French in England and English in France, at intervals 1962-67; wine merchant (Moët et Chandon and Harvey's of Bristol), 1962-65; Hon. Artillery Co., 1964-65 (fired salute at funeral of Sir Winston Churchill, 1965); Green Staff Officer at Investiture of the Prince of Wales, 1969; Rouge Croix Pursuivant, 1970-78, and on staff of Sir Anthony Wagner, Garter King of Arms, 1971-78. Member: Council, Heraldry Soc., 1973-; Bach Choir, 1979-; Madrigal Soc., 1980-. Lay Clerk, Southwark Cathedral, 1971-; Freeman, City of London, 1975. *Publications:* (Eng. lang. editor) C. A. von Volborth, Heraldry of the World, 1973; The Identification of Coats of Arms on British Silver, 1978; (with A. J. Robinson) The Green: a history of the heart of Bethnal Green, 1978; genealogical and heraldic articles in British Heritage and elsewhere. *Recreations:* singing, lecturing, gardening, mountain walking, motorcycling, squash. *Address:* 62 Malvern Road, E8 3LJ. *T:* 01-249 7777; College of Arms, Queen Victoria Street, EC4V 4BT. *T:* 01-248 1137. *Club:* Petit Club Français.

CHESTER, Bishop of, since 1982; **Rt. Rev. Michael Alfred Baughen;** *b* 7 June 1930; *s* of Alfred Henry and Clarice Adelaide Baughen; *m* 1956, Myrtle Newcomb Phillips; two *s* one *d. Educ:* Bromley County Grammar Sch; Univ. of London; Oak Hill Theol Coll. BD (London). With Martins Bank, 1946-48, 1950-51. Army, Royal Signals, 1948-50. Degree Course and Ordination Trng, 1951-56; Curate: St Paul's, Hyson Green, Nottingham, 1956-59; Reigate Parish Ch., 1959-61; Candidates Sec., Church Pastoral Aid Soc., 1961-64; Rector of Holy Trinity (Platt), Rusholme, Manchester, 1964-70; Vicar of All Souls, Langham Place, W1, 1970-75; Rector, 1975-82; Area Dean of St Marylebone, 1978-82; a Prebendary of St Paul's Cathedral, 1979-82. *Publications:* Moses and the Venture of Faith, 1979; The Prayer Principle, 1981; Bible Comes Alive—2 Corinthians, 1982; Editor: Youth Praise, 1966; Youth Praise II, 1969; Psalm Praise, 1973; consultant editor, Hymns for Today's Church, 1982. *Recreations:* music, railways, touring. *Address:* Bishop's House, Chester CH1 2JD. *T:* Chester 20864.

CHESTER, Dean of; *see* Cleasby, Very Rev. T. W. I.

CHESTER, Archdeacon of; *see* Williams, Ven. H. L.

CHESTER, Sir (Daniel) Norman, Kt 1974; CBE 1951; MA; Warden of Nuffield College, Oxford, 1954-78; Official Fellow of Nuffield College, 1945-54, Hon. Fellow, 1978; *b* 27 Oct. 1907; *s* of Daniel Chester, Chorlton-cum-Hardy, Manchester; *m* 1936, Eva (*d* 1980), *d* of James H. Jeavons. *Educ:* Manchester Univ. BA Manchester, 1930, MA 1933; MA Oxon, 1946. Rockefeller Fellow, 1935-36, Lecturer in Public Administration, 1936-45, Manchester Univ.; Mem. of Economic Section, War Cabinet Secretariat, 1940-45. Editor of jl of Public Administration, 1943-66. Mem. Oxford City Council, 1952-74. Chairman: Oxford Centre for Management Studies, 1965-75; Police Promotion Examinations Bd, 1969-; Cttee on Association Football, 1966-68; Football Grounds Improvement Trust, 1975-80; Dep. Chm., Football Trust, 1980-; Vice-Pres. (ex-Chm.), Royal Inst. of Public Administration; Past Pres., Internat. Political Science Assoc. Hon. LittD Manchester, 1968. Corresp. Mem., Acad. des Sciences Morales et Politiques, Institut de France, 1967. Chevalier de la Légion d'Honneur, 1976. *Publications:* Public Control of Road Passenger Transport, 1936; Central and Local Government: Financial and Administrative Relations, 1951; The Nationalised Industries, 1951; (ed) Lessons of the British War Economy, 1951; (ed) The Organization of British Central Government, 1914-56; (with Nona Bowring) Questions in Parliament, 1962; The Nationalisation of British Industry, 1945-51, 1975; The English Administrative System 1780-1870, 1981; articles in learned journals. *Address:* 136 Woodstock Road, Oxford. *Club:* Reform.

CHESTER, Dr Peter Francis, FInstP; Director, Central Electricity Research Laboratories, since 1973; *b* 8 Feb. 1929; *s* of late Herbert and of Edith Maud Chester (*née* Pullen); *m* 1953, Barbara Ann Collin; one *s* four *d. Educ:* Gunnersbury Grammar Sch.; Queen Mary College, London. BSc 1st Physics 1950; PhD London 1953. Post-doctoral Fellow, Nat. Research Council, Ottawa, 1953-54; Adv. Physicist, Westinghouse Res. Labs, Pittsburgh, 1954-60; Head of Solid State Physics Section, CERL, 1960-65; Head of Fundamental Studies Section, CERL, 1965-66; Res. Man., Electricity Council Res. Centre, 1966-70; Controller of Scientific Services, CEGB NW Region, 1970-73. Science Research Council: Mem., 1976-80; Mem., Science Bd, 1972-75; Chm., Energy Round Table and Energy Cttee, 1975-80. Vice-Pres., Inst. of Physics, 1972-76. A Dir, Fulmer Res. Inst., 1976-. *Publications:* original papers in solid state and low temperature physics, reports on energy and the environment. *Address:* Central Electricity Research Laboratories, Kelvin Avenue, Leatherhead, Surrey KT22 7SE.

CHESTER, Prof. Theodore Edward, CBE 1967; D.jur, MA (Econ) Manchester; Diploma in Commerce; Director, Management Programme for Clinicians, since 1979; Senior Research Fellow and Emeritus Professor,

1976-78, Professor of Social Administration, 1955-75, University of Manchester; Member, Council and Finance and General Purposes Committee, Manchester Business School, since 1964; *b* 28 June 1908; *m* 1940, Mimi; one *s*. Teaching and research in law and administration, 1931-39. Service with HM Forces, 1940-45. Asst Man. in London city firm, 1946-48; Acton Soc. Trust: Senior Research Worker, 1948-52; Dir, 1952-55; Dean, Faculty of Economic and Social Studies, Univ. of Manchester, 1962-63. Research work into problems of large-scale Administration in private and public undertakings including the hosp. and educn service in Britain and comparative studies abroad as well as into the problems of training managers and administrators. Vis. Prof. at many foreign univs and institutions, notably in the United States, Western Europe, Canada, and Australia, 1959-; Kenneth Pray Vis. Prof., Univ. of Pa, 1968; first Kellogg Vis. Prof., Washington Univ., St Louis, 1969 and 1970. Mem. Summer Fac., Sloan Inst. of Health Service Admin, Cornell Univ., 1972-. Ford Foundn Travelling Fellowships, 1960, 1967. WHO Staff Training Programme, 1963-; UN Res. Inst. for Economic and Social Studies, 1968. Member: National Selection Cttee for the recruitment of Sen. Hospital Administrative Staff, 1956-66; Advisory Cttee on Management Efficiency in the Health Service, 1959-65; Cttee of Inquiry into recruitment, training and promotion of clerical and administrative staffs in the Hospital Service, 1962-63; Programme Cttee of Internat. Hosp. Fedn and Chm. study group into problems of trng in hosp. admin, 1959-65; Pres. Corp of Secs, 1956-66; Trng Couns for Social Workers and Health Visitors, 1963-65; Cttee on Technical Coll. Resources, 1964-69; Adviser: Social Affairs Div., OECD, 1965-66; Turkish State Planning Org. on Health and Welfare Problems, 1964. Broadcasts on social problems in Britain and abroad. Golden Needle of Honour, Austrian Hosp. Dirs Assoc., 1970. The Grand Gold Komturcross for services to the Health Service (Austria), 1980. *Publications:* (for Acton Soc. Trust) Training and Promotion in Nationalised Industry, 1951; Patterns of Organisation, 1952; Management under Nationalization, 1953; Background and Blueprint: A Study of Hospital Organisation under the National Health Service, 1955; The Impact of the Change (co-author), 1956; Groups, Regions and Committees, 1957; The Central Control of the Service, 1958; (with H. A. Clegg): The Future of Nationalization, 1953; Wage Policy and the Health Service, 1957; Post War Growth of Management in Western Europe, 1961; Graduate Education for Hospital Administration in the United States: Trends, 1969; The British National Health Service, 1970; The Swedish National Health Service, 1970; Organisation for Change: preparation for reorganisation, 1974 (OECD); Editor and contrib. Amer. Coll. Hosp. Administrators; regular contribs to scientific and other jls. *Recreations:* travel, music, swimming, detective stories. *Address:* Lisvane, 189 Grove Lane, Hale, Altrincham, Cheshire. *T:* 061-980 2828.

CHESTER JONES, Prof. Ian, DSc; Professor of Zoology, University of Sheffield, 1958-81, now Emeritus Professor; Hon. Professor, Wolfson Institute for Research on Ageing, Hull, 1981; *b* 3 Jan. 1916; *s* of late H. C. Jones; *m* 1942, Nansi Ellis Williams; two *s* one *d*. *Educ:* Liverpool Institute High Sch. for Boys; Liverpool Univ. BSc 1938; PhD 1941; DSc 1958. Served in Army, 1941-46. Commonwealth Fund Fellow, Harvard Univ., 1947-49. Senior Lecturer in Zoology, Univ. of Liverpool, 1955. Chm., Soc. for Endocrinology, 1966 (Sir Henry Dale medal, 1976). Dr de l'Université de Clermont (*hc*), 1967. *Publications:* The Adrenal Cortex, 1957; Integrated Biology, 1971; General, Comparative and Clinical Endocrinology of the Adrenal Cortex, vol. 1, 1976, vol. 2, 1978, vol. 3, 1980. *Address:* Department of Zoology, University of Sheffield S10 2TN.

CHESTERFIELD, Archdeacon of; *see* Phizackerley, Ven. G. R.

CHESTERFIELD, Arthur Desborough, CBE 1962; Director: Singer & Friedlander (Holdings) Ltd, since 1967 (Chairman, 1967-76); Singer & Friedlander Ltd, since 1967 (Chairman, 1967-76); Clifford Property Co. Ltd, since 1973 (Chairman); Percy Bilton Ltd, since 1977; *b* 21 Aug. 1905; *s* of Arthur William and Ellen Harvey Chesterfield; *m* 1932, Betty (*d* 1980), *d* of John Henry Downey; two *s* three *d*. *Educ:* Hastings Grammar Sch. Entered Westminster Bank Ltd, 1923; Joint Gen. Manager, 1947; Chief Gen. Manager, 1950-65, retired; Director: Nat. Westminster Bank, 1963-69 (Local Dir, Inner London, 1969-74); Woolwich Equitable Bldg Soc., 1966-80 (Vice-Chm., 1976-80). Member: Export Guarantees Adv. Council, 1952-63; Nat. Savings Cttee, 1954-67; Chm., City of London Savings Cttee, 1962-72. FIB (Mem. Council, 1950-65). *Recreations:* music, gardening. *Address:* Coaters, Shirleys, Ditchling, Sussex. *T:* Hassocks 3514.

CHESTERMAN, Sir Clement (Clapton), Kt 1974; OBE 1919; Consulting Physician in Tropical Diseases, retired; *b* 30 May 1894; 5th *s* of late W. T. Chesterman, Bath, and Elizabeth Clapton; *m* 1917, Winifred Lucy (*d* 1981), *d* of late Alderman F. W. Spear; three *s* two *d*. *Educ:* Monkton Combe Sch.; Bristol Univ. MD London 1920; DTM and H, Cantab, 1920; FRCP 1952. Served European War, 1914-18 (despatches, OBE): Capt. RAMC (SR), 1917-19, Middle East. Medical Missionary, Belgian Congo, 1920-36; MO and Secretary, Baptist Missionary Soc., 1936-48. Lecturer in Tropical Medicine, Middlesex Hospital Medical Sch., 1944; Lecturer in Tropical Hygiene, University of London Institute of Education, 1956. Member Commn Royale Belge pour la Protection des Indigènes; Mem. Colonial Advisory Medical Cttee; Past Vice-Pres. Royal Society Tropical Medicine and Hygiene; Pres. Hunterian Society, 1967-68; Hon. Mem. Belgian Royal Society of Tropical Medicine. Occasional broadcasts on Medical Missions and Tropical Diseases. Hon. FRAM, 1972. Serbian Red Cross Medal, 1915; Chevalier, Ordre Royal du Lion, 1938. *Publications:* In the Service of Suffering, 1940; A Tropical

Dispensary Handbook (7th edn), 1960; articles in Transactions of Royal Society of Tropical Medicine and Hygiene, British Encyclopædia of Medical Practice, etc. *Recreation:* golf. *Address:* Kestrel Grove, Hive Road, Bushey Heath, Herts. *T:* 01-950 4329. *Clubs:* Royal Commonwealth Society; Highgate Golf.

CHESTERMAN, Sir Ross, Kt 1970; MSc, PhD; DIC; Warden of Goldsmiths' College (University of London), 1953-74; Hon. Fellow, 1980; Vice-Master of the College of Craft Education, since 1960 (Dean, 1958-60); *b* 27 April 1909; *s* of late Dudley and Ettie Chesterman; *m* 1938, Audrey Mary Horlick (*d* 1982); one *s* one *d*. *Educ:* Hastings Grammar Sch.; Imperial College of Science, London (scholar). Acland English Essay Prizeman, 1930; 1st class hons BSc (Chem.), 1930; MSc 1932; Lecturer in Chemistry, Woolwich Polytechnic; PhD 1937; Science master in various grammar schools; Headmaster, Meols Cop Secondary Sch., Southport, 1946-48. Chief County Inspector of Schools, Worcestershire, 1948-53. Educnl Consultant to numerous overseas countries, 1966-73. Ford Foundation Travel Award to American Univs, 1966. Chairman: Standing Cttee on Teacher Trng; Nat. Council for Supply and Trng of Teachers Overseas, 1971; Adv. Cttee for Teacher Trng Overseas, FCO (ODA), 1972-74. Fellow *hc* of Coll. of Handicraft, 1958. Liveryman and Freeman of Goldsmiths' Co., 1968. *Publications:* The Birds of Southport, 1947; chapter in The Forge, 1955; chapter in Science in Schools, 1958; Teacher Training in some American Universities, 1967; scientific papers in chemical journals and journals of natural history; articles in educational periodicals. *Recreations:* music, painting, travel. *Address:* Greenacre, 27 Greenhill Road, Otford, Sevenoaks, Kent TN14 5RR.

CHESTERS, Prof. Charles Geddes Coull, OBE 1977; BSc, MSc, PhD; FRSE; FLS; FInstBiol; Professor of Botany, University of Nottingham, 1944-69, now Emeritus Professor; *b* 9 March 1904; *s* of Charles and Margaret Geddes Chesters; *m* 1928, Margarita Mercedes Cathie Maclean; one *s* one *d*. *Educ:* Hyndland Sch.; Univ. of Glasgow. Lecturer in Botany, 1930, Reader in Mycology, 1942, Univ. of Birmingham. Chairman: Educn and other Cttees, Associated Exam. Bd; Jt Cttee, HNC Applied Biol. *Publications:* scientific papers on mycology and microbiology, mainly in Trans. British Myc. Soc., Ann. Ap. Biol., Jl Gen. Microb. *Recreations:* photography and collecting fungi. *Address:* Grandage Cottages, Quenington, near Cirencester, Glos GL7 5DB.

CHESTERS, Dr John Hugh, OBE 1970; FRS 1969; FEng; Consultant, since 1971; *b* 16 Oct. 1906; 2nd *s* of Rev. George M. Chesters; *m* 1936, Nell Knight, Minnesota, USA; three *s* one *d*. *Educ:* High Pavement Sch., Nottingham; King Edward VII Sch., Sheffield; Univ. of Sheffield. BSc Hons Physics, 1928; PhD 1931; DSc Tech 1945; Hon. DSc 1975. Metropolitan-Vickers Research Schol., Univ. Sheff., 1928-31. Robert Blair Fellowship, Kaiser-Wilhelm Inst. für Silikatforschung, Berlin, 1931-32; Commonwealth Fund Fellowship, Univ. of Illinois, 1932-34; United Steel Co Ltd: in charge of Refractories Section, 1934-45; Asst Dir of Research, 1945-62; Dep. Dir of Research, United Steel Cos Ltd, 1962-67, Midland Group, British Steel Corporation, 1967-70; Dir, Corporate Labs, BISRA, 1970-71. Chm., Watt Cttee on Energy, 1976-. President: Brit. Ceramic Soc., 1951-52; Inst. of Ceramics, 1961-63; Iron and Steel Inst., 1968-69; Inst. of Fuel, 1972-73. Foreign Associate, Nat. Acad. of Engineering, USA, 1977. Iron and Steel Inst., Bessemer Gold Medal, 1966; John Wilkinson Gold Medal, Staffs Iron and Steel Inst., 1971; American Inst. Met. Eng: Robert Hunt Award, 1952; Benjamin Fairless Award, 1973. Fellow, Fellowship of Engineering, 1978; SFInstF, FIM, FICeram; Fellow, Amer. Ceramic Soc. *Publications:* Steelplant Refractories, 1945, 2nd edn 1957; Iron and Steel, 1948; Refractories: production and properties, 1973; Refractories for Iron- and Steelmaking, 1974; numerous articles in Jl of Iron and Steel Inst., Trans Brit. Cer. Soc., Jl Amer. Cer. Soc., Jl Inst. of Fuel, etc. *Recreations:* foreign travel, fishing. *Address:* 21 Slayleigh Lane, Sheffield S10 3RF. *T:* Sheffield 301257.

CHESTERTON, Elizabeth Ursula, OBE 1977; architect and town planner; *b* 12 Oct. 1915; *d* of late Maurice Chesterton, architect, and Dorothy (*née* Deck). *Educ:* King Alfred Sch.; Queen's Coll., London; Architectural Assoc. Sch. of Architecture, London. AA Dipl. (Hons) 1939; ARIBA 1940; DistTP 1968; FRTPI 1967 (AMTPI 1943). Asst County Planning Officer, E Suffolk CC, 1940-47; Develt Control Officer, Cambs CC Planning Dept, 1947-51; Mem. Staff: Social Res. Unit, Dept of Town Planning, UCL, 1951-53; Architectural Assoc. Sch. of Architecture, 1954-61. Member: Council, Architectural Assoc., 1964-67; Royal Fine Art Commn, 1970-; Historic Buildings Council, 1973-. FRSA 1982. *Publications:* Report on Local Land Use for the Dartington Hall Trustees, 1957; (jtly) The Historic Core of King's Lynn: study and plan, 1964; Plan for the Beaulieu Estate, 1966; North West Solent Shore Estates Report, 1969; Snowdon Summit Report for Countryside Commission, 1974; Plans for Quarries and Rail Distribution Depots, Foster Yeoman and Yeoman (Morvern), 1974-; Central Area Study, Chippenham, for North Wiltshire District Council, 1975; The Crumbles, Eastbourne, for Chatsworth Settlement, 1976; Aldeburgh, Suffolk, for Aldeburgh Soc., 1976; Old Market Conservation and Redevelopment Study, for City of Bristol and Bristol Municipal Charities, 1978; Uplands Landscape Study, for Countryside Commission, 1980. *Recreations:* narrow boat owner; gardening; travel. *Address:* The Studio, Money's Yard, The Mount, NW3 6SZ. *T:* 01-435 0666 and 01-580 6396.

CHESTERTON, Sir Oliver (Sidney), Kt 1969; MC 1943; Consultant, Chestertons, Chartered Surveyors, London, since 1980 (Partner, 1936, Senior

Partner, 1945–80); Chairman, Woolwich Equitable Building Society, since 1976 (Vice-Chairman, 1969–76); Director: Property Growth Assurance, since 1972; London Life Association, since 1975; Estates Property Investment Company, since 1979; *b* 28 Jan. 1913; *s* of Frank and Nora Chesterton; *m* 1944, Violet Ethel Jameson; two *s* one *d. Educ:* Rugby Sch. Served War of 1939–45, Irish Guards. Vice-Chm., Council of Royal Free Med. Sch., 1964–77; Crown Estate Comr, 1969–. Past Pres., Royal Instn of Chartered Surveyors, Hon. Sec., 1972–79; Pres., Commonwealth Assoc. Surveying and Land Economy, 1969–77; first Master, Chartered Surveyors' Co., 1977–78. Governor, Rugby Sch., 1972–. *Recreations:* golf, fishing, National Hunt racing. *Address:* 19 Hornton Court, W8. *Clubs:* White's; Rye Golf.

CHESWORTH, Donald Piers; Warden, Toynbee Hall, since 1977; *b* 30 Jan. 1923; *s* of late Frederick Gladstone Chesworth and Daisy Radmore. *Educ:* King Edward VI Sch., Camp Hill, Birmingham; London Sch. of Economics. War of 1939–45: Nat. Fire Service; Royal Air Force. Chm., Nat. Assoc. of Labour Student Organisations, 1947; Student and Overseas Sec., Internat. Union of Socialist Youth, 1947–51. Contested (Lab) elections: Warwick and Leamington, 1945; Bromsgrove, 1950 and 1951; Mem. LCC (Kensington N Div.), 1952–65 (Whip and Mem., Policy Cttee); Labour Adviser: Tanganyika Govt (and Chm., Territorial Minimum Wages Bd), 1961–62; Mauritius Govt (and Chm., Sugar Wages Councils), 1962–65; Mem. Economics Br., ILO, Geneva, 1967; Dir, Notting Hill Social Council, 1967–77; Chm. (part time) Mauritius Salaries Commn, 1973–77; Co-opted Mem., ILEA Educn Cttee, 1970–74 and 1975–77; Alderman, Royal Borough of Kensington and Chelsea, 1971–77. Chm., Assoc. for Neighbourhood Councils, 1972–74. Member: Council, War on Want, 1965–76 (Chm., 1967, 1968, 1970–74); Exec. Bd, Voluntary Cttee on Overseas Aid and Devel't, 1969–76; Nat. Cttee, UK Freedom from Hunger Campaigns, 1969–76; S Metropolitan Conciliation Cttee, Race Relations Bd, 1975–77; Chm., World Development Political Action Trust, 1971–75; Trustee: UK Bangladesh Fund, 1971–72; Campden Charities, 1971–77; Internat. Extension Coll., 1972–; Attlee Meml Foundn, 1977– (Director, 1979–81); Mutual Aid Centre, London, 1977–. Mem. Bd of Visitors, Hewell Grange Borstal, 1950–52; Chm. Managers Mayford Home Office Approved Sch., 1952–58. Chairman of Governors: Isaac Newton Sch., N Kensington, 1971–77; Paddington Sch., 1972–76; Mem., Ct of Governors, LSE, 1973–78. *Publications:* Report Tanganyika Territorial Minimum Wages Board, 1961; Reports Mauritius Sugar Wages Councils, 1962–65; Reports Mauritius Salaries Commission, 1973–77; contribs Statutory Wage Fixing in Developing Countries (ILO), 1968; contrib. Internat. Labour Review. *Recreation:* travel. *Address:* Toynbee Hall, Universities' Settlement in East London, 28 Commercial Street, E1 6LS. *T:* 01-247 3633. *Clubs:* Reform, Royal Commonwealth Society.

CHESWORTH, Air Vice-Marshal George Arthur, CB 1982; OBE 1972; DFC 1954; Chief of Staff, Headquarters 18 Group, RAF, since 1980; *b* 4 June 1930; *s* of Alfred Matthew Chesworth and Grace Edith Chesworth; *m* 1951, Betty Joan Hopkins; two *d* (one *s* decd). *Educ:* Carshalton and Wimbledon. Joined RAF, 1948; commissioned, 1950; 205 Flying boat Sqdn, FEAF, 1951–53 (DFC 1954); RAF Germany, RAF Kinloss, RAF St Mawgan, 1956–61; RN Staff Coll., 1963; MoD, 1964–67; OC 201 Nimrod Sqdn, 1968–71 (OBE); OC RAF Kinloss, 1972–75; Air Officer in Charge, Central Tactics & Trials Orgn, 1975–77; Director, RAF Quartering, 1977–80. *Address:* c/o Lloyds Bank Ltd, 10 Hanover Square, W1R 0BT; Hill End, Pinner Hill, Pinner, Mddx HA5 3XT. *T:* 01-866 9529. *Club:* Royal Air Force.

CHETWODE, family name of **Baron Chetwode.**

CHETWODE, 2nd Baron *cr* 1945, of Chetwode; **Philip Chetwode;** Bt, 1700; *b* 26 March 1937; *s* of Capt. Roger Charles George Chetwode (*d* 1940; *o s* of Field Marshal Lord Chetwode, GCB, OM, GCSI, KCMG, DSO) and Hon. Molly Patricia Berry, *d* of 1st Viscount Camrose (she *m* 2nd, 1942, 1st Baron Sherwood, from whom she obtained a divorce, 1948, and *m* 3rd, 1958, late Sir Richard Cotterell, 5th Bt, CBE); *S* grandfather, 1950; *m* 1967, Mrs Susan Dudley Smith (diss. 1979); two *s* one *d. Educ:* Eton. Commissioned Royal Horse Guards, 1956–66. *Heir: s* Hon. Roger Chetwode, *b* 29 May 1968. *Address:* 31 Moore Street, SW3. *T:* 01-584 6300. *Club:* White's.

CHETWYN, Robert; *b* 7 Sept. 1933; *s* of Frederick Reuben Suckling and Eleanor Lavinia (*née* Boffee). *Educ:* Rutlish, Merton, SW; Central Sch. of Speech and Drama. First appeared as actor with Dundee Repertory Co., 1952; subseq. in repertory at Hull, Alexandra Theatre, Birmingham, 1954; Birmingham Repertory Theatre, 1954–56; various TV plays, 1956–59; 1st prodn, Five Finger Exercise, Salisbury Playhouse, 1960; Dir of Prodns, Opera Hse, Harrogate, 1961–62; Artistic Dir, Ipswich Arts, 1962–64; Midsummer Night's Dream, transf. Comedy (London), 1964; Resident Dir, Belgrade (Coventry), 1964–66; Assoc. Dir, Mermaid, 1966, The Beaver Coat, three one-act plays by Shaw; There's a Girl in My Soup, Globe, 1966 and Music Box (NY), 1967; A Present for the Past, Edinburgh Fest., 1966; The Flip Side, Apollo, 1967; The Importance of Being Earnest, Haymarket, 1968; The Real Inspector Hound, Criterion, 1968; What the Butler Saw, Queens, 1968; The Country Wife, Chichester Fest., 1968; The Bandwaggon, Mermaid, 1968 and Sydney, 1970; Cannibal Crackers, Hampstead, 1969; When We are Married, Strand, 1970; Hamlet, in Rome, Zurich, Vienna, Antwerp, Cologne, then Cambridge (London), 1971; Parents Day, Globe, 1972; Restez Donc Jusq'au Petit Dejeuner, Belgium, 1973; Who's Who, Fortune, 1973; At the End of the Day, Savoy, 1973; Chez Nous, Globe, 1974; Qui est Qui, Belgium, 1974; The Doctor's Dilemma, Mermaid, 1975; Getting Away with Murder,

Comedy, 1976; Private Lives, Melbourne, 1976; It's All Right If I Do It, Mermaid, 1977; A Murder is Announced, Vaudeville, 1977; Arms and The Man, Greenwich, 1978; LUV, Amsterdam, 1978; Brimstone and Treacle, Open Space, 1979; Bent, Royal Court and Criterion, 1979; Pygmalion, National Theatre of Belgium, 1979; Moving, Queen's, 1980; Eastward Ho!, Mermaid, 1981. Has produced and directed for BBC (incl. series Private Shulz, by Jack Pullman) and ITV. *Publication:* (jtly) Theatre on Merseyside (Arts Council report), 1973. *Recreations:* tennis, films, gardening. *Address:* 1 Wilton Court, Eccleston Square, SW1V 1PH.

CHETWYND, family name of **Viscount Chetwynd.**

CHETWYND, 10th Viscount *cr* 1717 (Ireland); **Adam Richard John Casson Chetwynd;** Baron Rathdowne, 1717 (Ireland); New Business Manager, Prudential Assurance Co. of South Africa Ltd, Harland House Branch, Johannesburg, since 1978; *b* 2 Feb. 1935; *o s* of 9th Viscount and Joan Gilbert (*d* 1979), *o c* of late Herbert Alexander Casson, CSI, Ty'n-y-coed, Arthog, Merioneth; *S* father, 1965; *m* 1st, 1966, Celia Grace (marr. diss. 1974), *er d* of Comdr Alexander Robert Ramsay, DSC, RNVR, Fasque, Borrowdale, Salisbury, Rhodesia; two *s* one *d* ; 2nd, 1975, Angela May, *o d* of Jack Payne McCarthy, 21 Llanberis Grove, Nottingham. With Colonial Mutual Life Assurance Soc. Ltd, Salisbury, Rhodesia, then Johannesburg, 1968–78. *Educ:* Eton. 2nd Lieut Cameron Highlanders, 1954–56. Freeman, Guild of Air Pilots and Air Navigators. Qualifying Mem., Million Dollar Round Table, 1980; Holder, Internat. Quality Award, 1978–80. *Recreations:* shooting, flying. *Heir: s* Hon. Adam Douglas Chetwynd, *b* 26 Feb. 1969. *Address:* c/o J. G. Ouvry Esq., Lee Bolton & Lee, 1 The Sanctuary, Westminster, SW1P 3JT.

CHETWYND, Sir Arthur (Ralph Talbot), 8th Bt *cr* 1795; President, Brocton Hall Communications Ltd, Toronto, since 1978; Chairman, Board of Directors, Chetwynd Films Ltd, Toronto, since 1977; *b* Walhachin, BC, 28 Oct. 1913; *o s* of Hon. William Ralph Talbot Chetwynd, MC, MLA (*d* 1957) (*b* of 7th Bt), and of Frances Mary, *d* of late James Jupe; *S* uncle, 1972; *m* 1940, Marjory May McDonald, *er d* of late Robert Bruce Lang, Vancouver, BC, and Glasgow, Scotland; two *s. Educ:* Vernon Preparatory School, BC; University of British Columbia (Physical Education and Recreation). Prior to 1933, a rancher in interior BC; Games Master, Vernon Prep. School, BC, 1933–36, also Instructor, Provincial Physical Education and Recreation; Chief Instructor, McDonald's Remedial Institute, Vancouver, 1937–41; Director of Remedial Gymnastics, British Columbia Workmen's Compensation Board, 1942; RCAF, 1943–45; Associate in Physical and Health Education, Univ. of Toronto, also Publicity Officer, Univ. of Toronto Athletic Assoc., 1946–52. Dir, NZ Lamb Co. Ltd. Vice Chm., Toronto Branch, Royal Commonwealth Soc.; Member: Monarchist League of Canada; St George's Soc. of Canada; Dir, Duke of Edinburgh's Award in Canada. KCLJ. *Recreations:* golf, swimming. *Heir: er s* Robin John Talbot Chetwynd [*b* 21 Aug. 1941; *m* 1967, Heather Helen, *d* of George Bayliss Lothian; one *s* one *d*]. *Address:* 402-95 Thorncliffe Park Drive, Toronto, Ontario M4H 1L7. *T:* (416) 423-0367. *Clubs:* Naval and Military; Albany, Empire of Canada (Pres., 1974–75), Canadian, Board of Trade, Toronto Hunt (all in Toronto).

CHETWYND-TALBOT, family name of **Earl of Shrewsbury and Waterford.**

CHETWYND-TALBOT, Richard Michael Arthur; *see* Talbot.

CHEVELEY, Stephen William, OBE 1946; farmer; with Cheveley & Co., Agricultural Consultant, since 1959; *b* 29 March 1900; *s* of George Edward Cheveley and Arabella Cheveley; *m* 1926, Joan Hardy (*d* 1977); two *s* one *d. Educ:* Leeds Modern Sch.; Leeds Univ. (BSc 1922; MSc). Served War, HAC, 1917–18. Min. of Agric. Scholarship, Farm Costings Res., 1922–23. British Sulphate of Ammonia Fedn, 1924–26; ICI Ltd, 1927–59; Chm., ICI Central Agricultural Control, 1952–59; Man. Dir, Plant Protection Ltd, 1945–51. Min. of Agric., Technical Devel't Cttee, 1941–46; Chm., Foot and Mouth Res. Inst., 1950–58. Governor, Wye Coll., 1963–78, Fellow, 1977; Chm., Appeal Cttee, Centre for European Agric. Studies, 1973–75. Chm., Farmers' Club, 1956. Master, Worshipful Co. of Farmers, 1961. *Publications:* Grass Drying, 1937; Out of a Wilderness, 1939; A Garden Goes to War, 1940; (with O. T. W. Price) Capital in UK Agriculture, 1956. *Recreations:* farming, fishing, painting. *Address:* Dunorlan Farm, Tunbridge Wells, Kent. *T:* Tunbridge Wells 26632. *Clubs:* Athenaeum, Farmers'.

CHEVRIER, Hon. Lionel, CC (Canada) 1967; PC (Can.); QC (Can.); Member, Legal Firm of Geoffrion, Prud'homme, Chevrier, Cardinal, Marchessault, Mercier & Greenstein, 500 Place d'Armes, Montreal; *s* of late Joseph Elphège Chevrier and late Malvina DeRepentigny; *m* 1932, Lucienne, *d* of Thomas J. Brulé, Ottawa; three *s* three *d. Educ:* Cornwall College Institute; Ottawa Univ.; Osgoode Hall. Called to bar, Ontario, 1928; KC 1938; called to Bar, Quebec, 1957. MP for Stormont, Canada, 1935–54; MP for Montreal-Laurier, 1957–64. Dep. Chief Government Whip, 1940; Chm., Special Parly Sub-Cttee on War Expenditures, 1942; Parliamentary Asst to Minister of Munitions and Supply, 1943; Minister of Transport, 1945–54; Pres., St Lawrence Seaway Authority, 1954–57; Minister of Justice, 1963–64; High Commissioner in London, 1964–67. Delegate, Bretton Woods Conf., 1945; Chm., Canadian Delegn, UN General Assembly, Paris, 1948; Pres., Privy Council, Canada, 1957. Comr-Gen. for State Visits to Canada, 1967; Chairman: Canadian Economic Mission to Francophone Africa, 1968; Mission to study Canadian Consular Posts in USA, 1968; Seminar to study river navigation for Unitar, Buenos Aires, 1970. Hon. degrees: LLD: Ottawa, 1946; Laval, 1952; Queen's, 1956; DCL, Bishops', 1964. *Publication:* The St Lawrence Seaway, 1959. *Recreations:* walking and reading. *Address:* 500 Place d'Armes, Montreal 126, Canada.

CHEW, Victor Kenneth, TD 1958; Fellow of the Science Museum, London; *b* 19 Jan. 1915; *yr s* of Frederick and Edith Chew. *Educ:* Christ's Hospital; Christ Church, Oxford (Scholar). 1st class, Final Honours School of Natural Science (Physics), 1936; BA (Oxon) 1936, MA 1964. Asst Master, King's Sch., Rochester, 1936-38; Winchester Coll., 1938-40. Served War: Royal Signals, 1940-46. Asst Master, Shrewsbury Sch., 1946-48 and 1949-58; Lecturer in Education, Bristol Univ., 1948-49. Entered Science Museum as Asst Keeper, 1958; Deputy Keeper and Sec. to Advisory Council, 1967; Keeper, Dept of Physics, 1970-78. *Publications:* official publications of Science Museum. *Recreations:* choral singing, mountain walking, photography. *Address:* 701 Gilbert House, Barbican, EC2.

CHEWTON, Viscount; James Sherbrooke Waldegrave; *b* 8 Dec. 1940; *e s* of 12th Earl Waldegrave, *qv. Educ:* Eton Coll.; Trinity Coll., Cambridge. *Address:* West End Farm, Chewton Mendip, Bath. *Clubs:* Brooks's, Beefsteak.

CHEYNE, Major Sir Joseph (Lister Watson), 3rd Bt *cr* 1908; OBE 1976; Curator, Keats Shelley Memorial House, Rome, since 1976; *b* 10 Oct. 1914; *e s* of Sir Joseph Lister Cheyne, 2nd Bt, MC, and Nelita Manfield (*d* 1977), *d* of Andrew Pringle, Borgue; *S* father, 1957; *m* 1st, 1938, Mary Mort (marr. diss. 1955; she *d* 1959), *d* of late Vice-Adm. J. D. Allen, CB; one *s* one *d* ; 2nd, 1955, Cicely, *d* of late T. Metcalfe, Padiham, Lancs; two *s* one *d. Educ:* Stowe Sch.; Corpus Christi Coll., Cambridge. Major, The Queen's Westminsters (KRRC), 1943; Italian Campaign. 2nd Sec. (Inf.), British Embassy, Rome, 1968, 1st Sec., 1971, 1st Sec. (Inf.), 1973-76. *Heir: s* Patrick John Lister Cheyne [*b* 2 July 1941; *m* 1968, Helen Louise Trevor, *yr d* of Louis Smith, Southsea; one *s* three *d*]. *Address:* Leagarth, Fetlar, Shetland; Via Aventina 30, Rome, Italy. *T:* Rome 572238. *Clubs:* Boodles; Circolo della Caccia (Rome).

CHEYSSON, Claude, Officer Legion of Honour 1962; Croix de Guerre (5 times); Minister for External Relations, France, since 1981; *b* 13 April 1920; *s* of Pierre Cheysson and Sophie Funck-Brentano; *m* 1969, Danièle Schwarz; one *s* two *d* (and two *s* one *d* by former marrs). *Educ:* Coll. Stanislas, Paris; Ecole Polytechnique; Ecole Nationale d'Administration. Escaped from occupied France, 1943; Tank Officer, Free French Forces, France and Germany, 1944-45. Liaison Officer with German authorities, Bonn, 1948-52; Political Adviser to Viet Nam Govt, Saigon, 1952-53; Personal Adviser: to Prime Minister of France, Paris, 1954-55; to French Minister of Moroccan and Tunisian Affairs, 1956; Sec.-Gen., Commn for Techn. Cooperation in Africa, Lagos, Nairobi, 1957-62; Dir-Gen., Sahara Authority, Algiers, 1962-66; French Ambassador in Indonesia, 1966-69; Pres., Entreprise Minière et Chimique, 1970-73; European Comr (relations with Third World), 1973-81. Grand Cross, Nat. Orders of Guinea, Japan, Liberia, Portugal, Saudi Arabia and Tunisia, Grand Officer, Nat. Orders of Cameroun, Chad, Ivory Coast, Lebanon, Niger, Senegal, Togo, Upper Volta; Comdr, Nat. Orders of Central African Rep., Gabon, Indonesia, and Mali; US Presidential Citation. Dr *hc* Univ. of Louvain; Joseph Bech Prize, 1978. *Publications:* Une idée qui s'incarne, 1978; articles on Europe, and develt policies. *Recreation:* ski-ing. *Address:* 37 quai d'Orsay, 75007 Paris, France.

CHIANG KAI-SHEK, Madame (Mayling Soong Chiang); Chinese sociologist; *y d* of C. J. Soong; *m* 1927, Generalissimo Chiang Kai-Shek (*d* 1975). *Educ:* Wellesley Coll., USA. LHD, John B. Stetson Univ., Deland, Fla, Bryant Coll., Providence, RI, Hobart and William Smith Colls, Geneva, NY; LLD, Rutgers Univ., New Brunswick, NJ, Goucher Coll., Baltimore, MD, Wellesley Coll., Wellesley, Mass, Loyola Univ., Los Angeles, Cal., Russell Sage Coll., Troy, NY, Hahnemann Medical Coll., Philadelphia, Pa, Wesleyan Coll., Macon, Ga, Univ. of Michigan, Univ. of Hawaii; Hon. FRCS. First Chinese woman appointed Mem. Child Labor Commn; Inaugurated Moral Endeavor Assoc.; established schools in Nanking for orphans of Revolutionary Soldiers; former Mem. Legislative Yuan; served as Sec.-General of Chinese Commission on Aeronautical Affairs; Member Chinese Commission on Aeronautical Affairs; Director-General of the New Life Movement and Chairman of its Women's Advisory Council; Founder and Director: National Chinese Women's Assoc. for War Relief; National Assoc. for Refugee Children; Chinese Women's Anti-Aggression League; Huashing Children's Home; Cheng Hsin Medical Rehabilitation Center for Post Polio Crippled Children. Chm., Fu Jen Catholic University. Governor, Nat. Palace Museum. Frequently makes inspection tours to all sections of Free China where personally trained girl workers carry on war area and rural service work; accompanies husband on military campaigns; first Chinese woman to be decorated by National Govt of China. Recipient of highest military and Civil decorations; Hon. Chm., British United Aid to China Fund, China; Hon. Chm., Soc. for the Friends of the Wounded; Hon. President, American Bureau for Medical Aid to China; Patroness, International Red Cross Commn; Hon. President, Chinese Women's Relief Assoc. of New York; Hon. Chairman, Canadian Red Cross China Cttee; Hon. Chairman, Board of Directors, India Famine Relief Cttee; Hon. Mem., New York Zoological Soc.; Hon. Pres., Cttee for the Promotion of the Welfare of the Blind; Life Mem., San Francisco Press Club and Associated Countrywomen of the World;

Mem., Phi Beta Kappa, Eta Chapter; first Hon. Member, Bill of Rights Commemorative Society; Hon. Member, Filipino Guerrillas of Bataan Assoc. Medal of Honour, New York City Federation of Women's Clubs; YWCA Emblem; Gold Medal, New York Southern Soc.; Chi Omega Nat. Achievement Award for 1943; Gold Medal for distinguished services, National Institute for Social Sciences; Distinguished Service Award, Altrusa Internat. Assoc.; Churchman Fifth Annual Award, 1943; Distinguished Service Citation, All-American Conf. to Combat Communism, 1958; Hon. Lieut-Gen. US Marine Corps. *Publications:* China in Peace and War, 1939; China Shall Rise Again, 1939; This is Our China, 1940; We Chinese Women, 1941; Little Sister Su, 1943; Ten Eventful Years, for Encyclopædia Britannica, 1946; Album of Reproduction of Paintings, vol. I, 1952, vol. II, 1962; The Sure Victory, 1955; Madame Chiang Kai-Shek Selected Speeches, 1958-59; Madame Chiang Kai-shek Selected Speeches, 1965-66; Album of Chinese Orchid Paintings, 1971; Album of Chinese Bamboo Paintings, 1972; Album of Chinese Landscape Paintings, 1973; Album of Chinese Floral Paintings, 1974. *Address:* Shihlin, Taipei, Taiwan.

CHIASSON, Most Rev. Donat; *see* Moncton, Archbishop of, (RC).

CHIBNALL, Albert Charles, FRS 1937; PhD (London); ScD (Cantab); Fellow of Clare College, Cambridge; Fellow of the Imperial College of Science and Technology, London; *b* 28 Jan. 1894; *s* of G. W. Chibnall; *m* 1st, 1931 (wife *d* 1936); two *d* ; 2nd, 1947, Marjorie McCallum Morgan (*see* M. McC. Chibnall); one *s* one *d. Educ:* St Paul's Sch.; Clare Coll., Cambridge; Imperial Coll. of Science and Technology; Yale Univ., New Haven, Conn. 2nd Lieut, ASC 1914; Capt., 1915; attached RAF, 1917-19, served Egypt and Salonika. Huxley Medal, 1922; Imperial Coll. Travelling Fellow, 1922-23; Seessel Fellow, Yale Univ., 1923-24; Hon. Asst in Biochemistry, University Coll., London, 1924-30; Asst Prof. 1930-36, Prof. 1936-43, Emeritus Prof. 1943, of Biochemistry, Imperial Coll.; Sir William Dunn Prof. of Biochemistry, Univ. of Cambridge, 1943-49. Silliman Lectr, Yale Univ., 1938; Bakerian Lectr, Royal Society, 1942. Hon. Mem., Biochem. Soc.; Vice-Pres., Bucks Record Soc. Hon. DSc St Andrews, 1971. *Publications:* Protein Metabolism in the Plant, 1939; Richard de Badew and the University of Cambridge, 1315-1340, 1963; Sherington, fiefs and fields of a Buckinghamshire village, 1965; Beyond Sherington, 1979; papers in scientific journals on plant biochemistry. *Address:* 6 Millington Road, Cambridge. *T:* Cambridge 353923.

CHIBNALL, Marjorie McCallum, MA, DPhil; FSA; FBA 1978; Fellow of Clare Hall, Cambridge, since 1975; *b* 27 Sept. 1915; *d* of J. C. Morgan, MBE; *m* 1947, Prof. Albert Charles Chibnall, *qv* ; one *s* one *d* and two step *d. Educ:* Shrewsbury Priory County Girls' Sch.; Lady Margaret Hall, Oxford; Sorbonne, Paris. BLitt, MA, DPhil (Oxon); PhD (Cantab). Amy Mary Preston Read Scholar, Oxford, 1937-38; Goldsmiths' Sen. Student, 1937-39; Nursing Auxiliary, 1939; Susette Taylor Research Fellow, Lady Margaret Hall, Oxford, 1940-41; Asst Lectr, University Coll., Southampton, 1941-43; Asst Lectr, 1943-45, Lectr, 1945-47, in Medieval History, Univ. of Aberdeen; Lectr in History, later Fellow of Girton Coll., Cambridge, 1947-65; Research Fellow, Clare Hall, Cambridge, 1969-75; Leverhulme Emeritus Fellowship, 1982. Hon. DLitt Birmingham, 1979. *Publications:* The English Lands of the Abbey of Bec, 1946; Select Documents of the English Lands of the Abbey of Bec, 1951; The *Historia Pontificalis* of John of Salisbury, 1956; The Ecclesiastical History of Orderic Vitalis, 6 vols, 1969-80; Charters and Custumals of the Abbey of Holy Trinity Caen, 1982; numerous articles and reviews, principally in English and French historical jls. *Address:* Clare Hall, Cambridge. *T:* Cambridge 353923. *Club:* University Women's.

CHICHESTER, family name of **Marquess of Donegall.**

CHICHESTER, 9th Earl of, *cr* 1801; **John Nicholas Pelham;** Bt 1611; Baron Pelham of Stanmer, 1762; *b* (posthumous) 14 April 1944; *s* of 8th Earl of Chichester (killed on active service, 1944) and Ursula (she *m* 2nd, 1957, Ralph Gunning Henderson; marr. diss. 1971), *o d* of late Walter de Pannwitz, de Hartekamp, Bennebroek, Holland; *S* father, 1944; *m* 1975, Mrs June Marijke Hall. *Recreations:* music, flying. *Heir: kinsman* Richard Anthony Henry Pelham, *b* 1st Aug. 1952. *Address:* Little Durnford Manor, Salisbury, Wilts.

CHICHESTER, Bishop of, since 1974; **Rt. Rev. Eric Waldram Kemp,** MA Oxon, DD; *b* 27 April 1915; *o c* of Tom Kemp and Florence Lilian Kemp (*née* Waldram), Grove House, Waltham, Grimsby, Lincs; *m* 1953, Leslie Patricia, 3rd *d* of late Rt Rev. K. E. Kirk, sometime Bishop of Oxford; one *s* four *d. Educ:* Brigg Grammar Sch., Lincs; Exeter Coll., Oxford; St Stephen's House, Oxford. Deacon 1939; Priest 1940; Curate of St Luke, Southampton, 1939-41; Librarian of Pusey House, Oxford, 1941-46; Chaplain of Christ Church Oxford, 1943-46; Actg Chap., St John's Coll., Oxford, 1943-45; Fellow, Chaplain, Tutor, and Lectr in Theology and Medieval History, Exeter Coll., Oxford, 1946-69; Dean of Worcester, 1969-74. Exam. Chaplain: to Bp of Mon, 1942-45; to Bp of Southwark, 1946-50; to Bp of St Albans, 1946-69; to Bp of Exeter, 1949-69; to Bp of Lincoln, 1950-69. Proctor in Convocation for University of Oxford, 1949-69. Bp of Oxford's Commissary for Religious Communities, 1952-69; Chaplain to the Queen, 1967-69. Canon and Prebendary of Caistor in Lincoln Cathedral, 1952; Hon. Provincial Canon of Cape Town, 1960-; Bampton Lecturer, 1959-60. FRHistS 1951. *Publications:* (contributions to) Thy Household the Church, 1943; Canonization and Authority in the Western Church, 1948; Norman Powell Williams, 1954;

Twenty-five Papal Decretals relating to the Diocese of Lincoln (with W. Holtzmann), 1954; An Introduction to Canon Law in the Church of England, 1957; Life and Letters of Kenneth Escott Kirk, 1959; Counsel and Consent, 1961; The Anglican-Methodist conversations: A Comment from within, 1964; (ed) Man: Fallen and Free, 1969; Square Words in a Round World, 1980; contrib. to English Historical Review, Jl of Ecclesiastical History. *Recreations:* music, travel. *Address:* The Palace, Chichester, W Sussex PO19 1PY. *T:* Chichester 782161. *Club:* National Liberal.

CHICHESTER, Dean of; *see* Holtby, Very Rev. R. T.

CHICHESTER, Archdeacon of; *see* Hobbs, Ven. Keith.

CHICHESTER, Sir (Edward) John, 11th Bt *cr* 1641; *b* 14 April 1916; *s of* Comdr Sir Edward George Chichester, 10th Bt, RN, and late Phyllis Dorothy, *d* of late Henry F. Compton, Minstead Manor, Hants; *S* father, 1940; *m* 1950, Hon. Mrs Anne Rachel Pearl Moore-Gwyn, *widow* of Capt. Howel Moore-Gwyn, Welsh Guards, and *d* of 2nd Baron Montagu of Beaulieu and of Hon. Mrs Edward Pleydell-Bouverie; two *s* two *d* (and one *d* decd). *Educ:* Radley; RMC Sandhurst. Commissioned RSF, 1936. Patron of one living. Served throughout War of 1939-45. Was employed by ICI Ltd, 1950-60. A King's Foreign Service Messenger, 1947-50. Formerly Capt., Royal Scots Fusiliers and Lieut RNVR. *Heir:* s James Henry Edward Chichester, *b* 15 Oct. 1951. *Address:* Battramsley Lodge, Boldre, Lymington, Hants. *Club:* Naval.

CHICHESTER-CLARK, family name of **Baron Moyola.**

CHICHESTER-CLARK, Sir Robert, (Sir Robin Chichester-Clark), Kt 1974; Director: Alfred Booth and Co.; Welbeck Group Ltd; management consultant; *b* 10 Jan. 1928; *s* of late Capt. J. L. C. Chichester-Clark, DSO and Bar, DL, MP, and Mrs C. E. Brackenbury; *m* 1st, 1953, Jane Helen Goddard (marr. diss. 1972); one *s* two *d* ; 2nd, 1974, Caroline, *d* of Anthony Bull, *qv* ; two *s*. *Educ:* Royal Naval Coll.; Magdalene Coll., Cambridge (BA Hons Hist. and Law). Journalist, 1950; Public Relations Officer, Glyndebourne Opera, 1952; Asst to Sales Manager, Oxford Univ. Press, 1953-55. MP (UU) Londonderry City and Co., 1955-Feb. 1974; PPS to Financial Secretary to the Treasury, 1958; Asst Government Whip (unpaid), 1958-60; a Lord Comr of the Treasury, 1960-61; Comptroller of HM Household, 1961-64; Chief Opposition Spokesman on N Ireland, 1964-70, on Public Building and Works, 1965-70; Minister of State, Dept of Employment, 1972-74. Hon. FIWM 1972. *Recreations:* fishing, reading. *Club:* Brooks's.
See also Baron Moyola.

CHIEF RABBI; *see* Jakobovits, Rabbi Sir Immanuel.

CHIEPE, Hon. Gaositwe Keagakwa Tibe, PMS 1975; MBE 1962; FRSA; Minister for Mineral Resources and Water Affairs, since 1977; *b* 20 Oct. 1922; *d* of late T. Chiepe. *Educ:* Fort Hare, South Africa (BSc, EdDip); Bristol Univ., UK (MA (Ed)). Asst Educn Officer, 1948-53; Educn Officer and Schools Inspector, 1953-62; Sen. Educn Officer, 1962-65; Dep. Dir of Educn, 1965-67; Dir of Educn, 1968-70; Diplomat, 1970-; High Comr to UK and Nigeria, 1970-74; Ambassador: Denmark, Norway, Sweden, France and Germany, 1970-74; Belgium and EEC, 1973-74 Minister of Commerce and Industry, 1974-77. Member: Botswana Society; Botswana Girl Guide Assoc.; Internat. Fedn of University Women. Hon. LLD Bristol, 1972. FRSA 1973. *Recreations:* gardening, a bit of swimming (in Botswana), reading. *Address:* Ministry of Mineral Resources and Water Affairs, Private Bag 0018, Gaborone, Botswana. *Club:* Notwane (Botswana).

CHILCOT, John Anthony; Assistant Under-Secretary of State, Director of Personnel and Finance, Prison Department, Home Office, since 1980; *b* 22 April 1939; *s* of Henry William Chilcot and Catherine Chilcot (*née* Ashall); *m* 1964, Rosalind Mary Forster. *Educ:* Brighton Coll. (Lyon Scholar); Pembroke Coll., Cambridge (Open Scholar; MA). Assistant Principal, Home Office, 1963; Asst Private Sec. to Home Secretary (Rt Hon. Roy Jenkins), 1966; Principal, 1967; seconded to Civil Service Dept, 1969; Private Sec. to Head of Civil Service (late Baron Armstrong of Sanderstead), 1971; Asst Sec., Home Office, 1973; Principal Private Secretary to Home Secretary (Rt Hon. Merlyn Rees; Rt Hon. William Whitelaw), 1978-80. *Recreations:* reading, music and opera, travel, hill-walking. *Address:* Home Office, 50 Queen Anne's Gate, SW1.

CHILCOTT, C. M.; *see* Fordyce, C. M.

CHILD, Christopher Thomas; National President, Bakers' Union, 1968-77; Consultant to Baking Industry, Industrial Relations Officer and Training Officer, Baking Industry and Health Food Products; *b* 8 Jan. 1920; *s* of late Thomas William and Penelope Child; *m* 1941, Lilian Delaney; two *s* one *d*. *Educ:* Robert Ferguson Sch., Carlisle; Birmingham Coll. of Food and Domestic Science. Apprenticed baker, 1936-41; gained London City and Guilds final certificates in Breadmaking, Flour Confectionery and Bakery Science, 1951, and became Examiner in these subjects for CGLI. Full-time trade union official in Birmingham, 1958. Former Chairman: Nat. Council Baking Education; Nat. Joint Apprenticeship Council for Baking. Mem., Industrial Training Bd, Food, Drink and Tobacco, 1968-78; former Vice-Pres., EEC Food Group and Mem., EEC Cttees on Food Products, Vocational Training, and Food Legislation; former Sec., Jt Bakers' Unions of England,

Scotland and Ireland. Mem., TEC C4 programme Cttee, Hotel, Food, Catering and Institutional Management. *Recreations:* fishing, gardening, climbing in English Lake District. *Address:* 200 Bedford Road, Letchworth, Herts SG6 4EA. *T:* Letchworth 72170.

CHILD, Clifton James, OBE 1949; MA, PhM, FRHistS; Administrative Officer, Cabinet Office Historical Section, 1969-76, retired; *b* Birmingham, 20 June 1912; *s* of late Joseph and Georgina Child; *m* 1938, Hilde Hurwitz; two *s*. *Educ:* Moseley Grammar Sch.; Universities of Birmingham, Berlin and Wisconsin. Univ. of Birmingham: Entrance Schol., 1929; Kenrick Prizeman, 1930; BA 1st class hons, 1932; Francis Corder Clayton Research Schol., 1932-34; MA 1934. Univ. of Wisconsin: Commonwealth Fund Fellow, 1936-38; PhM 1938. Educn Officer, Lancs Community Council, 1939-40. Joined Foreign Office, 1941; Head of American Section, FO Research Dept, 1946-58; African Section, 1958-62; Dep. Librarian and Departmental Record Officer, 1962; Librarian and Keeper of the Papers, FO, 1965-69; Cabinet Office, 1969-76. FRHistS 1965. *Publications:* The German-Americans in Politics, 1939; (with Arnold Toynbee and others) Hitler's Europe, 1954; contribs to learned periodicals in Britain and US. *Recreations:* gardening, foreign travel. *Address:* Westcroft, Westhall Road, Warlingham, Surrey. *T:* Upper Warlingham 2540.

CHILD, Sir (Coles John) Jeremy, 3rd Bt *cr* 1919; actor; *b* 20 Sept. 1944; *s* of Sir Coles John Child, 2nd Bt, and Sheila (*d* 1964), *e d* of Hugh Mathewson; *S* father, 1971; *m* 1971, Deborah Jane (*née* Snelling) (marr. diss. 1976); one *d* ; *m* 1978, Jan, *y d* of B. Todd, Kingston upon Thames; one *s* one *d*. *Educ:* Eton; Univ. of Poitiers (Dip. in Fr.). Trained at Bristol Old Vic Theatre Sch., 1963-65; Bristol Old Vic, 1965-66; repertory at Windsor, Canterbury and Colchester; Conduct Unbecoming, Queen's, 1970; appeared at Royal Court, Mermaid and Bankside Globe, 1973; Oh Kay, Westminster, 1974; Donkey's Years, Globe, 1977; Hay Fever, Lyric, Hammersmith, 1980; *films include:* Privilege, 1967; Oh What a Lovely War!, 1967; The Breaking of Bumbo, 1970; Young Winston, 1971; The Stud, 1976; Quadrophenia, 1978; Sir Henry at Rawlinson's End, 1979; Chanel Solitaire, 1980; High Road to China, 1982; *TV series:* Father, Dear Father, Glittering Prizes, Wings, Backs to the Land, Edward and Mrs Simpson, When the Boat Comes In, Sapphire and Steel, Play for Tomorrow, Bird of Prey, Crown Court. *Recreations:* travel, squash, flying, photography. *Heir:* s Coles John Alexander Child, *b* 10 May 1982. *Address:* 26 Madrid Road, Barnes, SW13. *Club:* Roehampton.

CHILD, Sir Jeremy; *see* Child, Sir C. J. J.

CHILD, Ven. Kenneth; Archdeacon of Sudbury since 1970; *b* 6 March 1916; *s* of late James Child, Wakefield; *m* 1955, Jane, *d* of late G. H. B. Turner and of Mrs Turner, Bolton; one *s* two *d*. *Educ:* Queen Elizabeth's School, Wakefield; University of Leeds (BA); College of the Resurrection, Mirfield. Deacon 1941, Priest 1942, Manchester; Curate of St Augustine, Tonge Moor, 1941-44; Chaplain to the Forces, 1944-47; Vicar of Tonge Moor, 1947-55; Chaplain of Guy's Hospital, 1955-59; Rector of Newmarket, 1959-69; Rector of Great and Little Thurlow with Little Bradley, 1969-80; Rural Dean of Newmarket, 1963-70. Proctor in Convocation, 1964-; Hon. Canon of St Edmundsbury, 1968-. Hon. CF, 1947. *Publications:* Sick Call, 1965; In His Own Parish, 1970. *Recreation:* travel. *Address:* 6/7 College Street, Bury St Edmunds, Suffolk. *T:* Bury St Edmunds 703035. *Club:* Subscription Rooms (Newmarket).

CHILD-VILLIERS, family name of **Earl of Jersey.**

CHILDS, Rt. Rev. Derrick Greenslade; *see* Monmouth, Bishop of.

CHILDS, Hubert, CMG 1951; OBE 1943; *b* 6 July 1905; 3rd *s* of late Dr W. M. Childs, first Vice-Chancellor of the University of Reading. *Educ:* Oakham Sch.; University College, Oxford. Colonial Administrative Service, Nigeria, 1928-46, Sierra Leone, 1946-58. On Military service, 1941-46. Chief Comr, Protectorate, Sierra Leone, 1950-58. UK Plebiscite Administrator for Southern Cameroons, 1960-61. *Address:* c/o National Westminster Bank, Newbury, Berks.

CHILE, Bishop of, since 1977; **Rt. Rev. Colin Frederick Bazley;** *b* 27 June 1935; *s* of Reginald Samuel Bazley and Isabella Davies; *m* 1960, Barbara Helen Griffiths; three *d*. *Educ:* Birkenhead School; St Peter's Hall, Oxford (MA); Tyndale Hall, Bristol. Deacon 1959, priest 1960; Assistant Curate, St Leonard's, Bootle, 1959-62; Missionary of S American Missionary Society in Chile, 1962-69; Rural Dean of Chol-Chol, 1962-66; Archdeacon of Temuco, 1966-69; Assistant Bishop for Cautin and Malleco, Dio. Chile, Bolivia and Peru, 1969-75; Assistant Bishop for Santiago, 1975-77; Bishop of Chile, Bolivia and Peru, 1977; diocese divided, Oct. 1977; Bishop of Chile and Bolivia until Oct. 1981; Presiding Bishop of the Anglican Council for South America, 1977. *Recreations:* football (Liverpool supporter) and fishing on camping holidays. *Address:* Iglesia Anglicana, Casilla 675, Santiago, Chile. *T:* 2292158.

CHILSTON, 4th Viscount *cr* 1911, of Boughton Malherbe; **Alastair George Akers-Douglas;** Baron Douglas of Baads, 1911; film producer; *b* 5 Sept. 1946; *s* of Ian Stanley Akers-Douglas (*d* 1952) (*g s* of 1st Viscount) and of Phyllis Rosemary (who *m* 2nd, John Anthony Cobham Shaw, MC), *d* of late Arthur David Clere Parsons; *S* cousin, 1982; *m* 1971, Juliet Anne, *d* of Lt-Col Nigel Lovett, Glos Regt; three *s*. *Educ:* Eton College; Madrid Univ.

Recreation: sailing. *Heir:* s Hon. Oliver Ian Akers-Douglas, b 13 Oct. 1973. *Address:* The Old Rectory, Twyford, near Winchester, Hants. *T:* Twyford 712300.

CHILTON, Air Marshal Sir (Charles) Edward, KBE 1959 (CBE 1945); CB 1951; RAF (retired); o s of J. C. Chilton; m 1st, 1929, Betty Ursula (d 1963), 2nd d of late Bernard Temple Wrinch; one s; 2nd, 1964, Joyce Cornforth. Royal Air Force general duties branch; Air Commodore, 1950; Air Vice-Marshal, 1954; Air Marshal, 1959. Dep. Air Officer i/c Administration, Air Command, SE Asia, 1944; AOC Ceylon, 1946; Imperial Defence Coll., 1951; AOC Gibraltar, 1952; Asst Chief of the Air Staff (Policy), 1953-54; SASO, HQ Coastal Command, 1955; AOC Royal Air Force, Malta, and Dep. Comdr-in-Chief (Air), Allied Forces Mediterranean, 1957-59; AOC-in-C, Coastal Command and Maritime Air Commander Eastern Atlantic Area, and Commander Maritime Air, Channel and Southern North Sea, 1959-62. Consultant and Dir, IBM (Rentals) UK, 1963-78. Specialist navigator (Air Master navigator certificate) and Fellow (Vice-Pres. 1949-51, 1959-61, 1963-65), Royal Institute of Navigation. Pres. RAF Rowing Club, 1956; Vice-Adm. and Hon. Life Mem. RAF Sailing Assoc.; Hon. Vice-Pres. RAF Swimming Assoc. Vice Patron, Regular Forces Employment Assoc. FInstD. Grand Cross of Prince Henry the Navigator (Portugal), 1960; Order of Polonia Restituta, Poland, 1980. *Publications:* numerous contributions to Service and other journals, on maritime-air operations and air navigation, and biographical papers on Rear-Adm. Sir Murray Sueter, CB, and Wing Comdr J. C. Porte, CMG. *Recreations:* sailing, sea fishing and country walking. *Address:* 11 Charles House, Phyllis Court Drive, Henley-on-Thames, Oxon. *Clubs:* Royal Air Force; (Vice-Patron) Royal Gibraltar Yacht; Phyllis Court (Henley).

CHILTON, Brig. Sir Frederick Oliver, Kt 1969; CBE 1963 (OBE 1957); DSO 1941 and bar 1944; Chairman, Repatriation Commission, Australia, 1958-70; b 23 July 1905. *Educ:* Univ. of Sydney (BA, LLB). Solicitor, NSW, 1929. Late AIF; served War of 1939-45, Libya, Greece, New Guinea and Borneo (despatches, DSO and bar); Controller of Joint Intelligence, 1946-48; Asst Sec., Dept of Defence, Australia, 1948-50; Dep. Sec., 1950-58. *Address:* Clareville Beach, NSW, Australia. *Clubs:* Melbourne, Union, Naval and Military (Melbourne); Imperial Service (Sydney).

CHILVER, Sir (Amos) Henry; see Chilver, Sir H.

CHILVER, Elizabeth Millicent, (Mrs R. C. Chilver); Principal of Lady Margaret Hall, Oxford, 1971-79, Honorary Fellow, 1979; b 3 Aug. 1914; o d of late Philip Perceval Graves and late Millicent Graves (née Gilchrist); m 1937, Richard Clementson Chilver, qv. *Educ:* Benenden Sch., Cranbrook; Somerville Coll., Oxford (Hon. Fellow, 1977). Journalist, 1937-39; temp. Civil Servant, 1939-45; Daily News Ltd, 1945-47; temp. Principal and Secretary, Colonial Social Science Research Council and Colonial Economic Research Cttee, Colonial Office, 1948-57; Director, Univ. of Oxford Inst. of Commonwealth Studies, 1957-61; Senior Research Fellow, Univ. of London Inst. of Commonwealth Studies, 1961-64; Principal, Bedford Coll., Univ. of London, 1964-71, Fellow, 1974. Mem. Royal Commn on Medical Education, 1965-68. Trustee, British Museum, 1970-75; Mem. Governing Body, SOAS, Univ. of London, 1975-80. Médaille de la Reconnaissance française, 1945. *Publications:* articles on African historical and political subjects. *Address:* 108 Clifton Hill, NW8. *T:* 01-624 2702.

CHILVER, Sir Henry, Kt 1978; FRS 1982; FEng 1977; FBIM 1976; Vice-Chancellor, Cranfield Institute of Technology, since 1970; Chairman, Advisory Council for Applied Research and Development (ACARD), since 1982; Hon. Fellow, Corpus Christi College, Cambridge; Director: English China Clays Ltd, since 1973; National Westminster Bank, South-East Region, since 1975; Delta Metal Co., since 1977; Powell Duffryn Co., since 1979; TR Technology Investment Trust, since 1982; b 30 Oct. 1926; e s of A. H. Chilver and A. E. Mack; m 1959, Claudia M. B. Grigson, MA, MB, BCh, o d of Sir Wilfrid Grigson; three s two d. *Educ:* Southend High Sch.; Bristol Univ. (Albert Fry Prize 1947). Structural Engineering Asst, British Railways, 1947; Asst Lecturer, 1950, Lecturer, 1952, in Civil Engineering, Bristol Univ.; Demonstrator, 1954, Lectr, 1956, in Engineering, Cambridge Univ.; Fellow of Corpus Christi Coll., Cambridge, 1958-61; Chadwick Prof. of Civil Engineering, UCL, 1961-69. Director: Centre for Environmental Studies, 1967-69; Node Course (for civil service and industry), 1974-75; De La Rue Co., 1973-81; SKF (UK), 1972-80. Chairman: PO, 1980-81; Higher Educn Review Body, NI, 1978-81; Univs' Computer Bd, 1975-78; RAF Trng and Educn Adv. Cttee, 1976-80; Adv. Council, RMCS, Shrivenham, 1978-; Working Gp on Advanced Ground Transport, 1978-81; Electronics EDC, 1980-. Member: Ferrybridge Enquiry Cttee, 1965; Management Cttee, Inst. of Child Health, 1965-69; ARC, 1967-70 and 1972-75; SRC, 1970-74; Beds Educn Cttee, 1970-74; Planning and Transport Res. Adv. Council, 1972-79; Cttee for Ind. Technologies, 1972-76; ICE Special Cttee on Educn and Trng, 1973 (Chm.); CNAA, 1973-76; Royal Commn on Environmental Pollution, 1976-81; Standing Commn on Energy and the Environment, 1978-81; Adv. Bd for Res. Councils, 1982-. Vice-Pres., Standing Conf. on Schools Sci. and Technol.; Assessor, Inquiry on Lorries, People and the Envt, 1979-80. Pres., Inst. of Management Services, 1982-; Vice-Pres., ICE, 1981-; Mem., Smeatonian Soc. of Civil Engrs. Member Council: Birkbeck Coll., 1980-82; Cheltenham Coll., 1980-. STC Communications Lectr, 1981. Telford Gold Medal, ICE, 1962; Coopers Hill War Meml Prize, ICE, 1977. Hon. DSc Leeds. *Publications:* Problems in Engineering Structures (with R. J. Ashby),

1958; Strength of Materials (with J. Case), 1959; Thin-walled Structures (ed), 1967; papers on structural theory in engineering journals. *Address:* Cranfield Institute of Technology, Cranfield, Bedford MK43 0AL. *T:* Bedford 750111. *Clubs:* Athenæum, United Oxford & Cambridge University.

CHILVER, Richard Clementson, CB 1952; b 1912; yr s of Arthur Farquhar Chilver; m 1937, Elizabeth Chilver, qv. *Educ:* Winchester; New Coll., Oxford. Entered HM Civil Service, 1934; Under-Sec., Air Ministry, 1946; Deputy Sec., Cabinet Office, 1955; MoD, 1957; Min. of Transport, 1960; DOE, 1965-72. Administrative Director, Insurance Technical Bureau, 1972-76. *Address:* 108 Clifton Hill, NW8. *T:* 01-624 2702.
See also B. Davidson.

CHINNERY, Charles Derek; Controller, Radio 1, BBC, since 1978; b 27 April 1925; s of Percy Herbert and Frances Dorothy Chinnery; m 1953, Doreen Grace Clarke. *Educ:* Gosforth Grammar School. Youth in training, BBC, 1941; RAF Cadet Pilot, 1943. BBC: Technical Asst, 1947; Programme Engineer, 1948; Studio Manager, 1950; Producer, 1952; Executive Producer, 1967; Head of Radio 1, 1972. *Recreation:* DIY. *Address:* c/o BBC, Broadcasting House, W1. *T:* 01-580 4468. *Club:* BBC.

CHIONA, Most Rev. James; see Blantyre, Archbishop of, (RC).

CHIPIMO, Elias Marko; Chairman, Standard Bank Zambia Ltd, 1976-80 (Deputy Chairman, 1975); b 23 Feb. 1931; s of Marko Chipimo, Zambia (then Northern Rhodesia); m 1959, Anna Joyce Nkole Konie; four s three d. *Educ:* St Canisius, Chikuni, Zambia; Munali; Fort Hare Univ. Coll., SA; University Coll. of Rhodesia and Nyasaland. Schoolmaster, 1959-63; Sen. Govt Administrator, 1964-67; High Comr for Zambia in London, and Zambian Ambassador to the Holy See, 1968-69; Perm. Sec., Min. of Foreign Affairs, 1969. Chairman: Zambia Stock Exchange Council, 1970-72; Zambia Nat. Bldg Soc., 1970-71; Dep. Chm., Development Bank of Zambia Ltd, 1973-75; Director: Zambia Airways Corp., 1975-81; Zambia Bata Shoe Co. Ltd, 1977-. Mem., Nat Council for Sci. Res., 1977-. Pres., Lusaka Branch, Zambia Red Cross, 1970-75; Vice-Pres., Zambia Red Cross Soc., 1976-; Mem., Zambia Univ. Council, 1970-76; Dir, Internat. Sch. of Lusaka, 1970-76. Cllr, Lusaka City Council, 1974-80. *Publication:* Our Land and People, 1966. *Recreations:* rose gardening, reading, general literature, linguistics, philosophy, politics, economics, discussions, chess, growing roses. *Address:* PO Box 32115, Lusaka, Zambia.

CHIPP, David Allan; Editor in Chief of The Press Association since 1969; b 6 June 1927; s of late Thomas Ford Chipp and late Isabel Mary Ballinger; unmarried. *Educ:* Geelong Grammar Sch., Australia; King's Coll., Cambridge (MA). Served with Middlesex Regt, 1944-47; Cambridge, 1947-50. Joined Reuters as Sports Reporter, 1950; Correspondent for Reuters: in SE Asia, 1953-55; in Peking, 1956-58; various managerial positions in Reuters, 1960-68; Editor of Reuters, 1968. *Recreations:* coaching rowing (Steward of Henley Royal Regatta, 1975); listening to Wagner. *Address:* Mile House, Ibstone, Bucks. *T:* Turville Heath 348. *Clubs:* Garrick; Leander (Henley-on-Thames).

CHIPPERFIELD, Geoffrey Howes; Deputy Secretary, Department of the Environment, since 1982; b 20 April 1933; s of Nelson Chipperfield and Eleanor Chipperfield; m 1959, Gillian James; two s. *Educ:* Cranleigh; New Coll., Oxford. Called to the Bar, Gray's Inn, 1955. Joined Min. of Housing and Local Govt, 1956; Harkness Fellow, Inst. of Govtl Studies, Univ. of Calif, Berkeley, 1962-63; Principal Private Sec., Minister of Housing, 1968-70; Sec., Greater London Develt Plan Inquiry, 1970-73; Under Sec., 1976. *Recreations:* reading, gardening. *Address:* Department of the Environment, 2 Marsham Street, SW1. *Club:* United Oxford & Cambridge University.

CHIRAC, Jacques René; President, Rassemblement des Français pour la République, 1976-81 and since 1982; Mayor of Paris, since 1977; b Paris, 29 Nov. 1932; s of François Chirac and Marie-Louise (née Valette); m 1956, Bernadette Chodron de Courcel; two s. *Educ:* Lycée Carnot and Lycée Louis-le-Grand, Paris; Ecole Nationale d'Administration. Diploma of Inst. of Polit. Studies, Paris, and of Summer Sch., Harvard Univ., USA. Served Army in Algeria. Auditor, Cour des Comptes, 1959; Head Dept: Sec.-Gen. of Govt, 1962; Private Office of Georges Pompidou, 1962-67; Counsellor, Cour des Comptes, 1965; State Sec.: Employment Problems, 1967-68; Economy and Finance, 1968-71; Minister for Parly Relations, 1971-72; Minister for Agriculture and Rural Development, 1972-74; Home Minister, March-May 1974; Prime Minister, 1974-76; Sec.-Gen., UDR, Dec. 1974-June 1975. Deputy from Corrèze, elected 1967, 1968, 1973, 1976 (UDR), 1978 (RFR), and 1981; Member from Meymac, Conseil Général of Corrèze, 1968-, Pres. 1970-79. Mem., European Parlt, 1979-80. Holds several civil and military awards, etc. *Publication:* a thesis on development of Port of New Orleans, 1954. *Address:* 57 rue Boissière, 75116 Paris, France.

CHISHOLM, Prof. Alexander William John; Research Professor in Engineering, University of Salford, since 1982; b 18 April 1922; s of Thomas Alexander Chisholm and Maude Mary Chisholm (née Robinson); m 1945, Aline Mary (née Eastwood); one s one d. *Educ:* Brentwood Sch., Essex; Northampton Polytechnic; Manchester Coll. of Science and Technology; Royal Technical Coll., Salford (BSc(Eng) London). CEng, FIMechE, FIProdE. Section Leader, Res. Dept, Metropolitan Vickers Electrical Co. Ltd, 1944-49; Sen. Scientific Officer, then Principal Scientific Officer, Nat. Engrg

Lab., 1949-57; UK Scientific Mission, British Embassy, USA, 1952-54; Head of Dept of Mechanical Engrg, then Prof. of Mechanical Engrg, Royal Coll. of Advanced Technology, Salford, 1957-67; Prof. of Mech. Engineering, Univ. of Salford, 1967-82 (Chm., Industrial Centre, 1962-82). Visitor, Cambridge Univ. Engrg Dept and Vis. Fellow, Wolfson Coll., 1973-74. Chm., Industrial Admin and Engrg Prodn Gp, IMechE, 1960-62. Nat. Council for Technological Awards: Chm., Mechanical/Prodn Engrg Cttee, 1960-63; Vice-Chm., Bd of Studies in Engrg and Governor, 1963-65. Member: Technology Cttee, UGC, 1969-74; Council, Internat. Inst. of Prodn Engrg Res., 1972-75 (Chm., UK Bd, 1977-); Engrg Profs Conf. (Chm., 1976-80); Court, Cranfield Inst. of Technology, 1974-. Whitworth Prize, IMechE, 1965. *Publications:* numerous on production process technology, manufacturing systems, organization of industrial research, internat. comparisons of educn and training of engineers. *Recreations:* hill walking, sailing. *Address:* 12 Legh Road, Prestbury, Macclesfield, Cheshire SK10 4HX. *T:* Prestbury 829412. *Club:* Athenæum.

CHISHOLM, Archibald Hugh Tennent, CBE 1946; MA; *b* 17 Aug. 1902; 2nd *s* of late Hugh Chisholm and Mrs Chisholm (*née* Harrison), Rush Park, Co. Antrim; *m* 1939, Josephine, *e d* of J. E. Goudge, OBE, ICS; one *s* one *d* (and one *d* decd). *Educ:* Westminster; Christ Church, Oxford. Wall Street Journal of NY, 1925-27; The British Petroleum Co. (then Anglo-Persian/Anglo-Iranian Oil Co.), Iran and Kuwait, 1928-36 and London, 1945-72. Editor of The Financial Times, 1937-40; Army, 1940-45 (despatches twice, CBE). FZS; FInstPet. Chevalier, Légion d'Honneur. *Publication:* The First Kuwait Oil Concession Agreement: a Record of the Negotiations, 1911-1934, 1975. *Address:* 27 Strawberry Hill Road, Twickenham, Mddx. *T:* 01-892 6545. *Clubs:* Athenæum, Naval and Military, MCC; Cork and County.

CHISHOLM, Prof. Michael Donald Inglis; Professor of Geography, University of Cambridge, since 1976; Professorial Fellow, St Catharine's College, Cambridge, since 1976; *b* 10 June 1931; *s* of M. S. and A. W. Chisholm; *m* 1959, Edith Gretchen Emma (*née* Hoof) (marr. diss. 1981); one *s* two *d*. *Educ:* St Christopher Sch., Letchworth; St Catharine's Coll., Cambridge (MA). MA Oxon. Nat. Service Commn, RE, 1950-51. Deptl Demonstrator, Inst. for Agric. Econs, Oxford, 1954-59; Asst Lectr, then Lectr in Geog., Bedford Coll., London, 1960-64; Vis. Sen. Lectr in Geog., Univ. of Ibadan, 1964-65; Lectr, then Reader in Geog., Univ. of Bristol, 1965-72; Prof. of Economic and Social Geography, Univ. of Bristol, 1972-76. Associate, Economic Associates Ltd, consultants, 1965-77; Mem. SSRC, and Chm. of Cttees for Human Geography and Planning, 1967-72; Member: Local Govt Boundary Commn for England, 1971-78; Develt Commn, 1981-. Mem. Council, Inst. of British Geographers, 1961 and 1962, Junior Vice-Pres., 1977, Sen. Vice-Pres., 1978, Pres. 1979. Conservator of River Cam, 1979-. Gill Memorial Prize, RGS, 1969. Geography Editor for Hutchinson Univ. Lib., 1973-. *Publications:* Rural Settlement and Land Use: an essay in location, 1962; Geography and Economics, 1966; (ed jtly) Regional Forecasting, 1971; (ed jtly) Spatial Policy Problems of the British Economy, 1971; Research in Human Geography, 1971; (ed) Resources for Britain's Future, 1972; (jtly) Freight Flows and Spatial Aspects of the British Economy, 1973; (jtly) The Changing Pattern of Employment, 1973; (ed jtly) Studies in Human Geography, 1973; (ed jtly) Processes in Physical and Human Geography: Bristol Essays, 1975; Human Geography: Evolution or Revolution?, 1975; papers in Farm Economist, Oxford Econ. Papers, Trans Inst. British Geographers, Geography, Applied Statistics, Area, etc. *Recreations:* gardening, swimming, theatre, opera, interior design. *Address:* Department of Geography, Downing Place, Cambridge CB2 3EN.

CHISHOLM, Roderick Æneas, CBE 1946; DSO 1944; DFC and bar; AE; ARCS; BSc; *b* 23 Nov. 1911; *s* of Edward Consitt Chisholm and Edith Maud Mary Cary Elwes; *m* 1945, Phillis Mary Sanchia, *d* of late Geoffrey A. Whitworth, CBE; one *s* two *d*. *Educ:* Ampleforth Coll.; Imperial Coll. of Science and Technology, London. AAF, 1932-40; Royal Air Force, 1940-46 (Air Cdre). *Publication:* Cover of Darkness, 1953. *Address:* Ladywell House, Alresford, Hants.

CHISWELL, Rt. Rev. Peter; see Armidale, Bishop of.

CHISWELL, Maj.-Gen. Peter Irvine, CBE 1976 (OBE 1972; MBE 1965); Commander, Land Forces Northern Ireland, since 1982; *b* 19 April 1930; *s* of late Col Henry Thomas Chiswell, OBE (late RAMC) and of Gladys Beatrice Chiswell; *m* 1958, Felicity Philippa, *d* of R. F. Martin, Esher, Surrey; two *s. Educ:* All hallows School; RMA Sandhurst. Commissioned Devonshire Regt, 1951; transf. Parachute Regt, 1958; DAAG HQ Berlin Inf. Bde, 1963-65; Brigade Major, 16 Para Bde, 1967-68; GSO1 (DS), Staff Coll., 1968-69; CO 3 Para, 1969-71; Col GS (Army Training), 1971-74; Comdr British Contingent DCOS UN Force Cyprus, 1974-76; Comdr, 44 Para Bde, 1976-78; ACOS (Operations), HQ Northern Army Gp, 1978-81. *Recreations:* travel and sailing. *Address:* British Forces Post Office 825.

CHITNIS, family name of **Baron Chitnis.**

CHITNIS, Baron *cr* 1977 (Life Peer), of Ryedale, N Yorks; **Pratap Chidamber Chitnis;** Chief Executive and Director, Joseph Rowntree Social Service Trust, since 1975 (Secretary, 1969-75); *b* 1 May 1936; *s* of late Chidamber N. Chitnis and Lucia Mallik; *m* 1964, Anne Brand; one *s* decd. *Educ:* Penryn Sch.; Stonyhurst Coll.; Univs of Birmingham (BA) and Kansas

(MA). Admin. Asst, Nat. Coal Board, 1958-59; Liberal Party Organisation: Local Govt Officer, 1960-62; Agent, Orpington Liberal Campaign, 1962; Trng Officer, 1962-64; Press Officer, 1964-66; Head of Liberal Party Organisation, 1966-69. Mem., Community Relations Commn, 1970-77; Chm., BBC Immigrants Programme Adv. Cttee, 1979- (Mem., 1972-77). *Publications:* Local Government Handbook, 1960; (ed) Liberal Election Agents Handbook, 1962. *Address:* Beverley House, Shipton Road, York. *T:* York 25744.

CHITTY, Beryl; see Chitty, M. B.

CHITTY, (Margaret) Beryl, CMG 1977; HM Diplomatic Service, retired; Appeal Director, St Peter's College, Oxford, since 1982; *b* 2 Dec. 1917; *d* of Wilfrid and Eleanor Holdgate; *m* 1949, Keith Chitty, FRCS (*d* 1958). *Educ:* Belvedere Sch. (GPDST), Liverpool; St Hugh's Coll., Oxford (BA, MA; Hon. Fellow, 1982). Dominions Office, 1940; Private Sec. to Parly Under-Sec. of State, 1943-45; Principal, 1945; CRO, 1947-52; First Sec., Commonwealth Office, 1958; UK Mission to UN, New York, 1968-70; FCO, 1970-71; Dep. British High Comr in Jamaica, 1971-75; Head of Commonwealth Co-ord. Dept, FCO, 1975-77. Appeal Sec., St Hugh's Coll., Oxford, 1978-81. Non-Press Mem., Press Council, 1978-80. Mem., Governing Body, Queen Elizabeth House, Oxford, 1977-80. *Address:* 79 Bainton Road, Oxford OX2 7AG.

CHITTY, Susan Elspeth, (Lady Chitty); author; *b* 18 Aug. 1929; *d* of Rudolph Glossop and Mrs E. A. Hopkinson; *m* 1951, Sir Thomas Willes Chitty, Bt, *qv* ; one *s* three *d. Educ:* Godolphin Sch., Salisbury; Somerville Coll., Oxford. Mem. editorial staff, Vogue, 1952-53; subseq. journalist, reviewer, broadcaster and lecturer. *Publications:* novels: Diary of a Fashion Model, 1958; White Huntress, 1963; My Life and Horses, 1966; *biographies:* The Woman who wrote Black Beauty, 1972; The Beast and the Monk, 1975; Charles Kingsley and North Devon, 1976; Gwen John 1876-1939, 1981; *non-fiction:* (with Thomas Hinde) On Next to Nothing, 1976; (with Thomas Hinde) The Great Donkey Walk, 1977; *edited:* The Intelligent Woman's Guide to Good Taste, 1958; The Puffin Book of Horses, 1975; The Young Rider, 1979. *Recreations:* riding, travel. *Address:* Bow Cottage, West Hoathly, Sussex RH19 4QF. *T:* Sharpthorne 810269.

CHITTY, Sir Thomas Willes, 3rd Bt *cr* 1924; author (as Thomas Hinde); *b* 2 March 1926; *e s* of Sir (Thomas) Henry Willes Chitty, 2nd Bt, and Ethel Constance (*d* 1971), *d* of S. H. Gladstone, Darley Ash, Bovingdon, Herts; *S* father, 1955; *m* 1951, Susan Elspeth (see S. E. Chitty); one *s* three *d. Educ:* Winchester; University Coll., Oxford. Royal Navy, 1944-47. Shell Petroleum Co., 1953-60. Granada Arts Fellow, Univ. of York, 1964-65; Visiting Lectr, Univ. of Illinois, 1965-67; Vis. Prof., Boston Univ., 1969-70. *Publications:* novels: Mr Nicholas, 1952; Happy as Larry, 1957; For the Good of the Company, 1961; A Place Like Home, 1962; The Cage, 1962; Ninety Double Martinis, 1963; The Day the Call Came, 1964; Games of Chance, 1965; The Village, 1966; High, 1968; Bird, 1970; Generally a Virgin, 1972; Agent, 1974; Our Father, 1975; Daymare, 1980; *non-fiction:* (with wife, as Susan Hinde) On Next to Nothing, 1976; (with Susan Chitty) The Great Donkey Walk, 1977; The Cottage Book, 1979; *autobiography:* Sir Henry and Sons, 1980; *biography:* A Field Guide to the English Country Parson, 1982; *anthology:* Spain, 1963. *Heir: s* Andrew Edward Willes Chitty, *b* 20 Nov. 1953. *Address:* Bow Cottage, West Hoathly, Sussex RH19 4QF. *T:* Sharpthorne 810269.

CHLOROS, Prof. Alexander George; Judge of the Court of Justice of the European Communities, at Luxembourg, since 1981; *b* Athens, 15 Aug. 1926; *yr s* of late George Chloros and of Pipitsa Chloros (*née* Metaxas, now Salti), Athens; *m* 1st, 1951, Helen Comninos, London (*d* 1956); one *d* ; 2nd, 1965, Jacqueline Destouche, Marseilles (marr. diss.); one *d* ; 3rd, 1979, Katerina Meria, Athens. *Educ:* Varvakeion Model Sch., Athens; University Coll., Oxford. BA Oxon 1951; MA Oxon 1955; LLD London 1972; FKC 1981. Asst Lectr in Law, 1951-54, and Lectr in Law, 1954-59, University Coll. of Wales, Aberystwyth; University of London, King's College: Lectr in Laws, 1959-63; Reader in Comparative Law, 1963-66, Prof., 1966-81; Dir, Centre of European Law, 1974-81; Hon. Vis. Prof., 1981-82. Hayter Scholar, Inst. of Comparative Law, Belgrade, Yugoslavia, 1963-64; Vice-Dean, Internat. Univ. of Comparative Sciences, Luxembourg, 1962-66; Dean of the Faculty of Laws, King's Coll., London, 1971-74; Adviser to Seychelles Government, for: recodification and reform of Code Napoléon, 1973; recodification and reform of Commercial Code, 1975. Visiting Professor: (Professeur associé), Faculty of Law, Univ. of Paris I, 1974-75; Uppsala Univ., 1976; Fribourg, 1977; Athens Univ., 1978-80. Member: Soc. of Public Teachers of Law; UK Cttee on Comparative Law, Inst. Advanced Legal Studies; Brit. Inst. Internat. and Comparative Law; UK deleg. and Vice-Pres., Council of Europe Sub-Cttee on Fundamental Legal Concepts; UK deleg., Conf. of European Law Faculties, Council of Europe, Strasbourg, 1968; Leader of UK delegn to 2nd Conf., 1971, 1st Vice-Pres., 3rd Conf., 1974, Pres., 4th Conf., 1976; exch. Lecturer, Faculty of Law, Univ. of Leuven, Belgium; Director: Brit. Council scheme for foreign lawyers; Student Exchange Scheme with Univ. of Aix-en-Provence; UK deleg. representing Cttee of Vice-Chancellors and Principals at Preparatory Cttee, European Inst. in Florence, and UK Mem., Prov. Academic Cttee. Mem., Central Negotiating Cttee, Entry of Greece in the European Communities. Hon. Bencher, Gray's Inn, 1981; Hon. Vis. Prof., King's Coll., London, 1981-82. Corresp. Member: Acad. of Athens, 1976; Royal Uppsala Acad., 1977. Associate Mem., Internat. Acad. of Comparative Law, 1976. Medal of Univ. of Zagreb, Yugoslavia, 1972. Chevalier 1st cl.,

Royal Order of Polar Star, Sweden, 1977; Officier, Ordre des palmes académiques, 1979. Gen. Editor, European Studies in Law, 1976-. *Publications:* Editor, Vol. IV (Family Law) and contributor to Internat. Encyc. of Comparative Law, Max Planck Inst. of Internat. and For. Law, Hamburg; Ch. 2 in Graveson, Law and Society, 1967; Yugoslav Civil Law, 1970; ed, A Bibliographical Guide to the Law of the United Kingdom, the Channel Is and Isle of Man, 2nd edn, 1973; ed jtly (with K. H. Neumayer) Liber Amicorum Ernst J. Cohn, 1975; Codification in a Mixed Jurisdiction, 1977; The EEC Treaty (Greek trans.), 1978; (ed) The EEC Treaty and the Act of Accession of Greece (official texts), 1981; contrib. various British and foreign learned periodicals on Comparative Law and legal philosophy. *Recreations:* photography, swimming, travel, European history, coins, icons. *Address:* The Court of Justice of the European Communities, BP 1406, Kirchberg, Luxembourg. *T:* 43031. *Clubs:* Athenæum, Royal Commonwealth Society; Fondation Universitaire (Brussels).

CHOLERTON, Frederick Arthur, CBE 1978; *b* 15 April 1917; *s* of Frederick Arthur Cholerton and Charlotte (*née* Wagstaffe); *m* 1939, Ethel (*née* Jackson); one *s* decd. *Educ:* Penkhull Secondary Sch., Stoke-on-Trent. Locomotive driver, British Rail, 1934-77; Trade Union work with ASLEF, 1934-71. City of Stoke-on-Trent: Councillor, 1951-; Leader of Council, 1976-; Lord Mayor, 1971-72; Staffordshire County Council: Councillor, 1973-; Vice-Chm., 1973-76; Chm., 1977 and 1981-82; Opposition Leader, 1977. JP Stoke-on-Trent, 1956-74. *Recreations:* sports, gardening, politics, voluntary work for charities, particularly RNIB. *Address:* 12 Werburgh Drive, Trentham, Stoke-on-Trent ST4 8JP. *T:* Stoke-on-Trent 657457.

CHOLMELEY, Francis William Alfred F.; *see* Fairfax-Cholmeley.

CHOLMELEY, John Adye, FRCS; Surgeon, Royal National Orthopædic Hospital, 1948-70, Hon. Consultant Surgeon, since 1970; Chairman of Joint Examining Board for Orthopædic Nursing; *b* 31 Oct. 1902; *s* of Montague Adye Cholmeley and Mary Bertha Gordon-Cumming; unmarried. *Educ:* St Paul's Sch.; St Bartholomew's Hosp. MRCS, LRCP 1926; MB, BS London 1927; FRCS 1935; Resident appts St Bart's Hosp, 1928-30; Asst MO: Lord Mayor Treloar Cripples' Hosp., Alton, 1930-32; Alexandra Orth. Hosp., Swanley, 1933-34; Resident Surg. and Med. Supt, Country Br., Royal Nat. Orth. Hosp., Stanmore, 1940-48 (Asst Res. Surg., 1936-39); former Orthopædic Surg., Clare Hall Hosp., Neasden Hosp. Mem. Internat. Soc. of Orthopædic Surgery and Trauma (Société Internationale de Chirurgie Orthopédique et de Traumatologie, SICOT; FRSocMed (Pres. Orthopædic Sect., 1957-58); Fellow Brit. Orth. Assoc. *Publications:* articles on orthopædic subjects, particularly tuberculosis and poliomyelitis in med. jls. *Address:* 14 Warren Fields, Valencia Road, Stanmore, Mddx. *T:* 01-954 6920.

CHOLMELEY, Sir Montague (John), 6th Bt *cr* 1806; Captain, Grenadier Guards; *b* 27 March 1935; *s* of 5th Bt and Cecilia, *er d* of W. H. Ellice; *S* father, 1964; *m* 1960, Juliet Auriol Sally Nelson; one *s* two *d. Educ:* Eton. Grenadier Guards, 1954-64. *Heir: s* Hugh John Frederick Sebastian Cholmeley, *b* 3 Jan. 1968. *Address:* Church Farm, Burton le Coggles, Grantham, Lincs. *T:* Corby Glen 329. *Clubs:* White's, Cavalry and Guards.

CHOLMONDELEY, family name of **Marquess of Cholmondeley,** and of **Baron Delamere.**

CHOLMONDELEY, 6th Marquess of, *cr* 1815; **George Hugh Cholmondeley,** GCVO 1977; MC 1943; DL; Bt 1611; Viscount Cholmondeley, 1661; Baron Cholmondeley of Namptwich (Eng.), 1689; Earl of Cholmondeley, Viscount Malpas, 1706; Baron Newborough (Ire.), 1715; Baron Newburgh (Gt Brit.), 1716; Earl of Rocksavage, 1815; late Grenadier Guards; Lord Great Chamberlain of England since 1966; *b* 24 April 1919; *e s* of 5th Marquess of Cholmondeley, GCVO, and Sybil (CBE 1946), *d* of Sir Edward Albert Sassoon, 2nd Bt; *S* father, 1968; *m* 1947, Lavinia Margaret, *d* of late Colonel John Leslie, DSO, MC; one *s* three *d. Educ:* Eton; Cambridge Univ. Served War of 1939-45: 1st Royal Dragoons, in MEF, Italy, France, Germany (MC). Retd hon. rank Major, 1949. DL Chester, 1955. *Heir: s* Earl of Rocksavage, *qv. Address:* Cholmondeley Castle, Malpas, Cheshire. *T:* Cholmondeley 202. *Clubs:* Turf, Cavalry and Guards.

CHOLMONDELEY CLARKE, Marshal Butler; Master of the Supreme Court of Judicature (Chancery Division), since 1973; *b* 14 July 1919; *s* of Major Cecil Cholmondeley Clarke and Fanny Ethel Carter; *m* 1947, Joan Roberta Stephens; two *s. Educ:* Aldenham. Admitted a solicitor, 1943; Partner, Burton Yeates & Hart, Solicitors, London, WC2, 1946-72. Pres., City of Westminster Law Soc., 1971-72; Mem. Council, Law Soc., 1966-72; Chm., Family Law Cttee, 1970-72; Chm., Legal Aid Cttee, 1972; Chancery Procedure Cttee, 1968-72; Ecclesiastical Examiner, Dio. London; Trustee, United Law Clerks' Soc.; Mem. Council, Inc. Soc. The Church Lads' and Girls' Brigade. *Recreation:* reading. *Address:* 51 Ovington Street, SW3. *Club:* Turf.

CHOMSKY, Prof. (Avram) Noam, PhD; Institute Professor, Massachusetts Institute of Technology, since 1976 (Ferrari P. Ward Professor of Modern Languages and Linguistics, 1966-76); *b* Philadelphia, 7 Dec. 1928; *s* of late William Chomsky and of Elsie Simonofsky; *m* 1949, Carol Doris Schatz; one *s* two *d. Educ:* Central High Sch., Philadelphia; Univ. of Pennsylvania (PhD). Massachusetts Institute of Technology: Asst Prof., 1955-58; Associate Prof., 1958-61; Prof. of Modern Langs, 1961-66. Res. Fellow, Harvard Cognitive

Studies Center, 1964-65. Vis. Prof., Columbia Univ., 1957-58; Nat. Sci. Foundn Fellow, Inst for Advanced Study, Princeton, 1958-59; Linguistics Soc. of America Prof., Univ. of Calif, LA, 1966; Beckman Prof., Univ. of Calif, Berkeley, 1966-67; Vis. Watson Prof., Syracuse Univ., 1982; Lectures: Shearman, UCL, 1969; John Locke, Oxford, 1969; Bertrand Russell Meml, Cambridge 1971; Nehru Meml, New Delhi, 1972; Whidden, McMaster Univ., 1975; Huizinga Meml, Leiden, 1977; Woodbridge, Columbia, 1978; Kant, Stanford, 1979. Member: Nat. Acad. of Scis; Amer. Acad of Arts and Scis; Linguistics Soc. of America; Amer. Philosophical Assoc.; Bertrand Russell Peace Foundn; Utrecht Soc. of Arts and Scis; Deutsche Akademie der Naturforscher Leopoldina; Aristotelian Soc., GB; Corresp. Mem., British Acad., 1974. Fellow, Amer. Assoc. for Advancement of Science. Mem., Council, Internat. Confedn for Disarmament and Peace, 1967. Hon. DLitt: London, 1967; Visva-Bharati, West Bengal, 1980; Hon. DHL: Chicago, 1967; Loyola Univ., Chicago, 1970; Swarthmore Coll., 1970; Bard Coll., 1971; Delhi, 1972; Massachusetts, 1973. *Publications:* Syntactic Structures, 1957; Current Issues in Linguistic Theory, 1964; Aspects of the Theory of Syntax, 1965; Cartesian Linguistics, 1966; Topics in the Theory of Generative Grammar, 1966; Language and Mind, 1968; (with Morris Halle) Sound Pattern of English, 1968; American Power and the New Mandarins, 1969; At War with Asia, 1970; Problems of Knowledge and Freedom, 1971; Studies on Semantics in Generative Grammar, 1972; For Reasons of State, 1973; The Backroom Boys, 1973; Peace in the Middle East?, 1974; (with Edward Herman) Bains de Sang, 1974; Reflections on Language, 1975; The Logical Structure of Linguistic Theory, 1975; Essays on Form and Interpretation, 1977; Human Rights and American Foreign Policy, 1978; Language and Responsibility, 1979; (with Edward Herman) Political Economy of Human Rights, 1979; Rules and Representations, 1980; Lectures on Government and Binding, 1981; Towards a New Cold War, 1982. *Recreation:* gardening. *Address:* Department of Linguistics, Massachusetts Institute of Technology, Massachusetts Avenue, Cambridge, Mass 02139, USA. *T:* 617-253-7819.

CHOPE, Robert Charles; His Honour Judge Chope; a Circuit Judge (formerly Judge of County Courts), since 1965; *b* 26 June 1913; *s* of Leonard Augustine and Ida Florence Chope; *m* 1946, Pamela Durell; one *s* two *d. Educ:* St Paul's Sch.; University Coll., London. Called to Bar, Inner Temple, 1938. Served Royal Artillery, 1939-45. Dep. Chm., Cornwall QS, 1966-71. *Address:* 12 King's Bench Walk, Temple, EC4; Carclew House, Perranarworthal, Truro, Cornwall.

CHORLEY, family name of **Baron Chorley.**

CHORLEY, 2nd Baron *cr* 1945, of Kendal; **Roger Richard Edward Chorley,** FCA; Partner in Coopers & Lybrand, Chartered Accountants, since 1967; Visiting Professor, Department of Management Sciences, Imperial College of Science and Technology, University of London, since 1979; *b* 14 Aug. 1930; *er s* of 1st Baron Chorley, QC, and of Katherine Campbell, *d* of late Edward Hopkinson, DSc; *S* father, 1978; *m* 1964, Ann, *d* of late A. S. Debenham; two *s. Educ:* Stowe Sch.; Gonville and Caius Coll., Cambridge (BA). Pres., CU Mountaineering Club. Expedns to Himalayas, 1954 (Rakaposhi), 1957 (Nepal); joined Cooper Brothers & Co. (later Coopers & Lybrand), 1955; New York office, 1959-60; Pakistan (Indus Basin Project), 1961; Hon. Sec., Climbers Club, 1963-67; seconded to Nat. Bd for Prices and Incomes as accounting adviser, 1965-68; Mem. Management Cttee, Mount Everest Foundn, 1968-70; Hon. Treas., Alpine Club, 1968-78 (Vice-Pres., 1975-76); Member: Finance Cttee, National Trust, 1970-; Royal Commn on the Press, 1974-77; Finance Act 1960 Tribunal, 1974-79; Ordnance Survey Rev. Cttee, 1978-79; British Council Rev. Cttee, 1979-80; Nat. Theatre Bd, 1980-; Top Salaries Review Body, 1981-; Bd, British Council, 1981-; Council, City and Guilds of London Inst. *Recreation:* mountains. *Heir: s* Hon. Nicholas Rupert Debenham Chorley, *b* 15 July 1966. *Address:* 69 Bedford Gardens, W8 7EF. *Clubs:* Reform, Alpine.

CHORLEY, (Charles) Harold, CB 1959; Second Parliamentary Counsel, 1968-69; *b* 10 June 1912; *o s* of late Arthur R. Chorley; *m* 1941, Audrey (*d* 1980), *d* of R. V. C. Ash, MC; two *d. Educ:* Radley; Trinity Coll., Oxford. Called to Bar (Inner Temple), 1934. Joined Office of Parliamentary Counsel, 1938; one of the Parliamentary Counsel, 1950-68. *Address:* Paddock Wood, Tisbury, Salisbury, Wilts. *T:* Tisbury 870325.

CHORLEY, Prof. Richard John; Professor of Geography, University of Cambridge, since 1974; *b* 4 Sept. 1927; *s* of Walter Joseph Chorley and Ellen Mary Chorley; *m* 1965, Rosemary Joan Macdonald More; one *s* one *d. Educ:* Minehead Grammar Sch.; Exeter Coll., Oxford. MA (Oxon), ScD (Cantab). Lieut, RE, 1946-48. Fulbright Schol., Columbia Univ., 1951-52; Instructor: in Geography, Columbia Univ., 1952-54; in Geology, Brown Univ., 1954-57; Cambridge Univ.: Demonstrator in Geography, 1958-62; Lectr in Geography, 1962-70, Reader, 1970-74. British rep. on Commn on Quantitative Techniques of Internat. Geographical Union, 1964-68; Dir, Madingley Geog. Courses, 1963-. First Hon. Life Mem., British Geomorphological Res. Gp, 1974. Gill Meml Medal, RGS, 1967; Hons Award, Assoc. of Amer. Geographers, 1981. *Publications:* co-author of: The History of the Study of Landforms, Vols I and II, 1964, 1973; Atmosphere, Weather and Climate, 1968; Network Analysis in Geography, 1969; Physical Geography, 1971; Environmental Systems, 1978; co-editor of: Frontiers in Geographical Teaching, 1965; Models in Geography, 1967; editor of: Water, Earth and Man, 1969; Spatial Analysis in Geomorphology, 1972; Directions in Geography, 1973; contribs to: Jl of Geology, Amer. Jl of Science, Bulletin of Geolog. Soc.

of Amer., Geog. Jl, Geol. Magazine, Inst. of Brit. Geographers, etc. *Recreation:* gardening. *Address:* 76 Grantchester Meadows, Newnham, Cambridge CB3 9JL.

CHOUFFOT, Geoffrey; Deputy Chairman, Civil Aviation Authority, since 1980. Formerly Group Director, Safety Services, Civil Aviation Authority, 1978-80. *Address:* Civil Aviation Authority, 45-59 Kingsway, WC2B 6TE.

CHOWDHURY, Abu Sayeed; President of Bangladesh, 12 Jan. 1972 - 24 Dec. 1973; unanimously elected President of Republic of Bangladesh from April 1973, for five year term, resigned December 1973; Foreign Minister of Bangladesh, 1975; Member, United Nations Sub-Commission on Prevention of Discrimination and Protection of Minorities, since 1978, re-elected 1981 (Chairman, Working Group on Slavery Practices, 1978); *b* 31 Jan. 1921; *s* of late Abdul Hamid Chowdhury (formerly Speaker, the then East Pakistan Assembly); *m* 1948, Khurshid Chowdhury; two *s* one *d*. *Educ:* Presidency Coll.; Calcutta Univ. (MA, BL). Called to the Bar, Lincoln's Inn, 1947. Gen.-Sec., Presidency Coll. Union, 1941-42; Pres. British Br. of All India Muslim Students' Fedn, 1946. Mem., Pakistan Delegn to Gen. Assembly of the UN, 1959; Advocate-Gen., E Pakistan, 1960; Mem., Constitution Commn, 1960-61; Judge, Dacca High Court, July 1961-72; Chm., Central Bd for Develt of Bengali, 1963-68; Leader, Pakistan Delegn to World Assembly of Judges and 4th World Conf. on World Peace through Law, Sept. 1969; Vice-Chancellor, Dacca Univ., Nov., 1969-72, in addition to duties of Judge of Dacca High Court; Mem., UN Commn on Human Rights, 1971; Ambassador-at-large for Govt of Bangladesh, designated by Bangladesh Govt as High Comr for UK and N Ireland, 1971, and Head of the Bangladesh Missions at London and New York, April 1971-11 Jan. 1972; Chancellor, all Bangladesh Univs, 1972-73. Special Rep. of Bangladesh, 1973-75; Leader, Bangladesh Delegns: Conf. on Humanitarian Law, Geneva, 1974, 1975 (Chm., Drafting Cttee); World Health Assemblies, Geneva, 1974, 1975; Internat. Labour Confs, Geneva, 1974, 1975 (Chm., Human Resources Cttee); Confs on Law of the Sea, Caracas, 1974, Geneva, 1975; Gen. Conf. Internat. Atomic Energy Agency, Vienna, 1974; Non-aligned Foreign Ministers' Conf., Lima, 1975; UN Special Session, Sept. 1975, NY; 30th Session of Gen. Assembly, UN, 1975; Islamic Foreign Ministers' Conf., Jeddah, 1975; led goodwill missions to: Saudi Arabia, Egypt, Syria, Lebanon and Algeria, 1974; Turkey, 1975. Minister of Shipping and Ports, 8-21 Aug. 1975. Hon. Fellow, Open Univ., 1977. Hon. Deshikottama Viswabharati (Shantiniketan), India, 1972; Hon. LLD Calcutta, 1972. *Recreations:* reading, gardening. *Address:* 2 Paper Buildings, Temple, EC4. *T:* 01-353 9119. *Clubs:* Athenæum, Royal Over-Seas League, Royal Commonwealth Society; (Hon.) Rotarian, Rotary (Dacca).

CHRÉTIEN, Hon. Jean, PC (Canada); MP (L) St Maurice, Canada, since 1963; Minister of Energy, since 1982; *b* 11 Jan. 1934; *s* of Wellie Chrétien and Marie Boisvert Chrétien; *m* 1957, Aline Chaine; two *s* one *d*. *Educ:* Trois-Rivières; Joliette; Shawinigan; Laval Univ. (BA, LLL). Called to the Bar, and entered Shawinigan law firm of Chrétien, Landry, Deschênes, Trudel and Normand, 1958; Director: Shawinigan Sen. Chamber of Commerce, 1962; Bar of Trois-Rivières, 1962-63. Govt of Canada: Parly Sec. to Prime Minister, 1965, and to Minister of Finance, 1966; Minister of State, 1967; Minister of National Revenue, Jan. 1968; Minister of Indian and Northern Affairs, July 1968; Pres., Treasury Bd, 1974; Minister of Industry, Trade and Commerce, 1976; Minister of Finance, 1977-79; Minister of Justice, Attorney General, Minister of State for Social Develt, 1980-82. *Recreations:* skiing, fishing, squash. *Address:* House of Commons, Ottawa, Ont, Canada. *Club:* Knights of Columbus.

CHRIMES, Henry Bertram, DL; Chairman, Liverpool Daily Post and Echo Ltd, since 1976; *b* 11 March 1915; *s* of Sir Bertram Chrimes, CBE, and Mary (*née* Holder); *m* 1946, Suzanne, *d* of W. S. Corbett-Lowe, Sodylt Hall, Ellesmere; one *s* three *d*. *Educ:* Oundle; Clare Coll., Cambridge. Served War of 1939-45: RA, India and Burma, Bde Major (despatches). Cooper & Co.'s Stores Ltd, 1945-60 (Man. Dir, 1954-60); Ocean Transport & Trading Ltd, 1960- (Dep. Chm., 1971-75); Liverpool Daily Post & Echo Ltd, 1963-; Member, Liverpool Bd, Barclays Bank Ltd, 1972-. Member: Council, Univ. of Liverpool, 1951- (Pres., 1975-; Pro-Chancellor, 1981); Univ. Authorities Panel, 1976-; Dir, Univs Superannuation Scheme Ltd, 1980-; Vice-Pres., Liverpool Sch. of Tropical Medicine, 1981-; Mem., 1951-, Vice-Pres., 1973-, Liverpool Council of Social Service (Chm., 1964-76); Pres., Royal Liverpool Seamen's Orphan Instn, 1980. DL 1974, High Sheriff 1978-79, Merseyside. *Recreations:* books, bees, gardening. *Address:* Bracken Bank, Heswall, Merseyside L60 4RP. *T:* 051-342 2397. *Club:* Reform.

CHRIMES, Prof. Stanley Bertram, MA, PhD, LittD; Professor of History and Head of Department of History, University College, Cardiff, 1953-74, now Emeritus; Director, University College, Cardiff, Centenary History Project, 1975-81; Deputy Principal, 1964-66; Dean of Faculty of Arts, 1959-61; *b* 23 Feb. 1907; *yr s* of late Herbert Chrimes and Maude Mary (*née* Rose); *m* 1937, Mabel Clara, *o d* of late L. E. Keyser. *Educ:* Purley County Sch., Surrey; King's Coll., London (Lindley Student, BA, MA); Trinity Coll., Cambridge (Research Studentship, Senior Rouse Ball Student, PhD, LittD). Lectr, 1936, Reader, 1951, in Constitutional History, University of Glasgow. Temp. Principal, Ministry of Labour and National Service, 1940-45. Alexander Medal, Royal Hist. Society, 1934. *Publications:* English Constitutional Ideas in the XVth century, 1936 (American repr. 1965, 1976); (translated) F. Kern's Kingship and Law in the Middle Ages, 1939 (repr. 1948,

1956; paperback edn 1970); (ed and trans.) Sir John Fortescue's De Laudibus Legum Anglie, 1942 (repr. 1949); English Constitutional History, 1948 (4th rev. edn 1967; edn in Japan, 1963); (ed) The General Election in Glasgow, February 1950, 1950; An Introduction to the Administrative History of Mediæval England, 1952 (3rd rev. edn 1966); Some Reflections on the Study of History, 1954; (ed and cont. 7th edn) Sir W. Holdsworth's History of English Law, Vol. I, 1957; (ed, with A. L. Brown) Select Documents of English Constitutional History, 1307-1485, 1961; Lancastrians, Yorkists, and Henry VII, 1964 (2nd rev. edn 1966); King Edward I's Policy for Wales, 1969; ed (with C. D. Ross and R. A. Griffiths) and contrib., Fifteenth-Century England, studies in politics and society, 1972; Henry VII, 1972, repr. 1977; articles and reviews in Trans Royal Hist. Soc., English Historical Review, Law Quarterly Review, etc. *Address:* 24 Cwrt-y-vil Road, Penarth, South Glamorgan.

CHRIST CHURCH, Dublin, Dean of; *see* Salmon, Very Rev. T. N. D. C.

CHRIST CHURCH, Oxford, Dean of; *see* Heaton, Very Rev. E. W.

CHRISTCHURCH, Bishop of, since 1966; **Rt. Rev. William Allan Pyatt,** MA; *b* Gisborne, NZ, 4 Nov. 1916; *e s* of A. E. Pyatt; *m* 1942, Mary Lilian Carey; two *s* one *d*. *Educ:* Gisborne High Sch.; Auckland Univ.; St John's Coll., Auckland; Westcott House, Cambridge. BA 1938 (Senior Sch. in Hist.); MA 1939. Served War of 1939-45: combatant service with 2 NZEF; Major, 2 IC 20 NZ Armd Regt 1945. Ordained, 1946; Curate, Cannock, Staffs, 1946-48; Vicar: Brooklyn, Wellington, NZ, 1948-52; Hawera, 1952-58; St Peter's, Wellington, 1958-62; Dean of Christchurch, 1962-66. *Publications:* contribs to NZ Jl of Theology. *Recreations:* Rugby referee; political comment on radio; golf. *Address:* Bishopscourt, 100 Park Terrace, Christchurch, NZ. *T:* 62.653. *Club:* Canterbury Officers (Christchurch).

CHRISTENSEN, Arent Lauri, (A. Lauri Chris); Norwegian painter and etcher; *b* 30 April 1893; *m* 1933, Hjordis Charlotte Lohren (Lill Chris), painter. *Educ:* The Royal Drawing Sch., Oslo. Began career as etcher and painter in Oslo; later travelled in the South, especially in Provence and Italy, and made a series of decorative landscape-etchings, which were exhibited in several countries; his interest in classic antiquity-especially the Grecian and Egyptian culture- inspired him to make various figure-compositions with incidents from the life in the antiquity and from Homer's Iliad; these compositions have been exhibited throughout Europe and America. Decorated Asker High Sch. with wall-paintings. Invented a new graphic method Chrisgrafia. The following museums have bought his works: British Museum, Victoria and Albert Museum, National Galleriet, Oslo, New York Free Arts Library Museum, Bibliothèque Nationale, Paris, Brooklyn Museum, Brooklyn, etc; Mem. of the Soc. of Graphic Art, London, 1926. *Address:* Villa Chriss, Fjeldstadvn 16, Nesbru, Norway.

CHRISTENSEN, Christian Neils, CBE 1970; ERD; *b* 10 Dec. 1901; *m* 1928, Elsie Florence Hodgson; one *s* one *d*. Army service, France, N Africa, Sicily, Italy, 1939-45 (Lt-Col, despatches twice); Officer, Legion of Merit, USA, 1944); Man. Dir, North Western Transport Services Ltd and Dir, Transport Services (BTC) Ltd, 1945-49; Road Haulage Executive: Eastern Divisional Man., 1950-55; Midland Divisional Man., 1955-63; Man. Dir, British Road Services Ltd, and Chm., BRS (Contracts) Ltd, 1963-68; Chm., Road Air Cargo Express (International) Ltd, 1968-71, retired. FCIT. *Recreation:* gardening. *Address:* Ellesmere, 22 Greensleeves Avenue, Broadstone, Dorset, BH18 8BL. *T:* Broadstone 694501.

CHRISTENSEN, Eric Herbert, CMG 1968; Chairman, Atlantic Hotel Ltd, since 1980; Director: Gambia Industrial Fishing Co., since 1980; Seagull Cold Stores, since 1980; *b* 29 Oct. 1923; *s* of George Vilhelm Christensen and Rose Fleury; *m* 1951, Diana, *d* of Rev. J. Dixon-Baker; four *s* three *d*. Trained, St Augustine's Sec. Sch., Bathurst, 1941-43; Military Service, W African Air Corps (RAF), Bathurst, 1944-45; Clerk, The Secretariat, Bathurst, 1946-47; Head of Chancery, then Vice-Consul, French Consulate, Bathurst, 1947-60; acted as Consul on several occasions; Attaché, Senegalese Consulate-Gen., Bathurst, 1961-65, acted as Consul-Gen. on several occasions; Asst Sec. (Ext. Affairs), Gambia Govt, 1965; Principal Asst Sec., Prime Minister's Office, Bathurst, 1966-67; Sec.-Gen., President's Office, Perm. Sec., Min. of External Affairs, and Sec. to the Cabinet, The Gambia, 1967-78; also Hd, Public Service, 1967-78. Foreign decorations include: Grand Officer, Order of the Brilliant Star of China (Taiwan), 1966; Officer, Order of Merit of Islamic Republic of Mauritania, 1967; Knight Commander's Cross, Badge and Star, Order of Merit of Federal Republic of Germany, 1968; Order of Republic of Nigeria, 1970; Grand Officer, National Order of Republic of The Gambia, 1970; Order of Diplomatic Merit, Republic of Korea, 1970, and also those from Egypt, Republic of Guinea and Republic of Liberia; Comdr, Nat. Order of the Lion, Senegal, 1972; Chevalier de la Légion d'Honneur, 1975. *Recreations:* reading, photography, philately, chess. *Address:* Pipeline Road, Latrikunda, The Gambia. *T:* Serekunda 2222.

CHRISTENSEN, Jens; Commander First Class, Order of the Dannebrog; Hon. GCVO; Chairman, Danish Oil and Natural Gas Company, since 1981; *b* 30 July 1921; *s* of Christian Christensen and Sophie Dorthea Christensen; *m* 1950, Tove (*née* Jessen); one *s* two *d*. *Educ:* Copenhagen Univ. (MPolSc 1945). Joined Danish Foreign Service, 1945; Head of Section, Econ. Secretariat of Govt, 1947; Sec. to OECD Delegn in Paris, 1949 and to NATO Delegn,

1952; Hd of Sect., Min. of Foreign Affairs, 1952, Actg Hd of Div., 1954; Chargé d'Affaires a.i. and Counsellor of Legation, Vienna, 1957; Asst Hd of Econ.-Polit. Dept, Min. of For. Affairs, 1960; Dep. Under-Sec., 1961; Under-Sec. and Hd of Econ.-Polit. Dept, 1964-71; Hd of Secretariat for Europ. Integration, 1966; Ambassador Extraord. and Plenipotentiary, 1967; State Sec. for Foreign Econ. Affairs, 1971; Ambassador of Denmark to the Court of St James's, 1977-81. Governor for Denmark, The Asian Development Bank, 1967-73. Knight Grand Cross: Order of Icelandic Falcon; Order of Northern Star, Sweden; Order of St Olav, Norway; Royal Victorian Order. *Address:* Agern Allé 24-26, 2970 Hørsholm, Denmark.

CHRISTIAN, Clifford Stuart, CMG 1971; consultant in environmental matters; *b* 19 Dec. 1907; *s* of Thomas William and Lilian Elizabeth Christian; *m* 1933, Agnes Robinson; four *d. Educ:* Univ. of Queensland (BScAgr); Univ. of Minnesota (MS). Officer-in-charge: Northern Australia Regional Survey Section, 1946-50; Land Research and Regional Survey Section, CSIRO, 1950-57; Chief, Div. of Land Research, CSIRO, 1957-60; Mem. Executive, CSIRO, 1960-72. Adviser, Ranger Uranium Environmental Inquiry, 1975-76. Farrer Memorial Medal, 1969. FAIAS; FWA; Fellow, Aust. Acad. of Technological Sciences. Hon. DScAgr Queensland, 1976. *Publications:* A Review Report, Alligator Rivers Study (with J. Aldrick), 1977; chapter contribs to books; articles in various pubns mainly concerning natural resources. *Recreation:* photography. *Address:* 6 Baudin Street, Forrest, ACT 2603, Australia. *T:* 062 952495. *Club:* Commonwealth (Canberra).

CHRISTIAN, Prof. John Wyrill, FRS 1975; Professor of Physical Metallurgy, Oxford University, since 1967; Fellow of St Edmund Hall, Oxford, since 1963; *b* 9 April 1926; *e s* of John Christian and Louisa Christian (*née* Crawford); *m* 1949, Maureen Lena Smith; two *s* one *d. Educ:* Scarborough Boys' High Sch.; The Queen's Coll., Oxford. BA 1946, DPhil 1949, MA 1950. Pressed Steel Co. Ltd Research Fellow, Oxford University, 1951-55; Lectr in Metallurgy, 1955-58; George Kelley Reader in Metallurgy, 1958-67. Visiting Prof.: Univ. of Illinois, 1959; Case Inst. of Technology, USA, 1962-63; MIT and Stanford Univ., 1971-72. Lectures: Williams, MIT, 1971; Hume-Rothery Meml, 1976; Inst. of Metals, AIME, 1981; Campbell Meml, ASM, 1982. Rosenhain medallist of Inst. of Metals, 1969; Mehl Medallist of AIME, 1981. *Publications:* Metallurgical Equilibrium Diagrams (with others), 1952; The Theory of Transformations in Metals and Alloys, 1965, 2nd rev. edn, 1975; (Editor) Progress in Materials Science, 1970-; (Editor) Jl Less Com. Metals, 1976-; contribs to scientific jls. *Address:* 11 Charlbury Road, Oxford OX2 6UT. *T:* Oxford 58569.

CHRISTIAN, Prof. Reginald Frank; Professor of Russian, St Andrews University, since 1966; *b* Liverpool, 9 Aug. 1924; *s* of late H. A. Christian and late Jessie Gower (*née* Scott); *m* 1952, Rosalind Iris Napier; one *s* one *d. Educ:* Liverpool Inst.; Queen's Coll., Oxford (Open Scholar; MA). Hon. Mods Class. (Oxon), 1943; 1st cl. hons Russian (Oxon), 1949. Commnd RAF, 1944; flying with Atlantic Ferry Unit and 231 Sqdn, 1943-46. FO, British Embassy, Moscow, 1949-50; Lectr and Head of Russian Dept, Liverpool Univ., 1950-55; Sen. Lectr and Head of Russian Dept, Birmingham Univ., 1956-63; Vis. Prof. of Russian, McGill Univ., Canada, 1961-62; Prof. of Russian, Birmingham Univ., 1963-66; Exchange Lectr, Moscow, 1964-65. Mem. Univ. Ct, 1971-73 and 1981-, Associate Dean, Fac. of Arts, 1972-73, Dean, Fac. of Arts, 1975-78, St Andrews Univ. Pres., British Univs Assoc. of Slavists, 1967-70; Member, Internat. Cttee of Slavists, 1970-75. *Publications:* Korolenko's Siberia, 1954; (with F. M. Borras) Russian Syntax, 1959, 2nd rev. edn, 1971; Tolstoy's War and Peace: a study, 1962; (with F. M. Borras) Russian Prose Composition, 1964, 2nd rev. edn, 1974; Tolstoy: a critical introduction, 1969; Tolstoy's Letters, 2 vols, 1978; numerous articles and reviews in Slavonic and E European Review, Slavonic and E European Jl, Mod. Languages Review, Survey, Forum, Birmingham Post, Times Lit. Supp., Oxford Slavonic Papers, etc. *Recreations:* squash, fell-walking, violin. *Address:* The Roundel, St Andrews, Fife. *T:* St Andrews 73322; Scioncroft, Knockard Road, Pitlochry, Perthshire. *T:* Pitlochry 2993.

CHRISTIANSEN, Michael Robin; bookseller; *b* 7 April 1927; *e s* of Arthur and Brenda Christiansen; *m* 1st, 1948, Kathleen Lyon (marr. diss.); one *s* one *d* ; 2nd, 1961, Christina Robinson; one *s* one *d. Educ:* Hill Crest, Frinton; St Luke's, Conn., USA. Reporter, Daily Mail, 1943; Royal Navy, 1945-47; Chief Sub-Editor: Daily Mail, 1950; Daily Mirror, 1956; Dep. Editor, Sunday Pictorial, 1961; Asst Editor, Daily Mirror, 1961-64; Editor, Sunday Mirror, 1964-72; Dep. Editor, Daily Mirror, 1972-74, Editor, 1975. *Recreations:* golf, coarse cricket. *Address:* 2 Armstrong Close, Danbury, Essex.

CHRISTIANSON, Alan, CBE 1971; MC 1945; Deputy Chairman, South of Scotland Electricity Board, 1967-72; retired; *b* 14 March 1909; *s* of Carl Robert Christianson; *m* 1936, Gladys Muriel Lewin, *d* of William Barker; two *d. Educ:* Royal Grammar Sch., Newcastle upon Tyne; FCA, CompIEE. Served as Major, RA, 1939-45: comd Field Battery, 1943-45. Central Electricity Bd, 1934-48; Divisional Sec., British Electricity Authority, SW Scotland Div., 1948-55; Dep. Sec., S of Scotland Electricity Bd, 1955-62; Chief Financial Officer, 1962-65; Gen. Man., Finance and Administration, 1965-67. *Recreation:* golf. *Address:* Tynedale, Lennox Drive East, Helensburgh, Dunbartonshire. *T:* Helensburgh 4503.

CHRISTIE, Ann Philippa; *see* Pearce, A. P.

CHRISTIE, Charles Henry; Director of Studies, Britannia Royal Naval College, Dartmouth, since 1978; *b* 1 Sept. 1924; *s* of late Lieut-Comdr C. P. Christie and Mrs C. S. Christie; *m* 1950, Naida Joan Bentley; one *s* three *d. Educ:* Westminster Sch. (King's Scholar); Trinity Coll., Cambridge (Exhibitioner). Served 1943-46, RNVR (despatches, 1945). Trinity Coll., Cambridge, 1946-49; Asst Master, Eton Coll., 1949-57; Under Master and Master of Queen's Scholars, Westminster Sch., 1957-63; Headmaster, Brighton Coll., 1963-71; Warden, St Edward's Sch., Oxford, 1971-78. *Address:* Ashford House, Britannia Royal Naval College, Dartmouth, Devon TQ6 0HJ.

CHRISTIE, George William Langham; Chairman, Glyndebourne Productions Ltd; *b* 31 Dec. 1934; *o s* of John Christie, CH, MC, and Audrey Mildmay Christie; *m* 1958, Patricia Mary Nicholson; three *s* one *d. Educ:* Eton. Asst to Sec. of Calouste Gulbenkian Foundation, 1957-62. Chm. of Glyndebourne Productions, 1956-, and of other family companies. Founder Chm., The London Sinfonietta. *Address:* Glyndebourne, Lewes, E Sussex. *T:* Ringmer 812250.

CHRISTIE, Herbert; Under Secretary, HM Treasury, since 1978; *b* 26 Sept. 1933; *s* of Brig.-Gen. H. W. A. Christie, CB, CMG, and Mary Ann Christie. *Educ:* Methodist Coll., Belfast; Univ. of St Andrews (MA). Asst Lectr, Univ. of Leeds, 1958-60; Econ. Asst, HM Treasury, 1960-63; First Sec., Washington, DC, 1963-66; Econ. Adviser, J. Henry Schroder Wagg and Co. Ltd, 1966-71, with secondment as Econ. Adviser, NBPI, 1967-71; Sen. Econ. Adviser, Min. of Posts and Telecommunications, 1971-74, and Dept of Prices and Consumer Protection, 1974-76; Econ. Adviser, EEC Commn, Brussels, 1976-78. *Publications:* contrib. to books and learned jls. *Recreations:* languages, foreign travel. *Address:* 23 Brunswick Gardens, W8. *T:* 01-233 4246.

CHRISTIE, Prof. Ian Ralph, FBA 1977; Astor Professor of British History, University College London, since 1979; *b* 11 May 1919; *s* of John Reid Christie and Gladys Lilian (*née* Whatley). *Educ:* privately; Worcester Royal Grammar Sch.; Magdalen Coll., Oxford, 1938-40 and 1946-48 (MA). Served War, RAF, 1940-46. University Coll. London: Asst Lectr in Hist., 1948; Lectr, 1951; Reader, 1960; Prof. of Modern British History, 1966; Dean of Arts, 1971-73; Chm. History Dept, 1975-79. Jt Literary Dir, Royal Hist. Soc., 1964-70, Mem. Council, 1970-74. Mem. Editorial Bd, History of Parliament Trust, 1973-. *Publications:* The End of North's Ministry, 1780-1782, 1958; Wilkes, Wyvill and Reform, 1962; Crisis of Empire: Great Britain and the American Colonies, 1754-1783, 1966; (ed) Essays in Modern History selected from the Transactions of the Royal Historical Society, 1968; Myth and Reality in late Eighteenth-century British Politics, 1970; (ed) The Correspondence of Jeremy Bentham, vol. 3, 1971; (with B. W. Labaree) Empire or Independence, 1760-1776, 1976; (with Lucy M. Brown) Bibliography of British History, 1789-1851, 1977; Wars and Revolutions: Britain, 1760-1815, 1982; contrib. to jls. *Recreation:* walking. *Address:* 10 Green Lane, Croxley Green, Herts. *T:* Rickmansworth 73008. *Club:* Royal Commonwealth Society.

CHRISTIE, John Arthur Kingsley; Under-Secretary, Ministry of Agriculture, Fisheries and Food, 1970-75; *b* 8 Feb. 1915; *s* of Harold Douglas Christie and Enid Marian (*née* Hall); *m* 1951, Enid Margaret (*née* Owen); one *s* two *d. Educ:* Rugby Sch.; Magdalen Coll., Oxford. BA (1st cl. Hon. Mods, 1st cl. Litt. Hum.). Asst Principal, Min. of Agriculture, 1937-41; Sub-Lt, RNVR, 1941-45; Asst Private Sec. to Lord President of the Council, 1945-47; Min. of Agriculture: Principal, 1947-52; Asst Sec., 1952-70. *Recreations:* music, travel. *Address:* Westfield, 16 Knole Road, Sevenoaks, Kent. *T:* Sevenoaks 451423.

CHRISTIE, John Belford Wilson, CBE 1981; Sheriff of Tayside, Central and Fife (formerly Perth and Angus) at Dundee, since Nov. 1955; *b* 4 May 1914; *o s* of late J. A. Christie, Advocate, Edinburgh; *m* 1939, Christine Isobel Syme, *o d* of late Rev. J. T. Arnott; four *d. Educ:* Merchiston Castle Sch.; St John's Coll., Cambridge; Edinburgh Univ. Admitted to Faculty of Advocates, 1939. Served War of 1939-45, in RNVR, 1939-46. Sheriff-Substitute of Western Div. of Dumfries and Galloway, 1948-55. Mem., Parole Bd for Scotland, 1967-73; Mem., Queen's Coll. Council, Univ. of St Andrews, 1960-67; Mem. Univ. Court, 1967-75, and Hon. Lectr, Dept of Private Law, Univ. of Dundee. Hon.LLD Dundee, 1977. *Recreations:* curling, golf. *Address:* Annsmuir Farm, Ladybank, Fife. *T:* Ladybank 30480. *Clubs:* New (Edinburgh); Royal and Ancient (St Andrews).

CHRISTIE, John Rankin, CB 1978; Deputy Master and Comptroller of the Royal Mint, 1974-77; *b* 5 Jan. 1918; *s* of Robert Christie and Georgina (*née* Rankin); *m* 1941, Constance May, *d* of Henry Gracie; one *s* two *d. Educ:* Ormskirk Gram. Sch.; London Sch. of Economics. War Office, 1936-39; Min. of Supply, 1939; Royal Artillery, 1943-47; Min. of Supply, 1947; Admin. Staff Coll., 1949; Air Ministry, 1954; Private Sec. to Ministers of Supply, 1955-57; Asst Sec., 1957; British Defence Staffs, Washington, 1962-65; Under-Sec., Min. of Aviation, 1965-67, Min. of Technology, 1967-70, Min. of Aviation Supply, 1970-71; Asst Under-Sec. of State, MoD, 1971-74. *Recreations:* travel, bird-watching. *Address:* Twitten Cottage, East Hill, Oxted, Surrey. *T:* Oxted 3047.

CHRISTIE, Julie (Frances); actress; *b* 14 April 1940; *d* of Frank St John Christie and Rosemary Christie (*née* Ramsden). *Educ:* Convent; Brighton Coll. of Technology; Central Sch. of Speech and Drama. *Films:* Crooks Anonymous, 1962; The Fast Lady, 1962; Billy Liar, 1963; Darling, 1964

(Oscar, NY Film Critics Award, Br. Film Academy Award, etc); Young Cassidy, 1964; Dr Zhivago, 1965 (Donatello Award); Fahrenheit 451, 1966; Far from the Madding Crowd, 1966; Petulia, 1967; In Search of Gregory, 1969; The Go-Between, 1971; McCabe and Mrs Miller, 1972; Don't Look Now, 1973; Shampoo, 1974; Heaven Can Wait, 1978; Memoirs of a Survivor, 1981; The Animals Film, 1982; Return of the Soldier, 1982. Motion Picture Laurel Award, Best Dramatic Actress, 1967; Motion Picture Herald Award, Best Dramatic Actress, 1967. *Address:* c/o ICM Ltd, 22 Grafton Street, W1. *T:* 01-629 8080.

CHRISTIE, Ronald Victor, MD (Edin.); MSc (McGill); DSc (London); FACP; FRCP(C); FRCP; Professor of Medicine and Chairman of the Department, McGill University, 1955-64; now Emeritus Professor; Dean of the Faculty of Medicine, 1964-68; formerly Director Medical Professorial Unit and Physician, St Bartholomew's Hospital; Professor of Medicine, University of London, 1938-55; *b* 1902; *s* of late Dr Dugald Christie, CMG; *m* 1st, 1933, Joyce Mary Ervine (*d* 1967); one *s* one *d*; 2nd, 1976, Manette S. Loomis. *Educ:* in China and later at George Watson's Coll.; Edinburgh Univ. House Physician and House Surg., Royal Infirmary, Edinburgh; Asst in Medicine, Rockefeller Institute for Medical Research, NY; Asst in Dept of Pathology, Freiburg Univ.; Research Associate, McGill Univ. Clinic, Royal Victoria Hosp., Montreal; Asst Dir of the Med. Unit and Asst Physician, London Hosp. Harveian Orator, RCP, 1969. Hon. FRCPEd; Hon. ScD, Dublin, 1962; Hon. DSc: Edinburgh, 1970; McGill, 1978; Hon. LLD Otago, 1975. *Publications:* papers in medical and scientific journals. *Address:* Box 11147, 1055 W Georgia, Vancouver, BC V6E 3P3, Canada.

CHRISTIE, Hon. Sir Vernon (Howard Colville), Kt 1972; Speaker of the Legislative Assembly, Victoria, 1967-73; MLA (L) for Ivanhoe, Victoria, 1955-73; *b* Manly, NSW, 17 Dec. 1909; *s* of C. Christie, Sydney; *m* 1936, Joyce, *d* of F. H. Hamlin; one *s* one *d*. Chm. Cttees, Legislative Assembly, 1956-61, 1965-68; Director: Australian Elizabethan Theatre Trust, 1969-78; Australian Ballet Foundn; Qld Ballet. Hon. Life Mem., Victoria Br., CPA. AASA; FCIS; AFAIM. *Recreations:* bowls, sailing, music, ballet and the arts, conservation, fly fishing. *Address:* Rothes, Gray Street, Redland Bay, Queensland 4165, Australia. *Club:* Queensland (Brisbane).

CHRISTIE, Walter Henry John, CSI 1948; CIE 1946; OBE 1943; *b* 17 Dec. 1905; *s* of late H. G. F. Christie and Mrs L. M. Christie (*née* Humfrey); *m* 1934, Elizabeth Louise, *d* of late H. E. Stapleton; two *s* two *d*. *Educ:* Eton (KS, Newcastle Medallist); King's Coll., Cambridge (Winchester Reading Prize; MA). Joined Indian Civil Service, 1928 and served in Bengal and New Delhi; Joint Private Sec. to the Viceroy, 1947; Adviser in India to Central Commercial Cttee, 1947-52; Vice-Chm., British India Corp. Ltd, 1952-58; Commonwealth Develt Finance Co. Ltd, 1959-68; Adviser, E African Develt Bank, 1969-70. Pres., Upper India Chamber of Commerce, 1955-56; Vice-Pres., Employers' Federation of India, 1956; Pres., UK Citizens Assoc., 1957; Steward, Indian Polo Assoc., 1951. *Publications:* contribs to Blackwood's Magazine. *Address:* The Lawn House, Quarry Road, Oxted, Surrey. *Clubs:* East India, Devonshire, Sports and Public Schools; Achilles.

CHRISTIE, Sir William, KCIE 1947 (CIE 1941); CSI 1945; MC; retired as Chairman, Bailey Meters & Controls Ltd Croydon and Cornhill Insurance Co. Ltd; former Director, Thomas Tilling Ltd; *b* 29 Feb. 1896; *s* of late Rev. Alexander Mackenzie Christie; *m* Marjorie Haughton, 2nd *d* of late Henry Hall Stobbs; one *s* one *d*. *Educ:* Perth Acad., Perth; Bell Baxter Sch., Cupar, Fife; St Andrews Univ.; Clare Coll., Cambridge. Served Royal Scots, 1914-19 (MC). Joined Indian Civil Service, 1920; Finance Sec., UP, 1938-44; Chief Sec., UP, 1944-45; Chief Comr, Delhi, 1945-47. *Address:* 3 Hartley Court, East Common, Gerrards Cross, Bucks. *T:* Gerrards Cross 82246. *Club:* Caledonian.

CHRISTIE, Sir William, Kt 1975; MBE 1970; JP; Lord Mayor of Belfast, 1972-75; a Company Director; *b* 1 June 1913; *s* of Richard and Ellen Christie, Belfast; *m* 1935, Selina (*née* Pattison); one *s* two *d* (and one *s* decd). *Educ:* Ward Sch., Bangor, Northern Ireland. Belfast City Councillor, 1961; High Sheriff of Belfast, 1964-65; Deputy Lord Mayor, 1969; Alderman, 1973-77. JP Belfast, 1951; DL Belfast, 1977. Salvation Army Order of Distinguished Auxiliary Service, 1973. *Recreations:* travel, walking, boating, gardening. *Address:* 9 Ballymullan Road, Crawfordsburn, Bangor, Co. Down BT19 1JG.

CHRISTIE, William James; Sheriff of Tayside, Central and Fife at Kirkaldy, since 1979; *b* 1 Nov. 1932; *s* of William David Christie and Mrs Anne Christie; *m* 1957, Maeve Patricia Gallacher; three *s*. *Educ:* Holy Cross Acad., Edinburgh; Edinburgh Univ. LLB. Nat. Service, 1954-56; commnd Royal Scots. Private Practice, 1956-79. Mem. Council, Law Soc. of Scotland, 1975-79; President: Soc. of Procurators of Midlothian, 1977-79; Soc. of Solicitors in the Supreme Court, 1979. *Recreations:* music, reading, shooting. *Address:* White Lodge, Barnton Avenue, Edinburgh. *T:* 031-336 2603. *Club:* New (Edinburgh).

CHRISTISON, Gen. Sir (Alexander Frank) Philip, 4th Bt *cr* 1871; GBE 1948 (KBE 1944); CB 1943; DSO 1945; MC (and Bar); DL; *b* 17 Nov. 1893; 2nd *s* of Sir Alexander Christison, 2nd Bt and Florence (*d* 1949), *d* of F. T. Elworthy; *S* half-brother, *m* 1st, 1916, Betty (*d* 1974), *d* of late Rt Rev. A. Mitchell, Bishop of Aberdeen and Orkney; (one *s* killed in action in Burma, 7 March 1942) two *d* (and one *d* decd); 2nd, 1974, Vida Wallace Smith, MBE.

Educ: Edinburgh Academy; Oxford Univ. (BA); Hon. Fellow, University Coll., Oxford, 1973. 2nd Lieut Cameron Highlanders, 1914; Capt. 1915; Bt Major, 1930; Bt Lt-Col 1933; Lt-Col Duke of Wellington's Regt, 1937; Col 1938; comd Quetta Bde, 1938-40; Comdt Staff Coll., Quetta, 1940-41; Brig. Gen. Staff, 1941; Maj.-Gen. 1941; Lt-Gen. 1942; Gen. 1947; comd XXIII and XV Indian Corps, 1942-45; Temp. Comdr 14th Army, 1945; C-in-C, ALFSEA, 1945; Allied Comdr Netherland East Indies, 1945-46; GOC-in-C Northern Command, 1946; GOC-in-C Scottish Command and Governor of Edinburgh Castle, 1947-49; ADC Gen. to the King, 1947-49; retired pay, 1949. Col, The Duke of Wellington's Regt, 1947-57; Col, 10th Princess Mary's Own Gurkha Rifles, 1947-57; Hon. Col, 414 Coast Regt Royal Artillery, 1950-57. Dir, Cochran and Co. Ltd, 1951-66; Chm., Alban Timber Ltd, 1953-78. Fruit farmer, 1949-. President: Scottish Unionist Party, 1957-58; Army Cadet Force, Scotland; Vice-President: Burma Star Assoc.; Officers' Assoc.; Scottish Salmon Angling Fedn, 1969; Chm., Lodge Trust for Ornithology, 1969; Chm. and Pres., Clarsach Soc., 1947-. DL Roxburghshire, 1956. FSA Scot, 1957. Chinese Order of Cloud and Banner with Grand Cordon, 1949. Hon. Fellow, Mark Twain Soc., USA, 1977. *Publications:* Birds of Northern Baluchistan, 1940; Birds of Arakan (with Aubrey Buxton), 1946. *Heir:* none. *Recreations:* ornithology, Celtic languages, field sports. *Address:* The Croft, Melrose, Roxburghshire. *T:* Melrose 2456. *Club:* New (Edinburgh).

CHRISTMAS, Arthur Napier, BSc(Eng), CEng, FIEE, FRAeS; Chief Scientific Officer and Director of Materials Quality Assurance, Ministry of Defence, 1971-74, retired; *b* 16 May 1913; *s* of Ernest Napier and Florence Elizabeth Christmas; *m* 1940, Betty Margaret Christmas (*née* Bradbrook); one *s* one *d*. *Educ:* Holloway Sch.; Northampton Technical Coll., London (BSc (Hons)). BEAIRA, 1934-37; Post Office Research Station, 1937-46; Prin. Scientific Officer, Min. of Supply, 1946-51; Sec., British Washington Guided Missile Cttee, 1951-54; Sen. Prin. Scientific Officer, Armament Research and Develt Estabt, 1954-59; DCSO, 1959; Dir, Guided Weapons Research and Techniques, Min. of Aviation, 1959-62; Dir for Engrg Develt, European Launcher Develt Org., 1962-67; Prin. Supt, Royal Armament Research and Develt Estabt, 1967-71. *Recreations:* sailing, mountain walking, music. *Address:* Old Farm Cottage, Itchenor, Sussex. *T:* Birdham 512224. *Clubs:* Itchenor Sailing, Island Sailing, Chichester Cruiser Racing.

CHRISTODOULOU, Anastasios, CBE 1978; Secretary-General, Association of Commonwealth Universities, since 1980; *b* Cyprus, 1 May 1932; *s* of Christodoulos and Maria Haji Yianni; *m* 1955, Joan P. Edmunds; two *s* two *d*. *Educ:* St Marylebone Grammar Sch.; The Queen's Coll., Oxford (MA). Colonial Administrative Service, Tanganyika (Tanzania), 1956-62; served as District Commissioner and Magistrate. Univ. of Leeds Administration, 1963-68: Asst Registrar, 1963-65; Dep. Sec., 1965-68; Secretary, Open Univ., 1969-80. Vice-Chm., Commonwealth Inst., 1981-. DUniv: Open, 1981; Athabasca, 1981. *Recreations:* sport, music, bridge; international and Commonwealth relations. *Address:* 22 Kensington Court Gardens, W8. *T:* 01-937 4626. *Clubs:* Athenæum, Royal Commonwealth Society.

CHRISTOFAS, Kenneth Cavendish, CMG 1969; MBE 1944; HM Diplomatic Service, retired; Director General in the Secretariat of the Council of Ministers of the European Communities, 1973-82; *b* 18 Aug. 1917; *o* *s* of late Edward Julius Goodwin and of Lillian Christofas (*step-s* of late Alexander Christofas); *m* 1948, Jessica Laura (*née* Sparshott); two *d*. *Educ:* Merchant Taylors' Sch.; University Coll., London (Fellow, 1976). Served War of 1939-45 (MBE): commissioned in The Queen's Own Royal West Kent Regt, 1939; Adjt 1940; Staff Capt. 1941; DAAG 1942; Staff Coll., Quetta, 1944; AAG 1944; GSO1, War Office, 1944. Resigned from Army with Hon. rank of Lieut-Col and joined Sen. Br. of HM Foreign Service, 1948 (HM Diplomatic Service after 1965); served in Foreign Office, 1948-49 and 1951-55; Rio de Janeiro, 1949-51; Rome, 1955-59 and as Dep. Head of UK Delegn to European Communities, Brussels, 1959-61; seconded to CRO for service as Counsellor in the British High Commn, Lagos, 1961-64 and to Colonial Office as Head of Economic Dept, 1965-66; on sabbatical year at Univ. of London, 1964-65; Counsellor in Commonwealth Office, then in FCO, 1966-69; Minister and Dep. Head of UK Delegn to EEC, 1969-72 (acting Head, March-Oct. 1971); Cabinet Office, on secondment, 1972-73. Order of Polonia Restituta (Poland), 1944. *Recreations:* railways and motoring. *Address:* 3 The Ridge, Bolsover Road, Eastbourne, Sussex BN20 7JE. *T:* Eastbourne 22384. *Club:* East India, Devonshire, Sports and Public Schools.

CHRISTOFF, Boris; opera singer (bass); *b* Plovdiv, near Sofia, Bulgaria, 18 May 1919; *s* of Kyryl and Rayna Teodorova; *m* Franca, *d* of Raffaello de Rensis. *Educ:* Univ. of Sofia (Doctor of Law). Joined Gussla Choir and Sofia Cathedral Choir as soloist. Obtained scholarship, through King Boris III of Bulgaria, to study singing in Rome under Riccardo Stracciari; made concert début at St Cecilia Academy in Rome, 1946 and operatic début, 1946; Covent Garden début, 1950, as Boris Godunov and Colline; subsequently has appeared at all leading European and American opera houses; American début, Metropolitan Opera House, 1950; as Boris Godunov, San Francisco, 1956. Principal rôles include: Boris Godunov, King Philip, Galitzky, Konchak, Don Quixote, Dositheus, Ivan the Terrible, Ivan Susanin, Mephistopheles, Moses, Don Basilio, Pizarro, Simon Boccanegra. Has made numerous recordings, including opera and songs, winning many prix du disque; these include particularly the complete lyric works of the five great Russian composers.

Hon. Mem. Théâtre de l'Opéra, Paris, Mem. La Scala, Milan. Holds foreign decorations. Commendatore della Repubblica Italiana.

CHRISTOPHER, Ann, ARA 1980; sculptor; *b* 4 Dec. 1947; *d* of William and Phyllis Christopher; *m* 1969, Kenneth Cook. *Educ:* Harrow School of Art (pre-Diploma); West of England College of Art (DipAD Sculpture). Prizewinner, Daily Telegraph Young Sculptors Competition, 1971; Arts Council grants, 1973-76. *Exhibitions include:* Oxford Gallery, Oxford, 1973, 1974, 1978; Festival Gall., Bath, 1973; London Group exhibns, 1975, 1977; Park Street Gall., Bristol, 1978, 1980; Royal Academy, Summer Exhibns, 1971-81 incl. *Work in Collections:* Bristol City Art Gallery; Contemporary Arts Soc.; Chantrey, London. *Recreation:* cinema. *Address:* The Stable Block, Hay Street, Marshfield, near Chippenham, Wilts SN14 8NL. *T:* Marshfield 717.

CHRISTOPHER, Anthony Martin Grosvenor; General Secretary, Inland Revenue Staff Federation, since 1976; *b* 25 April 1925; *s* of George Russell Christopher and Helen Kathleen Milford Christopher (*née* Rowley); *m* 1962, Adela Joy Thompson. *Educ:* Cheltenham Grammar Sch.; Westminster Coll. of Commerce. Articled Pupil, Agric. Valuers, Gloucester, 1941-44; RAF, 1944-48; Inland Revenue, 1948-57; Asst Sec. 1957-60, Asst Gen. Sec. 1960-74, Jt Gen. Sec. 1975, Inland Revenue Staff Fedn; Member: TUC General Council, 1976-; TUC Economic Cttee, 1977-; TUC Education Cttee, 1977-; TUC Employment Policy and Organisation Cttee, 1979-. Member: Tax Reform Cttee, 1974-80; Tax Consultative Cttee, 1980-; Royal Commn on Distribution of Income and Wealth, 1978-79; IBA, 1978-. Director: Civil Service Building Soc., 1958- (Chm., 1978-); Trades Union Unit Trust, 1981-; Mem. Bd, Civil Service Housing Assoc., 1958-. Mem. Council, Nat. Assoc. for Care and Resettlement of Offenders, 1956 (Chm., 1973-); Mem., Home Sec.'s Adv. Council for Probation and After-care, 1967-77; Mem., Inner London Probation and After-care Cttee, 1966-79; Chm., Alcoholics Recovery Project, 1970-76; Mem., Home Sec.'s Working Party on Treatment of Habitual Drunken Offenders, 1969-71. Vis. Fellow, Univ. of Bath, 1981-. *Publications:* (jtly) Policy for Poverty, 1970; (jtly) The Wealth Report, 1979. *Recreations:* gardening, reading, music. *Address:* Douglas Houghton House, 231 Vauxhall Bridge Road, SW1V 1EH. *T:* 01-834 8254.

CHRISTOPHER, John Anthony, FRICS; Chief Valuer, Valuation Office, Inland Revenue, since 1981; *b* 19 June 1924; *s* of John William and Dorothy Christopher; *m* 1947, Pamela Evelyn Hardy; one *s* one *d* (and one *s* decd). *Educ:* Sir George Monoux Grammar Sch., Walthamstow; BSc Estate Management (London). Chartered Surveyor; LCC Valuation Dept, 1941. Served War, RAF, 1943-47. Joined Valuation Office, 1952; District Valuer and Valuation Officer, Lincoln, 1965; Superintending Valuer, Darlington, 1972; Asst Chief Valuer, 1974; Dep. Chief Valuer, Valuation Office, Inland Revenue, 1978. *Recreation:* golf. *Address:* Valuation Office, New Court, Carey Street, WC2A 2JE.

CHRISTOPHERSON, Sir Derman (Guy), Kt 1969; OBE 1946; FRS 1960; DPhil (Oxon) 1941; MICE, FIMechE; Master, Magdalene College, Cambridge, since 1979; *b* 6 Sept. 1915; *s* of late Derman Christopherson, Clerk in Holy Orders, formerly of Blackheath, and Edith Frances Christopherson; *m* 1940, Frances Edith, *d* of late James and Martha Tearle; three *s* one *d*. *Educ:* Sherborne Sch.; University Coll., Oxford (Hon. Fellow, 1977). Henry Fellow at Harvard Univ., 1938; Scientific Officer, Research and Experiments Dept, Ministry of Home Security, 1941-45; Fellow, Magdalene Coll., Cambridge, 1945 (Hon. Fellow 1969); Bursar, 1947; University Demonstrator, Cambridge Univ. Engineering Dept, 1945, Lecturer, 1946; Professor of Mechanical Engineering, Leeds Univ., 1949-55; Prof. of Applied Science, Imperial Coll. of Science and Technology, 1955-60; Vice-Chancellor and Warden, Durham Univ., 1960-78. Mem. Council of Institution of Mechanical Engineers, 1950-53; Clayton Prize, Instn of Mechanical Engineers, 1963. Chairman: Cttee of Vice-Chancellors and Principals, 1967-70; Central Council for Educn and Training in Social Work, 1971-79; CNAA (Chm., Educn Cttee), 1966-74; Board of Washington New Town Develt Corp., 1964-78; Science Research Coun., 1965-70. Mem. Council, Royal Soc., 1975; Chm., Royal Fine Art Commn, 1980- (Mem., 1978-). Fellow, Imperial Coll. of Science and Technology, 1966. Hon. DCL: Kent, 1966; Newcastle, 1971; Hon DSc: Aston, 1967; Sierra Leone, 1970; Hon. LLD: Leeds, 1969; Royal Univ. of Malta, 1969; DTech Brunel, 1979. *Publications:* The Engineer in The University, 1967; The University at Work, 1973; various papers in Proc. Royal Soc., Proc. IMechE, Jl of Applied Mechanics, etc. *Address:* Magdalene College, Cambridge. *Club:* United Oxford & Cambridge University.

CHRISTOPHERSON, Sir Harald Fairbairn, CMG 1978; a Senior Clerk, Committee Office, House of Commons, since 1980; *b* 12 Jan. 1920; *s* of late Captain H. and Mrs L. G. L. Christopherson; *m* 1947, Joyce Winifred Emmett (*d* 1979); one *s* two *d*. *Educ:* Heaton Grammar Sch., Newcastle upon Tyne; King's Coll., Univ. of Durham (BSc and DipEd). Served in RA, 1941-46, Captain 1945. Teacher and lecturer in mathematics, 1947-48. Entered administrative class, Home CS, Customs and Excise, 1948; seconded to Trade and Tariffs Commn, W Indies, 1956-58; Asst Sec., 1959; seconded to Treasury, 1965-66; Under Sec., 1969; Comr of Customs and Excise, 1970-80. *Recreations:* music, travel. *Address:* 57a York Road, Sutton, Surrey SM2 6HN. *T:* 01-642 2444.

CHRISTY, Ronald Kington, CB 1965; HM Chief Inspector of Factories, 1963-67; *b* 18 Aug. 1905; *s* of William and Edna Christy; *m* 1931, Ivy, *y d*

of W. Hinchcliffe, Whitchurch, Salop; one *s* one *d*. *Educ:* Strand Sch.; King's Coll., Univ. of London. Appointed HM Inspector of Factories, 1930; HM Superintending Inspector of Factories, 1953-59; HM Dep. Chief Inspector of Factories, 1959-63. Mem., Nuclear Safety Advisory Cttee, 1963-67. *Recreations:* gardening, travelling. *Address:* 6 Tyne Walk, Bembridge, IoW. *T:* Bembridge 2255.

CHUBB, family name of **Baron Hayter**.

CHUBB, Prof. Frederick Basil, MA, DPhil, LittD; Professor of Political Science, Dublin University, Trinity College, since 1960; *b* 8 Dec. 1921; *s* of late Frederick John Bailey Chubb and Gertrude May Chubb, Ludgershall, Wilts; *m* 1946, Margaret Gertrude, *d* of late George Francis and Christina Rafther; no *c*. *Educ:* Bishop Wordsworth's Sch., Salisbury; Merton Coll., Oxford. BA 1946; MA Oxon; MA Dublin; DPhil Oxon 1950; LittD Dublin 1976. Lecturer in Political Science, Trinity Coll., Dublin, 1948; Fellow in Polit. Sci., 1952; Reader in Polit. Sci., 1955; Bursar, 1957-62. Vice-Pres. Inst. of Public Administration, 1958; Chm., Comhairle na n-Ospidéal, 1972-78; Chm., Employer-Labour Conf., 1970; MRIA 1969. *Publications:* The Control of Public Expenditure, 1952; (with D. E. Butler (ed) and others) Elections Abroad, 1959; A Source Book of Irish Government, 1964; (ed with P. Lynch) Economic Development and Planning, 1969; The Government and Politics of Ireland, 1970, 2nd edn 1982; Cabinet Government in Ireland, 1974; The Constitution and Constitutional Change in Ireland, 1978; articles in learned jls. *Recreation:* fishing. *Address:* 19 Clyde Road, Ballsbridge, Dublin 4. *T:* 684625.

CHUBB, John Oliver, CMG 1976; HM Diplomatic Service, retired; Counsellor, Foreign and Commonwealth Office, 1973-80; *b* 21 April 1920; *s* of Clifford Chubb and Margaret Chubb (*née* Hunt); *m* 1945, Mary Griselda Robertson (marr. diss. 1980); one *s* two *d*. *Educ:* Rugby; Oxford (MA). Served War, Scots Guards, 1940-46. Joined Diplomatic Service, 1946; Beirut, 1947; Bagdad, 1948-49; Canal Zone, 1950-52; Cyprus, 1953; FO, 1954-56; Tokyo, 1957-61; FO, 1961-63; Hong Kong, 1964-66; FO, 1967. Chm., St John's Wood Soc., 1978-. *Recreations:* reading, spectator sports, golf, gardening, sailing. *Address:* 42 Clifton Hill, NW8 0QG. *T:* 01-624 2794. *Clubs:* Athenæum, MCC; Berkshire Golf, Senior Golfers' Society.

CHUNG, Kyung-Wha, Korean Order of Merit; concert violinist; *b* 26 March 1948; *d* of Chun-Chai Chung and Won-Sook (Lee) Chung. *Educ:* Juilliard Sch. of Music, New York. Moved from Korea to New York, 1960; 7 years' study with Ivan Galamian, 1960-67; New York début with New York Philharmonic Orch., 1967; European début with André Previn and London Symphony Orch., Royal Festival Hall, London, 1970. First prize, Leventritt Internat. Violin Competition, NY, 1967. *Address:* c/o Harrison Parrott, 12 Penzance Place, W11 4PA.

CHUNG, Hon. Sir Sze-yuen, Kt 1978; CBE 1975 (OBE 1968); DSc; PhD; CEng, FIMechE, FIProdE; CBIM; JP; Senior Unofficial Member, Hong Kong Executive Council, since 1980 (Member, 1972-80); Chairman: Hong Kong Polytechnic, since 1972; Planning Committee for the Second Polytechnic, since 1982; Sonca Industries Ltd, since 1978; Standing Commission on Civil Service Salaries and Conditions of Service, since 1980; *b* 3 Nov. 1917; *m* 1947, Nancy Cheung (*d* 1977); one *s* two *d*. *Educ:* Hong Kong Univ. (BScEng 1st Cl. Hons, 1941); Sheffield Univ. (PhD 1951). CEng, FIMechE 1957; FIProdE 1958. CBIM (FBIM 1978). Consulting engr, 1952-56; Gen. Man., Sonca Industries, 1956-60, Man. Dir 1960-77. Dir of cos. Mem., Hong Kong Legislative Council, 1965-74; Sen. Unofficial Mem., 1974-78. Chairman: Hong Kong Productivity Council, 1974-76; Asian Product. Org., 1969-70; Hong Kong Industrial Design Council, 1969-75; Fedn of Hong Kong Industries, 1966-70 (Hon. Life Pres. 1974); Hong Kong Metrication Cttee, 1969-73. Pres., Engrg Soc. of Hong Kong, 1960-61; Hon. Fellow, Hong Kong Instn of Engrs, 1976. DSc (*hc*) Hong Kong Univ., 1976. JP Hong Kong, 1964. Defence Medal, 1948; Silver Jubilee Medal, 1977; Gold Medal, Asian Productivity Orgn, 1980. *Publications:* contrib. Proc. IMechE, Jl Iron and Steel Inst., and Jl Engrg Soc. of Hong Kong. *Recreations:* swimming, hiking, badminton. *Address:* House 25, Bella Vista, Silverstrand, Beach Road, Kowloon, Hong Kong. *T:* Hong Kong 3-213506. *Clubs:* Hong Kong, Royal Hong Kong Jockey, Kowloon Cricket (Hong Kong).

CHURCH, John Carver, MBE 1970; HM Diplomatic Service; Consul-General, Naples, since 1981; *b* 8 Dec. 1929; *s* of Richard Church, CBE, FRSL, and Catherina Church; *m* 1953, Marie-Geneviève Vallette; two *s* two *d*. *Educ:* Cranbrook Sch., Kent; Ecole Alsacienne, Paris; Christ's Coll., Cambridge (MA 1953). Reuters News Agency, 1953-59; Central Office of Information, 1959-61; Commonwealth Relations Office: Information Officer, Calcutta, 1961-65; Foreign and Commonwealth Office: Second Secretary (Commercial) Rio de Janeiro, 1966-69; First Sec. (Information) Tel Aviv, 1969-74; First Sec., News Dept, FCO, 1974-77; Consul (Commercial) Milan, 1977-78; Consul-Gen., São Paulo, 1978-81. *Recreations:* reading, swimming, skiing. *Address:* c/o Foreign and Commonwealth Office, SW1; 8 Bramshill Gardens, NW5 1JH. *T:* 01-272 6240.

CHURCH, Prof. Ronald James H.; *see* Harrison-Church.

CHURCHER, Maj.-Gen. John Bryan, CB 1952; DSO 1944, Bar 1946; retired; Director and General Secretary, Independent Stores Association, 1959-71; *b* 2 Sept. 1905; *s* of late Lieut-Col B. T. Churcher, Wargrave, Berks, and Beatrice Theresa Churcher; *m* 1937, Rosamond Hildegarde Mary, *y d* of late Frederick Parkin, Truro Vean, Truro, Cornwall; one *s* two *d. Educ:* Wellington Coll., Berks; RMC Sandhurst. Commissioned DCLI, 1925; Lieut, 1927; Capt. KSLI, 1936; Staff Coll., 1939; served War of 1939-45 (despatches, DSO and Bar); commanded: 1 Bn Hereford Regt, 1942-44; 159 Inf. Bde, 1944-46; 43 Div., 1946; Northumbrian Dist., 1946; 2 Div., 1946; 3 Div., 1946-47; 5 Div., 1947-48; Brig., Imperial Defence Coll., 1948; BGS, Western Command, 1949-51; Chief of Staff, Southern Comd, 1951-54; GOC, 3rd Inf. Div., 1954-57; Dir of Military Training at the War Office, 1957-59; retired, 1959. ADC to King George VI, 1949-52; ADC to the Queen to 1952. *Address:* Tudor Barn, Stanway, near Colchester, Essex. *T:* Colchester 210294. *Club:* Army and Navy.

CHURCHHOUSE, Prof. Robert Francis, CBE 1982; PhD; Professor of Computing Mathematics, University College, Cardiff, since 1971; *b* 30 Dec. 1927; *s* of Robert Francis Churchhouse and Agnes Howard; *m* 1954, Julia McCarthy; three *s. Educ:* St Bede's Coll., Manchester; Manchester Univ. (BSc 1949); Trinity Hall, Cambridge (PhD 1952). Royal Naval Scientific Service, 1952-63; Head of Programming Gp, Atlas Computer Lab., SRC, 1963-71. Vis. Fellow, St Cross Coll., Oxford, 1972-. Chm., Computer Bd for Univs and Res. Councils, 1979-. *Publications:* (ed jtly) Computers in Mathematical Research, 1968; (ed jtly) The Computer in Literary and Linguistic Studies, 1976; Numerical Analysis, 1978; papers in math. and other jls. *Recreations:* cricket, astronomy. *Address:* 15 Holly Grove, Lisvane, Cardiff CF4 5UJ. *T:* Cardiff 750250. *Club:* Challenor.

CHURCHILL; see Spencer-Churchill.

CHURCHILL, 3rd Viscount *cr* 1902; **Victor George Spencer;** Baron 1815; Investment Manager, Central Board of Finance of the Church of England and Charities Official Investment Fund; Director, Local Authorities' Mutual Investment Trust; *b* 31 July 1934; *s* of 1st Viscount Churchill, GCVO, and late Christine Sinclair (who *m* 3rd, Sir Lancelot Oliphant, KCMG, CB); *S* half-brother, 1973. *Educ:* Eton; New Coll., Oxford (MA). Lieut, Scots Guards, 1953-55. Morgan Grenfell & Co. Ltd, 1958-74. *Heir* (to Barony only): Richard Harry Ramsay Spencer [*b* 11 Oct. 1926; *m* 1958, Antoinette Rose-Marie de Charrière; one *s* one *d*]. *Address:* 6 Cumberland Mansions, George Street, W1.

CHURCHILL, Diana (Josephine); actress, stage and screen; *b* Wembley, 21 Aug. 1913; *d* of Joseph H. Churchill, MRCS, LRCP and Ethel Mary Nunn; *m* Barry K. Barnes (*d* 1965); *m* 1976, Mervyn Johns. *Educ:* St Mary's Sch., Wantage; Guildhall Sch. of Music (scholarship). First professional appearance in Champion North, Royalty, 1931; subsequently in West End and in Repertory. Old Vic Season, 1949-50, New Theatre, as Rosaline in Love's Labour's Lost, Miss Kate Hardcastle in She Stoops to Conquer, Lizaveta Bogdanovna in A Month in the Country and Elise in The Miser; High Spirits, London Hippodrome, 1953; The Desperate Hours, London Hippodrome, 1955; Hamlet, Stratford-on-Avon Festival, 1956; Lady Fidget in The Country Wife, Royal Court Theatre, 1956; The Rehearsal, Globe Theatre, 1961; The Winter's Tale, Cambridge, 1966; The Farmer's Wife, Chichester, 1967; Heartbreak House, Chichester, later Lyric, 1967. Has also appeared in several films. *Address:* c/o Stella Richards Management, 42 Hazlebury Road, SW6.

CHURCHILL, Hon. Gordon, PC (Canada); DSO 1945; ED; QC; Canadian barrister, retired; *b* Coldwater, Ont, 8 Nov. 1898; *s* of Rev. J. W. and Mary E. Churchill; *m* 1922, Mona Mary, *d* of C. W. McLachlin, Dauphin, Man.; one *d. Educ:* Univ. of Manitoba. MA 1931, LLB 1950. Served European War, 1916-18, France; served War of 1939-45 (DSO), commanded First Canadian Armoured Carrier Regt, NW Europe. Principal of a Manitoba High Sch., 1928-38; Mem. Manitoba Legislature, 1946-49; called to Manitoba Bar, 1950; Member Federal Parlt for Winnipeg South Centre, 1951-68, retired; Federal Minister: for Trade and Commerce, 1957-60; of Veterans' Affairs, 1960-63; of National Defence, Feb.-April 1963. Hon. LLD Winnipeg 1976. *Address:* 2469 Mill Bay Road, Mill Bay, BC V0R 2P0, Canada.

CHURCHILL, John George Spencer; mural and portrait, townscape, landscape painter; sculptor, lecturer and author since 1932; *b* 31 May 1909; *s* of John Strange Spencer Churchill and Lady Gwendoline Bertie; *m* 1st, 1934, Angela Culme Seymour; one *d*; 2nd, 1941, Mary Cookson; 3rd, 1953, Kathlyn Tandy (*d* 1957); 4th, 1958, Lullan Boston (marr. diss. 1972). *Educ:* Harrow School; Pembroke Coll., Oxford; Royal Coll. of Art; Central Sch. of Art; Westminster Sch. of Art; Ruskin Sch. of Art, Oxford; private pupil of Meninsky, Hubbard, Nicholson and Lutyens. Stock Exchange, 1930-32. Served War, Major GSO, RE, 1939-45. Mural and portrait, townscape and landscape paintings in England, France, Spain, Portugal, Italy, Switzerland, Belgium and America, 1932-80. Lectr in America, 1961-69. *Work includes:* incised relief carving on slate and cement cast busts, in Marlborough Pavilion at Chartwell, Westerham, Kent (National Trust), 1949; reportage illustrations and paintings of Spanish Revolution, 1936, and Evacuation of BEF from Dunkirk, 1940 (in Illustrated London News). Mem., Soc. of Mural Painters. *Publications:* Crowded Canvas, 1960; A Churchill Canvas, 1961 (USA), serialised in Sunday Dispatch and Atlantic Monthly, USA; contrib. illustr.: Country Life, Connoisseur, etc. *Recreations:* music, travel. *Address:* (professional) Oscar Court, 17 Tite Street, SW3 4JR. *T:* 01-352 2352; (domicile) Appartement Churchill, 83360 Grimaud, France. *T:* 94.43.21.31. *Clubs:* Press; Cincinatti (Washington, DC, USA).

CHURCHILL, Very Rev. John Howard; Dean of Carlisle, since 1973; *b* 9 June 1920; *s* of John Lancelot and Emily Winifred Churchill; *m* 1948, Patricia May, *d* of late John James and Gertrude May Williams; one *s* two *d. Educ:* Sutton Valence Sch.; Trinity Coll., Cambridge (Exhibitioner); Lincoln Theological Coll. BA 1942, MA 1946. Deacon, 1943; priest, 1944; Asst curate St George, Camberwell, 1943-48; All Hallows', Tottenham, 1948-53; Chaplain and Lectr in Theology, King's Coll., London, 1953-60; Vicar of St George, Sheffield, 1960-67; Lectr in Education, Univ. of Sheffield, 1960-67; Canon Residentiary of St Edmundsbury, 1967-73; Director of Ordinands and Clergy Training, Diocese of St Edmundsbury and Ipswich, 1967-73. Lady Margaret Preacher, Univ. of Cambridge, 1969; Proctor in Convocation 1970-; Mem., Dioceses Commn, 1978-. Fellow of King's Coll., London, 1982. *Publications:* Prayer in Progress, 1961; Going Up: a look at University life 1963; Finding Prayer, 1978. *Recreation:* walking. *Address:* The Deanery, Carlisle CA3 8TZ. *T:* Carlisle 23335.

See also A. E. C. Green.

CHURCHILL, Maj.-Gen. Thomas Bell Lindsay, CB 1957; CBE 1949; MC *b* 1 Nov. 1907; 2nd *s* of late Alec Fleming Churchill, of PWD, Ceylon and Hong Kong, and late Elinor Elizabeth (*née* Bell); *m* 1934, Gwendolen Janie (*d* 1962), *e d* of late Lewis Williams, MD; one *s* one *d*; *m* 1968, Penelope Jane Ormiston (marr. diss. 1974). *Educ:* Dragon Sch., Oxford; Magdalen Coll Sch., Oxford; RMC Sandhurst. Gained Prize Cadetship to RMC Sandhurst 1926; Prize for Mil. Hist., 1927. 2nd Lieut, Manchester Regt, 1927; Burma Rebellion, 1930-31 (despatches, MC); Adjt, 1931-34; instructor in interpretation of air photographs, RAF Sch. of Photography, 1934-39 Company Comdr, France, 1939-40; GSO1 Commandos, Sicily and Salerno Landings, 1943; comd 2nd Commando Bde, Italy, 1943; with Marshal Tito and Yugoslav Partisans, 1944 (Partisan Star with Gold Wreath); Albania 1944; comd 11th and 138th Inf Bdes, Austria, 1945-46; Zone Comdr, Austria 1947-49; student, Imperial Def. Coll., 1952; Maj.-Gen. i/c Admin., GHQ, Far ELF, 1955-57; Vice-Quartermaster-Gen. to the Forces, 1957-60; Deputy Chief of Staff, Allied Land Forces, Central Europe, 1960-62, retd. Col The Manchester Regt, 1952-58; Col The King's Regt (Manchester and Liverpool) 1958-62. A Vice-Pres., British-Jugoslav Soc., 1975-. *Publications:* Manual of Interpretation of Air Photographs, 1939; articles to Yorks Archæolog. Jl, 1935 to Army Quarterly and to Jl of RUSI. *Recreations:* genealogy, heraldry; fine arts. *Address:* Lower Minchindgown Farm, Black Dog, near Crediton, Devon EX17 4QX. *T:* Witheridge 474.

CHURCHILL, Winston Spencer; MP (C) Stretford (Lancs) since 1970 author; journalist; company director; Chairman and Managing Director Gatwick Air Taxis Ltd; *b* 10 Oct. 1940; *s* of late Randolph Frederick Edward Spencer Churchill, MBE and of Mrs Averell Harriman, *e d* of 11th Baron Digby, KG, DSO, MC, TD; *m* 1964, Mary Caroline d'Erlanger, *d* of late Sir Gerard d'Erlanger, CBE, Chairman of BOAC; two *s* two *d. Educ:* Eton Christ Church, Oxford (MA). Correspondent in: Yemen, Congo and Angola 1964; Borneo and Vietnam, 1966; Middle East, 1967; Czechoslovakia, 1968 Nigeria, Biafra and Middle East, 1969. Correspondent of The Times, 1969-70 Lecture tours of the US and Canada, 1965, 1969, 1971, 1973, 1975, 1978, 1980 1981. Contested Gorton Div. of Manchester in Bye-election, Nov. 1967. PPS to Minister of Housing and Construction, 1970-72, to Minister of State, FCO 1972-73; Sec., Cons. Foreign and Commonwealth Affairs Cttee, 1973-76 Conservative Party front-bench spokesman on Defence, 1976-78; Vice-Chm. Cons. Defence Cttee, 1979-; Cons. Party Co-ordinator for Defence and Multilateral Disarmament, 1982-. Mem., Exec. of Cons. 1922 Cttee, 1979- Sponsored Motor Vehicles (Passenger Insce) Act 1972. Pres., Trafford Park Indust. Council, 1971-. Trustee: Winston Churchill Meml Trust, 1968-; Nat Benevolent Fund for the Aged, 1973-; Governor, English-Speaking Union 1975-80; Vice-Pres., British Technion Soc., 1976-. Hon. Fellow, Churchill Coll., Cambridge, 1969. Hon. LLD, Westminster Coll., Fulton, Mo, USA *Publications:* First Journey, 1964; (with late Randolph Churchill) Six Day War, 1967; Defending the West, 1981. *Recreations:* tennis, sailing, ski-ing *Address:* House of Commons, SW1A 0AA. *Clubs:* White's, Buck's, Press.

CHURSTON, 4th Baron *cr* 1858; **Richard Francis Roger Yarde-Buller;** B 1790; VRD; Lieut-Comdr RNVR, retired; *b* 12 Feb. 1910; *er s* of 3rd Baron and Jessie (who *m* 2nd, 1928, Theodore William Wessel), *o d* of Alfred Smither; *S* father, 1930; *m* 1st, 1933, Elizabeth Mary (from whom he obtained a divorce, 1943, and who *m* 1943, Lieut-Col P. Laycock; she *d* 1951), 2nd *d* of late W. B. du Pre; one *s* one *d*; 2nd, 1949, Mrs Jack Dunfee (*d* 1979) *Educ:* Eton Coll. *Heir: s* Hon. John Francis Yarde-Buller [*b* 29 Dec. 1934 *m* 1973, Alexandra, *d* of A. Contomichalos; one *s* one *d*]. *Address* Woodcote, St Andrew, Guernsey, Channel Isles. *Club:* Royal Yacht Squadron.

See also Earl Cadogan, Sir G. A. Lyle, Bt.

CHUTE, Marchette; author; *b* 16 Aug. 1909; *d* of William Young Chute and Edith Mary Pickburn; unmarried. *Educ:* Univ. of Minnesota (BA). Doctor of Letters: Western Coll., 1952; Carleton Coll., 1957; Dickinson Coll., 1964 Mem., American Acad. of Arts and Letters. Outstanding Achievement Award Univ. of Minnesota, 1958; co-winner of Constance Lindsay Skinner Award 1959. *Publications:* Rhymes about Ourselves, 1932; The Search for God, 1941 Rhymes about the Country, 1941; The Innocent Wayfaring, 1943; Geoffrey Chaucer of England, 1946; Rhymes about the City, 1946; The End of the Search, 1947; Shakespeare of London, 1950; An Introduction to Shakespeare 1951 (English title: Shakespeare and his Stage); Ben Jonson of Westminster 1953; The Wonderful Winter, 1954; Stories from Shakespeare, 1956; Around and About, 1957; Two Gentle Men: the Lives of George Herbert and Robert Herrick, 1959; Jesus of Israel, 1961; The Worlds of Shakespeare (with Ernestine Perrie), 1963; The First Liberty: a history of the right to vote in America, 1619-1850, 1969; The Green Tree of Democracy, 1971; PEN American Center: a history of the first fifty years, 1972; Rhymes About Us, 1974; various articles in Saturday Review, Virginia Quarterly Review, etc. *Recreations*: walking, reading, talking. *Address*: 450 East 63rd Street, New York, NY 10021, USA. *T*: Templeton 8-8920. *Clubs*: Royal Society of Arts; PEN, Renaissance Society of America (New York).

CHWATT, Professor Leonard Jan B.; *see* Bruce-Chwatt.

CHYNOWETH, David Boyd; County Treasurer, South Yorkshire County Council, since 1973; *b* 26 Dec. 1940; *s* of Ernest and Blodwen Chynoweth; *m* 1968, Margaret Slater; one *s* two *d*. *Educ*: Simon Langton Sch., Canterbury; Univ. of Nottingham (BA). IPFA. Public Finance posts with Derbs CC, 1962 and London Borough of Ealing, 1965; Asst County Treas., Flints CC, 1968; Dep. County Treas., West Suffolk CC, 1970. Mem. Investment Protection Cttee, Nat. Assoc. of Pension Funds; Financial Advisor to Assoc. of Metropolitan Authorities; Pres., Assoc. of Public Service Finance Officers, 1981-82. *Recreations*: sailing, photography. *Address*: County Offices, Regent Street, Barnsley, S Yorks S70 2DX. *T*: Barnsley 86141. *Club*: Royal Over-Seas League.

CHYNOWETH, Rt. Rev. Neville James; *see* Gippsland, Bishop of.

CILENTO, Sir Raphael West, Kt 1935; MD, BS (Adelaide); DTM&H (England); (life) FRSanI (London); FRHistSoc, Queensland; Director-General of Health and Medical Services, Queensland, Australia, 1934-45; Hon. Professor of Tropical and Social Medicine, University of Queensland, 1937-45; Barrister Supreme Court, Queensland, since 1939; *b* 2 Dec. 1893; *s* of Raphael Ambrose Cilento and Frances Ellen Elizabeth West; *m* 1920, Phyllis Dorothy, *d* of late C. T. McGlew; three *s* three *d*. *Educ*: Adelaide High Sch.; Prince Alfred Coll., South Australia; Univ. of Adelaide. Colonial Medical Service (Federated Malay States), 1920-21; Duncan and Lalcaca medals, London Sch. of Tropical Medicine, 1922; Dir, Australian Inst. of Tropical Medicine, Townsville, North Queensland, 1922-28; Dir of Public Health, New Guinea, 1924-28; Rep. (Brit.) League of Nations Mission on Health Conditions in the Pacific with Dr P. Hermant (French rep.), 1928-29; Dir for Tropical Hygiene, Commonwealth of Australia, and Chief Quarantine Officer (General) NE Div., 1928-34, Brisbane, Qld; Pres., Royal Society Qld, 1933-34; Chm., State Nutritional Advisory Board, 1937; Pres., Med. Board of Qld, 1939; Assessor, Med. Assessment Tribunal, 1940; Senior Administrative Officer, Commonwealth Dept of Health, Canberra, ACT; Mem., Army Medical Directorates Consultative Cttee, 1941-45; Chm., National Survey, Health of Coal Miners, Australia, 1945; UNRRA Zone Dir, British occupied area Germany, Maj.-Gen., with assimilated status, BAOR, 1945-46; Dir, Div. of Refugees, 1946, of Div. of Social Activities, 1947-50, UN, NY. Pres., Royal Hist. Soc. of Queensland, 1934-35, 1943-44, 1953-68; Pres., Nat. Trust of Queensland, 1967-71. *Publications*: Malaria, 1924; White Man in the Tropics, 1925; Factors in Depopulation; NW Islands of the Mandated Territory of New Guinea, 1928; Health Problems in the Pacific, 1929; Anne Mackenzie Oration, 1933; Second Sir Herbert Maitland Oration, 1937; Tropical Diseases in Australasia, 1940 (and 1942); Blueprint for the Health of a Nation, 1944. *Recreations*: international affairs, reading history. *Address*: Altavilla, 56 Glen Road, Toowong, Queensland 4066, Australia. *Clubs*: Johnsonian (Brisbane); Australasian Pioneers (Sydney).
See also Sean Connery.

CITRINE, family name of **Baron Citrine.**

CITRINE, 1st Baron *cr* 1946, of Wembley; **Walter McLennan Citrine,** PC 1940; GBE 1958 (KBE 1935); Comp. IEE; *b* Liverpool, 22 Aug. 1887; *m* 1913, Doris Slade (*d* 1973); two *s*. Mersey District Sec. of Electrical Trades Union, 1914-20; Pres., Fed. Engineering and Shipbuilding Trades, Mersey District, 1917-18; Sec., 1918-20; Asst Gen. Sec., Electrical Trades Union, 1920-23; Asst Sec., TUC, 1924-25, Gen. Sec., 1926-46; Mem., Nat. Coal Board, 1946-47; Chm., Miners' Welfare Commn, 1946-47. Pres., Internat. Fed. of Trade Unions, 1928-45; Dir, Daily Herald (1929) Ltd, 1929-46; Mem., Nat. Production Advisory Council, 1942-46 and 1949-57; Past Mem., Reconstruction Jt Advisory Council; Treasury Consultative Council; Visiting Fellow, Nuffield Coll., 1939-47; Trustee of Imperial Relations Trust, 1937-49; Nuffield Trust for the Forces, 1939-46; Mem. of Cinematograph Films Council, 1938-48; Exec. Cttee of Red Cross, and St John War Organisation, 1939-46; Chm. of Production Cttee on Regional Boards (Munitions), 1942; Mem., Royal Commission on W Indies, 1938; Pres., British Electrical Development Assoc., 1948-52; Chm. Central Electricity Authority, 1947-57; Pres., Electrical Research Assoc., 1950-52 and 1956-57; Pres. (1955) and Mem. of Directing Cttee, Union Internationale des Producteurs et Distributeurs d'Energie Electrique; Part-time Mem., Electricity Council, 1958-62. Part-time Mem. of UK Atomic Energy Authority, 1958-62. Hon. LLD, Manchester. *Publications*: ABC of Chairmanship; The Trade Union Movement of Great Britain; Labour and the Community; I Search for Truth in Russia, 1936 and 1938; My Finnish Diary; My American Diary, 1941; In Russia Now, 1942; British Trade Unions, 1942; Men and Work, 1964; Two Careers, 1967, etc. *Heir*: *s* Hon. N. A. Citrine, *qv*. *Address*: Gorse Cottage, Victoria Road, Brixham, Devon.

CITRINE, Hon. Norman Arthur, LLB; solicitor in general practice; author, editor, lecturer; *b* 27 Sept. 1914; *e s* and *heir* of 1st Baron Citrine, *qv*; *m* 1939, Kathleen Alice Chilvers; one *d*. *Educ*: University Coll. Sch., Hampstead; Law Society's Sch., London. Admitted solicitor of Supreme Court (Hons), 1937; LLB (London), 1938. Served War of 1939-45, Lieut RNVR, 1940-46. Legal Adviser to Trades Union Congress, 1946-51; entered general legal practice, 1951. *Publications*: War Pensions Appeal Cases, 1946; Guide to Industrial Injuries Acts, 1948; Trade Union Law, 1950, 3rd edn, 1968; Editor, ABC of Chairmanship, 1952-. *Recreations*: boating, engineering, painting, carpentry. *Address*: Gorse Cottage, Berry Head, Brixham, Torbay, Devon. *T*: Brixham 51091.

CIVIL, Alan; Principal Horn, BBC Symphony Orchestra, since 1966; *b* 13 June 1928; *m* Shirley Jean Hopkins; three *s* three *d*. *Educ*: Northampton, various schools. Principal Horn, Royal Philharmonic Orchestra, 1953-55; Philharmonia Orchestra, 1955-66. Guest Principal, Berlin Philharmonic Orchestra; international horn soloist; Prof. of Horn, Royal Coll. of Music, London; composer; founder of Alan Civil Horn Trio. Member: London Wind Soloists; London Wind Quintet; Music Group of London. *Recreations*: brewing, gardening, Baroque music. *Address*: Downe Hall, Downe, Kent. *T*: Farnborough (Kent) 52982. *Club*: Savage.

CLAGUE, Ven. Arthur Ashford; Archdeacon of the Isle of Man, 1978-82; Vicar of Lezayre, 1969-82; *b* 12 Jan. 1915; *s* of John James and May Clague; *m* 1940, Kathleen Louise (*née* Delaney); one *d*. *Educ*: King William's Coll., Isle of Man; St John's Coll., Durham Univ. (BA 1938, MA 1941). Deacon 1938, priest 1939, Manchester; Curate, St Mary, Crumpsall, Manchester, 1938-40; Lecturer, Bolton Parish Church, 1940-44; Rector, Christ Church, Harpurhey, Manchester, 1945-49; Rector of Golborne, Dio. Liverpool, 1949-69. Rural Dean of Ramsey, 1972; Diocesan Canon, 1977. *Recreation*: golf. *Address*: The Old Coach House, Northumberland Street, Alnmouth, Alnwick, Northumberland NE66 2RJ. *Clubs*: Royal Commonwealth Society; Raven (I of M).

CLAMAGERAN, Alice Germaine Suzanne; Director, School of Social Workers, Centre Hospitalier Universitaire de Rouen, 1942-73; President, International Council of Nurses, 1961-65; *b* 5 March 1906; *d* of William Clamageran, shipowner at Rouen and of Lucie Harlé. *Educ*: Rouen. Nursing studies: Red Cross School of Nurses, Rouen; Ecole Professionnelle d'Assistance aux Malades, Paris. Tutor, Red Cross Sch. for Nurses, Rouen, 1931-42 (leave, for course in Public Health at Florence Nightingale Internat. Foundn, London, 1934-35). War service (6 months), 1939-40. President: Bd of Dirs, Fondation Edith Seltzer (Sanatorium Chantoiseau, Briançon) for Nurses, Social Workers and Medical Auxiliaries; Assoc. Médico-Sociale Protestante de Langue Française; Hon. Pres. Nat. Assoc. of Trained Nurses in France. Hon. Fellow, Royal Coll. of Nursing of UK, 1977. Médaille de Bronze de l'Enseignement Technique, 1960; Officier dans l'Ordre de la Santé Publique, 1961; Chevalier, Légion d'Honneur, 1962. *Address*: Hautonne, 27310 Bourg-Achard, France.

CLANCARTY, 8th Earl of, *cr* 1803; **William Francis Brinsley Le Poer Trench;** Baron Kilconnel, 1797; Viscount Dunlo, 1801; Baron Trench (UK), 1815; Viscount Clancarty (UK), 1823; Marquess of Heusden (Kingdom of the Netherlands), 1818; author; *b* 18 Sept. 1911; 5th *s* of 5th Earl of Clancarty and of Mary Gwatkin, *d* of late W. F. Rosslewin Ellis; *S* half-brother, 1975; *m* 1st, 1940, Diana Joan (marr. diss. 1947), *yr d* of Sir William Younger, 2nd Bt; 2nd, 1961, Mrs Wilma Dorothy Millen Belknap (marr. diss. 1969), *d* of S. R. Vermilyea, USA; 3rd, 1974, Mrs Mildred Alleyn Spong (*d* 1975); 4th, 1976, May, *widow* of Commander Frank M. Beasley, RN and *o d* of late E. Radonicich. *Educ*: Nautical Coll., Pangbourne. Founder Pres., Contact International; Chm., House of Lords UFO Study Gp. *Publications*: (as Brinsley Le Poer Trench): The Sky People, 1960; Men Among Mankind, 1962; Forgotten Heritage, 1964; The Flying Saucer Story, 1966; Operation Earth, 1969; The Eternal Subject, 1973; Secret of the Ages, 1974. *Recreations*: Ufology, travel, walking. *Heir*: *nephew* Nicholas Power Richard Le Poer Trench, *b* 1 May 1952. *Address*: 6 Lyall Street, Belgravia, SW1. *Club*: Buck's.

CLANCY, Most Rev. Edward Bede; *see* Canberra and Goulburn, Archbishop of, (RC).

CLANFIELD, Viscount; Ashton Robert Gerard Peel; *b* 16 Sept. 1976; *s* and *heir* of 3rd Earl Peel, *qv*.

CLANMORRIS, 7th Baron (Ireland), *cr* 1800; **John Michael Ward Bingham;** *b* 3 Nov. 1908; *o s* of 6th Baron Clanmorris; *S* father, 1960; *m* 1934, Madeleine Mary, *d* of late Clement Ebel, Copyhold Place, Cuckfield, Sussex; one *s* one *d*. *Educ*: Cheltenham Coll.; France and Germany. *Publications*: as John Bingham: My Name is Michael Sibley, 1952; Five Roundabouts to Heaven, 1953; The Third Skin, 1954; The Paton Street Case, 1955; Marion, 1958; Murder Plan Six, 1958; Night's Black Agent, 1960; A Case of Libel, 1963; A Fragment of Fear, 1965; The Double Agent, 1966; I Love, I Kill, 1968; Vulture in the Sun, 1971; The Hunting Down of Peter Manuel, 1974; God's Defector, 1976; The Marriage Bureau Murders, 1977; Brock the Defector, 1981. *Heir*: *s* Hon. Simon John Ward Bingham [*b* 25 Oct. 1937; *m* 1971, Gizella Maria, *d* of Sandor Zverkó; one *d*]. *Address*: c/o Coutts & Co., 10 Mount Street, W1. *Club*: Press.
See also Hon. Charlotte Bingham.

CLANWILLIAM, 6th Earl of, *cr* 1776; **John Charles Edmund Carson Meade;** Bt 1703; Viscount Clanwilliam, Baron Gilford, 1766; Baron Clanwilliam (UK), 1828; Major Coldstream Guards (retired); HM Lord-Lieutenant for Co. Down, 1975-79 (HM Lieutenant, 1962-75); *b* 6 June 1914; *o s* of late Earl of Clanwilliam; *S* father, 1953; *m* 1948, Catherine, *y d* of late A. T. Loyd, Lockinge, Wantage, Berks; six *d. Educ:* Eton; RMC Sandhurst. Adjt, 1939-42; Staff Coll., Haifa, 1942; Bde Major, 201 Guards Motor Brigade, 1942-43; Bde Major, 6 Guards Tank Brigade, 1944; Command and Gen. Staff Sch., Fort Leavenworth, USA, 1944; served in Middle East and France (despatches twice); retd, 1948. *Heir: cousin* John Herbert Meade [*b* 27 Sept. 1919; *m* 1956, Maxine, *o d* of late J. A. Hayden-Scott; one *s* two *d*]. *Address:* Rainscombe Park, Oare, Marlborough, Wilts. *T:* Pewsey 3491. *Clubs:* Carlton, Pratt's.

CLAPHAM, Prof. Arthur Roy, CBE 1969; FRS 1959; MA, PhD Cantab; FLS; Professor of Botany in Sheffield University, 1944-69, Professor Emeritus 1969; Pro-Vice-Chancellor, 1954-58, Acting Vice-Chancellor, 1965; Member of the Nature Conservancy, 1956-72 (Chairman, Scientific Policy Committee, 1963-70); Chairman, British National Committee for the International Biological Programme, 1964-75; President, Linnean Society, 1967-70; *b* 24 May 1904; *o s* of George Clapham, Norwich; *m* 1933, Brenda North Stoessiger; one *s* two *d* (and one *s* decd). *Educ:* City of Norwich Sch.; Downing Coll., Cambridge (Foundation Scholar). Frank Smart Prize, 1925; Frank Smart Student, 1926-27; Crop Physiologist at Rothamsted Agricultural Experimental Station, 1928-30; Demonstrator in Botany at Oxford Univ., 1930-44. Mem., NERC, 1965-70; Trustee, British Museum (Natural History), 1965-75. Hon. LLD Aberdeen, 1970; Hon. LittD, Sheffield, 1970. Linnean Gold Medal (Botany), 1972. *Publications:* (with W. O. James) The Biology of Flowers, 1935; (with T. G. Tutin and E. F. Warburg) Flora of the British Isles, 1952, 1962; Excursion Flora of the British Isles, 1959, 3rd rev. edn 1981; (with B. E. Nicholson) The Oxford Book of Trees, 1975; various papers in botanical journals. *Address:* The Parrock, Arkholme, Carnforth, Lancs. *T:* Hornby 21206.

CLAPHAM, Brian Ralph; His Honour Judge Clapham; a Circuit Judge, South East Circuit, since 1974; *b* 1 July 1913; *s* of Isaac Clapham and Laura Alice Clapham (*née* Meech); *m* 1961, Margaret Warburg; two *s. Educ:* Tonbridge Sch.; Wadham Coll., Oxford; University Coll. London (LLB, LLM 1976). Called to Bar, Middle Temple, 1936. Contested (Lab): Tonbridge, 1950; Billericay, 1951, 1955; Chelmsford, 1959. Councillor, Tonbridge and Southborough UDCs, 1947-74; Chm., Tonbridge UDC, 1959-60. Governor, West Kent Coll. Corresp. Mem., British Psychological Soc. Freeman of City of London. BA Open, 1981. *Recreations:* walking and talking.

CLAPHAM, Sir Michael (John Sinclair), KBE 1973; Chairman: IMI Ltd, 1974-81; BPM Holdings Ltd, 1974-81; *b* 17 Jan. 1912; *s* of late Sir John Clapham, CBE and Lady Clapham, Cambridge; *m* 1935, Hon. Elisabeth Russell Rea, *d* of 1st Baron Rea of Eskdale; three *s* one *d. Educ:* Marlborough Coll.; King's Coll., Cambridge (MA). Apprenticed as printer with University Press, Cambridge, 1933-35; Overseer and later Works Man., Percy Lund Humphries & Co. Ltd, Bradford, 1935-38; joined ICI Ltd as Man., Kynoch Press, 1938; seconded, in conseq. of developing a diffusion barrier, to Tube Alloys Project (atomic energy), 1941-45; Personnel Dir, ICI Metals Div., 1946; Midland Regional Man., ICI, 1951; Jt Man. Dir, ICI Metals Div., 1952; Chm. 1959; Dir, ICI, 1961-74, Dep. Chm. 1968-74; served as Overseas Dir; Dir, ICI of Austr. & NZ Ltd, 1961-74; Director: Imp. Metal Industries Ltd, 1962-70; Lloyds Bank Ltd, 1971-82 (Dep. Chm., 1974-80); Grindlay's Bank Ltd, 1975-; Associated Communications Corp., 1982-. Mem., General Motors European Adv. Council, 1975-82. Dep. Pres., 1971-72, Pres., 1972-74, CBI. Member: IRC, 1969-71; Standing Adv. Cttee on Pay of Higher Civil Service, 1968-71; Review Body on Doctors' and Dentists' Remuneration, 1968-70; Birmingham Educn Cttee, 1949-56; W Mids Adv. Coun. for Techn., Commercial and Art Educn, and Regional Academic Bd, 1952; Life Governor, Birmingham Univ., 1955 (Mem. Coun., 1956-61); Member: Court, Univ. of London, 1969-; Govt Youth Service Cttee (Albemarle Cttee), 1958; CNAA, 1964-77 (Chm., 1971-77); NEDC, 1971-76; Pres., Inst. of Printing, 1980-82. Hon. DSc Aston, 1973; Hon. LLD CNAA, 1978. *Publications:* Printing, 1500-1730, in The History of Technology, Vol. III, 1957; Multinational Enterprises and Nation States, 1975; various articles on printing, personnel management and education. *Recreations:* sailing, canal boating, cooking. *Address:* 26 Hill Street, W1X 7FU. *T:* 01-499 1240. *Clubs:* Royal Yacht Squadron, Royal Cruising.
See also B. D. Till.

CLARE, Ernest Elwyn S.; *see* Sabben-Clare.

CLARE, Herbert Mitchell N.; *see* Newton-Clare.

CLARENDON, 7th Earl of, 2nd *cr* 1776; **George Frederick Laurence Hyde Villiers;** a Managing Director, Seccombe Marshall and Campion Ltd, since 1962; *b* 2 Feb. 1933; *o s* of Lord Hyde (*d* 1935) and Hon. Marion Féodorovna Louise Glyn, Lady Hyde (*d* 1970), *er d* of 4th Baron Wolverton; *S* grandfather, 1955; *m* 1974, Jane Diana, *d* of late E. W. Dawson; one *s* one *d.* Page of Honour to King George VI, 1948-49; Lieut RHG, 1951-53. *Heir: s* Lord Hyde, *qv. Address:* 8 Chelsea Square, SW3 6LF. *T:* 01-352 6338.

CLARFELT, Jack Gerald; Director, FMC Ltd (Executive Deputy Chairman, 1975-79); *b* 7 Feb. 1914; *s* of Barnett Clarfelt and Rene (*née* Frankel); *m* 1948, Baba Fredman; one *s* one *d. Educ:* Grocers' Co. Sch.; Sorbonne. Practised as Solicitor in own name, 1938-40; Man. Dir, Home Killed Meat Assoc., 1940-43 and 1945-54; Queen's Royal Surreys, 1940-45; Man. Dir, Fatstock Marketing Corp., 1954-60; Chm., Smithfield & Zwanenberg Gp Ltd, 1960-75; Dir, Macpherson Train & Co. Ltd, 1975-. Farming, Hampshire. Master, Worshipful Co. of Butchers, 1978. *Recreations:* golf, swimming. *Address:* Linhay Meads, Timsbury, Romsey, Hants. *T:* Braishfield 68243. *Clubs:* City Livery, Farmers'.

CLARINGBULL, Sir (Gordon) Frank, Kt 1975; BSc, PhD, FGS, FInstP, FMA; Director, British Museum (Natural History), 1968-76; *b* 21 Aug. 1911; *s* of William Horace Claringbull and Hannah Agnes Cutting; *m* 1st, 1938, Grace Helen Mortimer (*d* 1953); one *s* one *d*; 2nd, 1953, Enid Dorothy Phyllis, *d* of late William Henry Lambert. *Educ:* Finchley Grammar Sch.; Queen Mary Coll., Univ. of London (Fellow 1967). British Museum (Natural Hist.): Asst Keeper, 1935-48; Princ. Scientific Officer, 1948-53; Keeper of Mineralogy, 1953-68. Explosives res., Min. of Supply, 1940-43; special scientific duties, War Office, 1943-45. Mineralogical Soc.: Gen. Sec., 1938-59; Vice-Pres, 1959-63; Pres., 1965-67; For. Sec., 1967-71, Managing Trustee, 1969-77; Gemmological Assoc.: Vice-Pres., 1970-72, Pres., 1972-. Mem., Commn on Museums and Galleries, 1976-. *Publications:* Crystal Structures of Minerals (with W. L. Bragg); papers in journals of learned societies on mineralogical and related topics. *Recreations:* craftwork, gardening, photography. *Address:* Langley House, Main Street, Ash, Martock, Somerset TA12 6PB. *T:* Martock 822983. *Club:* Athenæum.

CLARK; *see* Chichester-Clark.

CLARK, family name of Baron Clark.

CLARK, Baron *cr* 1969 (Life Peer); **Kenneth Mackenzie Clark,** OM 1976; CH 1959; KCB 1938; CLit 1974; FBA 1949; *b* 13 July 1903; *o s* of late Kenneth McKenzie Clark and Margaret McArthur; *m* 1st, 1927, Elizabeth Martin (*d* 1976); two *s* one *d*; 2nd, 1977, Mme Nolwen de Janzé-Rice. *Educ:* Winchester; Trinity College, Oxford (Hon. Fellow, 1968). Worked for two years with Mr Bernard Berenson, Florence; Keeper of Dept of Fine Art, Ashmolean Museum, Oxford, 1931-33; Director of National Gallery, 1934-45; Surveyor of the King's Pictures, 1934-44; Director of Film Div., later Controller, Home Publicity, Ministry of Information, 1939-41; Slade Professor of Fine Art, Oxford, 1946-50, and October 1961-62; Prof. of the History of Art, Royal Academy, 1977-. Chancellor, Univ. of York, 1969-79. Chairman: Arts Council of Great Britain, 1953-60; ITA, 1954-57. Former Trustee, British Museum. Member: Conseil Artistique des Musées Nationaux; Amer. Academy; Swedish Academy; Spanish Academy; Florentine Acad.; French Acad., 1973; Institut de France. Hon. Mem., American Inst. of Architects. Hon. Degrees from Universities: Oxford, Cambridge, London, Glasgow, Liverpool, Sheffield, York, Warwick, Bath, Columbia (NY), Brown (Rhode Island). Hon. FRIBA; Hon. FRCA. Serena Medal of British Academy (for Italian Studies), 1955; Gold Medal and Citation of Honour New York University; US Nat. Gall. of Arts Medal, 1970; Gold Medal, NY City, 1977; Gold Medal, Academie des Beaux-Arts. HRSA. Comdr, Legion of Honour, France; Comdr, Lion of Finland; Order of Merit, Grand Cross, 2nd Cl., Austria. *Publications:* The Gothic Revival, 1929; Catalogue of Drawings of Leonardo da Vinci in the collection of His Majesty the King at Windsor Castle, 1935; One Hundred Details in the National Gallery, 1938; Leonardo da Vinci, 1939, new edn 1967; Last Lectures by Roger Fry, edited with an introduction, 1939; L. B. Alberti on Painting, 1944; Constable's Hay Wain, 1944; (Introduction to) Praeterita, 1949; Landscape into Art, 1949; Piero della Francesca, 1951; Moments of Vision, 1954; The Nude, 1955; Looking, 1960; Ruskin Today, 1964; Rembrandt and the Italian Renaissance, 1966; A Failure of Nerve, 1967; Civilisation, 1969; Looking at Pictures, 1972; (jtly) Westminster Abbey, 1972; The Artist Grows Old (Rede Lecture), 1972; The Romantic Rebellion, 1973; Another Part of the Wood (autobiog.), 1974; Henry Moore Drawings, 1974; The Drawings by Sandro Botticelli for Dante's Divine Comedy, 1976; The Other Half (autobiog.), 1977; Animals and Men, 1977; An Introduction to Rembrandt, 1978; The Best of Aubrey Beardsley, 1979; Feminine Beauty, 1980. Numerous TV programmes, 1965-68; TV series: Civilisation, 1969; Romantic versus Classic Art, 1973; Moments of Vision, 1981. *Address:* The Garden House, Castle Road, Saltwood, Hythe, Kent.
See also Hon. A. K. M. Clark.

CLARK, Rt. Rev. Alan Charles; *see* East Anglia, Bishop of, (RC).

CLARK, Hon. Alan Kenneth McKenzie; MP (C) Plymouth Sutton, since Feb. 1974; historian; *b* 13 April 1928; *s* of Baron Clark, *qv* ; *m* 1958, Caroline Jane Beuttler; two *s. Educ:* Eton; Christ Church, Oxford (MA). Household Cavalry (Training Regt), 1946; RAuxAF, 1952-54. Barrister, Inner Temple, 1955. Mem., Inst. for Strategic Studies, 1963. Vice-Chm., Parly Defence Cttee, 1980-. Mem., RUSI. *Publications:* The Donkeys, A History of the BEF in 1915, 1961; The Fall of Crete, 1963; Barbarossa, The Russo-German Conflict, 1941-45, 1965; Aces High: the war in the air over the Western Front 1914-18, 1973; (ed) A Good Innings: the private papers of Viscount Lee of Fareham, 1974. *Address:* Saltwood Castle, Kent. *T:* Hythe 67190. *Clubs:* Brooks's, Pratt's.

CLARK, Albert William; His Honour Judge Clark; a Circuit Judge, since 1981; *b* 23 Sept. 1922; *s* of William Charles Clark and Cissy Dorothy Elizabeth Clark; *m* 1951, Frances Philippa, *d* of Dr Samuel Lavington Hart, Tientsin; one *s* one *d. Educ:* Christ's Coll., Finchley. War service, 1941-46, Royal Navy. Called to Bar, Middle Temple, 1949; Clerk of Arraigns, Central Criminal Court, 1951-56; Clerk to the Justices, E Devon, 1956-70; Acting Dep. Chm., Inner London QS, 1971; Dep. Circuit Judge, 1972-80; Metropolitan Magistrate, 1970-80. Mem., Central Council of Probation and After-Care Cttees, 1975-81. *Recreations:* fly-fishing, walking, etc. *Address:* Coombe Cottage, Renfrew Road, Kingston Hill, Surrey. *T:* 01-942 8100.

CLARK of Herriotshall, Arthur Melville, MA (Hons); DPhil; DLitt; FRSE; FRSA; Reader in English Literature, Edinburgh University, 1946-60; *b* 20 Aug. 1895; 4th *s* of late James Clark and Margaret Moyes McLachlan, Edinburgh. *Educ:* Stewart's Coll., Edinburgh; Edinburgh Univ. (Sibbald Bursar and Vans Dunlop Scholar); Oriel Coll., Oxford (Scholar); MA First Class Hons and twice medallist, DLitt Edinburgh; DPhil Oxford. Lectr in English Language and Literature, Reading, 1920; Tutor to Oxford Home Students, 1921; Sec. of Oxford Union Soc., 1923; Pres. of Speculative Soc., 1926-29; Lectr in English Literature, Edinburgh Univ., 1928-46; Dir of Studies, Edinburgh Univ., 1931-47; Editor of Edinburgh University Calendar, 1933-45; External Examiner in English, St Andrews Univ., 1939-43, and Aberdeen Univ., 1944-46. Pres. of Scottish Arts Club, 1948-50. Pres. of Edinburgh Scott Club, 1957-58. Exhibitor RSA, SSA. Knight's Cross, Order of Polonia Restituta, 1968; GCLJ 1977. *Publications:* The Realistic Revolt in Modern Poetry, 1922; A Bibliography of Thomas Heywood (annotated), 1924; Thomas Heywood, Playwright and Miscellanist, 1931; Autobiography, its Genesis and Phases, 1935; Spoken English, 1946; Studies in Literary Modes, 1946; Two Pageants by Thomas Heywood, 1953; Sonnets from the French, and Other Verses, 1966; Sir Walter Scott: The Formative Years, 1969; Murder under Trust, or The Topical Macbeth, 1982; contribs to Encyc. Brit., Collier's Encyc., Encyc. of Poetry and Poetics, Cambridge Bibl. of Eng. Lit., Library, Mod. Lang. Review, Classical Review, etc. *Recreations:* walking, pastel-sketching. *Address:* 3 Woodburn Terrace, Edinburgh EH10 4SH. *T:* 031-447 1240; Herriotshall, Oxton, Berwickshire. *Clubs:* New, Scottish Arts (Edinburgh); Union Society (Oxford).

CLARK, Charles David Lawson; Chief Executive, Hutchinson Ltd, since 1980; Chairman, Hutchinson Publishing Group, since 1980 (Managing Director, 1972); *b* 12 June 1933; *s* of Alec Fulton Charles Clark, CB, and of Mary Clark; *m* 1960, Fiona McKenzie Mill; one *s* three *d. Educ:* Edinburgh Acad.; Jesus Coll., Oxford (Exhibnr; MA). Called to the Bar, Inner Temple, 1960. Second Lieut 4th Regt RHA. Editor: Sweet and Maxwell, 1957-60; Penguin Books, 1960-66; Managing Director: Penguin Educn, 1966-72; Allen Lane the Penguin Press, 1967-69; Dir, LWT (Holdings) Ltd, 1982-. Chairman: Bookrest, 1975-78; Book Marketing Council, 1979-81. Member: Book Trade Working Party, 1972; Council, Publishers Assoc., 1976-82 (Chm. Copyright Panel, 1976-79); Brit. Copyright Council, 1976-79; Council of Management, MIND, the Nat. Assoc. of Mental Health, 1970-79 (Chm. MIND, 1976-79, Vice-Pres., 1980-). *Publications:* (ed) Publishing Agreements, 1980; articles on publishing topics. *Recreations:* singing lieder, golf. *Address:* 19 Offley Road, SW9 0LR. *T:* 01-735 1422. *Club:* Arts.

CLARK, Rt. Hon. Charles Joseph, (Joe); PC (Canada); MP (Progressive C) Rocky Mountain, later Yellowhead, Constituency, since 1972; Leader of HM's Loyal Opposition, in the House of Commons of Canada, since 1980; *b* 5 June 1939; *s* of Charles and Grace Clark; *m* 1973, Maureen McTeer (she retained her maiden name); one *d. Educ:* High River High Sch.; Univ. of Alta (BA History); Univ. of Alberta (MA Polit. Sci.). Journalist, Canadian Press, Calgary Herald, Edmonton Jl, High River Times, 1964-66; Prof. of Political Science, Univ. of Alberta, Edmonton, 1966-67; Exec. Asst to Hon. Robert L. Stanfield, Leader of HM's Loyal Opposition, 1967-70. Leader of HM's Loyal Opposition, Canada, 1976-79; Prime Minister of Canada, 1979-80. Hon. LLD New Brunswick, 1976. *Recreations:* riding, reading, walking, film going. *Address:* Stornoway, 541 Acacia Avenue, Ottawa, Ont, Canada. *T:* 996-5084.

CLARK, Col Charles Willoughby, DSO 1918; OBE 1945; MC 1916; DL; *b* 6 April 1888; *m* 1916; one *s* (one *d* deced). *Educ:* Atherstone Grammar Sch. Apprentice, Alfred Herbert Ltd, Coventry, 1904; Dir, 1934 (Chm. 1958-66). Served European War, 1914-18, France, Machine Gun Corps, Royal Tank Corps (MC, DSO, despatches twice). Chm. Coventry Conservative Assoc., 1945-48; Pres. Coventry Chamber of Commerce, 1951-53; Chm. Manufacturers' Section Cttee of Machine Tool Trades Assoc., 1946-55. Mem. Bd of Trade Machine Tool Advisory Council, 1957-66. Freeman of the City of London. Fellow Royal Commonwealth Society; FInstD; Mem. Inst of Export. DL Warwickshire, 1965. *Recreations:* shooting, fishing, travelling. *Address:* Flat 41, Regency House, Newbold Terrace, Leamington Spa, Warwickshire. *T:* Leamington Spa 24004; Brooklands Close, Ablington, near Bibury, Glos. *T:* Bibury 326. *Club:* Royal Automobile.

CLARK, Colin Grant, MA, DLitt (Oxon); Corresponding Fellow, British Academy; Research Consultant, Queensland University; Director of Institute for Research in Agricultural Economics, Oxford, 1953-69; Fellow of the Econometric Society; *b* 2 Nov. 1905; *s* of James Clark, merchant and manufacturer, Townsville and Plymouth; *m* 1935, Marjorie Tattersall; eight *s* one *d. Educ:* Dragon Sch.; Winchester; Brasenose Coll., Oxford; MA 1931, DLitt 1971; MA Cantab 1931; took degree in chemistry; Frances Wood

Prizeman of the Royal Statistical Soc., 1928; Asst to late Prof. Allyn Young of Harvard; worked on the New Survey of London Life and Labour, 1928-29, and Social Survey of Merseyside, 1929-30; on Staff of Economic Advisory Council, Cabinet Offices, 1930-31; University Lectr in Statistics, Cambridge, 1931-37. Contested (Lab): North Dorset, 1929; Wavertree (Liverpool), 1931; South Norfolk, 1935. Visiting Lectr at Univs of Melbourne, Sydney, and Western Australia, 1937-38. Under-Sec. of State for Labour and Industry, Dir of Bureau of Industry, and Financial Adviser to the Treasury, Qld, 1938-52. Hon. ScD, Milan; Hon. DEcon, Tilburg. *Publications:* The National Income, 1924-31, 1932; (with Prof. A. C. Pigou) Economic Position of Great Britain, 1936; National Income and Outlay, 1937; (with J. G. Crawford) National Income of Australia, 1938; Critique of Russian Statistics, 1939; The Conditions of Economic Progress, 1940 (revised edns 1951 and 1957); The Economics of 1960, 1942; Welfare and Taxation, 1954; Australian Hopes and Fears, 1958; Growthmanship, 1961; Taxmanship, 1964; (with Miss M. R. Haswell) The Economics of Subsistence Agriculture, 1964; Economics of Irrigation, 1967, 2nd rev. edn (with Dr D. I. Carruthers), 1981; Population Growth and Land Use, 1967; Starvation or Plenty?, 1970; The Value of Agricultural Land, 1973; Regional and Urban Location, 1982; other pamphlets and numerous articles in Economic periodicals. *Recreations:* walking, gardening. *Address:* Department of Economics, University of Queensland, St Lucia, Qld 4067, Australia. *Club:* Johnsonian (Brisbane).

CLARK, David Allen Richard; *b* 18 July 1905; *s* of David Richard Clark and Sarah Ann Clark (*née* Clark); *m* 1932, Mary Kathleen, *y d* of Samuel Finney and Mary Ellen Finney (*née* Bagnall), Burslem, Stoke-on-Trent; three *s. Educ:* West Felton, Oswestry, C of E Sch.; Oswestry Boys' High Sch.; Oswestry Technical Coll.; Faculty of Technology, Manchester Univ. Stoney Prizeman, 1930; BScTech 1931; MScTech 1932. Apprentice fitter and turner, GWR Co., Oswestry Works, 1921-27; Asst. Surveyor's Office, Oswestry RDC, 1929; Draughtsman, Sentinel Steam Wagon Co. Ltd., Shrewsbury, 1930; Part-time Lectr, Manchester Coll. of Technology, 1931-32; Lectr, Heanor Mining and Technical Coll., 1932-36; Senior Lectr, Kingston-upon-Thames Technical Coll., 1936-39; Head of Engineering Dept, Luton Technical Coll., 1939-47; Principal, Constantine Technical Coll., Middlesbrough, 1947-55; Principal, Nottingham Regional Coll. of Technology, 1955-65. CEng, FIMechE. *Publications:* Materials and Structures, 1941; Advanced Strength of Materials, 1951; articles in technical and educational journals. *Recreation:* collection of old English pottery and porcelain, historical documents, autographs, etc. *Address:* 50 Manor Drive, Upton, Wirral, Merseyside.

CLARK, David (George); MP (Lab) South Shields, since 1979; *b* 19 Oct. 1939; *s* of George and Janet Clark; *m* 1970, Christine Kirkby; one *d. Educ:* Manchester Univ. (BA(Econ), MSc); Sheffield Univ. (PhD 1978). Forester, 1956-57; Laboratory Asst in Textile Mill, 1957-59; Student Teacher, 1959-60; Student, 1960-63; Pres., Univ. of Manchester Union, 1963-64; Trainee Manager in USA, 1964; University Lecturer, 1965-70. Contested Manchester (Withington), Gen. Elec. 1966; MP (Lab) Colne Valley, 1970-Feb. 1974; contested Colne Valley, Oct. 1974; Opposition spokesman on Agriculture and Food, 1973-74, on Defence, 1980-81, on the Environment, 1981-. *Publications:* The Industrial Manager, 1966; Colne Valley: Radicalism to Socialism, 1981; various articles on Management and Labour History. *Recreations:* fell-walking, ornithology. *Address:* House of Commons, SW1A 0AA.

CLARK, David S.; *see* Stafford-Clark.

CLARK, Desmond; *see* Clark, John Desmond.

CLARK, Douglas Henderson, MD, FRCSEd, FRCSGlas, FRCPEd; Consultant Surgeon, Western Infirmary, Glasgow, since 1950; *b* 20 Jan. 1917; *s* of William and Jean Clark; *m* 1950, Morag Clark (decd); three *s. Educ:* Ayr Acad.; Glasgow Univ. (ChM 1950, MD Hons 1956). FRCSEd, FRCSGlas 1947, FRCPEd 1982. Captain RAMC, 1941-47. Miners Welfare Scholar, 1936; Fulbright Scholar, 1952; William Stewart Halsted Fellow, Johns Hopkins Hosp., 1952-53. Vis. Lectr in America, S Africa, Australia and NZ. Pres., RCPGlas, 1980-; Dir, James IV Assoc. of Surgeons, 1979-. Hon. FRCS 1982, Hon. FRCSI 1982. *Publications:* papers on gastro-enterology and thyroid disease; chapters in text-books. *Address:* 36 Southbrae Drive, Glasgow G13 1PZ. *T:* 041-959 3556.

CLARK, Elisabeth, (Mrs Edward Clark); *see* Lutyens, Elisabeth.

CLARK, Sir Fife; *see* Clark, Sir T. F.

CLARK, Lt-Gen. Findlay; *see* Clark, Lt-Gen. S. F.

CLARK, (Francis) Leo, QC 1972; **His Honour Judge Leo Clark;** a Circuit Judge, since 1976; *b* 15 Dec. 1920; *s* of Sydney John Clark and Florence Lilian Clark; *m* 1st, 1957, Denise Jacqueline Rambaud; one *s* ; 2nd, 1967, Dr Daphne Margaret Humphreys. *Educ:* St Peter's Coll., Oxford (MA). Called to Bar, Lincoln's Inn, 1947. Dep. Chm., Oxford County QS, 1970; a Recorder of the Crown Court, 1972-76. *Recreations:* tennis, travel. *Address:* The Ivy House, Charlbury, Oxon. *T:* Charlbury 810242. *Clubs:* Hurlingham; Union (Oxford).

CLARK, Sir George Anthony, 3rd Bt *cr* 1917; DL; Captain Reserve of Officers, Black Watch, 1939-64; Senator, N Ireland Parliament, 1951-69; *b*

24 Jan. 1914; *e s* of Sir George Ernest Clark, 2nd Bt and Norah Anne (*d* 1966), *d* of W. G. Wilson, Glasgow; *S* father 1950; *m* 1949, Nancy Catherine, 2nd *d* of George W. N. Clark, Carnabane, Upperlands, Co. Derry; one *d*. *Educ:* Canford. DL Belfast, 1961. Pres., Ulster Unionist Council, 1980. *Recreations:* golf, tennis. *Heir: b* Colin Douglas Clark, MC, MA [*b* 20 July 1918; *m* 1946, Margaret Coleman, *d* of late Maj.-Gen. Sir Charlton Watson Spinks, KBE, DSO, and *widow* of Major G. W. Threlfall, MC; one *s* two *d*]. *Address:* Tullygirvan House, Ballygowan, Newtownards, Co. Down, Northern Ireland BT23 6NR. *T:* Ballygowan 267. *Clubs:* Naval and Military; Royal Ulster Yacht (Bangor, Co. Down).

CLARK, Gerald Edmondson; HM Diplomatic Service; Commercial Counsellor, Peking, since 1981; *b* 26 Dec. 1935; *s* of Edward John Clark and Irene Elizabeth Ada Clark (*née* Edmondson); *m* 1967, Mary Rose Organ; two *d*. *Educ:* Johnston Grammar School, Durham; New College, Oxford. MA. Foreign Office, 1960; Hong Kong, 1961; Peking, 1962-63; FO, 1964-68; Moscow, 1968-70; FCO, 1970-73; Head of Chancery, Lisbon, 1973-77; Asst Sec., Cabinet Office, 1977-79; seconded to Barclays Bank International, 1979-81. *Recreations:* architecture, economics and politics. *Address:* c/o Foreign and Commonwealth Office, SW1. *Club:* Athenæum.

CLARK, Sir (Gordon Colvin) Lindesay, AC 1975; KBE 1968; CMG 1961; MC; BSc; MME; Mining Engineer, Australia; *b* 7 Jan. 1896; *s* of late Lindesay C. Clark, Launceston, Tas.; *m* 1922, Barbara J., *d* of A. C. Walch; one *s* two *d*. *Educ:* Church of England Grammar Sch., Launceston, Tasmania; Universities of Tasmania and Melbourne. Deputy-Controller of Mineral Production, Dept of Supply, Australia, 1942-44. Chairman: Western Mining Corp. Ltd, 1952-74 (Dir, 1974-78); Central Norseman Gold Corp. NL, 1952-74; Gold Mines of Kalgoorlie (Aust.) Ltd, 1952-74; BH South Ltd, 1956-74 (Dir, 1974-78); Alcoa of Australia Ltd, 1961-70, Dep. Chm. 1970-72; Director: Broken Hill Associated Smelters Pty Ltd, 1944-67; North Broken Hill Ltd, 1953-71; Beach Petroleum NL, 1964-72. Pres., Australasian Inst. of Mining and Metallurgy, 1959. Life Mem., Nat. Gallery of Victoria. Pres., The Art Foundn of Victoria, 1976-. Hon. DEng, Melbourne Univ., 1961; Hon. LLD, Monash Univ., 1975. Australasian Inst. of Mining and Metallurgy Medal, 1963; Kernot Meml Medal, Melbourne Univ., 1964. *Recreation:* golf. *Address:* Western Mining Corporation, 360 Collins Street, Melbourne, Victoria 3001, Australia; 8 Moralla Road, Kooyong, Victoria 3144, Aust. *T:* 20.2675. *Clubs:* Melbourne, Australian (Melbourne); Tasmanian (Hobart); Weld (Perth); Explorers' (New York).

CLARK, Grahame; *see* Clark, J. G. D.

CLARK, Henry Maitland; Assistant Controller, Council for Small Industries in Rural Areas, since 1977; *b* 11 April 1929; *s* of Major H. F. Clark, Rockwood, Upperlands, Co. Londonderry; *m* 1972, Penelope Winifred Tindal; one *s* two *d*. *Educ:* Shrewsbury Sch.; Trinity Coll., Dublin; Trinity Hall, Cambridge. Entered Colonial Service and appointed District Officer, Tanganyika, 1951; served in various Districts of Tanganyika, 1951-59; resigned from Colonial Service, 1959. MP (UU) Antrim North (UK Parliament), Oct. 1959-1970; Chm. Conservative Trade and Overseas Develt Sub-Cttee; Member: British Delegation to Council of Europe and WEU, 1962-65; Advisory Council Food Law Res. Centre, Univ. of Brussels; Exec. Cttee, Lepra (British Leprosy Relief Assoc.); Select Cttee on Overseas Aid and Develt, 1969-70; Grand Jury, Co. Londonderry, 1970. A Commonwealth Observer, Mauritius General Election, 1967. Wine merchant, IDV Ltd and Cock Russell Vintners, 1972-76. Vice-Pres., Dublin Univ. Boat Club. *Recreations:* rowing coach, sailing, shooting, golf, collecting old furniture. *Address:* Rockwood, Upperlands, Co. Derry, Northern Ireland. *T:* Maghera 42237; Staddles Cottage, Hindon Lane, Tisbury, Wilts. *T:* Tisbury 870330. *Clubs:* Leander; Kildare Street and University (Dublin); Royal Portrush Golf.

See also H. W. S. Clark.

CLARK, (Henry) Wallace (Stuart), MBE 1970; DL; Director, Wm Clark & Sons, Linen Manufacturers, since 1972; Chairman, Everbond Interlinings, London, since 1969; Director, Lintrend Developments Ltd, since 1981; *b* 20 Nov. 1926; *s* of Major H. F. Clark, MBE, JP, RA, Rockwood, Upperlands, and Sybil Emily (*née* Stuart); *m* 1957, June Elisabeth Lester Deane; two *s*. *Educ:* Shrewsbury School. Lieut, RNVR, 1945-47 (bomb and mine disposal); Cattleman, Merchant Navy, 1947-48. District Comdt, Ulster Special Constabulary, 1955-70; Major, Ulster Defence Regt, 1970-81. Foyle's Lectr, USA tour, 1964. Led Church of Ireland St Columba commemorative curragh voyage, Derry to Iona, 1963. DL 1962, High Sheriff 1969, Co. Londonderry. FSA Scotland. *Publications:* (jtly) North and East Coasts of Ireland, 1957; (jtly) South and West Coasts of Ireland, 1962, 2nd edn 1970; Guns in Ulster, 1967; Rathlin Disputed Island, 1972; Sailing Round Ireland, 1976; Linen on the Green, 1982; numerous newspaper and magazine articles. *Recreations:* various. *Address:* Gorteade Cottage, Upperlands, Co. Londonderry, N Ireland. *T:* Maghera 42737. *Clubs:* Royal Cruising, Irish Cruising (Cdre 1962).

See also H. M. Clark.

CLARK, Most Rev. Howard Hewlett, CC (Canada) 1970; DD; Chancellor, University of Trinity College, Toronto, since 1972; *b* 23 April 1903; *s* of Douglass Clark and Florence Lilian Hewlett; *m* 1935, Anna Evelyn Wilson; one *s* three *d*. *Educ:* University of Toronto; Trinity College, Toronto. BA 1932. Christ Church Cathedral, Ottawa: Curate 1932. Priest-in-Charge, 1938, Rector 1939-54, Canon 1941; Dean of Ottawa, 1945; Bishop of Edmonton,

1954, Archbishop of Edmonton, 1959-61; Primate of Anglican Church of Canada, 1959-70; Metropolitan and Archbishop of Rupert's Land, 1961-69; Episcopal Canon of St George's Collegiate Church, Jerusalem, 1964-70. DD (*jure dignitatis*) Trinity College, Toronto, 1945; subsequently awarded numerous honorary doctorates in divinity and in civil law, both in Canada and abroad. *Publication:* The Christian Life According to the Prayer Book, 1957. *Address:* 252 Glenrose Avenue, Toronto, Ont M4T 1K9, Canada.

CLARK, Ian Robertson, CBE 1979; Member, British National Oil Corporation; Chairman, BNOC (Ventures) Ltd, since 1979; *b* 18 Jan. 1939; *s* of Alexander Clark and Annie Dundas Watson; *m* 1961, Jean Scott Waddell Lang; one *s* one *d*. *Educ:* Dalziel High Sch., Motherwell. FCCA, IPFA, FRVA. Trained with Glasgow Chartered Accountant; served in local govt, 1962-76, this service culminating in the post of Chief Executive, Shetland Islands Council. Hon. LLD Glasgow, 1979. *Publications:* Reservoir of Power, 1980; contribs to professional and religious periodicals. *Recreations:* theology, general reading, walking. *Address:* 48 Auchingramont Road, Hamilton, Lanarks. *Club:* Royal Scottish Automobile.

CLARK, James Leonard; Under Secretary, Establishment Personnel Division, Departments of Industry and Trade Common Services, since 1980 (Under Secretary, Department of Trade, since 1978); *b* 8 Jan. 1923; *s* of James Alfred and Grace Clark; *m* 1954, Joan Pauline Richards. *Educ:* Mercers' School. Lieut (A), Fleet Air Arm, 1942-46. Clerical Officer, HM Treasury, 1939; Private Sec. to successive First Secs of State, 1964-67; Cabinet Office, 1969-71; Asst Sec., Price Commn, 1973-75; Dept of Industry, 1975-78. *Recreation:* motoring. *Address:* 4 Westcott Way, Cheam, Surrey SM2 7JY. *T:* 01-393 2622.

CLARK, James McAdam, CVO 1972; MC 1944; HM Diplomatic Service, retired; *b* 13 Sept. 1916; *er s* of late James Heriot Clark of Wester Coltfield, and late Ella Catherine McAdam; *m* 1946, Denise Thérèse, *d* of late Dr Léon Dufournier, Paris; two *d*. *Educ:* Edinburgh Univ. BSc (Hons) Tech. Chemistry, 1938. Asst Lectr, Edinburgh Univ., 1938-39. Served Royal Artillery, 1939-46 (MC), rank of Capt.; Royal Mil. Coll. of Science, 1945-46 (pac). Min. of Fuel and Power, 1947-48. Entered Foreign (now Diplomatic) Service, 1948; FO, 1948-50; Head of Chancery, Quito, 1950-53; FO, 1953-56; Head of Chancery, Lisbon, 1956-60; Counsellor, UK Rep. to and Alternate Gov. of Internat. Atomic Energy Agency, Vienna, 1960-64; Head of Scientific Relations Dept, FO, 1964-66; Counsellor on secondment to Min. of Technology, 1966-70; Consul-Gen., Paris, 1970-77. Officer Order of Christ of Portugal, 1957. *Publications:* a number of poems and articles. *Recreations:* golf, sailing, music, disputation. *Address:* Hill Lodge, Aldeburgh, Suffolk. *Clubs:* Aldeburgh Yacht, Aldeburgh Golf.

CLARK, Rt. Hon. Joe; *see* Clark, Rt Hon. C. J.

CLARK, Sir John (Allen), Kt 1971; Chairman and Chief Executive, The Plessey Company Ltd, since 1970; *b* 14 Feb. 1926; *e s* of late Sir Allen Clark and Lady (Jocelyn) Clark, *d* of late Percy and Madeline Culverhouse; *m* 1952, Deirdre Kathleen (marr. diss. 1962), *d* of Samuel Herbert Waterhouse and Maeve Murphy Waterhouse; one *s* one *d* ; *m* 1970, Olivia, *d* of H. Pratt and of Mrs R. S. H. Shepard; twin *s* one *d*. *Educ:* Harrow; Cambridge. Received early industrial training with Metropolitan Vickers and Ford Motor Co.; spent over a year in USA, studying the electronics industry. Served War of 1939-45; commissioned RNVR. Asst to Gen. Manager, Plessey International Ltd, 1949; Dir and Gen. Man., Plessey (Ireland) Ltd, and Wireless Telephone Co. Ltd, 1950; appointed to main board, The Plessey Co. Ltd, 1953; Gen. Man., Plessey Components Group, 1957; Man. Dir, 1962-70, and Dep. Chm., 1967-70, The Plessey Co. Ltd. Director: International Computers Ltd, 1968-79; Banque Nationale de Paris Ltd, 1976-. Pres., Telecommunication Engineering and Manufacturing Assoc., 1964-66, 1971-73; Vice-President: Inst. of Works Managers; Engineering Employers' Fedn. Member: Nat. Defence Industries Council; Engineering Industries Council, 1975-. CompIEE; FIM. Order of Henry the Navigator, Portugal, 1973. *Recreations:* horseriding, shooting. *Address:* The Plessey Co. plc, Millbank, SW1P 4QP. *T:* 01-834 9641. *Club:* Carlton.

See also Michael W. Clark.

CLARK, John Anthony, DL, JP; *b* 19 July 1908; *s* of John Bright Clark and Caroline Susan (*née* Pease); *m* 1930, Eileen Mary Cousins; three *s* two *d*. *Educ:* Leighton Park School; New Coll., Oxford. Director, 1931-74, Chairman, 1967-74, C. & J. Clark Ltd and subsidiary companies, retired. Somerset County Council: Councillor, 1952-; Alderman, 1965; Vice-Chm., 1968 (Chm., Agriculture Cttee and Police Authority). Governor, Millfield Sch., 1953 (Chm. of Governors, 1965). JP 1934, DL 1971, High Sheriff 1970, Somerset. Hon. LLD Bath, 1972. *Recreations:* hunting, golf, farming. *Address:* Home Orchard, Street, Somerset BA16 0HX. *T:* Street 42042. *Club:* Somerset County.

CLARK, Prof. J(ohn) Desmond, CBE 1960; PhD, ScD; FBA 1961; FSA 1952; FRSSAf 1959; Professor of Anthropology, University of California, Berkeley, USA, since 1961; *b* London, 10 April 1916; *s* of late Thomas John Chown Clark and Catharine (*née* Wynne); *m* 1938, Betty Cable, *d* of late Henry Lea Baume and late Frances M. S. (*née* Brown); one *s* one *d*. *Educ:* Monkton Combe Sch.; Christ's Coll., Cambridge. PhD in Archaeology (Cambridge), 1950; ScD Cantab 1975. Dir, Rhodes-Livingstone Museum, Livingstone, N Rhodesia, 1938-61. Has conducted excavations in Southern,

East and Equatorial Africa, the Sahara, Ethiopia, Syria, 1938-, incl. India, 1980-82. Military Service in East Africa, Abyssinia, The Somalilands and Madagascar, 1941-46. Founder Mem. and Sec., N Rhodesia Nat. Monuments Commn, 1948-61. Corr. Mem. Scientific Coun. for Africa South of the Sahara, 1956-64, etc. Faculty Res. Lectr, Berkeley, 1979; Raymond Dart Lectr, Johannesburg, 1979. Fellow, Amer. Acad. of Arts and Sciences, 1965. Huxley Medal, RAI, 1974. Comdr, Nat. Order of Senegal, 1968. *Publications:* The Prehistoric Cultures of the Horn of Africa, 1954; The Prehistory of Southern Africa, 1959; The Stone Age Cultures of Northern Rhodesia, 1960; Prehistoric Cultures of Northeast Angola and their Significance in Tropical Africa, 1963; (ed) Proc. 3rd Pan-African Congress on Pre-history, 1957; (comp.) Atlas of African Pre-history, 1967; (ed, with W. W. Bishop) Background to Evolution in Africa, 1967; Kalambo Falls Prehistoric Site, vol. I, 1969, vol. II, 1973; The Prehistory of Africa, 1970; contribs to learned journals on prehistoric archaeology. *Recreations:* gardening, walking, photography. *Address:* 1941 Yosemite Road, Berkeley, Calif. 94707, USA. *T:* 525/4519 Area Code 415. *Club:* Royal Commonwealth Society.

CLARK, Sir John (Douglas), 4th Bt *cr* 1886; *b* 9 Jan. 1923; *s* of Sir Thomas Clark, 3rd Bt and of Ellen Mercy, *d* of late Francis Drake; *S* father, 1977; *m* 1969, Anne, *d* of Angus and Christina Gordon, Aberfawn, Beauly, Invernessshire. *Educ:* Gordonstoun School; Edinburgh University. Entered firm of T. & T. Clark, Publishers, Edinburgh, 1953; Partner, 1958; retired through ill-health. Founder Mem., Roseburn Literary Soc., Hon. Pres., 1968. *Recreations:* gardening, reading, chess, listening to music, watching Rugby football. *Heir:* b Francis Drake Clark [*b* 16 July 1924; *m* 1958, Mary, *d* of late John Alban Andrews, MC, FRCS; one *s*]. *Address:* 52 Ormidale Terrace, Edinburgh EH12 6EF. *T:* 031-337 5610.

CLARK, John Edward; Secretary, National Association of Local Councils, since 1978; *b* 18 Oct. 1932; *s* of Albert Edward Clark and Edith (*née* Brown); *m* 1969, Judith Rosemary Lester; one *d* decd. *Educ:* Royal Grammar Sch., Clitheroe; Keble Coll., Oxford (MA, BCL). Called to the Bar, Gray's Inn, 1957; practised at the Bar, 1957-61. Dep. Sec., National Assoc. of Local (formerly Parish) Councils, (part-time) 1959-61, (full-time) 1961-78. *Publications:* chapters on local govt, public health, and theatres, in Encyclopaedia of Court Forms, 2nd edn 1964 to 1975. *Recreations:* gardening, walking; indoor games, making and playing. *Address:* 71 Stradella Road, SE24 9HL. *T:* 01-274 1381.

CLARK, Prof. (John) Grahame (Douglas), CBE 1971; FBA 1951; MA, PhD, ScD (Cantab); Master of Peterhouse, 1973-80 (Fellow, 1950-73, Honorary Fellow, 1980); *b* 28 July 1907; *s* of Lt-Col Charles Douglas Clark and Maude Ethel Grahame Clark (*née* Shaw); *m* 1936, Gwladys Maude (*née* White); two *s* one *d*. *Educ:* Marlborough Coll.; Peterhouse, Cambridge. Served War of 1939-45, RAFVR, in Photographic Interpretation, 1941-43, and Air Historical Br., 1943-45. Research Student, 1930-32, and Bye-Fellow, 1933-35, of Peterhouse; Faculty Asst Lectr in Archæology, Cambridge, 1935-46, and Univ. Lectr, 1946-52; Disney Prof. of Archæology, Cambridge, 1952-74; Head of Dept of Archæology and Anthropology, Cambridge, 1956-61 and 1968-71. Lectures: Munro, in Archæology, Edinburgh Univ., 1949; Reckitt, British Acad. 1954; Dalrymple in Archæology, Glasgow Univ., 1955; G. Grant MacCurdy, Harvard, 1957; Mortimer Wheeler Meml, New Delhi, 1978; William Evans Vis. Prof., Univ. of Otago, NZ, 1964; Commonwealth Vis. Fellow, Australia, 1964; Hitchcock Prof., Univ. of California, Berkeley, 1969; Leverhulme Vis. Prof., Uppsala, 1972. Member: Ancient Monuments Board, 1954-77; Royal Commn on Historical Monuments, 1957-69; a Trustee, BM, 1975-80; Pres., Prehistoric Soc., 1958-62; Vice-Pres., Soc. of Antiquaries, 1959-62. Hon. Editor, Proceedings Prehistoric Soc., 1935-70. Hon. Corr. Mem., Royal Soc. Northern Antiquaries, Copenhagen, 1946, and of Swiss Prehistoric Soc., 1951; Fellow, German Archæological Inst., 1954; Hon. Member: RIA, 1955; Archæol. Inst. of America, 1977; Foreign Member: Finnish Archæological Soc., 1958; Amer. Acad. of Sciences (Hon.) 1964; Royal Danish Acad. of Sciences and Letters, 1964; Royal Netherlands Acad. of Sciences, 1964; For. Fellow, Royal Society of Sciences, Uppsala, 1964; For. Associate, Nat. Acad. of Sciences, USA, 1974; Royal Soc. of Humane Letters, Lund, 1976. Hon. DLitt: Sheffield, 1971; National Univ. of Ireland, 1976; Fil dr, Uppsala, 1977. Hodgkins Medal, Smithsonian Institution, 1967; Viking Medal, Wenner-Gren Foundn, 1971; Lucy Wharton Drexel Gold Medal, Museum, Univ. of Pennsylvania, 1974; Gold Medal, Soc. of Antiquaries, 1978; Chanda Medal, Asiatic Soc., Calcutta, 1979. Comdr, Order of the Danebrog, 1961. *Publications:* The Mesolithic Settlement of Northern Europe, 1936; Archæology and Society 1939, 1947 and 1957; Prehistoric England, 1940, 1941, 1945, 1948, 1962; From Savagery to Civilization, 1946; Prehistoric Europe, The Economic Basis, 1952; Excavations at Star Carr, 1954; The Study of Prehistory, 1954; World Prehistory, An Outline, 1961; (with Stuart Piggott) Prehistoric Societies, 1965; The Stone Age Hunters, 1967; World Prehistory, a new outline, 1969; Aspects of Prehistory, 1970; The Earlier Stone Age Settlement of Scandinavia, 1975; World Prehistory in New Perspective, 1977; Sir Mortimer and Indian Archaeology (Wheeler Memorial Lectures, 1978), 1979; Mesolithic Prelude, 1980; The Identity of Man (as seen by an archaeologist), 1982; numerous papers in archæological journals. *Recreations:* gardening, travel, contemporary art. *Address:* 36 Millington Road, Cambridge CB3 9HP. *Club:* United Oxford & Cambridge University.

CLARK, Sir John S.; *see* Stewart-Clark.

CLARK, Ven. Kenneth James, DSC 1944; Archdeacon of Swindon, since 1982; *b* 31 May 1922; *er s* of Francis James Clark and Winifred Adelaide Clark (*née* Martin); *m* 1948, Elisabeth Mary Monica Helen Huggett; three *s* three *d*. *Educ:* Watford Grammar School; St Catherine's Coll., Oxford (MA); Cuddesdon Theological Coll. Midshipman RN, 1940; Lieutenant RN, 1942; served in submarines, 1942-46. Baptist Minister, Forest Row, Sussex, 1950-52; Curate of Brinkworth, 1952-53; Curate of Cricklade with Latton, 1953-56; Priest-in-Charge, then Vicar (1959), of Holy Cross, Inns Court, Bristol, 1956-61; Vicar: Westbury-on-Trym, 1961-72; St Mary Redcliffe, Bristol, 1972-82; Hon. Canon of Bristol Cathedral, 1974. Member, Gen. Synod of C of E, 1980-. *Recreations:* music, travel, gardening. *Address:* 70 Bath Road, Swindon, Wilts SN1 4AY. *T:* Swindon 695059.

CLARK, Leo; *see* Clark, F. L.

CLARK, Leslie Joseph, CBE 1977; BEM 1942; Chairman, Victor Products (Wallsend) Ltd, 1977-79; Special Adviser on the international gas industry to the Chairman of British Gas, since 1975; Chairman, Northern Gas Region (formerly Northern Gas Board), 1967-75; *b* 21 May 1914; *s* of Joseph George Clark and Elizabeth (*née* Winslow); *m* 1940, Mary M. Peacock; one *s* one *d*. *Educ:* Stationers' Company's Sch.; King's Coll., London, BSc(Eng), 1st Cl. Hons, 1934; MSc 1948. Engineer, Gas Light & Coke Co., then North Thames Gas Board. Chief Engineer, North Thames Gas Board, 1962-65 (pioneered work for development of sea transp. of liquefied natural gas, 1954-63), Dep. Chm., 1965-67. Pres., Instn of Gas Engineers, 1965-66; Pres., IGU, 1973-76 (Vice-Pres., 1970-73). Member: Court, Univ. of Newcastle upon Tyne, 1972-; Council, Univ. of Durham, 1975-78. Fellow, Fellowship of Engineering. CEng, FICE, FIMechE, FIGasE, FInstF, MIEE, AMIChemE. Founder Fellow, Fellowship of Engineering, 1976. Elmer Sperry Award, USA, 1979. *Publications:* technical papers to Instns of Gas Engineers and Mech. Engrs, Inst. of Fuel, World Energy Conf., Internat. Gas Union, etc. *Recreations:* model engineering, walking, photography, music. *Address:* Hillway, New Ridley Road, Stocksfield, Northumberland. *T:* Stocksfield 2339.

CLARK, Sir Lindesay; *see* Clark, Sir G. C. L.

CLARK, Marjorie, (Pen-name, Georgia Rivers); journalist, writer of fiction; *b* Melbourne; *d* of George A. and Gertrude M. Clark. *Educ:* Milverton Girls' Grammar Sch. *Publications:* Jacqueline, 1927; Tantalego, 1928; The Difficult Art, 1929; She Dresses for Dinner, 1933; 12 full-length serials, numerous short stories and articles. *Recreation:* music. *Address:* Flat 2, 374 Auburn Road, Hawthorn, Victoria 3122, Australia. *Club:* PEN (Melbourne Centre).

CLARK, Gen. Mark Wayne, DSC (US); DSM (3 Oak Leaf Clusters) (US Army); DSM (US Navy); US Army, retired; President Emeritus, The Citadel, Military College of South Carolina (President, 1954-65); *b* Madison Barracks, New York, USA, 1 May 1896; *s* of Col Charles Carr and Rebecca Clark; *m* 1st, 1924, Maurine Doran (*d* 1966); one *s* (one *d* decd); 2nd, 1967, Mrs Mary Millard Applegate, Muncie, Ind. *Educ:* United States Mil. Acad. (BS 1917); Infantry Sch. (grad. 1925); Comd and Gen. Staff Sch. (grad. 1935); Army War Coll. (grad. 1937). Served European War, 1917-18 (wounded); Dep. Chief of Staff, Civilian Conservation Corps, 1936-37; Mem. Gen. Staff Corps, March-June 1942; Chief of Staff for Ground Forces, May 1942; C-in-C Ground Forces in Europe, July 1942; led successful secret mission by submarine to get information in N Africa preparatory to Allied invasion, 1942; Comdr Fifth Army in Anglo-American invasion of Italy, 1943, capture of Rome, June 1944; Commanding Gen. 15th Army Group, Dec. 1944; Gen., 1945; US High Commissioner and Comdg Gen. US Forces in Austria, 1945-47; dep. US Sec. of State, 1947; sat in London and Moscow with Council of Foreign Ministers negotiating a treaty for Austria, 1947; Comdg Gen. 6th US Army, HQ San Francisco, 1947-49; Chief, US Army Field Forces, Fort Monroe, Virginia, 1949-52; 1952-53: Comdr-in-Chief, United Nations Command; C-in-C, Far East; Commanding Gen., US Army Forces in the Far East; Governor of the Ryukyu Islands. Thanks of US House of Representatives, 1945. Hon. KCB 1955; Hon. KBE 1944. Hon. DCL Oxford, 1945; many other awards and honours, both American and foreign. *Publications:* Calculated Risk, 1950; From the Danube to the Yalu, 1954. *Recreations:* fishing, hunting, golfing and hiking. *Address:* 17 Country Club Drive, Charleston, South Carolina 29412, USA. *T:* 795-5333.

CLARK, Michael Lindsey, PPRBS; sculptor; *b* 1918; *s* of late Phillip Lindsey Clark, DSO, FRBS, and Truda Mary Calnan; *m* 1942, Catherine Heron; five *s* three *d*. *Educ:* Blackfriars Sch.; City of London Art School. ARBS 1949; FRBS 1960; Pres., RBS, 1971-76. Otto Beit Medal for Sculpture, 1960 and 1978, and Silver Medal, 1967, RBS. *Address:* Barford Court Farm, Lampard Lane, Churt, Surrey GU10 2HJ.

CLARK, Michael William, CBE 1977; Deputy Chairman and Deputy Chief Executive, Plessey Co. Ltd; Chairman, Plessey Electronic Systems Ltd; *b* 7 May 1927; *yr s* of late Sir Allen Clark and late Jocelyn Anina Maria Louise Clark (*née* Emerson Culverhouse); *m* 1955, Shirley (*née* MacPhadyen) (*d* 1974); two *s* two *d*. *Educ:* Harrow. 1st Foot Guards, Subaltern, 1945-48. Ford Motor Co., 1948-49; Bendix Aviation (USA), 1949-50; Plessey Co. Ltd, 1950- (Exec. Dir, 1951; formed Electronics Div., 1951; Main Bd Dir, 1953); formed Plessey (UK) Ltd (Chm. and Man. Dir, 1962, Dir responsible for Corporate Planning, 1965, Man. Dir, Telecommunications Gp, 1967); formed Plessey Electronics Systems Ltd, 1976. Member: Electronics EDC, 1975-80; Council,

Inst. of Dirs; Nat. Electronics Council; Ct of Univ. of Essex. Comp. IEE, 1964; Comp. IERE, 1965. *Recreations:* fishing, forestry. *Address:* Braxted Park, Witham, Essex. *Club:* Boodle's.

See also Sir J. A. Clark.

CLARK, Oswald William Hugh, CBE 1978; Assistant Director-General, Greater London Council, 1973-79; *b* 26 Nov. 1917; *s* of late Rev. Hugh M. A. Clark and Mabel Bessie Clark (*née* Dance); *m* 1966, Diana Mary (*née* Hine); one *d. Educ:* Rutlish Sch., Merton; Univ. of London (BA; BD Hons). Local Govt Official, LCC (later GLC), 1937-79. Served War, HM Forces, 1940-46: Major, 2nd Derbyshire Yeo., Eighth Army, Middle East, NW Europe. Member: Church Assembly (later General Synod), dio. of Southwark, 1948- (Chm., House of Laity, 1970-); Standing and Legislative Cttees, 1950-; Standing Orders Cttee (Chm.), 1950-; Chm., House of Laity, 1979- (Vice-Chm., 1970-79); a Church Commissioner, 1958-, Mem. Bd of Governors, 1966-68, 1969-73, 1977-; Chm. of Council, Queen Victoria Clergy Fund, 1970-. Vice-Pres., Corp. of Church House, 1981-; Mem., Guild of Guide Lectrs, 1960-. *Recreations:* London's history and development, commemorative and Goss china, heraldry. *Address:* 63 Broadhurst, Ashtead, Surrey KT21 1QD. *T:* Ashtead 72663. *Club:* Cavalry and Guards.

CLARK, Paul Nicholas Rowntree; a Recorder, since 1981; *b* 17 Aug. 1940; *s* of late Henry Rowntree Clark and of Gwendoline Victoria Clark; *m* 1967, Diana Barbara Bishop; two *s* one *d. Educ:* Bristol Grammar Sch.; New Coll., Oxford (Open Schol.; MA (Lit. Hum.)). Called to the Bar, Middle Temple, 1966 (Harmsworth Schol.), Bencher 1982; in practice since, on Midland and Oxford (formerly Oxford) Circuit. *Address:* 2 Harcourt Buildings, Temple, EC4Y 9DB. *T:* 01-353 8549.

CLARK, Percy, CBE 1970; Managing Director, Stainforth-Clark PR Ltd; *b* 18 May 1917; *s* of Perceval Harold Clark and Grace Lilian Clark; *m* 1st, 1941, Nan Dalgleish (*d* 1970); two *s* two *d;* 2nd, 1972, Doreen Stainforth. Early career in newspapers: owner South Lancs News Agency, 1936-47. Labour Party: Publications Officer, 1947; Regional Publicity Dir, 1957; Dep. Dir, Information, 1960, Dir, 1964-79. MIPR. *Recreation:* music. *Address:* Barrow Moor, Longnor, Buxton, Derbyshire SK17 0QP. *T:* Buxton 83292. *Club:* MCC.

CLARK, Petula (Sally Olwen); singer, actress; *b* 15 Nov. 1934; *d* of Leslie Clark; *m* 1961, Claude Wolff; one *s* two *d.* Own BBC radio series, Pet's Parlour, 1943; early British films include: Medal for the General, 1944; I Know Where I'm Going, 1945; Here Come the Huggetts, 1948; Dance Hall, 1950; White Corridors, 1951; The Card, 1951; Made in Heaven, 1952; The Runaway Bus, 1953; That Woman Opposite, 1957. Began career as singer in France, 1959. Top female vocalist, France, 1962; Bravos du Music Hall award for outstanding woman in show business, France, 1965; Grammy awards for records Downtown and I Know A Place. Numerous concert and television appearances in Europe and USA including her own BBC TV series. *Films:* Finian's Rainbow, 1968; Goodbye Mr Chips, 1969; *musical:* The Sound of Music, Apollo Victoria, 1981. *Address:* c/o PROGENAR, 82 rue de Lausanne, Fribourg 1701, Switzerland.

CLARK, Ramsey; lawyer, New York City, since 1970; *b* Dallas, Texas, 18 Dec. 1927; *s* of late Thomas Campbell Clark, Associate Justice, US Supreme Court, and of Mary Ramsey; *m* 1949, Georgia Welch, Corpus Christi, Texas; one *s* one *d. Educ:* Public Schs, Dallas, Los Angeles, Washington; Univ. of Texas (BA); Univ. of Chicago (MA, JD). US Marine Corps, 1945-46. Engaged private practice of law, Dallas, 1951-61; Asst Attorney Gen., Dept of Justice, 1961-65; Dep. Attorney Gen., 1965-67, Attorney Gen., 1967-69. Adjunct Professor: Howard Univ., 1969-72; Brooklyn Law Sch., 1973-. *Publication:* Crime in America, 1970. *Address:* Clark, Wulf, Levine and Peratis, 113 University Place, New York, NY 10003, USA; 37 West 12th Street, New York, NY 10011, USA.

CLARK, Sir Robert (Anthony), Kt 1976; DSC 1944; Chairman: Hill Samuel & Co. Ltd, since 1974; Hill Samuel Group Ltd, since 1980 (Chief Executive, 1976-80); IMI, since 1981; Deputy Chairman, UDS Group, since 1982; a Director, Bank of England, since 1976; *b* 6 Jan. 1924; *yr s* of John Clark and Gladys Clark (*née* Dyer); *m* 1949, Andolyn Marjorie Lewis; two *s* one *d. Educ:* Highgate Sch.; King's Coll., Cambridge. Served War, Royal Navy, 1942-46 (DSC). Partner with Slaughter and May, Solicitors, 1953; became a director of merchant bankers, Philip Hill, Higginson, Erlangers Ltd (now known as Hill Samuel & Co. Ltd), 1961-; Director: British Leyland Ltd, 1977-; Shell Transport and Trading Co., plc, 1982-; Chairman: Industrial Development Adv. Bd, 1973-80; Review Body on Doctors' and Dentists' Remuneration, 1979-; Council, Charing Cross Hosp. Med. Sch., 1981-. *Recreations:* reading, music. *Address:* Munstead Wood, Godalming, Surrey. *T:* Godalming 7867; Hill Samuel & Co. Ltd, 100 Wood Street, EC2P 2AJ. *T:* 01-628 8011. *Clubs:* Pratt's, Travellers'.

CLARK, Prof. Robert Bernard, DSc, PhD; FIBiol, FRSE; Professor of Zoology, University of Newcastle upon Tyne, since 1966; *b* 13 Oct. 1923; *s* of Joseph Lawrence Clark and Dorothy (*née* Halden); *m* 1st, 1956, Mary Eleanor (*née* Laurence) (marr. diss.); 2nd, 1970, Susan Diana (*née* Smith); one *s* one *d. Educ:* St Marylebone Grammar Sch.; Chelsea Polytechnic (BSc London 1944); University Coll., Exeter (BSc 1950); Univ. of Glasgow (PhD 1956); DSc London 1965. FIBiol 1966, FLS 1969, FRSE 1970. Asst Experimental Officer, DSIR Road Research Laboratory, 1944; Asst to Prof.

of Zoology, Univ. of Glasgow, 1950; Asst Prof., Univ. of California (Berkeley), 1953; Lectr in Zoology, Univ. of Bristol, 1956; Head of Dept of Zoology and Director of Dove Marine Laboratory, Univ. of Newcastle upon Tyne, 1966-77, Director of Research Unit on Rehabilitation of Oiled Seabirds, 1967-76. Member: Natural Environment Research Council, 1971-77; Royal Commn on Environmental Pollution, 1979-; Mem. Council, Nature Conservancy, 1975. *Publications:* Neurosecretion (ed, jtly), 1962; Dynamics in Metazoan Evolution, 1964, corrected repr. 1967; Practical Course in Experimental Zoology, 1966; (jtly) Invertebrate Panorama, 1971; (jtly) Synopsis of Animal Classification, 1971; (ed, jtly) Essays in Hydrobiology, 1972. Founder, 1968, and ed, Marine Pollution Bulletin; numerous papers in learned jls. *Recreations:* architecture, music, unambitious gardening, reading undemanding novels. *Address:* Department of Zoology, The University, Newcastle upon Tyne NE1 7RU. *T:* Newcastle upon Tyne 28511; Highbury House, Highbury, Newcastle upon Tyne NE2 3LN. *T:* Newcastle upon Tyne 814672.

CLARK, Rev. Canon Robert James Vodden; *b* 12 April 1907; *s* of Albert Arthur Clark and Bessie Vodden; *m* 1934, Ethel Dolina McGregor Alexander; one *d. Educ:* Dalry Normal Practising Episcopal Church Sch., Edinburgh; Church Army Coll.; Coates Hall Theol. Coll. Ordained, 1941. Men's Social Dept, Church Army, 1926; varied work in homes for men; special work in probation trng home under Home Office, 1934-39; St Paul and St George, Edinburgh, 1941-44; Rector, St Andrew's, Fort William, 1944-47; seconded to Scottish Educn Dept as Warden-Leader of Scottish Centre of Outdoor Trng, Glenmore Lodge, 1947-49; Curate i/c St David's, Edinburgh, 1949-54; Rector of Christ Church, Falkirk, 1954-69; Rector of St Leonards, Lasswade, 1969-79; Canon, Edinburgh, 1962; Dean of Edinburgh, 1967-76; Hon. Canon, Edinburgh, 1976; retd 1979. Mem., Royal Highland and Agric. Soc. *Recreations:* mountaineering (Mem., Scottish Mountaineering Club); photography. *Address:* 15 North Street, St Andrews, Fife, Scotland KY16 9PW.

CLARK, Lt-Gen. (Samuel) Findlay, CBE 1945; CD 1950; MEIC; MCSEE, PEng; *b* 17 March 1909; *m* 1937, Leona Blanche Seagram. *Educ:* Univ. of Manitoba (BScEE); Univ. of Saskatchewan (BScME). Lieut, Royal Canadian Signals, 1933. Assoc. Prof. of Elec. and Mechan. Engrg (Capt.) at RMC Kingston, 1938. Overseas to UK, Aug. 1940 (Major); Comd 5th Canadian Armd Div. Sigs Regt (Lt-Col), 1941. GSO1 Can. Mil. HQ, London, 1942; Staff Course, Camberley, England (Col), 1942-43; CSO, HQ 2nd Canadian Corps until end of War (Brig. 1943). Dep. Chief of Gen. Staff, 1945; Imperial Defence Coll., 1948; Canadian Mil. Observer on Western Union Mil. Cttee; Maj.-Gen. 1949; Canadian Mil. Rep. NATO, London, 1949; Chm., Joint Staff. CALE, London, 1951; QMG of Canadian Army, 1951; GOC Central Comd, 1955; CGS, Sept. 1958-61. Chm., Nat. Capital Commission, 1961-67 Past Col Comdt, Royal Canadian Corps of Signals; Hon. Lt-Col, 741 Comm. Sqn. FRCGS. Legion of Merit (USA), 1945; Comdr Order of Orange Nassau (Netherlands), 1945. OStJ 1975. *Address:* 301-1375 Newport Avenue, Victoria, BC V8S 5E8, Canada. *T:* 592 4338. *Club:* Union (Victoria).

CLARK, Ven. Sidney H.; see Harvie-Clark.

CLARK, Stuart Ellis; *b* 6 Feb. 1899; *s* of Robert and Susanah Clark, Dartford, Kent; *m* 1st, 1923, Mabel Olive Winspear (*d* 1932); one *s*; 2nd, 1935, Joan Bulley. *Educ:* Wilson's Sch. Acting Sec., Southern Rly Co., 1944; Asst Docks and Marine Manager, Southern Rly Co., Southampton Docks, 1947; Sec. Docks Executive, 1948; Sec., Docks and Inland Waterways Board of Management, British Transport Commission, 1950-55. *Recreations:* golf, swimming. *Address:* Knapp Cottage, Wambrook, near Chard, Somerset. *T:* Chard 2442.

CLARK, Terence Joseph, CVO 1978; HM Diplomatic Service; Deputy Leader, UK Delegation to the Conference on Security and Co-operation in Europe, Madrid, since 1982; *b* 19 June 1934; *s* of Joseph Clark and Mary Clark; *m* 1960, Lieselotte Rosa Marie Müller; two *s* one *d. Educ:* Thomas Parmiter's London. RAF (attached to Sch. of Slavonic Studies, Cambridge), 1953-55 Pilot Officer, RAFVR, 1955. HM Foreign Service, 1955; ME Centre for Arab Studies, 1956-57; Bahrain, 1957-58; Amman, 1958-60; Casablanca 1961-62; FO, 1962-65; Asst Polit. Agent, Dubai, 1965-68; Belgrade, 1969-71 Hd of Chancery, Muscat, 1972-73; Asst Hd of ME Dept, FCO, 1974-76 Counsellor (Press and Information), Bonn, 1976-79; Chargé d'Affaires Tripoli, Feb.-March 1981; Counsellor, Belgrade, 1979-82. Commander's Cross, Order of Merit of Fed. Republic of Germany, 1978. *Recreations* aquatic sports, amateur dramatics. *Address:* c/o Foreign and Commonwealth Office, SW1A 2AH; 33 Lovelace Road, West Dulwich, SE21.

CLARK, Sir (Thomas) Fife, Kt 1965; CBE 1949; retired; formerly Director General, Central Office of Information; *b* Thornaby-on-Tees, 29 May 1907 *m* 1945, Joan (*d* 1977), *d* of late Captain James Mould, DSO, MC; two *s* one *d. Educ:* Middlesbrough High Sch. (North Riding Scholar). Reporter sub-editor, Parly lobby corresp. and diplomatic correspondent, Westminster Press provincial newspapers, 1924-39; Public Relations and Principal Press Officer, Min. of Health, 1939-49 (resp. for national publicity on diphtheria immunisation scheme and gen. health educn, and the launching of the NHS) Controller, Home Publicity, COI, 1949-52; Adviser on Govt Public Relations and Adviser on Public Relations to Prime Ministers Sir Winston Churchill and Sir Anthony Eden, 1952-55; Advr on Public Relations to Earl Marshal Coronation, 1953; as Dir Gen, COI, 1954-71, responsible on behalf of FCC for organisation of British Pavilions at World Exhibitions in Brussels, 1958, Montreal, 1967 and Osaka, 1970; acted as Chief Officer, Nov. 1956-March 1957, to first Cabinet Minister, Dr Charles Hill, to co-ordinate Govt inf. services home and overseas. Consultant on External Relations to Crown Agents for Overseas Govts and Administrations, 1971-75, and to Trident Television Gp of Cos, 1976-78. First Pres., 1955-57, Mem. Emeritus, 1978, Internat. Public Relations Assoc. Fellow and Past Pres., Inst. of Public Relations (President's Medal, 1967); Pres., Civil Service Horticultural Fedn, 1959-70. Mem., Coun. of Management, Brighton Arts Festival, 1966-. *Publication:* The Central Office of Information, 1971. *Recreations:* gardening, walking, watching ships and horses. *Address:* Wave Hill, Nevill Road, Rottingdean, Sussex. *T:* Brighton 33020. *Clubs:* Athenæum; Marina Yacht (Brighton).

CLARK, Prof. Timothy John Hayes, FRCP; Professor of Thoracic Medicine, Guy's Hospital Medical School, since 1977; Dean Elect, 1982; Consultant Physician: to Guy's Hospital, since 1968; to Brompton Hospital, since 1970; *b* 18 Oct. 1935; *s* of John and Kathleen Clark; *m* 1961, Elizabeth Ann Day; two *s* two *d*. *Educ:* Christ's Hospital; Guy's Hospital Medical Sch. BSc 1958; MB BS (Hons) 1961, MD 1967 London. FRCP 1973 (LRCP 1960, MRCP 1962); MRCS 1960. Fellow, Johns Hopkins Hosp., Baltimore, USA, 1963; Registrar, Hammersmith Hosp., 1964; Lecturer and Sen. Lectr, Guy's Hospital Med. Sch., 1966. Member: Lambeth, Southwark and Lewisham AHA (Teaching), 1978-82, Lewisham and N Southwark Health Authority, 1982-; School Council, St Thomas' Hosp., 1980-; Governor, St Saviour's and St Olave's Grammar Sch., 1981-; Specialist Adviser to Social Services Cttee, 1981-. *Publications:* (jtly) Asthma, 1977; (jtly) Topical Steroid Treatment of Asthma and Rhinitis, 1980; (ed) Clinical Investigation of Respiratory Disease, 1982; (ed) Small Airways in Health and Disease, 1979; articles in British Medical Jl, Lancet, and other specialist scientific jls. *Recreation:* cricket. *Address:* 8 Lawrence Court, Mill Hill, NW7 3QP. *T:* 01-959 4411. *Club:* MCC.

CLARK, Wallace; *see* Clark, H. W. S.

CLARK, William Donaldson; President, International Institute for Environment and Development, since 1980; *b* 28 July 1916; *y s* of John McClare Clark and Marion Jackson; unmarried. *Educ:* Oundle Sch.; Oriel Coll., Oxford (MA). 1st class Hons Mod. Hist., Gibbs Prize. Commonwealth Fellow and Lectr in Humanities, Univ. of Chicago, 1938-40; Min. of Information, and Brit. Inf. Services, Chicago, 1941-44; Press Attaché, Washington, 1945-46; London Editor, Encyclopædia Britannica, 1946-49; Diplomatic Corresp., Observer, 1950-55; Public Relations Adviser to Prime Minister, 1955-56; toured Africa and Asia for BBC and Observer, 1957; Editor of "The Week" in Observer, 1958-60; Dir, Overseas Development Inst., 1960-68; Dir of Information and Public Affairs, IBRD, 1968-73; International Bank for Reconstruction and Development (World Bank): Dir, External Relns, 1973-74; Vice-Pres. for External Relns, 1974-80; an independent Dir, Observer, 1981-. Frequent broadcasts and television appearances, including original Press Conference series (BBC), and Right to Reply (ATV). *Publications:* Less than Kin: a study of Anglo-American relations, 1957; What is the Commonwealth?, 1958; Number 10 (novel and (with Ronald Miller) play), 1966; Special Relationship (novel), 1968. *Recreations:* writing, talking, travel. *Address:* IIED, 10 Percy Street, W1P 0DR; K5, Albany, W1. *T:* 01-734 1182; The Mill, Cuxham, Oxford OX9 5NF. *T:* Watlington 2381; Biniparell, Menorca, Baleares, Spain. *T:* (3471) 367683. *Clubs:* Athenæum, Savile.

CLARK, Sir William (Gibson), Kt 1980; MP (C) Croydon South, since 1974 (E Surrey, 1970-74); *b* 18 Oct. 1917; *m* 1944, Irene Dorothy Dawson Rands; three *s* one *d*. *Educ:* London. Mem. Association of Certified Accountants, 1941. Served in Army, 1941-46 (UK and India), Major. Mem. Wandsworth Borough Council, 1949-53 (Vice-Chm. Finance Cttee). Contested (C) Northampton, 1955; MP (C) Nottingham South, 1959-66. Opposition Front Bench Spokesman on Economics, 1964-66; Chairman: Select Cttee on Tax Credits, 1973; Cons. Back Bench Finance Cttee, 1979-. Jt Deputy Chm., Conservative Party Organisation, 1975-77 (Jt Treasurer, 1974-75). Hon. Nat. Dir, Carrington £2 million Appeal, 1967-68. *Recreations:* tennis, gardening. *Address:* The Clock House, Box End, Bedford. *T:* Bedford 852361; 3 Barton Street, SW1. *T:* 01-222 5759. *Clubs:* Carlton, Buck's.

CLARK, William P.; Assistant to the President of the United States of America for National Security Affairs, since 1982; *b* 23 Oct. 1931; *s* of William and Bernice Clark; *m* 1955, Joan Brauner; three *s* two *d*. *Educ:* Stanford Univ., California; Loyola Law Sch., Los Angeles, California. Admitted to practice of law, California, 1959; Sen. Member, law firm, Clark, Cole & Fairfield, Oxnard, Calif, 1959-67. Served on Cabinet of California, Governor Ronald Reagan, first as Cabinet Secretary, later as Executive Secretary, 1967-69; Judge, Superior Court, State of California, County of San Luis Obispo, 1969-71; Associate Justice: California Court of Appeal, Second District, Los Angeles, 1971-73; California Supreme Court, San Francisco, 1973-81; Dep. Secretary, Dept of State, Washington, DC, 1981-82. *Publications:* judicial opinions in California Reports, 9 Cal. 3d through 29 Cal. 3d. *Recreations:* ranching, horseback riding, outdoor sports. *Address:* The White House, Washington, DC 20500, USA. *T:* 202/456-2255. *Clubs:* California Cattleman's Association; Rancheros Visitadores (California).

CLARK HUTCHISON; *see* Hutchison.

CLARK-KENNEDY, Archibald Edmund, MD (Cantab); FRCP; Fellow of Corpus Christi College, Cambridge, since 1919; Physician to the London Hospital, 1928-58; Dean of the London Hospital Medical College, 1937-53; *s* of late Rev. A. E. Clark-Kennedy (RN retired), Rector of Ewhurst, Surrey; *m* 1918, Phyllis (*d* 1978), *d* of late Charles Howard Jeffree, Howard Lodge, Clapham Park; one *s* one *d*. *Educ:* Wellington Coll.; Corpus Christi Coll., Cambridge (exhibitioner, scholar). 1st class hons in Natural Science Tripos. Lieut, Queen's Royal West Surrey Regt (5th Territorial Bn), Aug. 1914; served as a combatant officer in India, then in Mesopotamia with IEF, D; returned to England, 1917; obtained diploma of MRCS and LRCP; commd in RAMC, 1918; served in France as MO to 158th Army RFA Bde. MRCP 1922; FRCP 1930. *Publications:* Stephen Hales, DD, FRS, an Eighteenth Century Biography, 1929; Medicine (two vols): Vol. I, The Patient and his Disease, 1947; Vol. II, Diagnosis, Prognosis and Treatment; Medicine in its Human Setting, 1954; Patients as People, 1957; Human Disease (a Pelican medical book), 1957; How to Learn Medicine, 1959; Clinical Medicine, The Modern Approach, 1960; The London: A Study in the Voluntary Hospital System (two vols): Vol. I, The First Hundred Years, 1740-1840, 1962; Vol. II, The Second Hundred Years, 1840-1948, 1963; Edith Cavell, Pioneer and Patriot, 1965; Man, Medicine and Morality, 1969; Attack the Colour! the Royal Dragoons in the Peninsula and at Waterloo, 1975; papers in medical and scientific journals. *Recreations:* mountaineering, sailing, hunting. *Address:* 7 Maitland House, Barton Road, Cambridge. *T:* Cambridge 352323.

CLARKE, Prof. Alan Douglas Benson, CBE 1974; Professor of Psychology, University of Hull, since 1962; *b* 21 March 1922; *s* of late Robert Benson Clarke and late Mary Lizars Clarke; *m* 1950, Dr Ann Margaret (*née* Gravely); two *s*. *Educ:* Lancing Coll.; Univs of Reading and London. 1st cl. hons BA Reading 1948; PhD London 1950; FBPsS. Reading Univ., 1940-41 and 1946-48. Sen. Psychol., 1951-57 and Cons. Psychol., 1957-62, Manor Hosp., Epsom. Dean of Faculty of Science, 1966-68, and Pro-Vice-Chancellor 1968-71, Univ. of Hull. Rapporteur, WHO Expert Cttee on Organization of Services for Mentally Retarded, 1967; Mem. WHO Expert Adv. Panel on Mental Health, 1968-; Lectures: Maudsley, Royal Medico-Psychol Assoc., 1967; Stolz, Guy's Hosp., 1972; Chm., Trng Council for Teachers of Mentally Handicapped, 1969-74; Hon. Vice-Pres., Nat. Assoc. for Mental Health, 1970-; President, Internat. Assoc. for Sci. Study of Mental Deficiency, 1973-76, Hon. Past-Pres., 1976-; Mem., Personal Social Services Council, 1973-77; Mem., DHSS/SSRC Organizing Gp Transmitted Deprivation, 1974-; Chm. 1978-; Cons., OECD/NZ Conf. on Early Childhood Care and Educn, 1978; Chm., Sec. of State's Adv. Cttee on Top Grade Clinical Psychologist Posts and Appts, NHS, 1981-82. Hon. Life Mem., Amer. Assoc. on Mental Deficiency, 1975 (Research award, 1977, with Ann M. Clarke). Pres., BPsS, 1977-78. Editor, Brit. Jl Psychol., 1973-79; Mem., Editorial Bds of other jls. *Publications* (with Ann M. Clarke): Mental Deficiency: the Changing Outlook, 1958, 3rd edn 1974; Mental Retardation and Behavioural Research, 1973; Early Experience: myth and evidence, 1976; numerous in psychol and med. jls. *Address:* 55 Newland Park, Hull HU5 2DR. *T:* Hull 444141.

CLARKE, Anthony Peter, QC 1979; *b* 13 May 1943; *s* of Harry Alston Clarke and Isobel Clarke; *m* 1968, Rosemary (*née* Adam); two *s* one *d*. *Educ:* Oakham Sch.; King's Coll., Cambridge (Econs Pt I, Law Pt II; MA). Called to the Bar, Middle Temple, 1965. *Recreations:* golf, tennis, holidays. *Address:* 2 Essex Court, Temple, EC4Y 9AP. *T:* 01-583 8381.

CLARKE, Arthur Charles; *b* 16 Dec. 1917; *s* of Charles Wright Clarke and Nora Mary Willis; *m* 1953, Marilyn Mayfield (marr. diss. 1964). *Educ:* Huish's Grammar Sch., Taunton; King's Coll., London (BSc); FKC 1977. HM Exchequer and Audit Dept, 1936-41. Served RAF, 1941-46. Instn of Electrical Engineers, 1949-50. Techn. Officer on first GCA radar, 1943; originated communications satellites, 1945. Chm., British Interplanetary Soc., 1946-47, 1950-53. Asst Ed., Science Abstracts, 1949-50. Since 1954 engaged on underwater exploration in Gt Barrier Reef of Australia and coast of Ceylon. Extensive lecturing, radio and TV in UK and US. Chancellor, Moratuwa Univ., Sri Lanka, 1979-; Vikram Sarabhai Prof., Physical Research Lab., Ahmedabad, 1980; Marconi Fellowship, 1982. Unesco, Kalinga Prize, 1961; Acad. of Astronautics, 1961; World Acad. of Art and Science, 1962; Stuart Ballantine Medal, Franklin Inst., 1963; Westinghouse-AAAS Science Writing Award, 1969; Amer. Inst. of Aeronautics and Astronautics: Aerospace Communications Award, 1974; Hon. Fellow, 1976; Nebula Award, Science Fiction Writers of America, 1972, 1974, 1979; John Campbell Award, 1974; Hugo Award, World Science Fiction Convention, 1974. *Publications: non-fiction:* Interplanetary Flight, 1950; The Exploration of Space, 1951; The Young Traveller in Space, 1954 (publ. in USA as Going into Space); The Coast of Coral, 1956; The Making of a Moon, 1957; The Reefs of Taprobane, 1957; Voice Across the Sea, 1958; The Challenge of the Spaceship, 1960; The Challenge of the Sea, 1960; Profiles of the Future, 1962; Voices from the Sky, 1965; (with Mike Wilson): Boy Beneath the Sea, 1958; The First Five Fathoms, 1960; Indian Ocean Adventure, 1961; The Treasure of the Great Reef, 1964; Indian Ocean Treasure, 1964; (with R. A. Smith) The Exploration of the Moon, 1954; (with Editors of Life) Man and Space, 1964; (ed) The Coming of the Space Age, 1967; The Promise of Space, 1968; (with the astronauts) First on the Moon, 1970; Report on Planet Three, 1972; (with Chesley Bonestell) Beyond Jupiter, 1973; The View from Serendip, 1977; (with Simon Welfare and John Fairley) Arthur C. Clarke's Mysterious World, 1980 (also TV Series); *fiction:* Prelude to Space, 1951; The Sands of Mars, 1951; Islands in the Sky, 1952; Against the Fall of Night, 1953; Childhood's End, 1953; Expedition to Earth, 1953; Earthlight, 1955; Reach for Tomorrow, 1956; The City and the Stars, 1956; Tales from the White Hart, 1957; The Deep Range, 1957; The Other Side of the Sky, 1958; Across the Sea of Stars, 1959; A Fall of Moondust, 1961; From the Ocean, From the Stars, 1962; Tales of Ten Worlds, 1962; Dolphin Island, 1963; Glide Path, 1963; Prelude to Mars, 1965; The Nine Billion Names of God, 1967; (with Stanley Kubrick) novel and screenplay, 2001: A Space Odyssey, 1968; The Lost Worlds of 2001, 1972; Of Time and Stars, 1972; The Wind from the Sun, 1972; Rendezvous with Rama, 1973; The Best of Arthur C. Clarke, 1973; Imperial Earth, 1975; The Fountains of Paradise, 1979; 2010: Space Odyssey II, 1982; papers in Electronic Engineering, Wireless World, Wireless Engineer, Aeroplane, Jl of British Interplanetary Soc., Astronautics, etc. *Recreations:* diving, photography, table-tennis. *Address:* 25 Barnes Place, Colombo 7, Sri Lanka. *T:* Colombo 94255; c/o David Higham Associates, 5 Lower John Street, Golden Square, W1R 3PE. *Club:* British Sub-Aqua.

CLARKE, Brig. Arthur Christopher L. S.; *see* Stanley-Clarke.

CLARKE, Arthur Grenfell, CMG 1953; *b* 17 Aug. 1906; *m* 1st, 1934, Rhoda McLean Arnott (*d* 1980); 2nd, 1980, Violet Louise Riley. *Educ:* Mountjoy Sch., Dublin; Dublin Univ. Appointed Cadet Officer, Hong Kong, 1929; entered service of Hong Kong Government, 1929; interned in Stanley Camp during Japanese occupation; Financial Sec., 1952-62; retired, 1962. *Address:* Foxdene, Brighton Road, Foxrock, Co. Dublin. *T:* 894368.

CLARKE, Dr Arthur S.; Keeper, Department of Natural History, Royal Scottish Museum, since 1980; *b* 11 Feb. 1923; *yr s* of late Albert Clarke and Doris Clarke (*née* Elliot); *m* 1951, Joan, *er d* of Walter Andrassy; one *s* one *d*. *Educ:* Leeds Boys' Modern School; Aireborough Grammar School; Leeds Univ. (BSc 1948, PhD 1951). Pilot, RAF, 1943-46. Assistant Lecturer, Glasgow Univ., 1951; Asst Keeper, Royal Scottish Museum, 1954; Deputy Keeper, 1973. *Address:* 27 Queen's Crescent, Edinburgh EH9 2BA.

CLARKE, Captain Arthur Wellesley, CBE 1946; DSO 1943; RN; *b* 16 April 1898; *s* of late Captain Sir Arthur W. Clarke, KCVO, KBE, and Lady Clarke; *m* 1926, Kate Cicely Lance; one *s*. *Educ:* Merton Court Prep. Sch.; RN Colls Osborne and Dartmouth; Emmanuel Coll., Cambridge (6 months 1919). Midshipman, 1914; Lieut 1918; Comdr 1933; Captain 1939; retired list, 1948 and re-employed at Admiralty. Served at sea throughout European War, 1914-18; Dardanelles, 1915 (despatches); Battle of Jutland, 1916; Atlantic and North Sea convoys. Between wars qualified as Navigating and Staff Officer; served at sea including in command at home and abroad; Asst Sec., Cttee of Imperial Defence, 1933-36. War of 1939-45: War Cabinet office, 1940, and later Addtl Naval Attaché, USA; commanded HMS Sheffield, Atlantic, North Russian and Malta convoys, N African landings and Barents Sea battle, 1941-43; Chief of Staff to Governor and C-in-C Malta, and later Naval Liaison Officer to Comdr, 8th Army, 1943; Chief of Staff to Head of Brit. Admty Delegn USA, 1944-46; comd HMS Ocean, 1946-48; Chief of Naval Information, Admty, 1948-57. Vice-President: King George's Fund for Sailors; Younger Brother, Trinity House. Officer, Legion of Merit (USA), 1946. *Recreation:* gardening. *Address:* 16 Yarborough Road, Southsea, Hants. *T:* Portsmouth 24539. *Club:* Naval (Hon. Mem.).

CLARKE, Sir Ashley; *see* Clarke, Sir H. A.

CLARKE, Bernard; *see* Clarke, J. B.

CLARKE, Prof. Bryan Campbell, DPhil; FRS 1982; Foundation Professor of Genetics, University of Nottingham, since 1971; *b* 24 June 1932; *s* of Robert Campbell Clarke and Gladys Mary (*née* Carter); *m* 1960, Ann Gillian, *d* of Prof. John Jewkes, *qv*; one *s* one *d*. *Educ:* Fay Sch., Southborough, Mass, USA; Magdalen Coll. Sch., Oxford; Magdalen Coll., Oxford (MA, DPhil). FLS 1980. National Service, 1950-52 (Pilot Officer, RAF). Nature Conservancy Res. Student, Oxford Univ., 1956; Asst 1959, Lectr 1963, Reader 1969, Dept of Zoology, Univ. of Edinburgh. Carnegie Fellow, USA, 1964; National Science Foundn Fellow, USA, 1964 and 1968; Res. Fellow, Stanford Univ., 1973; SRC Sen. Res. Fellow, 1976-81. Joint Founder, Population Genetics Gp, 1967; Vice-Pres., Genetical Soc., 1981. Scientific expeditions to: Morocco, 1955; Polynesia, 1962, 1967, 1968 and 1980. Lectures: Special, London Univ., 1973; Official Visitor, Australian Genetics Soc., 1979; Nelson, Rutgers Univ., 1980. *Publications:* Berber Village, 1959; contrib. scientific jls, mostly on ecological genetics and evolution. *Recreations:* sporadic painting and gardening; archaeology, computing. *Address:* Linden Cottage, School Lane, Colston Bassett, Nottingham NG12 3FD. *T:* Kinoulton 243. *Club:* Royal Air Force.

CLARKE, Sir (Charles Mansfield) Tobias, 6th Bt *cr* 1831; *b* Santa Barbara, California, 8 Sept. 1939; *e s* of Sir Humphrey Orme Clarke, 5th Bt, and Elisabeth (*d* 1967), *d* of Dr William Albert Cook; *S* father, 1973; *m* 1971, Charlotte (marr. diss. 1979), *e d* of Roderick Walter. *Educ:* Eton; Christ Church, Oxford (MA); Univ. of Paris; New York Univ. Graduate Business Sch. Vice-Pres., Bankers Trust Co., NY, 1974-80. Hon. Treasurer, Standing Council of the Baronetage, 1980-. *Recreations:* fox hunting, gardening, photography and meeting people; Pres., Bibury Cricket Club; Vice-Pres., Bibury Association Football Club. *Heir: half b* Orme Roosevelt Clarke [*b* 30 Nov. 1947; *m* 1971, Joanna Valentine, *d* of John Barkley Schuster, TD; one *s*]. *Address:* 80A Campden Hill Road, W8 7AA. *T:* 01-937 6213; The Church House, Bibury, Glos GL7 5NR. *T:* Bibury 225. *Clubs:* Boodle's, Pratt's; Pilgrims; Jockey (Paris); The Brook, Racquet & Tennis (New York).

CLARKE, Cyril Alfred Allen, MA; Headmaster, Holland Park Secondary School, 1957-71; *b* 21 Aug. 1910; *s* of late Frederick John Clarke; *m* 1934, Edna Gertrude Francis; three *s*. *Educ:* Langley Sch., Norwich; Culham Coll. of Educn, Oxon; Birkbeck Coll., Univ. of London; King's Coll., Univ. of London. Entered London Teaching Service, 1933; Royal Artillery, 1940-46; Staff Officer (Major) in Educn Br. of Mil. Govt of Germany, 1945-46; Asst Master, Haberdashers' Aske's Hatcham Boys' Sch., 1946-51; Headmaster: Isledon Sec. Sch., 1951-55; Battersea Co. Sec. Sch., 1955-57. *Recreations:* photography, reading, archaeology. *Address:* 1 Youl Grange, Link Road, Eastbourne, E Sussex BN20 7TR. *T:* Eastbourne 20792.

CLARKE, Prof. Sir Cyril (Astley), KBE 1974 (CBE 1969); FRS 1970; MD, ScD, FRCP, FRCOG; FIBiol; Emeritus Professor and Hon. Nuffield Research Fellow, Department of Genetics, University of Liverpool (Professor of Medicine, 1965-72, Director, Nuffield Unit of Medical Genetics, 1963-72, and Nuffield Research Fellow, 1972-76); Consultant Physician, United Liverpool Hospitals (David Lewis Northern, 1946-58, Royal Infirmary since 1958) and to Broadgreen Hospital since 1946; *b* 22 Aug. 1907; *s* of Astley Vavasour Clarke, MD, JP, and Ethel Mary Clarke, *d* of H. Simpson Gee; *m* 1935, Frieda (Féo) Margaret Mary, *d* of Alexander John Campbell Hart and Isabella Margaret Hart; three *s*. *Educ:* Wyggeston Grammar Sch., Leicester; Oundle Sch.; Gonville and Caius Coll., Cambridge; Guy's Hosp. (Schol.). 2nd Class Hons, Natural Science Tripos Pt I; MD Cantab 1937; ScD Cantab 1963. FRCP 1949; FRCOG 1970; FRACP 1973; FRCPI 1973; FRSA 1973; FFCM 1974; FACP 1976; Fellow Ceylon Coll. of Physicians 1974; FRCPE 1975; FRCP(C) 1977; Fellow Linnean Soc. 1981. House Phys., Demonstr in Physiology and Clin. Asst in Dermatology, Guy's Hosp., 1932-36. Life Insurance practice, Grocers' Hall, EC2, 1936-39. Served, 1939-46, as Med Specialist, RNVR: HM Hosp. Ship Amarapoora (Scapa Flow and N Africa), RNH Seaforth and RNH Sydney. After War, Med. Registrar, Queen Elizabeth Hosp., Birmingham. Visiting Prof. of Genetics, Seton Hall Sch. of Med., Jersey City, USA, 1963; Lectures: Lumleian, RCP, 1967; Ingleby, Univ. of Birmingham, 1968; Foundn, RCPath, 1971; Inaugural Faculty, Univ. of Leeds, 1972; P. B. Fernando Meml, Colombo, 1974; Marsden, Royal Free Hosp., 1976; Linacre, 1978; New Ireland, UCD, 1979; William Meredith Fletcher Shaw, RCOG, 1979; Harveian Oration, RCP, 1979; Sir Arthur Hall Meml, Sheffield, 1981. Examr in Med., Dundee Univ., 1965-69. Pres., RCP, 1972-77 (Censor, 1967-69, Sen. Censor, 1971-72, Dir, Med. Services Study Group, 1977-); Pres. Liverpool Med. Instn, 1970-71; Chm., British Heart Foundn Council, 1982-; Member: MRC Working Party, 1966; Sub-Cttee of Dept of Health and Social Security on prevention of Rhesus hæmolytic disease, 1967 (Chm., 1973-); Bd of Governors, United Liverpool Hosps, 1969; Assoc. of Hungarian Medical Socs, 1973; Pres., Harveian Soc.; Governor and Councillor, Bedford Coll., 1974, Chm. of Council, 1975. Chm., Cockayne Trust Fund, Natural History Museum, 1974-. Hon. Fellow, Caius Coll. Cambridge, 1974; Leverhulme Emeritus Fellow, 1980. Hon. FRCPE 1981; Hon FRCPath 1981; Hon. FRSM 1982; Hon. Mem., Liverpool Med. Inst, 1981. Hon. DSc: Edinburgh, 1971; Leicester, 1971; East Anglia, 1973; Birmingham, Liverpool and Sussex, 1974; Hull, 1977; Wales, 1978; London, 1980. Gold Medal in Therapeutics, Worshipful Soc. of Apothecaries, 1970; James Spence Medal, Brit. Paediatric Assoc., 1973; Addingham Medal, Leeds, 1973; John Scott Medal and Award, Philadelphia, 1976; Fothergillian Medal, Med. Soc., 1977; Gairdner Award, 1977; Ballantyne Prize, RCPEd, 1979; (jtly) Albert and Mary Lasker Foundn Award, 1980; Linnean Medal for Zoology, 1981; Artois-Baillet Latour Health Prize, 1981. *Publications:* Genetics for the Clinician, 1962; (ed) Selected Topics in Medical Genetics, 1969; Human Genetics and Medicine, 1970, 2nd edn, 1977; (with R. B. McConnell) Prevention of Rhesus Hæmolytic Disease, 1972; (ed) Rhesus Hæmolytic Disease: selected papers and extracts, 1975; many contribs med. and scientific jls, particularly on prevention of Rhesus hæmolytic disease and on evolution of mimicry in swallowtail butterflies. *Recreations:* small boat sailing, breeding swallowtail butterflies. *Address:* Duncan Buildings, Royal Liverpool Hospital, Prescot Street, Liverpool L7 8XP. *T:* 051-709 0141; 43 Caldy Road, West Kirby, Wirral; Merseyside L48 2HF. *T:* 051-625 8811; 126 Albert Street, NW1 7NF. *T:* 01-267 6111. *Clubs:* Athenæum; Explorers' (New York); Oxford and Cambridge Sailing Society (Pres., 1975-77); West Kirby Sailing, Royal Mersey Yacht; United Hospitals Sailing (Pres.).

CLARKE, David Clive; a Recorder, since 1981; *b* 16 July 1942; *s* of Philip George Clarke and José Margaret Clarke; *m* 1969, Alison Claire, *d* of Rt Rev. Percy James Brazier, *qv*; three *s*. *Educ:* Winchester Coll.; Magdalene Coll., Cambridge. BA 1964, MA 1968. Called to the Bar, Inner Temple, 1965. In practice, Northern Circuit, 1965-. *Recreations:* exploring inland waterways, industrial archaeology. *Address:* Refuge Assurance House, Derby Square, Liverpool. *T:* 051-709 4222.

CLARKE, Denzil Robert Noble; Chairman, British-American Tobacco Co. Ltd, 1966-70 (Director, 1954-70; Vice-Chairman, 1962); Director, Sun Life Assurance Society, 1966-79; *b* 9 July 1908; *er s* of late R. T. Clarke, ICS, LLD and late Mrs M. M. G. Clarke (*née* Whyte); *m* 1942, Ismay Elizabeth, *e d* of late Lt-Col Hon. R. M. P. Preston, DSO; one *s* two *d*. *Educ:* Stonyhurst Coll. Articled Clerk, Singleton Fabian & Co., Chartered Accountants, 1926; ACA 1932; FCA 1960. Joined British-American Tobacco Co. Ltd, 1932. War service, 1941-45; Far East; Lt-Col 1944. *Recreations:* gardening, tennis. *Address:* Puffins, South Drive, Wokingham, Berks. *T:* Wokingham 780975. *Clubs:* Special Forces, Army and Navy.

See also Maj.-Gen. D. A. B. Clarke.

CLARKE, Maj.-Gen. Desmond Alexander Bruce, CB 1965; CBE 1961 (OBE 1944); *b* 15 July 1912; *yr s* of late R. T. Clarke, ICS, LLD, Weybridge and late Mrs R. T. Clarke (*née* Whyte), Loughbrickland, Co. Down; *m* Madeleine, 2nd *d* of Rear-Adm. Walter Glyn Petre, DSO, Weybridge; three *s* two *d*. *Educ*: Stonyhurst Coll.; RMA Woolwich. Commissioned RA, 1932. Served War of 1939-45 (OBE; despatches 4 times); Middle East, India, France, Germany; AA and QMG, 59 (Staffs) Div., 1943; AA and QMG, 43 (Wessex) Div., Dec. 1944. Brig. i/c Administration, Southern Command, 1960-62; Dir of Personal Services, War Office, 1962-64; Dir of Personal Services (Army), Min. of Defence, 1964-66; retd Oct. 1966. Chevalier, Order of the Crown (Belgium), 1945; Croix de Guerre (Belgium), 1945. *Address*: Elm Cottage, Caldbeck, near Wigton, Cumbria. *T*: Caldbeck 433.
   See also D. R. N. Clarke.

CLARKE, His Honour Edward, QC 1960; a Circuit Judge (Judge of the Central Criminal Court), 1964-81; *b* 21 May 1908; *s* of William Francis Clarke; *m* 1948, Dorothy May, *d* of Thomas Leask, Richmond, Surrey; three *s* one *d*. *Educ*: Sherborne Sch.; King's Coll., London. Called to Bar, Lincoln's Inn, 1935. Served War, 1943-46 in France, Belgium, Holland and Germany, Lieut-Col, Judge Advocate-General's Staff. Bencher, 1955, Treasurer, 1973, Lincoln's Inn; Dep. Chm., Herts Quarter Sessions, 1956-63; Dep. Chm., London Quarter Sessions, 1963-64. FKC, 1965. President: King's Coll. London Assoc., 1972-73, 1978-79; Old Shirburnian Soc., 1975-76. *Publications*: (with Derek Walker Smith) The Life of Sir Edward Clarke; Halsbury's Laws of England (Criminal Law). *Recreations*: lawn tennis, criminology. *Address*: 19 Old Buildings, Lincoln's Inn, WC2. *T*: 01-405 2980. *Clubs*: Garrick, MCC.

CLARKE, Edwin (Sisterson), MD, FRCP; Research Associate, Wellcome Institute for the History of Medicine, since 1980; *b* Felling-on-Tyne, 18 June 1919; *s* of Joseph and Nellie Clarke; *m* 1st, 1949, Margaret Elsie Morrison (marr. diss.); two *s*; 2nd, 1958, Beryl Eileen Brock (marr. diss.); one *d*. *Educ*: Jarrow Central Sch.; Univ. of Durham Med. Sch. (MD); Univ. of Chicago Med. Sch. (MD). Neurological Specialist, RAMC, 1946-48; Nat. Hosp., Queen Square, 1950-51; Postgrad. Med. Sch. of London, 1951-58; Lectr in Neurology and Consultant Neurologist to Hammersmith Hosp., 1955-58; Asst Sec. to Wellcome Trust, 1958-60; Asst Prof., History of Medicine, Johns Hopkins Hosp. Med. Sch., 1960-62; Vis. Assoc. Prof., History of Medicine, Yale Univ. Med. Sch., 1962-63; Med. Historian to Wellcome Historical Med. Library and Museum, 1963-66; Sen. Lectr and Head of Sub-Dept of History of Medicine, University Coll. London, 1966-72, Reader, 1972-73; Dir, Wellcome Inst. for the History of Medicine, 1973-79. *Publications*: (jtly) The Human Brain and Spinal Cord, 1968; (ed) Modern Methods in the History of Medicine, 1971; (jtly) An Illustrated History of Brain Function, 1972; (trans.) Die historische Entwicklung der experimentellen Gehirn- und Rückenmarksphysiologie vor Flourens, by M. Neuburger, 1981; articles in jls dealing with neurology and with history of medicine. *Address*: Wellcome Institute for History of Medicine, Wellcome Building, Euston Road, NW1. *T*: 01-387 4477.

CLARKE, Elizabeth Bleckly, CVO 1969; MA; JP; Headmistress, Benenden School, Kent, 1954-Dec. 1975; *b* 26 May 1915; *d* of Kenneth Bleckly Clarke, JP, MRCS, LRCP, Cranborne, Dorset, and Dorothy Milborough (*née* Hasluck). *Educ*: Grovely Manor Sch., Boscombe, Hants; St Hilda's Coll., Oxford, 1933-37. BA 1936, BLitt and MA 1940. Asst Mistress, The Grove Sch., Hindhead, 1937-39; Benenden Sch., 1940-47; called to the Bar, Middle Temple, 1949; Vice-Principal, Cheltenham Ladies' Coll., 1950-54. JP, County of Kent, 1956. *Recreations*: walking, gardening. *Address*: The Old Oast, Stream Lane, Hawkhurst, Kent TN18 4RD. *T*: Hawkhurst 2566. *Club*: English-Speaking Union.

CLARKE, Sir Ellis (Emmanuel Innocent), TC 1969; GCMG 1972 (CMG 1960); Kt 1963 (but does not use the title within Republic of Trinidad and Tobago); President of Trinidad and Tobago, since 1976 (Governor General and C-in-C, 1973-76); *b* 28 Dec. 1917; *o c* of late Cecil Clarke and of Mrs Elma Clarke; *m* 1952, Eyrmyntrude (*née* Hagley); one *s* one *d*. *Educ*: St Mary's Coll., Trinidad (Jerningham Gold Medal, 1936, and other prizes). London Univ. (LLB 1940); called to the Bar, Gray's Inn, 1940. Private practice at Bar of Trinidad and Tobago, 1941-54; Solicitor-Gen., Oct. 1954; Dep. Colonial Sec., Dec. 1956; Attorney-Gen., 1957-62; Actg Governor, 1960; Chief Justice designate, 1961; Trinidad and Tobago Perm. Rep. to UN, 1962-66; Ambassador: to United States, 1962-73; to Mexico, 1966-73; Rep. on Council of OAS, 1967-73. Chm. of Bd, British West Indian Airways, 1968-72. KStJ 1973. *Address*: President's House, Port of Spain, Trinidad. *Clubs*: Queen's Park Cricket (Port of Spain); Trinidad Turf, Arima Race (Trinidad); Tobago Golf (President, 1969-75).

CLARKE, Geoffrey, RA 1976 (ARA 1970); ARCA; artist and sculptor; *b* 28 Nov. 1924; *s* of John Moulding Clarke and Janet Petts; two *s*. *Educ*: Royal College of Art (Hons). Exhibitions: Gimpel Fils Gallery, 1952, 1955; Redfern Gallery, 1965; Tranman Gallery, 1975, 1976. Works in public collections: Victoria and Albert Museum; Tate Gallery; Arts Council; Museum of Modern Art, NY; etc. Prizes for engraving: Triennial, 1951; London, 1953, Tokyo, 1957. Commissioned work includes: iron sculpture, Time Life Building, New Bond Street; cast aluminium relief sculpture (1000 sq. ft), Castrol House, Marylebone Road; mosaics, Liverpool Univ. Physics Block and Basildon New Town; stained glass windows for Treasury, Lincoln Cathedral; bronze sculpture (80 ft high), Thorn Electric Building, Upper St Martin's Lane; relief sculpture on Canberra and Oriana; 3 (70 ft high) stained glass windows, high altar, cross and candlesticks (10 ft high cast silver), the flying cross and crown of thorns, all in Coventry Cathedral; sculpture, Nottingham Civic Theatre; UKAEA Culham; Westminster Bank, Bond Street; Univs of Liverpool, Exeter, Cambridge, Oxford, Manchester, Lancaster and Loughborough; screens in Royal Military Chapel, Birdcage Walk. Further work at Chichester, Newcastle, Manchester, Plymouth, Ipswich, Canterbury, Taunton, Winchester, St Paul, Minnesota, Lincoln, Nebraska, Newcastle Civic Centre, Wolverhampton, Leicester, Churchill Coll., Aldershot, Suffolk Police HQ, All Souls, W1, The Majlis, Abu Dhabi. *Address*: Stowe Hill, Hartest, Bury St Edmunds, Suffolk. *T*: Hartest 319.

CLARKE, Guy Hamilton, CMG 1959; HM Ambassador to Nepal, 1962-63, retired; *b* 23 July 1910; 3rd *s* of late Dr and Mrs Charles H. Clarke, Leicester. *Educ*: Wyggeston Grammar Sch., Leicester; Trinity Hall, Cambridge. Probationer Vice-Consul, Levant Consular Service, Beirut, 1933; transf. to Ankara, 1936; Corfu, 1940; Adana, 1941; Baltimore, 1944; has since served at: Washington, Los Angeles (Consul 1945), Bangkok, Jedda, Kirkuk (Consul 1949), Bagdad, Kirkuk (Consul-Gen. 1951); Ambassador to the Republic of Liberia, 1957-60, and to the Republic of Guinea, 1959-60; Mem. United Kingdom Delegation to United Nations Gen. Assembly, New York, 1960; HM Consul-General, Damascus, Feb. 1961, and Chargé d'Affaires there, Oct. 1961-Jan. 1962. *Address*: 10 Fairlawn House, Christchurch Road, Winchester, Hants.

CLARKE, Sir (Henry) Ashley, GCMG 1962 (KCMG 1952; CMG 1946); GCVO 1961; Vice-Chairman, Venice in Peril Fund, since 1970; Member: General Board, Assicurazioni Generali of Trieste, since 1964; Director, Royal Academy of Music, since 1973; *b* 26 June 1903; *e s* of H. R. Clarke, MD; *m* 1st, 1937, Virginia (marr. diss. 1960), *d* of Edward Bell, New York; 2nd, 1962, Frances, *d* of John Molyneux, Stourbridge, Worcs. *Educ*: Repton; Pembroke Coll., Cambridge. Entered Diplomatic Service, 1925; 3rd Sec., Budapest and Warsaw; 2nd Sec., Constantinople, FO and Gen. Disarmament Conf, Geneva; 1st Sec., Tokyo; Counsellor, FO; Minister, Lisbon and Paris; Deputy Under-Sec., FO; Ambassador to Italy, 1953-62, retd. London Adviser, Banca Commerciale Italiana, 1962-71; Sec.-Gen., Europa Nostra, 1969-70. Governor: BBC, 1962-67; Brit. Inst. of Recorded Sound, 1964-67; Member: Council, British Sch. at Rome, 1962-78; Exec. Cttee, Keats-Shelley Assoc., 1962-71; D'Oyly Carte Trust, 1964-71; Governing Body, Royal Acad. of Music, 1967-73; Adv. Council, V&A Mus., 1969-73; Nat. Theatre Bd, 1962-66; Chairman: British-Italian Soc., 1962-67; Italian Art and Archives Rescue Fund, 1966-70; Royal Acad. of Dancing, 1964-69. Hon. Dr of Political Science, Genoa, 1956; Hon. Academician, Accademia Filarmonica Romana, 1962; Hon. Fellow: Pembroke Coll., Cambridge, 1962; Ancient Monuments Soc., 1969 (Vice-Pres., 1982); Royal Acad. of Music, 1971; Ateneo Veneto, 1973. Pietro Torta Prize, 1974 and Bolla Award, 1976 (for conservation in Venice). Knight Grand Cross of the Order of Merit of the Republic of Italy, 1957; Knight Grand Cross, Order of St Gregory the Great, 1976; Knight of St Mark, 1979. *Publication*: Restoring Venice: The Madonna dell'Orto (with P. Rylands), 1977. *Recreation*: music. *Address*: The Glebe House, Halstock, near Yeovil, Som BA22 9SG; Fondamenta Bonlini 1113, Dorsoduro, 30123 Venice, Italy. *Clubs*: Athenæum, Garrick.

CLARKE, Sir Henry O.; see Osmond-Clarke.

CLARKE, Hilton Swift; Chairman: Atlantic International Bank Ltd, since 1973; Exco International plc, since 1981; Astley & Pearce, since 1981; *b* 1 April 1909; *yr s* of Fredrick Job Clarke; *m* 1934, Sibyl Muriel, *d* of late C. J. C. Salter; one *s*. *Educ*: Highgate School. FIB. Bank of England, 1927-67; former Director: Charterhouse Group Ltd to 1982 (Chm. Charterhouse Japhet Ltd, 1971-73); United Dominions Trust Ltd, 1967-81; Guthrie Corp., 1967-79; Bank of Scotland Ltd (London Bd), 1967-79. Freeman, City of London, 1973. Hon. FRCGP 1975. *Recreations*: gardening, golf. *Address*: Hedges, Peaslake, Guildford, Surrey. *T*: Dorking 730757. *Clubs*: City of London, Overseas Bankers'; Royal Fowey Yacht; Effingham Golf.

CLARKE, James Samuel, MC 1943 and Bar 1944; Under-Secretary and Principal Assistant Solicitor, Inland Revenue, 1970-81, retired; *b* 19 Jan. 1921; *s* of James Henry and Deborah Florence Clarke; *m* 1949, Ilse Cohen; two *d*. *Educ*: Reigate Grammar Sch.; St Catharine's Coll., Cambridge (MA). Army Service, 1941-45: Royal Irish Fusiliers; served 1st Bn N Africa and Italy; Major 1943. Called to Bar, Middle Temple, 1946. Entered Legal Service (Inland Rev.), 1953; Sen. Legal Asst, 1958; Asst Solicitor, 1965. *Recreations*: gardening, sailing. *Address*: Dormers, The Downs, Givons Grove, Leatherhead, Surrey. *T*: Leatherhead 78254. *Club*: National Liberal.

CLARKE, (John) Bernard; Leader, Greater Manchester County Council, since 1981; *b* 10 March 1934; *s* of John Clarke and Alice (*née* Hewitt); *m* 1955, Patricia Powell; four *s* two *d*. *Educ*: St Mary's RC Sch., Stockport. Employed by National Carriers Ltd. Mem., Stockport Metrop. Bor. Council, 1963-74 (Leader, 1972-74); Mem., Greater Manchester CC, 1973- (Leader of Labour Gp, 1978-). *Recreations*: angling, gardening. *Address*: 22 Fallowfield Road, North Reddish, Stockport SK5 6XT.

CLARKE, Sir Jonathan (Dennis), Kt 1981; His Honour Judge Sir Jonathan Clarke; a Circuit Judge, since 1982; *b* 19 Jan. 1930; *e s* of late Dennis Robert Clarke, Master of Supreme Court, and of Caroline Alice (*née* Hill); *m* 1956, Susan Margaret Elizabeth (*née* Ashworth); one *s* three *d*. *Educ*:

Kidstones Sch.; University Coll. London. Admitted Solicitor, 1956; partner in Townsends solicitors, 1959-82; a Recorder of the Crown Court, 1972-82. Mem. Council, Law Soc., 1964-, Pres., 1980-81; Sec., Nat. Cttee of Young Solicitors, 1962-64; Member: Matrimonial Causes Rule Cttee, 1967-78; Legal Studies Bd, CNAA, 1968-75; Judicial Studies Bd, 1979-; Governor, College of Law, 1970-, Chm. of Governors, 1982-. *Recreation:* sailing. *Address:* West Lodge, Westlecot Road, Swindon, Wilts. *T:* Swindon 27695. *Clubs:* Carlton, Farmers'; Law Society Yacht.

CLARKE, Kenneth Harry; QC 1980; MP (C) Rushcliffe Division of Nottinghamshire since 1970; Minister of State (Minister for Health), Department of Health and Social Security, since 1982; *b* 2 July 1940; *e c* of Kenneth Clarke, Nottingham; *m* 1964, Gillian Mary Edwards; one *s* one *d*. *Educ:* Nottingham High Sch.; Gonville and Caius Coll., Cambridge (BA, LLB). Chm., Cambridge Univ. Conservative Assoc., 1961; Pres., Cambridge Union, 1963; Chm., Fedn Conservative Students, 1963. Called to Bar, Gray's Inn 1963; practising Mem., Midland Circuit, 1963-. Research Sec., Birmingham Bow Group, 1965-66; contested Mansfield (Notts) in General Elections of 1964 and 1966. PPS to Solicitor General, 1971-72; an Asst Govt Whip, 1972-74 (Govt Whip for Europe, 1973-74); a Lord Comr, HM Treasury, 1974; Parly Sec., DoT, later Parly Under Sec. of State for Transport, 1979-82. Mem., Parly delegn to Council of Europe and WEU, 1973-74; Sec., Cons. Parly Health and Social Security Cttee, 1974; Opposition Spokesman on: Social Services, 1974-76; Industry, 1976-79. *Publications:* New Hope for the Regions, 1979; pamphlets published by Bow Group, 1964-. *Recreations:* modern jazz music; watching Association Football and cricket. *Address:* House of Commons, SW1.

CLARKE, Dr Malcolm Roy, FRS 1981; Senior Principal Scientific Officer, Marine Biological Association of the UK, since 1978; *b* 24 Oct. 1930; *s* of Cecil Dutfield Clarke and Edith Ellen Woodward; *m* 1958, Dorothy Clara Knight; three *s* one *d*. *Educ:* eleven schools and finally Wallingford County Grammar Sch.; Hull Univ. BSc 1955, PhD 1958, DSc 1978. National Service, Private, RAMC, 1949-50. Teacher, 1951; Hull Univ., 1951-58; Whaling Inspector in Antarctic, 1955-56; Scientific Officer, later PSO, Nat. Inst. of Oceanography, 1958-71; led Oceanographic Expedns on RRS Discovery, RRS Challenger and RV Sarsia; PSO, Marine Biol Assoc. of UK, 1972-78. *Publications:* papers on squids and whales in Jl of Marine Biol Assoc. etc, and a Discovery Report, 1980. *Recreations:* boating, painting. *Address:* Ridge Court, Court Road, Newton Ferrers, S Devon PL8 1DD. *T:* Plymouth 872738. *Club:* Yealm Yacht (Newton Ferrers).

CLARKE, Marshal Butler C.; *see* Cholmondeley Clarke.

CLARKE, Prof. Martin Lowther; *b* 2 Oct. 1909; *s* of late Rev. William Kemp Lowther Clarke; *m* 1942, Emilie de Rontenay Moon, *d* of late Dr R. O. Moon; two *s*. *Educ:* Haileybury Coll.; King's Coll., Cambridge. Asst, Dept of Humanity, Edinburgh Univ., 1933-34; Fellow of King's Coll., Cambridge, 1934-40; Asst Lecturer in Greek and Latin, University Coll., London, 1935-37. Foreign Office, 1940-45. Lecturer, 1946-47, and Reader, 1947-48, in Greek and Latin, University Coll., London; Prof. of Latin, University Coll. of North Wales, 1948-74, Vice-Principal, 1963-65, 1967-74. *Publications:* Richard Porson, 1937; Greek Studies in England, 1700 to 1830, 1945; Rhetoric at Rome, 1953; The Roman Mind, 1956; Classical Education in Britain, 1500-1900, 1959; George Grote, 1962; Bangor Cathedral, 1969; Higher Education in the Ancient World, 1971; Paley, 1974; The Noblest Roman, 1981. *Address:* Lollingdon House, Cholsey, Wallingford OX10 9LS. *T:* Cholsey 651389.

CLARKE, Mary; Editor, Dancing Times, since 1963; *b* 23 Aug. 1923; *d* of Frederick Clarke and Ethel Kate (*née* Reynolds); unmarried. *Educ:* Mary Datchelor Girls' School. London Corresp., Dance Magazine, NY, 1943-55; London Editor, Dance News, NY, 1955-70; Asst Editor and Contributor, Ballet Annual, 1952-63; joined Dancing Times as Asst Editor, 1954. Dance critic, The Guardian, 1977-. *Publications:* The Sadler's Wells Ballet: a history and an appreciation, 1955; Six Great Dancers, 1957; Dancers of Mercury: the story of Ballet Rambert, 1962; (with Clement Crisp) Ballet, an Illustrated History, 1973; (with Clement Crisp) Making a Ballet, 1974; (with Clement Crisp) Introducing Ballet, 1976; ed (with David Vaughan) Encyclopedia of Dance and Ballet, 1977; (with Clement Crisp) Design for Ballet, 1978; (with Clement Crisp) Ballet in Art, 1978; (with Clement Crisp) The History of Dance, 1981; contrib. Encycl. Britannica. *Address:* 11 Danbury Street, Islington, N1 8LD. *T:* 01-226 9209. *Club:* Gautier.

CLARKE, Norman, OBE 1982; Secretary and Registrar, Institute of Mathematics and its Applications, since 1965; *b* 21 Oct. 1916; *o s* of late Joseph Clarke and of Ellen Clarke, Oldham; *m* 1940, Hilda May Watts; two *d*. *Educ:* Hulme Grammar Sch., Oldham; Univ. of Manchester (BSc). FInstP, FIMA. Pres., Manchester Univ. Union, 1938-39. External Ballistics Dept, Ordnance Bd, 1939-42; Armament Res. Estabt, Br. for Theoretical Res., 1942-45; Dep. Sec., Inst. Physics, 1945-65; Hon. Sec., Internat. Commn on Physics Educn, 1960-66. Southend-on-Sea County Borough Council: Mem., 1961-74; Alderman, 1964-74; Chm. of Watch Cttee, 1962-69 and of Public Protection Cttee, 1969-78; Vice-Chm., Essex Police Authority, 1969-; Member: Essex CC, 1973-; Southend-on-Sea Borough Council, 1974- (Mayor, 1975-76). *Publications:* papers on educn; editor and contributor: A Physics Anthology: (with S. C. Brown) International Education in Physics; Why Teach Physics; The Education of a Physicist; contributor: A Survey of the Teaching of

Physics in Universities (Unesco); Metrication. *Recreations:* music, boating, cricket, gastronomy. *Address:* 106 Olive Avenue, Leigh-on-Sea, Essex SS9 3QE. *T:* Southend-on-Sea 558056; Institute of Mathematics and its Applications, Maitland House, Warrior Square, Southend-on-Sea, Essex SS1 2JY. *T:* Southend-on-Sea 612177.

CLARKE, Norman Eley; Under Secretary, Department of Health and Social Security, since 1976; *b* 11 Feb. 1930; *s* of Thomas John Laurence Clarke and May (*née* Eley); *m* 1953, Pamela Muriel Colwill; three *s* one *d*. *Educ:* Hampton Grammar Sch. Grade 5 Officer, Min. of Labour and National Service, 1948-56; Asst Principal, National Assistance Bd, 1957-61 (Private Sec. to Chm., 1960-61); Principal, Nat. Asstnce Bd, subseq. Min. of Social Security, and DHSS, 1961-69; Private Sec. to Minister without Portfolio, Jan.-June 1970; Principal, DHSS, 1970-71; Asst Sec., 1971-75; Under Sec., Dir of Estabts and Personnel (HQ), Jan.-Sept. 1976, Dir of Estabts and Personnel (Departmental), 1976-82. *Recreations:* reading, tennis, watching Queens Park Rangers, talking. *Address:* Winton, Guildford Lane, Woking, Surrey. *T:* Woking 64453.

CLARKE, Prof. Patricia Hannah, DSc; FRS 1976; Professor of Microbial Biochemistry, University College, University of London, since 1974; *b* 29 July 1919; *d* of David Samuel Green and Daisy Lilian Amy Willoughby; *m* 1940, Michael Clarke; two *s*. *Educ:* Howells Sch., Llandaff; Girton Coll., Cambridge (BA). DSc London. Armament Res. Dept, 1940-44; Wellcome Res. Labs, 1944-47; National Collection of Type Cultures, 1951-53; Lectr, Dept of Biochemistry, UCL, 1953; Reader in Microbial Biochemistry, 1966. Hon. Gen. Sec., Soc. for General Microbiology, 1965-70; Mem., CNAA, 1973-79. Lectures: Royal Soc. Leeuwenhoek, 1979; Marjory Stephenson, Soc. for Gen. Microbiology, 1981. A Vice-Pres., Royal Soc., 1981. *Publications:* Genetics and Biochemistry of Pseudomonas (ed with M. H. Richmond), 1975; papers on genetics, biochemistry and enzyme evolution in Jl of Gen. Mcrobiol. and other jls. *Recreations:* walking, gardening, dress-making. *Address:* Department of Biochemistry, University College London, Gower Street, WC1E 6BT. *T:* 01-387 7050.

CLARKE, Paul (Henry Francis); His Honour Judge Paul Clarke; a Circuit Judge since 1974; *b* 14 Oct. 1921; *s* of Dr Richard Clarke, FRCP, Clifton, Bristol; *m* 1955, Eileen Sheila, *d* of Lt-Col J. K. B. Crawford, Clifton Coll.; two *s* one *d*. *Educ:* Clifton Coll.; Exeter Coll., Oxford (MA). Served War, Gloucester Regt and Royal Engineers, 1940-46. Called to Bar, Inner Temple, 1949, practising as Barrister from Guildhall Chambers, Bristol, 1949-74. *Address:* Saffron House, Chudleigh, Devon TQ13 0EE.

CLARKE, Peter, PhD, CChem, FRSC, FInstPet; Principal, Robert Gordon's Institute of Technology, Aberdeen, since 1970; *b* 18 March 1922; *er s* of Frederick John and Gladys May Clarke; *m* 1947, Ethel Jones; two *s*. *Educ:* Queen Elizabeth's Grammar Sch., Mansfield; University Coll., Nottingham (BSc). Industrial Chemist, 1942; Sen. Chemistry Master, Buxton Coll., 1947; Lectr, Huddersfield Technl Coll., 1949; British Enka Ltd, Liverpool, 1956; Sen. Lectr, Royal Coll. of Advanced Tech., Salford, 1962; Head of Dept of Chemistry and Biology, Nottingham Regional Coll. of Technology, 1963; Vice-Principal, Huddersfield Coll. of Technology, 1965-70. Member: SERC (formerly SRC), 1978-; Council for Professions Supplementary to Medicine, 1977-; Scottish Technical Educn Council, 1982-. Chm., Assoc. of Principals of Colleges (Scotland), 1976-78; Pres., Assoc. of Principals of Colleges, 1980-81 (Vice-Pres., 1979-80); Chm., Cttee of Principals and Directors of Central Instns, 1974-75, 1980-; Pres., Aberdeen Business and Professional Club, 1976-77. Burgess of Guild, City of Aberdeen, 1973. *Publications:* contribs to Jl of Chem. Soc., Chemistry and Industry. *Recreations:* gardening, swimming. *Address:* Tulloch Lodge, West Cults, Aberdeen AB1 9ES.

CLARKE, Major Peter Cecil, CVO 1969; Chief Clerk, Duchy of Lancaster, and Extra Equerry to HRH Princess Alexandra, the Hon. Mrs Angus Ogilvy; *b* 9 Aug. 1927; *s* of late Captain E. D. Clarke, CBE, MC, Binstead, Isle of Wight; *m* 1950, Rosemary Virginia Margaret Harmsworth, *d* of late T. C. Durham, Appomattox, Virginia, USA; one *s* two *d*. *Educ:* Eton; RMA, Sandhurst. 3rd The King's Own Hussars and 14th/20th King's Hussars, 1945-64. Seconded as Asst Private Secretary to HRH Princess Marina, Duchess of Kent, 1961-64; Comptroller, 1964-68; Comptroller to HRH Princess Alexandra, 1964-69. *Recreations:* golf, fishing. *Address:* 6 Gordon Place, W8. *T:* 01-937 0356. *Club:* Cavalry and Guards.

CLARKE, Peter James; Secretary of the Forestry Commission, since 1976; *b* 16 Jan. 1934; *s* of Stanley Ernest Clarke and Elsie May (*née* Scales); *m* 1966, Roberta Anne, *y d* of Robert and Ada Browne; one *s* one *d*. *Educ:* Enfield Grammar Sch.; St John's Coll., Cambridge (MA). Exec. Officer, WO, 1952-62 (univ., 1957-60), Higher Exec. Officer, 1962; Sen. Exec. Officer, Forestry Commn, 1967, Principal 1972; Principal, Dept of Energy, 1975. *Recreations:* gardening, hill walking, sailing. *Address:* 5 Murrayfield Gardens, Edinburgh EH12 6DG. *T:* 031-337 3145.

CLARKE, Reginald Arnold, CMG 1962; OBE 1960; DFC 1945; Director of Compensation, International Bank for Reconstruction and Development (World Bank), Washington, DC, since 1979; *b* 6 May 1921; *s* of late John Leonard Clarke; *m* 1949, Doritchea Nanette Oswald; three *s* one *d*; *m* 1979, Serena Kwang Ok Han. *Educ:* Doncaster Grammar Sch. Royal Air Force, 1939-46; Provincial Administration, Nigeria, 1947-52; Financial Secretary's Office, Nigeria, 1952-57; Federal Ministry of Finance, Nigeria, 1957,

Permanent Sec., 1958-63, retd. Asst Dir of Administration, IBRD, 1964-70, Dir of Personnel, 1970-79. *Recreations:* travel, tennis, bridge. *Address:* c/o Midland Bank, Gosforth, Cumbria; 8104 Hamilton Spring Road, Bethesda, Maryland 20817, USA.

CLARKE, Robin Mitchell, MC 1944; JP; Chairman, Gatwick Airport Consultative Committee, since 1982; *b* 8 Jan. 1917; *e s* of Joseph and Mary Clarke; *m* 1946, Betty Mumford; twin *s* and *d. Educ:* Ruckholt Central Sch., Leyton. Middleton and St Bride's Wharf, Wapping, 1932-34; Town Clerk's Office, City of Westminster, 1935-40. War of 1939-45: 12th Regt, RHA (HAC) and 142 (Royal Devon Yeomanry) Fd Regt, RA; Major, 1944; served Sicily and Italy (wounded, despatches, MC). Town Clerk's Office, Westminster, 1946-48; Crawley Development Corporation, 1948-62; Manager, Crawley, Commn for the New Towns, 1962-78; Chief Exec., New Towns Commn, 1978-82. ACIS 1949; FCIS 1959 (Mem. Nat. Council, 1968-; Pres., 1978). JP Crawley, 1971. FRSA 1980. *Address:* Hillcrest, 40 Mount Close, Pound Hill, Crawley, Sussex. *T:* Crawley 882266. *Club:* Army and Navy.

CLARKE, Roger Simon Woodchurch, JP; Chairman, The Imperial Tobacco Co. Ltd, 1959-64; *b* 29 June 1903; *s* of late Charles S. Clarke, Tracy Park, Wick, Bristol; *m* 1936, Nancy Lingard (*d* 1980), *d* of late William Martin, formerly of St Petersburg; no *c. Educ:* RN Colleges, Osborne and Dartmouth. Joined The Imperial Tobacco Co., 1922; Dir, 1944-68. Pro-Chancellor, Bristol Univ., 1975-. JP Bristol, 1964. Hon. LLD Bristol, 1975. *Address:* The Little Priory, Bathwick Hill, Bath. *T:* Bath 63103.

CLARKE, Major Sir Rupert William John, 3rd Bt *cr* 1882; MBE 1943; late Irish Guards; Director: Conzinc Riotinto of Australia Ltd, since 1962; P&O Australia Ltd, since 1980; Cadbury Schweppes Ltd, since 1977; Custom Credit Corporation; Vice-Chairman, National Bank of Australasia, since 1978 (Director, since 1955); Chairman: United Distillers Co. since 1960; Cadbury Schweppes Australia Ltd (formerly Schweppes (Australia)); Victory Reinsurance Co. of Australia; International Ranch Management Services Pty Ltd; Bain Dawes Australia Ltd; Morganite Australia Pty Ltd; *b* 5 Nov. 1919; *s* of 2nd Bt and Elsie Florence (who *m* 2nd, 1928, 5th Marquess of Headfort), *d* of James Partridge Tucker, Devonshire; *S* father, 1926; *m* 1947, Kathleen, *d* of P. Grant Hay, Toorak, Victoria, Australia; two *s* one *d* (and one *s* decd). *Educ:* Eton; Magdalen Coll., Oxford (MA). Hon. Fellow, Trinity Coll., Melbourne, 1981. Served War of 1939-45 (despatches, MBE). Vice-Pres., Royal Humane Soc. of Australasia. Chm., Vict. Amateur Turf Club. Hon. Consul General for Monaco, 1975- (Hon. Consul, 1961). Chevalier de la Légion d'Honneur, 1979. *Heir: s* Rupert Grant Alexander Clarke [*b* 12 Dec. 1947; *m* 1978, Susannah, *d* of Sir Robert Law-Smith, *qv*]. *Address:* Bolinda Vale, Clarkefield, Vic 3430, Australia; Richmond House, 56 Avoca Street, South Yarra, Vic 3141. *Clubs:* Cavalry and Guards, Lansdowne; Melbourne, Athenæum, Australian (Melbourne); Union (Sydney); Queensland (Brisbane).

CLARKE, Samuel Harrison, CBE 1956; MSc; Hon. MIFireE; *b* 5 Sept. 1903; *s* of Samuel Clarke and Mary Clarke (*née* Clarke); *m* 1st, 1928, Frances Mary Blowers (*d* 1972); one *s* two *d* ; 2nd, 1977, Mrs Beryl N. Wood; two step *d. Educ:* The Brunts Sch., Mansfield; University Coll., Nottingham (MSc London). Forest Products Res. Laboratory of DSIR, 1927; Fire Research Div., Research and Experiments Dept, Ministry of Home Security, 1940; Dir of Fire Research, DSIR, and Fire Offices Cttee, 1946-58; Dir of Fuel Research Station, DSIR, 1958; Dir, Warren Spring Laboratory, DSIR, 1958-63; Careers Officer, Min. of Technology, 1963-67 (DSIR, 1964-65). Mem. Stevenage Development Corporation, 1962-71; Chm., Herts Assoc. for Care and Resettlement of Offenders, 1974-78. *Publications:* papers in scientific and technical jls. *Recreations:* exchanging ideas, painting. *Address:* 35 Lonsdale Court, Lonsdale Road, Stevenage, Herts SG1 5EL.
See also S. L. H. Clarke.

CLARKE, Samuel Laurence Harrison, CEng, FIEE; Assistant Technical Director, GEC plc (Computing & Automation), since 1981; *b* 16 Dec. 1929; *s* of Samuel Harrison Clarke, *qv*; *m* 1952, Ruth Joan Godwin, *yr d* of Oscar and Muriel Godwin; one *s* three *d. Educ:* Westminster Sch.; Trinity Coll., Cambridge (BA). Director, Elliott Process Automation Ltd, 1965-69; Technical Dir, GEC-Elliott Automation Ltd, 1970-74; Technical Dir (Automation), GEC-Marconi Electronics Ltd, 1974-87; Director, GEC Computers Ltd, 1971-. Chairman, Information Engineering Cttee, SERC, 1981-; Member, Engineering Board, SERC, 1981-. *Publications:* various papers in learned and technical jls. *Recreations:* skiing, Scottish dancing, sailing. *Address:* The Old Bakery, Danbury Common, Essex CM3 4ED. *T:* Danbury 2728.

CLARKE, Stanley George, CBE 1975; Chief Inspector of the Prison Service, 1971-74; Member: Prisons Board, 1971-74; Parole Board, 1975-78; *b* Dunfermline, 5 May 1914; *s* of Stanley and Catherine Clarke; *m* 1940, Mary Preston Lewin; one *s* one *d. Educ:* Sutton High Sch., Plymouth (school colours: cricket, Rugby, soccer). Civil Service Clerk: Dartmoor Prison, 1931; Lowdham Grange Borstal, 1933; North Sea Camp, 1935; Borstal Housemaster: Portland, 1937; North Sea Camp, 1939. Served War, 1941-45 (despatches). Sqdn Ldr, RAF. Borstal Housemaster: Hollesley Bay Colony, 1945; Gaynes Hall, 1946. Dep. Governor, Manchester Prison, 1947; Governor: Norwich Prison, 1949; Nottingham Prison, 1952; Eastchurch Prison, 1955; Liverpool Prison, 1959. Asst Dir of Prisons, in charge of North Region, 1964; Asst

Controller, Prison Dept, 1970. *Address:* 17 Grundy's Lane, Malvern Wells, Worcs.

CLARKE, Mrs Stella Rosemary, JP; a Governor of the BBC, 1974-81; *b* 16 Feb. 1932; *m* 1952, Charles Nigel Clarke; four *s* one *d. Educ:* Cheltenham Ladies' Coll.; Trinity Coll. Dublin. Long Ashton RDC: Councillor, Chm. Council, Housing and Public Health Cttees, 1955-73; Mem., Wood Spring Dist Council, 1973-; co-opted Mem., Somerset CC, Social Services and Children's Cttee, 1957-73. Chm., Project for Girls at Risk, Bristol, 1971-. Purchased and restored Theatre Royal, Bath, with husband, 1974-76. JP Bristol, 1968. *Recreations:* family and the variety of life. *Address:* Gatcombe Court, Flax Bourton, near Bristol BS19 1PX. *T:* Long Ashton 3141.

CLARKE, Brig. Terence Hugh, CBE 1943; *b* 17 Feb. 1904; *e s* of late Col Hugh Clarke, AM, Royal Artillery, and of Mrs Hugh Clarke, Bunces, Kennel Ride, Ascot; *m* 1928, Eileen Armistead, Hopelands, Woodville, NZ; two *d. Educ:* Temple Grove; Haileybury Coll.; RMA Sandhurst. 2nd Lieut Glos Regt, 1924; served India, 1924-27; China, 1928; India, 1928-31, in IA Ordnance Corps; England, 1931-33, Glos Regt; transferred to RAOC, 1933; Norway, 1940 (despatches); DDOS 1st Army, 1942, as Brig. (despatches, CBE); DDOS 2nd Army, 1944; Normandy to Luneberg, Germany (despatches); comd RAOC Training Centre, 1946; DDOS Southern Command, 1948-50; retired from Army, 1950, to enter industry as a Dir of public and private companies. MP (C) Portsmouth West, 1950-66; Parly Cand. (C) Portsmouth West, 1966, 1970. *Recreations:* capped six times for the Army at Rugby and boxed heavyweight for Army; sailing, ski-ing and horse racing. *Address:* Hollybank House, Emsworth, Hants PO10 7UE. *T:* Emsworth 2256.

CLARKE, Thomas, CBE 1980; JP; MP (Lab) Coatbridge and Airdrie, since 1982; *b* 10 Jan. 1941; *s* of James Clarke and Mary (*née* Gordon). *Educ:* All Saints Primary Sch., Airdrie; Columba High Sch., Coatbridge; Scottish College of Commerce. Started working life as office boy with Glasgow Accountants' firm; Asst Director, Scottish Council for Educational Technology, before going to Parliament. Councillor: (former) Coatbridge Council, 1964; (reorganised) Monklands District Council, 1974; Provost of Monklands, 1975-77, 1977-80, 1980-82. Vice-President, Convention of Scottish Local Authorities, 1976-78, President, 1978-80. Director, award winning amateur film, Give Us a Goal, 1972; former President, British Amateur Cinematographers' Central Council. JP County of Lanark, 1972. *Recreations:* films, reading, walking. *Address:* 12 Lugar Street, Coatbridge, Lanarkshire. *T:* Coatbridge 22550. *Clubs:* Coatbridge Municipal Golf, Easter Moffat Golf.

CLARKE, Thomas Ernest Bennett, OBE 1952; screenwriter; *b* 7 June 1907; 2nd *s* of late Sir Ernest Michael Clarke; *m* 1932, Joyce Caroline Steele; one *d* (one *s* decd). *Educ:* Charterhouse; Clare Coll., Cambridge. Staff writer on Answers, 1927-35; editorial staff Daily Sketch, 1936; subsequently free-lance journalist. Wrote screen-plays of films: Johnny Frenchman, Hue and Cry, Against the Wind, Passport to Pimlico, The Blue Lamp, The Magnet, The Lavender Hill Mob (Academy and Venice Awards), The Titfield Thunderbolt, The Rainbow Jacket, Who Done It?, Barnacle Bill, A Tale of Two Cities, Gideon's Day, The Horse Without a Head. Other screen credits include For Those in Peril, Halfway House, Champagne Charlie (lyrics), Dead of Night, Train of Events, Encore, Law and Disorder, Sons and Lovers, A Man Could Get Killed. *Play:* This Undesirable Residence. *Publications:* Go South-Go West, 1932; Jeremy's England, 1934; Cartwright Was a Cad, 1936; Two and Two Make Five, 1938; What's Yours?, 1938; Mr Spirket Reforms, 1939; The World Was Mine, 1964; The Wide Open Door, 1966; The Trail of the Serpent, 1968; The Wrong Turning, 1971; Intimate Relations, 1971; This is Where I Came In (autobiog.), 1974; The Man Who Seduced a Bank, 1977; Murder at Buckingham Palace, 1981. *Recreations:* racing, gardening. *Address:* Tanners Mead, Oxted, Surrey. *T:* Oxted 2183.

CLARKE, Sir Tobias; see Clarke, Sir C. M. T.

CLARKE, Tom; freelance screenwriter, playwright; *b* 7 Nov. 1918; *s* of Herman C. Clarke and May Dora Carter; *m* 1st, 1945, B. D. Gordon; two *s* two *d* ; 2nd, 1953, J. I. Hampton; two *s* ; 3rd, 1960, Ann Wiltshire; one *d. Educ:* Tonbridge School. Served War, Royal Artillery, 1939-46 (Captain). Called to Bar, Gray's Inn, 1951. Freelance writer, 1958-. TV plays and films include: Mad Jack, 1971; Stocker's Copper, 1972; Billion Dollar Bubble, 1975; Muck and Brass, 1982; stage play, Come Again, 1983. Grand Prize, Monte Carlo TV Festival, 1972, UNRRA Silver Dove, 1972, Mention d'Honneur, Prague TV Festival, 1973, Writer's Guild Award, 1973, BAFTA Award, 1973. *Recreations:* nursing hypochondria and awaiting fulfilment of optimistic astrological predictions. *Address:* c/o Judy Daish Associates, 122 Wigmore Street, W1H 9FE. *T:* 01-486 5404.

CLARKE, William Malpas, CBE 1976; Director General and Deputy Chairman, Committee on Invisible Exports, since 1976 (Director, 1966-76); *b* 5 June 1922; *o s* of late Ernest and Florence Clarke; *m* 1st, 1946, Margaret Braithwaite; two *d* ; 2nd, 1973, Faith Elizabeth Dawson. *Educ:* Audenshaw Grammar Sch.; Univ. of Manchester. Served Royal Air Force, 1941-46; Flying Instructor, 1942-44; Flight-Lieut, 1945. Editorial Staff, Manchester Guardian, 1948-55; The Times, 1955-66: City Editor, 1957-62; Financial and Industrial Editor, 1962-66; Editor, The Banker, March-Sept. 1966, Consultant 1966-76. Director: Grindlays Bank plc; Grindlays Bank, Jersey (Chm., 1981-); Grindlay

Brandts plc; Swiss Reinsurance Co (UK) plc; UK Provident Instn; Cincinnati Milacron plc; Trade Indemnity Co. Ltd (Dep. Chm., 1980-); Euromoney Publications; Romney Trust plc; City Communications Orgn (Dep. Chm.); Chairman: Harold Wincott Financial Journalist Press Award Panel; City Telecommunications Cttee. Governor, The Hospitals for Sick Children. *Publications:* The City's Invisible Earnings, 1958; The City in the World Economy, 1965; Private Enterprise in Developing Countries, 1966; (ed, as Director of Studies) Britain's Invisible Earnings, 1967; (with George Pulay) The World's Money, 1970; Inside the City, 1979. *Recreations:* books, theatre. *Address:* 37 Park Vista, Greenwich, SE10. *T:* 01-858 0979. *Club:* Reform.

CLARKE HALL, Denis; architect; President, Architectural Association, 1958-59; Chairman, Architects Registration Council of the UK, 1963-64; *b* 4 July 1910; *m* 1936, Mary Garfitt; one *s* two *d. Educ:* Bedales. Holds AA Dip. *Address:* Moorhouse, Iping, Midhurst, W Sussex.

CLARKSON, Prof. Brian Leonard, PhD; Principal, University College of Swansea, since 1982; *b* 28 July 1930; *s* of L. C. Clarkson; *m* 1953, Margaret Elaine Wilby; three *s* one *d. Educ:* Univ. of Leeds (BSc, PhD). FRAeS; Fellow, Soc. of Environmental Engineers; FInst Acoustics. George Taylor Gold Medal, RAeS, 1963. Dynamics Engineer, de Havilland Aircraft Co., Hatfield, Herts, 1953-57; Southampton University: Sir Alan Cobham Research Fellow, Dept of Aeronautics, 1957-58; Lectr, Dept of Aeronautics and Astronautics, 1958-66; Prof. of Vibration Studies, 1966-82; Dir, Inst. of Sound and Vibration Res., 1967-78; Dean, Faculty of Engrg and Applied Science, 1978-80; Deputy Vice-Chancellor, 1980-82. Sen. Post Doctoral Research Fellow, Nat. Academy of Sciences, USA, 1970-71 (one year's leave of absence from Southampton). Sec., Internat. Commn on Acoustics, 1975-. *Publications:* author of sections of two books: Technical Acoustics, vol. 3 (ed Richardson) 1959; Noise and Acoustic Fatigue in Aeronautics (ed Mead and Richards), 1967; (ed) Stochastic Problems in Dynamics, 1977; technical papers on Jet Noise and its effect on Aircraft Structures, Jl of Royal Aeronautical Soc., etc. *Recreations:* walking, gardening, travelling, golf. *Address:* University College of Swansea, Singleton Park, Swansea SA2 8PP. *T:* Swansea 205678.

CLARKSON, Derek Joshua, QC 1969; **His Honour Judge Clarkson;** a Circuit Judge, since 1977; *b* 10 Dec. 1929; *o s* of Albert and Winifred Charlotte Clarkson (*née* James); *m* 1960, Peternella Marie-Luise Ilse Canenbley; one *s* one *d. Educ:* Pudsey Grammar Sch.; King's Coll., Univ. of London. LLB (1st cl. Hons) 1950. Called to Bar, Inner Temple, 1951; Nat. Service, RAF, 1952-54 (Flt Lt). In practice as Barrister, 1954-77; Prosecuting Counsel to Post Office on North-Eastern Circuit, 1961-65; Prosecuting Counsel to Inland Revenue on North-Eastern Circuit, 1965-69; Recorder of Rotherham, 1967-71; Recorder of Huddersfield, 1971; a Recorder of the Crown Court, 1972-77. Mem., Gen. Council of the Bar, 1971-73. Inspector of companies for the Department of Trade, 1972-73, 1975-76. *Recreations:* theatre-going, walking, book collecting. *Address:* 24 John Islip Street, Westminster, SW1; 26 Cornwall Road, Harrogate, N Yorks. *Club:* Reform.

CLARKSON, Prof. Geoffrey Peniston Elliott, PhD; Professor of Business Administration, since 1980, and Dean, College of Business Administration, since 1977, Northeastern University, Boston; Visiting Professor, Sloan School of Management, Massachusetts Institute of Technology, since 1975; *b* 30 May 1934; *s* of George Elliott Clarkson and Alice Helene (*née* Manneberg); *m* 1960, Eleanor M. (*née* Micenko); two *d. Educ:* Carnegie-Mellon Univ., Pittsburgh, Pa (BSc, MSc, PhD). Asst Prof., Sloan Sch. of Management, MIT, 1961-65, Associate Prof., 1965-67. Vis. Ford Foundn Fellow, Carnegie-Mellon Univ., 1965-66; Vis. Prof., LSE, 1966-67; Nat. Westminster Bank Prof. of Business Finance, Manchester Business Sch., Univ. of Manchester, 1967-77. Dir of and consultant to public and private manufng and financial services cos, 1969-. *Publications:* Portfolio Selection: a simulation of trust investment, USA 1962 (Ford Dissertation Prize, 1961); The Theory of Consumer Demand: a critical appraisal, USA 1963; Managerial Economics, 1968; (with B. J. Elliott) Managing Money and Finance, 1969 (2nd edn 1972); Jihad, 1981. *Recreations:* fishing, sailing, reading. *Address:* College of Business Administration, Northeastern University, Boston, Mass 02115, USA. *Clubs:* Royal Automobile, Crockfords.

CLASEN, Andrew Joseph, Hon. GCVO 1968; Grand Cross, Adolphe Nassau; Commander Order of the Oaken Crown; Grand Cross: Order of Orange Nassau; Iceland Falcon; Luxembourg Ambassador in London, 1955-71 (Minister, 1944-55); *b* 5 Sept. 1906; *yr s* of late Bernard Clasen and Claire Duchscher; *m* 1944, Joan Mary Luke; one *s* one *d. Educ:* Beaumont Coll.; Univs of Oxford, London and Aix-la-Chapelle. DrIng, BSc; ARSM; Hon. FIC. Acting Sec.-Gen. Luxembourg Foreign Affairs Ministry, Consul-Gen., Chargé d'Affaires, 1940-44. Luxembourg Delegate to Red Cross, UNRRA, European Council, UN, NATO and WEU. Grand Officer, Order of Tunisian Republic. *Address:* The Manor House, Rotherfield, Sussex. *Club:* Turf.

CLATWORTHY, Robert, RA 1973 (ARA 1968); sculptor; *b* 31 Jan. 1928; *s* of E. W. and G. Clatworthy; *m* 1954, Pamela Gordon (marr. diss.); two *s* one *d. Educ:* Dr Morgan's Grammar Sch., Bridgwater. Studied West of England Coll. of Art, Chelsea Sch. of Art, The Slade. Teacher, West of England Coll. of Art, 1947-71. Visiting Tutor, RCA, 1960-72; Mem., Fine Art Panel of Nat. Council for Diplomas in Art and Design, 1961-72; Governor, St Martin's Sch. of Art, 1970-71; Head of Dept of Fine Art, Central

Sch. of Art and Design, 1971-75. Exhibited: Hanover Gall., 1954, 1956; Waddington Galls, 1965; Holland Park Open Air Sculpture, 1957; Battersea Park Open Air Sculpture, 1960, 1963; Tate Gallery, British Sculpture in the Sixties, 1965; British Sculptors 1972, Burlington House; Basil Jacobs Fine Art Ltd, 1972; Diploma Galls, Burlington Ho., 1977; Photographers Gall., 1980. Work in Collections: Arts Council, Contemporary Art Soc., Tate Gallery, Victoria and Albert Museum, Greater London Council. *Address:* 15 Park Street, SE1.

CLAUDE, Prof. Albert; creating a Cancer Research Laboratory, L'Université Libre de Bruxelles; Professor, Catholic University of Louvain; *b* Longlier, Belgium, 24 Aug. 1898; an American citizen. *Educ:* Liège Univ. Med. Sch. (Dr in Med. and Surgery, 1928); Inst. für Krebsforschung, Berlin Univ.; Kaiser Wilhelm Inst., Berlin-Dahlem. Professor: Rockefeller Inst., later Univ., 1929, Emeritus, 1972; Univ. Libre de Bruxelles, 1948, Emeritus, 1969; Dir, Jules Bordet Inst., later Lab. de Biologie Cellulaire et Cancérologie, Brussels, 1948-71, now Emeritus. Vis. Res. Prof., Johnson Res. Foundn, 1967. Founder of modern cell biol.; first to isolate a cancer virus by chemical analysis and characterize it as a RNA virus. Member: Royal Acad. of Medicine, Belgium; Nat. Acad. of Medicine, France; Internat. Soc. of Cell Biology; Associate Member: Royal Acad. of Scis, Letters and Fine Arts, Belgium; Inst. de France; Hon. Member: Amer. Acad. of Arts and Sciences; Koninklijke Acad. voor Geneeskunde, Belgium; Soc. Française de Microscopie Electronique; Amer. Assoc. for Cancer Res.; French Biol. Soc.; Belgian Soc. of Cell Biol. Hon. doctorates: Modena, 1963; J. Purkinje Univ., Brno, 1971; Rockefeller, 1971; Liège, 1975; Univ. Catholique de Louvain, 1975; Rigksuniv. of Gent, 1975. Prix Baron Holvoet, Fonds Nat. de la Recherche Scientifique, 1965; Medal, Belgian Acad. of Medicine, 1965; Louisa G. Horowitz Prize, Columbia Univ., 1970; Paul Ehrlich and Ludwig Darmstädter Prize, Frankfurt, 1971; (jtly with Prof. Christian de Duve and Prof. George Emil Palade) Nobel Prize for Medicine or Physiology, 1974 (he carried out initial work and they developed his findings). Grand Cordon, Order of Léopold II)Belgium); Comdr, Palmes académiques (France). *Address:* Laboratoire de Biologie Cellulaire, rue des Champs Elysées 62, 1050 Brussels, Belgium; Rockefeller University, 1230 York Avenue, New York, NY 10021, USA.

CLAUSEN, Alden Winship, (Tom); President, The World Bank, since 1981; *b* 17 Feb. 1923; *s* of Morton and Elsie Clausen; *m* 1950, Mary Margaret Crasswoller; two *s. Educ:* Carthage Coll. (BA 1944); Univ. of Minnesota (LLB 1949); Grad. Harvard Advanced Management Program, 1966. Admitted to Minnesota Bar, 1949. Joined Bank of America, 1949: Vice-Pres., 1961-65; Sen. Vice-Pres., 1965-68; Exec. Vice-Pres., 1968-69; Vice-Chm. of Bd, 1969; Pres. and Chief Exec. Officer, 1970-81. President: Fed. Adv. Council, 1972; Internat. Monetary Conf., Amer. Bankers' Assoc., 1977. Former Director: US-USSR Trade and Econ. Council, 1974-81; Nat. Council for US-China Trade, 1974-81; Co-Chm., Japan-California Assoc., 1973-80. Hon. LLD: Carthage, 1970; Lewis and Clark, 1978; Ganzaga Univ., 1978; Univ. of Notre Dame, 1981; Hon. DPS Univ. Santa Clara, 1981. *Address:* The World Bank, 1818 H Street NW, Washington, DC 20433, USA.

CLAXTON, Rt. Rev. Charles Robert, MA, DD; Assistant Bishop, Diocese of Exeter since 1971; *b* 16 Nov. 1903; *s* of Herbert Bailey and Frances Ann Claxton; *m* 1930, Agnes Jane Stevenson; two *s* two *d. Educ:* Monkton Combe Sch.; Weymouth Coll.; Queen's Coll., Cambridge. Deacon, 1927; Priest, 1928; Curate, St John's, Stratford, E15, 1927-29; St John, Redhill, 1929-33; St Martin-in-the-Fields, 1944-46; Vicar Holy Trinity, Bristol, 1933-38; Hon. Canon of Bristol Cathedral, 1942-46; Hon. Chaplain to Bishop of Bristol, 1938-46; Hon. Chaplain to Bishop of Rochester, 1943-46; Rector of Halsall, near Ormskirk, Lancs, 1948-59; Suffragan Bishop of Warrington, 1946-60; Bishop of Blackburn, 1960-71. Hon. Officiating Chaplain, RN, 1978. *Recreation:* golf. *Address:* St Martins, Budleigh Salterton, Devon. *T:* Budleigh Salterton 2193.

CLAXTON, John Francis, CB 1969; Deputy Director of Public Prosecutions 1966-71; *b* 11 Jan. 1911; *s* of late Alfred John Claxton, OBE, and Dorothy Frances O. Claxton (*née* Roberts); *m* 1937, Norma Margaret Rawlinson; no *c. Educ:* Tonbridge Sch.; Exeter Coll., Oxford (BA). Called to Bar, 1935. Joined Dept of Dir of Public Prosecutions, 1937; Asst Dir, 1956-66. *Recreations:* model making, gardening. *Address:* The White Cottage, 9 Lock Road, Marlow, Bucks. *T:* Marlow 2744.

CLAXTON, Maj.-Gen. Patrick Fisher, CB 1972; OBE 1946; General Manager, Regular Forces Employment Association, 1971-81; *b* 13 March 1915; *s* of late Rear-Adm. Ernest William Claxton and Kathleen O'Callaghan Claxton, formerly Fisher; *m* 1941, Jóna Gudrún Gunnarsdóttir (*d* 1980); two *d. Educ:* Sutton Valence Sch.; St John's Coll., Cambridge (BA). Served GHQ, India, 1943-45; Singapore, 1945-46; WO, 1946-48; British Element Trieste Force, 1949-51; HQ, BAOR, 1952-54; RASC Officers' Sch., 1955-56; Amphibious Warfare HQ and Persian Gulf, 1957-58; Col, WO, 1959-60; Brig., WO, 1961-62; DST, BAOR, 1963-65; CTO, BAOR, 1965-66; Comdt, Sch. of Transport, and ADC to the Queen, 1966-68; Transport Officer-in-Chief (Army), 1969-71, retired; Col. Comdt, RCT, 1972-80. Governor and Mem. Administrative Bd, Corps of Commissionaires, 1977-. FCIT. *Address:* The Lodge, Beacon Hill Park, Hindhead, Surrey GU26 6HU. *T:* Hindhead 4437. *Club:* MCC.

CLAY, Charles John Jervis; *b* 19 March 1910; *s* of late Arthur J. Clay and Bridget Clay (*née* Parker-Jervis); *m* 1935, Patricia Agnes, *d* of late James and

Dorothy Chapman; one s two d. *Educ:* Eton; New College, Oxford; Pitmans Business College. Served War, 1939-45, Rifle Bde (Officer), and PoW (despatches). Antony Gibbs & Sons Ltd, 1933-70 (Man. Dir, 1952-70); Dir, Internat. Commodities Clearing House Ltd, 1952-, Man. Dir, 1971-75, Dep. Chm., 1975-77; Dir, R. J. Rouse & Co. Ltd, 1961-74; Dir-Gen., Accepting Houses Cttee, 1971-76. Chairman: Anton Underwriting Agencies Ltd, 1958-76; Wool Testing Services International Ltd, 1961-74; Automated Real-Time Investments Exchange Ltd, 1972-; London Bd, National Mutual Life Assoc. of Australasia Ltd, 1969-; Quality Control International Ltd, 1974-; Mem. London Cttee, Ottoman Bank, 1955-; Dir, A. P. Bank Ltd, 1977-. Member: Public Works Loans Bd, 1958-70; ECGD Adv. Council, 1965-70. Mem. Executive Cttee, BBA, 1973-76; Mem. Council, CBI, 1972-76. *Publications:* Modern Merchant Banking, 1976; papers and speeches on Commodity Futures Trading and Clearing. *Recreations:* sailing, archery, gardening. *Address:* Lamberts, Hascombe, Godalming, Surrey. *T:* Hascombe 240. *Clubs:* Brooks's, MCC.

CLAY, Sir Henry Felix, 6th Bt *cr* 1841; consultant to McLellan and Partners, Consulting Engineers; *b* 8 Feb. 1909; *s* of Sir Felix Clay, 5th Bt, and late Rachel, *er d* of Rt Hon. Henry Hobhouse; *S* father, 1941; *m* 1933, Phyllis Mary, *yr d* of late R. H. Paramore, MD, FRCS; one s two d. *Educ:* Gresham's Sch.; Trinity Coll., Cambridge. *Heir:* s Richard Henry Clay [*b* 2 June 1940; *m* 1963, Alison Mary, *o d* of Dr J. Gordon Fife; three s two d]. *Address:* Wheelwrights, Cocking, Midhurst, Sussex GU29 0HJ.

CLAY, John Lionel, TD 1961; **His Honour Judge Clay;** a Circuit Judge, since 1977; *b* 31 Jan. 1918; *s* of Lionel Pilleau Clay and Mary Winifred Muriel Clay; *m* 1952, Elizabeth, *d* of Rev. Canon Maurice and Lady Phyllis Ponsonby; one s three d. *Educ:* Harrow Sch.; Corpus Christi Coll., Oxford (MA). Served War of 1939-45 (despatches): in 1st Bn Rifle Bde, N Africa (8th Army), Italy, 1941-44; Instr, Infantry Heavy Weapons Sch., 1944-45; 1st Bn Rifle Bde, Germany, 1945-46. London Rifle Bde Rangers (TA); Major, 2nd i/c Bn and 23 SAS (TA), 1948-60. Called to the Bar, Middle Temple, 1947; a Recorder of the Crown Court, 1975-76. Chm., Horserace Betting Levy Appeal Tribunal for England and Wales, 1974-77. Freeman of City of London, 1980; Liveryman, Gardeners' Co., 1980. *Recreations:* gardening, fishing, shooting. *Address:* Newtimber Place, Hassocks, Sussex BN6 9BU.

CLAY, John Martin; Deputy Chairman, Hambros Bank Ltd, since 1972 (Director, since 1961); Director, Bank of England, since 1973; *b* 20 Aug. 1927; *s* of late Sir Henry Clay and Gladys Priestman Clay; *m* 1952, Susan Jennifer, *d* of Lt-Gen. Sir Euan Miller, *qv*; four s. *Educ:* Eton; Magdalen Coll., Oxford. Chairman: Johnson & Firth Brown Ltd; Hambro Life Assurance Ltd. Mem., Commonwealth Develt Corp., 1970-. FBIM 1971. *Recreation:* sailing. *Address:* 41 Bishopsgate, EC2. *Club:* Royal Thames Yacht.

CLAY, Trevor; General Secretary to the Royal College of Nursing of the United Kingdom since 1982 (Deputy General Secretary, 1979-82); *b* 10 May 1936; *s* of Joseph Reginald George and Florence Emma Clay. *Educ:* Nuneaton and Bethlem Royal and Maudsley Hosps. (SRN 1957; RMN 1960); MPhil Brunel Univ. 1976. Staff Nurse and Charge Nurse, Guy's Hosp., London, 1960-65; Asst Matron in charge of Psychiatric Unit, Queen Elizabeth II Hosp., Welwyn Garden City, 1965-67; Asst Regional Nursing Officer, NW Metropolitan Regional Hosp. Board, 1967-69; Director of Nursing, Whittington Hosp., London, 1969-70; Chief Nursing Officer, N London Group HMC, 1970-74; Area Nursing Officer, Camden and Islington Area Health Authority, 1974-79. *Publication:* thesis on The Workings of the Nursing and Midwifery Advisory Committees in the NHS since 1974. *Recreations:* work, good friends, Mozart. *Address:* The Royal College of Nursing, Cavendish Square, W1M 0AB.

CLAYDEN, Rt. Hon. Sir (Henry) John, PC 1963; Kt 1958; *b* 26 April 1904; *s* of Harold William and Florence Hilda Clayden; *m* 1948, Gwendoline Edith Lawrance. *Educ:* Diocesan Coll., Capetown; Charterhouse; Brasenose Coll., Oxford. Called to Bar, Inner Temple, 1926; Advocate, South Africa, 1927; practised Johannesburg. Served War with S African Engineer Corps and SA Staff Corps, 1940-45. Apptd KC 1945; Judge, Supreme Court of South Africa, Transvaal Provincial Div., 1946-55, 1964-65. Judge of Federal Supreme Court, 1955; Chief Justice, Federation of Rhodesia and Nyasaland, Dec. 1960-April 1964. Chm., Industrial Tribunals, 1967-77. Chm. Southern Rhodesia Capital Commission, 1955; Federal Delimitation Commission, 1958; Hammarskjöld Accident Commission, 1962. Acting Gov.-Gen., Federation of Rhodesia and Nyasaland, May-June 1961. Hon. LLD Witwatersrand. *Address:* 8 Walton Street, SW3 1RE. *T:* 01-589 1300. *Clubs:* Athenæum; Rand (Johannesburg); Salisbury (Zimbabwe).

CLAYDON, Geoffrey Bernard; Principal Assistant Treasury Solicitor and Legal Adviser, Department of Energy, since 1980; *b* 14 Sept. 1930; *s* of Bernard Claydon and Edith Mary (*née* Lucas); unmarried. *Educ:* Leeds Modern; King Edward's, Birmingham; Birmingham Univ. (LLB). Articled at Pinsent & Co., Birmingham, 1950; admitted Solicitor, 1954. Legal Asst, 1959, Sen. Legal Asst, 1965, Treasury Solicitor's Dept; Asst Solicitor, DTI, 1973; Asst Treasury Solicitor, 1974. Sec., National Tramway Museum, 1958- (Vice-Chm., 1969-); Vice-Pres., Light Rail Transit Assoc. (formerly Light Railway Transport League), 1968- (Chm. of League, 1963-68); Chairman: Tramway and Light Railway Soc., 1967-; Consultative Panel for Preservation of British Transport Relics, 1982; Mem., Inst. of Traffic Admin., 1972-.

Recreations: rail transport, travel. *Address:* 23 Baron's Keep, W14 9AT. *T:* 01-603 6400. *Club:* Royal Automobile.

CLAYSON, Christopher William, CBE 1974 (OBE 1966); retired; *b* 11 Sept. 1903; *s* of Christopher Clayson and Agnes Lilias Montgomerie Hunter; *m* Elsie Webster Breingan. *Educ:* George Heriot's Sch.; Edinburgh University. MB, ChB 1926; DPH 1929; MD (Gold Medal) Edinburgh 1936; FRCPE 1951; FRCP 1967. Physician: Southfield Hosp., Edinburgh, 1931-44; Edinburgh City Hosp., 1939-44; Lectr in Tuberculosis Dept, Univ. of Edinburgh, 1939-44; Med. Supt, Lochmaben Hosp., 1944-48; Consultant Phys. in Chest Medicine, Dumfries and Galloway, 1948-68; retd from clinical practice, 1968. Served on numerous Govt and Nat. Health Service cttees, 1948-; Chairman: Scottish Licensing Law Cttee, 1971-73; Scottish Council for Postgrad. Med. Educn, 1970-74. Pres., RCPE, 1966-70; Mem., Scottish Soc. of Physicians; Mem., Thoracic Soc.; Hon. FACP 1968; Hon. FRACP 1969; Hon. FRCPGlas 1970; Hon. FRCGP 1971. William Cullen Prize, RCPE, 1978. *Publications:* various papers on tuberculosis problem and on alcoholism in leading medical jls. *Recreations:* gardening, fishing. *Address:* Cockiesknowe, Lochmaben, Lockerbie, Dumfriesshire. *T:* Lochmaben 231. *Clubs:* Caledonian; New (Edinburgh).

CLAYSON, Sir Eric (Maurice), Kt 1964; DL; *b* 17 Feb. 1908; *yr s* of late Harry and Emily Clayson; *m* 1933, Pauline Audrey Wright; two s. *Educ:* Woodbridge Sch. Chartered Accountant, 1931; Birmingham Post & Mail Group Ltd: Dir, 1944-74; Man. Dir, 1947; Jt Man. Dir, 1957; Chm., 1957-74; Director: Associated TV Ltd, 1964-75; ATV Network Ltd, 1966-78; Sun Alliance & London Insurance Group, 1965-75 (Chm., Birmingham Area Bd, 1967-80); Birmingham Reg. Bd, Lloyds Bank Ltd, 1966-78. President: Birmingham Publicity Assoc., 1948-49 (Chm., 1947-48); W Midlands Newspaper Soc., 1949-50; The Newspaper Soc., 1951-52 (Hon. Treasurer, 1956-60); Birmingham Branch, Incorporated Sales Managers' Assoc., 1953-54; Birmingham and Midland Inst., 1967-68. Vice-Pres., Fédération Internationale des Editeurs de Journaux et Publications, 1954-67. Chairman: Exec. Cttee, British Industries Fair, 1956-57; Midlands Regular Forces Resettlement Cttee, 1961-70 (Mem., 1958-70). Director: The Press Assoc. Ltd, 1959-66 (Chm., 1963-64); Reuters Ltd, 1961-66. Member: Council, Birmingham Chamber of Commerce, 1951- (Vice-Pres., 1953-54, Pres., 1955-56); Gen. Council of the Press, 1953-72; BBC Midland Regional Adv. Council, 1954-57; W Midland Regional Economic Planning Council, 1965-68. Governor, The Royal Shakespeare Theatre, Stratford-upon-Avon, 1963- (Mem. Exec. Council, 1963-74); Life Governor, Birmingham Univ., 1956-, Mem. Council, 1959-71; Mem. Convocation, Univ. of Aston in Birmingham, 1967-. President: Radio Industries Club of the Midlands, 1965-69; Midland Counties Golf Assoc., 1960-62; Vice-Pres., Professional Golfers' Assoc., 1959-. Guardian, Standard of Wrought Plate in Birmingham, 1969-. DL West Midlands, 1975. *Recreation:* reading newspapers. *Address:* The Poor's Piece, Linthurst Road, Barnt Green, Birmingham B45 8JJ. *T:* 021-445 1209.

CLAYTON, Sir Arthur Harold, 11th Bt of Marden, *cr* 1732; DSC 1945; Lt-Comdr RNR; *b* 14 Oct. 1903; *s* of Sir Harold Clayton, 10th Bt, and Leila Cecilia (*d* 1976), *d* of Francis Edmund Clayton; *S* father, 1951; *m* 1st, 1927, Muriel Edith (*d* 1929), *d* of Arthur John Clayton; 2nd, 1931, Alexandra Andreevsky (marr. diss. 1954); one s one d; 3rd, 1954, Dorothy (Jill) (*d* 1964), *d* of Arthur John Greenhalgh; 4th, 1965, Diana Bircham, *d* of late Charles Alvery Grazebrook. *Educ:* Haileybury Coll. In business in London, 1923-41, 1946-50. Served War of 1939-45, RNVR, 1941-46 (despatches, DSC). *Recreation:* continental driving. *Heir:* s David Robert Clayton [*b* 12 Dec. 1936; *m* 1971, Julia Louise, *d* of late C. H. Redfearn; one s]. *Address:* Colonsay, Kingswear, Dartmouth, Devon. *T:* Kingswear 243. *Clubs:* Royal Naval Sailing Association Portsmouth; Royal Yachting Association; Brixham Yacht (Brixham); Royal Dart Yacht (Kingswear); Shore Line (Lifeboat).

CLAYTON, Prof. Barbara Evelyn, (Mrs W. Klyne), MD, PhD; FRCP, FRCPath; Professor of Chemical Pathology and Human Metabolism, University of Southampton, since 1979; *b* 2 Sept. 1922; *m* 1949, William Klyne; one s one d. *Educ:* Univ. of Edinburgh (MD, PhD). FRCP 1972; FRCPath 1971. Consultant in Chem. Pathology, Hosp. for Sick Children, London, 1959-70; Prof. of Chem. Pathology, Inst. of Child Health, Univ. of London, 1970-78, Hon. Sen. Lectr, 1979-. Mem., Royal Commn on Environmental Pollution, 1981-. *Publications:* contrib. learned jls, incl. Jl Endocrinol., Arch. Dis. Childhood, and BMJ. *Recreations:* natural history, walking. *Address:* 16 Chetwynd Drive, Bassett, Southampton SO2 3HZ. *T:* Southampton 769937.

CLAYTON, Prof. Frederick William; Professor of Classics, 1948-75, and Public Orator, 1965-73, University of Exeter; *b* 13 Dec. 1913; *s* of late William and Gertrude Clayton, Liverpool; *m* 1948, Friederike Luise Büttner-Wobst; two s two d. *Educ:* Liverpool Collegiate Sch.; King's Coll., Cambridge. Members' Essay Prizes (Latin and English), Porson Prize, Browne Medal, 1933; Craven Scholar in Classics, 1934; Chancellor's Medal for Classics, 1935; Fellow of King's Coll., 1937. Served War, Nov. 1940-Oct. 1946, Signals, Field Security, RAF Intelligence, India. *Publications:* The Cloven Pine, 1942; various articles. *Address:* Halwill, Clydesdale Road, Exeter, Devon. *T:* Exeter 71810.
See also G. Clayton.

CLAYTON, Air Marshal Sir Gareth (Thomas Butler), KCB 1970 (CB 1962); DFC 1940, and Bar, 1944; Air Secretary, Ministry of Defence, 1970-72, retired; *b* 13 Nov. 1914; *s* of Thomas and Katherine Clayton; *m* 1938, Elisabeth Marian Keates; three *d. Educ:* Rossall Sch. Entered RAF, 1936; served in various Bomber and Fighter Squadrons, 1936–44; RAF Staff Coll., 1944; Air Attaché, Lisbon, 1946–48; various command and staff appts, 1948–58; idc 1959; Air Ministry, 1960–61; Air Officer Commanding No. 11 Group, RAF, 1962–63; Chief of Staff, Second Allied Tactical Air Force, Germany, 1963–66 Dir-Gen., RAF Personal Services, 1966–69; Chief of Staff, HQ RAF Strike Command, 1969–70. Life Vice-Pres., RAFA (Chm., 1978–80). *Address:* c/o Lloyds Bank Ltd, 263 Tottenham Court Road, W1. *Club:* Royal Air Force.

CLAYTON, Prof. George; Newton Chambers Professor of Applied Economics, University of Sheffield, since 1967, Pro-Vice-Chancellor, since 1978; *b* 15 July 1922; *s* of late William Clayton and late Gertrude Alison Clarke Clayton; *m* 1948, Rhiannon Jones, JP; two *s* two *d. Educ:* Liverpool Collegiate Sch.; King's Coll., Cambridge. Served War of 1939–45: Pilot, RAF, 1941–45; Pilot, Fleet Air Arm, 1945, Acting Sqdn Ldr. Univ. of Liverpool: Asst Lectr, 1947–50; Lectr, 1950–57; Sen. Lectr, 1957–60 and 1961–63; Sen. Simon Res. Fellow, Univ. of Manchester, 1960–61; Prof. and Head of Dept of Econs, UCW Aberystwyth, 1963–67. Member: Council, Royal Econ. Soc., 1965–68; (part-time) East Midland Gas Bd, 1967–70; Crowther Cttee on Consumer Credit, 1968–70; Scott Cttee on Property Bonds and Equity-linked Insce, 1970–72; Econs Cttee, SSRC, 1978– (Vice-Chm., 1979–). Non-exec. Director: Pioneer Mutual Assurance Co.; Wagon Finance Corp. Ltd. Chm., British, Canadian and Amer. Mission to British Honduras, 1966; Econ. Adviser: Govt of Tanzania, 1965–66; Govt of Gibraltar, 1973–. Chm., Assoc. of Univ. Teachers of Economics, 1973–78. *Publications:* (contrib.) A New Prospect of Economics, ed G. L. S. Shackle, 1956; (contrib.) Banking in Western Europe, ed R. S. Sayers, 1959; Insurance Company Investment, 1965; Problems of Rail Transport in Rural Wales: Two Case Studies, 1967; Monetary Theory and Monetary Policy in the 1970s, 1971; British Insurance, 1971; articles in Econ. Jl, etc. *Recreations:* tennis, sailing, theatre, fell walking. *Address:* 108 Westbourne Road, Sheffield S10 2GT. *T:* Sheffield 681833. *Club:* Hawks (Cambridge).
See also Prof. F. W. Clayton.

CLAYTON, Jack; film director; *b* 1921; *m* Christine Norden (marr. diss.); *m* Katherine Kath (marr. diss.). Entered film industry, 1935. Served War of 1939–45, RAF Film Unit. Production Manager: An Ideal Husband; Associate Producer: Queen of Spades; Flesh and Blood; Moulin Rouge; Beat the Devil; The Good Die Young; I am a Camera; Producer and Director: The Bespoke Overcoat, 1955; The Innocents, 1961; Our Mother's House, 1967; Director: Room at the Top, 1958; The Pumpkin Eater, 1964; The Great Gatsby, 1974. *Address:* c/o William Morris Agency (UK) Ltd, 147/149 Wardour Street, W1.

CLAYTON, John Pilkington, MVO 1975; MA, MB, BChir; Apothecary to HM Household at Windsor since 1965; Surgeon Apothecary to HM Queen Elizabeth the Queen Mother's Household at the Royal Lodge, Windsor, since 1965; Senior Medical Officer, Eton College, since 1965 (MO, 1962–65); *b* 13 Feb. 1921; *s* of late Brig.-Gen. Sir Gilbert Clayton, KCMG, KBE, CB, and Enid, *d* of late F. N. Thorowgood. *Educ:* Wellington Coll.; Gonville and Caius Coll., Cambridge; King's Coll. Hospital. RAFVR, 1947–49; Sqdn Ldr 1949. Senior Resident, Nottingham Children's Hosp., 1950. MO, Black and Decker Ltd, 1955–70; Divnl Surgeon, St John's Ambulance Bde, 1955–75; MO, 1953–62, SMO 1962–81, Royal Holloway Coll. *Address:* Town End House, Eton College, Windsor. *T:* Windsor 62257.

CLAYTON, Prof. Keith Martin; Professor of Environmental Sciences, University of East Anglia, since 1967; *b* 25 Sept. 1928; *s* of Edgar Francis Clayton and Constance Annie (*née* Clark); *m* 1st, 1950 (marr. diss. 1976); three *s* one *d*; 2nd, 1976. *Educ:* Bedales Sch.; Univ. of Sheffield (MSc). PhD London. Demonstrator, Univ. of Nottingham, 1949–51. Served RE, 1951–53. Lectr, London Sch. of Economics, 1953–63; Reader in Geography, LSE, 1963–67; Univ. of E Anglia: Founding Dean, Sch. of Environmental Scis, 1967–71; Pro-Vice-Chancellor, 1971–73; Dir, Centre of E Anglian Studies, 1974–81; Vis. Professor, State Univ. of New York at Binghamton, 1960–62. Member: Natural Environment Res. Council, 1970–73; UGC, 1973–; Nat. Radiological Protection Bd, 1980–; Nat. Adv. Bd for Local Authority Higher Educn, 1982–. *Publications:* Editor and publisher, Geo Abstracts, 1966–. *Recreations:* gardening, work. *Address:* Well Close, Pound Lane, Thorpe, Norwich NR7 0UA. *T:* Norwich 33780.

CLAYTON, Lucie; *see* Kark, Evelyn F.

CLAYTON, Michael Thomas Emilius, CB 1976; OBE 1958; *b* 15 Sept. 1917; *s* of Lt-Col Emilius Clayton, OBE, RA and Irene Dorothy Constance (*née* Strong); *m* 1942, Mary Margery Pate; one *d. Educ:* Bradfield College, Berks. Attached War Office, 1939 and Ministry of Defence, 1964–76. *Recreations:* philately, country pursuits generally. *Address:* Hillside Cottage, Marshwood, Bridport, Dorset. *T:* Hawkchurch 452.

CLAYTON, Richard Henry Michael, (William Haggard); writer; *b* 11 Aug. 1907; *o s* of late Rev. Henry James Clayton and late Mabel Sarah Clayton (*née* Haggard); *m* 1936, Barbara, *e d* of late Edward Sant, Downton, Wilts; one *s* one *d. Educ:* Lancing; Christ Church, Oxford. Indian Civil Service, 1931–39; Indian Army, 1939–46 (GSO1 1943); BoT, 1947–69 (Controller of Enemy Property, 1965–69). *Publications:* Slow Burner, The

Telemann Touch, 1958; Venetian Blind, 1959; Closed Circuit, 1960; The Arena, 1961; The Unquiet Sleep, 1962; The High Wire, 1963; The Antagonists, 1964; The Hard Sell, The Powder Barrel, 1965; The Power House, 1966; The Conspirators, The Haggard Omnibus, 1967; A Cool Day For Killing, 1968; The Doubtful Disciple, Haggard For Your Holiday, 1969; The Hardliners, 1970; The Bitter Harvest, 1971; The Protectors, 1972; The Little Rug Book (non-fiction), 1972; The Old Masters, 1973; The Kinsmen, 1974; The Scorpion's Tail, 1975; Yesterday's Enemy, 1976; The Poison People, 1977; Visa to Limbo, 1978; The Median Line, 1979; The Money Men, 1981; The Mischief Makers, 1982. *Address:* 15 Court Gardens, Camberley, Surrey GU15 2HY. *Club:* Travellers'.

CLAYTON, Adm. Sir Richard (Pilkington), GCB 1980 (KCB 1978); Commander-in-Chief, Naval Home Command, 1979–81; Flag ADC to the Queen, 1979–81; retired; with General Electric Co., since 1981; *b* July 1925; *s* of late Rear-Adm. John Wittewronge Clayton and Florence Caroline Schuster. *Educ:* Horris Hill, Newbury; RNC Dartmouth. Midshipman, HMS Cumberland, 1942–43; various destroyers, 1944; Home Fleet destroyers, 1944–46; HMS Comus, Far East, 1946–49; Trng Sqdn destroyers, 1949–53; HMS Striker, Suez, 1956; psc 1957; comd HMS Puma, 1958–59; Admty, 1959–61; HMS Lion, 1962–64; MoD, 1964–66; Captain of Dockyard, Gibraltar, 1967–68; comd HMS Kent and HMS Hampshire, 1968–69; MoD, 1970–72; Flag Officer Second Flotilla, 1973–74; Sen. Naval Mem., Directing Staff, RCDS, 1975; Controller of the Navy, 1976–79. *Recreations:* winter sports, motor cycling. *Address:* c/o Coutts & Co., 1 Cadogan Place, Sloane Street, SW1X 9PX. *Club:* Royal Naval and Royal Albert Yacht (Portsmouth).

CLAYTON, Sir Robert (James), Kt 1980; CBE 1970 (OBE 1960); FEng, FIEE, FInstP, FRAeS, FIERE, FIEEE; Technical Director, The General Electric Co. plc, since 1968; GEC Director, since 1978; *b* 30 Oct. 1915; *m* 1949, Joy Kathleen King; no *c. Educ:* Cambridge Univ. (Scholar, Christ's Coll.; MA). GEC Research Labs, 1937; Manager, GEC Applied Electronics Labs, 1955; Dep. Dir, Hirst Research Centre, 1960; Man. Dir, GEC (Electronics), 1963; Man. Dir, GEC (Research), 1966. Member: Adv. Council for Applied R&D, 1976–80 (Chm. of Groups producing reports on Applications of Semiconductors, Computer Aided Design and Manufacture, and Inf. Technology); Adv. Council on R&D for Fuel and Power, 1976–; NEB, 1978–80; Science Mus. Adv. Council, 1980–; British Library Bd, 1981–; UGC, 1982–; Chm., Computer Systems and Electronics Requirements Bd, DoI, 1978–81; Chm., Electronics Engrg Assoc., 1965; Pres., 1975-76, IEE (Chm., Electronics Div., 1968–69); Pres., Inst. of Physics, 1982–; Vice-Pres., Fellowship of Engineering, 1980-82; Vis. Prof., Electrical Engrg Dept, Imperial Coll. of Science and Technology, 1971–77; Lectures: IEE Faraday; CEI Graham Clarke; Christopher Hinton, Fellowship of Engineering. Hon. DSc: Aston, 1979; Salford, 1979; City, 1981. *Publications:* papers in Proc. IEE (premium awards). *Address:* GEC Hirst Research Centre, East Lane, Wembley, Mddx. *T:* 01-904 1262. *Club:* United Oxford & Cambridge University.

CLAYTON, Prof. Robert Norman, FRS 1981; Professor, Departments of Chemistry and of the Geophysical Sciences, University of Chicago, since 1966; *b* 20 March 1930; *s* of Norman and Gwenda Clayton; *m* 1971, Cathleen Shelburne Clayton; one *d. Educ:* Queen's Univ., Canada (BSc, MSc); California Inst. of Technol. (PhD). Res. Fellow, Calif. Inst. of Technol., 1955-56; Asst Prof., Pennsylvania State Univ., 1956-58; University of Chicago: Asst Prof., 1958-62; Associate Prof., 1962-66. *Publications:* over 100 papers in geochemical journals. *Address:* 5201 South Cornell, Chicago, Ill 60615, USA. *T:* 312-643-2450.

CLAYTON, Prof. Sir Stanley (George), Kt 1974; MD, MS London; FRCP; FRCS; FRCOG; FKC 1976; Professor of Obstetrics and Gynæcology, King's College Hospital Medical School, 1967–76, now Emeritus; Hon. Consulting Surgeon: King's College Hospital; Queen Charlotte's Hospital; Chelsea Hospital for Women; *b* 13 Sept. 1911; *s* of Rev. George and Florence Clayton; *m* 1936, Kathleen Mary Willshire; one *s* one *d. Educ:* Kingswood Sch.; King's Coll. Hosp. Med. Sch. Qualified, 1934; FRCS 1936; Sambrooke Schol., Jelf Medal, Hallett Prize. Surg. EMS; Major RAMC. Obstetric Surg., Queen Charlotte's Hosp., 1946; Surg., Chelsea Hosp. for Women, 1953; Obstetric and Gynæcological Surg., King's Coll. Hosp., 1947-63; Prof. of Obst. and Gyn., Postgrad. Inst. of Univ. of London, 1963-67. Vice-Pres., RCOG, 1971, Pres., 1972-75; Chm., Conf. of Royal Colls, 1975; Mem. Council, RCS, 1975-78; Chm., Adv. Cttee on Distinction Awards, 1976–. Pres., Nat. Assoc. of Family Planning Doctors, 1974-76; Vice-Pres., FPA, 1976. Mem., Adv. Cttee on Med. Training, EEC, 1976-81. Examiner, Univs of London, Oxford, Cambridge, Birmingham, Dublin, Wales, Hong Kong, Singapore, W Indies and RCOG. Editor, Jl of Obstetrics and Gynaecology, 1963-75. Hon. Fellow, Amer. Assoc. of Obstetricians and Gynecologists, 1975; Hon. FCOG (SA); Hon. Fellow, S Atlantic Assoc. of Obst. and Gyn., 1973; For. Mem., Belgian Soc. of Obst. and Gyn., 1965; Beecham Lectr, Inst. of Obst. and Gyn., 1973; Joseph Price Orator, Amer. Assoc. Obst. & Gyn., 1974; Simpson Orator, RCOG, 1978. *Publications:* Pocket Gynaecology, 1948, 9th edn 1979; Pocket Obstetrics, 9th edn 1979; jointly: Queen Charlotte's Text-Book, 11th edn 1965; Ten Teachers' Obstetrics, 13th edn 1980; Ten Teachers' Gynaecology, 13th edn 1980; British Obstetric and Gynæcological Practice, 3rd edn 1964; contrib. Encyclopædia Britannica, 1974; articles in med. jls. *Address:* Fir Tree Lodge, Fir Tree Road, Leatherhead, Surrey.

CLAYTON, Stanley James; Town Clerk of the City of London 1974-82; *b* 10 Dec. 1919; *s* of late James John Clayton and late Florence Clayton; *m* 1955, Jean Winifred, *d* of Frederick Etheridge; one *s* one *d. Educ:* Ensham Sch.; King's Coll., London (LLB). Served War of 1939-45, commnd RAF. Admitted Solicitor 1958. City of Westminster, 1938-52; Camberwell, 1952-60; Asst Solicitor, Holborn, 1960-63; Deputy Town Clerk: Greenwich, 1963-65; Islington, 1964-69; City of London, 1969-74. Comdr, Order of Dannebrog (Denmark); holds other foreign orders. *Address:* Redriff, 215 East Dulwich Grove, SE22 8SY. *T:* 01-693 1019.

CLEALL, Charles; HM Inspector of Schools, since 1972; *b* 1 June 1927; *s* of Sydney Cleal and Dorothy Bound; *m* 1953, Mary, *yr d* of G. L. Turner, Archery Lodge, Ashford, Mddx; two *d. Educ:* Hampton Sch.; Univ. of London (BMus); Univ of Wales (MA); Jordanhill Coll. of Educn, Glasgow. ADCM, GTCL, FRCO(CHM), LRAM, HonTSC. Command Music Adviser, RN, 1946-48; Prof., TCL, 1949-52; Conductor, Morley Coll. Orch., 1949-51; Organist and Choirmaster, Wesley's Chapel, City Road, EC4, 1950-52; Conductor, Glasgow Choral Union, 1952-54; BBC Music Asst, Midland Region, 1954-55; Music Master, Glyn County Sch., Ewell, 1955-66; Conductor, Aldeburgh Festival Choir, 1957-60; Organist and Choirmaster: St Paul's, Portman Sq., W1, 1957-61; Holy Trinity, Guildford, 1961-65; Lectr in Music, Froebel Inst., 1967-68; Adviser in Music, London Borough of Harrow, 1968-72; Warden, Music in Education Section, ISM, 1971-72. Delivered two papers at study-conf. of teachers of singing, The Maltings, Snape, 1976, and papers at: Nat. Course on Develt of Young Children's Musical Skills, Univ. of Reading Sch. of Educn, 1979; annual conf., Scottish Fedn of Organists, 1980. Internat. Composition Prizeman of Cathedral of St John the Divine, NY; Limpus Fellowship Prizeman of RCO. *Publications:* Voice Production in Choral Technique, 1955 (2nd edn, 1970); The Selection and Training of Mixed Choirs in Churches, 1960; Music and Holiness, 1964; Plainsong for Pleasure, 1969; Guide to Vanity Fair, 1982. *Recreations:* learning anything; correspondence; etymology; indexing; post codes; thought. *Address:* 29 Colthill Circle, Milltimber, Aberdeen AB1 0EH.

CLEARY, Denis Mackrow, CMG 1967; HM Diplomatic Service, retired; *b* 20 Dec. 1907; *s* of late Francis Esmonde Cleary and late Emmeline Marie Cleary (*née* Mackrow); *m* 1st, 1941, Barbara Wykeham-George (*d* 1960); 2nd, 1962, Mary Kent (*née* Dunlop), widow of Harold Kent; one step-*d. Educ:* St Ignatius Coll. and St Olave's Sch.; St John's Coll., Cambridge (Major Schol.). 1st Class Hons Pts I and II, Math. Tripos; BA 1930; MA 1934. Asst Principal, India Office, 1931; Principal, 1937; seconded to Min. of Home Security, 1940-44; Dep. Principal Officer to Regional Commissioner, Cambridge, March 1943-Sept. 1944; seconded to Foreign Office (German Section) as Asst Sec., 1946-49; transferred to CRO and posted to Delhi as Counsellor, 1949-51; Dep. High Commissioner, Wellington, 1955-58; Mem. of British Delegn to Law of the Sea Conf., Geneva, 1960; Dep. High Comr, Nicosia, 1962-64; Head of Atlantic Dept, Commonwealth Office, 1964-68 (Mem., Cttee for Exports to the Caribbean, 1965-67); retd 1968; re-employed in Internat. Div., DHSS, 1968-72; UK Delegate to Public Health Cttees, Council of Europe, 1968-72; Chm., Council of Europe Med. Fellowships Selection Cttee, 1972-74. *Recreations:* gardening, walking. *Address:* High Gate, Burwash, East Sussex TN19 7LA. *T:* Burwash 882712.

CLEARY, Frederick Ernest, CBE 1979 (MBE 1951); FRICS; Chairman and Founder, Haslemere Estates Ltd, since 1973; Chairman and Founder, City & Metropolitan Building Society, 1948, President since 1972; *b* 11 April 1905; *s* of Frederick George and Ada Kate Cleary; *m* 1st, 1929, Norah Helena (decd); two *d*; 2nd, 1968, Margaret Haworth (decd). *Educ:* Dame Alice Owen's Sch. FRICS 1929. Common Councilman, Corporation of London (Coleman Street Ward), 1959-; Deputy Mayor, Borough of Hornsey, 1951; Chairman, Metropolitan Public Gardens Assoc., 1954-; Past Master, Worshipful Co. of Gardeners, 1969-70. Hon. Fellow, Magdalene Coll., Cambridge, 1975. President: Dover and Deal Constituency Cons. Assoc.; Council, CPRE (Kent). Officier de la Légion d'Honneur, 1976. *Publications:* Beauty and the Borough, 1949; The Flowering City, 1969, 7th edn 1977; I'll Do It Yesterday (autobiog.), 1979. *Recreations:* lawn tennis, swimming, the environment. *Address:* 33 Grosvenor Square, W1. *T:* 01-499 2717; South Sands House, St Margaret's Bay, near Dover, Kent. *T:* Dover 852106. *Clubs:* MCC, City Livery (Pres., 1956-66).

CLEARY, Jon Stephen; novelist; *b* 22 Nov. 1917; *s* of Matthew Cleary and Ida (*née* Brown); *m* 1946, Constantine Lucas; two *d. Educ:* Marist Brothers' Sch., Randwick, NSW. Variety of jobs, 1932-40; served with AIF, 1940-45; freelance writer, 1945-48; journalist with Australian News and Information Bureau: London, 1948-49; New York, 1949-51; subseq. full-time writer. *Publications:* These Small Glories (short stories), 1946; You Can't See Round Corners, 1947; The Long Shadow, 1949; Just Let Me Be, 1950; The Sundowners, 1952; The Climate of Courage, 1953; Justin Bayard, 1955; The Green Helmet, 1957; Back of Sunset, 1959; North from Thursday, 1960; The Country of Marriage, 1962; Forests of the Night, 1963; A Flight of Chariots, 1964; The Fall of an Eagle, 1964; The Pulse of Danger, 1966; The High Commissioner, 1967; The Long Pursuit, 1967; Season of Doubt, 1968; Remember Jack Hoxie, 1969; Helga's Web, 1970; Mask of the Andes, 1971; Man's Estate, 1972; Ransom, 1973; Peter's Pence, 1974; The Safe House, 1975; A Sound of Lightning, 1976; High Road to China, 1977; Vortex, 1977; The Beaufort Sisters, 1979; A Very Private War, 1980; The Golden Sabre, 1981; The Faraway Drums, 1981; Spearfield's Daughter, 1982. *Recreations:* cricket,

tennis, reading. *Address:* c/o Wm Collins Sons & Co. Ltd, 14 St James's Place, SW1.

CLEARY, Rt. Rev. Joseph Francis; Auxiliary Bishop of Birmingham, (RC), and Titular Bishop of Cresima, since 1965; *b* 4 Sept. 1912; *s* of William Cleary and Ellen (*née* Rogers). *Educ:* Dublin; Oscott Coll., Sutton Coldfield. Ordained Priest 1939. Asst, St Chad's Cathedral, 1939-41; Archbishop's Sec., 1941-51; Parish Priest, SS Mary and John's, Wolverhampton, 1951-; Diocesan Treasurer, 1963-65; Provost of Diocesan Chapter, 1966-. Pres., RC Internat. Justice and Peace Commn of England and Wales, 1978-80. *Address:* Presbytery, Snow Hill, Wolverhampton WV2 4AD. *T:* Wolverhampton 21676.

CLEARY, Sir Joseph Jackson, Kt 1965; *b* 26 Oct. 1902; *s* of Joseph Cleary, JP; *m* 1945, Ethel McColl. *Educ:* Holy Trinity C of E Sch., Anfield, Liverpool; Skerry's Coll., Liverpool. Alderman, 1941, JP, 1927 for Liverpool; Lord Mayor of Liverpool, 1949-50. Contested East Toxteth Div., Liverpool, March 1929 and May 1929; West Derby, Oct. 1931; MP (Lab) Wavertree Div. of Liverpool, Feb.-Oct. 1935. Lecture tour to Forces in Middle East, 1945. Freeman, City of Liverpool, 1970. *Recreations:* football (Association), tennis. *Address:* 115 Riverview Heights, Liverpool L19 0LQ. *T:* 051-427 2133.

CLEASBY, Very Rev. Thomas Wood Ingram; Dean of Chester, since 1978; *b* 27 March 1920; *s* of T. W. Cleasby, Oakdene, Sedbergh, Yorks, and Jessie Brown Cleasby; *m* 1st, 1956, Olga Elizabeth Vibert Douglas (*d* 1967); one *s* one *d* (and one *d* decd); 2nd, 1970, Monica, *e d* of Rt Rev. O. S. Tomkins, *qv*; one *d. Educ:* Sedbergh Sch., Yorks; Magdalen Coll., Oxford; Cuddesdon Coll., Oxford. BA, MA (Hons Mod. History) 1947. Commissioned, 1st Bn Border Regt, 1940; served 1st Airborne Div., 1941-45, Actg Major. Ordained, Dio. Wakefield, 1949 (Huddersfield Parish Church). Domestic Chaplain to Archbishop of York, 1952-56; Anglican Chaplain to Univ. of Nottingham, 1956-63; Archdeacon of Chesterfield, 1963-78; Vicar of St Mary and All Saints, Chesterfield, 1963-70; Rector of Morton, Derby, 1970-78. *Recreations:* fell-walking, bird-watching, gardening, fishing. *Address:* The Deanery, 7 Abbey Street, Chester CH1 2JF. *T:* Chester 25920.

CLEAVER, Leonard Harry, FCA; JP; Director: A. W. Phillips Ltd; Outersport Ltd; Nor. E. Sport (Wholesale) Ltd; *b* 27 Oct. 1909; *s* of late Harry Cleaver, OBE, JP; *m* 1938, Mary Richards Matthews; one *s. Educ:* Bilton Grange and Rugby. Chartered Accountant: articled Agar, Bates, Neal & Co., Birmingham; Sec. and Chief Accountant, Chance Bros Ltd, 1935-51; Partner, Heathcote & Coleman, 1951-59. MP (C) Yardley Div. of Birmingham, 1959-64; PPS to Parly Sec. to Min. of Housing and Local Govt, 1962-64; contested Yardley Div. of Birmingham, 1964, 1966. Member: Smethwick Nat. Savings Cttee, 1939-45; Birmingham Probation Cttee, 1955-73; Central Council, Probation and After-Care Cttees for England and Wales, 1966-73. Treasurer: Deritend Unionist Assoc., 1945-48; Yardley Div. Unionist Assoc., 1971-73 (Chm., 1973-74). Governor, Yardley Educnl Foundn, 1966-70. JP Birmingham, 1954; City Councillor, Birmingham, 1966-70. *Recreations:* Rugby football, fishing, philately. *Address:* 19 Cherry Orchard Close, Chipping Campden, Glos GL55 6DH. *T:* Evesham 840870.

CLEAVER, Air Vice-Marshal Peter (Charles), CB 1971; OBE 1945; *b* 6 July 1919; *s* of William Henry Cleaver, Warwick; *m* 1948, Jean, *d* of J. E. B. Fairclough, Ledbury; two *s. Educ:* Warwick Sch.; Coll. of Aeronautics (MSc). Staff Coll., Haifa, 1945; idc 1966. HM Asst Air Attaché, Bucharest, 1947-49; Coll. of Aeronautics, Cranfield, 1950-52; Structural Research, RAE Farnborough, 1952-55; Min. of Supply, 1955-57; HQ FEAF, 1957-60; Maintenance Comd, 1960-63; OC, Central Servicing Develt Estabt, 1963-64; Air Officer Engineering: HQ Flying Trg Comd, 1964-66; HQ FEAF, 1967-69; Air Support Command, 1969-72; retired 1972. Sec., Cranfield Inst. of Technology, 1973-78. Governor, Warwick Schs Foundn, 1978-; Chm. Governors, Warwick Sch., 1980-. CEng, FRAeS. *Recreations:* shooting, gardening. *Address:* Willow House, Watling Street, Little Brickhill, Milton Keynes MK17 9LS. *Club:* Royal Air Force.

CLEAVER, William Benjamin, CEng, FIMinE; JP; Deputy Director, South Wales Area, National Coal Board, since 1969; Vice-Chairman, Welsh Arts Council, and Member, Arts Council of Great Britain, since 1980; *b* 15 Sept. 1921; *s* of David John Cleaver and Blodwen (*née* Miles); *m* 1943, Mary Watkin (*née* James); one *s* two *d. Educ:* Pentre (Rhondda) Grammar Sch.; University Coll. Cardiff (BSc Hons). National Coal Board: Manager: N Celynen Collieries, Gwent, 1947; Oakdale Colliery, Gwent, 1950; Production Manager (Group), S Wales, 1953; Area General Manager, No 2 S Wales Area, 1958. Sec., Contemporary Art Soc. for Wales, 1972-; Mem., Welsh Arts Council, 1977-; Founder Pres., Cardiff Jun. Ch. of Commerce, 1953. Rugby Union Football: Cardiff RFC, 1940-50; Welsh Rugby International, 1947-50 (14 caps); British Lion to NZ and Aust., 1950; Barbarian Rugby Club, 1946; Founder Chm., Welsh Youth Rugby Union, 1949-57. JP Cardiff 1973. *Recreations:* theatre, fine arts. *Address:* 24 Millwood, Lisvane, Cardiff CF4 5TL. *T:* Cardiff 757400. *Clubs:* Savile; Cardiff and County (Cardiff).

CLEDWYN OF PENRHOS, Baron *cr* 1979 (Life Peer), of Holyhead in the Isle of Anglesey; **Cledwyn Hughes,** CH 1977; PC 1966; Deputy Leader of the Opposition, House of Lords, since 1981; *b* 14 Sept. 1916; *er s* of Rev. Henry David and Emily Hughes; *m* 1949, Jean Beatrice Hughes; one *s* one *d. Educ:* Holyhead Grammar Sch.; University Coll. of Wales, Aberystwyth

(LLB). Solicitor, 1940. Served RAFVR, 1940–45. Mem. Anglesey County Council, 1946–52. Contested (Lab) Anglesey, 1945 and 1950; MP (Lab) Anglesey, 1951–79; Opposition spokesman for Housing and Local Govt, 1959–64; Minister of State for Commonwealth Relations, 1964–66; Sec. of State for Wales, 1966–68; Min. of Agriculture, Fisheries and Food, 1968–70; Opposition spokesman on Agriculture, Fisheries and Food, 1970–72; Commissioner of the House of Commons, 1979; Chm., House of Lords Select Cttee on Agriculture and Food, 1980–. Chairman: Welsh Parliamentary Party, 1953–54; Welsh Labour Group, 1955–56; Parly Labour Party, Oct. 1974–1979 (Vice-Chm., March–Oct. 1974). Member: Cttee of Public Accounts, 1957–64; Cttee of Privileges, 1974–79. Jt Chm. TUC/Labour Party Liaison Cttee, 1974–79. Vice-Pres., Britain in Europe, 1975. Mem. Parly Delegn to Lebanon, 1957; represented British Govt at Kenya Independence Celebrations, 1964; led UK Delegn to The Gambia Independence celebrations, 1965; Mission to Rhodesia, July 1965; led UK Mission on Contingency Planning to Zambia, 1966; led Parliamentary Delegn to USSR, 1977; Prime Minister's Envoy to Southern Africa, Nov.–Dec. 1978. Director: Shell UK Ltd, 1980–; Anglesey Aluminium Ltd, 1980–; Holyhead Towing Ltd, 1980–; a Regional Advr in Midland Bank, with special responsibilities for Wales, 1979–. Member, County Councils' Assoc., 1980–; Chm., Welsh Theatre Co., 1981–; President: Housing and Town Planning Council, 1980–; Age Concern, Wales, 1980–; Soc. of Welsh People Overseas, 1979–; UCW, Aberystwyth, 1976–. Hon. Freedom of Beaumaris, 1972; Freeman, Borough of Anglesey, 1976. Hon. LLD Wales, 1970. Alderman, Anglesey CC, 1973. *Publication:* Report on Conditions in St Helena, 1958. *Address:* Swynol Le, Trearddur, Holyhead, Gwynedd. *T:* Trearddur 544. *Club:* Travellers'.

CLEERE, Henry Forester; FSA; Director, Council for British Archaeology, since 1974; *b* 2 Dec. 1926; *s* of late Christopher Henry John Cleere and Frances Eleanor (*née* King); *m* 1st, 1950, Dorothy Percy (marr. diss.); one *s* one *d* ; 2nd, 1975, Pamela Joan Vertue; two *d. Educ:* Beckenham County Sch.; University Coll. London (BA Hons 1951); Univ. of London Inst. of Archaeology (PhD 1981). FBIM. Commissioned Royal Artillery, 1944–48. Successively, Production Editor, Asst Sec., Man. Editor, Dep. Sec., Iron and Steel Inst., 1952–71; Industrial Development Officer, UN Industrial Develt Org., Vienna, 1972–73. Mem. Exec. Cttee, ICOMOS. Winston Churchill Fellow, 1979. FSA 1967. *Publications:* papers in British and foreign jls on aspects of early ironmaking, Roman fleets, etc. *Recreations:* gardening, beekeeping, cookery. *Address:* Acres Rise, Lower Platts, Ticehurst, Wadhurst, East Sussex TN5 7DD. *T:* Ticehurst 200752. *Club:* Athenæum.

CLEESE, John Marwood; writer and actor; *b* 27 Oct. 1939; *s* of Reginald and Muriel Cleese; *m* 1st, 1968, Connie Booth (marr. diss. 1978); one *d* ; 2nd, 1981, Barbara Trentham. *Educ:* Clifton Sports Acad.; Downing College, Cambridge (MA). Started making jokes professionally, 1963; started on British television, 1966; TV series have included: The Frost Report, At Last the 1948 Show, Monty Python's Flying Circus, Fawlty Towers. Films include: Interlude, The Magic Christian, And Now For Something Completely Different, Monty Python and the Holy Grail, Romance with a Double Bass, Life of Brian. Hon. LLD St Andrews. *Publication:* (with Connie Booth) Fawlty Towers, 1977. *Recreations:* gluttony, sloth. *Address:* c/o David Wilkinson, 8 Waterloo Place, SW1.

CLEGG, Sir Alec, (Alexander Bradshaw Clegg), Kt 1965; Chief Education Officer, West Riding County Council, 1945–74, retired; *b* 13 June 1909; *s* of Samuel and Mary Clegg, Sawley, Derbs; *m* 1940, Jessie Coverdale Phillips, West Hartlepool; three *s. Educ:* Long Eaton Gram. Sch.; Bootham Sch., York; Clare Coll., Cambridge (BA); London Day Training Coll.; King's Coll., London (MA), FKC 1972. Asst Master, St Clement Danes Gram. Sch., London, 1932–36; Admin. Asst Birmingham Educn Cttee, 1936–39; Asst Educn Officer, Ches CC, 1939–42; Dep. Educn Officer, Worcs CC, 1942–45; West Riding, Jan.–Sept. 1945. Chm. of Governors, Centre for Information and Advice on Educational Disadvantage, 1976–79. Hon. LLD Leeds, 1972; Hon DLitt: Loughborough, 1972; Bradford, 1978. Chevalier de l'ordre de L'Étoile Noire, 1961. *Publications:* The Excitement of Writing, 1964, USA 1972; (with B. Megson) Children in Distress, 1968; (ed) The Changing Primary School, 1972; About our Schools, 1981. *Address:* Saxton, Tadcaster, N Yorks. *T:* Barkston Ash 288.

CLEGG, Sir Alexander Bradshaw; *see* Clegg, Sir Alec.

CLEGG, Brian George Herbert; Chairman, Northern Region of British Gas Corporation, 1975–82; *b* 10 Dec. 1921; *s* of Frederic Bradbury Clegg and Gladys Butterworth; *m* 1st, 1949, Iris May Ludlow; one *s* one *d* ; 2nd, 1976, Anne Elizabeth Robertson. *Educ:* Manchester Grammar Sch.; Trinity Coll., Cambridge (Open Math. Schol., MA). FIS, FIM, CEng, FIGasE, MBIM. Sci. Officer, Min. of Supply, 1942 (Hon. Flt-Lt); Statistician, Liverpool Gas Co., 1946; Market and Operational Res. Man., Southern Gas Bd, 1957; Commercial Man., Southern Gas Bd, 1961; Dep. Dir of Marketing, Gas Council, 1968; Dir of Marketing, British Gas Corp., 1972. *Publications:* numerous articles and papers on marketing and fuel matters. *Recreations:* swimming, ice-skating, ski-ing, electronic organ. *Address:* The Grove, Balcombe Road, Poole, Dorset.

CLEGG, Sir Cuthbert (Barwick), Kt 1950; TD; JP; *b* 9 Aug. 1904; *s* of Edmund Barwick Clegg, DL, JP, Shore, Littleborough, Lancs; *m* 1930, Helen Margaret, *y d* of Arthur John Jefferson, MD; one *s. Educ:* Charterhouse; Trinity Coll., Oxford (MA). Pres., British Employers Confederation, 1950–

52; JP Lancs, 1946, Sheriff, 1955; Sheriff of Westmorland, 1969; Major (retired), Duke of Lancaster's Own Yeomanry. Member: Cotton Industry Working Party, 1946; Cotton Manufacturing Commission, 1947–49; Anglo-American Council on Productivity, 1948–52; Economic Planning Bd, 1949–53; British Productivity Council, 1952–54; Leader, UK Cotton Industry Mission to India, Hong Kong and Pakistan, 1957. Hon. Life Governor, The Cotton, Silk and Man-Made Fibres Research Association (Pres., 1962–67); President: UK Textile Manufacturers' Assoc., 1960–69; Overseas Bankers' Club, 1966–67; Inst. of Bankers, 1968–69. Chm., Martins Bank Ltd, 1964–69; Dir, Barclays Bank Ltd, 1968–75; Dep. Chm., Barclays Bank Trust Co. Ltd, 1969–76; Vice-Chm., Halifax Building Soc., 1971–76 (Dir, 1960–76). *Address:* Willow Cottage, Arkholme, Carnforth, Lancs. *T:* Hornby 21205.

See also R. N. B. Clegg.

CLEGG, Professor Edward John, MD, PhD; FIBiol; Regius Professor of Anatomy, University of Aberdeen, since 1976; *b* 29 Oct. 1925; *s* of Edward Clegg and Emily Armistead; *m* 1958, Sheila Douglas Walls; two *d* (and one *d* decd). *Educ:* High Storrs Grammar Sch., Sheffield; Univ. of Sheffield (MB, ChB Hons 1948, MD 1964). PhD Liverpool, 1957; FIBiol 1974. RAMC, 1948–50 and RAMC (TA), 1950–61; Major, RAMC (RARO). Demonstr, Asst Lectr and Lectr in Anatomy, Univ. of Liverpool, 1952–63; Lectr, Sen. Lectr and Reader in Human Biology and Anatomy, Univ. of Sheffield, 1963–77. MO, British Kangchenjunga Expedn, 1955; Sci. Mem., Chogolungma Glacier Expedn, 1959; Leader, WHO/IBP Expedn, Simien Mountains, Ethiopia, 1967. *Publications:* The Study of Man: an introduction to human biology, 1968 (2nd edn 1978); papers on anatomy, endocrinology and human biology. *Recreations:* mountaineering, fishing, sailing, music. *Address:* c/o Department of Anatomy, Marischal College, Aberdeen AB9 1AS. *T:* Aberdeen 40241, ext. 233M. *Clubs:* Alpine; Wayfarers (Liverpool).

CLEGG, Hugh Anthony, CBE 1966; MA, MB Cantab; Hon. MD (TCD); Hon. DLit QUB; FRCP; retired; *b* 19 June 1900; *s* of Rev. John Clegg and Gertrude, *d* of John Wilson; *m* 1932, Baroness Kyra Engelhardt, *o d* of late Baron Arthur Engelhardt, Smolensk, Russia; one *s* one *d. Educ:* Westminster Sch. (King's Schol.); Trinity Coll., Cambridge (Westminster Exhibr, Senior Schol., in Nat. Science); St Bartholomew's Hospital. 1st Class Hons Part 1 Nat. Sci. Tripos; House Physician at St Bartholomew's Hosp.; House Physician at Brompton Hosp. for Diseases of the Chest; Medical Registrar, Charing Cross Hosp.; Sub-editor, British Medical Journal, 1931–34; Deputy Editor, 1934–46; Editor, 1947–65; Dir, Office for Internat. Relations in Med., RSM, 1967–72; Founder and Editor, Tropical Doctor, a jl of med. practice in the Tropics, 1971–72. Hon. Fellow: American Medical Assoc.; Alpha Omega Alpha Honor Med. Soc. Late Chm., UNESCO Cttee on Co-ordination of Abstracting in the Medical and Biological Sciences. Initiator and Sec., First World Conf. on Med. Educn, London, 1953, and Ed. of its Proceedings, 1954; Editor, Medicine a Lifelong Study (Proceedings of the Second World Conf. on Med. Educn, Chicago, 1959). Vice-Pres., L'Union Internationale de la Presse Médicale, and Pres. of its Third Congress, 1957; Member: Med. Panel, British Council to 1965; Council, World Medical Assoc., 1957–61 (Chm., Cttee on Medical Ethics and author of first draft of code of ethics on human experimentation, subsequently modified as Declaration of Helsinki); RCP Cttees on air pollution and health, and smoking tobacco and health, 1969–77. Gold Medal of BMA, 1966. *Publications:* What is Osteopathy? (jointly), 1937; Brush up your Health, 1938; Wartime Health and Democracy, 1941; contributed medical terms Chambers's Technical Dictionary, 1940; How to Keep Well in Wartime (Min. of Information), 1943; Medicine in Britain (British Council), 1944; revised Black's Medical Dictionary, 1944–44; Advisory Editor medical section of Chambers's Encyclopædia. *Recreation:* reading reviews of the books I should like to read but haven't the time to. *Address:* 42 Cloncurry Street, Fulham, SW6 6DU. *T:* 01-736 3445.

CLEGG, Prof. Hugh Armstrong; Titular Professor and Leverhulme Research Fellow, University of Warwick, since 1979; *b* 22 May 1920; *s* of late Rev. Herbert Hobson Clegg and of Mabel (*née* Duckering); *m* 1941, Mary Matilda (*née* Shaw); two *s* two *d. Educ:* Kingswood Sch., Bath; Magdalen Coll., Oxford. Served War, 1940–45; Official Fellow, Nuffield Coll., Oxford, 1949–66, Emeritus Fellow, 1966–; Prof. of Industrial Relns, Univ. of Warwick, 1967–79. Chm., Civil Service Arbitration Tribunal, 1968–71; Dir, Industrial Relations Res. Unit, SSRC, 1970–74; Member: Royal Commn on Trade Unions and Employers' Assocs, 1965–68; Cttee of Inquiry into Port Transport Industry, 1964–65; Ct of Inquiry into Seamen's Dispute, 1966–67; Nat. Board for Prices and Incomes, 1966–67; Ct of Inquiry into Local Authorities' Manual Workers' Pay Dispute, 1970; Council, ACAS, 1974–79; Chm., Standing Commn on Pay Comparability, 1979–80. *Publications:* Labour Relations in London Transport, 1950; Industrial Democracy and Nationalisation, 1951; The Future of Nationalisation (with T. E. Chester), 1953; General Union, 1954; Wage Policy in the Health Service (with T. E. Chester), 1957; The Employers' Challenge (with R. Adams), 1957; A New Approach to Industrial Democracy, 1960; Trade Union Officers (with A. J. Killick and R. Adams), 1961; General Union in a Changing Society, 1964; A History of British Trade Unions (with A. Fox and A. F. Thompson), Vol. I, 1964; The System of Industrial Relations in Great Britain, 1970; How to run an Incomes Policy and Why we made such a Mess of the Last One, 1971; Workplace and Union (with I. Boraston and M. Rimmer), 1975; Trade Unionism under Collective Bargaining, 1976; The Changing System of Industrial Relations in Great Britain, 1979. *Recreations:* walking, beer. *Address:* 48 Amherst Road, Kenilworth, Warwicks. *T:* Kenilworth 54825.

CLEGG, Richard Ninian Barwick, QC 1979; a Recorder of the Crown Court, since 1978; *b* 28 June 1938; *o s* of Sir Cuthbert Clegg, *qv* ; *m* 1963, Katherine Veronica, *d* of A. A. H. Douglas; two *s* one *d*. *Educ:* Aysgarth; Charterhouse; Trinity Coll., Oxford (MA). Captain of Oxford Pentathlon Team, 1959. Called to Bar, Inner Temple, 1960. Chm., NW section of Bow Group, 1964-66; Vice-Chm., Bow Group, 1965-66; Chm., Winston Circle, 1965-66; Pres., Heywood and Royton Conservative Assoc., 1965-68. *Publication:* (jtly) Bow Group pamphlet, Towards a New North West, 1964. *Recreations:* sport, music, travel. *Address:* The Old Rectory, Brereton, via Sandbach, Cheshire CW11 9RY. *T:* Holmes Chapel 32358; 5 Essex Court, Temple, EC4. *T:* 01-353 4365. *Club:* Lansdowne.

CLEGG, Sir Walter, Kt 1980; MP (C) North Fylde since 1966; *b* 18 April 1920; *s* of Edwin Clegg; *m* 1951, Elise Margaret Hargreaves. *Educ:* Bury Grammar Sch.; Arnold Sch., Blackpool; Manchester Univ. Law Sch. Articled to Town Clerk, Barrow-in-Furness, 1937. Served in Royal Artillery, 1939-46 (commnd 1940). Qualified as Solicitor, 1947; subsequently in practice. Lancashire CC, 1955-61. Opposition Whip, 1967-69; a Lord Comr, HM Treasury, 1970-72; Vice-Chamberlain, HM Household, 1972-73; Comptroller, 1973-74; an Opposition Whip, March-Oct. 1974. Chm., Cons. NW Members Group, 1977-; Vice-Chm., Assoc. of Conservative Clubs, 1969-71; Hon. Sec., Cons. Housing and Local Govt Cttee, 1968-69; President: Assoc. of Cons. Clubs, 1977-78; Cons. NW Area Clubs; Mem. Exec., 1922 Cttee, 1975-76, Hon. Treasurer, 1976-; Chm., Parly All-Party Solicitors Gp. *Recreation:* reading. *Address:* Beech House, Raikes Road, Little Thornton, near Blackpool, Lancs. *T:* Cleveleys 76131. *Clubs:* Garrick, Carlton.

CLEGG-HILL, family name of **Viscount Hill.**

CLELAND, Dame Rachel, DBE 1980 (CBE 1966; MBE 1960); *b* Peppermint Grove, Jan. 1906; *d* of W. H. Evans, Perth, WA; *m* 1928, Sir Donald Cleland, *s* of E. D. Cleland; two *s*. *Educ:* Methodist Ladies' Coll., Perth, WA; Kindergarten Training Coll. Pres., Girl Guide Assoc., Papua and New Guinea, 1952-66; President: Red Cross, Papua and New Guinea, 1952-66; Branch of Aust. Pre-Sch. Assoc. (TPNG), 1952-66. *Recreations:* gardening, bird-watching. *Address:* 155r Forrest Street, Peppermint Grove, WA 6011, Australia. *Clubs:* Queen's, Royal Sydney Golf.

CLELAND, William Paton, FRCP, FRCS, FACS; Consulting Surgeon, Brompton Chest Hospital; Consulting Thoracic Surgeon, King's College Hospital; Emeritus Consultant to the RN; late Adviser in Thoracic Surgery to the Department of Health and Social Security; *b* 30 May 1912; *o s* of late Sir John Cleland, CBE; *m* 1940, Norah, *d* of George E. Goodhart; two *s* one *d*. *Educ:* Scotch Coll., Adelaide; Univ. of Adelaide, S Australia. MB, BS (Adelaide). Resident appts, Royal Adelaide and Adelaide Children's Hosps, 1935-36; MRCP 1939; House Physician and Resident Surgical Officer, Brompton Chest Hosp., 1939-41. Served in EMS as Registrar and Surgeon, 1939-45. FRCS 1946. Consulting Thoracic Surg., 1948-; Surgeon, Brompton Chest Hospital, 1948; Sen. Lectr in Thoracic Surgery, Royal Postgrad. Med. Sch., 1949; former Dir, Dept of Surgery, Cardio-Thoracic Inst., Brompton Hosp. Member: Assoc. Thoracic Surgeons of Gt Brit. and Ire.; Thoracic Soc.; British Cardiac Soc. Editor, Jl of Cardiovascular Surgery, 1978-. Comdr, Order of Lion of Finland; Comdr, Order of Icelandic Falcon. *Publications:* (jt author) Medical and Surgical Cardiology, 1969; chapters on thoracic surgery in British Surgical Practice, Diseases of the Chest (Marshall and Perry), Short Practice of Surgery (Bailey and Love), and Operative Surgery (Rob and Rodney Smith); articles on pulmonary and cardiac surgery in medical literature. *Recreations:* fishing, photography, gardening. *Address:* 50 Shrewsbury House, Cheyne Walk, Chelsea, SW3 5LW. *T:* 01-352 6530; Green Meadows, Goodworth Clatford, Andover, Hants SP11 7HH. *T:* Andover 4327.

CLEMENS, Clive Carruthers, MC 1946; HM Diplomatic Service; High Commissioner in Lesotho, since 1981; *b* 22 Jan. 1924; British; *s* of late M. B. Clemens, Imperial Bank of India, and late Margaret Jane (née Carruthers); *m* 1947, Philippa Jane Bailey; three *s*. *Educ:* Blundell's Sch.; St Catharine's Coll., Cambridge. War Service 1943-46: commissioned in Duke of Cornwall's Light Infantry; served in India and Burma, 1944-45. Entered HM Foreign Service and apptd to FO, 1947; Third Sec., Rangoon, 1948; Third (later Second) Sec., Lisbon, 1950; FO, 1953; First Sec., Budapest, 1954; Brussels, 1956; Seoul, 1959; FO, 1961; Strasbourg (UK Delegn to Council of Europe), 1964; Counsellor, Paris, 1967; Principal British Trade Comr, Vancouver, 1970-74; Dep. Consul-Gen., Johannesburg, 1974-78; Consul-Gen., Istanbul, 1978-81. *Recreations:* birdwatching, photography. *Address:* c/o Foreign and Commonwealth Office, SW1.

CLEMENT, David James; Under Secretary, Department of the Environment, Northern Ireland, since 1980; *b* 29 Sept. 1930; *s* of James and Constance Clement; *m* 1958, Margaret Stone; two *s* one *d*. *Educ:* Chipping Sodbury Grammar Sch.; Univ. of Bristol (BA). IPFA. Internal Audit Asst, City of Bristol, 1953-56; Accountancy/Audit Asst, 1956-60, Chief Accountancy Asst, 1960-65, City of Worcester; Dep. Chief Finance Officer, Runcorn Devlt Corp., 1965-68; Chief Finance Officer, Antrim and Ballymena Devlt Commn, 1968-72; Asst Sec., Dept of Finance, NI, 1972-75, Dep. Sec., 1975-80. *Recreations:* lawn tennis, Association football, contract bridge, philately.

CLEMENT, David Morris, CBE 1971; FCA, IPFA; Chairman: Joint Mission Hospital Equipment Board Ltd, since 1978; Redwood-Corex Services Ltd, since 1978; *b* 6 Feb. 1911; 2nd *s* of Charles William and Rosina Wannell Clement, Swansea; *m* 1938, Kathleen Mary, *o d* of Ernest George Davies, ACA, Swansea; one *d*. *Educ:* Bishop Gore's Grammar Sch., Swansea. Mem. Inst. Chartered Accountants, 1933. A. Owen John & Co., Swansea, and Sissons Bersey Gain Vincent & Co., London, Chartered Accts, 1928-35; ICI Ltd, Lime Gp, 1935-40; Chloride Electrical Storage Co. Ltd, 1941-46; National Coal Board: Sec., North Western Div., 1946-49; Chief Acct, Northern and Durham Divs, 1950-55; Dep. Dir-Gen. of Finance, 1955-61; Dir-Gen. of Finance, 1961-69; Bd Mem., 1969-76; Chm., NCB (Ancillaries) Ltd, 1973-79. Chm., Public Corporations Finance Gp, 1975-76. Dep. Chm., Horizon Exploration Ltd, 1978-80. Member: Aircraft and Shipbuilding Industries Arbitration Tribunals, 1980-; Council, CIPFA, 1975-76; Council, CGLI (Hon. Treas., 1978-82). *Recreations:* golf, photography. *Address:* 19 The Highway, Sutton, Surrey. *T:* 01-642 3626. *Clubs:* Royal Automobile, Directors'.

CLEMENT, John; Chairman, Unigate Group, since 1977; non-executive Chairman, The Littlewoods Organisation, since 1982; Director, Eagle Star Holdings, since 1981; *b* 18 May 1932; *s* of Frederick and Alice Eleanor Clement; *m* 1956, Elisabeth Anne (née Emery); two *s* one *d*. *Educ:* Bishop's Stortford College. Howards Dairies, Westcliff on Sea, 1949-64; United Dairies London Ltd, 1964-69; Asst Managing Director, Rank Leisure Services Ltd, 1969-73; Chairman, Unigate Foods Div., 1973; Chief Executive, Unigate Group, 1976. CBIM (FBIM 1977). *Recreations:* tennis, shooting, sailing, skiing, bridge, Rugby. *Address:* Tuddenham Hall, Tuddenham, Ipswich, Suffolk IP6 9DD. *T:* Witnesham 217. *Clubs:* MCC, Farmers', Royal Automobile, London Welsh Rugby Football.

CLEMENT, John Handel, CB 1980; Under-Secretary, Welsh Office, 1971-81, and Director, Industry Department, 1976-81; *b* 24 Nov. 1920; *s* of late William Clement and Mary Hannah Clement; *m* 1946, Anita Jones; one *d* (and one *d* decd). *Educ:* Pontardawe Grammar Sch. RAF, 1940-46, Flt Lt (despatches). Welsh Board of Health: Clerical Officer, 1938; Exec. Officer, 1946; Higher Exec. Officer, 1948; Sen. Exec. Officer, 1956; Principal, Welsh Office, Min. of Housing and Local Govt, 1960, and Sec., 1966. Private Sec. to Sec. of State for Wales, 1966. Sec., Council for Wales, 1955-59; Chm., Welsh Planning Bd, 1971-76. Hon. MA Wales, 1982. *Recreations:* Welsh Rugby, fishing. *Address:* 6 St Brioc Road, Heath, Cardiff. *T:* Cardiff 64192.

CLÉMENT, René; Chevalier de la Légion d'Honneur; Officier, Ordre National du Mérite; Commandeur des Arts et des Lettres; film director; *b* Bordeaux, 18 March 1913; *s* of Jean Clément and Marguérite Clément (née Bayle); *m* 1940, Bella Gurwich. *Educ:* Lycée de Bordeaux; Ecole nationale supérieure des beauxarts. *Films:* Soigne ton Gauche (short), 1936; *documentaries:* L'Arabie Interdite, 1937; La Grande Chartreuse, 1938; La Bièvre, 1939; Le Tirage, 1940; Ceux du Rail, 1942; La Grande Pastorale, 1943; Chefs de Demain, 1944; *feature films:* La Bataille du Rail, 1946 (Cannes Fest. Prize); Le Père Tranquille, 1946; Les Maudits, 1947 (Cannes Fest. Prize); Au-delà des Grilles, 1948 (US Academy Award, British award); Le Chateau de Verre, 1950; Jeux Interdits, 1952 (US Academy Award, British award, Cannes Fest. Prize and Grand Internat. Prize Venice Biennale); Monsieur Ripois, 1954 (Cannes Fest. Prize); Gervaise, 1955 (Venice Internat. Prize); Barrage contre le Pacifique, 1958; Plein Soleil, 1959; Quelle Joie de Vivre, 1961; Le Jour et l'Heure, 1962; Les Félins, 1964; Paris, Brûle-t-il?, 1966 (Prix Europa); Le Passager de la Pluie, 1969; La Maison sous les Arbres, 1971; La Course du lièvre à travers les champs, 1971; The Baby Sitter, 1975. Founder Mem., Institut des hautes études cinématographiques. *Publication:* (with C. Audry) Bataille du rail, 1947. *Recreations:* antiques, painting, music. *Address:* 10 Avenue de St Roman, Monte Carlo, Monaco. *T:* 50-59-35; 91 Avenue Henri Martin, 75016 Paris. *T:* 504-30-93.

CLEMENTS, Clyde Edwin, CMG 1962; OBE 1958; Director: C. E. Clements & Co. Pty Ltd, since 1926; C. E. Clements (Holdings) Ltd; President, Clements Peruana SA; *b* 2 Aug. 1897; *e s* of late Edwin Thomas Clements and late Mrs Clements; *m* 1919, Doris Gertrude Garrett; one *d*. *Educ:* Devonport Grammar Sch., Tasmania; Queen's Coll., Hobart, Tas. Served European War, 1914-18. Vice-Pres. Young Christian Workers, 1943-66; Dir Young Christian Workers Co-operative Soc. Ltd, 1948-62. Pres. Austr. AA, 1956-57; Mem. Bd, Austr. Nat. Travel Assoc., 1956-57; Mem. Bd, Tourist Develt Authority of Victoria, 1958-69; Vice-Pres. (OTA) World Touring Organization, 1958; Chm., British motoring Conf., 1964-69. Mem. Board of Management, Sir Colin MacKenzie Sanctuary, Healesville, Vic, 1962. Hon. Consul of Peru. Hon. FAIEx. *Recreations:* golf, angling. *Address:* 11 Cosham Street, Brighton, Vic 3186, Australia. *T:* 92.3974. *Clubs:* Royal Automobile of Victoria (Vice-Pres. 1942-44, 1952-53; Pres. 1955-61); RACV Country; Victoria Golf; West Brighton (Vic).

CLEMENTS, Sir John (Selby), Kt 1968; CBE 1956; FRSA; Actor, Manager, Producer; *b* 25 April 1910; *s* of late Herbert William Clements, Barrister-at-Law, and Mary Elizabeth (née Stephens); *m* 1st, 1936, Inga Maria Lillemor Ahlgren (marr. diss. 1946); 2nd, 1946, Dorothy Katharine (Kay Hammond) (*d* 1980), *d* of late Sir Guy Standing, KBE, and Dorothy Frances Plaskitt. *Educ:* St Paul's Sch.; St John's Coll., Cambridge. British Actors' Equity: Mem. Council, 1948, 1949; Vice-Pres., 1950-59; Trustee, 1958. Member: Arts Council Drama Panel, 1953-58; Council, RADA, 1957-. First stage appearance, Out of the Blue, Lyric, Hammersmith, 1930; subsequently appeared in: She Stoops to Conquer, Lyric; The Beaux' Stratagem, Royalty, 1930; The Venetian, Little, 1931; Salome, Gate Theatre, 1931; many

Shakespearian parts under management of late Sir Philip Ben Greet; founded The Intimate Theatre, Palmers Green, London, 1935, and ran it as weekly repertory theatre until 1940, directing most of and appearing in nearly 200 plays; produced Yes and No, Ambassadors, 1937; appeared in: Skylark, Duchess, 1942; They Came to a City, Globe, 1943; (also produced) Private Lives, Apollo, 1944; (with Old Vic Co.) played Coriolanus, Petruchio and Dunois, New, 1947–48; appeared in Edward My Son, Lyric, 1948–49; as Actor-Manager-Producer, has presented and played in: The Kingmaker; Marriage à la Mode, St James's, 1946; The Beaux' Stratagem, Phoenix and Lyric, 1949–50; Man and Superman, New and Princes, 1951; (also author) The Happy Marriage, Duke of York's, 1952–53; Pygmalion, St James's 1953–54; The Little Glass Clock, Aldwych, 1954–55; personal management of Saville Theatre, 1955–57, where presented and played in: The Shadow of Doubt; The Wild Duck, 1955–56; The Rivals, 1956; The Seagull; The Doctor's Dilemma; The Way of the World, 1956–57; Adviser on Drama to Associated Rediffusion Ltd, 1955–56, where produced films including: A Month in the Country; The Wild Duck; played in: (also co-presented and directed) The Rape of the Belt, Piccadilly, 1957–58; (also presented) Gilt and Gingerbread, Duke of York's, 1959; The Marriage-Go-Round, Piccadilly, 1959–60; produced Will You Walk a Little Faster?, Duke of York's, 1960; played in: J. B., Phœnix, 1961; The Affair, Strand, 1961; The Tulip Tree, Haymarket, 1962; Old Vic American tour, 1962; played in: (also co-presented and directed) The Masters, Savoy, 1963; Robert and Elizabeth, Lyric, 1964; dir and played in, The Case in Question, Haymarket, 1975. Director, Chichester Festival Theatre, 1966–73; 1966 season, presented: The Clandestine Marriage; (also played in) The Fighting Cock (subseq. Duke of York's); The Cherry Orchard; (also played) Macbeth; 1967 season, directed: The Farmer's Wife; (also played Shotover) Heartbreak House (subseq. Lyric); presented: The Beaux' Stratagem; An Italian Straw Hat; 1968 season, presented: The Unknown Soldier and His Wife; The Cocktail Party (subseq. Wyndham's); (played Prospero) The Tempest; The Skin of our Teeth; 1969 season, presented: The Caucasian Chalk Circle; (also directed and played in) The Magistrate (subseq. Cambridge); The Country Wife; (also played Antony) Antony and Cleopatra; 1970 season, presented: Peer Gynt; Vivat! Vivat! Regina!; (also directed) The Proposal; Arms and the Man; The Alchemist; 1971 season presented: (also directed and played in) The Rivals; (also played in) Dear Antoine (subseq. Piccadilly); Caesar and Cleopatra; Reunion in Vienna; 1972 Season, presented: The Beggar's Opera; (also directed and played in) The Doctor's Dilemma; 1973 Season, presented: (also directed and played in) The Director of the Opera; (also directed) Dandy Dick; dir, Waters of the Moon, Chichester, 1977; The Devil's Disciple (General Burgoyne), The Importance of Being Earnest (Canon Chasuble), Chichester, 1979; entered films, 1934; films include: Things to Come; Knight Without Armour; South Riding; Rembrandt; The Four Feathers; Convoy; Ships With Wings; Undercover; They Came to a City; Train of Events; The Silent Enemy; The Mind Benders; Oh What a Lovely War!. *Address:* Rufford Court, 109 Marine Parade, Brighton, E Sussex BN2 1AT. *T:* Brighton 603026. *Club:* Garrick.

CLEMENTS, Julia; *see* Seton, Lady, (Julia).

CLEMENTS, Rt. Rev. Kenneth John; *b* 21 Dec. 1905; *s* of John Edwin Clements and Ethel Evelyn Clark; *m* 1935, Rosalind Elizabeth Cakebread; one *s* two *d. Educ:* Highgate Sch., London; St Paul's Coll., University of Sydney. BA (Hons) 1933; ThD 1949. Registrar, Diocese of Riverina, 1933–37; Rector of: Narrandera, NSW, 1937–39; Tumbarumba, NSW, 1939–43; Gunning, NSW, 1943–44; Director of Studies, Canberra Grammar Sch., Canberra, ACT, 1945; Registrar Diocese of Canberra and Goulburn, 1946–56; Archdeacon of Goulburn, 1946–56; Asst Bishop of Canberra and Goulburn, 1949–56; Bishop of Grafton, NSW, 1956–61; Bishop of Canberra and Goulburn, 1961–71; retired, 1971. *Address:* Mons School Road, Buderim, Qld 4556, Australia.

CLEMENTS, Richard Harry; Political Adviser to the Leader of the Opposition, since 1982; *b* 11 Oct. 1928; *s* of Harry and Sonia Clements; *m* 1952, Bridget Mary MacDonald; two *s. Educ:* King Alfred Sch., Hampstead; Western High Sch., Washington, DC; Regent Street Polytechnic. Middlesex Independent, 1949; Leicester Mercury, 1951; Ed., Socialist Advance (Labour Party Youth paper), 1953; industrial staff, Daily Herald, 1954; joined Tribune, 1956, Editor, 1961–82. *Publication:* Glory without Power: a study of trade unions, 1959. *Recreation:* woodwork. *Address:* 53B Hendon Lane, N3.

CLEMINSON, Sir James (Arnold Stacey), Kt 1982; MC 1945; Chairman, Reckitt & Colman Ltd, since 1977 (Chief Executive, 1973–80); *b* 31 Aug. 1921; *s* of Arnold Russel Cleminson and Florence Stacey; *m* 1950, Helen Juliet Measor; one *s* two *d. Educ:* Rugby Sch. Served War, 1940–46, mainly in Parachute Regt. Reckitt & Colman, 1946–: Overseas Co., 1946; Dir, Reckitt & Colman Overseas, 1957; Chm., Food and Wine Div., Norwich, 1970. Vice-Chm., Norwich Union, 1981–(Dir, 1979-). Mem., Food EDC, 1976–; Pres., Food Manufrs Fedn, 1980–82. Mem., CBI Council, 1978–; Jt Chm., Netherlands British Chamber of Commerce Council, 1978-. Chm., Council of Endeavour Trng; Trustee, Airborne Forces Security Fund. *Recreations:* hunting, shooting, tennis, golf, fishing. *Address:* Loddon Hall, Hales, Norfolk. *Club:* Aldeburgh.

CLEMITSON, Ivor Malcolm; *b* 8 Dec. 1931; *s* of Daniel Malcolm Clemitson and Annie Ellen Clemitson; *m* 1960, Janet Alicia Meeke; one *s* one *d. Educ:* Harlington Primary Sch.; Luton Grammar Sch.; London Sch. of Economics (BScEcon); Bishops Theol College. Deacon 1958, Priest 1959. Curate: St

Mary's (Bramall Lane), Sheffield, 1958–61; Christ Church, Luton, 1962–64; Industrial Chaplain, Dio. St Albans, 1964–69; Dir of Industrial Mission, Dio. Singapore, 1969–70; Research Officer, National Graphical Assoc., 1971–74. MP (Lab) Luton East, Feb. 1974–1979. *Publication:* (with George Rodgers) A Life to Live, 1981. *Recreations:* watching football, theatre, travel. *Address:* 49 Marlborough Road, Luton, Beds. *T:* Luton 419198.

CLEMO, George Roger, DSc; FRS 1937; FIC; Professor of Organic Chemistry, King's College, University of Durham, 1925–54, Professor Emeritus, 1954; Director of Department of Chemistry, 1932-54. *Educ:* University Coll., Exeter; Queen's Coll., Oxford. Late asst to Prof. W. H. Perkin at Oxford; was in charge of the Research Department of the British Dyestuffs Corporation, Manchester. *Address:* Cherryburn, Mickley, Stocksfield, Northumberland NE43 7DD.

CLEMOES, Prof. Peter Alan Martin, PhD (Cantab); FRHistS; Elrington and Bosworth Professor of Anglo-Saxon, Cambridge University, since 1969; Official Fellow of Emmanuel College, Cambridge, 1962-69, Professorial Fellow since 1969; Fellow, Queen Mary College, London University, since 1975; *b* 20 Jan. 1920; *o s* of Victor Clemoes and Mary (*née* Paton); *m* 1956, Jean Elizabeth, *yr d* of Sidney Grew; two *s. Educ:* Brentwood Sch.; Queen Mary Coll., London; King's Coll., Cambridge. BA London (1st Cl. Hons English) 1950; Soley Student, King's Coll., Cambridge, 1951-53; Research Fellow, Reading Univ., 1954-55; PhD Cambridge 1956. Lectr in English, Reading Univ., 1955-61; Lectr in Anglo-Saxon, Cambridge Univ., 1961-69; Coll. Lectr in English, 1963-69 and Dir of Studies in English, 1963-65; Tutor, 1966-68; Asst Librarian, 1963-69. Mem., Council of Early English Text Soc., 1971-. Founder and Chief Editor, Anglo-Saxon England, 1972-. *Publications:* The Anglo-Saxons, Studies . . . presented to Bruce Dickins (ed and contrib.), 1959; General Editor of Early English Manuscripts in Facsimile (Copenhagen), 1963-74, and co-editor of vol. XIII, 1966, vol. XVIII, 1974; Rhythm and Cosmic Order in Old English Christian Literature (inaug. lecture), 1970; England before the Conquest: Studies . . . presented to Dorothy Whitelock (co-ed and contrib.), 1971; textual and critical writings, especially on the works of Ælfric. *Address:* 14 Church Street, Chesterton, Cambridge. *T:* Cambridge 358655.

CLEOBURY, Stephen John, FRCO; Fellow, Director of Music and Organist, King's College, Cambridge, since 1982; *b* 31 Dec. 1948; *s* of John Frank Cleobury and Brenda Julie (*née* Randall); *m* 1971, Penelope Jane (*née* Holloway); two *d. Educ:* King's Sch., Worcester; St John's Coll., Cambridge (MA, MusB). FRCO 1968. Organist, St Matthew's, Northampton, 1971-74; Sub-Organist, Westminster Abbey, 1974-78; Master of Music, Westminster Cathedral, 1979-82. Hon. Sec., RCO, 1981-. *Recreations:* playing chess, watching cricket, reading railway timetables. *Address:* 85 Gough Way, Newnham, Cambridge CB3 9LN. *T:* Cambridge 59461, (King's College) Cambridge 350411, ext. 224.

CLERK, Sir John Dutton, 10th Bt *cr* 1679; CBE 1966; VRD; FRSE 1977; JP; Lord-Lieutenant of Midlothian since 1972 (Vice-Lieutenant, 1965-72); Cdre RNR; retd; *b* 30 Jan. 1917; *s* of Sir George James Robert Clerk, 9th Bt, and Hon. Mabel Honor (*d* 1974), *y d* of late Col Hon. Charles Dutton and *sister* of 6th Baron Sherborne, DSO; *S* father, 1943; *m* 1944, Evelyn Elizabeth Robertson; two *s* two *d. Educ:* Stowe. Brig., Queen's Body Guard for Scotland, Royal Company of Archers, 1973. JP 1955, DL 1956, Midlothian. *Heir: s* Robert Maxwell Clerk [*b* 3 April 1945; *m* 1970, Felicity Faye, *yr d* of George Collins, Bampton, Oxford; one *s* one *d*]. *Address:* Penicuik House, Penicuik, Midlothian, Scotland. *T:* Penicuik 74318. *Clubs:* Royal Over-Seas League; New (Edinburgh).

CLERKE, Sir John Edward Longueville, 12th Bt *cr* 1660; Captain Royal Wilts Yeomanry, RAC, TA; *b* 29 Oct. 1913; *s* of late Francis William Talbot Clerke, *e s* of 11th Bt, and Albinia Mary, *er d* of Edward Henry Evans-Lombe (she *m* 3rd, 1923, Air Chief Marshal Sir Edgar Rainey Ludlow-Hewitt, GCB, GBE, CMG, DSO, MC); *S* grandfather, 1930; *m* 1948, Mary, *d* of Lt-Col I. R. Beviss Bond, Prosperity, Natal, S Africa and The Old Rectory, North Newnton, Marlborough, Wilts; one *s* two *d. Heir: s* Francis Ludlow Longueville Clerke, *b* 25 Jan. 1953. *Address:* Holly Tree House, Pound Pill, Corsham, Wilts. *T:* Corsham 713760.

CLEVELAND, Archdeacon of; *see* Southgate, Ven. J. E.

CLEVELAND, (James) Harlan; Director, Hubert H. Humphrey Institute of Public Affairs, University of Minnesota, since 1980; *b* 19 Jan. 1918; *s* of Stanley Matthews Cleveland and Marian Phelps (*née* Van Buren); *m* 1941, Lois W. Burton; one *s* two *d. Educ:* Phillips Acad., Andover, Mass; Princeton Univ.; Oxford Univ. Farm Security Admin., Dept of Agric., 1940-42; Bd of Econ. Warfare (subseq. Foreign Econ. Admin.), 1942-44; Exec. Dir Econ. Sect., 1944-45, Actg Vice-Pres., 1945-46, Allied Control Commn, Rome; Mem. US Delegn, UNRRA Council, London, 1945; Dept Chief of Mission, UNRRA Italian Mission, Rome, 1946-47; Dir, UNRRA China Office, Shanghai, 1947-48; Dir, China Program, Econ. Coop. Admin., Washington, 1948-49; Dept Asst Adminstr, 1949-51; Asst Dir for Europe, Mutual Security Agency, 1952-53; Exec. Editor, The Reporter, NYC, 1953-56, Publisher, 1955-56; Dean, Maxwell Sch. of Citizenship and Pub. Affairs, Syracuse Univ., 1956-61; Asst Sec. for Internat. Orgn Affairs, State Dept, 1961-65; US Ambassador to NATO, 1965-69; Pres., Univ. of Hawaii, 1969-74; Dir, Program in Internat. Affairs, Aspen Inst. for Humanistic Studies, 1974-80.

Distinguished Vis. Tom Slick Prof. of World Peace, Univ. of Texas at Austin, 1979. Chm., Weather Modification Adv. Bd, US Dept of Commerce, 1977-78. Holds hon. degrees and foreign orders; US Medal of Freedom, 1946. Woodrow Wilson Award, Princeton Univ. *Publications:* The Obligations of Power, 1966; NATO: the Transatlantic Bargain, 1970; The Future Executive, 1972; (ed jtly) The Art of Overseasmanship, 1957; (jtly) The Overseas Americans, 1960; (ed) The Promise of World Tensions, 1961; (ed jtly) The Ethic of Power, 1962; (ed jtly) Ethics and Bigness, 1962; China Diary, 1976; The Third Try at World Order, 1977; (jtly) Humangrowth: an essay on growth, values and the quality of life, 1978; (ed) Energy Futures of Developing Countries, 1980; (ed jtly) Bioresources for Development, 1980; (ed) The Management of Sustainable Growth, 1981. *Address:* Hubert H. Humphrey Institute of Public Affairs, 909 Social Sciences, 267 19th Avenue South, Minneapolis, Minn 55455, USA. *Clubs:* Century, Princeton (NY); International (Washington); Edina Country (Minn); Waikiki Yacht (Honolulu).

CLEVERDON, (Thomas) Douglas (James); publisher and radio producer; *b* 17 January 1903; *er s* of Thomas Silcox Cleverdon, Bristol; *m* 1944, Elinor Nest, *d* of Canon J. A. Lewis, Cardiff; two *s* one *d* (and one *s* decd). *Educ:* Bristol Grammar Sch.; Jesus Coll., Oxford. Bookseller, and publisher of fine printing, Bristol, 1926-39. Free-lance acting and writing for BBC West Region, 1935-39; joined BBC (Children's Hour), 1939; W Regional Features Producer, 1939-43; Features Producer, London, 1943, until retirement in 1969; free-lance producer, 1969-80. Devised and co-produced BBC Brains Trust, 1941. BBC War Corresp. in Burma, 1945; from 1947, mainly concerned with productions for Third Programme including radio works by Max Beerbohm, J. Bronowski, Bill Naughton, George Barker, David Gascoyne, Ted Hughes, David Jones, Stevie Smith, Henry Reed, Dylan Thomas (Under Milk Wood), Peter Racine Fricker, Elizabeth Poston, Humphrey Searle and other poets and composers. Directed first stage prods of Under Milk Wood, in Edinburgh and London, 1955, and in New York, 1957. Directed: Poetry Festivals, Stratford-upon-Avon, 1966-70; Cheltenham Festival of Literature, 1971. Compiled exhibition of paintings, engravings and writings of David Jones, NBL, 1972. Publisher, Clover Hill Edns (illustrated by contemporary engravers), 1964-. Pres., Private Libraries Assoc., 1978-80. *Publications:* Engravings of Eric Gill, 1929; Growth of Milk Wood, 1969; (ed) Sixe Idyllia of Theocritus, 1971; (ed) Under Milk Wood (Folio Soc.), 1972; (ed) Verlaine, Femmes/Hombres, 1972; The Engravings of David Jones: a survey, 1981. *Recreations:* book-collecting; visual arts. *Address:* 27 Barnsbury Square, N1. *T:* 01-607 7392. *Clubs:* Savile, Double Crown.

CLEVERLEY FORD, Rev. Preb. Douglas William; Chaplain to The Queen since 1973; *b* 4 March 1914; *yr s* of late Arthur James and Mildred Ford; *m* 1939, Olga Mary, *er d* of late Dr Thomas Bewley Gilbart-Smith; no *c*. *Educ:* Great Yarmouth Grammar Sch.; Univ. of London. BD, MTh, ALCD (1st cl.). Deacon 1937, Priest 1938. London Coll. of Divinity: Tutor, 1937-39; Lectr, 1942-43 and 1952-58; Lectr, Church Army Trng Coll., 1953-60. Curate of Bridlington, Yorks, 1939-42; Vicar of Holy Trinity, Hampstead, 1942-55; Vicar of Holy Trinity with All Saints Church, South Kensington, 1955-74; Senior Chaplain to Archbishop of Canterbury, 1975-80; Hon. Dir, Coll. of Preachers, 1960-73; Rural Dean of Westminster, 1965-74; Prebendary of St Paul's Cathedral, 1968, now Prebendary Emeritus; Provincial Canon of York, 1969-; Lectr, Wey Inst. of Religious Studies, 1980-; Tutor, Southwark Ordination Course, 1980-. Six Preacher, Canterbury Cathedral, 1982-. Chm., Queen Alexandra's House, Kensington Gore, 1966-74; Mem. Governing Body, Westminster City Sch. and United Westminster Schs, 1965-74; Hon. Life Governor: British and Foreign Bible Soc., 1948; Church's Ministry among the Jews. Queen's Jubilee Medal, 1977. *Publications:* An Expository Preacher's Notebook, 1960; The Christian Faith Explained, 1962; A Theological Preacher's Notebook, 1962; A Pastoral Preacher's Notebook, 1965; A Reading of St Luke's Gospel, 1967; Preaching at the Parish Communion, Vol. 1 1967, Vol. 2 1968, Vol. 3 1969; Preaching Today, 1969; Preaching through the Christian Year, 1971; Praying through the Christian Year, 1973; Have You Anything to Declare?, 1973; Preaching on the Special Occasions, 1974, Vol. 2 1981; Preaching at the Parish Communion (Series III), 1975; New Preaching from the Old Testament, 1976; New Preaching from the New Testament, 1977; The Ministry of the Word, 1979; Preaching through the Acts of the Apostles, 1979; More Preaching from the New Testament, 1982; contrib. Churchman's Companion 1967, Expository Times. *Recreations:* maintenance of country cottage and garden, music, languages. *Address:* Rostrevor, Lingfield, Surrey RH7 6BZ. *Club:* Athenæum.

CLEWES, Howard Charles Vivian; novelist; *b* York, 27 Oct. 1912; British parentage; *m* 1946, Renata Faccincani; one *d*. *Educ:* Merchant Taylors' Sch. Various advertising agents, 1931-37. Served War of 1939-45, infantry company Comdr Green Howards, then Major G2; Chief Press and Information Officer, Milan, Italy, 1945-47. Professional novelist, resident Florence, Rome, London, 1948-. *Publications:* (in UK, USA, etc) Dead Ground, 1946; The Unforgiven, 1947; The Mask of Wisdom, 1948; Stendhal, 1949; Green Grow the Rushes, 1950; The Long Memory, 1951; An Epitaph for Love, 1952; The Way the Wind Blows, 1954; Man on a Horse, 1964; I, the King, 1978; *plays:* Quay South, 1947; Image in the Sun, 1955; *films:* The Long Memory, Steel Bayonet, The One that Got Away, The Day They Robbed the Bank of England, Mutiny on the Bounty, The Holiday, Up from the Beach, William the Conqueror, The Novice, The 40 Days of Musa Dagh, etc. *Recreations:* writing, fishing. *Address:* Wildwood, North End, NW3. *T:* 01-455 7110.

CLEWS, Michael Arthur; Master of the Supreme Court Taxing Office, since 1970; *b* Caudebec, France, 16 Sept. 1919; *s* of late Roland Trevor Clews and late Marjorie (*née* Baily); *m* 1947, Kathleen Edith, *d* of late Adam Hollingworth, OBE, JP, and Gertrude (*née* Bardsley); three *c*. *Educ:* Epworth Coll., Rhyl; Clare Coll., Cambridge (MA). Served in Indian Army (Major, RA and V Force), 1940-46. Solicitor, 1953; Partner, W. H. House & Son, and Knocker & Foskett, Sevenoaks, 1957-70. Mem., Lord Chancellor's Adv. Cttee on Legal Aid, 1977-. *Address:* Royal Courts of Justice, Strand, WC2.

CLIBBORN, Donovan Harold, CMG 1966; HM Diplomatic Service, retired; *b* 2 July 1917; *s* of Henry Joseph Fairley Clibborn and Isabel Sarah Jago; *m* 1st, 1940, Margaret Mercedes Edwige Nelson (*d* 1966); one *s* two *d*; 2nd, 1973, Victoria Ondiviela Garvi. *Educ:* Ilford High Sch.; St Edmund Hall, Oxford (MA). Laming Travelling Fellow, Queen's Coll., Oxford, 1938-40. Entered Consular Service, 1939; Vice-Consul, Genoa, 1939-40. Army Service, 1940-45: Intelligence Corps and Royal Signals, Western Desert, Sicily, Italy, NW Europe (despatches); Major, 1944. Foreign Office, 1945-46; Consul, Los Angeles, 1946-48; Foreign Office, 1948-50; 1st Sec. (UK High Commn, India), Madras, 1950-52; 1st Sec. (Information), Rio de Janeiro, 1952-56; 1st Sec. (Commercial), Madrid, 1956-60; Consul (Commercial), Milan, 1960-62; Counsellor (Economic), Tehran, 1962-64; Counsellor, Rio de Janeiro, 1964-66; Consul-General, Barcelona, 1966-70; Ambassador, El Salvador, 1971-75. *Recreations:* reading, music, perpetrating light verse. *Address:* Paseo del Dr Moragas 188, Atico 1A, Barberá del Vallés, Prov. Barcelona, Spain. *T:* Barcelona 7185377.

CLIBBORN, Rt. Rev. Stanley Eric Francis B; *see* Manchester, Bishop of.

CLIBURN, Van, (Harvey Lavan Cliburn Jr); Pianist; *b* Shreveport, La, 12 July 1934; *o c* of Harvey Lavan Cliburn and Rildia Bee (*née* O'Bryan). *Educ:* Kilgore High Sch., Texas; Juilliard Sch. of Music, New York. Made début in Houston, Texas, 1947; subsequently has toured extensively in United States and Europe. Awards include first International Tchaikovsky Piano Competition, Moscow, 1958, and every US prize, for pianistic ability. *Recreation:* swimming. *Address:* 455 Wilder Place, Shreveport, La 71104, USA.

CLIFFORD, family name of **Baron Clifford of Chudleigh.**

CLIFFORD OF CHUDLEIGH, 13th Baron *cr* 1672; **(Lewis) Hugh Clifford,** OBE 1962; DL; Count of The Holy Roman Empire; farmer and landowner; President: Devon Branch, Country Landowners Association, 1973-75; Devon Branch, Royal British Legion, 1969-80; *b* 13 April 1916; *o s* of 12th Baron and Amy (*d* 1926), *er d* of John A. Webster, MD; *S* father, 1964; *m* 1945, Hon. Katharine Vavasseur Fisher, 2nd *d* of 2nd Baron Fisher; two *s* two *d*. *Educ:* Beaumont Coll.; Hertford Coll., Oxford (BA). 2nd Lieut, Devonshire Regt, 1935. Served War of 1939-45: North Africa; Major, 1941 (prisoner of war, escaped). Retd, 1950. Lieut-Col, 1959; Col, 1961. ADC (TA), 1964-69. Hon. Col, The Royal Devon Yeomanry/1st Rifle Volunteers, RAC, T&AVR (formerly the Devonshire Territorials, RAC), 1968-71; Dep. Hon. Col, The Wessex Yeomanry, 1971-72, Hon. Col D Sqdn, 1972-. Pres., Devon Co. Agricultural Assoc., 1973-74. DL Devon, 1964. *Recreations:* shooting, sailing. *Heir: s* Hon. Thomas Hugh Clifford [*b* 17 March 1948; *m* 1980, Suzanne Austin, *yr d* of Mrs Campbell Austin, Limerick, Eire. Commnd Coldstream Guards, 1967, retired 1977 (Captain)]. *Address:* (seat) Ugbrooke Park, Chudleigh, South Devon TQ13 0AD; Morella, Montrose, Vic, Australia. *Clubs:* Army and Navy; Royal Yacht Squadron.

CLIFFORD, Clark McAdams; Senior Partner, Clifford, Warnke, since 1969; Special Counsel and Special Envoy of the President of the United States; *b* 25 Dec. 1906; *s* of Frank Andrew Clifford and Georgia (*née* McAdams); *m* 1931, Margery Pepperell Kimball; three *d*. *Educ:* Washington Univ., St Louis (LLB). Served US Naval Reserve, 1944-46 (Naval Commendation Ribbon). Practised law in St Louis, 1928-43; specialised in trial cases, corporation and labour law; Special Counsel to President of US, 1946-50; Senior Partner, Clifford & Miller, 1950-68; Secretary of Defense, USA, 1968-69. Director: Knight-Ridder Newspapers; Financial General Bankshares. Medal of Freedom with Distinction, USA, 1969. *Recreation:* golf. *Address:* 815 Connecticut Avenue, Washington, DC 20006, USA.

CLIFFORD, Sir (Geoffrey) Miles, KBE 1949 (OBE 1939); CMG 1944; ED; Médaille de la Résistance Française avec Rosette; *b* 1897; *m* 1st, 1920, Ivy Dorothy ("Peta") (decd), *y d* of Arthur Robert Eland, Thrapston, Northants; no *c*; 2nd, Mary, *e d* of late Thomas Turner, Shelbyville, Ill., USA. *Educ:* privately. Diploma in Anthropology, UCL; Fellow, UCL. Served European War (France and Flanders), 1914-18; Army of the Rhine, 1919-20. Comd Nigerian European Defence Force, 1938-40 (Special Duty, 1941-42). Entered Colonial Administrative Service (Nigeria), 1921; Acting Resident, Adamawa, 1934-37; Principal Asst Sec., 1938-41; seconded as Colonial Sec., Gibraltar, 1942-44; Senior Resident, Nigeria, 1944; Chm. Salaries Commn, Cyprus, 1945; attached CO, 1946; Governor and C-in-C of Falkland Islands, 1946-54. Chief Warden, Westminster, 1954-57; Mem., LCC, 1955-58; Hon. Organiser, Mental Health Research Fund, 1954-56; Dir, Leverhulme Trust, 1956-65; Cttee of Management, Trans-Antarctic Expedition, 1954; Mem., Antarctic Sub-Cttee, International Geophysical Year; Chm., British National Cttee on Antarctic Research, 1964-78; Cttee of Management, British Trans-Arctic Expedn, 1967; a Vice-Pres., RGS, 1956-62; St Paul's Cathedral Trust Council,

1962-78; a Trustee of Toc H; Vice-Pres., African Medical and Research Foundn; Life Gov., Imperial Cancer Research Fund; Trustee, E Grinstead Res. Trust; Mem., Management Cttee (co-opted), Inst. of Basic Med. Sciences; Hon. Treasurer, Soc. for Health Educn; Mem., Porritt Working Party on Med. Aid to Developing Countries and Chm. Anglo-Amer. Conf. on same theme, Ditchley, 1966; Chm. Planning Cttee, Chelsea Group of Post-graduate Hospitals; Chm. Cttee of Management, Inst. Latin American Studies, London Univ., 1964-78; Mem. Council Voluntary Service Overseas. Chm., Nigerian Electricity Supply Corp., 1957-77. Member: Inst. of Dirs; Ct of Patrons, RCS; a Governor, Sutton Valence Sch. Hon. FRCS; Hon. FDS, RCS. *Publications:* A Nigerian Chiefdom; Notes on the Bassa-Komo Tribe; book reviews and occasional contribs to the Press. *Address:* Kingswood Lodge, Trinity Close, Tunbridge Wells, Kent. *Clubs:* Athenæum; Antarctic (Hon. Mem.); Explorers' (New York) (Fellow).

CLIFFORD, Graham Douglas, CMG 1964; FCIS; Director, The Institution of Electronic and Radio Engineers, 1937-78, Hon. Fellow 1978; *b* 8 Feb. 1913; *s* of John William Clifford and Frances Emily Reece; *m* 1937, Marjory Charlotte Willmot; two *d* (one *s* decd). *Educ:* London schs and by industrial training. Molins Machine Co. Ltd, 1929; Columbia Graphophone Co. Ltd, 1931; American Machinery Co. Ltd, 1934. Secretary: Radio Trades Exam. Bd, 1942-65 (Hon. Mem. 1965); Nat. Electronics Council, 1961-70 (Hon. Treasurer, 1971-). For 40 years Editor of The Radio and Electronic Engineer and Electronics Rev. Hon. Mem., Assoc. of Engineers and Architects, Israel, 1966; Hon. Treasurer, UK Cttee for the Gandhi Centenary, 1969; Hon. Sec. and Governor, Nehru Meml Trust. Comdr, Order of Merit, Research and Invention, France, 1967. *Publications:* A Twentieth Century Professional Institution, 1960; (ed) Nehru Memorial Lectures, 1973; contribs to various technical journals. *Recreations:* photography, genealogy, music, but mainly work. *Address:* 45 West Park Lane, West Worthing, W Sussex BN12 4EP. *T:* Worthing 41423. *Club:* Royal Automobile.

CLIFFORD, Sir Miles; *see* Clifford, Sir G. M.

CLIFFORD, Rev. Paul Rowntree, MA; President, Selly Oak Colleges, Birmingham, 1965-79; *b* 21 Feb. 1913; *s* of Robert and Harriet Rowntree Clifford; *m* 1947, Marjory Jean Tait; one *s* one *d. Educ:* Mill Hill Sch.; Balliol Coll., Oxford; Mansfield and Regents Park Colls, Oxford. MA (Oxon) 1939. West Ham Central Mission, London: Asst Minister, 1938-43; Supt Minister, 1943-53; McMaster Univ., Hamilton, Canada: Asst Prof. of Homiletics and Pastoral Theology, 1953-59; Dean of Men and Chm. of Dept of Religion, 1959-64; Prof. of Religion, 1964-65. Hon. Treas., Internat. Assoc. for Mission Studies, 1974-; Sec., Foundn for Study of Christianity and Society, 1980-. Chm. Trustees and Governors, Fircroft Coll., Birmingham, 1979-. *Publications:* The Mission of the Local Church, 1953; The Pastoral Calling, 1959; Now is the Time, 1970; Interpreting Human Experience, 1971; The Death of the Dinosaur, 1977; articles in Jl of Religion, Metaphysical Review, Dialogue, Canadian Jl of Theology, Scottish Jl of Theology, Foundations, Religious Studies. *Recreations:* golf, gardening. *Address:* Crinan Cottage, Moss Road, Dalbeattie, Dumfries DG5 4NW. *Club:* Reform.

CLIFFORD, Sir Roger (Charles Joseph Gerrard), 6th Bt *cr* 1887; Manager, Rod Weir & Co. Ltd, Waikanae Stock and Station Agents, retired 1979; *b* 28 May 1910; *s* of Charles William Clifford, *d* 1939 (3rd *s* of 1st Bt) and Sicele Agnes (*d* 1948), *d* of Sir Humphrey de Trafford, 2nd Bt; *S* brother, 1970; *m* 1st, 1934, Henrietta Millicent Kiver (*d* 1971); two *s* one *d*; 2nd, 1973, Gretchen Patrice Pollock. *Educ:* Beaumont College, Old Windsor; Harper Adams Agricultural College. *Heir: er s* Roger Joseph Clifford [*b* 5 June 1936; *m* 1968, Joanna Theresa, *d* of C. J. Ward, Christchurch, NZ; one *d*]. *Address:* 8 Kea Street, Waikanae, New Zealand.

CLIFFORD, Timothy Peter Plint, BA, AMA; Director, Manchester City Art Galleries, since 1978; *b* 26 Jan. 1946; *s* of Derek Plint Clifford and Anne (*née* Pierson); *m* 1968, Jane Olivia, *yr d* of Sir George Paterson, *qv* ; one *d. Educ:* Sherborne, Dorset; Perugia Univ. (Dip. Italian); Courtauld Inst., Univ. of London (BA Hons, History of Art). Dip. Fine Art, Museums Assoc., 1972. Asst Keeper, Dept of Paintings, Manchester City Art Galleries, 1968-72, Acting Keeper, 1972; Asst Keeper (First Class), Dept of Ceramics, Victoria and Albert Mus., London, 1972-76; Asst Keeper (First Class), Dept of Prints and Drawings, British Mus., London, 1976-78. Member: Manchester Diocesan Adv. Cttee for Care of Churches, 1978-; NACF Cttee (Cheshire and Gtr Manchester Br.), 1978-; North Western Museum and Art Gall. Service Jt Adv. Panel, 1978-; Cttee, ICOM (UK), 1980-82; Chm., Internat. Cttee for Museums of Fine Art, ICOM, 1980-; Founder and Committee Member: Friends of Manchester City Art Galls, 1978-; Patrons and Associates, Manchester City Art Galls, 1979-. FRSA. *Publications:* (with Derek Clifford) John Crome, 1968; (with Dr Ivan Hall) Heaton Hall, 1972; (with Dr T. Friedmann) The Man at Hyde Park Corner: sculpture by John Cheere, 1974; Vues Pittoresques de Luxembourg ... par J. M. W. Turner, (Luxembourg) 1977; Ceramics of Derbyshire 1750-1975 (ed, H. G. Bradley), 1978; J. M. W. Turner, Acquerelli e incisioni, (Rome) 1980; Turner at Manchester, 1982; contrib. Burlington Magazine, etc. *Recreations:* shooting, bird watching, collecting butterflies and moths. *Address:* City of Manchester Art Galleries, Mosley Street, Manchester M2 3JL. *T:* 061-236 9422; The Clock House, Peover Park, Peover Superior, Knutsford, Cheshire. *T:* Lower Peover 2758. *Clubs:* Turf, Beefsteak; Literary and Philosophical Society (Manchester).

CLIFFORD, William Henry Morton, CB 1972; CBE 1966; Legal Consultant, Civil Service College, 1974-79, retired; *b* 30 July 1909; *s* of Henry Edward Clifford, FRIBA, Glasgow, and Margaret Alice, *d* of Dr William Gibson, Campbeltown, Argyll; *m* 1936, Katharine Winifred, *d* of Rev. H. W. Waterfield, Temple Grove, Eastbourne; one *s* two *d. Educ:* Tonbridge Sch.; Corpus Christi Coll., Cambridge. Admitted a solicitor, 1936. Entered Solicitor's Department, GPO, 1937. Served in Army, 1939-45: Major GS, Army Council Secretariat, WO, 1944-45. Transferred to Solicitor's Office, Min. of National Insurance, 1945; Assistant Solicitor, Min. of Pensions and Nat. Insurance (later Min. of Social Security), 1953; Solicitor, DHSS (formerly Min. of Social Security), 1968-74. *Recreations:* reading, listening to music (especially opera), genealogy, walking, sailing. *Address:* Woodbrook, 9 Lake Road, Tunbridge Wells, Kent. *T:* Tunbridge Wells 21612.

CLIFFORD-TURNER, Raymond; Senior Partner, Clifford-Turner, solicitors; *b* 7 Feb. 1906; *s* of Harry Clifford-Turner, solicitor; *m* 1933, Zoë Vachell; one *s* two *d. Educ:* Rugby Sch.; Trinity Coll., Cambridge. Solicitor, 1930; Partner, Clifford-Turner & Co., 1931. Dir, Transport Holding Co., 1962-73. Wing Commander, RAFVR. *Recreations:* golf, racing. *Address:* 86 Eaton Place, SW1. *T:* 01-235 2443; Childown, Stonehill Road, Longcross, Surrey. *Clubs:* Portland; Berkshire; Swinley.

See also Hon. A. G. Berry.

CLIFT, Richard Dennis; HM Diplomatic Service; Head of Hong Kong and General Department, Foreign and Commonwealth Office, since 1979; *b* 18 May 1933; *s* of late Dennis Victor Clift and of Helen Wilmot Clift (*née* Evans); *m* 1957, Barbara Mary Travis (marr. diss. 1982); three *d*; *m* 1982, Jane Rosamund Barker (*née* Homfray). *Educ:* St Edward's Sch., Oxford; Pembroke Coll., Cambridge. BA 1956. FO, 1956-57; Office of British Chargé d'Affaires, Peking, 1958-60; British Embassy, Berne, 1961-62; UK Delegn to NATO, Paris, 1962-64; FO, 1964-68; Head of Chancery, British High Commn, Kuala Lumpur, 1969-71; FCO, 1971-73; Counsellor (Commercial), Peking, 1974-76; Canadian Nat. Defence Coll., 1976-77; seconded to NI Office, 1977-79. *Recreations:* sailing, walking. *Address:* c/o Foreign and Commonwealth Office, SW1A 2AL. *Club:* Royal Commonwealth Society.

CLIFTON, Lord; Ivo Donald Stuart Bligh; *b* 17 April 1968; *s* and *heir* of 11th Earl of Darnley, *qv*.

CLIFTON, Bishop of (RC), since 1974; **Rt. Rev. Mervyn Alban Newman Alexander,** DD; *b* London, 29 June 1925; *s* of William Paul Alexander and Grace Evelyn Alexander (*née* Newman). *Educ:* Bishop Wordsworth School, Salisbury; Prior Park College, Bath; Gregorian University, Rome (DD 1951). Curate at Pro-Cathedral, Clifton, Bristol, 1951-63; RC Chaplain, Bristol University, 1953-67; Parish Priest, Our Lady of Lourdes, Weston-super-Mare, 1967-72; Auxiliary Bishop of Clifton and Titular Bishop of Pinhel, 1972-74; Vicar Capitular of Clifton, 1974. *Address:* St Ambrose, Leigh Woods, Bristol BS8 3PW. *T:* Bristol 33072.

CLIFTON, Lt-Col Peter Thomas, CVO 1980; DSO 1945; DL; JP; Standard Bearer, HM Body Guard of Honourable Corps of Gentlemen at Arms, 1979-81; *b* 24 Jan. 1911; *s* of Lt-Col Percy Robert Clifton, CMG, DSO, TD, Clifton Hall, Nottingham; *m* 1st, 1934, Ursula (marr. diss. 1936), *d* of Sir Edward Hussey Packe; 2nd, 1948, Patricia Mary Adela (who *m* 1935, Robert Cobbold, killed in action 1944), *d* of Major J. M. Gibson-Watt, Doldowlod, Radnorshire; two *d. Educ:* Eton; RMC Sandhurst. 2nd Lieut Grenadier Guards, 1931; served War of 1939-45: France, 1939-40; Italy, 1944-45; Lt-Col 1944; Palestine, 1945-47. Mem. HM Body Guard of Hon. Corps of Gentlemen at Arms, 1960-81 (Clerk of the Cheque and Adjutant, 1973-79). DL Notts 1954; JP Notts 1952-59, Hants 1964. *Address:* Dummer House, Basingstoke, Hants. *T:* Dummer 306. *Clubs:* Cavalry and Guards, White's; Royal Yacht Squadron.

See also Baron Gibson-Watt, Baron Wrottesley.

CLIFTON-BROWN, Anthony George, TD; late Major RA; formerly Director: Royal Exchange Assurance; Westminster Bank Ltd; Westminster Foreign Bank Ltd; Bank of New South Wales (London Board); one of HM Lieutenants for City of London, 1950-60; *b* 11 Feb. 1903; *y s* of late Edward Clifton-Brown; *m* 1st, 1930, Delia Charlotte (*d* 1947), *y d* of late George Edward Wade; three *d*; 2nd, 1949, Phyllis Adrienne McCulloch, (Bridget) (*d* 1977), *d* of late Francis Harvey, Dublin. *Educ:* Eton; Trinity Coll., Cambridge. Mem. of Court of Assistants, Merchant Taylors' Company (Master, 1945-46; First Upper Warden, 1955-56); Sheriff of the City of London, 1957-58; Alderman of Broad Street Ward, 1950-60. Chm., Management Cttee, Royal London Homœopathic Hosp., 1948-61. Commandatore of Order of Merit of Italian Republic. *Address:* Via del Moro 7, 00153 Rome, Italy.

CLIFTON-BROWN, Lt-Col Geoffrey Benedict; *b* 25 July 1899; *m* 1927, Robina Margaret (*d* 1979), *d* of late Rowland Sutton; two *s* (one *d* decd). *Educ:* Eton; RMC Sandhurst. 2nd Lieut 12th Lancers, 1918; Major, 1935; Lt-Col, 1940; served with 12th Lancers in France and Belgium, 1939-40, evacuated Dunkirk (despatches). MP (C) Bury St Edmunds Div. of West Suffolk, 1945-50. *Address:* Little Bradley House, near Haverhill, Suffolk. *T:* Thurlow 261.

CLIFTON-TAYLOR, Alec, OBE 1982; FSA; architectural historian and critic; *b* 2 Aug. 1907; *o s* of Stanley E. Taylor and E. E. Clifton Hills. *Educ:* Bishop's Stortford Coll.; Queen's Coll., Oxford (MA); Courtauld Inst. of Art, London (BA 1st Cl. Hons History of Art); Sorbonne, Paris (Dip.). FSA 1963; Hon. Brother, Art Workers Guild, 1976; Hon. FRIBA, 1979. Served War, Admiralty, 1940-46: Private Sec. to Parly Sec., 1943-46. Lectr, Univ. of London Inst. of Educn, and RCA, 1934-39; extra-mural lectr, London, 1946-57; Ferens Lectr in Fine Art, Univ. of Hull, 1981; since 1956 has lectured extensively all over Britain and (for univs, museums and art galls, British Council, and E-SU) in every continent, incl. 32 states of USA; occasional talks and television progs for BBC. Pres., Kensington Soc., 1979-; Vice-President: Men of the Stones; Soc. for Italic Handwriting; Patron, Avoncroft Mus. of Buildings; Trustee, Historic Churches Preservation Trust. *Publications:* The Pattern of English Building, 1962 (3rd edn 1972); The Cathedrals of England, 1967; English Parish Churches as Works of Art, 1974 (also transcribed into Braille); (with R. W. Brunskill) English Brickwork, 1977; *based on BBC TV series:* Spirit of the Age (contrib.), 1975; Six English Towns, 1978; Six More English Towns, 1981; contrib to over 20 books and to art jls, esp. The Connoisseur. *Recreations:* gazing at mountains, quizzing old churches and houses, painting, gardening, writing limericks, looking up other people in Who's Who. *Address:* 15 Clareville Grove, SW7 5AU. *T:* 01-373 7222. *Club:* Oxford Union (Oxford).

CLINCH, David John; Secretary, Open University, since 1981; *b* 14 Feb. 1937; *s* of Thomas Charles Clinch and Madge Isabel Clinch (*née* Saker); *m* 1963, Hilary Jacques; one *s* one *d. Educ:* Nautical Coll., Pangbourne; Univ. of Durham (BA); Indiana Univ. (MBA). National Service, Royal Navy (Sub-Lieut), Supply and Secretariat, 1955-57. Administrator, Univ. of Sussex, 1963-69; Deputy Secretary and Registrar, Open University, 1969-81. *Recreations:* music, reading, walking. *Address:* 39 Tudor Gardens, Stony Stratford, Milton Keynes MK11 1HX. *T:* Milton Keynes 562475.

CLINTON, 22nd Baron *cr* 1299 (title abeyant 1957-65); **Gerard Nevile Mark Fane Trefusis;** JP; DL; landowner; *b* 7 Oct. 1934; *s* of Capt. Charles Fane (killed in action, 1940); assumed by deed poll, 1958, surname of Trefusis in addition to patronymic; *m* 1959, Nicola Harriette Purdon Coote; one *s* two *d. Educ:* Gordonstoun. Took seat in House of Lords, 1965. Mem., Prince of Wales's Councils, 1968-79. JP Bideford, 1963; DL Devon, 1977. *Recreations:* shooting, fishing, forestry. *Heir: s* Hon. Charles Patrick Rolle Fane Trefusis, *b* 21 March 1962. *Address:* Heanton Satchville, near Okehampton, North Devon. *T:* Dolton 224, *Club:* Boodle's.

CLINTON, (Francis) Gordon, FRCM; FBSM; Hon. RAM; ARCM; baritone; Member, Board of Professors, Royal College of Music, since 1975; *b* 19 June 1912; *s* of Rev. F. G. Clinton, Broadway, Worcs; *m* 1939, Phyllis Jarvis, GRSM, ARCM; two *s* one *d. Educ:* Evesham Grammar Sch.; Bromley Sch. for Boys. Open Schol. RCM, 1935; Vicar Choral, St Paul's Cathedral, 1937-49; served War of 1939-45 in RAF; demobilised as Flt-Lieut. Appearances at over 2,000 major concerts and festivals (50 in Royal Albert Hall, 30 in Festival Hall, inc. inaugural concerts), 1946-; soloist, Beecham 70th birthday concert, 1949; joined staff, RCM, 1949; Principal, Birmingham Sch. of Music, 1960-74; Chorus Master, City of Birmingham Symph. Orch. Chorus, 1974-80. Examr to Associated Board, 1956-. Tours of America, Canada, Europe, Africa, Australasia, Scandinavia, Far East (singing, adjudicating, lecturing). *Recreations:* sport, wild-life. *Address:* 42 Pembroke Croft, Hall Green, Birmingham. *T:* 021-744 3513.

CLINTON, Robert Alan; Executive Member of Post Office Board (Member for Network and Developments), since 1981; *b* 12 July 1931; *s* of John and Leah Clinton; *m* 1956, Valerie Joy Falconer. *Educ:* George Dixon Grammar Sch., Edgbaston, Birmingham. On leaving school, joined the Post Office, 1948; Postal Headquarters: Member, North Western Postal Board, 1970; Asst Director (Personnel), London, 1975; Asst Director (Operations), London, 1976; Director of Eastern Postal Region, Colchester, 1978; Director of Postal Operations, London, 1979; Post Office Headquarters: Mem. Post Office Board, 1981-. FCIT 1982. Mem., Worshipful Company of Carmen; Freeman of City of London, 1979. *Recreations:* music, walking. *Address:* Binders, Colchester Road, St Osyth, Clacton-on-Sea, Essex CO16 8HA. *T:* St Osyth 820375. *Club:* City Livery.

CLITHEROE, 1st Baron *cr* (June) 1955, of Downham; Bt *cr* 1945 (succeeded to Btcy Sept. 1955); **Ralph Assheton,** PC 1944; KCVO 1977; KStJ; FSA; JP; DL; Lord-Lieutenant of Lancashire, 1971-76 (Vice-Lieutenant, 1956-71); High Steward of Westminster since 1962; *b* 24 Feb. 1901; *o s* of Sir Ralph Assheton, 1st Bt; *m* 1924, Hon. Sylvia Benita Frances Hotham, FRICS, FLAS, *d* of 6th Baron Hotham; two *s* one *d. Educ:* Eton (Oppidan Schol.); Christ Church, Oxford (MA). Called to Bar, Inner Temple, 1925; MP (Nat. U) Rushcliffe Div. of Notts, 1934-45; City of London, 1945-50; Blackburn West, 1950-55. Parly Sec., Min. of Labour and Min. of National Service, 1939-42; Parly Sec., Min. of Supply, 1942-43; Financial Sec. to the Treasury, 1943-44; Chm. Conservative Party Organisation, 1944-46; Chm. Public Accounts Cttee, 1948-50; Chm. Select Cttee on Nationalised Industries, 1951-53; Mem. Royal Commission on West Indies, 1938-39. Chm., Borax (Holdings) Ltd, 1958-69 (Dir, 1947-); Deputy Chairman: (Jt) National Westminster Bank Ltd until 1971 (formerly a Dep. Chm. National Provincial Bank); John Brown & Co. Ltd until 1971; Director: The Mercantile Investment Trust Ltd (Chm. 1958-71); Coutts & Co., 1955-71; formerly Director: Tube Investments Ltd (Dep. Chm.); Rio Tinto Zinc; Tanganyika Concessions Ltd; and other cos.

Pres., NW of England and IoM TAVR, 1973-75. DL 1955, JP 1934, Lancashire; Mem. Council, Duchy of Lancaster, 1956-77. *Heir: s* Hon. Ralph John Assheton [*b* 3 Nov. 1929; *m* 1961, Juliet, *d* of Christopher Hanbury; two *s* one *d. Educ:* Eton; Christ Church (Scholar), Oxford (MA)]. *Address:* 17 Chelsea Park Gardens, SW3. *T:* 01-352 4020; Downham Hall, Clitheroe, Lancs. *T:* Chatburn 210. *Clubs:* Carlton, Royal Automobile, MCC.
See also Sir W. M. J. Worsley, Bt.

CLITHEROW, Rt. Rev. Richard George, MA Cantab; *b* 1 Oct, 1909; *s* of H. G. Clitherow, MRCS, and Elizabeth Willis Clitherow; *m* 1941, Diana, *d* of H. St J. Durston; two *s* one *d. Educ:* Dulwich College; Corpus Christi College, Cambridge; Wells Theological College. Asst Curate, St Augustine, Bermondsey, 1936-40. Chaplain to the Forces, 1940-46 (despatches). Canon Residentiary, Guildford Cathedral, 1946-58; Bishop Suffragan of Stafford, 1958-74. *Recreations:* fishing and gardening. *Address:* 37 Fairbanks Walk, Swynnerton, Stone, Staffs.

CLIVE, Eric McCredie; a Scottish Law Commissioner, since 1981; *b* 24 July 1938; *s* of Robert M. Clive and Mary L. D. Clive; *m* 1962, Kay M. McLeman; one *s* three *d. Educ:* Univs of Edinburgh (MA, LLB with dist.); Michigan (LLM); Virginia (SJD). Solicitor. Lecturer 1962-69, Sen. Lectr 1969-75, Reader 1975-77, Professor of Scots Law 1977-81, Univ. of Edinburgh. *Publications:* (jtly) Law of Husband and Wife in Scotland, 1974; (jtly) Scots Law for Journalists, 1965, 3rd edn 1976; articles and notes in legal jls. *Recreations:* gardening, beekeeping. *Address:* 14 York Road, Edinburgh EH5 3EH. *T:* 031-552 2875.

CLIVE, Nigel David, CMG 1967; OBE 1959; MC 1944; TD; Editorial Consultant of Institute for the Study of Conflict, 1981-82; *b* 13 July 1917; *s* of late Horace David and Hilda Mary Clive; *m* 1949, Maria Jeanne Tambakopoulou. *Educ:* Stowe; Christ Church, Oxford (Scholar). Commissioned 2nd Mddx Yeomanry, 1939; served in Middle East and Greece. Joined Foreign Office, 1946; served Athens, 1946-48; Jerusalem, 1948; FO, 1948-50; Baghdad, 1950-53; FO, 1953-58; Tunis, 1958-62; Algiers, 1962-63; FO, 1964-65; Head of Information Research Dept, FCO (formerly FO), 1966-69; Adviser to Secretary-General of OECD, 1970-80. *Recreations:* reading, travel. *Address:* Flat 2, 41 Lowndes Square, SW1. *T:* 01-235 1186. *Clubs:* Brooks's, MCC.

CLOAKE, John Cecil, CMG 1977; HM Diplomatic Service, retired; *b* 2 Dec. 1924; *s* of late Dr Cecil Stedman Cloake, Wimbledon, and Maude Osborne Newling; *m* 1956, Margaret Thomure Morris, Washington, DC, USA; one *s. Educ:* King's Coll. Sch., Wimbledon; Peterhouse, Cambridge. Served in Army, 1943-46 (Lieut RE). Foreign Office, 1948; 3rd Sec., Baghdad, 1949, and Saigon, 1951; 2nd Sec., 1952; FO, 1954; Private Sec. to Permanent Under-Sec., 1956, and to Parly Under-Sec., 1957; 1st Sec., 1957; Consul (Commercial) New York, 1958; 1st Sec., Moscow, 1962; FO, 1963; DSAO, 1965; Counsellor, 1966; Head of Accommodation Dept, 1967; Counsellor (Commercial), Tehran, 1968-72; Fellow, Centre for International Studies, LSE, 1972-73; Head of Trade Relations and Exports Dept, FCO, 1973-76; Ambassador to Bulgaria, 1976-80. Member: Council, British Inst. for Persian Studies, 1981-; Cttee of Honour for Bulgarian 1300th Anniv., 1981. *Recreations:* gardening, painting, architecture, local history, geneaology. *Address:* 4 The Terrace, Richmond Hill, Richmond, Surrey TW10 6RN. *Club:* Travellers'.

CLODE, Dame (Emma) Frances (Heather), DBE 1974 (CBE 1969; OBE 1955; MBE 1951); Chairman, Women's Royal Voluntary Service, 1971-74; *b* 12 Aug. 1903; *d* of Alexander and Florence Marc; *m* 1927, Colonel Charles Clode (then Captain in Royal Norfolk Regt); one *s. Educ:* privately. Joined WRVS, 1939; served in Cambridge, 1940-45; WRVS Headquarters, 1945; Vice-Chm. 1967. CStJ 1973. *Address:* 1 Willow Close, Pershore, Worcs WR10 1JN. *Club:* Lansdowne.

CLOGHER, Bishop of, since 1980; **Rt. Rev. Gordon McMullan;** *b* 1934; *m* 1957, Kathleen Davidson; two *s. Educ:* Queen's Univ., Belfast (BSc Econ 1961, PhD 1971); Ridley Hall, Cambridge. ACIS 1957. Dipl. of Religious Studies (Cantab) 1978. Deacon 1962, priest 1963, dio. Down; Curate of Ballymacarrett, 1962-67; Central Adviser on Christian Stewardship to Church of Ireland, 1967-70; Curate of St Columba, Knock, Belfast, 1970-71; Rector of St Brendan's, East Belfast, 1971-76; Rector of St Columba, Knock, Belfast, 1976-80; Archdeacon of Down, 1979-80. *Address:* The See House, Thornfield, Fivemiletown, Co. Tyrone.

CLOGHER, Bishop of, (RC), since 1979; **Most Rev. Joseph Duffy,** DD; *b* 3 Feb. 1934; *s* of Edward Duffy and Brigid MacEntee. *Educ:* St Macartan's College, Monaghan; Maynooth College. MA, BD, HDipEd. Ordained priest, 1958; Teacher, 1960-72; Curate, 1972-79. *Publications:* Patrick in his own words, 1972; Lough Derg Guide, 1980. *Recreations:* local history, travel. *Address:* Bishop's House, Monaghan, Ireland. *T:* 047-81019.

CLOSE, Roy Edwin, CBE 1973; Director General, British Institute of Management, since 1976; *b* 11 March 1920; *s* of Bruce Edwin and Minnie Louise Close; *m* 1947, Olive Joan Forty; two *s. Educ:* Trinity Grammar Sch., N London. Served Army, 1939-46; SAS, 1943-46 (Captain). Editorial Staff, The Times; Asst Editor, The Times Review of Industry, 1949-56; Executive, Booker McConnell GP; Dir, Bookers Sugar Estates, 1957-65; Directing Staff, Admin. Staff Coll., Henley, 1965; Industrial Adviser, NEDO, 1966-69;

Industrial Dir, NEDO, 1969-73; MSc Univ. of Aston in Birmingham, 1973; Chm., Univ. of Aston Management Centre; Dean of Faculty of Management, 1973-76. CBIM (FBIM 1979); FIIM (FIWM 1979); FRSA 1980. *Publications:* various articles on industrial, economic subjects. *Recreations:* swimming, walking, reading, listening to music. *Address:* 5 Chester Mews, SW1. *T:* 01-235 3879; Cathedral Cottage, North Elmham, Norfolk. *Clubs:* Reform, Special Forces.

CLOSE-SMITH, Charles Nugent, TD 1953; Underwriting Member of Lloyd's (Deputy Chairman, 1970); *b* 7 July 1911; 2nd *s* of Thomas Close Smith, Boycott Manor, Buckingham, and Mary Morgan-Grenville, *d* of 11th Baroness Kinloss; *m* 1946, Elizabeth Vivien, *d* of late Major William Kinsman, DSO, Dublin; three *s. Educ:* Eton; Magdalene Coll., Cambridge. Entered Lloyd's, 1932; 2nd Lt, Royal Bucks Yeomanry, 1938. Served War of 1939-45 France and Burma (despatches); retd as Lt-Col, RA. Chairman Lloyd's Non-Marine Underwriters Assoc., 1965; elected to Committee of Lloyd's, 1967-70. *Recreation:* horticulture. *Address:* The Heymersh, Britford, Salisbury, Wilts. *T:* Salisbury 6760. *Clubs:* Boodle's, Gresham.

CLOSS, Prof. August, MA, DPhil; Professor of German and Head of German Department, University of Bristol, 1931-64, now Emeritus; Dean of the Faculty of Arts, 1962 and 1963; *b* 9 Aug. 1898; 4th *s* of late A. Closs; *m* 1931, Hannah Margaret Mary (*d* 1953), novelist and art-critic, *d* of late Robert Priebsch, Prof. and Medievalist at UCL; one *d. Educ:* Berlin, Vienna, Graz, London. Lectured at Sheffield Univ., 1929-30; at University Coll., London, 1930-31. Guest-Prof. at univs of Amsterdam, Ghent, Berlin, Heidelberg, Frankfurt A/M, Bern, Vienna, Rome, Florence, etc, and in the USA at Univs of Columbia, Princeton, Yale, California and at Canadian and Indian Univs. Hon. Fellow Hannover Univ.; Korresp. Mitglied der Deutschen Akademie; Membre Corresp. de l'Institut International des Arts et des Lettres (Zürich); Fellow of PEN. FRSL. Comdr, Cross of Order of Merit, West Germany; Austrian Cross of Merit *Litteris et Artibus. Publications:* Medieval Exempla: (Dame World) Weltlohn, 1934; The Genius of the German Lyric, 1938 (enlarged 2nd edn 1962, paperback edn 1965); German Lyrics of the Seventeenth Century, 1940, 1947; Hölderlin, 1942, 1944; Tristan und Isolt, 1944, 1974; Die Freien Rhythmen in der deutschen Dichtung, 1947; Novalis-Hymns to the Night, 1948; Die neuere deutsche Lyrik vom Barock bis zur Gegenwart, 1952, 1957; Deutsche Philologie im Aufriss; Woge im Westen, 1954; Medusa's Mirror; Reality and Symbol, 1957; The Harrap Anthology of German Poetry, 1957, new edn 1969; Reality and Creative Vision in German Lyrical Poetry (Symposium), 1963; Introductions to German Literature (4 vols), 1967; Twentieth Century German Literature, 1969, 2nd edn 1971; The Sea in the Shell, 1977; (ed) Briefwechsel, 1979; contribs to Times Literary and Educ. Supplements, German Life and Letters, Modern Lang. Rev., Euphorion, Reallexikon, Deutsches Literatur-Lexikon, Aryan Path, Germanistik, Universitas, and American journals. *Recreations:* music, collecting first editions. *Address:* 40 Stoke Hill, Stoke Bishop, Bristol BS9 1EX. *T:* Bristol 682244. *Club:* University of Bristol.

CLOTHIER, Sir Cecil (Montacute), KCB 1982; QC 1965; Parliamentary Commissioner for Administration, and Health Service Commissioner for England, Wales and Scotland, since 1979; *b* 28 Aug. 1919; *s* of Hugh Montacute Clothier, Liverpool; *m* 1943, Mary Elizabeth, *o d* of late Ernest Glover Bush; one *s* two *d. Educ:* Stonyhurst Coll.; Lincoln Coll., Oxford (BCL, MA). Served 1939-46, 51 (Highland) Div.; British Army Staff, Washington, DC; Hon. Lt-Col Royal Signals. Called to Bar, Inner Temple, 1950, Bencher, 1973. Recorder of Blackpool, later of the Crown Court, 1965-78; Judge of Appeal, IoM, 1972-78. A Legal Assessor to Gen. Medical and Gen. Dental Councils, 1972-78; Mem., Royal Commn on NHS, 1976-78. *Address:* Church House, Great Smith Street, SW1P 3BW. *T:* 01-212 7676.

CLOTWORTHY, Stanley Edward, CBE 1959; Chairman, Alcan Aluminium (UK) Ltd, 1969-74; *b* 21 June 1902; *s* of Joseph and Fanny Kate Clotworthy; *m* 1927, Winifred Edith, *d* of J. Mercer Harris; one *s* one *d. Educ:* Peter Symonds Sch., Winchester; University Coll., Southampton. Student apprenticeship with B. T. H. Ltd, Rugby, 1923-26; Macintosh Cable Co., Liverpool, 1926-27; Alcan Industries Ltd (formerly Northern Aluminium Co.), 1927-67. Pro-Chancellor, Southampton Univ., 1972-. Hon. DSc Southampton, 1969. *Recreations:* shooting, gardening. *Address:* Kemano, Warreners Lane, St George's Hill, Weybridge, Surrey. *T:* Weybridge 42904.

CLOUDSLEY-THOMPSON, Prof. John Leonard, MA, PhD (Cantab), DSc (London); FRES, FLS, FZS, FIBiol, FWA; Professor of Zoology, Birkbeck College, University of London, since 1972 (Reader 1971-72); *b* Murree, India, 23 May 1921; *s* of Dr Ashley George Gyton Thompson, MA, MD (Cantab), DPH, and Muriel Elaine (*née* Griffiths); *m* 1944, Jessie Anne Cloudsley, MCSP, DipBS, LCAD; three *s. Educ:* Marlborough Coll.; Pembroke Coll., Univ. of Cambridge. War of 1939-45: commissioned into 4th Queen's Own Hussars, 1941; transf. 4th Co. of Lond. Yeo. (Sharpshooters); N Africa, 1941-42 (severely wounded); Instructor (Capt.), Sandhurst, 1943; rejoined regt for D Day, escaped from Villers Bocage, Caen Offensive, etc, 1944 (Hon. rank of Capt. on resignation). Lectr in Zoology, King's Coll., Univ. of London, 1950-60; Prof. of Zoology, Univ. of Khartoum, and Keeper, Sudan Nat. Hist. Museum, 1960-71. Nat. Science Foundn Sen. Res. Fellow, Univ. of New Mexico, Albuquerque, USA, 1969; Vis. Prof., Univ. of Kuwait, 1978, Univ. of Nigeria, Nsukka, 1981. Took part in: Cambridge Iceland Expedn, 1947; Expedn to Southern Tunisia, 1954; univ.

expedns with his wife to various parts of Africa, 1960-73, incl. Trans-Sahara crossing, 1967. Chairman: British Naturalists' Assoc., 1974-83; Biological Council, 1977-82. Pres., British Arachnological Soc., 1982-. Vice-Pres., Linnean Soc., 1975-76 and 1977-78. Liveryman, Worshipful Co. of Skinners, 1952-. Royal African Soc's Medal, 1969. Silver Jubilee Medal and Hon. DSc, Khartoum, 1981. Editor, Jl of Arid Environments (assisted by wife). *Publications:* Biology of Deserts (ed), 1954; Spiders, Scorpions, Centipedes and Mites, 1958 (2nd edn 1968); Animal Behaviour, 1960; Rhythmic Activity in Animal Physiology and Behaviour, 1961; Land Invertebrates (with John Sankey), 1961; Life in Deserts (with M. J. Chadwick), 1964; Desert Life, 1965; Animal Conflict and Adaptation, 1965; Animal Twilight: man and game in eastern Africa, 1967; Microecology, 1967; Zoology of Tropical Africa, 1969; The Temperature and Water Relations of Reptiles, 1971; Desert Life, 1974; Terrestrial Environments, 1975; Insects and History, 1976; Evolutionary Trends in the Mating of Arthropoda, 1976; (ed jtly) Environmental Physiology of Animals, 1976; Man and the Biology of Arid Zones, 1977; The Water and Temperature Relations of Woodlice, 1977; The Desert, 1977; Animal Migration, 1978; Why the Dinosaurs Became Extinct, 1978; Wildlife of the Desert, 1979; Biological Clocks: their functions in nature, 1980; Tooth and Claw: defensive strategies in the animal world, 1980; contribs to Encyclopædia Britannica, Encyclopedia Americana; shorter monographs and children's books; many scientific articles in learned jls, etc. *Recreations:* music (especially opera), photography, travel. *Address:* Department of Zoology, Birkbeck College, Malet Street, WC1E 7HX; (home) Flat 9, 4 Craven Hill, W2 3DS; Little Clarkes, Little Sampford, Saffron Walden, Essex CB10 2SA.

CLOUGH, (John) Alan, CBE 1972; MC 1945; Chairman and Joint Managing Director, British Mohair Spinners Ltd, since 1980 (Deputy Chairman, 1970-80, Chief Executive, 1977-80); *b* 20 March 1924; *s* of John Clough and late Yvonne (*née* Dollfus); *m* 1st, 1949, Margaret Joy Catton (marr. diss.); one *s* two *d*; 2nd, 1961, Mary Cowan Catherwood; one *s* one *d. Educ:* Marlborough Coll.; Leeds Univ. HM Forces, Queen's Bays, 1942-47, N Africa and Italy (Captain); TA Major, Yorkshire Hussars, 1947-55. Director: Robert Clough (Keighley) Holdings Ltd; Smith (Allerton) Ltd; Keighley Fleece Mills Co. Ltd; Jeremiah Ambler Ltd, 1970-; Christopher Waud Ltd, 1970-; Worsted Spinners Fedn, 1964-; Crofton Yarns Ltd, 1968-; Stork Brothers Ltd; Jeremiah Ambler (Ulster) Ltd; Jarol Ltd; McHarg & Aird. Mayor, Co. of Merchants of Staple of England, 1969-70. Chm., Wool Industries Res. Assoc., 1967-69; Chm., Wool Textile Delegn, 1969-72; Member: Wool Textile EDC, 1967-72; Jt Textile Cttee, NEDO, 1972-74; President: Comitextil (Co-ordinating Cttee for Textile Industries in EEC), Brussels, 1975-77 (Pres. d'honneur, 1977-); British Textile Confedn, 1974-77; Textile Inst., 1979-81; Confedn of British Wool Textiles, 1982-. CompTI 1975. *Recreations:* fishing, gardening, travel. *Address:* Spitalcroft Green, Knaresborough, N Yorks. *T:* Harrogate 863232. *Club:* Boodle's.

CLOUGH, Prunella; painter; *b* 1919; *d* of Eric Clough Taylor, poet and civil servant, and Thora Clough Taylor. *Educ:* privately; Chelsea Sch. of Art. Exhibited at Leger Gallery, 1947; Roland Browse & Delbanco, 1949; Leicester Galleries, 1953; Whitechapel Gallery, 1960; Grosvenor Gallery, 1964, 1968; Graves Art Gallery, Sheffield, 1972; New Art Centre, 1975, 1979; Serpentine Gallery, 1976; Warwick Arts Trust, 1982. City of London Midsummer Prize, 1977. *Address:* 65 Moore Park Road, SW6.

CLOUSTON, Air Cdre (retd) Arthur Edmond, CB 1957; DSO 1943; DFC 1942; AFC and Bar, 1939; RAF retd; *b* 7 April 1908; *s* of R. E. Clouston, mining engineer, Motueka, Nelson, NZ; *m* 1937, Elsie, *d* of late S. Markham Turner, Farnborough, Hants; two *d. Educ:* Rockville Sch.; Bainham Sch. Joined Royal Air Force, 1930. Record Flight, London-Capetown-London, 1937 (Seagrave Trophy); Record Flight, London-NZ-London, 1938 (Britannia Trophy). Served War of 1939-45 (DFC, DSO), engaged in Research Test Flying, Fighter Comd, Coastal Comd; Comdt, Empire Test-Pilots Sch., Farnborough, 1950-53; AOC, Singapore, 1954-57; Comdt, Aeroplane and Armament Experimental Establishment, Boscombe Down, Amesbury, 1957-60. Group Capt. 1947; Air Cdre 1954. *Publication:* The Dangerous Skies (autobiography), 1954. *Address:* Wings, Constantine Bay, Padstow, Cornwall.

CLOUTMAN, Air Vice-Marshal Geoffrey William, CB 1980; FDSRCS; Director of Dental Services, Royal Air Force, 1977-80; *b* 1 April 1920; *s* of Rev. Walter Evans Cloutman and Dora Cloutman; *m* 1949, Sylvia Brown; three *d. Educ:* Cheltenham Grammar Sch.; Queen Mary Coll., and The London Hosp., Univ. of London. LDSRCS 1942, FDSRCS 1954. House Surg., London Hosp., 1942; joined RAFVR, 1942; War Service, UK and India; specialisation in preventive dentistry, 1948-55; dental hygiene trng; oral surgery appts, 1955-73: RAF Hosps, Fayid, Akrotiri, Aden, Wegberg, Wroughton, Uxbridge; Principal Dental Off., Strike Comd, 1973; QHDS, 1976-80. *Publications:* papers in Brit. Dental Jl and Dental Practitioner. *Recreations:* English church music, cricket, Rugby. *Address:* Willo-Bridge, Easton, Wells, Somerset. *T:* Priddy 580. *Club:* Royal Air Force.

CLOVER, His Honour Robert Gordon, TD 1951; QC 1958; JP; a Circuit Judge (formerly Judge of County Courts), 1965-82; *b* 14 Nov. 1911; *m* 1947, Elizabeth Suzanne (*née* McCorquodale); two *s. Educ:* Lancing Coll.; Exeter Coll., Oxford. MA, BCL Oxford. Called to Bar, Lincoln's Inn, 1935. Served in RA, 1939-45 (despatches, 1944). Practised on Northern Circuit, 1935-61; Recorder of Blackpool, 1960-61; Dep. Comr for purposes of Nat. Insurance

Acts, 1961-65; Dep. Chm., Bucks QS, 1969-71; Chm., Marlow Magistrates Court, 1972-79. JP Bucks, 1969. *Address:* 18 St Nicholas Place, Sheringham, Norfolk NR26 8LF.

CLOWES, A. W.; General Secretary, Ceramic and Allied Trades Union, since 1980; *b* 17 Dec. 1931. Has been in the Industry since leaving school. Asst Gen. Sec., Ceramic and Allied Trades Union, 1975-80. *Address:* Ceramic and Allied Trades Union, Hillcrest House, Garth Street, Hanley, Stoke-on-Trent, Staffordshire ST1 2AB. *T:* Stoke-on-Trent 24201.

CLOWES, Col Sir Henry (Nelson), KCVO 1981 (CVO 1977); DSO 1945; OBE 1953; *b* 21 Oct. 1911; *yr s* of late Major E. W. Clowes, DSO, Bradley Hall, Ashbourne, Derbs; *m* 1941, Diana Katharine, MBE, *er d* of late Major Basil Kerr, DSC; one *s. Educ:* Eton; Sandhurst. Served in Scots Guards, 1931-57: Adjt RMA Sandhurst, 1940-41; psc 1941; Bde Major 4th Inf. Bde, 1942-44; comd 2nd Bn Scots Guards, 1944-46; jssc 1947; cmd 1st Bn Scots Guards, 1947-50; War Office (AG4), 1950-52; AAG Scottish Comd, 1952-54; Lt-Col comdg Scots Guards, 1954-57; retired 1957. Mem. Her Majesty's Body Guard, 1961; Clerk of the Cheque and Adjt, 1966; Standard Bearer, 1973-76; Lieut, 1976-81. *Recreations:* shooting, fishing. *Address:* 57 Perrymead Street, SW6 3SN. *T:* 01-736 7901. *Clubs:* Cavalry and Guards, Pratt's, Shikar.

CLOYNE, Bishop of, (RC), since 1957; **Most Rev. John J. Ahern;** *b* 31 Aug. 1911; *s* of James Ahern and Ellen Mulcahy. *Educ:* St Colman's Coll., Fermoy; St Patrick's Coll., Maynooth; Irish Coll., Rome. Ordained, 1936. Prof. at St Colman's Coll., Fermoy, 1940-44; St Patrick's Coll., Maynooth, 1946-57. *Address:* Bishop's House, Cobh, Co. Cork, Ireland.

CLUCAS, Sir Kenneth (Henry), KCB 1976 (CB 1969); Permanent Secretary, Department of Trade, 1979-82; *b* 18 Nov. 1921; *o s* of late Rev. J. H. Clucas; *m* 1960, Barbara, *e d* of Rear-Adm. R. P. Hunter, USN (Retd), Washington, DC; two *d. Educ:* Kingswood Sch.; Emmanuel Coll., Cambridge. Royal Signals, 1941-46 (despatches). Joined Min. of Labour as Asst Principal, 1948; 2nd Sec. (Labour), British Embassy, Cairo, 1950; Principal, HM Treasury, 1952; Min. of Labour, 1954; Private Sec. to Minister, 1960-62; Asst Sec., 1962; Under-Sec., 1966-68; Sec., Nat. Bd for Prices and Incomes, 1968-71; First Civil Service Comr, and Dep. Sec., CSD, 1971-73; Dep. Sec., DTI, 1974; Permanent Sec., Dept of Prices and Consumer Protection, 1974-79. Director: Gestetner Holdings plc, 1982-; Carreras Rothmans Ltd, 1982-. Chm., Surrey and W Sussex Area Cttee, Nat. Assoc. of Citizens' Advice Bureaux, 1982-; Mem. Management Cttee, Godalming CAB, 1982-. *Address:* Cariad, Knoll Road, Godalming, Surrey. *T:* Godalming 6430. *Club:* Athenæum.

CLUFF, Algy; Chairman, since 1979, and Chief Executive, since 1971, Cluff Oil; Proprietor of The Spectator, since 1981; *b* 19 April 1940; *s* of Harold Cluff, Waldeshare House, Waldeshare, Kent. *Educ:* Stowe Sch. 2/Lieut, Grenadier Guards, 1959; Captain, Guards Independent Parachute Co., 1963; served W Africa, Cyprus, Malaysia, retd 1964. Ionian Bank Ltd, 1964-65. Contested (C) Ardwick (Manchester) Gen. Elec., 1966. Founded Cluff Oil, 1971; Chairman: Cluff Oil (Hong Kong) Ltd, 1980-; Cluff Oil (Pacific), 1982-. Member: Council, RGS, 1977-78; Council, Inst. of Directors, 1981-. *Recreations:* collecting travel books and 20th Century British paintings. *Address:* 10 Barton Street, SW1; Clova House, Lumsden, West Aberdeenshire AB5 4YJ. *T:* Lumsden 336. *Clubs:* White's, Brooks's, Beefsteak, Turf; Royal St George's (Sandwich); Travellers' (Paris).

CLUFF, John Gordon; *see* Cluff, Algy.

CLUSKEY, Frank; TD Dublin South Central, 1965-81 and since 1982; Member (Lab) from Ireland, European Parliament, since 1981; *b* April 1930; *m* Eileen Gillespie (decd); one *s* two *d. Educ:* St Vincent's Sch., Glasnevin; Harvard Univ., USA. A Branch Sec., Workers' Union of Ireland, 1954-68; Member, Dublin City Council, 1960-63; Lord Mayor of Dublin, 1968-69. Member: Cttee of Public Accounts and Cttee of Procedure, 1965-69 and 1970-73; Parly Sec. to Min. of Social Welfare, 1973-77; former Labour Opposition Front Bench Spokesman on Justice, Social Welfare, and Labour; Leader of the Labour Party, Ireland, 1977-81. *Address:* 1 Glasnevin Park, Dublin 11, Ireland.

CLUTTERBUCK, Vice-Adm. Sir David Granville, KBE 1968; CB 1965; *b* Gloucester, 25 Jan. 1913; *m* 1937, Rose Mere Vaile, Auckland, NZ; two *d.* Joined RN, 1929. Served War of 1939-45 (despatches twice): navigating officer of cruisers HMS Ajax, 1940-42, HMS Newfoundland, 1942-46 (present Japanese surrender at Tokyo). Subsequently commanded destroyers Sluys and Cadiz; Naval Attaché at British Embassy, Bonn; Capt. (D) of Third Training Squadron in HMS Zest, Londonderry, 1956-58; commanded cruiser HMS Blake; Chief of Staff to C-in-C Home Fleet and C-in-C Allied Forces Eastern Atlantic, 1963-66; Rear-Adm., 1963; Vice-Adm. 1966; Dep. Supreme Allied Comdr, Atlantic, 1966-68. Administrative Dir, Business Graduates Assoc. Ltd, 1969-. *Address:* 29 Elvaston Place, SW7. *Club:* Army and Navy.

CLUTTERBUCK, Edmund Harry Michael, OBE 1957; Director, Scottish & Newcastle Breweries Ltd, 1960-80 (Deputy Chairman, 1973-77); *b* 22 July 1920; *s* of Maj.-Gen. W. E. Clutterbuck, *qv*; *m* 1945, Anne Agatha Woodsend; one *s* three *d. Educ:* Winchester Coll.; New Coll., Oxford (MA). HM Forces, 1940-46. Joined William Younger & Co. Ltd, 1947; Dir, Scottish Brewers Ltd, 1955; Scottish & Newcastle Breweries Ltd: Techn. Man. Dir,

1965; Jt Man. Dir, 1970; Director: Scottish American Mortgage Co., 1962; Scottish Eastern Investment Trust, 1965; Scottish Widows' Fund, 1965 (Chm., 1979-81; Dep. Chm., 1981-82); Pres., European Brewery Convention, 1971-; Member: Heriot-Watt Univ. Court, 1959; Herring Industry Bd, 1963-81; White Fish Authority, 1973-81; Dep. Chm., Royal Inst. of Internat. Affairs (Scottish Br.), 1969. *Recreations:* music, fishing, shooting, travel, languages. *Address:* Greystane, 4 Kinellan Road, Edinburgh EH12 6ES. *T:* 031-337 6027. *Club:* New (Edinburgh).

CLUTTERBUCK, Maj.-Gen. Richard Lewis, CB 1971; OBE 1958; Senior Lecturer in Politics, University of Exeter, since 1972; *b* London, 22 Nov. 1917; *s* of late Col L. St J. R. Clutterbuck, OBE, late RA, and late Mrs I. J. Clutterbuck; *m* 1948, Angela Muriel Barford; three *s. Educ:* Radley Coll.; Pembroke Coll., Cambridge. MA Cantab (Mech. Scis); PhD (Econ. and Pol.), London Univ., 1971. Commd in RE, 1937; War Service: France, 1940; Sudan and Ethiopia, 1941; Western Desert, 1941-43; Italy, 1944; subseq. service in: Germany, 1946 and 1951-53; Italy, 1946; Palestine, 1947; Malaya, 1956-58; Christmas Island (Nuclear Trials), 1958; USA, 1961-63; Singapore, 1966-68. Instructor, British Army Staff Coll., 1953-56; Instructor, US Army Staff Coll., 1961-63; idc 1965; Chief Engr, Far East Land Forces, 1966-68; Engr-in-Chief (Army), 1968-70; Chief Army Instructor, Royal Coll. of Defence Studies, 1971-72, retired. Col Comdt, RE, 1972-77. FICE. *Publications:* Across the River (as Richard Jocelyn), 1957; The Long Long War, 1966; Protest and the Urban Guerrilla, 1973; Riot and Revolution in Singapore and Malaya, 1973; Living with Terrorism, 1975; Guerillas and Terrorists, 1977; Britain in Agony, 1978, rev. edn 1980; Kidnap and Ransom, 1978; The Media and Political Violence, 1981; contribs to British and US jls. *Address:* Department of Politics, University of Exeter, Exeter. *Clubs:* Royal Commonwealth Society, Army and Navy.

CLUTTERBUCK, Maj.-Gen. Walter Edmond, DSO 1943; MC; *b* 17 Nov. 1894; *s* of E. H. Clutterbuck, JP, Hardenhuish Park, Chippenham, Wilts; *m* 1919, Gwendolin Atterbury (*d* 1975), *o d* of H. G. Younger, JP, Benmore, Argyllshire; one *s* three *d. Educ:* Horris Hill; Cheltenham Coll.; RMC Sandhurst. Commissioned Royal Scots Fusiliers, 1913; served European War, 1914-19, France, Gallipoli, Egypt, Palestine, and S Russia (wounded twice, MC and bar, Crown of Italy, 1914 Star and clasp, despatches twice); Bt Lt-Col 1939; War of 1939-45 commanded: 1st Royal Scots Fusiliers, 1939-40; 10th Inf. Bde, 1940-41; 1st Div., 1941-43, N Africa and Pantellaria (DSO, Legion of Honour); an Inf. Div. Home Forces, 1943. Chief of British Military Mission to Egypt, 1945-46; retired pay, 1946. *Recreations:* hunting, fishing, shooting. *Address:* Hornby Castle, Bedale, N Yorks. *T:* Richmond 811579. *Club:* Naval and Military.

See also E. H. M. Clutterbuck.

CLUTTON, Rafe Henry, FRICS; Partner in Cluttons, Chartered Surveyors, London, since 1955; *b* 13 June 1929; *s* of late Robin John Clutton and Rosalie Muriel (*née* Birch); *m* 1954, Jill Olwyn Evans; four *s* one *d. Educ:* Tonbridge Sch., Kent. FRICS 1959. Director, Legal & General Assurance Soc. Ltd, 1972-. Member: National Theatre Bd, 1976-; Salvation Army London Adv. Bd, 1971-. Governor, Royal Foundn of Grey Coat Hosp., 1967-. *Recreations:* occasional sailing and perpetual gardening. *Address:* Fairfield, North Chailey, Sussex. *T:* Newick 2431. *Clubs:* Royal Thames Yacht, City of London.

CLUTTON-BROCK, Arthur Guy; independent social worker, 1965-72, retired; *b* 5 April 1906; *s* of late Henry Alan Clutton-Brock and late Rosa Clutton-Brock; *m* 1934, Francys Mary Allen; one *d. Educ:* Rugby Sch.; Magdalene Coll., Cambridge (Hon. Fellow, 1973). Cambridge House, 1927; Rugby House, 1929; Borstal Service, 1933; Principal Probation Officer for the Metropolitan Police Court District, 1936; Head of Oxford House, 1940; Christian Reconstruction in Europe, 1946; Agricultural Labourer, 1947; Agriculturalist at St Faith's Mission, 1949; Field Worker of African Development Trust, 1959-65; deported from Rhodesia by rebel regime, 1971. Treasurer, Cold Comfort Farm Soc., 1966. *Publications:* Dawn in Nyasaland, 1959; Cold Comfort Confronted, 1973. *Address:* Gelli Uchaf, Llandyrnog, Clwyd LL16 4HR.

CLUVER, Eustace Henry, ED; MA; DM, ChB Oxon; DPH London; FRSH; Emeritus Professor of Medical Education, University of the Witwatersrand, Johannesburg, SA, since 1963; *b* 28 Aug. 1894; *s* of late Dr F. A. Cluver, Stellenbosch; *m* 1929, Eileen Ledger; three *d. Educ:* Victoria Coll., Stellenbosch; Hertford Coll., Oxford (Rhodes scholar). 1st class Final Hon. Sch. of Physiology, 1916. Elected to a Senior Demyship at Magdalen Coll., 1917; King's Coll. (Burney Yeo Scholarship, 1918). Served European War, 1914-18 (Capt. S Af. Med. Corps, BEF, France); War of 1939-45 (Col Dir of Pathology, S Af. Med. Corps). Prof. of Physiology, Univ. of the Witwatersrand, Johannesburg, 1919-26; Sec. for Public Health and Chief Health Officer for the Union of South Africa, 1938-40; Dir of S African Inst. for Med. Research and Prof. of Preventive Medicine, Univ. Witwatersrand, 1940-59. LLD (*hc*) Witwatersrand, 1974. KStJ. *Publications:* Public Health in South Africa, 1934 (Textbook), 6th edn 1959; Social Medicine, 1951; Medical and Health Legislation in the Union of South Africa, 1949, 2nd edn 1960; papers in scientific and medical journals. *Address:* Mornhill Farm, PO Box 226, Walkerville, Transvaal, 1876, South Africa.

CLWYD, 2nd Baron *cr* 1919; **John Trevor Roberts;** Bt, 1908; Assistant Secretary of Commissions, Lord Chancellor's Department of House of Lords, 1948-61; *b* 28 Nov. 1900; *s* of 1st Baron and Hannah (*d* 1951), *d* of W. S.

Caine, MP; S father, 1955; m 1932, Joan de Bois, d of late Charles R. Murray, Woodbank, Partickhill, Glasgow; one s one d. Educ: Gresham's Sch.; Trinity Coll., Cambridge. BA 1922. Barrister, Gray's Inn, 1930. JP County of London, 1950. Recreation: fishing. Heir: s Hon. (John) Anthony Roberts [b 2 Jan. 1935; m 1969, Geraldine, yr d of C. E. Cannons, Sanderstead; three s]. Address: 15 Aubrey Road, W8. T: 01-727 7911; Trimmings, Gracious Street, Selborne, Hants.

CLWYD, Ann, (Ann Clwyd Roberts); journalist and broadcaster; Member (Lab) Mid and West Wales, European Parliament, since 1979; b 21 March 1937; d of Gwilym Henri Lewis and Elizabeth Ann Lewis; m 1963, Owen Dryhurst Roberts, Assistant to Head of Programmes, BBC Wales. Educ: Halkyn Primary Sch.; Holywell Grammar Sch.; The Queen's Sch., Chester; University Coll., Bangor. Former: Student-teacher, Hope Sch., Flintshire; BBC Studio Manager; freelance reporter, producer; Welsh corresp., The Guardian and The Observer, 1964-79; Vice-Chm., Welsh Arts Council, 1975-79. Member: Welsh Hospital Board, 1970-74; Cardiff Community Health Council, 1975-; Royal Commn on NHS, 1976-79; Working Party, report, Organisation of Out-Patient Care, for Welsh Hosp. Bd; Working Party, Bilingualism in the Hospital Service; Labour Party Study Gp., People and the Media; Arts Council of Gt Britain, 1975-80; Chm., Cardiff Anti-Racialism Cttee, 1978-. Member: NUJ; TGWU. Contested (Lab): Denbigh, 1970; Gloucester, Oct. 1974. Address: 1 Lon Werdd, St Fagans, Cardiff. T: Cardiff 593492.

CLYDE, James John, QC (Scot.) 1971; b 29 Jan. 1932; s of Rt Hon. Lord Clyde; m 1963, Ann Clunie Hoblyn; two s. Educ: Edinburgh Academy; Corpus Christi Coll., Oxford (BA); Edinburgh Univ. (LLB). Called to Scottish Bar, 1959; Advocate-Depute, 1973-74. Contested (C) Dundee East, 1974. Chancellor to Bishop of Argyll and the Isles, 1972-. Mem., Scottish Valuation Adv. Council, 1972-; Chm., Med. Appeal Tribunal, 1974-; a Judge of the Courts of Appeal of Jersey and Guernsey, 1979-. Publications: (ed jtly) Armour on Valuation, 3rd edn, 1961, 4th edn, 1971. Recreations: music, golf, walking. Address: 9 Heriot Row, Edinburgh EH3 6HU. T: 031-556 7114. Club: New (Edinburgh).

CLYDESMUIR, 2nd Baron cr 1948, of Braidwood; Ronald John Bilsland Colville, KT 1972; CB 1965; MBE 1944; TD; Lord High Commissioner to the General Assembly, Church of Scotland, 1971 and 1972; Lord-Lieutenant, Lanarkshire, since 1963; Lieutenant, Royal Company of Archers, Queen's Body Guard for Scotland; b 21 May 1917; s of 1st Baron Clydesmuir, PC, GCIE, TD, and Agnes Anne (d 1970), CI 1947, Kaisar-i-Hind Gold Medal; S father, 1954; m 1946, Joan Marguerita, d of Lt-Col E. B. Booth, DSO, Darver Castle, Co. Louth; two s two d. Educ: Charterhouse; Trinity Coll., Cambridge. Served in The Cameronians (Scottish Rifles), 1939-45 (MBE, despatches). Commanded 6/7th Bn The Cameronians, TA, 1953-56. Director: Colvilles Ltd, 1958-70; British Linen Bank (Governor, 1966-71); Bank of Scotland (Dep. Governor, 1971-72, Governor, 1972-81); Scottish Provident Instn, 1954-; Scotbits Securities Ltd, 1960-; The Scottish Western Investment Co., 1965-78; BSC Strip Mills Div., 1970-73; Caledonian Offshore Co. Ltd, 1971-; Barclays Bank, 1972-; Chm., North Sea Assets Ltd, 1972-. President: Scottish Council (Development and Industry), 1978- (Chm., Exec. Cttee, 1966-78); Scottish Council of Physical Recreation, 1964-72; Scottish Br., National Playing Fields Assoc.; Chm., Council, Territorial, Auxiliary and Volunteer Reserve Assocs, 1969-73, Pres., 1974-81; Chm., Lanarkshire T&AFA, 1957-63, Pres. 1963-68; Pres. Lowland TA&VRA. Hon. Colonel: 6th/7th (Territorial) Bn, The Cameronians (Scottish Rifles), 1967-71; 52 Lowland Volunteers, T&AVR, 1970-75. Chm., Scottish Outward Bound Assoc. Trustee, MacRobert Trusts. DL Lanarkshire, 1955, Vice-Lieut, 1959-63. Hon. LLD Strathclyde, 1968; Hon. DSc Heriot-Watt, 1971. Recreations: shooting, fishing. Heir: s Hon. David Ronald Colville [b 8 April 1949; m 1978, Aline Frances, er d of Peter Merriam, Holton Lodge, Holton St Mary, Suffolk]. Address: Langlees House, Biggar, Lanarkshire. T: Biggar 20057. Clubs: Caledonian; New (Edinburgh).
See also Captain N. E. F. Dalrymple Hamilton.

COADY, Aubrey William Burleton, CMG 1959; Chairman, Electricity Commission of NSW, 1959-75 (Member since 1950); b Singleton, NSW, 15 June 1915; s of W. A. Coady, Belmont; m 1964, Phyllis K., d of late G. W. Mathews. Educ: Newcastle High Sch.; Sydney Univ. (BA, BEc). Under-Sec. and Comptroller of Accounts, NSW Treasury, 1955-59. Address: 42 Rickard Avenue, Mosman, NSW 2088, Australia.

COAKER, Maj.-Gen. Ronald Edward, CB 1972; CBE 1963; MC 1942; b 28 Nov. 1917; s of late Lieut-Col Vere Arthur Coaker, DSO, and Cicely Annie Coaker (née Egerton), Richard's Hill, Battle, Sussex; m 1946, Constance Aimée Johanna, d of Francis Newton Curzon, Lockington Hall, Derby; one s two d. Educ: Wellington; RMC, Sandhurst. 2nd Lieut IA (Skinner's Horse), 1937; served War of 1939-45, Middle East, Italy and Burma; transf. 17th/21st Lancers, 1947; Lt-Col 1954; GSO1, 7th Armoured Div., 1954-56; comd 17th/21st Lancers, 1956-58; Col GS to Chief of Defence Staff, 1958-60; Brig. 1961; Commandant RAC Centre, 1961-62; Dir of Defence Plans (Army), 1964-66; Assistant Chief of Staff (Intelligence), SHAPE, 1967-70; Dir of Military Operations, MoD, 1970-72. Maj.-Gen. 1966; retired 1972. Col 17th/21st Lancers, 1965-75. DL Rutland, 1973; High Sheriff of Leicestershire, 1980. Recreations: agriculture, field sports, bridge. Address: Daleacre House, Lockington, Derby DE7 2RH. T: Kegworth 3339. Club: Cavalry and Guards.

COALES, Prof. John Flavell, CBE 1974 (OBE 1945); FRS 1970; FEng; Professor of Engineering (Control), Cambridge University, 1965-74, now Emeritus; Fellow of Clare Hall, 1964-74, now Emeritus; b 14 Sept. 1907; s of John Dennis Coales and Marion Beatrice Coales (née Flavell); m 1936, Mary Dorothea Violet, d of Rev. Guthrie Henry Lewis Alison; two s two d. Educ: Berkhamsted Sch.; Sidney Sussex Coll., Cambridge (MA). Admty Dept of Scientific Res., 1929-46; Res. Dir, Elliott Bros (London) Ltd, 1946; Engrg Dept, Cambridge Univ.: Asst Dir of Res., 1953; Lectr, 1956; Reader in Engrg, 1958; Prof., 1965. Part-time Mem., E Electricity Bd, 1967-73. Director: Tube Investments Technological Centre, 1955-60; TI R&D Bd, 1960-65; BSA Metal Components, 1967-73; BSA Gp Res. Bd (Chm.), 1967-73; Delta Materials Research Ltd, 1974-77. Mackay Vis. Prof. of Electrical Engrg, Univ. of Calif., Berkeley, 1963. Internat. Fedn of Automatic Control: MEC, 1957; Vice-Pres., 1961; Pres., 1963. Brit. Conf. on Automation and Computation: Gp B Vice-Chm., 1958; Chm., 1960. UK Automation Council: Chm. Res. and Develt Panel, 1960-63; Chm. For. Relations Panel, 1960-64; Vice-Chm., 1961-63; Chm., 1963-66. Instn of Electrical Engrs: Mem. Council, 1953-55, 1964-77; Chm., Measurement Section, 1953; Chm., Control and Automation Div., 1965, etc; Vice-Pres., 1966-71; Pres., 1971-72. Council of Engineering Institutions: Vice-Chm., 1974; Chm., 1975 (Mem. Council for Envtl Sci. and Engrg, 1973-); World Environment and Resources Council, Pres., 1973-74. Pres., Soc. of Instrument Technology, 1958. Past Member, Gen. Bd and Exec. Cttee of Nat. Physical Laboratory; Member: Adv. Council, RMCS, 1963-73; Educn Adv. Cttee for RAF, 1967-76; Trng and Educn Adv. Cttee of RAF, 1976-; Court of Cranfield Inst. of Technology, 1970-; Governing Body, Nat. Inst. of Agric. Engrg, 1970-75; Envtl Design and Engrg Res. Cttee, DoE Bldg Res. Estab., 1973-; British Council Sci. Adv. Cttee, 1973-75; Engrg and Bldgs Bd, ARC, 1973-77; British Library Adv. Council, 1975-; Chm., IFAC Pubns Managing Bd, 1976-. Governor: Hatfield Coll. of Technology, 1951-68; Hatfield Polytechnic, 1969-70 (Hon. Fellow, 1971-). FICE, FIEE (Pres., IEE, 1971-72), FIEEE, FIAgrE, FInstP; Founder Fellow, Fellowship of Engineering, 1976 (Mem., Exec. Cttee and Chm., Activities Cttee, 1976-80); Hon. Mem., Inst. of Measurement and Control, 1971. For. Mem., Serbian Acad. of Scis, 1981. Hon. DSc City Univ., 1970; Hon. DTech Loughborough, 1977; Hon. DEng Sheffield, 1978. Harold Hartley Medal, 1971; Giorgio Quazza Medal, IFAC, 1981 (first recipient); Honda Prize, 1982. Publications: (ed) Automatic and Remote Control (Proc. First Congr. of Internat. Fedn of Automatic Control), 1961; original papers on radio direction finding, radar, information theory, magnetic amplifiers, automatic control, automation and technical education. Recreations: mountaineering, farming, gardening. Address: 4 Latham Road, Cambridge CB2 2EQ. Clubs: Athenæum, Alpine.

COATE, Maj.-Gen. Sir Raymond Douglas, KBE 1967; CB 1966; Chairman, Royal Homes for Officers' Widows and Daughters, Queen Alexandra's Court, Wimbledon, since 1969; b 8 May 1908; s of Frederick James and Elizabeth Anne Coate; m 1939, Frances Margaret Varley; two s. Educ: King Edward's Sch., Bath; RMC Sandhurst. Commissioned into Devonshire Regt, 1928; transferred to Royal Army Pay Corps, 1937; Paymaster-in-Chief, 1963-67; Col Comdt RAPC, 1970-74. Address: 18 Roehampton Close, SW15 5LU.

COATES, Sir Anthony Robert M.; see Milnes Coates.

COATES, Edith, OBE 1977; Principal Dramatic Mezzo-Soprano, Royal Opera, Covent Garden, 1947; b Lincoln, 31 May 1908; d of Percy and Eleanor Coates, Leeds; m 1933, Harry Powell Lloyd. Educ: Trinity Coll. of Music, London. Principal Mezzo, Sadler's Wells, 1935 (Carmen, Delilah, Azucena, Ortrud, Amneris, etc); Principal Mezzo, Covent Garden, 1937 (first appearance there under Sir Thomas Beecham, and in The Ring under Furtwängler, in Coronation season and 1938, 1939); Sadler's Wells, New Theatre and Provinces, singing many roles during War of 1939-45 and in Germany after war. Created role of Auntie in Britten's Peter Grimes, Sadler's Wells, 1945, and afterwards sang it at Paris Opera, Monnaie, Brussels and Covent Garden; has sung over 60 roles in opera; many oratorios, Royal Albert Hall, BBC and Provinces; many concerts and broadcasts; sang title role in Covent Garden in Tchaikowsky's Queen of Spades under Kleiber, 1950-51; sang in first English performances of Berg's Wozzeck, 1952; sang in first performance of Tippett's Midsummer Marriage, Covent Garden, 1955, Janacek's Jenufa, Covent Garden, 1956, and John Gardner's Moon and Sixpence, Sadler's Wells, 1957; played in Candide (Hillman-Bernstein after Voltaire), Saville, 1959; Countess in Queen of Spades, Covent Garden, 1961; sang in first performances of Grace Williams' Opera, The Parlour, Welsh National Opera, Cardiff, 1966; English Opera Group, 1963, 1965, 1967. Hon. FTCL. Recreations: reading, walking. Address: Montrose, Cross Lane, Findon, Worthing, West Sussex. T: Findon 2040. Club: Lansdowne.

COATES, Sir Ernest (William), Kt 1973; CMG 1970; State Director of Finance and Permanent Head of Victoria Treasury, Australia, 1959-77; b 30 Nov. 1916; s of Thomas Atlee Coates; m 1st, 1943, Phyllis E. Morris (d 1971); one s three d ; 2nd, 1974, Patricia Ann, d of late C. A. Fisher, Herts. Educ: Ballarat High Sch.; Univ. of Melbourne. BCom. Member: Bd of State Savings Bank of Victoria, 1960-77; Nat. Debt Commn, Australia, 1963-78; Australian Universities Commn, 1968-77; Aust. Administrative Appeals Tribunal, 1978-. Director: Kinnears Ltd; Equity Trustees Executors and Agency Co. Ltd. Chairman: Australian Selection Cttee, Harkness Fellowships; Rhodes Scholarship Selection Cttee (Victoria), 1981 (Mem., 1977-81). Hon. LLD Melbourne, 1979. Recreations: golf, music. Address: 64 Molesworth Street,

Kew, Victoria 3101, Australia. *T:* 8618226. *Clubs:* Melbourne (Melbourne); Green Acres Golf, Lorne Golf.

COATES, Brig. Sir Frederick (Gregory Lindsay), 2nd Bt *cr* 1921; *b* 19 May 1916; *o s* of Sir William Frederick Coates, 1st Bt, Belfast, N Ireland; *S* father, 1932; *m* 1940, Joan Nugent, *d* of late Maj.-Gen. Sir Charlton Spinks, KBE, DSO; one *s* two *d. Educ:* Eton; Sandhurst. Commissioned Royal Tank Regt, 1936; Served War of 1939-45, North Africa and NW Europe. Min. of Supply, 1947-53; Asst Military Attaché, Stockholm, 1953-56; British Joint Services Mission, Washington, 1956-58; Comdt, RAC School of Tank Technology, 1958-61; Asst Dir of Fighting Vehicles, and Col GS, War Office and MoD, 1961-66; Brig., British Defence Staff, Washington, DC, 1966-69; Mil. Dep. to Head of Defence Sales, 1969-71; retired 1971. *Heir:* s David Charlton Frederick Coates [*b* 16 Feb. 1948; *m* 1973, Christine Helen, *d* of Lewis F. Marshall; two *s. Address:* Launchfield, Briantspuddle, Dorchester, Dorset DT2 7HN. *Clubs:* Royal Yacht Squadron; RMYC; Island Sailing; RAC Yacht.

COATES, Prof. Geoffrey Edward, MA, DSc; Professor of Chemistry, University of Wyoming, since 1968; *b* 14 May 1917; *er s* of Prof. Joseph Edward Coates, OBE; *m* 1951, Winifred Jean Hobbs; one *s* one *d. Educ:* Clifton Coll.; Queen's Coll., Oxford. Research Chemist, Magnesium Metal Corp., 1940-45; Univ. of Bristol: Lecturer in Chemistry, 1945-53; Sub-Warden of Wills Hall, 1946-51; Prof. of Chemistry, Univ. of Durham, 1953-68. *Publications:* Organo-metallic Compounds (monograph), 1956, 4th edn (in 3 vols), 1979-; Principles of Organometallic Chemistry, 1968; papers in scientific journals. *Address:* Chemistry Department, University of Wyoming, Laramie, Wyoming 82071, USA. *Club:* Royal Commonwealth Society.

COATES, James Richard; Director, London Region Property Services Agency, since 1979; *b* 18 Oct. 1935; *s* of William Richard Coates and Doris Coral (*née* Richmond); *m* 1969, Helen Rosamund Rimington; one *s* one *d. Educ:* Nottingham High Sch.; Clare Coll., Cambridge (MA). Joined Ministry of Transport, 1959; Private Sec. to Permanent Sec., 1962-63; Principal, 1963; Private Sec. to Secretary of State for Local Govt and Regional Planning, 1969, and to Minister of Transport, 1970-71; Asst Sec., Dept of the Environment, 1971; Under Secretary, 1977. *Recreations:* listening to music, gardening, renovating old houses. *Address:* 10 Alwyne Road, Canonbury, N1 2HH. *T:* 01-359 7827.

COATES, John Francis, OBE 1955; FRINA; Deputy Director, Ship Design, Ministry of Defence, 1977-79, retired; *b* 30 March 1922; *s* of Joseph Edward Coates and Ada Maria Coates; *m* 1954, Jane Waymouth; two *s. Educ:* Clifton Coll.; Queen's Coll., Oxford (MA 1946). RCNC; FRINA 1969. Entered RCNC, 1943; Constructor: Chatham Dockyard, 1951; Naval Construction Res. Estabt, Dunfermline, 1953; Ship Dept, MoD, 1957; Chief Constructor, Fleet Maintenance, 1964; Hd of Forward Design, Ship Dept, 1970; RCDS, 1971; Supt, Naval Construction Res. Estabt, Dunfermline, 1974. *Recreation:* nautical research. *Address:* Sabinal, Lucklands Road, Bath BA1 4AU. *T:* Bath 23696.

COATES, Michael Arthur, FCA; Chairman, Price Waterhouse, World Firm, since 1982; *b* 12 May 1924; *yr s* of Joseph Michael Smith Coates, OBE, Elmfield, Wylam, Northumberland, and late Lillian Warren Coates (*née* Murray); *m* 1st, 1952, Audrey Hampton Thorne (marr. diss. 1970); one *s* two *d*; 2nd, 1971, Sally Rogers (marr. diss. 1980). *Educ:* Uppingham Sch. Admitted Mem., Inst. of Chartered Accountants, 1951. Served RA, mainly in ME and Italy, 1942-47. Articled with Price Waterhouse & Co., Newcastle, 1942; returned to Price Waterhouse, 1947; transf. to London, 1954; Partner, Price Waterhouse & Co., 1959-82, Dep. Sen. Partner, 1974-75, Sen. Partner, 1975-82; Chm., Price Waterhouse Internat. Manpower Cttee, 1971-74; Mem., Policy Cttee, 1974-. *Recreations:* diverse, including music, modern painting, antiques, gardens, reading, railways, photography. *Address:* The Old Rectory, Avon Dassett, Leamington Spa, Warwicks. *T:* Farnborough (Banbury) 472; 20 Wilton Crescent, SW1. *T:* 01-235 4423.

COATES, Patrick Devereux; Editor for British Academy of Chinese records at Public Record Office, since 1978; *b* 30 April 1916; *s* of late H. H. H. Coates, OBE, and late Mrs F. J. Coates; *m* 1946, Mary Eleanor, *e d* of late Capt. Leveson Campbell, DSO, RN and late Mrs Campbell; one *s* one *d. Educ:* Trinity Coll., Cambridge. Entered Consular Service and served at Peking, Canton and Kunming, 1937-41; attached to Chinese 22nd Div. in Burma (despatches) and to Chinese forces in India, 1941-44; Actg Chinese Sec. to HM Embassy in China, 1944-46; 1st Sec., Foreign Office, 1946-50; transf. to Min. of Town and Country Planning, 1950; Asst Sec., Min. of Housing and Local Govt, 1955; Asst Under-Sec. of State, Dept of Economic Affairs, 1965-68, Min. of Housing and Local Govt, 1968-70, Dept of the Environment, 1970-72. Hon. Vis. Fellow, SOAS, Univ. of London, 1973-76. *Recreations:* Chinese studies, getting into the fresh air. *Address:* Lewesland Cottage, Barcombe, near Lewes, Sussex BN8 5TG. *T:* Barcombe 400407.

COATES, Reginald Charles, FEng 1978; Professor and Head of Department of Civil Engineering, Papua New Guinea University of Technology, Lae, since 1982; *b* 28 June 1920; *s* of Wilfrid and Margaret Anne Coates; *m* 1942, Doris Sheila (*née* Sharrad); two *s* one *d. Educ:* New Mills Grammar Sch.; The Herbert Strutt Sch., Belper, Derbyshire; University Coll., Nottingham. Served War of 1939-45, Corps of Royal Engineers. Univ. of Nottingham: Lectr in Civil Engineering, 1946; Sen. Lectr, 1953; Prof. and Head of Dept of Civil

Engrg, 1958-82; Dep. Vice-Chancellor, 1966-69. Member: Council, Instn of Civil Engineers, 1967-72 (Vice-Pres., 1975-78, Pres., 1978-79); Sheffield Regional Hosp. Bd, 1971-74; Notts AHA, 1974-75; Council, Construction Industry Research and Information Assoc., 1978-82 (Mem. Research Cttee, 1973-78, Chm., 1980-82); Adv. Cttee, Books for Overseas, British Council, 1974-82; Construction and Housing Res. Adv. Council, DoE, 1976-79. *Publications:* (with M. G. Coutie and F. K. Kong) Structural Analysis, 1972; occasional articles in technical press. *Recreations:* cooking and idling. *Address:* Department of Civil Engineering, Papua New Guinea University of Technology, PO Box 793, Lae, Papua New Guinea.

COATS, Sir Alastair Francis Stuart, 4th Bt, *cr* 1905; *b* 18 Nov. 1921; *s* of Lieut-Col Sir James Stuart Coats, MC, 3rd Bt and Lady Amy Coats (*d* 1975), *er d* of 8th Duke of Richmond and Gordon; *S* father, 1966; *m* 1947, Lukyn, *d* of Capt. Charles Gordon; one *s* one *d. Educ:* Eton. Served War of 1939-45, Coldstream Guards (Capt.). *Heir:* s Alexander James Coats, *b* 6 July 1951. *Address:* Birchwood House, Durford Wood, Petersfield, Hants. *T:* Liss 2254.

COATS, William David; Chairman, Coats Patons Ltd, since 1981 (Deputy Chairman, 1979-81); *b* 25 July 1924; *s* of Thomas Heywood Coats and Olivia Violet Pitman; *m* 1950, Hon. Elizabeth Lilian Graham Macandrew; two *s* one *d. Educ:* Eton Coll. Entered service of Coats Patons Ltd, 1948; Director: The Central Agency Ltd (subsid. co.), 1953-; Coats Patons Ltd, 1960-. Hon. LLD Strathclyde, 1977. *Recreations:* shooting and golf. *Address:* The Cottage, Symington, Ayrshire KA1 5QG. *T:* Symington 830287. *Club:* Western (Glasgow).

See also Baron Macandrew.

COBB, Henry Stephen, FSA; FRHistS; Clerk of the Records, House of Lords, since 1981; *b* 17 Nov. 1926; *y s* of Ernest Cobb and Violet Kate Cobb (*née* Sleath), Wallasey; *m* 1969, Eileen Margaret Downer. *Educ:* Birkenhead Sch.; London School of Economics (BA, MA); Liverpool Univ. (Dip. Archive Admin). Archivist, Church Missionary Soc., 1951-53; Asst Archivist, House of Lords, 1953-59, Asst Clerk of the Records, 1959-73, Dep. Clerk, 1973-81. Mem. Council: British Records Assoc., 1978-81; Society of Archivists, 1970-80 (Vice-Chm., 1980-). Lecturer in Palaeography, School of Librarianship, North London Polytechnic, 1973-77. FSA 1967; FRHistS 1970. *Publications:* (ed) The Local Port Book of Southampton 1439-40, 1961; contribs to Economic History Rev., Jl of Soc. of Archivists, Archives, etc. *Recreations:* music, historical research. *Address:* 1 Child's Way, Hampstead Garden Suburb, NW11 6XU. *T:* 01-458 3688.

COBB, Richard Charles, CBE 1978; FBA 1967; Professor of Modern History, University of Oxford, since 1973; Fellow of Worcester College, Oxford; *b* 20 May 1917; *s* of Francis Hills Cobb, Sudan Civil Service, and Dora Cobb (*née* Swindale); *m* 1963, Margaret Tennant; four *s* one *d. Educ:* Shrewsbury Sch.; Merton Coll., Oxford (Hon. Fellow 1980). Postmastership in History, Merton, 1934. HM Forces, 1942-46. Research in Paris, 1946-55; Lectr in History, UCW Aberystwyth, 1955-61; Sen. Simon Res. Fellow, Manchester, 1960; Lectr, University of Leeds, 1962; Fellow and Tutor in Modern History, Balliol Coll., 1962-72, Hon. Fellow, 1977; Reader in French Revolutionary History, Oxford, 1969-72. Vis. Prof. in the History of Paris, Collège de France, 1971. Lectures: Ralegh, British Academy, 1974; Zaharoff, Oxford, 1976; Helmsley, Brandeis, 1981. DUniv Essex, 1981. Chevalier des Palmes Académiques, 1956; Officier de l'Ordre National du Mérite, 1977. *Publications:* L'armée révolutionnaire à Lyon, 1952; Les armées révolutionnaires du Midi, 1955; Les armées révolutionnaires, vol. 1, 1961, vol. 2, 1963; Terreur et Subsistances, 1965; A Second Identity: essays on France and French history, 1969; The Police and the People: French Popular Protest 1789-1820, 1970; Reactions to the French Revolution, 1972; Paris and its Provinces 1792-1802, 1975; A Sense of Place, 1975; Tour de France, 1976; Death in Paris 1795-1801, 1978 (Wolfson Prize, 1979); Streets of Paris, 1980; Promenades, 1980. *Address:* Worcester College, Oxford. *Club:* Beefsteak.

COBB, Timothy Humphry, MA; *b* 4 July 1909; *s* of Humphry Henry Cobb and Edith Muriel (*née* Stogdon); *m* 1952, Cecilia Mary Josephine, *d* of W. G. Chapman; two *s* one *d. Educ:* Harrow; Magdalene Coll., Cambridge. Asst Master, Middlesex Sch., Concord, Mass, USA, 1931-32; Bryanston Sch., Blandford, Dorset, 1932-47, Housemaster, Head of Classics, Estate Bursar; Headmaster of King's Coll., Budo, Kampala, Uganda, 1947-58; formerly Sec., Uganda Headmasters' Association; Headmaster, Dover College, 1958-73. *Publication:* Certificate English Language Practice, 1958. *Recreations:* music, railway photography, producing vegetables. *Address:* Parkgate Farm, Framlingham, Woodbridge, Suffolk. *T:* Badingham 672. *Clubs:* MCC, Royal Commonwealth Society.

COBBAN, Sir James (Macdonald), Kt 1982; CBE 1971; TD; MA; DL; JP; Headmaster of Abingdon School, 1947-70; *b* 14 Sept. 1910; *s* of late A. M. Cobban, MIStructE, Scunthorpe, Lincs; *m* 1942, Lorna Mary (*d* 1961), *er d* of late G. S. W. Marlow, BSc, FRIC, barrister-at-law, Sydenham; four *d* (one *s* decd). *Educ:* Pocklington Sch.; Jesus Coll., Cambridge (Scholar); Univ. of Vienna. Classical Tripos, Part I, 1931, Part II, 1932; Sandys Student, 1932: Thirlwall Medallist and Gladstone Prizeman, 1933; MA, Cambridge; MA, Oxford (Pembroke Coll.). Asst Master, King Edward VI Sch., Southampton, 1933-36; Class. Sixth Form Master, Dulwich Coll., 1936-40, 1946-47. Intelligence Corps (TA), 1941; GSO3, Directorate of Mil. Intelligence, 1941; Intermediate War Course, Staff Coll., 1943; DAQMG, Combined Ops HQ,

1943; Staff Officer, CCG, 1944 (Lt-Col 1945). Rep. Diocese of Oxford on Gen. Synod, 1970- (Vice-Pres., Dio. Synod, 1975-82; Panel of Chairmen, 1979-81); Chm., Abingdon Co. Bench, 1964-74; Member: Cttee GBA, 1972- (Dep. Chm., 1976-82; Hon. Life Mem., 1981); Direct Grant Schs Jt Cttee, 1966-80 (Chm., 1975-80); Cttee, GBSA, 1976-81; Council, Ind. Schs Careers Orgn, 1972-80; Cttee, United Soc. Christian Lit., 1974-; Thames Valley Police Authority, 1973-80; Vale of White Horse DC, 1973-76; Governor: Stowe Sch., 1970-; Wellington Coll., 1970-81; Campion Sch., Athens, 1980-; Sch. of St Helen and St Katharine, 1954-80 (Chm., 1958-67); Abingdon Coll. of Further Education, 1974-80; St Stephen's House, Oxford, 1982-. JP Berks, 1950, Oxon, 1974; DL Berks, 1966, Oxon, 1974. *Publications:* Senate and Provinces, 78-49 BC, 1935; (in collaboration) Civis Romanus, 1936; Pax et Imperium, 1938; Church and School, 1963. *Address:* The Old Vicarage, Steventon, Oxon OX13 6SJ. *T:* Abingdon 831444.

COBBETT, David John, TD 1973; ERD 1962; Director, Strategic Studies, British Railways Board, since 1978; *b* 9 Dec. 1928; *m* 1952, Beatrix Jane Ogilvie Cockburn; three *s. Educ:* Royal Masonic Sch. FCIT. Gen. Railway admin. and managerial positions, 1949-67; Divl Movements Manager, Liverpool Street, 1967; Divl Manager, Norwich (British Railways Bd), 1968-70; Asst Managing Dir, Freightliners Ltd, 1970-73; Dep. Gen. Manager, British Railways Bd Scottish Region, 1973; Gen. Manager, British Railways Scottish Region, 1974-76; Chm., British Transport Ship Management, Scotland, 1974-76; Gen. Manager, BR Eastern Region, 1976-77; Export Dir (Special Projects), British Rlys Bd, 1977-78. Dir, Transmark, 1978. Dep. Chm., Railway Benevolent Instn, 1981-. Bt Col, Royal Corps of Transport (RARO), 1974. *Recreations:* military matters, historical reading, games. *Address:* The Grange, Strensall, York YO3 5XA. *T:* York 490334. *Club:* Army and Navy.

COBBOLD, family name of **Baron Cobbold.**

COBBOLD, 1st Baron *cr* 1960, of Knebworth; **Cameron Fromanteel Cobbold,** KG 1970; PC 1959; GCVO 1963; DL; Lord Chamberlain of HM Household, 1963-71; Chancellor of the Royal Victorian Order, 1963-71; Governor of Bank of England, 1949-61; one of HM Lieutenants for the City of London; *b* 14 Sept. 1904; *s* of late Lt-Col Clement Cobbold; *m* 1930, Lady (Margaret) Hermione (Millicent) Bulwer-Lytton, *er d* of 2nd Earl of Lytton, KG, PC, GCSI, GCIE; two *s* one *d. Educ:* Eton; King's Coll., Cambridge. Entered Bank of England as Adviser, 1933; Exec. Dir, 1938; Dep. Governor, 1945. Dir, BIS, 1949-61. A Permanent Lord in Waiting to the Queen, 1971-. Vice-Pres., British Heart Foundn (Pres. to 1976); Chm., Middlesex Hosp. Board of Governors and Med. Sch. Council, 1963-74. High Sheriff of County of London for 1946-47. Hon. Fellow Inst. of Bankers, 1961; Fellow of Eton, 1951-67; Steward of the Courts, Eton, 1973-. Chm. Malaysia Commission of Enquiry, 1962. Hon. LLD, McGill Univ., 1961. Hon. DSc (Econ.), London Univ., 1963. DL Herts, 1972. *Heir: s* Hon. David Antony Fromanteel Lytton-Cobbold [*b* 14 July 1937; assumed by deed poll, 1960, the additional surname of Lytton; *m* 1961, Christine Elizabeth, 3rd *d* of Major Sir Dennis Frederic Bankes Stucley, 5th Bt, *qv* ; three *s* one *d*]. *Address:* Lake House, Knebworth, Herts. *T:* Stevenage 812310.

COBBOLD, (Michael) David (Nevill), MA; DL; Senior Partner, Stileman, Neate & Topping, since 1959; Leader of Westminster City Council, since 1976; *b* 21 Oct. 1919; *s* of late Geoffrey Wyndham Nevill Cobbold and Cicely Helen Cobbold; *m* 1949, Ann Rosemary Trevor; two *s* one *d* (and one *s* decd). *Educ:* Charterhouse; New Coll., Oxford (MA); RMA, Sandhurst. War of 1939-45: commissioned and served with 2nd Bn, The Buffs, 1940-45. Admitted Solicitor, 1949. Westminster City Council: Member, 1949-; Leader, 1964-65; Alderman, 1962-78; Mayor of Westminster, 1958-59; Lord Mayor and Dep. High Steward of Westminster, 1973-74. Hon. Treasurer, London Boroughs Assoc., 1977- (Chm., Gen. Purposes Cttee, 1978-); Member: DoE Housing Act Gp, 1970-76; Adv. Cttee on Local Govt Audit, 1979-82. Pres., Beckenham Conservative Assoc., 1974-. DL Greater London, 1967-. *Recreations:* gardening, minding grandchildren. *Address:* 31 Ashley Court, Morpeth Terrace, SW1P 1EN. *T:* 01-834 5020.

COBBOLD, Patrick Mark; brewery director, free trade, since 1962; *b* 20 June 1934; *s* of late Captain J. M. Cobbold and of Lady Blanche Cobbold. *Educ:* Eton. Served Scots Guards, 1953-57; ADC to the Governor of the Bahamas, 1957-60; Tolly Cobbold Breweries, 1961-. *Recreations:* fishing, shooting, football. *Address:* Glemham Hall, Woodbridge, Suffolk. *T:* Wickham Market 746219. *Clubs:* White's, Pratt's.

COBHAM, 11th Viscount *cr* 1718; **John William Leonard Lyttelton;** Bt 1618; Baron Cobham 1718; Lord Lyttelton, Baron of Frankley 1756 (renewed 1794); Baron Westcote (Ire.) 1776; Partner of Hagley Hall Farms, since 1976; *b* 5 June 1943; *e s* of 10th Viscount Cobham, KG, PC, GCMG, GCVO, TD, and of Elizabeth Alison Viscountess Cobham, *d* of J. R. Makeig-Jones, CBE; *S* father, 1977; *m* 1974, Penelope Ann, *e d* of late Roy Cooper, Moss Farm, Ollerton, near Knutsford, Cheshire. *Educ:* Eton; Christ's College, New Zealand; Royal Agricultural College, Cirencester. *Recreations:* cricket, shooting. *Heir: b* Hon. Christopher Charles Lyttelton [*b* 23 Oct. 1947; *m* 1973, Tessa Mary, *d* of late Col A. G. J. Readman, DSO; one *s* one *d*]. *Address:* Hagley Hall, near Stourbridge, West Midlands DY9 9LG. *T:* Hagley 885823; 20 Kylestrome House, Cundy Street, Ebury Street, SW1. *T:* 01-730 5756. *Clubs:* Buck's, MCC.

COBHAM, Barony of; (abeyant).

COBHAM, Ven. John Oldcastle, MA; Archdeacon of Durham and Canon Residentiary of Durham Cathedral, 1953-69, now Archdeacon Emeritus; Licence to Officiate Diocese of St Edmundsbury and Ipswich, 1969-82; *b* 11 April 1899; *s* of late Ven. John Lawrence Cobham; *m* 1934, Joan (*d* 1967), *d* of late Rev. George Henry Cobham; no *c. Educ:* St Lawrence Coll., Ramsgate; Tonbridge Sch.; Corpus Christi Coll., Cambridge; Univ. of Marburg; Westcott House, Cambridge; Académie Goetz. Served in Royal Field Artillery, 1917-19; Curate at St Thomas', Winchester, 1926-30; Vice-Principal of Westcott House, Cambridge, 1930-34; Principal of The Queen's Coll., Birmingham, 1934-53; Vicar of St Benet's, Cambridge, 1940-45; Recognised Lectr, Dept of Theology, Birmingham Univ., 1946-53; Hon. Canon, Derby Cathedral, 1950-53. Chaplain to the Forces (EC), 1943-45. Select Preacher: Univ. of Cambridge, 1933 and 1940; Univ. of Birmingham, 1938; Univ. of Oxford, 1952-53; Examining Chaplain to the Bishop of Durham, 1953-66, to the Bishop of Wakefield, 1959-68. Member: Liturgical Commn, 1955-62; Archbishop of Canterbury's Commn on Roman Catholic Relations, 1964-69. George Craig Stewart Memorial Lecturer, Seabury-Western Theological Seminary, Evanston, Ill., 1963. *Publications:* Concerning Spiritual Gifts, 1933; co-translator of K. Barth in Revelation, a Symposium, 1937; contributor to: The Parish Communion, 1937; No Other Gospel, 1943; The Significance of the Barmen Declaration for the Oecumenical Church, 1943; DNB 1931-40 (E. C. Hoskyns), 1949; Theological Word Book of the Bible, 1950. *Recreation:* sketching. *Address:* 16 Hillcrest Park, Exeter EX4 4SH. *T:* Exeter 74390.

COBHAM, Michael John, CBE 1981; FRAeS; CBIM; Chairman and Managing Director, Flight Refuelling (Holdings) Ltd, since 1969; *b* 22 Feb. 1927; *s* of Sir Alan John Cobham, KBE, AFC, and Lady (Gladys) Cobham; *m* 1st, 1954, June Oakes (marr. diss. 1972); 2nd, 1973, Nadine Felicity, *e d* of William Abbott, Wimborne, Dorset; one *d. Educ:* Malvern; Trinity Coll., Cambridge (BA 1949, MA 1965). Served RN, 1945-47. Called to the Bar, Inner Temple, 1952; practised, 1954-55. Flight Refuelling Ltd: Dir, 1952; Man. Dir, 1964-77; Chm., 1969-. *Recreations:* ski-ing, sailing. *Address:* Long Meadow, Iwerne Stepleton, Blandford, Dorset DT11 8PP. *T:* Child Okeford 860397. *Clubs:* Naval and Military; Royal Southern Yacht (Hamble).

COBURN, Prof. Kathleen; OC 1974; Professor of English, Victoria College, University of Toronto, 1953-71, now Emeritus; author; *b* 1905; *d* of Rev. John Coburn and Susannah Coburn. *Educ:* University of Toronto (MA); Oxford University (BLitt). Imperial Order of the Daughters of the Empire (IODE) Travelling Scholarship, 1930-31. Formerly Lectr, Asst Prof., and Assoc. Prof. of English, Victoria College, University of Toronto. University Women's Internat. Senior Fellowship, 1948-49; John Simon Guggenheim Memorial Fellowship, 1953-54, renewed, 1957-58; Commonwealth Visiting Fellowship (Univ. of London), 1962-63. FRSC 1958. Rose Mary Crawshay Prize for English Literature (Brit. Acad.), 1959. Hon. Fellow, St Hugh's Coll., Oxford, 1970; Hon. Fellow, Champlain Coll., Trent Univ., Ont., 1972; Corresp. FBA, 1973. DHL Haverford, 1972; Hon. LLD, Queen's Univ., Kingston, Ontario, 1964; Hon. DLitt: Trent Univ., 1972; Cambridge, 1975; Toronto, 1978. *Publications:* The Philosophical Lectures of S. T. Coleridge, 1949; Inquiring Spirit, 1951, revd edn 1979; The Letters of Sara Hutchinson, 1954; The Notebooks of S. T. Coleridge, vol. i, 1957, vol. ii, 1961, vol. iii, 1973; Coleridge: A Collection of Critical Essays, 1967; The Self-Conscious Imagination (Riddell Meml Lectures), 1972; Discourse, Royal Institution, 1972; In Pursuit of Coleridge, 1977; Experience into Thought: perspectives in the Coleridge notebooks, 1979; general editor, The Collected Coleridge, 1968-. *Address:* Victoria College, 91 Charles Street W, Toronto, Ontario M5S 1K7, Canada.

COCHRAN, William; PhD, MA; FRS 1962; Professor of Natural Philosophy, University of Edinburgh, since 1975; *b* 30 July 1922; *s* of James Cochran and Margaret Watson Cochran (*née* Baird); *m* 1953, Ingegerd Wall; one *s* two *d. Educ:* Boroughmuir Sch., Edinburgh; Edinburgh Univ. Asst Lectr, Edinburgh Univ., 1943-46; Demonstrator and Lectr, Univ. of Cambridge, 1948-62; Reader in Physics, Univ. of Cambridge, 1962-64. Fellow of Trinity Hall, Cambridge, 1951-64; Prof. of Physics, Univ. of Edinburgh, 1964-75, Dean, Faculty of Science, 1978-81. Research fellowships abroad, 1950-51, 1958-59, 1970. Hon. Fellow, Fitzwilliam Coll., Cambridge, 1982. Guthrie medallist, Inst. Physics and Phys. Soc., 1966; Hughes medallist, Royal Soc., 1978. *Publications:* Vol. III of The Crystalline State (with Prof. H. Lipson), 1954, new edn 1966; Dynamics of Atoms in Crystals, 1973. *Recreations:* Scots verse, family history. *Address:* Department of Physics, The University, The King's Buildings, Edinburgh EH9 3JZ; 71 Clermiston Road, Edinburgh.

COCHRANE, family name of **Earl of Dundonald** and **Baron Cochrane of Cults.**

COCHRANE OF CULTS, 3rd Baron *cr* 1919; **Thomas Charles Anthony Cochrane;** *b* 31 Oct. 1922; *s* of 2nd Baron Cochrane of Cults, DSO, and Hon. Elin Douglas-Pennant (*d* 1934), *y d* of 2nd Baron Penrhyn; *S* father, 1968. *Educ:* privately. Founder and Trustee, Gardeners' Memorial Trust, 1980-. *Heir:* Hon. (Ralph Henry) Vere Cochrane [*b* 20 Sept. 1926; *m* 1956, Janet Mary Watson, *d* of late Dr W. H. W. Cheyne; two *s*]. *Address:* Balgownie, 18 Cliff Terrace, Buckie, Banffshire.

COCHRANE, Lord; Iain Alexander Douglas Blair Cochrane; *b* 17 Feb. 1961; *s* and *heir* of 14th Earl of Dundonald, *qv. Educ:* Wellington College. *Recreations:* shooting, fishing, skiing, sailing. *Address:* Lochnell Castle, Ledaig, Argyll.

COCHRANE, (Alexander John) Cameron, MA; Headmaster, Fettes College, Edinburgh, since 1979; *b* 19 July 1933; *s* of Dr Alexander Younger Cochrane and Jenny Johnstone Cochrane; *m* 1958, Rosemary Aline, *d* of late Robert Alexander Ogg and of Aline Mary Ogg; one *s* two *d. Educ:* The Edinburgh Academy; University Coll., Oxford (BA English Lang. and Lit. 1957, MA 1961). National Service in RA, 1952-54. Asst Master, St Edward's Sch., Oxford, 1957-66; Warden, Brathay Hall, Ambleside, Cumbria, 1966-70; Asst Dir of Educn, City of Edinburgh, 1970-74; Headmaster, Arnold Sch., Blackpool, 1974-79. Member: Lancashire CC Educn Cttee, 1976-79; Council, Outward Bound Trust, 1979-; RA Council for Scotland; Scottish Cttee, Duke of Edinburgh's Award; Chairman: Ullswater Outward Bound Mountain Sch., 1979-; Lothian Fedn of Boys' Clubs, 1981-. Governor: Ardvreck Sch.; Clifton Hall Sch. Hon. Fellow, Dept of Educnl Studies, Univ. of Edinburgh, 1973-74. *Recreations:* Rugby football, cricket, golf and other games; mountains; Rotary. *Address:* The Lodge, Fettes College, Edinburgh. *Clubs:* Public Schools; MCC; Vincent's (Oxford); New (Edinburgh).

COCHRANE, Sir (Henry) Marc (Sursock), 4th Bt *cr* 1903; *b* 23 Oct. 1946; *s* of Sir Desmond Oriel Alastair George Weston Cochrane, 3rd Bt, and of Yvonne Lady Cochrane (*née* Sursock); *S* father, 1979; *m* 1969, Hala (*née* Es-Said); two *s* one *d. Educ:* Eton; Trinity Coll., Dublin (BBS, MA). Director Hambros Bank Ltd, 1979. Hon. Consul General of Ireland in Beirut. *Recreations:* skiing, target shooting, electronics. *Heir:* *s* Alexander Desmond Cochrane, *b* 7 May 1973. *Address:* Woodbrook, Bray, Co. Wicklow, Ireland. *T:* 821421; Palais Sursock, PO Box 154, Beirut, Lebanon. *T:* 331607.

COCHRANE, Dr Robert Greenhill, CMG 1969; MD, FRCP, DTM&H; Regional Leprosy Officer, Shinyanga Region, Tanzania, 1969-72; Medical Superintendent, Kola Ndoto Leprosarium, Tanzania, 1969-72; retired; *b* 11 Aug. 1899; *s* of Dr Thomas Cochrane and Grace Hamilton Cochrane (*née* Greenhill); *m* 1st, 1927, Ivy Gladys Nunn (*d* 1966); two *s* one *d* ; 2nd, 1968, Dr Martha Jeane Shaw. *Educ:* Sch. for Sons of Missionaries, Blackheath (now Eltham Coll.); Univ. of Glasgow; St Bartholomew's Hosp., London; London Sch. of Tropical Medicine. Med. Sec., BELRA (now LEPRA), 1928-33; Med. Supt, Leprosy Hosp., Chingleput, S India, 1933-44 and 1948-51; Dir, Leprosy Campaign and Dir of Leprosy Research, Madras State, India, 1941-51; Dir and Prin. Prof. of Medicine and Dermatology, and Dir, Rural Medicine, Christian Med. Coll., Vellore, S India, 1944-48; Adviser in Leprosy to Min. of Health, London, 1951-65; Vis. Med. Officer, Homes of St Giles, E Hanningfield, Essex, 1951-66; Tech. Med. Adviser, Amer. Leprosy Mission, Inc., 1953-64; Dir, Leprosy Study Centre, London, 1953-65; Med. Supt, Leprosy Hosp., Vadathorasalur, S Arcot, Madras, 1966-68. Pres., Internat. Leprosy Assoc., 1963-68, since when Pres. Emeritus. Kaisar-i-Hind gold medal (India), 1935; Damien-Dutton Award, 1964. *Publications:* A Practical Textbook of Leprosy, 1947; Leprosy in Theory and Practice, 1959, 2nd edn, 1964; Biblical Leprosy, A Suggested Interpretation, 1961; contribs to Internat. Jl of Leprosy, Leprosy Review. *Address:* 606 Swede Street, Norristown, Pa 19401, USA. *Club:* Royal Commonwealth Society.

COCKAYNE, Dame Elizabeth, DBE 1955; Chief Nursing Officer, Ministry of Health, 1948-58, retired; *d* of William and Alice Cockayne, Burton-on-Trent. *Educ:* Secondary Sch., Burton-on-Trent, and privately. Gen. Hospital Training, Royal Infirmary, Sheffield; Fever Training, Mount Gold Hospital, Plymouth; Midwifery Training, Maternity Hospital, Birmingham. Former experience includes: Supervisor of Training Sch., LCC; Matron of West London Hosp., St Charles' Hosp., Royal Free Hosp. *Recreation:* gardening. *Address:* Rushett Cottage, Little Heath Lane, Cobham, Surrey.

COCKBURN, Prof. Forrester, MD; FRCPGlas; FRCPE; Samson Gemmell Professor of Child Health, University of Glasgow, since 1977; *b* 13 Oct. 1934; *s* of Forrester Cockburn and Violet E. Bunce; *m* 1960, Alison Fisher Grieve; two *s. Educ:* Leith Acad.; Univ. of Edinburgh (MD). DCH Glasg. FRCPE 1971; FRCPGlas 1978. Med. trng, Royal Infirmary of Edinburgh, Royal Hosp. for Sick Children, and Simpson Memorial Maternity Pavilion, Edinburgh, 1959-63; Huntingdon Hertford Foundn Res. Fellow, Boston Univ., Mass, 1963-65; Nuffield Sen. Res. Fellow, Univ. of Oxford, 1965-66; Wellcome Trust Sen. Med. Res. Fellow, Univ. of Edin. and Simpson Meml Maternity Pavilion, 1966-71; Sen. Lectr, Dept of Child Life and Health, Univ. of Edin., 1971-77. *Publications:* Neonatal Medicine, 1974; The Cultured Cell in Inherited Metabolic Disease, 1980; contrib. Foetal and Neonatal Nutrition. *Recreations:* sailing, fishing. *Address:* University Department of Child Health, Royal Hospital for Sick Children, Yorkhill, Glasgow G3 8SJ. *T:* 041-339 8888.

COCKBURN, Sir John (Elliot), 12th Bt of that Ilk, *cr* 1671; Managing Director, Cellar Management Ltd; *b* 7 Dec. 1925; *s* of Lieut-Col Sir John Cockburn, 11th Bt of that Ilk, DSO and Isabel Hunter (*d* 1978), *y d* of late James McQueen, Crofts, Kirkcudbrightshire; *S* father, 1949; *m* 1949, Glory Patricia, *er d* of Nigel Tudway Mullings; three *s* two *d. Educ:* RNC Dartmouth; Royal Agricultural Coll., Cirencester. Served War of 1939-45, joined RAF, July 1944. *Recreation:* reading. *Heir:* *s* Charles Christopher Cockburn [*b* 19 Nov. 1950; *m* 1978, Beverley, *d* of B. Stangroom]. *Address:* 48 Frewin Road, SW18. *Club:* Naval and Military.

COCKBURN, Sir Robert, KBE 1960 (OBE 1946); CB 1953; PhD, MSc, MA; Senior Research Fellow, Churchill College, Cambridge, 1970-77; Chairman, National Computing Centre, 1970-77; *b* 31 March 1909; 2nd *s* of late Rev. R. T. Cockburn, Columba Manse, Belford, Northumberland; *m* 1935, Phyllis Hoyland; two *d. Educ:* Southern Secondary Sch. and Municipal Coll., Portsmouth; London Univ. BSc 1928, MSc 1935, PhD 1939, London; MA Cantab 1973. Taught Science at West Ham Municipal Coll., 1930-37; research in communications at RAE Farnborough, 1937-39; in radar at TRE Malvern, Worcs, 1939-45; in atomic energy at AERE Harwell, 1945-48; Scientific Adviser to Air Min., 1948-53; Princ. Dir of Scientific Research (Guided Weapons and Electronics), Ministry of Supply, 1954-55; Deputy Controller of Electronics, Ministry of Supply, 1955-56; Controller of Guided Weapons and Electronics, Ministry of Supply, 1956-59; Chief Scientist of Ministry of Aviation, 1959-64; Dir, RAE, Farnborough, 1964-69. Chairman: Television Adv. Cttee for Posts and Telecommunications, 1971-; BBC Engineering Adv. Cttee, 1973-81. Hon. Fellow, RAeS, 1970. Congressional Medal for Merit, 1947. *Publications:* scientific papers. *Recreation:* sailing. *Address:* 21 Fitzroy Road, Fleet, Hants. *T:* Fleet 5518. *Club:* Athenæum.

COCKBURN, William; Board Member for Finance, Counter Services and Planning, Post Office, since 1982; *b* 28 Feb. 1943. Entered Post Office, 1961; held various junior and middle management positions; Personal Assistant to Chm. of PO, 1971-73; Asst Dir of Finance and Planning, 1973-77; Dir, Central Finance Planning, 1977-78; Dir, Postal Finance, 1978-79; Dir, London Postal Region, 1979-82; apptd Mem., PO Board, 1980. *Address:* Postal Headquarters, St Martins le Grand, EC1A 1HQ.

COCKBURN-CAMPBELL, Sir Thomas; *see* Campbell.

COCKCROFT, Dr Janet Rosemary, OBE 1975; Chairman, Bottoms Mill Co. Ltd, Todmorden, since 1980 (Director, since 1961, Deputy Chairman, 1974-80); *b* 26 July 1916; *er d* of late Major W. G. Mowat, MC, TD, JP, of Buchollie, Lybster, Caithness, Scotland, and late Mary Mowat; *m* 1942, Major Peter Worby Cockcroft (*d* 1980); two *s* one *d. Educ:* Glasgow Univ. MB, ChB 1938. Ho. Surg. and Ho. Phys., Glasgow Royal Infirmary, 1938-39; GP, 1939-43; Asst MOH, Co. of Caithness, 1943-46; MO, Maternity and Child Welfare, Halifax, 1950-53; Part-time MOH, WRCC, 1953-67; MO, Family Planning Assoc., 1947-75 (Halifax and Sowerby Bridge Clinics); MO, British Red Cross, Halifax, 1960-66; Chairman: N Midlands FPA Doctors' Gp, 1966-68; Halifax FPA Clinic, 1963-75. Mem., Food Additives and Contaminants Cttee, MAFF, 1972-81; Chm., Consumers' Cttees for England and Wales and for GB, MAFF, 1975-; Vice-Pres., 1969-70, Pres., 1970-72, Nat. Council of Women of GB; Vice-Pres., Internat. Council of Women, 1973-76; UK Rep., UN Status of Women Commn, 1973-79 (Vice Chm., 1976; Chm., 1978-80); Member: BBC Northern Adv. Council, 1975-79; Gen. Adv. Council, BBC, 1980-. Elder, United Reformed Church, 1973-. *Recreations:* travel, reading. *Address:* Dalemore, Savile Park, Halifax, W Yorks HX1 3EA. *T:* Halifax 52621. *Club:* Naval and Military.

COCKCROFT, John Hoyle; Microelectronical Economist, Statham Duff Stoop, stockbrokers, since 1978; Director: RSJ Aviation, since 1979; Spalding Asset Management Services, since 1982; *b* 6 July 1934; *s* of Lionel Fielden Cockcroft and Jenny Hoyle; *m* 1971, Tessa Fay Shepley; three *d. Educ:* Primary, Trearddur House; Gundle; St John's Coll., Cambridge (Sen. Maj. Scholar (History), 1953). MA Hons History and Econs 1958; Pres., Cambridge Union, 1958. Royal Artillery, 1953-55. Feature Writer and Investment Analyst, Financial Times, 1959-61; Economist, GKN, 1962-67; seconded to Treasury, Public Enterprises Div., 1965-66; Econ. Leader-writer, Daily Telegraph, 1967-74; Historian and Consultant, GKN, 1971-76; Financial Public Relations Internat. Consultant, Petcliff Ltd, 1975-76; Economic Consultant, Rowe Rudd, 1977-78; Consultant, Edmund Gp, 1976-77; MP (C) Nantwich, Feb. 1974-1979; Mem., Select Cttee on Nationalised Industries, 1975-79; Company Secretaries Bill (Private Member's), 1978. Consultant: Inst. of Chartered Secretaries, 1977-79; Mail Users' Assoc., 1976-. Member Council: European Movement, 1973-74; Conservative Gp for Europe, 1980-; Member: Cttee, Assoc. of Youth Clubs, 1970-74; Cons. Foreign Affairs Forum, 1980-; Treasurer, Cambridge Univ. Cons. Assoc., 1978. Columnist, MicroScope, 1982-. *Publications:* Why England Sleeps, 1971; (jtly) An Internal History of Guest Keen and Nettlefolds; Westminster Commentary, Investment Report, 1978-79; Political Commentary, Commerce, I. White, 1979-80; Microelectronics (booklet), 1979; leader page articles, Daily and Sunday Telegraphs, 1979-. *Recreations:* walking, reading, swimming, entertaining. *Address:* Mitchell's Farmhouse, Stapleford Tawney, Essex.

COCKCROFT, Dr Wilfred Halliday; Vice-Chancellor, The New University of Ulster, since 1976; *b* 7 June 1923; *s* of Wilfred Cockcroft and Bessie Halliday; *m* 1949, Barbara Rhona Huggan; two *s* ; *m* 1982, Vivien, *o d* of Mr and Mrs David Lloyd. *Educ:* Keighley Boys' Grammar Sch.; Balliol Coll., Oxford (Williams Exhibnr, 1941, Hon. Scholar, 1946). MA, DPhil Oxon; FIMA. Technical Signals/Radar Officer, RAF, 1942-46. Asst Lectr, Univ. of Aberdeen, 1949, Lectr 1950; Lectr, Univ. of Southampton, 1957, Reader 1960; G. F. Grant Prof. of Pure Mathematics, Univ. of Hull, 1961; Vis. Lectr and Prof., Univs of Chicago, Stanford, State Univ. of NY, 1954, 1959, 1967. University Grants Committee: Mem., 1973-76; Mem., Math. Sciences Subcttee, 1967-72, Chm. 1973-76; Chm., Educn Subcttee, 1973-76; Mem., Management and Business Studies Subcttee, and Educnl Technology Subcttee, 1973-76. Science and Engineering Research Council (formerly Science Research Council): Mem., 1978-82; Mem. Maths Sub-Cttee, 1964-68

(Chm., 1969-73); Mem. Science Bd, 1969-73; Chm., Postgraduate Trng Cttee, 1979-82. Chairman: Nuffield Maths Project Consultative Cttee, 1963-71; Specialist Conf. on Maths in Commonwealth Schs, Trinidad, 1968; Member: Council, London Math. Soc., 1973-76; Council, Inst. of Maths and its Applications, 1974-77; US/UK Educational Commn, 1977-80; Computer Bd for Univs and Res. Councils, 1975-76; Chairman: Cttee to review Rural Planning Policy, DoE, NI, 1977-78; Cttee to consider teaching of maths in schs in England and Wales, 1978-82; Standing Conference on Univ. Entrance, 1979-82. *Publications:* Your Child and Mathematics, 1968; Complex Numbers, 1972. *Recreations:* golf, swimming, sketching, bad piano playing. *Address:* The New University of Ulster, Coleraine, Northern Ireland. *T:* Coleraine 4141.

COCKER, Prof. Ralph, CBE 1968; MB, ChB, LDS (Victoria University Manchester), FRCS, FDSRCS; Professor Emeritus of Dental Surgery in the University of London, ex-Director of Dental Studies, and Sub-Dean, King's College Hospital Medical School, University of London, 1947-73 (FKCHMS 1981), Consultant Dental Surgeon and Director of Dental Department, King's College Hospital, 1947-73, Hon. Consultant Dental Surgeon, since 1973; *b* 18 April 1908; *er s* of Frank Barlow Cocker and Mary Wildman; *m* 1942, Margaret (*née* Jacques); one *s* two *d. Educ:* William Hulme's Grammar Sch., Manchester; Manchester Univ. Preston Prize and Medallist, Manchester Univ., 1930. Private Practice, 1930-36; Asst Hon. Dental Surg., Manchester Dent. Hosp., 1933-36; Lectr in Clin. Dental Surg., Manchester Univ., 1936-45; Industrial Health Service (ICI Ltd), 1940-45; Lectr in Periodontia, Manchester Univ., 1945-47; Actg Cons. Dental Surg., Manchester Royal Infirmary, 1945-47; Past Examr in Dental Surgery, Univs of Manchester, London, Birmingham, Bristol, Sheffield, St Andrews; Chm. Bd of Examrs for Statutory Exam. (GDC), 1964-73; Member: Bd of Faculty, RCS, 1955-71 (Vice-Dean, 1964-65) and Examr to Coll. for Dipl. and Final Fellowship in Dental Surgery; Standing Dental Adv. Cttee of Dept. of Health and Social Security, 1963-74 (Vice-Chm. 1965-74); GDC, 1963-74 (Chm., Educn Cttee, 1970-74, Chm. Central Examining Bd for Dental Hygienists, 1967-74); Sec., Odontolog. Section, RSM, 1961-63 (Vice-Pres. 1971-73); Mem., Dental Educn Adv. Coun. of Gt Brit., 1947-73 (Chm., 1956-57; Treas., 1957-73; Sec., 1967-73); Mem. and Chm., Assoc. of British Dental Hospitals, 1947-73; Mem., Dental Industry Standards Cttee (BSI); Founder Mem., King's Coll. Hosp. Med. Sch. Council and King's Coll. Hosp. Bd of Govs, 1948-73; Mem. Bd of Dental Studies, London Univ., 1948-73 (Chm., 1966-71); Adviser in Dental Surgery to Dept. of Health and Social Security, 1968-74; Temp. Adviser, WHO, 1970-72. *Recreations:* mountaineering, ski-ing, photography, ornithology. *Address:* Broad Mead, Westwell Leacon, Charing, Kent TN27 0EN. *T:* Charing 2437. *Club:* Alpine.

COCKERAM, Eric (Paul); JP; MP (C) Ludlow, since 1979; *b* 4 July 1924; *er s* of Mr and Mrs J. W. Cockeram; *m* 1949, Frances Irving; two *s* two *d. Educ:* The Leys Sch., Cambridge. Served War, 1942-46: Captain The Gloucestershire Regt; "D Day" landings (wounded and discharged). MP (C) Bebington, 1970-Feb. 1974. PPS: to Minister for Industry, 1970-72; to Minister for Posts and Telecommunications, 1972; to Chancellor of Exchequer, 1972-74. Mem., Select Cttee on Corporation Tax, 1971, on Industry and Trade, 1979-. Pres., Menswear Assoc. of Britain, 1964-65. Mem., Bd of Governors, United Liverpool Hosps, 1965-74; Chm., Liverpool NHS Exec. Council, 1970. Chm., Watson Prickard Ltd; Director: Liverpool Building Soc., 1975- (Vice-Chm., 1981-); TSB (NW), 1968-; Midshires Building Soc.; Member of Lloyd's. Liveryman, Worshipful Co. of Glovers, 1969-, Mem. Court, 1979-. Freeman: City of London; City of Springfield, Ill. JP, City of Liverpool, 1960. *Recreations:* bridge, shooting, country walking. *Address:* House of Commons, SW1. *Clubs:* Carlton, Royal Automobile.

COCKERELL, Sir Christopher (Sydney), Kt 1969; CBE 1966; MA; FRS 1967; Chairman, Wavepower Ltd, since 1974 (former Joint Managing Director); *b* 4 June 1910; *s* of late Sir Sydney Cockerell; *m* 1937, Margaret Elinor Belsham; two *d. Educ:* Gresham's; Peterhouse, Cambridge (Hon. Fellow, 1974). Pupil, W. H. Allen & Sons, Bedford, 1931-33; Radio Research, Cambridge, 1933-35; airborne and navigational equipment research and development, Marconi Wireless Telegraph Co. Ltd, 1935-50; inventor of and engaged on hovercraft since 1953; Consultant (hovercraft), Ministry of Supply, 1957-58. Consultant: Hovercraft Development Ltd, 1958-70 (Dir, 1959-66); British Hovercraft Corp., 1973-79; Chm., Ripplecraft Co. Ltd, 1950-79. Foundn Pres., Internat. Air Cushion Engrg Soc., 1969-71 (Vice-Pres., 1971-); Pres., UK Hovercraft Soc., 1971-; Member, Min. of Technology's Adv. Cttee for Hovercraft, 1968-70. A Trustee of National Portrait Gallery, 1967-79. Hon. Fellow: Swedish Soc. of Aeronautics, 1963; Soc. of Engineers, 1966; Manchester Inst. of Sci. and Tech., 1967; Downing Coll., Cambridge, 1969. Hon. Mem., Southampton Chamber of Commerce, 1967. Hon. DSc: Leicester, 1967; Heriot-Watt, 1971; London, 1975; Hon. Dr RCA, 1968. Hon. Freeman, Borough of Ramsgate, 1971. Viva Shield, Worshipful Co. of Carmen, 1961; RAC Diamond Jubilee Trophy, 1962. Thulin Medal, Swedish Soc. of Aeronautics, 1963; Howard N. Potts Medal, Franklin Inst., 1965; Albert Medal, RSA, 1966; Churchill Medal, Soc. of Engineers, 1966; Royal Medal, Royal Soc., 1966; Mitchell Memorial Medal, Stoke-on-Trent Assoc. of Engineers, 1967; Columbus Prize, Genoa, 1968; John Scott Award, City of Philadelphia, 1968; Elmer A. Sperry Award, 1968; Gold Medal, Calais Chamber of Commerce, 1969; Bluebird Trophy, 1969; James Alfred Ewing Medal, ICE, 1977. *Recreations:* the visual arts, gardening, fishing. *Address:* 16 Prospect Place, Hythe, Hants SO4 6AU.

COCKERELL, Sydney (Morris), OBE 1980; FSA; bookbinder; Senior Partner in Cockerell Bindery (formerly D. Cockerell & Son), since 1946; *b* 6 June 1906; *er s* of late Douglas Cockerell and Florence Arundel; *m* 1932, Elizabeth Lucy Cowlishaw; one *s* two *d. Educ:* St Christopher Sch., Letchworth. Partnership with Douglas Cockerell, 1924. Vis. Lectr, Sch. of Library, Archive and Information Studies, UCL, 1945-76. Assisted with repair and binding of Codex Sinaiticus Manuscript at British Museum, 1934; has repaired and bound many early and medieval manuscripts including Codex Bezae Book of Cerne, Book of Deer, Thornton Romances, Fitzwilliam Virginal Book, Handel's Conducting Score of Messiah, and repaired and treated, amongst others, papers of Wordsworth, Milton, Tennyson, Isaac Newton, Captain Cook's First Circumnavigation of the Globe; mounted Hereford Mappa Mundi; designed and made numbers of tooled bindings for collectors. Revived and developed craft of marbling paper; designed and made tools and equipment for binding and marbling. Visited Ceylon, Ethiopia, Italy, Canada, Tunisia, Portugal, USA, Greece and Jordan to advise on book conservation. Hon. Member: Soc. of Scribes and Illuminators, 1956; Double Crown Club (Pres., 1976-77); Fellow International Institute for Conservation of Historic and Artistic Works, 1959; Master, Art Workers Guild, 1961. Hon. LittD Cantab, 1982. *Publications:* Marbling Paper, 1934; Appendix to Bookbinding and the Care of Books, 1943, revised and repr. 1973; The Repairing of Books, 1958; contributor to: The Calligrapher's Handbook, 1956; Encyclopædia Britannica, 1963. *Recreation:* keeping the house up and the weeds down. *Address:* Riversdale, Grantchester, Cambridge. *T:* Cambridge 840124.

COCKERILL, Geoffrey Fairfax, CB 1980; Secretary, University Grants Committee, 1978-82; *b* 14 May 1922; *e s* of late Walter B. Cockerill and Mary W. Cockerill (*née* Buffery); *m* 1959, Janet Agnes Walters, JP, MA, *d* of late Archibald J. Walters, MBE, and Elsie Walters; two *s. Educ:* Humberstone Foundation Sch.; UC Nottingham. BA London 1947. Royal Artillery, 1941-45 (Captain). Min. of Labour, 1947; Min. of Educn, 1952; Private Sec. to last Minister of Educn and Secs of State for Educn and Science, 1963-65; Asst Sec., 1964; Sec., Public Schools Commn, 1966-68; Jt Sec., Schools Council for Curriculum and Examinations, 1970-72; Under-Sec., DES, 1972-77; Dep. Sec., 1978. Chairman: Anglo-Amer. Primary Educ. Project, 1970-72; Working Party on Nutritional Aspects of School Meals, 1973-75; Mem., Adv. Gp on London Health Services, 1980-81. Reviewed Educational Visits and Exchanges for Govt, 1982-83; Hon. Senior Research Fellow, KCL, 1982-. *Recreations:* gardening, photography. *Address:* 29 Lovelace Road, Surbiton, Surrey KT6 6NS. *T:* 01-399 0125. *Clubs:* Athenæum, Royal Commonwealth Society.

COCKERTON, Rev. John Clifford Penn; Rector of Wheldrake, since 1978; *b* 27 June 1927; *s* of late William Penn Cockerton and Eleanor Cockerton; *m* 1974, Diana Margaret Smith, *d* of Mr and Mrs W. Smith, Upper Poppleton, York. *Educ:* Wirral Grammar Sch.; Univ. of Liverpool; St Catherine's Society, Oxford; Wycliffe Hall, Oxford. Asst Master, Prenton Secondary Sch., 1949-51; Deacon 1954; Priest 1955; Asst Curate, St Helens Parish Church, 1954-58; Tutor 1958-60, Chaplain 1960-63, Cranmer Hall, Durham; Vice-Principal, St John's Coll., Durham, 1963-70; Principal, St John's College and Cranmer Hall, Durham, 1970-78. Examining Chaplain to Bishop of Durham, 1971-73. *Recreation:* music. *Address:* The Rectory, 3 Church Lane, Wheldrake, York YO4 6AW. *T:* Wheldrake 230. *Club:* Royal Commonwealth Society.

COCKETT, Frank Bernard, MS, FRCS; Consulting Surgeon to: St Thomas' Hospital; King Edward VII Hospital for Officers, London; *b* Rockhampton, Australia, 22 April 1916; *s* of late Rev. Charles Bernard Cockett, MA, DD; *m* 1945, Felicity Ann (*d* 1958), *d* of Col James Thackeray Fisher, DSO, Frieston, near Grantham, Lincs; one *s* two *d*; *m* 1960, Dorothea Anne Newman; twin *s. Educ:* Bedford Sch.; St Thomas's Hosp. Med. Sch. BSc (1st Cl. Hons), 1936; MRCS, LRCP 1939; MB, BS (London) 1940; FRCS Eng 1947; MS (London) 1953. Sqdn Ldr (Surgical Specialist) RAFVR, 1942-46; Surgical Registrar, St Thomas' Hosp., 1947-48; Resident Asst Surg., St Thomas' Hosp., 1948-50, Consultant, 1954-81; Senior Lecturer in Surgery, St Thomas's Hosp. Med. Sch., 1950-54; Consultant, King Edward VII Hosp. for Officers, 1974-81. Fellow Assoc. of Surgs of Gt Brit.; Mem. European Soc. of Cardiovascular Surgery; Pres., Vascular Surgical Soc. of GB and Ireland, 1980. *Publications:* The Pathology and Surgery of the Veins of the Lower Limb, 1956, 2nd edn 1976; several contribs to Operative Surgery (ed. C. G. Rob and Rodney Smith), 1956; various papers in medical and surgical journals. *Recreations:* sailing, tennis, squash, gardening, collecting marine paintings. *Address:* 61 Harley Street, W1. *T:* 01-580 3612; 14 Essex Villas, Campden Hill, Kensington, W8. *T:* 01-937 9883. *Clubs:* Little Ship; Island Sailing.

COCKFIELD, family name of **Baron Cockfield.**

COCKFIELD, Baron *cr* 1978 (Life Peer), of Dover in the County of Kent; **Francis Arthur Cockfield,** Kt 1973; PC 1982; Secretary of State for Trade, since 1982; *b* 28 Sept. 1916; 2nd *s* of late Lieut C. F. Cockfield and Louisa (*née* James); *m* Aileen Monica Mudie, choreographer. *Educ:* Dover County; London Sch. of Economics (LLB, BSc (Econ.)). Called to Bar, Inner Temple, 1942. Home Civil Service, Inland Revenue, 1938; Asst Sec. to Board of Inland Revenue, 1945; Commissioner of Inland Revenue, 1951-52; Dir of Statistics and Intelligence to Board of Inland Revenue, 1945-52; Boots Pure Drug Co. Ltd: Finance Dir, 1953-61; Man. Dir, and Chm. Exec. Management Cttee,

1961-67. Chm., Price Commn, 1973-77. Minister of State, HM Treasury, 1979-82. Mem., NEDC, 1962-64, 1982-; Advr on Taxation Policy to Chancellor of Exchequer, 1970-73. Mem., Court of Governors, Univ. of Nottingham, 1963-67. Pres., Royal Statistical Soc., 1968-69. Hon. Fellow, LSE, 1972. *Address:* House of Lords, SW1.

COCKIN, Rt. Rev. George Eyles Irwin; Assistant Bishop, Diocese of York, since 1969; *b* 15 Aug. 1908; *s* of late Charles Irwin Cockin, Solicitor, and Judith Cockin. *Educ:* Repton; Leeds University (BA); Lincoln Theological College. Tutor, St Paul's College, Awka, Nigeria, 1933-40; Supervisor, Anglican Schools, E Nigeria, 1940-52. Deacon, 1953, Priest, 1954; Curate, Kimberworth, Rotherham, 1953-55; Sen. Supervisor, Anglican Schools, E Nigeria, 1955-58; Canon, All Saints Cathedral, Onitsha, 1957; first Bishop of Owerri, 1959-69. Rector of Bainton, dio. York, 1969-78; Rural Dean of Harthill, 1973-78. *Address:* 42 Carr Lane, Willerby, Hull. *T:* Hull 653086.

COCKING, Prof. John Martin, MA; Leverhulme Emeritus Research Fellow, 1975-77; Fellow, since 1965 and Emeritus Professor, since 1975, King's College, University of London; *b* 9 Nov. 1914; *s* of Matthew Maddern Bottrell Cocking and Annie Cocking; *m* 1941, May Parsons Wallis; one *s*. *Educ:* Penzance County Sch. for Boys; King's Coll., London; Sorbonne; British Institute in Paris. BA (Hons) French, 1935; Teacher's Diploma (London), 1936; Diplôme d'Etudes Universitaires (Sorbonne), 1937; MA (London), 1939. Lecturer in English Literature, British Institute in Paris, 1937-38, Lecturer in English and Asst to the Dir, 1938-39; Asst Lecturer in French, King's Coll., London, 1939-46 (including 5 years' absence on war service in the Army); Lecturer in French, 1946-52; Prof. of French Lang. and Literature, 1952-75, King's Coll., London. Officier de l'ordre national du mérite (France), 1973. *Publications:* Marcel Proust, 1956; Proust: collected essays on the writer and his art, 1982; articles in journals and reviews. *Address:* 8 Marlborough Court, Pinehurst, Grange Road, Cambridge CB3 9BQ. *T:* Cambridge 51740.

COCKRAM, Sir John, Kt 1964; Director, 1952-79, General Manager, 1941-73, The Colne Valley Water Company; Director since 1970, Chairman since 1971, Rickmansworth and Uxbridge Valley Water Co.; *b* 10 July 1908; *s* of Alfred John and Beatrice Elizabeth Cockram; *m* 1937, Phyllis Eleanor, *d* of Albert Henning; one *s* two *d*. *Educ:* St Aloysius Coll., Highgate. Chartered Accountant. Member: Herts CC, 1949-74 (Chm. 1961-65); Thames Conservancy, 1954-74; Exec. Cttee, British Waterworks Assoc., 1948-74 (Pres., 1957-58); Water Companies Assoc., 1950- (Chm., 1950-79, Dep. Pres., 1979-); Central Advisory Water Cttee, 1955-73; Thames Water Authy, 1973-76. Life Governor, Haileybury. *Recreations:* fishing, gardening. *Address:* Rebels' Corner, The Common, Chorleywood, Hertfordshire. *Club:* MCC.

COCKS, family name of **Baron Somers.**

COCKS, Sir Barnett; see Cocks, Sir T. G. B.

COCKS, Rt. Rev. Francis William, CB 1959; *b* 5 Nov. 1913; *o s* of late Canon W. Cocks, OBE, St John's Vicarage, Felixstowe; *m* 1940, Irene May (Barbara), 2nd *d* of H. Thompson, Bridlington; one *s* one *d*. *Educ:* Haileybury; St Catharine's Coll., Cambridge; Westcott House. Played Rugby Football for Cambridge Univ., Hampshire and Eastern Counties, 1935-38. Ordained, 1937. Chaplain RAFVR, 1939; Chaplain RAF, 1945; Asst Chaplain-in-Chief, 1950; Chaplain-in-Chief, and Archdeacon, Royal Air Force, 1959-65; Rector and Rural Dean of Wolverhampton, 1965-70; Bishop Suffragan of Shrewsbury, 1970-80. Mem. of Council, Haileybury and Imperial Service Coll., 1949-. Hon. Chaplain to HM the Queen, 1959-65. Prebendary of S Botolph in Lincoln Cathedral, 1959; Canon Emeritus, 1965-70; Prebendary of Lichfield Cathedral, 1968-70; Select Preacher, Univ. of Cambridge, 1960; Hon. Canon of Lichfield Cathedral, 1970-. Dir, Mercia Television, 1980-81. Fellow, Woodard Schools, 1969-; Mem. Council: Denstone Sch., 1970-72; Shrewsbury Sch., 1971-80; Ellesmere Coll., 1971-80. Archbishops' Advr to HMC, 1975-80. President: Shropshire Horticultural Soc., 1979; Shropshire and W Midlands Agric. Soc., 1980; Buccaneers CC, 1965-. *Recreations:* cricket, tennis, golf. *Address:* 41 Beatrice Avenue, Felixstowe, Suffolk IP11 9HB. *T:* Felixstowe 283574. *Clubs:* MCC, Royal Air Force; Hawks (Cambridge).

COCKS, Freda Mary, OBE 1972; JP; Lord Mayor of Birmingham, 1977-78; *b* 30 July 1915; *d* of Frank and Mary Wood; *m* 1942, Donald Francis Melvin, *s* of Melvin J. Cocks; one *d* (and one *d* decd). *Educ:* St Peter's Sch., Harborne; Queen's Coll., Birmingham. Birmingham Council, 1957-78: Alderman, 1965-74; Dep. Chm., Housing Cttee, 1968-70, Chm. 1970-72. Founder Sec., Birmingham Sanatoria League of Friends, 1950-68; Founder, Birm. Hosps Broadcasting Assoc., 1952-78; Mem., Little Bromwich Hosp. Management Cttee, 1953-68. Conservative Women's Central Council: Chm., 1968-71; Chm., Gen. Purposes Cttee, 1978; service on housing, finance, policies, and land cttees; Pres., Edgbaston Conservative Assoc. JP Birmingham, 1968. *Recreations:* hospitals and housing. *Address:* 332-4 Hagley Road, Edgbaston, Birmingham B17 8BH. *T:* 021-420 1140.

COCKS, Rt. Hon. Michael Francis Lovell, PC 1976; MP (Lab) Bristol South since 1970; *b* 19 Aug. 1929; *s* of Dr H. F. Lovell Cocks; *m* 1954, Janet Macfarlane; two *s* two *d*. *Educ:* Bristol University. Various posts in education from 1954; Lectr, Bristol Polytechnic, 1968. Contested (Lab): Bristol West, 1959; South Gloucestershire, 1964, 1966. An Asst Govt Whip, 1974-76; Parly

Sec. to the Treasury and Govt Chief Whip, 1976-79. *Recreations:* swimming, listening to music, reading. *Address:* House of Commons, SW1.

COCKS, Sir (Thomas George) Barnett, KCB 1963 (CB 1961); OBE 1949; Clerk of the House of Commons, 1962-73, retired; *b* 1907; *m* 1952, Iris Mary Symon (*née* Coltman); one *s* one step *d*. *Educ:* Blundells Sch.; Worcester Coll., Oxford. Clerk in the House of Commons, from 1931; temporarily attached Min. of Home Security, 1939. Hon. Sec. and later a Trustee of the History of Parliament; Mem., Assoc. of Secretaries-General of Parliaments, 1959-73; Pres., Governing Bd, Internat. Centre of Parliamentary Documentation, Geneva, 1972. Hon. Officer, Saskatchewan Parlt, 1977. *Publications:* The Parliament at Westminster, 1949; (with Strathearn Gordon) A People's Conscience, 1952; The European Parliament, 1973; Mid-Victorian Masterpiece, 1977; Editor: Erskine May's Parliamentary Practice, 15th, 16th, 17th and 18th edns; Council of Europe Manual of Procedure, seven edns. *Address:* 13 Langford Green, SE5 8BX. *T:* 01-274 5448.

COCKSHUT, Mrs Gillian; see Avery, G. E.

CODRINGTON, John Ernest Fleetwood, CMG 1968; *b* 1919; *s* of late Stewart Codrington; *m* 1951, Margaret, *d* of late Sir Herbert Hall Hall, KCMG; three *d*. *Educ:* Haileybury; Trinity Coll., Cambridge. Served RNVR, 1940-42: HMS Enchantress, HMS Vanity; Royal Marines, 1942-46: 42 (RM) Commando; Colonial Administrative Service, 1946: Gold Coast (later Ghana), 1947-58; Nyasaland, 1958-64; Financial Sec., Bahamas, 1964-70; Bahamas Comr in London, 1970-73, acting High Comr, 1973-74; Financial Sec., Bermuda, 1974-77. *Recreation:* sailing. *Address:* Chequers Close, Lymington, Hants. *Clubs:* Army and Navy; Royal Lymington Yacht.

CODRINGTON, Kenneth de Burgh; Professor Emeritus of Indian Archæology in University of London (Institute of Archæology and School of Oriental and African Studies); *o s* of late Col H. de B. Codrington, IA; *m* 1927, Philippa Christine, *y d* of late E. V. Fleming, CB; one *s* one *d*. *Educ:* Sherborne Sch.; Cadet Coll., Wellington, India; Corpus Christi Coll., Cambridge; Wadham Coll., Oxford. Indian Army, 33rd QVO Light Horse, 1917; invalided, 1921; BA 1921; MA 1926. RAF Educational Staff, Cranwell, 1922; Prof. of Archæology and Fellow of the Graduate Sch., Univ. of Cincinnati, USA, 1925-26; Hon. Lecturer, University Coll., London and School of Oriental and African Studies, 1931; Prof., 1948-66. Mem. Cttee of Management, Inst. of Archæology, 1944-67; Keeper, Indian Section, Victoria and Albert Museum, South Kensington, 1935-48. London Division RNVR, 1924-39; Commander (S) retd, 1946. Joined J. Hackin, Dir of the French Archæological Delegation in Afghanistan, 1940; Dir, Anaradhapura Excavations, Sri Lanka, 1972. Catalogued and hung Burlington Fine Arts Club Exhibn of Indian Art (with Laurence Binyon), 1930; organised Tagore Society's Exhibn of Indian Art, London, 1944; Mem. Selection and Hanging Cttee, Royal Academy Exhibn of Art of India and Pakistan, Burlington House, 1947. Served on Councils of the Royal Asiatic Soc., Royal Anthropological Inst. (Sec., India Res. Cttee, 1927-39), and Museums Assoc.; Hon. Fellow, School of Oriental and African Studies. Chm., Civil Service Retirement Fellowship, SE Kent. Served on County Youth Cttee (Training). Mem., Geographical Club, 1944; Hon. Mem., Mark Twain Soc., 1977. *Publications:* Ancient India, 1926; An Introduction to the Study of Medieval Indian Sculpture, 1929; rev. edns of Vincent Smith's History of Indian Fine Art, 1930, 1961, 1969; An Introduction to the Study of Islamic Art in India (India Soc.), 1934; The Wood of the Image, 1934; Cricket in the Grass, 1959; Birdwood and the Arts of India (Birdwood Lecture, RSA), 1969; papers on art, archæology and anthropology, incl. Art for Archaeologists (Bull. of John Rylands Liby vol. 48 no 1, 1965). *Address:* Rose Cottage, Appledore, Kent. *T:* Appledore 388.

CODRINGTON, Sir Simon (Francis Bethell), 3rd Bt *cr* 1876; *b* 14 Aug. 1923; *s* of Sir Christopher William Gerald Henry Codrington, 2nd Bt, and Joan Mary Hague-Cook (*d* 1961); *S* father, 1979; *m* 1st, 1947, Joanne (marr. diss. 1959), *d* of J. W. Molineaux and *widow* of William Humphrey Austin Thompson; 2nd, 1959, Pamela Joy Halliday Wise (marr. diss 1979); three *s* ; 3rd, 1980, Sarah Gwynne Gaze (*née* Pennell). *Educ:* Eton. Late Coldstream Guards. *Heir:* *s* Christopher George Wayne Codrington, *b* 20 Feb. 1960. *Address:* Dodington, Chipping Sodbury, Bristol. *T:* Chipping Sodbury 312354.

CODRINGTON, Sir William (Alexander), 8th Bt *cr* 1721; FNI; in command with Worldwide Shipping; Port Captain, Hong Kong, for Worldwide Shipping Agency, since 1979; *b* 5 July 1934; *e s* of Sir William Richard Codrington, 7th Bt, and Joan Kathleen Birellu, *e d* of Percy E. Nicholas, London, NW; *S* father, 1961. *Educ:* St Andrew Coll., S Africa; S African Naval Coll., General Botha. Joined Merchant Navy, 1952; joined Union Castle Mail Steamship Co., 1960; Master Mariner's Certificate of Competency, 1961. Joined Worldwide Shipping 1976. Mem., Hon. Co. of Master Mariners. Pres., Tooting and Balham Sea Cadet Unit. *Recreations:* model engineering, sailing. *Heir:* *b* Giles Peter Codrington, *b* 28 Oct. 1943. *Address:* 99 St James Drive, Wandsworth Common, SW17. *Club:* Royal Southern Yacht.

CODRON, Michael Victor; theatrical producer; *b* 8 June 1930; *s* of I. A. Codron and Lily (*née* Morgenstern). *Educ:* St Paul's Sch.; Worcester Coll., Oxford (BA). Director: Hampstead Theatre; Theatres Mutual Insurance Co.; Theatres Consolidated Ltd. Productions include: Share My Lettuce, Breath of

Spring, 1957; Dock Brief and What Shall We Tell Caroline?, The Birthday Party, Valmouth, 1958; Pieces of Eight, 1959; The Wrong Side of the Park, The Caretaker, 1960; Three, Stop It Whoever You Are, One Over the Eight, The Tenth Man, Big Soft Nellie, 1961; Two Stars for Comfort, Everything in the Garden, Rattle of a Simple Man, 1962; Next Time I'll sing to You, Private Lives (revival), The Lovers and the Dwarfs, Cockade, 1963; Poor Bitos, The Formation Dancers, Entertaining Mr Sloane, 1964; Loot, The Killing of Sister George, Ride a Cock Horse, 1965; Little Malcolm and his Struggle against the Eunuchs, The Anniversary, There's a Girl in my Soup, Big Bad Mouse, 1966; The Judge, The Flip Side, Wise Child, The Boy Friend (revival), 1967; Not Now Darling, The Real Inspector Hound, 1968; The Contractor, Slag, The Two of Us, The Philanthropist, 1970; The Foursome, Butley, A Voyage Round my Father, The Changing Room, 1971; Veterans, Time and Time Again, Crown Matrimonial, My Fat Friend, 1972; Collaborators, Savages, Habeas Corpus, Absurd Person Singular, 1973; Knuckle, Flowers, Golden Pathway Annual, The Norman Conquests, John Paul George Ringo . . . and Bert, 1974; A Family and A Fortune, Alphabetical Order, A Far Better Husband, Ashes, Absent Friends, Otherwise Engaged, Stripwell, 1975; Funny Peculiar, Treats, Donkey's Years, Confusions, Teeth 'n' Smiles, Yahoo, 1976; Dusa, Stas, Fish & Vi, Just Between Ourselves, Oh, Mr Porter, Breezeblock Park, The Bells of Hell, The Old Country, 1977; The Rear Column, Ten Times Table, The Unvarnished Truth, The Homecoming (revival), Alice's Boys, Night and Day, 1978; Joking Apart, Tishoo, Stage Struck, 1979; Dr Faustus, Make and Break, The Dresser, Taking Steps, Enjoy, 1980; Hinge and Bracket at the Globe, Rowan Atkinson in Revue, House Guest, Quartermaine's Terms, 1981; Season's Greetings, Noises Off, 1982. *Recreations:* collecting Caroline memorabilia. *Address:* c/o 117 Regent Street, W1. *Club:* Garrick.

COE, Denis Walter; Assistant Director, Middlesex Polytechnic, since 1974; *b* 5 June 1929; *s* of James and Lily Coe, Whitley Bay, Northumberland; *m* 1953, Margaret Rae (marr. diss. 1979), *d* of William and Ida Chambers; three *s* one *d*; *m* 1979, Diana Rosemary, *d* of Maxwell and Flora Barr. *Educ:* Bede Trng Coll., Durham; London Sch. of Economics. Teacher's Certificate, 1952; BSc (Econ.) 1960; MSc (Econ.) 1966. National Service in RAF, 1947–50; Junior and Secondary Schoolmaster, 1952–59; Dep. Headmaster, Secondary Sch., 1959–61; Lectr in Govt, Manchester Coll. of Commerce, 1961–66. Contested (Lab) Macclesfield, 1964; MP (Lab) Middleton, Prestwich and Whitefield, 1966–70; Parly deleg. to Council of Europe and WEU, 1968–70. Dean of Students, NE London Polytechnic, 1970–74. Chm., Nat. Bureau for Handicapped Students, 1975–. Mem. Governing Council, Nat. Youth Theatre, 1968–. *Recreations:* music, drama, walking. *Address:* 35 Pinewood Close, St Albans, Herts.

COFFER, David Edwin, CBE 1973 (OBE 1963); General Secretary, The Royal British Legion, 1959–78; *b* 18 Sept. 1913; *s* of David Gilbertson Coffer and Florence Ellen Gard; *m* 1947, Edith Mary Moulton; three *d*. *Educ:* Colfe Grammar Sch. Mem., Supplementary Benefits Appeal Tribunals. Chm., Queen Mary's Roehampton Trust; Patron, SE County, Royal British Legion. *Address:* 47 Malvern Road, Orpington, Kent BR6 9HA. *T:* Orpington 29007.

COFFIN, Cyril Edwin; Director General, Food Manufacturers' Federation, since 1977; *b* 29 June 1919; *o s* of late Percy Edwin and Helena Constance Coffin; *m* 1947, Joyce Mary, *d* of C. R. Tobitt, Castle Hedingham; one *s* one *d* (and one *d* decd). *Educ:* King's Coll. Sch., Wimbledon; King's Coll., Cambridge (MA). Enlisted Royal Artillery, 1939; transf. Royal Scots, 1940; commnd RIASC, 1941. Temp. Asst Princ., Burma Office, 1946; Asst Princ., Min. of Food, 1947; Princ., 1948; jssc 1950; Asst, Sec., Min. of Agric., Fisheries and Food, 1957; seconded to Office of Minister for Science, 1963; Alternate UK Governor, Internat. Atomic Energy Agency, 1964. Under-Secretary: Min. of Technology, 1966, later DTI; Dept of Prices and Consumer Protection, 1974–77. *Recreations:* music, learning languages. *Address:* 54 Cambridge Avenue, New Malden, Surrey. *T:* 01-942 0763. *Clubs:* Athenæum; Union (Cambridge).

COGGAN, Baron *cr* 1980 (Life Peer), of Canterbury and of Sissinghurst in the County of Kent; **Rt. Rev. and Rt. Hon. (Frederick) Donald Coggan;** PC 1961; Royal Victorian Chain, 1980; MA; DD; *b* 9 Oct. 1909; *s* of late Cornish Arthur Coggan and late Fannie Sarah Coggan; *m* 1935, Jean Braithwaite Strain; two *d*. *Educ:* Merchant Taylors' School; St John's College, Cambridge; Wycliffe Hall, Oxford. Late Schol. of St John's Coll., Cambridge, 1st cl. Or. Lang. Trip. pt i, 1930; BA (1st cl. Or. Lang. Trip. pt ii) and Jeremie Sep. Prize, 1931, Naden Div. Student, 1931; Tyrwhitt Hebrew Schol. and Mason Prize, 1932; MA 1935. Asst Lectr in Semitic Languages and Literature, University of Manchester, 1931–34; Curate of St Mary Islington, 1934–37; Professor of New Testament, Wycliffe College, Toronto, 1937–44; Principal of the London College of Divinity, 1944–56; Bishop of Bradford, 1956–61; Archbishop of York, 1961–74; Archbishop of Canterbury, 1974–80. Chairman of the Liturgical Commission, 1960–64. President, Society for Old Testament Studies, 1967–68; first Life President, Church Army, 1981. Pro-Chancellor, York Univ., 1962–74, Hull Univ., 1968–74. Prelate, Order of St John of Jerusalem, 1967–. Hon. DD: Cambridge; Leeds, 1958; Aberdeen, 1963; Tokyo, 1963; Saskatoon, 1963; Huron, 1963; Hull, 1963; Manchester, 1972; Moravian Theol Seminary, 1976; Virginia Theol Seminary, 1979. Hon. LLD Liverpool, 1972; HHD Westminster Choir Coll., Princeton, 1966; Hon. DLitt Lancaster, 1967; STD (*hc*) Gen. Theol Seminary, NY, 1967; Hon. DCL Kent,

1975; DUniv York, 1975; FKC, 1975. *Publications:* A People's Heritage, 1944; The Ministry of the Word, 1945; The Glory of God, 1950; Stewards of Grace, 1958; Five Makers of the New Testament, 1962; Christian Priorities, 1963; The Prayers of the New Testament, 1967; Sinews of Faith, 1969; Word and World, 1971; Convictions, 1975; On Preaching, 1978; The Heart of the Christian Faith, 1978; The Name above All Names, 1981; Sure Foundation, 1981; Mission to the World, 1982; contributions to Theology, etc. *Recreations:* gardening, motoring, music. *Address:* Kingshead House, Sissinghurst, Kent. *T:* Cranbrook 714443. *Club:* Athenæum.

COGHILL, John Percival, CBE 1951; Foreign Service, retired; Minister to Republic of Honduras, 1954–55; *b* 29 Nov. 1902; *s* of Percy de Geiger Coghill and Dr Agnes Irene Sinclair Coghill. *Educ:* Loretto Sch.; Cheltenham Coll.; Emmanuel Coll., Cambridge. Served at various Foreign Service posts in China. *Recreation:* walking. *Club:* Royal Commonwealth Society.

COGHILL, Sir Joscelyn (Ambrose Cramer), 7th Bt *cr* 1778; retired; *b* 30 Sept. 1902; 3rd *s* of Sir Egerton Bushe Coghill, 5th Bt and Elizabeth Hildegarde Augusta (*d* 1954), *d* of Lt-Col Thomas Henry Somerville; *S* brother, 1981; *m* 1st, 1926, Elizabeth Gwendoline Atkins (marr. diss. 1949; she *d* 1980); one *s* one *d*; 2nd, 1949, Louise Berdonneau (marr. diss. 1971; she *d* 1978); three *d*. *Educ:* Osborne; RNC Dartmouth; Haileybury; Sandhurst. 1st Lt South Wales Borderers (24th Foot), 1922–25; tea and coffee planting, Kenya, 1926–28; Colonial Service, Kenya, 1929–32; as Lt-Comdr RNVR, served in Aden, Beirut and S France, 1940–46; UNO, London, 1946–47; Allied Control Commission, Germany, 1947–50; also engaged in various businesses and in film acting. *Heir:* *s* Egerton James Nevill Tobias Coghill [*b* 26 March 1930; *m* 1958, Gabriel Nancy, *d* of Major Dudley Claud Douglas Ryder; one *s* one *d*]. *Address:* Bishopmill House, Elgin, Morayshire.

COGMAN, Rev. Canon Frederick Walter; Dean of Guernsey, 1967–78; Rector of St Peter Port, Guernsey, 1976–78; *b* 4 March 1913; *s* of William Frederick Cogman and Mabel Cozens; *m* 1940, Rose Hélène Mauger; one *s* one *d*. *Educ:* Rutlish Sch., Merton; King's Coll., London. Asst Priest, Upton-cum-Chalvey, Slough, 1938–42; Chaplain and Housemaster, St George's Sch., Harpenden, 1942–48; Rector of St Martin, Guernsey, 1948–76. *Recreations:* music, painting. *Address:* Oriana Lodge, Rue des Fontenelles, Forest, Guernsey, CI.

COHAN, Robert Paul; Artistic Director and Principal Choreographer, Contemporary Dance Trust; *b* 27 March 1925; *s* of Walter and Billie Cohan. *Educ:* Martha Graham Sch., NYC. Joined Martha Graham Sch., 1946; Partner, 1950; Co-Dir, Martha Graham Co., 1966; Artistic Dir, Contemporary Dance Trust Ltd, 1967; Artistic Dir and Principal Choreographer, London Contemp. Dance Theatre, 1969–83; Artistic Advr, Batsheva Co., Israel, 1980; Director: York Univ., Toronto Choreographic Summer Sch., 1977; Gulbenkian Choreographic Summer Sch., Univ. of Surrey, 1978. With London Contemporary Dance Theatre has toured Britain, E and W Europe, S America, N Africa and USA; Dir, Banff Sch. of Fine Arts Choreographic Seminar, Canada, 1980; major works created: Cell, 1969 (recorded for BBC TV, 1982); Stages, 1971; People Together, 1973; Waterless Method of Swimming Instruction, 1974 (recorded for BBC TV); Class, 1975; Stabat Mater, 1975 (recorded for BBC TV); Masque of Separation, 1975; Khamsin, 1976; Nympheas, 1976 (recorded for BBC TV, 1983); Forest, 1977 (recorded by BBC TV); Eos, 1978; Songs, Lamentations and Praises, 1979; Field, 1980; Dances of Love and Death, 1981. Hon. Fellow, York Univ., Toronto. Evening Standard Award for most outstanding achievement in ballet, 1975; Soc. of West End Theatres Award for most outstanding achievement in ballet, 1978. *Recreation:* dancing. *Address:* The Place, 17 Dukes Road, WC1. *T:* 01-387 0161.

COHEN; *see* Waley-Cohen.

COHEN, His Honour Arthur; *see* Cohen, His Honour N. A. J.

COHEN, Sir Edward, Kt 1970; Director; Solicitor; Consultant, Paveys, Melbourne, Australia; Chairman: E Z Industries Ltd; Electrolytic Zinc Co. of Australasia Ltd; National Commercial Union Ltd; Commercial Union Properties (Australia) Pty Ltd; Derwent Metals Pty Ltd; Emu Bay Railway Co. Ltd; CUB Fibre Containers Pty Ltd; Carlton & United Breweries Ltd; Deputy Chairman, Associated Pulp & Paper Mills Ltd, 1981 (Director, 1951); Director of other cos; *m* 1939, Meryl D. Fink; one *s*. *Educ:* Scotch Coll., Melbourne; (Exhibnr in Greek and Roman History) Ormond Coll., Univ. of Melbourne (LLB). Served, 1940–45: AIF, 2/12 Fd Regt, 9th Div. Artillery, Captain 1942. Director: Herald and Weekly Times Ltd, 1974–77 (Vice-Chm., 1976–77); Michaelis Bayley Ltd, 1964–80. Past Member: Faculty of Law of Melbourne Univ., Council of Legal Education, and Bd of Examiners. Chm., Pensions Cttee of Melbourne Legacy, 1959–; Mem. Council Law Inst. of Victoria, 1959–68, Pres. 1965–66. *Address:* Orrong Road, Toorak, Victoria 3142, Australia; (office) 360 Collins Street, Melbourne, Victoria 3000, Australia. *Clubs:* Naval and Military, Victoria Racing, Royal Automobile (all in Melbourne).

COHEN, George Cormack; Sheriff-Substitute of the Lothians and Peebles at Edinburgh, 1955–66; *b* 16 Dec. 1909; *s* of J. Cohen and Mary J. Cormack, Melfort House, Bearsden, Dunbartonshire; *m* 1939, Elizabeth, *d* of James H. Wallace, Malvern; one *s* one *d*. *Educ:* Kelvinside Academy, Glasgow; Glasgow Univ. MA 1930, LLB 1934, Admitted to Scottish Bar, 1935; Sheriff-Substitute of Caithness at Wick, 1944-51; of Ayr and Bute at Kilmarnock, 1951-55. *Recreations:* travel, gastronomy, philately, gardening. *Address:* 51 Grange Road, Edinburgh EH9 1UF. *T:* 031-668 1689.

COHEN, Prof. John, PhD; Professor of Psychology, University of Manchester, 1952-78, now Emeritus; *b* 20 Jan. 1911; *s* of Joseph and Rebecca Cohen, Tredegar, Mon.; *m* 1st, 1939; one *s* one *d* ; 2nd, 1955, Rosemarie Loss; three *s. Educ:* Tredegar Elementary and County Schs.; University Coll., London (MA, PhD). Research at: University Coll., London, 1933-40; Institute of Experimental Psychology, Oxford, 1940. RAC, 1940-41; attached to Offices of War Cabinet and Central Statistical Office, 1941-48; Joint Sec., Expert Cttee on Work of Psychologists and Psychiatrists in the Services, 1942-45; Mem., Working Party on Recruitment and Training of Nurses, 1946-47; Tech. Sec., Internat. Preparatory Commn for World Congress on Mental Health, 1948; Mem., Inter-professional Advisory Cttee to World Fedn for Mental Health, 1949-52; Consultant to UNESCO, 1948, 1950, 1967; Lectr in Psychology, Univ. of Leeds, 1948-49; Prof. of Psychology, Univ. of Jerusalem, 1949-51; Lectr in Psychology, Birkbeck Coll., Univ. of London, 1951-52. Mem. of Council, Brit. Psychological Soc., 1956-59. Hon. MA (Manchester), FBPsS 1943. Fellow, World Academy of Art and Science; Corr. Mem., Centre de Recherches de Psychologie Comparative. Member: Internat. Editorial Bd of Medikon; Editorial Cttee of IKON Revue Internationale de Filmologie; Adv. Bd, Internat. Soc. for Study of Time. *Publications:* Human Nature, War and Society, 1946; Report on Recruitment and Training of Nurses, 1948; co-editor: Human Affairs, 1937; Educating for Democracy, 1939; co-author: Risk and Gambling, 1956; Humanistic Psychology, 1958; Chance, Skill and Luck, 1960; Readings in Psychology (ed), 1964; Behaviour in Uncertainty, 1964; Human Robots in Myth and Science, 1966; A New Introduction to Psychology, 1966; Psychological Time in Health and Disease, 1967; Psychology: An Outline for the intending Student (ed), 1967; Causes and Prevention of Road Accidents (with B. Preston), 1968; (with I. Christensen) Information and Choice, 1970; Elements of Child Psychology, 1970; Homo Psychologicus, 1971; Psychological Probability, 1972; Everyman's Psychology, 1973; (with J. H. Clark) Medicine, Mind and Man, 1980; The Lineaments of Mind, 1981; numerous papers in psychological, medical, psychiatric and other learned jls. *Recreations:* travel, music. *Address:* 15 Didsbury Park, Didsbury, Manchester M20 0LH. *T:* 061-445 3024.

COHEN, John Michael, FRSL 1957; critic and translator; *b* 5 Feb. 1903; *s* of late Arthur Cohen and Elizabeth (*née* Abrahams); *m* 1928, Audrey Frances Falk; four *s. Educ:* St Paul's Sch.; Queens' Coll., Cambridge. After short spell in publishing, joined family manufacturing business, 1925-40; war-time Schoolmaster, 1940-46; writing and translating from that date. *Publications: translations:* Don Quixote, 1950; Rousseau's Confessions, 1953; Rabelais, 1955; Life of Saint Teresa, 1957; Montaigne's Essays, 1958; Pascal's Pensées, 1961; Bernal Diaz, The Conquest of New Spain, 1963; The Spanish Bawd, 1964; Zarate, The Discovery and Conquest of Peru, 1968; The Four Voyages of Christopher Columbus, 1969; Sent off the Field, 1974; *criticism and biography:* Robert Browning, 1952; History of Western Literature, 1956; Life of Ludwig Mond, 1956; Poetry of This Age, 1959 (2nd, revised edn, 1966); Robert Graves, 1960; English Translators and Translations, 1962; The Baroque Lyric, 1963; En tiempos dificiles (a study of the new Cuban poetry), 1971; J. L. Borges, 1974; Journeys down the Amazon, 1975; (with J.-F. Phipps) The Common Experience, 1979; *anthologies:* Penguin Book of Comic & Curious Verse, 1952; More Comic & Curious Verse, 1956; Penguin Book of Spanish Verse, 1956; Yet More Comic & Curious Verse, 1959; Latin American Writing Today, 1967; Writers in the New Cuba, 1967; A Choice of Comic and Curious Verse, 1975; *dictionaries:* (with M. J. Cohen) Penguin Dictionary of Quotations, 1960; (with M. J. Cohen) Penguin Dictionary of Modern Quotations, 1971, rev. edn 1981; other translations. *Recreations:* meditation; listening to music; gardening. *Address:* Knappswood, Upper Basildon, Reading, Berks. *T:* Upper Basildon 282.

COHEN, Comdr Kenneth H. S., CB 1954; CMG 1946; RN; European Adviser to United Steel Companies, 1953-66; Vice-President: European League for Economic Co-operation, since 1972; Franco-British Society, since 1972 (Chairman, 1967-72); *b* 15 March 1900; *s* of late Herman Cohen, Barrister-at-Law, Inner Temple; *m* 1932, Mary Joseph, *d* of late Ernest Joseph, CBE, FRIBA; one *s* one *d. Educ:* Elstree Sch.; Eastbourne Coll. "Special Entry" RN Cadet, 1918, Midshipman, HMS Iron Duke; specialised in Torpedo Duties, 1926; RN Staff Coll., 1932; interpreter in French and Russian; retired (Lt-Comdr), 1935; appointed HMS President, 1939; Comdr 1940. Attached Foreign Office, 1945. Councillor, RIIA, Chatham House, 1963-75. Officier de la Légion d'Honneur; Croix de Guerre avec palmes (France); Legion of Merit, Degree of Officer (USA); Officier de la Couronne (Belgium); Order of the White Lion (Czechoslovakia); Commandeur de l'Etoile Noire (France), 1960. *Publications:* articles in national press on problems of European integration. *Address:* 33 Bloomfield Terrace, SW1. *T:* 01-730 3228. *Club:* Garrick.

COHEN, Laurence Jonathan, FBA 1973; Fellow and Praelector in Philosophy, Queen's College, since 1957, and British Academy Reader in Humanities, since 1982 Oxford University; *b* 7 May 1923; *s* of Israel and Theresa Cohen; *m* 1953, Gillian Mary Slee; three *s* one *d. Educ:* St Paul's Sch., London; Balliol Coll., Oxford (MA 1947). Served War: Naval Intell. in UK and SEAC, 1942-45, and Lieut (Sp.) RNVR. Asst in Logic and Metaphysics, Edinburgh Univ., 1947; Lectr in Philosophy, St Andrews Univ. at Dundee, 1950; Commonwealth Fund Fellow in Logic at Princeton and Harvard Univs,

1952-53. Vis. Lectr, Hebrew Univ. of Jerusalem, 1952; Visiting Professor: Columbia Univ., 1967; Yale Univ., 1972; British Acad. Philosophical Lectr, 1975; Fry Lectr, Bristol Univ., 1976; Vis. Fellow, ANU, 1980; Austin Lectr, UK Assoc. for Legal and Social Philos., 1982. Sec., Internat. Union of History and Philosophy of Science (Div. of Logic Methodology and Philosophy of Science), 1975-; Pres., British Soc. for Philosophy of Science, 1977-79. General Editor, Clarendon Library of Logic and Philosophy, 1973-. *Publications:* The Principles of World Citizenship, 1954; The Diversity of Meaning, 1962; The Implications of Induction, 1970; The Probable and the Provable, 1977; (ed jtly) Applications of Inductive Logic, 1980; Logic, Methodology and Philosophy of Science, 1982. *Recreations:* gardening; work for Council for Protection of Rural England. *Address:* Queen's College, Oxford OX1 4AW.

COHEN, Hon. Leonard Harold Lionel; barrister-at-law; *b* 1 Jan. 1922; *s* of Rt Hon. Lord Cohen, PC (Life Peer), and Adelaide, Lady Cohen (*née* Spielmann); *m* 1949, Eleanor Lucy Quixano Henriques; two *s* one *d. Educ:* Eton Coll.; New Coll., Oxford (MA). War Service, Rifle Bde (wounded), Captain, 1941-45. Called to Bar, Lincoln's Inn, 1948; practised at Chancery Bar, 1949-61. Dir, M. Samuel & Co. Ltd (subseq. Hill Samuel & Co. Ltd), 1961-76; Dir-Gen., Accepting Houses Cttee, 1976-82; Chm., United Services Trustee, 1976-. Master of the Skinners' Co., 1971-72. Hon. Col, 39th (City of London) Signal Regt (V), 1973-78. *Recreations:* shooting, golf, reading, opera. *Address:* 57 Bedford Gardens, W8 7EF. *T:* 01-229 6401. *Club:* White's.

COHEN, Dr Louis; Executive Secretary, Institute of Physics, since 1966; *b* 14 Oct. 1925; *s* of late Harry Cohen and Fanny Cohen (*née* Abrahams); *m* 1948, Eve G. Marsh; one *s* two *d. Educ:* Manchester Central High Sch.; Manchester Univ.; Imperial Coll., London. BSc, PhD, FInstP. Research Physicist, Simon-Carves Ltd, 1953-63; Research Manager, Pyrotenax Ltd, 1963-66. Hon. Sec., Council of Science and Technology Insts, 1969-; Treasurer, European Physical Soc., 1968-73; Corresp. Mem., Manchester Literary and Philosophical Soc., 1963. FRSA. *Publications:* papers and articles on physics and related subjects. *Recreations:* cooking, books, music, the theatre. *Address:* 9 Limewood Close, W13 8HL. *T:* 01-997 2001.

COHEN, Lt-Col Mordaunt, TD 1954; Regional Chairman of Industrial Tribunals, since 1976 (Chairman, 1974-76); *b* 6 Aug. 1916; *s* of Israel Ellis Cohen and Sophie Cohen; *m* 1953, Her Honour Judge Myrella Cohen, *qv* ; one *s* one *d. Educ:* Bede Collegiate Sch. for Boys, Sunderland. Admitted solicitor, 1938. Served War, RA, 1940-46: seconded RWAFF; despatches, Burma campaign; served TA, 1947-55: CO 463(M) HAA Regt, RA(TA), 1954-55. Alderman, Sunderland Co. Bor. Council, 1967-74; Chm., Sunderland Educn Cttee, 1970-72; Chm., NE Council of Educn Cttees, 1971; Councillor, Tyne and Wear CC, 1973-74; Dep. Chm., Northern Traffic Comrs, 1973-74. Chairman: Mental Health Review Tribunal, 1967-76; Governors, Sunderland Polytechnic, 1969-72; Mem. Court, Univ. of Newcastle upon Tyne, 1968-72. Pres., Sunderland Law Soc., 1970; Trustee and past Pres., Sunderland Hebrew Congregation; Mem., Bd of Deputies of British Jews (Vice-Chm., Provincial Cttee); former Mem., Chief Rabbinate Council; Trustee: Ajex Charitable Trust; Ashbrooke Foundn. *Recreations:* watching sport but playing bowls; gardening, communal service, promoting inter-faith understanding. *Address:* c/o Regional Office of Industrial Tribunals, Watson House, Pilgrim Street, Newcastle upon Tyne NE1 6RB. *T:* Newcastle upon Tyne 28865.

COHEN, Myrella, QC 1970; Her Honour Judge Myrella Cohen; a Circuit Judge, since 1972; *b* 16 Dec. 1927; *d* of late Samuel and Sarah Cohen, Manchester; *m* 1953, Lt-Col Mordaunt Cohen, *qv* ; one *s* one *d. Educ:* Manchester High Sch. for Girls; Colwyn Bay Grammar Sch.; Manchester Univ. (LLB 1948). Called to the Bar, Gray's Inn, 1950. Recorder of Hull, 1971. *Address:* c/o Crown Court, Moot Hall, Newcastle upon Tyne NE1 1RT. *Club:* Soroptimist Club of Great Britain.

COHEN, Nat; Director and Consultant, EMI Films Ltd (Chairman, 1970-78); *b* 1906. Entered film industry, 1930. Director: EMI Film Productions Ltd, 1970-79; EMI Film & Theatre Corporation Ltd, 1970-79. *Films produced include:* Carry On Sergeant, and 12 other Carry On films; A Kind of Loving; Billy Liar; Darling; Far From the Madding Crowd; Murder on the Orient Express; Death on the Nile. *Address:* EMI Films Ltd, 30 Golden Square, W1A 4QX.

COHEN, Lt-Col Nathan Leslie, TD 1949; JP; *b* 13 Jan. 1908; *s* of Reuben and Maud Cohen; unmarried. *Educ:* Stockton-on-Tees Grammar Sch.; Clifton Coll. In private practice as a Solicitor until 1939; called to the Bar, Lincoln's Inn, 1954. War Service, Aug. 1939-May 1945. Senior Legal Officer (Lt-Col), Military Govt, Carinthia, Austria, 1945-49; Pres. of Sessions Courts, Malaya, 1949-57; Justice of the Special Courts, Cyprus, 1958-59; Judge of HM Court of Sovereign Base Areas of Akrotiri and Dhekalia, Cyprus, 1960-67; Adjudicator under Immigration Appeals Act, 1970-71. Mem., Cleveland Co. Social Services Cttee 1978-80. Vice-President: Northern Area, British Legion; Durham and Cleveland British Legion; Cleveland Co. British Red Cross Soc.; Pres., St John Ambulance Assoc., Stockton. Associate SBStJ, 1980. JP Stockton-on-Tees, 1967. Diamond Jubilee Medal (Johore), 1955; Colonial Police Medal, 1956; Royal Brit. Legion Gold Badge, 1979; Badge of Honour, British Red Cross Soc., 1981. *Recreations:* travelling, reading. *Address:* 35

Richmond Road, Stockton-on-Tees, Cleveland. *Club:* Royal Over-Seas League.

COHEN, His Honour (Nathaniel) Arthur (Jim), JP; County Court Judge, Circuit No 38, 1955-56, Circuit No 43, 1956-60, Circuit No 56, 1960-70, retired; *b* 19 Jan. 1898; 2nd *s* of late Sir Benjamin Arthur Cohen, KC, and Lady Cohen; *m* 1st, 1927, Judith Luard (marr. diss.); two *s*; 2nd, 1936, Joyce Collingridge. *Educ:* Rugby; CCC, Oxford (BA). Served European War, 1916-19, Royal Navy. Called to Bar, Inner Temple, 1923. War of 1939-45: recalled to RN and placed on Emergency List with rank of Commander. Legal Adviser to UNRRA, 1946-49; Dep. Chm., Foreign Compensation Commn, 1950-55. JP Surrey, 1958. *Recreations:* golf, music. *Address:* Bay Tree Cottage, Crockham Hill, Edenbridge, Kent. *Club:* United Oxford & Cambridge University.

COHEN, Percy, CBE 1936; Joint Director, Conservative Research Department, 1948-59; *b* London, 25 Dec. 1891; *e s* of late M. Cohen; *m* 1917, Rosa Abrams (*d* 1973); one *s* one *d. Educ:* Central Foundation Sch., London. Entered service of Conservative Central Office, 1911; Head of Library and Information Dept, 1928-48. Served first European War, France. Worked in 12 General Elections; Editor, Constitutional Year Book, 1929-39; Editor, Notes on Current Politics, 1942-59. Sec. to several post-war problems Cttees, 1944-45. *Publications:* British System of Social Insurance, 1932; Unemployment Insurance and Assistance in Britain, 1938; (ed) Conservative Election Handbook, 1945; (ed) Campaign Guide, 1950, 1951, 1955 and 1959. *Recreation:* walking. *Address:* Sunridge Court, 76 The Ridgeway, NW11. *T:* 01-455 5203. *Club:* St Stephen's Constitutional.

COHEN, Sir Rex (Arthur Louis), KBE 1964 (OBE 1944); Director, Tribune Investment Trust; *b* 27 Nov. 1906; *s* of Rex David Cohen, Condover Hall, Shrewsbury; *m* 1932, Nina Alice Castello; one *d. Educ:* Rugby Sch.; Trinity Coll., Cambridge (BA). Served KSLI, 1938-45. Past Mem., BoT Cttee for Consumer Protection. Past Chairman: Lewis's Investment Trust Group, 1958-65 (Joint Man. Dir, 1945); NAAFI, 1961-63; Higgs & Hill Ltd, 1966-72; Meat and Livestock Commn, 1967-72. Officer, Order of Orange Nassau (Netherlands), 1944. *Recreations:* racing, horse breeding, shooting. *Address:* Ruckmans Farm, Oakwood Hill, near Dorking, Surrey. *T:* Oakwood Hill 255. *Clubs:* White's; Jockey (Newmarket).

COHEN, Dr Richard Henry Lionel, CB 1969; Chief Scientist, Department of Health and Social Security, 1972-73, retired; *b* 1 Feb. 1907; *y s* of Frank Lionel and Bertha Hendelah Cohen; *m* 1934, Margaret Clarkson Deas; one *s. Educ:* Clifton Coll.; King's Coll., Cambridge; St Bartholomew's Hospital. Miscellaneous hosp. appts, 1940-46; MRC, 1948-62; Dep. Chief Med. Off., MRC, 1957-62; Dept of Health and Social Security (formerly Min. of Health), 1962-73. *Address:* The End House South, Lady Margaret Road, Cambridge. *Club:* Reform.

COHEN, Prof. Robert Donald, MD, FRCP; Professor of Medicine and Director, Academic Medical Unit, London Hospital Medical College, University of London, since 1981 (Professor of Metabolic Medicine, 1974-81); *b* 11 Oct. 1933; *s* of Dr Harry H. and Ruby Cohen; *m* 1961, Dr Barbara Joan Boucher; one *s* one *d. Educ:* Clifton Coll.; Trinity Coll., Cambridge. MA, MD (Cantab). Hon. Cons. Physician, London Hosp., 1967; Chm., Editorial Bd, Clinical Science and Molecular Medicine, 1973-74; Dir, Academic Unit of Metabolism and Endocrinology, London Hosp. Med. Coll., 1974; Chairman: Adv. Cttee on the Application of Computing Science to Medicine and the Nat. Health Service, 1976-77; DHSS Computer R&D Cttee, 1977-80. *Publications:* Clinical and Biochemical Aspects of Lactic Acidosis (with H. F. Woods), 1976; papers in Clin. Sci. and Molecular Med., BMJ, Lancet, Biochemical Journal. *Address:* The London Hospital, Whitechapel Road, E1 1BB. *T:* 01-247 5454.

COHEN, Ruth Louisa, CBE 1969; MA; Principal, Newnham College, Cambridge, 1954-72; University Lecturer in Economics, Cambridge, 1945-74; Governor, Hebrew University of Jerusalem; *b* 10 Nov. 1906; *d* of late Walter Samuel Cohen and late Lucy Margaret Cohen. *Educ:* Hayes Court, Kent; Newnham Coll., Cambridge. Commonwealth Fund Fellow, Stanford and Cornell Univs., USA, 1930-32; Research Officer, Agricultural Economics Research Inst., Oxford, 1933-39; Fellow of Newnham Coll., Cambridge, 1939-54; Min. of Food, 1939-42; Board of Trade, 1942-45. Lay Mem., Gen. Medical Council, 1961-76. City Cllr, Cambridge, 1973-. *Publications:* History of Milk Prices, 1936; Economics of Agriculture, 1939; articles in Economic Journal, etc. *Address:* 25 Gough Way, Cambridge. *T:* Cambridge 62699. *Club:* University Women's.

COHEN, Stanley; MP (Lab) Leeds (South East) since 1970; *b* 31 July 1927; *s* of Thomas and Teresa Cohen; *m* 1954, Brenda P. Rafferty; three *s* one *d. Educ:* St Patrick's and St Charles' Schools, Leeds. Served in Royal Navy, 1947-49. Employed in Clothing Industry, 1943-47 and 1949-51; Clerical Officer with British Railways, 1951-70. Mem. Leeds City Council, 1952-; elected Alderman, 1968. Parly Candidate (Lab) Barkston Ash County Constituency, 1966. PPS to Minister of State, DES, 1976-79. Mem., Duke of Edinburgh's Commonwealth Study Conf. to Australia, 1968. *Recreations:* walking, camping, driving. *Address:* 164 Ring Road, Halton, Leeds LS15 7AE. *T:* Leeds 649568. *Clubs:* Crossgates Recreational; Irish Centre (Leeds).

COHEN, Prof. Stanley, PhD; Professor of Criminology, Hebrew University, Jerusalem, since 1981; *b* 23 Feb. 1942; *s* of Ray and Sie Cohen; *m* 1963, Ruth Kretzmer; two *d. Educ:* Univ. of Witwatersrand, Johannesburg (BA); LSE, Univ. of London (PhD). Psychiatric social worker, 1963-64; Lectr in Sociology: Enfield Coll., 1965-67; Univ. of Durham, 1967-72; Sen. Lectr in Sociol., Univ. of Essex, 1972-74, Prof. of Sociol., 1974-81. *Publications:* Images of Deviance, 1971; Folk Devils and Moral Panics, 1972; Psychological Survival, 1972; The Manufacture of News, 1973; Escape Attempts, 1976; Prison Secrets, 1978. *Address:* Institute of Criminology, Hebrew University, Jerusalem 91905, Israel.

COHEN, Prof. Sydney, CBE 1978; FRS 1978; Professor of Chemical Pathology, Guy's Hospital Medical School, since 1965; *b* Johannesburg, SA, 18 Sept. 1921; *s* of Morris and Pauline Cohen; *m* 1950, June Bernice Adler, JP, *d* of Dr and Mrs L. D. Adler; one *s* one *d. Educ:* King Edward VIIth Sch., Johannesburg; Witwatersrand and London Univs. MD, PhD. Lectr, Dept of Physiology, Witwatersrand Univ., 1947-53; Scientific Staff, Nat. Inst. for Med. Research, London, 1954-60; Reader, Dept of Immunology, St Mary's Hosp. Med. Sch., 1960-65. Mem., MRC, 1974-76; Chm., Tropical Med. Research Bd, MRC, 1974-76; Chm., WHO Scientific Gp on Immunity to Malaria, 1976-81; Mem., WHO expert adv. panel on malaria, 1977-; Mem. Council, Royal Soc., 1982-. Nuffield Dominion Fellow in Medicine, 1954; Founder Fellow, RCPath, 1964. *Publications:* papers on immunology and parasitic diseases in sci. jls. *Recreations:* golf, gardening, forestry. *Address:* 4 Frognal Rise, NW3 6RD. *T:* 01-435 6507. *Club:* Royal and Ancient (St Andrews).

COHN, Prof. Norman, MA; DLitt; FBA 1978; FRHistS; historian; Astor-Wolfson Professor, University of Sussex, 1973-80, now Professor Emeritus; *b* London, 12 Jan. 1915; *yr s* of late August Cohn, barrister-at-law, Middle Temple, and Daisy (*née* Reimer); *m* 1941, Vera, *d* of late Mark and Eva Broido, St Petersburg; one *s. Educ:* Gresham's Sch., Holt (Scholar); Christ Church, Oxford (Scholar). 1st Class Hons, Sch. of Medieval and Mod. Languages, 1936; DLitt Glasgow, 1957. Served War of 1939-45, Queen's Royal Regt and Intell. Corps. Lectr in French, Glasgow Univ., 1946-51; Professor of French: Magee Univ. Coll. (then associated with TCD), 1951-60; King's Coll., Durham Univ., 1960-63; changed career to become Dir, Columbus Centre, Gen. Ed., Columbus Centre's Studies in the Dynamics of Persecution and Extermination, and Professorial Fellow, Sussex Univ., 1966-73. Hugh Le May Fellow, Rhodes Univ., 1950; Fellow, Center for Advanced Study in the Behavioral Sciences, Stanford, Calif, 1966; Vis. Fellow, Center for Humanities, Wesleyan Univ., Conn, 1971; Fellow, Netherlands Inst. for Advanced Study, 1975-76; Vis. For. Scholar, Concordia Univ., Montreal, 1982. *Publications:* Gold Khan and other Siberian legends, 1946; The Pursuit of the Millennium: revolutionary millenarians and mystical anarchists of the middle ages, 1957, rev. edns 1961, 1970; Warrant for Genocide: the myth of the Jewish world-conspiracy and the Protocols of the Elders of Zion, 1967, rev. edn 1981 (Anisfield-Wolf Award in Race Relations, 1967); Europe's Inner Demons: an enquiry inspired by the great witch-hunt, 1975, rev. edn 1976; contributor to various symposia, learned jls, and reviews. *Recreations:* walking, travel, looking at pictures, butterfly-watching. *Address:* 61 New End, NW3 1HY. *T:* 01-435 5755. *Club:* Athenæum.

COHN, Prof. Paul Moritz, FRS 1980; Professor of Mathematics in the University of London, at Bedford College, since 1967; *b* Hamburg, 8 Jan. 1924; *o c* of late James Cohn and late Julia Cohn (*née* Cohen); *m* 1958, Deirdre Sonia Sharon; two *d. Educ:* Trinity Coll., Cambridge. BA 1948, MA, PhD 1951. Chargé de Recherches, Univ. de Nancy, 1951-52; Lectr, Manchester Univ., 1952-62; Reader, London Univ., at Queen Mary Coll., 1962-67. Visiting Prof.: Yale Univ., 1961-62; Univ. of California (Berkeley), 1962; Univ. of Chicago, 1964; State Univ. of New York (Stony Brook), 1967; Rutgers Univ., 1967-68; Univ. of Paris, 1969; Tulane Univ., 1971; Indian Inst. of Technology, Delhi, 1971; Univ. of Alberta, 1972; Carleton Univ., Ottawa, 1973; Technion, Haifa, 1975; Iowa State Univ., 1978; Univ. of Bielefeld, 1979. Sec., London Mathematical Soc., 1965-67; Member: Council, London Math. Soc., 1968-71, 1972-75; 1979-; Mathematics Cttee, SRC, 1977-80; Editor, London Math. Soc. Monographs, 1968-77, 1980-. Lester R. Ford Award (Mathematical Assoc. of America), 1972; Senior Berwick Prize, London Mathematical Soc., 1974. *Publications:* Lie Groups, 1957; Linear Equations, 1958; Solid Geometry, 1961; Universal Algebra, 1965, 2nd edn 1981 (trans foreign langs); Free Rings and their Relations, 1971; Algebra, vol. I, 1974, 2nd edn 1982, vol. II, 1977; Skewfield Constructions, 1977; papers on algebra in various mathematical periodicals. *Recreations:* linguistics, etymology. *Address:* Department of Mathematics, Bedford College, Regent's Park, NW1 4NS. *T:* 01-486 4400.

COILEY, John Arthur, PhD; Keeper, National Railway Museum, York, since 1974; *b* 29 March 1932; *o s* of Arthur George Coiley and Stella Coiley (*née* Chinnock); *m* 1956, Patricia Anne Coiley, BA, (*née* Dixon); two *s* one *d. Educ:* Beckenham and Penge Grammar Sch.; Selwyn Coll., Cambridge (BA, PhD Metallurgy). Scientific Officer, UKAEA, Harwell, 1957-60; Aeon Laboratories, Egham, 1960-65; Development Manager, Fulmer Research Laboratories, 1965-73; Asst Keeper, Science Museum, 1973-74. Vice-President, Internat. Assoc. of Transport Museums, 1977-. *Publication:* (jtly) Images of Steam, 1968, 2nd edn 1974. *Recreations:* photography, motoring. *Address:* 4 Beech Close, Farnham, Knaresborough, N Yorkshire HG5 9JJ. *T:* Copgrove 497.

COKAYNE, family name of **Baron Cullen of Ashbourne.**

COKE, family name of **Earl of Leicester.**

COKE, Viscount; Edward Douglas Coke, DL; *b* 6 May 1936; *s* and *heir* of 6th Earl of Leicester, *qv*; *m* 1962, Valeria Phyllis, *e d* of late L. A. Potter; two *s* one *d*. *Educ*: St Andrew's, Grahamstown, CP, S Africa. DL Norfolk, 1981. *Recreations*: skiing, sailing, shooting. *Heir*: *s* Hon. Thomas Edward Coke, *b* 6 July 1965. *Address*: Holkham, Wells-next-the-Sea, Norfolk. *Clubs*: Brooks's, White's, Farmers'; Norfolk (Norwich).

COKE, Dorothy Josephine, RWS 1943 (ARWS 1935); artist; an official war artist, 1940, Women's Services subjects; *d* of Joseph Charles Coke and Edith Mary Price. *Educ*: The Slade School. Mem. of the New English Art Club. *Address*: 11 Eley Crescent, Rottingdean, Brighton, E Sussex.

COKE, Gerald Edward, CBE 1967; JP; DL; *b* 25 Oct. 1907; *o s* of late Major the Hon. Sir John Coke, KCVO, and late Hon. Mrs Coke; *m* 1939, Patricia, *e d* of late Rt Hon. Sir Alexander Cadogan, PC, OM, GCMG, KCB; two *s* one *d* (and one *s* decd). *Educ*: Eton; New Coll., Oxford (MA). Served War of 1939-45, Lieut-Col. Treas., Bridewell Royal Hosp. (King Edward's Sch., Witley), 1946-72; Chm., Glyndebourne Arts Trust, 1955-75; Dir, Royal Acad. of Music, 1957-74; Dir, Royal Opera House, Covent Garden, 1958-64; a Governor, BBC, 1961-66. Director: Rio Tinto-Zinc Corp., 1947-75 (Dep. Chm. 1962-66; Chm. Rio Tinto Co., 1956-62); S. G. Warburg & Co., 1945-75; United Kingdom Provident Instn, 1952-74. JP 1920, DL 1974, Hants. Hon. FRAM 1968. *Address*: Jenkyn Place, Bentley, Hants. *T*: Bentley 23118. *Club*: Brooks's.

COKER, Dame Elizabeth, DBE 1979; DL; Chairman: Mid-Essex District Health Authority (formerly Essex Area Health Authority), since 1973; Basildon Development Corporation, since 1981 (Member, since 1971; Deputy Chairman, 1980); *d* of William Lowe and Ellen Elizabeth (*née* Winnington); *m* 1947, Frank L. Coker, LDS RCS; one *d*. *Educ*: Grove Park Sch., Wrexham; Queen Mary Coll., Univ. of London (BSc Hons). Member: Essex CC, 1959- (Chm., 1971-74); Essex Cttee, Assoc. of Educn Cttees, 1965-74 (Vice-Pres., 1972-74); County Councils Assoc., 1968-74; Assoc. of County Councils, 1974- (Chm., Exec. Council, 1976-79); Council of Local Educn Authorities, 1974-79 (Chm., 1974-75); Eastern Electricity Bd, 1973-77; Chm., Harlow Development Corporation, 1979-80. Mem. Council, Essex Univ., 1965- (Treasurer, 1982-); Fellow and Governor, Queen Mary Coll.; Governor: United World Coll. of the Atlantic, St Donats, 1980; Felsted and Brentwood Schs. DL Essex, 1974. *Recreation*: travel. *Address*: Winnington House, Danbury, Chelmsford, Essex. *T*: Danbury 2555.

COKER, Peter Godfrey, RA 1972 (ARA 1965); ARCA 1953; *b* 27 July 1926; *m* 1951, Vera Joyce Crook; one *s*. *Educ*: St Martin's Sch. of Art; Royal Coll. of Art (Royal Schol.). Brit. Inst. Schol., 1954. Arts Council Award to Artists, 1976. One-man Exhibitions: Zwemmer Gall., 1956, 1957, 1959, 1964, 1967; Magdalene Street Gall., Cambridge, 1968; Stone Gall., Newcastle, 1969; Thackeray Gall., London, 1970, 1972, 1974, 1975, 1976, 1978; Gallery 10, 1980. Retrospective Exhibitions: Minories, Colchester, 1972; Victoria Gall., Bath, 1972; Morley Gall., London, 1973; Mappin Art Gall., Sheffield, 1973; Chelmsford and Essex Museum, 1978; Royal Acad., 1979. Represented in Group Exhibitions: Tate Gall., 1958; Jordan Gall., Toronto, 1958; Northampton, 1960; Europaisches Forum, Alpbach, Austria, 1960; Neue Galerie, Linz, 1960; RCA, 1952-62; Painters in E Anglia, Arts Council, 1966; Bicentenary Exhibn, Royal Acad., 1768-1968, 1968; British Painting 1900-1960, Sheffield and Aberdeen, 1975-76; British Painting 1952-77, RA. Works in permanent collections: Tate Gall.; Arts Council; Contemp. Art Soc., GB; Contemp. Art Soc., Wales; Chantrey Bequest; Nat. Portrait Gall.; V&A; Stedelijk Museum Ostend; Eastern Arts Assoc.; Rugby Library and Museum; Chelmsford and Essex Museum; Art Galls and Mus. of Carlisle, Ipswich, Leicester, Rochdale; Art Galls of Bath (Victoria), Batley, Birmingham, Coventry (Herbert), Kettering, Leeds City, Sheffield City, Southport (Atkinson); RCA; RA; Educn Cttees of Nottingham, Essex, Derbyshire, Lancs, ILEA; Liverpool Univ. *Publication*: Etching Techniques, 1976. *Recreation*: music. *Address*: The Red House, Mistley, Manningtree, Essex. *T*: Manningtree 2179.

COLAHAN, Air Vice-Marshal William Edward, CB 1978; CBE 1973; DFC 1945; retired; Officer Careers Counsellor (Royal Air Force), since 1978; *b* 7 Aug. 1923; *er s* of Dr W. E. and Dr G. C. J. Colahan; *m* 1949, Kathleen Anne Butler; one *s* two *d*. *Educ*: Templeton High Sch., S Africa; Univ. of Cape Town. S African Air Force, 1941-46; service in Italy, France (Temp. Captain); Royal Air Force, 1947-: Flt-Lt 1947; Sqdn Ldr 1952; psa 1957; Wing Comdr 1959; jssc 1962; Gp Captain 1965; Air Cdr 1970; idc 1970; Air Comdr Malta, 1971-73; Air Vice-Marshal 1973; ACAS (Operations), 1973-75; AOC and Commandant, RAF College Cranwell, 1975-78. Mem. Council, St Dunstans, 1978-. *Recreation*: shooting. *Address*: OCC (RAF), RAF College, Cranwell, Sleaford, Lincs NG34 8HB. *T*: Sleaford 302489. *Club*: Royal Air Force.

COLBECK-WELCH, Air Vice-Marshal Edward Lawrence, CB 1961; OBE 1948; DFC 1941; Royal Air Force, retired; *b* 29 Jan. 1914; *s* of Major G. S. M. Colbeck-Welch, MC, Collingham, Yorks; *m* 1938, Doreen, *d* of T. G. Jenkin, Sliema, Malta; one *s* two *d*. *Educ*: Leeds Grammar Sch. Commnd RAF, 1933; No. 22 Sqdn, RAF, 1934-37; CFS Instructor Course, 1937; Flying Instr RAuxAF Sqdns, 1937-39; Staff duties, 1940; OC No. 29 Night Fighter Sqdn, 1941-42; Staff Coll., 1942; Staff duties, 1943-44; Staff duties in 2nd TAF and OC No. 139 (Bomber) Wing, 1944-45; Air Min. Dep. Dir Air Defence, 1945-47; Staff duties in USA, 1947-50; OC Fighter Stations (2), 1950-53; Air Min. Personnel Staff duties, 1954-55; student, idc 1956; Comdt Central Fighter Estab., 1957-58; SASO, HQ No 13 (F) Group, 1959; SASO, HQ Fighter Comd RAF, 1960-63. *Recreation*: sailing. *Address*: La Cote au Palier, St Martin, Jersey, CI. *Clubs*: Royal Air Force Yacht, Royal Channel Islands Yacht, St Helier Yacht.

COLBERT, Claudette; stage and film actress; *b* Paris, 13 Sept. 1905; *d* of Georges Chauchoin and Jeanne Loew; *m* 1st, Norman Foster (marr. diss.); 2nd, Dr Joel J. Pressman (*d* 1968). Went to America, 1908. First appearances: New York Stage, 1925; London stage, 1928. Returned to Broadway stage, 1958-60. After success on Broadway, entered films, 1929. *Plays include*: Wild Westcotts, The Marionette Man, We've Got to Have Money, The Cat Came Back, Leah Kleschna, High Stakes, A Kiss in the Taxi, The Ghost Train, The Pearl of Great Price, The Barker, The Mulberry Bush, La Gringa, Within the Law, Fast Life, Tin Pan Alley, Dynamo, See Naples and Die, The Marriage-Go-Round. *Films include*: For the Love of Mike, The Lady Lies, Manslaughter, The Smiling Lieutenant, Sign of the Cross, Cleopatra, Private Worlds, Maid of Salem, It Happened One Night (Academy Award, 1934), The Gilded Lily, I Met Him in Paris, Bluebeard's Eighth Wife, Zaza, Midnight, Drums Along the Mohawk, Skylark, Remember the Day, Palm Beach Story, No Time for Love, So Proudly We Hail, Without Reservations, The Secret Heart, The Egg and I, Sleep My Love, Three Came Home, The Secret Fury, The Planter's Wife, Destiny, Versailles, Parrish. *Address*: Bellerive, St Peter, Barbados, West Indies.

COLBURN, Oscar Henry, CBE 1981; JP; farmer; *m* 1950, Helen Joan (*née* Garne); one *s* two *d*. Crown Estates Commission, 1976-; Chairman, Consultative Board of Joint Consultative Organisation for Research and Development in Agriculture and Food, 1981-; Chairman, Grasslands Research Institute. Former Chm., Regional Panel, MAFF; former Mem., Northfield Cttee; past Mem. Council, RASE. Pioneer breeder of Poll Hereford cattle; during 1960s developed Colbred sheep, first new British breed of sheep for over a century. JP Northleach (Chm., 1976-); High Sheriff of Glos, 1980-81. Hon. FRAgS, 1982. Summers Trophy, NFU Glos Br., 1956; George Hedley Meml Award, for services to Sheep Industry, 1963; Bledisloe Lecture, 1972; Bath and West Bi-Annual Lecture, 1981. *Address*: Crickley Barrow, Northleach, near Cheltenham, Glos GL54 3QA. *Clubs*: MCC, Farmers', Brooks's.

COLCHESTER, Suffragan Bishop of, since 1966; **Rt. Rev. Roderic Norman Coote,** DD; *b* 13 April 1915; *s* of late Comdr B. T. Coote and late Grace Harriet (*née* Robinson); *m* 1964, Erica Lynette, *d* of late Rev. E. G. Shrubbs, MBE; one *s* two *d*. *Educ*: Woking County Sch.; Trinity Coll., Dublin. Curate Asst, St Bartholomew's, Dublin, 1938-41; Missionary Priest in the Diocese of Gambia and the Rio Pongas, 1942; Bishop of Gambia and the Rio Pongas, 1951-57; Suffragan Bishop of Fulham, 1957-66; Archdeacon of Colchester, 1969-72. Member, General Synod of Church of England, 1969-72. *Recreations*: tennis; squash; piano (composer and broadcaster); Irish Champion 120 yds Hurdles. *Address*: The Bishop's House, 32 Inglis Road, Colchester, Essex.

COLCHESTER, Archdeacon of; *see* Roxburgh, Ven. J. W.

COLCHESTER, Rev. Halsey Sparrowe, CMG 1968; OBE 1960; MA Oxon; Priest in Charge at Great Tew, Oxfordshire, since 1981; *b* 5 March 1918; *s* of late Ernest Charles Colchester; *m* 1946, Rozanne Felicity Hastings Medhurst, *d* of late Air Chief Marshal Sir Charles Medhurst, KCB, OBE, MC; four *s* one *d*. *Educ*: Uppingham Sch.; Magdalen Coll., Oxford. Served Oxf. and Bucks Lt Inf., 1940-43; 2nd SAS Regt, 1944-46 (despatches); Captain. Joined Diplomatic Service, 1947; FO 1948-50; 2nd Sec., Istanbul, 1950-54; FO 1954-56; Consul, Zürich, 1956-60; 1st Sec., Athens, 1960-64; FO 1964-68; Counsellor, Paris, 1968-72; retired from Diplomatic Service, 1972; Ordinand at Cuddesdon Theological Coll., 1972-73; Deacon, 1973; Priest, 1974; Curate, Minchinhampton, Glos, 1973-76; Vicar of Bollington, Cheshire, 1976-81. *Recreations*: walking, theatre-going, wild flowers. *Address*: Great Tew Vicarage, Oxfordshire OX7 4AG. *T*: Great Tew 293. *Club*: Travellers'.

COLCHESTER, Trevor Charles, CMG 1958; *b* London, 18 April 1909; *s* of Charles Colchester; *m* 1937, Nancy Joan Russell; one *d*. *Educ*: Corpus Christi Coll., Cambridge (MA). Colonial Service, 1931-64; in Kenya, Zanzibar, and Northern Rhodesia. Sec. to Cabinet, Kenya, 1954-57; Permanent Sec., Kenya, 1957-61. Sec., Commonwealth Assoc. of Architects, 1964-74. Hon. FRIBA 1975. *Recreations*: conservation, gardening. *Address*: Plomesgate, Aldeburgh, Suffolk.

COLDRICK, Albert Percival, OBE 1974; FCIT 1972; Member, Industrial Tribunal, since 1975; Chairman: National Health Service SE Thames Appeals Tribunal, since 1974; Executive Committee, Industrial Participation Association, since 1974; *b* 6 June 1913; *s* of Albert Percival and Florence Coldrick; *m* 1938, Esther Muriel Blades; three *s*. *Educ*: Britannia Bridge Elementary Sch.; Wigan Mining and Technical College. Railway Controller, 1933-47; Transport Salaried Staffs' Assoc.: full-time Officer, 1948-62; Sen. Asst Sec., 1962-66; Asst Gen. Sec., 1967; Gen. Sec., 1968-73. Mem., General Council, TUC, 1968-73. Mem., Midlands and West Region Rlys Bd,

1975-77. Chm., Foundn for Industrial Understanding, 1979-. Jt Editor, International Directory of the Trade Union Movement, 1977-. *Recreations:* reading, walking, photography. *Address:* 10 Murray Avenue, Bromley, Kent. *T:* 01-464 4089. *Club:* Reform.

COLDSTREAM, Sir George (Phillips), KCB 1955 (CB 1949); KCVO 1968; QC 1960; *b* 20 Dec. 1907; *s* of late Francis Menzies Coldstream; *m* 1st, 1934, Mary Morna (marr. diss. 1948), *o d* of Major A. D. Carmichael, Meigle, Perthshire; one *d* (and one *d* decd); 2nd, Sheila Hope, *widow* of Lt-Col J. H. H. Whitty, DSO, MC. *Educ:* Rugby; Oriel Coll., Oxford. Called to the Bar, Lincoln's Inn, 1930. Bencher, 1954; Asst to Parly Counsel to Treasury, 1934-39; Legal Asst, Lord Chancellor's Office, 1939-44; Dep. Clerk of the Crown, 1944-54; Clerk of the Crown in Chancery and Permanent Sec. to the Lord Chancellor, 1954-68. Member: British War Crimes Commn, 1944-46; British team, Anglo-Amer. Legal Exchanges, 1961-69; Royal Commn on Assizes and Quarter Sessions, 1967-70; Top Salaries Review Body, 1971-82. Special Consultant, Amer. Inst. of Judicial Admin, NY, 1968-71. Part-time Chm., Industrial Tribunals, 1975-80. Chm., Council of Legal Educn, 1970-73. Pres., Old Rugbeian Soc., 1978-80. Hon. Fellow, Amer. Coll. of Trial Lawyers, 1969. Hon. LLD Columbia Univ., 1966. *Address:* The Gate House, Seaford, East Sussex. *T:* Seaford 892801. *Clubs:* Athenæum; Royal Cruising.

COLDSTREAM, Prof. John Nicolas, FSA; FBA 1977; Professor of Aegean Archaeology, Bedford College, University of London, since 1975; *b* 30 March 1927; *s* of Sir John Coldstream and Phyllis Mary Hambly; *m* 1970, Imogen Nicola Carr. *Educ:* Eton; King's College, Cambridge (Class. Tripos, BA 1951, MA 1956). FSA 1964. Nat. Service, Buffs and HLI (Egypt and Palestine), 1945-48. Asst Master, Shrewsbury Sch., 1952-56; Temp. Asst Keeper, Dept of Greek and Roman Antiquities, BM, 1956-57; Macmillan Student, British Sch. at Athens, 1957-60; Bedford College, London: Lectr, 1960-66; Reader, 1966-75. Mem., Managing Cttee, British Sch. at Athens, 1966-. Chm., Nat. Organizing Cttee, XI Internat. Congress of Classical Archaeol., London, 1978. Mem., Deutsches Archäologisches Inst., 1978. Editor, Annual of the British School at Athens, 1968-73. *Publications:* Greek Geometric Pottery, 1968; (with G. L. Huxley) Kythera: Excavations and Studies, 1972; Knossos: The Sanctuary of Demeter, 1973; Geometric Greece, 1977; articles in British and foreign classical and archaeological journals. *Recreations:* music, travel. *Address:* 180 Ebury Street, SW1.

COLDSTREAM, Sir William (Menzies), Kt 1956; CBE 1952; painter; Slade Professor of Fine Art, at University College, University of London, 1949-75; Vice-Chairman, Arts Council of Great Britain, 1962-70 (Member, 1953); Fellow of University College, London; Senior Fellow, Royal College of Art; *b* 28 Feb. 1908; *yr s* of George Probyn Coldstream, MB, CM, and Lilian Mercer Tod; *m* 1st, 1931, Nancy Culliford Sharp (marr. diss. 1942); two *d* ; 2nd, 1961, Monica Mary Hoyer, *d* of A. E. Monrad Hoyer; one *s* two *d*. *Educ:* privately; Slade Sch. of Fine Art, University Coll., London. Member: London Artists Assoc., 1931; London Group, 1933; work represented in exhibitions of: World's Fair, NY, 1938; British Art Since Whistler, Nat. Gallery, 1939; UN Internat. Exhibition, Paris, 1946; Retrospective Exhibition, South London Gallery, 1962; Painting and Sculpture of a Decade, Tate Gallery, 1964 (represented). Pictures in the collections of: Tate Gallery, National Gallery of Canada, National Museum of Wales, Ashmolean Museum, Imperial War Museum, Arts Council, British Council, Bristol Art Gallery, etc. Works purchased by Contemporary Art Soc. and Chantrey Bequest, 1940. In association with Claude Rogers and Victor Pasmore founded the Sch. of Drawing and Painting, Euston Road, 1937. Served War of 1939-45 with RE; official War Office Artist, Middle East and Italy, 1943-45. Trustee of National Gallery, 1948-55, 1956-63; Trustee of Tate Gallery, 1949-55, 1956-63; a Dir of Royal Opera House, Covent Garden, 1957-62; Chairman: Art Panel of Arts Council, 1953-62; Nat. Adv. Council on Art Education, 1958-71; British Film Institute, 1964-71; Hon. DLitt: Nottingham, 1961; Birmingham, 1962; Hon. DEd CNAA, 1975. *Address:* University College London, Gower Street, WC1. *T:* 01-387 7050. *Clubs:* Athenæum, MCC. *See also* J. W. D. Margetson.

COLE, family name of **Earl of Enniskillen.**

COLE, Viscount; Andrew John Galbraith Cole; pilot, and company director; Captain Irish Guards, 1965; *b* 28 April 1942; *s* and *heir* of 6th Earl of Enniskillen, *qv* ; *m* 1964, Sarah, *o d* of Maj.-Gen. J. Keith-Edwards, CBE, DSO, MC, Nairobi; three *d*. *Educ:* Eton. Man. Dir, Kenya Airways, 1979-81. *Address:* c/o Williams & Glyn's Bank Ltd, 9 Pall Mall, SW1.

COLE, (Alexander) Colin, CVO 1979 (MVO 1977); TD 1972; FSA; Garter Principal King of Arms, since 1978; *b* 16 May 1922; *er s* of late Capt. Edward Harold Cole, and of Blanche Ruby Lavinia (*née* Wallis); *m* 1944, Valerie, *o d* of late Capt. Stanley Walter Card; four *s* three *d*. *Educ:* Dulwich; Pembroke Coll. Cambridge; Brasenose Coll., Oxford. BCL Oxon; MA Oxon. Served War of 1939-45, Capt. Coldstream Guards. Barrister-at-law (Inner Temple), 1949. Fitzalan Pursuivant of Arms Extraordinary, 1953; Portcullis Pursuivant of Arms, 1957; Windsor Herald of Arms, 1966. One of the Court of Assistants of the Hon. Artillery Company; Major, 6th (Volunteer) Bn, Queen's Regt, 1971-73, Lt-Col RARO (Brevet, 1973); Hon. Col, 6/7 Bn, Queen's Regt, 1981-. Mem. Court of Common Council of City of London (Castle Baynard Ward), 1964-; Sheriff, City of London, 1976-77. Freeman of City of London, Freeman and Liveryman, Scriveners', Basketmakers and

Painter Stainers Companies of London. A Governor, Museum of London. Fellow Heraldry Soc.; Hon. Heraldic Adviser, Monumental Brass Soc.; Registrar and Librarian, College of Arms, 1967-74. Officer of Arms attendant, Imperial Soc. of Knights Bachelor. FRSA 1979. OStJ. *Publications:* articles on heraldry and kindred subjects in their appropriate journals; illus. Visitations of London (1568) and Wiltshire (1623) (Harleian Soc.). *Recreations:* art, archæology, architecture, parenthood and wine-bibbing. *Address:* College of Arms, Queen Victoria Street, EC4. *T:* 01-248 1188; Holly House, Burstow, Surrey. *Clubs:* Cavalry and Guards, City Livery.

COLE, Prof. Boris Norman, BSc(Eng) (London), PhD (Birmingham), WhSch, CEng, FIMechE; Professor of Mechanical Engineering and Head of Department of Mechanical Engineering, University of Leeds, since 1962; *b* 8 Jan. 1924; *s* of James Edward Cole and Gertrude Cole; *m* 1945, Sibylle Duijts; two *s* one *d*. *Educ:* King Edward's Sch., Birmingham. Apprenticed to Messrs Belliss and Morcom Ltd, Engineers, Birmingham. Dept of Mech. Engrg, Univ. of Birmingham: Lectr, 1949-55; Sen. Lectr, 1955-58; Reader, 1958-62; Chm. of Faculty Bd of Applied Sciences, Birmingham Univ., 1955-57 and 1959-62. Member: Smethwick Co. Borough Educn Cttee, 1957-60; Engrg Materials Res. Requirements Bd, 1974-78, and various other govt cttees; Governor, Engrg Industries Training Bd, Leeds Training Centre, 1967-. Prizewinner, IMechE, 1953 and 1962. *Publications:* numerous in fields of solid and fluid mechanics and in engineering education. *Recreations:* walking, music, social history of engineering. *Address:* 399 Gledhow Lane, Leeds LS7 4NQ. *T:* Leeds 621306.

COLE, (Claude Neville) David, CBE 1977; JP; Chairman and Chief Executive, Thomson Information Services, since 1982; Chairman: Thomson Books, since 1980; Rainbird Publishing Group, since 1980; Janes Publishing Co., since 1981; Thomson Directories, since 1982; Hamish Hamilton, since 1982; Joint Deputy Managing Director, International Thomson Organisation plc, since 1980; Member, Council, Newspaper Society, since 1974 (President, 1982); *b* 4 June 1928; 2nd *s* of late W. J. Cole and of Mrs M. J. Cole; *m* 1951, Alma Gwlithyn Williams; one *s* one *d* (one *s* decd). *Educ:* Royal Masonic School; Harvard Business Sch. Journalist: Merthyr Express; South Wales Echo; Daily Graphic (Manchester); Daily Sketch (London); Daily Recorder; Empire News (Cardiff); Editor, Western Mail, Cardiff, 1956-59; Managing Director (now Chairman): Western Mail and Echo Ltd, 1959-67; Newcastle Chronicle and Journal Ltd, 1967-69; Thomson Regional Newspapers Ltd: Asst Man. Dir and Editorial Dir, 1969-72; Man. Dir and Chief Exec., 1972-82; Chm., 1980-82. Director: Thomson Organisation (Exec. Bd), 1973-80; Reuters Ltd, 1976-81; Scotsman Publications Ltd; Press Consultancy Services Ltd; Press Assoc. (Chm. 1976-77, 1977-78); Welsh Nat. Opera Co. Ltd, 1960-71; Chairman: Celtic Press Ltd. Chm., Cole Cttee on Recruitment of Nurses in Wales, 1961-63; Chm., Working Party on Welsh Tourism, 1963-64; Member: Press Council, 1976-80; Court of Governors of Univ. of Wales, 1962-; Council of Univ. of Wales, 1962-; Council of Welsh National Sch. of Medicine, 1964-67; Governing Body of Cardiff Coll. of Music and Drama, 1963-67; Council of Cardiff New Theatre Trust, 1964-67; Welsh Nat. Theatre Cttee; Aberfan Disaster Fund, 1966-67; Welsh Hospitals Bd, 1962-67. Vice-Patron, Coun. for Wales, Brit. Empire and Commonwealth Games. Pres., Tenovus. OStJ. FBIM. *Publications:* This and Other Worlds (poems), 1975; Meeting Places and other poems, 1977; Mount of Angels (poems), 1978. *Recreations:* two of the three R's. *Address:* 71 Ashley Gardens, Westminster, SW1. *T:* 01-828 1792. *Club:* East India, Devonshire, Sports and Public Schools.

COLE, Colin; *see* Cole, A. C.

COLE, David; *see* Cole, C. N. D.

COLE, Sir David (Lee), KCMG 1975 (CMG 1965); MC 1944; HM Diplomatic Service, retired; *b* 31 Aug. 1920; *s* of late Brig. D. H. Cole, CBE, LittD, and Charlotte Cole (*née* Wedgwood); *m* 1945, Dorothy (*née* Patton); one *s*. *Educ:* Cheltenham Coll.; Sidney Sussex Coll., Cambridge. MA (1st Cl. Hons History). Served Royal Inniskilling Fusiliers, 1940-45. Dominions Office, 1947; seconded to Foreign Office for service with UK Delegn to UN, New York, 1948-51; First Sec., Brit. High Commn, New Delhi, 1953-56; Private Sec. to Rt Hon. the Earl of Home (Sec. of State for Commonwealth Relations and Lord President of the Council), 1957-60; Head of Personnel Dept, CRO, 1961-63; British Dep. High Comr in Ghana, 1963-64; British High Comr in Malawi, 1964-67; Minister (Political), New Delhi, 1967-70; Asst Under-Sec. of State, FCO, 1970-73; Ambassador to Thailand, 1973-78. *Publication:* Thailand: Water Colour Impressions, 1977. *Recreation:* watercolour painting (exhibited RI, RBA). *Address:* 49 Drayton Gardens, SW10.

COLE, Eileen Marie Lucy; Chief Executive, Research International (Unilever Ltd), since 1973 (in Rotterdam, 1973-77); Director (non-executive), Post Office, since 1980; *b* 22 April 1924; *d* of Arthur Walter Cole and Mary Agnes Boyd. *Educ:* grammar schs; Girton Coll., Cambridge (BA Hons Econ.). Joined Unilever as trainee, 1948; with associated cos and market res. div. of Unilever, 1948-60; Market Research Controller, Lever Bros Ltd, 1960-64; Research Bureau Ltd: Dir, 1966-67; Chm. and Man. Dir, 1967-72. Vice-Pres., 1979-, and Full Mem., UK Market Res. Soc. (Chm., 1977-79); Council Mem., Women in Management, 1971-; Mem., Careers Advisory Services: Cambridge Univ., 1968-75, 1979-; Reading Univ., 1970-76, 1979-. FBIM; Mem., Inst. of Dirs. *Publications:* various in learned jls connected with market research.

Recreations: gardening, cooking, reading, theatre. *Address:* Research International, Bridgwater House, 5/13 Great Suffolk Street, SE1 0NP; Nicholas Farm, Lower Wield, Alresford, Hants.

COLE, Maj.-Gen. Eric Stuart, CB 1960; CBE 1945; retired; Consultant Director, Granger Associates Ltd, Weybridge; *b* 1906; *s* of John William Cole; *m* 1941, Doris Cole. Served Palestine, 1936-39; War of 1939-45 in Italy, France, Greece (despatches, CBE); Maj.-Gen., 1958; Dir of Telecommunications, War Office, 1958-61. Col Comdt Royal Corps of Signals, 1962-67. Pres., Radio Soc. of GB, 1961. Pres., Army Golf Soc., 1971-73. *Address:* 28 Royal Avenue, Chelsea, SW3. *Clubs:* Army and Navy, MCC, Roehampton.

COLE, Frank; *see* Cole, (George) Francis.

COLE, George; actor on stage, screen, radio and television; *b* 22 April 1925; *m* 1st, 1954, Eileen Moore (marr. diss. 1966); one *s* one *d*; 2nd, 1967, Penelope Morrell; one *s* one *d. Educ:* Surrey County Council Secondary Sch., Morden. Made first stage appearance in White Horse Inn, tour and London Coliseum, 1939; Cottage to Let, Birmingham, 1940; West End and on tour, 1940-41; subseq. West End plays included Goodnight Children, New, 1942; Mr Bolfry, Playhouse, 1943. Served in RAF, 1943-47. Returned to stage in Dr Angelus, Phoenix, 1947; The Anatomist, Westminster, 1948; Mr Gillie, Garrick, 1950; A Phoenix too Frequent and Thor with Angels, Lyric, Hammersmith, 1951; Misery Me, Duchess, 1955; Mr Bolfry, Aldwych, 1956; Brass Butterfly, Strand, 1958; The Bargain, St Martin's, 1961; The Sponge Room and Squat Betty, Royal Court, 1962; Meet Me on the Fence (tour), 1963; Hedda Gabler, St Martin's, 1964; A Public Mischief, St Martin's, 1965; Too True To Be Good, Strand, 1965; The Waiting Game, Arts, 1966; The Three Sisters, Royal Court, 1967; Doubtful Haunts, Hampstead, 1968; The Passionate Husband, 1969; The Philanthropist, Mayfair, 1971; Country Life, Hampstead, 1973; Déjà Revue, New London, 1974; Motive (tour), 1976; Banana Ridge, Savoy, 1976; The Case of the Oily Levantine, Guildford, 1977; Something Afoot, Hong Kong, 1978; Brimstone and Treacle, Open Space, 1979; Liberty Hall, Greenwich, 1980. *Films include:* Cottage to Let, 1941; Morning Departure, Laughter in Paradise, Scrooge, Top Secret, 1949-51; Will Any Gentleman?, The Intruder, 1952; Happy Ever After, Our Girl Friday, 1953; Belles of St Trinian's, 1954; Quentin Durward, 1955; The Weapon, It's a Wonderful World, The Green Man, 1956; Blue Murder at St Trinian's, Too Many Crooks, Don't Panic Chaps, The Bridal Path, 1957-59; The Pure Hell of St Trinian's, Cleopatra, Dr Syn, 1961-62; One Way Pendulum, Legend of Dick Turpin, 1964; Great St Trinian's Train Robbery, 1965; The Green Shoes, 1969; Vampire Lovers, 1970; Girl in the Dark, 1971; The Blue Bird, 1975. TV Series include Life of Bliss (also radio), A Man of our Times, Don't Forget to Write, Minder (3 series), The Bounder, The Pirates of Penzance. *Address:* Donnelly, Newnham Hill Bottom, Nettlebed, Oxon.

COLE, George Francis, (Frank); Chairman: James Cooke & Son Ltd, since 1976; Stokes Bomford (Holdings) Ltd, since 1979; Aero Needles Group, since 1981; Arbuthnot Engineering, since 1982; Virgocrest (Franklin Medical Products), since 1982; F. J. Neve & Co., since 1982; Debenholt, since 1982; Director: G. Clancey Ltd; Armstrong Equipment Ltd; Reed Stenhouse UK Ltd; Frank Cole (consultancy) Ltd; *b* 3 Nov. 1918; *m* ; two *s* one *d. Educ:* Manchester Grammar Sch. Dir and Gen. Manager, Clarkson Engineers Ltd, 1944-53; Gen. Man., Ariel Motors Ltd (BSA Group), 1953-55; Dir, then Man. Dir, Vono Ltd, 1955-67. Past Chairman: Grovewood Products Ltd; Portways Ltd; R. & W. H. Symington Holdings Ltd; National Exhibition Centre Ltd; Crane's Screw (Hldgs); Past Director: Duport Ltd; Shipping Industrial Holdings Ltd. Pres., Birmingham Chamber of Commerce and Industry, 1968-69. Leader of Trade Missions to West Germany, Yugoslavia, Romania and Hungary. CBIM; Life Governor, Birmingham Univ.; Liveryman of City of London. Radio and Television appearances. *Publications:* press articles on economics, exports, etc. *Recreations:* tennis, oil painting. *Address:* Northcot, 128 Station Road, Balsall Common, Coventry, West Midlands CV7 7FF. *T:* Berkswell 32105.

COLE, Dr Herbert Aubrey, CMG 1967; Controller, Fisheries Research and Development, Ministry of Agriculture, Fisheries and Food, 1972-74; *b* 24 Feb. 1911; *s* of Edwin Aubrey Cole, Farmer; *m* 1936, Elizabeth Lloyd; two *s* one *d. Educ:* Friars Sch., Bangor, N Wales; Univ. Coll. of N Wales. Entire career in Fishery Research, Min. of Agric., Fisheries and Food, Dir of Fishery Research, 1959-72. *Publications:* numerous articles in learned jls. *Recreation:* gardening. *Address:* Forde House, Moor Lane, Hardington Mandeville, Yeovil, Somerset BA22 9NW. *T:* West Coker 2090.

COLE, Humphrey John Douglas; Chief Economic Adviser, Departments of the Environment and Transport, since 1976; *b* 30 Jan. 1928; *s* of late G. D. H. Cole and Dame Margaret I. Cole, DBE; *m* 1955, Hilda Annette Robinson; two *s* one *d. Educ:* Winchester Coll.; Trinity Coll., Cambridge. Fellow, Oxford Inst. of Statistics, 1950-61; Head, Economic Indicators and Foreign Trade, OECD Statistics Div., 1961-66; Dept of Economic Affairs: Senior Economic Adviser (Regional), 1966-67; Asst Dir of Economics, 1967-69; Dir of Economics, Min. of Technology, 1969-70; Dir of Econs (Urban and Highways), DoE, 1970-72; Dir Gen., Econs and Resources, DoE, 1972-76. *Publications:* articles in Bulletin of Inst. of Statistics, 1950-61. *Recreations:* walking, family. *Address:* 3 The Mead, W13. *T:* 01-997 8285.

COLE, James S.; *see* Stuart-Cole.

COLE, John Morrison; Political Editor, BBC, since 1981; *b* 23 Nov. 1927; *s* of George Cole and Alice Jane Cole; *m* 1956, Margaret Isobel, *d* of Mr and Mrs John S. Williamson, Belfast; four *s. Educ:* Fortwilliam and Skegoneill Primary Schs, Belfast; Belfast Royal Acad.; London Univ. (BA External). Belfast Telegraph, 1945-56: successively reporter, industrial, municipal and political correspondent; The Guardian: Reporter, 1956-57; Labour Correspondent, 1957-63; News Editor, 1963-69; Dep. Editor, 1969-75; The Observer: Asst Editor, 1975; Dep. Editor, 1976-81. *Publications:* The Poor of the Earth, 1976; contrib. to books on British and Irish politics. *Recreations:* reading, travel, tennis. *Address:* BBC Office, House of Commons, Westminster, SW1A 0AA. *T:* 01-219 4765. *Club:* Athenæum.

COLE, John Sydney Richard, QC (Somaliland); MA; FIArb; Barrister-at-Law; Senior Lecturer, Law School, University of Dublin, 1966-77; *b* 24 Jan. 1907; *o s* of late Rev. R. Lee Cole, MA, BD, Dublin; *m* 1st, 1931, Doreen Mathews (*d* 1966); one *s* one *d*; 2nd, 1968, Mrs Deirdre Gallet. *Educ:* Methodist Coll., Belfast; Cork Gram. Sch.; Trinity Coll., Dublin (Scholar and Moderator). Master, Royal Coll., Mauritius, 1930-36; Education Officer, Nigeria, 1936-40; Crown Counsel, Nigeria, 1940-46; Attorney-Gen., Bahamas, 1946-51; Somaliland Protectorate, 1951-56; Attorney-Gen. and Minister for Legal Affairs, Tanganyika, 1956-61; retired, 1961. English Legal Draftsman to Government of Republic of Sudan, 1962-65. Reid Prof. of Penal Legislation, Univ. of Dublin, 1965-66. *Publication:* (with W. N. Denison) Tanganyika-the Development of its Laws and Constitution, 1964; Irish Cases on the Law of Evidence, 1972, 2nd edn 1979; Irish Cases on Criminal Law, 1975. *Recreations:* walking, swimming. *Address:* 2 Rus in Urbe, Glenageary, Dublin. *T:* 801993. *Club:* Kildare Street and University (Dublin).

COLE, Leslie Barrett, MA, MD Cantab, FRCP; Hon. Consultant Physician, Addenbrooke's Hospital, Cambridge; Fellow of King's College, Cambridge, 1949-66; Dean of Post Graduate Medical School, University of Cambridge, 1957-65; *b* 1898; *s* of Samuel Barrett Cole and Annie Gammon; *m* 1927, Mary, *d* of late Surg. Capt. H. W. Finlayson, DSO; three *s. Educ:* Leighton Park Sch.; King's Coll., Cambridge (Exhibitioner). Served European War, 1916-18, RFA, India and Mesopotamia; RAMC 1939-41, BEF France. St Thomas's Hosp. (Medical Registrar and Resident Asst Physician; Mead Medal and Toller Prize); formerly Physician: W Suffolk Hosp.; Papworth Hosp. Assessor, MD Cttee, Univ. of Cambridge, 1958-65; Late Examiner: Medicine for MRCP and to Univs of Oxford, Cambridge and Bristol, also Conjoint Board; in Pharmacology, to Univ. of Cambridge; in Pathology to Conjoint Board. Royal College of Physicians: Councillor, 1950; Censor, 1960-62; Sen. Censor and Sen. Vice-Pres., 1964-65. Hon. Lt-Col RAMC. *Publications:* Dietetics in General Practice, 1939; numerous contribs to medical journals on cardiology, diabetes and general medical subjects and on tetanus to Quart. Jl of Medicine, Index of Treatment, British Encyclopædia of Medical Practice and Surgery of Modern Warfare. *Recreations:* riding, sailing. *Address:* 57 De Freville Avenue, Cambridge. *T:* Cambridge 50836. *Club:* Athenæum.

COLE, Prof. Monica M.; Professor of Geography, since 1964 and Director of Research in Geobotany, Terrain Analysis and related Resource Use, since 1975, Bedford College, University of London; *b* 5 May 1922; *d* of William Henry Parnall Cole and Dorothy Mary Cole (*née* Thomas). *Educ:* Wimbledon County Grammar Sch.; Bedford Coll., Univ. of London. Research Asst, Min. of Town and Country Planning, Cambridge, 1944-45; Postgrad. study, Univ. of London, 1945-46; Lectr in Geography: Univ. of Capetown, 1947; Univ. of Witwatersrand, 1948-51, Univ. of Keele, 1951-64. Assoc. Prof., Univ. of Idaho summer sch., 1952; Vis. Lectr, Univs of Queensland, Melbourne, and Adelaide, 1960. Mem. British delegn Internat. Geographical Congress in: Washington, 1952; Rio de Janeiro, 1956; London, 1964; New Delhi, 1968; Montreal, 1972; Tokyo, 1980. Research: vegetation/soils/geomorphology: S Africa, 1948-51; Brazil, 1956, 1965; Central and E Africa, 1959; Australia, 1960, 1962, 1963, 1965, 1966, 1967, 1968, 1971, 1972, 1975, 1976, 1980; Venezuela, 1964; Southern Africa, 1967, 1968, 1978, 1979, 1980; plant indicators of mineralization: Australia, Africa, Brazil, UK, 1964-73; remote sensing for terrain analysis: Australia, UK, 1970-76, China, 1981. *Publications:* The Transvaal Lowveld, 1956; South Africa, 1961, 1966; contribs to Geograph. Jl, Geography, Trans. Inst. Brit. Geographers, S African Geograph. Jl, Trans. Instn Mining and Metallurgy, Proc. Royal Soc., Jl Applied Ecology, ESRO, Jl Biogeography, S Africa Geol Soc. *Recreations:* painting, photography, tennis, squash, walking, climbing. *Address:* Bedford College, Regent's Park, NW1.

COLE, Richard Raymond Buxton; solicitor; a Recorder of the Crown Court, since 1976; *b* 11 June 1937; *s* of Raymond Buxton Cole, DSO, TD, DL, and Edith Mary Cole; *m* 1962, Sheila Joy Rumbold; one *s* one *d. Educ:* Dragon School, St Edward's, Oxford. Admitted as Solicitor 1960; Partner in Cole & Cole Solicitors, Oxford, 1962-. Mem., Parole Bd, 1981-. Pres., Berks, Bucks and Oxon Law Soc., 1981-82. Mem. Governing Body, Dragon Sch., 1975-. Chm., Burford Parish Council, 1976-79, first Town Mayor, 1979. *Recreations:* sport, gardening. *Address:* Tanners Close, Burford, Oxon. *T:* Burford 3102. *Clubs:* MCC; Frewen (Oxford).

COLE, Sir (Robert) William, Kt 1981; Chairman, Public Service Board, Australia, since 1978; *b* 16 Sept. 1926; *s* of James Henry and Rita Sarah Cole; *m* 1956, Margaret Noleen Martin; one *s* one *d. Educ:* Univ. of Melbourne (BCom). Joined Australian Public Service, 1952; Res. Officer, Treasury, 1952-57; Technical Asst, IMF, Washington, 1957-59; various positions,

Treasury, 1959-70; Dir, Bureau of Transport Econs, Dept of Shipping and Transport, 1970-72; First Asst Sec., Gen. Financial and Economic Policy Div., Treasury, 1972-76; Australian Statistician, 1976; Sec., Dept of Finance, 1977-78. *Recreations:* reading, fishing, wine. *Address:* 8 Scarborough Street, Red Hill, ACT 2603, Australia. *T:* Canberra 957089. *Club:* Commonwealth (Canberra).

COLE, Ven. Ronald Berkeley; *b* 20 Oct. 1913; *s* of James William and Florence Caroline Cole; *m* 1943, Mabel Grace Chapman; one *s* one *d. Educ:* Bishop's Coll., Cheshunt. Registrar, London County Freehold and Leasehold Properties Ltd, 1934-40. Deacon, 1942; Priest, 1943; Curate, Braunstone, Leicester, 1942-48; Succentor, Leicester Cathedral, 1948-50; Vicar of St Philip, Leicester, 1950-73; Archdeacon of Loughborough, 1952-63, of Leicester, 1963-80; Residentiary Canon of Leicester Cathedral, 1977-80. Hon. Chaplain, 1949-53, Examining Chaplain, 1956-80, to Bishop of Leicester. Hon. DLitt Geneva Theol. Coll., 1972. *Recreations:* gardening, motoring. *Address:* Harland Rise, 70 Cromer Road, Sheringham, Norfolk.

COLE, Sir William; *see* Cole, Sir R. W.

COLE, William Charles, MVO 1966; DMus; FSA, FRAM, FRCM; FRCO; The Master of the Music at the Queen's Chapel of the Savoy since 1954; Member Council, Royal College of Organists, since 1960 (Hon. Treasurer since 1964; President, 1970-72); Member, Central Music Library Committee, since 1964, Chairman 1973; *b* 9 Oct. 1909; *s* of Frederick George Cole and Maria (*née* Fry), Camberwell, London; *m* 1st, Elizabeth Brown Caw (*d* 1942); three *d*; 2nd, Winifred Grace Mitchell; one *s. Educ:* St Olave's Grammar Sch.; RAM. Organist and Choirmaster, Dorking Parish Church, 1930; Music Master, Dorking County Sch., 1931; served War of 1939-45, in Air Ministry; Hon. Musical Dir, Toynbee Hall, 1947-58; Prof. of Harmony and Composition, and Lectr in History of Music, Royal Academy of Music, 1945-62; Royal Academy of Dancing: Lectr, 1948-62; Chm. Music Cttee, 1961-68; Mem. Exec. Council, 1965-68; Mem., Grand Council, 1976-; Conductor: People's Palace Choral Soc., 1947-63; Leith Hill Musical Festival, 1954-77; Sec., Associated Bd of Royal Schools of Music, 1962-74; Hon. Sec., Royal Philharmonic Soc., 1969-80. President: Surrey County Music Assoc., 1958-76; The London Assoc. of Organists, 1963-66. Member: Governing Cttee, Royal Choral Soc., 1972- (Chm., Music Cttee, 1975-78); Exec. Cttee, Musicians' Benevolent Fund, 1972-. Mem. Education Cttee, Surrey CC, 1951-62. *Publications:* Rudiments of Music, 1951; chapter on Development of British Ballet Music, in The Ballet in Britain, 1962; The Form of Music, 1969; articles in various musical jls and in various learned jls on stained glass. *Recreation:* stained glass. *Address:* Packways, Hindhead, Surrey. *T:* Hindhead 4917. *Club:* Garrick.

COLE, Maj.-Gen. William Scott, CB 1949; CBE 1946; Army Officer, retired; *b* 29 March 1902; *s* of late William Scott Cole; *m* 1st, 1948, Kathleen Winifred Coleing (marr. diss. 1970); one *d*; 2nd, 1971, Alice Rose Pitts, *widow* of Dr G. T. Pitts. *Educ:* Victoria Coll., Jersey; RMA Woolwich. Commissioned into the Corps of Royal Engineers, 1921. Served War of 1939-45; Temp. Brig., 1943; Substantive Col, 1945; Subs. Brig., 1951; temp. Maj.-Gen., 1955; Subs. Maj.-Gen., 1956; retd 1958. *Club:* Army and Navy.

COLE-HAMILTON, John, CBE 1954; DL; *b* 15 Oct. 1899; *s* of late Col A. R. Cole-Hamilton; *m* 1930, Gladys Cowie; one *s* two *d. Educ:* Royal Academy, Irvine. Served European War, 1914-19, with RFC and RAF. Major, Home Guard, 1942. DL for County of Ayr, 1951. *Address:* Beltrim House, Kilwinning, Ayrshire.

COLEBROOK, Philip Victor Charles, CEng, AMIChemE; Managing Director of Pfizer Ltd since 1958; Vice-President, Pfizer International, since 1967; Managing Director, Imperial Continental Gas Association, since 1973 (Director, 1971; Director, CompAir Ltd, since 1980); *b* 8 March 1924; *s* of Frederick Charles Colebrook and Florence Margaret (*née* Cooper); *m* 1946, Dorothy Ursula Kemp; one *s* three *d. Educ:* Andover Grammar Sch.; Guildford Technical Coll.; Battersea Polytechnic, London. Served War of 1939-45, RNVR. Joined Pfizer as Works and Production Manager, 1952; appointed Dir, Pfizer Ltd, 1956; Chm. and Man. Dir, Pfizer Gp, 1961-69; Man. Dir, Calor Gas Holding Co., 1969-80. Member: NHS Affairs Cttee, Assoc. of the British Pharmaceutical Industry, 1963-67; CBI Cttee on State Intervention in Private Business, 1975-78. Trustee and Mem. of Steering Cttee, Univ. of Kent at Canterbury, 1964-65. *Publication:* Going International, 1972. *Recreations:* sailing, ski-ing, golf. *Address:* Kestrels, Easterton, Wilts. *Clubs:* Royal Automobile; Royal Cinque Ports Yacht.

COLEBY, Anthony Laurie; Assistant Director, Bank of England, since 1980; *b* 27 April 1935; *s* of Dr Leslie James Moger Coleby and Laurie Coleby (*née* Shuttleworth); *m* 1966, Rosemary Melian Elisabeth, *d* of Sir Peter Garran, *qv*; one *s* two *d. Educ:* Winchester; Corpus Christi, Cambridge (BAEcon, MA). Bank of England: joined, 1961; Assistant Chief, Overseas Dept, 1969; Adviser, Overseas Dept, 1972; Dep. Chief Cashier, 1973. Personal Asst to Managing Director, International Monetary Fund, 1964-67. *Recreations:* choral singing, railways and transport. *Address:* Bank of England, EC2R 8AH. *T:* 01-601 4444. *Club:* Overseas Bankers'.

COLECLOUGH, Peter Cecil; Chairman, Howard Machinery Ltd, 1969-82 (Director, 1950-82); Director: National Westminster Bank (Chairman SE

Region); NCR Ltd; *b* 5 March 1917; *s* of late Thomas James Coleclough and of Hilda Emma (*née* Ingram); *m* 1944, Pamela Beresford (*née* Rhodes); two *s. Educ:* Bradfield. Served War, Cheshire Yeomanry, 1939; commnd into Roy. Warwickshire Regt, 1940; served until 1946. Mem., FBI/CBI Council, 1962-72; Chm., E Region, CBI, 1971-72; Mem., FBI Mission to Sudan, 1962; Leader, OECD/BIAC Investment Gp to Ceylon, 1968 and 1969; Chm., Meat and Livestock Commn, 1971-74; Pres., Agricl Engrs Assoc., 1971-72; Pres., Royal Warrant Holders Assoc., 1971-72. Chm., Appeals and Management Cttee, S Essex Medical Educn and Research Trust, 1969-75 (Patron, 1975-). *Recreation:* fishing. *Address:* Longlands Hall, Stonham Aspal, Stowmarket, Suffolk IP14 6AR. *T:* Stonham 242. *Club:* Naval and Military.

COLEGATE, Raymond, CBE 1982; Member, Civil Aviation Authority, since 1974; Group Director, Economic Regulation, since 1977; *b* 31 Aug. 1927; *s* of Ernest William and Violet Colegate; *m* 1961, Sally Healy; one *s* one *d. Educ:* County Sch. for Boys, Gravesend; LSE. BA London (Hons History). Joined BoT, 1949; seconded to Central Statistical Office, 1952-53; Asst Private Sec. to President, 1955-56; seconded to Treasury, 1957-59; seconded to EFTA Secretariat, Geneva and Brussels, 1960-64; CRE Dept, BoT, 1964-67; Aviation Dept, BoT/DTI, 1967-72; Head, Economic Policy and Licensing Div., CAA, 1972-75; Head, Economic Dept, CAA, 1975-77. *Publications:* all anonymous. *Recreations:* music, travel, thinking. *Address:* 40 Lebanon Park, Twickenham TW1 3DG.

COLEMAN, Arthur Percy; Deputy Director and Secretary to the Board of Trustees, British Museum (Natural History), 1976-82 (Museum Secretary, 1965-76); *b* 8 Feb. 1922; *s* of late Percy Coleman and Gladys May Coleman (*née* Fisher); *m* 1948, Peggy (*née* Coombs); two *d. Educ:* Wanstead Co. High Sch.; Bristol Univ. War Service in 1st King George V Own Gurkha Rifles, 1943-47; Min. of Public Building and Works, 1948-61; HM Treasury, 1961-64. *Recreations:* wild life, music. *Address:* Candleford, Hurst, Beaminster, Dorset. *T:* Beaminster 862155.

COLEMAN, Bernard; HM Diplomatic Service; High Commissioner to Tonga, since Nov. 1980; *b* 3 Sept. 1928; *s* of William Coleman and Ettie Coleman; *m* 1950, Sonia Dinah (*née* Walters); two *d. Educ:* Alsop High Sch., Liverpool. HM Forces (RAEC), 1946-48. Entered Foreign (later Diplomatic) Service, 1950; FO, 1950-53; Lima, 1953-56; Detroit, 1956-59; Second Secretary (Information): Montevideo, 1959-62; Caracas, 1962-64; First Sec. (Inf.), Caracas, 1964-66; FCO, 1967-69; First Sec. (Inf.), Ottawa, 1969-73; FCO, 1973-74; seconded to DTI, 1974-75; Consul-Gen., Bilbao, 1976-78; First Sec. (Commercial), Dublin, 1979-80. *Recreations:* golf, reading, walking, travel. *Address:* c/o Foreign and Commonwealth Office, SW1. *Club:* Royal Commonwealth Society.

COLEMAN, Prof. Donald Cuthbert, LittD; FBA 1972; Professor of Economic History, Cambridge University, 1971-81, now Emeritus; Fellow of Pembroke College, Cambridge; *b* 21 Jan. 1920; *s* of Hugh Augustus Coleman and Marian Stella Agnes Cuthbert; *m* 1954, Jessie Ann Matilda Child (*née* Stevens). *Educ:* Haberdashers' Aske's, Hampstead (now Elstree); London Sch. of Economics, Univ. of London. Worked in London, in insurance, 1937-39; admitted LSE, 1939. Served War, in Army, 1940-46: commissioned Royal Warwickshire Regt, 1941; transf. RA, 1942; active service in N Africa, Italy and Greece. Returned to LSE, 1946; BSc(Econ), 1st Cl. Hons. 1949; Leverhulme Research Studentship, 1949-51; PhD 1951. Lectr in Industrial History, LSE, 1951-58; Reader in Economic History, 1958-69; Prof. of Economic History, 1969-71. Visiting Associate Prof. of Economics, Yale Univ., 1957-58. English Editor, Scandinavian Economic History Review, 1952-61; Editor, Economic History Review, 1967-73. FRHistS. *Publications:* The British Paper Industry, 1495-1860, 1958; Sir John Banks: Baronet and Businessman, 1963; Courtaulds: an economic and social history, vols 1 & 2, 1969, vol. 3, 1980; What Has Happened to Economic History? (Inaug. Lect.), 1972; Industry in Tudor and Stuart England, 1975; The Economy of England 1450-1750, 1977; (ed with A. H. John) Trade, Government and Economy in Pre-Industrial England, 1977; numerous articles in: Economic History Review, Economica, Historical Jl, etc. *Recreations:* music, cricket, coarse gardening. *Address:* Over Hall, Cavendish, Sudbury, Suffolk. *T:* Glemsford 280325.

COLEMAN, Donald Richard, CBE 1979; MP (Lab) Neath since 1964; *b* 19 Sept. 1925; *s* of late Albert Archer Coleman and of Winifred Marguerite Coleman; *m* 1949, Phyllis Eileen (*née* Williams) (*d* 1963); one *s*; *m* 1966, Margaret Elizabeth Morgan; one *d. Educ:* Cadoxton Boys' Sch., Barry; Cardiff Technical Coll. Laboratory Technician, Welsh National Sch. of Medicine, Cardiff, 1940-42; Central Tuberculosis Laboratory, Cardiff, 1942-46; Sen. Technician, Swansea Technical Coll., 1946-50; University Coll., Swansea, 1950-54; Metallurgist, Research Dept, Steel Co. of Wales Ltd, Abbey Works, Port Talbot, 1954 until election to Parliament. PPS to Minister of State for Wales (later Secretary of State for Wales), 1967-70; an Opposition Whip, 1970-74; a Lord Comr, HM Treasury, 1974-79, Vice-Chamberlain of the Household, 1978-79. Delegate to Council of Europe and WEU, 1968-73. *Address:* Penderyn, 18 Penywern Road, Bryncoch, Neath, West Glamorgan. *T:* Neath 4599.

COLEMAN, John Ennis; Under Secretary (Legal), Departments of Industry and Trade, since 1980; *b* 12 Nov. 1930; *o s* of late Donald Stafford Coleman and Dorothy Jean Balieff (*née* Ennis); *m* 1958, Doreen Gwendoline Hellinger; one *s* one *d. Educ:* Dean Close Sch., Cheltenham; Dulwich Coll.; Worcester

Coll., Oxford (MA). Solicitor (Hons), 1957. Legal Asst, Treasury Solicitor's Dept, 1958; Senior Legal Asst, 1964; Asst Solicitor, 1971. *Address:* 2 Penrith Close, Reigate, Surrey RH2 0LP. *T:* Redhill 63347.

COLEMAN, Laurence Vail; Director Emeritus, American Association of Museums, since 1958; *b* 19 Sept. 1893; *s* of Thaddeus Vail Coleman and Kate Pratt; *m* 1917, Martine Weeks (decd); three *s* ; *m* 1939, Susannah Armstrong. *Educ:* B. S. College of City of New York, 1915; MA Yale Univ., 1919; grad. work, Harvard Univ., 1919. Research Asst, NY State Commn on Ventilation, 1915; Asst in public health, American Museum Natural History, 1916; Asst in Zoology, Peabody Museum Natural History, 1917; US Army, 1918; Chief of Exhibits, American Museum Natural History, 1919-21; Dir, Safety Inst. America, 1921-23; Exec. Sec., American Assoc. of Museums, 1923-26; Dir, 1927-58. Trustee, Edward MacDowell Assoc., 1939-47; Hill-Stead Museum Trust, Connecticut, 1946-49; Mem. Executive Cttee, Internat. Museums Office, Paris, 1930-36; Educational Advisory Cttee, Pan-American Union, 1929-34; Jt Cttee on Materials for Research of American Council of Learned Societies and Social Science Research Council, 1931-40; Nat Cttee of USA on Intellectual Co-operation of the League of Nations, 1932-46; Cttee on Conservation of Cultural Resources, of National Resources Planning Board, 1941-43; US Nat. Cttee of Internat. Council of Museums, 1948-51. Hon. Fellow, The Museums Assoc. (British); Fellow, Rochester Museum Assoc.; Mid-west Museums Conf., USA; Charter Mem., Nat. Trust for Historical Preservation. Surveys of Museums in: USA, 1924 and 1932-34; Europe, 1927 and 1938; South America, 1928 and 1937; Canada, 1942. Received Alumni Service Medal, 1933, and Townsend Harris Medal, 1944, of College of City of New York; Distinguished Service Award of American Assoc. of Museums, 1940. *Publications:* Manual for Small Museums, 1927; Museums in South America, 1929; Historic House Museums, 1933; The Museum in America (3 vols), 1939, repr. 1970; College and University Museums, 1942; Company Museums, 1942; Museum Buildings (vol. 1), 1950; (with Beardsley Ruml) Manual of Corporate Giving, 1952; contribs to educational magazines in US and Europe. *Address:* 1600 S Eads Street, 321 N, Arlington, Va 22202, USA. *Clubs:* Cosmos (Emeritus Mem.) (Washington); Lake Placid (NY State).

COLEMAN, Ven. Peter Everard; Archdeacon of Worcester, since 1981; *b* 28 Aug. 1928; *s* of Geoffrey Everard Coleman and Lilian Coleman; *m* 1960, HSH Princess Elisabeth-Donata Reuss; two *s* two *d. Educ:* Haileybury; King's Coll., London Univ. (LLB, AKC); Bristol Univ. (MLitt). Called to the Bar, Middle Temple, 1965. Ordained, Bristol, 1955; Chaplain and Lectr, King's Coll., London, 1960-66; Vicar of St Paul's, Clifton, and Chaplain, Bristol Univ., 1966-71; Canon Residentiary and Dir of Training, Bristol, 1971-81. Clerical Member, Court of Arches, 1980-; Mem. General Synod, 1971-81. Jt Editor, Theology, 1982-. *Publications:* Experiments with Prayer, 1961; A Christian Approach to Television, 1968; Christian Attitudes to Homosexuality, 1980. *Recreations:* film making, fishing. *Address:* 7 College Yard, Worcester WR1 2LA. *T:* Worcester 25046. *Club:* Royal Commonwealth Society.

COLEMAN, Ronald Frederick, DSc; CChem, FRSC; Government Chemist, since 1981; *b* 10 Nov. 1931; *s* of late Frederick George Coleman and of Dorothy Alice Coleman (*née* Smith); *m* 1954, Maureen Mary Salt; one *s* one *d. Educ:* King Edward VI Sch., Birmingham; College of Technology, Birmingham (BSc, DSc). Chance Brothers Glassworks, Smethwick, 1949-54; UKAEA: Aldermaston, 1954-71; Harwell, 1972; Laboratory of the Government Chemist, 1973-77 and 1981-; National Physical Laboratory, 1977-81. Visiting Professor, Kingston Polytechnic, 1981-. *Publications:* various papers on analytical chemistry, nuclear chemistry and forensic science. *Recreations:* music, squash, gardening. *Address:* 23 Clare Avenue, Wokingham, Berks RG11 1EB. *T:* Wokingham 788546.

COLEMAN, Terry, (Terence Francis Frank); reporter and author; *b* 13 Feb. 1931; *s* of J. and D. I. B. Coleman; *m* 1st, 1954, Lesley Fox-Strangeways Vane (marr. diss.); two *d* ; 2nd, 1981, Vivien Rosemary Lumsdaine Wallace. *Educ:* 14 schs. LLB London. Formerly: Reporter, Poole Herald; Editor, Savoir Faire; Sub-editor, Sunday Mercury, and Birmingham Post; Reporter and then Arts Corresp., The Guardian, 1961-70, Chief Feature Writer, 1970-74; Special Writer with Daily Mail, 1974-76; Chief Feature Writer, The Guardian, 1976-79, writing mainly political interviews, inc. last seven British Prime Ministers. *Publications:* The Railway Navvies, 1965 (Yorkshire Post prize for best first book of year); A Girl for the Afternoons, 1965; (with Lois Deacon) Providence and Mr Hardy, 1966; The Only True History: collected journalism, 1969; Passage to America, 1972; (ed) An Indiscretion in the Life of an Heiress (Hardy's first novel), 1976; The Liners, 1976; The Scented Brawl: collected journalism, 1978; Southern Cross, 1979; Thanksgiving, 1981. *Recreations:* cricket, opera, circumnavigation. *Address:* c/o A. D. Peters, 10 Buckingham Street, WC2. *Clubs:* National Liberal; MCC.

COLEMAN, Rt. Rev. William Robert, DD; Professor of Humanities, York University, Toronto; *b* Ulverton, Quebec, 16 Aug. 1917; *s* of Rev. Stanley Harold Coleman and Mary Ann Coleman (*née* Armstrong); *m* 1947, Mary Elizabeth Summers, *er d* of Thomas Summers and Marion Wilson; one *s* two *d. Educ:* St Mary's Collegiate Inst.; Brantford Collegiate Inst.; University Coll. and Wycliffe Coll. (BD); Univ. of Toronto (MA); Union Theological Seminary, New York (STM); Univs of Cambridge and Edinburgh. Deacon, 1942; Priest, 1943; Curate, Church of the Epiphany, Sudbury, Ont., 1942-43; Priest-in-charge, 1943-45; post-graduate study, 1945-47; Prof. of Religious Philosophy and Ethics, Wycliffe Coll., 1947-50; Dean of Divinity and Harold Prof., Bishop's Coll., Lennoxville, Quebec, 1950-52; Principal, Huron Coll.,

London, Ont., 1952-61; Bishop of Kootenay, 1961-65. FRSA, London. DD Wycliffe Coll., 1951. DD (Hon.) Huron Coll., 1961; DD (Hon.) Trinity Coll., Toronto, 1962. *Publications:* contributed to: In Such an Age (ed W. C. Lockhart), 1951; The Church in the Sixties (ed. P. Jefferson), 1962. *Address:* 25 Four Winds Drive, Apartment 903, Downsview, Ontario, Canada.

COLERAINE, 2nd Baron *cr* 1954, of Haltemprice; **James Martin Bonar Law;** *b* 8 Aug. 1931; *s* of 1st Baron Coleraine, PC, and Mary Virginia (*d* 1978), *d* of A. F. Nellis, Rochester, NY; *S* father, 1980; *m* 1st, 1958, Emma Elizabeth (marr. diss.), *o d* of late Nigel Richards; two *d* ; 2nd, 1966, Patricia, *yr d* of Major-Gen. R. H. Farrant, *qv* ; one *s* two *d. Educ:* Trinity College, Oxford. *Heir:* *s* Hon. James Peter Bonar Law, *b* 23 Feb. 1975. *Address:* 5 Kensington Park Gardens, W11.

COLERIDGE, family name of Baron Coleridge.

COLERIDGE, 4th Baron *cr* 1873, of Ottery St Mary; **Richard Duke Coleridge,** KBE 1971 (CBE 1951; OBE 1944); DL; Captain Royal Navy, retired; *b* 24 Sept. 1905; *e s* of 3rd Baron Coleridge and Jessie Alethea Mackarness (*d* 1957); *S* father, 1955; *m* 1936, Rosamund, *er d* of Admiral Sir W. W. Fisher, GCB, GCVO; two *s. Educ:* RNC Osborne and Dartmouth. Entered RN, 1919; RN Staff Course, 1938; invalided off Med. station and retd, 1939; rejoined, 1940, Offices of War Cabinet and of Minister of Defence, with appt to GQG Vincennes, France; War Cabinet Office in London, July 1940-May 1941; Jt Staff Mission, Washington, May 1941; Brit. Jt Staff and Combined Chiefs of Staff, 1942-45, and attended the Confs of Washington, Quebec (1942 and 1943), Cairo, Malta and Yalta; Council of Foreign Ministers, London Conf., Sept. 1945; UN Assembly in London, Jan. 1946; Mil. Staff Cttee of UN, New York, 1946-48; Brit. Jt Services Mission in Washington, 1948, and also Chief Staff Officer to Marshal of the RAF Lord Tedder (Chm. of Brit. Chiefs of Staff Cttee and Brit. Rep. on Standing Gp of NATO, 1950-51); rep. Brit. Chiefs of Staff on Temp. Cttee of Council of NATO, in Paris, 1951; attended Lisbon Conf., 1952; Exec. Sec., NATO, 1952-70. Chairman: Devon and Exeter Savings Bank, 1971-75; SW Trustee Savings Bank, 1975-80 (Pres., 1980-). Chm., Devon Historic Churches Trust, 1972-. DL Devon 1973. US Legion of Merit. *Heir:* *s* Hon. William Duke Coleridge, Major Coldstream Guards, retired [*b* 18 June 1937; *m* 1962, Everild, (Judy) (marr. diss. 1977), *o d* of Lt-Col and Mrs Beauchamp Hambrough, Wisper's Farm, Nairobi; one *s* two *d*]. *Address:* The Chanter's House, Ottery St Mary, S Devon. *T:* Ottery St Mary 2417. *Club:* Army and Navy.

COLERIDGE, Lady (Marguerite) Georgina; *b* 19 March 1916; *d* of 11th Marquess of Tweeddale; *m* 1941, Arthur Coleridge, *yr s* of John Duke Coleridge; one *d. Educ:* home, abroad as a child. Joined National Magazine Co.: Circulation Dept, 1937; Advertisement Dept., 1938; joined Country Life, 1945; Editor of Homes and Gardens, 1949-63; Chm., Inst. of Journalists (London District), 1954, Fellow 1970; Chm., Women's Press Club, 1959 (Pres., 1965-67). Dir, Country Life Ltd, 1962-74; Dir, George Newnes Ltd, 1963-69; Publisher: Homes and Gardens; Woman's Journal, 1969-71; Ideal Home, 1970-71; Dir, Special Projects, IPC Women's Magazines, 1971-74; Consultant: IPC Women's Magazines, 1974-82; Public Relations Counsel Ltd, 1974- (Dir, 1978-). Mem., Internat. Assoc. of Women and Home Page Journalists, 1968-74; Associate, Women in Public Relations, 1972-; Associate Mem., Ladies Jockeys Assoc. of GB, 1973-; Founder Mem., Media Soc. Ltd (Inst. of Journalists Foundn), 1973-76; Member: Information Cttee, Brit. Nutrition Foundn, 1975-79; Information Cttee, RCP, 1977-81; Vice-Pres., Greater London Fund for the Blind, 1981; Pres., Friends of Moorfields, 1981. Freeman, Worshipful Co. of Stationers and Newspapermakers, 1973. *Publications:* Grand Smashional Pointers (book of cartoons), 1934; I Know What I Like (clichés), 1959; That's Racing, 1978. *Recreations:* racing, writing, cooking; nothing highbrow. *Address:* 33 Peel Street, W8 7PA. *T:* 01-727 7732.

COLES, Arthur John; HM Diplomatic Service; Private Secretary to the Prime Minister, since 1981; *b* 13 Nov. 1937; *s* of Arthur Strixton Coles and Doris Gwendoline Coles; *m* 1965, Anne Mary Sutherland Graham; two *s* one *d. Educ:* Magdalen Coll. Sch., Brackley; Magdalen Coll., Oxford (BA 1960). Served HM Forces, 1955-57. Joined HM Diplomatic Service, 1960; Middle Eastern Centre for Arabic Studies, Lebanon, 1960-62; Third Sec., Khartoum, 1962-64; FO (later FCO), 1964-68; Asst Political Agent, Trucial States (Dubai), 1968-71; FCO, 1971-75; Head of Chancery, Cairo, 1975-77; Counsellor (Developing Countries), UK Perm. Mission to EEC, 1977-80; Head of S Asian Dept, FCO, 1980-81. *Recreations:* walking, cricket, bird-watching, reading, music. *Address:* c/o Foreign and Commonwealth Office, King Charles Street, SW1. *Club:* United Oxford & Cambridge University.

COLES, Sir Arthur (William), Kt 1960; *b* 6 Aug. 1892; *s* of George and Elizabeth Coles; *m* 1919, Lilian Florence Knight; two *s* three *d* (and one *s* decd). *Educ:* State Sch.; Geelong Coll. Served European War, 1914-18: 6th Bn, 1914, Gallipoli and France; commissioned, 1916; wounded thrice. Original partner in retail firm of G. J. Coles & Co., 1919; Dir and Gen. Man. on formation of Company, 1921; Managing Dir, 1931-44. JP 1934; Mem. Melbourne City Council, 1934-44; Lord Mayor of Melbourne, 1938-39-40; MP, Henty, Vic., 1940, resigned, 1946. Mem. Commonwealth War Workers Housing Trust, 1941-45; Chairman: Commonwealth War Damage Commn, 1942-48; Commonwealth Rationing Commn, 1942-50; Austr. Nat. Airlines

Commn, 1946-50; British Commonwealth Pacific Airlines, 1946-50; Geelong Coll. Council, 1939-69; Austr. Trustees, Northcote Trust Fund, 1952-75. Vice-Chm., Trusts Corp. of Presbyterian Church of Vic., 1957-77; Mem., Commonwealth Immigration Planning Council, 1948-68; Part-time Mem. of Executive, CSIRO, 1956-65; Mem. Advisory Council, CSIRO, 1965-70; Australian Delegations to Commonwealth Agricultural Bureaux: Quinquennial Conf., London, 1960; Leader Delegn, 1965. *Recreation:* golf. *Address:* 3 Majella Court, Kew, Victoria 3101, Australia. *Clubs:* Athenæum, Peninsula Country Golf (both in Victoria, Australia).
See also Sir K. F. Coles, Sir N. C. Coles.

COLES, Prof. Bryan Randell, DPhil; FInstP; Professor of Solid State Physics, Imperial College, University of London, since 1966; *b* 9 June 1926; *s* of Charles Frederick Coles and Olive Irene Coles; *m* 1955, Merivan Robinson; two *s. Educ:* Canton High Sch., Cardiff; Univ. of Wales, Cardiff (BSc); Jesus Coll., Univ. of Oxford (DPhil). FInstP 1972. Lectr in Metal Physics, Imperial Coll., London, 1950; Res. Fellow, Carnegie Inst. of Technol., Pittsburgh, 1954-56. Vis. Prof., Univ. of Calif, San Diego, 1962 and 1969. Vice-Pres., Inst. of Physics, 1968-72; Mem. Physics Cttee, SRC, 1972-76 (Chm. 1973-76). Chm. Bd of Dirs, Taylor & Francis Ltd (Scientific Publishers), 1976–. *Publications:* Electronic Structures of Solids (with A. D. Caplin), 1976; papers on structure, electrical properties, superconductivity and magnetic properties of metals and alloys in Philosoph. Magazine, Advances in Physics, Jl of Physics. *Recreations:* music, natural history, theatre. *Address:* 61 Courtfield Gardens, SW5. *T:* 01-373 3539.

COLES, Gerald James Kay, QC 1976; a Recorder of the Crown Court, since 1972; *b* 6 May 1933; *o s* of James William Coles and Jane Elizabeth Coles; *m* 1958, Kathleen Yolande, *e d* of Alfred John Hobson, FRCS, and Kathleen Elizabeth Hobson; three *s. Educ:* Coatham Sch., Redcar; Brasenose Coll., Oxford; Harvard Law Sch., Harvard Univ. Meritorious Award, Hastings Schol., Queen's Coll., Oxford, 1949; Akroyd Open Schol. 1950; BA 1954, BCL 1955, Oxon; Westengard Schol., Harvard Law Sch., 1955; LLM 1956. Called to Bar, Middle Temple, 1957; practised at Bar, London and NE Circuit, 1957–; Prosecuting Counsel to Inland Revenue, 1971-76. *Recreations:* music, theatre, photography. *Address:* The Old Rectory, Sessay, Thirsk, N Yorks. *T:* Hutton Sessay 218; (chambers) 4 Paper Buildings, Temple, EC4Y 7DN. *T:* 01-353 8408; 2 Park Square, Leeds LS1 2NE. *T:* Leeds 33277/8/9. *Clubs:* Carlton; Leeds (Leeds).

COLES, Prof. John Morton, ScD, PhD; FBA 1978; Professor of European Prehistory, University of Cambridge, since 1980; Fellow of Fitzwilliam College, since 1963; *b* 25 March 1930; *s* of Edward John Langdon Coles and Alice Margaret (née Brown); *m* 1958, Mona McLellan Shiach; two *s* two *d. Educ:* Woodstock, Ontario; Univ. of Toronto (BA); Univ. of Cambridge (MA, ScD); Univ. of Edinburgh (PhD). Research Fellow, Univ. of Edinburgh, 1959-60; Asst Lectr, 1960-65, Lectr, 1965-76, Reader, 1976-80, Univ. of Cambridge. President, Prehistoric Soc., 1978-82. FSA 1963. *Publications:* The Archaeology of Early Man (with E. Higgs), 1969; Field Archaeology in Britain, 1972; Archaeology by Experiment, 1973; The Bronze Age in Europe (with A. Harding), 1979; Experimental Archaeology, 1979; Prehistory of the Somerset Levels (with B. Orme), 1980; contrib. Proc. Prehist. Soc., Antiquaries Jl, Antiquity, Somerset Levels Papers, etc. *Recreations:* music, tennis. *Address:* 89 Long Road, Cambridge CB2 2HE. *T:* Cambridge 840354.

COLES, Sir Kenneth (Frank), Kt 1957; Chairman, G. J. Coles & Co. Ltd, 1956-63; *b* 19 April 1896; *s* of George and Elizabeth Coles; *m* 1925, Marjorie Evelyn Tolley; one *s* two *d.* Entered G. J. Coles & Co. Ltd, 1921; London Manager, 1927-28; State Manager for NSW, 1933-53; Dir, 1926-76; Dep. Chm., 1945-56; Chm., Aust. Oil and Gas Corp., 1954-67. Pres., Internat. Soc. for Welfare of Cripples, 1957-60. *Recreation:* golf. *Address:* 81A Victoria Road, Bellevue Hill, Sydney, Australia. *T:* 36 4728. *Clubs:* Australian, Elanora Country, Royal Sydney Golf (Sydney).
See also Sir A. W. Coles, Sir N. C. Coles, K. G. Coles.

COLES, Kenneth George, BE; CEng, FIMechE, FAIM; Chairman, Conveyor Co. of Australia Pty Ltd, since 1957; *b* Melbourne, 30 June 1926; *s* of Sir Kenneth Coles, *qv*; *m* 1950, Thalia Helen (marr. diss. 1980); one *s* two *d. Educ:* The King's Sch., Parramatta, NSW; Sydney Univ. (BE 1948). MIE (Aust); FIMechE 1969; FAIM 1959. Gained engrg experience in appliance manufacturing and automotive industries Nuffield Aust. Pty Ltd, Gen. Motors Holdens Pty Ltd and Frigidaire, before commencing own business manufacturing conveyors, 1955; Chm & Man. Dir, K. G. Coles & Co. Pty Ltd, 1955-76, Chm. 1976–; Chm. & Man. Dir, K. G. C. Magnetic Tape Pty Ltd, 1973-80. Director: Australian Oil & Gas Corp. Ltd, 1969–; A. O. G. Minerals Ltd, 1969–; G. J. Coles & Coy Ltd, 1976–; Electrical Equipment Ltd, 1976–; Permanent Trustee Co. Ltd, 1978–. Gen. Councillor, NSW Br., Metal Trades Industries Assoc. of Australia, 1976– (Section Councillor, Alexandria, 1974-76); Mem., Internat. Solar Energy Soc., 1957–. Councillor and Mem. Bd of Governors, Ascham Sch., 1972–; Employers' Rep., NSW Secondary Schs Bd, 1979–. *Recreations:* tennis, skiing, bridge. *Address:* 24 Rosemont Avenue, Woollahra, NSW 2025, Australia. *T:* 328.6084. *Clubs:* Union (Sydney); Royal Sydney Golf; RACV (Melbourne).

COLES, Dame Mabel Irene, DBE 1971 (CBE 1965); President: Royal Women's Hospital, Melbourne, 1968-72; Australian Women's Liberal Club, since 1965; Director, Asthma Foundation of Victoria, 1965; *d* of late E.

Johnston; *m* 1927, Sir Edgar Coles (*d* 1981); one *s* two *d.* Associated with Royal Women's Hosp. for 30 years; Chairman: Ladies Cttee for (two) $1,000,000 appeals; (two) Door Knock Appeals; Asthma Ladies' Appeal Cttee; Patroness: Family Planning Assoc. of Vic.; Rheumatism and Arthritis Assoc. of Vic.; 3Rs Assoc.; Frankston Musical Soc., National Theatreites; Trustee, Mayfield Centre. *Recreations:* dogs, horses, walking. *Address:* Hendra, Williams Road, Mount Eliza, Vic. 3930, Australia. *Clubs:* Alexandra, Peninsula Country (Melbourne).

COLES, Norman, CB 1971; Consultant; *b* 29 Dec. 1914; *s* of Fred and Emily Coles; *m* 1947, Una Valerie Tarrant; five *s. Educ:* Hanson High Sch., Bradford; Royal College of Science; City and Guilds Coll. Head, Armament Dept, RAE, 1959; Dir Gen. Equipment Research and Development, Min. of Aviation, 1962; Dep. Controller: of Aircraft (RAF), Min. of Technology, 1966-68; of Guided Weapons, Min. of Technology, 1968-69; Dep. Chief Adviser (Research and Studies), MoD, 1969-71; Dep. Controller, Establishments and Research, MoD, 1971-75. *Recreations:* carpentry, crossword puzzles. *Address:* Castle Gate, 27 Castle Hill, Banwell, Weston-super-Mare, Avon. *T:* Banwell 822019.

COLES, Sir Norman (Cameron), Kt 1977; Chairman, G. J. Coles & Co. Ltd, Melbourne, 1968-79; *b* 10 Sept. 1907; *s* of George Coles and Annie Cameron Coles; *m* 1932, Dorothy Verna Deague; one *s* one *d. Educ:* Launceston C of E Grammar Sch., Tas; Trinity Grammar Sch., Kew, Vic. AASA, FCIS. Joined G. J. Coles & Co. Ltd, Australia, 1924: Company Secretary, 1933; Director, 1949-79; Finance Dir, 1963-67; Man. Dir, 1967-75. Dir, Multiple Sclerosis Soc. (Victoria), 1975–; Mem., Victorian Plastic Surgery Unit, 1978–. *Recreations:* golf, gardening. *Address:* (office) G. J. Coles & Co. Ltd, 236 Bourke Street, Melbourne, Vic 3000, Australia. *T:* 667-4603; (home) 28 Somers Avenue, Malvern, Vic 3144, Australia. *Clubs:* Athenæum (Melbourne); Melbourne Cricket, Victoria Racing, Peninsula Golf (all Victoria).
See also Sir A. W. Coles, Sir K. F. Coles.

COLFOX, Sir (William) John, 2nd Bt *cr* 1939; JP; DL; *b* 25 April 1924; *yr* and *o* surv. *s* of Sir (William) Philip Colfox, 1st Bt, MC, and Mary (Frances) Lady Colfox (*d* 1973); *S* father, 1966; *m* 1962, Frederica Loveday, *d* of Adm. Sir Victor Crutchley, *qv* ; two *s* three *d. Educ:* Eton. Served in RNVR, 1942-46, leaving as Lieut. Qualified Land Agent, 1950. Chm., Land Settlement Assoc., 1980-81. JP Dorset, 1962, High Sheriff of Dorset, 1969, DL Dorset, 1977. *Heir:* *s* Philip John Colfox, *b* 27 Dec. 1962. *Address:* Symondsbury House, Bridport, Dorset. *T:* Bridport 22956.

COLGATE, Dennis Harvey, MM 1944; Registrar of Family Division of Supreme Court since 1975; *b* 9 Oct. 1922; *s* of Charles William and Marjorie Colgate; *m* 1961, Kathleen (née Marquis); one *d. Educ:* Varndean Sch., Brighton; Univ. Coll. of South West, Exeter; King's Coll., London (LLB). HM Forces, 1942-47; Principal Probate Registry, 1947-64 (Estabt Officer 1959-64); District Probate Registrar at High Court, Manchester, 1964-75. Consulting Editor, Tristram and Coote's Probate Practice. *Publications:* (ed jtly) Rayden on Divorce, 7th edn 1958 and 8th edn 1960; (ed jtly) Atkin's Court Forms (Probate), 2nd edn 1974. *Recreations:* walking, camping, do-it-yourself. *Address:* 10 Frogmore Close, Hughenden Valley, High Wycombe, Bucks HP14 4LN. *T:* Naphill 2659.

COLGRAIN, 3rd Baron *cr* 1946, of Everlands; **David Colin Campbell;** a Director, Antony Gibbs Holdings Ltd, since 1954; *b* 24 April 1920; *s* of 2nd Baron Colgrain, MC, and of Margaret Emily, *d* of late P. W. Carver; *S* father, 1973; *m* 1st, 1945, Veronica Margaret (marr. diss. 1964), *d* of late Lt-Col William Leckie Webster, RAMC; one *s* one *d* ; 2nd, 1973, Mrs Sheila M. Hudson. *Educ:* Eton; Trinity Coll., Cambridge. Served War of 1939-45, 9th Lancers. Manager, Grindlays Bank Ltd, India and Pakistan, 1945-49; joined Antony Gibbs and Sons Ltd, 1949. Jt Treasurer, Royal Assoc. for Disability and Rehabilitation. *Heir:* *s* Hon. Alastair Colin Leckie Campbell [*b* 16 Sept. 1951; *m* 1979, Annabel Rose, *yr d* of Hon. Robin Warrender, *qv*]. *Address:* Flat 4, 51 Winchester Street, SW1; Bushes Farm, Weald, Sevenoaks, Kent.

COLHOUN, Prof. John; Barker Professor of Cryptogamic Botany, University of Manchester, 1960-80, now Emeritus; Dean, Faculty of Science, 1974 and 1975; Pro-Vice-Chancellor, 1977-80; *b* 15 May 1913; *yr s* of late James Colhoun and Rebecca Colhoun, Castlederg, Co. Tyrone; *m* 1949, Margaret, *e d* of late Prof. Gilbert Waterhouse, LittD, and Mary Elizabeth, *e d* of Sir Robert Woods; three *d. Educ:* Edwards Sch., Castlederg, Co. Tyrone; The Queen's Univ. of Belfast; Imperial Coll. of Science, London Univ. BSc, MAgr (Belfast), PhD, DSc (London), MSc (Manchester), DIC. Min. of Agriculture for Northern Ireland: Research Asst, 1939-46; Senior Scientific Officer, 1946-50; Principal Scientific Officer, 1951-60. The Queen's Univ., Belfast: Asst Lecturer in Agricultural Botany, 1940-42; Asst Lectr 1942-45, Jun. Lectr 1945-46, Lectr 1946-54, Reader 1954-60, in Mycology and Plant Pathology. Warden of Queen's Chambers, 1942-49. FLS 1955. FIBiol 1963. Pres., British Mycological Soc., 1963; Chm., Fedn of British Plant Pathologists, 1968. Jt Editor, Phytopathologische Zeitschrift, 1973–. *Publications:* Diseases of the Flax Plant, 1947; Club Root Disease of Crucifers caused by *Plasmodiophora Bassicae* Woron, 1958; numerous papers in Annals of Applied Biology, Annals of Botany, Trans Brit. Mycological Soc., Nature, Phytopath. Z. *Address:* 12 Southdown Crescent, Cheadle Hulme, Cheshire SK8 6EQ. *T:* 061-485 2084. *Club:* Athenæum.

COLIN, Rt. Rev. Gerald Fitzmaurice, MA; an Assistant Bishop, Diocese of Lincoln, since 1979; *b* 19 July 1913; *s* of Frederick Constant Colin and Jemima Fitzmaurice; *m* 1941, Iris Susan Stuart Weir; three *s* two *d*. *Educ:* Mountjoy Sch.; Trinity Coll., Dublin. MA (TCD) 1946. Deacon, 1936; Priest, 1937. St George's, Dublin, 1938; Chancellor's Vicar, St Patrick's Cathedral, Dublin, 1938; RAFVR, 1939-47; Vicar of Frodingham, Dio. of Lincoln, 1947-66; Bishop Suffragan of Grimsby, 1966-78. Canon of Lincoln Cathedral, 1960; Rural Dean of Manlake, 1960; Proctor in Convocation, 1960-65, 1966-70. *Recreation* : fishing. *Address:* Orchard Close, St Mary's Lane, Louth, Lincs. *T:* Louth 602600.

COLLAR, Prof. (Arthur) Roderick, CBE 1964; MA, DSc; FRS 1965; FEng 1976; Sir George White Professor of Aeronautical Engineering, University of Bristol, 1945-73, now Emeritus; Pro-Vice-Chancellor, 1967-70 (Vice-Chancellor 1968-69); *b* 22 Feb. 1908; *s* of late Arthur Collar, JP, and Louie Collar; *m* 1934, Winifred Margaret Moorman; two *s*. *Educ:* Simon Langton Sch., Canterbury; Emmanuel Coll., Cambridge (Scholar). Aerodynamics Dept, Nat. Physical Laboratory, 1929-41; Structural and Mechanical Engineering Dept, Royal Aircraft Establishment, 1941-45. Pres., Royal Aeronautical Soc., 1963-64; Chairman: Aeronautical Research Council, 1964-68; Chm. Council, Rolls-Royce Technical Coll.; Mem. Adv. Council, Royal Military Coll. of Science, Shrivenham, 1964-80 (Chm., 1970-78). Member: Clifton Coll. Council, 1969-79; Council, Royal Society, 1971-73; Bd of Governors, United Bristol Hosps, 1968-74; Academic Adv. Council, Cranfield Inst. of Technology, 1970-75; SW Regional Hosp. Bd, 1969-74. FAIAA. Liveryman, Guild of Air Pilots and Air Navigators. Hon. LLD Bristol, 1969; Hon. DSc: Bath, 1971; Cranfield, 1976. R38 Memorial Prize (joint), 1932; George Taylor Gold Medal, 1947; Orville Wright Prize, 1958; J. E. Hodgson Prize, 1960, 1979; Gold Medal, RAeS, 1966; Hon. FRAeS 1973; Hon FCASI 1980. *Publications:* Elementary Matrices (joint), 1938; (joint ed.) Hypersonic Flow; numerous papers in technical press. *Recreations:* sport (onlooker), poetry, music. *Address:* 12 Rockleaze, Bristol BS9 1NE. *T:* Bristol 681491. *Clubs:* Royal Commonwealth Society; Bristol Savages.

COLLARD, Douglas Reginald, OBE 1976; HM Diplomatic Service, retired; Director, Anglo-Arab Association, since 1976; Director, Arab British Centre; *b* 7 April 1916; *s* of late Hebert Carthew Collard and late Mary Ann (*née* Pugh); *m* 1947, Eleni Alkmini Kiortsi (marr. diss. 1969), Greece; two *s* three *d*. *Educ:* Wallasey Grammar Sch.; privately. Army Service, 1940-46 (despatches); UNRRA, Greece, 1946-47; Asst Commercial Adviser, British Econ. Mission to Greece, 1947; Consul, Patras, Greece, 1947-52; Develt Div., Beirut, 1952-54; 2nd Sec. (Commercial); Khartoum, 1954-56; Copenhagen, 1958-61; FCO, 1956-58 and 1967-69; 1st Sec. (Commercial): Tripoli, 1961-65; Lahore, 1965-67; Montevideo, 1969-71; 1st Sec., later Counsellor (Commercial), Algiers, 1971-73; Consul-Gen., Bilbao, 1973-76. *Recreations:* reading, walking. *Address:* 21 Collingham Road, SW5 0NU. *T:* 01-373 8417.

COLLARD, Prof. Patrick John, JP; MD, FRCP; Professor of Bacteriology and Director of Department of Bacteriology and Virology, University of Manchester, 1962-80, now Professor Emeritus; *b* 22 April 1920; *s* of Rupert John Collard; *m* 1st, 1948, Jessie Robertson (marr. diss. 1955); one *s* one *d*; 2nd, 1956, Kathleen Sarginson; one *s* one *d*. *Educ:* St Bartholomew's Medical Coll., Univ. of London. Qualified MB, BS, 1942; MD 1951. House Appts, 1942-44. RAMC, 1944-48. Registrar, Westminster Hospital, 1948-50; Lectr, Guy's Hosp. Med. Sch., 1950-54; Prof. of Bacteriology, University Coll., Ibadan, Nigeria, 1954-62; Vis. Prof., London Sch. of Hygiene and Tropical Medicine, 1979. FRCP 1972. JP Manchester, 1973. *Publications:* The Development of Microbiology, 1976; papers in: BMJ, Lancet, Jl Soc. Gen. Microbiol., Jl of Hygiene, West African Med. Jl, etc. *Recreations:* talking, reading, playing chess, silver-smithing. *Address:* Honor Oak Cottage, Kingham, Oxford. *T:* Kingham 335. *Club:* Athenæum.

COLLENS, John Antony; Deputy Secretary, Exchequer and Audit Department, since 1979; *b* 19 Nov. 1930; *s* of John Collens and Emily Charlotte Collens (*née* Gomm); *m* 1957, Josephine Stark; three *s*. *Educ:* Harrogate Grammar Sch. Mem. CIPFA, 1979. National Service, 1950-52. Exchequer and Audit Department: Asst Auditor, 1949; Sen. Auditor, 1962; Dep. Dir of Audit, 1973; Dir of Audit, 1977. *Recreations:* cricket, tennis, walking. *Address:* 141 Park Avenue, Orpington, Kent BR6 9ED. *T:* Orpington 29133.

COLLETT, Sir Ian (Seymour), 3rd Bt *cr* 1934; *b* 5 Oct. 1953; *s* of David Seymour Collett (*d* 1962), and of Sheila Joan Collett (who *m* 1980, James William Miskin, *qv*), *o d* of late Harold Scott; *S* grandfather, 1971; *m* 1982, Philippa, *o d* of James R. I. Hawkins, Preston St Mary, Suffolk. *Educ:* Lancing College, Sussex. *Recreations:* fishing, sailing, cricket, shooting. *Heir:* uncle Christopher Collett [*b* 10 June 1931; *m* 1959, Christine Anne, *o d* of late Oswald Hardy Griffiths; two *s* one *d*]. *Address:* 75 Engadine Street, SW18. *Clubs:* Hurlingham, MCC, Flyfishers'.

COLLETT, Sir (Thomas) Kingsley, Kt 1968; CBE 1956; formerly Director, Adams Bros & Shardlow Ltd (Creative Printers), London and Leicester, retired 1971; *b* 7 March 1906; 6th *s* of late Sir Charles Collett, 1st Bt, Bromley, Kent (Lord Mayor of London, 1933-34); *m* 1930, Beatrice Olive, *d* of late Thomas H. Brown, Bickley, Kent. *Educ:* Bishop's Stortford Coll. Mem., City of London Territorial Auxiliary and Volunteer Reserve Assoc. Forces Association. HM Lieut for City of London, 1958. Freeman, City of London,

1930; Liveryman, Worshipful Co. of Distillers, 1934 (Master, 1960-61); Mem., Ct of Common Coun., City of London (Ward of Bridge), 1945-; Chairman: City of London Freemen's Sch. Cttee, 1949-52; Port of London Health Authority, 1953; City Lands Cttee and Chief Commoner, 1955; Special Cttee, 1956-66; Policy and Parly Cttee, 1967-70. Corp. of London Rep. on Bd of Port of London Authority, 1959-67; Mem., Pollution Control Cttee, PLA, 1966-73; Chm., Lord Mayor's Appeal Cttee; Kennedy Mem. Fund, 1964; Churchill Fund, 1965; Vice-Chm., Lord Mayor's Appeal Cttee: cleaning St Paul's Cath, 1963-64; Attlee Meml Fund, 1967. Governor, Royal Hospitals; Chm., Governing Council, Bishop's Stortford Coll., 1964-76; Life Mem., Court of The City Univ., 1970-, Hon. DLitt 1980. Chm., East India and Sports Club, 1959-66; Pres., City Pickwick Club. Dep. Governor, Irish Soc., 1975. Chevalier, Mil. Order of Christ (Portugal), 1956. *Recreation:* shooting. *Address:* 5 Moorlands, Wilderness Road, Chislehurst, Kent. *Club:* East India, Devonshire, Sports and Public Schools.

COLLEY, Surg. Rear-Adm. Ian Harris, OBE 1963; *b* 14 Oct. 1922; *s* of Aubrey James Colley and Violet Fulford Colley; *m* 1952, Joy Kathleen (*née* Goodacre). *Educ:* Hanley Castle Grammar Sch.; King's Coll., London and King's Coll. Hosp. MB, BS 1948; DPH; MFOM; FFCM. Royal Naval Medical Service, 1948-80: MO HMS Cardigan Bay and HMS Consort, 1949-52; service with Fleet Air Arm, 1955-78: as PMO HMS Centaur; MO i/c Air Med. Sch.; Pres., Central Air Med. Bd; Comd MO to Flag Officer, Naval Air Comd; Surg. Rear Adm. (Ships and Estabs), 1978-80, retired. QHP 1978-80. Consultant in Aviation Medicine; former Examr to Conjoint Bd, Royal College of Surgeons and Royal College of Physicians for Dip.Av.Med. Hon. Consultant in Occup. Medicine to Royal Nat. Life-Boat Instn. CStJ 1980. *Publications:* papers in field of aviation medicine. *Address:* c/o Lloyds Bank Limited, 222 Strand, WC2.

COLLEY, Thomas, MB, ChB (Victoria); MRCS, LRCP, FRCSE; DOMS; Emeritus Cons. Ophthalmologist, Wessex Regional Hospital Board; late Director of Ophthalmology to West Dorset Group of Hospitals; late Hon. Surgeon to Weymouth and Dorset County Royal Eye Infirmary; late Hon. Ophthalmic Surgeon to Dorset County Hospital, Dorchester and Weymouth and District Hospital; Ophthalmic Surgeon to EMS Hospital, Portwey, Weymouth (War Years); late Cons. Oculist to the Dorset CC and Weymouth Education Committee; *b* Dec. 1894; *s* of Thomas and Esther Colley, Preston; *m* Eleanor Mary, *e d* of late Rev. D. J. Thomas, OBE, MA, JP; two *d*. *Educ:* privately; Manchester Univ. (Dumville Surgical Prize, Medical Clinical Prize); Edinburgh University. House appointments Royal Infirmary, Manchester, Central Branch Royal Infirmary, Manchester, Hospital for Sick Children, Great Ormond Street, London, Royal London Ophthalmic Hospital (Moorfields). Chm., W Dorset Group Med. Adv. Cttee, 1948-54; Member: Med. Adv. Cttee to SW Metropolitan Regional Hosp. Bd, 1949-51, (Mem., Med. Adv. Cttee of Western Area, 1948-53); W Dorset Group Hospitals Management Cttee, 1948-61. FRSM (Mem. of Council, Section of Ophthalmology, 1938-42); Mem. of Ophthalmological Soc., BMA, etc. *Publications:* papers in medical journals. *Recreation:* philately. *Address:* Anchor House, Eaton Crescent, Clifton, Bristol.

COLLICK, Percy Henry; Assistant General Secretary, Associated Society of Locomotive Engineers, 1940-57 (Organising Secretary, 1934-40). Contested (Lab) Reigate Division of Surrey, 1929 and 1931; MP (Lab) West Birkenhead, 1945-50, Birkenhead, 1950-64. General Purposes Cttee, TUC, 1930-34; National Executive, Labour Party, 1944; Joint Parly Sec., Min. of Agriculture, 1945-47. Mem. Council, Royal College of Veterinary Surgeons, 1949-53. Hon. Freeman of Birkenhead, 1965. *Address:* 142 Hendon Way, NW2.

COLLIE, Alexander Conn, MBE 1979; JP; Lord Provost of the City of Aberdeen, since 1980; Lord Lieutenant of the City of Aberdeen, since 1980; *b* 1 July 1913; *s* of late Donald and Jane Collie; *m* 1942, Elizabeth Keith Macleod; two *s*. *Educ:* Ferryhill Sch., Aberdeen; Ruthrieston Sch., Aberdeen. Councillor, Aberdeen Town Council, 1947- (Chm., Leisure and Recreation Cttee, 1956-80); Member: Aberdeen Harbour Board, 1947-74; North of Scotland Hydro-Electric Consultative Council, until Oct. 1980; Past Member: Scottish Sports Council; Scottish Bakers' Union Exec. Council. JP Aberdeen, 1956. OStJ 1981. *Address:* (home) 43 Brimmond Place, Aberdeen AB1 3EN. *T:* Aberdeen 874972; (office) Town House, Aberdeen AB9 1LP. *T:* Aberdeen 23456.

COLLIER, family name, **Monkswell Barony.**

COLLIER, Air Vice-Marshal Sir (Alfred) Conrad, KCB 1947 (CB 1943); CBE 1941; retired as Chief Executive, Guided Weapons Division, English Electric Aviation Ltd, 1960; *b* 16 Nov. 1895; *m* 1st, 1920, G. M. C. Luis (*d* 1961); two *s* one *d*; 2nd, 1963, Kathleen, *d* of late Joseph Donaghy, JP, Londonderry. *Educ:* Sherborne Sch. 2nd Lieut 9th King's Own (RL) Regt, 1914; RFC, 1915 with subsequent continuous service in RFC and RAF; Air Attaché, Moscow, 1934-37; Dep. Dir of Plans, Air Min., 1938; Dir of Allied Air Co-operation, Air Min., 1940; Head of Air Section, British Military Mission to Moscow, 1941; Air Officer i/c Administration, AHQ, India, 1942-43; Deputy AOC-in-C Transport Comd, 1943-45; AOC No. 3 Group, Bomber Comd, 1946; Dir-Gen. of Technical Services, Min. of Civil Aviation, 1946-47; Air Vice-Marshal, 1946; Controller of Technical and Operational Services, Min. of Civil Aviation, 1947, resigned, 1948. A Governor, National Hospitals for Nervous Diseases, 1961-64. DL Kent, 1952-64. FRAeS. Order of White Lion, 2nd Class (Czechoslovakia); Grand Officer, Order of Orange

Nassau (Netherlands); Officer, Legion of Honour, and Croix de Guerre (France). *Address:* c/o Lloyds Bank Ltd, Walton-on-Thames, Surrey. *Club:* Royal Air Force.

COLLIER, Andrew James, CB 1976; Deputy Secretary, Department of Health and Social Security, since 1973; *b* 12 July 1923; *s* of Joseph Veasy Collier and Dorothy Murray; *m* 1950, Bridget, *d* of George and Edith Eberstadt, London; two *d. Educ:* Harrow; Christ Church, Oxford. Served Army, 1943-46. Entered HM Treasury, 1948; Private Sec. to: Sir Henry Wilson Smith, 1950; Sir Leslie Rowan, 1951; Chancellors of the Exchequer, 1956-59; Asst Sec., 1961; Under-Sec., 1967; Under-Secretary: Civil Service Dept, 1968-71; DHSS, 1971-73. *Address:* 82 Old Church Street, SW3. *T:* 01-352 5150. *Club:* Athenæum.

COLLIER, Andrew John; Chief Education Officer, Lancashire County Council, since 1980; *b* 29 Oct. 1939; *s* of Francis George Collier and Margaret Nancy (*née* Nockles); *m* 1964, Gillian Ann (*née* Churchill); two *d. Educ:* University College Sch.; St John's Coll., Cambridge (MA). Assistant Master, Winchester Coll., 1962-68; Hampshire County Educn Dept, 1968-71; Buckinghamshire County Educn Dept, 1971-77; Dep. Chief Educn Officer, Lancashire, 1977-80. Mem., Technician Educn Council, 1982. Liveryman, Worshipful Company of Wheelwrights, 1972. Mem. Council, Univ. of Lancaster, 1981. *Recreations:* music, walking, gardening. *Address:* County Hall, Preston, Lancs PR1 8RJ. *T:* Preston 54868. *Club:* Leander (Henley-on-Thames).

COLLIER, Air Vice-Marshal Sir Conrad; *see* Collier, Sir A. C.

COLLIER, Kenneth Gerald; *b* 1910; *m* 1938, Gwendoline Halford; two *s. Educ:* Aldenham Sch.; St John's Coll., Cambridge. MA 1935; Diploma in Education (Oxon) 1945. Technical translation, Stockholm, 1931-32; Schoolmaster, 1933-41; Royal Ordnance Factories, 1941-44; Physics Master, Lancing Coll., 1944-49; Lectr, St Luke's Coll., Exeter, 1944-59; Principal, College of the Venerable Bede, Durham, 1959-75. Editor, Education for Teaching, 1953-58. Chm., Assoc. Teachers in Colls and Depts of Education, 1964-65. Vis. Prof. of Education, Temple Univ., Philadelphia, 1965, 1968. Seconded to Nat. Council for Educational Technology, 1971. Hon. Research Fellow, Univ. of East Anglia, 1978-81. *Publications:* The Science of Humanity, 1950; The Social Purposes of Education, 1959; New Dimensions in Higher Education, 1968; (ed) Innovation in Higher Education, 1974; (ed) Values and Moral Development in Higher Education, 1974; (ed) Evaluating the New BEd, 1978; (ed) Peer-group Study in Higher Education, 1982; (contrib.) Sixth Form Citizens, 1950; Religious Faith and World Culture (New York), 1951; articles in educational and other jls. *Recreations:* local history; music; the film. *Address:* Lumley Park House, Chester-le-Street, Co. Durham DH3 4EY. *T:* Chester-le-Street 883355.

COLLIER, Lesley Faye, (Mrs Nicholas Dromgoole); Principal Dancer with the Royal Ballet, since 1972; *b* 13 March 1947; *d* of Roy and Mavis Collier; *m* 1977, Nicholas Arthur Dromgoole. *Educ:* The Royal Ballet School, White Lodge, Richmond. Joined Royal Ballet, 1965; has danced most principal roles in the Royal repertory. *Address:* c/o Royal Ballet Company, 155 Talgarth Road, W14.

COLLIER, Prof. Leslie Harold, MD, DSc; FRCP, FRCPath; Professor of Virology and Senior Lecturer, Joint Department of Virology, London Hospital Medical College and St Bartholomew's Hospital Medical College, since 1978; Head, Department of Virology, London Hospital Medical College, since 1982; Hon. Consultant in Virology, City and East London Area Health Authority (Teaching); *b* 9 Feb. 1921; *s* of late Maurice Leonard Collier and Ruth (*née* Phillips); *m* 1942, Adeline Barnett; one *s. Educ:* Brighton Coll.; UCH Med. Sch. MD London 1953; DSc London 1968; MRCP 1969; FRCPath 1975; FRCP 1980. House Phys., UCH, 1943; served RAMC, 1944-47; Asst Pathologist, St Helier Hosp., Carshalton, 1947; Lister Inst. of Preventive Medicine, 1948-78: Head, Dept of Virology, 1955-74; Dep. Dir, 1968-74; Dir, Vaccines and Sera Laboratories, 1974-78. Hon. Dir, MRC Trachoma Unit, 1957-73. Chibret Gold Medal, Ligue contre le Trachome, 1959; Luys Prize, Soc. de Médecine de Paris, 1963. *Publications:* papers in med. and scientific jls. *Recreations:* various. *Address:* Brontë Cottage, 89 South End Road, NW3 2RJ. *T:* 01-794 6331.

COLLIER, Dr William Adrian Larry; District Medical Officer for Falmouth, Jamaica, since 1980; *b* 25 Nov. 1913; *s* of Hon. Gerald Collier, 2nd *s* of 2nd Baron Monkswell, and Lily Anderson; *S* uncle as 4th Baron Monkswell, 1964; disclaimed title, 7 April 1964; *m* 1945, Helen (*née* Dunbar, now Mrs Kemp); two *s*; *m* 1951, Nora Selby; one *s* one *d. Educ:* Fellowship Sch.; Odenwald Schule; Summerhill; Univs of Queensland, Edinburgh, London and Cambridge. IB 1937; MB, ChB Edinburgh 1943; DPH London 1947, PHLS (Trainee), 1947-50. Mem., Halstead UDC, 1954-67; Essex CC, 1958-61. General Practitioner: Halstead, Essex, 1951-69; Hackney, 1970. Member: Amenity Cttee, Nat. Assoc. River Authorities, 1970-72; Council, Forest School Camps; Council, Centreprise 1973. *Publications:* World Index of Imprints used on Tablets and other Solid Dose Forms, 1964, 6th edn (now known as IMPREX), 1976; contribs to Lancet, Pharmaceutical Journal, Drug Intelligence and Clinical Pharmacy (washington DC). *Recreations:* swimming, camping, kids, local government, Essex River Authority. *Heir:* (to disclaimed barony); *s* Gerard Collier, *b* 28 Jan. 1947. *Address:* 1 Brett Manor,

Brett Road, E8. *T:* 01-986 8837; Falmouth Health Centre (Hospital), Trelawny, Jamaica. *T:* 0 954 2346; (home) 0 954 2284.

COLLIER-WRIGHT, John Hurrell, CBE 1966; Member, British Transport Docks Board, 1974-77; *b* 1 April 1915; *s* of John Robert Collier Collier-Wright and Phyllis Hurrell Walters; *m* 1940, Pauline Beatrice Platts; three *s* (and one *s* decd). *Educ:* Bradfield Coll.; Queen's Coll., Oxford (MA). FCIT. Traffic Apprentice, LNER, 1936-39. Served War of 1939-45, RE, France, Iraq and Iran (Lt-Col; US Legion of Merit). East African Railways and Harbours, 1946-64; Chief Commercial Supt; joined British Transport Docks Bd, 1964; Chief Commercial Man., 1964-70; Asst Man. Dir, 1970-72; Dep. Man. Dir, 1972-77; Dir, British Transport Advertising, 1966-81. *Address:* Laurel Cottage, 71 Main Street, Mursley, Bucks MK17 0RT. *Club:* Nairobi (Kenya).

COLLIGAN, John Clifford, CBE 1963 (OBE 1957); Director-General, Royal National Institute for the Blind, 1950-72; Secretary, British Wireless for the Blind Fund, since 1950; Hon. Treasurer and Life Member, World Council for the Blind, since 1969 (British Representative, 1954-69); *b* 27 Oct. 1906; *s* of John and Florence Colligan, Wallasey, Cheshire; *m* 1st, 1934, Ethel May Allton (*d* 1948); one *s* one *d*; 2nd, 1949, Frances Bird. *Educ:* Liscard High Sch., Wallasey. Dep. Sec., National Institute for the Blind, 1945-49. *Publications:* The Longest Journey, 1969; various articles on blind welfare. *Recreations:* fishing, gardening. *Address:* 3 Jonathans, Dene Road, Northwood, Mddx. *T:* Northwood 21988.

COLLIN, Maj.-Gen. Geoffrey de Egglesfield, CB 1975; MC 1944; DL; *b* 18 July 1921; *s* of late Charles de Egglesfield Collin and Catherine Mary Collin; *m* 1949, Angela Stella (*née* Young); one *s* three *d. Educ:* Wellington Coll., Berks. Served War of 1939-45: commissioned as 2nd Lt, RA, 1941; in India and Burma, 1942-45. Qualified as Army Pilot, 1946; attended Staff Coll., Camberley, 1951; Instructor at RMA, Sandhurst, 1954-56; served Kenya, 1956-58; JSSC, 1958; Instructor at Staff Coll., Camberley, 1960-62; comd 50 Missile Regt, RA, 1962-64; CRA, 4th Div., 1966-67; attended Imperial Defence College, London, 1968; Comdt, Royal School of Artillery, 1969-71; Maj.-Gen. RA, HQ BAOR, 1971-73; GOC North East District, York, 1973-76; retired 1976. Col Comdt, RA, 1976-83. Part-time Chm., CS Selection Bd (Mem., 1978). Hon. Dir, Great Yorks Show, 1976-. DL N Yorks, 1977. *Recreations:* fishing, ornithology, music, photography. *Address:* Old Vicarage, Roecliffe, York YO5 9LY. *Club:* Army and Navy.

COLLIN, Jack, MA, MD; FRCS; Clinical Reader in Surgery, University of Oxford, and Fellow of Trinity College, Oxford, since 1980; *b* 23 April 1945; *s* of John Collin and Amy Maud Collin; *m* 1971, Christine Frances Proud; two *s* one *d. Educ:* Univ. of Newcastle (MB BS, MD); Mayo Clinic, Minn. University of Newcastle: Demonstrator in Anatomy, 1969-70; Sen. Res. Associate, 1973-75; Registrar in Surgery, Royal Victoria Infirmary, Newcastle, 1971-80; Mayo Foundn Fellow, Mayo Clinic, Minn, 1977. Moynihan Fellow, Assoc. of Surgeons of GB and Ire., 1980. Arris and Gale Lectr, RCS, 1976. Jacksonian Prize, RCS, 1977. *Publications:* papers on intestinal myoelectrical activity and absorption, parenteral nutrition and pancreatic transplantation. *Recreations:* gardening, walking. *Address:* Nuffield Department of Surgery, John Radcliffe Hospital, Oxford. *T:* Oxford 64711.

COLLINGRIDGE, Jean Mary, (Mrs A. R. Collingridge); Chief Executive, Employment Service Division of the Manpower Services Commission, 1979-82; *b* 9 March 1923; *d* of Edgar and Elsie Bishop; *m* 1951, Albert Robert Collingridge; one *d. Educ:* County High School, Loughton, Essex; University College London (BSc Econ); LSE (Social Science Course). Asst Personnel Officer, C. and J. Clark, 1945-49; Personnel Manager, Pet Foods Ltd, 1949-50; Ministry of Labour/Department of Employment: Personnel Management Adviser and Industrial Relations Officer, 1950-65; Regl Industrial Relations Officer/Sen. Manpower Adviser, 1965-71; Assistant Secretary, Office of Manpower Economics 1971-73, Pay Board 1973-74, Dept of Employment HQ 1974-76; Dep. Chief Exec., Employment Service Div. of Manpower Services Commn, 1976-79. *Publication:* (jointly) Personnel Management in the Small Firm, 1953. *Recreations:* home and garden. *Address:* 104 Silverdale Road, Sheffield S11 9JL. *T:* Sheffield 350839. *Club:* Royal Commonwealth Society.

COLLINGS, Juliet Jeanne d'Auvergne; HM Diplomatic Service; Counsellor, Jakarta, since 1982; *b* 23 May 1935; *d* of Maj.-Gen. Wilfred d'Auvergne Collings, qv. *Educ:* a variety of schools; Lady Margaret Hall, Oxford. BA. Joined Foreign Office 1957; Common Market Delegation, Brussels, 1961-63; FO, 1963-64; Second, later First Secretary, Bangkok, 1964-66; News Dept, FO, 1967-70; Head of Chancery, The Hague, 1970-74; European Integration Dept, FCO, 1974-77; Counsellor (Inf.), Paris, 1977-80; RCDS, 1981. *Address:* c/o Foreign and Commonwealth Office, SW1. *Club:* United Oxford & Cambridge University.

COLLINGS, Maj.-Gen. Wilfred d'Auvergne, CB 1946; CBE 1941; *b* Guernsey, 8 Aug. 1893; 5th *s* of C. d'Auvergne Collings, MD, and Laura Josephine Williams; *m* 1928, Nancy Draper Bishop; two *s* one *d. Educ:* Elizabeth Coll., Guernsey; RMC Sandhurst. Commissioned ASC 1914. Served in France, Gallipoli and Mesopotamia, 1914-18 (despatches twice); seconded for service with Egyptian Army, 1923-24 and Sudan Defence Force, 1925-30; on active service in Palestine, 1937-39; Dep. Dir of Supplies and

Transport, Western Desert Force, 1940, British Forces in Greece, 1941, Eighth Army, 1941; Dir of Supplies and Transport, Persia and Iraq Force, 1942-43, 21st Army Group, 1944-45, and British Army of the Rhine, 1945-46; retired 1948. Chief of Supply and Transport Div., UN Relief and Works Agency in the Near East, 1949-53. Maj.-Gen. 1944. Commander, Order of Leopold II (Belgium); MC of Greece, Croix de Guerre of France and Belgium. *Address:* La Verdure, Clifton, St Peter Port, Guernsey. *Club:* Army and Navy.

See also J. J. d'A. Collings.

COLLINGWOOD, Adrian Redman, CBE 1975; TD 1953; Chairman of the Eggs Authority, 1971-78; *b* Driffield, Yorks, 26 Feb. 1910; *s* of Bernard Joseph Collingwood and Katherine Mary Collingwood; *m* 1939, Dorothy Strong; two *d. Educ:* Hull Technical College. FIB. Served War of 1939-45, E Yorks Regt (50th Div.) (Major; despatches, 1944); wounded in Western Desert; POW for a year, then escaped by means of tunnel. Midland Bank: Asst Man., Whitefriargate Branch, Hull, 1947-51; Branch Supt, 1951-55; Gen. Manager's Asst, 1955-59; Gen. Manager (Agriculture), 1959-66; retd from bank, 1971. *Publications:* lectures. *Recreations:* previously rugger, cricket, tennis; now golf, bridge, fishing. *Address:* Flat 6, Burrells, 25 Court Downs Road, Beckenham, Kent. *T:* 01-650 2265. *Clubs:* Farmers'; Rugby (Rugby); (Chm.) Langley Park Golf.

COLLINGWOOD, Lt-Gen. Sir George; *see* Collingwood, Lt-Gen. Sir R. G.

COLLINGWOOD, John Gildas, FEng, FIChemE; Director: Unilever Ltd, 1965-77; Unilever NV, 1965-77; Head of Research Division of Unilever Ltd, 1961-77; *b* 15 June 1917; *s* of Stanley Ernest Collingwood and Kathleen Muriel (*née* Smalley); *m* 1942, Pauline Winifred (*née* Jones); one *s* one *d. Educ:* Wycliffe Coll., Stonehouse, Glos; University Coll. London (BSc). English Charcoal, 1940-41; British Ropeway Engrg Co, 1941-44; De Havilland Engines, 1944-46; Olympia Oil and Cake Mills Ltd, 1946-49; British Oil and Cake Mills Ltd, 1949-51; Mem., UK Milling Group of Unilever Ltd, 1951-60; Dir, Advita Ltd, 1951-60; Dir, British Oil & Cake Mills Ltd, 1955-60. Instn of Chemical Engrs: Mem. Research Cttee, 1963-68; Mem. Council, 1964-67. Mem. Council of Univ. of Aston, 1971- (Chm., Academic Advisory Cttee, 1964-71); Mem., Research Cttee, CBI, 1970-71; Member: Council for Scientific Policy, 1971-72; Exec. Cttee, British Nutrition Foundn, 1978- (Council, 1970-); Food Standards Cttee, 1972-; Royal Commn on Environmental Pollution, 1973-79; Standing Commn on Energy and the Environment, 1978-. A Gen. Sec., British Assoc. for Advancement of Science, 1978-. Hon. DSc, Aston, 1966; Fellow, University Coll. London, 1970. *Recreations:* sailing, music. *Address:* 54 Downs Road, Coulsdon, Surrey. *T:* Downland 54817. *Club:* Athenæum.

COLLINGWOOD, Lawrance Arthur, CBE 1948; *b* 14 March 1887; *s* of J. H. Collingwood; *m* 1914, Anna Koenig, St Petersburg, Russia; two *s* two *d. Educ:* Westminster Abbey Choir Sch.; Exeter Coll., Oxford; St Petersburg Conservatoire. For 50 years associated with work for EMI (HMV); for 25 years associated with work of The Old Vic and Sadler's Wells, first as repetiteur, then conductor; musical dir of Sadler's Wells Opera Co., 1940-47. *Address:* Annalac, Rynachulig, Killin, Perthshire, Scotland.

COLLINGWOOD, Lt-Gen. Sir (Richard) George, KBE 1959 (CBE 1951); CB 1954; DSO 1944; *b* 7 Oct. 1903; 4th *s* of Col C. G. Collingwood, Lilburn Tower and Glanton Pyke, Northumberland. *Educ:* RN Colls Osborne and Dartmouth; RMC Sandhurst. Entered Cameronians, 1923; Brigadier, 1944; served in Middle East and Burma. GOC 52 Lowland Division and Lowland District, Oct. 1952-55; Maj.-Gen. 1953; GOC, Singapore District, 1957-58; GOC-in-C, Scottish Command, 1958-61; Gov. of Edinburgh Castle, 1958-61; retired, 1961. Col, The Cameronians (Scottish Rifles), 1964-68. A Mem. of the Jockey Club (Steward, 1960). Knight Grand Cross, Order of the Sword (Sweden), 1964. *Recreations:* hunting, shooting, racing. *Address:* Abbey Lands, Alnwick, Northumberland. *T:* Alnwick 602220. *Club:* Boodle's.

COLLINGWOOD, Brig. Sydney, CMG 1957; CBE 1945; MC 1917; retired; *b* 10 July 1892; *s* of late Sir William Collingwood, KBE, MICE, JP, Dedham Grove, near Colchester, Essex; *m* 1st, 1915, Charlotte Annie (decd), *d* of Colonel James Charles Oughterson, late 18th Royal Irish, Greenock; two *s* one *d*; 2nd, 1940, Eileen Mary (*d* 1977), *widow* of late Major W. D. G. Batten, 3rd Gurkha Rifles, and *d* of A. Willson, Waldegrave Park, Twickenham. *Educ:* Liverpool Coll.; Royal Military Academy. 2nd Lieut, RA, 1912. Served European War, 1914-18. Major, 1930; Bt Lieut-Col 1934; Col, 1938; Brig., 1940; BGS, Southern Command, 1940-42; DDPS, War Office, 1942-46; retd, 1946. Regional Dir, Southern Region, Imperial War Graves Commission (Headquarters, Rome), 1946-57. Croix de Guerre, 1917. *Recreation:* rural preservation. *Address:* Cliffordine House, Rendcomb, Cirencester, Glos.

COLLINS, Sir Arthur (James Robert), KCVO 1980; *b* 10 July 1911; *s* of Col William Fellowes Collins, DSO, and Lady Evelyn Collins (*née* Innes Ker), OBE; *m* 1965, Elizabeth, *d* of Rear-Adm. Sir Arthur Bromley, Bt, and *widow* of 6th Baron Sudeley (*died* on war service, 1941). *Educ:* Eton; Christ Church Oxford (MA). Admitted a Solicitor, 1935; Partner, Withers, 1937, Sen. Partner, 1962-81, now Consultant. Served with Royal Horse Guards, 1938-46; Adjt, 2nd Household Cavalry Regt, 1940-44 (despatches), Major 1943. *Address:* Kirkman Bank, Knaresborough, N Yorks HG5 9BT. *T:*

Harrogate 863136; 38 Clarence Terrace, NW1. *T:* 01-723 4198. *Clubs:* Turf, White's.

COLLINS, Arthur John, OBE 1973; HM Diplomatic Service; High Commissioner in Papua New Guinea, since 1982; *b* 17 May 1931; *s* of Reginald and Margery Collins; *m* 1952, Enid Maureen, *d* of Charles and Sarah Stableford; one *s* one *d. Educ:* Purley Grammar Sch. Served RAF, 1949-51. Min. of Health, 1951-68 (Private Sec. to Perm. Sec., 1960-61, and to Parly Sec., 1962-63); transf. to HM Diplomatic Service, 1968; FCO, 1968-69; First Secretary and Head of Chancery: Dacca, 1970-71; Brasilia, 1972-74; Asst Head of Latin America and Caribbean Depts, FCO, 1974-77; Counsellor, UK Del. to OECD, Paris, 1978-81. *Recreation:* dabbling in archaeology. *Address:* c/o Foreign and Commonwealth Office, SW1. *Club:* Royal Commonwealth Society.

COLLINS, Basil Eugene Sinclair; Deputy Chairman and Group Chief Executive, Cadbury Schweppes Ltd, since 1980; *b* 21 Dec. 1923; *s* of Albert Collins and Pauline Alicia (*née* Wright); *m* 1942, Doris Slott; two *d. Educ:* Great Yarmouth Grammar School. Accountant, L. Rose & Co. Ltd, 1945, Sales Man. 1955; Export Dir, Schweppes (Overseas) Ltd, 1958; Group Admin Dir, Schweppes Ltd, 1964, Chm. of Overseas Gp 1968; Chm. of Overseas Gp, Cadbury Schweppes Ltd, 1969, Dep. Man. Dir 1972, Man. Dir 1974; Dir, Thomas Cook Gp, 1980-. Royal College of Nursing: Chm., Finance and General Purposes Cttee, 1970; Hon. Treasurer, 1970; Vice-Pres., 1972. Fellow Inst. of Dirs, 1974; FZS 1975; CBIM (FBIM 1976); FIGD; Fellow, Amer. Chamber of Commerce. *Recreations:* music, languages, travel, English countryside. *Address:* Wyddial Parva, Buntingford, Herts SG9 0EL. *Club:* Carlton.

COLLINS, Bernard John, CBE 1960; town planner, retired; Controller (formerly Director) of Planning and Transportation, Greater London Council, 1969-74; *b* 3 July 1909; *s* of late John Philip and Amelia Bounevialle Collins; *m* 1937, Grete Elisabeth, *e d* of H. A. Piehler; one *s* three *d. Educ:* Ampleforth. Served Royal Artillery, 1939-45, North Africa (despatches) and Italy. Ryde Memorial Prizeman, RICS, 1937. President: Royal Town Planning Inst., 1957-58; International Fedn of Surveyors, 1967-69; Mem. Bureau, Internat. Fedn for Housing and Planning, 1962-66; Vice-Pres., 1968-73, Sen. Vice-Pres., 1973-74, Pres., 1974-75, RICS; Mem. Board of Governors, Coll. of Estate Management, 1959-69; Vice-Chm. of Executive, Town and Country Planning Assoc., 1951-62; Chm., Assoc. of County Planning Officers, 1954-58; County Planning Officer, Middx, 1947-62; Sec. and Chief Exec. Commn for the New Towns, 1962-64; Dir of Planning, GLC, 1964-69; responsible for preparation of Greater London Develt Plan, 1969. Chairman, Technical Panel: Conf. on London and SE Regional Planning, 1964-74; Greater London and SE Regional Sports Council, 1966-74; advised on reorganisation of planning system, City of Jerusalem, 1971. Described by William Hickey of Daily Express as probably the world's top town planner. Pres. Honoraire, Fédération Internationale des Géomètres, 1970-; Hon. Mem., Deutscher Verein für Vermessungswesen (German Soc. of Surveyors), 1965-; Membre d'honneur, Union Belge des Géomètres-experts Immobiliers, 1976-. *Publications:* Development Plans Explained (HMSO), 1951; Middlesex Survey and Development Plan, 1952; numerous addresses, articles and papers on town planning. *Address:* Foxella, Matfield, Kent TN12 7ET. *Club:* Athenæum.

COLLINS, Sir Charles Henry, Kt 1947; CMG 1941; *b* 10 Feb. 1887; *s* of late C. H. Collins, Torquay; *m* 1913, Florence E. Campkin (*d* 1968); one *d* (one *s* and one *d* decd). *Educ:* King's Coll., Univ. of London. BA 1909. Entered Ceylon Civil Service, 1910; Dep. Chief Sec., 1940; Acting Financial Sec. in 1935, 1936, 1937, 1940, and 1943; Acting Chief Sec. in 1944, 1945 and 1947; adviser to govt on changes in administration and procedure in connection with introduction of new constitution, 1946; retired, 1948. *Publications:* Public Administration in Ceylon, 1951; Public Administration in Hong Kong, 1952. *Recreations:* historical and archæological studies. *Address:* Devoncroft, Clandon Road, West Clandon, Guildford, Surrey GU4 7TL. *T:* Guildford 222542. *Club:* Royal Over-Seas League.

COLLINS, Sir David (Charles), Kt 1975; CBE 1969; Consultant, Westland Aircraft Ltd; Director, Normalair-Garrett (Holdings) Ltd; *b* 23 Jan. 1908; *s* of Richard and Margaret Collins; *m* 1936, Dorothy Bootyman. Joined Westland Aircraft Ltd as Works Dir, 1951; Dep. Man. Dir, 1959; Man. Dir, 1965; Chief Exec. and Chm. subsidiary cos, 1968; Chm., 1970-77. FEng, FIMechE, FIProdE, FRAeS. Hon. DSc. *Recreations:* golf, fishing. *Address:* Little Gables, Redwood Road, Sidmouth, Devon EX10 9AB. *T:* Sidmouth 6756. *Club:* Honiton Golf.

COLLINS, Sir Geoffrey Abdy, Kt 1952; *b* 5 June 1888; *y s* of Philip George and Susan Kate Collins; *m* 1936, Joan Mary, 2nd *d* of Albert Edward and Margaret Alice Ratcliffe; one *s* four *d. Educ:* Rugby; Christ's Coll., Cambridge (BA, LLB). Admitted solicitor, 1913. Served European War, 1914-18, in The Rifle Brigade (Capt.). Member: Royal UK Beneficent Assoc. Cttee, 1926-54 (Chm., 1950-54); Council of The Law Society, 1931-56, Pres., 1951-52. Past Master, Tylers and Bricklayers Co. *Address:* Mullion, 20 Ballard Estate, Swanage, Dorset. *T:* Swanage 2030.

COLLINS, Gerard; *see* Collins, John G.

COLLINS, Henry Edward, CBE 1948; Consulting Mining Engineer; *b* 4 Oct. 1903; *s* of James Collins; *m* 1934, Cecilia Harris (*d* 1975); no *c. Educ:*

Rotherham Grammar Sch.; Univ. of Sheffield (MEng). Sen. Lectr in Mining, Univ. of Sheffield, 1935-38; Manager, Rossington Main Colliery, Doncaster, 1939-42; Agent, Markham Colliery, Doncaster, 1942-44; Chief Mining Agent, Doncaster Amalgamated Collieries Ltd, 1944-45; Dir Coal Production, CCG, 1945-47; British Chm., UK/US Coal Control Gp, Germany (later Combined Coal Control Gp), 1947-50; Production Dir, Durham Div., NCB, 1950-56; Dir-Gen. of Reconstruction, NCB, 1956-57; Board Mem. for Production, NCB, 1957-67; Consultant to NCB, 1967-69. Mem., Govtl Cttee on Coal Derivatives, 1959-60; Chairman: NCB Opencast Executive, 1961-67; NCB Brickworks Executive, 1962-67; Whittlesea Central Brick Co. Ltd, 1966-67; Field Research Steering Cttee, Min. of Power, 1964-67; Past Director: Omnia Concrete Sales Ltd; Bradley's (Concrete) Ltd; Powell Duffryn Technical Services Ltd; Inter-Continental Fuels Ltd. Member: Minister of Power's Adv. Council on Research and Develt, 1963-67; Min. of Power Nat. Jt Pneumoconiosis Cttee, 1964-67; Safety in Mines (Adv.) Bd; Mining Qualifications Bd, 1962-69. Pres., Inst. of Mining Engineers, 1962. *Publications:* numerous papers on mining engineering subjects. *Address:* Rising Sun, 22a West Side, Wimbledon Common, SW19 4UF. *T:* 01-946 3949. *Club:* Athenæum.

COLLINS, James Gerard; TD (FF) Limerick West, since 1967; Minister for Foreign Affairs, Ireland, since 1982; *b* Abbeyfeale, Co. Limerick, 16 Oct. 1938; *s* of late James J. Collins, TD and Margaret Collins; *m* 1969, Hilary Tattan. *Educ:* University Coll., Dublin (BA). Teacher. Asst Gen. Sec., Fianna Fáil, 1965-67. Parly Sec. to Ministers for Industry and Commerce and for the Gaeltacht, 1969-70; Minister for Posts and Telegraphs, 1970-73; opposition front-bench spokesman on agriculture, 1973-75; spokesman on justice, 1975-77; Minister for Justice, 1977-81. Mem., Consultative Assembly, Council of Europe, 1973-77. Mem., Limerick CC, 1974-77. *Address:* Department of Foreign Affairs, 80 St Stephen's Green, Dublin 2; The Hill, Abbeyfeale, Co. Limerick.

COLLINS, Vice-Adm. Sir John (Augustine), KBE 1951; CB 1940; RAN retired; *b* Deloraine, Tasmania, 7 Jan. 1899; *s* of Michael John Collins, MD; *m* 1930, Phyllis Laishley, *d* of A. J. McLachlan; one *d. Educ:* Royal Australian Naval Coll. Served European War with Grand Fleet and Harwich Force, 1917-18; thereafter in various HM and HMA Ships abroad and in Australian waters; Squadron Gunnery Officer, HMA Squadron; Liaison Officer for visit of Duke and Duchess of York to Australia; in command HMAS Anzac; staff course; Asst Chief of Naval Staff, Australia; Capt. HMAS Sydney (CB), 1939-41; Asst Chief of Staff to C-in-C, China, 1941 (despatches); Cdre comdg China Force, 1942 (Comdr of Order of Orange Nassau); Capt. HMAS Shropshire, 1943-44; Cdre comdg HM Australian Sqdn (wounded), 1944-46; idc 1947; Chief of Naval Staff and First Naval Mem., Australian Commonwealth Naval Bd, Melbourne, 1948-55; Australian High Comr to New Zealand, 1956-62. Officer of Legion of Merit (US); Royal Humane Society's Certificate for Saving Life at Sea. *Publication:* As Luck Would Have It, 1965. *Recreation:* golf. *Address:* 13 Dumaresq Road, Rose Bay, Sydney, NSW 2029, Australia. *Club:* Royal Sydney Golf.

COLLINS, John Ernest Harley, MBE 1944; DSC 1945 and Bar 1945; DL; Chairman: Morgan Grenfell Holdings Ltd, 1974-79; Guardian Royal Exchange Assurance since 1974; *b* 24 April 1923; *o s* of late G. W. Collins, Taynton, Glos; *m* 1946, Gillian (*d* 1981), *e d* of 2nd Baron Bicester; one *s* one *d. Educ:* King Edward's Sch., Birmingham; Birmingham Univ. Royal Navy, 1941-46. Morgan Grenfell & Co. Ltd, 1946, Dir 1957. Director: Royal Exchange Assce, 1957; Rank Hovis McDougall Ltd; Charter Consolidated Ltd; Hudson's Bay Co., 1957-74. Chm. United Services Trustee, 1968-76. DL Oxon, 1975; High Sheriff, Oxon, 1975. *Recreations:* shooting, stalking, fishing. *Address:* Tusmore Park, Bicester, Oxon. *T:* Fritwell 209. *Clubs:* Brooks's, White's, Pratt's.

COLLINS, (John) Martin, QC 1972; a Recorder of the Crown Court, since 1972; *b* 24 Jan. 1929; *s* of John Lissant Collins and Marjorie Mary Collins; *m* 1957, Daphne Mary, *d* of George Martyn Swindells, Prestbury; two *s* one *d. Educ:* Uppingham Sch.; Manchester Univ. (LLB). Called to Bar, Gray's Inn, 1952, Bencher, 1981. Dep. Chm., Cumberland QS, 1969-72. Mem., Senate of Inns of Court and Bar, 1981-. *Address:* 2 Pump Court, Temple, EC4; Pott Hall, Pott Shrigley, Macclesfield, Cheshire. *Clubs:* Athenæum, Carlton.

COLLINS, John Morris; a Recorder of the Crown Court, since 1980; *b* 25 June 1931; *s* of late Emmanuel Cohen, MBE, and of Ruby Cohen; *m* 1968, Sheila Brummer; one *d. Educ:* Leeds Grammar Sch.; The Queen's Coll., Oxford (MA LitHum). Called to Bar, Middle Temple, 1956, Member of North Eastern Circuit; a Deputy Circuit Judge, 1970. *Publications:* Summary Justice, 1963; various articles in legal periodicals, etc. *Recreation:* walking. *Address:* (home) 14 Sandhill Oval, Leeds LS17 8EA. *T:* Leeds 686008; (professional) Pearl Chambers, East Parade, Leeds LS1 5BZ. *T:* Leeds 451986.

COLLINS, Maj.-Gen. Joseph Clinton, CB 1953; CBE 1951 (OBE 1946); *b* 8 Jan. 1895; British; *m* 1925, Eileen Patricia Williams; two *d. Educ:* London Hosp. Served European War, 1914-18, France and Belgium, 1914; Surgeon Probationer, RNVR, 1915-16; Lieut, RAMC, 1917; Egyptian Army, 1923-33; DDMS, BAOR, 1946-49; DMS Far ELF, 1949-51; DMS Northern Command, 1951-53; KHS 1951-54; Dir Medical Services, BAOR, 1953-Dec.

1954, retired. CStJ 1948. 3rd Class Order of Nile. *Address:* c/o Williams & Glyn's Bank Ltd, Whitehall, SW1.

COLLINS, Gen. (retd) J(oseph) Lawton, DSM 1942 (Oak Leaf Cluster, 1943, 1944, 1953); Silver Star, 1943 (Army Oak Leaf Cluster, and Navy Gold Star, 1944); Legion of Merit, 1943 (Oak Leaf Cluster, 1945); Bronze Star Medal, 1944; Director, Chas Pfizer & Co. Inc., 1957-72; Vice-Chairman, Pfizer International Subsidiaries 1957-72; *b* New Orleans, La, 1 May 1896; *s* of Jeremiah Bernard Collins and Catherine Lawton; *m* 1921, Gladys Easterbrook; one *s* two *d. Educ:* Louisiana State Univ.; US Military Academy. 2nd Lieut, Infantry, 1917; 22nd Infantry, Fort Hamilton, NY, until Jan. 1918; graduated Inf. Sch. of Arms, Fort Sill, Oklahoma, 1918; went overseas and took command of bn of 18th Inf., Coblenz, 1919; Asst Chief of Staff, Plans and Training Div., American Forces in Germany, until 1921; Instr, US Mil. Acad., 1921-25; graduated: Inf. Sch., Fort Benning, Ga, 1926; Advanced Course, Field Artillery Sch., Fort Sill, Oklahoma, 1927; Instr, Inf. Sch., 1927-31; student, Comd and Gen. Staff Sch., Fort Leavenworth, Kansas, 1931-33; with 23rd Bde (Philippine Scouts), Fort William McKinley, and Asst Chief of Staff, Ops and Mil. Intell., Philippine Div., until 1936; Student: Army Industrial Coll., 1936-37; Army War Coll., 1937-38; Instr there, 1938-40. Served War of 1939-45; Office of Sec., War Dept Gen. Staff, 1940-41; Chief of Staff, VII Army Corps, 1941; Chief of Staff, Hawaiian Dept, 1941; Comdg Gen., 25th Inf. Div. in Guadalcanal ops, New Georgia Campaign, 1942-43; comd VII Army Corps, European Theater, for Invasion of France, 1944; and subseq. campaigns to end of hostilities, 1945; Dep. Comdg Gen. and Chief of Staff, HQ, Army Ground Forces, 1945; Dir of Information, War Dept, 1945; Dep. Chief of Staff, US Army, 1947, and Vice Chief of Staff (upon creation of that post), 1948; Chief of Staff, US Army, 1949-53; US Rep., Standing Group, NATO and US Mem. Mil. Cttee, 1953-56; US Special Rep. in Viet Nam with personal rank Ambassador, Nov. 1954-May 1955. Holds hon. degrees. Army of Occupation Medal, Germany, European War, 1914-18, and War of 1939-45; American Defense Service Medal; Asiatic-Pacific Medal; European-African-Middle Eastern Campaign Ribbon. (In addition to above US decorations) Hon. CB (British) 1945; Order of Suvorov, 2nd Class, twice (Russian); Croix de Guerre with Palm, Legion of Honor, Degree of Grand Officer (French); Order of Leopold II, Grand Officer Croix de Guerre with Palm (Belgian). *Address:* 4000 Massachusetts Avenue, NW, Washington, DC 20016, USA. *T:* 362-0971. *Club:* Chevy Chase (Md).

COLLINS, Kenneth Darlingston; Member (Lab) East Strathclyde, European Parliament, since 1979; *b* 12 Aug. 1939; *s* of Nicholas Collins and Ellen Williamson; *m* 1966, Georgina Frances Pollard; one *s* one *d. Educ:* St John's Grammar Sch.; Hamilton Acad.; Glasgow Univ. (BSc Hons); Strathclyde Univ. (MSc). Left school, 1956; steelworks apprentice, 1956-59; univ., 1960-65; planning officer, 1965-66; WEA Tutor-Organiser, 1966-67; Lecturer: Glasgow Coll. of Bldg, 1967-69; Paisley Coll. of Technol., 1969-79. Dep. Leader, Labour Gp, Eur. Parlt, 1979-. Chairman: Environment Cttee, Eur. Parlt, 1979-; NE Glasgow Children's Panel, 1974-76. Member: East Kilbride Town and Dist Council, 1973-79; Lanark CC, 1973-75; East Kilbride Develt Corp., 1976-79. *Publications:* occasional papers on local govt and town planning. *Recreations:* Labour Party, music, boxer dogs, cycling, reading. *Address:* 11 Stuarton Park, East Kilbride, Lanarkshire. *T:* East Kilbride 37282.

COLLINS, Rear-Adm. Kenneth St Barbe, CB 1959; OBE 1945; DSC 1942; *b* 9 June 1904; *s* of late Charles Bury Collins, Col RE and late Ethel St Barbe; *m* 1932, Helen Mary Keen; one *s* one *d. Educ:* Lydgate House Sch., Hunstanton, Norfolk; RN Colls Osborne and Dartmouth. Midshipman, HMS Warspite, 1922, Vimiera, 1923; Sub-Lt, HMS Fitzroy, 1925; Lt and Lt-Comdr surveying ships, 1927-37; Seaplane Carrier, HMS Albatross, 1939; (as Comdr) Staff of Allied Naval Expeditionary Force, North Africa, 1942; staff of Allied Naval Expeditionary Force, Europe, 1943; surveying, 1947-54; Hydrographer of the Navy, 1955-60; Rear-Adm., 1957; retd 1960. Consultant to the Survey and Mapping Branch of Dept of Mines and Technical Surveys, Ottawa, 1960-63. *Address:* The Old Parsonage, Bentley, near Farnham, Surrey. *T:* Bentley 3227.

COLLINS, Lesley Elizabeth; *see* Appleby, L. E.

COLLINS, Rev. Canon Lewis John; President, International Defence and Aid Fund, since 1964; Canon of St Paul's Cathedral, 1948-81, now Emeritus; *b* 23 March 1905; *s* of Arthur Collins and Hannah Priscilla; *m* 1939, Diana Clavering Elliot; four *s. Educ:* Cranbrook Sch.; Sidney Sussex Coll. and Westcott House, Cambridge. Curate of Whitstable, 1928-29; Chaplain, Sidney Sussex Coll., Cambridge, 1929-31; Minor Canon of St Paul's Cathedral, 1931-34; a Dep. Priest-in-Ordinary to HM the King, 1931-34, Priest-in-Ordinary, 1934-35; Vice-Principal, Westcott House, Cambridge, 1934-37; Chaplain RAFVR, 1940-45; Dean of Oriel Coll., Oxford, 1938-48; Fellow Lecturer and Chaplain, 1937-48. St Paul's Cathedral: Chancellor, 1948-53; Precentor, 1953-70; Treasurer, 1970-81. Chairman: Campaign for Nuclear Disarmament, 1958-64; Martin Luther King Foundn, 1969-73; President, Christian Action, 1959- (Chairman, 1946-73). Order of Grand Companion of Freedom, Third Div., Zambia, 1970; Commander, Order of the Northern Star, Sweden, 1976. Gold Medal of UN Special Cttee against Apartheid, for significant contribution to internat. campaign against apartheid, 1978. *Publications:* The New Testament Problem, 1937; A Theology of Christian Action, 1949; Faith Under Fire, 1966; contributor, Three Views of

Christianity, 1962. *Address:* Mill House, Chappel Road, Mount Bures, Bures, Suffolk.

COLLINS, Margaret Elizabeth, RRC; QHNS; Matron-in-Chief, Queen Alexandra's Royal Naval Nursing Service, since 1980; *b* 13 Feb. 1927; *d* of James Henry Collins and Amy Collins. *Educ:* St Anne's Convent Grammar Sch., Southampton. RRC 1978 (ARRC 1965); QHNS 1980. Royal Victoria Hosp., Bournemouth, SRN 1949; West Middlesex Hosp., CMB Part 1; entered QARNNS as Nursing Sister, 1953; accepted for permanent service, 1958; Matron, 1972; Principal Matron, 1976. SSStJ 1978. *Recreations:* gardening, theatre-going. *Address:* Lancastria, First Marine Avenue, Barton-on-Sea, Hants BH25 6JA. *T:* New Milton 374.

COLLINS, Martin; *see* Collins, J. M.

COLLINS, Michael; Vice President, Vought Corporation, since 1980; former NASA Astronaut; Command Module Pilot, Apollo 11 rocket flight to the Moon, July 1969; *b* Rome, Italy, 31 Oct. 1930; *s* of Maj.-Gen. and Mrs James L. Collins, Washington, DC, USA; *m* 1957, Patricia M. Finnegan, Boston, Mass; one *s* two *d. Educ:* St Albans Sch., Washington, DC (grad.). US Mil. Academy, West Point, NY (BSc); advanced through grades to Colonel; Harvard Business Sch. (AMP), 1974. Served as an experimental flight test officer, Air Force Flight Test Center, Edwards Air Force Base, Calif; he was one of the third group of astronauts named by NASA in Oct. 1963; served as backup pilot for Gemini 7 mission; as pilot with John Young on the 3-day 44-revolution Gemini 10 mission, launched 18 July 1966, he shared record-setting flight (successful rendezvous and docking with a separately launched Agena target vehicle; completed two periods of extravehicular activity); Command Module Pilot for Apollo flight, first lunar landing, in orbit 20 July 1969, when Neil Armstrong and Edwin Aldrin landed on the Moon. Asst Sec. of State for Public Affairs, US, 1970-71; Dir, Nat. Air and Space Museum, Smithsonian Institution, 1971-78; Under Sec., Smithsonian Inst., 1978-80. Maj. Gen. Air Force Reserve. Dir, AF Historical Foundn; Member: Bd of Trustees, Rand Corp.; Bd of Dirs, Children's Hosp. Nat. Med. Center; Washington Historical Monument Soc.; Bd of Trustees, Theodore Von Karman Meml Foundn Inc.; General Thomas D. White USAF Space Trophy Cttee; Soc. of Experimental Test Pilots; Internat. Acad. of Astronautics of Internat. Astronautical Fedn; Washington Inst. of Foreign Affairs. FAIAA; Fellow, Amer. Astronautical Soc. Member, Order of Daedalians. Hon. degrees from: Stonehill Coll.; St Michael's Coll.; Northeastern Univ.; Southeastern Univ. Presidential Medal of Freedom, NASA; FAI Gold Space Medal; DSM (NASA); DSM (AF); Exceptional Service Medal (NASA); Astronaut Wings; DFC. *Publications:* Carrying the Fire (autobiog.), 1974; Flying to the Moon and Other Strange Places (for children), 1976. *Recreations:* fishing, handball. *Address:* Vought Corporation, 1745 Jefferson Davis Highway, Suite 612, Arlington, Va 22202. *Clubs:* Cosmos, Alfalfa, Alibi (all Washington, DC).

COLLINS, Miss Nina; *see* Lowry, Mrs N. M.

COLLINS, Pauline; actress (stage and television); *b* Exmouth, Devon, 3 Sept. 1940; *d* of William Henry Collins and Mary Honora Callanan; *m* John Alderton, *qv* ; two *s* one *d. Educ:* Convent of the Sacred Heart, Hammersmith, London; Central Sch. of Speech and Drama. *Stage:* 1st appearance in A Gazelle in Park Lane, Theatre Royal, Windsor, 1962; 1st London appearance in Passion Flower Hotel, Prince of Wales, 1965; The Erpingham Camp, Royal Court, 1967; The Happy Apple, Hampstead, 1967, and Apollo, 1970; Importance of Being Earnest, Haymarket, 1968; The Night I chased the Women with an Eel, 1969; Come As You Are (3 parts), New, 1970; Judies, Comedy, 1974; Engaged, National Theatre, Old Vic, 1975; Confusions, Apollo, 1976; Rattle of a Simple Man, Savoy, 1980; *television,* 1962-: series: Upstairs Downstairs; No Honestly; P. G. Wodehouse; Thomas and Sarah; play: Long Distance Information, 1979. *Address:* c/o Nems Management Ltd, 29-31 King's Road, SW3.

COLLINS, Peter G., RSA 1974 (ARSA 1966); painter in oil; lecturer, Duncan of Jordanstone College of Art, Dundee; *b* Inverness, 21 June 1935; *s* of E. G. Collins, FRCSE; *m* 1959, Myra Mackintosh (marr. diss. 1978); one *s* one *d. Educ:* Fettes Coll., Edinburgh; Edinburgh Coll. of Art. Studied in Italy, on Andrew Grant Major Travelling Scholarship, 1957-58. Work in permanent collections: Aberdeen Civic; Glasgow Civic; Scottish Arts Council. *Recreations:* music and procrastination. *Address:* Royal Scottish Academy, The Mound, Edinburgh; Jasmine Cottage, Newbigging Road, Tealing, Tayside.

COLLINS, Prof. Philip Arthur William; Professor of English, University of Leicester, since 1964; *b* 28 May 1923; *er s* of Arthur Henry and Winifred Nellie Collins; *m* 1st, 1942, Mildred Lowe (marr. diss. 1964); 2nd, 1965, Joyce Dickins; two *s* one *d. Educ:* Brentwood Sch.; Emmanuel Coll., Cambridge (Sen. Schol.). MA 1948. Served War (RAOC and Royal Norfolk Regt), 1942-45. Leicester: Staff Tutor in Adult Educn, 1947; Warden, Vaughan Coll., 1954; Sen. Lectr in English, 1962-64; Prof., 1964; Head, English Dept, 1971-76, 1981-; Public Orator, 1975-78, 1980-. Visiting Prof.: Univ. of California, Berkeley, 1967; Columbia, 1969; Victoria Univ., NZ, 1974. Sec., Leicester Theatre Trust Ltd, 1963-; Member: Drama Panel, Arts Council of Gt Britain, 1970-75; National Theatre Bd, 1976-. Many overseas lecture-tours; performances, talks and scripts for radio and television. *Publications:* James Boswell, 1956; (ed) English Christmas, 1956; Dickens and Crime, 1962;

Dickens and Education, 1963; The Canker and the Rose (Shakespeare Quater-centenary celebration) perf. Mermaid Theatre, London, 1964; The Impress of the Moving Age, 1965; Thomas Cooper the Chartist, 1969; A Dickens Bibliography, 1970; Dickens's Bleak House, 1971; (ed) Dickens, the Critical Heritage, 1971; (ed) A Christmas Carol: the public reading version, 1971; Reading Aloud: a Victorian Métier, 1972; (ed) Dickens's Public Readings, 1975; Dickens's David Copperfield, 1977; (ed) Dickens: Interviews and Recollections, 1981; (ed) Thackeray: Interviews and Recollections, 1982. contrib. to: Encyclopaedia Britannica, Dickensian, Essays and Studies, Notes and Queries, Listener, Review of English Studies, TLS. *Recreations:* theatre, theatricals, music. *Address:* 26 Knighton Drive, Leicester LE2 3HB. *T:* Leicester 706026.

COLLINS, Stuart Verdun, CB 1970; retired; Chief Inspector of Audit, Department of the Environment (formerly Ministry of Housing and Local Government), 1968-76; *b* 24 Feb. 1916; *m* 1st, 1942, Helen Simpson (*d* 1968); two *d* ; 2nd, 1970, Joan Mary Walmsley (widow); one *step s* two *step d. Educ:* Plymouth Coll. Entered Civil Service as Audit Assistant in the District Audit Service of the Ministry of Health, 1934; appointed District Auditor for the London Audit District, 1958. IPFA, FBCS. *Recreations:* golf, do-it-yourself, sailing. *Address:* Kemendine, Court Wood, Newton Ferrers, Devon.

COLLINS, Brig. Thomas Frederick James, CBE 1945 (OBE 1944); JP; DL; *b* 9 April 1905; *s* of Capt. J. A. Collins and Emily (*née* Truscott); *m* 1942, Marjorie Morwenna, *d* of Lt-Col T. Donnelly, DSO; one *d. Educ:* Haileybury; RMC, Sandhurst. Gazetted to Green Howards, 1924; Staff College, 1938. Served War of 1939-45 (despatches twice, OBE, CBE): France, 1940, NW Europe, 1944-45. Retired, with rank of Brig., 1948. Essex County Council: CC, 1960; Vice-Chm., 1967; Chm., 1968-71. JP 1968, DL 1969, Essex. Comdr, Order of Leopold II (Belgium), 1945. *Recreation:* shooting. *Address:* Ashdon Hall, Saffron Walden, Essex. *T:* Ashdon 232. *Club:* Army and Navy.

COLLINS, William Janson; Chairman, William Collins Sons & Co. (Holdings) Ltd, 1976-81; *b* 10 June 1929; *s* of late Sir William Alexander Roy Collins, CBE, and Lady Collins (Priscilla Marian, *d* of late S. J. Lloyd); *m* 1951, Lady Sara Elena Hely-Hutchinson, *d* of 7th Earl of Donoughmore; one *s* three *d. Educ:* Magdalen Coll., Oxford (BA). Joined William Collins Sons & Co. Ltd, 1952; Dir, then Man. Dir, 1967; Vice-Chm., 1971; Chm., 1976. *Recreations:* Royal tennis, shooting, fishing, tennis, golf. *Address:* House of Craigie, by Kilmarnock, Ayrshire KA1 5NA. *T:* Craigie 246. *Clubs:* Boodle's; All England Lawn Tennis and Croquet.

COLLINSON, Prof. Patrick, PhD; FBA 1982; FRHistS, FAHA; Professor of History, University of Kent at Canterbury, since 1976; *b* 10 Aug. 1929; *s* of William Cecil Collinson and Belle Hay (*née* Patrick); *m* 1960, Elizabeth Albinia Susan Selwyn; two *s* two *d. Educ:* King's Sch., Ely; Pembroke Coll., Cambridge (Exhibnr 1949, Foundn Scholar 1952). BA 1952, 1st Cl. Hons Hist. Tripos Pt II; Hadley Prize for Hist., 1952). PhD London, 1957; FRHistS 1967 (Mem. Council, 1977); FAHA 1974. University of London: Postgrad. Student, Royal Holloway Coll., 1952-54; Res. Fellow, Inst. of Hist. Res., 1954-55; Res. Asst, UCL, 1955-56; Lectr in Hist., Univ. of Khartoum, 1956-61; Asst Lectr in Eccles. Hist., King's Coll., Univ. of London, 1961-62; Lectr, 1962-69 (Fellow 1976); Prof. of Hist., Univ. of Sydney, 1969-75. Vis. Fellow, All Souls Coll., Oxford, 1981. Ford's Lectr in Eng. Hist., Univ. of Oxford, 1978-79; Birkbeck Lectr, Univ. of Cambridge, 1981. Chm., Adv. Editorial Bd, Jl of Ecclesiastical History, 1982. *Publications:* The Elizabethan Puritan Movement, 1967 (USA 1967); Archbishop Grindal 1519-1583: the struggle for a Reformed Church, 1979 (USA 1979); The Religion of Protestants: the Church in English Society 1559-1625 (Ford Lectures, 1979), 1982; articles and revs in Bull. Inst. Hist. Res., Eng. Hist. Rev., Hist., Jl Eccles. Hist., Studies in Church Hist., TLS. *Recreations:* mountains, fishing, music, gardening. *Address:* 73 Beaconsfield Road, Canterbury, Kent. *T:* Canterbury 55121.

COLLINSON, Richard Jeffreys Hampton; His Honour Judge Collinson; a Circuit Judge, since 1975; *b* 7 April 1924; *s* of Kenneth Hampton Collinson and Edna Mary Collinson; *m* 1955, Gwendolen Hester Ward; two *s* two *d. Educ:* Heath Grammar Sch., Halifax; Wadham Coll., Oxford (BCL, MA). Sub-Lieut, RNVR, 1944-46. Called to Bar, Middle Temple, 1950; Northern Circuit. Councillor, then Alderman, Wallasey County Borough Council, 1957-74, Leader of Council, 1965-72. *Address:* Merehaven, 2 Mere Lane, Wallasey, Merseyside L45 3HY. *T:* 051-639 5818.

COLLIS, John Stewart; author; *b* 16 Feb. 1900; *s* of W. S. Collis and Edith (*née* Barton), Irish; *m* 1929, Eirene Joy; two *d* ; *m* 1974, Lady Beddington-Behrens. *Educ:* Rugby Sch.; Balliol Coll., Oxford (BA). FRSL. *Publications:* include: Shaw, 1925; Forward to Nature, 1927; Farewell to Argument, 1935; The Sounding Cataract, 1936; An Irishman's England, 1937; While Following the Plough, 1946; Down to Earth, 1947 (Heinemann Foundation Award); The Triumph of the Tree, 1950; The Moving Waters, 1955; Paths of Light, 1959; An Artist of Life, 1959; Marriage and Genius, 1963; The Life of Tolstoy, 1969; Bound upon a Course (autobiog.), 1971; The Carlyles, 1972; The Vision of Glory, 1972; The Worm Forgives the Plough, 1973; Christopher Columbus, 1976; Living with a Stranger: a discourse on the human body, 1978; (contrib) Holroyd: The Genius of Bernard Shaw, 1979. *Recreation:* tennis. *Address:* Park House, Abinger Common, Dorking, Surrey. *T:* Dorking 730412.

COLLISON, family name of **Baron Collison.**

COLLISON, Baron (Life Peer) *cr* 1964, of Cheshunt; **Harold Francis Collison,** CBE 1961; Chairman, Supplementary Benefits Commission, 1969-75; *b* 10 May 1909; *m* 1946, Ivy Kate Hanks. *Educ:* The Hay Currie LCC Sch.; Crypt Sch., Gloucester. Firstly, worked in a commercial office in London; farm worker in Glos, 1934-53. National Union of Agricultural Workers (later Nat. Union of Agricultural and Allied Workers): District Organiser in Gloucester and Worcs, 1944; Nat. Officer, 1946; General Secretary, 1953-69. Mem., TUC Gen. Coun., 1953-69, Chm., 1964-65; Chm., Social Insce and Industrial Welfare Cttee of TUC, 1957-69. President: Internat. Fedn of Plantation, Agricultural and Allied Workers, 1960-76; Assoc. of Agriculture, 1976-; Member: Coun. on Tribunals, 1959-69; Nat. Insce Adv. Cttee, 1959-69; Governing Body of ILO, 1960-69; Pilkington Cttee on Broadcasting, 1960-62; Central Transport Consultative Cttee, 1962-70; Agric. Adv. Council, 1962-80; Adv. Cttee on Agricultural Educn, 1963; Royal Commn on Trades Unions and Employers' Assocs, 1965-68; Home-Grown Cereals Authority, 1965-78; Industrial Health Adv. Cttee; Economic Develt for Agriculture; Industrial Consultative Cttee, Approach to Europe; Overseas Labour Consultative Cttee; Agric. Productivity Cttee, British Productivity Council; Chairman: Land Settlement Assoc., 1977-79 (Vice-Chm., 1964-77); Agric. Apprenticeship Council, 1968-74; Mem., N Thames Gas Board (part-time), 1961-72. *Recreations:* gardening, chess. *Address:* Honeywood, 163 Old Nazeing Road, Broxbourne, Herts. *T:* Hoddesdon 63597.

COLLISON, Lewis Herbert, TD; MA; Headmaster of Liverpool College, 1952-70; *b* 30 July 1908; *s* of late Mr and Mrs W. H. Collison; *m* 1934, Edna Mollie Ivens; two *d. Educ:* Mill Hill Sch.; St John's Coll., Cambridge. Asst Master of Sedbergh Sch., 1931-40; Major in King's Own Royal Regt, 1940-45; Housemaster of Sedbergh Sch., 1946-52. Mem. Council, University of Liverpool, 1963-69. JP Liverpool, 1958-70. *Recreations:* pottery, sailing. *Address:* 22 Riverview, Melton, near Woodbridge, Suffolk IP12 1QU. *Club:* Hawks (Cambridge).

COLMAN, Anthony David, QC 1977; barrister-at-law; *b* 27 May 1938; *s* of Solomon Colman and Helen Colman; *m* 1964, Angela Glynn; two *d. Educ:* Harrogate Grammar Sch.; Trinity Hall, Cambridge (MA). Called to the Bar, Gray's Inn, 1962. *Publication:* 2nd edn, Mathew's Practice of the Commercial Court (1902), 1967. *Recreations:* cricket, music, gardening, the 17th Century, Sifnos. *Address:* 4 Essex Court, Temple, EC4Y 9AJ. *T:* 01-353 6771.

COLMAN, Anthony John; Director, Burton Group PLC, Chief Executive, Development and Concessions for Burton, Top Man, Top Shop, Dorothy Perkins, Peter Robinson and Evans; *b* 24 July 1943; *s* of late William Benjamin Colman and Beatrice (*née* Hudson); *m* Rita Mary Ann Hoss; four *s* two *d. Educ:* Paston Grammar Sch.; Magdalene Coll., Cambridge (MA); Univ. of E Africa, 1964-69; LSE, 1966. United Africa Co., 1964-69; Burton Group, 1969- (beginning of Top Shop). Member: Price Commn, 1977-79; Exec., 1972 Industry Gp. Mem., Labour Party NEC Prices and Consumer Affairs Sub-Cttee, 1975-79, Industrial Policy Sub-Cttee, 1975-, Planning Working Gp, 1980-82, Trade Policy Working Gp, 1980-. Contested (Lab), SW Herts, 1979. *Address:* Phoebus, 4 Helme Close, SW19 7EB. *T:* 01-879 0045. *Club:* Reform.

COLMAN, David Stacy, MA; retired; *b* Broughty Ferry, Angus, 1 May 1906; *yr s* of Dr H. C. Colman; *m* 1934, Sallie Edwards (*d* 1970). *Educ:* Shrewsbury Sch.; Balliol Coll., Oxford (Scholar). 1st Class Hon. Mods, 1926; 1st Class Lit. Hum., 1928. Asst Master at Shrewsbury Sch., 1928-31 and 1935-36; Fellow of Queen's Coll., Oxford and Praelector in Classics and Ancient History, 1931-34; Headmaster, C of E Grammar Sch., Melbourne, 1937-38; Shrewsbury School: Asst Master, 1938-46; Master of Day Boys, 1949-61; Librarian, 1961-66. Mem Council, Soc. for Promotion of Roman Studies, 1958-61, Classical Assoc., 1961-64. *Publication:* Sabrinae Corolla: The Classics at Shrewsbury School under Dr Butler and Dr Kennedy, 1950. *Address:* 19 Woodfield Road, Shrewsbury SY3 8HZ. *T:* 53749. *Clubs:* National Liberal; Leander; Salop (Shrewsbury).

COLMAN, Elijah Alec, JP; Chairman: E. Alec Colman Group of Companies; Langham Life Assurance Co. Ltd; *b* Tipton, Staffs, 7 Jan. 1903; *s* of Abraham and Leah Colman; *m* 1956, Eileen Amelia Graham; no *c. Educ:* Tipton Green Coun. Sch., Staffs. Dir of numerous charitable organisations; concerned with rehabilitation of refugees throughout the world; Pres., British Friends of Bar-Ilan Univ.; Exec. Mem., Jt Palestine Appeal; Vice Pres., British-Israel (formerly Anglo-Israel) Chamber of Commerce. Mem. Ct, Patternmakers Co. JP Inner London, 1962. Hon. PhD, Bar-Ilan Univ., 1974. *Recreations:* reading, philosophy. *Clubs:* East India, Devonshire, Sports and Public Schools, City Livery, Royal Automobile.

COLMAN, Sir Michael (Jeremiah), 3rd Bt *cr* 1907; *b* 7 July 1928; *s* of Sir Jeremiah Colman, 2nd Bt, and Edith Gwendolyn Tritton; *S* father, 1961; *m* 1955, Judith Jean Wallop, *d* of Vice-Adm. Sir Peveril William-Powlett, *qv* ; two *s* three *d. Educ:* Eton. Director: Reckitt & Colman Ltd; Waterer's Sons & Crisp Ltd. Mem., Council of Royal Warrant Holders, 1977-. Capt., Yorks Yeomanry, RARO, 1967. *Recreations:* farming, shooting. *Heir:* *s* Jeremiah Michael Powlett Colman, *b* 23 Jan. 1958. *Address:* Malshanger, Basingstoke, Hants. *T:* Basingstoke 780241; Tarvie, Bridge of Cally, Blairgowrie, Perthshire. *T:* Strathardle 264. *Clubs:* Cavalry and Guards, Lansdowne.

COLMAN, Timothy James Alan; Lord-Lieutenant of Norfolk, since 1978; *b* 19 Sept. 1929; 2nd but *o* surv. *s* of late Captain Geoffrey Russell Rees Colman and Lettice Elizabeth Evelyn Colman, Norwich; *m* 1951, Lady Mary Cecelia (Extra Lady in Waiting to Princess Alexandra), twin *d* of late Lt-Col Hon. Michael Claude Hamilton Bowes Lyon and Elizabeth Margaret, Glamis; two *s* three *d. Educ:* RNC, Dartmouth and Greenwich. Lieut RN, 1950, retd 1953. Chm., Eastern Counties Newspapers Group Ltd; Director: Reckitt & Colman plc; Whitbread & Co. PLC. Chm., Carnegie UK Trust; Pro-Chancellor and Chm. Council, Univ. of E Anglia, 1973-; Chm., Trustees, Norfolk and Norwich Triennial Festival. Member: Countryside Commn, 1971-76; Water Space Amenity Commn, 1973-76; Adv. Cttee for England, Nature Conservancy Council, 1974-80; Eastern Regional Cttee, National Trust, 1967-71. President: Norfolk Naturalists Trust, 1962-78; Royal Norfolk Agricultural Assoc., 1982. JP 1958, DL 1968, High Sheriff 1970, Norfolk. Hon. DCL E. Anglia, 1973. KStJ 1979. *Address:* Bixley Manor, Norwich, Norfolk NR14 8SJ. *T:* Norwich 25298. *Clubs:* Turf, Pratt's; Norfolk (Norwich).

COLOMBO, Archbishop of, (RC), since 1977; **Most Rev. Nicholas Marcus Fernando,** STD; *b* 6 Dec. 1932. *Educ:* St Aloysius Seminary, Colombo; Universitas Propaganda Fide, Rome. BA (London); PhL (Rome); STD (Rome). Chairman, Episcopal Commission for Seminaries, Sri Lanka. *Address:* Archbishop's House, Colombo 8, Sri Lanka. *T:* 595471/2/3.

COLOMBO, Emilio; Minister of Foreign Affairs, Italy, since 1980; *b* Potenza, Italy, 11 April 1920. *Educ:* Rome Univ. Deputy: Constituent Assembly, 1946-48; Italian Parliament (Christian Democrat), 1948-; Under-Secretary: of Agriculture, 1948-51; of Public Works, 1953-55; Minister: of Agriculture, 1955-58; of Foreign Trade, 1958-59; of Industry and Commerce, 1959-60, March-April 1960, July 1960-63; of the Treasury, 1963-70, Feb.-May 1972, 1974-76; Prime Minister, 1970-72; Minister of State for UN Affairs, 1972-73; Minister of Finance, 1973-74. European Parliament: Mem., 1976-80; Chm., Political Affairs Cttee, 1976-77; Pres., 1977-79. Formerly Vice-Pres., Italian Catholic Youth Assoc. *Address:* Camera dei Deputati, Rome, Italy; Via Aurelia 239, Rome, Italy.

COLQUHOUN, Maj.-Gen. Sir Cyril (Harry), KCVO 1968 (CVO 1965); CB 1955; OBE 1945; late Royal Artillery; Secretary of the Central Chancery of the Orders of Knighthood, 1960-68; Extra Gentleman Usher to the Queen since 1968; *b* 1903; *s* of late Capt. Harry Colquhoun; *m* 1930, Stella Irene, *d* of late W. C. Rose, Kotagiri, India, and Cheam, Surrey; one *s.* Served War of 1939-45 (despatches, OBE); Palestine, 1946-48 (despatches); Comdr, 6th, 76th and 1st Field Regiments; CRA 61st Div., 1945; CRA 6th Airborne Div., 1947-48; CRA 1st Infantry Div., 1949-50; Comdt, Sch. of Artillery, 1951-53; GOC 50th (Northumbrian) Infantry Div. (TA), and Northumbrian District, 1954-56; GOC Troops, Malta, 1956-59; retired 1960. Col Commandant: Royal Artillery, 1962-69; Royal Malta Artillery, 1962-70. *Recreations:* gardening, shooting. *Address:* Longwalls, Shenington, Banbury, Oxon OX15 6NQ. *T:* Edgehill 246. *Club:* Army and Navy.

COLQUHOUN, Rev. Canon Frank, MA; Canon Residentiary of Norwich Cathedral, 1973-78, Canon Emeritus, since 1978; Vice-Dean, 1974-78; *b* 28 Oct. 1909; *s* of Rev. R. W. Colquhoun; *m* 1st, 1934, Dora Gertrude Hearne Slater; one *s* one *d* ; 2nd, 1973, Judy Kenney. *Educ:* Warwick Sch.; Durham Univ. LTh 1932, BA 1933, MA 1937. Durham. Deacon, 1933; Priest, 1934; Curate, St Faith, Maidstone, 1933-35; Curate, New Malden, Surrey, 1935-39; Vicar, St Michael and All Angels, Blackheath Park, SE3, 1939-46; Editorial Sec., Nat. Church League, 1946-52; Priest-in-Charge, Christ Church, Woburn Square, WC1, 1952-54; Vicar of Wallington, Surrey, 1954-61; Canon Residentiary of Southwark Cathedral, 1961-73; Principal, Southwark Ordination Course, 1966-72. Editor, The Churchman, 1946-53. *Publications:* Harringay Story, 1954; Your Child's Baptism, 1958; The Gospels, 1961; Total Christianity, 1962; The Catechism, 1963; Lent with Pilgrim's Progress, 1965; Christ's Ambassadors, 1965; (ed) The Living Church in the Parish, 1952; (ed) Parish Prayers, 1967; (ed) Hard Questions, 1967; Preaching through the Christian Year, 1972; Strong Son of God, 1973; Preaching at the Parish Communion, 1974; Contemporary Parish Prayers, 1975; (ed) Moral Questions, 1977; Hymns that Live, 1980; Prayers that Live, 1981; New Parish Prayers, 1982. *Recreations:* writing, listening to music. *Address:* 21 Buckholt Avenue, Bexhill-on-Sea, East Sussex N40 2RS. *T:* Bexhill 221138.

COLQUHOUN OF LUSS, Captain Sir Ivar (Iain), 8th Bt *cr* 1786; JP; DL; Hon. Sheriff (formerly Hon. Sheriff Substitute); Chief of the Clan; Grenadier Guards; *b* 4 Jan. 1916; *s* of Sir Iain Colquhoun, 7th Bt, and Geraldine Bryde (Dinah) (*d* 1974), *d* of late F. J. Tennant; *S* father, 1948; *m* 1943, Kathleen, 2nd *d* of late W. A. Duncan and of Mrs Duncan, 53 Cadogan Square, SW1; one *s* one *d* (and one *s* decd). *Educ:* Eton. JP 1951, DL 1952, Dunbartonshire. *Heir:* *s* Malcolm Rory Colquhoun, Younger of Luss [*b* 20 Dec. 1947; *m* 1978, Susan Timmerman]. *Address:* Camstraddan, Luss, Dunbartonshire; Eilean da Mheinn, Crinan, Argyllshire; 37 Radnor Walk, SW3. *Clubs:* White's, Royal Ocean Racing.
See also Duke of Argyll.

COLQUHOUN, Ms Maureen Morfydd; writer; Member, Hackney Borough Council (New River Ward), since 1982; *b* 12 Aug. 1928; *m* 1949, Keith Colquhoun (marr. diss. 1980); two *s* one *d.* Partner, 1975-, Ms Barbara Todd; extended family, two *d.* Mem. Labour Party, 1945-; Councillor: Shoreham UDC, 1965-74; Adur District Council, 1973-81; County Councillor, West

Sussex, 1973–81. MP (Lab) Northampton North, Feb. 1974–1979; Information Officer, Gingerbread, 1980–82. *Publication:* A Woman In the House, 1980. *Recreations:* walking, jazz, opera, theatre, collecting primitive and naieve paintings. *Address:* 19 Vicars Close, E9 7HT. *T:* 01-986 6573.

COLSTON, Colin Charles; QC 1980; a Recorder of the Crown Court, since 1978; *b* 2 Oct. 1937; *yr s* of late Eric Colston, JP, and Catherine Colston; *m* 1963, Edith Helga, *d* of Dr and Mrs Wilhelm Hille, St Oswald/Freistadt, Austria; two *s* one *d. Educ:* Rugby Sch.; The Gunnery, Washington, Conn, USA; Trinity Hall, Cambridge (BA 1961, MA 1964). National Service, RN, 1956-58; commissioned, RNR, 1958-64. Called to the Bar, Gray's Inn, 1962; Midland and Oxford Circuit (formerly Midland Circuit); Recorder of Midland Circuit, 1968-69; Member, Senate of Inns of Court and the Bar, 1977-80. *Address:* Punchardon Hall, Willian, Letchworth, Herts SG6 2AE. *T:* Letchworth 5074.

COLSTON, Michael; Chairman and Managing Director, Charles Colston Group Ltd, since 1969; *b* 24 July 1932; *s* of Sir Charles Blampied Colston, CBE, MC, DCM, FCGI and Lady (Eliza Foster) Colston, MBE; *m* 1st, 1956, Jane Olivia Kilham Roberts (marr. diss.); three *d* ; 2nd, 1977, Judith Angela Briggs. *Educ:* Ridley Coll., Canada; Stowe; Gonville and Caius Coll., Cambridge. Joined 17th/21st Lancers, 1952; later seconded to 1st Royal Tank Regt for service in Korea. Founder Dir Charles Colston Group Ltd (formerly Colston Appliances Ltd) together with late Sir Charles Colston, 1955; Chm. and Man. Dir, Colston Domestic Appliances Ltd, 1969-79. Chairman: Tallent Engineering Ltd, 1969; ITS Rubber Ltd, 1969; Dishwasher Council, 1970-75. Chm., Assoc. Manufrs of Domestic Electrical Appliances, 1976-79. Member Council: Inst. of Directors (Chm., Thames Valley Br.); British Electrotechnical Approvals Bd, 1976-79. *Recreations:* fishing, shooting, tennis; founder Cambridge Univ. Water Ski Club. *Address:* Ewelme Park, Nettlebed, Oxfordshire RG9 6DZ. *T:* Nettlebed 641279.

COLT, Sir Edward (William Dutton), 10th Bt *cr* 1694; MB, MRCP, FACP; Consultant in Endocrinology, St Barnabas Hospital, Bronx, New York; Assistant Attending Physician, St Luke's Hospital, New York; Associate in Clinical Medicine, Columbia University, New York; *b* 22 Sept. 1936; *s* of Major John Rochfort Colt, North Staffs Regt (*d* 1944), and of Angela Miriam Phyllis (*née* Kyan; she *m* 1946, Capt. Robert Leslie Cock); *S* uncle, 1951; *m* 1966, Jane Caroline (marr. diss. 1972), *d* of James Histed Lewis, Geneva and Washington, DC; *m* 1979, Suzanne Nelson (*née* Knickerbocker). *Educ:* Stoke House, Seaford; Douai Sch.; University Coll., London. Lately: Medical Registrar, UCH; House Physician, Brompton Hosp. Mem., BMA. FACP. *Recreations:* the arts, skiing, lawn tennis, jogging. *Heir:* none. *Address:* 12 E 88 Street, New York, NY 10028, USA; c/o Cock, 11 Stafford Road, Seaford, East Sussex.

COLTART, James Milne; Chairman: Scottish Television Ltd, 1969-75 (Managing Director, 1957-61, Deputy Chairman, 1961-69); Highland Printers Ltd, since 1959; Deputy Chairman: The Thomson Organisation Ltd, 1964-76 (Managing Director, Thomson Newspapers Ltd, 1959-61); Thomson Television (International) Ltd, since 1962; The Scotsman Publications Ltd, since 1962 (Managing Director, 1955-62); Director, Thomson Printers Ltd and various other newspaper and television companies in Britain and overseas; Chairman of Trustees, The Thomson Foundation, since 1969 (Trustee since 1962); *b* 2 Nov. 1903; *s* of Alexander Coltart and Alice Moffat; *m* 1927, Margaret Shepherd (*d* 1966); one *s* ; *m* 1961, Mary Fryer; one *s* one *d. Educ:* Hamilton Cres., Glasgow. Accountant: Ioco Rubber Co. Ltd, 1926; Weir Housing Co. Ltd, 1927; Dir and Sec., Marr Downie & Co. Ltd, 1937; Man. Dir, Reid Bros Ltd, 1939; Asst Gen. Manager, Scottish Daily Express, 1950; Gen. Manager, Evening Citizen Ltd, 1955. Hon. LLD Strathclyde Univ., 1967. *Recreations:* golf, fishing. *Address:* (business) 16th Floor, International Press Centre, Shoe Lane, EC4. *T:* 01-353 6718; Manor Cottage, Smithwood Common, Cranleigh, Surrey. *T:* Cranleigh 3633.

COLTHURST, Sir Richard La Touche, 9th Bt *cr* 1744; *b* 14 Aug. 1928; *er s* of Sir Richard St John Jefferyes Colthurst, 8th Bt, and Denys Maida Hanmer West (*d* 1966), *e d* of Augustus William West; *S* father, 1955; *m* 1953, Janet Georgina, *d* of L. A. Wilson-Wright, Coolcarrigan, Co. Kildare; three *s* one *d. Educ:* Harrow; Peterhouse, Cambridge (MA). Dir, Lindsey Underwriting Agencies Ltd. Liveryman of Worshipful Company of Grocers. *Recreations:* forestry, cricket, tennis, swimming. *Heir:* s Charles St John Colthurst [*b* 21 May 1955. *Educ:* Eton; Magdalene Coll., Cambridge (MA); University Coll., Dublin]. *Clubs:* City University, MCC.

COLTMAN, (Arthur) Leycester (Scott); HM Diplomatic Service; Counsellor (Political and Economic), Mexico City, since 1979; *b* 24 May 1938; *s* of late Arthur Cranfield Coltman and Vera Vaid; *m* 1969, Maria Piedad Josefina Cantos Aberasturi; two *s* one *d. Educ:* Rugby School; Magdalene Coll., Cambridge. Foreign Office, 1961-62; Third Secretary, British Embassy, Copenhagen, 1963-64; Second Secretary, Cairo 1964-65, Madrid 1966-69; Manchester Business School, 1969-70; Foreign Office, 1970-74; Commercial Secretary, Brasilia, 1974-77; Foreign Office, 1977-79. *Recreations:* tennis, squash, chess, bridge, music. *Address:* c/o Foreign and Commonwealth Office, King Charles Street, SW1A 2AH.

COLTON, Cyril Hadlow, CBE 1970; *b* 15 March 1902; *yr s* of Albert Edward Colton and Kate Louise; *m* 1932, Doree Beatrice Coles; one *s* two *d. Educ:* Reigate Grammar School. Man-made fibres industry from 1921: Fabrique de Soie Artificiel de Tubize, 1921; British Celanese Ltd, 1923: Dir, 1945; Chm., 1964; Pres., 1968; Courtaulds Ltd, 1957: Marketing Dir, 1962-67; Dir, Samuel Courtauld Ltd, 1959-64; Dir, Courtaulds SA, 1962-68; Consultant, Courtaulds Ltd, 1967-78. Chm., Rayon Allocation Cttee, 1940-49; Member: Council, British Rayon Research Assoc., 1946-61; BoT Utility Cloth Cttee, 1950-52; BoT Mission to Middle East, 1954; Pres., Textile Inst., 1954-55. Chairman: British Man-Made Fibres Fedn, 1967-75; British Man-Made Fibres Producers Cttee, 1965-72; Silk and Man-Made Fibres Users Assoc., 1968-70; BSI Textile Div., 1969-72; Pres., Bureau International pour la Standardisation de la Rayonne et des Fibres Synthetiques, 1969-72; Vice-Pres., Cttee Internat. des Fibres Synthetiques, 1969-72; Pres., British Display Soc., 1966-79; Mem. Council, Cotton, Silk and Man-Made Fibres Research Assoc. (Shirley Inst.), 1969-72; Dep. Chm., Textile Council, 1969-71; Mem., Crowther Cttee on Consumer Credit, 1968-71. CompTI; FRSA; FInstM. Liveryman, Worshipful Co. of Weavers. *Address:* Appin House, Cobham, Surrey. *T:* Cobham 4477.

COLTON, Gladys M.; Head Mistress, City of London School for Girls, 1949-72; *b* 1909; *er d* of William Henry Colton. *Educ:* Wycombe High Sch.; University Coll., London. BA Hons, History; Postgrad. DipEd, London. Asst Mistress: Slepe Hall, St Ives, 1932-37; Beaminster Grammar Sch., 1937-41; Senior History Mistress, Ealing Girls' Grammar Sch., 1941-49. Mem. Governing Body, City of London Coll., 1957-62. Mem., St Bartholomew's Hosp. Nurse Educn Cttee, 1962-72. FRSA 1953 (Mem. Council, 1969-73). *Recreations:* music, gardening. *Address:* Four Winds, Westleton, Saxmundham, Suffolk. *T:* Westleton 402.

COLVILLE, family name of **Viscount Colville of Culross** and of **Baron Clydesmuir.**

COLVILLE OF CULROSS, 4th Viscount *cr* 1902; **John Mark Alexander Colville;** QC; 14th Baron (Scot.) *cr* 1604; 4th Baron (UK) *cr* 1885; *b* 19 July 1933; *e s* of 3rd Viscount and Kathleen Myrtle, OBE 1961, *e d* of late Brig.-Gen. H. R. Gale, CMG, RE, Bardsey, Saanichton, Vancouver Island; *S* father, 1945; *m* 1st, 1958, Mary Elizabeth Webb-Bowen (marr. diss. 1973); four *s* ; 2nd, 1974, Margaret Birgitta, Viscountess Davidson, *o d* of Maj.-Gen. C. H. Norton, *qv* ; one *s. Educ:* Rugby (Scholar); New Coll., Oxford (Scholar) (MA). Lieut Grenadier Guards Reserve. Barrister-at-law, Lincoln's Inn, 1960 (Buchanan prizeman); QC 1978. Minister of State, Home Office, 1972-74. Director: Rediffusion Television Ltd, 1961-68; British Electric Traction Co. Ltd, 1968-72, 1974- (Dep. Chm., 1980-81); Thames TV Ltd, 1981-. UK rep., UN Human Rights Commn, 1980-; Mem., UN Working Gp on Disappeared Persons, 1980- (Chm., 1981-); Mem. Council, Univ. of E Anglia, 1968-72. Mem., Royal Company of Archers (Queen's Body Guard for Scotland). Hon. Mem., Rating and Valuation Assoc. *Heir:* s Master of Colville, *qv. Address:* House of Lords, SW1A 0PW.

See also Baron Carrington.

COLVILLE, Master of; Hon. Charles Mark Townshend Colville; *b* 5 Sept. 1959; *s* and *heir* of 4th Viscount Colville of Culross, *qv. Educ:* Rugby; Univ. of Durham. *Address:* Rookyards, Spexhall, near Halesworth, Suffolk. *T:* Ilketshall 318.

COLVILLE, Sir Cecil; see Colville, Sir H. C.

COLVILLE, Sir (Henry) Cecil, Kt 1962; MS (Melbourne), FRACS; private surgical practice, Melbourne; *b* 27 Aug. 1891; *s* of John William Colville and Mary Newman; *m* 1916, Harriet Elizabeth Tatchell; two *d. Educ:* Melbourne Church of England Grammar Sch. MB, BS (Melbourne) 1914; MS (Melbourne) 1920; FRACS 1931. War service, RAMC and AAMC, 1915-17. Pediatric Surg., Alfred Hospital, Melbourne, 1924-51. Pres., Federal Council of BMA, 1955-62; Pres. AMA, 1962-64. *Address:* 1045 Burke Road, Hawthorn, Vic 3123, Australia. *T:* Melbourne 82-5252. *Club:* Naval and Military.

COLVILLE, Sir John (Rupert), Kt 1974; CB 1955; CVO 1949; Director: Grindlays Bank; Provident Life Association; Deputy Chairman, London Committee, Ottoman Bank; Chairman: Thames Valley Broadcasting; Eucalyptus Pulp Mills Ltd; *b* 28 Jan. 1915; *s* of late Hon. George Colville and Lady Cynthia Colville; *m* 1948, Lady Margaret Egerton (*see* Lady Margaret Colville); two *s* one *d. Educ:* Harrow; Trinity Coll., Cambridge. Page of Honour to King George V, 1927-31. 3rd Sec., Diplomatic Service, 1937; Asst Private Sec. to Mr Neville Chamberlain, 1939-40; to Mr Winston Churchill, 1940-41 and 1943-45, and to Mr Clement Attlee, 1945. Served War of 1939-45, Pilot, RAFVR, 1941-44. Private Sec. to Princess Elizabeth, 1947-49; 1st Sec., British Embassy, Lisbon, 1949-51; Counsellor, Foreign Service, 1951; Joint Principal Private Sec. to the Prime Minister, 1951-55. President: New Victoria Hospital, 1978-; Prayer Book Soc., 1981; Vice-Pres., National Assoc. of Boys' Clubs. Hon. Fellow, Churchill Coll., Cambridge, 1971. Officier, Légion d'Honneur. *Publications:* Fools' Pleasure, 1935; contrib. to Action This Day-Working with Churchill, 1968; Man of Valour, 1972; Footprints in Time, 1976; The New Elizabethans, 1977; The Portrait of a General, 1980; The Churchillians, 1981. *Address:* The Close, Broughton, near Stockbridge, Hampshire. *T:* Broughton 331. *Clubs:* White's, Pratt's.

COLVILLE, Lady Margaret; b 20 July 1918; d of 4th Earl of Ellesmere; m 1948, Sir John Rupert Colville, qv; two s one d. Served War of 1939-45 in ATS (Junior Subaltern). Lady in Waiting to the Princess Elizabeth, Duchess of Edinburgh, 1946-49. Address: The Close, Broughton, near Stockbridge, Hants. T: Broughton 331.
See also Duke of Sutherland.

COLVIN, David; Chief Adviser in Social Work, The Scottish Office, since 1980; b 31 Jan. 1931; s of James Colvin and Mrs Crawford Colvin; m 1957, Elma Findlay; two s three d. Educ: Whitehill Sch., Glasgow; Glasgow and Edinburgh Univs. Probation Officer, Glasgow City, 1955-60; Psychiatric Social Worker, Scottish Prison and Borstal Service, Scottish Home and Health Dept, 1960-61; Sen. Psychiatric Social Worker, Crichton Royal Hosp., Child Psychiatric Unit, 1961-65; Director, Family Casework Unit, Paisley, 1965-66; Welfare Officer, SHHD, 1966-68; Social Work Adviser, Social Work Services Gp, Scottish Educn Dept, 1968, and subseq. At various times held office in Howard League for Penal Reform, Assoc. of Social Workers and Inst. for Study and Treatment of Delinquency. Sen. Associate Research Fellow, Brunel Univ., 1978. Recreations: collector; swimming, climbing, golf, gardens, social affairs. Address: Sea Brae, Marine Terrace, Gullane, East Lothian EH31 2AZ. T: Gullane 842139.

COLVIN, Howard Montagu, CBE 1964; FBA 1963; MA; Fellow of St John's College, Oxford, since 1948, Librarian since 1950, Tutor in History, 1957-78; Reader in Architectural History, Oxford University, since 1965; Member: Historic Buildings Council for England, since 1970; Royal Commission on Ancient and Historical Monuments of Scotland, since 1977; Royal Commission on Historical Manuscripts, since 1981; Reviewing Committee on the Export of Works of Art, since 1982; Royal Fine Art Commission, 1962-72; Royal Commission on Historical Monuments, England, 1963-76; President, Society of Architectural Historians of Great Britain, 1979-81; b 15 Oct. 1919; s of late Montagu Colvin; m 1943, Christina Edgeworth, d of late H. E. Butler, Prof. of Latin at University Coll., London; two s. Educ: Trent Coll.; University Coll., London (Fellow, 1974). Served in RAF, 1940-46 (despatches); Asst Lecturer, Dept of History, University Coll., London, 1946-48. Hon. FRIBA. DUniv York, 1978. Wolfson Literary Award, 1978. Publications: The White Canons in England, 1951; A Biographical Dictionary of English Architects 1660-1840, 1954; (General Editor and part author) The History of the King's Works, 6 Vols, 1963-82; A History of Deddington, 1963; Catalogue of Architectural Drawings in Worcester College Library, 1964; Architectural Drawings in the Library of Elton Hall (with Maurice Craig), 1964; (ed with John Harris) The Country Seat, 1970; Building Accounts of King Henry III, 1971; A Biographical Dictionary of British Architects 1600-1840, 1978; (introduction) The Queen Anne Churches, 1980; (ed with John Newman) Roger North, Of Architecture, 1981; articles on mediæval and architectural history in Archaeological Journal, Architectural Review, etc. Recreation: gardening. Address: 50 Plantation Road, Oxford. T: Oxford 57460.

COLVIN, John Horace Ragnar, CMG 1968; HM Diplomatic Service, retired; Vice-President and Director for International Relations (Asia/Pacific), Chase Manhattan Bank, since 1980; b Tokyo, 18 June 1922; s of late Adm. Sir Ragnar Colvin, KBE, CB and of Lady Colvin; m 1st, 1948, Elizabeth Anne Manifold (marr. diss., 1963); one s one d; 2nd, 1967, Moranna Sibyl de Lerisson Cazenove; one s one d. Educ: RNC Dartmouth; University of London. Royal Navy, 1935-51. Joined HM Diplomatic Service, 1951; HM Embassies, Oslo, 1951-53 and Vienna, 1953-55; British High Commn, Kuala Lumpur, 1958-61; HM Consul-General, Hanoi, 1965-67; Ambassador to People's Republic of Mongolia, 1971-74; HM Embassy, Washington, 1977-80. Address: The Old Parsonage, Pamber Heath, Hants. T: Silchester 253; Chase Manhattan Bank, 280 Gloucester Road, Hong Kong. Club: Brooks's.

COLVIN, Brigadier Dame Mary Katherine Rosamond, DBE 1959 (OBE 1947); TD; Extra Lady in Waiting to the Princess Royal, 1964-65 (Lady in Waiting, 1962-64); b 25 Oct. 1907; d of Lt-Col F. F. Colvin, CBE. Commissioned 1939; Commanded Central Ordnance Depot, ATS Gp, Weedon, Northants, 1943-44; subsequently held staff appointments in Military Government, Germany; Comdt WRAC Sch. of Instruction, 1948-51; Asst Dir, WRAC, HQ. Scottish Comd, 1951-54; Inspector of Recruiting (Women's Services), War Office, 1954-56; Dep. Dir, WRAC, HQ Eastern Command, 1956-57; Dir of the Woman's Royal Army Corps, 1957-61. Hon. ADC to the Queen, 1957-61, retd. Address: Pasture House, North Luffenham, Oakham, Rutland LE15 8JU.

COLVIN, Michael Keith Beale; MP (C) Bristol North West, since 1979; b 27 Sept. 1932; s of late Captain Ivan Beale Colvin, RN, and Mrs Joy Colvin, OBE; m Hon. Nichola, e d of Baron Cayzer, qv; one s two d. Educ: Eton; RMA, Sandhurst; Royal Agricultural Coll., Cirencester. Served Grenadier Guards, 1950-57: Temp. Captain; served BAOR, Berlin, Suez campaign, Cyprus. J. Walter Thompson & Co. Ltd, 1958-63. Landowner and farmer. Councillor: Andover RDC, 1965-72; Test Valley Bor. Council, 1972-74 (first Vice Chm.); Dep. Chm., Winchester Constituency Conservative Assoc., 1973-76; Mem. (part-time), Cons. Res. Dept, 1975-79. Chm., Conservative Aviation Cttee, 1982-; Vice-Chm., Conservative Smaller Businesses Cttee, 1980-; Mem., Select Cttee on Employment, 1981-; Secretary: Cttee of West Country Conservative MPs; Conservative Shipping and Shipbuilding Cttee. President: Hampshire Young Farmers Clubs, 1973-74; Test Valley Br., CPRE, 1974-; Mem., Southern Sports Council, 1970-74. Governor, Enham Village

Settlement. Address: Tangley House, near Andover, Hants SP11 0SH. T: Chute Standen 215. Club: Turf.

COLWYN, 3rd Baron, cr 1917; **Ian Anthony Hamilton-Smith;** Bt 1912; Dental Surgeon since 1966; b 1 Jan. 1942; s of 2nd Baron Colwyn and Miriam Gwendoline, d of Victor Ferguson; S father 1966; m 1st, 1964, Sonia Jane (marr. diss. 1977), d of P. H. G. Morgan, The Eades, Upton-on-Severn; one s one d; 2nd, 1977, Nicola Jeanne, d of Arthur Tyers, The Avenue, Sunbury-on-Thames; one d. Educ: Cheltenham Coll.; Univ. of London. BDS London 1966; LDS, RCS 1966. Recreations: Rugby Union, motoring, music. Heir: s Hon. Craig Peter Hamilton-Smith, b 13 Oct. 1968. Address: (practice) 53 Wimpole Street, W1.

COLYER, John Stuart, QC 1976; b 25 April 1935; s of Stanley Herbert Colyer, MBE, and late Louisa (née Randle); m 1961, Emily Warner, o d of Stanley Leland Dutrow and Mrs Dutrow, Blue Ridge Summit, Pa, USA; two d. Educ: Dudley Grammar Sch.; Shrewsbury; Worcester Coll., Oxford (Open History Scholarship; BA 1955, MA 1961). 2nd Lieut RA, 1954-55. Called to the Bar, Middle Temple, 1959; Instructor, Univ. of Pennsylvania, Philadelphia, 1959-60, Asst Prof., 1960-61; practised English bar, Midland and Oxford Circuit (formerly Oxford Circuit), 1961-; Lectr (Law of Landlord and Tenant), Council of Legal Educn, 1970-. Chm., Lawyers' Christian Fellowship, 1981-. Publications: (ed jtly) Encyclopaedia of Forms and Precedents (Landlord and Tenant), vol. XI, 1965, vol. XII, 1966; A Modern View of the Law of Torts, 1966; Landlord and Tenant, in Halsbury's Laws of England, 4th edn, 1981; articles in Conveyancer. Recreations: entertaining my children; opera; cultivation of cacti and of succulents (esp. Lithops); gardening generally; travel. Address: 11 King's Bench Walk, Temple, EC4. T: 01-353 2484.

COLYER-FERGUSSON, Sir James Herbert Hamilton, 4th Bt, cr 1866; b 10 Jan. 1917; s of Max Christian Hamilton Colyer-Fergusson (d on active service, 1940) and Edith Jane (d 1936), singer, d of late William White Miller, Portage la Prairie, Manitoba; S grandfather, 1951. Educ: Harrow; Balliol Coll., Oxford. BA 1939; MA 1945. Formerly Capt., The Buffs; served War of 1939-45 (prisoner-of-war, 1940). Entered service of former Great Western Railway Traffic Dept, 1947, later Operating Dept of the Western Region of British Rlys. Personal Asst to Chm. of British Transport Commission, 1957; Passenger Officer in SE Division of Southern Region, BR, 1961; Parly and Public Correspondent, BRB, 1967; Deputy to Curator of Historical Relics, BRB, 1968. Retired. Heir: none. Address: 61 Onslow Square, SW7. Club: Naval and Military.
See also Sir Lingard Goulding, Bt, Viscount Monckton of Brenchley.

COLYTON, 1st Baron, cr 1956, of Farway and of Taunton; **Henry Lennox d'Aubigné Hopkinson,** PC 1952; CMG 1944; b 3 Jan. 1902; e s of late Sir Henry Lennox Hopkinson, KCVO; m 1st, 1927, Alice Labouisse (d 1953), d of Henry Lane Eno, Bar Harbor, Maine, USA; one s; 2nd, 1956, Mrs Barbara Addams, d of late Stephen Barb, New York. Educ: Eton Coll.; Trinity Coll., Cambridge (BA History and Modern Languages Tripos). Entered Diplomatic Service, 1924; 3rd Sec., Washington, 1924; 2nd Sec., Foreign Office, 1929; Stockholm, 1931; Asst Private Sec. to Sec. of State for Foreign Affairs, 1932; Cairo, 1934; 1st Sec., 1936; Athens, 1938; War Cabinet Secretariat, 1939; Private Sec. to Permanent Under-Sec. for Foreign Affairs, 1940; Counsellor and Political Advr to Minister of State in the Middle East, 1941; Minister Plenipotentiary, Lisbon, 1943; Dep. Brit. High Comr in Italy, and Vice-Pres. Political Sect., Allied Control Commn, 1944-46. Resigned from Foreign Service to enter politics, 1946; Head of Conservative Parly Secretariat and Jt Dir, Conservative Research Dept, 1946-50; MP (C) Taunton Div. of Somerset, 1950-56; Sec. for Overseas Trade, 1951-52; Minister of State for Colonial Affairs, 1952-Dec. 1955; Mem., Consultative Assembly, Council of Europe, 1950-52; Delegate, General Assembly, United Nations, 1952-55; Chairman: Anglo-Egyptian Resettlement Board, 1957-60; Joint East and Central African Board, 1960-65; Tanganyika Concessions Ltd, 1966-72. Royal Humane Society's Award for saving life from drowning, 1919. OStJ 1959. Grand Cross, Order of Prince Henry the Navigator (Portugal), 1972; Dato, Order of the Stia Negara (Brunei), 1972; Grand Star, Order Paduka Stia Negara Brunei, 1978; Commander, Order of the Zaire (Congo) 1971. Heir: s Hon. Nicholas Henry Eno Hopkinson [b 18 Jan. 1932; m 1957, Fiona Margaret, o d of Sir Torquil Munro, qv; two s]. Address: Le Formentor, avenue Princesse Grace, Monte Carlo, Monaco. T: (93) 30 92 96. Clubs: Buck's, White's, Beefsteak; Monte Carlo.

COMAY, Michael; Fellow, Leonard Davis Institute for International Affairs, Jerusalem; b Cape Town, 17 Oct. 1908; s of Alexander and Clara Comay; m 1935, Joan Solomon; one s one d. Educ: Univ. of Cape Town (BA, LLB). Barrister, 1931-40. Served with S African Army, Western Desert and UK, 1940-45 (Major). Settled Palestine as representative S African Zionist Fedn, 1945; Adviser, Political Dept Jewish Agency, 1946-48; Dir, British Commonwealth Div., Israel Foreign Min., 1948-51; Asst Dir-Gen., Israel For. Min., 1951-53 and 1957-59; Minister, then Ambassador to Canada, 1953-57; Perm. Rep. and Ambassador of Israel to UN, 1960-67; Political Adviser to For. Minister and Ambassador-at-Large, 1967-70; Ambassador of Israel to the Court of St James's, 1970-73. Associate Gen. Chm., Chaim Weizmann Centenary. Recreations: walking, painting. Address: 47 Harav Berlin Street, Jerusalem, Israel.

COMBER, Ven. Anthony James; Archdeacon of Leeds, since 1982; *b* 20 April 1927; *s* of late Norman Mederson Comber and of Nellie Comber. *Educ:* Leeds Grammar School; Leeds Univ. (MSc Mining); St Chad's Coll., Durham (DipTh); Munich Univ. Colliery underground official, 1951-53. Vicar: Oulton, 1960-69; Hunslet, 1969-77; Rector of Farnley, 1977-82. *Publication:* (contrib.) Today's Church and Today's World, 1977. *Recreations:* politics; walking in Bavaria. *Address:* 712 Foundry Lane, Leeds LS14 6BL. *T:* Leeds 602069.

COMBERMERE, 5th Viscount, *cr* 1826; **Michael Wellington Stapleton-Cotton;** Bt 1677; Baron Combermere, 1814; Lecturer in Biblical and Religious Studies, University of London, Department of Extra-Mural Studies, since 1972; *b* 8 Aug. 1929; *s* of 4th Viscount Combermere and Constance Marie Katherine (*d* 1968), *d* of Lt-Col Sir Francis Dudley W. Drummond, KBE; *S* father, 1969; *m* 1961, Pamela Elizabeth, *d* of Rev. R. G. Coulson; one *s* two *d*. *Educ:* Eton; King's Coll., Univ. of London. Palestine Police, 1947-48; Royal Canadian Mounted Police, 1948-50; Short-service commn as gen. duties Pilot, RAF, 1950-58, retd as Flt-Lt; Sales Rep., Teleflex Products Ltd, 1959-62; read Theology, KCL, 1962-67 (BD, MTh). *Heir:* *s* Hon. Thomas Robert Wellington Stapleton-Cotton, *b* 30 Aug. 1969. *Address:* 46 Smith Street, SW3. *T:* 01-352 1319. *Club:* Royal Automobile.

COMBS, Sir Willis (Ide), KCVO 1974; CMG 1962; HM Diplomatic Service, retired; *b* Melbourne, 6 May 1916; *s* of Willis Ide Combs, Napier, New Zealand; *m* 1942, Grace Willis; two *d*. *Educ:* Dannevirke High Sch.; Victoria Coll., NZ; St John's Coll., Cambridge. Served in HM Forces, 1940-46. Apptd Mem. Foreign Service, 1947; transf. to Paris as 2nd Sec. (Commercial), Dec. 1947; 1st Sec., Nov. 1948; transf. to Rio de Janeiro, as 1st Sec., 1951; to Peking as 1st Sec. and Consul, 1953 (Chargé d'Affaires, 1954); Foreign Office, 1956; to Baghdad as Counsellor (Commercial), 1959; Diplomatic Service Inspector, 1963; Counsellor, British Embassy, Rangoon, 1965; Asst Under-Sec. of State, FCO, 1968; Ambassador to Indonesia, 1970-75. *Address:* Sunset, Wadhurst Park, Wadhurst, East Sussex. *Club:* United Oxford & Cambridge University.

COMFORT, Alexander, PhD, DSc; physician; poet and novelist; Consultant psychiatrist, Brentwood VA Hospital, Los Angeles, since 1978; Adjunct Professor, Neuropsychiatric Institute, UCLA, since 1980; *b* 10 Feb. 1920; *s* of late Alexander Charles and Daisy Elizabeth Comfort; *m* 1st 1943, Ruth Muriel Harris (marr. diss. 1973); one *s*; 2nd, 1973, Jane Tristram Henderson. *Educ:* Highgate Sch.; Trinity Coll., Cambridge (Robert Styring Scholar Classics, and Senior Scholar, Nat. Sciences); London Hospital (Scholar). 1st Cl. Nat. Sc. Tripos, Part I, 1940; 2nd Cl. Nat. Sc. Tripos, 1st Div. (Pathology), 1941; MRCS, LRCP 1944; MB, BCh Cantab 1944; MA Cantab 1945; DCH London 1945; PhD London 1949 (Biochemistry); DSc London 1963 (Gerontology). Refused military service in war of 1939-45. Lectr in Physiology, London Hospital Medical Coll., 1948-51; Hon. Research Associate, Dept of Zoology, 1951-73, and Dir of Research, Gerontology, 1966-73, UCL; Clin. Lectr, Dept Psychiatry, Stanford Univ., 1974-; Sen. Fellow, Inst. for Higher Studies, Santa Barbara, Calif, 1975-; Prof., Dept of Pathol., Univ. of Calif Sch. of Med., Irvine, 1976-78 Pres., Brit. Soc. for Research on Ageing, 1967; Member: RSocMed.; Amer. Psychiatric Assoc. *Publications:* The Silver River, 1937; No Such Liberty (novel), 1941; Into Egypt (play), 1942; France and Other Poems, 1942; A Wreath for the Living (poems), 1943; Cities of the Plain (melodrama), 1943; The Almond Tree (novel), 1943; The Powerhouse (novel), 1944; Elegies, 1944; The Song of Lazarus (poems, USA), 1945; Letters from an Outpost (stories), 1947; Art and Social Responsibility (essays), 1947; The Signal to Engage (poems), 1947; Gengulphus (play), 1948; On this side Nothing (novel), 1948; First Year Physiological Technique (textbook), 1948; The Novel and Our Time (criticism), 1948; Barbarism and Sexual Freedom (essays), 1948; Sexual Behaviour in Society (social psychology), 1950; The Pattern of the Future (broadcast lectures), 1950; Authority and Delinquency in the Modern State (social psychology), 1950; And all but He Departed (poems), 1951; A Giant's Strength (novel), 1952; The Biology of Senescence (textbook), 1956 (2nd edn 1964, 3rd edn 1978); Darwin and the Naked Lady (essays), 1961; Come Out to Play (novel), 1961; Haste to the Wedding (poems), 1961; Are you Sitting Comfortably? (songs), 1962; Sex and Society (social psychology), 1963; Ageing, the Biology of Senescence (textbook), 1964; The Koka Shastra (translation), 1964; The Process of Ageing (science), 1965; Nature and Human Nature (science), 1966; The Anxiety Makers (med. history), 1967; The Joy of Sex (counselling), 1973; More Joy (counselling), 1974; A Good Age, 1976; (ed) Sexual Consequences of Disability, 1978; I and That: notes on the Biology of Religion, 1979; Poems, 1979; (with Jane T. Comfort) The Facts of Love, 1979; A Practise of Geriatric Psychiatry, 1979; Tetrarch (trilogy of novels), 1980; What is a Doctor? (essays), 1980. *Address:* 683 Oak Grove Drive, Santa Barbara, Calif 93108, USA.

COMFORT, Anthony Francis; HM Diplomatic Service, retired; *b* Plymouth, 12 Oct. 1920; *s* of Francis Harold Comfort and Elsie Grace (*née* Martin); *m* 1948, Joy Margaret Midson; two *s* one *d*. *Educ:* Bristol Grammar Sch.; Oriel Coll., Oxford. Entered Foreign Service, 1947; 2nd Sec. (Commercial), Athens, 1948-51; Consul, Alexandria, 1951-53; 1st Sec. (Commercial), Amman, 1953-54; Foreign Office, 1954-57; seconded to Colonial Office, 1957-59; 1st Sec. (Commercial), Belgrade, 1959-60; 1st Sec. and Consul, Reykjavik, 1961-65; Inspector of Diplomatic Establishments, 1965-68, retired 1969. *Recreations:* walking, gardening. *Address:* Garliford, Bishop's Nympton, South Molton, Devon.

COMFORT, Dr Charles Fraser, OC; CD; RCA; artist and author; Emeritus Director, National Gallery of Canada, 1965; *b* Edinburgh, 22 July 1900; *m* 1924, Louise Chase, Winnipeg; two *d*. *Educ:* Winnipeg Sch. of Art and Art Students' League, New York. Cadet Officer, Univ. of Toronto Contingent of Canadian OTC, 1939; Commnd Instr in Infantry Weapons, 1940; Sen. Canadian War Artist (Army) Major, 1942-46 (UK, Italy and NW Europe). Head of Dept of Mural Painting, Ontario Coll. of Art, 1935-38; Associate Prof., Dept of Art and Archaeology, Univ. of Toronto, 1946-60 (Mem. staff, 1938); Dir, Nat. Gall. of Canada, 1959. Gold Medal and cash award, Great Lakes Exhibn, Albright Gall., Buffalo, NY, 1938; has travelled widely in Europe; Royal Society Fellowship to continue research into problems of Netherlandish painting, 1955-56; studied under Dr William Heckscher of Kunsthistorisch Inst., Utrecht. *Works include:* landscape painting and portraiture (oils and water colour); mural paintings and stone carvings in many public buildings. Pres., Royal Canadian Academy of Arts, 1957-60; Past Pres., Canadian Soc. of Painters in Water Colour; Past Pres. and Charter Mem., Canadian Group of Painters; Mem., Ontario Soc. of Artists. Dr of Laws *hc:* Mount Allison Univ., 1958; Royal Military Coll., Canada, 1980. Medaglia Benemerito della cultura (Italy), 1963; Univ. of Alberta National Award in painting and related arts, 1963. Centennial Decoration, 1967; OC 1972; Queen's Jubilee Medal, 1978. *Publications:* Artist at War, 1956 (Toronto); contrib. to Royal Commission Studies Report on National Development in the Arts, Letters and Sciences, Vol. II, 1951; contrib. various art and literary publications. *Address:* 1201, 100 Bronson Avenue, Ottawa, Ont. K1R 6G8, Canada.

COMINO, Demetrius, OBE 1963; President, Dexion-Comino International Ltd, 1973 (Chairman, 1947-73); *b* Australia, 4 Sept. 1902; *s* of John and Anna Comino, Greek origin, naturalized British; *m* 1935, Katerina Georgiadis; one *d*. *Educ:* University Coll., London. BSc 1st cl. hons Engrg 1923. Student Apprentice with The British Thompson Houston Co. Ltd, Rugby, until 1926; started own business, Krisson Printing Ltd, 1927; started present company, 1947. FRSA 1971; FBIM; Fellow, UCL, 1971. Golden Cross, King George I (Greece), 1967. *Publications:* contribs to official jl of Gk Chamber of Technology and to New Scientist. *Recreations:* thinking; preparing a book on result getting and problem solving and another on basic unifying concepts, and an educational foundation on the basis of these concepts. *Address:* Silver Birches, Oxford Road, Gerrards Cross, Bucks. *T:* Gerrards Cross 83170.

COMMAGER, Henry Steele, MA Oxon; MA Cantab; Professor of American History, Amherst College, since 1956; Professor of History, Columbia University, 1938-56; Hon. Professor, University of Santiago de Chile; *b* 25 Oct. 1902; *s* of James W. Commager and Anna Elizabeth Dan; *m* 1928; Evan Carroll; one *s* two *d*. *Educ:* Univ. of Chicago; Univ. of Copenhagen. AB, Univ. of Chicago, 1923; MA, 1924; PhD, 1928; Scholar Amer-Scand. Foundation, 1924-25; taught History New York Univ., 1926-29; Prof. of History, 1929-38. Lectr on American History, Cambridge Univ., 1942-43; Hon. Fellow, Peterhouse; Pitt Prof. of Amer. Hist., Cambridge Univ., 1947-48; Lectr, Salzburg Seminar in Amer. Studies, 1951; Harold Vyvyan Harmsworth Prof. of American History, Oxford Univ., 1952; Gotesman Lectr, Upsala Univ., 1953; Special State Dept lectr to German Univs, 1954; Zuskind Prof., Brandeis Univ., 1954-55; Prof., Univ. of Copenhagen, 1956; Visiting Prof., Univ. of Aix-Provence, summer 1957; Lectr, Univ. of Jerusalem, summer 1958; Commonwealth Lectr, Univ. of London, 1964; Harris Lectr, Northwestern Univ., 1964; Visiting Prof., Harvard, Chicago, Calif, City Univ. NY, Nebraska, etc. Editor-in-Chief, The Rise of the American Nation; Consultant, Office War Information in Britain and USA; Mem. US Army War Hist. Commn; Mem. Historians Commn on Air Power; special citation US Army; Consultant US Army attached to SHAEF, 1945. Trustee; American Scandinavian Foundation; American Friends of Cambridge Univ. Mem. of the Amer. Acad. of Arts and Letters, USA (Gold Medal for History, 1972). Hon degrees: EdD Rhode I; LittD: Washington, Ohio Wesleyan, Pittsburgh, Marietta, Hampshire Coll., 1970; Adelphi Coll., 1974; DLitt: Cambridge, Franklin-Marshall, W Virginia, Michigan State; LHD: Brandeis, Puget Sound, Hartford, Alfred; LLD: Merrimack, Carleton; Dickinson Coll., 1967; Franklin Pierce Coll., 1968; Columbia Univ., 1969; Ohio State, 1970; Wilson Coll., 1970; W. C. Post Coll., 1974; Alassa Univ., 1974; DHL: Maryville Coll., 1970; Univ. of Mass, 1972. Knight of Order of Dannebrog (Denmark), 1957 (1st cl.). *Publications:* Theodore Parker, 1936; Growth of the American Republic, 1930, 2 vols 1939; sub-ed (with S. E. Morison) Documents of American History, 1934, 9th edn 1974; Heritage of America (with A. Nevins), 1939; America: Story of a Free People (with A. Nevins), 1943, new edn 1966; Majority Rule and Minority Rights, 1944; Story of the Second World War, 1945; ed Tocqueville, Democracy in America, 1947; ed America in Perspective, 1947; ed The St Nicholas Anthology, 1947; The American Mind, 1950; The Blue and the Gray, 2 vols 1950; Living Ideas in America, 1951; Robert E. Lee, 1951; Freedom, Loyalty, Dissent, 1954 (special award, Hillman Foundation); Europe and America since 1942 (with G. Bruun), 1954; Joseph Story, 1956; The Spirit of Seventy-Six, 2 vols (with R. B. Morris); Crusaders for Freedom; History: Nature and Purpose, 1965; Freedom and Order, 1966; Search for a Usable Past, 1967; Was America a Mistake?, 1968; The Commonwealth of Learning, 1968; The American Character, 1970; The Use and Abuse of History, 1972; Britain Through American Eyes, 1974; The Defeat of America, 1974; Essays on the Enlightenment, 1974; The Empire of Reason, 1978; edited: Atlas of American Civil War; Winston Churchill, History of the English Speaking Peoples; Why the Confederacy Lost the Civil War; Major Documents of the Civil War; Theodore Parker, an Anthology; Immigration in American History;

Lester Ward and the Welfare State; The Struggle for Racial Equality; Joseph Story, Selected Writings and Judicial Opinions; Winston Churchill, Marlborough, 1968. *Recreation:* music. *Address:* Amherst College, Mass 01002, USA; (summer) Linton, Cambs, England. *Clubs:* Savile, Lansdowne (London); Century, Lotos (New York); St Botolph (Boston); (former Pres.) PEN (American Centre).

COMPSTON, Nigel Dean, CBE 1981; MA, MD, FRCP; Consulting Physician, retired; Royal Free Hospital, 1954–83; Royal Masonic Hospital, 1960–82; St Mary Abbot's Hospital, 1957–73; King Edward VII Hospital for Officers, since 1965; *b* 21 April 1918; *s* of George Dean Compston and Elsie Muriel Robinson; *m* 1942, Diana Mary (*née* Standish); two *s* one *d*. *Educ:* Royal Masonic Sch.; Trinity Hall, Cambridge; Middlesex Hospital. BA Cantab 1939; MRCS, LRCP 1942; MB, BCh Cantab 1942; MRCP 1942; MA, MD Cantab 1947; FRCP 1957. RAMC, 1942–47 (Temp. Lt-Col). Research Fellow, Middlesex Hosp. Medical Sch., 1948–51; E. G. Fearnsides Scholar, Cambridge, 1951; Mackenzie Mackinnon Research Fellow, RCP, 1951; Asst Prof. Medicine, Middlesex Hosp., 1952–54; Treasurer, RCP, 1970 (formerly Asst Registrar). Examiner: Pharmacology and Therapeutics, Univ. of London, 1958–63, Medicine, 1968; Medicine, RCP, 1965–; Medicine, Univ. of Cambridge, 1971–. Vice-Dean, Royal Free Hosp. Sch. of Medicine, 1968–70; Mem. Bd of Governors, The Royal Free Hosp., 1963–74. Hon. Editor Proc. RSM, 1966–70. *Publications:* Multiple Sclerosis (jtly), 1955; Recent Advances in Medicine (jtly), 1964, 1968, 1973, 1977, 1981. Contributions to learned jls. *Recreation:* golf. *Address:* Puckstye Cottage, Holtye Common, Cowden, Kent. *T:* Cowden 789. *Club:* Highgate Golf.

COMPSTON, Vice-Adm. Sir Peter (Maxwell), KCB 1970 (CB 1967); *b* 12 Sept. 1915; *s* of Dr G. D. Compston; *m* 1st, 1939, Valerie Bocquet (marr. diss); one *s* one *d*; 2nd, 1953, Angela Brickwood. *Educ:* Epsom Coll. Royal Navy, 1937; specialised in flying duties. Served 1939–45, HMS Ark Royal, Anson, Vengeance; HMCS Warrior, 1946; HMS Theseus, 1948–50 (despatches); Directorate of RN Staff Coll., 1951–53; Capt. 1955; in comd HMS Orwell and Capt. 'D' Plymouth, 1955–57; Imperial Defence Coll., 1958; Naval Attaché, Paris, 1960–62; in comd HMS Victorious, 1962–64; Rear-Adm., Jan. 1965; Chief of British Naval Staff and Naval Attaché, Washington, 1965–67; Flag Officer Flotillas, Western Fleet, 1967–68; Dep. Supreme Allied Comdr, Atlantic, 1968–70, retired. Dep. Chm., Cttee of Management, RNLI; Mem., Cttee, Royal Humane Soc. *Recreations:* theatre, country life. *Address:* Holmwood, Stroud, near Petersfield, Hants. *Club:* Army and Navy.

COMPTON, family name of **Marquess of Northampton.**

COMPTON, Earl; Daniel Bingham Compton; *b* 16 Jan. 1973; *s* and *heir* of Marquess of Northampton, *qv*.

COMPTON, Denis Charles Scott, CBE 1958; professional cricketer, retired 1957; Sunday Express Cricket Correspondent, since 1950; BBC Television Cricket Commentator, since 1958; *b* 23 May 1918; *m* 1st; one *s*; 2nd; two *s*; 3rd, 1975, Christine Franklin Tobias; one *d*. *Educ:* Bell Lane Sch., Hendon. First played for Middlesex, 1936. First played for England *v* New Zealand, 1937; *v* Australia, 1938; *v* West Indies, 1939; *v* India, 1946; *v* S Africa, 1947. Played in 78 Test matches; made 123 centuries in first-class cricket. Association football: mem. of Arsenal XI; England XI, 1943; Editor, Denis Compton's Annual, 1950–57. *Publications:* Playing for England, 1948; Testing Time for England, 1948; In Sun and Shadow, 1952; End of an Innings, 1958; Denis Compton's Test Diary, 1964; (jtly) Cricket and All That, 1978. *Recreation:* golf. *Address:* Royds House, Mandeville Place, W1M 6AE. *T:* 01-935 7733. *Clubs:* MCC; Wanderers (Johannesburg).

COMPTON, Sir Edmund (Gerald), GCB 1971 (KCB 1965, CB 1948); KBE 1955; MA; *b* 30 July 1906; *er s* of late Edmund Spencer Compton, MC, Pailton House, Rugby; *m* 1934, Betty Tresyllian, 2nd *d* of late Hakewill Tresyllian Williams, DL, JP, Churchill Court, Kidderminster; one *s* four *d*. *Educ:* Rugby (Scholar); New Coll., Oxford (Scholar); 1st Class Lit. Hum., 1929; Hon. Fellow 1972. Entered Home Civil Service, 1929; Colonial Office, 1930; transf. to HM Treasury, 1931; Private Sec. to Financial Sec. to Treasury, 1934–36; seconded to Min. of Aircraft Production as Private Sec. to Minister, 1940; Min. of Supply, 1941; Asst Sec., HM Treasury, 1942, Under-Sec., 1947, Third Sec., 1949–58; Comptroller and Auditor General, Exchequer and Audit Dept, 1958–66; Parly Comr for Administration, 1967–71, and in NI, 1969–71. Chm., English Local Govt Boundary Commn, 1971–78. Chairman: Irish Sailors and Soldiers Land Trust, 1946–; Miliburn Trust, 1968–; BBC Programmes Complaints Commn, 1972–81; Governing Body, Royal Acad. of Music, 1975–81. *Recreation:* music. *Address:* 1/80 Elm Park Gardens, SW10. *T:* 01-351 3790. *Clubs:* Athenæum, Boodle's.
See also Viscount De L'Isle.

COMPTON, Michael Graeme; Keeper of Museum Services, Tate Gallery, since 1970; *b* 29 Sept. 1927; *s* of Joseph Nield Compton, OBE, and Dorothy Margaret Townsend Compton; *m* 1952, Susan Paschal Benn; two *d*. *Educ:* Courtauld Institute, London (BA Hons History of Art). Asst to Director, Leeds City Art Gallery and Templenewsam, 1954–57; Keeper of Foreign Schools, Walker Art Gallery, Liverpool, 1957–59; Dir, Ferens Art Gall., Hull, 1960–65; Asst Keeper, Modern Collection, Tate Gall., 1965–70. Mem., Fine Arts Adv. Cttee, British Council. *Publications:* Optical and Kinetic Art, 1967; Pop Art, 1970; (jtly) Catalogue of Foreign Schools, Walker Art Gallery, 1963;

articles in art jls, exhibn catalogues. *Address:* Michaelmas Lodge, Rockfield Road, Oxted, Surrey RH8 0HB.

COMPTON, Robert Edward John; DL; Chairman, Time-Life International Ltd, since 1979; *b* 11 July 1922; *yr s* of late Major Edward Robert Francis Compton, JP, DL, and Sylvia Farquharson of Invercauld; *m* 1951, Ursula Jane Kenyon-Slaney; two *s*. *Educ:* Eton; Magdalen Coll., Oxford, 1940–41. Served War, Coldstream Guards, 1941–46 (4 medals, wounded); Mil. Asst to British Ambassador, Vienna (temp. Major), 1946. Studied fruit growing and horticulture (Diploma), 1946–48; with W. S. Crawford Ltd, Advertising Agency, 1951–54; Sen. Acct Exec., Crawfords Internat., 1954; joined Time International, 1954; advertising sales, 1954–58, UK Advtsg Dir, 1958–62; also Dir, Time-Life Internat. Ltd, 1958–79; New Projects Dir, Time-Life Internat. Europe, 1962–65; Public Affairs Dir, Europe, Time-Life Internat. Ltd, 1965. Chairman: Newby Hall Estate Co., 1964–69; CXL UK Ltd, 1971–73; Bd Dir, Extel Corp., Chicago, 1973–80; Dir, Transtel Communications Ltd, Slough, 1974–. FInstD 1958. Vice-Chm., National Trust, Yorks, 1970–, also Mem. Properties Cttee and Gardens Panel, London, 1970–, and Pres., Dales Centre Nat. Trust, 1979–; Pres., Ripon Tourist Assoc., 1977–. High Sheriff, 1978–79, DL 1981, N Yorks. *Recreations:* gardening, shooting, golf. *Address:* Newby Hall, Ripon, Yorkshire. *T:* Boroughbridge 2583; 42 Ennismore Gardens, SW7. *Clubs:* White's, Buck's; Swinley Forest (Ascot).
See also Captain A. A. C. Farquharson of Invercauld.

COMPTON, Robert Herbert K.; *see* Keppel-Compton.

COMPTON, Air Vice-Marshal William Vernon C.; *see* Crawford-Compton.

COMPTON MILLER, Sir John (Francis), Kt 1969; MBE (mil.) 1945; TD; MA Oxon; Barrister-at-Law; Senior Registrar, The Family Division (formerly Probate, Divorce and Admiralty Division), 1964–72 (Registrar, 1946–64), retired 1972; *b* 11 May 1900; 3rd *s* of Frederic Richard Miller, MD and Effie Anne, *d* of Samson Rickard Stuttaford; *m* 1st, 1925, Alice Irene Mary (*d* 1931), *er d* of John Scales Bakewell; one *s*; 2nd, 1936, Mary, *e d* of Rev. Alexander MacEwen Baird-Smith; one *s* one *d*. *Educ:* Colet Court; St Paul's Sch.; New Coll., Oxford. Called to Bar, Inner Temple, 1923; went the Western Circuit, practised Criminal, Common Law, Probate and Divorce Courts. Major, Inns of Court Regt, TA, 1936; OC No 21 Recep. Unit; Asst Comdt, Army Tech. Sch. (Boys), Chepstow. A Deputy Judge Advocate, United Kingdom and North West Europe, 1969. Examiner, Council of Legal Education, 1951–64. UK Rep., Council of Europe Sub-Cttee on Registration of Wills, 1970. *Publications:* I Tried My Hand at Verse, 1968; Further Verse, 1970; The Miraculous Cornfield, 1978; The Chinese Saucer, 1980; Poems '81, 1981; Selected Poems, 1982. *Recreations:* painting (Dip., City of London Art Exhibn, 1979), versing, heraldic art. *Address:* 2 Crown Office Row, Temple, EC4. *T:* 01-583 1352. *Club:* Garrick.

COMRIE, Rear-Adm. Alexander Peter, CB 1982; Director General Aircraft (Navy), since 1981; *b* 27 March 1924; *s* of Robert Duncan Comrie and Phyllis Dorothy Comrie; *m* 1945, Madeleine Irene (*née* Bullock); one *s* one *d*. *Educ:* Sutton Valence Sch., Kent; County Technical Coll., Wednesbury, Staffs, and in the Royal Navy. Joined Royal Navy, 1945; served in cruisers, frigates, minesweepers and RN air stations; RCDS 1973; Captain HMS Daedalus, 1974; Director of Weapons Coordination and Acceptance (Naval), 1975; Deputy Controller Aircraft, MoD, 1978–81. IEE Electronics Divisional Bd, 1976; IEE Membership Panel, 1977; Mem. Council, IEE, 1981. FIEE 1975; FRAeS 1978. *Recreations:* sailing, swimming, DIY. *Address:* c/o National Westminster Bank Ltd, 23 West Street, Havant, Hants PO9 1EU. *Clubs:* Army and Navy, Royal Commonwealth Society; Hayling Island Sailing.

COMYN, Hon. Sir James, Kt 1978; **Hon. Mr Justice Comyn;** Judge of the High Court of Justice, Queen's Bench Division, since 1979 (Family Division, 1978–79); *b* Co. Dublin, 8 March 1921; *o s* of late James Comyn, QC, Dublin and late Mary Comyn; *m* 1967, Anne, *d* of late Philip Chaundler, MC, Biggleswade, and of Mrs Chaundler, Cambridge; one *s* one *d*. *Educ:* Oratory Sch.; New Coll., Oxford (MA). Ex-Pres. of Oxford Union. Inner Temple, 1942; called to Irish Bar, 1947; QC 1961. Recorder of Andover, 1964–71; Hon. Recorder of Andover, 1972; a Recorder of the Crown Court, 1972–77. Master of the Bench, Inner Temple, 1968–; Mem. and Chm., Bar Council, 1973–74. A Governor of the Oratory Sch., 1964. Owner of the "Clareville" herd of pedigree Aberdeen-Angus and the "Beaufield" herd of pedigree Herefords. *Publications:* Their Friends at Court, 1973; Irish at Law: a selection of famous and unusual cases, 1981. *Recreations:* farming, golf. *Address:* Royal Courts of Justice, Strand, WC2; Belvin, Tara, Co. Meath, Ireland. *T:* Navan 25111. *Clubs:* Athenæum, Royal Dublin Society.

COMYNS, Jacqueline Roberta; a Metropolitan Stipendiary Magistrate, since 1982; *b* 27 April 1943; *d* of late Jack and of Belle Fisher; *m* 1963, Malcolm John Comyns, medical practitioner; one *s*. *Educ:* Hendon County Grammar Sch.; London Sch. of Econs and Pol. Science (LLB Hons 1964). Called to the Bar, Inner Temple, 1969. Practised on South Eastern Circuit. *Recreations:* theatre, bridge, travel. *Address:* 4 Brook Way, Chigwell, Essex IG7 6AA. *T:* 01-500 3020.

CONAN DOYLE, Air Comdt Dame Jean (Lena Annette), (Lady Bromet), DBE 1963 (OBE 1948); Director of the Women's Royal Air Force, 1963–66, retired; *b* 21 Dec. 1912; *d* of late Sir Arthur Conan Doyle and Lady Conan Doyle (née Jean Leckie); *m* 1965, Air Vice-Marshal Sir Geoffrey Bromet, *qv. Educ:* Granville House, Eastbourne. Joined No 46 (Co. of Sussex) ATS, RAF Company, Sept. 1938; commnd in WAAF, 1940; served in UK, 1939-45; commnd in RAF, 1949; Comd WRAF Admin Officer: BAFO, Germany, 1947-50; HQ Tech. Trg. Comd, 1950-52 and 1962-63; Dep. Dir, 1952-54 and 1960-62; OC, RAF Hawkinge, 1956-59; Inspector of the WRAF, 1954-56 and 1959-60. Hon. ADC to the Queen, 1963-66. A Governor, Star and Garter Home; Vice-Pres., Officers Pension Soc.; Pres., Not Forgotten Assoc. Holder of USA copyright on her father's literary works publd 1907-26. *Address:* Flat 6, 72 Cadogan Square, SW1; Home Green, Littlestone-on-Sea, New Romney, Kent. *Clubs:* Naval and Military, Royal Air Force.

CONANT, Sir John (Ernest Michael), 2nd Bt *cr* 1954; farmer and landowner, since 1949; *b* 24 April 1923; *s* of Sir Roger Conant, 1st Bt, CVO, and Daphne, Lady Conant, *d* of A. E. Learoyd; *S* father, 1973; *m* 1950, Periwinkle Elizabeth, *d* of late Dudley Thorp, Kimbolton, Hunts; two *s* two *d* (and one *s* decd). *Educ:* Eton; Corpus Christi Coll., Cambridge (BA Agric). Served in Grenadier Guards, 1942-45; at CCC Cambridge, 1946-49. Farming in Rutland, 1950-; High Sheriff of Rutland, 1960. *Recreations:* fishing, shooting, tennis. *Heir: s* Simon Edward Christopher Conant, *b* 13 Oct. 1958. *Address:* Lyndon Hall, Oakham, Rutland LE15 8TU. *T:* Manton 275.

CONCANNON, Rt. Hon. John Dennis, (Rt. Hon. Don Concannon), PC 1978; MP (Lab) Mansfield, since 1966; *b* 16 May 1930; *m* 1953, Iris May Wilson; two *s* two *d. Educ:* Rossington Sec. Sch. Coldstream Guards, 1947-53; Mem. Nat. Union of Mineworkers, 1953-66; Branch Official, 1960-65. Mem., Mansfield Town Council, 1962-66. Asst Govt Whip, 1968-70; Opposition Whip, 1970-74; Vice-Chamberlain, HM Household, 1974; Parly Under-Sec. of State, NI Office, 1974-76; Minister of State, NI Office, 1976-79; Opposition Spokesman for Defence, 1979-80, for NI, 1980-. *Recreations:* cricket, basket-ball. *Address:* 69 Skegby Lane, Mansfield, Notts. *T:* Mansfield 27235.

CONDON, Denis David, OBE 1964; retired; Senior Representative at Lloyd's of London for Neilson McCarthy, Consultants, 1968-75; *b* 23 Oct. 1910; *s* of Capt. D. Condon and Mary A. E. Condon; *m* 1933, Mary Marson; one *d. Educ:* Paston Grammar Sch., North Walsham, Norfolk. Journalist until 1939. War Service with Royal Artillery, UK and Burma (Major). Joined India Office, 1946; CRO, 1947; served India, Ceylon, Australia, Nigeria; Head of News Dept, CO, 1967-68. *Recreations:* fishing, bird-watching, gardening. *Address:* Rose Cottage, Weir, Dulverton, Somerset. *T:* Dulverton 23309. *Clubs:* Gymkhana (Delhi); Australasian Pioneers (Sydney).

CONGLETON, 8th Baron *cr* 1841; **Christopher Patrick Parnell**; Bt 1766; *b* 11 March 1930; *s* of 6th Baron Congleton (*d* 1932) and Hon. Edith Mary Palmer Howard (MBE 1941) (she *m* 2nd, 1946, Flight Lieut A. E. R. Aldridge, who died 1950), *d* of late R. J. B. Howard and late Lady Strathcona and Mount Royal; *S* brother, 1967; *m* 1955, Anna Hedvig, *d* of G. A. Sommerfelt, Oslo, Norway; two *s* three *d. Educ:* Eton; New Coll., Oxford. Mem., Salisbury and Wilton RDC, 1964-74; Vice-President: RDCA, 1973-74; Assoc. of District Councils, 1974-79; Chm., Salisbury and S Wilts Museum, 1972-77; Pres., Nat. Ski Federation of GB, 1976-81. *Heir: s* Hon. John Patrick Christian Parnell, *b* 17 March 1959. *Address:* Ebbesbourne Wake, Salisbury, Wilts.

CONGREVE, Ambrose, CBE 1965; responsible for Humphreys & Glasgow Ltd, since 1939; *b* London, 4 April 1907; *s* of Major John Congreve, DL, JP, and Helena Blanche Irene Ponsonby, *d* of 8th Earl of Bessborough; *m* 1935, Marjorie, *d* of Dr Arthur Graham Glasgow, London, and Richmond, Virginia, and Margaret, *d* of John P. Branch, President of Virginia's Merchants National Bank. *Educ:* Eton; Trinity Coll., Cambridge. Employed by Unilever Ltd, in England and China, 1927-36; joined Humphreys & Glasgow Ltd, as Director, 1936; responsible for the company, 1939-, in succession to Dr Glasgow who founded the firm in 1892. Served War of 1939-45: Air Intelligence for Plans and Bomber Command, then Min. of Supply. Hon. Fellow IChemE 1967. *Recreation:* collection and large-scale outdoor cultivation in Ireland of plant species and hybrids from all over the world. *Address:* Mount Congreve, Waterford, Ireland. *T:* Waterford 84103; (London office) 22 Carlisle Place, SW1P 1JA. *T:* 01-828 1234. *Club:* Beefsteak.

CONI, Peter Richard Carstairs, QC 1980; *b* 20 Nov. 1935; *s* of late Eric Charles Coni and Leslie Sybil Carstairs (née Pearson). *Educ:* Uppingham; St Catharine's Coll., Cambridge (MA). Called to the Bar, Inner Temple, 1960. Steward, Henley Royal Regatta, 1974 (Chm. Cttee of Management, 1977-); Vice-Pres., London Rowing Club, 1977-; Member: Exec. Cttee, Amateur Rowing Assoc., 1968- (Chm., 1970-77); Exec. Cttee, Central Council of Physical Recreation, 1978-80; Thames Water Authority, 1978-. *Recreations:* rowing, sports administration, good food, modern art. *Address:* 3 Churton Place, SW1. *T:* 01-828 2135. *Clubs:* Athenæum, Garrick, London Rowing; Leander (Henley-on-Thames).

CONINGSBY, Thomas Arthur Charles; Chancellor of the Diocese of York, since 1977; Vicar General of the Province of York, since 1980; *b* 21 April 1933; *s* of Francis Charles and Eilleen Rowena Coningsby; *m* 1959, Elaine Mary Coningsby; two *s* three *d. Educ:* Epsom; Queens' Coll., Cambridge (MA). Called to the Bar, Gray's Inn, 1957. Member, General Synod, 1970-.

Recreation: lawn tennis. *Address:* Leyfields, Chipstead, Surrey CR3 3SG. *T:* Downland 53304.

CONLAN, Bernard; MP (Lab) Gateshead (East) since 1964; Engineer; *b* 24 Oct. 1923; *m* ; one *d. Educ:* Manchester Primary and Secondary Schs. Mem., AEU, 1940-, Officer, 1943-. City Councillor, Manchester, 1954-66. Joined Labour Party, 1942; contested (Lab) High Peak, 1959. A Vice-Chm., Parly Lab. Party Trade Union Gp, 1974-. Member: House of Commons Expenditure Cttee (since inception), 1971-79; Select Cttee on Defence, 1979-. *Address:* House of Commons, SW1; 33 Beccles Road, Sale, Cheshire.

CONN, Edward, CBE 1979; Chief Veterinary Officer, Department of Agriculture, Northern Ireland, since 1958 (Veterinary Officer, 1947); *b* 25 March 1918; *s* of late Edward and Elizabeth Conn; *m* 1st, 1943, Kathleen Victoria Sandford (*d* 1974); three *d* ; 2nd, 1975, Lilian Frances Miley. *Educ:* Coleraine Academical Instn; Royal (Dick) Veterinary Sch., Edinburgh Univ. Qual. Vet. Surgeon, 1940; Diploma; MRCVS 1940. Gen. practice, Coleraine, 1940-43; Chief Vet. Officer to Hampshire Cattle Breeders, 1943-47. Governor, Coleraine Academical Instn, 1972-. *Recreations:* golf, walking; watching all sports, particularly Rugby and athletics. *Address:* Dunedin, 4 Brooklyn Avenue, Bangor, N Ireland BT20 5RB. *T:* Bangor 2383. *Clubs:* Clandeboye Golf; Bangor Rugby and Athletic.

CONN, Prof. John Farquhar Christie, DSc; CEng; FRINA; John Elder Professor of Naval Architecture, University of Glasgow, 1957-73; *b* 5 July 1903; *s* of Alexander Aberdein Conn and Margaret Rhind Wilson; *m* 1935, Doris Maude Yeatman; one *s* one *d. Educ:* Robert Gordon's Coll., Aberdeen; Glasgow Univ. Apprenticeship at Alexander Hall and Co. Ltd, Aberdeen, 1920-25; employed in several shipyards; Scientific staff, Ship Div., National Physical Laboratory, 1929-44; Chief Naval Architect, British Shipbuilding Research Association, 1945-57. Hon. Vice-Pres., RINA. *Publications:* various papers in Trans. of Royal Instn of Naval Architects and other learned societies. *Recreations:* music, reading. *Address:* 14 Elm Walk, Bearsden, Glasgow G61 3BQ. *T:* 041-942 4640.

CONNALLY, John Bowden; lawyer; *b* 27 Feb. 1917; *s* of John Bowden Connally and Lela (née Wright); *m* 1940, Idanell Brill; two *s* one *d. Educ:* Univ. of Texas (LLB). Served US Navy, 1941-46. Pres. and Gen. Manager, KVET radio stn, 1946-49; Admin. Asst to Lyndon Johnson, 1949; employed with Powell, Wirtz & Rauhut, 1950-52; Attorney to Richardson & Bass, oil merchants, 1952-61; Sec. US Navy, 1961; Governor of Texas, 1962-68; Secretary of the Treasury, USA, 1971-72. Member: President's Adv. Cttee on Exec. Organisation, 1969-70; President's Foreign Intelligence Adv. Bd, 1972-74 and 1976-; US Adv. Cttee on reform of Internat. Monetary System, 1973-74; Partner, Vinson Elkins, 1972-; Director: Falconbridge Nickel Mines, 1973-; First City Bancorporation of Texas, 1974-; Justin Industries Inc., 1975-; First City National Bank of Floresville, Texas, 1975-; Dr Pepper Company, 1977-; The American Trauma Soc., 1977-; The Methodist Hospital, 1977-; Continental Airlines Inc., 1978-. Mem. and Trustee, Andrew W. Mellon Foundn, 1973-. *Address:* c/o Vinson Elkins, First City National Bank Building, Houston, Texas 77002, USA.

CONNELL, Sir Charles (Gibson), Kt 1952; Consultant, Connell & Connell, WS, 10 Dublin Street, Edinburgh; *b* 11 March 1899; *s* of late Sir Isaac Connell, SSC, and Mary Jane (née Gibson); *m* 1927, Constance Margaret Weir (*d* 1976); one *s* one *d. Educ:* Melville Coll., Edinburgh; Edinburgh Univ. 2nd Lieut RFA, 1917-19. WS 1923; BL Edinburgh, 1923. JP City of Edinburgh, 1933. Secretary: Royal Scottish Agricultural Benevolent Instn, 1935-66; Scottish Agricultural Arbiters Assoc., 1935-66; Dir, The Edinburgh Building Soc., 1937-79; Life Governor, Melville Coll. Trust. Member: Nature Conservancy, 1961-73 (Chm., Scottish Cttee, 1961-72); Dept Cttee on Registration of Title to Land in Scotland, 1963; Pres., Scottish Wildlife Trust; Hon. Vice-Pres., Selborne Soc. Pres., Scottish Unionist Assoc., 1944-45 (Joint Hon. Sec., 1938-54); Hon. Pres., Scottish Ornithologists Club. Hon. FRZSScot 1979. Hon. LLD Dundee, 1976. *Publications:* (ed) 3rd, 4th and 5th Edns (1961) of Connell on the Agricultural Holdings (Scotland) Acts. *Recreations:* wildlife conservation, gardening. *Address:* 12 Abbotsford Park, Edinburgh EH10 5DZ. *T:* 031-447 2026. *Clubs:* Caledonian, New (Edinburgh).

CONNELL, Charles Percy; Puisne Judge, Kenya Colony, 1951-64, retired; *b* 1 Oct. 1902; *s* of late C. R. Connell, Barrister-at-Law and late K. Adlard; *m* 1946, Mary O'Rourke. *Educ:* Charterhouse; New Coll., Oxford (Hons, Jurisprudence). Called to Bar, Lincoln's Inn, 1927. Joined Kenya Judicial Service, 1938 (Resident Magistrate). Served War of 1939-45 (8th Army Clasp and war medals); commissioned King's African Rifles, 1941; British Military Administration (Legal and Judicial), Eritrea and Tripolitania, 1942-46. Acting Puisne Judge, Kenya, 1950, retired 1964. *Recreations:* tennis, cricket and trout fishing. *Address:* c/o National Westminster Bank, 14 Sloane Square, SW1.

CONNELL, George Edward, PhD; FRSC 1975; President and Vice-Chancellor, University of Western Ontario, since 1977; *b* 20 June 1930; *m* 1955, Sheila Horan; two *s* two *d. Educ:* Univ. of Toronto (BA, PhD Biochemistry). Post-doctoral Fellow, Div. of Applied Biol., National Res. Council, Ottawa, Ont, 1955-56; Fellow, National Science Foundn (US), Dept of Biochem., New York University Coll. of Medicine, 1956-57; University of Toronto: Asst Prof. of Biochem., 1957-62; Associate Prof. of Biochem., 1962-65; Prof. and Chm. Dept of Biochem., 1965-70; Associate Dean, Faculty of Med., 1972-74; Vice-Pres., Res. and Planning, 1974-77. Mem., MRC of Canada, 1965-70. *Publications:* scientific papers in jls incl. Canadian Jl of Biochem., Biochemical Jl (UK), and Jl of Immunol. *Recreations:* squash, skiing. *Address:* University of Western Ontario, London, Ont, Canada. *T:* 679-2322. *Clubs:* London Hunt and Country, University of London (London, Ont).

CONNELL, John MacFarlane; Member of Management Committee, The Distillers Company plc, since 1971; Chairman, United Glass Ltd, since 1979; *b* 29 Dec. 1924; *s* of late John Maclean Connell and Mollie Isobel MacFarlane; *m* 1949, Jean Matheson Sutherland Mackay, *d* of late Major George Sutherland Mackay and late Christine Bourne; two *s. Educ:* Stowe; Christ Church, Oxford. Joined Tanqueray, Gordon & Co. Ltd, 1946, Export Dir 1954, Man. Dir 1962-70; Dir, Distillers Co. Ltd, 1965; Chm., Gin Rectifiers and Distillers Assoc., 1968-71. Pres., Royal Warrant Holders Assoc., 1975. *Recreations:* golf, shooting. *Address:* 20 St James's Square, SW1Y 4JF. *T:* 01-930 1040. *Club:* Royal and Ancient (St Andrews).

CONNELL, Michael Bryan, QC 1981; barrister-at-law; a Recorder of the Crown Court, since 1980; *b* 6 Aug. 1939; *s* of Lorraine Connell and of late Joan Connell; *m* 1965, Anne Joan Connell; three *s* one *d. Educ:* Harrow; Brasenose Coll., Oxford (MA Jurisprudence). Called to the Bar, Inner Temple, 1962. *Recreations:* steeplechasing, cricket, foxhunting. *Address:* Whitewalls, Kinsbourne Green, Harpenden, Herts. *T:* Harpenden 68667. *Clubs:* Buck's, Royal Automobile.

CONNELL, Dame Ninette; *see* de Valois, Dame Ninette.

CONNELL, Philip Henry; Physician, The Bethlem Royal Hospital and The Maudsley Hospital, since 1963; *b* 6 July 1921; *s* of George Henry Connell and Evelyn Hilda Sykes; *m* 1st, 1948, Marjorie Helen Gilham; two *s* ; 2nd, 1973, Cecily Mary Harper. *Educ:* St Paul's Sch.; St Bartholomew's Hosp., London. MD, BS, MRCS, FRCP, FRCPsych, DPM (academic). St Stephen's Hosp., Fulham Road, 1951-53; Bethlem Royal and the Maudsley Hosp., 1953-57; Cons. Psychiatrist, Newcastle Gen. Hosp. and Physician i/c Child Psychiatry Unit, Newcastle Gen. Hosp. in assoc. with King's Coll., Durham Univ., and Assoc. Phys., Royal Victoria Infirm., 1957-63. Extensive nat. and internat. work on drug addiction and dependence (incl. work for WHO, Council of Europe and CENTO), and on maladjusted and psychiatrically ill children and adolescents. Mem. numerous adv. cttees, working parties, etc; Consultant Adviser (Addiction) to DHSS, 1968-71 and 1981-; Pres., Soc. for Study of Addiction, 1973-76; Chairman: Inst. for Study of Drug Dependence, 1975-; Scientific and Professional Adv. Bd, Internat. Council on Alcohol and Addictions, 1971-79; Member: Council, RMPA, 1962-67; GMC, 1979-; Vice-Pres., RCPsych, 1979-81 (Chm., Child and Adolescent Specialist Section, 1971-74). Mem., editorial bds, various jls. *Publications:* Amphetamine Psychosis (monograph), 1958; (ed jtly) Cannabis and Man, 1975; numerous chapters in books, papers in sci. jls and proc. sci. confs. *Recreations:* theatre, bridge, tennis. *Address:* 25 Oxford Road, Putney, SW15 2LG. *T:* 01-788 1416; 21 Wimpole Street, W1M 7AD. *T:* 01-636 2220. *Club:* Athenæum.

CONNELL-SMITH, Prof. Gordon Edward, PhD; FRHistS; Professor of Contemporary History, University of Hull, since 1973; *b* 23 Nov. 1917; 2nd *s* of George Frederick Smith and Margaret Smith (*née* Woolerton); surname changed to Connell-Smith by deed-poll, 1942; *m* 1954, Wendy Ann, *o d* of John Bertram and Kathleen Tomlinson; one *s* one *d. Educ:* Richmond County Sch., Surrey; University Coll. of SW of England, Exeter (BA); Birkbeck Coll., London (PhD). FRHistS 1959. Served War, RA and Staff, 1940-46 (Staff Major). Julian Corbett Prize, Inst. of Historical Res., 1949; University of Hull: Staff Tutor/Lectr in Adult Educn and History Depts, 1952-63; Sen. Lectr, 1963-69; Reader in Contemp. Internat. History, 1969-73. Mem., Ctteeof Management, Univ. of London Inst. of Latin Amer. Studies, 1973-. Chm., Latin American Newsletters, Ltd, London, 1969-72. *Publications:* Forerunners of Drake, 1954; Pattern of the Post-War World, 1957; The Inter-American System, 1966 (Spanish edn 1971); (co-author) The Relevance of History, 1972; The United States and Latin America, 1974 (Spanish edn 1977); contrib. to Bull. Inst. of Historical Res., Contemp. Rev., Econ. History Rev., Eng. Historical Rev., History, Internat. Affairs, Jl of Latin Amer. Studies, World Today, etc. *Recreations:* travel, sport. *Address:* Department of History, The University, Cottingham Road, Hull HU6 7RX. *T:* Hull 46311.

CONNELLY, Thomas John; Director of Services, General and Municipal Workers' Union, since 1978; *b* 24 Dec. 1925; *s* of William and Jane Connelly; *m* 1952, Naomi Shakow; one *s* one *d. Educ:* Priory St Elementary Sch., Colchester; Ruskin Coll.; Lincoln Coll., Oxford. BA 1955. Research Officer: Amalgamated Soc. of Woodworkers, 1955-63; G&MWU, 1963-66; Adviser, Industrial Relations Prices and Incomes Bd, 1966-68; various posts, finally as Chief Officer, Race Relations Bd, 1968-77; apptd Chief Executive, Commn for Racial Equality, 1977, but withdrew from appt. *Publication:* The Woodworkers 1860-1960, 1960. *Recreations:* reading, walking. *Address:* 4 Grena Gardens, Richmond, Surrey. *T:* 01-940 0471.

CONNER, Rearden; (pen-name of Patrick Reardon Connor), MBE 1967; novelist and short-story writer; *b* 19 Feb. 1907; *s* of John and Bridie Connor; *m* 1942, Malinka Marie Smith; no *c. Educ:* Christian Brothers Schs: Presentation Coll., Cork. Worked in Min. of Aircraft Production, during War, in Research and Development of Equipment. Carried on this field, after war, in Min. of Supply, and later in Min. of Aviation and Min. of Technology. Critic of fiction, The Fortnightly, 1935-37, also on Books of the Month; Reader of fiction for Cassell, 1948-56. Work has been included in: Best Short Stories Anthology (twice); Pick of To-Day's Short Stories; Whit Burnett anthology (USA), Stories of the Forties. *Publications:* Shake Hands with The Devil, 1933 (Literary Guild Selection in USA; filmed, 1958); Rude Earth, 1934; Salute to Aphrodite, 1935 (USA); I am Death, 1936; Time to Kill, 1936 (USA); Men Must Live, 1937; The Sword of Love, 1938; Wife of Colum, 1939; The Devil Among the Tailors, 1947; My Love to the Gallows, 1949; Hunger of the Heart, 1950; The Singing Stone, 1951; The House of Cain, 1952; (under *pseudonym* Peter Malin): To Kill is My Vocation, 1939; River, Sing Me a Song, 1939; Kobo the Brave, 1950. *Recreations:* listening to music; going to the theatre. *Address:* 79 Balsdean Road, Woodingdean, Brighton, Sussex BN2 6PG. *T:* Brighton 34032.

CONNERY, Sean, (Thomas Connery); actor; *b* 25 Aug. 1930; *s* of Joseph and Euphamia Connery; *m* 1st, 1962, Diane (marr. diss. 1974), *d* of Sir Raphael West Cilento, *qv*, and Lady Cilento; one *s* (and one step *d*); 2nd, 1975, Micheline Roquebrune. Served Royal Navy. Dir, Tantallon Films Ltd, 1972-. Has appeared in films: No Road Back, 1956; Action of the Tiger, 1957; Another Time, Another Place, 1957; Hell Drivers, 1958; Tarzan's Greatest Adventure, 1959; Darby O'Gill and the Little People, 1959; On the Fiddle, 1961; The Longest Day, 1962; The Frightened City, 1962; Woman of Straw, 1964; The Hill, 1965; A Fine Madness, 1966; Shalako, 1968; The Molly Maguires, 1968; The Red Tent (1st Russian co-production), 1969; The Anderson Tapes, 1970; The Offence, 1973; Zardoz, 1973; Ransom, 1974; Murder on the Orient Express, 1974; The Wind and the Lion, 1975; The Man Who Would Be King, 1975; Robin and Marian, 1976; The Great Train Robbery, 1978; Cuba, 1978; Meteor, 1979; Outland, 1981; The Man with the Deadly Lens, 1982; *as James Bond:* Dr No, 1963; From Russia With Love, 1964; Goldfinger, 1965; Thunderball, 1965; You Only Live Twice, 1967; Diamonds are Forever, 1971. Hon. DLitt Heriot-Watt, 1981. *Recreations:* oil painting, golf, reading, cooking. *Address:* Michael S. Ovitz, Creative Artists Agency Inc., Suite 1400, 1888 Century Park East, Los Angeles, Calif 90067, USA.

CONNOR, Jeremy George; Metropolitan Stipendiary Magistrate, since 1979; *b* 14 Dec. 1938; *s* of Joseph Connor and Mabel Emmeline (*née* Adams), ARCA. *Educ:* Beaumont; University Coll., London (LLB). Called to the Bar, Middle Temple, 1961; S Eastern Circuit. Apptd to Treasury List, Central Criminal Court, 1973; a Chm., Inner London Juvenile Cts, 1980-; Member: Exec. Council, British Acad. of Forensic Scis, 1980-; Central Council of Probation and After-Care Cttees for England and Wales, 1981-. Underwriting Mem. of Lloyd's. Freeman, City of London, 1980; Liveryman, Fanmakers' Co., 1981. *Publications:* chapter in Archbold, Criminal Pleading, Evidence and Practice, 38th and 39th edns. *Recreations:* travel, theatre, occasional broadcasting. *Address:* Marlborough Street Magistrates' Court, WC2. *Clubs:* Garrick, Royal Society of Medicine.

CONNOR, Patrick Reardon; *see* Conner, Rearden.

CONOLLY, Mrs Yvonne Cecile; Inspector of Primary Schools, Inner London Education Authority, since 1981; *b* 12 June 1939; *d* of Hugh Augustus and Blanche Foster; *m* 1965, Michael Patrick Conolly; one *d. Educ:* Westwood High Sch., Jamaica; Shortwood Coll., Jamaica (Teachers' CertEd); Polytechnic, N London (BEd Hons Primary Educn). Primary school teacher: Jamaica, 1960-63; London, 1963-68; Head Teacher, London, 1969-78; ILEA Inspector, Multi-ethnic Education, 1978-81. Member: Home Secretary's Adv. Council on Race Relations, 1977-; IBA, 1982-; Consumer Protection Adv. Cttee, 1974-75. Governor, former Centre for Information and Advice on Educnl Disadvantage, 1975-80; (first) Chm., Caribbean Teachers' Assoc., 1974-76. *Publication:* (contributor) Mango Spice, book of 44 Caribbean songs for schools, 1981. *Recreations:* special interest in the activities of ethnic minority groups; travelling, conversing. *Address:* 10 Beatrice Road, N4 4PD. *T:* (office) 01-499 4141.

CONOLLY-CAREW, family name of **Baron Carew.**

CONQUEST, (George) Robert (Acworth), OBE 1955; writer; *b* 15 July 1917; *s* of late Robert Folger Westcott Conquest and Rosamund, *d* of H. A. Acworth, CIE; *m* 1st, 1942, Joan Watkins (marr. diss. 1948); two *s* ; 2nd, 1948, Tatiana Mihailova (marr. diss. 1962); 3rd, 1964, Caroleen Macfarlane (marr. diss. 1978); 4th, 1979, Elizabeth, *d* of late Col Richard D. Neece, USAF. *Educ:* Winchester; Magdalen Coll., Oxford. MA Oxon 1972; DLitt 1975. Oxf. and Bucks LI, 1939-46; Foreign Service, 1946-56; Fellow, LSE, 1956-58; Fellow, Univ. of Buffalo, 1959-60; Literary Editor, The Spectator, 1962-63; Fellow: Columbia Univ., 1964-65; Woodrow Wilson International Center, 1976-77; Hoover Instn, 1977-79 and 1981-; Distinguished Vis. Scholar, Heritage Foundn, 1980-81. FRSL 1972. *Publications:* Poems, 1955; A World of Difference, 1955; (ed) New Lines, 1956; Common Sense About Russia, 1960; Power and Policy in the USSR, 1961; Courage of Genius, 1962; Between Mars and Venus, 1962; (ed) New Lines II, 1963; (with Kingsley Amis) The Egyptologists, 1965; The Great Terror, 1968; Arias from a Love Opera, 1969; The Nation Killers, 1970; Lenin, 1972; Kolyma, 1978; The Abomination of Moab, 1979; Present Danger, 1979; Forays, 1979; We and They, 1980. *Address:* c/o Brown Shipley & Co., Founder's Court, Lothbury, EC2. *Club:* Travellers'.

CONRAN, (George) Loraine, FMA; Director, Manchester City Art Galleries, 1962-76; *b* 29 March 1912; *o s* of Col George Hay Montgomery Conran; *m* 1st, 1938, Jacqueline Elspeth Norah Thullier O'Neill Roe (marr. diss. 1970); one *s* one *d* (and one *d* decd); 2nd, 1970, Elizabeth Margaret Johnston; one *d. Educ:* RNC Dartmouth. Museum and Art Gallery, Birmingham, 1935; Walker Art Gallery, Liverpool, 1936; Southampton Art Gallery, 1938; Curator, The Iveagh Bequest, Kenwood, 1950. Pres., Museums Assoc. (Hon. Sec., 1959-64); Hon. Sec., Contemporary Art Soc., 1959-65. Chm., Jt Cttee of Museums Assoc. and Carnegie UK Trust; Member: British Nat. Cttee, Internat. Council of Museums, 1959-71; Ct, RCA. Hon. MA Manchester, 1973. Served War of 1939-45 (despatches). *Address:* 31 Thorngate, Barnard Castle, Co. Durham DL12 8QB.

CONRAN, Shirley Ida; writer; *b* 21 Sept. 1932; *d* of W. Thirlby Pearce and Ida Pearce; *m* 1955, Terence Conran; two *s. Educ:* St Paul's Girls' Sch.; Southern College of Art, Portsmouth. Fabric Designer and Director of Conran Fabrics, 1956-62; Member, Selection Cttee, Design Centre, 1961-69. Journalist; (first) Woman's Editor, Observer Colour Magazine, 1964; Woman's Editor, Daily Mail, 1969; Life and Style Editor, Over 21, 1972-74. *Publications:* Superwoman, 1975; Superwoman Year Book, 1976; Superwoman in Action, 1977; (with E. Sidney) Action Woman, 1979; Lace (novel), 1982; Shirley Conran's Magic Garden, 1983. *Recreations:* reading, swimming, Yoga. *Address:* c/o Coutts Bank, 14 Lombard Street, EC4.

CONRAN, Terence Orby; Chairman: Habitat Group Ltd, since 1971; Conran Associates, since 1971; Habitat France SA, since 1973; Conran Stores Inc., since 1977; J. Hepworth & Son Ltd, since 1981 (Director, since 1979); Habitat/Mothercare PLC, since 1982; Director: Conran Ink Ltd, since 1969; The Neal Street Restaurant, since 1972; Conran Roche Ltd, since 1982; Electra Risk Capital, since 1981; *b* 4 Oct. 1931; *m* ; two *s* ; *m* 1963, Caroline Herbert; two *s* one *d. Educ:* Bryanston, Dorset. Chm., Conran Holdings Ltd, 1965-68; Jt Chm., Ryman Conran Ltd, 1968-71. Mem., Royal Commn on Environmental Pollution, 1973-76. Member: Council, RCA, 1978-81; Adv. Council, V&A Mus., 1979-. RSA Presidential Medal for Design Management to Conran Group; RSA Presidential Award for Design Management to Habitat Designs Ltd, 1975; SIAD Medal, 1981. *Publications:* The House Book, 1974; The Kitchen Book, 1977; The Bedroom & Bathroom Book, 1978; (with Caroline Conran) The Cook Book, 1980. *Recreations:* gardening, cooking. *Address:* Barton Court, Kintbury, Newbury, Berks. *T:* Kintbury 200.

CONS, Hon. Derek; Hon. Mr Justice Cons; Justice of Appeal, Supreme Court of Hong Kong, since 1980; *b* 15 July 1928; *s* of Alfred Henry Cons and Elsie Margaret (*née* Neville); *m* 1952, Mary Roberta Upton Wilkes. *Educ:* Rutlish; Birmingham Univ. (LLB (Hons)). Called to Bar, Gray's Inn, 1953. RASC (2nd Lieut), 1946-48. Magistrate, Hong Kong, 1955-62, Principal Magistrate, 1962-66; District Judge, 1966-72; Judge of Supreme Court of Hong Kong, 1972-80. *Recreations:* golf, skiing. *Address:* The Supreme Court, Hong Kong; Mulberry Mews, Church Street, Fordingbridge, Hants. *Clubs:* Bramshaw Golf (Hants); Hong Kong, Royal Hong Kong Yacht, Shek O Country (Hong Kong).

CONSTABLE, Sir Robert Frederick S.; *see* Strickland-Constable.

CONSTANT, Antony; Group Archivist, the Delta Group plc (formerly Delta Metal Co. Ltd); *b* 1918; *s* of Frederick Charles and Mary Theresa Constant; *m* 1947, Pamela Mary Pemberton; one *s. Educ:* Dover Coll.; King's Coll., Cambridge. Asst master, Oundle Sch., 1939-45; Staff of Dir of Naval Intelligence, Admiralty, 1940-44; Educational Adviser to the Control Commission, Germany, 1945. Asst Master, and Asst House Master of School House, Rugby Sch., 1945-49; Rector of Royal Coll., Mauritius, 1949-53; Dir of Studies, RAF Coll., Cranwell, 1953-59; Educational Adviser to the Ministry of Defence and Chm. of Joint-Services Working Party, 1959-62; joined Delta Group of Companies, 1963, as Head of Training Dept; later Group Management Develt Executive. Mem. Bd for Postgraduate Studies, and Mem. Faculty Bd, Management Centre, Univ. of Aston, 1973-77. *Publications:* various papers on historical geography. *Recreations:* ornithology, sailing. *Address:* Delta Group plc, Group Archives Office, Argyle Street, Birmingham B7 5TH.

CONSTANTINE, family name of Baron Constantine of Stanmore.

CONSTANTINE OF STANMORE, Baron *cr* 1981 (Life Peer), of Stanmore in Greater London; **Theodore Constantine;** Kt 1964; CBE 1956; AE 1945; DL; *b* 15 March 1910; *er s* of Leonard and Fanny Louise Constantine; *m* 1935, Sylvia Mary, *y d* of Wallace Henry Legge-Pointing; one *s* one *d. Educ:* Acton Coll. Personal Asst to Chm. of public company, 1926-28; Executive in industry, 1928-38; Managing Dir of public company subsidiary, 1938-39. Served War of 1939-45, Auxiliary Air Force. Resumed pre-war Directorships, Oct. 1945. Dir of Industrial Holding Company, 1956-59; Chm. of Public Companies, 1959-75. Organisational work for Conservative Party as Constituency Chm., Area Chm., Mem. Nat. Exec. Cttee, Policy Cttee, Nat. Advisory Cttee on Publicity. Chm., Nat. Union Cons. and Unionist Assocs, 1967-68, Pres. 1980. Trustee, Sir John Wolstenholme Charity; Master, Worshipful Co. of Coachmakers, 1975; Freeman of City of London. High Sheriff of Greater London, 1967; DL Greater London, 1967. *Recreations:* watching motor racing, reading, walking. *Address:* Hunters Beck, Uxbridge Road, Stanmore, Mddx. *T:* 01-954 0624. *Clubs:* Carlton, Brooks's; British Automobile Racing.

CONSTANTINE, Air Chief Marshal Sir Hugh (Alex), KBE 1958 (CBE 1944); CB 1946; DSO 1942; Co-ordinator, Anglo-American Community Relations, Ministry of Defence (Air), 1964-77; *b* 23 May 1908; *s* of Fleet Paymaster Henry Constantine, RN, and Alice Louise Squire; *m* 1937, Helen, *d* of J. W. Bourke, Sydney, Australia; one *d. Educ:* Christ's Hosp.; Royal Air Force Coll., Cranwell. Pilot Officer in RAF, 1927; 56 (F) Sqdn, 1928-29; Flying Instructor, RAF Coll., 1930-31; CFS Instructor, 1932-33 and 1936-37; No 1 Armoured Car Co. (Iraq), 1934-36 (Palestine, despatches); Sqdn Ldr, 1936; 214 Bomber Sqdn, 1936-38; graduated Staff Coll., Andover, 1940; served in Bomber Comd, 1940-45 (despatches, four times); Gp Capt. 1941; comd RAF Elsham Wolds, 1941-42; SASO No 1 (B) Gp, 1943; Dep. SASO Bomber Comd, 1944; Air Vice-Marshal, Jan. 1945, and commanded No 5 (B) Group Bomber Command; Chief Intelligence Officer, BAFO and Control Commission, Germany, 1946; idc, 1947; SASO, 205 Gp (Egypt), 1948-49; Dir of Intelligence, Air Min., 1950-51; AO i/c A, Fighter Comd, 1952-54; AOC No 25 Group, Flying Training Command, 1954-56; Deputy Chief of Staff (Plans and Operations), SHAPE, NATO, 1956-59; AOC-in-C, Flg Trg Comd, 1959-61; Commandant, Imperial Defence Coll., 1961-64. Air Marshal, 1958; Air Chief Marshal, 1961. Governor and Almoner, Christ's Hospital, 1963-. Hon. LLD Warwick, 1978. Order of Polonia Restituta (2nd Class), 1945. *Recreations:* Rugby (English Trial, 1934), Eastern Counties, RAF and Leicester; golf. *Address:* 4 Chester Row, SW1W 9JH. *T:* 01-730 0700. *Club:* Royal Air Force.

CONTI, Rt. Rev. Mario Joseph; *see* Aberdeen, Bishop of, (RC).

CONTI, Tom; actor, since 1960; director; *b* Scotland, 1942; *m* Kara Wilson; one *d.* London appearances include: Savages, Royal Court and Comedy, 1973; The Devil's Disciple, RSC Aldwych, 1976; Whose Life is it Anyway?, Mermaid and Savoy, 1978, NY 1979 (SWET Award for Best Actor in a new play, Variety Club of GB Award for Best Stage Actor, 1978, Tony Award for Best Actor, 1979); They're Playing Our Song, Shaftesbury, 1980; *Directed:* Last Licks, Broadway, 1979; Before the Party, Oxford Playhouse and Queen's, 1980; The Housekeeper, Apollo, 1982; *films include:* Galileo, Flame, 1974; Eclipse, 1975; Full Circle, The Duellists, 1977; The Wall, 1980; *television appearances include:* Madame Bovary, The Norman Conquests, Glittering Prizes. *Address:* c/o Chatto and Linnit, Globe Theatre, Shaftesbury Avenue, W1.

CONTOGEORGIS, George; Member, Commission of the European Communities, since 1981; *b* 21 Nov. 1912; *s* of Leonidas and Angeliki Contogeorgis; *m* 1949, Mary Lazopoulou. *Educ:* Athens Sch. (now University) of Economic and Commercial Sciences. Ministry of Trade, Greece: Administrator, 1937; Chief of Section, 1945; Dir, 1952; Dir Gen., 1964-77, resigned. Gen. Sec., Tourism, Govt of Nea Dimokratia, 1974; Dep. Minister of Co-ordination (Econs), 1974-77; Minister for EEC Affairs, 1977-81. MP, 1977-81. Grand Comdr, Order of the Phoenix, 1966. *Address:* Avenue de Tervueren 308, Bruxelles 1150, Belgium. *T:* (02) 762.70.67; Rue Anagnostopouloy 26, Athens 136, Greece. *T:* 361.68.44.

CONWAY, Most Rev. Dominic J.; *see* Elphin, Bishop of, (RC).

CONWAY, Hugh Graham, CBE 1964; *b* 25 Jan. 1914; *s* of G. R. G. Conway; *m* 1937, Eva Gordon Simpson (*d* 1980); two *s. Educ:* Merchiston Castle Sch., Edinburgh; Cambridge Univ. Joined aircraft industry, 1938; Man. Dir, Bristol Engine Division, Rolls Royce Ltd, 1964-70; Dir, Rolls-Royce Ltd, 1966-70, Rolls-Royce (1971) Ltd, 1971; Gp Managing Dir, Gas Turbines, Rolls-Royce Ltd, 1970-71. Member: Decimal Currency Board, 1967-71; Design Council, 1971-76 (Dep. Chm., 1972-76). *Publications:* Engineering Tolerances, 1948; Fluid Pressure Mechanisms, 1949; Landing Gear Design, 1958; Bugatti, 1963; Grand Prix Bugatti, 1968. *Recreation:* vintage motoring. *Address:* 33 Sussex Square, W2.

CONWAY, Dr John Horton, FRS 1981; Reader in Pure Mathematics and Mathematical Statistics, since 1973, and Fellow of Gonville and Caius College, since 1968, Cambridge University. *Educ:* Gonville and Caius Coll., Cambridge. BA 1959; MA 1963; PhD 1964. Univ. Lectr in Pure Maths, Cambridge, to 1973; Fellow, Sidney Sussex Coll., Cambridge, to 1968. *Publications:* Regular Algebra and Finite Machines, 1971; On Numbers and Games, 1976. *Address:* Gonville and Caius College, Cambridge.

CONYNGHAM, family name of Marquess Conyngham.

CONYNGHAM, 7th Marquess *cr* 1816; **Frederick William Henry Francis Conyngham;** Baron Conyngham, 1781; Viscount Conyngham, 1789; Earl Conyngham, Viscount Mount Charles, 1797; Earl of Mount Charles, Viscount Slane, 1816; Baron Minster (UK), 1821; late Captain Irish Guards; *b* 13 March 1924; *e s* of 6th Marquess Conyngham and Antoinette Winifred (*d* 1966), *er d* of late J. W. H. Thompson; *s* father, 1974; *m* 1st, 1950, Eileen Wren (marr. diss. 1970), *o d* of Capt. C. W. Newsam, Ashfield, Beauparc, Co. Meath; three *s* ; 2nd, 1971, Mrs Elizabeth Anne Rudd; 3rd, 1980, Mrs D. G. A. Walker. *Educ:* Eton. *Heir:* *s* Earl of Mount Charles, *qv. Address:* Bifrons, near Canterbury; Cronk Ghennie House, Ramsey, Isle of Man. *Club:* Royal St George Yacht.

COOK, Prof. Alan Hugh, FRS 1969; Jackson Professor of Natural Philosophy, since 1972, and Head of Department of Physics, since 1979, Cambridge University; *b* 2 Dec. 1922; *s* of late Reginald Thomas Cook, OBE, and of Ethel Cook; *m* 1948, Isabell Weir Adamson; one *s* one *d*. *Educ:* Westcliff High Sch. for Boys; Corpus Christi Coll. Cambridge. MA, PhD, ScD. Admty Signal Estabt, 1943-46; Research Student, then Res. Asst, Dept of Geodesy and Geophysics, Cambridge, 1946-51; Metrology Div., Nat. Physical Laboratory, Teddington, 1952. Vis. Fellow, Jt Inst. for Laboratory Astrophysics, Boulder, Colorado, 1965-66; Supt, Standards (subseq. Quantum Metrology) Div., Nat. Physical Laboratory, 1966-69; Prof. of Geophysics, Univ. of Edinburgh, 1969-72. FInstP; FRSE 1970; Foreign Fellow, Acad. Naz. dei Lincei, 1971. Pres., RAS, 1977-79. Fellow, Explorers' Club, NY, 1980. C. V. Boys Prize, Inst. of Physics, 1967. *Publications:* Gravity and the Earth, 1969; Global Geophysics, 1970; Interference of Electromagnetic Waves, 1971; Physics of the Earth and Planets, 1973; Celestial Masers, 1977; Interiors of the Planets, 1980; many contribs learned jls on gravity, artificial satellites, precise measurement, fundamental constants of physics and astronomy. *Recreations:* amateur theatre, travel, painting. *Address:* Cavendish Laboratory, Madingley Road, Cambridge CB3 0HE. *T:* Cambridge 66477; King's College, Cambridge. *T:* Cambridge 50411; 8 Wootton Way, Cambridge CB3 9LX. *T:* Cambridge 356887.

COOK, Alexander Edward, CMG 1955; *b* 3 April 1906; *s* of Edward Arthur Cook and M. J. Cook (*née* Wreford); *m* 1936, Ethel Catherine Margaret (*née* Mayo); one *s* two *d*. *Educ:* Imperial Service Coll., Windsor; Pembroke Coll., Cambridge. Entered Colonial Service as a Cadet, Nigeria, 1928; Asst District Officer, District Officer, Asst Sec.; Financial Sec., Gibraltar, 1945; Financial Sec., Eastern Region, Nigeria, 1953; Permanent Sec., Ministry of Finance, Eastern Region, Nigeria, 1954; retired 1956; Mem., British Caribbean Federal Capital Commn, 1956. Attached Fed. Govt of UK of Libya as Economic Adviser, under auspices of UN Tech. Assistance Admin., 1959-60. *Recreations:* fishing and golf. *Address:* The White Cottage, Whitby Road, Milford-on-Sea, near Lymington, Hants. *T:* Milford-on-Sea 3526. *Club:* United Oxford & Cambridge University.

COOK, (Alfred) Melville, MusDoc, FRCO; Organist and Choirmaster of the Metropolitan United, Toronto, since 1967; *b* 18 June 1912; *s* of Harry Melville and Vera Louis Cook; *m* 1944, Marion Weir Moncrieff; no *c*. *Educ:* King's Sch., Gloucester. Chorister, 1923-28, Asst Organist, 1932-37, Gloucester Cathedral. Organist and Choirmaster: All Saints, Cheltenham, 1935-37; Leeds Parish Church, 1937-56. MusDoc Durham, 1940. Served War in RA, 1941-46. Organist and Master of the Choristers, Hereford Cathedral, 1956-66. Conductor, Three Choirs Festival, Hereford, 1958, 1961, 1964; Conductor, Hereford Choral Soc., 1957-66. Organist and Choirmaster, All Saints', Winnipeg; Conductor of the Winnipeg Philharmonic Choir, Canada, 1966. *Recreations:* walking, swimming. *Address:* Metropolitan United Church, 51 Bond Street, Toronto, Canada.

COOK, Ann; see Christopher, A.

COOK, Arthur Herbert, FRS 1951; DSc, PhD, FRIC; Director, Brewing Industry Research Foundation, Nutfield, Surrey, 1958-71 (Assistant Director, 1949-58), retired 1971; *b* London, 10 July 1911; *s* of Arthur Cook, London. *Educ:* Owen's Sch., Islington, London; Universities of London (Imperial Coll. of Science and Technology) and Heidelberg. Joined staff of Imperial Coll., 1937; Asst Prof. and Reader in the University, 1947-49. Hon. DSc Heriot-Watt. *Publications:* (with late Prof. F. Mayer) Chemistry of the Natural Colouring Matters. Numerous articles, mainly in Journal of Chemical Soc. Editor, The Chemistry and Biology of Yeasts, 1958; Barley and Malt: Biology, Biochemistry, Technology, 1962. *Recreations:* gardening, photography. *Address:* Merrylands, Lympstone, Devon. *T:* Exmouth 71426. *Club:* Athenæum.

COOK, Maj.-Gen. Arthur Thompson, FRCP, FRCPE; Director of Army Medicine, 1977-81; *b* 21 Oct. 1923; *s* of Thomas and Mabel Elizabeth Cook; *m* 1960, Kathleen Lane; two *s* one *d*. *Educ:* China Inland Mission Sch., Chefoo, N China; City of London Sch.; St Thomas' Hosp., London (MB). FRCP 1955, FRCPE 1954. Joined RAMC, 1948. QHP, 1977-81. *Address:* Askham, 18A Firwood Drive, Camberley, Surrey GU15 3QD. *T:* Camberley 63043.

COOK, Bernard Christopher Allen, CMG 1958; OBE 1945; *b* 20 July 1906; *s* of late Sir Edward Cook, CSI, CIE; *m* 1933, Margaret Helen Mary, *d* of Rt Rev. C. E. Plumb, DD; two *d* (and one *s* decd). *Educ:* Radley Coll. (Open Scholarship); Brasenose Coll., Oxford (Open Scholarship). ICS 1929; held various posts in UP; Govt of India: Finance and Commerce Cadre, 1938; Custodian of Enemy Property, 1939-41; Actg Joint Sec., Finance Dept, and Mem. Central Legislative Assembly, 1946; Indian Trade Comr, London, 1946-47; Foreign Service, 1947; Control Commn, Germany (currency reform), 1948-49; Political Adviser, Asmara, 1949-51; First Sec. (Commercial), Paris, 1951-53; Counsellor (Commercial), Rangoon, 1953-57; Counsellor (Commercial), HBM Embassy, Mexico City, 1957-59; HM Consul-General, Barcelona, 1959-66; retired, 1966; re-employed, 1967-69. *Address:* 11 Priory Court, Granville Road, Eastbourne BN20 7ED.

COOK, Mrs Beryl Frances; painter; *b* 10 Sept. 1926; *d* of Adrian Lansley and Ella Farmer-Francis; *m* 1948, John Victor Cook; one *s*. *Educ:* Kendrick Girls' Sch., Reading, Berks. *Exhibitions:* Plymouth Arts Centre, 1975; Whitechapel Art Gallery, London, 1976; The Craft of Art, Walker Art Gallery, 1979; Musée de Cahors, 1981; Chelmsford Museum, 1982. *Publications:* The Works, 1978; Private View, 1980; Seven Years and a Day (illustrations), 1980; One

Man Show, 1981; Bertie and the Big Red Ball (illustrations), 1982. *Recreation:* reading. *Address:* Glanville House, 3 Athenæum Street, The Hoe, Plymouth PL1 2RQ. *T:* Plymouth 661324.

COOK, Brian Francis, FSA; Keeper of Greek and Roman Antiquities, British Museum, since 1976; *b* 13 Feb. 1933; *yr s* of late Harry Cook and Renia Cook; *m* 1962, Veronica Dewhirst. *Educ:* St Bede's Grammar Sch., Bradford; Univ. of Manchester (BA); Downing Coll. and St Edmund's House, Cambridge (MA); British Sch. at Athens. FSA 1971. Dept of Greek and Roman Art, Metropolitan Museum of Art, New York: Curatorial Asst, 1960; Asst Curator, 1961; Associate Curator, 1965-69; Asst Keeper, Dept of Greek and Roman Antiquities, BM, 1969-76. Corr. Mem., German Archaeol. Inst., 1977. *Publications:* Inscribed Hadra Vases in the Metropolitan Museum of Art, 1966; Greek and Roman Art in the British Museum, 1976; articles and revs on Greek, Etruscan and Roman antiquities in Brit. and foreign periodicals. *Recreations:* reading, gardening. *Address:* 4 Belmont Avenue, Barnet, Herts. *T:* 01-440 6590. *Club:* Challoner.

COOK, Brian Hartley K.; see Kemball-Cook.

COOK, Charles Alfred George, MC 1945; GM 1945; FRCS; Consultant Ophthalmic Surgeon: Guy's Hospital, 1954-73; Moorfields Eye Hospital, 1956-73; Teacher of Ophthalmology, University of London (Guy's Hospital and Institute of Ophthalmology), 1955-73; *b* 20 Aug. 1913; *s* of late Charles F. Cook and Beatrice Grist; *m* 1939, Edna Constance Dobson; one *s* one *d*. *Educ:* St Edward's Sch., Oxford; Guy's Hospital. MRCS LRCP, 1939; DOMS (Eng.), 1946; FRCS, 1950. Capt. and Major RAMC, 1939-45. Moorfields Eye Hospital: Clinical Asst, 1946-47; Ho. Surg., 1948-49; Sen. Resident Officer, 1950; Chief Clin. Asst, 1951-55. Sen. Registrar, Eye Dept, Guy's Hospital, 1951-55; Moorfields Research Fellow, Inst. of Ophthalmology, 1951-58; Ophthalmic Surg., West Middlesex Hospital, 1954-56. Mem., Court of Examrs, RCS; Examr for DOMS, RCP and RCS; Examr Brit. Orthoptic Board; Sec., Ophthalmological Soc. of UK, 1956-57; Vice-Dean, Inst. of Ophthalmology, 1959-62; Member: Council, Coll. of Opth. Opticians; Bd of Governors, Faculty of Dispensing Opticians. Governor: Royal Nat. Coll. for Blind; Moorfields Eye Hosp., 1962-65. Renter Warden, Upper Warden, then Master, Worshipful Co. of Spectacle Makers, 1975-81. Freeman, City of London. *Publications:* (ed) S. Duke Elder, Embryology, vol. 3, 1963; (contrib.) Payling, Wright and Symers, Systematic Pathology, 1966; (jt) May and Worth, Diseases of the Eye, 1968; articles in Brit. Jl of Ophthalmology, Trans Ophthalmological Soc., Jl of Pathology and other Med. Jls. *Recreations:* swimming, reading; an interest in all outdoor recreations. *Address:* 13 Clarence Terrace, Regents Park, NW1. *T:* 01-723 5111. *Clubs:* Athenæum, Garrick.

COOK, Sir Christopher Wymondham Rayner Herbert, 5th Bt *cr* 1886; company director since 1979; Director, Diamond Guarantees Ltd, since 1980; *b* 24 March 1938; *s* of Sir Francis Ferdinand Maurice Cook, 4th Bt and Joan Loraine, *d* of John Aloysius Ashton-Case; *S* father, 1978; *m* 1st, 1958, Mrs Malina Gunasekera (from whom he obtained a divorce, 1975); 2nd, 1975, Mrs Margaret Miller, *d* of late John Murray; one *s* one *d*. *Educ:* King's School, Canterbury. *Recreation:* golf. *Address:* La Fontenelle, Ville au Roi, St Peter Port, Guernsey, CI.

COOK, David Somerville; solicitor; Lord Mayor of Belfast, 1978-79; *b* 25 Jan. 1944; *s* of Francis John Granville Cook, *qv* ; *m* 1972, Mary Fionnuala Ann Deeny; four *s* one *d*. *Educ:* Campbell Coll., Belfast; Pembroke Coll., Cambridge (MA). Alliance Party of Northern Ireland: Founder Member, 1970; Hon. Treasurer, 1972-75; Central Executive Cttee, 1970-78, 1980-; Dep. Leader, 1980-. Chm., NI Voluntary Trust, 1979-. Elected to Belfast City Council, 1973; re-elected, 1977, 1981; contested (Alliance) Belfast South, gen. election, Feb. 1974 and 1982. Trustee, Ulster Museum, 1974-; Vice Pres., NI Council on Alcohol, 1978-; Mem. NI Council, European Movement, 1980-. Dir, Ulster Actors' Co. Ltd, 1981-; Mem., Council of Management, Belfast City Marathon Ltd, 1982. *Recreations:* football, hill walking, marmalade making. *Address:* 31 Rugby Road, Belfast 7, N Ireland.

COOK, Air Vice-Marshal Eric, DFC 1945; Fellow, Hughes Hall, Cambridge, since 1975; *b* 30 April 1920; *s* of late Thomas Cook and Sara Elizabeth Cook (*née* Hunnam); *m* 1953, Thelma, *o d* of late Alfred and Isabelle Burns Withnell, Chorley, Lancs; one *s*. *Educ:* Sunderland Technical Coll. MA Cantab. Served War, Bomber Command Sqdns, 1940-45 (despatches twice). Command, MEAF VIP Sqdn, 1951; Staff, HQ Transport Comd, 1953; Sqdn Comdr, Training Comd, 1955-57; Sen. Personnel Staff Officer, MEAF, 1959-60; Chief Instr, Jet Provost Wing, 1961; Sen. Air Staff Officer, Ghana Air Force, 1963; AOA, RAF Germany, 1968-71; Dir of Flying Training, 1971-72; Dir-Gen. RAF Training, 1972-75. *Recreations:* outdoor activities, music. *Address:* Hawkwood, Madeley Court, Hemingford Grey, Cambridgeshire. *T:* St Ives 63647. *Clubs:* Royal Air Force, MCC.

COOK, Eric William; HM Diplomatic Service, retired; *b* 24 Feb. 1920; *s* of Ernest Gordon Cook and Jessie (*née* Hardy); *m* 1949, Pauline Elizabeth Lee; one *s*. *Educ:* various private estabts. RAF, 1940-46. GPO, 1947-49; FO (later FCO), 1949-; Consul, Belgrade, 1961-64; Vice-Consul, Leopoldville, 1964-65; Consul, Cleveland, Ohio, 1967-69; also served at Rome, Moscow, Peking and Djakarta; Consul Gen., Adelaide, 1974-76; FCO, 1977-80. *Recreations:* music, writing and photography. *Address:* 11 St Ann's Court, Nizells Avenue, Hove, East Sussex BN3 1PR. *T:* Brighton 776100.

COOK, Vice-Adm. Eric William L.; see Longley-Cook.

COOK, Francis John Granville, MA Cantab; Headmaster of Campbell College, Belfast, 1954-71; *b* 28 Jan. 1913; *o s* of late W. G. Cook and Nora Braley; *m* 1942, Jocelyn McKay, *d* of late John Stewart, Westholm, Dunblane, Perthshire; one *s* two *d. Educ:* Wyggeston Sch.; Downing Coll., Cambridge. Historical Tripos, Law Tripos; Squire Scholar; Tancred Studentship, Lincoln's Inn. Asst Master, Rossall Sch., 1937; served War, 1940-46, with Royal Navy; Headmaster of Junior Sch., Rossall Sch., 1949-54. *Recreations:* gardening, fishing, savouring retirement. *Address:* Via Brugnago 19, 22070 Capiago Intimiano, P. Como, Italy. *T:* 031.461579. *Club:* Naval.
See also D. S. Cook.

COOK, Frank Patrick; Member, Commission for Local Administration in England; *b* 28 March 1920; *o c* of Frank Cook, FRCS, FRCOG and Edith Harriet (*née* Reid); *m* 1st, 1945, Rosemary Eason (marr. diss. 1975); two *s* one *d* ; 2nd, 1975, Margaret Rodgers, 2nd *d* of Dr J. W. Rodgers, PhD; one *s. Educ:* Rugby; Trinity Hall, Cambridge (Open Schol.); LSE (Personnel Management). Royal Marines, 1939-46; Courtaulds Ltd, 1946-56; Nat. Coal Board, 1956-61; Venesta Ltd, 1961-64; Principal, British Transport Staff Coll., 1964-69; First Chief Exec., English Tourist Board, 1970-74; Local Ombudsman, 1974-. Chm., Microtest Research Ltd, 1982-; A Vice President: IPM, 1965-67; RCN, 1973-; Member: Nat. Nursing Staff Cttee, 1967-72; Brighton and Lewes HMC, 1972-74; Ombudsman Adv. Bd, Internat. Bar Assoc., 1975-; Exec. Cttee, Fawcett Soc., 1975-77; Council, Univ. of York, 1979-; Merchant Taylors' Co. of York, 1981-. *Publications:* Shift Work, 1954; Ombudsman (autobiog.), 1981; articles on personnel management. *Address:* 5 Malton Way, Clifton, York. *Club:* Naval and Military.

COOK, George Steveni L.; see Littlejohn Cook.

COOK, Sir Halford; see Cook, Sir P. H.

COOK, Harold James; a Metropolitan Stipendiary Magistrate, since 1975; *b* 25 Jan. 1926; *s* of Harold Cook and Gwendoline Lydia (*née* List); *m* 1952, Mary Elizabeth (*née* Edwards); one *s. Educ:* The John Lyon Sch., Harrow; Edinburgh Univ. RN, 1944-47. Civil Service, 1947-52. Called to the Bar, Gray's Inn, 1952; Dep. Chief Clerk, Bow Street, and later Thames, Magistrates' Courts, 1952-54; Inner London QS, 1955; Dep. Clerk to Justices, Gore Div., Mddx, 1956-60; Clerk to Justices, Highgate Div., 1961, and also Barnet and South Mymms Divs, 1968. *Publications:* contrib. legal jls. *Address:* West London Magistrates' Court, Southcombe Street, W14.

COOK, Rt. Rev. Henry George; retired; *b* Walthamstow, London, England, 12 Oct. 1906; *s* of Henry G. Cook and Ada Mary Evans; *m* 1935, Opal May Thompson, Sarnia, Ont, *d* of Wesley Thompson and Charity Ellen Britney; two *s* one *d. Educ:* Ingersoll Collegiate Inst., Ont; Huron Coll. (LTh); Univ. of Western Ont, London, Canada (BA). Deacon, 1935, Priest, 1936; Missionary at Fort Simpson, 1935-43; Canon of Athabasca, 1940-43; Incumbent S Porcupine, Ont., 1943-44; Archdeacon of James Bay, 1945-48; Principal, Bp Horden Sch., Moose Factory, 1945-48; Mem., Gen Synod Exec., 1943-47; Supt of Indian Sch. Admin., 1948-62; Bishop Suffragan of the Arctic, 1963-66, of Athabasca, 1966-70 (the area of Mackenzie having been part first of one diocese and then of the other, constituted an Episcopal District, 1970); Bishop of Mackenzie, 1970-74. RCN(R) Chaplain, 1949-56. Hon. DD Huron Coll. and Univ. of Western Ont. 1946. *Recreations:* fishing, coin collecting, model carving. *Address:* 15 Plainfield Court, Stittsville, Ont K0A 3G0, Canada.

COOK, Cdre Henry Home; *b* 24 Jan. 1918; Director, C. Gold Associates Ltd, since 1974; *o s* of George Home Cook, Edinburgh; *m* 1943, Theffania, *yr d* of A. P. Saunders, Gerrards Cross; two *s* two *d. Educ:* St Lawrence Coll., Ramsgate; Pangbourne College. Entered RN as Paymaster Cadet, 1936; Comdr 1955; Captain 1963; Cdre 1970. Naval Sec. to Vice-Adm. Sir Guy Sayer, 1953-59; Sqdn Supply Officer, 1st S/m Sqdn, 1959; Comdr, RNC Greenwich, 1961; Naval Attaché, Ankara, 1964; Dir of Public Relations (RN), 1966; Defence Adviser to British High Comr, and Head of British Defence Liaison Staff, Ottawa, 1970-72; retired, 1973. ADC to HM the Queen, 1971-72. Dir, Ellerman City Liners Ltd, 1973-80. Pres., Anchorites, 1978. FInstAM 1973 (Chm., 1982). DipCAM 1975. *Recreations:* fencing, swimming, sailing. *Address:* Ramblers Cottage, Layters Green, Chalfont St Peter, Bucks. *T:* Gerrards Cross 83724. *Club:* Army and Navy.

COOK, Rear-Adm. James William Dunbar, CB 1975; Appeals Director, Royal Star and Garter Home for Disabled Sailors, Soldiers and Airmen, Richmond, since 1981; *b* 12 Dec. 1921; *s* of James Alexander Cook, Pluscarden, Morayshire; *m* 1949, Edith May Williams; one *s* two *d. Educ:* Bedford Sch.; HMS Worcester. CO, HM Ships Venus, Dido and Norfolk; Sen. British Naval Officer, S Africa, 1967-69 (as Cdre); Dir RN War College, 1969-71; Asst Chief of Naval Staff (Ops), 1973-75; retired from RN, 1975. Comdr 1957; Captain 1963; Rear-Adm. 1973; jssc 1958; sowc 1970. *Recreations:* golf, gardening. *Address:* Springways Cottage, Farnham Lane, Haslemere, Surrey. *T:* Haslemere 3615. *Club:* Army and Navy.

COOK, Dr John Barry; Headmaster of Epsom College, since 1982; *b* 9 May 1940; *er s* of Albert Edward and late Beatrice Irene Cook, Gloucester; *m* 1964, Vivien Margaret Roxana Lamb, *o d* of Victor and Marjorie Lamb, St Albans; two *s* one *d. Educ:* Sir Thomas Rich's Sch., Gloucester; King's Coll., Univ.

of London (BSc 1961, AKC 1961); Guy's Hosp. Med. Sch. (PhD 1965). Guy's Hospital Medical School: Biophysics research, 1961-64; Lectr in Physics, 1964-65; Haileybury College: Asst Master, 1965-72; Senior Science Master and Head of Physics Dept, 1967-72; Headmaster of Christ Coll., Brecon, 1973-82. Mem., Governing Body of Church in Wales. *Publications:* (jtly) Solid State Biophysics, 1969; Multiple Choice Questions in A-level Physics, 1969; Multiple Choice Questions in O-level Physics, 1970; papers in Nature, Molecular Physics, Internat. Jl of Radiation Biology, Jl of Scientific Instruments, Educn in Science, Conference and Trends in Education. *Recreations:* sports, philately. *Address:* Headmaster's House, Epsom College, Epsom, Surrey KT17 4JQ. *T:* Epsom 22118.

COOK, John Edward E.; see Evan-Cook.

COOK, Prof. John Manuel, FSA; FBA 1974; Professor of Ancient History and Classical Archæology, Bristol University, 1958-76 (formerly Reader); *b* 11 Dec. 1910; *s* of late Rev. C. R. Cook; *m* 1st, 1939, Enid May (*d* 1976), *d* of Dr W. A. Robertson; two *s* ; 2nd, 1977, Nancy Easton Law, MA, *widow* of Ralph Hamilton Law. *Educ:* Marlborough; King's Coll., Cambridge. Sir William Browne's Medal for Greek Ode, 1933; Members' Latin Essay Prize, 1933; Augustus Austen Leigh Student in King's Coll., 1934; Asst in Humanity and Lectr in Classical Archæology, Edinburgh Univ., 1936-46; Dir of British Sch. of Archæology at Athens, 1946-54; Dean, Faculty of Arts, 1966-68, Pro-Vice-Chancellor, 1972-75, Bristol Univ. C. E. Norton Lectr of the Archaeological Inst. of America, 1961-62; Visiting Prof., Yale Univ., 1965; Gray Memorial Lectr, Cambridge, 1969; Geddes-Harrower Prof., Univ. of Aberdeen, 1977. Served in Royal Scots, Force 133, and HQ Land Forces, Greece. *Publications:* The Greeks in Ionia and the East, 1962; (with W. H. Plommer) The Sanctuary of Hemithea at Kastabos, 1966; The Troad, an archaeological and historical study, 1973; chapters in: Cambridge Ancient History; Cambridge History of Iran. *Address:* 8 Dalrymple Crescent, Edinburgh EH9 2NU.

COOK, Joseph, CChem, FRSC; management consultant; *b* 7 April 1917; *y s* of Joseph Cook, MBE, JP, and Jane Cook (*née* Adams), Cumberland; *m* 1950, Betty, *d* of James and Elizabeth Barlow, Standish, Lancs; two *d. Educ:* Whitehaven Grammar Sch.; Univ. of Liverpool (BSc, DipEd). RAF, 1939-40. Posts in Ministries of Supply, Aviation, Technology and Defence 1941-59; Dir, ROF Burghfield, 1959-65; Gp Dir, Ammunition Factories, 1966; Dir Gen. (Prodn), ROF, 1966-74; Man. Dir, Millbank Tech. Services Ordnance Ltd, 1974-77 (on secondment from MoD). *Recreations:* swimming, golf. *Address:* Abbots-wood, Bramley Road, Pamber End, near Basingstoke, Hants. *T:* Basingstoke 850304.

COOK, Melville; see Cook, Alfred Melville.

COOK, Michael John; Senior Partner, Ward Bowie, Solicitors, since 1965; a Recorder of the Crown Court, since 1980; *b* 20 June 1930; *s* of George Henry Cook and Nora Wilson Cook (*née* Mackman); *m* 1st, 1958, Anne Margaret Vaughan; three *s* one *d* ; 2nd, 1974, Patricia Anne Sturdy; one *d. Educ:* Leeds Grammar Sch.; Worksop Coll.; Univ. of Leeds (LLB 2(1) Cl. Hons). Admitted Solicitor, 1953. National Service, commnd Royal Artillery, 1954. Willey Hargrave & Co., Solicitors, to 1957; Ward Bowie, Solicitors, 1957-. Past Hon. Sec. and Pres., London Solicitors' Litigation Assoc.; Member: Solicitors Disciplinary Tribunal, 1975-; Law Society sub-cttees and working parties. Speaker at professional seminars, broadcaster on Commercial and BBC radio and BBC TV and ITV. *Publications:* The Courts and You, 1976; The Taxation of Contentious Costs, 1979; contrib. The Solicitor's Practice, 1981; articles and reviews in cassette tapes on Divorce, Family Law and Costs; Law Society's Gazette. *Recreations:* squash, gardening, theatre. *Address:* Clement House, 99 Aldwych, WC2B 4JF. *T:* 01-405 2885. *Clubs:* Athenæum, Law Society, United and Cecil.

COOK, Norman Charles, BA; FSA, FMA; Hon. Curator, Wells Museum, Somerset, since 1972; *b* 24 Jan. 1906; *s* of George and Emily Cook; *m* 1934, Dorothy Ida Waters; one *s* one *d. Educ:* Maidstone Grammar Sch. Maidstone Museum, 1924-37; Morven Institute of Archaeological Research, Avebury, 1937-39; Curator, Southampton Museum, 1947-50; Director: Guildhall Museum, 1950-71; Museum of London, 1970-72. Hon. Sec., 1954-59, Pres., 1964-65, Museums Assoc. Vice-Pres., Soc. of Antiquaries, 1967-72. *Recreation:* archæology. *Address:* 8 Cathedral Green, Wells, Somerset BA5 2UE.

COOK, Norman Edgar, CBE 1980; writer and media consultant; *b* 4 March 1920; *s* of Edgar James and Kate Cook; *m* 1942, Mildred Warburton; three *s. Educ:* Cowley Grammar Sch., St Helens. TA (Royal Corps of Signals), 1939; served war, UK, Sierra Leone, Gold Coast. Min. of Information, 1943-45; Editor, Northwich Guardian, 1945-47; Liverpool Daily Post, 1947-49; Information Officer, Air Ministry, 1949-53; Liverpool Daily Post and Echo: Night News Editor, 1953-55; Dep. News Editor, 1955-59; London Editor, 1959-72; Exec. News Editor, 1972-77; Editor, Liverpool Daily Post, 1978-79. *Publications:* numerous articles and reviews. *Recreations:* walking and gardening, interspersed with the study of political biographies. *Address:* 15 Ormskirk Road, Rainford, St Helens, Merseyside WA11 8DY. *T:* Rainford 2331. *Club:* Athenæum (Liverpool).

COOK, Peter Edward; writer; entertainer; *b* 17 Nov. 1937; *s* of Alexander and Margaret Cook; *m* 1st, 1964, Wendy Snowden; two *d* ; 2nd, 1973, Judy

Huxtable. *Educ:* Radley Coll.; Pembroke Coll., Cambridge (BA). Part-author and appeared in: *revues:* Pieces of Eight, 1958; One Over the Eight, 1959; Beyond the Fringe, 1959-64 (London and New York); Behind the Fridge, 1971-72 (Australia and London); Good Evening, 1973-75 (US); *television:* Not Only but Also (four series, BBC), 1965-71; Revolver (ITV series), 1978. *Films:* The Wrong Box, 1965; Bedazzled, 1967; Monte Carlo or Bust, 1969; The Bed-Sitting Room, 1970; The Rise and Rise of Michael Rimmer, 1971; The Hound of the Baskervilles, 1978. *Publication:* Dud and Pete: The Dagenham Dialogues, 1971. *Recreations:* gambling, gossip, golf. *Address:* c/o Wright & Webb, 10 Soho Square, W1. *T:* 01-734 9641.

COOK, Sir (Philip) Halford, Kt 1976; OBE 1965; retired; *b* 10 Oct. 1912; *s* of Rev. R. Osborne Cook and May Cook; *m* 1945, Myra V., *d* of M. A. Dean; one *s* one *d. Educ:* Wesley Coll., Melbourne; Queen's Coll., Univ. of Melbourne; University Coll., Univ. of London; Columbia and Kansas Univs, USA. MA Melbourne, 1938; PhD Kansas, 1941. FBPsS 1943; FAPsS 1968, Hon. FAPsS 1972. Lectr, Industrial Relations, Univ. of Melbourne, 1945-46, Lectr, Indust. Admin, 1947-50; Professional Staff, Tavistock Inst. of Human Relations, London, 1950-51; Asst Sec., 1952-63, First Asst Sec., 1963-68, Sec., 1968-72, Aust. Dept of Labour and Nat. Service; Ambassador and Special Labour Advr in Europe, Australian Permanent Mission, Geneva, 1973-77. Chm., Governing Body, ILO, 1975-76. Fellow, Queen's Coll., Univ. of Melbourne, 1972. *Publications:* Theory and Technique of Child Guidance, 1944; Productivity Team Technique, 1951; articles in jls on psychology and on indust. relations. *Recreations:* reading and travel. *Address:* 11 Boisdale Street, Surrey Hills, Victoria 3127, Australia. *T:* Melbourne 884793. *Club:* Athenæum (Melbourne).

COOK, Reginald, FCA; Chairman, South Wales Electricity Board, 1977-81; Member, Electricity Council, 1977-81; *b* 29 Dec. 1918; *s* of Harold Cook and Gwendolyn Cook, Birmingham; *m* 1945, Constance Irene Holt, Norden, Lancs; one *s* one *d. Educ:* Rochdale High Sch.; Manchester Univ. (BA); Admin. Staff Coll. Served War, 1939-46; Staff Captain, RA. Local Govt Service with Corporations of Manchester, West Bromwich and York, 1946-52; Midlands Electricity Board: accountancy posts, 1952-59; Chief Accountant, 1959-69; Exec. Mem., 1964-69; Dep. Chm., S Wales Electricity Bd, 1969-77. FBIM; CompIEE. Gold Medal, IMTA, 1949. *Recreations:* countryside activities, gardening, golf, bridge. *Address:* Heppleshaw, Itton, Chepstow, Gwent. *T:* Shirenewton 265.

COOK, Brig. Richard Arthur, CBE 1961; *b* 26 May 1908; *m* 1940, Sheila Mary Ostell Prosser; two *s. Educ:* St Paul's; RMA, Woolwich. Commissioned, Royal Artillery, 1928. Posted to India, 1933. Served War of 1939-45 in India and Burma: Staff Coll., 1941; Regimental Comd, 1943; Joint Services Staff Coll., 1947; Col, 1948; Col Administrative Plans, GHQ, MELF, 1948-51; CRA (Brig.) 16th Airborne Div., 1954-56; NATO Defence Coll., 1957; BGS, Southern Command, 1958-61; retired from Army, 1961. *Address:* Drove End House, West Grimstead, near Salisbury, Wilts. *T:* Farley 205. *Club:* Army and Navy.

COOK, Robert Finlayson, (Robin F. Cook); MP (Lab) Edinburgh Central, since Feb. 1974; *b* 28 Feb. 1946; *s* of Peter Cook, headmaster and Christina Cook (*née* Lynch); *m* 1969, Margaret K. Whitmore, medical consultant; two *s. Educ:* Aberdeen Grammar Sch.; Univ. of Edinburgh. MA Hons English Lit. Tutor-Organiser with WEA, 1970-74. Chm., Scottish Assoc. of Labour Student Organisations, 1966-67; Sec., Edinburgh City Labour Party, 1970-72; Mem., Edinburgh Corporation, 1971-74; Chm. Housing Cttee, 1973-74. An Opposition Treasury spokesman, 1980-; Mem., Tribune Group. *Recreations:* eating, reading, talking. *Address:* c/o House of Commons, SW1A 0AA. *T:* 01-219 5120. *Club:* Abbotsford (Edinburgh).

COOK, Prof. Robert Manuel, FBA 1976; Laurence Professor of Classical Archaeology, University of Cambridge, 1962-76; *b* 4 July 1909; *s* of Rev. Charles Robert and Mary Manuel Cook; *m* (killed *d* 1979), *d* of James Frank and Ellen Hardman Porter. *Educ:* Marlborough Coll.; Cambridge Univ. Walston Student, Cambridge Univ., 1932; Asst Lectr in Classics, Manchester Univ., 1934; Lectr, 1938; Sub-warden, St Anselm's Hall, Manchester, 1936-38; Laurence Reader in Classical Archaeology, Cambridge Univ., 1945, Ord. Mem., German Archaeological Inst., 1953. *Publications:* Corpus Vasorum Antiquorum, British Museum 8, 1954; Greek Painted Pottery, 1960, 2nd edn 1972; The Greeks till Alexander, 1962; (with Kathleen Cook) Southern Greece: an archaeological guide, 1968; Greek Art, 1972; Clazomenian Sarcophagi, 1981. *Address:* 15 Wilberforce Road, Cambridge CB3 0EQ. *T:* Cambridge 352863.
See also Prof. J. M. Cook.

COOK, Robin; see Cook, R. F.

COOK, William Birkett, MA; Master of Magdalen College School, Oxford, since 1972; *b* 30 Aug. 1931; *e s* of late William James and Mildred Elizabeth Cook, Headington, Oxford; *m* 1958, Marianne Ruth, *yr d* of late A. E. Taylor, The Schools, Shrewsbury; one *s* one *d* (and one *d* decd). *Educ:* Dragon Sch.; Eton (King's Schol.); Trinity Coll., Cambridge (Schol.). National Service, 1950-51 (commnd in RA). Porson Prizeman, 1953; 1st cl. Classical Tripos Pt I, 1953, Pt II, 1954; Henry Arthur Thomas Student, 1954; MA Oxon by incorporation, 1972. Asst Master, Shrewsbury Sch., 1955-67, and Head of Classical Faculty, 1960-67; Headmaster of Durham Sch., 1967-72. Governor,

Oxford High Sch., 1979-. *Recreations:* music, gardening. *Address:* Magdalen College School, Oxford. *T:* Oxford 42191.

COOK, Sir William (Richard Joseph), KCB 1970 (CB 1951); Kt 1958; FRS 1962; Director, Buck & Hickman Ltd, since 1970; *b* 10 April 1905; *s* of John Cook; *m* 1929, Grace (*née* Purnell); one *d*; *m* 1939, Gladys (*née* Allen); one *s* one *d. Educ:* Trowbridge High Sch.; Bristol Univ. Entered CS, 1928; various scientific posts in Research Estabs of WO and Min. of Supply, 1928-47; Dir of Physical Research, Admiralty, 1947-50; Chief of Royal Naval Scientific Service, 1950-54; Deputy Dir, Atomic Weapons Research Establishment, Aldermaston, 1954-58; Mem. for Reactors, Atomic Energy Authority, 1961-64 (Mem. for Development and Engineering, 1959-61, for Engineering and Production, 1958-59); Dep. Chief Scientific Adviser, Ministry of Defence, 1964-67; Chief Adviser (Projects and Research) MoD, 1968-70. Director: Rolls-Royce (1971) Ltd, 1971-76; GEC-Marconi Electronics Ltd, 1972-79; Chm., Marconi International Marine Co., 1971-75. Hon. DSc: Strathclyde, 1967; Bath, 1975. *Address:* Adbury Springs, Newbury, Berks. *T:* Newbury 40409. *Club:* Athenæum.

COOKE, (Alfred) Alistair, KBE (Hon.) 1973; journalist and broadcaster; *b* 20 Nov. 1908; *s* of Samuel Cooke and Mary Elizabeth Byrne; *m* 1st, 1934, Ruth Emerson; one *s*; 2nd, 1946, Jane White Hawkes; one *d. Educ:* Blackpool Grammar Sch.; Jesus Coll., Cambridge (Scholar); Yale Univ.; Harvard. Founded Cambridge University Mummers, 1928; First Class, English Tripos, 1929; Second Class, 1930. Editor, The Granta, 1931; Commonwealth Fund Fellow, 1932-34. BBC Film Critic, 1934-37; London Correspondent for NBC, 1936-37; Commentator on American Affairs for BBC, 1938-; Special Correspondent on American Affairs, The London Times, 1938-40; American Feature Writer, The Daily Herald, 1941-43; UN Correspondent of the Manchester Guardian (which changed name to Guardian, 1959), 1945-48; Chief Correspondent in US of The Guardian, 1948-72. Master of ceremonies: Ford Foundation's television programme, Omnibus, 1952-61; UN television programme, International Zone, 1961-67; Masterpiece Theatre, 1971-. Wrote and narrated, America: a personal history of the United States, BBC TV, 1972-73 (Peabody Award for meritorious services to broadcasting, 1972; Writers' Guild of GB award for best documentary of 1972; Dimbleby Award, Soc. of Film and TV Arts, 1973; four Emmy awards of (US) Nat. Acad. of TV Arts and Sciences, 1973). Hon. LLD: Edinburgh, 1969; Manchester, 1973; Hon. LittD St Andrews, 1975. Peabody Award for internat. reporting, 1952; Benjamin Franklin Medal, RSA, 1973; Howland Medal, Yale Univ., 1977. *Publications:* (ed) Garbo and the Night Watchmen, 1937, repr. 1972; Douglas Fairbanks: The Making of a Screen Character, 1940; A Generation on Trial: USA v Alger Hiss, 1950; Letters from America, 1951; Christmas Eve, 1952; A Commencement Address, 1954; (ed) The Vintage Mencken, 1955; Around the World in Fifty Years, 1966; Talk about America, 1968; Alistair Cooke's America, 1973; Six Men, 1977; The Americans: fifty letters from America on our life and times, 1979; (with Robert Cameron) Above London, 1980; Masterpieces, 1982. *Recreations:* golf, photography, music, travel. *Address:* 1150 Fifth Avenue, New York City; Nassau Point, Cutchogue, Long Island, NY, USA. *Clubs:* Athenæum; Royal and Ancient (St Andrews); National Press (Washington); Players (New York); San Francisco Golf.

COOKE, Alistair; see Cooke, Alfred A.

COOKE, Rear-Adm. Anthony John, CB 1980; Private Secretary to Lord Mayor of London, since 1981; *b* 21 Sept. 1927; *s* of Rear-Adm. John Ernest Cooke, CB; *m* 1951, Margaret Anne, *d* of Frederick Charles Hynard; two *s* three *d. Educ:* St Edward's Sch., Oxford. Entered RN 1945; specialised in navigation, 1953; Army Staff Coll., 1958; Sqdn Navigating Officer, HMS Daring, Second Destroyer Sqdn, 1959-61; Staff Navigating Officer to Flag Officer, Sea Trng, 1961; Comdr 1961; Directorate of Naval Ops and Trade, 1961-63; i/c HMS Brighton, 1964-66; Directorate of Navigation and Tactical Control, 1966; Captain 1966; Captain of Dockyard and Queen's Harbourmaster, Singapore, 1967-69; Captain 1st Destroyer Sqdn, Far East, later Divnl Comdr 3rd Div. Western Fleet, i/c HMS Galatea, 1969-71; Dir, Royal Naval Staff Coll., 1971-73; Cdre Clyde i/c Clyde Submarine Base, 1973-75; Rear-Adm. 1976; Senior Naval Mem., Directing Staff, RCDS, 1975-78; Adm. Pres., RNC Greenwich, 1978-80, retd. Police Found, 1980-81. A Younger Brother, Trinity House. Freeman, City of London, 1979; Liveryman, Shipwrights' Co., 1980. *Recreation:* philately. *Address:* Chalkhurst, Eynsford, Kent. *T:* Farningham 862789. *Club:* City Livery.

COOKE, Dr Arthur Hafford, MBE 1946; Warden of New College, Oxford, since 1976; *b* 13 Dec. 1912; *er s* of late Sydney Herbert Cooke and Edith Frances (*née* Jee); *m* 1939, Ilse (*d* 1973), *d* of late Prof. Hans Sachs; two *s. Educ:* Wyggeston Grammar Sch., Leicester; Christ Church, Oxford (MA, DPhil). Research Lectr, Christ Church, 1939. Radar research for Admiralty, 1940-45. Fellow of New Coll., Oxford, 1946-76; University Lectr in Physics, 1944-71; Reader in Physics, 1971-76. Member: Gen. Bd of the Faculties, 1962-72 (Vice-Chm., 1969-71); Hebdomadal Council, 1969-. Hon. DSc Leicester, 1979. *Publications:* articles in scientific jls on magnetism and low temperature physics. *Address:* New College, Oxford. *T:* Oxford 48451. *Club:* United Oxford & Cambridge University.

COOKE, Brian; Secretary of Commissions, Lord Chancellor's Department, since 1982; *b* 16 Jan. 1935; *s* of Norman and Edith Cooke; *m* 1958, Edith Mary Palmer; two *s* one *d. Educ:* Manchester Grammar Sch.; University Coll. London (LLB). Served Royal Air Force, 1956-59. Called to Bar, Lincoln's

Inn, 1959; Dept of Director of Public Prosecutions, 1960-68; Deputy Clerk of the Peace, Inner London Quarter Sessions, 1968-71; Dep. Circuit Administrator, North Eastern Circuit, 1971-81, Circuit Administrator 1981-82. *Recreations:* tennis, walking, theatre, music. *Address:* Lord Chancellor's Department, House of Lords, SW1A 0PW. *Clubs:* Army and Navy; Leeds (Leeds).

COOKE, Prof. Brian Ernest Dudley; Professor of Oral Medicine and Oral Pathology, University of Wales, Dean of Welsh National School of Medicine Dental School and Consultant Dental Surgeon to University Hospital of Wales, 1962-82; *b* 12 Jan. 1920; *e s* of Charles Ernest Cooke and Margaret Beatrice Wood; *m* 1948, Marion Neill Orkney Hope; one *s* one *d*. *Educ:* Merchant Taylors' Sch.; London Univ. LDSRCS 1942; LRCP, MRCS 1949; FDSRCS 1952; MDSU London 1959; MRCPath 1965, FR.CPath 1974. Served RNVR (Dental Br.), 1943-46. Nuffield Dental Fellow, 1950-52; Trav. Nuffield Fellow, Australia, 1964. Lectr 1952-57, Reader in Dental Med. 1958-62, Guy's Hosp. Dental School. Rep. Univ. of Wales on Gen. Dental Council, 1964-82; Mem. Bd of Faculty of Dental Surgery, RCS England, 1964-72 (Vice-Dean 1971-72); Chm., Dental Educn Adv. Council, GB, 1975-78 (Mem. 1962-82); Sec.-Gen., Assoc. for Dental Educn in Europe, 1982-. Adviser in Dental Surgery to Welsh Hosp. Bd, 1962-74; Civilian Consultant in Dental Surgery to RN, 1967-. Hon. Adviser, Editorial Bd, British Jl of Dermatology, 1967-76. Mem., S Glamorgan AHA, 1974-76. Mem. Bd of Governors: United Cardiff Hosps, 1965-71; HMC (Cardiff) Univ. Hosp. of Wales, 1971-74. Vice-Provost, Welsh Nat. Sch. of Medicine, 1974-76. Examr in Dental Surgery and Oral Pathology, Liverpool, Manchester and London Univs; Examr for Primary Fellowship in Dental Surgery, RCS, 1967-73. Hon. Mem., Pierre Fauchard Acad., 1967. Charles Tomes Lectr, RCS, 1963; Guest Lectr, Students' Vis. Lectrs Trust Fund, Witwatersrand Univ., 1967. Pres., Section of Odontology, R.SocMed, 1975; Founder Pres., British Soc. for Oral Medicine, 1981. Cartwright Prize and Medal, RCS, 1955; Chesterfield Prize and Medal, St John's Hosp. for Diseases of Skin, 1955. *Publications:* (jtly) Oral Histopathology, 1959, 2nd edn 1970; scientific contribs to medical and dental jls. *Recreations:* various. *Address:* 4 Mill Place, Lisvane, Cardiff. *T:* Cardiff 756110.

COOKE, Cecil; *see* Cooke, R. C.

COOKE, Sir Charles Fletcher F.; *see* Fletcher-Cooke.

COOKE, Cynthia Felicity Joan, CBE 1975; RRC 1969; Matron-in-Chief, Queen Alexandra's Royal Naval Nursing Service, 1973-76; *b* 11 June 1919; *d* of late Frank Alexander Cooke, MBE, DCM, and of Ethel May (*née* Buckle). *Educ:* Rosa Bassett Sch. for Girls; Victoria Hosp. for Children, Tite Street, Chelsea; RSCN, 1940; University Coll. Hosp., London, SRN, 1942; Univ. of London, Sister Tutor Diploma, 1949. Joined QARNNS, 1943; served in: Australia, 1944-45; Hong Kong, 1956-58; Malta, 1964-66. HMS: Collingwood, Gosling, Goldcrest; RN Hospitals: Chatham, Plymouth, Haslar. Principal Tutor, Royal Naval School of Nursing, 1967-70; Principal Matron, RN Hosp., Haslar, 1970-73. QHNS 1973-76. Dep. County Supt, Hampshire, St John Ambulance Bde. CStJ 1975. *Address:* 3 Glebe Court, Fleet, Hampshire. *T:* Fleet 28893.

COOKE, Lt-Col Sir David (William Perceval), 12th Bt *cr* 1661; Assistant Quartermaster-General, Ministry of Defence, since 1980; *b* 28 April 1935; *s* of Sir Charles Arthur John Cooke, 11th Bt, and of Diana, *o d* of late Maj.-Gen. Sir Edward Maxwell Perceval, KCB, DSO; *S* father, 1978; *m* 1959, Margaret Frances, *o d* of Herbert Skinner, Knutsford, Cheshire; three *d*. *Educ:* Wellington College; RMA Sandhurst; Open Univ. (BA). FCIT, MBIM, AMInstTA. Commissioned 4/7 Royal Dragoon Guards, 1955; served BAOR, 1955-58; transferred to RASC, 1958; served: BAOR, 1958-60; France, 1960-62; Far East, 1962-65; UK. Transferred to RCT on formation, 1965, and served UK, 1965-76, and BAOR, 1976-80. Operational service: Brunei, 1962; Malay Peninsula, 1964-65; N Ireland, 1971-72. Attended Staff Coll., Camberley, 1968 and Advanced Transport Course, 1973-74. Lt-Col 1977. Queen's Jubilee Medal, 1977. *Recreations:* fishing, shooting, ornithology, military history. *Heir: cousin* Edmund Harry Cooke-Yarborough [*b* 25 Dec. 1918; *m* 1952, Anthea Katharine, *e d* of J. A. Dixon; one *s* one *d*]. *Address:* c/o Midland Bank, Knutsford, Cheshire. *Clubs:* Royal Aeronautical Society, Royal Over-Seas League.

COOKE, George Venables, CBE 1978; General Secretary, Society of Education Officers, since 1978; *b* 8 Sept. 1918; *s* of William Geoffrey Cooke and Constance Eva (*née* Venables); *m* 1941, Doreen (*née* Cooke); one *s* two *d*. *Educ:* Sandbach Sch., Cheshire; Lincoln Coll., Oxford, 1936-39 and 1946. MA, DipEd (Oxon). Served Army, 1939-46 (Major). Teacher, Manchester Grammar Sch., 1947-51; Professional Asst (Educn), W Riding of Yorkshire CC, 1951-53; Asst Dir of Educn, Liverpool, 1953-58; Dep. Dir of Educn, Sheffield, 1958-64; Dir of Educn, Lindsey (Lincs) CC, 1965-74; County Educn Officer, Lincolnshire CC, 1974-78. Secretary of State's Adv. Cttee on Handicapped Children, 1973-74; Vice-Chm., Nat. Cttee of Enquiry into Special Educn (Warnock Cttee), 1974-78; Mem., Jt Adv. Cttee on Agricultural Educn (Hudson Cttee), 1971-74. Pres., Soc. of Educn Officers, 1975-76; Chm., County Educn Officers' Soc., 1976-77 (Hon. Sec. 1970-73). *Recreations:* golf, gardening. *Address:* White House, Grange Lane, Riseholme, Lincoln LN2 2LQ. *T:* Lincoln 22667. *Club:* Royal Over-Seas League.

COOKE, George William, CBE 1975; FRS 1969; Chief Scientific Officer, Agricultural Research Council, 1975-81, retired; *b* 6 Jan. 1916; *s* of late William Harry Cooke and late Sarah Jane Cooke (*née* Whittaker); *m* 1944, Elizabeth Hannah Hill; one *s* one *d*. *Educ:* Loughborough Grammar Sch.; University Coll., Nottingham. BSc (Chem.) London Univ., 1937, PhD London, 1940. Awarded Min. of Agric. Research Schol., tenable at Rothamsted Experimental Station, 1938; apptd Scientific Officer there, 1941, and Prin. Sc. Officer, 1951; Head of Chemistry Dept, 1956-75; Deputy Dir, 1962-75 (acting Dir, 1972-73). Chm., Agriculture Group of Soc. of Chem. Industry, 1956-58; President: Fertiliser Soc., London, 1961-62; British Soc. of Soil Science, 1976-78. Lectures: Amos Meml, East Malling Res. Station, 1967; Francis New Meml, Fertiliser Soc., 1971; Clive Behrens, Univ. of Leeds, 1972-73; Scott Robertson Meml, QUB, 1973; Macaulay, Macaulay Inst. for Soil Res., 1979; Blackman, Oxford Univ., 1980; Boyd Orr Meml, Nutrition Soc., 1981. Hon. MRIA, 1980; Hon. FRAgS 1981; For. Mem., Lenin All-Union Acad. of Agric. Scis, USSR, 1972. Research Medal of Royal Agricultural Soc., 1967. *Publications:* Fertilizers and Profitable Farming, 1960; The Control of Soil Fertility, 1967; Fertilizing for Maximum Yield, 1972, 3rd edn 1982; many papers in scientific jls on soil science, crop nutrition and fertilizers. *Recreation:* boats. *Address:* 33 Topstreet Way, Harpenden, Herts. *T:* Harpenden 2899. *Club:* Farmers'.

COOKE, Gilbert Andrew, FCA; Chairman and Chief Executive, C. T. Bowring & Co. Ltd, since 1982; Director, Marsh & McLennan Companies Inc., since 1980; *b* 7 March 1923; *s* of Gilbert N. Cooke and Laurie Cooke; *m* 1949, Katherine Margaret Mary McGovern; one *s* one *d*. *Educ:* Bournemouth Sch. FCA 1950. Sen. Clerk, chartered accountants, 1950-54; Bowmaker Ltd: Chief Accountant, 1955; Dir, 1968; Man. Dir, 1968; Dep. Chm. and Chief Exec., 1972; C. T. Bowring & Co. Ltd: Dir, 1969; Gp Man. Dir, 1976-82. Chm., Finance Houses Assoc., 1972-74. *Recreations:* music, reading. *Address:* Kilmarth, Onslow Road, Burwood Park, Walton-on-Thames, Surrey. *T:* Walton-on-Thames 40451.

COOKE, Rev. Canon Greville (Vaughan Turner), MA, MusB Cantab; FRAM; FSA; Canon Emeritus, Peterborough Cathedral, since 1956; Composer, Author, Poet, Broadcaster; Adjudicator at Musical Festivals; *b* 14 July 1894; *s* of William Turner Cooke, Chief Clerk of Central Office of Royal Courts of Justice, London, and Adeline Hannah, *d* of David Johnson, MD. *Educ:* Hamilton House, Ealing; Royal Academy of Music (Schol., Exhibitioner, Prizewinner); Christ's Coll., Cambridge (Stewart of Rannoch Schol., 1913, Organ Schol.); Ridley Hall, Cambridge (Theol. Studentship); ARAM 1913; BA 1916; MusBac 1916; MA 1920. Ordained, 1918; Curate, Tavistock, 1918, Ealing, 1920; Dep. Minor Canon of St Paul's Cathedral, 1920-21; Vicar of Cransley, Northants, 1921-56; Rector of Buxted, 1956-71. Canon Non-residentiary of Peterborough Cathedral, 1955. Prof., Royal Academy of Music, 1925-59, FRAM 1927; FSA 1962. Elected FRSA by Council, 1958; Mem., Athenæum, 1931-53. Dir of Music, London Day Training Coll. Examiner for LRAM Diploma, Associated Board Exams, 1927; Lectr for London Univ., Royal Institution of Great Britain, League of Arts, Music Teachers' Association, Sussex Archæological Soc. (Mem. Council), London Appreciation Soc., RSCM, RSA, Shell-Mex, IBM. *Publications:* The Theory of Music, 1928; Art and Reality, 1929; Tonality and Expression, 1929; Poems, 1933; Cransley Broadcast Sermons, 1933; The Light of the World, 1949 (USA 1950, paperback 1965); A Chronicle of Buxted, 1960 (paperback 1965); The Grand Design, 1964; Thus Saith the Lord: a Biblical anthology, 1967; Jenny Pluck Pears, 1972; Night Fancies and other poems, 1976; The Heresies of Orthodoxy, 1980; Who Wrote the Fourth Gospel?, 1981; An Easter Offering, 1982; musical publications include: *orchestral:* Prelude for Strings; *songs:* Three Songs; Day-dreams; The Shepherdess; Bereft; Eileen Aroon; But Yesterday; Your Gentle Care; My Heaven; Weep you no more; The Bells of Heaven; Shepherd Boy's Song; *choral:* Nobody Knows; Deep River; Jillian of Berry; Oh, to be in England; How can I help England; Claribel; Oh, Hush Thee My Baby; Cobwebs; *anthems:* Drop, Slow Tears; Let us with a gladsome mind; This Joyful Eastertide; Bread of the World; Lo! God is Here; *pianoforte:* High Marley Rest; Time Keepers; Meadowsweet; La Petite; Pets' Corner; Up the Ladder; A Day at the Sea; Bargain Basement; Reef's End; Cormorant Crag: Song Prelude; Whispering Willows; Haldon Hills; In the Cathedral; Gothic Prelude; *violin and piano:* High Marley Rest; *cello and piano:* Sea Croon. Composer of several Hymns and contributor to Hymns Ancient and Modern, 1950, BBC Hymn Book, Baptist Hymn Book, Methodist Hymn Book, etc. *Address:* Waveney, West Close, Middleton-on-Sea, West Sussex.

COOKE, Jean Esme Oregon, RA 1972 (ARA 1965); (professional name Jean E. Cooke); Lecturer in Painting, Royal College of Art, 1964-74; *b* 18 Feb. 1927; *d* of Arthur Oregon Cooke, Grocer, and of Dorothy Emily Cooke (*née* Cranefield); *m* 1953, John Randall Bratby (marr. diss.), *qv*; three *s* one *d*. *Educ:* Blackheath High Sch.; Central Sch. of Arts and Crafts, Camberwell; City and Guilds; Goldsmiths' Coll. Sch. of Art; Royal Coll. of Art. NDD in Sculpture, 1949. Pottery Workshop, 1950-53. Purchase of self-portrait, 1969, and portrait of John Bratby (called Lilly, Lilly on the Brow), 1972, by Chantry Bequest; portraits of Dr Egon Wellesz and Dr Walter Oakshott for Lincoln Coll., Oxford; portrait of Mrs Bennett, Principal, for St Hilda's Coll., Oxford, 1976. Television film: Portrait of John Bratby, BBC, 1978. One-man shows: Establishment Club, 1963; Leicester Gall., 1964; Bear Lane Gall., Oxford, 1965; Arun Art Centre, Arundel; Ashgate Gall., Farnham; Moyan Gall., Manchester; Bladon Gall., Hampshire, 1966; Lane Gall., Bradford, 1967; Gallery 66, Blackheath, 1967; Motley Gall., Lewisham, 1968; Phoenix,

Suffolk, 1970; New Grafton Gall., 1971; Ansdell Gall., 1974; Woodlands Gall., Blackheath, 1976; J. K. Taylor Gall., Cambridge, 1976; open studio for: Greenwich Festival, 1977, 1978, 1980, 1981, 1982; Norwich Gall., 1979, 1980; Blackheath High Sch. Art Fund, 1979; Imp. Coll. Gall., 1980; Bakehouse Gall., Blackheath, 1980; open studio in aid of Royal Acad. Trust, 1982. Works exhibited: annually, RA, 1956–; Furneaux Gall., 1968; Upper Grosvenor Gall., 1968; Ashgate Gall., 1973; Agnews, 1974; Gall. 10, Richmond Hill, 1974; Leonie Jonleigh Gall., 1976; Dulwich Coll. Picture Gall., 1976; British Painting 1952–77, Royal Acad., 1977; Business Art Galleries, 1978; New Ashgate Gall., 1979; Tate Gall., 1979; Grosvenor Street Gall., 1979, 1980; Patrick Seale Gall., Belgravia, 1981. *Publications:* Contemporary British Artists; The Artist, 1980. *Recreations:* gardening, biology, swimming, walking. *Address:* 7 Hardy Road, Blackheath, SE3. *T:* 01-858 6288.

COOKE, Sir John F.; *see* Fletcher-Cooke.

COOKE, Air Vice-Marshal John Nigel Carlyle, OBE 1954; QHP 1979; Dean of Air Force Medicine, since 1979; *b* 16 Jan. 1922; *s* of Air Marshal Sir Cyril Bertram Cooke, KCB, CBE and Phyllis Amelia Elizabeth Cooke; *m* 1958, Elizabeth Helena Murray Johnstone; two *s* one *d. Educ:* Felsted Sch.; St Mary's Hosp., Paddington (MD, BS(London)). FRCP, FRCPEd, MRCS. House Physician, St Mary's, Paddington, 1945; RAF medical Br., 1945–; Sen. Registrar, St George's, London, 1956–58; Consultant Physician, RAF, 1958–; overseas service in Germany, Singapore, Aden; Prof. of Aviation Medicine, 1974–79. UK Mem., Medical Adv. Bd, European Space Agency, 1978–; Consultant to CAA, UK, 1972–; Chm., Defence Med. Services Postgrad. Council, 1980–. *Publications:* articles on metabolic and aviation medicine subjects in numerous medical jls. *Recreations:* gliding, fly fishing. *Address:* 4 Lincoln Close, Stoke Mandeville, Bucks HP22 5YS. *T:* Stoke Mandeville 3852. *Club:* Royal Air Force.

COOKE, Kenneth; *see* Cooke, R. K.

COOKE, Peter; *see* Cooke, W. P.

COOKE, Peter Maurice; Regional Administrator, Oxford Regional Health Authority, since 1980; *b* Feb. 1927; *s* of late Reginald and Grace Cooke; *m* 1956, Daphne Joyce (*née* Annoot); two *s. Educ:* Bristol Grammar Sch.; Corpus Christi Coll., Oxford (MA). 3rd Royal Tank Regt, 1946–48. FHA, MRSH. Admin. Assistant, Central Middlesex and Taunton HMCs, 1951–59; Asst Sec., NW Met Regional Hosp. Bd, 1959–63; Group Secretary: W Suffolk and Ipswich and District HMCs, 1963–73; Area Administrator, Suffolk AHA, 1973–80. *Recreations:* golf, choral singing. *Address:* Haremire House, Buckland, near Faringdon, Oxon SN7 8QS. *T:* Buckland 603.

COOKE, Randle Henry, MVO 1971; *b* 26 April 1930; *o s* of Col H. R. V. Cooke, Dalicote Hall, Bridgnorth, Salop and late Mrs E. F. K. Cooke, Brodawel, Tremeirchion, N Wales; *m* 1961, Clare Bennett; one *s* one *d. Educ:* Heatherdown, Ascot; Eton College. 2nd Lieut, 8th King's Royal Irish Hussars, 1949; served Korea, 1950–53 with Regt and USAF (POW); ADC to GOC 7th Armoured Div., 1955; Regimental Adjt, 1957; Instructor, RMA Sandhurst, 1960; Sqdn Comdr, Queen's Royal Irish Hussars, Malaya, Borneo and Germany, 1963; GSO3 (SD), HQ 1st Div., 1965. Equerry to the Duke of Edinburgh, 1968–71; Private Sec. to Lord Mayor of London, 1972–74. *Recreations:* most things to do with water. *Address:* Coney Hill House, Great Missenden, Bucks. *T:* Great Missenden 2147. *Club:* Cavalry and Guards.

COOKE, (Richard) Kenneth, OBE 1945; **His Honour Judge Cooke;** a Circuit Judge, since 1980; *b* 17 March 1917; *s* of Richard and Beatrice Mary Cooke; *m* 1945, Gwendoline Mary Blad; no *c. Educ:* Sebright Sch., Wolverley; Birmingham Univ. Admitted Solicitor (Hons), 1939; Birmingham Law Soc. Prizeman. Sqdn Leader, RAFVR, 1939–45. Solicitor in private practice specialising in Magistrates' Courts, 1945–52; Clerk: to Prescot and St Helens Justices, 1952–57; to Rotherham County Borough and WR Justices, 1957–64; to Bradford City Justices, 1964–70; Metropolitan Stipendiary Magistrate, 1970–80; a Recorder of the Crown Court, 1972–80. Mem. Council, Magistrates' Assoc., 1973– (Vice-Chm. Legal Cttee; Hon. Sec. Inner London Branch; a Dep. Chm., 1981–82); Mem., Lord Chancellor's Adv. Cttee on the Training of Magistrates, 1978–. Reader, Rochester Dio., 1970–. *Publications:* contribs to Criminal Law Review, Justice of the Peace and Local Govt Review, etc. *Recreations:* fishing, choral singing, sampling bin ends. *Address:* 8 St Paul's Square, Church Road, Bromley, Kent. *T:* 01-464 6761.

COOKE, Sir Robert (Gordon), Kt 1979; MA (Oxon); Special Adviser on the Palace of Westminster to the Secretary of State for the Environment, since 1979; *b* 29 May 1930; *er s* of late Robert V. Cooke, FRCS, and Dr Elizabeth Mary Cowie; *m* 1966, Jenifer Patricia Evelyn, *yr d* of Evelyn Mansfield King, *qv; s* one *d. Educ:* Harrow; Christ Church, Oxford. Pres., Oxford Univ. Conservative Assoc., 1952; Editor, Oxford Tory, 1952–53. Councillor, City and Co. of Bristol, 1954–57; contested Bristol SE at Gen. Election, 1955; MP (C) Bristol West, March 1957–1979; Parliamentary Private Secretary to: Minister of State, Home Office, 1958–59; Minister of Health, 1959–60; Minister of Works, 1960–62; introduced: Fatal Accidents Act, 1959; Historic Buildings Bill, 1963; Motorways Commn Bill, 1968; Owner Occupiers Under-occupied Housing Bill, 1973 and 1974. State Dept Foreign Leader Visitor in USA, 1961. Chairman: Cons. Broadcasting and Communications Cttee, 1962–64, 1973–76; Arts and Heritage Cttee of Cons. Party, 1970–79

(Vice-Chm., 1959–62 and 1964–70); House of Commons Administration Cttee, 1974–79; a Commissioner, 1978; Vice-Chm., Media Cttee, 1976–79; Member: Services Cttee, House of Commons, 1967–79; Select Cttee on Wealth Tax, 1974–75 (Chm. Nat. Heritage Sub-Cttee); Select Cttee, Broadcasting Proceedings of Parlt, 1977–79; Parly delegn to Brazil, 1975; Sudan, 1978; Hungary, 1978; Council of Europe, Athens, 1976; Historic Buildings Council for England, 1970–80; Board, BTA, 1980– (Chm., British Heritage Cttee, 1981–). Trustee: Nat. Heritage Meml Fund, 1980–; Primrose League. Director, Westward Television, 1970–81. Chm., Parish Meeting of Athelhampton. FRSA. *Publications:* West Country Houses, 1957; Government and the Quality of Life, 1974. *Recreations:* architecture, building, gardening. *Address:* Athelhampton, Dorchester, Dorset. *T:* Puddletown 363. *Clubs:* Carlton, Pratt's, Farmer's, Garrick, MCC.

COOKE, Brig. Robert Thomas, CBE 1943; psc†; *b* 23 Jan. 1897; *o s* of Capt. Robert George Cooke and Sarah Louisa, *d* of Thomas Connolly, Dundalk, Co. Louth; *m* 1922, Löie Howard (*d* 1979), *d* of Frank Shawcross-Smith, Buxton, Derbyshire; two *d. Educ:* Warwick Sch.; RMC Sandhurst; Staff Coll., Camberley. 2nd Lieut ASC, 1915; Capt., 1926; Bt Major, 1937; Major, 1938; Lieut-Col, 1940; Col, 1942; Brig., 1943. Served France, Belgium, Egypt and Syria, 1914–19 (severely wounded twice). Staff Coll., 1930–31; Staff Appointments: Aldershot Command, 1932–34; Southern Command, 1934–36; Active Service, Palestine Rebellion, 1937–38; GSO2, War Office, 1938–40. AA&QMG, Narvik, March 1940; AA&QMG 54 Div., July 1940; AQMG (ops) Eastern Command, 1941; DQMG 1st Army, Aug. 1942; DQMG, AFHQ, N Africa, Dec. 1942; DA&QMG 9 Corps BNAF, March 1943; Brig. "Q" 15 Army Group, July 1943; DA&QMG 5 Army, Italy, Sept. 1943; Brig. i/c Administration, HQ L of C 21st Army Group, Nov. 1943–Feb. 1945; Col i/c Admin S Wales District, 1945–46; Brig. "Q" GHQ, Middle East, 1946–47; Brig. i/c Administration, British Troops in Egypt, 1947; invalided out of Army as result of war wounds, 1949. Croix de Guerre, 1944. *Address:* c/o Mrs Thom, 215 South Lambeth Road, SW8 1XR. *T:* 01-735 3541. c/o Lloyds Bank Ltd, Bournemouth, Dorset.

COOKE, Rt. Hon. Sir Robin (Brunskill), Kt 1977; PC 1977; PhD; **Rt. Hon. Mr Justice Cooke;** Judge, Court of Appeal of New Zealand, since 1976; *b* 9 May 1926; *s* of Philip Brunskill Cooke and Valmai Digby Gore; *m* 1952, Phyllis Annette Miller; three *s. Educ:* Wanganui Collegiate Sch.; Victoria University Coll., Wellington (LLM); Gonville and Caius Coll., Cambridge (MA, PhD). Trav. Scholarship in Law, NZ, 1950; Fellow, Gonville and Caius Coll., Cambridge, 1952 (Yorke Prize, 1954). Called to the Bar, Inner Temple, 1954; practised at NZ Bar, 1955–72; QC 1964; Judge of Supreme Court, 1972. Chm., Commn of Inquiry into Housing, 1970–71. *Publications:* (ed) Portrait of a Profession (Centennial Book of NZ Law Society), 1969; articles in Law Qly Rev. and NZ Law Jl. *Recreations:* running, golf. *Address:* 4 Homewood Crescent, Karori, Wellington, New Zealand. *T:* 768-059. *Clubs:* United Oxford & Cambridge University; Wellington, Wellington Golf (NZ).

COOKE, (Roland) Cecil, CMG 1959; CBE 1952; Director of Exhibitions, Central Office of Information, 1946–61, retired; *b* 28 June 1899; *m* 1924, Doris Marjorie, *d* of Reginald Fewings. Architectural Asst, LCC, 1921; Dir of Publicity, Catesbys, Ltd, 1935; Dir of Exhibitions Div., Ministry of Information, 1945. Dir of Exhibitions, Festival of Britain, 1949–51; Dir, Festival Gardens Co., 1951; Dir of Exhibitions, British Government Pavilion, Brussels, 1958; UK representative, International Jury, Brussels Exhibition, 1958. Comr Gen., British Pavilion, Seattle World's Fair. *Publications:* contrib. to periodicals and press, illustrated stories for children, political and strip cartoons. *Recreation:* painting. *Address:* 6 Wells Close, Eastbourne, East Sussex BN20 7TX. *T:* Eastbourne 30258.

COOKE, Roy, MA; JP; Director of Coventry School Foundation, since 1977; *b* Manchester, 6 May 1930; *s* of Reginald Herbert Cooke and Alice Cooke; *m* 1957, Claire Marion Medlicott Woodward, *d* of Lt-Col C. S. Woodward, CBE, JP, DL and Irene Anne Woodward, Glamorgan; three *s. Educ:* Manchester Grammar Sch. (schol.); Trinity Coll., Oxford (schol.; BA 1951; MA 1955; DipEd). Army service, 1951–54; commnd RAEC; Staff Officer in Germany (Captain, actg Major). Assistant Master: Gillingham Grammar Sch., Kent, 1955–56; Woking Grammar Sch., Surrey, 1956–58; Manchester Grammar Sch., 1958–64; Head of For. Langs, Stockport Sch., 1964–68; Headmaster: Gravesend Sch. for Boys, 1968–74; King Henry VIII Sch., Coventry, 1974–77. JP Kent, 1972, W Midlands, 1976. *Recreations:* photography, gardening, fell-walking, music. *Address:* 10 Stivichall Croft, Coventry CV3 6GN.

COOKE, Thomas Fitzpatrick, TD 1946; DL; Lord Lieutenant, City of Londonderry, since 1975; *b* 10 July 1911; *s* of Thomas Fitzpatrick Cooke and Aileen Frances Cooke; *m* 1946, Ruth, *d* of Rt Hon. Sir Anthony Brutus Babington, QC; one *s* one *d. Educ:* Stowe; Trinity Coll., Dublin (Dip. in Commerce). Served War, 1939–46, Captain, RA. Chm., Londonderry Port and Harbour Commissioners, 1967–73. Alderman, Londonderry Corp., 1946–52; High Sheriff, County of Londonderry, 1949; DL 1950, High Sheriff, 1971–72, City of Londonderry. *Recreations:* gardening, shooting, fishing. *Address:* The Lodge, 5 Edenreagh Road, Eglinton, Londonderry BT47 3AR. *T:* Eglinton 810256. *Club:* Northern Counties (Londonderry).

COOKE, Tom Harry; Group Editorial Director, St Regis Newspapers Ltd (publishers of the Bolton Evening News, and weekly newspapers in Lancashire, South Yorkshire and north-east England), 1979–81, retired; *b* 26

March 1923; *er s* of Tom Cooke and Dorothy Cooke; *m* 1952, Jean Margaret Taylor; four *d. Educ:* Bacup and Rawtenstall Grammar Sch. Served RAF, 1942-47. Journalist on weekly, evening and morning papers in Lancs, 1939-51; Parly and Lobby Corresp. with Kemsley (now Thomson) Newspapers, 1951-59; Asst Editor, Evening Telegraph, Blackburn, 1959-64; Dep. Editor, The Journal, Newcastle upon Tyne, 1964-65; Editor-in-Chief, Bolton Evening News and Lancashire Journal Series, 1965-79. Pres., Guild of Brit. Newspaper Editors, 1975-76; Mem., Press Council, 1976-. *Recreations:* music, esp. opera; travel, reading. *Address:* 2 Hill Side House, Hill Side, Bolton BL1 5DT. *T:* Bolton 492170. *Club:* Royal Over-Seas League.

COOKE, Victor Alexander, OBE 1981; CEng, FIMechE; Chairman and Managing Director: Henry R. Ayton Ltd, Belfast, since 1970; Springvale Polyproducts Ltd, since 1964; Director: Harland & Wolff Ltd, since 1970; Northern Ireland Airports Ltd, since 1970; *b* 18 Oct. 1920; *s* of Norman Victor Cooke and Alice Harman Cooke (*née* Peavey); *m* 1951, Alison Sheila Casement; two *s* one *d. Educ:* Marlborough Coll., Wilts; Trinity Coll., Cambridge (MA). Engineer Officer, Royal Navy, 1940-46 (Lieut (E) RN). Henry R. Ayton Ltd, Belfast, 1946-; Chairman: Belfast Savings Bank, 1963; Harland & Wolff Ltd, 1980-May 1981. Member: Senate, Parliament of N Ireland, 1960-68; N Ireland Economic Council, 1974-78; Commissioner, Belfast Harbour, 1968-79. *Recreations:* sailing, shooting. *Address:* Islandreagh House, Dunadry, Antrim, N Ireland BT41 2HF. *T:* Templepatrick 32388. *Clubs:* Naval; Ulster (Belfast).

COOKE, (William) Peter; Associate Director and Head of Banking Supervision, Bank of England, since 1982; *b* 1 Feb. 1932; *s* of late Douglas Edgar Cooke, MC (Chief Educn Officer for Bucks) and of Florence May (*née* Mills); *m* 1957, Maureen Elizabeth, *er d* of late Dr E. A. Haslam-Fox; two *s* two *d. Educ:* Royal Grammar Sch., High Wycombe; Kingswood Sch., Bath; Merton Coll., Oxford (MA). Entered Bank of England, 1955; Bank for Internat. Settlements, Basle, 1958-59; Personal Asst to Man. Dir, IMF, Washington, DC, 1961-65; Sec., City Panel on Takeovers and Mergers, 1968-69; First Dep. Chief Cashier, Bank of England, 1970-73; Adviser to Governors, 1973-76; Hd of Banking Supervision, 1976-82. Chairman: City EEC Cttee, 1973-80; Group of Ten Cttee on Banking Regulations and Supervisory Practices at BIS, Basle, 1977-. *Recreations:* music, golf, travel. *Address:* Heathside, Fulmer Way, Gerrards Cross, Bucks. *Club:* Overseas Bankers.

COOKSLEY, Clarence Harrington, CBE 1973; QPM 1969; DL; one of HM Inspectors of Constabulary, 1975-77; *b* 16 Dec. 1915; *e s* of late Clarence Harrington Cooksley and Elsie Cooksley, Nottingham; *m* 1940, Eunice May White, Nottingham; two *s. Educ:* Nottingham. Joined Nottinghamshire Constabulary, 1938. Served Duke of Wellington's Regt and Dep. Asst Provost Marshal, Special Investigation Branch, Royal Corps of Military Police, 1942-46. Dir. of Dept of Law, Police Coll., Bramshill, 1961; Dep. Chief Constable of Hertfordshire, 1961-63; Chief Constable: Northumberland County Constabulary, 1963-69; Northumberland Constabulary, 1969-74; Northumbria Police, 1974-75. DL Northumberland 1971. OStJ 1966. *Address:* 8 Sandringham Way, Ponteland, Newcastle upon Tyne NE20 9AE.

COOKSON, Catherine; author, since 1950; *b* 20 June 1906; *d* of Catherine Fawcett; *m* 1940, Thomas Cookson. Mem., Writers' and Authors' Guild. *Publications:* Kate Hannigan, 1950; The Fifteen Streets; Colour Blind, 1953; Maggie Rowan, 1954; A Grand Man, 1954 (filmed as Jacqueline, 1956); The Lord and Mary Ann, 1956; Rooney, 1957 (filmed 1958); The Menagerie, 1958; The Devil and Mary Ann, 1958; Slinky Jane, 1959; Fanny McBride, 1959; Fenwick Houses, 1960; Love and Mary Ann, 1961; The Garment, 1962; Life and Mary Ann, 1962; The Blind Miller, 1963; Hannah Massey, 1964; Marriage and Mary Ann, 1964; The Long Corridor, 1965; Mary Ann's Angels, 1965; Matty Doolin, 1965; The Unbaited Trap, 1966; Katie Mulholland, 1967; Mary Ann and Bill, 1967; The Round Tower, 1968 (RSL Winifred Holtby Award for Best Regional Novel); Joe and the Gladiator, 1968; Our Kate (autobiog.), 1969; The Nice Bloke, 1969; The Glass Virgin, 1970; The Invitation, 1970; The Nipper, 1970; The Dwelling Place, 1971; Feathers in the Fire, 1971; Pure as the Lily, 1972; Blue Baccy, 1972; The Mallen Streak, 1973; The Mallen Girl, 1974; The Mallen Litter, 1974; Our John Willie, 1974; The Invisible Cord, 1975; The Gambling Man, 1975; The Tide of Life, 1976; Mrs Flannigan's Trumpet, 1976; The Girl, 1977; Go Tell It To Mrs Golightly, 1977; The Cinder Path, 1978; The Man Who Cried, 1979; Tilly Trotter, 1980; Lanky Jones, 1980; Tilly Trotter Wed, 1981; Tilly Trotter Widowed, 1982; The Whip, 1983; *as Catherine Marchant:* Heritage of Folly, 1962; Fen Tiger, 1963; House of Men, 1964; Martha Mary Crawford, 1975; The Slow Awakening, 1976; The Iron Façade, 1977. *Recreations:* painting, gardening. *Address:* Bristol Lodge, Langley on Tyne, Northumberland. *Club:* PEN (English Centre).

COOKSON, Prof. Richard Clive, FRS 1968; MA, PhD, FRSC; Professor of Chemistry in the University of Southampton since 1957; *b* 27 Aug. 1922; *s* of late Clive Cookson; *m* 1948, Ellen Fawaz; two *s. Educ:* Harrow Sch.; Trinity Coll., Cambridge. BA 1944; MA, PhD Cantab 1947. Research Fellow, Harvard Univ., 1948; Research Div. of Glaxo Laboratories Ltd, 1949-51; Lectr, Birkbeck Coll., London Univ., 1951-57. *Publications:* papers, mainly in Jl Chem. Soc. *Address:* Chemistry Department, The University, Southampton SO9 5NH. *T:* 559122.

COOKSON, Roland Antony, CBE 1974 (OBE 1946); Chairman, Lead Industries Group Ltd (until 1967 known as Goodlass Wall & Lead Industries Ltd), 1962-73 (Director, 1948-80, a Managing Director, 1952-62); Chairman, Consett Iron Co. Ltd, 1966-67 (Director 1955; Acting Chairman 1964); Director of Lloyds Bank Ltd, 1964-79 (Chairman, Northern Regional Board, 1965-79); *b* 12 Dec. 1908; *s* of late Bryan Cookson; *m* 1st, 1931, Rosamond Gwladys (*d* 1973), *er d* of late Sir John S. Barwick, 2nd Bt; one *d*; 2nd, 1974, Dr Anne Aitchison, *widow* of Sir Stephen Charles de Lancey Aitchison, 3rd Bt. *Educ:* Harrow; Magdalen Coll., Oxford. Vice-Chm., Northern Regional Board for Industry, 1949-65; Mem., Northern Economic Planning Council, 1965-68; Pres., Tyneside Chamber of Commerce, 1955-57; Chm., Northern Regional Council, CBI, 1970-72 (Vice-Chm., 1968-70); Mem., Port of Tyne Authority, 1968-74. Mem., Court and Council, Univ. of Newcastle upon Tyne; Chm., Careers Adv. Board, Univs of Newcastle upon Tyne and Durham, 1962-73. Hon. DCL Newcastle, 1974. *Recreations:* music, fishing. *Address:* The Brow, Wylam, Northumberland NE41 8DQ. *T:* Wylam 3888. *Clubs:* Brooks's; Northern Counties (Newcastle upon Tyne).

COOLEY, Sir Alan (Sydenham), Kt 1976; CBE 1972; FIE; Secretary, Department of Productivity, 1977-80, retired 1981; *b* 17 Sept. 1920; *s* of Hector William Cooley and Ruby Ann Cooley; *m* 1949, Nancie Chisholm Young; four *d. Educ:* Geelong Grammar Sch.; Melbourne Univ. (BEngSc). Cadet Engr, Dept of Supply, 1940-43; Engrg Rep., London, 1951-52; Manager, Echuca Ball Bearing Factory, 1953-55; Supply Rep., Washington, 1956-57; Manager, Small Arms Factory, Lithgow, 1958-60; Dept of Supply: First Asst Sec. (Management Services and Planning), 1961-62; Controller-Gen. (Munitions Supply), 1962-66; Sec., 1966-71; Chm., Australian Public Service Bd, 1971-77. *Recreations:* golf, fishing. *Address:* 330 Canadian Bay Road, Mt Eliza, Vic 3930, Australia. *Clubs:* Commonwealth (Canberra); Melbourne, Melbourne Cricket (Vic).

COOLS-LARTIGUE, Sir Louis, Kt 1968; OBE 1955; Governor of Dominica, 1967-78; *b* 18 Jan. 1905; *s* of Theodore Cools-Lartigue and Emily (*née* Giraud); *m* 1932, Eugene (*née* Royer); two *s* four *d. Educ:* Convents, St Lucia and Dominica; Dominica Grammar Sch. Clerk, Dominica Civil Service, 1924; Chief Clerk to Administrator and Clerk of Councils, 1932; Colonial Treas., Dominica, 1940, St Vincent, 1945; Asst Administrator, St Lucia, 1949; Chief Sec., Windward Is, 1951, retd, 1960 on abolition of office; performed duties of Governor's Dep., Windward Is, over fifty times; Speaker of Legislative Council, Dominica, 1961-67; Speaker of House of Assembly, Dominica, March-Oct. 1967. KStJ 1975. *Recreations:* tennis, swimming. *Address:* 7 Virgin Lane, Roseau, Commonwealth of Dominica, West Indies.

COOMBE, Michael Rew; Senior Treasury Counsel at the Central Criminal Court, since 1978; a Recorder of the Crown Court, since 1976; *b* 17 June 1930; *s* of John Rew Coombe and late Phyllis Mary Coombe; *m* 1961, Elizabeth Anne Hull; two *s* one *d* (and one *s* decd). *Educ:* Berkhamsted; New Coll., Oxford. MA (Eng. Lang. and Lit.). Called to Bar, Middle Temple, 1957. 2nd Prosecuting Counsel to the Inland Revenue at Central Criminal Court and 5 Courts of London Sessions, 1971; 2nd Counsel to the Crown at Inner London Sessions, Sept. 1971; 1st Counsel to the Crown at Inner London Crown Court, 1974; 4th Junior Treasury Counsel at Central Criminal Court, 1974, 2nd Jun. Treasury Counsel, 1975, 1st Jun. Treasury Counsel, 1977. *Recreations:* theatre, antiquity, art and architecture, printing. *Address:* 112 Lupus Street, SW1V 4AJ. *T:* 01-828 8742; 2 Harcourt Buildings, Temple, EC4Y 9DB. *T:* 01-353 2112.

COOMBS, Derek Michael; political journalist; *b* 12 Aug. 1937; *m* Patricia O'Toole; one *s* one *d. Educ:* Rydal Prep. Sch.; Bromsgrove. Chairman: S&U Stores plc, 1976- (Dir, 1960; Jt Man. Dir, 1970-76); Hardanger Properties plc, 1976-; Bressel Properties plc, 1976-; Home Video (Holdings) plc, 1981-; Director: Birmingham City FC, 1974-; Metalrax Holdings plc, 1975-. MP (C) Birmingham, Yardley, 1970-Feb. 1974. Successfully introduced unsupported Private Member's Bill for relaxation of Earnings Rule, 1972, establishing parly record for a measure of its kind; author of new Cons. rate scheme for Oct. 1974 Gen. Election; specialist on economic affairs. Lectured on foreign affairs at Cons. weekend confs. Active pro-European. Governor, Royal Hosp. and Home for Incurables. Sponsor: Save the Children Fund; Riding for the Disabled. *Publications:* numerous articles on home, economic and foreign affairs. *Recreations:* friends, tennis, skiing. *Address:* 14 Chester Street, SW1. *T:* 01-235 8765; Squalls Farm Estate, Tisbury, Wilts. *T:* Tisbury 870245.

COOMBS, Douglas Stafford, PhD; Controller, Books Division, British Council, since 1980; *b* 23 Aug. 1924; *s* of Alexander John Coombs and Rosina May (*née* Stafford); *m* 1950, Valerie Nyman; one *s* three *d. Educ:* Royal Liberty Sch., Romford; University College of Southampton; University College London (BA Hons, PhD). Served Royal Air Force, 1943-47. Lecturer in History, University College of the Gold Coast (subseq. Univ. of Ghana), 1952-60; British Council, 1960-: Nigeria, 1960-62; Overseas Student Centre, London, 1962-67; Bombay, 1967-73; Representative: Zambia, 1973-76; Yugoslavia, 1976-79; Visiting Fellow, Postgrad. School of Librarianship and Information Science, Univ. of Sheffield, 1979-80. *Publications:* The Conduct of the Dutch, 1958; The Gold Coast, Britain and The Netherlands, 1963; articles in historical jls. *Recreations:* travel, slow jogging, watching cricket. *Address:* 94 East Sheen Avenue, SW14 8AU. *T:* 01-876 9013. *Club:* Royal Commonwealth Society.

COOMBS, Herbert Cole, MA, PhD; FAA; FAHA; FASSA; Visiting Fellow, Centre for Resource and Environmental Studies, Australian National University, since 1976; *b* 24 Feb. 1906; *s* of Francis Robert Henry and Rebecca Mary Coombs; *m* 1931, Mary Alice Ross; three *s* one *d. Educ:* Univ. of Western Australia, Perth, WA (MA); LSE (PhD). Asst Economist, Commonwealth Bank of Australia, 1935; Economist to Commonwealth Treasury, 1939; Mem., Commonwealth Bank Board, 1942; Dir of Rationing, 1942; Dir-Gen. of Post-War Reconstruction, 1943; Governor, Commonwealth Bank of Australia, 1949-60; Chm., Commonwealth Bank Board, 1951-60; Governor and Chm. of Board, Reserve Bank of Australia, 1960-68; Chancellor, ANU, 1968-76. Chairman: Australian Elizabethan Theatre Trust, 1954-68; Australian Council for Arts, 1968-74; Australian Council for Aboriginal Affairs, 1968-76; Royal Commn on Australian Govt Admin, 1974-76. Hon. LLD: Melbourne; ANU; Sydney; Hon. DLitt WA; Hon. Fellow LSE, 1961. *Publications:* The Fragile Pattern, 1970; Other People's Money, 1971; Kulinma: Listening to Aboriginal Australians, 1978; Trial Balance—issues in my working life, 1981. *Recreations:* golf, squash, theatre-going. *Address:* 119 Milson Road, Cremorne, NSW 2090, Australia.

COOMBS, Ven. Peter Bertram; Archdeacon and Borough Dean of Wandsworth, since 1975; *b* 30 Nov. 1928; *s* of Bertram Robert and Margaret Ann Coombs; *m* 1953, Catherine Ann (*née* Buckwell); one *s* one *d. Educ:* Reading Sch.; Bristol Univ. (MA 1960); Clifton Theological Coll. Curate, Christ Church, Beckenham, 1960-64; Rector, St Nicholas, Nottingham, 1964-68; Vicar, Christ Church, New Malden, 1968-75; Rural Dean of Kingston upon Thames, 1970-75. *Recreations:* walking, sketching. *Address:* 68 Wandsworth Common North Side, SW18 2QX. *T:* 01-874 5766.

COOMBS, Prof. Robert Royston Amos, ScD; FRS 1965; FRCPath 1969; Quick Professor of Biology, and Head, Immunology Division, Department of Pathology, University of Cambridge, since 1966; Fellow of Corpus Christi College, since 1962; *b* 9 Jan. 1921; *s* of Charles Royston Amos and Edris Owen Amos (formerly Coombs); *m* 1952, Anne Marion Blomfield; one *s* one *d. Educ:* Diocesan Coll., Cape Town; Edinburgh and Cambridge Univs. BSc, MRCVS Edinburgh 1943; PhD Cambridge 1947; Stringer Fellow, King's Coll., Cambridge, 1947. Asst Director of Research, Dept of Pathology, University of Cambridge, 1948; Reader in Immunology, University of Cambridge, 1963-66. Foreign Corres., Royal Belgium Acad. of Medicine, 1979. Hon. FRCP 1973; Hon. Fellow, Amer. Coll. of Allergists, 1979. Hon. MD Linköping Univ. 1973; Hon. dr med. vet. Copenhagen, 1979; Hon. DSc Guelph, 1981. Landsteiner Award, Amer. Assoc. of Blood Banks, 1961; Gairdner Foundn Award, 1965; Henry Steele Gold Medal, RCVS, 1966; James Calvert Spence Medal, British Paediatric Assoc., 1967. *Publications:* (with Anne M. Coombs and D. G. Ingram) Serology of Conglutination and its relation to disease, 1960; (ed with P. G. H. Gell) Clinical Aspects of Immunology, 1963, 3rd edn (also with P. J. Lachmann), 1975; numerous scientific papers on immunology. *Recreation:* retreat to the country. *Address:* 6 Selwyn Gardens, Cambridge. *T:* Cambridge 352681.

COONEY, Raymond George Alfred, (Ray Cooney); actor, author, director, theatrical producer; *b* 30 May 1932; *s* of Gerard Cooney and Olive (*née* Clarke); *m* 1962, Linda Dixon; two *s. Educ:* Alleyn's Sch., Dulwich. First appeared in Song of Norway, Palace, 1946; toured in Wales, 1954-56; subseq. played in: Dry Rot and Simple Spymen, Whitehall; Mousetrap, Ambassador; Charlie Girl, Adelphi; Not Now Darling, Savoy (also film); Not Now Comrade (film). Productions (some jointly) include: Thark (revival); Doctor at Sea; The Queen's Highland Servant; My Giddy Aunt; Move Over Mrs Markham; The Mating Game; Lloyd George Knew My Father; That's No Lady-That's My Husband; Say Goodnight to Grandma; Two and Two Make Sex; At the End of the Day; Why Not Stay for Breakfast?; A Ghost on Tiptoe; My Son's Father; The Sacking of Norman Banks; The Bedwinner; The Little Hut; Springtime for Henry; Saint Joan; The Trials of Oscar Wilde; The Dame of Sark; Jack the Ripper; There Goes the Bride (and played leading role, Ambassadors, 1974); Ipi Tombi; What's a Nice Country Like US Doing In a State Like This?; Some of My Best Friends Are Husbands; Banana Ridge; Fire Angel; Elvis; Whose Life is it Anyway? (London and NY); Clouds; Chicago; Bodies; Beatlemania; Not Now Darling (revival); Hello Dolly (revival); Duet for One (London and NY); They're Playing Our Song; Children of a Lesser God. *Publications:* (with H. and M. Williams) Charlie Girl, 1965; *plays:* (with Tony Hilton) One for the Pot, 1961; Chase Me Comrade, 1964; (with Tony Hilton) Stand by your Bedouin, 1966; (with John Chapman) Not Now Darling, 1967; (with John Chapman) My Giddy Aunt, 1968; (with John Chapman) Move Over Mrs Markham, 1969; (with Gene Stone) Why Not Stay for Breakfast?, 1970; (with John Chapman) There Goes the Bride, 1973; Two into One, 1981. *Recreations:* tennis, swimming, golf. *Address:* 1-3 Spring Gardens, Trafalgar Square, SW1. *Club:* Dramatists'.

COOP, Sir Maurice (Fletcher); Kt 1973; Solicitor; *b* 11 Sept. 1907; *s* of George Harry and Ada Coop; *m* 1948, Elsie Hilda Brazier. *Educ:* Epworth Coll., Rhyl; Emmanuel Coll., Cambridge (BA). Admitted Solicitor of Supreme Court, 1932. Sec., Dunlop Rubber Co. Ltd, 1948-68; Dir, Dunlop Rubber Co. Ltd, 1966-70. Chm., Standing Adv. Cttee to Govt on Patents, 1972-74. *Recreations:* Association football, cricket. *Address:* 39 Hill Street, Berkeley Square, W1X 7FG. *T:* 01-491 4549. *Club:* United Oxford & Cambridge University.

COOPER, family name of Viscount Norwich and Baron Cooper of Stockton Heath.

COOPER; see Ashley-Cooper.

COOPER OF STOCKTON HEATH, Baron *cr* 1966, of Stockton Heath (Life Peer); **John Cooper**, MA; General Secretary and Treasurer, National Union of General and Municipal Workers, 1962-73; National Water Council, 1973-77; *b* 7 June 1908; *s* of late John Ainsworth Cooper and of Annie Lily Cooper (*née* Dukes); *m* 1934, Nellie Spencer (marr. diss. 1969); three *d* ; *m* 1969, Mrs Joan Rogers. *Educ:* Stockton Heath Council Sch.; Lymm Grammar Sch., Cheshire. Employed Crosfields Soap Works, Warrington, 1924-28; NUGMW, 1928-73, District Sec., Southern Dist, 1944-61; Chm., 1952-61. Member: Manchester CC, 1936-42; LCC, 1949; Alderman, 1952-53; London Labour Party Executive; MP (Lab) Deptford, 1950-51; PPS to Sec. of State for Commonwealth Relations, 1950-51. Member: NEC Labour Party, 1953-57; TUC Gen. Council, 1959-73 (Pres., TUC, 1970-71). Chm., British Productivity Council, 1965-66; Mem., Thames Conservancy, 1955-74. Governor various instns, etc. MA Oxon. Prix de la Couronne Française, 1970. *Address:* 23 Kelvin Grove, Chessington, Surrey. *T:* 01-397 3908.

COOPER, Very Rev. Alan; *see* Cooper, Very Rev. W. H. A.

COOPER, Sqdn Ldr Albert Edward, MBE 1946; formerly: Managing Director, Dispersions Ltd; Director, Ault & Wiborg International Ltd; *b* 23 Sept. 1910; *s* of Albert Frederick Smith and Edith Alice Cooper, Withernsea, Yorks; *m* 1st, 1933, Emily Muriel (*decd*), *d* of William John Nelder, Launceston; one *d* ; 2nd, 1978, Margaret de Gignac, *d* of Edward Gerrard Rabette, Portarlington, Queen's Co., Eire. *Educ:* London Coll. for Choristers; Australia. Entered politics, 1935, when elected to Ilford Borough Council; Chairman: Electricity and Lighting Cttee; Education (Finance) and Legal and Parliamentary Cttees; Alderman, 1947. Served War of 1939-45; enlisted in RAF, 1940, and served as navigator in Coastal Command. Contested (C) Dagenham, Gen. Election, 1945; MP (C) Ilford South, 1950-66, 1970-Feb. 1974; PPS to President of the Board of Trade, 1952-54. *Recreations:* cricket, swimming, bridge, and motoring. *Address:* 156 Park West, W2.

COOPER, Rev. Albert Samuel; Moderator, Free Church Federal Council, 1973-74; *b* 6 Nov. 1905; *s* of Samuel and Edith Cooper; *m* 1936, Emily, *d* of Hugh and Emily Williams; one *s* one *d. Educ:* Birkenhead Inst.; London Univ. (external student; BA Hons Philosophy); Westminster Coll., Cambridge (DipTheol); Fitzwilliam House, Cambridge (BA Theol Tripos, MA). Ordained 1936. Pastoral charges: St Columba's Presbyterian Church, Grimsby, 1936-41; Blundellsands Presbyt. Ch., Liverpool, 1941-44; St Columba's Presbyt. Ch., Cambridge, 1944-60; St Columba's Presbyt. (later United Reformed) Ch., Leeds, 1960-72, retd 1972. Free Church Chaplain, Fulbourn Mental Hosp., Cambridgeshire, 1950-60. Moderator, Presbyt. Ch. of England, 1968-69. *Address:* 10 Thorpe Bank, Rock Ferry, Birkenhead, Merseyside L42 4NP. *T:* 051-645 0418.

COOPER, Andrew Ramsden, CBE 1965; FEng 1978; Industrial Consultant, since 1966; Member for Operations and Personnel, Central Electricity Generating Board, 1959-66; *b* 1 Oct. 1902; *s* of Mary and William Cooper, Rotherham, Yorks. *Educ:* Rotherham Grammar Sch.; Sheffield Univ. Colliery Engineer, Yorks and Kent, 1916-28; Chief Electrical Engineer, Pearson & Dorman Long, 1928; Personal Asst to G. A. Mower, London, 1934; joined Central Electricity Board Operation Dept, NW England and N Wales, 1935; transf. to HQ, 1937; Operation Engineer, SE and E England, 1942; Chief Operation Engineer to Central Electricity Board, 1944; Controller, Merseyside and N Wales Div. (Central Electricity Authority), 1948-52; NW Div., 1952-54; N West, Merseyside and N Wales Div., 1954-57; Mem., Ops and Personnel, CEGB, 1957-66. Inventor, ARCAID Deaf/Blind Conversation Machine; Pres., Electrical Industries Benevolent Assoc., 1964-65; Mem., GB-USSR Cttee. Faraday Lectr, 1952-53. CEng, FIEE; SFInstE; FIEEE. Pres., CIGRE, 1966-72. Bernard Price Meml Lectr, S African Inst. of Electr. Engrg, 1970; Meritorious Service Award, Power Engrg Soc. of America, 1972; Willans Medal, IEE, 1952; Thornton Medal, AMEME, 1961; Donor, Power/Life Award, Power Engrg Soc. Hon. Mem., Batti-Wallahs Assoc. Hon. MEng Liverpool Univ., 1954. *Publications include:* Load Dispatching, with Special Reference to the British Grid System (a paper receiving John Hopkinson Award, 1948, and Willans Medal, 1952, IEE). *Recreations:* golf, art, music, writing, broadcasting. *Address:* 4 Exeter House, Putney Heath, SW15 3SU. *T:* 01-788 5544. *Clubs:* Savile, Energy Industries, 25, Dynamcables; Royal Wimbledon Golf.

COOPER, Beryl Phyllis, QC 1977; a Recorder of the Crown Court, since 1977; *b* 24 Nov. 1927; *o c* of late Charles Augustus Cooper and of Phyllis Lillie (*née* Burrows). *Educ:* Surbiton High Sch.; Univ. of Birmingham (BComm 1950; Hon. Sec., Guild of Undergrads, 1949-50). Called to the Bar, Gray's Inn, 1960. Hosp. Adminstr, Royal Free Hosp., 1951-57. Formerly: Councillor, St Pancras Metrop. Bor. Council; Mem., Homeopathic Hosp. Cttee; Mem., Bd of Visitors, Wandsworth Prison. Conservative Party Candidate, Stepney, 1966; Founder Mem., Bow Gp (former Sec. and Council Mem.); Mem. Exec. Cttee, Soc. of Cons. Lawyers, 1981-. Member: Cripps Cttee, Women and the Law; Home Office Cttee on Criminal Statistics (Perks Cttee); Housing Corp., 1976-78; Criminal Injuries Compensation Bd, 1978-; Lambeth, Southwark and Lewisham AHA (Teaching), 1980-82. *Publications:* pamphlets for CPC; articles on social, criminal and local govt matters.

Recreations: travel, swimming, golf. *Address:* 31 Alleyn Park, Dulwich, SE21 8AT. *T:* 01-670 7012; 2 Dr Johnson's Buildings, Temple, EC4Y 7AY. *T:* 01-353 5371; 8d South Cliff Tower, Eastbourne, Sussex. *Clubs:* English-Speaking Union; Caledonian (Edinburgh); Royal Eastbourne Golf, Dulwich and Sydenham Hill Golf.

COOPER, Sir Charles (Eric Daniel), of Woollahra, 5th Bt, *cr* 1863; *b* 5 Oct. 1906; *s* of Sir Daniel Cooper, 4th Bt, and Lettice Margaret, *y d* of 1st Viscount Long; *S* father 1954; *m* 1st, 1931, Alice Estelle (*d* 1952), *y d* of late William Manifold, Victoria, Australia; 2nd, 1953, Mary Elisabeth, *e d* of Capt. J. Graham Clarke, Frocester Manor, Glos; two *s. Educ:* Harrow; RMC Sandhurst. Lieut 1st The Royal Dragoons, 1926; Capt., 1935; Major, 1945. Served War of 1939-45. *Recreations:* hunting and shooting. *Heir: s* William Daniel Charles Cooper, *b* 5 March 1955. *Address:* Cranbourne Grange, Sutton Scotney, Winchester SO21 3NA. *Club:* Cavalry and Guards.

COOPER, Lady Diana, (Diana, Viscountess Norwich); 3rd *d* of 8th Duke of Rutland, KG (*d* 1925), and Violet Lindsay (*d* 1937); *m* 1919 (as Lady Diana Manners) A. Duff Cooper, 1st Viscount Norwich (*cr* 1952), PC, GCMG, DSO (*d* 1954); one *s* (*see* 2nd Viscount Norwich). Nurse at Guy's Hospital during European War, 1914-18. Took leading part in Max Reinhardt's play, The Miracle, that showed, on and off, for 12 years in London and provincial towns, in USA (New York and all the great cities), and on the Continent (Prague, Buda-Pest, Vienna, Dortmund, Salzburg). Pres., Order of Charity. *Publications:* The Rainbow Comes and Goes, 1958; The Light of Common Day, 1959; Trumpets from the Steep, 1960. *Address:* 10 Warwick Avenue, W2.

COOPER, Douglas; Art Historian and Critic: Slade Professor of Fine Art, Oxford University, 1957-58; *b* London, 20 Feb. 1911. *Educ:* various European Univs. Dep.-Dir, Monuments and Fine Arts Branch, Control Commn for Germany, 1944-46; Lectr, Courtauld Institute of Art; Flexner Lectr, Bryn Mawr, 1961; Mem., Real Patronato of Prado Mus., Madrid; Fellow (*hc*), Fogg Mus., Harvard Univ.; Chevalier de la Légion d'Honneur. *Publications:* Letters of Van Gogh to Emile Bernard, 1937; The Road to Bordeaux, 1940; Paul Klee, 1949; Turner, 1949; Juan Gris, 1949; Leger, 1949; Degas Pastels, 1954; Catalogue of the Courtauld Collection, 1954; Van Gogh Water Colours, 1955; Toulouse-Lautrec, 1956; Graham Sutherland, 1961; De Staël, 1962; Picasso: Les Déjeuners, 1962; Picasso: Theatre, 1968; The Cubist Epoch, 1971; Braque: The Great Years, 1973; Juan Gris: catalogue raisonné, 1977; The Letters of Paul Gauguin to the Brothers Van Gogh, 1982. *Address:* Monte Carlo Star, Monte Carlo.

COOPER, Sir Francis Ashmole, (Sir Frank), 4th Bt *cr* 1905; Chairman, Ashmole Investment Trust Ltd, 1969-74; *b* 9 Aug. 1905; *s* of Sir Richard Ashmole Cooper, 2nd Bt, and Alice Elizabeth (*d* 1963), *d* of Rev. E. Priestland, Spondon; *S* brother, 1970; *m* 1933, Dorothy F. H., *d* of Emile Deen, Berkhamsted, and Maggie Louise Deen; one *s* two *d* (and one *d* decd). *Educ:* Lancing Coll.; King's Coll., Cambridge (MA); University Coll., London (PhD). Joined Cooper, McDougall and Robertson Ltd, 1926; on leave to University College, 1931-36; Technical Director, 1940-62; retired, 1962. *Recreation:* yachting. *Heir: s* Richard Powell Cooper [*b* 13 April 1934; *m* 1957, Angela Marjorie, *e d* of Eric Wilson, Norton-on-Tees; one *s* two *d*]. *Address:* La Bastide de la Maraouro, 06490 Tourrettes sur Loup, France. *Clubs:* Carlton, Royal Thames Yacht; Royal Motor Yacht (Sandbanks, Poole).

COOPER, Sir Frank, GCB 1979 (KCB 1974; CB 1970); CMG 1961; Permanent Under Secretary of State, Ministry of Defence, 1976-82; *b* 2 Dec. 1922; *s* of late V. H. Cooper, Fairfield, Manchester; *m* 1948, Peggie, *d* of F. J. Claxton; two *s* one *d. Educ:* Manchester Grammar Sch.; Pembroke Coll., Oxford (Hon. Fellow, 1976). War of 1939-45: Pilot, Royal Air Force, 1941-46. Asst Principal, Air Ministry, 1948; Private Secretary: to Parly Under-Sec. of State for Air, 1949-51; to Permanent Under-Sec. of State for Air, 1951-53; to Chief of Air Staff, 1953-55; Asst Sec., Head of the Air Staff, Secretariat, 1955-60; Dir of Accounts, Air Ministry, 1961-62; Asst Under-Sec. of State, Air Min., 1962-64, Min. of Defence, 1964-68; Dep. Under-Sec. of State, Min. of Defence, 1968-70; Dep. Sec., CSD, 1970-73; Permanent Under-Sec. of State, NI Office, 1973-76. Commodore, Civil Service Sailing Assoc., 1976. *Recreations:* tennis, sailing. *Club:* Athenæum.

COOPER, Wing-Comdr Geoffrey; free-lance writer; *b* 18 Feb. 1907; *s* of Albert Cooper, Leicester, and Evelyn J. Bradnam, Hastings. *Educ:* Wyggeston Gram. Sch., Leicester; Royal Grammar School, Worcester. Accountancy, business management. Auxiliary Air Force, 1933; BOAC, 1939. Royal Air Force 1939-45, Pilot (mentioned in despatches). MP (Lab) for Middlesbrough West Div., 1945-51. Captain, 56th London Boys' Brigade. *Publications:* Cæsar's Mistress (exposé of BBC and nationalisation); articles in England, Bahamas and USA on civil aviation, business management and government methods. *Recreations:* portrait and landscape painting, swimming, tennis, horse riding. *Address:* PO Box N1673, Nassau, Bahamas; 9 Rosenau Crescent, SW11. *Club:* Royal Air Force.

COOPER, George A.; Marketing and Business Consultant; Chairman, Independent Television Publications Ltd, since 1971; *b* 9 Oct. 1915; *s* of late Joseph Cooper; *m* 1944, Irene Burns; one *d.* Exec. with internat. publishing gp; served War of 1939-45, Royal Artillery (Captain); Exec., Hulton Press, 1949-55; Director: ABC Television Ltd, 1955-77; Thames Television Ltd, 1968 (Man. Dir, 1974-77); Independent Television News, 1976-77; Chm.,

Network Programme Cttee of Independent Television, 1975-77. *Recreations:* golf, walking. *Address:* 43 Rivermill, 151 Grosvenor Road, SW1V 3JN. *T:* 01-821 9305. *Clubs:* Royal Automobile, Thirty.

COOPER, George Edward; Chairman, North Thames Gas Region (formerly North Thames Gas Board), 1970-78; Part-time Member, British Gas Corporation, 1973-78; *b* 25 Jan. 1915; *s* of H. E. Cooper and R. A. Jones, Wolverhampton; *m* 1941, Dorothy Anne Robinson; one *s. Educ:* Wolverhampton Municipal Grammar Sch. Wolverhampton and Walsall Corp., 1933-40. Served War, 1940-45, with RA in Middle East (Bimbashi Sudan Defence Force), Captain. Qualified as Accountant, Inst. of Municipal Treasurers and Accountants (now Chartered Inst. of Public Accountants), 1947; Hemel Hempstead Development Corp., 1948-50; W Midlands Gas Bd (finally Dep. Chm.), 1950-70. IPFA (FIMTA 1965); CIGasE 1968. OStJ 1976. *Recreations:* photography, geology, golf. *Club:* City Livery.

COOPER, Gen. Sir George (Leslie Conroy), KCB 1979; MC 1953; Adjutant-General, since 1981; Aide-de-Camp General to the Queen, since 1982; *b* 10 Aug. 1925; *s* of late Lt-Col G. C. Cooper and Mrs Y. V. Cooper, Bulmer Tye House, Sudbury; *m* 1957, Cynthia Mary Hume; one *s* one *d. Educ:* Downside Sch.; Trinity Coll., Cambridge. Commnd 1945; served with Bengal Sappers and Miners, 1945-48; Korea, 1952-53; psc 1956; jssc 1959; Instructor, RMA Sandhurst, 1959-62 and Staff Coll., Camberley, 1964; GSO1, 1st Div., 1964-66; CRE, 4th Div., 1966-68; MoD, 1968-69; Comdr, 19th Airportable Bde, 1969-71; Royal Coll. of Defence Studies, 1972; Dep. Dir Army Trng, 1973-74; GOC SW District, 1974-75; Dir, Army Staff Duties, 1976-79; GOC SE District, 1979-81. Colonel Commandant: RE, 1980-; RPC, 1981-; Col, Queen's Gurkha Engineers, 1981-. Chm., Infantile Hypercalcæmia Foundn, 1980-. *Recreations:* ski-ing, sailing, tennis, shooting, gardening. *Address:* c/o Barclays Bank Ltd, 3-5 King Street, Reading, Berks. *Club:* Army and Navy.

COOPER, Sir Gilbert (Alexander), Kt 1972; CBE 1964; ED 1943; MLC, Bermuda, 1968-72, retired; *b* 31 July 1903; *s* of Alexander Samuel and Laura Ann Cooper. *Educ:* Saltus Grammar Sch., Bermuda; McGill Univ., Canada (BCom). Mem., Corp. of Hamilton, Bermuda, 1946-72; Mayor of Hamilton, 1963-72. Mem., House of Assembly, 1948-68 (Chm. House Finance Cttee, 1959-68). *Recreations:* music, painting, sailing, swimming. *Address:* Shoreland, Pembroke, Bermuda. *T:* 5-4189. *Clubs:* Royal Bermuda Yacht, Royal Hamilton Amateur Dinghy, Bermuda Police.

COOPER, Henry, OBE 1969; company director since 1972; *b* 3 May 1934; *s* of Henry William Cooper and late Lily Nutkins; *m* 1960, Albina Genepri; two *s. Educ:* Athelney Street Sch., Bellingham. Professional boxer, 1954-71. KSG 1978. *Film:* Royal Flash, 1975. *Publications:* Henry Cooper: an autobiography, 1972; The Great Heavyweights, 1978. *Recreation:* golf. *Address:* 36 Brampton Grove, NW4.

COOPER, Jilly, (Mrs Leo Cooper); Columnist, Sunday Times, since 1969; *b* 21 Feb. 1937; *d* of Brig. W. B. Sallitt, OBE, and Mary Elaine Whincup; *m* 1961, Leo Cooper; one *s* one *d. Educ:* Godolphin Sch., Salisbury. Reporter, Middlesex Independent, Brentford, 1957-59; followed by numerous short-lived jobs as account executive, copy writer, publishers' reader, receptionist, puppy fat model, switchboard wrecker, and very temporary typist. *Publications:* How to Stay Married, 1969: How to Survive from Nine to Five, 1970 (new edn as Work and Wedlock, 1978); Jolly Super, 1971; Men and Super Men, 1972; Jolly Super Too, 1973; Women and Super Women, 1974 (new edn as Super Men and Super Women, 1977); Jolly Superlative, 1975; Super Jilly, 1977; Class, 1979; The British in Love, 1980; (with Tom Hartman) Violets and Vinegar, 1980; Supercooper, 1980; Intelligent and Loyal, 1981; Jolly Marsupial, 1982; *novels:* Emily, 1975; Bella, 1976; Harriet, 1976; Octavia, 1977; Prudence, 1978; Imogen, 1978; *short stories:* Love and Other Heartaches, 1981; *for children:* Little Mabel, 1980; Little Mabel's Great Escape, 1981; Little Mabel Wins, 1982. *Recreations:* merry-making, wild flowers, music, mongrels. *Address:* The Sunday Times, Thomson House, 200 Gray's Inn Road, WC1X 8EZ. *T:* 01-837 1234.

COOPER, Joan Davies, CB 1972; Hon. Research Fellow, University of Sussex, since 1979; *b* 12 Aug. 1914; *d* of late Valentine Holland Cooper and of Wynnefred Louisa Cooper; unmarried. *Educ:* Fairfield High Sch., Manchester; University of Manchester (BA). Asst Dir of Educn, Derbyshire CC, 1941; Children's Officer, E Sussex CC, 1948; Chief Inspector, Children's Dept, Home Office, 1965-71; Dir, Social Work Service, DHSS, 1971-76; Nat. Inst. for Social Work, 1976-77. Mem., SSRC, 1973-76. Vice Pres., Nat. Children's Bureau, 1964; Chairman: NACRO Community Alternatives for Young Offenders, 1978; Adv. Council on Juvenile Crime, 1982; Parents for Children, 1979; Trustee, Homestart, 1981; Sponsor, Inst. of Family Therapy, 1981. FRAI 1972. *Publications:* Patterns of Family Placement, 1978; Social Groupwork with Elderly Patients, 1981; contribs to professional and social work journals. *Recreation:* gardening. *Address:* 2A Gallows Bank, Abinger Place, Lewes, East Sussex BN7 2QA. *T:* Lewes 2604. *Club:* University Women's.

COOPER, Ven. John Leslie; Archdeacon of Aston and Canon Residentiary of St Philip's Cathedral, Birmingham, since 1982; *b* 16 Dec. 1933; *s* of Iris and Leslie Cooper; *m* 1959, Gillian Mary Dodds; two *s* one *d. Educ:* Tiffin School, Kingston, Surrey; Chichester Theological Coll. BD 1965, MPhil 1978, London Univ. (External Student). National Service, RA; commissioned,

1952-54; 292 Para. Field Regt, RA (TA), 1954–58; 21 SAS (Artists Rifles) (TA), 1958–59. General Electric Co. management trainee, 1954–59; Chichester Theolog. Coll., 1959–62; Asst Curate, All Saints, Kings Heath, Birmingham, 1962–65; Asst Chaplain, HM Prison, Wandsworth, 1965–66; Chaplain: HM Borstal, Portland, Dorset, 1966–68; HM Prison, Bristol, 1968–72; Research Fellow, Queen's Coll., Birmingham, 1972–73; Priest-in-Charge 1973–81, Vicar 1981–82, St Paul's, Balsall Heath, Birmingham. Examining Chaplain to Bishop of Birmingham, 1981–. *Recreations:* music, reading, squash, walking, travel, carpentry, gardening. *Address:* 51 Moor Green Lane, Moseley, Birmingham B13 8NE. *T:* 021–449 0766.

COOPER, Prof. John Philip, DSc; FRS 1977; FIBiol; Director, Welsh Plant Breeding Station, University College of Wales, Aberystwyth, since 1975; *b* Buxton, Derbyshire, 16 Dec. 1923; *o s* of Frank Edward and Nora Goodwin Cooper; *m* 1951, Christine Mary Palmer; one *s* three *d*. *Educ:* Stockport Grammar Sch.; Univ. of Reading (BSc 1945, PhD 1953, DSc 1964); FitzWilliam House, Cambridge (DipAgrSc 1946). Scientific Officer, Welsh Plant Breeding Station, 1946–50; Lectr, Univ. of Reading, 1950–54; Plant Geneticist, 1950–59, and Head of Dept of Develtl Genetics, Welsh Plant Breeding Station, 1959–75. Consultant, FAO Headquarters, Rome, 1956; Nuffield Royal Society Bursary, CSIRO, Canberra, 1962; Visiting Professor: Univ. of Kentucky, 1965; Univ. of Khartoum, 1975. Member: UK Seeds Exec., 1979–; Internat. Bd for Plant Genetics Resources, 1981–. *Publications:* (ed, with P. F. Wareing) Potential Crop Production, 1971; (ed) Photosynthesis and Productivity in Different Environments, 1975; various papers on crop physiology and genetics in sc. jls. *Recreations:* gardening, walking. *Address:* Bronsiriol, Bryn-y-mor, Aberystwyth, Dyfed. *T:* Aberystwyth 617644. *Club:* Farmers'.

COOPER, Joseph, OBE 1982; Pianist and Broadcaster; *b* 7 Oct. 1912; *s* of Wilfrid Needham and Elsie Goodacre Cooper; *m* 1st, 1947, Jean (*d* 1973), *d* of late Sir Louis Greig, KBE, CVO; no *c* ; 2nd, 1975, Carol, *d* of Charles and Olive Borg. *Educ:* Clifton Coll. (music schol.); Keble Coll., Oxford (organ schol.). MA (Oxon), ARCM (solo piano). Studied piano under Egon Petri, 1937–39. Served War, in RA, 1939–46. Solo pianist debut, Wigmore Hall, 1947 (postponed, Oct. 1939, owing to War); concerto debut, Philharmonia Orchestra, 1950; BBC debut Promenade Concerts Royal Albert Hall, 1953. Since then has toured in: British Isles, Europe, Africa, India, Canada. Many solo piano records. Chm., BBC TV prog., Face The Music, 1971–79. Hon. Chm., Barclaycard Composer of the Year Competition, 1983. Liveryman, Worshipful Co. of Musicians, 1963–; Mem., Music Panel of Arts Council (and Chm. piano sub-cttee), 1966–71; Trustee, Countess of Munster Musical Trust, 1975–80. Governor, Clifton College. Ambrose Fleming award, Royal Television Soc., 1961; Music Trades Assoc. Record Award, 1976. *Publications:* Hidden Melodies, 1975; More Hidden Melodies, 1976; Still More Hidden Melodies, 1978; Facing the Music (autobiog.), 1979; Arrangement of Vaughan Williams Piano Concerto for 2 pianos (in collab. with composer). *Recreations:* walking, church architecture. *Address:* Octagon Lodge, Ranmore, near Dorking, Surrey. *T:* East Horsley 2658. *Club:* Garrick.
See also A. C. N. Borg.

COOPER, Prof. Kenneth Ernest; Emeritus Professor of Bacteriology, Bristol University, 1968; *b* 8 July 1903; *s* of E. Cooper; *m* 1930, Jessie Griffiths; no *c*. *Educ:* Tadcaster Grammar Sch.; Leeds Univ. BSc 1925, PhD 1927 Leeds; LRCP MRCS 1936; FIBiol. Leeds University: Research Asst in Chemotherapy, 1928–31; Research Asst in Bacteriology, 1931–36; Lectr in Bacteriology, 1936–38; Bristol University: Lectr in Bacteriology, 1938–46; Reader in Bacteriology, 1946–50; Prof. of Bacteriology, 1951–68; Dep. Dean of the Faculty of Science, 1955–58. Hon. Gen. Sec. of Soc. for Gen. Microbiology, 1954–60, Hon. Treas., 1961–68, Hon. Mem., 1969. *Publications:* numerous papers in medical, chemical and bacteriological journals. *Recreations:* golf, chess. *Address:* Fairfield, 50 Clevedon Road, Tickenham, Clevedon, Avon BS21 6RB. *T:* Nailsea 2375.

COOPER, Kenneth Reginald; Director General, National Federation of Building Trades Employers, since 1979; *b* 28 June 1931; *s* of Reginald and Louisa May Cooper; *m* 1955, Olga Ruth (*née* Harvey); two *s* two *d*. *Educ:* Queen Elizabeth's Grammar Sch., Barnet; New Coll., Oxford (MA). FIPM; FITD (Pres., 1981–). Various appointments, Min. of Labour, 1954–62; Principal, HM Treasury, 1962–65; Principal Private Secretary to Minister of Labour, 1966–67; Asst Sec. for Industrial Training, Min. of Labour, 1967–70; Chief Executive: Employment Services Agency, 1971–75; Training Services Agency, 1975–79. *Recreations:* music, Rugby football. *Address:* 82 New Cavendish Street, W1M 8AD.

COOPER, Prof. Leon N., PhD ; Thomas J. Watson, Sr, Professor of Science, Brown University, Providence, RI, since 1974; Co-Director, Center for Neural Science; *b* NYC, 28 Feb. 1930; *s* of Irving Cooper and Anna Cooper (*née* Zola); *m* 1969, Kay Anne Allard; two *d*. *Educ:* Columbia Univ. (AB 1951, AM 1953, PhD 1954). Nat. Sci. Foundn post-doctoral Fellow, and Mem., Inst. for Advanced Study, 1954–55; Res. Associate, Univ. of Illinois, 1955–57; Asst Prof., Ohio State Univ., 1957–58; Associate Prof., Brown Univ., 1958–62, Prof., 1962–66, Henry Ledyard Goddard Prof., 1966–74. Consultant, various governmental agencies, industrial and educational organizations. Lectr, Summer Sch., Varenna, Italy, 1955; Visiting Professor: Brandeis Summer Inst., 1959; Bergen Internat. Sch. Physics, Norway, 1961; Scuola Internazionale di Fisica, Erice, Italy, 1965; Ecole Normale Supérieure, Centre Universitaire Internat., Paris, 1966; Cargèse Summer Sch., 1966; Radiation Lab., Univ. of Calif. at Berkeley, 1969; Faculty of Scis, Quai St Bernard, Paris, 1970, 1971; Brookhaven Nat. Lab., 1972; Chair of Math. Models of Nervous System, Fondation de France, 1978–. Alfred P. Sloan Foundn Res. Fellow, 1959–66; John Simon Guggenheim Meml Foundn Fellow, 1965–66. Fellow: Amer. Physical Soc.; Amer. Philosoph. Soc.; Amer. Acad. of Arts and Sciences; Nat. Acad. of Sciences. Comstock Prize, Nat. Acad. of Scis, 1968; (jtly) Nobel Prize for Physics, 1972; Award of Excellence, Grad. Fac. Alumni, Columbia Univ., 1974; Déscartes Medal, Acad. de Paris, Univ. René Déscartes, 1977. Hon. DSc: Columbia, 1973; Sussex, 1973; Illinois, 1974; Brown, 1974; Gustavus Adolphus Coll., 1975; Ohio State Univ., 1976; Univ. Pierre et Marie Curie, Paris, 1977. *Publications:* Introduction to the Meaning and Structure of Physics, 1968; (contrib.) The Physicist's Conception of Nature, 1973; contrib. The Many Body Problem, 1963; contrib. to numerous jls incl. Physics Rev., Amer. Jl Physics, Biological Cybernetics. *Recreations:* music, theatre, skiing. *Address:* 49 Intervale Road, Providence, RI 02906, USA. *T:* (401)–421–1181; Physics Department, Brown University, Providence, RI 02912, USA. *T:* (401)–863–2172. *Club:* University Faculty (Providence, RI).

COOPER, Dr Leslie Hugh Norman, OBE 1973; FRS 1964; CChem, FRSC, FIBiol, FGS; formerly Deputy Director, Marine Biological Laboratory, Plymouth, retired 1972; *b* 17 June 1905; *s* of Charles Herbert Cooper and Annie Cooper (*née* Silk), Prestatyn, Clwyd; *m* 1935, Gwynedd Daloni Seth Hughes, Bangor, Gwynedd; four *s* one *d*. *Educ:* John Bright Grammar Sch., Llandudno; University Coll. of North Wales, Bangor. PhD 1927, DSc 1938, Univ. of Wales. Chemist, Rubber Research Assoc., 1927–29; Chemist, Imperial Chemical Industries, 1929–30; Chemist at the Marine Biological Laboratory, Plymouth, engaged on the study of the physics and chemistry of the ocean as a biological environment, 1930–72; continuing research at Plymouth on quaternary oceanography and on the application of plate tectonics to biological problems. Hon. DSc Exon, 1974. *Publications:* numerous papers on oceanography. *Address:* 2 Queens Gate Villas, Lipson, Plymouth PL4 7PN. *T:* Plymouth 661174.

COOPER, Louis Jacques B.; see Blom-Cooper.

COOPER, Prof. Malcolm McGregor, CBE 1965; Emeritus Professor, University of Newcastle upon Tyne, since 1972; *b* Havelock North, New Zealand, 17 Aug. 1910; *s* of Laurence T. Cooper, farmer, and Sarah Ann Cooper; *m* 1937, Hilary Mathews, Boars Hill, Oxford; three *d*. *Educ:* Napier Boys High Sch., NZ; Massey Agricultural Coll., Palmerston North, NZ; University Coll., Oxford. BAgrSc (NZ), 1933; Rhodes Scholarship, 1933; Oxford, 1934–37; Diploma Rural Econ., 1935; BLitt in Agric. Economics, 1937. Returned to NZ 1937; Mem. of Staff, Dept of Scientific and Industrial Research, till 1940, when appointed Lecturer in Dairy Husbandry at Massey Agric. Coll. Served War of 1939–45, with NZ Mil. Forces, 1941–46; in Italy with 2 NZ Div. in an Infantry battalion, 1943–45; rank of Major on demobilisation; returned to Massey as Head of Dept of Dairy Husbandry, 1946; Prof. of Agriculture, Univ. of London, 1947–54; Prof. of Agriculture and Rural Economy, and Dean, Fac. of Agriculture, Univ. of Newcastle upon Tyne, 1954–72; Pro-Vice-Chancellor, Univ. of Newcastle upon Tyne, 1971–72. Nat. Res. Coordinator, Instituto Nacional Investigaciones Agrarias, Spain, 1972–75. President: British Grassland Soc., 1958–59; British Soc. of Animal Production, 1972–73; formerly Member: Nature Conservancy Council; Agricultural Advisory Council; Advisory Board, Pig Industry Development Authority; Agricultural Research and Advisory Cttee for Government of Sudan; Scientific Advisory Panel of the Minister of Agriculture; Agricultural Cttee of UGC; Chm., Beef Recording Assoc. (UK) Ltd. Hon. Life Mem., British Soc. of Animal Production, 1979. FRSE 1956, Hon. FRASE 1969. Hon. Fellow, Wye Coll., London Univ., 1979. Massey Ferguson Award for services to agriculture, 1970. Hon DSc Massey Univ., NZ, 1972. *Publications:* (in collaboration) Principles of Animal Production (New Zealand), 1945; Beef Production, 1953; Competitive Farming, 1956; Farm Management, 1960; Grass Farming, 1961; Sheep Farming, 1965; (with M. B. Willis) Profitable Beef Production, 1972; technical articles on agricultural topics. *Recreations:* Rugby football (Rugby Blue, 1934, 1935 and 1936; Capt. OURFC 1936, and Sec. 1935; capped for Scotland, 1936); summer sports, reading, farming. *Address:* Holme Cottage, Longhoughton, Alnwick, Northumberland. *Club:* Farmers'.

COOPER, Margaret Jean Drummond, OBE 1980; Chief Education Officer, General Nursing Council for England and Wales, 1974–82; *b* 24 March 1922; *d* of Canon Bernard R. Cooper and A. Jean Cooper (*née* Drackley). *Educ:* School of St Mary and St Anne, Abbots Bromley; Royal College of Nursing. SRN, SCM, RNT. Nursing trng and early posts, Leicester Royal Infirmary, 1941–47; Midwifery trng, General Lying-in Hosp., SW1 and Coventry and Warwicks Hosp.; Nurse Tutor, Middlesex Hosp., 1953–55; Principal Tutor: General Hosp., Northampton, 1956–63; Addenbrooke's Hosp., Cambridge, 1963–68; Principal, Queen Elizabeth Sch. of Nursing, Birmingham, 1968–74. Chm., General Nursing Council for England and Wales, 1971–74 (Mem., 1965 and 1970). *Recreations:* birds, books, buildings. *Address:* 28 Lambert Cross, Saffron Walden, Essex CB10 2DP.

COOPER, Martin Du Pré, CBE 1972; Music Editor of the Daily Telegraph, 1954–76; *b* 17 Jan. 1910; *s* of late Cecil Henry Hamilton Cooper, and late Cecil Stephens; *m* 1940, Mary, *d* of late Lieut-Col Douglas Stewart, DSO, and late Mabel Elizabeth Ponsonby; one *s* three *d*. *Educ:* Winchester; Oxford (BA). Studied music in Vienna, 1932–34, with Egon Wellesz; Asst Editor, Royal Geographical Soc. Journal, 1935–36; Music Critic: London Mercury, 1934–39;

Daily Herald, 1945-50; The Spectator, 1946-54; joined music staff of Daily Telegraph, 1950; Editor of Musical Times, 1953-56. Pres., Critics' Circle, 1959-60. Mem., Editorial Bd of New Oxford History of Music, 1960-. Hon. FTCL; Hon. FRAM 1976. *Publications:* Gluck, 1935; Bizet, 1938; Opéra Comique, 1949; French Music from the death of Berlioz to the death of Fauré, 1950; Russian Opera, 1951; Les Musiciens anglais d'aujourd'hui, 1952; Ideas and Music, 1966; Beethoven-the Last Decade, 1970. *Address:* 34 Halford Road, Richmond, Surrey.

COOPER, Nigel Cookson; General Secretary, British Amateur Athletic Board, since 1982; *b* 7 May 1929; *s* of Richard and Violet Sarah Cooper; *m* 1972, Elizabeth Gillian Smith; two *s* one *d. Educ:* Leeds Training Coll., Leeds Univ. (LLB); State Univ. of Iowa, USA (MA). Teacher, primary and secondary schools, 1950-59; Lecturer: Trent Park Training Coll., 1959-61; Loughborough Training Coll., 1961-64; Provincial Supervisor (Schools and Community) for Nova Scotia, Canada, 1964-65; County Organiser of Schools for Norfolk, 1965-68; Asst Education Officer for Oldham, 1970-72; Asst Director of Educn for British Families Educn Service in Europe, 1972-78; Registrar, Kelvin Grove College of Advanced Education, Brisbane, Australia, 1978-82. *Recreations:* playing the trumpet, squash, jogging. *Address:* c/o British Amateur Athletic Board, Francis House, Francis Street, SW1P 1DL. *T:* 01-828 9326.

COOPER, Sir Patrick Graham Astley, 6th Bt *cr* 1821; Director, Crendon Concrete Co. Ltd, Long Crendon, since 1973; *b* 4 Aug. 1918; *s* of late Col C. G. A. Cooper, DSO, RA and I. M. M. A. Cooper, Abergeldie, Camberley, Surrey; *S* cousin, Sir Henry Kelvin Cooper, 5th Bt, 1959; *m* Audrey Ann Jervoise, *d* of late Major D. P. J. Collas, Military Knight of Windsor; one *s* two *d. Educ:* Marlborough Coll. Qualified RICS, 1949; Sen. Asst Land Comr, Min. of Agric., Fisheries and Food, 1950-59. Joined Crendon Concrete Co. Ltd, 1959. Served 1939-40, Gunner, RA, 52 AA Bde TA (invalided out). *Recreations:* golf, tennis. *Heir: s* Alexander Paston Astley Cooper [*b* 1 Feb. 1943; *m* 1974, Minnie Margaret, *d* of Charles Harrison]. *Address:* Monkton Cottage, Monks Risborough, Aylesbury, Bucks. *T:* Princes Risborough 4210. *Club:* Farmers'.

COOPER, Philip John; Under Secretary, Research and Technology Requirements and Space Division, Department of Industry, since 1979; *b* 15 Sept. 1929; *s* of Charles Cooper and Mildred Annie Marlow; *m* 1953, Dorothy Joan Chapman; two *d. Educ:* Deacon's Sch., Peterborough; University Coll., Leicester. BSc (Chem. 1st Cl. Hons). CChem, FRSC. Joined Dept (later Laboratory) of Govt Chemist, 1952; Nat. Service, 2nd Lt, R Signals, 1953-55; Dept of Scientific and Ind. Res., 1956-67; Principal, Min. of Technology, 1967; Prin. Private Sec. to Minister for Industrial Develt, 1972-73; Asst Sec., Dept of Industry, 1973-79. *Publications:* various papers on analytical and chemical matters. *Address:* 8 Edenfield Gardens, Worcester Park, Surrey. *T:* 01-337 1035.

COOPER, Robert George; Chairman, Northern Ireland Fair Employment Agency, since 1976; Member: Equal Opportunities Commission for Northern Ireland, since 1976; Northern Ireland Standing Advisory Commission on Human Rights, since 1976; *b* 24 June 1936; *er s* of William Hugh Cooper and Annie (*née* Pollock); *m* 1974, Patricia, *yr d* of Gerald and Sheila Nichol, Belfast; one *s* one *d. Educ:* Foyle Coll., Londonderry; Queen's Univ., Belfast (LLB). Industrial Relations, International Computers Ltd, Belfast, 1958-63; Asst Sec., Engineering Employers' Fedn, NI, 1963-67, Sec. 1967-72; Gen. Sec., Alliance Party of Northern Ireland, 1972-73. Member (Alliance): West Belfast, NI Assembly, 1973-75; West Belfast, NI Constitutional Convention, 1975-76; Minister, Manpower Services, NI, 1974. *Address:* Lynwood, 104 Bangor Road, Holywood, Co. Down, N Ireland. *T:* Holywood 2071.

COOPER, Ronald Cecil Macleod, CB 1981; Deputy Secretary, Principal Establishment and Finance Officer, Departments of Industry and Trade, since 1979; *b* 8 May 1931; *s* of Cecil Redvers Cooper and Norah Agnes Louise Cooper (*née* Macleod); *m* 1st, 1953, June Bicknell (marr. diss. 1967); 2nd, 1967, Christine Savage; one *s* two *d. Educ:* Royal Grammar Sch., Newcastle upon Tyne; St Edmund Hall, Oxford (MA). Asst Principal, Min. of Supply, 1954-59; Principal, Min. of Aviation, 1959-62; on loan to European Launcher Develt Org., Paris, 1962-67; Asst Sec., Min. of Technology, 1968-70, DTI, 1970-73; Under Sec., Dept of Trade, 1973-78; Sec., Price Commn, 1979. *Recreations:* music, reading. *Address:* Departments of Industry and Trade, Sanctuary Buildings, 16-20 Great Smith Street, SW1P 3DB. *Club:* United Oxford & Cambridge University.

COOPER, Sidney G.; *see* Grattan-Cooper.

COOPER, Sidney Pool; Head of Public Services, British Museum, 1973-76; *b* 29 March 1919; *s* of late Sidney Charles Henry Cooper and Emily Lilian Baptie; *m* 1940, Denise Marjorie Peverett; two *s* one *d. Educ:* Finchley County Sch.; Northern Polytechnic (BSc); University Coll. London (MSc). Laboratory of the Government Chemist, 1947; Asst Keeper, National Reference Library of Science and Invention, British Museum, 1963; Dep. Keeper, NRLSI, 1969. *Recreations:* gardening, golf. *Address:* 98 King's Road, Berkhamsted, Herts. *T:* Berkhamsted 4145. *Club:* City Glee.

COOPER, Susie, (Mrs Susan Vera Barker), OBE 1979; RDI 1940; FRSA; Senior Designer for Josiah Wedgwood & Sons Ltd, since 1966; *b* 29 Oct. 1902; *d* of John Cooper and Mary-Ann (*née* Adams); *m* 1938, Cecil Barker; one

s. Educ: Burslem School of Art, Mollart House, Hanley. Resident designer, Gray's Pottery, 1924; founded Susie Cooper Pottery, 1929; designed and produced tableware for Royal Pavilion, Festival of Britain, on South Bank, 1951. *Recreation:* boat-building. *Address:* The Orchard Cottage, Dilhorne, Stoke-on-Trent, Staffs. *T:* Blythe Bridge 2221.

COOPER, Hon. Warren Ernest; Minister of Foreign Affairs and Overseas Trade, New Zealand, since 1981; *b* Dunedin, 21 Feb. 1933; *s* of William Cooper; *m* 1959, Lorraine Margaret, *d* of Angus T. Rees; three *s* two *d. Educ:* Musselburgh Sch.; King's High Sch., Dunedin. Formerly Postmaster-Gen., Minister of Tourism, Minister of Broadcasting, Minister of Regional Develt, Associate Minister of Finance. Member: Dominion Council, National Party, 1973-; Exec., S Island Publicity Assoc., 1971. Mayor of Queenstown, 1968-71. JP Queenstown. *Address:* Parliament House, Wellington, New Zealand; 12 Stanley Street, Queenstown.

COOPER, Dame Whina, DBE 1981 (CBE 1974; MBE 1953); JP; New Zealand President, Maori Land Rights, since 1975; *b* 9 Dec. 1895; *d* of Heremia Te Wake, JP (a Chief of Ngati-Manawa hapu of Te Rarawa tribe) and Kare Pouro; *m* 1st, 1916, Richard Gilbert (decd); one *d* (one *s* decd); 2nd, 1935, William Cooper (decd); two *s* two *d. Educ:* St Joseph's Coll., Greenmeadows, Napier, NZ. Proficiency Cert.; qualified as school teacher. Teacher, Pawarenga Sch., Northland, 1917; postmistress and storekeeper, Panguru, 1940 (Pres., Panguru Federated Farmers, 1940). Active in Maori land develt schemes, 1930; President: (first), Maori Women's Welfare League, 1952; Te Unga Waka Marae Soc., 1960; Maori Progressive Cultural Org., 1966; Pres. and Maori Land Rights Leader who led the Great Maori Land March to Parliament, 1975. Had the honour of being the first woman to cross the threshold of Waitangi House, 1949. Pres., Hokianga Rugby Union, 1947; Mem., Whangarei Gun Club, 1930-38. JP Auckland, 1952. *Publication:* Notable New Zealanders, 1979. *Recreations:* hockey, netball, table tennis. *Address:* 4 McCulloch Road, Panmure, Auckland, New Zealand. *T:* Auckland 578-534.

COOPER, William, (Harry Summerfield Hoff); novelist; Adjunct Professor of English Literature, Syracuse University, London Centre, since 1977; *b* 1910; *m* 1951, Joyce Barbara Harris; two *d.* Assistant Commissioner, Civil Service Commission, 1945-58; Personnel Consultant to: UKAEA, 1958-72; CEGB, 1958-72; Commn of European Communities, 1972-73; Asst Dir, Civil Service Selection Bd, 1973-75; Mem. Bd of Crown Agents, 1975-77; Personnel Advr, Millbank Technical Services, 1975-77. *Publications:* (as H. S. Hoff) Trina, 1934; Rhéa, 1935; Lisa, 1937; Three Marriages, 1946; (as William Cooper) Scenes from Provincial Life, 1950; The Struggles of Albert Woods, 1952; The Ever-Interesting Topic, 1953; Disquiet and Peace, 1956; Young People, 1958; C. P. Snow (British Council Bibliographical Series, Writers and Their Work, No 115) 1959; Prince Genji (a play), 1960; Scenes from Married Life, 1961; Memoirs of a New Man, 1966; You Want The Right Frame of Reference, 1971; Shall We Ever Know?, 1971; Love on the Coast, 1973; You're Not Alone, 1976; Scenes from Metropolitan Life, 1982. *Address:* 22 Kenilworth Court, Lower Richmond Road, SW15. *Club:* Savile.

COOPER, Maj.-Gen. William Frank, CBE 1971; MC 1945; Deputy Quarter-Master-General, 1973-76; retired 1976; *b* 30 May 1921; *s* of Allan Cooper, Officer of Indian State Railways, and Margaret Cooper; *m* 1945, Elisabeth Mary Finch; one *s* one *d. Educ:* Sherborne Sch.; RMA Woolwich. Commnd in RE, 1940; served N Africa and Italy (MC; despatches 1944); Malaya, 1956-58 (despatches); S Arabia, 1963-65 (OBE); Chief Engr FARELF, 1968-70; Dep. Dir Army Staff Duties, MoD, 1970-72; Dir, Mil. Assistance Office, 1972-73. Col Comdt, RE, 1978-. *Recreations:* tennis, golf, birdwatching, theatre. *Address:* c/o Lloyds Bank Ltd, High Street, Guildford, Surrey. *Club:* Army and Navy.

COOPER, Very Rev. (William Hugh) Alan; Priest-in-charge of Chrishall, since 1981; *b* 2 June 1909; *s* of William and Ethel Cooper; *m* 1st, 1940, Barbara (*née* Bentall); one *s* two *d*; 2nd, 1980, Muriel Barnes. *Educ:* King's Coll. Sch., Wimbledon; Christ's Coll., Cambridge; St John's Hall, London. Curate of Lee, 1932-36; Holy Trinity, Cambridge, 1936-38; CMS Missionary and Diocesan Missioner of Dio. Lagos, 1938-41; Curate of Farnham, 1941-42; Rector of Ashtead, 1942-51; Vicar of St Andrew, Plymouth, 1951-62; Preb. of Exeter Cathedral, 1958-62; Provost of Bradford, 1962-77; Hon. Assistant to Bishop of Karachi, 1977-80. *Address:* The Vicarage, 5 Engleric, Crawley End, Chrishall, near Royston, Herts; 1 Barton Wood Road, New Milton, Hants BH25 7NN.

COOPER, Prof. Sir William M.; *see* Mansfield Cooper.

COORAY, His Eminence Thomas Benjamin, Cardinal, OMI; BA, PhD, DD; Archbishop of Colombo (RC), 1947-76, now Archbishop Emeritus; *b* 28 Dec. 1901. *Educ:* St Joseph's Coll., Colombo; University Coll., Colombo; The Angelicum, Rome. Pres., Sri Lanka Bishops' Conference, 1947-76; created Cardinal, 1965; Member, Pontifical Commn for Canon Law, 1970-. *Address:* Cardinal's Residence, Tewatta, Ragama, Sri Lanka. *T:* 538.208.

COOTE, Sir Christopher (John), 15th Bt *cr* 1621; Senior Baronetcy of Ireland in use; *b* 22 Sept. 1928; *s* of Rear-Adm. Sir John Ralph Coote, 14th Bt, CB, CBE, DSC, and of Noreen Una, *o d* of late Wilfred Tighe; *S* father, 1978; *m* 1952, Anne Georgiana, *d* of Lt-Col Donald Handford; one *s* one *d.*

Educ: Winchester; Christ Church, Oxford (MA 1957). Coffee and tea merchant. *Heir:* s Nicholas Patrick Coote [b 28 July 1953; m 1980, Mona, d of late Moushegh Bedelian]. *Address:* Russets, Blackpond Lane, Farnham Royal, Bucks; Knockanattin, Ardnaboha, Belgooly, Co. Cork.

COOTE, John Oldham; Captain, RN; Consultant, Boeing Marine Systems, since 1980; *b* 13 Aug. 1921; *o s* of F. Stanley Coote, OBE, KStJ and Edith F. Coote; *m* 1944, Sylvia Mary (*née* Syson); three *d. Educ:* China Inland Mission Sch., Chefoo; Felsted. Royal Navy, as submarine specialist, 1940-60 (despatches 1944). Joined Beaverbrook Newspapers, 1960 (Vice-Chm. and Man. Dir, 1968-74; Dep. Chm. and Gp Man. Dir, 1974-75). Mem., Newspaper Publishers Assoc., 1968-75; Chm., Newsvendors Benevolent Inst. Festival Appeal, 1974. Dir Gen., British Film Prodn Assoc., 1976-77; Dir, Talking Pictures Ltd, 1975-. Mem. Council, King George's Fund for Sailors, 1968-; Trustee: Submarine Meml Museum, 1968-; Devas Boys' Club. *Publications:* (ed) Shell Pilot to the South Coast Harbours, 1982; contrib. defence and yachting pubns. *Recreations:* performing arts, offshore sailing, Real tennis. *Address:* 47 Caversham Street, SW3 4AF. *Clubs:* Garrick, Royal Ocean Racing; Royal Yacht Squadron; Cruising of America.

COOTE, Rt. Rev. Roderic Norman; *see* Colchester, Suffragan Bishop of.

COPAS, Most Rev. Virgil; *see* Kerema, Archbishop of, (RC).

COPE, David Robert, MA; Headmaster, The British School of Paris, since 1981; *b* 24 Oct. 1944; *yr s* of Dr C. L. Cope; *m* 1966, Gillian Margaret Peck; one *s* two *d. Educ:* Winchester Coll. (Scholar); Clare Coll., Cambridge (Scholar). 1st Cl. Hons Hist. Tripos Part II, 1965; BA 1965; MA 1972. Asst Master, Eton Coll., 1965-67; Asst British Council Rep. (Cultural Attaché), Mexico City, 1968-70; Asst Master, Bryanston Sch., 1970-73; Headmaster, Dover College, 1973-81. FRSA. *Recreations:* music, tennis, travel. *Address:* The British School of Paris, 38 Quai de l'Ecluse, 78290 Croissy-sur-Seine, France. *T:* 976-2900; Les Azalées, Hameau de la Jonchère, 92500 Rueil-Malmaison, France. *T:* 708-3761. *Club:* Athenæum.

COPE, Prof. F(rederick) Wolverson, DSc, FGS, CEng, FIMinE; Consultant Geologist; Professor of Geology and Head of Geology Department, University of Keele, 1950-76, now Professor Emeritus; *b* 30 July 1909; *e s* of late Fred and Ida Mary Cope (*née* Chappells), Macclesfield; *m* 1st, 1935, Ethel May Hitchens, BSc (*d* 1961); one *s* two *d* ; 2nd, 1962, Evelyn Mary Swales, BA, AKC, *d* of late John Frederick and Ada Mary Swales, Kingston-upon-Hull; one *d. Educ:* The King's Sch., Macclesfield; Univs of Manchester (DSc 1946) and London. Brocklehurst Medal, 1928; John Dalton Prize, 1930; BSc with First Class Honours in Geology, 1931; MSc, Mark Stirrup Scholar, Manchester, 1932. Demonstrator in Geology, Bedford Coll., Univ. of London, 1933-34; Daniel Pidgeon Fund, Geol. Soc. of London, 1937; Prin. Geologist in Geological Survey of GB, 1934-50; Murchison Award of Geol. Soc. of London, 1948; Vis. Prof. of Geology, Univ. of Pisa, 1964. FGS 1934; CEng 1968; FIMinE 1969. *Publications:* The North Staffordshire Coalfields, in Coalfields of Great Britain (ed by late Sir Arthur Trueman), 1954; Geology Explained in the Peak District, 1976; various research publications mainly in the fields of stratigraphy and palaeontology. *Recreations:* landscape sketching, cars, ornithology, Italy, reading and speaking Italian. *Address:* 6 Boley Drive, Clacton-on-Sea, Essex CO15 6LA. *T:* Clacton-on-Sea 21829.

COPE, Hon. James Francis, CMG 1978; Speaker of the Australian House of Representatives, 1973-75; *b* 26 Nov. 1907; *s* of G. E. Cope; *m* 1931, Myrtle Irene, *d* of S. J. Hurst; one *d. Educ:* Crown Street Public Sch., NSW. Hon. Treaurer, NSW Br., Aust. Glass Workers' Union; Delegate to Federal Council, 1953-55. MHR (Lab) for divs of: Cook, 1955; Watson, 1955-69; Sydney, 1969-75. *Recreations:* billiards, horse racing, cricket, football. *Address:* 1/38-40 Fontainebleau Street, Sans Souci, NSW 2219, Australia.

COPE, John Ambrose; MP (C) South Gloucestershire since Feb. 1974; a Government Whip, since 1979 and a Lord Commissioner of HM Treasury, since 1981; *b* 13 May 1937; *s* of George Cope, MC, FRIBA, Leicester; *m* 1969, Djemila Lovell Payne, *d* of Col P. V. L. Payne, Martinstown, Dorset and Mrs Tanetta Blackden; two *d. Educ:* Oakham Sch., Rutland. Chartered Accountant; Company Director. Commnd RA and RE, Nat Service and TA. Conservative Research Dept, 1965-67; Personal Asst to Chm. of Conservative Party, 1967-70; contested (C) Woolwich East, 1970; Special Asst to Sec. of State for Trade and Industry, 1972-74. Formerly Secretary: Cons. Parly Finance Cttee; Parly Gp for Concorde; Vice Chm., Cons. Parly Smaller Business Cttee. *Publication:* (with Bernard Weatherill) Acorns to Oaks (Policy for Small Business), 1967. *Recreation:* woodwork. *Address:* House of Commons, SW1; Bluegates, Berkeley, Glos. *Clubs:* Carlton, St Stephen's Constitutional; Tudor House (Chipping Sodbury).

COPE, John Wigley, MA, MB, BChir Cantab, FRCS; Retired; formerly Surgeon in charge Ear, Nose and Throat Department, St Bartholomew's Hospital; *b* 1 Nov. 1907; *o s* of J. J. Cope, Widney Manor, Warwicks; *m* 1937, Muriel Pearce Brown, Reading; two *s* one *d. Educ:* King Edward's Sch., Birmingham; Trinity Coll., Cambridge; St Bartholomew's Hosp., London. Demonstrator in Anatomy, St Bartholomew's Med. Coll., 1935. Served with RAFVR (Med. Branch) as Aural Specialist, 1940-45 (Sqdn-Ldr). Aural Surgeon, Royal Waterloo Hosp., 1946; Surgeon, Royal National Throat, Nose and Ear Hosp., 1946. Dean, St Bartholomew's Hosp. Med. Coll., 1962-68. Pres., Section of Otology, RSM, 1970-71 (formerly Sec.).

Recreations: shooting, rock-climbing, gardening, golf. *Address:* Owls Hatch Cottage, Seale, near Farnham, Surrey. *T:* Runfold 2456.

COPE, Maclachlan Alan Carl S.; *see* Silverwood-Cope.

COPELAND, Mrs Roy; *see* Bracewell, J. W.

COPEMAN, Harold Arthur; Under-Secretary, HM Treasury, 1972-76; *b* 27 Jan. 1918; *s* of H. W. M. and G. E. Copeman; *m* 1948, Kathleen (Kay) Gadd; one *s. Educ:* Manchester Grammar Sch.; The Queen's Coll., Oxford. BA, 1st Cl. Hons in PPE, 1939. Served War, Army: Cheshire Regt, RA (Instructor in gunnery) and Ordnance Board (Applied Ballistics Dept), 1940-45. HM Treasury, 1946-76. Vis. Fellow, Warwick Univ., 1976. Consultant, Fiscal Affairs Dept, IMF, 1982. *Publications:* (jtly) Health Care: priorities and management, 1980; The National Accounts: a short guide, 1981. *Recreations:* music, gardening, photography. *Address:* The Limes, Avon Dassett, Leamington Spa, Warwicks. *T:* Farnborough (Banbury) 245.

COPISAROW, Alcon Charles, DSc; FInstP; CEng; FIEE; Member, British National Oil Corporation, since 1980; *b* 25 June 1920; *o s* of late Dr Maurice Copisarow, Manchester; *m* 1953, Diana, *y d* of Ellis James Castello, MC, Bucklebury, Berks; two *s* two *d. Educ:* Manchester Central Grammar Sch.; University of Manchester; Imperial Coll. of Science and Technology; Sorbonne, Paris. Council of Europe Research Fellow. Served War, 1942-47; Lieut RN, 1943-47; British Admiralty Delegn, Washington, 1945. Home Civil Service, 1946-66; Office of Minister of Defence, 1947-54. Scientific Counsellor, British Embassy, Paris, 1954-60. Dir, Forest Products Research Laboratory, Dept of Scientific and Industrial Research, 1960-62; Chief Technical Officer, Nat. Economic Development Council, 1962-64; Chief Scientific Officer, Min. of Technology, and Head of Internat. Div. and Electrical, Chemical Plant and Materials Industries Div., 1964-66. Dir and Vice-Pres., McKinsey & Co. Inc., 1966-76; non-exec. Dir, British Leyland, 1976-77. Chairman: Commonwealth Forest Products Conf., Nairobi, 1962; CENTO Conf. on Investment in Science, Teheran, 1963; Cttee for Research on Dental Materials and Equipment, 1966; Member: Scientific Manpower Cttee, Advisory Council on Scientific Policy, 1963-64; Econ. Develt Cttees for Electronics Industry, 1963-64, and for Heavy Electrical Industry, 1966-67; Trop. Prod. Adv. Cttee, 1965-66; Press Council, 1975-81; Cabinet (Official) Cttees. A Chm., Gen. Comrs for Income Tax, 1975-. Dep. Chm., Bd of Governors, English-Speaking Union, 1976-; Trustee, Duke of Edinburgh's Award, 1978-; Mem., Admin. Council, Royal Jubilee Trusts, 1981-; Governor, Benenden Sch.; Dir, Atlas Electric & General Trust. Hon. FTCL. *Address:* The White House, Denham Village UB9 5BE. *Clubs:* Athenæum, MCC.

COPLAND, Aaron; American composer; *b* Brooklyn, NY, 14 Nov. 1900; *s* of Harris M. Copland and Sarah Mittenthal; unmarried. *Educ:* Boys' High Sch., Brooklyn, NY; studied music privately; Fontainebleau Sch. of Music, France; Paris (with Nadia Boulanger). Guggenheim Fellow, 1925, 1926. Lecturer on music, New School for Social Research, NY, 1927-37; organised Copland-Sessions Concerts, which presented American music, 1928-31; tour of Latin-American countries, as pianist, conductor and lecturer in concerts of American music, 1941 and 1947; Charles Eliot Norton Prof. of Poetry, Harvard Univ., 1951-52. *Principal works:* Symphony for Organ and Orchestra, 1924; First Symphony (orch.), 1928; Short Symphony (No. II), 1933; El Salon Mexico (orch.), 1936; Billy the Kid (ballet), 1938; Piano Sonata, 1941; Lincoln Portrait (speaker and orch.), 1942; Rodeo (ballet), 1942; Sonata for Violin and piano, 1943; Appalachian Spring (ballet, Pulitzer Prize), 1944; Third Symphony, 1946; Clarinet Concerto, 1948; Piano Quartet, 1950; Twelve Poems of Emily Dickinson, 1950; The Tender Land (Opera), 1954; Symphonic Ode (1929, rev. 1955); Piano Fantasy, 1957; Orchestral Variations 1958; Nonet, 1960; Connotations for Orchestra, 1962; Dance Panels, 1962; Music for a Great City, 1964; Emblems for Symphonic Band, 1964; Inscape for Orchestra, 1967; Duo for flute and piano, 1971; Three Latin-American Sketches, 1972; various film scores. Pres., American Acad. Arts and Letters, 1971; Member: National Institute of Arts and Letters; American Academy of Arts and Sciences; President of the Edward MacDowell Assoc., 1962; American Soc. of Composers, Authors and Publishers; Hon. Mem., Accademia Santa Cecilia, Rome; Hon. Mem., RAM, 1959; Hon. Dr of Music, Princeton Univ., 1956, Harvard Univ., 1961; Hon. Dr of Humane Letters, Brandeis Univ., 1957. FRSA 1960. Presidential Medal of Freedom, Washington, 1964; Howland Prize, Yale Univ., 1970; Haendel Medallion, NY, 1970; Chancellor's Medal, Syracuse Univ., 1975; Creative Arts Award, Brandeis Univ., 1975. *Publications:* What to listen for in music, 1939 (revised 1957); Our New Music, 1941; Music and Imagination, 1952; Copland on Music, 1960; The New Music 1900-1960, 1968. *Address:* c/o Boosey and Hawkes, 24 West 57 Street, New York, USA. *Clubs:* Harvard, Century Association (New York).

COPLAND, Rev. Canon Charles McAlester; *b* 5 April 1910; *s* of Canon Alexander Copland and of Violet Williamina Somerville McAlester; *m* 1946, Gwendoline Lorimer Williamson; two *d. Educ:* Forfar Academy; Denstone Coll.; Corpus Christi Coll., Cambridge (MA); Cuddesdon College. Reserve of Officers, 1933-38. Curate, Peterborough Parish Church, 1934-38; Mission Priest, Chanda, CP, India, 1938-53 (Head of Mission, 1942-53); Canon of Nagpur, 1952; Rector, St Mary's, Arbroath, 1953-59; Canon of Dundee, 1953; Provost of St John's Cathedral, Oban, 1959-79, also Dean of Diocese of Argyll and The Isles, 1977-79; Hon. Canon of Oban, 1979. *Recreations:* formerly

Rugby football, athletics; rifle shooting (shot for Cambridge, for Scotland 1932–81). *Address:* Fir Cottage, South Crieff Road, Comrie, Perthshire. *T:* Comrie 70185.

COPLESTON, Ernest Reginald, CB 1954; Secretary, Committee of Enquiry into the Governance of the University of London, 1970–72; *b* 16 Nov. 1909; *s* of F. S. Copleston, former Chief Judge of Lower Burma; *m* Olivia Green. *Educ:* Marlborough Coll.; Balliol Coll., Oxford. Inland Revenue Dept, 1932; Treasury, 1942; Under-Sec., 1950; Dep. Sec., 1957–63, Sec., 1963–69, UGC; retired. *Address:* Holland Hill, Bulmer, Sudbury, Suffolk. *T:* Twinstead 356.

COPLESTON, Rev. Frederick Charles, SJ; MA Oxon, DPhil Rome, Gregorian Univ.; FBA 1970; Principal of Heythrop College, University of London, 1970–74; Emeritus Professor of University of London, 1974; Dean, Faculty of Theology, 1972–74; *b* 10 April 1907; *s* of F. S. Copleston, former Chief Judge of Lower Burma, and N. M. Little. *Educ:* Marlborough Coll.; St John's Coll., Oxford (Hon. Fellow, 1975). Entered Catholic Church, 1925; Soc. of Jesus, 1930; ordained 1937. Prof. of History of Philosophy: Heythrop Coll., Oxford, 1939–70, and Univ. of London, 1972–74; Gregorian Univ., Rome, 1952–68; Dean of Faculty of Theology, Univ. of London, 1972–74; Visiting Professor: Univ. of Santa Clara, Calif., 1974–75 and 1977–82; Univ. of Hawaii, 1976; Gifford Lectr, Univ. of Aberdeen, 1979–80. *Publications:* Friedrich Nietzsche, Philosopher of Culture, 1942, new edn 1975; St Thomas and Nietzsche, 1944; Arthur Schopenhauer, Philosopher of Pessimism, 1946; A History of Philosophy (vol. 1, Greece and Rome, 1946; revised 1947; vol. 2, Augustine to Scotus, 1950; vol. 3, Ockham to Suárez, 1953; vol. 4, Descartes to Leibniz, 1958; vol. 5, Hobbes to Hume, 1959; vol. 6, Wolff to Kant, 1960; vol. 7, Fichte to Nietzsche, 1963; vol. 8, Bentham to Russell, 1966; vol. 9, Maine de Biran to Sartre, 1975); Medieval Philosophy, 1952; Existentialism and Modern Man, 1948; Aquinas (Pelican), 1955; Contemporary Philosophy, 1956, rev. edn 1972; A History of Medieval Philosophy, 1972; Religion and Philosophy, 1974; Philosophers and Philosophies, 1976; On the History of Philosophy, 1979; Philosophies and Cultures, 1980; Religion and the One, 1982; articles in learned journals. *Address:* Campion Hall, Oxford OX1 1QS. *T:* Oxford 40861.

COPLESTONE-BOUGHEY, John Fenton; His Honour Judge Coplestone-Boughey; a Circuit Judge (formerly Judge of the County Courts), since 1969; *b* 5 Feb. 1912; *o s* of late Comdr A. F. Coplestone-Boughey, RN; *m* 1944, Gilian Beatrice, *e d* of late H. A. Counsell, Appleby; one *s* one *d. Educ:* Shrewsbury School; Brasenose Coll., Oxford (Open Exhibitioner, Matthew Arnold Prizeman). Inner Temple, Entrance Scholar 1934, Barrister 1935. Legal Assistant, Min. of Health, 1937–40. Royal Artillery, 1940–46; Advanced Class, Military Coll. of Science, 1945. Chester Chronicle & Associated Newspapers, Ltd: Dir, 1947–56; Dep. Chm., 1956–65. Chairman, Nat. Insurance Tribunals (SW London), 1951–69; Referee, Nat. Service and Family Allowances Acts, 1957–69. Battersea etc Hospital Management Cttee: Member 1960–69, Chairman 1969–74; Mem., Wandsworth etc AHA, 1973–. Governor, St Thomas' Hosp., 1971–74; Special Trustee, St George's Hospital, 1974–. Mem. Council, Queen's Coll., London, 1976–. *Publications:* contrib. to Halsbury's Laws of England. *Recreations:* walking, travel. *Address:* 82 Oakley Street, SW3. *T:* 01-352 6287. *Club:* Athenæum.

COPLEY, John (Michael Harold); Principal Resident Producer, Royal Opera, Covent Garden, since 1975; *b* 12 June, 1933; *s* of Ernest Harold Copley and Lilian Forbes. *Educ:* King Edward's, Five Ways, Birmingham; Sadler's Wells Ballet Sch.; Central Sch. of Arts and Crafts, London (Dip. with Hons in Theatre Design). Appeared as the apprentice in Britten's Peter Grimes for Covent Garden Opera Co, 1950; stage managed: both opera and ballet companies at Sadler's Wells, in Rosebery Avenue, 1953–57; also various musicals, plays, etc, in London's West End, incl. The World of Paul Slickey and My Fair Lady. Joined Covent Garden Opera Co.: Dep. Stage Manager, 1960; Asst Resident Producer, 1963; Associate Resident Producer, 1966; Resident Producer, 1972. *Productions include:* at Covent Garden: Suor Angelica, 1965; Cosi fan Tutte, 1968, 1981; Orpheo ed Euridice, 1969; Le Nozze di Figaro, 1971; Don Giovanni, 1973; La Bohème, 1974; Faust, 1974; L'elisir d'amore, 1975, 1981; Benvenuto Cellini, 1976; Ariadne auf Naxos, 1976; Maria Stuarda; Royal Silver Jubilee Gala, 1977; Werther, 1979; La Traviata, Lucrezia Borgia, 1980; Alceste, 1981; at London Coliseum (for Sadler's Wells, subseq. English Nat. Opera): Carmen, Il Seraglio, Il Trovatore, La Traviata, Mary Stuart; Rosenkavalier, La Belle Hélène, 1975; Werther, 1977; Manon, Aida, Julius Caesar, Les Mamelles de Tirésias, 1979; Macbeth, Athens Festival; Lucia, Netherlands Opera; Lucia, Opera National de Belge; La Clemenza di Tito and L'Infedelta delusa, for Wexford Festival; Lucia, Dallas Civic Opera, Texas and Chicago Lyric Opera, Canadian Opera, Toronto; Madame Butterfly and Otello, Greek Nat. Opera; Fidelio, Nozze di Figaro, Rigoletto, Magic Flute, Jenufa, Ariadne auf Naxos, Madame Butterfly, Fra Diavolo, Macbeth, La Traviata, Manon Lescaut, Lucia di Lammermoor, Tosca, for Australian Opera; La Traviata, Falstaff, Peter Grimes, Tosca for Welsh National Opera Co.; Les Mamelles de Tirésias for English Opera North; Lucia, Ballo in Maschera, Dido and Aeneas, for Scottish Opera; Acis and Galatea for English Opera Group productions in Stockholm, Paris, New York, Ottawa, Vancouver. Sang as soloist in Bach's St John Passion, Bremen, Germany, 1965; appeared as Ferdy in John Osborne's play, A Patriot for Me, at Royal Court Theatre, 1965. Co-directed (with Patrick

Garland) Fanfare for Europe Gala, Covent Garden, 3 Jan. 1973. *Recreation:* cooking. *Address:* 9D Thistle Grove, SW10 9RR.

COPP, Darrell John Barkwell, OBE 1981; General Secretary, Institute of Biology, 1951-82; *b* 25 April 1922; *s* of J. J. H. Copp and L. A. Hoad; *m* 1944, Margaret Henderson; two *s* one *d. Educ:* Taunton's Sch., Southampton; Southampton Univ. (BSc). FIBiol. Scientific Officer, Admty Signals Estabt, 1942-45; Asst Sec., British Assoc. for Advancement of Science, 1947-51. Sec., Council for Nature, 1958-63; originator and co-ordinator of first National Nature Week, 1963. Hon. Treas., Parly and Scientific Cttee, 1980-; Sec., European Community Biologists' Assoc., 1978-. Hon. MTech Bradford, 1975. *Publications:* reports and reviews in scientific jls. *Recreations:* mountain walking, renovating country cottages. *Address:* Duke's Mount, Woldingham, Surrey. *T:* Woldingham 2374.

COPP, Prof. (Douglas) Harold, CC 1980 (OC 1971); MD, PhD; FRS 1971; FRSC; FRCP(C); Professor of Physiology, University of British Columbia, Canada, since 1950; *b* 16 Jan. 1915; *s* of Charles J. Copp and Edith M. O'Hara; *m* 1939, Winnifred A. Thompson; three *d. Educ:* Univ. of Toronto, Canada (BA, MD); Univ. of California, Berkeley, Calif (PhD); British Columbia College of Physicians and Surgeons (Lic.). Asst Prof. of Physiology, Calif, 1945-50. Co-ordinator, Health Scis, Univ. of British Columbia, 1976-77; Head of Dept of Physiology, Univ. of British Columbia, 1950-80. FRSC 1959 (Mem. Council, 1973-75, 1977-; Vice-Pres., and Pres. Academy of Science, 1978-); FRCP(C) 1974. Hon. LLD: Queen's Univ., Kingston, Ont, 1970; Univ. of Toronto, 1970; Hon. DSc: Univ. of Ottawa, 1973; Acadia Univ., 1975; Univ. of British Columbia, 1980. Discovered calcitonin (ultimobranchial hormone) and teleocalcin (corpuscles of Stannius). *Recreation:* gardening. *Address:* 4755 Belmont Avenue, Vancouver, British Columbia V6T 1A8, Canada. *T:* 604-224-3793.

COPPEN, Dr Alec James, MD, DSc; FRCP, FRCPsych; Director, Medical Research Council Neuropsychiatry Laboratory, and Consultant Psychiatrist, West Park Hospital, Epsom, Surrey, since 1974; *b* 29 Jan. 1923; *y s* of late Herbert John Wardle Coppen and Marguerite Mary Annie Coppen; *m* 1952, Gunhild Margareta, *y d* of late Albert and Sigrid Andersson, Bastad, Sweden; one *s. Educ:* Dulwich Coll.; Univ. of Bristol (MB, ChB 1953; MD 1958; DSc 1978); Maudsley Hosp.; Univ. of London (DPM 1957); MRCP 1975, FRCP 1980, FRCPsych 1971. Registrar, then Sen. Registrar, Maudsley Hosp., 1954-59; MRC Neuropsychiatry Research Unit, 1959-74, MRC External Staff, 1974-; Consultant Psychiatrist: St Ebba's Hosp., 1959-64; West Park Hosp., 1964-; Hon. Cons. Psychiatrist, St George's Hosp., 1965-70. Head of WHO designated Centre for Biological Psychiatry in UK, 1974-; Consultant, WHO, 1977-; Examiner, Royal Coll. of Psychiatry, 1973-77; Andrew Woods Vis. Prof., Univ. of Iowa, 1981; Lectr to learned socs and univs in Europe, N and S America and Africa. Mem. Council, RMPA (Chm., Research and Clinical Section), 1965-70; Chairman, Biolog. Psychiatry Section, World Psychiatric Assoc., 1972; President, British Assoc. of Psychopharmacology, 1975; Member: Internat. Coll. Neuropsychopharm., 1960- (Mem. Council, 1979); RSM, 1960-; British Pharmacol. Soc., 1977-; Special Health Auth., Bethlem Royal and Maudsley Hosp., 1982; Hon. Member: Mexican Soc. for Biolog. Psychiatry, 1973-; Mexican Inst. of Culture, 1974-; Swedish Psychiatric Assoc., 1977-; Corresp. Mem., Amer. Coll. of Neuropsychopharm., 1977-; Distinguished Fellow, APA, 1981. Freeman, City of London, 1980; Yeoman, Soc. of Apothecaries, 1980. Anna Monika Prize, 1969. *Publications:* (jtly) Recent Developments in Schizophrenia, 1967; (jtly) Recent Developments in Affective Disorders, 1968; (jtly) Psychopharmacology of Affective Disorders, 1979; contribs to text books; papers in Nature, Lancet, BMJ, etc (Current Contents Citation Classic, 1978, Biochemistry of the Affective Disorders). *Recreations:* golf, music, photography. *Address:* 5 Walnut Close, Epsom, Surrey KT18 5JL. *T:* Epsom 20800. *Club:* Athenæum.

COPPLESTONE, Frank Henry; Managing Director, Southern Television Ltd; *b* 26 Feb. 1925; 2nd *s* of late Rev. Frank T. Copplestone; *m* 1st, 1950, Margaret Mary (*d* 1973), *d* of late Edward Walker; three *s*; 2nd, 1977, Penelope Ann Labovitch, *d* of Ben and Eve Perrick; one step *s* one step *d. Educ:* Truro Sch.; Nottingham Univ. (BA). Royal Horse Artillery, 1943-47. Pres., Univ. of Nottingham Union, 1952-53; Pres., Nat. Union of Students, 1954-56; Internat. Research Fellow, 1956-58; Regional Officer, Independent Television Authority, 1958-62; Head of Regional Services, ITA, 1962-63; Head of Programme Services, ITA, 1963-67; Controller, ITV Network Programme Secretariat, 1967-73; Dir, ITV Programme Planning Secretariat, 1973-75; Man. Dir, Southern Television, 1976-; Director: Independent Television News Ltd, 1977-81; Independent Television Publications Ltd, 1976-81. Mem., Broadcasters' Audience Res. Bd, 1981. *Recreations:* sailing, reading, music. *Address:* 44 Charleville Road, W14. *Clubs:* Reform; Royal Fowey Yacht, Fowey Gallants Sailing.

COPPOCK, Prof. John Terence, FBA 1975; FRSE 1976; Ogilvie Professor of Geography, University of Edinburgh, since 1965; *b* 2 June 1921; *s* of late Arthur Coppock and of Valerie Margaret Coppock (*née* Phillips); *m* 1953, Sheila Mary Burnett; one *s* one *d. Educ:* Penarth County Sch.; Queens' Coll., Cambridge. MA (Cantab), PhD (London). Civil Servant: Lord Chancellor's Dept, Min. of Works, Board of Customs and Excise, 1938-47. Served War, Army (commissioned Welch Regt, 1941), 1939-46. Cambridge Univ., 1947-50. University Coll. London (Dept of Geography): successively, Asst Lecturer, Lecturer, Reader, 1950-65. Member: Scottish Sports Council, 1976-;

Ordnance Survey Rev. Cttee, 1978-79. FRSA 1980. *Publications:* The Changing Use of Land in Britain (with R. H. Best), 1962; An Agricultural Atlas of England and Wales, 1964, 2nd edn 1976; Greater London (ed, with H. C. Prince), 1964; An Agricultural Geography of Great Britain, 1971; Recreation in the Countryside: a Spatial Analysis (with B. S. Duffield), 1975; Spatial Dimensions of Public Policy (ed, with W. R. D. Sewell), 1976; An Agricultural Atlas of Scotland, 1976; Second Homes: Curse or Blessing? (ed), 1977; Public Participation in Planning (ed, with W. R. D. Sewell), 1977; Land Use and Town and Country Planning (with L. F. Gebbett), 1978; Land Assessment in Scotland (ed, with M. F. Thomas), 1980; numerous papers: mainly in geographical, but also historical, planning and agricultural periodicals, mainly on theme of rural land use in Great Britain. *Recreations:* listening to music, natural history. *Address:* 57 Braid Avenue, Edinburgh EH10 6EB. *T:* 031-447 3443.

CORBEN, Albert Edward; Assistant Under Secretary of State, Radio Regulatory Department, Home Office, since 1980; *b* 25 Nov. 1923; *s* of Ebenezer Joseph James Corben and Frances Flora (*née* Orchard); *m* 1953, Doris Dodd; two *s. Educ:* Portsmouth Grammar Sch.; Sir John Cass Technical Inst. Served Royal Artillery, 1943-47. Entered Home Office, as Executive Officer, 1947; Higher Executive Officer, 1955-62; Sen. Executive Officer, 1962-66; Principal, 1966-70; Secretary to Advisory Council on Penal System, 1966-68; Sen. Principal, 1972-73; Asst Sec., 1973-80. *Recreations:* swimming, tennis, walking. *Address:* 1a Winchester Road, Bromley, Kent BR2 0PZ. *T:* 01-460 4106.

CORBET, Mrs Freda (Kunzlen), (Mrs Ian McIvor Campbell), BA; JP; *b* 1900; *d* of James Mansell; *m* 1925, William Corbet (*d* 1957); *m* 1962, Ian McIvor Campbell (*d* 1976). *Educ:* Wimbledon County Sch.; University Coll., London. Called to Bar, Inner Temple, 1932. MP (Lab) NW Camberwell, later Peckham Div. of Camberwell, 1945-Feb. 1974. Awarded Freedom of Southwark, 1974. JP, Co. London, 1940. *Address:* 39 Gravel Road, Bromley, Kent.

CORBET, Dr Gordon Barclay; Head, Department of Central Services, British Museum (Natural History), since 1976; *b* 4 March 1933; *s* of George and Mary Corbet; *m* 1959, Elizabeth Urquhart; one *s* one *d. Educ:* Morgan Acad., Dundee; Univ. of St Andrews. BSc, PhD. Asst Lectr in Biology, Sir John Cass Coll., London, 1958-59; Sen., later Principal, Scientific Officer, Dept of Zoology, British Museum (Natural History), 1960-71; Dep. Keeper of Zoology, 1971-76. *Publications:* The Terrestrial Mammals of Western Europe, 1966; Finding and Identifying Mammals in Britain, 1975; The Handbook of British Mammals (with H. N. Southern), 1977; The Mammals of the Palaearctic Region, 1978. *Recreations:* bird-watching, walking. *Address:* 27 Farnaby Road, Bromley, Kent BR1 4BL. *T:* 01-460 2439.

CORBET, Lieut-Col Sir John (Vincent), 7th Bt, *cr* 1808; MBE 1946; DL; JP; RE (retired); *b* 27 Feb. 1911; *s* of Archer Henry Corbet (*d* 1950) and Anne Maria (*d* 1951), *d* of late German Buxton; *S* kinsman, Sir Gerald Vincent Corbet, 6th Bt, 1955; *m* 1st, 1937, Elfrida Isobel Francis; 2nd, 1948, Doreen Elizabeth Stewart (*d* 1964), *d* of Arthur William Gibbon Ritchie; 3rd, 1965, Annie Elizabeth Lorimer, MBE, MSc, Dunedin, NZ. *Educ:* Shrewsbury Sch.; RMA; Magdalene Coll., Cambridge. BA 1933, MA 1972. 2nd Lieut, RE, 1931; served North-West Frontier, India, 1935, and War of 1939-45 in India, Burma and Malaya (despatches, MBE); Lieut-Col, 1953; retd 1955. DL County of Salop, 1961; JP 1957; High Sheriff of Salop, 1966; CC Salop, 1963-81. OStJ; Mem., Church Assembly, later General Synod, 1960-75; former Chm., Board of Visitors, Stoke Heath Borstal. *Address:* Acton Reynald, near Shrewsbury, Salop SY4 4DS. *T:* Clive 259. *Club:* Royal Thames Yacht.

CORBET, Air Vice-Marshal Lancelot Miller, CB 1958; CBE 1944; RAF retired; *b* Brunswick, Vic, Australia, 19 April 1898; *s* of late John Miller and late Ella Beatrice Corbet, Caulfield, Vic, Australia; *m* 1924, Gwenllian Elizabeth, *d* of late Thomas Powell and late May Maria Bennett, Claremont, Western Australia; one *s. Educ:* Melbourne High Sch.; Scotch Coll., Melbourne; Melbourne Univ. (MB, BS 1922). RMO, Perth (WA) Hospital, 1922-23, Perth Children's Hospital 1923; Hon. Asst Anæsthetist, Perth Hospital, 1931; Clinical Asst to Out-Patient Surgeon, Perth Hospital, 1931-32. Was Major AAMC; commanded 6th Field Hygiene Sect., 1930-32; entered RAF 1933; served in UK and India, 1933-37; Principal MO, W Africa, 1941-43; Principal MO, Transport Command, RAF, 1943-45; Principal MO, Malaya, 1945-46; Principal MO, British Commonwealth Air Forces, Japan, 1946-48; OC, RAF Hospital, Nocton Hall, 1949-52; Principal MO, HQBF, Aden, 1952-54; Principal MO, 2nd Tactical Air Force, 1954-56; Dep. Dir-Gen. of Medical Services, Air Ministry, 1956-58, retired. Hon. Life Member: BMA; AMA; Aviation Med. Soc. of Aust. and NZ; Aust. Air Force Assoc. KStJ. *Recreations:* lacrosse, tennis, squash, golf, etc. *Address:* 6 Goldsmith Avenue, Ringwood North, Victoria 3134, Australia. *T:* Melbourne 870 7762.

CORBETT, family name of **Baron Rowallan.**

CORBETT, Rev. Canon Charles Eric; Canon-Treasurer of Liverpool Cathedral, since 1979. *Educ:* Jesus College, Oxford (BA 1939, MA 1943); Wycliffe Hall, Oxford. Deacon 1940, priest 1941, St Asaph; Curate of Gresford, 1940-44; CF, 1944-47; Curate of Eglwys-Rhos, 1947-49; Rector of Harpurhey, 1949-54; Vicar of St Catherine's, Wigan, 1954-61; Vicar of St Luke, Farnworth, 1961-71; Rural Dean of Farnworth, 1964-71; Archdeacon of Liverpool, 1971-79. *Address:* 20 Garth Drive, Liverpool L18 6HW.

CORBETT, Captain Hugh Askew, CBE 1968; DSO 1945; DSC 1943; RN; Warden of University Centre, Cambridge University, since 1969; *b* 25 June 1916; *s* of late Rev. F. St John Corbett, MA, FRSL, FRHistS and late Elsie L. V. Askew; *m* 1945, Patricia Nancy, *d* of late Thomas Patrick Spens, OBE, MC, LLD; three *s. Educ:* St Edmund's Sch., Canterbury. Joined Royal Navy, 1933; IDC 1960; HMS Cæsar as Capt. (D), 8th Destroyer Sqdn, 1961-63; HMS Fearless, 1965-67 (Capt.); Head of Naval Manpower Future Policy Div., 1967-69. FBIM. *Address:* Holly Cottage, 3 Clare Road, Cambridge. *T:* Cambridge 357735.

CORBETT, Prof. John Patrick, MA; Professor of Philosophy, University of Bradford, 1972-76; *b* 5 March 1916; *s* of E. S. H. and K. F. Corbett; *m* 1st, 1940, Nina Angeloni; two *s* ; 2nd, 1968, Jan Adams; two *d. Educ:* RNC, Dartmouth; Magdalen Coll., Oxford. Lieut, RA, 1940; POW in Germany, 1940-45. Fellow of Balliol, 1945-61; Prof. of Philosophy, Univ. of Sussex, 1961-72; Jowett Lectr in Philosophy. Council of Europe Fellow, 1957; Visiting Lectr, Yale Univ., 1958; NATO Fellow, 1960; Vis. Prof., Univ. of Toronto, 1968. *Publications:* Europe and the Social Order, 1959; Ideologies, 1965. *Address:* Pervolia, Larnaca, Cyprus.

CORBETT, Prof. Peter Edgar; Yates Professor of Classical Art and Archaeology in the University of London (University College), since 1961; *b* 19 June 1920; 2nd *s* of Ernest Oliver Corbett and Margaret Edgar. *Educ:* Bedford Sch.; St John's Coll., Oxford. Royal Artillery, 1940-41, RAFVR, 1942-45. Thomas Whitcombe Greene Scholar, and Macmillan Student of British School at Athens, 1947-49; Asst Keeper in Dept of Greek and Roman Antiquities, British Museum, 1949-61. Lectr in Classics, Univ. of Calif, Los Angeles, 1956. Pres., Soc. for Promotion of Hellenic Studies, 1980-. *Publications:* The Sculpture of the Parthenon, 1959; (with A. Birchall) Greek Gods and Heroes, 1974; articles in Jl of Hellenic Studies, Hesperia, Annual of Brit. School at Athens, BM Quarterly, Bulletin of the Inst. of Classical Studies. *Address:* University College, Gower Street, WC1E 6BT.

CORBETT, Robin; communication and public affairs consultant; *b* 22 Dec. 1933; *s* of Thomas Corbett and Marguerite Adele Mainwaring; *m* 1970, Val Hudson; one *d. Educ:* Holly Lodge Grammar Sch., Smethwick. Newspaper and magazine journalist, 1950-69; Editoral Staff Develt Exec., IPC Magazines, 1969-72; Sen. Lab. Adviser, IPC Magazines, 1972-74. Mem. Nat. Union of Journalists Nat. Exec. Council, 1965-69. MP (Lab) Hemel Hempstead, Oct. 1974-1979. Chm., PLP Agric. Gp, 1977-78; Sec., PLP Civil Liberties Gp, 1974-79; Mem., Expenditure Cttee, 1976-79; Vice Chm., All-Party Animal Welfare Gp, 1976-79. Mem. Food and Agriculture Sub-Cttee, Labour Party Nat. Exec. Cttee, 1974-79; Chm., farm animal welfare co-ordinating exec., 1977-. Fellow, Industry and Parlt Trust, 1979. *Recreations:* visiting North Wales; pottering. *Address:* 96 Piccotts End, Hemel Hempstead, Herts. *T:* Hemel Hempstead 52866. *Clubs:* Hemel Hempstead Cricket; Robin Sports and Social.

CORBETT, Rupert Shelton, MA, MChir Cantab; FRCS; retired 1961; *b* 11 Feb. 1893; 2nd *s* of late Henry Shelton Corbett. *Educ:* Diocesan Coll., South Africa; Stubbington House, Hampshire; Cambridge Univ.; St Bartholomew's Hosp., London. MRCS, LRCP 1917; FRCS; MA Cantab 1922; BCh 1922; MB 1923; MChir 1927; formerly: Surgeon, St Bartholomew's Hosp.; Surgeon, St Andrew's Hosp., Dollis Hill; Consulting Surgeon, Chalfonts and Gerrards Cross Hosp.; Examiner in Surgery, Universities of Cambridge and London; Mem. of Examining Board, Royal Coll. of Surgeons; Mayo Lectr, Ann Arbor, USA, 1955; First Gordon-Watson Memorial Lectr, 1958; Mem. Council, Assoc. of Surgeons of Great Britain and Ireland, 1957-59; Pres., Chiltern Medical Soc., 1960-61. Chm., Jersey District Nursing Assoc. Central Cttee, 1971-. Vice-President: Jersey Branch, Royal Commonwealth Soc.; St John Ambulance Assoc., Jersey. OStJ 1977 (SBStJ 1971). *Publications:* contributions in British Surgical Practice; various articles in med. jls. *Address:* Katrina, Beaumont Hill, St Peter, Jersey. *T:* Central 20065.

CORBETT, Lt-Col Uvedale, DSO 1944; *b* 12 Sept. 1909; *s* of Major C. U. Corbett, Stableford, Bridgnorth, Shropshire; *m* 1st, 1935, Veronica Marian Whitehead (marr. diss., 1952); two *s* one *d* ; 2nd, 1953, Mrs Patricia Jane Walker. *Educ:* Wellington (Berks); RMA, Woolwich. Commissioned Royal Artillery, 1929; relinquished command 3rd Regt RHA 1945; retired. MP (C) Ludlow Div. of Shropshire, 1945-51. Chm., Sun Valley Poultry Ltd, 1961-. *Address:* Shobdon Court, Leominster, Herefordshire. *T:* Kingsland 260. *Club:* Army and Navy.

CORBETT-WINDER, Col John Lyon, OBE 1949; MC 1942; JP; Lord-Lieutenant of Powys, since 1974 (of Montgomeryshire, 1960-74); *b* 15 July 1911; *o s* of Major W. J. Corbett-Winder, Vaynor Park, Berriew, Montgomery (Lord Lieutenant of Montgomeryshire, 1944-50); *m* 1944, Margaret Ailsa, *d* of Lt-Col J. Ramsay Tainsh, CBE, VD; one *s* two *d. Educ:* Eton; RMC Sandhurst. 2nd Lieut, 60th Rifles, 1931; Lt-Col, 1942. Served War of 1939-45, Western Desert and N Africa, 1939-43 (despatches twice); Commanded: 44 Reconnaissance Regt; 1st Bn 60th Rifles; GSO1 Infantry Directorate, WO, 1944-47; commanded 2nd Bn 60th Rifles, Palestine, 1947-48 (despatches); AAG, HQ Southern Command, 1948-51; GSO1, HQ 53 Welsh Inf. Div., 1952-55; Col Gen. Staff, SHAPE Mission to Royal Netherlands Army, 1955-57; Dep. Mil. Sec., HQ, BAOR, 1957-58; retd 1959;

RARO, 1958-69. Mem., Parly Boundary Commn for Wales, 1963-79. Pres., TA & VR Assoc. for Wales, 1977-81. Chm., Dyfed-Powys Police Authority, 1978-80 (Vice-Chm., 1976-78). JP Powys (formerly Montgomeryshire), 1959. Commander, Order of Orange Nassau, 1958. KStJ 1970 (CStJ 1966). *Recreations:* gardening, forestry. *Address:* Vaynor Park, Berriew, Welshpool, Powys SY21 8QE. *T:* Berriew 204.

CORBIN, Maurice Haig Alleyne; Hon. Mr Justice Corbin; Justice of Appeal, Supreme Court, Trinidad and Tobago, since 1972; *b* 26 May 1916; *s* of L. A. Corbin; *m* 1943, Helen Jocelyn Child; one *s* two *d* ; *m* 1968, Jean Barcant. *Educ:* Harrison Coll., Barbados; Queen's Royal Coll., Trinidad. Solicitor, 1941; appointed Magistrate, Trinidad, 1945; called to the Bar, Middle Temple, 1949; Crown Counsel, 1953; Registrar, Supreme Court, 1954; Puisne Judge, Supreme Court, 1957-72. *Recreation:* tennis. *Address:* 6 Antigua Drive, Federation Park, Trinidad, West Indies. *Club:* Queen's Park Cricket (Port of Spain, Trinidad).

CORBY, (Frederick) Brian, FIA; Chief General Manager, since 1982, and Director, since 1981, Prudential Assurance Co. Ltd; Chief Executive, Prudential Corporation plc, since 1982; *b* 10 May 1929; *s* of Charles Walter and Millicent Corby; *m* 1952, Elizabeth Mairi McInnes; one *s* two *d. Educ:* Kimbolton Sch.; St John's Coll., Cambridge (MA). Joined Prudential Assce Co. Ltd, 1952; Dep. Gen. Manager, 1974; Gen. Manager, 1976-79; Gp Gen. Manager, Prudential Corp. Ltd, 1979-82. Vice-President, Inst. of Actuaries, 1979-. *Publications:* contribs to Jl of Inst. of Actuaries. *Recreations:* reading, golf, squash. *Address:* Fairings, Church End, Albury, Ware, Herts SG11 2JG. *T:* Albury 337.

CORBY, George Arthur; International meteorological consultant; *b* 14 Aug. 1917; *s* of Bertie John Corby and Agnes May (*née* Dale); *m* 1951, Gertrude Anne Nicoll; one *s* one *d. Educ:* St Marylebone Grammar Sch.; Univ. of London (BSc Special Maths 1st Cl.). Architect's Dept. LCC, 1936-42; entered Met. Office, 1942; Flt Lt, RAFVR, 1943; Sqdn Leader, Dep. Chief Met. Officer, ACSEA, 1945-46; Sen. Met. Off., Northolt Airport, 1947-53; research, 1953-73; Dep. Dir for Communications and Computing, 1973-76; Dir of Services and Dep. Dir Gen., 1976-78. Vice-Pres., Royal Meteorol Soc., 1975-77. *Publications:* official scientific pubns and res. papers on mountain airflow, dynamical meteorol., and numerical forecasting. *Recreations:* music, photography. *Address:* Kings Barn, High Street, Harwell, Oxon. *T:* Harwell 7883.

CORCORAN, Hon. James Desmond, AO 1982; MP (Labor) Hartley, South Australia, since 1977; *b* 8 Nov. 1928; *s* of James and Catherine Corcoran; *m* 1957, Carmel Mary Campbell; four *s* four *d. Educ:* Tantanoola Public School. Enlisted Australian Regular Army, 1950; served Korea, Japan, Malaya and New Guinea (despatches twice); discharged, rank of Captain, 1962. Entered politics, contested and won House of Assembly seat of Millicen, S Aust. Parliament, 1962, Member for Coles, 1975; held portfolios of Minister of Lands, Irrigation, Repatriation, Immigration and Tourism, in Labor Govt, 1965-68; Dep. Leader of Opposition, 1968-70; Dep. Premier, Minister of Works and Minister of Marine, 1970-77, additionally Minister of Environment, 1977-79; Premier, Treasurer, and Minister of Ethnic Affairs, of S Australia, Feb.-Sept. 1979. *Address:* 1 Aringa Court, Rostrevor, SA 5073, Australia.

CORCORAN, Percy John; His Honour Judge Corcoran; a Circuit Judge (formerly County Court Judge), since 1970; *b* 26 Nov. 1920; *s* of Michael Joseph and Sarah Corcoran, Macclesfield, S Australia; *m* 1949, Jean, JP, MSc, LCST; one *s* one *d. Educ:* Christian Brothers' Coll., Adelaide. Royal Australian Air Force, 1941-47. Called to Bar, Gray's Inn, 1948; practised as Barrister, 1948-70; Deputy Judge Advocate, 1953-57; Asst Recorder: Blackpool, 1959-70; Blackburn, 1962-70; Chm., Mental Health Tribunal, NW Area, 1962-70. Pres., Caterham District Scout Council. *Recreations:* golf, walking, music. *Address:* 18 Stanstead Road, Caterham, Surrey. *T:* Caterham 42423.

CORDEIRO, His Eminence Cardinal Joseph; *see* Karachi, Archbishop of, (RC).

CORDINGLEY, Maj-Gen. John Edward, OBE 1959; *b* 1 Sept. 1916; *s* of Air Vice-Marshal Sir John Cordingley, KCB, KCVO, CBE, and late Elizabeth Ruth Carpenter; *m* 1st, 1940, Ruth Pamela (marr. diss. 1961), *d* of late Major S. A. Boddam-Whetham; two *s* ; 2nd, 1961, Audrey Helen Anne, *d* of late Maj-Gen. F. G. Beaumont-Nesbitt, CVO, CBE, MC; two step *d. Educ:* Sherborne; RMA, Woolwich. 2nd Lieut RA, 1936; served War of 1939-45, Europe and India. Brigade Comdr, 1961-62; Imperial Defence Coll., 1963; Dir of Work Study, Min. of Defence (Army), 1964-66; Dep. Dir, RA, 1967-68; Maj-Gen., RA, BAOR, 1968-71, retired. Controller, Royal Artillery Instn, 1975-82; Chm. Bd of Management, RA Charitable Fund, 1977-82. Col Comdt, RA, 1973-82. Bursar, Sherborne Sch., 1971-74. Fellow, Inst. of Work Study Practitioners, 1965; MBIM, 1966. *Recreations:* golf and gardening. *Address:* Church Farm House, Rotherwick, Basingstoke, Hants RG27 9BG. *T:* Hook 2734. *Clubs:* Army and Navy; Senior Golfers.

CORDLE, John Howard; *b* 11 Oct. 1912; *s* of late Ernest William Cordle; *m* 1st, 1938 (marr. diss., 1956); three *s* (one *d* decd); 2nd, 1957 (marr. diss. 1971), *e d* of late C. A. Maynard, OBE; one *s* three *d. Educ:* City of London Sch. Served RAF (commissioned), 1940-45. Member: Archbishops of

Canterbury and York Commission on Evangelism, 1945-46; Church Assembly, 1946-53; Oxford Trust of Churches Patronage Board, 1947-. Mem. of Lloyd's, 1952; Mem. Founders Livery Company and Freeman of City of London, 1956. Dir, Presswork Ltd. Prospective Parly Cand. (C) NE Wolverhampton, 1949; contested (C) Wrekin Div., 1951; MP (C) Bournemouth E and Christchurch, Oct. 1959-1974, Bournemouth E, 1974-77; Chm., West Africa Cttee, Conservative Commonwealth Council, 1964-77; Member UK Delegation to: Council of Europe, Strasbourg, 1974-77 (Vice-Chm., Parly and Public Relations Cttee); WEU, Paris, 1974-77. Life Governor: St Mary's and St Paul's Coll., Cheltenham; Epsom Coll.; Mem. Court of University of Southampton, 1960-77. Gold Staff Officer, Coronation, 1953. Grand Band, Order of the Star of Africa (Liberia), 1964. *Recreations:* shooting, tennis, golf, gardening. *Address:* Malmesbury House, The Close, Salisbury, Wilts. *T:* Salisbury 27027. *Clubs:* Carlton, National, English-Speaking Union, Royal Commonwealth Society.

COREN, Alan; Editor of Punch, since 1978; *b* 27 June 1938; *s* of Samuel and Martha Coren; *m* 1963, Anne Kasriel; one *s* one *d. Educ:* East Barnet Grammar Sch.; Wadham Coll., Oxford (Open scholar; BA); Yale; Univ. of California, Berkeley. Asst Editor, Punch, 1963-66, Literary Editor 1966-69, Dep. Editor 1969-77. TV Critic, The Times, 1971-78; Columnist: Daily Mail, 1972-76; Evening Standard, 1977; contributor to: Sunday Times, Atlantic Monthly, Listener, TLS, Observer, Tatler, London Review of Books. Commonwealth Fellowship, 1961-63. Rector, St Andrews Univ., 1973-76. *Publications:* The Dog It Was That Died, 1965; All Except the Bastard, 1969; The Sanity Inspector, 1974; The Bulletins of Idi Amin, 1974; Golfing For Cats, 1975; The Further Bulletins of Idi Amin, 1975; The Lady From Stalingrad Mansions, 1977; The Peanut Papers, 1977; The Rhinestone as Big as the Ritz, 1979; Tissues for Men, 1980; The Best of Alan Coren, 1980; The Cricklewood Diet, 1982; Present Laughter, 1982; (ed) The Pick of Punch (annual), 1979-; (ed) The Punch Book of Short Stories, Bk 1, 1979, Bk 2, 1980, Bk 3, 1981; The Arthur Books (for children), 1976-81. *TV series:* The Losers, 1978. *Recreations:* bridge, riding, broadcasting. *Address:* 23 Tudor Street, EC4.

CORFIELD, Rt. Hon. Sir Frederick (Vernon), PC 1970; Kt 1972; QC 1972; a Recorder of the Crown Court, since 1979; *b* 1 June 1915; *s* of late Brig. F. A. Corfield, DSO, OBE, IA, and M. G. Corfield (*née* Vernon); *m* 1945, Elizabeth Mary Ruth Taylor; no *c. Educ:* Cheltenham Coll. (Scholar); RMA, Woolwich. Royal Artillery, 1935; 8th Field Regt, RA, India, 1935-39; served War of 1939-45; Actg Captain and Adjutant, 23rd Field Regt, BEF, 3rd Div., 1939; 51st (Highland) Div., 1940 (despatches); prisoner of war, Germany, 1940-45. Called to Bar, Middle Temple, 1945; Bencher, 1980; JAG's Branch, WO, 1945-46; retired, 1946; farming, 1946-56. MP (C) South Gloucester, 1955-Feb. 1974; Jt Parly Sec., Min. of Housing and Local Govt, 1962-64; Minister of State, Board of Trade, June-Oct. 1970; Minister of Aviation Supply, 1970-71; Minister for Aerospace, DTI, 1971-72. Mem., British Waterways Bd, 1974- (Vice-Chm., 1980-82); Dir, Mid-Kent Water Co. Chm., London and Provincial Antique Dealers' Assoc., 1975-. *Publications:* Corfield on Compensation, 1959; A Guide to the Community Land Act, 1976; (with R. J. A. Carnworth) Compulsory Acquisition and Compensation, 1978. *Recreations:* gardening, fishing. *Address:* Wordings Orchard, Sheepscombe, near Stroud, Glos.; 2 Paper Buildings, Temple, EC4.

CORFIELD, Sir Kenneth (George), Kt 1980; Chairman, since 1979, and Managing Director, since 1969, Standard Telephones & Cables Ltd; Chairman, Standard Telephones and Cables (Northern Ireland), since 1974; Senior Officer, International Telephone and Telegraph Corporation (UK), since 1974; Vice-President, ITT Europe Inc., since 1967; Chairman, British Engineering Council, since 1981; *b* 27 Jan. 1924; *s* of Stanley Corfield and Dorothy Elizabeth (*née* Mason); *m* 1960; one *d. Educ:* South Staffs Coll. of Advanced Technology. CE, FEng, FIMechE, CBIM. Management Develt, ICI Metals Div., 1946-50; Man. Dir, K. G. Corfield Ltd, 1950-60; Exec. Dir, Parkinson Cowan, 1960-66; Dep. Chm., STC Ltd, 1969-79. Dir, Midland Bank Ltd, 1979-. Chm., EDC for Ferrous Foundries Industry, 1975-78. Member: Adv. Council, Science Museum, 1975-; ACARD, 1981-. President: TEMA, 1974-80; BAIE, 1975-79; Vice-Pres., Engineering Employers' Fedn, 1979-; Member Council: CBI, 1971-; Inst. of Dirs, 1981-; Vice-Pres., BIM, 1978-. CompIEE 1974. DUniv Surrey, 1976; Hon. DSc City, 1981. *Publication:* Product Design, Report for NEDO, 1979. *Recreations:* hunting, shooting, photography. *Address:* 14 Elm Walk, Hampstead, NW3 7UP.

CORI, Prof. Carl Ferdinand; Biochemist at Massachusetts General Hospital, Harvard Medical School, Boston, Mass, since 1967; Professor of Biochemistry, Washington University School of Medicine, St Louis, Mo, 1931-67; *b* Prague, Czechoslovakia, 5 Dec. 1896; *s* of Carl Cori and Maria Lippich; went to US, 1922; naturalised, 1928; *m* 1920, Gerty T. (*d* 1957), *d* of Otto Radnitz; one *s* ; *m* 1960, Anne Fitz-Gerald Jones. *Educ:* Gymnasium, Trieste, Austria; (German) University of Prague (MD). Asst in Pharmacology, University of Graz, Austria, 1920-21; Biochemist State Inst. for Study of Malignant Disease, Buffalo, NY, 1922-31. Mem. Nat. Acad. of Sciences, Royal Society etc. Hon. ScD: Western Reserve, 1946, Yale, 1946, Boston Univ., 1948, Cambridge, 1949; Brandeis, 1965; Gustavus Adolphus Coll., 1965; Washington Univ., 1966; St Louis Univ., 1966; Monash, 1966; Granada, 1967; Univ. of Trieste, 1971. Shared Nobel Prize in Medicine and Physiology, 1947. Mid-West Award, 1946; Squibb Award, 1947; Sugar Research Foundation Award, 1947 and 1950; Willard Gibbs Medal, 1948. *Publications:* articles in scientific journals. *Address:* Department of Biochemistry, Harvard Medical School, Boston, Mass 02115, USA.

CORISH, Brendan; TD Wexford since 1945; Member of Council of State since 1964; *m* 1949; three *s. Educ:* Christian Brothers' Sch., Wexford. Vice-Chm. of Labour Party, Republic of Ireland, 1946–49; Party Chm., 1949–53; Parly Party Whip, 1947–54; Parly Sec. to Minister for Local Govt and Defence, 1948–51; Minister for Social Welfare, 1954–57; Party Leader, 1960–77; Tanaiste (Deputy Prime Minister) and Minister for Health and Social Welfare, 1973–77. Mem., Wexford CC, 1979–; Alderman, Wexford Corp., 1979–. *Address:* Leinster House, Kildare Street, Dublin 2, Ireland.

CORK AND ORRERY, 13th Earl of, *cr* 1620; **Patrick Reginald Boyle;** Baron Boyle of Youghall, 1616; Viscount Dungarvan, 1620; Viscount Kinalmeaky, Baron Boyle of Bandon Bridge and Baron Boyle of Broghill (Ireland), 1628; Earl of Orrery, 1660; Baron Boyle of Marston, 1711; writer, artist and broadcaster; *b* 7 Feb. 1910; *s* of Major Hon. Reginald Courtenay Boyle, MBE, MC (*d* 1946), and Violet (*d* 1974), *d* of late Arthur Flower; *S* uncle, 12th Earl of Cork and Orrery, 1967; *m* 1952, Dorothy Kate (*d* 1978), *o d* of late Robert Ramsden, Meltham, Yorks; *m* 1978, Mary Gabrielle Walker, *widow* of Kenneth Macfarlane Walker and *o d* of late Louis Ginnett. *Educ:* Harrow Sch.; Royal Military College, Sandhurst. Royal Ulster Rifles, 1930–33; Capt. London Irish Rifles, Royal Ulster Rifles (TA), 1935–38. Served War of 1939–45 with Royal Ulster Rifles, Burma Rifles, Cameronians (Scottish Rifles) in Special Force (Chindits) (severely wounded) and Parachute Regt. Now Hon. Major, late Army Air Corps. Dep. Speaker and Dep. Chm. of Cttees, House of Lords, 1973–78; Mem., British Delegn to Inter-Parly Conf., Tokyo, 1974, Madrid, 1976. Pres. and Exec. Chm., British Cancer Council; Dir, Cancer Research Campaign; Mem., Council of Management, St Christopher's Hospice, Sydenham. Hereditary Life Governor and Exec. Chm., Christian Faith Soc.; Mem., Diocesan Assembly, Russian Orthodox Church in GB. FRSA 1947. *Publications:* (author and illustrator) Sailing in a Nutshell, 1935; (jointly) Jungle, Jungle, Little Chindit, 1946. Contribs to the Hibbert Jl. *Recreations:* sailing, oil-painting, gardening. *Heir:* *b* Hon. John William Boyle, DSC [*b* 12 May 1916; *m* 1943, Mary Leslie, *d* of late Gen. Sir Robert Gordon Finlayson, KCB, CMG, DSO; three *s*]. *Address:* Flint House, Heyshott, Midhurst, W Sussex. *Clubs:* Royal Thames Yacht; Cork and County (Cork).

CORK, CLOYNE, AND ROSS, Bishop of, since 1978; **Rt. Rev. Samuel Greenfield Poyntz;** *b* 4 March 1926; *s* of James and Katharine Jane Poyntz; *m* 1952, Noreen Henrietta Armstrong; one *s* two *d. Educ:* Portora Royal School, Enniskillen; Univ. of Dublin. Mod., Mental and Moral Sci. and Oriental Langs, 1948; 1st cl. Div. Test., 1950; MA 1951; BD 1953; PhD 1960. Deacon 1950, priest 1951; Curate Assistant: St George's, Dublin, 1950-52; Bray, 1952-55; St Michan and St Paul, Dublin, 1955-59; Rector of St Stephen's, Dublin, 1959-67; Vicar of St Ann's, Dublin, 1967-78; Archdeacon of Dublin, 1974-78; Exam. Chaplain to Archbishop of Dublin, 1974-78. Chm., Youth Dept, British Council of Churches, 1965-69. *Publications:* The Exaltation of the Blessed Virgin Mary, 1953; St Stephen's—One Hundred and Fifty Years of Worship and Witness, 1974; Journey towards Unity, 1975; St Ann's—the Church in the heart of the City, 1976; (ed) Church the Way, the Truth, and Your Life, 1955. *Recreations:* interest in Rugby football, stamp collecting. *Address:* The Palace, Bishop Street, Cork. *T:* Cork 21214.

CORK, Sir Kenneth (Russell), GBE 1978; FCA; Senior Partner, Cork Gully, Chartered Accountants, since 1980 (Senior Partner, W. H. Cork, Gully & Co., 1946-80); Lord Mayor of London for 1978-79; *b* 21 Aug. 1913; *s* of William Henry Cork and Maud Alice (*née* Nunn); *m* 1937, Nina Lippold; one *s* one *d. Educ:* Berkhamsted. ACA 1937, FCA 1946. Enlisted HAC, 1938; called up, 1939; served in North Africa and Italy, 1939-45 (rank Lt-Col). Common Councilman, City of London, 1951-70; Alderman, City of London (Ward of Tower), 1970; Sheriff, City of London, 1975-76; Liveryman: Worshipful Co. of Horners (Mem. Court, 1970, Renter Warden, 1978, Master, 1980); Worshipful Co. of Chartered Accountants in England and Wales. One of HM Lieutenants, City of London, 1979-. Chairman: EEC Bankruptcy Convention Adv. Cttee to Dept Trade, 1973; Insolvency Law Review Cttee, 1977-. Chairman: NI Finance Corpn, 1974-76; NI Develt Agency, 1976-77, Hon. Consultant, 1977-. Mem., Cttee to Review the Functioning of Financial Institutions, 1977-. Pres., Inst. of Credit Management Ltd. Mem. Council, Inst. of Dirs; Chm., City Branch, Inst. of Dirs, 1981-. Governor, Royal Shakespeare Theatre, 1967- (Chm., 1975-); Dir, Shakespeare Theatre Trust (Chm. 1967-75). Treas., Royal Concert, 1970. Hon. Treas., Nat. Assoc. of Youth Clubs. Chm. of Governors, Berkhamsted Sch. FRSA 1970; FICM; CBIM 1979 (Pres., S Bucks Br.); FCIS 1979; FInstD. Hon. DLitt City Univ., 1978. Hon. GSM. KStJ 1979. Commandeur de l'Ordre du Merite (France); Order of Rio Branco, cl. III (Brazil); Grande Oficiãl da Ordem Militaire de Cristo (Portugal); Order of Diplomatic Service Merit Gwanghwa Medal (Korea). *Recreations:* sailing, photography, painting. *Address:* Cherry Trees, Grimms Lane, Great Missenden, Bucks. *T:* Great Missenden 2628. *Clubs:* Royal Thames Yacht, City Livery, Little Ship; Hardway Sailing (Gosport); Bosham Sailing.

CORKERY, Michael, QC 1981; *b* 20 May 1926; *o s* of late Charles Timothy Corkery and of Nellie Marie Corkery; *m* 1967, Juliet Shore Foulkes, *o d* of late Harold Glyn Foulkes; one *s* one *d. Educ:* The King's Sch., Canterbury. Commissioned in Welsh Guards, 1945; served until 1948. Called to Bar, Lincoln's Inn, 1949, Bencher 1973; Mem., South Eastern Circuit; 3rd Junior Prosecuting Counsel to the Crown at the Central Criminal Court, 1959; 1st Junior Prosecuting Counsel to the Crown, 1964; 5th Senior Prosecuting Counsel to the Crown, 1970; 3rd Sen. Prosecuting Counsel, 1971; 2nd Sen.

Prosecuting Counsel, 1974; 1st Sen. Prosecuting Counsel, 1977-81. *Recreations:* shooting, sailing, gardening, music. *Address:* 5 Paper Buildings, Temple, EC4.

CORLETT, Ewan Christian Brew, MA, PhD; FEng; Chairman and Managing Director, Burness, Corlett & Partners Ltd, since 1954; *b* 11 Feb. 1923; *s* of Malcolm James John and Catherine Ann Corlett; *m* 1946, Edna Lilian Büggs; three *s. Educ:* King William's Coll., IOM; Oxford Univ. (MA Engrg Sci.); Durham Univ. (PhD Naval Architecture). Fellow, Fellowship of Engineering. Dept of Director of Naval Construction, Admiralty, Bath, 1944-46; Tipton Engrg Co., Tipton, 1946-47; Aluminium Develt Assoc. Research Scholar, Durham Univ., 1947-50; Naval Architect, British Aluminium Co., 1950-53; Design Dir, Burness, Corlett & Partners Ltd, 1953-54. Chm. Council, RINA, 1977-79, Vice-Pres., 1971-82, Hon. Vice-Pres., 1982. Home Office Assessor (Technical Inquiries), 1959-80; Mem. Board, Nat. Maritime Inst., 1978-82; Trustee, Nat. Maritime Museum, 1974-. *Publications:* The Iron Ship, 1976; The Revolution in Merchant Shipping 1950-1980, 1980. numerous papers to learned instns. *Recreations:* sailing, painting, astronomy. *Address:* Cottimans, Port-e-Vullen, Isle of Man. *T:* Ramsey, IOM, 814009. *Club:* Manx Sailing and Cruising.

CORLEY, Sir Kenneth (Sholl Ferrand), Kt 1972; Chairman and Chief Executive, Joseph Lucas (Industries) Ltd, 1969-73; *b* 3 Nov. 1908; *s* of late S. W. Corley and late Mrs A. L. Corley; *m* 1937, Olwen Mary Yeoman; one *s* one *d. Educ:* St Bees, Cumberland. Joined Joseph Lucas Ltd, 1927; Director, 1948. Pres., Birmingham Chamber of Commerce, 1964. Governor, Royal Shakespeare Theatre; Life Governor, Birmingham Univ.; Pres., Soc. of Motor Mfrs and Traders, 1971. Chm. Governors, St Bees Sch., 1978-. Chevalier, Légion d'Honneur, 1975. *Recreations:* fell-walking, bee-keeping, theatre. *Address:* 34 Dingle Lane, Solihull, West Midlands B91 3NG. *T:* 021-705 1597; Yewtree, Wasdale, Cumbria CA20 1EU. *T:* Wasdale 285. *Club:* Royal Automobile.

CORLEY, His Honour Michael Early Ferrand; a Circuit Judge (formerly County Court Judge), 1967-82; *b* 11 Oct. 1909; *s* of late Ferrand Edward Corley, Christian College, Madras, and Elsie Maria Corley. *Educ:* Marlborough; Oriel Coll., Oxford. Called to Bar, 1934. War Service, RNVR, 1940-46. *Address:* 3 Brockley Grove, Hutton, Brentwood, Essex.

CORMACK, Prof. Allan MacLeod; University Professor, Tufts University, since 1980; *b* 23 Feb. 1924; *s* of George Cormack and Amelia MacLeod; *m* 1950, Barbara Jeanne Seavey; one *s* two *d. Educ:* Univ. of Cape Town (BSc, MSc). Research Student, St John's Coll., Cambridge. Lecturer, Univ. of Cape Town, 1950-56; Research Fellow, Harvard Univ., 1956-57; Tufts University: Asst Prof., 1957-60; Associate Prof., 1960-64; Prof. of Physics, 1964-80; Chairman, Physics Dept, 1968-76. Fellow, Amer. Physical Soc., 1964; Fellow, Amer. Acad. of Arts and Sciences, 1980; Hon. Mem., Swedish Neuroradiological Soc., 1979. Ballou Medallist, Tufts Univ., 1978. Nobel Prize for Medicine (jtly), 1979. Hon. DSc Tufts Univ., 1980. *Publications:* articles on nuclear and particle physics, and computed tomography. *Address:* 18 Harrison Street, Winchester, Mass 01890, USA. *T:* 617-729-0735.

CORMACK, John, CB 1982; Fisheries Secretary, Department of Agriculture and Fisheries for Scotland, 1976-82; *b* 27 Aug. 1922; *yr s* of late Donald Cormack and of Anne Hunter Cormack (*née* Gair); *m* 1947, Jessie Margaret Bain; one *s* one *d* (and one *d* decd). *Educ:* Royal High Sch., Edinburgh. Served RAPC, 1941-46; Captain, 1946. Entered Department of Agriculture for Scotland, 1939: Principal, 1959; Private Sec. to Sec. of State for Scotland, 1967-69; Asst Sec., 1969; Under Sec., 1976. *Recreations:* golf, music. *Address:* 57 Craigmount Avenue North, Edinburgh EH12 8DN. *T:* 031-339 5420. *Club:* Royal Commonwealth Society.

CORMACK, Sir Magnus (Cameron), KBE 1970; *b* Caithness, Scotland, 12 Feb. 1906; *s* of William Petrie Cormack and Violet McDonald Cameron; *m* 1935, Mary Gordon Macmeiken; one *s* three *d. Educ:* St Peter's Sch., Adelaide, S Aust. Farmer and Grazier. Served War, 1940-44; Aust. Imperial Forces, SW Pacific Area, Major. Pres., Liberal Party Organisation, 1947-49; Senator for Victoria, 1951-53 and 1962-78; President of the Senate, 1971-74. *Recreation:* deep sea sailing. *Address:* 7 Market Court, Portland, Victoria 3305, Australia. *Clubs:* Australian, Naval and Military (Melbourne, Victoria); Hamilton (Victoria).

CORMACK, Patrick Thomas; MP (C) Staffordshire South West, since 1974 (Cannock, 1970-74); *b* 18 May 1939; *s* of Thomas Charles and Kathleen Mary Cormack, Grimsby; *m* 1967, Kathleen Mary McDonald; two *s. Educ:* St James' Choir School and Havelock School, Grimsby; Univ. of Hull. Second Master, St James' Choir School, Grimsby, 1961-66; Company Education and Training Officer, Ross Group Ltd, Grimsby, 1966-67; Assistant Housemaster, Wrekin College, Shropshire, 1967-69; Head of History, Brewood Grammar School, Stafford, 1969-70. Trustee, Historic Churches Preservation Trust; Member: Historic Buildings Council; Cons. Party Arts and Heritage Cttee (Chm.); Select Cttee on Educn, Science and Arts; Faculty Jurisdiction Commn; All Party Heritage Cttee (Chm.); Heritage in Danger (Vice-Chm.); Council for British archaeology; Royal Commn on Historical Manuscripts; Council for Independent Educn (Chm.); Lord Chancellor's Adv. Cttee on Public Records. FSA 1978. *Publications:* Heritage in Danger, 1976; Right Turn, 1978; Westminster: Palace and Parliament, 1981; Castles of Britain, 1982.

Recreations: fighting philistines, walking, visiting old churches. *Address:* House of Commons, SW1A 0AA. *Clubs:* Athenæum, Brooks's.

CORMACK, Robert Linklater Burke; HM Diplomatic Service; Counsellor (Economic and Commercial), Stockholm, since 1981; *b* 29 Aug. 1935; *s* of late Frederick Eunson Cormack, CIE, and Elspeth Mary (*née* Linklater), Dounby, Orkney; *m* 1962, Eivor Dorotea Kumlin; one *s* two *d. Educ:* Trinity Coll., Glenalmond; Trinity Hall, Cambridge (BA Agric.). National Service, The Black Watch, 1954-56. Dist Officer, Kenya (HMOCS), 1960-64; entered CRO (subseq. Diplomatic Service), 1964: Private Sec. to Minister of State, 1964-66; 1st Secretary: Saigon, 1966-68; Bombay, 1969-70; Delhi, 1970-72; FCO, 1972-77; Counsellor and Consul-Gen., Kinshasa, 1977-79; RCDS, 1980. *Address:* c/o Foreign and Commonwealth Office, SW1.

CORMIE, (John) David, MA, FCA; Chief Executive, building and home improvement product area, Reed International plc, since 1981; *b* 8 Dec. 1930; *s* of John George Cormie and Barbara Evelyn Cormie; *m* 1956, Margaret Killer; two *s* two *d. Educ:* City of London Sch.; Cambridge Univ. (MA). FCA 1958. National Service, 2nd Lieut RA. Articled Clerk, J. H. Hugill & Co., 1954-57; Procter & Gamble Ltd, 1957-60; Unilever, 1960-76: Commercial Dir, Lever Brothers Ltd, 1968; Chief Accountant, Unilever, 1970; Chm. and Chief Exec., Batchelors Foods, 1973; Finance Dir, Reed Internat. Ltd, 1976-81. Part-time Mem., British Telecom Bd 1981-. Inst. of Chartered Accountants in England and Wales: Mem. Council, 1971-; Dep. Pres., 1982-83. Governor, Royal Vet. Coll., 1980-. *Recreations:* theatre, golf, badminton, sailing, gardening, reading. *Address:* Colneford House, Earls Colne, Colchester CO6 2LG. *T:* Earls Colne 2026.

CORNBERG, Mrs Sol; *see* Gaskin, Catherine.

CORNELL, Ward MacLaurin; Deputy Minister, Ministry of Citizenship and Culture, province of Ontario, since 1980; *b* London, Ont, 4 May 1924; *m* Georgina Saxon; three *s* two *d. Educ:* Pickering Coll.; Univ. of Western Ontario. Lectr in English and History, Pickering Coll., Ont, 1949-54; Vis. Lectr, Conestoga Coll.; Gen. Manager, Broadcast Div. (Radio), Free Press Printing Co., 1954-67; Pres., Creative Projects in Communications, 1967-72; Agent-Gen. for Ont. in UK, 1972-78; Gen. Manager, European Ops, Lenroc Internat. Ltd, 1978-80. *Recreations:* reading, tennis, travelling. *Address:* RR1, Uxbridge, Ontario, Canada.

CORNER, Edred John Henry, CBE 1972; FRS 1955; FLS; Professor of Tropical Botany, University of Cambridge, 1966-73, now Emeritus; *b* 12 Jan. 1906; *s* of late Edred Moss Corner and Henrietta Corner (*née* Henderson); *m* 1953, Helga Dinesen Sondergoord; one *s* two *d* (by 1st *m*). *Educ:* Rugby Sch. Asst Dir, Gardens Dept, Straits Settlements, 1929-45; Principal Field Scientific Officer, Latin America, Unesco, 1947-48; Lecturer in Botany, Cambridge, 1949-59; Reader in Plant Taxonomy, 1959-65; Fellow, Sidney Sussex Coll., Cambridge, 1959-73. Member: American Mycological Soc.; Brit. Mycological Soc.; French Mycological Soc.; Fellow, American Assoc. for the Advancement of Science; Corr. Member: Botanical Soc. of America; Royal Netherlands Botanical Soc.; Hon. Mem., Japanese Mycological Soc. Mem., Governing Body of Rugby Sch., 1959-75. Darwin Medal, Royal Soc., 1960; Patron's Medal, RGS, 1966; Gold Medal, Linnean Soc. of London, 1970; Victoria Medal of Honour, RHS, 1974. *Publications:* Wayside Trees of Malaya (2 vols), 1940 and 1952; A Monograph of Clavaria and allied genera, 1950; Life of Plants, 1964; Natural History of Palms, 1966; Monograph of Cantharelloid Fungi, 1966; Boletus in Malaysia, 1972; Seeds of Dicotyledons, 2 vols, 1976; The Marquis: a tale of Syonan-to, 1981. *Address:* 91 Hinton Way, Great Shelford, Cambs CB2 5AH. *T:* Shelford 842167.

CORNER, Frank Henry, CMG 1980; part-retired New Zealand Civil Servant and Diplomat; *b* 17 May 1920; *y* *s* of Charles William Corner, Napier, NZ, and Sybil Corner (*née* Smith); *m* 1943, Lynette Robinson; two *d. Educ:* Napier Boys' High Sch.; Victoria Univ. of Wellington. MA, 1st cl. History; James Macintosh and Post-graduate Scholar. External Affairs Dept, NZ, and War Cabinet Secretariat, 1943; 1st Sec., NZ Embassy, Washington, 1948-51; Sen. Counsellor, NZ High Commn, London, 1952-58; Dep. Sec. NZ Dept of External Affairs, 1958-62; Perm. Rep. (Ambassador) to UN, 1962-67; Ambassador of NZ to USA, 1967-72; Permanent Head of Prime Minister's Dept, 1973-75; Secretary of Foreign Affairs, 1973-80; Administrator of Tokelau, 1976-. Mem., NZ Delegn to Commonwealth Prime Ministers' Meetings, 1944, 1946, 1951-57, 1973, 1975, 1977, 1979; Deleg. to UN Gen. Assembly, 1949-52, 1955, 1960-68, 1973, 1974; NZ Rep. to UN Trusteeship Council, 1962-66 (Pres., 1965-66; Chm., UN Vis. Mission to Micronesia, 1964); NZ Rep. on UN Security Coun., 1966; Adviser, NZ Delegn: Paris Peace Conf., 1946; Geneva Conf. on Korea, 1954; numerous other internat. confs as adviser or delegate. Chm., Bd of NZ-US Educnl Foundn, 1980-; Patron, Assoc. of NZ Art Socs, 1973-; Mem. Council, Victoria Univ. of Wellington, 1981-. FRSA. *Recreations:* the arts, gardening, wine. *Address:* 26 Burnell Avenue, Wellington 1, NZ. *T:* 737-022. *Club:* Wellington (New Zealand).

CORNER, Philip; Director General of Quality Assurance, Ministry of Defence Procurement Executive, since 1975; *b* 7 Aug. 1924; *s* of late William Henry Corner and of Dora (*née* Smailes); *m* 1948, Nora Pipes; no *c. Educ:* Dame Allan's Boys' Sch., Newcastle upon Tyne; Bradford Technical Coll.; RNEC Manadon; Battersea Polytechnic. BScEng (London); CEng, MIMechE, MIEE. Short Bros (Aeronautical Engrs), 1942-43; Air Br., RN,

Sub-Lieut RNVR, 1944-46; LNER Co., 1946-47; Min. of Works, 1947-50; Min. of Supply, 1950; Ministry of Defence: Dir of Guided Weapons Prodn, 1968-72; Dir of Quality Assurance (Technical), 1972-75. Member: Metrology and Standards Requirements Bd, DoI, 1974-; Adv. Council for Calibration and Measurement, DoI, 1975-; BSI Quality Assurance Council, 1979-; BSI Bd, 1980-. *Recreations:* gardening, listening to music. *Address:* 97 Dartnell Park Road, West Byfleet, Weybridge, Surrey KT14 6QE.

CORNESS, Colin Ross; Chairman, Redland PLC, since 1977 (Managing Director, 1967-82); *b* 9 Oct. 1931; *s* of Thomas Corness and Mary Evlyne Corness. *Educ:* Uppingham Sch.; Magdalene Coll., Cambridge (BA 1954, MA 1958); Graduate Sch. of Business Admin, Harvard, USA (Advanced Management Program Dip. 1970). Called to the Bar, Inner Temple, 1956. Dir, Taylor Woodrow Construction Ltd, 1961-64; Man. Dir, Redland Tiles Ltd, 1965-70. Director: Chubb & Son Ltd, 1974-; W. H. Smith and Son Ltd, 1980-. Chm., Building Centre, 1974-77; Member: EDC for Building, 1980-; Industrial Develt Adv. Bd, 1982-. *Recreations:* squash rackets, travel, music. *Address:* West Mare, Marehill, Pulborough, W Sussex. *T:* Pulborough 2159.

CORNFORD, Sir (Edward) Clifford, KCB 1977 (CB 1966); FEng 1980; Member, Post Office Board, since 1981; Vice Chairman, A. C. Cossor Ltd, and Chairman of several subsidiary companies, since 1982; *b* 6 Feb. 1918; *s* of John Herbert Cornford; *m* 1945, Catherine Muir; three *s* three *d. Educ:* Kimbolton Sch.; Jesus Coll., Cambridge (BA). Joined RAE, 1938. Operational Research with RAF, 1939-45. Guided Weapons Res. at RAE, 1945-60; jssc 1951; Head of Guided Weapons Dept, RAE, 1956-61; Min. of Defence: Chm., Def. Res. Policy Staff, 1961-63; Asst Chief Scientific Adviser, 1963-64; Chief Scientist (Army), Mem. Army Board, Ministry of Defence, 1965-67; Chm. Programme Evaluation Group, MoD, 1967-Jan. 1968 Dep. Chief Adviser (Research and Studies), MoD, 1968-69; Controller of Guided Weapons and Electronics, Min. of Technology, later Min. of Aviation Supply and MoD (Procurement Executive), 1969-72; Ministry of Defence (PE): Controller (Policy), 1972-74; Dep. Chief Exec., 1974-75; Chief Exec. and Permanent Under Sec. of State, 1975-77; Chief of Defence Procurement, MoD, 1977-80. FRAeS. *Publications:* on aeronautical subjects in jls of learned socs and technical publications. *Recreation:* travelling. *Address:* Beechurst, Shaftesbury Road, Woking, Surrey. *T:* 68919. *Club:* Athenæum.

CORNFORD, James Peters; Director, Nuffield Foundation, since 1980; *b* 1935; *s* of John Cornford and Rachel Peters; *m* 1960, Avery Amanda Goodfellow; one *s* three *d. Educ:* Winchester Coll.; Trinity Coll., Cambridge (MA). Fellow, Trinity Coll., Cambridge, 1960-64; Harkness Fellow, 1961-62; Univ. of Edinburgh: Lectr in Politics, 1964-68; Prof. of Politics, 1968-76; Dir, Outer Circle Policy Unit, 1976-80. Vis. Fellow, All Souls Coll., Oxford, 1975-76; Vis. Prof., Birkbeck Coll., Univ. of London, 1977-80. Dir, Job Ownership Ltd, 1979-. Literary Editor, The Political Quarterly, 1976-. *Publications: contrib.:* Cleavages, Ideologies and Party Systems, ed Allardt and Littunen, 1965; Ideas and Institutions of Victorian Britain, ed Robson, 1967; International Guide to Election Statistics, ed Meyriat and Rokkan, 1969; Government and Nationalism in Scotland, ed Wolfe, 1969; Mass Politics, ed Rokkan and Allardt, 1970; Philosophy, Politics and Society IV, ed Laslett, Runciman and Skinner, 1972; (ed) The Failure of the State, 1975; (ed) William Stubbs, The Constitutional History of England, 1979; contrib. to jls. *Address:* The Brick House, Wicken Bonhunt, Saffron Walden, Essex CB11 3UG. *T:* Saffron Walden 40348.

CORNFORTH, Sir John (Warcup), Kt 1977; CBE 1972; FRS 1953; DPhil; Royal Society Research Professor, University of Sussex, 1975-82, now Emeritus; *b* 7 Sept. 1917; *er s* of J. W. Cornforth, Sydney, Aust.; *m* 1941, Rita, *d* of W. C. Harradence; one *s* two *d. Educ:* Sydney High Sch.; Universities of Sydney and Oxford. BSc Sydney 1937; MSc Sydney, 1938; 1851 Exhibition Overseas Scholarship, 1939-42; DPhil Oxford, 1941; scientific staff of Med. Research Coun., 1946-62; Dir, Shell Research, Milstead Lab. of Chem. Enzymology, 1962-75. Assoc. Prof. in Molecular Sciences, Univ. of Warwick, 1965-71; Vis. Prof., Univ. of Sussex, 1971-75. Lectures: Pedler, Chem. Soc., 1968-69; Max Tishler, Harvard Univ., 1970; Robert Robinson, Chem. Soc., 1971-72; Sandin, Univ. of Alberta, 1977. Corday-Morgan Medal and Prize, Chem. Soc., 1953; (with G. J. Popjak) CIBA Medal, Biochem. Soc., 1965; Flintoff Medal, Chem. Soc., 1966; Stouffer Prize, 1967; Ernest Guenther Award, Amer. Chem. Soc., 1969; (with G. J. Popjak) Davy Medal, Royal Soc., 1968; Prix Roussel, 1972; (jtly) Nobel Prize for Chemistry, 1975; Royal Medal, Royal Soc., 1976; Copley Medal, Royal Soc., 1982. For. Hon. Mem., Amer. Acad., 1973; Corresp. Mem., Aust. Acad., 1977; For. Associate, Nat. Acad. of Scis of Amer., 1978; For. Mem., Royal Netherlands Acad. of Scis, 1978. Hon. DSc: ETH Zürich, 1975; Oxford, Warwick, Dublin and Liverpool, 1976; Aberdeen, Hull, Sussex, Sydney, 1977. Hon. Fellow, St Catherine's Coll., Oxford, 1976. Has been deaf since boyhood. *Publications:* numerous papers on organic chemical and biochemical subjects. *Recreations:* lawn tennis, chess, gardening. *Address:* Saxon Down, Cuilfail, Lewes, East Sussex BN7 2BE.

CORNISH, Jack Bertram; HM Civil Service; Under-Secretary, Department of Health and Social Security, 1976-78; *b* 26 June 1918; *s* of Bertram George John Cornish and Nora Jarmy; *m* 1946, Mary Milton; three *d. Educ:* Price's Grammar Sch., Fareham; Cotham Grammar Sch., Bristol. Admiralty, 1937-61: London, Bath, Plymouth, Singapore; DHSS, 1961-78. Supply Ships in Singapore and Newfoundland, 1941 and 1942. *Recreations:* music, painting, gardening. *Address:* 13 Kingsley Road, Kingsbridge, South Devon. *T:* Kingsbridge 2585.

CORNISH, Prof. Ronald James; *b* Exeter, Devon, 30 Dec. 1898; *s* of William Henry Cornish and Eva Maud Eliza (*née* Horrell); *m* 1927, Edith Oliver Oliver; twin *d. Educ:* Hele's Sch., Exeter; Exeter Sch., Exeter; Manchester Univ. RGA, 1917-19; engineer, Messrs Mather & Platt, Ltd, Manchester, 1922-25; Manchester University: Asst Lecturer, 1925-29; Lecturer, 1929-34; Head of Dept of Municipal Engineering, 1934-53; Prof. of Municipal Engineering, 1953-61; Prof. Emeritus, 1966; seconded, Jan.-June 1960, as Prof. of Engineering in University Coll. of Ibadan, Nigeria; Prof. of Civil Engineering, Indian Institute of Technology, Hauz Khas, New Delhi, 1961-66; Head of Civil Engrg Dept, Malta Coll. of Arts, Science and Technology, 1966-70. Consultant, Allott and Lomax, 1970-79. FICE (Ex-Mem. Council); FIStructE (Ex-Mem. Council, Hon. Librarian, 1972-74, Lewis E. Kent award, 1974); MIMechE; FIMunE; FIE (Ind.). Hon. FIPHE; FRSH (Ex-Mem. Council). Jubilee Medal, 1977. *Publications:* papers in Proc. Royal Soc., Philosophical Magazine, Jls of Engineering Instns. *Recreations:* photography, walking, gardening. *Address:* 20 Oakdene Road, Marple, Stockport SK6 6PJ. *T:* 061-427 2768.

CORNISH, William Herbert, CB 1955; Receiver for the Metropolitan Police District, 1961-67; *b* 2 Jan. 1906; *s* of late Rev. Herbert H. Cornish and Susan Emerson; *m* 1938, Eileen May Elizabeth Cooney; two *d. Educ:* Wesley Coll., Dublin; Trinity Coll., Dublin. Scholar, 1st Cl. Moderator with Large Gold Medal in Modern History and Political Science. Entered Home Office, 1930; Asst Sec., 1942; Asst Under-Sec. of State, 1952-60. *Recreations:* gardening and music. *Address:* 2 Tormead, Dene Road, Northwood, Mddx. *T:* Northwood 21933.

CORNISH, Prof. William Rodolph; Professor of English Law, London School of Economics, University of London, since 1970; *b* 9 Aug. 1937; *s* of Jack R. and Elizabeth E. Cornish, Adelaide, S Australia; *m* 1964, Lovedy E. Moule; one *s* two *d. Educ:* Univs of Adelaide (LLB) and Oxford (BCL). Lectr in Law, LSE, 1962-68; Reader in Law, Queen Mary Coll., London, 1969-70. *Publications:* The Jury, 1968; (Jt Editor) Sutton and Shannon on Contracts, 1970; (jtly) Encyclopedia of United Kingdom and European Patent Law, 1977; Intellectual Property, 1982; articles etc in legal periodicals. *Address:* 74 Palace Road, SW2.

CORNOCK, Maj.-Gen. Archibald Rae, CB 1975; OBE 1968; Chairman, London Electricity Consultative Council, 1980; *b* 4 May 1920; *s* of Matthew Cornock and Mrs Mary Munro MacRae; *m* 1951, Dorothy Margaret Cecilia; two *d. Educ:* Coatbridge. MBIM 1965. Interpreter in German, French and Hungarian. NW Frontier, 1940-42; Burma, 1942-43; transf. Royal Indian Navy, 1943; Burma (Arakan), 1944-46; Gordon Highlanders, 1947-50; transf. RAOC, 1950; psc 1954; GSO2 Intelligence, 1955-57; DAQMG Northern Army Gp, 1959-61; comd 16 Bn RAOC, 1961-64; SEATO Planning Staff, Bangkok, 1964; Defence Attaché, Budapest, 1965-67; Comdt 15 Base Ordnance Depot, 1967; DDOS Strategic Comd, 1968-70; Brig. Q (Maint.), MoD, 1970-72; Dir of Clothing Procurement, 1972; Dir of Army Quartering, 1973-75. Col Comdt, RAOC, 1976-80. Mem. Council, Back Pain Assoc., 1979-. *Recreations:* sailing, opera, languages, golf. *Address:* 20 Claremont, St Johns Avenue, Putney Hill, SW15 2AB. *T:* 01-789 5892. *Clubs:* Royal Thames Yacht, Army and Navy; Highland Brigade.

CORNWALL, Archdeacon of; *see* Wood, Ven. Arnold.

CORNWALL, Ian Wolfran, PhD London; Reader in Human Environment, University of London, 1965-74; *b* 28 Nov. 1909; *s* of Lt-Col J. W. Cornwall, CIE, IMS, and Effie E. C. (*née* Sinclair), *d* of Surg.-Gen. D. Sinclair, IMS; *m* 1st, 1937, Anna Margareta (*née* Callear) (*d* 1967); two *s*; 2nd, 1974, Mary L. Reynolds (*née* Miller). *Educ:* private sch.; Wellington Coll., Berks; St John's Coll., Cambridge (BA). Teaching, clerking, pharmaceutical manufacturing, selling, 1931-39; Postal and Telegraph Censorship, Press Censorship, MOI, 1939-45. London Univ. Inst. of Archaeology: Student, 1945-47 (Diploma, 1947); Secretary, 1948-51. University teacher and researcher, 1951-74, retd. (PhD London, 1952). Life Mem., Geologists' Assoc. Henry Stopes Memorial Medal, Geologists' Assoc., 1970. *Publications:* Bones for the Archaeologist, 1956, rev. edn 1975; Soils for the Archaeologist, 1958; The Making of Man, 1960 (Carnegie Medal of Library Assoc.); The World of Ancient Man, 1964; Hunter's Half Moon (fiction), 1967; Prehistoric Animals and their Hunters, 1968; Ice Ages, 1970. Contribs to specialist jls. *Recreations:* geology, gardening, photography. *Address:* Newlands, Cornworthy, Totnes, Devon TQ9 7ES.

CORNWALL, Gen. Sir J. H. M.; *see* Marshall-Cornwall.

CORNWALL, Rt. Rev. Nigel Edmund, CBE 1955; Assistant Bishop, Diocese of Winchester, and Canon Residentiary of Winchester Cathedral, 1963-73; retired; *b* 13 Aug. 1903; *s* of late Alan Whitmore Cornwall, priest, sometime Archdeacon of Cheltenham; *m* 1959, Mary (*d* 1981), *d* of Rev. C. R. Dalton. *Educ:* Marlborough Coll; Oriel Coll., Oxford. BA, 3rd class History, 1926; MA 1930. Cuddesdon Theological Coll., 1926-27; Deacon, Diocese of Durham, 1927; Curate, St Columba's, Southwick, Sunderland, 1927-30; Priest, Durham, 1928; Chaplain to Bishop of Colombo, 1931-38; Curate, St Wilfred's, Brighton, 1938-39; Missionary Priest of Diocese of Masasi, 1939-49; Headmaster, St Joseph's Coll., Chidya, 1944-49; Bishop of

Borneo, 1949-62. Commissary to Bishop of Kuching, in England, 1963-. *Address:* The Hermitage, Cheriton Road, Winchester. *T:* Winchester 55837.

CORNWALL-LEGH, C. L. S.; *see* Legh.

CORNWALLIS, family name of Baron Cornwallis.

CORNWALLIS, 3rd Baron *cr* 1927, of Linton, Kent; **Fiennes Neil Wykeham Cornwallis,** OBE 1963; DL; Director, Town and Country (formerly Magnet and Planet) Building Society, since 1975 (Deputy Chairman, 1975-77, and Chairman, 1977-81); *b* 29 June 1921; *s* of 2nd Baron Cornwallis, KCVO, KBE, MC, and Cecily Etha Mary (*d* 1943), *d* of Sir James Walker, 3rd Bt; *S* father, 1982; *m* 1st, 1942, Judith Lacy Scott (marr. diss. 1948); one *s* (one *d* decd); 2nd, 1951, Agnes Jean Russell Landale; one *s* three *d. Educ:* Eton. Served War, Coldstream Guards, 1940-44. Farmer, 1945. Pres., British Agricultural Contractors Assoc., 1952-54; Pres., Nat. Assoc. of Agricultural Contractors, 1957-63; Chm., Smaller Firms Council, CBI, 1978-81. Director: Checkers Ltd; Checkers Growers Ltd; County Quality (Promotion and Marketing) Ltd; Northinvest Ltd; Town & Country Building Soc., 1978 (Chm. 1978-81). Admin. Trustee, Chevening Estate, 1979-. DL Kent, 1976. *Recreation:* fishing. *Heir:* *s* Hon. (Fiennes Wykeham) Jeremy Cornwallis [*b* 25 May 1946; *m* 1969, Sara Gray de Neufville, *d* of Lt-Col Nigel Stockwell, Benenden, Kent; two *d*]. *Address:* Ruck Farm, Horsmonden, Tonbridge, Kent TN12 8DT. *T:* Brenchley 2267; 25B Queen's Gate Mews, SW7. *T:* 01-589 1167. *Clubs:* Brooks's, Farmers'.

CORNWELL, David John Moore, (John le Carré); writer; *b* 19 Oct. 1931; *s* of Ronald Thomas Archibald Cornwell and Olive (*née* Glassy); *m* 1954, Alison Ann Veronica Sharp (marr. diss. 1971); three *s*; *m* 1972, Valerie Jane Eustace; one *s. Educ:* Sherborne; Berne Univ.; Lincoln Coll., Oxford (1st cl. Modern Languages). Taught at Eton, 1956-58. Mem. of HM Foreign Service, 1960-64. *Publications:* Call for the Dead, 1961 (filmed as The Deadly Affair, 1967); A Murder of Quality, 1962; The Spy Who Came in from the Cold, 1963 (Somerset Maugham Award; Crime Writers' Assoc. Gold Dagger) (filmed); The Looking-Glass War, 1965 (filmed); A Small Town in Germany, 1968; The Naïve and Sentimental Lover, 1971; Tinker, Tailor, Soldier, Spy, 1974 (televised 1979); The Honourable Schoolboy, 1977 (James Tait Black Meml Prize; Crime Writers' Assoc. Gold Dagger); Smiley's People, 1980 (televised 1982); The Little Drummer Girl, 1983. *Address:* John Farquharson Ltd, Bell House, Bell Yard, WC2A 2JU.

CORRIE, John Alexander; MP (C) Bute and North Ayr, since Feb. 1974; *b* 29 July 1935; *s* of John Corrie and Helen Brown; *m* 1965, Jean Sandra Hardie; one *s* two *d. Educ:* Kirkcudbright Acad.; George Watson's Coll.; Lincoln Agric. Coll., NZ. Farmed in NZ, 1955-59, in Selkirk, 1959-65 and in Kirkcudbright, 1965-. Lectr for British Wool Marketing Bd and Agric. Trng Bd, 1966-74; Mem. Cttee, National Farmers Union, 1964-74 (Vice-Chm. Apprenticeship Council, 1971-74); Nuffield Scholar in Agriculture, 1972. District Officer, Rotary International, 1973-74 (Community service). Nat. Chm., Scottish Young Conservatives, 1964; contested (C) North Lanark, 1964 and Central Ayr, 1966; opposition spokesman on educn in Scotland, Oct. 1974-75; an Opposition Scottish Whip, 1975-76 (resigned over Devolution); PPS to Sec. of State for Scotland, 1979-81. Treas., Scottish Cons. Back Bench Cttee, 1980-; Leader, Cons. Gp on Scottish Affairs, 1982-; Sec., Cons. Backbench Fish-farming Cttee, 1982-. Mem. European Parlt, 1975-76 and 1977-79 (Mem. Cttees of Agriculture, Reg. Develt and Transport). Vice-President: EEC-Turkey Cttee, 1975-76; EEC Fisheries Cttee, 1977-79; EEC Mediterranean Agricl Cttee, 1977-79; Rapporteur for EEC Fisheries Policy, 1977-78. *Publications:* (jtly) Towards a European Rural Policy, 1978; Towards a Community Forestry Policy, 1979; Fish Farming in Europe, 1979; The Importance of Forestry in the World Economy, 1980. *Recreations:* shooting, fishing, riding, tennis, golf, curling, water ski-ing, hang gliding, bridge. *Address:* Park of Tongland, Kirkcudbright, Scotland DG6 4NE. *T:* Ringford 232; 3D Morpeth Terrace, SW1; Carlung Farm, West Kilbride, Ayrshire. *Clubs:* Beefsteak, Annabel's.

CORRIE, W(allace) Rodney, CB 1977; *b* 25 Nov. 1919; *o c* of late Edward and Mary Ellen Corrie; *m* 1952, Helen Margaret (*née* Morice), widow of Flt-Lt A. H. E. Kahn; one *s* one *d. Educ:* Leigh Grammar School; Christ's Coll., Cambridge (BA 1941, MA 1944). Served Royal Signals, 1940-46 (despatches). Entered Civil Service, Min. of Town and Country Planning, 1947; Min. of Housing and Local Govt, 1951; Asst Secretary, 1961; Assistant Under-Secretary of State, DEA, 1969; Under-Secretary: Min. of Housing and Local Govt, 1969; Dept of the Environment, 1970; Chm., NW Econ. Planning Bd, 1969-80, and Regl Dir (NW), DoE, 1971-80, Dept of Transport, 1976-80. *Recreations:* walking, exploring byways, catching up on things. *Address:* Brambledown, Chapel Lane, Hale Barns, Cheshire WA15 0AJ.

CORRIGAN-MAGUIRE, Maired; Initiator of Peace Movement in Northern Ireland, Aug. 1976; Chairman, Peace People Organisation, 1980-81; Co-Founder, Community of Peace People; *b* 27 Jan. 1944; *d* of Andrew and Margaret Corrigan; *m* 1981, Jackie Maguire; one *s* and three step *c. Educ:* St Vincent's Primary Sch., Falls Road, Belfast; Miss Gordon's Commercial Coll., Belfast. Secretarial qualification. Confidential Sec. to Managing Director, A. Guinness Son & Co. (Belfast) Ltd, Brewers, Belfast. Hon. Dr of Law, Yale Univ., 1976; Nobel Prize for Peace (jtly), 1976; Carl-Von-Ossietzky Medaille for Courage, Berlin, 1976. *Recreations:* voluntary community and youth work. *Address:* 224 Lisburn Road, Belfast 9, N Ireland. *T:* (business) 663465.

CORRIN, John Bowes; Chairman, Anglia Building Society, since 1981; Partner, Thornton Baker, since 1949; *b* 26 Oct. 1922; *s* of Harold R. Corrin and Mabel F. Corrin; *m* 1948, José M. Sharman; one *s* one *d. Educ:* Berkhampsted. FCA 1945 (Auditing Prize). Pres., Leics and Northants Soc. of Chartered Accountants, 1959; past Pres., Northampton Conservative Assoc. Mayor, Northampton, 1964-65; Hon. Freeman, Borough of Northampton, 1972. *Recreation:* golf. *Address:* Tynwald, Sandy Lane, Church Brampton, Northampton NN6 8AX. *T:* Northampton 845301. *Clubs:* Northampton County; Northamptonshire County Golf.

CORRIN, John William; HM Second Deemster, Isle of Man, since 1980; *b* 6 Jan. 1932; *s* of Evan Cain Corrin and Dorothy Mildred Corrin; *m* 1961, Dorothy Patricia, *d* of late J. S. Lace; one *d. Educ:* Murrays Road Primary Sch., Douglas; King William's Coll., IOM. Admitted to Manx Bar, 1954. Attorney Gen., IOM, 1974-80. Chairman (all IOM): Criminal Injuries Compensation Tribunal, 1980-; Licensing Appeal Court, 1980-; Prevention of Fraud (Unit Trust) Tribunal, 1980-; Manx Blind Welfare Soc.; Council, Postgrad. Med. Centre; Hon. Mem., IOM Med. Soc.; Pres., Island Bridge Club. *Recreations:* music, gardening, bridge. *Address:* Carla Beck, 28 Devonshire Road, Douglas, Isle of Man. *T:* Douglas 21806. *Club:* Ellan Vannin (Douglas) (Past Pres.).

CORRY; *see* Lowry-Corry, family name of Earl of Belmore.

CORRY, Sir James Perowne Ivo Myles, 3rd Bt, *cr* 1885; a Vice-President of King George's Fund for Sailors; The Royal Alfred Merchant Seamen's Society, and of Royal Merchant Navy School; *b* 10 June 1892; *s* of 2nd Bt and Charlotte, *d* of late J. Collins; *S* father, 1926; *m* 1st, 1921, Molly Irene (marr. diss., 1936), *y d* of late Major O. J. Bell; one *s* two *d*; 2nd, 1946, Cynthia, *widow* of Capt. David Polson, and *o d* of late Capt. F. H. Mahony and Mrs Francis Bliss; one *d. Educ:* Eton; Trinity Coll., Cambridge. *Heir: s* Lt-Comdr William James Corry, RN retd [*b* 1924; *m* 1945, Diana (*née* Lapsley); four *s* two *d*]. *Address:* Dunraven, Fauvic, Jersey, CI. *Clubs:* Lansdowne, Leander.

CORTAZZI, Sir (Henry Arthur) Hugh, KCMG 1980 (CMG 1969); HM Diplomatic Service; HM Ambassador to Japan, since 1980; *b* 2 May 1924; *m* 1956, Elizabeth Esther Montagu; one *s* two *d. Educ:* Sedbergh Sch.; St Andrews and London Univs. Served in RAF, 1943-47; joined Foreign Office, 1949; Third Sec., Singapore, 1950-51; Third/Second Sec., Tokyo, 1951-54; FO, 1954-58; First Sec., Bonn, 1958-60; First Sec., later Head of Chancery, Tokyo, 1961-65; FO, 1965-66; Counsellor (Commercial), Tokyo, 1966-70; Royal Coll. of Defence Studies, 1971-72; Minister (Commercial), Washington, 1972-75; Dep. Under-Sec. of State, FCO, 1975-80. Pres., Asiatic Soc. of Japan, 1982. *Publications:* trans. from Japanese, Genji Keita: The Ogre and other stories of the Japanese Salarymen, 1972; The Guardian God of Golf and other humorous stories, 1972, reprinted as The Lucky One, 1980. *Recreations:* Japanese studies, the arts including antiques. *Address:* c/o Foreign and Commonwealth Office, SW1. *Club:* Army and Navy.

CORVEDALE, Viscount; Benedict Alexander Stanley Baldwin; *b* 28 Dec. 1973; *s* and *heir* of 4th Earl Baldwin of Bewdley, *qv.*

CORY, (Charles) Raymond, CBE 1982; Chairman: John Cory & Sons Ltd, since 1965; South Glamorgan Health Authority, since 1974; Milford Haven Conservancy Board, since 1982; *b* 20 Oct. 1922; *s* of Charles and Ethel Cory; *m* 1946, Vivienne Mary Roberts, Kelowna, BC, Canada; three *d. Educ:* Harrow; Christ Church, Oxford. Served, RNVR, Ord. Seaman to Lieut, 1942-46. Vice-Chm., A. B. Electronic Components Ltd, 1978-; Chairman: SE Wales Pilotage Authority, 1974-80; Finance Cttee, Representative Body of the Church in Wales, 1975-; Vice-Chm., BTDB, 1969-79 (Mem., 1966-79); Pres., Cardiff Chamber of Commerce, 1959-60; Mem., Cttee of Management, RNLI, 1954- (Vice-Pres., 1969). *Publication:* A Century of Family Shipowning, 1954. *Recreations:* skiing, sailing, country. *Address:* The Coach House, Llanblethian, Cowbridge, South Glamorgan. *T:* Cowbridge 2251. *Club:* Cardiff and County.

CORY, Sir Clinton James Donald, 4th Bt, *cr* 1919; *b* 1 March 1909; 2nd *s* of Sir Donald Cory, 2nd Bt, shipowner of Llandaff, Glam, and Gertrude (*d* 1981), *d* of Henry Thomas Box; *S* brother, 1941; *m* 1935, Mary, *o d* of Dr A. Douglas Hunt, Park Grange, Derby; one *s. Educ:* Brighton Coll.; abroad. *Recreations:* shooting, fishing, gardening. *Heir: s* Clinton Charles Donald Cory, *b* 13 Sept. 1937. *Address:* 18 Cloisters Road, Letchworth, Herts SG6 3JS. *T:* Letchworth 77206.

CORY, Raymond; *see* Cory, C. R.

CORY-WRIGHT, Sir Richard (Michael), 4th Bt *cr* 1903; *b* 17 Jan. 1944; *s* of Capt. A. J. J. Cory-Wright (killed in action, 1944), and of Susan Esterel (who *m* 2nd, 1949, late Lt-Col J. E. Gurney, DSO, MC), *d* of Robert Elwes; *S* grandfather, 1969; *m* 1976, Veronica, *o d* of James Bolton; two *s. Educ:* Eton; Birmingham Univ. *Heir: s* Roland Anthony Cory-Wright, *b* 11 March 1979. *Address:* Cox's Farm, Winterbrook Lane, Wallingford, Oxon OX10 9RE.

COSGRAVE, Liam, SC; *b* April 1920; *s* of late William T. Cosgrave; *m* 1952, Vera Osborne; two *s* one *d. Educ:* Synge Street Christian Brothers; Castlenock College, Dublin; King's Inns. Served in Army during Emergency. Barrister-at-Law, 1943; Senior Counsel, 1958. Member, Dáil Eireann, 1943-81; Chairman Public Accounts Committee, 1945; Parliamentary Secretary to Taoiseach and Minister for Industry and Commerce, 1948-51; Minister for External Affairs, 1954-57; Leader, Fine Gael Party, 1965-77; Taoiseach (Head of Govt of Ireland), 1973-77; Minister for Defence, 1976. Leader first delegation from Ireland to the UN Assembly. Hon. LLD: Duquesne Univ., Pittsburg, Pa, and St John's Univ., Brooklyn, 1956; de Paul Univ., Chicago, 1958; NUI, 1974; Dublin Univ., 1974. Knight Grand Cross of Pius IX, 1956. *Address:* Beechpark, Templeogue, Co. Dublin.

COSGRAVE, Patrick John, PhD; writer; feature writer, Daily Express, since 1982; *b* 28 Sept. 1941; *s* of Patrick John Cosgrave and Margaret FitzGerald; *m* 1st, 1965, Ruth Dudley Edwards (marr. diss.); 2nd, 1974, Norma Alicia Green (marr. diss.); one *d*; 3rd, 1981, Shirley Ward. *Educ:* St Vincent's Sch., Dublin; University Coll., NUI, Dublin (BA, MA); Univ. of Cambridge (PhD). London Editor, Radio Telefis Eireann, 1968-69; Conservative Research Dept, 1969-71; Political Editor, The Spectator, 1971-75; Special Adviser to Rt Hon. Mrs Margaret Thatcher, 1975-79. *Publications:* The Public Poetry of Robert Lowell, 1969; Churchill at War: Alone, 1974; Cheyney's Law (novel), 1976; Margaret Thatcher, 1978, 2nd edn 1979; The Three Colonels (novel), 1979; R. A. Butler: an English Life, 1981; contribs to Proc. of Royal Irish Academy, Irish Historical Studies, Encounter. *Recreations:* thriller fiction, cooking, roses, cricket. *Address:* 59 Britannia Road, SW6 2JR. *T:* 01-731 2878.

COSGROVE, Hazel Josephine, (Mrs J. A. Cosgrove); *see* Aronson, H. J.

COSLETT, Air Marshal Sir (Thomas) Norman, KCB 1963 (CB 1960); OBE 1942; CEng, FIMechE; idc; psc; *b* 8 Nov. 1909; *s* of Evan Coslett; *m* 1938, Audrey Garrett. *Educ:* Barry Grammar Sch.; Halton; Cranwell. Dep. Dir of Engineering Plans, Air Ministry, 1954; Senior Technical Staff Officer, HQ Coastal Command, 1957; Commandant, No 1 School of Technical Training, 1958-61; AOC No 24 Group, 1961-63; AOC-in-C, RAF Maintenance Command, 1963-66. Air Cdre, 1957; Air Vice-Marshal, 1962; Air Marshal, 1963; retired, 1966. *Recreation:* farming. *Address:* c/o Barclays Bank, Sandton City, Sandton, Republic of South Africa.

COSSLETT, Dr Vernon Ellis, FRS 1972; Reader in Electron Physics, University of Cambridge, 1965-75, now Emeritus; Fellow of Corpus Christi College, Cambridge, since 1963; *b* 16 June 1908; *s* of Edgar William Cosslett and Anne Cosslett (*née* Williams); *m* 1st, 1936, Rosemary Wilson (marr. diss. 1940); 2nd, 1940, Anna Joanna Wischin (*d* 1969); one *s* one *d. Educ:* Cirencester Grammar Sch.; Bristol Univ. BSc Bristol 1929; PhD Bristol 1932; MSc London 1939; ScD Cambridge 1963. Research at: Bristol Univ., 1929-30; Kaiser-Wilhelm Institut, Berlin, 1930-31; University Coll., London, 1931-32; Research Fellow, Bristol Univ., 1932-35; Lectr in Science, Faraday House, London, 1935-39; Research (part-time), Birkbeck Coll., London, 1936-39; Keddey-Fletcher-Warr Research Fellow of London Univ. (at Oxford), 1939-41; Lectr in Physics, Electrical Laboratory, Oxford Univ., 1941-46; ICI Fellow, Cavendish Laboratory, Cambridge, 1946-49; Lectr in Physics, Univ. of Cambridge, 1949-65. Past Pres., Royal Microscopical Soc.; Past Vice-Pres., Inst. of Physics; Past Pres., Assoc. of Univ. Teachers. Hon. DSc Tübingen, 1963; Hon. MD Gothenburg, 1974. Royal Medal, Royal Soc., 1979. *Publications:* Introduction to Electron Optics, 1946 (1951); Practical Electron Microscopy, 1951; X-ray Microscopy (with W. C. Nixon), 1960; Modern Microscopy, 1966; many scientific papers. *Recreations:* gardening, mountain walking, listening to music. *Address:* 31 Comberton Road, Barton, Cambridge. *T:* Comberton 2428.

COSSONS, Neil, OBE 1982; FSA; FMA; Director, Ironbridge Gorge Museum Trust, since 1971; *b* 15 Jan. 1939; *s* of late Arthur Cossons and Evelyn Cossons (*née* Bettle); *m* 1965, Veronica Edwards; two *s* one *d. Educ:* Henry Mellish Sch., Nottingham; Univ. of Liverpool (MA). Leicester Museums, 1961; Swindon Museums, 1963; Curator of Technology, Bristol City Museum, 1964; Dep. Director, City of Liverpool Museums, 1969. Mem. Curatorium, Internat. Committee for the Conservation of the Industrial Heritage, 1973-78; President, Assoc. for Industrial Archaeology, 1977-80; Chairman, Assoc. of Independent Museums, 1975-; Pres., Museums Assoc., 1981-82. Midlands Press, Radio and Television Award, 1978. Hon. DSocSc Birmingham, 1979. *Publications:* Contractors' Locomotives GCR, 1963; (with R. A. Buchanan) Industrial Archaeology of the Bristol Region, 1968; (with K. Hudson) Industrial Archaeologists' Guide, 1969, 2nd edn 1971; Industrial Archaeology, 1975; (ed) Transactions of the First International Congress on the Conservation of Industrial Monuments, 1975; (ed) Rees's Manufacturing Industry, 1975; (with H. Sowden) Ironbridge-Landscape of Industry, 1977; (with B. S. Trinder) The Iron Bridge-Symbol of the Industrial Revolution, 1979; numerous papers in Museums Jl and elsewhere. *Recreations:* travel, design. *Address:* Church Hill, Ironbridge, Telford, Shropshire TF8 7PW. *T:* Ironbridge 2701; (office) Ironbridge 3522.

COSTAIN, Sir Albert (Percy), Kt 1980; MP (C) Folkestone and Hythe since 1959; *b* 5 July 1910; *s* of William Percy Costain and Maud May Smith; *m* 1933, Joan Mary, *d* of John William Whiter; one *s* one *d. Educ:* King James, Knaresborough; Coll. of Estate Management. Production Dir on formation

of Richard Costain Ltd, 1933; Chm., Richard Costain Ltd, 1966-69; Chm., Pre-stressed Concrete Development Group, 1952. London Treasurer, National Children's Home, 1950-60. FCIOB. Author of Home Safety Act, 1961; Parliamentary Private Secretary: to Minister of Public Bldg and Works, 1962-64; to Minister of Technology, 1970; to Chancellor of Duchy of Lancaster, 1970-72; to Sec. of State for the Environment, 1972-74. Member: Cttee of Public Accts, 1961-64, 1974-; Estimates Cttee, 1960-61, 1965-70; Estimates Sub-Cttee on Building and Natural Resources, 1965-; Chairmen's Panel, House of Commons, 1975-. Joint Vice-Chm., Conservative Party Transport Cttee, 1964. Jt Sec., Conservative Housing and Local Govt Cttee, 1964-65, Jt Vice-Chm., 1965-66; All Party Tourists and Resorts Cttee: Sec., 1964-66; Vice-Chm., 1966-69; Chm., 1970-71; Vice-Chm., Conservative Party Arts, Public Building and Works Cttee, 1965-70; Chm., Cons. Party Horticulture Cttee, 1976-77. Recreations: sailing, golf. Address: Inwarren, Kingswood, Surrey. T: Mogador 832443; 2 Albion Villas, Folkestone, Kent CT20 1RP. Clubs: Carlton; Walton Heath Golf.
See also P. J. Costain.

COSTAIN, Noel Leslie, OBE 1964; Director of Works, University of Sheffield, 1964-78; b 11 Jan. 1914; s of George Wesley Costain and Minnie Grace Pinson; m 1945, Marie José Elizabeth (née Bishton); two d. Educ: King Edward's Sch., Five Ways, Birmingham; Univ. of Birmingham (BSc). CEng, MICE, FINucE. Engineer with Sir R. MacAlpine & Sons, 1937-38; Epsom and Ewell BC, 1939; Air Min., Directorate-Gen. of Works; Section Officer, Orkneys and Shetlands, 1940-43; Prin. Works Officer, Sierra Leone, 1944-46; Superintending Engr, Air Ministry, 1946-51; RAF Airfield Construction Br.: Cmdg 5352 Wing, Germany, and OC, RAF Church Lawford, 1951-54; Superintending Engr, Works Area, Bristol, 1954-58; Chief Engr, MEAF, 1958-60; Chief Resident Engr, BMEWS, Fylingdales, 1960-63. Vice-Chm., Yorkshire Univs Air Squadron Cttee. Mem. Council, Instn of Nuclear Engineers, 1965; Vice-Pres., 1969; President, 1972-76. Recreations: travel, gardening. Address: Villa Marie José, Avenida 3 no 59, Urbanisation Hacienda/Las Chapas, Marbella, Málaga, Spain. Club: International Sporting.

COSTAIN, Peter John, FCA; Group Chief Executive, Costain Group Ltd, since 1980; b 2 April 1938; s of Sir Albert Costain, qv; m 1963, Victoria M. Pope; three s. Educ: Charterhouse. Peat Marwick Mitchell & Co., 1956-63; Richard Costain Ltd, 1963-65; Costain Australia Ltd, 1965-: Board Member, 1967; Managing Director, 1971; Chief Executive, 1973. FAIB. Recreations: sailing, skiing, golf. Address: Flat 6, 82 St George's Square, SW1. Clubs: Royal Corinthian Yacht; Royal Thames Yacht; Athenæum, Royal Brighton Yacht (Melbourne).

COSTANZI, Edwin J. B.; see Borg-Costanzi.

COSTAR, Sir Norman (Edgar), KCMG 1963 (CMG 1953); b 18 May 1909. Educ: Battersea Grammar School; Jesus Coll., Cambridge. Asst Principal, Colonial Office, 1932; Private Sec. to Permanent Under Sec., Dominions Office, 1935; served in UK High Commissioner's Offices, Australia, 1937-39, New Zealand, 1945-47. Principal, 1938; Asst Sec., 1946. Dep. High Commissioner, Ceylon, 1953-57; Asst Under-Sec., Commonwealth Relations Office, 1958-60; Dep. High Commissioner in Australia, 1960-62; High Commissioner: Trinidad and Tobago, 1962-66; Cyprus, 1967-69. Adjudicator, Immigration Appeals, 1970-81. Club: United Oxford & Cambridge University.

COSTELLO, Gordon John; Chief Accountant of the Bank of England, 1975-78; b 29 March 1921; s of late Ernest James Costello and Hilda May Costello; m 1946, Joan Lilian Moore; two s one d. Educ: Varndean Sch. Served War, 1939-45 (RA). Bank of England, 1946; worked in various Departments; Asst Chief Accountant, 1964; Asst Sec., 1965; Dep. Sec., 1968; Dep. Chief Cashier, 1970. Recreations: music, travel, walking, tennis. Address: 26 Peacock Lane, Brighton, Sussex BN1 6WA. T: Brighton 552344.

COTES, Peter, (Sydney Arthur Boulting); author, lecturer, play producer, film and television director; e s of Arthur Boulting and Rose Bennett; m 1st, 1938, Myfanwy Jones (marr. diss.); 2nd, 1948, Joan Miller. Educ: Taplow; Italia Conti and privately. Was for some years an actor; made theatrical debut, Portsmouth Hippodrome, in the arms of Vesta Tilley. Formed own independent play-producing co. with Hon. James Smith, 1949, presented Rocket to the Moon, St Martin's Theatre, and subsequently produced, in association with Arts Council of Great Britain, notable seasons in Manchester and at Embassy and Lyric Theatres, Hammersmith. Founded: New Lindsay, 1946; New Boltons, 1951. West-End Productions include: Pick Up Girl, 1946; The Animal Kingdom, 1947; The Master Builder, 1948; Miss Julie, 1949; Come Back, Little Sheba, 1951; The Father, 1951; The Biggest Thief in Town, 1951; The Mousetrap, 1952; The Man, 1952; A Pin to see the Peepshow, Broadway, 1953; Happy Holiday, 1954; Hot Summer Night, 1958; Epitaph for George Dillon (Holland), 1959; The Rope Dancers, 1959; Girl on the Highway, 1960; A Loss of Roses, 1962; The Odd Ones, 1963; Hidden Stranger, Broadway, 1963; What Goes Up. . .!, 1963; So Wise, So Young, 1964; Paint Myself Black, 1965; The Impossible Years, 1966; Staring at the Sun, 1968; Janie Jackson, 1968; The Old Ladies, 1969; Look, No Hands!, 1971. Films: The Right Person; Two Letters; Jane Clegg; Waterfront; The Young and the Guilty; has prod. and adapted numerous plays for BBC Television and ITV; was Sen. Drama Dir, AR-TV, 1955-58; producing stage plays and films, 1959-60; Supervising Producer of Drama Channel 7, Melbourne, 1961;

produced and adapted plays for Anglia TV, 1964; produced first TV series of P. G. Wodehouse short stories, on BBC; wrote George Robey centenary TV Tribute, BBC Omnibus series, 1969; wrote and dir. in One Pair of Eyes series, BBC TV, 1970; has written and narrated many productions for radio incl. Back into the Light, The Prime Minister of Mirth, Mervyn Peake, Portrait of an Actor; collaborated 1980-81 on: The Song is Ended, Who Were You With Last Night, Whose Your Lady Friend, The Black Sheep of the Family (BBC); solely scripted This Fabulous Genius, Wee Georgie Wood (BBC), 1980; collaborated 1981-82 on Evelyn and John (The Two Barbirollis). FRSA; Member: Theatrical Managers' Assoc.; Medico-Legal Soc.; Our Society; Guild of Drama Adjudicators. Publications: No Star Nonsense, 1949; The Little Fellow, 1951; A Handbook of Amateur Theatre, 1957; George Robey, 1972; The Trial of Elvira Barney, 1976; Circus, 1976; Origin of a Thriller, 1977; JP (The Man Called Mitch), 1978; Misfit Midget, 1979; Portrait of an Actor, 1980; various articles. Recreations: walking, writing letters, criminology. Address: 70 York Mansions, SW11. T: 01-622 8546. Club: Savage.

COTILL, John Atrill T.; see Templeton-Cotill.

COTRUBAS, Ileana, (Mme Manfred Ramin); opera singer; b Rumania; d of Vasile and Maria Cotrubas; m 1972, Manfred Ramin. Educ: Conservatorul Ciprian Porumbescu, Bucharest. Opera and concert engagements all over Europe, N America and Japan. Permanent guest at Royal Opera House, Covent Garden; Member, Vienna State Opera; also frequently sings in Scala, Milan, Munich, Berlin, Paris, Chicago, NY Metropolitan Opera. Main operatic roles: Susanna, Pamina, Gilda, Traviata, Manon, Tatyana, Mimi, Melisande, Amina. Has made numerous recordings. Kammersängerin, Austria, 1981. Address: c/o Royal Opera House, Covent Garden, WC2.

COTT, Hugh Bamford, ScD Cantab, DSc Glasgow; FRPS, FZS; Fellow of Selwyn College, Cambridge, since 1945; b 6 July 1900; s of late Rev. A. M. Cott, Ashby Magna; m 1928, Joyce Radford; one s one d. Educ: Rugby Sch.; RMC, Sandhurst; Selwyn Coll., Cambridge. Joined 1st Bn the Leics Regt; served in Ireland, 1919-21. 2nd class, Nat. Sciences Tripos, Pt I, 1925. Carried out zoological expeditions to SE Brazil, 1923; Lower Amazon, 1925-26; Zoological Society's Expedition to the Zambesi, 1927, Canary Islands, 1931, Uganda, 1952, Zululand, 1956, Central Africa, 1957; Lecturer in Hygiene, Bristol Univ., 1928-32; Asst and Lecturer in Zoology, Glasgow Univ., 1932-38; Strickland Curator and Lectr in the University of Cambridge, 1938-67; Lectr, 1945-67, and Dean, 1966-67, of Selwyn Coll., Cambridge. Founder Member, Soc. Wildlife Artists. War of 1939-45: Mem. Advisory Cttee on Camouflage, 1939-40; Capt. and Major (RE) MEF; served Western Desert, 1941 (despatches); Chief Instructor, Middle East Camouflage Sch., 1941-43; GSO 2 (Cam) Mountain Warfare Trg Centre, 1943-44. Publications: Adaptive Coloration in Animals, 1940; Zoological Photography in Practice, 1956; Uganda in Black and White, 1959; Looking at Animals: a zoologist in Africa, 1975; various scientific papers on adaptive coloration, feeding habits of tree frogs, camouflage, edibility of birds, ecology of crocodiles, etc published in Trans and Proc. of Zool Soc. London, Proc. R. Ent. Soc. London, Photographic Jl, Engineers' Jl etc. Recreations: travel, pen drawing, photography. Address: 10 Stoke Water House, Beaminster, Dorset. T: Beaminster 862798.

COTTENHAM, 8th Earl of, cr 1850; **Kenelm Charles Everard Digby Pepys;** Bt 1784 and 1801; Baron Cottenham, 1836; Viscount Crowhurst, 1850; b 27 Nov. 1948; s of 7th Earl of Cottenham and Lady Angela Isabel Nellie Nevill, d of 4th Marquess of Abergavenny; S father, 1968; m 1975, Sarah, d of Captain S. Lombard-Hobson, CVO, OBE, RN; one d. Educ: Eton. Heir: kinsman Charles Donald Leslie Pepys [b 25 Sept. 1909; g g s of 1st Earl of Cottenham; m 1941, Hon. Pamela Sophia Nadine Stonor, d of 5th Baron Camoys].
See also Baron McGowan.

COTTER, Lt-Col Sir Delaval James Alfred, 6th Bt, cr 1763; DSO 1944; late 13th/18th Royal Hussars; b 29 April 1911; s of 5th Bt and Ethel Lucy (d 1956), d of Alfred Wheeler; S father, 1924; m 1st, 1943, Roma (marr. diss., 1949), widow of Sqdn Ldr K. A. K. MacEwen and o d of late Adrian Rome, Dalswinton Lodge, Salisbury, SR; two d; 2nd, 1952, Mrs Eveline Mary Paterson, widow of Lieut-Col J. F. Paterson, OBE, and d of late E. J. Mardon, ICS (retired). Educ: Malvern Coll; RMC, Sandhurst. Served War of 1939-45 (DSO); retired, 1959. JP Wilts, 1962-63. Heir: n Patrick Laurence Delaval Cotter [b 21 Nov. 1941; m 1967, Janet, d of George Potter, Barnstaple; one s two d]. Address: Green Lines, Iwerne Courtney, Blandford Forum, Dorset. Club: Cavalry and Guards.

COTTERELL, Geoffrey; author; b 24 Nov. 1919; yr s of late Graham Cotterell and Millicent (née Crews). Educ: Bishops Stortford College. Served War of 1939-45, Royal Artillery, 1940-46. Publications: Then a Soldier, 1944; This is the Way, 1947; Randle in Springtime, 1949; Strait and Narrow, 1950; Westward the Sun, 1952 (repr. 1973); The Strange Enchantment, 1956 (repr. 1973); Tea at Shadow Creek, 1958; Tiara Tahiti, 1960 (filmed 1962, screenplay with Ivan Foxwell); Go, said the bird, 1966; Bowers of Innocence, 1970; Amsterdam, the life of a city, 1972. Recreation: golf. Address: 2 Fulbourne House, Blackwater Road, Eastbourne, Sussex. Clubs: Savage, Cooden Beach Golf.

COTTERELL, Sir John (Henry Geers), 6th Bt *cr* 1805; Chairman, Radio Wyvern, since 1981; *b* 8 May 1935; *s* of Sir Richard Charles Geers Cotterell, 5th Bt, CBE, and Lady Lettice Cotterell (*d* 1973), *d* of 7th Earl Beauchamp; *S* father, 1978; *m* 1959, Vanda Alexandra Clare, *d* of Major Philip Alexander Clement Bridgewater; three *s* one *d*. *Educ:* Eton; RMA Sandhurst. Officer, Royal Horse Guards, 1955-61. Vice-Chm. Hereford and Worcs CC, 1973-77, Chm., 1977-81. Dep. Pres., Nat. Fedn of Young Farmers Clubs, 1979-. *Recreations:* cricket, shooting. *Heir: s* Henry Richard Geers Cotterell, *b* 22 Aug. 1961. *Address:* Garnons, near Hereford. *T:* Bridge Sollars 232. *Club:* White's.

COTTERILL, Kenneth William, CMG 1976; Group Adviser on Export Credits, Barclays Bank International Ltd, since 1981; Deputy Chairman, Commercial and Political Risk Consultants Ltd, since 1981; Director: Tarmac International, since 1981; NEI International, since 1981; *b* 5 June 1921; *s* of William and Ada May Cotterill; *m* 1948, Janet Hilda Cove; one *d*. *Educ:* Sutton County Sch.; London School of Economics, BSc (Econ). Served War in Royal Navy, 1941-46. After the war, joined ECGD; Principal, 1956; Asst Sec., 1966; Under Sec., 1970; Dep. Head of Dept, 1976-81. *Recreations:* reading, walking, gardening. *Address:* 15 Minster Drive, Croydon CR0 5UP. *T:* 01-681 6700.

COTTESLOE, 4th Baron (UK) *cr* 1874; **John Walgrave Halford Fremantle,** GBE 1960; TD; Bt 1821; Baron of Austrian Empire, *cr* 1816; *b* 2 March 1900; *s* of 3rd Baron Cottesloe, CB and Florence (*d* 1956), *d* of Thomas Tapling; *S* father 1956; *m* 1st, 1926, Lady Elizabeth Harris (marr. diss., 1945), *o d* of 5th Earl of Malmesbury; one *s* one *d*; 2nd, 1959, Gloria Jean Irene Dunn; one *s* two *d*. *Educ:* Eton; Trinity Coll., Cambridge. BA (Hons) Mechanical Sciences 1921; MA 1924. Served as OC 251 (Bucks) AA Battery RA (TA), 1938-39; GSO 1 att. 2nd Armoured Division, 1940; Senior Military Liaison Officer to Regional Commissioner, NE Region, 1940-41; GSO 1 (Technical) AA Command, 1941-42; Commanding Officer, 20 LAA Regt RA, 1942-44; GSO 1 (Radar) War Office, 1944-45. Mem. LCC, 1945-55. Chm., Thomas Tapling & Co. Ltd; Vice-Chm., PLA, 1956-67. Chairman: Tate Gallery, 1959-60; Arts Council of Gt Britain, 1960-65; South Bank Theatre Bd (from inception), 1962-77; Adv. Council and Reviewing Cttee on Export of Works of Art, 1954-72; Heritage in Danger, 1973-; Royal Postgrad. Med. Sch., 1949-58 (Fellow); NW Met. Reg. Hosp. Bd, 1953-60; Hammersmith and St Mark's Hospital, 1968-74; Northwick Park Hosp. Adv. Cttee, 1970-74; a Governor, King Edward's Hosp. Fund for London. Chairman: British Postgraduate Medical Fedn, 1958-72; Nat. Rifle Assoc., 1960-72; Vice-Chm., City Parochial Foundn, 1972-77; Pres., Hospital Saving Assoc., 1973-; Hon. Sec. Amateur Rowing Assoc., 1932-46; a Steward of Henley Royal Regatta; Pres., Leander, 1957-62. Chm., The Dogs' Home, Battersea. Former DL County of London (later Greater London). *Recreations:* rowed in winning crews in Oxford and Cambridge Boat Race, 1921 and 1922 and in Grand Challenge Cup, Henley, 1922; Captain of English VIII at Bisley on 25 occasions and has shot in English VIII on 37 occasions and won Match Rifle Championship six times, with many other first prizes for long-range shooting. *Heir: s* Comdr Hon. John Tapling Fremantle, (RN retd) [*b* 22 Jan. 1927; *m* 1958, Elizabeth Ann, *d* of Lieut-Col Henry Shelley Barker, Walcote House, Walcote, Rugby; one *s* two *d*]. *Address:* 89 York Mansions, Prince of Wales Drive, Battersea Park, SW11 4BN. *T:* 01-622 9349. *Clubs:* Travellers'; Leander.

COTTON, Bernard Edward, CBE 1976; President, Samuel Osborn & Co. Ltd, 1978-80 (Chairman and Chief Executive, 1969-78); *b* 8 Oct. 1920; *s* of Hugh Harry Cotton and Alice Cotton; *m* 1944, Stephanie Anne, *d* of Rev. A. E. and Mrs Furnival; three *s*. *Educ:* Sheffield City Grammar Sch.; Sheffield Univ. Served Army, 1939-45, latterly as Lieut, Worcs Yeomanry (53rd Airlanding Light Regt RA). Joined Round Oak Steelworks, Brierley Hill, 1949, Sales Man., 1954-57; Gen. Man., Samuel Osborn (Canada) Ltd, Montreal, 1957-63; Sales Dir, Samuel Osborn & Co. Ltd, 1963-69, Man. Dir 1969. Director: Baker Perkins Ltd, 1978-; Renold Ltd, 1979-. Chairman: Yorks and Humberside Reg. Econ. Planning Council, 1970-79; Health Service Supply Council, 1980-; Mem., BR Eastern Bd, 1977-; Pres., Yorks and Humberside Develt Assoc., 1973-. Chm., BIM Working Party on Employee Participation, 1975. Mem. Council, Sheffield Univ. Master, Cutlers' Co. in Hallamshire, 1979-80. Hon. Fellow, Sheffield City Poly., 1980. CBIM. *Recreations:* gardening and other quiet pursuits. *Address:* Stubbin House, Carsick Hill Road, Sheffield SI0 3LU. *T:* Sheffield 303082; Flat No 1, The Manor House, Lympstone, Devon. *T:* Exmouth 5120. *Clubs:* Cavalry and Guards; The Club (Sheffield).

COTTON, Christopher P.; see Powell-Cotton.

COTTON, Prof. H., MBE 1918; DSc; *b* 17 June 1889; *s* of John Thomas and Sophia Cotton; *m* 1915, Lilian Hall (decd); one *s*. *Educ:* Manchester Univ.; resident at Hulme Hall. Asst Lecturer in Electrical Engineering and in Physics at Technical Coll., Huddersfield; Lecturer in Electrical Engineering at Technical Sch., St Helens; Lecturer at University Coll., Nottingham; Emeritus Prof. of Electrical Engineering at Nottingham Univ.; retired 1954; three years in France with the Meteorological Section RE during the war; practical training in Electrical Engineering at the Hanley Power Station and with the Westinghouse Electrical Co. Ltd. *Publications:* Electricity Applied to Mining; Mining Electrical Engineering; Design of Electrical Machinery; Advanced Electrical Technology; Electrical Transmission and Distribution; Electric Discharge Lamps; Principles of Illumination; Applied Electricity; Vector and Phasor Analysis of Electric Fields and Circuits; Basic Electrotechnology; contributor to Journal of Institution of Electrical Engineers, World Power, Electrician, Electrical Review and Electrical Times. *Publication:* Memoirs of an Army Meteorologist 1914-18 (in archives of Imperial War Museum and Meteorological Office). *Recreations:* music, painting. *Address:* St George's Lodge, Cherry Tree Road, Woodbridge, Suffolk. *T:* 3081.

COTTON, Henry; see Cotton, T. H.

COTTON, John Anthony; His Honour Judge Cotton; a Circuit Judge, since 1973; *b* 6 March 1926; *s* of Frederick Thomas Hooley Cotton and Catherine Mary Cotton; *m* 1960, Johanna Aritia van Lookeren Campagne; three *s* two *d*. *Educ:* Stonyhurst Coll.; Lincoln Coll., Oxford. Called to the Bar, Middle Temple, 1949; Dep. Chm., W Riding of Yorks QS, 1967-71; Recorder of Halifax, 1971; a Recorder and Hon. Recorder of Halifax, 1972-73. *Recreation:* golf. *Address:* 81 Lyndhurst Road, Sheffield S11 9BJ. *T:* Sheffield 585569.

COTTON, Sir John Richard, KCMG 1969 (CMG 1959); OBE 1947 (MBE 1944); retired from HM Diplomatic Service, 1969; Adjudicator, Immigration Appeals, 1970-81; *b* 22 Jan. 1909; *s* of late J. J. Cotton, ICS, and late Gigia Ricciardi Arlotta; *m* 1937, Mary Bridget Connors, Stradbally, County Waterford, Ireland; three *s*. *Educ:* Wellington Coll.; RMC, Sandhurst (prize Cadet and King's India Cadet). Commissioned 1929; 8th King George's Own Light Cavalry (IA), 1930-34; transferred to Indian Political Service, 1934; served in: Aden, Abyssinia (Attaché HM Legation, 1935), Persian Gulf, Rajputana, Hyderabad, Kathiawar, Baroda, New Delhi (Dep. Sec. Political Dept). Transferred to HM Foreign Service, 1947; served in Karachi (First Sec.), 1947-48, Foreign Office, 1949-51, Madrid (Counsellor [Commercial] HM Embassy), 1951-54; Consul-Gen., Brazzaville, 1954-55, Leopoldville, 1955-57; Counsellor (Commercial), HM Embassy, Brussels, 1957-62. Consul-Gen., São Paulo, Brazil, 1962-65; Ambassador to Kinshasa, Congo Republic (now Zaire), and to Burundi, 1965-69. *Recreations:* golf, Victorian paintings. *Address:* Lansing House, Hartley Wintney, Hants. *T:* Hartley Wintney 2681. *Club:* Army and Navy.

COTTON, Leonard Thomas, MChl; FRCS; Surgeon, King's College Hospital, since 1957; Surgeon, Queen Victoria Hospital, East Grinstead, and St Luke's Nursing Home for the Clergy; Dean, King's College Hospital Medical School, since 1978 (Vice-Dean, 1976-77); *b* 5 Dec. 1922; *s* of Edward Cotton and Elizabeth (*née* Webb); *m* 1946, Frances Joanna Bryan; one *s* two *d*. *Educ:* King's College Sch., Wimbledon; Oriel Coll., Oxford; King's Coll. Hospital. MRCS, LRCP 1946; BM, BCh Oxon 1946; FRCS 1950; MCh Oxon 1957. House Surgeon, King's College Hospital, 1946; Resident Surgical Officer, Royal Waterloo Hospital, 1947; Resident Surgical Officer, Weymouth and District Hospital, 1948; National Service, Surgical Specialist RAMC, 1949-51; Senior Registrar and Registrar, King's College Hospital, 1951-57; Surgical Tutor, King's Coll. Hospital Medical Sch., 1957-65. FRSM; Member: Surgical Research Soc., Assoc. of Surgeons; Vascular Surgical Soc.; Ct of Examiners, RCS. Hunterian Prof., RCS. *Publications:* (ed) Hey Groves' Synopsis of Surgery; co-author, short text-book of Surgery; contributions to medical journals. *Recreations:* gardening, reading, squash. *Address:* 126 College Road, SE19. *T:* 01-670 7156; Private Wing, King's College Hospital, Denmark Hill, SE5. *T:* 01-274 8670; 22 Harley Street, W1. *T:* 01-637 0491.

COTTON, Hon. Sir Robert Carrington, KCMG 1978; Australian Consul-General in New York, since 1978; *b* 29 Nov. 1915; *s* of H. L. Carrington Cotton; *m* 1937, Eve Elizabeth MacDougall; one *s* two *d*. *Educ:* St Peter's Coll., Adelaide, SA. FASA. State President of Liberal Party (NSW), 1956-59; Federal Vice-Pres., 1960-61; elected to Senate, 1965; Minister for Civil Aviation, 1969-72; Shadow Minister for Manufacturing Industry (in Opposition), 1972-75; Minister for Industry and Commerce, 1975-77. *Recreations:* swimming, writing. *Address:* Australian Consulate-General, International Building, 636 5th Avenue, New York, NY 10020, USA; 13 Cynthea Road, Palm Beach, NSW 2108, Australia. *T:* 919.5456. *Clubs:* The Brook, Economic (NY); Australian (Sydney), Royal Sydney Golf (Sydney); Commonwealth (Canberra, ACT).

COTTON, (Thomas) Henry, MBE 1946; late Flight Lieutenant RAFVR (invalided, 1943); golfer; Professional Golf Correspondent of Golf Monthly; Director and Founder Golf Foundation for development of youthful golfers; Golf Course Architect: Abridge, Felixstowe, Canons Brook, Ampfield, Megève and Deauville (France), Penina, Val de Lobo, Golf de Monte Gorda, and Monte Velho, Algarve (Portugal), Castle Eden Golf Club, Eaglescliffe, Stirling, Gourock, Windmill Hill, Bletchley, Sene Valley, Folkestone, Campo de Lagoa, Madeira, Ely, Cambs, etc; *b* Holmes Chapel, Cheshire, 26 Jan. 1907; *m* 1939, Mrs Maria Isabel Estanguet Moss. *Educ:* Alleyn's Sch. Played in first Boys' Golf Championship, 1921; asst at Fulwell, 1924; Rye, 1925; Cannes, 1926; professional Langley Park, 1927; Waterloo, Brussels, 1933; Ashridge, 1936; won Kent Professional Championship, 1926-27-28-29-30; Belgian Open, 1930, 1934, 1938; Mar del Plata, 1930; Dunlop Tournament, 1931, 1932, 1953, runner-up, 1959; News of the World Tournament, 1932 and 1939; British Open, 1934, 1937 and 1948 (1934 was First British win for 11 years); Italian Open, 1936; German Open, 1937-38-39; Silver King Tournament, 1937; Czechoslovak Open, 1937-38; Harry Vardon Trophy, 1938; Daily Mail £2000 Tournament, 1939; Penfold Tournament, 1939 and 1954; News Chronicle Tournament, 1945; Star Tournament, 1946; Prof. Golfers' Assoc.

Match Play Champion, 1946; French Open Champion, 1946 and 1947; Vichy Open Champion, 1946; represented Great Britain v America, 1929, 1937, 1947, 1953; Ryder Cup Team Capt., 1939, 1947 and 1953; Spalding Tournament, 1947; visited USA in 1929, 1931, 1947, 1948, 1956 and 1957; led US Open Qualifying, 1956; visited Argentine 1929, 1948, 1949 and 1950. Collected over £70,000 for Red Cross and other war charities in 130 matches organised by himself. Golf Consultant: Penina Golf Hotel, Portugal, 1968-75; Penina and Vale do Lobo Golf Clubs, 1978. Hon. Life Mem., Professional Golf Assoc. Vice-President: National Golf Clubs Advisory Bureau; Golf Writers' Assoc. *Publications:* Golf, 1932; This Game of Golf, 1948; My Swing, 1952; (Henry Cotton's) My Golfing Album, 1960; Henry Cotton Says, 1962; Studying the Golf Game, 1964; The Picture World of Golf, 1965; Golf in the British Isles, 1969; A History of Golf, 1973; Thanks for the Game, 1980. *Recreations:* painting, motoring, photography. *Address:* Penina, Golf Hotel, Portimao, Portugal.

COTTON, William Frederick, (Bill Cotton), OBE 1976; JP; Director of Programmes, Television, and Director of Development, BBC, since 1982; Chairman, BBC Enterprises, since 1982; *b* 23 April 1928; *s* of William Edward (Billy) Cotton and Mabel Hope; *m* 1st, 1950, Bernadine Maud (*née* Sinclair); three *d* ; 2nd, 1965, Ann Corfield (*née* Bucknall); one step *d. Educ:* Ardingly College. Jt Man. Dir, Michael Reine Music Co., 1952-56; BBC-TV: Producer, Light Entertainment Dept, 1956-62; Asst Head of Light Entertainment, 1962-67; Head of Variety, 1967-70; Head of Light Entertainment Gp, 1970-77; Controller, BBC 1, 1977-81; Dep. Man. Dir, 1981-82. JP Richmond, 1976. *Recreation:* golf. *Address:* 19 Model Cottages, East Sheen, SW14 7PH. *T:* 01-878 2430.

COTTON, STAPLETON-, family name of **Viscount Combermere.**

COTTRELL, Sir Alan (Howard), Kt 1971; FRS 1955; Master of Jesus College, Cambridge, since 1974; Vice-Chancellor, University of Cambridge, 1977-79; *b* 17 July 1919; *s* of Albert and Elizabeth Cottrell; *m* 1944, Jean Elizabeth Harber; one *s. Educ:* Moseley Grammar Sch.; University of Birmingham. BSc 1939; PhD 1942; ScD(Cantab) 1976. Lectr in Metallurgy, University of Birmingham, 1943-49; Prof. of Physical Metallurgy, University of Birmingham, 1949-55; retired March 1955. Deputy Head of Metallurgy Division, Atomic Energy Research Establishment, Harwell, Berks, 1955-58; Goldsmiths' Prof. of Metallurgy, Cambridge Univ., 1958-65; Dep. Chief Scientific Adviser (Studies), Min. of Defence, 1965-67, Chief Adviser, 1967; Dep. Chief Scientific Advr to HM Govt, 1968-71, Chief Scientific Advr, 1971-74. Part-time Mem., UKAEA, 1962-65; Member: Adv. Council on Scientific Policy, 1963-64; Central Adv. Council for Science and Technology, 1967-; Exec. Cttee, British Council, 1974-; Adv. Council, Science Policy Foundn, 1976-; Security Commn, 1981-. A Vice-Pres., Royal Society, 1964, 1976, 1977. FEng 1979; Fellow Royal Swedish Academy of Sciences; Hon. Fellow, Christ's Coll., Cambridge, 1970 (Fellow, 1958-70). Foreign Hon. Mem., American Academy of Arts and Sciences, 1960; Foreign Associate, Nat. Acad. of Sciences, USA, 1972; Hon. Mem., Amer. Soc. for Metals, 1972 (Fellow 1974); Foreign Associate, Nat. Acad. of Engrng, USA, 1976; Hon. Member: Metals Soc., 1977; Japan Inst. of Metals, 1981. FEng 1979. Hon. DSc: Columbia Univ., 1965; Newcastle Univ., 1967; Liverpool Univ., 1969; Manchester, 1970; Warwick, 1971; Sussex, 1972; Bath, 1973; Strathclyde, 1975; Cranfield, 1975; Aston, 1975; Oxford, 1979. Rosenhain Medallist of the Inst. of Metals; Hughes Medal, 1961, Rumford Medal, 1974, Royal Society; Inst. of Metals (Platinum) Medal, 1965; Réaumur Medal, Société Française de Métallurgie, 1964; James Alfred Ewing Medal, ICE, 1967; Holweck Medal, Société Française de Physique, 1969; Albert Sauveur Achievement Award, Amer. Soc. for Metals, 1969; James Douglas Gold Medal, Amer. Inst. of Mining, Metallurgy and Petroleum Engrs, 1974; Harvey Science Prize, Technion Israel Inst., 1974; Acta Metallurgica Gold Medal, 1976; Guthrie Medal and Prize, Inst. of Physics, 1977; Gold Medal, Amer. Soc. for Metals, 1980; Brinell Medal, Royal Swedish Acad. of Engrg Sciences, 1980. *Publications:* Theoretical Structural Metallurgy, 1948, 2nd edn 1955; Dislocations and Plastic Flow in Crystals, 1953; The Mechanical Properties of Matter, 1964; Theory of Crystal Dislocations, 1964; An Introduction to Metallurgy, 1967; Portrait of Nature, 1975; Environmental Economics, 1978; How Safe is Nuclear Energy?, 1981; scientific papers to various learned journals. *Recreation:* music. *Address:* The Master's Lodge, Jesus College, Cambridge. *T:* Cambridge 353310. *Club:* United Oxford & Cambridge University.

COTTRELL, Richard John; Member (C) Bristol, European Parliament, since 1979; *b* 11 July 1943; *s* of John Cottrell and Winifred (*née* Barter); *m* 1965, Dinah Louise (*née* David); two *d. Educ:* Court Fields Sch., Wellington, Somerset. Journalist: Wellington Weekly News, 1958; South Devon Jl, 1960; Topic (internat. news weekly), 1962; Evening Argus, Brighton, 1963; Lincolnshire Standard, 1964; Evening Post, Bristol, 1965; TWW, subseq. HTV, 1967-79. European Parliament: Sec., backbench cttee, European Dem. Gp, 1979; Member: Transport Cttee, 1979-; External Econ. Relns Cttee, 1979-82; Information Cttee, 1981-; ACP-EEC Convention, 1981-; Agriculture Cttee, 1982-; Rules Cttee, 1982-. European Vice-Pres., Assoc. of District Councils; Vice-Pres., Nat. Council on Inland Transport. *Publications:* Energy, the Burning Question for Europe (jtly), 1981; (ed and contrib.) Transport for Europe, 1982. *Recreations:* travel, reading, transport studies, appreciation of real ale. *Address:* 48 Silver Street, Midsomer Norton, Bath. *T:* Midsomer Norton 412100.

COTTRELL, Thomas Edward; Managing Director, Texaco Ltd, 1973-82; *b* 30 July 1920; *s* of O. P. Cottrell and Alva T. Cottrell; *m* 1942, Laura; four *d. Educ:* Colgate Univ., Hamilton, NY. BA Philosophy and Econs. Sales Management positions with Texaco Inc. in New England, the South, San Francisco and New York, 1946-69; Dep. Man. Dir, Regent Oil Co. Ltd, UK, 1969; Vice-Pres., Texaco Europe Ltd, Brussels, 1969-70; Gen. Man., International Sales, Texaco Inc., US, 1970-71; Asst to Sen. Vice-Pres. Sales Exec. Staff, 1971-73. *Recreations:* golf, fishing. *Clubs:* Roehampton; Wentworth Golf.

COTTS, Sir Crichton Mitchell; see Cotts, Sir R. C. M.

COTTS, Sir (Robert) Crichton Mitchell, 3rd Bt, *cr* 1921; *b* 22 Oct. 1903; *yr s* of Sir William Dingwall Mitchell Cotts, 1st Bt, KBE, MP (*d* 1932), and Agnes Nivison (*d* 1966), 2nd *d* of late Robert Sloane; *S* brother, 1964; *m* 1942, Barbara (*d* 1982), *o d* of late Capt. Herbert J. A. Throckmorton, Royal Navy; two *s* three *d*. Late Temp. Major, Irish Guards; USSR, White Sea, 1941-42. *Heir: s* Richard Crichton Mitchell Cotts, *b* 26 July 1946. *Address:* Valley Farm, Clopton, near Woodbridge, Suffolk.

COUCHMAN, Dame Elizabeth (May Ramsay), DBE 1961 (OBE 1941); JP; BA; *b* 19 April 1876; *d* of late Archibald Tannock and Elizabeth Ramsay Tannock; *m* 1917, Claude Ernest Couchman (decd). *Educ:* University of Western Australia (BA). President, Australian Women's National League, 1927-45; Mem., Australian Broadcasting Commission, 1932-42; Senior Vice-Pres., Royal Commonwealth Soc., 1950-61; office-bearer in many educational, patriotic and social-service organisations. Life Member: National Council of Women (Vic); Liberal Party (Vic). *Publications:* articles in the press on Liberal politics and current topics. *Club:* Australian Women's Liberal (Melbourne).

COUGHTRIE, Thomas, CBE 1958; Chairman, Bruce Peebles Industries Ltd, and Bruce Peebles Ltd, Edinburgh, 1961-67; *b* 28 Oct. 1895; *m* 1918, Mary Morrison; one *s* two *d. Educ:* Royal Coll. of Science, Glasgow. Founded Belmos Co. Ltd, Elect. Engrs, 1919 (merged with Bruce Peebles & Co. Ltd, Edinburgh, 1961); Mem. Royal Fine Art Commn for Scotland, 1962-67; Chm. Valuation Appeals Cttee, Co. Lanark, 1956-71; Director: Ailsa Investment Trust Ltd; Alva Investment Trust Ltd, 1958-63. Chm., Greentower Farms Ltd. JP Lanark, 1959. Hon. LLD Glasgow, 1959; Hon. DSc Heriot-Watt, 1968. *Recreations:* golf, gardening, reading. *Address:* Orchard House, Crossford, Carluke, Lanarkshire. *T:* Crossford 203. *Clubs:* Athenæum, East India, Devonshire, Sports and Public Schools; Western (Glasgow).

COULL, Prof. Alexander, PhD; FRSE; FICE, FIStructE; Regius Professor of Civil Engineering, University of Glasgow, since 1977; *b* 20 June 1931; *s* of William Coull and Jane Ritchie (*née* Reid); *m* 1962, Frances Bruce Moir; one *s* two *d. Educ:* Peterhead Acad.; Univ. of Aberdeen (BScEng, PhD). FRSE 1971; FICE 1972, FIStructE 1973; FASCE 1972. Res. Asst, MIT, USA, 1955; Struct. Engr, English Electric Co. Ltd, 1955-57; Lectr in Engrg, Univ. of Aberdeen, 1957-62; Lectr in Civil Engrg, Univ. of Southampton, 1962-66; Prof. of Struct. Engrg, Univ. of Strathclyde, 1966-76. Chm., Clyde Estuary Amenity Council, 1981-. *Publications:* Tall Buildings, 1967; Fundamentals of Structural Theory, 1972; author or co-author of 80 res. papers in scientific jls. *Recreations:* golf, hill walking. *Address:* 11 Blackwood Road, Milngavie, Glasgow G62 7LB. *T:* 041-956 1655. *Club:* Buchanan Castle Golf (Drymen).

COULSHAW, Rev. Leonard, CB 1949; MC 1917; FKC; *b* 24 Feb. 1896; *s* of late Percy Dean Coulshaw and late Alice Maud Hatt; *m* 1932, Yvonne Cecilia Joan, *d* of Rev. C. Hanmer-Strudwick, Rector of Slawston, Leics; no *c. Educ:* Southend-on-Sea High Sch. for Boys; King's Coll., London; Ely Theological Coll. Served European War, 1914-18, Essex Regiment, 1914-20 (MC, despatches); left Army with rank of Captain. Ordained, 1923; Curate, St Andrew's, Romford, Essex; commissioned as Chaplain, RN, 1927; served in HMS Cyclops, 1927-29; RN Barracks, Portsmouth, 1929; HMS Iron Duke, 1929-30; HMS Effingham (Flagship East Indies Station), 1930-32; Royal Hospital Sch., Holbrook, 1932-34; Senior Chaplain HMS Ganges, 1934-37; HMS Royal Sovereign, 1937 (present at Coronation Review, Spithead); HMS Revenge, 1937. Chaplain Royal Naval Hospital, Malta, 1937-40; RM Depot, Lympstone, 1940-42; Senior Chaplain, RN Base, Lyness, 1942-44; Chaplain HM Dockyard, Sheerness, 1944-46; RM Barracks, Portsmouth, 1946-47; Chaplain of the Fleet and Archdeacon of the Royal Navy, 1948-52; KHC, 1948-52; QHC, 1952; Vicar of: West End, Southampton, 1952-54; Frensham, 1954-65. *Address:* 4 Ashurst Court, Alverstoke, Gosport, Hants PO12 2TZ. *T:* Gosport 82467.

COULSHED, Dame (Mary) Frances, DBE 1953 (CBE 1949); TD 1951; Brigadier, Women's Royal Army Corps, retired; *b* 10 Nov. 1904; *d* of Wilfred and Maud Coulshed. *Educ:* Parkfields Cedars, Derby; Convent of the Sacred Heart, Kensington. Served War of 1939-45 (despatches); North-West Europe, 1944-45, with General Headquarters Anti-Aircraft Troops and at Headquarters Lines of Communications; Deputy Dir, Anti-Aircraft Command, 1946-50; Dep. Dir, War Office, July-Dec. 1950; Director, WRAC, 1951-54. ADC to the King, 1951, to the Queen, 1952-54. Order of Leopold I of Belgium with palm, Croix de Guerre with palm, 1946. *Address:* 815 Endsleigh Court, Upper Woburn Place, WC1.

COULSON, Mrs Ann Margaret; Service Planning and Development Co-ordinator, West Midlands Regional Health Authority, since 1980; *b* 11 March 1935; *d* of Sidney Herbert Wood and Ada (*née* Mills); *m* 1958, Peter James Coulson; two *s* one *d*. *Educ*: The Grammar Sch., Chippenham, Wilts; UCL (BScEcon); Univ. of Manchester (DSA); Wolverhampton Technical Teachers' Coll. (CertEd). Hosp. Admin, 1956-62; Lectr in Econs and Management, Bromsgrove Coll. of Further Educn, 1968-76; Asst Dir, North Worcestershire Coll., 1976-80. City of Birmingham Dist Council, 1973-79; special interest in Social Services. Mem., IBA, 1976-81. FBIM. *Recreations*: cooking, family camping and sailing. *Address*: 81 Westhill Road, Kings Norton, Birmingham B38 8TG. *T*: 021-458 2230.

COULSON, (James) Michael; Barrister-at-Law; a Recorder of the Crown Court, since 1981; a Chairman of Industrial Tribunals, since 1968; *b* 23 Nov. 1927; *s* of William Coulson, Wold Newton Hall, Driffield, E Yorks; *m* 1st, 1955, Dilys Adair Jones (marr. diss.); one *s* ; 2nd, 1977, Barbara Elizabeth Islay, *d* of Dr Roland Moncrieff Chambers; one *s*. *Educ*: Fulneck Sch., Yorks; Merton Coll., Oxford; Royal Agricultural Coll., Cirencester. Served E Riding Yeomanry (Wenlocks Horse); Queen's Own Yorks Yeomanry (Major). Called to Bar, Middle Temple, 1951; Mem. North Eastern Circuit; Asst Recorder of Sheffield, 1965-71; Dep. Chm., NR of Yorks QS, 1968-71. Dep. Chm., Northern Agricl Land Tribunal, 1967-. Former Mem., Tadcaster RDC. MP (C) Kingston-upon-Hull North, 1959-64; PPS to Solicitor Gen., 1962-64; Mem., Executive Cttee, Conservative Commonwealth Council. Sometime Sec., Bramham Moor and York and Ainsty Point to Point Race Meetings. *Recreations*: hunting, reading, travel. *Address*: The Tithe Barn, Wymondham, Melton Mowbray, Leics. *Club*: Cavalry and Guards.

COULSON, Sir John Eltringham, KCMG 1957 (CMG 1946); President, Hampshire Branch, British Red Cross Society, 1972-79; Secretary-General of EFTA, 1965-72, retired; *b* 13 Sept. 1909; *er s* of H. J. Coulson, Bickley, Kent; *m* 1944, Mavis Ninette Beazley; two *s*. *Educ*: Rugby; Corpus Christi Coll., Cambridge (Hon. Fellow 1975). Entered Diplomatic Service in 1932. Served in Bucharest, Min. of Econ. Warfare, War Cabinet Office, Foreign Office and Paris. Sometime Dep. UK representative to UN, New York; Asst Under-Sec., Foreign Office, 1952-55; Minister British Embassy, Washington, 1955-57; Asst to Paymaster-Gen., 1957-60; Ambassador to Sweden, 1960-63; Dep. Under-Sec. of State, Foreign Office, 1963-65; Chief of Administration of HM Diplomatic Service, Jan.-Sept. 1965. Director: Atlas Copco (GB), 1972-80; Sheerness Steel Co. *Recreations*: fishing, golf. *Address*: The Old Mill, Selborne, Hants. *Club*: Brooks's.

COULSON, Emeritus Prof. John Metcalfe; Professor of Chemical Engineering, University of Newcastle upon Tyne (formerly University of Durham), 1954-75 (on leave of absence to Heriot-Watt University, 1968-69), now Emeritus; *b* 13 Dec. 1910; *m* 1943, Clarice Dora Scott (*d* 1961); two *s* ; *m* 1965, Christine Gould; one *d*. *Educ*: Clifton Coll.; Christ's Coll., Cambridge; Imperial Coll. Royal Arsenal, Woolwich, 1935-39; Asst Lectr, Imperial Coll., 1939; Ministry of Supply (Royal Ordnance Factories), 1939-45; Lectr in Chem. Engineering, Imperial Coll., 1945-52; Reader, 1952-54. Hon. DSc Heriot-Watt, 1973. Davis Medal, IChemE, 1973. *Publications*: Chemical Engineering Vol. I and Vol. II (with Prof. J. F. Richardson), 1954 and 1955, 3rd edn 1977; contrib. Instn of Chem. Eng, Chem. Eng Science, etc. *Recreations*: chess, photography. *Address*: 2 Rosedale, Pannal, Harrogate, N Yorks.

COULSON, Michael; see Coulson, J. M.

COULSON, Prof. Noel James, MA; Professor of Oriental Laws, since 1967, and Head of Law Department, since 1981, School of Oriental and African Studies, University of London; *b* 18 Aug. 1928; *s* of George Frederick and Marjorie Elizabeth Coulson; *m* 1951, Muriel Ivatts; two *d*. *Educ*: Wigan Grammar Sch.; Keble Coll., Oxford (MA). Called to the Bar, Gray's Inn, 1961. Lieut, Parachute Regt, 1950-52. Lectr, 1954, and Reader, 1964, in Islamic Law, SOAS; Dean of Faculty of Law, Ahmadu Bello Univ., Nigeria, 1965-66; Visiting Professor of Comparative Law at Law Schools of American Universities: UCLA, 1961 and 1977; Chicago, 1968; Pennsylvania, 1970; Utah, 1977; Harvard, 1979. Chm., Bd of Studies in Laws, Univ. of London, 1980-82. *Publications*: A History of Islamic Law, 1964, repr. 1971, 1979; Conflicts and Tensions in Islamic Jurisprudence, 1969; Succession in the Muslim Family, 1971; numerous articles in jls of Law and Islamic Studies. *Recreation*: golf. *Address*: Oak Tree Cottage, Chase Lane, Haslemere, Surrey. *T*: Haslemere 2994. *Club*: Effingham Golf (Surrey) (Captain, 1976).

COULSON, Maj.-Gen. Samuel M.; see Moore-Coulson.

COULTASS, (George Thomas) Clive; Senior Keeper, Imperial War Museum, London, since 1979; Keeper of the Department of Film, since 1970; *b* 5 July 1931; *m* 1962, Norma Morris. *Educ*: Tadcaster Grammar Sch.; Univ. of Sheffield (BA Hons). Teacher in various London schools, 1955-62; Lectr/Sen. Lectr in History, James Graham Coll., Leeds, 1962-69; Keeper of Film Programming, Imperial War Museum, 1969-70. Vice-Pres., Internat. Assoc. for Audio-Visual Media in Hist. Res. and Educn, 1978-. *Publications*: section in The Historian and Film, 1976; articles in various historical jls. *Recreations*: travel, music, including opera. *Address*: 39 Fairfield Grove, SE7 8UA.

COULTER, Robert, MC 1945; Controller BBC Scotland, 1973-75, retired 1976; *b* 15 June 1914; *s* of John and Margaret Coulter, Glasgow; *m* 1940, Flora Macleod Bell; no *c*. *Educ*: Irvine Royal Academy; Glasgow Univ. MA Hons English Lit. and Lang. 1st Bn Royal Scots Fusiliers, India, UK, Madagascar and Burma, 1939-46 (Major). Principal English Master, Ayr Grammar Sch., 1946-48; Educn Administration, Belfast, 1948-53; BBC Northern Ireland, 1953-67: radio and TV producer; TV organiser; Asst Head of Programmes; Dir of Television, Uganda, 1967-69; Head of Programmes, BBC Scotland, 1969-73. IBA Res. Fellow at QUB, 1978 (Signposts report on youth employment and radio/TV special output, 1980). Broadcasting consultant, R. & F. M. Coulter Associates, 1980-. *Recreations*: Arts Council NI, resisting senior citizenship. *Address*: 18 Knockmore Park, Bangor, Co. Down, N Ireland. *T*: Bangor (Co. Down) 62510.

COULTHARD, Alan George Weall; His Honour Judge Alan Coulthard; a Circuit Judge since 1981; *b* Bournemouth, 20 Jan. 1924; *s* of late George Robert Coulthard and Cicely Eva Coulthard (*née* Minns); *m* 1948, Jacqueline Anna, *d* of late Dr T. H. James, Fishguard; two *s* two *d*. *Educ*: Watford Grammar Sch. Pilot, RAF, 1941-46 (Flt-Lt); 1st Officer, BOAC, 1946-48; Pilot and Staff Officer, RAF, 1948-58. Called to Bar, Inner Temple, 1959; practised at Bar, Swansea, 1959-81; Asst Recorder, 1970; a Recorder of the Crown Court, 1972-81; Hon. Recorder of Borough of Llanelli, 1975-81. Chm., Medical Appeals Tribunal for Wales, 1976-81. Contested (L) Pembrokeshire, 1964. Pres., Swansea Festival Patrons' Assoc., 1974-80. BBC sound and TV broadcasts, 1960-. *Recreations*: music, motor sport, ornithology, country life. *Address*: 3 Bolton Road, St John's Wood, NW8 0RJ. *T*: 01-328 8941. *Club*: Royal Air Force.
See also C. W. Coulthard.

COULTHARD, Air Vice-Marshal Colin Weall, CB 1975; AFC 1953 (Bar 1958); retired; *b* 27 Feb. 1921; *s* of late Wing Comdr George Robert Coulthard and Cicely Eva Coulthard (*née* Minns); *m* 1st, 1941, Norah Ellen Creighton (marr. diss.); one *s* two *d* ; 2nd, 1957, Eileen Pamela (*née* Barber); one *s*. *Educ*: Watford Grammar Sch.; De Havilland Aeronautical Tech. Sch. Commissioned RAF, 1941; Fighter Pilot, 1942-45 (dispatches, 1945); HQ Fighter Comd, 1948-49; RAF Staff Coll., 1950; OC 266 Sqn, Wunstorf, 1952-54, DFLS, CFE, 1955; OC Flying, 233(F) OCU, 1956-57; OC AFDS, CFE, 1957-59; HQ Fighter Comd, 1959-60; Stn Cdr, Gutersloh, 1961-64; MoD, 1964-66; SOA, AHQ Malta, 1966-67; DOR 1(RAF), MoD, 1967-69; Air Attaché, Washington, DC, 1970-72; Mil. Dep. to Head of Defence Sales, MoD, 1973-75. Governor, Truro Sch., 1981. FRAeS. *Recreations*: walking, shooting, motor sport. *Address*: Fiddlers, Old Truro Road, Goonhavern, Truro TR4 9NN. *T*: Zelah 312. *Club*: Royal Air Force.
See also A. G. W. Coulthard.

COULTHARD, William Henderson, CBE 1968; MSc, CEng, FIMechE, FRPS; Deputy Director, Royal Armament Research and Development Establishment, 1962-74; *b* 24 Nov. 1913; *s* of William and Louise Coulthard, Flimby, Cumberland; *m* 1942, Peggie Frances Platts Taylor, Chiselhurst; one *d* (one *s* decd). *Educ*: Flimby, Workington Schs; Armstrong Coll., University of Durham. Mather Schol., University of Durham, 1932. Linen Industry Research Assoc., 1934; Instrument Dept, Royal Aircraft Estabt, 1935; Air Ministry HQ, 1939; Sqdn Ldr RAFVR, 1944; Official German Translator, 1945; Air Photography Div., RAE, 1946; Supt, later Dep. Dir, Fighting Vehicles Research and Development Estabt, 1951. *Publications*: Aircraft Instrument Design, 1951; Aircraft Engineer's Handbook, 1953; (trans.) Mathematical Instruments (Capellen), 1948; (trans.) Gyroscopes (Grammel), 1950; articles in technical journals. *Recreations*: art history (Diploma in History of Art, London Univ., 1964); languages. *Address*: Argyll, Francis Close, Ewell, Surrey. *T*: 01-337 4909.

COUNSELL, Hazel Rosemary; Her Honour Judge Hazel Counsell; a Circuit Judge, since 1978; *b* 7 Jan. 1931; *d* of late Arthur Henry Counsell and Elsie Winifred Counsell. *Educ*: Clifton High Sch.; Switzerland; Univ. of Bristol (LLB). Called to the Bar, Gray's Inn, 1956; Western Circuit, 1956-; a Recorder of the Crown Court, 1976-77. Legal Dept, Min. of Labour, 1959-62. Governor, Colston Girls Sch. *Recreations*: flying, reading, swimming, travel. *Address*: The Penthouse, Wallcroft, Durdham Park, Bristol BS6 6XJ. *T*: Bristol 22144.

COUNSELL, John William, OBE 1975; Managing Director of the Theatre Royal, Windsor, since 1938; *b* 24 April 1905; *s* of Claude Christopher Counsell and Evelyn Counsell (*née* Fleming); *m* 1939, Mary Antoinette Kerridge; twin *d*. *Educ*: Sedbergh Sch.; Exeter Coll., Oxford. Mem. of the OUDS, 1923-26; formerly engaged as a tutor. First appearance on professional stage, Playhouse, Oxford, 1928; two tours of Canada with Maurice Colbourne in Shavian Repertory, 1928-29; leading juvenile, Northampton and Folkestone Repertory Cos, 1929-30; Stage Manager for Baliol Holloway's production of Richard III, New, 1930; Stage Dir, Scenic Artist and eventually Producer, Oxford Repertory Company, 1930-33; Producer and Joint Man.-Dir, Windsor Repertory Company, 1933-34; Lover's Leap, Vaudeville, 1934; toured as Tubbs in Sweet Aloes, 1936; toured S Africa in The Frog, 1936-37; refounded Windsor Repertory Co., 1938. Called to the Colours as Territorial reservist, 1940; served in N Africa, France and Germany, 1942-45; Mem. planning staff of SHAEF; demobilised, 1945, rank of Lieut-Col. Resumed direction of Theatre Royal, Windsor. Has, in addition, produced: Birthmark, Playhouse, 1947; Little Holiday, 1948; Captain Brassbound's Conversion, Lyric, Hammersmith, 1948; The Man with the Umbrella, Duchess, 1950; Who

Goes There!, Vaudeville, 1951; His House in Order, 1951; Waggon Load of Monkeys, Savoy, 1951; For Better for Worse, Comedy, 1952; Anastasia, St James's, 1953; Grab Me a Gondola, Lyric, 1956; Three Way Switch, Aldwych, 1958; How Say You?, Aldwych, 1959. *Publications:* Counsell's Opinion (autobiography), 1963; Play Direction: a practical viewpoint, 1973. *Recreations:* gardening, photography. *Address:* 3 Queen's Terrace, Windsor, Berks. *T:* Windsor 65344. *Club:* Green Room.

COUNSELL, Paul Hayward; His Honour Judge Counsell; a Circuit Judge since 1973; *b* 13 Nov. 1926; twin *s* of Frederick Charles Counsell and Edna Counsell; *m* 1959, Joan Agnes Strachan; one *s* two *d. Educ:* Colston Sch., Bristol; Queen's Coll., Oxford (MA). Served RAF, 1944–48. Admitted Solicitor, 1951; called to Bar, Inner Temple, 1962. Northern Rhodesia: Crown Solicitor, 1955–56; Crown Counsel, 1956–61; Resident Magistrate, 1958; Dir of Public Prosecutions, 1962–63; Solicitor General, 1963–64; QC 1963; Acting Attorney General, 1964; Solicitor-General, Zambia, 1964, MLC 1963–64. In chambers of Lord Hailsham, Temple, 1965–73; Dep. Circuit Judge, 1971–73. Chm., Industrial Tribunal, 1970–73. *Recreation:* model engineering. *Address:* c/o Hitchin County Court, Station House, Nightingale Road, Hitchin, Herts. *T:* Hitchin 50011.

COUPER, Sir (Robert) Nicholas (Oliver), 6th Bt *cr* 1841; *b* 9 Oct. 1945; *s* of Sir George Robert Cecil Couper, 5th Bt, and of Margaret Grace, *d* of late Robert George Dashwood Thomas; *S* father, 1975; *m* 1972, Curzon Henrietta, *d* of Major George Burrell MacKean, DL, JP; one *s* one *d. Educ:* Eton; RMA, Sandhurst. Major, Blues and Royals; retired, 1975. Now working with Savills as an estate agent. *Heir: s* James George Couper, *b* 27 Oct. 1977. *Address:* 39 Cloncurry Street, SW6. *Club:* Cavalry and Guards.

COUPLAND, Prof. Rex Ernest; Professor of Human Morphology, since 1967 and Dean of Medicine, since 1981, University of Nottingham; Hon. Consultant, Regional Hospital Board, since 1970; *b* 30 Jan. 1924; *s* of Ernest Coupland, company dir; *m* 1947, Lucy Eileen Sargent; one *s* one *d. Educ:* Mirfield Grammar Sch.; University of Leeds. MB, ChB with honours, 1947; MD with distinction, 1952; PhD 1954; DSc 1970. House appointments, Leeds General Infirmary, 1947; Demonstrator and Lecturer in Anatomy, University of Leeds, 1948, 1950–58; Asst Prof. of Anatomy, University of Minnesota, USA, 1955–56; Prof. of Anatomy, Queen's Coll., Dundee, University of St Andrews, 1958–67. Medical Officer, RAF, 1948–50. FRSE 1960. Member: Biological Research Board of MRC, 1964–70; Med. Adv. Bd, Crippling Diseases Foundn, 1971–75; Chm., MRC Non-Ionizing Radiations Cttee, 1970–; Derbyshire AHA, 1978–81; Trent RHA, 1981–; Chm., Nottingham Div., BMA, 1978–79; GMC, 1982–. President: Anat. Soc. GB and Ireland, 1976–78; British Assoc. of Clinical Anat., 1977–82. *Publications:* The Natural History of the Chromaffin Cell, 1965; (ed jtly) Chromaffin, Enterochromaffin and Related Cells, 1976; (ed jtly) Peripheral Neuroendocrine Interaction, 1978; papers in jls of anatomy, physiology, endocrinology, pathology and pharmacology on endocrine and nervous systems; chapters on: Anatomy of the Human Kidney, in Renal Disease (ed Black), 1962, 1968, 1973; The Chromaffin System, in Catecholamines (ed Blaschko and Muscholl), 1973; The Blood Supply of the Adrenal Gland, in Handbook of Physiology, 1974; The Adrenal Medulla, in The Cell in Medical Science (ed Beck and Lloyd), 1976; Endocrine System, in Textbook of Human Anatomy (ed W. J. Hamilton), 1976; (ed) Chromaffin, Enterochromaffin and Related Cells, 1976; (ed) Peripheral Neuroendocrine Interaction, 1978; Asst Editor, Gray's Anatomy (ed Davies), 1967. *Recreations:* shooting, gardening. *Address:* Foxhollow, Quaker Lane, Farnsfield, Newark, Notts NG22 8EE. *T:* Mansfield 882028.

COURAGE, Richard Hubert, JP; DL; *b* 23 Jan. 1915; *s* of Raymond Courage and Mildred Frances Courage (formerly Fisher); *m* 1st, 1941, Jean Elizabeth Agnes Watson (*d* 1977), *d* of late Sir Charles Cuningham Watson, KCIE, CSI, ICS; two *s* (and one *s* decd); 2nd, 1978, Phyllida Anne, *widow* of J. D. Derouet. *Educ:* Eton. Served War of 1939–45: Northants Yeomanry, 1939–46, Major (despatches). Director: Courage Ltd, 1948–75 (Chm., 1959–75); Imperial Group Ltd, 1972–75; Norwich Union Insce Group, 1975–80; Chm., London Adv. Bd, Norwich Union Insce Gp, 1975–80 (Dir, 1964–80). Chm. Governors, Brentwood Sch., Essex, 1976–. JP Essex, 1955; DL Essex, 1977. *Recreations:* yachting and shooting. *Address:* Chainbridge, Mountnessing, near Brentwood, Essex. *T:* Brentwood 222206.

COURATIN, Rev. Canon Arthur Hubert; Sixth Canon and Chapter Librarian, Durham Cathedral, 1962–74, Canon Emeritus since 1974; *b* 1902; *s* of Arthur Louis and Marian Couratin. *Educ:* Dulwich Coll.; Corpus Christi Coll., Oxford (Scholar); S Stephen's House, Oxford. 1st Cl. Classical Moderations; 2nd Cl. Literae Humaniores; 2nd Cl. Hons Sch. of Theology; BA 1925; MA 1927. Deacon, 1926; priest, 1927; Asst Curate, S Saviour's, Roath, 1926–30 (in charge of S Francis', Roath, 1927–30); Vice-Principal, Queen's Coll., Birmingham, 1930; Asst Curate, S Stephen's, Lewisham (in charge of Church of the Transfiguration, Lewisham), 1930–35; Chaplain, S Stephen's House, Oxford, 1935–36, Vice-Principal, 1936, Principal, 1936–62; Junior Chaplain, Merton Coll., Oxford, 1936–39. Hon. Canon of Christ Church, 1961–62. *Address:* 7 Pimlico, Durham DH1 4QW. *T:* Durham 64767.

COURCEL, Baron de; (Geoffroy Chodron de Courcel) Grand' Croix de la Légion d'Honneur, 1980; Compagnon de la Libération, 1943; Croix de

Guerre, 1939–45; Government Representative on Board of Directors, Compagnie Française des Pétroles, since 1977; President, France-GB Association, since 1978; *b* Tours, Indre-et-Loire, 11 Sept. 1912; *s* of Louis Chodron de Courcel, Officer, and Alice Lambert-Champy; *m* 1954, Martine Hallade; two *s. Educ:* Stanislas Coll.; University of Paris. DenDr, LèsL, Dip. Ecole des Sciences Politiques. Attaché, Warsaw, 1937; Sec., Athens, 1938–39; Armée du Levant, 1939; joined Free French Forces, June 1940; Chef de Cabinet, Gén. de Gaulle, London, 1940–41; Captain 1st Spahis marocains Regt, Egypt, Libya and Tunisia, 1941–43; Dep.-Dir of Cabinet, Gén de Gaulle, Algiers, 1943–44; Mem. Conseil de l'Ordre de la Libération, 1944; Regional Comr for Liberated Territories, 1944; in charge of Alsace-Lorraine Dept, Min. of Interior, 1944–45; Counsellor, 1945; in Min. of Foreign Affairs: Dep. Dir Central and N European Sections, 1945–47; First Counsellor, Rome, 1947–50; Minister Plen., 1951; Dir Bilateral Trade Agreements Section, 1951; Dir African and ME Section, 1953; Dir Gen., Polit. and Econ. Affairs, Min. of Moroccan and Tunisian Affairs, 1954; Perm. Sec., Nat. Defence, 1955–58; Ambassador, Perm. Rep. to NATO, 1958; Sec.-Gen. Présidence de la République, 1959–62; Ambassador to London, 1962–72; Sec.-Gen., Min. of For. Affairs, 1973–76. Ambassadeur de France, 1965; Hon. DCL Oxon, 1970; Hon. LLD Birmingham, 1972. MC (Great Britain) 1943; Grand Cross of Royal Victorian Order (Hon. GCVO), 1950, etc. *Publication:* L'influence de la Conférence de Berlin de 1885 sur le droit Colonial International, 1936. *Recreations:* shooting, swimming. *Address:* 7 rue de Médicis, 75006 Paris, France; La Ravinière, Fontaines en Sologne, 41250 Bracieux, France.

COURCY; *see* de Courcy.

COURNAND, André Frédéric, MD; Professor Emeritus of Medicine, Columbia University College of Physicians and Surgeons, New York, since 1964 (Professor of Medicine, 1951–60); *b* Paris, 24 Sept. 1895; *s* of Jules Cournand and Marguérite Weber; *m* 1st, Sibylle Blumer (*d* 1959); three *d* (one *s* killed in action, 1944); 2nd, 1963, Ruth Fabian (*d* 1973); 3rd, 1975, Beatrice Berle. *Educ:* Sorbonne, Paris. BA Faculté des Lettres, 1913; PCB Faculté des Sciences, 1914; MD Faculté de Médecine, 1930. Interne des Hôpitaux de Paris, 1925–30. Came to US in 1930; naturalized American Citizen since 1941. Director, Cardio-Pulmonary Laboratory, Columbia University Division, Bellevue Hospital; Visiting Physician, Chest Service, Bellevue Hospital, 1952. Member: American Physiological Soc.; Assoc. of Amer. Physicians; National Acad. of Sciences (USA), 1958; Hon. Member: British Cardiac Soc.; Swedish Soc. Internal Medicine; Swedish Cardiac Soc.; Soc. Médicale des Hôpitaux, Paris; Foreign Mem., Académie Royale de Médecine de Belgique, 1970; Foreign Member: Académie des Sciences, Institut de France, 1957; Académie Nationale de Médecine, Paris, 1958. Laureate: Andreas Retzius Silver Medal of Swedish Soc. Internal Medicine, 1946; Award, US Public Health Assoc., 1949. Croix de Guerre (1914–18) France, three stars; Commandeur de la Légion d'Honneur, 1970 (Officier, 1957). Nobel Prize for Medicine and Physiology (jointly), 1956; Jimenez Diaz Fondacion Prize, 1970; Trudeau Medal, 1971. Doctor (*hc*): University of Strasburg, 1957; University of Lyons, 1958; Université libre de Bruxelles 1959; University of Pisa, 1961; University of Birmingham, 1961; Gustaphus Adolphus, Coll., Minnesota, 1963; University of Brazil, 1965; Columbia Univ., 1965; Univ. of Nancy, 1968. *Publications:* Cardiac Catheterization in Congenital Heart Disease, 1949; L'Insuffisance cardiaque chronique, 1950; Shaping the Future, 1974; numerous articles on human physiopathology of lungs and heart and on the relation between science and society. *Recreations:* Groupe de la Haute Montagne du Club Alpin Français, 1929, and American Alpine Club. *Address:* 142 East 19th Street, New York, NY 10003, USA. *T:* 473 3660. *Club:* Century Association (New York).

COURT, Hon. Sir Charles (Walter Michael), KCMG 1979; Kt 1972; OBE 1946; MLA (Liberal Party) for Nedlands, 1953–82; Premier of Western Australia, 1974–82; also Treasurer, and Minister co-ordinating Economic and Regional Development, 1974–82; *b* Crawley, Sussex, 29 Sept. 1911; *s* of late W. J. Court, Perth; *m* 1936, Rita M., *d* of L. R. Steffanoni; five *s. Educ:* Leederville and Rosalie State Schs; Perth Boys' Sch. Chartered Accountant, 1933; Partner, Hendry, Rae & Court, 1938–70. Served AIF, 1940–46; Lt-Col. State Registrar, Inst. Chartered Accountants in Aust. (WA Br.), 1946–52; Mem. State Council, 1952–55. Dep. Leader, 1957–59, 1971–72, and Leader, 1972–74, of Opposition, WA; Minister, Western Australia: for Industrial Development and the NW, 1959–71; for Railways, 1959–67; for Transport, 1965–66. Chm., Adv. Cttee under WA Prices Control Act, 1948–52; Pres., WA Band Assoc., 1954–59. Hon. Colonel: WA Univ. Regt, 1969–75; SAS Regt, 1976–80. FCA; FCIS; FASA. Hon. FAIM 1980. Hon. LLD Univ. of WA, 1969; Hon. DTech WA Inst. of Technol., 1982. Manufacturers' Export Council Award, 1969; James Kirby Award, Inst. of Production Engrs, 1971. Life Member: Musicians Union, 1953; Returned Services League, 1981. *Publications:* many professional papers on accountancy, and papers on economic and resource development. *Recreations:* music, yachting. *Address:* 46 Waratah Avenue, Nedlands, WA 6009, Australia. *Clubs:* Commercial Travellers Association, Nedlands and Perth Rotary, Lions.

COURT, Emeritus Prof. Seymour Donald Mayneord, CBE 1969; MD; FRCP; *b* 4 Jan. 1912; *s* of David Henry and Ethel Court; *m* 1939, Dr Frances Edith Radcliffe; two *s* one *d. Educ:* Adams Grammar Sch., Wem; Birmingham Univ (MB, ChB, 1936; MD 1947). FRCP 1956. Resident Hosp. appts Birmingham Gen. Hosps, and Hosp. for Sick Children, London, 1936–38; Paediatric Registrar, Wander Scholar, Westminster Hosp., 1938–39; Physician, EMS, 1939–46; Nuffield Fellow in Child Health, 1946–47; Reader in Child Health, University of Durham, 1947-55; James Spence Prof. of Child Health, Univ. of Newcastle upon Tyne, 1955-72, Emeritus Professor, 1972. Chm., Child Health Services Cttee for Eng. and Wales, 1973-76. Pres., British Paediatric Assoc., 1973-76. James Spence Medal, British Paed. Assoc., 1978; Nils Rosén von Rosenstein Medal, Swedish Paed. Assoc., 1979. *Publications:* (jointly) Growing Up in Newcastle upon Tyne, 1960; (ed) The Medical Care of Children, 1963; (ed jointly) Paediatrics in the Seventies, 1972; (jointly) The School Years in Newcastle upon Tyne, 1974; (ed jtly) Fit for the Future, 1976; contributions to special jls and text books on respiratory infection in childhood. *Recreations:* walking, natural history, poetry. *Address:* 8 Towers Avenue, Jesmond, Newcastle upon Tyne NE2 3QE. *T:* Newcastle upon Tyne 814884.

COURTAULD, Rev. (Augustine) Christopher Caradoc; Vicar of St Paul's, Knightsbridge, since 1978; *b* 12 Sept. 1934; *s* of late Augustine Courtauld and of Lady Butler of Saffron Walden; *m* 1978, Dr Elizabeth Ann Molland, MD, MRCPath, *d* of late Rev. Preb. John W. G. Molland; two *d*. *Educ:* Trinity College, Cambridge (BA 1958, MA 1961); Westcott House, Cambridge. Deacon 1960, priest 1961, Manchester; Curate of Oldham, 1960-63; Chaplain: Trinity College, Cambridge, 1963-68; The London Hospital, 1968-78. *Recreation:* sailing. *Address:* St Paul's Vicarage, 32 Wilton Place, SW1.

COURTENAY, family name of **Earl of Devon.**

COURTENAY, Lord; Hugh Rupert Courtenay; Salaried Partner with Messrs Stratton & Holborow, Chartered Surveyors, Exeter; *b* 5 May 1942; *o s* of 17th Earl of Devon, *qv* ; *m* 1967, Dianna Frances, *er d* of J. G. Watherston, Jedburgh, Roxburghshire; one *s* three *d*. *Educ:* Winchester; Magdalene Coll., Cambridge (BA). ARICS. Captain, Wessex Yeomanry, retd. *Recreations:* riding, hunting, shooting. *Heir: s* Hon. Charles Peregrine Courtenay, *b* 14 Aug. 1975. *Address:* The Stables House, Powderham, near Exeter, Devon. *T:* Starcross 370. *Club:* University Pitt (Cambridge).

COURTENAY, Sir Harrison; *see* Courtenay, Sir W. H.

COURTENAY, Thomas Daniel, (Tom Courtenay); actor; *b* 25 Feb. 1937; *s* of Thomas Henry Courtenay and late Annie Eliza Quest; *m* 1973, Cheryl Kennedy (marr. diss. 1982). *Educ:* Kingston High Sch., Hull; University Coll., London. RADA, 1958-60; started acting professionally, 1960; Old Vic, 1960-61: Konstantin Trepleff, Poins, Feste and Puck; Billy Liar, Cambridge Theatre, June 1961-Feb. 1962 and on tour; Andorra, National Theatre (guest), 1964; The Cherry Orchard, and Macbeth, Chichester, 1966; joined 69 Theatre Co., Manchester, 1966: Charley's Aunt, 1966; Romeo, Playboy of the Western World, 1967; Hamlet (Edinburgh Festival), 1968; She Stoops to Conquer, (transferred to Garrick), 1969; Peer Gynt, 1970; Charley's Aunt, Apollo, 1971; Time and Time Again, Comedy, 1972 (Variety Club of GB Stage Actor Award, 1972); The Norman Conquests, Globe, 1974; The Fool, Royal Court, 1975; Prince of Homburg, The Rivals, Manchester (opening prods of The Royal Exchange), 1976; Otherwise Engaged, NY, 1977; Clouds, Duke of York's, 1978; Crime and Punishment, Manchester, 1978; The Dresser, Manchester and Queen's, 1980 (Drama Critics Award and New Standard Award for best actor, 1980), NY 1981; The Misanthrope, Manchester and Round House, 1981; Andy Capp, Manchester and Aldwych, 1982. Began acting in films, 1962. *Films:* The Loneliness of the Long Distance Runner; Private Potter; Billy Liar; King and Country (Volpi Cup, 1964); Operation Crossbow; King Rat; Dr Zhivago; The Night of the Generals; The Day the Fish Came Out; A Dandy in Aspic; Otley; One Day in the Life of Ivan Denisovitch; Catch Me a Spy. Has appeared on Television. Best Actor Award, Prague Festival, 1968; TV Drama Award (for Oswald in Ghosts), 1968. *Recreations:* listening to music (mainly classical and romantic); watching sport (and occasionally taking part in it, in a light-hearted manner). *Address:* Putney. *Club:* Garrick.

COURTENAY, Hon. Sir (Woldrich) Harrison, KBE 1973 (OBE 1950); LLD; QC 1974; Speaker, House of Representatives, Belize, (formerly British Honduras), 1963-74 (of Legislative Assembly, 1961-63); Chancellor of Anglican Diocese, since 1956, Registrar since 1946; Barrister-at-Law; *b* Belize City, 15 July 1904; *s* of William and Sarah Courtenay; *m* 1929, Josephine Robinson; four *s* one *d*. *Educ:* Belize High Sch., British Honduras; Lincoln's Inn, London. Mem. Civil Service, Belize (British Honduras Secretariat), 1920-37; acted on several occasions as Clerk of Legislative and Exec. Councils, and as Head of Educn Dept, 1930; Sec.-Accountant, British Honduras Govt Marketing Agency, 1925-33; also Sec. of Stann Creek Develt Bd. Left for UK, Nov. 1933, to read for the Bar; called to Bar, Lincoln's Inn, 1936; returned to British Honduras and resumed duty, July 1936; resigned, 1937, and entered into private practice; admitted Solicitor of Supreme Court, Belize, 1937; Magistrate, Belize, 1938-41. Was for many years Diocesan Sec. and Mem. Synod, 1926-, Dio. Brit. Honduras; Diocesan Treas.; and Sec.-Treas., Bd of Governors of St Hilda's Coll. (Elected) MLC, 1945-54; MEC, 1947-54; Past Mem., Electricity Bd; also served on several other Bds and Cttees. British Honduras rep. to Conf. on Closer Assoc. of the BWI, Montego Bay, 1947, also to 2nd and 3rd WI confs; Leader of first delegn from Legislative Council to Colonial Office on Constitutional Reform and Economic Develt, 1947. Member: Standing Closer Assoc. Cttee, which prod. first Federal Constitution, 1948-51; Brit. Section, Caribbean Commn, 1948-52; Alternate Mem., 1952-55; BWI Regional Economic Cttee, 1951-54; Council of University Coll. of the WI; Finance and General Purposes Cttee, Bd of Extra-Mural Studies, and Bd of Inst. of Social and Economic Research, 1948-58; Chm., constitutional

Reform Commn, 1949-51; Fiscal Revision Cttee, 1952-53. Representative: at Installation of Princess Alice as Chancellor of University Coll. of WI, 1950; CPA Confs, NZ 1950 and Canada 1952; on visits to Australia, Canada, Jamaica, etc, 1950-52; for visit of the Queen and the Duke of Edinburgh to Jamaica, 1953; to Sugar Conf., Grenada, 1950, and Trade Promotion Conf., Trinidad, 1954; (for BWI) on UK delegn to Conf. of Commonwealth Finance Ministers, Sydney, 1954; Chm., BWI Regional Parly Conf., Jamaica, 1952; Chm. and Constitutional Adviser to United Front Political delegn to London for constitutional talks, 1960; Chm., NEDC, 1962-66; Constitutional Adviser to Political delegn to London for constitutional talks, 1963; Adviser, British Honduras delegn to tripartite confs on Anglo-Guatemalan Dispute, and with Mediator in the dispute, 1962-67. Hon. LLD (Univ. of WI), 1972; Hon. Citizen of San Juan, Puerto Rico, 1948. *Recreations:* travel, reading, music. *Address:* Cloverleaf Park, Northern Highway, (PO Box 636) Belize. *Club:* Royal Commonwealth Society (West Indian).

COURTNEY, Comdr Anthony Tosswill, OBE 1949; RN; author and lecturer; Managing Director, New English Typewriting School Ltd, since 1969; *b* 16 May 1908; *s* of Basil Tosswill Courtney and Frances Elizabeth Courtney (*née* Rankin); *m* 1st, 1938, Elisabeth Mary Cortlandt Stokes (*d* 1961); no *c* ; 2nd, 1962, Lady (Elizabeth) Trefgarne (marr. diss. 1966); 3rd, 1971, Mrs Angela Bradford. *Educ:* Royal Naval Coll., Dartmouth. Midshipman, HMS Ramillies, 1925; world cruise in HMS Renown with the Duke and Duchess of York, 1927; Sub-Lieut HMS Cornwall, 1930; Lieut HMS Malaya, 1931-33; qualified as Interpreter in Russian after language study in Bessarabia, 1934; qualified in Signals and W/T at Signal Sch., Portsmouth, 1935; served at Admiralty and on staff of C-in-C, Plymouth, 1936; Flag Lieut to Rear-Adm. comdg Third Cruiser Sqdn, Mediterranean Fleet, 1937-39; Staff of Adm. comdg 3rd Battle Squadron and N Atlantic Escort Force, 1939-41; Naval Mission in Russia, 1941-42; Flag Lieut and Signals Officer to Adm. comdg Aircraft Carriers, 1943; Staff of Adm. comdg S Atlantic Station, 1944; Staff of Rear-Adm., Gibraltar, 1945; Intelligence Div., Naval Staff, Admiralty, 1946-48; Chief Staff Officer (Intelligence) Germany, 1949-51; qualified as Interpreter in German; Intelligence Div., Naval Staff, Admiralty, 1952-53; retd with rank of Comdr, 1953. Entered business as Export Consultant (ETG Consultancy Services), until 1965. Contested (C) Hayes and Harlington, 1955. MP (C) Harrow East, 1959-66. Vice-Chm. Conservative Navy Cttee, 1964. Chm. Parliamentary Flying Club, 1965; Mem. Exec. Council, Monday Club; Chm., Wilts Monday Club, 1977. *Publication:* Sailor in a Russian Frame, 1968. *Recreations:* shooting, music, fishing. *Address:* Mulberry House, Urchfont, Devizes, Wilts. *T:* Chirton 357. *Club:* White's.

COURTNEY, Prof. Edward, MA; Professor of Latin, King's College, University of London, since 1977; *b* 22 March 1932; *s* of George and Kathleen Courtney; *m* 1962, Brenda Virginia Meek; two *s*. *Educ:* Royal Belfast Academical Instn; Trinity Coll., Dublin (BA); BA (by incorporation) 1955, MA 1957, Oxford. University studentship, Dublin, 1954-55; Research Lectr, Christ Church, Oxford, 1955-59; Lectr in Classics, 1959, Reader in Classics, 1970, King's Coll., London. *Publications:* Valerius Flaccus, Argonautica (Leipzig), 1970; (jtly) Juvenal, Satires 1, 3, 10, 1977; (jtly) Ovid, Fasti (Leipzig), 1978; A Commentary on the Satires of Juvenal, 1980; many articles and reviews. *Recreation:* chess (schoolboy champion of Ireland, 1950). *Address:* 116 Farnaby Road, Bromley, Kent BR1 4BH. *T:* 01-460 5124.

COURTOWN, 9th Earl of, *cr* 1762; **James Patrick Montagu Burgoyne Winthrop Stopford;** Baron Courtown (Ire.), 1758; Viscount Stopford, 1762; Baron Saltersford (GB), 1796; *b* 19 March 1954; *s* of 8th Earl of Courtown, OBE, TD, DL, and of Patricia, 3rd *d* of Harry S. Winthrop, Auckland, NZ; *S* father, 1975. *Educ:* Eton College; Berkshire Coll. of Agriculture. *Heir: b* Hon. Jeremy Neville Stopford, *b* 22 June 1958. *Address:* Beechshade, Cambridge Road, Beaconsfield, Bucks.

COUSIN, Prof. David Ross; Emeritus Professor of Philosophy, University of Sheffield; *b* 28 Jan. 1904; *s* of John William Cousin and Marion Miller Young; *m* 1930, Beatrice Elizabeth Connell; three *s*. *Educ:* Merchiston Castle Sch., Edinburgh; The Queen's Coll., Oxford (BA). Class. Mods 1925; Lit Hum 1927; Philosophy, Politics and Economics, 1928. Asst, Dept of Logic, University of Glasgow, 1928; Lecturer, 1930; Senior Lecturer, 1948. Board of Trade (temp. Principal), 1941-45. Prof. of Philosophy, Univ. of Sheffield, 1949-69; Dean of Faculty of Arts, 1958-61. Vis. Prof., Dept of Philosophy, Univ. of Edinburgh, Oct.-Dec., 1974. *Publications:* contributions to learned jls. *Address:* 16 Cobden Crescent, Edinburgh EH9 2BG.

COUSINS, Brian Harry, CBE 1981; Assistant Under Secretary, Ministry of Defence, since 1981; *b* 18 July 1933; *s* of late William and Ethel Margaret Cousins; *m* 1957, Margaret (*née* Spark); two *s*. *Educ:* Devonport High School. Served RAF, pilot, 1952-54. Joined Ministry of Defence, 1954; Private Sec. to Permanent Secretary, 1962-65; Private Sec. Parliamentary Secretary, 1971-72; ndc 1972; Civil Sec., British Forces Germany, 1973-76. *Recreations:* tennis, gardening. *Address:* Churston, Church Street, Ewell, Surrey KT17 2AQ.

COUSINS, Rt. Hon. Frank, PC 1964; Chairman, Community Relations Commission, 1968-70; *b* Bulwell, Notts, 8 Sept. 1904; *m* 1930, Annie Elizabeth Judd; two *s* two *d*. *Educ:* King Edward Sch., Doncaster. Mem. Institute of Transport; Organiser, Rd Transport Section, TGWU, 1938; Nat. Officer (Rd Tr. Section), 1944; Nat. Sec. (Rd Tr. Section), 1948; Asst Gen. Sec. TGWU, 1955; General Secretary, TGWU, 1956-69 (seconded, as

Minister of Technology, Oct. 1964-July 1966). MP (Lab) Nuneaton, Jan. 1965-Dec. 1966. Elected Mem., Gen. Council of TUC, 1956-69. Member: British Transport Jt Consultative Council, 1955-63; Min. of Labour Nat. Jt Advisory Council, 1956; Exec. Council Internat. Transport Workers Federation, 1956 (Pres., 1958-60, 1962-64); Colonial Labour Advisory Cttee, 1957-62; London Travel Cttee, 1958-60; Political Economy Club, 1957; Council for Scientific and Industrial Research, 1960-64; National Economic Development Council; Central Advisory Council for Science and Technology, 1967-; Nat. Freight Corp., 1968-73; Governor, Nat. Inst. of Economic and Social Research, 1958; Chm., Central Training Council, 1968-. *Relevant publication:* The Awkward Warrior, by Geoffrey Goodman, 1979. *Recreations:* gardening, reading. *Address:* Danby Ridge, Top Street, North Wheatley, Retford, Notts DN22 9DE.

See also J. P. Cousins.

COUSINS, John Peter; Director of Personnel and Industrial Relations, John Brown & Co. Ltd, since 1981; *b* 31 Oct. 1931; *s* of Rt Hon. Frank Cousins, *qv* ; *m* 1976, Pauline Cousins (*née* Hubbard); three *d*. *Educ:* Doncaster Central Sch. Motor engineering apprentice, 1947-52; RAF Engineering, 1952-55; BOAC cabin crew and clerical work, 1955-63; Full Time Official, TGWU, 1963-75, Nat. Sec., 1966-75; Dir of Manpower and Industrial Relations, NEDO, 1975-79; Dir of Personnel, Plessey Telecommunications and Office Systems Ltd, 1979-81. Mem., Transport and Local Govt Cttees, TUC; UK Deleg., ILO; International Transport Workers Federation: Member: Aviation Sect.; Local Govt Cttee; Chemical Cttee; Civil Aviation Cttee; Mem. Industrial Training Bds. Member: Countryside Commn, 1972-; New Towns Commn, 1975-79; Sandford Cttee to review National Parks in England and Wales, 1972-73. Chm., British Council of Productivity Assocs, 1977. Travelling Fellow, Kingston Reg. Management Centre, 1977. *Recreations:* hill walking, trout fishing, 17th and 18th century music. *Address:* The Cottage, Round Hill, Sydenham, SE26. *T:* 01-291 2344.

COUSINS, Norman; Editor Emeritus, Saturday Review, since 1978; Adjunct Professor, University of California at Los Angeles Medical School, since 1978; *b* 24 June 1915; *s* of Samuel and Sara Cousins; *m* 1939, Ellen Kopf; four *d*. *Educ:* Teachers Coll., Columbia Univ. Educational Editor, New York Evening Post, 1935-36; Managing Editor, Current History Magazine, 1936-39 (World War II edn, USA); Editor: Saturday Review, 1940-71, 1975-78; World Magazine, 1972-73; Saturday Review/World, 1973-74. Chm., Conn Fact-Finding Commission on Education, 1948-51. Vice-Pres. PEN Club, American Center, 1952-55; National Press and Overseas Press Clubs; Lectr for US Dept of State; co-Chm., National Cttee for a Sane Nuclear Policy, 1957-63. Pres. United World Federalists, 1952-54 (Hon. Pres., 1955-). Pres., World Assoc. of World Federalists, 1965-66, 1976-77; Pres., World Federalist Assoc., 1977-. Chairman: Nat. Educational Television, 1969-70; Nat. Programming Council for Public Television; Mem. Bd of Directors: The Charles F. Kettering Foundn; The Samuel H. Kress Foundn; US Govt Rep. at dedication Nat. Univ., Addis Ababa, 1962; co-Chm., Citizens' Cttee for a Nuclear Test-Ban Treaty, 1963; Chm., Cttee for Culture and Intellectual Exchange, for International Co-operation Year, 1965; US Presidential Rep. at Inauguration of Pres. of Philippines, 1966; US Govt Rep. at Internat. Writers Conf., Finland, 1966. Chm. Mayor's Task Force on Air Pollution, NYC, 1966-. Holds various hon. degrees. Awards include: Benjamin Franklin Award for Public Service in Journalism, 1956; Eleanor Roosevelt Peace Award, 1963; Overseas Press Club Award for best interpretation of foreign affairs in magazine writing, 1965; Family of Man Award, 1968; Carr Van Anda Award for Enduring Contribs to Journalism, Ohio Univ., 1971; Peace Medal of UN, 1971; Nat Arts Club Gold Medal for Literature, 1972; Univ. of Missouri Honor Award for Conspicuous Contribs to Journalism, 1972; Drexel Univ. Distinguished Achievement Award, 1972; Irita Van Doren Book Award, 1972; Magazine Publishers Assoc. Award, 1973; Human Resources Award, Nightingale-Conant Corp., 1973; Delbert Clark Award, West Georgia Coll., 1974; Canadian Govt Environment Award, 1975; Medal of Amer. Coll. of Cardiology, 1978; Author of the Year, Soc. of Authors and Journalists, 1980. *Publications:* The Good Inheritance, 1941; (ed) A Treasury of Democracy, 1941; Modern Man is Obsolete, 1945; (ed jtly) Poetry of Freedom, 1946; Talks with Nehru, 1951; Who Speaks for Man?, 1953; Saturday Review Treasury (ed. sup.), 1957; In God We Trust (ed), 1958; March's Thesaurus (ed. sup.), 1958; Dr Schweitzer of Lambaréné, 1960; In Place of Folly, 1961; Present Tense, 1967; The Improbable Triumvirate, 1972; Celebration of Life, 1974; Anatomy of an Illness, 1979; Human Options, 1981; The Physician in Literature, 1982. *Recreations:* music (especially organ), sports, reading, chess. *Address:* (office) 2859 Slichter Hall, University of California, Los Angeles, Calif 90024, USA; (home) 2644 Eden Place, Beverly Hills, Calif 90210, USA.

COUSINS, Philip, CB 1982; Secretary, Exchequer and Audit Department, since 1979; *b* 5 Feb. 1923; *s* of Herbert and Ella Cousins; *m* 1948, Ruby Laura Morris; two *d*. *Educ:* Royal Liberty School, Romford. Served in Royal Air Force, 1943-47. Joined Treasury, 1949; Under Secretary, 1974-79. *Address:* 102 Philbeach Gardens, SW5. *T:* 01-373 6164.

COUSTEAU, Jacques-Yves; Commandeur, Légion d'Honneur; Croix de Guerre with Palm; Officier du Mérite Maritime; Chevalier du Mérite Agricole; Officier des Arts et des Lettres; marine explorer; *b* 11 June 1910; *s* of Daniel and Elizabeth Cousteau; *m* 1937, Simone Melchior; one *s* (and one *s* decd). *Educ:* Stanislas, Paris; Navy Academy, Brest. Lt de vaisseau, War of 1939-45. Was partly responsible for invention of the Aqualung, 1943, a

portable breathing device for divers. Established Undersea Research Group, 1946; Founder and President: Campagnes Océanographiques Françaises, 1950; Centre d'Etudes Marines Avancées, 1952; since 1951 has made annual oceanographic expdns on his ship Calypso, and has made film records of his undersea expdns since 1951; took part in making of the Bathyscaphe; promoted Conshelf saturation dive programme, 1962-65. Dir, Musée Océanographique, Monaco, Feb. 1957-; Gen. Sec., Internat. Commn for Scientific Exploration of the Mediterranean Sea, 1966. For. Assoc. Mem., Nat. Acad. Scis, USA, 1968; Corresp. Mem., Hellenic Inst. of Marine Archaeology, 1975. Hon. DSc: California 1970; Brandeis 1970; Rensselaer Polytechnic Inst., 1977; Harvard, 1979. Gold Medal, RGS, 1963; Pott's Medal, Franklin Inst., 1970; Gold Medal, Nat. Geographic Soc., and Gold Medal Grand Prix d'Océanographie Albert Ier, 1971; Grande Médaille d'Or, Soc. d'encouragement au Progrès, 1973; Award of New England Aquarium, 1973; Prix de la couronne d'or, 1973; Polena della Bravura, 1974; Gold Medal "Sciences" (Arts, Sciences, Lettres), 1974; Manley Bendall Prize, Marine Acad., 1976; Special Cervia prize, 1976; Internat. Pahlavi Environment Prize, 1977. *Publications:* Par 18 mètres de fond, 1946; La Plongée en Scaphandre, 1950; (with Frederic Dumas) The Silent World, 1953 (New York and London), first published in English, then in other languages; (ed with James Dugan) Captain Cousteau's Underwater Treasury, 1960 (London); The Living Sea, 1963 (London); World Without Sun, 1965 (film awarded Oscar, 1966); (with P. Cousteau) The Shark, 1970; with P. Diolé: Life and Death in a Coral Sea, 1971; Diving for Sunken Treasure, 1971; The Whale: mighty monarch of the sea, 1972; Octopus and Squid, 1973; Galapagos, The Blue Holes: three adventures, 1973; The Ocean World of Jacques Cousteau (20 vol encyclopedia), 1973; Diving Companions, 1974; Dolphins, 1975; articles in National Geographical Magazine, 1952-66. *Films:* The Silent World (Grand Prix, Gold Palm, Cannes 1956; Oscar, 1957); The Golden Fish (Oscar, best short film, 1959); World without Sun (Oscar, 1965); Voyage to the Edge of the World, 1975; *TV film series:* The Undersea World of Jacques Cousteau, 1968-76 (numerous Emmy awards); Oasis in Space series, 1977; The Cousteau Odyssey series, 1977-81. *Address:* Oceanographic Institute, Fondation Albert 1er, Prince de Monaco, Monaco. *Clubs:* Club des Explorateurs (Paris); Club Alpin Sous Marin; Yacht Club de France.

COUTTS; *see* Money-Coutts.

COUTTS, Frederick, CBE 1967; General of The Salvation Army, 1963-69; *b* 21 Sept. 1899; British; *m* 1st, 1925, Bessie Lee (*d* 1967); one *s* three *d* ; 2nd, 1969, Olive Gatrall. *Educ:* Leith Academy and Whitehill. RFC, 1917-18. Officer, The Salvation Army, 1920. Literary Sec. to the General, 1952. Training Principal, International Training Coll., 1953-57; Territorial Comdr, Eastern Australia, 1957-63. Hon. DD Aberdeen, 1981. *Publications:* The Timeless Prophets, 1944; He had no Revolver, 1944; The Battle and the Breeze, 1945; Portrait of a Salvationist, 1955; Jesus and Our Need, 1956; The Call to Holiness, 1957; Essentials of Christian Experience, 1969; The Better Fight: the history of the Salvation Army 1914-1946, 1973; No Discharge in This War, 1975; No Continuing City, 1976; Bread for my Neighbour, 1978; In Good Company, 1980; More Than One Homeland, 1982. *Recreations:* reading, music. *Address:* 3 Dubrae Close, St Albans, Herts. *T:* St Albans 59655.

COUTTS, Prof. John Archibald; Professor of Jurisprudence in the University of Bristol, 1950-75, now Emeritus; Pro-Vice Chancellor, 1971-74; *b* 29 Dec. 1909; *e s* of Archibald and Katherine Jane Coutts; *m* 1940, Katherine Margaret Alldis; two *s*. *Educ:* Merchant Taylors', Crosby; Downing Coll., Cambridge (MA, LLB). Barrister Gray's Inn, 1933; lectured in Law: University Coll., Hull, 1934-35; King's Coll., London, 1935-36; Queen's Univ., Belfast, 1936-37; Trinity Coll., Dublin, 1937-50; Prof. of Laws, University of Dublin, 1944-50. Fellow, Trinity College, Dublin, 1944-50. Visiting Professor: Osgoode Hall Law Sch., Toronto, 1962-63; Univ. of Toronto, 1970-71, 1975-76. *Publications:* The Accused (ed); contributions to legal journals. *Address:* 22 Hurle Crescent, Clifton, Bristol BS8 2SZ. *T:* Bristol 736984.

COUTTS, Thomas Gordon, QC (Scotland) 1973; *b* 5 July 1933; *s* of Thomas Coutts and Evelyn Gordon Coutts; *m* 1959, Winifred Katherine Scott, BSc, MA; one *s* one *d*. *Educ:* Aberdeen Grammar Sch.; Aberdeen Univ. (MA, LLB). Admitted Faculty of Advocates, 1959; Standing Junior Counsel to Dept Agric. (Scot.), 1965; Chm. Industrial Tribunals, 1972. *Recreations:* golf, stamp collecting. *Address:* 6 Heriot Row, Edinburgh EH3 6HU. *Club:* New (Edinburgh).

COUTTS, Sir Walter (Fleming), GCMG 1962 (KCMG 1961; CMG 1953); Kt 1961; MBE 1949; retired; Director, The Farmington Trust, 1971-78; Director: Inchcape (East Africa) Ltd, 1970-78; Assam Investments, 1964-78; Chairman, Grindlays (Commercial) Holdings, 1974-78; *b* Aberdeen, 30 Nov. 1912; *s* of late Rev. John William Coutts, MA, DD, and Mrs R. Coutts, Dollar; *m* 1942, Janet Elizabeth Jamieson, CStJ, 2nd *d* of late Mr and Mrs A. C. Jamieson; one *s* one *d*. *Educ:* Glasgow Academy; St Andrews Univ.; St John's Coll., Cambridge. MA St Andrews, 1934. District Officer Kenya, 1936; Secretariat Kenya, 1946; District Commissioner, 1947; Administrator, St Vincent, 1949; Minister for Education, Labour and Lands, Kenya, 1956-58, Chief Sec., 1958-61; Special Commissioner for African Elections, Feb. 1955; Governor of Uganda, Nov. 1961-Oct. 1962; Governor-Gen. and C-in-C, Uganda, 1962-63. Sec. to Dulverton Trust, 1966-69; Asst Vice-Chancellor (Administration), Univ. of Warwick, 1969-71. Chm., Pergamon Press, 1972-

74. *Recreation:* gardening. *Address:* 19 Malindi Street, Willetton, WA 6155, Australia. *T:* Perth 457 2995.

COUVE DE MURVILLE, Maurice; Commandeur de la Légion d'Honneur; Ambassadeur de France; Deputy, French National Assembly, Paris 7ème Arrondissement, since 1973; *b* 24 Jan. 1907; *m* 1932, Jacqueline Schweisguth; three *d*. *Educ:* Paris Univ. Inspecteur des finances, 1930; directeur des finances extérieures, 1940; membre du Comité français de la libération nationale (Alger), 1943; représentant de la France, Conseil consultatif pour l'Italie, 1944; Ambassador in Rome, 1945; directeur général des affaires politiques, Ministère des Affaires Etrangères, 1945-50; Ambassador in Egypt, 1950-54; French Permanent Rep., NATO, Sept. 1954-Jan. 1955; Ambassador in the US, 1955-56; Ambassador of France to the Federal Republic of Germany, 1956-58; Ministre des Affaires Etrangères, 1958-68, de l'Economie et des Finances, June-July 1968; Prime Minister of France, 1968-69. *Publication:* Une Politique étrangère 1958-69, 1973. *Address:* 44 rue du Bac, 75007 Paris, France.

COUVE DE MURVILLE, Most Rev. Maurice Noël Léon; *see* Birmingham, Archbishop of, (RC).

COUZENS, Sir Kenneth (Edward), KCB 1979 (CB 1976); Second Permanent Secretary (Overseas Finance), HM Treasury, since 1977; *b* 29 May 1925; *s* of Albert Couzens and May Couzens (*née* Biddlecombe); *m* 1947, Muriel Eileen Fey; one *s* one *d*. *Educ:* Portsmouth Grammar Sch.; Caius Coll., Cambridge. Inland Revenue, 1949-51; Treasury, 1951-68, and 1970-; Civil Service Dept, 1968-70. Private Sec. to Financial Sec., Treasury, 1952-55, and to Chief Sec., 1962-63; Asst Sec., 1963-69; Under-Secretary: CSD, 1969-70; Treasury, 1970-73; Dep. Sec., Incomes Policy and Public Finance, 1973-77. *Address:* Coverts Edge, Woodsway, Oxshott, Surrey. *T:* Oxshott 3207. *Club:* Reform.

COVACEVICH, Sir (Anthony) Thomas, Kt 1978; DFC 1943; Senior Partner, MacDonnells, Solicitors and Notaries Public, Cairns, Queensland, Australia, since 1963 (Partner, 1939); *b* 1 March 1915; *s* of Prosper and Ellen Covacevich; *m* 1944, Gladys Rose (*née* Bryant); one *s* one *d*. *Educ:* Townsville and Brisbane Grammar Schools. Admitted Solicitor, Supreme Court of Queensland, 1938. Formerly Director of five publicly listed Australian companies, including Foxwood Ltd, a timber company (Chm.). *Recreation:* fishing. *Address:* 17 Temora Close, Edge Hill, Cairns, Queensland, Australia. *T:* 51 4000; Box 5046, Cairns Mail Centre, Queensland 4870, Australia. *Clubs:* Johnsonian (Brisbane); North Queensland (Townsville, Qld).

COVEN, Major Edwina Olwyn, JP; HM Lieutenant, City of London, since 1981; *b* 23 Oct. 1921; *d* of Sir Samuel Instone, DL, and Lady (Alice) Instone; *m* 1951, Frank Coven, *qv*. *Educ:* Queen's Coll., London; St Winifred's, Ramsgate; Lycée Victor Duruy, Paris; Marlborough Gate Secretarial Coll., London (1st Cl. Business Diploma). Volunteered for Mil. Service, Private ATS; commnd ATS (subseq. WRAC); Army Interpreter (French); served UK and overseas, incl. staff appts, Plans and Policy Div., Western Union Defence Org. and NATO, Directorate Manpower Planning, WO, 1942-56. 1959-: Children's Writer, Fleetway Publications; Gen. Features Writer, National Magazine Co.; Reporter, BBC Woman's Hour; performer and adviser, children's and teenage progs, ITV. Mem. Adv. Council, Radio London (BBC), 1978-. Chm., Davbro Chemists, 1967-71; stores consultant on promotion and fashion, 1960-77; Mem., Women's Adv. Cttee (Clothing and Footwear Sub-Cttee), BSI, 1971-73. JP Inner London, North Westminster, 1965-72 (Dep. Chm., 1971-72); JP City of London Commn, 1969 (Dep. Chm., 1971-); Mem., Central Council Probation and After-Care Cttee, 1971; Chm., City of London Probation and After-Care Cttee, 1971-77. Dowgate Ward, City of London: Court of Common Council, 1972-; Alderman, 1973 and 1974; Deputy, 1975-. Freedom, City of London, 1967; Mem., Guild of Freemen, City of London, 1971; Freeman, Loriners Co., 1967; Liveryman, Spectacle Makers Co., 1972. Member: Council, WRAC Assoc., 1973-; TAVRA, City of London, 1979-; Associated Speakers, 1975-; London Home Safety Council, 1980; Bd of Governors, City of London Sch., 1972-; Chm., Bd of Governors, City of London Sch. for Girls, 1978-81; Mem., Royal Soc. of St George, 1972-; Chm., Vintry and Dowgate Wards Club, 1977. *Publication:* Tales of Oaktree Kitchen, 1959 (2nd edn 1960; adapted for ITV children's educnl series). *Recreations:* looking after much-loved husband and homemaking generally; lawn tennis; watching a variety of spectator sports. *Address:* 22 Cadogan Court, Draycott Avenue, SW3 3BX. *T:* 01-589 8286. *Clubs:* Queen's, Hurlingham; Devonshire (Eastbourne).

COVEN, Frank; London and European Director, The Nine Television Network of Australia, since 1974; *b* 26 April 1910; *s* of Isaac L. Coven and Raie Coven; *m* 1951, Edwina Coven (*née* Instone), *qv*. *Educ:* The Perse, Cambridge; France and Germany. Studied film prodn, UFA and EFA Studios, Berlin. TA (Ranks), 1938; War Service, 1939-45 (commnd 1941). Film admin and prodn, Gaumont British Studies, 1932; Studio Manager, Gainsborough Pictures, 1935; TV prodn, BBC/Daily Mail, 1937-38; Jt Dep. Organiser, Daily Mail Ideal Home Exhibition (radio, television, special features), 1945; Manager, Public Relations, Associated Newspapers, 1949; interviews, Wimbledon tennis commentaries, children's series "Write it Yourself" BBC TV, 1949-54 (subseq. ITV); TV Adviser, Bd of Associated Newspapers, 1953, Associated Rediffusion, 1954; London Rep., Television Corporation Ltd, Sydney, and Herald-Sun Pty, Melbourne, 1954; Dir, Compagnie Belge Transmarine SA and Imperial Stevedoring Co. SA, 1959; Head of Publicity

and Promotions, Associated Newspapers, 1961; 1962: Dir, Associated Newspapers Gp; Dir, Bouverie Investments Ltd; Managing Director: Northcliffe Developments Ltd; Frank Coven Enterprises Ltd, presenting (with John Roberts) plays in London, incl. The Professor, How's the World Treating You? and, with London Traverse Theatre Co., works by Saul Bellow and others, 1964-69; Gen. Man., United Racecourses Ltd (Epsom, Sandown Park, Kempton Park), 1970, Man. Dir 1970, Vice-Chm. 1972. Mem., Variety Club of GB. Mem., Royal Soc. of St George, 1972. *Publications:* various Daily Mail Guides to Television Development in UK. *Recreations:* lawn tennis, swimming, study of varied media (current affairs). *Address:* 22 Cadogan Court, Draycott Avenue, SW3 3BX. *T:* 01-589 8286. *Clubs:* Savage, Saints and Sinners; Hurlingham, Queen's; Devonshire (Eastbourne).

COVENEY, Prof. James; Professor of Modern Languages, University of Bath, since 1969; *b* 4 April 1920; *s* of James and Mary Coveney; *m* 1955, Patricia Yvonne Townsend; two *s*. *Educ:* St Ignatius Coll., Stamford Hill, London; Univ. of Reading (BA, 1st Cl. hons French, 1950); Univ. of Strasbourg (Dr Univ 1953). Clerical Officer, LCC, 1936-40. Served War of 1939-45: private, The Welch Regt, 1940; Commnd in Queen's Own Royal West Kent Regt; served subsequently as Pilot in RAF; demobilized as Flt-Lt, 1946. Univ. of Strasbourg: French Govt Research Scholar, 1950-51; Lecteur d'Anglais, 1951-53; Lectr in French, Univ. of Hull, 1953-58; Asst Dir of Exams (Mod. Langs), Civil Service Commn, 1958-59; UNO Secretariat, New York, 1959-61; NATO Secretariat, 1961-64; Sen. Lectr and Head of Mod. Langs, Univ. of Bath, 1964-68; Jt Dir, Centre for European Ind. Studies, Univ. of Bath, 1969-75; Vis. Prof., University Coll. at Buckingham, 1974-. Member: Nat. Council for Modern Languages, 1972-75 (Vice-72-74); Jt Sec., Assoc. of Univ. Profs of French, 1973-79. Member: British-French Mixed Cultural Commn, 1973-79; Cttee of Management, British Inst. in Paris, 1975-79; Council, Fédération Britannique de l'Alliance Française, 1976-81; Comité de Patronage, Centre Charles Maurras, Aix-en-Provence, 1976. Governor, Bell Educnl Trust, 1972-. FRSA 1974. Corresp. Mem., Académie des Sciences, Agriculture, Arts et Belles Lettres, Aix-en-Provence, 1975. Chevalier de l'Ordre des Palmes Académiques, 1978. *Publications:* La Légende de l'Empereur Constant, 1955; (jtly) Glossary of French and English Management Terms, 1972; International Organization Documents for Translation from French, 1972; (jtly) Le français pour l'ingénieur, 1974; (jtly) Glossary of German and English Management Terms, 1977; (jtly) Glossary of Spanish and English Management Terms, 1978; (jtly) Guide to French Institutions, 1978; articles in British, French and American periodicals. *Address:* 40 Westfield Close, Bath, Avon. *T:* Bath 316670.

COVENTRY, family name of Earl of Coventry.

COVENTRY, 11th Earl of, *cr* 1697; **George William Coventry;** Viscount Deerhurst, 1697; *b* 25 Jan. 1934; *o s* of 10th Earl and Hon. Nesta Donne Philipps, *e d* of 1st Baron Kylsant; *S* father, 1940; *m* 1st, 1955, Marie Farquhar-Medart (marr. diss. 1963); one *s*; 2nd, 1969, Ann (marr. diss. 1975), *d* of F. W. J. Cripps, Bickley, Kent; 3rd, 1980, Valerie Anne Birch, Southport. *Educ:* Eton; RMA, Sandhurst. *Heir:* *s* Viscount Deerhurst, *qv*. *Address:* Earls Croome Court, Earls Croome, Worcester.

See also Earl of Harrowby.

COVENTRY, Bishop of, since 1976; **Rt. Rev. John Gibbs;** *b* 15 March 1917; *s* of late A. E. Gibbs, Bournemouth; *m* 1943, G. Marion, *d* of late W. J. Bishop, Poole, Dorset; one *s* one *d*. *Educ:* Univ. of Bristol; Western Coll., Bristol; Lincoln Theological Coll. BA (Bristol); BD (London). In the ministry of the Congregational Church, 1943-49. Student Christian Movement: Inter-Collegiate Sec., 1949-51; Study Sec. and Editor of Student Movement, 1951-55. Curate of St Luke's, Brislington, Bristol, 1955-57; Chaplain and Head of Divinity Dept, Coll. of St Matthias, Bristol, 1957-64, Vice-Principal, 1962-64; Principal, Keswick Hall Coll. of Education, Norwich, 1964-73; Examining Chaplain to Bishop of Norwich, Hon. Canon of Norwich Cathedral, 1968-73; Bishop Suffragan of Bradwell, 1973-76. Member, Durham Commn on Religious Education, 1967-70; Chairman: C of E Children's Council, 1968-71; C of E Bd of Educn Publications Cttee, 1971-79, Education and Community Cttee, 1974-76. *Recreations:* music, sailing, bird watching. *Address:* Bishop's House, 23 Davenport Road, Coventry, W Midlands CV5 6PW.

COVENTRY, Archdeacon of; *see* Bridges, Ven. P. S. G.

COVENTRY, Provost of; *see* Semper, Very Rev. C. D.

COVENTRY, Rev. John Seton, SJ; Master, St Edmund's House, Cambridge, since 1976; *b* 21 Jan. 1915; *yr s* of late Seton and Annie Coventry, Barton-on-Sea, Hants. *Educ:* Stonyhurst; Campion Hall, Oxford. MA Oxon 1945. Entered Society of Jesus, 1932; ordained, 1947; Prefect of Studies, Beaumont, 1950; Rector, Beaumont, 1956-58; Provincial, English Province of Soc. of Jesus, 1958-64; Lectr in Theology, Heythrop Coll., 1965-76. *Publications:* Morals and Independence, 1946; The Breaking of Bread, 1950; Faith Seeks Understanding, 1951; The Life Story of the Mass, 1959; The Theology of Faith, 1968; Christian Truth, 1975; Faith in Jesus Christ, 1980. *Address:* St Edmund's House, Cambridge CB3 0BN. *T:* Cambridge 350398.

COWAN, Prof. Charles Donald, MA Cantab, PhD London; Professor of Oriental History in the University of London, since 1980; Director, School of Oriental and African Studies, London, since 1976; *b* London, 18 Nov. 1923; *s* of W. C. Cowan and Minnie Ethel (*née* Farrow); *m* 1st, 1945, Mary Evelyn, *d* of Otto Vetter, Perth, WA (marr. diss. 1960); two *d*; 2nd, 1962, Daphne Eleanor, *d* of Walter Rishworth Whittam, Rangoon. *Educ:* Kilburn Grammar Sch.; Peterhouse, Cambridge. Served Royal Navy, 1941-45. Lecturer in History, Raffles Coll., Singapore, 1947-48, and University of Malaya, 1948-50; Lectr in the History of South-East Asia, Sch. of Oriental and African Studies, University of London, 1950-60, Prof., 1961-80. Visiting Prof. of South-East Asian History, Cornell Univ., 1960-61. *Publications:* Nineteenth Century Malaya, 1961; (ed) The Economic Development of South-East Asia, 1964; (ed) The Economic Development of China and Japan, 1964; (with P. L. Burns) Sir Frank Swettenham's Malayan Journals, 1975; (with O. L. Wolters) Southeast Asian History and Historiography, 1976. *Address:* School of Oriental and African Studies, University of London, WC1.

COWAN, Brig. Colin Hunter, DL; Chief Executive, Cumbernauld Development Corporation, since 1970; *b* 16 Oct. 1920; *s* of late Lt-Col S. Hunter Cowan, DSO and Mrs Jean Hunter Cowan; *m* 1949, Elizabeth Williamson, MD; two *s* one *d*. *Educ:* Wellington Coll.; RMA Woolwich; Trinity Coll., Cambridge (MA). MICE. Comd Engineer Regt, 1960-63; Defence Adviser, UK Mission to the UN, 1964-66; Brigadier Engineer Plans, MoD (Army), 1968-70. DL Dunbartonshire, 1973. *Recreations:* music, photography. *Address:* Hillcroft, Dullatur by Glasgow G68 0AW. *T:* Cumbernauld 23242. *Club:* Army and Navy.

COWAN, Maj.-Gen. David Tennant, CB 1945; CBE 1945; DSO 1942, Bar 1944; MC; Indian Army (retired); late RARO; *b* 8 Oct. 1896; *s* of Charles Thomas and Kate Cowan; *m* 1st, 1920, Anne Elliot Dunlop (*d* 1973); one *d* (one *s* killed in action); 2nd, 1973, Frances Elisabeth Newall, *widow* of Lt-Col F. H. A. Stables. *Educ:* Reading; Glasgow Univ. 2nd Lieut Argyll and Sutherland Highlanders, 1915; Capt. 1920; Maj.-Gen. 1942. Served European War, 1914-18 with 2nd Bn, The Argyll and Sutherland Highlanders (despatches, MC); 3rd Afghan War; Waziristan Ops, 1919-20 (despatches) and 1937 (despatches). 6th Gurkha Rifles, 1917-40; Staff Coll., Quetta, 1927-28; Chief Instructor, Indian Military Academy, 1932-34; Comdt 1/6 Gurkha Rifles, 1939-40; DDMT GHQ, India, 1941; Offg DMT, GHQ, India, 1941-42. War of 1939-45 in Burma (despatches, DSO and bar, CBE, CB). GOC 17th Indian Div., 1942-45, and British and Indian Div., British Commonwealth Occupation Force, Japan, 1945-46. Retd 1947, RARO 1948. Commandant, Devon Army Cadet Force, 1948-58. Chm. Approved Sch., Devon, 1951-60; Sec. (part-time) Assoc. of Managers of Approved Schs, 1963-73. DL Devon, 1953-63. Captain and Manager, Indian Army Hockey Team, NZ and Australia Tour, 1926; Hon. Commandant Empire Village, VIth British Empire and Commonwealth Games, Wales, 1958. *Recreations:* games, fishing. *Address:* Ridgecoombe, Penton Grafton, Andover, Hants SP10 0RR. *Club:* Army and Navy.

COWAN, James Robertson, OBE 1974; CEng, FIMinE; Board Member, since 1977, Member for Industrial Relations, since 1980, a Deputy Chairman, since 1982, National Coal Board; *b* 12 Sept. 1919; *s* of John and Jean Cowan; *m* 1945, Harriet Good Forrest; two *d*. *Educ:* Dalziel High Sch., Motherwell; Glasgow Univ. (BSc 1st Cl. Hons). CEng, FIMinE 1971. National Coal Board: colliery manager, 1945; Area Prodn Man., 1956; Area Gen. Man., 1965; Dir, Scottish Area, 1970-80. Chm., Scottish Brick Corp., 1980- (Dir. 1974-); Dir, British Investment Trust, 1978-. Vis. Prof., Strathclyde Univ., 1978. CBIM. *Recreation:* golf. *Address:* Dale House, 31 Muirfield Park, Gullane, Scotland EH31 2DY. *T:* Gullane 843398. *Club:* Caledonian.

COWAN, Lionel David, (Nick Cowan); Director and Secretary, Federation of London Clearing Bank Employers, since 1980; Chairman, West Lambeth Health Authority, since 1982; *b* 18 Dec. 1929; *m* 1953, Pamela Ida, *e d* of Hubert and Winifred Williams, Totton, Hants; one *s* two *d*. *Educ:* Surbiton County Grammar Sch. FBIM 1972; CIPM 1979 (AMIPM 1965). Served Royal Navy, 1945-61: Fleet Air Arm Aircrew (Lieut), 1953; Sen. Instr, RAN, 1958-60. Training Officer, Shoe and Allied Trades Res. Assoc., 1961-62; Perkins Engines Gp, 1962-72: Training Officer, 1962; Employee Development Manager 1965; Gp Employee Resourcing Man. 1966; Industrial Relations Man. 1967; Dir of Personnel and Industrial Relns 1970-72; Dir of Personnel, Philips Electronic and Associated Industries, 1972-78; Gp Personnel Dir, Unigate Ltd, 1978-79. Member: Editorial Panel, Personnel Management, 1967-; BIM Adv. Bd on Industrial Relations, 1970-75; Employment Relns Cttee, IPM, 1971-81; Council, Independent Res. and Assessment Centre, 1975-; Engrg Industry Trng Bd, 1976-79; Employment Appeal Tribunal, 1976-; Editorial Panel, Industrial Relns Law Reports, 1977-; Employment Policy Cttee, CBI, 1978-; Civil Service Arbitration Tribunal, 1979-; CBI Council, 1980-; NEDO Enquiry, Industrial Relns Trng for Managers, 1976, Supply and Demand for Skilled Manpower, 1977. Vice-Pres. (Employee Relations), IPM, 1977-79. Director, Oxford Univ. Business Summer Sch., 1980. Lecturer and writer on personnel management and industrial relations. *Publications:* numerous articles, papers and other pubns on various aspects of personnel management and industrial relations. *Recreations:* the National Health Service, music and opera, chess, golf. *Address:* Pembroke Lodge, 35 Cranes Park, Surbiton, Surrey KT5 8AB. *T:* 01-390 0731. *Club:* Naval and Military.

COWAN, Robert; Chairman, Highlands and Islands Development Board, Inverness, since 1982; *b* 27 July 1932; *s* of Dr John McQueen Cowan and May

Cowan; *m* 1959, Margaret Morton (*née* Dewar); two *d*. *Educ:* Edinburgh Academy; Edinburgh Univ. (MA). Fisons Ltd, 1958-62; Wolsey Ltd, 1962-64; PA Management Consultants Ltd, 1965-82. *Recreation:* sailing. *Address:* The Old Manse, Farr, Invernessshire. *Clubs:* Royal Scottish Automobile; Hong Kong.

COWAN, William Graham, MBE 1943; Chairman and Managing Director, J. H. Carruthers & Co. Ltd, since 1981; *b* 29 April 1919; *s* of William Cowan, WS, Edinburgh, and Dorothy Isobel Horsbrugh; *m* 1960, Karen Wendell Hansen, Crestwood, NY; two *s* one *d*. *Educ:* Edinburgh Academy; Cambridge Univ. (MA). CEng, FIMechE, FSIAD, FRSA. Served 1940-46, Royal Engrs and Gen. Staff, Africa, Italy (Lt-Col). Asst Man. Dir, North British Locomotive Co. Ltd, 1947-50; Man. Dir, J. H. Carruthers and Co. Ltd, 1950-79. Dir, Glasgow Sch. of Art, 1979-82. Mem. Exec. Cttee, Scottish Council (Develt and Industry), 1972-74; Pres., Scottish Engrg Employers' Assoc., 1972. Mem., Design Council, 1974-78 (Chm., Scottish Cttee, 1976-78); Dir, Scottish Transport Group, 1977-80. *Address:* Bryans, Jackton, East Kilbride. *T:* East Kilbride 20012. *Club:* New (Edinburgh).

COWAN, Prof. William Maxwell, FRS 1982; Vice President and Director, Developmental Neurobiology, The Salk Institute, San Diego, since 1981; *b* 27 Sept. 1931; *s* of Adam Cowan and Jessie Sloan Cowan (*née* Maxwell); *m* 1956, Margaret Sherlock; two *s* one *d*. *Educ:* Univ. of the Witwatersrand, S Africa (BSc Hons); Oxford Univ. (MA, DPhil, BM, BCh). University Lecturer in Anatomy, Oxford, 1958-66; Fellow of Pembroke Coll., Oxford, 1958-66; Associate Prof., Univ. of Wisconsin, 1966-68; Professor and Head of Dept of Anatomy, Washington Univ. Sch. of Medicine, 1968-80; Director, Div. of Biological Sciences, Washington Univ., 1975-80; Non-Resident Fellow, Salk Institute for Biological Studies, 1977-80, Professor, 1980-. Foreign Associate, US National Academy of Sciences, 1981. *Publications:* The Use of Axonal Transport for Studies of Neuronal Connectivity, 1975; Aspects of Cellular Neurobiology, 1978; Studies in Developmental Neurobiology, 1981; annual reviews of Neuroscience, Vol. 1 1978, Vols 2, 3, 4, 5, 6, 1979-83. *Recreations:* photography, reading, travel. *Address:* The Salk Institute for Biological Studies, PO Box 85800, San Diego, California 92138, USA. *T:* (714) 453-4100.

COWANS, Harry Lowes; MP (Lab) Newcastle Central, since Nov. 1976; *b* 1932; *m* Margaret; one *s* three *d*. Was a Technician Officer, Signals and Telecommunications Dept, British Rail. Branch Sec., NUR; Mem. Exec. Cttee, Labour Party Northern Region. Member: Gateshead Metropolitan DC (Chm., Housing Cttee); Tyne and Wear Metropolitan CC (Mem. Management, Finance and Transport Cttees). Sec., Northern Group Labour MPs. *Address:* House of Commons, SW1A 0AA; 4 Station Cottages, Elysium Lane, Bensham, Gateshead NE8 2XH.

COWARD, David John, CMG 1965; OBE 1962; Registrar General, Kenya, since 1955; *b* 21 March 1917; *s* of late Robert J. Coward, Exmouth, Devon; *m* 1954, Joan, *d* of late Reginald Frank, Doncaster; three *d*. *Educ:* Exmouth Grammar Sch. and Law Society's Sch. of Law. Admitted a solicitor, 1938. Joined RN as a rating at outbreak of war, 1939; commissioned, 1941; demobilized as Lieut-Comdr (S) RNVR, 1947. ADC to Governor of Trinidad, 1947. Joined Colonial Legal Service, 1948, Asst Registrar Gen., Kenya; Dep. Registrar Gen., 1952; Registrar Gen., Official Receiver and Public Trustee, 1955. Acted as Permanent Sec. for Justice and Constitutional Affairs, 1963-64. Served in Kenya Police Reserve, 1949-63, latterly as Senior Superintendent i/c Nairobi Area. Chm., Working Party on future of Company Secretarial Profession in Kenya; Mem. Accountants' Registration Bd, 1978; Trustee, Nat. Museums of Kenya, 1979. Silver Medal, Internat. Olympic Cttee, 1981. *Recreation:* golf. *Address:* PO Box 40,231, Nairobi, Kenya. *T:* Nairobi 28094. *Clubs:* Naval; Nairobi and Limuru Country (Kenya).

COWARD, John Stephen; barrister-at-law; a Recorder of the Crown Court, since 1980; *b* 15 Nov. 1937; *s* of Frank and Kathleen Coward; *m* 1967, Ann Lesley Pye; four *d*. *Educ:* King James Grammar Sch., Almondbury, Huddersfield; University Coll. London (LLB). Lecturer in Law and Constitutional History, University Coll. London and Police Staff Coll., 1962-64; called to the Bar, Inner Temple, 1964; in practice on Midland and Oxford Circuit, 1964-. *Publications:* contrib. Criminal Law Review. *Recreation:* trying to grow calceolarias and a decent row of peas. *Address:* The Grange, Scaldwell, Northampton NN6 9JP. *T:* Northampton 880255. *Clubs:* Northampton and County (Northampton); Scaldwell (Scaldwell, Northants).

COWARD, Richard Edgar; retired; Director for Library Planning, OCLC Inc., 1980; *b* 1927; *s* of Edgar Frank Coward and Jean (*née* McIntyre); *m* 1949, Audrey Scott Lintern; one *s* two *d*. *Educ:* Richmond Grammar Sch., Surrey. FLA. Dir Gen., Bibliographic Servs Div., British Library, 1975-79. Member: Adv. Cttee on BBC Archives, 1976-79; Library Adv. Council (England), 1976-. *Address:* Gaios, Paxos, Greece; 12 Marylebone Mews, W1M 7LF. *T:* 01-486 7316.

COWBURN, Norman; Managing Director, Britannia Building Society, since 1970; *b* 5 Jan. 1920; *s* of Harold and Edith Cowburn; *m* 1945, Edna Margaret Heatley; two *s* one *d*. *Educ:* Queen Elizabeth's Grammar Sch., Blackburn. FCIS, FBS. Burnley Building Soc., 1936. Served War, 1940-46. Burnley Building Soc., 1946; Leek and Westbourne Building Soc., 1954 (re-named

Britannia Building Soc., Dec. 1975). *Recreations:* golf, gardening. *Address:* Greywoods, Birchall, Leek, Staffs. *T:* Leek 383214.

COWDEROY, Brenda; General Secretary, Girls' Friendly Society, since 1978; *b* 27 June 1925; *o c* of late Frederick Cowderoy and of Evelyn Cowderoy (*née* Land). *Educ:* Surbiton High Sch.; St Hugh's Coll., Oxford (MA). Called to Bar, Gray's Inn, 1949. John Lewis Partnership: Asst Legal Adviser, 1954-56; Head of Legal Dept, 1956-70; Nat. Gen. Sec., YWCA, 1971-77. FBIM. *Recreations:* history of art, golf. *Address:* 26 Rossetti Road, Birchington, Kent CT7 9ER. *Clubs:* Royal Commonwealth Society; Prince's (Sandwich).

COWDRAY, 3rd Viscount, *cr* 1917; **Weetman John Churchill Pearson,** TD; Bt, *cr* 1894; Baron, *cr* 1910; Captain, Sussex Yeomanry; Chairman, S. Pearson & Son Ltd, 1954-77; *b* 27 Feb. 1910 (twin); *s* of 2nd Viscount and Agnes Beryl (*d* 1948), *d* of Lord Edward Spencer Churchill; *S* father, 1933; *m* 1st, 1939, Lady Anne Bridgeman (from whom he obtained a divorce, 1950), *d* of 5th Earl of Bradford; one *s* two *d*; 2nd, 1953, Elizabeth Georgiana Mather, 2nd *d* of Sir Anthony Mather-Jackson, Bt, *qv*; one *s* two *d*. *Educ:* Eton; Christ Church, Oxford. Parliamentary Private Sec. to Under-Sec. of State for Air, 1941-42. *Recreations:* polo, shooting, fishing. *Heir: s* Hon. Michael Orlando Weetman Pearson [*b* 17 June 1944; *m* 1977, Ellen, *yr d* of late Hermann Erhardt]. *Address:* Cowdray Park, Midhurst, West Sussex. *T:* Midhurst 2461; Dunecht, Skene, Aberdeenshire. *T:* Lyne of Skene 244. *Clubs:* Cavalry and Guards, White's.

See also Duke of Atholl, Baron Cranworth.

COWDREY, (Michael) Colin, CBE 1972; Representative: Barclays Bank International; Whitbread & Co. Ltd; Director, Whitbread Fremlins; *b* 24 Dec. 1932; *s* of Ernest Arthur Cowdrey and Kathleen Mary Cowdrey (*née* Taylor); *m* 1956, Penelope Susan Cowdrey (*née* Chiesman); three *s* one *d*. *Educ:* Homefield, Sutton, Surrey; Tonbridge; Brasenose Coll., Oxford. Cricket: 5 years Tonbridge Sch. XI (Capt., 1949-50); Public Schs (Lord's) (Capt. 1950); (3 years) Oxford XI (Capt. 1954); Kent Cap, 1951 (Captain, 1957-71); 117 appearances for England, 1954-75; Capt. 23 times; 11 Overseas Tours; 107 centuries in first class cricket, of which 22 were Test centuries; on retirement in 1975, held record for most runs and most catches in Test Matches. Runner-up Amateur Rackets Title, Queen's Club, 1953 and Doubles, 1965. Member: Council, Britain Australia Soc.; Winston Churchill Memorial Trust. Mem. Court, Skinners' Co. Freeman, City of London, 1962. *Publications:* Cricket Today, 1961; Time for Reflection, 1962; Tackle Cricket This Way, 1969; The Incomparable Game, 1970; MCC: the Autobiography of a Cricketer, 1976. *Recreation:* golf. *Address:* 168 Fenchurch Street, EC3. *T:* 01-283 8989. *Club:* MCC.

COWDRY, Rt. Rev. Roy Walter Frederick; Assistant Bishop of Port Elizabeth, since 1970; Rector of St Cuthbert's, Port Elizabeth, since 1964; *b* 28 April 1915; *s* of Frederick William Thomas Cowdry and Florence Emma (*née* Roberts); *m* 1964, Elizabeth Melene, *d* of Rt Rev. B. W. Peacey; two *s*. *Educ:* King's Coll., London. Deacon, 1941; Priest, 1942. Asst Curate: St Nicholas, Perivale, 1941-44; Christ Church, Ealing, 1944-50; Domestic Chaplain to Archbishop of Cape Town, 1950-58; Asst Bishop of Cape Town, 1958-61; Bishop Suffragan of Cape Town, 1961-64; Asst Bishop of Grahamstown, 1965-70. Chaplain, Cape Town Gaol, 1951-57. Chaplain, OStJ, 1961. *Address:* St Cuthbert's Rectory, 24 Westbourne Road, Port Elizabeth 6001, S Africa. *T:* 332526. *Club:* Port Elizabeth.

COWE, (Robert George) Collin; Fellow and Senior Bursar, Magdalen College, Oxford, 1970-80; *b* 24 Sept. 1917; *s* of Peter and Annie Cowe, Berwick-upon-Tweed; *m* 1943, Gladys May, *d* of William Greenwood Wright and Jessie Wright, Bingley, Yorks; one *d*. *Educ:* The Duke's Sch., Alnwick; The Grammar Sch., Berwick-upon-Tweed; Edinburgh Univ. MA (Hons Classics) 1939; MA Oxon, 1970. Served Royal Regiment of Artillery, Field Branch, 1939-46; Major, RA, 1944-46. National Coal Board, 1947-70; Private Sec. to Chm., 1947-49; Principal Private Sec. to Chm., 1949-52; Sec., East Midlands Div., 1952-55; Staff Dir, North-Eastern Div., 1955-58; Dep.-Sec. to NCB, 1958-59; Sec., 1960-67; Man. Dir, Associated Heat Services Ltd (associate co. of NCB), 1967-69. *Recreations:* riding, swimming. *Address:* Brookside Cottage, Brook End, Chadlington, Oxford OX7 3NF. *T:* Chadlington 373.

COWELL, John Richard; Secretary, Royal Horticultural Society, since 1975; *b* 30 April 1933; *er s* of late Frank Richard Cowell, CMG, PhD, and Lilian Margaret (*née* Palin); *m* 1972, Josephine Suzanne Elizabeth, *d* of I.A.F. Craig, Leppington, Yorks; two *s* one *d*. *Educ:* Westminster Sch.; Trinity Coll., Cambridge (MA). Secretariat: London Chamber of Commerce, 1957-58; Royal Horticultural Soc., 1958-. *Recreations:* gardening, fishing. *Address:* Crowdleham House, Kemsing, Sevenoaks, Kent. *T:* Sevenoaks 61192. *Club:* Athenæum.

COWEN, Alan Biddulph, CMG 1961; OBE 1945; retired as Deputy Chairman of Standards Association of Rhodesia and Nyasaland; *b* 26 Sept. 1896; *m*; two *s*. *Educ:* St John's Coll., Johannesburg, S Africa; Sch. of Mines and Technology. Formerly Chm., Southern Rhodesian Electricity Supply Commission; Mem. of Federal Power Board. CEng; FIEE; F(SA)IEE. *Address:* 68 Forest Glade, Tokai Road, Tokai, 7966, S Africa.

COWEN, Rt. Hon. Sir Zelman, AK 1977; GCMG 1977 (CMG 1968); GCVO 1980; Kt 1976; PC 1981; QC; Provost of Oriel College, Oxford, since 1982; *b* 7 Oct. 1919; *s* of late Bernard and of Sara Cowen; *m* 1945, Anna Wittner; three *s* one *d*. *Educ:* Scotch Coll., Melbourne; Univ. of Melbourne; Oxford Univ. BA 1939, LLB 1941, LLM 1942, Melbourne; BCL, MA 1947, DCL 1968, Oxford. Lieut, RANVR, 1941-45. Called to Bar, Gray's Inn, 1947; Hon. Bencher, 1978; called to Vic (Aust.) Bar, 1951, Queensland Bar, 1971; QC 1972. Victorian Rhodes Schol., 1941; Vinerian Schol., Oxford Univ., 1947. Fellow and Tutor, Oriel Coll., Oxford, 1947-50, Hon. Fellow 1977; Prof. of Public Law and Dean of Faculty of Law, Univ. of Melbourne, 1951-66; Dominion Liaison Officer to Colonial Office (UK), 1951-66; Prof. Emer., Univ. of Melbourne, 1967; Vice-Chancellor and Professor, Univ. of New England, Armidale, NSW, 1967-70; Vice-Chancellor, Qld Univ., 1970-77; Governor-General of Australia, 1977-82. Vis. Professor: Univ. of Chicago, 1949; Harvard Law Sch. and Fletcher Sch. of Law and Diplomacy, 1953-54 and 1963-64; Univ. of Utah, 1954; Univ. of Illinois, 1957-58; Washington Univ., St Louis, 1959; Tagore Law Prof., Univ. of Calcutta, 1975. For. Hon. Mem., Amer. Acad. of Arts and Sciences, 1965. Broadcaster on radio and TV on nat. and internat. affairs; Mem. and Chm., Victorian State Adv. Cttee of Australian Broadcasting Commn (at various times during 1950's and 1960's); Mem., Chief Justice's Law Reform Cttee, 1951-66; President: Asthma Foundn of Victoria, 1963-66; Adult Educn Assoc. of Australia, 1968-70; Aust. Inst. of Urban Studies, 1973-77; Mem., Law Reform Commn, Australia, 1976-77; Chm., Aust. Vice-Chancellors' Cttee, 1977; Pres., ANZAAS, 1981-82. Mem., Club of Rome, 1974-77. Hon. LLD: Hong Kong, 1967; Queensland, 1972; Melbourne, 1973; Western Australia, 1981; Turin, 1981; Hon. DLitt: New England, 1979; Sydney, 1980; Hon. DHL Hebrew Union Coll., Cincinnati, 1980; DUniv.: Newcastle, 1980; Griffith, 1981; FRSA 1971; Hon. FASSA 1977; Hon. FACE 1978; Hon. FRAIA 1978; Hon. FTS 1979; Hon. FRACP 1979; Hon. FAAH 1980; Hon. FASA 1980; Hon. FRACMA 1981; Hon. FRACOG 1981; FICCA 1981; Hon. Fellow: New Coll. Oxford 1978; ANU 1978; University House, ANU, 1978. KStJ (A) 1977. *Publications:* (ed jtly) Dicey's Conflict of Laws, 1949; Australia and the United States: Some Legal Comparisons, 1954; (with P. B. Carter) Essays on the Law of Evidence, 1956; American-Australian Private International Law, 1957; Federal Jurisdiction in Australia, 1959; (with D. M. da Costa) Matrimonial Causes Jurisdiction, 1961; Sir John Latham and other papers, 1965; British Commonwealth of Nations in a Changing World, 1964; Isaac Isaacs, 1967; The Private Man, 1969; Individual Liberty and the Law, 1977; articles and chapters in legal works in UK, US, Canada, Germany, Australia. *Recreations:* swimming, tennis, music, performing and visual arts. *Address:* Oriel College, Oxford. *T:* Oxford 41962. *Clubs:* Hon. Member: Queensland (Brisbane); Union, Tattersall's (Sydney); Athenæum (Melbourne); West Australian (Perth).

COWERN, Raymond Teague, RA 1968 (ARA 1957); RWS; RE; ARCA; RWA; painter, etcher and draughtsman; *b* 12 July 1913; *s* of George Dent Cowern and Elsie Ellen Teague; *m* Margaret Jean Trotman; one *s* two *d*. *Educ:* King Edward's Grammar Sch., Aston, Birmingham. Studied Central Sch. of Art, Birmingham, Royal Coll. of Art, London. Worked with Sakkarah Expedition of the Oriental Institute of Chicago; Rome Scholar in Engraving, 1937-39; commissioned by Pilgrim Trust Scheme for Recording Britain. Served in the Army, Infantry, Camouflage and Intelligence Corps, 1940-46. Principal, Brighton Coll. of Art, 1958-70; Associate Dir, and Dean of Faculty of Art and Design, Brighton Polytechnic, 1970-74. Represented by work at British Museum, V&A, Imperial War Mus. and in public collections Glasgow, Liverpool, Manchester, Birmingham, Oxford, Cambridge, Bristol and museums abroad. *Address:* 41 Irish Street, Whitehaven, Cumbria CA28 7BY. *T:* Whitehaven 61734.

COWEY, Prof. Alan, PhD; Professor of Physiological Psychology, University of Oxford, since 1981; *b* 28 April 1935; *s* of Harry and Mary Cowey; *m* 1959, Patricia Leckonby; three *s*. *Educ:* Bede Grammar Sch., Sunderland; Emmanuel Coll., Cambridge (MA, PhD). Rockefeller Foundn Fellow, Center for Brain Research, Univ. of Rochester, New York, 1961-62; Univ. Demonstrator in Experimental Psychology, Cambridge, 1962-67; Fellow and Coll. Tutor, Emmanuel Coll., Cambridge, 1964-67; Vis. Sen. Fulbright Fellow, Psychology Dept, Harvard Univ., 1967; Sen. Res. Officer, Inst. of Experimental Psychology, Univ. of Oxford, 1967-68; Nuffield Sen. Res. Fellow, Lincoln Coll., Oxford, 1968-81; Henry Head Res. Fellow of Royal Society, 1968-73; Reader in Physiolog. Psychology, Oxford Univ., 1973-81. Member: MRC Neurosciences Grants Cttee, 1974-77 (Chm., 1979-81); MRC Neurosciences Board, 1979-83 (Chm., 1981-83); Mem. Council, MRC, 1981-. Spearman Medal, British Psychological Soc., 1967. *Publications:* numerous articles in psychological and physiological jls. *Recreations:* squash, swimming, reading. *Address:* Department of Experimental Psychology, South Parks Road, Oxford OX1 3UD. *T:* Oxford 512251.

COWEY, Brig. Bernard Turing Vionnée, DSO 1945; OBE 1976; DL; *b* 20 Nov. 1911; *s* of late Lt-Col R. V. Cowey, DSO, RAMC and late Mrs B. A. Cowey (*née* Blancke); *m* 1947, Margaret Heath Dean (*née* Godwin). *Educ:* Wellington; RMC Sandhurst. Commnd The Welch Regt, 1931; served War of 1939-45: N Africa, 1939-41 (despatches 1941); psc 1941; India, 1942-43; Burma, 1944-45; CO 2 York and Lancs, 1944; CO 2 Welch, 1945-47; Co. Comdr RMA Sandhurst, 1947-49; Chief Instructor, Staff Coll., Quetta, 1952-53; CO 1 Welch, 1953-56; Comd (Brig.) 9 Indep. Armd Bde Gp TA, 1956 and 148 Inf. Bde Gp TA, 1956-58; Inspector of Intelligence, 1961-63; retd 1963. Sec., Notts T&AFA, 1965-67; TAVR Council (formerly TA

Council): Dep. Sec., 1967-72; Sec., 1973-75. Regional Organiser, Army Benevolent Fund, 1975-; Regional Sec., British Field Sports Soc., 1976-. DL Notts, 1973. *Recreations:* Rugby football (played for Wales, Barbarians and Army, 1934-35; Chm., Army Rugby Union Referees Soc., 1963-73); Arab horses (Hon. Show Dir, Arab Horse Show, 1968-81). *Address:* Trent Hills Farm, Flintham, Newark, Notts. *T:* 063-68 5274. *Clubs:* Army and Navy, British Sportsman's.

COWGILL, Bryan; Managing Director, Thames Television, since 1977; Chairman, Thames Television International, since 1982; *b* 27 May 1927; *m* 1966, Jennifer E. Baker; two *s. Educ:* Clitheroe Grammar School. Marine, subseq. Lieut, 3rd Royal Marine Commando Bde, SE Asia, 1943-47. Copy boy, then reporter, then feature writer with Lancashire Evening Post and Preston Guardian Group, 1942-50; edited local newspaper, Clitheroe, 1950-55; joined BBC TV as Outside Broadcasts prodn asst, 1955; produced Sportsview and Grandstand, 1957-63; Head of BBC Sport, 1963; Head of TV Outside Broadcasts Group, 1972; Controller, BBC1, 1974-77; Dir, News and Current Affairs, BBC, 1977. *Recreation:* golf. *Address:* Thames Television House, 306-316 Euston Road, NW1 3BB. *T:* 01-387 9494.

COWIE, Hon. Lord; William Lorn Kerr Cowie; a Senator of the College of Justice in Scotland, since 1977; *b* 1 June 1926; *s* of late Charles Rennie Cowie, MBE and Norah Slimmon Kerr; *m* 1958, Camilla Henrietta Grizel Hoyle; two *s* two *d. Educ:* Fettes Coll.; Clare Coll., Cambridge; Glasgow Univ. Sub-Lieut RNVR, 1944-47; Cambridge, 1947-49; Glasgow Univ., 1949-51; Mem., Faculty of Advocates, 1952; QC (Scotland) 1967. *Address:* 20 Blacket Place, Edinburgh EH9 1RL. *T:* 031-667 8238. *Club:* New (Edinburgh).

COWIE, Mervyn Hugh, CBE 1960; ED 1954; FCA, FZS; *b* 13 April 1909; *s* of Capt. Herbert Hugh Cowie, JP; *m* 1st, 1934, Erica Mary Beaty (*d* 1956); two *s* one *d* ; 2nd, 1957, Valori Hare Duke; one *s* one *d. Educ:* Brighton; Brasenose Coll., Oxford. Hon. Game Warden, 1932-; Mem. Nairobi District Council, 1932-36; KAR, Reserve of Officers, 1932-38 (3rd and 5th Battalions); Kenya Regt, 1939; served War of 1939-45; Abyssinia, Middle East, Madagascar (retd Lieut-Col). MLC Kenya, 1951-60; Dir of Manpower, Mau-Mau Emergency, 1953-56. Founder and Dir, Royal National Parks of Kenya, 1946-66. Vice-Pres. E African Tourist Travel Assoc., 1950-65; Mem. Nat. Parks Commn, Internat. Union for Conservation of Nature, 1959-66; Hon. Trustee, Uganda Nat. Parks, 1950-; Vice-Pres., Fauna Preservation Soc., London; Trustee, East African Wild Life Soc.; Financial Dir, African Med. and Res. Foundn (Flying Doctor Services), 1972-79. TV and Radio (BBC Natural History Section). Editor, Royal Nat. Parks of Kenya Annual Reports, 1946-65. Lectures (tours USA and Britain). Gold Medal, San Diego Zool Soc., 1972. Order of the Golden Ark, Netherlands, 1975. *Publications:* Fly Vulture, 1961; I Walk with Lions (USA), 1964; African Lion, 1965. Contributor to International Journals and Conferences. *Recreations:* flying and wild life conservation. *Address:* PO Box 15549, Mbagathi, Nairobi, Kenya. *Clubs:* Shikar; Explorer's (New York); Muthaiga Country (Nairobi).

COWIE, William Lorn Kerr; *see* Cowie, Hon. Lord.

COWLES, Virginia, OBE 1947; writer; *b* USA, 24 Aug. 1910; *d* of Florence Wolcott Jaquith and Edward Spencer Cowles; *m* 1945, Aidan M. Crawley, *qv* ; two *s* one *d. Educ:* privately. Newspaper correspondent, 1937-41 and 1943-45; Special Asst to the American Ambassador, American Embassy, London, 1942-43. *Publications:* Looking for Trouble, 1941; How America is Governed, 1944; No Cause for Alarm, 1949; Winston Churchill: The Era and the Man, 1953; Edward VII and His Circle, 1956; The Phantom Major, 1958; The Great Swindle, 1960; The Kaiser, 1963; 1913: The Defiant Swan Song, 1967; The Russian Dagger, 1969; The Romanovs, 1971; The Rothschilds, 1973; The Last Tsar and Tsarina, 1977; The Astors, 1979. *Recreation:* politics. *Address:* 19 Chester Square, SW1. *T:* 01-730 3030.

COWLEY, 7th Earl *cr* 1857; **Garret Graham Wellesley;** Baron Cowley, 1828; Viscount Dangan, 1857; Group Vice President and Director, International Investment Management Service, Bank of America NT&SA, London, since 1980; Director: Bank of America International Ltd, London, since 1978; BankAmerica Trust Co. (Hong Kong) Ltd, since 1980; Bank of America Banking & Trust Co. (Gibraltar), since 1981; Bank of America Trust Co. (Jersey), since 1982; Bank of America Banking & Trust Co. (Nassau), since 1982; Bank of America Banking & Trust Co. (Cayman), since 1982; *b* 30 July 1934; 3rd *s* of 4th Earl Cowley (*d* 1962) and of Mary (Elsie May), Countess Cowley; *S* nephew, 1975; *m* 1st, 1961, Elizabeth Suzanne Lennon (marr. diss. 1966), S Carolina; one *s* one *d* ; 2nd, 1968, Isabelle O'Bready, Quebec, Canada; 3rd, 1981, Paige Deming, Reno, Nevada. *Educ:* Univ. of S California (BSc Finance 1957); Harvard Univ. (MBA 1962). Investment Research Analyst: Wells Fargo Bank, San Francisco, 1962-64; Dodge & Cox, San Francisco, 1964-66; Asst Head, Investment Research Dept, Wells Fargo Bank, 1966-67; Vice-Pres., Investment Counsel, Thorndike, Doran, Paine & Lewis, Los Angeles, 1967-69; Sen. Vice-Pres., Exec. Cttee Mem., Securities, Real Estate and Company Acquisition Advisor, Shareholders Capital Corp., Los Angeles, 1969-74; Vice-Pres., and Sen. Investment Manager, Trust Dept, Bank of America, San Francisco, 1974-78. Served US Army Counter Intelligence Corps, primarily in France, 1957-60. *Heir:* *s* Viscount Dangan, *qv.* *Address:* 6 Eldon Road, W8. *T:* 01-937 8647. *Clubs:* Brooks's; Harvard (San Francisco).

COWLEY, Rev. Canon Colin Patrick; Rector of Wonston, Winchester, 1955-71; Canon of Winchester, 1950-55, Hon. Canon, 1955; Canon Emeritus, 1971; *b* 3 Aug. 1902; *er s* of Rev. H. G. B. Cowley; *m* 1930, Dorothea Minna Pott (*d* 1980); three *d. Educ:* Winchester; Hertford Coll., Oxford. Curate at St Mary's, Bridport, 1926-28; Curate at St Mary Abbots, Kensington, 1928-35; Rector of Shenfield, Essex, 1935-50. Chaplain to the Forces, 1940-45. *Recreation:* coping with old age. *Address:* Cheriton Lodge, 42 Cheriton Road, Winchester, Hants.

COWLEY, Denis Martin; AE 1945; QC 1965; a Recorder of the Crown Court, since 1974; Senior Judge, Sovereign Base Areas, Cyprus, since 1982 (Deputy Senior Judge, 1969-82); *b* 30 Jan. 1919; *s* of late Sir William Percy Cowley, CBE; *m* 1940, Margaret Hazel, *d* of Hugo Teare, Ramsey, Isle of Man; one *s* two *d. Educ:* Radley Coll.; Exeter Coll., Oxford (MA (Hons Jurisprudence)). Served RAFVR, 1939-45. Called to Bar, Inner Temple, 1946; Bencher, 1972. Midland and Oxford Circuit. *Recreations:* shooting, sailing. *Address:* 2a Huntingdon Drive, The Park, Nottingham. *T:* 42948; Ellan Vannin, The Quay, Castletown, Isle of Man. *T:* Castletown 3532; Francis Taylor Buildings, Temple, EC4. *T:* 01-353 9942. *Club:* United Oxford & Cambridge University.

COWLEY, Maj.-Gen. John Cain, CB 1971; Paymaster-in-Chief and Inspector of Army Pay Services, Ministry of Defence, 1967-72, retired; with de Zoete and Bevan, Stockbrokers, 1972-79; *b* 17 July 1918; *er s* of late Philip Richard and Eleanor Cowley, Ballaquane, Peel, Isle of Man; *m* 1948, Eileen Rosemary, CBE 1982, *d* of late George Percival Stewart, Aigburth, Liverpool; three *s. Educ:* Douglas School, Isle of Man. War of 1939-45: commissioned, RAPC, 1940; served: Palestine, Western Desert, Italy, France, Belgium, Holland, Germany. Dep. Asst Adj.-Gen., Middle East, 1949-51; GSOI, with Permanent Under Sec., War Office, 1952-54; West African Frontier Force, 1956-59; Dep. Paymaster-in-Chief: War Office, 1960-63; BAOR, 1963-65; Chief Paymaster, Eastern Command, 1965-67. Capt. 1946, Maj. 1953, Lt-Col 1955, Col. 1960, Brig. 1963, Maj.-Gen. 1967; psc, 1948; jssc, 1955; Administrative Staff Coll., 1960. Col Comdt, RAPC, 1974-79. *Recreations:* shooting, fishing, ornithology. *Address:* The Old Post Office, Nuthurst, Horsham, West Sussex. *T:* Lower Beeding 266. *Clubs:* Army and Navy, Flyfishers'.

COWLEY, Lt.-Gen. Sir John Guise, GC (AM 1935); KBE 1958 (CBE 1946; OBE 1943); CB 1954; late RE; Chairman, Polamco Ltd, since 1976; *b* 20 Aug. 1905; *s* of Rev. Henry Guise Beatson Cowley, Fourgates, Dorchester, Dorset; *m* 1941, Irene Sybil, *d* of Percy Dreuille Millen, Berkhamsted, Herts; one *s* three *d. Educ:* Wellington Coll.; RMA Woolwich. 2nd Lieut RE 1925; Capt. 1936; Major 1940; Lieut-Col 1941; Brig. 1943; Maj.-Gen. 1953; Lieut-Gen. 1957. Served War of 1939-45, Middle East, Italy, and North-West Europe (despatches four times, OBE). Chief of Staff, HQ, Eastern Command, 1953-56; Vice-QMG, 1956-57; Controller of Munitions, Ministry of Supply, 1957-60; Master-Gen. of the Ordnance, War Office, 1960-62; retd, 1962. Col Commandant: Royal Pioneer Corps, 1961-67; Royal Engineers, 1961-70. Chairman: Bowmaker Ltd, 1962-71; Wilverley Securities Ltd, 1970-73; Keith and Henderson Ltd, 1973-76; Director: British Oxygen Ltd, 1962-76; Alastair Watson Ltd, 1962-70; C. T. Bowring and Co. Ltd, 1969-71. Governor, Wellington Coll., 1960-76, Vice-Pres. and Chm. of Governors, 1969-76, Pres. OW Soc. 1979-; Chairman of Governors: Eagle House Sch., 1968-76; Bigshotte Sch., 1968-76; Brockenhurst Sixth Form Coll., 1977-. Knight Comdr Order of Orange Nassau (Netherlands). FRSA. *Recreations:* golf, bridge. *Address:* Whitemoor, Sandy Down, Boldre, Lymington, Hants. *T:* Lymington 23369. *Club:* Army and Navy.

COWLEY, Dr John Maxwell, FRS 1979; FAA; Galvin Professor of Physics, Arizona State University, USA, since 1970; *b* 18 Feb. 1923; *s* of Alfred E. and Doris R. Cowley; *m* 1951, Roberta J. (*née* Beckett); two *d. Educ:* Univ. of Adelaide (BSc 1942, MSc 1945, DSc 1957); MIT (PhD 1949). FAA 1961. Res. Officer, CSIRO, Australia, 1945-62; Prof. of Physics, Univ. of Melbourne, 1962-70. Mem. Exec. Cttee, Internat. Union of Crystallography, 1963-69. *Publications:* Diffraction Physics, 1975; approx. 200 articles in learned jls. *Recreations:* painting, music. *Address:* 1718 E Gaylon Drive, Tempe, Ariz 85282, USA. *T:* (602) 966-0071.

COWLEY, Kenneth Martin, CMG 1963; OBE 1956; *b* 15 May 1912; *s* of late Robert Martin Cowley, OBE, and late Mabel Priscilla Cowley (*née* Lee); *m* 1948, Barbara (*née* Tannahill); one *s* (and one step *s*). *Educ:* Merchant Taylors' Sch., Crosby; Exeter Coll., Oxford. District Officer, Kenya, 1935-44; Asst Sec., 1944-46; District Comr, 1946-49; Actg Native Courts Officer, 1949-53; Sec. for African Affairs, 1953-56; Provincial Commissioner, Southern Province, Kenya, 1956-63 (despatches, 1957); Sec., Kenya Regional Boundaries and Constituencies Commns, 1962; Sen. Administrative Manager, Express Transport Co. Ltd, Kenya, 1963-70. Sec., Overseas Service Pensioners' Assoc., 1971-79. *Recreation:* natural history. *Address:* Grasmere, 38 Wellington Avenue, Fleet, Hants. *T:* Fleet 5990. *Club:* Nairobi (Kenya).

COWLEY, Prof. Roger Arthur, FRS 1978; FRSE 1972; Professor of Physics, University of Edinburgh, since 1970; *b* 24 Feb. 1939; *s* of Cecil A. Cowley and Mildred S. Cowley; *m* 1964, Sheila J. Wells; one *s* one *d. Educ:* Brentwood Sch., Essex; Cambridge Univ. (MA,PhD). Fellow, Trinity Hall, Cambridge, 1962-64; Research Officer, Atomic Energy of Canada Ltd, 1964-70. Max Born Medal, 1973. *Address:* 54A St Albans Road, Edinburgh EH9 2LX. *T:* 031-667 7630.

COWLING, Richard John, ARICS; Deputy Chief Valuer, Inland Revenue Valuation Office, 1972-74; *b* 2 Feb. 1911; *s* of Sydney George and Madge Prentice Cowling, late of East Grinstead; *m* 1936, Doris Rosa, *o d* of Albert James Puttock, Guildford; one *s. Educ:* Skinners' Company's Sch. Articles and private practice as a surveyor, 1928-35; War Office Lands Branch, 1936; Inland Revenue Valuation Office, 1937. TA Commission, Green Howards, 1942. *Recreations:* golf, bridge, sailing. *Address:* 18 Gateways, Epsom Road, Guildford, Surrey GU1 2LF. *T:* Guildford 73473.

COWLING, Thomas George, FRS 1947; Professor of Applied Mathematics, Leeds University, 1948-70, now Professor Emeritus; *b* 17 June 1906; *s* of George and Edith Eliza Cowling; *m* 1935, Doris Moffatt; one *s* two *d. Educ:* Sir George Monoux Sch., Walthamstow; Oxford Univ. Teacher of mathematics, Imperial Coll. of Science, University Coll., Swansea, University Coll., Dundee, Manchester Univ., and at University Coll., Bangor (Prof. of Mathematics, 1945-48). Gold Medallist, Royal Astronomical Soc., 1956, Pres., 1965-67. Hon. Fellow, Brasenose Coll., Oxford, 1966. Halley Lectr, Oxford Univ., 1969. *Publications:* (with S. Chapman) The Mathematical Theory of Non-Uniform Gases, 1939; Molecules in Motion, 1950; Magneto-hydrodynamics, 1957, 2nd edn 1976; also a number of papers, chiefly astronomical and gas-theoretic. *Recreation:* gardening. *Address:* 19 Hollin Gardens, Leeds LS16 5NL. *T:* 785342.

COWPER, Brig. Anthony William, CBE 1964 (OBE 1945); company director; *b* 10 May 1913; *s* of Walter Taylor Cowper, solicitor, Southgate, London, and West Burton, Yorks; *m* 1949, Margaret Mary, *d* of Clarence W. Fry, Upminster, Essex; no *c. Educ:* Merchant Taylors' Sch. Joined Christie's, Fine Art Auctioneers, 1932. Commissioned from TA (HAC) into West Yorks Regt, Nov. 1939; War Service in India, Burma, Ceylon and Singapore, 1940-45 (OBE). Granted regular commn, 1947; served overseas almost continuously (mainly Far East) in Regtl and Staff appts (despatches, Malayan Emergency, 1954); Col 1961; Brig. 1965; Defence Adviser to British High Comr in Malaysia, 1967; retd 1969. Freeman of City of London. *Recreations:* fly fishing, small boat sailing, antiques, Far East affairs. *Address:* 97 Kingsway Gardens, 38 Kings Park Road, Perth, West Australia 6005. *T:* 3213373.

COWPER, Sir Norman (Lethbridge), Kt 1967; CBE 1958; *b* 15 Sept. 1896; *yr s* of Cecil Spencer de Grey Cowper; *m* 1925, Dorothea Huntly, *d* of Hugh McCrae; three *d. Educ:* Sydney Grammar Sch.; University of Sydney (BA, LLB). Served War of 1939-45, 2nd AIF, Lt-Col. Solicitor, Supreme Court of NSW, 1923. Partner, Allen, Allen & Hemsley, 1924-70. Dir, Australian Inst. of Polit. Science, 1932-69; Mem. Council, Australian National Univ., 1955-74; Mem. Board of Trustees, Sydney Grammar Sch., 1935-75 (Chm., 1951-75); Chm., Council on New Guinea Affairs, 1965. *Publications:* occasional articles: Australian Quarterly, Australian Outlook, Australian Dictionary of Biography. *Recreations:* reading, gardening. *Address:* Wivenhoe, Millewa Avenue, Wahroonga, Sydney, Australia. *T:* 48 2336. *Club:* Australian (Sydney).

COWPERTHWAITE, David Jarvis; Under-Secretary, Scottish Home and Health Department, 1974-81, retired; *b* 14 Sept. 1921; *s* of J. J. Cowperthwaite and Mrs J. W. B. Cowperthwaite (*née* Jarvis); *m* 1944, Patricia Stockdale; two *d. Educ:* Edinburgh Academy; Exeter Coll., Oxford (MA). Nigerian Admin. Service, 1942-48; joined Home Civil Service (Scottish Home Dept), 1948. *Recreations:* cricket, golf. *Address:* 69 Northumberland Street, Edinburgh EH3 6JG. *T:* 031-557 0215.
See also Sir J. J. Cowperthwaite.

COWPERTHWAITE, Sir John James, KBE 1968 (OBE 1960); CMG 1964; International Adviser to Jardine Fleming & Co. Ltd, Hong Kong, 1972-81; Financial Secretary, Hong Kong, 1961-71; *b* 25 April 1915; *s* of late John James Cowperthwaite and Jessie Wemyss Barron Jarvis Cowperthwaite; *m* 1941, Sheila Mary, *d* of Alexander Thomson, Aberdeen; one *s. Educ:* Merchiston Castle Sch.; St Andrews Univ; Christ's Coll., Cambridge. Entered Colonial Administrative Service, Hong Kong, 1941; seconded to Sierra Leone, 1942-45. *Address:* 25 South Street, St Andrews, Fife. *T:* St Andrews 74759. *Clubs:* Royal Hong Kong Jockey, Royal Hong Kong Golf; Royal and Ancient.
See also D. J. Cowperthwaite.

COWTAN, Maj.-Gen. Frank Willoughby John, CBE 1970 (MBE 1947); MC 1942 and Bar, 1945; *b* 10 Feb. 1920; *s* of late Air Vice-Marshal F. C. Cowtan, CB, CBE, KHS and late Mrs N. A. Cowtan (*née* Kennedy); *m* 1949, Rose Isabel Cope; one *s* one *d. Educ:* Wellington Coll.; RMA Woolwich. 2nd Lieut Royal Engineers, 1939; served War of 1939-45, BEF, N Africa, Italy, NW Europe (Captain); Palestine, Kenya, Middle East, 1945-50 (Major); psc 1951; Middle East, UK, BAOR, 1952-58; Liaison Officer to US Corps of Engrs, USA, 1958-60 (Bt Lt-Col); CO 131 Parachute Engr Regt, 1960-62; CO Victory Coll., RMA Sandhurst, 1962-65 (Lt-Col); Comd 11 Engr Bde, BAOR, 1965-67 (Brig.); ndc (Canada) 1967-68; Dir of Quartering (Army), 1968-70; Dep. QMG, MoD(AD), 1970-71; Comdt, RMCS, 1971-75, retired. Col Comdt RE, 1977-82. *Recreations:* golf, shooting, wildfowling, sailing, travel, languages. *Address:* Rectory Cottage, Coleshill, Swindon, Wilts. *Club:* Army and Navy.

COX; see Roxbee Cox.

COX, Alan Seaforth; Clerk to the Grocers' Company, 1965-81; Secretary, Grocers' Trust Company Ltd, 1968-81; *b* 15 Oct. 1915; *m* 1st, 1944, Jean Heriot-Maitland (marr. diss. 1952); one *s*; 2nd, 1954, Mary Thornton; three *s* one *d.* Served War: London Scottish and Gold Coast Regt, 1939-45; Staff Officer, WO, 1945-46. Farming and banking, Argentine (Patagonia), 1947-52; joined Grocers' Co., 1954. Sec., Governing Body of Oundle Sch., 1965-81. Hon. Mem. Ct, Grocers' Co., 1981-. *Recreations:* bridge, cribbage, dining and wining. *Address:* 33 Murray Road, Wimbledon Common, SW19 4PD. *T:* 01-946 4718.

COX, Albert Edward; His Honour Judge Edward Cox; a Circuit Judge, since 1977; *b* 26 Sept. 1916; *s* of Frederick Stringer Cox; *m* 1962, Alwyn Winifred Cox, JP. Admitted Solicitor, 1938; Principal Partner, Claude Hornby & Cox, 1946-76. A Recorder of the Crown Court, 1972-77. President: London Criminal Courts Solicitors' Assoc., 1967-68; British Acad. of Forensic Science, 1977-78; Mem., Parole Board, 1971-75; Chm., London (Metropolis) Licensing Planning Cttee, 1979. *Address:* 38 Carlton Hill, NW8 0JY. *Club:* Hurlingham.

COX, Anthony; see Cox, J. A.

COX, Anthony Wakefield, CBE 1972; FRIBA, AADip; Consultant, Architects' Co-Partnership, since 1980; *b* 18 July 1915; *s* of late William Edward Cox, CBE, and of Elsie Gertrude Wakefield; *m* 1943, Susan Babington Smith, ARIBA, AADip; two *d. Educ:* Mill Hill Sch.; Architectural Association Sch. of Architecture, London. RIBA Journal, 1938-39; Jt Editor of Focus, 1938-39; founder partner, Architects' Co-Partnership, 1939; Sir Alexander Gibb & Partners, ordnance factories and hostels, 1940-42. Served War: Royal Engineers, Western Europe and India, 1943-46; Hertfordshire CC Schools, 1946-47; reabsorbed in Architects' Co-Partnership, 1947; part-time teaching AA Sch. of Architecture, 1948-54; Mem. Council: Architectural Assoc., 1956-64 (Pres. 1962-63); RIBA, 1967-72; Member: Bd of Educn, RIBA, 1967-73; Royal Fine Art Commn, 1970-; Bd, Property Services Agency, 1979-81, Adv. Bd, 1981-. *Works include* Depts of: Chemistry at Univ. of Leicester and University Coll., London; Chemistry and Biochemistry at Imperial Coll. of Science and Technology; buildings for: Inst. of Psychiatry, London; the Maudsley Hosp., London. *Publication:* (jtly) Design for Health Care, 1981. *Recreations:* reading, listening, looking, making. *Address:* 5 Bacon's Lane, Highgate, N6. *T:* 01-340 2543.

COX, Prof. Archibald; Carl M. Loeb University Professor, Harvard University, since 1976; Chairman, Governing Board, Common Cause, since 1980; *b* 17 May 1912; *s* of Archibald Cox and Frances Bruen (*née* Perkins); *m* 1937, Phyllis Ames; one *s* two *d. Educ:* St Paul's Sch., Concord; Harvard Univ. AB 1934, LLB 1937. Admitted to Mass Bar, 1937. Gen. practice with Ropes, Gray, Best, Coolidge & Rugg, 1938-41; Office of Solicitor-Gen., US Dept of Justice, 1941-43; Assoc. Solicitor, Dept of Labor, 1943-45; Lectr on Law, Harvard, 1945-46, Prof. of Law, 1946-61; Solicitor-Gen., US Dept of Justice, 1961-65; Williston Prof. of Law, Harvard Law Sch., 1965-76. Pitt Prof., Univ. of Cambridge, 1974-75. Co-Chm., Constrn Industry Stablizn Commn, 1951-52; Chm., Wage Stablzn Bd, 1952; Mem. Bd Overseers, Harvard, 1962-65. Special Watergate Prosecutor, 1973. Hon. LLD: Loyola, 1964; Cincinnati, 1967; Rutgers, Amherst, Denver, 1974; Harvard, 1975; Michigan, 1976; Holyoke, 1977; Northeastern, 1978; Clark, 1980; Hon. LHD: Hahnemann Med. Coll., 1980; Univ. of Mass, 1981. *Publications:* Cases on Labor Law, 9th edn 1981; (jtly) Law and National Law or Policy, 1960; Civil Rights, the Constitution and the Courts, 1967; The Warren Court, 1968; The Role of the Supreme Court in American Government, 1976; Freedom of Expression, 1981; miscellaneous articles. *Address:* PO Box 393, Wayland, Mass 01778, USA; (office) Harvard Law School, Cambridge, Mass 02138. *T:* 1-617-495-3133. *Clubs:* Somerset (Boston, Mass); Century Association (New York).

COX, Arthur George Ernest S.; see Stewart Cox.

COX, Brian Robert Escott, QC 1974; a Recorder of the Crown Court, since 1972; *b* 30 Sept. 1932; *yr s* of late George Robert Escott Cox; *m* 1st, 1956; one *s* two *d*; 2nd, 1969, Noelle Gilormini; one *s* one *d. Educ:* Rugby Sch.; Oriel Coll., Oxford (BA, MA). Called to Bar, Lincoln's Inn, 1954. Midland and Oxford Circuit. *Address:* 1 King's Bench Walk, Temple, EC4. *T:* 01-353 8436.

COX, Prof. Charles Brian; John Edward Taylor Professor of English Literature, University of Manchester, since 1976; *b* 5 Sept. 1928; *s* of Hedley E. Cox and late Rose Thompson; *m* 1954, Jean Willmer; one *s* two *d. Educ:* Wintringham Sec. Sch.; Pembroke Coll., Cambridge (MA, MLitt). Lectr, Univ. of Hull, 1954-66; Prof. of English Lit., Univ. of Manchester, 1966-76. Vis. Associate Prof., Univ. of Calif, Berkeley, 1964-65; Brown Fellow, Univ. of the South, Sewanee, Tennessee, 1980. Co-editor: Critical Qly, 1959-; Black Papers on Education, 1969. *Publications:* The Free Spirit, 1963; (ed, with A. E. Dyson) Modern Poetry, 1963; (ed, with A. E. Dyson) Practical Criticism of Poetry, 1965; Joseph Conrad: the modern imagination, 1974; Every Common Sight (poems), 1981. *Recreations:* squash, walking. *Address:* 20 Park Gates Drive, Cheadle Hulme, Stockport SK8 7DF. *T:* 061-485 2162. *Club:* Lansdowne.

COX, Prof. David Roxbee, PhD; FRS 1973; Professor of Statistics, Imperial College of Science and Technology, since 1966; Head of Department of Mathematics, 1970-74; *b* 15 July 1924; *s* of S. R. Cox, Handsworth, Birmingham; *m* 1948, Joyce (*née* Drummond), Keighley, Yorks; three *s* one *d. Educ:* Handsworth Grammar Sch., Birmingham; St John's Coll., Cambridge (MA). PhD Leeds, 1949. Posts at Royal Aircraft Establishment, 1944-46; Wool Industries Research Assoc., 1946-50; Statistical Laboratory, Cambridge, 1950-55; Visiting Prof., University of N Carolina, 1955-56; Reader in Statistics, Birkbeck College, 1956-60, Professor of Statistics, 1961-66. President: Bernoulli Soc., 1979-81; Royal Statistical Soc., 1980-82. For. Hon. Mem., Amer. Acad. of Arts and Sciences, 1974. Editor of Biometrika, 1966-. *Publications:* Statistical Methods in the Textile Industry, 1949 (jt author); Planning of Experiments, 1958; (jtly) Queues, 1961; Renewal Theory, 1962; (jtly) Theory of Stochastic Processes, 1965; (jtly) Statistical Analysis of Series of Events, 1966; Analysis of Binary Data, 1970; (jtly) Theoretical Statistics, 1974; (jtly) Problems and Solutions in Theoretical Statistics, 1978; (jtly) Point Processes, 1980; (jtly) Applied Statistics, 1981; papers in Jl of Royal Statistical Society, Biometrika, etc. *Address:* Imperial College, SW7. *T:* 01-589 5111.

COX, Dennis George; Under-Secretary (Industrial Relations), Department of Employment, 1971-74; a Deputy Chairman, Central Arbitration Committee, since 1977; *b* 23 Feb. 1914; *s* of George and Amelia Cox; *m* 1938, Victoria Barraclough; two *s*. *Educ:* University College Sch.; Queens' Coll., Cambridge. Royal Navy, 1942-45; served with Netherlands and Norwegian navies, Lieut RNVR. Entered Min. of Labour, 1936; Asst Sec. 1966; Regional Controller, SW Region. *Recreations:* gardening, fishing. *Address:* 22 Ashley Court, Morpeth Terrace, SW1; Church Cottage, Laughton, Lewes, East Sussex. *T:* Ripe 382. *Club:* Army and Navy.

COX, Edward; see Cox, A. E.

COX, Sir (Ernest) Gordon, KBE 1964; TD; FRS 1954; FRSC; FInstP; DSc; Secretary of the Agricultural Research Council, 1960-71; *b* 24 April 1906; *s* of Ernest Henry Cox and Rosina Ring; *m* 1st, 1929, Lucie Grace Baker (*d* 1962); one *s* one *d*; 2nd, 1968, Prof. Mary Rosaleen Truter, DSc, *d* of Dr D. N. Jackman. *Educ:* City of Bath Boys' Sch.; University of Bristol. Research Asst, Davy-Faraday Laboratory, Royal Institution, 1927; Chemistry Dept, Univ. of Birmingham, 1929-41 (Reader in Chemical Crystallography, 1940); Prof. of Inorganic and Structural Chemistry, University of Leeds, 1945-60; commissioned in Territorial Army, 1936; special scientific duties, War Office, 1942-44; attached to HQ staff of 21 Army Group, France and Germany, as Technical Staff Officer, Grade I, 1944-45. Vice-Pres., Institute of Physics, 1950-53; Mem. Agric. Research Council, 1957-60. Hon. DSc: Newcastle, 1964; Birmingham, 1964; Bath, 1973; East Anglia, 1973; Hon. LLD Bristol, 1969; Hon. ARCVS, 1972. *Publications:* numerous scientific papers in jls of various learned societies, chiefly on the crystal structures of chemical compounds. *Recreations:* music, gardening, natural history. *Address:* 117 Hampstead Way, NW11 7JN. *T:* 01-455 2618. *Clubs:* Athenæum, English-Speaking Union, Lansdowne.
See also P. A. Cox.

COX, Sir Geoffrey (Sandford), Kt 1966; CBE 1959 (MBE 1945); Chairman: Upitn Inc., USA, 1975-81; London Broadcasting Co., since 1977; Director, The Observer, since 1981; *b* 7 April 1910; *s* of Sandford Cox, Wellington, NZ, and Mary Cox (*née* MacGregor); *m* 1935, Cecily Barbara Talbot Turner; two *s* two *d*. *Educ:* Southland High Sch., New Zealand; Otago Univ., New Zealand (MA); Rhodes Scholar, 1932-35; Oriel Coll., Oxford (BA). Reporter, Foreign and War Corresp. News Chronicle, 1935-37, Daily Express, 1937-40. Enlisted New Zealand Army, 1940; commissioned, Dec. 1940; served in 2 New Zealand Div., Greece, Crete, Libya, Italy; Major, Chief Intelligence Officer, Gen. Freyberg's staff (despatches twice). First Sec. and Chargé d'Affaires, NZ Legation, Washington, 1943; NZ Rep., first UNRRA Conf., 1943; Political Corresp., News Chronicle, 1945; Asst Editor, News Chronicle 1954. Regular Contributor, BBC radio and TV, 1945-56; Editor and Chief Exec., Independent Television News, 1956-68; founded News at Ten, 1967; Dep. Chm., Yorkshire Television, 1968-71; Chm., Tyne Tees Television, 1971-74. Trustee, Internat. Broadcast Inst. TV Producers' Guild Award Winner, 1962; Fellow, Royal TV Soc. (Silver Medal, 1963; Gold Medal, 1978); Fellow, British Kinematograph and TV Soc. *Publications:* Defence of Madrid, 1937; The Red Army Moves, 1941; The Road to Trieste, 1946; The Race for Trieste, 1977. *Recreations:* fishing, golf. *Club:* Garrick.

COX, Sir (George) Trenchard; see Cox, Sir Trenchard.

COX, Sir Gordon; see Cox, Sir E. G.

COX, Harry Bernard, CBE 1956; Deputy Chairman, Thos Wyatt Nigeria Ltd, since 1967; Consultant, Knight, Frank & Rutley (Nigeria), since 1967; *b* 29 Nov. 1906; *e* surv. *s* of Rev. Charles Henry Cox, BSc; *m* 1955, Joan, *e d* of P. Munn, Brighton; one *s* one *d*. *Educ:* Upholland Grammar Sch.; Keble Coll., Oxford. Colonial Administrative Service, Nigeria, 1930; Dir of Commerce and Industries, Nigeria, 1949; Acting Development Sec., Nigeria, 1953-54; Acting Commissioner for Nigeria, 1955; Principal Sec. to the Commissioner for Nigeria in the United Kingdom, 1955. John Holt & Co. (Liverpool) Ltd, 1958; Chm., John Holt (Nigeria) Ltd, 1962. Leader, Westminster Chamber of Commerce Mission to Nigeria, 1974. *Address:* 26 Church Lane, Oxted, Surrey RH8 9LB. *T:* Oxted 5136. *Club:* Oriental.

COX, Major Horace B. T.; see Trevor Cox.

COX, Ian Herbert, CBE 1952; MA; FRGS; FZS; *b* 20 Feb. 1910; *e s* of late Herbert Stanley Cox and Elizabeth Dalgarno; *m* 1945, Susan Mary, *d* of late Lieut Comdr N. G. Fowler Snelling and widow of Flt Lieut D. S. S. Low; two *s* two *d*. *Educ:* Oundle; Magdalene Coll., Cambridge (Exhibnr). Geologist, Oxford Univ. Hudson Straits Expedition, 1931; research, Dept of Geology, Cambridge, 1932-36; with BBC 1936-39; served War of 1939-45 (Comdr, RNVR); BBC 1946; Science Corresp., London Press Service, 1947-48; Dir of Sc., Festival of Britain Office, 1948-51; Shell Internat. Pet. Co., 1952-70 (Hd Sc. and Develt TR Div., Convener Shell Grants Cttee); Mem. Council: RGS, 1953-57, 1959-62; Overseas Develt Inst., 1966-74; British Assoc. for the Advancement of Science, 1960-73 (Gen. Treasurer, 1965-70); Chelsea Coll., Univ. of London, 1968-74; Mem. Management Cttee, Scott Polar Research Inst., 1955-57; Vice-Pres., Geol. Soc., 1966-68; Mem., Bd of Governors, and Vice-Pres., Exec. Cttee, European Cultural Foundn (Amsterdam); Mem. Court, RCA. Pres., Arctic Club, 1961. *Publications:* papers on geology and palæontology of the Arctic; (ed) The Queen's Beasts, 1953; The Scallop, 1957; monographs in World Land Use Survey. *Recreations:* working with wood and stone; gardening. *Address:* The Old Post Office, School Hill, Seale, Farnham, Surrey GU10 1HY. *T:* Runfold 2481. *Club:* Athenæum.

COX, Surgeon Rear-Adm. James, OBE 1964; QHS 1982; FFARCS; Surgeon Rear Admiral (Naval Medicine and Training), since 1982; *b* 4 Feb. 1928; *s* of James Wolseley Cox and Gladys May Cox (*née* Watkinson); *m* 1952, Elizabeth Jennings; one *s* one *d*. *Educ:* Durham Sch.; Durham Univ. (MB BS 1951). FFARCS 1960. HMS Birmingham, 1952-54; Consultant Anaesthetist, RN Hospitals: Plymouth, 1955-59; Chatham, 1959-61; Plymouth, 1962-65; Gibraltar, 1965-69; Plymouth, 1969-71; Principal Medical Officer, HMS Bulwark, 1971-72; Consultant Anaesthetist, RN Hospitals: Plymouth, 1972-75; Haslar, 1975-77; Staff Medical Officer to MGRM Commando Forces, 1977-80; Medical Officer in Charge, RN Hospital Stonehouse, 1980-82. *Recreations:* fishing, gardening. *Address:* c/o Westminster Bank plc, 87 Grey Street, Newcastle upon Tyne NE1 6ER. *Club:* Royal Naval and Royal Albert Yacht (Portsmouth).

COX, (James) Anthony; His Honour Judge Anthony Cox; a Circuit Judge, since 1976; *b* 21 April 1924; *s* of Herbert Sidney Cox and Gwendoline Margaret Cox; *m* 1950, Doris Margaret Fretwell; three *s* one *d*. *Educ:* Cotham Sch., Bristol; Bristol Univ. LLB Hons 1948. War Service, Royal Marines, 1943-46. Called to Bar, Gray's Inn, 1949; a Recorder of the Crown Court, 1972-76. *Recreations:* cricket, sailing, golf, the arts. *Address:* Haldonhay, Lower Court Road, Newton Ferrers, Plymouth, Devon PL8 1DE. *Clubs:* MCC; Clifton (Bristol); Royal Western Yacht (Plymouth).

COX, John; General Administrator, Scottish Opera, since 1982; *b* 12 March 1935; *s* of Leonard John Cox and Ethel M. (*née* McGill). *Educ:* Queen Elizabeth's Hosp., Bristol; St Edmund Hall, Oxford (BA). Freelance producer of plays, opera, revue and musicals in Britain and abroad, incl. La Scala, Milan, and Metropolitan Opera, New York, 1959-; Dir of Prodn, Glyndebourne Festival Opera, 1971-81. Productions include: *opera:* Glyndebourne: Richard Strauss cycle, Rake's Progress, The Magic Flute; ENO: Cosi Fan Tutte, Patience; Scottish Opera: L'Egisto; New York: Mastersingers, Don Giovanni, Barber of Seville; Sydney: Barber of Seville, Albert Herring, Patience; Arabella, Houston and San Francisco; Der Rosenkavalier, Houston and Amsterdam; *plays:* Never The Twain, Mermaid; Miss Julie, Twelfth Night, Greenwich; British Nat. Day Spectacular, Expo '67, Montreal. *Address:* 7 West Grove, SE10 8QT. *T:* 01-692 2450.

COX, Vice-Adm. Sir John Michael Holland, KCB 1982; Flag Officer Naval Air Command, since 1982; *b* Peking, China, 27 Oct. 1928; *s* of late Thomas Cox, MBE, and of Daisy Anne Cox; *m* 1962, Anne Garden Farquharson Seth-Smith; one *s* one *d*. *Educ:* Hilton Coll., Natal, SA. Joined BRNC, 1946; ADC to C-in-C Allied Forces, N Europe, 1952-53; ADC to Governor of Victoria, 1955; commanded HM Ships: Dilston, 1957 (despatches); Stubbington, 1958; sc Camberley, 1960; Cadet Trng Officer, BRNC Dartmouth, 1962; CSO, London Div., RNR, 1963; commanded HMS: Surprise, 1964; Naiad, 1965; Comdr, Sea Trng, Staff of Flag Officer Sea Trng, 1967; Naval Attaché, Bonn, 1969; comd HMS Norfolk, 1972; Dir, Naval Ops and Trade, 1973-75; Comdr, Standing Naval Force Atlantic, 1976-77; COS to C-in-C, Naval Home Command, 1977-79; Flag Officer Third Flotilla and Comdr Anti-Submarine Group Two, 1979-82. *Recreations:* tennis, skiing. *Club:* Lansdowne.

COX, Sir John (William), Kt 1951; CBE 1946; Member, 1930-68, and Speaker of the House of Assembly, Bermuda, 1948-68; *b* 29 April 1900; *s* of Henry James and Ellen Augusta Cox; *m* 1926, Dorothy Carlyle, *d* of J. D. C. Darrell; three *s*. *Educ:* Saltus Grammar Sch., Bermuda. Merchant; Pres., Pearman, Watlington & Co. Ltd, Hamilton, Bermuda, General and Commission Merchants. Comdr, Royal Netherlands Order of Orange Nassau, 1956. *Address:* The Grove, Devonshire Parish, Bermuda. *T:* 2-0303. *Clubs:* Royal Automobile; Royal Bermuda Yacht, Royal Hamilton Amateur Dinghy, Mid Ocean (Bermuda).

COX, Air Vice-Marshal Joseph, CB 1957; OBE 1950; DFC 1940; retired; *b* 25 Oct. 1904; *m* 1933, Dorothy Thomas; one *d*. *Educ:* Peter Symond's Sch., Winchester, Hants. Commissioned, RAF, 1928; various appts at home and abroad, 1929-39. War of 1939-45: Examining Officer (flying), Central Flying Sch., 1939-40; comd No 15 (Bomber) Sqdn, June-Dec. 1940; Chief Instructor

No 33 Service Flying Training Sch., Canada, 1941-42; commanded No 31 Bombing and Gunnery Sch., Canada, 1942-43; commanded No 12 Advanced (Pilot) Flying Unit, and Stn Comdr RAF Spitalgate (Grantham), 1943-45. Comd No 8302 Air Disarmament Wing in Germany, 1945-46; comd RAF Fuhlsbuttel (Hamburg), 1946-48; Senior Personnel Staff Officer, HQ Maintenance Comd, 1948-51; Stn Comdr RAF Finningley, 1951-52; AOC, RAF, Ceylon, 1952-55; Senior Air Staff Officer, Flying Training Command, 1955-58; retired, 1958. *Recreations:* tennis, swimming, cricket, (in younger days) soccer, hockey, squash, badminton, water polo, riding. *Address:* 45 Ellesmere Close, Derby Road, Caversham, Reading RG4 0HG. *T:* Reading 472761. *Clubs:* MCC, Royal Air Force; Adastrian Cricket.

COX, Dr Leonard Bell, CMG 1968; Consulting Neurologist since 1927; *b* 29 Aug. 1894; *s* of Rev. Edward Thomas Cox and Isabella Bell; *m* 1925, Nancy Compson Trumble; one *d* (and one *d* decd). *Educ:* Wesley Coll., Melbourne; Melbourne Univ. MB, BS Melbourne 1916; MRCPE 1919; MD Melbourne 1920; FRACP 1938. Hon. and Consulting Neurologist, Alfred Hosp., Melbourne, 1934-; Cons. Neurologist, Queen Victoria Hosp., 1948. Served European War, 1914-18, Capt. AAMC, 1917; War of 1939-45, Wing Comdr, Consultant in Neurology to RAAF. Foundation Pres., Aust. Assoc. of Neurologists, 1950. Chairman: Trustees of Nat. Gallery of Victoria, 1957-65; Nat. Gallery and Cultural Centre Building Cttee, 1957-64; Member: Commonwealth Research Adv. Cttee, 1948; Felton Bequests Cttee, 1958-; Nat. Soc. of Victoria, 1976. *Publications:* Ars Vivendi, 1942; (jt) Human Torulosis, 1946; The National Gallery of Victoria, 1861-1968: a search for a collection, 1970; articles on neurology and neuropathology in med. jls. *Recreations:* Chinese art, country gardening. *Address:* Folly Farm, Falls Road, Olinda, Vic 3788, Australia. *T:* 751-1101. *Clubs:* Melbourne, Melbourne Cricket (Melbourne).

COX, Sir Mencea Ethereal, Kt 1980; Member of the Senate, Barbados; *b* 28 Nov. 1906; *s* of James William Cox and Charlotte Matilda Cox, Plymouth Brethren. *Educ:* elementary and private (languages: English, Latin, French, Spanish). Formerly worked in carpentry, engineering and hired car driving, and as garage owner; also in wholesale and retail business. Elected to Parliament, 1944; Member of the then Governor's Exec. Council, 1948; following the introduction of ministerial system of Govt in 1954, apptd Minister of Communications, Works and Housing, 1954, then Minister of Trade, Industry, Tourism and Labour, 1956-61; concurrently, 1958-61, Dep. Premier and Leader of House of Assembly. *Recreations:* horse racing, cricket. *Address:* Ambury, Clapham St Michael, Barbados, WI. *T:* 77766.

COX, Norman Ernest, CMG 1973; MA; HM Diplomatic Service, retired; International Consultant; research student at London School of Economics and Colegio de México, since 1981; *b* 28 Aug. 1921; *s* of late Ernest William Cox and late Daisy Beatrice (née Edmonds); *m* 1945, Maruja Margarita (née Cruz); one *s* one *d*. *Educ:* Lycée Français de Madrid; King's Coll., London. Tax Officer, Inland Revenue, 1938-41; Army, Intell. Corps, 1941-45: Gibraltar, 1942-45; Attaché, Madrid, 1945-47; FO, 1947-50; 2nd Sec., Sofia, 1950-52; 2nd Sec., Montevideo, 1952-54; FO, 1954-57; Dep. Regional Information Officer for SE Asia, Singapore, 1957-60; FO, 1960-62: Laos Conf., Geneva, 1961; Sec. to UK Conf. Delegn to ECSC, Luxemburg, 1962-63; 1st Sec. (Commercial), Madrid, 1963-66; Counsellor (Information), Mexico, Regional Information Officer for Central American Republics, PRO to Duke of Edinburgh for 1968 Olympics, 1966-68; Counsellor (Commercial), Moscow, 1969-72; Inst. of Latin American Studies, London Univ., 1972-73; Diplomatic Service Inspector, 1973-74; Ambassador to: Ecuador, 1974-77; Mexico, 1977-81. *Recreations:* swimming, walking, climbing, travelling; archaeology, history, linguistics, comparative religion. *Address:* 36 Meadow Road, Malvern Link, Worcs WR14 2SD; Monte Himalaya 27-303, Balcones de la Herradura, Mexico 10 DF, Mexico. *Club:* Royal Automobile.

COX, Oliver Jasper, CBE 1982; RIBA; Partner, Shankland/Cox Partnership, since 1965; *b* 20 April 1920; *s* of William Edward and Elsie Gertrude Cox; *m* 1953, Jean; one *s* two *d*. *Educ:* Mill Hill Sch.; Architectural Association School of Architecture (AADip Hons). DistTP. Architects Dept, Herts CC, New Schools Division, 1948-49; Architects Dept, LCC Housing Division, 1950-59; Dep. Chief Architect, and Leader, Research and Development Gp, Min. of Housing and Local Govt, 1960-64. *Recreations:* painting, drawing and screen printing. *Address:* 22 Grove Terrace, NW5 1PL. *T:* 01-485 6929.
See also A. W. Cox.

COX, Patricia Ann; Under Secretary, Scottish Education Department, since 1976; *b* 25 May 1931; *d* of Sir (Ernest) Gordon Cox, *qv*. *Educ:* Leeds Girls' High Sch.; Newnham Coll., Cambridge (MA). Asst Principal, Dept of Health for Scotland, 1953; Principal: SHHD, 1959-62; HM Treasury, 1962-65; SHHD, 1965-67; Asst Sec., Scottish Educn Dept, 1967. *Publication:* Sandal Ash (novel for children), 1950. *Recreations:* opera, archaeology, needlework, walking. *Address:* 2 Gloucester Place, Edinburgh EH3 6EF. *T:* 031-225 6370.

COX, Peter Arthur, BSc Eng; FEng, FICE, FCGI; Senior Partner, Rendel Palmer & Tritton, Consulting Engineers, since 1978; President, Institution of Civil Engineers, Nov. 1980-81; *b* 30 Oct. 1922; *m* 1944, Rosemary; one *s* two *d*. *Educ:* Westcliff High Sch., Essex; City and Guilds Coll., Imperial Coll., London. Commissioned, Royal Engineers, 1942 (despatches). Lewis & Duvivier, Cons. Engrs, 1947; Rendel Palmer & Tritton, 1952; Peter Lind & Co. Ltd, 1954; Sir Bruce White Wolfe Barry & Partners, Cons. Engrs, 1955;

Rendel Palmer & Tritton, 1956, Partner, 1966. *Publications:* papers to Instn of Civil Engrs on Leith Harbour and Belfast Dry Dock; many papers to conferences. *Recreations:* walking, gardening. *Address:* 18 Ranmore Avenue, Croydon, Surrey CR0 5QA. *T:* (office) 01-928 8999. *Club:* East India.

COX, Peter Denzil John H.; see Hippisley-Cox, P. D. J.

COX, Peter Richmond, CB 1971; Deputy Government Actuary, 1963-74; *b* 3 Sept. 1914; *s* of Richard R. Cox, Civil Servant, and Nellie (née Richmond); *m* 1971, Faith Blake Schenk. *Educ:* King's Coll. Sch., Wimbledon. Entered Government Actuary's Dept, 1933. Qualified as Fellow, Institute of Actuaries, 1939. Joint Hon. Sec., Institute of Actuaries, 1962-64 (Vice-Pres., 1966-68). Pres., Eugenics Soc., 1970-72. Chm., CS Insurance Soc., 1973-78. Silver Medal, Inst. of Actuaries, 1975. *Publications:* Demography, 1950 (5 edns); (with R. H. Storr-Best) Surplus in British Life Assurance, 1962; (ed jtly) Population and Pollution, 1972; Resources and Population, 1973; Population and the New Biology, 1974; Equalities and Inequalities in Education, 1975; various papers on actuarial and demographic subjects. *Recreations:* music, painting, gardening. *Address:* The Level House, Mayfield, East Sussex TN20 6BW. *T:* Mayfield 2217. *Club:* Actuaries.

COX, Philip (Joseph), DSC 1943; QC 1967; a Recorder, and Honorary Recorder of Northampton, since 1972; *b* 28 Sept. 1922; *s* of Joseph Parriss Cox, Rugby; *m* 1951, Margaret Jocelyn Cox, *d* of R. C. H. Cox, Purley, Surrey; one *s* one *d*. *Educ:* Rugby Sch; Queens' Coll., Cambridge. RNVR, 1942-46 (Lieut). Called to Bar, Gray's Inn, 1949; Bencher, 1972; practised at Bar, Birmingham, 1949-67. Mem. County Court Rules Cttee, 1962-68; Dep. Chm., Northants QS, 1963-71; Dep. Chm., Warwicks QS, 1966-71; Leader, Midland and Oxford Circuit, 1975-79; Mem. Senate, Inns of Court and Bar, 1974-80. Legal Assessor to Disciplinary Cttee, RCVS, 1969-; Chm., Cttee of Enquiry into London Smallpox Outbreak, 1973; Chm. Code of Practice Cttee, British Pharmaceut. Assoc., 1978-. Pres., Edgbaston Liberal Assoc., 1974-. *Recreations:* sailing, golf, gardening, reading. *Address:* (home) 40 George Road, Edgbaston, Birmingham B15 1PL. *T:* 021-454 2656; (chambers) 1 King's Bench Walk, Temple, EC4. *Clubs:* Naval; Birmingham; Royal Cruising, Bar Yacht.

COX, Richard Charles, MBE 1961; HM Diplomatic Service, retired; *b* 27 May 1920; *s* of Charles Victor Cox and Marjorie Eleanor Cox (née Fox); *m* 1941, Constance (née Goddard); one *s*. *Educ:* Gravesend Grammar Sch. Served War of 1939-45, RAF; released with rank of Sqdn Leader, 1946. Entered Colonial Office, 1937; Dominions Office, 1946; High Commn, Colombo, 1949-52; Second Sec., Calcutta, 1953-54; CRO, 1954-56; First Sec., Bombay, 1956-59; CRO, 1960-63; First Sec., Valletta, 1964-68; FCO, 1968-72; NI Office, 1972-74; Dep. Sec. Gen., Cento, 1975-77. *Recreations:* swimming, gardening, watching Rugby football. *Address:* The Old Forge, Hartley, Kent. *T:* Longfield 2035.

COX, Ronald; Director-General, Greater Glasgow Passenger Transport Executive, 1973-74, retired; *b* St Helens, Lancs, 3 Feb. 1916; *s* of Frederick Nisbet Cox and Annie Cox; *m* 1941, Edna Frances Heaton; one *s* one *d*. *Educ:* Higher Grade Boys' Sch., St Helens, Lancs (Oxford Univ. Cert., 6 credits); Trainee Transport Officer, St Helens Corp. Transport (Endorsed Cert. in Commerce, NC Engrg). Served War, Flt Lt (Tech.), RAF Transport Command, 1940-46. Sen. Traffic Officer, St Helens Corp. Transport, 1946-48; Traffic Supt, Salford City Transport, 1948-53; Dep. Engr and Gen. Manager, Rochdale Corp. Transport, 1953-54, Engr and Gen. Manager, 1954-62; Gen. Manager, Bournemouth Corp. Transport, 1962-64; Transport Manager, Edinburgh Corp. Transport, 1964-73. President: Scottish Road Passenger Transport Assoc., 1973-74; Incorp. Assoc. of Public Passenger Transport, 1974-75. RSA Dip. (prizewinner transport subjects); MIRTE, MInstT, FCIT. *Recreation:* sailing. *Address:* 6 Stonehanger Court, Devon Road, Salcombe, Devon TQ8 8HJ. *T:* Salcombe 3456.

COX, Roy Arthur, JDipMA; FCA, FCMA, FCBSI, CBIM; Director since 1976 and Chief General Manager since 1970, Alliance Building Society; *b* 30 Nov. 1925; *s* of J. W. Arthur Cox; *m* 1951; one *s* one *d*. *Educ:* Isleworth Grammar Sch. FCA 1953; FCMA 1957; FCBSI (FBS 1971); CBIM 1980. War Service, 1944-47. Wells & Partners, Chartered Accountants, 1942-49; Colombo Commercial Co. Ltd, 1950-61; Urwick, Orr & Partners, Management Consultants, 1961-65; Alliance Building Society: Sec., 1965; Gen. Man., 1967. Dir, Southern Bd, Legal & General Assurance Soc. Ltd, 1972-. Building Societies Association: Chm., S Eastern Assoc., 1972-74; Mem. Council, 1973-; Chm., Gen. Purposes and Public Relations Cttee, 1975-77. Mem., Royal Commn on Distribution of Income and Wealth, 1974-78. *Recreations:* golf, bridge. *Address:* The Yett, 281 Dyke Road, Hove, E Sussex BN3 6PD.

COX, Thomas Michael; MP (Lab) Wandsworth, Tooting, since 1974 (Wandsworth Central, 1970-74); *b* London, 1930. *Educ:* state schools; London Sch. of Economics. Electrical worker. Former Mem., Fulham Borough Council; contested (Lab) GLC elections, 1967; contested (Lab) Stroud, 1966. An Asst Govt Whip, 1974-77; a Lord Comr of the Treasury, 1977-79. Member: ETU; Co-operative Party. *Address:* House of Commons, SW1.

COX, Thomas Richard Fisher, CMG 1955; Bursar, St Andrew's College, Dublin, 1962-79; *b* 21 Feb. 1907; *s* of late Rev. James Fisher Cox; *m* 1st, 1933, Doreen Alice Rae; one *s* two *d*; 2nd, 1968, Rowena Mary Figgis; three *s*.

Educ: Portora Royal Sch.; TCD; University Coll., Oxford. Provincial Admin., Uganda, 1930; acted as Sec. for African Affairs, 1949-50; Chm. Languages Board, Uganda, 1950-60; Provincial Comr, Uganda, 1950-61. *Publications:* articles in Uganda Jl and Jl of African Admin. *Recreations:* gardening; formerly boxing (boxed for Oxford Univ. v Cambridge Univ., 1930). *Address:* 21 Hyde Park, Dalkey, Co. Dublin. *T:* 804596; Ballinahinch, Ashford, Co. Wicklow. *T:* Wicklow 4112.

COX, Sir Trenchard, Kt 1961; CBE 1954; MA; FRSA (Vice-President 1964-68); FMA; FSA; Director and Secretary, Victoria and Albert Museum, 1956-66; *b* 31 July 1905; *s* of late William Pallett Cox and Marion Beverley; *m* 1935, Mary Désirée (*d* 1973), *d* of late Sir Hugh Anderson, Master of Gonville and Caius Coll., Cambridge. *Educ:* Eton; King's Coll., Cambridge. Worked as volunteer at the National Gallery and Brit. Museum (Dept of Prints and Drawings), 1929-32; spent a semester at the University of Berlin in the Dept of Arts, 1930; Asst to the Keeper, Wallace Collection, 1932-39; seconded for war-time duties, to Home Office, 1940-44; Dir of Birmingham Museum and Art Gallery, 1944-55. Member: Ancient Monuments Board for England, 1959-69; Standing Commn on Museums and Galleries, 1967-77. People's Warden, St Martin-in-the Fields, 1968-79. Hon. DLitt Birmingham, 1956. Hon. Fellow, Royal Acad., 1981. Chevalier, Légion d'Honneur, 1967. *Publications:* The National Gallery, a Room-to-Room Guide, 1930; Jehan Foucquet, Native of Tours, 1931; part editor of the Catalogue to the Exhibition of French Art at Burlington House, Jan.-March 1932; The Renaissance in Europe, 1933; A General Guide to the Wallace Collection, 1933; A Short Illustrated History of the Wallace Collection and its Founders, 1936; David Cox, 1947; Peter Bruegel, 1951; Pictures: a Handbook for Curators, 1956. *Recreations:* reading, travelling. *Address:* 33 Queen's Gate Gardens, SW7. *T:* 01-584 0231. *Club:* Athenæum.

COX, Maj.-Gen. William Reginald, CB 1956; DSO 1945; Director Territorial Army, Cadets and Home Guard, 1958-60, retired; *b* 13 June 1905; *e s* of late Major W. S. R. Cox; *m* 1947, Dorothy Irene Cox; no *c. Educ:* Wellington Coll. Commissioned KSLI, 1925; Adjutant, 2nd Bn, 1931-34; Staff Coll., Camberley, 1938; served War of 1939-45: Bde Major 114 Inf. Bde, 1940; Instr, Staff Coll., Camberley, 1941; GSO 1 Northern Comd, York, 1942; comd 1 Worcs. Regt, 1942-43; GSO 1, 21 Army Gp, 1943-44; comd 7 Green Howards, 1944; 131 Lorried Inf Bde, 1944; 129, 146 and 31 Inf. Bdes, 1945-47; BGS Western Comd, 1948; idc 1949; DAG, GHQ, MEF, 1950-52; Dep. Dir Infty, War Office, 1952-54; Chief of Staff, Southern Command, 1954-55; GOC 53rd (Welsh) Div., TA, and Mid-West District, 1955-58. Col, KSLI, 1957-63. Order of White Lion of Czechoslovakia (3rd Cl.); Military Cross of Czechoslovakia, 1945. *Recreations:* tennis, golf. *Address:* Mill House, Laverstock, Salisbury, Wilts. *Club:* Naval and Military.

COX, William Trevor; see Trevor, William.

COXETER, Harold Scott Macdonald, FRS 1950; PhD Cambridge, 1931; Professor of Mathematics, University of Toronto, 1948-80, now Emeritus Professor; *b* 9 Feb. 1907; *s* of Harold Samuel Coxeter and Lucy (*née* Gee); *m* 1936, Hendrina Johanna Brouwer, The Hague; one *s* one *d. Educ:* King Alfred Sch., London; St George's Sch., Harpenden; Trinity Coll., Cambridge. Entrance Scholar, Trinity Coll., 1926; Smith's Prize, 1931. Fellow Trinity Coll., Cambridge, 1931-36; Rockefeller Foundation Fellow, Princeton, 1932-33; Procter Fellow, Princeton, 1934-35; Asst Prof., 1936-43, Associate Prof., 1943-48, University of Toronto. Visiting Professor: Notre Dame, 1947; Columbia Univ., 1949; Dartmouth Coll., 1964; Univ. of Amsterdam, 1966; Univ. of Edinburgh, 1967; Univ. of E Anglia, 1968; ANU, 1970; Univ. of Sussex, 1972; Univ. of Warwick and Univ. of Utrecht, 1976; Calif. Inst. of Technology, 1977; Univ. of Bologna, 1978. Editor Canadian Jl of Mathematics, 1948-57. President: Canadian Mathematical Congress, 1965-67; Internat. Mathematical Congress, 1974. Foreign Mem., Koninklijke Nederlandse Akademie van Wetenschappen, 1975; Hon. Member: Mathematische Gesellschaft, Hamburg, 1977; Wiskundig Genootschap, Amsterdam, 1978; London Mathematical Soc., 1978. Hon. LLD: Alberta, 1957; Trent, 1973; Toronto, 1979; Hon. DMath Waterloo, 1969; Hon. DSc Acadia, 1971. *Publications:* Non-Euclidean Geometry, 1942 and 1965; Regular Polytopes, 1948, 1963 and 1973; The Real Projective Plane, 1949, 1955 and 1959; (with W. O. J. Moser) Generators and Relations, 1st edn, 1957, 4th edn, 1980; Introduction to Geometry, 1961 and 1969; Projective Geometry, 1964 and 1974; (with S. L. Greitzer) Geometry Revisited, 1967; Twelve Geometric Essays, 1968; Regular Complex Polytopes, 1974; (with W. W. Rouse Ball) Mathematical Recreations and Essays, 12th edn, 1974; (with R. W. Frucht and D. L. Powers) Zero-symmetric Graphs, 1981; various mathematical papers. *Recreations:* music, travel. *Address:* 67 Roxborough Drive, Toronto M4W 1X2, Canada.

COXWELL-ROGERS, Maj.-Gen. Norman Annesley, CB 1944; CBE 1943 (OBE 1933); DSO 1940; *b* 29 May 1896; *s* of late Henry Annesley Coxwell-Rogers, Asst Inspector-General Royal Irish Constabulary, Dowdeswell, Glos, and late Mary Georgina, *d* of Edmund Waller, Dundrum and Bray, Co. Dublin; *m* 1928, Diana Coston; one *s* one *d. Educ:* Cheltenham Coll.; Royal Military Academy, Woolwich. 2nd Lieut Royal Engineers, 1915; service at home, Gibraltar and India; served France and Belgium, 1915-18 (wounded, despatches twice); NW Frontier, Mohmand Operations, . . . served as Field Engineer in charge of construction of Gandab Road . . . patches); Mohmand Operations, 1935, as CRE (Bt Lieut-Col); War . . . France, Sept. 1939-June 1940, N Africa, Sicily, and Italy,

1943, Chief Engineer Allied Armies in Italy (despatches twice, DSO, CBE, CB, Legion of Merit (USA)); Colonel, 1941; Maj.-Gen. 1943; retired pay, 1946. Col Comdt RE, 1956-61. *Recreation:* field sports. *Address:* Rossley Manor, near Cheltenham, Glos. *T:* Andoversford 233. *Club:* Naval and Military.

COYNE, James Elliott; Canadian banker and financial consultant; *b* Winnipeg, 17 July 1910; *s* of James Bowes Coyne and Edna Margaret Coyne (*née* Elliott); *m* 1957, Meribeth Stobie; one *s* one *d. Educ:* University of Manitoba (BA); University of Oxford (BCL). RCAF (Flying Officer), 1942-44. Admitted to the Bar, Manitoba, 1934; solicitor and barrister in Manitoba, 1934-38; Financial Attaché, Canadian Embassy, Washington, DC, 1941; Mem. War-time Prices and Trade Board, Ottawa, 1942 (Dep.-Chm.). Bank of Canada, Ottawa: Asst to the Governors, 1944-49; Deputy-Governor, 1950-54; Governor, 1955-61. *Address:* 29 Ruskin Row, Winnipeg, Manitoba R3M 2R9, Canada.

COZENS, Brig. Dame (Florence) Barbara, DBE 1963; RRC 1958; *b* 24 Dec. 1906; *d* of late Capt. A. Cozens, S Staffs. *Educ:* Seabury Sch., Worthing. Nurse Training: The Nightingale Sch., St Thomas' Hosp., London, 1928-32. Joined QAIMNS, 1933. Served War of 1939-45, England and Continent. Lieut-Col 1954; Col 1958; Brig. 1960; Matron-in-Chief and Dir of Army Nursing Services, 1960-64, retd; Chief Nursing Officer to St John Ambulance Brigade, 1965-72. Col Commandant, QARANC, 1966-69. DStJ 1972.

COZENS, Air Cdre Henry Iliffe, CB 1946; AFC 1939; RAF retired; *b* 13 March 1904; *m* 1956, Gillian Mary, *o d* of Wing Comdr O. R. Pigott, Wokingham, Berks; one *s* two *d. Educ:* St Dunstan's Coll.; Downing Coll., Cambridge. MA 1934. Commissioned in RAF, 1923; Mem. of British Arctic Air Route Expedition, 1930-31. Served War of 1939-45 (AFC, CB). idc 1947. *Address:* Horley Manor, Banbury, Oxon. *Club:* Royal Air Force.

COZENS, Robert William, QPM 1981; Chief Constable, West Mercia Constabulary (Hereford, Worcester and Shropshire), since 1981; *b* 10 Nov. 1927; *s* of Sydney Robert and Rose Elizabeth Cozens; *m* 1952, Jean Dorothy Banfield; one *s* one *d. Educ:* Stoke C of E Sch., Guildford. Constable to Chief Superintendent, Surrey Constabulary, 1954-72; Asst Dir, Command Courses, Police Staff Coll., Bramshill, 1972-74; Asst Chief Constable, S Yorks Police, 1974-78; seconded to Federal Judicial Police in Mexico for advisory duties, 1975; Dep. Chief Constable, Lincs Police, 1978-81. *Recreations:* tennis, squash, badminton. *Address:* West Mercia Constabulary, Police Headquarters, Hindlip Hall, Worcester WR3 8SP. *T:* Worcester 27188.

CRABB, Rt. Rev. Frederick Hugh Wright; see Athabasca, Bishop of.

CRABBE, Kenneth Herbert Martineau, TD; *b* 4 Nov. 1916; *m* 1940, Rowena Leete (*d* 1981); one *s. Educ:* Stowe Sch. Commnd TA, 1937; psc; Major. Member, Stock Exchange, London, 1937-; Mem. Council, The Stock Exchange, 1963- (Dep. Chm., 1970-73). *Recreations:* golf, fishing, shooting, painting. *Address:* Spandrels, Walliswood, Ockley, Surrey RH5 5RJ. *T:* Oakwood Hill 275. *Clubs:* Boodle's, Ski Club of Great Britain; West Sussex Golf.

CRABBE, Mrs Pauline, (Mrs Joseph Benjamin), OBE 1969; JP; Secretary, London Brook Advisory Centres, since Nov. 1971; *b* 1 April 1914; *y d* of Cyril and Edith Henriques, Kingston, Jamaica; *m* 1st, 1936, Geoffrey Henebery (marr. diss. 1948); one *d*; 2nd, 1949, Neville Crabbe (marr. diss. 1960); one *s*; 3rd, 1969, Joseph Benjamin; three step *s. Educ:* Highgate Convent; London Academy of Music and Drama; London Univ. (extra-mural course in Psychology). Actress and broadcaster, 1945-53; secretarial work with British Actors' Equity and WEA, 1953-56; then with Old People's Welfare and London Council of Social Service, 1956-57; Welfare Sec. and Dep. Gen. Sec. to Nat. Council for Unmarried Mother and her Child, 1957-69; Conciliation Officer for Race Relations Bd, 1969-71. Founder Mem., Haverstock Housing Trust for Fatherless Families, 1966; Mem. Bd, Housing Corp., 1968-75; Member: Community Relations Commn, 1972-77; Standing Adv. Council on Race Relations, 1977-; Parole Bd, 1978-. Hon. Fellow, Manchester Polytechnic, 1979. Radio and TV broadcaster and panellist. JP London, 1967. FRSA 1972. *Publications:* articles and book reviews in social work jls. *Recreations:* entertaining, walking, indoor gardening, the theatre and the arts. *Address:* 27 Elgin Court, Elgin Avenue, W9 2NU. *T:* 01-289 0824. *Club:* Magistrates' Association.

CRABBE, Reginald James Williams, FIA, FSS; a Director, since 1956, and President, since 1982, Provident Life Association of London Ltd; Chairman: United Standard Insurance Co. Ltd, 1967-79; Vigilant Assurance Co. Ltd, 1970-79; Deputy Chairman, Cope & Timmins Holdings Ltd (formerly Cope & Timmins Ltd), since 1971 (Chairman 1975-77); *b* 22 June 1909; *e s* of late Harry James and Annie Martha Crabbe; *m* 1948, Phyllis Maud Smith; two *d. Educ:* Chigwell Sch., Essex. Entered National Mutual Life Assurance Soc., 1926; FIA 1933; joined Provident Life as Asst Actuary, 1935; Man. Dir, 1956-74; Chm., 1967-82. Chm., Life Offices' Assoc., 1965, 1966. *Publication:* (with C. A. Poyser, MA, FIA) Pension and Widows' and Orphans' Funds, 1953. *Recreations:* reading, gardening, music, art. *Address:* Fairways, 166 Lower Green Road, Esher, Surrey. *T:* Esher 62219.

CRABBIE, Mrs (Margaret) Veronica, CBE 1977; *b* 26 Nov. 1910; *d* of late Sir Christopher Nicholson Johnston (Lord Sands, Senator of the College of

Justice, Scotland), and Lady Sands; *m* 1938, John Patrick Crabbie; two *s* one *d*. *Educ:* St Denis Sch., Edinburgh; Queen Margaret's Sch., Escrick, York. Chairman: Edinburgh Home for Mothers and Infants, 1951-66; Walpole Housing Assoc., 1969-72; Scottish Council for the Unmarried Mother and her Child, 1966-72; WRVS, Scotland, 1972-77. *Recreation:* curling. *Address:* 17 Ravelston Dykes, Edinburgh EH4 3JE. *T:* 031-332 4489. *Club:* New (Edinburgh).

CRABTREE, Maj.-Gen. Derek Thomas; Director General of Weapons (Army), Ministry of Defence, since 1980; *b* 21 Jan. 1930; *s* of late William Edward Crabtree and of Winifred Hilda Burton; *m* 1960, Daphne Christine Mason; one *s* one *d*. *Educ:* St Brendan's Coll., Bristol. Commissioned, 1953; Regimental Service: 13th/18th Royal Hussars (QMO), UK and BAOR, 1953-56; Royal Berkshire Regt, UK, Malta and Cyprus, 1956-59; Technical Staff Course, RMCS, 1960-62; Regimental Service, 1st Bn Devonshire and Dorset Regt, UK and NI, 1963; *sc* Camberley, 1964; BM 11 Inf. Bde, BAOR, 1965-67; Regimental Service, 1st Bn Duke of Edinburgh's Royal Regt, 1967-69; CO 1st Bn Duke of Edinburgh's Royal Regt, UK and Berlin, 1970-72; DS RMCS, 1972-74; Col GS, MGO Secretariat, MoD, 1974-76; Dep. Comdr and Chief of Staff Headquarters British Forces Hong Kong, 1976-79; Dep. Comdt RMCS, 1979-80. *Recreations:* skiing, golf, tennis, shooting, sailing. *Address:* c/o Lloyds Bank Ltd, Brislington, Bristol. *Club:* Army and Navy.

CRABTREE, Jonathan; a Recorder of the Crown Court, since 1974; barrister-at-law; *b* 17 April 1934; *s* of Charles H. Crabtree and Elsie M. Crabtree; *m* 1st, 1957, Caroline Ruth Keigwin (*née* Oliver) (marr. diss., 1976); two *s* three *d*; 2nd, 1980, Wendy Elizabeth Hudson (*née* Ward). *Educ:* Bootham; St John's Coll., Cambridge (MA, LLB). Called to Bar, Gray's Inn, 1958. *Recreations:* cricket, cooking. *Address:* 7 Upper Price Street, York YO2 18J. *T:* York 22825.

CRABTREE, Prof. Lewis Frederick, PhD, FRAeS; Sir George White Professor of Aeronautical Engineering, University of Bristol, since 1973; *b* 16 Nov. 1924; *m* 1955, Averil Joan Escott; one *s* one *d*. *Educ:* Univ. of Leeds; Imperial Coll. of Science and Technology; Cornell Univ., USA. BSc (Mech Eng) Leeds, 1945; DIC (Aeronautics), 1947; PhD (Aero Eng), Cornell, 1952. Air Engr Officer, RNVR, 1945-46. Grad. apprentice, Saunders-Roe Ltd, E Cowes, IoW, 1947-50; ECA Fellowship, Grad. Sch. of Aero. Engrg, Cornell Univ., 1950-52; Aerodynamics Dept, RAE, Farnborough, 1952-73; Head of: Hypersonics and High temperature Gasdynamics Div., 1961-66; Low Speed Aerodynamics Div., 1966-70; Propulsion Aerodynamics and Noise Div., 1970-73. Visiting Prof., Cornell Univ., 1957. Pres., RAeS, 1978-79. AFAIAA. *Publications:* Elements of Hypersonic Aerodynamics, 1965; contributor to: Incompressible Aerodynamics, 1960; Laminar Boundary Layers, 1963; articles chiefly in Jl RAeS, Aeron. Quart., Jl Aeron. Sci., Jahrbuch der WGLR, and Reports and Memos of ARC. *Address:* Queen's Building, The University, Bristol. *T:* Bristol 24161.

CRABTREE, Simon; *see* Wharton, Michael B.

CRACKNELL, (William) Martin; Chief Executive, Glenrothes Development Corporation, since 1976; *b* 24 June 1929; *s* of John Sidney Cracknell and Sybil Marian (*née* Wood); *m* 1962, Gillian Goatcher; two *s* two *d*. *Educ:* St Edward's School, Oxford; RMA Sandhurst. Regular Army Officer, Royal Green Jackets, 1949-69; British Printing Industries Fedn, 1969-76. *Address:* Alburne Knowe, Orchard Drive, Glenrothes, Fife. *T:* Glenrothes 752413.

CRACROFT, Air Vice-Marshal Peter Dicken, CB 1954; AFC 1932; *b* 29 Nov. 1907; *s* of Lt-Col H. Cracroft, Bath; *m* 1932, Margaret Eliza Sugden Patchett; two *s*. *Educ:* Monkton Combe Sch., Bath. Commissioned RAF 1927; Fleet Air Arm, 1928-31; Central Flying Sch. Instructors' Course, 1931; Flying Instructor, Leuchars, 1931-35; Adjt HMS Courageous, 1936-37; Chief Flying Instructor, Oxford Univ. Air Sqdn, 1937-39; RAF Stn Mount Batten, 1939-40; Air Staff, Coastal Command, 1940-41; OC RAF Station, Chivenor, 1941-43; SASO 19 Gp (later 17 Gp), 1933-44; OC 111 Op. Trg Unit, Bahamas, 1944-45; SASO HQ Air Comd, SE Asia, Mil. Gov. Penang, 1945; AOC Bombay, 1945-46; SASO, HQ 19 Gp, 1946-48; RAF Dir and CO, Jt Anti-Submarine Sch., Londonderry, 1948-50; Sen. Air Liaison Officer, S Africa, 1950-52; AOC 66 Gp, Edinburgh, 1952-53; Senior Air Staff Officer, Headquarters Coastal Command, 1953-55; AOC Scotland and 18 Group, 1955-58; retired from RAF, Dec. 1958. *Recreations:* tennis, fishing, shooting. *Address:* Alderney House, Burton Bradstock, Bridport, Dorset DT6 4NQ. *Club:* Royal Air Force.

CRADDOCK, (William) Aleck; MVO 1981; Chairman since 1981, and Managing Director since 1980, Harrods Ltd; *b* Nov. 1924; *m* 1947, Olive May Brown; one *s* one *d*. *Educ:* City of London School. Joined Druce and Craddock, Craddock and Tomkins Ltd (family firm), Meat and Provision Merchants, Marylebone, London, 1946; joined Harrods Ltd as Asst Food Manager, 1954; Member of the Board, 1964; Director and General Manager, 1970; Asst Managing Director, 1975; Man. Dir, Harrods Ltd, also a Director of House of Fraser Ltd, 1980. Liveryman, Worshipful Company of Cooks, 1972. Cavaliere Official (Fourth Cl.), Order Al Merito Della Repubblica Italiana, 1980. *Address:* c/o Harrods Ltd, Knightsbridge, SW1X 7XL. *T:* 01-730 1234.

CRADOCK, Sir Percy, KCMG 1980 (CMG 1968); HM Ambassador to the People's Republic of China, since 1978; *b* 26 Oct. 1923; *m* 1953, Birthe Marie Dyrlund. Served Foreign Office, 1954-57; First Sec., Kuala Lumpur, 1957-61, Hong Kong, 1961, Peking, 1962; Foreign Office, 1963-66; Counsellor and Head of Chancery, Peking, 1966-68; Chargé d'Affaires, Peking, 1968-69; Head of Planning Staff, FCO, 1969-71; Under-Sec., Cabinet Office, 1971-75; Ambassador to German Democratic Republic, 1976-78. Leader, UK Delegn to Comprehensive Test Ban Discussions at Geneva, 1977-78. *Address:* c/o Foreign and Commonwealth Office, SW1. *Club:* Reform.

CRADOCK-HARTOPP, Sir J. E.; *see* Hartopp.

CRAFT, Professor Ian Logan, FRCS; Director of Gynaecology, The Cromwell Hospital, since 1982; *b* 11 July 1937; *s* of Reginald Thomas Craft and Lois Mary (*née* Logan); *m* 1959, Jacqueline Rivers Symmons; two *s*. *Educ:* Owens Sch., London; Westminster Med. Sch., Univ. of London (MB, BS). FRCS 1966; MRCOG 1970. Sen. Registrar, Westminster Hosp. Teaching Gp (Westminster Hosp. and Kingston Hosp.), 1970-72; Sen. Lectr and Consultant, Inst. of Obstetrics and Gynaecology, Queen Charlotte's Hosp., London, 1972-76; Prof. of Obstetrics and Gynaecology, Royal Free Hosp., London, 1976-82. FRSocMed. *Publications:* contrib. BMJ, Lancet and other medical jls. *Recreations:* art, music, ornithology, sports of most types. *Address:* 12 Coval Gardens, East Sheen, SW14 7DG. *T:* 01-876 5461.

CRAFT, Prof. Maurice, PhD; Professor of Education, and Head of Colleges Division, School of Education, University of Nottingham, since 1980; Dean, Faculty of Education, since 1981; *b* 4 May 1932; *er s* of Jack and Polly Craft, London; *m* 1957, Alma, *y d* of Elio and Dinah Sampson, Dublin; two *d*. *Educ:* LCC Elem. Sch. and Colfe's Grammar Sch., SE13; LSE, Univ. of London (BSc Econ); Sch. of Education, Trinity Coll., Univ. of Dublin (HDipEd); Inst. of Education, Univ. of London (AcadDipEd); Dept of Sociology, Univ. of Liverpool (PhD 1972). 2/Lt RAOC (Nat. Service), 1953-55. Asst Master, Catford Secondary Sch., SE6, 1956-60; Princ. Lectr and Head of Dept of Sociology, Edge Hill Coll. of Education, Ormskirk, Lancs, 1960-67; Sen. Lectr in Education, i/c Advanced Courses, Univ. of Exeter, 1967-73; Sub-Dean, Faculty of Educn, 1969-73; Prof. of Education, and Chairman, Centre for the Study of Urban Education, La Trobe Univ., Melbourne, 1973-75; Goldsmiths' Prof. of Education, Inst. of Educn, Univ. of London, and Head of Dept of Advanced Studies in Education, Goldsmiths' Coll., 1976-80. Adviser: Devon CC, 1970-72; Aust. Federal Poverty Commn, 1974-75; State Coll., Vict., Aust., 1974-75; SSRC, 1974-; Assoc. of Commonwealth Univs, 1976, 1979; CNAA, 1978-; Centre for Advice and Inf. on Eductl Disadvantage, 1979- (Chm., Teacher Educn Working Gp, 1979-80); Schools Council, 1979; CRE (Chm., Teacher Educn Adv. Gp, 1980-); H of C Home Affairs Cttee, 1981; Swann Cttee, 1982. Mem., British Delegn to EEC Colloquium on Ethnic Min. Educn, Brussels, 1979; UK deleg. to Council of Europe Seminars on Intercultural Trng of Teachers, Lisbon, 1981, Rome, 1982. Management Cttee, Sociology of Educn Abstracts, 1965-; Edtl Bd, Jl of Multilingual and Multicultural Develt, 1979-; Edtl Bd, Multicultural Educn Abstracts, 1981-; Chm., E Midlands Reg. Consultative Gp on Teacher Educn, 1980-. *Publications:* (ed jtly) Linking Home and School, 1967 (3rd edn, 1980); (ed jtly) Guidance and Counselling in British Schools, 1969 (2nd edn, 1974); (ed) Family, Class and Education: a Reader, 1970; Urban Education—a Dublin case study, 1974; School Welfare Provision in Australia, 1977; (ed) Teaching in a Multicultural Society: the Task for Teacher Education, 1981; contrib. to numerous books and to the following jls: Educnl Research, Internat. Review of Educn, Social and Econ. Admin., Educn for Teaching, Internat. Social Work, Aust. Jl of Social Work, Aust. Eductl Researcher, Higher Educn Jl, New Society, Administration, New Era, Studies. *Recreations:* music, walking. *Address:* School of Education, University of Nottingham, Nottingham NG7 2RD. *T:* Nottingham 56101.

CRAGG, Rt. Rev. (Albert) Kenneth, DPhil; *b* 8 March 1913; *yr s* of Albert and Emily Cragg; *m* 1940, Theodora Melita, *yr d* of John Wesley Arnold; three *s* (one *d* decd). *Educ:* Blackpool Grammar Sch.; Jesus Coll., Oxford; Tyndale Hall, Bristol. BA Oxon 2nd Cl. Hons Mod. Hist., 1934; MA Oxon 1938; DPhil 1950. Ellerton Theol. Essay Prize, Oxford, 1937; Green Moral Philos. Prize, Oxford, 1947. Deacon, 1936; Priest, 1937; Curate, Higher Tranmere Parish Church, Birkenhead, 1936-39; Chaplain, All Saints', Beirut, Lebanon, 1939-47; Warden, St Justin's House, Beirut, 1942-47; Asst Prof. of Philos., Amer. University of Beirut, 1942-47; Rector of Longworth, Berks, 1947-51; Sheriff's Chap., Berks, 1948; Prof. of Arabic and Islamics, Hartford Seminary, Conn, USA, 1951-56; Rockefeller Travelling Schol., 1954; Res. Canon, St George's Collegiate Church, Jerusalem, 1956-61; Fellow, St Augustine's Coll., Canterbury, 1959-60, Sub-Warden, 1960-61, Warden, 1961-67; Examng Chaplain to Archbishop of Canterbury, 1961-67; Hon. Canon of Canterbury, 1961-80; Asst Bishop to Archbishop in Jerusalem, 1970-74; Reader in Religious Studies, Sussex Univ., and Asst Bishop, dio. of Chichester, 1973-78; Vicar of Helme, W Yorks, and Asst Bishop, dio. Wakefield, 1978-81; Asst Bishop, dio. Oxford, 1982-. Select Preacher: Cambridge, 1961; Dublin, 1962; Oxford, 1974. Proctor in Convocation, Canterbury, 1965-68; Visiting Prof., Union Theological Seminary, New York, 1965-66; Lectr, Faculty of Divinity, Cambridge, 1966; Jordan Lectr, Sch. of Oriental and African Studies, University of London, 1967; Vis. Prof., University of Ibadan, Nigeria, 1968; Bye-Fellow, Gonville and Caius Coll., Cambridge, 1968-74. Editor, The Muslim World Quarterly, 1952-60. *Publications:* The Call of the Minaret, 1956; Sandals at the Mosque, 1959; The Dome and the Rock, 1964; Counsels in Contemporary Islam, 1965;

Christianity in World Perspective, 1968; The Privilege of Man, 1968; The House of Islam, 1969; Alive to God, 1970; The Event of the Qur'an, 1971; The Mind of the Qur'an, 1973; The Wisdom of the Sufis, 1976; The Christian and Other Religion, 1977; Islam from Within, 1979; This Year in Jerusalem, 1982; translated: City of Wrong, 1959; The Theology of Unity, 1965; A Passage to France, 1976; The Hallowed Valley, 1977; Contributor: Journal of World History, 1957; Religion in the Middle East, 1969. *Address:* Appletree Cottage, Ascott-under-Wychwood, Oxford OX7 6AG.

CRAGG, James Birkett; Emeritus Professor of Environmental Science, University of Calgary, Alberta; *b* 8 Nov. 1910; *s* of late A. W. Cragg, N Shields; *m* 1937, Mary Catherine Macnaughtan (marr. diss. 1968); five *s* (one *d* decd); *m* Jean Moore. *Educ:* private sch.; Tynemouth High Sch.; Durham Univ. BSc King's Coll., University of Durham, 1933; DThPT, 1934; MSc, 1937; DSc Newcastle, 1965. Demonstrator, Physiology Dept, Manchester Univ., 1935; Asst Lecturer, and later Lecturer, in Zoology, University Coll. of North Wales, 1937; seconded to Agricultural Research Council, 1942; Scientific Officer, ARC Unit of Insect Physiology, 1944; Reader in Zoology, Durham Colls, in University of Durham, 1946; Prof. of Zoology, University of Durham, 1950-61; Dir, Merlewood Research Station (Nature Conservancy, NERC), Grange-over-Sands, Lancs, 1961-66; Dir, Environmental Sciences Centre, and Prof. of Biology, 1966-72, Killam Meml Prof., 1966-76, Vice-Pres. (Academic), 1970-72, Univ. of Calgary, Alberta. Former Chairman: Commn for Ecology; Internat. Union for Conservation of Nature; Convenor, Internat. Biological Programme PT Cttee; Mem., Internat. Biological Programme Cttees; Consultant, Ford Foundation, 1965. Commonwealth Prestige Fellow (New Zealand), 1964. Jubilee medal, 1977. Hon. FIBiol 1981. *Publications:* papers in scientific periodicals; formerly Editor, Advances in Ecological Research. *Recreation:* books. *Address:* 2112 Uralta Road, Calgary, Alberta T2N 4B4, Canada. *Club:* Athenæum.

CRAGG, Rt. Rev. Kenneth; *see* Cragg, Rt. Rev. A. K.

CRAGGS, Prof. James Wilkinson, BSc, PhD; Professor of Engineering Mathematics, University of Southampton, 1967-81; *b* 3 Feb. 1920; *s* of Thomas Gibson Craggs and Margaret (*née* Wilkinson); *m* 1946, Mary Baker; two *s* one *d. Educ:* Bede Collegiate Sch., Sunderland; University of Manchester. BSc 1941, PhD 1948, Manchester; PhD Cambridge, 1953. Junior Lectr, Royal Military Coll. of Science, 1941-45; Asst Lectr, University of Manchester, 1947-49; Lecturer, Queen's Coll., Dundee, 1951-52; King's Coll., Newcastle upon Tyne: Lectr, 1952-56; Senior Lecturer, 1956-60; Reader in Mathematics, 1960-61; Prof. of Mathematics, University of Leeds, 1961-63; Prof. of Applied Mathematics, Melbourne Univ., 1963-67. *Publications:* contrib. learned journals regarding the mechanics of solids and fluids. *Recreation:* Methodist lay preacher. *Address:* 33 Pirrie Close, Southampton.

CRAGGS, Prof. John Drummond, MSc, PhD, FInstP; Professor of Electronic Engineering, University of Liverpool, 1955-82; *b* 17 May 1915; *s* of Thomas Lawson Craggs and Elsie Aidrienne Roberts; *m* 1941, Dorothy Ellen Margaret Garfitt; two *d. Educ:* Huddersfield Coll.; University of London. Research Student, King's Coll., London Univ., 1937-38; Metropolitan-Vickers High Voltage Research Laboratory, Manchester, 1938-48; University of California, Radiation Laboratory, 1944-45; apptd Sen. Lectr, 1948, and, later, Reader, Dept of Electrical Engineering, University of Liverpool. A Pro-Vice-Chancellor, Liverpool Univ., 1969-72. *Publications:* Counting Tubes, 1950 (with S. C. Curran); Electrical Breakdown of Gases, 1953; High Voltage Laboratory Technique, 1954 (with J. M. Meek); Electrical Breakdown of Gases (with J. M. Meek), 1978; papers in various professional jls. *Address:* Stone Cottage, Newton-cum-Larton, West Kirby, Wirral, Merseyside L48 1PG. *T:* 051-625 5055.

CRAIB, Douglas Duncan Simpson, CBE 1974; DL; FRAgS 1971; farmer and company director, since 1937; Member, Potato Marketing Board of Great Britain, since 1968; *b* 5 April 1914; *s* of Peter Barton Salsbury Simpson and Helen Duncan; changed name by deed poll, 1930; *m* 1939, Moyra Louise Booth; one *s* one *d. Educ:* Aberdeen Grammar Sch.; Dundee High School. Commerce, 1934. Captain, 7th Bn Seaforth Highlanders, 1939-42. Chm., Elec. Cons. Council, N Scotland Area, 1971-79; Mem., N of Scotland Hydro-Elec. Bd, 1971-79. Chm. of Directors, Royal Highland and Agric. Soc. of Scotland, 1967-69 (Hon. Sec. and Hon. Treas., 1970-74; Vice-Pres., 1978-79); Chm., Highland Agric. Exec. Cttee, 1970-72; Mem., Scottish Agric. Devel t Council, 1972-76; Governor: N of Scotland Coll. of Agriculture, 1970-; Rowett Res. Inst., Aberdeen, 1973-; Trustee, The MacRobert Trusts, Scotland, 1970-. DL Moray 1974. *Address:* Stynie House, Fochabers, Morayshire IV32 7LE. *T:* Fochabers 820231. *Club:* Farmers'.

CRAIG, family name of Viscount Craigavon.

CRAIG, Sir (Albert) James (Macqueen), KCMG 1981 (CMG 1975); HM Diplomatic Service; Ambassador to Saudi Arabia, since 1979; *b* 13 July 1924; *s* of James Craig and Florence Morris; *m* 1952, Margaret Hutchinson; three *s* one *d. Educ:* Liverpool Institute High Sch.; Univ. of Oxford. Queen's Coll., Oxford (Exhibr), 1942; 1st cl. Hon. Mods Classics, 1943 (Hon. Schol.); Army, 1943-44; 1st cl. Oriental Studies (Arabic and Persian), 1947; Sen. Demy, Magdalen Coll., 1947-48; Lectr in Arabic, Durham Univ., 1948-55; seconded to FO, 1955 as Principal Instructor at Middle East Centre for Arab Studies, Lebanon; joined Foreign Service substantively, 1956; served: FO, 1958-61; HM Political Agent, Trucial States, 1961-64; 1st Sec., Beirut, 1964-67;

Counsellor and Head of Chancery, Jedda, 1967-70; Supernumerary Fellow, St Antony's Coll., Oxford, 1970-71; Head of Near East and N Africa Dept, FCO, 1971-75; Dep. High Comr, Kuala Lumpur, 1975-76; Ambassador to Syria, 1976-79. *Address:* c/o Foreign and Commonwealth Office, SW1. *Club:* Travellers'.

CRAIG, Very Rev. Archibald Campbell, MC 1918; DD (Hon.); *b* 3 Dec. 1888; *yr s* of Rev. Alexander McRae Craig; *m* 1950, Mary Isobel Laidlaw, *d* of Rev. John Laidlaw; no *c. Educ:* Kelso High Sch.; Edinburgh Univ.; New Coll., Edinburgh. Served European War, 1914-18, 13th Royal Scots and Intelligence Corps, 1914-19. Pastorates in Galston and Glasgow, 1921-30; Chaplain to University of Glasgow, 1930-39; Sec. to the Churches' Commn of Internat. Friendship and Social Responsibility, 1939-42; Gen. Sec., British Council of Churches, 1942-46; Asst Leader, Iona Community, 1946-47; Lecturer in Biblical Studies, Glasgow Univ., 1947-57. Moderator of the Gen. Assembly of the Church of Scotland, May 1961-62. Hon. DD: Edinburgh, 1938; Glasgow, 1961; Dublin, 1961. *Publications:* University Sermons, 1937; Preaching in a Scientific Age (Warrack Lectures), 1954; God Comes Four Times, 1957. *Recreation:* gardening. *Address:* St John's, Doune, Perthshire. *T:* Doune 386.

CRAIG, Mrs Barbara Denise, MA Oxon; Principal of Somerville College, Oxford, 1967-80, Honorary Fellow, 1980; *b* 22 Oct. 1915; *o d* of John Alexander Chapman and Janie Denize (*née* Callaway); *m* 1942, Wilson James Craig; no *c. Educ:* Haberdashers' Aske's Girls' Sch., Acton; Somerville Coll., Oxford. Craven Fellow, 1938; Goldsmiths' Sen. Student, 1938; Woolley Fellow in Archæology of Somerville Coll., 1954-56. Temp. Asst Principal, Mins of Supply and Labour, 1939-40; Asst to Prof. of Greek, Aberdeen Univ., 1940-42; Temp. Asst Principal, Min. of Home Security, 1942; Temp. Principal, Min. of Production, 1943-45. Unofficial work as wife of British Council officer in Brazil, Iraq, Spain, Pakistan, 1946-65; from 1956, archæological work on finds from British excavations at Mycenae. *Recreations:* bird-watching (Mem. Brit. Ornithologists' Union); walking. *Address:* The Wynd, Gayle, Hawes, North Yorkshire DL8 3SD. *T:* Hawes 289. *Club:* University Women's.

CRAIG, Charles (James); opera singer (tenor); *b* 3 Dec. 1920; *s* of James and Rosina Craig; *m* 1946, Dorothy Wilson; one *s* one *d. Educ:* in London. Protégé of Sir Thomas Beecham; Principal Tenor with Carl Rosa Opera Co., 1953-56; joined Sadler's Wells Opera Co., 1956. Appears regularly at Internat. Opera Houses, incl. Covent Garden, Milan, Rome, Vienna, Paris, Berlin, Buenos Aires, etc; repertoire of 48 operas, incl. Otello, Aida, Turandot, Norma, Andrea Chenier, Die Walküre, Götterdämmerung, Lohengrin, etc. Concerts, TV and radio, and records. International Opera Medal Award, 1962. *Recreations:* motoring, cooking. *Address:* Whitfield Cottage, Whitfield, Northants.

CRAIG, Clifford, CMG 1951; radiologist; *b* 3 Aug. 1896; *s* of Dr W. J. Craig, Box Hill, Victoria, Australia; *m* 1927, Edith Nance Bulley; two *s* one *d. Educ:* Scotch Coll., Melbourne; University of Melbourne. MB, BS, 1924; MD Melbourne, 1926; MS Melbourne, 1930; FRACS 1930; DDR 1954. Surgeon Superintendent, Launceston General Hospital, 1926-31; Hon. Surgeon, Launceston General Hospital, 1932-41; Surgeon Superintendent, 1941-51. Pres., Tasmanian Branch, BMA, 1941; Mem. Federal Council, BMA, 1941-47. Pres. Rotary International, Launceston, 1950; Pres., Medical Council, Tasmania, 1954-66; Chairman, Tasmanian Cancer Cttee; President: Nat. Trust of Aust. (Tasmania), 1963-72; Aust. Cancer Soc., 1970-73. Gold Medal, Aust. Cancer Soc., 1981. Served European War, 1914-18, 1st AIF (Palestine), 1916-18; War of 1939-45, RAAF, 1940-45. *Publications:* The Engravers of Van Diemen's Land, 1961; Old Tasmanian Prints, 1964; History of the Launceston General Hospital, 1963; (jtly) Early Colonial Furniture in New South Wales and Van Diemen's Land, 1972; A Bibliographical Study of the Van Diemen's Land 'Pickwick Papers', 1973; Mr Punch in Tasmania, 1981; articles in medical jls. *Recreations:* Cricket Blue, Melbourne Univ.; tennis, golf. *Address:* 21 High Street, Launceston, Tasmania 7250, Australia. *T:* 319025. *Club:* Launceston (Launeston).

CRAIG, Air Marshal Sir David (Brownrigg), KCB 1981 (CB 1978); OBE 1967; Air Officer Commanding-in-Chief, RAF Strike Command and C-in-C UK Air Forces, since 1982; *b* 17 Sept. 1929; *s* of Major Francis Brownrigg Craig and Mrs Olive Craig; *m* 1955, Elisabeth June Derenburg; one *s* one *d. Educ:* Radley Coll.; Lincoln Coll., Oxford (MA). Commnd in RAF, 1951; OC RAF Cranwell, 1968-70; ADC to the Queen, 1969-71; Dir, Plans and Ops, HQ Far East Comd, 1970-71; OC RAF Akrotiri, 1972-73; ACAS (Ops), MoD, 1975-78; AOC No 1 Group, RAF Strike Command, 1978-80; Vice-Chief of Air Staff, 1980-82. *Recreations:* fishing, shooting, golf. *Address:* c/o Williams & Glyn's Bank Ltd, 9 Pall Mall, SW1. *Club:* Royal Air Force.

CRAIG, Prof. David Parker, FRS 1968; FAA 1969; FRIC; Professor of Chemistry, Australian National University, since 1967; Dean, Research School of Chemistry, 1970-73 and 1977-81; *b* 23 Dec. 1919; *s* of Andrew Hunter Craig, Manchester and Sydney, and Mary Jane (*née* Parker); *m* 1948, Veronica, *d* of Cyril Bryden-Brown, Market Harborough and Sydney; three *s* one *d. Educ:* Sydney Church of England Grammar Sch.; University of Sydney; University Coll., London. MSc (Sydney) 1941, PhD (London) 1950, DSc (London) 1956. Commonwealth Science Scholar, 1940. War Service: Capt., Australian Imperial Force, 1941-44. Lectr in Chemistry, University of Sydney, 1944-46; Turner and Newall Research Fellow, 1946-49, and Lectr in

Chemistry, University Coll., London, 1949-52; Prof. of Physical Chemistry, Univ. of Sydney, 1952-56; Prof. of Chemistry, University Coll., London, 1956-67, Vis. Prof., 1968-; Firth Vis. Prof., Univ. of Sheffield, 1973; Vis. Prof. University Coll., Cardiff, 1975-. Part-time Mem., CSIRO Exec., 1980-. Fellow of University Coll., London, 1964-. *Publications:* original papers on chemistry in scientific periodicals. *Address:* Research School of Chemistry, Australian National University, Box 4 PO Canberra, ACT 2600, Australia. *Club:* Athenæum.

CRAIG, Douglas, OBE 1965; Member of Executive, since 1979, and Editor, since 1980, Music Journal of Incorporated Society of Musicians; *b* 26 May 1916; *m* 1955, Dorothy Dixon; two *d*. *Educ:* Latymer Upper Sch.; St Catharine's Coll., Cambridge (MA). FRCM, FRSA. Winchester Prize, Cambridge, 1938. Intell. Corps, 1940-46, Major 1944. Baritone, Sadler's Wells Opera and elsewhere, 1946-; Artistic Dir, Opera for All, 1949-65; Stage Dir, Glyndebourne, 1952-55; Asst Gen. Man., Glyndebourne, 1955-59; Producer, Royal Coll. of Music, 1958-; Freelance Opera Producer, 1959-; Dep. Dir, London Opera Centre, 1965-66; Administrator, Welsh Nat. Opera, 1966-70; Dir, Sadler's Wells Theatre, 1970-78; Dir, Opera and Drama Sch., RCM, 1976-80. *Publication:* (ed) Delius: Koanga (opera), 1975. *Recreation:* travel. *Address:* 43 Park Road, Radlett, Herts WD7 8EG. *T:* Radlett 7240. *Clubs:* Garrick, Oxford and Cambridge Music.

CRAIG, Edward Anthony, (works also under name of Edward Carrick), FRSA; writer and lecturer, designer for film and theatre; independent film art director; *b* 3 Jan. 1905; *s* of late Edward Gordon Craig, CH; *m* 1960, Mary, *d* of late Lieut-Col H. A. Timewell, OBE. Studied art, the theatre and photography in Italy, 1917-26; has discovered numerous documents of great value to the history of the theatre; Art Dir to the Welsh Pearson Film Co., 1928-29; Art Dir for Associated Talking Pictures, 1932-36; Supervising Art Dir, Criterion Film, 1937-39; established AAT Film Sch., 1937; Art Dir to the Crown Film Unit (Ministry of Information), 1939-46; Executive Art Dir, Independent Producers (Rank), 1947-49; wood-engravings, oil paintings, and scene designs exhibited at: the St George's Gallery, 1927 and 1928; at the Redfern Gallery, 1929, 1931, 1938; The Grubb Group, 1928-38; also in the principal Galleries of Canada and North America; designer of scenes and costumes for numerous London productions and at Stratford-upon-Avon, 1949. *Official Purchasers:* the British Museum; Victoria and Albert Museum; Metropolitan Museum, New York; Yale Univ., USA; The University, Austin, Texas. *Publications:* Designing for Moving Pictures, 1941; Meet the Common People, 1942; Art and Design in British Films, 1948; Designing for Films, 1949; Gordon Craig, The Story of his Life, 1968; (in Italian) Fabrizio Carini Motta, 1972, Polish trans., 1977; William Nicholson's An Alphabet, 1978; Robinson Crusoe and Gordon Craig, 1979; William Nicholson's An Almanac, 1980; (ed) Gordon Craig: the last eight years, by Ellen Gordon Craig, 1982; Baroque Theatre Construction, 1982. *Illustrations:* The Georgics of Virgil, 1931, etc; books of verse by John Keats, Edith Sitwell, Edmund Blunden, W. H. Davies, etc. *Recreations:* books and music. *Address:* Cutlers Orchard, Bledlow, Aylesbury, Bucks HP17 9PA.

CRAIG, Hamish M.; *see* Millar-Craig.

CRAIG, Sir James; *see* Craig, Sir A. J. M.

CRAIG, Norman; Assistant Secretary, Lord Chancellor's Department, since 1979; *b* 15 May 1920; *s* of George Craig, OBE; *m* 1st, 1946, Judith Margaret Newling (marr. diss. 1957); one *s*; 2nd, 1960, Jane Hudson; two *s* one *d*. *Educ:* Penarth County Sch.; Cardiff Univ. Army Service, Royal Sussex Regt, 1940-47. Board of Trade, 1948; Min. of Supply, 1953; Private Sec. to Minister of Aviation, 1959-60; Sec. to Cttee of Inquiry into Aircraft Industry, 1964-65. Course at IDC, 1968; Asst Under-Sec. of State, MoD, 1972-79. *Publication:* The Broken Plume, 1982. *Address:* 51 Hayes Lane, Beckenham, Kent. *T:* 01-650 7916.

CRAIG, Rev. Prof. Robert, CBE 1981; Minister, St Andrew's Scots Memorial Church, Jerusalem, since 1980; Principal, 1969-80, Vice-Chancellor, 1970-80, Professor of Theology, 1963-80, University of Zimbabwe (formerly University of Rhodesia), now Emeritus; *b* 22 March 1917; *s* of late John Craig, stone-mason, and late Anne Peggie, linen-weaver; *m* 1950, Olga Wanda, *d* of late Michael and of Helena Strzelec; one *s* one *d*. *Educ:* Fife CC schs; St Andrews Univ. (Hon. Regent, 1982); Union Theol Seminary, NY. MA (Ordinary) 19 38, BD with distinction in Systematic Theology 1941, PhD 1950, St Andrews; STM *magna cum laude* Union Theol Seminary 1948. Pres., Students' Rep. Council, Chm. Union Debating Soc., Berry Schol. in Theology, St Andrews Univ., 1941; Asst Minister, St John's Kirk, Perth, 1941-42, ordained 1942; Chaplain (4th class), Army, 1942-47: infantry bns, NW Europe, 1944-45 (despatches, France, 1944); Palestine, Egypt, 1945-47; HCF 1947. Hugh Black Fellow and Instructor in Systematic Theology, Union Theol Seminary, 1947-48; Dep. Leader, Iona Community, Scotland, 1948-49; Natal Univ.: Prof. of Divinity, 1950-57; College Dean, Adviser of Students and personal rep. of Principal and Vice-Chancellor, 1953-54; Prof. of Religion, Smith Coll., Mass, 1958-63; UC Rhodesia and Nyasaland: Prof. of Theology, 1963; Dean, Faculty of Arts, 1965; Vice-Principal, 1966; Actg Principal, 1967 and 1969. External Examiner: Boston, Cape Town, McGill, Natal, Rhodes, S Africa Univs, various times, 1950-80. Vis. Lectr, Ecumenical Inst., Bossey, Switz., 1955; John Dewey Mem. Lectr, Vermont Univ., 1961; Ainslie Mem. Lectr, Rhodes Univ., 1965. Jerusalem appointments: Member: Ecumenical Theol Res. Fraternity, 1980-; Ecumenical Friends Gp, 1980-;

Council, Interfaith Cttee, 1981-; Bd of Dirs, Internat. YMCA, 1982-; Exec. Cttee, Spafford Community Centre, 1982-; Chm., Church of Scotland Israel Council, 1981-; Moderator, Presbytery of Jerusalem, 1982-. Brit. Council Commonwealth Interchange Fellow, Cambridge Univ., 1966. Hon. DD St Andrews, 1967; Hon. LLD: Witwatersrand 1979; Birmingham, 1980; Natal, 1981; Hon. DLitt Zimbabwe, 1981. Hon. Fellow, Zimbabwe Instn of Engineers, 1976. Golden Jubilee Medal, Witwatersrand Univ., 1977. *Publications:* The Reasonableness of True Religion, 1954; Social Concern in the Thought of William Temple, 1963; Religion: Its Reality and Its Relevance, 1965; The Church: Unity in Integrity, 1966; Religion and Politics: a Christian view, 1972; On Belonging to a University, 1974. *Recreations:* the cinema, theatre, contemporary and recent history, light classical music, listening and talking to people. *Address:* St Andrew's Scots Memorial Church, PO Box 14216, Jerusalem, Israel. *T:* (02) 714659. *Clubs:* Kate Kennedy, University Staff, Students' Union (St Andrews); YMCA, Rainbow (Jerusalem).

CRAIG, Thomas Rae, CBE 1969 (OBE 1945); TD; DL; retired; Deputy Governor, The Bank of Scotland, 1972-77; *b* 11 July 1906; *s* of Sir John Craig, CBE, and Jessie Craig (*née* Sommerville); *m* 1931, Christina Gay (*née* Moodie); three *s* one *d*. *Educ:* Glasgow Academy; Lycée Malherbe, Caen, Normandy. Served War of 1939-45: Lt-Col 6th Cameronians; AA and QMG 52nd (Lowland) Div. Dir of Colvilles Ltd, 1935; Man. Dir, 1958; Dep. Chm., 1961; Chm. and Man. Dir, 1965-68. Mem. Bd, BSC, 1967-72. Formerly Dir of companies. Member: Convocation of Strathclyde Univ.; Court of Glasgow Univ. DL Dunbartonshire, 1973. Hon. LLD: Strathclyde, 1968; Glasgow, 1970. OStJ. *Recreation:* farming. *Address:* Invergare, Rhu, Dunbartonshire. *T:* Rhu 820427. *Club:* Royal Scottish Automobile (Glasgow).

CRAIG, Rt. Hon. William, PC (N Ire.) 1963; solicitor and company director; *b* 2 Dec. 1924; *s* of late John Craig and Mary Kathleen Craig (*née* Lamont); *m* 1960, Doris Hilgendorff; two *s*. *Educ:* Dungannon Royal Sch.; Larne Grammar Sch.; Queen's Univ., Belfast. Served War of 1939-45, Royal Air Force, 1943-46. Qualified as solicitor, 1952. MP (U) Larne Div. of Antrim, NI Parliament, 1960-73; Mem. (Vanguard Unionist Progressive), N Antrim, NI Assembly, 1973-75; Mem. (UUC), E Belfast, NI Constitutional Convention, 1975-76; MP (UU) Belfast East, Feb. 1974-79. Chief Whip, Parliament of Northern Ireland, 1962-63; Minister of Home Affairs, 1963-64, and 1966-68; Minister of Health and Local Government, 1964; Minister of Development, 1965-66. Founder: Ulster Vanguard, 1972 (Leader, 1972-77); Vanguard Unionist Party, 1973 (Leader, 1973-77). Member: Council of Europe, 1976-79; WEU, 1976-79. *Recreations:* travel, motoring, shooting. *Address:* 23 Annadale Avenue, Belfast, Northern Ireland BT7 3JJ. *T:* Belfast 644096. *Club:* Royal North of Ireland Yacht (Cultra, Belfast).

CRAIG-McFEELY, Comdt Elizabeth Sarah Ann, CB 1982; Director, Women's Royal Naval Service, 1979-82; *b* 28 April 1927; *d* of late Lt-Col Cecil Michael Craig McFeely, DSO, OBE, MC, and late Nancy Sarah (*née* Mann, later Roberts). *Educ:* St Rose's Convent, Stroud, Glos; Anstey College of Physical Educn, Birmingham. DipPhysEducn London. Taught PE at St Angela's Ursuline Convent Sch., 1948-52; joined WRNS, 1952; Third Officer, 1953; served in various Royal Naval, Royal Marines and Royal Naval Reserve Estabts, 1952-67; in charge, WRNS, Far Eastern Fleet, 1967-69; various appts, MoD (Navy), 1969-74; HMS Centurion, 1974-76; Supt WRNS, 1977. Naval member, NAAFI Bd of Management, 1977-79; Hon. ADC to the Queen, 1979-82. CBIM. *Recreations:* gardening and country pursuits. *Address:* Moonrakers, Mockbeggar Lane, Biddenden, Kent TN27 8ES. *T:* Biddenden 291325.

CRAIGAVON, 3rd Viscount *cr* 1927, of Stormont, Co. Down; **Janric Fraser Craig;** Bt 1918; *b* 9 June 1944; *s* of 2nd Viscount Craigavon; *S* father, 1974. *Educ:* Eton; London Univ. (BA, BSc). FCA. *Heir:* none. *Address:* Flat 13, 65 Courtfield Gardens, SW5 0NQ. *T:* 01-373 9834.

CRAIGEN, Desmond Seaward; Chairman, Vanbrugh Life Assurance Co. Ltd, since 1982; Director, Prudential Corporation plc, since 1982; *b* 31 July 1916; *s* of late John Craigen and Ann Amelia Craigen (*née* Brebner); *m* 1961, Elena Ines (*née* Oldham Florez); one *s* one *d*. *Educ:* Holloway Sch.; King's Coll., London (BA Hons). Prudential Assurance Co. Ltd, 1934-; India, 1950-57; attached O&M Div., Treasury, 1957-58; Dep. General Manager, 1968-69; General Manager, 1969-78; Chief General Manager, 1979-81. Served War of 1939-45: 53rd Reconnaisance Regt RAC (Major). *Recreations:* tennis, music, reading. *Address:* Corrydon House, Blewbury, Oxon OX11 9PF. *T:* Blewbury 850426.

CRAIGEN, James Mark, JP; MP (Lab and Co-op) Glasgow Maryhill since Feb. 1974; *b* 2 Aug. 1938; *e s* of James Craigen, MA and Isabel Craigen; *m* 1971, Sheena Millar. *Educ:* Shawlands Academy, Glasgow; Strathclyde University. MLitt, Heriot-Watt, 1974. FBIM. Compositor, 1954-61. Industrial Relations Asst, Scottish Gas Bd, 1963-64; Head of Organisation and Social Services at Scottish TUC, 1964-68; Asst Sec., and Industrial Liaison Officer, Scottish Business Educn Council, 1968-74. Glasgow City Councillor, 1965-68, Magistrate, 1966-68; JP 1966-; Mem. Scottish Ambulance Service Bd, 1966-71; Mem. Police Adv. Bd for Scotland, 1970-74; contested Ayr constituency, 1970; PPS to Sec. of State for Scotland, 1974-76. Mem., UK Delegn to Council of Europe Assembly, 1976-80. Chairman: Co-op. Party Group, 1978-79; Scottish Group, Labour MPs, 1978-79; PLP Employment Gp, 1981-; Mem., House of Commons Employment Select

Cttee, 1979-. Mem. General and Municipal Workers Union. Fellow, Industry and Parliament Trust, 1978-79. *Publications:* contribs to Co-operative News. *Address:* House of Commons, SW1A 0AA.

CRAIGIE, Dr Hugh Brechin, CBE 1965; Principal Medical Officer, Mental Health Division, Scottish Home and Health Department, retired; *b* 19 May 1908; *s* of late Hugh Craigie; *m* 1st, 1933, Lillia Campbell (*d* 1958), *d* of Dr George Campbell Murray; three *s*; 2nd, 1962, Eileen (MBE 1950), *d* of F. S. Lyons. *Educ:* Manchester Grammar Sch.; Manchester Univ. House Physician, Manchester Royal Infirmary, 1931-32; Asst Medical Officer, Monsall Fever Hosp., Manchester, 1932-33; Senior Medical Officer, County Mental Hosp., Lancaster, 1933-46; Dep. Med. Supt, County Mental Hosp., Whittingham, 1946; HM Senior Medical Commissioner, General Board of Control for Scotland, 1947. Served War of 1939-45 (despatches), RAMC (Hon. Lieut-Col). *Publications:* various papers on psychiatry. *Address:* Saviskaill, Westerdunes Park, North Berwick.

CRAIGIE, John Hubert, OC 1967; FRS 1952; *b* 8 Dec. 1887; *s* of John Yorston Craigie and Elizabeth Mary Pollock; *m* 1926, Miriam Louise, *d* of Allen R. Morash and Clara Louise (*née* Smith). *Educ:* Harvard Univ. (AB); University of Minnesota (MSc); University of Manitoba (PhD). Dalhousie Univ., 1914. Served European War, 1914-18, Canadian Expeditionary Force, 1915-18; Indian Army, 1918-20. Canada Dept of Agriculture: Plant Pathologist, 1925-27; Senior Plant Pathologist, 1927-28; Officer-in-Charge (of Laboratory), Dominion Laboratory of Plant Pathology, Winnipeg, 1928-45; Associate Dir, Science Service, Canada Dept of Agriculture, Ottawa, 1945-52; retired 1952. Hon. DSc: University of British Columbia, 1946; University of Manitoba, 1959; Hon. LLD: University of Saskatchewan, 1948; Dalhousie Univ., 1951. *Publications:* papers in scientific journals. *Address:* 950 Bank Street, Ottawa, Ontario K1S 5G6, Canada.

CRAIGMYLE, 3rd Baron, *cr* 1929, of Craigmyle; **Thomas Donald Mackay Shaw;** Director of Inchcape & Co. Ltd; Chairman: Craigmyle & Co. Ltd; Claridge Mills Ltd; Walsham Mill Ltd; *b* 17 Nov. 1923; *s* of 2nd Baron and Lady Margaret Cargill Mackay (*d* 1958), *e d* of 1st Earl of Inchcape; *S* father, 1944; *m* 1955, Anthea Esther Christine, *y d* of late E. C. Rich; three *s* three *d*. *Educ:* Eton; Trinity Coll., Oxford (MA). Served RNVR, 1943-46. FRSA. Kt of Obedience, OStJ; SMO Malta (Hospitaller to British Assoc., 1962-73; Sec.-Gen., 1979-). *Publication:* (ed with J. Gould) Your Death Warrant?, 1971. *Recreation:* home baking. *Heir: s* Hon. Thomas Columba Shaw, *b* 19 Oct. 1960. *Address:* 18 The Boltons, SW10 9SY; Scottas, Knoydart, Inverness-shire PH41 4PL. *Clubs:* Caledonian; Royal Thames Yacht; Bengal (Calcutta).
See also W. B. Dean.

CRAIGTON, Baron, *cr* 1959 (Life Peer); **Jack Nixon Browne,** PC 1961; CBE 1944; *b* 3 Sept. 1904; *m* 1950, Eileen Nolan, *d* of late Henry Whitford Nolan, London. *Educ:* Cheltenham Coll. Served War of 1939-45, RAF (Balloon Command), Actg Group Capt. Contested (C) Govan Div., Glasgow, in 1945; MP (C) Govan Div., 1950-55; MP (C) Craigton Div. of Glasgow, 1955-Sept. 1959; Parly Private Sec. to Sec. of State for Scotland, 1952-April 1955; Parly Under-Sec., Scottish Office, April 1955-Oct. 1959; Minister of State, Scottish Office, Nov. 1959-Oct. 1964. City of Westminster Chamber of Commerce (formerly Westminster Chamber of Commerce): Mem., General Purposes Cttee, 1948; Mem., Exec. Cttee, 1950; Chm., 1954; Pres., 1966-. Chm., United Biscuits (Holdings) Ltd, 1967-72. Pres., Commercial Travellers Benevolent Instn, 1976-; Vice-Pres., World Wildlife Fund (British Nat. Appeal), 1979; Chm., Fauna Preservation Soc., 1981- (Vice-Chm., 1970-80); Chairman: Cttee for Environmental Conservation, 1972-; All-Party Conservation Cttee of both Houses of Parliament, 1972-; Fedn of Zoological Gardens, 1975-81. RSA: Mem. Council, 1975-81; Mem., Environment Cttee, 1975-. *Recreation:* gardening. *Address:* Friary House, Friary Island, Wraysbury, near Staines, Mddx. *T:* Wraysbury 2213. *Club:* Buck's.

CRAIK, Duncan Robert Steele, CB 1979; OBE 1971; FASA, FAIM; part-time Member, Administrative Appeals Tribunal, since 1981; *b* 17 Feb. 1916; *s* of Henry Steele Craik and Lilian Kate Ellis; *m* 1943, Audrey Mavis Ion; four *d*. *Educ:* Univ. of Sydney (BEc). FASA 1973, FAIM 1975. Commonwealth Bank, 1933-40; Taxation Br., 1940-60; Treasury: Asst Sec., 1960-66; First Asst Sec., 1966-69; Dep. Sec., 1969-73; Auditor-General for Australia, 1973-81. Mem. Council, ANU, 1981-. *Publications:* contrib. to Economic Record. *Recreations:* bowls, gardening. *Address:* 15 Meehan Gardens, Griffith, ACT 2603, Australia. *T:* 95 8512. *Club:* Commonwealth (Canberra).

CRAIK, Roger George, QC (Scot.) 1981; *b* 22 Nov. 1940; *s* of George and Frances Craik; *m* 1964, Helen Sinclair Sutherland; one *s* one *d*. *Educ:* Lockerbie Academy; Breadalbane Academy, Aberfeldy; George Watson's Boys' Coll.; Edinburgh Univ. (MA 1960, LLB 1962). Qualified as solicitor, 1962; worked for Orr Dignam & Co., Solicitors, Pakistan, 1963-65; called to Scottish Bar, 1966. Standing junior counsel to Min. of Defence (Army), 1974-80; Advocate Depute, 1980-. *Recreations:* Scottish antiquities, modern jazz. *Address:* Advocates' Library, Parliament House, Edinburgh EH1 1RF.

CRAM, Alastair Lorimer, MC 1945; Appellate Judge, Supreme Court of Appeal, Malawi, 1964-68, retired; in private practice at Scots Bar, Edinburgh; *b* 25 Aug. 1909; *m* 1951, Isobel Nicholson; no *c*. *Educ:* Perth Academy; Edinburgh University (LLB). Solicitor, 1933; private practice, 1935-39;

admitted Scots Bar, 1946. Served in HM Army, 1939-48: POW, successful escapes; RA, SAS, Intelligence Corps, Counsel War Crimes Group NW Europe, Major; GSO 2. Resident Magistrate, Kenya, 1948; Actg Puisne Judge, 1953-56; Sen. Resident Magistrate, Kenya, 1956; Temp. Puisne Judge, 1958-60; Puisne Judge, High Court of Nyasaland, 1960; acting Chief Justice and (briefly) Governor-General, Malawi, 1965; Legal Dept, Scottish Office, 1971-74. Athlete, climber, and traveller: in Alps, 1930-60, and Himalayas, 1960 and 1963; in African, Asian and South American deserts, 1940-66; in Amazon basin and Peruvian Andes, 1966; in Atlas Mts, 1971. *Publications:* Editor, Kenya Law Reports, 1952-56; contribs law reports, legal and mountaineering jls. *Recreations:* shooting, sound-recordings, photography (still and cine), orchid-collecting, languages. *Address:* 5 Upper Dean Terrace, Edinburgh. *T:* 031-332 5441. *Clubs:* Alpine; Scottish Mountaineering (Edinburgh).

CRAMER, Hon. Sir John (Oscar), Kt 1964; FREI; QRV; MHR (L) for Bennelong, New South Wales, 1949-74; Senior Partner, Cramer Brothers, real estate auctioneers; Managing Director, Higgins (Buildings) Ltd; *b* Quirindi, NSW, 18 Feb. 1897; *s* of J. N. Cramer, Quirindi; *m* 1921, Mary (Dame Mary Cramer, *qv*), *d* of William M. Earls; two *s* two *d*. *Educ:* state public schs; business coll. Mayor of North Sydney, 1940-41; Member: Sydney County Council, 1935- (Chm., 1946-49); Statutory Cttee on Public Works, 1949-56 (Chm., 1955-56); Executive Building Industry Congress of New South Wales; Executive of Liberal Party of Australia, NSW Division (a founder of Provisional Exec.). Minister for the Army, 1956-63. Patron: Anzac Meml Club, N Sydney; RSL, N Ryde, NSW. *Recreation:* bowls. *Address:* Unit 7, 47a Shirley Road, Wollstonecraft, NSW 2065, Australia. *T:* 43 5007. *Club:* Rotary.

CRAMER, Dame Mary (Theresa), DBE 1971; Past President of the Mater Hospital Auxiliary, Sydney, New South Wales, Australia; *d* of William M. Earls; *m* 1921, Hon. Sir John (Oscar) Cramer, *qv*; two *s* two *d*. Has been for many years in public life and interested in charitable activities; was closely associated with the Red Cross movement; during War of 1939-45 she was the first area officer of Women's Aust. Nat. Services on the North Shore. *Address:* Unit 7, 47a Shirley Road, Wollstonecraft, NSW 2065, Australia.

CRAMOND, Ronald Duncan; Under Secretary, Department of Agriculture and Fisheries for Scotland, since 1977; *b* 22 March 1927; *s* of Adam and Margaret Cramond; *m* 1954, Constance MacGregor; one *s* one *d*. *Educ:* George Heriot's Sch.; Edinburgh Univ. (MA). Sen. Medallist History 1949. FBIM; FSAScot 1978. Commnd Royal Scots, 1950. Entered War Office, 1951; Private Sec. to Parly Under-Sec. of State, Scottish Office, 1956; Principal, Dept of Health for Scotland, 1957; Mactaggart Fellow (Applied Econs), Glasgow Univ., 1962; Haldane Medallist in Public Admin, 1964; Asst Sec., Scottish Develt Dept, 1966, Under Sec., 1973. *Publication:* Housing Policy in Scotland, 1966. *Recreations:* golf, hill walking, Rugby refereeing. *Address:* c/o Department of Agriculture and Fisheries for Scotland, Chesser House, 500 Gorgie Road, Edinburgh EH11 3AW. *Club:* Royal Commonwealth Society.

CRAMOND, Dr William Alexander, OBE 1960; FRSE; Director of Mental Health Services, New South Wales, since 1980; *b* 2 Oct. 1920; *er s* of William James Cramond, MBE and of May Battisby, Aberdeen; *m* 1949, Bertine J. C. Mackintosh, MB, ChB, Dornoch; one *s* one *d*. *Educ:* Robert Gordon's Coll., Aberdeen; Aberdeen Univ. MB, ChB, MD, FRCPsych, FRANZCP, FRACP, DPM. Physician Supt, Woodilee Mental Hosp., Glasgow, 1955-61; Dir of Mental Health, S Australia, 1961-65; Prof. of Mental Health, Univ. of Adelaide, 1963-71; Principal Medical Officer in Mental Health, Scottish Home and Health Dept, 1971-72; Dean of Faculty of Medicine and Prof. of Mental Health, Univ. of Leicester, 1972-75; Principal and Vice-Chancellor, Stirling Univ., 1975-80. Hon. Prof. Clin. Psych. Sydney, 1980-. *Publications:* papers on psychosomatic medicine and on care of dying in Brit. Jl Psychiat., Lancet, BMJ. *Recreations:* walking, reading, theatre. *Address:* Health Commission for New South Wales, McKell Building, Rawson Place, Sydney, NSW 2000, Australia.

CRAMP, Prof. Rosemary Jean; Professor of Archaeology, University of Durham, since 1971; *b* 6 May 1929. *Educ:* St Anne's Coll., Oxford (MA, BLitt). Lectr, St Anne's Coll., Oxford, 1950-55; Lectr, Durham Univ., 1955, Sen. Lectr, 1966. Member: Ancient Monuments Board for England, 1974-; Royal Commn on Ancient and Historical Monuments of Scotland, 1975-. Vice-Pres., Soc. of Antiquaries of London, 1978-83; Trustee, British Museum, 1978-. *Publications:* contribs in the field of Early Monasticism, Anglo-Saxon Sculpture and Northern Archaeology. *Address:* Department of Archaeology, University of Durham, 46 Saddler Street, Durham DH1 3NU. *T:* Durham 64466.

CRAMPTON, (Arthur Edward) Seán, MC 1943; GM(mil.) 1944; FRBS 1965 (ARBS 1952, PPRBS); sculptor; *b* 15 March 1918; *e s* of late Joshua Crampton, architect, and Ethel Mary (*née* Dyas); *m* 3rd, 1959, Patricia, *e d* of L. J. Cardew Wood, Weybridge; one *s* one *d*; three *d* by former marriages. *Educ:* St Joseph de Cluny, Stafford; Vittoria Jun. Sch. of Art, Birmingham; Birmingham Central Coll. of Art; London; Paris. Served TA, London Irish Rifles, Western Desert, Sicily, Italy, 1938-46 (Captain). Prof. de Sculpture, Anglo-French Art Centre, 1946-50; won Nat. Comp. for RAC Meml, 1951; served on juries for Thomas More and Winston Churchill meml statues. Member, Art Workers Guild, 1971 (Master, 1978); Pres., RBS, 1966-71.

Mem., Accademia Italia, 1981. Governor, Camberwell Sch. of Arts and Crafts, 1970-. FRSA 1973. *Exhibitions: general:* RA and RI Galls, summer and winter salons, 1950-; *one-man:* London Gall., 1948; Ashley Gall., 1952; Alwin Gall. (Brook St.), 1965, 1966, 1968, 1970; Minories, Colchester, 1971; Alwin Gall. (Grafton St.), 1972, 1974, 1976, 1977, 1979, 1981. *Major heroic size works:* Persephone, Crowmallie, Aberdeen; Horseman (RBS Medal for best work of the year, 1965); Simon de Montfort, County Hall, Leics; Three Judges, Churchill Coll., Cambridge; Three Kings, Knochallachie, Aberdeen; Stability, Burgess Hill; Cascade, Duke of Westminster, Eaton, Chester; *works in RC churches:* St Mary and Child, Midhurst; Our Lady, St Michael and Crucifix, Wolverhampton; Crucifix, Church of Child Jesus, Birmingham; Risen Christ and sanctuary furniture, St Vincent's Convent, Mill Hill; Our Lady and Child, Convent of Sisters of Mercy, Brentwood; Crucifix, St Cedd's, Goodmayes; Our Lady, St Mary's Coll., Wallasey; Cross Motif, St Thomas More, Manor House; Risen Christ, St Albans, Derby. *Publications:* contribs to Apollo, Liturgical Arts, Studio Internat., Arts Rev. *Recreations:* fishing, gardening, painting. *Address:* Rookery Farmhouse, Calne, Wilts SN11 0LH. *T:* Calne 814068. *Clubs:* Athenæum, Chelsea Arts.

CRAMPTON SMITH, Alec; *see* Smith, Alexander C.

CRANBORNE, Viscount; Robert Michael James Cecil; MP (C) Dorset South, since 1979; *b* 30 Sept. 1946; *s* and *heir* of 6th Marquess of Salisbury, *qv*; *m* 1970, Hannah Ann, *er d* of Lt-Col William Joseph Stirling of Keir; two *s* three *d. Educ:* Eton; Oxford. *Heir: s* Hon. Robert Edward William Cecil, *b* 18 Dec. 1970. *Address:* Cranborne Lodge, Dorset.

CRANBROOK, 5th Earl of, *cr* 1892; **Gathorne Gathorne-Hardy;** Viscount Cranbrook, 1878; Baron Medway, 1892; *b* 20 June 1933; *er s* of 4th Earl of Cranbrook, CBE, and of the Dowager Countess of Cranbrook (Fidelity, OBE 1972, *o d* of late Hugh E. Seebohm); *S* father, 1978; *m* 1967, Caroline, *o d* of Col Ralph G. E. Jarvis, Doddington Hall, Lincoln; two *s* one *d. Educ:* Eton; Corpus Christi Coll., Cambridge (MA); University of Birmingham (PhD). Asst, Sarawak Museum, 1956-58; Fellow, Yayasan Siswa Lokantara (Indonesia), 1960-61; Sr Lectr in Zoology, Univ. of Malaya, 1961-70. Editor of Ibis, 1973-80. Member: Royal Commn on Environmental Pollution, 1981-; NERC, 1982-. Mem., Suffolk Coastal DC, 1974-; Governor, Thomas Mills High Sch., Framlingham, 1978; President: Suffolk Trust for Nature Conservation, 1979-; British Herpetological Soc., 1981-; Trustee, BM (Natural History), 1982-. Skinner and Freeman of the City of London. FLS; FZS; FRGS; FRSA; MBOU. OStJ. *Publications:* Mammals of Borneo, 1965, 2nd edn 1977; Mammals of Malaya, 1969, 2nd edn 1978; (with D. R. Wells) Birds of the Malay Peninsula, 1976. *Heir: s* Lord Medway, *qv. Address:* c/o National Westminster Bank, St James's Square, SW1Y 4JX.

CRANE, Prof. Francis Roger; Professor of Law, Queen Mary College, University of London, 1965-78, now Emeritus; *b* 19 Dec. 1910; *m* 1938, Jean Berenice Hadfield; two *s* one *d. Educ:* Highgate Sch.; University Coll., London. LLB 1933; Solicitor, 1934, Clifford's Inn Prize. Lecturer in Law; King's Coll. and private practice, 1935-38; Lecturer in Law, University of Manchester, 1938-46; Prof. of Law, University of Nottingham, 1946-52; Prof. of English Law, King's Coll., London, 1952-65; Dean of the Faculty of Law, QMC, London, 1965-76. University of London: Mem. Senate, 1969-71, 1973-78; Chm. Academic Council, 1975-78; Mem. Court, 1975-78. Visiting Professor: Tulane Univ., 1960; University of Khartoum, 1963; Dean of the Faculty of Law and Visiting Prof., University of Canterbury (New Zealand), 1964; Vis. Professor: Univ. of Melbourne, 1972; Monash Univ., 1972; Univ. of Sydney, 1980. Served War of 1939-45: Royal Corps of Signals, Major, 1944. Pres., Soc. of Public Teachers of Law, 1975-76. FKC 1976; Fellow QMC 1980. *Publications:* (jointly) A Century of Family Law, 1957; articles and notes in legal periodicals. *Address:* 25 Winston Drive, Isham, Kettering, Northants NN14 1HS. *T:* Kettering 723938.

CRANE, Geoffrey David; Director, Personnel Management and Training, Departments of the Environment and Transport, since 1981; *b* 13 Oct. 1934; *s* of Frederick David Crane and late Marion Doris Crane; *m* 1962, Gillian Margaret, *d* of late Harry Thomas Austin; one *d. Educ:* City of London Sch. (John Carpenter Schol.); Trinity Hall, Cambridge (Schol., MA). Served RAF, 1956-58, Flying Officer. Assistant Principal, Min. of Works, 1958; Asst Private Sec. to Minister of Works, 1961-62; Principal, 1962; Secretary, Historic Buildings Council for Scotland and Ancient Monuments Bd for Scotland, 1962-66; Private Sec. to Minister of Public Building and Works, 1968-69; Asst Sec., Machinery of Govt Div., CSD, 1970-72; Dep. Dir, Central Unit on Environmental Pollution, DoE, 1972-76; Personnel Management and Trng, DoE and Dept of Transport, 1976-78; Under Sec. and Dir of Res. Ops, DoE and Dept of Transport, 1978-80. *Recreations:* music, industrial archaeology, mathematics. *Address:* 6 The Paddock, Datchet, Berks SL3 9DL. *T:* Slough 43644. *Clubs:* Royal Air Force, Civil Service.

CRANE, Sir Harry (Walter Victor), Kt 1966; OBE 1949; JP; Industrial Relations Consultant since 1965; *b* 12 Feb. 1903; *s* of William and Ann Crane; *m* 1930, Winefride Mary, *d* of Thomas and Lucy Wing; one *s. Educ:* Nottingham. Engineer Fitter. NUGMW: District Officer, 1934; Nat. Officer, 1943; District Sec., 1957; retd from Union service, 1965. Member: Catering Commn, 1950-52; Catering Hygiene Cttee, 1949-52; Food Hygiene Adv. Coun., 1952-78; Workers' Travel Assoc. (now Galleon World Travel Assoc.) Management Cttee, 1960-; (pt-time) E Midlands Electricity Bd, 1965-73; Milk Marketing Bd, 1966-72. Director (part-time), Transport Holding Co.,

Ministry of Transport, 1966-73. Hon. Pres., Galleon World Travel, 1973-. Chairman: Labour Party Conference Arrangements Cttee, 1954-65; Industrial Injuries Advisory Council, 1967-73; Sec. or Chm. of Joint Industrial Councils during Trade Union career. FR.EconS 1944. JP 1961. *Recreations:* swimming, gardening, reading. *Address:* Riverain, 22 Cliff Drive, Radcliffe-on-Trent, Nottingham. *T:* Radcliffe-on-Trent 2683. *Clubs:* Royal Commonwealth Society, Civil Service.

CRANE, Sir James (William Donald), Kt 1980; CBE 1977; HM Chief Inspector of Constabulary, since 1979; *b* 1 Jan. 1921; *s* of late William James Crane and Ivy Winifred Crane; *m* 1942, Patricia Elizabeth Hodge; one *s* one *d. Educ:* Hampshire schs. Joined Metrop. Police, 1946; Comdr and Dep. Asst Comr, Fraud Squad and Commercial Br., 1970-76; Inspector of Constabulary, 1976-79. *Recreations:* gardening, walking, reading. *Address:* Home Office, 50 Queen Anne's Gate, SW1H 9AT. *Club:* Royal Commonwealth Society.

CRANE, Morley Benjamin, FRS 1947; Hon. FLS; VMH; formerly Deputy Director and Head of Pomology Department of the John Innes Horticultural Institution; *b* 17 March 1890. *Publications:* (with Sir Daniel Hall) The Apple, 1933; (with W. J. C. Lawrence) The Genetics of Garden Plants, 4th edn 1952; many research papers on origin, genetics and breeding of cultivated fruits and plants. Hon. Freedom, Fruiterer's Co., 1949; Freedom of City of London, 1949. *Address:* Plovers Dip, 22 Fishponds Way, Haughley, Suffolk.

CRANE, Prof. William Alfred James, MD; FRCP, FRCPGlas, FRCPath; Joseph Hunter Professor of Pathology, University of Sheffield, since 1965; Dean of Sheffield Medical School, 1976-79; Hon. Consultant Pathologist, since 1959; Hon. Director of Cancer Research, since 1968; *b* 27 June 1925; *s* of late William Crane and Margaret McGechie; *m* 1952, Yvonne Elizabeth Dann; one *s* one *d. Educ:* Univ. of Glasgow (MB ChB, MD Hons and Bellahouson Gold Medal). FRCPath 1971 (MRCPath 1963); FRCPGlas 1972 (MRCPGlas 1965); FRCP 1975 (MRCP 1967). RAMC, 1948-50; Hansen Scholar and Lectr, Univ. of Glasgow, 1951-56; Asst Prof., Univ. of Chicago, 1956-57; Lectr in Pathology, Univ. of Glasgow, 1957-59; Sen. Lectr in Pathology, Univ. of Sheffield, 1959-64; Associate Prof., Univ. of Chicago, 1962. Member: MRC Bd, 1970-76; Council, RCPath, 1970-73; Med. Sub-Cttee, UGC, 1979; GMC, 1979-; Sec., Path. Soc. of GB and Ire., 1969-74. Hon. Mem., Dutch Path. Soc., 1976. *Publications:* papers in scientific and med. jls on endocrinology and hypertension. *Recreations:* gardening, music. *Address:* 56 Stumperlowe Crescent Road, Fulwood, Sheffield S10 3PR.

CRANFIELD, Rev. Prof. Charles Ernest Burland, FBA 1982; Emeritus Professor of Theology, University of Durham, since 1980; *b* 13 Sept. 1915; *s* of Charles Ernest Cranfield and Beatrice Mary Cranfield (*née* Tubbs); *m* 1953, Ruth Elizabeth Gertrude, *d* of Rev. T. Bole; two *d. Educ:* Mill Hill Sch.; Jesus Coll., Cambridge; Wesley House, Cambridge. MA Cantab. Research in Basel, cut short before it properly began by outbreak of war. Probationer in Methodist Church, 1939; ordained 1941; Minister, Shoeburyness; Chaplain to the Forces, 1942-46; from end of hostilities worked with German prisoners-of-war and was first staff chaplain to POW Directorate, War Office; Minister, Cleethorpes, 1946-50; admitted to Presbyterian Church of England (now United Reformed Church) as a minister, 1954. Lecturer in Theology, Durham Univ., 1950-62; Sen. Lectr, 1962-66; Reader, 1966-78; Prof. of Theology (personal), 1978-80. Joint general editor, new series of International Critical Commentary, 1966-. Hon. DD Aberdeen, 1980. *Publications:* The First Epistle of Peter, 1950, 4th imp. 1958; The Gospel according to Saint Mark, 1959, supplemented and somewhat revised over the years, 7th imp. 1979; I and II Peter and Jude, 1960; A Ransom for Many, 1963; The Service of God, 1965; A Commentary on Romans 12-13, 1965; A Critical and Exegetical Commentary on the Epistle to the Romans, vol. 1 1975, 3rd (corrected) imp. 1980, vol. 2 1979, 2nd (corrected) imp. 1981; contribs to composite works and to various theological periodicals. *Address:* 30 Western Hill, Durham City DH1 4RL. *T:* Durham 43096.

CRANKSHAW, Edward, TD; FRSL; writer; Correspondent on Soviet Affairs for The Observer, 1947-68; *b* 3 Jan. 1909; *s* of Arthur and Amy Crankshaw; *m* 1931, Clare, *d* of late E. A. Carr. *Educ:* Bishop's Stortford Coll. Commissioned 4th Bn Queen's Own Royal West Kent Regt (TA), 1936; GSO1 attached Brit. Mil. Mission, Moscow, 1941-43. Ehrenkreuz für Wissenschaft und Kunst, 1st Class (Austria), 1964. *Publications:* Joseph Conrad: Aspects of the Art of the Novel, 1936; Vienna: the Image of a Culture in Decline, 1938; Britain and Russia, 1945; Russia and the Russians, 1947; Russia by Daylight, 1951; Gestapo: Instrument of Tyranny, 1956; Russia without Stalin, 1956; Krushchev's Russia, 1959; The Fall of the House of Habsburg, 1963; The New Cold War: Moscow v. Pekin, 1963; Krushchev: a Biography, 1966; Maria Theresa, 1969; The Habsburgs, 1971; Tolstoy: the making of a novelist, 1974; The Shadow of the Winter Palace: the drift to revolution, 1825-1917, 1976 (Yorkshire Post Prize, 1976; Heinemann Award, 1977); Bismarck, 1981; *novels:* Nina Lessing, 1938; What Glory?, 1939; The Creedy Case, 1954; many translations from German and French, incl. five plays by Ernst Toller; contribs to many periodicals and symposia in UK and USA. *Recreations:* fishing, music. *Address:* Church House, Sandhurst, Hawkhurst, Kent. *Club:* Brooks's.

CRANLEY, Viscount; Rupert Charles William Bullard Onslow; *b* 16 June 1967; *s* and *heir* of 7th Earl of Onslow, *qv*.

CRANMER, Philip, FRCO; Secretary, Associated Board of the Royal Schools of Music, 1974-83; *b* 1 April 1918; *s* of Arthur Cranmer and Lilian Phillips; *m* 1939, Ruth Loasby; one *s* three *d. Educ:* Wellington; Christ Church, Oxford (BMus, MA). Asst Music Master, Wellington Coll. 1938-40; served RA, 1940-46; Major, Education Officer, Guards Div., 1946; Dir of Music, King Edward's Sch., Birmingham, 1946; Staff Accompanist, Midland Region, BBC, 1948; Lectr in Music, Birmingham Univ., 1950; Hamilton Harty Prof. of Music, Queen's Univ., Belfast, 1954-70; Prof. of Music, Univ. of Manchester, 1970-74. Pres., Incorporated Soc. of Musicians, 1971; Chm., Musicians' Benevolent Fund, 1980-. FRCO 1947. Hon. RAM 1967; FRMCM 1974; FRCM 1976. Chevalier de l'Ordre de Léopold II, 1947; Croix de Guerre Belge, 1947. *Publications:* The Technique of Accompaniment, 1970; Sight-reading for Young Pianists, 1979; How to Follow a Score, 1982. *Address:* Quince Cottage, Underhill Lane, Clayton, Hassocks, W Sussex.

CRANSTON, Prof. Maurice (William); Professor of Political Science at the London School of Economics, since 1969 (seconded as Professor of Political Science, European University Institute, 1978-81); *b* 8 May 1920; *o c* of William Cranston and Catherine Harris; *m* 1958, Baroness Maximiliana von und zu Fraunberg; two *s. Educ:* London Univ.; St Catherine's, Oxford (MA, BLitt). London Civil Defence during war, 1939-45. Lecturer (part-time) in Social Philosophy, London Univ., 1950-59; Reader (previously Lecturer) in Political Science at London Sch. of Economics, 1959-69. Visiting Prof. of Government: Harvard Univ., 1965-66; Dartmouth Coll., USA, 1970-71; Univ. of British Columbia, 1973-74; Univ. of California, 1976; Ecole des Hautes Etudes, Paris, 1977; Woodrow Wilson Center, Washington, 1982. Pres., Institut International de Philosophie Politique, 1976-79; Vice-Pres. de l'Alliance Française en Angleterre, 1964-. Literary Adviser to Methuen Ltd, 1959-69. FRSL. Foreign Hon. Mem., Amer. Acad. of Arts and Sciences, 1970-. *Publications:* Freedom, 1953; Human Rights Today, 1954 (revised edn 1962); John Locke: a biography, 1957 (James Tait Black Memorial Prize); Jean-Paul Sartre, 1962; What Are Human Rights? (New York), 1963, 2nd rev. edn (London), 1973; Western Political Philosophers (ed), 1964; A Glossary of Political Terms, 1966; Rousseau's Social Contract, 1967; Political Dialogues, 1968; La Quintessence de Sartre (Montreal), 1969; Language and Philosophy (Toronto), 1969; The New Left (ed), 1970; (ed with R. S. Peters) Hobbes and Rousseau, 1972; The Mask of Politics, 1973; (ed with P. Mair) Idéologie et Politique, 1980; Langage et Politique, 1981; Culture et Politique, 1982. *Recreation:* walking. *Address:* 1A Kent Terrace, Regent's Park, NW1 4RP. *T:* 01-262 2698. *Club:* Garrick.

CRANSTON, Prof. William Ian; Professor of Medicine, St Thomas's Hospital Medical School, since 1964; *b* 11 Sept. 1928; *s* of Thomas and Margaret Cranston; *m* Pamela Isabel Pearson; four *s. Educ:* High Sch. for Boys, Glasgow; Aberdeen Grammar Sch.; Boys' High Sch., Oswestry; University of Aberdeen, FRCP London 1965 (MRCP 1952); MB, ChB (Hons), 1949; MD Aberdeen 1957; MA Oxon. 1962. Royal Infirmary, Aberdeen: House Physician, 1949-50; Medical Registrar, 1952-53; Asst in Medical Unit, St Mary's Hospital, Paddington, 1953-56; 1st Asst in Dept of Regius Prof. of Med., Radcliffe Inf., Oxford, 1961-64. Mem., Med. Res. Soc. *Recreations:* reading, gardening, painting. *Address:* St Thomas's Hospital Medical School, Albert Embankment, Westminster Bridge, SE1.

CRANSTONE, Bryan Allan Lefevre; Curator, Pitt Rivers Museum, Oxford, since 1976; *b* 26 Feb. 1918; *s* of late Edgar Arnold Cranstone and late Clarice Edith Cranstone; *m* 1941, Isabel May, *d* of W. Gough-Thomas; one *s. Educ:* Bootham Sch., York; St Catharine's Coll., Cambridge (MA). Hampshire Regt, 1939-46. Asst Keeper, Dept of Ethnography, BM, 1947-69; field work, New Guinea, 1963-64; Dep. Keeper, Dept of Ethnography, BM (later Museum of Mankind), 1969-76. Vis. Lectr, University Coll., London, 1955-71. Fellow, Linacre Coll., Oxford, 1976. Vice-Pres., RAI, 1980-. *Publications:* Melanesia: a short ethnography, 1961; The Australian Aborigines, 1973; (with D. C. Starzecka) The Solomon Islanders, 1974; articles in learned jls and encyclopaedias. *Address:* Pitt Rivers Museum, South Parks Road, Oxford OX1 3AP.

CRANWORTH, 3rd Baron, *cr* 1899; **Philip Bertram Gurdon;** Lieutenant, Royal Wiltshire Yeomanry; *b* 24 May 1940; *s* of Hon. Robin Gurdon (killed in action, 1942) and Hon. Yoskyl Pearson (she *m* 2nd, 1944, as his 2nd wife, Lieut.-Col. Alistair Gibb, and 3rd, 1962, as his 2nd wife, 1st Baron McCorquodale of Newton, PC, KCVO; she *d* 1979), *d* of 2nd Viscount Cowdray; *S* grandfather, 1964; *m* 1968, Frances Henrietta Montagu Douglas Scott, *d* of late Lord William Scott and of Lady William Scott, Beechwood, Melrose; two *s* one *d. Educ:* Eton; Magdalene Coll., Cambridge. *Heir: s* Hon. Sacha William Robin Gurdon, *b* 12 Aug. 1970. *Address:* Grundisburgh Hall, Woodbridge, Suffolk IP13 6TW.

See also Earl of Aboyne, C. M. T. Smith-Ryland.

CRATHORNE, 2nd Baron *cr* 1959; **Charles James Dugdale;** Bt 1945; consultant and lecturer in Fine Art; *b* 12 Sept. 1939; *s* of 1st Baron Crathorne, PC, TD, and Nancy, OBE (*d* 1969), *d* of Sir Charles Tennant, 1st Bt; *S* father, 1977; *m* 1970, Sylvia Mary, *yr d* of Brig. Arthur Herbert Montgomery, OBE, TD; one *s* two *d. Educ:* Eton College; Trinity Coll., Cambridge. MA Cantab (Fine Arts). Impressionist and Modern Painting Dept, Sotheby & Co., 1963-66; Assistant to the President, Parke-Bernet, New York, 1966-69; James Dugdale & Associates, London, Independent Fine Art Consultancy Service, 1969-; James Crathorne & Associates, 1980-. Director: Blakeney Hotels Ltd, 1980-; Windsor Court Ltd, USA. Member: Productions Cttee, Georgian

Theatre, Richmond, Yorks, 1969; Yorks Reg. Cttee, National Trust, 1978; Cttee, CLA, 1978. Pres., Friends of Cleveland Museums and Art Galls, 1974; Sec., All Party Parly Heritage Gp, 1981-. Director, Radio Tees, 1975-. Trustee, Captain Cook Trust, 1978. Mem., Standing Council of Baronetage, 1978. Annual lecture tours to America, 1970-; lecture series, Metropolitan Mus., NY, 1981. FRSA 1972. *Exhibition:* Photographs, Middlesbrough Art Gall., 1980. *Publications:* Edouard Vuillard, 1967; (co-author) Tennant's Stalk, 1973; contribs to Apollo and The Connoisseur. *Recreations:* photography, travel, collecting, shooting, fishing, golf, Royal Tennis. *Heir: s* Hon. Thomas Arthur John Dugdale, *b* 30 Sept. 1977. *Address:* Crathorne House, Yarm, Cleveland TS15 0AT. *T:* Stokesley 700431; 52 Lower Sloane Street, SW1W 8BS. *T:* 01-730 9131.

CRAUFURD, Sir Robert (James), 9th Bt *cr* 1781; Member of the London Stock Exchange; *b* 18 March 1937; *s* of Sir James Gregan Craufurd, 8th Bt and of Ruth Marjorie, *d* of Frederic Corder; *S* father, 1970; *m* 1964, Catherine Penelope, *yr d* of late Captain Horatio Westmacott, Torquay; three *d. Educ:* Harrow; University College, Oxford. Elected Member of the London Stock Exchange, 1969. *Recreations:* gardening, local history, music and Commonwealth coins. *Address:* Brightwood, Aldbury, Tring, Herts.

CRAVEN, family name of **Earl of Craven.**

CRAVEN, 7th Earl of, *cr* 1801; **Thomas Robert Douglas Craven;** Viscount Uffington, 1801; Baron Craven, 1665; *b* 24 Aug. 1957; *e s* of 6th Earl of Craven and of Elizabeth (*née* Johnstone-Douglas); *S* father, 1965. *Heir: b* Hon. Simon George Craven, *b* 16 Sept. 1961. *Address:* Hamstead House, Hamstead Marshall, Newbury, Berks.

CRAVEN, Archdeacon of; *see* Rogers, Ven. D. A.

CRAVEN, Marjorie Eadon, RRC 1941 (1st Class); *b* 21 March 1895; *yr d* of late John Alfred Craven and Susannah Eadon Craven, Sheffield, Yorks. *Educ:* Roedean Sch. SRN; SCM; RNT; Diploma in Nursing, Leeds Univ.; Health Visitor. Mem. St John VAD, 1915-17; Leeds Gen. Infirmary, 1917-26; studied nursing administration: Bedford Coll., London, Royal College of Nursing, 1926; Teachers' Coll., Columbia Univ., NY City, 1927-28. Matron, West London Hospital, 1929-38 and 1947-53; Matron and Principal Matron, TANS, 1939-44; Matron-in-Chief, British Red Cross Soc. and Joint Cttee, Order of St John and BRCS, 1953-62, retd. Vice-Pres., W. L. H. Nurses' League; Vice-Pres., National Florence Nightingale Memorial Cttee. Officer (Sister) Order of St John, 1957. Florence Nightingale Medal, 1961. *Recreation:* music. *Address:* Green Finches, 33 North Park, Gerrards Cross, Bucks SL9 8AT. *T:* Gerrards Cross 82349.

CRAVEN, Air Marshal Sir Robert Edward, KBE 1970 (OBE 1954); CB 1966; DFC 1940; *b* 16 Jan. 1916; *s* of Gerald Craven, Port Elizabeth, S Africa, and Edith Craven, York; *m* 1940, Joan Peters; one *s* one *d. Educ:* Scarborough Coll. MN, 1932-37; Pilot Officer, RAF, 1937; 201, 210, 228 Sqdns, 1937-41; RAF Staff Coll., 1942; Staff Appts: Coastal Command, 1942 (despatches thrice); Directing Staff, RAF Staff Coll., 1944; HQ, Mediterranean and Middle East, Cairo, 1945; CO Eastleigh, Kenya, 1946; RN Staff Coll., 1948; Directing Staff, Joint Services Staff Coll., 1949; Standing Group, NATO Washington, 1951; RAF St Eval, 1954; Directing Staff, RAF Staff Coll., 1957; Group Capt. 1957; CO RAF Lyneham, 1959; Director, Personal Services, RAF, 1961; Air Cdre 1961; Air Officer Admin., Transport Comd, 1964; Air Vice-Marshal, 1965; SASO, Flying Training Comd, 1967-68, Training Comd, 1968-69; Commander, Maritime Air Forces, 1969-72, retired. Order of Menelik (Ethiopia), 1955. *Recreations:* water fowl breeding, antique furniture restoration and reproduction. *Address:* Letcombe House, Letcombe Regis, Oxon. *Club:* Royal Air Force.

CRAWFORD, 29th Earl of, *cr* 1398, and **BALCARRES,** 12th Earl of, *cr* 1651; **Robert Alexander Lindsay,** PC 1972; Lord Lindsay of Crawford, before 1143; Lord Lindsay of Balcarres, 1633; Lord Balniel, 1651; Baron Wigan (UK), 1826; Baron Balniel (Life Peer), 1974; Premier Earl of Scotland; Head of House of Lindsay; DL; First Crown Estate Commissioner, since 1980; *b* 5 March 1927; *er s* of 28th Earl of Crawford and 11th of Balcarres, KT, GBE, and of Mary, 3rd *d* of late Lord Richard Cavendish, PC, CB, CMG; *S* father, 1975; *m* 1949, Ruth Beatrice, *d* of Leo Meyer-Bechtler, Zürich; two *s* two *d. Educ:* Eton; Trinity College, Cambridge. Served with Grenadier Guards, 1945-49. MP (C) Hertford, 1955-74, Welwyn and Hatfield, Feb.-Sept. 1974; Parliamentary Private Secretary: to Financial Secretary of Treasury, 1955-57; to Minister of Housing and Local Government, 1957-60; Minister of State for Defence, 1970-72; Minister of State for Foreign and Commonwealth Affairs, 1972-74. Chm., Lombard North Central Bank, 1976-80; Director: Nat. Westminster Bank, 1975-; Scottish American Investment Co., 1978-; a Vice-Chm., Sun Alliance & London Insurance Gp, 1975-. President, Rural District Councils Assoc., 1959-65; Chairman: National Association for Mental Health, 1963-70; Historic Buildings Council for Scotland, 1976-. DL Fife. *Heir: s* Lord Balniel, *qv. Address:* 107 Frognal, NW3. *T:* 01-431 1584.

CRAWFORD, Sir (Archibald James) Dirom, Kt 1957; Hon. Treasurer Western Area Conservative and Unionist Association since 1959 (President, 1956-59; Chairman, 1951-56); *b* 1899; *s* of Malcolm M. Crawford and Ethel Elizabeth Crawford, *d* of Andrew Wernicke; unmarried. *Educ:* Winchester; RMC Sandhurst. Served as Subaltern, 6th Inniskilling Dragoons, then

RARO; invalided out of Service, 1939. Chairman: Bridgwater Div. Conservative and Unionist Assoc., 1948-51; Somerset County Federation of Conservative and Unionist Assocs, 1950-51. Pres., Somerset County Cttee, British Legion, Dec. 1957- (Hon. Treasurer, 1953-57). *Address:* Park House, Over Stowey, Bridgwater, Somerset. *T:* Nether Stowey 269. *Club:* Cavalry and Guards.

CRAWFORD, Sir Dirom; *see* Crawford, Sir A. J. D.

CRAWFORD, Douglas; *see* Crawford, G. D.

CRAWFORD, Prof. Frederick William; Vice-Chancellor, University of Aston, since 1980; *b* 28 July 1931; *s* of William and Victoria Maud Crawford; *m* 1963, Béatrice Madeleine Jacqueline Hutter, LèsL, MA, PhD, Paris; one *s* one *d*. *Educ:* George Dixon Grammar Sch., Birmingham; Univ. of London (BSc Eng (1st cl. hons), MSc, DSc); Univ. of Liverpool (DipEd, PhD, DEng). Pres., Guild of Undergraduates, 1955-56; Mem. Court, 1955-62 and 1981-; Treas., NUS, 1957-59; Winner, NUS-Observer Fifth Nat. Student Debating Tourn., 1958. ACT Birmingham 1952; CEng, FIEE 1965; FIEEE 1972; FInstP 1964; FAPS 1965; FAAAS 1971; FIMA 1978. Research Trainee, J. Lucas Ltd, 1948-52; Scientist, NCB Mining Res. Estabt, 1956-57; Sen. Lectr in Elec. Engrg, CAT Birmingham, 1958-59; Stanford University, California, 1959-82: Res. Associate, W. W. Hansen Labs of Physics, 1959-64; Institute for Plasma Research: Adjunct Prof., 1964-67; Associate Prof., 1967-69; Prof., 1969-82; Chm., 1974-80; Dir, Centre for Interdisciplinary Res. and Associate Dean of Graduate Studies, 1973-77. Vis. Scientist, French Atomic Energy Commn, and Cons. to Comp. Française Thomson-Houston, 1961-62; Vis. Professor: Japan, 1969; Univ. of Paris, 1971; Australia and S Africa, 1972; Mathematical Inst., Oxford Univ., also Vis. Fellow, St Catherine's Coll., Oxford, 1977-78. Union Radio-Scientifique Internationale: Member: US Nat. Cttee, 1975-81; UK Nat. Cttee, 1969-; Commn H (Waves in Plasmas); US Chm., 1975-78; Internat. Chm., 1978-81; UK Rep., 1982-; Chm. Internat. Sci. Cttee, Internat. Conf. on Phenomena in Ionised Gases, 1979-81; Dir, Sigma Xi, 1976-78; Mem. Council, Amer. Assoc. of Univ. Profs, 1980-82; Univ. Space Research Association: Member: Council, 1973-81 (Chm. 1977-78); Bd of Trustees, 1975-81 (Chm. 1976-77); Mem. numerous cttees on Space Shuttle, NASA, 1972-80. Member: City of Birmingham Educn Cttee, 1980-; US-UK Educnl Commn, 1981-; Ct, Birmingham Univ., 1980-. Vice-Pres., Birmingham Br., E-SU, 1980-. Patron, Midlands Centre, Royal TV Soc., 1980-. Mem. Editorial Board: Jl of Applied Phys. and Appl. Phys. Letters, 1976-78; Oxford Univ. Press Engrg Science Series, 1979-. *Publications:* numerous papers on plasma physics in sci. books and jls. *Address:* Vice-Chancellor's Office, University of Aston, Birmingham B4 7ET. *T:* 021-359 3611. *Club:* Athenæum.

CRAWFORD, (George) Douglas; Director, Polecon Group of Cos, since 1970; *b* 1 Nov. 1939; *s* of Robert and Helen Crawford; *m* 1964, Joan Burnie; one *s* one *d*. *Educ:* Glasgow Academy; St Catharine's Coll., Cambridge (MA). Features Editor, Business, 1961-63; Industrial Corresp., Glasgow Herald, 1963-66; Editor, Scotland Magazine, 1966-70. MP (SNP) Perth and East Perthshire, Oct. 1974-1979. *Recreations:* hill-walking, playing piano and clavichord, watching cricket. *Address:* 5 Wemyss Place, Edinburgh EH3 6DH. *T:* 031-225 1667. *Clubs:* Savile; Scottish Arts, Press (Edinburgh).

CRAWFORD, Hon. Sir George (Hunter), Kt 1972; Judge of the Supreme Court of Tasmania 1958-81; *b* 12 Dec. 1911; *s* of Frederick Charles Crawford and Ruby Priscilla (née Simpson); *m* 1st, 1936, Helen Zoë (*d* 1976), *d* of Dr Bruce Arnold Anderson; two *s* one *d*; 2nd, 1979, Nancy Jean Garrott (née Findlay). *Educ:* East Launceston State Sch.; Launceston Church Grammar Sch.; Univ. of Tasmania (LLB). Barrister and Solicitor, 1934-58; Mem. Cttee, Northern Law Society, 1946-58 (Vice-Pres. 1957-58). Served (including War): AMF, 1929-40; AIF, 1940-44, Lt-Col. Councillor, Northern Br., Royal Soc. of Tasmania, 1954-72 (Chm., 1957-58 and 1966-68); Mem. Cttee, Tasmanian Historical Res. Assoc., 1960-62 (Chm., 1961-62); Mem. Bd, Launceston Church Grammar Sch., 1946-71 (Chm., 1958-65); Mem. Bd, Cradle Mountain-Lake St Clair Nat. Park; Mem. Adv. Cttee, Cradle Mountain, 1956-71; Pres., N Tasmania Branch, Roy. Commonwealth Soc., 1974-76. Col Comdt, Royal Regt of Australian Artillery, in Tasmania Command, 1972-78. *Recreations:* music, historical research. *Address:* 10A Wentworth Street, Launceston, Tasmania 7250, Australia. *T:* Launceston 311910. *Clubs:* Tasmanian (Hobart); Launceston (Launceston).

CRAWFORD, Maj.-Gen. George Oswald, CB 1956; CBE 1944; Director of Ordnance Services, War Office, 1958-61; *b* 1902; *s* of late Col Arthur Gosset Crawford, Nailsworth, Glos; *m* Sophie Cecilia (*d* 1974), *d* of J. C. Yorke, JP, Langton, Dwrbach, Pembs; two *s* one *d*; *m* 1974, Ella Brown. *Educ:* Bradfield; RMC. 2nd Lieut Glos Regt, 1922; transf. RAOC 1928. Served CMF, 1942-45; Lieut-Col 1942; Brig. 1943; Dep. Dir of Ordnance Services, Western Command, 1947-51; DDOS, Southern Command, 1951-55; ADC to the Queen, 1954-55; Maj.-Gen. 1955; Inspector, Royal Army Ordnance Corps, 1955-57; Commandant Mechanical Transport Organisation, Chilwell, 1957-58; Col Comdt RAOC, 1960-66. *Address:* Gwyers, Dinton, Wilts.
See also Wilson Stephens.

CRAWFORD, Sir John (Grenfell), AC 1978; Kt 1959; CBE 1954; MEc (Sydney); FAIAS; Chancellor, Australian National University, since 1976; Director, Australia-Japan Economic Research Project; *b* 4 April 1910; *s* of Henry and Harriet Crawford, Sydney; *m* 1935, Jessie Anderson Morgan; one *d*. *Educ:* Sydney Univ.; Harvard Univ.; Research Fellow, University of Sydney, 1933-35; Lectr, Agricultural Economics, University of Sydney (Part-time), 1934-41; Commonwealth Fund Fellow, USA, 1938-40; Economic Adviser, Rural Bank of NSW, 1935-43; Director, Commonwealth Bureau of Agricultural Economics, 1945-50; Sec., Dept of Commerce and Agriculture, 1950-56; Sec., Dept of Trade, Commonwealth of Australia, 1956-60; resigned from Civil Service, 1960. Dir and Prof. of Economics, Research Sch. of Pacific Studies, Australian National Univ., 1960-67, and Fiscal Adviser to the Univ.; Vice-Chancellor, ANU, 1968-73; Chancellor, Univ. of Papua and New Guinea, 1972-75. Vice-Chm., Commonwealth Cttee of Economic Enquiry, 1962-64, 1966-67. Mem. World Bank Economic Mission to India, 1964-65; Sen. Agricl Adviser to World Bank, Washington, 1967-81. Chairman: Technical Adv. Cttee to Consultative Gp of Internat. Agricultural Res., 1971-76; Australian Develt Adv. Board, 1975-77; Bd, Internat. Food Policy Res. Inst., 1976-; Mem. Bd, Internat. Fertilizer Develt Center, 1977-. Pres., ANZAAS, 1967-68 (Medallist, 1971). Hon. DSc Newcastle, NSW, 1966; Hon. DEc New England, NSW, 1969; Hon. LLD: Tasmania, 1971; Papua New Guinea, 1975; ANU, 1976; Hon. DSc Econ Sydney, 1972. *Publications:* Australian National Income (with Colin Clark), 1938; Australian Trade Policy 1942-1966, 1968; A Commission to Advise on Assistance to Industries (report to Aust. Govt), 1973; Report on Structural Adjustment in Industry, 1979; Report on Revitalisation of Australian Shipping, 1981; articles in Economic Record, Journal of Public Administration, Australian Outlook; several edited books on Australian Economic Affairs and several published lectures on trade and educn policy. *Recreation:* reading. *Address:* 32 Melbourne Avenue, Deakin, ACT 2600, Australia. *Clubs:* Commonwealth (Canberra); Melbourne (Melbourne).

CRAWFORD, John Michael; Chief Education Officer, Birmingham, since 1977; *b* 6 Dec. 1938; *s* of James and Emily Crawford; *m* 1962, Geraldine Kay Weaver; two *d*. *Educ:* Ipswich Sch.; University Coll., London (BA); Fitzwilliam House, Cambridge. Asst Master, Merchant Taylor's, Crosby, 1961-63; Admin. Asst, E Suffolk CC, 1963-66; Sen. Admin. Asst, Lancs CC, 1966-68; Asst Educn Officer, W Riding CC, 1968-73; Dep. Educn Officer, Birmingham, 1973-77. *Address:* July Green, Snuff Mill Walk, Bewdley, Worcs. *T:* Bewdley 400174.

CRAWFORD, Captain John Stuart, DSO 1940; OBE 1970; Royal Navy, retired; HM Consul, Tromsö, Norway, 1956-70, retired; *b* 24 March 1900; *s* of late John Crawford, MD, BS, and late Christian Patricia Blackstock; *m* 1927, Katherine Macdonald (*d* 1981); one *d* (and one *s* decd). *Educ:* Dollar Academy; RNC, Osborne and Dartmouth. Midshipman, 1916-18; HMS Valiant; Lieut, 1920; Lieut-Comdr, 1928; Comdr, 1934; Capt., 1940. Naval Attaché Angora, 1946-48; retired list, 1950. County Civil Defence Officer, Northants, 1951; Asst Commissioner of Police (in charge of Marine Police Branch), Malaya, 1951-55. Younger Brother of Trinity House, 1961-. *Address:* The Gardens, West Stafford, Dorchester, Dorset. *Club:* Naval and Military.

CRAWFORD, Michael; actor since 1955; *b* 19 Jan. 1942. *Educ:* St Michael's Coll., Bexley; Oakfield Sch., Dulwich. In orig. prodn of Britten's Noyes Fludde and of Let's Make an Opera; *stage appearances include:* Travelling Light, 1965; The Anniversary, 1966; No Sex Please, We're British, Strand, 1971; Billy, Drury Lane, 1974; Same Time, Next Year, Prince of Wales, 1976; Flowers for Algernon, Queen's, 1979; Barnum, Palladium, 1981. *Films include:* Soap Box Derby; Blow Your Own Trumpet; Two Left Feet; The War Lover; Two Living, One Dead; The Knack, 1964; A Funny Thing Happened on the Way to the Forum, 1965; The Jokers, How I Won the War, 1966; Hello Dolly, 1968; The Games, 1969; Hello and Goodbye, 1970; Alice in Wonderland, 1972; The Condorman, 1980. Numerous radio broadcasts and TV appearances; *TV series include:* Some Mothers Do 'Ave 'Em; Chalk and Cheese. *Address:* c/o Michael Linnit, Chatto & Linnit Ltd, Globe Theatre, Shaftesbury Avenue, W1. *T:* 01-439 4371.

CRAWFORD, Michael Hewson, FBA 1980; Lecturer, University of Cambridge, since 1969; *b* 7 Dec. 1939; *s* of Brian Hewson Crawford and Margarethe Bettina Crawford. *Educ:* St Paul's School; Oriel College, Oxford (BA, MA). Scholar, British School at Rome, 1962-64; Jane Eliza Procter Visiting Fellow, Princeton Univ., 1964-65; Research Fellow, Christ's Coll., Cambridge, 1964-69. Jt Dir, Excavations of Fregellae, 1980-. Chm., JACT Ancient History Cttee, 1978-; Vice-Pres., Roman Soc., 1981-. Editor: Papers of the British Sch. at Rome, 1975-79; Jl of Roman Studies, 1980-. *Publications:* Roman Republican Coin Hoards, 1969; Roman Republican Coinage, 1974; The Roman Republic, 1978; La Moneta in Grecia e a Roma, 1981; (with D. Whitehead) Archaic and Classical Greece, 1982; contribs to Annales, Economic History Rev., Jl of Roman Studies, etc. *Address:* Christ's College, Cambridge CB2 3BU. *T:* Cambridge 67641.

CRAWFORD, Peter John, QC 1976; a Recorder of the Crown Court, since 1974; *b* 23 June 1930; *s* of William Gordon Robertson and Doris Victoria Robertson (née Mann, subseq. Crawford); *m* 1st, 1955, Jocelyn Lavender; two *s* two *d*; 2nd, 1979, Ann Allen Travis. *Educ:* Berkhamsted Sch.; Brasenose Coll., Oxford (MA). Called to Bar, Lincoln's Inn, 1953. Mem., Paddington Borough Council, 1962-65; Chm., W London Family Service Unit, 1972-79; Mem., Family Service Units Nat. Council, 1975-81. *Recreation:* sailing. *Address:* 13 King's Bench Walk, Temple, EC4Y 7EN. *T:* 01-353 7204.

CRAWFORD, (Robert) Norman, CBE 1973; Divisional Head, Northern Ireland Development Agency, 1976–82, retired; *b* 14 June 1923; *s* of Wm Crawford and Annie Catherine (*née* Rexter); *m* 1948, Jean Marie Patricia (*née* Carson); one *s* five *d. Educ:* Foyle Coll., Londonderry; Queen's Univ., Belfast (BComSc). FCA. Sec./Accountant, John McNeill Ltd, 1948–60; Dep. Man. Dir, McNeill Group Ltd, 1960–66, Man. Dir 1966–68; Chairman: N Ireland Transport Holding Co., 1968–75; R. N. Crawford & Co., Merchant Bank Facilities, 1968–. Pres., N Ireland Chamber of Commerce and Industry, 1966–67; Chairman: N Ireland Regional Bd, BIM, 1966–69; Nature Reserves Cttee, 1967–; NI Outward Bound Assoc., 1969–76; Open Door Housing Assoc., 1979–; Retirement Assoc. of NI, 1982–83. Member Senate, Queen's University, Belfast (Pres., Queen's Univ. Assoc., 1982–83); Pres., Foyle Coll. Old Boys' Assoc., 1981–82. Mem. Council, Ulster Trust for Nature Conservation, 1979–81. FRSA. *Address:* 4 Fort Road, Helens Bay, Bangor, Co. Down BT19 1LD. *T:* Helens Bay 853661. *Clubs:* Ulster Reform (Belfast); Kildare Street and University (Dublin).

CRAWFORD, Sir (Robert) Stewart, GCMG 1973 (KCMG 1966; CMG 1951; CVO 1955; HM Diplomatic Service, retired; *b* 27 Aug. 1913; *s* of late Sir William Crawford, KBE, head of W. S. Crawford Ltd, advertising agents; *m* 1938, Mary Katharine, *d* of late Eric Corbett, Gorse Hill, Witley, Surrey; three *s* one *d* (and one *s* decd). *Educ:* Gresham's Sch., Holt; Oriel Coll., Oxford. Home Civil Service (Air Ministry), 1936; Private Sec. to Chief of Air Staff, 1940–46; Asst Sec., Control Office for Germany and Austria, 1946; Foreign Office, 1947; Counsellor, British Embassy, Oslo, 1954–56; Counsellor, later Minister, British Embassy, Baghdad, 1957–59; Dep. UK Delegate to OEEC Paris, 1959–60; Asst Under Sec., Foreign Office, 1961–65; Political Resident, Persian Gulf, 1966–70; Dep. Under-Sec. of State, FCO, 1970–73. Chm., Cttee on Broadcasting Coverage, 1973–74; Mem., BBC Gen. Adv. Council, 1976–; Chm., Broadcasters' Audience Res. Bd, 1980–. *Recreations:* opera, gardening, bookbinding. *Address:* Ruperts Elm, Northfield End, Henley-on-Thames, Oxon. *T:* Henley 4702. *Club:* United Oxford & Cambridge University.

CRAWFORD, Robert William Kenneth; Deputy Director, Imperial War Museum, since 1982; *b* 3 July 1945; *s* of late Hugh Merrall Crawford, FCA, and Mary Crawford (*née* Percival); *m* 1975, Vivienne Sylvia Polakowski. *Educ:* Culford Sch.; Pembroke Coll., Oxford (Cleoburey Schol.; BA). Joined Imperial War Museum as Research Asst, 1968: Head of Research and Information Office, 1971–; Keeper, Dept of Photographs, 1975–; Asst Director, 1979–82. *Address:* c/o Imperial War Museum, Lambeth Road, SE1 6HZ. *T:* 01-735 8922.

CRAWFORD, Prof. Sir Theodore, (Sir Theo), Kt 1973; Professor of Pathology in the University of London, 1948–77, Professor Emeritus, 1977; Director of Pathological Services, St George's Hospital and Medical School, 1946–77; *b* 23 Dec. 1911; *s* of late Theodore Crawford and late Sarah Mansfield; *m* 1st, 1938, Margaret Donald Green, MD (*d* 1973); two *s* three *d*; 2nd, 1974, Priscilla Leathley Chater. *Educ:* St Peter's Sch., York; Glasgow Academy; Glasgow Univ. BSc, 1932; MB, ChB, 1935; Hon. LLD, 1979. FRFPS, 1938; MD 1941; Bellahouston Gold Medal (Glasgow Univ.), 1941; MRCP 1960; FRCP Glas 1962; FRCPath 1963, FRCP 1964; Hall Tutorial and Research Fellow, 1936–38. Asst Physician, Glasgow, Royal Hosp. for Sick Children, 1936–38; Lecturer in Pathology (Glasgow Univ.), 1939–46. Served War of 1939–45, Major RAMC, 1941–45. Mem. of the Medical Research Council, 1960–64 (and Mem. Cell Board, 1974–78); Registrar, Coll. of Pathologists, 1963–68; Consultant Adviser in Pathology to Dept of Health and Social Security and Chm. of its Central Pathology Cttee, 1969–78. Royal Society of Medicine (Pres. Section of Pathology, 1961–62). Pres., Royal Coll. of Pathologists, 1969–72 (Vice-Pres., 1968–69); Mem., Pathological Soc. of Great Britain, etc.; Chm., Scientific Cttee, British Empire Cancer Campaign, 1969–78 (Hon. Sec., 1955–67; Hon. Sec. of the Campaign, 1967–70); Vice-Pres., Cancer Res. Campaign, 1979–. Member: Council Epsom Coll., 1949–71; Standing Medical Advisory Cttee, Health Services Council, 1964–69; Cttee on Safety of Medicines, 1969–77 (Vice-Chm., 1976–77); Army Pathology Adv. Cttee, 1970–75; DHSS Cttee on Smoking and Health, 1973–79. *Publications:* (ed) Modern Trends in Pathology, 1967; Pathology of Ischaemic Heart Disease, 1977; scientific papers in Lancet, British Medical Journal, British Journal of Surgery, Archives of Disease in Childhood, British Journal of Opthalmology, Journal of Pathology and Bacteriology, etc. *Recreations:* horticulture, growing trees, walking, music. *Address:* 9 Asher Reeds, Langton Green, Tunbridge Wells, Kent TN3 0AL. *T:* Langton 3341. *Club:* Sloane.

CRAWFORD, Vice-Adm. Sir William (Godfrey), KBE 1961; CB 1958; DSC 1941; *b* 14 Sept. 1907; *s* of late H. E. V. Crawford, Wyld Court, Axminster, and late Mrs M. E. Crawford; *m* 1939, Mary Felicity Rosa, *d* of late Sir Philip Williams, 2nd Bt; three *s* one *d. Educ:* RN Coll., Dartmouth. Lieut RN, 1929; specialised in gunnery, 1932; Lieut-Comdr, 1937; Gunnery Officer, HMS Rodney, 1940–42; Comdr Dec. 1941; Exec. Officer, HMS Venerable, 1944–46; Capt. 1947; in comd HMS Pelican and 2nd Frigate Flotilla, Med., 1948–49; Dep.-Dir RN Staff Coll., 1950–52; in comd HMS Devonshire, 1952–53; in comd RN Coll., Dartmouth, 1953–56; Rear-Adm. 1956; Imperial Defence Coll., 1956–58; Flag Officer, Sea Training, 1958–60; Vice-Adm. 1959; Comdr British Navy Staff and Naval Attaché Washington, 1960–62; retired list, 1963. Dir, Overseas Offices, BTA, 1964–72. *Recreations:* sailing, fishing. *Address:* Abbotsford, Uplyme, Lyme Regis, Dorset. *T:* Lyme Regis 2756. *Clubs:* Naval and Military; Cruising (Naval Member).

CRAWFORD, William Hamilton Raymund, QC 1980; a Recorder of the Crown Court, since 1979; *b* 10 Nov. 1936; *s* of Col Mervyn Crawford, DSO, DL, JP, and Martha Macmillan Crawford; *m* 1965, Marilyn Jean Colville; one *s* two *d. Educ:* West Downs, Winchester; Winchester Coll.; Emmanuel Coll., Cambridge (BA). Called to the Bar, Inner Temple, 1964; Dep. Chm., Agricultural Land Tribunal, 1978. *Recreations:* hill farming, fishing, shooting (shot for GB in Kolapore Match, and for Scotland in Elcho and Twenty Matches on several occasions; mem., Scottish Rifle Team, Commonwealth Games, Jamaica, 1966). *Address:* Jarbruck, Moniaive, Dumfriesshire. *T:* Moniaive 500. *Club:* Naval and Military.

CRAWFORD-COMPTON, Air Vice-Marshal William Vernon, CB 1965; CBE 1957; DSO 1943, Bar 1945; DFC 1941, Bar, 1942; RAF retired, 1969; *b* 2 March 1915; *s* of William Gilbert Crawford-Compton; *m* 1st, 1949, Chloe Clifford-Brown (marr. diss. 1978); two *d*; 2nd, 1978, Dolores Perle Goodhew, widow. *Educ:* New Plymouth High Sch., New Zealand. Joined RAF, 1939; served War of 1939–45 (DFC and Bar, DSO and Bar); 11 Group and 2nd TAF Group Capt., 1955; SASO, 11 (Fighter) Group; Student, Imperial Defence Coll., 1961; Air Officer in Charge of Administration, Near East Air Force, 1962–63; SASO 1963–66. Air Vice-Marshal, 1963. Legion of Honour (France); Croix de Guerre (France); Silver Star (USA). *Recreations:* golf, tennis, fishing. *Address:* Church House, Yapton, Arundel, West Sussex BN18 0EP.

CRAWLEY, Aidan Merivale, MBE; Chairman, London Weekend Television, 1967–71, President 1971–73; *b* 10 April 1908; *s* of late Canon A. S. Crawley; *m* 1945, Virginia Cowles, *qv* ; two *s* one *d. Educ:* Harrow; Oxford. Journalist, 1930–36; Educational Film Producer, 1936–39. AAF, 601 Sqdn, 1936–40; Asst Air Attaché, Ankara, Belgrade (resident Sofia), May 1940–May 1941; joined 73 (F) Sqdn, Egypt; shot down July 1941; prisoner until May 1945. MP (Lab) Buckingham Div. of Bucks, 1945–51; Parliamentary Private Sec. to successive Secs of State for the Colonies, 1945 and 1946–47; Parliamentary Under-Sec. of State for Air, 1950–51; resigned from the Labour Party, 1957; MP (C) West Derbyshire, 1962–68; Editor-in-Chief, Independent Television News Ltd, 1955–56; making television documentaries for BBC, 1956–60; Mem. Monckton Commission on Federation of Rhodesia and Nyasaland, 1960. Pres., MCC, 1973. *Publications:* Escape from Germany, 1956; De Gaulle: A Biography, 1969; The Rise of Western Germany 1945–72, 1973; Dial 200-200, 1980. *Recreation:* cricket; Co-Founder, Haig Nat. Village Cricket Championship, 1971. *Address:* 19 Chester Square, SW1. *T:* 01-730 3030. *Clubs:* White's, Buck's; MCC.

CRAWLEY, Charles William; Hon. Fellow of Trinity Hall, 1971; University Lecturer in History, 1931–66; Vice-Master of Trinity Hall, Cambridge, 1950–66, Emeritus Fellow, 1966; *b* 1 April 1899; *s* of Charles Crawley, barrister of Lincoln's Inn, and Augusta, *d* of Rt Rev. Samuel Butcher, Bishop of Meath; *m* 1930, Kathleen Elizabeth (*d* 1982), *d* of Lieut-Col H G. Leahy, OBE, RA; four *s* one *d. Educ:* Winchester (Scholar); Trinity Coll., Cambridge (Scholar). Fellow of Trinity Hall, 1924–66. Asst Tutor, 1927, Acting Senior Tutor, 1940, Senior Tutor, 1946–58. *Publications:* The Question of Greek Independence, 1821–1833, 1930, repr. 1973; (ed) New Cambridge Modern History, Vol. IX, 1965; John Capodistrias: unpublished documents, 1970; Trinity Hall: the history of a Cambridge College, 1350–1975, 1976. *Address:* 1 Madingley Road, Cambridge. *T:* 352849.
See also J. M. Crawley.

CRAWLEY, Desmond John Chetwode, CMG 1964; CVO 1961; HM Diplomatic Service, retired; *b* 2 June 1917; *s* of late Lieutenant-Colonel C. G. C. Crawley, OBE and late Agnes Luke; *m* 1945, Daphne Lesley, *y d* of late Sir Vere Mockett, MBE, and late Ethel Norah Gaddum Tomkinson; two *s* one *d. Educ:* King's Sch., Ely; Queen's Coll., Oxford. Entered Indian Civil Service, serving in Madras Presidency, 1939; entered Indian Political Service, serving in Baluchistan, 1946; entered Commonwealth Relations Office, 1947, and served in London, Calcutta, and on loan to the Foreign Office in Washington; Principal Private Secretary to Sec. of State for Commonwealth Relations, 1952–53; British Dep. High Commissioner in Lahore, Pakistan, 1958–61; Imperial Defence Coll., 1962; British High Commissioner in Sierra Leone, 1963–66; Ambassador to Bulgaria, 1966–70; Minister to Holy See, 1970–75. Coronation Medal, 1953. Knight Grand Cross, Order of St Gregory the Great, 1973. *Address:* 35 Chartfield Avenue, SW15. *T:* 01-788 9529. *Club:* United Oxford & Cambridge University.

CRAWLEY, John Cecil, CBE 1972 (MBE 1944); Chairman of Trustees of Visnews, since 1976; *b* 1909; *s* of John and Kathleen Crawley; *m* 1933, Constance Mary Griffiths; two *d. Educ:* William Ellis Sch. War Service, Army, 1939–45. Journalism: Reynolds, 1927; Central News Agency, 1928; National Press Agency, 1929; Press Secretaries, 1933; BBC: Sub-Editor, 1945; Foreign Correspondent, New York, 1959–63; Foreign News Editor, 1963–67; Editor of News and Current Affairs, 1967–71; Chief Asst to Dir-Gen., BBC, 1971–75. *Recreations:* walking, bird-watching. *Address:* 157 Clarence Gate Gardens, NW1. *T:* 01-723 6876.

CRAWLEY, John Maurice; Under Secretary, Inland Revenue; *b* 27 Sept. 1933; *s* of Charles William Crawley, *qv*; *m* 1978, Jane Meadows Rendel; two *s. Educ:* Rugby Sch.; New Coll., Oxford (MA). Assistant Principal, Inland Revenue, 1959; Principal, 1963; Asst Secretary, 1969; Under Sec., 1979; seconded to Cabinet Office (Central Policy Review Staff), 1973–76 and

1979-81. *Recreations:* music, walking. *Address:* 85 St Mark's Road, W10 6JS.

CRAWLEY, Virginia, (Mrs Aidan Crawley); *see* Cowles, Virginia.

CRAWLEY-BOEVEY, Sir Thomas (Michael Blake), 8th Bt *cr* 1784; Editor-in-Chief, Which?, since 1980 (Editor, 1976-80); *b* 29 Sept. 1928; *er s* of Sir Launcelot Valentine Hyde Crawley-Boevey, 7th Bt, and Elizabeth Goodeth (*d* 1976), *d* of Herbert d'Auvergne Innes, late Indian Police; *S* father, 1968; *m* 1957, Laura Coelingh (*d* 1979); two *s. Educ:* Wellington Coll.; St John's Coll., Cambridge (BA 1952, MA 1956). 2nd Lieut, Durham Light Infantry, 1948. With Shipping Agents, 1952-61; with Consumers' Association, 1961-; Editor, Money Which?, 1968-76. *Recreations:* gardening, bicycling. *Heir: er s* Thomas Hyde Crawley-Boevey, *b* 26 June 1958. *Address:* 41 Thornhill Road, N1. *T:* 01-607 5575.

CRAWSHAW, 4th Baron, *cr* 1892; **William Michael Clifton Brooks; Bt** *cr* 1891; *b* 25 March 1933; *s* of 3rd Baron and Sheila (*d* 1964), *o d* of late Lieut-Col P. R. Clifton, CMG, DSO; *S* father, 1946. *Educ:* Eton; Christ Church, Oxford. Jt Master, Oxford Univ. Drag Hounds, 1952-53. Treasurer, Loughborough Div. Conservative Assoc., 1954-58; County Commissioner, Leics Boy Scouts, 1958-. Pres., Leics Assoc. of the Disabled; Chm., Quorn Hunt Cttee, 1971-. Lord of the Manor of Long Whatton. Patron of the Living of Shepshed. *Heir: b* Hon. David Gerald Brooks [*b* 14 Sept. 1934; *m* 1970, Belinda Mary, *d* of George Burgess, Melbourne, and of Mrs J. P. Allen, Coleman's Hatch, Sussex; two *d. Educ:* Eton; Royal Agricultural College, Cirencester]. *Address:* Whatton, Loughborough, Leics. *TA:* Kegworth. *T:* Hathern 225. *Clubs:* Boodle's, MCC.

CRAWSHAW, Sir (Edward) Daniel (Weston), Kt 1964; QC (Aden) 1949; *b* 10 Sept. 1903; British; *m* 1942, Rosemary Treffry; one *s* two *d* (and one *s* decd). *Educ:* St Bees Sch.; Selwyn Coll., Cambridge. Solicitor, Supreme Court of Judicature, England, 1929; Barrister-at-Law, Gray's Inn, 1946; Solicitor, Northern Rhodesia, 1930-32; Colonial Legal Service, Tanganyika, 1933-39; Zanzibar, 1939-47; Attorney-Gen., Aden, 1947-52; Puisne Judge, Tanganyika, 1952-60; Justice of Appeal, Court of Appeal for Eastern Africa, 1960-65. Commissioner, Foreign Compensation Commission, 1965-75. Brilliant Star of Zanzibar, 1947; Coronation Medal, 1953. *Recreation:* golf. *Address:* 1 Fort Road, Guildford, Surrey. *T:* Guildford 76883. *Clubs:* Royal Over-Seas League; County (Guildford).

CRAWSHAW, Philip, CBE 1959 (MBE 1948); Director-General, Royal Over-Seas League, 1959-79; *b* 25 Nov. 1912; twin *s* of R. Crawshaw; *m* 1947, June Patricia, *d* of E. D. K. Mathews; two *d. Educ:* Repton. Travelling Sec., Over-Seas League, 1936; Asst Sec., 1940; Sec., 1946; Sec.-Gen., 1956. *Address:* 14 Champs Beulai, Longy Road, Alderney, CI. *Clubs:* Royal Over-Seas League; Alderney Golf, Alderney Sailing.

CRAWSHAW, Lt-Col Richard, OBE 1958; TD 1958; MA, LLB; DL; Barrister-at-Law; MP Toxteth Division of Liverpool since 1964 (Lab, 1964-81, SDP, since 1981); *b* 25 Sept. 1917; *s* of Percy Eli Lee Crawshaw and Beatrice Lavinia (*née* Barritt); *m* 1960, Audrey Frances Lima; no *c. Educ:* Pendleton Gram. Sch.; Tatterford Sch.; Pembroke Coll., Cambridge (MA); London Univ. (LLB). Clerk, 1931-33; Engineer, 1933-36; Theological Student, 1936-39; Royal Artillery and Parachute Regt, 1939-45; Pembroke Coll., Cambridge, 1945-47; called to Bar, Inner Temple, 1948; Northern Circuit. Liverpool City Council, 1948-65. Commanded 12/13th Bn, The Parachute Regt, TA, 1954-57. Mem., Speaker's Panel of Chairmen, 1971-79; Dep. Chm. of Ways and Means and Deputy Speaker, 1979-81. Estd world non-stop walking record of 255.8 miles, 1972; estd world non-stop walking record (literally non-stop) of 231 miles, 1974. DL Merseyside, 1970. *Recreations:* climbing, walking, free fall parachuting and youth activities. *Address:* The Orchard, Aintree Lane, Liverpool L10 8LE. *T:* 051-526 7886.

CRAWSHAY, Elisabeth Mary Boyd, (Lady Crawshay), JP, DL; Chairman, Local Government Boundary Commission, Wales, since 1979; Deputy Chief Commissioner, St John's Ambulance Brigade, Wales, since 1979; *b* 2 July 1927; *d* of Lt-Col Guy Franklin Reynolds, late 9th Lancers, and Katherine Isobel (*née* Macdonell); *m* 1950, Col Sir William (Robert) Crawshay, *qv. Educ:* Convent of Sacred Heart, Roehampton; St Anne's Coll., Oxford (MA). DL Gwent 1978; JP Abergavenny, 1972, Chm., Juvenile Bench, 1980-, Mem., Borstal Board of Visitors, 1975. DJStJ 1970. *Address:* Llanfair Court, Abergavenny, Gwent.

CRAWSHAY, Col Sir William (Robert), Kt 1972; DSO 1945; ERD; TD; Vice Lord-Lieutenant of Gwent, since 1979; *b* 27 May 1920; *o s* of late Captain J. W. L. Crawshay, MC, Caversham Park, Oxon, and late Hon. Mrs. George Egerton, Brussels; *m* 1950, Elisabeth Mary Boyd Reynolds (*see* Lady Crawshay). *Educ:* Eton. Served Royal Welch Fus.(SR), 1939-46; SOE 1944 (DSO, despatches twice); TA, 1947-62, Parachute Regt, Welch Regt, SW Brigade. ADC to HM the Queen, 1966-71. Hon. Colonel: 3rd RRW (V) Bn, 1970-82; Cardiff Univ. OTC, 1977-. Mem., Arts Council of GB, 1962-74; Chairman: Welsh Arts Council, 1968-74; Council, University Coll. of Cardiff, 1966; Member: Council and Court, Univ. of Wales, 1967; Welsh Council, 1966-69, 1970-; Pres., 1977- (Mem., Council and Court, 1966-), Nat. Museum of Wales. Pres., Royal British Legion, Wales Area, 1974-. Mem., Crafts Adv. Council, 1974-78. Hon. LLD, Univ. of Wales, 1975. DL

Glamorgan, 1964, Monmouthshire, 1970, Gwent, 1974. Chevalier, Légion d'honneur, 1956; Croix de Guerre (France) with Palms twice, 1944, 1945. KStJ (formerly KJStJ) 1969. *Address:* Llanfair Court, Abergavenny, Gwent. *Clubs:* White's; Cardiff and County (Cardiff).

CRAXTON, (Harold) Antony, CVO 1977 (MVO 1968); freelance television consultant; Executive Producer/Director, Precedent Productions Ltd, since 1979; *b* 23 April 1918; 2nd *s* of late Harold Craxton, OBE, and Essie Craxton; *m* 1944, Anne Sybil Cropper (marr. diss. 1978); one *s* one *d. Educ:* St George's Chapel Choir Sch., Windsor; Royal Acad. of Music; Gordonstoun Sch., Scotland. Joined BBC Radio, 1941; Home and Overseas Announcer, 1942-45; joined TV Service as Outside Broadcast Producer, 1951; resp. for coverage of all major Royal occasions, 1953-77, Jubilee Day being 200th broadcast involving the Queen and Royal Family; retd, 1977. Helped pioneer presentation of internat. cricket, Rugby and golf in early 50s; covered over 100 orchestral concert relays from many parts of country, 1953-71. Chief Royal Occasions: Queen's 1st Christmas Television Broadcast and Prince Philip's 1st major TV appearance, Round the World in 40 Minutes, 1957; Princess Margaret's Wedding, 1960; Duke of Kent's Wedding, 1961; Princess Alexandra's Wedding, 1963; State Funeral of Sir Winston Churchill, 1965; Investiture of Prince Charles as Prince of Wales, 1969; Lying in State of Duke of Windsor, 1972; Queen's Silver Wedding Celebrations, 1972; Princess Anne's Wedding, 1973; Funeral of Duke of Gloucester, 1974; Funeral of Field-Marshal Montgomery, 1976; Queen's Silver Jubilee Day Celebrations, 1977; 10 State visits abroad and 19 visits by Foreign Heads of State to Britain, 1954-76. News Chronicle Readers' Award for Prince Philip's Round the World Documentary, 1957; Guild of TV Producers' Award for Princess Alexandra's Wedding, 1963; French TV Internat. Award for Investiture of Prince Charles, 1970; BAFTA Award for Jubilee Day (1977), 1978. Silver Jubilee Medal, 1977. *Recreations:* golf, cricket, classical music. *Address:* 14 Kidderpore Avenue, NW3. *Clubs:* MCC, Lord's Taverners, Eccentric.

CREAGH, Maj.-Gen. Sir Kilner Rupert B.; *see* Brazier-Creagh.

CREAMER, Brian; Physician, St Thomas' Hospital, London, since 1959; Senior Lecturer in Medicine since 1959, and Dean, since 1979, St Thomas's Hospital Medical School; Hon. Consultant in Gastroenterology to the Army, since 1970; *b* 12 April 1926; *s* of late L. G. Creamer and Mrs Creamer, Epsom; *m* 1953, Margaret Holden Rees; two *s* one *d. Educ:* Christ's Hosp.; St Thomas' Hosp. MB, BS Hons London, 1948; MD London, 1952; FRCP 1966 (MRCP 1950); Research Asst, Mayo Clinic, Rochester, USA, 1955-56. Vis. Prof., 1977-78, Hon. Prof. of Medicine, 1978-, Shiraz Univ., Iran. Sir Arthur Hurst Memorial Lectr, 1968; Watson Smith Lectr, RCP, 1971. Member: British Soc. of Gastroenterology; Assoc. of Physicians of GB and NI; Exec. Subcttee, Univ. Hosps Assoc., 1981-. Member: Collegiate Council, Univ. of London, 1980-; Senate, Univ. of London, 1981-. *Publications:* (ed) Modern Trends in Gastroenterology, vol. 4, 1970; (ed) The Small Intestine, 1974; contributions to med. jls. *Recreations:* drawing and painting, gardening, and listening to music. *Address:* Tetherdown, Oxshott Rise, Cobham, Surrey KT11 2RN. *T:* Cobham 3994.

CREAN, Hon. Frank; *b* Hamilton, Vic, 28 Feb. 1916; *s* of J. Crean; *m* 1946, Mary, *d* of late A. E. Findlay; three *s. Educ:* Hamilton High Sch.; Melbourne High Sch.; Melbourne Univ. BA Hons; BCom. DPA; FASA. Income Tax Assessor, 1934-45. MLA: for Albert Park, Vic, 1945-47; for Prahran, 1949-51; MHR for Melbourne Ports, 1951-77; Mem. Exec., Federal Parly Labour Party, 1956-72, Dep. Leader, 1975-76; Mem., Jt Party Cttee on Public Accounts, 1952-55; Treasurer, Commonwealth of Australia, 1972-74; Minister for Overseas Trade, 1974-75, also Deputy Prime Minister, 1975. Chm., Council of Adult Educn, 1947-74. *Publication:* (with W. J. Byrt) Government and Politics in Australia, 1972. *Address:* 106 Harold Street, Middle Park, Vic 3206, Australia.

CREASEY, Gen. Sir Timothy (May), KCB 1978 (CB 1975); OBE 1966; Deputy Commander-in-Chief and Chief of Defence Staff, London since 1981; *b* 21 Sept. 1923; *s* of late Lt-Col G. M. Creasey and late Phyllis Creasey, *d* of Vice-Adm. F. C. B. Robinson, RN; *m* 1951, Ruth Annette, *y d* of Major J. I. H. Friend, OBE, MC, DL, JP, Northdown, Kent; one *s* one *d* (and one *s* decd). *Educ:* Clifton Coll. Commissioned Baluch Regt, IA, 1942. Served War: Far East, Italy, Greece, 1942-45. Transf. to Royal Norfolk Regt, 1946; Instructor, Sch. of Infantry, 1951-53; Bde Major, 39th Infantry Bde, Kenya and Ireland, 1955-56; Instr, Army Staff Coll., 1959-61; Instr, RMA, Sandhurst, 1963-64; commanded: 1 Royal Anglian, Aden and BAOR, 1965-67; 11th Armoured Bde, 1969-70; Student, IDC, 1971; Comdr, Sultan's Armed Forces, Oman, 1972-75; Dir of Infantry, 1975-77; GOC Northern Ireland, 1977-79; C-in-C, UKLF, 1980-81. Dep. Col, Royal Anglian Regt, 1976-81, Col, 1982-. Colonel Commandant: The Queen's Div., 1977-81; Small Arms Sch. Corps, 1977-81. Governor, Clifton Coll., 1979-. Jordanian Order of Independence, 1st class, 1974; Order of Oman, 2nd class, 1975. *Recreations:* shooting, golf. *Address:* c/o Williams & Glyn's Bank Ltd, Holt's Branch, Whitehall, SW1. *Clubs:* MCC, Army and Navy.

CREASY, Sir Gerald Hallen, KCMG 1946 (CMG 1943); KCVO 1954; OBE 1937; *b* 1 Nov. 1897; *y s* of Leonard and Ellen Maud Creasy; *m* 1925, Helen Duff, *y d* of Reginald B. Jacomb; one *s* one *d. Educ:* Rugby. On Military Service (RA), 1916-19; entered Colonial Office, 1920; Chief Sec. to the West African Council, 1945-47; Governor and C-in-C, Gold Coast, 1947-49; Governor and C-in-C, Malta, 1949-54, retired 1954. GCStJ 1970 (KStJ 1949).

LLD (*hc*) Royal University of Malta, 1954. *Address:* 2 Burlington Court, Eastbourne, East Sussex. *T:* Eastbourne 27147.

CREASY, Leonard Richard, CB 1972; OBE 1961; CEng, FICE, FIStructE; civil engineer in private practice since 1974; *b* 20 Dec. 1912; *s* of William and Ellen Creasy; *m* 1937, Irene Howard; one *s* one *d*. *Educ:* Wimbledon Technical Coll. BSc(Eng) London. Served War, RE, E Africa, 1944-46. Service in Industry, 1928-34; HM Office of Works, Asst Engr, 1935; Min. of Works, Suptg Engr, 1959; MPBW: Dir, Civil Engrg, 1966; Dir, Central Services, 1968; Dir of Civil Engrg Develt, Dept of the Environment, 1970-73. Concerned with Inquiries into disasters at Aberfan, Ronan Point and Brent, and with design of Radio Towers, London and Birmingham; Plant House, Royal Botanical Gardens, Edinburgh; Wind Tunnels, Bedford NAE; and other structures. Bronze Medal, Reinforced Concrete Assoc.; Manby and Telford Premiums, Instn Civil Engrs; Pres., Instn Struct. Engrs, 1973 (Bronze Medal and Certif. of Merit of the Instn). *Publications:* Pre-stressed Concrete Cylindrical Tanks, 1961; James Forrest Lecture, 1968; many other papers on civil and structural engrg projects and engrg economics. *Recreations:* music, opera, languages. *Address:* 5 The Oaks, Epsom, Surrey KT18 5HH. *T:* Epsom 22361.

CREDITON, Bishop Suffragan of, since 1974; **Rt. Rev. Philip John Pasterfield;** *b* 1920; *s* of Bertie James Pasterfield and Lilian Bishop Pasterfield (*née* Flinn); *m* 1948, Eleanor Maureen, *d* of William John Symons; three *s* one *d*. *Educ:* Denstone Coll., Staffs; Trinity Hall, Cambridge (MA); Cuddesdon Coll., Oxford. Army Service, 1940-46; commnd in Somerset Light Infantry. Deacon 1951, Priest 1952. Curate of Streatham, 1951-54; Vicar of West Lavington, Sussex, and Chaplain, King Edward VII Hosp., Midhurst, 1954-60; Rector of Woolbeding, 1955-60; Vicar of Oxton, Birkenhead, 1960-68; Rural Dean of Birkenhead, 1966-68; Canon Residentiary and Sub Dean of St Albans, 1968-74; Rural Dean of St Albans, 1972-74. *Recreations:* ornithology, music. *Address:* 10 The Close, Exeter EX1 1EZ. *T:* Exeter 73509.

CREE, Brig. Gerald Hilary, CBE 1946; DSO 1945; Colonel, The Prince of Wales's Own Regiment of Yorkshire, 1960-70; *b* 23 June 1905; *s* of late Maj.-Gen. Gerald Cree; *m* 1945, Joan Agnes, *d* of late Lt-Col W. R. Eden, RA; one *d*. *Educ:* Kelly Coll.; RMC Sandhurst. Commissioned, The West Yorks Regt, 1924; King's African Rifles, 1931-36; comd 2nd Bn West Yorks Regt, 1942-44; 1st Bn 1946-48; Comdr 25 (East African) Infantry Bde, 1944-45 and Brig. 1953. Served Palestine, East Africa, Abyssinia, Western Desert, Iraq, Burma, 1938-45. Commander 127 (East Lancs) Infantry Brigade (TA), 1953-56; Col, The West Yorks Regt, 1956-57, Col, PWO Regt of Yorkshire, 1960-70, retd. *Address:* Laurels, Sharpham Drive, Totnes, Devon. *Club:* Naval and Military.

CREED, Albert Lowry, MA; *b* 16 July 1909; *s* of Rev. Albert H. Creed; *m* 1943, Joyce Marian (*née* Hunter), Leeds; two *s* one *d*. *Educ:* Kingswood Sch.; Downing Coll., Cambridge. MA Cantab 1933. Asst Master: Stretford Grammar Sch., 1932-35; Bishop's Stortford Coll., 1935-39; Housemaster, Christ's Hospital, 1939-42; Headmaster: Staveley-Netherthorpe Grammar Sch., 1942-46; Truro Sch., Cornwall, 1946-59; Kingswood Sch., 1959-70; Volunteer with Botswana Min. of Educn, 1973-74. Chm., West Cornwall Hospital Management Cttee, 1957-59; Vice-Pres., Methodist Conf., 1962-63; a Dir, The Methodist Recorder. Pres., Kingswood Old Boys' Assoc., 1975-76. Hon. Sec., UK-Botswana Soc., 1981-. *Address:* Trevor House, Langford, near Lechlade, Glos. *T:* Filkins 392. *Club:* Royal Commonwealth Society.

CREEGGAN, Rt. Rev. Jack Burnett; *b* 10 Nov. 1902; *s* of Alfred Henry Creeggan and Mary Laura (*née* Sheffield); *m* 1931, Dorothy Jarman (*née* Embury); one *s* one *d*. *Educ:* Deseronto (Ont) Public and High Schs; Queen's Univ. (BA); Bishop's Univ. (LST). Priest, 1928; served in many parishes in Dio. Ontario; Canon, St George's Cathedral, Kingston, Ont, 1952; Archdeacon of: Ontario, 1953; Frontenac, 1962; Kingston, 1969; Bishop of Ontario, 1970-74. Prolocutor, Lower House, Provincial Synod of Ont., 1963. Hon. DCL, Bishop's Univ., Lennoxville, PQ, 1971. *Recreations:* curling, golf. *Address:* Apt 112, 32 Ontario Street, Kingston, Ontario K7L 2Y1, Canada. *T:* 542-5319.

CREESE, Nigel Arthur Holloway; Headmaster, Melbourne Grammar School, since 1970; *b* 4 June 1927; *s* of late H. R. Creese; *m* 1951, Valdai (*née* Walters); two *s* two *d*. *Educ:* Blundell's Sch.; Brasenose Coll., Oxford. Assistant Master: Bromsgrove Sch., 1952-55; Rugby Sch., 1955-63; Headmaster, Christ's Coll., Christchurch, NZ, 1963-70. *Address:* Melbourne Church of England Grammar School, Domain Road, South Yarra, Victoria 3141, Australia.

CREIGHTMORE, Peter Beauchamp; Master of Supreme Court, Queen's Bench Division, since 1975; *b* 15 Jan. 1928; *s* of Maximilian Louis Creightmore, MRCS, LRCP and Mary Arnell Beauchamp; *m* 1957, June Patricia, *d* of Harold William Hedley, Captain Suez Canal Co. (Pilote Majeur), and Gwendoline Pugh; one *s* one *d*. *Educ:* Geelong Grammar Sch. (H. H. Whittingham Student, 1945); Worcester Coll., Oxford (MA). O/Sig, RNVR, 1952, commnd 1955. Called to Bar, Inner Temple, 1954; Oxford, later Oxford and Midland, Circuit. *Recreations:* narrow-boating; music. *Address:* Royal Courts of Justice, Strand, WC2.

CREIGHTON, Harold Digby Fitzgerald; Chairman, 1967-75, Editor, 1973-75, The Spectator; *b* 11 Sept. 1927; *s* of late Rev. Digby Robert Creighton and Amy Frances Rohde; *m* 1964, Harriett Mary Falconer Wallace, *d* of late A. L. P. F. Wallace of Candacraig (Mem., Queen's Body Guard for Scotland); four *d*. *Educ:* Haileybury. National Service, Army (Lieut), India and ME, 1945-48. Consolidated Tin Smelters, Penang, 1950-52; Dir, machine tool companies, London, 1952-63; Chm., Scottish Machine Tool Corp. Ltd, Glasgow, 1963-68. *Recreations:* conversation, reading. *Address:* 11c Mount Street, W1. *Club:* Beefsteak.

CREMIN, Cornelius Christopher; Chairman, Irish delegation to 3rd UN Conference on the Law of the Sea, 1973-79; *b* 6 Dec. 1908; 2nd *s* of D. J. Cremin and Ann (*née* Singleton), Kenmare, Co. Kerry; *m* 1st, 1935, Patricia Josephine (decd), Killarney; one *s* three *d* ; 2nd, 1974, Dr Mary Eta Murphy, Beare Island. *Educ:* National Univ. of Ireland. BComm 1930; MA (Classics) 1931. Travelling studentship (Classics), NUI, 1931-34; Brit. Sch. at Athens and Rome, 1932; Dipl. in Class. Archaeol., Oxford, 1934; 3rd Sec., Dept of External Affairs, 1935; 1st Sec., Irish Legation, Paris, 1937-43; Chargé d'Affaires, Berlin, 1943-45; Chargé d'Affaires, Lisbon, 1945-46; Couns., Dept of External Affairs, Dublin, 1946-48; Asst Sec., 1948-50; Minister to France, March-Sept. 1950; Ambassador to France, 1950-54; Head of Irish Delegn, OEEC, 1950-54, and Vice-Chm. of OEEC Council (official), 1952-54; Ambassador to the Holy See, 1954-56; Sec. of the Dept of External Affairs, Dublin, 1958-62; Irish Ambassador to Britain, 1963-64 (and 1956-58); Irish Permanent Representative at UN, 1964-74. LLD *hc* National Univ. of Ireland, 1965. Grand Officer of the Legion of Honour, 1964; Knight Grand Cross of the Order of Pius, 1956; Grand Cross of Merit (Fed. Germany), 1960. *Recreations:* golf, boating. *Address:* Tuosist, Killarney, Ireland.

CREMONA, Hon. John Joseph; Chief Justice of Malta and President of the Constitutional Court, Court of Appeal and Court of Criminal Appeal, 1971-81; Judge, European Court of Human Rights, since 1965; Emeritus Professor, University of Malta, since 1965; *b* 6 Jan. 1918; *s* of late Dr Antonio Cremona, KM, MD and Anne (*née* Camilleri); *m* 1949, Marchioness Beatrice Barbaro of St George; one *s* two *d*. *Educ:* Malta Univ. (BA 1936, LLD *cum laude* 1942); Rome Univ. (DLitt 1939); London Univ. (BA 1st Cl. Hons 1946, PhD in Laws 1951). DrJur Trieste, 1972. Crown Counsel, 1947; Lectr in Constitutional Law, Malta Univ., 1947-65, Prof. of Criminal Law, 1959-65; Attorney-Gen., 1957-64; Vice-Pres., Constitutional Court and Court of Appeal, 1965-71; sometime Actg Governor General and Actg Pres., Republic of Malta. Chm., Human Rights Section, World Assoc. of Lawyers; Vice-Pres., Internat. Inst. of Studies, Documentation and Info. for the Protection of Envt, Italy; Member: Cttee of Experts of Human Rights and Cttee on State Immunity, Council of Europe, Strasbourg; Scientific Council, Revue des Droits de l'Homme, Paris; Patronage Cttee, Europäische Grundrechte Zeitschrift, Strasbourg; Scientific Council Centro Internazionale per Protezione dei Diritti dell' Uomo, Pesaro, Italy; Editorial Adv. Board: Checklist of Human Rights Documents, NY; Human Rights Law Jl, Arlington, Va; delegate and rapporteur, internat. confs. FRHistS; Fellow *ex titulo*, Internat. Acad. of Legal Medicine and Social Medicine; Hon. Fellow, LSE; Hon. Mem., Real Acad. de Jurisprudencia y Legislacion, Madrid. Kt Comdr, Order of Merit, Italy, 1968; Kt, Sovereign Military Order of Malta, 1966; KSG, 1972; Kt Comdr, 1971, Grand Cross of Merit, 1981, Constantinian Order of St George. *Publications:* The Treatment of Young Offenders in Malta, 1956; The Malta Constitution of 1835, 1959; The Doctrine of Entrapment in Theft, 1959; The Legal Consequences of a Conviction, 1962; The Constitutional Development of Malta, 1963; From the Declaration of Rights to Independence, 1965; Human Rights Documentation in Malta, 1966; articles in French, German, Italian and American law jls. *Recreation:* gardening. *Address:* Villa Barbaro, Main Street, Attard, Malta. *T:* 40818.

CRESPI, (Caesar) James; a Recorder of the Crown Court, since 1973. *Educ:* Trinity Hall, Cambridge (BA). Called to the Bar, Middle Temple, 1951, South Eastern Circuit. *Address:* 5 Paper Buildings, Temple, EC4Y 7HB. *T:* 01-353 7811. *Club:* Garrick.

CRESPIN, Régine; Officier de la Légion d'Honneur, 1981 (Chevalier, 1969); Chevalier de l'Ordre National du Mérite, 1965; Commandeur des Arts et des Lettres, 1974; soprano singer; Professor of Singing, Conservatoire National Supérieur de Musique de Paris, since 1976; *b* 23 Feb.; *d* of Henri Crespin and Marguerite (*née* Meirone); *m* 1962, Lou Bruder, French novelist, critic, poet, translator. *Educ:* Nîmes; Conservatoire National, Paris (Baccalauréat). Has been working at the Opera, Paris, from 1951, in all the famous opera houses of Europe and all over the world, giving concerts, recitals, etc.; *Operas include:* Otello, Tosca, Il Trovatore, Le Nozze di Figaro, Ballo in Maschere, Der Rosenkavalier, Tannhauser, Lohengrin, Die Walkuere, Parsifal, Les Troyens, Dialogues of the Carmelites, Tales of Hoffmann, Carmen. *Recreations:* sea, sun, sleep, books, theatre; and my dog! *Address:* 3 Avenue Frochot, 75009 Paris, France.

CRESSWELL, Rev. Amos Samuel; Chairman, Plymouth and Exeter District of the Methodist Church, since 1976; (designated) President of the Methodist Conference, June 1983-July 1984; *b* 21 April 1926; *s* of Amos and Jane Cresswell; *m* 1956, Evelyn Rosemary Marchbanks; two *s* one *d*. *Educ:* Queen Mary's Grammar School, Walsall; University College, Durham Univ.; Wesley House, Cambridge; Theological Seminary, Bethel bei Bielefeld, Westphalia. BA (Dunelm), Classics, 1947; BA (Cantab), Theology, 1952, MA (Cantab) 1956. Teacher of English and Latin, High School for Boys,

Colchester, 1947-49; Methodist Minister, Clitheroe Circuit, 1949-50; Asst Tutor in New Testament, Richmond Coll., London, 1953-56; Minister in Darlaston (Slater St), 1956-61; Tutor in New Testament, Cliff Coll., Derbyshire, 1961-66; Minister in Bramhall Circuit (Cheadle Hulme), 1966-73; Superintendent Minister, Welwyn Garden City, 1973-76. *Publications:* The Story of Cliff (a history of Cliff College), 1965; The Story They Told (a short study of the Passion Narratives in the Gospels), 1966; Life Power and Hope—a study of the Holy Spirit, 1972. *Recreations:* compulsive watching of sport (especially West Bromwich Albion); collecting Roman Imperial coins; reading about American Civil War; listening to music and to Shakespeare. *Address:* 18 Velwell Road, Exeter EX4 4LE. *T:* Exeter 72541.

CRESWELL, Jack Norman; Deputy Chairman of Lloyd's, 1972, 1974; *b* 20 April 1913; *s* of late Sydney and Dora Creswell; *m* 1938, Jean (Lilian Jane) Maxwell; two *s*. *Educ:* Highgate School. Served War, 1942-46, 2nd Household Cavalry Regt; Captain and Adjt, The Life Guards, 1945-46. Member of Lloyd's, 1946: Mem. Cttee, 1969-72, 1974; Mem. Cttee Lloyd's Underwriters Non-Marine Assoc., 1968-74, Chm. 1973. Dir, Ellinger Heath Western (Underwriting Agencies) Ltd. *Recreations:* photography, family croquet. *Address:* Lullington Court, near Polegate, E Sussex. *T:* Alfriston 870548. *Club:* Cavalry and Guards.

CRESWELL, Sir Michael Justin, KCMG 1960 (CMG 1952); Ambassador to Argentine Republic, 1964-69; retired; *b* 21 Sept. 1909; *s* of late Col Edmund William Creswell, RE; *m* 1st, 1939, Elizabeth Colshorn; one *s*; 2nd, 1950, Baroness C. M. thoe Schwartzenberg; one *s*. *Educ:* Rugby; New Coll., Oxford. Laming Travelling Fellow, Queen's Coll., Oxford, 1932. Entered Foreign Service, 1933; 3rd Sec., Berlin, 1935-38; 2nd Sec., Madrid, 1939-44, Athens, 1944; Foreign Office, 1944-47; Counsellor, Tehran, 1947-49; Singapore, 1949-51; Minister, British Embassy, Cairo, 1951-54; Ambassador to Finland, 1954-58; Senior Civilian Instructor, Imperial Defence Coll., 1958-60; Ambassador to Yugoslavia, 1960-64. Chm., Surrey Amenity Council, 1974-; Member: Waverley SC, 1974-; Surrey CC, 1977-. *Recreations:* travel, wild life. *Address:* Copse Hill, Ewhurst, near Cranleigh, Surrey. *T:* Ewhurst 311.

CRESWICK, Sir Alexander Reid, (Sir Alec Creswick), Kt 1974; company director and pastoralist, Australia; Chairman, Victoria Racing Club Committee, 1969-77 (Member, since 1959); *b* 1912; *s* of late H. F. Creswick; *m* 1st, Claudia, *d* of C. B. Palmer; two *s*; 2nd, Dinah Bingham Meeks, *d* of Anthony Hordern; one *d*. *Educ:* Melbourne Church of England Grammar Sch.; St John's Coll., Oxford. Served War of 1939-45, Australian Army Service Corps. Past Pres.: Victoria Polo Assoc.; Equestrian Fedn of Aust. Formerly: Master of Melbourne Hounds; Manager of Aust. Olympic Equestrian Teams: Rome, Stockholm, Montreal. Life Mem., Council of Royal Agricultural Soc. of Victoria. Director, Carlton and United Breweries Ltd, retd 1979. *Address:* Allanvale, Avenel, Victoria 3664, Australia; *c/o* 422 Collins Street, Melbourne, Vic. 3000, Australia. *Clubs:* VRC, Melbourne (Melbourne).

CRESWICK, Harry Richardson, MA; Librarian Emeritus of Cambridge University; *b* 1902; *m* Agnes Isabel (*d* 1982), *d* of late J. W. Stubbings. *Educ:* Barnet Grammar Sch.; Trinity Coll., Cambridge. On staff of University Library, Cambridge, 1926-38; Deputy Librarian, Bodleian Library, Oxford, 1939-45; Bodley's Librarian and Student of Christ Church, 1945-47; Librarian of Cambridge Univ. and Professorial Fellow of Jesus Coll., 1949-67, Emeritus Fellow, 1976. Hon. LittD, Trinity Coll., Dublin. *Address:* Gifford, East Lothian, Scotland.

CRETNEY, Stephen Michael; a Law Commissioner, since 1978; *b* 25 Feb. 1936; *s* of late Fred and of Winifred M. V. Cretney; *m* 1973, Antonia Lois Vanrenen; two *s*. *Educ:* Queen's Road Primary Sch., Cheadle Hulme; Cheadle Hulme Sch.; Magdalen Coll., Oxford (MA). Solicitor. Partner, Macfarlanes, London, 1964; Lecturer: Kenya Sch. of Law, Nairobi, 1966; Southampton Univ., 1968; Fellow and Tutor, Exeter Coll., Oxford, 1969-78. Chorley Lectr, 1980. A Gen. Comr of Income Tax, 1970-78. *Publications:* Theobald on Wills, (ed jtly) 13th edn 1970; Principles of Family Law, 1974, 3rd edn 1979; Family Law (Teach Yourself series), 1982; articles and notes in legal jls. *Recreations:* cooking, gardening, taking snapshots. *Address:* 41 Stapleton Road, Headington, Oxford OX3 7LX. *T:* Oxford 67160. Conquest House, 37/8 John Street, Theobald's Road, WC1N 2BQ. *T:* 01-242 0861. *Club:* United Oxford & Cambridge University.

CREW, Air Vice-Marshal Edward Dixon, CB 1973; DSO 1944 and Bar 1950; DFC 1941 and Bar 1942; FRAeS 1972; Planning Inspectorate, Department of the Environment, since 1973; *b* 24 Dec. 1917; *er s* of F. D. Crew, MB, MRCS, LRCP; *m* 1945, Virginia Martin; one *s*. *Educ:* Felsted Sch.; Downing Coll., Cambridge (MA). Commissioned RAFVR, 1939; served War of 1939-45: night fighter sqdns; 604 sqdn, 85 Sqdn; Comd 96 Sqdn; permanent commission, 1945. Malayan Emergency, Comd No 45 Sqdn, 1948-50; on exchange, RCAF, 1952-54; CFE, 1954-56; Comd RAF Brüggen, Germany, 1956-57; Comdr, Air Forces Borneo, 1965-66; AOC Central Reconnaissance Establt, 1968; Dep. Controller, Nat. Air Traffic Services, 1969-72; various Air Staff jobs at Air Min. and MoD; retd 1973. *Recreations:* shooting, tennis. *Address:* 13 Silver Street, Tetbury, Glos. *Club:* Royal Air Force.

CREWE, Albert V., PhD; Professor, Department of Physics and the Enrico Fermi Institute, since 1963 (Assistant Professor, 1956-59; Associate Professor, 1959-63; William E. Wrather Distinguished Service Professor, 1977), Dean of Physical Sciences Division, 1971-81, University of Chicago; *b* 18 Feb. 1927; *m* 1949, Doreen Patricia Blunsdon; one *s* three *d*. *Educ:* Univ. of Liverpool (BS, PhD). Asst Lectr, 1950-52, Lectr, 1952-55, Univ. of Liverpool; Div. Dir, Particle Accelerator Division, Argonne National Laboratory, 1958-61; Dir, Argonne National Laboratory, 1961-67. Member: Nat. Acad. of Sciences; Amer. Acad. of Arts and Sciences. Named Outstanding New Citizen by Citizenship Council of Chicago, 1962; received Immigrant's Service League's Annual Award for Outstanding Achievement in the Field of Science, 1962; Illinois Sesquicentennial Award, 1968; Industrial Research Award, 1970; Distinguished Award, Electron Microscope Soc. of America, 1976; Albert A. Michelson Award, Franklin Inst., 1977; Duddell Medal, Inst. of Physics, 1980. *Publications:* Research USA (with J. J. Katz), 1964; contribs to: Proc. Royal Soc.; Proc. Phys. Soc.; Physical Review; Science; Physics Today; Jl of Applied Physics; Reviews of Scientific Instruments, etc. *Address:* 63 Old Creek Road, Palos Park, Illinois, USA. *T:* Gibson 8-8738. *Clubs:* Cosmos (Washington DC); Quadrangle, Wayfarers' (Chicago).

CREWE, Ivor Martin; Director (professorial), Social Science Research Council Survey Archive, since 1977 (Director, since 1974); Co-Director, British Election Study, since 1974; *b* 15 Dec. 1945; *s* of Francis and Lily Crewe; *m* 1968, Jill Barbara (*née* Gadian); two *s* one *d*. *Educ:* Manchester Grammar Sch.; Exeter Coll., Oxford (BA); London School of Economics (MScEcon). Assistant Lecturer, Univ. of Lancaster, 1967-69; Junior Research Fellow, Nuffield Coll., Oxford, 1969-71; Lectr, Dept of Govt, Univ. of Essex, 1971-74. Editor, British Journal of Political Science and elections analyst for The Times, 1977-. *Publications:* (with A. H. Halsey) Social Survey of the Civil Service (HMSO), 1969; ed, British Political Sociology Yearbook, vol. 1 1974, vol. 2 1975; co-ed, Party Identification and Beyond, 1976; articles in British Jl of Pol. Sci. and others. *Recreations:* opera, psephology. *Address:* 141 Maldon Road, Colchester, Essex CO3 3BJ. *T:* Colchester 61695.

CREWE, Quentin Hugh; writer, journalist and farmer; *b* 14 Nov. 1926; *s* of Major Hugh Crewe and Lady Annabel Crewe; *m* 1st, 1956, Martha Sharp; one *s* one *d*; 2nd, 1961, Angela Huth; one *d* (one *s* decd); 3rd, 1970, Susan Cavendish; one *s* one *d*. *Educ:* Eton; Trinity Coll., Cambridge. Joined Evening Standard, 1953; subseq. worked for Queen, Vogue, Daily Mail, Sunday Mirror; freelance, 1970-, contrib. to Times, Sunday Times, Sunday Telegraph, and Spectator. *Publications:* A Curse of Blossom, 1960; Frontiers of Privilege, 1961; Great Chefs of France, 1978; Pocket Book of Food, 1980. *Recreation:* travel. *Address:* 52 Beauchamp Place, SW3.

CRIBB, Air Cdre Peter Henry, CBE 1957; DSO 1942, and Bar, 1944; DFC. 1941; JP; Planning and Property Manager, Slow Learning Children's Group of WA Inc., since 1980; *b* 28 Sept. 1918; *s* of late Charles B. Cribb and Mrs Ethel Cribb; *m* 1949, Vivienne Janet, *yr d* of late Col S. T. J. Perry, MC, TD, DL, Oxton, Birkenhead, Ches; three *s*. *Educ:* Bradford Grammar Sch.; Prince Henry's Sch., Otley. Flt Cadet, RAF Coll., 1936-38; Flying duties in Bomber Comd, 1938-45 (Comd No. 582 Sqdn, RAF Little Staughton); Comdg RAF Salbani, RAF Peshawar, India and Staff No. 1 Indian Gp, 1945-47; OC 203 Sqdn, 1947, and HQ Staff, 1950, Coastal Comd; RAF Staff Coll., Bracknell, 1951; Asst Dir Tech. Intell., Air Min., 1951-53; Gp Capt. Plans and Policy, HQ Bomber Comd, 1953-57; 2nd TAF, Germany (OC Oldenburg, Ahlhorn and Gutersloh), 1957-60; Air Min., Dep. Dir Air Staff Briefing, 1959-61, Dir, 1961-62; SASO, Air Forces, Middle East, 1962-63; DFC, 1964; Deputy to Asst Chief of Defence Staff (Joint Warfare), MoD 1965-66; retired, 1966. Administrative Manager, Goldsworthy Mining Ltd, 1966-68. Associate Fellow, Australian Inst. of Management, 1969; Past State Pres., Ryder-Cheshire Foundn of WA, Inc. JP Western Australia, 1968. *Recreations:* sailing, fishing, facetting gem stones. *Address:* The Oaks, 5 Peet Road, Roleystone, WA 6111, Australia.

CRICHTON, family name of Earl of Erne.

CRICHTON, Viscount; John Henry Michael Ninian Crichton; *b* 19 June 1971; *s* and *heir* of Earl of Erne, *qv*.

CRICHTON, Sir Andrew Maitland-Makgill-, Kt 1963; Director, P&OSN Co., since 1957; Vice-Chairman, Port of London Authority, 1967-76 (Member, 1964-67); *b* 28 Dec. 1910; *s* of late Lt-Col D. M.-M.-Crichton, Queen's Own Cameron Highldrs, and Phyllis (*née* Cuthbert); *m* 1948, Isabel, *d* of Andrew McGill, Sydney, NSW. *Educ:* Wellington Coll. Joined Gray, Dawes & Co., 1929; transf. India to Mackinnon Mackenzie & Co. (Agents of BI Co. and for P & O on Indian Continent and in parts of Far East), 1931. Joined IA, 1940; DDM (Shipping), Col, at GHQ India, 1944. Mackinnon Mackenzie, Calcutta, 1945-48; P&O Co., UK (Gen. Manager, 1951); Chm., Overseas Containers Ltd, 1965-73; former Director: Julian S. Hodge & Co. Ltd; Hodge Group Ltd; Director: Standard Chartered Group; Inchcape Insurance Hldgs Ltd; Amalgamated Tin Mines of Nigeria. Chairman: Nat. Assoc. Port Employers, 1958-65; EDC for GPO, 1965-70; Vice-Chm., British Transport Docks Bd, 1963-68; Member: Baltic Exchange; Nat. Freight Corp., 1969-73; Court of The Chartered Bank; Police Council for GB (Arbitrator), 1969-79; Industrial Arbitration Bd. FRSA; FCIT (a past Vice-Pres.). *Recreations:* golf, music. Freeman, Co. of Watermen and Lightermen. *Address:* 55 Hans Place, Knightsbridge, SW1. *T:* 01-584 1209; The Old Bakery, Yoxford, Suffolk. *T:* Yoxford 426. *Clubs:* City of London,

Caledonian.
See also Maj.-Gen. Edward Maitland-Makgill-Crichton.

CRICHTON, David George, MVO 1968; British Consul-General, Nice, 1970-74; *b* 31 July 1914; *e s* of late Col Hon. Sir George Crichton, GCVO; *m* 1941, Joan Fenella, *d* of late Col D. W. Cleaver, DSO; one *s* one *d*. *Educ:* Eton. Worked as journalist, Reading and Manchester, and on Daily Telegraph, Paris and London, 1933-39; served War of 1939-45 in Derbyshire Yeomanry (despatches); Major 1944; entered Foreign Service, 1946; served in Belgrade, Singapore, Alexandria, Miami, La Paz and Santiago. *Address:* Church House, Medstead, Alton, Hampshire. *T:* Alton 62632; Résidence Bois Joli, 06320-Cap d'Ail, France. *T:* 78 42 52. *Clubs:* Boodle's; MC (Monte Carlo). •
See also R. J. V. Crichton.

CRICHTON, Maj.-Gen. Edward Maitland-Makgill-, OBE 1948 (MBE 1945); GOC 51st Highland Division, 1966-68, retired; *b* 23 Nov. 1916; *s* of late Lt-Col D. E. Maitland-Makgill-Crichton, Queen's Own Cameron Highlanders and Phyllis (*née* Cuthbert); *m* 1951, Sheila Margaret Hibbins, Bexhill-on-Sea; three *s*. *Educ:* Bedford Sch.; RMC SAndhurst. 2nd Lieut Queen's Own Cameron Highlanders, 1937; Adjt 5th Bn Cameron Highlanders, 1939; served with 5th Cameron Highlanders and 51 (Highland) Div., N Africa, Sicily, Normandy, NW Europe, 1940-45; GSO 1, HQ British Commonwealth Occupation Force, Japan, 1946-47; Mobilisation Br., WO 1948-50; 1st Bn Cameron Highlanders, Tripoli and Canal Zone, 1950-52; Jt Services Staff Coll., 1953; GSO 1, 3rd Inf. Div. (UK Strategic Reserve), Canal Zone, Egypt, UK and Suez, 1953-57; with 1st Bn Cameron Highlanders, Aden, 1957; comd 1st Liverpool Scottish, 1958-61; Comdr 152 (Highland) Inf. Bde, 1962-64; Dep. Dir Army Staff Duties, MoD, 1965-66. *Recreations:* shooting, golf, gardening, fishing. *Address:* Clive House, Letham, Angus. *T:* Letham 391. *Club:* Army and Navy.
See also Sir Andrew Maitland-Makgill-Crichton.

CRICHTON, Sir (John) Robertson (Dunn), Kt 1967; Judge of the High Court of Justice, Queen's Bench Division, 1967-77; *b* 2 Nov. 1912; *s* of Alexander Cansh and Beatrice Crichton, Wallasey, Ches; *m* 1944, Margaret Vanderlip, *d* of Col Livingston Watrous, Washington, DC, and Nantucket, Mass, USA; two *s* one *d*. *Educ:* Sedbergh Sch.; Balliol Coll., Oxford. Called to the Bar, Middle Temple, 1936; Bencher, 1959. Served War of 1939-45, RA (TA). KC 1951; QC 1952. Recorder of Blackpool, 1952-60; Judge of Appeal of the Isle of Man, 1956-60; Recorder of Manchester and Judge of Crown Court at Manchester, 1960-67. *Recreations:* gardening, painting. *Address:* Hempfield, Dunham Massey, Altrincham, Cheshire. *T:* 061-928 6101. *Club:* United Oxford & Cambridge University.

CRICHTON, Col Richard John Vesey, MC 1940; *b* 2 Nov. 1916; *s* of late Col Hon. Sir George Crichton, GCVO, and Lady Mary Crichton; *m* 1948, Yvonne Avril Catherine, *d* of late Dr and Mrs H. E. Worthington; three *s*. *Educ:* Eton; RMC, Sandhurst. Commissioned 2/Lieut Coldstream Guards, 1936; served World War II: Belgium, 1940, Italy, 1943-44 (twice wounded, MC, despatches); Commanded: 1st Bn Coldstream Guards, 1954-57; Coldstream Guards, 1958-61, retired 1961. Comptroller, Union Jack Services Clubs, 1964-66; Member, HM Body Guard, Hon. Corps of Gentlemen at Arms, 1966-; Clerk of the Cheque and Adjutant, 1979-81; Lieutenant, 1981-. *Publication:* The Coldstream Guards 1946-1970, 1972. *Address:* Eglinton Lodge, Hartley Wintney, Hampshire. *T:* Hartley Wintney 2440. *Clubs:* Cavalry and Guards, Pratt's.
See also D. G. Crichton.

CRICHTON, Col Walter Hugh, CIE 1941; MB, ChB Edinburgh 1919; DPH London 1934; IMS (retired); *b* 24 July 1896; *m* 1920, Dorothy Martindale, Trinity, Edinburgh; one *s* one *d*. Apptd Indian Medical Service, 1920; Foreign Political Dept, 1930; Vice-Consul, Seistan, Persia; Agency Surgeon Kurram Valley, NWFP, 1932; MOH, Simla, 1934; Chief Health Officer, Delhi Prov., 1936; on active service Paiforce, 1941; ADMS, Basra, 1942; Mil. Gov., CMF, 1943; Dir PH Mil. Gov., 21 Army Group, BLA, 1944-45; Dir Public Health, CP and Behar, 1945-47; MOH Kent Co. Dists, 1948-50; Chief WHO Mission, Korea, 1950; PH Administrator WHO East Med. Region, until 1956; ACMO Norfolk; Freeman Naples City, 1944; Cross of Merit (1st Class) Order of Malta, 1944; Kt Comdr Order of Orange-Nassau, 1946. *Address:* Hillside Home, Great Cornard, Sudbury, Suffolk. *T:* Sudbury 78511. *Club:* Naval and Military.

CRICHTON-BROWN, Sir Robert, KCMG 1980; Kt 1972; CBE 1970; TD; *b* Melbourne, 23 Aug. 1919; *s* of late L. Crichton-Brown, Sydney; *m* 1941, Norah Isabelle, *d* of late A. E. Turnbull; one *s* one *d*. *Educ:* Sydney Grammar Sch. Served War, 1939-45, BEF; Major, Royal Artillery and Gen. Staff, France, Iceland, India, Burma (despatches twice). Chm. and Man. Dir, The Security & General Insurance Co. Ltd; Chairman: Edward Lumley Ltd; The Commercial Banking Co. of Sydney Ltd; CBC Savings Bank Ltd; Commercial and General Acceptance Ltd; Security Life Assurances Ltd; NEI Engrg Pacific Ltd; WestHam Dredging Co. Pty Ltd; Rothmans of Pall Mall (Aust.) Ltd; Director: Royal Prince Alfred Hosp.; Daily Mail and General Trust Ltd (UK); Edward Lumley Holdings Ltd (UK); Nat. Bank of Australasia Ltd; Rothmans International plc (UK). Fed. Pres., Inst. of Dirs in Aust., 1967-80 (Chm., NSW Branch, 1965-80; Hon. Life Mem.); Pres., Postgrad. Med. Res. Foundn; Hon. Life Governor, Aust. Postgraduate Fedn in Medicine; Member: Finance Cttee, RACP; Adv. Bd, Salvation Army; Adv.

Bd, Girl Guides Assoc. of Australia; Nat. Co-ordinator, Duke of Edinburgh's Award Scheme in Aust.; Nat. Councillor, Scout Assoc. of Aust. Underwriting Mem. of Lloyd's, 1946-. Mem., Australia's winning Admiral's Cup Team (Balandra), UK, 1967; winner, Hobart Yacht Race (Pacha), 1970. *Address:* 11 Castlereagh Street, Sydney, NSW 2000, Australia. *Clubs:* White's, Royal Cruising; Royal Yacht Squadron; Australian, Union (Sydney); Cruising Yacht Club of Australia, Royal Sydney Yacht Squadron, Royal Prince Alfred Yacht.

CRICHTON-MILLER, Donald, TD; MA; *b* 1906; *s* of late Hugh Crichton-Miller, MA, MD, FRCP; *m* 1931, Monica, *d* of late B. A. Glanvill, JP, Bromley, Kent; two *s* one *d*. *Educ:* Fettes Coll., Edinburgh; Pembroke Coll., Cambridge (Exhibitioner). Played Rugby Football for Cambridge and Scotland; Asst Master: Monmouth Sch., 1929-31; Bryanston Sch., 1931-34; Stowe Sch., 1934-36; Head Master: Taunton Sch., Somerset, 1936-45; Fettes Coll., 1945-58; Stowe Sch., 1958-63. Carried out education surveys in Pakistan, 1951, and Malta, 1956. HM Comr, Queen Victoria Sch., Dunblane. *Recreations:* games and sports of various kinds. *Address:* Westridge House, Compton, Berks RG16 0RE.

CRICHTON-STUART, family name of **Marquess of Bute.**

CRICK, Alan John Pitts, OBE 1956; *b* 14 May 1913; *er s* of Owen John Pitts Crick and Margaret Crick (*née* Daw), late of Minehead, Somerset; *m* 1941, Norah (*née* Atkins); two *d*. *Educ:* Latymer Upper Sch.; King's Coll., London Univ. (MA); Heidelberg Univ. (Dr.phil). Vice-Consul, British Consulate-Gen., Free City of Danzig, 1938-39. Served War, Army, 1939-46: Egypt and Libya, 1941-43, HQ Eighth Army; NW Europe, 1944-46 (despatches); Major, GSO2, Intell., SHAEF; HQ 21 Army Group and HQ BAOR. Min. of Defence Jt Intell. Bureau, 1946-63; jssc, 1948; British Jt Services Mission, Washington, 1953-56; Asst Dir, Jt Intell. Bureau, 1957-63; idc, 1960; Counsellor, British Embassy, Washington, 1963-65; Asst Sec., Cabinet Office, 1965-68; Def. Intell. Staff, MoD, 1968-73; Director of Economic Intelligence, MoD, 1970-73. Adviser to Commercial Union Assurance Co., 1973-78. *Recreations:* travel, antiquarian interests, books. *Address:* 16 Church Square, Rye, East Sussex. *T:* Rye 2050; Condat sur Trincou, 24530 Champagnac-de-Belair, France. *Clubs:* Naval and Military; Dormy House (Rye).
See also R. Pitts Crick.

CRICK, Prof. Bernard, BSc (Econ.), PhD (London); Professor of Politics, Birkbeck College, University of London, since 1971; *b* 16 Dec. 1929; *s* of Harry Edgar and Florence Clara Crick. *Educ:* Whitgift Sch.; University Coll., London. Research student, LSE, 1950-52; Teaching Fellow, Harvard, 1952-54; Asst Prof., McGill, 1954-55; Vis. Fellow, Berkeley, 1955-56; Asst Lectr, later Lectr, later Sen. Lectr, LSE, 1957-65; Prof. of Political Theory and Institutions, Sheffield Univ., 1965-71. Jt Editor, Political Quarterly, 1966-80. Joint Sec., Study of Parlt Gp, 1964-68. Hon. Pres., Politics Assoc., 1970-76; Mem., Council of the Hansard Soc., 1962-. *Publications:* The American Science of Politics, 1958; In Defence of Politics, 1962, 3rd edn 1982 (trans. German, Japanese, Spanish, Italian); The Reform of Parliament, 1964, 2nd edn 1968; (ed) Essays on Reform, 1967; (ed with W. A. Robson) Protest and Discontent, 1970; (ed) Machiavelli: The Discourses, 1971; Political Theory and Practice, 1972; (ed with W. A. Robson) Taxation Policy, 1973; Basic Forms of Government, 1973; Crime, Rape and Gin, 1975; (ed with Alex Porter) Political Education and Political Literacy, 1978; George Orwell: a Life, 1980, 2nd edn 1982; (ed) Unemployment, 1981. *Recreations:* polemicising, book- and theatre-reviewing, hill-walking. *Address:* Birkbeck College, Malet Street, WC1. *T:* 01-580 2275. *Club:* Savile.

CRICK, Francis Harry Compton, FRS 1959; BSc London, PhD Cantab; J. W. Kieckhefer Distinguished Professor, The Salk Institute, since 1977; Adjunct Professor of Biology and Chemistry, University of California, San Diego; *b* 8 June 1916; *e s* of late Harry Crick and late Annie Elizabeth (*née* Wilkins); *m* 1st, 1940, Ruth Doreen Dodd (divorced, 1947); one *s*; 2nd, 1949, Odile Speed; two *d*. *Educ:* Mill Hill Sch.; University Coll., London; Caius Coll., Cambridge (Hon. Fellow, 1976). Scientist in Admiralty, 1940-47; Strangeways Laboratory, Cambridge, 1947-49; MRC Lab. of Molecular Biology, Cambridge, 1949-77; Brooklyn Polytechnic, NY, USA, 1953-54. Vis. Lectr Rockefeller Inst., NY, USA, 1959; Vis. Prof., Chemistry Dept, Harvard, 1959; Fellow, Churchill Coll., Cambridge, 1960-61; Vis. Biophysics Prof., Harvard, 1962; Non-resident Fellow, Salk Inst. for Biological Studies, San Diego, 1962-73; Ferkauf Foundn Visiting Prof., Salk Inst., 1976-77; Fellow, UCL, 1962; For. Hon. Mem., Amer. Acad. of Arts and Sciences, 1962; Hon. Mem., Amer. Soc. Biological Chem., 1963; Hon. MRIA, 1964; Hon. Fellow: Churchill Coll., Cambridge, 1965; Caius Coll., Cambridge, 1976; FAAAS 1966; Hon. FRSE, 1966; For. Associate, US Nat. Acad. of Sciences, 1969; Mem., German Acad. of Science, Leopoldina, 1969; For. Mem., American Philos. Soc., Philadelphia, 1972; Hon. Mem., Hellenic Biochem. and Biophys. Soc., 1974. Associate For. Mem., French Acad. of Scis, 1978. Lectures: Bloor, Rochester, USA, 1959; (with J. D. Watson) Warren Triennial Prize, Boston, USA, 1959; Korkes Meml, Duke Univ., 1960; Herter, Johns Hopkins Sch. of Medicine, USA, 1960; Franklin Harris, Mount Zion Hosp., 1962; Holme, London, 1962; Henry Sidgewick Meml, Cambridge, 1963; Harveian, London, 1963; Graham Young, Glasgow, 1963; Robert Boyle, Oxford, 1963; James W. Sherrill, Scripps Clinic, 1964; Elisha Mitchel Meml, N Carolina, 1964; Vanuxem, Princeton, 1964; Charles West, London, 1964; William T. Sedgwick Meml, MIT, 1965; A. J. Carlson Meml, Chicago, 1965; Failing, Univ. of Oregon, 1965; Robbins, Pomona Coll., 1965; Telford

Meml, Manchester, 1965; Kinnaird, Regent St Polytechnic, 1965; John Danz, Univ. of Washington, 1966; Sumner, Cornell, 1966; Royal Society Croonian, 1966; Cherwell-Simon Meml, Oxford, 1966; Genetical Soc. Mendel, 1966; Rickman Godlee, UCL, 1968; Shell, Stanford Univ., 1969; Evarts A. Graham Meml, Washington Univ., St Louis Missouri; Gehrmann, Illinois Univ., 1973; Cori, Buffalo, NY, 1973; Jean Weigle Meml, Calif Inst. of Technology, 1976; John Stauffer Distinguished, Univ. of Southern Calif, 1976; Smith Kline and French, Univ. of Calif, SF, 1977; Henry Failing Distinguished, Oregon, 1977; Paul Lund, Northwestern, 1977; Steenbock, Wisconsin, 1977; 8th Sir Hans Krebs, and medal, FEBS, Copenhagen, 1977; Lynen, Miami, 1978; Briody Meml, New Jersey, 1979; Dupont, Harvard, 1979; Ferguson, Mo, 1980; George W. Gardiner Meml, New Mexico; Jean Weigle Meml, Geneva. Lasker Award (jointly), 1960; Prix Charles Léopold Mayer, French Académies des Sciences, 1961; Research Corp. Award (with J. D. Watson), 1961; Gairdner Foundation Award, Toronto, 1962; Nobel Prize for Medicine (jointly), 1962; Royal Medal, Royal Soc., 1972; Copley Medal, Royal Soc., 1976; Michelson-Morley Award, Cleveland, 1981. *Publications:* Of Molecules and Men, 1966; Life Itself, 1981; papers and articles on molecular and cell biology in scientific journals. *Address:* The Salk Institute for Biological Studies, PO Box 85800, San Diego, Calif 92138, USA; 337 Longden Lane, Calif 92075, USA.

CRICK, R(onald) Pitts, FRCS, DOMS; Senior Ophthalmic Surgeon, King's College Hospital, since 1950; Recognised Teacher in the Faculty of Medicine, University of London, since 1960; Chairman, Ophthalmic Post-Graduate Training, SE Thames Regional Health Authority, since 1972; *b* 5 Feb. 1917; *yr s* of James Pitts Crick and Margaret Daw, Minehead, Som; *m* 1941, Jocelyn Mary Grenfell Robins, *yr d* of Leonard A. C. Robins and Geraldine Grenfell, Hendon; four *s* one *d*. *Educ:* Latymer Upper Sch., London; King's Coll. and (Science Schol.) King's Coll. Hosp. Med. Sch., Univ. of London. MRCS, LRCP 1939. Surgeon, MN, 1939-40; Surg. Lieut, RNVR, 1940-46. Ophthalmic Registrar, King's Coll. Hosp., 1946-48; DOMS 1946. Surgical First Asst, Royal Eye Hosp., 1947-50; Ophth. Surg., Epsom County Hosp., 1948-49; Ophth. Registrar, Belgrave Hosp. for Children, 1948-50; Ophth. Surg., Sevenoaks Hosp., 1948-50; Sen. Ophthalmic Surg., Royal Eye Hosp., 1950-69; Ophthalmic Surg., Belgrave Hosp. for Children, 1950-66. Vis. Res. Fellow, Sussex Univ., 1976-. Examr to RCS for Diploma in Ophthalmology, 1961-68. FRCS, 1950. Hon. Ophth. Surg., Royal London Soc. for the Blind, 1954-57. FRSocMed, Vice-Pres. Ophthalmological Section, 1964, and Mem. Council Ophthalmolog. Section, 1953-54 and 1956-58. Member: Ophthalmolog. Soc. of the UK; Faculty of Ophthalmologists; Oxford Ophthalmolog. Congress; Southern Ophthalmolog. Soc. (Vice-Pres., 1969; Pres., 1970); Chm., Internat. Glaucoma Assoc., 1975; Charter Member Internat. Glaucoma Congress, USA, 1977-; Internat. Assoc. of Ocular Surgeons, 1981. *Publications:* Cardiovascular Affections, Arteriosclerosis and Hypertension (Section in Systemic Ophthalmology, ed A. Sorsby), 1950 and 1958; medical and opthalmic contribs to Brit. Jl Ophthalmology, BMJ, Jl RN Med. Service, Trans Ophthalmolog. Soc. of the UK, etc. *Recreations:* walking, motoring, sailing. *Address:* Private Consulting Rooms, King's College Hospital, SE5. *T:* 01-274 8570; Pembroke House, Sevenoaks, Kent. *T:* Sevenoaks 53633. *Clubs:* Royal Automobile; Royal Motor Yacht.
    See also A. J. P. Crick.

CRIDLAND, Charles Elliot Tapscott; Vice-Chairman, The Aero Group, 1969-70; *b* Glos, 21 July 1900; *s* of S. L. Cridland; *m* 1st, 1923, Kathleen (*d* 1957), *d* of Capt. Bell, Cheltenham; two *d*; 2nd, 1968, Joan Gardiner, *d* of late G. A. McLennan and Mrs E. Coy. *Educ:* Trent Coll., Long Eaton; Faraday House Engineering Coll., London. Chm. and Managing Director: Rye & Co., Lincoln, 1927-30; Eclair Doors Ltd, 1937-47; Aldis Bros Ltd, 1946-57; Automatic Changers Ltd, 1956-57; Chairman: Hawkes & Snow (Curtaincraft) Ltd, 1949-63; Portable Balers Ltd, 1953-61; Aero Heat Treatment Ltd, 1947-69; Hard Coating Ltd, 1951-69; Chisholm, Gray and Co. Ltd, 1956-69; Aerotaps Ltd, 1958-69; Aerocoldform Ltd, 1956-69; Broadstone Ballvalve Co. Ltd, 1959-69; Bendz Ltd, 1962-69; Quality Machined Parts, Ltd, 1964-69; Kinsman Ltd, 1965-69. Vice-Chm., Mercian Builders Merchants Ltd, 1965-67. Dir, A. D. Foulkes Ltd, 1958-65. Mem. Org. Cttee, Birmingham Productivity Assoc., 1955-63. Chm. Organisation Cttee, National Farmers' Union, Glos Branch, 1946; Chm., Steel Rolling Shutter Assoc., 1945-46. Scientific Instrument Manufacturers' Assoc. of Gt Brit. Ltd: Mem. Council, 1949-57, Vice-Pres., 1953 and 1957, Pres., 1954-56; Chm., Transport Users' Consultative Cttee, W Midlands Area, 1960-69; Mem., Central Transport Consultative Cttee, 1963-69. Mem. Court of Assistants, The Worshipful Co. of Scientific Instrument Makers, 1955; elected Master, 1956 and 1957; Freeman, City of London, 1955. *Ex-officio* Mem. Bd of Govs, Faraday House Engrg Coll., 1961-63; Vice-Pres. and Hon. Treas. Faraday House Old Students Assoc., 1960, Pres. 1962-63. Served War, RAF, 1918-19. *Recreations:* golf (played for Warwicks and Glos), and farming. *Address:* c/o National Westminster Bank Ltd, Prospect Hill, Douglas, Isle of Man.

CRIPPIN, Harry Trevor, FCIS; Chief Executive and Town Clerk, Cardiff City Council, since 1979; *b* 14 May 1929; *s* of Harry and Mary Elizabeth Crippin; *m* 1959, Hilda Green; one *s* one *d*. *Educ:* Leigh Grammar Sch., Lancs. DMA; FBIM; FCIS 1975. Asst Town Clerk, Manchester, 1970-74; City Sec., Cardiff CC, 1974-79. *Address:* 37 Ely Road, Llandaff, Cardiff CF5 2JF. *T:* Cardiff 564103.

CRIPPS, family name of **Baron Parmoor.**

CRIPPS, Anthony L.; *see* Cripps, M. A. L.

CRIPPS, Cyril Humphrey, MA; CChem, FRSC; Managing Director, Pianoforte Supplies Ltd, Roade, Northampton, since 1960, Chairman since 1979; Founder Member, Cripps Foundation, Chairman since 1979; Chairman: Velcro Industries NV, since 1973; Air BVI, since 1971; *b* 2 Oct. 1915; *o s* of Sir Cyril Thomas Cripps, MBE, and Lady (Amy) Cripps; *m* 1942, Dorothea Casson, *o d* of Reginald Percy Cook, architect; three *s* one *d*. *Educ:* Northampton Grammar Sch. (schol.); St John's Coll., Cambridge (Nat. Sci. Prelim. Cl. 1, Tripos Pts I and II, Cl. 2; BA, MA). FCS 1935; FRIC 1977; FRSC 1979. Founder of private businesses in UK, Australia, Canada and Brit. Virgin Islands. Member, Northamptonshire CC, 1963-74 (Leader of Independents, to 1974; formerly Vice-Chm., Educn and Planning Cttees); Mem., (new) Northants CC, 1973-81; Board Mem., Northampton Develt Corp. Life Mem., Ct, Univ. of Nottingham, 1953; Governor, Northampton Grammar Sch., 1963-74 (Vice-Chm. to 1974 and Vice-Chm. Foundn Trust, 1970-); Chm. of Governors: Northampton Sch. for Boys, 1977-; Northampton High Sch. for Girls, 1972-; Foundn Governor, Bilton Grange Prep. Sch., 1957-80. Trustee, Postgrad. Med. Centre, Sports and Recreation, Residence and Res., Northampton Gen. Hosp., 1969-; Mem. Trusts: Peterborough Cath., 1975-; All Saints Church, Northampton, 1975-. Hon. Fellow: Cambridge Univ.: St John's, 1966; Magdalene, 1971; Selwyn, 1971; Queens', 1979; Cripps Hall, Nottingham Univ., 1959; Hon. DSc Nottingham, 1975; Hon. LLD Cantab 1976; Pres., Johnian Soc., 1966. Liveryman, Worshipful Co. of Wheelwrights, 1957, Mem. Court 1970, Sen. Asst 1979, Renter Warden 1980, Upper Warden 1981, Master 1982; Freeman, City of London (by redemption), 1957. *Recreations:* travel, photography, natural history—entomological (espec. Rhopalocera), philately (Curator, Westwell Philatelic Collection). *Address:* Bull's Head Farm, Stoke Goldington, Newport Pagnell, Bucks. *T:* Stoke Goldington 223; Southwold House, Southwold, Suffolk.

CRIPPS, Sir John Stafford, Kt 1978; CBE 1968; Chairman, Countryside Commission, 1970-77; *b* 10 May 1912; *s* of late Rt Hon. Sir Stafford Cripps, PC, CH, FRS, QC, and Isobel (Dame Isobel Cripps, GBE); *m* 1st, 1936, Ursula (marr. diss. 1971), *d* of late Arthur C. Davy; four *s* two *d*; 2nd, 1971, Ann Elizabeth Farwell. *Educ:* Winchester; Balliol Coll., Oxford. 1st Class Hons Politics, Philosophy and Economics (Modern Greats). Editor, The Countryman, 1947-71. Filkins Parish Councillor; Witney Rural District Councillor, 1946-74; Chairman: Rural District Councils' Association, 1967-70; Rural Cttee of Nat. Council of Social Service; Member: Oxfordshire Planning Cttee, 1948-69; W Oxfordshire Technical Coll. Governors, 1951-70; South East Economic Planning Council, 1966-73; Nature Conservancy, 1970-73; Exec. Cttee, CPRE, 1963-69; Inland Waterways Amenity Advisory Council, 1968-73; Defence Lands Cttee, 1971-73; Water Space Amenities Commn, 1977-80; Development Commn, 1978-82. Pres., Camping Club of GB and Ireland, 1981-. Prepared report on Accommodation for Gypsies, 1976. *Address:* Fox House, Filkins, Lechlade, Glos GL7 3JQ. *TA:* Filkins. *T:* Filkins 209. *Club:* Farmers'.

CRIPPS, (Matthew) Anthony Leonard, CBE 1971; DSO 1943; TD 1947; QC 1958; a Recorder, since 1972 (Recorder of Nottingham, 1961-71); Deputy Senior Judge, British Sovereign Base Areas, Cyprus, since 1978; *b* 30 Dec. 1913; *s* of late Major Hon. L. H. Cripps; *heir-pres.* to 4th Baron Parmoor, *qv*; *m* 1941, Dorothea Margaret (Surrey CC 1965-67), *d* of G. Johnson Scott, Ashby-de-la-Zouch; three *s*. *Educ:* Eton; Christ Church, Oxford; Combined Army and RAF Staff Coll., 1944-45. Royal Leicestershire Regt, TA, 1933. Served War of 1939-45: Norway, Sweden, Finland, Iceland, N Africa, Italy, Egypt, 1939-44 (Capt. to Lt-Col); Staff Officer, Palestine and Syria, 1944-46. Barrister-at-law, Middle Temple, 1938 (Bencher 1965; Dep. Treas., 1982), Inner Temple, 1961, and Hong Kong, 1974. Hon. Judge of Court of Arches, 1969-80. Comr for Local Govt Petitions, 1978-. Chairman: Disciplinary Cttees, Milk Marketing Bd, 1956-, Potato and Egg Marketing Bds, 1956-67; Isle of Man Govt Commn on Agricultural Marketing, 1961-62; Home Sec.'s Adv. Cttee on Service Candidates, 1966- (Dep. Chm., 1965); Nat. Panel, Approved Coal Merchants Scheme, 1972-; Nat. Panel, Approved Solid Fuel Distributors Scheme; Legal Adv. Cttee, RSPCA, 1978-. Member: Agricultural Wages Bd, 1964-67; Northumberland Cttee of Inquiry into Foot and Mouth Disease, 1968-69; Cttee of Inquiry, Export of Live Animals for Slaughter, 1973-74. Dir, Caledonian African Investment Trust (Pty) Ltd (S Africa). Chm., Alpine Sun for British Children. *Publications:* Agriculture Act 1947, 1947; Agriculture Holdings Act, 1948, 1948; (ed) 9th edn, Cripps on Compulsory Purchase: Powers, Procedure and Compensation, 1950; legal articles, especially on agricultural matters, for Law Jl and Encyclopaedia Britannica. *Recreations:* family life and gardening. *Address:* Alton House, Felbridge, East Grinstead, Sussex RH19 2PP. *T:* 23238; 1 Harcourt Buildings, Temple EC4Y 9DA. *T:* 01-353 9421. *Clubs:* Brooks's, Lansdowne.

CRISHAM, Air Vice-Marshal William Joseph, CB 1953; CBE 1944; RAF, retired; *b* 19 Nov. 1906; Served War of 1939-45; Nos 13 and 23 Sqdns; Central Fighter Establishment, 1950-53; No 12 Group Fighter Command, 1953-56; RAF Levant MEAF, 1956-58; RAF Germany (2nd TAF), 1958-61; retired 1961. *Club:* Royal Air Force.

CRISP, Prof. Arthur Hamilton, MD, DSc; FRCP, FRCPE, FRCPsych; Professor of Psychiatry, University of London at St George's Hospital Medical School, since 1967, and Dean, Faculty of Medicine, University of London, 1976-80; *b* 17 June 1930; *s* of John and Elizabeth Crisp; *m* 1958, Irene Clare (*née* Reid); three *s*. *Educ:* Watford Grammar Sch.; Univ. of London (MD; DSc). FRCP 1973, FRCPE 1972, FRCPsych 1971. Previously Lectr, then

Sen. Lectr in Psych., Middlesex Hosp. Med. Sch., London. *Publications:* (jtly) Sleep, Nutrition and Mood, 1976; Anorexia Nervosa: Let Me Be, 1980; approx. 200 articles in learned jls. *Recreations:* golf, study of the River Wandle. *Address:* 113 Copse Hill, Wimbledon, SW20 0NT. *T:* 01-946 0976. *Clubs:* Athenæum; Royal Wimbledon Golf.

CRISP, Prof. Dennis John, CBE 1978; ScD; FRS 1968; Professor in Department of Marine Biology, University College of North Wales, since 1962; Hon. Director, Natural Environment Research Council Unit of Marine Invertebrate Biology, since 1965; *b* 29 April 1916; *m* 1944, Ella Stewart Allpress; one *s* one *d. Educ:* St Catharine's Coll., Cambridge. Research Asst, Dept of Colloid Science, Univ. of Cambridge, 1943-46; ICI (Paints Div.), i/c of Marine Paints Res. Stn, Brixham, Devon, 1946-51; Dir, Marine Science Laboratories, University Coll. of N Wales, 1951-70. *Publications:* (ed) Grazing in Terrestrial and Marine Environments, 1964; (ed) 4th European Marine Biology Symposium Volume (1969), 1971; papers in Proc. Royal Soc., Jl Marine Biol. Assoc., Jl Experimental Biology, Jl Animal Ecology, etc. *Recreations:* travel, photography. *Address:* Craig y Pîn, Llandegfan, Menai Bridge, Gwynedd. *T:* Menai Bridge 712775.

CRISP, Sir (John) Peter, 4th Bt *cr* 1913; *b* 19 May 1925; *o s* of Sir John Wilson Crisp, 3rd Bt, and Marjorie (*d* 1977), *d* of F. R. Shriver; *S* father, 1950; *m* 1954, Judith Mary, *d* of late H. E. Gillett; three *s* one *d. Educ:* Westminster. *Heir: s* John Charles Crisp, *b* 10 Dec. 1955. *Address:* Crabtree Cottage, Drungewick Lane, Loxwood, West Sussex. *T:* Loxwood 752374.

CRISP, Prof. Leslie Finlay; Professor of Political Science, Australian National University, 1950-77, now Emeritus Professor; Member since 1974, Chairman, since 1975, Board of Commonwealth Banking Corporation; *b* Melbourne, 19 Jan. 1917; *s* of Leslie Walter and Ruby Elizabeth Crisp; *m* 1940, Helen Craven Wighton; one *s* two *d. Educ:* St Peter's Coll., Adelaide; St Mark's Coll., Univ. of Adelaide (MA); Balliol Coll., Oxford (Rhodes Schol., MA). Australian Public Service, 1940-50: Dir-Gen., Dept of Post-War Reconstruction, 1949-50. Chm., Canberra Hosp. Bd, 1951-55; Mem., Prime Minister's Cttee on Future of Nat. Library and Archives, 1956; Chm., Prime Minister's Cttee on Integration of Data Bases, 1973-74. *Publications:* Parliamentary Government of the Commonwealth of Australia, 1949; Australian Federal Labour Party, 1955; Ben Chifley, 1961; Australian National Government, 1965; Peter Richard Heydon 1913-1971, 1972, etc. *Recreation:* golf. *Address:* 47 Stonehaven Crescent, Deakin, Canberra, ACT 2600, Australia. *T:* 81 3828. *Club:* Royal Canberra Golf.

CRISP, Hon. Sir (Malcolm) Peter, Kt 1969; retired; a Justice of the Supreme Court of Tasmania, 1952-71; Senior Puisne Judge, 1968-71; *b* Devonport, Tasmania, 21 March 1912; *s* of late T. M. Crisp, Burnie, (legal practitioner), and Myrtle May (*née* Donnelly); *m* 1935, Edna Eunice (*née* Taylor); two *d. Educ:* St Ignatius Coll., Riverview, Sydney; Univ. of Tasmania (LLB). Admitted legal practitioner, Tas, 1933; Crown Prosecutor, 1940. Served AIF, 1940-46 (in Australia, UK and Borneo, 2/1 Tank Attack Regt and Staff appts; rank of Colonel on discharge). Crown Solicitor, 1947-51; Solicitor-Gen. and KC, 1951. Lecturer in Law of Real Property, Univ. of Tasmania, 1947-52; Mem. Univ. Council, 1948-55; Chairman: State Library Bd, 1956-77; Council, Nat. Library of Aust., 1971 (Mem., 1960-71); Australian Adv. Council on Bibliographical Services, 1973-; Pres., Library Assoc. of Aust., 1963-66; Royal Commissioner, Fluoridation of Public Water Supplies, 1966-68. *Recreations:* cruising, angling. *Address:* 10 Anglesea Street, Hobart, Tasmania. *T:* Hobart 235639. *Clubs:* Tasmanian, Royal Yacht Club of Tasmania (Hobart).

CRISP, Sir Peter; *see* Crisp, Sir (John) P.

CRISP, Hon. Sir Peter; *see* Crisp, Hon. Sir M. P.

CRITCHETT, Sir Ian (George Lorraine), 3rd Bt *cr* 1908; BA Cantab; HM Diplomatic Service, retired; Counsellor, Foreign and Commonwealth Office, 1977-80; *b* 9 Dec. 1920; *s* of Sir Montague Critchett, 2nd Bt, and Innes, 3rd *d* of late Col F. G. A. Wiehe, The Durham Light Infantry; *S* father, 1941; *m* 1st, 1948, Paulette Mary Lorraine (*d* 1962), *d* of late Col H. B. Humfrey; 2nd, 1964, Jocelyn Daphne Margret, *e d* of Comdr C. M. Hall, Higher Boswarva, Penzance, Cornwall; one *s* one *d. Educ:* Harrow; Clare Coll., Cambridge. RAFVR, 1942-46. Joined Foreign Office, 1948; 3rd Sec. (Commercial), at Vienna, 1950-51; 2nd Sec. (Commercial) at Bucharest, 1951-53; 2nd Sec. at Cairo, 1956; First Sec., FO, 1962. *Heir: s* Charles George Montague Critchett, *b* 2 April 1965. *Address:* Uplands Lodge, Pains Hill, Limpsfield, Surrey. *Clubs:* Travellers', Pratt's, MCC.

CRITCHLEY, Julian Michael Gordon; MP (C) Aldershot, since 1974 (Aldershot and North Hants, 1970-74); writer and journalist; *b* 8 Dec. 1930; *s* of Dr Macdonald Critchley, *qv*; *m* 1955, Paula Joan Baron (divorced 1965); two *d; m* 1965, Mrs Heather Goodrick; one *s* one *d. Educ:* Shrewsbury; Sorbonne; Pembroke Coll., Oxford (MA). MP (C) Rochester and Chatham, 1959-64; contested Rochester and Chatham, 1966. Chm. of the Bow Group, 1966-67. Vice-Chairman: Cons. Party Broadcasting Cttee; Cons. Party Defence Cttee; Chm., Cons. Party Media Cttee, 1976-81. Delegate to WEU and Council of Europe; Chm., WEU Defence Cttee; Deleg. to N Atlantic Assembly. Pres., Atlantic Assoc. of Young Political Leaders, 1968-70. *Publications:* (with O. Pick) Collective Security, 1974; Warning and Response, 1978; The North Atlantic Alliance and the Soviet Union in the

1980s, 1982; various Bow Group and CPC pamphlets. *Recreations:* watching boxing, the country, reading military history, looking at churches. *Address:* The Brewer's House, 18 Bridge Square, Farnham, Surrey. *T:* Farnham 722075. *Club:* Carlton.

CRITCHLEY, Macdonald, CBE 1962; MD, ChB 1st Class Hons (Bristol); FRCP; MD (Zürich) *hc* ; D en M (Aix-Marseille) *hc* ; FACP (hon.); Consulting Neurologist; *s* of Arthur Frank and Rosina Matilda Critchley; *m* 1st, Edna Auldeth Morris (decd); two *s* ; 2nd, Eileen Hargreaves. *Educ:* Christian Brothers Coll.; Univ. of Bristol (Lady Haberfield Scholarship in Medicine, Markham Skerritt Prize for Original Research). Goulstonian Lectr, RCP, 1930; Hunterian Prof., RCS, 1935; Royal Coll. of Physicians: Bradshaw Lectr, 1942; Croonian Lectr, 1945; Harveian Orator, 1966; Pres., World Fedn of Neurology, 1965-73; Hon. Consulting Neurologist, King's Coll. Hosp.; Hon. Consulting Physician, National Hosp., Queen Square; formerly Dean, Inst. of Neurology; Neurological Physician, Royal Masonic Hosp.; formerly Neurologist to Royal Hosp. and Home for Incurables, Putney. Consulting Neurologist to Royal Navy, 1939-77; Long Fox Lectr, Univ. of Bristol, 1935; William Withering Lectr, Univ. of Birmingham, 1946; Tisdall Lectr, Univ. of Manitoba, 1951; Semon Lectr, Univ. of London, 1951; Sherrington Lectr, Univ. of Wisconsin; Orator, Medical Soc. of London, 1955. Pres. Harveian Soc., 1947. Hunterian Orator, 1957; Doyne Memorial Lectr, 1961; Wartenberg Lectr, 1961; Victor Horsley Memorial Lectr, 1963; Honyman Gillespie Lectr, 1963; Schorstein Lectr, 1964; Hughlings Jackson Lectr and Medallist, RSM, 1964; Gowers Lectr and Medallist, 1965; Veraguth Gold Medallist, Bern, 1968; Sam T. Orton Award for work on Dyslexia, 1974; Arthur Hall Memorial Lectr, 1969; Rickman Godlee Lectr, 1970; Cavendish Lectr, 1976. Pres. Assoc. of British Neurologists, 1962-64; Second Vice-Pres., RCP, 1964; Mem., GMC, 1957-73. Hon. Fellow, Pan-African Assoc. of Neurological Scis; Hon. Mem., RSM; Hon. Corresp. Mem. Académie de Médecine de France, Norwegian Academy of Science and Letters, Royal Academy of Medicine, Barcelona, and Neurological Socs of France, Switzerland, Holland, Turkey, Uruguay, US, Canada, Australia, Brazil, Argentine, Germany, Chile, Spain, Roumania, Norway, Czechoslovakia, Greece, Italy, Bulgaria, Hungary, Peru, Poland and Sweden. Visiting Prof., Univs of: Istanbul, 1949; California, 1950 and 1964; Hawaii, 1966. Master, Worshipful Soc. of Apothecaries, 1956-57. Served European War, 1917-18; Surgeon Captain RNVR, 1939-46. *Publications:* Mirror Writing; Neurology of Old Age; Observations on Pain; Language of Gesture; Shipwreck-survivors; Sir William Gowers; The Parietal Lobes; The Black Hole; Developmental Dyslexia; Aphasiology; The Dyslexic Child; Silent Language; (ed jtly) Music and the Brain, 1976; (jtly) Dyslexia defined, 1978; various articles on nervous diseases. *Address:* Private Consulting Room, National Hospital, Queen Square, WC1. *T:* 01-837 3611. *Clubs:* Athenæum, Garrick, Pilgrims.

See also J. M. G. Critchley.

CRITCHLEY, Philip; Under Secretary, Planning Land Use Policy Directorate, Department of the Environment, since 1980; *b* 31 Jan. 1931; *s* of Henry Stephen and Edith Adela Critchley; *m* 1962, Stella Ann Barnes; two *s* one *d. Educ:* Manchester Grammar Sch.; Balliol Coll., Oxford (MA, 2nd Classical Mods and Greats). National Service, Intelligence Corps, 1953-55. Joined Min. of Housing and Local Govt (now Dept of Environment), 1955-: Principal, 1960; Asst Sec., 1969. *Recreations:* cross country running, climbing, writing poetry. *Address:* Redstone House, Maidstone Road, Ashford, Kent TN25 4NP. *T:* Ashford 21037. *Clubs:* Blackheath Harriers; Oxford Union Society.

CRITCHLEY, Thomas Alan, JP; Assistant Under-Secretary of State, Home Office, 1972-76; *b* 11 March 1919; *y s* of Thomas Critchley and Annie Louisa Darvell; *m* 1942, Margaret Carol Robinson; one *s* two *d. Educ:* Queen Elizabeth's Grammar Sch., Barnet. Entered Civil Service, 1936. Served War, 1940-46 (commnd in RAOC). Asst Principal, Home Office, 1947; Principal, 1948; Cabinet Office, 1954-56; Principal Private Sec., to Home Secretary, 1957-60; Asst Sec., 1958; Sec., Royal Commn on Police, 1960-62; Sec. to Lord Denning's Enquiry into the Profumo Affair, 1963; Sec. of the Gaming Board for Great Britain, 1971-72; Director (and Mem.), Uganda Resettlement Board, 1972-74; held enquiry into UK Immigrants Adv. Service, 1976; Vice-Chm., WRVS, 1977-81. JP Middlesex 1977. *Publications:* The Civil Service Today, 1951; A History of Police in England and Wales, 1967, 2nd edn 1978 (Amer. edn, 1972); The Conquest of Violence, 1970; (with P. D. James) The Maul and the Pear Tree, 1971; contributor to: The Police We Deserve, 1973, and various jls. *Recreations:* reading, gardening, walking. *Address:* 26 Temple Fortune Lane, NW11. *T:* 01-455 4894.

CROAN, Thomas Malcolm; Sheriff of Grampian, Highland and Islands (formerly Aberdeen, Kincardine and Banff) at Banff and Peterhead, since 1969; *b* 7 Aug. 1932; *s* of John Croan and Amelia Sydney; *m* 1959, Joan Kilpatrick Law; one *s* one *d. Educ:* St Joseph's Coll., Dumfries; Edinburgh University. MA 1953; LLB 1955. Admitted to Faculty of Advocates, 1956; Standing Junior Counsel, to Scottish Develt Dept, 1964-65 and (for highways work) 1967-69; Advocate Depute, 1965-66. *Recreations:* sailing, reading. *Address:* Belvedere, Sandyhill Road, Banff. *T:* Banff 5861.

CROCKER, Antony James Gulliford, CB 1973; retired as Under-Secretary, Family Support Division, Department of Health and Social Security (1974-78); *b* 28 Oct. 1918; *s* of late Cyril James Crocker and Mabel Kate Crocker; *m* 1st, 1943, E. S. B. Dent; 2nd, 1949, Nancy Wynell, *d* of late Judge Gamon and Eleanor Margaret Gamon; two s one d. *Educ:* Sherborne Sch. (Scholar); Trinity Hall, Cambridge (Major Scholar, MA). Served War, 1939-46, Dorsetshire Regt (Major). Asst Princ. 1947, Princ. 1948, Min. of Nat. Insurance. Sec., Nat. Insce Advisory Cttee, 1955-56; Asst Sec., Min. of Pensions and Nat. Insce, 1956; Under-Secretary; War Pensions Dept, 1964 (Min. of Social Security, 1966-68); Supplementary Benefits Commn, 1968; Tax Credits Div., 1972; New Pensions Scheme, 1974. *Recreations:* horticulture, philately. *Address:* Wealdover, Guildown Avenue, Guildford, Surrey. *T:* 66555.

CROCKER, Peter Vernon; His Honour Judge Crocker; a Circuit Judge, since 1974; *b* 29 June 1926; *s* of Walter Angus Crocker and Fanny Victoria Crocker (*née* Dempster); *m* 1950, Nancy Kathleen Sargent. *Educ:* Oundle; Corpus Christi Coll., Cambridge (BA). Called to Bar, Inner Temple, 1949. *Recreations:* gardening, tennis, swimming.

CROCKER, Sir Walter (Russell), KBE 1978 (CBE 1955); Australian diplomat, retired 1970; Lieutenant-Governor of South Australia, 1973-82; *b* 25 March 1902; *e s* of late Robert Crocker and Alma Bray, Parnaroo, SA; *m* 1951, Claire (marr. diss. 1968), *y d* of F. J. Ward, Headmaster of Prince Alfred Coll., Adelaide, and *widow* of Dr John Gooden, Physicist; two s. *Educ:* University of Adelaide; Balliol Coll., Oxford; Stanford University, USA. Entered Colonial Administrative Service (Nigeria), 1930; transf. to League of Nations, 1934, and to ILO (Asst to Dir-Gen). Served War, 1940-45 (Lt.-Col, Croix de Guerre avec palme, Ordre royal du Lion, Belgium). Farming at Parnaroo, 1946; UN Secretariat (Chief of Africa Sect.), 1946-49; Prof. of Internat. Relations, Aust. Nat. Univ., 1949-52; Actg Vice-Chancellor, 1951; High Commissioner for Australia to India, 1952-55; Ambassador of Australia to Indonesia, 1955-57; High Comr to Canada, 1957-58; High Comr for Australia to India and Ambassador to Nepal, 1958-62; Amb. of Australia to the Netherlands and Belgium, 1962-65; Ambassador to Ethiopia and High Commissioner to Kenya and Uganda, 1965-67; Ambassador to Italy, 1967-70. Hon. Colonel, Royal South Australia Regt, 1977-. L'Ordre royal du Lion (Belgium), 1945; Cavaliere di Gr. Croce dell'Ordine al Merito (Italy), 1970; Order of Malta (Grand' Uffiziale del Merito Melitense), 1975. *Publications:* The Japanese Population Problem, 1931; Nigeria, 1936; On Governing Colonies, 1946; Self-Government for the Colonies, 1949; Can the United Nations Succeed?, 1951; The Race Question as a factor in International Relations, 1955; Nehru, 1965; Australian Ambassador, 1971; Memoirs, 1981. *Recreations:* gardening, walking, music; previously ski-ing, tennis. *Address:* 256 East Terrace, Adelaide, SA 5000, Australia. *Clubs:* United Oxford & Cambridge University, Reform; Adelaide.

CROCKFORD, Brig. Allen Lepard, CBE 1955 (OBE 1945); DSO 1943; MC 1916; TD 1942; late Hon. Colonel RAMC 54 and 56 Division (TA); *b* 11 Sept. 1897; *s* of late J. A. V. Crockford, West Worthing, Sussex; *m* 1924, Doris Ellen Brookes-Smith; one s two d. *Educ:* Gresham's Sch.; King's Coll., Cambridge; St Thomas's Hosp. Glos Regt, BEF (Capt.; wounded), 1915-19. BA Cantab, 1920; MA 1926; MB, BCh Cantab, 1922; Gen. Practice, 1924-39; RAMC (TA): served with 43rd, Guards Armoured, 46th and 56th Divs, BNAF and CMF (Col), 1939-45; Gen. Practice, 1945-46; Medical Sec., St Thomas's Hosp. Medical Sch., London, SE1, 1946-64. Col (TA), ADMS, 56 Armoured Div., 1947; Brig. (TA); DDMS AA Comd, 1949; KHS 1952; QHS 1952-57; OStJ 1954. *Recreations:* reading, gardening. *Address:* Holly Cottage, Humshaugh, Hexham, Northumberland NE46 4AG. *T:* Hexham 81298.

CROFT, family name of **Baron Croft.**

CROFT, 2nd Baron *cr* 1940, of Bournemouth; **Michael Henry Glendower Page Croft;** Bt 1924; *b* 20 Aug. 1916; *s* of 1st Baron Croft, PC, CMG, and Hon. Nancy Beatrice Borwick (*d* 1949), *y d* of 1st Baron Borwick; S father, 1947; *m* 1948, Lady Antoinette Fredericka Conyngham (*d* 1959), *o d* of 6th Marquess Conyngham; one s one d. *Educ:* Eton; Trinity Hall, Cambridge (BA). Served War of 1939-45, Capt. RASC. Called to the Bar, Inner Temple, 1952. Director: Henry Page & Co. Ltd, 1946-57; Ware Properties Ltd, 1958-65. Underwriting Mem., Lloyd's, 1971-. Mem. Exec. Cttee, Contemporary Arts Soc., 1960-68 and 1970- (Hon. Sec., 1971-76, Hon. Treasurer, 1976-80, Vice-Chm., 1980-81). FRSA. OStJ. *Heir: s* Hon. Bernard William Henry Page Croft [*b* 28 Aug. 1949. *Educ:* Stowe; Univ. of Wales, Cardiff. BScEcon]. *Address:* Croft Castle, near Leominster, Herefordshire; 19 Queen's Gate Gardens, SW7 5LZ. *Club:* Athenæum.

CROFT, Sir Bernard Hugh (Denman), 13th Bt *cr* 1671; *b* 24 Aug. 1903; *s* of Sir Hugh Matthew Fiennes Croft, 12th Bt, and Lucy Isabel, *e d* of Frederick Taylor, Terrible Vale, near Uralla, NSW; S father, 1954; *m* 1931, Helen Margaret, *d* of H. Weaver; three s two d. *Educ:* Armidale Sch., NSW. Rep. NSW Rugby Union in NZ, 1928. *Recreations:* football, tennis, golf. *Heir: s* Owen Glendower Croft [*b* 26 April 1932; *m* 1959, Sally, *d* of Dr T. M. Mansfield, Brisbane, Queensland; one s two d]. *Address:* Salisbury Court, Uralla, NSW 2358, Australia. *T:* Uralla 24.

CROFT, David Legh, QC 1982; *b* 14 Aug. 1937; *s* of late Alan Croft and of Doreen Mary Berry (*née* Mitchell); *m* 1963, Susan Mary (*née* Bagnall); two s. *Educ:* Haileybury and ISC; Nottingham Univ. (LLB). Called to the Bar, Middle Temple, 1960. *Recreations:* cookery, gossip. *Address:* Star Hill House, Rochester, Kent ME1 1XB.

CROFT, Ivor John, CBE 1982; painter in oils; Head of Home Office Research and Planning Unit, since 1981 (Head, Home Office Research Unit, 1972-81); *b* 6 Jan. 1923; *s* of Oswald Croft and Doris (*née* Phillips). *Educ:* Westminster Sch.; Christ Church, Oxford (MA); Inst. of Education, Univ. of London (MA); LSE. Temp. jun. admin. officer, FO, 1942-45; asst teacher, LCC, 1949-51; Inspector, Home Office Children's Dept, 1952-66; Sen. Research Officer, Home Office Research Unit, 1966-72. Mem., Criminological Scientific Council, Council of Europe, 1978-, Chm., 1981-. Governor, ILEA Secondary Schs, 1959-68. Mem. Exec. Cttee, English Assoc., 1966-77 (Hon. Treas. 1972-75). Group shows, 1958, 1963, 1967, 1968, 1969, 1973; one-man shows, 1970, 1971. *Publications:* Research in Criminal Justice, 1978; Crime and the Community, 1979; Crime and Comparative Research, 1979; Research and Criminal Policy, 1980; Managing Criminological Research, 1981; contrib. various learned jls. *Clubs:* Athenæum, Reform.

CROFT, Major Sir John (Archibald Radcliffe), 5th Bt *cr* 1818; Army Officer, retired 1956; *b* 27 March 1910; *s* of Tom Radcliffe Croft, OBE (*d* 1964) (6th s of 2nd Bt) and Louise (*d* 1964), *d* of Francis Sales; S cousin, 1979; *m* 1953, Lucy Elizabeth, *d* of late Major William Dallas Loney Jupp, OBE; one s. *Educ:* King's School, Canterbury. Commissioned The West Yorkshire Regt (PWO), 1935; served India, Burma, 1936-44; France and Germany, 1945. *Recreations:* shooting, fishing, golf. *Heir: s* Thomas Stephen Hutton Croft, *b* 12 June 1959. *Address:* Cornerways, Stodmarsh, Canterbury, Kent. *T:* Littlebourne 256. *Clubs:* Army and Navy; Kent and Canterbury (Canterbury).

CROFT, (John) Michael, OBE 1971; Director, National Youth Theatre, since 1956; *b* 8 March 1922. *Educ:* Plymouth Grove Elem. Sch. and Burnage Gram. Sch., Manchester; Keble Coll., Oxford (BA Hons). War Service in RAF and RN, 1940-45. After short career as actor, took up teaching, 1949; Asst English Master, Alleyn's Sch., 1950-55 (prod. series of Shakespeare plays with large schoolboy cos); founded Youth Theatre with group from Alleyn's Sch., 1956; this grew rapidly into nat. organisation with provincial branches; rep. Gt Brit. at Paris Festival, 1960 and W Berlin Festival, 1961; appeared at Old Vic, 1965. Also Dir Shakespeare for leading cos in Belgium and Holland, 1960-65; founded Dolphin Theatre Co., Shaw Theatre, 1971; productions include: Devil's Disciple, 1971; Romeo and Juliet, 1972; Antony and Cleopatra, 1977; Richard II, 1980; Nat. Youth Theatre Productions include: Zigger Zagger, Strand, 1968, Berlin Festival, 1968, Holland Festival, 1970, Shaw, 1981; Little Malcolm and his Struggle, Holland Festival, 1968; Fuzz, Berlin Festival, 1970; a series of plays by Peter Terson and Barrie Keeffe, during 1970s; Good Lads at Heart, tour of Canada, 1978; Brooklyn, NY, 1979; The Bread and Butter Trade, Shaw, 1982. *Publications:* (novel) Spare the Rod, 1954; (travel book) Red Carpet to China, 1958. *Recreations:* sport, travel. *Address:* 74 Bartholomew Road, NW5. *Club:* Savile.

CROFT, Michael; *see* Croft, J. M.

CROFT, Col Noel Andrew Cotton, DSO 1945; OBE 1970; MA Oxon; Essex Regiment; retired; *b* 30 Nov. 1906; *s* of late Rev. Canon R. W. Croft, MA; *m* 1952, Rosalind, 2nd *d* of late Comdr A. H. de Kantzow, DSO, RN; three d. *Educ:* Lancing Coll.; Stowe Sch.; Christ Church, Oxford (MA; Sch. of Technology, Manchester. Cotton Trade, 1929-32; Mem. British Trans-Greenland Expedition, 1933-34; ADC to Maharajah of Cooch Behar, India, 1934-35; Second-in-Command, Oxford Univ. Arctic Expedition to North-East Land, 1935-36; Ethnological Exped. to Swedish Lapland, 1937-38; Sec. to Dir of Fitzwilliam Museum, Cambridge, 1937-39. Served War of 1939-45, Capt. 1939; WO Mission to Finno-Russian War, 1939-40; Bde Intelligence Officer Independent Companies, Norwegian Campaign, 1940; Combined Ops, 1940-41; Major, 1941; Asst Mil. Attaché, Stockholm, 1941-42; sea or parachute ops in Tunisia, Corsica, Italy, France, and Denmark, 1943-45; Lieut-Col 1945; Asst Dir Scientific Research, War Office, 1945-49; WO Observer on Canadian Arctic Exercise "Musk-Ox", 1945-46, and on New Frontier Trials, India, 1946-47; attached Canadian Army, 1947-48. GSO1, War Office, 1949-51; Liaison Officer HQ Continental Army, USA, 1952-54; comd The Infantry Junior Leaders Bn, 1954-57; Comdt Army Apprentices Sch., Harrogate, 1957-60; Comdt, Metropolitan Police Cadet Corps, 1960-71. Chm., Women's Transport Service (FANY). Corresp. Fellow, Arctic Inst. of North America; Chm., Reindeer Council of UK. Polar Medal (clasp Arctic, 1935-36), 1942; Back Award, RGS, 1946. *Publications:* (with A. R. Glen) Under the Pole Star, 1937; Polar Exploration, 1939. *Recreations:* mountaineering, ski-ing, sailing, photography. *Address:* River House, Strand-on-the-Green, W4. *T:* 01-994 6359. *Clubs:* Alpine, Hurlingham, Special Forces.

CROFT, Roy Henry Francis; Deputy Secretary, Department of Industry, since 1980; *b* 4 March 1936; *s* of late William Henry Croft and Dorothy Croft; *m* 1961, Patricia Ainley; one s two d. *Educ:* Isleworth Grammar Sch.; Christ's Coll., Cambridge (MA). BoT, 1959; Treasury, 1961-62; DEA, 1964-67; Private Sec. to Pres. Bd of Trade, 1968-70; Cabinet Office, 1970-72; Civil Aviation Div., Dept of Trade, 1973-76; Economic Appraisal Div., DoI, 1976-79; Posts and Telecommunications Div., DoI, 1979-80. *Address:* Ashdown House, 123 Victoria Street, SWIE 6RB. *T:* 01-212 5808.

CROFT, Stanley Edward, TD 1951; Senior Associate, Abbey Life Assurance Company; formerly HM Diplomatic Service; *b* 18 Oct. 1917; *s* of Edward John and Alice Lucy Croft; *m* 1950, Joan Mary Kaye; four s two d. *Educ:* Portsmouth Grammar School. TA, 1939; served War of 1939-45, RA, Middle

East, Aden, Italy, Germany. Min. of Labour, 1935; Admty, 1937-39 and 1946-47; transf. to Diplomatic Service, 1947; Vice-Consul, Barcelona, 1950; 2nd Sec., Lahore, 1951; Washington, 1955; Madrid, 1956; 1st Sec., FO, 1960; Consul, Geneva, 1961; FO and CRO, 1965-70; Consul-Gen., Madrid, 1970; Counsellor and Consul-Gen., Luanda, 1974-77. *Recreations:* swimming, tennis, camping, fishing, carpentry. *Address:* South Lodge, Ruxbury Road, Chertsey, Surrey. *Clubs:* Royal Commonwealth Society; Foxhills (Ottershaw).

CROFTON, family name of **Baron Crofton.**

CROFTON, 6th Baron *cr* 1797; **Charles Edward Piers Crofton;** Bt 1758; Master Mariner, since 1978; *b* 27 April 1949; *s* of 5th Baron Crofton and of Ann, *e d* of Group Captain Charles Tighe, The Mill House, Kilbride, Co. Wicklow; *S* father, 1974; *m* 1976, Maureen Jacqueline, *d* of S. J. Bray, Taunton, Somerset. Ship Master, with Buries Markes (Ship Management) Ltd, 1979-. Mem., Nautical Institute, 1978. *Heir: b* Hon. Guy Patrick Gilbert Crofton [*b* 17 June 1951; commissioned 9/12 Royal Lancers, 1971]. *Address:* Longford House, Beltra, Co. Sligo, Eire.

CROFTON, Denis Hayes, OBE 1948 (MBE 1943); retired Home and Indian Civil Servant; Member, Panel of Inspectors, Department of the Environment, 1969-79; Chairman, Tunbridge Wells and District Branch, Civil Service Retirement Fellowship, since 1972; *b* 14 Dec. 1908; *s* of late Richard Hayes Crofton, Colonial Civil Service and Mabel Annie Crofton (*née* Smith); *m* 1933, Alison Carr, *d* of late Andrew McClure and Ethel McClure; three *s* one *d. Educ:* Tonbridge Sch.; Corpus Christi Coll., Oxford (Class. Mods, Lit. Hum., MA). Indian Civil Service, 1932; served in Bihar; subdivisional Magistrate, Giridih, 1934, Jamshedpur, 1935; Under-Sec. to Govt of Bihar, Polit. and Appt Depts, 1936; Under-Sec. to Govt of India, Dept of Labour, 1939; Private Sec. to Indian Mem., Eastern Gp Supply Council, 1941; Dist Mag. and Collector, Shahabad, Bihar, 1942; Sec. to Gov. of Bihar, 1944; apptd to Home Civil Service, 1947; Principal, Min. of Fuel and Power, Petroleum Div. 1948; Asst Sec., Petroleum Div. and Chm., OEEC Oil Cttee, Paris, 1950-53; Asst Sec., Monopolies and Restrictive Practices Commn, 1953; Asst Sec., Min. of Fuel and Power, Electricity Div., 1956; Petroleum Div., 1961; Accountant General and Under-Secretary for Finance, 1962-68. *Publications:* The Children of Edmonstown Park: memoirs of an Irish family, 1981; (ed) The Surgery at Aberffrwd: some encounters of a colliery doctor, by Francis Maylett Smith, 1982. *Recreations:* reading, gardening. *Address:* Tile Barn House, 147 Hadlow Road, Tonbridge, Kent. *T:* Tonbridge 353465. *Club:* Royal Commonwealth Society.

CROFTON, Sir John (Wenman), Kt 1977; retired; Professor of Respiratory Diseases and Tuberculosis, University of Edinburgh, 1952-77; *b* 1912; *s* of Dr W. M. Crofton; *m* 1945, Eileen Chris Mercer; two *s* three *d. Educ:* Tonbridge; Sidney Sussex Coll., Cambridge; St Thomas's Hosp. Medical qualification, 1936; War of 1939-45, RAMC; France, Middle East, Germany. Lecturer in Medicine, Postgraduate Medical Sch. of London, 1947-51, Senior Lecturer, 1951; Part-time Tuberculosis Unit, Medical Research Council, Brompton Hosp., 1947-50; Dean of Faculty of Medicine, 1964-66, and Vice-Principal, 1969-70, Univ. of Edinburgh. Vice-Pres., 1972-73, Pres., 1973-76, RCPE. Weber-Parkes Prize, RCP, 1966. *Publications:* (jt author) Respiratory Diseases, 1969, 3rd edn 1981; contributor to BMJ, Lancet, Thorax, etc. *Recreations:* conversation, family life, mountains. *Address:* 13 Spylaw Bank Road, Edinburgh EH13 0JW. *T:* 031-441 3730. *Club:* University Staff (Edinburgh).

CROFTON, Sir Malby (Sturges), 5th Bt *cr* 1838 (orig. *cr* 1661); Partner, Messrs Fenn & Crosthwaite; Member of the London Stock Exchange, 1957-75; *b* 11 Jan. 1923; *s* of Sir Malby Richard Henry Crofton, 4th Bt, DSO and Bar, and Katharine Beatrix Pollard; *S* father, 1962. *Educ:* Eton (King's Scholar); Trinity Coll., Cambridge (scholar). Served with Life Guards, 1942-46, in Middle East and Italy. Member: Kensington Borough Council, 1962, Leader, 1968-77, Mayor, Kensington and Chelsea, 1978-; GLC, 1970-73; ILEA, 1970-73; Ealing N, GLC, 1977-; Leader, GLC Scrutiny Cttee, 1977-78. *Recreations:* tennis, swimming, motoring, planting trees, farming. *Heir: kinsman* Henry Edward Melville Crofton [*b* 15 Aug. 1931; *m* 1955, Brigid, twin *d* of Gerald K. Riddle; two *s* one *d*]. *Address:* 51 Clareville Street, SW7 5AX; Longford House, Co. Sligo, Eire.

CROFTON, Sir Patrick Simon, 7th Bt *cr* 1801; *b* 2 Dec. 1936; *o s* of Major Morgan G. Crofton (*d* 1947); *S* grandfather, 1958; *m* 1967, Mrs Lene Eddowes, *d* of Kai Augustinus, Copenhagen, and Mrs R. Tonnesen, Port Elizabeth, SA; one *d. Educ:* Eton Coll. 2nd Lieut Welsh Guards, 1955-57. Entered Steel Industry, 1957; became Public Relations Consultant, 1961. Joint Managing Dir, Crofton Mohill Holdings Ltd; Dir, Blair Eames Suslak, Sir Patrick Crofton Ltd, Advertising Agents; Managing Dir, Sir Patrick Crofton Developments Ltd. *Recreations:* ski-ing, motoring, music, political argument. *Heir: uncle* Hugh Denis Crofton, *b* 10 April 1937. *Clubs:* Cavalry and Guards, East India, Devonshire, Sports and Public Schools.

CROHAM, Baron *cr* 1978 (Life Peer), of the London Borough of Croydon; **Douglas Albert Vivian Allen,** GCB 1973 (KCB 1967; CB 1963); an Industrial Adviser to the Governor, Bank of England, since 1978; Chairman, British National Oil Corporation, since 1982 (a Deputy Chairman BNOC, 1978-82); Head of the Home Civil Service and Permanent Secretary, Civil Service Department, 1974-77; *b* 15 Dec. 1917; *s* of late Albert Allen; *m* 1941,

Sybil Eileen Allegro, *d* of late John Marco Allegro; two *s* one *d. Educ:* Wallington County Grammar Sch.; London School of Economics. BSc (Econ.) First Class Hons, 1938. Entered Board of Trade, 1939; Royal Artillery, 1940-45; Cabinet Office, 1947; Treasury, 1948-58; Under-Secretary, Ministry of Health, 1958-60; Under-Secretary, Treasury, 1960-62, Third Secretary, 1962-64; Dept of Economic Affairs: Dep. Under-Sec. of State, 1964-66; Second Permanent Under-Sec. of State, May-Oct. 1966; Permanent Under-Sec. of State, 1966-68; Permanent Sec., HM Treasury, 1968-74. Dir, Pilkington Bros, 1978-. Pres., Inst. for Fiscal Studies, 1979. A Trustee, Anglo-German Foundn, 1977- (Chm., 1982-). FBIM 1969; FRSA 1975. Hon. Fellow, LSE, 1969; Hon DSc Southampton, 1977. *Recreations:* tennis, woodwork. *Address:* 9 Manor Way, South Croydon, Surrey. *T:* 01-688 0496. *Club:* Reform.
See also J. M. Allegro.

CROKER, Edgar Alfred; Secretary and Chief Executive of the Football Association, since 1973; *b* 13 Feb. 1924; *m* 1952, Kathleen Mullins; one *s* two *d. Educ:* Kingston Technical Coll. Served War: Flt Lieut, RAF, 1942-46. Flt Lieut, RAFVR, 1947-55. Professional footballer: Charlton Athletic, 1947-51; Headington United, 1951-56. Sales Dir, Douglas Equipment, 1956-61; Chairman and Managing Dir, Liner-Croker Ltd, 1961-73; Chairman, Liner Concrete Machinery Co. Ltd, 1971-73. King's commendation for brave conduct, 1946. *Recreations:* golf, tennis, bridge, squash. *Address:* South Court, The Park, Cheltenham, Glos. *T:* Cheltenham 27618. *Clubs:* Sportsman; New (Cheltenham).

CROLL, Hon. David Arnold, QC; BA, LLB; Senator; Chairman, Senate Committees on: Poverty; Aging; Retirement Policies; *b* Moscow, 12 March 1900; *s* of Hillel and Minnie Croll; *m* 1925, Sarah Levin; three *d. Educ:* public schs and Patterson Collegiate Institute, Windsor; Osgoode Hall, Toronto; University of Toronto. Emigrated to Canada with family, 1906, settling at Windsor, Ont; first and only commercial venture operation of news-stand, which greatly facilitated secondary education; after high school and course articled to solicitor; graduation from Osgoode Hall law sch. followed by practice at Windsor, 1925-30; presently senior partner in Croll and Croll, Windsor, Ont., and Croll and Godfrey, Toronto, Ont. Mayor of Windsor, Ont., 1930-34, 1939-40; Mem. for Windsor-Walkerville, Ont. Legislature, 1934-44; late Minister of Labour, Public Welfare and Municipal Affairs for the Province of Ont.; was youngest and first Jewish Cabinet Minister and first Jewish Senator, in Canada. Mem. of House of Commons for Toronto Spadina, 1945-55 when appointed to Senate. Served War of 1939-45, with Canadian Army overseas, enlisting as Private in Sept. 1939 and discharged in rank of Col in Sept. 1945. *Recreations:* golf and the more strenuous sports. *Address:* 1603 Bathurst Street, Suite 508, Toronto, Ont M5P 3J2, Canada. *Club:* Primrose (Toronto).

CROLY, Brig. Henry Gray, CBE 1958; JP; *b* 7 June 1910; *s* of late Lt-Col W. Croly, DSO, late RAMC, Ardvarna, Tralee; *m* 1939, Marjorie Rosanne, *er d* of late Major J. S. Knyvett, late R Warwickshire Regt, Clifford Manor Road, Guildford; two *s* two *d. Educ:* Sherborne Sch.; RMA Woolwich. 2nd Lieut RA, 1930; served in India: Mohmand Ops, 1935; Waziristan, 1936-37 (despatches); served War of 1939-45, mostly India and Burma; GSO1, British Mil. Mission to France, 1946-47; 2nd-in-Comd 26 Medium Regt RA, 1947-48; jssc 1949; GSO1, WO, 1950-51; Col GS, SHAPE, 1952; OC 26 Field Regt Suez Canal Zone, 1953-55; Dep. Sec., Chiefs of Staff Cttee, 1955-58; UK Nat. Mil. Rep. to SHAPE, 1959-61; retd 1962. Sec., Health Visitor Trng Council and Council for Trng in Social Work, 1963-66; Asst Sec. of Commns, Lord Chancellor's Office, 1966-74; Sec., Wolfenden Cttee on Voluntary Orgns, 1974-78. JP Surrey, 1968. *Recreations:* golf, reading. *Address:* 20 Middle Bourne Lane, Farnham, Surrey. *T:* Farnham 714851. *Clubs:* Army and Navy, MCC; Hankley Common Golf.

CROMARTIE, 4th Earl of, *cr* 1861 (re-creation, revival of peerage forfeited 1745/46); **Roderick Grant Francis Mackenzie,** MC 1945; TD 1964; JP; DL; Major Seaforth Highlanders, retired; Viscount Tarbat of Tarbat, Baron Castlehaven and Baron Macleod of Leod, *cr* 1861; Chief of the Clan Mackenzie; *b* 24 Oct. 1904; *er surv. s* of Lt-Col Edward Walter Blunt-Mackenzie, DL (*d* 1949) and Countess of Cromartie, (3rd in line); *S* mother, 1962, having discontinued use of surname of Blunt, for himself and son, and reverted to Mackenzie; *m* 1st, 1933, Mrs Dorothy Downing Porter (marr. diss. 1945), *d* of Mr Downing, Kentucky, USA; two *d*; 2nd, 1947, Olga (Mendoza) (marr. diss. 1962), *d* of late Stuart Laurance, Paris; one *s* ; 3rd, 1962, Lilias Richard, MB, ChB, *d* of Prof. (James) Walter MacLeod, OBE, FRS, FRSE. *Educ:* Charterhouse; RMC Sandhurst. Commissioned to 1st Bn Seaforth Highlanders in Ireland, 1924; transferred to 2nd Bn Seaforth Highlanders, in India, 1925; seconded to Nigeria Regt of RWAFF, 1928-29; rejoined 2nd Seaforth Highlanders, 1930; Operations North-West Frontier, India, 1930-31; in France in 1940 with 4th Seaforth Highlanders (MC). Sec., Scottish Peers Assoc., House of Lords. JP Ross and Cromarty, 1937, DL Ross and Cromarty, 1976; CC Ross and Cromarty, 1963-77 (Vice-Convener, 1970-71, Convener, 1971-75); Hon. Sheriff (formerly Hon. Sheriff Substitute); Convener, Ross and Cromarty District Council, 1975-77. FSAScot. Freeman of Ross and Cromarty, 1977. *Publication:* A Highland History, 1980. *Heir: s* Viscount Tarbat, *qv. Address:* Castle Leod, Strathpeffer, Ross and Cromarty, Scotland. *Clubs:* Army and Navy, Pratt's.

CROMARTIE, (Ronald) Ian (Talbot); HM Diplomatic Service; Ambassador and Leader, UK Delegation to Committee on Disarmament,

Geneva, since 1982; *b* 27 Feb. 1929; *s* of late Ronald Duncan Cromartie and of Mrs Margaret Talbot Cromartie; *m* 1962, Jennifer Frances, *er d* of late Captain Ewen Fairfax-Lucy and Mrs Margaret Fairfax-Lucy; two *s* one *d*. *Educ:* Sherborne; Clare Coll., Cambridge (MA, PhD). Scientific research at Univs of Cambridge and Tübingen, 1950-58; Univ. Demonstrator in Organic Chemistry, Cambridge, 1958-60. Entered Foreign (later Diplomatic) Service, 1961; served in: FO, 1961-62; Saigon, 1962-64; FO, 1964-67; UK Disarmament Delegn, Geneva, 1967-69; FCO, 1969-72; Counsellor, 1972-75, Counsellor (Scientific), 1975-78, Bonn; UK Resident Rep. to IAEA and UN Orgs in Vienna, 1978-82, with personal rank of Ambassador, 1981-82. *Publications:* papers in Jl of Chem. Soc. and other scientific periodicals. *Recreations:* walking, sailing, shooting. *Address:* 61 Ashley Gardens, SW1. *Club:* United Oxford & Cambridge University.

CROMBIE, Alistair Cameron, MA, BSc, PhD; Fellow of Trinity College, Oxford, since 1969; Lecturer in History of Science, University of Oxford, since 1953; *b* 4 Nov. 1915; 2nd *s* of William David Crombie and Janet Wilmina (née Macdonald); *m* 1943, Nancy Hey; three *s* one *d* (and one *s* decd). *Educ:* Geelong Grammar Sch.; Trinity Coll., Melbourne Univ.; Jesus Coll., Cambridge. Zoological Lab., Cambridge, 1941-46; Lectr in History and Philosophy of Science, University Coll., London, 1946-53, nominated Reader, resigned; Technischen Hochschule, Aachen, 1948; Vis. Prof., Univ. of Washington, 1953-54; All Souls Coll., Oxford, 1954-69; Princeton Univ., 1959-60; Council of Science Museum, London, 1962-66; Guest Vis., Australian Univs, 1963; Brit. Nat. Cttee for History of Science, 1963-69; Visiting Professor: Tokyo Univ. (guest of Japan Soc. for Promotion of Sci.), 1976; All-India Inst. of Med. Scis, and guest of Indian Nat. Sci. Acad., 1976; Virginia Mil. Inst., 1977; Kennedy Prof. in Renaissance, Smith Coll., Mass., 1982. Conseil Scientifique, Dépt d'Hist. et Philosophie de la Médecine, Univ. of Paris XII, 1981-. Editor: Brit. Jl Philos. Sci., 1949-54; Hist. Sci., 1961-; Dir, Oxford Univ. Symp. Hist. Sci., 1961; Pres., Brit. Soc. Hist. Sci., 1964-66; Pres., Internat. Acad. Hist. Sci., 1968-71; Member: Internat. Acad. Hist. Med.; Academia Leopoldina; FRHistS. Galileo Prize, 1969. Hon. DLitt Durham, 1979. *Publications:* Augustine to Galileo, 1952, 4th edn 1979; Robert Grosseteste and the Origins of Experimental Science, 1953, 3rd edn 1971; Scientific Change, 1963; The Mechanistic Hypothesis and the Scientific Study of Vision, 1967; contrib. Annals of Sci., Brit. Jl Hist. Sci., EHR, Isis, Jl Animal Ecol., Physis, Proc. Royal Soc. Lond., Rev. de Synthèse, TLS, Dict. Sci. Biogr., Encyc. Brit., New Cambridge Modern Hist., etc. *Recreations:* literature, travel, landscape gardening. *Address:* Orchard Lea, Boars Hill, Oxford. *T:* Oxford 735692. *Club:* Brooks's.

CROMBIE, Prof. Leslie, FRS 1973; CChem, FRSC; Sir Jesse Boot Professor of Organic Chemistry, University of Nottingham, since 1969; *b* 10 June 1923; *s* of Walter Leslie Crombie and Gladys May Crombie (née Clarkson); *m* 1953 Winifred Mary Lovell Wood; two *s* two *d*. *Educ:* Portsmouth Municipal Coll.; King's Coll., London. PhD, DSc, FKC 1978. Admiralty Chemical Lab., Portsmouth Naval Dockyard, 1941-46. Lectr, Imperial Coll., London, SW7, 1950-58; Reader in Organic Chemistry, King's Coll., London Univ., 1958-63, Fellow, 1978; Prof. of Organic Chemistry, University Coll. (Univ. of Wales), Cardiff, 1963-69. Pres., British Association, Section B, 1978. Tilden Lectr, Chem. Soc., 1970; Simonsen Lectr, 1975; Hugo Muller Lectr, 1977; Pedler Lectr, 1982; Pres., Perkin Div. of Chem. Soc., 1976-79. Natural Products Chemistry award, Royal Soc. of Chem., 1980. *Publications:* many original papers in learned chemical jls, especially those of Chem. Soc., London. *Recreation:* gardening. *Address:* 153 Hillside Road, Bramcote, Beeston, Nottingham. *T:* 259412. *Club:* Athenæum.

CROMER, 3rd Earl of, *cr* 1901; **George Rowland Stanley Baring**, KG 1977; GCMG 1974 (KCMG 1971); MBE (Mil) 1945; PC 1966; Baron Cromer, 1892; Viscount Cromer, 1899; Viscount Errington, 1901; Chairman, International Advisory Council, Morgan Guaranty Trust Co. of New York, since 1977; Advisor to Baring Brothers & Co. Ltd, since 1974; Member, European Advisory Council, IBM Corporation, NY, since 1967; International Advisor to Marsh & McLennan Cos, NY, since 1978; European Advisor to Government Research Corporation, Washington, DC, since 1974; *b* 28 July 1918 (HM King George V stood sponsor); *o s* of 2nd Earl of Cromer, PC, GCB, GCIE, GCVO, and Lady Ruby Elliot, 2nd *d* of 4th Earl of Minto, KG, PC, GCSI, GCMG; *S* father, 1953; *m* 1942, Hon. Esmé Harmsworth (CVO 1980), 2nd *d* of 2nd Viscount Rothermere and of Margaret Hunam (née Redhead); two *s* (one *d* decd). *Educ:* Eton Coll.; Trinity Coll., Cambridge. Page of Honour: to King George V, 1931-35; to Queen Mary at Coronation, 1937; Private Sec. to Marquess of Willingdon representing HMG on missions to Argentina, Uruguay, Brazil, 1938, and to NZ and Aust., 1940. Served War, 1939-45: Grenadier Guards; Staff Col., Camberley; NW Europe (despatches, MBE); demob. 1945, Lt-Col. Joined Baring Brothers & Co. Ltd, 1938, rejoined 1945; seconded to: J. P. Morgan & Co.; Kidder Peabody & Co.; Morgan Stanley & Co.; Chemical Bank (all of NYC); Man. Dir, Baring Brothers & Co. Ltd, 1948-61; Mem., Inter-Parly Mission to Brazil, 1954; Econ. Minister and Head of Treasury and Supply Delegn, Washington, 1959-61; UK Exec. Dir, IMF, IBRD, and IFC, 1959-61; Head, UK Delegn to Internat. Coffee Conf., Washington, 1960; Governor of Bank of England, 1961-66; UK Governor, IBRD, IFC, and IDA, 1961-66; Bank of Internat. Settlements, Basle, 1961-66; Sen. Partner and Man. Dir, Baring Brothers & Co. Ltd, 1967-70; HM Ambassador, Washington, 1971-74. Author of report for Pres. of BoT, 1967, and for Cttee of Lloyd's, 1968. Chairman: IBM (UK) Ltd, 1967-70 and 1974-79; London Multinational Bank Ltd, 1967-70; Security & Prosper Fund SA, Luxembourg, 1967-70; Hon. Chm.,

Harris & Partners Ltd, Toronto, 1967-70. Director, 1949-59: Anglo-Newfoundland Develt Co. Ltd; Royal Ins. Co. Ltd; Liverpool, London & Globe Ins. Co. Ltd; Lewis Investment Trust Ltd; Director: Daily Mail & Gen. Trust Ltd, 1949-61, 1966-70 and 1974-; Union Carbide Corp. of NY, 1967-70; Associated Financial Services, Geneva, 1967-70; Imperial Group Ltd, 1974-80; P & O Steam Navigation Co. Ltd, 1974-80; Shell Trans. & Trading Co. Ltd, 1974-; Compagnie Financiere de Suez, Paris, 1974-82; Robeco Gp of Investment Trusts, Rotterdam, 1977-; IBM World Trade (Eur./ME/Africa) Corp., NY, 1977-; Barfield Trust Co. Ltd, Guernsey, 1979-; Baring Henderson Gilt Fund, 1979-. Chairman: Accepting House Cttee, 1967-70; OECD High Level Cttee on Capital Movements, 1967-70; Churchill Meml Trust, 1979; Member: Inst. Internat. d'Etudes Bancaires, 1967-70; Special Cttee on Trans-national Corps, Internat. Chamber of Commerce, 1967-69; Finance Cttee, UCL, 1954-57; British Inst. in Paris, 1952-57. A Governor: Atlantic Inst. for Internat. Affairs; Member: The Pilgrims (Mem. Exec. Cttee); Overseas Bankers Club; Trustee: King George's Jubilee Trust; Brain Res. Trust; Comr, Trilateral Commn. HM Lieut, City of London, 1961-; Dep. Lieut, Kent, 1968-79. FIB; Hon. LLD New York Univ., 1966. *Heir: s* Viscount Errington, *qv. Address:* Beaufield House, St Saviour, Jersey. *T:* Jersey 61671. *Clubs:* White's, Brooks's, Beefsteak, MCC; Brook (NY); Metropolitan (Washington).

CROMPTON, Dr Gareth, FFCM; Chief Medical Officer, Welsh Office, since 1978; *b* 9 Jan. 1937; *s* of Edward Crompton, Drefach-Felindre, Dyfed; *m* 1965; one *d. Educ:* Llandysul Grammar Sch.; Welsh Nat. Sch. of Medicine. MB, BCh Wales, 1960; DObstRCOG 1962; DPH Wales, 1964; FFCM 1976; MRCP 1980. County Med. Officer, County Welfare Officer and Principal Sch. Med. Officer, Anglesey CC, 1966-73; Area Med. Officer, Gwynedd Health Authority, 1974-77. Specialty Advr, Health Service Comr for England and Wales, 1974-77; Advr in Wales, Faculty of Community Medicine, 1974-77. Chm., Anglesey Disablement Adv. Cttee, 1969-77; Sec., Fluoridation Study Gp, Soc. of Med. Officers of Health, 1969-73; Mem., Welsh Hosp. Bd, 1970-74. Med. Fellow, Council of Europe, 1971. *Publications:* papers on the effects of fluoridated water supplies on dental caries, and the epidemiology and management of chronic sickness and disablement. *Recreations:* cycling, golf, watching Rugby, reading contemporary Welsh verse. *Address:* Health and Social Work Department, Welsh Office, Cathays Park, Cardiff CF1 3NQ. *T:* Cardiff 823911.

CROMPTON, Air Cdre Roy Hartley, OBE 1962; Group Director, Home Defence College, Easingwold, York, since 1976; *b* 24 April 1921; *er s* of Frank and Ann Crompton, Bedford; *m* 1961, Rita Mabel Leslie; one *s* one *d. Educ:* Bedford Sch.; University Coll., London (BA Hons). PSO to C-in-C Fighter Comd, 1956-59; OC Flying No 5 FTS, 1959-61; jssc 1962; Chiefs of Staff Secretariat, 1962-64; Stn Comdr No 1 FTS, 1965-67; sowc 1967; Dep. Dir Defence Policy Staff, 1968-70; Gp Dir RAF Staff Coll., 1970; Project Officer, Nat. Defence Coll., 1970-71; AOC and Comdt, Central Flying Sch., RAF, 1972-74. Directing Staff, Home Defence Coll., York, 1974-76. *Publications:* contrib. RAF Quarterly. *Recreations:* golf, music, horticulture. *Address:* Sharnford Lodge, Huby, York YO6 1HT. *T:* Easingwold 810124. *Club:* Royal Air Force.

CROMPTON-INGLEFIELD, Col Sir John (Frederick), Kt 1963; TD; DL; *b* 1904; *e s* of Adm. Sir F. S. Inglefield, KCB, DL; *m* 1st, 1926, Rosemary (*d* 1978), *d* of Adm. Sir Percy Scott, 1st Bt, KCB, KCVO, LLD; three *d*; 2nd, 1979, Madeline Rose, widow of W. E. Dodds and *d* of Col. Conyers Alston, Seven Rivers, Cape Province, South Africa. *Educ:* RN Colls Osborne and Dartmouth. Retired from Royal Navy, 1926. Derbyshire Yeomanry (Armoured Car Co.), Lieut 1936, Major 1939. Served War of 1939-45, with 1st Derbyshire Yeo. and 79th Armoured Div. (despatches) Africa and Europe. Lt-Col Comdg Derbyshire Yeo., 1950-53; Bt Col 1954; Hon. Col, Leics and Derbyshire Yeo., 1962-70. Chm. W Derbyshire Conservative and Unionist Assoc., 1951-66; Vice-Chm., 1957-64, Chm., TA, Derbyshire, 1964-69. CC 1932-55, JP 1933, DL 1953, and High Sheriff, 1938, Derbyshire. OStJ. *Address:* 15 Beaufort Gardens, SW3. *T:* 01-589 0650. *Club:* Cavalry and Guards.

CROMWELL, 7th Baron *cr* 1375 (called out of abeyance, 1923); **Godfrey John Bewicke-Copley**; *b* 4 March 1960; *s* of 6th Baron Cromwell and of Vivian, *y d* of late Hugh de Lisle Penfold, Isle of Man; *S* father, 1982. *Heir: b* hon. Thomas David Bewicke-Copley, *b* 6 Aug. 1964. *Address:* The Manor House, Great Milton, Oxfordshire.

CRONIN, John Desmond, FRCS; Consultant Surgeon; *b* 1 March 1916; *s* of John Patrick Cronin and Beatrice Cronin (née Brooks); *m* 1941, Cora, *d* of Rowland Mumby-Croft; one *s* two *d. Educ:* London Univ. MRCS, LRCP 1939; MB, BS (London) 1940; FRCS 1947. House Surgeon, St Bartholomew's Hosp., 1939-40; Surgeon EMS, Royal Free Hosp., 1941-42. Served RAMC, 1942-46, France, Germany and Burma campaigns; Surgical Specialist, Major (Actg Lt-Col 1945). Asst Orthopædic Surgeon, Prince of Wales's Hosp., 1947-51; Orthopædic Surgeon, French Hosp., 1948-. Vice-Chm., North St Pancras Labour Party, 1950. Member LCC, 1952-55. MP (Lab) Loughborough, 1955-79; Opposition Whip, House of Commons, 1959-62. Director: Racal Electronics Ltd, 1965-; Knight Wegenstein Ltd, 1969-70. Officier, Légion d'Honneur, 1967 (Chevalier, 1960). *Publications:* contributions to British Med. Journal and Proceedings Royal Soc. Medicine, and to the national press; Report on the Medical Services of Malta (pub. Central Office of Information, Govt of Malta). *Recreations:* sailing, riding, running, cooking. *Address:* 14 Wimpole Street, W1. *T:* 01-580 2460; Longslade, Adlam's Lane, Sway, Lymington, Hants. *T:* Lymington 683022. *Club:* Royal Lymington Yacht (Lymington).

CRONIN, John Walton; Regional Chairman of Industrial Tribunals, since 1972; *b* 14 Oct. 1915; *s* of John and Alice Cronin; *m* 1947, Eileen Veronica Bale (*née* Rector); one *d*; one step *s*. *Educ:* Xaverian Coll., Manchester; Manchester Univ. Solicitor. Served War, 1940-46, Major, Indian Army, latterly Staff appt, DAQMG. Private practice, 1946-55; Resident Magistrate, High Court Registrar, Acting Sheriff, Registrar-General Patents, Trade Marks and Designs, Sen. Resident Magistrate, Acting High Court Judge, Adv. Comr to Governor on Detained Persons, N Rhodesia/Zambia, 1955-65; Circuit Justice, Stipendiary and Circuit Magistrate, Grand Bahama, 1965-71. SBStJ 1969, OStJ 1977. *Address:* Moyle Cottage, The Fairway, Hythe, Kent CT21 6AU. *T:* Hythe (Kent) 67879.

CRONIN, Vincent Archibald Patrick; author; *b* 24 May 1924; *s* of late Archibald Joseph Cronin, MD, MRCP, DPH and of Agnes Mary Gibson, MB, ChB; *m* 1949, Chantal, *d* of Comte Jean de Rolland; two *s* three *d*. *Educ:* Ampleforth; Harvard; Trinity Coll., Oxford. Rifle Bde, 1943-45. *Publications:* The Golden Honeycomb, 1954; The Wise Man from the West, 1955; The Last Migration, 1957; A Pearl to India, 1959; The Letter after Z, 1960; Louis XIV, 1964; Four Women in Pursuit of an Ideal, 1965; The Florentine Renaissance, 1967; The Flowering of the Renaissance, 1970; Napoleon, 1971; Louis and Antoinette, 1974; trans., Giscard d'Estaing, Towards a New Democracy, 1977; Catherine, Empress of all the Russias, 1978; The View from Planet Earth, 1981. *Address:* 44 Hyde Park Square, W2 2JT.

CRONNE, Prof. Henry Alfred; Professor of Medieval History in the University of Birmingham, 1946-70, now Emeritus Professor; Dean of the Faculty of Arts, 1952-55; *b* 17 Oct. 1904; *o c* of late Rev. James Kennedy Cronne, Portaferry, Co. Down, N Ireland; *m* 1936, Lilian Mey, *er d* of E. F. Seckler, Bishops Tawton, Barnstaple; one *d*. *Educ:* Campbell Coll., Belfast; Queen's Univ. of Belfast; Balliol Coll., Oxford; Inst. of Historical Research. MA Belfast; MA Oxon; MA Birmingham, *jure officii.* Asst Lecturer in History, QUB, 1928-31; Lecturer in Medieval History, King's Coll., London, 1931, and subsequently Lecturer in Palaeography and Reader in Medieval History. War of 1939-45, served in Home Guard and Somerset Special Constabulary. *Publications:* Bristol Charters, 1378-1499, 1946; (ed with Charles Johnson) Regesta Regum Anglo-Normannorum, Vol. II, 1100-1135, 1956, (ed with R. H. C. Davis), Vol. III, 1135-1154, 1968, and Vol. IV, Facsimiles and Diplomatic, 1135-54, 1969; The Reign of Stephen, 1970; contribs to historical jls. *Recreations:* writing, drawing. *Address:* Winswood Cottage, Cheldon, Chulmleigh, N Devon EX18 7JB. *T:* Chulmleigh 80567.

CROOK, family name of **Baron Crook.**

CROOK, 1st Baron *cr* 1947, of Carshalton, Surrey; **Reginald Douglas Crook;** *b* 2 March 1901; *s* of Percy Edwin Crook; *m* 1922, Ida G. Haddon; one *s*. *Educ:* Strand Sch. Local Govt Service; Organising Sec. of Poor Law Officers' Union and Ed., Poor Law Gazette, 1920-24; Gen. Sec., Min. of Labour Staff Assoc., 1925-51, and Ed., Civil Service Argus, 1929-51; Sec., Fedn of Min. of Labour Staff, 1944-51; Mem., National Whitley Council for Civil Service, 1925-51; Mem., Min. of Labour Departmental Whitley Council, 1925-51; Hon. Sec., Labour Parliamentary Assoc., 1945-47; a Dep. Chm. of Cttees, House of Lords, 1949-75; Mem., Ecclesiastical Cttee of Parliament, 1949-75; Chm. of Interdeptl Cttee of Enquiry as to Optical Services, appointed by Min. of Health, 1949-52, leading to Opticians Act, 1958; Mem., Parl. Delegn to Denmark, 1949; Deleg. to Finland, 1950; Mem., Police Wages Council, 1951; Chm., National Dock Labour Board, 1951-65, also Chm., National Dock Labour Board (Nominees) Ltd and Chm., National Dock Labour Board Pensions Trustees Ltd; Member: London Electricity Board, 1966-72, General Practice Finance Corp., 1972-76; Chm., London Electricity Consultative Council, 1966-72; Delegate, United Nations General Assembly, 1950; Mem., United Nations Administrative Tribunal, 1951-71, Vice-Pres., 1952-71; Mem., UK Goodwill Mission to 350th Anniversary of Virginia, 1957; President: (also Fellow) Brit. Assoc. of Industrial Editors, 1953-61; Assoc. of Optical Practitioners, 1959- (Mem., 1951-); Cystic Fibrosis Research Foundation Trust; The Pre-Retirement Assoc.; Sutton Talking Newspaper, 1975-; Vice-Pres., Royal Soc. for the Prevention of Accidents; Vice-Pres. and Fellow, Inst. of Municipal Safety Officers. Mem., Inst. of Neurology. Master, Worshipful Co. of Spectacle Makers, 1963-65; an Apothecary, 1951-, and Freeman, 1948-, of City of London. Warden, 1968, Senior Warden, 1971, Master, 1972, Guild of Freemen of City of London. JP Surrey. KStJ 1955. Mem. Chapter-Gen. of St John, 1957-. *Heir: s* Hon. Douglas Edwin Crook [*b* 19 Nov. 1926; *m* 1954, Ellenor Rouse; one *s* one *d*]. *Address:* Breedene, Princes Avenue, Carshalton, Surrey. *T:* 01-643 2620.

CROOK, Arthur Charles William; Consultant to Times Newspapers, since 1974; Editor, The Times Literary Supplement, 1959-74; *b* 16 Feb. 1912; *m* 1948, Sarita Mary Vivien Bushell (marr. diss.); one *s* two *d*. Editorial staff of The Times, 1941-; Asst Editor, The Times Literary Supplement, 1951-59. *Recreation:* theatre. *Address:* 70 Regent's Park Road, NW1. *T:* 01-722 8446. *Club:* Garrick.

CROOK, Eric Ashley, FRCS; Consulting Surgeon; *b* 25 April 1894; *s* of Thomas Ashley and Emma Daisy Crook; *m* 1924, Elizabeth Grace Garratt (*d* 1978); one *s* one *d*. *Educ:* Winchester; New Coll., Oxford (MA, MCh). FRCS 1922. Cons. Surgeon: Charing Cross Hosp., Gordon Hosp., Putney Hosp., Royal Masonic Hosp. Served European War, 1914-18, Surg. Lieut, RN. *Address:* The Old Rectory, Sixpenny Handley, near Salisbury, Wilts. *See also* W. H. C. Frend.

CROOK, Maj.-Gen. James Cooper, MD, FRCPath; late RAMC, retired 1981; Civilian Medical Specialist, Army Blood Supply Depot, Aldershot, since 1982; *b* 19 March 1923; *s* of late Francis William Crook and late Mary Catherine Perry, *d* of late Sir Edwin Cooper Perry, GCVO, MD, Superintendent of Guy's Hospital and Vice-Chancellor of London Univ.; *m* 1950, Ruth, *d* of late W. A. Bellamy of Santa Cruz, Tenerife; one *s* two *d*. *Educ:* Worksop Coll.; Guy's Hosp. Med. Sch., Univ. of London. MB BS 1946, MD 1953; DTM&H 1952; FRCPath 1968. Guy's and Pembury Hosps, 1946; Commnd RAMC 1946; served Egypt and N Africa, 1946-49; Pathologist, Queen Alexandra's Mil. Hosp., 1950; David Bruce Laboratories, 1953; med. liaison officer to MRC Radiobiology Unit, AERE, 1954; Asst Dir of Pathology, Middle East, 1957; Cons. in Pathology, 1958; RAMC Specialist, Chem. Defence Estab., Porton, 1960; Asst Dir of Pathology, Eastern Comd, 1963; ADGMS, 1966; Comd Cons. in Pathology, BAOR, 1969; Prof. of Pathology, Royal Army Med. Coll., 1974; Dir of Army Pathology and Consulting Pathologist to the Army, 1976-81; Hon. Physician to HM The Queen, 1978-81. Hon. Col, 380 Blood Supply Unit RAMC, TAVR, 1982-. FRSM; Mem., BMA. *Publications:* articles in Jl of Clinical Path., Nature, Med. Sci. and the Law, Jl of RAMC, British Jl of Radiology. *Recreations:* gardening, travelling, history and art. *Address:* Danebury, 2 Wilmerhatch Lane, Epsom, Surrey KT18 7EQ. *T:* Epsom 20967.

CROOK, Prof. John Anthony, MA; Professor of Ancient History, University of Cambridge, since 1979; Fellow of St John's College, Cambridge, since 1951; *b* 5 Nov. 1921; *s* of Herbert Crook and Hilda Naomi (*née* Flower). *Educ:* St Mary's C of E Sch., Balham; Dulwich Coll.; St John's Coll., Cambridge 1939-41 and 1945-47 (John Stewart of Rannoch Scholar); BA 1947, Craven Student, 1947; Research Student of Balliol Coll., Oxford, 1947-48; MA (Cantab) 1949. Served War, Private and Corporal, 9th Royal Fusiliers, 1941-43 (PoW Stalag VIIIB, 1943-45); Sgt, RAEC, 1945. Univ. Asst Lectr in Classics, Reading Univ., 1948, Lectr, 1949-51; St John's Coll., Cambridge: Tutor, 1956-64; President, 1971-75; Univ. Asst Lectr in Classics, Cambridge Univ., 1953, Lectr, 1955-71, Reader in Roman History and Law, 1971-79, and Brereton Reader, 1974-79. FBA 1970-80. *Publications:* Consilium Principis, 1955; Law and Life of Rome, 1967. *Address:* St John's College, Cambridge CB2 1TP. *T:* Cambridge 61621.

CROOK, Prof. Joseph Mordaunt; Professor of Architectural History, Bedford College, University of London, since 1981; *b* 27 Feb. 1937; *e s* of late Austin Mordaunt Crook and Irene Woolfenden; *m* 1st, 1964, Margaret, *o d* of late James Mulholland; 2nd, 1975, Susan, *o d* of late F. H. Mayor. *Educ:* Wimbledon Coll.; Brasenose Coll., Oxford. BA (1st cl. Mod. Hist.) 1958; DPhil 1961, MA 1962, Oxon; FSA 1972. Research Fellow: Inst. of Historical Res., 1961-62; Bedford Coll., London, 1962-63; Warburg Inst., London, 1970-71; Asst Lectr, Univ. of Leicester, 1963-65; Lectr, Bedford Coll., London, 1965-75, Reader in Architectural Hist., 1975-81. Slade Prof. of Fine Art, Oxford Univ., 1979-80; Vis. Fellow, Brasenose Coll., Oxford, 1979-80. Member: Exec. Cttee, Soc. Architect. Historians of Gt Britain, 1964-77; RIBA Drawings Cttee, 1969-75; Exec. Cttee, Georgian Gp, 1970-77; Exec. Cttee, Victorian Soc., 1970-77, Council, 1978-; Historic Buildings Council, DoE, 1974-80; Council, Soc. of Antiquaries, 1980-82. Editor, Architectural History, 1967-75; Adv. Editor, British Studies Monitor, 1974-. *Publications:* (contrib.) Concerning Architecture, 1967; The Greek Revival, 1968; (contrib.) The Country Seat, 1970; (ed) Eastlake, A History of the Gothic Revival, 1970, revd edn, 1978; Victorian Architecture: A Visual Anthology, 1971; The British Museum, 1972; (contrib.) The Age of Neo Classicism, 1972; The Greek Revival: Neo-Classical Attitudes in British Architecture 1760-1870, 1972; (ed) Emmet, Six Essays, 1972; (ed) Kerr, The Gentleman's House, 1972; (jtly) The History of the King's Works, Vol. VI, 1782-1851, 1973 (Hitchcock Medallion, 1974), Vol. V, 1660-1782, 1976; The Reform Club, 1973; (contrib.) The Building of Early America, 1976; (contrib.) Seven Victorian Architects, 1976; William Burges and the High Victorian Dream, 1981; (ed) The Strange Genius of William Burges, 1981; (contrib.) The Ruskin Polygon, 1982; numerous articles in Architect. History, Architect. Review, Country Life, History Today, Jl Royal Soc. Arts, RIBA Jl, Antiquaries Jl, TLS, etc. *Recreation:* strolling. *Address:* 55 Gloucester Avenue, NW1. *T:* 01-485 8280. *Club:* Athenæum.

CROOK, Kenneth Roy, CMG 1978; HM Diplomatic Service, retired; Ambassador to Afghanistan, 1976-79; *b* 30 July 1920; *s* of Alexander Crook, Prescot, Lancs, and Margaret Kay Crook; *m* 1943, Freda Joan Vidler; two *d*. *Educ:* Prescot Grammar Sch., Lancs; Skerry's Coll., Liverpool. Appointed to: Board of Trade, 1937; Min. of War Transport, 1939. Royal Navy, 1941-46. Board of Trade, 1946-49; Commonwealth Relations Office, 1949; Second Sec., Canberra, 1951-54; First Sec., Madras, 1956-59; Deputy High Commissioner: Peshawar, W Pakistan, 1962-64; Dacca, E Pakistan, 1964-67; Counsellor, FCO, 1967; Head of Information Research Dept, FCO, 1969-71; Governor, Cayman Is, 1971-74; Canadian Nat. Defence Coll., 1974-75; Head of Science and Technology Dept, FCO, 1975-76. *Recreations:* walking, gardening, golf. *Address:* 16 Burntwood Road, Sevenoaks, Kent. *T:* Sevenoaks 452774.

CROOK, Brig. Paul Edwin, CBE 1965 (OBE 1946); DSO 1957; *b* 19 April 1915; *s* of late Herbert Crook and Christine Crook, Lyme Regis; *m* 1st, 1944, Joan (marr. diss. 1967), *d* of late William Lewis; one *d*; 2nd, 1967, Betty, *d* of late John William Wyles. *Educ:* Uppingham Sch.; Emmanuel Coll., Cambridge. BA 1936, MA 1956. Commnd into QORWK Regt, 1935; served: India and Palestine, 1937-39; War of 1939-45, Africa, NW Europe, Burma; Chief Civil Affairs Officer (Col), Netherlands East Indies, 1946; comd 3rd Bn The Parachute Regt, 1954-57; Suez Ops, 1956; comd Army Airborne Trng and Develt Centre, 1959-62; Comdr and Chief of Staff, Jamaica Defence Force, 1962-65; Security Ops Advisor to High Comr for Aden and S Arabia, 1965-67; Comdr, Rhine Area, 1969-70. Col, 1959; Brig., 1963; retired 1971. ADC to The Queen, 1965. Hon. Col, 1974-79, Dep. Hon. Col, 1979-, 16 Lincoln Co. Parachute Regt (VR). Bronze Star (US), 1945. *Recreations:* cricket, golf, jazz. *Address:* Frieston House, Caythorpe, Grantham, Lincs NG32 3DA. *T:* Loveden 72060. *Clubs:* Naval and Military, MCC; Jamaica (W Indies).

CROOKENDEN, Maj.-Gen. George Wayet Derek; Fellow and Senior Bursar, Peterhouse, Cambridge, since 1975; *b* 11 Dec. 1920; *o s* of late Lt-Col John Crookenden and Iris Margherita Gay; *m* 1948, Elizabeth Mary Angela Bourke; one *s* one *d. Educ:* Winchester Coll.; Christ Church, Oxford. Commnd Royal Artillery, 1941. GSO1, SHAPE, 1961-62; CO, 19 Field Regt, RA, 1962-64; Comdr, 7 Artillery Bde, 1964-67; Exercise Controller, CICC (West), 1969-71; Chief, British Commanders-in-Chief Liaison Mission, 1971-72; C of S, Contingencies Planning, SHAPE, 1972-75. Col Comdt, RA, 1977-82. *Address:* c/o Lloyds Bank Ltd, 95-97 Regent Street, Cambridge CB2 1BQ. *Club:* Army and Navy.

CROOKENDEN, Lt.-Gen. Sir Napier, KCB 1970 (CB 1966); DSO 1945; OBE 1954; DL; Lieutenant, HM Tower of London, 1975-81; *b* 31 Aug. 1915; 2nd *s* of late Col Arthur Crookenden, CBE, DSO; *m* 1948, Patricia Nassau, *d* of 2nd Baron Kindersley, CBE, MC, and of Nancy Farnsworth, *d* of Dr Geoffrey Boyd; two *s* two *d. Educ:* Wellington Coll.; RMC, Sandhurst. Commissioned, Cheshire Regt, 1935; Bde Major, 6th Airlanding Bde, 1943-44; CO, 9th Bn, The Parachute Regt, 1944-46; GSO1 (Plans) to Dir of Ops, Malaya, 1952-54; Comdr, 16th Parachute Bde, 1960-61; idc 1962; Dir, Land/Air Warfare MoD (Army Dept), 1964-66; Commandant, RMCS, Shrivenham, 1967-69; GOC-in-C, Western Comd, 1969-72. Col, The Cheshire Regt, 1969-71; Col Comdt, The Prince of Wales Div., 1971-74. Director: SE Regional Bd, Lloyds Bank Ltd, 1973-; Flextech Ltd, 1978-. A Trustee, Imperial War Museum, 1973-. Chm., SS&AFA, 1974-; a Vice-Pres., RUSI, 1978-. DL Kent, 1979. *Publications:* Dropzone Normandy, 1976; Airborne at War, 1978; Battle of the Bulge 1944, 1980. *Address:* Sissinghurst Place, Cranbrook, Kent TN17 2JP. *T:* Cranbrook 712863. *Clubs:* Army and Navy; Ski Club of Great Britain.

CROOKS, Very Rev. John Robert Megaw; Dean of Armagh and Keeper of the Library, since 1979; *b* 9 July 1914; *s* of Canon the Rev. Louis Warden Crooks, OBE, MA, and Maria Kathleen Megaw; *m* 1941, Elizabeth Catherine Vance; two *s. Educ:* Campbell College, Belfast; Trinity College Dublin (MA). Deacon, 1938; priest, 1939; Curate Assistant, St Peter's, Dublin, 1938-43; Hon. Vicar Choral, St Patrick's Cathedral, Dublin, 1939-43; Catechist, High School, Dublin, 1939-43; Curate Assistant, Leighlin, 1943-44; Incumbent, Killylea, Dio. Armagh, 1944-56; Vicar Choral, St Patrick's Cathedral, 1956-73; Diocesan Sec., 1963-79; Hon. Clerical Sec., General Synod, 1970-; Prebendary of Ballymore, 1971, of Mullabrack 1972; Archdeacon of Armagh, 1973-79. *Recreation:* golf. *Address:* 44 Abbey Street, Armagh. *T:* 522540. *Club:* University (Dublin).

CROOKS, Air Vice-Marshal Lewis M.; *see* Mackenzie Crooks.

CROOKS, Very Rev. Samuel Bennett, OBE 1981; TD 1964; SCF 1963; Dean of Belfast since 1970; *b* 20 Jan. 1920; 3rd *s* of Rev. S. B. Crooks, Rector of St Stephen's, Belfast; *m* 1945, Isabel Anne (*née* Kennedy), Belfast; one *s* one *d. Educ:* Down High Sch., Downpatrick, Co. Down; Trinity Coll. Dublin. BA 1943, MA 1947. Dean's Vicar, 1943-47, Vicar Choral, 1947-49, Minor Canon, 1952-61, Belfast Cathedral. Rector of St John's, Orangefield, Belfast, 1949-63; Rural Dean of Hillsborough, 1953-63; Rector of Lurgan, 1963-70; Archdeacon of Dromore, 1964-70. Chaplain to the Houses of Parliament, 1970-74. ChStJ 1976. *Address:* The Deanery, 5 Deramore Drive, Belfast BT9 5JQ. *T:* Belfast 660980.

CROOM, Sir John (Halliday), Kt 1975; TD 1946; FRCP, FRCPE; Chairman, Executive Committee, St Columba's Hospice (Vice-Chairman, Board of Management); *b* 2 July 1909; *s* of David Halliday Croom and Eleanor Addey Blair Cunynghame; *m* 1940, Enid Valerie Samuel, actress (known as Valerie Tudor); one *s* one *d. Educ:* Trinity Coll., Glenalmond; Gonville and Caius Coll., Cambridge; Univ. of Edinburgh. BA Cantab, MB, ChB Edin.; FRCPE 1940 (MRCPE 1936), FRCP 1972, FFCM 1972. Served War, RAMC (Lt-Col), France, ME, Malta, Italy, 1939-45 (despatches). Consultant Phys.: Royal Infirmary, Edinburgh, 1946-74; Chalmers Hosp., Edin., 1960-66. Royal Coll. of Phys., Edin.: Sec., Councillor and Vice-Pres., 1950-70; Pres., 1970-73. Principal MO, Standard Life Ass. Co., 1946-; Med. Adviser: Royal Bank of Scotland, 1965-; Northern Lighthouse Bd, 1952-; Hon. Cons. Phys. to Army in Scotland, 1970-75. Chairman: Scottish Cttee of

Action on Smoking and Health, 1972-77; Scientific Adv. Gp, 1975-78, and Cancer Programme Planning Gp, 1976-79, of Planning Council, Scotland; Scottish Health Services Scientific Council, 1972-75; Scottish Council for Postgrad. Medical Education, 1974-79; Edinburgh Crematorium Bd, 1972-80. Has served on numerous NHS cttees. Hon. FRACP 1972; Hon. FACP 1973. *Publications:* several articles in sci. jls. *Recreations:* racing, fishing, golf. *Address:* 18 Succoth Avenue, Edinburgh EH12 6BU. *T:* 031-337 2033. *Clubs:* Army and Navy; New (Edinburgh), Hon. Company of Edinburgh Golfers.

CROOM-JOHNSON, Hon. Sir David Powell, Kt 1971; DSC 1944; VRD 1953; **Hon. Mr Justice Croom-Johnson;** Judge of Queen's Bench Division, High Court of Justice, since 1971; *b* 28 Nov. 1914; 3rd *s* of late Hon. Sir Reginald Powell Croom-Johnson, sometime a Judge of the High Court, and late Lady (Ruby) Croom-Johnson; *m* 1940, Barbara Douglas, *y d* of late Erskine Douglas Warren, Toronto; one *d. Educ:* The Hall, Hampstead; Stowe Sch.; Trinity Hall, Cambridge (MA). RNVR (London Div.) 1936-53; served with Royal Navy, 1939-46; Lt-Comdr RNR (retired). Called to Bar, Gray's Inn, 1938, Master of the Bench, 1964, Treasurer, 1981-; Western Circuit. QC 1958; Recorder of Winchester, 1962-71; Judge of Courts of Appeal, Jersey and Guernsey, 1966-71. Member: Gen. Council of the Bar, 1958-62; Senate of Inns of Court, 1966-70. Vice-Chm., Home Office Cttee on Mentally Abnormal Offenders, 1972-75; Chm., Crown Agents Tribunal, 1978-82. Mem., Council, Oakdene Sch., 1956-79; Chm., Knightsbridge Assoc., 1965-71. *Recreations:* books, music. *Address:* Royal Courts of Justice, WC2. *Club:* Garrick.
See also H. P. Croom-Johnson.

CROOM-JOHNSON, Henry Powell, CMG 1964; CBE 1954 (OBE 1944); TD 1948; *b* 15 Dec. 1910; *e s* of late Hon. Sir Reginald Croom-Johnson, sometime Judge of High Court, and of late Lady (Ruby) Croom-Johnson; *m* 1947, Jane, *er d* of late Archibald George Mandry; two *s. Educ:* Stowe Sch.; Trinity Hall, Cambridge. Asst Master, Bedford Sch., 1932-34. Joined staff of British Council, 1935. Served with Queen's Westminsters and King's Royal Rifle Corps, 1939-46 (staff Sicily, Italy, Greece; Lt-Col). Rejoined British Council, 1946: Controller Finance Div., 1951; Controller European Div., 1956; Representative in India, 1957-64; Controller, Overseas Div. B, 1964; Asst Dir-Gen., 1966-72, retired 1973. *Recreations:* climbing, books, music. *Address:* 3a Ravenscourt Square, W6. *T:* 01-748 3677; The Cottage, Hillesden, Buckingham. *T:* Steeple Claydon 391. *Club:* Savile.
See also Sir D. P. Croom-Johnson.

CROOME, (John) Lewis, CMG 1957; *b* 10 June 1907; *s* of John and Caroline Croome; *m* 1st, 1931, Honoria Renée Minturn (*née* Scott; as Honor Croome, Editorial Staff of The Economist) (*d* 1960); four *s* one *d* (and one *s* decd); 2nd, 1961, Pamela Siola, *o d* of Lt-Col Tyrrel Hawker, Hurstbourne Priors, Hants; one *s. Educ:* Henry Thornton Sch., Clapham; London Sch. of Economics. Imperial Economic Cttee, 1931-39; Ministry of Food, 1939-48; Deputy (later Head), British Food Mission, Ottawa, 1942-46; HM Treasury (Central Economic Planning Staff), 1948-51; Min. of Food, 1951-54; UK Delegation to OEEC, Paris, 1954-57; Ministry of Agriculture, Fisheries and Food, 1957-58; Chief Overseas Relations Officer, UKAEA, 1958-72, retired. *Recreations:* painting, gardening. *Address:* Pearmain, Ruxley, Claygate, Surrey. *T:* Esher 62597.

CROSBIE, Hon. John Carnell; PC (Canada); MP (PC) St John's West, Newfoundland, since 1976; *b* 30 Jan. 1931; *s* of Chesley Arthur Crosbie and Jessie Carnell; *m* 1952, Jane Furneaux; two *s* one *d. Educ:* Bishop Field Coll., St John's, Nfld; St Andrew's Coll., Aurora, Ont.; Queen's Univ., Kingston, Ont. (Pol. Sc. and Econs); Dalhousie Univ., Halifax, NS (Law); LSE, London, Eng. Joined Newfoundland Law Soc. and Newfoundland Bar; entered law practice, St John's, 1957; Mem. City Council, St John's, 1965; Dep. Mayor, 1966; Minister of Municipal Affairs and Housing, Province of Newfoundland, (Lib. Admin), July 1966; MHA, Prov. of Newfoundland, Sept. 1966; Minister of Health, 1967; resigned from Govt, 1968; re-elected Member for St John's West (Progressive Conservative), Provincial election, 1971; Minister of Finance, Pres. of Treasury Bd and Minister of Econ. Develt, 1972-74; Minister of Fisheries, Min. for Intergovtl Affairs and Govt House Leader, 1974-75; Minister of Mines and Energy and Minister for Intergovtl Affairs, 1975-76; resigned from Newfoundland Govt, Sept. 1976. Elected to House of Commons for St John's West, Oct. 1976; re-elected 1979 and 1980; Chm. of Progressive Conservative Caucus Cttee on Energy, 1977; PC parly critic for Industry, Trade and Commerce, 1977-79; Minister of Finance, 1979-80; Party Finance Critic, 1980-. *Address:* 16 Circular Road, St John's, Newfoundland; Room 531C, House of Commons, Ottawa, Ontario.

CROSBIE, William, RSA 1973; RGI 1977; artist; *b* Hankow, China, 31 Jan. 1915; *s* of Archibald Shearer Crosbie, marine engineer, and Mary Edgar, both Scottish; *m* 1st, 1944, M. G. McPhail (decd); one *d* (and one *d* decd); 2nd, 1975, Margaret Anne Roger. *Educ:* Chinese Tutor; Renfrew primary sch.; Glasgow Academy; Glasgow Sch. of Art, Glasgow Univ. (4 yrs under Forrester Wilson). Haldane Travelling Schol., 1935, for 3 yr period of study in British Schs in Athens, Rome and Paris (Beaux Arts); studied history and theory of techniques, in Beaux Arts and Sorbonne, and finally took a post-grad. qualif. in these (continues to acquire craftsmanship); passed into studio of Fernand Leger, Paris, and remained until war declared. Served War of 1939-45: ambulance service, WVS driving pool, and at sea. Has exhibited, on average, every two yrs, 1946-; principally one-man exhibns: Glasgow, Edinburgh, London, etc; also in USA, Brussels, Hamburg, etc. *Works in:*

Kelvingrove Galls, Glasgow; Scottish provincial galls; Edinburgh City Arts Centre (mural), 1980; Scottish Gall. of Modern Art, 1980; Sydney State Gall., Australia; Wellington, NZ; Royal collection, UK, etc; also in many private collections. *Recreation:* sailing. *Address:* Studio, 12 Ruskin Lane, Glasgow G12 8EA. *T:* 041-334 4573; Rushes House, 10 Winchester Road, Petersfield, Hants GU32 3BY. *Clubs:* Glasgow Art; Royal Northern and Clyde Yacht (Rhu).

CROSBY, John Michael, MVO 1976; HM Diplomatic Service; Counsellor and Deputy High Commissioner, Dar es Salaam, since 1981; *b* 2 Aug. 1940; *s* of Rev. B. Crosby and Norah Crosby (*née* Copeland); *m* 1963, Mary Collinge Smethurst; one *s* one *d. Educ:* Kingswood Sch., Bath; Magdalene Coll., Cambridge (MA). Social work in North Kensington and for SCM in Schools, 1962-65; entered Diplomatic Service, 1965; Third, later Second, Secretary, Addis Ababa, 1966-70; Second, later First, Secretary, FCO, 1970-73; seconded to Cabinet Office, 1973; First Secretary and Head of Chancery: Luxembourg, 1973-76; Mexico City, 1977-79; First Secretary, FCO, 1979-81. *Recreations:* sport, history, travel, good food. *Address:* c/o Foreign and Commonwealth Office, SW1A 2AH. *Club:* United Oxford & Cambridge University.

CROSBY, Theo, ARA 1982; RIBA, FSIAD; Partner, Pentagram Design, since 1972; *b* 3 April 1925; *s* of N. J. Crosby and N. J. A. Goosen; *m* 1960, Finella Anne Buchanan; one *s* one *d. Educ:* Univ. of the Witwatersrand (BArch 1947). RIBA 1948; FSIAD 1964. Technical Editor, Architectural Design, 1953-62; now engaged in private architectural practice in exhibns, interiors and conservation. Mem., Berlin Acad., 1977-. Triennale of Milan Gran Premio, 1964; 2 Architectural Heritage Year Awards, 1973. *Publications:* Architecture: City Sense, 1965; The Necessary Monument, 1970; How to Play the Environment Game, 1973. *Recreation:* art. *Address:* Tower 3, Whitehall Court, SW1A 2EL. *T:* 01-930 0730 and 01-402 5511.

CROSFIELD, Very Rev. George Philip Chorley; Provost of St Mary's Cathedral, Edinburgh, since 1970; *b* 9 Sept. 1924; *s* of James Chorley Crosfield and Marjorie Louise Crosfield; *m* 1956, Susan Mary Jullion (*née* Martin); one *s* two *d. Educ:* George Watson's Coll., Edinburgh; Selwyn Coll., Cambridge. Royal Artillery, 1942-46 (Captain). Priest, 1952; Asst Curate: St David's, Pilton, Edinburgh, 1951-53; St Andrew's, St Andrews, 1953-55; Rector, St Cuthbert's, Hawick, 1955-60; Chaplain, Gordonstoun School, 1960-68; subseq. Canon and Vice Provost, St Mary's Cathedral, Edinburgh. *Recreations:* walking, reading, carpentry. *Address:* 8 Lansdowne Crescent, Edinburgh, EH12 5EQ. *T:* 031-225 2978.

CROSS, family name of Viscount Cross and Baron Cross of Chelsea.

CROSS, 3rd Viscount, *cr* 1886; Assheton Henry Cross; late Lieut Scots Guards; *b* 7 May 1920; *e s* of 2nd Viscount and Maud Evelyn (who *m* 2nd, 1944, Guy Hope Coldwell (*d* 1948), Stoke Lodge, Ludlow, Salop; she *d* 1976), *d* of late Maj.-Gen. Inigo Jones, CVO, CB, Kelston Park, Bath; *S* father, 1932; *m* 1952, Patricia Mary (marr. diss., 1957; she *m* 1960, Comdr G. H. H. Culme-Seymour), *e d* of E. P. Hewetson, JP, The Craig, Windermere, Westmorland; two *d* ; *m* 1972, Mrs Victoria Webb (marr. diss. 1977). *Educ:* Shrewsbury; Magdalene Coll., Cambridge. *Heir:* none. *Club:* Cavalry and Guards.

CROSS OF CHELSEA, Baron *cr* 1971 (Life Peer), of the Royal Borough of Kensington and Chelsea; (Arthur) Geoffrey (Neale) Cross, PC 1969; Kt 1960; a Lord of Appeal in Ordinary, 1971-75; Chairman, Appeals Committee, Takeover Panel, 1976-81; *b* 1 Dec. 1904; *e s* of late Arthur George Cross and Mary Elizabeth Dalton; *m* 1952, Joan, *d* of late Major Theodore Eardley Wilmot, DSO, and *widow* of Thomas Walton Davies; one *d. Educ:* Westminster; Trinity College, Cambridge. Craven Scholar, 1925. Fellow of Trinity College, 1927-31, Hon. Fellow, 1972; called to the Bar, Middle Temple, 1930, Master of the Bench, 1958, Reader, 1971; QC 1949. Chancellor of the County Palatine of Durham, 1959. A Judge of the High Court of Justice, Chancery Div., 1960-69; a Lord Justice of Appeal, 1969-71. *Publications:* Epirus, 1932; (with G. R. Y. Radcliffe) The English Legal System (6th edn 1977). *Address:* The Bridge House, Leintwardine, Craven Arms, Shropshire. *T:* Leintwardine 205.

CROSS, Alexander Galbraith, MA, MD, FRCS; Ophthalmic Surgeon; lately Dean of the Medical School, St Mary's Hospital; Civilian Consultant in Ophthalmology, RN, 1946-76; Consultant Surgeon, Moorfields Eye Hospital, 1947-73; Consultant Ophthalmic Surgeon, St Mary's Hospital, 1946-73; Consultant Ophthalmic Surgeon, Royal National Throat, Nose, and Ear Hospital, 1954-73; Ophthalmic Surgeon, St Dunstan's, since 1946; Hon. Consultant Ophthalmologist, Royal National Institute for the Blind, 1968-82; *b* 29 March 1908; *er s* of late Walter Galbraith Cross and Mary Stewart Cross, Wimbledon; *m* 1939, Eileen Longman, twin *d* of late Dr H. B. Corry, Liss, Hants; one *d. Educ:* King's Coll. Sch.; Gonville and Caius Coll., Cambridge; St Mary's Hosp., London (University Scholar). Meadows Prize, 1932, Broadbent and Agnes Cope Prizes, 1933, Cheadle Gold Medallist, 1933, St Mary's Hospital. House Phys. and House Surg., St Mary's, 1933-35; House Surg. and Sen. Res. Officer, Moorfields Eye Hosp., 1937-39; Opthalmic Surgeon: West Middlesex Hosp., 1938-48; Tite Street Children's Hosp., 1939-48; Princess Beatrice Hosp., 1939-47; Royal Masonic Hosp., 1961-71. Wing Comdr, RAFVR, 1941-46 and Adviser in Ophthalmology, South-East Asia Air Forces. Examiner in Fellowship and in Diploma of Ophthalmology

for RCS and in Ophthalmology for Univ. of Bristol; Recognised Teacher of Ophthalmology, University of London. Co-opted Mem. Council RCS, 1963-68. Mem. Bd of Governors: St Mary's Hosp., 1951-60; Moorfields Eye Hosp., 1962-65 and 1968-75. Mem. Paddington Group Hosp. Management Cttee, 1952-60. Pres. Ophthalmological Soc. of UK, 1975-77 (Sec. 1949-51; Vice-Pres., 1963-66); Member: RSocMed (Sec., Ophthalmic Section, 1951; Vice-Pres., 1960; Hon. Mem. 1979); BMA (Sec., Ophthalmic Section, 1948; Vice-Pres., 1957). Chm., Ophthalmic Gp Cttee, 1963-75; Mem. Council, Faculty of Ophthalmologists, 1963-72, Vice-Pres. 1964, Pres. 1968-71; Dean, Inst. of Ophthalmology, 1967-75 (Deputy Dean, 1966-67); Mem., Orthoptists Bd, 1970, Vice-Chm. 1971, Chm. 1972-75. *Publications:* 12th Edn, May and Worth's Diseases of the Eye; articles in British Jl of Ophthalmology, the Lancet, and other med. jls, dealing with ophthalmology. *Recreations:* gardening, lawn tennis, golf, squash racquets. *Address:* 4 Cottenham Park Road, Wimbledon, SW20. *T:* 01-946 3491.

CROSS, Alexander Urquhart, TD 1959; JP; Lord Provost of Perth, 1972-75; *b* 24 Dec. 1906; *m* 1936; one *s* one *d. Educ:* Univ. of Glasgow (MA). Owner of private school, 1931-70 (except war years, 1939-45). JP 1972, DL 1972-75, Hon. Sheriff, 1974-, Perth. CStJ 1981. *Address:* 6 Craigie Road, Perth. *T:* Perth 25013.

CROSS, Dr Barry Albert, CBE 1981; FRS 1975; Director, ARC Institute of Animal Physiology, since 1974; *b* 17 March 1925; *s* of Hubert Charles and Elsie May Cross; *m* 1949, Audrey Lilian Crow; one *s* two *d. Educ:* Reigate Grammar Sch.; Royal Veterinary Coll. London, MRCVS, BSc (Vet Sci); St John's Coll. Cambridge, BA Hons, MA, PhD. ScD 1964. ICI Research Fellow, Physiological Lab., Cambridge, 1949-51, Gedge Prize 1952; Demonstrator, Zoological Lab., Cambridge, 1951-55; Lectr, 1955-58; Rockefeller Fellow at UCLA, 1957-58; Lectr, Dept. of Anatomy, Cambridge 1958-67; Supervisor in Physiology at St John's Coll., 1955-67; Corpus Christi College, Cambridge: Fellow, 1962-67, 1974-; Tutor for Advanced Students, 1964-67; Warden of Leckhampton, 1975-80; WHO Consultant, Geneva 1964; Prof. and Head of Dept of Anatomy, Univ. of Bristol, 1967-74, and Chm., Sch. of Preclinical Studies, 1969-73. Lectures: Share Jones, RCVS, 1967; Charnock Bradley, Edinburgh Univ., 1968; Glaxo, 1975; Entwhistle, Cambridge, 1976; McFadyean, London Univ., 1976; Wilmott, 1978, Long Fox, 1980, Bristol Univ. Member: Council, Anatomical Soc., 1968-73 (Vice Pres. 1973-74); Council, Assoc. for Study of Animal Behaviour, 1959-62, 1973-75 (Asst Editor 1952-58); Cttee, Soc. for Study of Fertility, 1961-65 (Mem. Editorial Bd 1962-); Cttee, Physiological Soc., 1971-75 (Chm. 1974-75); Internat. Soc. for Neuroendocrinology (Vice-Pres., 1972-75, Pres. 1976-80); Mem. Farm Animals Welfare Advr. Cttee, MAFF, 1975-78. FIBiol 1975; FRVC 1979. Chevalier, Order of Dannebrog, 1968; Comdr d'honneur de l'Ordre du Bontemps de Médoc et des Graves, 1973. *Publications:* sci. papers on neuroendocrine topics in various biol. jls. *Address:* 6 Babraham Road, Cambridge. *Club:* Athenæum.

CROSS, Beverley; playwright; *b* 13 April 1931; *s* of George Cross, theatrical manager, and Eileen Williams, actress; *m* 1st, 1955, Elizabeth Clunies-Ross (marr. diss.); two *d* ; 2nd, 1965, Gayden Collins (marr. diss.); one *s* ; 3rd, 1975, Maggie Smith, *qv. Educ:* Nautical Coll., Pangbourne; Balliol Coll., Oxford. Mem. Shakespeare Memorial Theatre Company, 1954-56; then began writing plays. One More River, Duke of York's, 1959; Strip the Willow, Arts, Cambridge, 1960 (Arts Council Drama Award for both, 1960); The Singing Dolphin, Oxford, 1960; The Three Cavaliers, Birmingham Rep., 1960; Belle, or The Ballad of Dr Crippen, Strand, 1961; Boeing-Boeing, Apollo, 1962; Wanted On Voyage, Marlowe, Canterbury, 1962; Half A Sixpence, Cambridge, London, 1963; Jorrocks, New, London, 1966; The Owl on the Battlements, Nottingham, 1971; Catherine Howard, York, 1972; The Great Society, Mermaid, 1974; Hans Andersen, Palladium, 1974; Happy Birthday, Apollo, 1979; Haworth, Birmingham Rep., 1981. *Libretti:* The Mines of Sulphur, Sadler's Wells, 1965; All the King's Men, 1969; Victory, Covent Garden, 1970; The Rising of the Moon, Glyndebourne, 1970; A Capital Transfer, British Council, London, 1981. *Screen plays of:* Jason and the Argonauts, 1962; The Long Ships, 1963; Genghis Khan, 1965; Half A Sixpence, 1966; (with Carlo Lizzani) Mussolini: Ultimo Atto, 1973; Sinbad and the Eye of the Tiger, 1977; The Clash of the Titans, 1981. *Television plays:* The Nightwalkers, 1960; The Dark Pits of War, 1960; Catherine Howard, 1969; March on, Boys!, 1975; A Bill of Mortality, 1975. *Directed:* Boeing-Boeing, Sydney, 1964; The Platinum Cat, Wyndham's, 1965. *Publications:* Mars in Capricorn, 1955; The Nightwalkers, 1956; Plays For Children, 1960. *Address:* c/o Curtis Brown Ltd, 1 Craven Hill, W2 3EW. *T:* 01-262 1011.

CROSS, Clifford Thomas, CB 1977; Commissioner, Customs and Excise, 1970-79; *b* 1 April 1920; *o s* of late Arthur and Helena Cross; *m* 1942, Ida Adelaide Barker; one *s* two *d. Educ:* Latymer Upper Sch., Hammersmith; Univ. of London (LLB). Joined Inland Revenue, 1939; Customs and Excise, 1946; Asst Sec. 1959; Comr 1970. *Recreations:* squash rackets, bonsai culture, watching television, etc. *Address:* Monkton Combe, 10 Drake Road, Westcliff-on-Sea, Essex. *T:* 01-626 1515.

CROSS, Rt. Rev. David Stewart; *see* Blackburn, Bishop of.

CROSS, Sir Eugene, Kt 1979; MBE 1954; MM 1918; retired steel works manager; *b* 13 Sept. 1896; *s* of Eugene and Hannah Cross; *m* 1923, Ada M. Caswell; one *s. Educ:* local school, Ebbw Vale. Served War of 1914-18, Fifth

Army, 1st Welsh Field Ambulance (Gallipoli, 101st Bridge, France). Iron and Steel Works Manager, 1936, until retirement. (The first Hot Strip and Cold Reduction Mills in the world (outside USA) built at Ebbw Vale commenced rolling Oct. 1939). Elected Mem. Ebbw Vale Hospital Cttee, 1926 (during National Strike); Trustee, Chm. of the Trusteeship, and Chm. Hosp. Bd and Medical Fund, Ebbw Vale, 1934; Mem. Wales Hosp. Bd, 1949, for 19 years (Vice-Chm.). JP Ebbw Vale 1941, served 27 years, Chm. 18 years. *Recreations:* Rugby, cricket, etc. *Address:* Ty Coed, Hospital Drive, Ebbw Vale, Gwent NP3 6PW.

CROSS, Hannah Margaret, (Mrs E. G. Wright); barrister-at-law; *b* 25 April 1908; *o d* of late F. J. K. Cross and Eleanor Mary Cross (*née* Phillimore); *m* 1936, Edmund Gordon Wright, Barrister-at-Law (*d* 1971); one *s* one *d. Educ:* Downe House Sch.; St Hilda's Coll., Oxford. BA 1929. Called to Bar, Lincoln's Inn, 1931; first woman Mem. of Gen. Council of Bar, 1938–45; Civil Defence, 1939–45. *Address:* The Quay House, Sidlesham, near Chichester, West Sussex. *T:* Sidlesham 258.

CROSS, James Richard, (Jasper), CMG 1971; Under-Secretary, Principal Establishment Officer, Department of Energy, 1978–80; *b* 29 Sept. 1921; *s* of J. P. Cross and Dinah Cross (*née* Hodgins); *m* 1945, Barbara Dagg; one *d. Educ:* King's Hosp., Dublin; Trin. Coll., Dublin. Scholar, First Cl. Moderatorship Economics and Polit. Science. RE (Lieut). Asst Principal, Bd of Trade, 1947; Private Sec. to Parly Sec., 1947–49; Principal, 1950; Trade Commissioner: New Delhi, 1953–56; Halifax, 1957–60; Winnipeg, 1960–62; Asst Sec., 1962; Sen. Trade Comr, Kuala Lumpur, 1962–66; Bd of Trade, 1966–67; Under Sec., 1968; Sen. British Trade Comr, Montreal, 1968–70 (kidnapped by terrorists and held for 59 days, Oct.–Dec. 1970); Under-Sec., Export Planning and Develt Div., DTI, 1971–73; Sec., British Overseas Trade Bd, 1972; Coal Div., DTI, later Dept of Energy, 1973–78. *Recreations:* theatre, bridge, the New Forest. *Address:* The Small House, Queen Katherine Road, Lymington, Hants.

CROSS, Joan, CBE 1951; opera singer; *b* Sept. 1900. *Educ:* St Paul's Girls' Sch. Principal soprano, Old Vic and Sadler's Wells, 1924–44; Dir of Opera, Sadler's Wells, 1941–44; subsequently Principal, National Sch. of Opera (Ltd), Morley Coll., London, resigned. *Address:* 4 The Timberyard, Great Glemham, Saxmundham, Suffolk.

CROSS, Air Chief Marshal Sir Kenneth (Brian Boyd), KCB 1959 (CB 1954); CBE 1945; DSO 1943; DFC 1940; *b* 4 Oct. 1911; *s* of Pembroke H. C. Cross and Jean Cross; *m* 1945, Brenda Megan, *d* of Wing-Comdr F. J. B. Powell; two *s* one *d. Educ:* Kingswood Sch., Bath. Pilot Officer, RAF, 1930; Flying Badge, 1931; 25 Fighter Sqdn, 1931; Flying Officer, 1932; Flying Instructor, No 5 FTS Sealand and Cambridge Univ. Air Sqdn, 1934; Flt Lt 1935; Sqdn Ldr 1938; commanded No 46 Fighter Sqdn UK, Norway, 1939–40; Wing Comdr 1940; posted Middle East, 1941; Actg Group Capt. 1941; Actg Air Commodore, 1943; Director Overseas Operations, Air Ministry, 1944; Imperial Defence Coll., 1946; reverted Group Capt., 1946; Group Capt. Operations HQ BAFO Germany, 1947; OC Eastern Sector Fighter Command, 1949; Dir of Weapons, Air Ministry, 1952; subs. Air Cdre, 1953; Dir of Ops, Air Defence, 1954–Dec. 1955; Air Vice-Marshal, 1956; AOC No 3 (Bomber) Group, 1956–59; Air Marshal, 1961; AOC-in-C, Bomber Comd, 1959–63; Air Chief Marshal, 1965; AOC-in-C, Transport Comd, 1963–66, retd, 1967. Director: Suffolk Branch, 1968, London Branch, 1974, British Red Cross Soc. Norwegian War Cross, 1941; USA Legion of Merit, 1944; French Legion of Honour, 1944; French Croix de Guerre, 1944; Dutch Order of Orange Nassau, 1945. *Recreations:* Rugby football and golf (colours RAF). *Address:* 12 Callow Street, Chelsea, SW3. *Club:* Royal Air Force.

CROSS, Prof. Kenneth William, MB, DSc, FRCP; Professor of Physiology, London Hospital Medical College, 1960–81, now Emeritus; Hon. Physiologist to The London Hospital; *b* 26 March 1916; *s* of late George Cross, Ealing; *m* 1942, Joyce M. Wilson (*née* Lack, *d* 1970); one step *d* ; *m* 1970, Dr Sheila R. Lewis. *Educ:* St Paul's Sch.; St Mary's Hospital Medical Sch. Qualified, 1940; House appointments in St Mary's Hospital Sector; graded Physician EMS Amersham Emergency Hosp. 1945; Friends' Ambulance Unit, China, 1946–47. Lecturer in Physiology, 1947, Reader, 1952, St Mary's Hosp. *Publications:* contrib. to Journal of Physiology.

CROSS, Brig. Lionel Lesley, CBE 1950; *b* 7 June 1899; *yr s* of Charles Frederick Cross, FRS, and Edith, *d* of Maj.-Gen. Charles Stainforth, CB; *m* 1940, Rose Blanche Margaret (*d* 1976), *d* of Sir Robert Taylor, Kytes, Herts; no *c. Educ:* Wellington Coll.; RMA Woolwich. Commissioned RFA, 1918; France and Belgium, 1918. Adjutant Bucks and Berks Yeo. Artillery, 1925–29; retd 1929. Rejoined Army, 1939; Staff Capt. RA 1939; France and Belgium, 1940; Major 1941; Lieut-Col 1942; Asst Dir of Public Relations, War Office, 1942–46; Brig. 1946; Dep. Dir of Public Relations, War Office, 1946–50; Chief of Public Information, SHAPE, 1954–58 (Dep., 1951–54); retired, 1958. Sec., Commonwealth Press Union, 1959–70. *Recreations:* racing, bridge. *Address:* 15 Cedar House, Marloes Road, W8. *T:* 01-937 0112. *Club:* Army and Navy.

CROSS, Mrs Margaret Natalie; *see* Smith, Maggie.

CROSS, Prof. Robert Craigie, CBE 1972; MA Glasgow, MA Oxford; Regius Professor of Logic, 1953–78, Vice-Principal, 1974–77, University of Aberdeen; *b* 24 April 1911; *s* of Matthew Cross and Margaret Dickson; *m* 1943, Peggy Catherine Elizabeth Vernon; two *d. Educ:* Glasgow Univ.; Queen's Coll., Oxford. MA 1st Cl. Hons Classics, Glasgow, 1932; 1st Cl. Hons Classical Mods, Oxford, 1934; 1st Cl. Lit. Hum., Oxford, 1936. Fellow and Tutor in Philsophy, Jesus Coll., Oxford, 1938; served War, 1941–45, Navy and Admiralty; Senior Tutor, Jesus Coll., Oxford, 1948–53. Trustee, Scottish Hospital Endowments Research Trust, 1968–80; Mem., University Grants Cttee, 1965–74; Mem., North Eastern Regional Hospital Bd, 1958–65. *Publications:* (with A. D. Woozley) Plato's Republic: A Philosophical Commentary, 1964; contributions to learned jls. *Address:* Heatherlands, Ancrum, Roxburghshire. *T:* Ancrum 282.

CROSSE, Gordon; composer; *b* 1 Dec. 1937; *s* of Percy and Marie Crosse; *m* 1965, Elizabeth Bunch. *Educ:* Cheadle Hulme Sch.; St Edmund Hall, Oxford; Accad. di S Cecilia, Rome. Music Fellow, Essex Univ., 1969–74; Composer in residence, King's Coll., Cambridge, 1974–76; Vis. Lectr, Univ. of Calif at Santa Barbara, 1977–78. Hon. RAM, 1980. *Operas:* Purgatory, 1966; The Grace of Todd, 1967; The Story of Vasco, 1970; Potter Thompson, 1973; *ballets:* Playground, 1979; Wildboy, 1981; *other compositions:* Concerto da Camera, 1962; Meet My Folks, 1963; "Symphonies", 1964; Second Violin Concerto, 1970; Memories of Morning: Night, 1972; Ariadne, 1973; Symphony 2, 1975; Wildboy (clarinet concerto), Play Ground, 1977; Dreamsongs, 1978; Cello Concerto, 1979; String Quartet, 1980; Dreamcanon (chorus), 1981; much other orchestral, vocal and chamber music. *Address:* Brant's Cottage, Wenhaston, Halesworth, Suffolk.

CROSSLAND, Anthony, FRCO; Organist and Master of the Choristers, Wells Cathedral, since 1971; *b* 4 Aug. 1931; *s* of Ernest Thomas and Frances Elizabeth Crossland; *m* 1960, Barbara Helen Pullar-Strecker; one *s* two *d. Educ:* Christ Church, Oxford. MA, BMus (Oxon), FRCO (CHM), ARCM. Asst Organist: Christ Church Cathedral, Oxford, 1957–61; Wells Cathedral, 1961–71. *Recreations:* music, reading, photography. *Address:* 15 Vicars' Close, Wells, Somerset. *T:* Wells (Somerset) 73526.

CROSSLAND, Prof. Bernard, CBE 1980; MSc (London); PhD (Bristol); DSc (Nottingham); FRS 1979; FEng 1979; MRIA; FIMechE; FIProdE; FIW; Research Professor, Department of Mechanical and Industrial Engineering, The Queen's University, Belfast, since 1982 (Professor and Head of Department, 1959–82; Pro-Vice-Chancellor, 1978–82); *b* 20 Oct. 1923; *s* of R. F. Crossland and K. M. Rudduck; *m* 1946, Audrey Elliott Birks; two *d. Educ:* Simon Langton's, Canterbury. Apprentice, Rolls Royce Ltd, 1940–41; Nottingham Univ., 1941–43; Technical Asst, Rolls Royce, 1943–45; Asst Lectr, Lectr and then Senior Lectr in Mechanical Engineering, Univ. of Bristol, 1946–59. Mem., ARC, 1981–. Chm., Youth Careers Guidance Cttee, N Ireland, 1975–79, 1979–81; Member: NI Training Council, 1964–76, 1977–81; NI Economic Council, 1981–; NI Manpower Adv. Cttee, 1981; NI Industrial Develt Bd, 1982–. Chm., Engineering Sciences Div., IMechE, 1980–; George Stephenson and Thomas Hawksley Medals, IMechE. *Publications:* An Introduction to the Mechanics of Machines, 1964; Explosive Welding and its Application, 1982; various papers on fatigue of metals and effect of very high fluid pressures on properties of materials; strength of thick-walled vessels, explosive welding, friction welding, and design. *Recreation:* walking. *Address:* Ashby Institute, Stranmillis Road, Belfast BT9 5AH; The Queen's University, Belfast BT7 1NN. *T:* Belfast 661111. *Club:* Athenæum.

CROSSLAND, Sir Leonard, Kt 1969; Chairman: Eaton Ltd (UK), since 1972; Ford Motor Co. Ltd, 1968–72; Energy Research and Development Ltd (formerly Sedgeminster Technical Developments Ltd), since 1974; *b* 2 March 1914; *s* of Joseph and Frances Crossland; *m* 1st, 1941, Rhona Marjorie Griffin; two *d* ; 2nd, 1963, Joan Brewer. *Educ:* Penistone Grammar Sch. Purchase Dept, Ford Motor Co. Ltd, 1937–39. Royal Army Service Corps, 1939–45. Ford Motor Co. Ltd: Purchase Dept. 1945–54; Chief Buyer, Tractor and Implement Dept, 1954–57; Chief Buyer, Car and Truck Dept, 1957–59; Asst Purchase Manager, 1959–60; Purchase Manager, 1960–62; Exec. Dir, Supply and Services, 1962–66; Dir, Manufacturing Staff and Services, 1966; Asst Man. Dir, 1966–67; Man. Dir, 1967; Dep. Chm., 1967; Chm., Autolite Motor Products Ltd; Director: Henry Ford & Son Ltd, Cork; Eaton Corp. (US), 1974–81. Farmer. *Recreations:* shooting, fishing, golf. *Address:* Abbotts Hall, Great Wigborough, Colchester, Essex. *T:* Peldon 456. *Clubs:* City Livery, Royal Automobile, British Racing Drivers'; American.

CROSSLAND, Prof. Ronald Arthur, FSA 1982; Professor of Greek, University of Sheffield, since 1958; *b* 31 Aug. 1920; *s* of late Ralph Crossland, BSc, and late Ethel Crossland (*née* Scattergood). *Educ:* Stanley Road Elementary Sch., Nottingham; Nottingham High Sch.; King's Coll., Cambridge. Major Scholar in Classics, King's Coll., Cambridge, 1939–41 and 1945–46. National Service in Royal Artillery, 1941–45. Henry Fellow, Berkeley Coll., Yale Univ., 1946–47; Instructor in Classics, Yale Univ., 1947–48; Senior Student of Treasury Cttee for Studentships in Foreign Languages and Cultures (for research in Hittite Philology and Linguistics), 1948–51; Hon. Lectr in Ancient History, University of Birmingham, 1950–51; Lecturer in Ancient History, King's Coll., University of Durham, Newcastle upon Tyne, 1951–58. Harris Fellow of King's Coll., Cambridge, 1952–56. Vis. Prof., Univ. Texas, 1962; Collitz Vis. Prof., Univ. Michigan, 1967. Pres., South Shields Archaeological and Historical Soc., 1976–77. *Publications:* (with A. Birchall) Bronze Age Migrations in the Aegean, 1973; chapter, Immigrants from the North, in Cambridge Ancient History, rev. edn, 1967; Teaching Classical Studies, 1976; articles in Trans Philological Soc., Archivum Linguisticum, Studia Balcanica, Past and Present. *Recreations:* music, travel.

Address: 103 Vernon Crescent, Ravenshead, Notts NG15 9BP. *T:* (private) Blidworth 5124; (office) Sheffield 78555 ext. 4603.

CROSSLEY, family name of **Baron Somerleyton.**

CROSSLEY, Sir Christopher John, 3rd Bt *cr* 1909; Lieutenant-Commander Royal Navy, retired; *b* 25 Sept. 1931; *s* of late Lt-Comdr Nigel Crossley, RN (*s* of late Eric Crossley, OBE, 2nd *s* of 1st Bt); *S* great uncle (Sir Kenneth Crossley, 2nd Bt), 1957; *m* 1959, Carolyne Louise (marr. diss. 1969), *d* of late L. Grey Sykes; two *s* ; *m* 1977, Lesley, *e d* of late Dr K. A. J. Chamberlain. *Educ:* Canford Sch. Entered Royal Navy, 1950. *Recreations:* royal tennis, squash. *Heir: s* Nicholas John Crossley, *b* 10 Dec. 1962. *Address:* PO Box 100, Heliopolis, Egypt.

CROSSLEY, Geoffrey Allan, CMG 1974; HM Diplomatic Service, retired; Director, External Relations, Continuing Education, European Institute of Business Administration, INSEAD, Fontainebleau; *b* 11 Nov. 1920; *s* of Thomas Crossley and Winifred Mary Crossley (*née* Ellis); *m* 1945, Aline Louise Farcy; two *s* one *d. Educ:* Penistone; abroad; Gonville and Caius Coll., Cambridge (Scholar). Served War of 1939-45: Min. of Supply, 1941-; Foreign Office, 1942-; in Algeria and France. Foreign Service, 1945-: Second Sec., Paris, 1945-48; FO, 1948-49; Alternate UK Deleg. on UN Balkans Commn, Greece, 1949-52; Dep. Regional Inf. Officer with Commissioner-Gen. for SE Asia, Singapore, 1952-55; FO, 1955-57; Consulate-Gen., Frankfurt, for Saar Transition from France to Germany, 1957-59; Political Office, NE Command, Cyprus (later in charge), 1959-61; Head of Chancery, Berne, 1961-65; on secondment to Min. of Overseas Development, as Head of W and N African Dept, 1965-67; Dep. High Comr, Lusaka, 1967-69; Counsellor, Oslo, 1969-73; Ambassador to Colombia, 1973-77; Envoy to the Holy See, 1978-80. *Recreations:* various. *Address:* INSEAD, 77305 Fontainebleau, Cedex, France.

CROSSLEY, Harry; DL; Chief Executive, Derbyshire County Council, 1974-79, retired; *b* 2 Sept. 1918; *s* of late Percy Crossley and Nellie McMinnies Crossley, Burnley, Lancs; *m* 1949, Pamela, *e d* of late Ald. E. A. C. Woodcock, Kettering, Northants; two *s. Educ:* Burnley Grammar Sch. Solicitor. LAM RTPI. War service, RA, attached Indian Army (Major), 1939-46. Private practice and local govt service as solicitor; Derbyshire CC: Dep. Clerk of Peace and of CC, 1960-69; Clerk of Peace and of CC, 1969-74. Clerk to Derbyshire Lieutenancy, 1969-79; Sec., Lord Chancellor's Adv. Cttee for Derbyshire, 1969-79. Clerk, Peak Park Planning Bd, 1969-74. DL Derbyshire, 1978. *Publications:* articles for legal and local govt jls. *Recreations:* golf, tennis, gardening. *Address:* Alpine, Bracken Lane, Holloway, Matlock DE4 5AS. *T:* Dethick 382.

CROSSLEY, Wing-Comdr Michael Nicholson, DSO 1940; OBE 1946; DFC; Fighter Command; farming in South Africa since 1955; *b* 29 May 1912; *s* of late Major E. Crossley, OBE; *m* 1957, Sylvia Heyder (*d* 1975); one *s* two *d* ; *m* 1977, Moyra Birkbeck, widow of Maj.-Gen. T. H. (John) Birkbeck. *Educ:* Eton Coll.; Munich. Commissioned in RAF, 1935. *Recreation:* golf. *Address:* Loughrigg, White River 1240, E Transvaal, S Africa. *Clubs:* Army and Navy; Rand (Johannesburg).

CROSSMAN, Sir (Douglas) Peter, Kt 1982; TD 1944; DL; Chairman, Huntingdon Steeplechases Ltd, since 1970; *b* 25 Sept. 1908; *s* of late Percy Crossman, Gt Bromley Hall, Colchester; *m* 1st, 1932, Monica, *d* of late C. F. R. Barnett; two *s* one *d* ; 2nd, 1939, Jean Margaret, *d* of late Douglas Crossman, Cokenach, Royston. *Educ:* Uppingham; Pembroke Coll., Cambridge. Commission Warwicks Yeomanry, 1934-45. Chairman: Mann Crossman Paulin Ltd, 1961-65; Watney Mann Ltd, 1965-70. President: Licensed Victuallers' Sch., 1958; Shire Horse Soc., 1958; Beer and Wine Trade Benev., 1960; Licensed Victuallers' Nat. Homes, 1963; Hunts Agricultural Soc., 1965; Chairman: Govs, Dame Alice Owen's Sch., 1951-65; Hunts Conservative Assoc., 1954-61; Eastern Area, Nat. Union of Conservative Party, 1965; Nat. Union of Conservative Party, 1969. Master, Brewers' Co., 1950. Chairman, Brewers' Soc., 1968, 1969. DL Huntingdonshire, 1958. Master: Essex and Suffolk Foxhounds, 1938-40; Cambridgeshire Foxhounds, 1947-49. *Recreations:* hunting, shooting, fishing, gardening. *Address:* Tetworth Hall, Sandy, Beds. *T:* Gamlingay 212. *Club:* Cavalry and Guards.

CROSTHWAIT, Timothy Leland, CMG 1964; MBE 1944; HM Diplomatic Service, retired; *b* 5 Aug. 1915; *s* of Lt-Col L. G. Crosthwait, Survey of India; *m* 1959, Anne Marjorie, *d* of Col T. M. M. Penney. *Educ:* Wellington Coll.; Peterhouse, Cambridge (MA). Appointed to Indian Civil Service, 1937; Asst Private Sec. to Viceroy, 1942-44; Air Min., 1948-55; Commonwealth Relations Office, 1955; British Deputy High Commissioner in Ceylon, 1957-61; Asst Sec., CRO, 1961-63; British High Commissioner, Zanzibar, 1963-64; British Deputy High Commissioner, Malta, 1965-66; British High Commissioner, Guyana, 1966-67; Ambassador, Malagasy Republic, 1970-75. *Address:* 39 Eaton Terrace, SW1. *T:* 01-730 9553. *Club:* United Oxford & Cambridge University.

CROSTHWAITE, Sir (Ponsonby) Moore, KCMG 1960 (CMG 1951); *b* 13 Aug. 1907; *o s* of late P. M. Crosthwaite, MICE, and late Agnes Alice, *y d* of J. H. Aitken, Falkirk, Stirlingshire. *Educ:* Rugby; CCC, Oxford. Laming Fellowship, Queen's Coll., 1931. Entered Diplomatic Service, 1932; has served in Bagdad, Moscow, Madrid, Athens and Foreign Office; Deputy UK Representative to United Nations, New York, 1952-58; Ambassador to the Lebanon, 1958-63; Ambassador to Sweden, 1963-66. *Recreations:* travel, the arts. *Address:* 17 Crescent Grove, SW4. *Club:* Athenæum.

CROUCH, David (Lance); MP (C) Canterbury since 1966; Director: David Crouch & Co. Ltd; Pfizer Ltd; Burson-Marsteller Ltd; Foster Crouch (Consultants) Ltd; *b* 23 June 1919; *s* of late Stanley Crouch and Rosalind Kate Crouch (*née* Croom); *m* 1947, Margaret Maplesden, *d* of Major Sydney Maplesden Noakes, DSO and Norah Parkyns Maplesden Noakes (*née* Buckland), Shorne, Kent; one *s* one *d. Educ:* University Coll. Sch. Served in City of London Yeomanry (TA), 1938-39; served War of 1939-45, Royal Artillery: Major 1943; attached RAF Staff (GSO2), 1944-45. Joined British Nylon Spinners Ltd, 1946; ICI Ltd, 1950; Dir of Publicity, Internat. Wool Secretariat, 1962-64. Formed own co., David Crouch & Co. Ltd, as international marketing and public relations consultants (Chairman, 1964-). Contested (C) West Leeds, 1959. Chairman: Anglo-Egyptian Party Gp; All-Party Gp for the Chemical Industry; All-Party Gp for Energy Studies; Member: Select Cttee for Nationalized Industries, 1966-74; Public Accounts Cttee, 1974-79. Trustee, Theatres Trust, 1977- (Dep. Chm., 1979-). Member: SE Thames RHA; Soc. of Chemical Industry; Council Univ. of Kent; Council, RSA, 1974- (Fellow, 1971). *Recreations:* cricket, tennis, golf. *Address:* 3 Tufton Court, Tufton Street, SW1; The Oast House, Fisher Street, Badlesmere, Faversham, Kent. *Club:* Athenæum.

CROUT, Dame Mabel, DBE 1965; JP; Alderman, London Borough of Greenwich, 1964-71; *b* 6 Jan. 1890. Member of Woolwich Borough Council, 1919-64 (Mayor, 1936-37); Mem. of London Borough of Greenwich, 1964-71. JP, London, 1920-. Mem. of London County Council, 1949-55. Freeman of Woolwich, 1959. *Address:* 17 Beulah Road, Tunbridge Wells, Kent.

CROWDEN, James Gee Pascoe, JP, DL; FRICS, FCIArb; Senior Partner, Grounds & Co., since 1974; *b* 14 Nov. 1927; *yr s* of late Lt-Col R. J. C. Crowden, MC, and late Mrs Crowden; *m* 1955, Kathleen Mary, widow of Captain F. A. Grounds and *d* of late Mr and Mrs J. W. Loughlin, Upwell; one *s. Educ:* Bedford Sch.; Pembroke Coll., Cambridge (MA). Chartered surveyor; FRICS 1959; FCIArb 1977. Commnd Royal Lincs Regt, 1947. Rowed in Oxford and Cambridge Boat Race, 1951 and 1952 (Pres., 1952); Captain, Great Britain VIII, European Championships, Macon, 1951 (Gold Medallists); also rowed in 1950 European Championships and 1952 Olympics; coached 20 Cambridge crews; Steward and Mem., Cttee of Management, Henley Royal Regatta; Mem. Council, Amateur Rowing Assoc., 1957-77; Freeman, Co. of Watermen and Lightermen of River Thames. Chm., Appeal Exec. Cttee, Peterborough Cathedral. JP Wisbech, 1969; DL Cambridgeshire, 1971; High Sheriff, Cambridgeshire and Isle of Ely, 1970. *Recreations:* rowing, shooting. *Address:* 19 North Brink, Wisbech, Cambridgeshire PE13 1JR. *T:* Wisbech 583320. *Clubs:* East India, Devonshire, Sports and Public Schools; Hawks', University Pitt, Cambridge County (Cambridge); Leander (Henley-on-Thames).

CROWDER, F(rederick) Petre, QC 1964; a Recorder (formerly Recorder of Colchester), since 1967; Barrister-at-Law; *b* 18 July 1919; *s* of late Sir John Ellenborough Crowder; *m* 1948, Hon. Patricia Stourton, *d* of 25th Baron Mowbray, MC (also 26th Baron Segrave and 22nd Baron Stourton); two *s. Educ:* Eton; Christ Church, Oxford. Served War of 1939-45; joined Coldstream Guards, 1939, and served in North Africa, Italy, Burma; attained rank of major. Called to the Bar, Inner Temple, 1948, Master of the Bench, 1971. South Eastern Circuit; North London Sessions. Recorder of Gravesend, 1960-67; Herts QS: Dep. Chm., 1959-63; Chm., 1963-71. Contested (C) North Tottenham, by-elec. 1945; MP (C) Ruislip-Northwood, 1950-74, Hillingdon, Ruislip-Northwood, 1974-79; PPS to Solicitor-Gen., 1952-54; PPS to Attorney General, 1954-62. *Address:* 2 Harcourt Buildings, Temple, EC4. *T:* 01-353 2112; 8 Quarrendon Street, SW6 3SU. *T:* 01-731 6342; Pond House, Charlestown, St Austell, Cornwall PL25 3NN. *T:* St Austell 61515. *Clubs:* Carlton, Pratt's, Turf.

CROWDER, Prof. Michael, FRHistS; Professor of History, University College of Botswana, University of Botswana and Swaziland; *b* 9 June 1934; *s* of Henry Cussons Crowder and late Molly Gladys Elizabeth Crowder (*née* Burchell). *Educ:* Mill Hill Sch.; Hertford Coll., Oxford (BA 1st Cl. Hons PPE, MA). 2/Lieut, Middx Regt, seconded to Nigeria Regt, 1953-54. Editor, Nigeria Magazine, Lagos, 1959-62; Secretary, Inst. of African Studies, Univ. of Ibadan, Nigeria, 1962-64; Vis. Lectr in African History, Univ. of Calif, Berkeley, 1964-65; Director, Inst. of African Studies, Fourah Bay Coll., Univ. of Sierra Leone, 1965-67; Research Prof. and Dir, Inst. of African Studies, Univ. of Ife, Nigeria, 1968-71; Prof. of History, Ahmadu Bello Univ., 1971-75 (Head, Dept of History, Kano Campus, 1971-74; Dean, Faculty of Arts and Islamic Studies, 1972-73; Dir, Univ. Centre for Nigerian Cultural Studies, 1972-75); Research Prof. in History, Centre for Cultural Studies, Univ. of Lagos, 1975-78; Editor, 1979-81, Consultant Editor, 1981-82, History Today; Jt Hon. Dir, Internat. African Inst., 1981-82. Visiting Professor: Columbia Univ., 1964, 1965; Ibadan Univ., 1967, Georgetown Univ., 1970; Vis. Fellow, Centre for Internat. Studies, LSE, 1981-82. Hon Exec. Sec., Internat. Congress of Africanists, 1962-68 (jtly with Prof. Lalage Bown, 1965-68); Member Council: African Studies Assoc. of UK, 1979-; Minority Rights Gp, 1980-; Mem. Exec. Council, International African Inst., 1979- (Chm., Publication Cttee, 1979-). General Editor, Hutchinson University Library for Africa, 1976-. Officer, National Order of Senegal, 1964. FRHistS, 1979. *Publications:* The Story of Nigeria, 1962, 4th edn 1977;

Senegal: a study in French assimilation policy, 1962, 2nd edn 1967; West Africa under Colonial Rule, 1968; ed jtly, West African Chiefs, 1970; West African Resistance, 1971, 2nd edn 1981; ed jtly, History of West Africa, vol. I 1971, 2nd edn 1976, vol. II 1974; Revolt in Bussa: a study in British 'Native' Administration in Nigerian Borgu 1902-1936, 1973; Colonial West Africa: collected essays, 1978; Nigeria: an introduction to its history, 1979; West Africa: 1000 AD to the present day, 1980; Jt Gen. Editor, Cambridge Encyclopaedia of Africa, 1981. *Recreations:* music, travelling. *Address:* 13 Addington Square, SE5 7JZ. *T:* 01-703 8938; Dar Demdam, rue Merrouche, Casbah, Tangier, Morocco. *Club:* Travellers'.

CROWDY, Maj.-Gen. Joseph Porter; QHP 1981; Commandant and Postgraduate Dean, Royal Army Medical College, since 1981; *b* 19 Nov. 1923; *s* of late Lt-Col Charles R. Crowdy and Kate Crowdy (*née* Porter); *m* 1948, Beryl Elisabeth Sapsford; four *d. Educ:* Gresham's Sch.; Edinburgh Univ. MB, ChB 1947, DTM&H 1956, DPH 1957, DIH 1957; FFCM 1974; MFOM 1981. House Surgeon, Norfolk and Norwich Hosp., 1947-48; joined RAMC, 1949; North Africa, 1952-55; Singapore, 1960-62; Head of Applied Physiology, Army Personnel Res. Estabt, 1963-73; Prof. of Army Health, Royal Army Med. Coll., 1973-76; SMO, Land Forces Cyprus, 1976-78; Dir, Army Preventive Medicine, 1978-81. Editor, RAMC Jl, 1978-. *Publications:* articles in medical jls, on smoking and health, nutrition, physical fitness and obesity. *Address:* Royal Army Medical College, Millbank, SW1P 4RJ; 5 Atterbury Street, SW1P 4RQ. *T:* 01-821 7086.

CROWE, Brian Lee; HM Diplomatic Service; Counsellor and Head of European Community Department (External), Foreign and Commonwealth Office, since 1982; *b* 5 Jan. 1938; *s* of Eric Crowe and Virginia Crowe; *m* 1969, Virginia Willis; two *s. Educ:* Sherborne; Magdalen Coll., Oxford (1st Cl. Hons PPE). Joined FO, 1961; served: Moscow, 1962-64; London, 1965-67; Aden, 1967; Washington, 1968-73; Bonn, 1973-76; FCO, 1976-78; Counsellor and Hd of Chancery, UK Perm. Representation to EEC, Brussels, 1979-81. *Recreations:* winter sports, tennis, riding. *Address:* c/o Foreign and Commonwealth Office, SW1.

CROWE, Sir Colin Tradescant, GCMG 1973 (KCMG 1963; CMG 1956); HM Diplomatic Service, retired; *b* 7 Sept. 1913; *s* of late Sir Edward Crowe, KCMG; *m* 1938, Bettina Lum. *Educ:* Stowe Sch.; Oriel Coll., Oxford. Served at HM Embassy, Peking, 1936-38 and 1950-53; Shanghai, 1938-40; HM Embassy, Washington, 1940-45; Foreign Office, 1945-48, 1953-56; UK Delegn to OEEC, Paris, 1948-49; HM Legation, Tel Aviv, 1949-50; Imperial Defence Coll., 1957; Head, British Property Commn, Cairo, 1959; British Chargé d'Affaires, Cairo, 1959-61; Deputy UK Representative to the UN, New York, 1961-63; Ambassador to Saudi Arabia, 1963-64; Chief of Administration, HM Diplomatic Service, 1965-68; High Comr in Canada, 1968-70; UK Permanent Rep. to UN, 1970-73. Supernumerary Fellow, St Antony's Coll., Oxford, 1964-65. Dir, Grindlay's Bank Ltd, 1976-. Chm., Marshall Aid Commemoration Commn, 1973-. Chm. Council, Cheltenham Ladies Coll., 1974-. Vice-Chm. Council, UCL, 1978-. *Address:* Pigeon House, Bibury, Glos. *Club:* Travellers'.

CROWE, Gerald Patrick, QC 1973; **His Honour Judge Crowe;** a Circuit Judge, since 1980; *b* 3 April 1930; *y s* of Patrick Crowe and Ethel Maud Crowe (*née* Tooth); *m* 1954, Catherine Mary, *d* of Joseph and Rose Murphy, Newry, N Ireland. *Educ:* St Francis Xavier's Coll.; Liverpool Univ. (LLB). Called to Bar, Gray's Inn, 1952; practised Northern Circuit. A Recorder of the Crown Court, 1976-80. *Recreations:* golf, fishing. *Address:* The Spinney, Long Hey Road, Caldy, Cheshire. *T:* 051-625 8848; Goldsmith Building, Temple, EC4Y 7BL.

CROWE, Prof. Ralph Vernon, FRIBA; Professor of Architecture and Head of Department, School of Architecture, The University, Newcastle upon Tyne, 1976-81, now Professor Emeritus; now in private practice; *b* 30 Sept. 1915; *s* of Sidney John Crowe and Sarah Emma (*née* Sharp); *m* 1943, Nona Heath Eggington; two *s* one *d. Educ:* Westminster City Sch.; Architectural Assoc., London (AA Dipl. Hons); Sch. of Planning and Res. for Reg. Develt. MA Newcastle upon Tyne; ARIBA 1945; MRTPI 1949. War Service, 1941-45: Captain, RE. Govt Architect and Planning Officer, Govt of Barbados, BWI, 1947-50; teaching, Arch. Assoc., 1950-52; Basildon New Town, 1952-53; LCC, 1953-58; County Architect: Shropshire, 1958-66; Essex, 1966-76. *Publications:* contribs to professional and tech. jls. *Recreations:* music (flute), hill walking. *Address:* Holly Hall Barn, Sandhoe, Hexham, Northumberland NE46 4LX. *Club:* Savage.

CROWE, Dame Sylvia, DBE 1973 (CBE 1967); landscape architect in private practice since 1945; *b* 1901; *d* of Eyre Crowe; unmarried. *Educ:* Berkhamsted; Swanley Hort. Coll. Designed gardens, 1927-39. Served FANY and ATS, 1939-45. Since 1945, private practice as landscape architect has included: work as consultant to: Harlow and Basildon New Town Corporations; Wimbleball and Rutland Water reservoirs; Central Electricity Generating Board, for Trawsfynydd and Wylfa Nuclear Power Stations; Forestry Commission; reclamation of land after 1952 floods and design of public gardens at Mablethorpe and Sutton on Sea; gardens for Oxford Univ., various Colls and Commonwealth Inst., London; Sec., Internat. Federation Landscape Architecture, 1948-59; Vice-Pres., 1964; Pres., Inst. Landscape Architects, 1957-59; Corresp. Mem., Amer. Soc. of Landscape Architects, 1960; Hon. Fellow, Aust. Inst. of Landscape Architects, 1978. Chm., Tree Council, 1974-76. Hon. FRIBA, 1969; Hon. FRTPI, 1970. Hon. DLitt: Newcastle,

1975; Heriot-Watt, 1976; Hon. LLD Sussex, 1978. *Publications:* Tomorrow's Landscape, 1956; Garden Design, 1958, 2nd edn 1981; The Landscape of Power, 1958; Landscape of Roads, 1960; Forestry in the Landscape, 1966; The Landscapes of Forests and Woodlands, 1979. *Recreations:* walking and gardening. *Address:* 59 Ladbroke Grove, W11 3AT. *T:* 01-727 7794.

CROWFOOT, Brig. Anthony Bernard, CBE 1982 (MBE 1974); Student, US Army War College, 1982-83; *b* 12 Aug. 1936; *s* of Thomas Bernard Crowfoot and Gladys Dorothy Crowfoot; *m* 1960, Bridget Sarah Bunting; three *s* one *d. Educ:* King Edward VII Sch., Norfolk; Royal Military Academy, Sandhurst, psc. Commissioned 1956; 1 E Yorks 1PWO: BAOR, UK, Aden, Gibraltar, 1956-60; Instructor, School of Infantry, 1960-62; 1PWO: BAOR, UK, Aden, 1962-66; Army Staff Coll. 1967; Brigade Major, HQ 5 Inf. Bde, 1968-69; Coy Comd 1PWO, Cyprus, 1970-71; DAAG, MoD, 1971-73; CO 1PWO: UK, BAOR, N Ireland, 1973-76; Instructor, Army Staff College, 1976-77; Col GS, MoD, 1977-80; Comd 39 Inf. Bde, N Ireland, 1980-82. *Recreations:* sailing, philately, golf. *Address:* c/o National Westminster Bank Ltd, 45 Park Street, Camberley, Surrey GU15 3PA. *T:* Camberley 65171. *Club:* Army and Navy.

CROWLEY, Sir Brian Hurtle, Kt 1969; MM; Chairman, 1962-74 (Member 1944-74), Australian Jockey Club Committee; *m* 1922, Dorothy, *d* of L. Sweet; one *s* two *d. Educ:* Scots College, Sydney. Served with Aust. Imperial Forces, 1916-19. *Address:* 3 Bedford Crescent, Collaroy, NSW 2097, Australia. *Clubs:* Union, Australian, Elanora Country (all Sydney).

CROWLEY, Rear-Adm. George Clement, CB 1968; DSC 1942, and Bar 1944; Official Fellow and Domestic Bursar of Corpus Christi College, Oxford University, 1969-75; *b* 9 June 1916; *s* of Charles Edmund Lucas Crowley and Beatrice Cicely Crowley; *m* 1948, Una Margaret Jelf; two *s. Educ:* Pangbourne Coll. Cadet, HMS Frobisher, 1933; served in China and New Zealand, 1934-39; served War of 1939-45, destroyers; comdg HMS Walpole, 1943-45; comdg HMS Tenacious, 1945-46 (despatches); RN Staff Course, 1947; Staff appts, 1948-53; Exec. Off., HMS Newfoundland, 1953-55; Drafting Comdr, Chatham, 1955-57; Asst Dir Plans, 1957-59; Capt. (D) 7th Destroyer Sqdn, 1959-61; CO New Entry, Trng Estab. HMS Raleigh, 1961-63; Capt. of Fleet to Flag Off. C-in-C Far East Fleet, 1963-64; Staff of Jt Exercise Unison, 1964-65; Staff of Defence Operational Analysis Estab., W Byfleet, 1965-66; Director-General, Naval Personal Services, 1966-68. Capt. 1957; Rear-Adm. 1966. *Recreations:* fishing, tennis, gardening. *Address:* Windrush, Shroton, Blandford, Dorset.

CROWLEY, Niall, FICAI; Chairman: Allied Irish Banks Ltd Group, since 1977; Irish Life Assurance Co. Ltd, since 1974; President, Dublin Chamber of Commerce, 1983-84; *b* 18 Sept. 1926; *s* of Vincent Crowley and Eileen (*née* Gunning); *m* 1953, Una Hegarty; five *s* one *d. Educ:* Xavier Sch.; Castle Knock Coll. FICAI 1955. Entered father's accounting firm, Stokes Kennedy Crowley & Co., as articled clerk, 1944: qualified, 1949; Partner, 1950, subseq. Managing Partner; Consultant to the firm, which also represents Peat Marwick Mitchell & Co. in Ireland, 1977-. President, Inst. of Chartered Accountants in Ireland, 1971-72. Member, Company of Goldsmiths of Dublin, 1973-. Hon. LLD NUI, 1982. *Recreations:* bridge, golf. *Address:* 18 Herbert Park, Ballsbridge, Dublin 4. *T:* 683637. *Clubs:* Stephens Green; Portmarnock Golf; Milltown Golf; Fitzwilliam Lawn Tennis (Dublin).

CROWLEY, Thomas Michael, CMG 1970; Assistant Secretary, Ministry of Defence, 1971-77; *b* 28 June 1917; *s* of late Thomas Michael Crowley; *m* 1965, Eicke Laura, *d* of late Carl Jensen; one *s. Educ:* Forres Acad.; Aberdeen Univ. Entered Civil Service in 1940; Assistant Secretary: Min. of Technology, 1953-70; DTI, 1970; Min. of Aviation Supply, 1970-71. *Address:* 116 Barnett Wood Lane, Ashtead, Surrey.

CROWLEY-MILLING, Air Marshal Sir Denis, KCB 1973; CBE 1963; DSO 1943; DFC 1941, Bar 1942; Gentleman Usher of the Scarlet Rod to the Order of the Bath, since 1979; Controller, RAF Benevolent Fund, 1975-81; *b* 22 March 1919; *s* of T. W. and G. M. Crowley-Milling (*née* Chinnery); *m* 1943, Lorna Jean Jeboult (*née* Stuttard); two *d* (one *s* decd). *Educ:* Malvern Coll., Worcs. Rolls Royce apprentice and RAF Volunteer Reserve, 1937-39; served with Fighters and Fighter Bombers, Nos 615, 242, 610 and 181 Sqdns, 1939-44; Air Ministry Operational Requirements, 1945-47; OC No 6 Sqdn, Middle East, 1947-50; Personal Staff Officer C-in-C Fighter Comd, 1950-52; Wing Comdr Flying, RAF Odiham, 1952-54; Directing Staff, RAF Staff Coll., Bracknell, 1954-57; Flying Coll., RAF Manby, 1957-58; Plans Staff Fighter Comd, 1958-59; Group Capt. Operations Central Fighter Establishment, 1959-62; Station Comdr, RAF Leconfield, 1962-64; AOC RAF Hong Kong, 1964-66; Dir Operational Requirements, MoD (Air), 1966-67; Comdr, RAF Staff and Principal Air Attaché, Washington, 1967-70; AOC No 38 Gp, RAF Odiham, 1970-72; AOC 46 Gp RAF Upavon, 1973; UK Rep., Perm. Mil. Deputies Gp, Cento, 1974-75. *Recreations:* golf and shooting. *Address:* c/o Barclays Bank Ltd, 46 Park Lane, W1A 4EE. *Club:* Royal Air Force.

CROWLEY-MILLING, Michael Crowley, CMG 1982; CEng, FIEE; Consultant to CERN (European Organization for Nuclear Research), since 1982; *b* 7 May 1917; *s* of Thomas William Crowley-Milling and Gillian May (*née* Chinnery); *m* 1958, Gee Dickson. *Educ:* Radley Coll.; St John's Coll., Cambridge (MA 1943). CEng, FIEE 1956. R&D on radar systems, Metropolitan-Vickers Electrical Co. Ltd, Manchester, 1938-46; design and

develt of electron linear accelerators for physics, medical and irradiation purposes, 1946-63; contrib. to construction of electron synchrotron, Daresbury Nuclear Physics Lab., Warrington, 1963-71; CERN, Geneva: resp. for control system for Super Proton Synchrotron (SPS), 1971-75; SPS Div. Leader, 1977-78; Dir, Accelerator Prog., 1979-80. Crompton Premium, IEE, 1959; Glazebrook Medal, Inst. of Physics, 1980. Captain LMBC, 1938. *Publications:* articles and chapters in books on particle accelerators and computer control systems. *Recreations:* vintage cars, sailing. *Address:* 7 Avenue Pictet de Rochemont, 1207 Geneva, Switzerland. *T:* Geneva 36-04-91.
   See also Sir Denis Crowley-Milling.

CROWSON, Richard Borman; HM Diplomatic Service; Counsellor for Hong Kong Affairs, British Embassy, Washington, since 1977; *b* 23 July 1929; *s* of late Clarence Borman Crowson and Cecilia May Crowson (*née* Ramsden); *m* 1960, Sylvia Cavalier (marr. diss. 1974); one *s* one *d. Educ:* Downing Coll., Cambridge (MA). FCIS. HMOCS, Uganda, 1955-62; Foreign Office, 1962-63; First Sec. (Commercial), Tokyo, 1963-68; Dep. High Commissioner, Barbados, 1968-70; FCO, 1970-75; Counsellor (Commercial and Aid), Jakarta, 1975-77. *Recreations:* music, drama, travel. *Address:* c/o Foreign and Commonwealth Office, SW1; 67 Crofton Road, Orpington, Kent. *T:* Orpington 30781; 2841 29th Place, NW, Washington, DC 20008. *T:* (202) 332-4494. *Club:* Royal Commonwealth Society.

CROWTHER, Eric (John Ronald), OBE 1977; Metropolitan Magistrate, since 1968; *b* 4 Aug. 1924; *s* of Stephen Charles Crowther, company secretary, and Olive Beatrix Crowther (*née* Selby); *m* 1959, Elké Auguste Ottilie Winkelmann; one *s* one *d. Educ:* University College Sch., Hampstead. Royal Navy, 1943-47 (Medit. Area of Ops). Awarded Tancred Studentship in Common Law, 1948; Called to Bar, Lincoln's Inn, 1951; winner of Inns of Court Contest in Advocacy, 1951; Lectr and Student Counsellor, British Council, 1951-81; Lecturer on Elocution and Advocacy for Council of Legal Educn, 1955-; Dir of Studies, Post-Final Gps, Council of Legal Educn, 1975-77. Joined Inner Temple *ad eundem,* 1960. Practised at Criminal Bar, 1951-68. Chairman: Inner London Magistrates' Assoc. Trng Sub-Cttee, 1981-; Prisoners' Wives Service, 1982-. Mem., Bd of Academic Studies, St Catherine's, Cumberland Lodge, 1977-; Trustee, Professional and Academic Regional Visits Organisation, 1977-. Mem. Cttee, RADA, 1979-. Hon. Officer, Internat. Students' Hse, 1981-. Editor, Commonwealth Judicial Jl, 1973-77. *Recreations:* travel, transport, the theatre, debating, student welfare, Scottish dancing. *Address:* 21 Old Buildings, Lincoln's Inn, WC2.

CROWTHER, Fráncis Harold; retired from Diplomatic Service, 1966; *b* Umtali, Southern Rhodesia, 25 May 1914; *s* of A. D. Crowther; *m* 1952, Mary Eleanor, *d* of F. G. Forman; two *d. Educ:* Plumtree Sch., Southern Rhodesia; Univ. of Cape Town; Christ Church, Oxford. Entered Consular Service, Japan, 1938; served in Japan, India, Ceylon, Singapore, Indochina, Korea, Foreign Office, Yugoslavia, Morocco, Mozambique and the Netherlands. *Address:* 59 Sloane Gardens, SW1.

CROWTHER, (Joseph) Stanley; MP (Lab) Rotherham, since June 1976; *b* 30 May 1925; *s* of Cyril Joseph Crowther and Florence Mildred (*née* Beckett); *m* 1948, Margaret Royston; two *s. Educ:* Rotherham Grammar Sch.; Rotherham Coll. of Technology. Royal Signals, 1943-47. Journalist: Rotherham Advertiser, 1941-43 and 1947-50; Yorkshire Evening Post, 1950-51; freelance, 1951-. Mem., Rotherham Borough Council, 1958-59, 1961-76; Mayor of Rotherham, 1971-72, 1975-76; Chm., Yorkshire and Humberside Develt Assoc., 1972-76; Exec. Mem., Town and Country Planning Assoc., 1973-. *Recreations:* walking, singing, listening to jazz. *Address:* 15 Clifton Crescent South, Rotherham S65 2AR. *T:* Rotherham 64559. *Clubs:* Central Labour, Eastwood View Working Men's (Rotherham).

CROWTHER, Thomas Rowland, QC 1981; Barrister-at-law; a Recorder of the Crown Court, since 1980; *b* 11 Sept. 1937; *s* of Kenneth Vincent Crowther, MB, BCh, and Winifred Anita Crowther, MPS; *m* 1969, Gillian Jane (*née* Prince); one *s* one *d. Educ:* Newport High Sch.: Keble Coll., Oxford (MA). President, Oxford Univ. Liberal Club, 1957; Editor, Oxford Guardian, 1957. Called to the Bar, Inner Temple, 1961; Junior and Wine Steward, Wales and Chester Circuit, 1974; a Recorder, Wales and Chester Circuit, 1980-. Contested (L) General Elections: Oswestry, 1964 and 1966; Hereford, 1970. Founder mem., Gwent Area Broadcasting. *Recreation:* garden. *Address:* Lansor, Llandegfedd, Caerleon, Gwent NP6 1LS. *T:* Tredunnock 224. *Clubs:* Cardiff and County; Newport Golf.

CROWTHER, Sir William (Edward Lodewyk Hamilton), Kt 1964; CBE 1955; DSO 1919; VRD; FRACP; medical practitioner; President of Medical Council of Tasmania, 1953-54; *b* 9 May 1887; *s* of Edward L. Crowther, MD; *m* 1915, Joyce Nevett Mitchell, Tunallock, NSW; one *s. Educ:* Buckland's School; Ormond Coll., University of Melbourne. Late CO 5th Field Ambulance AIF (despatches, wounded, DSO, 1914-15 star, two medals). Pres., Tasmanian Br., BMA, 1934-42. Hon. Consulting Physician, Hobart Gen. Hosp. Halford Oration, 1933; Archibald Watson Memorial Lecture, 1951; Roentgen Oration, 1953. Hon. Advisor, Australian Bibliography Library Bd, State Library of Tasmania, 1965. *Publications:* series on the extinct Tasmanian race and on history of medicine in Tasmania, to scientific journals. *Recreations:* yachting, historical research. *Address:* 190 Macquarie Street, Hobart, Tasmania 7000. *T:* 23.6003. *Clubs:* Tasmanian (Life Mem.), Naval and Military (Hobart).

CROWTHER, William Ronald Hilton; QC 1980; *b* 7 May 1941; *s* of Ronald Crowther and Ann Bourne Crowther; *m* 1964, Valerie Meredith (*née* Richards); one *s. Educ:* Univ. of Oxford (BA Jurisprudence). Called to the Bar, Inner Temple, 1963. *Recreations:* bird-watching and all aspects of natural history. *Address:* 83 South End Road, NW3. *T:* 01-794 4619.

CROWTHER-HUNT, family name of **Baron Crowther-Hunt.**

CROWTHER-HUNT, Baron *cr* 1973 (Life Peer), of Eccleshill in the West Riding of the County of York; **Norman Crowther Crowther-Hunt,** PhD; Rector, Exeter College, Oxford, since 1982; *b* 13 March 1920; *s* of late Ernest Angus Hunt, and of Florence Hunt, Bradford, Yorks; *m* 1944, Joyce, *d* of late Rev. Joseph Stackhouse, Walsall Wood, Staffs; three *d. Educ:* Wellington Road Council Sch.; Belle Vue High Sch., Bradford; Sidney Sussex Coll., Cambridge. Exhibitioner, 1939-40, Open Scholar, 1945-47, Sidney Sussex Coll.; MA 1949, PhD 1951; Hon. Fellow, 1982. Served RA, 1940-45; War Office (GSO3), 1944-45. First Cl. Hist. Tripos, 1946 and 1947; Res. Fellow, Sidney Sussex Coll., 1949-51; Commonwealth Fund Fellow, Princeton Univ., USA, 1951-52; Fellow and Lectr in Politics, 1952-82, Domestic Bursar, 1954-70, Exeter Coll., Oxford. Deleg., Oxford Univ. Extra-Mural Delegacy, 1956-70; Vis. Prof., Michigan State Univ., 1961. Constitutional Adviser to the Govt, March-Oct. 1974; Minister of State: DES, 1974-76; Privy Council Office, 1976. Member: Cttee on the Civil Service (Fulton Cttee), 1966-68 (Leader of Management Consultancy Group); Commn on the Constitution, 1969-73 (principal author of the Memorandum of Dissent); Civil Service Coll. Adv. Council, 1970-74. Mem. Council, Headington Sch., Oxford, 1966-74. Hon. DLitt Bradford, 1974. *Publications:* Two Early Political Associations, 1961; (ed) Whitehall and Beyond, 1964; (ed with Graham Tayar) Personality and Power 1970; (with Peter Kellner) The Civil Servants, 1980. *Recreations:* playing tennis, squash and the piano; broadcasting. Cambridge Univ. Assoc. Football XI, 1939-40. *Address:* 14 Apsley Road, Oxford. *T:* Oxford 58342; Exeter College, Oxford. *T:* Oxford 44681.

CROXTON-SMITH, Claude; President, Institute of Chartered Accountants in England and Wales, June 1970-71; *b* 24 Aug. 1901; *m* 1928, Joan Norah Bloss Watling; two *d. Educ:* Dulwich Coll.; Gonville and Caius Coll., Cambridge. The Sales Staff, Anglo American Oil Co. Ltd, 1924-31; Articled Clerk, Inst. of Chartered Accountants in England and Wales, 1932-36; Chartered Accountant, 1936-39. Served War of 1939-45, RAOC (Major). Chartered Accountant in Public Practice (Bristol), 1946-. *Recreations:* walking, reading. *Address:* 5 Wanscow Walk, Henleaze, Bristol BS9 4LE. *T:* Bristol 623385. *Club:* Bristol (Bristol).

CROYDON, Bishop Suffragan of, since 1977; **Rt. Rev. Geoffrey Stuart Snell;** Bishop to the Forces; *b* 25 Oct. 1920; *s* of Charles James and Ellen Snell; *m* 1948, Margaret Lonsdale Geary; two *s* one *d. Educ:* Exeter School; St Peter's College, Oxford (MA 2nd cl. Hons PPE). Called to the Bar, Inner Temple, 1957. UK Civil Service, 1937-39. Served Army, 1939-46, Major, Supplies and Transport. University, 1946-49; Overseas Admin. Civil Service, 1950-54; Managing Governor, Gabbitas-Thring Educational Trust, 1954-61. Deacon and priest, Church of England, 1962; Fellow, Central College of the Anglican Communion, Canterbury, 1964-67; Founder/Director, Christian Organisations Research and Advisory Trust, 1968-75, of Africa, 1975-77. *Publication:* Nandi Customary Law, 1955. *Recreations:* music, travel. *Address:* 52 Selhurst Road, S Norwood SE25 5QD. *T:* 01-689 0767. *Clubs:* East India, Devonshire, Sports and Public Schools; United Kenya (Nairobi).

CROYDON, Archdeacon of; *see* Hazell, Ven F. R.

CROYDON, Rear-Adm. John Edward Kenneth, CEng, FIEE; Director General Weapons (Naval), since 1981; *b* 25 Feb. 1929; *s* of late Kenneth P. Croydon and Elizabeth V. Croydon; *m* 1953, Brenda Joyce Buss, MA; one *s* two *d. Educ:* King Edward's Sch., Birmingham; Selwyn Coll., Cambridge (MA). BA London; CEng, FIEE 1975; jssc 1969. RN Special Entry Cadet (L), 1947; HMS Verulam and HMS Undine, 1954-55; Royal Naval Coll., Dartmouth, 1959-61; HMS Devonshire, 1961-64; HMS London, 1970-72; MoD, 1972-74; Captain Weapon Trials, 1974-77; Dir, Underwater Weapon Projects (Naval), 1978-80. Rear Cdre (Dinghies), Royal Naval Sailing Assoc., 1980. *Recreations:* sailing, music, walking. *Clubs:* Royal Naval Sailing Association; Weymouth Sailing.

CROZIER, Brian Rossiter; writer and consultant on international affairs; Columnist, National Review, New York, since 1978; Co-founder Institute for the Study of Conflict, 1970, and Director, 1970-79; *b* 4 Aug. 1918; *s* of R. H. Crozier and Elsa (*née* McGillivray); *m* 1940, Mary Lillian Samuel; one *s* three *d. Educ:* Lycée, Montpellier; Peterborough Coll., Harrow; Trinity Coll. of Music, London. Music and art critic, London, 1936-39; reporter-sub-editor, Stoke-on-Trent, Stockport, London, 1940-41; aeronautical inspection, 1941-43; sub-editor: Reuters, 1944-43; News Chronicle, 1944-48; and writer, Sydney Morning Herald, 1948-51; corresp., Reuters-AAP, 1951-52; features editor, Straits Times, 1952-53; leader writer and corresp., Economist, 1954-64; commentator, BBC English, French and Spanish overseas services, 1954-66; Chm., Forum World Features, 1965-74; Columnist, Now!, 1979-81. *Publications:* The Rebels, 1960; The Morning After, 1963; Neo-Colonialism, 1964; South-East Asia in Turmoil, 1965 (3rd edn 1968); The Struggle for the Third World, 1966; Franco, 1967; The Masters of Power, 1969; The Future of Communist Power (in USA: Since Stalin), 1970; De Gaulle, vol. 1 1973, vol. 2 1974; A Theory of Conflict, 1974; The Man Who Lost China (Chiang

Kai-shek), 1976; Strategy of Survival, 1978; The Minimum State, 1979; Franco: crepúsculo de un hombre (Spanish orig.), 1980; The Price of Peace, 1980; contrib. jls in many countries. *Recreations:* piano, taping stereo, Polaroid photography. *Address:* Kulm House, Dollis Avenue, Finchley, N3 1DA. *T:* 01-346 8124. *Clubs:* Royal Commonwealth Society, Royal Automobile.

CROZIER, Eric John; writer and theatrical producer; *b* 14 Nov. 1914; *s* of John and Ethel Mary Crozier, London; *m* 1st, 1936, Margaret Johns (marriage dissolved, 1949); two *d* ; 2nd, 1950, Nancy Evans. *Educ:* University Coll. Sch., London; Royal Academy of Dramatic Art; British Institute, Paris. Play producer for BBC Television Service, 1936-39. Produced plays and operas for Sadler's Wells Opera, Stratford-on-Avon Memorial Theatre, Glyndebourne Opera and other theatres, 1944-46. Closely associated with Benjamin Britten as producer or author of his operas, 1945-51, and was co-founder with him of The English Opera Group, 1947, and The Aldeburgh Festival of Music and the Arts, 1948. *Publications:* Christmas in the Market Place (adapted from French of Henri Ghéon), 1944; The Life and Legends of Saint Nicolas, 1949; Noah Gives Thanks, a play, 1950; (with Benjamin Britten): Albert Herring, a comic opera in three acts, 1947; Saint Nicolas, a cantata, 1948; Let's Make an Opera, an entertainment for children, 1949; (with E. M. Forster and Benjamin Britten) Billy Budd, an opera in four acts, 1951; opera translations include: The Bartered Bride, Otello, Falstaff, La Traviata, Idomeneo, Salome, The Woman without a Shadow. *Recreation:* listening to music. *Address:* Church Field Cottage, Great Glemham, Saxmundham, Suffolk. *T:* Rendham 471.

CRUDDAS, Rear-Adm. Thomas Rennison, CB 1974; Director, Pressure Vessels Quality Assurance Board, since 1977; *b* 6 Feb. 1921; *s* of late Thomas Hepple Wheatley Cruddas, MBE, and Lily (*née* Rennison); *m* 1943, Angela Elizabeth Astbury; one *s* one *d. Educ:* Queen Elizabeth Grammar Sch., Darlington; RN Engineering College, Keyham. Joined RN 1938; RNEC, 1939-42. Served War, 1939-45: in Mediterranean and E Indies, in HM Ships Unicorn and Valiant. HMS Cardigan Bay, 1948-50; specialised Aero. Engrg, 1950; RNAY Donibristle, 1951-53; Comdr, 1953; HMS Ark Royal, 1953-55; RNAY Fleetlands, 1956-58; Admty, 1958-61; Staff of Flag Officer Aircraft Carriers, 1961-63; Captain, 1963; Asst Dir Ship Production, 1964-66; service with USN, Washington, DC, as Programme Manager UK Phantom Aircraft, 1967-69; Command Engr Officer, Staff FONAC, 1970-72; Rear-Adm. Engineering, Naval Air Comd, 1972; Dep. Controller Aircraft B, MoD (PE), 1973-76, retired. FIMechE. *Recreations:* golf, horticulture. *Address:* Beeches Close, Bishop's Waltham, Hants. *T:* Bishop's Waltham 2335. *Club:* Corhampton Golf.

CRUFT, John Herbert; Hon. Treasurer, Royal Society of Musicians; Trustee, Loan Fund for Musical Instruments; Governor, London Festival Ballet Trust Ltd; *b* 4 Jan. 1914; *er s* of late Eugene and Winifred Cruft; *m* 1938, Mary Margaret Miriam, *e d* of late Rev. Pat and Miriam McCormick; two *s. Educ:* Westminster Abbey Choir Sch.; Westminster Sch.; Royal College of Music (K. F. Boult Conducting Scholar). Oboist in BBC Television, London Philharmonic and Suisse Romande Orchestras, 1936-40. Served with Royal Corps of Signals, 1940-46. London Symphony Orchestra: Oboist, 1946-49; Sec., 1949-59. British Council: Dir of Music Dept, 1959-61; Dir of Drama and Music Dept, 1961-65; Music Dir, Arts Council of GB, 1965-79. FRCM, Hon. RAM. *Address:* 7 Phene Street, Chelsea, SW3. *T:* 01-352 7817.

CRUICKSHANK, Andrew John Maxton, MBE 1945; actor; *b* 25 Dec. 1907; *m* 1939, Curigwen Lewis; one *s* two *d. Educ:* Aberdeen Grammar Sch. Hon. DLitt St Andrews, 1977. With Baynton Shakespearean Company, 1929; appeared in Richard of Bordeaux, New York, 1934; Mary Tudor, London Playhouse, 1935; Lysistrata, Gate, 1936; Macbeth, Old Vic, 1937 (Mem. of Old Vic Company, 1937-40). Served Royal Welch Fus., and GS, 1940-45. Spring 1600, Lyric, Hammersmith, 1945-46; The White Devil, Duchess, 1947; The Indifferent Shepherd, Criterion, 1949; Memorial Theatre, Stratford (Parts included Wolsey, Kent and Julius Caesar), 1950; St Joan, Cort Theatre, New York, 1951; Dial M for Murder, Westminster Theatre, 1952; Dead on Nine, Westminster, 1955; The House by the Lake, Duke of York's, 1956; Inherit The Wind, 1960; Look Homeward Angel, 1960; The Lady From the Sea, Queen's, 1961; The Master Builder, Ashcroft Theatre, Croydon, 1963; Alibi for a Judge, Savoy, 1965; Lloyd George Knew my Father, Savoy, 1973; When We Dead Awaken, Haymarket Leicester, 1975; *National Theatre:* The Woman, 1978; Strife, 1978; The Fruits of Enlightenment, 1979; The Wild Duck, 1980; Sisterly Feelings, 1980. Has appeared in many films, also in radio and on television; TV series, Dr Finlay's Casebook; author of play, Games, 1975. *Address:* 33 Carlisle Mansions, Carlisle Place, SW1. *Club:* Garrick.

CRUICKSHANK, Charles Greig, MA, DPhil; FRHistS; author; *b* 10 June 1914; *s* of late George Leslie Cruickshank, Fyvie; *m* 1943, Maire Kissane; three *s. Educ:* Aberdeen Grammar Sch.; Aberdeen Univ.; Hertford Coll., Oxford; Edinburgh Univ. Min. of Supply, 1940-46; BoT, 1946-51; Trade Comr, Ceylon, 1951-55 (economic mission to Maldive Is, 1953); Canada, 1955-58; Sen. Trade Comr, NZ, 1958-63; Exec. Sec., Commonwealth Econ. Cttee, 1964-66; Dir, Commodities Div., Commonwealth Secretariat, 1967-68; BoT (Regional Export Dir, London and SE), 1969-71; Inspector, FCO, 1971-72; CAA, 1972-73; Asst Sec., DTI, 1973. Official historian, SOE in Far East, 1980. *Publications:* Elizabeth's Army, 1966; Army Royal, 1969; The English Occupation of Tournai, 1971; (jtly) A Guide to the Sources of British Military History, 1971; The German Occupation of the Channel Islands (official

history), 1975; Greece 1940-41, 1976; The V-Mann Papers, 1976; The Tang Murders, 1976; The Fourth Arm: psychological warfare, 1938-45, 1977; The Ebony Version, 1978; The Deceivers, 1978; Deception in World War II, 1979; Kew for Murder, 1979; contrib. to English Historical Review, Army Quarterly, History Today, Punch, War Monthly, etc. *Recreation:* golf. *Address:* 15 McKay Road, Wimbledon Common, SW20 0HT. *T:* 01-947 1074. *Club:* Royal Wimbledon Golf.

CRUICKSHANK, Prof. Durward William John, PhD, ScD; FRS 1979; CChem, FRSC; Professor of Chemistry (Theoretical Chemistry), University of Manchester Institute of Science and Technology, since 1967; *b* 7 March 1924; *s* of William Durward Cruickshank, MB, ChB, and Margaret Ombler Meek, MA, MRCS, LRCP; *m* 1953, Marjorie Alice Travis, MA, PhD; one *s* one *d. Educ:* St Lawrence Coll., Ramsgate; Loughborough Coll. (DLC 1944; BScEng 1st Cl. Hons London, 1944); Cambridge Univ. (Wrangler, Math. Tripos, 1949; Dist. Pt III Math. Tripos, 1950; BA 1949, MA 1954, ScD 1961). PhD Leeds, 1952; CChem, FRIC 1971. Engrg Asst, WO and Admiralty (Naval Opl Res.), 1944-46; Leeds University: Res. Asst, Chemistry Dept, 1946-47; Lectr, 1950-57; Reader in Math. Chemistry, 1957-62; Fellow, St John's Coll., Cambridge, 1953-56; Joseph Black Prof. of Chem. (Theor. Chem.), Glasgow Univ., 1962-67; Dep. Principal, UMIST, 1971-72. Treasurer, 1966-72, and Gen. Sec., 1970-72, Internat. Union of Crystallography. 1977 Chemical Soc. Award for Struct. Chem., 1978. *Publications:* scientific papers on crystallography, molecular structure determination and theoretical chemistry in Acta Cryst., Proc. Royal Soc., and Jl Chem. Soc. *Recreation:* golf. *Address:* 105 Moss Lane, Alderley Edge, Cheshire SK9 7HW. *T:* Alderley Edge 582656; Chemistry Department, University of Manchester Institute of Science and Technology, Manchester M60 1QD. *T:* 061-236 3311.

CRUICKSHANK, Prof. Eric Kennedy, OBE 1961; MD; FRCP, FRCPGlas; Dean of Postgraduate Medicine, University of Glasgow, 1972-80; *b* 29 Dec. 1914; *s* of John Cruickshank, CBE, and Jessie (*née* Allan); *m* 1st, 1951, Ann Burch; two *s* two *d* ; 2nd, 1969, Josephine Williams. *Educ:* Aberdeen Grammar Sch.; Univ. of Aberdeen (MB, ChB Hons, 1937; MD Hons and gold medal, 1948). Fellow, Harvard and Massachusetts Gen. Hosp., USA, 1938-39; Lectr, then Sen. Lectr, Dept of Medicine, Univ. of Aberdeen, 1939-50; Hon. Consultant in Medicine, NHS, 1948-50; First Dean, Medical Faculty, and Prof. of Medicine, Univ. of West Indies, Kingston, Jamaica, 1950-72. Served War of 1939-45: Captain RAMC, Medical Specialist, Changi Prisoner of War Camp, Singapore (despatches twice). WHO Consultant in Medical Educn, 1959-, Nutrition, 1955-; Member: GMC, 1972-80; Inter-Univ. Council, 1972-; Greater Glasgow Health Bd, 1972-80. Hon. FACP 1969. *Publications:* on nutrition, neurology, medical educn. *Recreations:* tennis, golf, gardening, ornithology. *Address:* Parsonage House, Oare, Wilts SN8 4JA.

CRUICKSHANK, Herbert James, CBE 1969; CEng, MIMechE; FIOB; *b* 12 July 1912; *s* of late James William Cruickshank and of Dorothy Adeline Cruickshank; *m* 1939, Jean Alexandra Payne (*d* 1978); no *c. Educ:* Charlton Central Sch.; Regent Street Polytechnic (Schol.). Bovis Ltd: Staff Trainee, 1931; Plant and Labour Controller, 1937; Gilbert-Ash Ltd: (formed within Bovis Gp), 1945; Director, 1949; Civil Engineering Works in Nyasaland, 1949-55; Managing Dir, UK, 1960-63; Chm. and Man. Dir, 1964; Dir, Bovis Holdings, 1964-72; Group Man. Dir, 1966, Dep. Chm. 1970-72. Chm., House-Building Adv. Bureau, 1981-. Member: Metrication Bd, 1969-73; SE Thames RHA, 1972-78; BSI Quality Assurance Council, 1976-81. FRSA. *Recreations:* amateur theatre, photography, sketching. *Address:* 45 Bidborough Ridge, Tunbridge Wells, Kent. *T:* Tunbridge Wells 27270. *Clubs:* Oriental, MCC.

CRUICKSHANK, Prof. John; Professor of French, University of Sussex, since 1962; *b* Belfast, N Ireland, 18 July 1924; *s* of Arthur Cruickshank, parliamentary reporter, and Eva Cruickshank (*née* Shummacher); *m* 1st, 1949, Kathleen Mary Gutteridge; one *s* ; 2nd, 1972, Marguerite Doreen Penny. *Educ:* Royal Belfast Academical Institution; Trinity Coll., Dublin. Awarded Mod. Lang. Sizarship, TCD, 1943; Cryptographer in Mil. Intell., 1943-45; 1st class Moderatorship in Mod. Langs (French and German) and 2nd class Moderatorship (Mental and Moral Science), TCD, 1948; Lecteur d'Anglais, Ecole Normale Supérieure, Paris, 1948-49; Asst Lectr in French and German, Univ. of Southampton, 1951; Sen. Lectr in French, Univ. of Southampton, 1961. Mem., UGC, 1970-77. *Publications:* Albert Camus and the Literature of Revolt, 1959; Critical Readings in the Modern French Novel, 1961; The Novelist as Philosopher, 1962; Montherlant, 1964; (ed) French Literature and Its Background: vols 1-6, 1968-70; Benjamin Constant, 1974; Variations on Catastrophe, 1982; articles in: French Studies; Modern Language Review; Times Literary Supplement; Times Higher Education Supplement, etc. *Recreations:* bird-watching, painting in oils, watching cricket. *Address:* Woodpeckers, East Hoathly, Sussex BN8 6QL. *T:* Halland 364.

CRUICKSHANK, Flight-Lieut John Alexander, VC 1944; late RAF; with Grindlay's Bank Ltd, London, 1952-76; retired; *b* 20 May 1920; *s* of James C. Cruickshank, Aberdeen, and Alice Bow, Macduff, Banffshire; *m* 1955, Marion R. Beverley, Toronto, Canada. *Educ:* Aberdeen Grammar Sch.; Daniel Stewart's Coll., Edinburgh. Entered Commercial Bank of Scotland, 1938; returned to banking, 1946. Mem. of Territorial Army and called for service, Aug. 1939, in RA; transferred to RAF 1941 and commissioned in 1942; all RAF service was with Coastal Command. ADC to Lord High Commissioner to the Gen. Assembly of the Church of Scotland, 1946–48. *Address:* 34 Frogston Road West, Edinburgh EH10 7AH. *T:* 031-445 1215.

CRUIKSHANK, John Merrill, CMG 1951; OBE 1937; *b* 4 Sept. 1901; *s* of J. P. and J. E. Cruikshank (*née* Crombie); *m* 1930, Elaine Strong; one *s. Educ:* McGill Univ. (MD, CM, DPH). Colonial Medical Service; Surgeon, Bahamas, 1928–30; Chief Medical Officer, Bahamas, 1930–40; DMS Bahamas Military Forces, 1939–41; RCAF, 1941–46; Asst Medical Adviser, Colonial Office, 1946–48; Insp.-Gen., S Pacific Health Service, and DMS, Fiji, 1948–56; WHO Area Representative for S Pacific, 1956–59. Subseq. Dir, Medical Services, Belmont, Calif; retd. Certificate Tropical Medicine, London; Fellow: Amer. Coll. Surgeons; Amer. Coll. Physicians; Royal Sanitary Inst. OStJ 1950. *Publications:* articles in medical journals. *Recreation:* electronics. *Address:* 401-33 Avenue SW, Calgary, Alberta T2S 0S8, Canada. *T:* 2436691. *Club:* Corona.

CRUMP, Maurice, CBE 1959; *b* 13 Jan. 1908; *s* of William Hamilton Crump and Jean Morris Alan Crump (*née* Esplen); *m* 1946, Mary Arden, *d* of Austin Stead, Montreal, PQ, Canada. *Educ:* Harrow; Oxford. Called to Bar, Inner Temple, 1931, practised Western Circuit. RAF Reserve, 1929–35; recommissioned RAF Volunteer Reserve, 1940; served War of 1939–45, as pilot, 1940–45; Capt. in Command on North Atlantic Return Ferry, 1944–45. In Dept of Dir of Public Prosecutions, 1945; Asst Dir, 1951–58, Deputy Dir, 1958–66. *Recreations:* flying, travelling. *Address:* Dorval, Punta de la Mona, Almuñecar, P. de Granada, Spain. *Clubs:* United Oxford & Cambridge University, Royal Air Force.

CRUMP, Rt. Rev. William Henry Howes; *b* London, Ontario, Canada, 13 March 1903; *m* 1932, Betty Margaret Dean Thomas; one *s* one *d. Educ:* London, Ontario; University of Western Ontario; Huron College; Trinity College, Toronto. Ordained Deacon, 1926; Curate, Wawanesa, Manitoba, 1926; Priest, 1927. Rector: Glenboro, Manitoba, 1927; Holland, Manitoba, 1931; Boissevain, Manitoba, 1933; St Aidan's, Winnipeg, 1933–44; Christ Church, Calgary, 1944–60; Canon of St Paul, Diocese of Calgary, 1949; Bishop of Saskatchewan, 1960–71. *Address:* 552 Academy Road, Winnipeg, Manitoba R3N 0E3, Canada.

CRUMP, William Maurice Esplen; *see* Crump, Maurice.

CRUMPTON, Michael Joseph, PhD; FRS 1979; Deputy Director of Research, Imperial Cancer Research Fund Laboratories, London, since 1979; *b* 7 June 1929; *s* of Charles E. and Edith Crumpton; *m* 1960, Janet Elizabeth Dean; one *s* two *d. Educ:* Poole Grammar Sch., Poole; University Coll., Southampton; Lister Inst. of Preventive Medicine, London. BSc, PhD, London. Member, scientific staff, Microbiological Research Estabt, Porton, Wilts, 1955–58; Visiting Scientist Fellowship, Nat. Insts of Health, Bethesda, Maryland, USA, 1959–60; Research Fellow, Dept of Immunology, St Mary's Hosp. Med. Sch., London, 1960–66; Mem., scientific staff, Nat. Inst. for Med. Research, Mill Hill, 1966–79, Head of Biochemistry Div., 1977–79. Visiting Fellow, John Curtin Sch. for Med. Research, ANU, Canberra, 1973–74. Member: Cell Board, MRC, 1979; EMBO, 1982. Mem. Sci. Council, Celltech Ltd, 1980–. *Publications:* contribs to Biochemical Jl and various other learned scientific jls. *Recreations:* gardening, reading. *Address:* 33 Homefield Road, Radlett, Herts WD7 8PX. *T:* Radlett 4675.

CRUTCHLEY, Brooke, CBE 1954; Printer of the University of Cambridge, 1946–74; Fellow of Trinity Hall, 1951–73, Emeritus Fellow, 1977 (Vice-Master, 1966–70); Honorary Fellow of St Edmund's House, Cambridge, since 1980; *b* 31 July 1907; *yr s* of late Ernest Tristram Crutchley, CB, CMG, CBE, and Anna, *d* of James Dunne; *m* 1936, Diana, *d* of late Lt-Col Arthur Egerton Cotton, DSO, and Beryl Marie (who *m* 2nd, John Lee Booker); two *s* one *d. Educ:* Shrewsbury; Trinity Hall, Cambridge. Editorial Staff of Yorkshire Post, 1929–30; Asst Univ. Printer at Cambridge, 1930–45; Secretary's Dept of the Admiralty, 1941–45. Pres., Inst. of Printing, 1972–74. Hon. Col, Commonwealth of Kentucky, 1974. Bicentenary Medal, RSA, 1977. *Publication:* To be a printer, (autobiog.), 1980. *Address:* 2 Courtyards, Little Shelford, Cambridge CB2 5ER. *T:* Cambridge 842389. *Club:* Double Crown.

CRUTCHLEY, Adm. Sir Victor Alexander Charles, VC 1918; KCB 1946 (CB 1945); DSC 1918; RN retired; DL; *b* 2 Nov. 1893; *s* of late Percy Edward Crutchley and late Hon. Frederica Louisa, 2nd *d* of 3rd Baron Southampton; *m* 1930, Joan Elizabeth Loveday (*d* 1980), *d* of late William Coryton, Pentillie Castle, Cornwall, and late Mrs William Coryton; one *s* one *d. Educ:* Osborne and Dartmouth. Served European War in HMS Centurion, Battle of Jutland; in HMS Brilliant in attempt to block Ostend Harbour, 22-23 April 1918 (DSC); in HMS Vindictive in similar attempt, 9-10 May 1918 (VC, Croix de Guerre); commanded HMS Diomede, New Zealand; Senior Officer, First Minesweeping Flotilla, 1935–36; Capt. Fishery Protection and Minesweeping Flotilla, 1936–37; commanded HMS Warspite, 1937–40; Commodore RN Barracks, Devonport, 1940–42; commanded Australian Naval Squadron, 1942–44; Flag Officer Gibraltar, 1945–47; retired, 1947, as Adm. DL Dorset, 1957. Chief Comdr Legion of Merit (USA), 1944; Polonia Restituta, 1942. *Address:* Mappercombe Manor, Nettlecombe, Bridport, Dorset DT6 3SS.

See also Sir William John Colfox, Bt.

CRUTHERS, Sir James (Winter), Kt 1980; Chairman and Managing Director, TVW Enterprises Ltd, Perth, Western Australia, 1976–81; *b* 20 Dec. 1924; *s* of James William and Kate Cruthers; *m* 1950, Alwyn Sheila Della; one *s* one *d. Educ:* Claremont Central State Sch.; Perth Technical College. Started as junior in Perth Daily News, 1939; war service, AIF and RAAF (Pilot), 1942; Journalist, Perth Daily News, 1946; Editor, Weekly Publications, West Australian Newspapers Ltd, 1953; TVW Ltd: General Manager, 1958; Managing Director, 1969; Dep. Chairman, 1974. Western Australian Citizen Of The Year, Industry and Commerce, 1980. *Recreations:* golf, jogging. *Address:* Post Office Box 7, Tuart Hill, Western Australia 6060. *T:* 349.7777. *Clubs:* Weld (Perth); Lake Karrinyup Country.

CRUTTWELL, Mrs Geraldine; *see* McEwan, Geraldine.

CRUTTWELL, Hugh (Percival); Principal of Royal Academy of Dramatic Art since 1966; *b* 31 Oct. 1918; *s* of Clement Chadwick Cruttwell and Grace Fanny (*née* Robin); *m* 1953, Geraldine McEwan, *qv* ; one *s* one *d. Educ:* King's Sch., Bruton; Hertford Coll., Oxford. *Address:* 8 Ranelagh Avenue, Barnes, SW13. *T:* 01-878 0695.

CRYER, (George) Robert; MP (Lab) Keighley, since Feb. 1974; *b* 3 Dec. 1934; *m* 1963, Ann (*née* Place); one *s* one *d. Educ:* Salt High Sch., Shipley; Hull Univ. BSc Econ Hons, Certif. Educn. Secondary Sch. Teacher, Hull, 1959, Bradford, 1961 and Keighley, 1962; Asst Personnel Officer, 1960; Dewsbury Techn. Coll., 1963; Blackburn Coll. of Technology, 1964–65; Keighley Techn. Coll., 1965–74. Parly Under-Sec. of State, DoI, 1976–78. Contested (Lab) Darwen Div. of Lancs, 1964; Labour Councillor, Keighley Borough Council, 1971–74. *Publications:* Steam in the Worth Valley, Vol. 1 1969, Vol. 2 1972. *Recreation:* working on Worth Valley Railway. *Address:* Holyoake, Providence Lane, Oakworth, Keighley, W Yorks. *T:* Haworth 42595. *Club:* Workers Union Social (Keighley).

CRYSTAL, Prof. David; Professor of Linguistic Science, University of Reading, since 1975; *b* 6 July 1941; *s* of Samuel Cyril Crystal and Mary Agnes Morris; *m* 1st, 1964, Molly Irene Stack (*d* 1976); one *s* two *d* (and one *s* decd); 2nd, 1976, Hilary Frances Norman; one *s. Educ:* St Mary's Coll., Liverpool; University Coll. London (BA 1962); London Univ. (PhD 1966). Res. Asst, UCL, 1962–63; Asst Lectr, UCNW, 1963–65; University of Reading: Lectr, 1965–69; Reader, 1969–75. Vis. Prof., Bowling Green State Univ., 1969. Sec., Linguistics Assoc. of GB, 1965–70. Mem., Academic Bd, Coll. of Speech Therapists, 1972–79. Editor: Language Res. in Progress, 1966–70; Jl of Child Language, 1973–; The Language Library, 1978–; Applied Language Studies, 1980–; Adv. Editor, Penguin Linguistics, 1968–75; Associate Editor, Jl of Linguistics, 1970–73; Co-Editor, Studies in Language Disability, 1974–. Has broadcast BBC talks on English language and linguistics. *Publications:* Systems of prosodic and paralinguistic features in English (with R. Quirk), 1964; Linguistics, language and religion, 1965; (ed jtly) Proceedings, Modern approaches to language teaching at university level, 1967; What is linguistics?, 1968, 4th edn 1981; Prosodic systems and intonation in English, 1969; (with D. Davy) Investigating English style, 1969; (ed with W. Bolton) The English Language, vol. 2, 1969; Linguistics, 1971; Basic linguistics, 1973; Language acquisition, 1973; The English tone of voice, 1975; (with D. Davy) Advanced conversational English, 1975; (with J. Bevington) Skylarks, 1975; (jtly) The grammatical analysis of language disability, 1976; Child language, learning and linguistics, 1976; Working with LARSP, 1979; Introduction to language pathology, 1980; A first dictionary of linguistics and phonetics, 1980; (ed) Eric Partridge: in his own words, 1980; Clinical Linguistics, 1981; Directions in applied linguistics, 1981; Profiling linguistic disability, 1982; (ed) Linguistic Controversies, 1982; (with J. L. Foster) Databank series: Heat, Light, Sound, Roads, Railways, Canals, Manors, Castles, Money, Monasteries, Parliament, Newspapers, 1979; The Romans, The Greeks, The Ancient Egyptians, 1981; Air, Food, Volcanoes, 1982; contributions to: The Library of Modern Knowledge, 1978; A Dictionary of Modern Thought, 1978; and to numerous volumes on language, style, prosody, communication, religion, handicap, teaching and reading; symposia and proceedings of learned socs; articles and reviews in jls on linguistics, English language, speech pathology and education. *Recreations:* cinema, music, bibliophily. *Address:* The School House, Forest Road, Wokingham, Berks RG11 5SD. *T:* Bracknell 23359.

CUBBON, Sir Brian (Crossland), KCB 1977 (CB 1974); Permanent Under Secretary of State, Home Office, since 1979; *b* 9 April 1928; *m* 1956, Elizabeth Lorin Richardson; three *s* one *d. Educ:* Bury Grammar Sch.; Trinity Coll., Cambridge. Entered Home Office, 1951; Cabinet Office, 1961–63, 1971–75; Private Sec. to Home Sec., 1968–69; Permanent Under-Sec. of State, Northern Ireland Office, 1976–79. *Address:* c/o Home Office, SW1. *Club:* United Oxford & Cambridge University.

CUBBON, Maj.-Gen. John Hamilton, CB 1962; CBE 1958 (OBE 1940); DL; *b* 15 March 1911; *s* of Joseph Cubbon; *m* 1935, Amelia Margaret Yates; two *s* one *d. Educ:* St Bees Sch.; RMC Sandhurst. 2nd Lieut Ches Regt, 1931; Commanded: 1st Bn The Parachute Regt, 1946–49; 1st Bn The Ches Regt, 1951–54; 18th Infantry Bde, Malaya, 1956–57. Maj.-Gen. 1960; GOC SW Dist, 1960–63; GOC Land Forces, Middle East Command, 1963–65. DL Devon, 1969. *Recreation:* sailing. *Address:* The Hayes, Harpford, Sidmouth, Devon.

CUBITT, family name of **Baron Ashcombe.**

CUBITT, Hugh Guy, CBE 1977; FRICS; JP; DL; Director: National Westminster Bank (Chairman, Outer London Region); Property Security Investment Trust; Chairman: Lombard North Central PLC, since 1980; The Housing Corporation, since 1980; *b* 2 July 1928; *s* of late Col Hon. (Charles) Guy Cubitt, CBE, DSO, TD, and of Rosamund Mary Edith, *d* of Sir Montagu Cholmeley, 4th Bt; *m* 1958, Linda Ishbel, *d* of late Hon. Angus Campbell, CBE; one *s* two *d*. *Educ:* RNC Dartmouth and Greenwich. Lieut RN, 1949; served in Korea, 1949-51; Flag Lieut to Adm., BJSM Washington, 1952 and to C-in-C Nore, 1953; retd 1953. Qual. Chartered Auctioneer and Estate Agent, 1958; Chartered Surveyor (FRICS) 1970. Partner: Rogers Chapman & Thomas, 1958-67; Cubitt & West, 1962-79. Mem. Westminster City Council, 1963-78; Chairman: Highways Cttee, 1968-71; Town Planning Cttee, 1971-72; Leader of Council, 1972-76; Alderman, 1974-78; Lord Mayor and dep. High Steward of Westminster, 1977-78. Hon. Treas., London Boroughs Assoc., 1974-77. Mem. Home Office Cttee on London Taxicab Trade (Stamp Cttee), 1967-70. Governor: Cranleigh Sch. (Chm. of Governors, 1981); West Heath Sch.; Mem. Governing Body, RAM. Hon. Steward, Westminster Abbey, 1978. Mem., Bd of Green Cloth Verge of Palaces, 1980-. FRSA. JP Surrey, 1964; Dep. Chm., Dorking PSD, 1974-; High Sheriff of Surrey, 1983-84. DL Greater London, 1978. Liveryman, Needlemakers' Co. *Recreations:* country sports, travel, photography. *Address:* Chapel House, West Humble, Dorking, Surrey. *T:* Dorking 882994. *Club:* Boodle's.

CUBITT, James William Archibald, MBE 1945; FRIBA; architect, sculptor; Senior Partner of James Cubitt and Partners, London, Nigeria, Malaya, since 1948; *b* 1 May 1914; *s* of James Edward and Isabel Margaret Cubitt; *m* 1st, 1939, Ann Margaret Tooth (marr. diss. 1947); one *s* one *d*; 2nd, 1950, Constance Anne (*née* Sitwell) (marr. diss. 1972; she *d* 1981); one *s*; 3rd, 1973, Eleni Collard (*née* Kiortsis). *Educ:* Harrow; Brasenose Coll., Oxford; Architectural Association Sch. of Architecture. BA Oxon 1935; ARIBA 1940; FRIBA 1955. Army, 1940-45. In private practice as architect from 1948. Main works in England: exhibition and shop design; schools for Herts CC, W Riding CC, LCC, Leeds Corporation. Has also designed many public buildings, schools, offices and private houses in Ghana; now works in Nigeria, Brunei and Libya. Architect for the Universities of Libya and Nigeria; photographs and drawings of Univ. of Garyounis, Benghazi, Libya exhibited at Venice Biennale, 1982. Chm., Mortimer and Burghfield Local Labour Party, 1974-. Writes articles and reviews. Council of Architectural Assoc., 1960- (Pres., 1965-66). Sculpture: one-man show, John Whibley Gallery, 1962; Burgos Gallery, NY, 1966; Ellingham Mill Art Soc. exhibn, 1978. *Address:* 25 Gloucester Place, W1. *T:* 01-935 0288.

CUCKNEY, Sir John (Graham), Kt 1978; Chairman: Thomas Cook Group, since 1978; Brooke Bond Group plc, since 1981 (Vice-Chairman, 1980; Director, since 1978); Deputy Chairman, John Brown plc, since 1982 (Director, since 1981); Director: Midland Bank plc, since 1978; Royal Insurance plc, since 1979; *b* 12 July 1925; *s* of late Air Vice-Marshal E. J. Cuckney, CB, CBE, DSC; *m* 2nd, 1960, Muriel, *d* of late Walter Scott Boyd. *Educ:* Shrewsbury; St Andrews Univ. (MA). War Service, Royal Northumberland Fusiliers, King's African Rifles, followed by attachment to War Office (Civil Asst, Gen. Staff), until 1957; Chm. and Dir of various industrial and financial cos, since 1957, including: Man. Dir, Standard Industrial Gp, 1966-70; Chm., Standard Industrial Trust, 1966-70; Director: Lazard Bros & Co., 1964-70; J. Bibby & Sons, 1970-72; Dep. Chm., Stanley Gibbons International, 1974-76; Public appointments include: Chm., Mersey Docks and Harbour Board, 1970-72; Chief Executive (Second Perm. Sec.), Property Services Agency, DoE, 1972-74; Chm., International Military Services Ltd (an MoD company), 1974-; Sen. Crown Agent and Chm. of Crown Agents, for Oversea Governments and Administrations, 1974-78. Independent Mem., Railway Policy Review Cttee, 1966-67; special Mem., Hops Marketing Bd, 1971-72; Chairman: EDC for Building, 1976-80; PLA, 1977-79; Internat. Maritime Bureau, Internat. Chamber of Commerce, 1981-; Mem., Docklands Joint Cttee, 1977-79. Governor, Centre for Internat. Briefing, Farnham Castle, 1974-. Elder Brother of Trinity House, 1980. *Address:* 45 Berkeley Street, W1. *Clubs:* Athenæum, Travellers'.

CUDLIPP, family name of **Baron Cudlipp.**

CUDLIPP, Baron *cr* 1974 (Life Peer), of Aldingbourne, W Sussex; **Hugh Cudlipp,** Kt 1973; OBE 1945; Chairman: International Publishing Corporation Ltd, 1968-73 (Deputy Chairman, 1964-68); International Publishing Corporation Newspaper Division, 1970-73; Deputy Chairman (editorial), Reed International Board, 1970-73; Director, Associated Television Ltd, 1956-73; *b* 28 Aug. 1913; *s* of William Cudlipp, Cardiff; *m* 2nd, 1945, Eileen Ascroft (*d* 1962); 3rd, 1963, Jodi, *d* of late John L. Hyland, Palm Beach, Fla, and Mrs D. W. Jones, Southport. *Educ:* Howard Gardens Sch., Cardiff. Provincial newspapers in Cardiff and Manchester, 1927-32; Features Ed., Sunday Chronicle, London, 1932-35; Features Ed., Daily Mirror, 1935-37; Ed., Sunday Pictorial, 1937-40. Military Service, 1940-46; CO, British Army Newspaper Unit, CMF, 1943-46. Ed., Sunday Pictorial, 1946-49; Managing Ed., Sunday Express, 1950-52; Editorial Dir, Daily Mirror and Sunday Pictorial, 1952-63; Joint Managing Dir, Daily Mirror and Sunday Pictorial, 1959-63; Chm., Odhams Press Ltd, 1961-63; Chm., Daily Mirror Newspapers Ltd, 1963-68. Mem., Royal Commn on Standards of Conduct in Public Life, 1974-76. *Publications:* Publish and be Damned!, 1955; At Your Peril, 1962; Walking on the Water, 1976; The Prerogative of the Harlot, 1980.

Address: The Dene, Hook Lane, Aldingbourne, West Sussex. *Club:* Garrick.

CUDLIPP, Michael John; Director of Information, International Thomson Organisation (formerly The Thomson Organisation), since 1979; *b* 24 April 1934; *o s* of late Percy Cudlipp and Mrs Gwendoline May Cudlipp; *m* 1957, Margaret Susannah Rees (marr. diss. 1975); one *d*. *Educ:* Tonbridge Sch., Kent. Trainee reporter, feature writer, gossip columnist, sub-editor, South Wales Echo, Cardiff, 1953-57; Sub-editor, Evening Chronicle, Manchester (various freelance jobs on daily and Sunday newspapers in Manchester), 1957-58; News Editor and Asst Editor (News), Sunday Times, 1958-67; Asst Editor (Night), Jt Man. Editor and sen. Dep. Editor, The Times, 1967-73; Chief Editor, London Broadcasting Co., 1973-74; Consultant on Public Relations to NI Office (temp. Civil Servant with rank of Under-Sec.), 1974-75; Dir of Information, Nat. Enterprise Bd, 1975-78. *Recreations:* Arts, Welsh rugby football, urban pigeon shooting. *Address:* Thomson House, 4 Stratford Place, W1A 4YG.

CUDLIPP, Reginald; Director, Anglo-Japanese Economic Institute, London, since 1961; *b* Cardiff, 11 Dec. 1910; *s* of William Cudlipp, Cardiff; *m* 1945, Rachel Joyce Braham. *Educ:* Cardiff Technical Coll. Began journalistic career on Penarth News, Glamorgan; Sub-Ed., Western Mail, Cardiff; joined News of the World Sub-Editorial Staff, 1938; served War, 1940-46; rejoined News of the World and became Special Correspondent in USA, 1946-47; Features Ed., 1948-50, Dep. Ed., 1950-53, Ed., 1953-59; Dir, News of the World Ltd, 1955-60. Extensive industrial tours and on-the-spot economic study of Japan regularly, 1962-. Member: Japan Soc.; RSAA; RSA; RIIA; Royal Commonwealth Soc. Life Mem., NUJ, 1929-. Editor, Japan (quarterly review and monthly survey), and special publications on the Japanese scene. Lecturer and writer on Japan's past, present and future; also first-hand research on developing nations and economic co-operation, especially in Africa and Asia. Order of the Sacred Treasure, Japan, 1982. *Publications:* numerous contribs to newspapers and periodicals, on Japan and Anglo-Japanese affairs. *Recreations:* music, travel, and reading, writing and talking about Japan. *Address:* 342 Grand Buildings, Trafalgar Square, WC2. *T:* 01-930 5567.

CULHANE, Rosalind, (Lady Padmore), MVO 1938; OBE 1949; Treasury Welfare Adviser, 1943-64; *y d* of late F. W. S. Culhane, MRCS, LRCP, Hastings, Sussex; *m* 1964, Sir Thomas Padmore, *qv*. Joined Treasury in 1923 and attached to office of Chancellor of Exchequer; Asst Private Sec. to Mr Chamberlain, 1934, Sir John Simon, 1937, Sir Kingsley Wood, 1940. *Address:* 39 Cholmeley Crescent, N6. *T:* 01-340 6587.

CULLEN OF ASHBOURNE, 2nd Baron *cr* 1920; **Charles Borlase Marsham Cokayne,** MBE 1945; a Lord in Waiting (Government Whip), 1979-82; Major, Royal Signals; *b* 6 Oct. 1912; *e s* of 1st Baron and Grace Margaret (*d* 1971), *d* of Rev. Hon. John Marsham; *S* father, 1932; *m* 1942, Valerie Catherine Mary (marr. diss. 1947), *o d* of late W. H. Collbran; one *d*; *m* 1948, Patricia Mary, *er d* of late Col S. Clulow-Gray and late Mrs Clulow-Gray, formerly of Clare Priory, Suffolk. *Educ:* Eton. Served War of 1939-45 (MBE). Amateur Tennis Champion, 1947, 1952. One of HM Lieutenants, City of London, 1976-. *Heir:* b Hon. Edmund Willoughby Marsham Cokayne [*b* 18 May 1916; *m* 1943, Janet Manson, *d* of late William Douglas Watson and of Mrs Lauritson, Calgary]. *Address:* 75 Cadogan Gardens, SW3. *T:* 01-589 1981. *Clubs:* MCC, Queen's.

CULLEN, Prof. Alexander Lamb, OBE 1960; DSc(Eng); FRS 1977; FEng 1977, FIEE, FIEEE, FInstP, FCGI; SERC (formerly SRC) Senior Research Fellow, Department of Electronic and Electrical Engineering, University College London, since 1980; *b* 30 April 1920; *s* of Richard and Jessie Cullen, Lincoln; *m* 1940, Margaret, *er d* of late Alexander Lamb, OBE; two *s* one *d*. *Educ:* Lincoln Sch.; City and Guilds Coll., London. Staff of Radio Dept, RAE Farnborough, working on development of radar, 1940-46; Lectr in Electrical Engineering, University Coll., London, 1946-55 (title of Reader conferred 1955); Prof. of Electrical Engineering, University of Sheffield, 1955-67; Pender Prof. of Electrical Engineering, University College London, 1967-80. Hon. Prof., Northwestern Polytechnical Univ., Xian, China, 1981. Mem., IBA, 1979. Kelvin premium of IEE, 1952; Extra premium of IEE, 1953 (with Prof. H. M. Barlow and Dr A. E. Karbowiak); Radio Sect. premium of IEE, 1954; Ambrose Fleming premium of IEE, 1956 (with J. C. Parr), 1975 (with Dr J. R. Forrest); Duddell premium of IEE, 1957 (with Dr H. A. French); Electronics and Communications Sect. premium of IEE, 1959. Chm., Brit. Nat. Cttee, URSI, Vice-Pres., 1981. Hon. DSc, Chinese Univ. of Hong Kong, 1981. *Publications:* Microwave Measurements (jointly with Prof. H. M. Barlow), 1950; a number of papers on electromagnetic waves and microwave measurement techniques in IEE proceedings and elsewhere. *Recreations:* music and reading. *Address:* Department of Electronic and Electrical Engineering, University College London, Torrington Place, WC1E 7JE.

CULLEN, Douglas; see Cullen, W. D.

CULLEN, Gordon; see Cullen, T. G.

CULLEN, James Reynolds; *b* 13 June 1900; *s* of Rev. James Harris Cullen, London Missionary Society; *m* 1931, Inez (*d* 1980), *e d* of M. G. Zarifi, MBE; one *s* two *d*. *Educ:* Weimar Gymnasium; Tonbridge Sch.; Balliol Coll., Oxford (Scholar). Hertford Schol., 1919; Craven Schol., 1920; 1st class Hon.

Mods, 1920; 2nd class Lit. Hum. 1922; MA 1925. Asst Master, Winchester Coll., 1922-30; archæological expeditions to Asia Minor, 1925, and Mytilene, 1930; Dir of Education, Cyprus, 1930-45; Dir of Education, Uganda, 1945-52; Asst Master, Oundle Sch., 1953-60, Cranbrook and Benenden Schs, 1960-68. *Address:* Weathercock House, Hawkhurst, Kent TN18 4QA. *Club:* Royal Commonwealth Society.

CULLEN, Raymond; Chairman, The Calico Printers' Association Ltd and subsidiaries, 1964-68; *b* 27 May 1913; *s* of late John Norman Cullen and Bertha (*née* Dearden); *m* 1940, Doris, *d* of A. W. Paskin; two *d. Educ:* King's Sch., Macclesfield; St Catharine's Coll., Cambridge (Scholar, MA). Joined The Calico Printers' Assoc. Ltd Commn Printing, 1934; transf. overseas, 1938; service in India and China. Dir, W. A. Beardsell & Co. (Private) Ltd, Madras, 1946 (Chm. and Man. Dir, 1949-55); Chm. and Man. Dir, Mettur Industries Ltd, 1949-55; Chm. and Man. Dir, Marshall Fabrics Ltd, 1955-62; Director: Calico Printers' Assoc. Ltd, 1962-68; Barclays Bank Ltd Manchester Local Bd, 1965-69. Member: Textile Coun., 1967-69; Coun., Inst. of Directors, 1967-69; NW Economic Planning Coun., 1968-69; Governor, Manchester Grammar Sch. *Recreations:* fishing, golf (Pres., Cheshire Union of Golf Clubs). *Address:* Cranford, Ladybrook Road, Bramhall, Cheshire SK7 3NB. *T:* 061-485 3204.

CULLEN, Terence Lindsay Graham, QC 1978; *b* 29 Oct. 1930; *s* of Eric Graham Cullen and Jean Morrison Hunter (*née* Bennett); *m* 1958, Muriel Elisabeth Rolfe; three *s. Educ:* RNC, Dartmouth. RN, 1948-55; Prestige Group Ltd, 1955-61. Called to the Bar, Lincoln's Inn, 1961. *Recreation:* the Turf. *Address:* 13 Old Square, Lincoln's Inn, WC2A 3UA. *T:* 01-404 4800; The Limes, East Malling, Kent.

CULLEN, (Thomas) Gordon, CBE 1978; RDI 1976; planning consultant, artist and writer; *b* 9 Aug. 1914; *s* of Rev. T. H. Cullen and Mary Anne (*née* Moffatt); *m* 1955, Comtesse Jacqueline de Chabameix du Chambon; three *d. Educ:* Prince Henry's Grammar Sch., Otley, Yorks; Regent Street Polytechnic Sch. of Architecture, London. Fraternal Delegate, Runcorn Trades Council, 1942; Mem. Planning Div., Develt and Welfare, Barbados, 1944-46; Asst Editor, Architectural Rev., 1946-56. Townscape Consultant: with Ford Foundn, New Delhi, 1960, and Calcutta, 1962; Liverpool, Llantrisant, Tenterden, Peterborough and Ware, 1962-76. Exhib. drawings, Paris Salon, Royal Acad.; One-Man Exhibn, Sweden and Holland, 1976. Member: Eton RDC, 1963-73; Wraysbury Parish Council, 1960-. Hon. FRIBA 1972. Hon. LittD Sheffield, 1975; Dr-IngEh Munich, 1973. Amer. Inst. of Architects Gold Medal, 1976. *Publications:* Townscape, 1964; planning reports. *Recreations:* observation, writing poetry, sleep. *Address:* 29 The Drive, Wraysbury, Staines, Mddx TW19 5ES. *T:* Wraysbury 2147. *Club:* Wraysbury Village Club and Institute (Wraysbury).

CULLEN, William Douglas, QC (Scotland) 1973; Advocate-depute, 1978-81; *b* 18 Nov. 1935; *s* of late Sheriff K. D. Cullen and Mrs G. M. Cullen; *m* 1961, Rosamond Mary Downer; two *s* two *d. Educ:* Dundee High Sch.; St Andrews Univ. (MA); Edinburgh Univ. (LLB). Called to the Scottish Bar, 1960. Standing Jun. Counsel to HM Customs and Excise, 1970-73. Chm., Medical Appeal Tribunal, 1977-. *Publication:* The Faculty Digest Supplement 1951-60, 1965. *Recreations:* gardening, natural history. *Address:* 62 Fountainhall Road, Edinburgh EH9 2LP. *T:* 031-667 6949. *Club:* New (Edinburgh).

CULLIMORE, Charles Augustine Kaye; HM Diplomatic Service; Counsellor and Head of Chancery, British High Commission, New Delhi, since 1979; *b* 2 Oct. 1933; *s* of Charles Cullimore and Constance Alicia Kaye Cullimore (*née* Grimshaw); *m* 1956, Val Elizabeth Margot (*née* Willemsen); one *s* one *d. Educ:* Portora Royal Sch., Enniskillen; Trinity Coll., Oxford (MA). N Ireland Short Service Commn, 1955-57. HMOCS, Tanganyika, 1958-61; ICI Ltd, 1961-71; joined HM Diplomatic Service, 1971; FCO, 1971-73; Bonn, 1973-77; FCO, 1977-79. *Recreations:* theatre, walking, tennis. *Address:* c/o Foreign and Commonwealth Office, SW1A 2AH. *Club:* Royal Commonwealth Society.

CULLIMORE, Colin Stuart, CBE 1978; Managing Director, J. H. Dewhurst Ltd, since 1976; *b* 13 July 1931; *s* of Reginald Victor Cullimore and May Maria Cullimore; *m* 1952, Kathleen Anyta Lamming; one *s. Educ:* Westminster Sch.; National Coll. of Food Technol. Commnd Royal Scots Fusiliers, 1951; seconded Parachute Regt; transf. when perm. officer cadre formed; Major 1956; 10th Bn Parachute Regt TA, 1960. Gen. Man., Payne & Son (Butchers) Ltd, 1960; Asst Gen. Man., J. H. Dewhurst Ltd, 1965, Gen. Man. 1969. Chairman: Retail Consortium Food Cttee, 1973-74; Multiple Shops Fedn, 1977-78. Vice-Chairman: Multiple Food Retailers Assoc., 1972-74; Governors, Coll. for Distributive Trades, 1976-79, 1980-; Vice-Pres., British Multiple Retailers Assoc., 1978-. Dep. Chm., Meat Promotion Exec., 1975-78. Member: Distribn and Consumer Cttees, Meat and Livestock Commn, 1969-72; EDC for Distrib. Trades, 1972-80; Council, Inst. of Meat. Gold Medal: Inst. of Meat, 1956; Butchers' Co., 1956. *Recreations:* golf, wine. *Address:* Barons, Chobham, Woking, Surrey. *T:* Chobham 8645. *Clubs:* Naval and Military, Institute of Directors.

CULLINGFORD, Rev. Cecil Howard Dunstan, MA; FRSA; *b* 13 Sept. 1904; *s* of Francis James and Lilian Mabel Cullingford; *m* 1st, 1933, Olive Eveline (*d* 1971), *d* of Lt-Col P. H. Collingwood, Clifton, Bristol; one *s* one *d*; 2nd, 1972, Penelope Wood-Hill, *e d* of Dr H. Wood-Hill, Beccles. *Educ:*

City of London Sch.; Corpus Christi Coll., Cambridge (Foundation Scholar). 1st Class Hons in Classical Tripos, Parts 1 and 2, and Historical Tripos, Part 2. VIth Form Master, Brighton Coll., 1928-32; Vice-Principal, Clifton Theological Coll., 1932-34; Chaplain of Oundle Sch., 1935-46. Army Chaplain, 1939-45; Guards Armoured Div., 1939-43; Staff Chaplain, 21st Army Group, 1943-44; Senior Chaplain, 79th Armoured Div., 1944-45. Headmaster of Monmouth Sch., 1946-56; Lectr in Naval History at Britannia, RNC Dartmouth, 1957-60; Chaplain: St John's Sch., Leatherhead, 1960-64; St Michael's Sch., Limpsfield, 1964-67; Vicar of Stiffkey with Morston, 1967-72; Rural Dean of Beccles, 1973-76. Pres., Silleren Ski Club, 1966; Vice-Pres., Wessex Cave Club; Hon. Member: Cave Res. Group of GB; British Speleological Assoc.; British Cave Res. Assoc. *Publications:* Exploring Caves, 1951; (ed) British Caving: an Introduction to Speleology, 1953 (2nd edn 1961); (ed) A Manual of Caving Techniques, 1969; The Thornhill Guide to Caving, 1976; (ed) The Science of Speleology, 1976. *Recreations:* hockey, pot-holing, music, archæology. *Address:* The Staithe, Beccles, Suffolk. *T:* Beccles 712182.
See also E. C. M. Cullingford.

CULLINGFORD, Eric Coome Maynard, CMG 1963; *b* 15 March 1910; *s* of Francis James and Lilian Mabel Cullingford; *m* 1938, Friedel Fuchs; two *s* one *d. Educ:* City of London Sch.; St Catharine's Coll., Cambridge (Exhibitioner). Entered Ministry of Labour as Third Class Officer, 1932; Principal, 1942. Served with Manpower Div. of CCG, 1946-50. Asst Sec., Min. of Labour, 1954. Labour Attaché, Bonn, 1961-65, 1968-72. Regional Controller, Eastern and Southern Region, Dept of Employment and Productivity, 1966-68; retired 1973. *Publication:* Trade Unions in West Germany, 1976. *Address:* Oaklands, 21 Furze Field, Oxshott, Surrey.
See also Rev. C. H. D. Cullingford.

CULLINGWORTH, Prof. (John) Barry; Professor of Planning, University of Toronto, since 1982; Visiting Professor, University of Strathclyde; *b* 11 Sept. 1929; *s* of Sidney C. and Winifred E. Cullingworth; *m* 1951, Betty Violet (*née* Turner); one *s* two *d. Educ:* High Pavement Sch., Nottingham; Trinity Coll. of Music, London; London Sch. of Economics. Research Asst, Asst Lectr and Lectr, Univ. of Manchester, 1955-60; Lectr, Univ. of Durham, 1960-63; Sen. Lectr and Reader, Univ. of Glasgow, 1963-66; Dir, Centre for Urban and Regional Studies, Univ. of Birmingham, 1966-72. Dir, Planning Exchange, Scotland, 1972-75; Official Historian, Cabinet Office, 1975-77. Chm., Dept of Urban and Regional Planning, 1977-80, Res. Prof., Centre for Urban and Community Studies, 1980-82, Univ. of Toronto. Vice-Chm., Scottish Housing Adv. Cttee; Chairman: Cttee on Community Facilities in Expanding Towns (Report, The Needs of New Communities, 1967); Cttee on Unfit Housing in Scotland (Report, Scotland's Older Houses, 1967); Cttee on Allocation of Council Houses (Report, Council Housing: Purposes, Procedures and Practices, 1968); Adv. Cttee on Rent Rebates and Rent Allowances, 1973-77. Mem., Ont. Council of Health, 1979-. Vice-Pres., Housing Centre Trust. FRSA 1974; Hon. MRTPI. *Publications:* Housing Needs and Planning Policy, 1960; Housing in Transition, 1963; Town and Country Planning in England and Wales, 1964, 8th edn 1982; English Housing Trends, 1965; Housing and Local Government, 1966; Scottish Housing in 1965, 1967; A Profile of Glasgow Housing, 1968; (with V. Karn) Ownership and Management of Housing in New Towns, 1968; Housing and Labour Mobility, (Paris) 1969; Problems of an Urban Society (3 vols), 1973; Environmental Planning—Reconstruction and Land Use Planning, 1975; Essays on Housing Policy, 1979; New Towns Policy, 1980; Canadian Housing Policy Research, 1980; Land Values, Compensation and Betterment, 1981. *Address:* Department of Geography, University of Toronto, 100 St George Street, Toronto M5S 1A1, Canada.

CULLIS, Prof. Charles Fowler; Professor of Physical Chemistry since 1967, Head of Chemistry Department since 1973, a Pro-Vice-Chancellor since 1980, City University, London; *b* 31 Aug. 1922; 2nd *s* of late Prof. C. G. Cullis, Prof. of Mining Geology, Univ. of London, and Mrs W. J. Cullis (*née* Fowler); *m* 1958, Marjorie Elizabeth, *er d* of late Sir Austin Anderson and of Lady Anderson; two *s* two *d. Educ:* Stowe Sch. (Open Schol.); Trinity Coll., Oxford. BA 1944, BSc 1st Cl. Hons Chem. 1945, DPhil 1948, MA 1948, DSc 1960; FRSC (FRIC 1958). ICI Research Fellow in Chem., Oxford, 1947-50; Lectr in Phys. Chem., Imperial Coll., London, 1950-59; Sen. Lectr in Chem. Engrg and Chem. Tech., Imperial Coll., 1959-64; Reader in Combustion Chemistry, Univ. of London, 1964-66. Vis. Prof., College of Chem., Univ. of California, Berkeley, 1966; Vis. Scientist, CSIRO, Sydney, 1970. Mem. Council, Chem. Soc., 1969-72, 1975-78; Mem., Chem. Soc. Publications Bd, 1976-81; Hon. Sec., Brit. Sect. of Combustion Inst., 1969-74; Mem., Rockets Sub-cttee, 1968-73, and of Combustion Sub-cttee, 1969-72, Aeronautical Research Council; Member: Navy Dept Fuels and Lubricants Adv. Cttee (Fire and Explosion Hazards Working Gp), 1967-; Safety in Mines Research Adv. Bd, 1973- (Chm., 1980-); Chem. Cttee, Defence Sci. Adv. Council, 1979-; Scientific Editor, Internat. Union of Pure and Applied Chem., 1976-78. Governor, City of London Polytechnic, 1982-. Joseph Priestley Award, 1974, Combustion Chem. Medal and Award, 1978, Chem. Soc. *Publications:* The Combustion of Organic Polymers (jtly with M. M. Hirschler), 1981; numerous sci. papers in Proc. Royal Soc., Trans Faraday Soc., Jl Chem. Soc., etc, mainly concerned with chemistry of combustion reactions. *Recreations:* music, travel. *Address:* Chieveley, Black Hill, Lindfield, Sussex RH16 2HF. *T:* Lindfield 2188; Chemistry Department, City University, Northampton Square, EC1V 0HB. *T:* 01-253 4399, ext. 367.

Club: Athenæum.
See also M. F. Cullis.

CULLIS, Michael Fowler, CVO 1955; HM Diplomatic Service, retired; consultant for academic and institutional fund-raising, also on European parliamentary affairs; *b* 22 Oct. 1914; *s* of late Prof. Charles Gilbert Cullis, Imperial Coll. of Science and Technology, London Univ., and late Winifred Jefford Cullis (*née* Fowler); *m* Catherine Robertson, Arbroath, Scotland; no *c. Educ:* Wellington Coll. (scholar); Brasenose Coll., Oxford (Hulme Open Scholar). MA, classics. Law (Lincoln's Inn), and journalism, 1938-39. Military Intelligence, Gibraltar, 1939-40; served Min. of Economic Warfare (London, Spain and Portugal), 1940-44; joined FO as head of Austrian Section, 1945; Political Adviser on Austrian Treaty negotiations (London, Moscow, Vienna, Paris, New York), 1947-50; Special Asst, Schuman Plan, 1950; First Sec., British Embassy, Oslo, 1951-55; Regional (Information) Counsellor for the five Nordic countries, British Embassy, Copenhagen, 1955-58; Dep. Gov. of Malta, 1959-61; Sen. Research Associate, Atlantic Institute, Paris, 1962-65; writing, lecturing, etc, at various European centres, 1965-66; Dir, Arms Control and Disarmament Res., FO, then FCO, 1967-74; Advr on relations with non-govtl bodies, FCO, 1974-79. Unsuccessful candidate (C), European Elections, 1979. FRSA. Chevalier (1st cl.) Order of Dannebrog, 1957. *Publications:* articles and broadcasts on international affairs. *Recreations:* music, chess, Siciliana. *Address:* County End, Bushey Heath, Herts. *T:* 01-950 1057. *Club:* Athenæum.
See also C. F. Cullis.

CULLITON, Hon. Edward Milton, CC 1981; QC; retired; Chief Justice of Saskatchewan, 1962-81; *b* Grand Forks, Minnesota, USA, 9 April 1906; *s* of John J. Culliton and Katherine Mary Kelly, Canadians; *m* 1939, Katherine Mary Hector. *Educ:* Primary educn in towns in Saskatchewan; Univ. of Saskatchewan. BA 1926, LLB 1928. Practised law in Gravelbourg, Sask., 1930-51. Served War: Canadian Armed Forces (active, overseas, Judges' Advocate Br.), 1941-46. MLA for Gravelbourg, 1935-44, re-elected, 1948; Mem. Opposition until 1951; Provincial Sec., 1938-41; Minister without portfolio, 1941-44. Apptd Judge of Court of Appeal for Sask., 1951. Chm., Sask. Jubilee Cttee, 1952-55. Univ. of Sask.: Mem. Bd of Governors, 1955-61; Chancellor, 1963-69; Mem. Bd, Can. Nat. Inst. for the Blind, 1955- (Pres. Sask. Div., 1962-); Chm., Adv. Bd, Martha House (unmarried mothers), 1955-; Chm., Sask. Revision of Statutes Cttee, 1963-65, and again 1974 until completion 1975-76. Mem., Knights of Columbus, 1930-. Hon. DCL Saskatchewan, 1962. Kt Comdr of St Gregory (Papal) 1963. *Recreations:* golf, curling; interested in football. *Address:* 1303-1830 College Avenue, Regina, Saskatchewan S4P 1C2, Canada. *T:* 569-1758. *Clubs:* Wascana Country, Assiniboia, Royal United Services Institute (all Regina, Sask.).

CULME-SEYMOUR, Comdr Sir Michael; *see* Seymour.

CULSHAW, John Douglas; Director, Defence Operational Analysis Establishment, and Assistant Chief Scientific Adviser (Studies), Ministry of Defence, since 1979; *b* 22 Oct. 1927; *s* of Alfred Henry Douglas Culshaw and Dorothy Yeats Culshaw (*née* Hogarth); *m* 1951, Hazel Speirs Alexander; one *s* one *d. Educ:* Alderman Smith Grammar Sch., Washington, Co. Durham; University Coll., Nottingham. BSc London 1949; MSc Nottingham 1950. Joined Weapons Dept, Royal Aircraft Estabt, Min. of Supply, Farnborough, 1950; OC (Scientific) 6 Joint Services Trials Unit RAF (UK), 1956; OC (Sci.) 16 JSTU RA Weapons Research Estabt, Salisbury, S Australia, 1961; Co-ordinating Research and Development Authority Technical Project Officer, RAE, 1964; Supt Mine Warfare Br., Royal Armament R&D Estabt, MoD, Sevenoaks, 1967; Director, Scientific Adv. Br., Home Office, 1970; Dept of Chief Scientific Adviser (Army), 1972; Head of Mathematics and Assessment Dept, RARDE, MoD, Sevenoaks, 1974; Head of Defence Science II, MoD, 1975; RCDS 1976; Dep. Dir, Scientific and Technical Intelligence, 1977. *Recreations:* war games, wine-making, folk-song collecting, bee-keeping. *Club:* Civil Service.

CULVER, Roland Joseph, OBE 1980; actor; *b* 31 Aug. 1900; *s* of Edward Culver and Florence Tullege; *m* 1st, 1934, Daphne Rye (marr. diss.); two *s*; 2nd, 1947, Nan Hopkins. *Educ:* Highgate Coll.; Royal Academy of Dramatic Art. First appearance on stage, Hull Rep. Theatre, as Paul, in Peter and Paul, 1925; first London appearance, Century Theatre, with Greater London Players, 1925; there followed continuous parts in plays in West End theatres. Played Lieut-Comdr Rogers, in French Without Tears, Criterion, Nov. 1936 until 1939; Ford, in Believe It or Not, New, 1940; Viscount Goring, in An Ideal Husband, Westminster, 1943; George Wayne, in Another Love Story, Phoenix, 1944. First English actor to go to Hollywood after end of 1939-45 War; on returning to England appeared as Ronald Knight, MA, in Master of Arts, Strand, 1949; Oscar, in Who is Sylvia?, Criterion, 1950; William Collyer, in The Deep Blue Sea, Duchess, 1952; prod revival of Aren't We All?, Haymarket, 1953. First appearance on New York stage at Coronet, 1953, as Philip, in The Little Hut; Simon Foster in Simon and Laura, Strand, London, 1954; Stanley Harrington in Five Finger Exercise, Comedy Theatre, London, 1958, New York and US tour, 1959-61; Sir Robert Conyngham, PC, MP, in Shout for Life, Vaudeville, 1963; Dr Parker in Carving a Statue, Haymarket, 1964; Lebedyev in Ivanov, Phoenix, 1965, New York and United States tour 1966; Getting Married, Strand, 1967; Hay Fever, Duke of York's, 1968; His, Hers and Theirs, Apollo, 1969; My Darling Daisy, Lyric, 1970; Trelawny, Prince of Wales, 1972; The Bedwinner, Royalty, 1974; Polonius, in Hamlet, Nat. Theatre, 1975; Agamemnon in Troilus and Cressida, Nat.

Theatre, 1976. Wrote and appeared in his own play, A River Breeze, 1956. Has appeared on BBC TV and ITV; since 1972 various television plays and serials including: Wives and Daughters; Cranford; The Pallisers (as The Duke of Omnium); Way Up to Heaven; The Inquisitor, in Shaw's St Joan. Entered films, 1931, and has appeared in numerous successful pictures. *Films include:* French without Tears, On Approval, The First of the Few, Secret Mission, To Each His Own, Down to Earth, Emperor Waltz, Trio, Quartette, The Greek Tycoon, No Longer Alone. *Publications:* A River Breeze (play), 1957; Not Quite a Gentleman (memoirs), 1979. *Recreations:* painting, golf, hacking and writing. *Address:* 18A Maunsel Street, SW1. *T:* 01-828 1484. *Clubs:* Garrick, Green Room, MCC, Lord's Taverners.

CULYER, Prof. Anthony John; Professor of Economics, University of York, since 1979; *b* 1 July 1942; *s* of late Thomas Reginald Culyer and Betty Ely (*née* Headland); *m* 1966, Sieglinde Birgit; one *s* one *d. Educ:* King's Sch., Worcester; Exeter Univ. (BA Hons); Univ. of California at Los Angeles. Tutor and Asst Lectr, Exeter Univ., 1965-69; Lectr, Sen. Lectr and Reader, Univ. of York, 1969-79; Deputy Director, Inst. of Social and Economic Research, Univ. of York, 1971-82. Sen. Research Associate, Ontario Economic Council, 1976, Vis. Professorial Lectr, Queen's Univ., Kingston, 1976; William Evans Vis. Professor, Otago Univ., 1979; Vis. Fellow, Australian National Univ., 1979. *Publications:* The Economics of Social Policy, 1973; (with M. H. Cooper) Health Economics, 1973; Economic Policies and Social Goals, 1974; Need and the National Health Service, 1976; (with J. Wiseman and A. Walker) Annotated Bibliography of Health Economics, 1977; (with V. Halberstadt) Human Resources and Public Finance, 1977; Measuring Health: Lessons for Ontario, 1978; (with K. G. Wright) Economic Aspects of Health Services, 1978; The Political Economy of Social Policy, 1980; articles in Oxford Econ. Papers, Economica, Scottish Jl of Political Economy, Public Finance, Jl of Public Economics, Kyklos, Qly Jl of Economics, Jl Royal Statistical Soc., and others. *Recreation:* church music. *Address:* The Laurels, Barmby Moor, York YO4 5EJ. *T:* Pocklington 2639.

CUMBER, John Alfred, CMG 1966; MBE 1954; TD; Director-General, Save the Children Fund, since 1976; *b* 30 Sept. 1920; *s* of A. J. Cumber, FRIBA, AMICE; *m* 1945, Margaret Anne Tripp; two *s. Educ:* Richmond County Sch.; LSE. Served War of 1939-46 (Major). HMOCS, Kenya, 1947-63 (Sen. District Comr); Administrator of the Cayman Islands, 1964-68; Comr in Anguilla, 1969; Dep. Election Comr, Southern Rhodesia/Zimbabwe, 1979-80. *Recreations:* art, music. *Address:* 6 Hawcroft Court, 19-21 York Street, W1H 1DY. *Club:* Royal Commonwealth Society.

CUMBERBATCH, Arthur Noel, CMG 1953; CBE 1942 (MBE 1933); Minister (Commercial), Cairo, 1948-54, retired from Foreign Service, 1954; *b* 25 Dec. 1895. *Educ:* King's Coll. Sch.; Paris. Served European War, 1914-18 (despatches). Employed in Commercial Secretariat, Athens, 1920; Asst to the Commercial Sec., Athens, 1931; Commercial Secretary, Athens, 1934. Served, later, in Cairo, Tehran and again in Athens. *Address:* 64 Chesterfield House, Chesterfield Gardens, W1. *T:* 01-493 7148.

CUMBERLEGE, Julia Frances, JP; Lay Member, Press Council, since 1977; *b* 27 Jan. 1943; *d* of Dr L. U. Camm and late M. G. G. Camm; *m* 1961, Patrick Francis Howard Cumberlege; three *s. Educ:* Convent of the Sacred Heart, Tunbridge Wells. Mem., East Sussex AHA, 1977-81; Chm., Brighton DHA, 1981-; Mem. Council, NAHA. Member: Lewes DC, 1966-79 (Leader, 1977-78); East Sussex CC, 1974- (Chm., Social Services Cttee, 1979-). Mem., Social Security Adv. Cttee, 1980-. JP East Sussex, 1973. *Recreations:* tennis, other people's gardens. *Address:* Vuggles Farm, Newick, Lewes, Sussex. *T:* Barcombe 400453.

CUMING, Frederick George Rees, RA 1974 (ARA 1969); ARCA 1954; NDD 1948; NEAC 1960; painter; *b* 16 Feb. 1930. *Educ:* University School, Bexley Heath; Sidcup Art School; Royal College of Art; travelling schol., Italy. Exhbns in Redfern, Walker, New Grafton, Thackeray, Fieldborne Galleries; Group shows at NEAC, RA, Schools' Exhbn, John Moores London Group; One Man exhbns at Thackeray Gall., galls in Chichester, Lewes, Eastbourne, Guildford, Durham, Chester, Folkstone, Canterbury, New York; works in collections: Dept. of Envt; Treasury; Chantrey Bequest; RA; Kendal Mus.; Scunthorpe Mus.; Bradford; Carlisle; Nat. Mus. of Wales; Brighton and Hove Mus.; Maidstone Mus.; Towner Gall., Eastbourne; Monte Carlo Mus.; works in galls in Canada, France, Germany, Greece, Holland. *Address:* 36 Earlsfield Road, Hythe, Kent.

CUMING, Mariannus Adrian, CMG 1962; Chairman, Cuming Smith & Co. Ltd, Melbourne, 1945-78, and formerly associated fertiliser companies; formerly Director: Broken Hill Pty Co. Ltd and subsidiaries; Imperial Chemical Industries of Australia and New Zealand Ltd; *b* 26 Nov. 1901; *s* of J. Cuming, Melbourne; *m* 1926, Wilma Margaret, *d* of W. C. Guthrie; three *s* one *d. Educ:* Melbourne Grammar Sch.; Melbourne Univ. (BSc); Imperial Coll., London (Dip.). Dir, Alfred Hospital, Melbourne, 1945-76. *Recreations:* golf, fishing. *Address:* 29 Stonnington Place, Toorak, Vic 3142, Australia. *T:* Melbourne 20 5319. *Clubs:* Australian, Melbourne, Royal Melbourne Golf (Melbourne); Weld (Perth).

CUMMING; *see* Gordon Cumming and Gordon-Cumming.

CUMMING, (John) Alan, CA, FCBSI, CBIM; Chief General Manager since 1976, and Director since 1978, Woolwich Equitable Building Society; *b* 6 March 1932; *s* of John Cumming; *m* 1958, Isobel Beaumont Sked; three *s*. *Educ:* George Watson's Coll., Edinburgh. CA 1956; FCBSI 1971; CBIM (FBIM 1976). Woolwich Equitable Building Society, 1958-: Gen. Manager's Asst, 1965; Asst Gen. Man., 1967; Gen. Man., 1969. Pres., Bldg Socs Inst., 1973-74; Chm., Metrop. Assoc. of Bldg Socs., 1977-78; Mem. Council: Bldg Socs Assoc. (Chm., 1981-); Internat. Union of Bldg Socs and Savings Assocs; European Fedn of Bldg Socs; Eur. Community Mortgage Fedn. *Recreations:* golf, bridge. *Address:* 8 Prince Consort Drive, Chislehurst, Kent BR7 5SB. *T:* 01-467 8382. *Club:* Caledonian.

CUMMING, Lt-Col Malcolm Edward Durant, CB 1961; OBE 1945; attached War Office, 1934-65; *b* 27 Sept. 1907. *Educ:* Eton; Royal Military Coll., Sandhurst. Served with 60th Rifles, 1927-34. *Recreations:* fishing and rural interests generally. *Address:* c/o Lloyds Bank Ltd, Cox & King's Branch, 6 Pall Mall, SW1. *Club:* Greenjackets.

CUMMING, Lt-Col Sir Ronald Stuart, Kt 1965; TD; Chairman, Distillers Company Ltd, 1963-67 (Dir 1946-67); *b* April 1900; *s* of John F. Cumming, OBE, DL, JP, Aberlour, Banffshire; *m* 1925, Mary, OBE 1953, *d* of late Col Wm Hendrie, Hamilton, Canada; two *d. Educ:* Uppingham; Aberdeen Univ. Grenadier Guards, 1918-19; Dir, John Walker & Sons Ltd, 1931-39; Joint Man. Dir, James Buchanan & Co. Ltd, 1939-46; served Seaforth Highlanders (TA), 1939-45; Man. Dir, James Buchanan & Co. Ltd, 1946-51; Chm., Booth's Distilleries Ltd, 1953-63; Chm., John Walker & Sons Ltd, 1957-63; Chm. Council, Scotch Whisky Assoc., 1961-67. Hon. LLD Strathclyde, 1967. *Recreations:* fishing, shooting, golf. *Address:* Sourden, Rothes, Morayshire. *Clubs:* Boodle's; New (Edinburgh).

CUMMING, Ronald William, ME; CEng, MIEAust, MRAeS; FTS; Director, Caulfield Institute of Technology, 1979-82; *b* 9 April 1920; *s* of John Borland Cumming and Muriel Cumming (*née* Hackford); *m* 1945, Betty Lovell Gent; two *s* two *d. Educ:* Sydney Univ. (BEAero); Univ. of Michigan (AMPsychol); Univ. of Melbourne (ME). FHFS; FAPsS, ABPsS. Research Scientist, Aeronautical Research Labs, Melbourne, 1941-55; Head, Human Engineering Gp, Aero Res. Labs, 1956-66 (research on human factors in aviation); set up Human Factors Cttee of Aust. Road Research Bd, 1962 (Chm. to 1969); Reader in Mechanical Engrg, Univ. of Melbourne, 1966-71; Prof. of Psychology, Monash Univ., 1971-78. Pt-time Comr, Road Safety & Standards Authority, 1975-76; Member, Adv. Council, CSIRO, 1973-78. Pres., Australian Psychological Soc., 1972-73. *Publications:* various research papers in jls. *Recreations:* classical music, flying. *Address:* 65 Beddoe Avenue, Clayton, Victoria 3168, Australia. *T:* (03) 544 2681. *Club:* Sciences (Melbourne).

CUMMING, William Richard, CVO 1954; Chairman, Public Lending Right Committee, Department of Home Affairs and Environment, Australia, since 1976; *b* 15 Oct. 1911; *s* of late George Cumming, Coorparoo, Qld; *m* 1939, Evelyn Joyce, *o d* of late George Paul, Epping, NSW; one *s* one *d. Educ:* Gregory Terr., Brisbane; Univs of Queensland and Sydney. BA Queensland, LLB, DipPubAd Sydney. Admitted to NSW Bar, 1941. Enlisted in AIF and served War of 1939-45 with AAPC, Major. Adviser, Federal Taxation Dept, 1947-51; part-time Lectr, Commercial Law, Political Science, Canberra University Coll., Univ. of Melbourne, 1949-53; Prime Minister's Dept, Australia: Senior Exec. Officer, 1951-55, Asst Secretary, 1955-60, and 1966-70; Official Sec., Australian High Commn, London, 1960-66, 1970-73, and acting Dep. High Comr; (various periods); Cultural Counsellor, Aust. High Commn, London, 1973-74; Chm., Aust. Musical Soc., London, 1973-74; Consultant, Australia Council, 1974-76. Extra Gentleman Usher to the Queen, 1962-66, 1971-74; Dir, Royal Visits, ACT, 1953-54, 1956, 1957-58; Dir-Gen., Australia, Royal Visit, 1959. Secretary: Commonwealth Literary Fund, 1955-60, 1966-70; Commonwealth Historic Memorials Cttee, 1955-60, 1966-70; Commonwealth Art Advisory Bd, 1955-60, 1966-70; Commonwealth Assistance to Australian Composers, 1967-70; Council, Australian Nat. Gallery, 1968-70; Member: Council, Nat. Library of Australia, 1967-70; Council, Australian Inst. of Aboriginal Studies, 1969-70. S. H. Ervin Gall. Cttee, 1978-; Norman Lindsay Gall. Cttee, 1978-. *Recreations:* collecting antiques and Australian art, Australiana, motoring. *Address:* 2 Eric Street, Wahroonga, NSW 2076, Australia. *Clubs:* Oriental; University (Sydney).

CUMMING-BRUCE, Rt. Hon. Sir (James) Roualeyn Hovell-Thurlow-, PC 1977; Kt 1964; MA; **Rt. Hon. Lord Justice Cumming-Bruce;** a Lord Justice of Appeal, since 1977; *b* 9 March 1912; *s* of 6th Baron Thurlow and Grace Catherine, *d* of Rev. Henry Trotter; *m* 1955, Lady (Anne) Sarah Alethea Marjorie Savile, *d* of 6th Earl of Mexborough; two *s* one *d. Educ:* Shrewsbury; Magdalene Coll., Cambridge (Hon. Fellow, 1977). Barrister, Middle Temple, 1937 (Harmsworth Scholar); Master of the Bench, 1959; Treasurer, 1975. Served War of 1939-45 (Lt-Col RA). Chancellor of Diocese of Ripon, 1954-57; Recorder of Doncaster, 1957-58; Recorder of York, 1958-61; Junior Counsel to the Treasury (Common Law), 1959-64; Judge of the High Court, Family Div. (formerly Probate, Divorce and Admiralty Div.), 1964-77; Judge of the Restrictive Practices Court, 1968; Presiding Judge, North Eastern Circuit, 1971-74. *Address:* 1 Mulberry Walk, Chelsea, SW3. *T:* 01-352 5754. *Clubs:* Pratt's, United Oxford & Cambridge University.

See also Baron Thurlow.

CUMMINGS, Constance, CBE 1974; actress; *b* Seattle, USA; *d* of Kate Cummings and Dallas Vernon Halverstadt; *m* 1933, Benn Wolfe Levy, MBE (*d* 1973); one *s* one *d. Educ:* St Nicholas Girls Sch., Seattle, Washington, USA. Began stage work, 1932; since then has appeared in radio, television, films and theatre; joined National Theatre Co., 1971. Member: Arts Council, 1965-71; Council, English Stage Co., 1978-; Chm., Young People's Theatre Panel, 1966-70. *Plays include:* Goodbye, Mr Chips, 1938; The Taming of the Shrew, 1938; The Good Natured Man, 1939; St Joan, 1939; Romeo and Juliet, 1939; The Petrified Forest, 1942; Return to Tyassi, 1952; Lysistrata, 1957; The Rape of the Belt, 1957; JB, 1961; Who's Afraid of Virginia Woolf?, 1964; Justice is a Woman, 1966; Fallen Angels, 1967; A Delicate Balance, 1969; Hamlet, 1969; Children, 1974; Stripwell, 1975; All Over, 1976; Wings, 1978; Hay Fever, 1980; *National Theatre:* Coriolanus, Amphitryon 38, 1971; A Long Day's Journey into Night, 1972; The Cherry Orchard, The Bacchae, 1973; The Circle, 1974-75. Has appeared Albert Hall, performing with orchestra Peter and the Wolf and Honegger's Jeanne d'Arc au Bûcher. *Recreations:* anthropology and music. *Address:* 68 Old Church Street, SW3. *T:* 01-352 0437.

CUMMINS, Frank; Headmaster, Thomas Telford High School, Sandwell, West Midlands, since 1973; *b* 20 Jan. 1924; *s* of Archibald Ernest and Ruth Elizabeth Cummins; *m* 1st, 1943, Joyce Swale (marr. diss.); three *s*; 2nd, 1973, Brenda Valerie Swift. *Educ:* Whitgift Middle Sch., Croydon; London School of Economics and Institute of Education, London Univ. Served Royal Signals, 1943-46. Assistant Teacher, Shireland Boys' Sch., Smethwick, 1949; Dep. Headmaster, 1956, Headmaster, 1961, Sandwell Boys' Sch., Smethwick. Vice-Chm., Exams Cttee, W Midlands Exams Bd, 1980-. Chairman, Community Relations Councils: Warley, 1969, Sandwell, 1974; part-time Commissioner for Racial Equality, 1977-82; Chm., Schools Council Steering Group on Educn in a Multi-Cultural Soc., 1981-. *Recreations:* cooking, camping, walking, theatre, City of Birmingham Symphony Orchestra. *Address:* 21 Green Street, Smethwick, Warley, West Midlands B67 7EB. *T:* (home) 021-558 8484; (school) 021-553 2615.

CUNARD, Major Sir Guy (Alick), 7th Bt *cr* 1859; Licensed Trainer for Steeple Chases and Hurdle Races; *b* 2 Sept. 1911; *s* of Captain Alick May Cunard (*d* 1926) (*s* of William Samuel Cunard, *g s* of 1st Bt) and Cecil Muriel (*d* 1964), *d* of late Guy St Maur Palmes, Lingcroft, York; *S* brother, 1973; unmarried. *Educ:* Eton; RMC, Sandhurst. Gazetted 16/5th Lancers, 1931; transferred to 4/7th Royal Dragoon Guards, 1933; Captain, 1939; Major, 1946; active service France and Belgium, 1940, and Western Desert; retired, 1949. *Recreations:* steeplechasing, point-to-pointing, hunting, cricket. *Heir:* none. *Address:* The Garden House, Wintringham, Malton, N Yorks. *T:* Rillington 286.

CUNEO, Terence Tenison; portrait and figure painter, ceremonial, military and engineering subjects; *b* 1 Nov. 1907; *s* of Cyrus Cuneo and Nell Marion Tenison; *m* 1934, Catherine Mayfield Monro (*d* 1979), *yr d* of Major E. G. Monro, CBE; one *d. Educ:* Sutton Valence Sch.; Chelsea and Slade. Served War of 1939-45: RE, and as War Artist; special propaganda paintings for Min. of Information, Political Intelligence Dept of FO, and War Artists Advisory Cttee; representative of Illustrated London News, France, 1940. Royal Glasgow Inst. of Fine Arts; Pres. of Industrial Painters Group; Exhibitor, RA, RP, ROI Paris Salon (Hon. Mention, 1957). Has painted extensively in North Africa, South Africa, Rhodesia, Canada, USA, Ethiopia and Far East; one-man exhibition, Underground Activities in Occupied Europe, 1941; one-man exhibitions: RWS Galleries, London, 1954 and 1958; Sladmore Gall., 1971, 1972, 1974. Best known works include: Meml Paintings of El Alamein and The Royal Engineers, King George VI at The Royal Artillery Mess, Woolwich, King George VI and Queen Elizabeth at The Middle Temple Banquet, 1950; Meml Painting of The Rifle Brigade, 1951; Visit to Lloyd's of Queen Elizabeth II with the Duke of Edinburgh to lay Foundation Stone of Lloyd's New Building, 1952; Queen's Coronation Luncheon, Guildhall, The Duke of Edinburgh at Cambridge, 1953; Portraits of Viscount Allendale, KG, as Canopy Bearer to Her Majesty, 1954; Coronation of Queen Elizabeth II in Westminster Abbey (presented to the Queen by HM's Lieuts of Counties), 1955; Queen's State Visit to Denmark, Engineering Mural in Science Museum, 1957; Queen Elizabeth II at RCOG, 1960; Queen Elizabeth II at Guildhall Banquet after Indian Tour, 1961; Equestrian Portrait of HM the Queen as Col-in-Chief, Grenadier Guards, 1963; Garter Ceremony, 1964; Commonwealth Prime Ministers' Banquet, Guildhall, 1969; first official portraits of Rt Hon. Edward Heath, 1971, of Field Marshal Viscount Montgomery of Alamein, 1972; HM the Queen as Patron of Kennel Club, 1975; King Hussein of Jordan, 1980. *Publications:* (autobiog.) The Mouse and his Master, 1977; articles in The Studio, The Artist. *Recreations:* writing, sketching, travel, riding. *Address:* 201 Ember Lane, East Molesey, Surrey. *T:* 01-398 1986. *Club:* Junior Carlton.

CUNINGHAME, Sir John Christopher Foggo M.; *see* Montgomery Cuninghame, Sir J. C. F.

CUNINGHAME, Sir William Alan F.; *see* Fairlie-Cuninghame.

CUNLIFFE, family name of Baron Cunliffe.

CUNLIFFE, 3rd Baron *cr* 1914, of Headley; **Roger Cunliffe,** RIBA; MBIM; Principal, CUNLIFFE/SCP, since 1977; *b* 12 Jan. 1932; *s* of 2nd Baron and Joan Catherine Lubbock (*d* 1980); *S* father, 1963; *m* 1957, Clemency Ann

Hoare; two s one d. *Educ:* Eton; Trinity Coll., Cambridge (MA); Architectural Association (AA Dipl.); Open Univ. With various architectural firms in UK and USA, 1957-65; Associate, Robert Matthew, Johnson-Marshall & Partners, 1966-69; Dir, Architectural Assoc., 1969-71; Partner, SCP, 1973-78. Mem., Urban Motorways Cttee, 1969-72. Governor: Lancing Coll., 1967-; Goldsmiths' Coll., 1972-78. *Publications:* (with Leonard Manasseh) Office Buildings, 1962; contrib. various professional jls. *Recreations:* photography, skiing, taxonomy. *Heir: s* Hon. Henry Cunliffe, *b* 9 March 1962. *Address:* 1 Hurst Avenue, N6 5TX.

CUNLIFFE, Prof. Barrington Windsor, FBA 1979; FSA; Professor of European Archaeology, Oxford University, and Fellow of Keble College, since 1972; *b* 10 Dec. 1939. *Educ:* Portsmouth; St John's Coll., Cambridge (MA, PhD, LittD). Lecturer, Univ. of Bristol, 1963-66; Prof. of Archæology, Univ. of Southampton, 1966-72. Mem., Ancient Monuments Bd for England, 1976-; Pres., Council for British Archaeology, 1979; Vice-Pres., Soc. of Antiquaries, 1982-. *Publications:* Fishbourne, a Roman Palace and its Garden, 1971; Roman Bath Discovered, 1971; The Cradle of England, 1972; The Making of the English, 1973; The Regni, 1973; Iron Age Communities in Britain, 1974; Rome and the Barbarians, 1975; Hengistbury Head, 1978; Rome and her Empire, 1978; The Celtic World, 1979; contribs to several major excavation reports and articles to Soc. of Antiquaries, and in other learned jls. *Recreation:* mild self-indulgence. *Address:* Keble College, Oxford.

CUNLIFFE, His Honour Christopher Joseph; a Circuit Judge (formerly County Court Judge), 1966-82; *b* 28 Feb. 1916; *s* of Lt-Col E. N. Cunliffe, OBE, RAMC, Buckingham Crescent, Manchester, and Harriet Cunliffe (*née* Clegg); *m* 1942, Margaret Hamer Barber; two *d. Educ:* Rugby Sch.; Trinity Hall, Cambridge. BA 1937. Called to the Bar, Lincoln's Inn, 1938. Legal Cadet, Br. North Borneo Civil Service. 1939-40. Served RAFVR, 1941-46; Intelligence, Judge Advocate General's Branch. Practised on Northern Circuit, 1946; Dep. Coroner, City of Liverpool, 1953; Chairman: National Insurance Tribunal, Bootle, 1956-; Mental Health Review Tribunal for SW Lancs and W Ches, 1961-. *Recreations:* golf, gardening.

CUNLIFFE, Sir David Ellis, 9th Bt *cr* 1759; *b* 29 Oct. 1957; *s* of Sir Cyril Henley Cunliffe, 8th Bt and of Lady Cunliffe (Eileen, *d* of Frederick William and Nora Anne Parkins); *S* father, 1969. *Heir: b* Andrew Mark Cunliffe, *b* 17 April 1959. *Address:* 17 Gurney Court Road, St Albans, Herts.

CUNLIFFE, Lawrence Francis; MP (Lab) Leigh, since 1979; *b* 1929. Engr, NCB, 1949-79. Contested (Lab) Rochdale, Oct. 1972 and Feb. 1974. *Address:* House of Commons, SW1.

CUNLIFFE, Prof. Marcus Falkner; University Professor, George Washington University, Washington DC, since 1980; *b* 5 July 1922; *s* of Keith Harold and Kathleen Eleanor Cunliffe. *Educ:* Oriel Coll., Oxford. Commonwealth Fund Fellow, Yale Univ., 1947-49; Lectr in American Studies, 1949-56, Sen Lectr, 1956-60, Prof. of Amer. Hist. and Instns, 1960-64, Univ. of Manchester; Prof. of Amer. Studies, Univ. of Sussex, 1965-80. Fellow, Center for Advanced Study in the Behavioral Sciences, Stanford, Calif., 1957-58; Vis. Prof. in American History, Harvard Univ., 1959-60; Vis. Prof., Michigan Univ., 1973; Fellow, Woodrow Wilson Internat. Centre, Washington DC, 1977-78. Member: Massachusetts Historical Soc.; Soc. of American Historians. Hon. Dr Humane Letters: Univ. of Pennsylvania, 1976; New England Coll., 1979. *Publications:* The Literature of the United States, 1954; George Washington: Man and Monument, 1958; The Nation Takes Shape, 1789-1837, 1959; (ed) Weems' Life of Washington, 1962; Soldiers and Civilians: The Martial Spirit in America, 1775-1865, 1968; American Presidents and the Presidency, 1969; (ed with R. Winks) Pastmasters: some essays on American historians, 1969; (ed) Sphere History of Literature, Vols 8 and 9 (American Literature), 1974-75; The Age of Expansion 1848-1917, 1974; (ed) The Divided Loyalist: Crèvecoeur's America, 1978; Chattel Slavery and Wage Slavery, 1979. *Recreation:* the pursuit of happiness. *Address:* 1823 Lamont Street NW, Washington, DC 20010, USA. *T:* 202-387-4459.

CUNLIFFE, Peter Whalley, CBE 1980; Chairman, Pharmaceuticals Division, Imperial Chemical Industries Ltd, since 1976; *b* 29 Oct. 1926; *s* of Fred Cunliffe and Lillie Whalley; *m* 1951, Alice Thérèse Emma Brunel; one *d. Educ:* Queen Elizabeth's Grammar Sch., Blackburn; Trinity Hall, Cambridge (Scholar; BA 1st Class Hons, 1948). Joined ICI Ltd, Pharmaceuticals Div., 1950; Services Dir, 1968; Overseas Dir, 1970; Dep. Chm., 1971. Pres., Assoc. of British Pharmaceutical Industry, 1981-; Member: Council, Internat. Fedn of Pharmaceutical Manufrs Assoc., 1979- (Vice Pres., 1982-); Exec. Cttee, European Fedn of Pharmaceutical Industries Assocs, 1982-. FRSA 1981. *Recreations:* reading, walking. *Address:* Breck Cottage, Sugar Lane, Adlington, near Macclesfield, Cheshire SK10 5SH. *T:* Bollington 72213.

CUNLIFFE, Captain Robert Lionel Brooke, CBE 1944; Royal Navy, retired; *b* 15 March 1895; *s* of Col Foster Cunliffe and Mrs Cunliffe (*née* Lyon); *m* 1st, 1926, Barbara Eleanor Cooper (*d* 1970); three *d* ; 2nd, 1971, Christina Cooper. *Educ:* RN Colls Osborne and Dartmouth. Comdr 1930; Capt. 1936; commanded HMS Milford, 1938-39; RNC Dartmouth, 1939-42; Commodore, Dover, 1942; commanded HMS Illustrious, 1942-44 (despatches); Cdre, RN Barracks, Devonport, 1944-46; Retd, 1946. Naval Asst to UK High Comr, Canada, 1946-48. Grand Officer Order of Leopold II, Belgium, 1948. *Recreations:* cricket, shooting. *Address:* The Garden House,

Pakenham, Bury St Edmunds, Suffolk. *T:* Pakenham 30236. *Club:* Army and Navy.
See also Baron Sackville.

CUNLIFFE, Stella Vivian; consultant statistician; *b* 12 Jan. 1917; *d* of Percy Cunliffe and Edith Blanche Wellwood Cunliffe. *Educ:* privately, then Parsons Mead, Ashtead; London School of Economics (BScEcon). Danish Bacon Co, 1939-44; Voluntary Relief Work in Europe, 1945-47; Arthur Guinness Son and Co. Ltd, 1947-70; Head of Research Unit, Home Office, 1970-72; Dir of Statistics, Home Office, 1972-77. Statistical Adviser to Cttee of Enquiry into Engineering Profession, 1978-80. Pres., Royal Statistical Soc., 1975-77. *Recreations:* work with youth organisations; gardening; prison after-care. *Address:* 69 Harriotts Lane, Ashtead, Surrey. *T:* Ashtead 72343.

CUNLIFFE, His Honour Thomas Alfred; a Circuit Judge (formerly County Court Judge), 1963-75; *b* 9 March 1905; *s* of Thomas and Elizabeth Cunliffe, Preston; *m* 1938, Constance Isabella Carden; one *s* one *d. Educ:* Lancaster Royal Grammar Sch.; Sidney Sussex Coll., Cambridge (Classical Scholar). Inner Temple: Profumo Prize, 1926; Paul Methven Prize, 1926. Called to the Bar, Inner Temple, 1927; Yarborough Anderson Scholar, 1927. Practised Northern Circuit, 1927-63; Dep. Chm., Lancs County Quarter Sessions, 1961-63; Recorder, Barrow-in-Furness, 1962-63. RAFVR (Squadron Leader), 1940-45. *Recreations:* music, gardening. *Address:* Wycoller, 3 Downham Road North, Heswall, Wirral, Merseyside L61 6UR. *T:* 051-342 3949.

CUNLIFFE-JONES, Rev. Prof. Hubert, DD (Hon.); Professor of Theology, University of Manchester, 1968-73, now Professor Emeritus; *b* Strathfield, Sydney, NSW, Australia, 30 March 1905; *s* of Rev. Walter and Maud Cunliffe-Jones; *m* 1933, Maude Edith Clifton, BSc, DipEd Sydney; two *s* two *d. Educ:* Newington Coll., Sydney; Sydney and Oxford Univs; Camden Coll., Sydney; Mansfield Coll., Oxford. Congregational Minister, Warrnambool, Vic., Australia, 1928-29; Travelling Sec., Australian SCM 1929-30; Congregational Minister, Witney, Oxon, 1933-37; Tutor in Systematic Theology, Yorks United Independent Coll., Bradford, 1937-47; Principal Yorks United Independent Coll., Bradford, 1947-58; Associate Principal, Northern Congregational Coll., Manchester, 1958-66; Prof., History of Doctrine, Univ. of Manchester, 1966-68 (Lectr, 1958-66). Chm. of the Congregational Union of England and Wales, 1957-58. Hon. DD Edinburgh, 1956. *Publications:* The Holy Spirit, 1943; The Authority of the Biblical Revelation, 1945; Deuteronomy, 1951; Jeremiah, 1960; Technology, Community and Church, 1961; Christian Theology since 1600, 1970; (ed) History of Christian Doctrine, 1979; articles in Theology, Expository Times, etc. *Recreation:* drama. *Address:* 5 Wood Road, Manchester M16 9RB.

CUNLIFFE-LISTER, family name of **Baroness Masham of Ilton** and **Earl of Swinton.**

CUNLIFFE-OWEN, Sir Dudley (Herbert), 2nd Bt, *cr* 1920; Managing Director: Palace Hotel & Casino Ltd; Palace Entertainments Ltd, since 1965; *b* 27 March 1923; 2nd (but *o* surv.) *s* of Sir Hugo Cunliffe-Owen, 1st Bt and Helen Elizabeth Cunliffe-Owen (*d* 1934), *d* of James Oliver, New York; *S* father 1947; *m* 1st, 1947, Mary Maud (*d* 1956), *e d* of R. R. Redgrave; 2nd, 1956, Hon. Juliana Eveline Nettlefold (*née* Curzon) (marr. diss. 1962), 3rd *d* of 2nd Viscount Scarsdale, TD; one *d* ; 3rd, 1964, Jean, *o d* of late Surg. Comdr A. N. Forsyth, RN; one *s* one *d. Educ:* RN Coll., Dartmouth. Served War, 1939-46 (despatches); Lieut Royal Navy; retired 1947. *Recreation:* yachting. *Heir: s* Hugo Dudley Cunliffe-Owen, *b* 16 May 1966. *Address:* Eyreton House, Quarterbridge, Douglas, Isle of Man. *T:* Douglas 4545. *Club:* Royal Thames Yacht.

CUNNANE, Most Rev. Joseph; see Tuam, Archbishop of, (RC).

CUNNINGHAM, Gen. Sir Alan Gordon, GCMG 1948; KCB 1941 (CB 1941); DSO 1918; MC 1915; LLD; *b* 1 May 1887; *s* of Prof. D. J. Cunningham, FRS, and Elizabeth Cumming Browne; *m* 1951, Margery, widow of Sir Harold Edward Snagge, KBE. *Educ:* Cheltenham; Royal Military Academy, Woolwich. First commission, 1906; served European War, France, 1914-18; Brigade Major and Gen. Staff Officer 2nd Grade (despatches 5 times, DSO and MC); Gen. Staff Officer, Straits Settlements, 1919-21; passed Naval Staff Coll., 1925; Brevet Lt-Col 1928; Instructor, Machine Gun Sch., 1928-31; Lt-Col 1935; Imperial Defence Coll., 1937; Comdr Royal Artillery, 1st Div., 1937-38; Maj.-Gen., 1938; Comdr 5th Anti-Aircraft Div. TA, 1938; commanded 66th, 9th and 51st Divs, 1940; GOC East Africa Forces, 1940-41; GOC-in-C 8th Imperial Army in Middle East, 1941; Commandant Staff College, Camberley, 1942; Lt-Gen. 1943; GOC Northern Ireland, 1943-44; GOC-in-C Eastern Command, 1944-45; Gen., 1945; High Commissioner and C-in-C for Palestine, 1945-48; Col Commandant Royal Artillery, 1944-54. Pres., Council of Cheltenham Coll., 1951-63. Comdr American Legion of Merit, 1945; Brilliant Star of Zanzibar (1st class), 1941; Ordre de la Couronne (1st Class), Belgium, 1950; Order of Menelik (1st Class), 1954, etc. *Recreations:* gardening, fishing. *Club:* Army and Navy.

CUNNINGHAM, Alexander Alan; A Vice President, General Motors, since 1976; *b* Bulgaria, 7 Jan. 1926; naturalised citizen, US; *m* 1955, Dorothy Ilene; one *s* three *d. Educ:* General Motors Inst., Michigan. BSc (Industrial Engrg) 1951. Served War of 1939-45, navigation electronics radar specialist, RAF. General Motors: Jun. Process Engr, Frigidaire Div., 1951; Asst to Frigidaire

Man., NY, Gen. Motors Overseas Ops, 1952; Prodn Planning Technician for Adam Opel AG, Germany, 1953; Exec. Asst to Man. Dir, GM Ltd, London, 1956; Master Mechanic, Gen. Motors do Brasil, 1957; Works Man. 1958; Works Man., Gen. Motors Argentina SA, 1962; Man. Dir, Gen. Motors do Brasil, 1963; Man., Adam Opel's Bochum plant, 1964; Asst Gen. Manufrg Man., Adam Opel AG, 1966, Gen. Manufrg Man. 1969; Man. Dir, Adam Opel AG, 1970; Gen. Dir, European Organisations, Gen. Motors Overseas Corp., 1974-76. *Address:* General Motors Corporation, 767 Fifth Avenue, New York 10022, USA. *T:* (212) 486-2400.

CUNNINGHAM, Sir Charles (Craik), GCB 1974 (KCB 1961; CB 1946); KBE 1952; CVO 1941; *b* Dundee, 7 May 1906; *s* of late Richard Yule Cunningham, Abergeldie, Kirriemuir, and Isabella Craik; *m* 1934, Edith Louisa Webster; two *d. Educ:* Harris Acad., Dundee; University of St Andrews. Entered Scottish Office, 1929; Private Sec. to Parliamentary Under Sec. of State for Scotland, 1933-34; Private Sec. to Sec. of State for Scotland, 1935-39; Asst Sec., Scottish Home Dept, 1939-41; Principal Asst Sec., 1941-42; Dep. Sec., 1942-47; Sec., 1948-57; Permanent Under-Sec. of State, Home Office, 1957-66; Dep. Chm., UKAEA, 1966-71; Chm., Radiochemical Centre Ltd, 1971-74. Dir, Securicor Ltd, 1971-81. Chm., Uganda Resettlement Bd, 1972-73. Mem., Nat. Radiological Protection Bd, 1971-74. Hon. LLD St Andrews, 1960. *Address:* Bankside, Peaslake, Surrey GU5 9RL. *T:* Dorking 730402. *Clubs:* Reform; New (Edinburgh).

CUNNINGHAM, David; Solicitor to the Secretary of State for Scotland, since 1980; *b* 26 Feb. 1924; *s* of Robert Cunningham and Elizabeth (*née* Shields); *m* 1955, Ruth Branwell Crawford; one *s* two *d. Educ:* High School of Glasgow; Univ. of Glasgow (MA, LLB). Served war, 1942-47: commnd, Cameronians, 1943; Intelligence Corps (Captain), and Control Commission for Germany, 1945-47. Admitted Solicitor, 1951; entered Office of Solicitor to Secretary of State for Scotland as Legal Asst, 1954; Sen. Legal Asst, 1960; Asst Solicitor, 1966; Cabinet Office Constitution Unit, 1975-77; Dep. Solicitor, 1978-80. *Recreations:* hill walking, reading, theatre, motor-cars. *Address:* 5 Crarae Avenue, Edinburgh, Scotland EH4 3JD. *T:* 031-332 4082. *Clubs:* Royal Commonwealth Society; Scottish Arts (Edinburgh).

CUNNINGHAM, George, BA, BSc; MP Islington South and Finsbury, since 1974 (South West Islington, 1970-74) (Lab 1970-81, Ind, 1981-82, SDP since 1982); *b* 10 June 1931; *s* of Harry Jackson Cunningham and Christina Cunningham, Dunfermline; *m* 1957, Mavis, *d* of Harold Walton; one *s* one *d. Educ:* Dunfermline High Sch.; Blackpool Grammar Sch.; Univs of Manchester and London. Nat. Service in Royal Artillery (2nd Lieut), 1954-56; on staff of Commonwealth Relations Office, 1956-63; 2nd Sec., British High Commn, Ottawa, 1958-60; Commonwealth Officer of Labour Party, 1963-66; Min. of Overseas Development, 1966-69. Mem., Parlt of European Community, 1978-79. Opposition front bench spokesman on home affairs, 1979 till resignation from Labour Party, Nov. 1981. Contested (Lab) Henley Div. of Oxfordshire, 1966. *Publications:* (Fabian pamphlet) Rhodesia, the Last Chance, 1966; (ed) Britain and the World in the Seventies, 1970; The Management of Aid Agencies, 1974. *Address:* 28 Manor Gardens, Hampton, Middlesex. *T:* 01-979 6221.

CUNNINGHAM, Prof. George John, MBE 1945; Professor and Chairman, Department of Academic Pathology, Virginia Commonwealth University, Richmond, 1974-77, now Emeritus Professor; Conservator of Pathological Collection, Royal College of Surgeons; Consultant Pathologist to South East and South West Regional Health Authorities; *b* 7 Sept. 1906; *s* of George S. Cunningham and Blanche A. Harvey; *m* 1957, Patricia Champion, Brisbane, Australia. *Educ:* Royal Belfast Academical Institution; Dean Close Sch., Cheltenham; St Bartholomew's Hospital Medical Coll. MRCS, LRCP, 1931; MB, BS London, 1933; MD London, 1937; FRCPath 1964. Asst Pathologist, Royal Sussex County Hosp., Brighton, 1934-42. War Service, RAMC, Middle East and Italy (temp. Lt-Col). Senior Lectr in Pathology, St Bartholomew's Hosp., London, 1946-55; Sir William Collins Prof. of Pathology, Univ. of London, at RCS, 1955-68; Prof. of Pathology, Medical Coll. of Virginia, and Chief Laboratory Service, McGuire VA Hosp., Richmond, 1968-74. Dorothy Temple Cross Travelling Fellow in America, 1951-52; Vis. Prof., New York State Univ., 1961; Vis. Prof., Cairo Univ., 1963. Past Pres., Assoc. Clin. Path., Internat. Acad. of Pathology, Quekett Microscopical Club. Freeman, City of London. *Publications:* chap. on Gen. Pathology of Malignant Tumours in Cancer, Vol. 2, 1957; chap. on Microradiography, in Tools of Biological Research, Vol. 2, 1960; and several articles on Pathology, in medical press. *Recreation:* golf. *Address:* 300 West Franklin Street, Apartment 1203-E, Richmond, Va 23220, USA. *T:* 804 643-1012. *Clubs:* National Liberal; Surrey County Cricket; Royal Blackheath Golf; Downtown (Richmond, Va).

CUNNINGHAM, Lt-Gen. Sir Hugh (Patrick), KBE 1975 (OBE 1966); Director: Fairey Holdings Ltd, since 1978; Fairey Engineering Ltd, since 1981; MEL, since 1982; *b* 4 Nov. 1921; *s* of late Sir Charles Banks Cunningham, CSI; *m* 1955, Jill, *d* of J. S. Jeffrey, East Knoyle; two *s* two *d. Educ:* Charterhouse. 2nd Lieut, RE, 1942; served War of 1939-45, India, New Guinea, Burma; Greece, 1950-51; Egypt, 1951-53; Instructor, Sch. of Infantry, 1955-57, RMA Sandhurst, 1957-60; Cameroons, 1960-61; CRE 3 Div., Cyprus and Aden, 1963-66; comd 11 Engr Bde, BAOR, 1967-69; comd Mons OCS, 1969-70; Nat. Defence Coll., Canada, 1970-71; GOC SW District, 1971-74; ACGS (OR), 1974-75; DCDS (OR), 1976-78, retired. Col, Queen's Gurkha Engineers (formerly Gurkha Engrs), 1976-81; Col Comdt, RE,

1976-81; Col, Bristol Univ. OTC, 1977-. Master, Glass Sellers' Co., 1981. *Recreations:* bird-watching, opera, golf. *Address:* Little Leigh, East Knoyle, Salisbury, Wilts. *T:* East Knoyle 281; 406 Howard House, Dolphin Square, SW1. *T:* 01-821 7960. *Clubs:* Athenæum, Army and Navy, MCC.

CUNNINGHAM, Group Captain John, CBE 1963 (OBE 1951); DSO 1941; DFC; Executive Director, British Aerospace, Hatfield, 1978-80; *b* 27 July 1917; *s* of late A. G. Cunningham and of E. M. Cunningham. *Educ:* Whitgift. Apprenticed to De Havilland Aircraft Co., Hatfield, 1935-38; employed, 1938-Aug. 1939, with De Havillands, Light Aircraft Development and Test Flying. Called up Aug. 1939; joined AAF, 1935; commanded 604 Sqdn, 1941-42; Staff job, 1942-43; commanded 85 Sqdn, 1943-44 (DSO and two bars, DFC and bar); Group Capt. Night Operations HQ 11 Group, 1944. Chief Test Pilot, de Havilland Aircraft Co., 1946-77; Exec. Dir, Hawker Siddeley Aviation, 1963-77. International Record Flight, 16 Oct. 1957: London to Khartoum direct; distance 3,064 statute miles in 5 hrs 51 mins, by Comet 3; average speed 523 statute mph. Derry and Richards Memorial Medal of Guild of Air Pilots and Air Navigators for 1965; Segrave Trophy, 1979; Air League Founders' Medal, 1979. *Address:* Canley, Kinsbourne Green, Harpenden, Herts.

CUNNINGHAM, Dr John A.; MP (Lab) Whitehaven, Cumbria, since 1970; *b* 4 Aug. 1939; *s* of Andrew Cunningham; *m* 1964, Maureen; one *s* two *d. Educ:* Jarrow Grammar Sch.; Bede Coll., Durham Univ. Hons Chemistry, 1962; PhD Chemistry, 1966. Formerly: Research Fellow in Chemistry, Durham Univ.; School Teacher; Trades Union Officer. PPS to Rt Hon. James Callaghan, 1972-76; Parly Under-Sec. of State, Dept of Energy, 1976-79; Opposition Spokesman on Industry, 1979-. *Recreations:* fell walking, squash, gardening, classical and folk music, reading, listening to other people's opinions. *Address:* House of Commons, SW1.

CUNNINGHAM, Robert Kerr, PhD; FIBiol; FRSC; Chief Natural Resources Adviser, Overseas Development Administration, since 1976; *b* 7 June 1923; *s* of John Simpson Cunningham and Agnes Stewart Cunningham; *m* 1947, Jean Sinclair (*née* Brown); one *s* one *d. Educ:* Bathgate Acad., Scotland; Edinburgh Univ. (BSc); London Univ. (PhD). FRIC 1964. Served War, RAF, 1942-46. Science Teacher, W Lothian County Educn Cttee, 1947-50; Science Lectr and Chemist, Govt of Bahamas, 1950-55; Colonial Res. Fellowship, Rothamsted Experimental Stn, 1955-56; Res. Off., W African Cocoa Res. Inst., Gold Coast and Ghana, 1956-60; Principal Scientific Off., Rothamsted Experimtl Stn, 1960-64; Prof. of Chemistry and Soil Science, Univ. of WI, Trinidad, 1964-67; Adviser on Res. and Nat. Resources, Min. of Overseas Develt, 1967-76. *Publications:* many scientific papers dealing mainly with soil chem. and plant nutrition in jls; several reports on organisation of R&D in developing countries; (co-author) reports on Brit. and internat. aid in natural resources field. *Recreations:* walking, reading, golf. *Address:* 35 Clarence Road, Harpenden, Herts AL5 4AH. *T:* Harpenden 4203. *Club:* Royal Air Force.

CUNYNGHAME, Sir Andrew (David Francis), 12th Bt *cr* 1702; FCA; *b* 25 Dec. 1942; *s* of Sir (Henry) David St Leger Brooke Selwyn Cunynghame, 11th Bt, and of Hon. Pamela Margaret Stanley, *qv* ; *S* father, 1978; *m* 1972, Harriet Ann, *d* of C. T. Dupont, Montreal. *Educ:* Eton. *Heir: b* John Philip Henry Michael Selwyn Cunynghame, *b* 9 Sept. 1944. *Address:* 69 Hillgate Place, W8; The School House, Williamscote, Banbury, Oxon. *Club:* Brooks's.

CUNYNGHAME, Sir James Ogilvy B.; *see* Blair-Cunynghame.

CURE, (George) Nigel C.; *see* Capel Cure.

CURIE, Eve, (Mrs Henry R. Labouisse), writer and journalist; *b* Paris, 6 Dec. 1904; *d* of late Marie and Pierre Curie; *m* 1954, Henry Richardson Labouisse, *qv. Educ:* by governesses, generally Polish; Sévigné College; Bachelor of Science and Bachelor of Philosophy. Accompanied her mother in her tour of the US 1921; devoted several years to the study of the piano and gave her first concert in 1925 in Paris; later she took up musical criticism and under a pseudonym acted for several years as musical critic of the weekly journal Candide; after the death of her mother in 1934 she collected and classified all the papers, manuscripts, and personal documents left by Mme Curie and went to Poland in 1935 to obtain material as to Mme Curie's youth; wrote Mme Curie's biography; went to America again in 1939 and has gone several times since on lecture tours; was a co-ordinator of the women's war activities at the Ministry of Information in Paris at the beginning of the war, until she went on a lecture tour in the USA; came back to Paris 2 May 1940; after the French capitulation went to live in London for six months, then to America for her third lecture tour; Vichy Govt deprived her of French citizenship in April 1941; in 1942, travelled, as a war correspondent to the battlefronts of Libya, Russia, China; enlisted in the Fighting French corps, Volontaires Françaises, 1943, as a private; received basic training in England; 2nd Lieut 1943; 1st Lieut 1944. Co-publisher of Paris-Presse, an evening paper in Paris, 1944-49. Special Adviser to the Sec. Gen. of NATO, Paris, Aug. 1952-Nov. 1954. *Publications:* Madame Curie (in US), 1937 (trans. into 32 langs); Journey Among Warriors, 1943. *Recreation:* swimming. *Address:* 1 Sutton Place South, New York, New York 10022, USA.

CURLE, Sir John (Noel Ormiston), KCVO 1975 (CVO 1956); CMG 1966; Director of Protocol, Hong Kong, since 1976; *b* 12 Dec. 1915; *s* of Major W.

S. N. Curle, MC, Melrose, Scotland; *m* 1st, 1940, Diana Deane; one *s* one *d*; 2nd, 1948, Pauline, *widow* of Capt. David Roberts; one step *s* two step *d*. *Educ:* Marlborough; New Coll., Oxford. 1st Class Hons, MA, Laming Travelling Fellow of Queen's Coll. Diplomatic Service, 1939; Irish Guards, 1939; War Cabinet Secretariat, 1941–44. Has served in Lisbon, Ottawa, Brussels, Stockholm (Counsellor), Athens (Counsellor); Boston (Consul-Gen., 1962–66); Ambassador to: Liberia, 1967–70 and Guinea, 1968–70; the Philippines, 1970–72; Vice Marshal of Diplomatic Corps, 1972–75; retired 1975. Liveryman, Masons Company. *Recreations:* skiing (represented Oxford *v* Cambridge, and British Univs *v* Swiss Univs), polo. *Address:* Appletree House, near Aston-le-Walls, Daventry, Northants NN11 6UG. *T:* Chipping Warden 211; Government Secretariat, Hong Kong. *Clubs:* Cavalry and Guards, Beefsteak; Hong Kong.

CURLEWIS, His Honour Judge Sir Adrian (Herbert), Kt 1967; CVO 1974; CBE 1962; retired as Judge of the District Court, New South Wales, Australia, (1948–71); *b* 13 Jan. 1901; *s* of late Judge Herbert R. Curlewis and late Ethel Turner, Authoress; *m* 1928, Beatrice Maude Carr; one *s* one *d*. *Educ:* Sydney Church of England Grammar Sch.; Univ. of Sydney. Called to Bar of NSW, 1927. Served War of 1939–45, Capt. 8 Div. AIF, Malaya. President: Surf Life Saving Assoc. of Australia, 1933–75 (Life Governor, 1975); International Surf Life Saving Council, 1956–71; Patron, World Life Saving, 1971–74; Life Patron, NSW RSL Youth Clubs, 1978; Chairman: Australian Outward Bound Trust (Founder and Past Pres.), 1956–; National Fitness Council, New South Wales, 1948–71; National Co-ordinator, Duke of Edinburgh's Award in Australia, 1958–73; Pres., Royal Humane Soc. (NSW), 1968–. Youth Policy Adv. Cttee to NSW Government, 1961–63. Chm. and Royal Commissioner on various Government Enquiries. *Recreations:* surfing, gardening. *Address:* 5 Hopetoun Avenue, Mosman, NSW 2088, Australia. *T:* 969-8365. *Club:* University (Sydney).

CURNOW, Elizabeth Ann Marguerite; Senior Treasury Counsel, Central Criminal Court, since 1981; Fifth Senior Prosecuting Counsel to the Crown, since 1981; *b* 5 June 1935; *d* of Cecil Curnow and Doris Curnow (*née* Behr); *m* 1981, William Neil Denison, *qv*. *Educ:* St Hilda's Sch., Whitby, Yorks; King's Coll., London (LLB). Called to the Bar, Gray's Inn, 1957. Treasury Counsel, Mddx Crown Court, 1972–77; Junior Treasury Counsel, Central Criminal Court, 1977–81; a Recorder, S Eastern Circuit, 1980–. *Recreations:* reading, gardening, listening to music, walking and (recently) tapestry. *Address:* 6 King's Bench Walk, Temple, EC4Y 7DR. *T:* 01-583 0410.

CURRALL, Alexander, CB 1970; CMG 1965; Director: Renold Ltd, since 1977; National Counties Building Society, since 1977; Applied Photophysics Ltd, since 1980 (Chairman, since 1981); Photophysics Research Ltd, since 1980 (Chairman, since 1981); Grantham House Ltd, since 1980 (Chairman, since 1981); *b* 30 Jan. 1917; *s* of late R. T. Currall, Edinburgh; *m* 1940, Madeleine Crombie Saunders; one *s*. *Educ:* George Watson's Coll., Edinburgh; Edinburgh Univ. Min. of Supply, 1939–40; Royal Artillery and Indian Artillery, 1940–46. Successively in Min. of Supply, Min. of Materials and Board of Trade, concerned mainly with internat. economic negotiations, excepting the period 1950–54, when responsible for public trading in non-ferrous metals, and 1954–55, when holding a Commonwealth Fellowship for travel and study in USA. Seconded to Foreign Office as Dep. Consul-Gen., New York, and Dir of British Industrial Development Office, 1960–62; Minister (Commercial), British High Commn, Ottawa, 1962–66; Under-Secretary: Board of Trade, 1966–67; DEA, 1967–68; Dir, Dept for Nat. Savings, 1968–72; Man. Dir (Posts), Post Office, 1972–77. Manager, Royal Instn, 1972–75, 1977–80, 1981–. *Address:* Fairlawn, Buckden, Skipton, North Yorkshire BD23 5JA. *Club:* Caledonian.

CURRAN, Desmond, CBE 1961; FRCP; Lord Chancellor's Medical Visitor, 1967–75; Hon. Consulting Psychiatrist, St George's Hospital, since 1967; formerly Professor of Psychiatry, St George's Hospital Medical School, University of London, 1961–67, now Emeritus Professor; Civil Consultant in Psychological Medicine to the Royal Navy, 1946–61; *b* 14 Feb. 1903; *s* of late J. P. Curran; *m* 1938, Marguerite (*née* Gothard); two *s*. *Educ:* Wellington Coll.; Trinity Coll., Cambridge; St George's Hosp.; Johns Hopkins Hosp., Baltimore. MB, BChir Cambridge, 1928; MRCP 1928, FRCP 1937; MRCS, LRCP 1927; DPM London 1930; House jobs, St George's, 1927–28; HP, Bethlem, 1928–29; RMO and Registrar, Maida Vale Hosp. for Nervous Diseases, 1929–30; Intern, Phipps Clinic, Baltimore, 1930–31; Rockefeller Travelling Fellowship, 1930–31; AMO, Maudsley Hosp., 1931–34 (and later part-time); Gaskell Gold Medal Psychological Medicine, 1933. Consultant Psychiatrist: St George's Hosp., 1934–67; Maida Vale Hosp. for Nervous Diseases, 1934–46. War of 1939–45: Consultant in Psychological Medicine to Royal Navy (Temp. Surg. Capt. RNVR), 1939–46. Mem. SW Metropolitan Hosp. Bd, 1948. Croonian Lecturer, RCP 1948. President: Psychiatric Section, RSM, 1951–52; Royal Med. Psychological Assoc., 1963–64. Member: (Franklin) Deptl Cttee on Punishments, Prisons and Borstals, etc, 1948–51; (Wolfenden) Deptl Cttee on Homosexuality and Prostitution, 1954–57; (Representative RCP), Gen. Med. Council, 1961–67. Examiner in Psychiatry: RCP; Univs of London, Edinburgh, Newcastle; NUI. Distinguished Fellow, Amer. Psychiatric Assoc., 1966. Hon. FRCPsych, 1972. *Publications:* (jointly) Psychological Medicine, 1943, 9th rev. edn (by P. B. Storey), 1980; articles and papers in medical text books and journals. *Address:* 51 Cottesmore Court, Stanford Road, W8 5QW. *T:* 01-937 4763. *Clubs:* Athenæum, United Oxford & Cambridge University.

CURRAN, Harry Gibson, CMG 1953; *b* 1901; *s* of late James P. and Jessie M. Curran; *m* 1962, Betty, *d* of Harold Beazley. *Educ:* Royal Naval College, Dartmouth; University College, Oxford (MA). Served War of 1914–18 in Grand Fleet; served War of 1939–45, Middle East (despatches). Treasury Representative, South Asia, India, 1946–53; Canada, 1953–56; Head of Economic Mission, Ecuador, 1956–58; Representative World Bank, India, 1959–61; Dep. Dir, European Office, World Bank, 1961–66. *Address:* Fairmile, St Mark's Avenue, Salisbury, Wilts. *Club:* Travellers'.

CURRAN, Rt. Hon. Sir Lancelot (Ernest), PC (N Ireland) 1957; Kt 1964; BA, LLB (QUB); Lord Justice of Appeal, Supreme Court of Judicature, Northern Ireland, 1956–75; *b* 8 March 1899; 4th *s* of late Miles Curran, Myrtlefield Park, Belfast; *m* 1st, 1924, Doris Lee; two *s* (one *d* decd); 2nd, 1976, Mrs Margaret P. Curran. *Educ:* Royal Belfast Academical Institution. Barrister, King's Inns, 1923; QC (NI) 1943; Bencher, Inn of Court of N Ireland, 1946. MP Carrick Div., Co. Antrim, NI Parlt, April 1945 (re-elected June 1945)–1949; Parly Sec., Min. of Finance and Chief Whip, 1945. Served European war, 1917–18, RFC and RAF; War of 1939–45, Major, Army. Lecturer in Contract and Tort, Queen's Univ., Belfast; Chm. Court of Referees and Dep. Umpire under Unemployment Pensions Acts, 1926–45; Senior Crown Prosecutor for Co. Down; Attorney-Gen., NI, 1947–49; Judge of High Courts of Justice, NI, 1949–56. *Recreation:* golf. *Address:* Rock Cottage, Tullyard, Co. Down. *T:* Drumbo 600. *Club:* Royal Co. Down Golf.

CURRAN, Leo Gabriel Columbanus, CEng, FIMechE, FIMarE; Chairman, Camac Transport Co. Ltd, since 1981; *b* 23 Nov. 1930; *s* of B. L. Curran and R. Fanning; *m* 1957, Margaret Hickey; one *s* two *d*. *Educ:* St Malachy's Coll., Belfast; Dublin Coll. of Higher Technol. CEng 1974, FIMechE 1969; FIMarE 1974; MIProdE 1970. Managing Director: British Silverware Ltd, 1970–71; Delta Electrical (South African Delta Metal Electrical Pty) Ltd, 1971–73; Gen. Man. and Dir, Harland & Wolff Ltd, 1973–76; Man. Dir, Plessey Hydraulics International Ltd, 1976–79; Bd Mem. for Enginebuilding and Gen. Engrg, British Shipbuilders, 1979–80. *Recreations:* music, walking. *Address:* The Mews, 37 Waterloo Lane, Dublin 4, Ireland. *Club:* Institute of Directors.

CURRAN, Prof. Robert Crowe, MD; FRSE 1962; Leith Professor of Pathology, Birmingham University, since 1966; Hon. Consultant Pathologist to the Central Birmingham Health District; *b* 28 July 1921; *s* of John Curran and Sarah Crowe, Netherton, Wishaw, Lanarkshire; *m* 1947, Margaret Marion Park; one *s* one *d*. *Educ:* Glasgow Univ. MB, ChB 1943, MD 1956; FRCPath 1967; FRCP 1969. RAMC, 1945–47. Lectr in Pathology, Glasgow Univ., 1950–55. Sen. Lectr and Cons. Pathologist, Sheffield Univ., 1955–58; Prof. of Pathology, St Thomas's Hospital Medical Sch., 1959–66. Registrar, Royal Coll. of Pathologists, 1968–73, Vice-Pres., 1977–80, Pres., 1981–; Mem., GMC, 1979–. *Publications:* Colour Atlas of Histopathology, 1966, 1972; The Pathological Basis of Medicine, 1972; Gross Pathology—a Colour Atlas, 1974; scientific papers on lymphoid tissue, disorders of connective tissue, etc. *Recreations:* golf, music. *Address:* 12 Hintlesham Avenue, Edgbaston, Birmingham B15 2PH.
See also Sir S. C. Curran.

CURRAN, Sir Samuel (Crowe), Kt 1970; FRS 1953; FRSE 1947; Visiting Professor in Energy Studies at the University of Glasgow, since 1980; Principal and Vice-Chancellor, University of Strathclyde, 1964–80; *b* 23 May 1912; *s* of John Curran, Kinghorn, Fife, and Sarah Owen Crowe, Ballymena, Ulster; *m* 1940, Joan Elizabeth, *yr d* of Charles William Strothers and Margaret Beatrice (*née* Millington); three *s* one *d*. *Educ:* Glasgow Univ.; St John's Coll., Cambridge (Hon. Fellow 1971). DSc Glasgow 1950; MA; BSc, PhD Glasgow, 1937; Cavendish Laboratory, 1937–39; PhD Cantab, 1941; RAE, 1939–40; Min. of Aircraft Production and Min. of Supply, 1940–44; Manhattan Project (Min. of Supply), Univ. of California, 1944–45 (Invention of Scintillation Counter, 1944). Natural Philosophy, Glasgow Univ. 1944–55; UK Atomic Energy Authority, 1955–58; Chief Scientist, AWRE, Aldermaston, Berks, 1958–59. Principal, Royal Coll. of Science and Technology, Glasgow, 1959–64. Pres., Scottish Soc. for the Mentally Handicapped, 1954–. Member: Council for Scientific and Industrial Research, 1962–65; Science Research Council, 1965–68; Adv. Council on Technology, 1965–70; Chairman: Adv. Cttee on Med. Research, 1962–75; Adv. Bd on Relations with Univs, 1966–70; Electricity Supply Res. Council, 1978–80 (Dep. Chm., 1980–82); Dep. Chm., Electricity Council, 1977–79; Chief Scientific Adviser to the Sec. of State for Scotland, 1967–77; Member: Oil Develt Council for Scotland, 1973–78; Adv. Cttee on Safety of Nuclear Installations, 1977–80; Radioactive Waste Management Adv. Cttee, 1978–; Adv. Council of A Power for Good (APG), 1978–; UK Nat. Commn for Unesco, and Educn Adv. Cttee, 1978–. Director: Scottish Television, 1964–82; Hall Thermotank Ltd, 1969–76; Cetec Systems Ltd, 1965–77; Internat. Res. & Develt Co. Ltd, 1970–78; Gen. Steels Div., BSC, 1970–73. Hon. President: Scottish Polish Cultural Assoc., 1972–; St Andrews' Soc., Glasgow, 1982– FRCPS (Hon.) 1964; Hon. LLD: Glasgow, 1968; Aberdeen, 1971; Hon. ScD Lodz, 1973; Hon. DSc Strathclyde, 1980; Hon. DEng Nova Scotia, 1982. Freeman: Motherwell and Wishaw, 1966; City of Glasgow, 1981. DL Glasgow, 1969. St Mungo Prize, 1976. Comdr, St Olav (Norway), 1966; Comdr, Order Polish People's Republic, 1976. *Publications:* (with J. D. Craggs) Counting Tubes, 1949; Luminescence and the Scintillation Counter, 1953; Alpha, Beta and Gamma Ray Spectroscopy, 1964; (jt) Energy Resources and the Environment, 1976; (with J. S. Curran) Energy and Human Needs, 1979; papers on nuclear researches and education in Proc. Royal Society.

Recreations: horology, golf. *Address:* 93 Kelvin Court, Glasgow G12 0AH. *Clubs:* Caledonian; Royal Scottish Automobile (Glasgow).
See also R. C. Curran.

CURREY, Rear-Adm. Edmund Neville Vincent, CB 1960; DSO 1944; DSC 1941; *b* 1 Oct. 1906; *s* of Dr and Mrs E. F. N. Currey, Lismore, Co. Waterford, Ireland; *m* 1941, Rosemary Knight; one *d. Educ:* Royal Naval Colls, Osborne and Dartmouth. Joined RNC Osborne 1920; served in submarines and destroyers as junior officer; served War of 1939-45; commanded HM ships Wrestler, Escapade and Musketeer; Comdr, 1942; Capt., 1949; subsequently served with British Naval Mission to Greece; Naval Asst to Adm. Commanding Reserves; in command of HMS Bermuda; Naval Asst to Second Sea Lord; Rear-Adm., 1958; Chief of Staff to C-in-C, Portsmouth, 1958-61, retired. Polish Gold Cross of Merit, with swords, 1943. *Recreation:* golf. *Address:* 11 George Street, Bathwick Hill, Bath, Avon. *T:* Bath 63743.

CURREY, Ronald Fairbridge, MC, MA, Hon. LLD; *b* 23 Oct. 1894; *s* of late Hon. H. L. Currey and Ethelreda (*d* 1942), *d* of late C. A. Fairbridge; *m* 1924, Dorothy White; three *s. Educ:* Diocesan Coll., Rondebosch; S Andrews Coll., Grahamstown; Rhodes Univ. Coll., Grahamstown; Trinity Coll., Oxford; Rhodes Scholar, 1912. Served 1914-18, Argyll and Sutherland Highlanders (attached Black Watch), France and Belgium (MC and Bar); Asst Master, Rugby Sch., 1920-21; S Andrews Coll., Grahamstown, 1922-26; Joint Headmaster, Ridge Preparatory Sch., Johannesburg, 1927-30; Rector of Michaelhouse, Balgowan, Natal, 1930-38; Headmaster of S Andrews Coll., Grahamstown, S Africa, 1939-55; Headmaster, Ruzawi Sch., Marandellas, S Rhodesia, 1956-61; Lectr in Classics, Rhodes Univ., Grahamstown, until 1965. *Publications:* (with others) Coming of Age-Studies in South African Politics, Economics, and Citizenship, 1930; Some Notes on The Future of the South African Church Schools, 1942; Rhodes: a Biographical Footnote, 1946; (with others) The South African Way of Life, 1953; S Andrews College, 1855-1955, 1955; Rhodes University, 1904-1970, 1970. *Address:* 34 Hill Street, Grahamstown, South Africa.

CURRIE, Prof. Sir Alastair (Robert), Kt 1979; FRCP, FRCPE, FRCP Glasgow, FRSE; Professor of Pathology, Edinburgh University, since 1972; Pathologist, Royal Infirmary of Edinburgh; Consultant Pathologist, Lothian Health Board; *b* 8 Oct. 1921; *s* of late John Currie and Maggie Mactaggart; *m* 1944, Jeanne Marion Clarke, MB, ChB; three *s* two *d. Educ:* High Sch. and Univ. of Glasgow. BSc 1941; MB, ChB Glasgow, 1944; MRCPE 1947, FRCPE 1957; MCPath 1963; FRCPath 1965; FRCP Glasgow, 1964; FRSE 1964; MRCP 1966; FRCP 1971; FRCSE 1973. RAMC 1949-51; Lectr in Pathology, Univ. of Glasgow 1947-54; Sen. Lectr in Pathology, Univ. of Glasgow, and Cons. Pathologist, Royal Infirmary, Glasgow, 1954-59; Head, Div. of Pathology, Imperial Cancer Research Fund, London, 1959-62; Regius Prof. of Pathology, Univ. of Aberdeen, 1962-72. Visiting Professor: Boston, 1969; Queensland, 1970; Nairobi, 1974; McGill, 1978. Chairman: Standing Adv. Cttee on Laboratory Services, 1968-72; Biomedical Res. Cttee, 1975-78; Jt MRC and NRPB Cttee on Radiological Protection, 1974-81; MRC/CRC Cttee for Jtly Supported Insts, 1978-80; CRC/MRC Cttee for Inst. of Cancer Research, 1980-; Co-ordinating Cttee for Cancer Res., 1980-81; Member: MRC, 1964-68 and 1976-80 (Chm., Cell Biology and Disorders Bd, 1976-78); Scottish NE Regional Hosp. Bd, 1966-71; Council, RCPath, 1968-71; Scottish Health Services Council, 1969-72; Chief Scientist's Cttee, Scottish Home and Health Dept, 1974-78; Court, Edinburgh Univ., 1975-78; Bd of Dirs, Inveresk Research International, 1980-; Sci. Adv. Council, Alberta Heritage Foundn for Med. Res., 1982-. Cancer Research Campaign: Mem., 1969-, Chm., 1978-. Scientific Cttee; Mem. Exec. Cttee and Council, 1977-. *Publications:* papers in scientific and med. jls. *Address:* 42 Murrayfield Avenue, Edinburgh EH12 6AY. *T:* 031-337 3100; Grianan, Strathlachlan, Strachur, Argyll. *T:* Strachur 769. *Club:* Army and Navy.

CURRIE, Sir Alick Bradley, 6th Bt *cr* 1847; retired; *b* 8 June 1904; *s* of George Hugh Currie (*d* 1951) (*g s* of 1st Bt) and Grace, *d* of A. F. Miller, Farmington, New Mexico, USA; *S* kinsman, Sir Walter Mordaunt Cyril Currie, 5th Bt, 1978. Formerly in Radio Communications with US Navy and Federal Aviation, 1923-50; US Representative, ICAO, 1945-50, attending numerous world-wide confs. *Heir:* nephew Donald Scott Currie [*b* 1930; *m* 1st, 1948, Charlotte (marr. diss. 1951), *d* of Charles Johnstone; one *s* two *d*; 2nd, 1952, Barbara Lee, *d* of A. P. Garnier; one *s* two *d*]. *Address:* Tenacre Ranch, 13467 County Road 501, Bayfield, Colorado 81122, USA.

CURRIE, Austin; see Currie, J. A.

CURRIE, Sir George (Alexander), Kt 1960; retired as Vice-Chancellor, University of New Zealand (May 1952-Dec. 1961); *b* Banffshire, Scotland, 13 Aug. 1896; *s* of George Currie, farmer, and Mary Currie; *m* 1923, Margaret, *d* of Alexander Smith; two *s. Educ:* University of Aberdeen (BscAg, DSc). War Service, Gordon Highlanders, 1915-18. Manager, Salter Estate Co. Ltd, N Queensland, 1923-26; Scientific Officer, Dept Agric., Queensland, 1926-29; Principal Research Officer, Council for Scientific and Industrial Research, Australia, 1929-39; Prof. of Agriculture, University of Western Australia, 1939-40; Vice Chancellor, Univ. of Western Australia, 1940-52. Chm. Commn on Higher Educn for Papua and New Guinea, 1963-64. Hon. LLD: Aberdeen, 1948; Melbourne, 1954; Dalhousie, Canada, 1958; Papua, New Guinea, 1967. Hon. DLitt, University of Western Australia, 1952. *Publications:* The Origins of CSIRO, 1901-26, 1966; some 20 bulletins,

pamphlets and articles on scientific research; articles on univ. educn and admin. *Address:* 20 Chermside Street, Canberra, ACT 2600, Australia.
See also Sir N. S. Currie.

CURRIE, Sir James, KBE 1967 (OBE 1950); CMG 1958; retired from HM Diplomatic Service, 1967; *b* 6 May 1907; *o s* of Charles Howat Currie and Rebecca Ralston, Glasgow; *m* 1945, Daisy Mowat; one *s. Educ:* Glasgow Academy; Glasgow Univ.; Balliol Coll., Oxford; London School of Economics. Did not take up appt at UCL, 1931; William Hollins & Co. Ltd, 1931-34; National Milk Publicity Council, 1934-39; taught Working Mens' Coll.; Ministry of Economic Warfare, 1939. Commercial Secretary: Rio de Janeiro, 1941; Ankara, 1944; First Secretary (Commercial), Istanbul, 1945; Santiago, Chile, 1947; British Rep., ECLA, 1948-49; Commercial Counsellor, Washington, 1949; Commercial Counsellor and Consul-General, Copenhagen, 1952; Consul-General: São Paulo, 1956; Johannesburg, 1962. Commonwealth Foundn, 1967-70; Civil Service Commn, 1967-77; London Council of Univ. of Witwatersrand, 1969-78; Community Relations Commn, 1970-73. FRSA 1955. *Publications:* Professional Organisations in the Commonwealth, 1970; reviews for TLS, The Times and other jls. *Recreations:* fishing and golf. *Address:* Juniper House, Tostock, Bury St Edmunds, Suffolk. *Club:* Reform.

CURRIE, (Joseph) Austin; Research Fellow, Faculty of Economic and Social Studies, Trinity College, Dublin, 1977-78; *b* 11 Oct. 1939; *s* of John Currie and Mary (*née* O'Donnell); *m* 1968, Anne Ita Lynch; two *s* three *d. Educ:* Edendork Sch.; St Patrick's Academy, Dungannon; Queen's Univ., Belfast (BA). MP (Nat) Tyrone, Parlt of N Ireland, 1964-72; Mem. (SDLP), Fermanagh and S Tyrone, NI Assembly, 1973-75, NI Constitutional Convention, 1975-76; Minister of Housing, Planning and Local Govt, 1974. *Address:* Tullydraw, Donaghmore, Co. Tyrone.

CURRIE, Sir Neil (Smith), Kt 1982; CBE 1977; Australian Ambassador to Japan, since 1982; *b* 20 Aug. 1926; *s* of Sir George Currie, *qv; m* 1951, Geraldine Evelyn; two *s* two *d. Educ:* Wesley Coll., Perth, W Australia; Univ. of Western Australia (BA). Department of External Affairs, 1948-59; Dept of Trade and Industry, 1959-71; Secretary: Dept of Supply, 1971-74; Dept of Manufacturing Industry, 1974-76; Dept of Industry and Commerce, 1976-82. *Recreations:* golf, tennis. *Address:* Australian Embassy, 1-14 Mita 2-Chome, Minato-Ku, Tokyo. *T:* 453-0251/9. *Clubs:* Commonwealth, Federal Golf (Canberra).

CURRIE, Rev. Piers William Edward, MC 1945; Hon. Curate of Holt with Edgefield; Deputy Master, Court of Protection, 1971-77; *b* 26 Feb. 1913; *e c* of late P. A. Currie, OBE and of Mrs L. A. Currie; *m* 1956, Ella Rosaleen, *y c* of late Rev. W. and Mrs Bennett-Hughes; no *c. Educ:* Rugby Sch.; Brasenose Coll., Oxford (MA). Solicitor, admitted Dec. 1939. Served War, 1940-45, in 4th Regt RHA. Sen. Legal Asst, Nat. Coal Bd, 1946-53; Asst Sec., 1953-55; Sec., W Midlands Divisional Bd, 1955-60; Sec. and Legal Adviser, 1960-62; Dep. Sec., NCB, 1962-67; Legal Adviser, Land Commission, 1967-71. Ordained deacon, 1980; priest, 1981. *Recreations:* church affairs, gardening, natural history. *Address:* Westward House, Woodlands Close, Holt, Norfolk. *Club:* United Oxford & Cambridge University.

CURRIE, Rear-Adm. Robert Alexander, CB 1957; DSC 1944, bar 1945; DL; *b* 29 April 1905; 5th *s* of John Currie, Glasgow, and Rachel Thomson, Dundee; *m* 1944, Lady (Edith Margaret) Beevor, *widow* of Sir Thomas Beevor, 6th Bt, and *d* of Frank Agnew, Eccles, Norfolk; one step *s* (*see* Sir Thomas Beevor, 7th Bt) three step *d. Educ:* RN Colleges, Osborne and Dartmouth. Specialised in Gunnery, 1930. Served War, 1939-45: HMS Hood; HMS Warspite, 2nd Battle of Narvik; Plans Division, Admiralty; Convoy Escort Comdr; Assault Gp Comdr, Far East; Captain RN, 1945; Captain (D) Fifth Flotilla, 1948-49; idc 1950; Director, Royal Naval Staff Coll., 1951-52; Comdg Officer, HMS Cumberland, 1953; Rear-Adm., 1954; Chief of Staff to Chairman, British Joint Service Mission, Washington, DC, 1954-57; retired, 1957. Member: Cttee of Enquiry into the Fishing Industry, 1958-60; W Suffolk County Council, 1962-74. DL, Suffolk, 1968. King Haakon VII Liberty Cross, Norway, 1945. *Recreations:* shooting, fishing, painting. *Address:* Thorpe Morieux Hall, near Bury St Edmunds. *T:* Cockfield Green 828 276.

CURRIE, Prof. Ronald Ian, CBE 1977; FIBiol; FRSE; Director and Secretary, Scottish Marine Biological Association, since 1966; *b* 10 Oct. 1928; *s* of Ronald Wavell Currie and Elizabeth Currie; *m* 1956, Cecilia, *d* of William and Lilian de Garis; one *s* one *d. Educ:* The Univ., Glasgow (BSc 1st Cl. Hons Zool., 1949); Univ. of Copenhagen. FIBiol 1967; FRSE 1969. Hon. Prof., Heriot-Watt Univ., 1979-. Joined Royal Naval Scientific Service, 1949; seconded to National Inst. of Oceanography; Head of Biol. Dept, 1962-66. William Scoresby Expedn, S Africa, 1950; Discovery Expedn, Antarctica, 1951; res. voyages, N Atlantic, 1955-64; Chm., Biol. Planning Cttee, Internat. Indian Ocean Expedn, 1960; Indian Ocean Expedn, 1963 and 1964. Secretary: Internat. Assoc. for Biol Oceanography, 1964-66 (Pres., 1966-70); Scientific Cttee on Oceanic Res., Internat. Council of Scient. Unions, 1972-78. Chm., Adv. Cttee on Internat. Ocean. Affairs; Mem., Scottish Adv. Cttee, Nature Conservancy Council. Hon. Sec., Challenger Soc., 1956-. *Publications:* (with T. J. Hart) The Benguela Current (Discovery Report), 1960; scientific papers on organic prodn in the sea and fertility of the ocean. *Recreations:* cooking, hill walking, shooting, local history. *Address:*

Kilmore House, Kilmore, by Oban, Argyll. *T:* Kilmore 248. *Club:* Royal Over-Seas League.

CURRY, Dr Alan Stewart; Controller, Forensic Science Service, Home Office, 1976-82; *b* 31 Oct. 1925; *s* of late Richard C. Curry and of Margaret Curry; *m* 1973, J. Venise Hewitt; one *s* (by previous marriage). *Educ:* Arnold Sch., Blackpool; Trinity Coll., Cambridge (Scholar). MA, PhD, CChem, FRSC, FRCPath. Served War of 1939-45 with RAF. Joined Home Office Forensic Science Service, 1952; served in NE Region, 1952-64; Dir, Nottingham Forensic Sci. Lab., 1964-66; Dir, Home Office Central Research Estabt, Aldermaston, 1966-76. Pres., Internat. Assoc. of Forensic Toxicologists, 1969-75; UN Consultant in Narcotics; Hon. Consultant in Forensic Toxicology to RAF. Fellow, Indian Acad. of Forensic Scis; Mem., Amer. Acad. of Forensic Scis; Hon. Mem., Belg. Pharmaceutical Soc. *Publications:* Poison Detection in Human Organs, 1962 (3rd edn 1976); Advances in Forensic and Clinical Toxicology, 1973; (ed, with wife) The Biochemistry of Women, Clinical Concepts; Methods for Clinical Investigation, 1964; (ed) Methods of Forensic Sciences, Vols 3 and 4; many papers in med. and sci. jls. *Recreations:* sailing, amateur radio. *T:* Reading 581481. *Clubs:* Athenæum, Safari.

CURRY, David Maurice; Member (C) Essex North East, European Parliament, since 1979 (Chairman, Agriculture Committee, since 1982); *b* 13 June 1944; *s* of Thomas Harold Curry and Florence Joan (*née* Tyerman); *m* 1971, Anne Helene Maud Roullet; one *s* two *d. Educ:* Ripon Grammar Sch.; Corpus Christi Coll., Oxford (MA Hons); Kennedy Sch. of Govt, Harvard (Kennedy Scholar, 1966-67). Reporter, Newcastle Jl, 1967-70; Financial Times: Trade Editor, Internat. Cos Editor, Brussels Corresp., Paris Corresp., and European News Editor, 1970-79. Sec., Anglo-American Press Assoc. of Paris, 1978; Founder, Paris Conservative Assoc., 1977. *Recreations:* digging, cycling, playing with the children. *Address:* Newland End, Arkesden, Essex CB11 4HF. *T:* Clavering 368.

CURRY, John Anthony, OBE 1976; professional skater; *b* 9 Sept. 1949; *s* of Joseph Henry Curry and Rita Agnes Pritchard. *Educ:* Solihull Sch. British, European, World, and Olympic Figure Skating Champion, 1976. Founder and Director: John Curry Theatre of Skating, 1977; John Curry Sch. of Skating, 1978. *Publication:* (with photographs by Keith Money) John Curry, 1978. *Recreation:* theatre.

CURRY, Thomas Peter Ellison, QC 1966, 1973; *s* of Maj. F. R. P. Curry; *m* 1950, Pamela Joyce, *d* of late Group Capt. A. J. Holmes, AFC, JP; two *s* two *d. Educ:* Tonbridge; Oriel Coll., Oxford. BA 1948; MA 1951. Served War of 1939-45; enlisted 1939; commnd, 1941; 17th Indian Div., India and Burma, 1941-45. War Office, 1946. Called to Bar, Middle Temple, 1953, Bencher, 1979. QC 1966. Solicitor, 1968; partner in Freshfields, Solicitors, 1968-70; returned to Bar; re-appointed QC 1973. Pres., Aircraft and Shipbuilding Industries Arbitration Tribunal, 1978-80. Hon. Treas., Barristers' Benevolent Assoc., 1964-71; Chm., Chancery Bar Assoc., 1980-. Rep. Army, Oxford and Sussex at Squash Racquets (described as fastest mover in squash, 1947; triple blue, Oxford; twice cross country winner); World Student Games (5000 m), 1947; British Steeplechase champion 1948, Olympic Games, 1948. Served on AAA Cttee of Inquiry, 1967. Holder of French certificate as capitaine-mécanicien for mechanically propelled boats. *Publications:* (Joint Editor) Palmer's Company Law, 1959; (Joint Editor) Crew on Meetings, 1966, 1975. *Recreations:* work, gardening, the Turf. *Address:* Rickhurst Farm, Dunsfold, Surrey. *T:* Dunsfold 356. *Club:* Army and Navy.

CURSON, Bernard Robert, CMG 1967; HM Diplomatic Service, retired; *b* 14 Nov. 1913; *e s* of late Robert and Mabel Curson; *m* 1949, Miriam Olive Johnson, Lynchburg, Virginia; one *s. Educ:* University Coll. Sch. Asst Private Sec. to Sec. of State for India, 1943-44, and 1945-46; Mem., UK Delegn to UN Assembly, 1946, 1947, 1948; Private Sec. to Sec. of State for Commonwealth Relations, 1948-50; Office of High Comr, Ceylon, 1950-52; Mem., UK Delegn to UN Wheat Conf., Geneva, 1956; Mem., UK Delegn to Colombo Plan Consultative Cttee, Wellington, 1956, and Saigon, 1957; British Information Services, Canada, 1958-64; Consul-Gen., Atlanta, USA, 1970-73. *Address:* 3804 Peachtree Road, NE, Atlanta, Ga 30319, USA. *Club:* Travellers'.

CURTEIS, Ian Bayley; television playwright; *b* 1 May 1935; *m* 1964, Dorothy Joan, *d* of late C. S. Armstrong, Sydney, Australia; two *s.* Uneducated. Director and actor in theatres all over Great Britain, and BBC-tv script reader, 1956-63; BBC and ATV staff director (drama), directing plays by John Betjeman, John Hopkins, William Trevor and others, 1963-67. Writing screenplay for Sir Richard Attenborough's film, Tom Paine, 1982-. Chm., Cttee on Censorship, Writers' Guild of GB, 1981-. *Television plays:* Beethoven, Sir Alexander Fleming (BBC's entry at 1973 Prague Fest.), Mr Rolls and Mr Royce, Long Voyage out of War (trilogy), The Folly, The Haunting, Second Time Round, A Distinct Chill, The Portland Millions, Philby, Burgess and Maclean (British entry 1978 Monte Carlo Fest.), Hess, The Atom Spies, Churchill and the Generals (BAFTA nomination; Grand Prize, Best Programme of 1980, NY Internat. Film and TV Fest.), Suez 1956 (BAFTA nomination), Miss Morison's Ghosts, The Mitford Girls. Also originated and wrote numerous popular television drama series; *film screenplay:* Andre Malraux's La Condition humaine, 1982; *play:* A Personal Affair, Globe, 1982. *Publications:* plays: Long Voyage out of War (trilogy), 1971; Churchill and the Generals, 1979; Suez 1956, 1980. *Recreation:* avoiding

television. *Address:* Mumford House, Kingsnorth, near Ashford, Kent; 45 Moreton Terrace, SW1.

CURTIN, Rt. Rev. Mgr. Canon Jeremiah John, DD; Priest-Director and Ecclesiastical Adviser, Universe Enquiry Bureau, since 1953; Canon of Southwark Diocesan Chapter, 1958; Domestic Prelate to HH Pope John XXIII, 1961, Protonotary Apostolic, 1972; Canon Theologian, Metropolitan Chapter, 1981; *b* Sileby, Leics, 19 June 1907; *e s* of late Jeremiah John Curtin and Mary Bridget Curtin (*née* Leahy). *Educ:* Battersea Polytechnic; Wimbledon Coll.; St Joseph's Coll., Mark Cross; St John's Seminary, Wonersh; Gregorian Univ., Rome. BA London 1927; DD Rome 1933 (Gregorian Univ.). Priest, 1931; Prof. of Philosophy and Theology, St John's Seminary, Wonersh, 1933-48; Vice-Rector, 1947-48; Parish Priest, St Paul's, Hayward's Heath, 1948-56; Parish Priest, Our Lady of Ransom, Eastbourne, 1956-61; Rector, Pontificio Collegio Beda, Rome, 1961-72. *Recreations:* archæology, music. *Address:* 48 Castle Street, Farnham, Surrey GU9 7JQ. *T:* Farnham 714659. *Club:* Athenæum.

CURTIS, Colin Hinton Thomson, CVO 1970; ISO 1970; Chairman, Metropolitan Public Abattoir Board, 1971-81; Member, Queensland Meat Industry Authority, 1972-78; *b* 25 June 1920; *s* of A. Curtis, Brisbane; *m* 1943, Anne Catherline Drevesen; one *s. Educ:* Brisbane Grammar School. RANR Overseas Service, 1940-45. Sec. and Investigation Officer to Chm., Sugar Cane Prices Board, 1948-49; Asst Sec. to Central Sugar Cane Prices Board, 1949; Sec. to Premier of Queensland, 1950-64; Mem., Qld Trade Missions to SE Asia, 1963 and 1964; Asst Under-Sec., Premier's Dept, 1961-64; Assoc. Dir and Dir of Industrial Development, 1964-66; Under-Sec., Premier's Dept and Clerk of Exec. Council, 1966-70; State Dir, Royal Visit, 1970; Agent-General for Queensland in London, 1970-71. *Recreations:* squash, yachting, swimming. *Address:* 117 Carlton Terrace, Manly, Qld 4179, Australia. *Clubs:* RSL Memorial, Tattersalls, Royal Queensland Yacht, Rugby League (Queensland).

CURTIS, Prof. David Roderick, FRS 1974; FAA 1965; Professor of Pharmacology, John Curtin School of Medical Research, Australian National University, since 1973; *b* 3 June 1927; *s* of E. D. and E. V. Curtis; *m* 1952, Lauris Sewell; one *s* one *d. Educ:* Univ. of Melbourne; Australian National Univ. MB, BS Melbourne 1950, PhD ANU 1957. Dept of Physiology, John Curtin Sch., ANU: Research Scholar, 1954-56; Research Fellow, 1956-57; Fellow, 1957-59; Sen. Fellow, 1959-62; Professorial Fellow, 1962-66; Prof. of Pharmacology, 1966-68; Prof. of Neuropharmacology, 1968-73. *Publications:* papers in fields of neurophysiology, neuropharmacology in Jl Physiology, Jl Neurophysiol., Brain Research, Exper. Brain Research, etc. *Recreation:* tennis. *Address:* 7 Patey Street, Campbell, Canberra City, ACT 2601, Australia. *T:* Canberra (062) 48-5664: John Curtin School of Medical Research, Australian National University, PO Box 334, ACT 2601. *T:* Canberra (062) 49-2757.

CURTIS, Sir (Edward) Leo, Kt 1965; Lord Mayor of Melbourne, Australia, 1963-64 and 1964-65; *b* London, 13 Jan. 1907; *m* 1938, Elvira Lillian Prahl. Joined Melbourne City Council, Dec. 1955; retired March 1975. Past President of Retail Traders Association of Victoria. *Address:* 168 Kooyong Road, Toorak, Vic. 3142, Australia. *Clubs:* Athenæum, Kelvin (Melbourne); various sporting.

CURTIS, Most Rev. Ernest Edwin, CBE 1976; Hon. Assistant Bishop of Portsmouth, since 1976; *b* 24 Dec. 1906, *s* of Ernest John and Zoe Curtis; *m* 1938, Dorothy Anne Hill (*d* 1965); one *s* one *d* ; *m* 1970, Evelyn Mary Josling. *Educ:* Sherborne; Foster's Sch.; Royal College of Science, London. BSc (hons Chem.) London, 1927; ARCSc 1927; Dipl. Educn, London, 1928. Asst Master, Lindisfarne Coll., Westcliff, 1928-31; Wells Theol Coll., 1932-33; Asst Curate, Holy Trinity, Waltham Cross, 1933-36; Chaplain i/c parishes Rose Hill and Bambous, and Principal, St Paul's Theol Coll., Mauritius, 1937-44; Missions to Seamen Chaplain, Port Louis, 1944; Priest i/c St Wilfrid, Portsmouth, 1945-47; Vicar, All Saints, Portsmouth, and Chaplain, Royal Portsmouth Hospital, 1947-55; Priest i/c St Agatha, Portsmouth, 1954-55; Vicar, St John Baptist, Locks Heath, 1955-66; Warden of Readers, Dio. Portsmouth, 1956-66; Rural Dean of Alverstoke, 1964-66; Bishop of Mauritius and Seychelles, 1966-72, of Mauritius, 1973-76; Archbishop of the Indian Ocean, 1973-76; Priest-in-charge of St Mary, Whitwell, 1976-82. *Recreations:* walking, hill-climbing, piano. *Address:* 5 Elizabeth Gardens, Havenstreet, Ryde, Isle of Wight PO33 4DU. *T:* Isle of Wight 883049.

CURTIS, Brig. Francis Cockburn, CBE 1945; MA; MIEE; Fellow Emeritus, Trinity Hall, Cambridge, since 1961; *b* 2 May 1898; *s* of late Lieut-Col J. G. C. Curtis, Oxford and Bucks Light Infantry, Walmer, Kent; *m* 1933, Dorothy Joan Grant; two *s* one *d. Educ:* Bedales Sch.; RMA, Woolwich; King's Coll., Cambridge (entered 1924; Starred First in Mech. Scis Tripos, 1926). Commissioned RE 1917; served in Flanders (despatches), Iraq and Palestine; transferred to Royal Signals, 1923; served on General Staff in War Office and Aldershot Command, and in Home Office (ARP Dept), and Office of the Lord Privy Seal; OC 38th (Welsh) Divisional Signals, 1940-41; Army Council Secretariat (Secretary Standing Cttee on Army Administration), 1941; Joint Planning Staff, 1942; Colonel 1943; Dep. Director of Military Operations, 1943-44; Director of Post-Hostilities Plans, War Office, 1944; Brigadier, General Staff (Plans and Ops), GHQ, MELF, 1945-48; Director for European Inter-Allied Planning, War Office, 1948-51; retired 1951; Fellow and Bursar, Trinity Hall, Cambridge, 1952-59; Treasurer, 1959-61. Former

Mem., Eagle Ski Club. *Recreation:* fishing. *Address:* 16 Marlborough Court, Cambridge CB3 9BQ. *T:* Cambridge 350664.

CURTIS, Frank; see Curtis, R. F.

CURTIS, John Henry, CB 1981; FAIM, FTS; Chairman, D. Richardson & Sons Ltd; Commissioner, Overseas Telecommunications Commission (Australia), since 1974; *b* 20 March 1920; *s* of K. H. and E. M. Curtis; *m* 1943, Patricia Foote; one *s* one *d*. *Educ:* Ipswich Grammar Sch.; Queensland Univ. (BE Hons 1950, BSc 1951, BA 1957). FIEAust 1981; FAIM 1970; FTS 1979. Dir of Posts and Telegraphs, Qld, 1971-73; Dep. Dir Gen., Postmaster-Gen.'s Dept, 1973-75; Man. Dir, Australian Telecommunications Commn, 1975-81. Pres., Victorian Div., Aust. Inst. of Management, 1979-81. *Address:* 36 Boyd Street, Blackburn, Vic 3130, Australia. *T:* 877 4848.

CURTIS, John S.; see Sutton Curtis.

CURTIS, Sir Leo; see Curtis, Sir E. L.

CURTIS, Michael Howard; Executive Aide to HH The Aga Khan; Director, Nation Printers and Publishers, Nairobi, Kenya, since 1959, Chairman, 1976-77; *b* 28 Feb. 1920; *e s* of Howard and Doris May Curtis; *m* 1st, 1947, Barbara Winifred Gough; two *s* two *d*; 2nd, 1961, Marian Joan Williams. *Educ:* St Lawrence Coll.; Sidney Sussex Coll., Cambridge (MA). Eastern Daily Press, Norwich, 1945; News Chronicle: Leader Writer, 1946; Dep. Editor, 1952; Editor, 1954-57; Dir, News Chronicle Ltd, 1954-57; Personal Aide to HH The Aga Khan, 1957-59. *Address:* La Vieille Maison, Villemetrie, 60300 Senlis, France. *Clubs:* Garrick, East India; Muthaiga (Nairobi).

CURTIS, Percy John, CB 1960; CBE 1955; Secretary, Exchequer and Audit Department, 1955-63; *b* 3 Oct. 1900; *s* of J. H. Curtis, Trimdon, Co. Durham; *m* 1st, 1924, Dorothy Hilda Ford Hayes (*d* 1954); one *s*; 2nd, 1958, Joyce Irene Potter. *Educ:* Rye Grammar Sch. Entered Exchequer and Audit Dept, 1920. *Address:* 2 Rigault Road, SW6. *T:* 01-736 4072. *Club:* Reform.

CURTIS, Peter; see Lofts, Norah.

CURTIS, His Honour Philip; a Circuit Judge (formerly a Judge of County Courts), 1969-79; *b* 29 April 1908; *s* of James William and Emma Curtis; *m* 1937, Marjorie Lillian Sharp; two *s* one *d*. *Educ:* St Mary's RC, Denton, Lancs; Manchester Grammar; Brasenose Coll., Oxford. Called to the Bar, Gray's Inn, 1944. *Address:* Mottram Hall Farm, Mottram St Andrew, near Macclesfield, Cheshire. *T:* Prestbury 829509.

CURTIS, Richard Herbert, QC 1977; a Recorder of the Crown Court, since 1974. *Educ:* Oxford Univ. (MA). Called to Bar, Inner Temple, 1958. Hon. Recorder, City of Hereford, 1980. *Address:* 1 King's Bench Walk, Temple, EC4. *T:* 01-353 8436.

CURTIS, Richard James Seymour, OBE 1962; *b* 22 Oct. 1900; *s* of late Sir George Curtis, KCSI, ICS, and of late Lady Curtis, OBE, La Frégate, Dinard, France; *m* 1929, Mary Margaret, *o d* of late Rev. and Mrs H. J. Boyd, St Paul's Vicarage, St Leonards-on-Sea; one *s* one *d*. *Educ:* Haileybury; King's Coll., Cambridge; University of Caen. Hons degree in History, Cambridge, 1922. Appointed Assistant Anglais at Lycée Corneille, Rouen, by Board of Education, Oct. 1922; Asst Master, Hurst Court, Sept. 1923, Partner, 1926, Headmaster, 1933-61. Incorporated Assoc. of Preparatory Schools (Vice-Chm. IAPS, 1946; Chm. 1957). Asst Sec. and Sec., Common Entrance Examination Board, 1961-67. Mem. Hastings Borough Council, 1952-61; President Soc. of Schoolmasters, 1962. *Publications:* (with A. R. Slater) Latin and French Revision Papers, 1948. Translator of The Revolutionaries, by Louis Madelin; Russia Unveiled, by Panait Istrati; Murder Party, by Henry Bordeaux; The Corsairs of St Malo, by Dupont. *Address:* The Wychert, Haddenham, Bucks. *T:* Haddenham 291136.

CURTIS, Prof. (Robert) Frank, PhD, DSc; FRSC, FIFST; Director, Agricultural Research Council Food Research Institute, and Professor, University of East Anglia, since 1977; *b* 8 Oct. 1926; *s* of late William John Curtis, Somerset, and Ethel Irene Curtis, Bath; *m* 1954, Sheila Rose, *y d* of Bruce Rose, Huddersfield; two *s* one *d*. *Educ:* City of Bath Sch.; Univ. of Bristol (BSc 1949, PhD 1952, DSc 1972). FRIC 1966, FIFST 1977. Johns Hopkins University: W. H. Grafflin Fellow, 1952; Instr in Chemistry, 1953; Technical Officer, ICI Ltd, Manchester, 1954-56; Res. Fellow, Univ. of WI, 1956-57; Lectr in Chem., University Coll., Swansea, 1957-62, Sen. Lectr 1962-69; Reader, Univ. of Wales, 1969-70; Head, Chem. Div., ARC Food Res. Inst., 1970-77. Chm., Food Standards Cttee, MAFF, 1979-. *Publications:* res. papers on chemistry and food science in jls of learned socs. *Address:* Manor Barn, Colton, Norwich NR9 5BZ. *T:* Norwich 880379. *Club:* Savage.

CURTIS, Very Rev. Wilfred Frank; Provost of Sheffield, since 1974; *b* 24 Feb. 1923; *s* of W. A. Curtis, MC and Mrs M. Curtis (*née* Burbidge); *m* 1951, Muriel (*née* Dover); two *s* two *d*. *Educ:* Bishop Wordsworth's Sch., Salisbury; King's Coll., London (AKC). Served in RA, 1942-47; Major 1946. London Univ., 1947-52; Curate of High Wycombe, 1952-55; staff of Church Missionary Soc., 1955-74: Area Sec., Devon and Cornwall, 1955-65; Adviser in Rural Work, 1957-65; SW Regional Sec., 1962-65; Home Sec., 1965-74. Vice-Pres., Church Missionary Soc., 1977-; Mem., General Synod, 1977-. Chaplain to Master Cutler, 1976, 1978. Hon. Fellow, Sheffield City

Polytechnic, 1980. *Recreations:* walking, photography, nature study. *Address:* Provost's Lodge, 22 Hallam Gate Road, Sheffield S10 5BS. *T:* Sheffield 662373 or 753434. *Club:* Sheffield.

CURTIS, Wilfred Harry, CB 1953; CBE 1950; *b* 23 May 1897; retired as Assistant Under-Secretary of State, War Office, 1958. *Educ:* Summerleaze, Harptree, Somerset. JP County of London, 1950-58. *Address:* Ashton, Dunsfold, Surrey. *T:* Dunsfold 384.

CURTIS, Sir William (Peter), 7th Bt *cr* 1802; *b* 9 April 1935; *s* of Sir Peter Curtis, 6th Bt, and of Joan Margaret, *d* of late Reginald Nicholson; *S* father, 1976. *Educ:* Winchester College; Trinity College, Oxford (MA); Royal Agricultural College, Cirencester. *Heir: cousin* Major Edward Philip Curtis, 16th/5th The Queen's Royal Lancers (retd) [*b* 25 June 1940; *m* 1978, Catherine, *d* of H. J. Armstrong, Christchurch, NZ; one *s* one *d*. *Educ:* Bradfield; RMA Sandhurst]. *Address:* Oak Lodge, Bank Street, Bishop's Waltham, Hants.

CURTIS-RALEIGH, Nigel Hugh; His Honour Judge Curtis-Raleigh; a Circuit Judge (formerly Judge of County Courts), since 1966; *b* 8 Nov. 1914; *s* of late Capt. H. T. R. Curtis-Raleigh; *m* 1964, Jean Steadman, MB, MRCPsych; five *s*. *Educ:* Wellington; Queen's Coll., Oxford (History Exhibitioner, Kitchener Scholar). Called to the Bar, Middle Temple (Harmsworth Law Scholar), 1939. Served HAC, 1939-40. *Recreations:* music, chess, poker.

CURTISS, Air Marshal Sir John (Bagot), KCB 1981 (CB 1979); KBE 1982; Air Officer Commanding No 18 Group, RAF, since 1980; *b* 6 Dec. 1924; *s* of Major E. F. B. Curtiss, RFC; *m* 1946, Peggy Drughorn Bowie; three *s* one *d*. *Educ:* Radley Coll.; Wanganui Collegiate Sch., NZ; Worcester Coll., Oxford. Served War: Oxford Univ. Air Sqdn, 1942-43; Bomber Comd, 578 and 158 sqdns, 1944-45; Transport Comd, 51 and 59 sqdn, 1945-49; Training Comd, 1950-53; Fighter Comd, 29 and 5 sqdns, 1953-64; Dir, RAF Staff Coll., 1967-69; Stn Comdr RAF Bruggen, RAFG, 1970-72; Gp Capt Ops, HQ Strike Comd, 1972-74; SASO, HQ 11 Gp, 1974-75; Dir-Gen. Organisation, RAF, 1975-77; Comdt, RAF Staff Coll., 1977-80; Air Comdr, South Atlantic Operations, 1982. Mem., RUSI, 1967-. CBIM 1981. *Recreations:* squash, sailing, cricket; President: RAF Cricket Assoc.; Combined Services Cricket Assoc., 1979-80. *Address:* c/o Coutts & Co., 1 Old Park Lane, W1Y 4BS. *Clubs:* MCC, Royal Air Force, Pilgrims; Royal Lymington Yacht; Keyhaven Yacht.

CURWEN, Christopher Keith, CMG 1982; HM Diplomatic Service; Counsellor, Foreign and Commonwealth Office, since 1980; *b* 9 April 1929; *s* of late Rev. R. M. Curwen and Mrs M. E. Curwen; *m* 1st, 1956, Noon Tai (marr. diss. 1977); one *s* two *d*; 2nd, 1977, Helen Anne Stirling; one *s* one *d*. *Educ:* Sherborne Sch.; Sidney Sussex Coll., Cambridge (BA). Served HM Forces, 4th Queen's Own Hussars, 1948-49 (despatches). Joined FO, 1952; Bangkok, 1954; Vientiane, 1956; FO, 1958; Bangkok, 1961; Kuala Lumpur, 1963; FO, 1965; Washington, 1968; FCO, 1971; Geneva, 1977. *Recreations:* books, gardening, motoring. *Address:* c/o Foreign and Commonwealth Office, SW1. *Club:* Travellers'.

CURZON; see Roper-Curzon.

CURZON, family name of **Earl Howe** and **Viscount Scarsdale.**

CURZON, Leonard Henry, CB 1956; *b* 4 Jan. 1912; *s* of late Frederick Henry Curzon; *m* 1935, Greta, *e d* of late Willem and Anny van Praag; one *s*. *Educ:* Sir Walter St John's Sch.; Jesus Coll., Cambridge (Scholar, BA, LLB). Civil Servant, 1934-72: Import Duties Adv. Cttee; Air Ministry, Ministries of Aircraft Production, Supply, Aviation and Defence. IDC 1947. *Address:* Southease, Derringstone Hill, Barham, Kent. *T:* Barham 449.

CUSACK, Henry Vernon, CMG 1955; CBE 1947; HM Overseas Civil Service (retired); Deputy Director General of the Overseas Audit Service, 1946-55; *b* 26 June 1895; 2nd *s* of late Edward Cusack, Bray, Co. Wicklow, and of Constance Louisa Vernon, *e d* of late Col Vernon, DL, JP, Clontarf Castle, Dublin; unmarried. *Educ:* Aravon Sch., Ireland. Served European War, 1914-19 (General Service and Victory medals), France, Belgium and North Russia, as Captain, RASC, attached RGA; entered Colonial Audit Service, 1920; Asst Auditor: Sierra Leone, 1920-22, Nigeria, 1922-28; Sen. Asst Auditor, Nyasaland, 1928-33; Asst Director, Central Office, Colonial Audit Dept London, 1933-37; Auditor, Gold Coast, 1937-46; a Governor of the King's Hospital Sch., Dublin (Chm., 1964-69). FRGS. Coronation Medal, 1953. *Address:* Our Lady's Manor, Bulloch Castle, Dalkey, Co. Dublin. *Clubs:* Naval and Military; Kildare Street and University (Dublin); Royal St George Yacht (Dun Laoghaire, Co. Dublin).

CUSDIN, Sidney Edward Thomas, OBE 1946; DSc (Hong Kong); FRIBA, AADip; Consultant to Firm of Cusdin, Burden and Howitt, Architects; *b* 28 July 1908; *s* of Sidney Herbert Cusdin, London; *m* 1936, Eva Eileen (Peggy), *d* of F. P. Dorizzi, London; no *c*. *Educ:* Municipal School of Arts and Crafts, Southend-on-Sea, Essex; Architectural Assoc., London. AA Holloway Scholarship, 1927; Fifth Year Travelling Studentship, 1929; joined staff of Stanley Hall & Easton and Robertson: British Pavilions at Brussels Internat. Exhibition and Johannesburg Exhibition; elected Member of AA Council, 1937, and worked on RIBA Cttees. Served War of 1939-45, RAF, on staff of HQ, No. 26 Group (despatches twice, OBE). Re-joined firm of Easton & Robertson, 1946 (firm later known as Easton & Robertson, Cusdin, Preston and Smith, until 1965 when this partnership was dissolved). Pres. AA, 1950-51; Mem. Council RIBA, 1950-51. Awarded Henry Saxon Snell Prize and Theakston Bequest, 1950; Principal works: London: Development of the Hosp. for Sick Children, Great Ormond Street, British Postgraduate Medical Fedn, and London Univ., Inst. of Child Health; Medical Coll. of St Bartholomew's Hosp., New Hostel and Labs; Middlesex Hosp. Medical Sch.; New Sch. Buildings and Astor Coll.; National Inst. for Medical Research Develt, Mill Hill; Cambridge: Dept of Engineering, New Workshops and Laboratories; Univ. Chemistry Laboratories; United Cambridge Hosps, Addenbrooke's Hosp., Hills Rd, New Develt; MRC, extension of Lab. of Molecular Biology; Harlow: Princess Alexandra Hosp.; Belfast: Queen's Univ. of Belfast, Inst. of Clin. Science; Royal Victoria Hosp. Develt; Royal Belfast Hosp. for Sick Children, alterations and additions; Malaya: plans for Develt of Univ. of Malaya; Hong Kong; plans for develt of Univ. of Hong Kong; Cons. Architect for: Queen Elizabeth Hosp., Hong Kong (awarded RIBA Bronze Medal); Faculty of Medicine, Univ. of Riyad, Saudi Arabia; Cons. Architect to The Imperial Cancer Research Fund, London. Chm., British Consultants Bureau, 1972-74. *Publications:* (with James Crooks) Suggestions and Demonstration Plans for Hospitals for Sick Children, 1947. *Recreations:* theatre, travel, fishing; spending time in believing that "WS" was Shakespeare. *Address:* 27 Devonshire Close, W1N 1LG. *T:* 01-637 1891; 34 Ringshall, Little Gaddesden, near Berkhamsted, Herts. *Clubs:* Savile, Royal Air Force, The Sette of Odd Volumes.

CUSHING, David Henry, DPhil; FRS 1977; Deputy Director, Fisheries Research, England and Wales, 1974-80; *b* 14 March 1920; *s* of W. E. W. Cushing and Isobel (*née* Batchelder); *m* 1943, Diana R. C. Antona-Traversi; one *d. Educ:* Duke's Sch., Alnwick; Newcastle upon Tyne Royal Grammar Sch.; Balliol Coll., Oxford (MA, DPhil). RA, 1940-45; 1st Bn, Royal Fusiliers, 1945-46. Fisheries Lab., 1946-80. *Publications:* The Arctic Cod, 1966; Fisheries Biology, 1968 (USA); Detection of Fish, 1973; Fisheries Resources and their Management, 1974; Marine Ecology and Fisheries, 1975; Science and the Fisheries, 1977. *Address:* 198 Yarmouth Road, Lowestoft, Suffolk. *T:* Lowestoft 65569.

CUST, family name of **Baron Brownlow.**

CUSTANCE, Michael Magnus Vere, CB 1959; *b* 3 Jan. 1916; *e s* of late Mrs Arthur Long (Marjorie Bowen, novelist); *m* ; one *s* one *d. Educ:* St Paul's (schol.); The Queen's Coll., Oxford (open hist. schol., BA Hons, 1st cl., Mod. Hist., 1937). Asst Principal, Board of Trade, 1938; Ministry of Shipping, 1939; Royal Air Force, 1941-45; Principal, Ministry of War Transport, 1943; Asst Sec., Min. of Transport, 1948; Under-Sec., Min. of Transport and Civil Aviation, 1956; Dep. Sec., Min. of Transport and Civil Aviation, 1958; in Ministry of Aviation, 1959-63; in Ministry of Transport, 1963-66; in Min. of Social Security, later DHSS, 1966-75; Chief Advr to Supplementary Benefits Commn, 1968-75. IDC (1952 Course). *Address:* The Patch, Lodsworth, Petworth, Sussex.

CUSTIS, Patrick James, CBE 1981; FCA, FCMA, FCIS; *b* 19 March 1921; *er s* of late Alfred and Amy Custis; *m* 1954, Rita, *yr d* of late Percy and Annie Rayner; one *s. Educ:* The High Sch., Dublin. JDipMA. FCA 1951; FCMA 1950; FCIS 1945. Served articles with Josolyne Miles & Co., Chartered Accountants, Cheapside, London, 1945-51; Asst to Gen. Man., Rio Tinto Co. Ltd, London, 1952-54; Gp Chief Accountant and Dir of subsid. cos, Glynwed Ltd, W Midlands, 1955-66; Guest Keen & Nettlefolds Ltd, W Midlands, 1967-81 (Dir of Finance, 1974-81); various sen. appts prior to 1974. Mem., Birmingham and W Midlands Reg. Bd, Lloyds Bank plc, 1979-; Director: New Court Property Fund Managers Ltd, 1978-; Turriff Corp. plc, 1981-; Associated Heat Services plc, 1981; Cayzer Gartmore Investments, 1982-; Leigh Interests plc, 1982-; Wolseley Hughes plc, 1982-. Mem., HM Prisons Bd, Home Office, 1980-. Co-opted Mem. Council, Inst. of Chartered Accountants in England and Wales, 1979-; Liveryman, Worshipful Co. of Chartered Accountants in England and Wales. *Recreations:* walking, gardening, reading. *Address:* 3 Stonehouse Drive, Little Aston Park, Sutton Coldfield, West Midlands B74 3AL. *T:* 021-353 8467. *Club:* Royal Over-Seas League.

CUSTIS, Ronald (Alfred); Director, Energy Industries Council, since 1981; *b* 28 Feb. 1931; *m* 1957, Enid (Angela) Rowe; one *s* one *d. Educ :* The High Sch., Dublin. Joined HM Treasury, 1947; DES, 1964; Min. of Technology, 1964-70: Private Sec. to Permanent Under Sec., 1964-66; Principal, 1967; Sec. to Cttee of Inquiry into the Brain Drain, 1967-68; Min. of Aviation Supply, later MoD (Procurement Exec.), 1970-74: Private Sec. to Sec. of State for Defence, 1971-73; Asst Sec., 1973; Dept of Energy, 1974-81: Private Sec. to successive Secs of State for Energy, 1974-75; Under Sec., 1978; Dir Gen., Offshore Supplies Office, 1980-81. *Recreations:* reading, hill walking, listening to music. *Address:* 7 Rockwells Gardens, SE19 1HW. *T:* 01-670 5769.

CUTHBERT, Prof. Alan William, PhD; FRS 1982; Sheild Professor of Pharmacology, University of Cambridge, since 1979; Fellow of Jesus College, Cambridge, since 1968; *b* 7 May 1932; *s* of Thomas William Cuthbert and late Florence Mary (*née* Griffin); *m* 1957, Harriet Jane Webster; two *s. Educ:* Leicester Coll. of Technol.; St Andrews Univ. (BSc); London Univ. (BPharm, PhD). MA Cantab. Res. Fellow, then Asst Lectr, Dept of Pharmacology, Sch.

of Pharmacy, Univ. of London, 1959-63; Demonstrator in Pharmacol., 1963-66, Lectr, 1966-73, and Reader, 1973-79, Dept of Pharmacol., Univ. of Cambridge. Chm. Editorial Bd, British Jl of Pharmacology, 1974-. Pereira Medal in Materia Medica, Pharmaceutical Soc. of GB, 1953; Sir James Irvine Medal in Chemistry, St Andrews Univ., 1955. *Publications:* scientific papers in pharmacol and physiol jls. *Recreations:* screen printing, painting, squash, Duodecimos. *Address:* 7 Longstanton Road, Oakington, Cambridge. *T:* Histon 3676.

CUTHBERT, Lady, (Betty Wake), CBE 1946 (OBE 1943); OStJ 1944; *d* of Guy Shorrock and Emma Wake; *m* 1928, Vice-Adm. Sir John Cuthbert, *qv* ; no *c.* Joined Auxiliary Fire Service, London, as driver, 1938; Fire Staff, Home Office, 1941; Chief Woman Fire Officer, National Fire Service, 1941-46. Nat. Chm., Girls' Venture Corps, 1946-67 (Pres. 1967). Mem., Hampshire CC, 1967-74. *Address:* Ibthorpe Manor Farm, Hurstbourne Tarrant, Andover, Hants.

CUTHBERT, Ian Holm; *see* Holm, Ian.

CUTHBERT, Vice-Adm. Sir John (Wilson), KBE 1957 (CBE 1945); CB 1953; DL; *b* 9 April 1902; *s* of William Cuthbert, Glasgow; *m* 1928, Betty Wake, *d* of Guy Shorrock (*see* Lady Cuthbert); no *c. Educ:* Kelvinside Acad.; RN Colleges. Midshipman, 1919; Commander, 1936; Captain, 1941; Rear-Adm., 1951; Vice-Adm., 1954. Commanded: HMS Glasgow, 1942; Ajax, 1944-46; Vengeance, 1949-50; Joint Planning Staff, London, 1942-44; Deputy Controller Admiralty, 1951-53; Flag Officer Flotillas, Home Fleet, 1953-54. Admiral Commanding Reserves, 1955-56; Flag Officer, Scotland, 1956-58. Retired List, 1958. Member Royal Company of Archers (Queen's Body Guard for Scotland). DL Hants 1977. *Address:* Ibthorpe Manor Farm, Hurstbourne Tarrant, near Andover, Hants. *T:* Hurstbourne Tarrant 237. *Club:* Naval and Military.

CUTHBERTSON, Sir David (Paton), Kt 1965; CBE 1957; MD, DSc Glasgow; FRSE, FRCPE; Hon. Senior Research Fellow in Pathological Biochemistry, Glasgow University, and Hon. Consultant in the Biochemical Department of the Royal Infirmary, Glasgow; late Director Rowett Research Institute, 1945-65; *b* 9 May 1900; *s* of John Cuthbertson, MBE, Kilmarnock; *m* 1928, Jean Prentice, *d* of late Rev. Alexander P. Telfer, MA, Tarbet, Dunbartonshire; two *s* one *d. Educ:* University of Glasgow. BSc 1921; MB, ChB, 1926; DSc, 1931; MD, 1937. Bellahouston Gold Medallist. 2nd Lieut (temp.) Royal Scots Fusiliers, 1919. Lecturer in Pathological Biochemistry and Clinical Biochemist, Royal Infirmary and University of Glasgow, 1926-34; Grieve Lecturer in Physiological Chemistry, University of Glasgow, 1934-45; Arris and Gale Lecturer Royal College of Surgeons, 1942. Lieut-Col and Zone Medical Advisor (No. 1) Glasgow Home Guard, 1941-43; seconded to Administrative Headquarters, Medical Research Council, 1943-45. Consultant Director Commonwealth Bureau of Animal Nutrition, 1945-65; Hon. Consultant in Physiology and Nutrition to the Army, 1946-65. Member: UK Agricultural Mission to Canada, 1950; Tech. Cttee, Scottish Agricultural Improvement Council, 1951-64; Advisory Cttee on Pesticides and other Toxic Chemicals, 1966-71. Chairman: General and Organising Cttees, 9th International Congress of Animal Production, 1966; ARC Tech. Cttee on Nutrient Requirements of Livestock, 1959-65. President: International Union of Nutritional Sciences, 1960-66 (Hon. Pres., 1972-); Sect. I (1953) and Sect. M (1958) of British Assoc.; Nutrition Soc., 1962-65; British Soc. of Animal Production, 1966-67. Scientific Governor, British Nutrition Foundn, 1968-76 (Pres., 1976-79; Hon. Pres., 1979-82). Baxter Lectr, American Coll. of Surgeons, 1959; 1st W. H. Sebrell Jr Internat. Nutrition Lectr, 1974; Mackdougall-Brisbane Prize Lectr, RSE, 1975; 2nd Jonathan E. Rhoads Lectr, Amer. Soc. Parenteral and Enteral Nutrition, 1979. Hon. Member: European Soc. of Parenteral and Enteral Nutrition, 1981 (Sir David Cuthbertson Lectureship founded 1979); American Institute of Nutrition; Society Biochemistry, Biophysics et Microbiol. Finland; British Soc. of Animal Production; British Nutrition Soc. Hon. DSc Rutgers, 1958; Hon. LLD: Glasgow, 1960; Aberdeen, 1972; Dr *hc* Zagreb, 1969. Hon. FRCSE 1967; Hon. FRCPath 1970; Hon. FRCPS Glas; Hon. FIFST 1972. *Publications:* papers on Physiology of Protein Nutrition and Metabolism and on Metabolic Response to Injury, Ruminant Digestion, etc. *Recreations:* water-colour painting and golf. *Address:* Glenavon, 11 Willockston Road, Troon, Ayrshire. *T:* Troon 312028. *Club:* Athenæum.

CUTHBERTSON, Prof. Joseph William, DSc, FIM, CEng, FIEE; retired as Cripps Professor of Metallurgy, University of Nottingham (1954-66), now Emeritus Professor; *b* 27 Feb. 1901; *s* of late William Edward Cuthbertson, MRCS, LRCP, and late Kathleen Cuthbertson; *m* 1933, Milly Beatrix Nelson (*d* 1980); no *c. Educ:* Manchester Grammar Sch., University of Manchester. Asst, ultimately Senior Lecturer, Dept of Metallurgy, Manchester Univ., 1939-44; seconded to Ministry of Supply, 1942-46; Asst Director of Research, Tin Research Institute, 1944-54. *Publications:* numerous scientific papers, progress reviews, and articles on metallurgy and electro-metallurgy. *Recreations:* motoring, gardening. *Address:* Flat 1, Belvedere, The Esplanade, Grange-over-Sands, Cumbria LA11 7HH. *T:* Grange-over-Sands 3344.

CUTLER, Sir (Arthur) Roden, VC; AK 1981; KCMG 1965; KCVO 1970; CBE 1957; Governor of New South Wales, 1966-81; company director; Chairman, State Bank of New South Wales, since 1981; *b* 24 May 1916; *s* of Arthur William Cutler and Ruby Daphne (*née* Pope); *m* 1946, Helen Gray Annetta (*née* Morris), AC 1980; four *s. Educ:* Sydney High Sch.; University of Sydney (BEc). Public Trust Office (NSW), 1935-42; War of 1939-45 (VC). State Secretary, RSS & AILA (NSW), 1942-43; Mem., Aliens Classification and Adv. Cttee to advise Commonwealth Govt, 1942-43; Asst Dep. Dir, Security Service, NSW, 1943; Asst Comr Repatriation, 1943-46; High Comr for Australia to New Zealand, 1946-52; High Comr for Australia to Ceylon, 1952-55; HM's Australian Minister to Egypt, 1955-56; Secretary General, SEATO Conference, 1957; Chief of Protocol, Dept of External Affairs, Canberra, 1957-58; State President of RSL, formerly RSSAILA (ACT), 1958; Australian High Comr to Pakistan, 1959-61; Australian Representative to Independence of Somali Republic, 1960; Australian Consul-General, New York, 1961-65; Ambassador to the Netherlands, 1965. Delegate to UN General Assembly, and Australian Rep., Fifth Cttee. 1962-63-64. Hon. Col, Royal New South Wales Regt, 1966; Hon. Col, Sydney Univ. Regt, 1966; Hon. Air Cdre RAAF. Hon. LLD, Univ. of Sydney; Hon. DSc: Univ. of New South Wales; Univ. of Newcastle; Hon. DLitt Univ. of New England. KStJ 1965. *Recreations:* swimming, shooting, yachting. *Address:* 22 Ginahgulla Road, Bellevue Hill, NSW 2023, Australia.

CUTLER, Hon. Sir Charles (Benjamin), KBE 1973; ED 1960; Director, since 1976, Chairman, since 1978, Sun Alliance (Australia); *b* Forbes, NSW, 20 April 1918; *s* of George Hamilton Cutler and Elizabeth Cutler; *m* 1943, Dorothy Pascoe (OBE 1976); three *s* one *d. Educ:* rural and high schs, Orange, NSW. MLA for Orange, NSW, 1947; Leader of Country Party (NSW), 1959; Dep. Premier and Minister for Educn, 1965; Dep. Premier, 1972-76, Minister for Local Govt, 1972-76, and Minister for Tourism, 1975-76, NSW. Chm., United World Colls (Aust.) Trust, 1977. Hon. DLitt Newcastle Univ., NSW, 1968. *Recreation:* golf. *Address:* 52 Kite Street, Orange, NSW 2800, Australia. *T:* 62-6418. *Clubs:* Royal Automobile, Imperial Service, Union (Sydney); Orange Golf.

CUTLER, Sir Horace (Walter), Kt 1979; OBE 1963; DL; Member of Greater London Council for Harrow West since 1964; *b* London, N16, 28 July 1912; *s* of Albert Benjamin and Mary Ann Cutler; *m* 1957, Christiane, *d* of Dr Klaus Muthesius; one *s* three *d* (and one *s* of previous marriage). *Educ:* Harrow Grammar Sch.; Hereford. Served War of 1939-45: RNVR, 1941-46, Lieut. Harrow Borough Council: elected 1952; Chm. Planning Cttee, 1954; Chm. Housing Cttee, 1955-58; Dep. Mayor, 1958; Alderman, 1959; Mayor, 1959-60; Leader of Council, 1961-65; Chm., Gen. Purposes Cttee, 1962-65; Middlesex CC: elected, 1955; Vice-Chm., Estates and Housing Cttee, 1957; Chm. Planning Cttee, 1961-65; Dep. Leader of CC, 1962; Leader, 1963-65; Greater London Council: Dep. Leader of Opposition, 1964-67 and 1973-74; Dep. Leader, 1967-73; Leader of Opposition, 1974-77 and 1981-82; Leader, 1977-81; Chm. Housing Cttee, 1967-70; Policy and Resources Cttee, 1970-73. Member: Milton Keynes New City Devlt Corp. (Chm., Central Milton Keynes Shopping Management Co. Ltd); Central Housing Adv. Cttee, Min. of Housing and Local Govt, 1967-74; Nat. Housing and Town Planning Exec. Cttee, 1967-74 (Vice-Chm., London Region, 1968); Dir, S Bank Theatre Bd; Mem., Nat. Theatre Bd, 1975-. Trustee, Nat. Theatre, 1976-. Contested (C) Willesden East, 1970; Pres., Harrow West Conservative Assoc., 1964- (Chm., 1961-64). Freeman of Harrow, and City of London. DL Greater London, 1981. FRSA. OStJ. *Publication:* The Cutler Files, 1982. *Recreations:* golf, ski-ing, classical music, travel. *Address:* Hawkswood, Hawkswood Lane, Gerrards Cross, Bucks. *T:* Fulmer 3182. *Clubs:* Carlton, Constitutional, United & Cecil.

CUTLER, Ivor; humorist, since 1957; *b* 1923; *s* of Jack and Polly Cutler; two *s. Educ:* Shawlands Academy. *Radio and television:* Monday Night at Home, Radio 4, 1959-63; John Peel, Radio 1, 1971-81, *et seq* ; 15 radio plays, Radio 3, 1979-82; Magical Mystery Tour, TV, 1967. Establishment Club, 1961-62; An Evening of British Rubbish, Comedy Th., 1963. Cartoonist, Private Eye and Observer, 1962-63. *Gramophone records:* Ivor Cutler of Y'hup, 1959; Get Away from the Wall, 1961; Who Tore Your Trousers?, 1961; Ludo, 1967; Dandruff, 1974; Velvet Donkey, 1975; Jammy Smears, 1976; Life in a Scotch Sitting Room, vol. 2, 1978. *Publications: stories:* Gruts, 1961; Cockadoodle don't, 1967; *children's books:* (illustr. Helen Oxenbury): Meal One, 1971; Balooky Klujypop, 1974; The Animal House, 1977; *poetry:* Many Flies Have Feathers, 1973; A Flat Man, 1977; Private Habits, 1981. *Recreations:* fighting noise pollution, nuclear profusion, race hatred; cycling, conversation. *Address:* c/o BBC, Broadcasting House, W1A 1AA.

CUTLER, Sir Roden; see Cutler, Sir A. R.

CUTT, Rev. Canon Samuel Robert; Canon Residentiary and Chancellor of Wells Cathedral, and Diocesan Director of Ordinands, Bath and Wells, since 1979; Examining Chaplain to the Bishop of Bath and Wells, since 1980; *b* 28 Nov. 1925; *er s* of Robert Bush Cutt and Lilian Elizabeth Cutt (*née* Saint); *m* 1972, Margaret Eva (*d* 1975), *yr d* of Norman and Eva McIntyre. *Educ:* Skegness Grammar Sch.; Selwyn Coll., Cambridge; Cuddesdon Coll., Oxford. BA Cantab 1950, MA 1954. Deacon 1953, Priest 1954. Asst Curate, St Aidan, West Hartlepool, 1953-56; Tutor for King's Coll. London at St Boniface Coll., Warminster, 1956-59; Sub-Warden for KCL at St Boniface Coll., 1959-65; Lectr and Tutor of Chichester Theol Coll., 1965-71; Priest Vicar of Chichester Cath., 1966-71; Minor Canon, 1971-79, and Succentor, 1974-79, St Paul's Cathedral, and Warden, Coll. of Minor Canons, 1974-79; part-time Lectr, Theological Dept, KCL, 1973-79; Priest in Ordinary to the Queen, 1975-79. OStJ 1981. *Recreations:* walking, music, biographical studies, heraldry, cooking. *Address:* 8 The Liberty, Wells, Somerset BA5 2SU. *T:* Wells 78763.

CUTTELL, Rev. Canon Colin, OBE 1977; Vicar of All Hallows, Barking-by-the-Tower, Guild Church of Toc H, 1963-76; *b* 24 Sept. 1908; *s* of late Maurice John Cuttell, Cheltenham, Glos, and Blanche Vickers; unmarried. *Educ:* Bishop's Univ., Lennoxville (BA; STM 1968). Deacon, 1937; Priest, 1938. Missioner of Wabamun, Canada, 1937-42; Domestic Chaplain to the Archbishop of Quebec, 1942-43; Chaplain to the Forces, 1943-44; Priest Vicar, Southwark Cathedral, 1945-49; Bishop of Southwark's Chaplain for Industrial Relations, 1948-63; Commissary for Bishop of Qu'Appelle, 1951; Founder and Senior Chaplain, S London Industrial Mission, 1950. Canon Residentiary and Librarian of Southwark Cathedral, 1954-63. Acting Chaplain, Lincoln Coll., Oxford. Sabbatical year, 1960; Acting Provost, Southwark, 1961. Field Commissioner, Toc H, 1962; Deputy Admin. Padre, Toc H, 1963. Editor of Over the Bridge, 1948. *Publication:* Ministry Without Portfolio, 1962. *Recreations:* swimming, sketching, walking.

CUTTER, Prof. Elizabeth Graham, PhD, DSc; FRSE; FLS; George Harrison Professor of Botany, University of Manchester, since 1979; *b* 9 Aug. 1929; *d* of Roy Carnegie Cutter and Alexandra (*née* Graham). *Educ:* Rothesay House Sch., Edinburgh; Univ. of St Andrews (BSc, DSc); Univ. of Manchester (PhD). Asst Lecturer in Botany, 1955-57, Lectr in Botany, 1957-64, Univ. of Manchester; Associate Professor of Botany, 1964-68, Professor of Botany, 1968-72, Univ. of California, Davis; Sen. Lectr in Cryptogamic Botany, 1972-74, Reader in Cryptogamic Botany, 1974-79, Univ. of Manchester. *Publications:* Trends in Plant Morphogenesis (principal editor), 1966; Plant Anatomy: Experiment and Interpretation, pt 1, Cells and Tissues, 1969, 2nd edn 1978; pt 2, Organs, 1971. *Recreations:* photography, fishing. *Address:* 8 Huxley Close, Bramhall, Stockport, Cheshire SK7 2PJ. *T:* 061-439 1566. *Club:* Royal Over-Seas League.

CUTTS, Rt. Rev. Richard Stanley; see Argentina and Eastern South America, Bishop in.

CYPRUS AND THE GULF, Bishop in; see Ashton, Rt Rev. L. J.

CYRIAX, James Henry, MD; Visiting Professor in Orthopaedic Medicine, University of Rochester, New York, USA, since 1975; *b* 27 Oct. 1904; *s* of Edgar Ferdinand Cyriax, MD, and Anna Kellgren, LRCP; *m* 1947, Patricia Jane McClintock; three *s* one *d. Educ:* University College Sch., London; Gonville and Caius Coll., Cambridge; St Thomas's Hosp., London. LRCP 1929, MD 1938, MRCP 1954. Orthopaedic Physician, St Thomas' Hosp., London, 1947-69. Civil Consultant: Min. of Aviation; BA. First Fellow., British Assoc. of Manipulative Medicine; Patron, Irish Soc. of Orthopaedic Medicine; Président d'Honneur, Societé française de Medicine Orthopédique; Hon. Member: Norwegian Soc. of Manual Medicine; Swedish Soc. of Manual Medicine; North American Acad. of Manipulative Medicine; Purkyne Med. Soc. of Czechoslovakia; Hon. Fellow, NZ Soc. of Physiotherapy. Freeman, City of London; Liveryman, Worshipful Co. of Apothecaries. *Publications:* Textbook of Orthopaedic Medicine (two vols), 1947, vol. I, 8th edn, 1982, vol. II, 10th edn, 1980; Hydrocortisone, 1956; The Shoulder, 1957; Cervical Spondylosis, 1971; The Slipped Disc, 1970, 3rd edn 1980; Manipulation: past and present, 1975; contrib. BMJ, Lancet, Jl of Bone and Joint Surgery. *Recreation:* sailing. *Address:* Clarence Cottage, Park Village West, NW1. *T:* 01-388 2226. *Clubs:* Savile; Faculty (Rochester, NY, USA).

CZIFFRA; Pianist; *b* Budapest, Hungary; *m* 1942, Madame Soleyka Cziffra; one *s. Educ:* Conservatoire of Music Franz Liszt, Budapest. Has given recitals and taken part in concerts at the Festival Hall, London, and throughout the world: USA, Canada, France, Israel, Benelux, Italy, Switzerland, Japan, S America, also BBC and BBC Television, London. Records for HMV: Liszt, Grieg, Tchaikowski, Beethoven, Schumann, paraphrases by G. Cziffra, etc. Founded, 1968, biennial Concours International de Piano, Versailles, for young pianists; Founder, with son, Festival of La Chaise Dieu; undertook the creation, in the Chapelle Royale Saint Frambourg, Senlis, of an Auditorium Franz Liszt, 1973; Pres., Foundation Cziffra, 1975- (created for young artists). Chevalier de la Légion d'Honneur, 1973. Comdr, Ordre des Arts et des Lettres, 1975. *Address:* 4 rue Saint Pierre, 60300 Senlis, France.

D

d'ABREU, Francis Arthur, ERD 1954; Surgeon, since 1946, Consultant Surgeon, since 1969, Westminster Hospital; Surgeon, 1950-69, now Emeritus, Hospital of St John and St Elizabeth; Surgeon to Jockey Club and National Hunt Committee, since 1964; *b* 1 Oct. 1904; *s* of Dr John Francis d'Abreu and Teresa d'Abreu; *m* 1945, Margaret Ann Bowes-Lyon; one *s* two *d. Educ:* Stonyhurst Coll.; Birmingham Univ. MB, ChB Birmingham 1929; MRCS, LRCP 1929; FRCS, 1932; ChM Birmingham 1935. House Surgeon, Gen. Hosp., Birmingham, 1929; Res. Surgical Officer, Gen. and Queen's Hosps, Birmingham, 1930-34; Surg. Registrar, St Bartholomew's Hosp., London, and Westminster Hosp., 1934-39. Formerly: Examiner to Soc. of Apothecaries; Examiner to Univs of Cambridge and London; Mem., Ct of Examiners, RCS. Mem. Bd of Management, Inst. of Sports Medicine. Lieut RAMC (Supp. Reserve), 1939. Served War of 1939-45: Major, RAMC, 1939, Lt-Col

1942-45. Kt of Magistral Grace, Sov. and Mil. Order of Malta; Kt Comdr, Order of St Gregory (Holy See), 1977. *Publications:* contrib. to various medical jls. *Recreations:* ski-ing, squash, tennis. *Address:* 36 Cumberland Terrace, Regent's Park, NW1. *Club:* Hurlingham.

DACCA, Archbishop of, (RC), since 1978; **Most Rev. Michael Rozario,** STL; *b* Solepore, Dacca, Bangladesh, 18 Jan. 1926; *s* of Urban Rozario. *Educ:* Little Flower Seminary, Dacca, Bangladesh; St Albert Seminary, Ranchi, India. Jagannath Coll., Dacca, Bangladesh, 1948-50; Univ. of Notre Dame, USA, 1951-53; Urbano Univ., Rome, 1953-57. Ordained priest, 1956; Bishop of Dinajpur, 1968. Pres., Catholic Bishops' Conf. of Bangladesh. *Address:* Archbishop's House, PO Box 3, Dacca 2, Bangladesh.

DACIE, Prof. Sir John (Vivian), Kt 1976; FRS 1967; MD, FRCP; Professor of Haematology, Royal Post-graduate Medical School of London, University of London, 1957-77, now Emeritus; *b* 20 July 1912; British; *s* of John Charles and Lilian Maud Dacie, Putney; *m* 1938, Margaret Kathleen Victoria Thynne; three *s* two *d. Educ:* King's Coll. Sch., Wimbledon; King's Coll., London: King's Coll. Hospital, London. MB, BS London 1935; MD 1952; MRCP 1936; FRCP 1956; MD (Hon.): Uppsala, 1961; Marseille, 1977; FRCPath (Pres., 1973-75); Pres., RSM, 1977. Various medical appointments, King's Coll. Hospital, Postgraduate Medical Sch. and Manchester Royal Infirmary, 1936-39. Pathologist, EMS, 1939-42; Major, then Lieut-Col, RAMC, 1943-46. Senior Lecturer in Clinical Pathology, then Reader in Haematology, Postgraduate Medical Sch., 1946-56. Chm., Med. and Scientific Adv. Panel, Leukaemia Research Fund, 1975-82. *Publications:* Practical Haematology, 1950, 2nd edn, 1956, 5th edn (jointly), 1975; Haemolytic Anaemias, 1954, 2nd edn, Part I, 1960, Part II, 1962, Parts III and IV, 1967; various papers on anaemia in medical journals. *Recreations:* music, entomology, gardening. *Address:* 10 Alan Road, Wimbledon, SW19. *T:* 01-946 6086.

da COSTA, Harvey Lloyd, CMG 1962; **Hon. Mr Justice da Costa;** Judge of Appeal, Court of Appeal for Bahamas and Bermuda, since 1982; *b* 8 Dec. 1914; *s* of John Charles and Martha da Costa. *Educ:* Calabar High Sch., Jamaica; St Edmund Hall (Sen. Exhibnr; Rhodes Schol.), Oxford. BA (Hons) London; MA, BLitt Oxon. Practised at Chancery Bar, 1950-52; Crown Counsel, Jamaica, 1952-54; Sen. Crown Counsel, Jamaica, 1954-56; Asst Attorney-Gen., Jamaica, 1956-59; QC Jamaica 1959; Attorney-Gen. of West Indies, 1959-62; practised Private Bar, Jamaica, 1962-77; Puisne Judge 1978-80, Chief Justice, 1980-81, Bahamas Supreme Court. Mem., Anguilla, British Virgin Is and Seychelles Commns. *Recreation:* swimming. *Address:* c/o Supreme Court, PO Box N167, Nassau, Bahamas.

da COSTA, Sergio Corrêa, GCVO; Brazilian Permanent Representative to United Nations in New York, since 1975; *b* 19 Feb. 1919; *s* of Dr I. A. da Costa and Lavinia Corrêa da Costa; *m* 1943, Zazi Aranha; one *s* two *d. Educ:* Law Sch., Univ. of Brazil; post grad. UCLA; Brazilian War Coll. Career diplomat; Sec. of Embassy, Buenos Ayres, then Washington, 1944-48; Acting Deleg., Council of OAS, Wash., 1946-48; Inter-American Econ. and Social Coun., Washington, 1946-48; Dep. Head, Economic Dept, Min. of Ext. Relations, 1952; Actg Pres., Braz. Nat. Techn. Assistance Commn, 1955-58; Minister-Counsellor, Rome, 1959-62; Permanent Rep. to FAO, Rome, 1960; Mem., Financial Cttee of FAO, 1962-63; Ambassador to Canada, 1962-65; Asst Sec.-Gen. for Internat. Organizations at Min. Ext. Relations, 1966; Sec.-Gen., Min. of Ext. Relations, 1967-68; Ambassador to UK, 1968-75. Grand Officer: Military Order of Aeronautical Merit, Brazil, 1967; Order of Naval Merit, Brazil, 1967; Grand Cross of Victorian Order (Hon. GCVO), Gt Britain, 1968; also numerous Grand Crosses, etc, of Orders, from other countries, 1957-. *Publications:* (mostly in Brazil): As 4 Coroas de Pedro I, 1941; Pedro I e Metternich, 1942; Diplomacia Brasileira na Questao de Leticia, 1943; A Diplomacia do Marechal, 1945; Every Inch a King-A biography of Pedro I, Emperor of Brazil, 1950 (NY 1964, London 1972). *Recreations:* reading, writing, boating. *Address:* 123 East 79th Street, New York, NY 10021, USA. *Clubs:* White's, Travellers' (London); Rideau, Country (Ottawa); Circolo della Caccia (Rome).

DACRE, Baroness (27th in line), *cr* 1321; **Rachel Leila Douglas-Home;** *b* 24 Oct. 1929; *er* surv. *d* of 4th Viscount Hampden, CMG (*d* 1965) (whose Barony of Dacre was called out of abeyance in her favour, 1970) and of Leila Emily, *o d* of late Lt-Col Frank Evelyn Seely; *m* 1951, Hon. William Douglas-Home, *qv* ; one *s* three *d. Heir: s* Hon. James Thomas Archibald Douglas-Home, *b* 16 May 1952. *Address:* Drayton House, East Meon, Hants.

DACRE OF GLANTON, Baron *cr* 1979 (Life Peer), of Glanton in the County of Northumberland; **Hugh Redwald Trevor-Roper;** Master of Peterhouse, Cambridge, since 1980; *b* 15 January 1914; *er s* of late Dr B. W. E. Trevor-Roper, Glanton and Alnwick, Northumberland; *m* 1954, Lady Alexandra Howard-Johnston, *e d* of late Field-Marshal Earl Haig, KT, GCB, OM. *Educ:* Charterhouse; Christ Church, Oxford. Research Fellow Merton Coll., 1937-39 (Hon. Fellow, 1980). Student of Christ Church, Oxford, 1946-57; Censor 1947-52; Hon. Student, 1979; Regius Prof. of Modern Hist., and Fellow of Oriel Coll., Oxford Univ., 1957-80 (Hon. Fellow, 1980). Dir, Times Newspapers Ltd, 1974-. Chevalier, Legion of Honour, 1975. *Publications:* Archbishop Laud, 1940; The Last Days of Hitler, 1947; The Gentry, 1540-1640, 1953; (ed) Hitler's Table Talk, 1953; (ed with J. A. W. Bennett) The Poems of Richard Corbett, 1955; Historical Essays, 1957; (ed) Hitler's War Directives, 1939-45, 1964; (ed) Essays in British History

Presented to Sir Keith Feiling, 1964; The Rise of Christian Europe, 1965; Religion, The Reformation and Social Change, 1967; (ed) The Age of Expansion, 1968; The Philby Affair, 1968; The European Witch-Craze of the 16th and 17th Centuries, 1970; The Plunder of the Arts in the Seventeenth Century, 1970; Princes and Artists, 1976; A Hidden Life, 1976; (ed) The Goebbels Diaries, 1978. *Address:* Master's Lodge, Peterhouse, Cambridge; Chiefswood, Melrose. *Clubs:* Athenæum, Savile, Beefsteak.

See also Earl Haig, P. D. Trevor-Roper.

da CUNHA, John Wilfrid, JP; **His Honour Judge da Cunha;** a Circuit Judge (formerly Judge of County Courts), since 1970; *b* 6 Sept. 1922; 2nd *s* of Frank C. da Cunha, MD, DPH, and Lucy (*née* Finnerty); *m* 1953, Janet, MB, ChB, *d* of Louis Savatard, (Hon.) MSc, LSA, and Judith Savatard, MB, BS; one *s* four *d. Educ:* Stonyhurst Coll., Lancs; St John's Coll., Cambridge. MA Cantab 1954. Served 1942-47, 23rd Hussars (RAC) and Judge Advocate Gen. (War Crimes), Hon. Major. Called to Bar, Middle Temple, 1948; Northern Circuit. Chm., Local Appeal Tribunal, Min. of Social Security (Wigan), 1964-69. Asst Recorder, Oldham County Borough QS, 1966-70; Chm., Industrial Tribunals, 1966-70; Dep. Chm., Lancs County QS, 1968-71. Comr, NI (Emergency Provisions) Act, 1973; Member: Appeals Tribunal; Parole Bd, 1976-78. JP Lancs 1968. *Recreations:* gardening, pottering. *Address:* c/o Circuit Administrator, Aldine House, New Bailey Street, Salford M3 5EU. *Club:* Manchester.

DAENIKER, Dr Armin; Swiss Ambassador to the Court of St James's, 1957-63, retired; *b* 24 Feb. 1898; *m* 1938; no *c. Educ:* Universities of Zürich, Berne, Geneva, London Sch. of Economics (doctor juris utriusque, Zürich). Vice-Consul, Riga, 1927; Shanghai, 1930; Swiss Chargé d'Affaires, Tokio, 1933, Teheran, 1936; Head of Administrative Div., Federal Political Dept, Berne, 1946; Swiss Minister, New Delhi, 1948, and concurrently in Bangkok, 1950; Swiss Minister, Stockholm 1952; Swiss Mem., Neutral Nations Commn for Repatriation of Prisoners of War in Korea, 1953-54; Swiss Minister to the Court of St James's, 1955; Mem. Council, Swiss Winston Churchill Foundation.

D'AETH, Air Vice-Marshal Narbrough Hughes, CB 1951; CBE 1943; Licentiate to Officiate, Diocese of Bath and Wells, 1976; *b* 7 Jan. 1901; *s* of late Capt. Reginald Hughes D'Aeth and late Lady Nina Hughes D'Aeth; *m* 1934, Mary Colbeck, *d* of late E. W. Davis; three *d. Educ:* Royal Naval Colls, Osborne and Dartmouth. Served European War, 1914-18, with Grand Fleet, 1917-19; transferred to RAF, 1920; Malta, 1924; China, 1926-28; British Arctic Air Route Expedn in E Greenland, 1930-31; Polar Medal, 1932; Aden, 1934-36; War of 1939-45 in UK and N Africa (despatches thrice, CBE); AOC, RAF, Malta, 1949-52 (CB); AO i/c Administration at HQ, Technical Training Command, 1952-54; SASO, HQ Home Command, 1954-56. Group Capt., 1941; Air Commodore, 1943; Air Vice Marshal, 1950; retired, 1956. Lincoln Theological Coll., 1956-57. Ordained Deacon, Dec. 1957; Curate, St John the Baptist, Crowthorne, Dec. 1957-59; Rector: East Langdon with Guston, Kent, 1959-60; Flinders Islands, 1960-67; Priest-in-Charge, Midland and Swan Parishes, Perth, 1967-71; Licentiate to Officiate: dio. of Perth, 1971-72; dio. of Exeter, 1972-76. American Legion of Merit, 1945; Czechoslovak Medal of Merit, 1945. *Address:* Knowlton Cottage, 11 Exmoor Way, Minehead, Somerset TA24 8AZ.

D'AETH, Prof. Richard, PhD; President, Hughes Hall, Cambridge, since 1978; *b* 3 June 1912; *e s* of Walter D'Aeth and Marion Turnbull; *m* 1943, Pamela Straker; two *d. Educ:* Bedford Sch.; Emmanuel Coll., Cambridge (Scholar; 1st Cl. Hons Nat. Sci., PhD); Harvard Univ. (Commonwealth Fellow; AM). Served War, RAF, 1941-46 (Wing Comdr). Master, Gresham's Sch., 1938-40; HM Inspector of Schs, 1946-52; Prof. of Education: University Coll. of West Indies, 1952-58; Univ. of Exeter, 1958-77. Mem., Internat. Assoc. for Advancement of Educnl Res. (Pres., Warsaw, 1969); sometime mem. cttees of Schools Council, BBC, Schs Broadcasting Council, and Royal Coll. of Nursing. *Publications:* Education and Development in the Third World, 1975; articles in jls. *Address:* Hughes Hall, Cambridge CB1 2EW.

DAHL, Rev. Canon Murdoch Edgcumbe; Canon Emeritus, since 1979; *b* 11 March 1914; *s* of Oscar Horace and Edith Gladys Dahl; *m* 1940, Joan, *d* of Daniel Charles and Edith Marion Woollaston; three *s. Educ:* Royal Grammar Sch., Newcastle upon Tyne; Armstrong Coll. (subsq. King's Coll.), Newcastle upon Tyne; St John's Coll., Durham. BA 1936, MA 1956, Durham. Deacon 1937; Priest 1938. Curate of: St Paul, Astley Bridge, 1937-39; Fallowfield, 1939-43; Harpenden, 1943-49; Vicar of Arlesey and Rector of Astwick, 1949-51; Minister, St Oswald's, Croxley Green, 1951-56; Vicar of Great with Little Hormead and Rector of Wyddial, 1956-65; Examining Chaplain to Bishop of St Albans, 1959-; Hon. Canon of St Albans, 1963-65, Canon Residentiary, 1965-68, Canon Theologian, 1968-79. *Publications:* Resurrection of the Body, 1962; Sin Streamlined, 1966; The Christian Materialist, 1968; Final Loss—Final Gain, 1980. *Address:* 52 Fleet Street, Beaminster, Dorset DT8 3EH.

DAHL, Roald; writer; *b* 13 Sept. 1916; *s* of Harald Dahl and Sofie Magdalene Hesselberg; *m* 1953, Patricia Neal; one *s* three *d* (and one *d* decd). *Educ:* Repton. Public Schools Exploring Soc. expedn to Newfoundland, 1934; Eastern Staff of Shell Co., 1934-39, served in Dar-es-Salaam; RAF flying trng, Nairobi and Habbanyah, 1939-40; No 80 Fighter Sqdn, Western Desert, 1940 (wounded); Greece, 1941; Syria, 1941; Asst Air Attaché, Washington, 1942-43; Wing Comdr, 1943; British Security Co-ordination, N America, 1943-45.

Edgar Allan Poe Award, Mystery Writers of America, 1954 and 1959. *Publications: short stories:* Over to You, 1945; Someone Like You, 1953; Kiss Kiss, 1960; Switch Bitch, 1974; Tales of the Unexpected, 1979; More Tales of the Unexpected, 1980; *novels:* Sometime Never (A Fable for Supermen), 1948; My Uncle Oswald, 1979; *children's books:* (with Walt Disney) The Gremlins, 1943; James and the Giant Peach, 1962; Charlie and the Chocolate Factory, 1964; The Magic Finger, 1966; Fantastic Mr Fox, 1970; Charlie and the Great Glass Elevator, 1972; Danny, the Champion of the World, 1975; The Wonderful Story of Henry Sugar and Six More, 1977; The Enormous Crocodile, 1978; The Twits, 1980; George's Marvellous Medicine, 1981; Revolting Rhymes, 1982; The BFG, 1982; *play:* The Honeys, 1955; *screenplays:* You Only Live Twice, 1967; Chitty Chitty Bang Bang, 1968; Willy Wonka and the Chocolate Factory, 1971; *television series:* Tales of the Unexpected, 1979; contrib. New Yorker, Harper's Magazine, Atlantic Monthly, Saturday Evening Post, Colliers, etc. *Recreations:* drinking fine wine, collecting paintings, furniture and antique objects of all kinds. *Address:* Gipsy House, Great Missenden, Bucks HP16 0PB. *T:* Great Missenden 2757. *Club:* Ritz Casino.

DAHL, Robert Henry, TD 1950; MA Oxford; Head Master of Wrekin College, 1952-71; *b* 21 April 1910; *y s* of Murdoch Cameron Dahl, London, and Lilian May Edgcumbe; *m* 1936, Lois Helen Allanby; three *s. Educ:* Sedbergh Sch.; Exeter Coll., Oxford. Asst Master (Modern Langs) at Merchant Taylors' Sch., 1934-38. Asst Master and Housemaster at Harrow Sch., 1938-52. Served War of 1939-45: Intelligence Corps, Middle East, 1941-43; Major, 1943; Political Intelligence Dept of Foreign Office, 1943-46. FRSA 1969. *Publication:* Joint Editor, Selections from Albert Schweitzer, 1953. *Recreations:* golf, music, painting. *Address:* 72 Eastgate Street, Bury St Edmunds, Suffolk IP33 1YR.

DAHLGAARD, Tyge; Comdr, Order of the Dannebrog, 1971; Ambassador of Denmark to the Court of St James's, since 1981; *b* 8 April 1921; *s* of Bertel Dahlgaard and Dorthea (*née* Poulsen); *m* 1947, Tove (*née* Jørgensen); two *d. Educ:* Copenhagen Univ. (graduated in Econs and Polit. Science, 1947). Joined Min. of Agriculture, 1947 and Min. for Foreign Affairs, 1949; Perm. Deleg., UN, Geneva, 1949-50; Min. for For. Affairs, Copenhagen, 1950-57; Econ. Counsellor, Danish OEEC Mission, Paris, 1957-59, and Danish Embassy, Washington, 1959; Ambassador to EEC, Euratom and ECSC, 1964-Sept. 1966; Minister of Commerce and for Nordic Affairs and Eur. Market Affairs, 1966-67; Ambassador: Belgrade, 1968-Sept. 1972 (also accredited in Tirana, 1970); Tokio and Seoul, 1972-Nov. 1976; The Hague, 1976-Feb. 1981. *Recreations:* music in particular. *Address:* Royal Danish Embassy, 55 Sloane Street, SW1X 9SR. *T:* 01-235 1255.

DAHRENDORF, Prof. Ralf, Hon. KBE 1982; DrPhil; FBA 1977; Director, London School of Economics and Political Science, since 1974; *b* Hamburg, 1 May 1929; *s* of Gustav Dahrendorf and Lina Dahrendorf (*née* Witt); *m* 1980, Ellen Joan (*née* Krug). *Educ:* several schools, including Heinrich-Hertz Oberschule, Hamburg; studies in philosophy and classical philology, Hamburg, 1947-52; DrPhil 1952; postgrad. studies at London Sch. of Economics, 1952-54; Leverhulme Research Schol., 1953-54; PhD 1956. Habilitation, and University Lecturer, Saarbrücken, 1957; Fellow at Center for Advanced Study in the Behavioural Sciences, Palo Alto, USA, 1957-58; Prof. of Sociology, Hamburg, 1958-60; Vis. Prof. Columbia Univ., 1960; Prof. of Sociology, Tübingen, 1960-64; Vice-Chm., Founding Cttee of Univ. of Konstanz, 1964-66; Prof of Sociology, Konstanz, 1966-69; Parly Sec. of State, Foreign Office, W Germany, 1969-70; Member: Commn of European Communities, Brussels, 1970-74; Hansard Soc. Commn on Electoral Reform, 1975-76; Royal Commn on Legal Services, 1976-79; Commn to Review Functioning of Financial Instns, 1977-80. Trustee, Ford Foundn, 1976-. Vis. Prof. at several Europ. and N American univs. Reith Lecturer, 1974. Hon. Fellow: LSE; Imperial Coll. Hon. MRIA 1974; Fellow, St Antony's Coll., Oxford, 1976. Foreign Hon. Member: Amer. Acad. of Arts and Sciences, 1975-; Nat. Acad. of Sciences, USA, 1977; Amer. Philosophical Soc., 1977; FRSA 1977; Hon. FRCS 1982. Hon. DLitt: Reading, 1973; Dublin, 1975; Hon. LLD: Manchester, 1973; Wagner Coll., NY, 1977; York, Ontario, 1979; Hon. DHL: Kalamazoo Coll., 1974; Johns Hopkins, 1982; Hon. DSc: Ulster, 1973; Bath, 1977; DUniv: Open, 1974; Maryland, 1978; Surrey, 1978; Hon. Dr Univ. Catholique de Louvain, 1977. Journal Fund Award for Learned Publication, 1966. Grand Croix de l'Ordre du Mérite du Sénégal, 1971; Grosses Bundesverdienstkreuz mit Stern und Schulterband (Federal Republic of Germany), 1974; Grand Croix de l'Ordre du Mérite du Luxembourg, 1974; Grosses goldenes Ehrenzeichen am Bande für Verdienste um die Republik Österreich (Austria), 1975; Grand Croix de l'Ordre de Léopold II (Belgium), 1975. *Publications include:* Marx in Perspective, 1953; Industrie- und Betriebssoziologie, 1956 (trans. Italian, Spanish, Dutch, Japanese, Chinese); Soziale Klassen und Klassenkonflikt, 1957 (Class and Class Conflict, 1959; also trans. French, Italian, Spanish, Finnish, Japanese); Homo Sociologicus, 1959 (trans. English, Italian, Portuguese, Finnish); Die angewandte Aufklärung, 1963; Gesellschaft und Demokratie in Deutschland, 1965 (Society and Democracy in Germany, 1966; also trans. Italian); Pfade aus Utopia, 1967 (Uscire dall'Utopia, 1971); Essays in the Theory of Society, 1968; Konflikt und Freiheit, 1972; Plädoyer für die Europäische Union, 1973; The New Liberty, 1975 (trans. German, Italian, Urdu, Arabic, Japanese, Korean); Life Chances, 1979 (trans. German, Japanese, Italian). *Address:* London School of Economics and Political Science, Houghton Street, Aldwych, WC2A 2AE. *T:* 01-405 7686. *Clubs:* PEN, Reform, Political Economy.

DAICHES, David, MA Edinburgh; MA, DPhil Oxon; PhD Cantab; FRSL; FRSE; Director, Institute of Advanced Studies in the Humanities, Edinburgh University, since 1980; Professor of English, University of Sussex, 1961-77, and Dean of the School of English Studies, 1961-68; now Emeritus Professor; *b* 2 Sept. 1912; *s* of Rabbi Dr Salis Daiches and Flora Daiches (*née* Levin); *m* 1st, 1937, Isobel J. Mackay (*d* 1977); one *s* two *d* ; 2nd, 1978, Hazel Neville (*née* Newman). *Educ:* George Watson's Coll., Edinburgh; Edinburgh Univ. (Vans Dunlop Schol., Elliot Prize); Balliol Coll., Oxford (Elton Exhibnr). Asst in English, Edinburgh Univ., 1935-36; Andrew Bradley Fellow, Balliol Coll., Oxford, 1936-37; Asst Prof. of English, Univ. of Chicago, 1939-43; Second Sec., British Embassy, Washington, 1944-46; Prof. of English, Cornell Univ., USA, 1946-51; University Lecturer in English at Cambridge, 1951-61; Fellow of Jesus Coll., Cambridge, 1957-62. Visiting Prof. of Criticism, Indiana Univ., USA, 1956-57; Elliston Lectr, University of Cincinnati, Spring 1960; Whidden Lectr, Mcmaster Univ., Canada, 1964; Hill Foundation Visiting Prof., Univ. of Minnesota, Spring 1966; Ewing Lectr, Univ. of California, 1967; Lectures: Carpenter Meml, Ohio Wesleyan Univ., 1969; Alexander, Univ. of Toronto, 1980; Gifford, Univ. of Edinburgh, 1983. Hon. Prof., Stirling Univ., 1980. Fellow, Centre for the Humanities, Wesleyan Univ., Middletown, Conn, 1970. Hon. Fellow, Sunderland Polytechnic, 1977. Hon. LittD, Brown Univ; Docteur *hc* Sorbonne; Hon. DLitt: Edinburgh, 1976; Sussex, 1978; DUniv Stirling, 1980. *Publications:* The Place of Meaning in Poetry, 1935; New Literary Values, 1936; Literature and Society, 1938; The Novel and the Modern World, 1939 (new edn, 1960); Poetry and the Modern World, 1940; The King James Bible: A Study of its Sources and Development, 1941; Virginia Woolf, 1942; Robert Louis Stevenson, 1947; A Study of Literature, 1948; Robert Burns, 1950 (new edn 1966); Willa Cather: A Critical Introduction, 1951; Critical Approaches to Literature, 1956; Two Worlds (autobiog.), 1956; Literary Essays, 1956; John Milton, 1957; The Present Age, 1958; A Critical History of English Literature, 1960; George Eliot's Middlemarch, 1963; The Paradox of Scottish Culture, 1964; (ed) The Idea of a New University, 1964; English Literature (Princeton Studies in Humanistic Scholarship), 1965; More Literary Essays, 1968; Some Late Victorian Attitudes, 1969; Scotch Whisky, 1969; Sir Walter Scott and his World, 1971; A Third World (autobiog.), 1971; (ed) The Penguin Companion to Literature: Britain and the Commonwealth, 1971; Robert Burns and his World, 1971; (ed with A. Thorlby) Literature and Western Civilization, vol. I, 1972, vols II and V, 1973, vols III and IV, 1975; vol. VI, 1976; Charles Edward Stuart: the life and times of Bonnie Prince Charlie, 1973; Robert Louis Stevenson and his World, 1973; Was, 1975; Moses, 1975; James Boswell and his World, 1976; Scotland and the Union, 1977; Glasgow, 1977; Edinburgh, 1978; (with John Flower) Literary Landscapes of the British Isles: a narrative atlas, 1979; (ed) Selected Writings and Speeches of Fletcher of Saltoun, 1979; (ed) Selected Poems of Robert Burns, 1979; (ed) A Companion to Scottish Culture, 1981; Literature and Gentility in Scotland, 1982; Robert Fergusson, 1982; Gen. Editor, Studies in English Literature, 1961-. *Recreations:* talking, music. *Address:* 9 Randolph Crescent, Edinburgh EH3 7TT.
See also L. H. Daiches.

DAICHES, Lionel Henry, QC (Scot) 1956; *b* 8 March 1911; *s* of late Rev. Dr. Salis Daiches, Edinburgh, and Mrs Flora Daiches; *m* 1947, Dorothy Estelle Bernstein (marr. diss. 1973); two *s. Educ:* George Watson's Coll., Edinburgh; Edinburgh Univ. (MA, LLB). Pres., Edinburgh Univ. Diagnostic Soc., 1931; Convener of Debates, Edinburgh Univ. Union, 1933; Editor, The Student, 1933. Served 1940-46 in N Stafford Regt and Major, JAG Branch in N Africa and Italy, including Anzio Beach-head. Admitted Scots Bar, 1946. Standing Junior Counsel to Board of Control, Scotland, 1950-56; Sheriff-Substitute of Lanarkshire at Glasgow, 1962-67. Fellow, Internat. Acad. of Trial Lawyers, 1976. Contested (L) Edinburgh South, 1950. *Publication:* Russians at Law, 1960. *Recreations:* walking and talking. *Address:* 10 Heriot Row, Edinburgh. *T:* 031-556 4144. *Clubs:* Puffin's, Scottish Arts (Edinburgh); RNVR (Scotland).
See also D. Daiches.

DAIN, Rt. Rev. Arthur John; Assistant Bishop, Diocese of Sydney, since 1965; Senior Assistant Bishop and Chief Executive Officer, since 1980; *b* 13 Oct. 1912; *s* of Herbert John Dain and Elizabeth Dain; *m* 1939, Edith Jane Stewart, MA, *d* of Dr Alexander Stewart, DD; four *d. Educ:* Wolverhampton Gram. Sch.; Ridley Coll., Cambridge. Missionary in India, 1935-40; 10th Gurkha Rifles, 1940-41; Royal Indian Navy, 1941-47; Gen. Sec., Bible and Medical Missionary Fellowship, formerly Zenana Bible and Medical Mission, 1947-59; Overseas Sec., British Evangelical Alliance, 1950-59; Federal Sec., CMS of Australia, 1959-65; Hon. Canon of St Andrew's Cathedral, 1963. *Publications:* Mission Fields To-day, 1956; Missionary Candidates, 1959. *Recreation:* sport. *Address:* 3 Mitchell Place, 4 Mitchell Road, Darling Point, NSW 2027, Australia. *T:* 328 7940.

DAIN, David John Michael; HM Diplomatic Service; Counsellor, Nicosia, since 1981; *b* 30 Oct. 1940; *s* of John Gordon Dain and Gladys Ellen (*née* Connop); *m* 1969, Susan Kathleen Moss; one *s* four *d. Educ:* Merchant Taylors' Sch.; St John's Coll., Oxford (MA Lit.Hum.). Entered HM Diplomatic Service, 1963; Third, later Second Sec., Tehran and Kabul, 1964-68; seconded to Cabinet Office, 1969-72; First Sec., Bonn, 1972-75; FCO, 1975-78; First Sec., Athens, 1978-81. *Recreations:* tennis, bridge, walking, natural history. *Address:* c/o Foreign and Commonwealth Office, SW1; Manor Cottage, Frant, Tunbridge Wells, Kent TN3 9DR.

DAINTON, Sir Frederick (Sydney), Kt 1971; FRS 1957; MA, BSc Oxon, PhD, ScD Cantab; Chancellor, Sheffield University, since 1978; *b* 11 Nov. 1914; *y s* of late George Whalley and Mary Jane Dainton; *m* 1942, Barbara Hazlitt, JP, PhD, *o d* of late Dr W. B. Wright, Manchester; one *s* two *d. Educ:* Central Secondary Sch., Sheffield; St John's Coll., Oxford; Sidney Sussex Coll., Cambridge. Open Exhibitioner, 1933; Casberd Prizeman, 1934, Casberd Scholar, 1935, Hon. Fellow 1968, St John's Coll., Oxford; Goldsmiths' Co. Exhibitioner, 1935, 1st class Hons Chemistry, 1937, University of Oxford; Research Student, 1937, Goldsmiths' Co. Senior Student, 1939, University Demonstrator in Chemistry, 1944, H. O. Jones Lecturer in Physical Chemistry, 1946, University of Cambridge. Fellow, 1945, Praelector, 1946, Hon. Fellow 1961, St Catharine's Coll., Cambridge. Prof. of Physical Chemistry, University of Leeds, 1950-65; Vice-Chancellor, Nottingham Univ., 1965-70; Dr Lee's Prof. of Chemistry, Oxford University, 1970-73; Chm., UGC, 1973-78. Vis. Prof., Univ. Toronto, 1949; Tilden Lectr, 1950, Faraday Lectr, 1973, Chem. Soc.; Peter C. Reilly Lectr, Univ. of Notre Dame, Ind., USA, 1952; Arthur D. Little Visiting Prof., MIT, 1959; George Fisher Baker Lectr, Cornell Univ., 1961; Boomer Lectr, Univ. of Alberta, 1962; Rede Lectr, Cambridge, 1981; Crookshank Lectr, RCR, 1981. Chm., Cttee on Swing away from Science (report published as Enquiry into the Flow of Candidates in Science and Technology into Higher Education, Cmnd 3541, 1968). Chairman: Assoc. for Radiation Research, 1964-66; Nat. Libraries Cttee, 1968-69; Adv. Cttee on Sci. and Tech. Information, 1966-70; Adv. Bd for Res. Councils, 1972-73; British Cttee, Harkness Fellowship, 1977-81 (Mem., 1973-); British Library Bd, 1978-; Nat. Radiological Protection Bd, 1978-. President: Faraday Soc., 1965-67; Chemical Soc., 1972-73; Assoc. for Science Education, 1967; Library Assoc., 1977; BAAS, 1980. Member: Council for Scientific Policy, 1965- (Chm. 1969-72); Central Advisory Council for Science and Technology, 1967-70; Trustee, Natural Hist. Museum, 1974-. Chm. Council, Royal Post-grad. Med. Sch., 1980-; Prime Warden, Goldsmiths' Co. Foreign Member: Swedish Acad. of Sci., 1968; Amer. Acad. of Arts and Scis, 1972; Acad. of Scis, Göttingen, 1975. Sylvanus Thompson Medal, British Institute of Radiology, 1958; Davy Medal, Royal Soc., 1969; Crookshank Medal, RCR, 1981. Hon. ScD: Lódz, 1966; Dublin, 1968; Hon. DSc: Bath Univ. of Technology, 1970; Loughborough Univ. of Technology, 1970; Heriot-Watt, 1970; Warwick, 1970; Strathclyde, 1971; Exeter, 1971; QUB, 1971; Manchester, 1972; E Anglia, 1972; Leeds, 1973; McMaster, 1975; Uppsala, 1977; Liverpool, Salford, 1979; Kent, 1981; Hon. LLD: Nottingham, 1970; Aberdeen, 1972; Sheffield, Cambridge, 1979. Hon. FRCP, 1979. *Publications:* Chain Reactions, 1956; Choosing a British University, 1981 (contrib.) The Parliament of Science, 1981; papers on physico-chemical subjects in scientific jls. *Recreations:* walking, colour photography. *Address:* Fieldside, Water Eaton Lane, Oxford OX5 2PR. *T:* Kidlington 5132. *Club:* Athenæum.

DAKERS, Lionel Frederick, DMus; FRCO; Director, Royal School of Church Music (Special Commissioner, 1958-72), since 1972; Examiner to the Associated Board of the Royal Schools of Music, since 1958; *b* Rochester, Kent, 24 Feb. 1924; *o s* of late Lewis and Ethel Dakers; *m* 1951, Mary Elisabeth, *d* of Rev. Claude Williams; four *d. Educ:* Rochester Cathedral Choir Sch. Studied with H. A. Bennett, Organist of Rochester Cathedral, 1933-40, with Sir Edward Bairstow, Organist of York Minster, 1943-45, and at Royal Academy of Music, 1947-51. Organist of All Saints', Frindsbury, Rochester, 1939-42. Served in Royal Army Educational Corps, 1943-47. Cairo Cathedral, 1945-47; Finchley Parish Church, 1948-50; Asst Organist, St George's Chapel, Windsor Castle, 1950-54; Asst Music Master, Eton Coll., 1952-54; Organist of Ripon Cathedral, 1954-57; Conductor Ripon Choral Soc. and Harrogate String Orchestra, 1954-57; Hon. Conductor, Exeter Diocesan Choral Association, 1957; Lectr in Music, St Luke's Coll., Exeter, 1958-70; Organist and Master of the Choristers, Exeter Cathedral, 1957-72; Conductor: Exeter Musical Soc., 1957-72; Exeter Chamber Orchestra, 1959-65. President: Incorporated Assoc. of Organists, 1972-75; London Assoc. of Organists, 1976-78; Mem. Council, Royal Coll. of Organists, 1967- (Pres., 1976-78). Sec., Cathedral Organists' Assoc., 1972-. Chm., Organs Adv. Cttee of Council for Care of Churches of C of E, 1974. Hon. Mem., US Assoc. of Anglican Musicians. ARCO, 1944; FRCO, 1945; ADCM, 1952; BMus Dunelm, 1951; ARAM 1955; FRAM, 1962; FRSCM 1969; DMus Lambeth, 1979; FRCM 1980. Fellow, St Michael's Coll., Tenbury, 1973. Hon. Fellow, Westminster Choir Coll., USA, 1975. Compositions: church music, etc. *Publications:* Church Music at the Crossroads, 1970; A Handbook of Parish Music, 1976; Making Church Music Work, 1978; (ed) Music and the Alternative Service Book, 1980; (ed) The Choristers Companion, 1980; (ed) The Psalms—their use and performance today, 1980; The Church Musician as Conductor, 1982. *Recreations:* book collecting, gardening, continental food, travel. *Address:* Addington Palace, Croydon CR9 5AD. *T:* 01-654 7676. *Clubs:* Athenæum; St Wilfrid's (NYC) (Hon. mem.).

DAKIN, Dorothy Danvers, OBE 1982; Chairman, Independent Schools' Information Service Association, since 1982; *b* 22 Oct. 1919; *d* of Edwin Lionel Dakin, chartered civil engr and Mary Danvers Dakin (*née* Walker), artist. *Educ:* Sherborne Sch. for Girls; Newnham Coll., Cambridge. MA Geography. 2nd Officer WRNS (Educn), 1943-50; Housemistress, Wycombe Abbey Sch., 1950-60; Headmistress, The Red Maids' School, Bristol, 1961-81. President: West of England Br., Assoc. of Headmistresses, 1969-71; Assoc. of Headmistresses of Girls' Boarding Schs, 1971-73; Girls' Schs Assoc. (Independent and Direct Grant), 1973-75; Chm., Council, Independent Schs Information Service, 1977-. Governor: Bath High Sch.; Greenway

Comprehensive Sch. for Boys. *Recreations:* fencing, painting, travel, embroidery. *Address:* Crofton, 8 Chapel Lane, Old Sodbury, Bristol.

DALAL, Maneck Ardeshir Sohrab; Managing Director, Tata Ltd, SW1, since 1977; Director, Tata Industries, Bombay, since 1980; *b* 24 Dec. 1918; *s* of Ardeshir Dalal and Amy Dalal; *m* 1947, Kathleen Gertrude Richardson; three *d. Educ:* Trinity Hall, Cambridge (MA). Called to the Bar, Middle Temple, 1945. Manager: Air-India New Delhi, 1946-48; Air-India London, 1948-53; Regional Traffic Manager, 1953-59; Regional Director, 1959-77; Minister for Tourism and Civil Aviation, High Commn for India, 1973-77. President: Indian Chamber of Commerce in Great Britain, 1959-62; Indian Management Assoc. of UK, 1960-63; Vice-Pres., Friends of Vellore, 1979-; Chairman: Foreign Airlines Assoc. of UK, 1965-67; Indian YMCA in London, 1972-; Bharatiya Vidhya Bhavan in London (Indian Cultural Inst. of Gt Britain), 1975-; Vice-Chm., Fest. of India in GB, 1980-; Member: Sub-Cttee on Transport, Industrial Trng Bd of Gt Britain, 1975-; Central Council, Royal Over-Seas League, 1974-. FCIT 1975; FBIM. *Recreations:* squash rackets, reading. *Address:* Tall Trees, Marlborough Road, Hampton, Mddx. *T:* 01-979 2065. *Clubs:* Oriental, Hurlingham, Royal Over-Seas League.

DALBY, Dr (Terry) David (Pereira); Reader in West African Languages, School of Oriental and African Studies, University of London, since 1967; *b* 7 Jan. 1933; *s* of Ernest Edwin Dalby and Rose Cecilia Dalby; *m* 1957, Winifred Brand; two *d. Educ:* Cardiff High Sch.; Queen Mary Coll., London (BA 1954, PhD 1961). Served to Lieut, Intell. Corps, 1954-56. United Africa Co. Ltd, London and W Africa, 1957-60; Lectr in Mod. Languages, University Coll. of Sierra Leone, 1961-62; Lectr in W African Langs, SOAS, Univ. of London, 1962-67. Hanns Wolff Vis. Prof., Indiana Univ., 1969. Chm., Centre for Afr. Studies, Univ. of London, 1971-74; Dir, Internat. African Inst., 1974-80; Chairman: Internat. Conf. on Manding Studies, 1972, and Drought in Africa Conf., 1973; Standing Cttee on Univ. Studies of Africa, 1978- (Dep. Chm., 1975-78). Vice-Pres., UNESCO Meeting on Cultural Specificity in Africa, Accra, 1980. Member: Governing Body, SOAS, 1969-70; Council, African Studies Assoc. of UK, 1970-73; Cttee of Management, British Inst. in Paris, 1975-; Comité d'Honneur, Société d'Etudes Linguistiques et Anthropologiques de France, 1980-; Conseil Internat. de Recherche et d'Etude en Linguistique Fondamentale et Appliquée, 1980-. Editor, African Language Review, 1962-72; Co-editor: Africa, 1976-80; African Languages/Langues Africaines, 1979-. *Publications:* Lexicon of the Mediaeval German Hunt, 1965; Black through White: patterns of communication in Africa and the New World, 1970; (ed) Language and History in Africa, 1970; (ed jtly) Drought in Africa, 1st vol. 1973, 2nd vol. 1978; Language Map of Africa and the adjacent islands, 1977; articles in linguistic and other jls. *Recreations:* cartography, rock-gardening. *Address:* 6 Rothamsted Avenue, Harpenden, Herts. *T:* Harpenden 5190.

DALDRY, Sir Leonard (Charles), KBE 1963 (CBE 1960); Chairman, St Loye's College for the Disabled, Exeter, since 1969; *b* 6 Oct. 1908; *s* of Charles Henry Daldry; *m* 1938, Joan Mary (*d* 1976), *d* of John E. Crisp; no *c*; *m* 1976, Monica Mary, *d* of late G. E. Benson and of Helen Benson, Moretonhampstead, Devon; one *s* one *d.* Joined Barclays Bank DCO 1929. Local Dir in W Africa at Lagos, 1952. Assoc. Inst. of Bankers, 1936. Mem. Nigerian Railway Corp., 1955-60; Special Mem., Nigerian House of Reps, 1956-59; Senator, Federal Legislature, Nigeria, 1960-61; Chm., Nigeria Bd, Barclays Bank DCO, 1961-63. *Address:* Prospect House, Budleigh Salterton, Devon. *Club:* Athenæum.

DALE, David Kenneth Hay, CBE 1976; Governor, Montserrat, West Indies, since 1980; *b* 27 Jan. 1927; *s* of Kenneth Hay Dale and Francesca Sussana Hoffman; *m* 1956, Hanna Szydlowska; one *s. Educ:* Dorchester Grammar Sch. Joined Queen's Royal Regt, 1944; 2/Lieut 8th Punjab Regt, 1945; Lieut 4 Bn (PWO) 8th Punjab Regt, 1946; Lieut Royal Regt of Artillery, 1948; Captain 1955: served Kenya and Malaya (despatches); Dist Officer, Kenya, 1960, Dist Comr, 1962; Admin Officer Cl. B, subseq. Cl. A, Anglo-French Condominium, New Hebrides, W Pacific, 1965-73; Perm. Sec., Min. of Aviation, Communications and Works, Seychelles, 1973-75; Dep. Governor, Seychelles, 1975; Sec. to Cabinet, Republic of Seychelles, 1976; FCO, 1977-80. *Recreations:* birdwatching, walking. *Address:* Government House, Montserrat, West Indies; Chatley Cottage, Batcombe, near Shepton Mallet, Somerset BA4 6AF. *T:* Upton Noble 449. *Club:* East India, Devonshire, Sports and Public Schools.

DALE, Jim; actor, singer, composer, lyricist; *b* 15 Aug. 1935; *m*; three *s* one *d. Educ:* Kettering Grammar School. Music Hall comedian, 1951; singing, compering, directing, 1951-61; films, 1965-, include: Lock Up Your Daughters, The Winter's Tale, The Biggest Dog in the World, National Health, Adolf Hitler-My Part in his Downfall, Joseph Andrews, Pete's Dragon, Bloodshy, The Spaceman and King Arthur. Joined Frank Dunlop's Pop Theatre for Edinburgh Festival, 1967-68; National Theatre, 1969-71: main roles in National Health, Love's Labour's Lost, Merchant of Venice, Good-natured Man, Captain of Kopenick; also appeared at Young Vic in Taming of the Shrew, Scapino (title rôle and wrote music); title rôle in musical The Card, 1973; Compère of Sunday Night at the London Palladium, 1973-74; Scapino (title rôle), Broadway, 1974-75 (Drama Critics' and Outer Circle Awards for best actor; Tony award nomination for best actor); Barnum, Broadway, 1980 (Tony award for best actor in a musical). Composed film music for: The Winter's Tale, Shaliko, Twinky, Georgy Girl (nominated for

Academy Award), Joseph Andrews. *Recreation:* escapology. *Address:* 9 Orme Court, W2. *T:* 01-727 0625.

DALE, Sir William (Leonard), KCMG 1965 (CMG 1951); International legal consultant; Fellow, Cambridge University Centre of International Studies; Director of Studies: Government Legal Officers Course; Cambridge Vacation Course in International Law; *b* 17 June 1906; *e s* of late Rev. William Dale, Rector of Preston, Yorks; *m* 1966, Mrs Gloria Spellman Finn, Washington, DC; one *d. Educ:* Hymers Coll., Hull; London (LLB); Barrister, Gray's Inn, 1931. Asst Legal Adviser, Colonial and Dominions Offices, 1935; Min. of Supply, 1940-45; Dep. Legal Adviser, Colonial and Commonwealth Relations Offices, 1945; Legal Adviser, United Kingdom of Libya, 1951-53; Legal Adviser: Min. of Educn, 1954-61; CRO, subseq. CO, 1961-66. Special Asst to the Law Officers, 1967-68; Gen. Counsel, UNRWA, Beirut, 1968-73. Hon. LLD Hull, 1978. *Publications:* Law of the Parish Church, 1932 (5th edn, 1975); Legislative Drafting: a new approach, 1977; contributions to journals. *Recreation:* music (except Wagner). *Address:* 20 Old Buildings, Lincoln's Inn, WC2A 3TL. *T:* 01-242 9365. Lamb Building, Temple, EC4. *Club:* Travellers'.

DALGARNO, Prof. Alexander, PhD; FRS 1972; Phillips Professor of Astronomy, since 1977, Chairman of Department of Astronomy, 1971-76, Associate Director of Centre for Astrophysics, 1973-80, Harvard University; Member of Smithsonian Astrophysical Observatory, since 1967; *b* 5 Jan. 1928; *s* of William Dalgarno; *m* 1st, 1957, Barbara Kane (marr. diss. 1972); two *s* two *d*; 2nd, 1972, Emily Izsák. *Educ:* Southgate Grammar Sch.; University Coll., London (Fellow 1976). BSc Maths, 1st Cl. Hons London, 1947; PhD Theoretical Physics London, 1951; AM Harvard, 1967. The Queen's University of Belfast: Lectr in Applied Maths, 1952; Reader in Maths, 1956; Dir of Computing Lab, 1960; Prof. of Quantum Mechanics, 1961; Prof. of Mathematical Physics, 1966-67; Prof. of Astronomy, Harvard Univ., 1967-77; Acting Dir, Harvard Coll. Observatory, 1971-73. Chief Scientist, Geophysics Corp. of America, 1962-63. Editor, Astrophysical Journal Letters, 1973–. Fellow: Amer. Acad. of Arts and Sciences, 1968; Amer. Geophysical Union, 1972; Amer. Physical Soc., 1980; Corresp. Mem., Internat. Acad. Astronautics, 1972. Hon. DSc QUB, 1980. Prize of Internat. Acad. of Quantum Molecular Sci., 1969; Hodgkins Medal, Smithsonian Instn, 1977; Davisson-Germer Prize, Amer. Physical Soc., 1980. *Publications:* numerous papers in scientific journals. *Recreations:* squash, books. *Address:* c/o Harvard-Smithsonian Center for Astrophysics, 60 Garden Street, Cambridge, Mass 02138, USA.

DALGLISH, Captain James Stephen, CVO 1955; CBE 1963; *b* 1 Oct. 1913; *e s* of late Rear-Adm. Robin Dalglish, CB; *m* 1939, Evelyn Mary, *e d* of late Rev. A. Ll. Meyricke, Vicar of Aislaby, near Whitby; one *s* one *d. Educ:* RN Coll., Dartmouth. Commanded HMS Aisne, 1952-53; HM Yacht Britannia, 1954, HMS Woodbridge Haven and Inshore Flotilla, 1958-59; HMS Excellent, 1959-61; HMS Bulwark, 1961-63; jssc 1950; idc 1957; retired from RN, 1963. Welfare Officer, Metropolitan Police, 1963-73. *Recreations:* gardening, painting. *Address:* Park Hall, Aislaby, Whitby, North Yorks. *T:* Whitby 810213.

DALHOUSIE, 16th Earl of, *cr* 1633; **Simon Ramsay**, KT 1971; GCVO 1979; GBE 1957; MC 1944; LLD; Baron Ramsay, 1619; Lord Ramsay, 1633; Baron Ramsay (UK), 1875; Lord Chamberlain to the Queen Mother, 1965; Lord-Lieutenant of Angus, since 1967; Chancellor, Dundee University, since 1977; *b* 17 Oct. 1914; 2nd *s* of 14th Earl (*d* 1928) and Lady Mary Adelaide Heathcote Drummond Willoughby (*d* 1960), *d* of 1st Earl of Ancaster; *S* brother, 1950; *m* 1940, Margaret Elizabeth, *d* of late Brig.-Gen. Archibald and Hon. Mrs Stirling of Keir; three *s* two *d. Educ:* Eton; Christ Church, Oxford. Served TA, Black Watch, 1936-39; embodied, 1939. MP (C) for County of Angus, 1945-50; Conservative Whip, 1946-48 (resigned). Governor-General, Fedn of Rhodesia and Nyasaland, 1957-63. Hon. LLD: Dalhousie, 1952; Dundee, 1967. *Heir: e s* Lord Ramsay, *qv. Address:* Brechin Castle, Brechin. *T:* Brechin 2176; 5 Margaretta Terrace, SW3. *T:* 01-352 6477. *Club:* White's. *See also Earl of Scarbrough.*

DALI, Salvador (Felipe Jacinto); Marquis of Pubol, 1982; Spanish painter; stage-designer; book-illustrator; writer; interested in commercial art and films; *b* Figueras, Upper Catalonia, 11 May 1904; *s* of Salvador Dali, notary and Felipa Dome (Doménech); *m* 1935, Gala (*d* 1982) (*née* Elena Diaranoff); she *m* 1st, Paul Eluard. *Educ:* Academy of Fine Arts, Madrid; Paris. First one-man show, Barcelona, 1925; became prominent Catalan painter by 1927; Began surrealist painting in Paris, 1928; first one-man show, Paris, Nov. 1929; first one-man show, New York, Nov. 1933. Visited United States, 1934, 1939, 1940; lectured in Museum of Modern Art, New York, 1935; later, came to London; first visited Italy, 1937. Designer of scenery and costumes for ballet, etc., also of film scenarios. Has held exhibitions of paintings in many American and European Cities; Exhibition of jewels, London, 1960; major exhibition, Rotterdam, 1970; retrospective, Paris, and Tate Gallery, 1980. *Publications:* Babaouo (ballet and film scenarios), 1932; Secret Life of Salvador Dali, 1942; Hidden Faces (novel), 1944; Fifty Secrets of Magic Craftsmanship, 1948; Diary of a Genius, 1966; The Unspeakable Confessions of Salvador Dali, 1976. *Address:* Hotel St Regis, 5th Avenue, and 55th Street, New York, NY 10022, USA; Port-Lligat, Cadaqués, Spain.

DALITZ, Prof. Richard Henry, FRS 1960; Royal Society Research Professor at Oxford University, since 1963; *b* 28 Feb. 1925; *s* of Frederick W. and Hazel B. Dalitz, Melbourne, Australia; *m* 1946, Valda (*née* Suiter) of

Melbourne, Australia; one *s* three *d. Educ:* Scotch Coll., Melbourne; Univ. of Melbourne; Trinity Coll., Univ. of Cambridge, PhD Cantab, 1950. Lecturer in Mathematical Physics, Univ. of Birmingham, 1949-55; Research appointments in various Univs, USA, 1953-55; Reader in Mathematical Physics, Univ. of Birmingham, 1955-56; Prof. of Physics, Univ. of Chicago, 1956-66. Mem. Council, Royal Soc., 1979-81. Corresp. Mem., Australian Acad. of Science, 1978; For. Mem., Polish Acad. of Sci., 1980. Maxwell Medal and Prize, Institute of Physics and the Physical Soc., 1966; Bakerian Lectr and Jaffe Prize, The Royal Soc., 1969; Hughes Medal, The Royal Soc., 1975; J. Robert Oppenheimer Meml Prize, Univ. of Miami, 1980. *Publications:* Strange Particles and Strong Interactions, 1962 (India); Nuclear Interactions of the Hyperons, 1965 (India); numerous papers on theoretical physics in various British and American scientific jls. *Recreations:* mountain walking, travelling. *Address:* 1 Keble Road, Oxford OX1 3NP; All Souls College, Oxford.

DALKEITH, Earl of; Richard Walter John Montagu Douglas Scott; *b* 14 Feb. 1954; *s* and *heir* of 9th Duke of Buccleuch, *qv*; *m* 1981, Lady Elizabeth Kerr, *d* of Marquess of Lothian, *qv. Educ:* Eton; Christ Church, Oxford. A Page of Honour to HM the Queen Mother, 1967-69. *Address:* Bowhill, Selkirk. *T:* Selkirk 20732; 1 Pembridge Crescent, W11. *T:* 01-221 7322.

DALLARD, Berkeley Lionel Scudamore, CMG 1948; FCA; JP; *b* Waikari, Christchurch, New Zealand, 27 Aug. 1889; *s* of Geo. Joseph Dallard, Settler, born Tewkesbury, England, and Sarah Maria, born Cheltenham, England; *m* 1915, Agnes Rowan Inglis; three *d. Educ:* Waikari Public Sch.; Rangiora High Sch.; Victoria University Coll. Entered Civil Service, NZ, 1907; served in Stamp Office, Audit Office, Board of Trade, Public Service Commissioner's Office (Asst Public Service Commr, 1929), Justice Dept; Controller Gen. of Prisons, and Chief Probation Officer, NZ, 1925-49; Under Sec. for Justice and Registrar Gen., NZ, 1934-49, retd, 1949. Govt Mem. of Govt Service Tribunal, 1949-60, retd. City Councillor, Wellington, 1949-62. Chairman: Wellington Hospital Board, 1962-66; Combined Purchasing Cttee for NZ Hosps, 1963-71. *Publications:* Fettered Freedom, 1980; miscellaneous brochures on Criminology and Law. *Address:* 94 Upland Road, Kelburn, Wellington, NZ. *TA* and *T:* Wellington 759209. *Clubs:* (Past Pres.) Savage, (Past Pres.) Rotary (Wellington, NZ).

DALLEY, Christopher Mervyn, CMG 1971; MA Cantab; CEng; Director: London and Scottish Marine Oil Co. Ltd, since 1979; Viking Resources Trust Ltd, since 1973; *b* 26 Dec. 1913; *er s* of late Christopher Dalley; *m* 1947, Elizabeth Alice, *yr d* of late Lt-Gen. Sir James Gammell, KCB, DSO, MC; one *s* three *d. Educ:* Epsom Coll., Surrey; Queens' Coll., Cambridge. Served in RN, 1939-45. Joined British Petroleum Co., 1946; joined Iranian Oil Operating Companies in Iran 1954: Asst Gen. Managing Dir, 1958; joined Iraq Petroleum Co. and associated companies, 1962, Man. Dir, 1963, Chm., 1970-73; Chm., Oil Exploration Holdings Ltd, 1973-79. Pres., Inst. of Petroleum, 1970; Mem. Council, World Petroleum Congress, 1970. Mem., Governing Body, Royal Medical Foundn (Epsom Coll.), 1970. Order of Homoyoun (Iran), 1963. *Address:* Mead House, Woodham Walter, near Maldon, Essex. *T:* Danbury 2404; 6 Godfrey Street, SW3. *T:* 01-352 8260. *Club:* Athenæum.

DALMENY, Lord; Harry Ronald Neil Primrose; *b* 20 Nov. 1967; *s* and *heir* of 7th Earl of Rosebery, *qv*.

DALRYMPLE, family name of **Earl of Stair.**

DALRYMPLE, Viscount; John David James Dalrymple; *b* 4 Sept. 1961; *s* and *heir* of 13th Earl of Stair, *qv*.

DALRYMPLE, Sir Hew (Fleetwood) Hamilton-, 10th Bt, *cr* 1697; CVO 1974; late Major, Grenadier Guards; Vice-Lieutenant of East Lothian, since 1973; Director: Scottish & Newcastle Breweries; Scottish American Investment Company; *b* 9 April 1926; *er s* of Sir Hew (Clifford) Hamilton-Dalrymple, 9th Bt, JP; *S* father, 1959; *m* 1954, Lady Anne-Louise Mary Keppel, *d* of 9th Earl of Albemarle, MC, and of (Diana Cicely) Countess of Albemarle, *qv*; four *s. Educ:* Ampleforth. Staff Coll., Camberley, 1957; DAAG HQ 3rd Div., 1958-60; Regimental Adjt, Grenadier Guards, 1960-62; retd 1962. Adjt, 1964–, and Lieut, Queen's Body Guard for Scotland (Royal Company of Archers). President: E Lothian Scout Council; E Lothian Council for Voluntary Services. DL East Lothian, 1964. *Heir: e s* Hew Richard Hamilton-Dalrymple [*b* 3 Sept. 1955. *Educ:* Ampleforth; Corpus Christi Coll., Oxford (MA); Clare Coll., Cambridge (MPhil)]. *Address:* Leuchie, North Berwick, East Lothian. *T:* North Berwick 2903. *Club:* Cavalry and Guards.

DALRYMPLE, Ian Murray, FRSA; Film Producer, Writer and Director; *b* 26 Aug. 1903; *s* of late Sir William Dalrymple, KBE, LLD; *m* 2nd, Joan Margaret, *d* of late James Douglas Craig, CMG, CBE; one *s* and one *d* of previous marriage and two *s. Educ:* Rugby Sch.; Trinity Coll., Cambridge (Editor of The Granta, 1924-25). Executive Producer, Crown Film Unit, Min. of Information, 1940-43; subseq. op. through Wessex Film Productions Ltd and Ian Dalrymple (Advisory) Ltd. Chm. Brit. Film Acad., 1957-58. Film Editor, 1927-35. Screen writer, 1935-39, films including The Citadel, South Riding, Storm in a Teacup, The Lion Has Wings. Produced for Crown Film Unit; Fires Were Started, Western Approaches, Coastal Command, Ferry Pilot, Close Quarters, Wavell's 30,000, Target for To-Night, London Can

Take It, etc. Independent productions: The Woman in the Hall, Esther Waters, Once a Jolly Swagman, All Over The Town, Dear Mr Prohack, The Wooden Horse, Family Portrait, The Changing Face of Europe (series), Royal Heritage, Raising a Riot, A Hill in Korea. Commissioned productions include: The Heart of the Matter, The Admirable Crichton, A Cry from the Streets, Bank of England (Educational Films), The Boy and the Pelican. Film Adviser, Decca Ltd, 1967-68. Supervising Film Projects, Argo Record Co. (Div. of Decca Ltd), 1969. Prod Chaucer's Tale, 1970. *Address:* 3 Beaulieu Close, Cambridge Park, Twickenham TW1 2JR.

DALRYMPLE-HAMILTON of Bargany, Captain North Edward Frederick, CVO 1961; MBE 1953; DSC 1943; JP; DL; Royal Navy; *b* 17 Feb. 1922; *s* of Admiral Sir Frederick Dalrymple-Hamilton of Bargany, KCB; *m* 1949, Hon. Mary Colville (*d* 1981), *d* of 1st Baron Clydesmuir, PC, GCIE, TD; two *s. Educ:* Eton. Entered Royal Navy, 1940; Comdr 1954; Captain 1960. Comdg Officer HMS Scarborough, 1958; Executive Officer, HM Yacht Britannia, 1959; Captain (F) 17th Frigate Squadron, 1963; Dir of Naval Signals, 1965; Dir, Weapons Equipment Surface, 1967; retd, 1970. Brig., Royal Company of Archers, Queen's Body Guard for Scotland. DL 1973, JP 1980, Ayrshire. *Address:* Lovestone House, Bargany, Girvan, Ayrshire KA26 9RF. *T:* Old Dailly 227. *Clubs:* Pratt's, MCC; New (Edinburgh).

DALRYMPLE-HAY, Sir James Brian, 6th Bt, *cr* 1798; estate agent; Partner, Whiteheads, Estate Agents, since 1967; *b* 19 Jan. 1928; *e s* of Lt-Col Brian George Rowland Dalrymple-Hay (*d* on active service, 1943) and Beatrice (*d* 1935), *d* of A. W. Inglis; *S* cousin, 1952; *m* 1958, Helen Sylvia, *d* of late Stephen Herbert Card and of Molly M. Card; three *d. Educ:* Hillsbrow Preparatory Sch., Redhill; Blundell's Sch., Tiverton, Devon. Royal Marine, 1946-47; Lieut Royal Marine Commando, 1947-49; Palestine Star, 1948. Estate Agent and Surveyor's Pupil, 1949; Principal, 1955-67. *Heir: b* John Hugh Dalrymple-Hay [*b* 16 Dec. 1929; *m* 1962, Jennifer, *d* of late Brig. Robert Johnson, CBE; one *s*]. *Address:* The Red House, Church Street, Warnham, near Horsham, W Sussex.

DALRYMPLE-SMITH, Captain Hugh, RN (retired); *b* 27 Sept. 1901; *s* of late Arthur Alexander Dalrymple-Smith and late Mary Glover; *m* 1939, Eleanor Mary Hoare; two *s* one *d. Educ:* Ovingdean; Osborne; Dartmouth. Midshipman, 1917; Ronald Megaw Prize for 1921-22; qualified gunnery 1925, advanced course, 1928. Capt. 1941 (despatches); Admiralty Operations Div., 1942-43; commanding HMS Arethusa, including Normandy landings, 1943-45 (despatches). Naval Attaché, Nanking, 1946-48; commanding HMS King George V, 1948-49. Retired, Dec. 1950, and recalled as Actg Rear-Adm.; Chief of Staff to C-in-C Allied Forces, Northern Europe, 1951-53; retired as Captain. Dir, Television Audience Measurement Ltd, 1958-66. *Recreation:* painting. *Address:* Dale Cottage, Bridge Street, Wickham, Hants PO17 5JE. *T:* Wickham 833103.

DALRYMPLE-WHITE, Sir Henry Arthur Dalrymple, 2nd Bt, *cr* 1926; DFC 1941 and Bar 1942; *b* 5 Nov. 1917; *o s* of Lt-Col Sir Godfrey Dalrymple-White, 1st Bt, and late Hon. Catherine Mary Cary, *d* of 12th Viscount Falkland; *S* father 1954; *m* 1948, Mary (marr. diss. 1956), *o d* of Capt. Robert H. C. Thomas; one *s. Educ:* Eton; Magdalene Coll., Cambridge; London Univ. Formerly Wing Commander RAFVR. Served War of 1939-45. *Heir: s* Jan Hew Dalrymple-White, *b* 26 Nov. 1950. *Address:* c/o Brown, Shipley Ltd, Founders Court, Lothbury, EC2.

DALSAGER, Poul; Member, Commission of the European Communities, since 1981; *b* 5 March 1929; *m* 1951, Betty Jørgensen; two *s. Educ:* grammar sch. Bank employee, 1945-64; Mem. (Social Democrat), Danish Parliament, 1964-81; Chm., Market Cttee of Parlt, 1971-73; Chm., Social-Democratic Gp in Parlt, 1978-79; Minister for: Agriculture and Fisheries, 1975-77 and 1979-81; Agriculture, 1977-78. Mem. and Vice Pres., European Parlt, 1973 and 1974. Delegate to UN Gen. Assembly, 1969-71. *Address:* 200 rue de la Loi, 1049 Brussels, Belgium. *T:* Brussels 235 1111; Gram Mikkelsensvej 12, 9800 Hjørring, Denmark.

DALTON, Sir Alan (Nugent Goring), Kt 1977; CBE 1969; DL; Deputy Chairman, English China Clays Ltd, since 1968; Managing Director, English Clays, Lovering & Pochin & Co. Ltd, since 1961; *b* 26 Nov. 1923; *s* of Harold Goring Dalton and Phyllis Marguerite (*née* Ash). *Educ:* Shendish Prep. Sch., King's Langley; King Edward VI Sch., Southampton. Chm., British Railways (Western) Bd, 1978-; Member: Sun Alliance & London Assurance Group Bd, 1976-; SW Reg. Bd, Nat. Westminster Bank Ltd, 1977-. FBIM; FRSA. DL Cornwall, 1982. *Recreations:* sailing, painting, reading. *Address:* English China Clays Ltd, John Keay House, St Austell, Cornwall.

DALTON, Alfred Hyam, CB 1976; Deputy Chairman, Board of Inland Revenue, 1973-82 (Commissioner of Inland Revenue, 1970-82); *b* 29 March 1922; *m* 1946, Elizabeth Stalker; three *d. Educ:* Merchant Taylors' Sch., Northwood; Aberdeen Univ. Served War, REME, 1942-45 (despatches). Entered Inland Revenue, 1947; Asst Sec., 1958; Sec. to Board, 1969. *Recreation:* bridge. *Address:* 10 Courtmead Close, Burbage Road, SE24 9HW. *T:* 01-733 5395.

DALTON, Maj.-Gen. Sir Charles (James George), Kt 1967; CB 1954; CBE 1949 (OBE 1941); *b* 28 Feb. 1902; *s* of late Maj.-Gen. James Cecil Dalton, Col Comdt, RA, and late Mary Caroline, *d* of late Gen. Sir George Barker, GCB; *m* 1936, Daphne, *d* of Col Llewellyn Evans, and late Mrs F. A.

Macartney; one *s* two *d* (and one *s* decd). *Educ:* Aysgarth Sch., Yorks; Cheltenham Coll.; RMA Woolwich. Commissioned, RA, 1921; Staff Coll., Camberley, 1935-36; served in Egypt and India, 1922-39; staff appts in India and Burma, 1939-45 (CRA 26 Ind. Div., BGS 33 Ind. Corps, CRA 14 Ind. Div.); served with CCG, 1946; War Office (Brig. AG Coordination), 1946-49; Comdr 8 AA Bde, 1949-51; Services Relations Adviser to UK High Comr Control Commn for Germany, 1951-54; Dir of Manpower Planning, War Office, 1954-57, retired. Capt. 1934, Major 1939, Lt-Col 1946, Col 1947, Brig. 1951, Maj.-Gen. 1954. Col Comdt RA, 1960-65. Dir-Gen. of Zoological Soc. of London, 1957-67. High Sheriff of Yorks 1972. CStJ. *Recreations:* shooting and fishing. *Address:* The Hutts, Grewelthorpe, Ripon, North Yorks. *T:* Kirkby Malzeard 355.

DALTON, Rear-Adm. Geoffrey Thomas James Oliver; Assistant Chief of Naval Staff (Policy), since 1981; *b* 14 April 1931; *s* of late Jack Rowland Thomas Dalton and Margaret Kathleen Dalton; *m* 1957, Jane Hamilton (*née* Baynes); four *s. Educ:* Parkfield, Sussex; Reigate Grammar Sch.; RNC Dartmouth. Midshipman 1950; served in HM Ships Illustrious, Loch Alvie, Cockade, Virago, Flag Lieut to C-in-C The Nore, and HMS Maryton, 1950-61; served HMS Murray, RN Staff Course and HMS Dido, 1961-66; served HMS Relentless (in Comd), RN Sch. of PT, HMS Nubian (in Comd), Staff of Flag Officers Second in Comd Far East Fleet and Second Flotilla, 1966-72; Asst Dir of Naval Plans, 1972-74; RCDS, 1975; Captain RN Presentation Team, 1976-77; in Comd HMS Jupiter, 1977-79 and HMS Dryad, 1979-81. Commander, 1966; Captain, 1972. *Recreations:* squash, fishing, gardening, walking. *Address:* c/o Lloyds Bank Ltd, Cox's and King's Branch, Pall Mall, SW1.

DALTON, Irwin; Member for Personnel Services, National Bus Company, since 1981; *b* 25 July 1932; *s* of Harry Farr Dalton and Bessie Dalton; *m* 1954, Marie Davies; two *d. Educ:* Cockburn High Sch., Leeds. FCA 1973; FCIT 1978. Accountancy profession, 1947-62; Asst Company Sec., 1962-67, Company Sec., 1968-70, West Riding Automobile, Wakefield; Company Sec., Crosville Motor Services, 1971-74; Dir and Gen. Manager, Ribble Motor Services, 1974-76; Regional Dir, Nat. Bus Co., 1977-81. *Recreations:* golf, other sporting activities. *Address:* Westview, 1 Birling Park Avenue, Birling Road, Tunbridge Wells, Kent TN2 5LQ. *T:* Tunbridge Wells 33459. *Club:* Tunbridge Wells Golf.

DALTON, Vice-Adm. Sir Norman (Eric), KCB 1959 (CB 1956); OBE 1944; *b* 1 Feb. 1904; *s* of late William John Henry Dalton, Portsmouth; *m* 1927, Teresa Elizabeth, *d* of late Richard Jenkins, Portsmouth; one *s* one *d. Educ:* RN Colls Osborne and Dartmouth. Joined RN, 1917; Capt. 1946; Rear-Adm. 1954; Vice-Adm. 1957. Deputy Engineer-in-Chief of the Fleet, 1955-57; Engineer-in-Chief of the Fleet, 1957-59; Dir-Gen. of Training, 1959-60; retired 1960. *Address:* New Lodge, Peppard Lane, Henley-on-Thames, Oxon. *T:* Henley 5552. *Club:* Army and Navy.

DALTON, Peter Gerald Fox, CMG 1958; *b* 12 Dec. 1914; *s* of late Sir Robert (William) Dalton, CMG; *m* 1944, Josephine Anne Helyar; one *s* one *d. Educ:* Uppingham Sch.; Oriel Coll., Oxford. HM Embassy, Peking 1937-39; HM Consulate-Gen., Hankow, 1939-41; HM Embassy, Chungking, 1941-42; Foreign Office, 1942-46; HM Legation, Bangkok, 1946; HM Embassy, Montevideo, 1947-50; Foreign Office, 1950-53; Political Adviser, Hong Kong, 1953-56; Foreign Office, 1957-60; HM Embassy, Warsaw, 1960-63; HM Consul-General: Los Angeles, 1964-65; San Francisco, 1965-67; Minister, HM Embassy, Moscow, 1967-69; retd from HM Diplomatic Service, 1969. *Address:* Rotherdale Cottage, Fir Toll Road, Mayfield, Sussex. *T:* Mayfield 873421.

DALTON, Philip Neale; Vice President, Immigration Appeal Tribunal, 1970-82; *b* 30 June 1909; *o s* of late Sir Llewelyn Dalton, MA; *m* 1947, Pearl, *d* of Mark Foster, Kenya; one *s* two *d. Educ:* Downside Sch.; Trinity Coll., Cambridge. Barrister-at-law. Inner Temple, 1933; Resident Magistrate, Ghana, 1937; military service, 1939-45; Crown Counsel, Ghana, 1945-51; Solicitor-Gen., Fiji, 1951-53; Attorney-Gen., British Solomon Islands, and Legal Adviser, Western Pacific High Commission, 1953-56; Attorney-Gen., Zanzibar, 1957-63; Puisne Judge, Kenya, 1963-69. Order of the Brilliant Star (second class) Zanzibar, 1963. *Recreations:* cricket, golf. *Address:* Spring Lane, Aston Tirrold, Oxon. *Clubs:* Royal Commonwealth Society; Nairobi (Nairobi).

DALY, Most Rev. Cahal Brendan; *see* Ardagh and Clonmacnois, Bishop of, (RC).

DALY, Hon. Francis Lenton; Hon. Mr Justice Daly; Chief Justice, Solomon Islands, since 1980; *b* 23 June 1938; *s* of Sydney Richard Daly and Lilian May Daly (*née* Lindholm); *m* 1964, Joyce Brenda (*née* Nicholls). *Educ:* Forest School; London School of Economics (LLB). Called to Bar, Gray's Inn, 1961 (Lord Justice Holker Exhibn). English Bar, 1961-66; Legal Secretary, Lord Chancellor's Office, 1966; Bermudian Bar, 1966-72; Asst Judge Advocate General to the Forces, UK, 1972-78; Principal Magistrate, Malaita, Solomon Islands, 1978; Attorney General, Solomon Islands, 1979. *Publications:* contribs to International and Comparative Law Qly, Commonwealth Judicial Jl. *Recreations:* tennis, rowing, reading. *Address:* High Court, Honiara, Solomon Islands. *T:* 632. *Clubs:* Royal Commonwealth Society; Tenavatu (Guadalcanal).

DALY, Harry John, CMG 1966; FRACP 1946; FFARCS 1949; FFARACS; Retired Anæsthetist; *b* 3 Aug. 1893; *s* of Henry and Victoria Daly, both Irish; *m* 1921, Jean Edmunds, Sydney. *Educ:* St Ignatius Coll., Sydney, Australia, MB, ChM Sydney, 1918; FFARACS Melbourne 1952. Gen. Practice, Haberfield NSW; Specialist Anæsthetist, Sydney, 1929; Hon. Consulting Anæsthetist to Lewisham, Sydney and St Vincent's Hospitals. Dean, Faculty of Anæsthetists, RACS, 1954. Hon. Member: Royal Society of Medicine; Liverpool Soc. Anæsthetists, 1935. Orton Medallion, RACS, 1969. Hon. FRACS, 1973. *Publications:* numerous scientific articles in med. jls, 1932-56. *Recreations:* fishing, gardening. *Address:* 8 The Parapet, Castlecrag, NSW 2068, Australia. *T:* 955957. *Club:* Royal Sydney Golf.

DALY, Rt. Rev. John Charles Sydney; Assistant to the Bishop of Coventry, 1968-75, and Vicar of Bishop's Tachbrook, 1970-75; *b* 13 Jan. 1903; *s* of S. Owen Daly. *Educ:* Gresham's Sch., Holt; King's Coll., Cambridge; Cuddesdon Coll., Oxford. Curate, St Mary's Church, Tyne Dock, South Shields, 1926-29; Vicar, Airedale with Fryston, Yorks, 1929-35; Bishop of Gambia, 1935-51; Bishop of Accra, 1951-55; Bishop in Korea, 1955-65, of Taejon (Korea), 1965-68; Priest-in-charge of Honington with Idlicote and Whatcote, 1968-70. *Address:* Rye Croft, Honington, Shipston-on-Stour, Warwicks CV36 5AA. *T:* Shipston-on-Stour 62140.

DALY, Lawrence; General Secretary, National Union of Mineworkers, since 1968; *b* 20 Oct. 1924; *s* of James Daly and late Janet Taylor; *m* 1948, Renée M. Baxter; four *s* one *d*. *Educ:* primary and secondary schools. Glencraig Colliery (underground), 1939; Workmen's Safety Inspector, there, 1954-64. Part-time NUM lodge official, Glencraig, 1946; Chm., Scottish NUM Youth Committee, 1949; elected to Scottish Area NUM Exec. Cttee, 1962; Gen. Sec., Scottish NUM, 1964; National Exec., NUM, 1965. Mem., TUC General Council, 1978-81. *Publications:* (pamphlets): A Young Miner Sees Russia, 1946; The Miners and the Nation, 1968. *Recreations:* literature, politics, folk-song. *Address:* 222 Euston Road, NW1. *T:* 01-387 7631. *Club:* Railway (Euston, London).

DALY, Dame Mary Dora, DBE 1951 (CBE 1949; OBE 1937); Victorian President of Catholic Welfare Organisation since 1941; Federal President, Australian Association of Ryder-Cheshire Foundations, 1976-78; *b* Cootamundra, NSW; *d* of late T. P. MacMahon, Darling Point, Sydney; *m* 1923, Dr John J. Daly, Melbourne; one *s* one *d*. *Educ:* Loreto Abbey, Ballarat, Vic. War of 1939-45; Mem. of finance and advisory cttees, Australian Comforts Fund; Mem. executive cttees, Lord Mayor of Melbourne's appeals for food for Britain, toys for Britain, Victorian Government fat for Britain drive. Member: National Council, Aust. Red Cross Soc. (Long Service Medal and Bar, 1950; Hon. Life Mem., 1971); Executive and Council (1936-), Victorian Div., Red Cross Soc.; Council, Nat. Heart Foundn of Australia (Victorian Div.); Victorian Council, Assoc. of Ryder-Cheshire Foundns; Council and Executive, Ryder-Cheshire Foundn (Victoria); Victorian Council Girl Guides Assoc., 1954; Anti-Cancer Council (Victoria); Lady Mayoress's (Melbourne) Cttee for Metropolitan Hosps and charities; Foundation Mem., Cttee of the Most Excellent Order of the British Empire (Victorian Assoc.); Patron: Nat. Boys Choir; Yooralla Hosp. Sch., for Crippled Children (Pres., DMD Cttee); Wattle Day Child Care Soc.; Austral Salon for advancement of music, literature and fine arts. Pres., Australian Catholic Relief, Archdiocese of Melbourne, 1966-75. Comr for Affidavits, State of Victoria. Cross, Pro Ecclesia et Pontifice, 1952. *Publications:* Marie's Birthday Party, 1934; Cinty, 1961; Timmy's Christmas Surprise, 1967; Holidays at Hillydale, 1974; articles in several magazines. *Recreations:* music, reading, gardening. *Address:* 6 Henry Street, Kew, Vic 3101, Australia; Finavarra, Stevens Street, Queenscliff, Victoria.

DALY, Michael de Burgh, MA, MD, ScD Cambridge; FRCP; Professor of Physiology in the University of London, at St Bartholomew's Hospital Medical College, since 1958; *b* 7 May 1922; *s* of late Dr Ivan de Burgh Daly, CBE, FRS; *m* 1948, Beryl Esmé, *y d* of late Wing Commander A. J. Nightingale; two *s*. *Educ:* Loretto Sch., Edinburgh; Gonville and Caius Coll., Cambridge; St Bartholomew's Hospital. Nat. Science Tripos. Part I, 1943, Part II, 1944, Physiology. House-physician, St Bartholomew's Hospital, 1947; Asst Lecturer, 1948-50, and Lecturer, 1950-54, in Physiology, University Coll., London. Rockefeller Foundation Travelling Fellowship in Medicine, 1952-53; Locke Research Fellow of Royal Soc., 1955-58; Vis. Prof. of Physiology, Univ. of NSW, 1966; Vis. Lectr, Swedish Univs, 1961. Member: Adv. Panel for Underwater Personnel Res., MoD; MRC/RN Personnel Res. Cttee, Underwater Physiology Sub-Cttee. Chm., Editorial Bd of Monographs of Physiological Soc.; former Co-Editor of Journal of Physiology. FRSM. Member: Soc. of Experimental Biol.; Physiological Soc.; Osler Med. Club; European Underwater Biomed. Soc.; Undersea Med. Soc. Inc. Schafer Prize in Physiology, University Coll., London, 1953; Thruston Medal, Gonville and Caius Coll., 1957; Sir Lionel Whitby Medal, Cambridge Univ., 1963. *Publications:* contributor to: Lippold and Winton, Human Physiology; Starling, Principles of Human Physiology; Bell, Emslie-Smith and Paterson, Textbook of Physiology; papers on the integrative control of respiration and the cardiovascular system in Journal of Physiology; contrib. to film on William Harvey and the Circulation of the Blood. *Recreation:* model engineering. *Address:* 7 Hall Drive, Sydenham, SE26 6XL. *T:* 01-778 8773.

DALY, Michael Francis; HM Diplomatic Service; Ambassador to Ivory Coast, Upper Volta and Niger, since 1978; *b* 7 April 1931; *s* of late William Thomas

Daly and of Hilda Frances Daly; *m* 1st, 1963, Sally Malcolm Angwin (*d* 1966); one *d*; 2nd, 1971, Juliet Mary Siragusa (*née* Arning); one step-*d*. *Educ:* Downside; Gonville and Caius Coll., Cambridge (BA Hons). Mil. Service, 1952-54: 2nd Lieut, Intell. Corps. E. D. Sassoon Banking Co., London, 1954; Transreef Industrial & Investment Co., Johannesburg, 1955-66; General Electric Co., London, 1966; HM Diplomatic Service: 1st Sec., FCO, 1967; 1st Sec. (Commercial), Rio de Janeiro, 1969; 1st Sec. (Inf.) and Head of Chancery, Dublin, 1973; Asst, Cultural Relations Dept, FCO, 1976; Counsellor, Consul-Gen. and Head of Chancery, Brasilia, 1977-78. *Recreations:* skiing, sailing, theatre, golf. *Address:* c/o Foreign and Commonwealth Office, SW1; 45 Priory Road, Kew Gardens, Richmond, Surrey. *Club:* Country (Johannesburg).

DALY, Lt.-Gen. Sir Thomas (Joseph), KBE 1967 (CBE 1953; OBE 1944); CB 1965; DSO 1945, Chief of the General Staff, Australia, 1966-71; *b* 19 March 1913; *s* of late Lt-Col T. J. Daly, DSO, VD, Melbourne; *m* 1946, Heather, *d* of late James Fitzgerald, Melbourne; three *d*. *Educ:* St Patrick's Coll., Sale; Xavier Coll., Kew, Vic; RMC, Duntroon (Sword of Honour). 3rd LH, 1934; attached for training 16/5 Lancers, India, 1938; Adj, 2/10 Aust. Inf. Bn, 1939; Bde Major, 18 Inf. Bde, 1940; GSO2 6 Aust. Div., 1941; GSO1 5 Aust. Div., 1942; Instructor, Staff Sch. (Aust.), 1944; CO 2/10 Inf. Bn, AIF, 1944; Instr, Staff Coll., Camberley, UK, 1946; Joint Services Staff Coll., Latimer, 1948; Dir of Mil. Art, RMC Duntroon, 1949; Dir of Infantry, AHQ, 1951; Comd 28 Brit. Commonwealth Inf. Bde, Korea, 1952; Dir, Ops and Plans, AHQ, 1953; IDC, London, 1956; GOC Northern Command, Australia, 1957-60; Adjt Gen., 1961-63; GOC, Eastern Command, Australia, 1963-66. Col Comdt, Royal Australian Regt, and Pacific Is Regt, 1971-75. Director: Jennings Industries Ltd, 1974-; Fruehauf Trailers (Aust.) Ltd, 1974-; Associated Merchant Bank (Singapore), 1975-77. Mem., Nat. Council, Australian Red Cross, 1972-75; Chm., Council, Australian Nat. War Memorial, 1974-82 (Mem., 1966-74); Councillor, Royal Agricl Soc. of NSW, 1972-. Legion of Merit (US), 1953. *Recreations:* golf, tennis, cricket, ski-ing. *Address:* 16 Victoria Road, Bellevue Hill, NSW 2023, Australia. *Clubs:* Australian (Sydney); Naval and Military (Melbourne); Royal Sydney Golf, Melbourne Cricket, Ski Club of Australia (Sydney).

DALYELL, Tam; MP (Lab) West Lothian, since 1962; *b* 9 Aug. 1932; *s* of late Gordon and Eleanor Dalyell; *m* 1963, Kathleen, *o d* of Baron Wheatley, *qv*; one *s* one *d*. *Educ:* Eton; King's Coll., Cambridge; Moray House Teachers' Training Coll., Edinburgh. Trooper, Royal Scots Greys, 1950-52; Teacher, Bo'ness High Sch., 1956-60. Contested (Lab) Roxburgh, Selkirk, and Peebles, 1959. Dep.-Director of Studies on British India ship-school, Dunera, 1961-62. Member Public Accounts Cttee, House of Commons, 1962-66; Secretary, Labour Party Standing Conference on the Sciences, 1962-64; PPS to Minister of Housing, 1964-65; Opposition spokesman on science, 1980-82; Chairman: PLP Education Cttee, 1964-65; PLP Sports Group, 1964-74; PLP Foreign Affairs Gp, 1974-75; Vice-Chairman: PLP Defence and Foreign Affairs Gps, 1972-74; Scottish Labour Group of MPs, 1973-75; Parly Lab. Party, Nov. 1974-; Sub-Cttee on Public Accounts; Member: European Parlt, 1975-79; European Parlt Budget Cttee, 1976-79; European Parlt Energy Cttee, 1979; Member: House of Commons Select Cttee on Science and Technology, 1967-69; Liaison Cttee between Cabinet and Parly Labour Party, 1974-76; Council, National Trust for Scotland; PPS to late R. H. S. Crossman, MP, 1964-70. Mem. Scottish Council for Devlt and Industry Trade Delegn to China, Nov. 1971. Political columnist, New Scientist. *Publications:* The Case of Ship-Schools, 1960; Ship-School Dunera, 1963; Devolution: the end of Britain?, 1977. *Recreations:* tennis, swimming. *Address:* The Binns, Linlithgow, Scotland. *T:* Philipstoun 255.

DALZELL-PAYNE, Maj.-Gen. Henry Salusbury Legh, CBE 1973; *b* 1929; *s* of late Geoffrey Legh Dalzell-Payne; *m* 1963, Serena Helen (marr. diss. 1980), *d* of Col Clifford White Gourlay, MC, TD; two *d*. *Educ:* Cheltenham; RMA Sandhurst. Commissioned, 7th Hussars, 1949; Major, Sultan of Muscat's Armed Forces, 1959-60; Staff Coll., Camberley, 1961; BM 20 Armd Brigade Gp, 1962-64; Queen's Own Hussars, 1964-65; Instructor, Staff Coll., Camberley, 1966; Comd 3rd Dragoon Guards, 1967-69; Gen. Staff, Mil. Ops, MoD, 1970-72; student, RCDS, 1973; Comdr, 6th Armoured Brigade, 1974-75; Chief of Staff, 1 (BR) Corps, 1976-78; GOC 3 Armoured Div., 1978-80. *Clubs:* White's, Cavalry and Guards, Turf.

DALZIEL, Geoffrey Albert; British Commissioner, Leader of Salvation Army activities in Gt Britain, 1974-80; *b* 10 Dec. 1912; *s* of Alexander William and Olive Mary Dalziel; *m* 1937, Ruth Edith Fairbank; two *s* one *d*. *Educ:* Harrow Elementary Sch. Commissioned Salvation Army Officer, 1934; Corps Officer in Gt Britain, to 1946; on Internat. Trng Coll. Staff, 1946-51; Divisional Youth Sec., 1951-59; Trng Coll. Principal, Melbourne, Aust., 1959-64; Chief Side Officer, Internat. Trng Coll., London, 1964-66; Chief Secretary: Sydney, Aust., 1966-68; Toronto, Canada, 1968-70; Territorial Comdr, Kenya, Uganda and Tanzania, E Africa, 1970-74. *Recreations:* walking, gardening, reading. *Address:* 407 Wickham Road, Shirley, Croydon, Surrey CR0 8DP.

DALZIEL, Ian Martin; Member (C) Lothians, European Parliament, since 1979; *b* 21 June 1947; *s* of John Calvin Dalziel and Elizabeth Roy Dalziel, *e d* of Rev. Ian Bain, FRS(Scot) and Mrs Christian Stuart Fisher Bain, Gairloch; *m* 1972, Nadia Maria Iacovazzi; two *s*. *Educ:* Daniel Stewart's Coll., Edinburgh; St John's Coll., Cambridge (BA Hons 1968, LLB Hons 1969); Université Libre de Bruxelles (Weiner Anspach Foundation Scholarship,

1970). MA 1972. Mullens & Co., 1970-72; Manufacturers Hanover Ltd, 1972-. Mem., Richmond upon Thames Council, 1978-79. *Publications:* contribs on political matters to Scottish newspapers and magazines. *Recreations:* reading, golf. *Address:* 21 Greenhill Gardens, Edinburgh EH10 4BL. *T:* 031-447 3441. *Club:* New (Edinburgh).

DALZIEL, Dr Keith, FRS 1975; Reader in Biochemistry, University of Oxford, since 1978; Fellow of Wolfson College since 1970; *b* 24 Aug. 1921; *s* of late Gilbert and Edith Dalziel; *m* 1945, Sallie Farnworth; two *d. Educ:* Grecian Street Central Sch., Salford; Royal Techn. Coll., Salford; 1st cl. hons BSc London 1944; PhD London; MA Oxon. Lab. Technician, Manchester Victoria Meml Jewish Hosp., 1935-44, Biochemist 1944-45; Asst Biochemist, Radcliffe Infirmary, Oxford, 1945-47; Res. Asst, Nuffield Haematology Res. Fund, Oxford, 1947-58; Rockefeller Trav. Fellowship in Medicine, Nobel Inst., Stockholm, 1955-57; Sorby Res. Fellow of Royal Soc., Sheffield Univ., 1958-63; Univ. Lectr in Biochem., Oxford, 1963-78. Vis. Prof. of Biochemistry, Univ. of Michigan, 1967. Member: Enzyme Chem. and Tech. Cttee, SRC, 1974; Council, Royal Soc., 1979-80; Editorial Bds, European Jl of Biochemistry and Biochimica Biophysica Acta, 1971-74; Adv. Bd, Jl Theor. Biol., 1976-79. *Publications:* sci. papers in Biochem. Jl, European Jl of Biochemistry, etc. *Recreations:* music, walking. *Address:* Department of Biochemistry, South Parks Road, Oxford. *T:* Oxford 511261; 25 Hampden Drive, Kidlington, Oxford. *T:* Kidlington 2623.

DAMER; *see* Dawson-Damer.

DAMERELL, Derek Vivian; Governor and Chief Executive, BUPA, since 1974; *b* 4 Aug. 1921; *s* of William James Damerell (Lt-Col), MBE and Zoe Damerell; *m* 1942, Margaret Isabel Porritt, *d* of Prof. B. D. Porritt; two *s* three *d. Educ:* ISC; Edinburgh Univ.; Harvard Business Sch. Parent Bd, BPB Industries, 1953-64; Regional Dir, Internat. Wool Secretariat, 1965-73. Governor, Nuffield Nursing Homes Trust, 1974-80; Dir, The Medical Centre; Founder, Independ. Hosp. Gp (Chm., 1975-80); Pres., Internat. Fedn of Voluntary Health Service Funds, 1981- (Dep. Pres., 1980-81); Mem. Bd of Governors, Assoc. Internat. de la Mutualité. *Recreations:* sailing (jt founder, BCYC, 1947); travel. *Address:* Stodham Park, Liss, Hants. *T:* Liss 2316. *Clubs:* various yacht.

DAMMERS, Very Rev. Alfred Hounsell; Dean of Bristol, since 1973; *b* 10 July 1921; *s* of late B. F. H. Dammers, MA, JP; *m* 1947, Brenda Muriel, *d* of late Clifford Stead; two *s* two *d. Educ:* Malvern Coll. (Schol.); Pembroke Coll., Cambridge (Schol., MA); Westcott House, Cambridge. Served RA (Surrey and Sussex Yeo.), 1941-44. Asst Curate, Adlington, Lancs, 1948; Asst Curate S Bartholomew's, Edgbaston, Birmingham, and Lectr at Queen's Coll., Birmingham, 1950; Chaplain and Lectr at S John's Coll., Palayamkottai, S India, 1953; Vicar of Holy Trinity, Millhouses, Sheffield, and Examining Chaplain to Bishop of Sheffield, 1957; Select Preacher at Univ. of Cambridge, 1963; Select Preacher at Univ. of Oxford, 1975; Chairman, Friends of Reunion, 1965; Canon Residentiary and Director of Studies, Coventry Cathedral, 1965. Founder and Central Correspondent, The Life Style Movement, 1972. Companion, Community of the Cross of Nails, 1975. *Publications:* Great Venture, 1958; Ye Shall Receive Power, 1958; All in Each Place, 1962; God is Light, God is Love, 1963; AD 1980, 1966; Lifestyle: a parable of sharing, 1982. *Recreations:* travel (home and abroad); walking, candle making, sailing. *Address:* The Deanery, 20 Charlotte Street, Bristol BS1 5PZ. *T:* Bristol 22443.

DANCE, Brian David, MA; Headmaster, St Dunstan's College, Catford, since 1973; *b* 22 Nov. 1929; *s* of late L. H. Dance and of Mrs M. G. Dance (*née* Shrivelle); *m* 1955, Chloe Elizabeth, *o d* of J. F. A. Baker, *qv* ; two *s* two *d. Educ:* Kingston Grammar Sch.; Wadham Coll., Oxford. BA 1952, MA 1956. Asst Master, Kingston Grammar Sch., 1953-59; Sen. History Master: Faversham Grammar Sch., 1959-62; Westminster City Sch., 1962-65; Headmaster: Cirencester Grammar Sch., 1965-66; Luton Sixth Form Coll., 1966-73. Cambridge Local Examination Syndicate, 1968-73; Headmasters' Assoc. Council, 1968-76 (Exec. Cttee, 1972-76, Hon. Legal Sec. 1975-76). *Publications:* articles in: Times Educnl Supp.; Headmasters' Assoc. 'Review'. *Recreations:* most ball games (especially cricket and Rugby football), music, philately. *Address:* Headmaster's House, St Dunstan's College, Catford SE6 4TY. *T:* 01-690 1277. *Club:* East India, Devonshire, Sports and Public Schools.

DANCKWERTS, Prof. Peter Victor, GC 1940; MBE 1943; FRS 1969; FEng; Shell Professor of Chemical Engineering, Cambridge University, 1959-77, now Emeritus; Fellow of Pembroke College, Cambridge, 1959-77, now Emeritus; *b* 14 Oct. 1916; *s* of late Vice-Adm. V. H. Danckwerts, CMG, and Joyce Danckwerts; *m* 1960, Lavinia, *d* of late Brig.-Gen. D. A. Macfarlane, CB, DSO, KOSB. *Educ:* Winchester Coll.; Balliol Coll., Oxford; Massachusetts Inst. of Technology. BA (chemistry) Oxon, 1938; SM (Chemical Engineering Practice), MIT, 1948; MA Cantab 1948. RNVR, 1940-46. Commonwealth Fund Fellow, MIT, 1946-48; Demonstrator and Lecturer, Dept of Chemical Engineering, Cambridge Univ., 1948-54; Deputy Director of Research and Development, Industrial Group, UK Atomic Energy Authority, 1954-56; Prof. of Chemical Engineering Science, Imperial College of Science and Technology, 1956-59. MIChemE 1955 (President, 1965-66); Hon. FIChemE. Hon. DTech Bradford, 1978; Hon. DSc Loughborough, 1981. For. Hon. Mem., Amer. Acad. of Arts and Scis, 1964;

For. Associate, Nat. Acad. of Engineering, USA, 1978. *Address:* The Abbey House, Abbey Road, Cambridge CB5 8HQ. *T:* Cambridge 357275.

d'ANCONA, John Edward William; Director General, Offshore Supplies Office of the Department of Energy, since 1981; *b* 28 May 1935; *o s* of Adolph and Margaret d'Ancona; *m* 1958, Mary Helen, *o d* of late Sqdn-Ldr R. T. Hunter and late Mrs Hunter; three *s. Educ:* St Edward's Coll., Malta; St Cuthbert's Grammar Sch., Newcastle upon Tyne. BA (Hons) Mod. History, DipEd (Durham). Teacher, 1959-61; Civil Service, 1961-: Asst Principal, Dept of Educn and Science, 1961; Private Sec. to Minister of State, DES, 1964-65; Principal: DES, 1965-67; Min. of Technology and DTI, 1967-74; Asst Sec., DoE, 1974; Under Sec., DoE OSO, 1981. *Recreations:* cricket, philately, wine-bibbing. *Address:* c/o Department of Energy, Thames House South, Millbank, SW1.

DANCY, Prof. John Christopher, MA; Professor of Education, University of Exeter, since 1978; *b* 13 Nov. 1920; *e s* of late Dr J. H. Dancy and Dr N. Dancy; *m* 1944, Angela Bryant; two *s* one *d. Educ:* Winchester (Scholar); New Coll., Oxford (Scholar, MA). 1st Class, Classical Hon. Mods., 1940; Craven Scholar, 1946; Gaisford Greek Prose Prize, 1947; Hertford Scholar, 1947; Arnold Historical Essay Prize, 1949. Served in Rifle Brigade, 1941-46; Capt. GSO(3)I, 30 Corps, 1945; Major, GSO(2)I, 1 Airborne Corps, 1945-46. Lecturer in Classics, Wadham Coll., 1946-48; Asst Master, Winchester Coll., 1948-53; Headmaster of Lancing Coll., 1953-61; Master, Marlborough Coll., 1961-72; Principal, St Luke's Coll. of Educn, Exeter, 1972-78. Member, Public Schools' Commission, 1966-68. *Publications:* Commentary on 1 Maccabees, 1954; The Public Schools and the Future, 1963; Commentary on Shorter Books of Apocrypha, 1972. *Address:* 7 Baring Crescent, Exeter EX1 1TL.

DANGAN, Viscount; Garret Graham Wellesley; *b* 30 March 1965; *s* and *heir* of 7th Earl Cowley, *qv.*

DANIEL, Gerald Ernest, FCA, IPFA, FRVA; MAAT; County Treasurer, Nottinghamshire County Council, since 1974; Director, Horizon Travel Ltd, since 1975; *b* 7 Dec. 1919; *s* of Ernest and Beata May Daniel; *m* 1942, Ecila Roslyn Dillow; one *s* one *d. Educ:* Huish's Grammar Sch., Taunton. Served War, 1939-46, Somerset LI. Various appts in Borough Treasurers' Depts at Taunton, Bexhill and Scunthorpe, 1935-50; Cost and machine accountant, subseq. Chief Accountant, City Treasury, Bristol, 1950-60; Dep. Borough Treasurer, Reading, 1960-64; Borough Treasurer, West Bromwich, 1965-68; City Treasurer, Nottingham, 1968-74. President: Nottingham Soc. of Chartered Accountants, 1976; Assoc. of Public Service Finance Officers, 1978; Soc. of County Treasurers, 1979; Member Council: CIPFA, 1971-; Assoc. of Accounting Technicians, 1981-. *Recreations:* gardening, music. *Address:* County Hall, West Bridgford, Nottingham NG2 7QP. *T:* Nottingham 863366; 242 Melton Road, Edwalton, Nottingham. *T:* Nottingham 231025. *Club:* Royal Over-Seas League.

DANIEL, Prof. Glyn Edmund, MA, LittD; FBA 1982; Fellow of St John's College, Cambridge, since 1938; Disney Professor of Archæology, University of Cambridge, 1974-81, Emeritus Professor since 1981 (Lecturer, 1948-74); *b* 23 April 1914; *o s* of John Daniel and Mary Jane (*née* Edmunds); *m* 1946, Ruth, *d* of late Rev. R. W. B. Langhorne, Exeter. *Educ:* Barry County Sch.; University College, Cardiff; St John's Coll., Cambridge (Scholar; BA 1st Class Hons with Distinction, Archaeological and Anthropological Tripos). Strathcona Student, 1936; Allen Scholar, 1937; Wallenberg Prizeman, 1937; Research Fellowship, St John's Coll., 1938; PhD 1938; MA 1939; LittD 1962. Intelligence Officer, RAF, 1940-45; in charge Photo Interpretation, India and SE Asia, 1942-45 (despatches); Wing Comdr, 1943. Faculty Asst Lectr in Archaeology, 1945-48; Steward of St John's Coll., 1946-55; Leverhulme Research Fellow, 1948-50. Lecturer: Munro, Archaeology, Edinburgh Univ., 1954; Rhys, British Acad., 1954; O'Donnell, Edinburgh Univ., 1956; Josiah Mason, Birmingham Univ., 1956; Gregynog University College, Wales, 1968; Ballard-Matthews, University Coll. of North Wales, 1968; George Grant MacCurdy, Harvard, 1971. Visiting Prof., Univ. Aarhus, 1968; Ferrens Prof., Univ. Hull, 1969. Pres., South Eastern Union of Scientific Socs, 1955. President: Bristol and Gloucestershire Archaeological Soc., 1962-63; RAI, 1977-79. Fellow, UC Cardiff, 1981. Hon. Mem. Istituto Italiano di Preistoria e Protostoria; Corresponding Fellow, German Archaeological Institute; Corresponding Mem., Jutland Archaeological Soc.; Foreign Hon. Mem., Archaeol Inst. of Amer. Editor, Ancient Peoples and Places, and of Antiquity, since 1958. Director: Anglia Television, Ltd, 1959-81; Antiquity Publications Ltd; Trustee, Cambridge Arts Theatre. FSA 1942. Knight (First Class) of the Dannebrog, 1961. *Publications:* The Three Ages, 1942; A Hundred Years of Archaeology, 1950; The Prehistoric Chamber Tombs of England and Wales, 1950; A Picture Book of Ancient British Art (with S. Piggott), 1951; Lascaux and Carnac, 1955; ed Myth or Legend, 1955; Barclodiad y Gawres (with T. G. E. Powell), 1956; The Megalith Builders of Western Europe, 1958; The Prehistoric Chamber Tombs of France, 1960; The Idea of Prehistory, 1961; The Hungry Archaeologist in France, 1963; New Grange and the Bend of the Boyne (with late S. P. O'Riordain), 1964; (ed with I. Ll. Foster), Prehistoric and Early Wales, 1964; Man Discovers his Past, 1966; The Origins and Growth of Archaeology, 1967; The First Civilisations, 1968; Archaeology and the History of Art, 1970; Megaliths in History, 1973; (ed jtly) France before the Romans, 1974; A Hundred and Fifty Years of Archaeology, 1975; Cambridge and the Back-Looking Curiosity: an inaugural lecture, 1976; A Short History of Archaeology, 1981; (ed) Towards a History of Archaeology,

1981; and articles in archaeological journals. *Recreations:* travel, walking, swimming, food, wine, writing detective stories (The Cambridge Murders, 1945; Welcome Death, 1954). *Address:* The Flying Stag, 70 Bridge Street, Cambridge. *T:* 356082; La Marnière, Zouafques-par-Tournehem, 62890 France. *T:* Calais 35.61.40. *Club:* United Oxford & Cambridge University.

DANIEL, Sir Goronwy Hopkin, KCVO 1969; CB 1962; DPhil Oxon; HM Lieutenant for Dyfed, since 1978; Principal, Aberystwyth University College, 1969-79; Vice-Chancellor, University of Wales, 1977-79; *b* Ystradgynlais, 21 March 1914; *s* of David Daniel; *m* 1940, Lady Valerie, *d* of 2nd Earl Lloyd George; one *s* two *d*. *Educ:* Pontardawe Secondary Sch.; Amman Valley County Sch.; University College of Wales, Aberystwyth; Jesus Coll., Oxford (Hon. Fellow, 1979). Fellow of University of Wales; Meyricke Scholar, Jesus Coll.; Oxford Institute of Statistics, 1937-40; Lecturer, Dept of Economics, Bristol Univ., 1940-41; Clerk, House of Commons, 1941-43; Ministry of Town and Country Planning, 1943-47; Ministry of Fuel and Power, Chief Statistician, 1947-55; Under-Sec., Coal Div., 1955-62, Gen. Div., 1962-64; Permanent Under-Sec. of State, Welsh Office, 1964-69. Chm., British Nat. Conf. on Social Welfare, 1970; Pres., West Wales Assoc. for the Arts, 1971-; Chm., Welsh Fourth TV Channel Authority, 1981-; Member: Welsh Language Council, 1974-78; Gen. Adv. Council, BBC, 1974-79; Adv. Council on Energy Conservation, 1977-79; SSRC, 1980-; Dep. Chm., Prince of Wales Cttee, 1980-. Dir, Commercial Bank of Wales, 1972-. Chairman: Home-Grown Timber Adv. Cttee, 1974-81; Cttee on Water Charges in Wales, 1974-75. Hon. LLD, Univ. of Wales, 1980. Hon. Freeman, City of London, 1982. *Publications:* papers in statistical, fuel and power, and other journals. *Recreations:* country pursuits, sailing. *Address:* Ridge Farm, Letterston, Dyfed. *T:* Letterston 586. *Club:* Travellers'.

DANIEL, Gruffydd Huw Morgan; a Recorder of the Crown Court, since 1980; *b* 16 April 1939; *s* of Prof. John Edward Daniel, MA, and Catherine Megan Daniel; *m* 1968, Phyllis Margaret (*née* Bermingham); one *d*. *Educ:* Ampleforth; University College of Wales (LLB); Inns of Court School of Law. Commissioned 2nd Lieut First Bn Royal Welch Fusiliers, 1959; Captain 6/7 Bn Royal Welch Fusiliers (TA), 1965. Called to the Bar, Gray's Inn, 1967; Wales and Chester Circuit (Circuit Junior, 1975). *Publication:* contributor to Ampleforth Country, 1957. *Recreations:* gardening, shooting, fishing, sailing. *Address:* (residence) Wern Isaf, Halfway Bridge, Bangor, Gwynedd; Sedan House, Stanley Place, Chester. *T:* Chester 20480; 10 Stanley Place, Chester. *Clubs:* Reform; Royal Anglesey Yacht.

DANIEL, Jack; *see* Daniel R. J.

DANIEL, Norman Alexander, CBE 1974 (OBE 1968); PhD; General Secretary, Coptic Archaeological Society, Cairo, and Planning Adviser, Hassan Khalifa, since 1979; *b* 8 May 1919; *s* of George Frederick Daniel and Winifred Evelyn (*née* Jones); *m* 1941, Marion Ruth (*d* 1981), *d* of Harold Wadham Pethybridge; one *s*. *Educ:* Frensham Heights Sch.; Queen's Coll., Oxford (BA); Edinburgh Univ. (PhD). Asst Dir, British Inst., Basra, 1947; British Council Asst Representative: Baghdad, 1948; Beirut, 1952; Edinburgh, 1953; Dir, Brit. Inst., Baghdad, 1957; Dep. Rep., Brit. Council, Scotland, 1960; Brit. Council Rep., Sudan, 1962; Vis. Fellow, University Coll., Cambridge, 1969-70; Dir, Visitors Dept, Brit. Council, London, 1970; Cultural Attaché, Cairo, 1971; British Council Rep. and Cultural Counsellor, British Embassy, Cairo, 1973-79. Egyptian Order of Merit, 2nd class, 1977. *Publications:* Islam and the West: the making of an image, 1960, 3rd edn 1966, repr. 1980; Islam, Europe and Empire, 1966; The Arabs and Mediaeval Europe, 1975, enlarged and rev. edn 1979; The Cultural Barrier, 1975; (contrib.) History of the Crusades, vol. 5 (Wisconsin, in progress); (contrib.) Islam: Past Influence and Future Challenge (ed Cachia), 1979; contrib. to learned jls. *Recreations:* gardening, mediaeval history, history of intercultural relations. *Address:* 1 rue Masna al-Tarabich, Abbasiah, Cairo, Egypt; Landmark, Flimwell, Wadhurst, East Sussex TN5 7PA. *T:* Flimwell 325.

DANIEL, Prof. Peter Maxwell, MA, MB, BCh Cambridge; MA, DM Oxon; DSc London; FRCP; FRCS; FRCPath; FRCPsych; FLS; FInstBiol; Senior Research Fellow, Department of Applied Physiology and Surgical Science, Institute of Basic Medical Sciences, Royal College of Surgeons, since 1976; Emeritus Professor, lately Professor of Neuropathology, University of London, at the Institute of Psychiatry, Maudsley Hospital, 1957-76; Hon. Consultant Neuropathologist, the Bethlem Royal and Maudsley Hospitals, 1956-76; *b* 14 Nov. 1910; *s* of Peter Daniel, FRCS, surgeon to Charing Cross Hospital, and Beatrice Laetitia Daniel; *m* 1st, Sarah Shelford; two *s* three *d*; 2nd, F. Dawn Bosanquet; one *s*; 3rd, Marion F. Bosanquet. *Educ:* Westminster Sch.; St John's Coll., Cambridge; New Coll., Oxford. Hon. Consultant Pathologist, Radcliffe Infirmary, 1948-56; Senior Research Officer, University of Oxford, 1949-56; Hon. Consultant in Neuropathology to the Army at Home, 1952-76. Emeritus Fellow, Leverhulme Trust, 1978-80; Vis. Sen. Res. Fellow, St Thomas's Hosp. Med. Sch., 1981-; Hon. Librarian, RCPath, 1981-. John Hunter Medal and Triennial Prize, 1946-48, and Erasmus Wilson Lectr, 1964, RCS. Editorial Board of: Jl of Physiology, 1958-65; Jl of Neurology, Neurosurgery and Psychiatry, 1953-64; Journal of Neuroendocrinology, 1966-77; Brain, 1974-76; Qly Jl Exp. Physiol., 1980-. President: British Neuropathological Society, 1963-64; Neurological Section, RSM, 1970-71; Harveian Soc. London, 1966 (Trustee, 1971-); Section of Hist. of Med., RSM, 1979-82; Osler Club, 1979-82; Mem. Council: Royal Microscopical Soc., 1968-72; Neonatal Soc., 1959-61; Assoc. of British

Neurologists, 1966-69; Med. Soc. of London, 1981-. Hon. Mem., Physiological Soc., 1981. Member: Bd of Govs, Bethlem Royal and Maudsley Hosps, 1966-75; Council, Charing Cross Hosp. Medical Sch., 1972-. Chm., Academic Bd, Inst. of Psychiatry, 1966-70; Vice-Chm., Central Academic Council, British Postgrad. Med. Fedn, 1975-76. Life Mem., Anatomical Soc. (of GB. Liveryman, Soc. of Apothecaries, 1952-. *Publications:* (jointly) Studies of the Renal Circulation, 1947; The Hypothalamus and Pituitary Gland, 1975; papers in various medical and scientific journals. *Address:* 5 Seaforth Place, Buckingham Gate, SW1E 6AB. *T:* 01-834 3087. *Clubs:* Athenæum, Garrick, Savage, Green Room.

DANIEL, (Reginald) Jack, OBE 1958; FEng, FRINA, FIMarE; RCNC; Member of the Board, British Shipbuilders, 1979, Managing Director, Warshipbuilding, 1980; *b* 27 Feb. 1920; *o s* of Reginald Daniel Daniel and Florence Emily (*née* Woods); *m* 1st, Joyce Earnshaw (marr. diss.); two *s*; 2nd, 1977, Elizabeth, *o d* of George Mitchell, Long Ashton, Som. *Educ:* Royal Naval Engineering Coll., Keyham; Royal Naval Coll., Greenwich. Grad., 1942; subseq. engaged in submarine design. Served War of 1939-45; Staff of C-in-C's Far East Fleet and Pacific Fleet, 1943-45. Atomic Bomb Tests, Bikini, 1946; Admty, Whitehall, 1947-49; Admty, Bath, Aircraft Carrier Design, 1949-52; Guided Missile Cruiser design, 1952-56; Nuclear and Polaris Submarine design, 1956-65; IDC, 1966; Materials, R&D, 1967-68; Head of Forward Design, 1968-70; Director, Submarine Design and Production, 1970-74; Dir-Gen. Ships and Head of RCNC, MoD, 1974-79. Vice Pres., RINA, 1982. Liveryman, Worshipful Co. of Shipwrights, 1980. Hon. Res. Fellow, UCL, 1974; Founder Fellow, Fellowship of Engineering, 1976. *Publications:* Warship Design, New Concepts and New Technology, Parsons Meml Lecture, 1976; papers for RINA, etc. *Recreations:* gardening, motoring, music. *Address:* Meadowland, Cleveland Walk, Bath BA2 6JU.

DANIELL, Brig. Averell John, CBE 1955; DSO 1945; *b* 19 June 1903; *s* of late Lt-Col Oswald James Daniell, QO Royal West Kent Regt, and late May Frances Drummond Daniell (*née* Adams); *m* 1934, Phyllis Kathleen Rhona Grove-Annesley; two *s* one *d*. *Educ:* Wellington Coll.; RM Acad., Woolwich. Commissioned, Royal Field Artillery, 1923; Captain, RA, 1936; Major, 1940; Lt-Col, 1943. Served War of 1939-45; Middle East, Iraq, Burma. Col, 1948; Brig., 1952; retired, 1955. Administrative Officer, Staff Coll., Camberley, 1955-61. Colonel Commandant, Royal Artillery, 1956-66. *Address:* Oak Lodge, Hillside Street, Hythe, Kent. *T:* Hythe 66494.

DANIELL, Sir Peter (Averell), Kt 1971; TD 1950; DL; Senior Government Broker, 1963-73; *b* 8 Dec. 1909; *s* of R. H. A. Daniell and Kathleen Daniell (*née* Monsell); *m* 1935, Leonie M. Harrison; two *s* one *d*. *Educ:* Eton Coll.; Trinity Coll., Oxford (MA). Joined Mullens & Co., 1932, Partner, 1945; retd 1973. Served KRRC, 1939-45, Middle East and Italy. Master, Drapers' Co., 1980-81. DL Surrey 1976. *Recreations:* shooting, fishing, golf. *Address:* Glebe House, Buckland, Surrey. *T:* Betchworth 2320. *Clubs:* Brooks's, Alpine.

DANIELL, Ralph Allen, CBE 1965 (OBE 1958); HM Diplomatic Service, retired; *b* 26 Jan. 1915; 2nd *s* of late Reginald Allen Daniell; *m* 1943, Diana Lesley (*née* Tyndale); one *s* three *d*. *Educ:* Lancing Coll.; University Coll., Oxford. Appointed to Board of Trade, 1937. Joined HM Forces, 1942; served with Royal Tank Regt in North Africa and Italian campaigns, 1943-45. Appointed to HM Foreign Service as First Sec., 1946; Mexico City, 1946; Rome, 1949; Foreign Office, 1951; Helsinki, 1953; Counsellor, 1958; Washington, 1958; New York, 1959; Cairo, 1962; Wellington, 1967; Consul-Gen., Chicago, 1972-74. *Address:* The Old Forge, Poulner, Ringwood, Hants BH24 1TY.

DANIELL, Roy Lorentz, CBE 1957; Barrister-at-Law; Charity Commissioner, 1953-62; *s* of late Edward Cecil Daniell, Abbotswood, Speen, Bucks; *m* 1936, Sheila Moore-Gwyn, *d* of late Maj. Moore-Gwyn, Clayton Court, Liss, Hants. *Educ:* Gresham's Sch., Holt; New Coll., Oxford. *Address:* Common Side, Russell's Water, Henley on Thames, Oxon. *T:* Nettlebed 641696. *Club:* United Oxford & Cambridge University.

DANIELLI, Prof. James Frederic, FRS 1957; PhD, DSc, MIBiol; Director, Danielli Associates, since 1980; *b* 13 Nov. 1911; *s* of James Frederic Danielli; *m* 1937, Mary Guy; one *s* one *d*. *Educ:* Wembley County Sch.; London, Princeton and Cambridge Univs. Commonwealth Fund Fellow, 1933-35; Beit Medical Research Fellow, 1938-42; Fellow of St John's Coll., Cambridge, 1942-45; Physiologist to Marine Biological Assoc., 1946; Reader in Cell Physiology, Royal Cancer Hospital, 1946-49; Prof. of Zoology, King's Coll., London, 1949-62; Chm., Dept of Biochemical Pharmacology, Univ. of Buffalo, 1962-65; Provost for Faculty of Natural Sciences and Mathematics, 1967-69; State Univ. of NY at Buffalo (formerly Univ. of Buffalo, NY); Prof. and Chm., Life Scis Dept, Worcester Polytechnic Inst., Mass, 1974-80. *Publications:* Permeability of Natural Membranes (with H. Davson), 1943; Cell Physiology and Pharmacology, 1950; Cytochemistry: a critical approach, 1953; Editor: Journal of Theoretical Biology; Jl of Social and Biol Structures; Internat. Review of Cytology; Progress in Surface and Membrane Science. *Address:* Danielli Associates Inc., 185 Highland Street, Worcester, Mass 01609, USA; Tangnefedd, Dinas Cross, Dyfed, Wales.

DANIELS, David Kingsley, CBE 1963 (OBE 1945); retired as Secretary-General, Royal Commonwealth Society (1958-67); *b* 17 Feb. 1905; *y s* of late E. Daniels and Anne M. Daniels; unmarried. *Educ:* Kent Coll., Canterbury;

St Edmund Hall, Oxford. Colonial Administrative Service, Tanganyika, 1928; King's African Rifles, 1940; Chief Staff Officer, Military Admin., Somalia, 1941 (despatches); Senior Civil Affairs Officer, Reserved Areas, Ethiopia, 1943-45 (OBE); Chief Secretary (Colonel), Military Administration, Malaya, 1945-46; Principal Asst Secretary, Singapore, 1947-49; Under Secretary, Singapore, 1950-52; Dep. Chief Secretary, Federation of Malaya, 1952-55; Dir, Malayan Students Dept in UK, 1956-58. *Address:* Lord's Acre, Red Lane, Cloudside, near Congleton, Cheshire. *Clubs:* Royal Commonwealth Society, MCC.

DANIELS, George, MBE 1982; FSA, FBHI; author, watch maker, horological consultant; *b* 19 Aug. 1926; *s* of George Daniels and Beatrice (*née* Cadou); *m* 1964, Juliet Anne (*née* Marryat); one *d*. *Educ:* elementary. 2nd Bn E Yorks Regt, 1944-47. Started professional horology, 1947; restoration of historical watches, 1956-; hand watch making to own designs, 1969-. President: British Horological Inst., 1980 (Fellow, 1951); British Clock and Watchmakers' Benevolent Soc., 1980. Worshipful Co. of Clockmakers: Liveryman, 1968; Warden, 1977; Master, 1980; Tompion Gold Medal, 1981; Asst Hon. Surveyor. FSA 1976. Arts, Sciences and Learning Award, City Corporation, London, 1974; Victor Kullberg Medal, Stockholm Watch Guild, 1977; Gold Medal, British Horol Inst., 1981. *Publications:* Watches (jtly), 1965 (3rd edn 1978); English and American Watches, 1967; The Art of Breguet, 1975 (2nd edn 1978); (jtly) Clocks and Watches of the Worshipful Company of Clockmakers, 1975; Sir David Salomons Collection, 1978; Watchmaking, 1981. *Recreations:* vintage cars, fast motorcycles, opera, Scotch whisky. *Address:* 34 New Bond Street, W1A 2AA.

DANIELS, Harold Albert; *b* 8 June 1915; *s* of Albert Pollikett Daniels and Eleanor Sarah Maud Daniels (*née* Flahey); *m* 1946, Frances Victoria Jerdan; one *s*. *Educ:* Mercers' Sch.; Christ's Coll., Cambridge. BA 1937; Wren Prize 1938; MA 1940. Asst Principal, Post Office, 1938; Admiralty, 1942; Post Office, 1945; Principal, 1946; Asst Sec., 1950; Under-Sec., 1961; Min. of Posts and Telecommunications, 1969. Asst Under Sec. of State, Home Office, 1974-76. *Address:* Lyle Court Cottage, Bradbourne Road, Sevenoaks, Kent. *T:* Sevenoaks 454039.

DANIELS, Prof. Henry Ellis, FRS 1980; Professor of Mathematical Statistics, University of Birmingham, 1957-78, now Emeritus Professor; Senior Research Associate, Statistical Laboratory, University of Cambridge, 1978-81; *b* 2 Oct. 1912; *s* of Morris and Hannah Daniels; *m* 1950, Barbara Edith Pickering; one *s* one *d*. *Educ:* Sciennes Sch., Edinburgh; George Heriot's Sch., Edinburgh; Edinburgh Univ.; Clare Coll., Cambridge. MA Edinburgh 1933, BA Cantab 1935, PhD Edinburgh 1943. Statistician, Wool Industries Research Assoc., 1935-47; Ministry of Aircraft Production, 1942-45; Lecturer in Mathematics, University of Cambridge, 1947-57; Fellow, King's Coll. Cambridge, 1975-76. Pres., Royal Statistical Soc., 1974-75; Fellow Inst. of Mathematical Statistics; elected Mem. Internat. Statistical Inst., 1956. Freeman, Clockmakers' Co., 1981. Guy Medal (Silver) Royal Statistical Society. *Publications:* papers in Journal of the Royal Statistical Society, Annals of Mathematical Statistics, Biometrika, etc. *Recreations:* playing the English concertina, repairing watches. *Address:* 12 Kimberley Road, Cambridge CB4 1HH. *T:* Cambridge 313402.

DANIELS, Jeffery; Director, Geffrye Museum, London, since 1969; *b* 13 July 1932; *s* of John Henry and Edith Mary Daniels. *Educ:* Milford Haven Grammar Sch.; Balliol Coll., Oxford. Read Modern History; MA Oxon. Heal & Son Ltd, 1953-56; Teaching (ILEA), 1956-69. Member: Internat. Consultative Cttee for Mostra di Sebastiano Ricci, Udine, 1976-; History of Art and Complementary Studies Bd, CNAA, 1975-80; Hon. Sec., London Fedn of Museums and Art Galls. Member: AICA (Pres., British Section, 1980-); Assoc. of Art Historians; Cttee, Thirties Soc., 1979-. *Publications:* Architecture in England, 1968; Biography and catalogue raisonné of Sebastiano Ricci, 1976 (Italian edn, L'Opera Completa di Sebastiano Ricci, 1976); Michelangelo, 1982; contrib. to: The Times, The Connoisseur, Apollo, The Burlington Magazine, The Listener; Art News (USA). *Recreations:* opera, ballet, Venice. *Address:* 5 Edith Grove, Chelsea, SW10 0JZ. *T:* 01-352 7692. *Club:* Society of Authors.

DANIELS, Laurence John, CB 1979; OBE 1970; Secretary, Department of Capital Territory, Australia, 1977-81, retired; *b* 11 Aug. 1916; *s* of Leslie Daniels and Margaret (*née* Bradley); *m* 1943, Joyce Carey; two *s* eight *d*. *Educ:* Rostrevor Coll., South Australia; Sydney Univ. (BEc 1943). AASA 1939. Commonwealth (Australian) Taxation Office, 1934-53; Commonwealth Dept of Health, 1953-72; Director-General, Dept of Social Security, 1973-77. *Address:* 5 Nares Crest, Forrest, ACT 2603, Australia. *T:* 062-95 1896.

DANILOVA, Alexandra, lecturer, teacher and choreographer, actress; *b* Pskoff, Russia, 20 Nov. 1906; *d* of Dionis Daniloff and Claudia Gotovzeffa; *m* 1st, 1931, Giuseppe Massera (*d* 1936); 2nd, 1941, Kazimir Kokic (marr. annulled, 1949). *Educ:* Theatrical Sch., Petrograd. Maryinski Theatre, Leningrad, 1923-24; Diaghileff Company, 1925-29; Waltzes from Vienna, 1931; Colonel de Basil Company, 1933-37; Prima Ballerina, Ballet Russe de Monte Carlo, 1938-58. Teacher (on Faculty) of School of American Ballet. Guest artist Royal Festival Hall, London, 1955; Ballerina in Oh Captain (Musical), New York, 1958. With own Company has toured West Indies, Japan, Philippines, USA, Canada and S Africa. Capezio Award (for outstanding services to Art of the Dance), 1958; Guest Choreographer Metropolitan Opera House, Guest Teacher and Choreographer, Germany

(Krefeld Festival of Dance) and Amsterdam, 1959-60; Choreographed Coppelia for La Scala di Milano, 1961; Lecture performances throughout US; Guest Choreographer, Washington Ballet, 1962-64. Choreographed Coppelia (with George Balanchine), NY City Ballet, 1975. Screen acting debut in film, The Turning Point, 1977. *Recreations:* needlework, ping-pong, gardening. *Address:* Carnegie House, 100 West 57 Street, New York, NY 10019, USA.

DANINOS, Pierre; French Author; *b* Paris, 26 May 1913; *m* 1st, 1942, Jane Marrain; one *s* two *d*; 2nd, 1968, Marie-Pierre Dourneau. *Educ:* Lycée Janson de Sailly, Paris. Began to write for newspapers, 1931; reporter for French press in England, USA, etc. Liaison agent with British Army, Dunkirk, 1940. Published first book in Rio de Janeiro, 1940; returned to France, 1941, from South America, Chronicler for Le Figaro. *Publications:* Les Carnets du Bon Dieu (Prix Interallié 1947); L'Eternel Second, 1949; Sonia les autres et moi (Prix Courteline, 1952) (English trans., Life with Sonia, 1958); Les Carnets du Major Thompson, 1954 (English trans., Major Thompson Lives in France, 1955); Le Secret du Major Thompson, 1956 (English trans., Major Thompson and I, 1957); Vacances à Tous Prix, 1958; Un certain Monsieur Blot, 1960 (English trans., 1961); Le Jacassin, 1962; Snobissimo, 1964; Le 36ème dessous, 1966; Le Major Tricolore, 1968; Ludovic Morateur, 1970; Le Pyjama, 1972; Les Touristocrates, 1974; Made in France, 1977; La Composition d'Histoire, 1979; Le Veuf Joyeux, 1981. *Recreations:* tennis, ski-ing, collecting British hobbies. *Address:* 81 rue de Grenelle, Paris 7e, France.

DANKERT, Pieter; President of the European Parliament, since 1982 (Member, since 1977); *b* Jan. 1934; *m* 1962, Paulette Puig; one *s* two *d*. *Educ:* Amsterdam Free Univ. Mem. (Partij van de Arbeid) Tweede Kamer, Netherlands; formerly: Internat. Sec., Partij van de Arbeid; Mem., NATO Assembly, WEU Assembly and Assembly of Council of Europe. *Address:* Secretariat of the European Parliament, Post Box 1601, Centre Européen, Kirchberg, Luxembourg; Hoogstraat 1, 1135 BZ Edam, Netherlands.

DANKS, Sir Alan (John), KBE 1970; Chairman, (NZ) University Grants Committee, 1966-77, retired; Director (non-executive): ICI (NZ); Norwich Winterthur (NZ); Norwich Union Life (NZ); *b* 9 June 1914; *s* of T. E. Danks; *m* 1943, Loma Beryl Hall (*née* Drabble). *Educ:* West Christchurch High Sch.; Univ. of Canterbury, NZ. Teaching profession, 1931-43; Economics Dept of Univ. of Canterbury, 1943-66; Prof., 1962; Pro-Vice Chancellor of Univ. of Canterbury, 1964. Hon. LLD Canterbury, 1973. *Address:* 116 Upland Road, Wellington, New Zealand. *Club:* Wellington, NZ.

DANKWORTH, Mrs C. D.; *see* Laine, Cleo.

DANKWORTH, John Philip William, CBE 1974; FRAM 1973; musician; *b* 20 Sept. 1927; British; *m* 1958, Cleo Laine, *qv*; one *s* one *d*. *Educ:* Monoux Grammar Sch. Studied Royal Academy of Music, 1944-46. ARAM 1969. Closely involved with post-war development of British jazz, 1947-60; formed large jazz orchestra, 1953. Composed works for combined jazz and symphonic musicians including: Improvisations (with Matyas Seiber, 1959); Escapade (commissioned by Northern Sinfonia Orch., 1967); Tom Sawyer's Saturday, for narrator and orchestra (commissioned by Farnham Festival), 1967; String Quartet, 1971; Piano Concerto (commissioned by Westminster Festival, 1972). Many important film scores (1964-) including: Saturday Night and Sunday Morning, Darling, The Servant, Morgan, Accident; other works include: Palabras, 1970; dialogue and lyrics for Colette, Comedy, 1980. Variety Club of GB Show Business Personality Award (with Cleo Laine), 1977. Hon. MA Open Univ., 1975. *Recreations:* driving, household maintenance. *Address:* The Old Rectory, Wavendon, Milton Keynes MK17 8LT; World Wide Management, Laurie Mansfield, International Artistes Representation, 235 Regent Street, W1. *T:* 01-439 8401.

DANN, Howard Ernest, CBE 1965; Director, Snowy Mountains Engineering Corporation, 1970-74, and Commissioner, Snowy Mountains Hydro-Electric Authority, 1967-74; *b* 27 April 1914; *m* 1946, Marjorie Bush; two *s*. *Educ:* Brighton Grammar Sch. (Dux); University of Melbourne (BMechE). AIF, 1940-44; Major RAEME. Supt. Engineer, Electric Authority of NSW, 1946-50; Member Commonwealth and States Snowy River Cttee, 1946-49 (NSW Representative, Techn. Cttee); Chief Engineer Investigations, Snowy Mountains Hydro-Electric Authority, prior to Associate Comr, Snowy Mountains Hydro-Electric Authority, 1959-67. FIEAust, MASCE. *Publications:* papers in journals of Instn of Engrs (Australia) and American Society of Civil Engineers. *Recreation:* golf. *Address:* 18 Rookwood Street, North Balwyn, Vic 3104, Australia. *T:* 859.4428.

DANN, Mrs Jill; *b* 10 Sept. 1929; *d* of Harold Norman Cartwright and Marjorie Alice Thornton; *m* 1952, Anthony John Dann; two *s* two *d* (and one *s* decd). *Educ:* Solihull High Sch. for Girls, Malvern Hall; Birmingham Univ. (LLB); St Hilda's Coll., Oxford (BCL). Called to the Bar, Inner Temple, 1952. Mayoress of Chippenham, 1964-65. Church Commissioner, 1968-; Member: General Synod of Church of England, and of its Standing Cttee, 1971-; Crown Appointments Commn, 1977-. Dir, Wiltshire Radio, 1981-. Chm., Chippenham Old People's Housing Assoc.; Pres., Inner Wheel, 1978-79. *Recreations:* reading, sport. *Address:* Harnish Mead, 30 Hardenhuish Lane, Chippenham, Wilts SN14 6HN. *T:* Chippenham 3142.

DANN, Most Rev. Robert William; *see* Melbourne, Archbishop of.

DANNATT, Prof. (James) Trevor, MA; ARA 1977; FRIBA; Senior Partner, Trevor Dannatt & Partners, Architects; Professor of Architecture, Manchester University, since 1975; *b* 15 Jan. 1920; *s* of George Herbert and Jane Ellen Dannatt; *m* 1953, Joan Howell Davies; one *s* one *d. Educ:* Colfes Sch.; Sch. of Architecture, Regent Polytechnic (Dip. Arch.). Professional experience in office of Jane B. Drew and E. Maxwell Fry, 1943-48; Architects Dept, LCC (Royal Festival Hall Gp), 1948-52; commenced private practice, 1952. Vis. Prof., Washington Univ., St Louis, 1976. Assessor for national and international architectural competitions; Mem., Cathedrals Adv. Commn. Editor, Architects' Year Book, 1945-62. Architectural work includes private houses, housing, school, university and welfare buildings, conservation and restoration; apptd Architects for British Embassy, Riyadh, 1980. Won internat. competition for conference complex in Riyadh, Saudi Arabia, 1974. *Publications:* Modern Architecture in Britain, 1959; Trevor Dannatt: Buildings and Interiors 1951-72, 1972; contribs to Architectural Rev., Architects' Jl, and various foreign journals. *Recreations:* the arts, including architecture. *Address:* 115 Crawford Street, W1. *T:* 01-486 6844. *Club:* Travellers'.

DANSON, Hon. Barnett Jerome, PC (Canada); Chairman, CSPG Consultants; Vice-Chairman, de Havilland Aircraft of Canada Ltd; Director, Victoria & Grey Trust Co.; *b* Toronto, Ont, 8 Feb. 1921; *s* of Joseph B. Danson and Saidie W. Danson, Toronto; *m* 1943, Isobel, *d* of Robert John Bull, London, England; four *s. Educ:* Toronto public and high schs. Served War: enlisted Queen's Own Rifles as Rifleman, 1939; commnd, 1943; wounded in France, 1944; retd 1945, Lieut. Manager, Jos. B. Danson & Sons Ltd, Toronto, 1945-50; Sales Man., Maple Leaf Plastics Ltd, 1950-53; Principal (Pres.), Danson Corp. Ltd, Scarborough, 1953-74. Active in Liberal Party, 1946-: MP (L) for York North, 1968-79; Parly Sec. to Prime Minister Trudeau, 1970-72; Minister of State for Urban Affairs, 1974-76; Minister of Nat. Defence, Canada, 1976-79; former Mem., Standing Cttee on Finance, Trade and Econ. Affairs, and Ext. Affairs and National Defence. Former Pres. and first Chm. Bd, Soc. of Plastics Engineers Inc. Former Member: Bd of Trade of Metrop. Toronto; Canadian Manufacturers Assoc.; Canadian Chamber of Commerce. *Recreations:* fishing, reading, music. *Address:* CSPG Consultants, 1804 Royal Trust Tower, Box 35, Toronto-Dominion Centre, Toronto M5K 1C4, Canada. *T:* 866-2800; 133 Seaton Street, Toronto M5A 2T2.

DANTZIC, Roy Matthew, CA; Member for Finance, British National Oil Corporation, since 1981; *b* 4 July 1944; *s* of David and Renee Dantzic; *m* 1969, Diane Clapham; one *s* one *d. Educ:* Brighton Coll., Sussex. CA 1968. Coopers & Lybrand, 1962-69; Kleinwort, Benson Ltd, 1970-72; Drayton Corporation Ltd, which merged in 1974 with Samuel Montagu & Co. Ltd, 1972-80 (Exec. Dir, 1975; Mem., Management Cttee, 1979); BNOC, Man. Dir, Finance and Planning, 1980-. *Recreations:* playing golf, watching cricket. *Address:* 12 Bedford Road, Moor Park, Northwood, Mddx HA6 2AZ. *Clubs:* MCC; Moor Park Golf.

DAR-ES-SALAAM, Archbishop of, (RC), since 1969; HE Cardinal Laurean Rugambwa; *b* Bukongo, 12 July 1912; *s* of Domitian Rushubirwa and Asteria Mukaboshezi. *Educ:* Rutabo, Rubya Seminary; Katigondo Seminary; Univ. of Propaganda, Rome (DCL 1951). Priest 1943; Bishop of Rutabo, 1952-60; Cardinal 1960; Bishop of Bukoba, 1960-69. Member: Knights of Columbus; Knights of St Peter Claver. Hon. Dr of Laws: Notre Dame, 1961; St Joseph's Coll., Philadelphia, 1961; Rosary Hill Coll., Buffalo, 1965; Hon. DHL New Rochelle, 1961; Hon. Dr Civil and Canon Law, Georgetown Univ. (Jesuits), 1961; Giving of the Scroll, Catholic Univ. of America, 1961. *Address:* Archbishop's House, PO Box 167, Dar-es-Salaam, Tanzania, East Africa.

DAR-ES-SALAAM, Bishop of, since 1965; Rt. Rev. John Sepeku. *Educ:* Hegongo Theological College. Deacon, 1938; priest, 1940; Curate, Diocese of Zanzibar, 1938-55; Priest-in-charge, 1955-60; Canon of Zanzibar, 1957-60; Archdeacon of Magila, 1960-63; Vicar-General of Zanzibar, 1963-65; Assistant Bishop of Zanzibar, 1963-65; Archbishop of Tanzania, 1970-78. *Address:* PO Box 25016, Ilala, Dar-es-Salaam, Tanzania, E Africa.

DARBISHIRE, David Harold, JP; Chairman, FMC plc, since 1975; *b* 23 Oct. 1914; *s* of H. D. Darbishire and Hester E. Bright (*g d* of Rt Hon. John Bright, MP); *m* 1939, Phebe Irene Lankester, *d* of Captain Felix Lankester, MC; three *d. Educ:* Sidcot; Wye Agric. Coll. (Wye DipAgric). Farmer; Vice-Pres., NFU, 1971-74. Mem., Metrication Bd, 1970-77. *Recreations:* hunting, fishing. *Address:* Manor Farm, Wormleighton, Leamington Spa CV33 0XW. *Club:* Farmers'.

DARBOURNE, John William Charles, CBE 1977; RIBA; Partner, Darbourne & Darke, Architects and Landscape Planners, since 1961; *b* 11 Jan. 1935; *s* of late William Leslie Darbourne and Violet Yorke; *m* 1960, Noreen Fifield; one *s* three *d. Educ:* Battersea Grammar Sch.; University Coll., London Univ. (BA Hons Arch. 1958); Harvard (MLA). RIBA 1960; AILA. Asst Architect in private practice, 1958-60; Post-grad. study in landscape arch. and planning, Harvard, 1960, completed degree course, 1964; estabd own practice with Geoffrey Darke (following successful entry in national architect. competition), 1961; practice moved to Richmond, 1963, and 1966-, has grown steadily to undertake several large commns, particularly public housing, laboratories and offices; in recent years practice has expanded into Europe (through internat. competitions) and is currently building in Stuttgart,

Hannover and Bolzano. Involved in professional and local cttees, and national confs. *Recreations:* working late, the piano; latterly tennis and squash and now the obsessive folly of golf. *Address:* 6A The Green, Richmond, Surrey. *T:* 01-940 7182; 10 Dynevor Road, Richmond, Surrey. *T:* 01-940 2241. *Club:* Athenæum.

DARBY, Dr Francis John, TD 1964; MRCGP; Chief Medical Adviser (Social Security), Department of Health and Social Security, since 1980; *b* 24 Feb. 1920; *o s* of Col John Francis Darby, CBE, late Royal Signals, and Georgina Alice (*née* Dean); *m* 1st, 1949, Joyce Helene Campbell Stewart (marr. diss.); one *s*; 2nd, 1969, Pamela Lisbeth, *o d* of Sydney Hill, Sutton Coldfield. *Educ:* Nottingham High Sch.; Edinburgh Acad.; Edinburgh Univ. (MB ChB 1950). MRCGP 1970; DIH 1963; DMJ 1965; MFOM RCP 1982. Commissioned, Royal Signals, 1938-46: N Africa (despatches), Italy and Egypt, 1942-46. House appts, 1950-51; general practice, Warwickshire, and member medical staff, Tamworth General Hosp. and St Editha's Hosp., Tamworth, 1951-64; MO, Min. of Pensions and Nat. Insurance, 1964-70; SMO, 1970-74, PMO, 1974-78, Dep. Chief Medical Advr, 1978-80, DHSS. Member: Medico-Legal Soc., 1967-; Anglo-German Med. Soc., 1968-. Mem., Worshipful Soc. of Apothecaries of London, 1978-; Freeman, City of London, 1979. FRSM 1974. QHP, 1980-. *Publications:* various papers on drug prescribing and medical administration. *Recreations:* sailing, literature. *Address:* 4 Berystede, Kingston Hill, Kingston-upon-Thames, Surrey KT2 7PQ. *T:* 01-549 5773; 92 Samber Close, Lymington, Hants. *Clubs:* Army and Navy; Royal Signals Yacht; Royal Lymington Yacht.

DARBY, Rt. Rev. Harold Richard; see Sherwood, Bishop Suffragan of.

DARBY, Henry Clifford, CBE 1978 (OBE 1946); LittD 1960; FBA 1967; Professor of Geography in the University of Cambridge, 1966-76, now Emeritus Professor; *b* 7 Feb. 1909; *s* of Evan Darby, Resolven, Glamorgan; *m* 1941, Eva Constance Thomson; two *d. Educ:* Neath County Sch.; St Catharine's Coll., Cambridge. 1st Class Geographical Tripos, Parts I, 1926, II, 1928; PhD 1931; MA 1932. Lecturer in Geography, University of Cambridge, 1931-45; Fellow, King's Coll., Cambridge, 1932-45, 1966-81; Intelligence Corps, 1940-41 (Capt.); Admiralty, 1941-45; John Rankin Prof. of Geography, University of Liverpool, 1945-49; Prof. of Geography, University Coll. London, 1949-66; Leverhulme Research Fellow, 1946-48; Visiting Prof. Univ. of Chicago, 1952, Harvard Univ., 1959, 1964-65, and Univ. of Washington, 1963; Mem., Royal Commission on Historical Monuments (England), 1953-77; Mem., National Parks Commn, 1958-63; Mem., Water Resources Board, 1964-68. Pres. Institute of British Geographers, 1961; Pres., Section E British Assoc., 1963; Chm., British National Cttee for Geography, 1973-78. Hon. Member: Croatian Geog. Soc., 1957; Royal Netherlands Geog. Soc., 1958; RGS, 1976; Inst. of British Geographers, 1977; Hon. Fellow, St Catharine's Coll., Cambridge, 1960. Victoria Medal, RGS, 1963. Daly Medal, American Geog. Soc., 1963; Honors Award, Assoc. of Amer. Geographers, 1977. Hon. degrees: Chicago, 1967; Liverpool, 1968; Durham, 1970; Hull, 1975; Ulster, 1977; Wales, 1979. *Publications:* An Historical Geography of England before AD 1800 (Editor, and Contributor), 1936; The Cambridge Region (Editor and Contributor), 1938; The Medieval Fenland, 1940; The Draining of the Fens, 2nd edn, 1956; The University Atlas (with H. Fullard), 19th edn 1978, 21st edn 1981; The Library Atlas (with H. Fullard), 13th edn 1978, 15th edn 1981; The New Cambridge Modern History Atlas (with H. Fullard), 1970; (ed and contrib.) A New Historical Geography of England, 1973; The Changing Fenland, 1983; General Editor and Contributor, The Domesday Geography of England, 7 vols, 1952-77; articles in geographical and historical journals. *Address:* 60 Storey's Way, Cambridge. *T:* Cambridge 354745.

DARBY, Peter Howard, CBE 1973; QFSM 1970; HM Chief Inspector of Fire Services, since 1981; *b* 8 July 1924; *s* of William Cyril Darby and Beatrice Colin; *m* 1948, Ellen Josephine Glynn; one *s* one *d. Educ:* City of Birmingham Coll. of Advanced Technology. Fire Brigades: Dep. Ch. Officer, Suffolk and Ipswich FB, 1963; Chief Officer, Nottingham FB, 1966; Chief Officer, Lancashire FB, 1967; County Fire Officer, Greater Manchester FB, 1974; Regional Fire Comdr (No 10) NW Region, 1974-76; Regional Fire Adviser (No 5) Greater London Region, 1977; Chief Officer of the London Fire Brigade, 1977-80. Pres., Chief and Asst Chief Fire Officers' Assoc., 1975-76; Fire Adviser, Assoc. of Metropolitan Authorities, 1975; Mem. Bd, Fire Service Coll., 1977; Mem. Adv. Council, Central Fire Brigades, 1977; Adviser, Nat. Jt Council for Local Authority Fire Brigades, 1977. Freeman, City of London; Liveryman, Worshipful Co. of Basketmakers. *Recreations:* fell-walking, golf, fishing, sailing. *Address:* Fire Service Inspectorate, 50 Queen Anne's Gate, SW1H 9AT. *T:* 01-213 3000. *Clubs:* City Livery, KSC.

D'ARCY, Surgeon Rear-Adm. Thomas Norman, CB 1953; CBE 1950; retired; *b* 12 Feb. 1896; *s* of Dr S. A. D'Arcy, Rosslea, County Fermanagh, Ireland; *m* 1922, Eleanor Lennox Broadbent (*d* 1982); two *s* two *d. Educ:* Royal School, Cavan; RCS Dublin. Qualified, 1919; Surgeon Probationer RNVR, 1915-18; Surgeon Lieut RN, 1919; Surgeon Lieut-Comdr 1925; Surgeon Comdr 1930; Surgeon Capt. 1943; Surgeon Rear-Adm., 1951; Medical Officer in Charge, RN Hospital, Plymouth, and Command Medical Officer, 1951-54. KHS 1951; QHS 1952-54. CStJ 1953. Gilbert Blane medal, 1929. *Publications:* surgical articles to Jl of RN Medical Service (Co-Editor, 1946-47). *Recreation:* hockey (old Irish International). *Address:* South Wind, Witley, Surrey GU8 5RB. *T:* Godalming 5751.

DARCY DE KNAYTH, Baroness (18th in line), *cr* 1332; **Davina Marcia Ingrams** (*née* **Herbert**); *b* 10 July 1938; *d* of late Squadron Leader Viscount Clive (*d* on active service, 1943), and of Vida, *o d* of late Capt. James Harold Cuthbert, DSO, Scots Guards (she *m* 2nd, 1945, Brig. Derek Schreiber, MVO (*d* 1972)); *S* to father's Barony, 1943; *m* 1960, Rupert George Ingrams (*d* 1964), *s* of late Leonard Ingrams and of Mrs Ingrams; one *s* two *d. Heir: s* Hon. Caspar David Ingrams, *b* 5 Jan. 1962. *Address:* Camley Corner, Stubbings, Maidenhead, Berks.

D'ARCY HART, P. M.; *see* Hart, P. M. D.

DARELL, Brig. Sir Jeffrey (Lionel), 8th Bt, *cr* 1795; MC 1945; *b* 2 Oct. 1919; *s* of late Lt-Col Guy Marsland Darell, MC (3rd *s* of 5th Bt); *S* cousin, 1959; *m* 1953, Bridget Mary, *e d* of Maj.-Gen. Sir Allan Adair, 6th Bt, *qv* ; one *s* two *d. Educ:* Eton; RMC, Sandhurst. Commissioned Coldstream Guards, July 1939; served War of 1939-45: ADC to GOC-in-C, Southern Comd, 1942; Bde Major, Guards Bde, 1953-55; Officer Comdg 1st Bn Coldstream Guards, 1957-59; GSO1, PS12, War Office, 1959; College Comdr RMA Sandhurst, 1961-64; Comdg Coldstream Guards, 1964-65; Comdr, 56 Inf. Brigade (TA), 1965-67; Vice-Pres., Regular Commns Bd, 1968-70; Comdt, Mons OCS, 1970-72; MoD, 1972-74; retd 1974. ADC to HM the Queen, 1973-74. *Recreations:* normal. *Heir: s* Guy Jeffrey Adair Darell, *b* 8 June 1961. *Address:* 55 Green Street, W1. *T:* 01-629 3860; Denton Lodge, Harleston, Norfolk. *T:* Homersfield 206. *Club:* Cavalry and Guards.

DARESBURY, 2nd Baron, *cr* 1927, of Walton, Co. Chester; **Edward Greenall,** Bt, *cr* 1876; late Life Guards; *b* 12 Oct. 1902; *o* surv. *s* of 1st Baron Daresbury, CVO, and late Frances Eliza, OBE 1945, *d* of Capt. Wynne-Griffith, 1st Royal Dragoons; *S* father 1938; *m* 1st 1925, Joan Madeline (*d* 1926), *d* of Capt. Robert Thomas Oliver Sheriffe, of Goadby Hall, Melton Mowbray; 2nd, 1927, Josephine (*d* 1958), *y d* of Brig.-Gen. Sir Joseph Laycock, KCMG, DSO; one *s* ; 3rd, 1966, Lady Helena Hilton Green (*née* Wentworth-Fitzwilliam) (*d* 1970), 4th *d* of 7th Earl Fitzwilliam. *Educ:* Wixenford; Eton. *Heir: s* Hon. Edward Gilbert Greenall [*b* 27 Nov. 1928; *m* 1952, Margaret Ada, *y d* of late C. J. Crawford and of Mrs Crawford, Wayside, St Andrews; three *s* one *d*]. *Address:* Altavilla, Askeaton, Co. Limerick, Eire. *T:* Limerick 64281.

DARGIE, Sir William Alexander, Kt 1970; CBE 1969 (OBE 1960); FRSA 1951; artist; portrait, figure and landscape painter; Chairman, Commonwealth Art Advisory Board, Prime Minister's Department, 1969-73 (Member, 1953-73); *b* 4 June 1912; *s* of Andrew and Adelaide Dargie; *m* 1937, Kathleen, *d* of late G. H. Howitt; one *s* one *d. Educ:* Melbourne, and in studio of A. D. Colquhoun. Official War Artist (Capt.) with AIF in Middle East, Burma, New Guinea, India, 1941-46. Dir, National Gallery of Victoria Art Schs, 1946-53. Member: Interim Council of Nat. Gallery Canberra, 1968-72; Nat. Capital Planning Cttee, Canberra, 1970-73; Aboriginal Arts Adv. Cttee, 1970-72; Trustee: Native Cultural Reserve, Port Moresby, Papua-New Guinea, 1970-73; Museum of Papua-New Guinea, 1970-73; Mem. Council, Nat. Museum, Victoria, 1978-; Chm., Bd of Trustees, McClelland Gall., 1981-. Archibald Prize for portraiture, 1941, 1942, 1945, 1946, 1947, 1950, 1952, 1956; Woodward Award, 1940; McPhillimy Award, 1940; McKay Prize, 1941. Painted portrait of The Queen for Commonwealth of Aust., 1954; the Duke of Gloucester, 1947; the Duke of Edinburgh for City of Melbourne, 1956. Portraits of Sir Macfarlane Burnet, Sir William Ashton, Sir Lionel Lindsay, acquired for Commonwealth Nat. Collection. Rep. in public and private collections in Aust., NZ, England and USA. One-man exhibition, Leger Galls, London, 1958. Exhibits with RA and Royal Soc. of Portrait Painters. *Publication:* On Painting a Portrait, 1956. *Recreations:* books, chess, tennis. *Address:* 19 Irilbarra Road, Canterbury, Victoria 3126, Australia. *T:* 836 3396 Melbourne. *Clubs:* Melbourne, Naval and Military (Melbourne).

DARK, Anthony Michael B.; *see* Beaumont-Dark.

DARKE, Geoffrey James, RIBA; Partner, Darbourne and Darke, Architects and Landscape Planners, since 1961; *b* 1 Sept. 1929; *s* of Harry James Darke and of late Edith Anne (*née* Rose); *m* 1959, Jean Yvonne Rose, ARCM; one *s* two *d. Educ:* Prince Henry's Grammar Sch., Evesham, Worcs; Birmingham School of Architecture (DipArch); ARIBA 1956. National Service, Malaya, commnd RE, 1954-56. Asst architect, Stevenage Development Corp., 1952-58; private practice, 1958-61; established present practice, with John Darbourne, 1961. Work includes several large commissions, particularly public buildings. Success in national and internat. competitions, latterly in Stuttgart, 1977, Hanover, 1979, W Germany, also in Bolzano, Italy, 1980; numerous medals and awards for architectural work; with John Darbourne, co-recipient of Fritz Schumacher Award, Hamburg, 1978, for services to architecture and townplanning. Mem. Council, RIBA, 1977-; Chm., RIBA Competitions Cttee, 1979-; has served on many professional committees. FRSA 1981. Mem., Aldeburgh Festival Snape Maltings Foundn, 1979-. *Recreation:* music. *Address:* 7 The Green, Richmond, Surrey TW9 1PL. *T:* 01-940 9873.

DARKE, Marjorie Sheila; writer, since 1962; *b* 25 Jan. 1929; *d* of Christopher Darke and Sarah Ann (*née* Palin); *m* 1952; two *s* one *d. Educ:* Worcester Grammar Sch. for Girls; Leicester Coll. of Art and Technol.; Central Sch. of Art, London. Worked in textile studio of John Lewis Partnership, 1950-54; mother and housewife, 1954-. *Publications:* Ride the Iron Horse, 1973; The Star Trap, 1974; A Question of Courage, 1975; The First of Midnight, 1977;

A Long Way to Go, 1978; Comeback, 1981; Tom Post's Private Eye, 1983; *for young children:* Mike's Bike, 1974; What Can I Do, 1975; Kipper's Turn, 1976; The Big Brass Band, 1976; My Uncle Charlie, 1977; Carnival Day, 1979; Kipper Skips, 1979. *Recreations:* reading, music, sewing, country walks, jogging. *Address:* c/o Kestrel Books, 536 King's Road, SW10 0UH. *Clubs:* Society of Authors; International PEN.

DARKIN, Maj.-Gen. Roy Bertram, CBE 1969; Commander Base Organisation RAOC, 1971-73, retired; *b* 3 Sept. 1916; *s* of late Bertram Duncan and of late Isobel Doris Darkin, Aylsham, Norfolk; *m* 1945, Louise Margaret, *d* of late Francis Charles Sydney Green and Lilian Green, Buckden, Hunts, and *widow* of Flt Lt J. C. D. Joslin, RAF (killed in action). no *c. Educ:* Felsted School. Commnd Baluch Regt, IA, 1940; war service, NW Frontier, Iraq, Persia (despatches); psc 1943; G2 HQ ALFSEA service, Burma; DAQMG India Office, 1945; transf. RAOC, 1946; Sen. Instructor, RAAOC Sch., Melbourne, 1952-54; DAQMG HQ Aldershot District, 1954-55; jssc 1955; AA&QMG Land Forces, Hong Kong, 1960-62; AAG (Col) MoD, 1962-65; Sen. Provision Officer, COD Bicester, 1965-66; Dir of Ordnance Services, FARELF (Brig.), 1966-69; Dep. Dir Ordnance Services MoD, 1969-71. Hon. Col, RAOC, T&AVR, 1971-73; Col Comdt, RAOC, 1975-79. FBIM. *Recreations:* travel, golf, philately. *Address:* c/o Lloyd's Bank Ltd, 75 Castle Street, Farnham, Surrey. *Clubs:* MCC; Hankley Common Golf.

DARLING, family name of **Barons Darling** and **Darling of Hillsborough.**

DARLING, 2nd Baron, *cr* 1924, of Langham; **Robert Charles Henry Darling;** DL; Major retired, Somerset Light Infantry; *b* 15 May 1919; *s* of late Major Hon. John Clive Darling, DSO; *S* grandfather, 1936; *m* 1942, Bridget Rosemary Whishaw, *d* of Rev. F. C. Dickson; one *s* two *d. Educ:* Wellington Coll.; RMC Sandhurst. Retired, 1955. Sec., later Chief Executive, Royal Bath and West and Southern Counties Soc., 1961-79. DL Somerset 1972, Avon 1974. *Recreations:* fishing, gardening. *Heir: s* Hon. Robert Julian Henry Darling, FRICS [*b* 29 April 1944; *m* 1970, Janet, *yr d* of Mrs D. M. E. Mallinson, Richmond, Yorks; two *s* one *d*]. *Address:* Puckpits, Limpley Stoke, Bath, Avon. *T:* Limpley Stoke 2146.

DARLING OF HILLSBOROUGH, Baron *cr* 1974 (Life Peer), of Crewe; **George Darling,** PC 1966; Journalist; *b* 1905; *s* of F. W. Darling, Co-operative shop asst; *m* 1932, Dorothy, *d* of T. W. Hodge, farmer; one *s* one *d. Educ:* Elementary Sch., Crewe; Liverpool and Cambridge Univs. MP (Co-op and Lab), Hillsborough Div. of Sheffield, 1950-Feb. 1974; Minister of State, BoT, 1964-68. Engineer; market research executive; newspaper reporter; BBC Industrial Correspondent, 1945-49; author. Pres., Inst. of Trading Standards Admin. *Recreation:* gardening. *Address:* 17 Amersham Road, Beaconsfield, Bucks. *T:* Beaconsfield 3352.

DARLING, Prof. Arthur Ivan, CBE 1971; Professor of Dental Medicine, University of Bristol, since 1959 (of Dental Surgery, 1947-59); Director of Dental Studies in the University of Bristol since 1947; *b* 21 Nov. 1916; *s* of John Straughan Darling and Henrietta Jeffcoat; *m* 1948, Kathleen Brenda Pollard; one *s* three *d. Educ:* Whitley Bay and Monkseaton Grammar Sch.; King's Coll., Univ. of Durham, LDS Dunelm, 1937, BDS Dunelm, 1938; Parker Brewis Research Fellow, 1938-41; MDS Dunelm, 1942; LRCP, MRCS 1947; FDSRCS 1948; DDSc Dunelm 1957; FFDRCSI 1964; FRCPath 1967. Lecturer: in Operative Dental Surgery, 1941, in Oral Anatomy, 1943, in Dental Materia Medica, 1945, University of Durham; Dean of Med. Faculty, Univ. of Bristol, 1963-66; Pro-Vice-Chancellor, Univ. of Bristol, 1968-72. Mem., Avon AHA (Teaching); Vice-Dean, Bd of Dental Faculty, RCS, 1977-78. Hon. Dir, Dental Unit of MRC, 1961-82. Hon. DSc Wales, 1981. *Publications:* scientific papers on professional subjects in journals. *Recreations:* fishing and music. *Address:* 7 Rylestone Grove, Bristol BS9 3UT. *Club:* Athenæum.

DARLING, Hon. Sir Clifford, Kt 1977; MP (Bahamas); Speaker, House of Assembly, Bahamas, since 1977; *b* Acklins Island, 6 Feb. 1922; *s* of Charles and Aremelia Darling; *m* Igrid Smith. *Educ:* Acklins Public Sch.; several public schs in Nassau. Became taxi-driver (Gen. Sec. Bahamas Taxicab Union for 8 yrs, Pres. for 10 yrs). An early Mem., Progressive Liberal Party; MHA for Englerston; Senator, 1964-67; Dep. Speaker, House of Assembly, 1967-69; Minister of State, Oct. 1969; Minister of Labour and Welfare, Dec. 1971; Minister of Labour and Nat. Insurance, 1974-77. Past Chm., Tourist Advisory Bd; instrumental in introd. of a comprehensive Nat. Insce Scheme in the Bahamas, Oct. 1974. Member: Masonic Lodge; Elks Lodge; Acklins, Crooked Is and Long Cays Assoc. *Address:* House of Assembly, Nassau, Bahamas.

DARLING, Gerald Ralph Auchinleck, RD 1967; QC 1967; MA; Lieutenant-Commander, retired; Judge, Admiralty Court of the Cinque Ports, since 1979; *b* 8 Dec. 1921; *er s* of late Lieut-Col R. R. A. Darling and Moira Moriarty; *m* 1954, Susan Ann, *d* of late Brig. J. M. Hobbs, OBE, MC; one *s* one *d. Educ:* Harrow Sch. (Reginald Pole Schol.); Hertford Coll., Oxford (Baring Schol., Kitchener Schol.; MA 1948). Served with RNVR, 1940-46: Fleet Fighter Pilot, N Africa, Sicily, Salerno landings, Malta convoys; Test Pilot, Eastern Fleet; Chief Test Pilot, British Pacific Fleet; RNR until 1967. Called to Bar, Middle Temple, 1950 (Harmsworth Law Schol.), Bencher, 1972; Barrister, Northern Ireland, 1957; QC Hong Kong 1968. Member: Panel of Lloyd's Arbitrators in Salvage Cases, 1967, Appeal Arbitrator, 1978; Panel of Wreck Commissioners, 1967. Freeman of City of London, 1968.

Publication: (contrib.) 3rd edn Halsbury's Laws of England (Admiralty and Ship Collisions). *Recreations:* fly fishing, shooting. *Address:* Crevenagh House, Omagh, Northern Ireland; Queen Elizabeth Building, Temple, EC4. *T:* 01-353 5728. *Clubs:* Naval and Military; Tyrone County (Omagh).

DARLING, Henry Shillington, CBE 1967; Director-General, International Centre for Agricultural Research in Dry Areas, 1977-81, retired; Fellow of Wye College, since 1982; *b* 22 June 1914; *s* of late J. S. Darling, MD, FRCS, and Marjorie Shillington Darling, BA, Lurgan, N Ireland; *m* 1940, Vera Thompson Chapman, LDS, Belfast; one *s* two *d. Educ:* Watts' Endowed Sch.; Greenmount Agric. Coll., N Ireland; Queen's Univ., Belfast; Imp. Coll. Tropical Agriculture, Trinidad. BSc (1st Hons), 1938, BAgr (1st Hons) 1939, MAgr 1950, Belfast; AICTA 1942; PhD London, 1959. Middle East Anti-Locust Unit, Iran and Arabia, 1942-44; Research Div., Dept of Agriculture: Uganda, 1944-47; Sudan, 1947-49; Faculty of Agriculture, University Coll., Khartoum, 1949-54; Head of Hop Research Dept, Wye Coll., London Univ., 1954-62; Prof. of Agriculture and Dir of Inst. for Agric. Research, Ahmadu Bello Univ., Zaria, Nigeria, 1962-68; Dep. Vice-Chancellor, Ahmadu Bello Univ., 1967-68; Principal, Wye College, Univ. of London, 1968-77. Technical Adviser, Parly Select Cttee for Overseas Develt, 1970-71. Chairman: Agricultural Panel, Intermediate Technology Develt Gp; British Council Agricl Adv. Panel; Member: Senate and Collegiate Council, London Univ. (Chm., Senate European Studies Cttee), and other univ. cttees; Council, Royal Veterinary Coll.; Council, Ahmadu Bello Univ. Exec. Cttee, and Acad. Policy Cttee, Inter-Univ. Council for Higher Educn Overseas (also Chm., W African Gp and Mem., working parties and gps); Kent Educn Cttee; Exec. Cttee East Malling Res. Station; Council S and E Kent Productivity Assoc. Pres., Agricultural Sect., British Assoc., 1971-72. Technical Adviser: Tear Fund; Methodist Missionary Soc.; Pres., Inter-Collegiate Christian Fellowship, 1971-72. FInstBiol 1968. Hon. DSc Ahmadu Bello Univ., 1968. Order of the Hop, 1959. *Publications:* many papers in jls and reports dealing with applied biology, entomology, agricultural science and rural development in the Third World. *Recreations:* reading, walking, Christian dialogue. *Address:* 9 Jemmett Road, Ashford, Kent. *Clubs:* Athenæum, Farmers'; Samaru (Nigeria).

DARLING, James Carlisle S.; see Stormonth Darling.

DARLING, Sir James Ralph, Kt 1968; CMG 1958; OBE 1953; MA Oxon; Hon. DCL, Hon. LLD; FACE; Headmaster, Geelong Church of England Grammar School, Corio, Victoria, Australia, 1930-61; *b* 18 June 1899; *s* of late Augustine Major Darling and Jane Baird Nimmo; *m* 1935, Margaret Dunlop, *er d* of late John Dewar Campbell; one *s* three *d. Educ:* Repton Sch.; Oriel Coll., Oxford. 2nd Lieut Royal Field Artillery, 1918-19, France and Germany; Asst Master Merchant Taylors' Sch., Crosby, Liverpool, 1921-24; Asst Master Charterhouse Sch., Godalming, 1924-29; in charge of Public Schs Empire Tour to NZ, 1929; Hon. Sec. Headmasters' Conference of Australia, 1931-45, Chm., 1946-48; Member: Melbourne Univ. Council, 1933-71 (Hon. MA Melbourne); Commonwealth Univs Commission, 1942-51; Commonwealth Immigration Advisory Council, 1952-68; Australian Broadcasting Control Board, 1955-61. President: Australian Coll. of Educn, 1959-63 (Hon. Fellow 1970); Australian Road Safety Council, 1961-70; Chairman: Australian Expert Gp on Road Safety, 1970-71; Australian Frontier Commission, 1962-71 (President, 1971-73); Australian Broadcasting Commission, 1961-67; Commonwealth Immigration Publicity Council, 1962-71; Pres., Elizabethan Trust. Hon. DCL Oxon, 1948; Hon. LLD Melbourne, 1973. *Publications:* The Education of a Civilized Man, 1962; Timbertop (with E. H. Montgomery), 1967; Richly Rewarding, 1978. *Address:* 3 Myamyn Street, Armadale, Victoria 3143, Australia. *T:* 20.6262. *Clubs:* Australian (Sydney); Melbourne (Melbourne).

DARLING, Gen. Sir Kenneth (Thomas), GBE 1969 (CBE 1957); KCB 1963 (CB 1957); DSO 1945; Commander-in-Chief, Allied Forces, Northern Europe, 1967-69, retired; *b* 17 Sept. 1909; *s* of late G. K. Darling, CIE; *m* 1941, Pamela Beatrice Rose Denison-Pender. *Educ:* Eton; Royal Military College, Sandhurst. Commissioned 7th Royal Fusiliers, 1929; jssc 1946; idc 1953. Served NW Europe, 1944-45: Comd 5th Parachute Bde, 1946; Comd Airborne Forces Depot, 1948; Comd 16th Parachute Bde, 1950; Brig. A/q 1st (Br) Corps, 1954; Chief of Staff 1st (Br) Corps, 1955; Chief of Staff 2nd Corps, 1956. Dep. Dir of Staff Duties (D), WO, 1957-58; GOC Cyprus District and Dir of Ops, 1958-60; Dir of Infantry, 1960-62; GOC 1st (Br) Corps, 1962-63; GOC-in-C, Southern Command, 1964-66. Colonel: The Royal Fusiliers (City of London Regt), 1963-68; The Royal Regt of Fusiliers, 1968-74; Col Comdt, The Parachute Regt, 1965-67. ADC Gen., 1968-69. *Recreation:* riding. *Address:* Vicarage Farmhouse, Chesterton, Bicester, Oxon. *T:* Bicester 2092. *Club:* Army and Navy.

DARLINGTON, Rear-Adm. Sir Charles (Roy), KBE 1965; BSc; Director of the Naval Education Service and Head of Instructor Branch, Royal Navy, Oct. 1960-Oct. 1965, retired; on staff of Haileybury, 1965-75; *b* 2 March 1910; *o s* of C. A. Darlington, Newcastle under Lyme, Staffs; *m* 1935, Nora Dennison Wright, Maulds Meaburn, Westmorland; one *s* one *d. Educ:* Orme Sch., Newcastle under Lyme; Manchester Univ. (BSc). Double First in Maths 1931; Sen. Maths Master, William Hulme's Gram. Sch., 1937-40. Entered Royal Navy, 1941 (Instructor Lieut); served in: HM Ships Valiant and Malaya during War, and later in HM Ships Duke of York, Implacable, Vanguard and Tyne. On Staff of C-in-C Home Fleet, 1954-55, as Fleet Meteorological Officer; for various periods in Admty, HMS Excellent and HMS Collingwood. Rear-Adm. 1960. *Recreations:* cricket, hill-walking,

mathematics and trying to avoid ignorance of the arts, and particularly of history. *Address:* 11 Freestone Road, Southsea, Hants. *T:* Portsmouth 25974.

DARLINGTON, Joyce, (Mrs Anthony Darlington); see Blow, Joyce.

DARNLEY, 11th Earl of, *cr* 1725; **Adam Ivo Stuart Bligh;** Baron Clifton of Leighton Bromswold, 1608; Baron Clifton of Rathmore, 1721; Viscount Darnley, 1723; *b* 8 Nov. 1941; *s* of 9th Earl of Darnley and of Rosemary, *d* of late Edmund Basil Potter; *S* half-brother, 1980; *m* 1965, Susan Elaine, *y d* of late Sir Donald Anderson; one *s* one *d. Educ:* Harrow; Christ Church, Oxford. *Heir:* *s* Lord Clifton, *qv. Address:* Hambledon House, near Portsmouth, Hants.

DARNLEY-THOMAS, Mrs John; see Hunter, Rita.

DART, Raymond Arthur; United Steelworkers of America Professor of Anthropology, The Institutes for the Achievement of Human Potential, Philadelphia, since 1966; Emeritus Professor since 1959, Professor of Anatomy, 1923-58, and Dean of the Faculty of Medicine, 1925-43, University of the Witwatersrand, Johannesburg; *b* Toowong, Brisbane, Australia, 4 Feb. 1893; *s* of Samuel Dart and Eliza Anne Brimblecombe; *m* 1936, Marjorie Gordon Frew, Boksburg, Transvaal; one *s* one *d. Educ:* Ipswich Grammar Sch., Queensland (Scholarship holder); University of Queensland (Scholarship holder and Foundation scholar); graduated BSc (Hons) 1913; MSc 1915; Sydney Univ., 1914-17; graduated MB, ChM (Hons) 1917; MD 1927; Demonstrator of Anatomy and Acting Principal of St Andrew's Coll., Sydney, 1917; House Surgeon at Royal Prince Alfred Hospital, Sydney, 1917-18; Capt., AAMC, Australia, England, France, 1918-19; Senior Demonstrator of Anatomy, University Coll., London, 1919-20; Fellow of Rockefeller Foundation, 1920-21; Senior Demonstrator of Anatomy and Lecturer in Histology, University Coll., London, 1921-22; Capt., SAMC, 1925; Major, 1928; Lieut-Col Reserve Officers, 1940; Pres. of Anthropological Section SAAAS, 1926 (Gold Medal, 1939); Vice-Pres., SAAAS, 1952; Vice-Pres. of Anthropological Section, BAAS, Johannesburg, 1929; Mem. of International Commission on Fossil Man since 1929; Fellow of Royal Society of South Africa, 1930, and Mem. of Council, 1938, Vice-Pres. 1938-39, 1939-40, 1950-51; Mem. Board, SA Institute for Medical Research, 1934-48; Mem. SA Med. Council, 1935-48, Executive Cttee, 1940-48; Mem. SA Nursing Council from its inception in 1944 until 1951; Mem. Medical Advisory Cttee, SA Council for Scientific and Industrial Research, 1946-48; Pres. Anthropological Section, First Pan-African Congress of Prehistory, 1947-51; guest-lecturer at The Viking Fund Seminar, New York, and public lecturer of The Lowell Inst., Boston, 1949; Inaugural Lecturer, John Irvine Hunter Memorial, Univ. of Sydney, NSW, 1950; Woodward Lecturer, Yale Univ., USA, 1958; Inaugural Van Riebeeck Lecturer; R. J. Terry Meml Lectr, Washington Univ. Sch. of Medicine, St Louis, 1971. SA Broadcasting Corp., 1959. Pres. SA Archaeological Soc., 1951; Pres. SA Assoc. for Advancement of Science, Bulawayo, S Rhodesia, 1953; Vice-Pres., Fourth Pan-African Congress of Prehistory, 1959-62; Pres. SA Museums Assoc., 1961-62; Vice-Pres., Assoc. Scientific and Technical Socs of S Africa, 1961-62, 1962-63, Pres., 1963-64; Pres. SA Soc. of Physiotherapy, 1961-68, Hon. Life Vice-Pres., 1968-; Mem., Internat. Primatological Cttee, 1963-; Mem., Municipal Library Advisory Cttee, Johannesburg, 1964-. Coronation Medal, 1953; Sen. Capt. Scott Memorial Medal, SA Biological Soc., 1955; Viking Medal and Award for Physical Anthropology, Wenner-Gren Foundation of New York, 1957; Simon Biesheuvel Medal (Behavioural Sciences), 1963; Gold Medal, SA Nursing Assoc., 1970; Silver Medal, SA Medical Assoc., 1972. Hon. DSc: Natal, 1956; Witwatersrand, 1964; La Salle, 1968. Fellow Odontological Soc. of SA, 1937; Fellow Institute of Biology, 1964; For. Fellow, Linnaean Soc., 1974. Raymond Dart Lectureship in Institute for Study of Man in Africa, estab. 1964; Museums of Man and Science, Johannesburg, initiated 1966, Board of Governors, 1968. Hon. Life Member: Dental Assoc. of South Africa, 1958, Medical Assoc. of South Africa, 1959, Anatomical Society of Great Britain and Ireland, 1961, Anatomical Soc. of Southern Africa, 1970, S African Nursing Assoc., 1970; Archaeological Soc. of SA, 1973. *Publications:* Racial Origins, chapter in The Bantu-speaking Tribes of South Africa, 1937; chapters on genealogy and physical characters, in Bushmen of the Southern Kalahari, 1937; (ed) Africa's Place in the Human Story, 1954; The Oriental Horizons of Africa, 1955; Adventures with the Missing Link, 1959; Africa's Place in the Emergence of Civilisation, 1960; Beyond Antiquity, 1965; over 250 articles on anthropological, archaeological, neurological and comparative anatomical subjects in scientific and lay periodicals. *Recreations:* swimming, music. *Address:* 20 Eton Park, Eton Road, Sandhurst, Sandton, Transvaal, 2196, South Africa. *Clubs:* Associated Scientific and Technical, Country (Johannesburg).

DARTMOUTH, 9th Earl of, *cr* 1711; **Gerald Humphry Legge;** Baron Dartmouth, 1682; Viscount Lewisham, 1711; *b* 26 April 1924; *s* of 8th Earl of Dartmouth, CVO, DSO; *S* father, 1962; *m* 1948, Raine (marr. diss. 1976), *d* of late Alexander McCorquodale; three *s* one *d* ; *m* 1980, Mrs G. M. Seguin. *Educ:* Eton. Served War, 1943-45, Coldstream Guards, Italy (despatches). FCA 1951. Dir, Rea Bros Ltd, Bankers, 1958. Hon. LLD Dartmouth Coll., USA, 1969. *Heir:* *s* Viscount Lewisham, *qv. Address:* The Manor House, Chipperfield, King's Langley, Herts WD4 9BN. *Clubs:* Buck's, Bath. *See also Baron Herschell.*

DARVALL, Sir (Charles) Roger, Kt 1971; CBE 1965; Director: Munich Reinsurance Company of Australia Ltd; L. M. Ericsson Pty Ltd; *b* 11 Aug. 1906; *s* of late C. S. Darvall; *m* 1931, Dorothea M., *d* of late A. C. Vautier; two *d. Educ:* Burnie, Tasmania. FASA. Gen. Manager, Australia & New Zealand Bank Ltd, Melbourne, 1961-67. *Recreations:* motoring, gardening, outdoors. *Address:* 2 Martin Court, Toorak, Vic 3142, Australia. *T:* 24-4647. *Clubs:* Athenæum, Melbourne (Melbourne).

DARVALL, Frank Ongley, CBE 1954; retired from HM Diplomatic Service, 1970; a Governor, Sulgrave Manor; Member Council of Haileybury and Imperial Service College; *b* 16 April 1906; 5th *s* of late R. T. Darvall and Annie E. Johnson, Reading; *m* 1931, Dorothy (*d* 1979), *er d* of Harry Edmonds and late Jane Quay, NY City; one *s* decd. *Educ:* Dover Coll.; Reading (BA); London (BA, PhD); Columbia (MA). President Nat. Union of Students, 1927-29; Commonwealth Fund Fellow, 1929-31; Assoc. Sec. for Internat. Studies, Internat. Students Service, 1931-32; Dir, Geneva Students Internat. Union, 1933. Lecturer in Economics and History, Queen's Coll., Harley Street, 1933-36; Director Research and Discussion, English-Speaking Union, 1936-39; Dep. Director American Div., Ministry of Information, 1939-45; British Consul, Denver, 1945-46; 1st Secretary HM Embassy, Washington, 1946-49; Vice-Chairman Kinsman Trust, 1949-56; Editor, The English-Speaking World, 1950-53; Director-General, English-speaking Union of the Commonwealth, 1949-57; Chairman, Congress of European-American Assoc., 1954-57. European Editor, World Review, 1958-59. Hon. Dir, UK Cttee, Atlantic Congress, 1959; Attached British High Commn, Cyprus, 1960-62; Dir, British Information Services, Eastern Caribbean, 1962-66; attached, British Consulate-Gen., Barcelona, 1966; Consul, Boston, 1966-68; FCO (formerly CO), 1968-70. Dean of Academics, Alvescot Coll., 1970-71, Vice-Pres., 1971-72. Contested (L) Ipswich, 1929, King's Lynn, 1935, Hythe bye-election, 1939. Extension Lecturer and Tutorial Classes Tutor, Cambridge and London Universities, 1933-39. *Publications:* Popular Disturbances and Public Order in Regency England, 1934; The Price of European Peace, 1937; The American Political Scene, 1939. *Address:* c/o Lloyds Bank Ltd, 1 Butler Place, SW1.

DARVALL, Sir Roger; *see* Darvall, Sir C. R.

DARWEN, 2nd Baron, *cr* 1946, of Heys-in-Bowland; **Cedric Percival Davies;** Publisher; President, Independent Publishers' Guild, since 1973; *b* 18 Feb. 1915; *e s* of 1st Baron and M. Kathleen Brown; *S* father 1950; *m* 1934, Kathleen Dora, *d* of George Sharples Walker; three *s* one *d. Educ:* Sidcot; Manchester Univ. BA Hons English Lit. and Language, Manchester, 1947. Engaged in Cotton Industry, 1932-40. On staff of school for Maladjusted Children, 1942-44. Manchester Univ., 1944-48, Teaching Diploma, 1948. Warden of Letchworth Adult Education Centre, 1948-51; Secretary to Training and Education Dept of National Assoc. for Mental Health, 1951-53; Founded Darwen Finlayson Ltd, Publishers, 1954, Chm., and Man. Dir, 1954-73; Dep. Editor of John O'London's, 1959-62. Chm., Hollybank Engineering Co. Ltd., 1957-70. *Publications:* designed and ed, Illustrated County History Series. *Recreations:* sailing, painting, cinéphotography. *Heir:* *s* Hon. Roger Michael Davies, [*b* 28 June 1938; *m* 1961, Gillian Irene, *d* of Eric G. Hardy, Bristol; two *s* three *d*]. *Address:* White Lodge, Sandelswood End, Beaconsfield, Bucks. *T:* Beaconsfield 3355.

DARWENT, Rt. Rev. Frederick Charles; *see* Aberdeen and Orkney, Bishop of.

DARWIN, Henry Galton, CMG 1977; MA; Deputy Legal Adviser, Foreign and Commonwealth Office, since 1976; *b* 6 Nov. 1929; *s* of late Sir Charles Darwin, KBE, FRS; *m* 1958, Jane Sophia Christie; three *d. Educ:* Marlborough Coll.; Trinity Coll., Cambridge. Called to Bar, Lincoln's Inn, 1953. Asst Legal Adviser, FO, 1954-60 and 1963-67; Legal Adviser, British Embassy, Bonn, 1960-63; Legal Counsellor: UK Mission to UN, 1967-70; FCO, 1970-73; a Dir-Gen., Legal Service, Council Secretariat, European Communities, Brussels, 1973-76. *Publications:* contribs in Report of a Study Group on the Peaceful Settlement of International Disputes, 1966 and International Regulation of Frontier Disputes, 1970; notes in British Yearbook of International Law and American Jl of International Law. *Address:* 30 Hereford Square, SW7. *T:* 01-373 1140. *Club:* Athenæum.

DARWIN, Kenneth; writer and lecturer; *b* 24 Sept. 1921; *s* of late Robert Lawrence and Elizabeth Darwin (*née* Swain), Ripon, Yorks. *Educ:* Elementary Sch.; Ripon Grammar Sch.; University Coll., Durham; Oflag VIIB (1943-45). BA 1947, MA 1948. Served 2nd Bn Lancs Fus., N Africa, (Captain) POW, 1942-46. Asst Keeper, Public Record Office (NI), 1948; Dep. Keeper of Records of N Ireland, 1955-70; Vis. Lectr in Archives, UC Dublin, 1967-71; Fellow Commoner, Churchill Coll., Cambridge, 1970; Asst Sec., Min. of Commerce (NI), 1970-74; Sen. Asst Sec., Dept of Finance (NI) and Dept of Civil Service (NI), 1974-77; Dep. Sec., Dept of Finance (NI), 1977-81. Member: Irish MSS Commn, Dublin, 1955-70; Adv. Bd for New History of Ireland, Royal Irish Acad., 1968-; Mem. Bd (sometime Administrator), Ulster Historical Foundn, 1956-; Trustee: Lyric Th., Belfast, 1966-69; Ulster Museum, 1982-. *Publications:* articles on archives, history and genealogy, in jls and Nat. Trust guides. *Recreations:* travel and fine arts; walking, gardening. *Address:* 18 Seymour Road, Bangor, Co. Down BT19 1BL. *T:* 60718. *Clubs:* Royal Commonwealth Society; Mahee Island Golf (Co. Down).

DARYNGTON, 2nd Baron, *cr* 1923, of Witley; **Jocelyn Arthur Pike Pease;** *b* 30 May 1908; *s* of 1st Baron Daryngton, PC and Alice (*d* 1948), 2nd *d* of Very Rev. H. Mortimer Luckock, sometime Dean of Lichfield; *S* father 1949. *Educ:* Eton; privately; Trinity Coll., Cambridge (MA). Member Inner Temple, 1932. *Heir:* none. *Address:* House of Lords, SW1.

DASGUPTA, Prof. Partha Sarathi, PhD; Professor of Economics, London School of Economics and Political Science, since 1978; *b* 17 Nov. 1942; *s* of Prof. Amiya Dasgupta and Shanti Dasgupta, Santiniketan, India; *m* 1968, Carol Margaret, *d* of Prof. James Meade, *qv* ; one *s* one *d. Educ:* Univ. of Delhi (BSc Hons 1962); Univ. of Cambridge (BA 1965, PhD 1968; Stevenson Prize, 1967). Res. Fellow, Trinity Hall, Cambridge, 1968-71; Supernumerary Fellow, 1971-74; Lectr, LSE, 1971-75, Reader, 1975-78. Vis. Professor: Stanford Univ., 1974-75; Delhi Univ., 1978. Consultant: on Proj. Planning, UNIDO, 1969-72; on Resource Management, World Bank, 1977; on Environmental Component of Natural Resource Pricing, UNCTAD, 1977-80. Member: Expert Panel on Environmtl Health, WHO, 1975-; Expert Gp on Management of Environmtl Resources, UNEP, 1979-. Fellow, Econometric Soc., 1975. *Publications:* (with S. Marglin and A. K. Sen) Guidelines for Project Evaluation, 1972; (with G. Heal) Economic Theory and Exhaustible Resources, 1979; The Control of Resources, 1982; articles on develt planning, optimum population, taxation and trade, welfare and justice, nat. resources, indust. org. and technical progress in Econ. Jl, Econometrica, Rev. of Econ. Stud., etc. *Address:* 96 Balham Park Road, SW12 8EA. *T:* 01-672 7891.

DASH, Sir Roydon Englefield Ashford, Kt 1945; DFC; Hon. LLD London; FRICS; Chairman of the Stevenage Development Corporation, 1953-62; *b* 3 March 1888; *s* of late Roland Ashford Dash, FSI; *m* 1933, Joan Pritchett Harrison. *Educ:* Haileybury Coll., Herts. Chief Valuer, Board of Inland Revenue, retired 1951. *Recreations:* golf and motoring. *Address:* 52 The Shimmings, Boxgrove Road, Guildford, Surrey.

DASHWOOD, Sir Francis (John Vernon Hereward), 11th Bt, *cr* 1707; (Premier Baronet of Great Britain); *b* 7 Aug. 1925; *s* of Sir John Lindsay Dashwood, 10th Bt, CVO, and Helen Moira Eaton; *S* father, 1966; *m* 1st, 1957, Victoria Ann Elizabeth Gwynne de Rutzen (*d* 1976); one *s* three *d* ; 2nd, 1977, Marcella (*née* Scarafia), formerly wife of Giuseppe Sportoletti Baduel and widow of Jack Frye, CBE; one step *s. Educ:* Eton; Christ Church, Oxford (BA 1948, MA 1953); Harvard Business Sch., USA. Foreign Office, 1944-45. Aluminium Company of Canada Ltd, 1950-51; EMI Ltd, 1951-53. Member of Buckinghamshire County Council, 1950-51; Member Lloyd's, 1956. Contested (C) West Bromwich, 1955, Gloucester, 1957. High Sheriff Bucks, 1976. *Heir:* *s* Edward John Francis Dashwood, *b* 25 Sept. 1964. *Address:* West Wycombe Park, Buckinghamshire. *T:* High Wycombe 23720. *Clubs:* White's, Brooks's.

DASHWOOD, Sir Richard (James), 9th Bt *cr* 1684, of Kirtlington Park; *b* 14 Feb. 1950; *s* of Sir Henry George Massy Dashwood, 8th Bt, and of Susan Mary, *er d* of late Major V. R. Montgomerie-Charrington, Hunsdon House, Herts; *S* father, 1972. *Educ:* Maidwell Hall Preparatory Sch.; Eton College. Commissioned 14/20th King's Hussars, 1969; T&AVR, 1973-. *Heir:* kinsman Alexander Thomas Whitburn Dashwood, *b* 1950. *Address:* Ledwell Cottage, Sandford St Martin, Oxfordshire OX5 4AN. *T:* Great Tew 267. *Club:* Cavalry and Guards.

da SILVA, John Burke, CMG 1969; HM Diplomatic Service, retired; Adviser, Commercial Union Assurance Co., since 1973; *b* 30 Aug. 1918; *o s* of late John Christian da Silva; *m* 1st, 1940, Janice Margaret (decd), *d* of Roy Mayor, Shrewsbury, Bermuda; one *d* ; 2nd, 1963, Jennifer Jane, *yr d* of late Capt. the Hon. T. T. Parker, DSC, RN, Greatham Moor, Hants; one *s* two *d. Educ:* Stowe Sch.; Trinity Coll., Cambridge (MA). Served Army, 1940-46: Major, Intell. Corps (despatches). Control Commission, Germany, 1946-50; Foreign Office, 1951; 2nd Sec., Rome, 1954; Consul, Hamburg, 1956; FO, 1958; 1st Sec., Bahrein, 1960; on Staff of C-in-C, Middle East, Aden, 1963; Counsellor, Washington, 1966; FCO, 1969-73. Chm., Governors, Virginia Water Junior Sch., 1973-. *Recreation:* Oriental Art. *Address:* Copse Close, Virginia Water, Surrey. *T:* Wentworth 2342. *Club:* Naval and Military.

DATE, William Adrian, CBE 1973; Chairman, Grenada Public Service Board of Appeal; Member, Judicial and Legal Services Commission, Organisation of Eastern Caribbean States; Vice-President: Grenada Building and Loan Association; Grenada Co-operative Bank; *b* 1 July 1908; *er s* of James C. Date; *m* 1933, Dorothy MacGregor Grant (*d* 1979); two *d* ; *m* 1981, Rhoda Elaine Minors. *Educ:* Queen's Royal Coll., Trinidad; Grenada Boys' Secondary Sch.; Lodge Sch., Barbados; Middle Temple, London. Magistrate and District Govt Officer, St Lucia, 1933-39; Crown Attorney, St Vincent, 1939-44; Legal Draughtsman, Jamaica, 1944-47; Chief Secretary, Windward Islands, 1947-50; Puisne Judge of the Supreme Court of the Windward and Leeward Islands, 1950-56; Puisne Judge, British Guiana, 1956-64, retd. *Recreations:* golf, tennis, bridge. *Address:* PO Box 133, St George's, Grenada, West Indies.

DAUBE, Prof. David, FBA 1957; MA, DCL, PhD, Dr jur; Director of the Robbins Hebraic and Roman Law Collections and Professor-in-Residence at the School of Law, University of California, Berkeley, 1970-81, Emeritus Professor of Law, since 1981; Emeritus Regius Professor, Oxford University, since 1970; Member, Academic Board, Institute of Jewish Studies, London, since 1953; b Freiburg, 8 Feb. 1909; 2nd s of Jakob Daube; m 1936 (marr. diss., 1964); three s. Educ: Berthold-gymnasium, Freiburg; Universities of Freiburg, Göttingen and Cambridge. Fellow of Caius Coll., 1938-46, Hon. Fellow, 1974; Lecturer in Law, Cambridge, 1946-51; Professor of Jurisprudence at Aberdeen, 1951-55; Regius Prof. of Civil Law, Oxford Univ., and Fellow of All Souls Coll., 1955-70, Emeritus Fellow, 1980. Senior Fellow, Yale Univ., 1962; Delitzsch Lecturer, Münster, 1962; Gifford Lecturer, Edinburgh, for 1962 and 1963 (lectures delivered, 1963-64); Olaus Petri Lecturer, Uppsala, 1963; Ford Prof. of Political Science, Univ. of California, Berkeley, 1964; Riddell Lectr, Newcastle, 1965; Gray Lectr, Cambridge, 1966; Lionel Cohen Lectr, Jerusalem, 1970; inaug. Frosty Gerard Lectr, UC Irvine, 1981. Vis. Prof. of History, 1966-78, Hon. Prof., 1980, Univ. of Constance. Pres., Classical Assoc. of GB, 1976-77. Corresp. Mem., Akad. Wiss., Göttingen, 1964, Bayer. Akad. Wiss., Munich, 1966; Hon. Mem. Royal Irish Acad., 1970; Fellow: Amer. Acad. of Arts and Sciences, 1971; World Acad. of Art and Sci., 1975; Amer. Acad. for Jewish Research, 1979; Hon. Fellow, Oxford Centre for Postgraduate Hebrew Studies, 1973. Hon. LLD: Edinburgh 1960; Leicester 1964; Cambridge 1981; Dr hc Paris 1963; Hon. DHL Hebrew Union Coll., 1971; Dr jur hc Munich, 1972. Publications: Studies in Biblical Law, 1947; The New Testament and Rabbinic Judaism, 1956; Forms of Roman Legislation, 1956; The Exodus Pattern in the Bible, 1963; The Sudden in the Scriptures, 1964; Collaboration with Tyranny in Rabbinic Law, 1965; He that Cometh, 1966; Roman Law, 1969; Civil Disobedience in Antiquity, 1972; Ancient Hebrew Fables, 1973; Wine in the Bible, 1975; Medical and Genetic Ethics, 1976; Duty of Procreation, 1977; Typologie im Werk des Flavius Josephus, 1977; Ancient Jewish Law, 1981; (ed) Studies in memory of F. de Zulueta, 1959; (with W. D. Davies) Studies in honour of C. H. Dodd, 1956, and articles; Festschriften: Daube Noster, 1974; Studies in Jewish Legal History in Honour of D.D., 1974; Donum Gentilicum, 1978. Address: School of Law, University of California, Berkeley, Calif 94720, USA.

DAULTANA, Mumtaz Mohammad Khan; Ambassador of Pakistan to the Court of St James's, 1972-78; b 23 Feb. 1916; o s of Nawab Ahmadyar Daultana; m 1943, Almas Jehan; one s one d. Educ: St Anthony's Sch., Lahore; Government Coll., Lahore (BA (Hons)); Corpus Christi Coll., Oxford (MA); Called to Bar, Middle Temple, 1940; 1st cl. 1st position in Bar exam. Mem., All India Muslim League, 1942-; unopposed election as Mem. Punjab Legislative Assembly, 1943; Gen. Sec., Punjab Muslim League, 1944; Sec., All India Muslim League Central Cttee of Action, 1945; Elected Member: Punjab Assembly, 1946; Constituent Assembly of India, 1947; Constituent Assembly, Pakistan, 1947; Finance Minister, Punjab, 1947-48; Pres., Punjab Muslim League, 1948-50; Chief Minister of Punjab, 1951-53; Finance Minister, West Pakistan, 1955-56; Defence Minister, Pakistan, 1957; Pres., Pakistan Muslim League, 1967-72. Elected Member: Nat. Assembly of Pakistan, 1970; Constitution Cttee of Nat. Assembly, 1972. Publications: Agrarian Report of Pakistan Muslim League, 1950; Thoughts on Pakistan's Foreign Policy, 1956; Kashmir in Present Day Context, 1965. Recreations: music, squash. Address: 8 Durand Road, Lahore, Pakistan. T: 302459 (Lahore), 532387 (Karachi). Clubs: United Oxford & Cambridge University; Gymkhana (Lahore).

DAUNT, Maj.-Gen. Brian, CB 1956; CBE 1953; DSO 1943; late RA; b 16 March 1900; s of Dr William Daunt, Parade House, Hastings; m 1938, Millicent Margaret, d of Capt. A. S. Balfour, Allermuir House, Colinton, Edinburgh; two d (one s decd). Educ: Tonbridge; RMA, Woolwich. Commissioned RA, 1920; served NW Frontier, India, 1929-30; War of 1939-45; France, 1940, as 2 i/c Regt; CO Anti-Tank Regt, 1941; Italy, as CO 142 Field Regt, RA, Royal Devon Yeo., 1943 (DSO); CRA: 1st Armoured Div., 1944; 46 Div., 1944; 10 Indian Div., 1946; Italy, 1945 (despatches). Has had various Brigadier's appts. Commandant Coast Artillery Sch. and Inspector Coast Artillery, 1950-53; General Officer Commanding Troops, Malta, 1953-Nov. 1956; retired, 1957; Controller, Home Dept, British Red Cross Society, 1957-66. Col Comdt RA, 1960-65. CStJ 1966. Recreations: gardening, music, drama. Address: Blackstone House, Sotwell, near Wallingford, Oxon OX10 0PX. T: Wallingford 37060. Club: Army and Navy.

DAUNT, Patrick Eldon; Head of Bureau for Action on behalf of Disabled People, since 1982; b 19 Feb. 1925; s of Dr Francis Eldon Daunt and Winifred Doggett Daunt (née Wells); m 1958, Jean Patricia, d of Lt-Col Percy Wentworth Hargreaves and of Joan (née Holford); three s one d. Educ: Rugby Sch.; Wadham Coll., Oxford. BA, 1st Cl. Hons Lit. Hum., 1949, MA 1954, Oxon. Housemaster, Christ's Hosp., 1959; Headmaster, Thomas Bennett Comprehensive Sch., Crawley, 1965. Chm., Campaign for Comprehensive Educn, 1971-73; Principal Administrator, EEC, 1974-82. Publication: Comprehensive Values, 1975. Recreation: family life. Address: Avenue des Cactus 29, 1150 Brussels, Belgium. T: Brussels 770-64-12; 4 Bourn Bridge Road, Little Abington, Cambridge. T: Cambridge 891485.

DAUNT, Timothy Lewis Achilles, CMG 1982; HM Diplomatic Service; Minister and Deputy UK Permanent Representative to NATO, Brussels, since 1982; b 11 Oct. 1935; m 1962, Patricia Susan Knight; one s two d. Educ: Sherborne; St Catharine's Coll., Cambridge. 8th KRI Hussars, 1957-59. Entered Foreign Office, 1959; Ankara, 1960; FO, 1964; Nicosia, 1967; Private Sec. to Permanent Under-Sec. of State, FCO, 1970; Bank of England, 1972; UK Mission, NY, 1973; Counsellor, OECD, Paris, 1975; Head of South European Dept, FCO, 1978-81; Associate at Centre d'étude et de recherches internationales, Paris, 1982. Address: c/o Foreign and Commonwealth Office, SW1.

DAUSSET, Prof. Jean Baptiste Gabriel Joachim; Officier de la Légion d'Honneur; Professeur de Medécine Expérimentale au Collège de France, since 1977; b 19 Oct. 1916; s of Henri Dausset and Elizabeth Brullard; m 1962, Rose Mayoral; one s one d. Educ: Lycée Michelet, Paris; Faculty of Medicine, University of Paris. Associate Professor, 1958-68, Professor of Immunohaematology, 1968-77, University of Paris. Institut Nationale de la Santé et de la Recherche Médicale: Director of Research Unit on Immunogenetics of Human Transplantation, 1968-; Centre National de la Recherche Scientifique: Co-Director, Oncology and Immuno-haematology Laboratory, 1968-. Gairdner Foundn Prize, 1977; Koch Foundn Prize, 1978; Wolf Foundn Prize, 1978; Nobel Prize for Physiology or Medicine, 1980. Publications: Immuno-hématologie biologique et clinique, 1956; (with F. T. Rapaport) Human Transplantation, 1968; (with G. Snell and S. Nathanson) Histocompatibility, 1976; (with M. Fougereau) Immunology 1980, 1980. Recreation: plastic art. Address: 9 rue de Villersexel, 75007 Paris, France. T: 222.18.82.

DAVENPORT, Brian John, QC 1980; a Law Commissioner, since 1981; b 17 March 1936; s of R. C. Davenport, FRCS, and Mrs H. E. Davenport; m 1969, Erica Tickell, yr d of Prof. E. N. Willmer, qv; two s one d. Educ: Bryanston Sch.; Worcester Coll., Oxford (MA). 2 Lieut RE, 1955-56. Called to the Bar, Gray's Inn, 1960 (Atkin Scholar). Junior Counsel: to Export Credit Guarantees Dept, 1971-74; to Dept of Employment, 1972-74; (Common Law), to Bd of Inland Revenue, 1974-80; (Common Law), to the Crown, 1978-80. Mem., Gen. Council of the Bar, 1969-73. Mem. Cttee of Management, Barristers Benevolent Assoc., 1963-78, Jt Hon. Sec. 1978-. Publications: (ed jtly with F. M. B. Reynolds) 13th and 14th edns of Bowstead on Agency. Address: 43 Downshire Hill, NW3 1NU. T: 01-435 3332; 7 King's Bench Walk, Temple, EC4Y 7DS. T: 01-353 3684.

DAVENPORT, Rear-Adm. Dudley Leslie, CB 1969; OBE 1954; b 17 Aug. 1919; s of Vice-Adm. R. C. Davenport, CB, Catherington, Hants; m 1950, Joan, d of Surg. Comdr H. Burns, OBE; two s. Educ: RNC, Dartmouth. Served in Destroyers, Mediterranean and Atlantic, 1939-45; commanded HMS Holmes, 1945 and HMS Porlock Bay, 1946; served in HMS Sheffield, 1947-48; at HMS Ganges, 1949-51; Naval Staff Course, 1951; Naval Instructor, Indian Defence Services Staff Coll., 1951-53; comd HMS Virago, 1954-55; NATO Defence Course, 1955-56; Comdr RN Barracks, Chatham, 1956-57; Captain, 1957; Staff of Admiral Comdg Reserves, 1958-60; Captain Inshore Flotilla Far East, 1960-62; Director Naval Officers Appointments (Seaman Officers), 1962-64; comd HMS Victorious, 1964-66; Rear-Admiral, 1967; Flag Officer, Malta, 1967-69; retd, 1969. Recreation: gardening. Address: Rose Cottage, Halnaker, Chichester, West Sussex. T: Chichester 773210. Club: Army and Navy.

DAVENPORT, Maurice Hopwood, FIB; Managing Director, Williams & Glyn's Bank, since 1982; Director, Royal Bank of Scotland Group, since 1982; b 19 March 1925; s of Richard and Elizabeth Davenport; m 1954, Sheila Timms; one s two d. Educ: Rivington and Blackrod Grammar Sch. FIB 1982. Served RN, 1943-46. Joined Williams Deacon's Bank, 1940; Sec., 1960; Asst Gen. Man., 1969; Dir, Williams & Glyn's Bank, 1978-. Recreations: walking, gardening, reading. Address: Pines, Dormans Park, East Grinstead, West Sussex RH19 2EN. T: Dormans Park 439.

DAVENPORT, Lt-Col Sir Walter Henry B.; see Bromley-Davenport.

DAVENPORT-HANDLEY, Sir David (John), Kt 1980; OBE 1962; JP; DL; Chairman, Clipsham Quarry Co., since 1947; b 2 Sept. 1919; s of John Davenport-Handley, JP; m 1943, Leslie Mary Goldsmith; one s one d. Educ: RNC Dartmouth. RN retd 1947. Chm., Rutland and Stamford Conservative Assoc., 1952-65; Treasurer, East Midlands Area Conservative Assoc., 1965-71, Chm. 1971-77; Vice-Chm., Nat. Union of Conservative & Unionist Assocs, 1977-79, Chm., 1979-80. Member: Consumers' Cttees for GB and for England and Wales, 1956-65; Parole Bd, 1981-. Governor, Swinton Conservative Coll., 1973-77; Chairman: Board of Visitors, Ashwell Prison, 1955-73; Governors, Casterton Community Coll., 1960-78; Trustee, Oakham Sch., 1970-. JP 1948, High Sheriff 1954, DL 1962, Vice-Lieutenant 1972, Rutland; Chm., Rutland Petty Sessional Div., 1957-; DL Leicestershire 1974. Recreations: gardening, shooting. Address: Clipsham Hall, Oakham, Rutland, Leics. T: Castle Bytham 204. Clubs: Carlton, English-Speaking Union.

DAVENTRY, 2nd Viscount, cr 1943; **Robert Oliver Fitz Roy,** Captain RN; retired; b 10 Jan. 1893; er s of late Captain Rt Hon. Edward Algernon Fitz Roy, MP and of 1st Viscountess Daventry, CBE; S mother, 1962; m 1916, Grace Zoë (d 1978), d of late Claude Hume Campbell Guinness; four d (and one d decd). Educ: Royal Naval Colleges, Osborne, Dartmouth. Joined Royal Navy, 1906; Captain, 1936. Served European War, 1914-18; served War of 1939-45: comd HMS Rodney (despatches). High Sheriff, Rutland, 1956-57. Heir: nephew Francis Humphrey Maurice FitzRoy Newdegate, qv. Address: 82 Swan Court, SW3. T: 01-352 7200. Club: Carlton.
See also Sir Geoffrey Bates, Bt.

DAVEY, David Garnet, OBE 1949; MSc, PhD; Research Director of Pharmaceuticals Division, Imperial Chemical Industries Ltd, 1969-75; b 8 Aug. 1912; y s of I. W. Davey, Caerphilly, Glamorgan; m 1938, Elizabeth Gale; one s two d. Educ: University Coll., Cardiff (1st cl. Hons Zoology; MSc 1935); Gonville and Caius Coll., Cambridge (PhD 1938); Harvard Univ. Med. Sch. (Research Fellow). Inst. of Animal Pathology, Univ. of Cambridge,

1938; Lectr, University Coll., Cardiff, 1939-40; Min. of Supply (Radar), 1941; joined ICI 1942; Biological Research Manager, Pharmaceuticals Div., 1957-69. Pres., European Soc. for Study of Drug Toxicity, 1964-69; Member: MRC, 1971-75; Cttee on Review of Medicines, 1975-81; Sub-cttee on Toxicity, Clinical Trials, and Therapeutic Efficacy, Cttee on Safety of Medicines, 1976-81. Chalmers Gold Medal, Royal Soc. Tropical Medicine and Hygiene, 1947; Therapeutics Gold Medal, Apothecaries Soc., 1947. *Publications:* contribs to Annals Trop. Med.; Trans Royal Soc. Tropical Medicine and Hygiene; British Med. Bulletin; Proc. European Soc. for Study of Drug Toxicity, etc. *Recreation:* gardening. *Address:* Aragon Lodge, Star Lane, Morcombelake, Dorset DT6 6DN. *T:* Chideock 458.

DAVEY, Francis, MA; Headmaster of Merchant Taylors' School, 1974-82; *b* 23 March 1932; *er s* of Wilfred Henry Davey, BSc and Olive (*née* Geeson); *m* 1960, Margaret Filby Lake, MA Oxon, AMA, *o d* of Harold Lake, DMus Oxon, FRCO; one *s* one *d. Educ:* Plymouth Coll.; New Coll., Oxford (Hon. Exhibr); Corpus Christi Coll., Cambridge (Schoolmaster Fellow Commoner). 1st cl. Class. Hon. Mods 1953, 2nd cl. Lit. Hum. 1955, BA 1955, MA 1958. RAF, 1950-51; Classical Upper Sixth Form Master, Dulwich Coll., 1955-60; Head of Classics Dept, Warwick Sch., 1960-66; Headmaster, Dr Morgan's Grammar Sch., Bridgwater, 1966-73. *Publications:* articles in Enciclopedia dello Spettacolo and Classical Review. *Recreations:* Rugby, swimming, gardening, travel. *Address:* Crossings Cottage, Dousland, Yelverton, S Devon PL20 6LU. *T:* Yelverton 853928. *Clubs:* East India, Devonshire, Sports and Public Schools; Union (Oxford).

DAVEY, Geoffrey Wallace; a Recorder of the Crown Court, since 1974; *b* 16 Oct. 1924; *s* of late Hector F. T. Davey and Alice M. Davey; *m* 1964, Joyce Irving Steel; two *s* one *d. Educ:* Queen Elizabeth Grammar Sch., Faversham; Wadham Coll., Oxford (MA). Called to Bar, Lincoln's Inn, 1954; admitted Ghana Bar, 1957; resumed practice NE Circuit, 1970. *Recreations:* golf, cooking, carpentry. *Address:* 22 Brompton Road, Northallerton, N Yorkshire. *T:* Northallerton 5943; 19 Baker Street, Middlesbrough, Cleveland. *T:* Middlesbrough 211310; 5 King's Bench Walk, Temple, EC4.

DAVEY, Idris Wyn; Under-Secretary, Welsh Office, 1972-77; Member, Sports Council for Wales, since 1978; Deputy Chairman, Local Government Boundary Commission for Wales, since 1979; *b* 8 July 1917; *m* 1943, Lilian Lloyd-Bowen; two *d. Educ:* Nantyglo Grammar Sch.; Cardiff Technical Coll.; London Univ. (BSc). Admiralty, 1940-47; Welsh Bd of Health: Asst Principal, 1948; Principal, 1951; Sec. Local Govt Commn for Wales, 1959-62; Welsh Office: Asst Sec. (in Min. of Housing and Local Govt), 1962; Establishment Officer, 1966-72; Under-Sec., 1972; seconded as Sec. and Mem., Local Govt Staff Commn for Wales and NHS Staff Commn for Wales, 1972-73. *Recreations:* watching Rugby football, gardening. *Address:* 4 Southgate Road, Pennard, Gower, West Glam. *T:* Bishopston 4320.

DAVEY, Jocelyn; see Raphael, Chaim.

DAVEY, Keith Alfred Thomas, CB 1973; Solicitor and Legal Adviser, Department of the Environment, 1970-82; *b* 1920; *s* of W. D. F. Davey; *m* 1949, Kathleen Elsie, *d* of Rev. F. J. Brabyn; one *s* one *d. Educ:* Cambridge and County High Sch.; Fitzwilliam House, Cambridge (MA). Served War of 1939-45, Middle East (Captain). Called to the Bar, Middle Temple, 1947. Principal Asst Solicitor, DHSS, 1968-70. *Recreations:* looking at churches, reading history, keeping cats and dogs. *Address:* 165 Shelford Road, Trumpington, Cambridge CB2 2ND. *Club:* Athenæum.

DAVEY, Roy Charles; Headmaster, King's School, Bruton, 1957-72; *b* 25 June 1915; *s* of William Arthur Davey and Georgina (*née* Allison); *m* 1940, Kathleen Joyce Sumner; two *d. Educ:* Christ's Hospital; Brasenose Coll., Oxford (Open Scholar). Asst Master, Weymouth Coll., 1937-40. War Service, Royal Artillery, 1940-46. Senior Master, 1946-49, Warden, 1949-57, The Village Coll., Impington. Vice Chm. Governors, St Hugh's Sch., Faringdon. FRSA. *Recreations:* poetry, botany, gardening, games. *Address:* Fir Trees, Buckland Newton, Dorchester, Dorset DT2 7BI. *T:* Buckland Newton 262. *Club:* East India, Devonshire, Sports and Public Schools.

DAVEY, Prof. William, CBE 1978; PhD; FRSC; President, Portsmouth Polytechnic, 1969-82; Honorary Professor, Polytechnic of Central London, since 1979; *b* Chesterfield, Derbyshire, 15 June 1917; *m* 1941, Eunice Battye; two *s. Educ:* University Coll., Nottingham; Technical Coll., Huddersfield. BSc, PhD (London, external). Chemist: ICI Scottish Dyes, 1940; Boots, 1941; Shell, 1942-44. Lectr and Sen. Lectr in Organic Chemistry, Acton Techn. Coll., 1944-53; Head of Dept of Chemistry and Biology, The Polytechnic, Regent Street, London, W1, 1953-59; Principal, Coll. of Technology, Portsmouth, 1960-69. FRSA, FRSC, CBIM. *Publications:* Industrial Chemistry, 1961; numerous original papers in: Jl Chem. Soc., Inst. Petroleum, Jl Applied Chem. *Recreations:* motoring, foreign travel. *Address:* 67 Ferndale, Waterlooville, Portsmouth PO7 7PH. *T:* Waterlooville 3014.

DAVID, family name of Baroness David.

DAVID, Baroness *cr* 1978 (Life Peer), of Romsey in the City of Cambridge; **Nora Ratcliff David;** JP; *b* 23 Sept. 1913; *d* of George Blockley Blakesley, JP, and Annie Edith Blakesley; *m* 1935, Richard William David, *qv*; two *s* two *d. Educ:* Ashby-de-la-Zouch Girls' Grammar School; St Felix, Southwold; Newnham Coll., Cambridge (MA). Mem. Bd, Peterborough

Develt Corp., 1976-78. A Baroness-in-Waiting (Government Whip), 1978-79; Opposition Whip, 1979-. Member: Cambridge City Council, 1964-67, 1968-74; Cambs County Council, 1974-78. JP Cambridge City, 1965-. *Recreations:* swimming, theatre. *Address:* 50 Highsett, Cambridge CB2 1NZ. *T:* Cambridge 350376; Cove, New Polzeath, Cornwall PL27 6UF.

DAVID, Brian Gurney; Deputy Receiver for the Metropolitan Police District, since 1976; *b* 25 Jan. 1926; *s* of Constantine and Gladys Emma David; *m* 1950, Jean Valerie (*née* Young). *Educ:* Alleyn's School, Dulwich. Joined Metropolitan Police Office, 1946; Private Secretary to Receiver for the Metropolitan Police District, 1958; Asst Secretary (Director of Finance), 1973. *Recreations:* cats, cooking, crossword puzzles. *Address:* New Scotland Yard, Broadway, SW1H 0BG. *T:* 01-230 1212.

DAVID, Mrs Elizabeth, OBE 1976; 2nd *d* of Rupert Sackville Gwynne, MP, and Hon. Stella Ridley; *m* 1944, Lt-Col Ivor Anthony David (marr. diss. 1960). DUniv Essex, 1979. Chevalier du Mérite Agricole (France), 1977. *Publications:* A Book of Mediterranean Food, 1950; French Country Cooking, 1951; Italian Food, 1954; Summer Cooking, 1955; French Provincial Cooking, 1960; English Cooking, Ancient and Modern: vol. I, Spices, Salt and Aromatics in the English Kitchen, 1970; English Bread and Yeast Cookery, 1977. *Address:* c/o Penguin Books Ltd, Harmondsworth, Middlesex.

DAVID, Richard (William), CBE 1967; formerly Publisher to the University, Cambridge University Press; Fellow of Clare Hall, Cambridge; *b* 28 Jan. 1912; *e s* of Rev. F. P. and Mary W. David, Winchester; *m* 1935, Nora (*see* Baroness David); two *s* two *d. Educ:* Winchester Coll. (Scholar); Corpus Christi Coll., Cambridge (Scholar). Joined editorial staff, CUP, 1936. Served RNVR, 1940-46, in Mediterranean and Western Approaches; qualified navigator, 1944; Lt-Comdr, 1945. Transferred to London Office of CUP, 1946; London Manager, 1948-63; Sec. to the Syndics of the Press, 1963-70. Member of Council of Publishers Assoc., 1953-63; Chairman of Export Research Cttee, 1956-59; President, 1959-61. Pres., Botanical Soc. of British Isles, 1979-81. *Publications:* The Janus of Poets, 1935; Love's Labour's Lost (The Arden Edition of Shakespeare), 1951; Shakespeare in the Theatre, 1978; (ed) Hakluyt's Voyages: a selection, 1981; (jtly) Review of the Cornish Flora, 1981; (jtly) Sedges of the British Isles, 1982; journal articles on the production of Shakespeare plays, and on botanical subjects, especially Carex. *Recreations:* music, botanising, fly-fishing. *Address:* 50 Highsett, Cambridge; Cove, New Polzeath, Wadebridge, Cornwall. *Club:* Garrick.

DAVID, Robin (Robert) Daniel George, QC 1968; DL; **His Honour Judge David;** a Circuit Judge (formerly Chairman, Cheshire Quarter Sessions), since 1968; *b* 30 April 1922; *s* of late Alexander Charles Robert David and late Edrica Doris Pole David (*née* Evans); *m* 1944, Edith Mary David (*née* Marsh); two *d. Educ:* Christ Coll., Brecon; Ellesmere Coll., Salop. War Service, 1943-47, Captain, Royal Artillery. Called to Bar, Gray's Inn, 1949; joined Wales and Chester Circuit, 1949. Dep. Chairman, Cheshire QS, 1961; Dep. Chairman, Agricultural Land Tribunal (Wales), 1965-68; Commissioner of Assize, 1970; Mem., Parole Bd for England and Wales, 1971-74. DL Cheshire 1972. *Recreation:* boating. *Address:* (home) Hallowsgate House, Kelsall, Cheshire. *T:* Kelsall 51456; (chambers) 4 Paper Buildings, Temple, EC4. *T:* 01-353 8408, 01-353 0196; (chambers) 40 King Street, Chester. *T:* Chester 23886.

DAVIDSON, family name of Viscount Davidson.

DAVIDSON, 2nd Viscount *cr* 1937, of Little Gaddesden; **John Andrew Davidson;** *b* 22 Dec. 1928; *er s* of 1st Viscount Davidson, PC, GCVO, CH, CB, and of Frances Joan, Viscountess Davidson, *qv*; *S* father, 1970; *m* 1st, 1956, Margaret Birgitta (marr. diss. 1974), *o d* of Maj.-Gen. C. H. Norton, *qv*; four *d* (including twin *d*); 2nd, 1975, Mrs Pamela Dobb (*née* Vergette). *Educ:* Westminster School; Pembroke College, Cambridge (BA). Served in The Black Watch and 5th Bn KAR, 1947-49. Director: Strutt & Parker (Farms) Ltd, 1960-75; Lord Rayleigh's Farms Inc., 1960-75; Member of Council: CLA, 1965-75; RASE, 1973; Chm., Management Committee, Royal Eastern Counties Hospital, 1966-72; Mem., East Anglia Economic Planning Council, 1971-75. *Recreation:* music. *Heir: b* Hon. Malcolm William Mackenzie Davidson [*b* 28 Aug. 1934; *m* 1970, Mrs Evelyn Ann Carew Perfect, *yr d* of William Blackmore Storey; one *s* one *d*]. *Address:* 63 Chester Row, SW1.

DAVIDSON, Dowager Viscountess; Frances Joan Davidson; Baroness (Life Peer), *cr* 1963, under title of **Baroness Northchurch;** DBE 1952 (OBE 1920); *y d* of 1st Baron Dickinson, PC, KBE; *m* 1919, 1st Viscount Davidson, PC, GCVO, CH, CB (*d* 1970); two *s* two *d.* MP (U) Hemel Hempstead Division of Herts, 1937-Sept. 1959. *Recreations:* gardening, walking. *Address:* 16 Lord North Street, Westminster, SW1. *T:* 01-222 2167.

DAVIDSON, Alan Eaton, CMG 1975; author; HM Diplomatic Service, retired; *b* 30 March 1924; *s* of William John Davidson and Constance (*née* Eaton); *m* 1951, Jane Macatee; three *d. Educ:* Leeds Grammar Sch.; Queen's Coll., Oxford. 1st class hons Class. Mods. and Greats. Served in RNVR (Ordinary Seaman, later Lieut) in Mediterranean, N Atlantic and Pacific, 1943-46. Member of HM Foreign Service, 1948; served at: Washington, 1950-53; The Hague, 1953-55; FO, 1955-59; First Secretary, British Property Commission, and later Head of Chancery, British Embassy, Cairo, 1959-61;

Head of Chancery and Consul, Tunis, 1962-64; FO, 1964; Counsellor, 1965; Head, Central Dept, FO, 1966-68; Head of Chancery, UK Delegn to NATO, Brussels, 1968-71; seconded, as Vis. Fellow, Centre for Contemporary European Studies, Univ. of Sussex, 1971-72; Head of Defence Dept, FCO, 1972-73; Ambassador to Vientiane, 1973-75. *Publications:* Seafish of Tunisia and the Central Mediterranean, 1963; Snakes and Scorpions Found in the Land of Tunisia, 1964; Mediterranean Seafood, 1972; The Role of the Uncommitted European Countries in East-West Relations, 1972; Fish and Fish Dishes of Laos, 1975; Seafood of South East Asia, 1976; (with Jane Davidson) Dumas on Food, 1978; North Atlantic Sea Food, 1979; (with Jennifer Davidson) Traditional Recipes of Laos, 1981. *Address:* 45 Lamont Road, World's End, SW10 0HU. *T:* 01-352 4209.

DAVIDSON, Alfred Edward; international lawyer; Vice-President, General Counsel, Technical Studies, 1957-70, and since 1975; *b* New York, 11 Nov. 1911; *s* of Maurice Philip Davidson and Blanche Reinheimer; *m* 1934, Claire H. Dreyfuss. *Educ:* Harvard Univ. (AB); Columbia Law Sch. (LLB). Advocate, Bar of New York, 1936; of Dist of Columbia, 1972; Asst to Gen. Counsel, US Dept of Labour, Wash., 1938-40; review section, Solicitor's Office, 1940-41; Legis. Counsel, Office of Emergency Management, in Exec. Office of President, 1941-43; Asst Gen. Counsel, Lend-Lease Admin. (later Foreign Economic Admin.), 1943-45; Gen. Counsel, 1945-; Gen. Counsel, UNRRA, Nov. 1945; Counsel, Preparatory Commn for Internat. Refugee Org., 1947; Dir, European Headqrs of UNICEF, 1947-51; Advisor, Office of Sec.-Gen. of UN, 1951-52; Gen. Counsel, UN Korean Reconstr. Agency, 1952-54; Exec. Asst to Chm., Bd of Rio Tinto of Canada, 1955-58; European Representative, Internat. Finance Corp., 1970-72; Counsel to Wilmer, Cutler & Pickering, Attorneys at Law, 1972-75. Dir, Channel Tunnel Study Gp, 1960-70; Dir, Gen. Counsel, Construction Capital Co., 1964-69. Hon. Chm., Democratic Party Cttee, France. Co-Founder, Assoc. for Promotion of Humor in Internat. Affairs; Co-Chm., Bipartisan Cttees on Medicare Overseas and Absentee Voting; Dir, Assoc. of American Residents Overseas; Hon. Chm., Common Cause. *Publications:* contribs. various periodicals and newspapers. *Recreations:* tennis, bridge, chess, reading. *Address:* 5 rue de la Manutention, 75116 Paris, France. *Clubs:* Queen's, Lansdowne (London); Standard (France).

DAVIDSON, Arthur; QC 1978; MP (Lab) Accrington since 1966; *b* 7 Nov. 1928. *Educ:* Liverpool Coll.; King George V Sch., Southport; Trinity Coll., Cambridge. Served in Merchant Navy. Barrister, Middle Temple, 1953. Trinity Coll., Cambridge, 1959-62; Editor of the Granta. Contested (Lab) Blackpool S, 1955, and Preston N, 1959. PPS to Solicitor-General, 1968-70; Chm., Home Affairs Gp, Parly Labour Party, 1971-74; Parly Sec., Law Officers' Dept, 1974-79; Opposition spokesman on Defence (Army), 1980-81, on legal affairs, 1981-; Member: Home Affairs Select Cttee, 1980-; Armed Forces Bill Select Cttee, 1981-. Member: Council, Consumers' Association, 1970-74; Exec. Cttee, Soc. of Labour Lawyers, 1981-; Nat. Exec., Fabian Soc.; Council, Nat. Youth Jazz Orchestra; Chm., House of Commons Jazz Club, 1973-. *Recreations:* lawn tennis, ski-ing, theatre, listening to good jazz and playing bad jazz; formerly Member Cambridge Univ. athletics team. *Address:* House of Commons, SW1. *Clubs:* James Street Men's Working (Oswaldtwistle); Free Gardeners (Rishton); King Street, Marlborough Working Men's (Accrington).

DAVIDSON, Basil Risbridger, MC 1945; author and historian; *b* 9 Nov. 1914; *s* of Thomas and Jessie Davidson; *m* 1943, Marion Ruth Young; three *s.* Served War of 1939-45 (despatches twice, MC, US Bronze Star, Jugoslav Zasluge za Narod); British Army, 1940-45 (Balkans, N Africa, Italy); Temp. Lt-Col demobilised as Hon. Major. Editorial staff of The Economist, 1938-39; The Star (diplomatic correspondent, 1939); The Times (Paris correspondent, 1945-47; chief foreign leader-writer, 1947-49); New Statesman (special correspondent, 1950-54); Daily Herald (special correspondent, 1954-57); Daily Mirror (leader-writer, 1959-62). Vis. Prof., Univ. of Ghana, 1964; Regents' Lectr, Univ. of California, 1971; Montagu Burton Vis. Prof. of Internat. Relations, Edinburgh Univ., 1972. A Vice-Pres., Anti-Apartheid Movement, 1969-. Freeman of City of Genoa, 1945. DLitt *hc* Ibadan, 1975; DUniv *hc:* Open, 1980; Edinburgh, 1981. Haile Selassie African Research Award, 1970; Medalha Amílcar Cabral, 1976. *Publications: novels:* Highway Forty, 1949; Golden Horn, 1952; The Rapids, 1955; Lindy, 1958; The Andrassy Affair, 1966; *non-fiction:* Partisan Picture, 1946; Germany: From Potsdam to Partition, 1950; Report on Southern Africa, 1952; Daybreak in China, 1953; The New West Africa (ed.), 1953; The African Awakening, 1955; Turkestan Alive, 1957; Old Africa Rediscovered, 1959; Black Mother, 1961, rev. edn 1980; The African Past, 1964; Which Way Africa?, 1964; The Growth of African Civilisation: West Africa AD 1000-1800, 1965; Africa: History of a Continent, 1966; A History of East and Central Africa to the late 19th Century, 1967; Africa in History: Themes and Outlines, 1968; The Liberation of Guiné, 1969; The Africans, An Entry to Cultural History, 1969; Discovering our African Heritage, 1971; In the Eye of the Storm: Angola's People, 1972; Black Star, 1974; Can Africa Survive?, 1975; Discovering Africa's Past, 1978 (Children's Rights Workshop Award, 1978); Africa in Modern History, 1978; Crossroads in Africa, 1980; Special Operations Europe, 1980; The People's Cause, 1980; No Fist is Big Enough, 1981. *Address:* c/o Barclays Bank Ltd, PO Box 175, EC4P 4DR. *Club:* Savile.

DAVIDSON, Brian, CBE 1965; *b* 14 Sept. 1909; *o s* of late Edward Fitzwilliam Davidson and late Esther Davidson (*née* Schofield); *m* 1935, Priscilla Margaret (*d* 1981), *d* of late Arthur Farquhar and Florence Chilver;

one *s* one *d* (and one *s* decd). *Educ:* Winchester Coll. (Scholar); New Coll., Oxford (Scholar). Gaisford Prize for Greek Verse; 1st class Honour Mods.; 2nd class LitHum; President, Oxford Union Society; President OU Conservative Assoc.; BA 1932. Cholmeley Student Lincoln's Inn; Barrister-at-Law, 1933; Law Society Sheffield Prize; Solicitor, 1939; Air Ministry and Ministry of Aircraft Production, 1940. With Bristol Aeroplane Co., 1943-68: Business Manager, 1946; Director, 1950-68; Director, Bristol Siddeley Engines Ltd, 1959-68. Solicitor with Gas Council, later British Gas Corp., 1969-75. Member: Monopolies Commission, 1954-68; Gloucestershire CC (and Chairman Rating Valuation Appeals Cttee), 1953-60; Cttee Wine Society, 1966-. *Recreations:* fox-hunting, sailing (represented Oxford Univ.), Scottish country dancing, bridge. *Address:* Sands Court, Dodington, Avon BS17 6SE. *T:* Chipping Sodbury 313077.
See also R. C. Chilver.

DAVIDSON, Charles Kemp, QC (Scot.) 1969; Procurator to the General Assembly of the Church of Scotland, since 1972; Dean of the Faculty of Advocates, since 1979; *b* Edinburgh, 13 April 1929; *s* of Rev. Donald Davidson, DD, Edinburgh; *m* 1960, Mary, *d* of Charles Mactaggart, Campbeltown, Argyll; one *s* two *d. Educ:* Fettes Coll., Edinburgh; Brasenose Coll., Oxford; Edinburgh Univ. Admitted to Faculty of Advocates, 1956; Vice-Dean, 1977-79; Keeper, Advocates' Library, 1972-76. *Address:* 22 Dublin Street, Edinburgh EH1 3PP. *T:* 031-556 2168.

DAVIDSON, Hon. Sir Charles (William), KBE 1964 (OBE 1945); retired; *b* 14 Sept. 1897; *s* of Alexander Black Davidson and Marion Perry; *m* 1929, Mary Gertrude Godschall Johnson; one *s* two *d. Educ:* Townsville Grammar Sch., Townsville. Served European War, 1914-18: 42 Bn AIF, 1916-19; Lieut; France (wounded); served War of 1939-45: 42 Bn AIF, 1939-44; Lt-Col; Hon. Colonel 42 Inf. Bn, 1955. Dairy farmer, 1921-25; sugar farming from 1925. MHR for Capricornia (Queensland), 1946-49, and for Dawson (Queensland), 1949-63, retired; Postmaster-General, 1956-63; Minister for Navy, 1956-58; Dep. Leader, Parliamentary Country Party, 1958-63. *Recreations:* bowls, golf, fishing, gardening. *Address:* 439 Brisbane Corso, Yeronga, Brisbane, Qld 4104, Australia. *T:* Brisbane 48.4264. *Clubs:* United Service, Masonic (Brisbane); Mackay Civic.

DAVIDSON, Francis, CBE 1961; Finance Officer, Singapore High Commission, London, 1961-71; *b* 23 Nov. 1905; *s* of James Davidson and Margaret Mackenzie; *m* 1937, Marial Mackenzie, MA; one *s* one *d. Educ:* Millbank Public Sch., Nairn; Nairn Academy. Commercial Bank of Scotland Ltd, 1923-29; Bank of British West Africa Ltd, 1929-41; Colonial Service (Treasury), 1941-61; retired from Colonial Service, Nov. 1961, as Accountant-General of Federation of Nigeria. *Recreation:* philately. *Address:* Woolton, Nairn, Scotland. *T:* Nairn 52187. *Club:* Royal Over-Seas League.

DAVIDSON, Howard William, CMG 1961; MBE 1942; *b* 30 July 1911; *s* of late Joseph Christopher Davidson, Johannesburg, and Helen, *d* of James Forbes; *m* 1st, 1941, Anne Elizabeth, *d* of late Captain R. C. Power; one *d;* 2nd, 1956, Dorothy (marr. diss. 1972), *d* of late Sir Wm Polson, KCMG; one step *s. Educ:* King Edward VII Sch., Johannesburg; Witwatersrand Univ.; Oriel Coll., Oxford (1st cl. Greats 1934). Cadet, Colonial Admin. Service, Sierra Leone, 1935; District Commissioner, 1942; Dep. Fin. Secretary, 1949; Fin. Secretary, Fiji, 1952; Fin. Secretary, N Borneo, 1958; State Financial Secretary and Member Cabinet, Sabah, Malaysia, 1963-64; Financial Adviser, 1964-65; Member of Inter-Governmental Cttee which led to establishment of new Federation of Malaysia; retired, 1965. Inspector (part-time) Min. of Housing and Local Government, 1967-70. Consultant with Peat, Marwick Mitchell & Co, to report on finances of Antigua, 1973. Appointed PDK (with title of Datuk) in first Sabah State Honours List, 1963, now SPDK. *Recreations:* cricket, gardening, learning. *Address:* Glebe Cottage, Tillington, Petworth, West Sussex. *Clubs:* East India, Devonshire, Sports and Public Schools; Sussex County Cricket.

DAVIDSON, Ian Douglas, CBE 1957; *b* 27 Oct. 1901; *s* of Rev. John Davidson, JP, and Elizabeth Helen (*née* Whyte); *m* 1st, 1936, Claire Louise (*d* 1937), *d* of E. S. Gempp, St Louis, Missouri; one *d;* 2nd, 1938, Eugenia, *d* of late Marques de Mohernando and Lorenza, Marquesa de Mohernando; one *d. Educ:* King William's Coll. Royal Dutch Shell Group of Companies, 1921-61; President: Mexican Eagle Oil Co., 1936-47; Cia Shell de Venezuela, 1953-57; Canadian Shell Ltd, 1957-61. Order of St Mark (Lebanon), 1957; Orden del Libertador (Venezuela), 1957. *Address:* One Benvenuto Place, Apt 105, Toronto, Ontario M4V 2L1, Canada. *Clubs:* Caledonian (London); York (Toronto); Links (NY).

DAVIDSON, Ian Thomas Rollo, QC 1977; a Recorder of the Crown Court, since Dec. 1974; *b* 3 Aug. 1925; *s* of late Robert Davidson and Margaret Davidson; *m* 1954, Gyöngyi, *d* of Prof. Cs. Anghi; one *s* one *d. Educ:* Fettes Coll.; Corpus Christi Coll., Oxford (Schol.). MA, Lit. Hum. Royal Armoured Corps, 1943-47, Lieut Derbs Yeomanry. Called to Bar, Gray's Inn, 1955. Asst Lectr, University Coll., London, 1959-60; Deputy Recorder, Nottingham, 1971. *Recreations:* music, golf, photography. *Address:* 1 Ludlow Avenue, Luton, Beds LU1 3RW. *T:* Luton 422624.

DAVIDSON, Ivor Macaulay; Chairman, D. O. Sanbiet Ltd, since 1980; *b* 27 Jan. 1924; *s* of late James Macaulay and Violet Alice Davidson; *m* 1948, Winifred Lowes; four *s* one *d. Educ:* Bellahouston Sch.; Univ. of Glasgow.

Royal Aircraft Establishment, 1943; Power Jets (R&D) Ltd, 1944; attached RAF, 1945; National Gas Turbine Establishment, 1946: Dep. Dir, 1964; Dir, 1970-74; Dir-Gen. Engines, Procurement Exec., MoD, 1974-79. *Publications:* numerous, scientific and technical. *Recreations:* music, gardening. *Address:* Monksway, Pirbright Road, Farnborough, Hants. *T:* Farnborough 544686.

DAVIDSON, James, MB, ChB, FRCP Edinburgh; FSAScot.; late Senior Lecturer on Pathology, University of Edinburgh and Consultant Pathologist to the Edinburgh Southern Hospitals and The Royal Victoria and Associated Hospitals; *b* 3 Feb. 1896; *s* of James Davidson and Isabella Slater Shaw; *m* 1927, Constance Ellen Cameron; two *d. Educ:* University of Edinburgh. House Physician, Royal Infirmary, Edinburgh; Tutor in Clinical Medicine, University of Edinburgh; Lecturer on Morbid Anatomy and Senior Asst to Prof. of Pathology, University of Edinburgh; Senior Pathologist to Royal Infirmary, Edinburgh; Asst to Prof. of Medical Jurisprudence, University of Edinburgh; Lecturer on Forensic Medicine, London Hospital Medical Coll.; Director of Metropolitan Police Laboratory, Hendon, NW9. *Publications:* various papers on subjects dealing with Pathology and Forensic Science; (joint) text-book, Practical Pathology, 1938. *Recreations:* gardening, golf and fishing. *Address:* Linton Muir, West Linton, Peebles-shire.

DAVIDSON, James Alfred, OBE 1971; Governor of the British Virgin Islands, 1978-81; *b* 22 March 1922; *s* of Lt-Comdr A. D. Davidson and Mrs (Elizabeth) Davidson; *m* 1955, Daphne (*née* While); two *d,* and two step *s. Educ:* Christ's Hospital; RN Coll., Dartmouth. Royal Navy, 1939-60 (war Service Atlantic, Mediterranean and Far East); commanded HM Ships Calder and Welfare; Comdr 1955; retd 1960. Holds Master Mariner's Cert. of Service. Called to the Bar, Middle Temple, 1960. Joined CRO (later FCO) 1960; served Port of Spain, Phnom Penh (periods as Chargé d'Affaires 1970 and 1971); Dacca (Chargé d'Affaires, later Dep. High Comr, 1972-73); Vis. Scholar, Univ. of Kent, 1973-74; British High Comr, Brunei, 1974-78; participated, Sept. 1978, in finalisation of Brunei Independence Treaty. *Publications:* Brunei Coinage, 1977; Indo-China: Signposts in the Storm, 1979. *Address:* Little Frankfield, Seal Chart, near Sevenoaks, Kent. *T:* Sevenoaks 61600. *Club:* Army and Navy.

DAVIDSON, James Duncan Gordon, MVO 1947; Chief Executive, Royal Highland and Agricultural Society of Scotland, since 1970; *b* 10 Jan. 1927; *s* of Alastair Gordon Davidson and M. Valentine B. Davidson (*née* Osborne); *m* 1st, 1955, Catherine Ann Jamieson; one *s* two *d* ; 2nd, 1973, Janet Stafford; one *s. Educ:* RN Coll., Dartmouth; Downing Coll., Cambridge. Active List, RN, 1944-55. Subseq. farming, and political work; contested (L) West Aberdeenshire, 1964; MP (L) West Aberdeenshire, 1966-70. Introduces Country Focus, Grampian TV. FRAgS; FBIM; MIEx. *Recreations:* family, farming, walking, ski-ing, music. *Address:* Tillychetly, Alford, Aberdeenshire. *T:* Alford 2246.

DAVIDSON, James Patton, CBE 1980; Chairman, Clyde Port Authority, since 1980; *b* 23 March 1928; *s* of Richard Davidson and Elizabeth Ferguson Carnichan. *Educ:* Rutherglen Acad.; Glasgow Univ. (BL). Mil. service, commissioned RASC, 1948-50. Clyde Navigation Trust, 1950; Asst Gen. Manager, 1958. Clyde Port Authority: Gen. Manager, 1966; Managing Dir, 1974; Dep. Chm. and Man. Dir, 1976. Chairman: Ardrossan Harbour Co. Ltd, 1976-; Clydeport Stevedoring Services Ltd, 1977-; Clyde Container Services Ltd, 1968-; S. & H. McCall Transport (Glasgow) Ltd, 1972-; Rhu Marina Ltd, 1976-80; Scotway Haulage Ltd, 1976-81; R. & J. Strang Ltd, 1976-81; Nat. Assoc. of Port Employers, 1974-79; British Ports Assoc., 1980- (Dep. Chm., 1978-80); Port Employers' & Registered Dock Workers' Pension Fund Trustee Ltd, 1978-; UK Dir, 1976- and Mem., Exec. Cttee, 1977-, Internat. Assoc. of Ports and Harbours; Mem., Pilotage Commn, 1979-; Dir, Iron Trades Insurance Gp, 1981-. FCIT, CBIM; FRSA. *Recreations:* golf, reading. *Address:* 44 Guthrie Court, Gleneagles Village, Gleneagles, Perthshire; Clyde Port Authority, 16 Robertson Street, Glasgow G2 8DS. *T:* 041-221 8733. *Clubs:* Oriental; Royal Scottish Automobile (Glasgow); Cambuslang Golf; Royal Troon Golf.

DAVIDSON, Prof. John Frank, FRS 1974; Shell Professor of Chemical Engineering, University of Cambridge, since 1978 (Professor of Chemical Engineering, 1975-78); *b* 7 Feb. 1926; *s* of John and Katie Davidson; *m* 1948, Susanne Hedwig Ostberg; one *s* one *d. Educ:* Heaton Grammar Sch., Newcastle upon Tyne; Trinity Coll., Cambridge. MA, PhD, ScD; FEng, FIChemE, MIMechE. 1st cl. Mech. Scis Tripos, Cantab, 1946, BA 1947. Engrg work at Rolls Royce, Derby, 1947-50; Cambridge Univ.: Research Fellow, Trinity Coll., 1949; research, 1950-52; Univ. Demonstrator, 1952; Univ. Lectr, 1954; Steward of Trinity Coll., 1957-64; Reader in Chem. Engrg, Univ. of Cambridge, 1964-75. Visiting Professor: Univ. of Delaware, 1960; Univ. of Sydney, 1967. Member: Flixborough Ct of Inquiry, 1974-75; Adv. Cttee on Safety of Nuclear Installations, HSE, 1977-. Pres., IChemE, 1970-71. Founder FEng, 1976. For. Associate, Nat. Acad. of Engrg, US, 1976. Dr *hc* Institut Nat. Polytech. de Toulouse, 1979. *Publications:* (with D. Harrison): Fluidised Particles, 1963; Fluidization, 1971; (with D. L. Keairns) Fluidization, 1978. *Recreations:* hill walking, gardening, mending cars and other domestic artefacts. *Address:* 5 Luard Close, Cambridge CB2 2PL. *T:* Cambridge 246104.

DAVIDSON, Maj.-Gen. Kenneth Chisholm, CB 1948; MC; psc; late Infantry; *b* 4 July 1897; *m* 1934, Diana Blanche Wilson; one *s* one *d. Educ:* Newbury Grammar Sch. 2nd Lieut Gordon Highlanders, 1915; served

European War, 1914-19 (wounded twice); War of 1939-45, Persia and Iraq Force (despatches), Sicily (despatches), Italy (despatches). Lieut-Col, 1942; Col, 1942; Brig., 1947; actg Maj.-Gen., 1946; retired pay, 1949 (with hon. rank of Maj.-Gen.). *Address:* Rooklands, Tangley, near Andover, Hants. *T:* Chute Standen 612.

DAVIDSON, Mrs Paul; see Cairns, Julia.

DAVIDSON, Roger Alastair McLaren, CMG 1947; Secretary of the Scottish Universities Entrance Board, 1953-66; *b* 6 Feb. 1900; *s* of late Rev. R. S. Davidson, The Manse, Kinfauns, Perthshire; *m* 1928, Elsie Stuart (*d* 1979); *d* of late J. A. Y. Stronach, Edinburgh; one *s* one *d. Educ:* Fettes Coll., Edinburgh; University of Edinburgh. Served European War, 1914-18, 2nd Lieut Royal Highlanders, 1918-19; entered Colonial Education Service, 1924; Nigeria, 1924-37; Asst Dir of Education, Tanganyika, 1937-40; seconded to Colonial Office, 1941-43; Asst Dir of Education, Southern Provinces, Nigeria, 1943-44; Dir of Education, Nigeria, 1944-51; Inspector-Gen. of Education, Nigeria, 1951-53. *Address:* 6 Hope Street, St Andrews. *T:* St Andrews 72345. *Club:* Royal and Ancient (St Andrews).

DAVIDSON, Air Vice-Marshal Sinclair Melville, CBE 1968; Secretary, The Institution of Electronic and Radio Engineers, since 1977; *b* 1 Nov. 1922; *s* of late James Stewart Davidson and Ann Sinclair Davidson (*née* Cowan); *m* 1944, Jean Irene, *d* of late Edward Albert Flay; one *s* (and one *s* decd). *Educ:* Bousfield Sch., Kensington; RAF Cranwell; RAF Techn. College. CEng, FRAeS, FIERE. War service with 209, 220 and 53 Sqdns RAF, 1941-45 (despatches); Staff RAF Coastal and Fighter Comds, 1943-53; Air Staff, Egypt, Iraq and Cyprus, 1954-55; psa 1956; Air Staff, Air Min., 1957-60; jssc 1960; Dirg Staff, RAF Staff Coll., Bracknell, 1961-63; Asst Comdt, RAF Locking, 1963-64; Chm. Jt Signal Bd (Middle East), 1965; Chief Signal Officer and Comd Electrical Engr, Near East Air Force, 1966-67; idc 1968; Dir of Signals (Air), MoD, 1969-71; AO Wales and Stn Comdr, RAF St Athan, 1972-74; Asst Chief of Defence Staff (Signals), 1974-77. *Address:* Moy Cottage, Fielden Lane, Crowborough, Sussex. *T:* Crowborough 4724. *Club:* Royal Air Force.

DAVIDSON, William Bird; a Deputy Chairman, National Westminster Bank Ltd, 1973-76 (Director and Chief Executive, 1970-72); Chairman, Lombard North Central, 1973-76; Director, Allied London Properties Ltd, since 1976; *b* 18 May 1912; 2nd *s* of late J. N. Davidson; *m* 1941, Christina M. Ireton; two *s. Educ:* Queen Elizabeth Grammar Sch., Penrith. War Service, Royal Artillery, 1939-45. Entered Nat. Provincial Bank, 1929; Jt Gen Manager, 1961; Chief Gen. Manager, 1967-68; Dir, 1968; Dir and Jt Chief Executive, Nat. Westminster Bank, 1968-70. FIB. *Recreation:* golf. *Address:* Rose Cottage, 9 Starrock Road, Coulsdon, Surrey. *T:* Downland 53687.

DAVIDSON-HOUSTON, Major Aubrey Claud; portrait painter since 1952; *b* 2 Feb. 1906; *s* of late Lt-Col Wilfred Bennett Davidson-Houston, CMG, and Annie Henrietta Hunt; *m* 1938, Georgina Louie Ethel (*d* 1961), *d* of late Capt. H. S. Dobson; one *d. Educ:* St Edward's Sch., Oxford; RMC, Sandhurst; Slade Sch. of Fine Art. 2nd Lieut, Royal Sussex Regt, 1925; ADC to Governor of Western Australia, 1927-30; Nigeria Regt, RWAFF, 1933-37; PoW (Germany), 1940-45; Sch. of Infty, 1946-47; MS Branch, WO, 1948-49; retd, 1949. Slade Sch. of Fine Art, 1949-52 (diploma). *Portraits include:* The Queen, for RWF; The Duke of Edinburgh, for 8th King's Royal Irish Hussars, for Duke of Edinburgh's Royal Regt, for the House of Lords, and for United Oxford & Cambridge University Club; Queen Elizabeth, The Queen Mother, for Black Watch of Canada; The Prince of Wales, for Royal Regt of Wales; The Princess Royal, for WRAC; The Duke of Gloucester, for Royal Inniskilling Fusiliers, for Scots Guards and for Trinity House; The Duchess of Kent for ACC; also portraits for Lincoln Coll. and Keble Coll., Oxford, and for Selwyn Coll., Cambridge; also for a number of other regts and for City Livery cos, schools, etc. Founder Trustee, Jt Educn Trust, 1971-. *Address:* Hillview, West End Lane, Esher, Surrey. *T:* Esher 64769; 4 Chelsea Studios, 412 Fulham Road, SW6. *T:* 01-385 2569. *Clubs:* Buck's, Naval and Military, MCC.

DAVIE, Alan, CBE 1972; HRSA 1977; painter, poet, jazz musician and designer of jewellery; *b* 1920. *Educ:* Edinburgh Coll. of Art. DA. Gregory Fellowship, Leeds Univ., 1956-59. One-man exhibitions, since 1946, in GB, USA and most European countries. Work represented in exhibitions: 4th Internat. Art Exhibn, Japan; Pittsburgh Internat.; Documenta II & III, Kassel, Germany; British Painting 1700-1960, Moscow; Salon de Mai, Paris; Peggy Guggenheim Collection; ROSC Dublin; Peter Styvesant Collection; British Painting and Sculpture 1960-1970, Washington; III Bienal de Arte Coltejer, Colombia; Hannover, 1973; British Paintings, 1974; Hayward Gall., 1974; Paris, 1975; Lausanne, 1975; 25 years of British Art, RA, 1977; South America, 1977; Kassell, 1977; Sydney, 1979; One-man exhbn, Edinburgh Fest., 1972. Works in Public Collections: Tate Gall., Gulbenkian Found'n London, Belfast, Bristol, Durham, Edinburgh, Hull, Leeds, Manchester, Newcastle, Wakefield; Boston, Buffalo, Dallas, Detroit, Yale New Haven, Phoenix, Pittsburgh, Rhode Island, San Francisco; Ottawa, Adelaide, Sydney, Auckland, São Paulo, Tel Aviv, Venice, Vienna, Baden-Baden, Bochum, Munich, Amsterdam, Eindhoven, The Hague, Rotterdam, Oslo, Basle, Stockholm, Gothenburg, St Paul de Vence and Paris. First public recital of music, Gimpel Fils Gall., 1971; music and lecture tour, Sydney, Melbourne, Canberra, 1979. Prize for Best Foreign Painter, VII Bienal de São Paulo, 1963; Saltire Award, RSA 1977.

Relevant Publication: Alan Davie (ed Alan Bowness), 1967. *Address:* Gamels Studio, Rush Green, Hertford.

DAVIE, Rev. Sir (Arthur) Patrick; *see* Ferguson Davie.

DAVIE, Cedric Thorpe, OBE 1955; FRSE 1978; FRSAMD 1978; FRAM; Master of Music, 1945-78, and Professor of Music, 1973-78, University of St Andrews, now Emeritus Professor; composer (especially for film, theatre, radio); *b* 30 May 1913; *s* of Thorpe and Gladys Louise Davie; *m* 1937, Margaret Russell Brown (*d* 1974); two *s. Educ:* High Sch. of Glasgow; Royal Scottish Academy of Music; Royal Academy of Music. Member: Scottish Arts Council, 1965-74; Arts Council of Great Britain, 1968-74. FRAM, 1949. Hon. Mem., Royal Scottish Acad., 1977. Hon. LLD Dundee, 1969. *Publications:* Musical Structure and Design, 1949; Oxford Scottish Song Book, 1969; Robert Burns: writer of songs, 1975; Scotland's Music, 1980; Catalogue of the Finzi Music Collection in the University Library, St Andrews, 1982; articles and reviews in learned jls. *Recreations:* eating and drinking; travel Northwards in search of sunshine. *Address:* 66 Main Street, Dalry, Castle Douglas DG7 3UW. *T:* Dalry (Kirkcudbrightshire) 293.

DAVIE, Prof. Donald Alfred; Andrew W. Mellon Professor of Humanities, Vanderbilt University, since 1978; *b* 17 July 1922; *s* of George Clarke Davie and Alice (*née* Sugden); *m* 1945, Doreen John; two *s* one *d. Educ:* Barnsley Holgate Gram. Sch.; St Catharine's Coll., Cambridge (Hon. Fellow, 1973). BA 1947; PhD 1951. Served with Royal Navy, 1941-46 (Sub-Lieut RNVR). Lecturer in Dublin Univ., 1950-57; Fellow of Trinity Coll., Dublin, 1954-57, Hon. Fellow, 1978; Visiting Prof., University of Calif., 1957-58; Lecturer, Cambridge Univ., 1958-64; Fellow of Gonville and Caius Coll., Cambridge, 1959-64; George Elliston Lecturer, University of Cincinnati, 1963; Prof. of Literature, University of Essex, 1964-68, and Pro-Vice-Chancellor, 1965-68; Prof. of English, 1968-74, Olive H. Palmer Prof. in Humanities, 1974-78, Stanford Univ. Clark Lectr, Trinity Coll., Cambridge, 1976. Hon. DLitt Univ. of Southern California, 1978. Fellow, Amer. Acad. of Arts and Scis, 1973. *Publications:* poetry: Brides of Reason, 1955; A Winter Talent, 1957; The Forests of Lithuania, 1959; A Sequence for Francis Parkman, 1961; Events and Wisdoms, 1964; Essex Poems, 1969; Six Epistles to Eva Hesse, 1970; Collected Poems, 1972; The Shires, 1975; In the Stopping Train, 1977; Three for Water-Music, 1981; criticism and literary history: Purity of Diction in English Verse, 1952; Articulate Energy, 1957, 2nd edn 1976; The Heyday of Sir Walter Scott, 1961; Ezra Pound: Poet as Sculptor, 1965; Introduction to The Necklace by Charles Tomlinson, 1955; Thomas Hardy and British Poetry, 1972; Pound, 1976; The Poet in the Imaginary Museum: essays of two decades, 1978; A Gathered Church: the literature of the English dissenting interest 1700-1930, 1978; Trying to Explain (essays), 1980; Dissentient Voice, 1982; anthologies: The Late Augustans, 1958; (with Angela Livingstone) Modern Judgements: Pasternak, 1969; Augustan Lyric, 1974; The New Oxford Book of Christian Verse, 1981. *Recreations:* verse-translation; literary politics; travel. *Address:* 4400 Belmont Park Terrace, Nashville, Tenn 37215, USA. *Clubs:* Savile; Union (Cambridge).

DAVIE, Sir Paul (Christopher), Kt 1967; *b* 30 Sept. 1901; *s* of Charles Christopher Davie and Beatrice Paulina Mabel (*née* Walrond); *m* 1938, Betty Muriel, *d* of late Captain Ronald Henderson, MP for Henley div. of Oxfordshire, 1924-32, of Studley Priory, Oxon; one *s* one *d. Educ:* Winchester; New Coll., Oxford. Called to Bar, Lincoln's Inn, 1925; 2nd Asst Legal Advisor, Home Office, 1936; Asst Legal Advisor, 1947. Remembrancer, City of London, 1953-67. Chairman: Nat. Deaf Children's Soc., 1970-74; Council and Gen. Develt Services Ltd, 1971-82. *Publications:* Silicosis and Asbestosis Compensation Schemes, 1932; Joint Managing Ed., Encyclopædia of Local Government Law and Administration, 1934. *Recreations:* history, gardening. *Address:* The Old Rectory, Bentley, Hants. *T:* Bentley 23128. *Club:* Travellers'.

DAVIE, Ronald, PhD; FBPsS; Director, National Children's Bureau, since 1982; *b* 25 Nov. 1929; *s* of late Thomas Edgar Davie and Gladys (*née* Powell); *m* 1957, Kathleen, *d* of William Wilkinson, Westhoughton, Lancs; one *s* one *d. Educ:* King Edward VI Grammar Sch., Aston, Birmingham; Univ. of Reading (BA 1954); Univ. of Manchester (PGCE and Dip. Deaf Educn 1955); Univ. of Birmingham (Dip. Educnl Psych. 1960); Univ. of London (PhD 1970). FBPsS 1973. Teacher, schs for normal and handicapped children, 1955-60; Co. Educnl Psychologist, IoW, 1961-64; Nat. Children's Bureau, London: Sen. Res. Officer, 1964; Dep. Dir, 1968; Dir of Res., 1972; Prof. of Educnl Psychology, Dept of Educn, UC Cardiff, 1974-81. Co-Dir, Nat. Child Develt Study, 1968-77; Pres., Links Assoc., 1977-; Chairman: Trng and Educn. Cttee, Nat. Assoc. Mental Health, 1969-72; Working Gp rep. nat. vol. orgs concerned with handicapped children, 1971-74; Assoc. for Child Psychol. and Psychiatry, 1972-73 (Hon. Sec. 1965-70); Working Gp rep. professional assocs in S Wales concerned with children, 1974-; Working Party, Children Appearing Before Juvenile Courts, Children's Reg. Planning Cttee for Wales, 1975-77; Wales Standing Conf. for Internat. Year of the Child, 1978-79; Steering Cttee, Child Health and Educn Study, 1979-. Member: Council of Management, Nat. Assoc. Mental Health, 1969-77; Working Party, Children at Risk, DHSS, 1970-72; Educn and Employment Cttee, Nat. Deaf Children's Soc., 1972-78; Management Cttee, Craig y Parc Sch., 1974-76; Local Authority Social Services Res. Liaison Gp, DHSS, 1975-77; Cttee, Welsh Br., Assoc. for Child Psychol. and Psychiatry, 1975-80; Mental Handicap Res.

Liaison Group, DHSS, 1977-81; Council, British Psychol. Soc., 1977-80; Experimental Panel on Children in Care, SSRC, 1978-79; Sci. Adviser, Mental Handicap in Wales Res. Unit, 1977-79; Bd of Assessors, Therapeutic Educn, 1975-. *Publications:* (co-author) 11,000 Seven-Year Olds, 1966; Directory of Voluntary Organisations concerned with Children, 1969; Living with Handicap, 1970; From Birth to Seven, 1972; chapters in books and papers in sci. and other jls on educn, psychol., child care and health. *Recreations:* photography, antiques, Rugby, athletics. *Address:* 3 Grange Grove, Canonbury Park, N1 2NP. *T:* 01-226 3761; (office) 8 Wakley Street, EC1. *Club:* Royal Over-Seas League.

DAVIES, family name of **Barons Darwen, Davies, Davies of Leek** and **Davies of Penrhys.**

DAVIES; *see* Edmund-Davies.

DAVIES; *see* Llewelyn-Davies.

DAVIES, 3rd Baron, *cr* 1932, of Llandinam; **David Davies,** MA; CEng, MICE, MBA; Chairman, Welsh National Opera Company, since 1975; *b* 2 Oct. 1940; *s* of 2nd Baron and Ruth Eldrydd (*d* 1966), 3rd *d* of Major W. M. Dugdale, CB, DSO; *S* father (killed in action), 1944; *m* 1972, Beryl, *d* of W. J. Oliver; one *s* two *d. Educ:* Eton; King's Coll., Cambridge. *Heir: s* Hon. David Daniel Davies, *b* 23 Oct. 1975. *Address:* Plas Dinam, Llandinam, Powys.

DAVIES OF LEEK, Baron *cr* 1970 (Life Peer), of Leek, Staffordshire; **Harold Davies,** PC 1969; Member, Executive Committee, Inter-Parliamentary Union, since 1975; *b* 31 July 1904; *m* Jessie Elizabeth Bateman, BSc (*d* 1979); one *d. Educ:* Lewis Grammar Sch., Pengam, Glam. Trained for teaching; Schoolmaster and Tutor in Adult Education; several lecture tours in USA and Canada; Lecturer to various organisations and Labour Movement. MP (Lab) Leek Div. of Staffs, 1945-70; formerly Member several Parliamentary Cttees; Joint Parliamentary Secretary, Ministry of Social Security, 1966-67 (Ministry of Pensions and National Insurance, 1965-66). Special Envoy of (Prime Minister) on Peace Mission to Hanoi, 1965. FRGS. Pres., Chatterly Whitfield Mining Museum, 1978-. Has travelled in most countries of Far East and SE Asia. *Publications:* various Press articles on Social and Educational Problems, etc.; numerous writings and pamphlets on Far East, SE Asia, etc. *Recreations:* was keen on all sports and played most of them, now interested in foreign affairs (Far East), agriculture, education, economic affairs. *Address:* 81 Trentham Road, Longton, Stoke-on-Trent, Staffs. *T:* Stoke-on-Trent 39976; 77 Montpelier Rise, NW11 9DU. *T:* 01-455 8015.

DAVIES OF PENRHYS, Baron *cr* 1974 (Life Peer), of Rhondda; **Gwilym Elfed Davies;** *b* 9 Oct. 1913; *s* of David Davies and Miriam Elizabeth (*née* Williams); *m* 1940, Gwyneth Rees, *d* of Daniel and Agnes Janet Rees; two *s* one *d. Educ:* Tylorstown Boys' Sch. Branch Official Tylortown Lodge, NUM, 1935-59. Member Glamorgan CC, 1954-61. Chairman Local Government Cttee, 1959-61. MP (Lab) Rhondda East, Oct. 1959-Feb. 1974; PPS to Minister of Labour, 1964-68, to Minister of Power, 1968. Part-time Mem., S Wales Electricity Bd, 1974-80. Mem., Nat. Sports Council for Wales, 1978-. Freeman, Borough of Rhondda, 1975. *Recreations:* Rugby football and cricket. *Address:* Maes-y-Ffrwd, Ferndale Road, Tylorstown, Rhondda, Glam. *T:* Ferndale 730254.

DAVIES, Air Commodore Adolphus Dan, CB 1953; CBE 1947; psa; *b* 14 Oct. 1902; *m* 1925, Kathleen Hobbs (*d* 1969); one *d.* Cranwell, 1921-23; Air Ministry, Dep. Directorate War Organisation, 1938; Commanded Scampton, Bomber Command, 1943; Fiskerton, Bomber Command, 1944; Air Ministry, Directorate Gen. of Manning, 1944; Air Officer Commanding Royal Air Force, Hong Kong, 1948; Air Cdre 1949; Air Officer in charge of Administration, Coastal Command, 1951-54; retired Aug. 1954. *Address:* 22 Ravenswood Park, Northwood, Mddx. *T:* Northwood 24290.

DAVIES, Air Marshal Sir Alan (Cyril), KCB 1979 (CB 1974); CBE 1967; Head of Support Area Economy Review Team, Royal Air Force, since 1981; *b* 31 March 1924; *s* of Richard Davies, Maidstone; *m* Julia Elizabeth Ghislaine Russell; two *s* (and one *s* decd). Enlisted RAF, 1941; commnd 1943; comd Joint Anti-Submarine School Flight, 1952-54; comd Air Sea Warfare Development Unit, 1958-59; comd No 201 Sqdn, 1959-61; Air Warfare Coll., 1962; Dep. Dir, Operational Requirements, MoD, 1964-66; comd RAF Stradishall, Suffolk, 1967-68; idc 1969; Dir of Air Plans, MoD, 1969-72; ACAS (Policy), MoD, 1972-74; Dep. COS (Ops and Intell.), HQ Allied Air Forces Central Europe, 1974-77; Dep. C-in-C, RAF Strike Command, 1977; Dir, internat. Mil. Staff, NATO, Brussels, 1978-81. *Address:* R3 Section, Lloyds Bank Ltd, 6 Pall Mall, SW1. *Club:* Royal Air Force.

DAVIES, Albert John; Chief Agricultural Officer, Agricultural Development and Advisory Service, Ministry of Agriculture, Fisheries and Food, 1971-79; *b* 21 Jan. 1919; *s* of David Daniel Davies and Annie Hilda Davies; *m* 1944, Winnifred Ivy Caroline Emberton; one *s* one *d. Educ:* Amman Valley Grammar Sch.; UCW Aberystwyth. BSc Hons Agric. 1940. FIBiol. Adv. Staff, UCW Aberystwyth, 1940-41; Asst Techn. Adviser, Montgomeryshire War Agricultural Cttee, 1941-44; Farm Supt, Welsh Plant Breeding Stn, 1944-47; Nat. Agricultural Adv. Service: Crop Husbandry Adviser Wales, 1947-51; Grassland Husbandry Adviser Wales, 1951-57 and E Mids, 1957-59; Dep. Dir Wales, 1959-64; Regional Dir SW Region, 1964; Chief Farm

Management Adviser, London Headquarters, 1964-67; Sen. Agric. Adviser, 1967-68; Dep. Dir, 1968-71. *Publications:* articles in learned jls and agric. press. *Recreations:* golf, Rugby, gardening. *Address:* Cefncoed, 38A Ewell Downs Road, Ewell, Surrey. *T:* 01-393 0069. *Clubs:* Farmers'; Epsom Golf.

DAVIES, (Albert) Meredith, CBE 1982; Principal, Trinity College of Music, since 1979; Conductor: Royal Choral Society, since 1972; Leeds Philharmonic Society, since 1975; Guest Conductor, Royal Opera House, Covent Garden, and Sadler's Wells; also BBC; *b* 30 July 1922; 2nd *s* of Reverend E. A. Davies; *m* 1949, Betty Hazel, *d* of late Dr Kenneth Bates; three *s* one *d. Educ:* Royal College of Music; Stationers' Company's Sch.; Keble Coll., Oxford; Accademia di S. Cecilia, Rome. Junior Exhibitioner, RCM, 1930; Organist to Hurstpierpoint Coll., Sussex, 1939; elected Organ Scholar, Keble Coll., 1940. Served War of 1939-45, RA, 1942-45. Conductor St Albans Bach Choir, 1947; Organist and Master of the Choristers, Cathedral Church of St Alban, 1947-49; Musical Dir, St Albans Sch., 1948-49; Organist and Choirmaster, Hereford Cathedral, and Conductor, Three Choirs' Festival (Hereford), 1949-56; Organist and Supernumerary Fellow of New Coll., Oxford, 1956; Associate Conductor, City of Birmingham Symphony Orchestra, 1957-59; Dep. Musical Dir, 1959-60; Conductor, City of Birmingham Choir, 1957-64; Musical Dir, English Opera Group, 1963-65; Musical Dir, Vancouver Symphony Orchestra, 1964-71; Chief Conductor, BBC Trng Orchestra, 1969-72. *Address:* c/o Trinity College of Music, Mandeville Place, W1M 6AQ.

DAVIES, Hon. Sir (Alfred William) Michael, Kt 1973; **Hon. Mr Justice Michael Davies;** a Judge of the High Court of Justice, Queen's Bench Division, since 1973; *b* 29 July 1921; *er s* of Alfred Edward Davies, Stourbridge; *m* 1947, Margaret, *y d* of Robert Ernest Jackson, Sheffield; one *s* three *d. Educ:* King Edward's Sch., Birmingham; University of Birmingham (LLB). Called to Bar, Lincoln's Inn, 1948, Bencher 1972; QC 1964; Dep. Chm. Northants QS, 1962-71; Recorder of: Grantham, 1963-65; Derby, 1965-71; Crown Court, 1972-73. Leader of Midland Circuit, 1968-71, Jt Leader of Midland and Oxford Circuit, 1971-73. Chm. Mental Health Review Tribunal, for Birmingham Area, 1965-71; Comr of Assize (Birmingham), 1970; Chancellor, Dio. of Derby, 1971-73; Mem., Gen. Council of the Bar, 1968-72. Chm., Hospital Complaints Procedure Cttee, 1971-73. *Recreations:* golf and the theatre. *Address:* Royal Courts of Justice, WC2. *Club:* Garrick.

DAVIES, Alun B. O.; *see* Oldfield-Davies.

DAVIES, Very Rev. Alun Radcliffe; Dean of Llandaff, since 1977; *b* 6 May 1923; *s* of Rev. Rhys Davies and Jane Davies; *m* 1952, Winifred Margaret Pullen; two *s* one *d. Educ:* Cowbridge Grammar Sch.; University Coll., Cardiff (BA 1945); Keble Coll., Oxford (BA 1947, MA 1951); St Michael's Coll., Llandaff. Curate of Roath, 1948-49; Lecturer, St Michael's Coll., Llandaff, 1949-53; Domestic Chaplain to Archbishop of Wales, 1952-57, to Bishop of Llandaff, 1957-59; Chaplain RNR, 1953-60; Vicar of Ystrad Mynach, 1959-75; Chancellor of Llandaff Cathedral, 1969-71; Archdeacon of Llandaff, 1971-77; Residentiary Canon of Llandaff Cathedral, 1975-77. *Address:* The Deanery, The Cathedral Green, Llandaff, Cardiff. *T:* Cardiff 561545.

DAVIES, Sir Alun Talfan, Kt 1976; QC 1961; MA; LLB; barrister-at-law; a Recorder, and Honorary Recorder of Cardiff, since 1972; Judge of the Courts of Appeal, Jersey and Guernsey, since 1969; *b* Gorseinon, 22 July 1913; *s* of late Rev. W. Talfan Davies, Presbyterian Minister, Gorseinon; *m* 1942, Eiluned Christopher, *d* of late Humphrey R. Williams, Stanmore, Middx; one *s* three *d. Educ:* Gowerton Gram. Sch.; Aberystwyth Univ. Coll. of Wales (LLB), Hon. Professorial Fellow, 1971; Gonville and Caius Coll., Cambridge (MA, LLB). Called to the Bar, Gray's Inn, 1939; Bencher, 1969-. Practised on Wales and Chester circuit. Contested (Ind.) University of Wales (by-elec.), 1943; contested (L): Carmarthen Div., 1959 and 1964; Denbigh, 1966. Mem. Court of University of Wales and of Courts and Councils of Aberystwyth and Swansea University Colls. Recorder: of Merthyr Tydfil, 1963-68; of Swansea, 1968-69; of Cardiff, 1969-71; Dep. Chm., Cardiganshire QS, 1963-71. Member: Commn on the Constitution, 1969-73; Criminal Injuries Compensation Bd, 1977-. President: Court of Nat. Eisteddfod of Wales, 1977-80; Court, Welsh Nat. Opera, 1978-. Dep. Chm., Commercial Bank of Wales, 1973- (Dir, 1971-); Vice-Chm., HTV (Group) Ltd (Chm., Welsh Bd). Chm. Trustees, Aberfan Fund (formerly Aberfan Disaster Fund), 1969-. Hon. LLD Wales: Aberystwyth, 1973. *Address:* 10 Park Road, Penarth, South Glam. *T:* Penarth 701341; 34 Park Place, Cardiff. *T:* Cardiff 22454. *Clubs:* Cardiff and County (Cardiff); Bristol Channel Yacht (Swansea).

DAVIES, Prof. Anna Elbina; Professor of Comparative Philology, Oxford University, since 1971; Fellow of Somerville College, Oxford, since 1971; *b* Milan, 21 June 1937; *d* of Augusto Morpurgo and Maria (née Castelnuovo); *m* 1962, J. K. Davies (marr. diss. 1978). *Educ:* Liceo-Ginnasio Giulio Cesare, Rome; Univ. of Rome. Dott.lett. Rome, 1959; Libera docente, Rome, 1963; MA Oxford, 1964. Asst in Classical Philology, Univ. of Rome, 1959-61; Junior Research Fellow, Center for Hellenic Studies, Harvard Univ., 1961-62; Univ. Lectr in Classical Philology, Oxford, 1964-71; Fellow of St Hilda's Coll., Oxford, 1966-71, Hon. Fellow, 1972. Visiting Professor: Univ. of Pennsylvania, 1971; Yale Univ., 1977; Collitz Prof. of Ling. Soc. of America, Univ. of South Florida, 1975. Pres., Philological Soc., 1976-80, Hon. Vice-Pres., 1980-. Hon. DLitt St Andrews, 1981. *Publications:* (as A. Morpurgo)

Mycenaeae Graecitatis Lexicon, 1963; articles and reviews on comparative and classical philology in Italian, German, British and American jls. *Address:* 22 Yarnells Hill, Oxford; Somerville College, Oxford. *T:* Oxford 57595.

DAVIES, Rear-Adm. Anthony, CB 1964; CVO 1972; Royal Navy, retired; *b* 13 June 1912; *s* of late James Arthur and Margaret Davies; *m* 1940, Lilian Hilda Margaret (*d* 1980), *d* of Admiral Sir Harold Martin Burrough, GCB, KBE, DSO, and late Nellie Wills Burrough; two *s* two *d. Educ:* Royal Naval College, Dartmouth. Midshipman, HMS Danae, 1930-32; Sub-Lieut, HMS Despatch, 1934; Lieut, HMS Duncan, 1935-37; Gunnery course, 1938; HMS Repulse, 1939; HMS Cossack 1940-41; Lieut-Comdr, HMS Indefatigable, 1943-45; Comdr, HMS Triumph, 1950; HMS Excellent, 1951-54; Capt., HMS Pelican, 1954-55; Dep. Dir, RN Staff Coll., 1956-57; Far East Fleet Staff, 1957-59; Dep. Dir, Naval Intelligence, 1959-62; Head of British Defence Liaison Staff, Canberra, Australia, 1963-65. Warden, St George's House, Windsor Castle, 1966-72. *Address:* Witts Piece, 11A South Street, Aldbourne, Marlborough, Wilts. *T:* Marlborough 40418.

DAVIES, Prof. Arthur; Reardon-Smith Professor of Geography, University of Exeter, 1948-71; Deputy Vice-Chancellor, University of Exeter, 1969-71; Dean of the Faculty of Social Studies, 1961-64; *b* 13 March 1906; *s* of Richard Davies, Headmaster, and Jessie Starr Davies, Headmistress; *m* 1933, Lilian Margaret Morris; one *d. Educ:* Cyfarthfa Castle Sch.; University Coll. of Wales, Aberystwyth, 1st cl. Hons in Geography and Anthropology, 1927; MSc Wales 1930; Fellow, University of Wales, 1929-30, Asst Lecturer in Geography, Manchester Univ., 1930-33; Lecturer in Geography, Leeds Univ., 1933-40. Served War of 1939-45, RA 1940-45, Normandy (despatches twice, Major); Mem., High Mil. Tribunal of Hamburg, 1945. *Publications:* Yugoslav Studies, Leplay Soc., London, 1932; Polish Studies, Leplay Soc., London, 1933; numerous papers in learned jls on Great Age of Discovery, Columbus, Drake (resolving California/San Francisco problem), etc. *Recreations:* gardening and architecture. *Address:* Morlais, Winslade Park, Clyst St Mary, Devon. *T:* Topsham 3296.

DAVIES, Sir Arthur; *see* Davies, Sir D. A.

DAVIES, Brian Meredith; *see* Davies, J. B. M.

DAVIES, Bryan; Secretary, Parliamentary Labour Party, since 1979; *b* 9 Nov. 1939; *s* of George William and Beryl Davies; *m* 1963, Monica Rosemary Mildred Shearing; two *s* one *d. Educ:* Redditch High Sch.; University Coll., London; Inst. of Education; London Sch. of Economics. BA Hons History London, Certif. Educn, BScEcons London. Teacher, Latymer Sch., 1962-65; Lectr, Middlesex Polytechnic at Enfield, 1965-74. MP (Lab) Enfield North, Feb. 1974-1979; an Asst Govt Whip, 1979; Member: Select Cttee on Public Expenditure, 1975-79; Select Cttee on Overseas Develt, 1975-79. Mem., MRC, 1977-79. *Recreations:* playing cricket, squash, tennis; reading non-modern poetry; going to the theatre. *Address:* 28 Churchfields, Broxbourne, Herts. *T:* Hoddesdon 66427. *Clubs:* Winchmore Hill Cricket, Enfield Highway Workingmen's.

DAVIES, Bryn, MBE 1978; Member, General Council, Wales Trades Union Congress, since 1974; *b* 22 Jan. 1932; *s* of Gomer and Ann Davies; *m* 1956, Esme Irene Gould; two *s. Educ:* Cwmlai School, Tonyrefail. Served HM Forces (RAMC), 1949-51; Forestry Commn, 1951-56; South Wales and Hereford Organiser, Nat. Union of Agricultural and Allied Workers, 1956-. Chm., Mid Glamorgan AHA, 1978-; Member: Welsh Council, 1965-81; Development Commn, 1975-81; Nat. Cttee (Wales), Forestry Commn, 1978-; Nat. Water Council, 1982-. *Recreations:* cricket and Rugby football. *Address:* Derwendeg, 36 Hall Drive, North Cornelly, Bridgend, Mid Glamorgan. *T:* Bridgend 740426. *Clubs:* Tonyrefail Rugby; Glamorgan CC.

DAVIES, Caleb William, CMG 1962; MRCS; LRCP; FFCM; DPH; Regional Specialist in Community Medicine, 1974-82 (Acting Regional Medical Officer, 1977-78, 1979-80), South Western Regional Health Authority; *b* 27 Aug. 1916; *s* of Caleb Davies, KIH, MB, ChB, and Emily (née Platt); *m* 1939, Joan Heath; three *s* one *d. Educ:* Kingswood Sch., Bath; University Coll. and University Coll. Hosp. Med. Sch., London; Edinburgh Univ.; London Sch. of Hygiene and Tropical Med. Kenya: MO, 1941; MOH, Mombasa, 1946; Tanganyika: Sen. MO, 1950; Asst Dir of Med. Services, 1952; Uganda: Dep. Dir of Medical Services, 1958; Permanent Sec. and Chief Medical Officer, Ministry of Health, 1960; retired 1963; South-Western Regional Hosp. Bd: Asst SMO, 1963-66; Principal Asst SMO, 1966-74. *Recreations:* swimming, photography. *Address:* Dolphins, Homefield Road, Saltford, Bristol BS18 3EG. *T:* Saltford 3522.

DAVIES, Ven. Carlyle W.; *see* Witton-Davies.

DAVIES, Christopher Evelyn K.; *see* Kevill-Davies.

DAVIES, (Claude) Nigel (Byam); *b* 2 Sept. 1920; unmarried. *Educ:* Eton. Studied at Aix en Provence University, 1937, and at Potsdam, 1938. PhD London (archaeology). Entered Sandhurst, 1939, and later commissioned Grenadier Guards. Served Middle East, Italy and Balkans, 1942-46. Formerly Managing Dir of Windolite Ltd from 1947. MP (C) Epping Div. of Essex, 1950-51. *Publications:* Los Señorios Independientes del Imperio Azteca, 1968; Los Mexicas: Primeras Pasos Hacia el Imperio, 1973; The Aztecs, 1973; The Toltecs, 1977; Voyagers to the New World: fact and fantasy, 1979; The Toltec

Heritage, 1980; Human Sacrifice, 1981. *Recreation:* travel. *Address:* Gelati 80, Mexico 18, Mexico. *T:* 2-774630. *Club:* Carlton.

DAVIES, Cyril James; Chief Executive, City of Newcastle upon Tyne, since 1980; *b* 24 Aug. 1923; *s* of James and Frances Davies; *m* 1948, Elizabeth Leggett; two *s* two *d. Educ:* Heaton Grammar Sch. CIPFA, ACIS, FRVA. Served RN, Fleet Air Arm, 1942-46. City Treasurer's Dept, Newcastle upon Tyne, 1946-: Dep. City Treas., 1964; City Treas., 1969; Treas., Tyne and Wear Co., 1973-80. Chm., Northern Sinfonia Orch. *Recreations:* theatre, walking, music. *Address:* 4 Mitchell Avenue, Jesmond, Newcastle upon Tyne NE2 3LA. *T:* Newcastle upon Tyne 815196. *Club:* Naval.

DAVIES, Dr David; Director, Dartington North Devon Trust, since 1980; *b* 11 Aug. 1939; *s* of Trefor Alun and Kathleen Elsie Davies; *m* 1968, Joanna Rachel Peace; one *s* two *d. Educ:* Nottingham High Sch.; Peterhouse, Cambridge. MA, PhD. Res. Scientist, Dept of Geophysics, Cambridge, 1961-69; Leader, Seismic Discrimination Gp, MIT Lincoln Laboratory, 1970-73; Editor of Nature, 1973-79. Rapporteur, Seismic Study Gp of Stockholm Internat. Peace Res. Inst. (SIPRI), 1968-73. Mem. Council, Internat. Disaster Inst., 1979. Musical Dir, Blackheath Opera Workshop, 1977-79. *Publications:* Seismic Methods for Monitoring Underground Explosions, 1968; numerous scientific papers. *Recreations:* orchestral and choral conducting. *Address:* Wester Ground, Chittlehamholt, N Devon.

DAVIES, Sir (David) Arthur, KBE 1980; Secretary-General Emeritus, World Meteorological Organization, Geneva, Switzerland, since 1980 (Secretary-General, 1955-79); Member, Welsh Centre for International Affairs, since 1981; *b* 11 Nov. 1913; *m* 1938, Mary Shapland; one *s* two *d. Educ:* University of Wales (MSc) (1st cl. Hons Maths; 1st cl. Hons Physics). Technical Officer, Meteorological Office, 1936-39. War Service, RAF, 1939-47 (despatches). Principal Scientific Officer, Met. Office, 1947-49; Dir, E African Met. Dept, Nairobi, 1949-55; Pres. World Meteorological Organization Regional Assoc. for Africa, 1951-55. United Nations Peace Medal, 1979. Hon. Member: Amer. Meteorological Soc., 1970; Hungarian Meteorol Soc., 1975. FInstP, FRMet Soc. Dr *hc* Univ. of Bucharest, 1970; Dr *hc* Univ. of Budapest, 1976; Dr è Sc *hc* Swiss Fed. Inst. of Technology, 1978; Hon. DSc Wales, 1981. Gold Medal of Merit, Czech. Acad. of Scis, 1978; Silver Medal, Royal Swedish Acad. of Science, 1979. *Publications:* various meteorological papers and articles. *Recreations:* music, Listener crossword. *Address:* 2 Ashley Close, Patcham, Brighton, East Sussex. *T:* Brighton 509437. *Club:* Anglo-Belgian.

DAVIES, David Cyril, BA, LLB; Headmaster, Crown Woods School, since 1971; *b* 7 Oct. 1925; *s* of D. T. E. Davies and Mrs G. V. Davies, JP; *m* 1952, Joan Rogers, BSc; one *s* one *d. Educ:* Lewis Sch., Pengam; UCW Aberystwyth, Asst Master, Ebbw Vale Gram. Sch., 1951-55; Head, Lower Sch., Netteswell Bilateral Sch., 1955-58; Sen. Master and Dep. Headmaster, Peckham Manor Sch., 1958-64; Headmaster: Greenway Comprehensive Sch., 1964-67; Woodberry Down Sch., 1967-71. *Recreations:* reading, Rugby and roughing it. *Address:* 9 Plaxtol Close, Bromley, Kent. *T:* 01-464 4187.

DAVIES, Sir David (Henry), Kt 1973; first Chairman, Welsh Development Agency, 1976-79; General Secretary, Iron and Steel Trades Confederation, 1967-75; *b* 2 Dec. 1909; British; *m* 1934, Elsie May Battrick; one *s* one *d* (and one *d* decd). *Educ:* Ebbw Vale, Mon. Organiser, 1950, Asst. Gen. Sec., 1953-66, Iron and Steel Trades Confederation. Chm., Jt Adv. Cttee on Safety and Health in the Iron and Steel Industry, 1965-67; Vice-Chm., Nat. Dock Labour Bd, 1966-68; Hon. Treas. WEA, 1962-69 (Mem. Central Coun. and Central Exec. Cttee, 1954-69); Hon. Treas., British Labour Party, 1965-67 (Chm., 1963; Mem. Nat. Exec., 1954-67); Hon. Sec., Brit. Sect., Internat. Metalworkers Federation, 1960-; Member: Ebbw Vale UDC, 1945-50; Royal Institute of International Affairs, 1954-; Iron and Steel Operatives Course Adv. Cttee, City and Guilds of London Institute Dept of Technology, 1954-68; Iron and Steel Industry Trng Bd, 1964-; Constructional Materials Gp, Economic Development Cttee for the Building and Civil Engrg Industries, 1965-68; Iron and Steel Adv. Cttee, 1967-; English Industrial Estates Corporation, 1971-; Vice-Pres., European Coal and Steel Community Consultative Cttee, 1975- (Pres., 1973-74). Governor: Ruskin Coll., Oxford, 1954-68; Iron and Steel Industry Management Trng Coll., Ashorne Hill, Leamington Spa, 1966-. Mem. TUC Gen. Coun., 1967-75. *Address:* 82 New House Park, St Albans, Herts. *T:* St Albans 56513.

DAVIES, Hon. Sir (David Herbert) Mervyn, Kt 1982; MC 1944; TD 1946; **Hon. Mr Justice Mervyn Davies;** a Judge of the High Court of Justice, Chancery Division, since 1982; *b* 17 Jan. 1918; *s* of Herbert Bowen Davies and Esther Davies, Llangunnor, Carms; *m* 1951, Zita Yollanne Angelique Blanche Antoinette, 2nd *d* of Rev. E. A. Phillips, Bale, Norfolk. *Educ:* Swansea Gram. Sch. Solicitor, 1939. 18th Bn Welch Regt and 2nd London Irish Rifles, Africa, Italy and Austria, 1939-45. Called to Bar, Lincoln's Inn, 1947; Bencher, 1974; QC 1967; a Circuit Judge, 1978-82. Mem., Bar Council, 1972; Mem., Senate of Inns of Court, 1975. *Address:* The White House, Great Snoring, Norfolk. *T:* Walsingham 575; 7 Stone Buildings, Lincoln's Inn, WC2. *T:* 01-242 8061.

DAVIES, David Hywel, MA, PhD, FIEE; Deputy Director-General for Science, Research and Development, Commission of the European Communities, Brussels, since 1982; *b* 28 March 1929; *s* of John and Maggie Davies; *m* 1961, Valerie Elizabeth Nott; one *s* two *d. Educ:* Cardiff High Sch.;

Christ's Coll., Cambridge. Radar Research Estabt, 1956; Head of Airborne Radar Group, RRE, 1970; Head of Weapons Dept, Admty Surface Weapons Estabt, 1972; Asst Chief Scientific Advr (Projects), MoD, 1976-79; Dir, RARDE, MoD, 1979-80; Dep. Controller, Res. Programmes, MoD, 1980-82. *Publications:* papers on electronics, radar and remote sensing, in Proc. IEE, etc. *Recreations:* do-it-yourself, photography, knots. *Address:* 52 Brittains Lane, Sevenoaks, Kent TN13 2JP. *T:* Sevenoaks 456359.

DAVIES, David John; Finance Director since 1973 and Vice Chairman since 1977, MEPC Ltd; *b* 1 April 1940; *s* of Stanley Kenneth Davies, *qv* ; *m* 1967, Deborah Frances Loeb (marr. diss.); one *s. Educ:* Winchester Coll., Winchester; New Coll., Oxford (MA); Harvard Business Sch. (Advanced Management Program). Chase Manhattan Bank, 1963-67; Hill Samuel Group, 1967-73: Dir, Hill Samuel Inc., New York, 1970-73; Dir, Hill Samuel Ltd, London, 1973. Chm., Wire Ropes Ltd, Wicklow, 1979-; Dir, Letheby & Christopher Ltd, 1979-. *Recreations:* farming, skiing, tennis, travel. *Address:* 73 Kensington Court, W8. *T:* 01-937 4389; Killoughter House, Ashford, Co. Wicklow, Ireland. *T:* Wicklow 4126. *Clubs:* Turf; Cardiff and County (Cardiff); Kildare Street and University (Dublin).

DAVIES, Rt. Hon. (David John) Denzil; PC 1978; MP (Lab) Llanelli since 1970; *b* 9 Oct. 1938; *s* of G. Davies, Conwil Elfed, Carmarthen; *m* 1963, Mary Ann Finlay, Illinois; one *s* one *d. Educ:* Queen Elizabeth Grammar Sch., Carmarthen; Pembroke Coll., Oxford. Bacon Scholar, Gray's Inn, 1961; BA (1st cl. Law) 1962; Martin Wronker Prize (Law), 1962. Teaching Fellow, Univ. of Chicago, 1963; Lectr in Law, Leeds Univ., 1964; called to Bar, Gray's Inn, 1964. Member: Select Cttee on Corporation Tax, 1971; Jt Select Cttee (Commons and Lords) on Delegated Legislation, 1972; Public Accounts Cttee, 1974-; PPS to the Secretary of State for Wales, 1974-76; Minister of State, HM Treasury, 1976-79; Opposition spokesman on Treasury matters, 1979-81, on foreign affairs, 1981-82, on defence, 1982-. *Address:* House of Commons, SW1.

DAVIES, Sir David (Joseph), Kt 1969; Chairman, Wales Tourist Board, 1965-70; *b* 30 Aug. 1896; *s* of David and Catherine Davies; *m* 1924, Eleanor Irene Davies (*née* Bowen); one *s. Educ:* Maesteg Higher Grade and Bridgend County Schools. Served in Welch Regt, 1915-19, Acting Captain. Mem. Court, University Coll., Cardiff, 1959-76; Mem. Court and Council, National Museum of Wales, 1961-73. *Address:* 28 Queen Anne Square, Cardiff CF1 3ED. *T:* Cardiff 22695. *Club:* Cardiff and County (Cardiff).

DAVIES, David Levric, CB 1962; OBE 1962; Under Secretary (Legal), Treasury Solicitor's Office, 1977-82; *b* 11 May 1925; *s* of Benjamin and Elizabeth Davies; *m* 1955, Beryl Justine Hammond. *Educ:* Llanrwst Grammar Sch.; University Coll. of Wales, Aberystwyth (LLB Hons). Called to the Bar, Middle Temple, 1949. Served War, 1943-46: Sub-Lt RNVR. Crown Counsel, Aden, 1950-55; Tanganyika: Asst to Law Officers, 1956-58; Parly Draftsman, 1958-61; Solicitor-Gen., 1961-64; Home Civil Service, 1964-82: seconded to Jamaica as Sen. Parly Draftsman, 1965-69, and to Seychelles as Attorney-Gen., 1970-72; Sen. Legal Asst, Treasury Solicitor's Office, 1972-73; Asst Treasury Solicitor, 1973-77. *Recreations:* gardening, loafing, reading. *Address:* 25 Downs Avenue, Epsom, Surrey. *T:* Epsom 27588. *Club:* RNVR.

DAVIES, David Lewis, CBE 1982; DM; Medical Director, The Newington Unit, Ticehurst House, since 1977; *b* 16 April 1911; *s* of late Harry Davies and the late Anne Davies; *m* 1945, Celia Marjorie Rapport, MB, FFA RCS; three *s. Educ:* Manchester Grammar Sch.; St John's Coll., Oxford (Scholar). BA Oxford (1st Cl. Hons Physiology), 1933; BM, BCh 1936; DPMEng 1943; MA 1944; DM 1948; MRCP 1946; FRCP 1970; FRCPsych 1971. RAMC (Temp. Major), 1942-46. Physician, Bethlem Royal and Maudsley Hosp., 1948, now Emeritus; Dean, Institute of Psychiatry, University of London, 1950-66. Med. Dir, Alcohol Educn Centre, 1973-80; Mem., Adv. Cttee on Alcoholism to DHSS; Chairman, Attendance Allowance Bd, 1976-82; Pres., Soc. for Study of Addiction. Patron, The Helping Hand Orgn. Hon. Mem., Venezuelan Psychiatric Association, 1964. Hon. FRCPsych 1982. Jellinek Meml Award (jtly), for res. into treatment of alcoholism, 1979. *Publications:* (ed jtly) Psychiatric Education, 1964; (ed jtly) Studies in Psychiatry, 1968; papers on psychiatric subjects in med. jls. Chapters in Louis Wain: the man who drew cats, 1968. Wrote script and commentary for film, Victorian Flower Paintings, 1967. *Recreations:* gardening, travel. *Address:* 152 Harley Street, W1N 1HH. *T:* 01-935 2477; 8 Tollgate Drive, College Road, SE21. *T:* 01-693 9380.

DAVIES, Prof. David Richard Seaborne, MA Cantab; LLB Wales; JP; Dean of the Faculty of Law, University of Liverpool, 1946-71, Professor of the Common Law, 1946-71, now Emeritus, Public Orator, 1950-55, Pro-Vice Chancellor, 1956-60, Warden of Derby Hall, 1947-71; *b* 26 June 1904; *er s* of late David S. and Claudia Davies, Pwllheli. *Educ:* Pwllheli Gram. Sch.; University Coll., Aberystwyth: St John's Coll., Cambridge. (McMahon and Strathcona Studentships). First Class Hons LLB (Wales); Law Tripos, 1927 (Class I, Div. I); Yorke Prize, Cambridge Univ., 1928; Lecturer, and later Reader, in English Law in University of London at London Sch. of Economics, 1929-45; Nationality Div., Home Office, 1941-45; Sec. of the Naturalization (Revocation) Cttee, 1944-48; Member: Oaksey Departmental Cttee on Police Conditions, 1948-49; Standing Cttee on Criminal Law Revision, 1959-72; Chm., Departmental Cttee on Agricultural Diploma Education in Wales, 1956; MP (L) Caernarvon Boroughs, April-July 1945.

Pres., Soc. of Public Teachers of Law, 1960-61. Lucien Wolf Memorial Lecturer, 1952. British delegate, SEATO Universities Conference, Pakistan, 1961. Cooley Lecturer, University of Mich., 1962. BBC (Wales) Annual Lecture, 1967. Examiner for many Universities, The Law Society, the Civil Service, etc. Chm., Liverpool Licensing Planning Cttee, 1960-63. Pres., Nat. Eisteddfod of Wales, 1955, 1973, 1975. Pres., Student Council, Univ. of Wales and UCW Aberystwyth; Hon. Life Pres., Liverpool Univ. Legal Soc.; Hon. Life Mem., Univ. Guild of Undergraduates; former Governor: Liverpool College; Rydal School; Life Pres., Liverpool Univ. RFC; Vice-Pres., London Welsh RFC; President: Pwllheli Sports Club; Pwllheli Choral Soc. JP Liverpool, later Caernarvonshire (Gwynedd); High Sheriff of Caernarvonshire, 1967-68. *Publications:* articles in Law Quarterly Review, Modern Law Review, Nineteenth Century, The Annual Survey of English Law, 1930-41. Journal of the Soc. of Public Teachers of Law, etc. *Recreation:* gardening. *Address:* Y Garn, Pwllheli, N Wales. *T:* Pwllheli 2109.

DAVIES, David Ronald, MB, BS, FRCS; Surgeon, University College Hospital, London, 1946-75, retired; *b* Clydach, Swansea, 11 May 1910; 3rd *s* of late Evan Llewelyn and Agnes Jane Davies; *m* 1940, Alice Christine, 2nd *d* of Rev. John Thomson; three *s. Educ:* University Coll. and University Coll. Hosp., London. MRCS, LRCP 1934; MB BS London, 1934; FRCS, 1937. House appts at UCH, Asst, Surgical Unit, UCH, 1937-39; Asst Surg. EMS at UCH and Hampstead Gen. Hosp., 1939-41; served RAMC, Surgical Specialist and Officer-in-Charge Surgical Div., 1941-46; Surgeon: Queen Mary's Hospital, Roehampton, 1947-69; Harrow Hosp., 1946-69. Mem., BMA. Fellow: University Coll. London; Assoc. of Surgeons; RSocMed; British Assoc. of Urological Surgeons; Internat. Assoc. of Urologists. *Publications:* The Operations of Surgery (with A. J. Gardham); various papers on surgical subjects. *Address:* 15 Camden Square, NW1 9UY; Newland Farm, Withypool, Somerset. *T:* Exford 352. *Club:* Oriental.

DAVIES, Prof. David Roy, PhD; Professor of Applied Genetics, University of East Anglia, since 1968, and Deputy Director, John Innes Institute, since 1978; *b* 10 June 1932; *s* of late J. O. Davies and A. Enid Davies; *m* 1957, Winifred Frances Davies, JP, BA (*née* Wills); two *s* two *d. Educ:* Llandyssul and Grove Park, Wrexham Grammar Schs; Univ. of Wales. BSc, PhD. UK Atomic Energy Authority, 1956-62 and 1963-68; US Atomic Energy Commn, 1962-63. Editor, Heredity, 1975-. *Publications:* papers on radiobiology and plant genetics in scientific jls. *Address:* 57 Church Lane, Eaton, Norwich. *T:* Norwich 51049.

DAVIES, Rt. Hon. Denzil; *see* Davies, Rt. Hon. David J. D.

DAVIES, Donald, CBE 1978 (OBE 1973); Board Member, National Coal Board, since 1973; *b* 13 Feb. 1924; *s* of late Wilfred Lawson Davies and Alwyne Davies; *m* 1948, Mabel (*née* Hellyar); two *d. Educ:* Ebbw Vale Grammar Sch.; UC Cardiff (BSc). CEng, FIMinE. Colliery Man., 1951-55; Gp Man., 1955-58; Dep. Prodn Man., 1958-60; Prodn Man., 1960-61; Area Gen. Man., 1961-67; Area Dir, 1967-73. Chairman: NCB Opencast Executive, 1973-; NCB (Ancillaries) Ltd, 1979-. FRSA, FBIM. *Recreations:* golf, walking. *Address:* Wendy Cottage, Dukes Wood Avenue, Gerrards Cross, Bucks SL9 7LA. *T:* Gerrards Cross 85083.

DAVIES, Duncan Sheppey, CB 1982; Technical Director, Tosco Inc. and BCRA Ltd, since 1982; consultant, Tate & Lyle, Unilever, US National Bureau of Standards, etc; Governor, Technical Change Centre, since 1982; *b* 20 April 1921; *o s* of Duncan S. Davies and Elsie Dora, Liverpool; *m* 1944, Joan Ann Frimston, MA; one *s* three *d. Educ:* Liverpool Coll.; Trinity Coll., Oxford (Minor Scholar). MA, BSc, DPhil. CEng, FIChemE, Hon. FIMechE. Joined ICI Dyestuffs Div., 1945; Research Dir, Gen. Chemicals Div., 1961; first Dir, ICI Petrochemical and Polymer Lab., 1962; Dep. Chm., Mond Div., 1967; Gen. Manager, Research, ICI, 1969-77; Chief Engineer and Scientist, DoI, 1977-82. Member: SERC (formerly SRC), 1969-73, 1977-82; SRC/SSRC, 1973-79 (Chm.); Adv. Bd for Res. Councils, 1977-82; Adv. Council on Applied R&D, NERC, 1977-82; Swann Manpower Working Gp, 1964-66; Council, Liverpool Univ., 1967-69; Council, QEC London, 1975-78; UK Nat. Commn for UNESCO, 1982-. Vis. Prof., Imperial Coll., 1968-70; Vis. Fellow, St Cross Coll., Oxford, 1970. Vis. Prof. Fellow, UC Swansea, 1974-79. DUniv Stirling, 1975; DUniv Surrey, 1980; Hon. DSc Bath, 1981. Castner Medal, SCI, 1967. Foreign Associate, Nat. Acad. of Engineering, USA, 1978. Hon. DSc Technion, Haifa, 1982. *Publications:* (with M. C. McCarthy) Introduction to Technological Economics, 1967; The Humane Technologist, 1976; various papers in engineering and economics, pure and applied chemistry jls. *Recreations:* music, writing. *Address:* 109 Southwood Lane, N6 5TB. *T:* 01-348 2011. *Clubs:* Athenæum, United Oxford & Cambridge University.

DAVIES, Ednyfed Hudson, BA (Wales); MA (Oxon); MP Caerphilly, since 1979 (Lab 1979-81, SDP since 1981); barrister; *b* 4 Dec. 1929; *s* of Rev. E. Curig Davies and Enid Curig (*née* Hughes); *m* 1972, Amanda Barker-Mill, *d* of Peter Barker-Mill and Elsa Barker-Mill; two *d. Educ:* Friars Sch., Bangor; Dynevor Grammar Sch., Swansea; University College of Swansea; Balliol Coll., Oxford. Called to the Bar, Gray's Inn, 1975. Lecturer in Dept of Extra-Mural Studies, University of Wales, Aberystwyth, 1957-61; Lecturer in Political Thought, Welsh Coll. of Advanced Technology, Cardiff, 1961-66. MP (Lab) Conway, 1966-70; Mem., H of C Select Cttee on Energy, 1980-; Sec., H of C All-Party Tourism Cttee, 1979-. Part-time TV and Radio Commentator and Interviewer on Current Affairs, 1962-66; on full-time

contract to BBC presenting Welsh-language feature programmes on overseas countries, 1970-76; Chm., Wales Tourist Board, 1976-78. *Address:* House of Commons, SW1A 0AA. *Club:* Cardiff and County (Cardiff).

DAVIES, (Edward) Hunter; author and journalist; *b* Renfrew, Scotland, 7 Jan. 1936; *s* of late John Hunter Davies and Marion (*née* Brechin); *m* 1960, Margaret Forster, *qv;* one *s* two *d. Educ:* Creighton Sch., Carlisle; Carlisle Grammar Sch.; University Coll., Durham. BA 1957, DipEd 1958; Editor of Palatinate. Reporter: Manchester Evening Chronicle, 1958-59; Sunday Graphic, London, 1959-60; Sunday Times, 1960-: Atticus, 1965-67; Chief Feature Writer, 1967; Editor, Look pages, 1970; Editor, Scene pages, 1975; Editor, Sunday Times Magazine, 1975-77; Columnist, Punch, 1979-. *Television:* The Playground (play), 1967; The Living Wall, 1974; George Stephenson, 1975; A Walk in the Lakes, 1979. *Publications:* Here We Go, Round the Mulberry Bush, 1965 (filmed, 1968); The Other Half, 1966; (ed) The New London Spy, 1966; The Beatles, 1968; The Rise and Fall of Jake Sullivan, 1970; (ed) I Knew Daisy Smuten, 1970; A Very Loving Couple, 1971; Body Charge, 1972; The Glory Game, 1972; A Walk Along the Wall, 1974; George Stephenson, 1975; The Creighton Report, 1976; (ed) Sunday Times Book of Jubilee Year, 1977; A Walk Around the Lakes, 1979; William Wordsworth, 1980; The British Book of Lists, 1980; The Grades, 1981; Father's Day, 1981; Beaver Book of Lists, 1981; A Walk Along the Tracks, 1982; England!, 1982; (with Frank Herrmann) Great Britain: a celebration, 1982; Flossie Teacake's Fur Coat, 1982. *Recreations:* stamps, railways, football, walking. *Address:* 11 Boscastle Road, NW5. *T:* 01-485 3785. *Clubs:* Railway Philatelic Group; Railway Ramblers.

DAVIES, Elidir (Leslie Wish), FRIBA, FRSA; Chartered Architect in private practice; *b* 3 Jan. 1907; *yr s* of late Rev. Thomas John Landy Davies and Hetty Boucher (*née* Wish); *m* 1st, Vera (*née* Goodwin) (*d* 1974); 2nd, 1976, Kathleen Burke-Collis. *Educ:* privately; Colchester Sch.; Bartlett Sch. of Architecture, University of London (under Prof. Albert Richardson). Min. of Supply Air Defence, 1939-44; Min. of Town and Country Planning, London and Wales, 1944-47; University Lectr and Cons. to Argentinian and Uruguay Govts on planning and low cost housing, 1947-49; private practice (Devereux and Davies); rebuilding of Serjeants' Inn, Fleet Street; Royal Vet. Coll., London Univ. (Research and Field Lab); King's Coll. Sch., Wimbledon (Jun. Sch. and Sci. Labs); St James's Hosp., Balham (Out-patients' and other Depts); St Benedict's Hosp. (Hydrotherapy Dept), 1950-61. West Indies: 5-year Hospital progr. for Trinidad (incl. new gen. and maternity hosps, trg schs, specialist depts, and hosp. services). Cons. Arch. Hosps to Govts of Guiana, Barbados and Grenada, 1957-63. Private practice (Elidir L. W. Davies & Partners). Architect to: St David's Coll., Lampeter, restoration and new bldgs; London Borough of Camden; Central Library, Shaw Theatre and arts centre; Mermaid Theatre; Dynevor Castle, Carmarthen, Wales; new arts centre for drama and films; Chigwell Central Public Library; church work: The Temple, White Eagle Lodge, Hants; rebuilding of Wren's church, St Michael Paternoster Royal; New Garden Hydrotherapy; upgrading and gen. maintenance, Burrswood Nursing Home of Healing, Groombridge, Kent; Cons. Architect to: St David's Trust, Welsh Nat. Arts Theatre Centre, Cardiff; Govt Offices, Century House, Waterloo; BP Offices, 100 Euston Road; private houses and housing developments in London and the country. Chm., Soc. of Theatre Consultants, 1969-71; Mem. of Exec., Assoc. of British Theatre Technicians, 1965-71. Bronze Medal, RIBA, 1953. *Publications:* lectures and articles; contrib. to pubn relating to hospital architecture. *Recreations:* theatre, travel, sailing, visual arts. *Address:* 100 Wigmore Street, W1. *T:* 01-486 3841; Hesmonds Oast, East Hoathly, Sussex. *T:* Halland 337. *Clubs:* Garrick, Art Workers' Guild.

DAVIES, Elwyn, MA; Hon. LLD Wales; MSc, PhD Manchester; President, National Library of Wales, since 1977 (Treasurer, 1959-64; Vice-President, 1970-77); Chairman: Library Advisory Council (Wales), 1973-79; Wales Regional Library Scheme, since 1973; Welsh Folk Museum, since 1974; *b* 20 Sept. 1908; *e s* of late Rev. Ben Davies, Llandeilo, Carms; *m* 1940, Margaret (*d* 1982), *o d* of late Matthew Henry Dunlop, Bury, Lancs; no *c. Educ:* Llandysul and Llandeilo Grammar Schs; Universities of Wales (Aberystwyth Coll.) and Manchester. Asst Lectr and Lectr in Geography, University of Manchester, 1934-45, seconded Intelligence Div. Naval Staff, 1941-45; Sec. to the Council, University of Wales, Sec. of the University Press Board and the Board of Celtic Studies, 1945-63; Sec. University Bd for Training Colls, 1945-48, and Univ. Educn Bd, 1948-49; Sec., Univ. Extension Bd, 1945-61; Permanent Sec., Welsh Dept, Min. of Educn, 1963-64; Sec. for Welsh Educn, DES, 1964-69. A Governor: National Museum of Wales, 1957- (Mem. Council, 1959-); University College of Wales, Aberystwyth, 1965- (Mem. Council, 1965-); Univ. of Wales, 1966-; Mem. Council, Welsh Nat. Sch. of Medicine, 1978-. Member: Bd of Celtic Studies, Univ. of Wales, 1972-; Local Govt Boundary Commn for Wales, 1974-79 (Dep. Chm., 1978-79); Adv. Council, British Library, 1975-79; Pilkington Cttee on Broadcasting, 1960-62; Standing Commission on Museums and Galleries, 1960-64. Hon. Fellow, UC Cardiff, 1970. *Publications:* Cyfarwyddiadau i Awduron (A Guide for Authors), 1954; (ed) A Gazetteer of Welsh Place-Names, 1957-75; (ed) Celtic Studies in Wales, 1963; (ed with Alwyn D. Rees) Welsh Rural Communities, 1960; papers in anthropological and geographical periodicals. *Recreations:* growing grapes and making wine. *Address:* Butts Field, Tenby, Dyfed SA70 8AQ.

DAVIES, Emlyn Glyndwr, MSc; Chief Scientific Officer, Controller, Forensic Science Service, Home Office, 1974-76; *b* 20 March 1916; *yr s* of late William and Elizabeth Davies; *m* 1940, Edwina, *d* of late Lemuel and Alice Morgan, Blaengarw; two *s*. *Educ:* Bargoed Grammar Sch.; Maesycwmmer Grammar Sch.; University Coll of Wales, Aberystwyth (MSc). Asst Master, Ardwyn Sch., 1939-42; Ministry of Supply, 1942-44; Forensic Science Laboratory, Cardiff, 1944-58; Director, Forensic Science Laboratories: Nottingham, 1958-59; Preston, 1959-63; Forensic Science Adviser, Home Office, 1963-74. Pres., Forensic Science Soc., 1975-77. *Publications:* contribs to scientific jls. *Recreation:* Rugby football. *Address:* 14 Church Hill Close, Llanblethian, Cowbridge, S Glamorgan CF7 7JH. *T:* Cowbridge 2234.

DAVIES, Emrys Thomas; HM Diplomatic Service; Foreign and Commonwealth Office, since 1982; *b* 8 Oct. 1934; *s* of Evan William Davies and Dinah Davies (*née* Jones); *m* 1960, Angela Audrey May; one *s* two *d*. *Educ:* Parmiters Foundation Sch.; assorted universities. RAF, 1953-55. Sch. of Oriental and African Studies, London Univ., 1955-56. Served Peking, 1956-59; FO, 1959-60; Bahrain, 1960-62; FO, 1962-63; Asst Political Adviser to Hong Kong Govt, 1963-68; First Sec., British High Commn, Ottawa, 1968-71; FCO, 1972-76; Commercial Counsellor, Peking, 1976-78 (Chargé, 1976 and 1978); NATO Defense Coll., Rome, 1979; Dep. High Comr, Ottawa, 1979-82. *Address:* c/o Foreign and Commonwealth Office, SW1A 2AH. *Club:* Royal Commonwealth Society.

DAVIES, Ernest Albert John; journalist, author; *b* London, 18 May 1902; *s* of late Alderman Albert Emil Davies; *m* 1st, 1926, Natalie Rossin, New York (marr. diss. 1944; she *d* 1955); two *s* one *d*; 2nd, 1944, Peggy Yeo (*d* 1963); one *d* (*decd*). *Educ:* Wycliffe Coll.; London Univ. (Diploma in Journalism). Managing Editor, Traffic Engineering and Control, 1960-76; Managing Editor, Antique Finder, 1962-72; Editor Clarion, 1929-32; Associate Editor, New Clarion, 1932. Served on Fabian Soc. Exec., 1940; Gov. National Froebel Foundation, 1938-40. With British Broadcasting Corporation, 1940-45, and its North American Service Organiser, 1944-45. Contested (Lab) Peterborough, 1935; MP (Lab) Enfield Division of Middx, 1945-50, East Enfield, 1950-59. Parl. Private Sec. to Min of State, 1946-50; Parliamentary Under-Sec. of State, Foreign Office, 1950-51. Chm. Transport Group Parliamentary Labour Party, 1945-50 and 1951-59; Jt Chm. Parliamentary Roads Study Group, 1957-59; Mem. Select Cttee on Nationalised Industries, 1952-59; Vice-Pres., British Yugoslav Soc., 1980- (Chm., 1957-80); Mem., Exec. Cttee, European-Atlantic Gp, 1958-65 (Vice-Pres., 1966-82). Mem. British Delegation to Gen. Assembly, UN, 1947, 1948-49 and 1950; Dep. Leader British Deleg. to UN Conf. on Freedom of Information, 1948; Mem. British Deleg. to London Conf. 1950; Leader UK Deleg., Economic Commn for Europe, Geneva, 1950; UK Representative at Foreign Ministers' Deputies' Four Power Talks, Paris, 1951. Vice-Chm., British Parking Assoc., 1969-71, 1976-77 (Pres., 1977-80; Hon. Sec. 1971-76; Mem. Council, 1968-80); Hon. FInstHE. Managing Dir, Printerhall Ltd. Orden de la Liberatión de España, Republican Govt, 1960; Ordenom Jugoslovenske Zvezde sa zlatnim vencem (Yugoslavia), 1976. *Publications:* How Much Compensation, 1935; National Capitalism, 1939; The State and the Railways, 1940; American Labour, 1943; British Transport, 1945; National Enterprise, 1946; Problems of Public Ownership, 1952; (ed) Roads and Their Traffic, 1960; Transport in Greater London, 1962; (ed) Traffic Engineering Practice, 1963, new edn 1968; Contrib. Encyclopaedia Britannica. *Address:* 16 Redcliffe Square, SW10 9JZ. *T:* 01-373 3962. *Clubs:* Wig and Pen, National Liberal.

DAVIES, Dr Ernest Arthur, JP; management consultant and lecturer; *b* 25 Oct. 1926; *s* of Daniel Davies and Ada (*née* Smith), Nuneaton; *m* 1st, 1956, Margaret Stephen Tait Gatt (marr. diss. 1967), *d* of H. Gatt, Gamesley, near Glossop; no *c*; 2nd, 1972, Patricia (marr. diss. 1980), *d* of S. Bates, Radford, Coventry; no *c*. *Educ:* Coventry Jun. Techn. Coll.; Westminster Trng Coll., London; St Salvator's Coll., University of St Andrews; St John's Coll., Cambridge. PhD Cantab 1959; MInstP 1959. RAF Aircraft Apprentice, 1942-43 (discharged on med. grounds). Westminster Trng Coll., 1946-48; Teacher, Foxford Sch., Coventry, 1948-50; University of St Andrews, 1950-54 (1st cl. hons Physics, Neil Arnott Prize, Carnegie Schol.); subseq. research in superconductivity, Royal Society Mond Lab., Cambridge; AEI Research Scientist, 1957-63; Lectr in Physics, Faculty of Technology, University of Manchester, 1963-66. Management Selection Consultant, MSL, 1970-81. MP (Lab) Stretford, 1966-70; Parliamentary Private Secretary to: PMG (Mr Edward Short), Nov.-Dec. 1967; Foreign Secretary (Mr George Brown), Jan.-Mar. 1968; Foreign and Commonwealth Sec. (Mr Michael Stewart), 1968-69; Jt Parly Sec., Min. of Technology, 1969-70. Co-Vice-Chm., Parly Labour Party's Defence and Services Group; Mem., Select Cttee on Science and Technology, 1966-67, 1967-68, 1968-69; Parly Deleg. to 24th Gen. Assembly of UN (UK Rep. on 4th Cttee). Councillor: Borough of Stretford, 1961-67; Borough of Southwark, 1974-82. JP Lancs, 1962. *Publications:* contribs to Proc. Royal Society, Jl of Physics and Chem. of Solids. *Recreations:* reading, walking. *Address:* Flat 3, 5 Rye Hill Park, Peckham, SE15.

DAVIES, Prof. Eurfil Rhys, FRCR, FRCPE; Professor of Radiodiagnosis, University of Bristol, since 1981; *b* 18 April 1929; *s* of late Daniel Haydn Davies and Mary Davies; *m* 1962, Zoë Doreen Chamberlain; three *s*. *Educ:* Rhondda Grammar Sch.; Llandovery Coll.; Clare Coll., Cambridge (MB, BChir 1953; MA); St Mary's Hosp., London. FRCPE 1971; FRCR 1975. Served RAMC, 1954-56. Sen. Registrar, St Mary's Hosp., 1963-66; Consultant Radiologist, United Bristol Hosps, 1966-81; Clinical Lectr, Univ. of Bristol, 1972-81. Royal Coll. of Radiologists: Sen. Examr, 1973-74; Mem.,

Fellowship Bd, 1974-76; Registrar, 1976-81; Chm., Nuclear Medicine Cttee, 1972-78. Pres., Nuclear Medicine Soc., 1974-76; Sec., Inter Collegiate Standing Cttee for Nuclear Medicine, 1980-82. Sen. Vis. Lectr, Univ. of Lagos, 1971. Hon. Fellow, Faculty of Radiologists, RCSI, 1978. *Publications:* (contrib.) Textbook of Radiology, ed Sutton, 1969, 3rd edn 1980; (contrib.) Textbook of Urology, ed J. P. Blandy, 1974; (jtly) Radioisotopes in Radiodiagnosis, 1976; (contrib.) Radiological Atlas of Biliary and Pancreatic Disease, 1978; papers in Clin. Radiology, British Jl of Radiology, Lancet. *Recreations:* theatre, walking, wine. *Address:* 22 Blenheim Road, Bristol BS6 7JP. *T:* Bristol 736093.

DAVIES, George Francis, CMG 1962; Chairman, Davies Brothers Ltd, since 1954; *b* 26 Jan. 1911; *yr s* of late C. B. Davies, CBE, MIEA, and late Ruby A. Davies; *m* 1935, Margaret Ingles; one *s* three *d*. *Educ:* Clemes Coll., Hobart, Tasmania. Director: Commercial Broadcasters Pty Ltd (Chm., 1950-); Australian Newsprint Mills Ltd, 1954-; Tasmanian Fibre Containers Pty Ltd (Chm., 1975-); Packaging Investments Pty Ltd (Chm., 1965-); Perpetual Trustees and Natural Executors Ltd, 1968-. *Recreations:* golf, fishing, racing. *Address:* 5/46 Marieville Esplanade, Sandy Bay, Tasmania 7005, Australia. *T:* 34.6411. *Clubs:* Tasmanian, Athenæum (Hobart).

DAVIES, George Peter H.; see Humphreys-Davies.

DAVIES, George Raymond, (Gerry), OBE 1977; FLA; Director, The Booksellers Association of Great Britain and Ireland, 1964-66 and 1970-81 (Hon. Life Member, 1981); *b* 3 Oct. 1916; *s* of George John Davies and Eva Florence Davies; *m* 1945, Sylvia Newling; one *s* one *d*. *Educ:* East Ham Grammar Sch. FLA 1948. Local govt service, 1934-40; land reclamation, 1940-45; estate under-bailiff, 1945-46; W Suffolk and Cambridge Public Libraries, 1947-54 (Dep. City Librarian, 1953); Gen. Sec., Booksellers Assoc., 1955-64; Man. Dir, Bowker Publishing Co. Ltd, 1966-67; Editor, Publishers Inf. Card Services Ltd, 1968-69; Jt Dep. Editor, The Bookseller, 1969-70. Founder-Mem., Internat. Community of Booksellers Assocs, 1956 (Mem. Council, 1972-78); Mem. Council, Internat. Booksellers Fedn, 1978- (Pres. 1978-81); Chairman: BA Service House Ltd, 1977-; Book Trade Benevolent Soc., 1974-. *Publications:* (ed jtly) Books are different, 1966; (contrib.) The Book of Westminster, 1964; Books and Their Prices, 1967; contrib. to Library Rev., Library World, Year's Work in Librarianship, Canadian Bookseller, American Bookseller, and The Bookseller. *Recreations:* estate management, writing words and music. *Address:* Crotchets, Mayfield, East Sussex. *T:* Mayfield 872356. *Club:* Savile.

DAVIES, Gwen F.; see Ffrangcon-Davies.

DAVIES, (Gwilym) E(dnyfed) Hudson; see Davies, Ednyfed H.

DAVIES, Gwilym Prys; Partner, Morgan Bruce & Nicholas, Solicitors, Cardiff, Pontypridd and Porth, since 1957; *b* 8 Dec. 1923; *s* of William and Mary Matilda Davies; *m* 1951, Llinos Evans; three *d*. *Educ:* Towyn Sch., Towyn, Merioneth; University College of Wales, Aberystwyth. Served RN, 1942-46. Faculty of Law, UCW, Aberystwyth, 1946-52; President of Debates, Union UCW, 1949; President Students' Rep. Council, 1950; LLB 1949; LLM 1952. Admitted Solicitor, 1956. Contested (Lab) Carmarthen, 1966. Special Adviser to Sec. of State for Wales, 1974-78; Chm., Welsh Hosps Bd, 1968-74; Member: Welsh Council, 1967-69; Welsh Adv. Cttee, ITA, 1966-69; Working Party on 4th TV Service in Wales, Home Office and Welsh Office, 1975-; Adv. Gp, Use of Fetuses and Fetal Material for Res., DHSS and Welsh Office, 1972; Econ. and Social Cttee, EEC, 1978-. OStJ. *Publications:* A Central Welsh Council, 1963; Y Ffermwr a'r Gyfraith, 1967. *Address:* Lluest, 78 Church Road, Tonteg, Pontypridd, Mid Glam. *T:* Newtown Llantwit 2462.

DAVIES, Rev. Gwynne Henton; Principal, Regent's Park College, Oxford, 1958-72; *b* 19 Feb. 1906; *m* 1935, Annie Bronwen (*née* Williams), BA Wales; two *d*. *Educ:* Perse Sch., Cambridge; University College of South Wales, Cardiff (BD, MA); St Catherine's and Regent's Park Colls, Oxford Univ. (MLitt, MA); Marburg/Lahn, Germany. Minister West End Baptist Church, London, W6, 1935-38; Tutor Bristol Baptist Coll., 1938-51; special Lecturer in Hebrew, University of Bristol, 1948-51; (First) Prof. of Old Testament Studies, Faculty of Theology, Durham Univ., 1951-58; Select Preacher to the Universities of Cambridge and Oxford. OT Editor, The Teachers' Commentary (revised 7th edn), 1955. Secretary, Society for Old Testament Study, 1946-62 (President, 1966); Vice-Pres., Baptist Union of GB and Ireland, 1970-71, Pres., 1971-72. OT Lecture, Pantyfedwen Foundn, 1975; Dist. Vis. Prof., Meredith Coll., USA, 1978, 1979. Hon. DD: Glasgow, 1958; Stetson, 1965. *Publications:* (with A. B. Davies) The Story in Scripture, 1960; Exodus, 1967; Who's Who in the Bible, 1970; Deuteronomy, in Peake's Commentary on the Bible, rev. edn, 1962; 20 articles in The Interpreter's Bible Dictionary, 1962; The Ark in the Psalms, in Promise and Fulfilment (ed F. F. Bruce), 1963; essay in R. Goldman's Breakthrough, 1968; Genesis, in The Broadman Bible Commentary, 1969; Gerhard von Rad, in O.T. Theology in Contemporary Discussion (ed R. Laurin). *Address:* Headlands, Broad Haven, Haverfordwest, Dyfed SA62 3JP. *T:* Broad Haven 339.

DAVIES, Handel, CB 1962; MSc; FEng; FRAeS; FAIAA; aeronautical engineering consultant; *m* 1942, Mary Graham Harris. *Educ:* Aberdare Grammar Sch.; University of Wales. Royal Aircraft Establishment and Ministry of Aircraft Production, 1936-47; Head of Aerodynamics Flight

Division, RAE, 1948-52. Chief Superintendent, Aeroplane and Armament Experimental Establishment, Boscombe Down, 1952-55; Scientific Adviser to Air Ministry, 1955-56; Director-General, Scientific Research (Air), Ministry of Supply, 1957-59; Dep. Director, RAE, Farnborough, 1959-63. Dep. Controller of Aircraft, (R&D), Ministry of Aviation, 1963-67, Ministry of Technology, 1967-69. Tech. Dir, British Aircraft Corp., 1969-77. Pres., RAeS, 1977-78. Chm., Standing Conf. on Schools Sci. and Technology, 1978-82. Fellow, University Coll., Cardiff, 1981. Gold Medal, RAeS, 1974. Wilbur and Orville Wright Meml Lectr, 1979. *Publications:* papers in Reports and Memoranda of Aeronautical Research Council and in Journal of Royal Aeronautical Society. *Recreation:* sailing. *Address:* Keel Cottage, Woodham Road, Horsell, Woking, Surrey. *T:* Woking 4192. *Clubs:* Naval and Military; Royal Air Force Yacht (Hamble).

DAVIES, Humphrey; *see* Davies, Morgan Wynn Humphrey.

DAVIES, Hunter; *see* Davies, E. H.

DAVIES, Ian Leonard, MA; CEng, FIEE; Director, Admiralty Underwater Weapons Establishment, since 1975; *b* 2 June 1924; *s* of late H. Leonard Davies and of Mrs J. D. Davies; *m* 1951, Hilary Dawson, *d* of late Rear-Adm. Sir Oswald Henry Dawson, KBE; two *s* two *d. Educ:* Barry County Sch.; St John's Coll., Cambridge. Mechanical Sciences Tripos, 1944, and Mathematical Tripos Pt 2, 1949. Telecommunications Research Estabt, 1944; Blind Landing Experimental Unit, 1946. TRE (later the Royal Radar Establishment), 1949-69; Imperial Defence Coll., 1970; Asst Chief Scientific Adviser (Projects), MoD, 1971-72; Dep. Controller Electronics, 1973, Dep. Controller Air Systems (D), 1973-75, MoD(PE). Mem. Council, IEE, 1974-77 (Chm., Electronics Div. Bd, 1975-76). Mem. Court, Univ. of Bath. *Publications:* papers on information theory, radar, and lasers. *Recreations:* music, sailing, walking. *Address:* 15 Bincleaves Road, Weymouth, Dorset. *T:* Weymouth 785891. *Club:* Athenæum.

DAVIES, Iforwyn Glyndwr; Formerly Senior Principal Medical Officer, Ministry of Health; QHP 1957-59; *b* 11 June 1901; *s* of Richard and Margaret Davies, Porth, South Wales; *m* 1930, Lillian May, *d* of Evan James, Cardiff, South Wales; one *s. Educ:* The County Sch., Porth; University College, Cardiff; St Bartholomew's Hospital, London. MRCS, LRCP, 1923; MB, BS London, 1924; MD London, 1944; MRCP, 1926; FRCP, 1954. Formerly: Tuberculosis Physician, City of Nottingham, 1933; Deputy MOH, City and County of Bristol, 1937; Lecturer in Public Health, University of Bristol, 1937; Dep. Director, Preventive Medicine Laboratories; Prof., of Public Health, University of Leeds, 1947, also Medical Officer of Health and School Medical Officer, City of Leeds. *Publications:* Text-Book: Modern Public Health for Medical Students, 1955 (2nd edn, 1963); contrib. to Lancet, Medical Officer, Public Health. *Recreation:* music. *Address:* Amberley, Well Meadows, Shaw, Newbury, Berks. *T:* Newbury 42055.

DAVIES, Ven. Ivor Gordon; Archdeacon of Lewisham, since 1972; Proctor in Convocation, since 1965; *b* 21 July 1917; *m* 1946, Kristine Wiley, SRN; one *s* two *d. Educ:* University of Wales (BA); Oxford; London (BD). Deacon 1941, Priest 1942, Llandaff; Curate of St Paul's, Cardiff, 1941-44; CF 1944-47; Curate of St John the Baptist, Felixstowe, 1947-49; Vicar of St Thomas', Ipswich, 1950-57; Residentiary Canon of Southwark Cathedral and Diocesan Missioner, 1957-72; Dean of Lewisham, 1970-72. *Address:* 2 St Austell Road, Lewisham Hill, SE13. *T:* 01-852 3649.

DAVIES, Jack Gale Wilmot, OBE 1946; Executive Director of the Bank of England, 1969-76; *b* 10 Sept. 1911; *s* of Langford George Davies, MD, BCh, MRCS, LRCP, and Lily Barnes Davies; *m* 1949, Georgette O'Dell (*née* Vanson); one *s. Educ:* Tonbridge Sch.; St John's Coll., Cambridge. Nat. Institute of Industrial Psychol., 1935-39. Regimental service, The Middlesex Regt, 1940-42; Chief Psychologist, Directorate for Selection of Personnel, War Office, 1942-46. Bureau of Personnel, UN Secretariat, 1946-48; Secretariat, Human Factors Panel, Cttee on Industrial Productivity, 1948-49; Staff Training Section, UN Secretariat, 1950-52; Secretary, Cambridge Univ. Appointments Board, 1952-68; Asst to the Governor, Bank of England, 1968. Dir, Portals Holdings Ltd, 1976-. FBPsS 1946. Fellow St John's Coll., Cambridge, 1959-68. Hon. DLitt City, 1976. *Publications:* articles in Occupational Psychology and similar journals. *Recreations:* cricket, golf, music. *Address:* 31 Wingate Way, Cambridge. *Clubs:* Royal Automobile, MCC.

DAVIES, Rev. Jacob Arthur Christian; Director, Personnel Division, FAO, since 1976 (Deputy Director, Agricultural Operations Division, 1975-76); *b* 24 May 1925; *s* of Jacob S. Davies and Christiana; *m* Sylvia Onikeh Cole; two *s* two *d. Educ:* Univ. of Reading (BSc 1950); Selwyn Coll., Cambridge; Imperial Coll. of Tropical Agriculture. Permanent Secretary, Min. of Agriculture and Natural Resources, 1961-63; Chief Agriculturist, 1962-67; Project Co-manager, UNDP, FAO, 1967-69; Chm., Public Service Commn, 1969-71; Ambassador to USA, 1971-72; High Comr for Sierra Leone in London, 1972-74; Non-resident Ambassador to Denmark, Sweden and Norway, 1972-74. *Recreations:* philately, sports. *Address:* Agricultural Operations Division, FAO, Viale delle Terme di Caracolla, Rome, Italy.

DAVIES, (James) Brian Meredith, MD, DPH, FFCM; Director of Social Services, City of Liverpool, 1971-81; Hon. Lecturer in (Preventive) Paediatrics, University of Liverpool, since 1964; *b* 27 Jan. 1920; *s* of late Dr

G. Meredith Davies and Caroline Meredith Davies; *m* 1944, Charlotte (*née* Pillar); three *s. Educ:* Bedford Sch.; Medical Sch., St Mary's Hosp., London Univ. MB, BS (London) 1943 MD (London) 1948, DPH 1948, MFCM 1972, FFCM 1974. Various hosp. appts. Served War, RAMC, Captain, 1944-47. Asst MOH, Lancashire CC, 1948-50; Dep. MOH, City of Oxford, 1950-53; Clin. Asst (infectious Diseases), United Oxford Hosps, 1950-53; Dep. MOH, 1953-69, Dir of Personal Health and Social Services, 1969-71, City of Liverpool. Chm., Liverpool div., BMA, 1958-59; Council of Europe Fellowship, to study Elderly: in Finland, Sweden, Norway and Denmark, 1964 (report awarded special prize); Mem. Public Health Laboratory Service Bd, 1966-71. Teaching Gp of Soc. of Community Med. (Sec. of Gp, 1958-72, Pres. Gp, 1972-73). Member: Personal Social Services Council, 1978-80; Mental Health Review Tribunal, Mersey Area, 1982-. Governor, Occupational Therapy Coll., Huyton, Liverpool, 1969-; Dir of MERIT (Merseyside Industrial Therapy Services Ltd), 1970-75; Mem. Council, Queen's Inst. of District Nursing, 1971-78; Assoc. of Dirs of Social Services: Chm., NW Br., 1971-73; Mem. Exec. Council, 1973-78; Pres. 1976-77; Mem. Exec. Cttee of Central Council for the Disabled, 1972-76; Adviser to Social Services Cttee of Assoc. of Metropolitan Authorities, 1974-81; Member: RCP Cttee on Rheumatism and Rehabilitation, 1974-; DES Cttee of Enquiry into Special Educn for Disabled Children, 1975-78; Exec. Cttee, Liverpool Personal Services Soc., 1973-81; Adv. Panel Inf. Service, Disabled Living Foundn, 1979-; UK Steering Cttee, Internat. Year for the Disabled, 1979-80; Jt Cttee on Mobility of Blind and Partially Sighted People, 1980-81; Exec. Cttee, N Regional Assoc. for the Blind, 1980-81. Vice Pres., MIND Appeal, 1978-79. Pres., Merseyside Ski Club, 1970-77. Mem. Council, Prospect Hall Coll., 1973-77; Chm., Bd of Governors, William Rathbone Staff Coll., Liverpool, 1961-75. *Publications:* Community Health, Preventative Medicine and Social Services, 4th edn 1979; Community Health and Social Services, 4th edn 1982; (contrib.) Going Home, 1981; The Disabled Child and Adult, 1982; numerous papers on Public Health, Physically and Mentally Handicapped and various social services, in scientific and other jls. *Recreations:* skiing, golf, fishing, gardening, music. *Address:* Tree Tops, Church Road, Thornton Hough, Wirral, Merseyside. *T:* 051-336 3435. *Clubs:* Royal Over-Seas League; Bromborough Golf.

DAVIES, Janet Mary H.; *see* Hewlett-Davies.

DAVIES, Dame Jean; *see* Lancaster, Dame J.

DAVIES, John; *see* Davies, L. J.

DAVIES, John Alun Emlyn; retired 1977; *b* 4 May 1909; *s* of Robert Emlyn and Mary Davies; *m* 1941, Elizabeth Boshier; three *s. Educ:* Ruabon Grammar Sch.; Trinity Coll., Cambridge (Scholar). BA 1st cl. Pts I and II, History Tripos. Called to Bar, Lincoln's Inn, 1936. Served War of 1939-45: DAA&QMG 2nd Parachute Bde, 1943; DAAG 1st Airborne Div., 1944. Joined BoT, 1946; Asst Solicitor, 1963; Principal Asst Solicitor, DTI, 1968-72; Asst Solicitor, Law Commn, 1972-74; part-time Asst, Law Commn, 1974-77. Asst Sec. to Jenkins Cttee on Company Law, 1959-62. *Recreations:* gardening, walking. *Address:* 29 Crescent Road, Sidcup, Kent. *T:* 01-300 1421. *Club:* Reform.

DAVIES, John Duncan, DSc, PhD; CEng, FICE, FIStructE; Director, Polytechnic of Wales, since 1978; *b* 19 March 1929; *s* of Ioan and Gertrude Davies; *m* 1949, Barbara, *d* of Ivor and Alice Morgan; three *d. Educ:* Pontardawe School; Treforest School of Mines. BSc, MSc, PhD, DSc, Univ. of London. Junior Engineer, Consulting Engineers, 1949; Site Engineer, Cleveland Bridge Co., 1950-54; Royal Engineers, 1952-53; Design Engineer, Local Authority, 1955-56; Asst Lectr, Manchester Univ., 1957-58; University College, Swansea: Lecturer, 1959; Senior Lecturer, 1965; Reader, 1968; Professor of Civil Engineering, 1971-76; Dean, 1974-76; Principal, West Glamorgan Inst. of Higher Education, 1976-77. Mem., Open University Delegacy, 1978-82. Mem., Manpower Services Cttee (Wales), 1980-82. *Publications:* contribs to Structural Mechanics. *Address:* Polytechnic of Wales, Treforest, Pontypridd, Mid Glamorgan CF37 1DL. *T:* Pontypridd 405133.

DAVIES, Rev. John Gordon, MA, DD; Edward Cadbury Professor of Theology and Head of Department of Theology, University of Birmingham, since Oct. 1960; Director of Institute for Study of Worship and Religious Architecture, University of Birmingham, since 1962; *b* 20 April 1919; *s* of late A. G. Davies and of Mrs Davies, Chester; *m* 1945, Emily Mary Tordoff; one *s* two *d. Educ:* King's Sch., Chester; Christ Church, Oxford; Westcott House, Cambridge. Curate of Rotherhithe, Dec. 1943-Sept. 1948; Univ. of Birmingham: Asst Lecturer in Theology, 1948-50; Lecturer, 1950-57; Senior Lecturer, 1957-59; Reader, 1959-60; Dean of Faculty of Arts, 1967-70. BA Oxon., 1942; MA 1945; BD 1946; DD 1956; MA (Official) Birmingham, 1952; Hon. DD St Andrews, 1968. Hereditary Freeman, City of Chester; Brother of Ancient and Worshipful Company of Skinners and Felt Makers. Bampton Lecturer, 1958. Hon. Canon, Birmingham, 1965. Hon. Mem., Guild for Religious Architecture, USA. Conover Memorial Award, New York, 1967. *Publications:* The Theology of William Blake, 1948 (USA 1966); The Origin and Development of Early Christian Church Architecture, 1952 (USA 1953); Daily Life in the Early Church: Studies in the Church Social History of the First Five Centuries, 1952 (repr. 1955); Daily Life of Early Christians, 1953 (trans. as La Vie quotidienne des premiers chrétiens, 1956); Social Life of Early Christians, 1954; The Spirit, the Church, and the Sacraments, 1954 (trans. as Der Heilige Geist, die Kirche, und die Sakramente, 1958); Members One of Another: Aspects of Koinonia, 1958; He Ascended into Heaven: a Study in the History of Doctrine (Bampton Lectures, 1958), 1958 (USA 1958); The Making of the Church, 1960; Intercommunion, 1961; The Architectural Setting of Baptism, 1962; Holy Week, a Short History, 1963 (USA 1963); The Early Christian Church, 1965 (USA 1965; trans. as La Chiesa delle Origini, 1966; As Origens do Cristianismo, 1967); A Select Liturgical Lexicon, 1965 (USA 1965; trans. as Liturgiskt Handlexikon, 1968); Worship and Mission, 1966 (USA 1967; Japan, 1968); Dialogue with the World, 1967 (trans. as Dialogo con el Mundo, 1967); The Secular Use of Church Buildings, 1968; Every Day God: encountering the Holy in World and Worship, 1973; Christians, Politics and Violent Revolution, 1976 (USA 1976; trans. as Los Christianos, la Politica y la Revolucion violenta, 1977; Kristendom, Politikk, Vold og Revolusjon, 1979); New Perspectives on Worship Today, 1978; Temples, Churches and Mosques: a guide to the appreciation of religious architecture, 1982; co-author: An Experimental Liturgy, 1958; translator: Essays on the Lord's Supper, 1958; The Eucharistic Memorial Vol. I, 1960, Vol. II, 1961; Mission in a Dynamic Society, 1968; editor: A Dictionary of Liturgy and Worship, 1972; Worship and Dance, 1975; The Recreational Use of Churches, 1978; contributor to: Becoming a Christian, 1954; The Teachers' Commentary, 1955; The Concise Encyclopædia of Living Faiths, 1959; Making the Building Serve the Liturgy, 1962; The Modern Architectural Setting of the Liturgy, 1964; A Manual for Holy Week, 1967; Preface to Christian Studies, 1971; Journal of Theological Studies; Journal of Hellenic Studies; Vigiliae Christianae; Harvard Theological Review; Encyclopædia Britannica, etc. *Recreation:* cooking. *Address:* 28 George Road, Edgbaston, Birmingham B15 1PJ. *T:* 021-454 6254.

DAVIES, John Henry Vaughan, CB 1981; Deputy Secretary, Ministry of Agriculture, Fisheries and Food, 1979-81; *b* 15 Sept. 1921; *s* of late Rev. James Henry Davies and Ethel Sarah Davies; *m* 1st, 1950, Dorothy Rosa Mary Levy (marr. diss.); 2nd, 1959, Claire Daphne Bates (marr. diss.); one *d* ; 3rd, 1971, Barbara Ann, *o d* of David L. Davies, Portland, Oregon. *Educ:* Monkton Combe Sch.; Worcester Coll., Oxford (MA). Served Royal Air Force, FO, 1942-46. Entered Ministry of Agriculture and Fisheries as Asst Principal, 1947; Principal, 1951; Asst Sec., 1964; Under Sec., 1970. Chairman, Joint FAO/WHO Codex Alimentarius Commn, 1968-70. *Publications:* contributor to The Country Seat, 1970; articles on architecture. *Recreations:* reading, architecture. *Address:* 17 Cherrywood Drive, SW15 6DS. *T:* 01-789 1529.

DAVIES, Rev. Canon John Howard; Director of Theological and Religious Studies, University of Southampton, since 1981; Canon Theologian of Winchester, since 1981; *b* 19 Feb. 1929; *s* of Jabez Howard and Sarah Violet Davies; *m* 1956, Ina Mary, *d* of Stanley William and Olive Mary Bubb; three *s* (and one *s* decd). *Educ:* Southall Grammar Sch.; St John's Coll., Cambridge (MA); Westcott House, Cambridge; Univ. of Nottingham (BD); FRCO 1952. Ordained deacon, 1955, priest 1956. Succentor of Derby Cathedral, 1955; Chaplain of Westcott House, 1958; Lectr in Theology, Univ. of Southampton, 1963, Sen. Lectr 1974. *Publication:* A Letter to Hebrews, 1967. *Recreations:* music, architecture, the countryside. *Address:* 13 Glen Eyre Road, Southampton SO2 3GA. *T:* Southampton 769359.

DAVIES, John Howard Gay; Editorial Director, Thomson Regional Newspapers Ltd, 1972-82; *b* 17 Jan. 1923; *er s* of late E. E. Davies, Nicholaston Hall, Gower, Glamorgan; *m* 1st, 1948, Eira Morgan (marr. dissolved, 1953); 2nd, 1955, Betty Walmsley; one *s.* *Educ:* Bromsgrove Sch.; Wadham Coll., Oxford. Welsh Guards, 1942-46 (despatches). Western Mail, 1950-52; Daily Telegraph, 1952-55; Deputy Editor, Western Mail, 1955-58; an Assistant Editor, Sunday Times, 1958-62; Exec. Assistant to Editorial Director, Thomson Newspapers Ltd, 1962-64; Editor, Western Mail, 1964, 1965. Mem., British Exec., IPI. *Address:* 41 Chartfield Avenue, SW15. *T:* 01-788 8685.

DAVIES, J(ohn) R(obert) Lloyd, CMG 1953; Principal, Training Services Agency, 1973-79; *b* 24 March 1913; *o s* of late J. R. and Mrs Davies, Muswell Hill; *m* 1943, Margery, *o d* of late Major and Mrs McClelland, Nottingham; one *s* one *d.* *Educ:* Highgate Sch.; Oriel Coll., Oxford. Joined staff of Ministry of Labour, 1936; Private Secretary to Sir Thomas Phillips, 1940. Served War of 1939-45: Royal Navy; Lieut RNVR; service in Far East; Dep. Labour Attaché, HM Embassy, Washington, 1945-47; Asst Secretary, Ministry of Labour, London, Oct. 1947; Labour Attaché, HM Embassy, Paris, 1956-60; Asst Sec., Dept of Employment, 1960-72; Counsellor (Labour), HM Embassy, Washington, DC, 1972-73. *Recreations:* music, geology and reading. *Address:* 5508 Glenwood Road, Bethesda, Md 20817, USA. *Club:* United Oxford & Cambridge University.

DAVIES, Prof. John Tasman, PhD, DSc London; MA, ScD Cantab; Professor of Chemical Engineering and Head of Department, University of Birmingham, since 1960; *b* 1 May 1924; *m* 1948, Ruth Batt; two *s.* *Educ:* Boys' High Sch., Christchurch, NZ; Canterbury University Coll.; London Univ. MA Cantab. 1955; PhD London 1949; DSc London 1955; ScD Cantab 1967. Worked with Sir Eric Rideal, FRS, Royal Institution London, 1946-48; Research Associate and Bristol-Myers Fellow, Stanford Univ., Calif. (USA) (worked with late Prof. J. W. McBain, FRS), 1948-49; Beit Mem. Fellow for Medical Research, Royal Instn and KCL, 1949-52; Lectr in: Chemistry, KCL, 1952-55; Chemical Engineering, Cambridge Univ., 1955-60. Overseas guest lecturer at Gordon Conference, USA, 1956, 1980. Visiting Professor: Univ. of Minnesota, 1963; Univ. of Auckland, NZ, 1976, 1980. Member: UN Consultative Commn to Indian Inst. of Petroleum, 1967-71; UNESCO Advisory Group on Petroleum Technology, Arab States, 1967; (part-time) West Midlands Gas Board, 1968-72. Member Sigma-Xi, 1949 (USA), FIChemE. *Publications:* (with Sir Eric Rideal, FRS) Interfacial Phenomena, 1961; The Scientific Approach, 1965, 2nd edn 1973; Turbulence Phenomena, 1972; many on Surface Phenomena and Chemical Engineering. *Address:* Department of Chemical Engineering, The University, Birmingham B15 2TT. *T:* 021-472 1301.

DAVIES, Joseph Marie, QC 1962; **His Honour Judge J. M. Davies;** a Circuit Judge (formerly Judge of County Courts), since 1971; *b* 13 Jan. 1916; *s* of Joseph and Mary Davies, St Helen's; *m* 1948, Eileen Mary (née Dromgoole); two *s* two *d.* *Educ:* Stonyhurst Coll.; Liverpool Univ. Called to Bar, Gray's Inn, Nov. 1938; practice in Liverpool. Recorder of Birmingham, 1970-71; Cumberland Co. QS: Dep. Chm., 1956-63, 1970-71; Chm., 1963-70. Served War of 1939-45; The King's Regt, Nov. 1939-Dec. 1941; RIASC and Staff Allied Land Forces, SE Asia, 1942-46. *Address:* 4 Elm Grove, Eccleston Park, Prescot, Lancs. *T:* 051-426 5415. *Clubs:* Athenæum (Liverpool); Cumberland County.

DAVIES, Kenneth; *see* Davies, S. K.

DAVIES, Kenneth Arthur, CMG 1952; OBE 1946; *b* 28 Jan. 1897; *s* of William and Alice Davies; *m* 1932, Edna Myfanwy, *d* of Rev. T. Rowlands; one *s.* *Educ:* Pontypridd Grammar Sch.; University Coll., Wales, Aberystwyth; Trinity Coll., Cambridge. Served European War, 1914-18, with RFA in France and Belgium, 1916-19; 1st Class Hons Geology BSc, University Coll., Aberystwyth. Research Scholar, 1923-26; Fellow of University of Wales, 1926; MSc 1925; PhD (Cantab.), 1928. Field Geologist, Govt of Uganda, 1929; Senior Geologist, 1936; Director, Geological Survey, 1939, retired 1951. Adviser on Mineral Development to Uganda Govt, 1952-54 and 1965; Commonwealth Geological Liaison Officer, 1954. Dep.-Dir Overseas Geological Surveys, 1957-65. Adviser to United Nations, 1966. Fellow, Geological Society, 1928; FIMM 1950. Murchison Medallist, Geological Society, 1954. *Publications:* various on Stratigraphy of Central Wales and graptolites in British Geological journals, and on African Geology in British and American journals. *Recreation:* gardening. *Address:* Park Cottage, Somerset Road, SW19.

DAVIES, Sir Lancelot Richard B.; *see* Bell Davies.

DAVIES, (Lewis) John, QC 1967; a Recorder of the Crown Court, since 1974; *b* 15 April 1921; *s* of William Davies, JP, and Esther Davies; *m* 1956, Janet Mary Morris; one *s* two *d.* *Educ:* Pontardawe Grammar Sch.; University College of Wales, Aberystwyth; Trinity Hall (Common Law Prizeman, 1943); Scholar, 1943-44), Cambridge. LLB Wales 1942 (1st cl.); BA Cantab (1st cl.); LLB Cantab (1st cl.). Asst Principal, HM Treasury, 1945-46; Senior Law Lecturer, Leeds Univ., 1946-48; Administrative Asst, British Petroleum, 1949-52. Called to the Bar, Middle Temple, 1948, Bencher, 1973; Mem., Bar Council, 1969-71; Mem., Senate, 1976-78. Mem., Council of Legal Educn, 1976-. Inspector, DoT, 1977. *Recreations:* gardening, golf. *Address:* Old Manor Cottage, 24 Park Road, Teddington, Mddx. *T:* 01-977 3975. *Club:* Travellers'.

DAVIES, Lewis Mervyn, CMG 1966; OBE 1962; Commissioner for Narcotics, Hong Kong, since 1983; *b* 5 Dec. 1922; *s* of late Rev. Canon L. C. Davies; *m* 1st, 1950, Ione Podger (*d* 1973); one *s* ; 2nd, 1975, Mona A. Birley; two steps *s. Educ:* St Edward's Sch., Oxford. Served with Fleet Air Arm, 1941-46: Lieut A, RNVR. District Commissioner, Gold Coast, 1948; Western Pacific: Senior Asst Secretary, 1956-62; Financial Secretary, 1962-65; Chief Secretary, 1965-70; Deputy Governor, Bahamas, 1970-73; Secretary for Security, Hong Kong, 1973-82. Lay Canon, Cathedral Church of St Barnabas, Honiara, 1965-70. Commandeur de l'Ordre National du Mérite, 1966. *Recreations:* sailing, tennis. *Address:* c/o Government Secretariat, Lower Albert Road, Hong Kong.

DAVIES, Lloyd; *see* Davies, J. R. L.

DAVIES, Col Lucy Myfanwy, CBE 1968 (OBE 1962); Deputy Controller Commandant, WRAC, 1967-77; *b* 8 April 1913; *d* of late Col A. M. O. Anwyl-Passingham, CBE, DL, JP, and late Margaret Anwyl-Passingham; *m* 1955, Major D. W. Davies, TD, RAMC (*d* 1959); no *c. Educ:* Frances Holland Graham Street Sch. Driver FANY, 1939; commnd ATS, 1941; served in Egypt, 1945-48; Asst Director, WRAC Middle East (Cyprus), 1957-59; Comdt WRAC Depot, 1961-64; Dep. Director WRAC, 1964-68; retired, 1968. An underwriting Member of Lloyd's, 1971-. OStJ 1938. *Recreations:* travel, racing, reading. *Address:* 6 Elm Place, SW7. *T:* 01-373 5731. *Club:* Lingfield Park.

DAVIES, Marcus John A.; *see* Anwyl-Davies.

DAVIES, Meredith; *see* Davies, Albert Meredith.

DAVIES, Hon. Sir Mervyn; *see* Davies, Hon. Sir D. H. M.

DAVIES, Hon. Sir Michael; *see* Davies, Hon. Sir A. W. M.

DAVIES, Michael John, CMG 1961; OBE 1957; Secretary, Imperial College of Science and Technology, and Clerk to the Governing Body, 1962–79, Fellow, since 1979, on retirement; *b* 7 Oct. 1918; *y s* of late David Alexander Davies; *m* 1949, Elizabeth Eve Burridge; two *s* one *d. Educ:* Diocesan Coll., Cape Town; University of Cape Town; Trinity Coll., Oxford. (MA) as a Rhodes Scholar. Appointed to Colonial Service in Tanganyika, as an Administrative Officer, 1940. Private Secretary to the Governor, 1943–47; seconded to the Colonial Office, 1947–49. Assistant Special Representative for Tanganyika at Trusteeship Council of United Nations, 1958 and 1959; Minister: for Constitutional Affairs in Tanganyika, 1959; for Security and Immigration, 1959–60; for Information Services, 1960–61 (until date of Self Government in Tanganyika, May 1st). Acting Chief Secretary May–Aug., 1960; retired from HM Overseas Civil Service, 1962. Médaille de la Belgique Reconnaissante (for services to Belgian Refugees), 1961. *Recreations:* watching Rugby football (Welsh International, 1938 and 1939); playing golf; gardening. *Address:* Barfield Cottage, Waldron, Heathfield, East Sussex. *T:* Heathfield 3704.

DAVIES, Prof. (Morgan Wynn) Humphrey, LLM, MSc; CEng, FIEE; FCGI; Professor of Electrical Engineering, Queen Mary College, University of London, 1956–79; Dean of Engineering, University of London, 1976–79; *b* 26 Dec. 1911; *s* of late Richard Humphrey Davies, CB; *m* 1944, Gwendolen Enid, *d* of late Canon Douglas Edward Morton, Camborne, Cornwall; one *s. Educ:* Hill Crest, Swanage; Westminster Sch.; University College of N Wales, Bangor; Charlottenburg Technische Hochschule, Berlin. Grad. Apprentice with Metropolitan-Vickers, 1933; Lecturer in Electrical Engineering, University of Wales, 1935–42; Commonwealth Fellow, MIT, 1938–39; University Lecturer in Electrical Engineering, College of Technology, Manchester, 1943; Education Officer to Instn of Electrical Engineers, 1944–47; Lecturer, 1947, and University Reader, 1952, in Electrical Engineering, Imperial Coll., University of London, 1947–56. Member: Council, IEE, 1948–51, 1958–61 (Chm., Science and Gen. Div. 1964–65). Council, City & Guilds of London Inst., 1952–62; Engineering Adv. Cttee, BBC, 1965–71; Computer Bd for Univs and Res. Councils, 1968–71; Council, University Coll. of N Wales, Bangor, 1976–; Chm., Bd of Univ. of London Computer Centre, 1968–79. *Publications:* Power System Analysis (with J. R. Mortlock), 1952; papers in Proc. of Instn of Electrical Engineers. *Recreation:* travel. *Address:* Church Bank, Beaumaris, Anglesey. *Club:* Athenæum.

DAVIES, Nigel; *see* Davies, Claude N. B.

DAVIES, (Norah) Olwen, MA; Headmistress, St Swithun's School, Winchester, since 1973; *b* 21 March 1926; *d* of late Rev. and Mrs E. A. Davies. *Educ:* Tregaron County Sch.; Walthamstow Hall, Sevenoaks; Edinburgh Univ. (MA). DipEd Oxon. Staff of Girls' Remand Home, Essex, 1948–50; Russell Hill Sch., Purley, 1950–53; Woodford House, NZ, 1953–57 (Dep. Headmistress); Westonbirt Sch., 1957–65; Headmistress, St Mary's Hall, Brighton, 1965–73. Pres., Girls' Schools Association, 1981–82. Governor: Hurstpierpoint Coll.; Tormead Sch., Guildford; St John's Special Sch., Brighton. *Address:* St Swithun's School, Winchester, Hants SO21 1HA. *T:* Winchester 61316.

DAVIES, Col Norman Thomas, MBE 1970; Registrar, General Dental Council, since 1981; *b* 2 May 1933; *s* of late Edward Ernest Davies and of Elsie Davies (*née* Scott); *m* 1961, Penelope Mary, *e d* of Peter Graeme Agnew, *qv*; one *s* one *d. Educ:* Holywell; RMA, Sandhurst; Open Univ. (BA 1979). Commnd RA, 1954; Regtl and Staff Appts, Malaya, Germany and UK, 1954–64; ptsc 1966; psc 1967; Mil. Asst to C of S Northern Army Gp, 1968–69; Commanded C Bty RHA and 2IC 3RHA, 1970–72; GSOI (DS), Staff Coll., Camberley, and Canadian Land Forces Comd and Staff Coll., 1972–74; Commanded 4 Field Regt, RA, 1975–77; Mil. Dir of Studies, RMCS, Shrivenham, 1977–80. *Recreations:* golf, gardening, wine. *Address:* Milestone House, 212 Farnborough Road, Farnborough, Hampshire GU14 7JW. *T:* Farnborough 544546.

DAVIES, Olwen; *see* Davies, N. O.

DAVIES, Oswald, CBE 1973; DCM 1944; JP; Chairman, Fairclough Construction Group Ltd (formerly Leonard Fairclough Ltd), since 1965 (Chief Executive, 1965–78); *b* 23 June 1920; *s* of George Warham Davies and Margaret (*née* Hinton); *m* 1942, Joyce Eaton; one *s* one *d. Educ:* Central Schs, Sale; Manchester Coll. of Technology. CBIM, FIHE, FIOB, FFB. Joined Leonard Fairclough Ltd at age of 15 years and became Agent/Engineer at 18. Served War of 1939–45: Sapper, bomb disposal squad, RE, Europe and ME, from 1940 (DCM (ME) 1944); returned to Europe, where involved with his unit in clearance of waterways, port, docks and bridge reconstruction. On release, Contracts Manager, area office, Stafford; then steel works near Chester. Dir, 1948, Jt Man. Dir, 1951, Leonard Fairclough Ltd. Dir, Nat. Building Agency, 1980–. JP 1969. *Recreations:* gardening, Rugby football, sport. *Address:* Dingle Bank, Church Road, Lymm, Cheshire WA13 0QD. *T:* Lymm 2701.

DAVIES, Oswald Vaughan L.; *see* Lloyd-Davies.

DAVIES, Patrick Taylor, CMG 1978; OBE 1967; HM Overseas Civil Service, retired; *b* 10 Aug. 1927; *s* of Andrew Taylor Davies and Olive Kathleen Mary Davies; *m* 1959, Marjorie Eileen (*née* Wilkinson); two *d. Educ:* Shrewsbury Sch.; St John's Coll., Cambridge (BA); Trinity Coll.,

Oxford. Lieut, RA, Nigeria, 1945–48. Colonial Admin. Service, Nigeria, 1952; Permanent Sec., Kano State, 1970; Chief Inspector, Area Courts, Kano State, 1972–79. *Address:* Rose Cottage, Childs Ercall, Salop TF9 2DB. *T:* Childs Ercall 255.

DAVIES, Percy Douglas, CB 1981; *b* 17 Sept. 1921; *s* of late Mr and Mrs Thomas Davies; *m* 1947, Renée Margaret Billings; one *s* one *d. Educ:* Liverpool Collegiate School. Clerical Officer, Ministry of Transport, 1938; served Royal Armoured Corps, 1941–46; Chief Executive Officer, Min. of Transport, 1963; Asst Secretary, 1966; Principal Establishment Officer, Under Secretary, Property Services Agency, Dept of the Environment, 1972–81; retired. *Recreations:* gardening, making things work. *Address:* 37 Byron Avenue, Coulsdon, Surrey CR3 2JS. *T:* 01-660 2789.

DAVIES, Peter; *see* Davies, R. P. H.

DAVIES, Peter Douglas Royston; HM Diplomatic Service; Counsellor, Kuala Lumpur, since 1982; *b* 29 Nov. 1936; *e s* of Douglas and Edna Davies; *m* 1967, Elizabeth Mary Lovett Williams; one *s* two *d. Educ:* Brockenhurst County High Sch.; LSE (BSc(Econ)). Joined HM Diplomatic Service, 1964; FO, 1964–66; Second Sec., Nicosia, 1966–67; FO, 1967–68; First Sec., Budapest, 1968–71; FCO, 1971–74; Consul (Commercial), Rio de Janeiro, 1974–78; Counsellor (Commercial), The Hague, 1978–82. *Address:* c/o Foreign and Commonwealth Office, SW1A 2AH. *Club:* Royal Commonwealth Society.

DAVIES, P(eter) Maxwell, CBE 1981; composer; *b* 8 Sept. 1934. *Educ:* Leigh Grammar Sch.; Manchester Univ.; Royal Manchester Coll. of Music. MusB (Hons), 1956; FRNCM 1978. Studied with Goffredo Petrassi in Rome (schol. 1957); Harkness Fellow, Grad. Music Sch., Princetown Univ., NJ, 1962. Dir of Music, Cirencester Grammar Sch., 1959–62; Lecture tours in Europe, Australia and New Zealand, 1965; Visiting Composer, Adelaide Univ., 1966; Co-Dir, with Harrison Birtwistle, of Pierrot Players, 1967–70; Dir, The Fires of London, 1971; has conducted many concerts with these ensembles in Britain and abroad; Dir of Music, Dartington Hall Summer Sch. of Music, 1979–. Series for Schools Broadcasts, BBC Television. Hon. Mem. RAM, 1978; Hon. DMus Edinburgh, 1979. *Publications:* Trumpet Sonata, 1955; Five Pieces for Piano, 1956; St Michael Sonata, for 17 Wind Instruments, 1957; Alma Redemptoris Mater for 6 Wind Instruments, 1957; Five Motets for Soprano, Contralto, Tenor and Bass soli, double Choir and Instruments, 1959; Prolation for Orchestra, 1959; Ricercar and Doubles on 'To Many a Well', 1959; O Magnum Mysterium, 1960 (Instrumental parts); Four Carols from O Magnum Mysterium for unaccompanied chorus, 1960; Fantasia on O Magnum Mysterium for organ, 1960; Te Lucis Ante Terminum, 1961; String Quartet, 1961; First Fantasia on an In Nomine of John Taverner, 1962 (commissioned by BBC); Leopardi Fragments, 1962; Sinfonia, 1962; The Lord's Prayer for SATB choir, 1962; Four Carols, 1962; Five Little Pieces for Piano Solo, 1962–64; Veni Sancte Spiritus for Soprano, Contralto and Bass soli, mixed Chorus and small Orchestra, 1963; Second Fantasia on John Taverner's In Nomine for Orchestra, 1964; Shakespeare Music for Chamber Ensemble, 1964; Ecce Manus Tradentis for mixed Chorus and Instruments, 1965; Seven in Nomine for Instruments, 1963–65; The Shepherd's Calender for Young Singers and Instrumentalists, 1965; Revelation and Fall for Soprano solo and Instruments, 1965; Shall I Die For Mannis Sake?, Carol for Soprano and Alto Voices and Piano, 1966; Five Carols for Soprano and Alto Voices, unaccompanied, 1966; Hymnos for Clarinet and Piano, 1967; Antechrist for Chamber Ensemble, 1967; L'Homme Armé for Chamber Ensemble, 1968; Fantasia and Two Pavans (Purcell, real. Davies), 1968–69; Eight Songs for a Mad King, 1969; St Thomas Wake—Foxtrot for Orchestra (commnd by City of Dortmund), 1969; Worldes Blis, 1969; Eram Quasi Agnus, 1969; Cauda Pavonis, 1969; Solita for flute solo, 1969; opera, Taverner, 1970; Hymn to St Magnus, 1972; Stone Litany, 1973; Ave Maris Stella for Chamber Ensemble, 1975; The Blind Fiddler for Soprano and Chamber Ensemble, 1976; opera, The Martyrdom of St Magnus, 1977; A Mirror Whitening Light, 1977; 1st Symphony, 1978; opera, The Two Fiddlers, 1978; Le Jongleur de Notre Dame, masque for mime, baritone, chamber ensemble and children's band, 1978; ballet score, Salome, 1979; Kirkwall Shopping Songs for young children, 1979; Solstice of Light, 1979; Black Pentecost for orchestra, mezzo and baritone, 1979; opera, The Lighthouse, 1979; pantomime opera for young people to perform, Cinderella, 1980; Symphony No 2, 1980; Piano Sonata, 1981; The Rainbow, 1981; The Medium, 1981; Hill Runes for solo guitar, 1981; film score, The Devils, 1971. *Address:* c/o Mrs Judy Arnold, 50 Hogarth Road, SW5.

DAVIES, Rhys Everson, QC 1981; a Recorder of the Crown Court, since 1980; *b* 13 Jan. 1941; *s* of Evan Davies and Nancy Caroline Davies (decd); *m* 1963, Katharine Anne Yeates; one *s* one *d. Educ:* Cowbridge Grammar School; Neath Grammar School; Victoria University of Manchester. LLB (Hons). Called to the Bar, Gray's Inn, 1964. On Northern Circuit. *Recreations:* music, conversation. *Address:* (chambers) 18 St John Street, Manchester M3 4EA. *T:* 061-834 9843; 6 Oakfield Road, Didsbury, Manchester M20 0XA. *T:* 061-445 1312.

DAVIES, Richard Harries, CVO 1982; CBE 1962; BSc; CEng, FIEE; Assistant Private Secretary to the Duke of Edinburgh, since 1977; *b* 28 June 1916; *s* of Thomas Henry Davies and Minnie Oakley (*née* Morgan); *m* 1st, 1944, Hon. Nan (*d* 1976), *e d* of 1st Baron Macpherson of Drumochter; two *s* two *d* ; 2nd, 1979, Mrs Patricia P. Ogier. *Educ:* Porth County Sch.; Cardiff

Technical Coll. Scientific Civil Service, 1939-46; British Air Commn, Washington, DC, 1941-45; Vice Pres., Ferranti Electric Inc., New York, 1948-63; Dir, Ferranti Ltd, 1970-76. Pres., British Amer. Chamber of Commerce, New York, 1959-62; Vice Pres., Manchester Chamber of Commerce, 1976. *Recreations:* gardening, sailing, amateur radio. *Address:* 50 Sussex Street, SW1 4RG. *T:* 01-834 2107; Comenden Manor, Cranbrook, Kent. *T:* Cranbrook 712840. *Clubs:* Athenæum; Blackwater Sailing (Essex).

DAVIES, Robert David, CB 1982; CVO 1977; RD 1963; JP; Under Secretary, Premier's Department, Western Australia, since 1975; Clerk of Executive Council, since 1975; *b* 17 Aug. 1927; *s* of late William Harold Davies and of Elsie Davies; *m* 1948, Muriel Patricia Cuff; one *s* one *d. Educ:* Fremantle Boys High Sch.; Perth Technical Coll. Senior AASA. Defence Service, 1945-47; Asst Commissioner, State Taxation Dept, 1973. Comdr, RANR, 1972. JP 1970. *Recreations:* fishing, sailing. *Address:* 82 Reynolds Road, Mount Pleasant, Western Australia 6153. *T:* 364-1596. *Clubs:* East Fremantle Football, WA Turf, Fremantle Sailing (Western Australia).

DAVIES, Rt. Rev. Robert Edward, CBE 1981; MA, ThD; *b* Birkenhead, England, 30 July 1913; *s* of late R. A. Davies, Canberra; *m* 1953, Helen M., *d* of H. M. Boucher; two *d. Educ:* Cessnock High School; Queensland University; St John's Theological College, Morpeth, NSW. Assistant Priest, Christ Church Cathedral, Newcastle, NSW, 1937-41. War of 1939-45: Toc H Army Chaplain, 1941-42; Chaplain, Royal Australian Air Force, Middle East and Mediterranean, 1942-46. Vice-Warden, St John's College, University of Queensland, Brisbane, 1946-48; Archdeacon of Canberra and Rector of Canberra, 1949-53; Archdeacon of Wagga Wagga, NSW, 1953-60; Assistant Bishop of Newcastle and Warden of St John's Theological College, Morpeth, NSW, 1960-63; Bishop of Tasmania, 1963-81. *Recreations:* golf, tennis. *Address:* 12 Elboden Street, Hobart, Tasmania 7000, Australia. *Clubs:* Tasmanian, Naval Military and Air Force of Tas. (Tas.).

DAVIES, Prof. Robert Ernest, FRS 1966; Benjamin Franklin Professor of Molecular Biology and University Professor, University of Pennsylvania, since 1977, and Chairman, Research Advisory Board, Institute for Environmental Medicine, School of Medicine, since 1970; *b* 17 Aug. 1919; *s* of William Owen Davies and Stella Davies; *m* 1961, Helen C. (*née* Rogoff); two *step s. Educ:* Manchester Grammar Sch.; Univ. of Manchester and Univ. of Sheffield. BSc(Chem.) Manchester, 1941; MSc Manchester 1942; PhD Sheffield 1949; DSc Manchester 1952; MA Oxon 1956; MA Penn 1971. Temp. Asst Lectr in Chemistry, Univ. of Sheffield. Half-time research (Ministry of Supply, Chemical Defence Research Dept), 1942; full-time research on temp. staff, Medical Research Unit for Research in Cell Metabolism, 1945; apptd to Estab. Staff of MRC, 1947; Hon. Lectr in Biochemistry, Univ. of Sheffield, 1948-54; Vis. Prof., Pharmacologisches Inst., Univ. Heidelberg, March-May 1954; University of Pennsylvania, 1955-: Prof. of Biochemistry, Sch. of Medicine, 1955-62, Grad. Sch. of Medicine, 1962-70; Prof. of Molecular Biology, 1970-77; Chm., Dept of Animal Biology, Sch. of Vet. Medicine, 1962-73; Chm., Grad. Group Cttee on Molecular Biology, 1962-72. Chm., Benjamin Franklin Professors, 1978-; Mem., Bd of Dirs, Assoc. for Women in Science Educnl Foundn, 1978-. Hon. Life Mem., NY Acad. of Scis. *Publications:* very many: in chemistry, biochemistry, physiology and biology journals concerning secretion, muscle contraction, kidneys, etc. *Recreations:* mountaineering, caving, underwater swimming, white water boating. *Address:* Department of Animal Biology, School of Veterinary Medicine, University of Pennsylvania, Philadelphia, Pa 19104, USA; 7053 McCallum Street, Philadelphia, Pa 19119, USA. *Clubs:* Fell and Rock-climbing Club of the English Lake District; Cave Diving Group; Manchester Univ. Mountaineering.

DAVIES, Robert Henry, MBE 1962; DFC 1943; HM Diplomatic Service, retired; *b* 17 Aug. 1921; *s* of John and Lena Davies; *m* 1st, 1945, Marion Ainsworth (marr. diss. 1973); one *s* one *d*; 2nd, 1973, Maryse Deuson. *Educ:* John Bright County Sch., Llandudno. RAF, 1940-46; flew with S African Air Force, N Africa, 1942-43. Joined Min. of Food, 1946; transf. to CRO, 1954; served in India, 1954-57 and Canada, 1959-62; HM Diplomatic Service, 1965; served in Brussels, 1967-70; Consul-Gen. and Counsellor (Admin), Moscow, 1973-75; FCO, 1975-76; Counsellor, Paris, 1976-81. *Recreations:* golf, birdwatching, reading. *Address:* 16 Beechcroft Drive, Guildford, Surrey. *Club:* Bramley Golf.

DAVIES, Prof. Rodney Deane, DSc, PhD, FInstP, FRAS; Professor of Radio Astronomy, University of Manchester, since 1976; *b* 8 Jan. 1930; *s* of Holbin James Davies and Rena Irene (*née* March), Mallala, S Australia; *m* 1953, Valda Beth Treasure; one *s* two *d* (and one *s* decd). *Educ:* Adelaide High Sch.; Univ. of Adelaide (BSc Hons, MSc); Univ. of Manchester (PhD, DSc). Research Officer, Radiophysics Div., CSIRO, Sydney, 1951-53; Univ. of Manchester: Asst Lectr, 1953-56; Lectr, 1956-67; Reader, 1967-76. Visiting Astronomer, Radiophysics Div., CSIRO, Australia, 1963. Member: Internat. Astronomical Union, 1958; Org. Cttee and Working Gps of various Commns; Council, Royal Astronomical Soc., 1972-75, 1978- (Vice-Pres. 1973-75; Sec., 1978-); Bd and various panels and cttees of Astronomy Space and Radio Bd and Science Bd of Science Research Council; British Nat. Cttee for Astronomy, 1974-77. *Publications:* Radio Studies of the Universe (with H. P. Palmer), 1959; Radio Astronomy Today (with H. P. Palmer and M. I. Large), 1963; The Crab Nebula (co-ed with F. G. Smith), 1971; numerous contribs to Monthly Notices of RAS and internat. jls on the galactic and extragalactic magnetic fields, structure and dynamics of the Galaxy and nearby external galaxies, using radio spectral lines. *Recreations:* cricket, gardening, fell-walking. *Address:* University of Manchester, Nuffield Radio Astronomy Laboratories, Jodrell Bank, Macclesfield, Cheshire SK11 9DL. *T:* Lower Withington 321.

DAVIES, (Roger) Peter (Havard), OBE 1978; Secretary, Anti-Slavery Society, since 1980; *b* 4 Oct. 1919; *s* of Arthur William Davies and Edith Mary Davies (*née* Mealand); *m* 1956, Ferelith Mary Helen Short; two *s* two *d. Educ:* Bromsgrove Sch., Worcs; St Edmund Hall, Oxford (MA). Army service, N Africa, Italy, NW Europe, Captain RA (AOP), 1939-46. Joined British Council, 1949; served Hungary, Israel, Sarawak, Finland, Chile, India (Calcutta); Director: Drama and Music Dept, 1965-69; Information Dept, 1974-75; retired, 1980. *Publications:* occasional articles and broadcasts. *Recreations:* family life, music, golf. *Address:* Ley Cottage, Elmore Road, Chipstead, Surrey CR3 3SG. *T:* Downland 53905. *Clubs:* Royal Commonwealth Society; Bengal (Calcutta).

DAVIES, Roy Dicker Salter, CBE 1967; a Chief Inspector of Schools, Department of Education and Science, 1958-68, retired; *b* 24 March 1906; *yr s* of Ernest Salter Davies, CBE, and Evelyn May Lile. *Educ:* Tonbridge Sch.; Magdalen Coll., Oxford (MA). Served RE, 1939-40, RA, 1940-45. Appointed HM Inspector of Schools, 1934; Staff Inspector, 1951. Mem., Departmental Cttee on Adult Educn, 1969-73. *Recreations:* watching Rugby football; cricket. *Address:* Wick House, Stogumber, Taunton, Somerset. *T:* Stogumber 422.

DAVIES, Rev. Rupert Eric; Warden, John Wesley's Chapel, Bristol, since 1976; *b* 29 Nov. 1909; *s* of Walter Pierce and Elizabeth Miriam Davies; *m* 1937, Margaret Price Holt; two *s* two *d. Educ:* St Paul's Sch.; Balliol Coll. (Class. Scholar), Oxford; Wesley House, Cambridge; Univ. of Tübingen, Germany. First cl. in Honour Mods, Classics, 1930; second cl. in Lit. Hum., 1932; first cl. in Theology, Pt II, 1934 (Wesley House); trav. schol. in Germany, 1934-35; BD (Cantab) 1946. Chaplain, Kingswood Sch., Bath, 1935-47; Methodist Minister, Bristol, 1947-52 and 1973-76; Tutor, Didsbury Coll., Bristol, 1952-67; Principal, Wesley Coll., Bristol, 1967-73. Pres., Methodist Conf., 1970-71. Select Preacher to Univs of: Cambridge, 1962; Oxford, 1969; Mem. Exec. Cttee, World Methodist Council, 1956-76; Mem., Anglican-Methodist Unity Commn, 1965-68; World Council of Churches: Faith and Order Commn, 1965-75; Deleg. to Fourth Assembly, 1968. *Publications:* The Problem of Authority in the Continental Reformers, 1946; Catholicity of Protestantism (ed), 1950; Approach to Christian Education (ed), 1956; John Scott Lidgett (ed), 1957; The Church in Bristol, 1960; Methodists and Unity, 1962; Methodism, 1963, rev. edn, 1976; History of the Methodist Church in Great Britain (ed), vol. I, 1965, vol. II, 1978; We Believe in God (ed), 1968; Religious Authority in an Age of Doubt, 1968; A Christian Theology of Education, 1974; What Methodists Believe, 1976; The Church in Our Times, 1979; (with M. P. Davies) Circles of Community, 1982. *Recreations:* gardening, theatre. *Address:* 6 Elmtree Drive, Bishopsworth, Bristol. *T:* Bristol 641087.

DAVIES, Ryland; opera singer; tenor; *b* 9 Feb. 1943; *s* of Gethin and Joan Davies; *m* 1966, Anne Elizabeth Howells (marr. diss. 1981), *qv. Educ:* Royal Manchester College of Music (Fellow, 1971) (studied with Frederic R. Cox, OBE). Début as Almaviva in The Barber of Seville, Welsh Nat. Opera, 1965; Glyndebourne Fest. Chorus, 1964-66: soloist rôles incl.: Belmonte in Il Seraglio, Ferrando in Così Fan Tutte, Flamand in Capriccio; rôles with Welsh Nat. Opera incl., Tamino in The Magic Flute, and with Scottish Opera, Ferrando; Sadler's Wells Opera: Almaviva, also Essex in Britten's Gloriana; Royal Opera: Hylas in The Trojans, Don Ottavio in Don Giovanni, Ferrando, Cassio in Otello, Ernesto in Don Pasquale, Lysander in A Midsummer Night's Dream, Almaviva. Overseas venues incl. Salzburg, as Cassio; S Francisco and Chicago, as Ferrando, also Paris; début NY Met., 1975, Ferrando and Almaviva; Vienna, Missa Solemnis; Bruxelles Opera, Werther. Concert works in UK incl.: Messiah, Saul, Beethoven's Ninth Symphony, Christ on the Mount of Olives, Verdi's Requiem, Dream of Gerontius, Dvorak's St Ludmila, J. C. Bach's Adriano in Siria; concert perfs in USA incl. Messiah and Die Fledermaus. Has sung with most leading orchestras in America. Many recordings, incl.: Il Seraglio, The Trojans, Saul, Così Fan Tutte, Thérèse, Monteverdi Madrigals, Idomeneo, Haydn's The Seasons, Messiah, L'Oracolo (Leone), Judas Maccabaeus, Il Matrimonio Segreto (Cimarosa). *Recreations:* antiques, art, cinema, sport. *Address:* Milestone, Broom Close, Esher, Surrey.

DAVIES, Sam; *see* Davies, Stanley Mason.

DAVIES, (Stanley) Kenneth, CBE 1951; Chairman: Wire Ropes Ltd, Wicklow; Westdore Ltd, Cardiff; *b* 25 April 1899; 2nd *s* of late Sir John Davies, CBE, JP; *m* 1938, Stephanie Morton (*d* 1979); one *s* one *d. Educ:* Christ Coll., Brecon; Blundell's; Royal Military Academy, Woolwich. Commnd RA, 1918; served France and Germany, 1918-19. Chairman and Managing Director: George Elliot & Co. Ltd; Bridgwater Wire Ropes Ltd; Somerset Wire Co. Ltd; Terrells Wire Ropes Ltd; Yacht and Commercial Rigging Co. Ltd; Hartlepool Wire Rope Co.; Excelsior Ropes Ltd (for varying periods between 1929 and 1960, when they were incorp. in British Ropes Ltd, now Bridon Ltd, or in GKN Ltd). Founder Member, Cardiff Aeroplane Club, 1929. Private pilot's licence, 1931-61. Formed Cambrian Air Services Ltd, 1935, Managing Director, 1935-51. Member Cttee Royal Aero

Club of United Kingdom, 1935 (Vice-Chm., 1948-51, Chm. 1952-58, Vice-Pres., 1958-); Member Board British European Airways Corporation, 1951-67; Dep. Chairman BEA Helicopters Ltd, 1965-67; Chairman Welsh Advisory Council for Civil Aviation, 1948-60; Chairman Cardiff Airport Consultative Cttee, 1956-63; Member Welsh Cttee of Arts Council of Great Britain, 1954-67; Member Consultative Cttee, Sadler's Wells Trust, 1962-; Chairman of Contemporary Art Society of Wales, 1966-72; Liveryman of the Guild of Air Pilots and Air Navigators; Vice-President, FAI (Federation Aeronautique Internationale), rep. UK; Member Cttee, Dublin Theatre Festival, 1967; Mem. Ct of Governors, National Theatre of Wales. Life Member: Iron & Steel Institute; S Wales Inst. of Engineers; Royal Agricultural Society; Royal Dublin Society. FRSA; FCIT. Coronation medal, 1953. *Recreations:* aviation and gastronomy (Vice-Pres., Internat. Wine and Food Society). *Address:* Killoughter, Ashford, Co. Wicklow. *T:* Wicklow 4126; Collingdon Road, Cardiff. *T:* 21693. *Clubs:* Athenæum, Brooks's, Naval and Military, Royal Automobile (among remaining 100 oldest members); County (Cardiff); Kildare Street and University (Dublin); Bristol Channel Yacht (Swansea).
    See also D. J. Davies.

DAVIES, Stanley Mason, (Sam Davies), CMG 1971; Director and Consultant, Vickers Ltd (Health Care) and other international medical firms, since 1977; *b* 7 Feb. 1919; *s* of late Charles Davies, MBE and Constance Evelyn Davies; *m* 1943, Diana Joan (*née* Lowe); three *d. Educ:* Bootle Grammar School. War Service, UK and W Europe, 1939-46; Royal Army Dental Corps, 1939-41 (Sgt); Corps of Royal Engineers, 1941-46 (Staff Captain). Clerical Officer, Min. of Labour, 1936; Exec. Officer, Inland Revenue, 1938; Higher Exec. Officer, Min. of Pensions, 1946-53; Min. of Health, 1953-68; Asst Sec., DHSS, 1968-75; Under Sec., Industries and Exports Div., DHSS, 1975-76. Mem., NY Acad. of Scis. FSAScot. Croix de Guerre (France), 1944. *Recreations:* reading, archæology, philately. *Address:* 31 Leverstock Green Road, Hemel Hempstead, Herts. *T:* Hemel Hempstead 54312. *Club:* Savile.

DAVIES, Stuart Duncan, CBE 1968; BSc; FEng; Hon. FRAeS; Past President, Royal Aeronautical Society, 1972-73 (President, 1971-72); *b* 5 Dec. 1906; *s* of William Lewis Davies and Alice Dryden Duncan; *m* 1935, Ethel Rosalie Ann Radcliffe; one *d. Educ:* Westminster City Sch.; London Univ. (BSc Eng.). Vickers (Aviation) Ltd, 1925-31; Hawker Aircraft Ltd, 1931-36; A. V. Roe and Co. Ltd, 1938-55, Chief Designer, 1945-55; with Dowty Group Ltd, 1955-58, as Managing Director of Dowty Fuel System Ltd; Technical Director: Hawker Siddeley Aviation Ltd, 1958-64; Dowty Rotol Ltd, 1965-72. British Gold Medal for Aeronautics, 1958. *Address:* Sheridans, Arun Way, Aldwick Bay, Bognor Regis, W Sussex.

DAVIES, Thomas Glyn, CBE 1966; *b* 16 Aug. 1905; *s* of Thomas Davies, Gwaelod-y-Garth, Cardiff; *m* 1935, Margaret Berry; one *d. Educ:* Pontypridd Grammar Sch.; Univ. of Wales, Cardiff (MA). Asst Master, Howard Gardens High Sch., Cardiff, 1927-37; Warden, Educational Settlement, Pontypridd, 1937-43; Director of Education: Montgomeryshire, 1943-58; Denbighshire, 1958-70, retd. Mem. ITA, later IBA, 1970-75. Member: Court and Council, UC Bangor; Court, UC Cardiff. *Recreations:* travel, music. *Address:* 42 Park Avenue, Wrexham, Clwyd LL12 7AH. *T:* Wrexham 52697.

DAVIES, Trevor Arthur L.; *see* Lloyd Davies.

DAVIES, Walter, OBE 1966; Secretary-General of The British Chamber of Commerce for Italy since 1961; *b* 7 Dec. 1920; *s* of late William Davies and late Frances Poole; *m* 1947, Alda, *d* of Tiso Lucchetta, Padua; two *d. Educ:* St Margaret's Higher Grade Sch., Liverpool; Liverpool Coll. of Commerce. Served War: RA, 1940-41; Scots Guards, 1942-47. Commendatore dell'Ordine al Merito della Repubblica Italiana, 1970. *Recreations:* good food, good company, fishing, motoring. *Address:* Via G. Dezza 27, 20144, Milan, Italy. *T:* Milan 4694391. *Club:* British American (Milan).

DAVIES, Wilfred Horace; Director, Eastern Telecommunications Philippines Inc., since 1974; Trustee, Cable & Wireless Pension Funds, since 1962; *b* 7 March 1917; *s* of late Gerald Edward Davies and Editha Lucy (*née* Sweet-Escott); *m* 1st, Helen Rose Gillam; one *s* one *d* ; 2nd, Eva Nancy Berry; two *s. Educ:* Aldenham Sch. Cable & Wireless Ltd, 1935: Asst Staff Manager, 1957; Dep. Staff Manager, 1961; Staff Manager, 1962; Dir, 1968-78; Chm., Cable and Wireless Systems (Hong Kong), 1973-78. Chm., Asiadata Ltd (Hong Kong), 1973-78; Chm., Fiji Telecommunications Ltd, 1976-79; Director: Nigeria External Telecommunications Ltd, 1969-73; Sierra Leone External Telecommunications Ltd, 1969-74; E African External Telecommunications Co. Ltd, 1969-74; Oceanic Wireless Network, Inc., Philippines, 1973-78; MBIM. *Recreations:* golf, gardening. *Address:* Hartrow, Sleepers Hill, Winchester, Hants. *T:* Winchester 3758. *Clubs:* Royal Commonwealth Society; Exiles (Twickenham).

DAVIES, William Llewellyn M.; *see* Monro Davies.

DAVIES, William Rupert R.; *see* Rees-Davies.

DAVIES, Dr Wyndham Roy; Consultant to the Pharmaceutical Industry; *b* 3 June 1926; *s* of late George Edward Davies, LLB, Llangadock, Carms, and of Ellen Theresa (*née* Merris), Treaford Hall, Birmingham. *Educ:* King Edward's, Birmingham; Birmingham and London Universities. LRCP 1948; MB, ChB, 1949; DPH 1958; DIH 1959. House Surgeon, General Hospital,

Birmingham, 1949; Receiving Room Officer, Children's Hospital, Birmingham, 1949; Resident Medical Officer, Little Bromwich Hospital, Birmingham, 1950. Entered RN, 1950; HMS Surprise, 1950-51; HMS St Angelo, 1951-53; Squadron Medical Officer, 4th Destroyer Sqdn, Home Fleet, 1953-54; Research Assistant, St George's Hospital Medical Sch. (MRC), 1955; Admiralty Medical Board and HMS Dauntless (WRNS), 1956-57; stood by building of HMS Albion, HMS Malcolm, 1957; HMS Glory, 1957; London School of Hygiene and Tropical Medicine, 1958; RN Medical Sch., 1958-59; habitability trials, HMS Centaur and HMS Bulwark, 1959-60; Joint Services Amphib. Warfare Centre, 1960-63; qual. shallow water diver, 1960; Chemical Defence Exper. Establishment, 1963; retired as Surgeon Lieut-Comdr, 1963. Adopted Prospective Parliamentary Candidate for Birmingham Perry Barr Div., 1963; MP (C) Perry Barr Div. of Birmingham, 1964-66; Joint Secretary, Party Educn and Sci. Cttee, 1965-66; Vice-President, Birmingham Cons. and Unionist Assoc., 1965-71. Dir, Medical Economic Res. Inst., 1968; Min. of Overseas Develt, Bahamas, 1969-72; Research on Immunology and Cancer, Rice Univ. and Univ. of Texas, 1976-78. Hon. Medical Adviser, British Sub-Aqua Club, 1959-66; Hon. Medical Adviser, British Safety Council, 1962-64; Governor, Royal Humane Society, 1962-; Chairman Organizing Cttee, World Congress of Underwater Activities, 1962; Cttee, Poole and Dorset Adventure Centre, 1961-64; Island Comdr for Sea Scouts, Malta, 1951-53; ADC, Boy Scouts, City of Westminster, 1957-62; Founder Member Old Edwardians BP Guild, 1948-; Hon. Secretary, Houses of Parliament BP Guild, 1964-66. Medical Officer British Schools Exploring Society Exped. to Labrador, 1958; Medical Commn on Accident Prevention, 1963-70; Founder, Society for Underwater Technology; BMA Rep., 1968-70, 1972-74; Exec. Council, Monday Club, 1965-69; Chairman: Health Cttee, 1965-69; University Liaison Cttee, 1967-68. Mem., Medical Cttee, SW Metropolitan Reg. Hosp. Bd, 1972. Dir, Brit. Cellular Therapy Soc., 1974; Mem., Deutsch Gesellschaft für Zelltherapie, 1972. Editor, Fellowship for Freedom in Medicine Bulletin, 1972-74. *Publications:* Expired Air Resuscitation, 1959; Skin Diving, 1959; Collectivism or Individualism in Medicine, 1965; Reforming the National Health Service, 1967; The Pharmaceutical Industry, A Personal Study, 1967; Health—or Health Service?, 1972; The Present Status of Cell Therapy, 1974; articles in The Practitioner and Physiological Journal. *Recreations:* all sports on, in or under water, travel, exploring, painting.

DAVIES-SCOURFIELD, Brig. Edward Grismond Beaumont, CBE 1966 (MBE 1951); MC 1945; General Secretary, National Association of Boys Clubs, 1973-82; *b* 2 Aug. 1918; 4th *s* of H. G. Davies-Scourfield and Helen (*née* Newton); *m* 1945, Diana Lilias (*née* Davidson); one *s* one *d. Educ:* Winchester Coll.; RMC Sandhurst. Commnd into KRRC, 1938; served War of 1939-45 (despatches 1945); psc; commanded: 3rd Green Jackets (Rifle Bde), 1960-62; Green Jackets Bde, 1962-64; British Jt Services Trng Team (Ghana), 1964-66; British Troops Cyprus and Dhekelia Area, 1966-69; Salisbury Plain Area, 1970-73; retd 1973. *Recreations:* country pursuits. *Address:* Old Rectory Cottage, Medstead, Alton, Hants. *T:* Alton 62133. *Clubs:* Army and Navy, MCC.

d'AVIGDOR-GOLDSMID, Maj.-Gen. Sir James (Arthur), 3rd Bt *cr* 1934; CB 1975; OBE 1955; MC 1944; *b* 19 Dec. 1912; *yr s* of Sir Osmond d'Avigdor-Goldsmid, 1st Bt, and Alice Lady d'Avigdor-Goldsmid; *S* brother, 1976; unmarried. *Educ:* Harrow; RMC, Sandhurst. 2nd Lieut 4th/7th Royal Dragoon Guards, 1932. Served War of 1939-45, France and Germany (wounded). Commanded: 4th/7th Royal Dragoon Guards, 1950-53; 20th Armoured Brigade Group, 1958-61; Director, Royal Armoured Corps, War Office, subseq. Ministry of Defence, 1962-65; President, Regular Commissions Board, Feb.-Sept. 1965; Director TA and Cadets, 1966-68; Col of 4th/7th Royal Dragoon Guards, 1963-73; Chm., SE TA&VRA, 1974-78; Hon. Col The Mercian Yeomanry, T&AVR, 1972-77. MP (C) Lichfield and Tamworth, 1970-Sept. 1974; Mem., Select Cttee on Estimates, 1971-74. Chairman: Racecourse Security Services Ltd, 1976-80; Tattersall's Cttee, 1980-; Exec. of Governors, Corps of Commissionaires, 1980-; Member: Horserace Betting Levy Bd, 1974-77; Council, Winston Churchill Meml Trust. Comr Royal Hosp. Chelsea, 1972-78. *Heir:* none. *Address:* 101 Mount Street, W1. *T:* 01-499 1989. *Clubs:* Cavalry and Guards, Turf, Jockey.

DAVIGNON, Viscount Etienne; Ambassador of HM the King of the Belgians; Member, since 1977 (currently with responsibility for internal market, customs union and industrial affairs), and Vice-President, since 1981 (with responsibility for industry, energy and research policies), Commission of the European Communities; *b* Budapest, 4 Oct. 1932; *m* 1959, Françoise de Cumont; one *s* two *d. Educ:* University of Louvain (LLD). Diplomat; Head of Office of Minister for Foreign Affairs, Belgium, 1963; Political Director, Ministry for Foreign Affairs, Belgium, 1969; Chm., Gov. Board, Internat. Energy Agency, 1974. *Recreations:* tennis, golf, skiing. *Address:* 200 rue de la Loi, 1049 Brussels, Belgium. *T:* 235.25.30.

DAVIN, Daniel Marcus, (Dan Davin), MBE 1945; Oxford Academic Publisher, and Deputy Secretary to Delegates of the Oxford University Press, 1974-78, retired; *b* 1 Sept. 1913; *s* of Patrick and Mary Davin; *m* 1939, Winifred Kathleen Gonley; three *d. Educ:* Marist Brothers Sch., Invercargill, NZ; Sacred Heart Coll., Auckland; Otago Univ. (MA); Balliol Coll., Oxford (First in Greats, 1939, MA 1945). Served War: Royal Warwickshire Regt, 1939-40; 2 NZEF, 1940-45; served in Greece and Crete (wounded 1941); Intell. GHQ, ME, 1941-42; NZ Div., N Africa and Italy, 1942-45 (despatches thrice, MBE). With Clarendon Press, 1945-78. Fellow of Balliol Coll., 1965-78, now Emeritus. FRSA. *Publications: novels:* Cliffs of Fall, 1945; For the Rest of Our Lives, 1947; Roads from Home, 1949; The Sullen Bell, 1956; No Remittance, 1959; Not Here, Not Now, 1970; Brides of Price, 1972; *short stories:* The Gorse Blooms Pale, 1947; Breathing Spaces, 1975; Selected Stories, 1981; *miscellaneous prose:* Introduction to English Literature (with John Mulgan), 1947; Crete (Official History), 1953 (Wellington, War Hist. Br., Dept of Internal Affairs); Writing in New Zealand: The New Zealand Novel (Parts One and Two, with W. K. Davin), 1956; Katherine Mansfield in Her Letters, 1959; Closing Times (Recollections of Julian Maclaren-Ross, W. R. Rodgers, Louis MacNeice, Enid Starkie, Joyce Cary, Dylan Thomas, Itzik Manger), 1975; *editions:* New Zealand Short Stories, 1953; English Short Stories of Today: Second Series, 1958; Katherine Mansfield, Selected Stories, 1963. *Recreations:* gardening, walking, talking. *Address:* 103 Southmoor Road, Oxford OX2 6RE. *T:* Oxford 57311.

DAVIS; *see* Lovell-Davis.

DAVIS, Allan; *see* Davis, W. A.

DAVIS, Andrew Frank; Artistic Director and Chief Conductor, Toronto Symphony Orchestra, since 1975; *b* 2 Feb. 1944; *m* 1970, Felicity Mary Vincent. *Educ:* Watford Grammar Sch.; King's Coll., Cambridge (MA, BMus); Accademia di S Cecilia, Rome. Assistant Conductor, BBC Scottish Symphony Orchestra, 1970-72; Asst Conductor, New Philharmonia Orchestra, 1973-77; Principal Guest Conductor, Royal Liverpool Philharmonic Orchestra, 1974-77. *Recreations:* kite flying, the study of mediaeval stained glass. *Address:* 1 Leighton Road, NW5.

DAVIS, Anthony Ronald William James; Editor-in-Chief, New World Publishers Ltd, Middle East Construction and Middle East Architectural Design, since 1978; *b* 26 July 1931; *e s* of Donald William Davis, Barnes and Mary Josephine Davis (*née* Nolan-Byrne), Templeogue Mill, Co. Dublin; *m* 1960, Yolande Mary June, *o d* of Patrick Leonard, retd civil engr; *one s two d* (and *one d* decd). *Educ:* Hamlet of Ratcliffe and Oratory; Regent Street Polytechnic. Joint Services School for Linguists on Russian course as National Serviceman (Army), 1953-55; Architectural Asst, Housing Dept, Mddx County Architect's Dept, 1956-58; Sub-Editor, The Builder, 1959; Editor: Official Architecture and Planning, 1964-70; Building, 1970-74; Dir, The Builder, subseq. Building, 1974-77; Member Board: Architecture and Planning Publications Ltd, 1966; Building (Publishers) Ltd, 1972. Mem. Council, Modular Soc., 1970-71. JP Berkshire, 1973-81. *Publications:* contribs to various, architectural and technical. *Recreations:* collecting porcelain, music and dreaming. *Address:* 8 Blake Close, Dowles Green, Wokingham, Berks. *T:* Wokingham 785046. *Club:* Architecture.

DAVIS, Arthur John, RD 1967; FIB; Chief General Manager, Lloyds Bank, since 1978; *b* 28 July 1924; *s* of Alan Wilfrid Davis and Emily Davis; *m* 1950, Jean Elizabeth Edna Hobbs; *one s one d* (and *one d* decd). *Educ:* grammar schs. FIB 1969. Served War, RN, 1942-46. Entered Lloyds Bank, 1941; Jt Gen. Manager, 1973; Asst Chief Gen. Man., 1973; Dep. Chief Gen. Man., 1976. *Recreations:* gardening, music, beagling. *Address:* Church Farm House, Aldbury, Tring, Herts. *T:* Aldbury Common 321. *Clubs:* Naval, Overseas Bankers.

DAVIS, Bette Ruth Elizabeth; Actress; *b* Lowell, Mass, 5 April 1908. *Educ:* Cushing Academy, Ashburnham, Mass. Stage experience in Wild Duck, Broken Dishes, Solid South; entered films, 1930. Pictures she has appeared in: Of Human Bondage, 1934; Border Town; Dangerous (Academy Award of 1935 won 1936); The Petrified Forest, The Golden Arrow, 1936; Marked Woman, Kid Galahad, It's Love I'm After, That Certain Woman, 1937; Jezebel (Academy Award of 1938 won 1939); The Sisters, 1938; Dark Victory, Juarez, The Old Maid, Private Lives of Elizabeth and Essex, 1939; All This and Heaven Too, 1940; The Letter, The Great Lie, The Bride came COD, The Man who came to Dinner, The Little Foxes, 1941; In This our Life, Watch on the Rhine, Old Acquaintance, 1942; Mr Skeffington, 1944; The Corn is Green, 1945; A Stolen Life, Deception, 1946; Winter Meeting; June Bride; The Story of a Divorce; All about Eve, 1950; Payment on Demand; Phone Call from a Stranger; Another Man's Poison; The Star, 1953; The Virgin Queen, 1955; Storm Center; The Catered Affair; John Paul Jones; Wedding Breakfast; The Scapegoat, 1959; Pocketful of Miracles; Whatever Happened to Baby Jane?; Dead Ringer; Painted Canvas; Where Love Has Gone; Hush . . . Hush, Sweet Charlotte, 1964; The Nanny, 1965; The Anniversary, 1967; Connecting Rooms, 1969; Bunny O'Hare, 1970; Madam Sin, 1971; The Game, 1972; Burnt Offerings, 1977; Death on the Nile, 1978; Watcher In The Woods, 1980. *TV Movies:* Sister Aimee, 1977; The Dark Secret of Harvest Home, 1978; Strangers, The Story of a Mother and Daughter, 1979 (Emmy Award); White Mama, 1980; Family Reunion, 1981; A Piano for Mrs Cimino, 1982. *Play:* The Night of the Iguana. Life Achievement Award, Amer. Film Institute, 1977. *Publication:* The Lonely Life, 1963. *Relevant Publication:* Mother Goddam by Whitney Stine, 1975 (footnotes by Bette Davis). *Recreations:* swimming and horseback riding. *Address:* c/o Gottlieb, Schiff, Ticktin, Sternklar & Harris, PC, 555 Fifth Avenue, New York, NY 10017, USA.

DAVIS, Brian; *see* ffolkes, Michael.

DAVIS, Rt. Rev. Brian Newton; *see* Waikato, Bishop of.

DAVIS, Maj-Gen. Brian William, CBE 1980 (OBE 1974); Chief of Staff, Logistic Executive (Army), since 1982; *b* 28 Aug. 1930; *s* of late Edward William Davis, MBE, and Louise Jane Davis (*née* Webber); *m* 1954, Margaret Isobel Jenkins; *one s one d. Educ:* Weston-super-Mare Grammar Sch.; Mons OCS, Aldershot. FBIM. Commissioned Royal Artillery, 1949; Regtl Duty, 1949-56 and 1960-61, UK/BAOR; Instr-in-Gunnery, 1956-59; Staff Coll. Camberley, 1962; DAA and QMG HQ 7 Armd Bde BAOR, 1963-66; GSO2 SD UN Force, Cyprus, 1966; Regtl Duty, 1967-69; Lt-Col 1969, Directing Staff, Staff Coll. Camberley, 1969-71; CO 32 Lt Regt RA BAOR/England/N Ireland, 1971-74; Col AQ Ops HQ BAOR, 1975; Brig. 1975; CRA 3 Div., 1976-77; RCDS 1978; Chief of Staff N Ireland, 1979-80; Chief of Comdrs-in-Chief Mission to Soviet Forces in Germany, 1981-82. *Recreations:* Rugby (President, RARFC, 1975-78), cricket, fishing, appreciating the countryside. *Address:* c/o Williams & Glyn's Bank, Lawrie House, Victoria Road, Farnborough, Hants. *Clubs:* Army and Navy, MCC; Somerset CCC.

DAVIS, Carl; composer; *b* 28 Oct. 1936; *s* of Isadore and Sara Davis; *m* 1972, Jean Boht; *two d. Educ:* New England Conservatory of Music; Bard Coll. (BA). *Major TV credits:* The Snow Goose, 1972; World at War, 1973; The Naked Civil Servant, 1973; Our Mutual Friend, 1976; Marie Curie, 1977; Prince Regent, The Old Curiosity Shop, 1979; Hollywood, Oppenheimer, The Sailor's Return, Fair Stood the Wind for France, 1980; The Commanding Sea, Private Schulz, 1981; The Last Night of the Poms, Home Sweet Home, La Ronde, 1982; *symphony:* Lines on London, 1980 (commnd by Capital Radio); *scores:* for RSC and National Theatre; *musicals:* The Projector, 1971; Pilgrim, 1975; Cranford, 1976; Alice in Wonderland, 1977; *opera:* Peace, 1978; *TV operas:* The Arrangement, 1967; Orpheus in the Underground, 1976; *West End:* Forty Years On, 1969; Habeas Corpus, 1974; *films:* Napoleon, 1980; The French Lieutenant's Woman (BAFTA Original Film Score Award), The Crowd, 1981; Five Days in Summer, 1982; *ballet:* Dances of Love and Death, 1981. Co-founder and partner with Terry Oates of Sundergrade Music Ltd. Mem. BAFTA, 1979-. First winner, BAFTA Award for Original TV Music, 1981. *Publications:* sheet music of television themes. *Recreations:* reading, gardening, playing chamber music, cooking. *Address:* 99 Church Road, Barnes, SW13. *T:* 01-741 0891.

DAVIS, Sir Charles (Sigmund), Kt 1965; CB 1960; Counsel to the Speaker (European Legislation), House of Commons, since 1974; *b* London, 22 Jan. 1909; *y s* of late Maurice Davis (*b* Melbourne, Australia) and Alfreda Regina Davis; *m* 1940, Pamela Mary, *er d* of late J. K. B. Dawson, OBE, and Phyllis Dawson; *two d. Educ:* Trinity Coll., Cambridge. Double 1st Cl. Hons, Law Tripos; Sen. Schol., Exhibitioner and Prizeman of Trinity, 1927-30; MA 1934. Called to the Bar, Inner Temple (Studentship and Certif. of Honour), 1930, and in Sydney Australia, 1931; practised as barrister in London, 1931-34; entered Legal Branch, Ministry of Health, 1934; held legal posts in various public offices, 1938-46 (Corporal, Home Guard, 1940-45); Asst Solicitor, Min. of Agric. and Fisheries, 1946-55; Prin. Asst Solicitor, MAFF, 1955-57; Legal Adviser and Solicitor, MAFF, and Forestry Commission, 1957-74, retired. *Recreations:* music (LRAM, ARCM) and much else. *Address:* 43 Wolsey Road, East Molesey, Surrey KT8 9EW.

DAVIS, Mrs Chloë Marion, OBE 1975; Chairman, Consumer Affairs Group of National Organisations, 1973-79; Member: Council on Tribunals, 1970-79; Consumer Standards Advisory Committee of British Standards Institution, 1965-78 (Chairman 1970-73); *b* Dartmouth, Devon, 15 Feb. 1909; *d* of Richard Henry Pound and Mary Jane Chapman; *m* 1928, Edward Thomas Davis, printer and sometime writer; *one s. Educ:* limited formal, USA and England. Various part-time voluntary social and public services from 1929; Birth Control Internat. Information Centre, 1931-38; voluntary activity in bombing etc emergencies, also cookery and domestic broadcasting during War of 1939-45; information service for Kreis Resident Officers, Control Commn for Germany, Berlin, 1946-48; regional Citizens Advice Bureaux office, London Council of Social Service, 1949-55; Sen. Information Officer to Nat. Citizens Advice Bureaux Council, 1956-69. Member: Nat. House-Building Council, 1973-76; Consumer Consultative Cttee, EEC, 1973-76; Exec. Cttee, Housewife's Trust, 1970-77. *Recreations:* reading present history in the morning in newspapers and past history in books in the evening; gardening, walking, talking with friends. *Address:* Auberville Cottage, 246 Dover Road, Walmer, Kent CT14 7NP. *T:* Deal 4038.

DAVIS, Clinton; *see* Davis, S. C.

DAVIS, Sir Colin (Rex), Kt 1980; CBE 1965; Musical Director, Royal Opera House, Covent Garden, since 1971; Principal Guest Conductor: Boston Symphony Orchestra, since 1972; London Symphony Orchestra, since 1974; Chief Conductor, Bavarian Radio Symphony Orchestra, from Sept. 1983; *b* 25 Sept. 1927; *s* of Reginald George and Lillian Davis; *m* 1949, April Cantelo (marr. diss., 1964); *one s one d; m* 1964, Ashraf Naini; *three s two d. Educ:* Christ's Hospital; Royal College of Music. Orchestral Conductor, Freelance wilderness, 1949-57; Asst Conductor, BBC Scottish Orchestra, 1957-59. Conductor, Sadler's Wells, 1959, Principal Conductor, 1960-65, Musical Director, 1961-65; Chief Conductor, BBC Symphony Orchestra, 1967-71, Chief Guest Conductor, 1971-75. Artistic Director, Bath Festival, 1969. Conducted at: Metropolitan Opera House, New York, 1969, 1970, 1972; Bayreuth Fest., 1977. *Recreations:* anything at all. *Address:* Royal Opera House, Covent Garden, WC2. *Club:* Athenæum.

DAVIS, Brig. Cyril Elliott, CBE 1941; *b* 15 March 1892; *y s* of late O. J. H. Davis, Ford Park, Plymouth, Devon; *m* 1st, 1918, Fay (*d* 1957), *y d* of Leathes Prior, Eaton, Norwich; two *s*; 2nd, 1958, Helen, *widow* of Rev. T. V. Garnier, OBE. *Educ:* Alton Sch.; Plymouth Coll. Regular Commission in ASC, 1912, from 3rd DCLI (SR); served European War, 1914-18, France, Belgium, Greek Macedonia, Serbia, Bulgaria, European Turkey, Egypt, Palestine (1914 Star and Clasp, BWM and Victory Medal); Palestine Campaign, 1937 (Palestine Gen. Service Medal); Lieut-Col 1939 and posted to Singapore. Temp. Col 1940; Col 1941; Dep. Dir of Supplies and Transport, Malaya Command (acting Brig.), 1941; transferred to S Western Pacific Command, Java, Jan. 1942; Ceylon, March 1942; retired April 1946. A General Comr of Income Tax, 1958-67. King George V Jubilee Medal, 1935; Comdr Order of Leopold II (Belgium), 1951. *Address:* Stour View Bridge, Sturminster Newton, Dorset. *T:* Sturminster Newton 72832.

DAVIS, David; *see* Davis, William Eric.

DAVIS, Prof. Derek Russell, MD, FRCP; Norah Cooke Hurle Professor of Mental Health, University of Bristol, 1962-79; *b* 20 April 1914; *s* of late Edward David Darelan Davis, FRCS, and of Alice Mildred (*née* Russell); *m* 1939, Marit, *d* of Iver M. Iversen, Oslo, Norway; one *s* one *d. Educ:* Stowe Sch., Buckingham; Clare Coll., Cambridge (major entrance and foundn schol.); Middlesex Hosp. Med. Sch. MA, MD; FRCP. Ho. Phys., Mddx Hosp., 1938; Addenbrooke's Hosp., Cambridge, 1939; Asst Physician, Runwell Hosp., 1939; Mem. Scientific Staff, MRC, 1940; Lectr in Psychopathology, Univ. of Cambridge, 1948; Reader in Clinical Psychology, 1950; Dir, Med. Psychology Research Unit, 1958; Consultant Psychiatrist, United Cambridge Hosps, 1948; Editor, Quarterly Jl of Experimental Psychology, 1949-57. Visiting Professor: Univ. of Virginia, 1958; Univ. of Dundee, 1976; Univ. of Otago, 1977. Fellow, Clare Coll., Cambridge, 1961. Dean of Medicine, Univ. of Bristol, 1970-72. Member: Avon AHA (Teaching), 1974-79; Council of Management, MIND, 1975-; Pres., Fedn of Mental Health Workers, 1972. Adolf Meyer Lectr, Amer. Psychiatric Assoc., 1967. FRCPsych, FBPsS. *Publications:* An Introduction to Psychopathology (3rd edn), 1972; many articles in scientific and med. jls. *Recreations:* Ibsen studies, theatre. *Address:* 9 Clyde Road, Bristol BS6 6RJ. *T:* Bristol 734744.

See also J. D. Russell-Davis.

DAVIS, Hon. Sir (Dermot) Renn, Kt 1981; OBE 1971; **Hon. Mr Justice Davis;** Chief Justice, Supreme Court of Gibraltar, since 1980; *b* 20 Nov. 1928; *s* of Captain Eric R. Davis, OBE and Norah A. Davis (*née* Bingham). *Educ:* Prince of Wales Sch., Nairobi; Wadham Coll., Oxford (BA Hons). Called to the Bar, Inner Temple, 1953; Daly and Figgis, Advocates, Nairobi, 1953-56; Attorney-General's Chambers, Kenya, 1956-62; Attorney-General, British Solomon Islands Protectorate, and Legal Advr to High Comr for Western Pacific, 1962-73; British Judge, New Hebrides Condominium, 1973-76; Chief Justice, Solomon Islands, 1976-80 and Chief Justice, Tuvalu, 1978-80. *Recreations:* music, reading, walking, riding, sailing, fishing, tennis, golf. *Address:* Chief Justice's Chambers, Supreme Court, Gibraltar. *T:* 4193. *Clubs:* United Oxford & Cambridge University; Muthaiga Country (Nairobi).

DAVIS, Sir (Ernest) Howard, Kt 1978; CMG 1969; OBE 1960; Deputy Governor, Gibraltar, 1971-78; Chairman, Gibraltar Broadcasting Corporation, 1981; *b* 22 April 1918; *m* 1948, Marie Davis (*née* Bellotti); two *s. Educ:* Christian Brothers Schs, Gibraltar and Blackpool; London Univ. (BA 1st cl. hons). Gen. Clerical Staff, Gibraltar, 1936-46; Asst Sec. and Clerk of Councils, 1946-54; seconded Colonial Office, 1954-55; Chief Asst Sec., Estabt Officer and Public Relations Officer (responsible for opening Radio Gibraltar), Gibraltar, 1955-62; Director of Labour and Social Security, 1962-65; Financial and Development Secretary, 1965-71; Acting Governor, various periods, 1971-77. Chairman, Committee of Enquiry: PWD, 1980-81; Electricity Dept, 1982. *Recreations:* cricket, gardening, bridge. *Address:* 36 South Barrack Road, Gibraltar. *T:* A.70358.

DAVIS, Godfrey Rupert Carless, CBE 1981; FSA; Secretary, Royal Commission on Historical Manuscripts, 1972-81; *b* 22 April 1917; *s* of late Prof. Henry William Carless Davis and Rosa Jennie Davis (*née* Lindup); *m* 1942, Dorothie Elizabeth Mary Loveband; one *s* two *d. Educ:* Highgate Sch.; Balliol Coll., Oxford (MA, DPhil). Rome Scholar in Ancient History, 1938. Army Service, 1939-46, Devon Regt and Intell. Corps, Captain 1942. Dept of MSS, British Museum: Asst Keeper, 1947; Dep. Keeper, 1961-72. FRHistS 1954 (Treas. 1967-74); FSA 1974. *Publications:* Medieval Cartularies of Great Britain, 1958; Magna Carta, 1963; contrib. British Museum Cat. Add. MSS 1926-1950 (6 vols); learned jls. *Address:* 214 Somerset Road, SW19 5JE. *T:* 01-946 7955.

See also R. H. C. Davis.

DAVIS, Harold Sydney, FRCP; Consultant Physician: Royal Free Hospital, London, 1954-73; King Edward VII Hospital, Windsor, 1945-73; Hampstead General Hospital, 1946-73; Florence Nightingale Hospital, London, since 1947; Hon. Physician to the Queen, T&AVR, 1967-68; *b* 6 Aug. 1908; *s* of Harold Adamson Davis and Edith May Davis, Jamaica, WI; *m* 1940, Molly, *d* of Herbert Percy Stimson, London; one *d. Educ:* Jamaica Coll., WI; Dulwich Coll., London; Gonville and Caius Coll., Cambridge; Charing Cross Hosp., London (Exhibr). BA 1930, MB, BChir 1935, MA 1936, Cantab.; LRCP, MRCS 1933; MRCP 1936; FRCP 1954. Held usual resident appts in various London hosps, 1933-39. Commissioned into RAMC, March 1939 (Lieut); seconded as Physician, Ashridge Hosp. (EMS), 1940. OC 308 (Co.

London) Gen. Hosp. RAMC/AER, 1964 (Col). Examr in Medicine, London Univ.; Lectr in Medicine, Royal Free Hosp. Sch. of Medicine, London Univ., 1962; Mem. Bd of Govs, Royal Free Hosp., 1963. Pres., Eagle Ski Club, 1960-63. *Publications:* contrib. learned jls. *Recreations:* ski-mountaineering, gardening. *Address:* Fingest Hill Cottage, Skirmett, near Henley-on-Thames, Oxon RG9 6TD. *T:* Turville Heath 275; 108 Harley Street, W1N 1AF. *T:* 01-935 8033. *Clubs:* Ski Club of Gt Britain (Vice-Pres. 1964), Kandahar Ski; Leander (Henley-on-Thames).

DAVIS, Sir Howard; *see* Davis, Sir E. H.

DAVIS, Ivor John Guest; Comptroller-General of Patents, Designs and Trade Marks, Patent Office, Department of Trade, since 1978; President, Administrative Council of The European Patent Office, since 1981; *b* 11 Jan. 1925; *s* of Thomas Henry Davis and Dorothy Annie Davis; *m* 1954, Mary Eleanor Thompson; one *s* one *d. Educ:* Devonport High Sch.; HM Dockyard Sch., Devonport. BSc London (ext.). Apprentice, HM Dockyard, Devonport, 1941-45, Draughtsman, 1946-47; Patent Office, Dept of Trade: Asst Examr, 1947; Examr, 1950; Sen. Examr, 1954; Principal Examr, 1967; Superintending Examr, 1972; Asst Comptroller, 1973. Governor, Centre d'études de la propriété industrielle, Strasbourg, 1979-. Mem., Editorial Adv. Bd, World Patent Information Journal, 1979-. *Recreations:* music, gardening. *Address:* c/o The Patent Office, 25 Southampton Buildings, WC2A 1AY. *T:* 01-405 8721.

DAVIS, James Gresham, FCIT; Director, Kleinwort, Benson Ltd, since 1973; *b* 20 July 1928; *s* of Col Robert Davis, OBE, JP and Josephine Davis; *m* 1973, Adrianna Johanna Verhoef; three *d. Educ:* Bradfield Coll.; Clare Coll., Cambridge (MA). FCIT 1969. Served RN, 1946-49. P&OSN Co., 1952-72: Calcutta, 1953; Kobe, Japan, 1954-56; Hong Kong, 1956-57; Director: P&O Lines, 1967-72; DFDS (UK) Ltd, 1975-; Vice Chairman: Pearl Cruises of Scandinavia Ltd, 1982-; Harley, Mullion Ltd (Shipbrokers), 1975-; Mem. Adv. Board: J. Lauritzen A/S, Copenhagen, 1981-; DFDS A/S, Copenhagen, 1981-. President: World Ship Soc., 1969 and 1971; CIT, 1981-82; Chm., Internat. Maritime Industries Forum, 1981-82; pt-time Mem., British Transport Docks Bd, 1981-; Member: Council, Missions to Seamen; Council, British Maritime League; Greenwich Forum. Liveryman, Worshipful Co. of Shipwrights. *Recreations:* golf, family. *Address:* 115 Woodsford Square, W14 8DT. *T:* 01-602 0675; Summer Lawn, Dovercourt, Essex, CO12 4EF. *T:* Harwich 2981. *Clubs:* Hurlingham, Golfers; Harwich & Dovercourt Golf.

DAVIS, Prof. John Allen, FRCP; Professor of Paediatrics, and Fellow of Peterhouse, Cambridge University, since 1979; *b* 6 Aug. 1923; *s* of Major H. E. Davis, MC, and Mrs M. W. Davis; *m* 1957, Madeleine Elizabeth Vinnicombe Ashlin; three *s* two *d. Educ:* Blundells Sch., Tiverton (Scholar); St Mary's Hosp. Med. Sch. (Scholar; MB, BS 1946; London Univ. Gold Medal); MSc Manchester, 1968; MA Cantab. FRCP 1967. Army Service, BAOR, 1947-49. House Physician: St Mary's Hosp., 1947; Gt Ormond St Hosp. for Sick Children, 1950; Registrar/Sen. Registrar, St Mary's Paediatric Unit and Home Care Scheme, 1951-57; Sen. Asst Resident, Children's Med. Centre, Boston, Mass, 1953; Nuffield Res. Fellowship, Oxford, 1958-59; Sen. Lectr, Inst. of Child Health, and Reader, Hammersmith Hosp., 1960-67; Prof. of Paediatrics and Child Health, Victoria Univ. of Manchester, 1967-79. Mem., Systems Bd, MRC, 1980-. Paediatric Editor of Medicine, 1975-. *Publications:* Scientific Foundations of Paediatrics (ed and contrib.), 1974 (2nd edn 1981); Place of Birth, 1978; papers in various medical and scientific jls. *Recreations:* collecting and painting watercolours, gardening, reading, music. *Address:* Department of Paediatrics, Addenbrooke's Hospital, Hills Road, Cambridge CB2 2QQ.

DAVIS, John Darelan R.; *see* Russell-Davis, J. D.

DAVIS, Air Chief Marshal Sir John (Gilbert), GCB 1968 (KCB 1964; CB 1953); OBE 1945; psc 1946; idc 1955; RAF, retired; Lieutenant-Governor and Commander-in-Chief of Jersey, 1969-74; *b* 24 March 1911; *e s* of late John Davis, Whitby, Yorks; *m* 1937, Doreen, *d* of Arthur Heaton, Hinckley, Leics; one *s* one *d. Educ:* Whitby Grammar Sch.; Queens' Coll., Cambridge, MA 1937. First Commnd RAF, 1934; served Bomber Sqdns 142 and 57, 1934-36; Instructor No 10 Flying Training Sch., 1936-37; Navigation Staff duties, 1938-39; served war of 1939-45 on anti-submarine duties in Mediterranean, Iceland, Azores, UK. Instructor RAF Staff Coll., 1948-50; Gp Captain Plans HQ MEAF, 1951-53; OC RAF Station, Topcliffe, 1953-54; Dir of Plans, Air Ministry, 1955-58; SASO, Bomber Command HQ, 1958-59; Air Officer Commanding No 1 Group, Bomber Command, 1959-61; Air Officer Commanding Malta, and Dep. Comdr-in-Chief (Air), Allied Forces Mediterranean, 1961-63; Air Mem. for Supply and Organisation, MoD, 1963-66; Air Officer Commanding-in-Chief: Flying Trng Comd, 1966-68; Trng Comd, 1968-69. Air ADC to the Queen, 1967-69. KStJ 1969. *Recreations:* ornithology, fishing. *Address:* The Stone House, Ruswarp, near Whitby, North Yorks. *Clubs:* Royal Air Force; Union Society (Cambridge).

DAVIS, Sir John (Gilbert), 3rd Bt *cr* 1946; Vice-President, Abitibi-Price Inc., Toronto, since 1976; *b* 17 Aug. 1936; *s* of Sir Gilbert Davis, 2nd Bt, and of Kathleen, *d* of Sidney Deacon Ford; *S* father, 1973; *m* 1960, Elizabeth Margaret, *d* of Robert Smith Turnbull; one *s* two *d. Educ:* Oundle School; Britannia RNC, Dartmouth. RN, 1955-56. Joined Spicers Ltd, 1956; emigrated to Montreal, Canada, 1957; joined Inter City Papers and progressed through the company until becoming Pres., 1967; transf. to parent co. in 1976. Director: Milmont Fibreboard; Hilroy; Canada Envelope; Inter City Papers; Canadian Arthritis Soc. *Recreations:* sports, golf, tennis, squash; music, reading. *Heir:* s Richard Charles Davis, b 11 April 1970. *Address:* 70 York Mills Road, Toronto, Ont M2P 1B7, Canada. *T:* 222-4916. *Clubs:* Donalda (Toronto); Badminton and Squash (Montreal); Kanawaki Golf; Rosedale Golf (Toronto).

DAVIS, Sir John (Henry Harris), Kt 1971; President, since 1977, The Rank Organisation plc, Subsidiary and Associated Cos (Chief Executive, 1962-74; Chairman, 1962-77); Joint President, Rank Xerox, since 1972 (formerly Joint Chairman); Chairman, National Centre of Films for Children; Director, Eagle Star Insurance Co. Ltd; b 10 Nov. 1906; s of David Myering Davis and Emily Harris; m 1926, Joan Buckingham; one s; m 1947, Marion Gavid; two d; m 1954, Dinah Sheridan (marr. diss. 1965); m 1976, Mrs Felicity Rutland. *Educ:* City of London Sch. British Thomson-Houston Group, 1931-38. Joined Odeon Theatres (predecessor of The Rank Organisation); Chief Accountant, Jan. 1938; Sec., June 1938; Jt Managing Dir, 1942; Man. Dir, 1948-62 and Dep. Chm., 1951-62, The Rank Organisation Ltd. Chm., Southern Television Ltd, 1968-76. Trustee, Westminster Abbey Trust (Chm., fund raising cttee, Westminster Abbey Appeal, 1973). Pres., The Advertising Assoc., 1973-76. FCIS 1939. Commandeur de l'Ordre de la Couronne (Belgium), 1974; KStJ. Hon. DTech Loughborough, 1975. *Recreations:* farming, gardening, reading, travel, music. *Address:* The Mill House, Four Elms, Edenbridge, Kent TN8 6NS. *Club:* Royal Automobile.

DAVIS, Leslie Harold Newsom, CMG 1957; b 6 April 1909; s of Harold Newsom Davis and Aileen Newsom Davis (née Gush); m 1950, Judith Anne, d of L. G. Corney, CMG; one s two d. *Educ:* Marlborough; Trinity Coll., Cambridge. Apptd to Malayan Civil Service, 1932; Private Sec. to Governor and High Comr, 1938-40; attached to 22nd Ind. Inf. Bde as Liaison Officer, Dec. 1941; interned by Japanese in Singapore, 1942-45; District Officer, Seremban, 1946-47; British Resident, Brunei, 1948; Asst Adviser, Muar, 1948-50; Sec. to Mem. for Education, Fed. of Malaya, 1951-52. Mem. for Industrial and Social Relations, 1952-53; Sec. for Defence and Internal Security, Singapore, 1953-55; Permanent Sec., Min. of Communications and Works, Singapore, 1955-57; Special Rep., Rubber Growers' Assoc. in Malaya, 1958-63. *Recreation:* golf. *Address:* Berrywood, Heyshott, near Midhurst, West Sussex. *Club:* United Oxford & Cambridge University.

DAVIS, Madeline; Regional Nursing Officer, Oxford Regional Health Authority, since 1973; b 12 March 1925; d of late James William Henry Davis, JP, and Mrs Edith Maude Davis; m 1977, Comdr William Milburn Gibson, RN. *Educ:* Haberdashers' Aske's Hatcham Girls' Sch.; Guy's Hosp. (SRN); British Hosp. for Mothers and Babies, Woolwich; Bristol Maternity Hosp. (SCM). Ward Sister, then Dep. Night Supt, Guy's Hosp., 1949-53; Asst Matron, Guy's Hosp., 1953-57; Admin. Sister then Dep. Matron, St Charles' Hosp., London, 1957-61; Asst Nursing Officer, 1962-68, Chief Regional Nursing Officer, 1968-73, Oxford Regional Hosp. Bd. Mem., Central Midwives Board. *Publication:* (with Mrs R. Sanders) article (Scheduling of Student Nurses with the Aid of a Computer) in The Hospital. *Recreations:* village community work, theatre, golf. *Address:* Cherry Holt, Middle Street, Islip, Oxon. *T:* Kidlington 4741. *Club:* North Oxford Golf.

DAVIS, Hon. Sir Maurice, Kt 1975; OBE 1953; QC 1965; Chief Justice of the West Indies Associated States Supreme Court, and of Supreme Court of Grenada, 1975-80; b St Kitts, 30 April 1912; m Kathleen; one s five d. Pres., St Kitts Bar Assoc., 1968-75. Mem. Legislature, St Kitts, 1944-57; Mem., Exec. Council, St Kitts; Dep. Pres., Gen. Legislative Council, and Mem., Fed. Exec. Council, Leeward Is. *Recreations:* cricket, football. *Address:* c/o Supreme Court, PO Box 316, Basseterre, St Kitts, West Indies.

DAVIS, Dr Michael; Director for Energy Saving, Alternative Sources of Energy, Electricity and Heat, Commission of European Communities, Brussels; b 9 June 1923; s of William James Davis and Rosaline Sarah (née May); m 1951, Helena Hobbs Campbell, e d of Roland and Catherine Campbell, Toronto. *Educ:* UC Exeter (BSc); Bristol Univ. (PhD). FIMM, FInstP. Radar Officer, Flagship, 4th Cruiser Sqdn, British Pacific Fleet, Lieut (Sp. Br.) RNVR, 1943-46 (despatches). Res. Fellow, Canadian Atomic Energy Project, Toronto Univ., 1949-51; Sen. Sci. Officer, Services Electronics Res. Lab., 1951-55; subseq. UKAEA: Commercial Dir and Techn. Adviser, 1956-73; Dir of Nuclear Energy, Other Primary Sources and Electricity, EEC, 1973-81. Chm., OECD Cttee on World Uranium Resources, 1969-73; Dir, NATO Advanced Study Inst., 1971; advised NZ Govt on Atomic Energy, 1967. McLaughlin Meml Lectr, Instn of Engineers of Ireland, 1977. *Publications:* (ed jtly) Uranium Prospecting Handbook, 1972; papers in various sci. jls. *Recreation:* sculpture. *Address:* 200 Rue de la Loi, 1049 Brussels, Belgium. *T:* 235.34.41. *Club:* United Oxford & Cambridge University.

DAVIS, Michael McFarland; Director for Wales, Property Services Agency, Department of the Environment, 1972-77; b 1 Feb. 1919; 2nd s of Harold McFarland and Gladys Mary Davis; m 1942, Aline Seton Butler; three d. *Educ:* Haberdashers' Aske's, Hampstead. Entered Air Ministry, 1936. Served War, RAF, 1940-45 (PoW, 1942-45). Private Sec. to Chiefs and Vice-Chiefs of Air Staff, 1945-49, and to Under-Secretary of State for Air, 1952-54; Harvard Univ. Internat. Seminar, 1956; Student, IDC, 1965; Command Sec., FEAF, 1966-69; on loan to Cabinet Office (Central Unit on Environmental

Pollution), 1970; transf. to Dept of Environment, 1971. Delegate to UN Conf. on Human Environment, Stockholm, 1972. *Recreations:* doing up old things, fishing, music, wine. *Address:* 3 Sidmount Gardens, Sidmouth, S Devon. *T:* Sidmouth 77123. *Clubs:* Ottery Fly Fishing, Sidmouth Croquet.

DAVIS, Morris Cael, CMG 1970; MD, FRACP; Consultant Physician, 110 Collins Street, Melbourne; b 7 June 1907; s of David and Sarah Davis; m 1933, Sophia Ashkenasy (d 1966); two s. *Educ:* Melbourne High Sch.; Univ. of Melbourne. MB, BS (1st cl. hons) Melbourne, 1930; MD 1932; MRCP 1938; FRACP 1946. Univ. of Melbourne: Prosector in Anatomy, 1927; Beaney Schol. in Pathology, 1932-33; Lectr in Pathology, 1933; Lectr in Medicine, Dental Faculty, 1940-63; Bertram Armytage Prize for Med. Res., 1934 and 1942; Fulbright Smith Mundt Schol., 1953-54. Alfred Hosp., Melbourne: Acting Pathologist, 1933-35; Physican to Out-Patients, 1938-46; Phys. to In-Patients, 1946-67; Cons. Phys., 1967-; Foundn Chm., Cardiovascular Diagnostic Service, 1959-67; Dir and Founder, Dept of Visual Aids, 1954-67; Chm. Drug Cttee, 1960-67. Med. Referee, Commonwealth Dept of Health. Travelled Nuffield Sponsorship, 1954; Litchfield Lectr, Oxford Univ., 1954; Hon. Consultant, Dental Hosp., Melbourne, 1946-. Mem., Curricular Planning Cttee, RMIT; Hon. Pres., Medico-Clerical Soc. of Victoria. Pres., Victorian Friends of Hebrew Univ., Jerusalem, 1953-64; Federal Pres., Australian Friends Hebrew Univ., 1964; Alternate Governor, Hebrew Univ., 1961-63, Governor, Bezalel Acad. of Art and Design, Israel. Founder, Australian Medical Assoc. Arts Group, Pres. 1959-; Hon. Life Pres., Bezalel Fellowship of Arts. Vice-Pres., Aust. Kidney Foundn Appeal, 1971; Mem., Epworth Hosp. Appeal Cttee, 1975-76. *Publications:* papers on medicine, medical philosophy and medical educn in Australian Med. Jl, Australian Dental Jl, student jls. *Recreations:* ceramics, painting, music, book collecting, garden. *Address:* 177 Finch Street, Glen Iris, Vic. 3146, Australia. *T:* Melbourne 509.2423. *Clubs:* University House, Australian American Association, Australian American Club, National Gallery Society (Melbourne).

DAVIS, Nathanael Vining; Chairman of the Board, since 1972, Director since 1947, Alcan Aluminium Limited (President, 1947-72, Chief Executive Officer, 1972-79); b 26 June 1915; s of Rhea Reineman Davis and Edward Kirk Davis; m 1941, Lois Howard Thompson; one s one d. *Educ:* Harvard Coll.; London Sch. of Economics. With Alcan group since 1939 with exception of 3 years on active duty with US Navy. Dir, Bank of Montreal. *Address:* Box 6090, Montreal, Quebec, Canada H3C 3H2. *T:* 877-2340. *Clubs:* Mount Royal, St James's (Montreal); University (New York); The Somerset Club (Boston, Mass).

DAVIS, Prof. Norman, MBE 1945; FBA 1969; Merton Professor of English Language and Literature, University of Oxford, 1959-80; Emeritus Fellow, Merton College, Oxford, since 1980; b Dunedin, NZ, 16 May 1913; s of James John and Jean Davis; m 1944, Magdalene Jamieson Bone; no c. *Educ:* Otago Boys' High Sch., Dunedin; Otago Univ.; Merton Coll., Oxford. MA NZ 1934; BA Oxon 1936, MA 1944; NZ Rhodes Scholar, 1934. Lecturer in English, Kaunas, Lithuania, 1937; Sofia, Bulgaria, 1938. Government service mainly abroad, 1939-46. Lecturer in English Language, Queen Mary Coll., University of London, 1946; Oriel and Brasenose Colls., Oxford, 1947; Oxford Univ. Lectr in Medieval English, 1948; Prof. of English Language, University of Glasgow, 1949. Hon. Dir of Early English Text Soc., 1957-. Jt Editor, Review of English Studies, 1954-63. R. W. Chambers Meml Lecturer, UCL, 1971. *Publications:* Sweet's Anglo-Saxon Primer, 9th edn 1953; The Language of the Pastons (Sir Israel Gollancz Memorial Lecture, British Academy, 1954), 1955; Paston Letters (a selection), 1958; Beowulf facsimile ed. Zupitza, 2nd edn 1959; English and Medieval Studies (ed with C. L. Wrenn), 1962; The Paston Letters (a selection in modern spelling), 1963; Glossary to Early Middle English Verse and Prose (ed J. A. W. Bennett and G. V. Smithers), 1966; rev. edn, Tolkien-Gordon: Sir Gawain, 1967; Non-Cycle Plays and Fragments (EETS), 1970; Paston Letters and Papers of the Fifteenth Century, Part I, 1971, Part II, 1977; (jtly) A Chaucer Glossary, 1979; Non-Cycle Plays and the Winchester Dialogues (facsimiles), 1979; reviews and articles in jls. *Address:* 191b Woodstock Road, Oxford OX2 7AB. *T:* Oxford 59634.

DAVIS, Prof. Ralph Henry Carless, FBA 1975; Professor of Medieval History, University of Birmingham, since 1970; b 7 Oct. 1918; s of late Prof. Henry William Carless Davis and Rosa Jennie Davis; m 1949, Eleanor Maud Megaw; two s. *Educ:* Leighton Park Sch.; Balliol Coll., Oxford. Friends' Ambulance Unit, 1939-45. Asst Master, Christ's Hosp., Horsham, 1947-48; Lectr, University Coll., London, 1948-56; Fellow and Tutor, Merton Coll., Oxford, 1956-70; Mem. Hebdomodal Council, Oxford Univ., 1967-69. Pres., Historical Assoc., 1979-82. Editor, History, 1968-78. *Publications:* The Mosques of Cairo, 1944; (ed) The Kalendar of Abbot Samson of Bury St Edmunds, 1954; A History of Medieval Europe, 1957; King Stephen, 1967; (ed with H. A. Cronne) Regesta Regum Anglo-Normannorum, vol. iii, 1968, vol. iv, 1969; The Normans and their Myth, 1976; (ed jtly) The Writing of History in the Middle Ages: essays presented to Richard William Southern, 1981; articles in historical and archæological jls. *Recreations:* travel, archæology, architecture. *Address:* 56 Fitzroy Avenue, Harborne, Birmingham B17 8RJ. *T:* 021-427 1711.
  See also G. R. C. Davis.

DAVIS, Hon. Sir Renn; see Davis, Hon. Sir D. R.

DAVIS, Air Vice-Marshal Robert Leslie; Commander, British Forces Cyprus and Administrator, Sovereign Base Areas, Cyprus, 1980-83; *b* 22 March 1930; *s* of Sidney and Florence Davis; *m* 1956, Diana, *d* of Edward William Bryant; one *s* one *d. Educ:* Woolsingham Grammar Sch., Co. Durham; Bede Sch. Collegiate, Sunderland, Co. Durham; RAF Coll., Cranwell. Commnd, 1952; served fighter units, exchange posting, USAF, Staff Coll., OR and Ops appts, MoD, DS Staff Coll., 1953-69; comd No 19 Sqdn, 1970-72; Dep. Dir Ops Air Defence, MoD, 1972-75; comd RAF Leuchars, 1975-77; Comdr RAF Staff, and Air Attaché, British Defence Staff, Washington, DC, 1977-80. *Recreations:* golf, antiques, music. *Address:* c/o Lloyds Bank, 54 Fawcett Street, Sunderland, Tyne and Wear.

DAVIS, Sir Rupert C. H.; *see* Hart-Davis.

DAVIS, S(tanley) Clinton; MP (Lab) Hackney Central since 1970; *b* 6 Dec. 1928; *s* of Sidney Davis; *m* 1954, Frances Jane Clinton Davis (*née* Lucas); one *s* three *d. Educ:* Hackney Downs Sch.; Mercers' Sch.; King's Coll., London University. LLB 1950; admitted Solicitor 1953. Mem. Exec. Council, Nat. Assoc. of Labour Student Organisations, 1949-50. Councillor, London Borough of Hackney, 1959; Mayor of Hackney, 1968. Contested (Lab): Langstone Div. of Portsmouth, 1955; Yarmouth, 1959 and 1964. Parly Under-Sec. of State, Dept of Trade, 1974-79; Opposition spokesman on trade, prices and consumer protection, 1979-. Mem., APEX. Pres., Hackney Br., Multiple Sclerosis Soc.; Vice-Pres., Hackney Assoc. for Disabled; Mem. Rotary Club, Hackney; Hon. Mem., Merchant Navy and Airline Officers' Assoc. *Recreations:* golf, Association football, reading biographical histories. *Address:* Essex Lodge, 354 Finchley Road, Hampstead, NW3. *T:* 01-435 4976.

DAVIS, Prof. Stanley Stewart, CChem, FRSC; Lord Trent Professor of Pharmacy, Nottingham University, since 1975; *b* 17 Dec. 1942; *s* of William Stanley and Joan Davis; two *s. Educ:* Warwick Sch.; London Univ. (BPharm, PhD, DSc). MPS. Lecturer, London Univ., 1976-80; Sen. Lectr, Aston Univ., 1970-75. Fulbright Scholar, Univ. of Kansas, 1978-79; various periods as visiting scientist to pharmaceutical industry. *Publications:* (co-ed) Radionuclide Imaging in Drug Research, 1982; over 200 research pubns in various scientific jls. *Recreations:* squash, tennis, travel. *Address:* 5 Wortley Hall Close, University Park, Nottingham. *T:* Nottingham 781601.

DAVIS, Terence Anthony Gordon, (Terry Davis); MP (Lab) Birmingham, Stechford, since 1979; *b* 5 Jan. 1938; *s* of Gordon Davis and Gladys (*née* Avery), Stourbridge, West Midlands; *m* 1963, Anne, *d* of F. B. Cooper, Newton-le-Willows, Lancs; one *s* one *d. Educ:* King Edward VI Grammar Sch., Stourbridge, Worcestershire; University Coll. London (LLB); Univ. of Michigan, USA (MBA). Company Executive, 1962-71. Motor Industry Manager, 1974-79. Joined Labour Party, 1965; contested (Lab) Bromsgrove, Gen. Election, 1970, By-election 1971, Gen. Elections Feb. and Oct. 1974; MP (Lab) Bromsgrove, May 1971-Feb. 1974; contested (Lab) Birmingham, Stechford, By-election, March 1977. Member, Assoc. of Scientific, Technical and Managerial Staffs. Member, Yeovil Rural District Council, 1967-68. *Address:* 48 Western Road, West Hagley, Stourbridge, West Midlands.

DAVIS, Hon. Sir Thomas (Robert Alexander Harries), KBE 1981; Pa Tu Te Rangi Ariki 1979; Prime Minister, Cook Islands, since 1978; *b* 11 June 1917; *s* of Sidney Thomes Davis and Maryanne Harries; *m* 1940, Myra Lydia Henderson; three *s* ; *m* 1979, Pa Tepaeru Ariki. *Educ:* King's Coll., Auckland, NZ; Otago Univ. Med. Sch. (MB, ChB 1945); Sch. of Tropical Medicine, Sydney Univ., Australia (DTM&H 1950); Harvard Sch. of Public Health (Master of Public Health 1952). FRSTM&H 1949. MO and Surg. Specialist, Cook Islands Med. Service, 1945-48; Chief MO, Cook Is Med. Service, 1948-52; Res. Staff, Dept of Nutrition, Harvard Sch. of Public Health, 1952-55; Chief, Dept of Environmental Medicine, Arctic Aero-medical Lab., Fairbanks, Alaska, 1955-56; Res. Physician and Dir, Div. of Environmtl Med., Army Medical Res. Lab., Fort Knox, Ky, 1956-61; Dir of Res., US Army Res. Inst. of Environmtl Med., Natick, 1961-63; Res. Exec., Arthur D. Little, Inc., 1963-71. Involved in biol aspects of space prog., first for Army, later for NASA, 1957-71. Formed Democratic Party, Cook Islands, 1971; private med. practice, Cook Islands, 1974-78. Mem., RSocMed, 1960; twice Pres., Med. and Dental Assoc., Cook Islands. Pres., Avatiu Sports Club. Silver Jubilee Medal, 1977; Order of Merit, Fed. Republic of Germany, 1978. *Publications:* Doctor to the Islands, 1954; Makutu, 1956; over 80 scientific and other pubns. *Recreations:* deep sea fishing, yacht racing, agriculture/planting, amateur radio. *Address:* Prime Minister's Department, Rarotonga, Cook Islands. *Club:* Harvard (Boston, Mass).

DAVIS, William; author, columnist and broadcaster; Editor and Publisher of High Life, since 1973; Chairman, Headway Publications, since 1977; Editorial Director, Executive World, since 1980; *b* 6 March 1933; *m* 1967, Sylvette Jouclas. *Educ:* City of London Coll. On staff of Financial Times, 1954-59; Editor, Investor's Guide, 1959-60; City Editor, Evening Standard, 1960-65 (with one year's break as City Editor, Sunday Express); Financial Editor, The Guardian, 1965-68; Editor, Punch, 1968-77; Editor-in-Chief, Financial Weekly, 1977-80. Presenter, Money Programme, BBC TV, 1967-69. Director, Fleet Publishing International, Morgan-Grampian, and Fleet Financial Publishing, 1977-80. *Publications:* Three Years Hard Labour: the road to devaluation, 1968; Merger Mania, 1970; Money Talks, 1972; Have Expenses, Will Travel, 1975; It's No Sin to be Rich, 1976; (ed) The Best of Everything, 1980; Money in the 1980s, 1981; The Rich: a study of the species,

1982. *Recreations:* drinking wine, travelling, playing tennis (badly), thinking about retirement. *Address:* Headway Publications, 66-68 Brewer Street, W1. *Clubs:* Garrick, Hurlingham.

DAVIS, (William) Allan, CA; Senior Partner, Armitage & Norton, London, since 1979 (Partner, 1976); *b* 19 June 1921; *s* of Wilfred Egwin Davis and Annie Helen Davis; *m* 1944, Audrey Pamela Louch; two *s* one *d. Educ:* Cardinal Vaughan Sch., Kensington. Mem., Inst. of Accountants and Actuaries, Glasgow (now Inst. of Chartered Accountants of Scotland), 1949; ATII. FRSA. Served War, Pilot RNVR FAA, 1940-44. Joined Barclays Bank, 1939; Dunn Wylie & Co.: apprentice, 1944; Partner, 1952; Sen. Partner, 1972-76. Director: Armitage Norton Consultants Ltd; Catholic Herald Ltd; Crowning Tea Co. Ltd; Dunkelman & Son Ltd; Fiat Auto (UK) Ltd; Forestry Ltd; Holco Trading Co. Ltd; Internatio-Muller UK Ltd; Wm H. Muller (UK) Ltd; Plantime Ltd. Common Councilman, Ward of Queenhithe, 1971-76; Alderman, Ward of Cripplegate, 1976-; Sheriff, City of London, 1982-83. Chairman: Port and City of London Health Cttee and Social Services Cttee, 1974-77; Management Cttee, London Homes for the Elderly, 1975-; Queenhithe Ward Club, 1976-77; Barbican Youth Club, 1979-; Mem. Court, HAC, 1976-. Hon. Treasurer: City of London Centre, St John Amb. Assoc., 1979-; Worshipful Co. of Painter-Stainers, 1962- (Liveryman, 1960; Mem. Court, 1962-). Governor: Bridewell Royal Hosp., 1976-; Cripplegate Foundn, 1976- (Chm., 1981-); Cardinal Vaughan Meml Sch., 1968-81; Lady Eleanor Holles Sch., 1979-; Trustee, St John Soane's Mus., 1979-; Patron, Barbican Lawn Tennis Club, 1979-; Vice Pres., Lancia Motor Club. KCSG 1979; KCHS 1977 (Kt, English Lieutenancy, 1972). *Recreations:* bridge, travel. *Address:* 540 Willoughby House, Barbican, EC2Y 8BN. *T:* 01-638 5354. *Clubs:* Oriental, Wig and Pen, City Livery, Players Theatre.

DAVIS, William Eric, (professionally known as David Davis), MBE 1969; MA Oxon; LRAM, ARCM; *b* 27 June 1908; *s* of William John and Florence Kate Rachel Davis; *m* 1935, Barbara de Riemer (*d* 1982); one *s* two *d. Educ:* Bishop's Stortford Coll.; The Queen's Coll., Oxford (MA). Schoolmaster, 1931-35; joined BBC as mem. of Children's Hour, 1935. Served with RNVR Acting Temp. Lieut, 1942-46. BBC, 1946-70; Head of Children's Hour, BBC, 1953-61; Head of Children's Programmes (Sound), BBC, 1961-64; Producer, Drama Dept, 1964-70, retired; *Publications:* various songs, etc. including: Lullaby, 1943; Fabulous Beasts, 1948; Little Grey Rabbit Song Book, 1952; *poetry:* A Single Star, 1973; various speech recordings, including The Tales of Beatrix Potter. *Recreations:* children, cats, growing roses. *Address:* 18 Mount Avenue, W5 2RG. *T:* 01-997 8156. *Club:* Garrick.

DAVIS, Hon. William Grenville, QC (Can.); Premier of Ontario, Canada, and President of the Council, Ontario, since 1971; Leader, Progressive Conservative Party; lawyer (former partner in law firm, Brampton); *b* Brampton, Ont., 30 July 1929; *s* of Albert Grenville Davis and Vera M. Davis (*née* Hewetson); *m* 1st, 1953, Helen MacPhee (*d* 1962), *d* of Hugh MacPhee, Windsor, Ontario; 2nd, 1963, Kathleen Louise, *d* of Dr R. P. Mackay, California; two *s* three *d. Educ:* Brampton High Sch.; University Coll., Univ. of Toronto (BA); Osgoode Hall Law Sch. (grad. 1955). Called to Bar of Ontario, 1955. Elected Mem. (C) Provincial Parlt (MPP) for Peel Riding, 1959, 1963, Peel North Riding, 1967, 1971, Brampton Riding, 1975. Mem., Select Cttee to examine and study admin. and exec. problems of Govt of Ontario, 1960-63; 2nd Vice-Chm., Hydro-Electric Power Commn of Ontario, Dec. 1961-Nov. 1962; Minister of Educn, Oct. 1962-March 1971; also Minister of Univ. Affairs, 1964-71. Holds hon. doctorates in Law from six Ontario Univs: Waterloo Lutheran, W Ontario, Toronto, McMaster, Queen's, Windsor; Hon. DUniv, Ottawa; Cert. of Merit, Edinboro Univ., Pa, USA. Amer. Transit Assoc. Man of the Year, 1973. A Freemason. *Publications:* Education in Ontario, 1965; The Government of Ontario and the Universities of the Province (Frank Gerstein Lectures, York Univ.), 1966; Building an Educated Society 1816-1966, 1966; Education for New Times, 1967. *Address:* Office of the Premier of Ontario, Parliament Buildings, Toronto, Ont., Canada; 61 Main Street South, Brampton, Ontario. *Clubs:* Kiwanis, Albany (both in Ont.).

DAVIS, William Herbert, TD; BSc; CEng, FIMechE, FIProdE; Consultant to BL, BL Europe & Overseas, Land Rover Ltd, since 1981; Director, Land Rover Santana (Spain), since 1981; *b* 27 July 1919; *s* of William and Dora Davis; *m* 1945, Barbara Mary Joan (*née* Sommerfield); one *d. Educ:* Waverley Grammar Sch.; Univ. of Aston in Birmingham (BSc). Austin Motor Co.: Engr Apprentice, 1935-39; Mech. Engr and Section Leader, Works Engrs, 1946-51; Supt Engr, 1951; Asst Production Manager, 1954; Production Manager, 1956; Dir and Gen. Works Manager, 1958. British Motor Corp. Ltd: Dir of Production, 1960; Dep. Managing Dir (Manufacture and Supply), 1961; Dep. Managing Dir, British Leyland (Austin-Morris Ltd), 1968; Chairman and Chief Executive, Triumph Motor Co. Ltd, 1970; Managing Dir, Rover Triumph BLUK Ltd, 1972; Dir (Manufacture), British Leyland Motor Corporation, 1973; Dir, Military Contracts and Govt Affairs, Leyland Cars, 1976-81. FIIM, FBIM, SME(USA). *Recreations:* riding, motoring, photography; interests in amateur boxing. *Address:* Arosa, The Holloway, Alvechurch, Worcs. *T:* Redditch 66187.

DAVIS, Most Rev. William Wallace; *b* 10 Dec. 1908; *s* of Isaac Davis and Margaret Dixon; *m* 1933, Kathleen Aubrey Acheson (*d* 1966); two *s* two *d* ; *m* 1968, Helen Mary Lynton. *Educ:* Bishop's Univ., Lennoxville, PQ. BA 1931, BD 1934; Deacon, 1932; Priest, 1932; Curate, St Matthew's, Ottawa, 1932-36; Rector, Coaticook, PQ, 1936-38; Rector, St Matthew's, Quebec,

1938-52; Archdeacon of Quebec, 1947-52; Dean of Nova Scotia, and Rector of the Cathedral Church of All Saints, Halifax, NS, 1952-58; Bishop Coadjutor of Nova Scotia, 1958-63; Bishop of Nova Scotia, 1963; Archbishop of Nova Scotia and Metropolitan of Ecclesiastical Province of the Atlantic, Canada, 1972-75. DD University of King's Coll., Halifax, 1954; Hon. DCL Bishop's Univ., Lennoxville, PQ, 1960; Hon. LLD St Francis Xavier Univ., Antigonish, Nova Scotia, 1974. *Address:* Apt 712, 1465 Baseline Road, Ottawa, Ont K2C 3L9, Canada.

DAVIS, Adm. Sir William (Wellclose), GCB 1959 (KCB 1956; CB 1952); DSO 1944, and Bar, 1944; DL; *b* 11 Oct. 1901; *s* of late W. S. Davis, Indian Political Service; *m* 1934, Lady Gertrude Elizabeth Phipps, 2nd *d* of 3rd Marquis of Normanby; two *s* two *d*. *Educ:* Summerfields, Oxford; Osborne and Dartmouth Naval Colls. Midshipman, 1917; Lieut, 1921; Comdr, 1935; Capt., 1940; Rear-Adm., 1950; Acting Vice-Adm. and Vice-Adm., 1953; Adm. 1956, Dep. Dir of Plans and Cabinet Offices, 1940-42; commanded HMS Mauritius, 1943-44; Dir of Under Water Weapons, Admiralty, 1945-46; Imperial Defence Coll., 1947; Chief of Staff to C-in-C Home Fleet, 1948-49. The Naval Sec., Admiralty, 1950-52; Flag Officer 2nd in Command Mediterranean, 1952-54; Vice-Chief of the Naval Staff, Admiralty, 1954-57; Comdr-in-Chief, Home Fleet, and NATO Comdr-in-Chief, Eastern Atlantic Area, 1958-60; First and Principal Naval ADC to the Queen, 1959-60, retired. Vice-Pres., King George's Fund for Sailors; Member: Royal Institution of GB (Vice-Pres.); Royal United Service Institution; European-Atlantic Group (Vice-Pres.); British Atlantic Cttee; Gloucestershire Community Council; Pres., Gloucestershire Outward Bound; Treasurer, Friends of Gloucester Cathedral; Mem., St Helena Assoc. DL Glos 1963. *Recreations:* fishing, shooting. *Address:* Coglan House, Longhope, Glos. *T:* Gloucester 830282. *Clubs:* Naval and Military; Ends of the Earth.
See also Comdr L. M. M. Saunders Watson.

DAVIS-GOFF, Sir Robert William; *see* Goff.

DAVIS-RICE, Peter; Regional Nursing Officer, North Western Regional Health Authority, since 1973; *b* 1 Feb. 1930; *s* of Alfred Davis-Rice and Doris Eva (*née* Bates); *m* 1967, Judith Anne Chatterton; one *s* two *d*. *Educ:* Riley High Sch., Hull; Royal Coll. of Nursing, Edinburgh; Harefield Hosp., Mddx; City Hosp., York. SRN; British Tuberculosis Assoc. Cert.; AMBIM; NAdmin (Hosp)Cert. Staff Nurse, Charge Nurse, St Luke's Hosp., Huddersfield, 1954-57; Theatre Supt, Hull Royal Infirmary, 1957-62; Asst Matron (Theatres), Walton Hosp., Liverpool, 1962-66; Matron, Billinge Hosp., Wigan, 1966-69; Chief Nursing Officer, Oldham and District HMC, 1969-73. Mem., Governing Body, Manchester Polytechnic, 1979-. *Publications:* contrib. Nursing Times. *Recreations:* badminton, tennis, do-it-yourself. *Address:* Riencourt, 185 Frederick Street, Oldham OL8 4DH. *T:* 061-624 2485.

DAVISON, family name of **Baron Broughshane.**

DAVISON, Arthur Clifford Percival, CBE 1974; FRAM 1966; Musical Director and Conductor: Little Symphony of London, since 1964; Virtuosi of England, since 1970; *b* Montreal, Canada; *s* of late Arthur Mackay Davison and Hazel Edith Smith; *m* 1st, 1950, Barbara June Hildred (marr. diss.); one *s* two *d* ; 2nd, 1978, Elizabeth Blanche. *Educ:* Conservatory of Music, McGill Univ.; Conservatoire de Musique, Montreal; Royal Associated Board Scholar at Royal Acad. of Music, London; later studies in Europe; LRSM 1947; ARCM 1950. A Dir and Dep. Leader, London Philharmonic Orch., 1957-65; Guest Conductor, Royal Danish Ballet, 1964; Asst Conductor, Bournemouth Symphony Orch., 1965-66. Guest Conductor of Orchestras: London Philharmonic; London Symphony; Philharmonia; Royal Philharmonic; BBC Orchs; Birmingham Symphony; Bournemouth Symphony and Sinfonietta; Ulster; Royal Liverpool Philharmonic; New York City Ballet; CBC Radio and Television Orchs; Royal Danish. Founder of Arthur Davison Concerts for Children, 1966; Dir and Conductor, Nat. Youth Orch. of Wales, 1966- (conducted Investiture Week Symphony concert in presence of HRH Prince of Wales, 1969; Guild for Promotion of Welsh Music Award for long and distinguished service, 1976); Mus. Dir, Corralls Concerts, Bournemouth Symphony, 1966-; conducted official Silver Jubilee concert, Fairfield Halls, 1977, and in presence of the Queen and HRH Duke of Edinburgh, Poole Arts Centre, Dorset, 1979; conducted Royal Over-Seas League 70th Anniversary concert, St James's Palace, in presence of HRH Princess Alexandra, 1980. Conductor and Lectr, London Univ., Goldsmiths' Coll., 1971-; Governor and Guest Lectr, Welsh Coll. of Music and Drama, 1973-; Conductor, Symphony Orchestra, Birmingham Sch. of Music, 1981. EMI/CFP award for sale of half a million classical records, 1973, Gold Disc for sale of one million classical records, 1977. Tour of Europe recorded for BBC TV. FRSA 1977. Hon. Master of Music, Univ. of Wales, 1974. *Publications:* various articles in musical jls. *Recreations:* reading, theatre-going, fishing, boating on Thames, antiques. *Address:* Glencairn, Shepherd's Hill, Merstham, Surrey RH1 3AD. *T:* Merstham 4434 and 2206. *Clubs:* Savage, Royal Over-Seas League.

DAVISON, Ian Frederic Hay, FCA; Senior Partner, Arthur Andersen & Co., Chartered Accountants, since 1982 (Managing Partner, 1966-82); *b* 30 June 1931; *s* of Eric Hay Davison, FCA, and late Inez Davison; *m* 1955, Maureen Patricia Blacker; one *s* two *d*. *Educ:* Dulwich Coll.; LSE (BScEcon); Univ. of Mich. ACA 1956, FCA 1966. Institute of Chartered Accountants: Mem. Cttee, London and Dist Soc., 1965-72; Mem., Technical Adv. Cttee, 1971-75; Mem. Council, 1975-; Mem., Auditing Practices Cttee, 1973-79; Mem.,

Inflation Accounting Steering Gp, 1975-79; Mem., Educn and Training Directorate, 1978-82; Chm., Tech. and Res. Cttee, 1979-82. Chm., Accounting Standards Cttee, 1982-. Indep. Mem., NEDC for Bldg Industry, 1971-77; Mem., Price Commn, 1977-79; Chairman: EDC for Food and Drink Manufg Industry, 1981-; Review Bd for Govt Contracts, 1981-. Dept of Trade Inspector, London Capital Securities, 1975-77; Inspector, Grays Building Soc., 1978-79. London Borough of Greenwich: Councillor and Alderman, 1961-73; Chm., Housing Cttee, 1968-70; Chm., London Boroughs Jt Computer Cttee, 1968-71. Governor, Greenwich Theatre, 1968-81 (Chm., 1968-74); Treasurer, Byam Shaw Sch. of Art, 1974-; Chairman: Stravinsky Festival Trust, 1978-79; Monteverdi Trust, 1979-. Governor and Mem. of Corp., LSE, 1982-. *Recreations:* theatre, music, squash, ski-ing. *Address:* 40 Earlham Street, WC2. *Clubs:* Carlton, Arts, MCC.

DAVISON, Sir John Alec B.; *see* Biggs-Davison.

DAVISON, Rt. Hon. Sir Ronald (Keith), GBE 1978; CMG 1975; PC 1978; **Rt. Hon. The Chief Justice Sir Ronald Davison;** Chief Justice of New Zealand, since 1978; *b* 16 Nov. 1920; *s* of Joseph James Davison and Florence May Davison; *m* 1948, Jacqueline May Carr; one *s* one *d* (and one *s* decd). *Educ:* Auckland Univ. (LLB). Admitted as barrister and solicitor, 1948; QC (NZ) 1963. Chairman: Environmental Council, 1969-74; Legal Aid Bd, 1969-78; Member: Council, Auckland Dist Law Soc., 1960-65 (Pres., 1965-66); Council, NZ Law Soc., 1966-68; Auckland Electric Power Bd (13 yrs); Aircrew Indust. Tribunal, 1970-78. Chm., Montana Wines Ltd, 1971-78; Dir, NZ Insurance Co. Ltd, 1975-78. *Recreations:* golf, fishing, bowls. *Address:* Chief Justice's Chambers, High Court, Wellington, New Zealand. *Clubs:* Wellington; Northern (Auckland, NZ).

DAVISON, William Norris; His Honour Judge Davison; a Circuit Judge (formerly a County Court Judge), since 1971; *b* 20 Aug. 1919; *s* of late Dr W. H. Davison; *m* 1947, Margaret, *d* of late G. H. Bettinson; one *s* two *d*. *Educ:* King Edward's High School, Birmingham; Trinity College, Dublin. RNVR, 1939-43; Royal Indian Naval Volunteer Reserve, 1943-46. Called to the Bar (Middle Temple), 1949; practised Midland Circuit, 1949-71. *Recreation:* collecting. *Address:* Kilsby, Llanwrtyd Wells, Powys LD5 4TL. *T:* Llanwrtyd Wells 281.

DAVITT, Cahir; President of the High Court, Eire, 1951-66, retired (Hon. Mr Justice Davitt); *b* 15 Aug. 1894; *s* of Michael Davitt and Mary Yore; *m* 1925, Sarah Gertrude Lynch; four *s* one *d*. *Educ:* O'Connell Sch. and University Coll., Dublin, BA, NUI, 1914; LLB, 1916; Barrister, King's Inns, Dublin, 1916, Bencher, 1927. Judge of the Dail Courts, 1920-22; Judge-Advocate Gen., Irish Free State Defence Forces, 1922-26; Temp. Judge, Circuit Court, 1926-27; Circuit Judge, City and County of Dublin, 1927-45; (Puisne) Judge of the High Court, 1945-51. Mem. of Judiciary Cttee, 1923-24, to advise Irish Free State Executive in relation to the establishment of Courts of Justice under the IFS Constitution; Chairman: Civil Service Compensation Board, 1929-66; Commission of Inquiry into Derating, 1930; Med. Bureau of Road Safety, 1969-74. President: Irish Rugby Football Union, 1936-37; Irish Squash Rackets Assoc., 1936. *Address:* 1 The Orchard, Booterstown Avenue, Co. Dublin. *Clubs:* Milltown Golf, Fitzwilliam Lawn Tennis (Dublin).

DAVSON, Sir Geoffrey Leo Simon, 2nd Bt; *see* Glyn, Sir Anthony, 2nd Bt.

DAVY, Brig. George Mark Oswald, CB 1945; CBE 1943; DSO 1941; US Legion of Merit; Gold Cross of Merit with Swords, Poland; Sculptor; Painter of horses in oils and of landscapes and seascapes in watercolours; Vice-President, Chelsea Art Society; Associate Member, National Society of Painters, Sculptors and Printmakers; *b* 22 Sept. 1898; *s* of late Capt. G. C. H. Davy; *m* 1932, Isabel Gwendolen (*d* 1970), *d* of late E. Alan Hay, Bengeo House, Hertford; one *s*. European War, 1914-18, France and Belgium: RFA and RHA; transferred to 3rd Hussars, 1931; Staff Coll., Camberley, 1932-33; Bde Major, 150 Inf. Bde, 1935-36; Company Comdr RMC, Sandhurst, 1937-38; Naval Staff Coll., Greenwich, 1939; France and Belgium, 1939-40; Western Desert, 1940-41; Greece, April 1941; commanded 3rd and 7th Armoured Bdes in Desert, 1941; Director of Military Operations GHQ, Middle East, 1942-44; Dep. Asst Chief of Staff (Operations), AFHQ Algiers, 1944; commanded Land Forces Adriatic, 1944-45; War Office representative with the Polish Forces, 1945-47; retd 1948; recommissioned for military service, 1956; retd again 1959. *Publication:* The Seventh and Three Enemies, 1953. *Recreation:* fishing. *Address:* Jordanstone House, Alyth, Blairgowrie, Perthshire. *Clubs:* Cavalry and Guards; New (Edinburgh).

DAVY, Humphrey Augustine A.; *see* Arthington-Davy.

DAWBARN, Sir Simon (Yelverton), KCVO 1980; CMG 1976; HM Diplomatic Service, retired; *b* 16 Sept. 1923; *s* of Frederic Dawbarn and Maud Louise Mansell; *m* 1948, Shelby Montgomery Parker; one *s* two *d*. *Educ:* Oundle Sch.; Corpus Christi Coll., Cambridge. Served in HM Forces (Reconnaissance Corps), 1942-45. Reckitt & Colman (Overseas), 1948-49. Joined Foreign Service, 1949. Foreign Office, 1949-53; Brussels, 1953; Prague, 1955; Tehran, 1957; seconded to HM Treasury, 1959; Foreign Office, 1961; Algiers, 1965; Athens, 1968; FCO, 1971-75. Head of W African Dept and concurrently non-resident Ambassador to Chad, 1973-75; Consul-General, Montreal, 1975-78; Ambassador to Morocco, 1978-82. *Address:* 44 Canonbury Park North, N1 2JT. *T:* 01-226 0659. *Club:* Travellers'.

DAWE, Donovan Arthur; Principal Keeper, Guildhall Library, London, 1967-73, retired; *b* 21 Jan. 1915; *s* of late Alfred Ernest and Sarah Jane Dawe, Wallington, Surrey; *m* 1946, Peggy Marjory Challen; two *d. Educ:* Sutton Grammar Sch. Associate, Library Assoc., 1938. Entered Guildhall Library as junior assistant, 1931. Served with Royal West African Frontier Force in Africa and India, 1941-46. Freeman of City of London and Merchant Taylors' Company, 1953. FRHistS 1954. *Publications:* Skilbecks; drysalters 1650-1950, 1950; 11 Ironmonger Lane: the story of a site in the City of London, 1952; The City of London: a select book list, 1972; contribs professional literature, Connoisseur, Musical Times, Genealogists' Magazine, etc. *Recreations:* the countryside, local history, musicology. *Address:* 46 Green Lane, Purley, Surrey CR2 3PJ. *T:* 01-660 4218.

DAWE, Roger James, OBE 1970; Director of Special Programmes, Manpower Services Commission, since 1981; *b* 26 Feb. 1941; *s* of Harry James and Edith Mary Dawe; *m* 1965, Ruth Day Jolliffe; one *s* one *d. Educ:* Hardyes Sch., Dorchester; Fitzwilliam House, Cambridge. BA Cantab. Entered Min. of Labour, 1962; Dept of Economic Affairs, 1964-65; Private Sec. to Prime Minister, 1966-70; Principal, Dept of Employment, 1970; Private Sec. to Secretary of State for Employment, 1972-74; Asst Sec., Dept of Employment, 1974-81; Under Sec., MSC, 1981. *Recreations:* tennis, Plymouth Argyle supporter. *Address:* 35 Cromwell Avenue, Bromley, Kent BR2 9AG.

DAWES, Prof. Edwin Alfred, FIBiol; CChem, FRSC; Reckitt Professor and Head of Biochemistry Department, University of Hull, since 1963; *b* 6 July 1925; *s* of late Harold Dawes and Maude Dawes (*née* Barker); *m* 1950, Amy Rogerson; two *s. Educ:* Goole Grammar Sch.; Univ. of Leeds. BSc, PhD, DSc. Asst Lectr, later Lectr, in Biochemistry, Univ. of Leeds, 1947-50; Lectr, later Sen. Lectr, Univ. of Glasgow, 1951-63; Hull University: Dean of Science, 1968-70; Pro-Vice-Chancellor, 1977-80. Visiting Lecturer: Meml Univ., Newfoundland, Dalhousie Univ., 1959; Univ. of Brazil, 1960, 1972; Univ. of S California, 1962; Univ. of Rabat, 1967; Univ. of Göttingen, 1972; Biochemical Soc. Lectr, Australia and NZ, 1975; Amer. Medical Alumni Lectr, Univ. of St Andrews, 1980-81. Editor, Biochemical Jl, 1958-65; Editor-in-Chief, Jl of Gen. Microbiol., 1976-81; Man. Editor, Fedn of European Microbiol Socs, 1982-. Chm., Scientific Adv. Cttee, Yorks Cancer Res. Campaign, 1978-. Pres., British Ring of Internat. Brotherhood of Magicians, 1972-73; Hon. Pres., Scottish Conjurers' Assoc.; Hon. Vice-Pres., Magic Circle (Mem., 1959-). Governor, Pocklington Sch., 1965-74; Mem. Council, Leeds Univ., 1974-. *Publications:* Quantitative Problems in Biochemistry, 1956, 6th edn 1980; (jtly) Biochemistry of Bacterial Growth, 1968, 3rd edn 1982; The Great Illusionists, 1979; Isaac Fawkes: fame and fable, 1979; The Biochemist in a Microbial Wonderland, 1982; numerous papers in scientific jls. *Recreations:* cricket, canoeing, conjuring, book-collecting. *Address:* Dane Hill, 393 Beverley Road, Anlaby, N Humberside HU10 7BQ. *T:* Hull 657998. *Club:* Savage.

DAWES, Prof. Geoffrey Sharman, CBE 1981; FRS 1971; Director of Nuffield Institute for Medical Research, Oxford, since 1948; *b* 21 Jan. 1918; *s* of Rev. W. Dawes, Thurlaston Grange, Derbyshire; *m* 1941, Margaret Monk; two *s* two *d. Educ:* Repton Sch.; New Coll., Oxford. BA 1939; BSc 1940; BM, BCh 1943; DM 1947. Rockefeller Travelling Fellowship, 1946; Fellow, Worcester Coll., Oxford, 1946; University Demonstrator in Pharmacology, 1947; Foulerton Research Fellow, Royal Society, 1948. Mem., MRC, 1978-; Chm., Physiological Systems and Disorders Bd, MRC, 1978-80. Governor of Repton, 1959, Chm., 1971-. A Vice-Pres., Royal Society, 1976, 1977. FRCOG, FRCP; Hon. FACOG. Max Weinstein Award, 1963; Gairdner Foundation Award, 1966; Maternité Award of European Assoc. Perinatal Medicine, 1976; Virginia Apgar Award, Amer. Acad. of Pediatrics, 1980. *Publications:* Foetal and Neonatal Physiology, 1968; various publications in physiological and pharmacological journals. *Recreation:* fishing. *Address:* 8 Belbroughton Road, Oxford. *T:* Oxford 58131.

DAWES, Ven. Peter Spencer; Archdeacon of West Ham, since 1980; *b* 1928; *s* of Jason Spencer Dawes and Janet Dawes; *m* 1954, Ethel Marrin; two *s* two *d. Educ:* Bickley Hall School; Aldenham School; Hatfield Coll., Durham (BA); Tyndale Hall, Bristol. Assistant Curate: St Andrew's, Whitehall Park, 1954-57; St Ebbe's, Oxford, 1957-60; Tutor, Clifton Theological Coll., 1960-65; Vicar, Good Shepherd, Romford, 1965-80. Examining Chaplain to Bishop of Chelmsford, 1970-; Member General Synod, 1970-, and of Standing Cttee, 1975-. *Address:* 15 Wallenger Avenue, Gidea Park, Romford, Essex RM2 6EP.

DAWICK, Viscount; Alexander Douglas Derrick Haig; *b* 30 June 1961; *s* and *heir* of 2nd Earl Haig, *qv. Educ:* Stowe School. *Address:* Bemersyde, Melrose, Scotland.

DAWKINS, Douglas Alfred; Assistant Director, Bank of England, since 1980; *b* 17 Sept. 1927; *s* of Arthur Dawkins and Edith Annie Dawkins; *m* 1953, Diana Pauline (*née* Ormes); one *s* one *d. Educ:* Edmonton County Secondary Sch.; University Coll. London (BA Hons). Entered Bank of England, 1950; Chief of Exchange Control, 1979. *Address:* 10 Woodmancourt, Godalming, Surrey GU7 2BT. *T:* Godalming 4643.

DAWNAY, family name of Viscount Downe.

DAWNAY, Lt-Col Christopher Payan, CBE 1946; MVO 1944; *s* of late Maj.-Gen. Guy P. Dawnay, CB, CMG, DSO, MVO, and Mrs Cecil Dawnay;

m 1939, Patricia, *d* of Sir Hereward Wake, 13th Bt, CB, CMG, DSO; two *s* two *d. Educ:* Winchester; Magdalen Coll., Oxford. With Dawnay Day & Co. Ltd, Merchant Bankers, 1933-39 and 1946-50. War service with Coldstream Guards and in various staff appointments, 1939-45. Partner Edward de Stein & Co., Merchant Bankers, 1951-60; Director Lazard Bros & Co. Ltd, 1960-74; Chairman: Guardian Assurance Co., 1967-68; Guardian Royal Exchange Assurance Co., 1970-74. One of HM Lieutenants, City of London. US Legion of Merit. *Recreations:* fishing, shooting. *Address:* Longparish House, Andover, Hants. *T:* Longparish 204. *Club:* Brooks's. *See also Captain O. P. Dawnay.*

DAWNAY, Hon. George William ffolkes, MC 1944; DL; Coldstream Guards; Director, Barclays Bank Ltd, 1956-79; Local Advisory Director, Barclays Bank Ltd, Norwich, retired 1979; *b* 20 April 1909; *s* of 9th Viscount Downe, CMG, DSO and Dorothy, *o c* of Sir William ffolkes, 3rd Bt; *m* 1945, Rosemary Helen (*d* 1969), *d* of late Lord Edward Grosvenor and of late Lady Dorothy Charteris; two *s* two *d. Educ:* Eton. DL Norfolk, 1961. *Address:* Hillington Hall, King's Lynn, Norfolk. *T:* Hillington 600304.

DAWNAY, Captain Oliver Payan, CVO 1953; *b* 4 April 1920; *s* of late Maj.-General Guy Payan Dawnay, CB, CMG, DSO, MVO; *m* 1st, 1944, Lady Margaret Dorothea Boyle (marr. diss. 1962), *y d* of 8th Earl of Glasgow, DSO; two *s* one *d* ; 2nd, 1963, Hon. Iris Irene Adele Peake, *e d* of 1st Viscount Ingleby, PC; one *d. Educ:* Eton; Balliol Coll., Oxford. Parliamentary and Press section, Ministry of Economic Warfare, 1939-40. Served War of 1939-45: Coldstream Guards, 1940-46; Adjt 1st Batt., 1943-44 (despatches 1944); seconded to Foreign Office, Conference Dept, 1945-46; demobilised, as Captain, 1946. Messrs Dawnay Day and Co., Merchant Bankers, 1946-50. Private Secretary and Equerry to Queen Elizabeth the Queen Mother, 1951-56; Extra Equerry, 1956-62. Partner, Grieveson, Grant & Co., Stockbrokers, 1961-80. *Address:* Flat 5, 32 Onslow Square, SW7; Wexcombe House, Marlborough, Wilts. *Clubs:* Brooks's, MCC. *See also Lt-Col C. P. Dawnay.*

DAWNAY, Vice-Adm. Sir Peter, KCVO 1961 (MVO 1939); CB 1958; DSC 1944; DL; Royal Navy, retired; an Extra Equerry to the Queen since 1958; *b* 14 Aug. 1904; *s* of Maj. Hon. Hugh and Lady Susan Dawnay; *m* 1936, Lady Angela Montagu-Douglas-Scott, *d* of 7th Duke of Buccleuch; one *s* one *d. Educ:* Osborne and Dartmouth. Legion of Merit (USA). In command HMS Saintes and 3rd Destroyer Flotilla, 1950-51; in command HMS Mercury (HM Signal Sch.), 1952-53; in command HMS Glasgow, 1954-56. Deputy Controller of the Navy, Admiralty, 1956-58; Flag Officer, Royal Yachts, 1958-62; retired, 1962. High Sheriff, Hants, 1973; DL Hants 1975. *Address:* The Old Post Cottage, Wield, Alresford, Hants SO24 9RS. *T:* Alton 63041.

DAWOOD, Nessim Joseph; Arabist and Middle East Consultant; Managing Director, The Arabic Advertising and Publishing Co. Ltd, London, since 1958; Director: Contemporary Translations Ltd, London, since 1962; Bradbury Wilkinson (Graphics) Ltd, 1975; *b* Baghdad, 27 Aug. 1927; 4th *s* of late Yousef Dawood, merchant, and Muzli (*née* Tweg); *m* 1949, Juliet, 2nd *d* of M. and N. Abraham, Baghdad and New York; three *s. Educ:* The American Sch. and Shamash Sch., Baghdad; Iraq State Scholar in England, UC Exeter, 1945-49; Univ. of London, BA (Hons). FIL 1959. Has written and spoken radio and film commentaries. *Publications:* The Muqaddimah of Ibn Khaldun, 1967 (US, 1969); Penguin Classics: The Thousand and One Nights, 1954; The Koran, 1956, 25th edn 1982, with parallel Arabic text, 1983; Aladdin and Other Tales, 1957; Tales from The Thousand and One Nights, 1973, 9th edn 1982; Arabian Nights (illus. children's edn), 1978; contribs to specialised and technical English-Arabic dictionaries; translated numerous technical publications into Arabic. *Recreation:* going to the theatre. *Address:* Berkeley Square House, Berkeley Square, W1X 5LE. *T:* 01-409 0953. *Club:* Hurlingham.

DAWS, Dame Joyce (Margaretta), DBE 1975; FRCS, FRACS; Surgeon, Queen Victoria Memorial Hospital, Melbourne, Victoria, Australia; Thoracic Surgeon, Prince Henry's Hospital, Melbourne, since 1975; President, Victorian Branch Council, Australian Medical Association, 1976; *b* 21 July 1925; *d* of Frederick William Daws and Daisy Ethel Daws. *Educ:* Royal School for Naval and Marine Officers' Daughters, St Margaret's, Mddx; St Paul's Girls' Sch., Hammersmith; Royal Free Hosp., London. MB, BS (London) 1949; FRCS 1952, FRACS. Ho. Surg., Royal Free Hosp.; SHMO, Manchester Royal Infirmary; Hon. Surg., Queen Victoria Meml Hosp., Melb. 1958; Asst Thoracic Surg., Prince Henry's Hosp., Melb., 1967-75. Pres., Bd of Management, After-Care Hosp., Melbourne, 1980-. Hon. Sec., Victorian Br., AMA, 1974. *Recreations:* opera, ballet, theatre, desert travel, swimming. *Address:* 26 Edwin Street, Heidelberg West, Victoria 3081, Australia. *T:* 452579. *Clubs:* Lyceum, Soroptimist International (Melbourne).

DAWSON, Anthony Michael, MD, FRCP; Physician to the Queen, since 1982 (to the Royal Household, 1974-82); Physician: St Bartholomew's Hospital, since 1965; King Edward VII Hospital for Officers, since 1968; King Edward VII Convalescent Home for Officers, Osborne, since 1975; *b* 8 May 1928; *s* of Leslie Joseph Dawson and Mabel Jayes; *m* 1956, Barbara Anne Baron Forsyth, *d* of late Thomas Forsyth, MB, ChB; two *d. Educ:* Wyggeston Sch., Leicester; Charing Cross Hosp. Med. Sch. MB, BS 1951, MB 1959, London; MRCP 1954, FRCP 1964. Jun. appts, Charing Cross Hosp., Brompton Hosp., Royal Postgrad. Med. Sch., Central Middlesex Hosp., 1951-57; MRC and US

Public Health Res. Fellow, Harvard Med. Sch. at Massachusetts Gen. Hosp., 1957-59; Lectr and Sen. Lectr in Medicine, Royal Free Hosp. Med. Sch., 1959-65. Hon. Sec., Assoc. of Physicians of Gt Britain and Ireland, 1973-78, Treasurer 1978. Examnr, London and Oxford, MRCP; Censor, RCP, 1977-78; Treasurer, St Bartholomew's Hosp. Med. Coll., 1976-79, Vice-Pres., 1979-; Member: Bd, BUPA Res. Co.; Bd of Management, King Edward's Hosp. Fund for London. *Publications:* contrib. med. books and jls. *Recreations:* music, gardening. *Address:* Flat 4, Stone House, 9 Weymouth Street, W1. *T:* 01-636 4121. *Club:* Garrick.
See also J. L. Dawson.

DAWSON, Christopher William, CMG 1947; *b* 31 May 1896; *s* of Rev. H. Dawson, MA, and Tertia Dean; *m* 1924, Jill, *d* of Prof. R. G. McKerron, Aberdeen Univ.; no *c. Educ:* Dulwich Coll.; Brasenose Coll., Oxford. Joined East Surrey Regt, 1915; served in India (NW Frontier) and Mesopotamia; demobilised with rank of Captain, 1919. Joined Malayan Civil Service 1920 and served in various parts of Malaya until 1942. Called to Bar, Gray's Inn, 1929. Secretary for Defence Malaya, 1941-42; interned by Japanese in Singapore, 1942-45; Chief Secretary and Officer Administering the Govt, Sarawak, 1946-50; retired, 1950; Deputy Chief Secretary, British Administration, Eritrea, 1951-52. President: British Assoc. of Malaya, 1957-58; Sarawak Assoc., 1962. *Address:* 11 Festival Court, Chichester, W Sussex. *T:* Chichester 780638.

DAWSON, Daryl Michael, CB 1980; QC (Australia) 1971; Solicitor-General for Victoria, since 1974; *b* 12 Dec. 1933; *s* of Claude Charles Dawson and Elizabeth May Dawson; *m* 1971, Mary Louise Thomas. *Educ:* Canberra High Sch.; Ormond Coll., Univ. of Melbourne (LLB Hons); LLM Yale. Sterling Fellow, Yale Univ., 1955-56. Mem. Council, Univ. of Melbourne, 1976-; Mem., Australian Motor Sport Appeal Court, 1970-. *Recreation:* squash. *Address:* Law Department, 221 Queen Street, Melbourne, Victoria 3000, Australia. *T:* (03)-602-0181. *Clubs:* Melbourne, Savage, RACV, Beefsteaks (Melbourne).

DAWSON, Sir (Hugh Halliday) Trevor, 3rd Bt *cr* 1920; *b* 6 June 1931; *s* of Sir Hugh Trevor Dawson, 2nd Bt, CBE, and of Vera Anne Loch, *d* of late Sir Frederick Loch Halliday, CIE, MVO; *S* father, 1976; *m* 1955, Caroline Jane, *d* of William Antony Acton, *qv*; two *s. Educ:* Harrow; RMA, Sandhurst. Joined Scots Guards, 1949; Major 1960; retired 1961. Dir, Arbuthnot Latham Holdings, 1969-81; Chairman: Arbuthnot Securities, 1976-81; Arbuthnot Govt Securities Trust, 1979-81. Mem., Exec. Cttee, Unit Trusts' Assoc., 1980. *Recreations:* racing, shooting. *Heir: s* Hugh Michael Trevor Dawson, *b* 28 March 1956. *Address:* 31 Eaton Square, SW1; China House, Pewsey, Wilts. *Clubs:* White's, Pratt's, Cavalry and Guards, Buck's, Turf, City of London, Royal Aero, MCC; Bembridge Sailing (IoW).

DAWSON, James Gordon, CBE 1981; FEng, FIMechE, FSAE; Consultant; *b* 3 Feb. 1916; *s* of James Dawson and Helen Mitchell (*née* Tawse); *m* 1941, Doris Irene (*née* Rowe); one *s* one *d. Educ:* Aberdeen Grammar Sch.; Aberdeen Univ. (BScEng Hons Mech. Eng, BScEng Hons Elect. Eng). Develt Test Engr, Rolls Royce Ltd, Derby, 1942; Chief Engr, Shell Research Ltd, 1946; Technical Dir, Perkins Engines Ltd, 1955; Dir, Dowty Group Ltd, 1966; Man. Dir, Zenith Carburetter Co. Ltd, 1969, Chm., 1977-81. Pres., IMechE, 1979-80. *Publications:* technical papers publd in UK and abroad. *Recreation:* golf. *Address:* Mildmay House, Apethorpe, Peterborough. *T:* Kingscliffe 348. *Club:* Caledonian.

DAWSON, James Lawrence, CEng, FICE; Director of Civil Engineering Services, Property Services Agency, since 1979; *b* 1 April 1924; *s* of Albert Lawrence Dawson and Margaret (*née* Howell); *m* 1947, Olive Joan (*née* Turner); three *s. Educ:* Sale High Sch.; Royal Naval Engineering Coll.; City Univ. (BSc). Engineer Cadet and RNVR, 1942-45. Engineer and Agent, West's Piling & Construction Co. Ltd, 1945-47; Civil Engineer, Air Ministry Works Directorate and Ministry of Public Building and Works, various positions in Iraq, Libya, Malta and UK, 1948-72; Suptg Engr, Roskill Commission on Third London Airport, 1968-70; Director of Naval Base Develt, Property Services Agency, 1972-79. *Publications:* papers to Instn of Civil Engrs and other professional bodies. *Recreations:* sailing, tennis, bridge, gardening. *Address:* Property Services Agency, Lunar House, 40 Wellesley Road, Croydon CR9 2EL.

DAWSON, John Alexander, CBE 1942; FICE; *b* 24 March 1886; *s* of Alexander Dawson, Aberdeen; *m* Margaret, *er d* of late Alexander M. Cruickshank, Bloemfontein, SA; two *s* one *d. Educ:* Robert Gordon's Coll., Aberdeen; Aberdeen and Glasgow Universities, BSc (Engineering) Glasgow. Entered Admiralty as Asst Civil Engineer, 1912; served at Portsmouth, Admiralty, Ostend (1919) and Rosyth; transferred to Air Ministry, 1921; served at Air Ministry, Inland Area, Singapore, Coastal Command; Chief Engineer Air Defence of Great Britain; Chief Engineer Bomber Command; Dep. Director of Works, 1938; Director of Works, Air Ministry, 1940-46; Ministry of Civil Aviation, 1946-48; Chief Resident Engineer, London Airport, 1948-54, retired 1954. *Address:* Belle Causey, Barnstaple, North Devon. *T:* Barnstaple 71112.

DAWSON, John Leonard, MB, MS; FRCS; Surgeon to HM Royal Household, since 1975; Surgeon: King's College Hospital, since 1964; Bromley Hospital, since 1967; King Edward VII Hospital for Officers, since 1975; *b* 30 Sept. 1932; *s* of Leslie Joseph Dawson and Mabel Annie Jayes; *m* 1958,

Rosemary Brundle; two *s* one *d. Educ:* Wyggeston Boys' Grammar Sch., Leicester; King's College Hosp., Univ. of London. MB, BS 1955, MS 1964; FRCS 1958. Served RAMC, 1958-60. Nuffield Scholarship, Harvard Univ., 1963-64; Sir Arthur Sims Travelling Prof., Australasia, 1981. Examiner in Surgery, Univs. of London and Cambridge, and Soc. of Apothecaries; Primary FRCS and Mem. Ct of Examrs, RCS. *Publications:* contribs to surgical text-books and jls on abdominal surgery. *Recreations:* squash, tennis, skiing, gardening, reading. *Address:* 107 Burbage Road, Dulwich, SE21 7AF. *T:* 01-733 3668.
See also A. M. Dawson.

DAWSON, (Joseph) Peter; General Secretary, National Association of Teachers in Further and Higher Education (NATFHE), since 1979; *b* 18 March 1940; *s* of Joseph Glyn and Winifred Olwen Dawson; *m* 1964, Yvonne Anne Charlton Smith; one *s* one *d. Educ:* Bishop Gore Grammar Sch., Swansea; University College of Swansea (BSc, DipEd). Assistant Master, Chiswick Grammar Sch., 1962; Field Officer, 1965, Sen. Field Officer, 1966, National Union of Teachers; Asst Sec., 1969, Negotiating Sec., 1974, Assoc. of Teachers in Technical Instns; Negotiating Sec., NATFHE, 1976. Vice-Pres., 1962-64, Sen. Treasurer, 1965-68, National Union of Students. *Recreations:* church activities, tennis, cricket. *Address:* NATFHE, Hamilton House, Mabledon Place, WC1H 9BH. *T:* 01-387 6806.

DAWSON, Ven. Peter; Archdeacon of Norfolk, since 1977; *b* 31 March 1929; *s* of Leonard Smith and Cicely Alice Dawson; *m* 1955, Kathleen Mary Sansome; one *s* three *d. Educ:* Manchester Grammar School; Keble Coll., Oxford (MA); Ridley Hall, Cambridge. Nat. service, Army, 1947-49; University, 1949-52; Theological College, 1952-54. Asst Curate, St Lawrence, Morden, Dio. Southwark, 1954-59; Vicar of Barston, Warwicks, Dio. Birmingham, 1959-63; Rector of St Clement, Higher Openshaw, Dio. Manchester, 1963-68; Rector of Morden, Dio. Southwark, 1968-77, and Rural Dean of Merton, 1975-77. *Recreations:* gardening, politics, the rural community, historical studies. *Address:* Intwood Rectory, Norwich NR4 6TG. *T:* Norwich 51946.

DAWSON, Peter; General Secretary, Professional Association of Teachers, since 1980; *b* 19 May 1933; *s* of Richard Dawson and Henrietta Kate Dawson (*née* Truman); *m* 1957, Shirley Margaret Pentland Johnson; two *d. Educ:* Beckenham Technical Sch.; Beckenham Grammar Sch.; London School of Economics (BScEcon); Westminster Coll. (Postgrad. CertEd). Schoolmaster Fellow Commoner, Keble Coll., Oxford, 1969, and Corpus Christi Coll., Cambridge, 1979. Asst Master, Roan Grammar School for Boys, Blackheath, 1957-62; Head of Upper School and Head of Religious Educn, Sedgehill Sch., Bellingham, SE, 1962-67; Second Master, Gateacre Comprehensive Sch., Liverpool, 1967-70; Headmaster, Eltham Green Sch., Eltham, 1970-80. *Publication:* Making a Comprehensive Work, 1981. *Recreations:* Methodist lay preaching, reading political biography, playing golf very badly. *Address:* (office) Professional Association of Teachers, 99 Friar Gate, Derby DE1 1EZ. *T:* Derby 372337; (home) 3 Lawn Heads Avenue, Littleover, Derby DE3 6DR.

DAWSON, Rex Malcolm Chaplin, FRS 1981; PhD, DSc; Deputy Director and Head of Biochemistry Department, Institute of Animal Physiology, Babraham, Cambridge, since 1969 (Principal Scientific Officer, 1955-69); *b* 3 June 1924; *s* of late James Dawson and Ethel Mary Dawson (*née* Chaplin); *m* 1946, Emily Elizabeth Hodder; one *s* one *d. Educ:* Hinckley Grammar Sch.; University Coll., London (BSc 1946, DSc 1960); Univ. of Wales (PhD 1951). MRC Fellowship followed by Beit Meml Fellowship, Neuropsychiatric Res. Centre, Whitchurch Hosp., Cardiff, 1947-52; Betty Brookes Fellow, Dept of Biochemistry, Univ. of Oxford, 1952-55. Vis. Res. Fellow, Harvard Univ., 1959; Vis. Prof., Northwestern Univ., Chicago, 1974. *Publications:* Metabolism and Physiological Significance of Lipids, 1964; Data for Biochemical Research, 1959, 2nd edn 1969; Form and Function of Phospholipids, 1973; numerous papers on structure, turnover and role of phospholipids in cell membranes in various scientific jls. *Recreations:* mercantile marine history, sailing, gardening. *Address:* Blue Cedars, 23 Cambridge Road, Little Abington, Cambs. *T:* Cambridge 891303.

DAWSON, Richard Leonard Goodhugh, MB, FRCS; Plastic Surgeon; *b* 24 Aug. 1916; *s* of L. G. Dawson and Freda Hollis; *m* 1945, Betty Marie Freeman-Mathews; two *s. Educ:* Bishop's Stortford Coll., Herts; University Coll., London; University College Hospital. MRCS, LRCP 1939; MB London 1940; FRCS 1947; BS London 1948. Royal Army Medical Corps, 1941-46; service in England and Far East (4 years); POW in Japanese hands, 1942-45. Plastic Surgeon, Mt Vernon Centre for Plastic Surgery, Northwood, 1953-81. Member, British Assoc. Plastic Surgeons (President, 1974). *Publications:* Chapters in Operative Surgery, 1957; numerous contributions to Lancet, BMJ, British Journal Plastic Surgery and other journals. *Recreations:* squash, golf, gardening. *Address:* (office) 69 Harley Street, W1. *T:* 01-935 0066; (home) Tara, Colley Hill Lane, Hedgerley, Bucks. *T:* Fulmer 2697.

DAWSON, Sir Trevor; see Dawson, Sir H. H. T.

DAWSON, Air Chief Marshal Sir Walter Lloyd, KCB 1954 (CB 1945); CBE 1943; DSO 1948; *b* 6 May 1902; *s* of late W. J. Dawson, Sunderland; *m* 1927, Elizabeth Leslie (*d* 1975), *d* of late D. V. McIntyre, MA, MB, ChB; one *s* one *d*. Enlisted in RAF as boy mechanic, 1919; commissioned from Cranwell, 1922; Station Comdr St Eval, Coastal Command, 1942-43; Dir,

Anti-U-Boat Operations, 1943; Dir of Plans, 1944-46; AOC Levant, 1946-48; Commandant, School of Land/Air Warfare, Old Sarum, 1948-50; idc, 1950-51 (RAF Instructor); Asst Chief of the Air Staff (Policy), 1952-53; Deputy Chief of Staff (Plans and Operations), SHAPE, 1953-56; Inspector-General of RAF, 1956-57; Air Member for Supply and Organisation, 1958-60, retired. Chm., Handley Page, 1966-69 (Vice-Chm., 1964-66). Dir, Southern Electricity Bd, 1961-72. *Address*: Woodlands, Heathfield Avenue, Sunninghill, Berks. *Club*: Royal Air Force.

DAWSON, Wilfred; retired; Under Secretary, Director, Manpower and Management Services, Departments of the Environment and Transport, 1978-80; *b* 11 Jan. 1923; *s* of Walter and Ivy Dawson; *m* 1944, Emily Louise Mayhew; two *d*. *Educ*: Riley High Sch., Hull. Civil Service: Air Min., 1939-49; Min. of Town and Country Planning, 1949; Principal, Min. of Housing and Local Govt, 1963; Asst Sec., DoE, 1970; Under-Sec., DoE, 1974-76; Under Sec., Dept of Transport, 1976-78. *Recreations*: walking, woodworking. *Address*: Reydon Grange, Wangford, Beccles, Suffolk.

DAWSON, William John Richard Geoffrey Patrick, CMG 1980; OBE 1967; HM Diplomatic Service; Counsellor, Foreign and Commonwealth Office, since 1977; *b* 21 Sept. 1926; *m* 1956, June Eaton Dangerfield; one *s* one *d*. Served HM Forces, 1942-45; joined FO, 1951; served in British Middle East Office, Tehran, Lomé, Dar es Salaam, 1952-72; FCO, 1972-73; Nairobi, 1973-77. *Address*: c/o Foreign and Commonwealth Office, SW1.

DAWSON-DAMER, family name of **Earl of Portarlington.**

DAWSON-MORAY, Edward Bruce, CMG 1969; *b* 30 June 1909; *s* of late Alwyn Bruce Dawson-Moray and late Ada (*née* Burlton); *m* 1st, 1933, Ursula Frances (*née* Woodbridge) (marr. diss.); one *s* one *d*; 2nd Beryl Barber. *Educ*: Cranbrook Sch.; University of London (BA Hons). Housemaster, Chillon Coll., Switzerland, 1938-42. British Legation, Berne, 1942; 3rd Secretary, 1944; 3rd Secretary and Vice-Consul, Rome, 1947-48; Consul: Leopoldville, 1948-50; Detroit, 1950-51; 1st Secretary and Consul, Rangoon, 1952-54; Information Officer and Consul, Naples, 1954-56; Foreign Office, 1956-60; Consul, Casablanca, 1960-63; Chief Establishment Officer, Diplomatic Wireless Service, 1963-69; Principal, Civil Service Dept, 1969-74; retired. Pre-retirement Training, CSD, 1975-82. Senior Editor, Foreign Office List, 1957-60. *Recreations*: literature, photography, opera, travel. *Address*: 2 Pennypiece, Cleeve Road, Goring-on-Thames, Reading, Berks RG8 9BY. *T*: Goring-on-Thames 873314.

DAWTRY, Sir Alan, Kt 1974; CBE 1968 (MBE (mil.) 1945); TD 1948; Chairman: Sperry Ltd, since 1977; Sperry (Ireland) Ltd, since 1977; President, London Rent Assessment Panel, since 1979; *b* 8 April 1915; *s* of Melancthon and Kate Nicholas Dawtry, Sheffield; unmarried. *Educ*: King Edward VII Sch., Sheffield; Sheffield Univ. (LLB). Served War of 1939-45: commissioned RA; campaigns France, N Africa, Italy (MBE, despatches twice); released with rank of Lt-Col. Admitted Solicitor, 1938; Asst Solicitor, Sheffield, 1938-48; Deputy Town Clerk, Bolton, 1948-52; Deputy Town Clerk, Leicester, 1952-54; Town Clerk, Wolverhampton, 1954-56; Chief Exec. (formerly Town Clerk), Westminster, 1956-77; Hon. Sec., London Boroughs Assoc., 1965-78. Member: Metrication Bd, 1969-74; Clean Air Council, 1960-75; CBI Council; Council of Management, Architectural Heritage Fund. Pres., Soc. of Local Authority Chief Execs, 1975-76. FBIM 1975; FRSA 1978. Foreign Orders: The Star (Afghanistan); Golden Honour (Austria); Leopold II (Belgium); Rio Branco (Brazil); Merit (Chile); Legion of Honour (France); Merit (W Germany); the Phœnix (Greece); Merit (Italy); Homayoun (Iran); The Rising Sun (Japan); the Star (Jordan); African Redemption (Liberia); Oaken Crown (Luxembourg); Loyalty (Malaysia); the Right Hand (Nepal); Orange-Nassau (Netherlands); the Two Niles (Sudan); the Crown (Thailand); Zaire (Zaire). *Address*: 806 Collingwood House, Dolphin Square, SW1. *T*: 01-828 6759.

DAY, Prof. Alan Charles Lynn; Professor of Economics, London School of Economics, University of London, since 1964; *b* 25 Oct. 1924; *s* of Henry Charles Day, MBE, and Ruth Day; *m* 1962, Diana Hope Bocking (*d* 1980); no *c*. *Educ*: Chesterfield Grammar Sch.; Queens' Coll., Cambridge. Asst Lecturer, then Lecturer, LSE, 1949-54; Economic Adviser, HM Treas., 1954-56; Reader in Economics, London Univ., 1956-64. Ed., National Inst. Econ. Review, 1960-62; Econ. Correspondent, The Observer, intermittently, 1957-81. Economic Adviser on Civil Aviation, BoT, later Dept of Trade and Industry, 1968-72; Economic Adviser, Civil Aviation Authority, 1972-78. Member: Council, Consumers' Assoc., 1963-; Board, British Airports Authority, 1965-68; SE Region Econ. Planning Council, 1966-69; Home Office Cttee on the London Taxicab Trade, 1967-70; Layfield Cttee on Local Govt Finance, 1974-76; Air Transport Users' Cttee, CAA, 1978-79. British Acad. Leverhulme Vis. Prof., Graduate Inst. for International Studies, Geneva, 1971. Governor, LSE, 1971-76, 1977-79, Pro-Director, 1979-. *Publications*: The Future of Sterling, 1954; Outline of Monetary Economics, 1956; The Economics of Money, 1959; (with S. T. Beza) Wealth and Income, 1960. *Address*: 2 Regent Square, WC1. *T*: 01-278 8326. *Club*: Reform.

DAY, Bernard Maurice; Assistant Under-Secretary of State (Programmes and Budget), Ministry of Defence, since 1980; *b* 7 May 1928; *s* of M. J. Day and Mrs M. H. Day; *m* 1956, Ruth Elizabeth Stansfield; two *s* one *d*. *Educ*: Bancroft's Sch.; London School of Economics (BScEcon). Army service, commmd RA, 1946-48. British Electric Traction Fedn, 1950-51; Asst

Principal, Air Ministry, 1951; Private Sec. to Air Mem. for Supply and Organisation, 1954-56; Principal, 1956; Cabinet Secretariat, 1959-61; Asst Sec., 1965; Sec., Meteorological Office, 1965-69; Estabt Officer, Cabinet Office, 1969-72; Head of Air Staff Secretariat, MoD, 1972-74; Asst Under Sec. of State, MoD, 1974; Civilian Staff Management, 1974-76; Operational Requirements, 1976-80. *Recreation*: swimming. *Address*: Burfield, Farmleigh Grove, Burwood Park, Walton-on-Thames, Surrey KT12 5BU. *T*: Walton-on-Thames 27416. *Club*: Royal Commonwealth Society.

DAY, Derek Malcolm, CMG 1973; HM Diplomatic Service; Deputy Under-Secretary of State, since 1980 and Chief Clerk, since 1982, Foreign and Commonwealth Office; *b* 29 Nov. 1927; *s* of late Mr and Mrs Alan W. Day; *m* 1955, Sheila Nott; three *s* one *d*. *Educ*: Hurstpierpoint Coll.; St Catharine's Coll., Cambridge. Royal Artillery, 1946-48; St Catharine's Coll., 1948-51. Entered HM Foreign Service, Sept. 1951; Third Sec., British Embassy, Tel Aviv, 1953-56; Private Sec. to HM Ambassador, Rome, 1956-59; Second, then First Sec., FO, 1959-62; First Sec., British Embassy, Washington, 1962-66; First Sec., FO, 1966-67; Asst Private Sec. to Sec. of State for Foreign Affairs, 1967-68; Head of Personnel Operations Dept, FCO, 1969-72; Counsellor, British High Commn, Nicosia, 1972-75; Ambassador to Ethiopia, 1975-78; Asst Under-Sec., FCO, 1979. *Recreations*: golf, gardening, and the family. *Address*: c/o Foreign and Commonwealth Office, SW1; Etchinghill, Goudhurst, Kent. *Club*: United Oxford & Cambridge University.

DAY, Graham; *see* Day, J. G.

DAY, James Wentworth; FRSA; author, journalist and publicist; Chairman and Managing Director of News Publicity Ltd; *b* Marsh House, Exning, Suffolk, 21 April 1899; *s* of J. T. Wentworth Day, Lacies Court, Abingdon, Berks, and Martha Ethel Staples of Landwade Hall, Exning and Wicken; *m* 1943, Marion Edith, *d* of late Hamish McLean, Mount Hutt Estates, S Island, NZ, and of Mrs Hamish McLean, Christchurch, NZ; one *d*. *Educ*: Newton Coll.; Cambridge (extra mural; English under Prof. Sir Arthur Quiller-Couch). Served European War, 1917-18; Daily Express, Editorial Manager and personal assistant to Lord Beaverbrook, 1923; Asst Editor Country Life, 1925; acting Editor of the Field, 1930-31; Dramatic Critic, Sunday Express, 1932, and Editor of English Life; as Personal Representative of Lady Houston, 1933-34, was on exec. of Houston-Mount Everest flight, negotiated purchase of Saturday Review (editor, 1934), conducted High Tory campaign in nine bye-elections. Editor, Illustrated Sporting and Dramatic News, 1935-36-37; Propaganda Adviser to Egyptian Government, 1938-39; Publicity Adviser to Anglo-Turk Relief Cttee, 1940; War Correspondent in France for Daily Mail and BBC, 1940, and with minesweepers; Near East Correspondent to BBC, 1941. Invalided out, 1943; fought press and parly campaign against extravagance and injustices of War Agricl Exec. Cttee system, which led to release of 17,000 acres of govt controlled farms in E Anglia and setting up of Land Appeal Tribunals; drafted Amendment to Pests Act 1954, which made it criminal offence to spread myxomatosis. Dir-Gen., 1100th Anniversary Festival, Bury St Edmunds. Contested (C) Hornchurch Div. of Essex, 1950 and 1951 (reducing Labour maj. from 11,000 to 134 votes). Editor, East Anglia Life, 1962-66; Country Correspondent, Daily Mail. Member Society of Authors; Member Inst. of Journalists; owns a large part of Adventurers' Fen and a few good Old Masters, mainly of the Wentworth family. Founded Essex Wildfowlers' Assoc., 1924; Hon. Life Mem., Wildfowlers' Assoc. of GB and Ireland. *Publications*: The Lure of Speed, 1929; The Life of Sir Henry Segrave, 1930; Speed, the Life of Sir Malcolm Campbell, 1931; My Greatest Adventure (for Sir Malcolm Campbell), 1932; Kaye Don—the Man, 1934; The Modern Fowler, 1934; A Falcon on St Paul's, 1935; King George V as a Sportsman, 1935; Sporting Adventure, 1937; The Dog in Sport, 1938; Sport in Egypt, 1939; Farming Adventure, 1943; Harvest Adventure, 1945; Gamblers' Gallery, 1948; Wild Wings, 1949; Coastal Adventure, 1949; Inns of Sport, 1949; Marshland Adventure, 1950; Broadland Adventure, 1951; The New Yeomen of England, 1952; Rural Revolution, 1952; The Modern Shooter, 1953; Norwich and the Broads, in quest of the Inn, 1953; The Wisest Dogs in the World, 1954; A History of the Fens, 1954; Ghosts and Witches, 1954; They Walk the Wild Places, 1956; Poison on the Land, 1957; The Angler's Pocket Book, 1957; The Dog Lover's Pocket Book, 1957; Lady Houston, DBE—The Woman Who Won the War, 1958; A Ghost Hunter's Game Book, 1958; Newfoundland—The Fortress Isle (for Newfoundland Govt; travelled further north than any British writer); 1959; HRH Princess Marina, Duchess of Kent (The First Authentic Life Story), 1962; The Queen Mother's Family Story, 1967 (republished 1979); Portrait of the Broads, 1967; In Search of Ghosts, 1969; Rum Owd Boys, 1975. Edited Best Sporting Stories (anthology). Contributions to Great Georgians; The English Counties; 50 Great Ghost Stories, 1966; 50 Great Horror Stories, 1969; Treasures of Britain (Readers Digest), 1968; Essex Ghosts, 1974; Norwich Through the Ages, 1976; King's Lynn and Sandringham Through the Ages, 1977; James Wentworth Day Book of Essex, 1980; has broadcast and written many articles on politics, the Near East, field sports, natural history, agriculture, dogs, flying, motoring, racing, shipping, etc, in the leading newspapers and journals. *Recreations*: taking the Left Wing intelligentsia at its own valuation; shooting (especially wildfowling), riding, fishing, sailing, natural history, and old furniture. *Address*: Ingatestone, Essex. *T*: Ingatestone 3035. *Clubs*: United Oxford & Cambridge University, Press, 1900.

DAY, John King, TD; MA, BSc; Principal, Elizabeth College, Guernsey, CI, 1958-71; *b* Ipoh, Perak, FMS, 27 Oct. 1909; *s* of Harold Duncan Day, Mining Engineer, and Muriel Edith Day; *m* 1935, Mary Elizabeth Stinton, *er d* of late Tom Stinton, Headmaster of the High Sch., Newcastle-under-Lyme; three *s. Educ:* Stamford Sch.; Magdalen Coll., Oxford. Demy 1928-32. Honour School of Natural Science (Chemistry) Class 2. Assistant Master, Kendal Sch., Westmorland, 1932; Asst Master and Housemaster, Gresham's Sch., 1933-57. Served Royal Norfolk Regt (7th Bn) and Military College of Science, 1939-45. *Recreations:* walking, fishing and sketching. *Address:* Sunnyside Cottage, Hunworth Green, Melton Constable, Norfolk. *T:* Holt 3435.

DAY, (Judson) Graham; Vice-President, Shipyards & Marine Development, Dome Petroleum Ltd, Calgary, since 1981; *b* 3 May 1933; *s* of Frank Charles Day and Edythe Grace (*née* Baker); *m* 1958, Leda Ann (*née* Creighton); one *s* two *d. Educ:* Queen Elizabeth High Sch., Halifax, NS; Dalhousie Univ., Halifax, NS (LLB). Private practice of Law, Windsor, Nova Scotia, 1956-64; Canadian Pacific Ltd, Montreal and Toronto, 1964-71; Cammell Laird Shipbuilders Ltd, Birkenhead, Eng., 1971-75; Dep. Chm., Organising Cttee for British Shipbuilders and Dep. Chm. and Chief Exec. designate, British Shipbuilders, 1975-76; Prof. of Business Studies and Dir, Canadian Marine Transportation Centre, Dalhousie Univ., NS, 1977-81. Director: Misener Hldgs; Atlantic Trustco of Canada; HMW Industries. Member: Nova Scotia Barristers' Soc.; Law Soc. of Upper Canada; Canadian Bar Assoc. Pres., Canadian Inst. of Marine Engrs; ARINA. *Recreations:* reading; lakeside chalet in Canada. *Address:* Dome Petroleum Ltd, 800 6th Avenue SW, Calgary, Alberta T2P 0N1, Canada.

DAY, Lance Reginald; Keeper, Science Museum Library, since 1976; *b* 2 Nov. 1927; *s* of late Reginald and of Eileen Day; *m* 1959, Mary Ann Sheahan; one *s* two *d. Educ:* Sherrardswood Sch., Welwyn Garden City; Alleyne's Grammar Sch., Stevenage; Northern Polytechnic and University Coll., London (MSc). Res. Asst, Science Museum Library, 1951-64, Asst Keeper 1964-73; Dep. Keeper, Science Museum, Dept of Chemistry, 1973-74; Keeper, Science Museum, Dept of Communications and Electrical Engrg, 1974-76. Sec., Nat. Railway Museum Cttee, 1973-75; Hon. Sec., Newcomen Soc., 1973-. *Publications:* reviews and articles. *Recreation:* music. *Address:* 10 Russellcroft Road, Welwyn Garden City, Herts. *T:* Welwyn Garden 22387.

DAY, Lucienne, RDI 1962; in freelance practice, since 1948; Consultant, with Robin Day, to John Lewis Partnership, since 1962; *b* 1917; *d* of Felix Conradi and Dulcie Lilian Duncan-Smith; *m* 1942, Robin Day, *qv*; one *d. Educ:* Convent Notre Dame de Sion, Worthing; Croydon School of Art; Royal Coll. of Art. ARCA 1940; FSIAD 1955; Mem. Faculty of Royal Designers for Industry, 1962. Teacher, Beckenham Sch. of Art, 1942-47; began designing full-time, dress fabrics and later furnishing fabrics, carpets, wallpapers, table-linen, 1947 for Edinburgh Weavers, Heal's Fabrics, Cavendish Textiles, Tomkinsons, Wilton Royal, Thos Somerset etc, and firms in Scandinavia, USA and Germany; also china decoration for Rosenthal China, Selb, Bavaria, 1956-68; work for Barbican Art Centre, 1979; currently also designing and making silk wall-hangings (silk mosaics). Work in permanent collections: V&A; Trondheim Museum, Norway; Cranbrook Museum, Michigan, USA. Member: Rosenthal Studio-line Jury, 1960-68; Cttee, Duke of Edinburgh's Prize for Elegant Design, 1960-63; Council, RCA, 1962-67; RSA Design Bursaries Juries. First Award, Amer. Inst. of Decorators, 1950; Gold Medal, 9th Triennale di Milano, 1951; Gran Premio, 10th Triennale di Milano, 1954; Design Council Awards, 1957, 1960, 1968. *Recreations:* growing vegetables, gardening. *Address:* 49 Cheyne Walk, Chelsea, SW3. *T:* 01-352 1455.

DAY, Peter Rodney, PhD; Director, Plant Breeding Institute, Trumpington, Cambridge, since 1979; Special Professor of Botany, University of Nottingham, since 1982; *b* 27 Dec. 1928; *s* of Roland Percy Day and Florence Kate (*née* Dixon); *m* 1950, Lois Elizabeth Rhodes; two *s* one *d. Educ:* Birkbeck Coll., Univ. of London (BSc, PhD). John Innes Institute, 1946-63; Associate Prof. of Botany, Ohio State Univ., 1963-64; Chief, Dept of Genetics, Connecticut Agricl Experiment Station, 1964-79. Commonwealth Fund Fellow, 1954; John Simon Guggenheim Meml Fellow, 1973. *Publications:* Fungal Genetics (with J. R. S. Fincham), 1963, 4th edn 1979; Genetics of Host-Parasite Interaction, 1974; contrib. Genetical Research, Genetics, Heredity, Nature, Proc. Nat. Acad. Sci., Phytopathology, etc. *Recreation:* Scottish country dancing. *Address:* Plant Breeding Institute, Maris Lane, Trumpington, Cambridge CB2 2LQ. *T:* Cambridge 840411.

DAY, Sir Robin, Kt 1981; Television and Radio Journalist; *b* 24 Oct. 1923; *s* of late William and Florence Day; *m* 1965, Katherine Mary, *d* of R. I. Ainslie, CBE, DSO, QC, Perth, WA; two *s. Educ:* Bembridge, Sch.; St Edmund Hall, Oxford. Military service, 1943-47; commd RA, 1944. Oxford, 1947-51: Union debating tour of American universities, 1949; President Union, 1950; BA Hons (Jurisprudence), 1951; MA. Middle Temple: Blackstone Entrance Scholar, 1951; Harmsworth Law Scholar, 1952-53; called to Bar, 1952. British Information Services, Washington, 1953-54; free-lance broadcasting and journalism, 1954-55; BBC Talks Producer (radio), 1955; Newscaster and Parliamentary Correspondent, Independent TV News, 1955-59; Guild of TV Producers' Merit Award, Personality of the Year, 1957; columnist in News Chronicle, 1959; ITV programmes, 1955-59: Roving Report (ITN); Tell the People (ITN); Under Fire (Granada); since 1959 chm. or contributor, BBC TV current affairs programmes including: Panorama, Gallery, People to Watch, Daytime, 24 Hours, Midweek, To-night, Sunday Debate, Talk-in, Newsday, Question Time. BBC radio programmes: It's Your Line, 1970-76; Politics in the Seventies, 1973; Election Call, 1974, 1979; The World at One, 1979-. Chm., Hansard Soc., 1981- (Mem. Council, 1977-);

Mem., Phillimore Cttee on Law of Contempt, 1971-74. Trustee, Oxford Literary and Debating Union Trust. Contested (L) Hereford, 1959. Richard Dimbleby Award for factual television, 1974; Broadcasting Press Guild Award, for Question Time, 1980. *Publications:* Television: A Personal Report, 1961; The Case for Televising Parliament, 1963; Day by Day: a dose of my own hemlock, 1975. *Recreations:* reading, talking, ski-ing. *Address:* c/o BBC TV Studios, Lime Grove, W12. *Clubs:* Garrick, Athenæum.

DAY, Robin, RDI 1959; FSIAD 1948; design consultant and freelance designer; *b* 25 May 1915; *s* of Arthur Day and Mary Shersby; *m* 1942, Lucienne Conradi (see Lucienne Day); one *d. Educ:* Royal Coll. of Art (ARCA). National scholarship to RCA, 1935-39; teacher and lectr for several yrs; Design Consultant: Hille International, 1948-; John Lewis Partnership, 1962-; Barbican Arts Centre, 1968-. Commissions include: seating for Royal Festival Hall, 1951; interior design of Super VC10 and other passenger aircraft for BOAC, 1963-74. Member: Duke of Edinburgh's Cttee for Prize for Elegant Design, 1961, 1970, 1971; juries for many national and internat. indust. design competitions. Governor, London Coll. of Furniture. Many awards for design work, including: 6 Design Centre awards; Gold Medal, Triennale di Milano, 1951, and Silver Medal, 1954; Designs Medal, SIAD, 1957. *Recreations:* mountaineering, skiing. *Address:* 49 Cheyne Walk, Chelsea, SW3 5LP. *T:* 01-352 1455. *Clubs:* Alpine, Alpine Ski, Climbers'.

DAY, Stephen Peter; HM Diplomatic Service; Ambassador to Qatar, since 1981; *b* 19 Jan. 1938; *s* of Frank William and Mary Elizabeth Day; *m* 1965, Angela Doreen (*née* Waudby); one *s* two *d. Educ:* Bancroft's School; Corpus Christi Coll., Cambridge. MA. Entered HMOCS as Political Officer, Western Aden Protectorate, 1961, transf. to FO, 1965; Senior Political Officer, South Arabian Federation, 1964-67; FO, 1967-70; First Sec., Office of C-in-C, Far East, Singapore, 1970-71; First Sec. (Press), UK Mission to UN, NY, 1971-75; FCO, 1976-77; Counsellor, Beirut, 1977-78; Consul-Gen., Edmonton, 1979-81. *Recreations:* walking, family. *Address:* c/o Foreign and Commonwealth Office, SW1; 92 West End Lane, Esher, Surrey. *T:* Esher 64138.

DAYMOND, Douglas Godfrey; Civil Service Commissioner, 1975-80; *b* 23 Nov. 1917; *s* of Samuel Kevern and Minnie Daymond; *m* 1945, Laura Vivien (*née* Selley); one *s* one *d. Educ:* Saltash Grammar Sch; London Univ. LLB Hons 1947. Called to Bar, Gray's Inn, 1952. Inland Revenue, 1935; Customs and Excise, 1939; War Service with Royal Engineers in Egypt, Greece and Crete, POW 1941-45; Inland Revenue, 1947; Asst Sec., Royal Commn on Taxation, 1951-55; Sec., Tithe Redemption Commn, 1959-60; Dep. Dir, CS Selection Bd, 1970; Under-Sec., Civil Service Dept, 1973. *Recreations:* gardening, theatre, music. *Address:* 55 Salisbury Road, Farnborough, Hants GU14 7AG. *T:* Farnborough (Hants) 42517; Flat 73, Fort Picklecombe, near Millbrook, Cornwall. *T:* Plymouth 822033.

DAYSH, Prof. George Henry John, CBE 1973; MLitt Oxon; DCL; Deputy Vice-Chancellor of University of Newcastle upon Tyne and Professor of Geography in the University, 1963-66; Emeritus Professor, since Oct. 1966 (Professor of Geography, King's College, University of Durham, Newcastle upon Tyne, 1943-63; Sub Rector, King's College, 1955-63); *b* 21 May 1901; *s* of Alfred John Daysh and Margaret (*née* Campbell); *m* 1927, Sheila Guthrie (*d* 1971), *er d* of Dr A. F. A. Fairweather; one *s* one *d. Educ:* Eggars Grammar Sch.; University College, Reading; Wadham Coll., Oxford. Housemaster, Pocklington Sch., E. Yorks, 1924-27; Lecturer in Geography, Bedford Coll., University of London, 1927-29; Lecturer-in-charge, Dept of Geography, 1930-38, Reader of Geography, 1938-43, King's Coll., Newcastle upon Tyne. Seconded for special duties with Dist Comr for special area of Cumberland, 1938; Senior Research Officer, Ministry of Town and Country Planning, 1943-45. Member of Exec. of NE Development Board, 1934-39, Vice-President NE Industrial and Development Assoc.; Chairman Research Cttee of NEIDA; Secretary Commn on Ports of International Geographic Union, 1947-51; Chairman University of Durham Matriculation and Sch. Examination Board, 1953-63. Part-time Member Northern Gas Board, 1956-70. Chairman, Newcastle upon Tyne Hospital Management Cttee, 1968-71. Visiting Prof. Fouad I Univ., 1951. Chairman, Triennial Grants Cttee, University College of Sierra Leone, 1960. Consultant to Cumberland Development Council, 1966-69. Chm., Tyne Tees Television, 1968-71; Dep. Chm., Trident Television Ltd, 1970-72; Dir, Solway Chemicals Ltd. Hon. DCL (Newcastle), 1964. FRSA; FRGS (Victoria Medal 1972). *Publications:* Southampton-Points in its Development, 1928; A Survey of Industrial Facilities of the North-East Coast, 1936 (rev., 1940 and 1949); West Cumberland with Alston-a Survey of Industrial Facilities, 1938 (revised 1951); (ed) Studies in Regional Planning, 1949; (ed) Physical Land Classification of North-East England, 1950; (with J. S Symonds) West Durham, 1953; (ed) A Survey of Whitby, 1958; contribs to Geographical Journal, Geography, Economic Geography, Geographical Review, etc. *Recreations:* gardening, field sports. *Address:* 2 Dunkirk Terrace, Corbridge, Northumberland. *T:* Corbridge-on-Tyne 2154.

DEACON, Lt-Col Edmund Henry; JP; *b* 1902; *s* of late Col E. Deacon, DL, Sloe House, Halstead, Essex; *m* 1927, Betty, *d* of late Brig.-Gen. J. E. C. Livingstone-Learmonth, CMG, DSO; one *d. Educ:* Wellington; Trinity Coll., Cambridge; Master Newmarket and Thurlow Hounds, 1934-42. Joint Master East Essex Hounds, 1947-50. Commanding 15 Bn Essex Home Guard, 1952; Chairman of Governors of Felsted Sch., 1952-65. DL 1953-78, JP 1954, Essex.

Address: The Old Rectory, Oxhill, Warwick CV35 0QR. *Club:* Cavalry and Guards.

DEACON, Sir George (Edward Raven), Kt 1971; CBE 1954; FRS 1944; FRSE 1957; FRAS; FRGS; DSc; Director, National Institute of Oceanography, 1949-71; Foreign Member, Swedish Royal Academy of Sciences, 1958; *b* 21 March 1906; *m* 1940, Margaret Elsa Jeffries (*d* 1966); one *d. Educ:* City Boys' Sch., Leicester; King's Coll., London. FKC. Vis. Prof. of Chemistry of the Environment, KCL, 1974. Served on Scientific Staff of the Discovery Cttee, in England and in the Royal Research Ships William Scoresby and Discovery II, 1927-39. Governor: Bridewell Royal Hosp., 1958-; King Edward's Sch., Witley, 1958-; Charterhouse Sch., 1959-81. Royal Society's National Committees: Oceanic Research, 1959-81 (Chm.); Geodesy and Geophysics, 1949-71 (Chm., 1955-60); Internat. Geophysical Year, 1953-60; Antarctic Research, 1959-81. Pres., Royal Inst. of Navigation, 1961-64; Vice-Pres., RGS, 1965-70. Hon. Member: Royal Soc. of NZ, 1964; Marine Biol Assoc. of UK, 1975; RMetS, 1982. Hon. DSc: Liverpool, 1961; Leicester, 1970. Polar Medal, 1942; Alexander Agassiz Medal, US National Academy of Sciences, 1962; Royal Medal, Royal Soc., 1969; Founder's Medal, RGS, 1971; Scottish Geographical Medal, 1972. *Publications:* Oceanographical papers in the Discovery Reports, etc. *Address:* Flitwick House, Milford, Surrey. *T:* Godalming 5929.

DEACON ELLIOTT, Air Vice-Marshal Robert, CB 1967; OBE 1954; DFC 1941 (2 mentions); *b* 20 Nov. 1914; *m* 1948, Grace Joan Willes, Leamington Spa; two *s* one *d. Educ:* Northampton. 72 Fighter Sqdn (Dunkirk and Battle of Britain), 1939-41; HQ Fighter Comd, 1942-43; 84 Group 2 ATAF, 1944-46; Air Ministry (OR 5), 1946-48; OC Flying Wing and OC 26 APC in Cyprus, 1948-51; HQ Fighter Comd, Head of Admin. Plans, 1951-54; Army Staff Coll., on Directing Staff, 1954-56; CO, RAF Leconfield, 1956-57; CO, RAF Driffield, 1957-58; Air University USAF, Maxwell AFB, USA, 1958-61; Commandant, Officer and Aircrew Selection Centre, 1962-65; AOC, RAF Gibraltar, 1965-66; AOC, RAF Malta, and Dep. C-in-C (Air), Allied Forces Mediterranean, 1966-68, retd; Bursar, Civil Service Coll., 1969-79. *Recreations:* squash rackets, shooting, photography. *Address:* Wild Rose Cottage, Little London, Andover, Hants SP11 6JE. *T:* Andover 64563. *Club:* Royal Air Force.

DEADMAN, Ronald; Fishery Warden, Kempton Park Reservoir; Editor, Teachers' World, 1968-76; Member of the Press Council, 1969-75; *s* of Thomas Deadman and Margaret Healey; *m* 1952, Joan Evans; no *c. Educ:* Hinguar Street Sch., Shoeburyness; Oakley Coll., Cheltenham. Served RAF, 1937-45. Teaching, 1950-66; Features Editor, The Teacher, 1966-67; Editor, Everyweek, 1967-68. Leverhulme Res. Fellow, 1975-77. Watchkeeper, M/T Aro, River Blackwater, 1977-78; Fishery Bailiff, Barn Elms Reservoir, 1978. *Publications:* Enjoying English, Bk 1, 1966; Bk 2, 1968; Bk 3 (Contrasts), 1971; Bk 4 (Perception), 1972; (novels for children): The Happening, 1968; Wanderbodies, 1972; The Pretenders, 1972; (ed, short stories) The Friday Story, 1966; Words in Your Ear, vols 1 and 2, 1972; Going My Way, vols 1, 2 and 3, 1973; (with Arthur Razzell) Ways of Knowing, 1977; Grandma George, 1977; Breadwinners, 1978; Firebirds, 1979; (ed) Round the World Folk Tales, Bks 1-12, 1981; contribs to New Statesman, The Times, British Clinical Jl, Guardian, BBC, Where magazine, Education and Training. *Recreation:* brooding. *Address:* Flat 1, Dawley House, 91 Uxbridge Road, Ealing, W5. *T:* 01-840 3627. *Club:* British Legion.

DEAKIN, Maj.-Gen. Cecil Martin Fothergill, CB 1961; CBE 1956; *b* 20 Dec. 1910; *m* 1934, Evelyn, *e d* of late Sir Arthur Grant, Bt of Monymusk, Aberdeenshire; one *s* one *d. Educ:* Winchester Coll. Commissioned into Grenadier Guards, 1931. Served with Regt NW Europe, 1944-45 (despatches). Commanded: 2nd Bn Grenadier Guards, 1945-46; 1st Bn, 1947-50; 32nd Guards Bde, 1953-55; 29th Infantry Bde, 1955-57 (Suez Expedition, despatches); Brigadier, General Staff, War Office, 1957-59; Director of Military Training, 1959; GOC 56th London Div., TA, 1960; Director Territorial Army, Cadets and Home Guard, 1960-62; Commandant of the JSSC, Latimer, 1962-65. *Recreations:* numerous. *Address:* Stocks Farm House, Beenham, Berks. *Club:* Royal Yacht Squadron.
See also Sir A. B. C. Edmonstone, Bt.

DEAKIN, Sir (Frederick) William (Dampier); *see* Deakin, Sir William.

DEAKIN, Michael; Director of Programmes, TV-am, since 1982; *b* 21 Feb. 1939; *s* of Sir William Deakin, qv, and Margaret Hodson (*née* Beatson-Ball). *Educ:* Bryanston; Univ. d'Aix-Marseille; Emmanuel Coll., Cambridge (MA Hons). Founding Partner, Editions Alecto, Fine Art Publishers, 1960-64; Producer, BBC Radio Current Affairs Dept, 1964-68; Producer, then Editor, Yorkshire Television Documentary Unit, 1968-81. Productions include: Out of the Shadow into the Sun—The Eiger; Struggle for China; The Children on the Hill; Whicker's World—Way Out West; The Japanese Experience; The Good, the Bad and the Indifferent; Johnny Go Home (British Academy Award, 1976); David Frost's Global Village; The Frost Interview—The Shah; Rampton—The Secret Hospital; also many others. Founding Mem., TV-am Breakfast Television Consortium, 1980. *Publications:* Restif de la Bretonne— Les Nuits de Paris (critical edn and trans. with Nicholas Deakin), 1968; Gaetano Donizetti—a biography, 1968; (for children) Tom Grattan's War, 1970, 2nd edn 1971; The Children on the Hill, 1972, 9th edn 1982; (with John Willis) Johnny Go Home, 1976; (with Antony Thomas) The Arab Experience, 1975, 2nd edn 1976; Flame in the Desert, 1976; (with David Frost)

I Could Have Kicked Myself, 1982. *Recreations:* travel, music, books, pictures, motorcycling. *Address:* 6 Glenhurst Avenue, NW5 1PS. *Club:* British Academy of Film and Television Arts.
See also N. D. Deakin.

DEAKIN, Prof. Nicholas Dampier; Professor of Social Policy and Administration, University of Birmingham, since 1980; *b* 5 June 1936; *s* of Sir (Frederick) William Deakin, qv and Margaret Ogilvy Hodson; *m* 1961, Rose Albinia Donaldson, *d* of Baron Donaldson of Kingsbridge, qv, and Frances Annesley Donaldson, qv; one *s* two *d. Educ:* Westminster Sch.; Christ Church Coll., Oxford. BA (1st cl. Hons) 1959, MA 1963, DPhil 1972. Asst Principal, Home Office, 1959-63, Private Sec. to Minister of State, 1962-63; Asst Dir, Nuffield Foundn Survey of Race Relations in Britain, 1963-68; Res. Fellow, subseq. Lectr, Univ. of Sussex, 1968-72; Head of Social Studies, subseq. Head of Central Policy Unit, GLC, 1972-80. Mem., BAFTA. *Publications:* (ed and trans.) Memoirs of the Comte de Gramont, 1965; Colour and the British Electorate 1964, 1965; Colour, Citizenship and British Society, 1969; (with Clare Ungerson) Leaving London, 1977; contribs to other vols and learned jls. *Recreations:* reading fiction, music. *Address:* Department of Social Administration, University of Birmingham, PO Box 363, Birmingham B15 2TT; 55 Estria Road, Birmingham B15 2LG. *T:* 021-440 6251.

DEAKIN, Rt. Rev. Thomas Carlyle Joseph Robert Hamish; *see* Tewkesbury, Bishop Suffragan of.

DEAKIN, Sir William, Kt 1975; DSO 1943; MA; Warden of St Antony's College, Oxford, 1950-68, retired; Hon. Fellow, 1969; *b* 3 July 1913; *e s* of Albert Witney Deakin, Aldbury, Tring, Herts; *m* 1st, 1935, Margaret Ogilvy (marr. diss. 1940), *d* of late Sir Nicholas Beatson Bell, KCSI, KCIE; two *s*; 2nd, 1943, Livia Stela, *d* of Liviu Nasta, Bucharest. *Educ:* Westminster Sch.; Christ Church, Oxford (Hon. Student, 1979). 1st Class, Modern History, 1934; Amy Mary Preston Read Scholar, 1935. Fellow and Tutor, Wadham Coll., Oxford, 1936-49; Research Fellow, 1949; Hon. Fellow, 1961. Served War of 1939-45; with Queen's Own Oxfordshire Hussars, 1939-41; seconded to Special Operations, War Office, 1941; led first British Military Mission to Tito, May 1943. First Secretary, HM Embassy, Belgrade, 1945-46. Hon. FBA, 1980. Russian Order of Valour, 1944; Chevalier de la Légion d'Honneur, 1953; Grosse Verdienstkreuz, 1958; Yugoslav Partisan Star (1st Class), 1969. *Publications:* The Brutal Friendship, 1962; (with G. R. Storry) The Case of Richard Sorge, 1964; The Embattled Mountain, 1971. *Address:* 83330 Le Beausset, Le Castellet, Var, France. *Clubs:* White's, Brooks's.
See also M. Deakin, N. D. Deakin.

DEAKINS, Eric Petro; MP (Lab) Waltham Forest, Walthamstow, since 1974 (Walthamstow West, 1970-74); *b* 7 Oct. 1932; *er s* of late Edward Deakins and Gladys Deakins. *Educ:* Tottenham Grammar Sch.; London Sch. of Economics. BA (Hons) in History, 1953. Executive with FMC (Meat) Ltd, 1956; General Manager, Pigs Div., FMC (Meat) Ltd, 1969. Parly Under-Sec. of State, Dept of Trade, 1974-76, DHSS, 1976-79. *Publication:* A Faith to Fight For, 1964. *Recreations:* writing, cinema, squash, football. *Address:* House of Commons, SW1. *T:* 01-219 3000.

DEALTRY, Thomas Richard; Director, Gulf Region Planning, Gulf Organization for Industrial Consulting, since 1978; *b* 24 Nov. 1936; *s* of George Raymond Dealtry and Edith (*née* Gardner); *m* 1962, Pauline (*née* Sedgwick); one *s* one *d. Educ:* Cranfield Inst. of Advanced Technol. (MBA). CEng, MIMechE; MInstM. National Service Commn, 1959-61: Temp. Captain 1960. Divl Exec., Tube Investments Ltd, 1967-71; Sen. Exec., Guest, Keen & Nettlefold Gp Corporate Staff, 1971-74; Dir, Simpson-Lawrence Ltd, and Man. Dir, BUKO BV, Holland, 1974-77; Under Sec./Industrial Adviser, Scottish Econ. Planning Dept, 1977-78. *Recreations:* golf, squash. *Address:* PO Box 5114, Doha, Qatar, Arabian Gulf; 35 Aldwark, York. *Club:* The Western (Glasgow).

DEAN, Anne (Mrs Stafford Dean); *see* Howells, Anne.

DEAN, (Arthur) Paul; MP (C) Somerset North since 1964; Company Director; *b* 14 Sept. 1924; *s* of Arthur Percival Dean and Jessie Margaret Dean (*née* Gaunt); *m* 1st, 1957, Doris Ellen Webb (*d* 1979); 2nd, 1980, Peggy Parker. *Educ:* Ellesmere Coll., Shropshire; Exeter Coll., Oxford (MA, BLitt). Former President Oxford Univ. Conservative Assoc. and Oxford Carlton Club. Served War of 1939-45, Capt. Welsh Guards; ADC to Comdr 1 Corps BAOR. Farmer, 1950-56. Resident Tutor, Swinton Conservative Coll., 1957; Conservative Research Dept, 1957-64, Assistant Director from 1962; a Front Bench Spokesman on Health and Social Security, 1969-70; Parly Under-Sec. of State, DHSS, 1970-74; Member: Exec. Cttee, CPA, UK Branch, 1975-; House of Commons Services Select Cttee, 1979-; House of Commons Chairman's Panel, 1979-; Chm., Conservative Health and Social Security Cttee, 1979-. Formerly, Member Governing Body of Church in Wales. *Publications:* contributions to political pamphlets. *Recreation:* fishing. *Address:* Bowman's Batch, Knightcott, Banwell, Weston-super-Mare, Avon; House of Commons, SW1. *Clubs:* St Stephen's Constitutional; Bath and County; Keynsham Conservative.

DEAN, Barbara Florence; Headmistress, Godolphin and Latymer School, Hammersmith, since 1974; *b* 1 Sept. 1924; *d* of Albert Sidney and Helen Catherine Dean. *Educ:* North London Collegiate Sch.; Girton Coll., Cambridge (MA); London Inst. of Educn (Teachers' Dipl.). Asst History

Mistress, Roedean Sch., 1947-49; Godolphin and Latymer School: Asst History Mistress and Head of Dept, 1949-70; Deputy Headmistress, 1970-73. *Address:* 9 Stuart Avenue, Ealing, W5 3QJ. *T:* 01-992 8324.

DEAN, Brenda; Secretary, SOGAT Manchester Branch, since 1976, and Member, National Executive Council, since 1977; *b* 29 April 1943; *d* of Hugh Dean and Lillian Dean. *Educ:* St Andrews Junior Sch., Eccles; Stretford High Sch. for Girls. Admin. Sec., SOGAT, 1959-72. Member: Printing and Publishing Trng Bd, 1974-; Women's National Commn, 1975-; Supplementary Benefits Commn, 1976-80; Price Commn, 1977-79. *Recreations:* sailing, reading, relaxing, thinking! *Address:* Sheridan House, 4/8 Great George Street, Salford, Lancs M3 6EH. *T:* 061-834 4786.

DEAN, (Cecil) Roy; HM Diplomatic Service; Director, Arms Control and Disarmament Research Unit, since 1976; *b* 18 Feb. 1927; *s* of Arthur Dean and Flora Dean (*née* Clare); *m* 1954, Heather Sturtridge; three *s*. *Educ:* Watford Grammar Sch.; London Coll. of Printing and Graphic Arts (diploma). Served RAF, 1945-48, India and Pakistan; Central Office of Information, 1948-58; Second, later First Sec., Colombo, 1958-62; Vancouver, 1962-64; Lagos, 1964-68; FCO, 1968-71; Consul, Houston, 1971, Acting Consul-Gen., 1972-73; FCO, 1973-76. Mem., UN Sec.-General's expert group on disarmament instns, 1980-81. Member: RUSI, 1977; Inst. of Public Relations, 1963. Editor, Arms Control and Disarmament, 1979-. *Publications:* Peace and Disarmament, 1982; chapter in Ethics and Nuclear Deterrence, 1982; numerous research papers; contribs to learned jls. *Recreations:* crosswords (Times national champion, 1970 and 1979); humour; songwriting. *Address:* c/o Foreign and Commonwealth Office, SW1; 14 Blyth Road, Bromley, Kent. *T:* 01-460 8159. *Club:* Royal Commonwealth Society.

DEAN, (Charles) Raymond, QC 1963; **His Honour Judge Dean;** a Circuit Judge (formerly Judge of County Courts), since 1971; *b* 28 March 1923; *s* of late Joseph Irvin Gledhill Dean and late Lilian Dean (*née* Waddington); *m* 1948, Pearl Doreen (*née* Buncall); one *s* one *d*. *Educ:* Hipperholme Grammar Sch.; The Queen's Coll., Oxford (1941-42 and 1945-47). RAF Flying Duties, 1942-45 (Flt Lieut). BA (Jurisprudence) 1947, MA 1948; called to Bar, Lincoln's Inn, 1948; Deputy Chairman, West Riding QS, 1961-65; Recorder: of Rotherham, 1962-65; of Newcastle upon Tyne, 1965-70; of Kingston-upon-Hull, 1970-71. *Recreations:* fishing, motoring, reading, Rugby Union (now non-playing), golf. *Address:* Inner Court, 248A High Street, Boston Spa, Yorks. *T:* Boston Spa 844155. *Club:* Leeds.

DEAN, David Edis; Director of Library Services, British Architectural Library, Royal Institute of British Architects, since 1969; *b* 18 June 1922; *y s* of Arthur Edis Dean, CBE, MA, MLitt, and Elsie Georgina Musgrave Wood; *m* 1944, Sylvia Mummery Gray. *Educ:* Bryanston; Wadham Coll., Oxford (MA); Reading Univ. (DipEd). ALA. Served War, RAF Photographic Interpretation, 1943-46. Schoolmaster, 1950-54; Cataloguer, then Dep. Librarian, Royal Commonwealth Soc., 1954-60; Dep. Librarian, RIBA, 1960-69. FRSA. *Publications:* English Shopfronts, 1970; articles, reviews. *Recreations:* book collecting, music, birdwatching. *Address:* 74 Vanbrugh Park, Blackheath, SE3. *T:* 01-858 1430. *Club:* Architecture.

DEAN, Col Donald John, VC 1918; OBE 1961; TD; DL; JP; *b* 1897; *m* 1923, Marjorie, *d* of late W. R. Wood; one *s* one *d*. Served European War, 1914-18 (despatches, VC); War of 1939-45 (despatches). JP 1951, DL 1957, Kent. Comdr Royal Danish Order of the Dannebrog. *Address:* 1 Park Avenue, Sittingbourne, Kent ME10 1QX.

DEAN, Eric Walter, CB 1968; CBE 1958; retired; *b* 5 March 1906; *s* of late Thomas W. Dean, London; *m* 1935, Joan Mary, *d* of late L. A. Stanley, Folkestone; one *d*. *Educ:* Forest Sch.; Exeter Coll., Oxford. Called to Bar, Inner Temple, 1931. Solicitors Dept, Board of Trade, 1935-68; Asst Solicitor, 1947-61; Principal Asst Solicitor, 1961-68, retired. *Recreations:* music, horse-racing. *Address:* 31 Hove Manor, Hove Street, Hove, Sussex BN3 2DG. *T:* Brighton 721783.

DEAN, (Frederick) Harold, CB 1976; QC 1979; Chairman, Disciplinary Appeal Committee, Institute of Chartered Accountants, since 1980; *b* 5 Nov. 1908; *o c* of late Frederick Richard Dean and Alice Dean (*née* Baron), Manchester; *m* 1st, 1939, Gwendoline Mary Eayrs Williams (marr. diss., 1966; she *d* 1975); 3rd *d* of late Rev. W. Williams, Kingsley, Staffs; one *s* one *d*; 2nd, 1966, Sybil Marshall Dennis (*d* 1977), *o c* of late Col F. B. M. Chatterton, CMG, CBE; 3rd, 1978, Mary-Rose Lester, *y d* of late Comdr F. L. Merriman, RN. *Educ:* Manchester Grammar Sch.; Manchester Univ. LLB 1930; LLM 1932. Called to Bar, Middle Temple, 1933. Practised on Northern Circuit, 1934-40 and 1945-50. Served in RAFVR, 1940-45 in UK, Iraq, Egypt and E Africa (Sqdn Ldr). AJAG, 1950; DJAG: Far East, 1954-57 and 1962-65; Middle East, 1958-61; Germany, 1967-68; Vice JAG, 1968-72; Judge Advocate General, 1972-79; a Comr, Duke of York's Royal Mil. Sch., 1972-79. *Publication:* Bibliography of the History of Military and Martial Law (in composite vol., Guide to the Sources of British Military History, 1971). *Recreations:* travel, walking, music, reading. *Address:* The Old Farmhouse, Lower Street, Quainton, Aylesbury, Bucks HP22 4BL. *T:* Quainton 263. *Club:* Athenæum.

DEAN, Sir John (Norman), Kt 1957; *b* 13 Dec. 1899; *s* of late George Dean; *m* 1st, 1935, Charlotte Helen Audrey (*d* 1973), *d* of late Thomas Atkinson Walker; one *s*; 2nd, 1974, Isabel Bothwell-Thomson. *Educ:* Felsted; King's

Coll., London University. BSc London (Hons Chemistry). Flying Officer, RNAS and RAF, 1916-19. Chairman: The Telegraph Construction and Maintenance Co. Ltd, 1954-61; Submarine Cables Ltd, 1960-63; Asst to President, General Cable Corporation of New York, USA, 1964-69, retd. ARIC; FIRI; Comp. IEE. *Publications:* various, to technical and scientific bodies. *Address:* Kiln Ridge, Ide Hill, Sevenoaks, Kent TN14 6JH. *T:* Ide Hill 245.

DEAN, Joseph Jabez; MP (Lab) Leeds West, since Feb. 1974; *b* 1923. Engineer; formerly Shop Steward, AUEW. Formerly Leader, Manchester City Council. PPS to Minister of State, CSD, 1974-77; an Asst Govt Whip, 1978-79; Lab Party Pairing Whip, 1982-. *Address:* House of Commons, SW1A 0AA.

DEAN, Joseph (Jolyon); His Honour Judge Joseph Dean; a Circuit Judge, South Eastern Circuit, since 1975; *b* 26 April 1921; *s* of late Basil Dean, CBE; *m* 1962, Hon. Jenefer Mills, *yr d* of 5th Baron Hillingdon, MC, TD; one *s* two *d*. *Educ:* Elstree Sch.; Harrow Sch.; Merton Coll., Oxford (MA Classics and Law). 51st (Highland) Div., RA, 1942-45. Called to the Bar, Middle Temple, 1947; Bencher 1972. *Publication:* Hatred, Ridicule or Contempt, 1953 (paperback edns 1955 and 1964). *Recreation:* domestic maintenance. *Address:* The Hall, West Brabourne, Ashford, Kent TN25 5LZ.

See also Winton Dean.

DEAN, Michael, QC 1981; *b* 2 Feb. 1938; *s* of late Henry Ross Dean and Dorothea Alicia Dean; *m* 1967, Diane Ruth Griffiths. *Educ:* Altrincham Co. Grammar Sch.; Univ. of Nottingham (LLB First Class Hons 1959). Lectr in Law, Univ. of Manchester, 1959-62; called to the Bar, Gray's Inn, 1962 (Arden Scholar and Holker Sen. Scholarship, 1962); practice at the Bar, Northern Circuit, Manchester, 1962-65; Lectr in Law, LSE, 1965-67; practice at the Bar, London, 1968-. *Publications:* articles in various legal periodicals. *Recreations:* conversation, music, theatre, sailing. *Address:* (chambers) 7 King's Bench Walk, Temple, EC4. *T:* 01-353 3684; (home) 15 Gayton Road, Hampstead, NW3. *T:* 01-794 0389.

DEAN, Sir Patrick (Henry), GCMG 1963 (KCMG 1957; CMG 1947); Director, Taylor Woodrow, since 1969; Amex Bank, since 1976; International Adviser, American Express, since 1969; Chairman of Governing Body, Rugby School, since 1972 (Member, since 1939); Chairman, English-Speaking Union, since 1973; *b* 16 March 1909; *o s* of late Professor H. R. Dean and Irene, *d* of Charles Arthur Wilson; *m* 1947, Patricia Wallace, *y d* of late T. Frame Jackson; two *s*. *Educ:* Rugby Sch.; Gonville and Caius Coll., Cambridge. Classical Scholar, Gonville and Caius Coll., 1928; First Class Hons, Classical Tripos Part I; Law Tripos Parts 1 and 2, 1929-32; Fellow of Clare Coll., Cambridge, 1932-35; called to the Bar, 1934; Barstow Law Scholar, Inns of Court, 1934; practised at Bar, 1934-39; Asst Legal Adviser, Foreign Office, 1939-45; Head of German Political Dept, FO, 1946-50; Minister at HM Embassy, Rome, 1950-51; Senior Civilian Instructor at Imperial Defence Coll., 1952-53; Asst Under-Secretary of State, Foreign Office, 1953-56; Dep. Under-Secretary of State, Foreign Office, 1956-60; Permanent Representative of the United Kingdom to the United Nations, 1960-64; Ambassador in Washington, 1965-69. Mem., Departmental Cttee to examine operation of Section 2 of Official Secrets Act, 1971. Chm., Cambridge Petroleum Royalties, 1975-82. Hon. Fellow, Clare Coll. and Gonville and Caius Coll., Cambridge, 1965. Hon. Bencher, Lincoln's Inn, 1965. Hon. LLD Lincoln Wesleyan Univ., 1961, Chattanooga Univ., 1962, Hofstra Univ., 1964, Columbia Univ., 1965, University of South Carolina, 1967, College of William and Mary, 1968. KStJ 1971. *Publications:* various articles and notes in the Law Quarterly Review. *Recreations:* mountains, walking, shooting. *Address:* 5 Bentinck Mansions, Bentinck Street, W1. *T:* 01-935 0881. *Club:* Brooks's.

See also Baron Roskill.

DEAN, Paul; *see* Dean, A. P.

DEAN, Dr Paul, CB 1981; Director, National Physical Laboratory, since 1977 (Deputy Director, 1974-76); *b* 23 Jan. 1933; *s* of late Sydney and Rachel Dean; *m* 1961, Sheila Valerie Gamse; one *s* one *d*. *Educ:* Hackney Downs Grammar Sch.; Queen Mary Coll., Univ. of London. BSc, PhD; FInstP, FIMA. National Physical Laboratory: Sen. Sci. Officer, Math. Div., 1957; Principal Sci. Officer, 1963; Sen. Principal Sci. Officer (Individual Merit), 1967; Head of Central Computer Unit, 1967; Supt, Div. of Quantum Metrology, 1969; Under-Sec., DoI (Head of Space and Air Res. and R&D Contractors Divs), 1976-77. Part-time Head, Res. Establts Management Div., DoI, 1979-82; Exec. Dep. Chm., Council of Res. Establts, 1979-82. *Publications:* numerous papers and articles in learned jls. *Recreations:* chess, music. *Address:* National Physical Laboratory, Teddington, Mddx.

DEAN, Rt. Rev. Ralph Stanley; Rector, Church of the Redeemer, Greenville, South Carolina, since 1979; *b* London, 1913; *m* 1939, Irene Florence, *er d* of late Alfred Bezzant Wakefield. *Educ:* Roan Sch., Greenwich; Wembley County Sch.; London Coll. of Divinity, BD London 1938; ALCD 1938; MTh 1944. Deacon 1938; Priest 1939; Curate of St Mary, Islington, 1938-41; Curate-in-charge, St Luke, Watford, 1941-45; Chaplain and Tutor, London Coll. of Divinity, 1945-47, Vice-Principal, 1947-51; Principal, Emmanuel Coll., Saskatoon, Canada, 1951-56; Incumbent of Sutherland and Hon. Canon of Saskatoon, 1955-56; Bishop of Cariboo, 1957; Anglican Executive Officer, 1964-69; Archbishop of Cariboo and Metropolitan of British Columbia, 1971-73; Theological Consultant, Christ Church,

Greenville, SC, 1973-79. Episcopal Secretary, Lambeth Conference, 1968. Hon. DD: Wycliffe Coll., Toronto, 1953; Emmanuel Coll., Saskatoon, 1957; Anglican Theolog. Coll., Vancouver, 1965; Huron Coll., Ont, 1965; Hon. STD, Hartford Coll., Conn, 1966. *Publications:* In the Light of the Cross, 1961; article on Anglican Communion, Encyclopædia Britannica. *Address:* 601 Wen Wood Circle, Greenville, South Carolina 29607, USA.

DEAN, Raymond; see Dean, C. R.

DEAN, Roy; see Dean, C. R.

DEAN, Dr William John Lyon, OBE 1959; Chairman, Herring Industry Board, 1971-81 (Member, 1963-81); *b* 4 Nov. 1911; *s* of William Dean, Lossiemouth; *m* 1st, 1938, Ellen Maud Mary (*d* 1977), *d* of Charles Weatherill, CBE; two *s* one *d*; 2nd, 1979, Rachel Marian, *e d* of Humphrey and Rebecca Lloyd, Wotton-under-Edge, Glos. *Educ:* Elgin Academy; Aberdeen Univ. (MB, ChB). Served RAF, 1935-43. Gen. med. practice, 1943-66. Provost of Lossiemouth, 1949-58; Chm., Jt CC of Moray and Nairn, 1964-71; Mem. NE Regional Hosp. Bd, 1947-58. Member: Cttee for Scotland and Northern Ireland White Fish Authority, 1954-81; White Fish Authority, 1963-81. *Publication:* Safety at Sea in Fishing Vessels, 1969 (FAO/ILO/WHO). *Recreation:* fishing (lobster, salmon, trout). *Address:* 6 Ravelston Heights, Edinburgh EH4 3LX. *T:* 031-332 9172. *Club:* New (Edinburgh).

DEAN, Winton (Basil), FBA 1975; author and musical scholar; *b* Birkenhead, 18 March 1916; *e s* of late Basil Dean, CBE, and Esther, *d* of A. H. Van Gruisen; *m* 1939, Hon. Thalia Mary Shaw, 2nd *d* of 2nd Baron Craigmyle; one *s* one adopted *d* (and two *d* decd). *Educ:* Harrow; King's Coll., Cambridge (MA). Translated libretto of Weber's opera Abu Hassan (Arts Theatre, Cambridge) 1938. Served War of 1939-45: in Admiralty (Naval Intelligence Div.), 1944-45. Member: Music Panel, Arts Council, 1957-60, Cttee of Handel Opera Society (London), 1955-60; Council, Royal Musical Assoc., 1965-(Vice-Pres., 1970-). Ernest Bloch Prof. of Music, 1965-66, Regent's Lectr, 1977, Universiy of California (Berkeley); Matthew Vassar Lectr, Vassar Coll., Poughkeepsie, NY, 1979. Member: Management Cttee, Halle Handel Soc., 1979-; Kuratorium, Göttingen Handel Fest., 1981-. Ed, with Sarah Fuller, Handel's opera Julius Caesar (Barber Inst. of Fine Arts, Birmingham), performed 1977. Hon. RAM 1971. *Publications:* The Frogs of Aristophanes (trans. of choruses to music by Walter Leigh), 1937; Bizet (Master Musicians), 1948 (3rd rev. edn, 1975); Carmen, 1949; Introduction to the Music of Bizet, 1950; Franck, 1950; Hambledon v Feathercombe, the Story of a Village Cricket Match, 1951; Handel's Dramatic Oratorios and Masques, 1959; Shakespeare and Opera (Shakespeare in Music), 1964; Georges Bizet, His Life and Work, 1965; Handel and the Opera Seria, 1969; Beethoven and Opera (in The Beethoven Companion), 1971; ed, Handel, Three Ornamented Arias, 1976; (ed) E. J. Dent, The Rise of Romantic Opera, 1976; contributed to Grove's Dictionary of Music and Musicians (5th and 6th edns), New Oxford History of Music and to musical periodicals and learned journals. *Recreations:* cricket, shooting; naval history. *Address:* Hambledon Hurst, Godalming, Surrey. *T:* Wormley 2644.
See also J. J. Dean.

DEANE, family name of Baron Muskerry.

DEANE, Dr Basil; Music Director, Arts Council, since 1980; *b* 27 May 1928; *s* of Canon Richard A. Deane and Lorna Deane; *m* 1955, Norma Greig; two *s*. *Educ:* Armagh Royal School; The Queen's Univ., Belfast (BA, BMus, PhD). Lecturer in Music, Glasgow Univ., 1953-59; Senior Lectr, Melbourne Univ., 1959-65; Lectr, Nottingham Univ., 1966-68; Prof., Sheffield Univ., 1968-74; Prof. of Music, Manchester Univ., 1975-80. Member of Arts Council, 1977-79 (Chairman, Music Advisory Panel, 1977-79); Chairman of Music Board, Council for Nat. Academic Awards, 1978-80. Hon. FRNCM. *Publications:* Albert Roussel, 1962; Cherubini, 1965; Hoddinott, 1979; contribs to periodicals. *Address:* c/o The Arts Council, 105 Piccadilly, W1V 0AU.

DEANE, Phyllis Mary, FBA 1980; Professor of Economic History, University of Cambridge, since 1981; Fellow of Newnham College since 1961; *b* 13 Oct. 1918; *d* of John Edward Deane and Elizabeth Jane Brooks; single. *Educ:* Chatham County Sch.; Hutcheson's Girls' Grammar Sch., Glasgow; Univ. of Glasgow. MA Hons Econ. Science Glasgow 1940; MA Cantab; FRHistS. Carnegie Research Scholar, 1940-41; Research Officer, Nat. Inst. of Econ. and Social Research, 1941-45; Colonial Research Officer, 1946-48; Research Officer: HM Colonial Office, 1948-49; Cambridge University: Dept of Applied Econs, 1950-61; Lectr, Faculty of Econs and Politics, 1961-71; Reader in Economic History, 1971-81. Vis. Prof., Univ. of Pittsburgh, 1969. Editor, Economic Jl, 1968-75. Pres., Royal Economic Soc., 1980-. *Publications:* (with Julian Huxley) The Future of the Colonies, 1945; The Measurement of Colonial National Incomes, 1948; Colonial Social Accounting, 1953; (with W. A. Cole) British Economic Growth 1688-1959, 1962; The First Industrial Revolution, 1965; The Evolution of Economic Ideas, 1978; papers and reviews in econ. jls. *Recreations:* walking, gardening. *Address:* 4 Stukeley Close, Cambridge CB3 9LT.

DEANE-DRUMMOND, Maj.-Gen. Anthony John, CB 1970; DSO 1960; MC 1942 and Bar, 1945; *b* 23 June 1917; *s* of late Col J. D. Deane-Drummond, DSO, OBE, MC; *m* 1944, Mary Evangeline Boyd; four *d*. *Educ:* Marlborough Coll.; RMA, Woolwich. Commissioned Royal Signals, 1937. War Service in Europe and N Africa; POW, Italy, 1941 (escaped, 1942); Staff Coll., 1945; Bde Major, 3rd Parachute Bde, 1946-47; Instructor, Sandhurst, 1949-51 and Staff Coll., 1952-55; CO, 22 Special Air Service Regt, 1957-60; Bde Comdr, 44 Parachute Bde, 1961-63; Asst Comdt, RMA, Sandhurst, 1963-66; GOC 3rd Division, 1966-68; ACDS (Operations), 1968-70, retired 1971. Col Comdt, Royal Corps of Signals, 1966-71. Director: Paper and Paper Products Industry Trng Bd, 1971-79; Wood Burning Centre, 1980-. British Gliding Champion, 1957; Pilot, British Gliding Team, 1958, 1960, 1963, 1965. *Publications:* Return Ticket, 1951; Riot Control, 1975. *Recreations:* conservation and saving energy, carpentry and carving, shooting. *Address:* c/o Williams & Glyn's Bank Ltd, Lombard Street, EC3. *Club:* Special Forces.

DEANS, Rodger William, CB 1977; Senior Chairman, Supplementary Benefit Appeal Tribunals in Scotland, since 1982; *b* 21 Dec. 1917; *s* of Andrew and Elizabeth Deans, Perth; *m* 1943, Joan Radley; one *s* one *d*. *Educ:* Perth Academy; Edinburgh Univ. Qual. Solicitor in Scotland, 1939. Served in RA and REME, 1939-46 (Major); Mil. Prosecutor, Palestine, 1945-46; Procurator Fiscal Depute, Edinburgh, 1946-47; entered Office of Solicitor to Sec. of State for Scotland, 1947; Scottish Office: Legal Asst, 1947-50; Sen. Legal Asst, 1951-62; Asst Solicitor, 1962-71; Solicitor to Secretary of State for Scotland and Solicitor in Scotland to HM Treasury, 1971-80. Consultant Editor, Green & Son, Edinburgh, 1981-82. *Recreations:* mountaineering, curling, golfing, etc. *Address:* 25 Grange Road, Edinburgh EH9 1UQ. *T:* 031-667 1893. *Clubs:* Royal Commonwealth Society; Scottish Arts (Edinburgh).

DEAR, Geoffrey James, QPM 1982; Assistant Commissioner, Metropolitan Police, since 1981 (Deputy Assistant Commissioner, 1980-81); *b* 20 Sept. 1937; *er s* of Cecil William Dear and Violet Mildred (*née* Mackney); *m* 1958, Judith Ann Stocker; one *s* two *d*. *Educ:* Fletton Grammar Sch., Hunts; University Coll., London (LLB). Joined Peterborough Combined Police after cadet service; Constable and Sgt, 1956-65; 1st Special Course, Staff Coll., Bramshill, 1962-63 (Distinction); Inspector, Mid-Anglia (now Cambridgeshire) Constab., 1965; Bramshill Scholarship, London Univ., 1965-68; Chief Inspector, 1969; Supt, 1970; i/c Cambridge City, 1970-72; 8th Sen. Comd Course, 1971; Asst Chief Constable (Ops), Notts (City and County), 1972-80; seconded as Dir of Comd Training, Bramshill, 1975-77; Asst Comr, D Dept (incl. Personnel/Training), Met. Police, 1981-. Member: Govt Adv. Cttee on Alcoholism, 1975-78; Council, RUSI, 1982- (Mem. Cttee, 1976-). Lecture tour of Eastern USA univs, 1978; visited Memphis, Tenn, USA to advise on reorganisation of Police Dept, 1979. SBStJ 1982. Queen's Commendation for Brave Conduct, 1979. *Publications:* (contrib.) The Police and the Community, 1975; articles in Police Jl and other pubns. *Recreations:* field sports, Rugby football (Chm., Met. Police RFC), fell-walking, reading, gardening, music. *Address:* New Scotland Yard, SW1H 0BG. *T:* 01-230 3228. *Club:* Naval and Military.

DEARE, Ronald Frank Robert; Head of Central and Southern Africa Department, Overseas Development Administration, Foreign and Commonwealth Office, since 1981; *b* 9 Oct. 1927; *s* of late Albert and Lilian Deare; *m* 1952, Iris Mann; one *s*. *Educ:* Wellington Sch., Somerset. RAF Service, 1945-48. CO 1948; Second Sec., UK Commn, Singapore, 1959; CO, 1962; Dept of Technical Cooperation, 1963; Principal, Min. of Overseas Develt, 1965; Private Sec. to Minister of Overseas Develt, 1971; Asst Sec., 1973; Counsellor (Overseas Develt), Washington, and Alternate Exec. Dir, World Bank, 1976-79; Head of W Indian and Atlantic Dept, FCO, 1980-81. *Recreations:* reading, gardening. *Address:* 10 Fairford Close, Haywards Heath, West Sussex RH16 3EF. *T:* Haywards Heath 450590. *Club:* Royal Commonwealth Society.

DEARING, Ronald Ernest, CB 1979; Chairman, Post Office Corporation, since 1981; *b* 27 July 1930; *s* of E. H. A. Dearing and M. T. Dearing (*née* Hoyle); *m* 1954, Margaret Patricia Riley; two *d*. *Educ:* Doncaster Grammar Sch.; Hull Univ. (BScEcon); London Business Sch. (Sloan Fellow). Min. of Labour and Nat. Service, 1946-49; Min. of Power, 1949-62; HM Treasury, 1962-64; Min. of Power, Min. of Technology, DTI, 1965-72; Regional Dir, N Region, DTI, 1972-74, and Under-Sec., DTI later Dept of Industry, 1972-76; Dep. Sec. on nationalised industry matters, Dept of Industry, 1976-80; Dep. Chm., Post Office, 1980-81. *Recreations:* gardening, Do it Yourself. *Address:* Postal Headquarters Building, St Martin's-le-Grand, EC1A 1PG.

DEARNLEY, Christopher Hugh, MA (Oxon), BMus, FRCO; Organist of St Paul's Cathedral since 1968; *b* 11 Feb. 1930; 3rd *s* of Rev. Charles Dearnley; *m* 1957, Bridget (*née* Wateridge); three *s* one *d*. *Educ:* Cranleigh Sch., Surrey; Worcester Coll., Oxford. Organ Scholar, Worcester Coll., Oxford, 1948-52. Asst Organist, Salisbury Cathedral, and Music Master, the Cathedral Sch., Salisbury, 1954-57; Organist and Master of the Choristers, Salisbury Cathedral, 1957-67. Pres., Incorporated Assoc. of Organists, 1968-70; Chm., Friends of Cathedral Music, 1971-. *Publications:* The Treasury of English Church Music, Vol. III, 1965; English Church Music 1650-1750, 1970. *Recreations:* sketching, bicycling, gardening. *Address:* 8B Amen Court, EC4.

DEAS, (James) Stewart, MA, BMus, Hon. FTCL; James Rossiter Hoyle Professor of Music in the University of Sheffield, 1948-68, Emeritus Professor, since 1969; Dean of the Faculty of Arts, University of Sheffield, 1955-58; *b* 19 June 1903; *e s* of John Mackenzie Deas, Asst Keeper HM General Register

House, Edinburgh and Elizabeth Bryce Cooper; *m* 1936, Hilda Jamieson; one *s* two *d*. *Educ:* George Watson's Coll.; Edinburgh Univ. MA 1924, BMus 1929, Bucher Scholar, 1926-30, in Berlin and Basle. Studied with Sir Donald Tovey and Felix Weingartner. Conductor Edinburgh Opera Co., 1931-33; music critic, Glasgow Evening Times, 1934-35; Director of South African Coll. of Music and Prof. of Music, University of Cape Town, 1935-38; war service Foreign Office and BBC (Caversham); music critic, The Scotsman, London, 1939-44, Edinburgh (Editorial Staff), 1944-48; Conductor Edinburgh Chamber Orchestra, 1946-48; Member BBC Scottish Music Advisory Cttee, 1947-48; Member Council, Programme Cttee, Edinburgh International Festival, 1946-48; has been Guest Conductor of various orchestras including Hallé, London Symphony, Royal Philharmonic, BBC Scottish, Cape Town Municipal and Hovingham Festival. Conductor, Sheffield Chamber Orchestra, 1951-68; Chairman, Sheffield Bach Society, 1959-63. Contributor, weekly music page, Country Life, 1966-73. Hon. Music Adviser, Southern Orchestral Concert Soc., 1979-. *Publications:* In Defence of Hanslick, 1940, 2nd edn 1973; Or Something, 1941; contrib. Felix Weingartner, 1976; articles in Music and Letters and other periodicals; occasional contribs to Country Life and Supplement of Oxford English Dictionary. *Address:* 1 The Slade, Froxfield, near Petersfield, Hants. *T:* Hawkley 346. *Clubs:* Savile, Arts.

DEAVE, John James; barrister-at-law; a Recorder of the Crown Court, since 1980; *b* 1 April 1928; *s* of Charles John Deave and Gertrude Debrit Deave; *m* 1958, Gillian Mary, *d* of Adm. Sir Manley Power, *qv*; one *s* one *d*. *Educ:* Charterhouse; Pembroke Coll., Oxford (MA). Served RA, 2nd Lieut, 1946-48; Pembroke Coll., 1948-51; called to the Bar, Gray's Inn, 1952; in practice at Nottingham, 1957-. *Recreations:* history, gardening. *Address:* (chambers) 24 The Ropewalk, Nottingham. *T:* Nottingham 42581. *Club:* Nottinghamshire United Services.

DEAVIN, Stanley Gwynne, CBE 1971 (OBE 1958); FCA; Chartered Accountant; Chairman, North Eastern Gas Board, 1966-71, retired (Dep. Chairman, 1961-66); *b* 8 Aug. 1905; *s* of Percy John Deavin and Annie (*née* Crayton); *m* 1934, Louise Faviell (*d* 1982); one *s* one *d*. *Educ:* Hymer's Coll., Hull. Firm of Chartered Accountants, 1921-33; Secretary and Accountant, Preston Gas Co., 1933-49; North Western Gas Board: Secretary, 1949-61; Member Board, 1960-61. OStJ. *Recreations:* cricket, Rugby football, theatre. *Address:* 50 Hookstone Drive, Harrogate, North Yorks. *T:* Harrogate 884301. *Clubs:* Royal Automobile; Yorks County Cricket.

DeBAKEY, Prof. Michael Ellis, MD, MS; Chancellor, Baylor College of Medicine, since 1979 (Professor of Surgery and Chairman of Department of Surgery since 1948, President, 1969-79, Chief Executive Officer, 1968-69, Baylor University College of Medicine; Vice-President for Medical Affairs, Baylor University, 1968-69); Surgeon-in-Chief, Ben Taub General Hospital, Houston, Texas; Director, National Heart and Blood Vessel Research and Demonstration Center; Consultant in Surgery to various Hospitals etc., in Texas, and to Walter Reed Army Hospital, Washington, DC; *b* 7 Sept. 1908; *s* of Shaker Morris and Raheeja Zerba DeBakey; *m* 1936, Diana Cooper (*d* 1972); four *s*. *Educ:* Tulane Univ., New Orleans, La, USA (Distinguished Alumnus of Year, 1974). Residency in New Orleans, Strasbourg, and Heidelberg, 1933-36; Instructor, Dept of Surgery, Tulane Univ., 1937-40; Asst Prof. of Surgery, 1940-46; Associate Prof. of Surgery, 1946-48. Colonel Army of US (Reserve). In Office of Surgeon-General, 1942-46, latterly Director Surgical Consultant Div. (Meritorious Civilian Service Medal, 1970). Chairman, President's Commission on Heart Disease, Cancer and Stroke, 1964; US Chm., Task for Mechanical Circulatory Assistance, Jt US-USSR Cttee, 1974; Dir, Cardiovascular Res. and Trng Center, Methodist Hosp. (Houston), 1968-75; has served on governmental and university cttees, etc., concerned with public health, research and medical education. Mem. Adv. Editorial Bds: Coeur, 1969-; Biomedical Materials and Artificial Organs, 1971-. Member and Hon. Member of medical societies, including: American Assoc. for Thoracic Surgery (Pres. 1959); Hon. Fellow, RCS, 1974; International Cardiovascular Society (Pres. 1959); BMA (Hon. Foreign Corresp. Member 1966); Royal Society Med., London; Acad. of Medical Sciences, USSR; US—China Physicians Friendship Assoc., 1974. Has received numerous awards from American and foreign medical institutions, and also honorary doctorates; Presidential Medal of Freedom with Distinction; Hektoen Gold Medal, Amer. Med. Assoc., 1970; Merit Order of the Republic, 1st class (Egypt), 1980; The Independence of Jordan Medal, 1st class, 1980; Sovereign Order of the Knights of the Hospital of St John (Denmark), 1980. *Publications:* The Blood Bank and the Technique and Therapeutics of Transfusions, 1942; (with B. M. Cohen) Buerger's Disease, 1962; A Surgeon's Diary of a Visit to China, 1974; The Living Heart, 1977; contributions to standard textbooks of medicine and surgery, Current Therapy, and many symposia; Editor, Year Book of General Surgery, etc.; numerous articles in medical journals. *Recreations:* hunting, music. *Address:* Baylor College of Medicine, 1200 Moursund Avenue, Houston, Texas 77030, USA. *T:* 790-9353; 5323 Cherokee, Houston, Texas 77005, USA. *Clubs:* Cosmos, University Federal (Washington, DC); River Oaks Country (Houston, Texas).

de BASTO, Hon. Gerald Arthur; Hon. Mr Justice de Basto; Judge of the High Court of Hong Kong, since 1982; *b* 31 Dec. 1924; *s* of Bernard and Lucie Marie de Basto; *m* 1961, Diana, *d* of Dr Frederick Osborne Busby Wilkinson; two *s*. *Educ:* Riverview Coll., Sydney, Australia; Univ. of Sydney (LLB). Called to the Bar: Supreme Court of New South Wales and High Court of Australia, 1952; Lincoln's Inn, 1955; called to the Hong Kong Bar, 1957;

Chairman, Hong Kong Bar, 1968-70, 1973; QC 1968; Judge of the District Court of Hong Kong, 1973. *Recreations:* travel, reading. *Address:* The High Court of Justice, Supreme Court Building, Hong Kong. *Clubs:* Carlton; Hong Kong, Shek O Country, Royal Hong Kong Jockey (Hong Kong).

de BEER, Esmond Samuel, CBE 1969; FBA 1965; FSA, FRSL, FRHistSoc; historical scholar, specialising in seventeenth-century English history; engaged in editing John Locke correspondence; *b* 15 Sept. 1895; *s* of I. S. de Beer and Emily, *d* of Bendix Hallenstein, Dunedin, NZ. *Educ:* Mill Hill Sch.; New Coll., Oxford (MA); University College, London (MA). Studied under late Sir Charles Firth. A Trustee, National Portrait Gallery, 1959-67. Independent Member, Reviewing Cttee on Export of Works of Art, 1965-70. Fellow University College, London, 1967. Hon. Fellow: New Coll., Oxford; Warburg Inst.; Hon. DLitt (Durham, Oxford); Hon. LittD (Otago). Hon. Vice-Pres., the Historical Association; Pres., Hakluyt Society, 1972-78 (Hon. Vice-Pres., 1966); Vice-Pres., Cromwell Assoc., 1980. *Publications:* first complete edition of Diary of John Evelyn, 1955; (ed) The Correspondence of John Locke, vols I-VII, 1976-82; articles and reviews in learned periodicals, etc. *Address:* 31 Brompton Square, SW3 2AE. *T:* 01-584 5687. *Club:* Athenæum.

DEBENHAM, Sir Gilbert Ridley, 3rd Bt, *cr* 1931; *b* 28 June 1906; 2nd *s* of Sir Ernest Ridley Debenham, 1st Bt, JP; *S* brother, Sir Piers Debenham, 2nd Bt, 1964; *m* 1935, Violet Mary, *e d* of late His Honour Judge (George Herbert) Higgins; three *s* one *d*. *Educ:* Eton; Trinity Coll., Cambridge. *Heir:* *s* George Andrew Debenham [*b* 10 April 1938; *m* 1969, Penelope Jane, *d* of John David Armishaw Carter; one *s* one *d*]. *Address:* Tonerspuddle Farm, Dorchester, Dorset.

DEBENHAM TAYLOR, John, CMG 1967; OBE 1959; TD 1967; HM Diplomatic Service, retired; *b* 25 April 1920; *s* of John Francis Taylor and Harriett Beatrice (*née* Williams); *m* 1966, Gillian May James; one *d*. *Educ:* Aldenham School. Eastern Counties Farmers Assoc. Ltd, Ipswich and Great Yarmouth, 1936-39. Commd in RA (TA), Feb. 1939; served War of 1939-46 in Finland, Middle East, UK and SE Asia (despatches, 1946). Foreign Office, 1946; Control Commn for Germany, 1947-49; 2nd Sec., Bangkok, 1950; Actg Consul, Songkhla, 1951-52; Vice-Consul, Hanoi, 1952-53; FO, 1953-54; 1st Sec., Bangkok, 1954-56; FO, 1956-58; Singapore, 1958-59; FO, 1960-64; Counsellor, 1964; Counsellor: Kuala Lumpur, 1964-66; FCO (formerly FO), 1966-69; Washington, 1969-72; Paris, 1972-73; FCO, 1973-77. *Recreations:* walking, reading, history. *Address:* Lloyds Bank, Butler Place, SW1. *Club:* Naval and Military.

de BOER, Anthony Peter, CBE 1982; Chairman: Anvil Petroleum Ltd (formerly Attock Oil Co.), since 1974; Tomatin Distillers Co. Ltd, since 1978; Steel Brothers Holdings, since 1980 (Director, since 1971); Channel Tunnel Developments (1981), since 1981; Director: Tarmac Ltd, since 1971; Chloride Group, since 1976; Burmah Oil Co. Ltd, since 1978; National Bus Co., since 1969; Member, Policy Committee, Price Waterhouse and Co., since 1979; Chairman: Keep Britain Tidy Group, 1969-79; British Road Federation, since 1972; *b* 22 June 1918; *s* of Goffe de Boer and Irene Kathleen (*née* Grist); *m* 1942, Pamela Agnes Norah Bullock; one *s*. *Educ:* Westminster School. Served War of 1939-45: RE (AA), 1939-40; Indian Army, 6th Gurkha Rifles, 1940-43; RIASC, 1944-46; Major 1944. Joined Royal Dutch/Shell Gp, 1937: served in China, Sudan, Ethiopia, Egypt, Palestine, 1946-58; Area Co-ordinator, Africa and Middle East, 1959-63; Chm., Shell Trinidad, 1963-64; Man. Dir, Marketing, Shell Mex & BP, 1964-67. Mem. Bd, British Travel Assoc., 1965-67; Dep. Chm., Wm Cory & Son, 1968-71; Dep. Chm., Associated Heat Services Ltd, 1969-76; Director: British Transport Advertising, 1973-; Internat. Road Fedn, 1974-; Mem. Council, CBI, 1980-; Mem. Council, Sussex Univ., 1969-; Chm., Indep. Schools Careers Org; Pres., Fuel Luncheon Club, 1967-69; Dir, Brighton and Hove Albion Football Club, 1969-72. Freeman, City of London; Liveryman, Coach Makers' and Coach Harness Makers' Co. FBIM 1970 (Mem. Council 1974). *Recreations:* football, racing, theatre. *Address:* Halletts Barn, Ditchling Common, Hassocks, Sussex. *T:* Hassocks 2442. *Clubs:* Garrick, Oriental.

de BONO, Dr Edward Francis Charles Publius; Lecturer in Medicine, Department of Medicine, University of Cambridge, since 1976; Director of The Cognitive Research Trust, Cambridge, since 1971; *b* 19 May 1933; *s* of late Prof. Joseph de Bono, CBE and of Josephine de Bono; *m* 1971, Josephine Hall-White; two *s*. *Educ:* St Edward's Coll., Malta; Royal Univ. of Malta; Christ Church, Oxford (Rhodes Scholar). BSc, MD Malta; DPhil Oxon; PhD Cantab. Research Asst, Dept of Regius Prof. of Medicine, Univ. of Oxford, 1958-60; Jun. Lectr in Med., Oxford, 1960-61; Asst Dir of Res., Dept of Investigative Medicine, Cambridge Univ., 1963-76. Research Associate: also Hon. Registrar, St Thomas' Hosp. Med. Sch., Univ. of London; Harvard Med. Sch., and Hon. Consultant, Boston City Hosp., 1965-66. TV series: The Greatest Thinkers, 1981; de Bono's Thinking Course, 1982. *Publications:* The Use of Lateral Thinking, 1967; The Five-Day Course in Thinking, 1968; The Mechanism of Mind; Lateral Thinking: a textbook of creativity, 1970; The Dog Exercising Machine, 1970; Technology Today, 1971; Practical Thinking, 1971; Lateral Thinking for Management, 1971; Beyond Yes and No, 1972; Children Solve Problems, 1972; Eureka!: an illustrated history of inventions from the wheel to the computer, 1974; Teaching Thinking, 1976; The Greatest Thinkers, 1976; Wordpower, 1977; The Happiness Purpose, 1977; The Case of the Disappearing Elephant, 1977; Opportunities: a handbook of business opportunity search, 1978; Future Positive, 1979; Atlas of Management Thinking, 1981; de Bono's Thinking Course, 1982; contribs to Nature, Lancet, Clinical Science, Amer. Jl of Physiology, etc. *Recreations:* polo, travel, toys, thinking. *Address:* Cranmer Hall, Fakenham, Norfolk. *Club:* Athenæum.

DEBRÉ, Michel Jean-Pierre; Deputy from La Réunion, French National Assembly, since 1963, re-elected 1967, 1968, 1973, 1978, 1981; *b* 15 Jan. 1912; *s* of late Prof. Robert Debré and Dr Jeanne Debré (*née* Debat-Ponsan); *m* 1936, Anne-Marie Lemaresquier; four *s*. *Educ:* Lycée Louis-le-Grand; Faculté de Droit de Paris (LLD); École Libre des Sciences Politiques; Cavalry Sch., Saumur. Auditeur, Conseil d'Etat, 1934; French Army, 1939-44; Commissaire de la République, Angers region, 1944-45; Saar Economic Mission, 1947; Secretary-General for German and Austrian Affairs, 1948. Senator from Indre et Loire, 1948, re-elected 1955; Minister of Justice, 1958-59; Prime Minister, 1959-62; Minister of Economic Affairs and Finances, 1966-68; Minister for Foreign Affairs, 1968-69; Minister for National Defence, 1969-73. Member, European Parliament, 1979-80. Mem. from Amboise, Conseil Général of Indre-et-Loire, 1951-70, 1976-. Member, Rassemblement pour la République. Officer Légion d'Honneur, Croix de Guerre, Rosette of Résistance, Free French Medal, Medal of Escaped Prisoners. *Publications:* Refaire la France 1944; Demain la Paix, 1945; La Mort de l'Etat Républicain, 1948; La République et son Pouvoir, 1950; La République et ses Problèmes, 1951; Ces Princes qui nous Gouvernent, 1957; Au Service de la Nation, 1963; Jeunesse, quelle France te faut-il?, 1965; Une certaine idée de la France, 1972; Français, choisissons l'espoir, 1979. *Recreation:* equitation. *Address:* 20 rue Jacob, 75006 Paris, France.

de BROGLIE, 7th Duc; Louis Victor de Broglie; Member of the Institut de France, Académie Française since 1944, Académie des Sciences since 1933; Professor, Faculté des Sciences, Paris, since 1932; Foreign Member Royal Society (London) since 1953; *b* Dieppe, 15 Aug. 1892; *s* of Victor, Duc de Broglie; *S* brother, Duc Maurice, 1960; unmarried. *Educ:* Lycée Janson de Sailly, Paris. Licencié ès Lettres, 1910; Licencié ès Sciences, 1913; served Radio-télégraphie Militaire, 1914-19; Docteur ès Sciences, 1924; Maître de Conférences, Faculté des Sciences, Paris, 1928. Permanent Sec., Académie des Sciences, 1942-75. Nobel Prize for Physics, 1929. *Publications:* Thèse de doctorat sur la théorie des Quanta, 1924; nombreux mémoires, articles, livres sur la physique, en particulier sur la théorie de Quanta et la mécanique ondulatoire et sur la philosophie des sciences. *Address:* 94 Perronet, 92 Neuilly-sur-Seine, France. *T:* Maillot 76.09.

de BROKE; *see* Willoughby de Broke.

de BRUYNE, Dirk, Commander, Order of Orange Nassau, 1982; Knight, Order of Netherlands Lion, 1976; Director, Royal Dutch Petroleum Co., The Hague, 1982 (President, 1977-82; Managing Director, 1974-77); Chairman, Committee of Managing Directors, Royal Dutch/Shell Group of Companies, 1979-82; *b* Rotterdam, Netherlands, 1 Sept. 1920; *s* of Dirk E. de Bruyne and Maria van Alphen, Rotterdam; *m* 1945,Geertje Straub; one *s* one *d*. *Educ:* Erasmus Univ., Rotterdam (Grad. Econ.). Joined Royal Dutch/Shell Gp of Companies, 1945: served in: The Hague, 1945-55; Indonesia, 1955-58; London, 1958-60 (Dep. Gp Treasurer); The Hague, 1960-62 (Finance Manager); Italy, 1962-65 (Exec. Vice-Pres., Shell Italiana); London, 1965-68 (Regional Co-ordinator: Oil, Africa); Germany, 1968-70 (Pres., Deutsche Shell); Dir of Finance, Shell Petroleum Co. Ltd, 1970; Man. Dir, Royal Dutch/Shell Gp of Cos, 1971-79; Director: Shell Transport & Trading Co. Ltd, 1971-74; Shell Canada Ltd, 1977-; Chm., Shell Oil Co., USA, 1977-82. *Recreations:* swimming, reading. *Address:* Shell Centre, SE1 7NA. *T:* 01-934 3868; 10 Kingston House, Princes Gate, SW7; De Schouwenburgh, Stoeplaan 9, Wassenaar, Netherlands. *Clubs:* Dutch (London); De Witte (The Hague).

de BRUYNE, Dr Norman Adrian, FRS 1967; Chairman, Techne Inc., since 1973 (President, 1967-73); *b* 8 Nov. 1904; *s* of Pieter Adriaan de Bruyne and Maud de Bruyne (*née* Mattock); *m* 1940, Elma Lilian Marsh; one *s* one *d*. *Educ:* Lancing Coll.; Trinity Coll., Cambridge. MA 1930, PhD 1930. Fellow of Trinity Coll., Cambridge, 1928-44. Managing Director: Aero Research Ltd, 1934-48; Ciba (ARL) Ltd, 1948-60; Techne (Cambridge) Ltd, 1964-67. Dir, Eastern Electricity Bd, 1962-67. Awarded Simms Gold Medal, RAeS, 1937. FInstP 1944; FRAeS 1955; Fellow, Fellowship of Engineering, 1976. *Recreation:* inventing. *Address:* 3700 Brunswick Pike, Princeton, New Jersey 08540, USA. *T:* 609-452 9275.

de BUNSEN, Sir Bernard, Kt 1962; CMG 1957; MA Oxon; Principal of Chester College, Chester, 1966-71; *b* 24 July 1907; *s* of late L. H. G. de Bunsen, and late Victoria de Bunsen (*née* Buxton); *m* 1975, Joan Allington Harmston, MBE. *Educ:* Leighton Park Sch.; Balliol Coll., Oxford. Schoolmaster, Liverpool Public Elementary Schools, 1930-34; Asst Director of Education, Wiltshire CC, 1934-38; HM Inspector of Schools, Ministry of Education, 1938-46; Director of Education, Palestine, 1946, until withdrawal of British administration, 1948; Professor of Education, Makerere University College, East Africa, 1948, acting Principal, Aug. 1949, Principal, 1950-64, Hon. Fellow, 1968. Vice-Chancellor of University of East Africa, 1963-65; Chairman: Africa Educational Trust, 1967-; Archbishops' Working Party on Future of Theological Colleges, 1967-68; Africa Bureau, 1971-77; Council for Aid to African Students, 1976-; Vice-President: The Anti-Slavery Soc., 1975-; Royal African Soc., 1977. Hon LLD St Andrews, 1963. *Address:* 3 Prince Arthur Road, NW3. *T:* 01-435 3521.

DE BUTTS, Brig. Frederick Manus, CMG 1967; OBE 1961 (MBE 1943); DL; *b* 17 April 1916; *s* of late Brig. F. C. De Butts, CB, DSO, MC, and K. P. M. O'Donnell; *m* 1944, Evelyn Cecilia, *d* of Sir Walter Halsey, 2nd Bt; one *s* one *d*. *Educ:* Wellington Coll.; Oriel Coll., Oxford. Commissioned into Somerset LI, 1937. Served War of 1939-45, in Middle East, Italy, France and Germany. Staff Coll., 1944; Joint Services Staff Coll., 1954; Bt Lieut-Colonel, 1957; Commanded 3rd Bn Aden Protectorate Levies, 1958-60; Bde Colonel, Light Infantry, 1961-64; Comdr, Trucial Oman Scouts, 1964-67; HQ Home Counties District, Shorncliffe, Kent, 1967-68; Defence Attaché, Cairo, 1968-71; retired 1971; employed on contract as COS (Brig.), MoD, United Arab Emirates, 1971-73; Hon. Brig. 1973. Mem., Dacorum DC, 1976-. Hon. Dir, Herts Soc., 1981-. County Chm., 1973-76, County Comr, 1976-81, Vice-Pres., 1981-, Herts Scouts; Vice-Pres., Herts Girl Guides, 1981-; Governor, Abbot's Hill School, 1971- (Chm., 1975-). DL Herts 1975. *Recreations:* tennis, hill-walking. *Address:* The Old Vicarage, Great Gaddesden, Hemel Hempstead, Herts. *T:* Hemel Hempstead 62129.

DEBY, John Bedford; QC 1980; a Recorder of the Crown Court, since 1977; *b* 19 Dec. 1931; *s* of Reginald Bedford Deby and Irene (*née* Slater). *Educ:* Winchester Coll.; Trinity Coll., Cambridge (MA). Called to the Bar, Inner Temple, 1954. *Address:* 11 Britannia Road, Fulham, SW6 2HJ. *T:* 01-736 4976. *Club:* The Club (Sheffield).

de CANDOLE, Eric Armar Vully, CMG 1952; CBE 1950; MA; Sudan Political Service (retired); *b* 14 Sept. 1901; *e s* of late Rev. Armar Corry Vully de Candole, Rector of Ayot Saint Lawrence, Hertfordshire and late Edith Hodgson; *m* 1932, Marian Elizabeth Pender, *d* of Maj. H. Constable Roberts, DSO, MVO; three *s*. *Educ:* Colet Court; Aldenham Sch.; Worcester Coll., Oxford (Exhibitioner). Class II Modern History, 1923, BA 1924, MA 1946. Joined Sudan Political Service, 1923; served in Education Dept as Tutor, Gordon Coll., 1923-27; Acting Warden, 1927-28; Berber, Khartoum and Darfur Provinces as Dist Comr and Magistrate, 1928-36; Resident, Dar Masalit, 1936-44; Bimbashi, SADF, 1940-44; Dep.-Governor, Northern Province, 1944-46; seconded to British Military Administration as Chief Secretary, Cyrenaica, 1946-48; Chief Administrator, Somalia, 1948; Chief Administrator, Cyrenaica, 1948-49; HBM's Resident in Cyrenaica, 1949-51. With Kuwait Oil Co. Ltd, 1952-66, BP Co. Ltd, 1966-69. Order of the Nile, Egypt (4th class), 1934; Order of Istiqlal, Libya (1st class), 1954. *Publications:* articles on Middle East. *Recreations:* gardening, travel. *Address:* Shootwood, Burley, Hants. *T:* Burley 2330. *Club:* Travellers'.

de CARDI, Beatrice Eileen, OBE 1973; retired 1973, but continuing archæological research in Lower Gulf countries; *b* 5 June 1914; *d* of Edwin Count de Cardi and Christine Berbette Wurrflein. *Educ:* St Paul's Girls' Sch.; University Coll. London (BA). Secretary (later Asst), London Museum, 1936-44; Personal Asst to Representative of Allied Supplies Exec. of War Cabinet in China, 1944-45; Asst UK Trade Comr: Delhi, 1946; Karachi, 1947; Lahore, 1948-49; Asst Sec. (title changed to Sec.), Council for British Archæology, 1949-73. Archæological research: in Kalat, Pakistan Baluchistan, 1948; in Afghanistan, 1949; directed excavations: in Kalat, 1957; at Bampur, Persian Baluchistan, 1966; survey in Ras al-Khaimah (then Trucial States), 1968; Middle East lecture tour for British Council, 1970; survey with RGS's Musandam Expedn (Northern Oman), 1971-72; directed archæological research projects: in Qatar, 1973-74; in Central Oman, 1974-76, 1978; survey in Ras al-Khaimah, 1977, 1982. Winston Churchill Meml Trust Fellowship for work in Oman, 1973. FSA 1950 (Vice-Pres., 1976-80; Dir, 1980-). *Publications:* Excavations at Bampur, a third millennium settlement in Persian Baluchistan, 1966; (contrib.) Vol. 51, Pt 3, Anthropological Papers of the American Museum of Natural History, 1970; contribs to Antiquity, Iran, Pakistan Archæology, East and West, Jl of Oman Studies. *Recreations:* archæological fieldwork, travel, cooking. *Address:* 1a Douro Place, Victoria Road, W8 5RW. *T:* 01-937 9740.

de CHAIR, Somerset; *b* 22 Aug. 1911; *s* of late Admiral Sir Dudley de Chair, Governor of NSW; *m* 1st, 1932, Thelma Arbuthnot (marr. diss. 1950); one *s* (and one *s* decd); 2nd, 1950, Carmen Appleton (*née* Bowen) (marr. diss. 1958); two *s*; 3rd, 1958, Mrs Margaret Patricia Manlove (*née* Field-Hart) (marr. diss. 1974); one *d*; 4th, 1974, Juliet, Marchioness of Bristol, *o d* of 8th Earl Fitzwilliam, DSC; one *d*. *Educ:* King's Sch., Paramatta, New South Wales; Balliol Coll., Oxford. MP (Nat C) for S. West Norfolk, 1935-45; Parliamentary Private Secretary to Rt Hon. Oliver Lyttelton MP, Minister of Production, 1942-44; MP (C) South Paddington, 1950-51. 2nd Lieut Supp. Res. RHG, 1938; served with Household Cavalry in the Middle East, during Iraqi and Syrian campaigns (wounded), IO to 4th Cavalry Bde, 1940-41; Captain GS (I), 1942; Chairman National Appeal Cttee of UN Assoc., and member of National Exec., 1947-50. *Publications:* The Impending Storm, 1930, and Divided Europe, 1931 (on International situation); Peter Public, 1932 (a political extravaganza); Enter Napoleon, 1935 (a novel); Red Tie in the Morning (a novel), 1937; The Golden Carpet (Iraq Campaign), 1943; The Silver Crescent (Syrian Campaign), 1943; A Mind on the March, 1945; Editor of Napoleon's Memoirs (2 vols), 1945; edited and translated Supper at Beaucaire by Napoleon, 1945; The First Crusade (edited and translated from Gesta Francorum), 1946; The Teetotalitarian State (a novel), 1947; The Dome of the Rock (a novel), 1948; The Millennium (poems), 1949; Julius Caesar's Commentaries (new edn), 1952; The Story of a Lifetime (novel), 1954; The Waterloo Campaign, 1957; Editor of Admiral de Chair's memoirs, The Sea is Strong, 1961; Bring Back the Gods (novel), 1962; Collected Verse, 1970; Friends, Romans, Concubines (novel), 1973; The Star of the Wind (novel),

1974; Legend of the Yellow River (novel), 1979. *Address:* St Osyth Priory, St Osyth, Essex; The Lake House, 46 Lake Street, Cooperstown, Otsego County, New York, USA. *Club:* Carlton.

DECIES, 6th Baron cr 1812; **Arthur George Marcus Douglas de la Poer Beresford;** Ex-Flying Officer, RAFVR (DFC, USA); b 24 April 1915; s of 5th Baron Decies and Helen Vivien (d 1931), d of late George Jay Gould; S father, 1944; m 1937, Ann Trevor (d 1945); m 1945, Mrs Diana Galsworthy; one s two d. *Heir:* s Hon. Marcus Hugh Tristram de la Poer Beresford [b 5 Aug. 1948; m 1970, Sarah Jane (marr. diss. 1974), o d of Col Basil Gunnell, New Romney, Kent]. *Address:* c/o Coutts & Co., 1 Old Park Lane, W1Y 4BS.

de CLIFFORD, 27th Baron cr 1299; **John Edward Southwell Russell;** b 8 June 1928; s of 26th Baron de Clifford, OBE, TD, and of Dorothy Evelyn, d of late Ferdinand Richard Holmes Meyrick, MD; S father, 1982; m 1959, Bridget Jennifer, yr d of Duncan Robertson, Llangollen, Denbighshire. *Educ:* Eton. *Heir:* b Hon. William Southwell Russell [b 26 Feb. 1930; m 1961, Jean Brodie, d of Neil Brodie Henderson; one s two d]. *Address:* Cliff House, Sheepy, Atherstone, Warwickshire. *Club:* Naval and Military.

de COURCY, family name of **Baron Kingsale.**

de COURCY, Kenneth Hugh; (Duc de Grantmesnil); Chancellor, Order of the Three Orders, since 1977; b 6 Nov. 1909; 2nd s of late Stephen de Courcy of Co. Galway and Hollinwood Mission (s of 8th Duc de Grantmesnil), and late Minnie de Courcy (née Schafer), d of late Frederick and Sophia Schafer; m 1950, Rosemary Catherine (marr. diss. 1973), o d of late Comdr H. L. S. Baker, OBE, RN (retired), Co. Roscommon, Eire; two s two d. *Educ:* King's College Sch. and by travelling abroad. 2nd Lieut, 3rd City of London Regt (Royal Fusiliers) TA (Regular Army Candidate), 1927. 2nd Lieut Coldstream Guards (Supplementary Reserve), 1930; Lieut and resigned, 1931; Hon. Secretary to late Sir Reginald Mitchell-Banks' unofficial cttee on Conservative policy, 1933; 1934, formed with late Earl of Mansfield, late Viscount Clive, late Lord Phillimore, and with Sir Victor Raikes, KBE, Imperial Policy Group and was Hon. Secretary 1934-39; travelled as Group's chief observer of Foreign Affairs in Europe and America, 1935-39; special visit of enquiry to Mussolini, Doctor Beneš, Dr Schuschnigg, 1936; to King Boris of Bulgaria, etc., 1938; to Italy and King Boris, 1939-40; FCO released 45 secret reports from 1936-40 to PRO, 1972; adviser on War Intelligence to United Steel Companies Ltd, 1944-45. Formerly published monthly serial memoranda on Foreign Affairs and Strategy, (1938-); Proprietor of: Intelligence Digest, 1938-76; The Weekly Review, 1951-76; Director, Ringrone Newspapers Ltd, 1966-68. Editor: Bankers Digest, 1969-72; Special Office Brief, 1973-; World Charts and Graphs, 1976-. Trustee, Marquis de Verneuil Trust, 1971-. Lord of the Manors of Stow-on-the-Wold and Maugersbury, Glos. Hon. Citizen of New Orleans, La, USA, 1950; Hon. Life Mem., Mark Twain Soc., 1977; Companion of Western Europe, 1979. *Publications:* Review of World Affairs (23 vols since 1938); various articles on Strategy and Foreign Affairs. *Recreation:* climbing. *Address:* Yeomans Cottage, Longborough, Moreton-in-Marsh, Glos; (office) 81 Merrion Square, Dublin 2, Ireland.

DE COURCY-IRELAND, Lt-Col Gerald Blakeney, MVO 1917; MC 1916; The Worcestershire Regt; b 1895; m 1924, Helen Beresford, e d of late John Stapleton-Martin, MA, barrister-at-law, and late Mrs Stapleton-Martin, Wood Hall, Norton, Worcester; one d. *Educ:* Sherborne; Clare Coll., Cambridge. Temp. 2nd Lieut King's Royal Rifle Corps, 1914; temp. Lieut 1915; temp. Captain, 1916; Acting Major, 1917; Adjutant, 9th Service Batt., 1918; relinquished Commission, 1920; Lieut The Worcestershire Regt, 1916; Captain, 1925; Major, 1938; retired pay, 1946, with hon. rank of Lt-Col. *Recreation:* shooting. *Address:* Greathed Manor, Ford Manor Road, Dormansland, Lingfield, Surrey RH7 6PA. *T:* Lingfield 833558.

de COURCY-IRELAND, Patrick Gault, CVO 1980; HM Diplomatic Service; Consul-General, Casablanca, since 1980; b 19 Aug. 1933; e s of late Lawrence Kilmaine de Courcy-Ireland and Elizabeth Pentland Gault; m 1957, Margaret Gallop; one s three d. *Educ:* St Paul's Sch.; Jesus Coll., Cambridge (MA). HM Forces (2nd Lieut), 1952-54. Joined Foreign Service, 1957; Student, ME Centre for Arab Studies, 1957-59; Third, later Second Sec., Baghdad, 1959-62; Private Sec. to HM Ambassador, Washington, 1963; Consul (Commercial), New York, 1963-67; UN (Polit.) Dept, 1967-69; Asst Head of Amer. Dept, 1969-71; First Sec. and Hd of Chancery, Kuwait, 1971-73; Asst Hd of SW Pacific Dept, 1973-76; Hd of Trng Dept and Dir, Diplomatic Serv. Language Centre, FCO, 1976-80. *Recreations:* book collecting, opera. *Address:* Foreign and Commonwealth Office, SW1A 2AH. *Clubs:* Athenæum; Hurlingham, MCC.

de COURCY LING, John; Member (C) Midlands Central, and Chief Whip, European Democratic Group, European Parliament, since 1979; farmer since 1978; Underwriting Member of Lloyds, since 1969; b 14 Oct. 1933; s of Arthur Norman Ling and Veronica de Courcy; m 1959, Jennifer Haynes; one s three d. *Educ:* King Edward's Sch., Edgbaston; Clare Coll., Cambridge. 2nd Lieut, Royal Ulster Rifles, 1956. FO, 1959; 2nd Sec., Santiago, 1963-66; 1st Sec., Nairobi, 1966-69; Chargé d'Affaires, Chad, 1973; Counsellor, HM Embassy, Paris, 1974-77. *Address:* Bellehatch Farm, Henley on Thames, Oxon. *T:* Henley on Thames 3878; 31 Chapel Street, Belgrave Square, SW1. *T:* 01-235

5655. *Clubs:* Beefsteak, Travellers'; Leander; Royal London Yacht (Cowes).

de DENEY, Geoffrey Ivor; Assistant Under Secretary of State, General Department, Home Office (and Registrar of the Baronetage), since 1980; b 8 Oct. 1931; s of Thomas Douglas de Deney and Violet Ivy de Deney (née Manwaring); m 1959, Diana Elizabeth Winrow; two s. *Educ:* William Ellis Sch.; St Edmund Hall, Oxford (MA, BCL); Univ. of Michigan. Home Office: joined, 1956; Asst Principal, 1956-61 (Private Sec. to Parly Under Sec. of State, 1959-61); Principal, 1961-69: Sec. to Graham Hall Cttee on maintenance limits in magistrates' courts; Sec. to Brodrick Cttee on Death Certification and Coroners; Private Sec. to Sec. of State, 1968; Asst Sec., 1969-1978: Cabinet Office, 1975; Asst Under Sec. of State, 1978-: Community Programmes and Equal Opportunities Dept, 1978-80. *Recreations:* books, walking. *Address:* 17 Ladbroke Terrace, W11. *T:* 01-229 6199.

DEDIJER, Vladimir, DJur, MA Oxon; Order of Liberation, of Yugoslavia, etc.; Yugoslav Author; b 4 Feb. 1914; m 1944, Vera Krizman; one s two d (and two s decd). *Educ:* Belgrade Univ. Served War from 1941, Tito's Army, Lieut-Colonel; Yugoslav Delegate to Peace Conference, Paris, 1946, and to UN General Assemblies, 1945, 1946, 1948, 1949, 1951, 1952. Member Central Cttee, League of Communists of Yugoslavia, 1952-54, when expelled (defended right of M Djilas to free speech, 1954; sentenced to 6 months on probation, 1955). Prof. of Modern History, Belgrade Univ., 1954-55. Simon Senior Fellow, Manchester Univ., 1960; Research Fellow, St Antony's Coll., Oxford, 1962-63; Research Associate, Harvard Univ., 1963-64; Visiting Prof.: Cornell Univ., 1964-65; MIT, 1969; Brandeis, 1970; Michigan, 1971, 1973, 1974. Hon. Fellow, Manchester Univ. President International War Crimes Tribunal, 1966; Hon. Pres., Internat. Tribunal on Afghanistan, 1981. Member, Serbian Acad. of Science. *Publications:* Partisan Diary, 1945; Notes from the United States, 1945; Paris Peace Conference, 1948; Yugoslav-Albanian Relations, 1949; Tito, 1952; Military Conventions, 1960; The Beloved Land, 1960; Road to Sarajevo, 1966; The Battle Stalin Lost, 1969; History of Jugoslavia, 1972; Novi prilozi za biografiju Josipa-Broza Tita, 1982 (New Documents for a Biography of J. B. Tito; banned in Yugoslavia). Contrib. to Acta Scandinavica. *Address:* 52395 Savudrija, Istria, Yugoslavia. *T:* 053-74-504.

de DUVE, Prof. Christian René Marie Joseph, Grand Cross Order of Leopold II 1975; Professor of Biochemistry, Catholic University of Louvain, since 1951; President, International Institute of Cellular and Molecular Pathology, Brussels, since 1975; Andrew W. Mellon Professor at Rockefeller University, New York, since 1962; b England, 2 Oct. 1917; s of Alphonse de Duve and Madeleine Pungs; m 1943, Janine Herman; two s two d. *Educ:* Jesuit Coll., Antwerp; Catholic Univ. of Louvain; Med. Nobel Inst., Stockholm; Washington Univ., St Louis. MD 1941, MSc 1946, Agrégé de l'Enseignement Supérieur 1945, Louvain. Lectr, Med. Faculty, Catholic Univ. of Louvain, 1947-51. Vis. Prof. at various univs. Mem. editorial and other bds and cttees; mem. or hon. mem. various learned socs, incl. For. Assoc. Nat. Acad. of Scis (US) 1975. Holds hon. degrees. Awards incl. Nobel Prize in Physiol. or Med., 1974. *Publications:* numerous scientific. *Recreations:* tennis, ski-ing, bridge. *Address:* Le Pré St Jean, 239 rue de Weert, 5988 Nethen (Grez-Doiceau), Belgium. *T:* (010)-866628; 80 Central Park West, New York, NY 10023, USA. *T:* (212)-724-8048.

DEE, Philip Ivor, CBE 1946 (OBE 1943); FRS 1941; MA Cantab; Professor of Natural Philosophy at University of Glasgow, 1943-72, now Professor Emeritus; b Stroud, Glos, 8 April 1904; s of Albert John Dee, Stroud; m 1929, Phyllis Elsie Tyte; two d. *Educ:* Marling Sch., Stroud; Sidney Sussex Coll., Cambridge (Scholar). Stokes Student at Pembroke Coll., Cambridge, 1930-33; Lecturer in Physics at Cavendish Laboratory and Fellow of Sidney Sussex Coll., Cambridge, 1934-43; Superintendent, Tele-communications Research Establishment, Ministry of Aircraft Production, 1939-45. Advisory Council DSIR, 1947-52. Hughes Medal of Royal Society, 1952. Hon. DSc Univ. of Strathclyde, 1980. *Publications:* scientific papers in Proceedings of Royal Society, etc. *Address:* Speedwell, Buchanan Castle Estate, Drymen, Stirlingshire. *T:* Drymen 60283.

DEED, Basil Lingard, OBE 1946; TD; MA; Headmaster of Stamford School, 1947-68; b 1909; s of late S. G. Deed, Maldon; m 1937, Elizabeth Mary, d of late S. P. Cherrington, Berkhamsted; four d. *Educ:* Haileybury Coll.; Peterhouse, Cambridge. 2nd Class Classical Tripos Part I; 1st class Classical Tripos Part II. Asst Master, Berkhamsted School, 1931-37; Asst Master, Shrewsbury Sch., 1937-47; served War of 1939-45, mostly on General Staff; Lt-Col MEF, 1943; Italy, 1944-45. Councillor (Ind.), 1972-, Vice-Chm., 1981-, Oxfordshire CC. *Address:* Bendor, Warborough, Oxon. *T:* Warborough 8514. *Club:* Blackwater Sailing.

DEEDES, Maj.-Gen. Charles Julius, CB 1968; OBE 1953; MC 1944; b 18 Oct. 1913; s of General Sir Charles Deedes, KCB, CMG, DSO; m 1939, Beatrice Murgatroyd, Brockfield Hall, York; three s. *Educ:* Oratory Sch.; Royal Military Coll., Sandhurst. Served War of 1939-45 (despatches); Asst Military Secretary, GHQ Middle East, 1945; Officer Comdg Glider Pilot Regt, 1948; GSO1 War Office, 1950; Officer Comdg 1st Bn KOYLI, 1954 (despatches); Colonel General Staff, War Office, 1956; Comd 146 Infantry Brigade (TA), 1958; Deputy Director, MoD, 1962; C of S, HQ Eastern Comd, 1965; C of S, HQ Southern Comd, 1968. Colonel of the KOYLI, 1966-68. Dep. Colonel, The Light Infantry (Yorks), 1968-72. Military Cross

(Norway), 1940. *Recreations:* riding, tennis. *Address:* Lea Close, Brandsby, York. *T:* Brandsby 239.

DEEDES, Rt. Hon. William Francis, PC 1962; MC 1944; DL; Editor, The Daily Telegraph, since Dec. 1974; *b* 1 June 1913; *s* of William Herbert Deedes; *m* 1942, Evelyn Hilary Branfoot; two *s* three *d. Educ:* Harrow. MP (C) Ashford Div. of Kent, 1950-Sept. 1974; Parliamentary Sec., Ministry of Housing and Local Government, Oct. 1954-Dec. 1955; Parliamentary Under-Sec., Home Dept., 1955-57; Minister without Portfolio, 1962-64. DL, Kent, 1962. *Address:* New Hayters, Aldington, Kent. *T:* Aldington 269. *Club:* Carlton.

DEEGAN, Joseph William, CMG 1956; CVO 1954; KPM; Inspector-General of Colonial Police, 1966-67; *b* 8 Feb. 1899; *s* of John and Sarah Deegan; *m* 1926, Elinor Elsie Goodson; one *s* two *d. Educ:* St Paul's and St Gabriel's Schs, Dublin. Army, 1919-25 (seconded to King's African Rifles, 1922-25); Tanganyika Police, 1925-38; Uganda Police, 1938-56 (Commissioner of Police, 1950-56); Dep. Inspector-Gen. of Colonial Police, 1956-61, 1963-65. Colonial Police Medal, 1942; King's Police Medal, 1950. *Address:* Tuffshard, Cuckmere Road, Seaford, East Sussex. *T:* Seaford 894180.

DEELEY, Michael; film producer; *b* 6 Aug. 1932; *s* of John Hamilton-Deeley and Anne Deeley; *m* 1955, Teresa Harrison; one *s* two *d*; *m* 1970, Ruth Stone-Spencer. *Educ:* Stowe. Entered film industry as film editor, 1952; Distributor, MCA TV, 1958-60; independent producer, 1961-63; Gen. Man., Woodfall Films, 1964-67; indep. prod., 1967-72; Man. Director: British Lion Films Ltd, 1973-76; EMI Films Ltd, 1976-77; Pres., EMI Films Inc., 1977-79. Academy Award, Best Picture Producer, 1978. Member: Prime Minister's Film Industry Working Party, 1975-76; Film Industry Interim Action Cttee, 1977-82. Films include: Robbery; The Italian Job; The Knack; Murphy's War; Conduct Unbecoming; The Man who fell to Earth; The Deer Hunter; Convoy; Blade Runner. *Address:* Little Island, Osterville, Mass 02655, USA; c/o Pickering Kenyon & Company, 23/24 Great James Street, WC1. *Clubs:* Garrick; California Yacht (Los Angeles); Wiannó Yacht (Mass).

DEER, Sir (Arthur) Frederick, Kt 1979; CMG 1973; Director: The Mutual Life and Citizens' Assurance Co Ltd, Australia, since 1956 (General Manager, 1955-74); Bowater-Scott Ltd; Dow Chemical (Aust.) Ltd; Glass Containers Ltd; Chairman, Expo Oil NL, since 1980; *b* 15 June 1910; *s* of Andrew and Maude Deer; *m* 1936, Elizabeth Christine, *d* of G. C. Whitney; one *s* three *d. Educ:* Sydney Boys' High Sch.; Univ. of Sydney (BA, LLB, BEc). Admitted to Bar of NSW, 1934. The Mutual Life and Citizens' Assurance Co Ltd: joined Company, 1930; apptd Manager for S Australia, 1943, and Asst to Gen. Manager, 1954. Chm., Life Offices' Assoc. for Australasia, 1960-61, 1967-68; Pres., Australian Insurance Inst., 1966. Chm., Cargo Movement Co-ordination Cttee, NSW, 1974-; Mem., Admin. Review Council, 1976-; Aust. Fellow, Senate of Univ. of Sydney, 1959- (Chm. Finance Cttee of the Univ., 1960-). Nat. Pres., Australia-Britain Soc., 1973-81; Chm., Salvation Army Sydney Adv. Bd. *Recreations:* golf, tennis. *Address:* 1179 Pacific Highway, Turramurra, NSW 2074, Australia. *T:* 44 2912. *Clubs:* Australian, Union, University, Athenæum, Avondale, Elanora (all in Australia).

DEER, Mrs Olive G.; Member of Grimsby Borough Council, 1964-67; *b* Grimsby, 31 July 1897; *m* 1916, George Deer, OBE (*d* 1974); one *s* one *d. Educ:* Barcroft Street Sch., Cleethorpes, Lincs. Member: Min. of Labour Exchange Cttees, 1921-45; Bd of Guardians, 1922-25; Bracebridge Mental Hosp. Cttee, 1933-47; Lincoln City Council, 1945-49; Sheffield Regional Hosp. Bd, 1948-50; Bd of Nat. Hosp., Queen Square, 1950; S Eastern Metrop. Regional Hosp. Bd, 1957. Dir, 1940-50, Chm., 1946-48, Lincoln Co-operative Soc. Alderman, LCC, 1952-58; Councillor, LCC (Shoreditch and Finsbury), 1958-64. Chm. LCC Welfare Cttee, 1955-62; Chm. of the London County Council, 1962-63. *Address:* Medina, Carlton Road, Manby, Louth, Lincs. *T:* S Cockerington 386.

DEER, Prof. William Alexander, MSc Manchester, PhD Cantab; FRS 1962; FGS; Professor of Mineralogy and Petrology, Cambridge University, 1961-78, now Emeritus; Master of Trinity Hall, Cambridge, 1966-75, Hon. Fellow, 1978; *b* 26 Oct. 1910; *s* of William Deer; *m* 1939, Margaret Marjorie (*d* 1971), *d* of William Kidd; two *s* one *d*; *m* 1973, Rita Tagg. *Educ:* Manchester Central High Sch.; Manchester Univ.; St John's Coll., Cambridge. Graduate Research Scholar, 1932, Beyer Fellow, 1933, Manchester Univ.; Strathcona Studentship, St John's Coll., Cambridge, 1934; Petrologist on British East Greenland Expedition, 1935-36; 1851 Exhibition Senior Studentship, 1938; Fellow, St John's Coll., Cambridge, 1939; served War of 1939-45, RE, 1940-45. Murchison Fund Geological Soc. of London, 1945 (Murchison Medal, 1974); Junior Bursar, St John's Coll., 1946; Leader NE Baffin Land Expedition, 1948; Bruce Medal, Royal Society of Edinburgh, 1948; Tutor, St John's Coll., 1946; Prof. of Geology, Manchester Univ., 1950-61; Fellow of St John's Coll., Cambridge, 1961-66, Hon. Fellow, 1969; Vice-Chancellor, Cambridge Univ., 1971-73. Percival Lecturer, Univ. of Manchester, 1953; Joint Leader East Greenland Geological Expedition, 1953; Leader British East Greenland Expedition, 1966. Trustee, British Museum (Natural History), 1967-75. President: Mineralogical Soc., 1967-70; Geological Soc., 1972-74; Member: NERC, 1968-71; Marshall Aid Commemoration Commn, 1973-. *Publications:* 79 books; papers in Petrology and Mineralogy. *Recreations:* gardening, bassoon playing. *Address:* Pastures, St Peters Street, Caxton, Cambridge.

DEERHURST, Viscount; Edward George William Omar Coventry; *b* 24 Sept. 1957; *s* and *heir* of 11th Earl of Coventry, *qv.*

de FARIA, Antonio Leite, Hon. GCVO 1973; Grand Cross of Christ (Portugal), 1949; Portuguese Ambassador to the Court of St James's, 1968-73; retired; *b* 23 March 1904; *s* of Dr Antonio B. Leite de Faria and Dona Lucia P. de Sequeira Braga Leite de Faria; *m* 1926, Dona Herminia Cantilo de Faria; two *s. Educ:* Lisbon University (Faculty of Law). Attaché to Min. of Foreign Affairs, 1926; Sec. to Portuguese Delegn, League of Nations, 1929-30; 2nd Sec., Rio de Janeiro, 1931, Paris, 1933, Brussels, 1934; 1st Sec., London, 1936; Counsellor, London, 1939; Minister to Exiled Allied Govts, London, 1944; Minister to The Hague, 1945; Dir Gen., Political Affairs, and Acting Sec. Gen., Min. of Foreign Affairs, 1947; Ambassador: Rio de Janeiro, 1950; NATO, 1958; Paris, 1959; Rome (Holy See), 1961; London, 1968. Holds many foreign decorations. *Address:* Rua da Horta Seca 11, Lisboa, Portugal. *T:* 32 25 38; Casa do Bom Retiro, S Pedro de Azurem, Guimarães, Portugal. *T:* (0023) 416418.

de FERRANTI, Basil Reginald Vincent Ziani; Member (C) Hampshire West, European Parliament, since 1979 (a Vice-President, 1979-82); Chairman, Ferranti plc; *b* 2 July 1930; *yr s* of Sir Vincent de Ferranti, MC, FIEE, and of Dorothy H. C. Wilson; *m* 1st, 1956, Susan Sara, *d* of late Christopher and of Lady Barbara Gore; three *s*; 2nd, 1964, Simone, *d* of late Col and of Mrs H. J. Nangle; one *d*; 3rd, 1971, Jocelyn Hilary Mary, *d* of late Wing Comdr and Mrs A. T. Laing. *Educ:* Eton; Trinity Coll., Cambridge. Served 4th/7th Royal Dragoon Guards, 1949-50. Man., Domestic Appliance Dept, Ferranti Ltd, 1954-57. Contested Exchange Div. of Manchester, Gen. Election, 1955; MP (C) Morecambe and Lonsdale Div. of Lancaster, Nov. 1958-Sept. 1964. Dir of overseas operations, Ferranti Ltd, 1957-62; Parliamentary Sec., Ministry of Aviation, July-Oct. 1962. Dep. Man. Dir, Internat. Computers and Tabulators, Sept. 1963 until Managing Dir, 1964; Dir, International Computers Ltd until 1972. Mem., Economic and Social Cttee, European Communities, 1973-79 (Chm., 1976-78); Chm., European Movement (British Council), since 1980. Pres., British Computer Soc., 1968-69. Hon. DSc City, 1970. *Publications:* In Europe, 1979; contrib. Brit. Computer Soc. Jl, Proc. IFIP, Proc. Royal Instn of GB. *Recreations:* ski-ing, sailing. *Address:* Ferranti Ltd, Millbank Tower, Millbank, SW1. *T:* 01-834 6611; The Old Manor, Church Lane, Ellisfield, Hants RG25 2QR. *Club:* Royal Yacht Squadron.

See also S. B. J. Z. de Ferranti.

de FERRANTI, Sebastian Basil Joseph Ziani; Chairman, Ferranti Ltd, 1963-82 (Managing Director, 1958-75; Director 1954); *b* 5 Oct. 1927; *er s* of Sir Vincent de Ferranti, MC, FIEE, and of Dorothy H. C. Wilson; *m* 1953, Mona Helen, *d* of T. E. Cunningham; one *s* two *d. Educ:* Ampleforth. 4th/7th Dragoon Guards, 1947-49. Brown Boveri, Switzerland, and Alsthom, France, 1949-50. President: Electrical Research Assoc., 1968-69; BEAMA, 1969-70; Centre for Educn in Science, Educn and Technology, Manchester and region, 1972-. Chm., Internat. Electrical Assoc., 1970-72. Member: Nat. Defence Industries Council, 1969-77; Council, IEE, 1970-73. Trustee, Tate Gallery, 1971-78. Chm., Civic Trust for the North-West, 1978-. Lectures: Granada, Guildhall, 1966; Royal Instn, 1969; Louis Blériot, Paris, 1970; Faraday, 1970-71. Hon. DSc: Salford Univ., 1967; Cranfield Inst. of Technology, 1973. Hon. Fellow, Univ. of Manchester Inst. of Science and Technology. *Address:* Henbury Hall, Macclesfield, Cheshire. *Clubs:* Cavalry and Guards, Pratt's.

See also B. R. V. Z. de Ferranti.

DEFFERRE, Gaston; Officier de la Légion d'honneur; Minister of State, Minister for the Interior and for Decentralisation, France, since 1981; Mayor of Marseilles, 1944-45 and since 1953; *b* 14 Sept. 1910; *s* of Paul and Suzanne Defferre; *m* 1st, 1935, Andrée Aboulker; 2nd, 1946, Marie-Antoinette Swaters; 3rd, 1973, Edmonde Charles-Roux, journalist. *Educ:* Lycée de Nîmes; Aix-en-Provence Univ. In practice as lawyer, Marseilles, 1931-51. During War, 1939-45, involved in resistance movement (Croix de guerre, Rosette de la Résistance). Dir, Le Provençal, 1951-. Deputy for Bouches-du-Rhône, 1946-58, 1962-81, re-elected June 1981; Senator, 1959-62; Sec. of State, Présidence du Conseil, 1946; Under Sec. of State, France Overseas, 1946-47; Minister: Merchant Marine, 1950-51; France Overseas, 1956-57; Leader, Socialist Group, Nat. Assembly, 1967-81. *Publications:* Un nouvel horizon, 1977; Si demain la gauche..., 1977. *Address:* Hôtel de Ville, 13002 Marseille, France.

de FISCHER-REICHENBACH, Henry-Béat, Dr jur.; Swiss Ambassador to the Court of St James's, 1964-66; *b* 22 July 1901; *s* of Henry B. de Fischer-Reichenbach, architect, bailiff-delegate of the Sov. Order of Malta in Switzerland, and Caroline Falck-Crivelli; *m* 1949, Madeleine de Graffenried, sculptress; three *d. Educ:* Stella Matutina Jesuit Coll., Feldkirch; Universities of Fribourg, Munich, Paris and Berne. Entered Federal Political Dept, Berne, 1929; Attaché, Swiss Legation, The Hague, 1931; Second Secretary, Buenos-Aires and Montevideo, 1933; First Secretary: Warsaw, 1939; Bucharest, 1940; Chargé d'affaires successively Riga, Kowno, Reval, Helsinki, 1940; Counsellor: Bucharest, 1941; Cairo and Beirut, 1947; Minister: Cairo, 1949; Ethiopia, 1952; Lisbon, 1954; Ambassador, Vienna, 1959-64. Mem. Board of Patrons, C. G. Jung Inst., Zürich, 1931-71. President: Fondation pour l'histoire des Suisses à L'étranger, 1969-79; Swiss Assoc., Knights of Malta, 1968-79; Comité exécutif international pour l'assistance aux lépreux de l'Ordre de Malte; European Anti-Leprosy Assoc., 1969-; Soc. des Amis suisses de Versailles, 1968-69. Lecture, The Sovereign Order of Malta, Hague Acad. of

Internat. Law, 1979. *Publications:* Contributions à la connaissance des relations suisses-égyptiennes, 1956; Dialogue luso-suisse, 1960 (Camões Prize, 1961); 2000 ans de présence suisse en Angleterre, 1980. *Recreations:* history, architecture, psychology. *Address:* Le Pavillon, Thunplatz 52, Berne. *T:* 031 44.15.09; Clos Soleil, Vufflens-le-Château, Vaud, Switzerland. *Clubs:* Travellers'; Grande Société (Berne).

de FRANCIA, Prof. Peter Laurent; Professor, School of Painting, Royal College of Art, London, since 1973; *b* 25 Jan. 1921; *s* of Fernand de Francia and Alice Groom. *Educ:* Academy of Brussels; Slade Sch., Univ. of London. Canadian Exhibition Commn, Ottawa, 1951; American Museum, Central Park West, NY, 1952-53; BBC, Television, 1953-55; Teacher, St Martin's Sch., London, 1955-63; Tutor, Royal College of Art, 1963-69; Principal, Dept of Fine Art, Goldsmiths Coll., 1969-72. *Publication:* Fernand Léger, 1969. *Address:* 44 Surrey Square, SE17 2JX. *T:* (home) 01-703 8361; (office) 01-584 5020.

de FREITAS-CRUZ, João Carlos Lopes Cardoso; Grand Cross, Order of Prince Henry the Navigator; Ambassador of Portugal to the Court of St James's, since 1980; *b* 27 March 1925; *s* of Jose A. de Freitas-Cruz and Maria A. L. C. de Freitas-Cruz; *m* 1955, Maria de Lourdes Soares de Albergaria; three *s. Educ:* Univ. of Lisbon (law degree). Joined Portuguese Foreign Service, 1948; Secretary, Portuguese Embassy, London, 1950-52; Portuguese Delegate to NATO, in Paris, 1952-57; Foreign Office, Lisbon, 1957-59; Sec., Portuguese Embassy, Pretoria, 1959-60; Chargé d'Affaires, Madagascar, 1960-62; Consul-General, New York, 1963-65; Consul-Gen., Salisbury, Rhodesia, 1965-70; Ambassador: to OECD, Paris, 1970-71; in Bonn, 1971-73; Dir-Gen. for Political Affairs, FO, Lisbon, 1973-74; Ambassador, Permanent Representative to NATO, Brussels, 1974-78; Minister for Foreign Affairs, 1978-80. Grand Cross, Order of Merit, Fed. Republic of Germany; Comdr, San Silvester, Holy See; Grand Officer, Légion d'Honneur, France; Grand Cross, Order of Flag, Hungary, and other foreign orders. *Recreations:* golf, hunting, reading. *Address:* 12 Belgrave Square, SW1. *T:* 01-235 3688. *Clubs:* Travellers', Royal Automobile, Hurlingham, Royal Wimbledon Golf.

DE FREYNE, 7th Baron *cr* 1851; **Francis Arthur John French;** Knight of Malta; *b* 3 Sept. 1927; *s* of 6th Baron and Victoria (*d* 1974), *d* of Sir J. Arnott, 2nd Bt; *S* father 1935; *m* 1954, Shirley Ann (marr. diss. 1978), *o c* of late D. R. Pobjoy; two *s* one *d* ; *m* 1978, Sheelin Deirdre, widow of William Walker Stevenson and *y d* of late Lt-Col H. K. O'Kelly, DSO. *Educ:* Ladycross, Glenstal. *Heir: s* Hon. Fulke Charles Arthur John French, *b* 21 April 1957. *Club:* Kildare Street and University (Dublin).

de GALE, Sir Leo (Victor), GCMG 1974; CBE 1969; Governor-General of Grenada, 1974-78; *b* 28 Dec. 1921; 3rd *s* of late George Victor and late Marie Leonie de Gale, Grenada; *m* 1953, Brenda Mary Helen (*née* Scott), Trinidad; five *s* two *d. Educ:* Grenada Boys' Secondary Sch.; Sir George Williams Univ., Canada. Dip. Accountancy, Dip. Business Admin, Qual. Land Surveyor. Served with 1st Canadian Survey Regt, 1940-45. Co-founder firm de Gale & Rapier, Auditors, 1949. Dir, Brit. Red Cross Br., Grenada, 1960-65; Chm. and Mem., Grenada Breweries Ltd, 1964-74; Dep. Chm., Grenada Banana Soc., 1965-69; Chm. Bd of Governors, Grenada Boys' Secondary Sch., 1960-65; Mem., West Indies Associated States Judicial and Legal Service Commn, 1970-73. *Recreations:* golf, fishing, reading. *Clubs:* St George's Men's (Grenada); Grenada Yacht.

De GEER, (William) Ross; Agent General for Ontario in the United Kingdom, since 1978; *b* 31 July 1936; *s* of late William Nelson De Geer and of Elizabeth De Geer; *m* Frances Eileen; one *s* two *d. Educ:* Weston Collegiate, Ontario. Vice-President and Director, St Lawrence Securities, Members of Toronto Stock Exchange, 1957-71. Executive Director, Progressive Conservative Party of Ontario, 1971-77; Principal Secretary to Premier of Ontario, Hon. William G. Davis, 1977-78. *Recreations:* golf, farming. *Address:* Flat 6, 12 Reeves Mews, W1. *T:* 01-629 6983. *Clubs:* East India, Devonshire, Sports and Public Schools; Board of Trade (Toronto); Albany of Toronto (past Pres.).

de GEX, Maj.-Gen. George Francis, CB 1964; OBE 1949; Director, Royal Artillery, 1964-66, retired; *b* 23 April 1911; *s* of late Brig.-Gen. F. J. de Gex, CB, CMG; *m* 1946, Ronda Marianne (*d* 1982), *d* of late C. F. Recaño; one *d. Educ:* Wellington Coll., Berks; Trinity Hall, Cambridge (MA). 2nd Lieut RA 1931; served War of 1939-45: BEF, 1940 (despatches); NW Europe, 1944. Lt-Col 1953; Col 1954; Brig. 1959; Comd 1 AGRA, 1958-59; DMS(B), War Office, 1959-60. Comd Artillery, Northern Army Group, 1961-64. Col Comdt, RA 1967-76. DSC (USA), 1945. *Recreations:* shooting, sailing. *Address:* Hyde House, Pilton, Shepton Mallet, Somerset. *Club:* Army and Navy.

de GREY, family name of **Baron Walsingham.**

de GREY, Roger, RA 1969 (ARA 1962); Principal, City and Guilds of London Art School, since 1973; *b* 18 April 1918; *s* of Nigel de Grey, CMG, OBE, and Florence Emily Frances (*née* Gore); *m* 1942, Flavia Hatt (*née* Irwin); two *s* one *d. Educ:* Eton Coll.; Chelsea Sch. of Art. Served War of 1939-45: Royal West Kent Yeomanry, 1939-42; RAC, 1942-45 (US Bronze Star, 1945). Lecturer, Dept of Fine Art, King's Coll., Newcastle upon Tyne, 1947-51; Master of Painting, King's Coll., 1951-53; Senior Tutor, later Reader in Painting, Royal Coll. of Art, 1953-73. Treasurer, RA, 1976. Pictures in the

following public collections: Arts Council; Contemporary Arts Society; Chantrey Bequest; Queensland Gallery, Brisbane; Manchester, Carlisle, Bradford and other provincial galleries. Hon. ARCA, 1959. *Address:* City and Guilds of London Art School, 124 Kennington Park Road, SW11 4DJ; 5 Camer Street, Meopham, Kent. *T:* 2327.

de HAVILLAND, Olivia Mary; actress; *b* Tokyo, Japan, 1 July 1916; *d* of Walter Augustus de Havilland and Lilian Augusta (*née* Ruse) (parents British subjects); *m* 1st, 1946, Marcus Aurelius Goodrich (marr. diss., 1953); one *s* ; 2nd, 1955, Pierre Paul Galante (marr. diss. 1979); one *d. Educ:* in California; won scholarship to Mills Coll., but career prevented acceptance. Played Hermia in Max Reinhardt's stage production of Midsummer Night's Dream, 1934. *Legitimate theatre* (USA): Juliet in Romeo and Juliet, 1951; Candida, 1951 and 1952; A Gift of Time, 1962. Began film career 1935, Midsummer Night's Dream. Nominated for Academy Award, 1939, 1941, 1946, 1948, 1949; Acad. Award, 1946, 1949; New York Critics' Award, 1948, 1949; San Francisco Critics' Award, 1948, 1949; Women's National Press Club Award for 1950; Belgian Prix Femina, 1957; British Films and Filming Award, 1967; Filmex Tribute, 1978; Amer. Acad. of Achievement Award, 1978. *Important Films:* The Adventures of Robin Hood, 1938; Gone With the Wind, 1939; Hold Back the Dawn, 1941; Princess O'Rourke, 1943; To Each His Own, 1946; The Dark Mirror, 1946; The Snake Pit, 1948; The Heiress, 1949; My Cousin Rachel, 1952; Not as a Stranger, 1955; The Ambassador's Daughter, 1956; Proud Rebel, 1957; The Light in the Piazza, 1961; Lady in a Cage, 1963; Hush . . . Hush, Sweet Charlotte, 1965; The Adventurers, 1969; Pope Joan, 1971; Airport '77, 1976; The Swarm, 1978. Also TV 1966, 1967, 1971; Roots, The Next Generations, 1979; 3 ABC Cable-TV Cultural Documentaries, 1981; Murder is Easy, 1982. US Lecture tours, 1971, 1972, 1973, 1974, 1975, 1976, 1978, 1979, 1980. Pres. of Jury, Cannes Film Festival, 1965. Took part in narration of France's BiCentennial Gift to US, Son et Lumière, A Salute to George Washington, Mount Vernon, 19 May 1976; read excerpts from Thomas Jefferson at BiCentennial Service, American Cathedral in Paris, 4 July 1976. Amer. Legion Humanitarian Medal, 1967; Freedoms Foundn Exemplar American Award, 1981. *Publications:* Every Frenchman Has One, 1962; (contrib.) Mother and Child, 1975. *Address:* BP 156, 75764 Paris, Cedex 16, France.

de HAVILLAND, Maj.-Gen. Peter Hugh, CBE 1945; DL; *b* 29 July 1904; *s* of late Hugh de Havilland, JP, CA, The Manor House, Gt Horkesley, Essex; *m* 1st, 1930, Helen Elizabeth Wrey (*d* 1976), *d* of late W. W. Otter-Barry, Horkesley Hall, Essex; two *s* ; 2nd, 1981, Mrs Angela Hoare. *Educ:* Eton; RMA, Woolwich. 2nd Lieut RA, 1925; Lieut RHA, 1933-36; Adjt 84th (East Anglian) Field Bde, RA (TA), 1936-38; served War of 1939-45 (despatches thrice, CBE); France, Middle East, N Africa, NW Europe; Brig. i/c Administration, 1 Corps, 1945-47; Dep. Regional Comr, Land Schleswig Holstein, 1948; Dep. Head, UK Deleg. Five Power Military Cttee, 1949; UK Mil. Rep., SHAPE, 1951; Chief of Staff, Northern Comd, 1953-55, retd 1955. DL Essex, 1962. Comdr Order of Leopold II, 1945. *Recreations:* shooting, flying. *Address:* Horkesley Hall, Colchester. *T:* Colchester 271 259. *Club:* Army and Navy.

DEHN, Conrad Francis, QC 1968; Barrister; a Recorder of the Crown Court, since 1974; *b* London, 24 Nov. 1926; *o s* of late C. G. Dehn, Solicitor and Cynthia (*née* Fuller: Francyn the painter); *m* 1st, 1954, Sheila (*née* Magan) (marr. diss.); two *s* one *d* ; 2nd, 1978, Marilyn, *d* of late Peter Collyer and of Constance Collyer. *Educ:* Charterhouse (Sen. Exhibr); Christ Church, Oxford. Served RA, 2nd Lieut 1947. 1st cl. hons PPE Oxon. 1950, MA 1952; Holt Schol., Gray's Inn, 1951; Pres., Inns of Court Students Union, 1951-52. WEA Tutor, 1951-55. Called to Bar, Gray's Inn, 1952; Bencher, 1977. Mem. Governing Body, United Westminster Schs, 1953-57. Chm., Bar Council Working Party on Liability for Defective Products, 1975-77; Mem., Foster Cttee of Inquiry into Operators' Licensing, Dept of Transport, 1978. Chm., Planning Cttee, Senate of Inns of Court and Bar, 1980-82. *Publication:* contrib. to Ideas, 1954. *Recreations:* theatre, travel, walking. *Address:* Fountain Court, Temple, EC4 9DH. *T:* 01-353 7356. *Club:* Reform.

de HOGHTON, Sir (Richard) Bernard (Cuthbert), 14th Bt *cr* 1611; KM; *b* 26 Jan. 1945; 3rd *s* of Sir Cuthbert de Hoghton, 12th Bt, and of Philomena, *d* of late Herbert Simmons; *S* half-brother, 1978; *m* 1974, Rosanna Stella Virginia (*née* Buratti); one *s* one *d. Educ:* Ampleforth College, York; McGill Univ., Montreal (BA Econs); Birmingham Univ. (MA); PhD (USA). Turner & Newall Ltd, 1967-70; international fund management, Vickers Da Costa & Co. Ltd, 1970-77; international institutional brokerage, de Zoete & Bevan & Co., 1977-; estate management, 1978-. *Recreations:* skiing, tennis, shooting, stamp collecting, travelling, writing. *Heir: s* Thomas James Daniel Adam de Hoghton, *b* 11 April 1980. *Address:* Hoghton Tower, Hoghton, Preston, Lancs. *T:* Hoghton 2986; 22 St Maur Road, SW6. *T:* 01-731 0130.

DEHQANI-TAFTI, Rt. Rev. Hassan Barnaba; Bishop in Iran, since 1961; President-Bishop of the Episcopal Church in Jerusalem and the Middle East, since 1976; Assistant Bishop of Winchester, since 1982; *b* 14 May 1920; *s* of Muhammad Dehqani-Tafti and Sakinneh; *m* 1952, Margaret Isabel Thompson; three *d* (one *s* decd). *Educ:* Stuart Memorial Coll., Isfahan, Iran; Tehran Univ.; Ridley Hall, Cambridge. Iran Imperial Army, 1943-45; layman in Diocese of Iran, 1945-47; theological coll., 1947-49; Deacon, Isfahan, 1949; Priest, Shiraz, 1950; Pastor: St Luke's Church, Isfahan, 1950-60; St Paul's Church, Tehran, 1960-61. Hon. DD, Virginia Theolog. Seminary, USA, 1981. *Publications:* many books in Persian; in English: Design of my World, 1959; The Hard

Awakening, 1981. *Recreations:* Persian poetry (primarily mystical); painting in water colours; walking. *Address:* Sohrab, 1 Camberry Close, Basingstoke, Hants RG21 3AG. *T:* Basingstoke 27457. *Club:* Royal Commonwealth Society.

DE-JA-GOU; *see* Gowda, Deve Javare.

De la BÈRE, Sir Cameron, 2nd Bt *cr* 1953; jeweller, Geneva; *b* 12 Feb. 1933; *s* of Sir Rupert De la Bère, 1st Bt, KCVO, and Marguerite (*d* 1969), *e d* of late Sir John Humphery; *S* father, 1978; *m* 1964, Clairemonde, *o d* of Casimir Kaufmann, Geneva; one *d. Educ:* Tonbridge, and on the Continent. Translator's cert. in Russian. British Army Intelligence Corps, 1951-53. Company director of Continental Express Ltd (subsid. of Hay's Wharf), 1958-64. Engaged in promotion of luxury retail jewellery stores, Switzerland and France, 1965-. Liveryman, Skinners' Co. *Recreations:* riding, swimming, history. *Heir:* b Adrian De la Bère, b 17 Sept. 1939. *Address:* 1 Avenue Theodore Flournoy, 1207 Geneva, Switzerland. *T:* (022) 31.26.86. *Clubs:* Hurlingham, Société Litéraire (Geneva).

DELACOMBE, Maj.-Gen. Sir Rohan, KCMG 1964; KCVO 1970; KBE 1961 (CBE 1951; MBE 1939); CB 1957; DSO 1944; Governor of Victoria, Australia, 1963-74; Administrator of the Commonwealth of Australia on four occasions; *b* 25 Oct. 1906; *s* of late Lieut-Col Addis Delacombe, DSO, Shrewton Manor, near Salisbury; *m* 1941, Eleanor Joyce (CStJ), *d* of late R. Lionel Foster, JP, Egton Manor, Whitby; one *s* one *d. Educ:* Harrow; RMC Sandhurst. 2nd Lieut The Royal Scots, 1926; served Egypt, N China, India and UK, 1926-37; active service Palestine, 1937-39 (despatches, MBE); France, Norway, Normandy, Italy, 1939-45; Lieut-Col comd 8th Bn and 2nd Bn The Royal Scots, 1943-45; GSO1, 2nd Infantry Div., Far East, 1945-47; Colonel GS, HQ, BAOR, 1949-50; Brig. Comd 5 Inf. Bde, 1950-53, Germany; Dep. Mil. Sec., War Office, 1953-55; Maj.-Gen. 1956. Col The Royal Scots, 1956-64; GOC 52 Lowland Div. and Lowland District, 1955-58; GOC Berlin (Brit. Sector) 1959-62. Mem. Queen's Body Guard for Scotland, Royal Company of Archers, 1957. Pres., Royal British Legion (Wilts). FRAIA. KStJ, 1963; Freeman, City of Melbourne, 1974. Hon. Col 1st Armoured Regt (Australian Army), 1963-74; Hon. Air Cdre RAAF. LLD *hc* Melbourne; LLD *hc* Monash. *Recreations:* normal. *Address:* Shrewton Manor, near Salisbury, Wilts. *T:* Shrewton 620253. *Clubs:* Army and Navy, Victoria Racing (Melbourne).

DELACOURT-SMITH OF ALTERYN, Baroness *cr* 1974 (Life Peer), of Alteryn, Gwent; **Margaret Delacourt-Smith;** *b* 1916; *d* of Frederick James Hando; *m* 1st, 1939, Charles Smith (subsequently Lord Delacourt-Smith, PC) (*d* 1972); one *s* two *d* ; 2nd, 1978, Professor Charles Blackton. *Educ:* Newport High School for Girls; St Anne's College, Oxford (MA). *Address:* 56 Aberdare Gardens, NW6 3QD.

de LACRETELLE, Jacques; French Writer; Member of Académie Française, since 1936; *b* 14 July 1888; *m* 1933, Yolande de Naurois; three *c.* First book published in 1920; Prix Femina, 1922; Grand Prix du roman de l'Académie Française, 1927. *Publications:* La Vie inquiète de Jean Hermelin, 1920; Silbermann, 1922; La Bonifas, 1925; Histoire de Paola Ferrani, 1929; Amour nuptial, 1929; Le Retour de Silbermann, 1930; Les Hauts Ponts (4 vols), 1932-35; L'Ecrivain public, 1936; Croisières en eaux troubles, 1939; Le Demi-Dieu ou le voyage en Grèce, 1944; Le Pour et le Contre, 1946; Une visite en été (play), 1952; Deux cœurs simples, 1953; Tiroir secret, 1959; Les Maîtres et les Amis, 1959; Grèce que j'aime, 1960; La Galerie des amants, 1963; L'Amour sur la place, 1964; Talleyrand, 1964; Racine, 1970; Portraits d'autrefois, figures d'aujourd'hui 1973; Journal de bord, 1974; Les Vivants et leur ombre, 1977; translation of Precious Bane by Mary Webb and Wuthering Heights by Emily Brontë. *Address:* 49 rue Vineuse, 75016 Paris, France. *T:* 553-79.87.

DELAFONS, John, CB 1982; Deputy Secretary, since 1979, and Chief Planner, since 1982, Department of the Environment; *b* 14 Sept. 1930; *m* 1957, Sheila Egerton; four *d. Educ:* Ardingly; St Peter's College, Oxford. 1st cl. Hons English. Asst Principal, Min. of Housing and Local Govt, 1953; Harkness Fellowship, Harvard, 1959-60; Principal, 1959-66; Principal Private Sec. to Minister, 1965-66; Department of the Environment: Assistant Sec., 1966-72; Under Sec., 1972-77; Under Sec., Cabinet Office, 1977-79. Chm., Royal Inst. of Public Admin. *Publication:* Land-Use Controls in the United States (Harvard/MIT), 1962, revd edn 1969. *Address:* Department of the Environment, SW1.

de la LANNE-MIRRLEES, Robin Ian Evelyn Stuart; *see* Mirrlees.

de la MARE, Sir Arthur (James), KCMG 1968 (CMG 1957); KCVO 1972; HM Diplomatic Service, retired; *b* 15 Feb. 1914; *s* of late Walter H. de la Mare, Trinity, Jersey, Channel Islands, and late Laura Vibert Syvret; *m* 1940, Katherine Elisabeth Sherwood; three *d. Educ:* Victoria Coll., Jersey; Pembroke Coll., Cambridge. Joined HM Foreign Service, 1936. HM Vice-Consul: Tokyo, 1936-38; Seoul, Korea, 1938-39; USA 1942-43; First Sec., Foreign Service, 1945; HM Consul, San Francisco, 1947-50; HM Embassy, Tokyo, 1951-53; Counsellor, HM Foreign Service, 1953-63; Head of Security Dept, Foreign Office, 1953-56; Counsellor, HM Embassy, Washington, 1956-60; Head of Far Eastern Dept, Foreign Office, 1960-63; Ambassador to Afghanistan, 1963-65; Asst Under-Sec. of State, Foreign Office, 1965-67; High Comr in Singapore, 1968-70; Ambassador to Thailand, 1970-73.

Chairman: Anglo-Thai Soc., 1976-82; Royal Soc. for Asian Affairs, 1978-; Jersey Soc. in London, 1980-81. *Recreation:* gardening. *Address:* The Birches, Onslow Road, Burwood Park, Walton-on-Thames, Surrey KT12 5BB. *Clubs:* Oriental, Royal Commonwealth Society; Tokyo (Tokyo, Japan).

de la MARE, Prof. Peter Bernard David, MSc NZ; PhD London; DSc London; FRSNZ; Professor of Chemistry, University of Auckland, New Zealand, 1967-82, now Emeritus (Head of Department, 1967-81); *b* 3 Sept. 1920; *s* of late Frederick Archibald and Sophia Ruth de la Mare, Hamilton, NZ; *m* 1945, Gwynneth Campbell, *yr d* of late Alexander and Daisy Gertrude Jolly, Hastings, NZ; two *d. Educ:* Hamilton High Sch., Hamilton, NZ; Victoria University Coll. (University of NZ); University Coll., London. BSc NZ, 1941; MSc NZ, 1942; PhD London, 1948; DSc London, 1955. Agricultural Chemist, NZ Govt Dept of Agriculture, 1942-45; Shirtcliffe Fellow (University of NZ) at University Coll. London, 1946-48; University Coll. London: Temp. Asst Lecturer, 1948; Lecturer, 1949; Reader, 1956; Prof. of Chemistry, Bedford Coll., University of London, 1960-67. FRSNZ 1970. *Publications:* (with J. H. Ridd) Aromatic Substitution-Nitration and Halogenation, 1959; (with W. Klyne) Progress in Stereochemistry 2, 1958, 3, 1962; (with R. Bolton) Electrophilic Addition to Unsaturated Systems, 1966, 2nd edn 1982; Electrophilic Halogenation, 1976; scientific papers and reviews. *Recreations:* chess, table tennis, etc. *Address:* Chemistry Department, University of Auckland, Auckland, New Zealand.

de la MARE, Richard Herbert Ingpen; President, Faber & Faber (Publishers) Ltd, since 1971 (Chairman, Faber & Faber Ltd, 1960-71); Chairman, Faber Music Ltd, 1966-71; *b* 4 June 1901; *e s* of late Walter John de la Mare, OM, CH, and Constance Elfrida Ingpen; *m* 1930, Amy Catherine (*d* 1968), *er d* of late Rev. S. A. Donaldson, DD, Master of Magdalene College, Cambridge; three *s* one *d. Educ:* Whitgift Sch., Croydon; Keble Coll., Oxford. Joined Faber & Gwyer Ltd, 1925, Dir 1928; succeeded by Faber & Faber Ltd, 1929, Dir 1929-45, Vice-Chm. 1945-60. *Publications:* essays and addresses on typography. *Recreations:* reading history and archaeology, listening to music, oriental art, gardening. *Address:* Tithe Barn House, High Street, Cumnor, Oxford OX2 9PE. *T:* Cumnor 3916. *Club:* Athenæum.
See also Baron Donaldson of Kingsbridge.

DELAMERE, 5th Baron *cr* 1821; **Hugh George Cholmondeley;** *b* 18 Jan. 1934; *s* of 4th Baron Delamere, and Phyllis Anne (*d* 1978), *e d* of late Lord George Scott, OBE; *S* father, 1979; *m* 1964, Mrs Ann Willoughby Tinne, *o d* of late Sir Patrick Renison, GCMG and of Lady Renison, Mayfield, Sussex; one *s. Educ:* Eton; Magdalene Coll., Cambridge. MA Agric. *Heir:* s Hon. Thomas Patrick Gilbert Cholmondeley, *b* 19 June 1968. *Address:* Soysambu, Elmenteita, Kenya.

DELANEY, Shelagh; playwright; *b* Salford, Lancs, 1939; one *d. Educ:* Broughton Secondary Sch. *Plays:* A Taste of Honey, Theatre Royal, Stratford, 1958 and 1959, Wyndhams, 1959, New York, 1960 and 1961 (Charles Henry Foyle New Play Award, Arts Council Bursary, New York Drama Critics' Award); The Lion in Love, Royal Court 1960, New York 1962. *Films:* A Taste of Honey, 1961 (British Film Academy Award, Robert Flaherty Award); The White Bus, 1966; Charlie Bubbles, 1968 (Writers Guild Award for best original film writing). *TV plays:* St Martin's Summer, LWT, 1974; Find Me First, BBC TV, 1979; *TV series:* The House that Jack Built, BBC TV, 1977 (stage adaptation, NY, 1979). *Radio plays:* So Does the Nightingale, BBC, 1980; Don't Worry About Matilda. *Publications:* A Taste of Honey, 1959 (London and New York); The Lion in Love, 1961 (London and New York); Sweetly Sings the Donkey, 1963 (New York), 1964 (London). *Address:* c/o Tessa Sayle, 11 Jubilee Place, SW3 3TE.

de LAROSIÈRE de CHAMPFEU, Jacques (Martin Henri Marie); Chevalier, Legion of Honour, 1977; Chevalier, National Order of Merit, 1970; Managing Director, International Monetary Fund, since 1978; *b* 12 Nov. 1929; *s* of Robert de Larosière and Hugayte de Champfeu; *m* 1960, France du Bos; one *s* one *d. Educ:* Institut d'Etudes Politiques, Paris (L ès L, licencié en droit); Nat. Sch. of Administration, Paris. Inspecteur des Finances, 1958; Inspecteur Général des Finances, 1980; appointments at: Inspectorate-General of Finance, 1961; External Finance Office, 1963; Treasury 1965; Asst Dir, Treasury, 1967; Dep. Dir then Head of Dept, Min. of Economics and Finance, 1971; Principal Private Sec. to Minister of Economics and Finance, 1974; Dir, Treasury, 1974-78. Director: Renault, 1971-74; Banque Nat. de Paris, 1973-78; Air France and French Railways, 1974-78; Société nat. industrielle aérospatiale, 1976-78. Director appointed by Treasury, General Council, Bank of France, 1974-78; Auditor: Crédit national, 1974-78; Comptoir des entrepreneurs, 1973-75; Crédit foncier de France, 1975-78. Vice Pres., Caisse nat. des télécommunications, 1974-78. Chairman: OECD Econ. and Develt Review Cttee, 1967-71; Deputies Group of Ten, 1976-78. *Address:* International Monetary Fund, 700 19th Street NW, Washington, DC 20431, USA. *T:* (202) 477-3057.

de la RUE, Sir Eric (Vincent), 3rd Bt, *cr* 1898; *b* 5 Aug. 1906; *s* of Sir Evelyn Andros de la Rue, 2nd Bt, and Mary Violet (*d* 1969), *e d* of John Liell Francklin of Gonalston, Notts; *S* father 1950; *m* 1st, 1945, Cecilia (*d* 1963), *d* of late Lady Clementine Waring; two *s* ; 2nd, 1964, Christine Schellin, Greenwich, Conn, USA; one *s. Educ:* Oundle. Served War of 1939-45. Capt. Notts Yeomanry, 1942-45. *Heir:* s Andrew George Ilay de la Rue, *b* 3 Feb. 1946. *Address:* Caldra, Duns, Scotland. *T:* Duns 3294.

de la TOUR, Frances; actress; *b* 30 July 1944; *d* of Charles de la Tour and Moyra (*née* Fessas); one *s* one *d*. *Educ:* Lycée français de Londres; Drama Centre, London. Royal Shakespeare Company, 1965-71: rôles include Audrey in As You Like It, 1967; Hoyden in The Relapse, 1969; Helena in A Midsummer Night's Dream (Peter Brooks's production), 1971; Belinda in The Man of Mode, 1971; Violet in Small Craft Warnings, Comedy, 1973 (Best Supporting Actress, Plays and Players Award); Ruth Jones in The Banana Box, Apollo, 1973; Isabella in The White Devil, Old Vic, 1976; appearances at Hampstead Theatre, and Half Moon Theatre incl. title rôle in Hamlet, 1979; Stephanie in Duet for One (written by Tom Kempinski), Bush Theatre and Duke of York's, 1980 (Best New Play, and Best Perf. by Actress, Drama Awards, Best Perf. by Actress in New Play, SWET Award, Best Actress, New Standard Award); Jean in Skirmishes, Hampstead, 1982 (also television, 1982); Sonya in Uncle Vanya, Haymarket, 1982. *Films:* include Our Miss Fred, 1972; To the Devil a Daughter, 1976; Rising Damp, 1979 (Best Actress, New Standard British Film Award, 1980). *Television:* Crimes of Passion, 1973; Play for Today (twice), 1973-75; Rising Damp (series), 1974, 1976; Cottage to Let, 1976; Flickers, 1980. *Address:* c/o John Cadell Ltd, 2 Southwood Lane, N6 5EE. *T:* 01-348 1914.

DE LA WARR, 10th Earl *cr* 1761; **William Herbrand Sackville,** DL; Baron De La Warr, 1299 and 1572; Viscount Cantelupe, 1761; Baron Buckhurst (UK), 1864; *b* 16 Oct. 1921; *e s* of 9th Earl De La Warr, PC, GBE, and Diana (*d* 1966), *d* of late Gerard Leigh; *S* father, 1976; *m* 1946, Anne Rachel, *o d* of Geoffrey Devas, Hunton Court, Maidstone; two *s* one *d*. *Educ:* Eton. Lieut Royal Sussex Regt, 1941-43; Lieut Parachute Regt, 1943; Capt. 1945-46. Contested (C) NE Bethnal Green, 1945; Chm. London Young Conservatives, 1946, Pres. 1947-49. Man. Dir, Rediffusion Ltd, 1974-79 (Dir, 1968-79); Director: British Electric Traction Co. Ltd, 1970-79; Wembley Stadium Ltd, 1972-79; Portals Hldgs Ltd, 1974-; Chm., Redifon, 1978-79. Hon. Col Sussex ACF, 1969-; Vice-Chm., South East TAVR Assoc. (and Chm. Co. of Sussex Cttee), 1968-74 and 1978-; Chairman: Sussex County Playing Fields Assoc., 1956-71; London and SE Resettlement Cttee for Ex-Regulars, 1969-74. DL East Sussex, 1975. *Heir: s* Lord Buckhurst, *qv*. *Address:* Buckhurst Park, Withyham, East Sussex. *T:* Hartfield 346; 93 Eaton Place, SW1. *T:* 01-235 7990; (office) 93 Eaton Place, SW1. *T:* 01-235 9227. *Clubs:* White's, Pratt's.

DE LA WARR, Sylvia Countess; Sylvia Margaret Sackville, DBE 1957; *d* of William Reginald Harrison, Liverpool; *m* 1st, 1925, David Patrick Maxwell Fyfe (later Earl of Kilmuir, *cr* 1962, PC, GCVO) (*d* 1967); two *d* (and one *d* decd); 2nd, 1968, 9th Earl De La Warr, PC, GBE (*d* 1976). *Address:* 23 The Priory, Prior Park, Blackheath, SE3.

DELAY, Professeur Jean, Commandeur de la Légion d'Honneur; Grand Officier de l'Ordre national du Mérite; Member of the Académie de Médecine since 1955; Member of the Académie Française, since 1959; *b* Bayonne, Pyrénées Atlantiques, 14 Nov. 1907; *m* 1933, Marie-Madeleine Carrez; two *d*. *Educ:* Faculté de Médecine and Faculté des Lettres Sorbonne. DèsL Sorbonne. Prof. of Mental Diseases, Faculté de Médecine de Paris, 1946-70; Director, L'Institut de Psychologie, Sorbonne, 1951-70. Mem. French Section Unesco. Hon. Member, Royal Society Med.; Mem., Royal Soc. of Sciences of Uppsala; Distinguished Fellow, APA, 1977. Dr hc Univs of Zürich, Montreal and Barcelona. Médaille d'Or, Congrès Mondial de Psycho-Pharmologie, 1971. *Publications:* scientific: Les Dissolutions de la mémoire, 1942; Les Dérèglements de l'humeur, 1946; Les Maladies de la mémoire, 1947; La Psycho-Physiologie humaine, 1945; Aspects de la psychiatrie moderne, 1956; Etudes de psychologie médicale, 1953; Méthodes biologiques, 1950, psychométriques, 1956, chimiothérapiques, 1961, en psychiatrie; Introduction a la médecine psychosomatique, 1961; Abrégé de psychologie, 1962; Les démences tardives, 1962; L'électroencéphalographie clinique, 1966; Le syndrome de Korsakoff, 1969; literary: La Cité grise, 1946; Hommes sans nom, 1948; Les Reposantes, 1947; La Jeunesse d'André Gide (grand prix de la Critique), Vol. 1, 1956, Vol. 2, 1957; Une Amitié (André Gide et Roger Martin du Gard), 1968; La Correspondance de Jacques Copeau et Roger Martin du Gard, 1972; Avant Mémoire, vol. 1, 1979, vol. 2, 1980. *Address:* 53 avenue Montaigne, 75008 Paris. *T:* 359 77-07.

DELFONT, family name of **Baron Delfont.**

DELFONT, Baron *cr* 1976 (Life Peer), of Stepney; **Bernard Delfont,** Kt 1974; Chairman and Chief Executive, Trusthouse Forte Leisure Ltd, since 1980; Director: EMI Films; EMI Cinemas Ltd; EMI Leisure Enterprises Ltd; EMI Elstree Studios; Bernard Delfont Organisation; Blackpool Tower Company; *b* Tokmak, Russia, 5 Sept. 1909; *s* of late Isaac and Olga Winogradsky; *m* Carole Lynne; one *s* two *d*. Entered theatrical management, 1941; assumed management of: Wimbledon Theatre, 1942; Whitehall Theatre and St Martin's Theatre, 1943; (with Mala de la Marr) Winter Garden, 1944; Saville Theatre, 1946 (now ABC 1 and 2); lease of Prince of Wales Theatre, 1958; assumed management of Comedy Theatre and Shaftesbury Theatre, 1964; New London Theatre, 1973; converted London Hippodrome into Talk of the Town Restaurant, 1958, and presents entertainment there; Chief Exec., EMI Ltd, May 1979-Dec. 1980; controls more than 30 cos (theatre, film, television, music, property interests). Presents many of West End's theatrical shows and summer shows in many cities and towns in Great Britain. Past Chief Barker (Pres.), Variety Club of GB, (1969); Life Pres., Entertainment Artistes' Benevolent Fund, for which presented annual Royal Variety Performance, 1958-78; Companion, Grand Order of Water Rats; Member, Saints and

Sinners; Pres., Printers Charitable Corp., 1979. *Address:* 17 Golden Square, W1R 3AG. *T:* 01-437 1695.
See also Baron Grade.

DELHI, Archbishop of, (RC), since 1967; **Most Rev. Angelo Fernandes;** Founder Member, Planetary Citizens, 1972; President, World Conference of Religion for Peace, since 1970; Member, General Council of World Synod of Catholic Bishops, since 1980; *b* 28 July 1913; *s* of late John Ligorio and Evelyn Sabina Fernandes. *Educ:* St Patrick's, Karachi; St Joseph's Seminary, Mangalore; Papal University, Kandy, Ceylon (STL). Secretary to Archbishop Roberts of Bombay, 1943-47; Administrator of Holy Name Cathedral, Bombay, 1947-59; Coadjutor Archbishop of Delhi, 1959-67; Sec. Gen., Catholic Bishops' Conf. of India, 1960-72. Member: Vatican Secretariat for Non-Believers, 1966-71; Vatican Justice and Peace Commn, 1967-76; Secretariat of Synod of Bishops, 1971-74; Office of Human Develt of Fedn of Asian Bishops' Confs, 1973-78 (Mem., Exec. Cttee for Ecumenism and Inter-Religious Affairs, 1981-). Hon. DD Vatican, 1959. *Publications:* Apostolic Endeavour, 1962; Religion, Development and Peace, 1971; Religion and the Quality of Life, 1974; Religion and a New World Order, 1976; Towards Peace with Justice, 1981; articles in Clergy Monthly, Vidyajyoti, World Justice, Religion and Society, Social Action, Reality, etc. *Recreations:* music, especially classical, and wide travel on the occasion of numerous meetings in many countries of the world. *Address:* Archbishop's House, Ashok Place, New Delhi 110001, India. *T:* 343457.

DELIGHT, Ven. John David; Archdeacon of Stoke, since 1982; *b* 24 Aug. 1925; *s* of late Rev. Sidney John Delight and of Elizabeth Ethel Tuckett; *m* 1952, Eileen Elsie Braden; four *s* two *d*. *Educ:* Christ's Hospital, Horsham; Liverpool Univ.; Oak Hill Theolog. Coll.; Open Univ. (BA). RNVR (Fleet Air Arm), 1943-46. Curate: Tooting Graveney, 1952-55; Wallington, 1955-58; Travelling Sec., Inter-Varsity Fellowship, 1958-61; Vicar, St Christopher's, Leicester, 1961-69; Chaplain, Leicester Prison, 1965-67; Rector of Aldridge, 1969-82. *Publication:* (contrib.) Families, Facts and Frictions, 1976. *Recreations:* birdwatching, walking, caravanning, farming, National Trust, music. *Address:* Sandon Vicarage, Stafford ST18 0DB. *T:* Sandon 261. *Club:* Christ's Hospital.

DE L'ISLE, 1st Viscount, *cr* 1956; **William Philip Sidney,** VC 1944; KG 1968; PC 1951; GCMG 1961; GCVO 1963; Baron De L'Isle and Dudley, 1835; Bt 1806; Bt 1818; Chairman, Property Growth Assurance, since 1977; Chancellor, Order of St Michael and St George, since 1968; Governor-General of Australia, 1961-65; *b* 23 May 1909; *o s* of 5th Baron De L'Isle and Dudley and Winifred (*d* 1959), *e d* of Roland Yorke Bevan and Hon. Agneta Kinnaird, 4th *d* of 10th Baron Kinnaird; *S* father, 1945; *m* 1st 1940, Hon. Jacqueline Corinne Yvonne Vereker (*d* 1962), *o d* of late Field Marshal Viscount Gort of Hamsterley, VC, GCB, CBE, DSO, MVO, MC; one *s* four *d*; 2nd 1966, Margaret Lady Glanusk, JP, *widow* of 3rd Baron Glanusk, DSO (whom she *m* 1942). *Educ:* Eton; Magdalene Coll., Cambridge. Commissioned Supplementary Reserve, Grenadier Guards, 1929, and served War of 1939-45 with Regt. MP (C) Chelsea, 1944-45; Parly Sec., Ministry of Pensions, 1945; Sec. of State for Air, Oct. 1951-Dec. 1955. Chm., Phoenix Assurance Co. Ltd, 1966-78; Director: Yorkshire Bank, 1970-80; Phoenix Assce Co. of NY, 1971-80; Radio-Tele-Luxembourg (UK), 1980-; Pan American Banks Inc., Miami. Pres., British Heart Foundn; Chm., Freedom Assoc., 1975-. Chm. of Trustees, Churchill Memorial Trust; Trustee, RAF Museum. Hon. Fellow Magdalene Coll., Cambridge, 1955. FCA; Hon. FRIBA. Hon. LLD Sydney, 1963. KStJ 1961. *Heir: s* Major Hon. Philip John Algernon Sidney, MBE 1977 [*b* 21 April 1945; *m* 1980, Isobel, *y d* of Sir Edmund Compton, *qv*. Grenadier Guards, 1966-79]. *Address:* Penshurst Place, near Tonbridge, Kent; Glanusk Park, Crickhowell, Brecon.
See also Baron Middleton, Sir E. H. T. Wakefield, Bt.

DELL, David Michael; Under Secretary, Department of Industry, since 1976; *b* 30 April 1931; *s* of late Montague Roger Dell and Aimée Gabrielle Dell; unmarried. *Educ:* Rugby Sch.; Balliol Coll., Oxford (MA). 2nd Lieut Royal Signals, Egypt and Cyprus, 1954-55. Admiralty, 1955-60; MoD, 1960-65; Min. of Technol., 1965-70; DTI, 1970; DoI, 1974. *Address:* 18 Shouldham Street, W1H 5FG.

DELL, Rt. Hon. Edmund, PC 1970; Chairman, Guinness Peat Group, since 1979 (Chief Executive, 1979-82); Chairman, Channel Four TV Co., since 1980; *b* 15 Aug. 1921; *s* of late Reuben and Frances Dell; *m* 1963, Susanne Gottschalk. *Educ:* Elementary schls; Owen's Sch., London; Queen's Coll., Oxford (Open Schol.). 1st Cl. Hons Mod. Hist., BA and MA 1947. War Service, 1941-45, Lieut RA (Anti-tank). Lecturer in Modern History, Queen's Coll., Oxford, 1947-49; Executive in Imperial Chemical Industries Ltd, 1949-63. Mem., Manchester City Council, 1953-60. Contested (Lab) Middleton and Prestwich, 1955. Pres., Manchester and Salford Trades Council, 1958-61. Simon Research Fellow, Manchester Univ., 1963-64. MP (Lab) Birkenhead, 1964-79; Parly Sec., Min. of Technology, 1966-67; Jt Parly Under-Sec. of State; Dept of Economic Affairs, 1967-68; Minister of State: Board of Trade, 1968-69; Dept of Employment and Productivity, 1969-70; Paymaster General, 1974-76; Sec. of State for Trade, 1976-78. Chm., Public Accts Cttee, 1973-74 (Acting Chm., 1972-73). Mem., Cttee of Three apptd by European Council to review procedures of EEC, 1978-79; Chairman: Hansard Soc. Commn on Financing of Politics, 1980-81; Working Party on Internat. Tax Avoidance, Inst. for Fiscal Studies, 1982. Boys' Chess Champion of London, 1936. *Publications:* (ed with J. E. C. Hill) The Good Old Cause,

1949; Brazil: The Dilemma of Reform (Fabian Pamphlet), 1964; Political Responsibility and Industry, 1973; (with B. Biesheuvel and R. Marjolin) Report on European Institutions, 1979; articles in learned journals. *Recreation:* listening to music. *Address:* 4 Reynolds Close, NW11 7EA.

DELL, Dame Miriam (Patricia), DBE 1980 (CBE 1975); JP(NZ); President, International Council of Women, since 1979; *b* 14 June 1924; *d* of Gerald Wilfred Matthews and Ruby Miriam Crawford; *m* 1946, Richard Kenneth Dell; four *d. Educ:* Epsom Girls Grammar Sch.; Univ. of Auckland (BA); Auckland Teachers' Coll. (Teachers' Cert. (Secondary Sch.)). Teaching, 1945-47, 1957-58 and 1961-71. Nat. Pres., Nat. Council of Women, 1970-74 (Vice-Pres., 1967-70); Chm., Cttee on Women, NZ, 1974-81. Member: Nat. Develt Council, 1969-74; Cttee of Inquiry into Equal Pay, 1971-72; Nat. Commn for UNESCO, 1974-; Social Security Appeal Authority, 1974-; Nat. Convenor, Internat. Women's Year, 1975. JP NZ 1975. Jubilee Medal, 1977. *Publications:* Role of Women in National Development, 1970; numerous articles in popular and house magazines, on role and status of women. *Recreations:* gardening, reading, handcrafts, beachcombing. *Address:* 98 Waerenga Road, Otaki, New Zealand. *T:* Otaki 47267; (office) PO Box 12-117, Wellington, New Zealand. *T:* 737623.

DELL, Ven. Robert Sydney; Archdeacon of Derby, since 1973; Canon Residentiary of Derby Cathedral, since 1981; *b* 20 May 1922; *s* of Sydney Edward Dell and Lilian Constance Palmer; *m* 1953, Doreen Molly Layton; one *s* one *d. Educ:* Harrow County Sch.; Emmanuel Coll., Cambridge (MA); Ridley Hall. Curate of: Islington, 1948; Holy Trinity, Cambridge, 1950; Asst Chaplain, Wrekin Coll., 1953; Vicar of Mildenhall, Suffolk, 1955; Vice-Principal of Ridley Hall, Cambridge, 1957; Vicar of Chesterton, Cambridge, 1966 (Dir, Cambridge Samaritans, 1966-69). Mem., Archbishops' Commn on Intercommunion, 1965-67; Proctor in Convocation and Mem. Gen. Synod of C of E, 1970-. Vis. Fellow, St George's House, Windsor Castle, 1981. *Publications:* Atlas of Christian History, 1960; contributor to: Charles Simeon, 1759-1836: essays written in commemoration of his bi-centenary, 1959; Jl of Ecclesiastical History. *Recreations:* reading, walking, travelling. *Address:* 72 Pastures Hill, Littleover, Derby DE3 7BB. *T:* Derby 512700. *Club:* Royal Commonwealth Society.

DELLAL, Jack; Chairman, Allied Commercial Exporters Ltd; *b* 2 Oct. 1923; *s* of Sulman and Charlotte Dellal; *m* 1952, Zehava Helmer; one *s* four *d. Educ:* Heaton Moor Coll., Manchester. Chm., Dalton, Barton & Co. Ltd, 1962-72; Dep. Chm., Keyser Ullman Ltd, 1972-74; Chm., Highland Electronics Group Ltd, 1971-76. Vice-Pres., Anglo-Polish Conservative Society. Officer, Order of Polonia Restituta, 1970. Freeman Citizen of Glasgow, 1971. *Recreations:* lawn tennis, squash, music, art. *Address:* 23 Ilchester Place, W14 8AA. *T:* 01-603 0981; Manor Farm, Brown Candover, Hants. *Clubs:* Royal Thames Yacht, Queen's, Lansdowne, Hurlingham.

DELLOW, John Albert, OBE 1979; Assistant Commissioner, B Department, Metropolitan Police, since 1982; *b* 5 June 1931; *s* of Albert Reginald and Lily Dellow; one *s* one *d. Educ:* William Ellis Sch., Highgate; Royal Grammar Sch., High Wycombe. Joined City of London Police, 1951; seconded Manchester City Police, 1966; Superintendent, Kent County Constabulary, 1966, Chief Supt, 1968; jssc 1969; Asst Chief Constable, Kent Co. Constabulary, 1969; Metropolitan Police: Dep. Assistant Commissioner: (Traffic Planning), 1973; (Personnel), 1975; No 2 Area, 1978; 'A' Dept Operations, 1979; Inspectorate, 1980. *Recreations:* walking, history, listening to wireless. *Address:* New Scotland Yard, Broadway, SW1H 0BG.

DEL MAR, Norman Rene, CBE 1975; freelance conductor; Conductor and Professor of Conducting, Royal College of Music; *b* 31 July 1919; *m* 1947, Pauline Mann; two *s. Educ:* Marlborough; Royal College of Music. Asst Sir Thomas Beecham, Royal Philharmonic Orchestra, 1947; Principal Conductor, English Opera Group, 1949-54; Conductor and Prof. of Conducting, Guildhall Sch. of Music, 1953-60; Conductor: Yorkshire Symphony Orchestra, 1954; BBC Scottish Orchestra, 1960-65; Royal Acad. of Music, 1974-77; Principal Conductor, Acad. of BBC, 1974-77. Artistic Dir, Norfolk and Norwich Triennial, 1979-. FRCM; FGSM; Hon. RAM. Hon. DMus: Glasgow, 1974; Bristol, 1978; Hon. DLitt Sussex, 1977. *Publications:* Richard Strauss, 3 vols, 1962-72; Mahler's Sixth Symphony: a study, 1980; Orchestral Variations, 1981; Anatomy of the Orchestra, 1981. *Recreations:* writing, chamber music. *Address:* Witchings, Hadley Common, Herts. *T:* 01-449 4836.

DELMAS, Jacques Pierre Michel C.; see Chaban-Delmas.

DELORS, Jacques Lucien Jean; Minister of the Economy and Finance, France, since 1981; *b* 20 July 1925; *s* of Louis and Jeanne Delors; *m* 1948, Marie Lephaille; one *s* one *d. Educ:* Paris Univ. Joined Banque de France, 1945; in office of Chief of Securities Dept, 1950-62, and in Sect. for the Plan and Investments, Conseil Economique et Social, 1959-61; Chief of Social Affairs, Gen. Commissariat of Plan Monnet, 1962-69; Gen. Sec., Interministerial Cttee for Professional Educn, 1969-73; Mem., Gen. Council, Banque de France, 1973-79, and Dir, on leave of absence, 1973-. Special Advr on Social Affairs to Prime Minister, 1969-72. Socialist Party spokesman on internat. econ. matters, 1976-. Mem., European Parlt, 1979-81 (Pres., Econ. and Financial Cttee). Associate Prof., Univ. of Paris-Dauphine, 1973-80, Dir, Work and Society Res. Centre, 1975-81. Founder, Club Echange et Projets, 1974. *Publications:* Les indicateurs sociaux, 1971; Changer, 1975; essays, articles and

UN reports on French Plan. *Address:* Ministère de l'Economie et des Finances, Paris, France; 93 rue de Rivoli, 75001, Paris, France.

de los ANGELES, Victoria; Cross of Lazo de Dama of Order of Isabel the Catholic, Spain; Condecoracion Banda de la Orden Civil de Alfonso X (El Sabio), Spain; Opera and Concert-Artiste (singing in original languages), Lyric-Soprano, since 1944; *b* Barcelona, Spain, 1 Nov. 1923; *m* 1948, Enrique Magriña; two *s. Educ:* Conservatorium of Barcelona; University of Barcelona. Studied until 1944 at Conservatorium, Barcelona; first public concert, in Barcelona, 1944; début at Gran Teatro del Liceo de Barcelona, in Marriage of Figaro, 1945; concert tours in Spain and Portugal, 1945 and 1946; winner of first prize at Concours International of Geneva, 1947; Paris Opera first appearance, and début at the Scala, Milan, also South-American concert-tour, 1949; first tour in Scandinavia, first appearance at Covent Garden, and Carnegie Hall Début, 1950; first United States concert tour, and Metropolitan Opera of New York season, 1951. Since 1951 has appeared at the most important opera theatres and concert halls of Europe, South and Central America and Canada; first tour in S Africa, 1953; first tour in Australia, 1956; first appearance, Vienna State Opera, 1957. Opening Festival, Bayreuth, with Tannhäuser, 1961. Gold Medal, Barcelona, 1958; Silver Medal, province of Barcelona, 1959; Medal Premio Roma, 1969, etc. *Address:* Victoria de los Angeles de Magriña, c/o E. Magriña, Paseo de Gracia, 87-7-D, Barcelona, Spain.

de LOTBINIÈRE, Lt-Col Sir Edmond; see Joly de Lotbinière.

de LOTBINIÈRE, Seymour Joly, CVO 1956; OBE 1953; *b* 21 Oct. 1905; *s* of late Brig.-Gen. H. G. Joly de Lotbinière, DSO; *m* 1944, Mona Lewis; one *s. Educ:* Eton; Trinity Coll., Cambridge. Called to Bar, Lincoln's Inn. On BBC staff, 1932-67. Governor, Bristol Old Vic Trust, 1963-67. CC West Suffolk, 1970-74. *Recreation:* gunflint research. *Address:* Brandon Hall, Brandon, Suffolk. *T:* Thetford 810227.
See also Lt-Col Sir Edmond Joly de Lotbinière.

DELVE, Sir Frederick (William), Kt 1962; CBE 1942; Chief Officer, London Fire Brigade, 1948-62, retired; Director and Vice-Chairman, Securicor Ltd, retired 1982; Director, Sound Diffusion Ltd; *b* 28 Oct. 1902; *s* of Frederick John Delve, Master Tailor, Brighton; *m* 1924, Ethel Lillian Morden (*d* 1980); no *c. Educ:* Brighton. Royal Navy, 1918-23; Fire Service since 1923; Chief Officer, Croydon Fire Brigade, 1934-41; Dep. Inspector-in-Chief of NFS, 1941-43; Chief Regional Fire Officer, No 5 London Region, National Fire Service, 1943-48. Pres., Institution of Fire Engineers, 1941-42; King's Police and Fire Services Medal, 1940. *Address:* 53 Ashley Court, Grand Avenue, Hove, East Sussex.

DELVIN, Lord; title borne by eldest son of Earl of Westmeath, *qv*; not at present used.

de MAJO, William Maks, (known as Willy), MBE (mil.) 1946; FSIAD; Chairman and Managing Director, W. M. de Majo Associates Ltd, since 1946; Sales Director, Cronmatch Ltd, since 1964; Consultant: Charles Letts & Co. Ltd, John Millar & Sons, Ti-Well Ltd; *b* 25 July 1917; *s* of Maks de Majo and Josefine (née Ganz); *m* 1941, Veronica Mary Booker (separated); three *d. Educ:* Commercial Academy, Vienna. Chartered Designer. In practice as graphic and industrial designer on continent, 1935-39; news typist and broadcaster with BBC Overseas Service, 1940-41; war service as pilot and liaison officer, Royal Yugoslav Air Force, UK, Africa, ME, 1942-45 (Actg Chief Air Sect.); transf. to RAF, SO SHAEF and CCG HQ, 1945-46; re-established practice London, on demobilisation, 1946. Cons. designer to various nat. and internat. cos; guest lectr on design; co-ordinating designer, Fest. of Britain, 1951 (Ulster farm and factory); guest speaker, Internat. Design Conf., Aspen, Colo, 1954; designer, Baden-Powell Mus., 1961; designer-in-chief and co-ordinator, internat. exhibits, 1950-75; Mem. Jury, Canada Olympic Coins Comp., 1976; work exhibited on 5 continents. Founder and past Pres., Internat. Council of Graphic Design Assocs, 1963-68; Mem. Internat. Relations Bd, SIAD. Hon. Member: Assoc. of Graphic Designers, Netherlands, 1959; Assoc. of Swedish Art Dirs and Designers, 1965; Chambre Belges des Graphistes, 1966. SIAD Design Medal 1969; winner of numerous nat. and internat. design competitions. *Publications:* contrib. Packaging (design of the gift pack), 1959 (Zürich); articles on graphic and industrial design to most leading jls in GB and abroad. *Recreations:* travelling, cooking, fostering good international relations. *Address:* 99 Archel Road, W14 9QL. *T:* 01-385 0394.

de MANIO, Jack, MC 1940; Broadcaster; *b* 26 Jan. 1914; *s* of Jean and Florence de Manio; *m* 1st, 1935, Juliet Gravaeret Kaufmann, New York (marr. diss., 1946); one *s*; 2nd, 1946, Loveday Elizabeth Matthews (widow, née Abbott). *Educ:* Aldenham. Served War of 1939-45, Royal Sussex Regt; 7th Bn, BEF, 1939-40; 1st Bn, Middle East Forces, 1940-44; Forces Broadcasting, Middle East, 1944-46. Joined Overseas Service, BBC, 1946; BBC Home Service, 1950; resigned to become freelance, 1964. Presenter BBC programmes: Today, 1958-71; Jack de Manio Precisely, 1971-78; With Great Pleasure, 1971-73; contributor Woman's Hour, 1979-. Dir, Neilson McCarthy. Radio Personality of Year Award, Variety Club of GB, 1964; Radio Personality Award of Year, British Radio Industries Club, 1971. *Publications:* To Auntie with Love, 1967; Life Begins Too Early, 1970; contrib to Punch and numerous other periodicals. *Recreation:* fishing. *Address:* 105 Cheyne Walk, SW10. *T:* 01-352 0889. *Clubs:* Brooks's, MCC.

DEMANT, Rev. Vigo Auguste, MA, DLitt Oxford; BSc, Hon. DD Durham; *b* 8 Nov. 1893; *s* of late T. Demant, linguist, of Newcastle on Tyne, and Emily Demant; *m* 1925, Marjorie, *d* of late George Tickner, FZS, Oxford; one *s* two *d. Educ:* Newcastle on Tyne; Tournan, France; Armstrong Coll., Durham Univ.; Manchester Coll. and Exeter Coll., Oxford; Ely Theological Coll. Curacies: S Thomas, Oxford, S Nicholas, Plumstead, S Silas, Kentish Town; Dir of Research to Christian Social Council, 1929-33; Vicar of S John-the-Divine, Richmond, Surrey, 1933-42; Canon Residentiary, 1942-49, Treasurer, 1948-49, of St Paul's Cathedral; Canon of Christ Church and Regius Professor of Moral and Pastoral Theology in Oxford University, 1949-71. Ex-Mem. Departmental Cttee on Homosexual Offences and Prostitution. Gifford Lecturer, St Andrews, 1957-58. *Publications:* This Unemployment, 1931; God, Man and Society, 1933; Christian Polity, 1936; The Religious Prospect, 1939; Theology of Society, 1947; Religion and the Decline of Capitalism, 1952; A Two-way Religion, 1957; Christian Sex Ethics, 1963. *Recreation:* carpentry. *Address:* 31 St Andrew's Road, Old Headington, Oxford. *T:* Oxford 64022.

DEMARCO, Richard, RWSScot, SSA; Director, The Richard Demarco Gallery Ltd, Edinburgh, since 1966; *b* 9 July 1930; *s* of Carmine Demarco and Elizabeth (*née* Fusco); *m* 1957, Anne Muckle. *Educ:* Holy Cross Academy, Edinburgh; Edinburgh College of Art. National Service, KOSB and RAEC, 1954-56. Art Master, Duns Scotus Academy, Edinburgh, 1956-67; Co-Founder, Traverse Theatre Club; Vice-Chm. and Director, Traverse Art Gall., 1963-67; appointed Dir, Richard Demarco Gall., Melville Crescent, Edinburgh, by co-founders John Martin, Andrew Elliott and James Walker, 1966; introduced contemporary visual arts into official Edinburgh Festival programme with Edinburgh Open 100 Exhibn, 1967; introduced work of 330 internat. artists to UK, mainly through Edinburgh Fest. exhibns, from Canada, 1968, W Germany, 1970, Romania, 1971, Poland, 1972 and 1979, France, 1973, Austria, 1973, Yugoslavia, 1976, incl. Joseph Beuys, 1970, and Tadeusz Kantor's Cricot Theatre, with prodns of The Water Hen, 1972, Lovelies and Dowdies, 1973, The Dead Class, 1976. Has presented, 1969-, annual programmes of theatre, music and dance prodns, incl. the freehold Company's Antigone, 1970, the Dublin Project Company's On Baille Strand, 1977. Director: Sean Connery's Scottish Internat. Educn Trust, 1972-74; Edinburgh Arts annual summer sch. and expedns, 1972-. Has directed annual exhib. prog. with Special Unit, HM Prison, Barlinnie, with partic. reference to sculpture of James Boyle, 1974-. Was subject of film, Walkabout Edinburgh, dir. by Edward McConnell, 1970; acted in feature films: Long Shot, 1978; That Sinking Feeling, 1980. Has broadcast regularly on television and radio, 1966-; has lectured in over 100 univs, art colls, schools, art galls; as water-colour painter and paintmaker is represented in over 1600 public and private collections, incl. Nat. Gall. of Modern Art of Scotland, V&A Museum, Scottish Arts Council. Contributing Editor, Studio International, 1982-. SSA 1964; RWSScot 1966. Gold Order of Merit, Polish People's Republic, 1976. *Publications:* The Artist as Explorer, 1978; The Road to Meikle Seggie, 1978. *Recreations:* exploring: the small and secret spaces in townscape; cathedrals, abbeys, parish churches; coastlines and islands and The Road to Meikle Seggie. *Address:* 29 Frederick Street, Edinburgh EH2 2ND. *T:* 031-225 5879. *Club:* Scottish Arts (Edinburgh).

de MARGERIE, Emmanuel; Chevalier de l'Ordre National de la Légion d'Honneur; Officier de l'Ordre National du Mérite; Commandeur de l'Ordre des Arts et des Lettres; French Ambassador to the Court of St James's, since 1981; *b* 25 Dec. 1924; *s* of Roland de Margerie, *qv*; *m* 1953, Hélène Hottinguer; one *s* one *d. Educ:* Lycée Français de Londres; Univ. Aurore, Shanghai; Sorbonne; Institut d'Etudes Politiques, Paris. Ecole Nat. d'Administration, 1949-51; joined Min. of Foreign Affairs, 1951; Sec., French Embassy, London, 1954-59; Moscow, 1959-61; Quai d'Orsay, 1961-67; Minister, Tokyo, 1967-70; Minister, Washington, 1970-72; Dir, European Dept, Quai d'Orsay, 1972-74; Dir Gen. of French Museums, 1975-77; Ambassador to Madrid, 1978-81. Grand Cross, Order of Isabel la Católica (Spain), 1980, and various other foreign orders. *Address:* French Embassy, 58 Knightsbridge, SW1. *Clubs:* Beefsteak, Garrick, Travellers', White's.

de MARGERIE, Roland, CVO 1938; Ambassador of France; Hon. Conseiller d'Etat; *b* 6 May 1899; *s* of late P. de Margerie, KBE, French Ambassador in Berlin, 1922-31, and Jeanne Rostand, sister of the Playwright Edmond Rostand, Mem. of the French Academy; *m* 1921, Jenny, *d* of Edmond Fabre-Luce, Vice-Chm. of the Crédit Lyonnais; two *s* one *d. Educ:* Sorbonne; Ecole des Sciences Politiques, Paris. Joined Foreign Office, 1917; Lieut 17th Bn of Chasseurs Alpins, 1918-21; Attaché to French Embassy, Brussels, 1921; Sec., Berlin, 1923; 1st Sec. to the French Embassy, London, 1933-39; mem. of the mission attached to their Majesties during their State visit to France, 1938; Counsellor, 1939; Captain 152nd Regt of the Line, Sept. 1939-Feb. 1940; ADC to Gen. Gamelin, Feb.-March 1940; Private Sec. to the Minister for Foreign Affairs, March 1940; French Consul-Gen., Shanghai, 1940-44; Chargé with the office of the French Embassy in Peking, 1944-46. Asst deleg. negotiations for Brussels Pact, 1948; Minister plenipotentiary, 1949; Director-Gen. of Political Affairs, France, 1955; French Ambassador to the Holy See, 1956-59; to Spain, 1959-62; to the Federal Republic of Germany, 1962-65; Conseiller d'Etat, 1965-70. Comdr Legion of Honour; holds various foreign orders. *Address:* 14 rue St Guillaume, 75007 Paris, France. *Club:* Jockey (Paris).

See also Emmanuel de Margerie.

de MAULEY, 6th Baron, *cr* 1838; **Gerald John Ponsonby;** *b* 19 Dec. 1921; *er s* of 5th Baron de Mauley and Elgiva Margaret, *d* of late Hon. Cospatrick Dundas and Lady Cordeaux; *S* father, 1962; *m* 1954, Helen Alice, *d* of late Hon. Charles W. S. Douglas and *widow* of Lieut-Col B. L. L. Abdy Collins, OBE, MC, RE. *Educ:* Eton; Christ Church, Oxford (MA). Served War of 1939-45, France; Lieut Leics Yeo., Captain RA. Called to Bar, Middle Temple, 1949. *Heir: b* Col Hon. Thomas Maurice Ponsonby, TD, late Royal Glos Hussars [*b* 2 Aug. 1930; *m* 1956, Maxine Henrietta, *d* of W. D. K. Thellusson; two *s*]. *Address:* Langford House, Little Faringdon, Lechlade, Glos.

de MAYO, Prof. Paul, FRS 1975; FRSC 1971; Professor of Chemistry, University of Western Ontario, since 1959; *b* 8 Aug. 1924; *s* of Nissim and Anna de Mayo; *m* 1949, Mary Turnbull; one *s* one *d. Educ:* Univ. of London. BSc, MSc, PhD London; DesS Paris. Asst Lectr, Birkbeck Coll., London, 1954-55; Lectr, Univ. of Glasgow, 1955-57; Lectr, Imperial Coll., London, 1957-59; Dir, Photochemistry Unit, Univ. of Western Ontario, 1969-72. Merck Lecture Award, 1966; Centennial Medal, 1967; Chemical Inst. of Canada Medal, 1982. *Publications:* Mono-and sesquiterpenoids, 1959; The Higher Terpenoids, 1959; (ed) Molecular Rearrangements, 1963; (ed) Rearrangements in Ground and Excited States, vols 1-3, 1980; numerous papers in learned jls. *Address:* 436 St George Street, London, Ontario, Canada. *T:* (office) 679-2473, (home) 679-9026.

de MILLE, Agnes George (Mrs W. F. Prude); Choreographer and Author; *b* New York City; *d* of William C. and Anna George de Mille; *m* 1943, Walter F. Prude; one *s. Educ:* University of Calif. (AB *cum laude*). Dance concerts USA, England, Denmark, France, 1929-40; Choreographed: Black Crook, 1929; Nymph Errant, 1933; Romeo and Juliet 1936; Oklahoma, 1943, 1980; One Touch of Venus, 1943; Bloomer Girl, 1944; Carousel, 1945; Brigadoon, 1947; Gentlemen Prefer Blondes, 1949; Paint Your Wagon, 1951; The Girl in Pink Tights, 1954; Oklahoma (film), 1955; Goldilocks, 1958; Juno, 1959; Kwamina, 1961; One Hundred and Ten in the Shade, 1963; Come Summer, 1968. Founded and directed Agnes de Mille Dance Theatre, 1953-54. Directed: Allegro, 1947; The Rape of Lucretia, 1948; Out of This World, 1950; Come Summer, 1968; Ballets composed: Black Ritual, 1940; Three Virgins and a Devil, 1941; Drums Sound in Hackensack, 1941; Rodeo, 1942; Tally-Ho, 1944; Fall River Legend, 1948; The Harvest According, 1952; The Rib of Eve, 1956; The Bitter Wierd, 1963; The Wind in the Mountains, 1965; The Four Marys, 1965; The Golden Age, 1966; A Rose for Miss Emily, 1970; Texas Fourth, 1976; A Bridegroom called Death; Agnes de Mille Heritage Dance Theater, 1973-74, etc. Television shows, for Omnibus, etc. Mem., Nat. Adv. Council of the Arts, 1965-66; Pres., Soc. for Stage Directors and Choreographers, 1966-67. Hon. Degrees: Mills Coll., 1952; Russell Sage College, 1953; Smith Coll., 1954; Northwestern Univ., 1960; Goucher Coll., 1961; University of Calif., 1962; Clark Univ., 1962; Franklin and Marshall Coll., 1966; Western Michigan Univ., 1967; Nasson Coll., 1971; Dartmouth Coll., 1974; Duke Univ.; Univ. of North Carolina; New York Univ. New York Critics Award, 1943, 1944, 1945; Antoinette Perry Award, 1962; Handel Medallion, 1976; Kennedy Curtis Award, 1981; and numerous other awards, 1943-58. *Publications:* Dance to the Piper, 1952; And Promenade Home, 1956; To a Young Dancer, 1962; The Book of the Dance, 1963; Lizzie Borden, Dance of Death, 1968; Dance in America, 1970; Russian Journals, 1970; Speak to me, Dance with me, 1973; Where the Wings Grow, 1978; America Dances, 1981; Reprieve, 1981; articles in Vogue, Atlantic Monthly, Good Housekeeping, New York Times, McCall's, Horizon, Esquire. *Club:* Merriewold Country (NY).

DE MOLEYNS; *see* Eveleigh-de-Moleyns.

de MONTEBELLO, (Guy) Philippe (Lannes); Director, Metropolitan Museum of Art, since 1978; *b* 16 May 1936; *s* of Roger Lannes de Montebello and Germaine (*née* Croisset); *m* 1961, Edith Bradford Myles; two *s* one *d. Educ:* Harvard Coll. (BA *magna cum laude*); New York Univ., Inst. of Fine Arts (MA). Curatorial Asst, European Paintings, Metropolitan Mus. of Art, 1963; Asst Curator, Associate Curator, MMA, until 1969; Director, Museum of Fine Arts, Houston, Texas, 1969-74; Vice-Director: for Curatorial Affairs, MMA, Jan. 1974-June 1974; for Curatorial and Educnl Affairs, 1974-77; Actg Dir, MMA, 1977-78. Gallatin Fellow, New York Univ., 1981; Hon. LLD: Lafayette Coll., East Pa, 1979; Bard Coll., Annandale-on-Hudson, NY, 1981. *Publication:* Peter Paul Rubens, 1968. *Address:* 1150 Fifth Avenue, New York, New York 10028, USA. *T:* 289 4475. *Club:* Knickerbocker (New York).

de MONTMORENCY, Sir Arnold (Geoffroy), 19th Bt *cr* 1631; Chairman, Contemporary Review Co. Ltd, since 1962, and Literary Editor since 1960; *b* 27 July 1908; *s* of Prof. James Edward Geoffroy de Montmorency (*d* 1934) and Caroline Maud Saumarez (*d* 1973), *d* of Maj.-Gen. James de Havilland; *S* cousin, 1979; *m* 1949, Nettie Hay Anderson (marr. annulled 1953, remarried 1972), *d* of late William Anderson and Janet Hay, Morayshire; no *c. Educ:* Westminster School (Triplett Exhibn); Peterhouse, Cambridge. BA 1930, LLB 1931, MA 1934. Harmsworth Law Scholar. Called to the Bar, 1932. Served War, RASC and staff in ME, Italy and Yugoslavia, 1940-45. Contested (L) Cambridge, 1959, Cirencester and Tewkesbury, 1964. Chm. (pt-time), Industrial Tribunals, 1975-81. Member, RIIA; Chm. of Council, Friends of Peterhouse. *Heir:* none. *Address:* 2 Garden Court, Temple, EC4Y 9BL. *Club:* National Liberal.

de MOURGUES, Prof. Odette Marie Hélène Louise, PhD, DLitt; Palmes Académiques 1964; Ordre National du Mérite 1973; Professor of French, University of Cambridge, since 1975; Lecturer, Research Fellow and Fellow, Girton College, Cambridge, since 1946; *b* 14 May 1914; *d* of Dr Pierre de Mourgues and Hélène Terle; *m* 1934 (marr. diss. 1943); one *s* decd. *Educ:* Lycée of Le Puy; Univs of Grenoble and Aix-en-Provence. Licence en droit, diplôme d'études supérieures de droit, LèsL, agrégation d'anglais; PhD, DLitt Cantab. Teaching posts, Valence, Digne and Marseille, 1942-45; Asst Lectr, Univ. of Aix-en-Provence, 1944-46; Lectr in French, 1952-68, Reader, 1968-75, Univ. of Cambridge. *Publications:* Metaphysical, Baroque and Précieux Poetry, 1953; Le Jugement Avant-dernier (fiction), 1954; L'Hortensia Bleu (fiction), 1956; La Fontaine: Fables, 1960; O Muse, fuyante Proie, 1962; An Anthology of French 17C Poetry, 1966; Racine or the Triumph of Relevance, 1967; Autonomie de Racine, 1967; Two French Moralists, 1978; essays, articles and revs. *Recreations:* travel, gardening. *Address:* 1 Marion Close, Cambridge. *T:* Cambridge 56865.

DEMPSEY, Andrew; *see* Dempsey, J. A.

DEMPSEY, (James) Andrew; Assistant Director of Exhibitions, Arts Council of Great Britain, since 1975; *b* 17 Nov. 1942; *s* of James Dempsey, Glasgow; *m* 1966, Grace, *d* of Dr Ian MacPhail, Dumbarton; one *s* one *d*. *Educ:* Ampleforth Coll.; Glasgow Univ. Whistler Research Asst, Fine Art Dept, Univ. of Glasgow, 1963-65; exhibn work for art dept of Arts Council, 1966-71; Keeper, Dept of Public Relations, V&A, 1971-75. *Address:* 105 Piccadilly, W1.

DEMPSTER, John William Scott; Principal Establishment and Finance Officer, Lord Chancellor's Department, since 1980; *b* 10 May 1938; *s* of late Dr David Dempster and Mrs M. C. Dempster; *m* 1965, Ailsa Newman (marr. diss. 1972). *Educ:* Plymouth Coll.; Oriel Coll., Oxford (MA(PPE)). HM Inspector of Taxes, Inland Revenue, 1961-65; Ministry of Transport: Asst Principal, 1965-66; Private Sec. to Parly Sec., 1966-67; Principal, 1967-73; Asst Sec., Property Services Agency, 1973-76; Principal Private Sec. to Sec. of State for the Environment, 1976-77; Asst Sec., 1977-79, Under Sec., 1979-80, Dept of Transport. *Recreations:* mountaineering, sailing, bridge, Munro collecting. *Address:* Lord Chancellor's Department, Neville House, Page Street, SW1. *T:* 01-211 7879. *Clubs:* Hampstead Cricket; Fell and Rock Climbing, Swiss Alpine.

DENBIGH, 11th Earl of, *cr* 1622 **AND DESMOND,** 10th Earl of, *cr* 1622; **William Rudolph Michael Feilding;** *b* 2 Aug. 1943; *s* of 10th Earl of Denbigh and Verena Barbara, *d* of W. E. Price; *S* father, 1966; *m* 1965, Caroline Judith Vivienne, *o d* of Lt-Col Geoffrey Cooke; one *s* two *d*. *Educ:* Eton. Heir: *s* Viscount Feilding, *qv. Address:* 21 Moore Park Road, SW6; Newnham Paddox, near Rugby, Warwickshire. *T:* Rugby 832173.

DENBIGH, Prof. Kenneth George, FRS 1965; MA Cantab, DSc Leeds; Director, Council for Science and Society, since 1977; Principal of Queen Elizabeth College, University of London, 1966-77; Professor Emeritus in the University of London, 1977; *b* 30 May 1911; *s* of late G. J. Denbigh, MSc, Harrogate; *m* 1935, Kathleen Enoch; two *s*. *Educ:* Queen Elizabeth Grammar Sch., Wakefield; Leeds University. Imperial Chemical Industries, 1934-38, 1945-48; Lecturer, Southampton Univ., 1938-41; Ministry of Supply (Explosives), 1941-45; Lecturer, Cambridge Univ., Chemical Engineering Dept, 1948-55; Professor of Chemical Technology, Edinburgh, 1955-60, of Chemical Engineering Science, London Univ., 1960-61; Courtauld's Prof., Imperial Coll., 1961-66. Fellow, Imperial Coll., 1976. Hon. DèsSc Toulouse, 1960; Hon. DUniv. Essex, 1967. *Publications:* The Thermodynamics of the Steady State, 1951; The Principles of Chemical Equilibrium, 1955; Science, Industry and Social Policy, 1963; Chemical Reactor Theory, 1965; An Inventive Universe, 1975; Three Concepts of Time, 1981; various scientific papers. *Address:* 19 Sheridan Road, Merton Park, SW19 3HW.

DENBY, Patrick Morris Coventry, CMG 1982; Assistant Director-General (Treasurer and Financial Comptroller), International Labour Office, Geneva, 1976-81; *b* 28 Sept. 1920; *s* of Robert Coventry Denby and Phyllis Denby (*née* Dacre); *m* 1950, Margaret Joy, *d* of Lt-Col C. L. Boyle; two *d* (and one *d* decd). *Educ:* Bradford Grammar Sch.; Corpus Christi Coll., Oxford (Open Scholar) (Honour Mods, Cl. II, MA). War service with Intelligence Corps, as Temp. Lieut RNVR, and with Foreign Office, 1941-46. Unilever Ltd, UK and Australia: management trainee and product manager, 1946-51; joined International Labour Office, 1951: Professional Officer, 1951; Chief of Budget and Control Div., 1959; Chief of Finance and General Services Dept, Treasurer and Financial Comptroller, 1970; Chm., Investments Cttee; Mem., UN Pension Board, 1971-75. *Recreations:* skiing, mountain walking, squash, tennis. *Address:* 1 avenue Dumas, 1206 Geneva, Switzerland. *Clubs:* United Oxford & Cambridge University, Ski Club of GB; Swiss Alpine.

DENBY, Sir Richard Kenneth, Kt 1978; President of the Law Society of England and Wales, 1977 (Vice-President, 1976); Senior Partner, A. V. Hammond & Co., Bradford; *b* 20 March 1915; *s* of John Henry and Emily Denby; *m* 1939, Eileen (*d* 1974), *d* of M. H. Pickles, CBE; one *s* two *d*. *Educ:* Ackworth School; Leeds Univ. (LLB). Admitted Solicitor, 1937 (First Cl. Hons and Clifford's Inn Prize). Served War of 1939-45: 2nd Lt, The Green Howards, 1940; AFHQ N Africa, 1942; War Office, DAMS MS1(b), 1944; AMS, Lt-Col Northern Command, 1945 (despatches). Pres., Bradford & Bingley Building Soc., 1982-; Chairman: Parkland Textile (Holdings) Ltd,

1979-; Pennine Radio (Bradford Community Radio Ltd), 1975-. Pres., Bradford Incorporated Law Soc., 1955. Mem., Criminal Injuries Compensation Bd, 1979-. Chm., Mental Health Review Tribunal, NE Region. *Recreations:* fishing, fell-walking. *Address:* Chilliswood, South Parade, Ilkley, W Yorks. *T:* Ilkley 609076. *Clubs:* Army and Navy, Carlton; Bradford.

DENCH, Judith Olivia, (Judi Dench), OBE 1970; **(Mrs Michael Williams);** actress (theatre, films and television); *b* 9 Dec. 1934; *d* of Reginald Arthur Dench and Eleanora Olave Dench (*née* Jones); *m* 1971, Michael Williams; one *d*. *Educ:* The Mount Sch., York; Central Sch. of Speech and Drama. *Theatre:* Old Vic seasons, 1957-61: parts incl.: Ophelia in Hamlet; Katherine in Henry V; Cecily in The Importance of Being Earnest; Juliet in Romeo and Juliet; also 1957-61: two Edinburgh Festivals; Paris-Belgium-Yugoslavia tour; America-Canada tour; Venice (all with Old Vic Co.). Subseq. appearances incl.: Royal Shakespeare Co., 1961-62: Anya in The Cherry Orchard; Titania in A Midsummer Night's Dream; Dorcas Bellboys in A Penny for a Song; Isabella in Measure for Measure; Nottingham Playhouse tour of W Africa, 1963; Oxford Playhouse, 1964-65: Irina in The Three Sisters; Doll Common in The Alchemist; Nottingham Playhouse, 1965: Saint Joan; The Astrakhan Coat (world première); Amanda in Private Lives; Variety London Critics' Best Actress of the Year Award for perf. as Lika in The Promise, Fortune, 1967; Sally Bowles in Cabaret, Palace, 1968; London Assurance, Aldwych, 1970, and New, 1972; Major Barbara, Aldwych, 1970; The Importance of Being Earnest, National, 1982; Associate Mem., Royal Shakespeare Co., Stratford-on-Avon, 1969-: Bianca in Women Beware Women, Viola in Twelfth Night, doubling Hermione and Perdita in The Winter's Tale, Portia in The Merchant of Venice, Viola in Twelfth Night, the Duchess in The Duchess of Malfi, Beatrice in Much Ado About Nothing, Lady Macbeth in Macbeth, Adriana in The Comedy of Errors, Regan in King Lear, Imogen in Cymbeline; The Wolf, Oxford and London, 1973; The Good Companions, Her Majesty's, 1974; The Gay Lord Quex, Albery, 1975; Too True to be Good, Aldwych, 1975, Globe, 1976; Pillars of the Community, The Comedy of Errors, Aldwych, 1977; The Way of the World, 1978; Juno and the Paycock, Aldwych, 1980 (Best Actress award, SWET, Evening Standard, Variety Club, and Plays and Players). Recital tour of W Africa, 1969; RSC tours: Japan and Australia, 1970; Japan, 1972. *Films:* He Who Rides a Tiger; A Study in Terror; Four in the Morning (Brit. Film Acad. Award for Most Promising Newcomer, 1965); A Midsummer Night's Dream; The Third Secret; Dead Cert. *Television* appearances include, 1957-: Talking to a Stranger (Best Actress of Year award, Guild of Television Dirs, 1967); Major Barbara; Hilda Lessways; Langrishe, Go Down; Macbeth; Comedy of Errors; On Giant's Shoulders; A Village Wooing; Love in a Cold Climate; A Fine Romance; The Cherry Orchard; Going Gently. Awards incl. British and foreign, for theatre, films and TV, incl. BAFTA award for best television actress, 1981. *Recreations:* sewing, drawing, catching up with letters.

DENHAM, 2nd Baron, *cr* 1937, of Weston Underwood; **Bertram Stanley Mitford Bowyer;** PC 1981; 10th Bt, *cr* 1660, of Denham; 2nd Bt, *cr* 1933 of Weston Underwood; Captain of the Gentlemen at Arms (Government Chief Whip in the House of Lords), since 1979; *b* 3 Oct. 1927; *s* of 1st Baron and Hon. Daphne Freeman-Mitford, 4th *d* of 1st Baron Redesdale; *S* father 1948; *m* 1956, Jean, *o d* of Kenneth McCorquodale, Fambridge Hall, White Notley, Essex; three *s* one *d*. *Educ:* Eton; King's Coll., Cambridge. Mem. Westminster CC, 1959-61. A Lord-in-Waiting to the Queen, 1961-64 and 1970-71; Captain of the Yeomen of the Guard, 1971-74. Opposition Dep. Chief Whip, 1974-78, Opposition Chief Whip, 1978-79. *Publication:* The Man who Lost his Shadow, 1979. *Recreations:* field sports. Heir: *s* Hon. Richard Grenville George Bowyer, *b* 8 Feb. 1959. *Address:* The Laundry Cottage, Weston Underwood, Olney, Bucks. *T:* Bedford 711535. *Clubs:* White's, Pratt's.

DENHAM, Ernest William; Deputy Keeper of Public Records, Public Record Office, 1978-82; *b* 16 Sept. 1922; *s* of William and Beatrice Denham; *m* 1957, Penelope Agatha Gregory; one *s* one *d*. *Educ:* City of London Sch.; Merton Coll., Oxford (Postmaster). MA 1948. Naval Intell., UK and SEAC, 1942-45. Asst Sec., Plant Protection Ltd, 1947-49; Asst Keeper 1949, Principal Asst Keeper 1967, Records Admin. Officer 1973, Public Record Office; Lectr in Palaeography and Diplomatic, UCL, 1957-73. *Recreation:* armchair criticism. *Address:* 27 The Drive, Northwood, Mddx. *T:* Northwood 27382.

DENHAM, Captain Henry Mangles, CMG 1945; RN, retired; *b* 9 Sept. 1897; *s* of Henry Mangles Denham and Helen Clara Lowndes; *m* 1924, Estelle Margaret Sibbald Currie; one *s* two *d*. *Educ:* RN Coll., Dartmouth. Went to sea at beginning of European War, serving at Dardanelles in HMS Agamemnon and destroyer Racoon; occupation of the Rhine in HM Rhine Flotilla; round the world cruise with the Prince of Wales in HMS Renown, 1921; served in Mediterranean for long period largely in HMS Queen Elizabeth and Warspite; at Staff Coll., 1935; Comdr of HMS Penelope, 1936-39. Naval Attaché, Scandinavian Countries, 1940; Naval Attaché, Stockholm, 1940-47; retd list, 1947. *Publications:* The Aegean, 1963, 4th edn, 1979; Eastern Mediterranean, 1964; The Adriatic, 1967; The Tyrrhenian Sea, 1969; The Ionian Islands to Rhodes, 1972; Ionian Islands to Anatolian Coast, 1982. *Recreation:* yachting. *Clubs:* Royal Automobile, Royal Cruising; Royal Yacht Squadron (Cowes).

DENHAM, Maurice; Actor since 1934; *b* 23 Dec. 1909; *s* of Norman Denham and Winifred Lillico; *m* 1936, Margaret Dunn (*d* 1971); two *s* one *d. Educ:* Tonbridge Sch. Hull Repertory Theatre, 1934-36; theatre, radio and television, 1936-39. Served War of 1939-45: Buffs, 1939-43; Royal Artillery, 1943-45; despatches, 1946. Theatre, films, radio and television, 1946-. *Recreations:* painting, conducting gramophone records, golf. *Address:* Flat 2, 44 Brunswick Gardens, W8. *Clubs:* Garrick, Green Room; Stage Golfing.

DENHOLM, Ian; *see* Denholm, J. F.

DENHOLM, John Ferguson, (Ian), CBE 1974; DL 1980; Chairman: Denholm Ship Management Ltd, since 1972; Denholm Line Steamers Ltd; J. & J. Denholm Ltd; P&O Steam Navigation Co., from June 1983 (a Deputy Chairman, 1980-83); *b* 8 May 1927; *s* of Sir William Lang Denholm, *qv* ; *m* 1952, Elizabeth Murray Stephen; two *s* two *d. Educ:* St Mary's Sch., Melrose; Loretto Sch., Musselburgh. Joined J. & J. Denholm Ltd, 1945. Pres., Chamber of Shipping of the UK, 1973-74; Member: Nat. Ports Council, 1974-77; Scottish Transport Gp, 1975-. Hon. Norwegian Consul in Glasgow, 1975-. DL Renfrewshire, 1980. *Recreation:* fishing. *Address:* Newton of Belltrees, Lochwinnoch, Renfrewshire PA12 4JL. *T:* Lochwinnoch 842406. *Clubs:* Royal Thames Yacht; Western (Glasgow).

DENHOLM, Col Sir William (Lang), Kt 1965; TD; DL; Chairman, J. & J. Denholm Ltd, 1966-74; Chairman, Shipping Federation, 1962-65; Joint Chairman, National Maritime Board, 1962-65; President, International Shipping Federation, 1962-67; *b* 23 Feb. 1901; *s* of John Denholm and Jane Miller, Greenock; *m* 1925, Dorothy Jane, *d* of Robert Ferguson, Greenock; two *s* one *d. Educ:* Greenock Academy; Greenock Collegiate. Joined family firm J. & J. Denholm Ltd, 1918. 2nd Lieut 77th (H) Field Regt, RA (TA), 1921; in command, 1939-40; Hon. Col 1945-60. Mem. Gen. Cttee, 1935-76 and Scottish Cttee, 1935-77, Lloyd's Register of Shipping. Mem. Council, Shipping Federation, 1936; Vice-Chm., 1950-62. Vice-Chm., Glasgow Royal Infirmary and Assoc. Hospitals, 1949-60; Chm., 1960-64. DL County of Renfrew, 1950. Chevalier of the Order of St Olav (Norway). *Recreation:* golf. *Address:* Glenmill, Kilmacolm, Renfrewshire. *T:* Kilmacolm 2535. *Club:* Royal Scottish Automobile (Glasgow).

See also J. F. Denholm.

DENINGTON, family name of **Baroness Denington.**

DENINGTON, Baroness *cr* 1978 (Life Peer), of Stevenage in the County of Hertfordshire; **Evelyn Joyce Denington,** DBE 1974 (CBE 1966); Chairman, Stevenage Development Corporation, 1966-80 (Member, 1950-80); Chairman, Greater London Council, 1975-76; *b* 9 Aug. 1907; *d* of Phillip Charles Bursill and Edith Rowena Bursill; *m* 1935, Cecil Dallas Denington. *Educ:* Blackheath High Sch.; Bedford Coll., London. Journalism, 1927-31; Teacher, 1933-45; Gen. Sec., Nat. Assoc. of Labour Teachers, 1938-47; Member: St Pancras Borough Council, 1945-59; LCC, 1946-65 (Chm. New and Expanding Towns Cttee, 1960-65); GLC, 1964-77 (Chm. Housing Cttee, 1964-67; Dep. Leader (Lab), Opposition, 1967-73; Chm., Transport Cttee, 1973-75); Central Housing Adv. Cttee, 1955-73 (Chm. Sub-Cttee prod. report Our Older Homes); SE Economic Planning Council, 1966-79; Chm., New Towns Assoc., 1973-75. Member: Sutton Dwellings Housing Trust, 1976-; North British Housing Assoc., 1976-; Greater London Secondary Housing Assoc., 1978-. Freeman, City of London. Hon. FRIBA; Hon. MRTPI. *Address:* Weale House, 29 Crescent Grove, Clapham, SW4 7AF. *T:* 01-622 1275.

DENISON, family name of **Baron Londesborough.**

DENISON, Dulcie Winifred Catherine, (Dulcie Gray); actress, playwright, authoress; *b* 20 Nov. 1920; *d* of late Arnold Savage Bailey, CBE, and of Kate Edith (*née* Clulow Gray); *m* 1939, Michael Denison, *qv. Educ:* England and Malaya. In Repertory in Aberdeen, 1st part Sorrel in Hay Fever, 1939; Repertory in Edinburgh, Glasgow and Harrogate, 1940; BBC Serial, Front Line Family, 1941; Shakespeare, Regents Park; Alexandra in The Little Foxes, Piccadilly; Midsummer Night's Dream, Westminster, 1942; Brighton Rock, Garrick; Landslide, Westminster, 1943; Lady from Edinburgh, Playhouse, 1945; Dear Ruth, St James's; Wind is 90, Apollo, 1946; on tour in Fools Rush In, 1946; Rain on the Just, Aldwych, 1948; Queen Elizabeth Slept Here, Strand, 1949; The Four-poster, Ambassadors, 1950 (tour of S Africa, 1954-55); See You Later (Revue), Watergate, 1951; Dragon's Mouth, Winter Garden, 1952; Sweet Peril, St James's, 1952; We Must Kill Toni, Westminster; The Diary of a Nobody, Arts, 1954; Alice Through the Looking Glass, Chelsea Palace, 1955, Ashcroft Theatre, Croydon, 1972; appeared in own play, Love Affair, Lyric Hammersmith, 1956; South Sea Bubble, Cape Town, 1956; Tea and Sympathy, Melbourne and Sydney, 1956; South Sea Bubble, Johannesburg, 1957; Double Cross, Duchess, 1958, Cambridge, 1960; Let Them Eat Cake, Cambridge, 1959; Candida, Piccadilly and Wyndham's, 1960; Heartbreak House, Wyndham's, 1961; A Marriage Has Been Arranged, and A Village Wooing (Hong Kong); Shakespeare Recital (Berlin Festival); Royal Gambit for opening of Ashcroft Theatre, Croydon, 1962; Where Angels Fear to Tread, Arts and St Martin's, 1963; An Ideal Husband, Strand, 1965; On Approval, St Martin's, 1966; Happy Family, St Martin's, 1967; Number 10, Strand, 1967; Out of the Question, St Martin's, 1968; Three, Fortune, 1970; The Wild Duck, Criterion, 1970; Clandestine Marriage (tour), 1971; Ghosts, York; Hay Fever (tour), 1972; Dragon Variation (tour), 1973; At the End of the Day, Savoy, 1973; The Sack Race, Ambassadors, 1974; The

Pay Off, Comedy, 1974, Westminster, 1975; Time and the Conways (tour), 1976; Ladies in Retirement (tour), 1976; The Cabinet Minister (tour), 1977; A Murder is Announced, Vaudeville, 1977; Bedroom Farce, Prince of Wales, 1979; The Cherry Orchard, Exeter, 1980; Lloyd George Knew my Father (tour), 1980; The Kingfisher, Windsor, 1980, Worthing and on tour, 1981; Relatively Speaking (tour), 1981; A Coat of Varnish, Haymarket, 1982; Cavell, Chichester Fest., 1982. *Films include:* They were Sisters, 1944; Wanted for Murder, 1945; A Man about the House, 1946; Mine Own Executioner, 1947; My Brother Jonathan, 1947; The Glass Mountain, 1948; The Franchise Affair, 1951; Angels One Five, 1952; There was a Young Lady, 1953; A Man Could Get Killed, 1965; The Trail of the Pink Panther, 1982; The Curse of the Pink Panther, 1982. Has appeared in television plays and radio serials. Queen's Silver Jubilee Medal, 1977. *Publications: play:* Love Affair; *books:* Murder on the Stairs; Murder in Melbourne; Baby Face; Epitaph for a Dead Actor; Murder on a Saturday; Murder in Mind; The Devil Wore Scarlet; No Quarter for a Star; The Murder of Love; Died in the Red; The Actor and His World (with Michael Denison); Murder on Honeymoon; For Richer, For Richer; Deadly Lampshade; Understudy to Murder; Dead Give Away; Ride on a Tiger; Stage-Door Fright; Death in Denims; Butterflies on my Mind (TES Senior Information Book Prize, 1978); Dark Calypso; The Glanville Women. *Recreations:* swimming, butterflies. *Address:* Shardeloes, Amersham, Bucks.

DENISON, Elizabeth Ann Marguerite, (Mrs W. N. Denison); *see* Curnow, E. A. M.

DENISON, John Law, CBE 1960 (MBE 1945); FRCM; Hon. RAM; Hon. GSM; Director, South Bank Concert Halls (formerly General Manager, Royal Festival Hall), 1965-76; Chairman: Arts Educational Schools; Royal Concert Committee, St Cecilia Festival; Member of Council, RCM, and Associated Board Royal Schools of Music; *b* 21 Jan. 1911; *s* of late Rev. H. B. W. and Alice Dorothy Denison; *m* 1st, 1936, Annie Claudia Russell Brown (marriage dissolved, 1946); 2nd, 1947, Evelyn Mary Donald (*née* Moir) (*d* 1958), *d* of John and Mary Scott Moir, Edinburgh; one *d* ; 3rd, 1960, Audrey Grace Burnaby (*née* Bowles) (*d* 1970); 4th, 1972, Françoise Charlotte Henriette Mitchell (*née* Garrigues). *Educ:* Brighton Coll.; Royal Coll. of Music. Played horn in BBC Symphony, London Philharmonic, City of Birmingham, and other orchestras, 1934-39. Served War of 1939-45; gazetted Somerset Light Inf., 1940; DAA and QMG 214 Inf. Bde and various staff appts, 1941-45 (despatches). Asst Dir, Music Dept, British Council, 1946-48; Music Dir, Arts Council of Great Britain, 1948-65. Chm., Cultural Programme, London Celebrations Cttee, Queen's Silver Jubilee; Hon. Treasurer, Royal Philharmonic Soc. Comdr, Order of Lion, Finland. *Publications:* articles for various musical publications. *Address:* 22 Empire House, Thurloe Place, SW7. *Club:* Army and Navy.

DENISON, (John) Michael (Terence Wellesley); Actor; *b* 1 Nov. 1915; *s* of Gilbert Dixon Denison and Marie Louise (*née* Bain); *m* 1939, Dulcie Gray (*see* D. W. C. Denison). *Educ:* Harrow; Magdalen Coll., Oxford (BA). Dramatic Sch., 1937-38; Westminster Theatre, 1938; Aberdeen Repertory, 1939. First film, 1940. Served War of 1939-45, Royal Signals and Intelligence Corps, 1940-46. Has appeared in following plays: Ever Since Paradise, 1946; Rain on the Just, 1948; Queen Elizabeth Slept Here, 1949; The Four-poster, 1950; Dragon's Mouth, 1952; Sweet Peril, 1952; The Bad Samaritan, 1953; Alice Through the Looking Glass, 1953, 1955 and 1972; We Must Kill Toni, 1954; tour of S Africa, 1954-55; All's Well That Ends Well, Twelfth Night, Merry Wives of Windsor, Titus Andronicus, Stratford-on-Avon, 1955; prod. and acted in Love Affair, 1956; A Village Wooing and Fanny's First Play (Edinburgh and Berlin festivals), 1956; Meet Me By Moonlight, 1957; Let Them Eat Cake, 1959; Candida, 1960; Heartbreak House, 1961; My Fair Lady, (Melbourne); A Village Wooing (Hong Kong); Shakespeare Recital (Berlin Festival), 1962; Where Angels Fear to Tread, 1963; Hostile Witness, 1964; An Ideal Husband, 1965; On Approval, 1966; Happy Family; Number 10, 1967; Out of the Question, 1968; Three, 1970; The Wild Duck, 1970; Clandestine Marriage, 1971; The Tempest, 1972; Twelfth Night, 1972, 1978; The Dragon Variation (tour), 1973; At the End of the Day, 1973; The Sack Race, 1974; Peter Pan, 1974; The Black Mikado, 1975; The First Mrs Fraser (tour), 1976; The Earl and the Pussycat (tour), 1976; Robert and Elizabeth (tour), 1976; The Cabinet Minister, 1977; The Lady's Not For Burning, Ivanov, 1978; Bedroom Farce, 1979; The Kingfisher, 1980-81; Venus Observed, 1980; Relatively Speaking (Far and Near East tour), 1981; A Coat of Varnish, Captain Brassbound's Conversion, 1982. *Films include:* My Brother Jonathan, 1947; The Glass Mountain, 1948; Landfall, 1949; The Franchise Affair, 1950; Angels One Five, The Importance of Being Earnest, 1951; The Truth About Women, 1957. Many television appearances including title role Boyd, QC, 1957-61 and 1963. Director: Allied Theatre Productions, 1966-75; Play Company of London, 1970-74; New Shakespeare Company, 1971-. On Council British Actors Equity Assoc., 1949-76 (Vice-Pres. 1952, 1961-63, 1973); Mem. Drama Panel, Arts Council, 1975-78. *Publications:* (with Dulcie Gray) The Actor and His World, 1964; Overture and Beginners, 1973. *Recreations:* golf, painting, watching cricket, gardening, motoring. *Address:* Shardeloes, Amersham, Bucks. *Clubs:* Richmond Golf (Richmond); MCC, Middlesex County Cricket.

DENISON, Michael; *see* Denison, J. M. T. W.

DENISON, William Neil, QC 1980; a Recorder of the Crown Court, since 1979; *b* 10 March 1929; *s* of William George Denison and Jean Brodie; *m* ;

three s ; m 1981, Elizabeth Ann Marguerite Curnow, qv. Educ: Queen Mary's Sch., Walsall; Univ. of Birmingham (LLB); Hertford Coll., Univ. of Oxford (BCL). Called to the Bar, Lincoln's Inn, 1952. Recreations: walking, reading rubbish. Address: 6 King's Bench Walk, Temple, EC4Y 7DR. T: 01-583 0410. Club: Garrick.

DENISON-PENDER, family name of **Baron Pender.**

DENMAN, family name of **Baron Denman.**

DENMAN, 5th Baron cr 1834; **Charles Spencer Denman,** CBE 1976; MC 1942; TD; Bt 1945; b 7 July 1916; e s of Hon. Sir Richard Douglas Denman, 1st Bt; S father, 1957 and to barony of cousin, 1971; m 1943, Sheila Anne, d of late Lt-Col Algernon Bingham Anstruther Stewart, DSO, Seaforth Highlanders, of Ornockenoch, Gatehouse of Fleet; three s one d. Educ: Shrewsbury. Served War of 1939-45 with Duke of Cornwall's Light Infantry (TA), India, Middle East, Western Desert and Dodecanese Islands; Major, 1943. Contested (C) Leeds Central, 1945. Chairman: Tennant Guaranty Ltd; Overseas Marketing Corporation Ltd; Tennant Budd Ltd. Chm., Marine and General Mutual Life Assurance Soc. Ltd; Deputy Chairman: C. Tennant Sons & Co. Ltd, 1973–; British Bank of the Middle East, 1977–; Director: Consolidated Gold Fields Ltd; Challenge Corporation Ltd. Chairman, Committee for Middle East Trade, 1971-75 (Mem., 1963-75); Member: Advisory Council of Export Credits Guarantee Department, 1963-68; British National Export Council, 1965; Cttee on Invisible Exports, 1965-67; Lord Kitchener Nat. Meml Fund. Governor, Windlesham House Sch. Heir: s Hon. Richard Thomas Stewart Denman, b 4 Oct. 1946. Address: Highden House, Washington, Pulborough, West Sussex. T: Findon 2102. Club: Brooks's.

DENMAN, Prof. Donald Robert; Professor of Land Economy, 1968-78 and Head of Department of Land Economy, 1962-78, Cambridge University; Fellow of Pembroke College, Cambridge, 1962-78, now Emeritus; b 7 April 1911; 2nd s of Robert Martyn Denman and Letitia Kate Denman, Finchley; m 1941, Jessica Hope, 2nd d of Richard H. Prior, Chichester; two s. Educ: Christ's Coll., Finchley. BSc 1938; MSc 1940; PhD 1945; MA 1948; Hon. DSc 1979; FRICS 1949; Dep. Exec. Off., Cumberland War Agricultural Exec. Cttee, 1939-46; University Lectr, Cambridge Univ., 1948-68. Land Management Cttee of Agricultural Improvement Coun., 1953-60; Member: Church Assembly, 1957-69; Standing Cttee of Istituto de Diritto Agrario Internazionale e Comparato, Florence, 1960–; Cttee of CNAA, 1966–; Nat. Commn of Unesco, 1972–; Advisor to Min. of Co-operation and Rural Affairs, Iran; Consultant, Internat. Union for Conservation of Nature and Nat. Resources, 1972; Chm. Marine Resource Development, 1981. Mem. Council, University Coll. at Buckingham, 1973-81. Member: Commonwealth Human Ecology Council, 1971–; Land Decade Educnl Council, 1981–; Acad. Adv. to Commonwealth Assoc. of Surveying and Land Economy, and on land economy to Universities of Science and Technology, Kumasi, West Indies, South Pacific and Universiti Teknologi, Malaysia. Patron, Small Farmers' Assoc. Hon. Fellow, Ghana Instn of Surveyors, 1970; Fellow, Royal Swedish Acad. of Forestry and Agriculture, 1971. Gold Medal, RICS, 1972. Ozo Order of Nobility of Iboland, Nigeria (Eze di Igbo Mma and other titles), 1971; Distinguished Order of Homayoun of the Imperial Court of Persia, 1974. Publications: Tenant Right Valuation: In History and Modern Practice, 1942; Tenant Right Valuation and Current Legislation, 1948; Estate Capital: The Contribution of Landownership to Agricultural Finance, 1957; Origins of Ownership: A Brief History of Landownership and Tenure, 1958; Bibliography of Rural Land Economy and Landownership 1900-1957 (et al), 1958; Farm Rents: A Comparison of Current and Past Farm Rents in England and Wales, 1959; (ed and contrib.) Landownership and Resources, 1960; (ed and contrib.) Contemporary Problems of Landownership, 1963; Land in the Market, 1964; (jtly) Commons and Village Greens: A Study in Land Use, Conservation and Management, 1967; (ed and contrib.) Land and People, 1967; Rural Land Systems, 1968; Land Use and the Constitution of Property, 1969; Land Use: An Introduction to Proprietary Land Use Analysis, 1971; Human Environment: the surveyor's response, 1972; The King's Vista (Persian Land reform), 1973; Prospects of Co-operative Planning (Warburton Lecture), 1973; Land Economy: an education and a career (British Assoc. lecture), 1975; The Place of Property, 1978; Land in a Free Society, 1980; The Fountain Principle, 1982; numerous monographs, articles and papers in academic and professional jls and nat. press in Britain and abroad. Recreation: travel. Address: Pembroke College, Cambridge; 12 Chaucer Road, Cambridge. T: Cambridge 357725. Clubs: Carlton, Farmers'.

DENMAN, Sir George Roy; see Denman, Sir Roy.

DENMAN, Sir Roy, KCB 1977 (CB 1972); CMG 1968; Head, Commission of European Communities Delegation in Washington, DC, since 1982; b 12 June 1924; s of Albert Edward and Gertrude Ann Denman; m 1966, Moya Lade; one s one d. Educ: Harrow Gram. Sch.; St John's Coll., Cambridge. War Service 1943-46; Major, Royal Signals. Joined BoT, 1948; Asst Private Sec. to successive Presidents, 1950-52; 1st Sec., British Embassy, Bonn, 1957-60; UK Delegn, Geneva, 1960-61; Counsellor, Geneva, 1965-67; Under-Sec., 1967-70, BoT; Deputy Secretary: DTI, 1970-74; Dept of Trade, 1974-75; Second Permanent Sec., Cabinet Office, 1975-77; Dir-Gen. for External Affairs, EEC Commn, 1977-82. Mem. negotiating delegn with European Communities, 1970-72. Mem., British Overseas Trade Bd, 1972-75. Address: 2100 M Street, NW (Suite 707), Washington, DC 20037, USA. Club: United Oxford & Cambridge University.

DENNELL, Prof. Ralph; Emeritus Professor of Zoology, University of Manchester, 1975; Beyer Professor of Zoology, 1963-74; b 29 Sept. 1907; m 1932, Dorothy Ethel Howard; no c. Educ: Leeds Grammar Sch.; University of Leeds. Demonstrator in Zoology, University of Leeds, 1929; Grisedale Research Student, University of Manchester, 1932; Asst Lecturer in Zoology, University of Manchester, 1935; Asst Lecturer in Zoology, and Lecturer in Zoology, Imperial Coll., 1937-46; Reader in Experimental Zoology, 1946-48, Prof. of Experimental Zoology, 1948-63, University of Manchester. Publications: papers on crustacea, insect physiology, and arthropod integuments, in various zoological periodicals. Address: Flat 9, 47 Kent Road, Harrogate, N Yorks HG1 2EU.

DENNING, Baron (Life Peer) cr 1957, of Whitchurch; **Alfred Thompson Denning,** PC 1948; Kt 1944; DL; Master of the Rolls, 1962-82; Hon. Fellow: Magdalen College, Oxford, 1948; Nuffield College, Oxford, 1982; Hon. LLD: Ottawa, 1955; Glasgow, 1959; Southampton, 1959; London, 1960; Cambridge, 1963; Leeds, 1964; McGill, 1967; Dallas, 1969; Dalhousie, 1970; Wales, 1973; Exeter, 1976; Columbia, 1976; Tilburg (Netherlands), 1977; W Ontario, 1979; British Columbia, 1979; Sussex, 1980; Hon. DCL Oxford, 1965; b 23 Jan. 1899; s of Charles and Clara Denning; m 1st, 1932, Mary Harvey (d 1941); one s ; 2nd, 1945, Joan, d of J. V. Elliott Taylor, and widow of J. M. B. Stuart, CIE. Educ: Andover Grammar Sch.; Magdalen Coll., Oxford (Demy). 1st Class Mathematical Moderations; 1st Class Mathematical Final School; 1st Class Final Sch. of Jurisprudence; Eldon Scholar, 1921; Prize Student Inns of Court; called to the Bar, 1923; KC 1938; Judge of the High Court of Justice, 1944; a Lord Justice of Appeal, 1948-57; a Lord of Appeal in Ordinary, 1957-62. Chancellor of Diocese of London, 1942-44; and of Southwark, 1937-44; Recorder of Plymouth, 1944; Bencher of Lincoln's Inn, 1944; Nominated Judge for War Pensions Appeals, 1945-48; Chm. Cttee on Procedure in Matrimonial Causes, 1946-47; Chm., Royal Commission on Historical MSS, 1962-. Held enquiry into circumstances of resignation of Mr J. D. Profumo, Sec. of State for War, 1963. Chairman: Cttee on Legal Education for Students from Africa; British Institute of International and Comparative Law. Pres., Birkbeck Coll.; Treas., Lincoln's Inn, 1964. Hon. Bencher: Middle Temple, 1972; Gray's Inn, 1979; Inner Temple, 1982. Dimbleby Lectr, BBC TV, 1980. Hon. FBA 1979. Served in RE 1917-19 (BEF France). DL Hants, 1978. Publications: Joint Editor of Smith's Leading Cases, 1929; of Bullen and Leake's Precedents, 1935; Freedom under the Law, (Hamlyn Lectures), 1949; The Changing Law, 1953; The Road to Justice, 1955; The Discipline of Law, 1979; The Due Process of Law, 1980; The Family Story, 1981; What Next in the Law, 1982. Address: The Lawn, Whitchurch, Hants. T: 2144. Club: Athenæum.
See also Lieut-Gen. Sir R. F. S. Denning.

DENNING, Lt-Gen. Sir Reginald (Francis Stewart), KCVO 1975; KBE 1946; CB 1944; Chairman, SSAFA, 1953-74; Vice-President, Liverpool School of Tropical Medicine, 1967-77; b 12 June 1894; 2nd s of Charles and Clara Denning, Whitchurch, Hants; m 1927, Eileen Violet (OBE 1969), d of late H. W. Currie, 12 Hyde Park Place, W2; two s one d. Educ: privately. 2nd Lieut Bedfordshire Regt, 1915; European War, 1914-18 (severely wounded, despatches). Adjutant, 1st Bedfs and Herts Regt, 1922-25; Adjutant, 2 Bedfs and Herts Regt, 1926-29; Student Staff Coll., Camberley, 1929-30; Bt Major, 1934; Bt Lt-Col, 1939; Brig., 1941; Subst. Col, 1942; Acting Maj.-Gen., 1943; Maj.-Gen., 1944; Lieut-Gen., 1949; Maj.-Gen. i/c Administration South-Eastern Command, 1943-44; Principal Administrative Officer to the Supreme Allied Commander, South-East Asia, 1944-46; Chief of Staff, Eastern Command, 1947-49; GOC Northern Ireland, 1949-52; retired pay, 1952. Col, Bedfs and Herts Regt, 1948 3rd East Anglian Regt (16th/44th Foot), 1958, Royal Anglian Regt, 1964-66 (formed Regt, 1964). DL, County of Essex, 1959-68. CStJ 1946; Commander Legion of Merit (USA), 1946. Recreations: hunting, polo, riding. Address: Delmonden Grange, Hawkhurst, Kent. T: 2286. Clubs: Army and Navy, MCC.
See also Baron Denning.

DENNINGTON, Dudley, FICE; FIStructE; FHKIE; Partner, Bullen & Partners, since 1972; b 21 April 1927; s of John Dennington and Beryl Dennington (née Hagon); m 1951, Margaret Patricia Stewart; two d. Educ: Clifton Coll., Bristol; Imperial Coll., London Univ. (BSc). ACGI 1947. National Service, 2nd Lieut, RE, 1947-49; Sandford Fawcett and Partners, Consulting Engineers, 1949-51; D. & C. Wm Press, Contractors, 1951-52; AMICE 1953; Manager, Design Office, George Wimpey & Co., 1952-65; GLC 1965-72: Asst Chief Engineer, Construction, 1965-67; Chief Engineer, Construction, 1967-70; Traffic Comr and Dir of Development, 1970-72. Vis. Prof., King's Coll., London Univ., 1978–. FICE 1966 (Mem. Council, 1975-78 and 1981–); FHKIE 1982. Recreations: sailing, mathematics, painting. Address: 25 Corkran Road, Surbiton, Surrey. T: 01-399 2977. Club: Reform.

DENNIS, Maj.-Gen. Alastair Wesley, OBE 1973; Director, Military Assistance Office, Ministry of Defence, since 1982; b 30 Aug. 1931; s of Ralph Dennis and Helen (née Henderson); m 1957, Susan Lindy Elgar; one s two d. Educ: Malvern Coll.; RMA, Sandhurst. Commanded 16th/5th The Queen's Royal Lancers, 1971-74; Col GS, Cabinet Office, 1974-75; Comd 20 Armoured Bde, 1976-77; Dep. Comdt, Staff Coll., 1978-80; Director of Defence Policy (B), MoD, Whitehall, 1980-82. Recreations: fishing, golf, gardening. Address: c/o Barclays Bank, 65 High Street, Camberley, Surrey GU15 3RQ.

DENNIS, Rt. Rev. John; see Knaresborough, Bishop Suffragan of.

DENNIS, Maxwell Lewis, CMG 1971; Chairman, South Australia Totalizator Agency Board, 1973-79; *b* 19 April 1909; *s* of Frank Leonard and Ethel Jane Dennis; *m* 1935, Bernice Abell; one *d* (one *s* decd). *Educ:* Gladstone High Sch., South Australia. FASA. Entered South Australian Public Service, 1924, Public Service Commissioner, 1965; Chm., Public Service Bd, 1968-73; Life Governor, Royal Soc. for the Blind. *Address:* 7/18 Patawalonga Frontage, Glenelg North, South Australia 5045.

DENNIS, Nigel Forbes; writer; *b* 1912; *s* of Lieut-Col M. F. B. Dennis, DSO, and Louise (*née* Bosanquet); *m* 1st, Mary-Madeleine Massias; 2nd, Beatrice Ann Hewart Matthew; two *d. Educ:* Plumtree Sch., S Rhodesia; Odenwaldschule, Germany. Secretary, Nat. Bd of Review of Motion Pictures, NY, 1935-36; Asst Editor and Book Reviewer, The New Republic, NY, 1937-38; Staff Book Reviewer, Time, NY, 1940-58; Dramatic Critic, Encounter, 1960-63; Staff Book Reviewer, Sunday Telegraph, 1961-; Joint Editor, Encounter, 1967-70. *Publications:* Boys and Girls Come out to Play, 1949; Cards of Identity, 1955; Two Plays and a Preface, 1958; Dramatic Essays, 1962; Jonathan Swift, 1964 (RSL Award, 1966); A House in Order, 1966; Exotics (poems), 1970; An Essay on Malta, 1971. *Plays:* Cards of Identity, Royal Court, 1956; The Making of Moo, Royal Court, 1957; August for the People, Royal Court and Edinburgh Festival, 1962. *Recreation:* gardening. *Address:* c/o A. M. Heath & Co., 40 William IV Street, WC2. *Club:* Casino Maltese (Malta).

DENNIS SMITH, Edgar; *see* Smith.

DENNISON, Mervyn William, CBE 1967; MC 1944; DL; a chairman of Industrial Tribunals, Northern Ireland; *b* 13 July 1914; *er s* of Reverend W. Telford Dennison and Hester Mary (*née* Coulter); *m* 1944, Helen Maud, *d* of Claud George Spiller, Earley, Berks; one *s* one *d. Educ:* Methodist Coll., Belfast; Queen's Univ., Belfast (BA); Middle Temple. Called to Bar of Northern Ireland, 1945; Middle Temple, 1964. Served War of 1939-45, with Royal Ulster Rifles and Parachute Regt (POW Arnhem, 1944). Crown Counsel, N Rhodesia, 1947; Legal Draftsman, 1952; Senior Crown Counsel and Parliamentary Draftsman, Federal Govt of Rhodesia and Nyasaland, 1953; Federal Solicitor-Gen., 1959; QC (N Rhodesia) 1960; also Chm. Road Service Bd, N Rhodesia, and Mem. Central African Air Authority. High Court Judge, Zambia, 1961-67. Secretary, Fermanagh CC, NI, 1967-73; Chief Comr, Planning Appeals Commn and Water Appeals Commn, 1973-80. Mem. Senate, Queen's Univ., Belfast 1979-. Hon. Col, The Zambia Regt, 1964-66. JP Co. Fermanagh, 1969-73, DL, 1972-. KStJ 1978 (CStJ 1964). *Recreations:* fishing, sailing. *Address:* Creevyloughgare, Saintfield, Ballynahinch, Co. Down BT24 7NB. *T:* Saintfield 510397. *Clubs:* Army and Navy; Salisbury (Rhodesia).

DENNISON, Stanley Raymond, CBE 1946; Vice-Chancellor, 1972-79, and Honorary Professor, 1974-79, University of Hull, now Emeritus Professor; Vice-Chairman, Committee of Vice-Chancellors and Principals of the United Kingdom, 1977-79; *b* 15 June 1912; *o s* of late Stanley Dennison and Florence Ann Dennison, North Shields; unmarried. *Educ:* University of Durham; Trinity College, Cambridge. Lecturer in Economics, Manchester University, 1935-39; Professor of Economics, University Coll. of Swansea, 1939-45; Lecturer in Economics, Cambridge Univ., 1945-58; Fellow of Gonville and Caius Coll., 1945-58; Prof. of Economics, Queen's Univ. of Belfast, 1958-61; David Dale Prof. of Economics, Univ. of Newcastle upon Tyne, 1962-72; Pro-Vice-Chancellor, 1966-72. Chief Economic Asst, War Cabinet Secretariat, 1940-46. Member: University Grants Cttee, 1964-68; North Eastern Electricity Board, 1965-72; Review Body on Remuneration of Doctors and Dentists, 1962-70; Verdon Smith Cttee on Marketing and Distribution of Fatstock and Carcase Meat, 1964; Scott Cttee on Land Utilisation in Rural Areas, 1942 (Minority Report); Beaver Cttee on Air Pollution, 1954; Waverley Cttee on Med. Services for the Armed Forces, 1955. Chm. of Wages Councils. Chm. Governors, Royal Grammar Sch., Newcastle upon Tyne, 1969-. Hon. LLD Hull, 1980. *Publications:* The Location of Industry and the Depressed Areas, 1939; (with Sir Dennis Robertson) The Control of Industry, 1960; various articles, etc, on economic questions. *Recreation:* music. *Address:* 17 Preston Avenue, North Shields, Tyne and Wear NE30 2BN. *Clubs:* Reform; Northern Counties (Newcastle upon Tyne).

DENNISS, Gordon Kenneth, CBE 1979; Senior Partner, Eastman & Denniss, Chartered Surveyors, London, since 1945; *b* 29 April 1915; *e s* of late Harold W. Denniss; *m* 1939, Violet Fiedler, Montreal; one *s* two *d. Educ:* Dulwich Coll.; Coll. of Estate Management. FRICS; MRSH. Articled to uncle, Hugh F. Thoburn, Chartered Surveyor, Kent, developing building estates, 1935, professional asst 1938; Eastman & Denniss: Junior Partner, 1943; sole principal, 1945. Crown Estate Comr, 1965-71. Governing Dir, London Consultants (Middle East), London, 1977-. Farming 1600 acres in E Sussex and Kent. *Recreations:* farming, cricket, fox-hunting, political economy. *Address:* 6 Belgrave Place, Belgravia, SW1. *T:* 01-235 4858; Lodgefield Farm, Blackham, East Sussex. *T:* Fordcombe 276. *Clubs:* Savile, Farmers', MCC; Surrey County Cricket.

DENNISTON, Rev. Robin Alastair; Academic and General Publisher, and Deputy Secretary to the Delegates, Oxford University Press, since 1980; *b* 25 Dec. 1926; *s* of late Alexander Guthrie Denniston, CMG, CBE, head of Govt code and cipher school, and late Dorothy Mary Gilliat; *m* 1950, Anne Alice Kyffin Evans, *y d* of late Dr Geoffrey Evans, MD, FRCP, consulting

Physician at St Bartholomew's Hosp., and late Hon. E. M. K. Evans; one *s* two *d. Educ:* Westminster Sch. (King's Schol.; Captain of School, 1945); Christ Church, Oxford (Classical Schol.; 2nd cl. Hons Lit. Hum.). National Service: commnd into Airborne Artillery, 1948. Editor at Collins, 1950-59; Man. Dir, Faith Press, 1959-60; Editor, Prism, 1959-61; Promotion Man., Hodder & Stoughton Ltd, 1960-64, Editorial Dir, 1966, Man. Dir, 1968-72; also Dir, Mathew Hodder Ltd (and subsid. cos); Dep. Chm., George Weidenfeld & Nicolson (and subsid. cos), 1973; Non-exec. Chm., A. R. Mowbray & Co., 1974-; Chairman: Sphere Books, 1975-76; Thomas Nelson & Sons (and subsid. cos), 1975; Michael Joseph Ltd, 1975; George Rainbird Ltd, 1975; Dir, Thomson Publications Ltd and Hamish Hamilton Ltd, 1975; Academic Publisher, OUP, 1978. Student of Christ Church, 1978-. Ordained Deacon, 1978, Priest, 1979; Hon. Curate in Parish of Clifton-on-Teme, 1978. *Publications:* The Young Musicians, 1956; Partly Living, 1967; (ed) Part Time Priests?, 1960. *Recreations:* farming, music, squash. *Address:* The Hope Farm, Clifton-on-Teme, Worcester WR6 6HE. *T:* Upper Sapey 248; 18 Dale Close, Oxford OX1 1TU. *T:* Oxford 44192. *Club:* United Oxford & Cambridge University.

DENNY, Sir Alistair (Maurice Archibald), 3rd Bt, *cr* 1913; *b* 11 Sept. 1922; *er s* of Sir Maurice Edward Denny, 2nd Bt, KBE and Lady Denny (*d* 1982), Gateside House, Drymen, Stirlingshire; *S* father 1955; *m* 1949, Elizabeth *y d* of Sir Guy Lloyd, Bt, *qv* ; two *s* (and one *s* decd). *Educ:* Marlborough. Started engineering training with William Denny & Bros. Served War in Fleet Air Arm, 1944-46. Continued engineering training with Alexander Stephen & Sons, Glasgow, and Sulzer Bros., Winterthur, Switzerland; returned to William Denny & Bros, 1948; left, Sept. 1963, when firm went into liquidation. Chm., St Andrews Links Management Cttee, 1980-81. *Recreations:* golf, ski-ing, gardening, photography. *Heir: s* Charles Alistair Maurice Denny [*b* 7 Oct. 1950; *m* 1981, Belinda, *yr d* of J. P. McDonald, Walkinstown, Dublin]. *Address:* Crombie Cottage, Abercrombie, by St Monans, Fife. *T:* St Monans 631. *Club:* Royal and Ancient Golf (St Andrews).

DENNY, Sir Anthony Coningham de Waltham, 8th Bt, *cr* 1782, of Tralee Castle, Co. Kerry, Ireland; designer; Partner in Verity and Beverley, Architects and Designers, since 1959; *b* 22 April 1925; *s* of Rev. Sir Henry Lyttleton Lyster Denny, 7th Bt, and Joan Lucy Dorothy, *er d* of Major William A. C. Denny, OBE; *S* father 1953; *m* 1949, Anne Catherine, *e d* of S. Beverley, FRIBA; two *s* one adopted *d. Educ:* Clayesmore Sch. Served War of 1939-45: Middle East, RAF (Aircrew), 1943-47. Anglo-French Art Centre, 1947-50; Mural Painter and Theatrical Designer, 1950-54. Hereditary Freeman of City of Cork. FRSA; MSIAD. *Recreations:* architecture and painting. *Heir: s* Piers Anthony de Waltham Denny, *b* 14 March 1954. *Address:* Daneway House, Sapperton, Cirencester, Glos. *T:* Frampton Mansell 232.

See also B. L. Denny.

DENNY, Barry Lyttelton, MVO 1979; HM Diplomatic Service; Counsellor, British Embassy, Oslo, since 1980; *b* 6 June 1928; *s* of Rev. Sir Henry Lyttelton Lyster Denny, 7th Bt, and late Joan Lucy Dorothy, *er d* of Major William A. C. Denny, OBE; *m* 1st, 1951 (marr. diss. 1968); one *s* one *d* ; 2nd, 1969, Anne Rosemary Jordon, *o d* of Col James F. White, MC; one *d. Educ:* Clayesmore Sch.; RMA, Sandhurst. Indian Army Cadet, 1946-47; commnd RA, 1949; retd from HM Forces as Captain (Temp. Major), 1960. Joined Foreign Office, 1962; First Sec., Nicosia, 1964; FO, later FCO, 1966; Kaduna, 1969; FCO, 1972; Vientiane, 1973; FCO, 1975; Kuwait, 1977. Comdr, Order of St Olav (Norway), 1981. *Recreations:* polo, collecting, photography. *Address:* c/o Foreign and Commonwealth Office, SW1A 2AH; British Embassy, Thomas Heftysgate 8, Oslo 2, Norway. *T:* 56 38 90.

See also Sir A. C. de W. Denny.

DENNY, Sir J(onathan) Lionel P(ercy), GBE 1966; Kt 1963; MC 1918; Hon. DSc; JP; Lord Mayor of London for 1965-66; *b* 5 Aug. 1897; *s* of J. Percy Denny, Putney; *m* 1920, Doris, *d* of R. George Bare, FSI, Putney; one *s. Educ:* St Paul's Sch. Served European War, 1915-19, Lieut E Surrey Regt; active service in France (wounded thrice, MC); Sqdn Leader RAFVR and RAF Regt, 1940-45. Mem. Court of Common Council, for Billingsgate Ward, 1941, Deputy 1951, Chief Commoner 1954, Alderman 1957-70. One of HM Lieuts for the City of London, 1951-70; JP Co. of London, 1951-; JP City of London, 1957-. Livery Companies: Barber-Surgeons (Master, 1938-39); Vintners' (Master, 1960-61); Company of Watermen and Lightermen (Master, 1967). Chm. London Court of Arbitration, 1958-59. Sheriff, City of London, 1961-62. First Chancellor, The City Univ., London, 1966; Hon. DSc. Jt Hon. Col 254 (City of London) Regt RA (TA), 1965-66. KStJ 1966 (OStJ 1961). Vicary Lecturer, RCS, 1972. Chevalier, Légion d'Honneur, 1967 and other orders from Liberia, Ivory Coast, Senegal, Austria and Jordan. *Address:* 901 Grenville House, Dolphin Square, SW1. *T:* 01-834 4048. *Clubs:* City Livery (Pres. 1959-60), Eccentric, Royal Thames Yacht.

DENNY, Margaret Bertha Alice, (Mrs E. L. Denny), OBE 1946; DL; Under Secretary, Ministry of Transport and Civil Aviation, 1957-58; *b* 30 Sept. 1907; *o d* of late Edward Albert Churchard and late Margaret Catherine (*née* Arnold) and step-*d* of late William Ray Lenanton, JP; *m* 1957, Edward Leslie Denny, JP, formerly Chm., William Denny Bros, Shipbuilders, Dumbarton. *Educ:* Dover County Sch.; Bedford Coll. for Women, London Univ. (BA Hons PhD). Entered Civil Service as Principal Ministry of Shipping, 1940; Asst Sec., 1946. Gov., Bedford Coll., University of London. Member: Scottish Adv. Coun. for Civil Aviation, 1958-67; Western Regional

Hospital Board, Scotland, 1960-74; Scottish Cttee, Council of Industrial Design, 1961-71; Gen. Advisory Council, BBC, 1962-66; Gen. Nursing Council, Scotland, 1962-78; Board of Management, State Hosp., Carstairs, 1966-76; Exec. Cttee, Nat. Trust for Scotland, 1974- (Mem. Council, 1973-78; Vice-Pres, 1981-); Vice-Chm., Argyll and Clyde Health Bd, 1974-77. County Comr, Girl Guides, Dunbartonshire, 1958-68. DL Dunbartonshire, 1973. Officer, Order of Orange Nassau, 1947. *Address:* Gartochraggan Cottage, Gartocharn, by Alexandria, Dunbartonshire. *T:* Gartocharn 272.

DENNY, Rev. Norwyn Ephraim; Chairman, Liverpool District Methodist Church, since 1975; President of the Methodist Conference, 1982-83; *b* 23 Oct. 1924; *s* of Percy Edward James Denny and Dorothy Ann Denny (*née* Stringer); *m* 1950, Ellen Amelia Shaw; three *d. Educ:* City of Norwich School; Wesley College, Bristol. BD (Hons), London Univ. Ordained Methodist Minister, 1951; Methodist Minister in Jamaica, 1950-54; Minister in Peterborough, 1955-61; Member of Notting Hill Group (Ecumenical) Ministry, 1961-75. *Publications:* (with D. Mason and G. Ainger) News from Notting Hill, 1967; Caring, 1976. *Recreations:* gardening, astronomy, association football. *Address:* 49 Queen's Drive, Mossley Hill, Liverpool L18 2DT. *T:* 051-722 1219.

DENNY, William Eric, QC 1975; a Recorder of the Crown Court, since 1974; *b* 2 Nov. 1927; *s* of William John Denny and Elsie Denny; *m* 1960, Daphne Rose Southern-Reddin; one *s* two *d. Educ:* Ormskirk Grammar Sch.; Liverpool Univ. (Pres., Guild of Undergraduates, 1952-53; LLB). Called to the Bar, Gray's Inn, 1953. Lectured at LSE, 1953-58. *Recreations:* music, sailing, gardening. *Address:* 1 Hare Court, Temple, EC4Y 7BE.

DENNYS, Cyril George, CB 1949; MC 1918; retired as Under-Secretary; *b* 25 March 1897; *s* of Lieut-Col A. H. Dennys, IA, and Lena Mary Isabel (*née* Harrison); *m* 1920, Sylvia Maitland (*née* Waterlow) (*d* 1980); two *d* (and one *d* decd). *Educ:* Malvern Coll.; Trinity Coll., Oxford. Served European War, 1914-18, as Lieut, RGA, 1917-18. Entered Ministry of Labour as Asst Principal, 1919; Principal Private Sec. to Minister of Labour, 1938; Asst Sec., 1938; Principal Asst Sec., Ministry of Supply, 1942-45; Under-Secretary: Ministry of Labour, 1946; Ministry of National Insurance, 1946; Ministry of Pensions and National Insurance, 1953; retired 1962. *Recreation:* golf. *Address:* 38 Belsize Grove, Hampstead, NW3. *T:* 01-722 3964. *Clubs:* United Oxford & Cambridge University; Hadley Wood Golf (Barnet).

DENNYS, Rodney Onslow, CVO 1982 (MVO 1969); OBE 1943; FSA, FSG; FRSA; Arundel Herald of Arms Extraordinary, since 1982 (Somerset Herald of Arms, 1967-82); *b* 16 July 1911; *s* of late Frederick Onslow Brooke Dennys, late Malayan Civil Service, and Claire (*née* de Paula); *m* 1944, Elisabeth Katharine (served FO 1938-41; GHQ MEF, 1941-44 (awarded certificate for outstandingly good service by C-in-C MEF)); Allied Forces HQ N Africa, Algiers, 1944, FO 1944-45), *d* of late Charles Henry Greene; one *s* two *d. Educ:* Canford Sch.; LSE. Apptd to FO, 1937; HM Legation, The Hague, 1937-40; FO, 1940-41. Commissioned in Intell. Corps, 1941; Lt-Col 1944; RARO, 1946. Reapptd, FO, 1947; 1st Sec. British Middle East Office, Egypt, 1948-50; 1st Sec. HM Embassy: Turkey, 1950-53; Paris, 1955-57; resigned, 1957. Asst to Garter King of Arms, 1958-61; Rouge Croix Pursuivant of Arms, 1961-67. Served on Earl Marshal's Staff for State Funeral of Sir Winston Churchill, 1965, and for the Prince of Wales' Investiture, 1969. Dep. Dir, Heralds' Museum, 1978-. Advised Queensland Govt on design of first Mace of Qld Leg. Assembly, and in attendance, in Tabard, on Governor of Qld for inauguration of Mace in Qld Parlt, 1978. Mem. Court, Sussex Univ., 1972-77. CPRE, 1972-: Mem., Nat. Exec., 1973-78; Chm., 1972-77, Vice-Pres., 1977, Sussex Br. Dir, Arundel Castle Trustees Ltd; Member: Exec. Cttee, Sussex Historical Churches Trust; Council Harleian Soc. (Chm. 1977-); Exec. Cttee, Soc. Genealogists; Devon Assoc.; Académicien, Académie Internationale d'Héraldique. Freeman of City of London; Liveryman and Freeman of Scriveners Co. High Sheriff E Sussex, 1983. *Publications:* Flags and Emblems of the World; (jt) Royal and Princely Heraldry of Wales, 1969; The Heraldic Imagination, 1975; Heraldry and the Heralds, 1982; articles in jls on heraldry and kindred subjects. *Recreations:* heraldry, ornithology. *Address:* College of Arms, EC4V 4BT. *T:* 01-248 1912; Heaslands, Steep, near Crowborough, Sussex. *T:* Crowborough 61328. *Clubs:* Garrick, City Livery; Sussex.

See also Graham Greene, Sir Hugh Greene, Raymond Greene.

DENSON, John Boyd, CMG 1972; OBE 1965; HM Diplomatic Service; Ambassador to Nepal, since 1977; *b* 13 Aug. 1926; *o s* of late George Denson and of Mrs Alice Denson (*née* Boyd); *m* 1957, Joyce Myra Symondson; no *c. Educ:* Perse Sch.; St John's Coll., Cambridge. Royal Regt of Artillery, 1944; Intelligence Corps, 1946; Cambridge, 1947-51 (English and Oriental Langs Triposes). Joined HM Foreign (now Diplomatic) Service, 1951. Served in Hong Kong, Tokyo, Peking, London, Helsinki, Washington, Vientiane; Asst Head of Far Eastern Dept, Foreign Office, 1965-68; Chargé d'Affaires, Peking, 1969-71; Royal Coll. of Defence Studies, 1972; Counsellor and Consul-Gen., Athens, 1973-77. *Recreations:* looking at pictures, the theatre, wine. *Address:* c/o Foreign and Commonwealth Office, SW1; 19 Gainsborough Court, College Road, Dulwich, SE21. *T:* 01-693 8361. *Club:* United Oxford & Cambridge University.

DENT, Harold Collett; *b* 14 Nov. 1894; *s* of Rev. F. G. T. and Susan Dent; *m* 1922, Loveday Winifred Martin; one *s* one *d. Educ:* Public elementary schs; Kingswood Sch., Bath; London Univ. (external student). Asst Master in secondary schs, 1911-25 (War Service, 1914-19); Head of Junior Dept, Brighton, Hove and Sussex Grammar Sch., 1925-28; first headmaster, Gateway School, Leicester, 1928-31; freelance journalist, 1931-35; asst ed., Book Dept Odhams Press, 1935-40; Ed., The Times Educational Supplement, 1940-51; Educational Correspondent, The Times, 1952-55; Professor of Education and Dir of the Inst. of Education, University of Sheffield, 1956-60; Senior Research Fellow, Inst. of Education, University of Leeds, 1960-62; Asst Dean, Inst. of Education, University of London, 1962-65; Visiting Prof., University of Dublin, 1966; BA; FRSA; Hon. FCP; Hon. FEIS. *Publications:* A New Order in English Education, 1942; The Education Act 1944, 1944; Education in Transition, 1944; To be a Teacher, 1947; Secondary Education for All, 1949; Secondary Modern Schools, 1958; The Educational System of England and Wales, 1961; Universities in Transition, 1961; British Education, 1962; 1870-1970, Century of Growth in English Education, 1970; The Training of Teachers in England and Wales 1700-1975, 1977; Education in England and Wales, 1977. *Recreation:* gardening. *Address:* Riccards Spring, Whatlington, Battle, East Sussex. *Club:* Athenæum.

DENT, John, CBE 1976 (OBE 1968); Chairman, Civil Aviation Authority, since 1982; *b* 5 Oct. 1923; *s* of Harry F. Dent; *m* 1954, Pamela Ann, *d* of Frederick G. Bailey; one *s. Educ:* King's Coll., London Univ. BSc(Eng), FEng, FRAeS, FIMechE, FIEE. Admty Gunnery Estabs at Teddington and Portland, 1944-45; Chief Engr, Guided Weapons, Short Bros & Harland Ltd, Belfast, 1955-60; Chief Engr, Armaments Div., Armstrong Whitworth Aircraft, Coventry, 1961-63; Dir and Chief Engr, Hawker Siddeley Dynamics Ltd, Coventry, 1963-67; Director: Engrg Gp, Dunlop Ltd, Coventry, 1968-76; Dunlop Holdings Ltd, 1970-82; Industrie Pirelli SpA, 1978-81; Dunlop AG, 1979-82; Pirelli Gen. plc, 1980-; Man. Dir, Dunlop Ltd, 1978-82. President: Coventry and District Engrg Employers' Assoc., 1971 and 1972; Engrg Employers' Fedn, 1974-76 (1st Dep. Pres., 1972-74). Member: Engineering Industries Council, 1975-76; Review Bd for Government Contracts, 1976-; Royal Dockyards Policy Bd, 1976-82; NCB, 1980-. *Recreations:* gardening, fishing, cabinet-making. *Address:* Civil Aviation Authority, CAA House, 45-59 Kingsway, WC2B 6TE.

DENT, Maj.-Gen. Jonathan Hugh Baillie, OBE 1974; Director General, Fighting Vehicles and Engineer Equipment, Ministry of Defence, since 1981; *b* 19 July 1930; *s* of Joseph Alan Guthrie Dent and Hilda Ina Dent; *m* 1957, Anne Veronica Inglis; one *s* three *d. Educ:* Winchester College. Commissioned, Queen's Bays, 1949; regtl and instructional employment in BAOR, UK, Jordan, Libya, 1949-61; Adjt 1958; Adjt Shropshire Yeomanry, 1959-60; Staff trng, RMCS, 1962-63; Staff Coll. Camberley, 1964; Sqdn Comd, Queen's Dragoon Guards, N Ireland and Borneo, 1965-66; MoD (Operational Requirements), 1967-69; Second in Comd, Queen's Dragoon Guards, 1970; Ministry of Defence: MGO Secretariat, 1971-74; Project Manager Chieftain, 1974-76; RCDS 1977; Defence R&D Attaché, British Embassy, Washington, 1978-80. *Recreations:* fishing, bird watching, walking, shooting. *Address:* c/o Lloyds Bank, 6 Pall Mall, SW1.

DENT, Major Leonard Maurice Edward, DSO 1914; Member: Council, Queen's College, London; Governing Body of Oundle School; Court of University of Reading (Treasurer, 1959-63); Berks Branch, Council for Preservation of Rural England (Chairman 1950-64); *b* 18 June 1888; *s* of Edward and Mabel P. Dent; *m* 1920, Hester Anita (*d* 1976), *d* of Col Gerard Clark, 4 Sussex Gardens, W2; one *s* four *d. Educ:* Eton; Trinity Coll., Cambridge, BA. Served European War, 1914-18 (wounded, despatches thrice, DSO, Chevalier Légion d'Honneur); Major R of O, retd. Chm. and Man. Dir., Abco Products Ltd, 1936-75. Master of the Grocers' Company, 1935-36; Berks CC, 1946-58; High Sheriff of Berks, 1948-49. Member: Executive Cttee, City and Guilds of London Institute, 1937-70; King's Coll. Hosp. Bd of Governors, 1950-63; Chairman: Belgrave Hosp. for Children, 1947-63; City and Guilds of London Art Sch. Cttee, 1958-70. *Recreations:* photography, music, art collecting (especially Rowlandsons). *Address:* Hillfields, Burghfield Common, near Reading. *T:* Burghfield Common 2495. *Clubs:* United Oxford & Cambridge University, MCC.

DENT, Sir Robert (Annesley Wilkinson), Kt 1960; CB 1951; *b* 27 Jan. 1895; *e s* of late R. W. Dent, JP, Flass, Maulds Meaburn, Penrith, and late Edith Vere, OBE, *d* of Rev. F. H. Annesley Clifford Chambers, Glos; *m* 1927, Elspeth Muriel, *d* of Sir Alfred Tritton, 2nd Bt, Upper Gatton Park, Reigate; one *s.* three *d. Educ:* Eton; Trinity Coll., Cambridge. Served European War, 1914-18, with King's Royal Rifle Corps (Lieutenant) in France and Flanders (wounded, despatches). Rejoined 1940 and served War of 1939-45, with GHQ Home Forces and at the War Office AQMG (Temporary Lieut-Col), 1943-45. Asst Clerk, House of Commons, 1920; Clerk of Public Bills, 1948-59. High Sheriff, Westmorland, 1960. *Recreation:* gardening. *Address:* Lyvennet Bank, Maulds Meaburn, Penrith, Cumbria CA10 3HN. *T:* Ravensworth (Penrith) 225.

DENT, (Robert) Stanley (Gorrell), RE 1946 (ARE 1935); ARCA (London) 1933; RWA 1954 (ARWA 1951); ASIA (Ed) 1967; Principal, Gloucestershire College of Art and Design, 1950-74; *b* 1 July 1909; *o c* of Robert and Hannah Dent; *m* Doris, *o c* of Clement and Mabel Wenban; two *s. Educ:* The Newport Technical Coll.; The Newport, Mon., Sch. of Art and Crafts; Royal College of Art. Volunteered for service in Royal Engineers, 1942, invalided out, 1944. Runner up in Prix-de-Rome Scholarship, 1935; awarded the British Institution Scholarship in Engraving for the year 1933; Works exhibited at the Royal Academy, The Royal Scottish Academy, The

Royal West of England Academy, The New English Art Club, The Royal Society of British Artists, The Art Institute of Chicago, The International Print Makers Exhibition, Calif., and other leading Art Exhibitions. Ministry of Education Intermediate Assessor, 1957-60. Panel Mem. (Fine Art), National Council for Diplomas in Art and Design, 1962-65; Chief Examiner A Level Art and Design, 1963-76. *Recreations:* travel, painting, music, gardening, spectator sports. *Address:* Wenbans, Ashley Road, Battledown, Cheltenham GL52 6QE. *T:* Cheltenham 24742.

DENT, Ronald Henry; Chairman, Cape Industries Ltd, 1962-79; *b* 9 Feb. 1913; *s* of late Henry Francis Dent, MA, and Emma Bradley; *m* 1939, Olive May, *d* of late George Wilby, FCA; one *s* one *d. Educ:* Portsmouth Grammar Sch. Chartered accountant, 1936. Served War, 1939-45: UK, France, India; War Office, 1942-45. Joined Cape Industries, 1947: Man. Dir, 1957-71. Director: English China Clays Ltd; Powell Duffryn Ltd, and other cos. Cancer Research Campaign: Mem. Grand Council, 1965-, Vice-Chm. 1975-; Chm., Finance Cttee, 1969-75; Chm., Exec. Cttee, 1975-. Dep. Chm., Finance Cttee, Union Internationale contre le Cancer, Geneva, 1978-; Dir, Internat. Cancer Foundn, 1978-. British Inst. of Management: Fellow 1965; Mem. Council, 1968-77; Mem., Bd of Fellows, 1971-77; Chm. Finance Cttee, and Vice-Chm. of Inst., 1972-76. Mem. Council, UK S Africa Trade Assoc., 1969-80. FRSA. *Recreations:* golf, gardening. *Address:* Badgers Copse, Birtley Green, Bramley, Surrey. *T:* Guildford 893649. *Clubs:* Army and Navy; St George's Hill Golf.

DENT, Stanley; *see* Dent, R. S. G.

DENT-BROCKLEHURST, Mrs Mary, JP; *b* 6 Feb. 1902; *d* of late Major J. A. Morrison, DSO, and late Hon. Mary Hill-Trevor; *m* 1924, Major John Henry Dent-Brocklehurst, OBE (*d* 1949), Sudeley Castle, Glos; three *d* (one *s* decd). *Educ:* at home. JP and CC, 1949, CA 1958, Glos; High Sheriff, County of Gloucester, 1967. *Recreations:* gardening, beekeeping, travelling, archæology. *Address:* Hawling Manor, Andoversford, Cheltenham, Glos GL54 5TA. *T:* Guiting Power 362.

DENTON, Dame Catherine Margaret Mary; *see* Scott, Dame M.

DENTON, Charles; Director of Programmes, Central Independent Television (formerly ATV Network), since 1981; Managing Director, Black Lion Films, since 1979; *b* 20 Dec. 1937; *s* of Alan Charles Denton and Mary Frances Royle; *m* 1961, Eleanor Mary Player; one *s* two *d. Educ:* Reading Sch.; Bristol Univ. BA History (Hons). Deckhand, 1960; advertising trainee, 1961-63; BBC TV, 1963-68; freelance television producer with Granada, ATV and Yorkshire TV, 1969-70; Dir, Tempest Films Ltd, 1969-71; ATV: Head of Documentaries, 1974-77; Controller of Programmes, 1977-81. *Recreations:* walking, music. *Address:* Manor Farm, Wolverton, Stratford upon Avon, Warwickshire. *T:* Snitterfield 373.

DENTON, Prof. Eric James, CBE 1974; FRS 1964; ScD; Director, Laboratory of Marine Biological Association, Plymouth, since 1974; Member, Royal Commission on Environmental Pollution, 1973-76; *b* 30 Sept. 1923; *s* of George Denton and Mary Anne (*née* Ogden); *m* 1946, Nancy Emily, *d* of Charles and Emily Jane Wright; two *s* one *d. Educ:* Doncaster Grammar Sch.; St John's Coll., Cambridge. Biophysics Research Unit, University Coll., London, 1946-48; Lectr in Physiology, University of Aberdeen, 1948-56; Physiologist, Marine Biological Assoc. Laboratory, Plymouth, 1956-74; Royal Soc. Res. Professor, Univ. of Bristol, 1964-74, Hon. Professor, 1975. Fellow, University Coll., London, 1965. Hon. Sec., Physiological Soc., 1963-69. Hon. DSc: Exeter, 1976; Göteborg, 1978. *Publications:* Scientific papers in Jl of Marine Biological Assoc., etc. *Recreation:* gardening. *Address:* Fairfield House, St Germans, Saltash, Cornwall PL12 5LS. *T:* St Germans (Cornwall) 30204; The Laboratory, Citadel Hill, Plymouth PL1 2PB. *T:* Plymouth 21761.

DENTON, Dame Margaret; *see* Scott, Dame M.

DENTON-THOMPSON, Aubrey Gordon, OBE 1958; MC 1942; Director, Fisheries Recruitment Ltd, Lymington, Hants; *b* 6 June 1920; *s* of late M. A. B. Denton-Thompson; *m* 1944, Ruth Cecily Isaac (*d* 1959); two *s* (one *d* decd); *m* 1961, Barbara Mary Wells. *Educ:* Malvern Coll. Served in RA 1940-44; seconded to Basutoland Administration, 1944; apptd to HM Colonial Service, 1945; transferred to Tanganyika as Asst District Officer, 1947; seconded to Colonial Office, 1948-50, District Officer; seconded to Secretariat, Dar es Salaam, as Asst Sec., 1950; Colonial Sec., Falkland Islands, 1955-60; Dep. Permanent Sec., Ministry of Agriculture, Tanganyika, 1960-62; retired from Tanganyika Civil Service, 1963. Man. Dir, Tanganyika Sisal Marketing Assoc. Ltd, 1966-68 (Sec. 1963). Sen. Agricl Advr, UNDP, 1968-78, and FAO Country Rep.: Korea, 1970-73, Indonesia, 1973-76, Turkey, 1976-78; Sen. Advr to Director General, FAO, Rome, July-Dec. 1978; retd Jan. 1979. *Address:* Octave Cottage, Ramley Road, Pennington, Lymington, Hants.

d'ENTRÈVES, Alexander Passerin; Professor Emeritus, University of Turin; *b* 26 April 1902; 4th *s* of Count Hector Passerin d'Entrèves et Courmayeur; *m* 1931, Nina Ferrari d'Orsara; one *s* one *d. Educ:* University of Turin, Italy; Balliol Coll., Oxford. Doctor of Law, Turin, 1922; DPhil Oxon, 1932; Lecturer, University of Turin, 1929; Prof. University of Messina, 1934, Pavia, 1935, Turin, 1938; Prefect of Aosta, April-May 1945; Mem. of Council of Val

d'Aosta, Dec. 1945. Serena Prof. of Italian Studies, University of Oxford, 1946-57; Fellow Magdalen Coll., Oxford, 1946-57; Prof. of Political Theory, Univ. of Turin, 1958-72. Vis. Prof., Harvard Univ., 1957; Yale Univ., 1960-64. FR.HistS; Fellow, Amer. Acad. Arts and Sciences; Member: Société Académique St Anselme, Aosta; Accademia delle Scienze, Turin; Accademia dei Lincei, Rome; Académie de Savoie, Chambéry. Hon. MA Yale, 1961; Dr *hc* Sorbonne, 1978. *Publications:* The Medieval Contribution to Political Thought, 1939; Reflections on the History of Italy, 1947; Aquinas, Selected Political Writings, 1948; Alessandro Manzoni, 1949; Natural Law, An Introduction to Legal Philosophy, 1951; Dante as a Political Thinker, 1952; The Notion of the State, An Introduction to Political Theory, 1967; other publications in Italian and French. *Recreation:* rambling in the Alps. *Address:* Strada ai Ronchi 48, Cavoretto, Torino 10133, Italy; Castello di Entrèves, Courmayeur, Val d'Aosta, Italy.

DENZA, Mrs Eileen; Counsellor (Legal Adviser), Office of the UK Permanent Representative to the European Communities, Brussels, since 1980; *b* 23 July 1937; *d* of Alexander L. Young and Mrs Young; *m* 1966, John Denza; two *s* one *d. Educ:* Aberdeen Univ. (MA); Somerville Coll., Oxford (MA); Harvard Univ. (LLM). Called to the Bar, Lincoln's Inn, 1963. Asst Lectr in Law, Bristol Univ., 1961-63; Asst Legal Adviser, FCO (formerly FO), 1963-74; Legal Counsellor, FCO, 1974-80. *Publications:* Diplomatic Law, 1976; contribs to: 5th edn Satow's Guide to Diplomatic Practice; Essays in Air Law; article in British Yearbook of Internat. Law. *Recreations:* music, piano playing. *Address:* c/o Foreign and Commonwealth Office, SW1A 2AH.

de OLLOQUI, Dr José Juan; Ambassador of Mexico to the Court of St James's, since 1979, and concurrently Ambassador to Ireland, since 1980; *b* 5 Nov. 1931; *m* 1962, Guillermina de Olloqui; three *s* one *d. Educ:* Autonomous Univ. of Mexico (LLB 1956, LLD 1979); Univ. of George Washington, Washington, DC (MEc 1970). Official, Bank of Mexico (with license at present), 1951-; Head of Dept of Banking, Currency and Investment, Min. of Finance, 1958-66; Exec. Dir, Interamerican Develt Bank, 1966-71 and also Dep. Dir General for Credit, Min. of Finance, 1966-70; Rep. of Mexico to Exec. Permanent Council of Interamerican Econ. and Social Commn, 1970-71; Chm., Nat. Securities Commn, 1970; Ambassador of Mexico to USA and concurrently Ambassador to Govt of Barbados, 1971-76; Under Sec. of State for Foreign Affairs, 1976-79. Prof. of History of Economic Thought, Faculty of Law, Nat. Autonomous Univ. of Mexico, 1964 (by open competition), Life Prof., 1966; Prof., Nat. Autonomous Univ. of Mexico and Universidad Iberoamericana, on Mexico's Econ. Problems, Econ. Theory and History of Econ. Thought. Mem., Bd of several credit instns and official bodies in Mexico, and has represented Mexico, Interamerican Develt Bank and Permanent Council of the Interamerican Econ. and Social Commn at various internat. confs. Pres. and Founder, Miner's Assoc. of Zacatecas, Zac. and Parral, Chihuahua, Mexico, 1963-71. A Vice-Pres., World Food Council. Member: Mexican Lawyer's Bar; Acad. of Political Sciences; Nat. Coll. of Economists; Mexican Acad. of Internat. Law. Dr *hc* in Human Letters St Mary's Coll. 1975. Holds numerous foreign decorations and awards. *Publications:* Mexico fuera de Mexico; several books, articles and bibliographical reviews on legal and econ. matters. *Address:* 48 Belgrave Square, SW1X 8QY. *T:* 01-235 6393/6.

de PASS, Col Guy Eliot, DSO 1918; OBE 1945; late 4th Dragoon Guards; *b* 30 Oct. 1898; *yr s* of late John de Pass; *m* 1925, Winifred Dorothy, *d* of late Westcot Featherstonehaugh and late Mrs Featherstonehaugh, Durban, Natal; three *d. Educ:* St Andrews, Eastbourne; Eton; Sandhurst. Served European War, 1914-18 (despatches, DSO), 4th Royal Dragoon Guards; Major 4th Batt. Oxford Bucks Light Infantry (TA), 1938; Military Asst to the Quartermaster-Gen. of the Forces, 1940; 2nd in Command 4th Bn Oxford and Bucks Light Infantry, 1939-40; Asst Commandant, Donnington, Salop, 1941; Sub-Area Comdr, Preston, 1943; Dep. Dir Labour 2nd Army (HQ), May 1943-45, NW Europe Campaign (OBE). *Recreation:* shooting. *Address:* Upper House Farm, near Henley-on-Thames, Oxfordshire. *T:* Rotherfield Greys 378. *Club:* Cavalry and Guards.

de PAULA, (Frederic) Clive, CBE 1970; TD 1950 and Clasp 1951; FCA, JDipMA, CBIM; Chairman, Tecalemit PLC, since 1980 (Director, 1972; Deputy Chairman, 1978); *b* 17 Nov. 1916; 2nd *s* of late F. R. M. de Paula, CBE, FCA; *m* 1950, Pamela Elizabeth Markham Quick (*née* Dean), widow of Joseph Bertram Telford Quick; one step *s. Educ:* Rugby Sch.; Spain and France. 2nd Lieut, TA, 1939; Liaison Officer, Free French Forces in London and French Equatorial Africa, 1940; Specially employed Middle East and E Africa, 1941; SOE Madagascar, 1942; comd special unit with 11th E African Div., Ceylon and Burma, 1943; Finance Div., Control Commn, Germany, 1945; demobilised as Major, 1946; Captain 21st Special Air Service Regt (Artists) TA, 1947-56. Joined Robson, Morrow & Co., management consultants, 1946; Partner, 1951; seconded to DEA then to Min. of Technology as an Industrial Adviser, 1967; Co-ordinator of Industrial Advisers to Govt, 1969; returned as Sen. Partner, Robson, Morrow & Co., 1970-71; Man. Dir, Agricultural Mortgage Corp. Ltd, 1972-81; Non-Exec. Dir, Green's Economiser Group plc, 1972-; Mem. Council, BIM, 1971-76; Mem., EDC for Agriculture, 1972-81. Gen. Comr of Income Tax, Winslow Div., Bucks, 1965-82. Vice Pres., Schoolmistresses and Governesses Benevolent Instn, 1982- (Hon. Treas., 1947-81); Chm., Internat. Wine and Food Soc., 1980-. *Publications:* Accounts for Management, 1954; Management Accounting in Practice, 1959; (with A. W. Willsmore) The Techniques of

Business Control, 1973; (with F. A. Attwood) Auditing: Principles and Practice, 1976, 1982. *Address:* c/o National Westminster Bank PLC, 5 Market Place, Glastonbury, Somerset BA6 9HB. *Club:* Enton Fly Fishers'.

de PEYER, Charles Hubert, CMG 1956; retired Under-Secretary, Ministry of Fuel and Power (served with Foreign Office, with rank of Minister in United Kingdom Delegation to European Coal and Steel Community, 1952-56); *b* 24 Oct. 1905; 2nd *s* of Everard Charles de Peyer and Edith Mabel Starkey; *m* 1st, 1930, Flora Collins, singer, New York; one *s* one *d* ; 2nd, 1953, Mary Burgess (*d* 1974); two *s* one *d*. *Educ:* Cheltenham Coll.; Magdalen Coll., Oxford (Hons PPE). Entered Civil Service, Mines Dept, 1930. *Recreations:* gardening, music. *Address:* 348 Chambersbury Lane, Leverstock Green, Hemel Hempstead, Herts. *Club:* Reform.
See also D. C. de Peyer.

de PEYER, David Charles; Under Secretary, Department of Health and Social Security, since 1979; *b* 25 April 1934; *s* of Charles de Peyer, *qv* and Flora (*née* Collins); *m* 1959, Ann Harbord. *Educ:* Rendcomb Coll., Cirencester; Magdalen Coll., Oxford (BA PPE). Asst Principal, Min. of Health, 1960; Sec., Royal Commn on NHS, 1976-79. *Address:* 21 Southwood Park, Highgate, N6 5SG. *T:* 01-340 0680.

de PEYER, Gervase; Solo Clarinettist; Conductor; Founder and Conductor, The Melos Sinfonia; Founder Member, The Melos Ensemble of London; Director, London Symphony Wind Ensemble; Associate Conductor, Haydn Orchestra of London; solo clarinettist, Chamber Music Society of Lincoln Center, New York, since 1969; Resident Conductor, Victoria International Festival, BC, Canada; *b* London, 11 April 1926; *m* 1st, 1950, Sylvia Southcombe (marr. diss. 1971); one *s* two *d* ; 2nd, 1971, Susan Rosalind Daniel (marr. diss. 1979); 3rd, 1980, Katia Perret Aubry. *Educ:* King Alfred's, London; Bedales; Royal College of Music. Served HM Forces, 1945 and 1946. Principal Clarinet, London Symphony Orchestra, 1955-72. ARCM; Hon. ARAM. Gold Medallist, Worshipful Co. of Musicians, 1948; Charles Gros Grand Prix du Disque, 1961, 1962; Plaque of Honour for recording, Acad. of Arts and Sciences of America, 1962. Most recorded solo clarinettist in world. *Recreations:* travel, cooking, kite-flying, sport, theatre. *Address:* 16 Langford Place, St John's Wood, NW8. *T:* 01-624 4098; 65 Central Park West, New York, NY 10023, USA. *T:* (212) 877 9789.

de PIRO, Alan C. H., QC 1965; FCIArb 1978; a Recorder, since 1972; *e s* of late J. W. de Piro; *m* 1947, Mary Elliot (deceased); two s ; *m* 1964, Mona Addington; one step *s* one step *d*. *Educ:* Repton; Trinity Hall, Cambridge (Sen. Scholar). MA 1947 (Nat. Sci. and Law). Royal Artillery, 1940-45 (Capt.); West Africa. Called to Bar, Middle Temple, 1947; Inner Temple, 1962; Bencher, Middle Temple, 1971; in practice at the Bar, London and Midlands. Member: Gen. Council of the Bar, 1961-65, 1966-70, 1971-73; Senate of the Inns of Court and the Bar, 1976-81; Dep. Chairman: Beds QS, 1966-71; Warwicks QS, 1967-71. Vice-Pres., L'Union Internationale des Avocats, 1968-73, Co-Pres., 1969. Member: Council Internat. Bar Assoc., 1967- (Chm., Human Rights Cttee, 1979-); Editorial Advisory Cttee, Law Guardian, 1965-73; Law Panel British Council, 1967-74. Legal Assessor, Disciplinary Cttee, RCVS, 1970-. *Recreations:* conversation, gardening, inland waterways. *Address:* 4 King's Bench Walk, Temple, EC4; 2 Fountain Court, Birmingham; The Toll House, Bascote Locks, near Southam, Warwicks. *Club:* Hawks (Cambridge).

de POLNAY, Peter; author; *b* 8 March 1906; *m* 1942, Margaret Mitchell-Banks (*d* 1950); one *s* ; *m* 1955, Maria del Carmen Rubio y Caparo. *Educ:* privately in England, Switzerland and Italy. Farmed in Kenya. First began to write in Kenya in 1932; was in Paris when Germans entered, worked with early French Resistance, escaped back to England after imprisonment under Vichy Government. *Publications:* Angry Man's Tale, 1938; Children My Children!, 1939; Boo, 1941; Death and Tomorrow, 1942; Water on the Steps, 1943; Two Mirrors, 1944; The Umbrella Thorn, 1946; A Pin's Fee, 1947; The Moot Point, 1948; Into an Old Room, a Study of Edward Fitzgerald, 1949; Somebody Must, 1949; An Unfinished Journey, 1952; Death of a Legend: The True Story of Bonny Prince Charlie, 1953; Fools of Choice, 1955; Before I Sleep, 1955; The Shorn Shadow, 1956; The Clap of Silent Thunder, 1957; Peninsular Paradox, 1958; The Crack of Dawn, 1960; The Gamesters, 1960; Garibaldi, 1961; No Empty Hands, 1961; The Flames of Art, 1962; A Man of Fortune, 1963; Three Phases of High Summer, 1963; The Plaster Bed, 1965; The World of Maurice Utrillo, 1967; Aspects of Paris, 1968; A Tower of Strength, 1969; The Patriots, 1969; A Tale of Two Husbands, 1970; Napoleon's Police, 1970; The Permanent Farewell, 1970; A T-Shaped World, 1971; A Life of Ease, 1971; The Grey Sheep, 1972; The Loser, 1973; The Price You Pay, 1973; The Crow and the Cat, 1974; Indifference, 1974; A Clump of Trees, 1975; None Shall Know, 1976; The Stuffed Dog, 1976; Driftsand, 1977; The Other Shore of Time, 1978; My Road (autobiog.), 1978; The Autumn Leaves Merchant, 1979; Make-Believe, 1980; The Talking House, 1980; A Minor Giant, 1981; Sea Mist, 1982. *Recreation:* French history. *Address:* c/o A. M. Heath & Co. Ltd, 40-42 William IV Street, WC2N 4DD.

DERAMORE, 6th Baron *cr* 1885; **Richard Arthur de Yarburgh-Bateson,** Bt 1818; Chartered Architect; *b* 9 April 1911; *s* of 4th Baron Deramore and of Muriel Katherine (*née* Duncombe); *S* brother, 1964; *m* 1948, Janet Mary, *d* of John Ware, MD, Askham-in-Furness, Lancs; one *d*. *Educ:* Harrow; St John's Coll., Cambridge. AA Diploma, 1935; MA Cantab 1936; ARIBA 1936.

Served as Navigator, RAFVR, 1940-45: 14 Sqdn, RAF, 1942-44 and 1945. County Architect's Dept, Herts, 1949-52. Member: Council, Queen Mary Sch., Duncombe Park, Helmsley, 1977-; Management Cttee, Purey Cust Nursing Home, York, 1976-; Manager, Heslington Sch., York, 1965-. Fellow, Woodard Schs (Northern Div.) Ltd, 1978. *Publications:* freelance articles and short stories. *Recreations:* walking, cycling, motoring, water-colour painting. *Heir:* none. *Address:* Heslington House, Aislaby, Pickering, North Yorks YO18 8PE. *Clubs:* Royal Air Force, Royal Automobile.

DE RAMSEY, 3rd Baron *cr* 1887; **Ailwyn Edward Fellowes,** KBE 1974; TD; DL; Captain RA; Lord Lieutenant of Huntingdon and Peterborough, 1965-68 (of Hunts, 1947-65); *b* 16 March 1910; *s* of late Hon. Coulson Churchill Fellowes and Gwendolen Dorothy, *d* of H. W. Jefferson; *S* grandfather, 1925; *m* 1937, Lilah, *d* of Frank Labouchere, 15 Draycott Avenue, SW; two *s* two *d*. Served War of 1939-45 (prisoner, Far East). Pres. Country Landowners' Assoc., Sept. 1963-65. Awarded KBE 1974 for services to agriculture. DL Hunts and Peterborough, 1973, Cambs 1974. *Heir:* s Hon. John Ailwyn Fellowes [*b* 27 Feb. 1942; *m* 1973, Phyllida Mary, *d* of Dr Philip A. Forsyth, Newmarket, Suffolk; one s]. *Address:* Abbots Ripton Hall, Huntingdon. *T:* Abbots Ripton 234. *Club:* Buck's.
See also Lord Ailwyn, Lord Fairhaven.

DERBY, 18th Earl of *cr* 1485; **Edward John Stanley,** MC 1944; DL; Bt 1627; Baron Stanley 1832; Baron Stanley of Preston, 1886; Major late Grenadier Guards; Constable of Lancaster Castle, since 1972; *b* 21 April 1918; *s* of Lord Stanley, PC, MC (*d* 1938), and Sibyl Louise Beatrix Cadogan (*d* 1969), *e d* of Henry Arthur, late Viscount Chelsea, and Lady Meux; *g s* of 17th Earl of Derby, KG, PC, GCB, GCVO; *S* grandfather, 1948; *m* 1948, Lady Isabel Milles-Lade, *yr d* of late Hon. Henry Milles-Lade, and sister of 4th Earl Sondes. *Educ:* Eton; Oxford Univ. Left Army with rank of Major, 1946. President: Merseyside and District Chamber of Commerce, 1972-; Liverpool Chamber of Commerce, 1948-71; NW Area Conservative Assoc., 1969-72. Pro-Chancellor, Lancaster Univ., 1964-71. Lord Lieut and Custos Rotulorum of Lancaster, 1951-68. Alderman, Lancashire CC, 1968-74. Commanded 5th Bn The King's Regt, TA, 1947-51, Hon. Col, 1951-67; Hon. Captain, Mersey Div. RNR, 1955; Hon. Colonel: 1st Bn The Liverpool Scottish Regt, TA, 1964-67; Lancastrian Volunteers, 1967-75; 5th/8th (V) Bn The King's Regt, 1975-; 4th (V) Bn The Queen's Lancashire Regt, 1975-; Chm., NW of England and IoM TAVR Assoc., 1979-. President: Rugby Football League, 1948-; Professional Golfers' Assoc., 1964-. DL Lancs 1946. Hon. LLD: Liverpool, 1949; Lancaster, 1972. Hon. Freeman, City of Manchester, 1961. *Heir:* b Captain Hon. Richard Oliver Stanley, *qv*. *Address:* Knowsley, Prescot, Merseyside L34 4AF. *T:* 051-489 6147; Stanley House, Newmarket, Suffolk. *T:* Newmarket 3011. *Clubs:* White's; Jockey (Newmarket).

DERBY, Bishop of, since 1969; **Rt. Rev. Cyril William Johnston Bowles;** *b* Scotstoun, Glasgow, 9 May 1916; *s* of William Cullen Allen Bowles, West Ham, and Jeanie Edwards Kilgour, Glasgow; *m* 1965, Florence Joan, *d* of late John Eastaugh, Windlesham. *Educ:* Brentwood Sch.; Emmanuel Coll., Jesus Coll. (Lady Kay Scholar) and Ridley Hall, Cambridge. 2nd cl., Moral Sciences Tripos, Pt. I, 1936; 1st cl., Theological Tripos, Pt. I, and BA, 1938; 2nd cl., Theological Tripos, Pt. II, 1939; MA 1941. Deacon 1939, Priest 1940, Chelmsford; Curate of Barking Parish Church, 1939-41; Chaplain of Ridley Hall, Cambridge, 1942-44; Vice-Principal, 1944-51; Principal, 1951-63; Hon. Canon of Ely Cathedral, 1959-63; Archdeacon of Swindon, 1963-69. Select Preacher: Cambridge, 1945, 1953, 1958, 1963; Oxford, 1961; Dublin, 1961. Exam. Chaplain to Bishop of Carlisle, 1950-63; to Bishops of Rochester, Ely and Chelmsford, 1951-63; to Bishop of Bradford, 1956-61; to Bishop of Bristol, 1963-69. Hon. Canon, Bristol Cathedral, 1963-69; Surrogate, 1963-69; Commissary to Bishop of the Argentine, 1963-69. Mem., Archbishops' Liturgical Commn, 1955-75. *Publications:* contributor: The Roads Converge, 1963; A Manual for Holy Week, 1967; The Eucharist Today, 1974. *Address:* The Bishop's House, 6 King Street, Duffield, Derby DE6 4EU. *T:* (office) Derby 46744; (home) Derby 840132. *Club:* English-Speaking Union.

DERBY, Provost of; see Lewers, Very Rev. B. H.

DERBY, Archdeacon of; see Dell, Ven. R. S.

DERBYSHIRE, Andrew George, FRIBA, FSIA; Partner in practice of Robert Matthew, Johnson-Marshall & Partners; *b* 7 Oct. 1923; *s* of late Samuel Reginald Derbyshire and late Helen Louise Puleston Derbyshire (*née* Clarke); *m*, Lily Rhodes (*née* Binns), widow of late Norman Rhodes; three *s* one *d*. *Educ:* Chesterfield Grammar Sch.; Queens' Coll., Cambridge; Architectural Assoc. MA (Cantab), AA Dip. (Hons). Admty Signals Estabt and Bldg Research Station, 1943-46. Farmer & Dark, 1951-53 (Marchwood and Belvedere power stations); West Riding County Architect's Dept, 1953-55 (bldgs for educn and social welfare). Asst City Architect, Sheffield, 1955-61; responsible for co-ord. of central area redevelt. Mem. Research Team, RIBA Survey of Architects' Offices, 1960-62. Since 1961, as Mem. RM, J-M & Partners, associated with: develt of Univ. of York, Central Lancs New Town, NE Lancs Impact Study, Univ. of Cambridge, West Cambridge Develt and New Cavendish Laboratory, Preston Market and Guildhall, London Docklands Study, Hillingdon Civic Centre, Cabtrack and Minitram feasibility studies, Suez Master Plan Study; Castle Peak Power Stations, and Harbour Reclamation and Urban Growth Study, Hong Kong. Member: RIBA Council, 1950-72, 1975-81 (Senior Vice-Pres., 1980); NJCC, 1961-65; Bldg Industry Communications Res. Cttee, 1964-66 (Chm. Steering Cttee); MoT

Urban Res. and Develt Gp, 1967; Inland Transport Res. and Develt Council, 1968; DoE Planning and Transport Res. Adv. Council, 1971-76; Standing Commn on Energy and the Environment, 1978-. Pt-time Mem., CEGB, 1973-; Mem. Bd, Property Services Agency, 1975-79. Hoffman Wood Prof. of Architecture, Univ. of Leeds, 1978-80; External Prof., Dept of Civil Engineering, Univ. of Leeds, 1981. Hon. DUniv York, 1972. FRSA 1981. *Publications:* (jointly) The Architect and his Office, 1962; broadcasts and contribs on auditorium acoustics, building economics, the planning and construction of univs and new towns, also new forms of public transport. *Recreation:* his family. *Address:* 4 Sunnyfield, Hatfield, Herts AL9 5DX. *T:* Hatfield 65903; 42 Weymouth Street, W1A 2BG. *T:* 01-486 4222.

DERHAM, Prof. Sir David (Plumley), KBE 1977 (MBE 1945); CMG 1968; BA, LLM Melbourne; Vice-Chancellor of the University of Melbourne, 1968-82; *b* 13 May 1920; *s* of late Dr A. P. Derham, CBE, MC, ED, MD, FRACP; *m* 1944, Rosemary, *d* of late Gen. Sir Brudenell White, KCB, KCMG, KCVO, DSO; one *s* two *d. Educ:* Scotch Coll., Melbourne; Ormond Coll., Melbourne Univ. AIF, 1941-45 (Major). Solicitor, 1948; Barrister, 1948-51; Melbourne University: Tutor in Law, Queen's Coll., and Independent Lectr, Constitutional Law, 1949-51; Prof. of Jurisprudence, 1951-64; Vis. Fellow, Wadham Coll., Oxford, 1953; Carnegie Trav. Fellow, 1953-54; Constitutional Consultant, Indian Law Inst., 1958-59; Sen. Res. Fellow and Vis. Lectr, Chicago Univ. Law Sch., 1961; Vis. Prof. Northwestern Univ. Law Sch., 1961; Dean of Faculty of Law, Monash Univ., 1964-68. Member: Victorian Chief Justice's Law Reform Cttee, 1951-68; Victorian Council of Legal Educn, 1951-68; Bd of Management, Royal Melbourne Hosp., 1958-; Commonwealth Cttee on Teaching Costs of Medical Hosps, 1961-65; Commonwealth Cttee on Future of Tertiary Educn in Australia, 1962-64; Australian Univs Commn, 1965-68; Bd of Management, Walter & Eliza Hall Inst. of Med. Res., 1968-. Chairman: Overseas Service Bureau, 1965-81; Melbourne Theatre Co. Bd of Management, 1973-82; Aust. Vice-Chancellors' Cttee, 1975-76. President: Medico-Legal Soc., Vic., 1963-64; Australasian Univs Law Schs Assoc., 1964-65. Fellow, Australian Acad. of Social Scis, 1964. Hon. LLD: Monash, 1968; Melbourne, 1982. *Publications:* (Ch. 1) Legal Personality and Political Pluralism, 1958; (Ch. 6) Essays on the Australian Constitution, 2nd edn 1961; Paton, Textbook of Jurisprudence (ed) 3rd edn 1964, 4th edn 1972; (with F. K. H. Maher and Prof. P. L. Waller) Cases and Materials on the Legal Process, 1966, 3rd edn 1979; (with F. K. H. Maher and Prof. P. L. Waller) An Introduction to Law, 1966, 4th edn 1982; articles in legal and other jls. *Recreations:* golf, tennis, lawn tennis. *Address:* 13 Selborne Road, Toorak, Vic 3142, Australia. *T:* 241-9329. *Clubs:* Melbourne, Naval and Military, Melbourne Beefsteak (Melbourne); Royal Melbourne Golf, Barwon Heads Golf.

DERHAM, Sir Peter (John), Kt 1980; Chairman, Advisory Board, Commonwealth Scientific and Industrial Research Organization, since 1981; *b* 21 Aug. 1925; *s* of John and Mary Derham; *m* 1950, Averil C. Wigan; two *s* one *d. Educ:* Melbourne Church of England Grammar School; Univ. of Melbourne (BSc 1958); Harvard Univ. (Advanced Management Programme). Served RAAF and RAN, 1944-46. Joined Moulded Products (Australasia) Ltd (later Nylex Corp.), 1943; Dir, 1953, Sales Dir, 1960, Gen. Manager, 1967, Man. Dir, 1972-80; Chairman: Armstrong-Nylex Pty Ltd; Internat. Pacific Corp. Ltd; Director: Cadillac Plastics (Australia) Pty Ltd; Lucas Industries Aust. Ltd; AMP Society (Victorian Branch Board); Station 3XY Pty Ltd; Radio 3XY Pty Ltd; Alternate Dir, Russell Armstrong Pty Ltd; Chairman: Australia New Zealand Foundn; Australian Canned Fruits Corp.; Nat. Training Council, 1971-80; Federal Pres., Inst. of Directors in Australia (Chm. Victorian Council, 1975-); Councillor: Yooralla Soc. of Victoria, 1972-79 (Chm. Workshops Cttee, 1972-81); Inst. of Public Affairs, 1971-80; Aust. Industries Develt Assoc., 1975-80; Melbourne Church of England Grammar Sch. Council, 1974-75, 1977-80; State Councillor, Industrial Design Council, 1967-73, Federal Councillor, 1970-73; Life Mem., Plastics Inst. of Australia Inc. (Victorian Pres., 1964-66; Nat. Pres., 1971-72); Chm., Australian Tourist Commn; Member: Manufacturing Industries Adv. Council, 1971-74; Victorian Econ. Develt Corp.; Board of Advisors, Inst. of Cultural Affairs, 1971-81; Rotary Club of Melbourne (Mem., Bd of Dirs, 1974-75, 1975-76); Victorian State Cttee, Child Accident Prevention Foundn of Australia; Appeal Cttee, Royal Victorian Eye and Ear Hosp.; Bd of Management, Alfred Hosp. and Caulfield Hosp.; Appeal Chm., Victorian Foundn on Alcoholism and Drug Dependence; Governor, Ian Clunies Ross Meml Foundn, 1979-; Dir, Enterprise Australia (Dep. Chm., 1975-78); Hon. Treasurer, Victorian Div., Liberal Party of Australia; Chairman: Trade & Industry Cttee, Victoria's 150th Anniv. Celebration; Police Toy Fund for Underprivileged Children; Pres., Old Melburnians, 1974-75; Life Governor, Assoc. for the Blind. *Recreations:* golf, sailing, tennis and gardening. *Address:* 12 Glenbervie Road, Toorak, Victoria 3142, Australia. *T:* (03) 509 8009. *Clubs:* Australian, Melbourne (Melbourne); Royal Melbourne Golf, Frankston Golf, Flinders Golf, Davey's Bay Yacht (Past Commodore), Royal South Yarra Lawn Tennis, Melbourne Cricket.

DERMOTT, William; Under Secretary, Head of Agricultural Science Service, Agricultural Development and Advisory Service, Ministry of Agriculture, Fisheries and Food, since 1976; *b* 27 March 1924; *s* of William and Mary Dermott; *m* 1946, Winifred Joan Tinney; one *s* one *d. Educ:* Univ. of Durham. BSc, MSc. Agricl Chemist, Univ. of Durham and Wye Coll., Univ. of London, 1943-46; Soil Scientist, Min. of Agriculture, at Wye, Bangor and Wolverhampton, 1947-70; Sen. Sci. Specialist, and Dep. Chief Sci. Specialist, MAFF, 1971-76. Pres., British Soc. of Soil Science, 1981-82.

Publications: papers on various aspects of agricultural chemistry in scientific journals. *Recreations:* gardening, the countryside. *Address:* 22 Chequers Park, Wye, Ashford, Kent. *T:* Wye 812694.

de ROS, 27th Baroness (in her own right; Premier Barony of England) *cr* 1264; **Georgiana Angela Maxwell;** *b* 2 May 1933; *er d* of Lieut-Comdr Peter Ross, RN (killed on active service, 1940) and *g d* of 26th Baroness de Ros (*d* 1956); *S* grandmother, 1958 (on termination of abeyance); *m* 1954, Comdr John David Maxwell, RN; one *s* one *d. Educ:* Wycombe Abbey Sch., Bucks; Studley Agricultural Coll., Warwicks. NDD 1955. *Heir: s* Hon. Peter Trevor Maxwell, *b* 23 Dec. 1958. *Address:* Old Court, Strangford, N Ireland.

de ROTHSCHILD; *see* Rothschild.

DERRETT, Prof. (John) Duncan (Martin), MA, PhD, DCL, LLD; Professor of Oriental Laws in the University of London, 1965-82, now Emeritus; *b* 30 Aug. 1922; *s* of John West Derrett and Fay Frances Ethel Kate (*née* Martin); *m* 1950, Margaret Esmé Griffiths; four *s* one *d. Educ:* Emanuel Sch., London; Jesus Coll., Oxford; Sch. of Oriental and Afr. Studies, London; Inns of Court School of Law. MA 1947, DCL 1966 (Oxon); PhD 1949, LLD 1971 (London). Called to the Bar, Gray's Inn, 1953. Lectr in Hindu Law, SOAS, 1949; Reader in Oriental Laws, 1956, Prof. of Oriental Laws, 1965, Univ. of London; Tagore Prof. of Law, Univ. of Calcutta, 1953 (lectures delivered, 1955); Vis. Professor: Univ. of Chicago, 1963; Univ. of Michigan, 1970; Wilde Lectr in Natural and Compar. Religion, Univ. of Oxford, 1978-81; Japan Soc. Prom. Sci. Fellow and Vis. Prof., Oriental Inst., Univ. of Tokyo, 1982. Mem., editorial bd, Zeitschrift für vergleichende Rechtswissenschaft, 1954, subseq. of Kannada Studies, Bharata Manisha, Kerala Law Times. Mem. Selection Cttee, Fac. of Law, Univs of Dacca and Rajshahi, 1978-. Mem., Stud. Novi Test. Soc., 1971. Barcelona Prize in Comparative Law, 1954; N. C. Sen-Gupta Gold Medal, Asiatic Soc. (Calcutta), 1977. *Publications:* The Hoysalas, 1957; Hindu Law Past and Present, 1957; Introduction to Modern Hindu Law, 1963; Religion, Law and the State in India, 1968; Critique of Modern Hindu Law, 1970; Law in the New Testament, 1970 (Ital. trans. 1983); Jesus's Audience, 1973; Dharmaśāstra and Juridical Literature, 1973; History of Indian Law (Dharmaśāstra), 1973; Henry Swinburne (?1551-1624) Civil Lawyer of York, 1973; Bhāruci's Commentary on the Manusmrti, 1975; Essays in Classical and Modern Hindu Law, vols I-IV, 1976-79; Studies in the New Testament, vols I-III, 1977-82; The Death of a Marriage Law, 1978; Beiträge zu Indischem Rechtsdenken, 1979; The Anastasis: the Resurrection of Jesus as an historical event, 1982; trans. R. Lingat, Classical Law of India, 1973; ed, Studies in the Laws of Succession in Nigeria, 1965; ed, Introduction to Legal Systems, 1968; (with W. D. O'Flaherty) The Concept of Duty in South Asia, 1978; contribs to learned jls; collab. with Yale Edn, Works of St Thomas More, Société Jean Bodin, Brussels, Fritz Thyssen Stiftung, Cologne, Institut für Soziologie, Heidelberg, and Sekai Kyusei Kyo, Atami. *Recreations:* listening to music, gardening, clocks. *Address:* Half Way House, High Street, Blockley, Moreton-in-Marsh, Glos GL56 9EX. *T:* Blockley 700828.

DERRICK, Patricia, (Mrs Donald Derrick); *see* Lamburn, P.

DERRY AND RAPHOE, Bishop of, since 1980; **Rt. Rev. James Mehaffey;** *b* 29 March 1931; *s* of John and Sarah Mehaffey; *m* 1956, Thelma P. L. Jackson; two *s* one *d. Educ:* Trinity College, Dublin (MA, BD); Queen's University, Belfast (PhD). Curate Assistant: St Patrick's, Belfast, 1954-56; St John's, Deptford, London, 1956-58; Minor Canon, Down Cathedral, 1958-60; Bishop's Curate, St Christopher's, Belfast, 1960-62; Incumbent: Kilkeel, Diocese of Dromore, 1962-66; Cregagh, Diocese of Down, 1966-80. *Address:* The See House, Culmore Road, Londonderry. *T:* Londonderry 51206.

DERRY, Thomas Kingston, OBE 1976; kt, Order of St Olav, Norway, 1981; MA, DPhil Oxon; *b* 5 March 1905; *y s* of late Rev. W. T. Derry, Wesleyan Minister; *m* 1930, Gudny, *e d* of late Hjalmar Wesenberg, Commander of Order of Vasa, Oslo, Norway. *Educ:* Kingswood Sch., Bath; Queen's Coll., Oxford (Bible Clerk and Taberdar). 1st Class, Classical Moderations, 1925; 1st Class, Final Sch. of Modern History, 1927; Senior George Webb Medley Scholar, 1927; Gladstone Prizeman, 1928; Sixth Form Master and Chief History Master, Repton Sch., 1929-37; Headmaster, Mill Hill School, 1938-40; Political Intelligence Dept of Foreign Office, 1941-45 (Chief Intelligence Officer, Scandinavia); Asst Master, St Marylebone Grammar Sch., 1945-65; Visiting Prof., Wheaton Coll., Mass, 1961-62. *Publications:* (with T. L. Jarman) The European World, 1950, rev. and extended edn 1975; The Campaign in Norway (official military history), 1952; A Short History of Norway, 1957; (with T. I. Williams) A Short History of Technology, 1960; The United Kingdom Today, 1961; A Short Economic History of Britain, 1965; (with E. J. Knapton) Europe 1815-1914, 1965; Europe 1914 to the Present, 1966; (with T. L. Jarman and M. G. Blakeway) The Making of Britain, 3 vols, 1956-69; A History of Modern Norway, 1814-1972, 1973; A History of Scandinavia, 1979; (with T. L. Jarman)Modern Britain, 1979. *Address:* Nils Lauritssons vei 27, Oslo 8, Norway.

DERRY, Warren, MA; *b* 19 Oct. 1899; *e s* of late Rev. W. T. Derry, Wesleyan minister; *m* 1930, Lorna Adeline, *yr d* of Reginald H. Ferard; one *s* two *d. Educ:* Kingswood Sch., Bath; Magdalen Coll., Oxford (Demy). 2nd Class Hons Classical Moderations, 1920; 1st Class Hons. Final Sch. of English Language and Literature, 1922; Passmore Edwards Scholar, 1922; Asst Master, the Edinburgh Academy, 1922-28; Headmaster Wolverhampton Grammar

Sch., 1929-56. *Publications:* Dr Parr, a Portrait of the Whig Dr Johnson, 1966; (ed) Journals and Letters of Fanny Burney, vols IX and X, 1982. *Address:* 11 Abbey Court, Edward Street, Bath.

DERWENT, 4th Baron cr 1881; **Patrick Robin Gilbert Vanden-Bempde-Johnstone,** CBE 1974; Bt 1795; *b* 26 Oct 1901; *y s* of late Hon. Edward Henry Vanden-Bempde-Johnstone, 2nd *s* of 1st Baron and Hon. Evelyn Agar-Ellis (*d* 1952), *d* of 5th Viscount Clifden; *S* brother 1949; *m* 1929, Marie-Louise, *d* of late Albert Picard, Paris; one *s. Educ:* Charterhouse; RMC, Sandhurst. Commissioned KRRC, 1921; Major, KRRC. Formerly Director: Yorkshire Insurance Co.; National Safe Deposit and Trustee Co. Ltd; past Chm., Reinsurance Corp.; ex-Mem., Horserace Totalisator Bd, Tote Investors Ltd; Past Chm., British Road Fedn. Junior Opposition Whip in House of Lords, 1950-51; Minister of State, Bd of Trade, 1962-63; Minister of State, Home Office, 1963-64; Deputy Speaker, House of Lords, 1970-. *Recreations:* shooting and fishing. *Heir: s* Hon. Robin Evelyn Leo Vanden-Bempde-Johnstone, MVO 1957 [*b* 30 Oct. 1930; *m* 1957, Sybille de Simard de Pitray, *d* of Vicomte de Simard de Pitray and Madame Jeannine Hennessy; one *s* three *d*]. *Address:* Hackness Hall, Scarborough, North Yorks; 48 Cadogan Place, SW1. *Club:* Beefsteak.
See also Earl of Listowel.

DERX, Donald John, CB 1975; Deputy Secretary, Department of Employment, since 1972; *b* 25 June 1928; *s* of John Derx and Violet Ivy Stroud; *m* 1956, Luisa Donzelli; two *s* two *d. Educ:* Tiffin Boys' Sch., Kingston-on-Thames; St Edmund Hall, Oxford (BA). Asst Principal, BoT, 1951; seconded to Cabinet Office, 1954-55; Principal, Colonial Office, 1957; Asst Sec., Industrial Policy Gp, DEA, 1965; Dir, Treasury Centre for Admin. Studies, 1968; Head of London Centre, Civil Service Coll., 1970; Under Sec., Dept of Employment, 1971-72. Governor, Ashridge Management Coll. *Address:* 40 Raymond Road, Wimbledon, SW19 4AP. *T:* 01-947 0682.

DESAI, Shri Morarji Ranchhodji, BA; Prime Minister of India, 1977-79; *b* Bhadeli, Gujarat, 29 Feb. 1896; *e s* of Shri Ranchhodji and Smt. Vajiyaben Desai. *Educ:* Wilson Coll., Bombay; Univ. of Bombay. Entered Provincial Civil Service of Govt of Bombay, 1918; resigned to join the Civil Disobedience Campaign of Mahatma Gandhi, 1930; convicted for taking part in the Movement during 1930-34; Sec., Gujarat Pradesh Congress Cttee, 1931-37 and 1939-46; Minister for Revenue, Co-operation, Agriculture and Forests, Bombay, 1937-39; convicted, 1940-41, and detained in prison, 1942-45; Minister for Home and Revenue, Bombay, 1946-52; Chief Minister of Bombay, 1952-56; Mem., 2nd, 3rd and 4th Lok Sabha, 1957-70; Minister of Commerce and Industry, Government of India, 1956-58; Treasurer, All India Congress Cttee, 1950-58; Minister of Finance, Government of India, 1958-63, resigned from Govt (under plan to strengthen Congress) Aug. 1963; Chm., Administrative Reforms Commn, Govt of India, 1966; Dep. Prime Minister and Minister of Finance, Government of India, 1967-69; Chm., Parly Gp, Congress Party (Opposition), 1969-77; elected to 5th Lok Sabha, 1971-79; detained in solitary confinement, 1975-77, under State of Emergency; Founder-Chairman, Janata Party, 1977. Hon. Fellow, College of Physicians and Surgeons, Bombay, 1956; Hon. LLD Karnatak Univ., 1957. *Publications:* books include: A View of the Gita; In My View; A Minister and His Responsibilities (Jawaharlal Nehru Meml Lectures); The Story of My Life (2 vols), 1978; Indian Unity: From Dream to Reality (Patel Meml Lectures); book on Nature Cure. *Recreations:* spinning on Charkha; follower of sport and classical Indian dancing. *Address:* 1 Safdarjung Road, New Delhi 110001, India; Oceana, Marine Drive, Bombay, India.

de STE CROIX, Geoffrey Ernest Maurice, DLitt; FBA 1972; Emeritus Fellow, New College, Oxford, since 1977; *b* 8 Feb. 1910; *s* of Ernest Henry de Ste Croix and Florence Annie (*née* Macgowan); *m* 1st, 1932, Lucile (marr. diss. 1959); one *d* (decd); 2nd, 1959, Margaret Knight; two *s. Educ:* Clifton Coll. (to 1925); University Coll. London (1946-50). BA 1st cl. Hons History, London, 1949; MA Oxon, 1953; DLitt Oxon, 1978. Solicitor, 1931. Served War, RAF, 1940-46. Asst Lectr in Ancient Economic History, London Sch. of Economics, and Part-time Lectr in Ancient History, Birkbeck Coll., London, 1950-53; Fellow and Tutor in Ancient History, New Coll., Oxford, 1953-77. J. H. Gray Lectr, Cambridge Univ., 1972-73; Vis. Prof., Univ. of Amsterdam, 1978. *Publications:* The Origins of the Peloponnesian War, 1972; The Class Struggle in the Ancient Greek World, from the Archaic Age to the Arab Conquests, 1981; contributions to: Studies in the History of Accounting, 1956; The Crucible of Christianity, 1969; Studies in Ancient Society, 1974; Debits, Credits, Finance and Profits, 1974; articles and reviews in various learned jls. *Recreations:* listening to music, walking. *Address:* Evenlode, Stonesfield Lane, Charlbury, Oxford OX7 3ER. *T:* Charlbury 810453.

DE SAUMAREZ, 6th Baron cr 1831; **James Victor Broke Saumarez;** Bt 1801; *b* 28 April 1924; *s* of 5th Baron de Saumarez and Gunhild, *d* of late Maj.-Gen. V. G. Balck, Stockholm; *S* father, 1969; *m* 1953, Julia, *d* of late D. R. Charlton, Gt Holland-on-Sea, Essex; twin *s* one *d. Educ:* Eton Coll.; Millfield; Magdalene Coll., Cambridge (MA). Farmer; Director, Shrubland Health Clinic Ltd. *Recreations:* swimming, gardening, photography. *Heir: s* Hon. Eric Douglas Saumarez [*b* 13 Aug. 1956; *m* 1982, Christine, *yr d* of B. N. Halliday]. *Address:* Shrubland Vista, Coddenham, Ipswich, Suffolk. *T:* Ipswich 830220.

DESCH, Stephen Conway; QC 1980; a Recorder of the Crown Court, since 1979; *b* 17 Nov. 1939; *o s* of Harold Ernest Desch and Gwendolen Lucy Desch;

m 1973, Julia Beatrice Little; two *d. Educ:* Dauntsey's Sch.; Magdalen Coll., Oxford (BCL, MA); Northwestern Univ., Chicago. Called to the Bar, Gray's Inn, 1962; joined Midland Circuit, 1964. *Recreations:* country pursuits, gardening, mountain walking. *Address:* 113 Knatchbull Road, SE5 9QY. *T:* 01-274 9639.

DESIO, Prof. Ardito; Professor of Geology (and Past Director of Institute of Geology), at the University of Milan, and of Applied Geology, at the Engineering School of Milan, 1931-72, now Emeritus; *b* 18 April 1897; *m* 1932; one *s* one *d. Educ:* Udine and Florence. Grad. Univ. of Florence in Nat. Sciences. Asst, University of Pavia, 1923, also Engineering Sch., Milan, 1924-25 to 1930-31; Lectr in Phys. Geography, University of Milan, 1929-30 and in Palaeontology there until 1935. Pres., Italian Geological Cttee, 1966-73. Dir., Rivista Italiana di Paleontologia e Stratigrafia, 1942-; Past Dir., Geologia Tecnica. Past Pres., Ital. Geolog. Soc.; Mem. (Hon. Pres.) Ital. Assoc. of Geologists; Past Pres., Ital. Order of Geologists; Mem., Ital. Order of Journalists; Hon. Member: Ital. Paleont. Soc.; Gesellschaft für Erdkunde zu Berlin, 1941; Italian Geog. Soc., 1955; Faculty of Sciences University of Chile, 1964; Geological Soc. of London, 1964; Indian Paleont. Soc.; Soc. Ital. Progresso delle Scienze, 1978; Ist. per il Medio ed Estremo Oriente, 1979; Corr. Mem., Soc. Géol. Belgique, 1952; Member: Institut d'Egypte, 1936; Accademia Naz. Lincei, 1948; Inst. Lombardo Accad. Scienze Lettre, 1949. In 1938 discovered first small deposits of natural oil and gas in subsoil of Libya and Mg-K salt deposit in Marada Oasis; led expedition to K2 (8611 m, 2nd highest peak in the World; reached on 31 July 1954), and 18 expeditions in Africa and Asia. Gold Medal of the Republic of Pakistan, 1954; Gold Medal of the Sciences, Letters and Arts, of Italy, 1956; Patrons medal of Royal Geog. Soc. of London, 1957; USA Antarctic Service Medal, 1974. Kt Grand Cross, Order of Merit, Italy, 1955. *Publications:* about 372, among them: La spedizione geografica Italiana al Karakoram 1929, 1936; Le vie delle sete, 1950; Geologia applicata all'ingegneria, 1949, 3rd edn 1973; Ascent of K2, 1956 (11 languages, 15 editions); Geology of the Baltoro Basin (Karakorum), 1970; Results of half-a-century investigation on the glaciers of the Ortler-Cevedale, 1973; La Geologia dell'Italia, 1973; Geology of Central Badakhshan (NE Afghanistan), 1975; Geology of the Upper Shaksgam Valley, Sinkiang, China, 1980. *Recreation:* alpinist. *Address:* (office) Piazzale Gorini 15, 20133-Milano. *T:* 292726; (residence) Viale Maino 14, 20129-Milano. *T:* 709845. *Clubs:* Alpine; Internat. Rotary; Panatlon; Himalayan (Hon. Sec. for Italy); Alpino, Touring (Italy); Explorers' (NY); Hon. Member Alpin Français; Excursionista Carioca.

DESPRÉS, Robert; Chairman of the Board, Atomic Energy of Canada Ltd, since 1980; *b* 27 Sept. 1924; *s* of Adrien Després and Augustine Marmen; *m* 1949, Marguerite Cantin; two *s* two *d. Educ:* Académie de Québec (BA 1943); Laval Univ. (MCom 1947); (postgrad. studies) Western Univ. Comptroller, Québec Power Co., 1947-63; Reg. Manager, Administration & Trust Co., 1963-65; Dep. Minister, Québec Dept of Revenue, 1965-69; Pres. and Gen. Man., Québec Health Insurance Bd, 1969-73; Pres., Université du Québec, 1973-78; Pres. and Chief Exec. Officer, National Cablevision Ltd, 1978-80, and Netcom Inc., 1978-. Mem. Board of Directors: Norcen Energy Resources Ltd; Campeau Corporation; Sidbec-Dosco Inc.; Domtar Inc.; Centre Internat. de Recherches et d'Etudes en Management; Canada Malting Co. Ltd; Manufacturers Life Insurance Co.; National Trust Co. Ltd; Sidbec; Canadian Union Insurance Co. Ltd; Corp. Falconbridge Copper; Drummond McCall Inc.; IAF Production Inc.; Netcom Inc.; Gaz Inter-Cité Québec Inc.; Foundation québécoise d'éducation économique. *Publications:* contrib. Commerce, and Soc. of Management Accountants Revue. *Recreations:* golf, tennis, reading. *Address:* 890 Dessane, Québec, Québec G1S 3J8, Canada. *T:* (418) 687-2100. *Clubs:* Mount Royal, Rideau, Cercle Universitaire; Lorette Golf.

de THIER, Jacques; Grand Officer, Order of Léopold II; Commander, Order of Léopold and Order of the Crown, Belgium; Civic Cross (1914-18); Grand Cross of Royal Victorian Order (Hon. GCVO); Director, Compagnie Financière et de Gestion pour l'Etranger (Cometra), Brussels, 1966-73; Counsellor, Cometra Oil Co.; *b* Heusy, Belgium, 15 Sept. 1900; *m* 1946, Mariette Negroponte (*d* 1973); three step *s. Educ:* University of Liège. Doctor of Laws (University of Liège), 1922; Mem. Bar (Liège and Verviers), 1923-29. Attached to Prime Minister's Cabinet, Brussels, 1929-32; entered Diplomatic Service, 1930; Attaché, Belgian Legation, Berlin, 1933; Chargé d'Affaires in Athens, 1935, Teheran, 1936; First Sec., Berlin, 1937-38; First Sec., then Counsellor, Washington, 1938-44; Chargé d'Affaires, Madrid, 1944-46; Asst to Dir-Gen., Polit. Dept, Min. of Foreign Affairs, Brussels, 1947, then Asst Head of Belgian Mission in Berlin; Consul-Gen. for Belgium, NY, 1948-55; Pres., Soc. of Foreign Consuls in New York, 1954; Belgian Ambassador: to Mexico, 1955-58; in Ottawa, 1958-61; Mem. Belgian Delegns to Gen. Assemblies of UN, 1956, 1957, 1959 and 1960; Belg. Rep. to Security Council, Sept. 1960; Belgian Ambassador to Court of St James's, 1961-65, and concurrently Belgian Perm. Rep. to Council of WEU, 1961-65. Holds foreign decorations. *Publication:* Dans l'Iran d'autrefois, and Souvenirs d'un diplomate belge, Washington, 1938-44; articles in La Revue Générale, Brussels. *Recreation:* golf. *Address:* 38 avenue des Klauwaerts, 1050 Brussels, Belgium. *Clubs:* Anglo-Belgian; Cercle Royal Gaulois, Cercle du Parc, Royal Golf de Belgique (Brussels).

de TRAFFORD, Dermot Humphrey, VRD 1963; Director, since 1977, Chairman, since 1982, Low & Bonar plc (Deputy Chairman, 1980-82); Chairman: GHP Group Ltd, 1965-77 (Managing Director, 1961); Calor Gas

Holding, since 1974; *b* 19 Jan. 1925; *s* and *heir* of Sir Rudolph de Trafford, Bt, *qv*, and June Lady Audley (*née* Chaplin), MBE (*d* 1977); *m* 1st, 1946, Patricia Mary Beeley (marr. diss. 1973); three *s* six *d* ; 2nd, 1973, Mrs Xandra Caradini Walter. *Educ*: Harrow Sch.; Christ Church, Oxford (MA). Trained as Management Consultant, Clubley Armstrong & Co. Ltd and Orr & Boss and Partners Ltd, 1949-52; Director: Brentford Transformers Ltd (now Brentford Electric Ltd); Hugh Smith & Co. (Possil) Ltd (now Hugh Smith (Glasgow) Ltd); Langley Alloys Ltd; Unerg SA; Imperial Continental Gas Assoc., 1963- (Dep. Chm., 1972-); Petrofina SA, 1971. *Recreations*: golf, ski-ing. *Address*: 59 Onslow Square, SW7 3LR. *T*: 01-589 2826. *Clubs*: White's, Royal Ocean Racing; Royal St George's Golf; Island Sailing.

de TRAFFORD, Sir Rudolph Edgar Francis, 5th Bt *cr* 1841; OBE 1919; *b* 31 Aug. 1894; *s* of Sir Humphrey Francis de Trafford, 3rd Bt and Violet Alice Maud (*d* 1925), *d* of James Franklin; *S* brother, 1971; *m* 1st, 1924, June (who obtained a divorce, 1938), *o d* of late Lieut-Col Reginald Chaplin; one *s* ; 2nd, 1939, Katherine, *e d* of W. W. Blake, Cincinnati, USA. *Educ*: Downside Sch.; Trinity Coll., Cambridge, BA. Served European War, 1914-18; Intelligence Corps and Gen. Staff GHQ. *Heir*: *s* Dermot Humphrey de Trafford, *qv*. *Address*: 70 Eaton Square, SW1. *T*: 01-235 1823. *Club*: White's.

DEUTSCH, André; Chairman and Managing Director, André Deutsch Ltd, since 1951; *b* 15 Nov. 1917; *s* of late Bruno and Maria Deutsch (*née* Havas); unmarried. *Educ*: Budapest; Vienna; Zurich. First job in publishing, with Nicholson & Watson, 1942; started publishing independently under imprint of Allan Wingate (Publishers) Ltd, 1945; started André Deutsch Limited, in 1951. Founded: African Universities Press, Lagos, Nigeria, 1962; East Africa Publishing House, Nairobi, Kenya, 1964. *Recreations*: travel, ski-ing, publishing, talking. *Address*: 5 Selwood Terrace, SW7. *Club*: Garrick.

de VALOIS, Dame Ninette, CH 1982; DBE 1951 (CBE 1947); Founder and Director of the Royal Ballet, 1931-63 (formerly the Sadler's Wells Ballet, Royal Opera House, Covent Garden, and the Sadler's Wells Theatre Ballet, Sadler's Wells Theatre); Founder of The Royal Ballet School (formerly The Sadler's Wells School of Ballet); *b* Baltiboys, Blessington, Co. Wicklow, 6 June 1898; 2nd *d* of Lieut-Col T. R. A. Stannus, DSO, Carlingford; *m* 1935, Dr A. B. Connell. Prima ballerina the Royal Opera Season Covent Garden (International), May to July 1919 and again in 1928. Première danseuse British National Opera Company, 1918; mem. The Diaghileff Russian Ballet, 1923-26; choreographic dir to the Old Vic, the Festival Theatre, Cambridge, and The Abbey Theatre, Dublin, 1926-30; Founder of The National Sch. of Ballet, Turkey, 1947. Principal choreographic works: Job, The Rake's Progress, Checkmate, and Don Quixote. Hon. MusDoc London, 1947; Hon. DLitt: Reading, 1951; Oxford, 1955; New Univ. of Ulster, 1979; Hon. DMus, Sheffield, 1955; Hon. MusD Trinity Coll., Dublin, 1957; Hon. DFA Smith Coll., Mass, USA, 1957; Hon. LLD: Aberdeen, 1958; Sussex, 1975; FRAD 1963. Chevalier of the Legion of Honour, 1950. Gold Albert Medal, RSA, 1964; (jtly) Erasmus Prize Foundn Award (first woman to receive it), 1974; Irish Community Award, 1980. *Publications*: Invitation to the Ballet, 1937; Come Dance with Me, 1957; Step By Step, 1977. *Address*: c/o Royal Ballet School, 153 Talgarth Road, W14.

DEVENPORT, Rt. Rev. Eric Nash; *see* Dunwich, Bishop Suffragan of.

DEVENPORT, Martyn Herbert, MA; Headmaster, Victoria College, Jersey, CI, since Sept. 1967; *b* 11 Jan. 1931; *s* of Horace Devenport and Marjorie Violet (*née* Fergusson); *m* 1957, Mary Margaret Lord; three *s* one *d*. *Educ*: Maidstone Gram. Sch.; Gonville and Caius Coll., Cambridge. Asst Master at Eton Coll., 1957-67. *Recreations*: photography, squash, sailing. *Address*: Victoria College, Jersey, CI. *T*: 37591.

DEVERELL, Sir Colville (Montgomery), GBE 1963 (OBE 1946); KCMG 1957 (CMG 1955); CVO 1953; retired from Government Service, Nov. 1962; Secretary-General, International Planned Parenthood Federation, 1964-69; *b* 21 Feb. 1907; *s* of George Robert Deverell and Maude (*née* Cooke); *m* 1935, Margaret Wynne, *d* of D. A. Wynne Wilson; three *s*. *Educ*: Portora Sch., Enniskillen, Ulster; Trinity Coll., Dublin (LLB); Trinity Coll., Cambridge. District Officer, Kenya, 1931; Clerk to Exec. and Legislative Councils, 1938-39; civil affairs Branch, E Africa Comd, 1941-46, serving Italian Somaliland, British Somaliland, Ethiopia; Mem. Lord de la Warr's Delegation, Ethiopia, 1944; seconded War Office in connection Italian Peace Treaty, 1946. Sec., Development and Reconstruction Authority, Kenya, 1946; acted as Financial Sec. and Chief Native Comr, 1949; Administrative Secretary, Kenya, 1949; Colonial Sec., Jamaica, 1952-55; Governor and Comdr-in-Chief, Windward Islands, 1955-59; Governor and Comdr-in-Chief, Mauritius, 1959-62. Chm. UN(FP) Mission to India, 1965; Mem., UN Mission on Need for World Population Inst., 1970; Chairman: UN Family Planning Evaluation Mission to Ceylon, 1971; UN Family Planning Assoc. Feasability Mission, Al Azhar Univ., Cairo, 1972. Constitutional Adviser: Seychelles, 1966; British Virgin Islands, 1973. LLD *jure dignitatis*, Dublin, 1964. *Recreations*: cricket, tennis, squash, golf and fishing. *Address*: 46 Northfield End, Henley-on-Thames, Oxon. *Clubs*: East India, Devonshire, Sports and Public Schools; MCC; Nairobi (Kenya).

DEVEREUX, family name of **Viscount Hereford.**

DEVEREUX, Alan Robert, CBE 1980; Director: Scottish Mutual Assurance, since 1976; Walter Alexander Ltd, since 1980; Chairman, Scottish Tourist Board, since 1980; *b* 18 April 1933; *s* of Donald Charles and Doris Louie Devereux; *m* 1959, Gloria Alma Hair; one *s*. *Educ*: Colchester School; Clacton County High School; Mid-Essex Technical Coll. CEng, FIProdE, FBIM. Apprentice 1950-55, Standards Engr 1955-56, Marconi's Wireless Telegraph Co.; Tech. Production Man., Halex Div. of British Xylonite Co., 1956-58; Tech. Sales Man., Spa Div., Sanitas Trust, 1958-65; Gen. Man., Dobar Engineering, 1965-67; Norcros Ltd: Man. Dir of Ward Brooke & Co., Norvic Electric Ltd, H. J. Reece, Aric Instruments, and Chief Exec. of Norcros Investment Cos, Beaudrey-Norcros, John Tinsley Ltd, 1967-69; Dir, Rowan & Boden Ltd, 1972-73; Gp Man. Dir 1969-78, Dep. Chm. 1978-80, Scotcros Ltd. President, 1977-79: Etablissements Pierre Remy SA; Remy SA; C.E.C.A. P.; L. Lieutaud et Cie. Directeur-General: Soc. Commerciale et Industrielle Due Triage au Parc, 1977-79; SCI St Remy Nonancourt, 1977-79; Scotcros Europe SA, 1976-79. Dep. Chm. 1975-77, Chm. 1977-79, CBI Scotland; CBI: Council Mem., 1972-; Mem. President's Adv. Cttee, 1979; UK Regional Chm., 1979. Scottish Free Enterprise Award, 1978. Chm., Small Industries Council for Rural Areas of Scotland, 1975-77. Member: Scottish Development Agency, 1977-; British Tourist Authority 1980-. Chairman: Nat. Children's Home Management Cttee; Police Dependant's Trust. Mem., Les Gastronomes de la Mer. *Recreations*: reading, work, running for aeroplanes. *Address*: 293 Fenwick Road, Giffnock, Glasgow G46 6UH. *Club*: East India, Devonshire, Sports and Public Schools.

de VESCI, 6th Viscount, *cr* 1776; **John Eustace Vesey;** *b* 25 Feb. 1919; *s* of Lt-Col Hon. Thomas (Eustace) Vesey (*d* 1946) (*b* of 5th Viscount), and Lady Cecily (Kathleen) Vesey (*d* 1976) (a Lady-in-Waiting to the Duchess of Gloucester, 1947-51, a Woman of the Bedchamber to Queen Mary, 1951-53, and an Extra Lady-in-Waiting to the Duchess of Gloucester from 1953), *d* of 5th Earl of Kenmare; *S* uncle 1958; *m* 1950, Susan Anne, *d* of late Ronald (Owen Lloyd) Armstrong Jones, MBE, QC, DL, and of Anne, *o d* of Lt-Col Leonard Messel, OBE (later Countess of Rosse); one *s* two *d* (and one *d* decd). *Educ*: Eton; Trinity Coll., Cambridge. Served War of 1939-45 with Irish Guards, Narvik (wounded), North Africa and Italy. Followed career of Land Agent; now managing own property. FLAS(O), FRICS. Kt of Honour and Devotion, Sovereign Mil. Order of Malta. *Heir*: *s* Hon. Thomas Eustace Vesey, *b* 8 Oct. 1955. *Address*: Abbeyleix, Ireland. *T*: Abbeyleix 31162. *Club*: White's.

DEVESI, Sir Baddeley, GCMG 1980; Governor-General of the Solomon Islands, since 1978; Chancellor, University of the South Pacific, since 1980; *b* 16 Oct. 1941; *s* of Mostyn Tagabasoe Norua and Laisa Otu; *m* 1969, June Marie Barley; four *s* two *d*. *Educ*: St Stephen's Sch., Auckland, NZ; Ardmore Teachers' Coll., Auckland, NZ. MLC and Mem. Exec. Council, 1967-69. Headmaster, St Nicholas Sch., Honiara, 1968; Educn Officer and Lectr, 1970-72; Dist. Officer, 1973; District Comr and Clerk to Malaita Council, 1974; Permanent Secretary, 1976. Dep. Chm., Solomon Islands Broadcasting Corp., 1976. Captain, Solomon Islands team, 2nd South Pacific Games, 1969. Comr, Boy Scouts Assoc., 1968. *Recreations*: reading, swimming, lawn tennis, cricket, snooker. *Address*: Government House, Honiara, Solomon Islands.

de VIGIER, William Alphonse, Hon. CBE 1978; Chairman and Managing Director (also founder), Acrow Ltd; Chairman: Acrow Australia Ltd; Acrow Engineers (Pty) Ltd, South Africa; Coles Cranes Ltd; *b* 22 Jan. 1912; *m* 1939, Betty Kendall; two *d*. *Educ*: La Chataigneraie, Coppet, Switzerland. Director: Vigier Cement SA, Switzerland; Acrow Argentina SA; Acrow Peru SA; Acrow India Ltd; Inland Steel Pty, South Africa; Acrow Corp. of America. Mem., British Airways Bd, 1973-78. Knight of Star of the North (Sweden); Grand Commander, Order of Star of Africa. *Recreations*: tennis, skiing, swimming. *Address*: Sommerhaus, Soleure, Switzerland; Tinkers Lodge, Marsh Lane, Mill Hill, NW7; Acrow Ltd, 8 South Wharf, W2. *T*: (business) 01-262 3456. *Club*: East India, Devonshire, Sports and Public Schools.

DE VILLE, Harold Godfrey, (Oscar), CBE 1979; Executive Deputy Chairman, BICC plc, since 1980 (Director, since 1971; Executive Vice-Chairman, 1978-80); *b* Derbyshire, 11 April 1925; *s* of Harold De Ville and Anne De Ville (*née* Godfrey); *m* 1947, Pamela Fay Ellis; one *s*. *Educ*: Burton-on-Trent Grammar Sch.; Trinity Coll., Cambridge (MA). Served RN, 1943-46. With Ford Motor Co. Ltd, 1949-65; Gen. Man., Central Personnel Relations, BICC Ltd, 1965-70. Member: Commn on Industrial Relations, 1971-74; Central Arbitration Cttee, 1976-77; Council, Advisory, Conciliation and Arbitration Service, 1976-; Council, CBI, 1977- (Chm., CBI Working Parties, Bullock Cttee, 1975-78, Pay Determination, 1976-78); Council, Industrial Soc., 1977-. *Recreations*: genealogy, fell-walking. *Address*: BICC plc, 21 Bloomsbury Street, WC1B 3QN. *T*: 01-637 1300.

de VILLIERS, 3rd Baron, *cr* 1910; **Arthur Percy de Villiers;** *b* 17 Dec. 1911; *s* of 2nd Baron and Adelheid, *d* of H. C. Koch, Pietermaritzburg, Natal; *S* father 1934; *m* 1939, Lovett (marr. diss. 1958), *d* of Dr A. D. MacKinnon, Williams Lake, BC; one *s* two *d*. *Educ*: Magdalen Coll., Oxford. Barrister, Inner Temple, 1938. Farming in New Zealand. Admitted as a barrister to the Auckland Supreme Court, 1949. *Heir*: *s* Hon. Alexander Charles de Villiers, *b* 29 Dec. 1940. *Address*: PO Box 66, Kumeu, Auckland, NZ.

de VILLIERS, Dawid Jacobus, DPhil; Minister of Industries, Commerce and Tourism, South Africa, since 1980; *b* 10 July 1940; *m* 1964, Suzaan Mangold; one *s* three *d*. *Educ*: Univ. of Stellenbosch (BA Hons Philosophy, 1963; BTh,

DPhil); Rand Afrikaans Univ. (MA Phil., 1972). Abe Bailey Scholar, 1963-64; Markotter Scholar, 1964. Part-time Lectr in Philosophy, Univ. of Western Cape, 1963-64; Minister of Dutch Reformed Church, Wellington, Cape, 1967-69; Lectr in Philosophy, 1969-72, and Pres. Convocation, 1973-, Rand Afrikaans Univ.; MP for Johannesburg W, 1972-79; Chm., Nat. Party's Foreign Affairs Cttee in Parlt; Ambassador of S Africa to London, 1979-80. Visited: USA on US Leaders Exchange Prog., 1974; UK as guest of Brit. Govt, 1975; Israel as guest of Israeli Govt, 1977. Represented S Africa in internat. Rugby in S Africa, UK, Ireland, Australia, NZ, France and the Argentine, 1962-70 (Captain, 1965-70). State President's Award for Sport, 1968 and 1970; S African Sportsman of the Year, 1968; Jaycee's Outstanding Young Man of the Year Award, 1971. *Recreations:* sports, reading. *Address:* Legal and General Building, Corner of Prinsloo and Pretorius Streets, Private Bag X274, Pretoria 0001, South Africa. *Clubs:* Royal Automobile, Les Ambassadeurs, Cavalry and Guards.

DEVINE, Hon. Grant; MLA for Estevan, since 1982; Premier of Saskatchewan, since 1982; Leader, Progressive Conservative Party of Saskatchewan, since 1979; *b* Regina, 15 July 1944; *m* 1966, Chantal Guillaume; two *s* two *d*. *Educ:* Saskatchewan Univ. (BScA 1967); Alberta Univ. (MSc 1969; MBA 1970); Ohio State Univ. (PhD 1976). Farming, 1962-; marketing specialist, Fed. Govt, Ottawa, 1970-72; Lectr in Agricl Econs, Saskatchewan Univ., 1976-79. Advisor: Food Prices Rev. Bd and Provincial Govts; Sask. Consumers' Assoc. Member: Amer. Econ. Assoc.; Amer. Marketing Assoc.; Amer. Assoc. for Consumer Res.; Canadian Agricl Econs Soc.; Consumers' Assoc. of Canada. *Recreations:* golf, ski-ing, baseball. *Address:* Office of the Premier, Legislative Building, 2405 Legislative Drive, Regina S4S 0B3, Canada.

DEVINE, Rt. Rev. Joseph; Titular Bishop of Voli and Auxiliary to the Archbishop of Glasgow, (RC), since 1977; *b* 7 Aug. 1937; *s* of Joseph Devine and Christina Murphy. *Educ:* Blairs Coll., Aberdeen; St Peter's Coll., Dumbarton; Scots Coll., Rome. Ordained priest in Glasgow, 1960; postgraduate work in Rome (PhD), 1960-64; Private Sec. to Archbishop of Glasgow, 1964-65; Assistant Priest in a Glasgow parish, 1965-67; Lecturer in Philosophy, St Peter's Coll., Dumbarton, 1967-74; a Chaplain to Catholic Students in Glasgow Univ., 1974-77. Papal Bene Merenti Medal, 1962. *Recreations:* general reading, music, Association football. *Address:* Nazareth House, 1647 Paisley Road West, Cardonald, Glasgow. *T:* 041-882 7888.

DE VITO, Gioconda; Violinist; Professor of Violin at Accademia Di Santa Cecilia, Rome, 1935; *b* 26 July 1907; *d* of Giacomo and Emilia De Vito (née Del Guidice), Martina Franca Puglia, Italy; *m* 1949, James David Bicknell; no *c*. *Educ:* Conservatorio Di Musica Rossini, Pesaro. Began to play violin at age of 8½; final examinations (distinction), Conservatorio Pesaro, 1921; first concert, 1921; first prize, Internat. Competition, Vienna, 1932. World wide musical activities since debut with London Philharmonic Orchestra, 1948, at concert conducted by Victor de Sabata; Royal Philharmonic Soc., 1950; Edinburgh Festival, 1949, 1951, 1953 (took part, 1953, in Festival of the Violin with Yehudi Menuhin and Isaac Stern), and played at Bath Fest. and Festival Hall with Yehudi Menuhin, 1955; Jury Tchaikowsky Internat. Violin Competition, Moscow, and recitals Moscow and Leningrad. 1958; Soloist, Adelaide Centenary Fest., and toured Australia, 1960; concerts, Buenos Aires, 1961; retired, 1961. Last concerts, Gt Brit., Swansea Festival, Oct. 1961; Continent, Basle Philharmonic, Nov. 1961. Diploma di Medaglia d'Oro del Ministero della Pubblica Istruzione for services to Art, 1957; Academician, Accademia Nazionale di Santa Cecilia, Rome, 1976. *Recreation:* bird watching. *Address:* Flint Cottage, Loudwater, Rickmansworth, Herts. *T:* 72865; Via Cassia 595, Rome. *T:* 3660937.

DEVITT, Lt-Col Sir Thomas Gordon, 2nd Bt, *cr* 1916; Partner of Devitt & Moore, Shipbrokers; *b* 27 Dec. 1902; *e s* of Arthur Devitt (*d* 1921) *e s* of 1st Bt and Florence Emmeline (*d* 1951), *e d* of late William Forbes Gordon, Manar, NSW; *S* grandfather, 1923; *m* 1st, 1930, Joan Mary (who obtained a divorce, 1936), 2nd *d* of late Charles Reginald Freemantle, Hayes Barton, Pyrford, Surrey; 2nd, 1937, Lydia Mary (marr. diss. 1953), *o d* of late Edward Milligen Beloe, King's Lynn, Norfolk; two *d* ; 3rd, 1953, Janet Lilian, *o d* of late Col H. S. Ellis, CBE, MC; one *s* one *d*. *Educ:* Sherborne; Corpus Christi Coll., Cambridge. 1939-45 War as Lt-Col, Seaforth Highlanders and OC Raiding Support Regt. Royal Order of Phœnix of Greece with swords. Chm. Macers Ltd, 1961-70. Chairman: Board of Governors, The Devitt and Moore Nautical Coll., Pangbourne, 1948-61; Nat. Service for Seafarers, 1948-77. Governor, Sherborne Sch., 1967-75. *Heir:* *s* James Hugh Thomas Devitt, *b* 18 Sept. 1956. *Recreations:* shooting, fishing. *Address:* 49 Lexden Road, Colchester, Essex CO3 3PY. *T:* Colchester 77958; 5 Rembrandt Close, Holbein Place, SW1. *T:* 01-730 2653. *Club:* MCC.

DEVLIN, family name of **Baron Devlin.**

DEVLIN, Baron (Life Peer) *cr* 1961, of West Wick; **Patrick Arthur Devlin,** PC 1960; Kt 1948; FBA 1963; High Steward of Cambridge University, since 1966; *b* 25 Nov. 1905; *e s* of W. J. Devlin; *m* 1932, Madeleine, *yr d* of Sir Bernard Oppenheimer, 1st Bt; four *s* twin *d*. *Educ:* Stonyhurst Coll.; Christ's Coll., Cambridge. President of Cambridge Union, 1926. Called to Bar, Gray's Inn, 1929; KC 1945; Master of the Bench, Gray's Inn, 1947; Treasurer of Gray's Inn, 1963. Prosecuting Counsel to the Mint, 1931-39. Legal Dept, Min. of Supply, 1940-42; Junior Counsel to the Ministries of War Transport, Food and Supply, 1942-45; Attorney-Gen., Duchy of Cornwall, 1947-48; Justice of

the High Court, Queen's Bench Div., 1948-60; Pres. of the Restrictive Practices Court, 1956-60; a Lord Justice of Appeal, 1960-61; a Lord of Appeal in Ordinary, 1961-64, retd; Chm. Wiltshire QS, 1955-71. A Judge of the Administrative Tribunal of the ILO, 1964-; Chm., Commn apptd under constn of ILO to examine complaints concerning observance by Greece of Freedom of Assoc. and similar Conventions, 1969-71. Chairman: Cttee of Inquiry into Dock Labour Scheme, 1955-56; Nyasaland Inquiry Commn, 1959; Cttee of inquiry into the port transport industry, 1964-65; Jt Bd for the Nat. Newspaper Industry, 1965-69; Commn of Inquiry into Industrial Representation, 1971-72; Cttee on Identification in criminal cases, 1974-76. Chm., Press Council, 1964-69. Chm. of Council, Bedford Coll., University of London, 1953-59. Pres., British Maritime Law Assoc., 1962-76; Chm. Assoc. Average Adjusters, 1966-67. Hon. LLD: Glasgow 1962; Toronto 1962; Cambridge 1966; Leicester, 1966; Sussex 1966; Durham, 1968; Liverpool, 1970; Hon. DCL Oxon, 1965. *Publications:* Trial by Jury, 1956 (Hamlyn Lectures); The Criminal Prosecution in England (Sherrill Lectures), 1957; Samples of Lawmaking (Lloyd Roberts and other lectures), 1962; The Enforcement of Morals, (Maccabean and other lectures), 1965; The House of Lords and the Naval Prize Bill, 1911 (Rede Lecture), 1968; Too Proud to Fight: Woodrow Wilson's Neutrality, 1974; The Judge (Chorley and other lectures), 1979. *Address:* West Wick House, Pewsey, Wilts; Casa da Colina, Praia da Luz, Algarve.

See also Tim Devlin, William Devlin, P. J. M. Kennedy.

DEVLIN, Alexander, OBE 1977; JP; Member, Glenrothes New Town Development Corporation, since 1958; *b* 22 Dec. 1927; *s* of Thomas Devlin and Jean Gibson; *m* 1949, Annie Scott Gordon. *Educ:* Cowdenbeath St Columba's High Sch.; National Council of Labour Colls (Local Govt and Public Speaking). Member: Fife CC, 1956-74; Fife Regional Council, 1974-78; Chm., Fife Educn Cttee, 1963-78; Vice-Chm., Educn Cttee of Convention of Scottish Local Authorities, 1974-78. Member: Dunning Cttee on Scottish System for Assessment of Pupils after 4 years Secondary Educn, 1974-77; Scottish Sports Council, 1964-74; Manpower Services Commn, 1978-79. JP Fife, 1963. *Recreation:* welfare of mentally handicapped. *Address:* 106 Woodside Road, Glenrothes, Fife KY7 4DS.

DEVLIN, (Josephine) Bernadette; *see* McAliskey, J. B.

DEVLIN, Stuart Leslie, CMG 1980; goldsmith, silversmith and designer in London since 1965; Goldsmith and Jeweller by appointment to HM The Queen, 1982; *b* 9 Oct. 1931; *m* 1962, Kim Hose. *Educ:* Gordon Inst. of Technology, Geelong; Royal Melbourne Inst. of Technology; Royal Coll. of Art. DesRCA (Silversmith), DesRCA (Industrial Design/Engrg). Art Teacher, Vic. Educn Dept, 1950-58; Royal Coll. of Art, 1958-60; Harkness Fellow, NY, 1960-62; Lectr, Prahran Techn. Coll., Melbourne, 1962; one-man shows of sculpture, NY and Sydney, 1961-64; Inspr Art in Techn. Schs, Vic. Educn Dept, 1964-65; exhibns of silver and gold in numerous cities USA, Australia, Bermuda, Middle East and UK, 1965-. Executed many commns in gold and silver: designed coins for Australia, Singapore, Cayman Is, Gibraltar, IoM, Burundi, Botswana, Ethiopia and Bhutan; designed and made: cutlery for State Visit to Paris, 1972; Duke of Edinburgh trophy for World Driving Championship, 1973; silver to commemorate opening of Sydney Opera House, 1973; Grand National Trophy, 1975, 1976; Australian Bravery Awards, 1975; Regalia for the Order of Australia, 1975-76; Queen's Silver Jubilee Medal, 1977. Freeman, City of London, 1966; Liveryman, Goldsmiths' Co., 1972. *Recreations:* work, travel. *Address:* 25 Conduit Street, W1. *T:* 01-408 0044.

DEVLIN, Tim; National Director, Independent Schools Information Service (ISIS), since 1977; *b* 28 July 1944; 3rd *s* of Rt Hon. Lord Devlin, *qv* ; *m* 1967, Angela Denise, *d* of Mr A. J. G. and late Mrs Laramy; two *s* two *d*. *Educ:* Winchester Coll.; University Coll., Oxford (Hons degree, History). Feature Writer, Aberdeen Press & Journal, 1966; Reporter, Scotsman, 1967; Educn Corresp., Evening Echo, Watford, 1968-69; Reporter, later News Editor, The Times Educnl Supplement, 1969-71; Reporter, The Times, 1971-73, Educn Corresp., 1973-77. *Publications:* (with Mary Warnock) What Must We Teach?, 1977; Good Communications Guide, 1980; Independent Schools—The Facts, 1981. *Recreations:* writing, art, tennis, children. *Address:* Jeakes House, Mermaid Street, Rye, East Sussex. *T:* Rye 2915.

DEVLIN, William; Actor; *b* Aberdeen, 5 Dec. 1911; *y s* of William John Devlin, ARIBA, and Frances Evelyn Crombie; *m* 1936, Mary Casson (marr. diss.); one *d* ; *m* 1948, Meriel Moore. *Educ:* Stonyhurst Coll.; Merton Coll., Oxford (BA). Sec. OUDS, 1932-33; studied at Embassy Theatre Sch., 1933-34. New Theatre with John Gielgud, 1934-35 (Hamlet and Noah); Old Vic Company, 1935-36 (Peer Gynt, Cassius, Richard III, Leontes, Lear, etc); except for war period has appeared for Old Vic in every year, 1935-53 (Shylock, Macbeth, Claudius, Brutus, Dogberry, Fluellen, etc.). Parnell in The Lost Leader, Abbey Theatre, Dublin, 1937; Zola, Clemenceau, Gladstone in biogr. plays about them, 1937-38; Ransom in Ascent of F6 and Seth in Mourning becomes Electra, New Theatre, 1938. Joined HM Forces, Sept. 1939, as a Trooper in Horsed Cavalry; commnd in Royal Wilts Yeom. and served with 8th Army in Africa and Italy for 4½ years; released as Major, Nov. 1945. Leading man with Old Vic at Theatre Royal, Bristol, 1945-48. Memorial Theatre, Stratford-on-Avon, seasons 1954 and 1955. First appeared in New York as Bohun, QC in You Never Can Tell, Martin Beck Theatre, 1948; subseq. at Boston as Lear and Macbeth. Played Clemenceau in The Tiger, the first play to be televised in 1936, and has appeared regularly in this medium and also in Sound Broadcasting. Mem., Equity Council, 1957-65. Mem., Monksilver Parish Council, 1967, Chairman 1971, and 1973-74. *Recreations:* golf and fishing. *Address:* Bird's Hill Cottage, Monksilver, Taunton, Som. *T:* Stogumber 389.

See also Baron Devlin.

DEVON, 17th Earl of, *cr* 1553; **Charles Christopher Courtenay,** Bt 1644; RARO Lieutenant (W/Captain) Coldstream Guards; *b* 13 July 1916; *o surv. s* of 16th Earl and Marguerite (*d* 1950), *d* of late John Silva; *S* father, 1935; *m* 1939, Venetia, Countess of Cottenham, *d* of Captain J. V. Taylor; one *s* one *d. Educ:* Winchester; RMC, Sandhurst. Served war of 1939-45 (despatches). *Recreations:* shooting and fishing. *Heir: s* Lord Courtenay, *qv. Address:* Powderham Castle, Exeter. *T:* Starcross 890253.

DEVONPORT, 3rd Viscount *cr* 1917, of Wittington, Bucks; **Terence Kearley,** RIBA, ALI; Bt 1908; Baron 1910; Architect, Landscape Architect, and Rural Consultant in private practice, Newcastle upon Tyne, since 1978; *b* 29 Aug. 1944; *s* of 2nd Viscount Devonport and of Sheila Isabel, *e d* of Lt-Col C. Hope Murray; *S* father, 1973; *m* 1968, Elizabeth Rosemary, *d* of late John G. Hopton (marr. diss. 1979); two *d. Educ:* Aiglon Coll., Vaud, Switzerland; Selwyn Coll., Cambridge (MA, DipArch); Newcastle Univ. (BPhil). Chartered Architect, RIBA. Nuclear Power Group, Dungeness site office, 1963; Fresco restorer, Massada, Israel, 1964; Cambridge Univ., 1964-67 and 1968-70; Waterside and US Pavilion, Expo '70, design teams, with Davis Brody, New York City, 1967-68; Architect, Rehabilitation Div., London Borough of Lambeth, 1971-72; with Barnett Winskell, 1972-75; Newcastle Univ., 1975-77; with Ralph Erskine, Byker, 1977-78. *Recreations:* naturalist, traveller and gourmet; a Turkophile; interests: archæology, shooting and fishing. *Address:* Linnheads House, West Woodburn, near Hexham, Northumberland NE48 2TU. *Clubs:* Royal Automobile, Beefsteak, Farmers'; Northern Counties (Newcastle upon Tyne).

DEVONS, Prof. Samuel; FRS 1955; Professor of Physics, Columbia University, New York, since 1960 (Chairman, Dept of Physics, 1963-67); Director, History of Physics Laboratory, Barnard College, Columbia University, since 1970; *b* 1914; *s* of Rev. David I. Devons and E. Edleston; *m* 1938, Celia Ruth Toubkin; four *d. Educ:* Trinity Coll., Cambridge. BA 1935; MA, PhD 1939. Exhibition of 1851 Senior Student, 1939. Scientific Officer, Senior Scientific Officer, Air Ministry, MAP, and Ministry of Supply, 1939-45. Lecturer in Physics, Cambridge Univ., Fellow and Dir of Studies, Trinity Coll., Cambridge, 1946-49; Prof. of Physics, Imperial Coll. of Science, 1950-55; Langworthy Prof. of Physics and Dir of Physical Laboratories, Univ. of Manchester, 1955-60. Royal Soc. Leverhulme Vis. Prof., Andhra Univ., India, 1967-68; Balfour Vis. Prof., History of Science, Weizmann Inst., Rehovot, Israel, 1973; Racah Vis. Prof. of Physics, Hebrew Univ., Jerusalem, 1973-74. Rutherford Medal and Prize, Inst. of Physics, 1970. *Publications:* Excited States of Nuclei, 1949; (ed) Biology and Physical Sciences, 1969; (ed) High Energy Physics and Nuclear Structure, 1970; contributions to Proc. Royal Society, Proc. Phys. Soc., etc. *Recreations:* plastic arts, travel. *Address:* Department of Physics, Columbia University, Morningside Heights, New York, NY 10027, USA.

DEVONSHIRE, 11th Duke of, *cr* 1694; **Andrew Robert Buxton Cavendish,** PC 1964; MC; Baron Cavendish, 1605; Earl of Devonshire, 1618; Marquess of Hartington, 1694; Earl of Burlington, 1831; Baron Cavendish (UK) 1831; Vice-Lord-Lieutenant of the County of Derby since 1957; Chancellor of Manchester University since 1965; *b* 2 Jan. 1920; *o surv s* of 10th Duke of Devonshire, KG, and Lady Mary Cecil (*see* Dowager Duchess of Devonshire), *d* of 4th Marquess of Salisbury, KG, GCVO; *S* father, 1950; *m* 1941, Hon. Deborah Vivian Freeman-Mitford, *d* of 2nd Baron Redesdale; one *s* two *d. Educ:* Eton; Trinity Coll., Cambridge. Served War of 1939-45, Coldstream Guards (MC). Contested (C) Chesterfield Div. of Derbyshire, 1945 and 1950. Parliamentary Under-Sec. of State for Commonwealth Relations, Oct. 1960-Sept. 1962; Minister of State, Commonwealth Relations Office, Sept. 1962-Oct. 1964 and for Colonial Affairs, 1963-Oct. 1964. Executive Steward of the Jockey Club, 1966-69. Mem., Horserace Totalisator Board, 1977-; a Trustee, Nat. Gallery, 1960-68; President: The Royal Hosp. and Home for Incurables, 1954-; Derbyshire Boy Scouts Assoc.; Arts Employed; Lawn Tennis Assoc., 1955-61; RNIB, 1979-; Nat Assoc. for Deaf Children, 1978-; East Midland Area, MENCAP; Vice-Pres., Building Societies Assoc. (Pres., 1954-61); Chairman: Grand Council, British Empire Cancer Campaign, 1956-81; Throughbred Breeders' Assoc., 1978-81. Mayor of Buxton, 1952-54. Hon. Col, Manchester and Salford Univs OTC, 1981-. Hon. LLD: Manchester; Sheffield; Liverpool; Hon. Dr Law, Memorial Univ. of Newfoundland. *Publication:* Park Top: a romance of the Turf, 1976. *Heir: s* Marquess of Hartington, *qv. Address:* 4 Chesterfield Street, W1. *T:* 01-499 5803; Chatsworth, Bakewell, Derbyshire. *T:* Baslow 2204; Lismore Castle, Co. Waterford, Eire. *T:* Lismore 54288. *Clubs:* Brooks's, Jockey, White's.

See also Rt Hon. Harold Macmillan.

DEVONSHIRE, Dowager Duchess of, (Mary Alice), GCVO 1955; CBE 1946; Mistress of the Robes to The Queen, 1953-66; Chancellor of the University of Exeter, 1956-70; *b* 29 July 1895; *d* of 4th Marquis of Salisbury, KG, PC, GCVO, and Lady Cicely Alice Gore (*d* 1955), 2nd *d* of 5th Earl of Arran; *m* 1917, as Lady Mary Cecil, 10th Duke of Devonshire, KG; one *s* (*see* 11th Duke of Devonshire) two *d* (*er s* killed in action, 1944). *Address:* 107 Eaton Square, SW1W 9AA. *T:* 01-235 8798; Moorview, Edensor, Bakewell, Derbyshire. *T:* Baslow 2204.

DEVONSHIRE, Michael Norman, TD 1969; Master of the Supreme Court, Taxing Office, since 1979; *b* 23 May 1930; *s* of late Norman George Devonshire and late Edith Devonshire (*née* Skinner); *m* 1962, Jessie Margaret Roberts. *Educ:* King's Sch., Canterbury. Military Service, 2nd Lt, RA, served Korea, 1953-55; 4/5 Bn Queen's Own Royal West Kent Regt TA and 7 Bn Queen's Regt TA, 1955-69; retired in rank of Major, 1969. Articled to H. D. Carter, 1948-53; admitted Solicitor, 1953; Partner, Doyle Devonshire Co., 1957-79. Pres., London Solicitors' Litigation Assoc., 1974-76; Mem., Law Soc. Family Law and Contentious Remuneration Cttees, 1969-79. Mem., Council, Royal Yachting Assoc., 1978- (Trustee, Seamanship Foundn, 1981-). *Publication:* (with M. J. Cook and W. H. Elliott) The Taxation of Contentious Costs, 1979. *Recreation:* sailing. *Address:* 17 Chestnut Avenue, Southborough, Tunbridge Wells, Kent. *T:* Tunbridge Wells 28672.

DE VRIES, Peter; writer; *b* Chicago, 27 Feb. 1910; *s* of Joost and Henrietta (*née* Eldersveld) de Vries; *m* 1943, Katinka Loeser; two *s* one *d. Educ:* Calvin College, Michigan (AB); Northwestern University. Editor, community newspaper, Chicago, 1931; free lance writer, 1931-; associate editor Poetry Magazine, 1938; co-editor, 1942; joined editorial staff New Yorker Magazine, 1944. Mem., Amer. Acad. and Inst. of Arts and Letters. *Publications:* No But I saw the Movie, 1952; The Tunnel of Love, 1954; Comfort Me with Apples, 1956; The Mackerel Plaza, 1958; The Tents of Wickedness, 1959; Through the Fields of Clover, 1961; The Blood of the Lamb, 1962; Reuben, Reuben, 1964; Let Me Count the Ways, 1965; The Vale of Laughter, 1967; The Cat's Pajamas and Witch's Milk, 1968; Mrs Wallop, 1970; Into Your Tent I'll Creep, 1971; Without a Stitch in Time, 1972; Forever Panting, 1973; The Glory of the Hummingbird, 1975; I Hear America Swinging, 1976; Madder Music, 1978; Consenting Adults, 1980; Sauce for the Goose, 1981. *Address:* c/o New Yorker Magazine, 25 W 43rd Street, New York, NY 10036, USA; (home) 170 Cross Highway, Westport, Conn 06880, USA.

DEW, Leslie Robert; Member, Bermuda Insurance Advisory Committee, since 1979; President and Managing Director, Britamco Ltd, since 1977; President, Insco Ltd, Bermuda (Gulf Oil Corporation Insurance Subsids), since 1980 (Executive Vice President-Underwriter, 1977-80); Chairman, 1971-77 and formerly Non-Marine Underwriter, Roy J. M. Merrett Syndicates; *b* 11 April 1914; *er s* of Robert Thomas Dew, RHA and Ellen Dora Frampton; *m* 1st, 1939, Vera Doreen Wills (marr. diss. 1956); 2nd, 1956, Patricia Landsberg (*née* Hyde); one *s. Educ:* privately. Underwriting Member of Lloyd's, 1950-; Mem. Cttee of Lloyd's, 1969-72, 1974-77; Dep. Chm. of Lloyd's, 1971, 1975, 1977; Mem. Cttee, Lloyd's Non-Marine Assoc., 1957-77 (Dep. Chm. 1963 and 1965, Chm. 1966); Chm., Lloyd's Common Market Working Gp, 1971-77; Dep. Chm., British Insurers' European Cttee, 1972-77. Binney Award for Civilian Bravery, 1975. *Recreations:* music, reading. *Address:* PO Box 268, Hamilton 5, Bermuda. *Clubs:* Metropolitan (NY), Royal Bermuda Yacht, Coral Beach and Tennis, Mid Ocean (Bermuda).

DEW, Prof. Ronald Beresford; Professor Emeritus, University of Manchester Institute of Science and Technology, since 1980; *b* 19 May 1916; *s* of Edwyn Dew-Jones, FCA, and Jean Robertson Dew-Jones, BA, (*née* McInnes); *m* 1940, Sheila Mary Smith, BA; one *s* one *d. Educ:* Sedbergh; Manchester Univ. (LLB); Cambridge Univ. (MA). Barrister-at-Law, Middle Temple, 1965. Lieut, RNVR, 1940-45. Asst Managing Dir, P-E Consulting Gp, 1952-62; Director: Kurt Salmon & Co., 1955-62; S. Dodd & Co., 1957-59. Visiting Prof. of Industrial Administration, Manchester Univ., 1960-63; Head of Dept of Management Sciences, Univ. of Manchester Inst. of Science and Technology, 1963-70 and 1974-77; Prof. of Industrial Administration, Manchester Univ., 1963-67; Prof. of Management Sciences, 1967-80. Mem. Council, Internat. Univ. Contact for Management Educn, 1966-71; Dir, Centre for Business Research, 1965-69; Dir, European Assoc. of Management Training Centres, 1966-71; Dep. Chm., Manchester Polytechnic, 1970-72; External Examiner, Univs of: Liverpool, 1967-70; Loughborough, 1968-73; Bath, 1970-73; Khartoum (Sudan), 1967-70. Co-Chm., Conf. of Univ. Management Schools (CUMS), 1970-73; Governor: Manchester Coll. of Commerce, 1966-70; Manchester Polytechnic, 1970-76; Member: Council of BIM, 1971-76 (Bd of NW Region, 1966-80); Council of Manchester Business School, 1967-76; Court of Manchester Univ., 1978-80; Trustee, European Foundation for Management Develt, 1975-77; Consultant on organisation and control, to various internat. cos. CBIM, FCA. *Publications:* (co-author) Management Control and Information, 1973; numerous papers in internat. jls, on management control systems. *Recreations:* archaeology, ornithology, bee-keeping, travel. *Address:* University of Manchester Institute of Science and Technology, Department of Management Sciences, Sackville Street, Manchester M60 1QD. *T:* 061-236 3311.

de WAAL, Constant Hendrik, CB 1977; Second Parliamentary Counsel since 1981; Barrister-at-law; *b* 1 May 1931; *s* of late Hendrik de Waal and Elizabeth von Ephrussi; *m* 1964, Julia Jessel; two *s. Educ:* Tonbridge Sch. (scholar); Pembroke Coll., Cambridge (scholar). 1st cl. Law Tripos, 1st cl. LLB. Called to the Bar, Lincoln's Inn, 1953; Buchanan Prize, Cassel Scholar. Fellow of Pembroke Coll., Cambridge, and Univ. Asst Lectr in Law, 1958-60. Entered Parliamentary Counsel Office, 1960; with Law Commission, 1969-71; Parly Counsel, 1971-. *Recreation:* remaining (so far as possible) unaware of current events. *Address:* 62 Sussex Street, SW1.

See also Very Rev. V. A. de Waal.

de WAAL, Rev. Hugo Ferdinand; Principal, Ridley Hall Theological College, Cambridge, since 1978; *b* 16 March 1935; *s* of Bernard Hendrik and

Albertine Felice de Waal; *m* 1960, Brigit Elizabeth Townsend Massingberd-Mundy; one *s* three *d*. *Educ:* Tonbridge School; Pembroke Coll., Cambridge (MA); Münster Univ., Germany; Ridley Hall, Cambridge. Curate, St Martin's-in-the Bull Ring, Birmingham, 1960; Chaplain, Pembroke Coll., Cambridge, 1964-68; Rector of Dry Drayton, Cambs, 1964-73; with Bar Hill Ecumenical Area, 1967-73; Vicar of St John's, Blackpool Parish Church, 1974-78. *Recreations:* music, tennis and squash, fly-fishing. *Address:* The Principal's Lodge, Ridley Hall, Cambridge CB3 9HG. *T:* Cambridge 58665.

de WAAL, Very Rev. Victor Alexander; Dean of Canterbury, since 1976; *b* 2 Feb. 1929; *s* of late Hendrik de Waal and of Elizabeth von Ephrussi; *m* 1960, Esther Aline Lowndes Moir, PhD; four *s*. *Educ:* Tonbridge School; Pembroke Coll., Cambridge (MA); Ely Theological College. With Phs van Ommeren (London) Ltd, 1949-50; Asst Curate, St Mary the Virgin, Isleworth, 1952-56; Chaplain, Ely Theological Coll., 1956-59; Chaplain and Succentor, King's Coll., Cambridge, 1959-63; Chaplain, Univ. of Nottingham, 1963-69; Chancellor of Lincoln Cathedral, 1969-76. *Publications:* What is the Church?, 1969; contrib.: Theology and Modern Education, 1965; Stages of Experience, 1965; The Committed Church, 1966; Liturgy Reshaped, 1982. *Recreations:* pottery, fishing. *Address:* The Deanery, Canterbury, Kent CT1 2EP. *T:* Canterbury 65983.
See also *C. H. de Waal.*

DEWAR, family name of **Baron Forteviot.**

DEWAR, David Alexander; Deputy Secretary, Exchequer and Audit Department, since 1981; *b* 28 Oct. 1934; *s* of James and Isabella Dewar; *m* 1959, Rosalind Mary Ellen Greenwood; one *s* one *d*. *Educ:* Leith Academy, Edinburgh. Entered Exchequer and Audit Dept, 1953; Chief Auditor, 1966; Deputy Director of Audit, 1973; Director of Audit, 1977. *Recreations:* gardening, golf. *Address:* 85 Orchard Drive, Horsell, Woking, Surrey GU21 4BS. *T:* Woking 5352.

DEWAR, Donald Campbell; MP (Lab) Glasgow, Garscadden, since April 1978; solicitor, with Ross Harper & Murphy, Glasgow; *b* 21 Aug. 1937; *s* of Dr Alasdair Dewar, Glasgow; *m* 1964, Alison McNair (marr. diss. 1973); one *s* one *d*. *Educ:* Glasgow Acad.; Glasgow Univ. (MA, LLB). MP (Lab) South Aberdeen, 1966-70; PPS to Pres. of Bd of Trade, 1967; Chm., Select Cttee on Scottish Affairs, 1979-81; front bench spokesman on Scottish Affairs, 1980-. *Address:* 23 Cleveden Road, Glasgow G12 0PQ.

DEWAR, George Duncan Hamilton; chartered accountant; Partner, Peat, Marwick, Mitchell & Co., Glasgow, 1949-81; *b* 11 Sept. 1916; *s* of George Readman Dewar and Elizabeth Garrioch Sinclair Hamilton; *m* 1940, Elizabeth Lawson Potts Lawrie; one *s* one *d*. *Educ:* High Sch. of Glasgow. Mem. Inst. Chartered Accountants of Scotland (admitted, 1940; Mem. Coun., 1960-65; Vice-Pres., 1969-70; Pres., 1970-71). Mem., Scottish Tourist Bd, 1977-80. *Recreations:* golf, gardening. *Address:* 82 Langside Drive, Glasgow G43 2SX. *T:* 041-637 1734. *Clubs:* Caledonian; Western, Royal Scottish Automobile (Glasgow).

DEWAR, Ian Stewart; Under-Secretary, Welsh Office, since 1973; *b* 29 Jan. 1929; *er s* of late William Stewart Dewar and of Eileen Dewar (*née* Godfrey); *m* 1968, Nora Stephanie House; one *s* one *d*. *Educ:* Penarth County Sch.; UC Cardiff; Jesus Coll., Oxford (MA). RAF, 1947-49. Asst Archivist, Glamorgan County Council, 1952-53. Entered Min. of Labour, 1953; Asst Private Sec. to Minister, 1956-58; Principal, Min. of Labour and Civil Service Commn, 1958-65; Asst Sec., Min. of Labour, Dept of Employment and Commn on Industrial Relations, 1965-70; Asst Sec., Welsh Office, 1973. *Address:* 59 Stanwell Road, Penarth, South Glamorgan. *T:* Cardiff 703255.

DEWAR, Prof. Michael James Steuart, FRS 1960; MA, DPhil Oxon; Robert A. Welch Professor of Chemistry, University of Texas, since 1963; *b* 24 Sept. 1918; *s* of Francis D. Dewar, ICS, and Nan B. Keith; *m* 1944, Mary Williamson; two *s*. *Educ:* Winchester Coll. (First Scholar); Balliol Coll., Oxford (Brackenbury, Frazer and Gibbs Scholar; Hon. Fellow, 1974). ICI Fellow in Chemistry, Oxford, 1945; Courtaulds Ltd, Fundamental Research Laboratory, 1945-51; Reilly Lecturer at Notre Dame Univ., USA, 1951; Prof. of Chemistry and Head of Dept of Chemistry at Queen Mary Coll., University of London, 1951-59; Prof. of Chemistry, University of Chicago, 1959-63. Visiting Prof. at Yale Univ., USA, 1957. Hon. Sec. Chemical Soc., 1957-59. Harrison Howe Award of Amer. Chem. Soc., 1961; (first) G. W. Wheland Meml Medal, Univ. of Chicago, 1976; Evans Award, Ohio State Univ., 1977; South West Regional Award, Amer. Chem. Soc., 1978. Lectures: Tilden, Chem. Soc., 1954; Falk-Plaut, Columbia Univ., 1963; Daines Memorial, Univ. of Kansas, 1963; Glidden Company, Western Reserve Univ., 1964; Marchon Visiting, Univ. of Newcastle upon Tyne, 1966; Glidden Company, Kent State Univ., 1967; Gnehm, Eidg. Tech. Hochschule, Zurich, 1968; Barton, Univ. of Oklahoma, 1969; Kahlbaum, Univ. of Basel, 1970; Benjamin Rush, Univ. of Pennsylvania, 1971; Venable, Univ. of N Carolina, 1971; Foster, State Univ. of NY at Buffalo, 1973; Robinson, Chem. Soc., 1974; Sprague, Univ. of Wisconsin, 1974; Bircher, Vanderbilt Univ., 1976; Faraday, Northern Illinois Univ., 1977; Priestley, Pennsylvania State Univ., 1980; Visiting Professor: Arthur D. Little, MIT, 1966; Maurice S. Kharasch, Univ. of Chicago, 1971; Firth, Sheffield, 1972; Dist. Bicentennial, Univ. of Utah, 1976; Pahlavi, Iran, 1977. Fellow, Amer. Acad. of Arts and Sciences, 1966. *Publications:* The Electronic Theory of Organic Chemistry, 1949;

Hyperconjugation, 1962; Introduction to Modern Chemistry, 1965; The Molecular Orbital Theory of Organic Chemistry, 1969; Computer Compilation of Molecular Weights and Percentage Compositions, 1970; The PMO Theory of Organic Chemistry, 1975; papers in scientific journals. *Address:* Department of Chemistry, University of Texas, Austin, Texas 78712, USA. *T:* (512) 471-5053.

DEWAR, Brig. Michael Preston Douglas, CB 1958; CBE 1956; retired; *b* 1 Oct. 1906; *s* of late Vice-Admiral R. G. D. Dewar, CBE, and Mrs S. E. Dewar (*née* Churchill); *m* 1935, Winifred Elizabeth, *née* Murphy (*d* 1971); one *s* one *d*. *Educ:* Winchester Coll. Commissioned 2nd Lieut, The Buffs, 1926; Captain, 1938; Staff Coll., 1939; Major, 1943; OC Home Counties Bde Trg Centre, 1946-47; GSO 1, 6th Airborne Div., 1947-48; Lt-Col, 1948; Jt Services Staff Coll., 1948-49; Col GS, E Africa, 1949-51; Col, 1951; Col Administrative Plans, GHQ, MELF, 1951-52; Dep. Dir Manpower Planning, War Office, 1952-55; Brig., 1955; UK Nat. Military Rep., SHAPE, 1955-58, retired 1959. *Recreations:* gardening, bridge. *Address:* Great Maytham Hall, Rolvenden, near Cranbrook, Kent. *T:* Rolvenden 375. *Club:* Army and Navy.

DEWAR, Robert James, CMG 1969; CBE 1964; Chief of Agricultural Division, Regional Mission for Eastern Africa of the World Bank, since 1974; *b* 1923; *s* of late Dr Robert Scott Dewar, MA, MB, ChB, Dumbreck, Glasgow, and of Mrs Roubaix Dewar, Aberdovey, N Wales; *m* 1947, Christina Marianne, *d* of late Olof August Ljungberger, Stockholm, Sweden; two *s* one *d*. *Educ:* High Sch. of Glasgow; Edinburgh Univ. (BSc, Forestry). Wadham Coll., Oxford. Asst Conservator of Forests, Colonial Forest Service, Nigeria and Nyasaland, 1944-55; Dep. Chief Conservator of Forests, Nyasaland, 1955-60; Chief Conservator of Forests, Dir of Forestry and Game, Nyasaland (now Malawi), 1960-64; Mem. Nyasaland Legislative Council, 1960. Permanent Secretary, Malawi: Min. of Natural Resources, 1964-67 and 1968-69; Min. of Economic Affairs, 1967-68; retd from Malawi CS, 1969; Sen. Agriculturalist, Agricl Projects Dept, IBRD, 1969-74. Mem. Nat. Development Council, Malawi, 1966-69. *Recreations:* golf, angling. *Address:* c/o World Bank, PO Box 30577, Nairobi, Kenya. *T:* Nairobi 891425. *Club:* Royal Commonwealth Society.

DEWAR, Thomas; His Honour Judge Dewar; a Circuit Judge (formerly Judge of the County Court), since 1962; Joint President, Council of Circuit Judges, 1980 (Vice-President, 1979); *b* 5 Jan. 1909; *s* of James Stewart Dewar and Katherine Rose Dewar; *m* 1950, Katherine Muriel Johnson; one *s*. *Educ:* Penarth Intermediate School; Cardiff Technical Coll.; Sch. of Pharmacy, University of London; Birkbeck Coll., University of London. Pharmaceutical Chemist, 1931; BPharm 1931, PhD 1934, BSc (Botany, 1st cl. hons) 1936, London. Called to Bar, Middle Temple, 1939; Blackstone Pupillage Prize, 1939. Admin. staff of Pharmaceutical Soc., 1936-40; Sec., Middx Pharmaceutical Cttee, 1940-41; Asst Dir, Min. of Supply, 1943; Sec., Wellcome Foundation, 1943-45. Mem. of Western Circuit, 1945-62; Judge of the County Court (circuit 59, Cornwall and Plymouth), 1962-65, (circuit 38, Edmonton, etc); 1965-66 (circuit 41, Clerkenwell), 1966-71; Circuit Judge, SE circuit, 1972-. Presided over inquiry into X-ray accident at Plymouth Hosp., 1962. Mem. Executive Council, Internat. Law Assoc., 1974-. Governor, Birkbeck Coll., 1944-46 and 1971-82. *Publications:* Textbook of Forensic Pharmacy, 1946 and four subsequent editions; scientific papers in Quarterly Jl of Pharmacy and Pharmacology. *Recreations:* horticulture, travel. *Address:* 1 Garden Court, Temple, EC4. *T:* 01-353 3326; Goldenhurst Cottage, Aldington, Kent. *T:* Aldington 420.

de WARDENER, Prof. Hugh Edward, CBE 1982 (MBE (mil.) 1946); MD, FRCP; Professor of Medicine, University of London, Charing Cross Hospital, 1960-81; Honorary Consultant Physician to the Army, 1975-80; *b* 8 Oct. 1915; *s* of Edouard de Wardener and Becky (*née* Pearce); *m* 1st, 1939, Janet Lavinia Bellis Simon (marr. diss. 1947); one *s*; 2nd, 1947, Diana Rosamund Crawshay (marr. diss. 1954); 3rd, 1954, Jill Mary Foxworthy (marr. diss. 1969); one *d*; 4th, 1969, Josephine Margaret Storey, MBE; two *s*. *Educ:* Malvern Coll. St Thomas's Hosp., 1933-39; RAMC, 1939-45; St Thomas's Hosp., 1945-60, Registrar, Senior Lecturer, Reader. MRCP 1946, MD 1949, FRCP 1958. Hon. MD, Univ. Pierre et Marie Curie, Paris, 1980. President: Internat. Soc. of Nephrology, 1969-72; Renal Assoc., 1973-76; Mem. Council, Imp. Cancer Res. Fund, 1981. *Publications:* The Kidney: An Outline of Normal and Abnormal Structure and Function, 1973. Papers in various scientific journals. *Recreations:* normal and scything. *Address:* 9 Dungarvan Avenue, Barnes, SW15. *T:* 01-878 3130.

DEWDNEY, Duncan Alexander Cox, CBE 1968; Director, The Coverdale Organisation, since 1973; *b* 22 Oct. 1911; *o s* of late Claude Felix Dewdney and Annie Ross Cox; *m* 1935, Ann, *d* of Walter Riley and Emily Sterratt; two *d*. *Educ:* Bromgrove Sch., Worcs; University of Birmingham (BSc Hons, Cadman Medallist). Served War of 1939-45; RAF, 1940-45 (Wing Comdr); Air Staff appts, Head RE8 Min. of Home Security (R&D Dept). British Petroleum Co., 1932-36; International Assoc. (Pet. Ind.) Ltd, 1936-40; Research Man., Esso Development Co., 1945-51; joined Esso Petroleum Co., 1951; Dir, 1957; Man. Dir, 1963-67; Vice-Chm., 1968. Seconded to NBPI as Jt Dep. Chm., 1965-66, part-time Mem. Bd, 1967-69. Exec. Dir, Rio Tinto Zinc Corporation, 1968-72; Chairman: Irish Refining Co. Ltd, 1958-65; Anglesey Aluminium, 1968-71; RTZ Britain, 1969-72; RTZ Development Enterprises, 1970-72; Dep. Chm., Manpower Services Commn, 1974-77; Dir, Esso Chemicals SA, 1964. Chairman: National Economic Develt Cttee for the

Mechanical Engrg Industry, 1964-68; Welsh Industrial Develt Bd, 1972-75; Underwater Training Centre, 1977-79. Legion of Merit, 1945. *Address:* Salters, Harestock, Winchester, Hants. *T:* Winchester 2034. *Club:* Travellers'.

DEWES, Sir Herbert (John Salisbury), Kt 1973; CBE 1954; DL; JP; Chairman, Cheshire County Council, 1968-74; *b* 30 June 1897; *s* of John Hunt Dewes, solicitor, Tamworth, Staffordshire; *m* 1923, Kathleen, *d* of W. Matthews, Nuneaton; two *s. Educ:* Aldenham. County Alderman for Cheshire, 1950; JP 1951, DL 1966, Cheshire. Presidential Award, RSA, 1973. *Address:* 2 Curzon Park North, Chester CH4 8AR. *T:* Chester 679798.

de WET, Dr Carel; South African Ambassador to the Court of St James's, 1964-67 and 1972-77; Director of companies; farmer; *b* Memel, OFS, S Africa, 25 May 1924; *g s* of Gen. Christian de Wet; *m* 1949, Catharina Elizabeth (Rina) Maas, BA; one *s* three *d. Educ:* Vrede High Sch., OFS; Pretoria Univ. (BSc); University of Witwatersrand (MB, BCh). Served at Nat. Hosp., Bloemfontein; subseq. practised medicine at Boksburg, Transvaal, at Winburg, OFS, and, from 1948, at Vanderbijlpark, Transvaal. Mayor of Vanderbijlpark, 1950-53; MP (Nat. Party) for Vanderbijlpark, 1953-64, for Johannesburg West, 1967-72; Mem. various Parly and Nat. Party Cttees, 1953-64; Minister of Mines and Health, Govt of S Africa, 1967-72. *Recreations:* beef ranching, golf, rugby, cricket, hunting, deep sea fishing. *Address:* Castrol House, PO Box 6424, Johannesburg 2000, South Africa. *T:* (office) 642-4343; (home) 706-6202. *Clubs:* Royal Automobile, East India, Institute of Directors, MCC, Les Ambassadeurs, Eccentric, Wentworth; Here XVII (Cape Town); Constantia (Pretoria); Club RSA, New, Rand Park Golf, Country (Johannesburg); Maccauvlei Country (Vereeniging), Emfuleni Golf (Vanderbijlpark); Brits Golf (Brits, Transvaal).

DEWEY, Sir Anthony Hugh, 3rd Bt, *cr* 1917; JP; *b* 31 July 1921; *s* of late Major Hugh Grahame Dewey, MC (*e s* of 2nd Bt), and of Marjorie Florence Isobell (who *m* 2nd, 1940, Sir Robert Bell, KCSI; he died 1953), *d* of Lieut-Col Alexander Hugh Dobbs; *S* grandfather, 1948; *m* 1949, Sylvia, *d* of late Dr J. R. MacMahon, Branksome Manor, Bournemouth; two *s* three *d.* JP Somerset, 1961. *Heir: s* Rupert Grahame Dewey [*b* 29 March 1953; *m* 1978, Suzanne Rosemary, *d* of late Andrew Lusk, Perthshire; one *s*]. *Address:* Silton Lodge, Gillingham, Dorset SP8 5AQ. *T:* Bourton 840324. *Club:* Army and Navy.

DEWHURST, Prof. Sir (Christopher) John, Kt 1977; FRCOG, FRCSE; Professor of Obstetrics and Gynaecology, University of London, at Queen Charlotte's Hospital for Women, since 1967; Dean, Institute of Obstetrics and Gynaecology, since 1979; *b* 2 July 1920; *s* of John and Agnes Dewhurst; *m* 1952, Hazel Mary Atkin; two *s* one *d. Educ:* St Joseph's Coll., Dumfries; Manchester Univ. MB, ChB. Surg. Lieut, RNVR, 1943-46. Sen. Registrar, St Mary's Hosp., Manchester, 1948-51; Lectr, Sen. Lectr and Reader, Sheffield Univ., 1951-67. Pres., RCOG, 1975-78. Hon. FACOG 1976; Hon. FRCSI 1977; Hon. FCOG (SA) 1978. Hon. DSc Sheffield, 1977; Hon. MD Uruguay, 1980. *Publications:* A Student's Guide to Obstetrics and Gynaecology, 1960, 2nd edn 1965; The Gynaecological Disorders of Infants and Children, 1963; (jtly) The Intersexual Disorders, 1969; (ed) Integrated Obstetrics and Gynaecology for Postgraduates, 1972, 3rd edn 1981; (jtly) A General Practice of Obstetrics and Gynaecology, 1977; Practical Paediatric and Adolescent Gynaecology, 1980; Royal Confinements, 1980. *Recreations:* cricket, gardening, music. *Address:* 39 Old Slade Lane, Iver, Bucks. *T:* Iver 653395.

DEWHURST, Keith Ward; His Honour Judge Dewhurst; a Circuit Judge, since 1972; *b* 11 March 1924; *s* of James Dewhurst, solicitor, and Mildred Catherine Dewhurst; *m* 1952, Norah Mary Hodgson (marr. diss. 1970); two *d. Educ:* Shrewsbury School; Trinity College, Oxford. Called to the Bar, Inner Temple, 1947. Practised on Northern Circuit. *Recreations:* reading, bridge. *Address:* 277 Garstang Road, Fulwood, Preston, Lancs. *T:* Preston 716850.

DEWHURST, Comdr Ronald Hugh, DSO 1940; RN retired; *b* 10 Oct. 1905; *s* of late Robert Paget Dewhurst, ICS, and late Florence Frances Maud Dewhurst; *m* 1928, Torquilla Macleod Lawrence (*d* 1953); one *s* one *d ; m* 1954, Marion Isabel Dahm; one *d. Educ:* Abberley Hall; Osborne; Dartmouth. Joined Royal Navy, 1919; served in submarines, 1927-53; commanded HM submarines H. 33, Seahorse, and Rorqual (DSO and two Bars); Amphion, Taciturn, and RN Detention Quarters, 1953-55; retired to New Zealand, 1955. *Recreations:* fishing, bridge. *Address:* 6 Wychwood Crescent, Rotorua, New Zealand.

DEWHURST, Timothy Littleton, MC 1945; Registrar of the High Court of Justice in Bankruptcy, since 1981; *b* 4 March 1920; *s* of late Robert Cyril Dewhurst and Rhoda Joan Dewhurst; *m* 1949, Pandora Laetitia Oldfield; four *d. Educ:* Stowe Sch.; Magdalen Coll., Oxford (MA). Called to Bar, Lincoln's Inn, 1950. Served with Rifle Brigade, 1941-46, N Africa and Italy (despatches 1944). Mem. Bar Council, 1977-79; Conveyancing Counsel of the Court, 1980-81. *Address:* Thomas More Building, Royal Courts of Justice, Strand, WC2.

de WINTER, Carl; Secretary General, Federation of British Artists, since 1978; *b* 18 June 1934; *s* of Alfred de Winter; *m* 1958, Lyndall Bradshaw; one *s* one *d. Educ:* Pangbourne. Purser, Orient Line, 1951-60. Art Exhibitions Bureau:

PA to Man. Dir, 1961-66; Director, 1967-; Royal Soc. of Portrait Painters: Asst Sec., 1962-; Royal Soc. of Miniature Painters, Sculptors and Gravers: Asst Sec., 1964-67; Sec., 1968-; Royal Soc. of Marine Artists: Asst Sec., 1964-70; Sec., 1971-78; Royal Soc. of British Artists: Asst Keeper, 1969-73; Keeper, 1974-; Royal Inst. of Oil Painters: Sec., 1973-; Royal Inst. of Painters in Watercolours: Sec., 1979-; National Soc. of Painters, Sculptors and Printmakers: Sec., 1973-; New English Art Club: Sec., 1973-; United Soc. of Artists: Sec., 1975-81. *Address:* 36 Winsham Grove, SW11. *T:* 01-228 7912. *Club:* Athenæum.

DE WOLF, Vice-Adm. Harry George, CBE 1946; DSO 1944; DSC 1944; *b* 1903; *s* of late Harry George De Wolf, Bedford, NS; *m* 1931, Gwendolen Fowle, *d* of Thomas St George Gilbert, Somerset, Bermuda; one *s* one *d.* Served War of 1939-45. Asst Chief of Naval Staff, Canada, 1944-47; Sen. Canadian Naval Officer Afloat, 1947-48; Flag Officer, Pacific Coast, 1948-50; Vice-Chief of Naval Staff, 1950-52; Chm. of Canadian Joint Staff, Washington, 1953-55; Chief of Naval Staff, Canada, 1956-60, retired. Hon. DSc (M), Royal Military College of Canada, 1966. *Address:* Apt 1006, 200 Rideau Terrace, Ottawa, Ont., Canada; Old Post Office, Somerset, Bermuda.

de WOLFF, Brig. Charles Esmond, CB 1945; CBE 1919 (OBE 1919); LLB; *b* 25 Nov. 1893; *s* of C. L. de Wolff; *m* 1920, Ada Marjorie, *d* of Henry Arnold, Hatch End. Served: European War, 1914-19 (despatches four times, OBE, CBE, Russian Order of Vladimir); Dardanelles and Salonika, South Russia, 1919; 2nd Lieut Royal Sussex Regiment, 1914; transferred RAOC War of 1939-45 (CB); France and Italy; retd pay, 1946. OStJ 1952. *Clubs:* Army and Navy; Union (Malta).

DEWS, Peter; Theatre and TV Director; *b* 26 Sept. 1929; *er s* of John Dews and Edna (Bloomfield); *m* 1960, Ann Rhodes. *Educ:* Queen Elizabeth Grammar Sch., Wakefield; University Coll., Oxford (MA). Asst Master, Holgate and District Grammar Sch., Barnsley, 1952-53; BBC Midland Region Drama Producer (Radio and TV), 1953-63; Dir, Ravinia Shakespeare Festival, Chicago, 1963-64; Artistic Director: Birmingham Repertory Theatre, 1966-72; Chichester Fest. Theatre, 1978-80. Directed: TV: An Age of Kings, 1960 (SFTA Award 1960); The Spread of the Eagle, 1963; Theatre: As You Like It, Vaudeville, 1967; Hadrian VII, Mermaid, 1968, Haymarket and NY, 1969 (Tony Award 1969); Antony and Cleopatra, Chichester, 1969; Vivat Vivat Regina, Chichester, 1970, Piccadilly and NY, 1972; The Alchemist, Chichester, 1970; Crown Matrimonial, Haymarket, 1972, NY 1973; The Director of the Opera, Chichester, 1973; The Waltz of the Toreadors, Haymarket, 1974; King John, Stratford, Ont, 1974; The Pleasure of His Company, Toronto, 1974; Coriolanus, Tel Aviv, 1975; Othello, Chichester, 1975; Equus, Vancouver, 1975; Number Thirteen Rue de l'Amour, Phœnix, 1976; The Circle, Chichester, transf. to Haymarket, 1976; The Pleasure of His Company, Phœnix, 1976; Man and Superman, Don Juan in Hell, When We Are Married, Ottawa, 1977; Julius Caesar, Chichester, 1977; A Sleep of Prisoners, Chichester Cathedral, 1978; Julius Caesar, A Sleep of Prisoners, Hong Kong Festival, 1979; The Devil's Disciple, The Importance of Being Earnest, Chichester, 1979; Terra Nova, Much Ado About Nothing, Chichester, 1980; Plenty, Toronto, 1981; The Taming of the Shrew, The Comedy of Errors, Stratford, Ont, 1981; Cards on the Table, Vaudeville, 1981; 56 Duncan Terrace, Edmonton, A Midsummer Night's Dream, Plymouth, and Terra Nova, Durban, 1982. *Recreation:* music. *Address:* c/o Larry Dalzell Associates Ltd, Goodwin's Court, St Martin's Lane, WC2N 4LL.

DEXTER, Harold; Organist; Professor and Head of General Musicianship Department, Guildhall School of Music and Drama; Organist, St Botolph's, Aldgate; Conductor, Southend Bach Choir; *b* 7 Oct. 1920; *s* of F. H. and E. Dexter; *m* 1942, Faith Grainger; one *d. Educ:* Wyggeston Grammar Sch., Leicester; Corpus Christi Coll., Cambridge, 1939-41 and 1946. ARCO 1938; College Organ Scholar, 1939; John Stewart of Rannoch Scholar, 1940; FRCO 1940; ARCM 1941. BA, MusB 1942; MA 1946; RCO Choirmaster's Diploma; John Brook Prize, 1946; ADCM, 1948. Royal Navy and RNVR, 1941-46. Organist, Louth Parish Church and Music-Master, King Edward VI Grammar Sch., Louth, 1947-49; Organist, Holy Trinity, Leamington Spa, 1949-56; Music Master, Bablake Sch., Coventry, 1952-56; Master of the Music, Southwark Cathedral, 1956-68. FGSM 1962, FRSCM 1964 (Hon. diplomas). *Address:* 8 Prince Edward Road, Billericay, Essex. *T:* Billericay 52042.

DEXTER, John; Production Adviser, Metropolitan Opera, New York, since 1981 (Director of Production, 1974-81); Joint Artistic Director, Mermaid Theatre, London, since 1982. Actor in repertory, television and radio, until 1957; Associate Dir, National Theatre, 1963. Best Dir of Drama Award, 1975; Shakespeare Prize, 1978. Plays directed: 15 plays, 1957-72, Royal Court, incl. The Old Ones, 1972; Pygmalion, King, 1974; *for National Theatre:* Saint Joan, 1963; Hobson's Choice, Othello, Royal Hunt of the Sun, 1964; Armstrong's Last Goodnight, Black Comedy, 1965; A Bond Honoured, The Storm, 1966; A Woman Killed With Kindness, Tyger, The Good Natur'd Man, 1971; The Misanthrope, Equus, The Party, 1973; Phaedra Britannica, 1975; As You Like It, 1979; The Life of Galileo, 1980; The Shoemakers' Holiday, 1981; *for Mermaid Theatre:* The Portage to San Cristobal of A. H., 1982; Valmouth, Chichester Fest., 1982; *in New York:* Chips With Everything, 1963; Do I Hear a Waltz?, 1965; Black Comedy and White Lies, The Unknown Soldier and His Wife, 1967; Equus, 1974; *in Los Angeles:*

Pygmalian, Ahmanson Th., 1979; *Film:* The Virgin Soldiers, 1968; *Opera:* Benvenuto Cellini, Covent Garden, 1966; House of the Dead, Boris Godunov, Billy Budd, Ballo in Maschera, I Vespri Siciliani, Hamburg; The Devils of Loudon, Sadler's Wells; La Forza Del Destino, 1975, Paris; *Opera for Metropolitan, NY:* I Vespri Siciliani, Aida, 1976; Le Prophète, Dialogues of the Carmelites, Lulu, Rigoletto, 1977; Don Pasquale, Billy Budd, The Bartered Bride, 1978; Don Carlo, Rise and Fall of the City of Mahagonny, Die Entführung aus dem Serail, 1979; Le Rossignol, Le Sacre du Printemps, Oedipus Rex (triple bill), 1981; Parade, 1981. *Recreation:* work. *Address:* c/o Metropolitan Opera, Lincoln Center, New York, NY 10023, USA.

DEXTER, Dr Keith, CB 1978; Director-General, Agricultural Development and Advisory Service, Ministry of Agriculture, Fisheries and Food, since 1975; Deputy Secretary (Agricultural Science); *b* 3 April 1928; *yr s* of Arthur William Dexter, farmer, and Phyllis Dexter; *m* 1954, Marjorie Billbrough; no *c. Educ:* Dixie Grammar Sch., Market Bosworth; Univs of Nottingham and Illinois. BSc London 1945; MS Illinois 1951; PhD Nottingham 1954; Nat. Diploma in Agric. 1948; FIBiol 1975. Asst Agric. Economist, Nottingham Univ., 1948-50; Booth Fellow, Illinois Univ., 1950-51; Fulbright Trav. Schol., 1950-51; Res. Schol. and Agric. Economist, Nottingham Univ., 1951-54; Agric. Economist, Min. of Agriculture, 1954-56; Principal Agric. Economist, 1956-62; Grade I Adviser, Nat. Agric. Adv. Service, 1962-64; Admin. Staff Coll., Henley, 1963; Sen. Principal Agric. Economist, 1964-68; Dep. Dir of Econs and Statistics, 1968-70; Head of Fatstock Div., 1970-71; Under-Sec. (Meat and Fatstock), MAFF, 1971-75; Dep. Sec. 1975. Member: ARC, 1975-; Court, Cranfield Inst. of Technology, 1980-. Mem. Duke of Edinburgh's 3rd Commonwealth Study Conf., Australia, 1968. *Publications:* (with Derek Barker) Farming for Profits, 1961, 2nd edn 1967; contribs to Jl Agric. Econs. *Recreations:* gardening, fishing. *Address:* c/o Ministry of Agriculture, Fisheries and Food, Whitehall Place, SW1A 2HH. *T:* 01-233 5360. *Club:* Farmers'.

DEXTRAZE, Gen. Jacques Alfred, CC, CBE, CMM, DSO (Bar), CD; Chairman, Canadian National Railways, since 1977; *b* 15 Aug. 1919; *s* of Alfred and Amanda Dextraze; *m* 1942, Frances Helena Pare; three *s* (and one *s* decd). *Educ:* St Joseph de Berthier; MacDonald Business Coll., Montreal; Univ. of Columbia. With Dominion Rubber Co, 1938-40. Served War of 1939-45: Fusiliers, Mt Royal, 1939-45, Lt-Col and Comdg Officer, 1944-45; Comdg Officer, Hastings and Prince Edward Regt, 1945. With Singer Mfg Co., 1945-50; Manager, Forest Ops, 1947-50. Resumed mil. career as Comdg Officer, 2nd Bn Royal 22e Regt, 1950-52; Chief of Staff HQ, UN ops in Congo, 1963-64; Chief of Personnel, Can. Forces HQ, 1970-72; Chief of Defence Staff, 1972-77, retired. Hon. ADC to the Governor-Gen., 1958. Hon. LLD Wilfred Laurier Univ.; Hon. PhD (Business Admin) Sherbrooke Univ. Cross of Grand Officer, Order of the Crown (Belgium), 1977. *Address:* Canadian National Railway System, 935 Lagauchetière Street, West Montreal, PQ H3C 3N4, Canada.

de YARBURGH-BATESON, family name of **Baron Deramore.**

d'EYNCOURT, Sir John Jeremy Eustace T.; *see* Tennyson d'Eyncourt.

de ZULUETA, Sir Philip Francis; *see* Zulueta.

DHAVAN, Shanti Swarup; Member, Law Commission of India, 1972-77; *b* 2 July 1905; *m* Shakuntala Kapur, *d* of Malik Basant Lal Kapur; two *s* one *d. Educ:* Punjab Univ.; Emmanuel Coll., Cambridge. BA, 1st Cl. Hons History, Punjab Univ., 1925. Hist. Tripos 1931, Law Tripos 1932, Cambridge Univ.; Pres. Cambridge Union, 1932. Called to the Bar, Middle Temple, 1934; Advocate of High Court, Allahabad, 1937, and Senior Advocate of Supreme Court of India, 1958; Lecturer in Commercial Law, Allahabad Univ., 1940-54; Senior Standing Counsel of Govt of Uttar Pradesh, 1956-58; Judge of Allahabad High Court, 1958-67; High Commissioner in UK, 1968-69; Governor of West Bengal, 1969-72. Founder-mem. and Sec., Bernard Shaw Soc., formed 1949. Pres. Indo-Soviet Cultural Soc., Uttar Pradesh Sect., 1965-67. Leader of cultural delegation to Soviet Union, 1966. Lal Bahadur Sastri Meml Lectr, Kerala Univ., Trivandrum, 1973; Pres., All-India Ramayana Conf., Trivandrum, 1973. *Publications:* The Legal system and theory of the State in Ancient India, 1962; Doctrine of sovereignty and colonialism, 1962; Secularism in Indian Jurisprudence, 1964; also papers on Indian Judicial system, UNO and Kashmir, and the Nehru Tradition. *Recreations:* study of Indian jurisprudence, journalism. *Address:* 28 Tashkent Marg, Allahabad Uttar Pradesh, 210001, India.

DHENIN, Air Marshal Sir Geoffrey (Howard), KBE 1975; AFC 1953 and Bar, 1957; GM 1943; MA, MD, DPH; FFCM 1975; FRAeS 1971; Director-General, Medical Services (RAF), 1974-78; *b* 2 April 1918; *s* of Louis Richard Dhenin and Lucy Ellen Dagg; *m* 1946, Claude Andree Evelyn Rabut; one *s* two *d* (and one *s* decd). *Educ:* Hereford Cathedral Sch.; St John's Coll., Cambridge; Guy's Hosp., London. Joined RAF; various sqdn and other med. appts, Bomber Comd, 2nd TAF, 1943-45 (despatches 1945); pilot trng, 1945-46; various med. officer pilot appts, 1946-58; Staff Coll., Bracknell, 1958-59; comd Princess Mary's RAF Hosp. Akrotiri, Cyprus, 1960-63; comd RAF Hosp. Ely, 1963-66; PMO Air Support Comd, 1966-68; Dir of Health and Research, RAF, 1968-70; Dep. DGMS, RAF, 1970-71; PMO Strike Comd, 1971-73. Fellow, Internat. Acad. of Aerospace Medicine, 1972. CStJ 1974. QHP 1970-78. Adviser to Saudi Arabian Nat. Guard, 1978-79. *Publication:* (ed) Textbook of Aviation Medicine, 1978. *Recreations:* golf,

ski-ing, sub-aqua. *Address:* Ruxbury Lodge, St Ann's Hill, Chertsey, Surrey. *T:* Chertsey 63624. *Clubs:* Royal Air Force, Wentworth.

DHRANGADHRA, Maharaja Sriraj of Halvad-, His Highness Shri Shaktimant Jhaladhip Mahamandlesvar Maharana Sriraj Meghrajji III, KCIE 1947; 45th Ruler (dynastic salute of 13 guns), Head of Jhala-Makhvana Clan and of Shaktimant Order; MP for Jhalwar (Gujarat State), since 1967; *b* 3 March 1923; *s* of HH Maharaja Sriraj Ghanshyamsinhji Saheb, GCIE, KCSI, late Ruler, and HH Maharani Srirajni Anandkunvarba Saheba, Rajmata Saheba; *S* to the Gaddi, 1942, assumed government 1943 on termination of political minority; *m* 1943, Princess Brijrakunvarba Sahiba, *d* of Air Cdre HH Raj-rajeshvar Sarmd-i-Hind Maharajadhiraj Shri Umaidsinhji, GCSI, GCIE, KCVO, Maharaja Sahib of Marwar (Jodhpur); three *s. Educ:* Heath Mount Sch.; Haileybury Coll.; St Joseph's Academy, Dehra Dun. Joined the Shivaji Military Sch., Poona, to train for joining Indian Mil. Acad., Dehra Dun; spent nearly a year acquiring administrative experience at Baroda, then at Dhrangadhra; philosophy course, Christ Church, Oxford, 1952-54; took Diploma in Social Anthropology, 1954-55; research in Indian Sociology, 1955-58 (BLitt Oxon.). FRAS, FRAI; Associate, Royal Historical Soc. Mem. Standing Cttee of Chamber of Princes, 1945; pursued active policy of social and economic reform; was prime mover in Confederation of States scheme, 1945; first state in Saurashtra to accept participation in Constituent Assembly of India; signed Instrument of Accession to India, 1947; First Mem. of Presidium of United State of Saurashtra, later Vice-Pres. Perm. Pres., Girassia Educ. Trust; Pres., Marwar Regency Council, 1965-68; and of Governing Council, Rajkumar Coll., Rajkot, 1966-; Chm. Board of Rulers, Saurashtra States Conf., 1966-; Promoter and Intendant General, Consultation of Rulers of Indian States in Concord for India, 1967-. Mem. Gujarat Legislative Assembly (from Dhrangadhra), Feb.-March 1967, resigned. *Heir: s* Tikaraj Saheb of Halvad-Dhrangadhra, Namdar Jhalavrit Maharajkumar Shri Sodhsalji, *cr* Tikaraj (Yuvaraj), 1961, *b* 22 March 1944. *Address:* Ajitniwas Palace, Dhrangadhra, Jhalawar, Gujarat State, India; Dhrangadhra House, Poona 16, India; A/6 Rashmi, Carmichael Road, Bombay 26, India; 108/E Malcha Marg, Diplomatic Enclave, New Delhi, 110021, India.

DIAMAND, Peter, Hon. CBE 1972; Consultant, Orchestre de Paris, since 1976; *b* 1913; *m* 1st, 1948, Maria Curcio, pianist (marr. diss. 1971); 2nd, Sylvia Rosenberg, violinist (marr. diss. 1979); one *s. Educ:* Schiller-Realgymnasium, Berlin; Berlin Univ. Studied Law and Journalism in Berlin. Left Germany, 1933; became Private Sec. to Artur Schnabel, pianist. Personal Asst to Dir of Netherlands Opera, Amsterdam, 1946, subsequently Artistic Adviser until 1965; Gen. Manager of Holland Festival, 1948-65; Dir, Edinburgh Internat. Festival, 1965-78; Dir and Gen. Manager, RPO, 1978-81. Mem. Board of Netherlands Chamber Orchestra, 1955-77. Hon. LLD Edinburgh, 1972. Knight, Order of Oranje Nassau, Holland, 1959; Grosses Ehrenzeichen fuer Verdienste, Austria, 1964; Medal of Merit, Czechoslovakia, 1966; Commander Italian Republic, 1973; Chevalier de l'Ordre des Arts et des Lettres, France. *Address:* 28 Eton Court, Eton Avenue, NW3. *T:* 01-586 1203.

DIAMOND, family name of **Baron Diamond.**

DIAMOND, Baron *cr* 1970 (Life Peer), of the City of Gloucester; **John Diamond,** PC 1965; FCA; Chairman: Royal Commission on Distribution of Income and Wealth, 1974-79; Industry and Parliament Trust, 1976-82; Trustee, Social Democratic Party, since 1981; *b* Leeds, 30 April 1907; *s* of Henrietta and Rev. S. Diamond, Leeds; *m* ; two *s* two *d. Educ:* Leeds Grammar Sch. Qualified as Chartered Accountant, 1931, and commenced practice as John Diamond & Co. MP (Lab) Blackley Div. of Manchester, 1945-51, Gloucester, 1957-70; Chief Secretary to the Treasury, 1964-70 (in the Cabinet, 1968-70); formerly PPS to Minister of Works; Deputy Chm. of Cttees, House of Lords, 1974. Chm. of Finance Cttee, Gen. Nursing Council, 1947-53; Dir of Sadler's Wells Trust Ltd, 1957-64; Hon. Treas., Fabian Soc., 1950-64. Hon. LLD Leeds, 1978. *Publications:* Socialism the British Way (jtly), 1948; Public Expenditure in Practice, 1975. *Recreations:* golf, ski-ing, music. *Address:* Aynhoe, Doggetts Wood Lane, Chalfont St Giles, Bucks.

DIAMOND, Anthony Edward John, QC 1974; *b* 4 Sept. 1929; *m* 1965, Joan Margaret Gee; two *d. Educ:* Rugby; Corpus Christi Coll., Cambridge (MA). Called to the Bar, Gray's Inn, 1953. *Recreation:* the visual arts. *Address:* 1 Cannon Place, NW3; 4 Essex Court, Temple, EC4. *T:* 01-583 9191.

DIAMOND, Prof. Aubrey Lionel; Professor of Law and Director, Institute of Advanced Legal Studies, University of London, since 1976; Solicitor; *b* 28 Dec. 1923; *s* of Alfred and Millie Diamond, London; *m* 1955, Dr Eva M. Bobasch; one *s* one *d. Educ:* elementary schs; Central Foundation Sch., London; London Sch. of Economics (LLB, LLM). Clerical Officer, LCC, 1941-48. Served RAF, 1943-47. Admitted a solicitor, 1951. Sen. Lectr, Law Society's Sch. of Law, 1955-57; Asst Lectr, Lectr and Reader, Law Dept, LSE, 1957-66; Prof. of Law in the Univ. of London (Queen Mary Coll.), 1966-71; Law Comr, 1971-76. Partner in Lawford & Co., Solicitors, 1959-71. Member: Central London Valuation Court, 1956-73; Consumer Advisory Council, BSI, 1961-63; Council, Consumers' Assoc., 1963-71; Consumer Council, 1963-66, 1967-71; Cttee on the Age of Majority, 1965-67; Estate Agents' Council, 1967-70; Council, Law Society, 1976-. Chairman: Social Sciences and the Law Cttee, SSRC, 1977-80; Hamlyn Trust, 1977-; Advertising Adv. Cttee, IBA, 1980-. Pres., Nat. Fedn of Consumer Groups, 1977-81 (Chm., 1963-67); Vice-Pres., Inst. of Trading Standards Administration, 1975-. Visiting Professor: University Coll. Dar es Salaam, Univ. of E Africa, 1966-67; Law

Sch., Stanford Univ., 1971; Melbourne Univ., 1977; Univ. of Virginia, 1982. Councillor, Stoke Newington BC, 1953-56. *Publications:* The Consumer, Society and the Law (with G. J. Borrie), 1963 (4th edn, 1981); Introduction to Hire-Purchase Law, 1967 (2nd edn. 1971); (ed) Instalment Credit, 1970; (co-ed) Sutton and Shannon on Contracts (7th edn) 1970; Commercial and Consumer Credit: an introduction, 1982; articles and notes in legal jls and symposia. *Address:* 17 Russell Square, WC1B 5DR. *T:* 01-637 1731.

DIAMOND, George Clifford, OBE 1955; MA; Head Master, Cardiff High School for Boys, retired 1966; *b* 27 Nov. 1902; *m* ; two *s. Educ:* Cardiff High Sch.; The Leys Sch., Cambridge; Queens' Coll., Cambridge (Scholar). English Tripos, Class I, History Tripos, Part II, Class II Div. I. Asst Master, Mill Hill Junior Sch., 1926-27; Senior English Master, The Leys Sch., 1927-34. Pres., Welsh Secondary Schools' Assoc., 1957. *Address:* Flat 9A, The Cathedral Green, Llandaff, Glamorgan.

DIAMOND, Prof. Jack, CBE 1969; Whitworth Scholar, MSc (Cambridge and Manchester); FCGI; FIMechE; Beyer Professor of Mechanical Engineering, Manchester University, 1953-77, now Emeritus; *b* 22 June 1912; *s* of late Alfred John Diamond and Jessie M. Kitchingham; *m* 1943, Iris Evelyn Purvis; three *d. Educ:* Chatham Technical Sch.; Royal Dockyard School, Chatham; City and Guilds Coll., London; St John's Coll., Cambridge. Engineering apprenticeship, HM Dockyard, Chatham, 1928-32; Whitworth Scholar, 1932; BSc, ACGI, Wh. Sch. (sen.), 1935. Research in Heat Transfer, University Eng. labs and St John's, Cambridge, 1935-37; MSc 1937; Univ. Demonstrator in Engineering, Cambridge, 1937-39. RN (temp. Engr Officer), 1939-44. RN Scientific Service on loan to Ministry of Supply in Canada and at AERE, Harwell, 1944-53. Member: Governing Board of Nat. Inst. for Research in Nuclear Science, 1957-60; UGC, 1965-73; NRDC, 1966-71; Council, IMechE, 1958-70 (Vice-Pres. 1967-70); Pres., Section G, British Assoc., 1970. Pro-Vice-Chancellor, Manchester Univ., 1970-77. FCGI 1968. Hon. DSc Heriot-Watt, 1975. *Publications:* various, in engineering publications. *Address:* 5 Chelford Road, Somerford, Congleton, Cheshire CW12 4QD. *Club:* Athenæum.

DIAMOND, (Peter) Michael, MA, FMA; Director, Birmingham City Museums and Art Gallery, since 1980; *b* 5 Aug. 1942; *s* of late William Howard and Dorothy Gladys Diamond; *m* 1968, Anne Marie; one *s* one *d. Educ:* Bristol Grammar Sch.; Queens' Coll., Cambridge (BA Fine Art 1964, MA 1966). Dip. of Museums Assoc. 1968, FMA 1980. Sheffield City Art Galleries: Art Asst, 1965; Keeper, Mappin Art Gall., 1967; Dep. Dir, 1969; City Arts and Museums Officer, Bradford, 1976. Mem. Exec. Cttee, Yorks Arts Assoc., 1977-80; Pres., Yorks Fedn of Museums, 1978-80; Chairman: Yorks Sculpture Park, 1978-; Crafts Council, 1980-. *Publications:* numerous exhibition catalogues incl. Victorian Paintings, 1968; Art and Industry in Sheffield 1850-75, 1975; articles in Museums Jl. *Recreations:* gardening, DIY, walking, music. *Address:* 40 Jordan Road, Four Oaks, Sutton Coldfield B75 5AB. *T:* 021-308 3287; Birmingham City Museums and Art Gallery, Chamberlain Square, Birmingham B3 3DH.

DIBBS, (Arthur Henry) Alexander; Director since 1970, and a Deputy Chairman, since 1977, National Westminster Bank Ltd; Joint Deputy Chairman, British Airways, since 1981; *b* 9 Dec. 1918; *s* of H. J. Dibbs and P. L. Dibbs (*née* Baker); *m* 1948, Helen Pearl Mathewson; two *d. Educ:* Dover Coll.; Whitgift Middle Sch., Croydon. FIB. AMP, Harvard Univ., 1963. Served with Army, 1939-46. Joined Westminster Bank Ltd, 1935; Manager, Croydon Br., 1960; Asst Gen. Man., 1963; Jt Gen. Man., 1966; National Westminster Bank Ltd: Gen. Man., Domestic Banking Div., 1968; Chief Exec. 1972-77. Mem., NEB, 1975-81. Mem. Bd of Governors, E-SU, 1976-. *Recreations:* golf; watching all sports. *Address:* The Orchard, Deans Lane, Walton on the Hill, Tadworth, Surrey. *Clubs:* Caledonian, MCC (Mem. Finance Cttee), Royal Automobile.

DICK, Air Vice-Marshal Alan David, CB 1978; CBE 1968; AFC 1957; FRAeS 1975; Secretary, British Association of Occupational Therapists, since 1979; *b* 7 Jan. 1924; *s* of late Brig. Alan MacDonald Dick, CBE, IMS(Retd), and Muriel Angela Dick; *m* 1951, Ann Napier Jeffcoat, *d* of late Col A. C. Jeffcoat, CB, CMG, DSO; two *s* two *d. Educ:* Fettes; Aitchison Coll., Lahore; King's Coll., Cambridge. MA. Joined RAF, 1942; SE Asia Command, 1943-45; Fighter Comd, 1945-46. Central Flying Sch., 1950-53; Empire Test Pilots Sch., 1953; Test Pilot, A&AEE, 1954-57; Fighter Comd, 1957-60; RAF Staff Coll., 1960-63; OC 207 Sqdn, Bomber Comd, 1963-64; Supt of Flying, A&AEE, 1964-68; Strike Comd, 1968-69; IDC 1970; MoD Air Staff, 1971-74; Comdt, A&AEE, 1974-75; Dep. Controller Aircraft/C, MoD(PE), 1975-78. *Recreations:* photography, walking, bird watching. *Address:* 44 St Peter's Avenue, Caversham, Reading, Berks RG4 7DD. *Club:* Royal Air Force.

DICK, Alick Sydney; industrial consultant; Purchasing Consultant to: Volkswagenwerk AG, Wolfsburg, Germany, since 1968; Audi NSU Auto Union AG, Ingolstadt, Germany, since 1968; *b* 20 June 1916; *s* of Dr W. Dick, Chichester, Sussex; *m* 1940, Betty Melinda Eileen Hill; three *s. Educ:* Chichester High Sch.; Dean Close, Cheltenham. Managing Dir, Standard Triumph International Ltd, Coventry, 1954-61. Pres. of Soc. of Motor Manufacturers and Traders, 1957. Governor: University of Birmingham, 1959-80; Coll. of Aeronautics, Cranfield, 1960-63. Benjamin Franklin Medal (RSA), 1961. Governor, Dean Close Sch., Cheltenham, 1964. *Recreation:* boats. *Address:* The Thatched Cottage, Hill Wootton, Warwick CV35 7PP. *T:* Kenilworth 54416.

DICK, Clare L.; *see* Lawson Dick.

DICK, Gavin Colquhoun; Under-Secretary, Department of Industry, since 1981; *b* 6 Sept. 1928; *s* of late John Dick and Catherine MacAuslan Henderson; *m* 1952, Elizabeth Frances, *e d* of late Jonathan Hutchinson; two *d. Educ:* Hamilton Academy; Glasgow Univ. (MA); Balliol Coll., Oxford (Snell Exhibnr, MA). National Service, 3rd RTR (Lieut), 1952-54. Asst Principal, BoT, 1954, Principal, 1958; UK Trade Comr, Wellington, NZ, 1961-64; Asst Sec., 1967; Jt Sec., Review Cttee on Overseas Representation, 1968-69; Under-Sec., 1975. Governor, Coll. of Air Training (Hamble), 1975-80. *Recreation:* words. *Address:* Fell Cottage, Bayley's Hill, Sevenoaks, Kent TN14 6NA. *T:* Sevenoaks 453704. *Club:* United Oxford & Cambridge University.

DICK, Prof. George (Williamson Auchinvole), MD (Edinburgh), DSc (Edinburgh), FRCPE, FRCP, FRCPath, MPH (Johns Hopkins); FIMLS, FIBiol; Emeritus Professor of Pathology, University of London; Chairman, Medical Advisory and Research Consultants Ltd, since 1981; *b* 14 Aug. 1914; *s* of Rev. David Auchinvole Dick and Blanche Hay Spence; *m* 1941, Brenda Marian Cook; two *s* two *d. Educ:* Royal High Sch., Edinburgh; Univ. of Edinburgh; The Johns Hopkins Univ., Baltimore, Md, USA. BSc 1939 (1st Cl. Hons Path.); Vans Dunlop Scholar; Buchanan Medal; MD (Gold Medal) 1949. Asst Pathologist, Royal Infirmary, Edinburgh, 1939-40; Pathologist, RAMC, 1940-46; OC Medical Div. (Lt-Col) (EA Comd), 1946; Pathologist, Colonial Med. Res. Service, 1946-51; Rockefeller Foundn Fellow (Internat. Health Div.), Rockefeller Inst., New York and Johns Hopkins Univ., 1947-48; Res. Fellow, Sch. of Hygiene and Public Health, Johns Hopkins Univ., Baltimore, Md, 1948-49; Scientific Staff, MRC, 1951-54; Prof. of Microbiology, QUB, 1955-65; Dir, Bland-Sutton Inst. and Sch. of Pathology, Middlesex Hosp. Med. Sch., Univ. of London, 1966-73; Bland-Sutton Prof. of Pathology, Univ. of London, 1966-73; Asst Dir, BPMF, and Postgraduate Dean, SW Thames, RHA, 1973-81; Prof. of Pathology, Univ. of London, and Hon. Lectr and Hon. Consultant, Inst. of Child Health, 1973-81. Examnr, Med. Schools in UK, Dublin, Nairobi, Kampala, Riyadh, Jeddah. Pres., Inst. of Med. Laboratory Technology, 1966-76; Member: Mid Downs Health Authority, W Sussex; Jt Bd of Clinical Nursing Studies; Assessor, HNC; Pres., Rowhook Med. Soc., 1975-. Treasurer, RCPath, 1973-78; Member: RSM; BMA; Internat. Epidemiol. Soc.; Path. Soc. GB and Ireland; Soc. of Scholars, Johns Hopkins Univ., 1979; Alpha Chapter, Delta Omega Hon. Soc., USA, 1981. Yeoman, Worshipful Co. of Apothecaries. Singapore Gold Medal, Edinburgh Univ., 1952 and 1958; Laurence Biedl Prize for Rehabilitation, 1958; Sims Woodhead Medal, 1976. *Publications:* Immunisation Update, 1978; Immunology of Infectious diseases MTP, 1979; Health on Holiday and other Travels, 1982; papers on yellow fever, Uganda S, Zika and other arbor viruses, Mengovirus, Marburgvirus, etc; encephalitis, poliomyelitis; hepatitis (MHV); multiple sclerosis and EHA (rabies) virus; smallpox, poliomyelitis, whooping cough and combined vaccines; vaccine reactions immunisation policies, subacute sclerosing panencephalitis etc. *Address:* Waterland, Rowhook, Horsham RH12 3PX. *T:* Slinfold 790549; MARC Ltd, Central House, 27 Park Street, Croydon, Surrey CR9 1TN. *T:* 01-681 2002. *Club:* Athenæum.

See also J. A. Dick.

DICK, James Brownlee, CB 1977; MA, BSc, FInstP, FCIBS, FIOB; consultant; *b* 19 July 1919; *s* of James Brownlee Dick and Matilda Forrest; *m* 1944, Audrey Moira Shinn; two *s. Educ:* Wishaw High Sch.; Glasgow Univ. Royal Naval Scientific Service, 1940. Building Research Station, later Building Research Establishment: Physics Div., 1947; Head of User Requirements Div., 1960; Head of Production Div., 1963; Asst Dir, 1964; Dep. Dir, 1969; Dir, 1969-79. Pres., Internat. Council for Building Res., 1974-77. *Publications:* papers in professional and scientific journals. *Recreations:* reading, gardening, golf. *Address:* 4 Murray Road, Berkhamsted, Herts. *T:* Berkhamsted 2580.

DICK, John Alexander, MC 1944; QC (Scotland) 1963; Sheriff Principal of Glasgow and Strathkelvin, since 1980; *b* 1 Jan. 1920; *y s* of Rev. David Auchinvole Dick and Blanche Hay Spence; *m* 1951, Rosemary Benzie Sutherland; no *c. Educ:* Waid Academy, Anstruther; University of Edinburgh. Enlisted in London Scottish, 1940; commissioned Royal Scots, 1942; Italy, 1944; Palestine, 1945-46; released 1946. MA (1st Cl. Hons Economics) 1947, LLB (with distinction) 1949, Univ. of Edinburgh. Called to Scots Bar, 1949; Lecturer in Public Law, Univ. of Edinburgh, 1953-60; Junior Counsel in Scotland to HM Commissioners of Customs and Excise, 1956-63; Comr under Terrorism (N Ireland) Order 1972, 1972-73; Sheriff of the Lothians and Borders at Edinburgh, 1969-78; Sheriff Principal of North Strathclyde, 1978-82. *Recreation:* hill-walking. *Address:* 66 Northumberland Street, Edinburgh EH3 6JE. *T:* 031-556 6081. *Club:* Royal Scots (Edinburgh).

See also Prof. George Dick.

DICK, John Kenneth, CBE 1972; FCA, FRSA; Director: N. M. Rothschild & Sons Ltd, since 1978; N. M. Rothschild (Leasing) Ltd, since 1978; *b* 5 April 1913; *s* of late John Dick and Beatrice May Dick (*née* Chitty); *m* 1942, Pamela Madge, 3rd *d* of late Maurice Salmon and Katie Salmon (*née* Joseph); two *s* (and one *s* decd). *Educ:* Sedbergh. Qual. with Mann Judd & Co., Chartered Accountants, 1936; Partner, Mann Judd & Co., 1947; Mitchell Cotts Group Ltd: Jt Man. Dir, 1957; Sole Man. Dir, 1959-78; Dep. Chm., 1964; Chm., 1966-78; Chm., Hume Holdings Ltd, 1975-80. Mem., Commonwealth Develt Corp., 1967-80; Gov., City of London Soc.; Member: British Nat. Export

Cttee, 1968-71; Covent Gdn Mkt Authority, 1976-; Chm., Cttee for Middle East Trade, 1968-71; Pres., Middle East Assoc., 1976-81 (a Vice-Pres., 1970-76). *Recreation:* golf. *Address:* Overbye, Church Street, Cobham, Surrey. *T:* (office) 01-623 1090; (home) Cobham (Surrey) 4393. *Clubs:* Caledonian, City of London; Rand (Johannesburg).

DICK, Air Cdre Ronald; Air Attaché, Washington, DC, since 1980; *b* Newcastle upon Tyne, 18 Oct. 1931; *s* of Arthur John Craig Dick and Lilian Dick; *m* 1955, Pauline Lomax; one *s* one *d. Educ:* Beckenham and Penge County Grammar Sch.; RAF Coll., Cranwell. Commnd 1952; served, 1953-69: No 64 Fighter Sqdn; Flying Instr, No 5 FTS; Central Flying Sch. Examg Wing and Type Sqdn; Flt Comdr, 3615th Pilot Trng Sqdn, USAF, and No IX Bomber Sqdn; Trng (Operational) 2a (RAF), MoD; RAF Staff Coll., Bracknell; Ops B2 (RAF), MoD; Jt Services Staff Coll.; OC No IX Bomber Sqdn, RAF Akrotiri, 1970-72; Staff, RCDS, 1972-74; PSO to Dep. SACEUR, SHAPE, 1974-77; OC RAF Honington, 1977-80. Sqdn Ldr 1961, Wing Comdr 1969, Gp Captain 1975, Air Cdre 1980. Wright Jubilee Aerobatic Trophy Winner, 1956. *Recreations:* wild life conservation, bird watching, private flying, military history, opera. *Address:* 5025 Rockwood Parkway NW, Washington, DC 20016, USA. *T:* 202-363-8525. *Club:* Royal Air Force.

DICK, Rear-Adm. Royer Mylius, CB 1951; CBE 1943; DSC 1918; *b* 14 Oct. 1897; *s* of Louis Henry Mylius Dick and Edith Alice Guy; *m* 1928, Agnes Mary Harben; one *d* (one *s* killed on active service); *m* 1955, Vera, *widow* of Col Bertram Pott. *Educ:* RN Colls, Osborne and Dartmouth. Midshipman, 1914; at sea, 1914-18 (DSC); Lieut 1918; Comdr 1933; Capt. 1940; Commodore 1st cl. 1942; Rear-Adm. 1949. Dep. Chief of Staff, Mediterranean Station, 1940-42; Naval Admty Delegn to Washington, 1942; Chief of Staff, Mediterranean Stn, 1942-44 (despatches twice, CBE); HMS Belfast, 1944-46; Dir Tactical and Staff Duties, Admiralty, 1947-48; Chief of Staff to Flag Officer, Western Europe, 1948-50; Naval ADC to the King, 1949; Flag Officer, Training Sqdn, 1951-52; Standing Group Liaison Officer to North Atlantic Council, 1952-55; Vice-Adm. (Acting), 1953; retired list, 1955. Dep. Comr-in-Chief, 1957-62, Comr-in-Chief, 1962-67, SJAB. Dep. Chm., Horticultural Marketing Council, 1960-63; Chairman: Royal United Service Institution, 1965-67; St John Council for London, 1971-75; a Vice-Pres., Royal UK Beneficent Assoc., 1979. KStJ 1961; Bailiff Grand Cross, Order of Hosp. of St John of Jerusalem, 1967. Officer Legion of Merit (US), 1943; Officer Legion of Honour, 1943; Croix de Guerre avec palme, 1946. *Address:* 15 Dorchester Court, Sloane Street, SW1. *Clubs:* Army and Navy, Royal Automobile.

DICK-LAUDER, Sir Piers Robert; *see* Lauder.

DICKENS, Prof. Arthur Geoffrey, CMG 1974; FBA 1966; Director, Institute of Historical Research and Professor of History in the University of London, 1967-77, now Emeritus Professor; *b* 6 July 1910; *er s* of Arthur James Dickens and Gertrude Helen Dickens (*née* Grasby), both of Hull, Yorks; *m* 1936, Molly (*d* 1978), *er d* of Walter Bygott; two *s. Educ:* Hymers Coll., Hull; Magdalen Coll., Oxford. Demy, 1929-32, Senior Demy, 1932-33, of Magdalen Coll.; BA with 1st Class Hons in Mod. Hist., 1932; MA 1936; DLit London, 1965. Fellow and Tutor of Keble Coll., Oxford, 1933-49, Hon. Fellow, 1971; Oxford Univ. Lecturer in Sixteenth Century English History, 1939-49. Served in RA, 1940-45; demobilised as Staff Capt. G. F. Grant Prof. of History, Univ. of Hull, 1949-62; Dep. Principal and Dean of Faculty of Arts, 1950-53; Pro-Vice-Chancellor, 1959-62; Prof. of History, King's Coll., Univ. of London, 1962-67; FKC, 1977. Mem. Senate and Academic Council, Univ. of London, 1974-77. Pres., Ecclesiastical History Soc., 1966-68. Member: Advisory Council on Public Records, 1968-76; Adv. Council on Export of Works of Art, 1968-76; Records Cttee, Essex CC, 1965-71; History of Medicine Adv. Panel, Wellcome Trust, 1974-79; Steering Cttee, Business History Unit, LSE, 1978-. Chm., Victoria History of the Counties of England, 1967-68. Sec., 1967-73, Chm. and Gen. Sec., 1973-79, British Nat. Cttee of Historical Sciences; Foreign Sec., British Acad., 1969-79 (Vice-Pres., 1971-72); Vice-Pres., British Record Soc., 1978-80; Hon. Vice-President: RHistS, 1977-(Vice-Pres., 1969-73); Historical Assoc., 1977-; Sec., Anglo-German Group of Historians 1969-76; Pres., German History Soc., 1979-. Editor, Bulletin of the Inst. of Historical Research, 1967-77. Visiting Prof., Univ. of Rochester, NY, 1953-54; Birkbeck Lectr, Trinity Coll., Cambridge, 1969-70. Fellow, 1954, Vis. Prof., 1972, Folger Library, Washington, DC; Strassberg Vis. Prof., Univ. of Western Australia, 1981; Lectures: James Ford Special, Univ. of Oxford, 1974; Neale, UCL, 1977; Bithell, Inst. of Germanic Studies, 1978; Stenton, Reading, 1980. Hon. Professorial Fellow, Univ. of Wales, Aberystwyth, 1979-. Governor, Highgate Sch., 1976-. FRHistS 1947; FSA 1962. Hon. DLitt: Kent, 1976; Hull, 1977; Leicester, 1978; Sheffield, 1978; Hon. LittD Liverpool, 1977. Comdr's Cross, Order of Merit, Fed. Repub. of Germany, 1980. *Publications:* Lübeck Diary, 1947; The Register of Butley Priory, 1951; The East Riding of Yorkshire, 1954; Lollards and Protestants, 1959; Thomas Cromwell, 1959; Tudor Treatises, 1960; Clifford Letters, 1962; The English Reformation, 1964; Reformation and Society in 16th Century Europe, 1966; Martin Luther and the Reformation, 1967; (ed jtly) The Reformation in England to the Accession of Elizabeth I, 1967; The Counter-Reformation, 1968; The Age of Humanism and Reformation, 1972, UK edn 1977; The German Nation and Martin Luther, 1974; (ed and contrib.) The Courts of Europe, 1977; Reformation Studies, 1982; (Gen. Editor) Documents of Modern History Series, 1966-; (Gen. Editor) A New History of England Series, 1975-; about 60 articles in: English Historical Review, Church

Quarterly Review, Yorkshire Archæological Jl, Cambridge Antiquarian Jl, Bodleian Library Record, Archiv für Reformationsgeschichte, Britain and the Netherlands, Victoria County History, York, Trans Royal Hist. Soc., Jl of Ecclesiastical History, Archæological Jl, Encycl. Britannica, Chambers's Encycl., etc. *Festschrift:* Reformation Principle and Practice: essays in honour of A. G. Dickens, ed P. N. Brooks, 1980. *Recreations:* travel, 20th Century British art. *Address:* c/o Institute of Historical Research, Senate House, WC1E 7HU. *Club:* Athenæum.

DICKENS, Frank, FRS 1946; MA Cambridge, DSc, PhD London; DIC; FIBiol; *b* 1899; *s* of late John Dickens and Elizabeth Dickens, Northampton; *m* 1925, Molly, *o d* of late Arthur W. and Norah Jelleyman, Northampton; two *d. Educ:* Northampton Grammar Sch.; Magdalene Coll., Cambridge (Scholar). Res. in Organic Chemistry at Imperial Coll. of Science, 1921-23; Lectr in Biochemistry, Middlesex Hospital Medical Sch., whole-time worker for MRC, 1929; Mem. Scientific Staff, MRC, 1931; Research Dir North of England Council of British Empire Cancer Campaign, 1933-46; Philip Hill Professor of Experimental Biochemistry, Middlesex Hosp. Med. Sch., 1946-67, now Emeritus; Dir, Tobacco Research Council Labs, Harrogate, 1967-69. Research for Royal Naval Personnel Cttee of MRC, Nat. Inst. for Medical Research, 1943-44. An Editor of Biochemical Journal, 1937-47; Chm., Biochemical Soc., 1950, Hon. Mem., 1967. Formerly Mem. Scientific Advisory Cttee of the British Empire Cancer Campaign. Chm., British Nat. Cttee for Biochemistry. Hon. Fellow: King's Coll. (University of Newcastle); Leeds Univ. Hon DSc Newcastle upon Tyne, 1972. *Publications:* Chemical and Physiological Properties of the Internal Secretions (with E. C. Dodds); translation of the Metabolism of Tumours (by O. Warburg); ed, Oxygen in the Animal Organism (with E. Neil); Carbohydrate Metabolism and its Disorders (with P. J. Randle and W. J. Whelan); Essays in Biochemistry (with P. N. Campbell); numerous scientific papers mainly in Biochemical Jl. *Recreations:* fishing, photography. *Address:* 9 Doone End, Ferring, West Sussex BN12 5PT. *T:* Worthing 43627.

DICKENS, Geoffrey Kenneth, JP; MP (C) Huddersfield West, since 1979; company director, engineering industry; *b* 26 Aug. 1931; *s* of John Wilfred and Laura Avril Dickens; *m* 1956, Norma Evelyn Boothby; two *s. Educ:* Park Lane and Byron Court Primary; East Lane Sch., Wembley; Harrow and Acton Technical Colls. Chairman: Sandridge Parish Council, 1968-69; St Albans Rural District Council, 1970-71 (Leader, 1967-70); Councillor, Hertfordshire CC, 1970-75; Hon. Alderman, City and District of St Albans, 1976. Contested (C): Teesside Middlesbrough, Feb. 1974, and Ealing North, Oct. 1974, general elections. Royal Humane Soc. Testimonial on Vellum for saving lives, 1972. JP St Albans, later Barnsley, 1968. *Address:* Water Hall, Water Hall Lane, Penistone, Sheffield, S Yorks S30 6EQ. *Clubs:* St Stephen's and Constitutional; Huddersfield County Conservative, Marsh Conservative (Huddersfield).

DICKENS, James McCulloch York; Director of Manpower and Training, National Water Council; *b* 4 April 1931; *e s* of A. Y. Dickens and I. Dickens (*née* McCulloch); *m* 1935, M. J. Grieve (marr. diss. 1965); 2nd, 1969, Mrs Carolyn Casey. *Educ:* Shawlands Academy, Glasgow; Newbattle Abbey Coll., Dalkeith, Midlothian; Ruskin Coll. and St Catherine's Coll., Oxford. Administrative Asst, National Coal Board, 1956-58; Industrial Relations Officer, National Coal Board, 1958-65; Management Consultant, 1965-66; MP (Lab) West Lewisham, 1966-70; Asst Dir of Manpower, Nat. Freight Corp., 1970-76; Asst Dir (Ind. Rel.), Manpower Services Div., Nat. Water Council, 1976-80. Prospective Parly Cand. (Lab), Newham North East, 1978-79. *Recreations:* music, theatre, the countryside. *Address:* 64 Woodbastwick Road, Sydenham, SE26 5LH. *T:* 01-778 7446.

DICKENS, Sir Louis (Walter), Kt 1968; DFC 1940; AFC 1938; DL; *b* 28 Sept. 1903; *s* of C. H. Dickens; *m* 1939, Ena Alice Bastable (*d* 1971); one *s* one *d. Educ:* Clongowes Wood Coll.; Cranwell Cadet Coll. Bomber Sqdn, 1923-27; Flying Trng, 1927; Egypt, 1932; Personnel, Air Min., 1932-35; subseq. Flying Instructor, Cranwell; Bomber Comd, France, 1940; Flying Instructor, Canada, 1941-42; Bomber Comd, 1943-44; SHAEF France, 1944-45; retired, 1947. Member: Berkshire CC, 1952-74 (Chm., 1965-68, Co. Alderman, 1959-73); Wokingham DC, 1974- (Chm., 1974-76). DL Berks, 1966. *Recreation:* golf. *Address:* Wayford, Bolney Avenue, Shiplake, Henley-on-Thames, Oxon. *Club:* Royal Air Force.

DICKENS, Monica Enid, (Mrs R. O. Stratton), MBE 1981; writer; Founder of The Samaritans, in the USA, Boston, Mass, 1974; *d* late Henry Charles Dickens, Barrister-at-law, and Fanny Runge; *m* 1951, Comdr Roy Olin Stratton, US Navy; two *d. Educ:* St Paul's Girls' Sch., Hammersmith. *Publications:* One Pair of Hands, 1939; Mariana, 1940; One Pair of Feet, 1942; The Fancy, 1943; Thursday Afternoons, 1945; The Happy Prisoner, 1946; Joy and Josephine, 1948; Flowers on the Grass, 1949; My Turn to Make the Tea, 1951; No More Meadows, 1953; The Winds of Heaven, 1955; The Angel in the Corner, 1956; Man Overboard, 1958; The Heart of London, 1961; Cobbler's Dream, 1963; Kate and Emma, 1964; The Room Upstairs, 1966; The Landlord's Daughter, 1968; The Listeners, 1970; The House at World's End, 1970; Summer at World's End, 1971; Follyfoot, 1971; World's End in Winter, 1972; Dora at Follyfoot, 1972; Spring Comes to World's End, 1973; Talking of Horses, 1973; Last Year when I was Young, 1974; The Horse of Follyfoot, 1975; Stranger at Follyfoot, 1976; An Open Book, 1978. *Recreations:* riding, gardening. *Address:* North Falmouth, Mass 02556, USA.

DICKENSON, Aubrey Fiennes T.; see Trotman-Dickenson.

DICKENSON, Lt-Col Charles Royal, CMG 1965; Postmaster-General of Rhodesia, 1964–68, retired; b 17 June 1907; e s of Charles Roland and Gertrude Dickenson; m 1950, Hendrika Jacoba Margaretha Schippers; two d. Educ: Shaftesbury Grammar Sch., Dorset. Entered British Post Office as Engineering Apprentice, 1923; British Post Office HQ, 1932–39. Served War in Royal Signals, 1939–45, attaining rank of Lieut-Col. BPO NW Regional HQ as Asst Controller of Telecommunications, 1945–47; BPO HQ, London, 1947–50; loaned to S Rhodesia Govt, 1950–54; Controller of Telecommunications. Ministry of Posts, Federation of Rhodesia and Nyasaland, 1954–57; Regional Controller for N Rhodesia, Fedn of Rhodesia and Nyasaland, 1957–61; Dep. Postmaster-Gen., Rhodesia and Nyasaland, 1961–62; Postmaster-Gen., Rhodesia and Nyasaland, 1962–63. Hon. Mem., S Africa Inst. of Electronic and Radio Engineers (Hon. M(SA) IERE), 1966. ICD, OLM, Rhodesia, 1979. Recreations: growing orchids, photography. Address: Koekoekstraat 50, Maassluis, Holland. T: Maassluis 21658.

DICKENSON, Joseph Frank, PhD, CEng, FIMechE; Director, North Staffordshire Polytechnic, since 1969; b 26 Nov. 1924; s of late Frank Brand Dickenson and late Maud Dickenson (née Beharrell); m 1948, Sheila May Kingston; two s one d. Educ: College of Technology, Hull. BSc (1st Cl. Hons) Engrg, PhD (both London). Engrg apprenticeship and Jun. Engr's posts, 1939–52; Lectr and Sen. Lectr, Hull Coll. of Technology, 1952–59; Head of Dept of Mechanical Engrg and later Vice-Principal, Lanchester Coll. of Technology, 1960–64; Principal, Leeds Coll. of Technology, 1964–69. Recreations: tennis, badminton, gardening. Address: Burntwood, Hookgate, Market Drayton, Salop. T: Ashley 2610.

DICKIE, Brian James; General Administrator, Glyndebourne Festival Opera, since 1981; b 23 July 1941; s of Robert Kelso Dickie and Harriet Elizabeth (née Riddell); m 1968; Victoria Teresa Sheldon (née Price); two s one d. Educ: Haileybury; Trinity Coll., Dublin. Admin. Asst, Glyndebourne Opera, 1962–66; Administrator, Glyndebourne Touring Opera, 1967–81; Opera Manager, Glyndebourne Fest. Opera, 1970–81. Artistic Dir, Wexford Fest., 1967–73. Chm., London Choral Soc., 1978–; Vice-Chm., TNC, 1980– (Chm., TNC Opera Cttee, 1976–). Address: Hayes Farmhouse, Barcombe Mills, Lewes, East Sussex BN8 5BP. T: Barcombe 400275. Club: Garrick.

DICKIE, Rev. Edgar Primrose, MC; MA, BD (Edinburgh); BA Oxon; Emeritus Professor of Divinity, St Mary's College, University of St Andrews, since 1967 (Professor, 1935–67, retired); Extra Chaplain to the Queen in Scotland since 1967 (Chaplain, 1956–67, retired); b 12 Aug. 1897; y and o surv. s of William Dickie, editor of Dumfries and Galloway Standard, and Jane Paterson; m 1927, Ishbel Graham Holmes, d of Andrew Frier Johnston and Magdalene Ross Holmes, Edinburgh. Educ: Dumfries Academy; Edinburgh University; Christ Church, Oxford; New Coll., Edinburgh; Marburg; Tübingen. Served with rank of Captain, 3rd and 1/5th KOSB, Palestine, Flanders, France (wounded, MC); mentioned in despatches. MA Edinburgh, First Class Hons in Classics; Vans Dunlop Scholar; BA Oxford, First Class in Literae Humaniores; at New Coll., Edinburgh, Hamilton Scholar; Fullarton Scholar in Hebrew; Tutor in Greek, 1925–26; Hons Diploma; Senior Cunningham Fellow, 1926; Asst Minister, New North Church, Edinburgh; Ordained, 1927; Minister of St Cuthbert's Church, Lockerbie, 1927–33; Minister of St Anne's Church, Corstorphine, Edinburgh, 1933–35; External Examiner in Biblical Criticism, Edinburgh Univ., 1931–34 and 1934–35; in New Testament Greek, New Coll., Edinburgh, 1931–34; in History of Doctrine, Univ. of Manchester, 1939–41; in Ethics, Queen's Univ., Belfast, 1941; in Systematic Theology, Univ. of Aberdeen, 1942; in Theology, Univ. of Glasgow, 1948, Belfast, 1953. Kerr Lectr in 1936–39; Murtle Lectr, Univ. of Aberdeen, 1941; Gen. Supt of work of Church of Scotland in BEF, 1940, and with BLA, 1944–45 (mentioned in despatches). Captain St Andrews Univ. OTC, 1941; Convener, Church of Scotland Youth Cttee, 1945–50. Founder-mem., Studiorum Novi Testamenti Societas, 1937. Pres. Scottish Sunday School Union, 1955–57; Vice-Pres. Scottish Universities Athletic Club. Governor, St Leonards Sch. Hon. DD Edinburgh, 1946; Hon. LLD St Andrews, 1969. Hon. Life Mem., Students' Union, St Andrews; Hon. Blue, Athletic Union, St Andrews. Companion of Merit and Canon, Order St Lazarus of Jerusalem. Publications: Psammyforshort: Rex. Imp.: A Nonsense Story, 1928; The New Divine Order, 1930; translation of Karl Heim's Die Neue Welt Gottes; The Seven Words from the Cross, 1931; Spirit and Truth, 1935; translation of Heim's Das Wesen des Evangelischen Christentums; God Transcendent; translation of Heim's Glaube und Denken (3rd edn); Revelation and Response, 1938; One Year's Talks to Children, 1940; Scottish Life and Character, 1942; A Second Year's Talks to Children, 1943; The Paper Boat, 1943; The Obedience of a Christian Man, 1944; Normandy to Nijmegen, 1946; The Fellowship of Youth, 1947; Mister Bannock: A Nonsense Story, 1947; I Promise (Girl Guides), 1949; It was New to me (Church of Scotland), 1949; God is Light: Studies in Revelation and Personal Conviction, 1953; Thou art the Christ, 1954; A Safe Stronghold, 1955; introductory essay to McLeod Campbell The Nature of the Atonement, 1959; The Unchanging Gospel, 1960; The Father Everlasting, 1965; Remembrance, 1966; occasional articles in Punch, The Scots Magazine, and other periodicals. Recreations: hill-walking, winter sports. Address: Surma, Hepburn Gardens, St Andrews, Fife. T: St Andrews 73617.

DICKINS, Aileen Marian, MD, FRCOG; Consultant Gynaecological and Obstetric Surgeon, University College Hospital, London, since 1967; b 17 Nov. 1917; d of Arthur George Dickins and Marian Helen Dickins. MD; FRCOG 1958. Obstetrician and Gynaecologist: Windsor Gp of Hosps, 1952–64; Ealing Hosp. and Perivale Maternity Hosp., 1951–. Jun. Vice Pres., RCOG, 1978–80, Sen. Vice-Pres., 1980–81. FRSM; Mem. Women's Visiting Gynaecological Club. Publications: contrib. to BMJ and Jl of Obs and Gyn. of Brit. Commonwealth. Recreations: skiing, gardening. Address: 97 Harley Street, W1N 1DF. T: 01-486 2523.

DICKINS, Basil Gordon, CBE 1952 (OBE 1945); BSc, ARCS, DIC, PhD; Deputy Controller of Guided Weapons, Ministry of Technology, 1966–68; b 1 July 1908; s of late Basil Dickins; m 1st, 1935, Molly Aileen (d 1969), d of late H. Walters Reburn; 2nd, 1971, Edith, widow of Warren Parkinson. Educ: Royal Coll. of Science, London. Royal Aircraft Establishment, 1932; Air Min., 1936, later Min. of Aircraft Production; Head of Operational Research Section, HQ Bomber Command, 1941; Asst Scientific Adviser, Air Ministry, 1945; Dir of Tech. Personnel Administration, Min. of Supply, 1948; Dep. Scientific Adviser to Air Ministry, 1952; Dir of Guided Weapons Research and Development, Min. of Supply, 1956; Dir-Gen. of Atomic Weapons, Min. of Supply, 1959; Dir-Gen. of Guided Weapons, Ministry of Aviation, 1962. Publications: papers in Proc. Royal Society and Reports and Memoranda of Aeronautical Research Council. Address: Villa Caprice, La Folie, Millbrook, Jersey; The Penthouse, Cassandra, Victoria Road, Clifton, Cape Town, South Africa.

DICKINSON, family name of Baron Dickinson.

DICKINSON, 2nd Baron cr 1930, of Painswick; Richard Clavering Hyett Dickinson; b 2 March 1926; s of late Hon. Richard Sebastian Willoughby Dickinson, DSO (o s of 1st Baron) and May Southey, d of late Charles Lovemore, Melsetter, Cape Province, S Africa; S grandfather, 1943; m 1957, Margaret Ann (marr. diss.1980), e d of Brig. G. R. McMeekan, CB, DSO, OBE; two s; m 1980, Rita Doreen Moir. Heir: s Hon. Martin Hyett Dickinson, b 30 Jan. 1961. Address: The Stables, Gloucester Road, Painswick, Stroud, Glos. T: Painswick 813204.
    See also Dowager Viscountess Davidson, Hon. P. M. de B. Dickinson.

DICKINSON, Basil Philip Harriman; Under Secretary, Department of the Environment (formerly Ministry of Transport), 1959–74; b 10 Sept. 1916; yr s of F. H. and I. F. Dickinson; m 1941, Beryl Farrow; three s one d. Educ: Cheltenham Coll.; Oriel Coll., Oxford. Address: c/o Child & Co., 1 Fleet Street, EC4Y 1BD.

DICKINSON, Sir Ben; see Dickinson, Sir S. B.

DICKINSON, Sir Harold (Herbert), Kt 1975; Director: Development Finance Corporation Ltd, since 1979; Australian Fixed Trusts Ltd, since 1979; Chairman, AFT Property Co. Ltd, since 1980; b 27 Feb. 1917; s of late William James Dickinson and Barwon Venus Clarke; m 1946, Elsie May Smith; two d. Educ: Singleton Public Sch.; Tamworth High Sch.; Univ. of Sydney (LLB, 1st Cl. Hons). Barrister-at-Law. Served War, 2nd AIF HQ 22 Inf. Bde, 1940–45 (despatches); Japanese POW (Sgt). Dept of Lands, NSW, 1933–40; NSW Public Service Bd, 1946–60: Sec. and Sen. Inspector, 1949–60; Chief Exec. Officer, Prince Henry Hosp., 1960–63; NSW Public Service Bd: Mem., 1963–70; Dep. Chm., 1970–71; Chm., 1971–79. Hon. Mem., NSW Univs Bd, 1967–71; Hon. Dir, Prince Henry, Prince of Wales, Eastern Suburbs Teaching Hosps, 1965–75, Chm. of Dirs, 1975–; Governor, NSW Coll. of Law, 1972–77. Publications: contribs to administration jls. Recreation: sailing. Address: 649 Old South Head Road, Rose Bay North, NSW 2030, Australia. T: 371-7475. Clubs: Union, Rotary (Sydney).

DICKINSON, Rt. Rev. John Hubert, MA; Vicar of Chollerton, 1959–71; Hon. Canon in Newcastle Cathedral, 1947–71; m 1937, Frances Victoria, d of late Rev. C. F. Thorp; two d. Educ: Jesus Coll., Oxford; Cuddesdon Coll. Deacon, 1925; Priest, 1926; Curate of St John, Middlesbrough, 1925–29; SPG Missionary, South Tokyo, 1929–31; Asst Bishop of Melanesia, 1931–37; Vicar of Felkirk-with-Brierley, 1937–42; Vicar of Warkworth, 1942–59. Address: Wingrove, Riding Mill, Northumberland.

DICKINSON, John Lawrence, (Bob), CBE 1973; DL; FCA; Chairman: SKF Steel Ltd, since 1974; Bofors Cos (UK), since 1974; General Manager, SKF Holding Co. (Holland), since 1975; b 16 Nov. 1913; s of Tom Dickinson and Jennie Louise Dickinson; m 1937, Bettine Mary Jenkins; two d. Educ: Taunton Sch. Qual. as Chartered Accountant, 1937; Chief Accountant, Lucas Industries, 1937–44; SKF (UK) Ltd: Finance Dir and Sec., 1944–62; Sales Dir, 1962–66; Man. Dir, 1967–75, retired; Chairman: Sheffield Twist Drill & Steel Co. Ltd, 1978–81 (Dep. Chm., 1974–78); Weyroc Ltd (subsid. of Swedish Match Co.), 1975–82; British Rail (Eastern) Bd, 1970–81; Mem., National Enterprise Bd, 1975–79; Chm., NEDO Industrial Engines Sector Working Party, 1976–79; Mem. Gen. Council, also Finance and Gen. Purposes Cttee, CBI, until 1977; first Chm., Eastern Regional Council. Dep. Chm., Cranfield Inst. Hon. Life Vice-Pres., Luton and District Chamber of Commerce and Industry. High Sheriff, Bedfordshire, 1972–73, DL Beds 1976–. Gold Medal, Royal Patriots Soc. (Sweden), 1975. Recreations: gardening, National Hunt racing. Address: Arkle House, Upton End, Shillington, Hitchin, Herts SG5 3PG. T: Shillington 554.

DICKINSON, Patric (Thomas); poet, playwright and freelance broadcaster; b 26 Dec. 1914; s of Major A. T. S. Dickinson, 51 Sikhs, FF, IA, and Eileen

Constance Kirwan; *m* 1946, Sheila Dunbar Shannon; one *s* one *d*. *Educ:* St Catharine's Coll., Cambridge (Crabtree Exhibitioner). Asst Schoolmaster, 1936-39. Artists' Rifles, 1939-40. BBC, 1942-48 (Feature and Drama Dept); Acting Poetry Editor, 1945-48. Sometime Gresham Prof. in Rhetoric at the City University. Atlantic Award in Literature, 1948; Cholmondeley Award for Poets, 1973. *Publications: poetry:* The Seven Days of Jericho, 1944; Theseus and the Minotaur and Poems, 1946; Stone in the Midst and Poems, 1948; The Sailing Race, 1952; The Scale of Things, 1955; The World I See, 1960; This Cold Universe, 1964; A Round of Golf Courses, 1951; Aristophanes Against War, 1957; Selected Poems, 1968; More Than Time, 1970; A Wintering Tree, 1973; The Bearing Beast, 1976; Our Living John (poems), 1979; Winter Hostages, 1980; *play:* A Durable Fire, 1962; *librettos:* (for Malcolm Arnold) The Return of Odysseus, 1977; (for Stephen Dodgson) The Miller's Secret, 1979; (for Alan Ridout) Good King Wenceslas, 1979; *autobiography:* The Good Minute, 1965; *translations:* The Aeneid of Vergil, 1960; Aristophanes, vols I and II, 1970; *anthologies:* Soldier's Verse, 1945; Byron (selected), 1949; Poems to Remember, 1958; (ed jtly) Poet's Choice, 1967; (ed and introd.) Selected Poems of Henry Newbolt, 1981. *Recreation:* golf, (Cambridge Blue, 1935). *Address:* 38 Church Square, Rye, East Sussex. *T:* Rye 2194. *Club:* Savile.

DICKINSON, Prof. Peter; composer, pianist; first Professor of Music, University of Keele, since 1974; *b* 15 Nov. 1934; *s* of late Frank Dickinson, contact lens specialist, and of Muriel Porter; *m* 1964, Bridget Jane Tomkinson; two *s*. *Educ:* The Leys Sch.; Queens' Coll., Cambridge (organ schol., Stewart of Rannoch schol., MA); Juilliard Sch. of Music, New York (Rotary Foundn Fellow). LRAM, ARCM; FRCO. Teaching and freelance work in New York, 1958-61, London and Birmingham, 1962-74; founded Centre for American Music, Keele Univ. Concerts, broadcasts and records as pianist, mostly with sister Meriel Dickinson, mezzo soprano, incl. French, American and British works, some specially commissioned, 1960-. FRSA 1981. *Publications: compositions include: orchestral:* Monologue for Strings, 1959; Five Diversions, 1969; Transformations—Homage to Satie, 1970; Organ Concerto, 1971; Concerto for Strings, Percussion and Electronic Organ, 1971; *chamber:* String Quartet No 1, 1958; Juilliard Dances, 1959; Fanfares and Elegies, 1967; Translations, 1971; Hymns, Blues and Improvisations, 1973; String Quartet No 2, 1975; works for solo organ, piano, clavichord, recorder and baryton; *vocal:* Four Auden Songs, 1956; A Dylan Thomas Cycle, 1959; Elegy, 1966; Five Poems of Alan Porter, 1968; Extravaganzas, 1969; An E. E. Cummings Cycle, 1970; Winter Afternoons, 1970; Three Comic Songs (Auden, 1972; Surrealist Landscape (Lord Berners), 1973; Lust (St Augustine), 1974; A Memory of David Munrow, 1977; Reminiscences (Byron), 1979; *choral:* Martin of Tours (Thomas Blackburn), 1966; The Dry Heart (Alan Porter), 1967; Outcry, 1969; Late Afternoon in November, 1975; *ballet:* Vitalitas, 1959; *musical drama:* The Judas Tree (Thomas Blackburn), 1965; various church music, music for children and for films; (ed) Twenty British Composers, 1975; Songs and Piano Music by Lord Berners, 1982; contrib. to Musical Times, Music and Musicians, Composer, Groves Dictionary, etc. *Recreation:* book collecting. *Address:* c/o Music Department, University of Keele, Keele, Staffs ST5 5BG. *T:* Newcastle (Staffs) 621111.

DICKINSON, Hon. Peter Malcolm de Brissac; author; *b* 16 Dec. 1927; *s* of Hon. Richard Sebastian Willoughby Dickinson and May Southey (Nancy) Lovemore; *m* 1953, Mary Rose Barnard; two *s* two *d*. *Educ:* Eton; King's Coll., Cambridge (BA). Asst Editor, Punch, 1952-69. Chm., Management Cttee, Soc. of Authors, 1978-80. *Publications: children's books:* The Weathermonger, 1968; Heartsease, 1969; The Devil's Children, 1970 (trilogy republished 1975 as The Changes); Emma Tupper's Diary, 1970; The Dancing Bear, 1972; The Gift, 1973; The Iron Lion, 1973; Chance, Luck and Destiny, 1975; The Blue Hawk, 1976; Annerton Pit, 1977; Hepzibah, 1978; Tulku, 1979 (Whitbread Prize; Carnegie Medal); The Flight of Dragons, 1979; City of Gold, 1980 (Carnegie Medal); The Seventh Raven, 1981; *TV series*, Mandog (Mandog, by Lois Lamplugh, 1972, is based on this series); *novels:* Skin Deep, 1968; A Pride of Heroes, 1969; The Seals, 1970; Sleep and His Brother, 1971; The Lizard in the Cup, 1972; The Green Gene, 1973; The Poison Oracle, 1974; The Lively Dead, 1975; King and Joker, 1976; Walking Dead, 1977; One Foot in the Grave, 1979; A Summer in the Twenties, 1981; The Last House-party, 1982. *Recreation:* manual labour. *Address:* 33 Queensdale Road, W11 4SB.
See also Baron Dickinson.

DICKINSON, Reginald Percy, OBE 1964; retired Under Secretary, Ministry of Defence; *b* 13 Feb. 1914; *s* of Percy and Nellie Dickinson; *m* 1943, Marjorie Ellen Lillistone; two *s*. *Educ:* Grammar school. BScEng London Univ., 1943; FRAeS, CEng. Air Min., Martlesham Heath, 1936; RAE, 1937; Aircraft and Armament Exper. Estabt, 1942: Supt of Performance, 1953, Supt Weapon Systems, 1962; Dir, Aircraft Develt (B), MoD, Project Dir, Lightning, Hercules, Victor, Buccaneer, Hawk etc, 1965-73; Dir Gen. Mil. Aircraft Projects, 1974-75. Chm., Flight Panel, AGARD, 1963-65; Mem., ARC and RAeS Cttees. Alston Medal for achievements in Flight Testing, 1961. *Recreations:* sailing, golf. *Address:* 1A Lingwood Avenue, Mudeford, Christchurch, Dorset BH23 3JS. *T:* Christchurch 482781. *Clubs:* Highcliffe Sailing; Highcliffe Castle Golf.

DICKINSON, Prof. Robert Eric; Professor of Geography, University of Arizona, 1967-75, retired; formerly Professor of Geography, University of Leeds, 1958, and Research Professor, 1963; *b* 9 Feb. 1905; *m* 1941, Mary Winwood; no *c*. *Educ:* Upholland Grammar Sch., near Wigan; Leeds University. BA Hons (1st Cl. Geog.), Leeds, 1925; DipEd, Leeds, 1926; MA (Geog.), Leeds, 1928; PhD London, 1932. Asst Lectr in Geography, University Coll., Exeter, 1926-28; University Coll., London: Asst Lectr, 1928-32, Lectr, 1932-41, Reader in Geog., 1941-47; Prof. of Geog., Syracuse Univ., NY, 1947-58. Visiting Prof. at Univs of: California, 1960-61; Washington, 1963; Nebraska, 1963; Kansas State Univ., 1964; Arizona, 1967; Laval, 1968. Rockefeller Fellow, 1931-32 (USA), 1936-37 (Europe); Guggenheim Fellow, 1957-58. *Publications:* Making of Geography, 1932, repr. 1977; The German Lebensraum, 1943; The Regions of Germany, 1944; City, Region and Regionalism, 1945; The West European City, 1951; Germany: A General and Regional Geography, 1952; The Population Problem of Southern Italy, 1955; City and Region, 1964; City and Region in Western Europe, 1967; Makers of Modern Geography, 1969; Regional Ecology, 1970; Regional Concept, 1975; Environments of America, 1975. *Address:* 636 Roller Coaster Road, Tucson, Arizona 85704, USA.

DICKINSON, Ronald Arthur, CMG 1964; Chairman, Exim Credit Management and Consultants, since 1971; *b* 7 Nov. 1910; *s* of J. H. Dickinson, JP, Cartmel and Oldham, Lancs; *m* 1939, Helen, *d* of Joseph Severs, Oldham, Lancs. *Educ:* schools and univs. Joined ECGD, Under-Sec., 1965-70. Governor, Sports Foundn, 1976-. Order of Merit, Admiral Class, Brazil, 1971. *Recreation:* any sport. *Address:* 86 Regency Lodge, NW3 5EB. *T:* 01-722 2655. *Club:* Overseas Bankers.

DICKINSON, Ronald Sigismund Shepherd, CMG 1967; Secretary, Air Travel Reserve Fund Agency, since 1975; *b* 30 March 1906; *o s* of Walter Sigismund Dickinson and Janet (*née* Shepherd); *m* 1932, Vida Evelyn, 4th *d* of Roger Hall and Maud (*née* Seaton); one *d*. *Educ:* Dulwich Coll.; London Sch. of Economics. AIB 1936. Min. of Aircraft Production, 1941; Principal, 1943; Civil Aviation Dept, Air Min., 1944; Min. of Civil Aviation, 1946; Asst Sec., 1947; Rees-Jeffreys Post-Graduate Research Student, LSE, 1950-51; Civil Air Attaché, British Embassy, Washington, 1952-54; Civil Aviation Adviser to Fedn of W Indies, Trinidad, 1961-62; UK Representative on Council of ICAO, Montreal, 1962-69. 1st Vice-Pres. of Council of ICAO, 1966-67. *Address:* Flat 1, 3 Sandrock Road, Tunbridge Wells, Kent TN2 3PX. *Club:* Royal Commonwealth Society.

DICKINSON, Sir Samuel Benson, (Sir Ben Dickinson), Kt 1980; Mining Advisor to South Australian Government, since 1975; *b* 1 Feb. 1912; *s* of Sydney Rushbrook Dickinson and Margaret Dickinson (*née* Clemes); *m* 1960, Dorothy Joan Weidenhofer; three *s* one *d*. *Educ:* Haileybury College, Melbourne; Univ. of Melbourne. MSc. N Australia Aerial Geological and Geophysical Survey, 1935-36; geologist: Electrolytic Zinc, Mt Lyell, Mt Isa, mining cos, 1937-41; S Australian Geological Survey, 1941-42. Dir of Mines, Govt Geologist, Sec. to Minister of Mines, Dep. Controller, Mineral Production, Chm. Radium Hill Mines, 1943-56; Director: Rio Tinto Mining Co. of Australia, 1956-60; Sir Frank Duval's Gp of Cos, 1960-62; Chief Technical Adviser, Pechiney Australia, 1962-65; Project Manager, Clutha Development Ltd and Daniel K. Ludwig Cos Australia, 1965-75. *Publications:* technical reports for Australian Dept of Mines, Inst. of Mining and Metallurgy and mining jls and bulletins. *Recreations:* golf, bowls. *Address:* PO Box 269, Stirling, SA 5152, Australia. *T:* (08) 339 5135. *Clubs:* Athenæum (Melbourne); American National (Sydney).

DICKINSON, Prof. Thorold (Barron), CBE 1973; Professor of Film in the University of London (Slade School of Fine Art), 1967-71, now Emeritus; *b* Bristol, 16 Nov. 1903; *s* of Ven. Charles Henry Dickinson, sometime Archdeacon of Bristol, and Beatrice Vindhya (*née* Thorold); *m* 1929, Irene Joanna Macfadyen, AA Dipl., RIBA (*d* 1979). *Educ:* Clifton Coll.; Keble Coll., Oxford. Entered film industry, 1926; film editor, subseq. film director and script writer. Directed (among others): Gaslight, 1940; The Next of Kin, 1941. Organised Army Kinematograph Service Production Group and produced 17 military training films, 1942-43. Directed Men of Two Worlds, 1944-45; collab. scripts of: Mayor of Casterbridge; Then and Now; directed: The Queen of Spades, 1949; Secret People, 1951; Hill 24 Doesn't Answer, 1953-55. Produced Power Among Men, 1958-59, and many short films for UN. Vice-Pres., Assoc. of Cine-Technicians, 1936-53. Mem. of Cttee, Nat. Film Archive, 1950-56; Chm., Brit. Film Acad., 1952-53; Mem., Cttee administering Brit. Film Inst. Experimental Fund, 1952-56; Chief, Film Services Office of Public Information, UN, NY, 1956-60; Senior Lecturer in Film, Slade School of Fine Art, UCL, 1960-67. Consultant to Amer. Film Inst., 1968; Hon. film consultant, CNAA, 1973-76; Vis. Prof. of Film, Univ. of Surrey, 1975-77. Mem. Board, New York Film Council, 1958-60. Pres., International Federation of Film Societies, 1958-66 (Hon. Pres., 1966); Hon. Mem., Assoc. of Ciné and TV Technicians, 1977; Hon. Life Member: British Univs Film Council, 1978-; Le Centre Internationale de Liaison des Ecoles de Cinéma et de Télévision (CILECT), 1978-. PhD Fine Arts/Film, University of London, 1971; DUniv Surrey, 1976. *Publications:* (with Catherine de la Roche) Soviet Cinema, 1948; A Discovery of Cinema, 1971; contribs to periodicals: Sight and Sound, Bianco e Nero, Geog. Mag., Soviet Studies, Screen Digest, Times Higher Educn Supplement, Film Comment (NY). *Recreations:* theatre, film, walking, reading. *Address:* Wing Cottage, Sheepdrove, Lambourn, Berks RG16 7UT. *T:* Lambourn 71393.

DICKINSON, William Michael, MBE 1960; publisher; Managing Director, Africa Research Ltd, since 1966; *b* 13 Jan. 1930; *s* of late Charles W. H. Dickinson, RN, and Ruth Sandeman Betts; *m* 1971, Enid Joy Bowers; one *s* two *d*. *Educ:* St Edward's Sch., Oxford. Army Service, 1948-51; 2/Lieut,

Ox. and Bucks LI, Sept. 1948; seconded Somaliland Scouts; Lieut 1950; Colonial Service Devonshire Course, 1951-52; Somaliland Protectorate: Admin. Officer, 1952; Dist. Officer, 1953-54; Asst Sec. (Political), 1955-56; seconded to British Liaison Org., Ethiopia, as Sen. Asst Liaison Officer, 1957-59; Brit. Liaison Officer in charge, 1959; transf. N Rhodesia as Dist Officer, 1960; Dist Comr, 1961; seconded to Foreign Office as HM Consul-Gen., Hargeisa, 1961-63; Principal, External Affairs Section, Office of Prime Minister, N Rhodesia, during 1964; Senior Principal, Ministry of Foreign Affairs, Government of Zambia. *Address:* c/o Africa Research Ltd, 18 Lower North Street, Exeter. *T:* Exeter 76190.

DICKSON, Alexander Graeme, (Alec), CBE 1967 (MBE 1945); MA Oxon; Hon. President, Community Service Volunteers, since 1982 (Hon. Director, 1962-82); *b* 23 May 1914; *y s* of late Norman Dickson and Anne Higgins; *m* 1951, Mora Hope Robertson, artist, author of numerous travel books and biographies. *Educ:* Rugby; New Coll., Oxford. Private Sec. to late Sir Alec Paterson, 1935; editorial staff: Yorkshire Post, 1936-37; Daily Telegraph, 1937-38, Germany; refugee relief, Czechoslovakia, winter 1938-39. Served War of 1939-45: Cameron Highlanders; 1st KAR (Abyssinian Campaign); led E Africa Comd mobile educn unit. Displaced Persons Directorate, Berlin, 1946-48; introd Mass Educn, Gold Coast, 1948-49; founded Man O' War Bay Training Centre, Cameroons and Nigeria, 1950-54; Chief Unesco Mission, Iraq, 1955-56; refugee relief, Austro-Hungarian frontier, winter 1956-57. Founder and first Dir, Voluntary Service Overseas, 1958-62; founded Community Service Volunteers, 1962, developing concept of 'A Year Between' for students, linking curriculum to human needs, promoting tutoring in schools, involving disadvantaged and unemployed young people in social service. Shared experience with US Peace Corps, 1961, 1969; India, 1968, 1972; Hong Kong, 1968, 1974, 1980; Israel, 1970, 1980; Nigeria, 1970, 1975, 1976; Malta, 1971; Nepal, 1972; New Zealand, 1972; Papua New Guinea, 1973; Bahamas, 1975; US Nat. Student Volunteer Program, Washington DC and Alaska, 1975; Ontario, 1975; Sri Lanka, Australia, 1976; Japan, 1976, 1980; Univ. of the South Pacific, 1978; W Germany, Denmark, 1979; Finland, 1980; Sweden, 1982. Consultant to Commonwealth Secretariat, 1974-77. Hon. LLD: Leeds, 1970; Bristol, 1980. Niwano Peace Foundn Award, 1982. *Publications:* (with Mora Dickson) A Community Service Handbook, 1967; School in the Round, 1969; A Chance to Serve, 1976; articles on community development and youth service. *Recreations:* identical with work - involving young people in community service, at home or overseas. *Address:* 19 Blenheim Road, W4. *T:* 01-994 7437; (office) 01-278 6601.
   See also M. G. Dickson.

DICKSON, Arthur Richard Franklin, CBE 1974; QC (Belize), 1979; Chairman, Industrial Tribunals (part-time), since 1972; Commissioner for Law Revision, Belize, 1978; *b* 13 Jan. 1913; *m* 1949, Joanna Maria Margaretha van Baardwyk; four *s. Educ:* Rusea's Secondary Sch. and Cornwall Coll., Jamaica. Called to the Bar, Lincoln's Inn, 1938. Judicial Service. HM Overseas Judiciary: Jamaica, 1941; Magistrate, Turks and Caicos Islands, 1944-47; Asst to Attorney-Gen., and Legal Draftsman, Barbados, 1947-49; Magistrate, British Guiana, 1949-52; Nigeria, 1952-62: Magistrate, 1952-54; Chief Magistrate, 1954-56; Chief Registrar, High Court, Lagos, 1956-58; Judge of the High Court, Lagos, 1958-62; retired. Temp. appointment, Solicitors Dept, GPO London, 1962-63; served Northern Rhodesia (latterly Zambia), 1964-67; Judge of the High Court, Uganda, 1967-71; Deputy Chm., Middlesex QS, July-Aug., 1971; Chief Justice, Belize, 1973-74; Judge of the Supreme Court, Anguilla (part-time), 1972-76. *Publication:* Revised Ordinances (1909-1941) Turks and Caicos Islands, 1944. *Recreations:* gardening, walking, swimming, riding. *Address:* No 1 The Pleasance, Kinsbourne Green, Harpenden, Herts AL5 3NA. *T:* Harpenden 3703. *Club:* Royal Commonwealth Society.

DICKSON, Bertram Thomas, CMG 1960; BA, PhD; *b* Leicester, 20 May 1886; *s* of J. T. Dickson of Leicester; *m* 1910, Florence (decd), *d* of W. Roberts; one *s* one *d. Educ:* Queen's Univ., Kingston, Ontario (BA); Cornell Univ.; McGill Univ., Montreal (PhD). Served European War, 1914-18: Agricultural Officer, 1st British Army, 1917-18; Commandant, 1st British Army Sch. of Agriculture, 1918-19. Professor of Economic Botany, McGill Univ., 1919-26; Prof. of Plant Pathology, McGill Univ., 1926-27; Chief, Division of Plant Industry, CSIRO, Canberra, 1927-51; Delegate, 2nd Session, FAO Conference, Copenhagen, 1946; Mem., UNESCO Arid Zone Advisory Cttee, 1952-57; UN Adviser, Desert Research Institute of Egypt, 1958-59. Pres., Canberra Repertory Soc., 1932-41; Exec. Mem., Australian National Research Council, 1932-47; Pres., Legacy Club, Canberra, 1933; Pres., Australian Institute of Agricultural Science, 1945-46 (Vice-Pres., 1935-39); Chm., Canberra Univ. Coll., 1954-60. *Address:* c/o Dr F. P. Dickson, 38 Trevellyan Street, Cronulla, NSW 2230, Australia.

DICKSON, Eileen Wadham, (Mrs C. F. Dickson); *d* of John Edward Latton, Librarian to Inner Temple, and Ethel Letitia Baker; *m* 1931, Charles Frederick Dickson, OBE. *Educ:* Convent of the Sacred Heart, Roehampton; Bruges, Belgium. Served War of 1939-45 with WVS and on Executive Council of Stage Door Canteen. Joined Harper's Bazaar, 1949; Fashion Editor, 1951; Editor, 1953-65. *Recreations:* theatre, reading, racing, gardens. *Address:* Grimsdyke, Aldworth, Reading, Berks. *T:* Compton 247; 4 Stack House, Ebury Street, SW1. *T:* 01-730 7675.

DICKSON, Prof. Gordon Ross; Professor of Agriculture, University of Newcastle upon Tyne, since 1973; Chairman, Agricultural Wages Board for England and Wales; Deputy Chairman, Central Council of Agricultural and

Horticultural Cooperation; *b* 12 Feb. 1932; *s* of T. W. Dickson, Tynemouth; *m* 1956, Dorothy Stobbs; two *s* one *d. Educ:* Tynemouth High Sch.; Durham Univ. BSc (Agric) 1st cl. hons 1953, PhD (Agric) 1958, Dunelm. Tutorial Research Student, Univ. Sch. of Agric., King's Coll., Newcastle upon Tyne, 1953-56; Asst Farm Dir, Council of King's Coll., Nafferton, Stocksfield-on-Tyne, 1956-58; Farms Director for the Duke of Norfolk, 1958-71; Principal, Royal Agric. Coll., Cirencester, 1971-73. *Address:* School of Agriculture, University of Newcastle upon Tyne, Newcastle upon Tyne NE1 7RU; Tyneholme, 44 Moor Crescent, Gosforth, Newcastle upon Tyne NE3 4AQ.

DICKSON, (Horatio Henry) Lovat, OC 1978; FRSC 1982; writer and publisher; *b* 30 June 1902; *s* of Gordon Fraser Dickson and Josephine Mary Cunningham; *m* 1934, Marguerite Isabella, *d* of A. B. Brodie, Montreal; one *s. Educ:* Berkhamsted Sch.; University of Alberta (MA). Lecturer in English, Univ. of Alberta, 1927-29; Associate Editor, Fortnightly Review, 1929-32; Editor of Review of Reviews, 1930-34; Managing Dir of Lovat Dickson Ltd (Publishers), 1932-38; Director: Macmillan & Co. (publishers), 1941-64; Pan Books Ltd, 1946-64; Reprint Soc., 1939-64. Hon. LLD Alberta, 1968; Hon. DLitt: Western Ontario, 1976; York Univ., Toronto, 1981. *Publications:* The Green Leaf, 1938; Half-Breed, The Story of Grey Owl, 1939; Out of the West Land, 1944; Richard Hillary, 1950; two vols of autobiog.: Vol. I, The Ante-Room, 1959; Vol. II, The House of Words, 1963; H. G. Wells, 1969; Wilderness Man, 1973; Radclyffe Hall at the Well of Loneliness, 1975. *Address:* 21 Dale Avenue, Toronto, Canada. *Club:* Arts and Letters (Toronto).

DICKSON, Jennifer (Joan), (Mrs R. A. Sweetman), RA 1976 (ARA 1970); RCA 1978; RE 1965; graphic artist, photographer and painter; *b* 17 Sept. 1936; 2nd *d* of late John Liston Dickson and of Margaret Joan Turner, S Africa; *m* 1962, Ronald Andrew Sweetman; one *s. Educ:* Goldsmith's College Sch. of Art, Univ. of London; Atelier 17, Paris. Taught at Eastbourne Sch. of Art, 1959-62 (French Govt Schol., to work in Paris under S. W. Hayter). Directed and developed Printmaking Dept, Brighton Coll. of Art, 1962-68; developed and directed Graphics Atelier, Saidye Bronfman Centre, Montreal, 1970-72. Has held appointments of Vis. Artist at following Universities: Ball State Univ., Muncie, Indiana, 1967; Univ. of the West Indies, Kingston, Jamaica, 1968; Univ. of Wisconsin, Madison, 1972; Ohio State Univ., 1973; Western Illinois Univ., 1973; Haystack Mountain Sch. of Crafts, Maine, 1973; Vis. Artist, Queen's Univ., Kingston, Ont., 1977; part-time Instructor of Drawing, Univ. of Ottawa, 1980-81. Founder Mem., Brit. Printmakers' Council. Prix des Jeunes Artistes (Gravure), Biennale de Paris, 1963; Major Prize, World Print Competition, San Francisco, 1974. *Publications:* suites of original etchings: Genesis, 1965; Alchemic Images, 1966; Aids to Meditation, 1967; Eclipse, 1968; Song of Songs, 1969; Out of Time, 1970; Fragments, 1971; Sweet Death and Other Pleasures, 1972; Homage to Don Juan, 1975; Body Perceptions, 1975; The Secret Garden, 1976; Openings, 1977; Three Mirrors to Narcissus, 1978; Il Paradiso Terrestre, 1980; Il Tempo Classico, 1981. *Address:* 508 Gilmour Street, Ottawa, Ontario K1R 5L4, Canada.

DICKSON, John Abernethy, CB 1970; Director-General and Deputy Chairman, Forestry Commission, 1968-76; *b* 19 Sept. 1915; *yr s* of late John and Williamina Dickson; *m* 1942, Helen Drummond, *o d* of Peter Drummond Jardine; two *d. Educ:* Robert Gordon's Coll., Aberdeen; Aberdeen Univ. MA 1936; BSc (For.) 1938. Joined Forestry Commn, 1938; District Officer, 1940; seconded to Min. of Supply, Home Grown Timber Production Dept, 1940-46; Divisional Officer, 1951; Conservator, 1956; Dir (Scotland), 1963; Comr Harvesting and Marketing, 1965. Director: Economic Forestry (Scotland), 1977-; Forest Thinnings Ltd, 1979- (Chm., 1981-). Chm., Standing Cttee on Commonwealth Forestry, 1968-76; Vice-Pres., Commonwealth Forestry Assoc., 1975- (Chm., 1972-75). Hon. LLD Aberdeen, 1969. FBIM 1975. *Recreation:* gardening. *Address:* 56 Oxgangs Road, Edinburgh EH10 7AY. *T:* 031-445 1067.

DICKSON, Leonard Elliot, CBE 1972; MC 1945; TD 1951; DL; Solicitor, Dickson, Haddow & Co., since 1947; *b* 17 March 1915; *s* of Rev. Robert Marcus Dickson, DD, Lanark, and Cordelia Elliot; *m* 1950, Mary Elisabeth Cuthbertson; one *s* one *d. Educ:* Uppingham, Rutland; Univ. of Cambridge (BA 1936); Univ. of Glasgow (LLB 1947). Served War, with 1st Bn Glasgow Highlanders, HLI, 1939-46. Clerk to Clyde Lighthouses Trust, 1953-65. Chm., Lowland TAVR, 1968-70; Vice-Chm. Glasgow Exec. Council, NHS, 1970-74. DL Glasgow, 1963. *Recreations:* travel, gardening. *Address:* Bridge End, Gartmore, by Stirling FK8 3RT. *T:* Aberfoyle 220. *Club:* Royal Scottish Automobile (Glasgow).

DICKSON, Lovat; *see* Dickson, H. H. L.

DICKSON, Murray Graeme, CMG 1961; *b* 19 July 1911; *s* of Norman and Anne Dickson. *Educ:* Rugby; New Coll., Oxford. Prison Service (Borstals), 1935-40. Served War of 1939-45, in Force 136. Entered Colonial Service, 1947; Education Officer, Sarawak, 1947, Deputy Dir of Education, 1952, Dir of Education, 1955-66; retd. Unesco adviser on educl planning to Govt of Lesotho, 1967-68. *Address:* Flat 150, Whitehall Court, SW1.
   See also A. G. Dickson.

DICKSON, Prof. Robert Andrew, MA Oxon, MB, ChM; FRCS, FRCSE; Professor and Head of Department of Orthopaedic Surgery, University of Leeds; Consultant Surgeon, St James's University Hospital, Leeds, and Leeds

General Infirmary, since 1981; *b* 13 April 1943; *s* of Robert Campbell Miller Dickson and Maude Evelyn Dickson; *m* 1980, Ingrid Irene Sandberg. *Educ:* Edinburgh Academy; Edinburgh Univ. (MB, ChB 1967, ChM 1973). FRCSE 1972; Moynihan Medal (Assoc. of Surgeons of GB and Ire.), 1977; FRCS *ad eund.* 1982. Lecturer, Nuffield Dept of Orthopaedic Surgery, Univ. of Oxford, 1972-75; Fellow in Spinal Surgery, Univ. of Louisville, Kentucky, 1975-76; Reader, Nuffield Dept of Orthopaedic Surgery, Univ. of Oxford, 1976-81. Fellow, Brit. Orthopaedic Assoc.; Member: Brit. Soc. for Surgery of the Hand; Brit. Orthopaedic Research Soc.; Brit. Scoliosis Soc. *Publications:* Surgery of the Rheumatoid Hand, 1979; papers on spinal surgery, hand surgery, and microsurgery. *Recreations:* squash, music. *Address:* 10 Whitechapel Close, Leeds LS8 2PT. *T:* Leeds 654491.

DICKSON, Dame Violet (Penelope), DBE 1976 (CBE 1964; MBE 1942); *b* Gautby, Lincs, 3 Sept. 1896; *d* of Neville Lucas-Calcraft and Emily Delmar Lindley; *m* 1920, Captain Harold Richard Patrick Dickson, CIE (*d* 1959); one *s* one *d*. *Educ:* Miss Lunn's High Sch., Woodhall Spa; Les Charmettes, Vevey, Switzerland. Mesopotamia, 1921-22; Quetta, Baluchistan, 1923-24; Bikaner, Rajputana, 1924-28; Bushire, Iran, 1928-29; Kuwait, 1929-. FRZS; Mem. RCAS. *Publications:* Wild Flowers of Kuwait and Bahrain, 1955; Forty Years in Kuwait, 1971. *Recreations:* shooting, riding, tennis, swimming. *Address:* Seef, Kuwait, Arabia. *T:* 432310.

DICKSON, Marshal of the Royal Air Force Sir William (Forster), GCB 1953 (KCB 1952; CB 1942); KBE 1946 (CBE 1945; OBE 1934); DSO 1918; AFC 1922; idc; psa; *b* 24 Sept. 1898; *s* of late C. C. Forster Dickson, Chancery Registrar's Office, Royal Courts of Justice, and of late Agnes Nelson Dickson, Northwood, Mddx; *m* 1932, Patricia Marguerite, *d* of late Sir Walter Allen, KBE; one *d* (and one *d* decd). *Educ:* Bowden House, Seaford; Haileybury Coll. Royal Naval Air Service, 1916-18 (DSO, despatches thrice); transferred to RAF, 1918; Permanent Commn in RAF, 1919; employed on Naval Flying work, 1919-21; Test Pilot, RAE, 1921-22; Air Ministry, 1923-26; No 56 (Fighter) Sqdn, 1926-27; RAF Staff Coll., Andover, 1927-28; posted to India, 1929; served on NW Frontier, 1929-30 and at HQ RAF Delhi (despatches); commanded RAF Station, Hawkinge, and No 25 (Fighter) Squadron, 1935-36; Directing Staff, Staff Coll., 1936-38; Imperial Defence Coll., 1939; Dir of Plans, Air Ministry, 1941-42; commanded Nos 9 and 10 Groups in Fighter Comd, 1942-43; commanded No 83 Group in TAF, 1943-44; commanded Desert Air Force, 1944; Asst Chief of Air Staff (Policy), Air Ministry, 1945-46; Vice-Chief of Air Staff, Air Council, Air Ministry, 1946-48; C-in-C, MEAF, 1948-50; Mem. for Supply and Organisation, Air Council, 1950-52; Chief of the Air Staff, 1953-56; Chm. of the Chiefs of Staff Cttee, 1956-59; Chief of Defence Staff, 1958-59. President: Royal Central Asian Soc., 1961-65; Ex-Services Mental Welfare Soc., 1960-76; Haileybury Soc., 1962; Forces Help Society and Lord Roberts Workshops, 1974-81. Master, The Glass Sellers' Co., 1964. Russian Order of Suvarov, 1944; USA Legion of Merit. *Address:* Foxbriar House, Cold Ash, Newbury, Berks. *Club:* Royal Air Force.

DICKSON MABON, Rt. Hon. Jesse; *see* Mabon, Rt Hon. J. D.

DIESKAU, Dietrich F.; *see* Fischer-Dieskau.

DIETRICH, Marlene; actress; *b* Berlin, 27 Dec. 1904; *d* of Eduard von Losch and Josephine Felsing; *m* 1924, Rudolph Sieber (*d* 1976); one *d*. *Educ:* Berlin; Weimar. Max Reinhardt Sch. of Theatre; Stage, Berlin and Vienna; First notable film, The Blue Angel; films in America since 1930, incl. Desire, Destry Rides Again, Foreign Affair, Garden of Allah, Golden Earrings, Rancho Notorious, Scarlet Empress, Shanghai Express, Stage Fright, Witness for the Prosecution, Just a Gigolo; naturalised as an American, 1937; numerous stage appearances in Europe, Great Britain, America and all continents; Special Tony Award, 1967-68. Officier, Légion d'Honneur, 1972; US Medal of Freedom. *Publication:* Marlene Dietrich's ABC, 1962. *Recreation:* tennis.

DIGBY, family name of **Baron Digby.**

DIGBY, 12th Baron (Ire.) *cr* 1620, and 5th Baron (GB) *cr* 1765; **Edward Henry Kenelm Digby,** JP; Vice Lord-Lieutenant, Dorset, since 1965; Captain, late Coldstream Guards; *b* 24 July 1924; *o s* of 11th and 4th Baron Digby, KG, DSO, MC, and Hon. Pamela Bruce, OBE (*d* 1978), *y d* of 2nd Baron Aberdare; *S* father, 1964; *m* 1952, Dione Marian (*see* Lady Digby); two *s* one *d*. *Educ:* Eton; Trinity Coll., Oxford; RMC. Served War of 1939-45. Capt., 1947; Malaya, 1948-50; ADC to C-in-C: FARELF, 1950-51; BAOR, 1951-52. Dep. Chm., SW Economic Planning Council, 1972-77; Mem. Council, Royal Agricultural Soc. England, 1954; Chm., Royal Agricultural Soc. of Commonwealth, 1966-77, Hon. Fellow 1977. Pres., 1976, Vice Pres., 1977, Royal Bath and West Soc. Dorchester Rural District Councillor, 1962; Dorset County Councillor, 1966 (Vice Chm. CC, 1977); Mem. Dorset Agric. Exec. Cttee. Dir, Brooklyns Westbrick Ltd. DL 1957, JP 1959, Dorset. *Recreations:* ski-ing, shooting, racing, tennis. *Heir:* *s* Hon. Henry Noel Kenelm Digby [*b* 6 Jan. 1954; *m* 1980, Susan, *er d* of Peter Watts]. *Address:* Minterne, Dorchester, Dorset. *T:* Cerne Abbas 370. *Club:* Pratt's.
See also W. A. Harriman.

DIGBY, Lady; Dione Marian Digby; *b* 23 Feb. 1934; *d* of Rear-Adm. Robert St Vincent Sherbrooke, VC, CB, DSO, and Rosemary Neville Sherbrooke (*née* Buckley), Oxton, Notts; *m* 1952, Baron Digby, *qv*; two *s* one *d*. *Educ:* Talindert State Sch., Victoria, Australia; Southover Manor Sch., Lewes,

Sussex. Chairman: Dorset Assoc. of Youth Clubs, 1966-73; Dorset Community Council, 1977-79; Standing Conf. of Rural Community Councils and Councils of Voluntary Service SW Region, 1977-79. Councillor (Ind.) W Dorset DC and Mem. Council's Planning Cttee 1976-; Mem. Dorset Small Industries Cttee, CoSIRA, 1977 (Chm. 1981). Mem. BBC/IBA Central Appeals Adv. Cttee, 1975-80; Governor, Dorset Coll. of Agriculture, 1978-; Mem. Council, Exeter Univ., 1981-. Founder Chairman, Hon. Sec., Summer Music Soc. of Dorset, 1963-; Mem. Bath Festival Soc. Council of Management, 1971- (Chm. of the Society, 1976-81); Chm. Bath Fest. Friends Trust, 1982-; Member: SW Arts Management Cttee, 1981-; Arts Council of Gt Britain, 1982-. *Recreations:* music and the arts, skiing, sailing, tennis; interest in local government, politics, history, people. *Address:* Minterne, Dorchester, Dorset DT2 7AU. *T:* Cerne Abbas 370.

DIGBY, Adrian, CBE 1964; MA Oxon; FSA; Keeper, Department of Ethnography, British Museum, 1953-69; excavated Maya site of Las Cuevas, British Honduras, 1957; *b* 13 June 1909; *s* of late William Pollard Digby, FInstP, MIME, MIEE; *m* 1939, Sylvia Mary, *d* of late Arnold Inman, OBE, KC; two *d*. *Educ:* Lancing; Brasenose Coll., Oxford. Entered British Museum as Asst Keeper, 1932. Hon. Asst Sec. of International Congress of Anthropological and Ethnological Sciences, London, 1934; Hon. Sec. of International Congress of Americanists, Cambridge, 1952. Served in Intelligence Division Naval Staff, Admiralty, 1942-44; Hydrographic Dept, Admiralty, 1944-45. Vis. Prof. in Archaeology, Univ. de Los Andes, Bogota, 1970. Pres. Sect. H of The British Association for the Advancement of Science, 1962; Vice-Pres. Royal Anthropological Inst., 1962-66. *Publications:* Ancient American Pottery (with G. H. S. Bushnell), 1955; Maya Jades, 1964; articles on anthropological subjects in Man and in Chambers's Encyclopædia. *Address:* The Paddocks, Eastcombe, Stroud, Glos GL6 7DR. *T:* Bisley (Glos) 409.

DIGBY, George F. Wingfield; retired Keeper Emeritus, Victoria and Albert Museum; *b* 2 March 1911; 2nd *s* of late Col F. J. B. Wingfield Digby, DSO; *m* 1935, Cornelia, *d* of Prof. H. Keitler, University of Vienna; one *s* (decd). *Educ:* Harrow; Trinity Coll., Cambridge; Grenoble Univ.; Sorbonne; Vienna. Asst Keeper, Dept of Textiles, Victoria and Albert Museum, 1934; seconded to Education Office, Jamaica (Jamaica Coll.), 1941-45; Asst Keeper (1st class), Victoria and Albert Museum, 1946; Keeper of Dept of Textiles, 1947-72; retired 1973. *Publications:* The Work of the Modern Potter in England, 1952; Meaning and Symbol in Three Modern Artists, 1955; Symbol and Image in William Blake, 1957; (jtly) History of the West Indian Peoples (4 vols for schools); (part author) The Bayeux Tapestry, 1957; (contributor) Brussels Colloque International: La Tapisserie flamande au XVII-XVIII siècle, 1959; (contributor) Colston Research Soc. Papers: Metaphor and Symbol, 1960; Elizabethan Embroidery, 1963; The Devonshire Hunting Tapestries, 1971; Tapestries, Mediaeval and Renaissance, 1980; (trans.) Islamic Carpets and Textiles in the Keir Collection, 1977. *Recreations:* oriental ceramics and contemporary hand-made pottery. *Address:* Raleigh Lodge, Castleton, Sherborne, Dorset.
See also S. W. Digby.

DIGBY, Very Rev. Richard Shuttleworth Wingfield, MA; Dean of Peterborough, 1966-80, Dean Emeritus since 1980; *b* 19 Aug. 1911; *s* of late Everard George Wingfield Digby and Dorothy (*née* Loughnan); *m* 1936, Rosamond Frances, *d* of late Col W. T. Digby, RE; two *s* one *d*. *Educ:* Nautical Coll., Pangbourne; Royal Navy; Christ's Coll., Cambridge; Westcott House, Cambridge. BA 1935; MA 1939. Asst Curate of St Andrew's, Rugby, 1936-46. Chaplain to the Forces (4th Cl. Emergency Commn), 1940-45; POW, 1940-45. Vicar of All Saints, Newmarket, 1946-53; Rector of Bury, Lancs, 1953-66; Rural Dean of Bury, 1962-66. Pres. and Chm., Bury Trustee Savings Bank, 1953-66; Dep. Chm., Trustee Savings Bank Assoc., North-West Area, 1965-66. Hon. Canon of Manchester Cath., 1965; Hon. Chaplain to Regt XX, The Lancs Fusiliers, 1965. Chm. CofE Council for Places of Worship, 1976-81. *Recreations:* walking, golf. *Address:* Byways, Higher Holton, near Wincanton, Somerset. *T:* Wincanton 32137. *Club:* Army and Navy.

DIGBY, Simon Wingfield, TD 1946; DL; MA; *b* 1910; *s* of late Col F. J. B. Wingfield Digby, DSO; *m* 1936, Kathleen Elizabeth, *d* of late Hon. Mr Justice Courtney Kingstone, Toronto, Canada; one *s* one *d*. *Educ:* Harrow Sch.; Trinity Coll., Cambridge. Delegate to International Studies Conference, 1934. Prospective Conservative Candidate for West Dorset, Jan. 1937-June 1941; MP (U) West Dorset, 1941-Feb. 1974; a Conservative Whip, 1948-51. Barrister-at-law, Inner Temple; served in Army (TA), Aug. 1939-June 1945 in UK and NW Europe; Major, 1943. Civil Lord of the Admiralty, 1951-57. Mem. of Empire Parl. Delegn to East Africa, 1948 and Inter-Parliamentary Union Delegation to Chile, 1962. Pres., Wessex Young Conservatives, 1947-50; Chairman: Conservative Forestry Sub-Cttee, 1959-67; Shipping and Shipbuilding Cttee, 1964-74. Member: Coastal Pollution Select Cttee, 1966-68; Select Cttee on Procedure; Public Accounts Cttee. Delegate (C), Council of Europe Assembly and Assembly of WEU, 1968-74 (Leader, 1972-74). Pres., Soc. of Dorset Men. DL Dorset, 1953. Order of Leopold and Order of White Lion. Medal of Council of Europe Assembly. *Recreations:* fishing, bloodstock breeding. *Address:* Sherborne Castle, Sherborne, Dorset. *T:* Gillingham 62650; Coleshill House, Coleshill, near Birmingham. *Club:* Carlton.
See also G. F. W. Digby, Sir Rupert Hardy, Bt.

DIGBY, Ven. Stephen Basil W.; *see* Wingfield-Digby.

DIGGINES, Christopher Ewart, CMG 1974; HM Diplomatic Service, retired; British High Commissioner, Port of Spain, Trinidad and Tobago, 1973-77; British High Commissioner (non-resident), Grenada, 1974-77; *b* 2 July 1920; *s* of late Sir William Diggines; *m* 1946, Mary Walls; one *s* one *d. Educ:* Haileybury Coll.; Trinity Coll., Oxford. Army, 1940-46. Senior History Master, Birkenhead Sch., 1948-49; apptd to CRO, 1949; Office of the UK High Comr in India (Madras), 1952-56; Canadian National Defence Coll., 1958-59; UK Mission to UN (1st Sec.), 1959-62; British Deputy High Commissioner, Kingston, Jamaica, 1962-64; Foreign and Commonwealth Office (formerly Commonwealth Office), 1964-69; Counsellor (Commercial), Lusaka, 1969-73. *Address:* 115 Middle Street, Deal, Kent. *Clubs:* United Oxford & Cambridge University, Royal Commonwealth Society.

DIGNAN, Maj.-Gen. Albert Patrick, CB 1978; MBE 1952; FRCS, FRCSI; Director of Army Surgery and Consulting Surgeon to the Army, 1973-78; Hon. Consultant Surgeon, Royal Hospital, Chelsea, 1973-78; Hon. Consultant in Radiotherapy and Oncology, Westminster Hospital, 1974-78; *b* 25 July 1920; *s* of Joseph Dignan; *m* 1952, Eileen White; two *s* one *d. Educ:* Trinity Coll., Dublin (Med. Schol.). MB, BCh, BAO, BA 1943, MA, MD 1968, FRCSI 1947, FRCS 1976. Prof. of Physiol. Prize, TCD. Posts in Dublin, Belfast and Wigan; subseq. NS Sen. Specialist in Surgery, Major RAMC Malaya; Sen. Registrar in Surgery, Bristol Royal Infirmary and Wanstead Hosp., Sen. Specialist in Surgery, BAOR Mil. Hosps and Consultant Surg., Brit. Mil. Hosps Singapore and Tidworth, 1953-68; Brig., and Consulting Surg., Farelf, 1969-70; Consultant Surg., Mil. Hosp. Tidworth, 1971-72; Consultant Surgeon, Queen Alexandra Mil. Hosp. Millbank, 1972-73; Consultant in Accident and Emergency, Ealing Dist, DHSS, 1978-79. Fellow, Association of Surgeons of GB and Ireland. QHS, 1974-78. *Publications:* papers in Brit. Jl Surgery, BMJ, Jl of RAMC, Postgrad. Med. Jl, Univ. Singapore Med. Soc. Med. Gazette. *Recreations:* gardening, golf. *Address:* 37 Queens Road, Beckenham, Kent BR3 4JJ.

DIKE, Prof. Kenneth Onwuka, MA, PhD; Andrew W. Mellon Professor of African History, Harvard University, since 1973; *b* 17 Dec. 1917; *s* of late Nzekwe Dike, merchant; *m* 1953, Ona Patricia, *d* of R. R. Olisa, MBE; two *s* three *d* (and one *d* decd). *Educ:* Dennis Memorial Grammar Sch., Onitsha; Achimota Coll., Ghana; Fourah Bay Coll., Sierra Leone; Univ. of Durham (BA); Univ. of Aberdeen (MA); London Univ. (PhD). Appointed Lectr in History, UC, Ibadan, 1950-52; Sen. Res. Fellow, W African Inst. of Social and Economic Res., 1952-54; University Coll., Ibadan: Sen. Lectr, Dept of History, 1954-56; Prof. of History, 1956-60; Vice-Principal, 1958-60; University of Ibadan: Vice-Chancellor, 1960-67; Dir, Inst. of African Studies, 1962-67; Chm., Planning Cttee, Univ. of Port Harcourt, 1967-71; Prof. of History, Harvard Univ., 1971-73. Founder and Dir. Nat. Archives of Nigeria, 1951-64; Chm. Nigerian Antiquities Commn, 1954-67; Pres., Historical Soc. of Nigeria, 1955-67; Chm., Assoc. of Commonwealth Univs, 1965-66. Chm., Commn for Review of Educational System in Eastern Region; Mem., Ashby Commn on Higher Educn in Nigeria; Chm. Organising Cttee, Internat. Congress of Africanists. FKC 1962. FRHistS 1956; Fellow Amer. Acad. of Arts and Scis, 1972. Hon. LLD: Aberdeen, 1961; Northwestern, 1962; Leeds, 1963; London, 1963; Columbia, 1965; Princeton, 1965; Michigan, 1979; Hon. DLitt: Boston, Mass, 1962; Birmingham, 1964; Ahmadu Bello, 1965; Ibadan; Ghana, 1979; Hon. DSc Moscow, 1963. *Publications:* Report on the Preservation and Administration of Historical Records in Nigeria, 1953; Trade and Politics in the Niger Delta 1830-1885, 1956; A Hundred Years of British Rule in Nigeria, 1957; The Origins of the Niger Mission, 1958; also articles in learned journals on Nigerian and West African history. *Address:* 275 Widener Library, Harvard University, Cambridge, Mass 02138, USA. *Clubs:* Royal Commonwealth Society; Metropolitan (Lagos, Nigeria); Odd Volumes (Boston, Mass).

DILHORNE, 2nd Viscount *cr* 1964, of Green's Norton; **John Mervyn Manningham-Buller;** Bt 1866; Baron 1962; Barrister-at-Law; *b* 28 Feb. 1932; *s* of 1st Viscount Dilhorne, PC, and of Lady Mary Lilian Lindsay, 4th *d* of 27th Earl of Crawford, KT, PC; *S* father, 1980; *m* 1955, Gillian Evelyn (marr. diss. 1973), *d* of Colonel George Stockwell; two *s* one *d* ; *m* 1981, Mrs Gilchrist. *Educ:* Eton; RMA Sandhurst. Called to the Bar, Inner Temple, 1979. Formerly Lieut, Coldstream Guards. Managing Director, Stewart Smith (LP&M) Ltd, 1970-74. Member, Wilts County Council, 1967-70. FTII (Mem. Council, 1967-). *Heir: s* Hon. James Edward Manningham-Buller, Lieut Welsh Guards [*b* 20 Aug. 1956. *Educ:* Harrow; Sandhurst]. *Address:* 58 Jubilee Place, SW3. *Clubs:* Pratt's, Buck's, MCC.

DILKE, Sir John Fisher Wentworth, 5th Bt *cr* 1862; *b* 1906; *e s* of Sir Fisher Wentworth Dilke, 4th Bt, and Ethel Clifford (*d* 1959); *S* father, 1944; *m* 1st, 1934, Sheila (marr. diss. 1949), *d* of late Sir William Seeds, KCMG; two *s* ; 2nd, 1951, Iris Evelyn, *d* of late Ernest Clark. *Educ:* Winchester; New Coll., Oxford. Foreign Office, 1929; Editorial Staff, The Times, 1936; rejoined Foreign Service, 1939 (economic warfare and shipping); Head of British official wireless news, 1942; political corresp., COI, 1946; BBC External Service, 1950. *Heir: s* Charles John Wentworth Dilke, *b* 1937. *Address:* Ludpits, Etchingham, Sussex.

DILKE, Mary Stella F.; *see* Fetherston-Dilke.

DILKS, Prof. David Neville, FRHistS; Professor of International History, University of Leeds, since 1970; *b* Coventry, 17 March 1938; *s* of Neville

Ernest Dilks and Phyllis Dilks; *m* 1963, Jill Medlicott; one *s. Educ:* Royal Grammar Sch., Worcester; Hertford Coll., Oxford (BA Modern Hist., Class II, 1959); St Antony's Coll., Oxford (Curzon Prizeman, 1960). Research Assistant to: Rt Hon. Sir Anthony Eden (later Earl of Avon), 1960-62; Marshal of the RAF Lord Tedder, 1963-65; Rt Hon. Harold Macmillan, 1964-67; Asst Lectr, then Lectr, in International History, LSE, 1962-70; Vis. Fellow, All Souls' Coll., Oxford, 1973; Chm., Sch. of History, Univ. of Leeds, 1974-79, Dean, Faculty of Arts, 1975-77. Chm., Commonwealth Youth Exchange Council, 1968-73; Mem., Adv. Council on Public Records, 1978-. Freeman of the Goldsmiths' Company, 1979. Hon. Sec., Edward Boyle Meml Trust, 1981-. Chm., Leeds Defence Studies Dining Club. Wrote and presented BBC TV series, The Loneliest Job, 1977. *Publications:* Curzon in India, Vol. I, 1969, Vol. II, 1970; (ed) The Diaries of Sir Alexander Cadogan, 1971; (contrib.) The Conservatives (ed Lord Butler of Saffron Walden), 1977; (ed and contrib.) Retreat from Power, vol. 1, 1906-1939, vol. 2, after 1939, 1981; (ed and contrib.) Britain and Canada (Commonwealth Foundn Paper), 1980; reviews and articles in English Historical Rev., Survey, History, Scandinavian Jl of History, etc. *Recreations:* ornithology, painting, railways, Bentley cars. *Address:* Wits End, Long Causeway, Leeds LS16 8EX. *T:* Leeds 673466. *Club:* Royal Commonwealth Society.

DILL, Sir (Nicholas) Bayard, Kt 1955; CBE 1951; Senior Partner, Conyers, Dill & Pearman, Barristers-at-Law, since 1948; *b* 28 Dec. 1905; *s* of Thomas Melville and Ruth Rapalje Dill; *m* 1930, Lucy Clare Dill; two *s. Educ:* Saltus Grammar Sch., Bermuda; Trinity Hall, Cambridge. Law Tripos Cantab, 1926. Mem. Colonial Parliament (for Devonshire Parish), 1938-68; Mem. HM Exec. Council, 1944-54; Chairman: Board of Trade, 1935-42, also Bd of Educn, 1940, and Board of Works, 1942-48, Bermuda; St David's Island Cttee, 1940-43; Public Works Planning Commn, 1942-49; Board of Civil Aviation, 1944-63; Bermuda Trade Development Bd, 1957-59; Mem., Legislative Council, Bermuda, 1968-73. Served as Capt., Bermuda Volunteer Engs, 1936-44. Chancellor of Diocese of Bermuda, 1950-. *Recreations:* sailing, golf. *Address:* Newbold Place, Devonshire, Bermuda. *T:* 2-4463. *Clubs:* Anglo-Belgian; Royal Thames Yacht; Royal Bermuda Yacht (Commodore, 1936-38), Mid-Ocean, Royal Hamilton Amateur Dinghy (Bermuda); India House, Canadian, Cruising of America (NYC).

DILLAMORE, Ian Leslie, PhD, DSc; CEng, FIM; Director of Technology, INCO Alloy Products Ltd, since 1982; *b* 22 Nov. 1938; *s* of Arthur Leslie Dillamore and Louise Mary Dillamore; *m* 1962, Maureen Birch; two *s. Educ:* Birmingham Univ. (BSc, MSc, PhD, DSc). ICI Research Fellow, Birmingham Univ., 1962-63, Lectr in Physical Metallurgy, 1963-69; Head of Phys. Metallurgy, BISRA, 1969-72; Head of Metals Technology Unit, British Steel Corp., 1972-76; Head of Metallurgy Dept, Aston Univ., 1976-81, Dean of Engineering, 1980-81; Director of Research and Development, INCO Europe, 1981-82. Hon. Professor of Metallurgy, Birmingham Univ., 1981-. Mem. Council: Metals Soc., 1980-; Instn of Metallurgists, 1981-; Mem. SRC Metallurgy Cttee, 1972-75, Materials Cttee, 1977-82; Chm., Processing Sub-Cttee, SRC, later SERC, 1979-82; Pres. Birmingham Metallurgical Assoc., 1980-81. Sir Robert Hadfield Medal and Prize, Metals Soc., 1976. *Publications:* numerous contribs to metallurgical and engrg jls. *Recreation:* industrial archaeology. *Address:* 65 Monmouth Drive, Sutton Coldfield B73 6JH. *T:* 021-355 5458.

DILLISTONE, Rev. Canon Frederick William, DD; Fellow and Chaplain, Oriel College, Oxford, 1964-70, Fellow Emeritus, 1970; Canon Emeritus of Liverpool Cathedral since 1964; *b* 9 May 1903; *s* of late Frederick Dillistone; *m* 1931, Enid Mary, *d* of late Rev. Cecil Francis Ayerst; two *s* one *d. Educ:* Brighton Coll.; BNC, Oxford (Scholar). BA 1924; BD 1933; DD 1951. Deacon, 1927; Priest, 1928; Vicar of St Andrew, Oxford, 1934-38; Prof. of Theology, Wycliffe Coll., Toronto, 1938-45; Prof. of Theology, Episcopal Theological Sch., Cambridge, Mass, 1947-52; Canon Residentiary and Chancellor of Liverpool Cathedral, 1952-56; Dean of Liverpool, 1956-63. Hulsean Preacher, Cambridge, 1953; Select Preacher, Oxford, 1953-55; Select Preacher, Cambridge, 1960; Stephenson Lectr, Univ. of Sheffield, 1966; Bampton Lectr, Univ. of Oxford, 1968; Vis. Fellow, Clare Hall, Cambridge, 1970; Zabriskie Lectr, Virginia Theol. Seminary, 1971. Asst Editor, Theology Today, 1951-61. Hon. DD: Knox Coll., Toronto, 1946; Episcopal Theological Sch., Cambridge, Mass, 1967; Virginia Theol Seminary, 1979. Chaplain OStJ, 1958. *Publications:* The Significance of the Cross, 1945; The Holy Spirit in the Life of To-day, 1946; Revelation and Evangelism, 1948; The Structure of the Divine Society, 1951; Jesus Christ and His Cross, 1953; Christianity and Symbolism, 1955; Christianity and Communication, 1956; The Novelist and the Passion Story, 1960; The Christian Faith, 1964; Dramas of Salvation, 1967; The Christian Understanding of Atonement, 1968; Modern Answers to Basic Questions, 1972; Traditional Symbols and the Contemporary World, 1972; Charles Raven: a biography, 1975; C. H. Dodd: a biography, 1977; Into all the World: a biography of Max Warren, 1980; Religious Experience and Christian Faith, 1982; Editor, Scripture and Tradition, 1955; Editor, Myth and Symbol, 1966; contributor to: The Doctrine of Justification by Faith, 1954; A Companion to the Study of St Augustine, 1955; Steps to Christian Understanding, 1958; The Ecumenical Era in Church and Society, 1959; Metaphor and Symbol, 1961; The Theology of the Christian Mission, 1961; Christianity and the Visual Arts, 1964; Mansions of the Spirit, 1966; Christianity in its Social Context, 1967; Studies in Christian History and Interpretation, 1967; Christ for us Today, 1968; Grounds of Hope, 1968; Man, Fallen and Free, 1969; Sociology, Theology and Conflict, 1969; Christ and Spirit in the New Testament, 1973; Religion and Art as Communication,

1974; Theolinguistics, 1981. *Recreation:* gardening. *Address:* 15 Cumnor Rise Road, Oxford OX2 9HD. *T:* Oxford 862071.

DILLON, family name of **Viscount Dillon.**

DILLON, 22nd Viscount *cr* 1622, of Castello Gallen, Co. Mayo, Ireland; **Henry Benedict Dillon;** Count in France, 1711; *b* 6 Jan. 1973; *s* of 21st Viscount Dillon and of Mary Jane, *d* of late John Young, Castle Hill House, Birtle, Lancs; *S* father, 1982. *Heir:* uncle Hon. Richard Arthur Louis Dillon [*b* 23 Oct. 1948; *m* 1975, Hon. Priscilla Frances Hazlerigg, *d* of 2nd Baron Hazlerigg, *qv*; one *d*]. *Address:* 83 Talfourd Road, SE15.

DILLON, Hon. Sir Brian; *see* Dillon, Hon. Sir G. B. H.

DILLON, C(larence) Douglas; Chairman, US & Foreign Securities Corporation; Managing Director, Dillon, Read & Co. Inc.; *b* Geneva, Switzerland, 21 Aug. 1909; *s* of Clarence Dillon; *m* 1931, Phyllis Ellsworth; two *d. Educ:* Groton Sch.; Harvard Univ. (AB). Mem., NY Stock Exchange, 1931-36; US and Foreign Securities Corporation and US and International Securities Corporation, 1937-53 (Dir, 1938-53; Pres., 1946-53); Dir, Dillon, Read & Co. Inc., 1938-53 (Chm. of Bd, 1946-53); American Ambassador to France, 1953-57; Under-Sec. of State for Economic Affairs, USA, 1957-59, Under-Sec. of State, USA, 1959-61; Sec. of the Treasury, USA, 1961-65. Served US Naval Reserve, 1941-45 (Lieut-Comdr; Air Medal, Legion of Merit). Dir, Council on Foreign Relations, 1965-78 (Vice-Chm. 1977-78); Pres., Board of Overseers, Harvard Coll., 1968-72; Chm., Rockefeller Foundn, 1971-75; Chm., Brookings Instn, 1971-75. Trustee, Metropolitan Museum of Art (President, 1970-77; Chm., 1977-). Hon. Dr of Laws: New York Univ., 1956; Lafayette Coll., 1957; Univ. of Hartford, Conn, 1958; Columbia Univ., 1959; Harvard Univ., 1959; Williams Coll., 1960; Rutgers Univ., 1961; Princeton Univ., 1961; University of Pennsylvania, 1962; Bradley Univ., 1964; Middlebury Coll., 1965. *Address:* Far Hills, New Jersey, USA.

DILLON, Rt. Hon. Sir (George) Brian (Hugh), Kt 1979; PC 1982; **Rt. Hon. Lord Justice Dillon;** a Lord Justice of Appeal, since 1982; *b* 2 Oct. 1925; *s* of late Captain George Crozier Dillon, RN; *m* 1954, Alisoun, *d* of late Hubert Samuel Lane, MC; two *s* two *d. Educ:* Winchester College; New College, Oxford. Called to the Bar, Lincoln's Inn, 1948; QC 1965; a Judge of the High Court of Justice, Chancery Division, 1979-82. *Address:* Royal Courts of Justice, WC2; Bridge Farm House, Grundisburgh, Woodbridge, Suffolk.

DILLON, Sir John (Vincent), Kt 1980; CMG 1974; Ombudsman for Victoria (Commissioner for Administrative Investigations), 1973-80; *b* 6 Aug. 1908; *s* of Roger Dillon and Ellen (*née* Egan); *m* 1935, Sheila Lorraine D'Arcy; three *s* one *d. Educ:* Christian Brothers Coll., Melbourne. AASA: Mem. Public Service Bd, 1941-54; Stipendiary Magistrate City Court, 1947-61; Chm., Medical Salaries Cttee, 1959-62; Under-Sec., Chief Sec.'s Dept, Vic, 1961-73; Chm., Racecourses Licences Bd, 1961-73. *Recreations:* racing, golf, reading. *Address:* 25 Kelvin Grove, Armadale, Vic 3143, Australia. *Clubs:* Athenæum, Green Room, Victoria Racing, Victoria Amateur Turf, Moonee Valley Racing, Melbourne Cricket, Metropolitan Golf (Melbourne).

DILLON, Sir Max, Kt 1979; *b* 30 June 1913; *s* of Cyril and Phoebe Dillon; *m* 1940, Estelle Mary Jones; one *s* one *d. Educ:* Wesley Coll., Melbourne; Melbourne Univ. (Faculty of Commerce). AASA (Sen.); ACIS; FAIM. General Manager, Cable Makers Australia Pty Ltd, 1957-70; Dep. Man. Dir, Metal Manufactures Ltd Gp, 1970-75. President: Aust. Council of Employer Fedns, 1967-69; Associated Chambers of Manufactures, 1974-77; Confedn of Aust. Industry, 1977-80; Chairman: Nat. Employers Policy Cttee, 1971-73 and 1975-78; Central Industrial Secretariat Council, 1972-77; Productivity Promotion Council, 1971-74; Member: Nat. Labour Adv. Council, 1966-72; Nat. Labour Consultative Council, 1977-80; Exec. Cttee, Aust. Manufacturing Council, 1978-80. *Recreations:* golf, swimming. *Address:* 33 Church Street, Pymble, NSW 2073, Australia. *T:* 44 3160. *Clubs:* Australian, Elanora Country (Sydney).

DILLON, Sir Robert William Charlier, 8th Bt *cr* 1801; Baron of the Holy Roman Empire, 1782; *b* 17 Jan. 1914; *s* of Robert Arthur Dillon (*d* 1925) and Laura Maud (*d* 1915), widow of J. Lachlin McCliver, New Zealand; *S* kinsman, 1925; *m* 1947, Synolda, *d* of late Cholmondeley Butler Clarke and of Mrs Cholmondeley-Clarke, late of Holywell, Co. Tipperary. *Heir:* none. *Address:* Overdene, Wentworth Place, Co. Wicklow, Ireland.

DILLON, Thomas Michael, QC 1973; a Recorder of the Crown Court since 1972; *b* 29 Nov. 1927; *yr s* of Thomas Bernard Joseph Dillon, Birmingham, and Ada Gladys Dillon (*née* Noyes); *m* 1956, Wendy Elizabeth Marshall Hurrell; two *s* one *d. Educ:* King Edward's Sch., Aston, Birmingham; Birmingham Univ. (LLB); Lincoln Coll., Oxford (BCL). Called to Bar, Middle Temple, 1952, Master of the Bench 1981. 2nd Lieut, RASC, 1953-54. In practice as barrister, 1954-; Part-time Chm. of Industrial Tribunals, 1968-74. *Recreations:* reading, listening to music. *Address:* 1 Fountain Court, Birmingham B4 6DR. *T:* 021-236 5721; 2 Dr Johnson's Buildings, Temple, EC4Y 7AH. *T:* 01-353 5371.

DILLWYN-VENABLES-LLEWELYN, Sir John Michael; *see* Venables-Llewelyn.

DILNOT, Mary, (Mrs Thomas Ruffle), OBE 1982; Director, IPC Women's Magazines Group, 1976-81; Editor, Woman's Weekly, 1971-81; *b* 23 Jan. 1921; 2nd *d* of George Dilnot, author, and Ethel Dilnot; *m* 1974, Thomas Ruffle. *Educ:* St Mary's Coll., Hampton. Joined Woman's Weekly, 1939. *Recreations:* home interests, reading, travel. *Address:* 28 Manor Road South, Hinchley Wood, Surrey.

DIMBLEBY, David; freelance broadcaster and newspaper proprietor; Managing Director: Dimbleby & Sons Ltd, since 1966; Wandsworth Borough News Ltd, since 1979; *b* 28 Oct. 1938; *e s* of (Frederick) Richard and Dilys Dimbleby; *m* 1967, Josceline Rose, *d* of Thomas Gaskell; one *s* two *d. Educ:* Glengorse Sch.; Charterhouse; Christ Church, Oxford (MA); Univs of Paris and Perugia. News Reporter, BBC Bristol, 1960-61; Presenter and Interviewer on network programmes on: religion (Quest), science for children (What's New?), politics (In My Opinion), Top of the Form, etc, 1961-63; Reporter, BBC2 (Enquiry), and Dir films, incl.: Ku-Klux-Klan, The Forgotten Million, Cyprus: Thin Blue Line, 1964-65; worked as asst to his father in family newspaper business at Richmond, Surrey, 1965, being apptd Managing Dir, 1966, on his father's death. Special Correspondent CBS News, New York; documentary film (Texas-England) and film reports for '60 minutes', 1966-; Reporter, BBC1 (Panorama), 1967-69; Commentator, Current Events, incl. President Nixon's visit to Britain, 1969; Presenter, BBC1 (24 Hours), 1969-72; various commentaries and films incl. Yesterday's Men, 1971; Chairman, The Dimbleby Talk-In, 1971-74; films for Reporter at Large, 1973; Presenter: BBC 1 (Panorama), 1974-77 1980-82, (Nationwide), 1982-; Election Campaign Report, 1974; BBC Election and Results programmes, 1979; film series, The White Tribe of Africa, 1979 (Royal TV Soc. Supreme Documentary Award). *Address:* 14 King Street, Richmond, Surrey TW9 1NF.

See also J. Dimbleby.

DIMBLEBY, Jonathan; freelance broadcaster, journalist; *b* 31 July 1944; *s* of Richard and Dilys Dimbleby; *m* 1968, Bel Mooney; one *s* one *d. Educ:* University Coll. London (BA Hons Philosophy). TV and Radio Reporter, BBC Bristol, 1969-70; BBC Radio, World at One, 1970-71; Thames TV, This Week, 1972-78; TV Eye, 1979; Jonathan Dimbleby in South America; series, Jonathan Dimbleby in Evidence, Yorkshire TV, 1979-. Society of Film and Television Arts Richard Dimbleby Award, for most outstanding contribution to factual TV, 1974. *Publications:* Richard Dimbleby, 1975; The Palestinians, 1979; contribs to New Statesman and other newspapers and magazines. *Recreations:* music, sailing, walking, postponing departures by air. *Address:* c/o David Higham Associates Ltd, 5 Lower John Street, W1.

See also D. Dimbleby.

DIMECHKIE, Nadim, GCVO (Hon.) 1978; Ambassador of Lebanon at large, and Senior Adviser on foreign affairs to the Foreign Secretary, Beirut, since 1979; *b* Lebanon, 5 Dec. 1919; *s* of Badr and Julia Dimechkie; *m* 1946, Margaret Alma Sherlock; two *s. Educ:* American Univ. of Beirut (BA, MA Economics). Deleg., Jt Supply Bd for Syria and Lebanon, 1942-44; Dir Gen., Min. of Nat. Economy, 1943-44; Counsellor, Lebanese Embassy, London, 1944-49; Consul-Gen., Ottawa, 1950; Dir, Economic and Social Dept, Min. of Foreign Affairs, 1951-52; Chargé d'Affaires, Cairo, 1952; Minister, 1953-55; Minister, Switzerland, 1955-57; Ambassador to USA, 1958-62; Dir, Economic Affairs, Min. of Foreign Affairs, 1962-66; Ambassador to UK, 1966-78, and Doyen of the Diplomatic Corps, 1977-78. Lebanese Order of Cedars, UAR Order of Ismail and Order of Merit; Syrian Order of Merit; Tunisian Order of Merit; Greek Order of Phoenix. *Address:* Ministry of Foreign Affairs, Beirut, Lebanon. *Clubs:* White's, Travellers', Hurlingham, Royal Automobile; Metropolitan, Chevy Chase (Washington); Golf, Aero (Beirut).

DIMMOCK, Peter, CVO 1968; OBE 1961; Vice-President, American Broadcasting Company Worldwide Syndication and Marketing TV Sports, and Managing Director, ABC Sports Worldwide Enterprises Ltd, since 1978; *b* 6 Dec. 1920; *e s* of late Frederick Dimmock, OBE, and of Paula Dimmock (*née* Hudd); *m* 1960, Mary Freya (Polly), *e d* of late Sir Richard Elwes, OBE, TD; three *d. Educ:* Dulwich Coll.; France. TA; RAF pilot, instr, and Air Ministry Staff Officer, 1939-45. After demobilisation became Press Association correspondent; joined BBC as Television Outside Broadcasts Producer and commentator, 1946; produced both studio and outside broadcasts, ranging from documentaries to sporting, theatrical and public events; has produced or commentated on more than 500 television relays, including Olympic Games 1948, Boat Race 1949, first international television relay, from Calais, 1950, King George VI's Funeral, Windsor, 1952. Produced and directed television outside broadcast of the Coronation Service from Westminster Abbey, 1953; first TV State Opening of Parliament, 1958; first TV Grand National, 1960; TV for Princess Margaret's Wedding, 1960. Created BBC Sportsview Unit and introduced new television programme Sportsview, 1954, regular host of this weekly network programme, 1954-64; Gen. Manager and Head of Outside Broadcasts, BBC TV, 1954-72; responsible for Liaison between BBC and Royal Family, 1963-77; Gen. Manager, BBC Enterprises, 1972-77. Sports Adviser, European Broadcasting Union, 1959-72. Mem., Greater London and SE Sports Council, 1972-77; Chm., Sports Develt Panel, 1976-77. *Publications:* Sportsview Annuals, 1954-65; Sports in View, 1964. Fellow, Royal Television Soc., 1978. *Recreations:* flying, gliding, winter sports, golf. *Address:* Le Mirabeau, 2 avenue des Citronniers, Monte Carlo, Monaco. *T:* (93) 50-62-18. *Clubs:*

Garrick, Turf, Hurlingham, National Liberal; Royal Mid-Surrey; New York Athletic.

DIMSON, Gladys Felicia, (Mrs S. B. Dimson), CBE 1976; Member of GLC for Battersea North, since 1973; Member, Inner London Education Authority, since 1970; *o d* of late I. Sieve, BA; *m* 1936, Dr S. B. Dimson, *e s* of late Rev. Z. Dimson; one *d*. *Educ*: Laurel Bank Sch., Glasgow; Glasgow Univ.; London Sch. of Economics. Voluntary social worker, mainly in E London, 1950-63; Co-opted Mem., Children's Cttee, LCC, 1958-65; Chm., gp of LCC Children's Homes and of a voluntary Hostel for Girls; Educn Counsellor, Marriage Guidance Council. Member: Home Office Advisory Cttee on Juvenile Delinquency, 1963-65 (Chm. Sub-Cttee on Transition from Sch. to Work); a Youth Employment Cttee, 1960-; Hendon Gp Hosp. Management Cttee, 1965-70; Exec., Greater London Labour Party, 1964-74; Toynbee Housing Soc., 1967- (Chm., 1976-); Bd of Governors, Nat. Hosp. for Nervous Diseases, 1976-79; Board of Management, Shelter, 1976- (Trustee, Shelter Housing Aid Centre); London Local Adv. Cttee, IBA, 1979-; Chm., East London Housing Assoc., 1979-. Mem., GLC Haringey, 1964-67, Wandsworth, 1970-73; (Vice-Chm.) GLC Ambulance Cttee; GLC Housing Cttee: Mem. (co-opted), 1968-70; Labour Spokesman, 1970-73, and 1977-81; Chm., 1973-75, 1981-82. Contested (Lab) Hendon South, at Gen. Election, 1970. Mem., Nat. and London Councils of Nat. Fedn of Housing Assocs, 1980-. FRSA 1977. *Recreations*: walking in the country, lazing in the sun; reading (incl. thrillers); theatre; watching TV. *Address*: 34 Sheldon Avenue, Highgate, N6 4JR.

DINEEN, Ven. Frederick George K.; see Kerr-Dineen.

DINEVOR; see Dynevor.

DINGLE, John Thomas, PhD, DSc; Director, Strangeways Research Laboratory, Cambridge, since 1979; Fellow of Corpus Christi College, Cambridge, since 1968; *b* 27 Oct. 1927; *s* of Thomas Henry and Violet Nora Dingle; *m* 1953, Dorothy Vernon Parsons; two *s*. *Educ*: King Edward Sch., Bath; London Univ. (BSc, DSc); Clare Coll., Cambridge (PhD). Royal National Hosp. for Rheumatic Diseases, Bath, 1951-59; Research Fellowship, Strangeways Research Laboratory, Cambridge, 1959-61; MRC External Staff, 1961-79; Head of Tissue Physiology Dept, Strangeways Research Laboratory, 1966, Dep. Dir of the Laboratory, 1970-79. Bursar of Leckhampton, 1972-80, Warden, 1980-. Visiting Professor: of Biochemistry, Royal Free Hosp. Med. Sch., 1975-78; of Rheumatology, New York Univ., 1977; of Pathology, Adelaide Univ. Med. Sch., Aust., 1981. Chm., British Connective Tissue Soc., 1980-; Chm. Editorial Bd, Biochemical Jl, 1975-. Trustee, Cambridge Univ. RFC, 1977-. Heberden Orator and Medalist, 1978; American Orthopaedic Assoc. Steindler Award, 1980. *Publications*: communications to learned jls. *Recreations*: Rugby football (playing member, Bath, Bristol, Somerset RFCs, 1943-57), sailing, golf. *Address*: Corpus Christi College, Cambridge. *T*: Cambridge 59418. *Clubs*: Hawks, Gog-Magog Golf (Cambridge); Royal Dart Yacht.

DINGLE, Prof. Robert Balson, PhD; FRSE; Professor of Theoretical Physics, University of St Andrews, since 1960; *b* 26 March 1926; *s* of late Edward Douglas Dingle and Nora Gertrude Balson; *m* 1958, Helen Glenronnie Munro; two *d*. *Educ*: Bournemouth Secondary Sch.; Cambridge University. PhD 1951. Fellow of St John's Coll., Cambridge, 1948-52; Theoretician to Royal Society Mond. Lab., 1951-52; Chief Asst in Theoretical Physics, Technical Univ. of Delft, Holland, 1952-53; Fellow, Nat. Research Council, Ottawa, 1953-54; Reader in Theoretical Physics, Univ. of WA, 1954-60. *Publications*: Asymptotic Expansions: their derivation and interpretation, 1973; contribs to learned journals. *Recreations*: music, local history, gastronomy. *Address*: 6 Lawhead Road East, St Andrews, Fife, Scotland. *T*: St Andrews 74287.

DINGWALL, Baroness; see Lucas of Crudwell and Dingwall.

DINGWALL, Eric John, MA, DSc (London), PhD (London, Faculty of Science); anthropologist; Hon. Assistant Keeper, The British Library (Reference Division); Hon. Vice-President, Magic Circle; *s* of Alexander Harvey Dingwall, Ceylon. *Educ*: privately; Pembroke Coll., Cambridge. Formerly on staff, Cambridge Univ. Library; Dir, Dept of Physical Phenomena, American Soc. for Psychical Research, New York, 1921; Research Officer, Soc. for Psychical Research, 1922-27, investigating many American and European mediums in New York, Boston, Paris, Copenhagen, Warsaw, Munich, Gratz, etc, publishing results in Proc. and Jl of the SPR; toured Spain, 1935; went to the West Indies, 1936, to study special social and religious conditions in Trinidad and Haiti with reference to abnormal mental phenomena; went to Poland, S America, W Indies, and USA, 1937. Attached to Ministry of Information and to a Dept, Foreign Office, 1941-45. *Publications*: Joint Editor, Revelations of a Spirit Medium, 1922; Studies in the Sexual Life of Ancient and Mediæval Peoples, I, Male Infibulation, 1925; How to Go to a Medium, 1927; Ghosts and Spirits in the Ancient World, 1930; The Girdle of Chastity, 1931; Artificial Cranial Deformation, 1931; How to Use a Large Library, 1933; Editor of English edn of Woman (Ploss-Bartels), 1935; Racial Pride and Prejudice, 1946; Some Human Oddities, 1947; Very Peculiar People, 1950; (with K. M. Goldney and T. H. Hall) The Haunting of Borley Rectory, 1956; (with J. Langdon-Davies) The Unknown-is it nearer?, 1956; The American Woman, 1956; (with T. H. Hall) Four Modern Ghosts, 1958; The Critics' Dilemma, 1966; Editor of and

contributor to: Abnormal Hypnotic Phenomena, 1967-68; contributions to English and foreign publications. *Recreation*: studying rare and queer customs. *Address*: 171 Marine Court, St Leonards-on-Sea, East Sussex. *Club*: National Liberal.

DINGWALL, John James, OBE 1964; HM Inspector of Constabulary for Scotland, 1966-70; *b* 2 Sept. 1907; *s* of late James Dingwall, Bannockburn, Stirling; *m* 1932, Jane Anne (*d* 1980), *d* of late James K. Halliday, Falkirk; two *d*. *Educ*: Bridge of Allan and Stirling. Stirlingshire Constabulary 1927-49; Stirling and Clackmannan Police Force, 1949-55; seconded to Directing Staff, Scottish Police Coll., 1953-55; Chief Constable of Angus 1955-66. *Recreations*: angling, shooting, golf. *Address*: 56 Carlogie Road Carnoustie, Angus.

DINGWALL, Walter Spender, MA; Secretary Chichester Diocesan Fund 1946-61, retired; *b* 14 Dec. 1900; *s* of late Rev. Walter Molyneux Dingwall and Sophia Spender; *m* 1932, Olive Mary Loasby; no *c*. *Educ*: Marlborough Coll.; Christ Church, Oxford. Sixth Form Master at St Edward's Sch. Oxford, 1923-37; nine years Bursar of the Sch., ten years Housemaster Headmaster, Hurstpierpoint Coll., Sussex, 1937-45; Hon. Sec. and Treasurer Public Schools Bursars' Assoc., 1931-38. *Address*: The White House Woodmancote, near Henfield, West Sussex BN5 9ST.

DINGWALL-SMITH, Ronald Alfred, CB 1977; *b* 24 Feb. 1917; *m* 1946; one *s* one *d*. *Educ*: Alleyn's Sch., Dulwich; London School of Economics (evening classes). Entered Civil Service as Clerical Officer, Ministry of Transport, 1934 Exchequer and Audit Dept, 1945-47; Scottish Educn Dept, 1947-65; Scottish Development Dept, 1965-70; Under-Sec. (Principal Finance Officer), Scottish Office, 1970-78. Sen. Res. Fellow, Glasgow Univ., 1979-81. Dir, St Vincent Drilling Ltd, 1979-80. Member: Management Cttee, Hanover (Scotland) Housing Assoc., 1979-; Commn for Local Auth. Accts in Scotland, 1980- Governor, Moray Hse Coll. of Educn, Edinburgh, 1980-. *Recreations*: golf bowls, gardening. *Address*: 3 Frogston Terrace, Edinburgh EH10 7AD. *T* 031-445 2727. *Club*: Royal Commonwealth Society.

DINKEL, Ernest Michael, RWS 1957; ARCA 1924; ARWA 1979; FGGE 1981; painter, glass engraver and sculptor; Head of The School of Design Edinburgh College of Art, 1947-60, retired; *b* 24 Oct. 1894; *s* of Charles and Lucy Dinkel; *m* 1st, 1929, Kathleen Hanks (*d* 1936); 2nd, 1941, Emmy Keet, ARCA, ARWA; two *s* two *d* (and one *s* decd). *Educ*: Huddersfield Sch. of Art; War Service abroad, 1916-19, on the Somme (general and war service medals). Royal Coll. of Art, 1921-25, Student. RIBA Owen Jones Scholarship, 1926. Asst to Prof. Robert Anning Bell and Prof. Tristram, at Royal Coll. of Art, 1925-40; Head of Stourbridge Sch. of Art, 1940-47 Exhibitor: Royal Academy, Royal Scottish Academy, Royal Society of Painters in Water Colours, Royal West Acad. and private exhibns; designer Royal Hunt Cup and Topham Trophy; work in Tate Gallery, Laing Art Gall. Newcastle upon Tyne, Dudley Art Gall. *Recreations*: pottery; wide interest in art subjects and music. *Address*: The Grange, Bussage, near Stroud, Glos *T*: Brimscombe 882368.

DINSDALE, Richard Lewis; Chairman, West of England Newspapers Ltd 1969-72; *b* 23 June 1907; *m* 1930, Irene Laverack; one *d*. *Educ*: Hull Technical Coll. Joined Hull Daily Mail as reporter, 1926; Editorial posts: Newcastle Evening World; Chief Sub-editor, Manchester Evening News; Dep. Chief Sub-editor, Daily Express, Manchester; Evening News, London; Daily Mirror, 1940-42; War Service, 1942-46; Copy-taster, Daily Mirror, 1946 successively Chief Sub-editor, Dep. Night Editor, Night Editor; Dep. Editor 1955; seconded Daily Herald as Editorial Adviser, 1961; Dep. Editor, Daily Herald, 1962; Dep. Editor, The Sun, 1964, Editor, 1965-69. *Recreations*: sea fishing, golf.

DINWIDDY, Thomas Lutwyche; Master of the Supreme Court (Chancery Division), 1958-73; *b* 27 Aug. 1905; *o c* of late Harry Lutwyche Dinwiddy Solicitor, and late Ethel Maude (*née* McArthur); *m* 1935, Ruth, *d* of late Charles Ernest Rowland Abbott, Barrister-at-Law and Bencher of Lincoln's Inn; three *s*. *Educ*: Winchester; New Coll., Oxford (BA). Solicitor, Dec. 1930 Partner in Frere Cholmeley & Co., 28 Lincoln's Inn Fields, WC2, 1933-57 Council of Law Soc., 1953-57. Served RA (TA), 1939-45; Staff Coll. Camberley, 1943; demobilised as Major. *Recreations*: golf, watching cricket motoring, gardening. *Address*: Northolme, 48 Saxmundham Road Aldeburgh, Suffolk.

DIONISOTTI-CASALONE, Carlo, FBA 1972; Professor of Italian, Bedford College (formerly Bedford College for Women), University of London 1949-70; *b* 9 June 1908; *s* of Eugenio Dionisotti-Casalone and Carla Cataneo; *m* 1942, Maria Luisa Pinna-Pintor; three *d* (and one *d* decd). *Educ*: Turin Italy. Dottore in lettere, Univ. of Turin, 1929; Libero Docente di Letteratur Italiana, Univ. of Turin, 1937; Asst di Letteratura Italiana, Univ. of Rome 1943; Italian Lectr, Univ. of Oxford, 1947; MA Oxon, 1947. *Publications* Indici del giornale storico della letteratura italiana (Turin), 1945; Guidiccioni orazione ai nobili di Lucca (Rome), 1946; Bembo-Savorgnan, Carteggio d'amore (Florence), 1950; Oxford Book of Italian Verse (revised edn), 1952 Bembo, Prose e Rime (Turin), 1960; Geografia e storia della letter. italiana (Turin), 1967; Gli Umanisti e il Volgare (Florence), 1968; Machiavellerie (Turin), 1980. *Address*: 44 West Heath Drive, NW11.

DI PALMA, Vera June, (Mrs Ernest Jones), FCCA, FTII; Director, Mobile Training & Exhibitions Ltd, since 1977; *b* 14 July 1931; *d* of late William Di Palma and of Violet Di Palma; *m* 1972, Ernest Jones. *Educ:* Haverstock Central Sch., London. Accountant in public practice, 1947-64; Taxation Accountant, Dunlop Co., 1964-67; Sen. Lectr in Taxation, City of London Polytechnic, 1967-71; taxation consultant, 1971-80. Pres., Assoc. of Certified Accountants, 1980-81 (Dep. Pres., 1979-80); Public Works Loan Comr, 1978-; Member: VAT Tribunals, 1977-; Air Travel Reserve Fund Agency, 1975-. *Publications:* Capital Gains Tax, 1972, 5th edn 1981; Your Fringe Benefits, 1978. *Recreations:* dog-walking, golf, tennis, gardening. *Address:* Temple Close, Sibford Gower, Banbury, Oxon OX15 5RX.

DIPLOCK, Baron (Life Peer) *cr* 1968, of Wansford; **(William John) Kenneth Diplock,** PC 1961; Kt 1956; a Lord of Appeal in Ordinary since 1968; *b* 8 Dec. 1907; *s* of W. J. Hubert Diplock, Croydon; *m* 1938, Margaret Sarah, *d* of George Atcheson, Londonderry. *Educ:* Whitgift; University Coll., Oxford. Barrister, Middle Temple, 1932, Bencher, 1956, Dep. Treas., 1973, Treas., 1974. Sec. to Master of the Rolls, 1939-48. Served War of 1939-45, RAF, 1941-45. KC 1948; Recorder of Oxford, Dec. 1951-Jan. 1956. Judge of High Court of Justice, Queen's Bench Div., 1956-61; a Lord Justice of Appeal, 1961-68. Judge of Restrictive Practices Court, 1960-61 (Pres., 1961). Mem., Lord Chancellor's Law Reform Cttee, 1952-69. Hon. Fellow of University Coll., Oxford, 1958. Pres., Nat. Assoc. of Parish Councils, 1962-66; Vice-Pres., Brit. Maritime Law Assoc., 1964, Pres., 1975-77; Chm., Inst. of Advanced Legal Studies, 1973-77. Chairman: Permanent Security Commn, 1971-82; Advisory Bd (Comparative Law), Brit. Inst. of Internat. and Comparative Law, 1959-67; Council of Legal Education, 1969-70 (Chm., Bd of Studies, 1963-69); Law Advisory Cttee, Brit. Council, 1966-80; Dep. Chm., Boundary Commn for England, 1958-61. Hon. Pres., Assoc. of Law Teachers, 1971-75; Pres., Inst. of Arbitrators, 1977-80. Hon. Fellow, American Bar Foundation, 1969. Hon. LLD: Alberta, 1972; London, 1979; Hon. DCL Oxon, 1977. *Address:* 1 Crown Office Row, Temple, EC4. *Club:* Athenæum.

DIRAC, Prof. Paul Adrien Maurice, OM 1973; FRS 1930; BSc Bristol, PhD Cantab; Lucasian Professor of Mathematics, Cambridge, 1932-69, now Professor Emeritus; Fellow of St John's College, Cambridge; Professor of Physics, Florida State University, since 1971; *b* 8 Aug. 1902; *m* 1937, Margit Wigner, Budapest. Mem. Pontifical Academy of Sciences, 1961. Nobel Prize in Physics for 1933; Royal Medal of Royal Society, 1939; Copley Medal of Royal Society, 1952. *Publications:* Principles of Quantum Mechanics, 1930; General Theory of Relativity, 1975; papers on quantum theory. *Address:* Department of Physics, Florida State University, Tallahassee, Florida 32306, USA; St John's College, Cambridge.

DISBREY, Air Vice-Marshal William Daniel, CB 1967; CBE 1945 (OBE 1943); AFC 1939; *b* London, 23 Aug. 1912; *s* of Horace William Disbrey; *m* 1939, Doreen Alice, *d* of William Henry Ivory, Stevenage; two *d. Educ:* Minchenden Sch. Joined RAF as an Apprentice, 1928; gained Cadetship to RAF Coll., Cranwell, 1931; No 3 Fighter Sqdn, 1933-34; Fleet Air Arm, 1934-37; Engr Specialist Course, Henlow, 1937-39; Engr Officer, No 13 Group HQ, 1940-41; Engr Officer, HQ Fighter Comd, 1941-43; Chief Engr Officer, 2nd TAF, 1943-46; Staff Coll. Course, 1946; CO, No 12 Sch. of Technical Training, Melksham, 1946-48; Sen. Technical Officer, Royal Indian Air Force, 1948-51; Min. of Supply, 1951-54; Chief Engr Officer, Bomber Comd, 1954-57; Imperial Defence Coll., 1957; Dir of Research and Development, Bombers, Min. of Aviation, 1958-61; Comdt, No 1 Radio Sch., Locking, 1961-64; Dir-Gen. of Engineering (RAF), 1964-67; AO Engineering, Bomber Comd, 1967, Strike Comd, 1968-70, retired. Manager, Tech. Trng Inst., Airwork Services, Saudi Arabia, 1970. CEng; FIMechE; FRAeS. *Recreations:* golf, sailing. *Address:* Old Heatherwode, Buxted, East Sussex. *T:* Buxted 2104. *Club:* Royal Air Force.

DISLEY, John Ivor, CBE 1979; Director: Fleetfoot Ltd; London Marathon Ltd; Silva UK Ltd; Silva Compasses Ltd; *b* Gwynedd, 20 Nov. 1928; *s* of Harold Disley and Marie Hughes; *m* 1957, Sylvia Cheeseman; two *d. Educ:* Oswestry High Sch.; Loughborough Coll. (Hon. DCL). Schoolmaster, Isleworth, 1951; Chief Instructor, CCPR Nat. Mountaineering Centre, 1955; Gen. Inspector of Educn, Surrey, 1958; Dir, Ski Plan, 1971. Member: Adv. Sports Council, 1964-71; Mountain Leadership Trng Bd, 1965-; Canal Adv. Bd, 1965-66; Internat. Orienteering Fedn, 1972-; Countryside Commn, 1974-77; Water Space Adv. Council, 1976-; Royal Commn on Gambling, 1976-78. Vice-Chm., Sports Council, 1974-82; Chm., Nat. Jogging Assoc., 1978-80. Mem., British athletics team, 1950-59; Brit. record holder steeplechase, 1950-56; Welsh mile record holder, 1952-57; bronze medal, Olympics, Helsinki, 1952; Sportsman of the Year, 1955; Athlete of the Year, 1955. *Publications:* Tackle Climbing, 1959; Young Athletes Companion, 1961; Orienteering, 1966; Expedition Guide for Duke of Edinburgh's Award Scheme, 1965; Your Way with Map and Compass, 1971. *Recreations:* running games, mountain activities. *Address:* Hampton House, Upper Sunbury Road, Hampton, Mddx TW12 2DW. *T:* 01-979 1707. *Clubs:* Climbers'; Ranelagh, Southern Navigators.

DISNEY, Harold Vernon, CBE 1956; Manager, Engineering Division, Reactor Group, UK Atomic Energy Authority, 1969-72, retired; *b* 2 July 1907; *s* of Henry Disney and Julia Vernon; *m* 1936, Lucy Quinton; two *d. Educ:* Hallcroft Higher Standard Sch., Ilkeston; Nottingham Univ. Coll. Internat. Combustion, 1931-35; ICI (Alkali), 1935-46. On loan to Min. of Supply (RFF's), 1941-46. Dept of Atomic Energy, 1946-54; UKAEA: Asst

Dir, Defence Projects, Industrial Gp, 1954; Dir of Engineering, Industrial Gp, 1958; Man. Dir, Engineering Gp, Risley, 1962. FIMechE 1947. *Recreation:* gardening. *Address:* 63 Vincent Drive, Westminster Park, Chester CH4 7RQ.

DISS, Eileen, (Mrs Raymond Everett), RDI 1978; freelance designer for theatre, film and television, since 1959; *b* 13 May 1931; *d* of Thomas and Winifred Diss; *m* 1953, Raymond Everett; two *s* one *d. Educ:* Ilford County High Sch. for Girls; Central Sch. of Art and Design. MSIAD; FRSA. BBC Television design, 1952-59. Television series and plays: Maigret, 1962-63; The Tea Party, 1964; Up the Junction, 1965; Somerset Maugham, 1969; Uncle Vanya, 1970; The Duchess of Malfi, and Candide, 1972; The Importance of Being Earnest, and Pygmalion, 1973; Caesar and Cleopatra, 1974; Moll Flanders, 1975; Ghosts, and The Winslow Boy, 1976; You Never Can Tell, 1977; The Rear Column, Hedda Gabler, 1980; The Potting Shed, 1981. Television opera: The Merry Widow, 1968; Tales of Hoffmann, 1969; Die Fledermaus, 1971; Falstaff, 1972; The Yeomen of the Guard, 1974. Television films: Cider with Rosie, 1971; Robinson Crusoe, 1974. Theatre: Exiles, 1969; Butley, 1971; The Caretaker, 1972; Otherwise Engaged, 1975; The Apple-cart, 1977; The Rear Column, The Homecoming, 1978; The Hothouse, 1980; Translations, 1981; Quartermaine's Terms, 1981; Incident at Tulse Hill, 1981. National Theatre: Blithe Spirit, 1976; The Philanderer, 1978; Close of Play, When We Are Married, 1979; Watch on the Rhine, 1980; The Caretaker, 1980; Measure for Measure, 1981. *Films:* Joseph Losey's A Doll's House, 1972; Sweet William, 1978; Harold Pinter's Betrayal, 1982. BAFTA Television Design Award, 1962, 1965 and 1974. *Recreations:* cooking, music, cinema. *Address:* 4 Gloucester Walk, W8 4HZ. *T:* 01-937 8794.

DITCHBURN, Robert William, FRS 1962; Professor of Physics, University of Reading, 1946-68, now Emeritus; *b* 14 Jan. 1903; *e s* of William and Martha Kathleen Ditchburn; *m* 1929, Doreen May, *e d* of Arthur Samuel Barrett; one *s* three *d. Educ:* Bootle Secondary Sch.; Liverpool Univ.; Trinity Coll., Cambridge (Entrance and Senior Scholar, Hooper Prizeman, Isaac Newton Student). Fellow of Trinity Coll., Dublin, 1928-46; Prof. of Natural and Experimental Philosophy in Dublin Univ., 1929-46; Temp. Principal Experimental Officer, Admiralty, 1942-45. Mem. of Royal Irish Academy, 1931; Registrar for Social Studies, Trinity Coll., Dublin, 1940-44; Vice-Pres. Physical Soc., 1958; Vice-Pres. Inst. of Physics and Physical Soc., 1960-62. FInstP. *Publications:* Light, 1952; Eye-Movements and Visual Perception, 1973; and scientific papers. *Recreations:* walking, music. *Address:* 9 Summerfield Rise, Goring, Reading RG8 0DS.

DIVER, Hon. Sir Leslie Charles, Kt 1975; President, Legislative Council, Western Australia, 1960-74; Member, Legislative Council (Country Party) for Central Province, Western Australia, 1952-74; *b* Perth, Australia, 4 Nov. 1899; *s* of late J. W. Diver; *m* 1st, 1922, Emma J., *d* of late F. Blakiston; one *s* two *d*; 2nd, 1971, Mrs Thelma May Evans. Farmer and grazier. Chairman: Kellerberrin Road Bd, 1940, 1942-46; Hon. Royal Commn on Retailing of Motor Spirits, 1956. Chm., Sixth Aust. Area Conf., Commonwealth Parly Assoc., 1961; Rep. WA Parlt, Town Planning Adv. Cttee. Warden, State War Meml, 1967-68. *Recreations:* bowls, Australian rules football. *Address:* 48 Sulman Avenue, Salter Point, Como, WA 6152, Australia. *Clubs:* Eastern Districts (Kellerberrin); Manning Memorial Bowling.

DIVERRES, Prof. Armel Hugh; Professor of French and Head of Department of Romance Studies, University College of Swansea, 1974-81; *b* Liverpool, 4 Sept. 1914; *o s* of late Paul Diverres and Elizabeth (*née* Jones); *m* 1945, Ann Dilys, *d* of late James and Enid Williams; one *s* two *d. Educ:* Swansea Grammar Sch.; University Coll., Swansea; Univ. of Rennes; Sorbonne, Paris. MA (Wales), LèsL (Rennes), Docteur de l'Université de Paris. Fellow of Univ. of Wales, 1938-40; served in RA and Int. Corps, 1940-46, Captain. Asst Lectr in French, 1946-49, Lectr, 1949-54, Univ. of Manchester; Sen. Lectr in French, 1954-57, Carnegie Prof., 1958-74, Dean, Faculty of Arts, 1967-70, Univ. of Aberdeen. Governor: Nat. Mus. of Wales, 1978-81; Centre for Information on Language Teaching and Res., 1977-82; Aberdeen Coll. of Education, 1971-74. Member: CNAA Lang. Board, 1965-78, Cttee for Res., 1975-82, Humanities Bd, 1978-81; Welsh Jt Educn Cttee, 1975-81. British Br., Internat. Arthurian Soc., 1978-80, Internat. Pres., 1979-81; Pres., Soc. French Stud., 1976-78. Officier des Palmes Académiques, 1971. *Publications:* Voyage en Béarn by Froissart (ed), 1953; La Chronique métrique attribuée à Geffroy de Paris (ed), 1956; Chatterton by A. de Vigny (ed), 1967; articles and reviews in learned journals. *Recreation:* hill walking. *Address:* 23 Whiteshell Drive, Langland, Swansea, W Glamorgan. *T:* Swansea 60322.

DIVINE, Arthur Durham, (David Divine), CBE 1976 (OBE 1946); DSM 1940; author and journalist; formerly War Correspondent and Defence Correspondent, Sunday Times (until 1975); *b* 27 July 1904; 2nd *s* of Arthur Henry and Mabel Divine, Cape Town; *m* 1931, Elizabeth Ann, 2nd *d* of Sir Ian MacAlister; two *d. Educ:* Rondebosch High Sch., Cape Town; Kingswood Coll., Grahamstown, S Africa. Cape Times, 1922-26 and 1931-35, where founded daily column of World Comment; has travelled extensively in Europe, Africa, Asia, N and S America, and the Pacific. *Publications:* Sea Loot, 1930; They Blocked the Suez Canal, 1936; The Pub on the Pool, 1938; Tunnel from Calais, 1943, new edn 1975; many other thrillers; The Merchant Navy Fights, The Wake of the Raiders, Behind the Fleets, 1940, in conjunction with Ministry of Information; Destroyer's War, 1942; Road to Tunis, 1944; Navies in Exile, 1944; Dunkirk, 1945, and many boys' books. Under pseudonym of

David Rame: Wine of Good Hope, 1939; The Sun Shall Greet Them, 1941. Under name of David Divine: The King of Fassarai, 1950; Atom at Spithead, 1953; The Golden Fool, 1954; Boy on a Dolphin, 1955; The Nine Days of Dunkirk, 1959, new edn 1976; These Splendid Ships, 1960; The Iron Ladies, 1961; The Daughter of the Pangaran, 1963; The Blunted Sword, 1964; The Broken Wing, 1966; The Stolen Seasons, 1967; The Key of England, 1968; The North-West Frontier of Rome, 1969; The Three Red Flares, 1970; Mutiny at Invergordon, 1970; Certain Islands, 1972; The Opening of the World, 1973; *Films:* Atom at Spithead; Boy on a Dolphin; Dunkirk. *Address:* 24 Keats Grove, Hampstead, NW3 2RS. *T:* 01-435 6928.

DIX, Alan Michael; Director General, Motor Agents' Association Ltd, since 1976; *b* 29 June 1922; *s* of late Comdr Charles Cabry Dix, CMG, DSO, RN, and Ebba Sievers; *m* 1955, Helen Catherine McLaren; one *s* one *d. Educ:* Stenhus Kostskole, Denmark. Escaped Nazi occupied Denmark to Scotland, 1943; joined RAF, commissioned 1944. President, Capitol Car Distributors Inc., USA, 1958-67; Gp Vice-Pres., Volkswagen of America, USA, 1967-68; Man. Dir, Volkswagen (GB) Ltd, London, 1968-72; Pres., Mid Atlantic Toyota Inc., USA, 1972-73; Dir Marketing, British Leyland International, 1973-74; Proprietor, Alan M. Dix Associates, 1974-76. Chm., Motor Agents Pensions Administrators Ltd, 1976-; Dir, Hire Purchase Information Ltd, 1977-. Freedom and Livery, Coachmakers' and Coach Harness Makers' Co., 1980. FIMI, FInstM, FIMH, FBIM. King Christian X war medal, 1947. *Publications:* contribs to automotive trade jls. *Recreations:* yachting, photography; the study of professional management (internat. speaker on management and organisation). *Address:* 112 Speed House, Barbican, EC2Y 8AU. *T:* 01-638 6571; Apartment 1.1, Edifici Hort del Sola, La Massana, Principality of Andorra. *T:* Andorra 35352. *Clubs:* Danish, Royal Air Force, Burkes; Royal Air Force Yacht (Hamble).

DIX, Bernard Hubert; Assistant General Secretary, National Union of Public Employees, since 1975; *b* 30 March 1925; *s* of Thomas Herbert John Dix and Gertrude Turner; *m* 1979, Eileen Veronica Smith; three *s*; two *s* one *d* by prev. *m. Educ:* LCC elem. schs; LSE (TUC Scholar). Engrg industry, 1939-55 (served Army, 1941-47); Deptl Asst, TUC, 1955-63; Res. Officer, NUPE, 1963-75. Member: Health Services Bd, 1976-80; Hotel and Catering Industry EDC, 1973-79; Local Govt Trng Bd; TUC Local Govt Cttee; TUC Hotel and Catering Industry Cttee; Labour Party NEC, 1981 (Mem., Social Policy Sub-Cttee and Econ. and Financial Policy Sub-Cttee); Labour Co-ordinating Cttee; Bd of Tribune. Governor, Ruskin Coll. *Publications:* (with Alan W. Fisher) Low Pay and How to End It: a trade union view, 1974; frequent contributor to Labour Monthly and Morning Star. *Address:* 58 Hartslock Drive, Thamesmead, SE2 9UT. *T:* 01-310 0624. *Club:* Pyramid (Thamesmead Community Association).

DIX, Geoffrey Herbert, OBE 1979; Secretary-General, The Institute of Bankers, 1971-82; *b* 1 March 1922; *o s* of late Herbert Walter and Winifred Ada Dix; *m* 1945, Margaret Sybil Outhwaite (*d* 1981), MA (Cantab); one *s. Educ:* Watford Grammar Sch.; Gonville and Caius Coll., Cambridge. MA (Mod. langs). Served War, 1942-45: commissioned into Royal Devon Yeomanry; later served with HQ 1st Airborne Corps. Inst. of Export, 1946-51; with Inst. of Bankers, 1951-: Asst Sec., 1956; Under-Sec. 1962; Dep. Sec. 1968. Mem., Jt Cttee for National Awards in Business Studies, 1960-76. *Recreations:* Mozart, theatre. *Address:* 102 Harestone Valley Road, Caterham, Surrey. *T:* Caterham 42837. *Clubs:* Overseas Bankers; Caterham Players.

DIX, Prof. Gerald Bennett, ARIBA; FRTPI; Lever Professor of Civic Design, University of Liverpool, since 1975; *b* 12 Jan. 1926; *s* of Cyril Dix and Mabel Winifred (*née* Bennett); *m* 1st, 1956, Ann Brough Worrall (marr. diss.); two *s*; 2nd, 1963, Lois Nichols; one *d. Educ:* Altrincham Grammar Sch.; Univ. of Manchester (BA (Hons Arch.), DipTP (dist.)); Harvard Univ. (MLA). Studio Asst, 1950-51, Asst Lectr in Town and Country Planning, 1951-53, Manchester Univ.; Smith Mundt and Fulbright awards to Harvard, 1952-53; Asst Architect, 1954; Chief Architect-Planner, Addis Ababa, and chief asst to Sir Patrick Abercrombie, 1954-56; Planning Officer, Singapore, 1957-59; Acting Planning Adviser, 1959. Sen. Research Fellow, Univ. of Science and Technol., Ghana, 1959-63; UN Planning Mission to Ghana, 1962; Planner, later Sen. Planner, BRS/ODM, 1963-65 (adv. missions to W Indies, W Africa, Aden, Bechuanaland, Swaziland, Cyprus); Lectr, Nottingham Univ., 1966-68, Sen. Lectr, 1968-70; Prof. of Planning, and Dir, Inst. of Planning Studies, 1970-75; Dir, Cyprus Planning Project, 1967-71; adv. visits on planning educn, to Uganda 1971, Nigeria 1972, Sudan 1975, Mexico 1978, Egypt 1980; UK Mem., Adv. Panel on planning Canal towns, Egypt, 1974, and Western Desert, 1975. Member: Professional Literature Cttee, RIBA, 1966-80, 1981- (Chm. 1975-80); Library Management Cttee, 1969-72, 1975-80; Vice-Pres., World Soc. for Ekistics, 1975-79. Editorial adviser, Ekistics (journal), 1972-; Chm. Management Bd, Town Planning Rev., 1976-; (Founder) Editor, Third World Planning Rev., 1978-. FRSA. *Publications:* ed, C. A. Doxiadis, Ecology and Ekistics, 1977, Boulder, Colo, 1978, Brisbane, 1978; numerous planning reports to govts in various parts of world; articles and reviews in Town Planning Rev., Third World Planning Rev., Ekistics, RIBA Jl, Arch. Rev. *Recreations:* photography, listening to music, travel. *Address:* Department of Civic Design, University of Liverpool, PO Box 147, Liverpool L69 3BX. *T:* 051-709 6022; Gamblegate, Meols Drive, West Kirby, Wirral, Merseyside L48 5DE. *T:* 051-632 1390. *Club:* Athenæum.

DIX, Victor Wilkinson, MA, MB, BChir Cantab, FRCS, MRCP; retired; Professor Emeritus, University of London. Assistant Surgeon, The London Hospital, 1930-37; Surgeon, The London Hospital, 1937-64. *Address:* 8 Shandon Close, Tunbridge Wells, Kent. *T:* Tunbridge Wells 30839.

DIXEY, Sir Frank, KCMG 1972 (CMG 1949); OBE 1929; DSc; FRS 1958; FEng; FGS; Geological Adviser and Director of Colonial Geological Surveys, Colonial Office, 1947-59; British Technical Aid Consultant to Water Development Department, Cyprus, 1967-73; Consultant Hydrologist, 1960-74, including service overseas with UN organisations and on geology and hydrogeology of Cyprus; *b* 7 April 1892; *m* 1919, Helen Golding (*d* 1961); one *d* (decd); *m* 1962, Cicely Hepworth. *Educ:* Barry Grammar Sch.; University of Wales; Fellow, University Coll., Cardiff, 1981. Served European War, 1914-18, RGA, 1915-18; Govt Geologist, Sierra Leone, 1918-21; Dir of Geological Survey, Nyasaland, 1921-39; Dir of Water Development, N Rhodesia, 1939-44; Dir of Geological Survey, Nigeria, 1944-47. Geological Soc. Murchison medallist, 1953; Geol. Soc. S Africa Draper medallist, 1945 and Hon. Mem., 1959; Corresponding Mem. Geological Soc., Belgium, 1947, Hon. Mem., 1958. Alexander du Toit Memorial Lecturer, Johannesburg, 1955. Hon. Fellow, Inst. Min. and Met., 1958; Founder Fellow, Fellowship of Engineering, 1976. *Publications:* Practical Handbook of Water Supply, 1931, 2nd edn 1950; official reports and scientific papers on geology, geomorphology, and mineral resources of African States. *Address:* Woodpecker Cottage, Bramber, Steyning, West Sussex BN4 3WE. *T:* Steyning 812313. *Club:* Athenæum.

DIXEY, John, OBE 1976; Production Director and Board Member, The Guardian, since 1979; *b* 29 March 1926; *s* of John Dixey and Muriel Doris Dixey; *m* 1948, Pauline Seaden; one *s* one *d. Educ:* Battersea Grammar Sch. Served Royal Marines and Royal Fusiliers, 1944-47. Press Telegraphist, Yorkshire Post and Glasgow Herald, 1948-59; Asst to Gen. Sec., Nat. Union of Press Telegraphists, 1959; Labour Officer, Newspaper Soc., 1959-63; Labour Adviser, Thomson Organisation Ltd, 1963-64; Asst Gen. Man., Liverpool Daily Post & Echo, 1964-67; Executive Dir, Times Newspapers, 1967-74; Special Adviser to Man. Dir, Thomson Org., 1974; Dir, Newspaper Publishers Assoc. Ltd, 1975-76; Employment Affairs Advr, IPA, 1977-79; Sec., Assoc. of Midland Advertising Agencies, 1977-79; Chm., Advertising Assoc. Trade Union Liaison Group; Mem., TUC New Daily Newspaper Advisory Group. Ward-Perkins Vis. Fellow, Pembroke Coll., Oxford, 1978. Former Mem., Printing and Publishing Industry Trng Bd; former Governor, London Coll. of Printing. *Recreations:* cooking, photography. *Address:* 23 West Hill, Sanderstead, Surrey. *T:* 01-657 7940.

DIXEY, Paul (Arthur Groser); Chairman of Lloyd's, 1973, 1974 (Deputy Chairman, 1967, 1969, 1972); *b* 13 April 1915; *e s* of late Neville Dixey, JP (Chairman of Lloyd's, 1931, 1934 and 1936), and Marguerite (*née* Groser); *m* 1939, Mary Margaret Baring, JP, 2nd *d* of late Geoffrey Garrod; four *s* one *d. Educ:* Stowe; Trinity Coll., Cambridge. Elected an Underwriting Mem. of Lloyd's, 1938. Served War of 1939-45, Royal Artillery. Member: London Insce market delegn to Indonesia, 1958; Dunmow RDC, 1958-64; Cttee, Lloyd's Underwriters' Assoc., 1962-74; Cttee, Salvage Assoc., 1962-74; Cttee, Lloyd's, 1964-70, 1972-75; Gen. Cttee, Lloyd's Register of Shipping, 1964-; Chm., Salvage Assoc., 1964-65. Chairman: Paul Dixey Underwriting Agencies Ltd, 1973-76; Pieri and Reynolds Underwriting Agencies Ltd, 1976-; Director, Merrett Dixey Syndicates Ltd, 1976-78. Mem. Council, Morley Coll., 1952-62; Chm. Governors, Vinehall Sch., 1966-73. Leader, Barn Boys' Club, 1949-61. Chm., Essex Hunt Cttee, 1981-. *Recreations:* riding, fly-fishing. *Address:* Little Easton Spring, Dunmow, Essex CM6 2JD. *T:* Great Dunmow 2840.

DIXIT, Prof. Avinash Kamalakar; Professor of Economics and International Affairs, Princeton University, USA, since 1981; *b* 8 June 1944; *s* of Kamalakar Ramchandra Dixit and Kusum Dixit (*née* Phadke). *Educ:* Bombay Univ. (BSc); Cambridge Univ. (BA, MA); Massachusetts Inst. of Technology (PhD). Acting Asst Professor, Univ. of California, Berkeley, 1968-69; Lord Thomson of Fleet Fellow and Tutor in Economics, Balliol Coll., Oxford, 1970-74; Professor of Economics, Univ. of Warwick, 1974-80. Fellow, Econometric Society, 1977-. Co-Editor, Bell Journal of Economics, 1981-. *Publications:* Optimization in Economic Theory, 1976; The Theory of Equilibrium Growth, 1976; (with Victor Norman) Theory of International Trade, 1980; several articles in professional jls. *Recreations:* listening to music (pre-Schubert only), watching cricket (when possible). *Address:* Woodrow Wilson School of Public and International Affairs, Princeton University, Princeton, New Jersey 08544, USA. *T:* (609) 452-5635.

DIXON, family name of **Baron Glentoran.**

DIXON; *see* Graham-Dixon.

DIXON, Bernard; Chairman, Dixon Group of Malting and Light Industrial Companies, Pampisford, Cambs, since 1960; *b* Redcar, Yorks, 23 Dec. 1906; 3rd *s* of late Capt. Thomas Robert Dixon and Lily Jane (*née* Barry), Triplow Place, near Royston, Herts; *m* 1930, Olive Marie, *d* of G. H. Watts, Cambridge; four *d. Educ:* Campbell Coll., Belmont, Belfast, NI; British Sch. of Malting and Brewing; University of Birmingham. Chm. and Man. Dir, Flowers Breweries Ltd, 1947-58. Sometime examiner, Institute of Brewing, Mem. Publications Cttee, Journal of Inst. of Brewing, Chm. London Section, Inst. of Brewing, 1939-40. Winner numerous awards at home and abroad for brewery products, including championship, London, 1929 and 1930 and Grand Prix, Brussels, Prague, Pilsen. Patentee of inventions used throughout brewing industry. Formerly Hon. Sec. Bedfordshire Brewers' Assoc. and Mem. Brewers' Soc. Cttee on Replanning. Commissioned, Cambs Regt, 1929; Sports Officer, 1930; commissioned, Home Guard, 1940. Breeder of pure-bred Arabian Horses which have been exported to Government studs in all parts of the world; a Governor of the Arab Horse Soc. Past Pres. Old Campbellian Soc. *Publications:* technical papers to various sections of Institute of Brewing and Incorporated Brewers' Guild. *Recreations:* hunting, farming, golf. *Address:* Pampisford Place, Pampisford, Cambs CB2 4EW. *Clubs:* Naval & Military, Royal Automobile; Kildare Street and University (Dublin).

DIXON, Dr Bernard; European Editor, Omni, since 1978; *b* Darlington, 17 July 1938; *s* of late Ronald Dixon and Grace Peirson; *m* 1963, Margaret Helena Charlton; two *s* one *d. Educ:* Queen Elizabeth Grammar Sch., Darlington; King's Coll., Univ. of Durham; Univ. of Newcastle upon Tyne. BSc, PhD. Luccock Res. Fellow, 1961-64, Frank Schon Fellow, 1964-65, Univ. of Newcastle; Asst Editor, 1965-66, Dep. Editor, 1966-68, World Medicine; Editor, New Scientist, 1969-79. Chm., Cttee, Assoc. of British Science Writers, 1971-72; Member: Soc. for General Microbiology, 1962; Council, BAAS, 1977- (Pres., Section X, 1979). MIBiol 1965. *Publications:* (ed) Journeys in Belief, 1968; What is Science For?, 1973; Magnificent Microbes, 1976; Invisible Allies, 1976; Beyond the Magic Bullet, 1978; contributor to: Animal Rights—A Symposium, 1979; The Book of Predictions, 1980; Development of Science Publishing in Europe, 1980; Medicine and Care, 1981; numerous articles in scientific and general press on microbiology, and other scientific topics; research papers in Jl of General Microbiology, etc, mostly on microbial biochemistry. *Recreation:* playing Scottish traditional music, collecting old books. *Address:* 81 Falmouth Road, Chelmsford, Essex. *T:* Chelmsford 58421.

DIXON, Bernard Tunbridge; Charity Commissioner, since 1981; *b* 14 July 1928; *s* of Archibald Tunbridge Dixon and Dorothy Dixon (*née* Cardinal); *m* 1962, Jessie Netta Watson Hastie; one *s* three *d. Educ:* Owen's Sch.; University Coll. London (LLB). Admitted Solicitor, 1952; Partner in Dixon & Co., Solicitors, 1952-59; Legal Asst/Sen. Legal Asst with Treasury Solicitor, 1959-67; Sen. Legal Asst with Land Commission, 1967-70; Sen. Legal Asst with Charity Comrs, 1970-74; Dep. Charity Comr, 1975-81. *Recreation:* photography. *Address:* c/o Charity Commission, Graeme House, Derby Square, Liverpool L2 7SB. *T:* 051-227 3191.

DIXON, Donald; MP (Lab) Jarrow, since 1979; *b* 6 March 1929; *s* of Christopher Albert Dixon and Jane Dixon; *m* Doreen; one *s* one *d. Educ:* Ellison Street Elementary School, Jarrow. Shipyard Worker, 1947-74; Branch Sec., GMWU, 1974-79. Chm., PLP Shipbuilding Group. Councillor, South Tyneside MDC, 1963-. Freeman of Jarrow, 1972. *Recreations:* football, reading. *Address:* 1 Hillcrest, Jarrow NE32 4DP. *T:* Jarrow 897635. *Clubs:* Jarrow Labour; Hastings (Hebburn).

DIXON, Sir (Francis Wilfred) Peter, KBE 1959 (CBE 1952); MB, BS, FRCS; Air Vice-Marshal retired; Consultant in Surgery to the RAF, retired 1966; *b* 4 Oct. 1907; *s* of late Frederick Henry Dixon, New Norfolk, Tas.; *m* 1940, Pamela Ruby, *d* of late Brig. Charles C. Russell, MC, RA (Retd), London; two *s* one *d. Educ:* Newman Coll.; Melbourne Univ. MB, BS, Melbourne, 1930; FRCS Ed. 1937; FRCS 1949; DO Oxford, 1936. House Surgeon, St Vincent's Hosp., Melbourne. Joined RAF 1930; Wing-Comdr 1943; served War of 1939-45 (despatches); Aden, Normandy, SW Pacific; Air Cdre 1949; Air Vice-Marshal, 1957. Civilian Consultant in Surgery, RAF, 1966-. Hon. Surgeon to King George VI, 1949-52, to Queen Elizabeth II, 1952-66. Lady Cade Medal, RCS, 1963. *Publications:* contribs to medical journals. *Recreation:* sailing. *Address:* Hill House, Snape Bridge, near Woodbridge, Suffolk. *T:* Snape 404.

DIXON, Prof. Gordon Henry, PhD; FRS 1978; FRSC; Professor of Medical Biochemistry, Faculty of Medicine, University of Calgary, since 1974; *b* 25 March 1930; *s* of Walter James Dixon and Ruth Nightingale; *m* 1954, Sylvia Weir Gillen; three *s* one *d. Educ:* Cambs High Sch. for Boys; Trinity Coll., Cambridge (BA Hons); Univ. of Toronto (PhD). FRSC 1970. Res. Asst Prof., Dept of Biochem., Univ. of Washington, Seattle, USA, 1954-58; Mem. staff, MRC Unit for res. in cell metabolism, Univ. of Oxford, 1958-59; Univ. of Toronto: Res. Associate, Connaught Med. Res. Lab., 1959-60; Associate Prof., Dept of Biochem., 1960-63; Prof., Dept of Biochem., Univ. of BC, Vancouver, 1963-72; Prof., Biochem. Group, Univ. of Sussex, 1972-74. Vis. Fellow Commoner, Trinity Coll., Cambridge, 1979-80. Pres., Canadian Biochemical Soc., 1982-83; Mem. Exec. Council, Pan-American Assoc. of Biochemical Socs, 1981-84. Flavelle Medal, RSC, 1980. *Publications:* 180 pubns in learned jls, incl. Jl Biol Chem., Proc. Nat. Acad. Sci. (US), Nature, and Biochemistry. *Recreations:* skiing, mountain walking, gardening. *Address:* 3424 Underwood Place NW, Calgary, Alberta T2N 4G7, Canada. *T:* 403-282-4394 or 403-284-6022.

DIXON, Guy Holford, JP; Barrister-at-Law; honorary Recorder of Newark-on-Trent, since 1972; *b* 20 March 1902; *s* of late Dr Montague Dixon, Melton Mowbray; unmarried. *Educ:* Abbotsholme Sch., Derbs; Repton Sch.; University Coll., Oxford. BA (History) Oxon, 1925. Called to the Bar, Inner Temple, 1929. Recorder of Newark-on-Trent, 1965-71; Deputy Chairman: Leics QS, 1960-71; Northampton County QS, 1966-71; a Recorder, 1972-75; a Dep. Circuit Judge, 1975-77. Lay Canon, Leicester Cathedral, 1962. JP Leics,

1960. *Recreation:* looking at and collecting pictures. *Address:* The Old Rectory, Brampton Ash, Market Harborough, Leics. *T:* Dingley 200; Burton Overy, Leics. *T:* Great Glen 2274. *Club:* Reform.

DIXON, Jack Shawcross, OBE 1969; HM Diplomatic Service, retired 1976; *b* 8 March 1918; *s* of Herbert Dixon and Helen (*née* Woollacott); *m* 1941, Ida Hewkin; one *d. Educ:* Oldham Hulme Grammar Sch.; London Sch. of Economics (BScEcon). Served in Royal Welch Fusiliers and RAOC attached Indian Army, 1940-46. Colonial Office, 1948; entered HM Foreign (subseq. Diplomatic) Service, 1949; FO, 1949; HM Political Agency, Kuwait, 1950; Rep. of Polit. Agent, Mina al Ahmadi, 1951; FO, 1952; 1st Sec., Singapore, 1956; HM Consul, Barcelona, 1959; FO, 1962; 1st Sec., Rome, 1966; FCO, 1971; Head of Treaty and Nationality Dept, FCO, 1973-76. *Recreations:* observing wildlife, photographing butterflies, philately. *Address:* 26 Brook Court, Meads Road, Eastbourne, E Sussex BN20 7PY. *Club:* Royal Commonwealth Society.

DIXON, Sir John George, 3rd Bt *cr* 1919; *b* 17 Sept. 1911; *s* of Sir John Dixon, 2nd Bt and Gwendolen Anne (*d* 1974), *d* of Sir Joseph Layton Elmes Spearman, 2nd Bt; *S* father, 1976; *m* 1947, Caroline, *d* of late Charles Theodore Hiltermann; one *d. Educ:* Cranleigh. *Heir: nephew* Jonathan Mark Dixon, *b* 1 Sept. 1949. *Address:* Avenue des Mousquetaires 19, La Tour de Peilz, Vaud, Switzerland.

DIXON, Jon Edmund, CMG 1975; Under Secretary, Ministry of Agriculture, Fisheries and Food, since 1971; *b* 19 Nov. 1928; *s* of Edmund Joseph Claude and Gwendoline Alice Dixon; *m* 1953, Betty Edith Stone; two *s* one *d* (and one *d* decd). *Educ:* St Paul's Sch., West Kensington; Peterhouse, Cambridge. Natural Sciences Tripos Part I and Part II (Physiology). Asst Principal, Min. of Agric. and Fisheries, 1952; Private Sec. to successive Parliamentary Secretaries, 1955-58; Principal, 1958; Asst Sec., 1966; Under-Sec., 1971; Minister in UK Delegn, subseq. Office of Permanent Rep., to EEC, 1972-75. *Recreations:* musical composition, oil painting, building harpsichords, gardening, walking. *Address:* Ministry of Agriculture, Fisheries and Food, Whitehall Place, SW1.

DIXON, Prof. Kendal Cartwright, MA, MD, PhD, FRCPath; Professor of Cellular Pathology, University of Cambridge, 1973-78, now Emeritus; Fellow of King's College, Cambridge, since 1937; *b* 16 Feb. 1911; *s* of late Prof. Henry H. Dixon, ScD, FRS, Dublin Univ., and Dorothea, *d* of late Sir John Franks, CB, Blackrock, Co. Dublin; *m* 1938, Anne , *d* of late F. D. Darley, Stillorgan, Co. Dublin; one *s* one *d. Educ:* St Stephen's Green Sch., Dublin; Haileybury; Trinity Coll., Dublin; King's Coll., Cambridge (Scholar); Dun's Hosp., Dublin; St Bartholomew's Hosp., London. 1st cl. Pt 1 1932, 1st cl. Pt 2 (Biochem.) 1933, Nat. Scis Tripos Cantab; MB, BChir Cantab 1939. Asst to Prof. of Physiol., Dublin Univ., 1936; RAMC, 1940-45, Specialist in Pathology; Univ. of Cambridge: Official Fellow of King's Coll., 1945; Univ. Demonstrator in Chem. Path., 1946, Lectr 1949; Tutor for Advanced Students, King's Coll., 1951-59; Dir of Studies in Medicine, King's Coll., 1959-73; Reader in Cytopathology, 1962-73. Vis. Prof. of Pathology, Columbia Univ., NY, 1978. Mem. European Soc. Pathology. *Publications:* chapters in books and articles in med. jls principally on cellular disorder and death, fatty change, and neuronal metabolism. *Recreation:* the mountains of Kerry. *Address:* King's College, Cambridge. *Club:* Kildare Street and University (Dublin).

DIXON, Kenneth Herbert Morley; Chairman, Rowntree Mackintosh Ltd, since 1981; *b* 19 Aug. 1929; *y s* of Arnold Morley Dixon and Mary Jolly; *m* 1955, Patricia Oldbury Whalley; two *s. Educ:* Cranbrook Sch., Sydney, Australia; Manchester Univ. (BA(Econ) 1952). Calico Printers Assoc., 1952-56; joined Rowntree Mackintosh Ltd, 1956; Dir, 1970; Dep. Chm., 1978-81; Chm., UK Confectionery Div., 1973-78. Member: Council, Incorporated Soc. of British Advertisers, 1971-79; Council, Cocoa, Chocolate and Confectionery Alliance, 1972-79; Council, Advertising Assoc., 1976-79; CBI, Companies Cttee, 1979-; BIM Econ. and Social Affairs Cttee, 1980-; Council, CBI, 1981-. *Recreations:* reading, music, fell walking. *Address:* Rowntree Mackintosh Ltd, York YO1 1XY. *T:* York 53071. *Club:* Yorkshire (York).

DIXON, Malcolm, FRS 1942; MA, PhD, ScD Cantab; Emeritus Professor of Enzyme Biochemistry, Cambridge University, since 1966; *b* 18 April 1899; *s* of Allick Page Dixon and Caroline Dewe Dixon (*née* Mathews). *Educ:* Emmanuel Coll., Cambridge. BA 1920; began research in biochemistry under Sir F. G. Hopkins, 1921; 1851 Exhibition Senior Student, 1924-27; Senior Demonstrator in Biochemistry, University of Cambridge, 1923-27; University Lecturer in Biochemistry, 1928-44; Reader in Enzyme Biochemistry, Cambridge University, 1945-65; Prof. of Enzyme Biochemistry, 1966; Dir of Sub-Dept of Enzyme Biochemistry, Cambridge Univ., 1945-66; Fellow of King's Coll., Cambridge, 1950-66, Hon. Fellow, 1968-. Pres. of the Commission on Enzymes of the Internat. Union of Biochemistry, 1956-61. *Publications:* Manometric Methods, 1934, 3rd edn 1951; Multi-enzyme Systems, 1949 (also Japanese edn); Enzymes (with Prof. E. C. Webb), 1958, 2nd edn 1964 (also Russian, Japanese and Italian edns), 3rd edn (with Prof. E. C. Webb, Dr C. J. R. Thorne and Prof. K. F. Tipton), 1979; numerous papers dealing with the subject of enzymes, with special reference to biological oxidation processes and cell-respiration. *Recreation:* music. *Address:* Biochemical Laboratory, Cambridge. *T:* Cambridge 51781. *Club:* Athenæum.

DIXON, Margaret Rumer H.; see Haynes Dixon.

DIXON, Michael George, OBE 1964; Chief Passport Officer, Foreign and Commonwealth Office, 1967–80, retired; *b* 10 March 1920; *s* of Sidney Wilfrid and Elsie Dixon. *Educ:* Enfield Grammar Sch. Foreign Office, 1937. HM Forces, 1940–46 (POW, Far East). MInstTM. *Recreation:* gardening. *Address:* 9 Ridge Crest, Enfield, Mddx. *T:* 01-363 3408.

DIXON, Sir Peter; see Dixon, Sir (F. W.) P.

DIXON, Peter Vibart; Secretary, National Economic Development Council, since 1982; *b* 16 July 1932; *s* of late Meredith Vibart Dixon and Phyllis Joan (*née* Hemingway); *m* 1955, Elizabeth Anne Howie Davison; three *s. Educ:* Summer Fields; Radley Coll.; King's Coll., Cambridge (BA Classics and Law 1955, MA 1959). Royal Artillery, 1951–52. Asst Principal, HM Treasury, 1955; Office of Lord Privy Seal, 1956; Treasury, 1956–62: Private Sec. to Economic Sec., 1959; Principal, 1960; Colonial Office, 1963; CS Selection Bd 1964–65; Treasury, 1965–72, Asst Sec., 1969; Counsellor (Economic), HM Embassy, Washington, 1972–75; Treasury, 1975–82: Press Sec., 1975–78; Under Sec., Industrial Policy, 1978–82. Mem., RIPA Council, 1976–82. *Address:* 17 Lauriston Road, Wimbledon SW19 4TJ. *T:* 01-946 8931.

DIXON, Piers; Stockbroker; *b* 29 Dec. 1928; *s* of late Sir Pierson Dixon (British Ambassador in New York and Paris) and of Lady (Ismene) Dixon; *m* 1st, 1960, Edwina (marr. diss. 1973), *d* of Rt Hon. Lord Duncan-Sandys, *qv*; two *s*; 2nd, 1976, Janet (marr. diss. 1981), *d* of R. D. Aiyar, FRCS, and *widow* of 5th Earl Cowley. *Educ:* Eton (schol.); Magdalene Coll., Cambridge (exhibnr); Harvard Business Sch. Grenadier Guards, 1948. Merchant banking, London and New York, 1954–64; Sheppards and Chase, stockbrokers, 1964–81; Underwriting Mem. of Lloyd's. Centre for Policy Studies, 1976–78. Contested (C) Brixton, 1966; MP (C) Truro, 1970–Sept. 1974; Sec., Cons. Backbenchers' Finance Cttee, 1970–71, Vice-Chm., 1972–74; sponsor of Rehabilitation of Offenders Act, 1974. *Publications:* Double Diploma, 1968; Cornish Names, 1973. *Recreations:* tennis, squash, modern history. *Address:* 22 Ponsonby Terrace, SW1. *T:* 01-828 6166. *Clubs:* Brooks's, Pratt's.

DIXON, Maj.-Gen. Roy Laurence Cayley, CB 1977; MC 1944; Chapter Clerk, College of St George, Windsor Castle, since 1981; *b* 19 Sept. 1924; *s* of Lt-Col Sidney Frank Dixon, MC and Edith Mary (Sheena) (*née* Clark). *Educ:* Haileybury; Edinburgh Univ. Commnd Royal Tank Regt, 1944; served in armd units and on staff; psc 1956; Instructor, Staff Coll., 1961–64; comd 5th Royal Tank Regt, 1966–67; Royal Coll. of Defence Studies, 1971; Comdr Royal Armd Corps, Germany, 1968–70; qual. helicopter pilot, 1973; Dir, Army Air Corps, 1974–76; Chief of Staff, Allied Forces Northern Europe, 1977–80. Col Comdt, RTR, 1978–. *Publications:* articles in mil. jls. *Recreations:* ski-ing, sailing, theatre, music. *Address:* 7 The Cloisters, Windsor Castle, Berks SL4 1NJ. *T:* Windsor 65538. *Club:* Army and Navy.

DIXON, Stanley; Chairman, Midland-Yorkshire Tar Distillers Ltd, 1968–71; *b* 12 Aug. 1900; *m* 1936, Ella Margaret Hogg; two *s. Educ:* Leeds Grammar Sch.; Queen's Coll., Oxford. Articled to Leather & Veale, Chartered Accountants in Leeds, 1924–27; Manager, Leather & Veale (later Peat, Marwick, Mitchell & Co.), Leeds, 1927–35; Sec., Midland Tar Distillers Ltd, 1935–66; Dir, Midland Tar Distillers Ltd (later Midland-Yorkshire Holdings Ltd), 1943–71. Pres., Inst. of Chartered Accountants in England and Wales, 1968–69. Hon. DSocSc Birmingham, 1972. *Publications:* The Case for Marginal Costing, 1967; The Art of Chairing a Meeting, 1975. *Recreations:* Church affairs, gardening and music. *Address:* 83 Norton Road, Stourbridge, West Midlands DY8 2TB. *T:* Stourbridge 5672.

DIXON, Group Captain William Michael, CBE 1972; DSO 1943; DFC 1941; AFC 1958; Bursar, Summer Fields School, Oxford, since 1975; *b* 29 July 1920; *s* of late William Michael Dixon; *m* 1944, Mary Margaret (*d* 1957), *d* of late William Alexander Spence, MC, MM; three *s.* Served War of 1939–45, Bomber Comd; Air Staff, Rhodesian Air Trng Gp, 1943–44; psa 1949; comd No 2 (Bomber) Sqdn RAAF, 1952–55; comd No 192 Sqdn RAF, 1955–58; jssc 1958; comd RAF Feltwell, 1961–63; Sen. Officer Admin No 1 (Bomber) Gp, 1963–66; Sen. Personnel SO HQ Air Support Comd, 1966–68; DCAS, Royal Malaysian Air Force, 1968–73; Dir of Aircraft Projects (RAF), MoD, 1972–75; ADC to the Queen, 1968–73. *Recreation:* natural history. *Address:* Lower Farm, Sutton, Oxford OX8 1RX. *T:* Oxford 881553. *Club:* Royal Air Force.

DIXON WARD, Frank, CBE 1979; Executive Director, Royal Society for the Prevention of Cruelty to Animals, since 1982; *b* 28 June 1922; *s* of Cecil Ward, LRAM, and Helen Cecilia Ward, Eastbourne; *m* 1960, Claire Collasius; one *s* one *d. Educ:* Eastbourne Grammar School. Solicitor (Hons), 1948. Articled to Town Clerk, Eastbourne, 1940. Served War, Royal Air Force, 1941–46. Solicitor posts, Peterborough, 1948–51, West Ham, 1952–54; Deputy Town Clerk, Hove, 1954–62; Chairman: Local Govt Legal Soc., 1957; Hove Round Table, 1961–62; Mem. Council, Sussex LTA, 1957–62; Town Clerk: Camberwell, 1963–65; Southwark, 1964–70; Chief Exec., Lambeth, 1970–81; Consultant, 1982; Chm., London Rent Assessment Cttees, 1982. Hon. Clerk: South London Housing Consortium, 1965–70; Social Service Cttee, London Boroughs Assoc., 1966–82; Hon. Legal Advr, Age Concern (Gtr London), 1965–82; Member official committees: London Welfare Services, 1963–65; NHS Reorganisation, 1969–74; Homelessness, 1970–72;

Citizens Advice Bureaux, 1973–74; Jt Approach to Social Policies, 1975–76. Chm., St Dunstan's College Soc., 1975–78. *Recreations:* music, lawn tennis. *Address:* RSPCA, Causeway, Horsham, West Sussex RH12 1HG. *T:* Horsham 64181.

DOBB, Erlam Stanley, CB 1963; TD; *b* 16 Aug. 1910; *m* 1937, Margaret Williams; no *c. Educ:* Ruthin; University Coll. of N Wales. Chartered Surveyor and Land Agent, Anglesey, Denbigh and Merioneth, 1930–35; Asst Land Comr, to Dir, Agricultural Land Service, MAFF, 1935–70; a Dep. Dir-Gen., Agricl Develt and Adv. Service, MAFF, 1971–73; Dir-Gen., 1973–75. Mem., ARC, 1973–75; Vice-Chm., Adv. Council for Agriculture and Horticulture in England and Wales, 1974–75. Chm. Trustees, T. P. Price Charity, Markshall Estate, Essex. Governor, Royal Agricultural College, 1960–75. Royal Welch Fusiliers (TA), 1938–46, Major. FRICS; FRAgS. *Publications:* professional contributions to journals of learned societies. *Recreations:* golf, gardening. *Address:* Churchgate, Westerham, Kent. *T:* Westerham 62294. *Clubs:* Farmers'; Crowborough Beacon Golf, Limpsfield Chart Golf.

DOBBIE, Mitchell Macdonald, CB 1951; *b* 2 Oct. 1901; *s* of James Dobbie, Ayr, and Jean Macdonald; *m* 1931, Evelyn Willison (*d* 1967), *e d* of R. W. Grieve, Edinburgh. *Educ:* Ayr Academy; University of Edinburgh (MA, LLB). Called to Bar, Gray's Inn, 1927. Entered Inland Revenue Dept, 1925; Ministry of Labour, 1928; Private Sec. to Parl. Sec., 1934; transferred to Dept of Health for Scotland, 1938; Asst Sec., 1939; Principal Asst Sec., 1945; seconded to Ministry of Home Security as Principal Officer, Scotland Civil Defence Region, 1943–45; Under-Sec., Min. of Housing and Local Govt, 1948; Principal Establishment Officer, 1956–63; retd 1963, and re-employed in Scottish Development Dept, 1963–66; Secretary of Commissions for Scotland, 1966–72. JP City of Edinburgh. *Address:* 13 Eton Terrace, Edinburgh EH4 1QD. *T:* 031-332 3150. *Clubs:* New, Scottish Arts (Edinburgh).

DOBBING, Prof. John, DSc, FRCP, FRCPath; Professor of Child Growth and Development, Department of Child Health, University of Manchester, and Honorary Consultant, United Manchester Hospitals, since 1968; *b* 14 Aug. 1922; *s* of Alfred Herbert Dobbing and May Gwendoline (*née* Cattell); *m* Dr Jean Sands. *Educ:* Bootham Sch., York; St Mary's Hosp., London (MSc, MB, BS). FRCPath 1976; FRCP 1981. Lectr in Path. and Gull Student, Guy's Hosp., 1954–61; Sen. Lectr in Physiol., London Hosp., 1961–64; Sen. Lectr, Inst. of Child Health, London, and Hon. Consultant, Hosp. for Sick Children, Gt Ormond Street, 1964–68. *Publications:* Applied Neurochemistry, 1968; Scientific Foundations of Paediatrics, 1974 (2nd edn 1981); Maternal Nutrition in Pregnancy: eating for two?, 1981; pubns on undernutrition and developing brain in scientific literature. *Recreations:* writing, travel, being critical of colleagues. *Address:* Higher Cliff Farm, via Birch Vale, via Stockport, Cheshire. *T:* New Mills 43220.

DOBBS, Bernard; see Dobbs, W. B. J.

DOBBS, Prof. (Edwin) Roland, PhD, DSc; Hildred Carlile Professor of Physics, University of London, and Head of Department of Physics, Bedford College, since 1973; *b* 2 Dec. 1924; *s* of late A. Edwin Dobbs, AMIMechE, and Harriet Dobbs (*née* Wright); *m* 1947, Dorothy Helena, *o d* of late Alderman A. F. T. Jeeves, Stamford, Lincs; two *s* one *d. Educ:* Ilford County High Sch.; Queen Elizabeth's Sch., Barnet; University College London. BSc Hons 1943, PhD 1949; DSc London 1977; FInstP 1964; FIOA 1977. Radar research, Admiralty, 1943–46; DSIR Res. Student, UCL, 1946–49; Lectr in Physics, QMC, Univ. of London, 1949–58; Res. Associate in Applied Maths, 1958–59, Associate Prof. of Physics, 1959–60, Brown Univ., USA; Mem., Gonville and Caius Coll., Cambridge, 1960–; AEI Fellow, Cavendish Lab., Univ. of Cambridge, 1960–64; Prof. and Head of Dept of Physics, Univ. of Lancaster, 1964–73. Mem., Nuclear Physics Bd, SRC, 1974–77. Visiting Professor: Brown Univ., 1966; Wayne State Univ., 1969; Univ. of Tokyo, 1977. Pres., Inst. of Acoustics, 1976–78; Hon. Sec., Inst. of Physics, 1976–. Hon. Fellow, Indian Cryogenics Council, 1977. *Publications:* research papers on metals and superconductors in Procs of Royal Soc., and on solid state physics and acoustics in Jl of Physics, Physical Rev. Letters, Physical Acoustics, etc. *Recreations:* travel, theatre, gardening. *Address:* Bedford College, Regent's Park, NW1 4NS. *Club:* Athenæum.

DOBBS, Joseph Alfred, CMG 1972; OBE 1957 (MBE 1945); TD 1945; HM Diplomatic Service, retired; *b* Abbeyleix, Ireland, 22 Dec. 1914; *s* of John L. Dobbs and Ruby (*née* Gillespie); *m* 1949, Marie, *d* of Reginald Francis Catton, Sydney; four *s. Educ:* Worksop Coll.; Trinity Hall, Cambridge (Schol.). Pres., Cambridge Union Soc., 1936. Served War of 1939–45, Major, Royal Artillery (despatches). Joined Foreign Office, 1946; served Moscow, 1947–51, 1954–57 and 1965–68; FO, 1951–54; Delhi, 1957–61; Warsaw, 1961–64; Rome, 1964–65; Consul-Gen., Zagreb, 1969–70; Minister, Moscow, 1971–74. *Recreations:* riding, gardening. *Address:* The Coach House, Charlton Musgrove, Wincanton, Somerset BA9 8ES. *T:* Wincanton 33356.

DOBBS, Mattiwilda; Order of North Star (Sweden), 1954; opera singer (coloratura soprano); Professor, Howard University, Washington, DC, since 1977; *b* Atlanta, Ga, USA; *d* of John Wesley and Irene Dobbs; *m* 1957, Bengt Janzon, Dir. of Information, Nat. Ministry of Health and Welfare, Sweden; no *c. Educ:* Spelman Coll., USA (BA); Columbia Univ., USA (MA). Studied voice in NY with Lotte Leonard, 1946–50; special coaching Paris with Pierre

Bernac, 1950-52. Marian Anderson Schol., 1948; John Hay Whitney Schol., 1950; 1st prize in singing, Internat. Comp., Geneva Conservatory of Music, 1951. Appeared Royal Dutch Opera, Holland Festival, 1952. Recitals, Sweden, Paris, Holland, 1952; appeared in opera at La Scala, Milan, 1953; Concerts, England and Continent, 1953; Glyndebourne Opera, 1953-54, 1956, 1961; Covent Garden Opera, 1953, 1954, 1956, 1958; command performance, Covent Garden, 1954. Annual concert tours: US, 1954-; Australia, New Zealand, 1955, 1959, 1968, 1972, 1977; Israel, 1957 and 1959; USSR concerts and opera (Bolshoi Theater), 1959; San Francisco Opera, 1955; début Metropolitan Opera, 1956; there annually, 1956-. Appearances Hamburg State Opera, 1961-63; Royal Swedish Opera, 1957 and subseq. annually; Norwegian and Finnish Operas, 1957-64. Vis. Prof., Univ. of Texas at Austin, 1973-74; Prof., Univ. of Illinois, 1975; Prof., Univ. of Georgia, 1976-77. Hon. Dr of Music: Spelman Coll., Atlanta, 1979; Emory Univ., Atlanta, 1980. *Address:* 1101 South Arlington Ridge Road, Apt 301, Arlington, Va 22202, USA.

DOBBS, Captain Richard Arthur Frederick; Lord-Lieutenant of County Antrim, 1975 (HM Lieutenant for County Antrim, 1959-75); *b* 2 April 1919; *s* of Senator Major Arthur F. Dobbs, DL, of Castle Dobbs, and Hylda Louisa Dobbs; *m* 1953, Carola Day, *d* of Christopher Clarkson, Old Lyme, Conn, USA; four *s* one *d*. *Educ:* Eton; Magdalene Coll., Cambridge (MA). Served War: 2nd Lieut Irish Guards (Supp. Reserve), 1939; Captain 1943. Called to Bar, Lincoln's Inn, 1947; Member, Midland Circuit, 1951-55. *Address:* Castle Dobbs, Carrickfergus, County Antrim, N Ireland. *T:* Whitehead 72238. *Club:* Cavalry and Guards.

DOBBS, Roland; see Dobbs, E. R.

DOBBS, (William) Bernard (Joseph); HM Diplomatic Service; Ambassador to Laos (Lao People's Democratic Republic), since 1982; *b* 3 Sept. 1925; *s* of late William Evelyn Joseph Dobbs and Maud Clifford Dobbs (*née* Bernard); *m* 1952, Brigid Mary Bilitch; one *s* one *d*. *Educ:* Shrewsbury Sch.; Trinity Coll., Dublin (BA Hons Mod. History). Served Rifle Bde/7th Gurkha Rifles, 1943-47 (Captain). Forbes Forbes Campbell and Co. Ltd, 1952-56; Examiner, Patent Office, 1957-61; British Trade Commission, 1961-65: Lagos, 1961-64; Freetown, 1964-66; HM Diplomatic Service: Freetown London, Rangoon, Milan, Kinshasa, Vientiane, 1965-. *Recreations:* reading, walking, writing. *Address:* c/o Foreign and Commonwealth Office, SW1. *T:* 01-233 3000. *Clubs:* Royal Automobile; Kildare Street and University (Dublin).

DOBREE, John Hatherley, MS, FRCS; Consultant in Ophthalmology, St Bartholomew's Hospital, London, EC1, since 1956; Senior Ophthalmic Surgeon, North Middlesex Hospital, N18, since 1947; *b* 25 April 1914; *s* of Hatherley Moor Dobree, OBE, and Muriel Dobree (*née* Hope); *m* 1941, Evelyn Maud Smyth; two *s*. *Educ:* Victoria Coll., Jersey; St Bartholomew's Hosp. MS London 1947; FRCS 1950. House Physician, Metropolitan Hosp., E8, 1938-39; House Surgeon, Western Ophthalm. Hosp., 1940. Served in RAMC, 1940-46, in MEF, as RMO and Ophthalmic Specialist. Chief Asst, Eye Dept, St Bartholomew's Hosp., 1946-51. FRSocMed (Past Sec., Sect. of Ophthalmology); Vice-Pres. and Past Hon. Sec. Ophthalmological Soc. of UK; Dep. Master, Oxford Ophth. Congress, 1976. *Publications:* The Retina, vol. x, in Sir Stewart Duke-Elder's System of Ophthalmology, 1967; (with E. S. Perkins) Differential Diagnosis of Fundus Conditions, 1971; (with E. Boulter) Blindness and Visual Handicap, the Facts, 1982. *Recreations:* archaeology, walking. *Address:* 113 Harley Street, W1. *T:* 01-935 9189; 2 Nottingham Terrace, NW1. *T:* 01-486 6227.

DOBROSIELSKI, Marian, PhD Zürich; Banner of Labour, 1st Class 1975 (2nd Class 1973); Knight Cross of the Order of Polonia Restituta, 1964; Professor of Philosophy, Warsaw University, since 1974; Ambassador *ad personam*, since 1973; *b* 25 March 1923; *s* of Stanislaw and Stefania Dobrosielski; *m* 1950; one *d*. *Educ:* Univ. of Zürich; Univ. of Warsaw. Served in Polish Army in France, War of 1939-45. With Min. of Foreign Affairs, 1948-81; Polish Legation, Bern, 1948-50; Head of Section, Min. of Foreign Affairs, 1950-54; Asst Prof., Warsaw Univ. and Polish Acad. of Sciences, 1954-57; Mem. Polish delegn to UN Gen. Assembly, 1952, 1953, 1958, 1966, 1972-76. First Sec., Counsellor, Polish Embassy in Washington, 1958-64; Min. of Foreign Affairs: Counsellor to Minister, 1964-69; Acting Dir, Research Office, 1968-69; Polish Ambassador to London, 1969-71; Dep. Minister of Foreign Affairs, 1978-81. Univ. of Warsaw: Associate Prof., 1966; Vice-Dean of Faculty of Philosophy, 1966-68; Dir, Inst. of Philosophy, 1971-73 (Chm. Scientific Council, 1969). Chm., Editorial Bd of Studia Filozoficzne, 1968-69; Sec., Polish Philos. Soc., 1955-57 and 1965-69; Dir, Polish Inst. of Internat. Affairs, 1971-80. Mem. Polish United Workers Party (Sec. Party Org., Univ. of Warsaw, 1956-57, 1968-69); Chm., Polish Cttee for European Security and Co-operation, 1973-79 (Vice-Chm., 1971-73). Hon. Vice-Pres., Scottish-Polish Cultural Assoc., Glasgow, 1969-71; Chm., Polish delegn to: 2nd stage Conf. on Security and Co-operation in Europe, 1973-75; CSCE Belgrade Meeting, 1977-78; CSCE Meeting, Madrid, 1980-81. *Publications:* A Basic Epistemological Principle of Logical Positivism, 1947; The Philosophical Pragmatism of C. S. Peirce, 1967; On some contemporary problems: Philosophy, Ideology, Politics, 1970; (trans. and introd) Selection of Aphorisms of G. C. Lichtenberg, Oscar Wilde, Karl Kraus, M. von Ebner-Eschenbach, 4 vols, 1970-74; On the Theory and Practice of Peaceful Coexistence, 1976; Belgrad 77, 1978; Chances and Dilemmas, 1980; numerous articles on philosophy and internat. problems in professional jls. *Recreation:* tennis. *Address:* Kozia Street 9-14, Warszawa, Poland.

DOBRY, George Leon Severyn, CBE 1977; QC 1969; **His Honour Judge George Dobry;** a Circuit Judge, since 1980; *b* 1 Nov. 1918; *m* 1948, Margaret Headley Smith (*d* 1978), *e d* of late Joseph Quartus Smith, JP, Bardfield, Saling, Essex; two *d*. *Educ:* Edinburgh Univ. (MA). Served War of 1939-45: Army, 1939-42; Air Force, 1942-46. Called to Bar, Inner Temple, 1946; Bencher 1977. A Recorder of the Crown Court, 1977-80. Mem. Council, Justice, 1956-68. Adviser to Sec. of State for Environment and Sec. of State for Wales on Develt Control, 1973-75; Mem., Docklands Jt Cttee, 1974-76. *Publications:* Woodfall's Law of Landlord and Tenant, 25th edition (one of the Editors), 1952; Blundell and Dobry, Town and Country Planning, 1962; Blundell and Dobry Planning Appeals and Inquiries, 1962, 2nd edn, 1970; Hill and Redman, Landlord and Tenant (Cons. Editor), 16th edn, 1976; Review of the Development Control System (Interim Report), 1974 (Final Report), 1975; (ed jtly) Development Gains Tax, 1975; (Gen. Editor) Encyclopedia of Development Law, 1976. *Address:* 1 Harcourt Buildings, Temple, EC4. *T:* 01-353 8131; Great Lodge, Great Bardfield, Essex. *T:* Thaxted 810776. *Clubs:* Travellers'; Garrick.

DOBSON, Maj.-Gen. Anthony Henry George, CB 1968; OBE 1953; MC 1944; BA Cantab; *b* 15 Dec. 1911; *s* of late Col Arthur Curtis Dobson, DSO, Royal Engineers, and late Susanna (*née* Oppenheim); *m* 1945, Nellie Homberger; two *s* two *d*. *Educ:* Cheltenham Coll.; Royal Military Academy, Woolwich; Clare Coll., Cambridge. Commissioned Royal Engineers, 1931; hons degree (mech. science), Cambridge, 1934; service in UK, 1934-37; seconded to RAF for survey duties, Iraq, 1938-39. Served War of 1939-45: Middle East (Egypt, Turkey, Iraq), 1939-42; Prisoner of War, Italy, 1942-43; interned in Switzerland after escape, 1944; North-West Europe (Holland and Germany), 1945. Germany, 1945-50; Manpower planning Dept, War Office, 1950-53; in comd, Engineer Regt, Hong Kong, 1953-56; Engr branch, War Office, 1956-59; Chief Engr, HQ Eastern Comd, UK, 1959-62; DQMG, HQ BAOR, 1962-64; Chief Engr, HQ North AG/BAOR, 1964-67, retd. Lt-Col 1945; Col 1956; Brig. 1959; Maj.-Gen. 1964. Planning Inspectorate, DoE, 1969-78. *Recreations:* travel, gardening. *Address:* Ramillies, Compton Way, Moor Park, Farnham, Surrey. *T:* Runfold 2350. *Clubs:* Army and Navy, Ski Club of Great Britain; Kandahar Ski.

DOBSON, Christopher Selby Austin, CBE 1976; FSA; Librarian, House of Lords, 1956-77; *b* 25 Aug. 1916; *s* of late Alban Tabor Austin Dobson, CB, CVO, CBE; *m* 1941, Helen Broughton, *d* of late Capt. E. B. Turner, Holyhead; one *s* one *d*. *Educ:* Clifton Coll.; Emmanuel Coll., Cambridge (BA). With National Council of Social Service, 1938-39. Served War of 1939-45, Lieut Middx Regt (despatches). Asst Principal (Temp.), Ministry of Education, 1946-47; Asst Librarian, House of Lords, 1947-56. *Publication:* (ed) Oxfordshire Protestation Returns 1641-42, 1955. *Recreations:* collecting books, stamps, etc. *Address:* Loxbeech, Mount Street, Battle, Sussex. *T:* Battle 4409. *Clubs:* Roxburghe; (Hon.) Rowfant (Cleveland).

DOBSON, Sir Denis (William), KCB 1969 (CB 1959); OBE 1945; QC 1971; Clerk of the Crown in Chancery and Permanent Secretary to the Lord Chancellor, 1968-77; *b* 17 Oct. 1908; *s* of late William Gordon Dobson, Newcastle upon Tyne; *m* 1st, 1934, Thelma (marr. diss. 1947), *d* of Charles Swinburne, Newcastle upon Tyne; one *s* one *d*; 2nd, 1948, Mary Elizabeth, *d* of J. A. Allen, Haywards Heath; two *s* one *d*. *Educ:* Charterhouse; Trinity Coll., Cambridge (MA, LLB). Solicitor, 1933. Served in RAF, 1940-45 (Desert Air Force, 1942-45). Called to the Bar, Middle Temple, 1951; Bencher, 1968. Dep. Clerk of the Crown in Chancery and Asst Permanent Sec. to Lord Chancellor, 1954-68. Mem., Adv. Council on Public Records, 1977-. *Address:* 50 Egerton Crescent, SW3. *T:* 01-589 7990. *Club:* Athenæum.

DOBSON, Prof. Eric John, MA, DPhil Oxon; MA Fhe BA 1973; Professor of English Language, Oxford University, 1964-80; *b* 16 Aug. 1913; *o s* of John and Lottie Frances Dobson; *m* 1940, Francis Margaret Stinton; two *s* one *d*. *Educ:* North Sydney High Sch.; Wesley Coll., Sydney Univ.; Merton Coll., Oxford. BA (1st cl. Hons English) Sydney, 1934; 1st in Final Hon. Sch. of English 1937, DPhil 1951, Oxford. Tutor in English, Sydney Univ., 1934-35; Wentworth Travelling Fellow of Sydney Univ., 1935-38; Harmsworth Sen. Schol. of Merton Coll., 1938-40; Lecturer in English, University of Reading, 1940-48. Served in Intelligence Div., Naval Staff, Admiralty, 1943-45. Lecturer in English, Jesus Coll. and St Edmund Hall, Oxford, 1948-54; Reader in English Lang., Oxford Univ., 1954-64 (title of Prof. from 1960); Professorial Fellow of Jesus Coll., Oxford, 1954-80, Emeritus Fellow, 1980-. Hon. Treas., Philological Soc., 1974-80. *Publications:* English Pronunciation 1500-1700, 1957, 2nd edn 1968; The Phonetic Writings of Robert Robinson, 1957; Edition of Hymn to the Virgin in Trans. of Cymmrodorion Soc., 1954; The Affiliations of the MSS of Ancrene Wisse, in English and Medieval Studies, 1962; The Date and Composition of Ancrene Wisse (Gollancz Memorial Lecture, Brit. Acad., 1966); The English Text of the Ancrene Riwle (MS Cleopatra C. vi), 1972; Moralities on the Gospels, 1975; The Origins of Ancrene Wisse, 1976; (with F. Ll. Harrison) Medieval English Songs, 1979; (with S. R. T. O. d'Ardenne) Seinte Katerine, 1981; articles and reviews in journals. *Address:* 50A Davenant Road, Oxford OX2 8BY. *T:* Oxford 56222.

DOBSON, Frank Gordon; MP (Lab) Holborn and St Pancras South, since 1979; *b* 15 March 1940; *s* of James William and Irene Shortland Dobson, York; *m* 1967, Janet Mary Alker; three *c*. *Educ:* Dunnington County Primary Sch., York; Archbishop Holgate's Grammar Sch., York; London School of Economics (BScEcon). Administrative jobs with Central Electricity

Generating Bd, 1962-70, and Electricity Council, 1970-75; Asst Sec., Commn for Local Administration (local Ombudsman's office), 1975-79. Member, Camden Borough Council, 1971-76 (Leader of Council, 1973-75); Chm., Coram's Fields and Harmsworth Meml Playground, 1977-. NUR sponsored MP; front bench spokesman on educn, 1981-. Chm., NHS Unlimited, 1981-. Member: Exec., Chile Solidarity Campaign, 1979-; Nat. Cttee, Anti Apartheid Movement, 1980-. *Address:* 22 Great Russell Mansions, Great Russell Street, WC1. *T:* 01-242 5760. *Clubs:* Covent Garden Community Centre; Camden Labour.

DOBSON, Commodore John Petter, CBE 1961; DSC 1940; RD 1940; RNR (retired); *b* 2 Sept. 1901; *s* of Lieut-Comdr John Dobson, RNR and Alice Martha (*née* Petter); *m* 1942, Edith Agnes Ferguson (*d* 1979); one *d*. *Educ:* Middlesbrough High Sch.; Liverpool Coll.; HMS Conway. Midshipman, RNR, 1917; Cadet, Canadian Pacific, 1919; Submarines, 1924; Navigator, RMS Empress of Australia; with Royal trip to Canada and US; subsequently called up, 1939. Minesweeping, 1939-42; Cdre of Convoys, 1942-44, including Normandy Landings; Admiralty Berthing Officer, Sydney, NSW, 1944-45. In command CPS, 1946-61; Master, Empress of Canada (Flagship of Canadian Pacific Steamships Ltd), 1961-62; retired, 1962. Mem., Hon. Company of Master Mariners. Freeman and Liveryman of City of London. *Address:* Sea View Cottage, Sandsend, Whitby, North Yorks. *T:* Whitby 83222. *Club:* Whitby Conservative.

DOBSON, Sir Patrick John H.; *see* Howard-Dobson.

DOBSON, Sir Richard (Portway), Kt 1976; President, BAT Industries Ltd, 1976-79; *b* 11 Feb. 1914; *s* of Prof. J. F. Dobson; *m* 1946, Emily Margaret Carver; one step *d*. *Educ:* Clifton Coll.; King's Coll., Cambridge. Flt-Lt, RAF, 1941-45 (Pilot). Joined British American Tobacco Co. Ltd, 1935: served in China, 1936-40; China, Rhodesia and London, 1946-76; Dir, 1955; Dep. Chm., 1962; Vice-Chm., 1968; Chm., 1970-76. Director: Molins Ltd, 1970-; Commonwealth Development Finance, 1974-79; Exxon Corporation (USA), 1975-; Davy Corp. Ltd, 1975-; Foseco Minsep, 1976-; Lloyds Bank International, 1976-; Chm., British Leyland Ltd, 1976-77. Chm., British-North American Res. Assoc., 1976-80. *Publication:* China Cycle, 1946. *Recreations:* fly fishing, golf. *Address:* 16 Marchmont Road, Richmond upon Thames, Surrey. *T:* 01-940 1504. *Clubs:* United Oxford & Cambridge University; Richmond Golf, Royal Wimbledon Golf.

DOCHERTY, Dr Daniel Joseph, JP; Manpower Services Commissioner, 1974-77; *b* 24 Oct. 1924; *s* of Michael Joseph Docherty and Ellen Stewart; *m* 1952, Dr Rosemary Catherine Kennedy; eight *s* two *d*. *Educ:* St Aloysius' Coll.; Anderson Coll. of Medicine; Glasgow Univ. LRCP, LRCS, LRFPS. Glasgow Town Councillor, 1959-75; Sen. Magistrate, City of Glasgow, 1964-65; Chm. of Police Cttee, 1967-68; Chm. of Educn Cttee, 1971-74. Chm. in Scotland, Job Creation Programme, 1975-78. Mem. Council, Open Univ., 1972-75. JP Glasgow, 1961. *Recreation:* travel. *Address:* 26 Newlands Road, Glasgow G43 2JE. *T:* 041-632 5031.

DOCKER, Rt. Rev. Ivor Colin; *see* Horsham, Bishop Suffragan of.

DODD, Air Vice-Marshal Frank Leslie, CBE 1968; DSO 1944; DFC 1945; AFC 1944 and Bars, 1955 and 1958; AE 1945; Administrator, MacRobert Trusts, since 1974; *b* 5 March 1919; *s* of Frank H. Dodd and Lillian (*née* Willis); *m* 1942, Joyce L. Banyard; one *s* three *d*. *Educ:* King Edward VI Sch., Stafford; Reading University. RAFVR, 1938; CFS course and Flying Instructor, 1940-44; No 544 Sqdn (photo-reconnaissance), 1944-46; CO 45 Sqdn (Beaufighters), 1947-48; CFS Staff and HQ Flying Trng Comd, 1948-52; pfc 1952-53; Chief Instructor CFS, 1953-55; psc 1955; CO 230 OCU Waddington (Vulcans), 1955-59; Gp Captain Trng HQ Bomber Comd, 1959-61; CO RAF Coningsby (Vulcans), 1961-63; idc 1964; AOC and Comdt CFS, 1965-68; MoD (Dir Estabs), 1968-70. Dir Gen., Linesman Project, 1970-74, retired. *Recreations:* golf, music. *Address:* The Lodge, Tarland, Aberdeenshire AB3 4TB. *T:* Tarland 304. *Clubs:* Royal Air Force; Royal Northern (Aberdeen).

DODD, Rev. Harold, MB, ChM (Liverpool), FRCS, LRCP; Hon. Curate, All Soul's Church, W1, 1970-81, retired; Emeritus Surgeon to: St Mary's Hospital Group, Paddington; King George Hospital, Ilford; Royal Hospital, Richmond; Royal London Homoeopathic Hospital; *b* 13 March 1899; *e s* of Alfred Ledward Dodd and Annie Elizabeth Marshall; *m* 1945, Mary, *yr d* of late R. H. Bond; one *s*. *Educ:* University of Liverpool; Guy's Hosp. RAF (pilot), 1917-19; MB, ChB (Distinction in Surgery) Liverpool, 1922, O. T. Williams Prizeman for 1923; House Surgeon, House Physician, Surgical Tutor and Registrar, Liverpool Royal Infirmary, 1923-26; Asst Medical Superintendent, St Luke's Hosp., Chelsea, 1926-28; Resident Medical Officer, Royal Northern Hosp., N7, 1928-30. Past Pres., Assoc. of Consultants and Specialists of Reg. Bd Hosps. Fellow, Assoc. of Surgeons of Great Britain; FRSM (Ex-Pres. Section of Proctology). *Publications:* (with F. B. Cockett) Pathology and Surgery of the Veins of the Lower Limb, 1956, 2nd edn, 1976; surgical papers in medical journals. *Address:* 8 Park Close, Ilchester Place, W14 8ND. *T:* 01-602 3024.

DODD, Prof. James Munro, DSc, PhD; FRS 1975; FRSE; Professor of Zoology, University College of North Wales, 1968-81, now Emeritus; Leverhulme Emeritus Fellowship, 1982-83; *b* 26 May 1915; *m* 1951, Margaret Helen Ingram Macaulay (*née* Greig), BSc (Aberdeen), PhD (Harvard); three

s. *Educ:* The White House Sch., Brampton, Cumberland; Univ. of Liverpool. BSc hons (Cl. 1) 1937; DipEd 1938. PhD St Andrews, 1953; DSc St Andrews, 1968. Biology Master, Cardigan Grammar Sch., 1938-40. Royal Air Force (Navigator and Staff Navigator), 1940-46. Asst in Zoology, Univ. of Aberdeen, 1946-47; Lectr in Zoology, Univ. of St Andrews, in charge of Gatty Marine Laboratory, 1947-57; Reader in Zoology, Univ. of St Andrews, and Dir of Gatty Marine Laboratory, 1957-60; Prof. of Zoology, Leeds Univ., 1960-68. Chm., British Nat. Cttee for Biology, 1972-. Assessor, ARC, 1981-82. Trustee, BM (Natural History), 1975-82. FRSE 1957. Associate Editor: Proceedings of the Royal Soc., series B; Philosophical Trans of the Royal Soc., series B. *Publications:* contributor to Marshall's Physiology of Reproduction, The Thyroid Gland, The Pituitary Gland, The Ovary, and to zoological and endocrinological jls. *Recreations:* fishing, photography, music. *Address:* Weirglodd Wen, Bulkeley Road, Bangor, Gwynedd.

DODD, Kenneth Arthur, (Ken Dodd), OBE 1982; professional entertainer, comedian, singer and actor, since 1957; *b* 1931; *s* of Arthur and late Sarah Dodd; unmarried. *Educ:* Holt High Sch., Liverpool. Frequently appears at the Palladium, London, etc. Pantomime, Robinson Crusoe, Coventry Theatre, 1969-70; Malvolio in Twelfth Night, Liverpool, 1971; HaHa, Liverpool, 1973. *Relevant publication:* How Tickled I Am: Ken Dodd, by Michael Billington, 1977. *Recreations:* racing, soccer, reading. *Address:* 76 Thomas Lane, Knotty Ash, Liverpool L14 5NX.

DODD, William Atherton; Chief Education Adviser, since 1978, and Under Secretary (Education Division), since 1980, Overseas Development Administration; *b* 5 Feb. 1923; *s* of Frederick Dodd and Sarah Atherton; *m* 1949, Marjorie Penfold; two *d*. *Educ:* Chester City Grammar Sch.; Christ's Coll., Cambridge (MA, CertEd). Served War, 1942-45: Captain, 8 Gurkha Rifles. Sen. History Master, Ipswich Sch., 1947-52; Educn Officer, Dept of Educn, Tanganyika, 1952-61; Sen. Educn Officer, Min. of Educn, Tanzania, 1961-65; Lectr, Dept of Educn in Developing Countries, Univ. of London Inst. of Educn, 1965-70; Educn Adviser, Min. of Overseas Develt, 1970-77. *Publications:* A Mapbook of Exploration, 1965; Primary School Inspection in New Countries, 1968; Education for Self-Reliance in Tanzania, 1969; Society, Schools and Progress in Tanzania, 1970; (ed) Teacher at Work, 1970. *Recreations:* walking, music, cricket. *Address:* 20 Bayham Road, Sevenoaks, Kent. *T:* Sevenoaks 454238. *Club:* MCC.

DODD, Rev. William Harold Alfred; *see* Dodd, Harold.

DODDERIDGE, Morris, CBE 1974 (OBE 1962); British Council Representative, Rome, 1970-75, retired; *b* 17 Oct. 1915; *s* of Reginald William Dodderidge and Amy Andrew; *m* 1941, Esme Williams; two *s* one *d*. *Educ:* Hertford Grammar Sch.; King's Coll., London; Inst. Educn, London. BA 1st cl. hons English 1937; Brewer Prize for Lit.; Teachers Dip. 1938; DipEd 1952. Asst Master, Hele's Sch., Exeter, 1938-40. War of 1939-45, Royal Signals; served N Africa, Italy, Austria (Captain, despatches). Joined British Council, 1946: Dir of Studies, Milan, 1947-53; Rep., Norway, 1953-57; Teaching of English Liaison Officer, 1957-59; Dir, Recruitment Dept, 1959-64; Controller: Recruitment Div., 1964-66; Overseas Div. A, 1966-67; Home Div. I, 1967-68; Appts Div., 1968-70. *Publications:* Man on the Matterhorn, 1940; (with W. R. Lee) Time for a Song, 1965. *Recreations:* golf, swimming, viticulture. *Address:* 35 St Catharine's Road, Broxbourne, Herts. *T:* Hoddesdon 62339.

DODDS, Denis George, CBE 1977; LLB (London); CompIEE; Solicitor; Chairman, British Approval Service for Electricity Cables Ltd, since 1982; *b* 25 May 1913; *s* of Herbert Yeaman Dodds and Violet Katharine Dodds; *m* 1937, Muriel Reynolds Smith; two *s* three *d*. *Educ:* Rutherford Coll., Newcastle upon Tyne; King's Coll., Durham Univ. Asst Solicitor and Asst Town Clerk, Gateshead, 1936-41. Served Royal Navy (Lieut RNVR), 1941-46. Dep. Town Clerk and Dep. Clerk of the Peace, City of Cardiff, 1946-48; Sec., S Wales Electricity Board, 1948-56; Chief Industrial Relations Officer, CEA and Industrial Relations Adviser, Electricity Council, 1957-59; Dep. Chm., 1960-62, Chm., 1962-77, Merseyside and N Wales Electricity Bd; Chairman: Merseyside Chamber of Commerce and Industry, 1976-78; Port of Preston Adv. Bd, 1978; Assoc. of Members of State Industry Boards, 1976-. Member: CBI Council for Wales, 1960-78; NW Economic Planning Council, 1971; Dir, Development Corporation for Wales, 1970. Mem., Nat. Adv. Council for Employment of the Disabled, 1978-. *Recreations:* music and gardening. *Address:* Corners, 28 Grange Park, Westbury on Trym, Bristol BS9 4BP. *T:* Bristol 621440.

DODDS, George Christopher Buchanan, CMG 1977; Assistant Under-Secretary of State, Ministry of Defence, 1964-76; *b* 8 Oct. 1916; *s* of George Hepple Dodds and Gladys Marion (*née* Ferguson), Newcastle upon Tyne; *m* 1944, Olive Florence Wilmot Ling; no *c*. *Educ:* Rugby; Gonville and Caius Coll., Cambridge (BA). Entered Secretary's Dept, Admiralty, 1939; Royal Marines, 1940-41; Private Sec. to Sec. of the Admiralty, 1941-43; Asst Private Sec. to Prime Minister, June-Aug. 1944; Asst Sec., 1951; idc, 1959. *Recreations:* bird-watching, walking, golf, bridge. *Address:* 5 Bryanston Square, W1. *T:* 01-262 2852. *Club:* Royal Mid-Surrey Golf.

DODDS, James Pickering, CB 1954; Under-Secretary, Department of Health and Social Security, 1968-73; *b* 7 Feb. 1913; *s* of James Thompson and Elizabeth Fingland Dodds; *m* 1942, Ethel Mary Gill; two *d*. *Educ:* Queen Elizabeth's Grammar Sch., Darlington; Jesus Coll., Cambridge. Entered

Ministry of Health, 1935; Nuffield Home Civil Service Travelling Fellowship, 1950; Under-Sec., 1951; Dir of Establishments and Orgn, 1965-68. *Address:* 21 Luttrell Avenue, Putney, SW15.

DODDS, Sir Ralph (Jordan), 2nd Bt *cr* 1964; *b* 25 March 1928; *o s* of Sir (Edward) Charles Dodds, 1st Bt, MVO, FRS, and Constance Elizabeth (*d* 1969), *o d* of late J. T. Jordan, Darlington; *S* father, 1973; *m* 1954, Marion, *er d* of late Sir Daniel Thomas Davies, KCVO; two *d. Educ:* Winchester; RMA, Sandhurst. Regular commission, 13/18th Royal Hussars, 1948; served UK and abroad; Malaya, 1953 (despatches); resigned, 1958. Underwriting Member of Lloyd's, 1964. *Address:* Picton House, Thames Ditton, Surrey. *Clubs:* Cavalry and Guards, Hurlingham.

DODDS-PARKER, Sir (Arthur) Douglas, Kt 1973; MA (Oxford); company director since 1946; *b* 5 July 1909; *o s* of A. P. Dodds-Parker, FRCS, Oxford; *m* 1946, Aileen, *d* of late Norman B. Coster and late Mrs Alvin Dodd, Grand Detour, Ill., USA; one *s. Educ:* Winchester; Magdalen Coll., Oxford. BA in Modern History, 1930; MA 1934. Entered Sudan Political Service, 1930; Kordofan Province, 1931-34; Asst Private Sec. to Governor-General, Khartoum, 1934-35; Blue Nile Province, 1935-38; Public Security Dept, Khartoum, 1938-39; resigned 1938; joined Grenadier Guards, 1939; employed on special duties, March 1940; served in London, Cairo, East African campaign, North Africa, Italy and France, 1940-45; Col, 1944 (despatches, French Legion of Honour, Croix de Guerre). MP (C): Banbury Div. of Oxon, 1945-Sept. 1959; Cheltenham, 1964-Sept. 1974; Jt Parly Under-Sec. of State for Foreign Affairs, Nov. 1953-Oct. 1954, Dec. 1955-Jan. 1957; Parly Under-Sec. for Commonwealth Relations, Oct. 1954-Dec. 1955. Chairman: British Empire Producers Organisation; Joint East and Central Africa Board, 1947-50; Conservative Commonwealth Council, 1960-64; Cons. Parly Foreign and Commonwealth Cttee, 1970-73; Europe Atlantic Gp, 1976-; Delegate to Council of Europe, North Atlantic and W European Assemblies, 1965-72; Mem., British Parly Delegn to European Parlt, Strasbourg, 1973-75. *Address:* 9 North Court, Great Peter Street, SW1; The Lighthouse, West Port, New York 12993, USA. *Clubs:* Carlton, Special Forces (Pres., 1977-81); Leander, Institute of Directors.

DODGE, John V.; Senior Editorial Consultant, Encyclopædia Britannica, since 1972; Chairman, Board of Editors, Encyclopædia Britannica Publishers, since 1977; *b* 25 Sept. 1909; *s* of George Dannel Dodge and Mary Helen Porter; *m* 1935, Jean Elizabeth Plate; two *s* two *d. Educ:* Northwestern Univ., Evanston, Ill., USA; Univ. of Bordeaux, Bordeaux, France. Free-lance writer, 1931-32; Editor, Northwestern Alumni News and official publications of Northwestern Univ., 1932-35; Exec. Sec., Northwestern Univ. Alumni Assoc., 1937-38; Asst Editor, Encyclopædia Britannica, and Associate Editor, Britannica Book of the Year, 1938-43. US Army, 1943-46 (Intelligence). Associate Editor, Ten Eventful Years and Asst Editor, Encyclopædia Britannica, 1946-50; Editor, Britannica World Language Dictionary, 1954; Managing Editor, Encyclopædia, 1950-60; Executive Editor, 1960-64; Senior Vice-Pres., Editorial, 1964-65; Senior Editorial Consultant, 1965-70; Vice-Pres., Editorial, 1970-72. Conseiller Editorial, Encyclopædia Universalis (Paris), 1968-; Editorial Advisor: Britannica Internat. Encyclopædia (in Japanese), Tokyo, 1969-; Enciclopedia Mirador (Rio de Janeiro) and Enciclopedia Barsa (Mexico City), 1974-. *Address:* 3851 Mission Hills Road, Northbrook, Ill 60062, USA. *T:* (312) 272-0254.

DODSON, family name of **Baron Monk Bretton.**

DODSON, Sir Derek (Sherborne Lindsell), KCMG 1975 (CMG 1963); MC 1945; HM Diplomatic Service, retired; *b* 20 Jan. 1920; *e* and *o* surv. *s* of late Charles Sherborne Dodson, MD, and Irene Frances Lindsell; *m* 1952, Julie Maynard Barnes; one *s* one *d. Educ:* Stowe; RMC Sandhurst. Commissioned as 2nd Lieut in Royal Scots Fusiliers, 1939, and served in Army until Feb. 1948. Served War of 1939-45 (MC): India, UK, Middle East, and with Partisans in Greece and N Italy. Mil. Asst to Brit. Comr, Allied Control Commn for Bulgaria, July 1945-Sept. 1946; GSO 3, War Office, Oct. 1946-Nov. 1947; apptd a Mem. HM Foreign Service, 1948; 2nd Sec., 1948; Acting Vice-Consul at Salonika, Sept. 1948; Acting Consul Gen. there in 1949 and 1950; Second Sec., Madrid, 1951; promoted First Sec., Oct. 1951; transferred to Foreign Office, Sept. 1953; apptd Private Sec. to Minister of State for Foreign Affairs, 1955; First Sec. and Head of Chancery, Prague, Nov. 1958; Chargé d'Affaires there in 1959, 1960, 1961, 1962; promoted and apptd Consul at Elisabethville, 1962; Transf. FO and apptd Head of the Central Dept, 1963; Counsellor, British Embassy, Athens, 1966-69; Ambassador: to Hungary, 1970-73; to Brazil, 1973-77; to Turkey, 1977-80. Chm., Anglo-Turkish Soc., 1982-. Mem., Bd of Governors, United World College of the Atlantic, 1982-. Order of the Southern Cross, Brazil. *Recreations:* shooting, fishing, walking. *Address:* 47 Ovington Street, SW3. *T:* 01-589 5055; Gable House, Leadenham, Lincoln. *T:* Loveden 72212. *Clubs:* Boodle's, Travellers'.

DODSWORTH, Geoffrey Hugh, FCA, JP; Joint Chief Executive, Oceanic Finance Corporation, since 1980; *b* 7 June 1928; *s* of late Walter J. J. Dodsworth and Doris M. Baxter; *m* 1st, 1949, Isabel Neale (decd); one *d* ; 2nd, 1971, Elizabeth Ann Beeston; one *s* one *d. Educ:* St Peter's Sch., York. MP (C) Herts SW, Feb. 1974-Oct. 1979, resigned. Mem. York City Council, 1959-65; JP York 1961, now JP Herts. Dir, Grindlays Bank Ltd, 1976-80; Chief Exec., Grindlay Brandts Ltd, 1977-80. *Recreation:* riding. *Address:*

Woodcote, Frithsden Copse, Berkhamsted, Herts. *T:* Berkhamsted 2323. *Club:* Carlton.

DODSWORTH, Sir John Christopher S.; *see* Smith-Dodsworth.

DODWELL, Prof. Charles Reginald, MA, PhD, LittD; FBA 1973; FRHistS, FSA; Pilkington Professor of History of Art and Director of Whitworth Gallery, University of Manchester, since 1966; *b* 3 Feb. 1922; *s* of William Henry Walter and Blanche Dodwell; *m* 1942, Sheila Juliet Fletcher; one *s* one *d. Educ:* Gonville and Caius Coll., Cambridge (MA, PhD, LittD). Served War, Navy, 1941-45. Research Fellow, Caius Coll., 1950-51. Sen. Research Fellow, Warburg Inst., 1950-53; Lambeth Librarian, 1953-58; Fellow, Lectr, Librarian, Trinity Coll., Cambridge, 1958-66. Visiting scholar, Inst. of Advanced Studies, Princeton, USA, 1965-66. *Publications:* The Canterbury School of Illumination, 1954; Lambeth Palace, 1958; The Great Lambeth Bible, 1959; The St Albans Psalter (section 2) 1960; Theophilus: De Diversis Artibus, 1961; Reichenau Reconsidered, 1965; Painting in Europe 800-1200, 1971; Early English Manuscripts in Facsimile, vol. xviii (section 2), 1972; Anglo-Saxon Art: a new perspective, 1982; articles in Burlington Magazine, Gazette des Beaux Arts, Atti del 18 Congresso Internazionale di studi sull'alto medioevo (Spoleto), Jumièges, Congrès Scientifique du 13 Centenaire, l'Archéologie, etc. *Recreations:* badminton, table-tennis. *Address:* The Old House, 12 Park Road, Cheadle Hulme, Cheshire SK8 7DA. *T:* 061-485 3923.

DOGGART, George Hubert Graham; Headmaster, King's School, Bruton, since 1972; *b* 18 July 1925; *e s* of Alexander Graham Doggart and Grace Carlisle Hannan; *m* 1960, Susan Mary, *d* of R. I. Beattie, Eastbourne; one *s* two *d. Educ:* Winchester; King's Coll., Cambridge. BA History, 1950; MA 1955. Army, 1943-47 (Sword of Honour, 161 OCTU, Mons, 1944); Coldstream Guards. On staff at Winchester, 1950-72 (exchange at Melbourne C of E Grammar Sch., 1963); Housemaster, 1964-72. HMC Schools rep. on Nat. Cricket Assoc., 1964-75; Pres., English Schools Cricket Assoc., 1965-; Member: Cricket Council, 1968-71, 1972; MCC Cttee, 1975-78, 1979-81 (Pres., 1981-82). *Publication:* (ed) The Heart of Cricket: memoir of H. S. Altham, 1967. *Recreations:* literary and sporting (captained Cambridge v Oxford at cricket, Association football, rackets and squash, 1949-50; played in Rugby fives, 1950; played for England v W Indies, two tests, 1950; captained Sussex, 1954). *Address:* Headmaster's House, King's School, Bruton, Somerset. *Clubs:* MCC, Lord's Taverners'; Hawks.

DOGGART, James Hamilton, MA, MD, FRCS; Consulting Surgeon, Moorfields, Westminster and Central Eye Hospital and Hospital for Sick Children, Great Ormond Street; Past Chairman, British Orthoptic Board; FRSM; Livery of the Society of Apothecaries of London; Ophthalmological Society, Société belge d'Ophtalmologie, Société française d'Ophtalmologie; Hon. Member: Australian, NZ and Peruvian Ophthalmological Societies; Oto-Neuro-Ophth. Soc. of the Argentine; Canadian Ophthalmological Society; formerly: Lecturer, Institute of Ophthalmology; Examiner: for British Orthoptic Board; (in Fellowship of Ophthalmology) RCSI; Faculty of Ophth. representative on Council of RCS; Examiner in Ophthalmology, Royal Coll. of Surgeons and Physicians, University of Belfast, and for FRCS, 1954-60; formerly Pres. and Mem. Council, Faculty of Ophthalmologists and Fellow and Councillor, Hunterian Society; Hon. Secretary, Editorial Committee, British Journal Ophthalmology; surgeon-oculist in London, 1929-72; *b* 22 Jan. 1900; *s* of late Arthur Robert Doggart, Bishop Auckland; *m* 1st, 1928, Doris Hilda Mennell; one *d* ; 2nd, 1938, Leonora Sharpley Gatti; one *s. Educ:* Bishop's Stortford Coll.; King's Coll., Cambridge (Scholar); St Thomas's Hospital. Surg. Sub-Lt, RNVR, 1918; Schol., King's Coll., Cambridge, 1919-22; Mem. Anglo-American Physiological Exped. to Andes, 1921; Ophth. Ho. Surg., St Thomas's Hosp., 1923-24; Ho. Surg., Casualty Officer, Royal Northern Hosp., 1925-26; appts at Royal Westminster Ophthalmic Hosp.; Clinical Asst, Refraction Asst, Chief Clin. Asst and Pathologist, 1926-30; appts at Moorfields Eye Hosp.; Clin. Asst, Refraction Asst, Chief Clin. Asst, 1927-34, Asst Med. Officer to Physico-Therapy Dept, 1930-31, Lang Research Schol., 1930-33; Clin. Asst, London Hosp., 1929-34; Ophth. Surg., East Ham Memorial Hosp., 1930-31; appts at St George's Hosp.: Asst Ophth. Surg., 1931-46, Ophth. Surg., 1946-49; Lectr in Ophthalmology, St George's Hosp. Med. Sch., University of London, 1931-49; Ophth. Surg., Lord Mayor Treloar Hosp., 1932-37; Asst Surgeon, Central London Ophthalmic Hosp., 1934-38; Ophth. Surg., Hosp. for Sick Children, Great Ormond Street, 1936-63; Lectr in Ophth., Inst. of Child Health, 1936-63; Hon. Secretary: Section of Ophthalmology, RSM, 1935-37; Ophthalmological Soc., 1939-40, 1946-47. Chm., Cttee of Horatian Soc., 1965-69. Sq/Ldr, W/Cdr, RAF, Med. Br., 1940-45. CStJ 1962. *Publications:* Diseases of Children's Eyes, 1947, 2nd edn, 1950; Children's Eye Nursing, 1948; Ocular Signs in Slit-Lamp Microscopy, 1949; Ophthalmic Medicine, 1949; Chapters in: Moncrieff's Nursing of Sick Children, 1948; Garrod Batten and Thursfield's Diseases of Children, 1949; Stallard's Modern Practice in Ophthalmology, 1949; Berens' Diseases of the Eye, 1949; Parsons and Barling's Diseases of Children, 1954; Treves and Rogers' Surgical Applied Anatomy, 1952; Gaisford and Lightwood's Pædiatrics for the Practitioner, 1955; Thérapeutique Médicale Oculaire; articles in British Encyclopædias of Medical and Surgical Practice; papers in Brit. Jl Ophth., etc. *Recreations:* walking, reading. *Address:* Albury Park, Albury, Guildford, Surrey. *T:* Shere 3289. *Clubs:* English-Speaking Union; Hawks (Cambridge).

DOGGETT, Frank John, CB 1965; retired; Deputy Chairman, UKAEA, 1971-76; Director, National Nuclear Corporation, 1973-76; *b* 7 Jan. 1910; *s* of Frank Hewitt and Charlotte Doggett; *m* 1st, 1940, Clare Judge (*d* 1956); one *d*; 2nd, 1957, Mary Battison. *Educ:* Mathematical Sch., Rochester; University of London (LLB). Inland Revenue, 1929; Air Ministry, 1938; MAP, 1940; MOS, 1946, Under-Sec., 1957-59; Under-Sec., Min. of Aviation. 1959-66, Dep. Sec., 1966-67; Dep. Sec. (A), Min. of Technology, 1967-70; Under-Sec., Dept of Trade and Industry, 1970-71. *Address:* The Jays, Ridgeway Road, Dorking, Surrey. *T:* Dorking 885819.

DOHA, Aminur Rahman S.; *see* Shams-ud Doha, A. R.

DOIG, Very Rev. Dr Andrew Beveridge; *b* 18 Sept. 1914; *s* of George and Hannah Doig; *m* 1st, 1940, Nan Carruthers (*d* 1947); one *d*; 2nd, 1950, Barbara Young; one *s* one *d*. *Educ:* Hyndland Secondary Sch., Glasgow; Glasgow Univ. (MA, BD; Hon. DD 1974); Union Theol Seminary, New York (STM). Ordained, 1938; Church of Scotland Missionary to Nyasaland, 1939-63; service included: Dist Missionary and Sec. of Mission Council; Sen. Army Chaplain, E Africa Comd, 1941-45; Mem., Legislative Council; Mem., Adv. Cttee on African Educn, University Coll. Council; Regional Sec., Nyasaland and N Rhodesia; seconded to represent African interests in Fed. Parlt, Rhodesias and Nyasaland, 1953-58; Gen. Sec., Synod of Ch. of Central Africa (Presbyterian), 1958-63; Minister, St John's and King's Park, Dalkeith, Scotland, 1963-72; Gen. Sec., National Bible Soc. of Scotland, 1972-82; Moderator of the Gen. Assembly of the Church of Scotland, 1981-82. *Address:* The Eildons, Moulin, Pitlochry. *T:* Pitlochry 2892.

DOIG, Sir James (Nimmo Crawford), Kt 1970; Director, UEB Industries Ltd; *b* 21 Aug. 1913; *s* of David Dickson Doig; *m;* two *s* one *d*; *m* 1976, Irene Evelyn Godden. *Educ:* Alan Glen's School and Royal Technical College, Glasgow. Managing Director, UEB Industries Ltd, 1948-73, Chairman 1965-79. *Recreations:* yachting, painting. *Address:* Rocky Bay, Waineke Island, Auckland, New Zealand. *Clubs:* Northern, Royal NZ Yacht Squadron (NZ); Royal Sydney Yacht Squadron.

DOIG, Peter Muir; *b* 27 Sept. 1911; *m* 1938, Emily Scott; two *s*. *Educ:* Blackness Sch., Dundee. Served RAF, 1941-46. Sales Supervisor with T. D. Duncan Ltd, Bakers, Dundee, until 1963. Mem., TGWU; joined Labour Party, 1930; Mem. of Dundee Town Council, 1953-63, Hon. Treasurer, 1959-63. Contested (Lab) S Aberdeen, 1959; MP (Lab) Dundee West, Nov. 1963-1979. *Recreation:* chess. *Address:* 29 Riverside Road, Wormit, Fife.

DOIG, Ralph Herbert, CMG 1974; CVO 1954; *b* 24 Feb. 1909; *s* of late William and Rose Doig; *m* 1937, Barbara Crock; two *s* four *d*. *Educ:* Guildford Grammar Sch.; University of Western Australia (BA, DipCom). Entered Public Service of WA, 1926; Private Sec. to various Premiers, 1929-41; Asst Under-Sec., Premier's Dept, 1941; Under-Sec., Premier's Dept, and Clerk of Executive Council, Perth, Western Australia, 1945-65; Public Service Comr, W Australia, 1965-71; Chm., Public Service Board, WA, 1971-74. State Director: visit to Western Australia of the Queen and the Duke of Edinburgh, 1954; visit of the Duke of Edinburgh for British Empire and Commonwealth Games, 1962; visit of the Queen and the Duke of Edinburgh, 1963. *Recreation:* bowls. *Address:* 3 Marapana Road, City Beach, WA 6015, Australia. *T:* 385-9640.

DOISY, Prof. Edward A.; Professor Emeritus of Biochemistry and Director Emeritus of Edward A. Doisy Department of Biochemistry, St Louis University School of Medicine, since 1965; *b* Hume, Ill., 13 Nov. 1893; *s* of Edward Perez and Ada Alley Doisy; *m* 1st, 1918, Alice Ackert (*d* 1964); four *s*; 2nd, 1965, Margaret McCormick. *Educ:* Univ. of Illinois (AB 1914, MS 1916); Harvard (PhD 1920). Hon. ScD: Yale, 1940; Washington, 1940; Chicago, 1941; Central Coll., 1942; Illinois, 1960; Gustavus Adolphus Coll., 1963; Hon. Dr. Paris, 1945; Hon. LLD, St Louis, 1955. Asst in Biochemistry, Harvard Medical Sch., 1915-17; Army Service, 1917-19; Instructor, Associate and Associate Prof. in Biochemistry, Washington Univ. Sch. of Medicine, 1919-23; Prof. of Biochemistry and Chm. of Dept, St Louis Univ. Sch. of Medicine, 1923-65, Distinguished Service Prof., 1951-65. Member: American Soc. of Biological Chemists (Pres. 1943-45); American Chem. Soc.; Endocrine Soc. (Pres. 1949-50); American Assoc. for the Advancement of Science; Soc. for Experimental Biology and Medicine (Pres. 1949-51); National Academy of Sciences; American Philosophical Soc.; Amer. Acad. Arts and Sci.; Pontifical Acad. of Sci.; Foundation or Memorial Lectr at New York, Kansas, Pittsburgh, Chicago, Cleveland, Minnesota, Rochester; several medals and awards; shared the Nobel Prize in Physiology and Medicine for 1943 with Dr Henrik Dam. *Publications:* more than 100 papers in medical and scientific journals. *Recreations:* golf, hunting and fishing. *Address:* Apt 4b, Colonial Village Apartments, Webster Groves, Mo 63119, USA; St Louis University School of Medicine, 1402 South Grand Boulevard, St Louis, Missouri 63104. *T:* 664-9800 ext. 121.

DOLBY, Ray Milton, PhD; engineering company executive; electrical engineer; Owner and President, Dolby Laboratories Inc., San Francisco and London, since 1965; *b* Portland, Ore, 18 Jan. 1933; *s* of Earl Milton Dolby and Esther Eufemia (*née* Strand); *m* 1966, Dagmar Baumert; two *s*. *Educ:* San Jose State Coll.; Washington Univ.; Stanford Univ. (Beach Thompson award, BS Elec. Engrg); Pembroke Coll., Cambridge (Marshall schol., 1957-60, Draper's studentship, 1959-61, NSF Fellow, 1960-61; PhD Physics 1961; Fellow, 1961-63; research in long-wave length x-rays, 1957-63). Electronic

technician/jun. engr, Ampex Corp., Redwood City, Calif, 1949-53. Served US Army 1953-54. Engr, 1955-57; Sen. Engr, 1957; UNESCO Advr, Central Sci. Instruments Org., Punjab, 1963-65; Cons., UKAEA, 1962-63. Inventions, research, pubns in video tape rec., x-ray microanalysis, noise reduction and quality improvements in audio and video systems; patentee. Fellow: Audio Engrg Soc. (Silver Medal, 1971; Governor, 1972-74; Pres., 1980-81); Brit. Kinematograph, Sound, TV Soc.; Soc. Motion Picture, TV Engrs (S. L. Warner award, 1978). MIEEE; Tau Beta Pi. Other Awards: Emmy (for contrib. to Ampex video recorder), 1957; Trendsetter, Billboard, 1971; Lyre, Inst. High Fidelity, 1972; Emile Berliner Assoc. Maker of Microphone award, 1972; Top 200 Execs Bi-Centennial, 1976; Sci. and Engrg, Acad. of Motion Picture Arts and Scis, 1979. Trustee, Univ. High Sch., San Francisco; Dir, San Francisco Opera; Governor, San Francisco Symphony. *Recreations:* yachting, skiing. *Address:* (home) 50 Walnut Street, San Francisco, Calif 94118, USA. *T:* (415) 563-6947; (office) 731 Sansome Street, San Francisco, Calif 94111. *T:* (415) 392-0300.

DOLCI, Danilo; Coordinator, Centro Studi e Iniziative, since 1958 (Founder); *b* Sesana, Trieste, 1924; *s* of Enrico Dolci and Mely Kontely. *Educ:* University of Rome; University of Milan. Came to Sicily to work for improvement of social conditions, 1952; arrested and tried for non-violent "reverse strike" to find work for unemployed, 1958. Mem. Internat. Council of War Resisters' International, 1963. Hon. DPhil, Univ. of Berne, 1968; Lenin Peace Prize, 1958; Gold Medal, Accademia Nazionale dei Lincei, 1969; Sonning Prize, 1971; Etna Taormina Poetry Prize, 1975; Viareggio Internat. Prize, 1979. *Publications:* Banditi a Partinico, 1955; Inchiesta a Palermo, 1956; Spreco, 1960; Racconti siciliani, 1963; Verso un mondo nuovo, 1964 (trans. A New World in the Making, 1965); Chi Gioca Solo, 1966; Chissà se i pesci piangono (documentazione di un'esperienza educativa), 1973; Non esiste il silenzio, 1974; Esperienze e riflessioni, 1974; Creatura di creature, 1979; Il ponte screpolato, 1979; Da bocca a bocca, 1981. *Address:* Centro Studi, Largo Scalia 5, Partinico (PA), Italy. *T:* 781905; Centro di formazione, Trappeto (PA). *T:* 788 312.

DOLE, John Anthony; Controller of Supplies, Property Services Agency, since 1982; *b* 14 Oct. 1929; *s* of Thomas Stephen Dole and Winifred Muriel (*née* Henderson); *m* 1952, Patricia Ivy Clements; two *s*. *Educ:* Bideford Grammar Sch.; Berkhamsted Sch. Air Ministry: Exec. Officer, 1950; Higher Exec. Officer, 1959; Principal, 1964; Ministry of Transport: Principal, 1965; Asst Sec. (Roads Programme), 1968; Administrator of Sports Council, 1972-75; Under Sec., Freight Directorate, 1976-78; Dir, Senior Staff Management, Depts of the Environment and Transport, 1978-82. *Publications:* plays: Cat on the Fiddle, 1964; Shock Tactics, 1966; Lucky for Some, 1968; Once in a Blue Moon, 1972; Top Gear, 1976. *Recreations:* writing, philately. *Address:* 240 Upton Road South, Bexley, Kent DA5 1QS.

DOLIN, Sir Anton, Kt 1981; dancer and choreographer; *b* Slinfold, Sussex, 27 July 1904; *s* of H. G. Kay and Helen Maude Kay (*née* Healey); changed name from Patrick Healey-Kay. Joined Diaghilev's Russian Ballet Company in 1923, creating a number of roles; in 1927 danced with Karsavina at the London Coliseum in Le Spectre de la Rose; and later in the year founded the Nemchinova-Dolin Ballet with Nemchinova; rejoined the Diaghilev Company in 1929 (prominently associated with the Camargo Soc.); principal dancer with the Vic-Wells Ballet Company, 1931-35; with Markova-Dolin Ballet Co., 1935-37; organised (with Julien Braunsweg) London's Festival Ballet, 1950; led Festival Ballet in 19-week tour of United States and Canada, 1954-55, and in tour of Europe, 1958; Indiana Univ., 1970-73; has danced principal rôle in all classical and many modern works; has worked also for films, and in revue, etc. His choreographic works for the ballet include: Hymn to the Sun, The Nightingale and the Rose, Rhapsody in Blue, Espagnol, The Pas de Quatre, Variations for Four, Ravel's Bolero, The Swan of Tuonela (Sibelius); choreography (with Lindsay Dolan) The Mitford Girls, Chichester, 1981. Guest Dir of Ballet, Rome Opera. Produced Nutcracker, Giselle, Swan Lake in many countries. The Queen Elizabeth Coronation award, 1954. Awarded The Order of The Sun by the Pres. of Peru, 1959. *Publications:* Divertissement, 1930; Ballet Go Round, 1939; Pas de Deux, 1950; Markova, 1953; Autobiography, 1960; The Sleeping Ballerina, 1966. *Recreation:* travel. *Address:* 3 Orme Court, W2 4RL. *T:* 01-727 1451.

DOLL, Sir Richard; *see* Doll, Sir W. R. S.

DOLL, Prof. Sir (William) Richard (Shaboe), Kt 1971; OBE 1956; FRS 1966; DM, MD, FRCP, DSc; first Warden, Green College, Oxford, 1979-Aug. 1983; *b* Hampton, 28 Oct. 1912; *s* of Henry William Doll and Mary Kathleen Shaboe; *m* 1949, Joan Mary Faulkner, MB, BS, MRCP, DPH; one *s* one *d*. *Educ:* Westminster Sch.; St Thomas's Hosp. Med. Sch., London. MB, BS 1937; MD 1945; FRCP 1957; DSc London 1958. RAMC, 1939-45. Appts with Med. Research Council, 1946-69; Mem. Statistical Research Unit, 1948; Dep. Dir, 1959; Dir, 1961-69. Hon. Associate Physician, Central Middlesex Hosp., 1949-69; Teacher in Medical Statistics and Epidemiology, University Coll. Hosp. Med. Sch., 1963-69; Regius Prof. of Medicine, Oxford Univ., 1969-79. Member: MRC, 1970-74; Royal Commn on Environmental Pollution, 1973-79; Standing Commn on Energy and the Environment, 1978-81; Scientific Council of Internat. Cancer Research Agency, 1966-70 and 1975-78; Council, Royal Society, 1970-71 (a Vice-Pres., 1970-71); Chairman: Adverse Reaction Sub-Cttee, Cttee on Safety of Medicines, 1970-77; UK Co-ordinating Cttee on Cancer Research, 1972-77. Hon. Lectr London Sch. of Hygiene and Tropical Med., 1956-62 (Hon. Fellow 1982); Milroy Lectr,

RCP, 1953; Marc Daniels Lectr, RCP, 1969; Harveian Orator, RCP, 1982; William Julius Mickle Fellow, Univ. of London, 1955. Hon DSc: Newcastle, 1969; Belfast, 1972; Reading, 1973; Newfoundland, 1973; Hon. DM Tasmania, 1976. David Anderson Berry Prize (jt), RSE 1958; Bisset Hawkins Medal, RCP, 1962; UN award for cancer research, 1962; Gairdner Award, Toronto, 1970; Buchanan Medal, Royal Soc., 1972; Presidential award, NY Acad. Sci., 1974; Prix Griffuel, Paris, 1976; Gold Medal, RIPH&H, 1977; Mott award, Gen. Motors' Cancer Res. Foundn, 1979; Bruce Medal, Amer. Coll. of Physicians, 1981; National Award, Amer. Cancer Soc., 1981. Hon. Foreign Member: Norwegian Acad. of Scis; American Acad. of Arts and Scis. *Publications:* Prevention of Cancer: pointers from epidemiology, 1967; Causes of Cancer, 1982; articles in scientific journals on aetiology of lung cancer, leukaemia and other cancers, also aetiology and treatment of peptic ulcer; author (jt) Med. Research Council's Special Report Series, 1951, 1957, 1964. *Recreations:* food and conversation. *Address:* 1A Observatory Street, Oxford.

DOLLERY, Prof. Colin Terence, FRCP; Professor of Clinical Pharmacology at Royal Postgraduate Medical School, University of London, since 1965; *b* 14 March 1931; *s* of Cyril Robert and Thelma Mary Dollery; *m* 1958, Diana Myra (*née* Stedman); one *s* one *d. Educ:* Lincoln Sch.; Birmingham Univ. (BSc, MB,ChB); FRCP 1968. House officer: Queen Elizabeth Hosp., Birmingham; Hammersmith Hosp., and Brompton Hosp., 1956-58; Hammersmith Hospital: Med. Registrar, 1958-60; Sen. Registrar and Tutor in Medicine, 1960-62; Consultant Physician, 1962-; Lectr in Medicine at Royal Postgrad. Med. Sch., 1962-65. Hon. Mem., Assoc. of Amer. Physicians. Chevalier de l'Ordre National du Mérite (France), 1976. *Publications:* The Retinal Circulation, 1971 (New York); numerous papers in scientific jls concerned with high blood pressure and drug action. *Recreations:* travel, amateur radio, work. *Address:* 101 Corringham Road, NW11 7DL. *T:* 01-458 2616. *Club:* Athenæum.

DOLLEY, Christopher; Chairman: Damis Group Ltd, since 1974; Vinopoly Ltd; Director, Glavki Trading Ltd, since 1982; *b* 11 Oct. 1931; *yr s* of late Dr Leslie George Francis Dolley and of Jessie, Otford, Kent; *m* 1966, Christine Elizabeth Cooper; three *s. Educ:* Bancrofts Sch.; Corpus Christi Coll., Cambridge. Joined Unilever, 1954; with Unilever subsidiaries, 1954-62: G. B. Ollivant Ltd, 1954-59; United Africa Co., 1959-62. Joined Penguin Books Ltd as Export Manager, 1962; became Dir, 1964, Man. Dir, 1970-73, Chm., 1971-73; Dir for Book Develt, IPC, 1973-77. Exec. Vice-Pres., Penguin Books Inc., Baltimore, 1966; Director: Penguin Publishing Co., 1969-73 (Jt Man. Dir, 1969); Pearson Longman Ltd, 1970-73; The Hamlyn Group, 1971-81; Farvise Ltd, 1976-80. Mem., Nat. Film Finance Corp., 1971-81; Dir, Nat. Film Trustee Corp., 1971-. *Publication:* (ed) The Penguin Book of English Short Stories, 1967. *Recreations:* golf, gardening, collecting. *Address:* Elm Place, 54 St Leonards Road, Windsor, Berkshire SL4 3BY. *T:* Windsor 66961. *Clubs:* Savile; 14 West Hamilton Street (Baltimore, Md).

DOLLEY, Michael, MRIA, FSA, FRHistS; Associate Professor in History, University of New England, Armidale, Australia, 1981, retired (Lecturer, 1978; Senior Lecturer, 1980); *b* 6 July 1925; *s* of late A. H. F. Dolley and Margaret (*née* Horgan); *m* 1950, (Phyllis) Mary Harris; two *s* four *d. Educ:* Wimbledon Coll.; King's Coll., Univ. of London (BA). MRIA 1964; FSA 1955; FRHistS 1965. Assistant Keeper: Nat. Maritime Museum, 1948-51; BM, 1951-63; Queen's Univ. of Belfast: Lectr in Med. Hist., 1963-69; Reader, Dept of Mod. Hist., 1969-75; Prof. of Historical Numismatics, 1975-78. Foreign Corresp. Mem., Royal Swedish Acad. of Letters, Hist. and Antiquities, 1970; Foreign Mem., Danish Acad. of Scis and Letters, 1979. *Publications:* Anglo-Saxon Pennies, 1964; Viking Coins of the Danelaw and of Dublin, 1965; The Hiberno-Norse Coins in the British Museum, 1966; The Norman Conquest and the English Coinage, 1966; Anglo-Norman Ireland, 1972; Medieval Anglo-Irish Coins, 1972; vols of jt authorship; papers in jls, mainly numismatic. *Recreations:* conversation and Irish and Manx history. *Address:* Mavis Bank, 33 Higher Brimley Road, Teignmouth, Devon. *T:* Teignmouth 2994.

DOLLING, Francis Robert; Vice-Chairman, Barclays Bank Ltd, since 1980; Chairman, Barclays Merchant Bank Ltd, since 1980; *b* 21 Jan. 1923; *s* of Frederick George Dolling and Edith Lilian Auriel; *m* 1949, Maisie Alice Noquet; two *d. Educ:* Tottenham County School. Served RAF, 1940-47. Joined Barclays Bank DCO, 1947; served in various overseas territories; Managing Director, Barclays National Bank Ltd, South Africa, 1974; Director and Sen. General Manager, Barclays Bank Internat. Ltd, and Director, Barclays Bank Ltd, 1976. *Recreations:* gardening, golf. *Address:* Rowan Cottage, The Ridgway, Pyrford, Surrey. *T:* Byfleet 43362. *Club:* Royal Automobile.

DOLMETSCH, Carl Frederick, CBE 1954; Director of Haslemere Festival since 1940; specialist and authority on early music and instruments; recording artist in England and abroad; *b* 23 Aug. 1911; *s* of Arnold Dolmetsch and Mabel Johnston; *m* ; one *s* two *d* (and one *s* decd). *Educ:* privately. Began studying music with Arnold Dolmetsch at age of 4; first performed in public at 7, first concert tour at 8, first broadcast on violin and viol, 1925, at 14 years of age; virtuoso recorder-player at 15. Toured and broadcast in America, 1935 and 1936; recorder recitals, Wigmore Hall, Feb. and Nov. 1939, and annually, 1946-; toured and broadcast on radio and TV in Holland, 1946; Italy and Switzerland, 1947; Sweden, 1949; New Zealand, 1953; France, 1956; America, 1957; Switzerland, Austria, Germany, Holland, 1958; Belgium, America, 1959; Sweden, Austria, Germany, 1960; Australia, 1965; Colombia, 1966; France,

Sweden, 1967; Alaska and Canada, 1969; Japan, 1974; America (yearly), 1961-. Frequent broadcasts in this country and abroad. Chm., Dolmetsch Musical Instruments, 1982-. Musical Dir of Soc. of Recorder Players, 1937; Musical Dir, Dolmetsch Internat. Summer School, 1970-; Mem. Incorporated Soc. of Musicians; Mem. Art Workers' Guild, 1953; Patron Early Music Soc., University of Sydney. Hon. Fellow of Trinity Coll. of Music, 1950. Hon. DLitt University of Exeter, 1960. Hon. Fellow London Coll. of Music, 1963. *Publications:* Recorder Tutors, 1957, 1962, 1970, 1977; edited and arranged numerous publications of 16th-, 17th- and 18th-century music; contrib. to many music jls. *Recreations:* ornithology, natural history. *Address:* Jesses, Haslemere, Surrey GU27 2BS. *T:* Haslemere 3818.

DOLTON, David John William; Assistant General Manager (Personnel), National Employers Mutual General Assurance Association Ltd, since 1979; *b* 15 Sept. 1928; *e s* of Walter William and Marie Frances Duval Dolton; *m* 1959, Patricia Helen Crowe; one *s* one *d. Educ:* St Lawrence Coll., Ramsgate. FCIS, FBIM, MIPM, MInstAM. Various appointments in Delta Metal Co. Ltd, 1950-76, incl. Commercial Director, Extrusion Division, and Director of Administration and Personnel, Rod Division, 1967-76; Chief Exec., Equal Opportunities Commn, 1976-78. Governor, The Queen's Coll., Birmingham, 1974-. Reader, Dio. Gloucester. Liveryman, Worshipful Co. of Gold and Silver Wyre Drawers. *Recreations:* music, reading, formerly mountaineering, now mountain and hill walking, swimming, travel. *Address:* Windrush, The Whiteway, Cirencester, Glos GL7 7BA. *T:* Cirencester 67739.

DOMB, Prof. Cyril, PhD; FRS 1977; Professor of Physics, Bar-Ilan University, since 1981; *m* Shirley Galinsky; three *s* three *d. Educ:* Hackney Downs Sch.; Pembroke Coll., Cambridge. Major Open Schol., Pembroke Coll., 1938-41; Radar Research, Admiralty, 1941-46; MA Cambridge, 1945; Nahum Schol., Pembroke Coll., 1946; PhD Cambridge, 1949; ICI Fellowship, Clarendon Laboratory, Oxford, 1949-52; MA Oxon, 1952; University Lecturer in Mathematics, Cambridge, 1952-54; Prof. of Theoretical Physics, KCL, 1954-81; FKC 1978. *Publications:* (ed) Clerk Maxwell and Modern Science, 1963; (ed) Memories of Kopul Rosen, 1970; (ed with M. S. Green) Phase Transitions and Critical Phenomena, vols 1 and 2, 1972, vol 3, 1974, vols 5a, 5b, 6, 1976; (ed, with A. Carmell) Challenge, 1976; articles in scientific journals. *Recreation:* walking. *Address:* Department of Physics, Bar-Ilan University, Ramat-Gan, Israel; 28 St Peter's Court, Queens Road, NW4.

DOMINGO, Placido; tenor singer; *b* Madrid, 21 Jan. 1941; *s* of Placido Domingo and Pepita (*née* Embil), professional singers; *m* Marta Ornelas, lyric soprano; three *s. Educ:* Instituto, Mexico City; Nat. Conservatory of Music, Mexico City. Operatic début, Monterrey, as Alfredo in La Traviata, 1961; with opera houses at Dallas, Fort Worth, Israel, to 1965; NY City Opera, 1965-; débuts: at NY Metropolitan Opera, as Maurizio in Adriana Lecouvreur, 1968; at La Scala, title role in Ernani, 1969; at Covent Garden, Cavaradossi in Tosca, 1971; sings, appears on TV, makes recordings, throughout USA and Europe. *Recreations:* piano, swimming. *Address:* Metropolitan Opera Company, Lincoln Center Plaza, New York, NY 10023, USA; 30 Herrick Avenue, Teaneck, NJ 07666.

DOMINIAN, Dr Jacobus, FRCPEd, FRCPsych; DPM; Senior Consultant Psychiatrist, Central Middlesex Hospital, since 1965; *b* 25 Aug. 1929; *s* of Charles Joseph Dominian and Mary Dominian (*née* Scarlatou); *m* 1955, Edith Mary Smith; four *d. Educ:* Lycée Leonin, Athens; St Mary's High Sch., Bombay; Stamford Grammar Sch., Lincs; Cambridge Univ.; Oxford Univ. MA, MB BChir (Cantab). Postgraduate work in medicine, various Oxford hosps, 1955-58, Maudsley Hosp. (Inst. of Psychiatry), 1958-64; training as psychiatrist at Maudsley Hosp.; Cons. Psychiatrist, Central Middlesex Hosp., 1965-; Director of Marital Research Centre, 1971. Hon. DSc Lancaster, 1976. *Publications:* Psychiatry and the Christian, 1961; Christian Marriage, 1967; Marital Breakdown, 1968; The Church and the Sexual Revolution, 1971; Cycles of Affirmation, 1975; Depression, 1976; Authority, 1976; (with A. R. Peacocke) From Cosmos to Love, 1976; Proposals for a New Sexual Ethic, 1977; Marriage, Faith and Love, 1981; contribs to Lancet, BMJ, the Tablet, TLS. *Recreations:* enjoyment of the theatre, music, reading and writing. *Address:* Pefka, The Green, Croxley Green, Rickmansworth, Herts WD3 3JA. *T:* Rickmansworth 77972.

DON-WAUCHOPE, Sir P. G.; *see* Wauchope.

DONALD, Alan Ewen, CMG 1979; HM Diplomatic Service; Assistant Under-Secretary of State, Foreign and Commonwealth Office, since 1980; *b* 5 May 1931; *2nd s* of Robert Thomson Donald and Louise Turner; *m* 1958, Janet Hilary Therese Blood; four *s. Educ:* Aberdeen Grammar Sch.; Fettes Coll., Edinburgh; Trinity Hall, Cambridge. BA, LLB. HM Forces, 1949-50. Joined HM Foreign Service, 1954: Third Sec., Peking, 1955-57; FO, 1958-61: Private Sec. to Parly Under-Sec., FO, 1959-61; Second, later First Sec., UK Delegn to NATO, Paris, 1961-64; First Sec., British Chargé d'Affaires Office, Peking, 1964-66; Personnel Dept, Diplomatic Service Admin. Office, later FCO, 1967-71; Counsellor (Commercial), British Embassy, Athens, 1971-73; Political Advr to Governor of Hong Kong, 1974-77; Ambassador to: Republics of Zaire, Burundi and Rwanda, 1977-80; People's Republic of the Congo, 1978-80. *Recreations:* music, military history, gentle golf. *Address:* c/o Foreign and Commonwealth Office, SW1A 2AH. *Clubs:* United Oxford & Cambridge University; Aula (London/Cambridge).

DONALD, Dr Alastair Geoffrey, OBE 1982; FRCGP, FRCPE; General Medical Practitioner, since 1952; Assistant Director, Edinburgh Postgraduate Board for Medicine, since 1970; Regional Adviser in General Practice, SE Scotland, since 1972; *b* 24 Nov. 1926; *s* of Dr Pollok Donald and Henrietta Mary (*née* Laidlaw); *m* 1952, Patricia Ireland; two *s* one *d*. *Educ:* Edinburgh Academy; Corpus Christi Coll., Cambridge (MA); Edinburgh Univ. (MB, ChB); Member: Cambridge and Edinburgh Univs Athletic Teams, RAF Medical Branch, 1952-54; general medical practice, Leith and Cramond (Edin.), 1954-; Lectr, Dept of General Practice, Univ. of Edinburgh, 1960-70. Royal College of General Practitioners: Vice-Chm. of Council, 1976-77, Chm., 1979-82; Chm., Bd of Censors, 1979-80; past Chm. and Provost, SE Scotland Faculty. Chairman: UK Conf. of Postgrad. Advisers in Gen. Practice, 1978-80; Jt Cttee on Postgrad. Trng for Gen. Practice, 1982-; Radio Doctor, BBC (Scotland), 1976-78. Chm. Court of Directors, Edinburgh Acad., 1978- (Dir, 1955-); President: Edinburgh Academical Club, 1978-81; Rotary Club of Leith, 1957-58. *Publications:* contribs to medical jls. *Recreations:* golf, family life, reading The Times. *Address:* 30 Cramond Road North, Edinburgh EH4 6JE. *T:* 031-336 3824. *Clubs:* Hawks (Cambridge); University of Edinburgh Staff (Edinburgh).

DONALD, Craig Reid Cantlie, CMG 1963; OBE 1959; *b* 8 Sept. 1914; *s* of Rev. Francis Cantlie and Mary Donald, Lumphanan, Aberdeenshire; *m* 1945, Mary Isabel Speid; one *d*. *Educ:* Fettes; Emmanuel Coll., Cambridge (Scholar). BA 1937, MA 1947. Administrative Officer, Cyprus, 1937. Military Service, 1940-46, Lieut-Col. Commissioner, Famagusta, 1948. Registrar, Cooperative Societies, 1951; Deputy Financial Sec., Uganda, 1951; Sec. to the Treasury, 1956-63. Bursar, Malvern Coll., 1964-79. *Recreation:* country pursuits. *Address:* 55 Geraldine Road, Malvern WR14 3NU. *T:* Malvern 61446. *Club:* Travellers'.

See also I. G. Gilbert.

DONALD, David William Alexander, OBE 1946; TD 1950; General Manager and Actuary, The Standard Life Assurance Company, 1970-79; *b* 3 Feb. 1915; *s* of David Donald and Wilhelmina Ewan. *Educ:* High Sch. of Dundee. FFA 1936. Commnd TA, 1937; served War of 1939-45, Black Watch (RHR), Britain and India; GSO2, Staff Duties, WO, 1943; GSO1, Staff Duties GHQ India, 1944; DAA&QMG 155 (L) Inf. Bde TA, 1949-56. Joined Standard Life Assce Co., 1932: Sen. Asst Actuary, 1946; Jt Actuary, 1949; Actuary, 1962; Dep. Gen. Man., 1969. Dir, Hammerson's Property and Investment Trust Ltd, 1970-. Pres. Faculty of Actuaries, 1969-71; Chm. Associated Scottish Life Offices, 1974-76; Chm. Bd of Governors, Red House Home, 1966-74; Mem. Council, Edinburgh Festival Soc. Ltd, 1977-81; Dir, Scottish Nat. Orchestra Soc. Ltd, 1977-. *Publications:* Compound Interest and Annuities-Certain, 1953; contrib. actuarial jls. *Recreations:* music, golf, wine and food. *Address:* 15 Hermitage Drive, Edinburgh EH10 6BX. *T:* 031-447 2562. *Clubs:* New, Hon. Company of Edinburgh Golfers (Edinburgh); Royal and Ancient (St Andrews).

DONALD, Prof. Ian, CBE 1973 (MBE 1946); MD; FRCSGlas; FRCOG; FCOG(SA); Regius Professor of Midwifery, University of Glasgow, 1954-76, now Emeritus Professor; Hon. Research Consultant, National Maternity Hospital, Dublin, since 1977; *b* 27 Dec. 1910; British; *m* 1937, Alix Mathilde de Chazal Richards; four *d*. *Educ:* Warriston Sch., Moffat; Fettes Coll., Edinburgh; Diocesan Coll., Rondebosch, Cape. BA Cape Town, 1930; MB, BS London, 1937; MD London, 1947; MRCOG 1947; FRCOG 1955; FRCSGlas 1958; FCOG(SA) 1967; Hon. FACOG 1976. Served War of 1939-45 with Royal Air Force (Medical), 1942-46 (despatches). Reader in Obstetrics and Gynæcology, St Thomas's Hosp. Medical Sch., 1951; Reader, University of London, Inst. of Obstetrics and Gynæcology, 1952; Leverhulme Research Scholar, 1953; Blair Bell Memorial Lecturer, RCOG, 1954. Hon. DSc London, 1981. Eardley Holland Gold Medal, 1970; Blair Bell Gold Medal, RSM, 1970; Victor Bonney Prize, RCS, 1970-72; MacKenzie Davidson Medal, BIR, 1975. *Publications:* Practical Obstetric Problems, 1955, 5th edn 1979; articles on respiratory disorders in the newborn, in Lancet and Jl of Obst. and Gynæc. Brit. Empire, and on ultrasonics in diagnosis, in Lancet. *Recreations:* sailing, music, painting. *Address:* Cobblers Row, East End, Paglesham, Essex SS4 2ER. *T:* Canewdon 616.

DONALD, Air Vice-Marshal John George, OBE 1972; Principal Medical Officer, RAF Strike Command, since 1981; *b* 7 Nov. 1927; *s* of John Shirran Donald and Janet Knox (*née* Napier); *m* 1954, Margaret Jean Walton; one *s* two *d*. *Educ:* Inverurie Acad.; Aberdeen Univ. (MB, ChB 1951); DTM&H Edin 1964; MRCGP 1971, FRCGP 1977; MFCM 1972; AFOM 1980. Commnd RAF, 1953; Senior Medical Officer: Colombo, Ceylon, 1954-57; RAF Stafford, 1957-60; RAF Waddington, 1960-63; student, RAF Staff Coll., 1965; SMO, HQ AFCENT, France and Holland, 1966-68; Dep. Dir, Medical Personnel (RAF), 1969-72; OC, The Princess Mary's RAF Hosp., Akrotiri, Cyprus, 1972-76; OC, RAF Hosp., Ely, 1976-78; PMO, RAF Germany, 1978-81. *Recreations:* golf, skiing, camping, ornithology. *Address:* 36 Bradenham Beeches, Walters Ash, High Wycombe, Bucks. *T:* Naphill 4104. *Club:* Royal Air Force.

DONALD, Prof. Kenneth William, DSC 1940; MA, MD, DSc, FRCP, FRCPE, FRSE; Professor of Medicine, University of Edinburgh, 1959-76, now Emeritus Professor; Senior Physician, Royal Infirmary, Edinburgh; Physician to the Queen in Scotland, 1967-76; *b* 25 Nov. 1911; *s* of Col William Donald, MC, RA and Julia Jane Donald, Sandgate; *m* 1942, Rêthe Pearl, *d* of D. H. Evans, Regents Park. *Educ:* Cambridge Univ.; St

Bartholomew's Hosp. Kitchener Scholar and State Scholar, 1930; Senior Scholar, Emmanuel Coll., Cambridge, 1933. Served with Royal Navy, 1939-45: Senior MO, 1st and 5th Flotilla of Destroyers; Senior MO, Admiralty Experimental Diving Unit. Chief Asst, Med. Prof. Unit and Cattlin Research Fellow, St Bartholomew's Hosp., 1946-48; Rockefeller Travelling Research Fellow, Columbia Univ., 1948-49; Senior Lecturer in Medicine, Inst. Diseases of the Chest, Brompton Hosp., 1949-50; Reader in Medicine, Univ. of Birmingham and Physician, Queen Elizabeth Hosp., Birmingham, 1950-59. Scientific Consultant to the Royal Navy. Physician to the Royal Navy in Scotland. Medical Consultant to Scottish Dept of Home and Health; Member: Commonwealth Scholarship Commn; Medical Sub-Cttee, UGC; RN Personnel Research Cttee (Chm.) of MRC; Scottish Adv. Cttee on Med. Research; Council and Scientific Adv. Cttee, British Heart Foundn; Scottish Gen. Nursing Council; Chairman: Under-Water Physiology Sub-Cttee of MRC; Adv. Gp to Sec. of State for Scotland on Health Care Aspects of Industrial Developments in North Sea. Governor, Inst. of Occupational Medicine, Edinburgh. *Publications:* contribs to scientific and medical jls concerning normal and abnormal function of the lungs, the heart and the circulation and high pressure physiology in relation to diving and submarines, drowning, resuscitation. *Recreations:* reading, theatre, fishing. *Address:* Nant-y-Celyn, Cloddiau, Welshpool, Powys SY21 9JE. *T:* Welshpool 2859. *Club:* Athenæum.

DONALDSON, family name of **Baron Donaldson of Kingsbridge.**

DONALDSON OF KINGSBRIDGE, Baron *cr* 1967 (Life Peer), of Kingsbridge; **John George Stuart Donaldson,** OBE 1943; retired farmer; *b* 9 Oct. 1907; *s* of Rev. S. A. Donaldson, Master of Magdalene, Cambridge, and Lady Albinia Donaldson (*née* Hobart-Hampden); *m* 1935, Frances Annesley Lonsdale (see F. A. Donaldson); one *s* two *d*. *Educ:* Eton; Trinity Coll., Cambridge. Pioneer Health Centre, Peckham, 1935-38; Road Transport, 1938-39. Royal Engineers, 1939-45. Farmed in Glos, and later Bucks. Mem., Glos Agric. Exec. Cttee, 1953-60. Parly Under-Sec. of State, NI Office, 1974-76; Minister for the Arts, DES, 1976-79. Joined SDP, 1981. Hon. Sec. Nat. Assoc. Discharged Prisoners Aid Socs, 1961; Chairman: Nat. Assoc. for the Care and Resettlement of Offenders, 1966-74; Bd of Visitors, HM Prison, Grendon, 1963-69; Consumer Council, 1968-71; EDC for Hotel and Catering Industry, 1972-74; Nat. Cttee Family Service Units, 1968-74; Cttee of Enquiry into conditions of service for young servicemen, 1969; British Fedn of Zoos; Pres., RSPB, 1975-80; Assoc. of Arts Instns, 1980; Confedn of Art and Design Assocs, 1982. Member, SE Regional Planning Council, 1966-69. Director: Royal Opera House, Covent Garden, 1958-74; Sadler's Wells, 1963-74; British Sugar Corp., 1966-74. *Recreations:* music in general, opera in particular. *Address:* 1 Chalcot Crescent, NW1. *Clubs:* Brooks's, Garrick.

See also R. H. I. de la Mare, N. D. Deakin.

DONALDSON OF KINGSBRIDGE, Lady; see Donaldson, Frances Annesley.

DONALDSON, David Abercrombie, RSA 1962 (ARSA 1951); RP 1964; RGI 1977; Painter; Head of Painting School, Glasgow School of Art, 1967-81; Her Majesty's Painter and Limner in Scotland, since 1977; *b* 29 June 1916; *s* of Robert Abercrombie Donaldson and Margaret Cranston; *m* 1949, Maria Krystyna Mora-Szorc; one *s* two *d*. *Educ:* Coatbridge Sec. Sch.; Glasgow Sch. of Art. Travelling Scholarship, 1938. Joined Staff of Glasgow Sch. of Art, 1940. Paintings in private collections in America and Europe and public collections in Scotland. Sitters include: The Queen, 1968; Sir Hector Hetherington; Dame Jean Roberts; Sir John Dunbar; Lord Binning; Rev. Lord McLeod; Mrs Winifred Ewing; Miss Joan Dickson; Earl of Haddo; Sir Samuel Curran; Roger Ellis. Hon. LLD Strathclyde, 1971. *Recreation:* painting. *Address:* Endrick Hill, Drymen, by Glasgow G63 0BG. *T:* Drymen 60569; 7 Chelsea Manor Studios, Flood Street, SW3. *T:* 01-352 1932. *Club:* Art (Glasgow).

DONALDSON, Sir Dawson, KCMG 1967; BSc; CEng, FIEE; Chairman, Commonwealth Telecommunications Board, 1962-69, retired; *b* 29 Dec. 1903; *s* of Dawson Donaldson and Ada M. Gribble; *m* 1928, Nell Penman; two *s* two *d*. *Educ:* Auckland Grammar Sch.; New Zealand Univ. New Zealand Post and Tels Dept, 1922-62; Executive Engineer, 1928-48; Superintending Engineer, 1948-54; Dep. Dir Gen., 1954-60; Dir Gen., 1960-62. *Recreations:* bowls and garden. *Address:* 2 Ridd Crescent, Karori, Wellington, New Zealand.

DONALDSON, Dorothy Mary, (Lady Donaldson), JP; Alderman, City of London Ward of Coleman Street, since 1975; *b* 29 Aug. 1921; *d* of late Reginald George Gale Warwick and Dorothy Alice Warwick; *m* 1945, Rt Hon. Sir John Francis Donaldson, *qv* ; one *s* two *d*. *Educ:* Portsmouth High Sch. for Girls (GPDST); Wingfield Morris Orthopædic Hosp.; Middlesex Hosp., London. SRN 1946. Chm., Women's Nat. Cancer Control Campaign, 1967-69; Vice-Pres., British Cancer Council, 1970; Member: NE Met. Regional Hosp. Bd, 1970-74; NE Thames RHA, 1976-81. Governor: London Hosp., 1971-74; Gt Ormond Street Hosp. for Sick Children, 1978-80; Mem., Cities of London and Westminster Disablement Adv. Cttee, 1974-. Mem., Inner London Educn Authority, 1968-71; Mem., City Parochial Foundn, 1969-75; Vice-Pres., Counsel and Care for the Elderly, 1980-; Governor: City of London Sch. for Girls, 1971-; Berkhampsted Schools, 1976-80; Mem., Governing Body, Charterhouse Sch., 1980-; Mem., Court of Common

Council, 1966-75, Sheriff, 1981-82, City of London; Mem. Guild of Freemen, City of London, 1970; Liveryman, Gardeners' Co., 1975. Hon. Mem., CIArb, 1981. Freedom City of Winnipeg, 1968; Order of Oman, 1982. JP Inner London, 1960; Mem., Inner London Juvenile Court Panel, 1960-65. *Recreations:* gardening, sailing, geriatric ski-ing. *T:* (home) 01-637 9658. *Clubs:* Royal Cruising, Royal Lymington Yacht, Bar Yacht.

DONALDSON, Air Cdre Edward Mortlock, CB 1960; CBE 1954; DSO 1940; AFC 1941 (and bar 1947); Air Correspondent, The Daily Telegraph, 1961-79; *b* 22 Feb. 1912; *s* of C. E. Donaldson, Malay Civil Service; *m* 1st, 1936, Winifred Constant (marr. diss., 1944); two *d*; 2nd, 1944, Estellee Holland (marr. diss., 1956); one *s*; 3rd, 1957, Anne, Sofie Stapleton (marr. diss., 1982). *Educ:* King's Sch., Rochester; Christ's Hosp., Horsham; McGill Univ., Canada. Joined RAF, 1931; 3 Sqdn, Upavon, Kenley and Sudan until 1936; won RAF air firing trophy, 1933 and 1934; Flight Comdr, 1 Sqdn, 1936-38; led flight aerobatic team, Hendon and Zürich, 1937; Flight-Lieut 1936; Sqdn Leader 1938; Comdr, 151 Squdn, 1938-40, Battle of Britain; Chief Instructor, 5 Flying Training Sch., 1941; Wing Comdr, 1940; went to US to build four air Gunnery Schs, 1941, and teach USAF combat techniques; Group Capt., 1942; Mem. USAF Board and Directing Staff at US Sch. of Applied Tactics, 1944; Comdr RAF Station, Colerne, RAF first jet station, 1944; in comd RAF Station, Milfield, 1946; in comd RAF High Speed Flight, 1946; holder of World's Speed Record, 1946; SASO, No. 12 Group, 1946-49; in comd Air Cadet Corps and CCF, 1949-51; in comd RAF Station, Fassberg, Germany, 1951-54; Joint Services Staff Coll., 1954; Dir of Operational Training, Air Ministry, 1954-56; Air Cdre, 1956; Dep. Comdr Air Forces, Arabian Peninsular Command, 1956-58; Commandant, Royal Air Force Flying Coll., Manby, 1958-61; retd. Legion of Merit (US), 1948. *Recreations:* shooting, sailing, golf. *Address:* 3 Fair Oak Court, Tower Close, Alverstoke, Gosport PO12 2TX. *Clubs:* Royal Air Force; Island Sailing (Cowes).

DONALDSON, Frances Annesley, (Lady Donaldson of Kingsbridge); *b* 13 Jan. 1907; *d* of Frederick Lonsdale and Leslie Lonsdale (*née* Hoggan); *m* 1935, John George Stuart Donaldson (*see* Lord Donaldson of Kingsbridge); one *s* two *d*. *Publications:* Approach to Farming, 1941, 6th edn 1946; Four Years' Harvest, 1945; Milk Without Tears, 1955; Freddy Lonsdale, 1957; Child of the Twenties, 1959; The Marconi Scandal, 1962; Evelyn Waugh: portrait of a country neighbour, 1967; Actor Managers, 1970; Edward VIII, 1974 (Wolfson History Award, 1975); King George VI and Queen Elizabeth, 1977; Edward VIII: the road to abdication, 1978; P. G. Wodehouse, 1982. *Recreations:* gardening, golf. *Address:* 1 Chalcot Crescent, NW1 8YE. *T:* 01-722 4695.
    See also N. D. Deakin.

DONALDSON, Prof. Gordon, FRSE 1978; FBA 1976; Professor of Scottish History and Palæography, University of Edinburgh, 1963-79, now Professor Emeritus; Historiographer to HM the Queen in Scotland, since 1979; *b* 13 April 1913; *s* of Magnus Donaldson and Rachel Hetherington Swan. *Educ:* Royal High Sch., Edinburgh; Universities of Edinburgh and London. Asst in HM Gen. Register House, Edinburgh, 1938; Lecturer in Scottish History, University of Edinburgh, 1947, Reader, 1955. Mem. Royal Commission on the Ancient and Historical Monuments of Scotland, 1964-82. Hon. DLitt Aberdeen, 1976. *Publications:* The Making of the Scottish Prayer Book of 1637, 1954; A Source Book of Scottish History, 1952-61; Register of the Privy Seal of Scotland, vols v-viii, 1957-82; Shetland Life under Earl Patrick, 1958; Scotland: Church and Nation through sixteen centuries, 1960, 2nd edn, 1972; The Scottish Reformation, 1960, repr. 1972; Scotland-James V to James VII, 1965, repr. 1971; The Scots Overseas, 1966; Northwards by Sea, 1966, repr. 1978; Scottish Kings, 1967, repr. 1977; The First Trial of Mary Queen of Scots, 1969; Memoirs of Sir James Melville of Halhill, 1969; (comp.) Scottish Historical Documents, 1970; Mary Queen of Scots, 1974; Who's Who in Scottish History, 1974; Scotland: The Shaping of a Nation, 1974, 2nd edn 1980; Dictionary of Scottish History, 1977; All the Queen's Men, 1982; contribs to Scottish Historical Review, English Historical Review, Transactions of Royal Historical Society, etc. *Address:* 6 Pan Ha', Dysart, Fife KY1 2TL. *T:* Kirkcaldy 52685.

DONALDSON, Rt. Hon. Sir John (Francis), Kt 1966; PC 1979; Master of the Rolls, since 1982; *b* 6 Oct. 1920; *er s* of late Malcolm Donaldson, FRCS, FRCOG, and late Evelyn Helen Marguerite Maunsell; *m* 1945, Dorothy Mary (*see* Dorothy Mary Donaldson); one *s* two *d*. *Educ:* Charterhouse; Trinity Coll., Cambridge. Sec. of Debates, Cambridge Union Soc., 1940; Chm. Federation of University Conservative and Unionist Assocs, 1940 (MA (Hons) 1941; MA 1959. Commissioned Royal Signals, 1941; served with Guards Armoured Divisional Signals, in UK and NW Europe, 1942-45; and with Military Government, Schleswig-Holstein, 1945-46; Hon. Lieut-Col, 1946. Called to Bar, Middle Temple, 1946; Harmsworth Law Scholar, 1946; QC 1961; Bencher 1966; Mem. Gen. Council of the Bar, 1956-61, 1962-66, Junior Counsel to Registrar of Restrictive Trading Agreements, 1959-61; Dep. Chm., Hants QS, 1961-66; Mem. Council on Tribunals, 1965-66; Judge of the High Court, Queen's Bench Div., 1966-79; Pres., Nat. Industrial Relations Court, 1971-74; a Lord Justice of Appeal, 1979-82. Mem. Croydon County Borough Council, 1949-53. President: Carthusian Soc., 1978-82; British Maritime Law Assoc., 1979- (Vice-Pres., 1978-79); British Insurance Law Assoc., 1979-81 (Dep. Pres., 1978-79). FCIArb 1980 (Pres., 1980-). Hon. Member: Assoc. of Average Adjusters, 1966 (Chm., 1981); Grain and Feed Trade Assoc., 1979; Liverpool Cotton Assoc., 1979. Governor, Sutton's Hosp. in Charterhouse, 1981-. *Publications:* Jt Ed., Lowndes and Rudolf on General

Average and the York-Antwerp Rules (8th edn), 1955, (9th edn), 1964 and (10th edn), 1975; contributor to title Insurance, in Halsbury's Laws of England (3rd edn), 1958. *Recreations:* sailing, do-it-yourself. *Address:* Royal Courts of Justice, Strand, WC2. *T:* 01-405 7641; (home) 01-637 9658. *Clubs:* Royal Cruising, Bar Yacht, Royal Lymington Yacht.

DONALDSON, Timothy Baswell, CBE 1973; Governor, Central Bank of the Bahamas, since 1974; *b* 2 Jan. 1934; *s* of late Rev. Dr T. E. W. Donaldson and of M. B. Donaldson; *m* 1957, Donna Ruth Penn; two *s*. *Educ:* Fisk Univ., Tennessee (BA Hons); Univ. of Minnesota; Columbia Univ. FIB. Lectr in Maths, Fisk Univ., 1957-58; Sen. Master, Clarendon Coll., Jamaica, 1959-61; Headmaster, Prince Williams High Sch., 1961-63; Sen. Inspector, Bahamas Min. of Educn, 1963-64; Asst Sec., 1964-66, Controller of Exchange, 1966-68, Min. of Finance, Bahamas; Manager, 1968-70, Chm., 1970-74, Bahamas Monetary Authority. Alternate Governor for Bahamas: IMF; Caribbean Develt Bank; Director: Intercontinental Diversified Corp.; Grand Bahama Port Authority. Chm., Duke of Edinburgh Awards Scheme, Nassau; Treasurer, Bahamas Assoc. for Mentally Retarded; Founder Mem., Rotary Club of E Nassau (Past Sec. and Vice Pres.). Mem., Bd of Trustees, Fisk Univ.; Founder Pres., Bahamas Br., Guild of Graduates; Pres., Gym Tennis Club. Pres. and Hon. Fellow, Bahamas Inst. of Bankers; FIB; Associate, Inst. of Dirs. Delta Chapter, Phi Beta Kappa, 1977. Hon. LLD London Inst. for Applied Research, 1972; Hon. PLD Pacific Northwestern Univ., 1979. *Publications:* numerous articles on international finance in periodicals and journals. *Recreations:* tennis, swimming. *Address:* (office) PO Box N-4868, Nassau, Bahamas. *T:* 22193; (home) PO Box ES-5116, Nassau, Bahamas. *T:* 43259.

DONALDSON, Rear-Adm. Vernon D'Arcy; *b* 1 Feb. 1906; *s* of Adm. Leonard Andrew Boyd Donaldson, CB, CMG, and of Mary Mitchell, *d* of Prof. D'Arcy Thompson, Queen's Coll., Galway; *m* 1946, Joan Cranfield Monypenny of Pitmilly, (The Lady Pitmilly), *d* of James Egerton Howard Monypenny. *Educ:* RN Colls, Osborne and Dartmouth. Entered Royal Navy, Sept. 1919; Midshipman, 1923; Sub-Lieut 1927, Lieut 1928; specialised in Torpedoes and served as Torpedo Officer in HMS Vernon, 8th Dest. Flot., China Stn, and HMS Glorious; Comdr Dec. 1939, and served in Plans Div. Admlty, as exec. officer HM Ships Birmingham and Frobisher in Eastern Fleet, and on staff of C-in-C Eastern Fleet; Capt. Dec. 1944. Asst-Dir, TASW Div., Naval Staff, 1945-47; Naval Attaché, China, 1948-49; commanded HMS Gambia, 1950-51; Dir TASW div., Naval Staff, 1952-54; ADC to the Queen, 1953-54; Dep. Chief of Supplies and Transport, Admiralty (acting Rear-Adm.), 1955-57; retired, 1957. *Address:* 36 Tregunter Road, SW10.

DONCASTER, Bishop Suffragan of, since 1982; **Rt. Rev. William Michael Dermot Persson;** *b* 27 Sept. 1927; *s* of Leslie Charles Grenville Alan and Elizabeth Mercer Persson; *m* 1957, Ann Davey; two *s* one *d*. *Educ:* Monkton Combe School; Oriel Coll., Oxford (MA); Wycliffe Hall Theological Coll. National service, Army, 1945-48; commissioned, Royal Signals. Deacon 1953, priest 1954; Curate: Emmanuel, South Croydon, 1953-55; St John, Tunbridge Wells, 1955-58; Vicar, Christ Church, Barnet, 1958-67; Rector, Bebington, Cheshire, 1967-79; Vicar, Knutsford with Toft, 1979-82. *Recreations:* gardening, writing poetry. *Address:* 5 Park Lane, Sheffield S10 2DU.

DONCASTER, Archdeacon of; *see* Harland, Ven. Ian.

DONEGALL, 7th Marquess of, *cr* 1791; **Dermot Richard Claud Chichester;** Viscount Chichester and Baron of Belfast, 1625; Earl of Donegall, 1647; Earl of Belfast, 1791; Baron Fisherwick (GB), 1790; Baron Templemore, 1831; Hereditary Lord High Admiral of Lough Neagh; late 7th Queen's Own Hussars; one of HM Bodyguard, Honourable Corps of Gentlemen at Arms, since 1966; *b* 18 April 1916; 2nd *s* of 4th Baron Templemore, PC, KCVO, DSO, and Hon. Clare Meriel Wingfield, 2nd *d* of 7th Viscount Powerscourt, PC Ireland (she *d* 1969); *S* father 1953, and to Marquessate of Donegall, 1975; *m* 1946, Lady Josceline Gabrielle Legge, *y d* of 7th Earl of Dartmouth, GCVO, TD; one *s* two *d*. *Educ:* Harrow; RMC, Sandhurst. 2nd Lt 7th Hussars, 1936; Lt 1939; served War of 1939-45 in Middle East and Italy (prisoner); Major, 1944; retired, 1949. *Recreations:* hunting, shooting, fishing. *Heir:* *s* Earl of Belfast, *qv*. *Address:* Dunbrody Park, Arthurstown, Co. Wexford, Eire. *T:* Waterford 89104. *Clubs:* Cavalry and Guards; Kildare Street and University (Dublin).

DONEGAN, Rt. Rev. Horace W(illiam) B(aden), Hon. CBE 1957; DD; *b* Matlock, Derbyshire, England, 17 May 1900; *s* of Horace George Donegan and Pembroke Capes Hand. *Educ:* St Stephen's, Annandale, NY; Oxford University, England; Harvard Divinity School; Episcopal Theological Seminary, Rector, Christ Church, Baltimore, 1929-33; Rector, St James' Church, NYC, 1933-47; Suffragan Bishop of New York, 1947-49; Bishop Coadjutor of New York, 1949-50. Bishop of New York, 1950-72. Vice-Pres., Pilgrims, USA; President: St Hilda's and St Hugh's Sch., NY; House of Redeemer, NY; Episcopal Actors Guild, NY; Chaplain, Veterans of Foreign Wars; Episcopal Visitor: Sisters of St Helena; Community of the Holy Spirit; Trustee: St Luke's Hosp., NY; Episcopal Sch., NY; Contemporary Club, NY. Award, Conf. of Christians and Jews; Medal of City of New York; Medal of Merit, St Nicholas Society, NY; Citation, NY Hospital Assoc.; Harlem Arts & Culture Award. Churchill Fellow, Westminster Coll., Fulton, Mo. Hon. degrees: DD: New York Univ., 1940; Univ. of South, 1949; Trinity, 1950; Bard, 1957; King's Univ., Halifax, 1958; Berkley Divinity School, New Haven, Conn., 1969; STD: Hobart, 1948; General Theological Seminary,

1949; Columbia Univ., 1960; DCL Nashotah, 1956; Sub Prelate OStJ, 1956; Grand Cross St Joanikije, 1956; Legion of Honour, France, 1957; Silver Medal of Red Cross of Japan, 1959; Holy Pagania from Armenian Church, 1960; Grand Kt, Order of St Denys of Zante (Greece), 1959. *Publications:* articles in religious publications. *Recreations:* golf, swimming, painting. *Address:* Manhattan House, 200 E 66th Street, New York, NY 10021. *Clubs:* Athenæum, Royal Automobile, American, Kennel (London); Union, Union League, Pilgrims, Century Association, Columbia Faculty, Tuxedo Park (all of New York).

DONERAILE, 9th Viscount, *cr* 1785; **Richard St John St Leger;** Baron Doneraile, 1776; *b* 29 Oct. 1923; *o s* of 8th Viscount and of Sylvia St Leger; *S* father 1957; *m* 1945, Melva Jean Clifton; three *s* two *d. Educ:* George Washington Sch., USA. In lumber business and real estate. *Heir: s* Hon. Richard Allen St Leger [*b* 17 Aug. 1946; *m* 1969, Kathleen Mary, *e d* of N. Simcox, Co. Cork; one *s* one *d*].

DONIACH, Prof. Israel, MD (London); FRCPath 1963; FRCP 1968; Professor of Morbid Anatomy in University of London, London Hospital, 1960–76, now Emeritus Professor; Hon. Lecturer in Histopathology, St Bartholomew's Hospital Medical School, since 1976; *b* 9 March 1911; *yr s* of late Aaron Selig and late Rahel Doniach; *m* 1933, Deborah Abileah; one *s* (one *d* decd). *Educ:* University Coll. and Hosp., London. Asst Pathologist, St Mary's Hosp., London, 1935–37; Clinical Pathologist and Cancer Research Asst, Mount Vernon Hosp., Northwood, 1937–43; Senior Lecturer in Morbid Anatomy, Postgraduate Medical Sch. of London, 1943–59, Reader, 1959–60. *Publications:* papers in morbid anatomy and experimental pathology in various journals. *Address:* 25 Alma Square, NW8 9PY. *T:* 01-286 1617.

DONKIN, Alexander Sim; HM Diplomatic Service; Counsellor (Administration), UK Mission to United Nations, and Deputy Consul-General, New York, since 1977; *b* 14 July 1922; *s* of Matthew Henderson Donkin and Margaret Donkin; *m* 1944, Irene Florence (*née* Willis); two *d. Educ:* Monkwearmouth Sch., Co. Durham. Served War, RAF, 1941–46: Sqdn Ldr. Civil Service, 1947–66; HM Diplomatic Service, 1966–: FCO, 1966–70; Washington, 1970–74; FCO, 1974–77. *Recreations:* music, walking, photography. *Address:* c/o Foreign and Commonwealth Office, SW1.

DONKIN, Air Cdre Peter Langloh, CBE 1946; DSO 1944; retired; *b* 19 June 1913; *s* of Frederick Langloh and Phyllis Donkin; *m* 1941, Elizabeth Marjorie Cox; two *d. Educ:* Sherborne; RAF Coll., Cranwell. Commissioned RAF, 1933; No. 16 Sqdn, 1933–38; British Mission in Poland, 1939; CO 225 Sqdn, 1940; CO 239 Sqdn, 1941–42; CO 35 Wing, 1943–44; Sch. Land Air Warfare, 1945; HQ, RAF Levant, 1946; RCAF Staff Coll., 1948–49; Exchange USAF, 1950; CO, RAF Chivenor, 1951–53; Air Attaché, Moscow, 1954–57; Asst Chief of Staff, HQ Allied Air Forces, Central Europe, 1957–58; idc, 1959; AOC, RAF, Hong Kong, 1960–62. *Recreations:* shooting, yachting. *Address:* Coombe Cross Cottage, Templecombe, Som. *Club:* Carlton.

DONLEAVY, James Patrick; Author; *b* 23 April 1926; *m* Valerie Heron (marr. diss.); one *s* one *d* ; *m* Mary Wilson Price; one *s* one *d. Educ:* schs in USA; Trinity Coll., Dublin. *Publications:* The Ginger Man (novel), 1955; Fairy Tales of New York (play), 1960; What They Did In Dublin With The Ginger Man (introd. and play), 1961; A Singular Man (novel), 1963 (play, 1964); Meet My Maker The Mad Molecule (short stories), 1964; The Saddest Summer of Samuel S (novella), 1966 (play, 1967); The Beastly Beatitudes of Balthazar B (novel), 1968 (play, 1981); The Onion Eaters (novel), 1971; The Plays of J. P. Donleavy, 1972; A Fairy Tale of New York (novel), 1973; The Unexpurgated Code: A Complete Manual of Survival and Manners, 1975; The Destinies of Darcy Dancer, Gentleman (novel), 1977; Schultz (novel), 1980. *Address:* Levington Park, Mullingar, Co. Westmeath, Ireland.

DONNE, David Lucas; Chairman: Dalgety, since 1977 (Deputy Chairman, 1975–77); Crest Nicholson, since 1973; *b* 17 Aug. 1925; *s* of late Dr Cecil Lucas Donne, Wellington, NZ, and of Marjorie Nicholls Donne; *m* 1st, 1957, Jennifer Margaret Duncan (*d* 1975); two *s* one *d* ; 2nd, 1978, Clare, *d* of Maj. F. J. Yates. *Educ:* Stowe; Christ Church, Oxford (MA Nat. Science). Called to the Bar, Middle Temple, 1949. Studied Business Admin, Syracuse Univ., 1952–53; Charterhouse Group, 1953–64; William Baird, 1964–67; Chm., Williams Lea, 1972–82. Director: M. L. Holdings; Royal Trust of Canada; Steetley (Dep. Chm., 1979–). Mem., Nat. Water Council, 1980–. Chm., Hellenic Travellers' Club. Mem., Council, Zool Soc. of London. *Recreations:* gun dogs, opera, sailing. *Address:* 19 Hanover Square, W1R 9DA. *Clubs:* Royal Thames Yacht; Vincent's (Oxford).

DONNE, Hon. Sir Gaven (John), KBE 1979; Chief Justice of, and Representative of the Queen in, the Cook Islands, 1975–82; Chief Justice of Niue, 1974–82; *b* 8 May 1914; *s* of Jack Alfred Donne and Mary Elizabeth Donne; *m* 1946, Isabel Fenwick, *d* of John Edwin Hall; two *s* two *d. Educ:* Palmerston North Boys' High Sch.; Hastings High Sch.; Victoria Univ., Wellington; Auckland Univ. (LLB New Zealand). Called to the Bar and admitted solicitor, 1938. Military Service, 2nd NZEF, Middle East and Italy, 1941–45. Stipendiary Magistrate, NZ, 1958–75; Puisne Judge, Supreme Court of Western Samoa, 1970–71; Chief Justice, Western Samoa, 1972–75, Mem. Court of Appeal of Western Samoa, 1975–82; Judge, High Court of Niue, 1973. Hon. Counsellor, Internat. Assoc. of Youth Magistrates, 1974–. Member: Takapuna Bor. Council, 1957–58; Auckland Town Planning Authority, 1958; Bd of Governors, Westlake High Sch., 1957–58. Grand Cross 2nd Cl., Order

of Merit of Fed. Republic of Germany, 1978. *Recreations:* golf, fishing, walking. *Address:* Otaramarae, Lake Rotoiti, Rotorua, New Zealand. *T:* Okere Falls 861; Government House, Rarotonga, Cook Islands. *Club:* University (Auckland).

DONNE, Sir John (Christopher), Kt 1976; Chairman, SE Thames Regional Health Authority, since 1973; *b* 19 Aug. 1921; *s* of late Leslie Victor Donne, solicitor, Hove, and Mabel Laetitia Richards (*née* Pike); *m* 1945, Mary Stuart (*née* Seaton); three *d. Educ:* Charterhouse. Royal Artillery, 1940–46 (Captain); served Europe and India. Solicitor, 1949; Notary Public; Partner, Donne Mileham & Haddock; Pres., Sussex Law Soc., 1969–70. Chm., SE (Metropolitan) Regional Hosp. Bd, 1971–74. Governor, Guy's Hosp., 1971–74, Guy's Hosp. Med. Sch., 1974–; Dep. Chm., RHA Chairmen, 1976–78 (Chm., 1974–76); Mem., Gen. Council and Management Cttee, King Edward's Hosp. Fund for London, 1972–; a Governing Trustee, Nuffield Provincial Hosp. Trust, 1975–; Dir, Nuffield Health and Soc. Services Fund, 1976–. Member: Council, Internat. Hosp. Fedn, 1979–; Council, Soc. for Study of Medical Ethics, 1980–; Court of Univ. of Sussex, 1979–; Ct of Assts, Hon. Company of Broderers, 1979; Editorial Bd, Jl Medical Ethics, 1977–79. *Recreations:* genealogy, gardening, photography, listening to music. *Address:* Copyhold, Partridge Green, Horsham, West Sussex. *T:* Partridge Green 710462. *Clubs:* Army and Navy, Pilgrims, MCC; Butterflies, Sussex Martlets.

DONNER, Frederic Garrett; Chairman of the Board of Trustees, Alfred P. Sloan Foundation, 1968–75, retired; Director, General Motors Corporation, 1942–74 (Chairman, 1958–67); *b* 1902; *s* of Frank Donner and Cornelia (*née* Zimmerman); *m* 1929, Eileen Isaacson; one *d* (and one *s* decd). *Educ:* University of Michigan, Ann Arbor, Michigan, USA. General Motors Corporation, 1926; Dir, Communications Satellite Corporation, 1964–77; Trustee, Sloan-Kettering Inst. for Cancer Research, NY, 1964–75. Holds hon. doctorates and foreign decorations. *Address:* 825 Fifth Avenue, New York, NY 10021, USA. *Clubs:* Links, University (NY City); Creek Country, North Hempstead Country (Long Island, NY).

DONNER, Sir Patrick William, Kt 1953; MA; DL; *b* 1904; *s* of late Ossian Donner and Violet Marion McHutchen, Edinburgh; *m* 1938, Hon. Angela Chatfield (*d* 1943), *er d* of 1st Baron Chatfield, GCB, OM, KCMG, CVO, Admiral of the Fleet; *m* 1947, Pamela *y d* of Rear Adm. Herbert A. Forster, MVO; one *s* two *d. Educ:* abroad and Exeter Coll., Oxford. Studied Imperial development and administration, 1928–30; MP (C) West Islington, 1931–35; Basingstoke Div. of Hants, 1935–55; Hon. Sec., India Defence League, 1933–35; Parliamentary Private Sec. to Sir Samuel Hoare, Home Sec., 1939; Mem. Advisory Cttee on Education in the Colonies, 1939–41; Parliamentary Private Sec. to Col Oliver Stanley, Sec. of State for the Colonies, 1944; Dir, National Review Ltd, 1933–47; Mem. Executive Council Joint East and Central African Board, 1937–54. Volunteered RAFVR 1939; served at HQ Fighter Command; Acting Sqdn Leader, 1941. Chm. Executive Cttee of the Men of the Trees, 1959–62. Mem., Art Panel of the Arts Council, 1963–66. High Sheriff of Hants, 1967–68; DL Hants 1971. *Recreations:* music, travel, landscape gardening. *Address:* Hurstbourne Park, Whitchurch, Hants. *T:* Whitchurch 2230.

DONNET, family name of **Baron Donnet of Balgay.**

DONNET OF BALGAY, Baron *cr* 1978 (Life Peer), of Balgay in the district of the City of Dundee; **Alexander Mitchell Donnet,** CBE 1975; FCIT 1979; JP; Chairman, Scottish Transport Group, 1978–80 (Member, 1969–80); *b* Dundee, 1916; *m* 1945, Mary, *d* of Gavin Mitchell Black; two *s* one *d. Educ:* Harris Academy, Dundee. Mem., G&MWU, 1935–; Regional Sec., Scottish Region, 1959–78; Nat. Chm., 1970–76; Pres., Scottish TUC, 1970–71; Mem. Gen. Council, TUC, 1972–76. An Asst Comr, Commn on the Constitution, 1969–73. Member: Scottish Economic Council, to 1981; Forestry Commn, 1973–78; Price Commn, 1977–79; Greater Glasgow Health Bd; Scottish Develt Agency, 1979–. JP Glasgow, 1961. *Address:* 8 Jordanhill Drive, Glasgow G13 1SA.

DONNISON, Prof. David Vernon; Professor of Town and Regional Planning, Glasgow University, since 1980; *b* 19 Jan. 1926; *s* of F. S. V. Donnison, *qv* ; *m* 1950, Jean Elizabeth (*née* Kidger); two *s* two *d. Educ:* Marlborough Coll., Wiltshire; Magdalen Coll., Oxford. Asst Lecturer and Lecturer, Manchester Univ., 1950–53; Lecturer, Toronto Univ., 1953–55; Reader, London Sch. of Economics, 1956–61; Prof. of Social Administration, 1961–69; Dir, Centre for Environmental Studies, 1969–76. Chairman: Public Schs Commission, 1968–70; Supplementary Benefits Commn, 1975–80. Hon. Doctorates: Bradford, 1973; Hull, 1980; Leeds, Southampton, 1981. *Publications:* The Neglected Child and the Social Services, 1954; Welfare Services in a Canadian Community, 1958; Housing since the Rent Act, 1961; The Government of Housing, 1967; An Approach to Social Policy, 1975; Social Policy and Administration Revisited, 1975; (with Paul Soto) The Good City, 1980; The Politics of Poverty, 1981; (with Clare Ungerson) Housing Policy, 1982. *Address:* 12 Holyrood Crescent, Glasgow G20 6HJ. *T:* 041-334 2827.

DONNISON, Frank Siegfried Vernon, CBE 1943; Indian Civil Service (retired); *b* 3 July 1898; *s* of Frank Samuel and of Edith Donnison; *m* 1923, Ruth Seruya Singer, MBE, JP (*d* 1968); one *s* one *d. Educ:* Marlborough Coll.; Corpus Christi Coll., Oxford. Served with Grenadier Guards, 1917–19;

ICS (Burma), 1922; Chief Sec. to Govt of Burma, 1946; military service, Burma, 1944-45 (despatches). Historian, Cabinet Office, Historical Section, 1949-66. *Publications:* Public Administration in Burma, 1953; British Military Administration in the Far East, 1943-46, 1956; Civil Affairs and Military Government, North-West Europe, 1944-46, 1961; Civil Affairs and Military Government, Central Organization and Planning, 1966; Burma, 1970. *Recreation:* music. *Address:* Lower Cross Farmhouse, East Hagbourne, Didcot OX11 9LD. *T:* Didcot 3314. *Club:* East India, Devonshire, Sports and Public Schools.
See also Professor D. V. Donnison.

DONOGHUE, Prof. Denis, MA, PhD; literary critic; Henry James Professor of Letters, New York University, since 1979; *b* 1928. *Educ:* University College, Dublin. BA 1949, MA 1952, PhD 1957; MA Cantab 1965. Admin. Office, Dept of Finance, Irish Civil Service, 1951-54. Asst Lectr, Univ. Coll., Dublin, 1954-57; Coll. Lectr, 1957-62; Visiting Schol., Univ. of Pennsylvania, 1962-63; Coll. Lectr, Univ. Coll., Dublin, 1963-64; University Lectr, Cambridge Univ., 1964-65; Fellow, King's Coll., Cambridge, 1964-65; Prof. of Modern English and American Literature, University Coll., Dublin, 1965-79. Mem. Internat. Cttee of Assoc. of University Profs of English. Mem. BBC Commn to monitor the quality of spoken English on BBC Radio, 1979. Reith Lectr, BBC, 1982. *Publications:* The Third Voice, 1959; Connoisseurs of Chaos, 1965; (ed jtly) An Honoured Guest, 1965; The Ordinary Universe, 1968; Emily Dickinson, 1968; Jonathan Swift, 1969; (ed) Swift, 1970; Yeats, 1971; Thieves of Fire, 1974; (ed) W. B. Yeats, Memoirs, 1973; Sovereign Ghost: studies in Imagination, 1978; Ferocious Alphabets, 1981; contribs to reviews and journals. *Address:* New York University, Washington Square, New York, NY 10003, USA; Gaybrook, North Avenue, Mount Merrion, Dublin, Ireland.

DONOUGHMORE, 8th Earl of, *cr* 1800; **Richard Michael John Hely-Hutchinson;** Baron Donoughmore, 1783; Viscount Hutchinson (UK), 1821; *b* 8 Aug. 1927; *er s* of 7th Earl of Donoughmore and of Dorothy Jean (MBE 1947), *d* of late J. B. Hotham; *S* father, 1981; *m* 1951, Sheila, *o c* of late Frank Frederick Parsons, and of Mrs Roy Smith-Woodward; four *s*. *Educ:* Winchester; New College, Oxford (MA; BM, BCh). *Heir: s* Viscount Suirdale, *qv*. *Address:* 13-15 rue des Huissiers, 92 Neuilly sur Seine, France. *Clubs:* Kildare Street and University (Dublin); Jockey, Interalliée (Paris).

DONOUGHUE, Bernard; *b* 1934; *s* of late Thomas Joseph Donoughue and of Maud Violet Andrews; *m* 1959, Carol Ruth Goodman; two *s* two *d*. *Educ:* Secondary Modern Sch. and Grammar Sch., Northampton; Lincoln Coll. and Nuffield Coll., Oxford. MA, DPhil (Oxon). FRHistS. Henry Fellow, Harvard, USA. Mem., Editorial Staff: The Economist, Sunday Times, Sunday Telegraph. Sen. Res. Officer, PEP, 1960-63; Lectr, Sen. Lectr, Reader, LSE, 1963-74; Sen. Policy Advr to the Prime Minister, 1974-79; Development Dir, Economist Intelligence Unit, 1979-81; Asst Editor, The Times, 1981-82. Member: Sports Council, 1965-71; Commn of Enquiry into Association Football, 1966-68; Ct of Governors, LSE, 1968-74, 1982-; Civil Service Coll. Adv. Council, 1976-; Adv. Bd, Wissenschaftzentrum, Berlin, 1978-; Bd of Nene Coll., Northampton, 1979-; Chm. Exec., London Symphony Orch., 1979-; Associate Mem., Nuffield Coll., Oxford, 1982-. *Publicatons:* (ed jtly) Oxford Poetry, 1956; Wage Policies in the Public Sector, 1962; Trade Unions in a Changing Society, 1963; British Politics and the American Revolution, 1964; (with W. T. Rodgers) The People into Parliament, 1966; (with G. W. Jones) Herbert Morrison: portrait of a politician, 1973. *Recreations:* politics, economics, music, the Gay Hussar. *Address:* 7 Brookfield Park, NW5.

DONOVAN, Charles Edward; Managing Director, Personnel, and Member, British Gas Corporation, since 1981; *b* 28 Jan. 1934; *s* of Charles and Sarah Donovan; *m* 1963, Robina Evelyn (*née* Anderson); three *s*. *Educ:* Camphill Sch., Paisley; Scottish Coll. of Commerce; Royal Technical Coll., Glasgow (now Univ. of Strathclyde). MIPM. Personnel Officer: HQ, BEA, 1962; London and SE, Richard Costain Ltd, Constr. and Civil Engrs, 1963; Sen. Personnel Officer, Engrg, W Midlands Gas Bd, 1966; Southern Gas: Personnel Planning Manager, 1970; Personnel Manager, 1973; Personnel Dir, 1975; Dir, Indust. Relations, British Gas, 1977. *Recreations:* sailing, hill walking, reading. *Address:* 65 Moss Lane, Pinner, Mddx HA5 3AZ. *T:* 01-866 3595.

DONOVAN, Prof. Desmond Thomas; Yates-Goldsmid Professor of Geology and Head of Department of Geology, University College, London, since 1966; *b* 16 June 1921; *s* of T. B. Donovan; *m* 1959, Shirley Louise Saward; two *s* one *d*. *Educ:* Epsom Coll.; University of Bristol. BSc 1942; PhD 1951; DSc 1960. Asst Lectr in Geology, University of Bristol, 1947; Lectr in Geology, Bristol, 1950; Prof. of Geology, University of Hull, 1962. Pres., Palaeontographical Soc., 1979-. *Publications:* Stratigraphy: An Introduction to Principles, 1966; (ed) Geology of Shelf Seas, 1968; papers on fossil cephalopods, Jurassic stratigraphy, Pleistocene deposits, marine geology. *Address:* University College, Gower Street, WC1E 6BT. *T:* 01-387 7050. *Club:* Athenæum.

DONOVAN, Hedley (Williams); *b* 24 May 1914; *s* of Percy Williams Donovan and Alice Dougan Donovan; *m* 1941, Dorothy Hannon (*d* 1978); two *s* one *d*. *Educ:* University of Minnesota; Hertford Coll., Oxford (Hon. Fellow, 1977). BA (*magna cum laude*) Minn., 1934; BA Oxon. 1936. US Naval Reserve, active duty, 1942-45 (Lieut-Comdr). Reporter, Washington Post, 1937-42; Writer and Editor, 1945-53, Managing Editor, 1953-59,

Fortune; Editorial Dir, Time Inc., 1959-64, Editor in Chief, 1964-79, Consultant, 1979-. Dir, Time-Life Books Inc. Trustee: New York Univ.; Mount Holyoke Coll.; Ford Foundn; Nat. Humanities Center; Asia Soc.; Aerospace Corp.; Carnegie Endowment for Internat. Peace; Mem., Council on Foreign Relations; Senior Advisor to the President, 1979-80. Fellow, Faculty of Govt, Harvard Univ., 1981-. Fellow, Amer. Acad. of Arts and Sciences. Phi Beta Kappa; Rhodes Scholar. Hon. LittD: Pomona Coll., 1966; Mount Holyoke, 1967; Boston, 1968; Hon DHL: South-Western at Memphis, 1967; Rochester, 1968; Transylvania, 1979; Hon LLD: Carnegie-Mellon, 1969; Lehigh, 1976; Allegheny Coll., 1979. *Address:* Harbor Road, Sands Point, NY 11050, USA. *Clubs:* University, Century, (both New York); Metropolitan, 1925 F Street (Washington DC); Manhasset Bay Yacht (Long Island); Sands Point Golf.

DOOGE, Prof. James Clement Ignatius; Professor of Civil Engineering, University College, Dublin, 1970-81, and since 1982; *b* 30 July 1922; *s* of Denis Patrick Dooge and Veronica Catherine Carroll; *m* 1946, Veronica O'Doherty; two *s* three *d*. *Educ:* Christian Brothers' Sch., Dun Laoghaire; University Coll., Dublin (BE, BSc 1942, ME 1952); Univ. of Iowa (MSc 1956). FICE; FASCE. Jun. Civil Engr, Irish Office of Public Works, 1943-46; Design Engr, Electricity Supply Bd, Ireland, 1946-58; Prof. of Civil Engrg, UC Cork, 1958-70; Minister for Foreign Affairs, Ireland, 1981-82. Pres., ICEI, 1968-69 (Hon. FICEI; Kettle Premium and Plaque, 1948; Mullins Medal, 1951, 1962). Fellow, Amer. Geophysical Union (Horton Award, 1959); MRIA. Hon. DrAgrSc Wageningen, 1978; Hon. DrTech. Lund, 1980. *Address:* University College, Earlsford Terrace, Dublin 2, Ireland.

DOOLITTLE, Lt-Gen. James H.; Hon. KCB 1945; Trustee, 1963-69 (Chairman of Executive Committee and Vice-Chairman, Board of Trustees, 1965-69), Aerospace Corporation; Chairman of Board, Space Technology Laboratories, Inc., 1959-62; Director: Mutual of Omaha Insurance Co.; United Benefit Life Insurance Co.; Companion Life Insurance Co.; Tele-Trip Co., Inc.; *b* 14 Dec. 1896; *s* of Frank H. Doolittle and Rosa C. Shephard; *m* 1917, Josephine E. Daniels; two *s*. *Educ:* University of California (AB); MIT (MS, ScD). US Army Air Force, 1917-30; Manager, Aviation Dept, Shell Oil Co., 1930-40; USAAF, 1940-45. Dir, Shell Oil Company, 1946-67 (Vice-Pres., 1946-59). *Publications:* various scientific. *Recreations:* shooting, fishing. *Address:* 1015 Cass Street, Monterey, Calif 93940, USA.

DORAN, John Frederick, CEng, FInstGasE, MInstM; Chairman, East Midlands Gas Region, 1974-77; *b* 28 July 1916; *s* of Henry Joseph and Clara Doran; *m* 1940, Eileen Brotherton; two *s*. *Educ:* Wandsworth Technical Coll.; Wimbledon Technical Coll. Served War, Fleet Air Arm, 1943-46. Various appts Gas Light & Coke Co (subseq. North Thames Gas Bd), 1935-53; Dist Manager, Hornsey Dist, North Thames Gas Bd, 1953; Regional Sales Manager, North Western Div., North Thames Gas Bd, 1955-57. Southern Gas Board: Regional Sales and Service Manager, Southampton Region and Dorset and Bournemouth Regions, 1957-65; Marketing Manager, 1965-67; Commercial Manager, 1968-69; Commercial Dir, 1970-71; Commercial Dir and Bd Mem., 1971-73. Dep. Chm., East Midlands Gas Region, 1973. Founder, John Doran Gas Museum, Leicester. *Publications:* technical papers to Instn Gas Engrs. *Recreations:* golf, gardening. *Address:* Heronshaw, 43 The Woodlands, Forest Park, Market Harborough, Leicestershire LE16 7BW. *T:* Market Harborough 2113.

DORATI, Antal; composer and conductor; Conductor Laureate for life: Royal Philharmonic Orchestra, 1978 (Principal Conductor, 1974-78); Detroit Symphony Orchestra, 1981 (Music Director, since 1977); Stockholm Philharmonic, 1981; *b* Budapest, 9 April 1906; *s* of Alexander Dorati and Margit (*née* Kunwald); *m* 1st, 1929, Klara Korody; one *d*; 2nd, 1971, Ilse von Alpenheim. *Educ:* Royal Academy of Music, Budapest; University of Vienna. Conductor: Royal Opera House, Budapest, 1924-28; Münster State Opera, 1929-32; Musical Director: Ballet Russe de Monte Carlo, 1932-40; Ballet Theatre, NY, 1940-42; New Opera Co., NY, 1942-43; Musical Dir and Conductor: Dallas Symph. Orch., 1944-49; Minneapolis Symph. Orch., 1944-60; Chief Conductor: BBC Symphony Orchestra, 1963-66; Stockholm Philharmonic Orch., 1966-74; Musical Dir, Nat. Symphony Orch., Washington, DC, 1970-77. Guest conductor of major orchestras of the world, Salzburg, Holland, Venice, Lucerne, Berlin Festivals, etc; London Symphony, New Philharmonia, London Philharmonic, Royal Philharmonic, Israel Philharmonic orchestras, etc. Holder of 26 recording awards in America and Europe. DrMus: Macalister Coll., St Paul, 1958; George Washington Univ., 1975; Dr (hc) Humanities Maryland, 1976. Member: Swedish Acad., 1967; Royal Swedish Academy of the Arts; Hon. Prof., Music Acad., Budapest, 1981. Comdr, Order of Vasa; Chevalier of Arts and Letters, France; Order of Letters and Arts, Austria; Order of the Flag, Hungary. Compositions include: The Way (dramatic cantata); Symphony I; Missa Brevis; The two enchantments of Li-Tai-Pe; String Quartet; Cello Concerto; Nocturne and Capriccio for oboe and strings; Magdalena (ballet); Seven Pictures for Orch.; Madrigal Suite; String Octet; Largo Concertato for String Orch.; 'Chamber-Music', Song Cycle for Sopr. and small orch.; Night Music for flute and small orch.; Variations on a theme of Bartok for piano, Piano Concerto; Threni for String Orch.; American Serenades for String Orch.; Ot Enek; Divertimento for Oboe and Orch.; The Voices (song cycle) for bass voice and Orch.; In the Beginning (five meditations) for baritone, oboe, cello and percussion; Sonata for Assisi for two flutes; String Quartet; Five Pieces for Oboe; Three Pieces for Mixed Choir; Of God, Man and Machine for Mixed Choir; Four Choruses for Female Choir. *Publication:* Notes of Seven Decades, 1979. *Recreations:*

painting sketching, reading, art collecting. *Address:* c/o Ibbs & Tillet, 450–452 Edgware Road, W2 1EG; c/o CAMI, 165 West 57th Street, New York, NY 10019, USA.

DORCHESTER, Bishop Suffragan of, since 1979; **Rt. Rev. Conrad John Eustace Meyer;** *b* 2 July 1922; *s* of William Eustace and Marcia Meyer; *m* 1960, Mary Wiltshire; no *c. Educ:* Clifton Coll.; Pembroke Coll., Cambridge; Westcott House. BA 1946, MA 1948. Served War of 1939–45: Royal Navy (commissioned from lower deck), 1942–46. Lieut (S) RNVR, post war, until apptd Chaplain, RNVR, 1950–54. Deacon, 1948; Priest, 1949; Asst Curate: St Francis, Ashton Gate, Bristol, 1948–51; Kenwyn, Truro, 1951; Falmouth Parish Church, 1954; Vicar of Devoran, Truro, 1956–65; Diocesan Youth Chaplain, 1956; Asst Dir of Religious Educn, 1958; Diocesan Sec. for Educn, 1960–69; Archdeacon of Bodmin, 1969–79; Hon. Canon of Truro, 1966–79; Examining Chaplain to Bishop of Truro, 1973–79. Hon. Diocesan Sec., Nat. Soc., 1960–69. Mem. Governing Body, SPCK, 1972–; Chairman: Cttee for Mission, SPCK, 1973–; Federation of Catholic Priests, 1976–79; Church Union Exec. Cttee, 1979–; Joint Group on Funerals at Cemeteries and Crematoria, 1980–. Fellow, Woodard Corp. of Schools, 1967; Provost, Western Div., Woodard Corp., 1970–. Mem., Inst. of Civil Defence. *Recreations:* swimming, walking, military history, civil defence, archaeology. *Address:* 151 Wroslyn Road, Freeland, Oxford OX7 2HR. *Club:* Royal Commonwealth Society.

DORE, Ronald Philip, FBA 1975; Assistant Director, Technical Change Centre, since 1982; *b* 1 Feb. 1925; *s* of Philip Brine Dore and Elsie Constance Dore; *m* 1957, Nancy Macdonald; one *s* one *d. Educ:* Poole Grammar Sch.; SOAS, Univ. of London (BA). Lectr in Japanese Instns, SOAS, London, 1951; Prof. of Asian Studies, Univ. of BC, 1956; Reader, later Prof. of Sociol., LSE, 1961 (Hon. Fellow, 1980); Fellow IDS, 1969–82. Hon. Foreign Mem., Amer. Acad. of Arts and Scis, 1978. *Publications:* City Life in Japan, 1958; Land Reform in Japan, 1959; Education in Tokugawa Japan, 1963; (ed) Aspects of Social Change in Modern Japan, 1967; British Factory, Japanese Factory, 1973; The Diploma Disease, 1976; Shinohata: portrait of a Japanese village, 1978; (ed with Zoe Mars) Community Development, Comparative Case Studies in India, The Republic of Korea, Mexico and Tanzania, 1981. *Recreation:* daydreaming. *Address:* 157 Surrenden Road, Brighton, East Sussex. *T:* Brighton 501370.

DORKING, Suffragan Bishop of, since 1968; **Rt. Rev. Kenneth Dawson Evans;** *b* 7 Nov. 1915; *s* of late Dr Edward Victor Evans, OBE; *m* 1939, Margaret, *d* of J. J. Burton; one *s. Educ:* Dulwich Coll.; Clare Coll., Cambridge. Ordained, 1938; Curate of: St Mary, Northampton, 1938–41; All Saints', Northampton, 1941–45; Rector of Ockley, 1945–49; Vicar of Dorking, 1949–63. Hon. Canon of Guildford, 1955–63 and 1979–. Ed., Guildford Diocesan Publications, 1947–61; Archdeacon of Dorking and Canon Residentiary of Guildford Cathedral, 1963–68. Mem., Bishop's Finance Commn, 1957. *Address:* 13 Pilgrims Way, Guildford, Surrey. *T:* Guildford 67978.

DORKING, Archdeacon of; *see* Hogben, Ven. P. G.

DORMAN, Lt-Col Sir Charles (Geoffrey), 3rd Bt *cr* 1923; MC 1942; *b* 18 Sept. 1920; *o s* of Sir Bedford Lockwood Dorman, 2nd Bart, CBE and Lady Constance Phelps Dorman (*née* Hay), (*d* 1946); *S* father 1956; *m* 1954, Elizabeth Ann (marr. diss. 1972), *d* of late George Gilmour Gilmour-White, OBE; one *d. Educ:* Rugby Sch.; Brasenose Coll., Oxford (MA). Commissioned, 1941; served with 3rd The King's Own Hussars at Alamein (MC) and in Italian Campaign; Commissioned to 13th/18th Royal Hussars (QMO), 1947; GSO1, 1961–70; retired. *Recreation:* gliding. *Heir:* cousin Philip Henry Keppel Dorman, *b* 19 May 1914. *Address:* Hutton Grange, Great Rollright, Chipping Norton, Oxon OX7 5SQ. *T:* Hook Norton 737535.

DORMAN, Sir Maurice Henry, GCMG 1961 (KCMG 1957; CMG 1955); GCVO 1961; DL; MA; Lord Prior, Order of St John of Jerusalem, since 1980; Chairman, Swindon District Health Authority (formerly of Wiltshire Area Health Authority), since 1974; Director, since 1972 and Vice-Chairman, since 1981, Ramsbury Building Society; *b* 7 Aug. 1912; *s* of late John Ehrenfried and late Madeleine Louise Dorman; *m* 1937, Florence Monica Churchward Smith, DStJ 1968; one *s* three *d. Educ:* Sedbergh Sch.; Magdalene Coll., Cambridge. Administrative Officer, Tanganyika Territory, 1935; Clerk of Councils, Tanganyika, 1940–45; Asst to the Lt-Governor, Malta, 1945; Principal Asst Sec., Palestine, 1947; Seconded to Colonial Office as Asst Sec., Social Services Dept, 1948; Dir of Social Welfare and Community Develt, Gold Coast, 1950; Colonial Sec., Trinidad and Tobago, 1952–56; Actg Governor of Trinidad, 1954, 1955; Governor, Comdr-in-Chief and Vice-Adm., Sierra Leone, 1956–61, after independence, Governor-Gen., 1961–62; Governor and Comdr-in-Chief, Malta, 1962–64, after independence, Governor-Gen., 1964–71. Dep. Chm., Pearce Commn on Rhodesian Opinion, 1971–72. Chm., Swindon HMC, 1972–74. Chm. Bd of Governors, Badminton Sch., 1975–81. A Trustee, Imperial War Museum, 1972–; Almoner, Venerable Order of St John, 1972–75; Chief Comdr, St John Ambulance, 1975–80. DL Wilts 1978. Hon. DCL Durham, 1962; Hon. LLD Royal Univ. Malta, 1966. GCStJ 1978 (KStJ 1957). Gran Croce Al Merito Melitense (Soc. Ordine Militaire di Malta), 1966. *Recreations:* once sailing, squash, and sometimes golf. *Address:* The Old Manor, Overton, Marlborough, Wilts. *T:* Lockeridge 600; 42 Lennox Gardens, SW1. *T:* 01-584 8698. *Clubs:* Athenæum; Casino

Maltese (Valletta).
See also R. B. Dorman.

DORMAN, Richard Bostock; HM Diplomatic Service; High Commissioner to Vanuatu, since 1982; *b* 8 Aug. 1925; *s* of late John Ehrenfried and late Madeleine Louise Dorman; *m* 1950, Anna Illingworth; one *s* two *d. Educ:* Sedbergh Sch.; St John's Coll., Cambridge. Army Service (Lieut, S Staffs Regt), 1944–48; Asst Principal, War Office, 1951; Principal, 1955; transferred to Commonwealth Relations Office, 1958; First Sec., British High Commission, Nicosia, 1960–64; Dep. High Commissioner, Freetown, 1964–66; SE Asia Dept, FO, 1967–69; Counsellor, Addis Ababa, 1969–73; Commercial Counsellor, Bucharest, 1974–77; Counsellor, Pretoria, 1977–82. *Address:* c/o Foreign and Commonwealth Office, SW1; 67 Beresford Road, Cheam, Surrey. *T:* 01-642 9627. *Club:* Royal Commonwealth Society.
See also Sir M. H. Dorman.

DORMAND, John Donkin; MP (Lab) Easington since 1970; *b* 27 Aug. 1919; *s* of Bernard and Mary Dormand; *m* 1963, Doris Robinson; one step *s* one step *d. Educ:* Bede Coll., Durham; Loughborough Coll.; Univs of Oxford and Harvard. Teacher, 1940–48; Education Adviser, 1948–52 and 1957–63; District Education Officer, Easington RDC, 1963–70. An Asst Govt Whip, 1974; a Lord Comr of HM Treasury, 1974–79; Chm., PLP, 1981–. *Recreations:* music, sport.

DORMER, family name of **Baron Dormer.**

DORMER, 16th Baron *cr* 1615; **Joseph Spencer Philip Dormer;** Bt 1615; landowner and farmer; *b* 4 Sept. 1914; *s* of 14th Baron Dormer, CBE, and Caroline May (*d* 1951), *y d* of Sir Robert Cavendish Spencer Clifford, 3rd Bt; *S* brother, 1975. *Educ:* Ampleforth; Christ Church, Oxford. Formerly Captain, Scots Guards; served War of 1939–45. Consultant, Thomas Comely & Sons Ltd. Member of Council, West Midlands Area Conservative Assoc. *Heir: cousin* Geoffrey Henry Dormer [*b* 13 May 1920; *m* 1st, 1947, Janet (marr. diss. 1957), *yr d* of James F. A. Readman; two *d* ; 2nd, 1958, Pamela, *d* of late Wallace Levick Simpson; two *s*]. *Address:* Grove Park, Warwick. *Club:* Cavalry and Guards.

DORNHORST, Antony Clifford, CBE 1977; MD, FRCP; Professor of Medicine, St George's Hospital Medical School, 1959–80; Civilian Consultant in Aviation Medicine to RAF, since 1973; *b* 2 April 1915; *s* of Ernst Dornhorst and Florence, *née* Partridge; *m* 1946, Helen Mary Innes; three *d. Educ:* St Clement Danes Sch.; St Thomas's Hosp. Medical Sch. MB BS London 1937; MD London 1939; FRCP 1955. Junior Appointments, St Thomas' Hosp., 1937–39. Served with RAMC, mostly in Mediterranean theatre, 1940–46. Reader in Medicine, St Thomas's Hosp. Medical Sch., 1949–59. Member: MRC, 1973–77; SW Thames RHA, 1974–82. *Publications:* papers in various journals on normal and abnormal physiology. *Recreation:* music. *Address:* 8 Albert Place, W8. *T:* 01-937 8782.

DORRELL, Ernest John; Secretary, Headmasters' Conference, 1975–79; General Secretary, Secondary Heads Association, 1978–79 (Secretary, Incorporated Association of Headmasters, 1975–77); *b* 31 March 1915; *s* of John Henry Whiting Dorrell and Amy Dorrell (*née* Roberts); *m* 1940, Alwen Irvona Jones; one *s* one *d. Educ:* Taunton Sch.; Exeter Coll., Oxford (Exhibr). Hon. Mods and Lit. Hum., MA. Served with 71 Field Regt and HQ 46 Div. RA, 1940–46. Asst Master, Dauntsey's Sch., 1937–40 and 1946–47; Admin. Asst, WR Educn Dept, 1947; Dep. Dir of Educn, Oxfordshire CC, 1950; Dir of Educn, Oxfordshire CC, 1970; Report on Educn in St Helena, 1974. *Recreations:* walking, travel, golf. *Address:* Swan Cottage, Shillingford, Oxford. *T:* Warborough 8342.

DORRELL, Stephen James; MP (C) Loughborough, since 1979; *b* 25 March 1952; *s* of Philip Dorrell; *m* 1980, Penelope Anne Wears, *y d* of Mr and Mrs James Taylor, Windsor. *Educ:* Uppingham; Brasenose Coll., Oxford. BA 1973. RAFVR, 1971–73. Dir, family's industrial clothing co. Personal asst to Rt Hon. Peter Walker, MBE, MP, Feb. 1974; contested (C) Kingston-upon-Hull East, Oct. 1974. Sec., Cons. Backbench Trade Cttee. *Recreations:* aviation, reading. *Address:* House of Commons, SW1.

DORSET, Archdeacon of; *see* Walton, Ven. G. E.

DORWARD, Ivor Gardiner Menzies Gordon, ARSA, FRIBA, FRIAS, RGI; Architect Principal in private practice, since 1960; Member, Royal Fine Art Commission for Scotland, since 1976; *b* 18 Oct. 1927; *s* of William Gordon Dorward and Jean Lawson Dorward (*née* Skinner); *m* 1954, Priscilla Purves Tindal, DA Edin.; two *d. Educ:* Royal High Sch., Edinburgh; Blackpool Grammar Sch.; Edinburgh Coll. of Art. DA 1953; FRIBA 1969. Served RAF, 1945–48. Various travelling scholarships in Europe and Africa, 1951, 1952 and 1953. Architect in private practice, Dorward, Matheson, Gleave & Partners, 1960–. Principal works include university, hospital, and both local and central government buildings. Royal Scottish Acad. Medal for Architecture, 1971. RGI 1978; ARSA 1979. *Recreations:* drawing, sailing, Bull Terriers. *Address:* 50 Sherbrooke Avenue, Glasgow G41 4SB. *T:* 041-427 1771; Kerryfern, Strone, Argyll PA23 8RR. *T:* Dunoon 84416. *Club:* Glasgow Art (Glasgow).

DORWARD, William, OBE 1977; Director of Trade, Industry and Customs and Member of Legislative Council, Hong Kong, since 1979; *b* 25 Sept. 1929;

s of Alexander and Jessie Dorward; m 1960, Rosemary Ann Smith; one s. Educ: Morgan Academy, Dundee. Colonial Office, 1951-53; Commerce and Industry Dept, Hong Kong Govt, 1954-74; Counsellor (Hong Kong Affairs) UK Mission, Geneva, 1974-76; Dep. Dir of Commerce and Industry, Hong Kong, 1974-77; Comr of Industry and Customs, Hong Kong, 1977-79. Hon. Vice Pres., Hong Kong Economics Soc.; Pres., Studio One (Film Soc. of Hong Kong). Address: A3101 Tregunter Mansions, Hong Kong. T: 5-246292; 38 Bingham Terrace, Dundee, Scotland. Clubs: Carlton; Hong Kong.

DOS SANTOS, Sir Errol Lionel, Kt 1946; CBE 1939; Consultant, Alstons Ltd; b 1 Sept. 1890; s of Solomon and Margaret dos Santos; m 1st, 1915; one s one d; 2nd, 1939, Enid Hilda Jenkin, Bath, England; two d. Educ: St Mary's Coll., Trinidad. Entered Trinidad Civil Service as a junior clerk in the Treasury; Financial Sec., 1941; Colonial Sec., 1947; retired from Colonial Service, 1948. Dir, Alstons Ltd, 1948, Chm. 1953-61. Address: Flat 3, 7 Bryanston Square, W1. Clubs: MCC; Union, Queen's Park Cricket, Portuguese (Trinidad).

DOSSER, Prof. Douglas George Maurice; Professor of Economics, University of York, 1965-81; retired, 1981; b 3 Oct. 1927; s of George William Dosser; m 1954, Valerie Alwyne Elizabeth, d of Leslie Jack Lindsey; three d. Educ: Latymer Upper School; London School of Economics. Lecturer in Economics, Univ. of Edinburgh, 1958-62; Vis. Prof. of Economics, Univ. of Washington, Seattle, 1960; Vis. Res. Prof. of Economics, Columbia Univ., NY, 1962; Reader in Economics, Univ. of York, 1963-65. Publications: Economic Analysis of Tax Harmonisation, 1967; (with S. Han) Taxes in the EEC and Britain, 1968; (with F. Andic) Theory of Economic Integration for Developing Countries, 1971; European Economic Integration and Monetary Unification, 1973; (with K. Hartley) The Collaboration of Nations, 1981; articles in Economic Jl, Economica, Rev. of Economic Studies. Recreations: art and antiques. Address: 16 New Walk Terrace, York YO1 4BG. T: York 54358.

DOSSOR, Rear-Adm. Frederick, CB 1963; CBE 1959; with Premmit Associates Ltd; b 12 March 1913; s of John Malcolm Dossor and Edith Kate Brittain; m 1951, Pamela Anne Huxley Newton; two d. Educ: Hymers Coll., Hull; Loughborough Coll. BSc(Eng.) London; FIEE. Post Graduate Apprentice and Junior Engineer, Metropolitan Vickers Electrical Co., Manchester, 1935-39; Dept of Dir of Electrical Engineering, Admiralty, 1939-50; Electrical Specialisation, Royal Navy, 1950-65; Chief Staff Officer (Technical), staff of Comdr-in-Chief, Portsmouth, 1961-63; Polaris Project Officer in the Ministry of Technology, 1963-67; Dir of Hovercraft, DTI (formerly Min. of Technology), 1968-71. Retired from Royal Navy, 1965. Recreation: gardening. Address: 1a Lynch Road, Farnham, Surrey. Club: Royal Commonwealth Society.

DOTRICE, Roy; actor (stage, films and television); b 26 May 1925; m 1946, Kay Newman, actress; three d. Educ: Dayton and Intermediate Schs, Guernsey, CI. Served War of 1939-45: Air Gunner, RAF, 1940; PoW, 1942-45. Acted in Repertory, 1945-55; formed and directed Guernsey Theatre Co., 1955; Royal Shakespeare Co., 1957-65 (Caliban, Julius Caesar, Hotspur, Firs, Puntila, Edward IV, etc); World War 2½, New Theatre, London, 1966; Brief Lives, Golden Theatre, New York, 1967; Latent Heterosexual and God Bless, Royal Shakespeare Co., Aldwych, 1968; Brief Lives (one-man play), Criterion, 1969 (over 400 perfs, world record for longest-running solo perf.), toured England, Canada, USA, 1973, Mayfair, 1974 (over 150 perfs); Broadway season, 1974; Australian tour, 1975; Peer Gynt, Chichester Festival, 1970; One At Night, Royal Court, 1971; The Hero, Edinburgh, 1970; Mother Adam, Arts, 1971; Tom Brown's Schooldays, Cambridge, 1972; The Hollow Crown, seasons in USA 1973 and 1975, Sweden 1975; Gomes, Queen's, 1973; The Dragon Variation, Duke of York's, 1977; Australian tour with Chichester Festival, 1978; Passion of Dracula, Queen's, 1978; Oliver, Albery, 1979; Mister Lincoln (one-man play on Abraham Lincoln), Washington, NY and TV special, 1980, Fortune, 1981; A Life, NY, 1980-81; Henry V, American Shakespeare Theatre, Stratford, Conn, 1981; Murder in Mind, Strand, 1982; films include: Heroes of Telemark, Twist of Sand, Lock up Your Daughters, Buttercup Chain, Tomorrow, One of Those Things, Nicholas and Alexandra; television: appearances in: Dear Liar, Brief Lives, The Caretaker (Emmy award), Imperial Palace, Misleading Cases, Clochemerle, Dickens of London, Stargazy on Zummerdown, Family Reunion (USA), etc. TV Actor of the Year Award, 1968. Recreations: fishing, riding. Address: Talbot House, St Martin's Lane, WC2. Club: Garrick.

DOUEK, Ellis Elliot, FRCS; Consultant Otologist since 1970, and Chairman, Hearing Research Group, since 1974, Guy's Hospital; b 25 April 1934; s of Cesar Douek and Nelly Sassoon; m 1964, Nicole Galante; two s. Educ: English School, Cairo; Westminster Medical School. MRCS, LRCP 1958; FRCS 1967. House appts, St Helier Hosp., 1959, and Whittington Hosp., 1963; nat. service, RAMC, 1960-62; ENT Registrar, Royal Free Hosp., 1966; Sen. Registrar, King's College Hosp., 1968. Mem., MRC working party on Hearing Research, 1975. Dalby Prize for hearing research, RSM, 1978. Publications: Sense of Smell—Its Abnormalities, 1974; Eighth Nerve, in Peripheral Neuropathy, 1975; Olfaction, in Scientific Basis of Otolaryngology, 1976; Cochlear Implant, in Textbook of ENT, 1980; papers on hearing and smell. Recreations: drawing and painting; studying history. Address: (home) 24 Reynolds Close, NW11. T: 01-455 6047; 97 Harley Street, W1. T: 01-935 7828.

DOUGAL, Malcolm Gordon; HM Diplomatic Service; Consul General, Lille, since 1981; b 20 Jan. 1938; s of Eric Gordon Dougal and Marie (née Wildermuth); m 1964, Elke (née Urban); one s. Educ: Ampleforth Coll., Yorkshire; The Queen's Coll., Oxford (MA Mod. History). National Service in Korea and Gibraltar with Royal Sussex Regt, 1956-58; Oxford, 1958-61; Contracts Asst, De Havilland Aircraft, Hatfield, 1961-64; Asst to Export Manager, Ticket Equipment Ltd (Plessey), 1964-66; Export Manager, Harris Lebus Ltd, 1967-69; entered HM Diplomatic Service, 1969; Foreign Office, 1969-72; 1st Secretary (Commercial): Paris, 1972-76; Cairo, 1976-79; Foreign Office, 1979-81. Recreations: natural history, walking, books, sport, wine. Address: c/o Foreign and Commonwealth Office, Whitehall, SW1.

DOUGAN, (Alexander) Derek; Chairman and Chief Executive, Wolverhampton Wanderers' Football Club, since 1982; Commercial Director, Professional Footballers' Association, since 1978 (Chairman, 1970-78); b 20 Jan. 1938; s of John and Josephine Dougan; m 1963, Jutta Maria; two s. Educ: Mersey Street primary sch., Belfast; Belfast Technical High School. Professional footballer with: Distillery, NI, 1953-57; Portsmouth, 1957-59; Blackburn Rovers, 1959-61; Aston Villa, 1961-63; Peterborough, 1963-65; Leicester, 1965-67; Wolverhampton Wanderers, 1967-75; Chief Exec., Kettering Town FC, 1975-78. Represented N Ireland at all levels, from schoolboy to full international, more than 50 times. Sports Presenter, Yorkshire Television. Publications: Attack! (autobiog.), 1969; The Sash He Never Wore (autobiog.), 1972; The Footballer (novel), 1974; On the Spot (football as a profession), 1974; Doog (autobiog.), 1980; How Not to Run Football, 1981. Recreations: watching football, playing squash. Address: Bayern House, 40 Keepers Lane, Codsall, Wolverhampton, West Midlands.

DOUGHERTY, Maj.-Gen. Sir Ivan Noel, Kt 1968; CBE 1946; DSO 1941 (bar, 1943); ED; b Leadville, NSW, 6 April 1907; m 1936, Emily Phyllis Lofts; two s two d (and one d decd). Educ: Leadville Primary Sch.; Mudgee High Sch.; Sydney Teachers' Coll.; Sydney Univ. (BEc). NSW Education Dept: Asst Teacher, 1928-32; Dep. Headmaster, 1933-39; Headmaster, 1946-47; Dist Inspector of Schs, 1948-53; Staff Inspector 1953-55. Commissioned Sydney Univ. Regt, 1927. Capt. 1931; Unattached List, 1932-34; transf. to 33/41 Bn. 1934; Major, 1938; Command, 33rd Bn, 1938; Lieut-Col 1939. Served War of 1939-45 (DSO and Bar, CBE, despatches thrice); Australian Imperial Force, Second-in-Command, 2/2 inf. Bn, 1939-40; Commanded 2/4 inf. Bn (Libya, Greece, Crete campaigns), 1940-42; Brig. 1942; commanded 23 Bde, 1942; commanded 21 Bde, South-West Pacific, 1942-45. R of O, 1946-47; commanded 8th Bde, Austr. Mil. Forces, 1948-52; Maj.-Gen., 1952; commanded 2nd Div., 1952-54; Citizen Military Forces Member, Australian Mil. Bd, 1954-57; R of O, 1957-64; Retired List, 1964; Hon. Col, Australian Cadet Corps, Eastern Command, 1964-70; Representative Hon. Col, Australian Cadet Corps, 1967-70. Dir of Civil Defence for NSW, 1955-73. Mem. Council, Nat. Roads and Motorists' Assoc., 1969-79. Mem. Senate, 1954-74, Dep. Chancellor, 1958-66, Hon. LLD 1976, Univ. of Sydney. Address: 4 Leumeah Street, Cronulla, NSW 2230, Australia. T: 523-5465. Club: Imperial Service (Sydney).

DOUGHTY, Dame Adelaide, DBE 1971 (CBE 1964); b 2 Dec. 1908; d of E. H. Shackell, Melbourne, Australia; m 1931, Charles John Addison Doughty, QC (d 1973); one s one d. Educ: St Catherine's Sch., Melbourne; St Hilda's Coll., Oxford (BA). Chm., Nat. Women's Advisory Cttee, Conservative Party, 1963-66; Chm., 1967, Pres., 1978, Nat. Union of Conservative and Unionist Party; Governor, English-Speaking Union, 1958-72 (Dep.-Chm. 1971-72). Mem. Grand Council, Cancer Res. Campaign, 1974. Address: Flat 4, 89 Onslow Square, SW7 3LT. T: 01-584 5126.

DOUGHTY, George Henry; General Secretary, Technical and Supervisory Section, Amalgamated Union of Engineering Workers, 1971-74, retired; Member, Central Arbitration Committee, since 1976; b 17 May 1911; British; m 1941, Mildred Dawson; two s. Educ: Handsworth Tech. Sch.; Aston Technical Coll. Draughtsman: trained at General Electric Co., Birmingham, 1927-32; employed as Design Draughtsman: English Electric, Stafford 1932-33; GEC Birmingham, 1934-46. With Draughtsmen's & Allied Technician's Assoc., 1946-71, General Secretary, 1952-71. Member: Gen. Council of TUC, 1968-74; Independent Review Cttee, 1976-; Chm., EDC for Electrical Engrg, 1974-82. Mem., Royal Commn on Distribution of Income and Wealth, 1974-78. Industrial Relns Advr, SIAD, 1977-. Publications: various technical and Trade Union publications. Recreation: photography. Address: Short Way, Whitton, Twickenham, Middx TW2 7NU. T: 01-894 0299.

DOUGLAS, family name of Viscount Chilston, Earl of Morton, and Marquess of Queensberry.

DOUGLAS AND CLYDESDALE, Marquess of; Alexander Douglas-Hamilton; b 31 March 1978; s and heir of Duke of Hamilton, qv.

DOUGLAS, Prof. Alexander Stuart; Regius Professor of Medicine, University of Aberdeen, since 1970; b 2 Oct. 1921; s of late Dr R. Douglas, MOH for Moray and Nairn; m 1954, Christine McClymont Stewart; one s one d. Educ: Elgin Academy, Morayshire. Mil. Service, RAMC, 1945-48 (despatches 1947). Research Fellow, Radcliffe Infirmary, Oxford, and Postgrad. Med. Sch., London, 1951-53; Lectr, Sen. Lectr and Reader in Medicine, Univ. Dept of Med., Royal Infirmary, Glasgow, 1953-64; Hon. Consultant status, 1957; Prof. of Med., Univ. of Glasgow, 1964-70;

secondment to Univ. of East Africa with hon. academic rank of Prof., 1965; Hon. Consultant Physician in Administrative Charge of wards, Royal Infirmary, Glasgow, 1968-70. *Publications:* scientific papers on blood coagulation, etc. *Recreations:* curling, travel. *Address:* Department of Medicine, Aberdeen Royal Infirmary, Foresterhill, Aberdeen AB9 2ZB. *T:* Aberdeen 681818 (ext 3349).

DOUGLAS, Arthur John Alexander, CMG 1965; OBE 1962; Assistant Secretary, Overseas Development Administration, Foreign and Commonwealth Office, (formerly Ministry of Overseas Development), 1975-80; *b* 31 May 1920; *s* of Alexander and Eileen Douglas; *m* 1948, Christine Scott Dyke; two *d. Educ:* Dumfries Academy; Edinburgh Univ. Royal Navy, 1940-45. District Officer, Basutoland, 1946; Seconded Colonial Office, 1957; Administration Sec., Bechuanaland, 1959; Government Sec. and Chief Sec. 1962-65; Dep. Commissioner for Bechuanaland, 1965-66; ODM, 1967-80. *Address:* 57 Lucastes Avenue, Haywards Heath, West Sussex. *Club:* Royal Commonwealth Society.

DOUGLAS, Prof. Charles Primrose, FRCOG; Professor of Obstetrics and Gynæcology, University of Cambridge, since 1976; Fellow, Emmanuel College, Cambridge, since 1979; *b* 17 Feb. 1921; *s* of Dr C. Douglas, Ayr, Scotland; *m* 1948, Angela Francis; three *s* one *d. Educ:* Loretto Sch.; Peterhouse; Edinburgh Univ. Surg. Lieut RNVR, 1944-47. Registrar and Sen. Registrar, Victoria Infirmary, Glasgow, 1950-59; William Waldorf Astor Foundn Fellow, 1957; Visiting Fellow, Duke Univ., NC, 1957; Sen. Lectr, Univ. of the West Indies, 1959-65; Prof. of Obst. and Gyn., Royal Free Hosp. Sch. of Medicine, 1965-76. Member: Bd of Governors, Royal Free Hosp., 1972-74; Camden and Islington AHA, 1974-76, Cambridge AHA, 1981-82; Council, RCOG, 1980-. *Publications:* contribs to BMJ, Amer. Heart Jl, Jl of Obst. and Gynæc. of Brit. Commonwealth, etc. *Recreations:* tennis, equestrian events, skin diving. *Address:* Old Mill House, Linton Road, Balsham, Cambs CB1 6HA. *Club:* United Oxford & Cambridge University.

DOUGLAS, Sir Donald (Macleod), Kt 1972; MBE 1943; ChM St Andrews, MS Minn, FRCSE; FRCS; FRSE 1973; Surgeon to the Queen in Scotland, 1965-76; an Extra Surgeon to the Queen in Scotland, since 1977; Professor of Surgery, University of Dundee (formerly Queen's College), 1951-76, Emeritus Professor, 1977; Surgeon, Ninewells Hospital, Dundee, 1951-76; *b* 28 June 1911; *s* of William Douglas and Christina Broom; *m* 1945, Margaret Diana Whitley; two *s* two *d. Educ:* Madras Coll.; Universities of St Andrews and Minnesota. Commonwealth Fellow in Surgery, Mayo Clinic, University of Minnesota, USA, 1937-39; First Asst in Surgery, British Postgraduate Medical Sch., 1939-40; RAMC, 1941-45; Reader in Experimental Surgery, University of Edinburgh, 1945-51; Asst Surgeon, Edinburgh Municipal Hospitals, 1945; formerly Surgeon, Royal Infirmary, Dundee. Assoc. Asst Surgeon, Royal Infirmary, Edinburgh. Dean of Faculty of Medicine, Univ. of Dundee, 1969-70. President: RCSE, 1971-73; Assoc. of Surgeons of GB and Ireland, 1964; Surgical Research Soc. of GB, 1966-69; Harveian Soc., 1974. Trustee, Thalidomide Trust, 1973- (Chm., Health and Welfare). Hon. FACS, 1972; Hon. FRCS (SA), 1972; Hon. FRCSI, 1973. Hon. DSc St Andrews, 1972. *Publications:* Wound Healing, 1965; The Thoughtful Surgeon, 1970; Surgical Departments in Hospitals, 1971. *Address:* The Whitehouse of Nevay, Newtyle, Angus. *T:* Newtyle 315.

DOUGLAS, Sir (Edward) Sholto, Kt 1977; Solicitor of the Supreme Court of Queensland, since 1934; *b* 23 Dec. 1909; *s* of Hon. Mr Justice E. A. Douglas and Annette Eileen Power; *m* 1939, Mary Constance Curr. *Educ:* St Ignatius Coll., Riverview, Sydney. Queensland Law Society Incorporated: Mem. Council, 1954-76; Actg Pres., 1960; Pres., 1962-64; Mem., Statutory Cttee, 1976-; Member: Legal Assistance Cttee, Qld, 1965-80; Solicitors' Bd, 1969-75; Exec. Mem., Law Council of Aust., 1973-75. President: Taxpayers Assoc. of Qld, 1955-58; Federated Taxpayers of Aust., 1957-58; Mem. Adv. Cttee, Terminating and Permanent Building Socs, 1966-77. Pres., Qld Div., Nat. Heart Foundn, 1976-77 (Vice-Pres., 1966-75); Vice-Pres., RSPCA, 1965-; Chm., Management Cttee, Currumbin Bird Sanctuary and Wildlife Reserve, 1978-80. *Recreations:* racing, gardening. *Address:* 81 Markwell Street, Hamilton, Brisbane, Qld 4007, Australia. *T:* 268.2759. *Clubs:* Queensland, Brisbane (Pres. 1965), Tattersalls, Royal Queensland Golf, Queensland Turf, Tattersalls Racing, Brisbane Amateur Turf (all Brisbane).

DOUGLAS, Gavin Stuart, RD 1970; QC (Scot.) 1971; *b* 12 June 1932; *y s* of late Gilbert Georgeson Douglas and Rosena Campbell Douglas. *Educ:* South Morningside Sch.; George Heriot's Sch.; Edinburgh Univ. MA 1953, LLB 1955. Qual. as Solicitor, 1955; nat. service with RN, 1955-57. Admitted to Faculty of Advocates, 1958; Sub-editor (part-time), The Scotsman, 1957-61; Mem. Lord Advocate's Dept in London (as Parly Draftsman), 1961-64; returned to practice at Scots Bar, 1964; Junior Counsel to BoT, 1965; Counsel to Scottish Law Commn, 1965; Hon. Sheriff in various sheriffdoms, 1965-71; a Chm. of Industrial Tribunals, 1966-78; Counsel to Sec. of State for Scotland under Private Legislation Procedure (Scotland) Act 1936, 1969-75, Sen. Counsel, 1975-. Editor, Session Cases, 1977-. *Recreations:* golf, ski-ing. *Address:* Parliament House, Parliament Square, Edinburgh 1. *Clubs:* Caledonian; University Staff (Edinburgh).

DOUGLAS, Henry Russell, FJI; Legal Manager, News Group Newspapers, since 1976; *b* Bishopbriggs, Lanarkshire, 11 Feb. 1925; 2nd *s* of late Russell Douglas and Jeanie Douglas Douglas (née Drysdale); *m* 1951, Elizabeth Mary,

d of late Ralph Nowell, CB; two *s* three *d. Educ:* various Scottish and English Grammar Schools; Lincoln Coll., Oxford (MA Hons). Served RNVR, 1943-46 (Sub-Lt, submarines). Merchant Navy, 1946-47; Oxford Univ. 1947-50; Liverpool Daily Post, 1950-69; The Sun, 1969-76. Inst of Journalists: 1956: Fellow, 1969; Pres., 1972-73; Chm. of Executive, 1973-76; Mem. Press Council, 1972-80; Founder Mem. and Treasurer, Media Society, 1973. *Recreations:* chess, travel, history. *Address:* Austen Croft, 31 Austen Road, Guildford, Surrey. *T:* Guildford 76960. *Club:* United Oxford & Cambridge University.

DOUGLAS, Very Rev. Hugh Osborne, KCVO 1981; CBE 1961; DD, LLD; Dean of the Chapel Royal in Scotland, 1974-81; Chaplain to The Queen 1959-81, Extra Chaplain to The Queen, since 1981; Minister at Dundee Parish Church (St Mary's), 1951-77; Moderator of the General Assembly of the Church of Scotland, May 1970- May 1971; *b* Glasgow, 11 Sept. 1911; *s* of Rev. Robert Baillie Douglas, DD, missionary in W India, and Mary Isabella Osborne; *m* 1939, Isabel Crammond, *d* of William Rutherford, Coldstream, Berwicks; one *s* two *d. Educ:* Glasgow Academy; Glasgow Univ.; Trinity Coll., Glasgow. MA 1st Cl. Hons (Classics), 1932. Licensed to preach by Presbytery of Glasgow, 1935; Asst, Govan Old Parish Church, 1935-39; Ordained, Glasgow, 1937; Minister: St John's Leven, 1939; North Leith, Edinburgh, 1942. Member: Legal Aid Central Cttee of Law Soc. of Scotland, 1955-80; Scottish Religious Advisory Cttee of BBC, 1956-58; Gen. Advisory Council of BBC, 1966-69; Convener of Gen. Assembly's Special Cttee on Fourth Centenary of the Reformation, 1955-60; Convener of Gen. Assembly's Special Cttee on Religious Education, 1960-64. Centenary Preacher, St Andrew's Church, Brisbane, 1962, Guest Preacher, 1977. Visiting Lectr, Christian Council of Ghana, 1967. Hon. Governor, Glasgow Acad., 1971. Hon. DD St Andrews, 1958; Hon. LLD Dundee, 1971. *Publications:* Coping with Life, 1964; various pamphlets and articles. *Recreation:* golf. *Address:* Broomlea, 7A Windmill Road, St Andrews. *T:* St Andrews 73232. *Club:* Royal and Ancient Golf (St Andrews).

DOUGLAS, James Albert Sholto, CMG 1966; Director, IDA/IBRD Education Project Implementation Unit, 1969-79; *b* 23 April 1913; *s* of Dr James Henry Sholto Douglas and Cécile Anne (née Brotherson); *m* 1945, Marjorie Lucille (née Reynolds); two *s. Educ:* privately in Guyana (Brit. Guiana); Culford Sch., England. Entered Brit. Guyana CS in Commissary's Dept 1932; various posts in Dist Admin, 1933-48; Asst Dist Comr, 1948; Dist Comr, 1953; seconded as a Local Govt Comr, 1957; Dep. Comr of Local Govt, 1960; Permanent Sec., Community Develt and Educn, 1961, Home Affairs 1961-66; Min. of Education, 1966; retired from Guyana Civil Service, 1972. *Recreations:* swimming, riding. *Address:* 93 Duke Street, Georgetown, Guyana. *T:* 61403. *Club:* Royal Commonwealth Society.

DOUGLAS, James Murray; Director, Country Landowners Association, since 1970; *b* 26 Sept. 1925; *s* of Herbert and Amy Douglas, Brechin; *m* 1950, Julie Kemmner; one *s* one *d. Educ:* Morrison's Acad., Crieff; Aberdeen Univ. (MA); Balliol Coll., Oxford (BA). Entered Civil Service, 1950; Treasury, 1960-63; Asst Sec., Min. of Housing and Local Govt, 1964; Sec. to Royal Commn on Local Govt, 1966-69; Vice-Pres., Confedn of European Agriculture, 1971; Mem., Econ. Develt Cttee for Agriculture, 1972. *Publications:* various articles on local govt and landownership. *Address:* 1 Oldfield Close, Bickley, Kent. *T:* 01-467 3213. *Club:* United Oxford & Cambridge University.

DOUGLAS, Kenneth, CEng, FRINA; Managing Director, Austin and Pickersgill Ltd, 1958-69, and since 1979; Chairman, Kenton Shipping Services, Darlington, since 1968; *b* 28 Oct. 1920; British; *m* 1942, Doris Lewer; one *s* two *d. Educ:* Sunderland Technical Coll. (Dip. Naval Architecture). CEng, FRINA. Dep. Shipyard Manager, Vickers Armstrong Naval Yard, Newcastle-upon-Tyne, 1946-53; Dir and Gen. Manager, Wm Gray & Co. Ltd, West Hartlepool, 1954-58; Man. Dir, Upper Clyde Shipbuilders Ltd, Chm., Simons Lobnitz Ltd and Chm., UCS Trng Co., 1969-72; Dep. Chm., Govan Shipbuilders, 1971-73; Chm., Douglas (Kilbride) Ltd, 1972-77; Chm. and Man. Dir, Steel Structures Ltd, 1974-76; Shiprepair Marketing Dir, British Shipbuilders, 1978-79. Fellow, Sunderland Poly., 1980. *Recreations:* fishing, golf. *Address:* 7 Birchfield Road, Sunderland, Tyne and Wear; Monks Cottage, Romaldkirk, Barnard Castle, Co. Durham. *Club:* Naval.

DOUGLAS, Prof. Mary; Avalon Foundation Professor in the Humanities, Northwestern University, since 1981; *b* 25 March 1921; *d* of Gilbert Charles Tew and Phyllis Twomey; *m* 1951, James A. T. Douglas, OBE; two *s* one *d. Educ:* Univ. of Oxford (MA, BSc, PhD). Returned to Oxford, 1946, to train as anthropologist; fieldwork in Belgian Congo, 1949-50 and 1953; Lectr in Anthropology, Univ. of Oxford, 1950; Univ. of London, 1951-78, Prof. of Social Anthropology, UCL, 1970-78. Res. Scholar, Russell Sage Foundn, NY, 1977-81. *Publications:* The Lele of the Kasai, 1963; Purity and Danger, 1966; Natural Symbols, 1970; Implicit Meanings, 1976; Evans-Pritchard, 1980. *Address:* 1738 Chicago Avenue, Evanston, Ill 60201, USA. *Club:* United Oxford & Cambridge University.

DOUGLAS, Richard Giles; MP (Lab and Co-op) Dunfermline, since 1979; Director, Ferguson Brothers (Port Glasgow), since 1975; *b* 4 Jan. 1932; *m* 1954, Jean Gray, *d* of Andrew Arnott; two *d. Educ:* Co-operative College, Stanford Hall, Loughborough; Univ. of Strathclyde. Engineer (Marine); Mem. AUEW. Tutor organiser in Adult Educn, Co-operative movement, 1957; Sectional Educn Officer, Scotland, 1958-61; Lectr in Economics, Dundee Coll. of Technol., 1964-70. Contested (Lab): South Angus, 1964,

Edinburgh West, 1966, Glasgow Pollok, March 1967; (Lab and Co-op) Clackmannan and E Stirlingshire, Oct. 1974; MP (Lab and Co-op) Clackmannan and E Stirlingshire, 1970-Feb. 1974. Hon. Lectr, Strathclyde, 1980-. Hon. Mem., Univ. of Strathclyde Staff Club. *Address:* Braehead House, High Street, Auchtermuchty, Fife.

DOUGLAS, Sir Robert (McCallum), Kt 1976; OBE 1956; President, Robert M. Douglas Holdings Limited, since 1980 (Director, since 1930; Chairman, 1952-77); *b* 2 Feb. 1899; *s* of John Douglas and Eugenia McCallum; *m* 1927, Millicent Irene Tomkys Morgan (*d* 1980); one *s* one *d. Educ:* Terregles Sch.; Dumfries Academy. Served Army, 1916-19. Served 10 years with civil engineering contracting co., 1920-30; founded Douglas Group of Companies, 1930. Mem., MPBW Midland Regional Jt Adv. Cttee, 1940-46. Federation of Civil Engineering Contractors: Chm., Midland Section, 1942-43 and 1947-48; Chm. Council, 1948-49; Pres., 1958-60. Patron, Staffs Agric. Soc. Hon. DSc Aston, 1977. *Recreations:* shooting, farming. *Address:* Dunstall Hall, Barton-under-Needwood, Burton-on-Trent, Staffordshire DE13 8BE. *T:* Barton-under-Needwood 2471. *Clubs:* Caledonian; Birmingham (Birmingham).

DOUGLAS, Ronald Albert Neale, DFC 1944; JP; Agent General for Western Australia in London, since 1982; *b* 18 Sept. 1922; *s* of Edwyn William Albert Douglas and Kate Maria Douglas; *m* 1st, 1944 (marr. diss. 1966); one *s* one *d* ; 2nd, Pamela Joy Carroll; one *s. Educ:* Albany High Sch., WA. Served War, RAAF, 1941-46 (Sqdn Ldr). Joined Shell Co. of Australia, 1938; sales rep., 1946-50; various appts, incl. Aviation Manager and Dist Manager, WA and NSW, 1950-60; appts with Shell Cos, France and USA, 1960-61; Sales Man., WA, 1961-65; Commercial Man., Shell Malaysia, 1965-66; Marketing Man. and Commercial Man., Shell Singapore, 1966-67; Retail Man., Vic/Tas, 1967-71; Chm.'s Rep. and Commercial Man., Shell Gp of Cos in WA, 1971-82. JP WA, 1982. *Recreations:* cricket, golf, fishing, farming. *Address:* 22 Lincoln Avenue, Wimbledon, SW19 5JT. *T:* 01-946 7833. *Clubs:* Weld, West Australian, Royal Aero (Perth); Lake Karrinyup Country (WA).

DOUGLAS, Prof. Ronald Walter, DSc, FInstP, FSGT; Professor of Glass Technology, University of Sheffield, 1955-75; *b* 28 March 1910; *s* of John H. P. and A. E. Douglas; *m* 1933, Edna Maud Cadle; two *s. Educ:* Latymer Upper Sch.; Sir John Cass Coll., London. Mem., Research Staff, Research Laboratories of General Electric Company, 1927-55. Pres., Internat. Commn on Glass, 1972-75. *Publications:* (with S. Frank) A History of Glassmaking, 1972; many papers on the physics of glass and semiconductors. *Address:* Burford Lea, Eymore, West Hill, Ottery St Mary, Devon.

DOUGLAS, Sir Sholto; see Douglas, Sir E. S.

DOUGLAS, Sir Sholto (Courtenay Mackenzie), 5th Bt, *cr* 1831; MC 1918; *b* 27 June 1890; *s* of Donald Sholto Mackenzie Douglas (*d* 1928), and Edith Elizabeth Anne (*d* 1933), *y d* of George Robinson, Bagatelle, Mauritius; *S* cousin 1954; *m* 1929, Lorna Tichborne, *d* of Captain Hugh Nangle; two *d.* Served European War, 1914-18 (MC) and War of 1939-45 with Seaforth Highlanders. *Heir:* none. *Address:* 192 Cooden Drive, Cooden, Sussex.

DOUGLAS, Rt. Hon. Sir William (Randolph), PC 1977; Kt 1969; Chief Justice of Barbados, since 1965; *b* Barbados, 24 Sept. 1921; *e s* of William P. Douglas and Emily Frances Douglas (*née* Nurse); *m* 1951, Thelma Ruth (*née* Gilkes); one *s* one *d. Educ:* Bannatyne Sch. and Verdun High Sch., Verdun, Que., Canada; McGill Univ. (BA, Hons); London Sch. of Economics (LLB). Private Practice at Barbados Bar, 1948-50; Dep. Registrar, Barbados, 1950; Resident Magistrate, Jamaica, 1955; Asst Attorney-Gen., Jamaica, 1959; Solicitor-Gen., Jamaica, 1962; Puisne Judge, Jamaica, 1962. Chm., Commonwealth Caribbean Council of Legal Education, 1971-77; Member: Internat. Labour Organisation's Cttee of Experts on the Application of Conventions and Recommendations; President: Barbados Assoc. for the Blind and Deaf; Barbados Council for the Handicapped; UN Assoc. of Barbados; Barbados Boy Scouts Assoc. *Address:* Leland, Pine Gardens, St Michael, Barbados. *T:* 92030. *Club:* Barbados Yacht.

DOUGLAS-HAMILTON, family name of Duke of Hamilton and Brandon and Earl of Selkirk.

DOUGLAS-HAMILTON, Lord James Alexander; MP (C) Edinburgh West since Oct. 1974; *b* 31 July 1942; 2nd *s* of 14th Duke of Hamilton, and *b* of 15th Duke of Hamilton, *qv* ; *m* 1974, Hon. Priscilla Susan Buchan, *d* of Baron Tweedsmuir, *qv* and late Baroness Tweedsmuir of Belhelvie, PC; four *s* (incl. twins). *Educ:* Eton College, Balliol Coll., Oxford (MA, Mod. History; Oxford Boxing Blue, 1961; Pres., Oxford Univ. Cons. Assoc., 1963; Pres., Oxford Union Soc., 1964); Edinburgh Univ. (LLB, Scots Law). Advocate at Scots Bar, 1968. Town Councillor, Murrayfield-Cramond, Edinburgh, 1972. Scottish Conservative Whip, 1977; a Lord Comr of HM Treasury, and Govt Whip for Scottish Cons. Mems, 1979-81. Captain Cameronian Co., 2 Bn Low Vols (TAVR), 1972. Hon. Pres., Scottish Amateur Boxing Assoc., 1975-; President: Royal Commonwealth Soc. in Scotland, 1979-; Scottish Council, UNA, 1981-. *Publications:* Motive for a Mission: The Story Behind Hess's Flight to Britain, 1971; The Air Battle for Malta: the diaries of a fighter pilot, 1981. *Recreations:* golf, forestry. *Address:* 3 Blackie House, Lady Stair's Close, Edinburgh. *T:* 031-225 1482. *Clubs:* New (Edinburgh); Hon. Company of Edinburgh Golfers.

DOUGLAS-HOME, family name of Baroness Dacre and Baron Home of the Hirsel.

DOUGLAS-HOME, Charles Cospatrick; Editor, The Times, since 1982; *b* 1 Sept. 1937; *s* of late Hon. Henry Douglas-Home and of Lady Margaret Spencer; *m* 1966, Jessica Violet Gwynne; two *s. Educ:* Eton (King's Scholar). Commissioned, Royal Scots Greys, 1956-57; ADC to Governor of Kenya, 1958-59; Military Correspondent, Daily Express, 1961-62, Political and Diplomatic Corresp., 1962-64; The Times: Defence Corresp., 1965-70; Features Editor, 1970-73; Home Editor, 1973-78; Foreign Editor, 1978-81; Deputy Editor, 1981-82. Dir, Times Newspapers Ltd, 1982-. Hon. FRCM (Councillor, 1975-). *Publications:* The Arabs and Israel, 1968; Britain's Reserve Forces, 1969; Rommel, 1973; Evelyn Baring: the last Proconsul, 1978. *Recreations:* outdoor sports, music, books. *Address:* 18 Mortimer Crescent, NW6 5NP. *T:* 01-624 6424. *Club:* Caledonian.

DOUGLAS-HOME, Hon. David Alexander Cospatrick; Director, Morgan Grenfell & Co. Ltd, since 1974; *b* 20 Nov. 1943; *o s* of Baron Home of the Hirsel, *qv* ; *heir* to Earldom of Home; *m* 1972, Jane Margaret, *yr d* of Col J. Williams-Wynne, *qv* ; two *d. Educ:* Eton College; Christ Church, Oxford (BA 1966). Director: Morgan Grenfell Egyptian Finance Co. Ltd, 1975-77; Morgan Grenfell (Asia) Ltd, 1978- (Dep. Chm., 1979-82); Morgan Grenfell (Scotland) Ltd, 1978-; Arab Bank Investment Co., 1979-; Agricultural Mortgage Corp., 1979-; Arab-British Chamber of Commerce, 1975-; Economic Forestry Group, 1981-. Member, Committee for Middle East Trade, 1973-75. Governor, Ditchley Foundn, 1977-. *Recreations:* outdoor sports. *Address:* 99 Dovehouse Street, SW3. *Club:* Turf.

DOUGLAS-HOME, Hon. William; see Home.

DOUGLAS-MANN, Bruce Leslie Home; Solicitor, in practice since 1954; *b* 23 June 1927; *s* of Leslie John Douglas-Mann, MC and Alice Home Douglas-Mann; *m* 1955, Helen Tucker; one *s* one *d. Educ:* Upper Canada Coll., Toronto; Jesus Coll., Oxford. Leading Seaman, RN, 1945-48; Oxford, 1948-51. Admitted solicitor, 1954. Contested (Lab): St Albans, 1964; Maldon, 1966; MP North Kensington, 1970-74, Merton, Mitcham and Morden, 1974-May 1982, resigned (Lab 1970-81, Ind 1981, SDP Jan.-May 1982); contested (SDP), Merton, Mitcham and Morden, June 1982. Chairman: PLP Housing and Construction Gp, 1974-79; PLP Environment Gp, 1979-81 (Vice-Chm., 1972-79); Parly Select Cttee on Environment, 1979-82. Vice-Pres., Soc. of Lab. Lawyers, 1980-81 (Chm., 1974-80). Mem. Bd, Shelter, 1974-. Mem., Kensington or Kensington and Chelsea Borough Council, 1962-68. *Publications:* pamphlets: (ed) The End of the Private Landlord, 1973; Accidents at Work—Compensation for All, 1974. *Address:* 33 Furnival Street, EC4A 1JQ. *T:* 01-405 7216.

DOUGLAS-MILLER, Robert Alexander Gavin; Chairman and Managing Director, Jenners (Princes St Edinburgh) Ltd; Chairman, Clarkson Puckle (Scotland) Ltd; Director: Kennington Leasing Ltd; Chamber Developments Ltd; *b* 11 Feb. 1937; *s* of F. G. Douglas Miller and Mora Kennedy; *m* 1963, Judith Madeleine Smith; three *s* one *d. Educ:* Harrow; Oxford Univ. (MA). 9th Lancers, 1955-57; Oxford, 1958-61. Treasurer, Queen's Body Guard for Scotland (Royal Company of Archers). *Recreations:* shooting, fishing. *Address:* Bavelaw Castle, Balerno, Midlothian. *T:* 031-449 3972. *Club:* New (Edinburgh).

DOUGLAS-PENNANT, family name of Baron Penrhyn.

DOUGLAS-SCOTT-MONTAGU, family name of Baron Montagu of Beaulieu.

DOUGLAS-WILSON, Ian, MD, FRCPE; Editor of the Lancet, 1965-76; *b* 12 May 1912; *o s* of late Dr H. Douglas-Wilson; *m* 1939, Beatrice May, *e d* of late R. P. Bevan; one *s* two *d. Educ:* Marlborough Coll.; Edinburgh Univ. MB ChB 1936; MD (commended) Edinburgh 1938; FRCP Edinburgh 1945. Served with RAMC, 1940-45 (temp. Major). House-physician, Royal Infirmary, Edinburgh, 1937; joined the Lancet staff, 1946; Asst Ed., 1952-62; Dep. Ed., 1962-64. Corresp. Mem., Danish Soc. of Int. Med., 1965. Dr (*hc*) Edinburgh, 1974. *Address:* 14 St Matthew's Drive, Bickley, Bromley, Kent. *T:* 01-467 1703.

DOUGLAS-WITHERS, Maj.-Gen. John Keppel Ingold, CBE 1969; MC 1943; *b* 11 Dec. 1919; *s* of late Lt-Col H. H. Douglas-Withers, OBE, MC, FSA, and late Mrs V. G. Douglas-Withers; *m* 1945, Sylvia Beatrice Dean, Croydon, Surrey; one *s* one *d. Educ:* Shrewsbury Sch.; Christ Church, Oxford. Diploma in French, Univ. of Poitiers, 1938; Associate of Inst. of Linguists, in French and German, 1939. Commissioned into RA, 1940; Service in UK, Iraq, Western Desert, N Africa and Italy, 1940-45. Instr in Gunnery, Sch. of Artillery, Larkhill, 1945-47; service in Canal Zone, 1948-49; attended Staff Coll., Camberley, 1950; Staff appt in WO (Mil. Ops), 1951-53; service in The King's Troop, RHA, 1954-55; Instr, Staff Coll., Camberley, 1956-58; Battery Comdr, G Bty, Mercers Troop, RHA, 1959-60; Staff appt in WO (Mil. Sec. Dept), 1961; commanded 49 Field Regt in BAOR and Hong Kong, 1962-64; student at IDC, 1965; Comd 6 Inf. Bde in BAOR, 1966-67; Chief of Staff, 1st Brit. Corps, 1968-69; GOC SW District, 1970-71; Asst Chief of Personnel and Logistics, MoD, 1972-74; retired 1974. Col Comdt, RA, 1974-82. Asst Dir and Gp Personnel Man., Jardine Matheson & Co. Ltd, Hong Kong, 1974-80; Matheson & Co. Ltd, London, 1980-. MPIM (Hong Kong),

1976. *Recreations:* golf, history, music. *Address:* The Pond House, Burmington, Shipston-on-Stour, Warwickshire. *Clubs:* East India, Devonshire, Sports and Public Schools; MCC.

DOULTON, Alfred John Farre, CBE 1973 (OBE 1946); TD 1954; psc 1943; MA Oxon; Head of Statistical Team and Comptroller, Independent Schools Information Service, 1974–80; *b* 9 July 1911; *s* of H. V. Doulton, Housemaster, Dulwich Coll., and Constance Jessie Farre, Dulwich; *m* 1940, Vera Daphne, *d* of A. R. Wheatley, Esher; four *s* one *d. Educ:* Dulwich Coll.; Brasenose Coll., Oxford (Classical Scholar). Asst Master, Uppingham School, 1934–40. Served War, 1940–46 (despatches twice); DAAG 11 Army Group, 1944; active service, Burma, Malaya, Java, 1945–46; DAQMG 4 Corps, AA&QMG 23 Indian Division, 1945–46. Burma Star, Far East and GS Medal with Java Clasp. Head of Classics and Housemaster of The Lodge, Uppingham Sch., 1946; Headmaster, Highgate Sch., 1955–74. Vice-Chm., HMC, 1967 (Hon. Treasurer, 1964–74). Alderman, Haringey, 1968–71 (Vice-Chm. Educn Cttee). Mem., Governing Bodies Assoc., 1977–80. Vice-Chm. and Chm. Finance Cttee, Kelly Coll.; Trustee, Uppingham Sch. Mem., Indep. Schools Careers Orgn Council, 1978–81. *Publications:* The Fighting Cock, 1951; Highgate School 1938–1944: the story of a wartime evacuation, 1976. *Recreations:* music, cricket, books, dinghy sailing, ornithology. *Address:* Field Cottage, Salcombe, Devon. *T:* Salcombe 2316. *Clubs:* Athenæum, MCC.

DOUNE, Lord; John Douglas Stuart; *b* 29 Aug. 1966; *s* and *heir* of 20th Earl of Moray, *qv.*

DOURO, Marquess of; Arthur Charles Valerian Wellesley; Member (C) Surrey, European Parliament, since 1979; Deputy Chairman, Thames Valley Broadcasting; Director: Eucalyptus Pulp Mills; *b* 19 Aug. 1945; *s* and *heir* of 8th Duke of Wellington, *qv* ; *m* 1977, Antonia von Preussen, *d* of late Prince Frederick of Prussia and of Lady Brigid Ness; one *s* one *d. Educ:* Eton; Christ Church, Oxford. Contested (C) Islington N, Oct. 1974. Dir., Antofagasta and Bolivia Railway Co., 1977–80. *Heir:* *s* Earl of Mornington, *qv. Address:* Apsley House, Piccadilly, W1V 9FA; The Old Rectory, Stratfield Saye, Reading RG7 2DA.

DOVE, Maj.-Gen. Arthur Julian Hadfield, CB 1948; CBE 1946 (MBE 1937); *b* Marton, New Zealand, 25 Aug. 1902; *s* of late Rev. J. Ll. Dove; *m* 1948, Betty Eyre Godson Bartholomew; one *d. Educ:* Haileybury Coll.; RMA, Woolwich. 2nd Lieut RE, 1922; served Palestine, 1936–38 (MBE, despatches, Bt Major). Served War of 1939–45, France, 1940; Dep. Director HQ, 1942; CRE Guards Armoured Div., 1942–43; Chief Engineer, Combined Ops., 1943–44; Dep. Director of Military Ops, 1944–47; WO rep. with Council of Foreign Ministers and at Peace Conference, 1946–47; Dep. Adjutant General, BAOR, 1948–50; Brigadier, General Staff (Staff Duties), GHQ, MELF, 1951–53; Director of Quartering, War Office, 1954–57; Technical Director, FBI, 1957–61; retired 1957. Colonel Comdt RE, 1961–66. *Recreation:* fencing. *Address:* Moors Farm, Reigate Heath, Surrey. *T:* Reigate 45436. *Club:* Royal Commonwealth Society.

DOVE, Sir Clifford (Alfred), Kt 1967; CBE 1960 (MBE 1944); ERD 1963; FCIT; Chairman, British Transport Docks Board, 1970–71; Director-General and Member, Mersey Docks and Harbour Board, Liverpool, 1965–69 (General Manager, 1962); Member: National Ports Council, 1967–71; Council Institute of Transport, 1963–66 (Vice-President, 1964–65); Chairman Merseyside and District Section, Institute of Transport, 1964–65; Council, Dock and Harbour Authorities Assoc., 1970–71 (Executive Committee, 1962–69, Chairman, 1965–67, Vice-President, 1971); *b* 1 Dec. 1904; *s* of Frederick George Dove and Beatrice Dove (*née* Warren); *m* 1936, Helen Taylor, *d* of Captain James Wilson; no *c. Educ:* Russell Sch.; West Ham Municipal Coll.; London School of Economics. Joined Port of London Authority, 1921; Asst Port Director, Calcutta, 1945–46; Asst to Gen. Manager, Tees Conservancy Comrs, 1947–52; Gen. Manager, Ports, Nigeria and British Cameroons, 1952–54; Chm. and Gen. Manager, Nigeria Ports Authority, 1954–61; Mem. Nigeria Railway Corp., 1955–61; Mem. Nigeria Coal Corp., 1956–61; Comr of St John, Nigeria, 1956–61; Vice-Chm., Nat. Stadium Board of Nigeria, 1959–61; First Chm., Inst. of Transport, Nigeria Sect., 1959–61. Member: NW Economic Planning Council, 1965–69; Economic Develt Cttee for Movement of Exports, 1965–69; Exec. Cttee, Nat. Assoc. of Port Employers, 1968–69. Served War, 1939–46 (despatches, MBE): enlisted RE as 2nd Lieut, 1939; BEF, 1940; Middle East, 1941–44; Military Dock Supt., Alexandria, 1942–44; Dep. Asst Director of Transportation, MEF, 1944; AQMG (Movements) India and Embarkation Comdt, Calcutta, 1946; Demob., as Lt-Col. Joined Suppl. Reserve, 1947; retd, 1956, as Lt-Col. OStJ 1956. FRSA 1967. *Publication:* (with late A. H. J. Bown) Port Operation and Administration, 1950. *Recreation:* golf. *Address:* Rubbles Edge Cottage, Burley, Ringwood, Hants. *T:* Burley 2384. *Clubs:* East India, Devonshire, Sports and Public Schools; Royal Lymington Yacht.

DOVER, Suffragan Bishop of, since 1980; **Rt. Rev. Richard Henry McPhail Third;** *b* 29 Sept. 1927; *s* of Henry McPhail and Marjorie Caroline Third; *m* 1966, Helen Illingworth; two *d. Educ:* Alleyn's Sch.; Reigate Grammar Sch.; Emmanuel Coll., Cambridge (BA 1950, MA 1955); Lincoln Theological Coll. Deacon 1952, priest 1953; Southwark; Curate: S Andrew, Mottingham, 1952–55; Sanderstead (in charge of St Edmund, Riddlesdown), 1955–59; Vicar of Sheerness, 1959–67; Vicar of Orpington, 1967–76; RD of Orpington, 1973–76; Hon. Canon of Rochester, 1974–76; Proctor in Convocation, 1975–76; Bishop Suffragan of Maidstone, 1976–80. *Recreations:*

music, walking. *Address:* Upway, St Martin's Hill, Canterbury, Kent CT1 1PR. *T:* Canterbury 64537.

DOVER, Den; MP (C) Chorley, since 1979; *b* 4 April 1938; *s* of Albert and Emmie Dover; *m* 1959, Anne Marina Wright; one *s* one *d. Educ:* Manchester Grammar Sch.; Manchester Univ. (BSc Hons). CEng, MICE. John Laing & Son Ltd, 1959–68; National Building Agency: Dep. Chief Executive, 1969–70; Chief Exec., 1971–72; Projects Dir, Capital and Counties Property Co. Ltd, 1972–75; Contracts Manager, Wimpey Laing Iran, 1975–77. Director of Housing Construction, GLC, 1977–79. Member, London Borough of Barnet Council, 1968–71. Mem., Commons Select Cttee on Transport, 1979–. *Recreations:* cricket, hockey, golf; Methodist. *Address:* 166 Furzehill Road, Boreham Wood, Herts. *T:* 01-953 5945; 30 Countess Way, Euxton, Chorley, Lancs.

DOVER, Sir Kenneth James, Kt 1977; DLitt; FRSE 1975; FBA 1966; President of Corpus Christi College, Oxford, since 1976; Chancellor, University of St Andrews, since 1981; *b* 11 March 1920; *o s* of P. H. J. Dover, London, Civil Servant; *m* 1947, Audrey Ruth Latimer; one *s* one *d. Educ:* St Paul's Sch. (Scholar); Balliol Coll., Oxford (Domus Scholar); Gaisford Prize, 1939; 1st in Classical Hon. Mods., 1940; DLitt 1974. Served War of 1939–45; Army (RA), 1940–45; Western Desert, 1941–43, Italy, 1943–45 (despatches). Ireland Scholar, 1946; Cromer Prize (British Academy), 1946; 1st in Litt. Hum., Derby Scholar, Amy Mary Preston Read Scholar, 1947; Harmsworth Sen. Scholar, Merton Coll., 1947 (Hon. Fellow, 1980); Fellow and Tutor, Balliol Coll., 1948–55 (Hon. Fellow, 1977); Prof. of Greek, Univ. of St Andrews, 1955–76. Visiting Lecturer, Harvard, 1960. Dean of the Faculty of Arts, St Andrews, 1960–63, 1973–75. Sather Prof. of Classical Literature, University of California, 1967. President: Soc. for Promotion of Hellenic Studies, 1971–74; Classical Assoc., 1975. Pres., British Acad., 1978–81. For. Hon. Mem., Amer. Acad. of Arts and Sciences, 1979; For. Mem., Royal Netherlands Acad. of Arts and Sciences, 1979. Hon. LLD: Birmingham, 1979; St Andrews, 1981; Hon. DLitt: Bristol, 1980; London, 1980; St Andrews, 1981. *Publications:* Greek Word Order, 1960; Commentaries on Thucydides, Books VI and VII, 1965; ed, Aristophanes' Clouds, 1968; Lysias and the Corpus Lysiacum, 1968; (with A. W. Gomme and A. Andrewes) Historical Commentary on Thucydides, vol. IV, 1970; (ed) Theocritus, select poems, 1971; Aristophanic Comedy, 1972; Greek Popular Morality in the Time of Plato and Aristotle, 1974; Greek Homosexuality, 1978; (ed) Plato, Symposium, 1980; (ed and co-author) Ancient Greek Literature, 1980; The Greeks, 1980 (contrib., The Greeks, BBC TV series, 1980); articles in learned journals; Co-editor, Classical Quarterly, 1962–68. *Recreations:* historical linguistics, country walking. *Address:* Corpus Christi College, Oxford. *Club:* Athenæum.

DOW, Christopher; see Dow, J. C. R.

DOW, Harold Peter Bourner; QC 1971; *b* 28 April 1921; *s* of late Col H. P. Dow and P. I. Dow; *m* 1943, Rosemary Merewether, *d* of late Dr E. R. A. Merewether, CB, CBE, FRCP; two *s* one *d. Educ:* Charterhouse; Trinity Hall, Cambridge (MA). Served RAF (Air Crew), 1941–42. Min. of Supply, 1943–45. Barrister, Middle Temple, 1946. *Publications:* Restatement of Town and Country Planning, 1947; National Assistance, 1948; Rights of Way (with Q. Edwards), 1951; ed, Hobsons Local Government, 1951 and 1957 edns. *Recreations:* music, painting. *Address:* 104 Valiant House, Vicarage Crescent, SW11; The Priory, Brandeston, near Woodbridge, Suffolk. *T:* Earl Soham 244.

DOW, James Findlay; Formerly: Consulting Physician, St George's Hospital, SW1; Physician to King Edward VII Hospital for Officers; *b* 13 May 1911; *s* of John Archibald Dow and Jetta Findlay; *m* 1952, Dr Jean Millbank; two *s* two *d. Educ:* Strathallan; St John's Coll., Cambridge; Middlesex Hospital. Resident posts at Middlesex and Brompton Hospitals until 1947; Consultant Physician, St George's Hospital, SW1, 1947–76. MB, BChir Cantab., MRCP 1938, FRCP 1948. Major, RAMC, 1947–49. Examiner in Medicine, Cambridge and London Universities, 1950–63. Member Board of Governors, St George's Hospital, 1962; Member Assoc. of Physicians; Member British Society of Gastro-Enterology. *Publications:* Papers in medical journals on gastro-enterology. *Recreations:* golf, fishing. *Address:* 149 Harley Street, W1. *T:* 01-935 4444. *Clubs:* Caledonian, MCC.

DOW, (John) Christopher (Roderick), FBA 1982; Adviser to the Governor of the Bank of England, since 1981; *b* 25 Feb. 1916; *s* of Warrender Begernie and Amy Langdon Dow; *m* 1960, Clare Mary Keegan; one *s* three *d. Educ:* Bootham Sch., York; Brighton, Hove and Sussex Grammar Sch.; University College London, Fellow 1973. Economic Adviser, later Senior Economic Adviser, HM Treasury, 1945–54; on staff, and Dep. Dir, National Inst. for Economic and Social Research, 1954–62; Treasury, 1962–63; Asst Sec.-Gen., OECD, Paris, 1963–73; Exec. Dir, Bank of England, 1973–81. *Publications:* The Management of the British Economy, 1945–1960, 1964; Fiscal Policy for a Balanced Economy (jointly), 1968. Various articles in learned jls. *Address:* c/o Bank of England, Threadneedle Street, EC2. *Club:* Reform.

DOW, His Honour R(onald) Graham; a Circuit Judge (formerly County Court Judge), 1959–80, retired; *b* 7 Dec. 1909; *s* of John Graham Dow and Bessie Graham Dow; *m* 1937, Dorothy May Christie; two *s. Educ:* Kelvinside Academy; Uppingham Sch.; University Coll., Oxford. Called to Bar, 1932.

Military Service, 1939-45. *Recreations:* golf and gardening. *Address:* 2 Kirkwick Avenue, Harpenden, Herts. *T:* Harpenden 2006.

DOWD, Ronald, AO 1976; tenor; with Australian Opera Company, since 1972; *b* Sydney, Australia, 23 Feb. 1914; *s* of Robert Henry Dowd and Henrietta (*née* Jenkins); *m* 1938, Elsie Burnitt Crute (English born); one *s* one *d. Educ:* Sydney. Prior to Army service in Australia, New Guinea and the Celebes, was a bank officer. Upon discharge, adopted full-time singing and performed for various opera organisations and Australian Broadcasting Commission in the Commonwealth. Came to UK for Sadler's Wells, 1956, and returned to Australia by arrangement with Elizabethan Theatre Trust; then rejoined Sadler's Wells, 1959, remaining for a year. Since then has been fully engaged in concerts and opera singing with leading conductors and organisations, including Royal Opera House. Toured NZ and Australia for Australian Broadcasting Commission, 1964; toured Continent with Sadler's Wells, 1963 and 1965. Chm., opera panel, Australian Council for the Arts, 1973-; Mem., Sydney Cultural Council, 1982. *Recreations:* squash and coin collecting. *Address:* 43 Ladbury Avenue, Penrith, NSW 2750, Australia. *Club:* Savage (London).

DOWDALLS, Hon. Sheriff Edward Joseph; Principal, Coatbridge Technical College, since 1973; *b* 6 March 1926; *s* of late Alexander Dowdalls and Helen Dowdalls; *m* 1953, Sarah Quinn; one *s. Educ:* Our Lady's High Sch., Motherwell; Glasgow Univ. (BSc). Member, Coatbridge Town Council, 1958, Provost, 1967. Mem., Scottish Economic Planning Council, 1968-71; Chm., Lanarkshire Area Health Bd, 1977-81 (Mem., 1974-81). Hon. Sheriff, S Strathclyde and Galloway, 1975-. *Recreations:* reading, watching sport. *Address:* 72 Drumpellier Avenue, Coatbridge, Lanarkshire ML5 1JS. *Clubs:* Drumpellier Cricket, Drumpellier Rugby (Coatbridge).

DOWDEN, Richard George; journalist, The Times, since 1980; *b* 20 March 1949; *s* of Peter Dowden and Eleanor Dowden; *m* 1976, Penny Mansfield; one *d. Educ:* St George's Coll., Weybridge, Surrey; London Univ. (BA History). Volunteer Teacher, Uganda, 1971-72; Asst Sec., Justice and Peace Commn, 1973-76; Editor, Catholic Herald, 1976-79. *Address:* 47 Highbury Hill, N5.

DOWDING, family name of **Baron Dowding.**

DOWDING, 2nd Baron *cr* 1943, of Bentley Priory; **Derek Hugh Tremenheere Dowding;** Wing Commander, RAF, retired; *b* 9 Jan. 1919; *s* of (Air Chief Marshal) 1st Baron Dowding, GCB, GCVO, CMG, and Clarice Maud (*d* 1920), *d* of Captain John Williams, IA; *S* father, 1970; *m* 1st, 1940, Joan Myrle (marr. diss. 1946), *d* of Donald James Stuart, Nairn; 2nd, 1947, Alison Margaret (marr. diss. 1960), *d* of Dr James Bannerman, Norwich and *widow* of Major R. M. H. Peebles; two *s*; 3rd, 1961, Odette L. M. S. Hughes, *d* of Louis Joseph Houles. *Educ:* Winchester; RAF College, Cranwell. Served War of 1939-45, UK and Middle East; in comd No 49 (B) Sqdn, 1950; Wing Commander, 1951. Gen. Sec., Sea Cadet Assoc. (formerly Navy League), 1977-. *Heir: s* Hon. Piers Hugh Tremenheere Dowding, *b* 18 Feb. 1948. *Address:* c/o Lloyds Bank Ltd, 6 Pall Mall, SW1.

DOWDING, Michael Frederick, CBE 1973; Chairman: Michael Dowding Associates Ltd, consulting engineers; Nautanuukki (UK) Ltd; Director: N. M. Rothschild & Sons (International) Ltd; Davy Loewy Ltd; Ashmore Benson Pease Ltd; James Armstrong & Co. Ltd; Hovair Ltd; *b* 19 Nov. 1918; *s* of late Guy Francis Dowding and of Frances Constance Dowding (*née* Bragger); *m* 1947, Rosemary, *d* of Somerville Hastings, MS, FRCS; one *s* two *d. Educ:* Westminster; Magdalene Coll., Cambridge. MA Cantab. CEng, FIMechE. Served War, 1939-45, Major RA (despatches, 1945). Joined Davy & United Engineering Co., 1946: Man. Dir, 1961-64; Chm., Davy Ashmore International, 1964-70; Dir, Davy Ashmore Ltd, 1962-72. Mem., Finnish British Technological Cttee, 1969. Vice-Pres., Iron and Steel Inst., 1965; Pres., The Metals Soc., 1978-79. Commander, Knights of Finnish Lion, 1st Class, 1969. *Publications:* various technical papers to Iron and Steel Inst. and foreign metallurgical socs. *Recreations:* painting, shooting, fishing. *Address:* 55 Drayton Gardens, SW10 9RV. *T:* 01-373 0380; Bod Isaf, Aberdaron, Gwynedd. *Clubs:* Brooks's, MCC.

DOWELL, Anthony (James), CBE 1973; Senior Principal, Royal Ballet, Covent Garden, since 1967; *b* 16 Feb. 1943; *s* of late Catherine Ethel and Arthur Henry Dowell; unmarried. *Educ:* Hampshire Sch., St Saviour's Hall, Knightsbridge; Royal Ballet Sch., White Lodge, Richmond, Surrey; Royal Ballet Sch., Barons Court. Joined Opera Ballet, 1960; 1st Company, for Russian Tour, 1961; created The Dream, 1964; Italian Tour, 1965; promoted Principal Dancer, 1966; Eastern Europe Tour, 1966; Japanese Tour, 1967; created Shadow Play, 1967; American Tours and Metropolitan Opera House, New York, 1968, 1969, 1972; created: Pavane, 1973; Manon, 1974. *Principal roles with Royal Ballet include:* La Fête Etrange, 1963; Napoli, 1965; Romeo and Juliet, 1965; Song of the Earth, 1966; Card Game, Giselle, Swan Lake, 1967; The Nutcracker, Cinderella, Monotones, Symphonic Variations, new version of Sleeping Beauty, Enigma Variations, Lilac Garden, 1968; Raymonda Act III, Daphnis and Chloe, La Fille Mal Gardée, 1969; Dances at a Gathering, 1970; La Bayadère, Meditation from Thaïs, Afternoon of a Faun, Anastasia, 1971; Triad, Le Spectre de la Rose, Giselle, 1972; Agon, Firebird, 1973; La Bayadère, 1973; Manon, 1974; Four Schumann Pieces, Les Sylphides, 1975; Four Seasons, 1975; Scarlet Pastorale, 1976; Rhapsody, 1981. Guest Artist with Amer. Ballet Theater, 1977-79; *performed in:* The

Nutcracker; Don Quixote; Other Dances; *created:* Contredanses; Solor in Makarova's La Bayadère; Fisherman in Le Rossignol (Ashton's choreography), NY Metropolitan Opera, 1981. Narrator in A Wedding Bouquet (first speaking role), Joffrey Ballet, 1977; guest appearances with Nat. Ballet of Canada (The Dream, Four Schumann Pieces), 1979 and 1981; Anthony Dowell Ballet Gala, Palladium, 1980 (for charity); narrated Oedipus Rex, NY Metropolitan Opera, 1981. *Television performances:* La Bayadère (USA); Swan Lake, Cinderella, Sleeping Beauty, A Month in the Country, The Dream, Les Noces (all BBC); All the Superlatives (personal profile), Omnibus, BBC. Dance Magazine award, NY, 1972. *Recreations:* painting, paper sculpture, theatrical costume design. *Address:* Royal Opera House, Covent Garden, WC2.

DOWER, E. L. G.; see Gandar Dower.

DOWLING, Sir Hallam (Walter), KBE 1978 (CBE 1968); barrister and solicitor, since 1933; Senior Partner, Dowling, Wacher & Co., Barristers and Solicitors, Napier, NZ; *b* 18 Aug. 1909; *s* of Walter Dowling, Bristol, and Catherine (*née* Shorney), Weston Super Mare; *m* 1936, Dorothea Agnes (*née* Nolan); two *s* two *d. Educ:* Wellington Coll.; Victoria Univ. of Wellington, NZ (LLB). Chairman, Hawke's Bay Hosp. Bd, to 1980 (Mem. Bd, 1944-80); Pres. and Chm., Hawke's Bay Med. Research Foundn Inc.; former Vice-Pres. and Councillor, Hosp. Bds Assoc. of NZ; Member: (representing all NZ hosps) Nursing Council of NZ; NZ Nurses Educn Adv. Cttee; Vice-Chm. and Foundn Trustee, Princess Alexandra Hosp. Trust Bd; Trustee, Hawke's Bay Alcohol and Drug Addiction Trust; Pres. and Chm., AA (Hawke's Bay) Inc., 1954- (Mem. Council, 1944-); Foundn Pres., NZ AA; Foundn Trustee and past Pres., Eastern and Central Savings Bank; former Councillor: NZ Law Soc.; Hawke's Bay Dist Law Soc. (also past Pres.); past Dep. Mayor and Councillor, Napier City Council; former Exec. Mem., No 5 (Hawke's Bay) Dist Roads Bd; Director: AA Mutual Insce Gp; NZ Motor World. *Recreations:* golf, trout fishing. *Address:* 48 Avondale Road, Taradale, Napier, New Zealand. *T:* (home) Napier 442-040. *Club:* Hawke's Bay (Napier, NZ).

DOWLING, Kenneth; Deputy Director of Public Prosecutions, since 1982; *b* 30 Dec. 1933; *s* of Alfred and Mary Dowling; *m* 1957, Margaret Frances Bingham; two *d. Educ:* King George V Grammar Sch., Southport. Called to the Bar, Gray's Inn, 1960. RAF, 1952-54. Immigration Branch, Home Office, 1954-61; joined DPP Dept: Legal Asst, 1961; Sen. Legal Asst, 1966; Asst Solicitor, 1972; Asst Dir, 1976; Princ. Asst Dir, 1978. *Recreation:* reading. *Address:* 4-12 Queen Anne's Gate, SW1H 9AZ. *T:* 01-213 5259.

DOWN AND CONNOR, Bishop of, (RC), since 1962; **Most Rev. William J. Philbin,** DD; *b* 26 Jan. 1907; *s* of late James Philbin and Brigid (*née* O Hora). *Educ:* St Nathy's Coll., Ballaghaderreen; St Patrick's, Maynooth. Priest, 1931; DD Maynooth, 1933. Curate, Eastbourne, 1933; Secondary teacher, Ballaghaderreen, 1934; Prof. of Dogmatic Theology, Maynooth, 1936; Bishop of Clonfert, 1953. *Publications:* Does Conscience Decide?, 1969; To You Simonides, 1973; pamphlets on socio-moral questions; Irish translation of St Patrick's writings. Contributor to The Irish Theological Quarterly, Studies, The Irish Ecclesiastical Record. *Address:* Lisbreen, Somerton Road, Belfast 15. *T:* 776185.

DOWN AND DROMORE, Bishop of, since 1980; **Rt. Rev. Robert Henry Alexander Eames;** *b* 27 April 1937; *s* of William Edward and Mary Eleanor Thompson Eames; *m* 1966, Ann Christine Daly; two *s. Educ:* Methodist Coll., Belfast; Queen's Univ., Belfast (LLB (hons), PhD); Trinity Coll., Dublin. Research Scholar and Tutor, Faculty of Laws, QUB, 1960-63; Curate Assistant, Bangor Parish Church, 1963-66; Rector of St Dorothea's, Belfast, 1966-74; Examining Chaplain to Bishop of Down, 1973; Rector of St Mark's, Dundela, 1974-75; Bishop of Derry and Raphoe, 1975-80. *Publications:* A Form of Worship for Teenagers, 1965; The Quiet Revolution—Irish Disestablishment, 1970; Through Suffering, 1973; Thinking through Lent, 1978; contribs to New Divinity, Irish Legal Quarterly, Criminal Law Review, The Furrow. *Address:* The See House, Knockdene Park, S Belfast.

DOWN, Sir Alastair (Frederick), Kt 1978; OBE 1944 (MBE 1942); MC 1940; TD 1951; Chairman, The Burmah Oil Co. Ltd, since 1975 (Chief Executive, 1975-80); *b* 23 July 1914; *e s* of Frederick Edward Down and Margaret Isobel Down (*née* Hutchison); *m* 1947, Bunny Mellon; two *s* two *d. Educ:* Edinburgh Acad.; Marlborough Coll. Commissioned in 7th/9th Bn, The Royal Scots (TA), 1935. CA 1938. Joined British Petroleum Co. Ltd in Palestine, 1938. Served War of 1939-45 (despatches twice, MC, MBE, OBE, Kt Comdr, Order of Orange Nassau, with swords, 1946): Middle East, N Africa, Italy and Holland, with Eighth Army and 1st Canadian Army as Lt-Col and full Col. Rejoined BP, in Iran, 1945-47; Head Office, 1947-54; Canada, 1954-62 (Chief Rep. of BP in Canada, 1954-57; Pres., BP Group in Canada, 1957-62); Pres. BP Oil Corp., 1969-70; Man. Dir, 1962-75 and Dep. Chm., 1969-75, British Petroleum Co. Ltd; Director: TRW Inc., USA, 1977-; Scottish American Investment Co. Ltd, 1980-; Royal Bank of Canada, 1981-; Chairman: British-North American Res. Assoc., 1980-; London American Energy NV, 1981-. Member: Review Body for pay of doctors and dentists, 1971-74; Television Adv. Cttee, 1971-72; Council, Marlborough Coll., 1979- (Chm. Council, 1982-); Hon. Treasurer, Field Studies Council, 1977-81. FRSA 1970; FBIM 1972; JDipMA (Hon.), 1966. Hambro British Businessman of the Year Award, 1980; Cadman Meml Medal, Inst. of Petroleum, 1981. *Recreations:* shooting, golf, fishing. *Address:* Stockleigh House, Stockleigh Pomeroy, near Crediton, Devon; 15 Rutland Gate, SW7. *Clubs:* Carlton;

Mount Royal (Montreal); York, Toronto (Toronto); Ranchmen's (Calgary).

DOWN, Antony Turnbull L.; see Langdon-Down.

DOWN, Barbara Langdon; see Littlewood, Lady (Barbara).

DOWN, Norman Cecil Sommers, CMG 1955; Senior Principal Inspector of Taxes, Inland Revenue, 1946-Dec. 1956, retired; *b* 9 Sept. 1893; *s* of late James Erskine Down; *m* 1st, 1917, Edith Gertrude (*née* Steddy) (*d* 1961); two *d*; 2nd, 1962, Agnes (*née* Sandham). *Educ:* St Lawrence Coll., Ramsgate. Inland Revenue since 1912; served European War, 1914-19, in 4th Gordon Highlanders, 51st Div. (Captain, despatches, wounded thrice). *Publications:* Temporary Heroes, 1918; Temporary Crusaders, 1919. *Address:* Binnlands, Swan Lane, Edenbridge, Kent TN8 6AJ. *T:* Edenbridge 863129.

DOWNE, 11th Viscount, *cr* 1680; **John Christian George Dawnay;** Bt 1642; Baron Dawnay of Danby (UK) *cr* 1897; DL; *b* Wykeham, 18 Jan. 1935; *s* of 10th Viscount Downe, OBE and Margaret Christine (*d* 1967), *d* of Christian Bahnsen, NJ; *S* father, 1965; *m* 1965, Alison Diana, *d* of I. F. H. Sconce, MBE; one *s* one *d. Educ:* Eton Coll.; Christ Church, Oxford. 2nd Lieut, Grenadier Guards, 1954-55. Non-marine broker at Lloyd's, 1957-65. Director: Brookdeal Electronics Ltd, 1962-; Dawnay Faulkner Associates Ltd, 1968-; Allen-Bradley Electronics Ltd, 1973-; Mill Feed Holdings Ltd, 1978-; George Rowney & Co. Ltd, 1978-, etc. President: Yorkshire Rural Community Council, 1979-; Aston Martin Owners Club, 1980-; Chairman: Friends of the Nat. Railway Museum, 1977-; York Technology Ltd, 1980-. DL N Yorks, 1981. *Publications:* contributions to various journals. *Recreation:* linear circuit design. *Heir:* s Hon. Richard Henry Dawnay, *b* 9 April 1967. *Address:* Wykeham Abbey, Scarborough, North Yorks. *T:* Scarborough 862404, *Telex:* 527192; 5 Douro Place, W8. *T:* 01-937 9449. *Clubs:* Pratt's, Cavalry and Guards'.

DOWNES, George Robert, CB 1967; Director of Studies, Royal Institute of Public Administration, since 1972; *b* 25 May 1911; *o s* of late Philip George Downes; *m* Edna Katherine Millar; two *d. Educ:* King Edward's Grammar School, Birmingham; Grocers', London. Entered GPO, 1928; Assistant Surveyor, 1937; Asst Principal, 1939. Served War of 1939-45: RNVR, in destroyers, 1942-45. Principal, GPO, 1946; Principal Private Sec. to: Lord President of the Council, 1948-50, Lord Privy Seal, 1951; Assistant Secretary, 1951; Imperial Defence College, 1952; Deputy Regional Director, GPO London, 1955; Dir, London Postal Region, 1960-65; Dir of Postal Services, 1965-67; Dir, Operations and Overseas, PO, 1967-71. *Recreations:* music, gardening. *Address:* Muircraig, Gordon Avenue, Stanmore, Mddx.

DOWNES, George Stretton, CBE 1976; Deputy Receiver for the Metropolitan Police District, 1976-79; retired; *b* London, 2 March 1914; *e s* of late George and Rosalind S. Downes; *m* 1939, Sheilah Gavigan; two *s* two *d. Educ:* Cardinal Vaughan Sch., Kensington. Joined Metropolitan Police Office, 1934; Secretary, 1969. *Recreations:* golf, gardening. *Address:* 45 Westbury Road, New Malden, Surrey.

DOWNES, Prof. (John) Kerry, FSA; Professor of History of Art, University of Reading, since 1978; *b* 8 Dec. 1930; *s* of Ralph William Downes, *qv*; *m* 1962, Margaret Walton. *Educ:* St Benedict's, Ealing; Courtauld Institute of Art. BA, PhD London. Library, Courtauld Inst. of Art, 1954-58; Librarian, Barber Inst. of Fine Arts, Univ. of Birmingham, 1958-66; Lectr in Fine Art, Univ. of Reading, 1966-71, Reader, 1971-78. Vis. Lectr, Yale Univ., 1968. Mem., Royal Commission on Historical Monuments (England), 1981-. *Publications:* Hawksmoor, 1959, 2nd edn 1979; English Baroque Architecture, 1966; Hawksmoor, 1969; Christopher Wren, 1971; Whitehall Palace, in Colvin and others, History of the King's Works, V, 1660-1782, 1976; Vanbrugh, 1977; The Georgian Cities of Britain, 1979; Rubens, 1980; The Architecture of Wren, 1982; contribs to Burlington Magazine, Architectural History, Architectural Rev., TLS, etc. *Recreations:* drawing, making music, learning electronics, procrastination. *Address:* Department of History of Art, University of Reading, London Road, Reading RG1 5AQ. *T:* Reading 875234.

DOWNES, M. P.; see Panter-Downes.

DOWNES, Ralph (William), CBE 1969; Organist, Brompton Oratory, 1936-78, now Organist Emeritus; Curator-Organist, Royal Festival Hall, since 1954; *b* 16 Aug. 1904; *s* of James William and Constance Edith Downes; *m* 1929, Agnes Mary (*née* Rix) (*d* 1980); one *s. Educ:* Derby Municipal Secondary Sch. (Scholar); Royal College of Music, London; Keble Coll., Oxford. ARCM 1925, MA 1931, BMus 1933. Asst Organist, Southwark Cathedral, 1924; Organ Scholar, Keble Coll., 1925-28; Director of Chapel Music and Lecturer, Princeton Univ., USA, 1928-35; Organ Prof., RCM, 1954-75. Organ Curator to LCC, 1949. Consultant to: the Corporation of Croydon, 1960; Cardiff City Council (St David's Hall), 1977; Designer and Supervisor of organs in: Buckfast Abbey, 1952; Royal Festival Hall, 1954; Brompton Oratory, 1954; St John's Cathedral, Valletta, Malta, 1961; Fairfield Halls, 1964; Paisley Abbey, 1968; Trinity Coll., Dublin, 1969; Gloucester Cathedral, 1971, and others. Recitals and performances in: Aldeburgh, 1948-76, Belgium, France, Germany, Holland, Italy, Switzerland, also radio and TV. Jury mem., organ festivals, Amsterdam, Haarlem, Munich, St Albans. Received into the Catholic Church, 1930. Hon. RAM 1965; Hon. FRCO

1966; FRCM 1969. KSG 1970. *Publications:* Baroque Tricks (Adventures with the Organ Builders), 1982; miscellaneous articles on the organ, compositions for keyboard and chorus. *Address:* 9 Elm Crescent, Ealing, W5 3JW. *T:* 01-567 6330.
See also J. K. Downes.

DOWNES, Dr Ronald Geoffrey, CB 1979; FTS; Scientific Consultant since 1979; *b* 3 Jan. 1916; *s* of Albert John Downes and Florence Maude Downes (*née* Davis); *m* Gwenyth Edith Dodds; three *s. Educ:* Univ. of Melbourne (BAgrSc 1937, MAgrSc 1939, DAgrSc 1972). CSIRO, Div. of Soils, 1939-50; Soils Adviser, US Corps of Engineers, New Guinea, 1942-43; Member, Soil Conservation Authority, Victoria, 1950-53; Dep. Chairman, 1953-61; Chm., 1961-73; Dir and Perm. Head, Min. for Conservation, 1973-79. Consultant, UN FAO: Israel, 1960, 1965; Iran, 1967; Lebanon, 1967; Algeria, 1972; Rome, 1969, 1974, 1979, 1980; Morocco, 1981. Harkness Fellow in US, 1954-55; Fellow: Aust. Inst. Agric. Sci., 1961; Soil Conservation Soc. America, 1965; Aust. Inst. of Management, 1977; (Foundn Fellow) Aust. Acad. of Technol Scis, 1976. Prescott Medal, Aust. Soc. Soil Sci., 1976; Aust. Medal of Agric., 1978; Hugh Hammond Bennett Award, Soil Conservation Soc. of Amer., 1981. Coronation Medal, 1953; Jubilee Medal, 1977. *Publications:* contribs to scientific jls, also separate publications and chapters in books on soils, land-use, and the ecological basis for conservation of natural resources and resource development. *Recreations:* lawn bowls, orchid and bonsai growing, model ships. *Address:* 3/84 The Righi, Eaglemont, Victoria 3084, Australia. *T:* (03) 458 2683 Melbourne. *Clubs:* Melbourne, Sciences (Melbourne).

DOWNEY, Anne Elisabeth; a Recorder of the Crown Court, since 1980; *b* 22 Aug. 1936; *d* of John James Downey and Ida May Downey. *Educ:* Notre Dame Convent, Liverpool; Liverpool Univ. LLB (Hons.). Called to the Bar, Gray's Inn, 1958. *Recreations:* antiques, reading. *Address:* Copperfield, 4 Pine Walk, Prenton, Merseyside. *T:* 051-608 2404.

DOWNEY, Gordon Stanley, CB 1980; Comptroller and Auditor General, since 1981; *b* 26 April 1928; *s* of Stanley William and Winifred Downey; *m* 1952, Jacqueline Goldsmith; two *d. Educ:* Tiffin's Sch.; London Sch. of Economics (BSc(Econ)). Served RA, 1946-48. Ministry of Works, 1951; entered Treasury, 1952; Asst Private Sec. to successive Chancellors of the Exchequer, 1955-57; on loan to Ministry of Health, 1961-62; Asst Sec., 1965, Under-Sec., 1972, Head of Central Unit, 1975; Dep. Sec., Treasury, 1976-81; on loan as Dep. Head, Central Policy Review Staff, Cabinet Office, 1978-81. *Recreations:* reading, tennis, visual arts. *Address:* Chinley Cottage, Eaton Park Road, Cobham, Surrey KT11 2JG. *T:* Cobham 7878. *Club:* Army & Navy.

DOWNEY, Air Vice-Marshal John Chegwyn Thomas, CB 1975; DFC 1945, AFC; Deputy Controller of Aircraft (C), Ministry of Defence, 1974-75, retired; *b* 26 Nov. 1920; *s* of Thomas Cecil Downey and Mary Evelyn Downey; *m* Diana, (*née* White); one *s* two *d. Educ:* Whitgift Sch. Entered RAF 1939; served War of 1939-45 in Coastal Command (DFC 1945 for his part in anti-U-boat ops). Captained Lincoln Aries III on global flight of 29,000 miles, during which London-Khartoum record was broken. RAF Farnborough 1956-58; commanded Bomber Comd Develt Unit 1959-60; head of NE Defence Secretariat, Cyprus, 1960-62; Comd RAF Farnborough, 1962-64; a Dir, Op. Requirements (RAF) MoD, 1965-67; IDC, 1968; Comdt, RAF Coll. of Air Warfare, Manby, Jan./Oct. 1969; Comdr Southern Maritime Air Region, 1969-71; Senior RAF Mem., RCDS, 1972-74. *Publication:* Management in the Armed Forces: an anatomy of the military profession, 1977. *Recreation:* sailing. *Address:* Windmill House, Windmill Field, Old Bosham, Chichester, West Sussex. *Club:* Royal Air Force.

DOWNEY, William George, CB 1967; *b* 3 Jan. 1912; *s* of late William Percy Downey; *m* 1936, Iris, *e d* of late Ernest Frederick Pickering; three *d. Educ:* Southend Grammar Sch. ACWA 1935, ACA 1937, FCA 1960. Ministry of Aircraft Production, 1940; Ministry of Supply, 1946 (Director of Finance and Administration, Royal Ordnance Factories, 1952-57); Ministry of Aviation, 1959; Under-Secretary, 1961; Chm., Steering Gp, Develt Cost Estimation, 1964-66; Min. of Technology, 1967, Min. of Aviation Supply, 1970; DTI, 1971; Management Consultant to Procurement Exec., MoD, 1972-74; Under Sec., NI Office, 1974-75; Dir, Harland and Wolff, 1975-81; Consultant to CAA, 1976-79, to Dept of Energy, 1980. *Address:* Starvelarks, Dawes Heath Road, Rayleigh, Essex. *T:* Rayleigh 774138.

DOWNIE, Prof. Allan Watt, FRCP 1982; FRS 1955; Professor of Bacteriology, Liverpool University, 1943-66, now Emeritus Professor; *b* 5 Sept. 1901; *s* of William Downie, Rosehearty, Aberdeenshire; *m* 1936, Nancy McHardy; one *s* two *d. Educ:* Fraserburgh Academy, Aberdeen Univ. MB, ChB, Aberdeen Univ., 1923; MD, 1929; DSc, 1937. Lecturer Aberdeen Univ., 1924-26, Manchester Univ., 1927-34; Senior Freedom Research Fellow, London Hospital, 1935-39; Member Scientific Staff, Nat. Institute Medical Research, 1939-43. Voluntary Asst, Rockefeller Inst. Med. Research, New York City, USA, 1934-35. Vis. Prof., Medical Sch., Univ. of Colorado, Denver, 1966-69, 1971, 1973. Founder Fellow, RCPath. Hon. LLD Aberdeen Univ., 1956. *Publications:* (Jt) Virus and Rickettsial Diseases of Man, 1950; numerous articles in scientific journals. *Recreations:* golf, fishing, ornithology. *Address:* 10 College Close, Birkdale, Merseyside. *T:* Southport 67269.

DOWNIE, Prof. Robert Silcock; Professor of Moral Philosophy, Glasgow University, since 1969; *b* 19 April 1933; *s* of late Robert Mackie Downie and late Margaret Barlas Downie; *m* 1958, Eileen Dorothea Flynn; three *d. Educ:* The High Sch. of Glasgow; Glasgow Univ.; The Queen's Coll., Oxford. MA, first cl. hons, Philosophy and Eng. Lit., Glasgow, 1955; Russian linguist, Intelligence Corps, 1955-57; Ferguson Schol., 1958; BPhil Oxford Univ., 1959; Lectr in Moral Philosophy, Glasgow Univ., 1959; Vis. Prof. of Philosophy, Syracuse Univ., NY, USA, 1963-64; Sen. Lectr in Moral Philosophy, Glasgow Univ., 1968. *Publications:* Government Action and Morality, 1964; Respect for Persons (jt), 1969; Roles and Values, 1971; Education and Personal Relationships (jt), 1974; Values in Social Works (jt), 1976; (jt) Caring and Curing, 1980; contribs to: Mind, Philosophy, Analysis, Aristotelian Society, Political Studies. *Recreation:* music. *Address:* Department of Moral Philosophy, University of Glasgow G12 8QQ. *T:* 041-339 8855.

DOWNING, Dr Anthony Leighton; Partner, Binnie & Partners, Consulting Engineers, since 1973; *b* 27 March 1926; *s* of Sydney Arthur Downing and Frances Dorothy Downing; *m* 1952, Kathleen Margaret Frost; one *d. Educ:* Arnold Sch., Blackpool; Cambridge and London Universities. BA Cantab. 1946; BSc Special Degree 2 (1) Hons. London, 1950; DSc London 1967. Joined Water Pollution Research Lab., 1946; seconded to Fisheries Research Lab., Lowestoft, 1947-48; granted transfer to Govt Chemist's Lab., 1948; returned to WPRL as Scientific Officer, 1950; subsequently worked mainly in field of biochemical engrg; Dir, Water Pollution Res. Lab., 1966-73. Vis. Prof., Imperial Coll. of Science and Technology, 1978. FIChemE 1975; FIWPC 1965 (Pres., 1979); FIBiol 1965; Hon. FIPHE 1965; FIWES 1975. FRSA. *Publications:* papers in scientific and technical journals. *Recreations:* golf, gardening. *Address:* 2 Tewin Close, Tewin Wood, Welwyn, Herts. *T:* Bulls Green 474. *Club:* Knebworth Golf.

DOWNING, David Francis, PhD; Assistant Director, Resources and Programmes B, Ministry of Defence, since 1981; *b* 4 Aug. 1926; *e s* of late Alfred William Downing, ARCO, and of Violet Winifred Downing; *m* 1948, Margaret Joan Llewellyn; one *s* one *d. Educ:* Bristol Grammar Sch.; Univ. of Bristol (BSc 1952, PhD 1955). Served Coldstream Gds and Royal Welch Fusiliers, 1944-48 (Lieut RWF, 1947). Student Mem. of delegn from Brit. univs to Soviet univs, 1954; Eli Lilley Res. Fellow, Univ. of Calif, LA, and Fulbright Travel Scholarship, 1955-56; Long Ashton Res. Stn, Univ. of Bristol, 1957-58; Chem. Def. Estab., 1958-63; Def. Res. Staff, Washington, 1963-66; Chem. Def. Estab., 1966-68; Counsellor (Scientific), British High Commn, Ottawa, 1968-73; Head, Management Services, RARDE, 1973-75, and Head, Pyrotechnics Br., 1975-78; Counsellor (Scientific), British Embassy, Moscow, 1978-81. Mem. Council, Internat. Disaster Inst., 1982. FRSA 1969. *Publications:* Psychotomimetic Compounds (monograph), in, Psychopharmacological Agents, 1964; scientific papers, mainly in Jl of Chem. Soc., and Qly Revs of Chem. Soc. *Recreations:* music, Arctic art, travel, bird watching, skiing. *Address:* 11 Cobhams, Speldhurst, Tunbridge Wells, Kent TN3 0QA. *T:* Langton 2930. *Club:* Army and Navy.

DOWNING, Henry Julian; HM Diplomatic Service, retired; *b* 22 March 1919; *o s* of Henry Julian Downing and Kate Avery; *m* 1951, Ruth Marguerite Ambler. *Educ:* Boys' High Sch., Trowbridge; Hertford Coll., Oxford. Indian Civil Service (Madras) 1941-47. Joined HM Foreign Service, 1947; 2nd Secretary, Madras and Dacca, 1947-50; Foreign Office, 1950-52; 1st Secretary (Commercial), Istanbul, 1952-56; Foreign Office, 1956-58; 1st Secretary and Head of Chancery, Kabul, 1958-62; Foreign Office, 1963-65; HM Consul-General, Lourenço Marques, 1965-69; Head of Claims Dept, 1969-71, of Migration and Visa Dept, 1971-73, FCO; Consul-Gen., Cape Town, 1973-77. *Recreations:* swimming, walking, bird watching. *Address:* 8b Greenaway Gardens, Hampstead, NW3. *T:* 01-435 2593. *Club:* United Oxford & Cambridge University.

DOWNS, Brian Westerdale, MA Cantab; Fellow (Master, 1950-63) of Christ's College, Cambridge; Professor of Scandinavian Studies, 1950-60; *b* 4 July 1893; *s* of late James Downs, OBE, JP; *m* Evelyn Wrangham (*née* Doubble) (*d* 1977). *Educ:* Abbotsholme Sch.; Christ's Coll., Cambridge (Entrance Scholar). First Class Honours (with distinction), Medieval and Modern Languages Tripos, 1915; Charles Oldham Shakespeare Scholar, 1914, and Allen Scholar, 1918. Lecturer in Modern Languages and English, Christ's Coll., Cambridge, 1918; Fellow, 1919, Tutor, 1928; Member of Council of Senate, Univ. of Cambridge, 1939-44, and 1954-60; Vice-Chancellor of Univ. of Cambridge, 1955-57; Founder Trustee, Churchill Coll., Cambridge. Representative of the British Council in the Netherlands, 1945-46. DLitt (*hc*), Hull. Commander, Royal Swedish Order of the North Star, 1954; Officier de la Légion d'Honneur, 1957; Chevalier, Royal Danish Order of Dannebrog, 1971. *Publications:* Cambridge Past and Present, 1926; Richardson, 1928; Ibsen, the Intellectual Background, 1946; (with Miss B. M. Mortensen) Strindberg, 1949; A Study of Six Plays by Ibsen, 1950; Norwegian Literature, 1860-1920, 1966; translations from the French, Dutch and German; editions of Shamela and Richardson's Familiar Letters. *Recreation:* walking. *Address:* 20 Marlborough Court, Grange Road, Cambridge CB3 9BQ; Christ's College, Cambridge CB2 3BU. *Club:* Athenæum.

DOWNS, Diarmuid, CBE 1979; FEng, FIMechE; Chairman and Managing Director, Ricardo Consulting Engineers plc, since 1976; *b* 23 April 1922; *s* of John Downs and Ellen McMahon; *m* 1951, Mary Carmel Chillman; one *s* three *d. Educ:* Gunnersbury Catholic Grammar Sch.; City Univ., London (BScEng). CEng, FIMechE 1961. Ricardo Consulting Engineers Ltd, 1942-: Head, Petrol Engine Dept, 1947; Dir, 1957; Man. Dir, 1967. Mem., Adv.

Council for Applied R&D, 1976-80; Member: SERC, 1981- (Chm., Engineering Bd); Design Council. President: Fédération Internationale des Sociétés d'Ingénieurs des Techniques de L'Automobile, 1978 (Vice-Pres., 1975); IMechE, 1978-79 (Vice-Pres., 1971-78); Assoc. of Indep. Contract Res. Organisations, 1975-77. Hon. DSc: City, 1978; Cranfield Inst. of Technol., 1981. *Publications:* paper on internal combustion engines in British and internat. engrg jls and conf. proc. *Recreation:* theatre. *Address:* The Downs, 143 New Church Road, Hove, East Sussex BN3 4DB. *T:* Brighton 419357. *Clubs:* St Stephen's; Hove (Hove).

DOWNS, Mrs George Wallingford; *see* Tureck, Rosalyn.

DOWNS, Leslie Hall, CBE 1942; MA Cantab; FIMechE; Chairman, 1936-71, Rose, Downs & Thompson Ltd, Old Foundry, Hull, retired; former Chairman, Rose Downs (Holdings) Ltd, Hull; *b* 6 June 1900; *s* of late Charles Downs, Hull and Bridlington; *m* 1930, Kathleen Mary Lewis; three *d. Educ:* Abbotsholme Sch., Derbys; Christ's Coll., Cambridge (Scholar, BA, 1922, MA, 1927). European War, Artists' Rifles; served engineering apprenticeship and subsequently employed in various positions with Rose, Downs & Thompson Ltd; Chm., Barnsley Canister Co. Ltd; former Vice-Chm., Davy-Ashmore Ltd; former Director: Blundell-Permoglaze (Holdings) Ltd; Ashmore Benson Pease & Co. Ltd; Power Gas Corp. Ltd. Past President Hull Chamber of Commerce and Shipping; Custodian Trustee, Hull Trustee Savings Bank; Former Treasurer and Member of Council, Hull Univ., retd 1976. Hon. DSc Hull Univ. *Recreations:* fly-fishing, cabinet making, reading. *Address:* King's Hall, Driffield, North Humberside. *T:* Driffield 43204; Rowling End Farm, Newlands, Keswick, Cumbria. *T:* Braithwaite 335.

DOWNSHIRE, 7th Marquess of, *cr* 1789; **Arthur Wills Percy Wellington Blundell Trumbull Sandys Hill;** Viscount Hillsborough, Baron Hill, 1717; Earl of Hillsborough, Viscount Kilwarlin, 1751; Baron Harwich (Great Britain), 1756; Earl of Hillsborough and Viscount Fairford, 1772; Hereditary Constable of Hillsborough Fort; late Lieut Berks Yeomanry; *b* 7 April 1894; *s* of 6th Marquess and Katherine, 2nd *d* of Hon. Hugh Hare, Forest House, Bracknell, Berks, and *g d* of 2nd Earl of Listowel; *S* father, 1918; *m* 1953, Mrs Noreen Gray-Miller, *d* of late William Barraclough. *Heir:* nephew (Arthur) Robin Ian Hill [*b* 10 May 1929; *m* 1957, Hon. Juliet Mary Weld-Forester, *d* of 7th Baron Forester, and of Marie Louise Priscilla, CStJ, *d* of Sir Herbert Perrott, 6th Bt, CH, CB; two *s* one *d*]. *Address:* Flat 5, 81 Onslow Square, SW7.

DOWNSIDE, Abbot of; *see* Roberts, Rt Rev. D. J.

DOWNWARD, Maj.-Gen. Peter Aldcroft, CB 1979; DSO 1967; DFC 1952; Lieutenant-Governor and Secretary, The Royal Hospital, Chelsea, since 1979; *b* 10 April 1924; *s* of late Aldcroft Leonard and Mary Downward; *m* 1st, 1953, Hilda Hinckley Wood (*d* 1976); two *s*; 2nd, 1980, Mrs Mary Boykett Procter (*née* Allwork). *Educ:* King William's Coll., Isle of Man. Enlisted 1942; 2nd Lieut, The South Lancashire Regt (Prince of Wales's Volunteers), 1943; served with 13th Bn (Lancs) Parachute Regt, NW Europe, India, Far East, 1944-46, Greece and Palestine, 1947; transf. to Glider Pilot Regt, 1948; Berlin Airlift, 1949, Korea, 1951-53; 1st Bn The South Lancs Regt (PWV) in Egypt and UK, 1953-54; instructor at Light Aircraft Sch., 1955-56; RAF Staff Coll., 1958; War Office, 1959-60; BAOR, 1961-63; Brigade Major 127 Bde, 1964; Comd 4th Bn The East Lancs Regt, 1965-66; Comd 1st Bn The Lancs Regt (PWV), Aden, 1966-67; Allied Forces N Europe, Oslo, 1968-69; instructor, Sch. of Infantry, 1970-71; Comd Berlin Inf. Bde. 1971-74; Comdt, Sch. of Infantry, 1974-76; GOC West Midland District, 1976-78; Col, The Queen's Lancashire Regt, 1978-; Col Comdt, The King's Division, 1979-; Hon. Col, Liverpool Univ. OTC, 1980-. *Recreations:* sailing, skiing, shooting. *Address:* Lieutenant-Governor's House, Royal Hospital, Chelsea, SW3 4SL. *Club:* Army and Navy.

DOWNWARD, Sir William (Atkinson), Kt 1977; Lord-Lieutenant of Greater Manchester, since 1974; Councillor, Manchester City Council, 1946-75; Alderman, Manchester, 1971-74; *b* 5 Dec. 1912; *s* of late George Thomas Downward; *m* 1946, Enid, *d* of late Ald. Charles Wood. *Educ:* Manchester Central High Sch.; Manchester Coll. of Technology. Mem., Court of Governors, Manchester Univ., 1969; Hon. LLD Manchester, 1977. FRSA 1978. Dir, Royal Exchange Theatre Co., 1976-; Chairman: Manchester Overseas Students Welfare Conf., 1972-; Peterloo Gall., 1974-. Lord Mayor of Manchester, 1970-71. DL Lancs, 1971. KStJ 1974. *Address:* 23 Kenmore Road, Northenden, Manchester M22 4AE. *T:* 061-998 4742; 061-247 3478.

DOWSE, Maj.-Gen. Sir Maurice Brian, KCVO 1953; CB 1952; CBE 1947 (OBE 1940); retired; *b* 10 Sept. 1899; *s* of late Bishop Charles Dowse, and of Mrs Charles Dowse; unmarried. *Educ:* Wellington Coll.; RMC, Sandhurst. 2nd Lieut 1918; Lieut 1920; Captain, 1927; Major, 1936; Lt-Col, 1941; Brigadier, 1943; Maj.-Gen. 1951. Served Royal Welch Fusiliers and on Staff at home and overseas, 1918-44; on Staff at home and Far East, 1944-53; retired, 1953. *Address:* 39 Hyde Park Gate, SW7. *Club:* Travellers'.

DOWSETT, Prof. Charles James Frank, MA, PhD Cantab; FBA 1977; Calouste Gulbenkian Professor of Armenian Studies, University of Oxford, and Fellow of Pembroke College, Oxford, since 1965; *b* 2 Jan. 1924; *s* of late Charles Aspinall Dowsett and Louise, *née* Stokes; *m* 1949, Friedel, *d* of Friedrich Lapuner, Kornberg, E Prussia. *Educ:* Owen's Sch.; St Catherine's

Society, Oxford, 1942-43; Peterhouse, Cambridge (Thomas Parke Scholar), 1947-50 (Mod. and Mediaeval Languages Tripos, Part I, 1st Class Russian, 1st Class German, 1948, Part II, Comparative Philology, 1st Class with distinction, 1949). Treasury Studentship in Foreign Languages and Cultures, 1949-54. Ecole Nationale des Langues Orientales Vivantes, Univ. de Paris, 1950-52 (diplôme d'arménien); Ecole des Langues Orientales Anciennes, Institut Catholique de Paris, 1950-53 (diplôme de géorgien); Lecturer in Armenian, School of Oriental and African Studies, University of London, 1954; Reader in Armenian, 1965. Vis. Prof., Univ. of Chicago, 1976. Member: Council, RAS, 1972-76; Philological Soc., 1973-77. *Publications:* The History of the Caucasian Albanians by Movses Dasxuranci, 1961; The Penitential of David of Ganjak, 1961; (with J. Carswell) Kütahya Armenian Tiles, vol. 1, The Inscribed Tiles, 1972; articles in Bulletin of the School of Oriental and African Studies, Le Muséon, Revue des Etudes Arméniennes, The Geographical Journal, W. B. Henning Memorial Volume, 1970, etc; translations from Flemish (Felix Timmermans' Driekoningentryptiek: "A Christmas Triptych", 1955, Ernest Claes' De Witte: "Whitey", 1970); as Charles Downing (children's books): Russian Tales and Legends, 1956; Tales of the Hodja, 1964; Armenian Folktales and Fables, 1972. *Address:* Pembroke College, Oxford. *Club:* United Oxford & Cambridge University.

DOWSON, Maj.-Gen. Arthur Henley, CB 1964; CBE 1961 (OBE 1945); Director-General, Ordnance Survey, 1961-65, retired; *b* 7 Dec. 1908; *s* of late Kenneth Dowson and Beatrice Mary (*née* Davis); *m* 1933, Mary Evelyn, *d* of Col. A. J. Savage, DSO; one *d. Educ:* Haileybury; RMA; King's Coll., Cambridge (BA). Commissioned in RE, 1928; War Service in NW Europe, N Africa, Italy. Director of Military Survey, War Office and Air Ministry, 1957. ADC to the Queen, 1958-61; Maj-Gen. 1961. Chm., Norfolk Broads Consortium Cttee, 1966-71. FRICS 1949. Bronze Star (USA) 1945. *Address:* 21 Berrow Court, Upton-upon-Severn, Worcs.

DOWSON, Prof. Duncan; Professor of Engineering Fluid Mechanics and Tribology, University of Leeds, since 1966, and Director of The Institute of Tribology, Department of Mechanical Engineering, Univ. of Leeds, since Dec. 1967; *b* 31 Aug. 1928; *o s* of Wilfrid and Hannah Dowson, Kirkbymoorside, York; *m* 1951, Mabel, *d* of Mary Jane and Herbert Strickland; one *s* (and one *s* decd). *Educ:* Lady Lumley's Grammar Sch., Pickering, Yorks; Leeds Univ. BSc Mech Eng. Leeds, 1950; PhD Leeds, 1952; DSc Leeds, 1971; FEng 1982. Research Engineer, Sir W. G. Armstrong Whitworth Aircraft Co., 1953-54; Univ. of Leeds: Lecturer in Mechanical Engineering, 1954; Sen. Lecturer, 1963; Reader, 1965; Prof. 1966. Chm., Tribology Group Cttee, IMechE, 1967-69. CEng, FIMechE, Fellow ASME. James Clayton Fund Prize (jtly), IMechE, 1963; Thomas Hawksley Gold Medal, IMechE, 1966; Gold Medal, British Soc. of Rheology, 1969; Nat. Award, ASLE, 1974; ASME Lubrication Div. Best Paper Awards (jt), 1975, 1976; ASME Melville Medal (jt), 1976; James Clayton Prize, IMechE, 1978; ASME Mayo D. Hersey Award, 1979; Tribology Gold Medal, IMechE, 1979. Hon. Mem. ASLE. Hon. DTech Chalmers Univ. of Technology, Göteborg, 1979. *Publications:* Elastohydrodynamic Lubrication—the fundamentals of roller and gear lubrication (jtly), 1966, 2nd edn 1977; History of Tribology, 1979; (jtly) An Introduction to the Biomechanics of Joints and Joint Replacement, 1981; (jtly) Ball Bearing Lubrication: The Elastohydrodynamics of Elliptical Contacts, 1981; papers on tribology and bio-medical engrg, published by: Royal Society; Instn of Mech. Engineers; Amer. Soc. of Mech. Engineers; Amer. Soc. of Lubrication Engineers. *Recreations:* travel, astronomy, photography. *Address:* 23 Church Lane, Adel, Leeds LS16 8DQ. *T:* Leeds 678933.

DOWSON, Graham Randall; Chairman, Erskine House Investments, since 1975; *b* 13 Jan. 1923; *o s* of late Cyril James Dowson and late Dorothy Celia (*née* Foster); *m* 1954, Fay Weston (marr. diss. 1974); two *d* ; *m* 1975, Denise Shurman. *Educ:* Alleyn Court Sch.; City of London Sch.; Ecole Alpina, Switzerland. Served War of 1939-45 (1939-43 and Africa Stars, Atlantic and Defence Medals, etc); RAF, 1941-46 (Pilot, Sqdn-Ldr). Sales, US Steel Corporation (Columbia Steel), Los Angeles, 1946-49; Sales and Senior Commentator, Mid South Network (MBS), radio, US, 1949-52; Dir, Rank Organization Ltd, 1960-75, Chief Exec., 1974-75; Chairman: Mooloya Investments, 1975-78; Pincus Vidler Arthur Fitzgerald Ltd, 1979-; Marinex Petroleum, 1981-; Deputy Chairman: Nimslo European Hldgs; Nimslo International Ltd; Nimslo Ltd, 1979- (Dir, 1978); Director: A. C. Nielsen Co., Oxford, 1953-58; Carron Co. (Holdings) Ltd, 1976-; Carron Investments Ltd, 1976-; Barrowmill Ltd, 1979-; Nimslo Corp. Chm., European League for Econ. Co-operation (British Section), 1972-. Vice-Pres., NPFA, 1974-. Liveryman, Distillers' Co. *Recreation:* sailing. *Address:* 193 Cromwell Tower, Barbican, EC2Y 8DD. *T:* 01-588 0396. *Clubs:* Brooks's, City Livery, Saints and Sinners, Thirty; Royal London Yacht (Ex-Commodore), Royal Cork Yacht, Royal Southern Yacht.

DOWSON, Sir Philip (Manning), Kt 1980; CBE 1969; ARA 1979; a Senior Partner, Ove Arup Partnership, since 1969; Founder architectural partner, Arup Associates, 1963; *b* 16 Aug. 1924; *s* of Robert Dowson and Ina Cowen Dowson; *m* 1950, Sarah Crewdson; one *s* two *d. Educ:* Gresham's Sch.; University Coll., Oxford; Clare Coll., Cambridge (MA). AA Dip., ARIBA. FSIAD 1982. Oxford, 1942-43; Lieut, RNVR, 1943-47; Cambridge, 1947-50; Architectural Association, 1950-53; joined Ove Arup & Partners, 1953. Work includes: Univ. development and college buildings (Oxford, Cambridge, Birmingham, Leicester); housing; new uses for old buildings; industrial and office developments. Member: Royal Fine Art Commn, 1971-; Craft Adv. Cttee, 1972-75. Governor, St Martin's Sch. of Art, 1975-. Trustee, The

Thomas Cubitt Trust, 1978-. Royal Gold Medal for Architecture, 1981. *Publications:* articles for technical press. *Recreation:* sailing. *Address:* 7 Soho Square, W1V 6QB. *T:* 01-734 8494; 1 Pembroke Studios, Pembroke Gardens, W8. *Club:* Garrick.

DOYLE, Rear-Adm. Alec Broughton, CBE 1937; Royal Australian Navy; *b* 5 Oct. 1888; *s* of James H. and Rebekah Doyle, Invermien, Scone, NSW; *m* 1917, Charlotte Madge, *d* of Dr Herbert Lillies, Armadale, Victoria, Australia; two *s. Educ:* Scone Grammar Sch., NSW; The King's Sch., Parramatta, NSW; Sydney Univ., NSW. Bachelor of Engineering, 1911; joined Royal Australian Navy, 1912; sea service, 1914-18; Squadron Engineer Officer, 1929-32; Engineer Manager, Royal Australian Naval Dockyard, Garden Island, and General Overseer, Naval Shipbuilding and Repair, Sydney, 1933-42; Engineer Captain, 1934; Director of Engineering (Naval), 1942-43; Engineer Rear-Admiral, 1943; Third Naval Member Australian Commonwealth Naval Board, Navy Office, Melbourne, and Chief of Construction, 1943-48; retired 1948. *Recreation:* reading. *Address:* Malgarai, Boggabilla, NSW 2409, Australia. *Clubs:* Union, University, Royal Sydney Golf (Sydney).

DOYLE, Bernard; see Doyle, F. B.

DOYLE, Brian André; Hon. Mr Justice B. A. Doyle; Judge, Botswana Court of Appeal, since 1973; *b* 10 May 1911; *s* of John Patrick Doyle, ICS and Louise Doyle (*née* Renard); *m* 1937, Nora (*née* Slattery); one *s* one *d. Educ:* Douai Sch.; Trinity Coll., Dublin. BA, LLB. Called to Irish Bar, 1932; Magistrate, Trinidad and Tobago, 1937; Resident Magistrate, Uganda, 1942; Solicitor-Gen., Fiji, 1948; Attorney-Gen., Fiji, 1949; KC (Fiji), 1950, later QC; Attorney-Gen., N Rhodesia, 1956; Minister of Legal Affairs and Attorney-Gen., Northern Rhodesia (Zambia, 1964), 1959-65, retired as minister, 1965; Chm., Local Govt Service Commn, Zambia, 1964; Justice of Appeal, 1965; Chief Justice and Pres., Supreme Court of Zambia, 1969-75. Dir, Law Develt Commn, Zambia, 1976-79; Chm., Delimitation Commn, Botswana, 1981-. *Recreations:* fishing, golf. *Address:* 41 Choumert Square, Peckham Rye, SE15 4RE. *Clubs:* Lusaka, Chainama Hills Golf; Dulwich and Sydenham Hill Golf.

DOYLE, (Frederick) Bernard; Chief Executive, Social Democratic Party, since 1981; *b* 17 July 1940; *s* of James Hopkinson Doyle and Hilda Mary Doyle (*née* Spotsworth); *m* 1963, Ann Weston; two *s* one *d. Educ:* St Bede's Coll.; Univ. of Manchester (BSc Hons); Harvard Business Sch., 1965-67 (MBA). CEng, FICE. Resident Civil Engineer with British Rail, 1961-65; Management Consultant with Arthur D. Little Inc., 1967-72; Booker McConnell Ltd: Secretary to Executive Cttee, 1973; Director, Engineering Div., 1973-76; Chairman, General Engineering Div., 1976-78; Chm. and Chief Exec., Booker McConnell Engineering, and Director, Booker McConnell, 1978-81. *Recreations:* sport, theatre, reading, travel. *Address:* Chiltern Cottage, 88 High Street, Prestwood, Bucks HP16 9EY. *T:* Great Missenden 4247; Sea Pie Cottage, Kilbeg, Union Hall, Co. Cork. *T:* Skibbereen 33164.

DOYLE, Air Comdt Dame Jean (Lena Annette) C.; see Conan Doyle.

DOYLE, Sir John (Francis Reginald William Hastings), 5th Bt, *cr* 1828; *b* 3 Jan. 1912; *s* of Col Sir Arthur Havelock James Doyle, 4th Bt, and Joyce Ethelreda (*d* 1961), 2nd *d* of Hon. Greville Howard; *S* father, 1948; *m* 1947, Diana (*d* 1980), *d* of late Col Steel, Indian Army; one *d. Educ:* Eton; RMC Sandhurst. Served Palestine, 1938 (medal with clasp); War of 1939-45, in France, Italy, Greece; Major, Cameronians and Royal Irish Fusiliers; retired, 1950. *Address:* Glebe House, Camolin, Co. Wexford.

DOYLE, William Patrick, QC (NI) 1968; **His Honour Judge Doyle;** a County Court Judge, Northern Ireland, since 1979; *b* 9 April 1927; *s* of John Joseph Doyle and Mary Doyle; *m* 1954, Nora Frances Morley; two *d. Educ:* Christian Brothers, Belfast; Coleraine Academical Instn; QUB (LLB 1947). Student, Gray's Inn, 1947-48; Inn of Court of NI, 1944-48; called to Bar of NI 1948. *Recreations:* fishing, golf, bridge. *Address:* 5 Broomhill Park, Belfast BT9 5JB. *T:* (Law Courts) Belfast 35111. *Clubs:* Lansdowne; University Common Room (Belfast).

D'OYLY, Sir John (Rochfort), 13th Bt, *cr* 1663; Commander, RN retired; *b* 19 April 1900; *s* of Sir (Hastings) Hadley D'Oyly, 11th Bt, and Beatrice, *d* of late Francis Bingham Clerk, JP; *S* brother, Sir Charles Hastings D'Oyly, 12th Bt, 1962; *m* 1930, Kathleen, *o d* of late Robert Brown Gillespie, Halgolle, Yatiyantota, Ceylon; two *d* (one *s* decd). *Educ:* Hill Brow, Eastbourne; Eastmans Royal Naval Academy, Southsea; HMS Conway. Served European War, 1916-18, with Grand Fleet; Baltic Operations, 1919. Gonville and Caius Coll., Cambridge, 1920-21. Specialised in physical and recreational training, 1921-22; Mediterranean, 1923-25; Term Officer at Royal Naval Coll., Dartmouth, 1925-27; East Indies, 1928-30; HMS St Vincent Boys' Training Establishment, 1930-32; Fleet Physical and Recreational Training Officer, Mediterranean, 1932-35; Asst Superintendent, RN Sch. of Physical and Recreational Training, Portsmouth, 1936-38. Served European War, 1939-45: Comdr of the Coll., RNC, Greenwich; Atlantic; East Indies; Pacific; retd, 1946. *Heir: half-brother,* Nigel Hadley Miller D'Oyly [*b* 6 July 1914; *m* 1940, Dolores (*d* 1971), *d* of R. H. Gregory; one *s* two *d*]. *Address:* c/o Lloyds Bank Ltd, 39 Piccadilly, W1. *Club:* Royal Naval and Royal Albert Yacht (Portsmouth).

D'OYLY CARTE, Dame Bridget, DBE 1975; Managing Director, Bridget D'Oyly Carte Ltd, since 1961; *b* 25 March 1908; *d* of late Rupert D'Oyly Carte and Lady Dorothy Milner Gathorne-Hardy; *m* 1926, 4th Earl of Cranbrook (marr. diss. 1931); resumed maiden name by deed poll, 1932. *Educ:* privately in England and abroad, and at Dartington Hall, Totnes (Dance-Drama Group). Savoy Hotel, 1933-39; evacuated nursery schools and child welfare work, 1939-47; Man. Director of D'Oyly Carte Opera Company, Director of Savoy Hotel Ltd and Savoy Theatre Ltd, 1948; Founder and Trustee of D'Oyly Carte Opera Trust Ltd, 1961. *Recreations:* country living and gardening; reading, theatre and music. *Address:* 1 Savoy Hill, WC2R 0BP. *T:* 01-836 4343.

DRABBLE, His Honour John Frederick, QC 1953; retired; a Circuit Judge (formerly County Court Judge) 1965-73; *b* 8 May 1906; *s* of late Joseph and Emily Drabble, Conisbrough, Yorks; *m* 1933, Kathleen Marie Bloor; one *s* three *d*. *Educ:* Mexborough Grammar Sch.; Downing Coll., Cambridge (MA). Called to Bar, 1931. Served War of 1939-45, RAF, 1940-45, finally as Sqdn Leader. Recorder of Huddersfield, 1955-57; of Kingston-upon-Hull, 1957-58. *Publications:* Death's Second Self, 1971; Scawsby, 1977. *Address:* St Mary's, Martlesham, Woodbridge, Suffolk. *T:* Ipswich 622615.
See also A. S. Byatt, Margaret Drabble, A. J. Langdon.

DRABBLE, Margaret, CBE 1980; author; *b* 5 June 1939; 2nd *d* of His Honour J.F. Drabble, *qv*; *m* 1960, Clive Walter Swift (marr. diss. 1975); two *s* one *d*; *m* 1982, Michael de Courcy Fraser Holroyd, *qv*. *Educ:* The Mount Sch., York; Newnham Coll., Cambridge. Lives in London. Chm., Nat. Book League, 1980-82 (Dep. Chm., 1978-80). E. M. Forster Award, Amer. Acad. of Arts and Letters, 1973. Hon DLitt Sheffield, 1976. Editor, Oxford Comp. to Eng. Lit., 1979-. *Publications:* A Summer Birdcage, 1963; The Garrick Year, 1964; The Millstone, 1966 (filmed, as A Touch of Love, 1969); Wordsworth, 1966; Jerusalem the Golden, 1967; The Waterfall, 1969; The Needle's Eye, 1972; (ed with B. S. Johnson) London Consequences, 1972; Arnold Bennett, a biography, 1974; The Realms of Gold, 1975; (ed) The Genius of Thomas Hardy, 1976; (ed jtly) New Stories 1, 1976; The Ice Age, 1977; For Queen and Country, 1978; A Writer's Britain, 1979; The Middle Ground, 1980. *Address:* c/o A. D. Peters, 10 Buckingham Street, WC2.

DRAIN, Geoffrey Ayrton, CBE 1981; JP; General Secretary, National and Local Government Officers Association, since 1973; *b* 26 Nov. 1918; *s* of Charles Henry Herbert Drain, MBE, and Ann Ayrton; *m* 1950, Dredagh Joan Rafferty (marr. diss. 1959); one *s*. *Educ:* Preston Grammar Sch.; Bournemouth Sch.; Skipton Grammar Sch.; Queen Mary Coll., Univ. of London (BA, LLB; Fellow, QMC, 1980). Called to Bar, Inner Temple, 1955. Served War, 1940-46. Asst Sec., Inst. of Hosp. Administrators, 1946-52; Exec., Milton Antiseptic Ltd, 1952-58; Dep. Gen.-Sec., NALGO, 1958-73; Mem. Gen. Council, TUC, 1973-; Pres., Nat. Fedn. of Professional Workers, 1973-75; Staff Side Sec., Health Service Admin. and Clerical Staffs Whitley Council, 1962-72. Dir, Bank of England, 1978-. Member: NW Metropolitan Regional Hosp. Bd and N London Hosp. Management Cttee, 1967-74; Lord Chancellor's Adv. Cttee on Legal Aid, 1974-76; Layfield Cttee of Inquiry into Local Govt Finance, 1974-76; NEDO Sector Working Party for Paper and Board Ind., 1976- (Chm.); Insolvency Law Review Cttee, 1976-; Council, Industrial Soc., 1974-; Energy Commn, 1977-79; NEDC, 1977-; Central Arbitration Cttee, 1977-; Cttee on Finance for Industry, 1978-; Engrg Council, 1981-; Exec. Cttee, Public Services Internat., 1981-. Member: Bd, Volunteer Centre, 1977-; British-North American Cttee, 1978-; Franco British Council, 1978-; Trilateral Commn, 1979-; Jt Hon. Treasurer, European Movement, 1979-; Trustee: Community Projects Foundn, 1974-; Trident Trust, 1979-. Hampstead Borough Councillor, 1956-58; contested (Lab), Chippenham, 1950; JP N Westminster, 1966. Freeman of City of London and Liveryman of Coopers' Company. *Publication:* The Organization and Practice of Local Government, 1966. *Recreations:* cricket, football, walking, studying birds, bridge. *Address:* Flat 3, Centre Heights, Swiss Cottage, NW3 6JG. *T:* 01-722 2081. *Clubs:* Reform, MCC.

DRAKE, Antony Elliot, CBE 1967 (OBE 1945); *b* 15 June 1907; *s* of Francis Courtney Drake and Mabel Grace (née Drake); *m* 1935, Moira Helen Arden Wall; one *s* one *d*. *Educ:* Aldenham Sch.; New Coll., Oxford. Indian Civil Service, 1930; Bihar and Orissa, 1931-37; seconded to Indian Political Service, 1937; served Rajputana, 1937-39; Baluchistan, 1939-43; Mysore (Sec. to Resident), 1943-46; Rajkot (Political Agent, E Kathiawar), 1946-47; appointed to Home Civil Service, HM Treasury, 1947; Asst Sec., 1950; on loan to UK Atomic Energy Authority as Principal Finance Officer, 1957; transferred permanently to UKAEA, 1960; Finance and Programmes Officer, 1964-69; retd, 1969. Member: Hosp. Management Cttee, Royal Western Counties Hosp. Group, 1970-74; Reg. Fisheries Adv. Cttee, SW Water Authority, 1975-81. *Recreation:* fishing. *Address:* Winneford Farm House, Awliscombe, Honiton, Devon. *T:* Honiton 2502. *Club:* Flyfishers'.

DRAKE, Sir (Arthur) Eric (Courtney), Kt 1970; CBE 1952; *b* 29 Nov. 1910; *e s* of Dr A. W. Courtney Drake; *m* 1st, 1935, Rosemary Moore; two *d*; 2nd, 1950, Margaret Elizabeth Wilson; two *s*. *Educ:* Shrewsbury; Pembroke Coll., Cambridge (MA; Hon. Fellow 1976). With The British Petroleum Co. Ltd, 1935-75: Man. Dir, 1958-62; Dep. Chm., 1962-69; Chm., 1969-75; Dep. Chm., P&O Steam Navigation Co., 1976-81. Pres., Chamber of Shipping, 1964; Hon. Mem., General Council of British Shipping, 1975-; Member: Gen. Cttee, Lloyd's Register of Shipping, 1960-81; MoT Shipping Adv. Panel, 1962-64; Cttee on Invisible Exports, 1969-75; Bd of Governors,

Pangbourne Nautical Coll., 1958-69; Court of Governors, London Sch. of Economics and Political Science, 1963-74; Governing Body of Shrewsbury Sch., 1969-; Cttee of Management, RNLI, 1975-; Life Mem., Court of City Univ., 1969-; Pres., City and Guilds Insignia Award Assoc., 1971-75; Hon. Petroleum Adviser to British Army, 1971-. Hon. Mem., Honourable Co. of Master Mariners, 1972; Hon. Elder Brother of Trinity House, 1975; Chm., Mary Rose Trust, 1979-; Freeman of City of London, 1974; one of HM Lieutenants, City of London. Hon. DSc Cranfield, 1971; Hon. Fellow, UMIST, 1974. Hambro British Businessman of the Year award, 1971; Cadman Meml Medal, Inst. of Petroleum, 1976. Comdr, Ordre de la Couronne, Belgium, 1969; Kt Grand Cross of Order of Merit, Italy, 1970; Officier, Légion d'Honneur, 1972; Order of Homayoun, Iran, 1974; Comdr, Ordre de Leopold, Belgium, 1975. *Address:* The Old Rectory, Cheriton, Alresford, Hants. *T:* Bramdean 334. *Clubs:* London Rowing; Royal Yacht Squadron, Leander, Royal Cruising.

DRAKE, Sir Eric; *see* Drake, Sir A. E. C.

DRAKE, Hon. Sir (Frederick) Maurice, Kt 1978; DFC 1944; **Hon. Mr Justice Drake;** a Judge of the High Court of Justice, Queen's Bench Division, since 1978; Presiding Judge, Midland and Oxford Circuit, since 1979; *b* 15 Feb. 1923; *o s* of late Walter Charles Drake and Elizabeth Drake; *m* 1954, Alison May, *d* of late W. D. Waterfall, CB; two *s* three *d*. *Educ:* St George's Sch., Harpenden; Exeter Coll., Oxford. MA Hons 1948. Served War of 1939-45, RAF 96 and 255 Squadrons. Called to Bar, Lincoln's Inn, 1950, QC 1968, Bencher, 1976. Dep. Chm., Beds QS, 1966-71; a Recorder of the Crown Court, 1972-78; Dep. Leader, Midland and Oxford Circuit, 1975-78. Standing Senior Counsel to RCP, 1972-78. Chm. Governors, Aldwickbury Prep. Sch. (Trust), 1969-80; Governor, St George's Sch., Harpenden, 1975-79. Hon. Alderman, St Albans DC, 1976-. *Recreations:* music, gardening, countryside. *Address:* The White House, West Common Way, Harpenden, Herts. *T:* Harpenden 2329; Royal Courts of Justice, Strand, WC2.

DRAKE, Jack Thomas Arthur H.; *see* Howard-Drake.

DRAKE, Sir James, Kt 1973; CBE 1962; Director, Fairclough Construction Group Ltd (formerly Leonard Fairclough Ltd), 1972-77; *b* 27 July 1907; *s* of James Drake and Ellen (née Hague); *m* 1937, Kathleen Shaw Crossley; two *d*. *Educ:* Accrington Grammar Sch.; Owens Coll.; Manchester Univ. (BSc). FEng, FICE, FIMunE, PPInstHE. Jun. Engrg Asst, Stockport Co. Borough, 1927-30; Sen. and Chief Engrg Asst, Bootle Co. Borough, 1930-37; Blackpool Co. Borough: Dep. Engr and Surveyor, 1937-38; Borough Engr and Surveyor, 1938-45; County Surveyor and Bridgemaster, Lancs CC, 1945-72 (seconded to Min. of Transport as Dir of NW Road Construction Unit, 1967-68). Hon. Fellow, Manchester Polytechnic, 1972. Hon. DSc Salford, 1973. *Publications:* Road Plan for Lancashire, 1949; Motorways, 1969. *Recreation:* golf. *Address:* 11 Clifton Court, St Annes-on-Sea, Lancs. *T:* St Annes 721635. *Clubs:* Royal Automobile; Royal Lytham and St Annes Golf, Blackpool North Shore Golf.

DRAKE, James Mackay Henry M.; *see* Millington-Drake.

DRAKE, Brig. Dame Jean Elizabeth R.; *see* Rivett-Drake.

DRAKE, John Edmund Bernard, CBE 1973; DSC 1945; *b* 15 Nov. 1917; *s* of late D. H. C. Drake, CIE; *m* 1942, Pauline Marjory Swift; three *s*. *Educ:* Blundells Sch.; Exeter Coll., Oxford (BA). Served War, RNVR. Executive, Burmah-Shell, India, 1945-57; Gen. Manager, Shell Co of Ceylon, 1955; Overseas Staff Manager, Burmah Shell, 1957-62; Gen. Manager Personnel, Shell Mex and BP, 1962-69; Special Advr on Personnel Management to CS, 1970-73; Partner, Tyzack & Partners Ltd, 1974-81. *Recreations:* travel, sailing, reading, music. *Address:* Farm House, Coldharbour Lane, Hildenborough, Kent. *T:* Hildenborough 832102.

DRAKE, Hon. Sir Maurice; *see* Drake, Hon. Sir F. M.

DRAKE-BROCKMAN, Hon. Sir Thomas Charles, Kt 1979; DFC 1944; Senator (Country Party) for West Australia, 1958-78; *b* 15 May 1919; *s* of R. J. Drake-Brockman; *m* 1st, 1942, Edith Sykes (marr. diss.); one *s* four *d*; 2nd, 1972, Mary McGinnity. *Educ:* Guildford Grammar School. Farmer, 1938; RAAF 1941. Minister for Air, 1969-72; Minister for Administrative Services and Minister for Aboriginal Affairs, Nov.-Dec. 1975; Dep. Pres. of the Senate, 1965-69, 1976-78. Gen. Pres., Nat. Country Party (WA) Inc., 1978-81; Federal Pres., Nat. Country Party of Aust., 1978-81. Former Wool President and Exec. Mem., WA Farmers' Union; Vice-Pres., Aust. Wool and Meat Producers' Fedn, 1956-57. State Pres., Australia-Britain Soc., 1982-. *Address:* 80 Basildon Road, Lesmurdie, WA 6076, Australia.

DRAPER, Alan Gregory; Chairman, NATO Budget Committees, 1977-81; Temporary Consultant, AGARD, Paris, May 1982; *b* 11 June 1926; *e s* of late William Gregory Draper and Ada Gertrude (née Davies); *m* 1st, 1953, Muriel Sylvia Cuss, FRSA (marr. diss.); three *s*; 2nd, 1977, Jacqueline Gubel; one *d*. *Educ:* Leeds Grammar Sch.; The Queen's Coll., Oxford (MA). RNVR, 1945; Sub-Lt, 1946-47. Admiralty: Asst Principal, 1950; Private Sec. to Civil Lord of the Admiralty, 1953-55; MoD, 1957-60; Head of Polit. Sect., Admiralty 1960-64; First Sec., UK Delegn to NATO, 1964-66; Asst Sec., MoD, 1966-; Counsellor, UK Delegn to NATO, 1974-77. *Recreations:* reading, travel, tennis, indifferent golf. *Address:* c/o Barclays Bank, 16 Whitehall, SW1A 2EA. *T:* 01-930 9323. *Club:* Naval.

DRAPER, Charles; *see* Draper, R. C.

DRAPER, Gerald Carter, OBE 1974; Member of the Board, since 1978 and Managing Director, Intercontinental Services Division, since 1982, British Airways; Chairman: British Airtours Ltd, since 1978; Silver Wing Surface Arrangements Ltd, since 1971; Deputy Chairman: Trust Houses Forte Travel Ltd, since 1974; ALTA Ltd, since 1977; *b* 24 Nov. 1926; *s* of Alfred Henderson Draper and Mona Violanta (*née* Johnson); *m* 1951, Winifred Lilian Howe; one *s* three *d. Educ:* Univ. of Dublin, Trinity Coll. (MA). FInstM, FCIT. Joined Aer Lingus, 1947; Advertising and PR Manager, 1950; Commercial Man., Central Afr. Airways, 1959; British European Airways: Advertising Man., 1964; Asst Gen. Man. (Market Develt), 1966; Gen. Man. and Dir, Travel Sales Div., 1970; British Airways: Dir, Travel Div., 1973; Marketing Dir, 1977; Dir, Commercial Ops, 1978. Member Board: Internat. Aeradio Ltd, 1971–; British Airways Associated Cos Ltd, 1972–; British Intercontinental Hotels Ltd, 1976–. Liveryman, Co. of Marketors, 1978. FRSA 1979. Chevalier de l'Ordre du Tastevin, 1980; l'Officier de l'Ordre des Coteaux de Champagne, 1982. *Recreations:* shooting, boating, tennis. *Address:* Old Chestnut, Onslow Road, Burwood Park, Walton-on-Thames, Surrey. *Clubs:* Canada (London); St George's Lawn Tennis (Weybridge).

DRAPER, Col Gerald Irving Anthony Dare, CBE 1965; a Chairman of Industrial Tribunals, since 1966; Barrister-at-law; *b* 30 May 1914; *o s* of late Harold Irving Draper and Florence Muriel Short; *m* 1951, Julia Jean, *e d* of late Captain G. R. Bald, RN. *Educ:* privately, and by late Hubert Brinton; King's Coll., London Univ. (Law Prizeman, 1933; LLB Hons 1935); LLM London 1938. Admitted Solicitor, 1936; called to the Bar, Inner Temple, 1946. Irish Guards, Ensign and Subaltern, 1941–44; seconded to Judge-Advocate-General's Office, 1945–48; Mil. Prosecutor (War Crimes Trials, Germany), 1945–49; Legal Advr, Directorate of Army Legal Staff, 1950–56; retd as Col, 1956. Lectr in Internat. Law, 1956, Reader, 1964, Univ. of London; Reader, 1967–76, Prof. of Law, 1976–79, Univ. of Sussex; Professor Emeritus, 1979. Vis. Prof., Cairo, 1965; Titular Prof., Internat. Inst. of Humanitarian Law, S Remo, 1976; Lionel Cohen Lectr, Hebrew Univ., Jerusalem, 1972; Vis. Lectr at UK Staff Colls, and Defence Acads, Vienna, Hamburg, Newport RI, and Tokyo. UK Deleg., Internat. Red Cross Confs, 1957-73; Legal Advr to UK Delegn, Diplomatic Conf. on Law of War, 1974–77. Mem., Medico-Juridical Commn, Monaco, 1977. Fellow of NATO, 1958. Hon. Mem., Faculty of US Army Judge-Advocate-General Sch. of Mil. Law. Mem. Editorial Bd, British Year Book of Internat. Law. *Publications:* Red Cross Conventions, 1958; Hague Academy Lectures, 1965, 1979; Civilians and NATO Status of Forces Agreement, 1966; (with HRH Prince Hassan) A Study on Jerusalem, 1979; (with HRH Prince Hassan) Palestinian Self-determination, 1981; articles in learned journals, incl. British Year Book of Internat. Law, Internat. Affairs, Internat., Comp. Law Qly, The Month, Acta Juridica. *Recreations:* Egyptology, history of Penitentials; (for leisure) sitting in the sun. *Address:* 16 Southover High Street, Lewes, Sussex. *T:* Lewes 2387; 2 Hare Court, Temple, EC4. *Clubs:* Beefsteak, Cavalry and Guards; Cercle de la Terrasse (Geneva).

DRAPER, (John Haydn) Paul; Senior Planning Inspector, Department of Environment, since 1977; *b* 14 Dec. 1916; *o c* of late Haydn Draper, clarinet player, and Nan Draper; *m* 1941, Nancy Allum, author and journalist; one *s* one *d* (and one *d* decd). *Educ:* LCC primary sch.; Bancroft's Sch.; University Coll. London. Engr in Post Office, 1939-48; Royal Signals, Signalman to Major, Middle East, N Africa, Sicily, NW Europe (despatches), 1940-46; MoT, 1948-64 and 1968-70; Jt Principal Private Sec. to Minister, 1956-58; Asst Sec., 1959; Counsellor (Shipping), British Embassy, Washington, 1964-67; BoT, 1967-68; Under-Sec., 1968; DoE, 1970-74; Senior Planning Inspector, 1973-74; Resident Chm., Civil Service Selection Bd, 1975-76. *Address:* 24 Gordon Mansions, Huntley Street, WC1E 7HF.

DRAPER, Michael William; Secretary, Diocese of Bath and Wells, since 1978; *b* 26 Sept. 1928; *s* of late John Godfrey Beresford Draper and Aileen Frances Agatha Draper (*née* Masefield); *m* 1952, Theodora Mary Frampton, *o d* of late Henry James Frampton; one *s* two *d. Educ:* St Edward's Sch., Oxford. FCA. Chartered Accountant, 1953; various posts in England, Ireland, Burma, Nigeria, Unilever Ltd, 1953-64; joined Civil Service, 1964; Principal, Min. of Power, 1964; Asst Sec., 1972, Under Sec., 1976-78, DHSS. *Recreations:* mountain walking, church affairs. *Address:* The Old Deanery, Wells, Somerset.

DRAPER, Paul; *see* Draper, J. H. P.

DRAPER, (Reginald) Charles, FIED, MInstPI; Senior Design Engineer and Project Engineer for Thames Barrier, since 1968; *b* 25 May 1932; *s* of Cecil Charles and Ada Beatrice Draper; *m* 1954, Diane Valerie (*née* Bunker) (*d* 1982). *Educ:* Enfield Technical Coll.; Westminster Technical Coll. Trainee draughtsman under agreement with Rendel, Palmer and Tritton, Cons. Engrs, 1949-53. National Service with RM and RE, 1953-55. Re-employed by Rendel, Palmer and Tritton on detailing many major bridges for Burma Railway, 1955-57; upgraded to Designer Draughtsman, developing and designing Radar Aerials, 1957-58; designing portions of large power stations, colliery winder towers and a slipway cradle, 1958-60; *designed:* off-shore oil loading manifold, from which present single buoy mooring manifold was

developed, 1961; motorway bridge for BR at Knutsford, 1962; all operating machinery for Bascule Bridge at Kidderpore, Calcutta; invented new constant mesh gear-box and a new tail locking device for bascule bridges, 1963; *designed:* various lock and dock gates and operating machinery for Belfast, Leith, Grangemouth, Haldia, India, 1964-67; oil rigs for North Sea, 1967-68. Initial member of Thames Barrier design group. Inventor of Rising Sector Gate and Operating machinery, 1970; Project Engr responsible for Gates for Thames Barrier. Engineer of the Year award from Engineering News Record in New York, for Thames Barrier Gates, 1978. *Publications:* two papers in Thames Barrier Design Symposium at Instn of Civil Engrs, 1977; various articles in technical jls. *Recreations:* swimming, walking, pot-holing, tennis, gardening, snooker, reading, painting. *Address:* 103 Heron Way, Highlands Ridge, Horsham, West Sussex RH13 6DN. *T:* Horsham 67644. *Club:* Horsham (W Sussex).

DRAYCOTT, Douglas Patrick, MA Oxon; QC 1965; a Recorder, since 1972 (Recorder of Shrewsbury, 1966-71); *b* 23 Aug. 1918; *s* of George Draycott and Mary Ann Draycott (*née* Burke); *m* Elizabeth Victoria Hall (marr. diss. 1974); two *s* three *d; m* 1979, Margaret Jean Brunton (*née* Speed). *Educ:* Wolstanton Grammar Sch.; Oriel Coll., Oxford (MA). War Service: Royal Tank Regiment and General Staff, 1939-46. Barrister, Middle Temple, 1950, Master of the Bench, 1972. Joined Oxford Circuit, 1950; Leader, Midland and Oxford Circuit, 1979-. *Recreations:* cruising on inland waterways. *Address:* 1 Essex Court, Temple, EC4Y 9AR. *T:* 01-353 6717; Devereux Chambers, Devereux Court, Strand, WC2R 3JJ. *T:* 01-353 1974; 11 Sir Harry's Road, Edgbaston, Birmingham B15 2UY. *T:* 021-440 1050.

DRAYCOTT, Gerald Arthur; a Recorder of the Crown Court, since 1972; *b* 25 Oct. 1911; *s* of Arthur Henry Seely Draycott and Maud Mary Draycott; *m* 1939, Phyllis Moyra Evans; two *s* one *d. Educ:* King Edward's Sch., Stratford-on-Avon. FCII. Called to Bar, Middle Temple, 1938. Served in RAF, 1939-46 (Sqdn Ldr; despatches). Practised at Bar, SE Circuit, from 1946. Chairman: Nat. Insurance Tribunal, Norwich, 1970-; E Anglia Med. Appeal Tribunal, 1978-. *Address:* Nethergate House, Saxlingham Nethergate, Norwich NR15 1PB. *T:* Hempnall 224. *Club:* Norfolk County (Norwich).

DRAYSON, George Burnaby; *b* 9 March 1913; *s* of late Walter Drayson, Stevenage, Herts, and Dorothy Dyott, *d* of late Captain Hugo Burnaby, RN; *m* 1939, Winifred Heath (marr. diss., 1958); one *d; m* 1962, Barbara Radonska-Chrzanowska, Warsaw. *Educ:* Borlasse Sch. Entered City, 1929; Mem. Stock Exchange, 1935-54; Company Director. Commnd Essex Yeomanry, 1931, Captain, 1938; served RA in Western Desert (TD, despatches, prisoner of war, June 1942-Sept. 1943, escaped twice, finally walked 500 miles to freedom). MP (C) Skipton, 1945-79. Member: Inter-Parliamentary Union Delegn to Turkey, 1947; CPA delegns to Caribbean, 1967, Ceylon, 1970, N Zealand, 1974; Leader, gp of parliamentarians to Morocco, 1979. Mem., Expenditure Cttee, 1970-74. Formerly: Chairman: Parly All Party East/West Trade Cttee; British-Polish Parly Gp; Vice-Chairman: British-Argentine, British-Bulgarian, British-Romanian, British-Czechoslovakian, British-Hungarian, British-German Democratic Republic, and British-Venezuelan Parly Gps; Sec., British-Equadorial Gp. *Recreations:* fishing, walking (completed London to Brighton walk, 1939); foreign travel. *Address:* 131A Hamilton Terrace, NW8 9QR. *T:* 01-624 7302; Linton House, Linton-in-Craven, Skipton, North Yorks. *T:* Grassington 752362. *Club:* Royal Automobile.

DRAYSON, Robert Quested, DSC 1943; MA; Resident Lay Chaplain to Bishop of Norwich, since 1979; *b* 5 June 1919; *s* of late Frederick Louis Drayson and late Elsie Mabel Drayson; *m* 1943, Rachel, 2nd *d* of Stephen Spencer Jenkyns; one *s* two *d. Educ:* St Lawrence Coll., Ramsgate; Downing Coll., Cambridge. Univ. of Cambridge: 1938-39, 1946-47; History Tripos, BA 1947, MA 1950. Served RNVR, 1939-46; Lieut in command HM Motor Torpedo Boats. Asst Master and Housemaster, St Lawrence Coll., 1947-50; Asst Master, Felsted Sch., 1950-55; Headmaster, Reed's Sch., Cobham, 1955-63; Headmaster of Stowe, 1964-79. Mem., HMC Cttee, 1975-79; Chm. of Governors, Riddlesworth Hall Sch., Diss; Governor: St Lawrence Coll.; Monkton Combe Sch.; Felixstowe Coll. FRSA 1968. *Recreations:* hockey (Cambridge Blue, 1946, 1947; Kent XI (Captain), 1947-56); golf. *Address:* St Martin-at-Palace Vicarage, Palace Plain, Norwich NR3 1RW. *T:* Norwich 614172. *Club:* Hawks (Cambridge).

DRENNAN, Alexander Murray, MD Edinburgh 1924; MB, ChB 1906; FRCPE 1914; FRSE 1932; Professor of Pathology, Edinburgh, 1931-54, retired; Professor Emeritus; *b* Jan. 1884; *s* of late Alexr Drennan, Dunalwyn, Helensburgh; *m* 1909; one *s* two *d. Educ:* Larchfield, Helensburgh; Kelvinside Academy Glasgow; Edinburgh Univ. Professor of Pathology, Otago Univ., Dunedin, NZ, 1914-28; Professor of Pathology, Queen's Univ. Belfast, 1928-31; Temporary Acting Lt-Comdr, RNVR (Sp.), 1942-47. *Publications:* various articles on pathological subjects, etc. *Recreations:* fishing, motoring, sailing. *Address:* Lochard Cottage, Kinlochard, Stirling FK8 3TL. *Club:* Royal Scottish Automobile (Glasgow).

DRENNAN, John Cherry, CBE 1959; JP; Senator, Northern Ireland, 1961-72; HM Lieutenant for Co. Londonderry, 1965-74; *b* 1899; *s* of late John Wallace Drennan, Carse Hall, Limavady, Co. Londonderry; *m* 1926, Margaret (*d* 1979), *d* of late Charles Macfarlane, West Hartlepool; two *d* (one *s* decd). *Educ:* Foyle Coll., Londonderry. JP 1923, High Sheriff, 1955, DL 1955, Co.

Londonderry. *Address:* Deerpark, Limavady, Co. Londonderry, N Ireland. *T:* Limavady 2321.

DRESCHFIELD, Ralph Leonard Emmanuel, CMG 1957; *b* 18 March 1911; *s* of late Henry Theodore and Jessie Mindelle Dreschfield; unmarried. *Educ:* Merchiston Castle Sch.; Trinity Hall, Cambridge (BA). Called to Bar, 1933; entered Colonial Service, 1938, and apptd resident Magistrate, Uganda; served in War of 1939-45, in 4th King's African Rifles; Crown Counsel, Uganda, 1948; Solicitor-Gen., Uganda, 1949; QC 1950; Attorney-Gen., Uganda, 1951-62. Chm. Trustees of Uganda National Parks, 1952-62. Sec., Community Council of Essex, 1963-76. Parly Counsel, Law Reform, Bermuda, 1976-. *Recreation:* yachting. *Address:* c/o Attorney General, Hamilton, Bermuda. *Clubs:* Royal Ocean Racing, Bar Yacht, Little Ship; West Mersea Yacht.

DREVER, James; Principal and Vice-Chancellor, University of Dundee, 1967-78; *b* 29 Jan. 1910; *s* of late Prof. James Drever; *m* 1936, Joan Isabel Mackay Budge; one *s* one *d. Educ:* Royal High Sch., Edinburgh; Universities of Edinburgh (MA Hons Philosophy, 1932) and Cambridge (MA Moral Science Tripos, 1934). LLD Dundee, 1979. FRSE. Asst, Dept of Philosophy, Edinburgh, 1934-38; Lecturer in Philosophy and Psychology, King's Coll., Newcastle, 1938-41; Royal Navy, 1941-45; Prof. of Psychology, Univ. of Edinburgh, 1944-66. Visiting Professor, Princeton Univ., 1954-55. Editor, British Journal of Psychology, 1954-58; President: British Psychological Soc., 1960-61; Internat. Union of Scientific Psychology, 1963-66. Member: Cttee on Higher Education, 1961-63; SSRC, 1965-69; Adv. Council, Civil Service Coll., 1973-; Oil Develt Council for Scotland, 1973-77; Perm. Cttee of Conf. of European Rectors, 1975-78; Chm., Advisory Council on Social Work, in Scotland, 1970-74. Dir, Grampian Television Ltd, 1973-80. *Publications:* papers and reviews. *Address:* East Ardblair, 494 Perth Road, Dundee DD2 1LR.

DREW, Sir Arthur (Charles Walter), KCB 1964 (CB 1958); JP; Chairman: Museums and Galleries Commission (formerly Standing Commission on Museums and Galleries), since 1978 (Member, since 1973); Ancient Monuments Board for England, since 1978; Voluntary Welfare Work Council, since 1979; Queen Mary College, University of London, 1982; *b* 2 Sept. 1912; *er s* of late Arthur Drew, Mexico City, and Louise Schulte-Umminger; *m* 1943, Rachel, *er d* of G. W. Lambert, *qv* ; one *s* three *d. Educ:* Christ's Hospital; King's Coll., Cambridge. Asst Principal, War Office, 1936; Private Sec. to successive Secs of State for War, 1944-49; IDC, 1949; International Staff, NATO, 1951-53; Dep. Under Sec. of State, Home Office, 1961-63; last Permanent Under Sec. of State, War Office, 1963-64; Permanent Under-Sec. of State (Army), MoD, 1964-68; Perm. Under-Sec. of State (Administration), MoD, and Mem., Admiralty, Army (from 1964) and Air Force Boards, 1968-72. Trustee: British Museum (Natural History), 1972-; British Museum, 1973-; Imperial War Museum, 1973-; Nat. Army Museum, 1975-; RAF Museum, 1976-; Member: Council, Nat. Trust, 1974-; Historic Houses Assoc., 1981-; Science Mus. Adv. Council, 1981-; Historic Buildings Council, 1982. Master, Drapers' Co., 1977-78. JP 1963, 1973-, Richmond. Coronation Medal, 1953. *Recreation:* following Baedeker. *Address:* 2 Branstone Road, Kew, Surrey TW9 3LB. *T:* 01-940 1210. *Club:* Reform.

DREW, Brig. Cecil Francis, DSO 1918; *b* 1890; *o s* of late Albert Francis Drew, JP of Foston, Farnham Royal, Bucks; *m* 1915, Elizabeth Seymour Hawker; one *s* (and one *s* decd). *Educ:* Highgate and Royal Milit. Acad.; Joined The Cameronians, 1910; served European War (despatches twice, DSO); temp. Lt-Col, 1917-19; Brevet Lt-Col, 1918; Lt-Col, 1936; Col, 1938; Brigadier, 1939; GSO 3, War Office, 1919-22; GSO 3, Scottish Command, 1924; DAA and QMG Highland Area, 1925-27; DAQMG South China Command, 1927-28; GSO 51st (Highland) Division, 1929-33; commanded 1st Bn The Cameronians, 1933-38; AAG War Office, 1938-39; Comd East Lancs Area, 1939-40; Comd 183 Inf. Brigade, 1940-42; Brigadier i/c Administration, 1st Corps District, 1942; AAG Southern Command, 1943; Gen. Staff, GHQ Home Forces, 1944-45; retired pay, 1945. JP Bucks, 1949. *Address:* Gatehouse Cottages, Framfield, near Uckfield, East Sussex. *Club:* Army and Navy.

DREW, Charles Edwin, MVO 1952; VRD 1960; FRCS; Surgeon, Westminster Hospital since 1951; Hon. Consultant Thoracic Surgeon, St George's Hospital; Civilian Consultant in Thoracic Surgery to the Royal Navy; Hon. Consultant in Thoracic Surgery to the Army; Hon. Consulting Thoracic Surgeon, King Edward VII Hospital, Midhurst; *b* 1916; *s* of Edwin Frank Drew, Croydon; *m* 1950, Doreen, *d* of Frederick James Pittaway, Stocksfield, Northumberland; one *s* one *d. Educ:* Westminster City Sch.; King's Coll., London. MB, BS London 1941; MRCS, LRCP 1941; FRCS 1946. Served War of 1939-45, RNVR (Surgeon-Comdr 1957). Formerly Chief Asst and Surg. Registrar, Westminster Hosp.; Chief Surgical Asst, Brompton Hosp. Mem. Soc. Thoracic Surgeons: FRSocMed. *Publications:* papers in med. jls. *Address:* 17 Rodway Road, SW15. *T:* 01-788 7030; 97/24 John Islip Street, SW1. *T:* 01-828 4709.

DREW, Sir Ferdinand (Caire), Kt 1960; CMG 1951; FASA; Under-Treasurer, South Australia and Chairman State Grants Committee, 1946-60, retired; *b* Adelaide, S Aust., 1 May 1895; *s* of late Charles H. Drew, Adelaide; *m* 1934, Chrissie A., *d* of George M. McGowan; one *s* two *d. Educ:* Rose Park Public Sch.; Muirden Coll. Asst Auditor-Gen., 1936-39; Asst Under-Treasurer, 1939-46. Chm. Supply and Tender Board, 1943-49; Mem. Industries Development Cttee, 1942-49; Board Member: State Bank of South Australia, 1948-73 (Dep. Chm. 1963); Adelaide Steamship Co. Ltd, 1962-70;

Cellular Aust. Ltd, 1948-59; Director: Unit Trust of SA; United Insurance Co. Ltd; Chrysler Aust. Ltd, 1963-74; Chm., Board of Electricity Trust, South Australia, 1949-70 (Mem., 1949-74). *Address:* 614 Anzac Highway, Glenelg East, SA 5045, Australia.

DREW, Prof. George Charles, MA; London University Professor of Psychology, University College, 1958-79, now Professor Emeritus; Honorary Fellow, 1979; *b* 10 Dec. 1911; *e s* of George Frederick Drew; *m* 1936, Inez Annie, *d* of F. Hulbert Lewis; one *s* one *d. Educ:* St George's Sch., Bristol; Bristol, Cambridge and Harvard Univs. Viscount Haldane of Cloan studentship, Cambridge, 1935-36; Rockefeller Fellowship, Harvard Univ., 1936-38; Rockefeller Research Fellowship, Cambridge, 1938-42; Psychological Adviser, Air Ministry, 1942-46; Lecturer in Psychology, University of Bristol, 1946-49, Reader, 1949-51, Prof. of Psychology, 1951-58. Mem. Science Research Council, 1965-67. Vis. Prof., University of Calif, Berkeley, USA, 1967-68. C. S. Myers Lectr, 1973. Founder Mem., Exper. Psych. Soc., 1946 (Pres. 1950-51, 1959-60); Pres., British Psych. Soc., 1962-63; Pres. and Chm., Org. Cttee, 19th Internat. Congress of Psychology, 1969. Dean of Science, UCL, 1973-76. *Publications:* articles on animal behaviour, learning, vision, and other psychological problems, in various British and American journals.

DREW, Harry Edward, CB 1970; Director, Quality Audit and Advisory Services, since 1973; *b* 18 Jan. 1909; 2nd *s* of W. H. Drew and F. E. Drew (*née* Brindley), Gillingham, Kent; *m* 1937, Phyllis (*née* Flippance); one *s. Educ:* Wesleyan Sch., Gillingham; RAF Apprentice Sch., Flowerdown, RAF, 1924-37; Air Min. Research Stn, Bawdsey, 1937; Works Man., Radio Prodn Unit, Woolwich, Min. of Supply, 1943; Officer i/c, Research Prototype Unit, W. Howe, Bournemouth, Min. of Aircraft Prodn, 1946; Asst Dir, 1951, Dir, 1959, Electronic Prodn, Min. of Supply, London; Dir of Techn. Costs, Min. of Aviation, London, 1961; Dir-Gen. of Quality Assurance, Min. of Technology, 1966-70; Chief Exec., Defence Quality Assurance Bd, MoD, 1970-72. FIERE (Mem. Charter Council; Pres., 1981-); FIProdE; FIIM (Nat. Chm., 1966-68, Vice-Pres., 1969-79, Pres., 1979-81). Hon. CGIA 1974. Past Master, Worshipful Co. of Scientific Instrument Makers, 1980- (Master, 1978-79). *Publications:* papers on training and quality and reliability. *Recreations:* photography, reading, gardening. *Address:* 18 Marten's Close, Shrivenham, Swindon, Wilts SN6 8BA. *Clubs:* Civil Service, City Livery.

DREW, Jane Beverly, FRIBA; architect; Partner in firm of Fry Drew and Partners, since 1946; *b* 24 March 1911; *m* 1st; two *d* ; 2nd, 1942, Edwin Maxwell Fry, *qv. Educ:* Croydon. Was in partnership with J. T. Alliston, 1934-39; independent practice, 1939-45; in partnership with Maxwell Fry, 1945-. Asst Town Planning Adviser to Resident Minister, West African Colonies, 1944-45; Senior Architect to Capital project of Chandigarh, Punjab, India, 1951-54; Beamis Prof. Mass Inst. of Techn., Jan.-June, 1961; Vis. Prof. of Architecture, Harvard, Feb-March 1970; Bicentennial Prof., Utah Univ., 1976. Completed work includes housing, hospitals, schools, and colleges in UK, West Africa, including Univs in Nigeria, Middle East and India; a section of Festival of Britain, 1951; town planning, housing and amenity buildings in Iran, W Africa and India. Past Pres., Architectural Association (1969). Hon. FAIA, 1978. Hon LLD Ibadan, 1966; DUniv Open Univ., 1973. *Publications:* (with Maxwell Fry) Architecture for Children, 1944; (with Maxwell Fry and Harry Ford) Village Housing in the Tropics, 1945; (Founder Editor, 1945-) Architects' Year Book; (with Maxwell Fry) Architecture in the Humid Tropics; Tropical Architecture, 1956; (with Maxwell Fry) Architecture and the Environment, 1976. *Recreations:* reading, writing, friends. *Address:* 63 Gloucester Place, W1. *T:* 01-486 2972; The Lake House, Rowfant, Sussex RH10 4TB. *T:* Crawley 882182. *Club:* Institute of Contemporary Arts.

DREW, Joanna Marie; Director of Art, Arts Council of Great Britain, since 1978; *b* Naini Tal, India, 28 Sept. 1929; *d* of Brig. Francis Greville Drew, CBE, and Sannie Frances Sands. *Educ:* Dartington Hall; Edinburgh Univ. (MA Hons Fine Art); Edinburgh Coll. of Art (DA). Arts Council of GB, 1952-: Asst Dir of Exhibns, 1970; Dir of Exhibns, 1975. Chevalier, l'Ordre des Arts et Lettres, 1979. *Address:* Arts Council of Great Britain, 105 Piccadilly, W1V 0AU.

DREW, John Alexander, CB 1957; *b* 19 July 1907; *s* of Charles Edward Drew, Okehampton, Devon, and Ethel Margaret Drew; *m* 1930, Edith Waud Marriott; two *s* (and one *s* decd). *Educ:* Gram. Sch., Okehampton. Entered CS, 1928; Secretaries' Office, HM Customs and Excise, 1935-40; employed on special duties, 1940-45; Asst Sec., Cabinet Office, 1945-48; Bd of Trade, 1948-50; Asst Under-Sec. of State, Ministry of Defence, 1951-67, retired, 1967. US Medal of Freedom with Bronze Palm, 1946. *Address:* 28 Montague Avenue, Sanderstead, Surrey. *T:* 01-657 3264.

DREW, Lt-Gen. Sir (William) Robert (Macfarlane), KCB 1965 (CB 1962); CBE 1952 (OBE 1940); KStJ 1977 (CStJ 1965); FRCP; company director, since 1977; *b* 4 Oct. 1907; *s* of late William Hughes Drew and Ethel Macfarlane; *m* 1934, Dorothy, *d* of late Alfred E. Dakingsmith, Bowral, NSW; one *s* (one *d* decd). *Educ:* Sydney Gram. Sch.; Sydney Univ. MB, BS, BSc Sydney, 1930; DTM&H (Eng.), 1938; MRCP 1938; FRCP 1945; FRCPEd, 1966; FRACP, 1966; Hon. FACP 1966; Hon. FRCS 1970. Joined RAMC, 1931; served India, France (Dunkirk), Iraq, MELF; MO, War Cabinet Offices, 1943-46; Consulting Physician to the Army, 1959-60; Commandant, Royal Army Medical Coll., 1960-63; Dir of Medical Services, British Army of the Rhine, 1963-64; Dir-Gen., Army Medical Services,

1965-69. Dep. Dir, British Postgraduate Med. Fedn, 1970-76 (Mem. Governing Body, 1954-56, 1967-69). QHP, 1959-69. Leishman Prize, Royal Army Medical Coll., 1938; Goulstonian Lecturer, RCP, 1946; Mitchener Medallist, RCS, 1955; Lettsomian Lecturer, Medical Soc., London, 1961. Prof. Medicine, Royal Faculty of Med., Baghdad, 1946-52; Lectr Westminster Med. Sch., 1954-59; Pres. Clin. Section, Royal Society of Medicine, 1968-70. Hon. Sec. and later Councillor: Royal Society of Tropical Medicine and Hygiene (Pres., 1971-73); Med. Soc. of London (Pres., 1967-68); Australia and NZ Med. Assoc. (Chm.); Councillor: Royal Society of Medicine; RCP (Vice-Pres., 1970-71); Hunterian Soc.; Mem. Bd of Governors: Hospital for Sick Children, Gt Ormond Street, London; Moorfields Eye Hosp.; Royal Sch. for Daughters of Officers of the Army; Member: Assoc. Physicians Gt Britain and Ireland; Exec. Cttee, Forces Help Soc.; Control Bd, Army Benevolent Fund; Bd, Kennedy Inst. of Rheumatology; Cttee, St John Ophthalmic Hospital of Jerusalem; Cttee of Management, Sir Oswald Stoll Foundn; Mem. Council, Royal Blind Soc., NSW, 1978-; Mem., Aust. Soc. of Genealogists, 1978-. HM Comr, The Royal Hosp., Chelsea, 1965-69 and 1970-76. Orator: York Med. Soc., 1963; Harrogate Med. Soc., 1963; Hunterian, Hunterian Soc., 1966. FRSA 1965. Extraordinary Mem., Assoc. of Clin. Pathologists; Hon. Member: Sydney Univ. Med. Soc., 1965; Anglo-German Med. Soc., 1970. Comdr Order of El-Rafidain (Iraq), 1951. *Publications:* Roll of Medical Officers in the British Army 1660-1960, 1968; articles in medical journals. *Recreations:* travel, gardening. *Address:* c/o Williams and Glyn's Bank, 22 Whitehall, SW1; 5B and 5C Wakefield, 26-28 Etham Avenue, Darling Point, NSW 2027, Australia. *Clubs:* Army and Navy; Australian, Royal Sydney Golf (Sydney).

DREW-SMYTHE, Henry James; *see* Smythe.

DREWE, Geoffrey Grabham, CIE 1947; CBE 1958 (OBE 1942); *b* 3 May 1904; 2nd *s* of late Alfred John Drewe, Bournemouth; *m* 1934, Christine Evelyn Isabel Young; two *d. Educ:* Cheltenham Coll.; Pembroke Coll., Oxford. Entered ICS, 1928; served in various parts of Sind and Bombay Provinces; Collector and Dist. Magistrate, Ahmedabad, 1938-43; Home Sec. to Government of Bombay, 1944-47; retired from Indian Civil Service, 1947. Asst to Hon. Treasurers of Cons. Party, 1948-70; Manager, Cons. Party Bd of Finance, 1965-70. *Recreation:* gardening. *Address:* Westering, Haven Road, Canford Cliffs, Poole, Dorset. *Club:* East India, Devonshire, Sports and Public Schools.

DREYER, Adm. Sir Desmond (Parry), GCB 1967 (KCB 1963; CB 1960); CBE 1957; DSC; JP; *b* 6 April 1910; *yr s* of late Adm. Sir Frederic Dreyer, GBE, KCB; *m* 1st, 1934, Elisabeth (*d* 1958), *d* of late Sir Henry Chilton, GCMG; one *s* one *d* (and one *s* decd); 2nd, 1959, Marjorie Gordon, *widow* of Hon. R. G. Whiteley. Served War of 1939-45 (DSC). Cdre First Class, 1955. Chief of Staff, Mediterranean, 1955-57; Asst Chief of Naval Staff, 1958-59; Flag Officer (Flotillas) Mediterranean, 1960-61; Flag Officer Air (Home), 1961-62; Comdr, Far East Fleet, 1962-65; Second Sea Lord, 1965-67; Chief Adviser (Personnel and Logistics) to Sec. of State for Defence, 1967-68. Principal Naval ADC to the Queen, 1965-68. Gentleman Usher to the Sword of State, 1973-80. Member: Nat. Bd for Prices and Incomes, 1968-71; Armed Forces Pay Review Body, 1971-79. President: RN Benevolent Trust, 1970-78; Officers' Pension Soc., 1978-; Regular Forces Employment Assoc., 1978-82. JP Hants 1968; High Sheriff for Hampshire, 1977-78. *Recreations:* fishing, golf. *Address:* Brook Cottage, Cheriton, near Alresford, Hants SO24 0QA. *T:* Bramdean 215.

DREYFUS, John Gustave, FIOP; typographical consultant and historian; *b* 15 April 1918; *s* of late Edmond and Marguerite Dreyfus; *m* 1948, Irène Thurnauer; two *d* (one *s* decd). *Educ:* Oundle Sch.; Trinity Coll., Cambridge (MA). FIOP 1977. Served War, Army, 1939-45. Joined Cambridge University Press as graduate trainee, 1939; Asst Univ. Printer, 1949-56; Typographical Adviser, 1956-; Typographical Adviser to Monotype Corp., 1955-; European Consultant to Limited Editions Club, USA, 1956-77; Dir, Curwen Press, 1970-82; Sandars Reader in Bibliography, Univ. of Cambridge, 1979-80. Helped plan exhibn, Printing and the Mind of Man, 1963 (also designed catalogues). Pres., Assoc. Typographique Internationale, 1968-73 (organised internat. congresses for Assoc.); Chm., Printing Historical Soc., 1974-77 (org. Caxton Internat. Congress, 1976). FRSA. Sir Thomas More Award, Univ. of San Francisco, 1979. *Publications:* The Survival of Baskerville's Punches, 1949; The Work of Jan van Krimpen, 1952; (ed series) Type Specimen Facsimiles, 1963-71; Italic Quartet, 1966; (ed with François Richaudeau) La Chose Imprimée (French encyc. on printing), 1977; A History of the Nonesuch Press, 1981; French Eighteenth Century Typography, 1982; contrib. The Library. *Recreations:* travel, theatre-going. *Address:* 38 Lennox Gardens, SW1X 0DH. *T:* 01-584 3510. *Club:* Garrick.

DREYFUS, Pierre; Grand Officier, Légion d'Honneur; *b* Paris, 18 Nov. 1907; *s* of Emmanuel Dreyfus, Banker, and Madeleine (*née* Bernard); *m* 1936, Laure Ullmo; one *d. Educ:* Lycée Janson-de-Sailly; Faculty of Law, Univ. of Paris (Dip., Dr of Law). Inspector-Gen. of Industry and Commerce, Chief of Gen. Inspectorate, and Dir of Cabinet to Minister of Industry and Commerce, M Robert Lacoste, 1947-49; Pres., Commn of Energy of the Plan, and Dir of the Cabinet to Minister of Industry and Commerce, M Bourgès-Maunoury, 1954. President: Houillères de Lorraine, 1950-55; Charbonnages de France, 1954; Société des Aciers Fins de l'Est, 1955. President Director-General, Régie Nationale des Usines Renault, 1955-75; Pres., Renault-Finance, 1976-80;

Minister for Industry, Finance, 1981-82. *Address:* 12 rue Duroc, 75007 Paris, France.

DRIDAN, Julian Randal, CMG 1955; retired; Chairman, Electricity Trust of South Australia, 1970-76 (Member, 1953-76); *b* 24 Nov. 1901; *s* of Sydney John Dridan and Eliza Gundry Dridan; *m* 1925, Ivy Viola Orr; two *d. Educ:* South Australian Sch. of Mines; University of Adelaide (BE). Entered service with Govt of S Australia, 1923; construction of locks and weirs on River Murray, 1923-34; District Engineer, 1934-44; Deputy Engineer-in-Chief, 1946; Engineer-in-Chief, 1949; Dir and Engineer-in-Chief, 1960-66. Mem. River Murray Commission, 1947-66. Coronation Medal, 1953; Jubilee Medal, 1978. *Recreations:* bowls, fishing. *Address:* 555 Fullarton Road, Mitcham, South Australia 6032. *Club:* Rotary (Adelaide).

DRINAN, Adam; *see* Macleod, Joseph T. G.

DRING, Lt-Col Sir (Arthur) John, KBE 1952; CIE 1943; JP; DL; *b* 4 Nov. 1902; *s* of late Sir William Dring, KCIE; *m* 1934, Marjorie Wadham (*d* 1943); two *d* ; *m* 1946, Alice Deborah, *widow* of Maj.-Gen. J. S. Marshall, CB, DSO, OBE, and *o d* of late Maj.-Gen. Gerald Cree, CB, CMG. *Educ:* Winchester Coll.; RMC, Sandhurst. Joined Guides Cavalry, 1923; Indian Political Service, 1927; Asst Private Sec. to Viceroy, 1930-32; Deputy Commissioner, Dera Ismail Khan, 1935-36; Sec. to Governor, NWFP, 1937-40; Political Agent, South Waziristan, 1940-42 (despatches); Sec. to NWFP Govt Development Depts; Revenue Commissioner, NWFP; Chief Sec. NWFP, 1947; Prime Minister of Bahawalpur, 1948-52; Adviser to Governor of Gold Coast on Togoland Plebiscite, 1955-56. Adviser to Governor-Gen. of Nigeria and the Governor of the Northern Region for the N & S Cameroons Plebiscite, 1959. JP 1954, DL 1973, Hants. *Recreations:* riding and gardening. *Address:* Ava Cottage, Purbrook, Hants. *T:* Waterlooville 3000.

DRING, (Dennis) William, RA 1955 (ARA 1944); RWS; *b* 26 Jan. 1904; *s* of William Henry Dring; *m* 1931, Grace Elizabeth Rothwell; one *s* two *d. Educ:* Slade Sch. of Fine Art. Portrait and landscape painter; during the war official war artist to Ministry of Information, Admiralty, and Air Ministry. *Address:* Windy Ridge, Compton, Winchester, Hants. *T:* Twyford, Hants 712181.

DRING, Lieut-Col Sir John; *see* Dring, Lieut-Col Sir A. J.

DRING, Richard Paddison; Editor of Official Report (Hansard), House of Commons, 1972-78; *b* 6 Nov. 1913; *s* of late Fred Dring and late Florence Hasleham Dring, East Sheen; *m* 1939, Joan Wilson, St Albans; one *s. Educ:* St Paul's School. Served Army, 1942-46. Herts Advertiser, 1932; Press Association, 1936; Official Report (Hansard), House of Commons, 1940: Asst Editor, 1954; Dep. Editor, 1970. *Recreation:* golf. *Address:* 24 Vicarage Drive, SW14 8RX. *T:* 01-876 2162. *Club:* Richmond Golf.

DRING, William; *see* Dring, D. W.

DRINKALL, John Kenneth, CMG 1973; HM Diplomatic Service, retired; High Commissioner in Jamaica, and Ambassador (non-resident) to Haiti, 1976-81; *b* 1 Jan. 1922; *m* 1961, Patricia Ellis; two *s* two *d. Educ:* Haileybury Coll.; Brasenose Coll., Oxford. Indian Army, 1942-45. Entered HM Foreign Service, 1947; 3rd Sec., Nanking, 1948; Vice-Consul, Tamsui, Formosa, 1949-51; Acting Consul, 1951; Foreign Office, 1951-53; 1st Sec., Cairo, 1953-56; Foreign Office, 1957-60; 1st Sec., Brasilia, 1960-62; Foreign Office, 1962-65. Appointed Counsellor, 1964; Counsellor: Nicosia, Cyprus, 1965-67; British Embassy, Brussels, 1967-70; FCO, 1970-71; Canadian Nat. Defence Coll., 1971-72; Ambassador to Afghanistan, 1972-76. *Recreations:* lawn tennis, golf, racquets and squash. *Address:* Bolham House, Tiverton, Devon EX16 7RA. *Clubs:* Royal Automobile, All England Lawn Tennis.

DRINKROW, John; *see under* Hardwick, Michael.

DRINKWATER, John Muir, QC 1972; a Recorder of the Crown Court, since 1972; *b* 16 March 1925; *s* of late Comdr John Drinkwater, OBE, RN (retd); *m* Jennifer Marion, *d* of Edward Fitzwalter Wright, Morley Manor, Derbs; one *s* four *d. Educ:* RNC Dartmouth. HM Submarines, 1943-47; Flag Lieut to C-in-C Portsmouth and First Sea Lord, 1947-50; Lt-Comdr 1952; invalided 1953. Called to Bar, Inner Temple, 1957, Bencher, 1979. Mem., Boundary Commn for England, 1977-80. Governor, St Mary's Hosp., 1960-64. *Recreations:* swimming, squash, travel. *Address:* Meysey Hampton Manor, Cirencester, Glos GL7 5JS. *T:* Poulton 366; 27 Kilmaine Road, SW6. *T:* 01-381 1279. *Club:* Garrick.

DRISCOLL, James; Director, Nationalised Industries' Chairmen's Group, since 1976; Chairman and Managing Director, Woodcote Consultants Ltd, since 1980; *b* 24 April 1925; *s* of Henry James Driscoll and Honorah Driscoll; *m* 1955, Jeanne Lawrence Williams, BA, CertEd; one *s* one *d. Educ:* Coleg Sant Illtyd, Cardiff; University Coll., Cardiff. BA (1st Cl. Hons). Chm., Welsh Young Conservatives, 1948-49; Nat. Dep. Chm., Young Conservatives, 1950; Dep. Chm., Univ. Cons. Fedn, 1949-50; Dep. Chm., NUS, 1951-53. Vice-Chm., European Youth Campaign, 1951-53. Contested (C) Rhondda West, 1950. Asst Lectr, UC Cardiff, 1950-53; Council of Europe Res. Fellowship, 1953. Joined British Iron and Steel Fedn, 1953; various econ. and internat. posts; Econ. Dir and Dep. Dir-Gen., 1963-67; various posts, British Steel Corporation, 1967-80; Man. Dir, Corporate

Strategy, 1971-76, Adviser, 1976-80. Member: Grand Council, FBI, 1957-65; CBI Council, 1970-; NEDC Co-ordinating Cttee, 1976-; Observer, NEDC, 1977-. Chm., Econ. Studies Cttee, Internat. Iron and Steel Inst., 1972-74. Mem., Court of Governors, UC, Cardiff, 1970-. *Publications:* various articles and pamphlets on econ. and internat. affairs, esp. steel affairs, European integration, wages policy and financing of world steel investment. *Recreations:* travel, reading. *Address:* Foxley Hatch, Birch Lane, Purley, Surrey CR2 3LH. *T:* 01-668 4081; 78 Burton Court, Franklin's Row, SW3. *T:* 01-730 6681.

DRISCOLL, Dr James Philip, CEng; Industrial Director, Welsh Office, since 1982; *b* 29 March 1943; *s* of Reginald Driscoll and Janetta Bridget Driscoll; *m* 1969, Josephine Klapper, BA; two *s* two *d. Educ:* St Illtyd's Coll., Cardiff; Birmingham Univ. (BSc 1964; PhD 1972); Manchester Business Sch. MIChemE 1975; MIGasE 1975; MInstF 1975. Taught at St Illtyd's Coll., Cardiff, 1964; res. posts with Joseph Lucas, Solihull, 1968-69; British Steel Corporation: res. posts, 1969-70; Commercial posts, 1971-79, incl. Manager, Divl Supplies, 1973; Reg. Manager, BSC (Industry), 1979-82; Dir, S Wales Workshops, 1980-82. Mem., S Wales Area Bd, MSC Special Progs Div., 1981-82. *Publications:* various technical papers. *Recreations:* family, sport. *Address:* 6 Cory Crescent, Wyndham Park, Peterston-super-Ely, S Glam. *T:* Peterston-super-Ely 760372. *Clubs:* Cardiff Athletic, Peterston Football (Cardiff).

DRIVER, Sir Arthur (John), Kt 1962; JP; *b* 1900; *s* of Percy John Driver, East Sheen, and Mary Amelie Driver; *m* 1937, Margaret, *d* of Hugh Semple McMeekin, Carnmoney, Northern Ireland; one *s* one *d.* Served in Royal Air Force, 1918. Pres. of Law Soc., 1961-62. Mem. Council, and Hon. Registrar, Imperial Soc. of Knights Bachelor, 1978-. Mem. Council, Univ. Coll., Buckingham. JP Supplementary List. *Address:* Frogmore Cottage, East Clandon, Surrey. *Club:* Reform.

DRIVER, Sir Eric (William), Kt 1979; Chairman, Mersey Regional Health Authority, 1973-82; Chairman, National Staff Committee, (Works), 1978-82; *b* 19 Jan. 1911; *s* of William Weale Driver and Sarah Ann Driver; *m* 1st, 1938, Winifred Bane; two *d* ; 2nd, 1972, Sheila Mary Johnson. *Educ:* Strand Sch., London; King's Coll., London Univ. (BSc). FICE. Civil Engr with ICI Ltd, 1938-73, retd as Chief Civil Engr Mond Div. *Recreations:* dinghy sailing (racing), hill walking, gardening. *Address:* Chapel House, Crowley, Northwich, Cheshire CW9 6NX. *Clubs:* Royal Yachting Association; Budworth Sailing.

DRIVER, Thomas; General Secretary, National Association of Teachers in Further and Higher Education, 1976-77, retired; *b* 9 Sept. 1912; *s* of Joseph and Eliza Driver; *m* 1936, Thora Senior; one *s* one *d. Educ:* Sheffield Univ. (BA, DipEd). FEIS 1977. Barnsley Central Sch., 1937-42; Keighley Jun. Techn. Sch., 1942-45; Barnsley Techn. Sch., 1945-47; Doncaster Coll. of Technology, 1947-68. Gen. Sec., Assoc. of Teachers in Technical Institutions, 1969-76. Hon. Fellow: Polytechnic of City of Sheffield, 1976; NE London Polytechnic, 1978. *Recreations:* walking, reading. *Address:* 20 Farndale Road, Doncaster, S Yorks DN5 8SH.

DROGHEDA, 11th Earl of, *cr* 1661 (Ireland); **Charles Garrett Ponsonby Moore,** KG 1972; KBE 1964 (OBE 1946); Baron Moore of Mellifont, 1616; Viscount Moore, 1621; Baron Moore of Cobham (UK), 1954; Chairman of the Financial Times Ltd, 1971-75 (Managing Director, 1945-70); Deputy Chairman, Economist Newspaper Ltd; Director, Earls Court & Olympia Ltd; Governor, The Royal Ballet; *b* 23 April 1910; *o s* of 10th Earl of Drogheda, PC, KCMG; *S* father, 1957; *m* 1935, Joan, *o d* of late William Henry Carr; one *s. Educ:* Eton; Trinity Coll., Cambridge. 2nd Lieut Royal Artillery (TA), 1939; Captain 1940. On staff of Ministry of Production, 1942-45. Chairman: Newspaper Publishers' Assoc., 1968-70; Royal Opera House, Covent Garden Ltd, 1958-74. Pres., Institute of Directors, 1975-76. Trustee, British Museum, 1974-77. Chm., London Celebrations Cttee, Queen's Silver Jubilee, 1977. Chm., Royal Ballet Sch. 1978-. Chairman: Henry Sotheran, 1977-; Clifton Nurseries, 1979-. Dir, Times Newspapers Hldgs Ltd, 1981-. Commander: Legion of Honour (France), 1960; Ordine al Merito (Italy), 1968; Grand Officier de l'Ordre de Léopold II (Belgium), 1974. *Publications:* Double Harness (memoirs), 1978; (jtly) Covent Garden Album, 1981. *Heir: s* Viscount Moore, *qv. Address:* Parkside House, Englefield Green, Surrey. *Club:* White's.
See also Sir Richard Latham, Bt.

DROMGOOLE, Jolyon; MA Oxon; Assistant Under-Secretary of State (Personnel and Logistics), Ministry of Defence, since 1979; *b* 27 March 1926; 2nd *s* of Nicholas and Violet Dromgoole; *m* 1956, Anthea, *e d* of Sir Anthony Bowlby, 2nd Bt, *qv* ; five *d* (incl. triplets). *Educ:* Christ's Hospital; Dulwich Coll.; University Coll., Oxford, 1944. 2nd Cl. Hons (History), MA. Entered HM Forces, 1944; commissioned 14/20 King's Hussars, 1946. University Coll., 1948-50. Entered Administrative Cl., Civil Service; assigned to War Office, 1950; Private Sec. to Permanent Under-Sec., 1953; Principal, 1955; Private Sec. to Sec. of State, 1964; Asst Sec., 1965; Command Sec., HQ FARELF, Singapore, 1968-71; Royal Coll. of Defence Studies, 1972; Under-Sec., Broadcasting Dept, Home Office, 1973-76; Asst Under-Sec. of State, Gen. Staff, MoD, 1976-79. *Recreations:* polo, literature. *Address:* 42 Upper Montagu Street, W1. *T:* 01-262 4904; Montreal House, Barnsley, Glos. *T:* Bibury 331. *Club:* Athenæum.

DROMGOOLE, Lesley Faye, (Mrs Nicholas Dromgoole); *see* Collier, L. F.

DROMORE, Bishop of, (RC), since 1976; **Most Rev. Francis Gerard Brooks,** DD, DCL; *b* Jan. 1924. Priest, 1949. Formerly President, St Colman's Coll., Violet Hill, Newry. *Address:* Bishop's House, Newry, Co. Down, N Ireland.

DRONFIELD, John, OBE 1971; MA Cambridge; JP; Headmaster of St Peter's School, York, 1937-67; *b* Heather, Leics, 23 Dec. 1898; *er s* of late Matthew H. Dronfield, Heather, Leics; *m* 1939, Sheila Mary Ross, *e d* of F. W. Williams, Greystones, Co. Wicklow; two *s* two *d. Educ:* Ashby-de-la-Zouch; Emmanuel Coll., Cambridge. War Service, 1917-19; 2nd Lieut in 2nd Hampshire Regt 1918; Asst Master and House Tutor at Stanley House Sch., Edgbaston, 1923-26; Asst Master at Worksop Coll., 1926-37; Housemaster of Talbot's House in 1927, and for six years Senior Housemaster and Sixth form Mathematical Master at Worksop; Acting Headmaster of Worksop, Aug.-Dec. 1935. JP City of York, 1942. *Address:* Askham Bryan, York. *T:* York 705757.

DRONFIELD, Ronald; Chief Insurance Officer for National Insurance, Department of Health and Social Security, since 1976; *b* 21 Dec. 1924; *m* 1966, Marie Renie (*née* Price). *Educ:* King Edward VII Sch., Sheffield; Oriel Coll., Oxford. RN, 1943-46. Entered Min. of National Insurance, 1949; Principal Private Sec. to Minister of Pensions and Nat. Insce, 1964-66; Cabinet Office, 1970-71. *Recreation:* reading, history mainly. *Address:* Cumberland House, Cumberland Place, Southampton. *T:* Southampton 34541. *Club:* Royal Commonwealth Society.

DROWLEY, Air Vice-Marshal Thomas Edward, CB 1947; CBE 1943 (OBE 1933); *b* 23 March 1894. Director of Equipment, RAF delegation, Washington, 1941-46; Director-General of Equipment, Air Ministry, 1946-49; retd 1949. Legion of Merit (Commander) USA. *Address:* Cedarwood, Christmas Lane, Farnham Common, Slough, Bucks. *T:* Farnham Common 4151.

DRUCKER, Prof. Peter (Ferdinand); writer and consultant; Clarke Professor of Social Science, Claremont Graduate School, Claremont, Calif, since 1971; Professorial Lecturer in Oriental Art, Claremont Colleges, since 1980; *b* 19 Nov. 1909; *s* of Adolph B. Drucker and Caroline (*née* Bond); *m* 1937, Doris Schmitz; one *s* three *d. Educ:* Austria, Germany, England. Investment banker, London, 1933-36; newspapers, 1937-41; Professor of Philosophy and Politics, Bennington Coll., Bennington, Vt, USA, 1942-49; Prof. of Management, NY Univ., 1950-72. Management Consultant (internat. practice among businesses and govts) (as well as Professorships), 1948-. Holds eleven hon. doctorates from Univs in Belgium, GB, Japan, Switzerland, USA. Hon. FBIM; FAAAS; Fellow: Amer. Acad. of Management; Internat. Acad. of Management. Order of Sacred Treasure, Japan; Grand Cross, Austria. *Publications:* End of Economic Man, 1939; Future of Industrial Man, 1942; Concept of Corporation, 1946; The New Society, 1950; Practice of Management, 1954; America's Next Twenty Years, 1959; Landmarks of Tomorrow, 1960; Managing for Results, 1964; The Effective Executive, 1967; The Age of Discontinuity, 1969; Technology, Management and Society, 1970; Men, Ideas and Politics, 1971; The New Markets . . . and other essays, 1971; Management: tasks, responsibilities, practices, 1974; The Unseen Revolution: how pension fund socialism came to America, 1976; Adventures of a Bystander, 1979; Managing in Turbulent Times, 1980; Toward the New Economics, 1981; The Changing World of the Executive (essays), 1982; The Last of All Possible Worlds (fiction), 1982. *Recreations:* mountaineering; Japanese history and paintings. *Address:* 636 Wellesley Drive, Claremont, Calif 91711, USA. *T:* (714) 621-1488.

DRUMALBYN, 1st Baron, *cr* 1963; **Niall Malcolm Stewart Macpherson,** PC 1962; KBE 1974; *b* 3 Aug. 1908; 3rd *s* of late Sir T. Stewart Macpherson, CIE, LLD, Newtonmore, Inverness-shire; *m* Margaret Phyllis (*d* 1979), *d* of late J. J. Runge and late Norah Cecil Runge, OBE, (she *m* 2nd, Dr T. A. Ross); two *d* (and one *d* decd). *Educ:* Edinburgh Academy; Fettes Coll.; Trinity Coll., Oxford (Scholar). First Class Honour Mods. 1929; First Class Litt Hum. 1931; MA; Rugby Football Blue, 1928. Business training with J. & J. Colman Ltd; Manager Turkish branch, 1933-35; Export branch, London, 1936-39. Commissioned Queen's Own Cameron Highlanders, TA June 1939: Staff Coll., 1942; Temp. Major 1942; MP (Nat L) 1945-50 (Nat L and U), 1950-63, Dumfriesshire. Scottish Whip, 1945-55; Chm., Commonwealth Producers' Organisation, 1952-55, Pres., 1967-70. Dep. Pres., Assoc. of British Chambers of Commerce, 1970. Member BBC General Advisory Council, 1950-55. Joint Under-Sec. of State for Scotland, 1955-60; Parly Sec., Board of Trade, 1960-62; Minister of Pensions and National Insurance, 1962-63; Minister of State, BoT, 1963-64; Minister without Portfolio, 1970-74. Chairman: Advertising Standards Authority, 1965-70, and 1974-77; Assoc. of Ind. Unionist (Conservative) Peers, 1975-80. *Heir:* none. *Address:* Claytons, Beeches Hill, Bishop's Waltham, Southampton SO3 1FU. *Club:* Royal Automobile.
See also R. T. S. Macpherson.

DRUMLANRIG, Viscount; Sholto Francis Guy Douglas; *b* 1 June 1967; *s* and *heir* of 12th Marquess of Queensberry, *qv.*

DRUMMOND, family name of **Earl of Perth.**

DRUMMOND, Lieut.-Gen. Sir Alexander; see Drummond, Lieut.-Gen. Sir W. A. D.

DRUMMOND, Maj.-Gen. Anthony John D.; see Deane-Drummond.

DRUMMOND, Dame (Edith) Margaret, DBE 1966 (OBE 1960); MA; Director of the Women's Royal Naval Service, 1964-67; b 4 Sept. 1917; d of Prof. Robert James Drummond and Marion (née Street). Educ: Park Sch., Glasgow; Aberdeen Univ. Joined WRNS, April 1941 and progressed through various ranks of the Service. Recreations: gardening, reading, concerts and friends. Address: Somersham Cottage, Saxlingham, Holt, Norfolk. Club: University Women's.

DRUMMOND, John Richard Gray; Director, Edinburgh International Festival, since 1978; Vice-Chairman, British Arts Festivals Association, since 1981; b 25 Nov. 1934; s of late Captain A. R. G. Drummond and Esther (née Pickering), Perth, WA. Educ: Canford; Trinity Coll., Cambridge (MA History). RNVR, 1953-55; BBC Radio and Television, 1958-78, latterly as Asst Head, Music and Arts. Programmes produced incl.: Tortelier Master Classes, 1964; Leeds Piano Comp., 1966 (1st Prize, Prague Fest., 1967); Diaghilev, 1967; Kathleen Ferrier, 1968; Music Now, 1969; Spirit of the Age, 1975; The Lively Arts, 1976-78. Mem. various adv. councils and cttees concerning music and dance. FRSA. Publication: (with Joan Bakewell) A Fine and Private Place, 1977. Recreations: conversation, looking at architecture, browsing in bookshops. Address: c/o Edinburgh Festival Society, 21 Market Street, Edinburgh. T: 031-226 4001. Clubs: New (Edinburgh), Scottish Arts.

DRUMMOND, Maldwin Andrew Cyril; JP; DL; farmer and author; Member, Countryside Commission, since 1980; b 30 April 1932; s of late Maj. Cyril Drummond, JP, DL, and Mildred Joan Quinnell; m 1st, 1955, Susan Dorothy Cayley (marr. diss. 1977); two d; 2nd, 1978, Gillian Turner-Laing; one s. Educ: Eton Coll.; Royal Agricl Coll., Cirencester; Univ. of Southampton (Cert. in Environmental Sci., 1972). 2nd Lieut, Rifle Bde, 1950-52; Captain, Queen Victoria's, later Queen's, Royal Rifles (TA), retd 1967. Verderer of New Forest, 1961-, now Sen. Elected Verderer. Member: Southampton Harbour Bd, 1967; British Transport Docks Bd, Southampton, 1968-74. Chairman: Sail Training Assoc., 1967-72; Maritime Trust, 1979-; Cutty Sark Soc., 1979-; Ships Preservation Trust, 1979-. Mem. Cttee of Management, RNLI; Trustee, World Ship Trust, 1980-. Mem., New Forest RDC, 1957-66; Hampshire: County Councillor, 1967-75; JP 1964; DL 1975; High Sheriff, 1980-81. Lord of the Manors of Cadland, Stanswood and Stone. Hon. Editor, Royal Cruising Club Jl. Publications: Conflicts in an Estuary, 1973; Tall Ships, 1976; Salt-Water Places, 1979; (with Paul Rodhouse) Yachtsman's Naturalist, 1980; (with Philip Allison) The New Forest, 1980. Recreations: cruising under sail and wondering about the sea. Address: Cadland House, Fawley, Southampton SO4 1AA. T: (office) Fawley 892039, (home) Fawley 891543; Wester Kames Castle, Port Bannatyne, Isle of Bute. T: Rothesay 3983. Clubs: White's, Pratt's, Royal Cruising; Royal Yacht Squadron (Cowes); Leander (Henley).

DRUMMOND, Dame Margaret; see Drummond, Dame E. M.

DRUMMOND, Lieut.-Gen. (Retd) Sir (William) Alexander (Duncan), KBE 1957 (CBE 1951; OBE 1945); CB 1954; SPk 1969; Director-General, Army Medical Services, War Office, 1956-61 (Deputy Director-General, 1954-56); late RAMC; b 16 Sept. 1901. Educ: Dundee Univ. MRCS, LRCP 1924; DLO Eng. 1932; FRCS 1947. Formerly: Registrar, Throat, Nose and Ear Hospital, Golden Square; Registrar, Throat, Nose and Ear Dept, Charing Cross Hosp. Served War of 1939-45 (despatches five times, OBE). Col Comdt RAMC, 1961-66. Formerly HM Comr, Royal Hospital, Chelsea. KStJ, 1959. Hon. LLD: Birmingham, 1959; Punjab, 1960. Publications: contributions to medical journals. Address: c/o Grindlay's Bank, 13 St James's Square, SW1; Chase Lodge, 27 Clapham Common North Side, SW4.

DRUMMOND, William Norman; Under Secretary (formerly Deputy Secretary), Department of Commerce, Northern Ireland, since 1979; b 10 July 1927; s of Thomas and Martha Drummond, Lurgan; m 1958, Pamela Joyce Burnham; two d. Educ: Lurgan Coll.; Queen's Univ. Belfast (BSc (Hons)). Physicist, Iraq Petroleum Co., Kirkuk, Iraq, 1950-54; Reed's Sch., Cobham, 1954-57; Northern Ireland Civil Service, 1957-; Dep. Sec., Dept of Manpower Services, NI, 1974-79. Recreations: gardening, reading. Address: Magheralave Park East, Lisburn, Northern Ireland. T: Lisburn 4104.

DRUON, Maurice Samuel Roger Charles; Officier de la Légion d'Honneur; Commandeur des Arts et Lettres; author; Member of the French Academy since 1966; Member: French Parliament (Paris), 1978-81; Assembly of Council of Europe, 1978-81; European Parliament, 1979-80; Franco-British Council, since 1972; b Paris, 23 April 1918; s of René Druon de Reyniac and Léonilla Jenny Samuel-Cros; m 1968, Madeleine Marignac. Educ: Lycée Michelet and Ecole des Sciences Politiques, Paris. Ecole de Cavalerie de Saumur, aspirant, 1940; joined Free French Forces, London, 1942; Attaché Commissariat à l'Intérieur et Direction de l'Information, 1943; War Correspondent, 1944-45; Lieut de réserve de cavalerie. Journalist, 1946-47; Minister for Cultural Affairs, France, 1973-74. Awarded Prix Goncourt, 1948, for novel Les Grandes Familles; Prix de Monaco, 1966. Member: Acad. of Morocco, 1980; Athènes' Acad., 1981. Commandeur du Phénix de Grèce; Grand Officier de l'Ordre de l'Honneur de Grèce; Grand Officier du Mérite de l'Ordre de Malte;

Commandeur de l'Ordre de la République de Tunisie; Grand Officier du Lion du Sénégal; Grand Croix du Mérite de la République Italienne; Grand Croix de l'Aigle Aztèque du Mexique; Grand Officier, Ouissam Alaouite (Morocco); Commandeur du Mérit de Monaco. Publications: Lettres d'un Européen, 1944; La Dernière Brigade (The Last Detachment), 1946 (publ. in England 1957); Les Grandes Familles, La Chute des Corps, Rendez-Vous aux Enfers, 1948-51 (trilogy publ. in England under title The Curtain falls, 1959); La Volupté d'Etre (Film of Memory), 1954 (publ. in England 1955); Les Rois Maudits (The Accursed Kings), 1955-60 (six vols: The Iron King, The Strangled Queen, The Poisoned Crown, The Royal Succession, The She-Wolf of France, The Lily and the Lion, publ. in England 1956-61); Tistou les pouces verts (Tistou of the green fingers), 1957 (publ. in England 1958); Alexandre le Grand (Alexander the God), 1958 (publ. in Eng. 1960); Des Seigneurs de la Plaine- (The Black Prince and other stories), 1962 (publ. in Eng. 1962); Les Mémoires de Zeus I (The Memoirs of Zeus), 1963 (in Eng. 1964); Bernard Buffet, 1964; Paris, de César à Saint Louis (The History of Paris from Caesar to St Louis), 1964 (in Eng. 1969); Le Pouvoir, 1965; Les Tambours de la Mémoire, 1965; Le Bonheur des Uns, 1967; L'Avenir en désarroi, 1968; Vézelay, colline éternelle, 1968; Nouvelles lettres d'un Européen, 1970; Une Eglise qui se trompe de siècle, 1972; La Parole et le Pouvoir, 1974; Oeuvres complètes, 25 vols, 1973-79; Quand un roi perd la France (Les Rois Maudits 7), 1977; Attention la France!, 1981; plays: Mégarée, 1942; Un Voyageur, 1953; La Contessa, 1962; song: Le Chant des Partisans (with Joseph Kessel and Anna Marly), 1943 (London). Recreations: riding, travel. Address: 73 rue de Varenne, 75007 Paris, France.

DRURY, (Alfred) Paul (Dalou), PPRE; etcher and painter; Principal, Goldsmiths' College School of Art, 1967-69, retired; b London, 14 Oct. 1903; s of late Alfred Drury, RA; m 1937, Enid Marie, painter, o c of late Victor Solomon; one s. Educ: King's Coll. Sch.; Bristol Grammar Sch.; Westminster Sch.; Goldsmiths' Coll. Sch. of Art (British Institution Scholarship in Engraving, 1924). Served War, 1939-45; Plaster (Orthopaedic) Dept, Queen Mary's Hosp., Roehampton. Since 1923 has exhibited etchings, paintings and drawings at the Royal Academy, galleries in England, and prints at representative exhibitions of British Art in Paris, Vienna, Florence, Stockholm, Buenos Aires, Tokyo, etc., and in Canada and the USA; etchings and drawings acquired by the Print Room, British Museum, Ashmolean, Imperial War Museum, Contemporary Art Soc., Boston, USA, and by various museums and galleries in the provinces and abroad. Fellow, Royal Soc. of Painter-Etchers and Engravers, 1926, President, 1970-75. Mem., Faculty of Engraving, British Sch. at Rome, 1948-74. Governor, West Surrey Coll. of Art, 1969-74. Recreations: music, writing. Address: Rangers Cottage, Nutley, Uckfield, East Sussex TN22 3LL. T: Nutley 2857. Club: Arts.

DRURY, Allen Stuart; Author; b Houston, Texas, 2 Sept. 1918; s of Alden M. and Flora A. Drury. Educ: Stanford Univ. (BA). Served with US Army, 1942-43. Ed., The Tulare (Calif) Bee, 1939-41; county ed., The Bakersfield Californian, Bakersfield, Calif, 1941-42; United Press Senate Staff, Washington, DC, 1943-45; freelance correspondent, 1946; Nation Ed., Pathfinder Magazine, Washington, DC, 1947-53; National Staff, Washington Evening Star, 1953-54; Senate Staff, New York Times, 1954-59. Sigma Delta Chi Award for Editorial Writing, 1942; hon. LitD, Rollins Coll., Winter Park, Fla, 1961. Publications: Advise and Consent, 1959 (Pulitzer Prize for Fiction, 1960); A Shade of Difference, 1962; A Senate Journal, 1963; That Summer, 1965; Three Kids in a Cart, 1965; Capable of Honor, 1966; "A Very Strange Society", 1967; Preserve and Protect, 1968; The Throne of Saturn, 1971; Courage and Hesitation: inside the Nixon administration, 1972; Come Nineveh, Come Tyre, 1973; The Promise of Joy, 1975; A God Against the Gods, 1976; Return to Thebes, 1977; Anna Hastings, 1977; Mark Coffin, USS, 1978; Egypt: the eternal smile, 1980; The Hill of Summer, 1981. Address: c/o Doubleday & Co., 245 Park Avenue, New York, NY 10167, USA. Clubs: Cosmos, University, National Press (Washington, DC); Bohemian (San Francisco).

DRURY, Charles Mills, OC 1981; CBE 1946 (MBE 1942); DSO 1944; ED 1956; Chairman, National Capital Commission, Canada, since 1978; b 17 May 1912; s of Victor Montague Drury, Montreal, and Pansy Jessie Mills, Ottawa; m 1939, Jane Ferrier Counsell (decd); two s two d. Educ: Bishops Coll. Sch., Lennoxville, Quebec; Royal Military Coll. of Canada, Kingston, Ontario; McGill Univ., Montreal (BCL); University of Paris, France. Practised at law, 1936-39; served War of 1939-45, Canadian Army (final rank Brig.). Chief of UNNRA Mission to Poland, 1945-46; Dept of External Affairs, Canada, 1947-48; Dep. Minister of National Defence, Canada, 1949-55; Pres. and Man. Dir, Provincial Transport Co., 1955-60; Pres., Avis Transport of Canada Ltd, 1960-62; MP, Montreal St Antoine-Westmount, 1962-78; Minister, Dept of Defence Production, and Minister of Industry, 1963-68; Pres., Treasury Bd, 1968-74; Minister of Public Works, Canada, and Minister of State for Science and Technol., 1974-76; responsible for Nat. Res. Council of Canada, 1963-76. Chevalier de la Légion d'Honneur (France), 1946; Order of Polonia Restituta (Poland), 1946. Address: (office) 161 Laurier Street West, Ottawa, Ont. K1P 6J6, Canada. Club: St James (Montreal).

DRURY, Rev. John Henry; Dean, since 1981, and Fellow, since 1982, King's College, Cambridge; b 23 May 1936; s of Henry and Barbara Drury; m 1972, (Frances) Clare Nineham; two d. Educ: Bradfield; Trinity Hall and Westcott House, Cambridge. MA (Hist. Pt 1, Cl. 1; Theol. Pt 2, Cl. 2/1). Curate, St John's Wood Church, 1963; Chaplain of Downing Coll., Cambridge, 1966; Chaplain and Fellow of Exeter Coll., Oxford, 1969; Res. Canon of Norwich

Cathedral and Examining Chaplain to Bp of Norwich, 1973-79; Vice-Dean of Norwich, 1978; Fleck Resident in Religion, Bryn Mawr Coll., USA, 1978; Lectr in Religious Studies, Sussex Univ., 1979-81. Examining Chaplain to Bp of Chichester, 1980-82. Mem., Doctrine Commn for C of E, 1978-. Jt Editor, Theology, 1976-. *Publications:* Angels and Dirt, 1972; Luke, 1973; Tradition and Design in Luke's Gospel, 1976; The Pot and The Knife, 1979; articles and reviews in Jl of Theol. Studies, Theology, Expository Times. *Recreations:* Mozart, gardening, reading. *Address:* King's College, Cambridge CB2 1ST.

DRURY, Paul; *see* Drury, A. P. D.

DRYDEN, Sir John (Stephen Gyles), 8th and 11th Bt *cr* 1795 and 1733; *b* 26 Sept. 1943; *s* of Sir Noel Percy Hugh Dryden, 7th and 10th Bt, and of Rosamund Mary, *e d* of late Stephen Scrope; *S* father, 1970; *m* 1970, Diana Constance, *o d* of Cyril Tomlinson, Highland Park, Wellington, NZ; one *s* one *d*. *Educ:* Oratory School. *Heir: s* John Frederick Simon Dryden, *b* 26 May 1976. *Address:* c/o Midland Bank Ltd, Redhill, Surrey.

DRYSDALE WILSON, John Veitch, CEng, FIMechE, FInstPet; Deputy Secretary, Institution of Mechanical Engineers, since 1979; *b* 8 April 1929; *s* of Alexander Drysdale Wilson and Winifred Rose (*née* Frazier); *m* 1954, Joan Lily, *e d* of Mr and Mrs John Cooke, Guildford; one *s* one *d*. *Educ:* Solihull School. Dennis Bros Ltd, Guildford: Engineer Apprentice, 1946-50; MIRA Research Trainee, 1949-50; Jun. Designer, 1950-51. National Service Officer, REME, 1951-53, Captain on Staff of CREME, 6th Armd Div. Management Trainee, BET Fedn, 1953-55; Technical Sales Engr, subseq. Head of Mechanical Laboratories, Esso Petroleum Co. Ltd, 1955-66; Chief Engr, R&D, Castrol Ltd, subseq. Burmah Oil Trading Ltd and Edwin Cooper Ltd, 1966-77; Projects and Res. Officer, Instn of Mechanical Engineers, 1977-79. Dir, Mechanical Engineering Publications Ltd, 1979-. MInstE; MSAE. *Publications:* numerous papers to learned societies in USA and Europe on subjects related to engine lubrication. *Recreations:* travel, gardening, horology. *Address:* Tungsten, Prior Road, Camberley, Surrey GU15 1DA. *T:* Camberley 26869. *Club:* East India, Devonshire, Sports and Public Schools.

DUBLIN, Archbishop of, and Primate of Ireland, since 1977; **Most Rev. Henry Robert McAdoo,** PhD, STD, DD; *b* 1916; *s* of James Arthur and Susan McAdoo; *m* 1940, Lesley Dalziel Weir; one *s* two *d*. *Educ:* Cork Grammar School; Mountjoy School, Dublin; Trinity College, Dublin. Deacon, 1939; Priest, 1940; Curate of Holy Trinity Cathedral, Waterford, 1939-43; Incumbent of Castleventry with Ardfield, 1943-48 (with Kilmeen, 1947-48); Rector of Kilmocomogue, Diocese of Cork, 1948-52; Rural Dean of Glansalney West and Bere, 1948-52; Canon of Kilbrittain in Cork Cathedral, and Canon of Donoughmore in Cloyne Cathedral, 1949-52; Dean of Cork, 1952-62; Canon of St Patrick's Cathedral, Dublin, 1960-62; Bishop of Ossory, Ferns and Leighlin, 1962-77. Member, Anglican-Roman Catholic Preparatory Commission, 1967-68; Jt Chm., Anglican-Roman Catholic International Commission, 1969-81 (Lambeth Cross). *Publications:* The Structure of Caroline Moral Theology, 1949; John Bramhall and Anglicanism, 1964; The Spirit of Anglicanism, 1965; Modern Eucharist Agreement, 1973; Modern Ecumenical Documents on Ministry, 1975. *Address:* The See House, 17 Temple Road, Milltown, Dublin 6. *Club:* Kildare Street and University (Dublin).

DUBLIN, Archbishop of, and Primate of Ireland, (RC), since 1972; **Most Rev. Dermot Ryan;** *b* 27 June 1924; *s* of Dr Andrew Ryan and Theresa (*née* McKenna). *Educ:* Belvedere Coll.; Holy Cross Coll., Clonliffe; UC Dublin; St Patrick's, Maynooth; St John Lateran Univ. and Gregorian Univ., Rome; Pontifical Biblical Inst., Rome. BA Dublin 1945; STL 1952, LSS 1954, Rome; MA NUI 1954. Priest, 1950; Chaplain: Mount Anville Convent, Dublin, 1950; Mater Hosp., Dublin, 1954; Prof. of Fundamental Dogmatic Theology, Clonliffe, and Asst Dean, 1955; Prof. (part-time) of Eastern Languages, UC Dublin, 1957; Prof. of Semitic Languages, UC Dublin, 1969. *Publications:* contrib. to The Furrow, Irish Theol Quarterly, Library of Catholic Knowledge, Catholic Commentary on Holy Scripture, etc. *Recreations:* golf, squash. *Address:* Archbishop's House, Dublin 9, Ireland. *T:* Dublin 373732.

DUBLIN, Auxiliary Bishop of, (RC); *see* Dunne, Most Rev. Patrick.

DUBLIN, (Christ Church), Dean of; *see* Salmon, Very Rev. T. N. D. C.

DUBLIN, (St Patrick's), Dean of; *see* Griffin, Very Rev. V. G. B.

du BOULAY; *see* Houssemayne du Boulay.

DU BOULAY, Prof. Francis Robin Houssemayne, FBA 1980; Professor of Mediæval History in the University of London, at Bedford Coll., since 1960; *b* 19 Dec. 1920; *er s* of Philip Houssemayne Du Boulay and Mercy Tyrrell (*née* Friend); *m* 1948, Cecilia Burnell Matthews; two *s* one *d*. *Educ:* Christ's Hospital; Phillip's Academy, Andover, Mass., USA; Balliol Coll., Oxford. Williams Exhibitioner at Balliol Coll., 1939; Friends' Ambulance Unit and subsequently Royal Artillery, 1940-45; MA 1947; Asst lecturer at Bedford Coll., 1947, Lecturer, 1949; Reader in Mediæval History, in University of London, 1955. FRHistS (Hon. Sec., 1961-65). *Publications:* The Register of Archbishop Bourgchier, 2 vols, 1953-55; Medieval Bexley, 1961; Documents Illustrative of Medieval Kentish Society, 1964; The Lordship of Canterbury,

1966; An Age of Ambition, 1970; (ed jtly) The Reign of Richard II, 1972; various essays and papers on late medieval subjects, English and German, in specialist journals and general symposia. *Address:* Broadmead, Riverhead, Sevenoaks, Kent. *Club:* Reform.

DuBRIDGE, Lee A(lvin); *b* 21 Sept. 1901; *s* of Frederick A. and Elizabeth Browne DuBridge; *m* 1st, 1925, Doris May Koht (*d* 1973); one *s* one *d*; 2nd, 1974, Arrola B. Cole. *Educ:* Cornell Coll., Mt Vernon, Ia (BA); University of Wisconsin (MA, PhD). Instructor in Physics, University of Wisconsin, 1925-26; Nat. Research Council Fellow at Calif. Inst. Tech., 1926-28; Asst Prof. Physics, Washington Univ. (St Louis, Mo.), 1928-33; Assoc. Prof., Washington Univ., 1933-34; Prof. of Physics and Dep. Chm., University of Rochester (NY), 1934-46; Dean of Faculty, University of Rochester, 1938-42; on leave from University of Rochester, 1940-45, as Dir of Radiation Lab. of Nat. Def. Research Comm. at MIT, Cambridge; Pres., California Inst. of Techn., Pasadena, 1946-69, Pres. Emeritus, 1969-; Science Adviser to President of USA, 1969-70. Hon. ScD: Cornell Coll.; Mt Vernon, Iowa, 1940; Weslyan Univ., Middletown, Conn., 1946; Polytechnic Inst. of Brooklyn, New York, 1946; University of Brit. Columbia, Can., 1947; Washington Univ., St Louis, Mo, 1948; Occidental Coll., 1952; Maryland, 1955; Columbia, 1957; Indiana, 1957; Wisconsin, 1957; Pennsylvania Mil. Coll., Chester, Pa, 1962; DePauw, Indiana, 1962; Pomona Coll., Claremont, Calif., 1965; Carnegie Inst. of Techn., Pittsburgh, 1965; Hon. LLD: California, 1948; Rochester, 1953; Southern California, 1957; Northwestern, 1958; Loyola, Los Angeles, 1963; Notre Dame, Indiana, 1967; Illinois Inst. Technology, 1968; Hon. LHD: University Judaism, Los Angeles, 1958; Redlands, 1958; Hon. DCL, Union Coll., Schenectady, NY, 1961; Hon. DSc: Rockefeller Institute, NY, 1965; Tufts Univ., 1969; Syracuse Univ., 1969; Rensselaer Polytech. Inst., 1970. King's Medal, 1946; Research Corp. Award, 1947; Medal for Merit of US Govt, 1948, Golden Key Award, 1959; Leif Erikson Award, 1959; Arthur Noble Award, 1961; Golden Plate Award, 1973; Vannevar Bush Award, 1982. *Publications:* Photoelectric Phenomena (with A. L. Hughes), 1932; New Theories of Photoelectric Effect (Paris), 1934; Introduction to Space, 1960; articles in various scientific and other journals. *Address:* 1730 Homet Road, Pasadena, Calif 91106, USA. *T:* 213 793-1683. *Clubs:* Sunset (Los Angeles); Bohemian (San Francisco).

DUBS, Alfred; MP (Lab) Wandsworth, Battersea South, since 1979; *b* Prague, Czechoslovakia, Dec. 1932; *m* ; one *s* one *d*. *Educ:* LSE. BSc (Econs). Local govt officer. Mem., Westminster CC, 1971-78; Chm., Westminster Community Relns Council, 1972-77; Mem., Kensington, Chelsea and Westminster AHA, 1975-78. Member: NALGO; GMWU; Co-operative Party. Contested (Lab) Cities of London and Westminster, 1970, Hertfordshire South, Feb. and Oct. 1974; Mem., Home Affairs Select Cttee. *Recreation:* walking in the Lake District. *Address:* House of Commons, SW1.

DUBUFFET, Jean; artist (exclusively since 1942); *b* Le Havre, 31 July 1901; *s* of George S. Dubuffet and Jeanne (*née* Paillette); *m* 1st, 1927, Paulette Bret (marr. diss., 1935); one *d*; 2nd, 1937, Emilie (Lili) Carlu. *Educ:* art schs, Paris. Settled at Vence, 1955, after travels. *Exhibitions* include: Galerie René Drouin, Paris, 1944, 1947; Pierre Matisse Gall., NY, 1947-78; Cercle Volney and Galerie Rive Gauche, Paris, 1954; ICA, London, 1955, 1966; Tooth, London, 1958, 1960; Daniel Cordier, Paris, 1959, 1960, 1962; Milan, 1960, 1961; Musée des Arts Décoratifs, Paris, 1960-76; Museum of Modern Art, NY, 1962, 1968, 1972; Robert Fraser, London, 1962, 1964, 1966; Venise, 1964; Tate Gall., London, 1966; Guggenheim Museum, NY, 1966-67, 1973; Galerie Jeanne Bucher, Paris, 1964-71; Galerie Claude Bernard, Paris, 1964, 1978; Galerie Beyeler, Bâle, 1968, 1975, 1976; Pace Gall., NY, 1968-79; Montréal, retrospective, 1969; Galerie Moos, Geneva, 1970; Centre national des arts contemporains, Paris, 1970, 1975; Kunsthalle and Kunstmuseum, Bâle, 1970; Arts Inst., Chicago, 1970; Waddington Gall., London, 1972, 1975, 1980; Grand Palais, Paris, 1973; Kröller-Müller, Holland, 1974; Städtische Kunsthalle, Düsseldorf, 1974; Fundacion Juan March, Madrid, 1976; Musée des Beaux Arts, Le Havre, 1977; Badischer Kunstverein, Karlsruhe, 1977; Galerie Rudolf Zwirner, Cologne, 1977, 1980; FIAT, Turin, 1978; Richard Gray Gall., Chicago, 1979. *Publications:* Prospectus aux amateurs de tout genre, 1946; Prospectus et tous écrits (2 vols), 1967; Asphyxiante culture, 1968; Edifices, 1968; L'homme du commun a l'ouvrage, 1973; La botte à nique, 1973; Catalogue intégral des travaux de Jean Dubuffet. *Address:* 51 rue de Verneuil, 75007 Paris, France.

DU CANE, John Peter, OBE 1964; Director: Amax Inc., since 1966; Australian Consolidated Minerals Pty, 1981; *b* 16 April 1921; *s* of Charles and Mathilde Du Cane; *m* 1945, Patricia Wallace (*née* Desmond); two *s*. *Educ:* Canford Sch., Wimborne. Pilot, Fleet Air Arm, RN, 1941-46. De Beers Consolidated Mines, 1946-54; Sierra Leone Selection Trust, 1955-63; Director: Consolidated African Selection Trust, 1963-81; Selection Trust Ltd, 1966-81 (Man. Dir, 1975-80; Chm., 1978-81); BP International Ltd, 1981; Chief Exec., BP Minerals Internat. Ltd, 1980-81. *Recreations:* sailing, fishing. *Address:* 20 Jameson Street, W8 7SH.

DU CANE, Comdr Peter, CBE 1964 (OBE 1942); CEng, FIMechE; FRINA; AFRAeS; FRSA; Royal Navy, retired; Consultant, Vosper Ltd, Shipbuilders, Portsmouth, (Managing Director, 1931-63; Deputy Chairman, 1963-73); *b* 18 March 1901; *s* of C. H. C. Du Cane, DL, Braxted Park, Essex, and Dorothy Blenkinsopp (*née* Coulson), Newbrough Park, Northumberland; *m* 1929, Victoria Geraldine Pole Carew; one *s* two *d*. *Educ:* RNC, Osborne,

Dartmouth, Keyham and Greenwich. Served as midshipman afloat, European War, 1917-18; Fleet Air Arm as pilot and technical officer, 1940-41. Specialised design and construction high speed craft including Bluebird II, holder of world's unlimited water speed record at 141.7 mph, for which awarded Segrave Medal for year 1939, also John Cobb's Crusader, first boat to exceed 200 mph, 1952. Designs include many Motor Torpedo Boats used by Royal Navy, Royal Barge, and High Speed Rescue Launches for RAF, also Tramontana, winner of Daily Express Internat. Offshore Power Boat Race, 1962; I and II winners of All British Daily Express Cowes/Torquay, 1964. *Publications:* High Speed Small Craft, 1951, 4th edn, 1974; An Engineer of Sorts, 1972. *Address:* Seamark, Glandore, Co. Cork, Ireland. *T:* Leap 95. *Clubs:* White's; Royal Yacht Squadron (Cowes).
See also Viscount Stuart of Findhorn.

du CANN, Col Rt. Hon. Edward Dillon Lott, PC 1964; MP (C) Taunton Division of Somerset since Feb. 1956; Director: Lonrho Ltd; Bow Group Publications Ltd; *b* 28 May 1924; *er s* of C. G. L. du Cann, Barrister-at-Law, and Janet (*née* Murchie); *m* 1962, Sallie Innes, *e d* of late James Henry Murchie, Caldy, Cheshire; one *s* two *d. Educ:* Colet Court; Woodbridge Sch.; St John's Coll., Oxford (MA, Law). Served with RNVR, 1943-46. Contested West Walthamstow Div., Gen. Election, 1951; Contested Barrow-in-Furness Div., Gen. Election, 1955. Vice-Pres., Somerset and Wilts Trustee Savings Bank, 1956-75; Founder, Unicorn Group of Unit Trusts, 1957; Chairman: Barclays Unicorn Ltd and associated cos, 1957-72; Keyser Ullman Holdings Ltd, 1970-75; Cannon Assurance Ltd, 1972-80. Chm., Association of Unit Trust Managers, 1961. Mem., Lord Chancellor's Adv. Cttee on Public Records, 1960-62; Joint Hon. Sec.: UN Parly Group, 1961-62; Conservative Parly Finance Group, 1961-62; Mem., Select Cttee on House of Lords Reform, 1962; Economic Sec. to the Treasury, 1962-63; Minister of State, Board of Trade, 1963-64; Founder Chm., Select Cttee on Public Expenditure, 1971-72; Mem., Select Cttee on Privilege, 1972-; Chairman: Select Cttee on Public Accounts, 1974-79; 1922 Cttee, 1972-; Liaison Cttee of Select Cttee Chairmen, 1974-; (founder) Select Cttee on Treasury and Civil Service Affairs, 1979-; Cons. Party Organisation, 1965-67; Buckie Club, 1973-79. President: (founder) Anglo-Polish Cons. Soc., 1972-74; Nat. Union of Conservative and Unionist Assocs, 1981-82; Vice-Chm., British American Parly Gp, 1978-81. Jt Leader, British-American Parly Gp delegns to USA, 1978, 1980; Leader, Jt British Parly Gp delegn to China, IPU, 1982. Dir, James Beattie Ltd, 1965-79; Vice-Pres., British Insurance Brokers Assoc., 1978-; Patron, Assoc. of Insurance Brokers, 1974-77. Visiting Fellow, Univ. of Lancaster Business School, 1970-82. Commodore, 1962, Admiral, 1974, House of Commons Yacht Club. Hon. Col, 155 (Wessex) Regt, RCT (Volunteers), 1972-82. Lecturer, broadcaster. Elected first Freeman of Taunton Deane Borough, 1977. *Publications:* Investing Simplified, 1959; articles on financial and international affairs (incl. The Case for a Bill of Rights, How to Bring Government Expenditure within Parliamentary Control, etc). *Recreations:* travel, gardening, sailing. *Address:* 9 Tufton Court, Tufton Street, SW1. *T:* 01-222 1922; Cothay Barton, Greenham, Wellington, Somerset. *Clubs:* Carlton, Pratt's; Royal Thames Yacht; Somerset County (Taunton).
See also R. D. L. Du Cann.

Du CANN, Richard Dillon Lott, QC 1975; a Recorder of the Crown Court, since 1982; *b* 27 Jan. 1929; *yr s* of C. G. L. du Cann; *m* 1955, Charlotte Mary Sawtell; two *s* two *d. Educ:* Steyning Grammar Sch.; Clare Coll., Cambridge. Called to Bar, Gray's Inn, 1953; Bencher, 1980; Treasury Counsel, Inner London QS, 1966-70; Treasury Counsel, Central Criminal Court, 1970-75. Chairman: Criminal Bar Assoc., 1977-79; Senate and Bar Council, 1980-81. *Publications:* (with B. Hayhoe) The Young Marrieds, 1954; The Art of the Advocate, 1964. *Address:* 29 Newton Road, W2 5AF. *T:* 01-229 3859.
See also Col Rt Hon. E. D. L. du Cann.

DUCAT, David; Chairman, The Metal Box Co. Ltd., 1967-70, retired (Managing Director 1949-66; Vice-Chairman 1952-66; Deputy Chairman 1966-67); *b* 1 June 1904; *s* of William John and Amy Ducat; *m* 1933, Hilary Mildred Stokes; three *s* one *d. Educ:* Merchant Taylors' Sch.; Gonville and Caius Coll., Cambridge (MA). ACIS 1935. Min. of Production, 1942-45. British Tin Box Manufacturers Fedn: Chm., 1952-61; Vice-Chm., 1961-69. Mem. Court of Assts, Merchant Taylors' Co., 1956- (Master, 1964). Vice-Pres., British Inst. of Management (Council Chm., 1966-68); Mem. Coun., City University, 1966-71. FCIS 1967. *Address:* Morar, 16 Sandy Lodge Road, Moor Park, Rickmansworth, Herts. *T:* Rickmansworth 73562.

DUCAT-AMOS, Air Comdt Barbara Mary, CB 1974; RRC 1971; Matron-in-Chief, Princess Mary's Royal Air Force Nursing Service, 1972-78, and Director of Royal Air Force Nursing Service, 1976-78; Medical Department, Cable and Wireless plc, since 1978; *b* 9 Feb. 1921; *d* of late Captain G. W. Ducat-Amos, Master Mariner, and late Mrs M. Ducat-Amos. *Educ:* The Abbey Sch., Reading; St Thomas's Hosp., London (The Nightingale Trng Sch.). SRN 1943; CMB Pt 1 1948. PMRAFNS, 1944-47: served in RAF Hosps, UK and Aden; further training; nursing in S Africa and SW Africa, 1948-52; rejoined PMRAFNS, 1952: served in RAF Hosps as General Ward and Theatre Sister, UK, Germany, Cyprus, Aden and Changi (Singapore); Matron 1967; Sen. Matron 1968; Principal Matron 1970. QHNS 1972-78. CStJ 1975. *Recreations:* music, theatre, travel. *Address:* c/o Barclays Bank Ltd, King Street, Reading, Berks RG1 2HD. *Club:* Royal Air Force.

DUCCI, Dr Roberto, Grand Cross, Italian Order of Merit; Ambassador of Italy to the Court of St James's, 1975-80; Counsellor of State, since 1980;

Visiting Professor of Political Science, Rome University, since 1982; *b* 8 Feb. 1914; *s* of Gino Ducci and Virginia Boncinelli; *m* 1951, Wanda Matyjewicz; two *s. Educ:* Univ. of Rome (Dr of Law). Entered Foreign Service, 1937; served: Ottawa, 1938; Newark, NJ, 1940; Italian Delegn to Peace Conf., 1946; Warsaw, 1947; Rio de Janeiro, 1949; Italian Delegn to NATO and OEEC, 1950-55; Chm., Drafting Cttee, Rome Treaties, 1956-57; Asst Dir, General Economic Affairs, 1955-57; Ambassador to Finland, 1958-62; Head, Italian Delegn to Brussels, UK-EEC Conf., 1961-63; Dep. Dir-Gen. for Political Affairs, 1963-64; Ambassador to: Yugoslavia, 1964-67; Austria, 1967-70; Director-General for Political Affairs, 1970-75. Mem. Bd, European Investment Bank, 1958-68. *Publications:* Prima Età di Napoleone, 1933; Questa Italia, 1948; L'Europa Incompiuta, 1971; D'Annunzio Vivente, 1973; Contemporanei, 1976; L'Innocenza (poems), 1978; 24 Hours at No 4 Grosvenor Square, 1979; Il Libro di Musica (poems), 1981; 1 Capintesta, 1982; Candidato a Morte, 1982; numerous political essays and articles. *Recreations:* riding, collecting frail things. *Address:* Via Belsiana 35, 00187 Rome, Italy. *Club:* Circolo della Caccia (Rome).

DUCHÊNE, Louis-François; Director for Western Europe, International Reporting Information Systems, Washington, DC, since 1982; *b* 17 Feb. 1927; *s* of Louis Adrien Duchêne and Marguerite Lucienne Duchêne (*née* Lainé); *m* 1952, Anne Margaret Purves; one *d. Educ:* St Paul's Sch.; London Sch. of Economics. Leader writer, Manchester Guardian, 1949-52; Press attaché, High Authority, European Coal and Steel Community, Luxembourg, 1952-55; Correspondent of The Economist, Paris, 1956-58; Dir, Documentation Centre of Action Cttee for United States of Europe (Chm. Jean Monnet), Paris, 1958-63; Editorial writer, The Economist, London, 1963-67. Director: Internat. Inst. for Strategic Studies, 1969-74; Sussex European Res. Centre (formerly Centre for Contemp. European Studies), Sussex Univ., 1974-82. *Publications:* (ed) The Endless Crisis, 1970; The Case of the Helmeted Airman, a study of W. H. Auden, 1972. *Address:* 3 Powis Villas, Brighton, East Sussex BN1 3HD. *T:* Brighton 29258.

DUCIE, 6th Earl of *cr* 1837; **Basil Howard Moreton;** Baron Ducie, 1763; Baron Moreton, 1837; *b* 15 Nov. 1917; *s* of Hon. Algernon Howard Moreton (2nd *s* of 4th Earl) (*d* 1951), and Dorothy Edith Annie, *d* of late Robert Bell; *S* uncle 1952; *m* 1950, Alison May, *d* of L. A. Bates, Pialba, Queensland; three *s* one *d. Heir: s* Lord Moreton, *qv. Address:* Tortworth House, Tortworth, Wotton-under-Edge, Glos.

DUCKER, Herbert Charles, BSc London; NDA; Field Officer Groundnut Research, under the Federal Ministry of Agriculture, Rhodesia and Nyasaland, now retired; *b* 13 May 1900; *s* of Charles Richard and Gertrude Louise Ducker; *m* 1925, Marjorie, *y d* of late Charles Tuckfield, AMICE; two *s* one *d. Educ:* Kingston Grammar Sch., Kingston-on-Thames; South-Eastern Agricultural Coll., Wye; Imperial Coll. of Science, South Kensington. British Cotton Industry Research Assoc. Laboratories; Asst Cotton Specialist, Nyasaland, 1922; Cotton Specialist, Empire Cotton Growing Corporation, Nyasaland, 1925-56; Superintendent-Curator of the National Botanic Gardens, Salisbury, Southern Rhodesia, under the Federal Ministry of Agriculture, of Rhodesia and Nyasaland, 1957. *Publications:* Annual Reports on Cotton Research work 1925-55, carried out in Nyasaland; articles on cotton growing. *Recreation:* fishing. *Address:* Pleasant Ways, MP 13, Mount Pleasant, Salisbury, Zimbabwe. *Club:* Royal Over-Seas League.

DUCKHAM, Prof. Alec Narraway, CBE 1950 (OBE 1945); Professor of Agriculture, University of Reading, 1955-69; *b* 23 Aug. 1903; *e s* of Alexander Duckham, FCS, and Violet Ethel Duckham (*née* Narraway); *m* 1932, Audrey Mary Polgreen (*d* 1969), St Germans, Cornwall; one *s* two *d. Educ:* Oundle Sch.; Clare Coll., Cambridge. MA (Hons) Cantab.: Cambridge Dip. Agric. Sci. (dist. in Animal Husbandry), 1926; FIBiol; Silver Research Medallist, Royal Agricultural Society, England, 1926. Research and Advisory work on Animal Husbandry at Cambridge, Aberdeen, Belfast, 1927-39. Chm. Home and Overseas Agric. Supplies Cttees and Dir of Supply Plans Div., Min. of Food, 1941-45. Agric. Attaché, Brit. Embassy, Washington, and Agric. Adviser to UK High Comr, Ottawa, 1945-50. Asst Sec. to Min. of Agriculture and Fisheries, 1950-54. Liaison Officer (SE Region), to the Minister of Agriculture, Fisheries and Food, 1965-70. Vice-Chm., Alex. Duckham and Co. Ltd, 1945-68. *Publications:* Animal Industry in the British Empire, 1932; American Agriculture, 1952 (HMSO); The Fabric of Farming, 1958; Agricultural Synthesis: The Farming Year, 1963; (with G. B. Masefield) Farming Systems of the World, 1970; (ed with J. G. W. Jones and E. H. Roberts) Food Production and Consumption, 1976. *Recreations:* painting and music. *Address:* Little Park House, Brimpton, Woolhampton, Berks. *Club:* Royal Automobile.

DUCKMANTON, Sir Talbot (Sydney), Kt 1980; CBE 1971; General Manager, Australian Broadcasting Commission, 1965-82 (Deputy General Manager, 1964-65); *b* 26 Oct. 1921; *s* of Sydney James Duckmanton. Joined Australian Broadcasting Commission, 1939. War Service: AIF and RAAF. President: Asia-Pacific Broadcasting Union, 1973-77; Commonwealth Broadcasting Assoc., 1975-. *Address:* PO Box E 148, St James, Sydney, NSW 2000, Australia. *Clubs:* Legacy, Australian, Tattersalls (Sydney).

DUCKWORTH, Arthur; see Duckworth, G. A. V.

DUCKWORTH, Brian Roy; a Recorder of the Crown Court, since 1972; *b* 26 July 1934; *s* of Roy and Kathleen Duckworth; *m* 1964, Nancy Carolyn

Holden; three s one d. *Educ:* Sedbergh Sch.; Worcester Coll., Oxford (MA). Called to Bar, Lincoln's Inn, 1958; Member: Northern Circuit; Bar Council, 1979-. Councillor, Blackburn RDC, 1960-74 (Chm. 1970-72). *Recreations:* golf, gardening, motor sport. *Address:* Close House, Abbey Village, Chorley, Lancs. *T:* Brinscall 830425. *Clubs:* St James's (Manchester); Pleasington Golf.

DUCKWORTH, (George) Arthur (Victor), JP; *b* 3 Jan, 1901; *e s* of Major A. C. Duckworth of Orchardleigh Park, Frome; *m* 1927, Alice, 3rd *d* of John Henry Hammond, New York; three *d*; *m* 1945, Elizabeth, *o d* of Alfred Ehrenfeld, Bridgeham Farm, Forest Green, Surrey; two *d*; *m* 1968, Mary, *y d* of Archdeacon Edmund Hope, and *widow* of Captain K. Buxton. *Educ:* Eton; Trinity Coll., Cambridge (BA). MP (C) Shrewsbury Div. of Salop, 1929-45; Parliamentary Private Sec. to Rt Hon. Sir Geoffrey Shakespeare, 1932-39. Served War of 1939-45, 36th (Middlesex) AA Bn RA, 1939-41. CC Somerset, 1949-64; JP Somerset, 1957. *Address:* Orchardleigh Park, Frome, Somerset. *T:* Frome 830306. *Clubs:* Travellers', Garrick.

DUCKWORTH, John Clifford; Chairman: IDJ Investment Services Ltd, since 1972; Lintott Control Equipment Ltd, since 1980; Clayton Goodfellow Ltd, since 1982; *b* 27 Dec. 1916; *s* of late H. Duckworth, Wimbledon, and of Mrs A. H. Duckworth (*née* Woods); *m* 1942, Dorothy Nancy Wills; three s. *Educ:* KCS, Wimbledon; Wadham Coll., Oxford. Telecommunications Research Establishment, Malvern: Radar Research and Development, 1939-46; National Research Council, Chalk River, Ont., 1946-47; Atomic Energy Research Establishment, Harwell, 1947-50; Ferranti Ltd: Chief Engineer, Wythenshawe Laboratories, 1950-54; Nuclear Power Engineer, Brit. Electricity Authority, 1954-58; Central Electricity Authority, 1957-58; Chief Research and Development Officer, Central Electricity Generating Board, 1958-59; Man. Dir., Nat. Research Develt Corp., 1959-70. Pres., Institute of Fuel, 1963-64; Vice-Pres., Parliamentary and Scientific Cttee, 1964-67. Chm., Science Mus. Adv. Council, 1972-. Vice-Pres., IEE, 1974-77. Director: Spear & Jackson International Ltd, 1972-; Bridon Ltd, 1970-; Rank Organisation, 1980-. *Recreations:* swimming, colour photography, cartography. *Address:* Suite 33, 140 Park Lane, W1. *Club:* Athenæum.

DUCKWORTH, Captain Ralph Campbell Musbury, CBE 1946 (OBE 1943); CEng; RN, retired; *b* 11 June 1907; 2nd *s* of Major Arthur Campbell Duckworth, DL, JP, Orchardleigh Park, Frome, Som; *m* 1945, Ruby Cortez, 2nd Officer WRNS (*d* 1979), *o d* of A. W. Ball, Sydenham, London. *Educ:* Royal Naval Colleges, Osborne and Dartmouth. War of 1939-45: served as Lieut-Comdr and Torpedo Officer of HMS Illustrious, 1940-41; Comdr 1941 and staff of C-in-C Mediterranean and C-in-C Levant, 1941-43; OBE for duties in planning and execution of operations for capture of Sicily; Dep. Chief of Staff (acting Capt.) to Vice-Adm. Administration, British Pacific Fleet, 1944-45 (CBE); Captain 1946; Dep. Dir Underwater Weapons Dept, Admiralty, 1946-48; Naval Attaché, British Embassy, Rio de Janeiro, 1949-51; Imperial Defence Coll., 1952; Capt., 1st Destroyer Sqdn, 1953-54; Staff of C-in-C, Mediterranean, 1954-55. Member: Northern Ireland Development Council, 1956-65; Dollar Exports Council, 1956-59; Manager, Industrial Engineering, Morgan Crucible Co. Ltd, 1956-58; Commercial Manager Elliott Bros (London) Ltd, 1959-61; Dir, British Mechanical Engrg Fedn, 1963-68. *Recreations:* gardening and travelling. *Address:* Westbury House, West Meon, near Petersfield, Hampshire.

DUCKWORTH, Major Sir Richard Dyce, 3rd Bt *cr* 1909; *b* 30 Sept. 1918; *s* of Sir Edward Dyce Duckworth, 2nd Bt, and Cecil Gertrude, *y d* of Robert E. Leman; *S* father, 1945; *m* 1942, Violet Alison, *d* of Lieut-Col G. B. Wauchope, DSO; two s. *Educ:* Marlborough Coll. Started business in 1937, retired 1969. *Recreations:* sailing, golf, squash, shooting. *Heir:* s Edward Richard Dyce Duckworth [*b* 13 July 1943; *m* 1976, Patricia, *o d* of Thomas Cahill]. *Address:* Dunwood Cottage, Shootash, Romsey, Hants. *T:* Romsey 513228.

DUCKWORTH, Walter Eric, PhD; FEng, FIM, FInstP, FIS; Managing Director, Fulmer Research Institute, since 1969; *b* 2 Aug. 1925; *s* of Albert Duckworth and Rosamund Biddle; *m* 1949, Emma Evans; one s. *Educ:* Cambridge Univ. (MA, PhD). Research Manager, Glacier Metal Co., 1955; Asst Director, BISRA, 1966; Chm., Yarsley Research Laboratories, 1973-; Dir, Ricardo Consulting Engineers plc, 1978-. Chm., Council of Science and Technology Insts, 1977-78; President: Instn of Metallurgists, 1974-75; Assoc. of Contract Res. Organisations, 1978-79; Hon. Treas., Metals Soc., 1981-. Chm., Christian Nationals Evangelism Commn, 1974-; Trustee, Comino Foundn, 1981-; Vice-Pres., St Mary's Hosp. Med. Sch., 1976-; Mem. Court, Brunel Univ., 1978-. Hon. DTech Brunel, 1976; DUniv. Surrey, 1980. *Publications:* A Guide to Operational Research, 1962, 3rd edn 1977; Statistical Techniques in Technological Research, 1968; Electroslag Refining, 1969; Manganese in Ferrous Metallurgy, 1976; *circa* 100 contribs to learned and other jls on many topics. *Recreations:* gardening, changing other people's attitudes. *Address:* Orinda, Church Lane, Stoke Poges, Bucks SL2 4NZ. *T:* Fulmer 2181.

du CROS, Sir Claude Philip Arthur Mallet, 3rd Bt *cr* 1916; *b* 22 Dec. 1922; *s* of Sir (Harvey) Philip du Cros, 2nd Bt, and of Dita, *d* of late Sir Claude Coventry Mallet, CMG; *S* father, 1975; *m* 1st, 1953, Mrs Christine Nancy Tordoff (marr. diss. 1974), *d* of late F. R. Bennett, Spilsby, Lincs; one s; 2nd, Mrs Margaret Roy Cutler, *d* of late R. J. Frater, Gosforth, Northumberland.

Heir: s Julian Claude Arthur Mallet du Cros, *b* 23 April 1955. *Address:* Long Meadow, Ballaugh Glen, IoM.

DUDBRIDGE, Bryan James, CMG 1961; retired from HM Overseas Civil Service, Nov. 1961; Deputy Director, formerly Associate Director, British Council of Churches Department of Christian Aid, 1963-72; *b* 2 April 1912; *o s* of late W. Dudbridge, OBE, and of Anne Jane Dudbridge; *m* 1943, Audrey Mary, *o d* of late Dr and Mrs Heywood, Newbury; two *s* one *d*. *Educ:* King's Coll. Sch., Wimbledon; Selwyn Coll., Cambridge. Appointed to Colonial Administrative Service as Cadet in Tanganyika, 1935; Asst Dist Officer, 1937; Dist Officer, 1947; Sen. Dist Officer, 1953; Actg Provincial Commr, Southern Province; Administrative Officer (Class IIA), 1955, and Actg Provincial Commissioner (Local Government); Provincial Commissioner, Western Province, 1957; Minister for Provincial Affairs, 1959-60, retd. *Publications:* contrib. Journal of African Administration, and Tanganyika Notes and Records. *Recreations:* natural history, and wildfowl. *Address:* Bridge Farm, High Halden, Ashford, Kent. *T:* High Halden 221. *Club:* Royal Commonwealth Society.

DUDDING, Sir John (Scarbrough), Kt 1964; DL; Her Majesty's Overseas Civil Service, retired; Chairman, Humberside Area Health Authority, 1974-82; *b* 28 Nov. 1915; *s* of Col Thomas Scarbrough Dudding, OBE, MRCS, LRCP, RAMC, and Maude Campbell Dudding; *m* 1945, Enid Grace Gardner, The Old Hall, Tacolneston, Norwich; one *s* one *d*. *Educ:* Cheltenham Coll.; Jesus Coll., Cambridge (BA Hons). Entered Colonial Service, posted to Nigeria, 1938. War service with Nigeria Regt of Royal West African Frontier Force, in Nigeria, India and Burma, 1940-45. Dep. Comr of the Cameroons and Actg Comr, 1956-58; Permanent Sec., Ministries Federal Nigerian Govt with responsibilities for Works, Surveys, Transport, Aviation, and Communications, 1959-63; retd, 1964. Chairman: Scunthorpe HMC, 1967-74; Lincolnshire Cttee VSO, 1966-73; Lincolnshire and Humberside Arts Assoc. (formerly Lincolnshire Regional Arts Assoc.), 1970-73, 1980-82; President: Winterton Agricl Soc.; S Humberside Br., CPRE. Lindsey CC, 1967-74; DL Lincoln, 1971-, Humberside 1974. FRSA 1971. Hon. LLD Hull, 1981. *Recreations:* gardening, local history and book-collecting. *Address:* Scarbrough House, Winteringham, Scunthorpe, South Humberside DN15 9ND. *T:* Scunthorpe 732 393. *Club:* Royal Commonwealth Society.

DUDGEON, Air Vice-Marshal Antony Greville, CBE 1955; DFC 1941; *b* 6 Feb. 1916; *s* of late Prof. Herbert William Dudgeon, Guy's Hosp. and Egyptian Government Service; *m* 1942, Phyllis Margaret, *d* of late Group Capt. John McFarlane, OBE, MC, AFC, Lowestoft, Suffolk; one *s* one *d*. *Educ:* Eton; RAF Cranwell; Staff Coll., Flying Coll.; Polytechnic London. RAF Service, 1933-68, in UK, Europe, Near, Middle and Far East, USA; personnel work, training, operations, flight safety, organisation of new formations, liaison with civilian firms and youth organisations; NATO Staff; 6 command appointments; 3,500 hours as pilot. Manager, Professional Staff Services, McKinsey & Co., Paris, 1968-78; representative, France, Grangersol Ltd, 1978-81. *Publications:* A Flying Command (under pen-name Tom Dagger), 1962; several stories contributed to Blackwood's Magazine. *Recreations:* writing, photography, swimming; (languages, French, Egyptian). *Address:* 43 Winchendon Road, SW6 5DH. *Club:* Royal Air Force.

DUDGEON, Henry Alexander, CMG 1976; HM Diplomatic Service, retired; *b* 12 Aug. 1924; *er s* of late John Brown Dudgeon and late Alison Dudgeon (*née* Winton); *m* 1952, Marjorie Patricia, *d* of Joseph Harvey, MD; no *c*. *Educ:* Knox Academy, Haddington; Magdalene Coll., Cambridge. Served in HM Forces, 1943-47; entered HM Foreign Service, 1949; served at: FO, 1949-52; Sofia, 1952-54; Amman, 1954-58; FO, 1958-61; 1st Sec. and Head of Chancery, Madrid, 1961-66; Counsellor and Head of Chancery, Havana, 1966-69; Civil Service Research Fellow at Glasgow Univ., 1969-70; Head of Marine and Transport Dept, FCO, 1970-74. Dep. Leader, UK Deleg to Third UN Conf. on Law of the Sea, 1974-75; Minister, Canberra, 1976-80. *Address:* 295 Fir Tree Road, Epsom Downs, Surrey. *T:* Burgh Heath 61983. *Club:* Travellers'.

DUDGEON, Prof. John Alastair, CBE 1977; MC 1942 and Bar 1943; TD 1947, Bars 1950 and 1956; DL; Consultant Microbiologist, Hospital for Sick Children, Great Ormond Street, 1960-81, Honorary Consulting Microbiologist, 1982; Professor of Microbiology, Institute of Child Health, University of London, 1972-82; *b* 9 Nov. 1916; *yr s* of late Prof. L. S. Dudgeon; *m* 1st, 1945, Patricia Joan Ashton (*d* 1969); two s; 2nd, 1974, Joyce Kathleen Tibbetts. *Educ:* Repton Sch.; Trinity Coll., Cambridge; St Thomas's Hosp., London. MB, BCh 1944; MA, MD Cantab 1947; FRCPath 1967; MRCP 1970; FRCP 1974. Served in London Rifle Bde and 7th Bn Rifle Bde, 1936-43; transf. to RAMC, 1944; Specialist in Pathology RAMC, 1945. Asst Pathologist, St Thomas's Hosp., 1947; Sen. Lectr, St George's Hosp. Med. Sch., 1953; Head of Virus Research, Glaxo Labs, 1958; Hosp. for Sick Children, Great Ormond Street: Asst Pathologist, 1948; Hon. Consultant Virologist, 1953; Mem. Bd of Governors, 1962-69, 1970-81; Mem. Cttee of Management, 1966-81, Dean, 1974-81, Inst. of Child Health (Univ. of London); Hon. Consultant in Pathology to Army, 1977-. Mem. Court of Assts, Soc. of Apothecaries of London, 1974. DL Greater London, 1973. OStJ 1958. *Publications:* Modern Trends in Paediatrics (contrib.); Immunization Procedures for Children; Viral Infections of the Fetus and Newborn (co-author). *Recreation:* sailing. *Address:* 1 Devonshire Place, W1N 1PA. *T:* 01-935 6703. *Clubs:* Army and Navy; Aldeburgh Yacht.

DUDLEY, 4th Earl of, *cr* 1860; **William Humble David Ward;** Baron Ward, 1644; Viscount Ednam, 1860; *b* 5 Jan. 1920; *e s* of 3rd Earl of Dudley, MC, TD, and Rosemary Millicent, RRC (*d* 1930), *o d* of 4th Duke of Sutherland; *S* father, 1969; *m* 1st, 1946, Stella (marr. diss., 1961), *d* of M. A. Carcano, KCMG, KBE; one *s* twin *d*; 2nd, 1961, Maureen Swanson; one *s* five *d*. *Educ:* Eton; Christ Church, Oxford. Joined 10th Hussars, 1941, Adjt, 1944-45; ADC to Viceroy of India, 1942-43. Served War of 1939-45 (wounded). Director: Baggeridge Brick Co. Ltd; Tribune Investment Trust Ltd. *Heir:* s Viscount Ednam, *qv. Address:* 6 Cottesmore Gardens, W8; Vention House, Putsborough, N Devon. *Clubs:* White's, Pratt's; Royal Yacht Squadron.

DUDLEY, Baroness (14th in line), *cr* 1439-1440 (called out of abeyance, 1916); **Barbara Amy Felicity Hamilton;** *b* 23 April 1907; *o d* of 12th Baron Dudley and Sybil Augusta (*d* 1958), *d* of late Rev. Canon Henry William Coventry; *S* brother, 1972; *m* 1929, Guy Raymond Hill Wallace (*d* 1967), *s* of late Gen. Hill Wallace, CB, RHA; three *s* one *d*; *m* 1980, Charles Anthony Crosse Hamilton. *Recreations:* floral water-colours (has exhibited Royal Watercolour Society, Conduit St]; gardening. *Heir: e s* Hon. Jim Anthony Hill Wallace [*b* 9 Nov. 1930; *m* 1962, Nicola Jane, *d* of Lt-Col Philip William Edward Leslie Dunsterville; two *s*]. *Address:* Hill House, Kempsey, Worcestershire. *T:* Worcester 820253.

DUDLEY, Bishop Suffragan of, since 1977; **Rt. Rev. Anthony Charles Dumper;** *b* 4 Oct. 1923; *s* of Charles Frederick and Edith Mildred Dumper; *m* 1948, Sibylle Anna Emilie Hellwig; two *s* one *d*. *Educ:* Surbiton Grammar School; Christ's Coll., Cambridge (MA); Westcott House, Cambridge. Relief Worker, Germany, 1946-47; ordained, 1947; Curate, East Greenwich, 1947-49; Vicar of South Perak, Malaya, 1949-57; Archdeacon of North Malaya, 1955-64; Vicar of Penang, Malaya, 1957-64; Dean of St Andrew's Cathedral, Singapore, 1964-70; Vicar of St Peter's, Stockton on Tees, and Rural Dean of Stockton, 1970-77. *Publication:* Vortex of the East, 1963. *Recreations:* walking, gardening. *Address:* Bishop's House, Halesowen Road, Cradley Heath, West Midlands. *T:* 021-550 3407.

DUDLEY, Archdeacon of; *see* Campling, Ven. C. R.

DUDLEY, Prof. Hugh Arnold Freeman, FRCSE, FRCS, FRACS; Professor of Surgery, St Mary's Hospital, London, since 1973; *b* 1 July 1925; *s* of W. L. and Ethel Dudley; *m* 1947, Jean Bruce Lindsay Johnston; two *s* one *d*. *Educ:* Heath Grammar Sch., Halifax; Edinburgh and Harvard Univs. MB, ChB Edin. 1947; ChM (Gold Medal and Chiene Medal) Edin. 1958; FRCSE 1951; FRACS 1965; FRCS 1974. Lecturer in Surgery, Edinburgh Univ., 1954-58; Sen. Lectr, Aberdeen Univ., 1958-63; Foundation Prof. of Surgery, Monash Univ., Melbourne, 1963-72. President: Surgical Res. Soc. of Australasia, 1968; Biol. Engrg Soc. of GB, 1978-80; Surgical Res. Soc. of GB, 1981-82. Chm., Editorial Board of Br. Jl of Surgery and of Br. Jl Surgery Soc. Ltd. *Publications:* Principles of General Surgical Management, 1958; Access and Exposure in Abdominal Surgery, 1963; (ed) Rob and Smiths Operative Surgery, 1976-; Hamilton Bailey's Emergency Surgery, 1977; Communication in Medicine and Biology, 1977; (jtly) Guide to House Surgeons in the Surgical Unit, 7th edn 1982; (ed) Aid to Clinical Surgery, 1978; papers in med. jls. *Recreations:* accidentally and unintentionally annoying others; surgical history. *Address:* 58 Westbourne Terrace, W2. *T:* 01-402 7507; Broombrae, Glenbuchat, Aberdeenshire. *T:* Glenkindie 341. *Club:* Flyfishers'.

DUDLEY, Prof. Norman Alfred, CBE 1977; PhD; FEng; Lucas Professor of Engineering Production, 1959-80, Emeritus Professor 1981, University of Birmingham; Head of Department of Engineering Production and Director of Lucas Institute of Engineering Production, 1956-80; Chartered Engineer; *b* 29 Feb. 1916; *s* of Alfred Dudley; *m* 1940, Hilda Florence, *d* of John Miles; one *s* two *d*. *Educ:* Kings Norton Grammar Sch.; Birmingham Coll. of Technology. BSc London, PhD Birmingham. FEng 1981. Industrial training and appts: H. W. Ward & Co. Ltd, 1932-39; Imperial Typewriter Co. Ltd, 1940-45; Technical Coll. Lectr, 1945-52; Sen. Lectr, Wolverhampton and Staffs, 1948-52; Lectr in Eng. Prod., 1952, Reader, 1956, University of Birmingham. Chm., Manufacturing Processes Div., Birmingham Univ. Inst. for Advanced Studies in Engineering Sciences, 1965-68. Director: Birmingham Productivity Services Ltd; West Midlands Low Cost Automation Centre. Member: SRC Manufacturing Technol. Cttee; SRC and DoI Teaching Company Cttee, 1977-80. Chm., Cttee of Hds of Univ. Depts of Production Studies, 1970-80. Governor: Dudley and Staffs Tech. Coll., and Walsall and Staffs Tech. Coll., 1955-60; Letchworth Coll. of Technol., 1964-66. Member: Council, West Midlands Productivity Assoc.; Council Internat. Univ. Contact for Management Education, 1957; Council, Instn of Prod. Engineers, 1959-61 (Chm., Research Cttee, 1965-66; Viscount Nuffield Meml Lectr, 1969]; UK Delegn to UNCSAT Geneva, 1963; W Midlands Economic Planning Council, 1970-78; Adv. Panel on Economic Develt, West Midlands Metropolitan CC, 1976-77; Council, Nat. Materials Handling Centre. Pres., Midlands Operational Research Soc., 1966-80. Member: Ergonomics Res. Soc. (Emeritus); Internat. Inst. of Production Engrg Research. FBIM; Hon. FIProdE. Hon. Member: Japanese Industrial Management Assoc.; Internat. Foundn of Prodn Research. Hon. DTech Loughborough, 1981. Editor, International Journal of Production Research,

1961-80. J. D. Scaife Medal, 1958. *Publications:* Work Measurement: Some Research Studies, 1968; (co-ed) Production and Industrial Systems, 1978; various papers on Engineering Production. *Address:* 37 Abbots Close, Knowle, Solihull, West Midlands. *T:* Knowle 5976. *Club:* Athenæum.

DUDLEY-SMITH, Rt. Rev. Timothy; *see* Thetford, Bishop Suffragan of.

DUDLEY-WILLIAMS, Sir Rolf (Dudley), 1st Bt, *cr* 1964; *b* 17 June 1908; *s* of Arthur Williams, Plymouth; assumed and adopted surname of Dudley-Williams, by Deed Poll, 1964; *m* 1940, Margaret Helen, *er d* of F. E. Robinson, OBE, AMIMechE; two *s*. *Educ:* Plymouth Coll.; Royal Air Force Coll., Cranwell. Gazetted, 1928, Flying Officer, 1930; Central Flying Sch., 1933, invalided from service, 1934. Founded Power Jets Ltd, 1936, to develop Whittle system of jet propulsion; Managing Dir, 1941. Mem. Council Soc. of British Aircraft Constructors, 1944; Companion Royal Aeronautical Society, 1944. Contested (C) Brierley Hill, 1950. MP (C) Exeter, 1951-66; PPS to Sec. of State for War, 1958; PPS to Minister of Agriculture, 1960-64. Chm., Western Area of National Union of Conservative Assocs, 1961-64. *Heir: s* Alastair Edgcumbe James Dudley-Williams [*b* 26 Nov. 1943; *m* 1972, Diana Elizabeth Jane, twin *d* of R. H. C. Duncan; three *d*]. *Address:* The Old Manse, South Petherton, Som. *T:* South Petherton 40143. *Club:* Royal Air Force.

DUDMAN, George Edward, CB 1973; *b* 2 Dec. 1916; *s* of William James Dudman and Nora Annie (*née* Curtis); *m* 1955, Joan Doris, *d* of late Frederick John Eaton; one *s* one *d*. *Educ:* Merchant Taylors' Sch., London; St John's Coll., Oxford (MA). Royal Artillery, 1940-46; Control Commn, Germany, 1946-49. Called to Bar, Middle Temple, 1950. Law Officers' Dept, 1951; Legal Sec., Law Officers' Dept, 1958; Legal Advr, DES, 1965-77; Editor, Statutes in Force, 1977-81. *Recreations:* painting, gardening, cooking, playing chess, studying philosophy. *Address:* 10 Viga Road, Grange Park, N21. *T:* 01-360 5129.

DUDMAN, Ven. Robert William; Archdeacon of Lindsey and Fourth Canon Residentiary of Lincoln Cathedral since 1971, Treasurer since 1975; *b* 4 Dec. 1925; *s* of late Robert and Jane Dudman, Basingstoke; *m* 1954, Betty Shannon; one *s* two *d*. *Educ:* King's Coll., Taunton; Lincoln Theol Coll.; Univ. of Hull (BA). Able Seaman, RN, 1944-47. Deacon, 1952; Priest, 1953. Curate: Shiregreen, Sheffield, 1952-53; Wombwell, 1953-55; Frodingham, Scunthorpe, 1955-57; Industrial Chaplain to Bp of Lincoln, 1957-71; Rector of Scotton, 1960-71; Canon and Prebend of Norton Episcopi, Lincoln Cath., 1968. *Address:* The Archdeaconry, Cantilupe Chantry, Lincoln LN2 1PX. *T:* Lincoln 25784.

DUESBERY, Rev. Canon Julian Percy T.; *see* Thornton-Duesbery.

DUFF, Rt. Hon. Sir (Arthur) Antony, GCMG 1980 (KCMG 1973; CMG 1964); CVO 1972; DSO 1944; DSC; PC 1980; Deputy Secretary, Cabinet Office, since 1980; *b* 25 Feb. 1920; *s* of late Adm. Sir Arthur Allen Morison Duff, KCB; *m* 1944, Pauline Marion, *d* of Capt. R. H. Bevan, RN, and *widow* of Flt-Lieut J. A. Sword; one *s* two *d* (and one step *s*). *Educ:* RNC, Dartmouth. Served in RN, 1937-46. Mem., Foreign (subseq. Diplomatic) Service, 1946; 3rd Sec., Athens, Oct. 1946; 2nd Sec., 1948; 2nd Sec., Cairo, 1949; 1st Sec., 1952; transferred Foreign Office, Private Sec. to Minister of State, 1952; 1st Sec., Paris, 1954; Foreign Office, 1957; Bonn, 1960; Counsellor, 1962; British Ambassador to Nepal, 1964-65; Commonwealth Office, 1965-68; FCO, 1968-69; Dep. High Comr, Kuala Lumpur, 1969-72; High Comr, Nairobi, 1972-75; Dep. Under-Sec. of State, 1975-80, Dep. to Perm. Under-Sec. of State, 1976-80, FCO. Dep. Governor, Southern Rhodesia, 1979-80. *Address:* c/o National Westminster Bank, 17 The Hard, Portsea, Hants. *Club:* Army and Navy.

DUFF, Patrick Craigmile, CMG 1982; *b* 6 Jan. 1922; *o s* of late Archibald Craigmile Duff, ICS, and Helen Marion (*née* Phillips); *m* 1st, 1947, Pamela de Villeneuve Graham (*osp*); 2nd, 1950, Elizabeth Rachel, *d* of late Rt Rev. R. P. Crabbe (Bishop of Mombasa, 1936-53) and Mrs Crabbe; two *d*. *Educ:* Wellington Coll., Berks; New Coll., Oxford (MA 1946). War service, 1941-42. HMOCS, 1942-63: Tanganyika; Kenya; CRO, 1964-65; ODM/ODA, 1966-74; Head, West Indian and Atlantic Dept, FCO, 1975-80; Head, British Develt for E Africa, FCO, 1980-82. *Recreations:* making music, fell walking, ball games. *Address:* 6 Christchurch Road, Winchester, Hants SO23 9SR. *T:* Winchester 65200. *Club:* Royal Commonwealth Society.

DUFF, Patrick William; Fellow of Trinity College, Cambridge; *b* 21 Feb. 1901; 3rd *s* of J. D. Duff, Fellow of Trinity College, Cambridge, and Laura, *d* of Sir William Lenox-Conyngham, KCB. *Educ:* Winchester; Trinity Coll., Cambridge; Munich Univ.; Harvard Law Sch. 1st Class, Classical Tripos Parts I and II; Craven and Whewell Scholar; Tancred Scholar of Lincoln's Inn; Fellow of Trinity, 1925; Lecturer, 1927; Tutor, 1938; Senior Tutor, 1945; Dean of Coll., 1950; Vice-Master, 1960. Regius Prof. of Civil Law, Cambridge, 1945-68. Barrister-at-Law, 1933. Cambridge Borough Councillor, 1947-51. Fellow of Winchester Coll., 1948-76; Warden, 1959-62. Pres. Soc. of Public Teachers of Law, 1957-58. Hon. Bencher of Lincoln's Inn, 1959. *Publications:* The Charitable Foundations of Byzantium (in Cambridge Legal Essays presented to Doctor Bond, Prof. Buckland and Prof. Kenny), 1926; The Personality of an Idol (in Cambridge Law Journal), 1927; Delegata Potestas Non Potest Delegari (in Cornell Law Quarterly), 1929; Personality in Roman Private Law, 1938; Roman Law Today (in Tulane Law Review), 1947. *Recreation:* scouting. *Address:* Trinity College, Cambridge.

DUFF, Col Thomas Robert G.; *see* Gordon-Duff.

DUFF GORDON, Sir Andrew (Cosmo Lewis), 8th Bt, *cr* 1813; *b* 17 Oct. 1933; *o s* of Sir Douglas Duff Gordon, 7th Bt and Gladys Rosemary (*d* 1933), *e d* of late Col Vivien Henry, CB; *S* father, 1964; *m* 1st, 1967, Grania Mary (marr. diss. 1975), *d* of Fitzgerald Villiers-Stuart, Ireland; one *s*; 2nd, 1975, Eveline Virginia, BA, *d* of S. Soames, Newbury; four *s. Educ:* Repton. Served with Worcs Regiment and 1st Bn Ches Regt, 1952-54. Mem. of Lloyd's, 1962-. *Recreations:* golf, shooting, skiing. *Heir: s* Cosmo Henry Villiers Duff Gordon, *b* 18 June 1968. *Address:* Downton House, Walton, Presteigne, Powys. *T:* New Radnor 223; 27 Cathcart Road, SW10. *Clubs:* City University; Kington Golf; Sunningdale Golf.

DUFFERIN AND AVA, 5th Marquess of, *cr* 1888; **Sheridan Frederick Terence Hamilton-Temple-Blackwood;** Baron Dufferin and Clandeboye, Ireland, 1800; Baron Clandeboye, UK, 1850; Earl of Dufferin, Viscount Clandeboye, 1871; Earl of Ava, 1888, and a Bt; *b* 9 July 1938; *o s* of 4th Marquess (killed in action, 1945) and Maureen (she *m* 1948, Major Desmond Buchanan, MC, from whom she obtained a divorce, 1954; *m* 1955, John Cyril Maude, *qv*), 2nd *d* of late Hon. (Arthur) Ernest Guinness; *S* father, 1945; *m* 1964, Serena Belinda Rosemary, *d* of Group Capt. (Thomas) Loel Evelyn Bulkeley Guinness, *qv. Educ:* Eton Coll.; Christ Church, Oxford. Trustee: Wallace Collection, 1973-; Nat. Gall., 1981-. Dir, Arthur Guinness PLC, 1979-. *Address:* 4 Holland Villas Road, W14. *T:* 01-603 8910; Clandeboye, Co. Down, Northern Ireland.

DUFFUS, Sir Herbert (George Holwell), Kt 1966; *b* 30 Aug. 1908; *e s* of William Alexander Duffus, JP, and Emily Henrietta Mary (*née* Holwell); *m* 1939, Elsie Mary (*née* Hollinsed); no *c. Educ:* Cornwall Coll., Jamaica. Admitted as Solicitor: Jamaica, 1930, England, 1948. Resident Magistrate, Jamaica, 1946-58; Called to the Bar, Lincoln's Inn, 1956; acted as Puisne Judge, Jamaica, 1956-58; Puisne Judge, Jamaica, 1958-62; Judge of Appeal, Jamaica, 1962-64; Pres. Court of Appeal, 1964-67; Chief Justice of Jamaica, 1968-73; Acting Governor General of Jamaica, 1973. Chairman: Commn of Enquiry into Prisons of Jamaica, 1954; Commn of Enquiry into the administration of justice and police brutality in Grenada, WI, 1974; Police Service Commission (Jamaica), 1958-68. Sole Commissioner, Enquiries into: Maffesanti Affair, 1968; Operations of Private Land Developers in Jamaica, 1975-76; Barbados Govt's Private Enterprises, 1977-78. Pres., Boy Scouts Assoc., Jamaica, 1967-70. Chancellor of the Church (Anglican) in Jamaica, 1973-76. *Address:* 6 Braywick Road, PO Box 243, Kingston 6, Jamaica. *T:* 92-70171.

DUFFY, (Albert Edward) Patrick, PhD; MP (Lab) Sheffield, Attercliffe, since 1970; *b* 17 June 1920. *Educ:* London Sch. of Economics (BSc(Econ.), PhD); Columbia Univ., Morningside Heights, New York, USA. Served War of 1939-45, Royal Navy, as an Officer (6 years service). Lecturer, University of Leeds, 1950-63, 1967-70. Visiting Prof., Drew Univ., Madison, NJ, 1966-70, Associate Prof., 1970-. Contested (Lab) Tiverton Division of Devon, 1950, 1951, 1955. MP (Lab) Colne Valley Division of Yorks, 1963-66; Chairman: Parly Labour Party Economic and Finance Gp, 1965-66, 1974-76; Trade and Industry Sub-Cttee of Select Cttee on Expenditure; PPS to Sec. of State for Defence, 1974-76; Parly Under-Sec. of State for Defence (Navy), MoD, 1976-79; opposition spokesman on defence, 1979-80. Mem., N Atlantic Assembly, 1979-. *Publications:* contrib. to Economic History Review, Victorian Studies, Manchester School, etc. *Address:* 153 Bennetthorpe, Doncaster, South Yorks. *Clubs:* Naval; Trades and Labour (Doncaster).

DUFFY, Antonia Susan, (Mrs P. J. Duffy); *see* Byatt, A. S.

DUFFY, Hugh Herbert White; *b* 24 Aug. 1917; *y s* of late Hugh Duffy and Catherine Duffy (*née* White); *m* 1946, Hylda, *y d* of Stanley Swales, Fleetwood; one *s. Educ:* Stonyhurst Coll.; Durham Univ. (LLB). Commnd 9th Bn, Durham LI (TA), 1937; BEF, 1940; wounded France, 1940; discharged owing to wounds, 1942. Admitted solicitor, 1943. Joined Public Trustee Office (Manchester Br.), 1944, transf. London, 1956; Chief Admin. Officer, 1970-73; Asst Public Trustee, 1973-75; Public Trustee, 1975. *Recreations:* reading, motoring, watching sport on TV. *Address:* One Stone, 19 Loughrigg Park, Ambleside, Cumbria. *T:* Ambleside 2478.

DUFFY, Most Rev. Joseph; *see* Clogher, Bishop of, (RC).

DUFFY, Maureen Patricia; author; *b* 1933; *o c* of Grace Rose Wright. *Educ:* Trowbridge High Sch. for Girls; Sarah Bonnell High Sch. for Girls; King's College, London (BA). Chm., Greater London Arts Literature Panel, 1979-81; Vice-Chm., British Copyright Council, 1981-. Co-founder, Writers' Action Group; Jt Chm., Writers Guild of GB, 1977-78. Vice-Pres., Beauty Without Cruelty. *Publications:* That's How It Was, 1962; The Single Eye, 1964; The Microcosm, 1966; The Paradox Players, 1967; Lyrics for the Dog Hour (poetry), 1968; Wounds, 1969; Rites (play), 1969; Love Child, 1971; The Venus Touch, 1971; The Erotic World of Faery, 1972; I want to Go to Moscow, 1973; A Nightingale in Bloomsbury Square (play), 1974; Capital, 1975; Evesong (poetry), 1975; The Passionate Shepherdess, 1977; Housespy, 1978; Memorials of the Quick and the Dead (poetry), 1979; Inherit the Earth, 1980; Gorsaga, 1981; *visual art:* Prop art exhibn (with Brigid Brophy, *qv*),

1969. *Address:* 14A Richmond Mansions, Old Brompton Road, SW5. *T:* 01-373 1020.

DUFFY, Patrick; *see* Duffy, A. E. P.

DUFFY, Terence; President, Amalgamated Union of Engineering Workers, since 1978; *b* 3 May 1922; *s* of John and Anne Duffy; *m* 1957, Joyce Sturgess; one *s* one *d. Educ:* St Joseph's RC Sch., Wolverhampton. Served War, Infantry, 1940-46 (1939-45 Star; African, Italian, Victory Decorations). Amalgamated Union of Engineering Workers: Divl Officer (full-time), Birmingham, 1969; Mem., Exec. Council, 1976. Member: TUC General Council, 1978-; NEDC, 1980-. *Recreations:* gardening, golf. *Address:* 9 Sunningdale Road, Bickley, Kent.

DUFTY, Arthur Richard, CBE 1971; FSA; Master of the Armouries in HM Tower of London, 1963-76; *b* 23 June 1911; *s* of T. E. Dufty, and Beatrice (*née* Holmes); *m* 1937, Kate Brazley (*née* Ainsworth); one *s* two *d. Educ:* Rugby; Liverpool School of Architecture. War service in RN. On staff of Royal Commn on Historical Monuments, 1937-73, Sec. and Gen. Editor 1962-73, with responsibility for Nat. Monuments Record, inc. Nat. Buildings Record, 1964-73. Sec., 1954-64, Vice-Pres. 1964-67, and 1975-78, Pres., 1978-81, Soc. of Antiquaries; Vice-Pres., Council for Brit. Archaeology, 1962-65. Member: Ancient Monuments Bd for England, 1962-73 and 1977-80; Council for Places of Worship, 1976-81; Council, Nat. Army Museum, 1963-; Historic Bldgs Adv. Cttee, GLC, 1964-67; Management Cttee of Inst. of Archaeology, Univ. of London, 1965-75; Royal Commn on Historical Monuments, 1975-. Vice-Chm., Cathedrals Advisory Commission (formerly Cathedrals Adv. Cttee), 1965-. Chairman: British Cttee, Corpus Vitrearum Medii Aevi, 1970- (sponsored by British Acad.); London Dio. Adv. Cttee, 1973-; Standing Cttee on Conservation of West Front of Wells Cathedral, 1974-. Trustee: Coll. of Arms Trust, 1978-; Marc Fitch Fund, 1978-. Directed, for Soc. of Antiquaries, repair and rehabilitation of Kelmscott, William Morris's home in Oxfordshire, 1964-67. Hon. Freeman, Armourers and Brasiers' Co., 1974. Hon. Mem., Art Workers' Guild, 1977. ARIBA 1935-74; FSA 1946. *Publications:* Kelmscott: an illustrated guide, 1970; ed 5 RCHM Inventories (incl. authorship of accounts of King's College Chapel, Corfe Castle, etc) and 5 occasional publications; Intr. Vol. to Morris's Story of Cupid and Psyche, 1974; articles in learned jls. *Recreations:* viewing sales; taking pleasure in Victoriana and Art Nouveau; music. *Address:* 46 Trafalgar Court, Farnham, Surrey. *Clubs:* Athenæum, Arts, Naval.

DUGARD, Arthur Claude, CBE 1969; Chairman, Cooper & Roe Ltd, 1952-79, retired (formerly Joint Managing Director); *b* 1 Dec. 1904; *s* of Arthur Thomas Turner Dugard, Nottingham; *m* 1931, Christine Mary Roe, Nottingham; two *s. Educ:* Oundle Sch., Northants. Joined Cooper & Roe Ltd, Knitwear manufacturers, 1923 (Dir, 1936; Man. Dir, 1947). President: Nottingham Hosiery Manufrs Assoc., 1952-53; Nat. Hosiery Manufrs Fedn, 1959-61; Nottingham Chamber of Commerce, 1961-62. First Chm., CBI North Midland Regional Council, 1965-66; Chm. British Hosiery & Knitwear Export Gp, 1966-68; Mem. East Midlands Economic Planning Council, 1967-72. Liveryman, Worshipful Co. of Framework Knitters, 1949-. *Recreation:* golf. *Address:* 16 Hollies Drive, Edwalton, Nottingham NG12 4BZ. *T:* Nottingham 233217.

DUGDALE, family name of **Baron Crathorne.**

DUGDALE, John Robert Stratford; Lord-Lieutenant of Salop, since 1975; *b* 10 May 1923; 2nd *s* of Sir William Francis Stratford Dugdale, 1st Bt, and Margaret, 2nd *d* of Sir Robert Gordon Gilmour, 1st Bt; *m* 1956, Kathryn Edith Helen (*see* K. E. H. Dugdale); two *s* two *d. Educ:* Eton; Christ Church, Oxford. Chm., Telford Develt Corp., 1971-75. KStJ 1976. *Recreation:* sleeping. *Address:* Tickwood Hall, Much Wenlock, Salop. *T:* Telford 882644. *Clubs:* Brooks's, White's, MCC.
See also Sir William Dugdale, Bt.

DUGDALE, Kathryn Edith Helen, CVO 1973; JP; a Woman of the Bedchamber to The Queen; *b* 4 Nov. 1923; *d* of Rt Hon. Oliver Stanley, PC, MC, MP and Lady Maureen Vane-Tempest Stewart; *m* 1956, John Robert Stratford Dugdale, *qv* ; two *s* two *d. Educ:* many and varied establishments. Served with WRNS. Temp. Woman of the Bedchamber to The Queen, 1955-60, Extra Woman of the Bedchamber 1960-72. JP Salop, 1964. Employee of Greater London Fund for the Blind. Comdr, Royal Order of North Star (Sweden), 1956. *Recreations:* gardening, reading, pottering. *Address:* Tickwood Hall, Much Wenlock, Salop. *T:* Telford 882644.
See also M. C. Stanley.

DUGDALE, Norman, CB 1974; Permanent Secretary, Department (formerly Ministry) of Health and Social Services, Northern Ireland, since 1970; *b* 6 Feb. 1921; *yr s* of William and Eva Dugdale, Burnley, Lancs; *m* 1949, Mary Whitehead. *Educ:* Burnley Grammar Sch.; Manchester Univ. (BA). Asst Principal, Bd of Trade, 1941; Min. of Commerce, NI, 1948; Asst Sec., Min. of Health and Local Govt, NI, 1955; Sen. Asst Sec., Min. of Health and Local Govt, NI, 1964; Second Sec., Min. of Health and Social Services, 1968. Governor, Nat. Inst. for Social Work, London, 1965-; Mem. Court, New University of Ulster, 1971. *Publications:* poems: The Disposition of the Weather, 1967; A Prospect of the West, 1970; Night-Ferry, 1974; Corncrake in October, 1978; Running Repairs, 1982; contribs to various literary periodicals. *Recreations:* procrastinating; next week-end.

DUGDALE, Peter Robin; Managing Director, Guardian Royal Exchange Assurance plc, since 1978; Chairman: Trade Indemnity plc, since 1980; Aviation and General Insurance Co. Ltd, since 1982; *b* 12 Feb. 1928; *s* of Dr James Norman Dugdale and Lilian (*née* Dolman); *m* 1957, Esmé Cyraine, *d* of L. Norwood Brown; three *s*. *Educ:* Canford; Magdalen Coll., Oxford (MA). Joined Union Insurance Soc. of Canton, Hong Kong, 1949; merged with Guardian Assurance, 1960; Marine and Aviation Underwriter, 1965; Pres., Guardian Insurance Company of Canada, 1973; Gen. Man., Guardian Royal Exchange, 1976. Chm., British Insurance Assoc., 1981-82. *Recreation:* flat-coated retrievers. *Address:* Trentham House, Emsworth, Hants PO10 7BH. *T:* Emsworth 2934. *Club:* Oriental.

DUGDALE, Sir William (Stratford), 2nd Bt *cr* 1936; CBE 1982; MC 1943; JP; DL; *b* 29 March 1922; *er s* of Sir William Francis Stratford Dugdale, 1st Bt, and Margaret, 2nd *d* of Sir Robert Gordon Gilmour, 1st Bt, of Liberton and Craigmillar; *m* 1st, 1952, Lady Belinda Pleydell-Bouverie (*d* 1961), 2nd *d* of 6th Earl of Radnor; one *s* three *d* ; 2nd, 1967, Cecilia Mary, *e d* of Sir William Malcolm Mount, 2nd Bt, *qv* ; one *s* one *d*. *Educ:* Eton; Balliol Coll., Oxford. Served War of 1939-45, Grenadier Guards (Captain). Admitted as Solicitor, 1949. Dir, Phoenix Assurance Co., 1968-. Mem., Warwicks County Council, 1964-76; Chairman: Severn Trent Water Authoirty, 1974-82; Birmingham Diocesan Board of Finance, 1979-; Governor, Lady Katherine Leveson's Hosp., Temple Balsall. High Steward, Stratford upon Avon, 1977. JP 1951, DL 1955, High Sheriff 1971, Warwicks. *Heir: s* William Matthew Stratford Dugdale, *b* 22 Feb. 1959. *Address:* Blyth Hall, Coleshill, near Birmingham. *T:* Coleshill 62203; Merevale Hall, Atherstone. *T:* Atherstone 3143; 24 Bryanston Mews West, W1. *T:* 01-262 2510. *Clubs:* Brooks's, White's, MCC; Jockey (Newmarket).
See also J. R. S. Dugdale.

DUGGAN, Gordon Aldridge; HM Diplomatic Service; Commercial and Economic Counsellor, Lagos, since 1981; *b* 12 Aug. 1937; *s* of Joseph Nathan Duggan and Elizabeth Aldridge; *m* 1969, Erica Rose Anderssen; one *s* two *d*. *Educ:* Liverpool Collegiate Sch.; Lincoln Coll., Oxford. BA, BPhil. FO, 1963-66; Canberra, 1966-69; FCO, 1969-72; Information Officer, Bonn, 1972-74; Head of Chancery, Jakarta, 1974-76; Canberra, 1976-79; FCO, 1979-80. *Recreations:* armchair sport, jazz, theatre, walking, countryside. *Address: c/o* Foreign and Commonwealth Office, King Charles Street, SW1; 1 Heads Mews, W11. *Club:* Metropolitan (Lagos).

DUGGAN, Rt. Rev. John Coote; *see* Tuam, Killala and Achonry, Bishop of.

DUGMORE, Rev. Prof. Clifford William, DD; Member, Advisory Editorial Board, The Journal of Ecclesiastical History, since 1979 (Editor, 1950-78); British Member of Editorial Board of Novum Testamentum, 1956-76; *b* 9 May 1909; *s* of late Rev. Canon William Ernest Dugmore, MA, RD, and late Frances Ethel Dugmore (*née* Westmore); *m* 1st, 1938, Ruth Mabel Archbould Prangley (*d* 1977); one *d* ; 2nd, 1979, Kathleen Mary Whiteley. *Educ:* King Edward VI Sch., Birmingham (foundation scholar); Exeter Coll., Oxford; Queens' Coll., Cambridge. Oxford: BA (Hons Sch. of Oriental Studies), 1932; MA and James Mew Rabbinical Hebrew Scholar, 1935; BD 1940; DD 1957. Cambridge: BA (by incorporation) 1933; MA 1936; Norrisian Prizeman 1940; Select Preacher 1956; Hulsean Lecturer, 1958-60. Deacon 1935, Priest 1936; Asst Curate of Holy Trinity, Formby, 1935-37; Sub-Warden St Deiniol's Library, Hawarden, 1937-38; Rector of Ingestre-with-Tixall, 1938-43; Chaplain of Alleyn's Coll. of God's Gift, Dulwich, 1943-44; Rector of Bredfield and Dir of Religious Education, dio. St Edmundsbury and Ipswich, 1945-47; Sen. Lecturer in Ecclesiast. Hist., University of Manchester, 1946-58; Tutor to Faculty of Theology, 1958; Prof. of Ecclesiastical History, King's Coll., Univ. of London, 1958-76, Emeritus Prof., 1976-. Chm. of British Sous-Commission of Commission Internationale d'Histoire Ecclésiastique, 1952-62; Pres. of the Ecclesiastical History Soc., 1963-64; Mem. of the Senate, 1964-71, Proctor in Convocation, 1970-75, Dean, Univ. Faculty of Theology, 1974-76, University of London. FKC 1965; FRHistS 1970. *Publications:* Eucharistic Doctrine in England from Hooker to Waterland, 1942; The Influence of the Synagogue upon the Divine Office, 1944 (2nd edn 1964); (ed) The Interpretation of the Bible 1944 (2nd edn 1946); The Mass and the English Reformers, 1958; Ecclesiastical History No Soft Option, 1959. Contributor to: Chambers's Encyclopædia, 1950 (Advisory Editor, 1960-); Weltkirchenlexikon 1960; Studia Patristica IV, 1961; Neotestamentica et Patristica, 1962; The English Prayer Book, 1963; A Companion to the Bible, 2nd revised edn, 1963; Studies in Church History I, 1964 (also ed); Studies in Church History II, 1965; Eucharistic Theology then and now, 1968; Man and his Gods, 1971; Aspects de l'Anglicanisme, 1974; Thomas More: through many eyes, 1978; Gen. Editor, Leaders of Religion, 1964-76; articles and reviews in Journal of Theological Studies, Journal of Ecclesiastical History, Theology, History, etc. *Recreations:* motoring and philately. *Address:* 77 The Street, Puttenham, Surrey GU3 1AT. *T:* Guildford 810460.

DUGUID, Prof. James Paris, CBE 1979; MD, BSc; FRCPath; Professor of Bacteriology, University of Dundee, since 1967; Consultant, Tayside Health Board, since 1963; *b* 10 July 1919; *s* of late Maj.-Gen. David Robertson Duguid, CB, and Mary Paris; *m* 1944, Isobel Duff; one *s* three *d*. *Educ:* Edinburgh Academy; Univ. of Edinburgh (MB ChB Hons 1942; BSc 1st Cl. Hons 1943; MD (Gold Medal) 1949); FRCPath 1966. Lectr, Sen. Lectr and Reader, Univ. of Edinburgh, 1944-62; Prof. of Bacteriology, Univ. of St

Andrews, 1963-67; Director of Postgrad. Medical Educn, Univ. of Dundee, 1968-71, Dean of Faculty of Medicine, 1971-74, Mem. Univ. Court, 1977-81. Cons. Adviser in Microbiology, Scottish Home and Health Dept, 1967-, Mem. Adv. Cttee on Medical Research, 1967-71; Member: Eastern Regional and Tayside Health Bds, 1967-77; Adv. Cttee on Laboratory Services, Scottish Health Serv. Council, 1967-74 (Chm., Epidemiology Sub-cttee, 1967-71); Scottish Health Services Planning Council, 1974-77 (Member: Adv. Cttee on New Developments in Health Care, 1976-; Scientific Services Adv. Gp, 1975-79; Chm., Microbiology and Clin. Immunology Cttees, 1975-77); Jt Cttee on Vaccination and Immunisation, Health Services Councils, 1967-74; GMC, 1975-81; Council for Professions Supp. to Medicine, 1978-. Asst Editor: Jl of Pathology and Bacteriology, 1959-68; Jl of Medical Microbiology, 1968-71. *Publications:* co-ed, Medical Microbiology, 11th edn 1969, 12th edn 1973, 13th edn 1978; scientific papers on bacterial fimbriae, adhesins, biotyping and phylogeny, airborne infection, and the action of penicillin. *Recreations:* gardening, atheism. *Address:* 69 Dalkeith Road, Dundee DD4 7HF. *T:* Dundee 44856; Hillside, Glenborrodale, Argyll.

du HEAUME, Sir (Francis) Herbert, Kt 1947; CIE 1943; OBE 1932; KPM 1924; Indian Police Medal; *b* 27 May 1897; *s* of George du Heaume, OBE; *m* 1923, Blanche Helen Learmonth Tainsh (*d* 1981); two *s*. Served European War, 1914-18, Captain, 15th London Regt; joined Indian Police, 1920; Principal, Police Training Sch., Punjab, 1934-42; Deputy Inspector-Gen. of Police, 1942-47. *Address: c/o* Grindlay's Bank Ltd, 13 St James's Square, SW1.

DUKE, family name of **Baron Merrivale.**

DUKE, Cecil Howard Armitage; Director of Establishments and Organisation, Ministry of Agriculture, Fisheries and Food, 1965-71; *b* 5 May 1912; *s* of late John William Duke and Gertrude Beatrice (*née* Armitage); *m* 1939, Eleanor Lucy (*née* Harvie); one *s* one *d*. *Educ:* Selhurst Gram. Sch.; LSE. RNVR, 1942-45 (Corvettes). Entered Civil Service, 1929; Asst Princ., 1940; Princ., 1945; Private Sec. to Lord Presidents of the Council, 1951-53; Asst Sec., Land Drainage Div. and Meat Div., 1953; Under-Sec., 1965. *Recreations:* walking, gardening, watching Sussex cricket. *Address:* 22 Fairways Road, Seaford, East Sussex. *T:* Seaford 894338.

DUKE, Maj.-Gen. Sir Gerald (William), KBE 1966 (CBE 1945); CB 1962; DSO 1945; DL; Chairman, M. A. M. Marinas Ltd, since 1972; *b* 12 Nov. 1910; *e s* of late Lieut-Col A. A. G. Duke, Indian Army; *m* 1946, Mary Elizabeth (*d* 1979), *er d* of late E. M. Burn, Church Stretton; one *s* one *d*. *Educ:* Dover Coll.; RMA Woolwich; Jesus Coll., Cambridge. Commissioned RE, 1931; served Egypt and Palestine, 1936-39; War of 1939-45, in Western Desert and Italy; BGS Eighth Army, 1944; North West Europe, Brig. Q (Movements), 21st Army Group, 1944; CRE 49th Div., 1945. Chief Engineer, Malaya Comd, 1946; idc 1948; Mil. Attaché, Cairo, 1952-54; Comdt Sch. of Mil. Engineering, 1956-59. Commodore Royal Engineer Yacht Club, 1957-60. DPS, WO, 1959-62; Engineer-in-Chief (Army), 1963-65; retired. Col Comdt, RE, 1966-75. Chm., SS&AFA, Kent, 1973-; Pres., Scout Assoc., Kent, 1974-; Vice-Pres., Hockey Assoc., 1965-. Governor of Dover Coll. FICE. DL Kent, 1970. *Recreations:* sailing, golf. *Address:* Little Barnfield, Hawkhurst, Kent. *T:* Hawkhurst 3214. *Clubs:* Royal Ocean Racing; Royal Burnham Yacht.

DUKE, Rt. Rev. Michael Geoffrey H.; *see* Hare Duke.

DUKE, Neville Frederick, DSO 1943; OBE 1953; DFC and Two Bars, 1942, 1943, 1944; AFC 1948; MC (Czech) 1946; Managing Director, Duke Aviation; Technical Adviser and Consultant Test Pilot; *b* 11 Jan. 1922; *s* of Frederick and Jane Duke, Tonbridge, Kent; *m* 1947, Gwendoline Dorothy Fellows. *Educ:* Convent of St Mary and Judds Sch., Tonbridge, Kent. Joined Royal Air Force (cadet), 1940, training period, 1940; 92 Fighter Sqdn, Biggin Hill, 1941; Desert Air Force: 112 Fighter Sqdn, Western Desert, 1941-42, 92 Fighter Sqdn, Western Desert, 1943, Chief Flying Instructor, 73 Operational Training Unit, Egypt, 1943-44, Commanding 145 Sqdn Italy (Fighter), 1944, 28 enemy aircraft destroyed. Hawker Aircraft Ltd test flying, 1945; Empire Test Pilots Sch., 1946; RAF high speed flight, 1946 (world speed record); test flying Aeroplane and Armament Experimental Estab., Boscombe Down, 1947-48; resigned from RAF as Sqdn Leader, 1948; test flying Hawker Aircraft Ltd, 1948; Commanding 615 (County of Surrey) Sqdn, Royal Auxiliary Air Force, Biggin Hill, 1950; Chief Test Pilot, Hawker Aircraft Ltd, 1951-56 (Asst Chief, 1948-51). FRSA 1970; ARAeS 1948. World records: London-Rome, 1949; London-Karachi, 1949; London-Cairo, 1950. World Speed Record, Sept. 1953. Closed Circuit World Speed Record, 1953. Gold Medal Royal Danish Aero Club, 1953; Gold Medal, Royal Aero Club, 1954; two De la Vaux Medals, FAI, 1954; Segrave Trophy, 1954; Queen's Commendation, 1955. Member: RAF Escaping Soc.; United Service & Royal Aero Club (Associate); Royal Aeronautical Soc. FRSA. *Publications:* Sound Barrier, 1953; Test Pilot, 1953; Book of Flying, 1954; Book of Flight, 1958; The Crowded Sky (anthology), 1959. *Recreations:* sporting flying, yachting. *Address:* 23 Needles Point, Milford-on-Sea, Hants. *Clubs:* Royal Air Force; Royal Cruising, Royal Naval Sailing, Royal Lymington Yacht.

DUKE, Robin Antony Hare, CVO 1975; CBE 1970 (OBE 1961); *b* 21 March 1916; *s* of late Reginald Franklyn Hare Duke, CBE, and Diana (*née* Woodforde); *m* 1945, Yvonne, *d* of late R. W. O. Le Bas, OBE; four *s* one *d*. *Educ:* Lancing Coll.; Brasenose Coll., Oxford (MA). Royal Artillery,

1939–46 (staff, ME, Italy, Greece, 1942–45; Political Adviser's Office, Athens, 1945–46). Joined British Council, 1947; Budapest, 1948–50; Dir, British Inst., Salonika, 1950–51; Athens, 1951–52; Dep. Dir, Visitors Dept, 1952–55; Representative, Chile, 1955–61; Dep. Controller, Books, Arts and Science Div., 1961–66; Controller, 1966–67; Rep., Japan, 1967–77, retd. Order of Sacred Treasure (Japan), 3rd Cl., 1975. *Publications:* introductions to Pillow Book of Sei Shonagon, 1979; The English Governess at the Court of Siam, 1980. *Recreations:* gardening, travel, theatre. *Address:* The Red House, Cavendish, Sudbury, Suffolk CO10 8BH. *T:* Glemsford 280058.

DUKES, Justin Paul; Managing Director, Channel Four Television Company Ltd, since 1981; *b* 19 Sept. 1941; *s* of John Alexander Dukes and Agnes Dukes; two *s* one *d. Educ:* King's Coll., Univ. of Durham. Dir, Financial Times Ltd, 1975–81; Chairman: Financial Times (Europe) Ltd and Fintel Ltd, 1978–81; C. S. & P. International Inc., NY, 1980–. Pres., Inst. of Information Scientists, 1982–83; Member: Council, Foundn for Management Educn, 1979–; Dept of Industry Steering Gp on Inf. Technology 1982, 1982. *Recreations:* changing institutions, walking. *Address:* c/o Channel Four Television Co. Ltd, 60 Charlotte Street, W1P 2AX.

DULBECCO, Dr Renato; Distinguished Research Professor, since 1977, Senior Clayton Foundation Investigator, since 1979, The Salk Institute for Biological Studies; *b* 22 Feb. 1914; *s* of late Leonardo Dulbecco and late Maria Virdia; *m* 1963, Maureen R. Muir Dulbecco; one *s* two *d. Educ:* Univ. of Turin Medical Sch. (MD). Assistente, Univ. of Turin: Inst. Pathology, 1940–46; Anatomical Inst., 1946–47; Res. Assoc., Indiana Univ., 1947–49; Sen. Res. Fellow, 1949–52, Assoc. Prof., 1952–54, Prof. 1954–63, California Inst. Technology; Vis. Prof., Rockefeller Inst., 1962; Royal Soc. Vis. Prof. at Univ. of Glasgow, 1963–64; Resident Fellow, Salk Inst., Calif, 1963–72, Fellow, 1972–77; Imperial Cancer Research Fund: Asst Dir of Res., 1972–74; Dep. Dir of Res., 1974–77; Prof. of Pathology and Medicine, Univ. of Calif San Diego Med. Sch., 1977–81. MNAS; Member: Fedn of Amer. Scientists; Amer. Assoc. for Cancer Research; Amer. Acad. of Arts and Scis; Internat. Physicians for Prevention of Nuclear War, Inc.; Chm., Internat. Assoc. for Breast Cancer Res.; Pres., Amer.-Ital. Foundn for Cancer Res. Trustee, La Jolla Country Day School. Foreign Member: Academia dei Lincei, 1969; Royal Society, 1974; Hon. Mem., Accademia Ligure di Scienze a Lettere. (Jtly) Nobel Prize for Medicine, 1975. Hon. DSc Yale, 1968; Hon. LLD Glasgow, 1970; *hc* Dr Med., Vrije Universiteit Brussel, Brussels, 1978. Numerous prizes and awards. *Publications:* (jtly) Microbiology, 1967; numerous in sci. jls. *Recreation:* music. *Address:* The Salk Institute, PO Box 85800, San Diego, Calif 92138, USA. *Club:* Athenæum.

DULVERTON, 2nd Baron, *cr* 1929, of Batsford; **Frederick Anthony Hamilton Wills,** CBE 1974; TD; DL; Bt 1897; MA Oxon; *b* 19 Dec. 1915; *s* of 1st Baron Dulverton, OBE, and Victoria May, OBE (*d* 1968), 3rd *d* of Rear-Adm. Sir Edward Chichester, 9th Bt, CB, CMG; *S* father, 1956; *m* 1st, 1939, Judith Betty (marr. diss., 1960), *e d* of late Lieut-Col Hon. Ian Leslie Melville, TD; two *s* two *d* ; 2nd, 1962, Ruth Violet, *o d* of Sir Walter Farquhar, 5th Bt. *Educ:* Eton; Magdalen Coll., Oxford (MA). Commissioned Lovat Scouts (TA), 1935; Major, 1943. President: Timber Growers' Orgn Ltd, 1976–78; Bath and West and Southern Counties Agric. Soc., 1973; British Deer Soc., 1973; Three Counties Agric. Soc., 1975; Gloucestershire Trust for Nature Conservation; Member, Red Deer Commn; Chairman: Forestry Cttee of GB, 1978–80; Dulverton Trust; Trustee: Wildfowl Trust; World Wildlife Fund (UK). Joint Master: N Cotswold Foxhounds, 1950–56; Heythrop Foxhounds, 1967–70. DL Gloucester, 1979. *Heir: s* Hon. (Gilbert) Michael Hamilton Wills [*b* 2 May 1944; *m* 1980, Rosalind van der Velde-Oliver; one *d*]. *Address:* Batsford Park, Moreton-in-Marsh, Glos. *T:* 50303; Fassfern, Kinlocheil, Fort William, Inverness-shire. *T:* Kinlocheil 232. *Club:* Boodle's.

DULY, Surgeon Rear-Adm. (D) Philip Reginald John, CB 1982; OBE 1971; QHDS 1978; Director of Naval Dental Services, since 1980; *b* 3 April 1925; *s* of Reginald and Minnie Duly; *m* 1948, Mary Walker Smith; two *s* one *d. Educ:* The London Hospital. LDSRCS 1947. Joined Royal Navy, Surgeon Lieut(D), 1948; Officer in Charge, Dental Training, 1965–70; Asst to Director of Naval Dental Services, 1970–72; Director of Dental Trng and Research, 1972–76; Comd Dental Surgeon: to Flag Officer Naval Air Comd, 1976–77; to C-in-C Naval Home Comd, 1977–80. Chairman of Examiners, General Dental Council Central Examining Board for Dental Hygienists, 1977–80. FRSM. *Recreation:* music, incl. church organ playing. *Address:* 13 The Avenue, Alverstoke, Gosport, Hants PO12 2JS. *T:* Gosport 80532; 1 Burton Lodge, Portinscale Road, Putney SW15 2HT. *T:* 01-870 2120. *Club:* Army and Navy.

DULY, Sidney John, MA; Consultant on the carriage of goods by sea; *b* London, 30 Oct. 1891; *s* of Henry Charles Duly; *m* 1916, Florence, *d* of William George Smith. *Educ:* St Olave's Gram. Sch.; Corpus Christi Coll., Cambridge; Berlin Univ. Till 1941 Head of the Dept for the Scientific Study of Commercial Products, City of London Coll. Visited Pacific Coast of N America for Furness Withy, to find cause of rusting of canned goods on voyage home, 1926; further voyages of investigation in 1927, 1929, 1930, 1932, 1933, 1934, 1935, 1936 and 1937. Mem., Shaef OKL Party to take surrender of and interrogate German Air Force Gen. Staff in Berchtesgaden and Chesham. A Governor, City of London College, 1950–70. Dir, Cargocaire Ltd, 1946–60. *Address:* 34 Sheldon Court, Bath Road, Worthing, West Sussex.

du MAURIER, Dame Daphne, DBE 1969; **(Lady Browning);** writer; *b* 1907; 2nd *d* of late Sir Gerald du Maurier; *m* 1932, Lieut-Gen. Sir Frederick A. M. Browning, GCVO, KBE, CB, DSO (*d* 1965); one *s* two *d. Educ:* privately; in Paris. Began writing short stories and articles in 1928; first novel appeared 1931. *Publications:* The Loving Spirit, 1931; I'll Never Be Young Again, 1932; The Progress of Julius, 1933; Gerald, a Portrait, 1934; Jamaica Inn, 1936; The du Mauriers, 1937; Rebecca, 1938; Frenchman's Creek, 1941; Hungry Hill, 1943; The King's General, 1946; The Parasites, 1949; My Cousin Rachel, 1951; The Apple Tree, 1952; Mary Anne, 1954; The Scapegoat, 1957; The Breaking Point, 1959; The Infernal World of Branwell Brontë, 1960; Castle Dor (continuation of MS left by late Sir Arthur Quiller-Couch (Q)), 1962; The Glassblowers, 1963; The Flight of the Falcon, 1965; Vanishing Cornwall, 1967; The House on the Strand, 1969; Not After Midnight, 1971; Rule Britannia, 1972; Golden Lads: a study of Anthony Bacon, Francis and their Friends, 1975; The Winding Stair: Francis Bacon, his Rise and Fall, 1976; The Rendezvous and other stories, 1980; The Rebecca Notebook and Other Memories, 1981; *autobiography:* Growing Pains, 1977; *drama:* The Years Between, 1945; September Tide, 1948; *edited:* The Young George du Maurier, 1951. *Recreations:* walking and swimming. *Address:* Kilmarth, Par, Cornwall.
See also Viscount Montgomery of Alamein.

DUMBELL, Dr Keith Rodney; Senior Specialist in Microbiology, Medical School, University of Cape Town, since 1982; *b* 2 Oct. 1922; *s* of late Stanley Dumbell and Dorothy Ellen (*née* Hewitt); *m* 1st, 1950, Brenda Margaret (*née* Heathcote) (*d* 1971); two *d* ; 2nd, 1972, Susan (*née* Herd); two *s. Educ:* Wirral Gram. Sch.; University of Liverpool, MB, ChB 1944; MD (Liverpool), 1950. FRCPath 1975. Asst Lecturer, Dept of Bacteriology, University of Liverpool, 1945–47; Mem. of Scientific Staff, MRC, 1947–50; Junior Pathologist, RAF, 1950–52; Asst in Pathology and Microbiology, Rockefeller Inst. for Medical Research (Dr Peyton Rous' laboratory), 1952–53; Lecturer in Bacteriology, University of Liverpool, 1952–58; Senior Lecturer, 1958–64; Prof. of Virology, Univ. of London at St Mary's Hosp. Med. Sch., 1964–81. *Publications:* articles in various medical and scientific journals. *Address:* Department of Medical Microbiology, Medical School, Observatory, Cape, 7925, South Africa.

DUMFRIES, Earl of; John Colum Crichton-Stuart; *b* 26 April 1958; *s* and heir of 6th Marquess of Bute, *qv. Address:* Mount Stuart, Rothesay, Isle of Bute. *T:* Rothesay 2730.

DUMMETT, (Agnes Margaret) Ann; Research Worker, Joint Council for the Welfare of Immigrants, since 1978; *b* 4 Sept. 1930; *d* of Arthur William Chesney and Kitty Mary Chesney; *m* 1951, Michael Anthony Eardley Dummett, *qv* ; three *s* two *d* (and one *s* one *d* decd). *Educ:* Guildhouse Sch., Pimlico; Ware Grammar Sch. for Girls; Somerville Coll., Oxford (MA). Pres., Oxford Univ. Liberal Club, 1949. Community Relations Officer, Oxford, 1966–69; teaching in further education, 1969–71; Research Worker: Inst. of Race Relations, 1971–73; Runnymede Trust, 1975, 1977. *Publications:* A Portrait of English Racism, 1973; Citizenship and Nationality, 1976; A New Immigration Policy, 1978; chapters in: Justice First (with Michael Dummett), 1969; Colloque de la Société Française pour le Droit International, 1979; Moral Philosophy, 1979; numerous articles and pamphlets. *Recreations:* walking about cities, theatregoing, popular music. *Address:* 54 Park Town, Oxford OX2 6SJ. *T:* Oxford 58698. *Club:* Royal Commonwealth Society.

DUMMETT, George Anthony, FEng, FIChemE; Chairman, Council of Engineering Institutions, 1976–77 (Vice-Chairman, 1975); *b* 13 Oct. 1907; *s* of George Herbert Dummett and Gertrude (*née* Higgins); *m* 1st, 1931, Peggy Schaeffer; 2nd, 1939, Ursula Margarete Schubert; two *s* one *d. Educ:* Rugby Sch.; Birmingham Univ.; Pembroke Coll., Cambridge. MA. Research in phys. chem., Cambridge Univ., 1930–32; Research Asst, Thorncliffe Coal Distillation Ltd, 1932–35; APV Co. Ltd (then Aluminium Plant and Vessel Co. Ltd): Technical Res. Asst, 1935; Laboratory Man., 1943; Chem. Engrg Dept Man., 1948; Scientific Man., 1949; Res. Dir, 1956; Dep. Man. Dir, 1965–72; Dir, APV (Holdings) Ltd, 1962–72; Dep. Chm., APV Internat., 1965–72; Dir, Diamond Power Specialty Ltd, 1958–. Chm., Res. Cttee, FBI, 1958–65; Pres., IChemE, 1968–69, Hon. Fellow, 1981. Fellow, Fellowship of Engineering, 1977. Chm., European Fedn Chemical Engrng, 1977–78. Hon. Member: Soc. de Chimie Ind., 1969; Dechema, 1976. *Publications:* From Little Acorns: a history of the APV company, 1981; numerous papers on chemical and biochemical engrg, metallurgy, etc. *Recreations:* music, mountaineering, gardening, stamp collecting. *Address:* Gowans, Possingworth Close, Cross-in-Hand, Heathfield, Sussex TN21 0TL. *T:* Heathfield 2085. *Clubs:* Alpine, Climbers.
See also M. A. E. Dummett.

DUMMETT, Michael Anthony Eardley, FBA 1968; Wykeham Professor of Logic in the University of Oxford, and Fellow of New College, Oxford, since 1979; *b* 27 June 1925; *s* of George Herbert Dummett and Iris Dummett (*née* Eardley-Wilmot); *m* 1951, Ann Chesney (see A. M. A. Dummett); three *s* two *d* (one *s* one *d* decd). *Educ:* Sandroyd Sch.; Winchester Coll. (1st Schol.); Christ Church, Oxford. Major hist. schol. (Ch. Ch.), 1942. Served in Army, 1943–47: in RA and Intell. Corps (India, 1945, Malaya, 1946–47, Sgt). Ch. Ch., Oxford, 1947–50, First Class Hons, PPE, 1950. Asst Lectr in Philosophy, Birmingham Univ., 1950–51; Commonwealth Fund Fellow, Univ. of California, Berkeley, 1955–56; Reader in the Philosophy of Mathematics,

Univ. of Oxford, 1962-74; All Souls College, Oxford: Fellow, 1950-79, Senior Research Fellow, 1974-79; Sub-Warden, 1974-76; Emeritus Fellow, 1980. Vis. Lectr, Univ. of Ghana, 1958; Vis. Professor: Stanford Univ., several occasions, 1960-66; Univ. of Minnesota, 1968; Princeton Univ., 1970; Rockefeller Univ., 1973; William James Lectr in Philosophy, Harvard Univ., 1976; Alex. von Humboldt-Stiftung vis. res. fellow, 1981. Founder Mem., Oxford Cttee for Racial Integration, 1965 (Chm., Jan.-May 1966); Member: Exec. Cttee, Campaign Against Racial Discrimination, 1966-67; Legal and Civil Affairs Panel, Nat. Cttee for Commonwealth Immigrants, 1966-68; Chairman: Jt Council for the Welfare of Immigrants, 1970-71 (Vice-Chm., 1967-69, 1973-75); unofficial cttee of enquiry into events in Southall 23 April 1979, 1979-80; shadow board, Barclays Bank, 1981-82. *Publications:* Frege: philosophy of language, 1973, 2nd edn 1981; The Justification of Deduction, 1973; Elements of Intuitionism, 1977; Truth and other Enigmas, 1978; Immigration: where the debate goes wrong, 1978; Catholicism and the World Order, 1979; The Game of Tarot, 1980; Twelve Tarot Games, 1980; The Interpretation of Frege's Philosophy, 1981; contrib. entry on Frege, to Encyclopedia of Philosophy (ed P. Edwards), 1967; (with Ann Dummett) chapter on Rôle of the Government, in Justice First (ed L. Donnelly), 1969; preface to R. C. Zaehner, The City Within the Heart, 1980; articles in: Aristotelian Soc. Proceedings, Philos. Review, Synthese, Inquiry, Econometrica, Jl of Symbolic Logic, Zeitschrift für mathematische Logik, Dublin Review, New Blackfriars, Clergy Review, Jl of Warburg and Courtauld Insts, Jl of Playing-Card Soc. *Recreations:* listening to the blues, investigating the history of card games, reading science fiction. *Address:* 54 Park Town, Oxford. *T:* Oxford 58698. *Club:* Royal Commonwealth Society.
See also G. A. Dummett.

DUMPER, Rt. Rev. Anthony Charles; *see* Dudley, Bishop Suffragan of.

DUNALLEY, 6th Baron *cr* 1800; **Henry Desmond Graham Prittie;** Lt-Col (retired) late The Rifle Brigade; *b* 14 Oct. 1912; *er s* of 5th Baron Dunalley, DSO, and Beatrix Evelyn (*d* 1967), *e d* of late James N. Graham of Carfin, Lanarkshire; *S* father, 1948; *m* 1947, Philippa, *o d* of late Hon. Philip Cary; two *s* one *d. Educ:* Stowe; RMC, Sandhurst. Retd 1953. *Recreation:* fishing. *Heir: s* Hon. Henry Francis Cornelius Prittie [*b* 30 May 1948; *m* 1978, Sally Louise, *er d* of Ronald Vere; one *d*]. *Address:* Fox Cottage, Middle Barton, Oxfordshire. *Club:* Kildare Street and University (Dublin); Christchurch (NZ) (Hon. Mem.).
See also Hon. T. C. F. Prittie.

DUNBAR, Alexander Arbuthnott; farmer; *b* 14 March 1929; *yr s* of Sir Edward Dunbar, 9th Bt; *m* 1965, Elizabeth Susannah, *d* of Rev. Denzil Wright; one *s* one *d. Educ:* Wellington Coll., Berks; Pembroke Coll., Cambridge (MA); Edinburgh Sch. of Agriculture, 1980-81. Mil. Service, Lieut QO Cameron Highlanders, 1947-49. Called to the Bar, Inner Temple, 1953. Joined ICI, 1954: Asst Sec., Wilton Works, 1959-63. Joined North Eastern Assoc. for the Arts, 1963, Sec. 1964, Dir 1967; Director: Northern Arts Assoc., 1967-69; UK and British Commonwealth Branch, Calouste Gulbenkian Foundn, 1970-71; Scottish Arts Council, 1971-80. *Publications:* contribs to various jls. *Recreations:* art, theatre, ski-ing, running. *Address:* Pitgaveny, Elgin, Moray.

DUNBAR of Northfield, Sir Archibald (Ranulph), 11th Bt *cr* 1700; *b* 8 Aug. 1927; *er s* of Sir (Archibald) Edward Dunbar, 9th Bt (by some reckonings 10th Bt) and Olivia Douglas Sinclair (*d* 1964), *d* of Maj.-Gen. Sir Edward May, KCB, CMG; *S* father, 1969; *m* 1974, Amelia Millar Sommerville, *d* of Horace Davidson; one *s* two *d. Educ:* Wellington Coll.; Pembroke Coll., Cambridge; Imperial Coll. of Tropical Agriculture, Trinidad. Mil. Service, 2nd Lt, Cameron (att. Gordon) Highlanders, 1945-48. Entered Colonial Agricultural Service, Uganda, as Agricultural Officer, 1953; retired, 1970. *Publications:* A History of Bunyoro-Kitara, 1965; Omukama Chwa II Kabarega, 1965; The Annual Crops of Uganda, 1969; various articles in Uganda Jl. *Recreations:* cross-country running, model railway. *Heir: s* Edward Horace Dunbar, Younger of Northfield, *b* 18 March 1977. *Address:* The Old Manse, Duffus, Elgin, Scotland. *T:* Hopeman 830270. *Club:* New (Edinburgh).

DUNBAR, Charles, CB 1964; Director, Fighting Vehicles Research and Development Establishment, Ministry of Defence, 1960-67; *b* 12 Jan. 1907; *s* of John Dunbar, Barrow-in-Furness, Lancs; *m* 1933, Mary Alice (*née* Clarke), Barnes, SW; two *d. Educ:* Grammar Sch., Barrow-in-Furness; Manchester Univ. (MSc). National Physical Laboratory, Dept of Scientific and Industrial Research, 1929-43; Tank Armament Research Establishment, Min. of Supply, 1943-47; Fighting Vehicles Research and Development Establishments, 1947-67, retired. *Publications:* contribs to learned journals. *Recreations:* golf, fishing. *Address:* Edenwood, 186 Upper Chobham Road, Camberley, Surrey. *T:* Camberley 26592.
See also Peter Graham.

DUNBAR, Sir David H.; *see* Hope-Dunbar.

DUNBAR of Durn, Sir Drummond Cospatrick Ninian, 9th Bt, *cr* 1697; MC 1943; Major Black Watch, retired; *b* 9 May 1917; *o s* of Sir George Alexander Drummond Dunbar, 8th Bt and Sophie Kathleen (*d* 1936), *d* of late J. Benson Kennedy; *S* father, 1949; *m* 1957, Sheila Barbara Mary, *d* of John B. de Fonblanque, London; one *s. Educ:* Radley Coll.; Worcester Coll.,

Oxford. BA 1938. Served War of 1939-45, Middle East, Sicily, Normandy (wounded twice, MC). Retired pay, 1958. *Heir: s* Robert Drummond Cospatrick Dunbar, Younger of Durn [*b* 17 June 1958. *Educ:* Harrow; Christ Church, Oxford; BA 1979]. *Address:* Town Hill, Westmount, Jersey, Channel Islands. *Club:* Naval and Military.

DUNBAR of Mochrum, Sir Jean Ivor, 13th Bt *cr* 1694; *b* 4 April 1918; *s* of Sir Adrian Ivor Dunbar of Mochrum, 12th Bt and Emma Marie (*d* 1925), *d* of Jean Wittevrongel; *S* father, 1977; *m* 1944, Rose Jeanne (marr. diss. 1979), *d* of Henry William Hertsch; two *s* one *d.* Formerly Sergeant, Mountain Engineers, US Army. *Recreation:* horsemanship. *Heir: s* Captain James Michael Dunbar, DDS, US Air Force [*b* 17 Jan. 1950; *m* 1978, Margaret Jacobs].

DUNBAR, John Greenwell; Secretary, Royal Commission on the Ancient and Historical Monuments of Scotland, since 1978; *b* 1 March 1930; *o s* of John Dunbar and Marie Alton; *m* 1974, Elizabeth Mill Blyth. *Educ:* University College Sch., London; Balliol Coll., Oxford (MA). FSA, FSAScot. Joined staff of Royal Commission on the Ancient and Historical Monuments of Scotland, 1953; Mem., Ancient Monuments Board for Scotland, 1978. *Publications:* The Historic Architecture of Scotland, 1966, revd edn 1978; numerous articles in archaeological jls, etc. *Recreations:* reading, gardening. *Address:* Patie's Mill, Carlops, By Penicuik, Midlothian. *T:* West Linton 250. *Club:* New (Edinburgh).

DUNBAR of Hempriggs, Dame Maureen Daisy Helen, (Lady Dunbar of Hempriggs), Btss (8th in line) *cr* 1706 (NS); *b* 19 Aug. 1906; *d* of Courtenay Edward Moore and Janie King Moore (*née* Askins); *m* 1940, Leonard James Blake (assumed the name of Dunbar, in lieu of Blake, on claiming succession to the Hempriggs baronetcy after death of kinsman, Sir George Cospatrick Duff-Sutherland-Dunbar, 7th Bt, in 1963; claim established and title recognised by Lyon Court, 1965); one *s* one *d. Educ:* Headington Sch.; Royal Coll. of Music. LRAM 1928. Music teacher at: Monmouth Sch. for Girls, 1930-33; Oxford High Sch., 1935-40; Malvern Coll., 1957-68. *Heir:* (to mother's Btcy) *s* Richard Francis Dunbar of Hempriggs, younger [*b* 8 Jan. 1945 (assumed the name of Dunbar, 1965); *m* 1969, Elizabeth Margaret Jane Lister; two *d*]. *Address:* 51 Gloucester Street, Winchcombe, Cheltenham, Glos. *T:* Winchcombe 602 122; Ackergill Tower, Wick, Caithness. *T:* Wick 2812.

DUNBAR-NASMITH, Rear-Adm. David Arthur, CB 1969; DSC 1942; retired 1972; Member: Highlands and Islands Development Board, since 1972 (Deputy Chairman, 1972-81; Chairman, 1981-82); British Waterways Board, since 1980; North of Scotland Hydro-Electric Board, since 1982; Vice-Lord-Lieutenant, Morayshire, since 1980; *b* 21 Feb. 1921; *e s* of late Admiral Sir Martin Dunbar-Nasmith, VC, KCB, KCMG, DL, and of late Justina Dunbar-Nasmith, CBE, DStJ; *m* 1951, Elizabeth Bowlby; two *s* two *d. Educ:* Lockers Park; RNC, Dartmouth. To sea as Midshipman, 1939. War Service, Atlantic and Mediterranean, in HM Ships Barham, Rodney, Kelvin and Petard. In comd: HM Ships Haydon 1943, Peacock 1945-46, Moon 1946, Rowena 1946-48, Enard Bay 1951, Alert 1954-56, Berwick, and 5th Frigate Squadron, 1961-63; Commodore, Amphibious Forces, 1966-67. RN and Joint Service Staff Colls, 1948-49; Staff of Flag Officer 1st Cruiser Squadron, 1949-51; NATO HQ, SACLANT, 1952-54 and SACEUR, 1958-60; Dir of Defence Plans, Min. of Defence, 1963-65; Naval Secretary, 1967-70; Flag Officer, Scotland and N Ireland, 1970-72. Comdr 1951; Capt. 1958; Rear-Adm. 1967. Mem., Countryside Commn for Scotland, 1972-76. Mem. Queen's Body Guard for Scotland (Royal Company of Archers), 1974-; Gentleman Usher of the Green Rod to the Order of the Thistle, 1979-. DL Moray, 1974. *Recreations:* sailing, ski-ing and shooting. *Address:* Glen of Rothes, Rothes, Moray. *T:* Rothes 216. *Clubs:* New (Edinburgh); Royal Ocean Racing.
See also J. D. Dunbar-Nasmith.

DUNBAR-NASMITH, Prof. James Duncan, CBE 1976; RIBA; PPRIAS; FRSA, FRSE; Professor and Head of Department of Architecture, Heriot-Watt University and Edinburgh College of Art, since 1978; Partner, The Law & Dunbar-Nasmith Partnership, architects, Edinburgh and Forres (founded 1957); *b* 15 March 1927; *y s* of late Adm. Sir Martin Dunbar-Nasmith, VC, KCB, KCMG, DL and of late Justina Dunbar-Nasmith, CBE, DStJ. *Educ:* Lockers Park; Winchester. Trinity Coll., Cambridge (BA); Edinburgh Coll. of Art (DA). ARIBA 1954. Lieut, Scots Guards, 1945-48. President: Royal Incorporation of Architects in Scotland, 1971-73; Edinburgh Architectural Assoc., 1967-69. Member: Council, RIBA, 1967-73 (a Vice-Pres., 1972-73; Chm., Bd of Educn, 1972-73); Council, ARCUK, 1976- (Vice-Chm., Bd of Educn, 1977); Royal Commn on Ancient and Historical Monuments of Scotland, 1972-; Ancient Monuments Bd for Scotland, 1969- (interim Chm., 1972-73); Historic Buildings Council for Scotland, 1966-; Dep. Chm., Edinburgh Internat. Festival; Trustee, Scottish Civic Trust, 1971-; Chm., Scottish Exec. Cttee of European Architectural Heritage Year. *Recreations:* music, theatre, ski-ing, sailing. *Address:* 16 Dublin Street, Edinburgh EH1 3RE. *T:* 031-556 8631. *Clubs:* Royal Ocean Racing; New (Edinburgh).
See also D. A. Dunbar-Nasmith.

DUNBOYNE, 28th Baron by Summons, 18th Baron by Patent; **Patrick Theobald Tower Butler; His Honour Judge The Lord Dunboyne;** a Circuit Judge, since 1972; *b* 27 Jan. 1917; *e s* of 27th Baron Dunboyne and Dora Isolde Butler (*d* 1977), *e d* of Comdr F. F. Tower; *S* father, 1945; *m* 1950, Anne Marie, *d* of late Sir Victor Mallet; one *s* three *d. Educ:* Winchester;

Trinity Coll., Cambridge (MA). Pres. of Cambridge Union. Lieut Irish Guards (Suppl. Res.); served European War, 1939-44 (prisoner, then repatriated); Foreign Office, 1945-46. Barrister-at-Law, Middle Temple (Harmsworth Scholar), Inner Temple, South-Eastern Circuit, King's Inns, Dublin. In practice 1949-71. Recorder of Hastings, 1961-71; Dep. Chm., Quarter Sessions: Mddx, 1963-65; Kent, 1963-71; Inner London 1971-72. Commissary Gen., Diocese of Canterbury, 1959-71. Pres., 1971-, Fellow 1982, Irish Genealogical Res. Soc. *Publications:* The Trial of J. G. Haigh, 1953; (with others) Cambridge Union, 1815-1939, 1953; Butler Family History, 1966. *Recreations:* rowing, lawn tennis, chess. *Heir: s* Hon. John Fitzwalter Butler [*b* 31 July 1951; *m* 1975, Diana Caroline, *yr d* of Sir Michael Williams, *qv*; two *d*]. *Address:* 36 Ormonde Gate, SW3 4HA. *T:* 01-352 1837. *Clubs:* Irish; International Lawn Tennis of Great Britain (Pres.); Forty Five Lawn Tennis (Pres.); All England Lawn Tennis (Wimbledon); Pitt, Union (Cambridge).

DUNCAN, Prof. Archibald Alexander McBeth; Professor of Scottish History and Literature, Glasgow University, since 1962; *b* 17 Oct. 1926; *s* of Charles George Duncan and Christina Helen McBeth; *m* 1954, Ann Hayes Sawyer, *d* of W. E. H. Sawyer, Oxford; two *s* one *d. Educ:* George Heriot's Sch.; Edinburgh Univ.; Balliol Coll., Oxford. Lecturer in History, Queen's Univ., Belfast, 1951-53; Lecturer in History, Edinburgh Univ., 1953-61; Leverhulme Research Fellow, 1961-62. Clerk of Senate, Glasgow Univ., 1978-. Mem. Royal Commn on the Ancient and Historical Monuments of Scotland, 1969-. *Publications:* Scotland: The Making of the Kingdom, 1975; (ed and revised) W. Croft Dickinson's Scotland from the Earliest Times to 1603, 3rd edn 1977. *Address:* 17 Campbell Drive, Bearsden, Glasgow G61 4NF.

DUNCAN, Prof. Archibald Sutherland, DSC 1943; FRCSE, FRCPE, FRCOG; Executive Dean of the Faculty of Medicine and Professor of Medical Education, Edinburgh University, 1966-76; *b* 17 July 1914; *y s* of late Rev. H. C. Duncan, K-i-H, DD and late Rose Elsie Edwards; *m* 1939, Barbara, *d* of late John Gibson Holliday, JP, Penrith, Cumberland. *Educ:* Merchiston Castle Sch.; Edinburgh Univ. MB, ChB Edinburgh, 1936. Resident hosp. appts in Edinburgh and London, 1936-41. Served RNVR Surg. Lieut-Comdr (surg. specialist), 1941-45 (DSC). Temp. Cons. in Obst. and Gynæc., Inverness, 1946; Lectr in Univ. and part-time Cons. Obstetr and Gynæcol., Aberdeen, 1946-50; Sen. Lectr, University of Edinburgh and Obstetr. and Gynæcol. to Western Gen. Hosp., Edinburgh 1950-53; Prof. of Obstetrics and Gynæcology in the Welsh National Sch. of Medicine, Univ. of Wales, 1953-66; Cons. Obstetrician and Gynæcologist, United Cardiff Hosps, 1953-66; Advisor in Obstetrics and Gynæcology to Welsh Hosp. Board, 1953-66. Member: Clin. Res. Bd of MRC, 1965-69; Council, RCSE, 1968-73; GMC, 1974-78; Lothian Health Bd, 1977-. Chm., Scottish Council on Disability, 1977-80. Hon. Pres., Brit. Med. Students Assoc., 1965-66. Mem. Court, Edinburgh Univ., 1979-. Mem., James IV Assoc. of Surgeons. Associate Editor, British Jl of Medical Education, 1971-75; Consulting Editor, Jl of Medical Ethics, 1975-81. *Publications:* (ed jtly) Dictionary of Medical Ethics, 2nd edn 1981; contribs on scientific and allied subjects in various med. jls. *Recreations:* mountains, photography. *Address:* 1 Walker Street, Edinburgh EH3 7JY. *T:* 031-225 7657. *Club:* New (Edinburgh).

DUNCAN, Sir Arthur (Bryce), Kt 1961; Convener Dumfriesshire County Council, 1961-68, retired; *b* 27 Aug. 1909; 2nd *s* of J. B. Duncan, Newlands, Dumfries; *m* 1936, Isabel Mary Kennedy-Moffat; four *s* one *d. Educ:* Rugby; St John's Coll., Cambridge. Chm., The Nature Conservancy, 1953-61, retd. Chm. of Dirs, Crichton Royal Hospital Bd, 1958-72. DL, Dumfriesshire, 1967-69, Lord Lieutenant 1967-69. *Recreations:* ornithology, entomology and shooting. *Address:* Castlehill, Kirkmahoe, Dumfries DG1 1RD.

DUNCAN, Brian Arthur Cullum, CB 1972; CBE 1963 (MBE 1949); QC 1972; Judge Advocate General of the Forces, 1968-72; *b* 2 Feb. 1908; *yr s* of late Frank Hubert Duncan, LDS, RCS, and late Edith Jane Duncan (*née* Cullum); *m* 1934, Irene Flora Templeman, *o c* of late John Frederick Templeman and late Flora Edith Templeman; two *s* two *d. Educ:* Queens' Coll., Cambridge (MA). Called to the Bar, Lincoln's Inn, 1931. Practised South Eastern Circuit, Central Criminal Court, North London Sessions, and Herts and Essex Sessions. Commissioned RAF, April 1940; relinqd commn, 1950 (Wing Comdr). Joined JAG's Dept, 1945. Dep. Judge Advocate Gen. (Army and RAF): Middle East, 1950-53; Germany, 1954-57; Far East, 1959-62; Vice Judge Advocate Gen., 1967-68. *Recreations:* tennis, swimming. *Address:* Culverlands, Neville Park, Baltonsborough, Glastonbury, Som.

DUNCAN, David Francis; HM Diplomatic Service, retired; *b* 22 Feb. 1923; *s* of late Brig. William Edmondstone Duncan, CVO, DSO, MC, and of Mrs Magdalene Emily Duncan (*née* Renny-Tailyour). *Educ:* Eton; Trinity Coll., Cambridge. Served War, RA, 1941-46 (despatches). Entered Foreign (later Diplomatic) Service, 1949; Foreign Office 1949-52; Bogotá, 1952-54; UK Delegn to ECSC, Luxembourg, 1954-55; FO, 1955-58; Baghdad, 1958; Ankara, 1958-60; FO, 1960-62; Quito, 1962-65; Phnom Penh, 1965 (as Chargé d'Affaires); FO (later Foreign and Commonwealth Office), 1965-70; Islamabad, 1970-71; Counsellor, UK Delegn to Geneva Disarm. Conf., 1971-74; Ambassador to Nicaragua, 1974-76; retired 1976. *Recreations:* skiing, walking, photography, travel. *Address:* 8 Eaton Mews South, SW1. *T:* 01-235 7761. *Club:* Travellers'.

DUNCAN, Rev. Denis Macdonald, MA, BD; Director, Highgate Counselling Centre, since 1969; *b* 10 Jan. 1920; *s* of late Rev. Reginald Duncan, BD, BLitt and late Clarice Ethel (*née* Hodgkinson); *m* 1942, Henrietta Watson McKenzie (*née* Houston); one *s* one *d. Educ:* George Watson's Boys' Coll., Edinburgh; Edinburgh Univ.; New Coll., Edinburgh. Minister of: St Margaret's, Juniper Green, Edinburgh, 1943-49; Trinity Duke Street Parish Church, Glasgow, 1949-57; Founder-editor, Rally, 1956-67; Managing Editor, British Weekly, 1957-70 (Man. Dir, 1967-70); Man. Dir, DPS Publicity Services Ltd, 1967-74; broadcaster and scriptwriter, Scottish Television, 1963-68; concert promotion at Edinburgh Festival and elsewhere, 1966-; Concert series "Communication through the Arts" poetry/music anthologies (with Benita Kyle), 1970-. Associate Dir and Trng Supervisor, Westminster Pastoral Foundn, 1971-79; Chm., Internat. Cttee of World Assocs of Pastoral Care and Counselling, 1977-79. FIBA (FIICS) 1976. *Publications:* (ed) Through the Year with William Barclay, 1971; (ed) Through the Year with Cardinal Heenan, 1972; (ed) Daily Celebration, vol. 1, 1972, vol. 2, 1974; Marching Orders I, 1973; (ed) Every Day with William Barclay, 1973; (ed) Through the Year with J. B. Phillips, 1974; Marching On, 1974; Here is my Hand, 1977; Creative Silence, 1980; A Day at a Time, 1980; Love, the Word that Heals, 1981. *Recreations:* cricket, badminton. *Address:* 1 Cranbourne Road, N10 2BT. *T:* 01-883 1831. *Club:* Arts.

DUNCAN, George; Chairman, Lloyds and Scottish plc, since 1976 (Director since 1973); Director, Lloyds Bank, since 1982; *b* 9 Nov. 1933; *s* of William Duncan and Catherine Gray Murray; *m* 1965, Frauke Ulrike; one *d. Educ:* London Sch. of Economics (BSc(Econ)); Wharton Sch.; Univ. of Pennsylvania (MBA). Mem., Inst. of Chartered Accountants (FCA); CBIM. Chief Executive, Truman Hanbury Buxton and Co. Ltd, 1967-71; Chief Executive, Watney Mann Ltd, 1971-72; Vice-Chm., Internat. Distillers and Vintners Ltd, 1972. Chm., CBI Companies Cttee, 1980-; Mem., CBI President's Cttee, 1980-. Freeman, City of London, 1971. *Recreations:* opera, tennis, riding. *Address:* Fisher's Gate, Withyham, Hartfield, East Sussex. *T:* Hartfield 246.

DUNCAN, George Alexander; Fellow Emeritus of Trinity College, Dublin, since 1967; Pro-Chancellor of the University of Dublin, 1965-72; *b* 15 May 1902; *s* of Alexander Duncan and Elizabeth Linn; *m* 1932, Eileen Stone, MSc, *d* of William Henry Stone and Sarah Copeland; one *d. Educ:* Ballymena Academy; Campbell Coll., Belfast; Trinity Coll., Dublin; University of North Carolina. BA, LLB 1923, MA 1926; Research Fellow on the Laura Spelman Rockefeller Memorial Foundation, 1924-25; Prof. of Political Economy in the University of Dublin, 1934-67; Registrar of TCD, 1951-52, and Bursar, 1952-57. Leverhulme Research Fellow, 1950; Visiting Fellow, Princeton Univ., 1963-64. Mem. of IFS Commissions of Inquiry into Banking, Currency and Credit, 1934-38; Agriculture, 1939; Emigration and Population, 1948. Planning Officer (temp.) in Ministry of Production, London, 1943-45; Economic Adviser to British National Cttee of Internat. Chambers of Commerce, 1941-47. Vice-Pres., Royal Dublin Society; Life Mem., Mont Pelerin Soc. Formerly Member: Irish National Productivity Cttee; Council Irish Management Inst.; Exec. Bd, Dublin Economic Research Inst.; Internat. Inst. of Statistics. *Publications:* numerous papers in the economic periodicals. *Recreations:* travel, walking. *Address:* 7 Braemor Park, Churchtown, Dublin 14. *T:* Dublin 970442. *Club:* Kildare Street and University (Dublin).

DUNCAN, Dr George Douglas; Regional Medical Officer, East Anglian Regional Health Authority, since 1973; *s* of late George Forman Duncan and Mary Duncan (*née* Davidson); *m* 1949, Isobel (*née* Reid); two *s* one *d. Educ:* Robert Gordon's Coll., Aberdeen; Aberdeen Univ. MB, ChB 1948, DPH 1952, FFCM 1972. Various hosp. appts; Asst MOH Stirlingshire, Divisional MO Grangemouth, 1953-57; Asst Sen. MO, Leeds RHB, 1957-60; Dep. Sen. Admin. MO, Newcastle RHB, 1960-68; Sen. Admin. MO, East Anglian RHB, 1968-73. Vice-Pres., FCM RCP, 1979-. *Address:* Clare House, Witchford, Ely, Cambs. *T:* Ely 2776; East Anglian Regional Health Authority, Union Lane, Chesterton, Cambridge. *T:* Cambridge 61212.

DUNCAN, Sir James (Blair), Kt 1981; Chairman, since 1975, and Chief Executive, since 1970, Transport Development Group; *b* 24 Aug. 1927; *s* of John Duncan and late Emily MacFarlane Duncan; *m* 1974, Dr Betty Psaltis, San Francisco. *Educ:* Whitehill Sch., Glasgow. Qualified as Scottish Chartered Accountant. Joined Transport Development Group, 1953; Dir, 1960. Member: London Exec. Cttee, Scottish Council, 1976-; LTE (part-time), 1979-; Council, CBI, 1980-. FCIT (Pres., 1980-81; Spurrier Meml Lectr, 1972; Award of Merit, 1973; Herbert Crow Medal, 1978); CBIM; FRSA 1977. *Publications:* papers on transport matters. *Recreations:* travel, reading, walking, swimming, theatre. *Address:* 17 Kingston House South, Ennismore Gardens, SW7. *T:* 01-589 3545. *Club:* Caledonian.

DUNCAN, Prof. James Playford, ME Adelaide, DSc Manchester; Professor of Mechanical Engineering, University of British Columbia, since 1966; *b* 10 Nov. 1919; *s* of late Hugh Sinclair Duncan and Nellie Gladys Duncan; *m* 1942, Jean Marie Booth; three *s* one *d. Educ:* Scotch Coll., Adelaide; University of Adelaide, S Australia. Executive Engineer, Richards Industries Ltd, Keswick, S Australia, 1941-46; Senior Physics Master, Scotch Coll., Adelaide, 1946-47; Lecturer in Mechanical Engineering, University of Adelaide, 1948-49, Senior Lecturer, 1950-51 and 1953-54; Turbine Engineer, Metropolitan Vickers Electrical Co., Trafford Park, Manchester, 1952; Turner and Newall Research Fellow, University of Manchester, 1955; Lecturer in Mechanical Engineering, University of Manchester, 1956; Prof. of Mechanical Engineering, University of Sheffield, 1956-66. *Recreations:* sailing, flautist. *Address:* 25 Oceanview Road, PO Box 137, Lions Bay, BC V0N 2E0, Canada. *T:* (604) 921-7191.

DUNCAN, James Stuart, CMG 1946; Hon. Air Commodore; company director; *b* 1893; *m* 1936, Victoria Martinez Alonso, Cordoba, Spain; one *s* two *d. Educ:* Coll. Rollin, Paris. Joined Massey-Harris Ltd, Berlin, 1909; went to Canada, 1911. Served with UK Forces in 1914-18 War, rising to be Capt. and Adjutant of 180th Brigade 16th Irish Divisional Artillery. Apptd Gen. Manager Massey-Harris Co., 1936; Pres. 1941; Chm. and Pres. 1949 until his resignation in 1956. Apptd Actg Dep. Minister of Defence for Air, 1940, when he took over leadership of Brit. Commonwealth Air Trg Plan; declined invitation of Prime Minister, in summer 1940, to join Federal Cabinet as Minister of Air. Chm., Combined Agricl & Food Cttee of UNRRA, 1941-42; Mem. Nat. Res. Council, Ottawa, during War Years. Past Chm.: Toronto Bd of Trade, Toronto Community Chest, Canadian Council of Internat. Chambers of Commerce, Montreal; Hon. Pres., Toronto section, "Free Fighting French"; Chm. Dollar Sterling Trade Council, 1949-61. First Canadian chosen by Nat. Sales Exec. Organization as "Canadian Businessman of the Year," 1956; Chm., Nat. Conf. on Engrg, Sci. and Tech. Manpower, NB, 1956; organizer and Dep. Chm. Canadian Trade Mission to the UK, 1957. On accepting Chairmanship of Hydro-Electric Power Commn of Ont., Nov. 1956, resigned from bd of many Canadian cos incl. Argus Corp. Ltd, Canada Cement, Ltd, Canadian Bank of Commerce, Internat. Nickel of Canada, Ltd, Page-Hersey Tubes; resigned from Chmship Hydro-Electric Power Commn of Ont., 1961. Upon establishing residence in Bermuda, Aug. 1961, resigned from Gov., University Toronto; Chm., Dollar Sterling Trade Coun.; Chm., Australian-Canadian Assoc.; Dir, Industrial Foundn on Educn; Dir, Atomic Energy of Canada, Ltd; Chm., Royal Conservatory of Music Cttee. Hon. LLD, Dartmouth Coll., NH, USA, 1957. Chevalier, French Legion of Honour; Croix de Lorraine; King Haakon VII Cross of Liberation. *Publications:* Russia's Bid for World Supremacy, 1955; The Great Leap Forward, 1959; Russia Revisited, 1960; In The Shadow of the Red Star, 1962; A Businessman Looks At Red China, 1965; Not a One-Way Street (autobiography), 1971. *Address:* Somerset House, Paget, Bermuda. *Clubs:* York (Toronto); Mid Ocean, Royal Bermuda Yacht (Bermuda); River (New York); Sotogrande (Spain).

DUNCAN, John Spenser Ritchie, CMG 1967; MBE 1953; HM Diplomatic Service, retired; High Commissioner in the Bahamas, 1978-81; *b* 26 July 1921; *s* of late Rev. J. H. Duncan, DD; *m* 1950, Sheila Conacher, MB, ChB, DObstRCOG; one *d. Educ:* George Watson's Boys' Coll.; Glasgow Acad.; Dundee High Sch.; Edinburgh Univ. Entered Sudan Political Service, 1941. Served in HM Forces, 1941-43. Private Sec. to Governor-Gen. of the Sudan, 1954; Dep. Adviser to Governor-Gen. on Constitutional and External Affairs, 1955; appointed to Foreign (subseq. Diplomatic) Service, 1956; seconded to Joint Services Staff Coll., 1957; Political Agent, Doha, 1958; Dep. Dir-Gen., British Information Services, New York, 1959-63; Consul-Gen., Muscat, 1963-65; Head of Personnel Dept, Diplomatic Service, 1966-68; Minister, British High Commn, Canberra, 1969-71; High Comr, Zambia, 1971-74; Ambassador to Morocco, 1975-78. *Publications:* The Sudan: A Record of Achievement, 1952; The Sudan's Path to Independence, 1957. *Recreation:* golf. *Address:* 9 Blackford Road, Edinburgh EH9 2DT. *Club:* New (Edinburgh).
See also K. P. Duncan.

DUNCAN, Dr Kenneth Playfair, FRCP; FRCPE; Deputy Director-General, Health and Safety Executive, since 1982; *b* 27 Sept. 1924; *s* of late Dr J. H. Duncan, MA, BPhil, DD, and H. P. Duncan (*née* Ritchie); *m* 1950, Dr Gillian Crow, MB, ChB; four *d. Educ:* Kilmarnock Acad.; Glasgow Acad.; Dundee High Sch.; St Andrews Univ. BSc, MB, ChB; DIH. FFOM 1978. House Surg., Dundee Royal Infirmary, 1947; RAMC, 1948-50; Gen. Practice, Brighton, 1950-51; Area MO, British Rail, 1951-54; Chief Medical Officer: SW Gas Bd, 1954-58; UKAEA, 1958-69; Head of Health and Safety, BSC, 1969-75; Dir of Medical Services, HSE, 1975-82. External Examiner in Occupational Health, Univ. of Dundee, 1970-74; Examiner in Occupational Health, Soc. of Apothecaries, 1974-79. Vis. Prof., London Sch. of Hygiene and Tropical Medicine, 1977-82. Mem., MRC, 1975-; Mem., IHAC, 1960-74. Pres., Soc. of Occupational Medicine, 1970. *Publications:* contrib. medical and scientific jls on radiological protection and gen. occupational health topics. *Recreation:* gardening. *Address:* Westfield, Steeple Aston, Oxon OX5 3SD. *T:* Steeple Aston 40277.
See also J. S. R. Duncan.

DUNCAN, Malcolm McGregor, WS; Chief Executive, City of Edinburgh District Council, since 1980; *b* 23 Jan. 1922; *s* of Rev. Reginald Duncan, BD, BLitt, and Clarice Ethel (*née* Hodgkinson); *m* 1954, Winifred Petrie (*née* Greenhorn); two *s* one *d. Educ:* George Watson's Coll., Edinburgh; Edinburgh Univ. (MA 1942; LLB 1948). Admitted Writer to the Signet, 1949. Served RAFVR, Flt Lieut, 1942-46. Edinburgh Corporation, 1952; Depute Town Clerk, 1971; Director of Administration, City of Edinburgh District Council, 1975-80. *Recreations:* playing golf, watching other sports, listening to music. *Address:* City Chambers, High Street, Edinburgh EH1 1YJ. *T:* 031-225 2424.
See also Rev. D. M. Duncan.

DUNCAN, Michael John Freeman; HM Diplomatic Service; Counsellor, Moscow, since 1982; *b* 9 Jan. 1926; *s* of late John Colley Duncan and of Blanche (*née* Freeman); *m* 1964, Sally Ilbert Crosse; one *s* one *d. Educ:* Hurstpierpoint (Scholar); Christ Church, Oxford (Scholar; MA); Ecole Nationale des Langues Orientales, Paris (Diplôme des Langues Slaves). Entered HM Diplomatic Service, 1951; Attaché, Moscow, 1949; FO, 1951; Germany, 1952; FO, 1954; Moscow, 1959; FO, 1961; UN Disarmament Conf., Geneva, 1964; FO, 1966; Caracas, 1969; FCO, 1973. Order of St Cecilia, Estado de Miranda, Venezuela, 1972. *Publications:* Ilf and Petrov, 1964; *translations:* Trotsky Papers, 1964; Paustovsky, Story of a Life, 1964; Lydia Ginzburg, Within the Whirlwind, 1981; various articles. *Recreations:* reading, linguistics, mushrooms, gardening. *Address:* c/o Foreign and Commonwealth Office, SW1; Whin Cottage, St Michaels Drive, Otford, Sevenoaks, Kent TN14 5SA.

DUNCAN, Maj.-Gen. Nigel William, CB 1951; CBE 1945; DSO 1945; DL; *b* 27 Nov. 1899; *s* of George William and Edith Duncan, Earlston, Guildford; *m* 1928, Victoria Letitia Troyte, *d* of late Capt. J. E. Acland, Wollaston House, Dorchester, Dorset; three *d. Educ:* Malvern Coll.; RMC Sandhurst. 2nd Bn The Black Watch, 1919; transf. Royal Tank Corps, 1923; Captain, 1931; Major, 1938; Lieut-Col, 1940; Col, 1943; Brig. 30 Armoured Bde, 1943, 2nd Armoured Bde, 1946; Comdr Royal Armoured Corps Centre, 1947; Maj.-Gen., 1949; Dir Royal Armoured Corps, WO, 1949-52; retired pay, 1952. Col Comdt Royal Tank Regt, 1952-58. Lieut-Governor Royal Hospital, Chelsea, 1953-57. DL Dorset, 1959. *Address:* The Paddock, West Stafford, Dorchester, Dorset. *T:* Dorchester 64145. *Club:* Army and Navy.

DUNCAN, Stanley Frederick St Clare; HM Diplomatic Service; Ambassador to Bolivia, since 1981; *b* 13 Nov. 1927; *yr s* of late Stanley Gilbert Scott Duncan and of Louisa Elizabeth Duncan; *m* 1967, Jennifer Jane Bennett; two *d. Educ:* Latymer Upper Sch. FRGS. India Office, 1946; CRO, 1947; Private Sec. to Parly Under-Sec. of State, 1954; Second Sec., Ottawa, 1954-55; Brit. Govt Information Officer, Toronto, 1955-57; Second Sec., Wellington, 1958-60; First Sec., CRO, 1960; seconded to Central African Office, 1962-64; Mem., Brit. Delegn to Victoria Falls Conf. on Dissolution of Fedn of Rhodesia and Nyasaland, 1963; First Sec., Nicosia, 1964-67; FCO, 1967-70; FCO Adviser, Brit. Gp, Inter-Parly Union, 1968-70; Head of Chancery and First Sec., Lisbon, 1970-73; Consul-General and subsequently Chargé d'Affaires in Mozambique, 1973-75; Counsellor (Political), Brasilia, 1976-77; Head of Consular Dept, FCO, 1977-80; Canadian Nat. Defence Coll., 1980-81. Officer, Military Order of Christ (Portugal), 1973. *Recreations:* countryside pursuits. *Address:* c/o Foreign and Commonwealth Office, SW1.

DUNCAN, William Barr Mckinnon, CBE 1972; FEng, FIMechE; FRSE; Chairman and Chief Executive, Rolls Royce Ltd, from April 1983 (Director since 1982); *b* 16 Dec. 1922; *m* 1951, Christina Boyd Worth; one *s* two *d. Educ:* Ardrossan Acad.; Glasgow Univ.; Royal Coll. of Science and Technology (1st Cl. Hons Mech Eng). Joined ICI, 1941; engrg duties, Billingham Div., 1950; Chief Engr and Engrg Dir, Agricl Div., 1961; Gp Gen. Manager, Man Services, 1964; Pres., ICI America, 1966; Dir, Can. Ind. Ltd, 1968; Pres. and Chief Exec., ICI North America Ltd, 1970; Dir, Fib. Ind. Inc., 1970; Dir, ICI Ltd, 1971; Chm., ICI Americas Inc., 1974; Dep. Chm., ICI Ltd, 1977-83; Director: NEB, 1975-78; Legal & General Gp, 1979. Pres., Soc. of Chemical Industry, 1980 (Vice-Pres., 1977). Vis. Prof., Strathclyde Univ., 1978-. FEng 1978 (Mem. Council, 1981-); Hon. LLD Strathclyde, 1978. *Recreations:* golf, tennis, music, bridge. *Address:* Rolls Royce Ltd, 65 Buckingham Gate, SW1E 6AT.

DUNCAN MILLAR, Ian Alastair, CBE 1978; MC; CEng, MICE; JP, DL; Director: Macdonald Fraser & Co. Ltd, Perth, since 1961; Member, Royal Company of Archers (Queen's Body Guard for Scotland), since 1956; *b* 22 Nov. 1914; *s* of late Sir James Duncan Millar and Lady Duncan Millar (*née* Forester Paton); *m* 1945, Louise Reid McCosh; two *s* two *d. Educ:* Gresham's Sch., Holt; Trinity Coll., Cambridge (MA). Served with Corps of Royal Engineers, 1940-45 (Major; wounded; despatches): 7th Armoured Div., N Africa and Normandy; 51 (Highland) Div., France and Germany. Contested Parly Elections (L): Banff, 1945; Kinross and W Perthshire, 1949 and 1963. Depute Chm., North of Scotland Hydro-Electric Bd, 1970-72 (Mem., 1957-72). Chm., United Auctions (Scotland) Ltd, 1967-74. Dir, Hill Farming Research Organisation, 1966-78; Chm., Consultative Cttee to Sec. of State for Scotland under 1976 Freshwater and Salmon Fisheries Act, 1981. Mem. Ct, Dundee Univ., 1975-78. Perth CC 1945-75: Chm. Planning Cttee, 1954-75; Convener, 1970-75; Chm. Jt CC of Perth and Kinross, 1970-75; Tayside Regional Council: Councillor and Chm., 1974-75; Convener, 1975-78. DL 1963, JP 1952, Perthshire. *Recreations:* studying and catching salmon, shooting, meeting people. *Address:* Remony, Aberfeldy, Perthshire. *T:* Kenmore 209. *Club:* Royal Golfing Society (Perth).

DUNCAN-SANDYS, family name of **Baron Duncan-Sandys.**

DUNCAN-SANDYS, Baron *cr* 1974 (Life Peer); **Duncan Edwin Duncan-Sandys,** CH 1973; Founder, Civic Trust and President, since 1956; President, Europa Nostra, since 1969; Chairman, Lonrho Ltd, since 1972; *b* 24 Jan. 1908; *o s* of Captain George Sandys, formerly MP for Wells, and Mildred, *d* of Duncan Cameron, Ashburton, New Zealand; *m* 1st, 1935, Diana (marr. diss. 1960; she *d* 1963), *d* of late Rt Hon. Sir Winston Churchill; one *s* two *d* ; 2nd, 1962, Marie-Claire, *d* of Adrien Schmitt, Paris, and formerly Viscountess Hudson; one *d. Educ:* Eton; Magdalen Coll., Oxford (MA). Entered Diplomatic Service, 1930; served in Foreign Office and British Embassy,

Berlin; MP (C) Norwood Div. of Lambeth, 1935-45, Streatham, 1950-Feb. 1974; Political Columnist of Sunday Chronicle, 1937-39; Member Nat. Exec. of Conservative Party, 1938-39; Commissioned in Territorial Army (Royal Artillery), 1937; Co-founder, Air Raid Protection Inst. (later Inst. of Civil Defence), 1938; served in Expeditionary Force in Norway, 1940; Lt-Col 1941; disabled on active service, 1941; Financial Sec. to War Office, 1941-43; Parly Sec., Ministry of Supply, responsible for armament production, 1943-44; Chm., War Cabinet Cttee for defence against German flying bombs and rockets, 1943-45; Minister of Works, 1944-45; Minister of Supply, Oct. 1951-Oct. 1954; Minister of Housing and Local Govt, Oct. 1954-Jan. 1957; Minister of Defence, Jan. 1957-Oct. 1959; Minister of Aviation, Oct. 1959-July 1960; Secretary of State for Commonwealth Relations, July 1960-Oct. 1964, and also Secretary of State for the Colonies, July 1962-Oct. 1964. Founded European Movement, 1947, Chm. International Executive until 1950; Chm., Parly Council of European Movement, 1950-51 (Pres. of Honour, European Movement, 1980-); Mem. Parly Assembly of Council of Europe and of WEU, 1950-51, 1965- (Leader British Delegns, 1970-72); Chm. British Section, Franco British Council, 1972-78; Chm. Internat. Organising Cttee, European Architectural Heritage Year, 1975. Mem., Gen. Adv. Council, BBC, 1947-51. Director, Ashanti Goldfields Corporation, 1947-51 and 1966-72. Vice-Pres., Assoc. of District Councils, 1979-. Hon. Vice-Pres., Nat. Chamber of Trade, 1951-. Hon. MRTPI, 1956; Hon. FRIBA, 1968. Mem. of Magic Circle. Freeman of Bridgetown, Barbados, 1962. Grand Cross, Order of Merit, Italy, 1960; Order of Sultanate of Brunei, 1973; Medal of Honour, City of Paris, 1974; Gold Cup of European Movement, 1975; Goethe Gold Medal, Hamburg Foundn, 1975; Grand Cross of Order of Crown, Belgium, 1975; Commandeur, Légion d'Honneur, France, 1979; Grand Cross, Order of Merit, Fed. Rep. of Germany, 1981. *Publications:* European Movement and the Council of Europe, 1949; The Modern Commonwealth, 1961. *Recreation:* abstract painting. *Address:* 86 Vincent Square, SW1P 2PG. *T:* 01-834 5886. *Club:* Pratt's.

DUNCOMBE, family name of **Baron Feversham.**

DUNCOMBE, Sir Philip (Digby) Pauncefort-, 4th Bt *cr* 1859; DL; one of HM Body Guard, Honorable Corps of Gentlemen-at-Arms, since 1979; *b* 18 May 1927; *o s* of Sir Everard Pauncefort-Duncombe, 3rd Bt, DSO, and of Evelyn Elvira, *d* of Frederick Anthony Denny; *S* father, 1971; *m* 1951, Rachel Moyra, *d* of Major H. G. Aylmer; one *s* two *d. Educ:* Stowe. 2nd Lieut, Grenadier Guards, 1946; served in Palestine, 1947-48; Malaya, 1948-49; Cyprus, 1957-59; Hon. Major, retired 1960, Regular Army Reserve. County Comdt, Buckinghamshire Army Cadet Force, 1967-70. DL Bucks 1971. *Heir: s* David Philip Henry Pauncefort-Duncombe, *b* 21 May 1956. *Address:* Great Brickhill Manor, Milton Keynes, Bucks MK17 9BE. *T:* Great Brickhill 205. *Club:* Cavalry and Guards.

DUNCUMB, Dr Peter, FRS 1977; Director and General Manager, Tube Investments Research Laboratories, since 1979 (Assistant Director, 1972-79); *b* 26 Jan. 1931; *s* of late William Duncumb and of Hilda Grace (*née* Coleman); *m* 1955, Anne Leslie Taylor; two *s* one *d. Educ:* Oundle Sch.; Clare Coll., Cambridge (BA 1953, MA 1956, PhD 1957). DSIR Res. Fellow, Cambridge Univ., 1957-59; Res. Scientist and Gp Leader, Tube Investments Res. Labs, 1959-67, Head, Physics Dept, 1967-72. Hon. Mem., Microbeam Analysis Soc. of America, 1973. C. V. Boys Prize, Inst. of Physics, 1966. *Publications:* numerous on electron microscopy and analysis in Jl of Inst. of Physics. *Recreations:* hill walking, family genealogy. *Address:* 5 Woollards Lane, Great Shelford, Cambridge. *T:* Cambridge 843064.

DUNDAS, family name of **Viscount Melville,** and of **Marquess of Zetland.**

DUNDAS, Lord; Robin Lawrence Dundas; *b* 5 March 1965; *s* and *heir* of Earl of Ronaldshay, *qv.*

DUNDAS, Group Captain Hugh Spencer Lisle, CBE 1977; DSO 1944 and Bar 1945; DFC 1941; RAF retired; DL; Chairman: British Electric Traction Co. PLC, since 1982 (Managing Director, 1973-82, Deputy Chairman, 1981-82); BET Omnibus Services Ltd, since 1978; BET Investments Ltd, since 1978; Rediffusion plc, since 1978; A-R Television PLC (formerly Rediffusion Television Ltd), since 1978 (Deputy Chairman, 1970-78); Thames Television Ltd, since 1981 (Director, since 1968); Director: BET Leisure Holdings Ltd (formerly Rediffusion Holdings Ltd); Wembley Stadium Ltd; *b* 22 July 1920; *s* of late Frederick James Dundas and Sylvia Mary (*née* March-Phillipps); *m* 1950, Hon. Enid Rosamond Lawrence, 2nd *d* of 1st Baron Oaksey and 3rd Baron Trevethin; one *s* two *d. Educ:* Stowe. Joined 616 (S Yorks) Sqdn AAF 1939; served in UK Fighter Comd Sqdn, 1939-43; N Africa, Malta, Sicily, Italy, 1943-46; perm. commn 1944; comd 244 Wing, Italy, 1944-46 (Gp Captain; despatches 1945); retd 1947. Comd 601 (Co. London) Sqdn RAuxAF, 1947-50. Beaverbrook Newspapers, 1948-60: various editorial and managerial posts; joined Exec. Staff, Rediffusion Ltd, 1961: Dir, 1966; Dep. Man. Dir, 1968; Man. Dir 1970-74. Chairman: Humphries Hldgs Ltd, 1975-77; Redifon Ltd, 1970-78. Vice-Chm. (Air) South East, TAVRA, 1973-; Mem. Council, and Finance and General Purposes Cttee, RAF Benevolent Fund, 1976-; Mem. Council, Nat. Soc. for Cancer Relief, 1976- (Vice-Chm.). DL Surrey, 1969. *Address:* 55 Iverna Court, W8 6TU. *T:* 01-937 0773; The Schoolroom, Dockenfield, Farnham, Surrey. *T:* Frensham 2331. *Clubs:* White's, Royal Air Force.

DUNDAS, Robert Giffen, CBE 1961; HM Diplomatic Service, retired 1969; *b* 4 March 1909; *s* of James Dundas and Grace Haxton Giffen; *m* 1938, Pauleen Gosling; three *s* one *d. Educ:* Edinburgh Univ. Entered Levant Consular Service, 1931; Vice-Consul: Beirut, 1931; Cairo, 1932; Third Sec., Ankara, 1934; Vice-Consul: Casablanca, 1936; Alexandria, 1938; Suez, 1939; Baghdad, 1941; Consul, Tangier, 1944; assigned to Foreign Office, 1947; Consul, Kermanshah, 1949; Consul-General: Tabriz, 1950; Salonika, 1952; New Orleans, 1955; Stuttgart, 1958; Alexandria, 1961; HM Counsellor and Consul-Gen., Benghazi, 1963-66; Consul-Gen., Amsterdam, 1966-69. *Publications:* The House on the Vecht, 1979; contrib. (fiction) to Argosy etc. *Address:* 43 Imber Close, Ember Lane, Esher, Surrey KT10 8ED. *T:* 01-398 7040.

DUNDEE, 11th Earl of, *cr* 1660 (Scotland); **Henry James Scrymgeour-Wedderburn,** PC; LLD; JP, DL; Viscount Dudhope and Lord Scrymgeour, *cr* 1641 (Scotland); Lord Inverkeithing, *cr* 1660 (Scotland); Lord Glassary, *cr* 1954 (UK); Hereditary Royal Standard-Bearer for Scotland; *b* 3 May 1902; *s* of Col Henry Scrymgeour-Wedderburn, *de jure* 10th Earl and Edith (*d* 1968), *d* of John Moffat, CE, Ardrossan, and Jessie Fulton Arthur; *S* father 1924 (claim admitted by Cttee for Privileges, House of Lords, as Viscount, 1952, as Earl, 1953); *m* 1946, Patricia Katherine, *widow* of Lieut-Col (Hon.) David Scrymgeour-Wedderburn, and *d* of late Col Lord Herbert Montagu Douglas Scott; one *s* (and two step *d*). *Educ:* Winchester; Balliol Coll., Oxford. Pres. Oxford Union, Oct. 1924; MP (U) Western Renfrew, 1931-45; Parliamentary Under-Sec. of State for Scotland, 1936-39; served with 7th Black Watch, 1939-41; Additional Parl. Under-Sec. of State, Scottish Office 1941-42. Minister without Portfolio, 1958-61; Minister of State for Foreign Affairs, 1961-62; Asst Dep. Leader, 1960-62, Dep. Leader, 1962-64, House of Lords. Hon. LLD St Andrews, 1954. *Heir: s* Lord Scrymgeour, *qv. Address:* Birkhill, Cupar, Fife. *TA:* Gauldry. *T:* Gauldry 209. *Clubs:* Carlton, Travellers', White's, Pratt's; New (Edinburgh).

See also Sir Iain Moncreiffe of that Ilk, Bt, Baron Teynham.

DUNDEE (St Paul's Cathedral), **Provost of;** *see* Rogan, Very Rev. J.

DUNDERDALE, Comdr Wilfred Albert, CMG 1942; MBE 1920; RNVR, retired; *b* 24 Dec. 1899; *s* of late Richard Albert Dunderdale, Shipowner, and Sophie Dunderdale; *m* 1952, Dorothy Brayshaw Hyde (*d* 1978); *m* 1980, Deborah, *d* of Eugene B. Jackson, Boston, Mass and *widow* of Harry McJ. McLeod. Trained as Naval Architect, 1914-17; served with Mediterranean Fleet, 1918-22 (despatches twice); Lieut RNVR, 1920; transferred to British Embassy, Constantinople, 1922-26; Paris, 1926-40; Comdr, 1939. Russian Order of St Anne; Polonia Restituta; French Legion of Honour (Officer); French Croix de Guerre with palm; United States Legion of Merit (Officer). *Recreations:* yachting, tennis. *Address:* Castlefield, Bletchingley, Surrey RH1 4LB. *T:* Godstone 843121. *Clubs:* Boodle's; Royal Harwich Yacht (Harwich).

DUNDONALD, 14th Earl of, *cr* 1669, **Ian Douglas Leonard Cochrane;** Lord Cochrane of Dundonald, 1647; Lord Cochrane of Paisley and Ochiltree, 1669; Chairman, Secure Holdings Ltd, de Jersey & Co. (Finland) Ltd and associated companies; a Representative Peer for Scotland, 1959-63; *b* 6 Dec. 1918; *s* of late Hon. Douglas Robert Hesketh Roger Cochrane (2nd *s* of 12th Earl) and of Hon. Mrs Douglas Cochrane (*d* 1960), Hawkhurst, Kent; *S* uncle 1958; *m* 1960, Aphra Farquhar (*d* 1972), *d* of late Comdr George Fetherstonhaugh; one *s* one *d*; *m* 1978, Ann Margaret, *d* of late Sir Joseph Harkness, and of Lady Harkness, Tenterden, Kent. *Educ:* Wellington Coll.; RMC, Sandhurst. Joined 1 Battalion The Black Watch, 1938; Adjutant, 16 DLI, 1940-41; Staff Capt. 139 Inf. Bde, 1941-42; Staff Coll., Camberley, 1942 (psc); Asst Mil. Landing Officer, 51 (H) Div., 1943; GSO 3 and GSO 2, HQ Eighth Army, 1943; Company Comdr 6 Bn The Black Watch, 1944-45; Bde Major, 180 Inf. Bde, 1946-47; GSO 2, Army Air Transport Development Centre, 1947-49; Company Comdr 1 Bn The Black Watch, 1949-51; DAQMG, SHAPE, 1951; GSO 2, SD3, War Office and GSO 2, Army Council Secretariat, 1952-53; retired 1953. North American Representative, Atlantic Shipbuilding Co., 1953-54. Mem., UK Delegn to NATO Citizens Convention, Paris, 1962. Chm. Anglo-Chilean Soc., 1958-65. Pres., Ayr and Bute Assoc. of Youth Clubs. Vice-Pres., Royal Caledonian Schs. Mem. Council, Anglo-Finnish Soc. *Recreations:* shooting, sailing, ski-ing, golf. *Heir: s* Lord Cochrane, *qv. Address:* Lochnell Castle, Ledaig, Argyll; Beacon Hall, Benenden, Cranbrook, Kent. *Club:* Carlton.

DUNEDIN, Bishop of, since 1976; **Rt. Rev. Peter Woodley Mann;** *b* 25 July 1924; *s* of Edgar Allen and Bessie May Mann; *m* 1955, Anne Victoria Norman; three *d. Educ:* Prince Alfred Coll., Adelaide; St John's Coll., Auckland (Fellow); Univ. of London (BD). Deacon, Dio. Waiapu, 1953; priest, 1954; Curate: Waiapu Cathedral, 1953-55; Rotorua, 1955-56; Vicar: Porangahau, 1956-61; Dannevirke, 1961-66; Vicar of Blenheim and Archdeacon of Marlborough, 1966-71; Vicar of St Mary's and Archdeacon of Timaru, 1971-75; Vicar of St James' Lower Hutt, 1975-76. *Recreations:* tennis, athletics. *Address:* Bishop's House, 10 Claremont Street, Roslyn, Dunedin, NZ. *T:* 772694.

DUNGEY, Prof. James Wynne, PhD; Professor of Physics, Imperial College, University of London, since 1965; *b* 30 Jan. 1923; *s* of Ernest Dungey and Alice Dungey; *m* 1950, Christine Scotland (*née* Brown); one *s* one *d. Educ:* Bradfield; Magdalene Coll., Cambridge (MA, PhD). Res. Fellow, Univ. of Sydney, 1950-53; Vis. Asst Prof., Penn State Coll., 1953-54; ICI Fellow, Cambridge, 1954-57; Lectr, King's Coll., Newcastle upon Tyne, 1957-59; Sen.

Principal Scientific Officer, AWRE, Aldermaston, 1959-63; Res. Fellow, Imperial Coll., London, 1963-65. Fellow, Amer. Geophysical Union, 1973. Chapman Medal, RAS, 1982. *Publications:* Cosmic Electrodynamics, 1958; papers on related topics. *Recreations:* music, sailing. *Address:* 35 Kensington High Street, W8 5BA. *T:* 01-937 1181.

DUNGLASS, Lord (courtesy title used by heirs to Earldom of Home before title was disclaimed); *see under* Douglas-Home, Hon. D. A. C.

DUNHAM, Cyril John; Director, Nationwide (formerly Co-operative Permanent) Building Society, since 1944 (President, 1959-69); *b* 22 April 1908; *m* 1936, Vera Georgia; one *s* two *d. Educ:* Watford Gram. Sch.; Coll. of Estate Management. FRICS 1929. Technical Adviser, War Damage Commn, 1941; Vice-Chm., Peterborough New Town Develt Corp., 1968-73; Vice-President: Building Societies Assoc. (Chm., 1961-63); Internat. Union of Building Socs. (Hon. Life Mem., 1980-). Has also served on: Wembley Borough Council; Nat. House-Builders Registration Council; Town and Country Planning Assoc. FRSA. *Address:* 15 Turner Close, Hampstead, NW11 6TU. *T:* 01-455 8348.

DUNHAM, Sir Kingsley (Charles), Kt 1972; FRS 1955; FRSE; PhD Dunelm, 1932; SD Harvard, 1935; FGS; Hon FIMM; Director, Institute of Geological Sciences, 1967-75; *b* Sturminster Newton, Dorset, 2 Jan. 1910; *s* of Ernest Pedder and Edith Agnes Dunham; *m* 1936, Margaret, *d* of William and Margaret Young, Choppington, Northumberland; one *s. Educ:* Durham Johnston Sch.; Hatfield Coll., Durham Univ.; Adams House, Harvard Univ. Temporary Geologist, New Mexico Bureau of Mines, 1934; HM Geological Survey of Great Britain; Geologist, 1935-45; Senior Geologist 1946; Chief Petrographer, 1948; Prof. of Geology, Univ. of Durham, 1950-66, Emeritus, 1968-; Sub-Warden of Durham Colls, 1959-61; Miller Prof., University of Ill., 1956; Member: Council, Royal Society, 1965-66 (Foreign Sec., A Vice-Pres., 1971-76; Royal Medal, 1970); Council for Scientific Policy (Min. of Ed. & Sci.), 1965-66. President: Instn Mining and Metallurgy, 1963-64 (Gold Medal, 1968); Yorks Geological Soc., 1958-60 (Sorby Medal, 1964); Internat. Union of Geological Sciences, 1969-72; Geological Soc. of London, 1966-68 (Council 1949-52, 1960-64; Bigsby Medal, 1954; Murchison Medal, 1966; Wollaston Medal, 1976); Brit. Assoc. for Advancement of Science, 1972-73; Mineralogical Soc., 1975-77. Trustee, British Museum (Natural History), 1963-66. Member Geology-Geophysics Cttee (NERC) 1965-70; Chairman: Internat. Geol. Correlation Project (IUGS-UNESCO), 1973-76; Council for Environmental Science and Engineering, 1973-75. Mem. Council and UK Rep., 1972-77, Hon. Scholar, 1977, Internat. Inst. for Applied Systems Analysis, Laxenburg, Vienna. Pres., Durham Univ. Soc., 1973-75. Founder Fellow, Fellowship of Engineering, 1976. Hon. Member: Royal Geol Soc. Cornwall (Bolitho Medal 1972); Geol. Soc. of India, 1972; Hon. Foreign Fellow, Geol. Soc. of America; Corr. Foreign Mem., Austrian Acad. of Scis, 1971; Hon. Foreign Member: Société Géologique de Belge, 1974; Bulgarian Geological Soc., 1975. Fellow, Imperial Coll., 1976. Hon. DSc: Dunelm, 1946; Liverpool, 1967; Birmingham, 1970; Illinois, 1971; Leicester, 1972; Michigan, 1973; Canterbury, 1973; Edinburgh, 1974; Exeter, 1975; Hull, 1978; Hon. ScD Cantab, 1973; DUniv Open, 1982. Haidinger Medaille der Geologischen Bundesanstalt, 1976; von Buch Medal, Deutsche Geol. Ges., 1981. Hon. Citizen of Texas, 1975. *Publications:* Geology of the Organ Mountains, 1935; Geology of the Northern Pennine Orefield, 1948; (as Editor) Symposium on the Geology, Paragenesis and Reserves of the Ores of Lead & Zinc, 2nd edn, 1950; Fluorspar, 1952; Geology of Northern Skye (with F. W. Anderson) 1966; (with W. C. C. Rose) Geology and Hermatite Deposits of South Cumbria, 1977; articles in Quarterly Jl of Geological Soc., Mineralogical Magazine, Geological Magazine, American Mineralogist, etc. *Recreations:* music (organ and pianoforte); gardening. *Address:* Charleycroft, Quarryheads Lane, Durham DH1 3DY. *T:* Durham 48977. *Clubs:* Athenæum; Geological Society's.

DUNICAN, Peter Thomas, CBE 1977; FEng, FICE, FIStructE, FIEI; Chairman, Ove Arup Partnership, since 1977; Chairman, National Building Agency, 1978-82 (part-time Director, 1964-82); *b* 15 March 1918; *s* of Peter Dunican and Elsie Alice McKenzie; *m* 1942, Irene May Jordan; two *s* one *d* (and one *d* decd). *Educ:* Central Sch., Clapham; Battersea Polytechnic. FICE 1971, FIStructE 1959, FIEI 1970. Asst, S. H. White & Son, Civil Engineers, 1936-43; Structural Engr, Ove Arup & Partners, Consulting Engineers, 1943-49, Sen. Partner 1956-. Instn of Structural Engineers: Mem. Council, 1964-; Vice-Pres., 1971-77; Pres., 1977-78. Member: LCC Adv. Cttee on London Bldg Act and Byelaws, 1957; Min. of Housing Working Party to revise Model Bldg Byelaws, 1960; Bldg Regulations Adv. Cttee, 1962-65; Council, Architect. Assoc., 1968-69; Chm., Ground and Structures Res. Cttee, BRE, 1979. Univ. Science and Technol. Bd of Science Research Council: Mem., Aeronaut. and Civil Eng Cttee, 1968-71; Mem., National Jt Consultative Cttee, 1974; Chm., Jt Bldg Gp, 1973-76. FEng 1978. *Publications:* professional, technical and philosophical papers to jls dealing with construction industry in general and struct. eng in particular. *Recreations:* working in the garden and going to the opera. *Address:* 60 Ryecroft Road, SW16 3EH. *T:* 01-670 7056. *Clubs:* Athenæum, Danish.

DUNITZ, Prof. Jack David, FRS 1974; Professor of Chemical Crystallography at the Swiss Federal Institute of Technology (ETH), Zürich, since 1957; *b* 29 March 1923; *s* of William Dunitz and Mildred (*née* Gossman); *m* 1953, Barbara Steuer; two *d. Educ:* Hillhead High Sch., Glasgow; Hutcheson's Grammar Sch., Glasgow; Glasgow Univ. (BSc, PhD). Post-

doctoral Fellow, Oxford Univ., 1946-48, 1951-53; California Inst. of Technology, 1948-51, 1953-54; Vis. Scientist, US Nat. Insts of Health, 1954-55; Sen. Res. Fellow, Davy Faraday Res. Lab., Royal Instn, London, 1956-57. Vis. Prof., Iowa State Univ., 1965; British Council Lectr, 1965; Treat B. Johnson Meml Lectr, Yale Univ., 1965; 3M Lectr, Univ. of Minnesota, 1966; Vis. Prof., Tokyo Univ., 1967; Overseas Fellow of Churchill Coll., Cambridge, 1968; Vis. Prof., Technion, Haifa, 1970; Lectures: Reilly, Univ. Notre Dame, US, 1971; Kelly, Purdue Univ., 1971; Gerhard Schmidt Meml, Weizmann Inst. of Sci., 1973; George Fisher Baker, Cornell Univ., 1976; Centenary, Chem. Soc., 1977; Appleton, Brown Univ., 1979; H. J. Backer, Gröningen Univ., 1980; Havinga, Leiden Univ., 1980; Karl Folkers, Wisconsin Univ., 1981. For. Mem., Royal Netherlands Acad. of Arts and Sciences, 1979; Mem., Leopoldina Acad., 1979; Fellow AAAS, 1981. Jt Editor, Perspectives in Structural Chemistry, 1967-71; Mem. Editorial Bd: Helvetica Chimica Acta, 1971-; Structure and Bonding, 1971-81. *Publications:* X-ray Analysis and the Structure of Organic Molecules, 1979; papers on various aspects of crystal and molecular structure in Acta Crystallographica, Helvetica Chimica Acta, Jl Chem. Soc., Jl Amer. Chem. Soc., etc. *Recreation:* walking. *Address:* (office) Organic Chemistry Laboratory, ETH, Universitätstrasse 16, CH-8092 Zürich, Switzerland. *T:* CH (01) 256 2892; (home) Obere Heslibachstrasse 77, 8700 Kusnacht, Switzerland. *T:* CH (01) 9101723.

DUNK, Sir William (Ernest), Kt 1957; CBE 1954; retired as Chairman Commonwealth of Australia Public Service Commission (1947-62); formerly Commissioner, British Phosphates Commission and Christmas Island Phosphates Commission; Director, General Television Corporation and other companies; *b* S Australia, 11 Dec. 1897; *s* of Albert L. Dunk; *m* 1922, Elma K. Evans; one *s* one *d. Educ:* Kapunda High Sch., Australia. Australian Public Service from 1914; Auditor-General's Office, 1914-39, Adelaide, New Guinea, London, Sydney; Treasury, 1939-45, as Asst Sec., Special War Services, Dir Reverse Lend Lease, 1943-45; Permanent Sec., Dept of External Affairs, 1945-46. *Address:* 7 Tintern Avenue, Toorak, Victoria 3142, Australia. *Club:* Melbourne (Melbourne).

DUNKEL, Arthur; Director General, General Agreement on Tariffs and Trade (GATT), since 1980; *b* 28 Aug. 1932; *s* of Walter Dunkel and Berthe Lerch; *m* 1957, Christiane Müller-Serda; one *s* one *d. Educ:* Univ. of Lausanne (LèsSc écon. et comm.). Federal Office for external economic affairs, 1956: successively Head of sections for OECD matters, 1960; for cooperation with developing countries, 1964; for world trade policy, 1971; Permanent Representative of Switzerland to GATT, with rank of Minister, 1973; Delegate of Federal Council for Trade Agreements, rank of Ambassador, 1976; in this capacity, head of Swiss delegations to multilateral (GATT, UNCTAD, UNIDO, etc) and bilateral negotiations in the fields of trade, development, commodities, transfer of technology, industrialisation, agriculture, etc. Dr *hc* rer. pol. Fribourg, 1980. *Publications:* various articles and studies in economic, commercial, agricl and development fields. *Address:* rue des Granges 4, 1204 Geneva, Switzerland.

DUNKELD, Bishop of, (RC), since 1981; **Rt. Rev. Vincent Logan;** *b* 30 June 1941; *s* of Joseph Logan and Elizabeth Flannigan. *Educ:* Blairs College, Aberdeen; St Andrew's Coll., Drygrange, Melrose. Ordained priest, Edinburgh, 1964; Asst Priest, St Margaret's, Davidson's Mains, Edinburgh, 1964-66; Corpus Christi Coll., London, 1966-67 (DipRE); Chaplain, St Joseph's Hospital, Rosewell, Midlothian, 1967-77; Adviser in Religious Education, Archdiocese of St Andrews and Edinburgh, 1967; Parish Priest, St Mary's, Ratho, 1977-81; Episcopal Vicar for Education, Archdiocese of St Andrews and Edinburgh, 1978. *Address:* Bishop's House, 29 Roseangle, Dundee DD1 4LX. *T:* Dundee 24327.

DUNKERLEY, Harvey John, CBE 1953; Controller, Midland Region, BBC, 1948-64, retired; *b* 10 Oct. 1902; *s* of Joseph Braithwaite Dunkerley and Rose Maria (*née* Harvey); *m* 1st, 1928, Kay Hargreaves (*d* 1958); 2nd, 1961, Thelma Couch; one *s* three *d. Educ:* Owen's Sch., London; Magdalen Coll., Oxford (2nd class Hons Mod. Hist.). Announcer, BBC, Savoy Hill, 1924; Asst, BBC Relay Station, Liverpool, 1924; Education Officer, BBC, Manchester, 1928; Programme Dir, BBC Midland Region, 1933; BBC European Service, Sept. 1939, latterly as Dep. to Controller. *Recreation:* country life. *Address:* Gallipot House, Broadway, Worcs. *T:* Evesham 830395. *Club:* Farmers'.

DUNKLEY, Captain James Lewis, CBE 1970 (OBE 1946); RD 1943; Marine Manager, P&O Lines, 1971-72 (Marine Superintendent, 1968-71); *b* 13 Sept. 1908; *s* of William E. Dunkley, Thurlaston Grange, Warwickshire; *m* 1937, Phyllis Mary Cale; one *d. Educ:* Lawrence Sheriff Sch., Rugby; Thames Nautical Training Coll., HMS Worcester. Junior Officer, P&O Line, 1928; Captain, 1954; Cdre, 1964. RNR: Sub-Lt, 1931; Comdr, 1951; Captain, 1956. Master, Honourable Co. of Master Mariners, 1970. *Recreations:* gardening, collecting. *Address:* 1 Collindale Gardens, Clacton-on-Sea, Essex. *T:* Clacton 813950. *Club:* City Livery.

DUNKLEY, Philip Parker, MC and Bar 1944; Executive Chairman, 1978-82, Chairman and Chief Executive, since 1982, Mitchell Cotts Group plc; *b* 23 March 1922; *s* of late Frederick and Rachel Dunkley; *m* 1948, Barbara Patricia Baxter; one *d. Educ:* King's School, Macclesfield, Cheshire. Served War, 1940-46 (despatches); commnd 10th Gurkha Rifles, 1942; Burma Campaign, 1942-46 (Major). F. Dunkley & Co., 1946-56; Man. Dir, John Shields & Co., 1956-59; joined Mitchell Cotts Group Ltd, 1959; Dir 1963; Man. Dir 1965;

Dep. Chm. 1973. Director: Bestobell Ltd, 1971 (Dep. Chm. 1976); Consolidated Gold Fields Ltd, 1979; Samuel Montagu & Co. Ltd, 1980. Chm., United Kingdom South Africa Trade Assoc., 1976-79. *Recreations:* fishing, shooting. *Address:* Hamptons Farm House, Shipbourne, near Tonbridge, Kent. *T:* Plaxtol 547. *Clubs:* East India, Devonshire, Sports and Public Schools, Oriental.

DUNLAP, Air Marshal Clarence Rupert, CBE 1944; CD; RCAF retired; *b* 1 Jan. 1908; *s* of late Frank Burns Dunlap, Truro, Nova Scotia; *m* 1935, Hester, *d* of late Dr E. A. Cleveland, Vancouver, BC; one *s*. *Educ:* Acadia Univ.; Nova Scotia Technical Coll. Joined RCAF 1928 as Pilot Officer; trained as pilot and specialised in aerial survey; later specialised in armament; Dir of Armament, RCAF HQ Ottawa on outbreak of War; commanded: RCAF Station, Mountain View, Ont., Jan.–Oct. 1942; RCAF Station, Leeming, Yorks, Dec. 1942-May 1943; 331 Wing NASAF, Tunisia, May-Nov. 1943; 139 Wing TAF, Nov. 1943-Feb. 1945; 64 Base, Middleton St George, Feb.-May 1945; Dep., AMAS, AFHQ, Ottawa, 1945-48; Air Mem. for Air Plans, AFHQ, Ottawa, 1948-49; AOC North-West Air Command, Edmonton, Alberta, 1949-51; Commandant of National Defence Coll., Kingston, Ont., 1951-54; Vice Chief of the Air Staff, AFHQ, Ottawa, 1954-58; Dep. Chief of Staff, Operations, SHAPE, Paris, 1958-62; Chief of Air Staff, AFHQ, Ottawa, 1962-64; Dep. C-in-C, N Amer. Air Def. Comd, 1964-67. Hon. DCL Acadia Univ., 1955; Hon. DEng Nova Scotia Technical Coll., 1967. *Address:* 203-1375 Newport Avenue, Victoria, BC V8S 5E8, Canada. *Clubs:* Union (Victoria); Victoria Golf; Royal Ottawa Golf (Ottawa).

DUNLEATH, 4th Baron, *cr* 1892; **Charles Edward Henry John Mulholland,** TD; DL; Chairman: Carreras Rothmans of NI, since 1974; Dunleath Estates Ltd; Northern Ireland Independent Television Ltd; Ulster & General Holdings Ltd; *b* 23 June 1933; *s* of 3rd Baron Dunleath, CBE, DSO, and of Henrietta Grace, *d* of late Most Rev. C. F. D'Arcy, Archbishop of Armagh; *S* father, 1956; *m* 1959, Dorinda Margery, *d* of late Lieut-Gen. A. E. Percival, CB, DSO and Bar, OBE, MC. *Educ:* Eton; Cambridge Univ. Served with 11th Hussars, 1952-53, with N Irish Horse, 1954-69, Lt-Col 1967-69; Captain, Ulster Defence Regt, 1971-73; Lt-Col, NIH, RARO, 1973-, Hon. Col 1981-. Member (Alliance): N Down, NI Assembly, 1973-75; N Down, NI Constitutional Convention, 1975-76; resigned from Alliance Party, 1979, rejoined 1981; Mem., Ards Borough Council, 1977-81 (Independent 1979-81). Governor of BBC for N Ireland, 1967-73; Mem. Admin. Council, King George's Jubilee Trust, 1974-75; Pres., Royal Ulster Agric. Soc., 1973-76. CBIM. DL, Co. Down, 1964-. *Recreations:* vintage motoring, mixtures and mutations, steam, B flat cornet. *Heir:* cousin Major Sir Michael Mulholland, Bt, *qv*. *Address:* Ballywalter Park, Newtownards, Co. Down, Northern Ireland. *T:* Ballywalter 203. *Clubs:* Cavalry and Guards; Ulster (Belfast).

DUNLEAVY, Philip, OBE 1978; JP; company director since 1975; Leader, Cardiff City Council, 1974-76 and since 1979; *b* 5 Oct. 1915; *s* of Michael and Bridget Dunleavy; *m* 1936, Valerie Partridge; two *s* two *d*. *Educ:* St Cuthbert's Sch., Cardiff. Served War, TA (Sgt), 1939-46. Post Office, 1930-39 and 1946-75 (Executive Officer, 1960-75). Member: Cardiff City Council, 1962-; South Glamorgan County Council, 1974-. JP 1960. *Recreations:* youth, conservation, local historical research, local govt political activity. *Address:* 35 Merches Gardens, Grangetown, Cardiff CF1 7RF.

DUNLOP, Rear-Adm. Colin Charles Harrison, CB 1972; CBE 1963; DL; Director General: Cable Television Association, since 1977; National Television Rental Association, since 1977; *b* 4 March 1918; *s* of late Engr Rear-Adm. S. H. Dunlop, CB; *m* 1941, Moyra Patricia O'Brien Gorges; two *s* (and one *s* decd). *Educ:* Marlborough Coll. Joined RN 1935; served War of 1939-45 at sea in HM Ships Kent, Valiant, Diadem and Orion; subseq. HMS Sheffield, 1957-59; Sec. to 1st Sea Lord, 1960-63; comd HMS Pembroke, 1964-66; Programme Evaluation Gp, MoD, 1966-68; Director, Defence Policy (A), MoD, 1968-69; Comdr, British Navy Staff, Washington, 1969-71; Chief Naval Supply and Secretariat Officer, 1970-74; Flag Officer, Medway, and Port Adm., Chatham, 1971-74, retd 1974. DL Kent 1976. *Recreations:* cricket, shooting. *Address:* Chanceford Farm, Sand Lane, Frittenden, near Cranbrook, Kent. *T:* Frittenden 242. *Clubs:* Army and Navy; MCC, I Zingari, Free Foresters, Incogniti, RN Cricket, Band of Brothers.

DUNLOP, Cdre David Kennedy B.; *see* Buchanan-Dunlop.

DUNLOP, Prof. Douglas Morton; Professor of History, Columbia University, New York, 1963-77, now Emeritus; *b* 25 Feb. 1909; *o s* of Rev. H. Morton Dunlop and Helen Oliver, *e d* of W. D. Dunn; *m* 1948, Margaret Sinclair, *y d* of Major A. R. Munro, TD, Hillend, Edinburgh. *Educ:* Glasgow Academy; Glasgow Univ.; University Coll. Oxford. Scholar, 1928-32; Vans Dunlop Scholar in Medicine, Edinburgh Univ., 1933; Trinity Coll., Glasgow, 1934-37; Brown Downie Fellow, 1937; Maclean Scholar, 1937 and 1938; University of Bonn, 1937-39; BA Oxon 1939, MA 1960. Trinity Hall, Cambridge (MA) 1950; DLitt Glasgow, 1955. Travelled in Turkey and Syria, 1938; Syria (Jabal Ansariyah), 1939; Asst to Prof. of Hebrew, Glasgow Univ., 1939-46. NFS 1942-44. Asst to Prof. of Oriental Langs, 1947-48, Lectr in Semitic Langs, 1948-50, St Andrews Univ.; Mem. CCG, 1948; Lectr in Islamic History, Cambridge Univ., 1950-62. Visiting Prof. of History, Columbia Univ., 1962-63. FRAS; FIAL. *Publications:* The History of the Jewish Khazars, 1954; The Fusul al-Madani (Aphorisms of the Statesman) of al-

Farabi, 1961; Arabic Science in the West, 1965; Arab Civilization to AD 1500, 1971; The Muntakhab Siwan al-Hikmah of Abu Sulaiman al-Sijistani, 1979; original papers and reviews in British and foreign Orientalist publications, and articles in encyclopædias. *Recreations:* hill-walking, Scottish history. *Address:* 46 Owlstone Road, Cambridge. *T:* 354147. *Club:* Royal and Ancient Golf (St Andrews).

DUNLOP, Sir (Ernest) Edward, Kt 1969; CMG 1965; OBE 1947; Consultant Surgeon; Consultant, Royal Melbourne Hospital, since 1967; *b* Wangaratta, Australia, 12 July 1907; *s* of James Henry and Alice Emily Maud Dunlop; *m* 1945, Helen Raeburn Ferguson, *d* of Mephan Ferguson; two *s*. *Educ:* Benalla High Sch.; Victorian Coll. of Pharmacy, Melbourne; Ormond Coll., Melbourne Univ.; St Bartholomew's, London. Qual. in Pharmacy, Gold Medallist, 1928; MB, BS Melbourne Univ., 1st Cl. Hons and Exhibn 1934; MS Melbourne 1937; FRCS 1938; FRACS 1947; FACS 1964. Membre Titulaire, Internat. Soc. of Surgeons; Mem., James IV Assoc. of Surgeons, 1971. Ho. Surg. and Registrar, Royal Melbourne Hosp., 1935-36; Royal Children's, Melbourne, 1937; Brit. Post-Grad. Med. Sch., Hammersmith, 1938; Specialist Surgeon, EMS London, St Mary's, Paddington, 1939. Served War, 1939-46 (despatches, OBE); RAAMC (Capt. to Col), Europe. Middle East and Far East. Hon. Surg. Royal Melbourne Hosp., 1946, Senior Hon. Surg. 1964-67; Hon. Surg. Victorian Eye and Ear Hosp., 1949, Hon. Life Governor, 1967; Cons. Surg., Peter MacCallum Clinic, Cancer and Repatriation Dept. Colombo Plan Adviser, Thailand and Ceylon 1956, India 1960-64; Team Leader, Australian Surgical Team, South Vietnam, 1969-75; CMO, British Phosphate Commn, 1974. Pres., Victorian Anti-Cancer Council, 1980- (Vice-Pres.-1966-74, Chm. Executive, 1975-80); Vice-Pres., Internat. Soc. of Surgeons, 1981-. Cecil Joll Prize and Lectr, RCS 1960; Gordon Taylor Lectr, Malaysia, 1978; Chapman Meml Lecture and Medal, Australian Instn of Engineers, 1978. Pres. Aust.-Asian Assoc., Victoria, 1965-; Pres. Ex-POW and Relatives Assoc., Victoria, 1946-; Hon. Life Mem., RSL, 1979; Chm., Prime Minister's POW Relief Fund; President: Australian Ex-POW Assoc., 1971-73; Victorian Foundn on Alcoholism and Drug Dependence; Chm., Adv. Cttee on Drug Educn, Victorian Min. of Health, 1970, 1977; Patron, Australian Foundn on Alcoholism and Drug Dependency; Member: Standing Cttee on Health Problems of Alcohol, Nat. Health and Medical Res. Council, 1973; Council, Ormond Coll.; Cttee, Nurses' Meml Centre, Melbourne; Exec., Vict. Red Cross Soc.; Victorian Cttee, Queen's Jubilee Appeal, 1977; Dir, Queen Elizabeth II Silver Jubilee Trust for Young Australians, 1977-; Vice-President: 3rd Asian Pacific Congress of Gastroenterology, 1968; Melbourne Scots Soc., 1974-77. Vice Pres., Victorian Rugby Union, 1946-. Australian of the Year Award, 1977. Hon. Mem., Assoc. of Surgeons of India, 1974. Hon. Fellow Pharmaceutical Soc. of Victoria; Hon. Fellow AMA, 1973. Hon. DSc (Punjab), 1966. Freedom of City, Wanganui, NZ, 1962. KStJ 1981. *Publications:* Carcinoma of the Oesophagus; Reflections upon Surgical Treatment, 1960; Appendix of Into the Smother, 1963; contribs to med. and surg. jls. *Recreations:* farming, travelling, golf; Rugby Union football (Blue, Aust. Caps 1932-34, British Barbarians 1939); formerly boxing (Blue). *Address:* (home) 605 Toorak Road, Toorak, Victoria 3142, Australia. *T:* 20 4749; (professional) 14 Parliament Place, East Melbourne, Victoria 3002, Australia. *T:* 63 1214. *Clubs:* Melbourne, Naval and Military, Peninsula Golf, Melbourne Cricket (Melbourne); Barbarian Football.

DUNLOP, Frank, CBE 1977; Founder, 1969, Director, 1969-78 and since 1980, The Young Vic (Consultant, 1978-80); *b* 15 Feb. 1927; *s* of Charles Norman Dunlop and Mary Aarons. *Educ:* Kibworth Beauchamp Grammar Sch.; University Coll., London (Fellow, 1979). BA Hons, English. Postgrad. Sch. in Shakespeare, at Shakespeare Inst., Stratford-upon-Avon; Old Vic Sch., London. Served with RAF before going to University. Director of: (own young theatre co.) Piccolo Theatre, Manchester, 1954; The Enchanted, for Bristol Old Vic Co., 1955; Arts Council Midland Theatre Co., 1955; Associate Dir, Bristol Old Vic, 1956; Writer and Dir, Les Frères Jacques', Adelphi, 1960; Director: Théâtre de Poche, Brussels, 1959-60; London première, The Bishop's Bonfire, Mermaid, 1960; Nottingham Playhouse, 1961-63; Schweyk, Mermaid, 1963; New Nottingham Playhouse, 1963-64; The Taming of the Shrew, Univ. Arts Centre, Oklahoma, 1965; Any Wednesday, Apollo, 1965; Too True to be Good, Edinburgh Fest., also Strand and Garrick, 1965; Saturday Night and Sunday Morning, Prince of Wales, 1966; (Founder and Dir) Pop Theatre, 1966; The Winter's Tale and The Trojan Women, Edin. and Venice Festivals, also Cambridge Theatre, London, 1966; The Burglar, Vaudeville, 1967; Getting Married, Strand, 1967; A Midsummer Night's Dream and The Tricks of Scapin, Edin. Fest. and Saville Theatre, London, 1967; A Sense of Detachment, Royal Court, 1972; Sherlock Holmes, Aldwych, 1974, NY 1974, Oslo, 1980; Habeas Corpus, NY 1975; The New York Idea, The Three Sisters, NY 1977; The Devil's Disciple, LA and NY, 1978; The Play's the Thing, Julius Caesar, NY, 1978; The Last of Mrs Cheyney, USA, 1978; Rookery Nook, Birmingham and Her Majesty's, 1979; Camelot, USA, 1980; Sherlock Holmes, Norwegian Nat. Th., Oslo, 1980; Lolita, NY, 1981; Assoc. Dir, 1967-71 and Admin. Dir, 1968-71, The Nat. Theatre; productions: *Nat. Theatre:* Edward II (Brecht and Marlowe); Home and Beauty; Macrune's Guevara; The White Devil; Captain of Kopenick; *Young Vic:* (author and Dir) Scapino 1970, 1977, NY 1974, LA 1975, Australia 1975, Oslo 1975; The Taming of the Shrew, 1970, 1977; The Comedy of Errors, 1971; The Maids, Deathwatch, 1972; The Alchemist, 1972; Bible One, 1972; French Without Tears, 1973; Joseph and the Amazing Technicolor Dreamcoat (Roundhouse and Albery Theatre), 1973, NY 1976; Much Ado About Nothing, 1973; Macbeth, 1975; Antony and Cleopatra,

1976; King Lear, 1980; Childe Byron, 1981; Masquerade, 1982; *for Théâtre National de Belgique:* Pantagleise, 1970; Antony and Cleopatra, 1971; Pericles, 1972. Mem., Arts Council Young People's Panel, 1968. Governor, Central School of Arts and Crafts, 1970. Hon. Fellow of Shakespeare Inst. Hon. Dr of Theatre, Philadelphia Coll. of Performing Arts, 1978. *Recreation:* travel. *Address:* The Young Vic Theatre, The Cut, SE1 8LP.

DUNLOP, Rev. Canon Ian Geoffrey David, FSA; Canon and Chancellor of Salisbury Cathedral, since 1972; *b* 19 Aug. 1925; *s* of late Walter N. U. Dunlop and Marguerite Irene (*née* Shakerley); *m* 1957, Deirdre Marcia, *d* of late Dr Marcus Jamieson; one *s* one *d. Educ:* Winchester Coll.; New Coll., Oxford (MA); Strasbourg Univ. (Diploma); Lincoln Theol Coll. FSA 1965. Served Irish Guards, 1944-46 (Lieut). Curate, Hatfield, 1956-60; Chaplain, Westminster Sch., 1960-62; Vicar of Bures, Suffolk, 1962-72. Member: Gen. Synod, 1975-; Cathedrals' Adv. Commn, 1981-. Trustee, Historic Churches Preservation Trust, 1969-. *Publications:* Versailles, 1956, 2nd edn 1970; Palaces and Progresses of Elizabeth I, 1962; Chateaux of the Loire, 1969; Companion Guide to the Ile de France, 1979; Cathedrals Crusade, 1981; weekly column in Church Times. *Recreations:* painting, bird watching. *Address:* 24 The Close, Salisbury, Wilts SP1 2EH. *T:* Salisbury 6809. *Club:* Army and Navy.

DUNLOP, John; MP (UUUP) Mid-Ulster since 1974; *b* 20 May 1910; *s* of Martin T. and Agnes Dunlop, Belfast; *m* 1st, 1936, Ruby Hunter; two *s* (and one *s* decd); 2nd, 1970, Joyce Campbell. *Educ:* primary sch. and techn. college. Apprentice multiple grocers, 1926; assumed management, 1934; acquired own business, 1944. Mem. (VULC), Mid-Ulster, NI Assembly, 1973-74. Civil Defence Medal and ribbon 1945. *Recreations:* music, choral singing, amateur soccer. *Address:* Turnaface Road, Moneymore, Magherafelt, Co. Londonderry BT4 7YP. *T:* 064-874. 594.

DUNLOP, Sir John (Wallace), KBE 1971; Australian Company Director; Chairman, Edwards Dunlop and Co. Ltd; Director: Australian Industry Development Corporation; Australian Bank Ltd; Rothmans of Pall Mall (Australia) Ltd; Lansing Australia Pty Ltd; Senior Adviser on Australian Affairs, Banque de Paris et des Pays-Bas, Paris; *b* 20 May 1910; *s* of late W. P. Dunlop, Sydney; *m* 1st, 1932, Phyllis Haley; one *s* decd; 2nd, 1960, Patricia Lloyd Jones. *Educ:* Tudor House; Geelong Grammar Sch.; Univ. of Sydney. Member (Bd or Cttee): Inst. of Directors in Australia, 1968-; Sydney Advisory Bd, the Salvation Army, 1970. *Address:* 275 George Street, Sydney, NSW 2000, Australia. *T:* 20222. *Clubs:* Australian, Union, Royal Sydney Golf (all Sydney).

DUNLOP, Norman Gordon Edward; Chief Financial Officer, British Airways, since 1982; *b* 16 April 1928; *s* of Ross Munn Dunlop, CA and May Dunlop; *m* 1952, Jean (*née* Taylor); one *s* one *d. Educ:* Trinity Coll., Glenalmond. CA 1951, Scotland. Thompson McLintock & Co., Glasgow, 1945-56; De Havilland and Hawker Siddeley Aviation Companies, 1956-64; Commercial Union Assce Co. Ltd, 1964-77, Chief Exec., 1972-77; Dir, Inchcape Berhad, Singapore, 1979-82. *Recreations:* gardening, fishing, ski-ing, ballet. *Address:* 40 Addisland Court, Holland Villas Road, W14 8DA. *T:* 01-602 3503. *Club:* Caledonian.

DUNLOP, Richard B.; *see* Buchanan-Dunlop.

DUNLOP, Sir Thomas, 3rd Bt, *cr* 1916; Partner, Thomas Dunlop & Sons, Ship & Insurance Brokers, Glasgow, since 1938; *b* 11 April 1912; *s* of Sir Thomas Dunlop, 2nd Bt; *S* father, 1963; *m* 1947, Adda Mary Alison, *d* of T. Arthur Smith, Lindsaylands, Biggar, Lanarks; one *s* one *d* (and one *d* decd). *Educ:* Shrewsbury; St John's Coll., Cambridge (BA). Chartered Accountant, 1939. Former Chm., Savings Bank of Glasgow. Member: Cttee of Princess Louise Scottish Hosp., Erskine; Vice-Pres., Royal Alfred Seafarers' Soc. OStJ 1965. *Recreations:* shooting, fishing, golf. *Heir: s* Thomas Dunlop, *b* 22 April 1951. *Address:* The Corrie, Kilmacolm, Renfrewshire. *T:* Kilmacolm 3239. *Club:* Western (Glasgow).

DUNLOP, Sir William (Norman Gough), Kt 1975; JP; Managing Director, Dunlop Farms Ltd; *b* 9 April 1914; *s* of Norman Matthew Dunlop and Alice Ada Dunlop (*née* Gough); *m* 1940, Ruby Jean (*née* Archie); three *s* three *d. Educ:* Waitaki Boys' High Sch. Farmer in Canterbury, NZ. President: Federated Farmers, NZ, 1973-74; Coopworth Sheep Soc., NZ, 1971-74; Member: Agriculture Adv. Council, NZ, 1970-74; Immigration Adv. Council, NZ, 1971-; Transport Adv. Council, NZ, 1971-76; Trustee, Todd Foundn, 1973-; Chm., Neurological Foundn (Canterbury), 1975-77; Dep. Chm., NZ Meat and Wool Board Electoral Coll., 1973; Director: Rural Bank & Finance Corp., NZ, 1974-81; New Zealand Light Leathers, 1973-80. Trustee: Todd Foundn, 1973-81; Lincoln Coll. Foundn, 1977- (Chm. Bd). Internat. Visitors Award, US Dept of State, 1971. JP 1972. *Recreations:* music, gardening. *Address:* 242 Main Road, Monks Bay, Christchurch 8, New Zealand. *T:* Christchurch 849056. *Clubs:* Civil Service (Wellington); Canterbury (Christchurch).

DUNLUCE, Viscount; *see under* Antrim, 14th Earl of (who succeeded 1977, but is still known as Viscount Dunluce).

DUNMORE, 11th Earl of, *cr* 1686; **Kenneth Randolph Murray;** Viscount Fincastle, Lord Murray, 1686; Baron Dunmore (UK), 1831; retired; *b* 6 June 1913; *s* of Arthur Charles Murray (*d* 1964) (*g g s* of 4th Earl), and Susan Maud

(*d* 1922), *d* of Edward Richards, Tasmania; *S* brother, 1981; *m* 1938, Margaret Joy (*d* 1976), *d* of late P. D. Cousins, Burnie, Tasmania; two *s. Educ:* Tasmanian State School. Sgt, 12th/50th Bn, AIF, 1939-45. Former Postmaster, Tasmania. Past Master, Tamar Valley Masonic Lodge 42 Tasmanian Constitution, 1957-58. JP Beaconsfield, Tasmania, 1963. *Recreation:* lawn bowls. *Heir: s* Viscount Fincastle, *qv. Address:* Gravelly Beach, Tasmania, Australia. *T:* 944275. *Club:* Exeter RSL (Exeter, Tasmania).

DUNN, Air Vice-Marshal Eric Clive, CB 1981; BEM 1951; Air Officer Engineering, HQ Strike Command, since 1981; *b* 27 Nov. 1927; *s* of W. E. and K. M. Dunn; *m* 1951, Margaret Gray; three *d. Educ:* Bridlington Sch. CEng, MRAeS; MBIM. RAF aircraft apprentice, 1944-47; commnd Engr Br., 1954; Staff Coll., 1964; Jt Services Staff Coll., 1967; Sen. Engrg Officer, RAF Boulmer, 1968; MoD, 1969-70; Comd Electrical Engr, NEAF, 1971-72; Dir of Engrg Policy (RAF), 1973-75; RCDS, 1976; AO Wales, and Stn Comdr RAF St Athan, 1977; Air Officer Maintenance, RAF Support Comd, 1977-81. *Recreations:* golf, sailing. *Address:* RAF Strike Command, High Wycombe, Bucks HP14 4UE. *Club:* Royal Air Force.

DUNN, Lt-Col Sir (Francis) Vivian, KCVO 1969 (CVO 1954; MVO 1939); OBE 1960; FRAM; RM Retd; *b* 24 Dec. 1908; *s* of Captain William James Dunn, (Paddy), MVO, MC, Director of Music, Royal Horse Guards, and Beatrice Maud Dunn; *g s* of Sgt Thomas Dunn, Band Sgt, 1st Bn 33rd (W Riding) Regt of Foot (over a century in succession in military music); *m* 1938, Margery Kathleen Halliday; one *s* two *d. Educ:* Winchester; Konservatorium der Musik, Cologne; Royal Acad. of Music. ARAM 1932, FRAM 1953. Played with Queen's Hall Prom. Orch., 1927, BBC Symph. Orch., 1930 (founder mem., 1st violin section). Lieut RM and Director of Music, 1931; addtl duties in cypher work, War of 1939-45; with HMS Vanguard for Royal Tour of S Africa, 1947; toured Canada and USA, 1949; Lt-Col and Principal Director of Music, RM, 1953; Royal Tour of Commonwealth countries, 1953; retired 1968. Liveryman, Worshipful Co. of Musicians, 1956. Hon. Mem., Amer. Bandmasters' Assoc., 1969; Pres., International Military Music Soc., 1977-. EMI Golden Disc Award, 1969. Guest conductor with principal British orchestras and in Univs in Canada and USA; composer and arranger of ceremonial music for RM. *Address:* 16 West Common, Haywards Heath, Sussex RH16 2AH. *T:* Haywards Heath 412987. *Club:* Army and Navy.

DUNN, Col George Willoughby, CBE 1959; DSO 1943 and Bar 1944; MC 1943; TD 1949; DL; Partner, Clark & Oliver, Solicitors, Arbroath; Chairman: The Alliance Trust; The Second Alliance Trust; Member of Queen's Body Guard for Scotland (Royal Company of Archers); *b* 27 March 1914; *s* of Willoughby Middleton Dunn, coal owner, Lanarkshire; *m* 1944, Louise Wilson, er *d* of Alexander Stephen MacLellan, LLD, ship builder and engr, Glasgow; two *d. Educ:* Trinity Coll., Glenalmond; Glasgow Univ. BL 1937; Solicitor, 1937. Served War of 1939-45 with 51st Highland Div., Middle East, N Africa, Sicily and NW Europe; Col late TA The Black Watch. Chm., Royal British Legion Scotland, 1971-74. DL Angus 1971. *Recreations:* golf, fishing. *Address:* Letham House, St Vigeans, Arbroath, Angus DD11 4RF. *T:* Arbroath 72538. *Clubs:* Naval and Military; New (Edinburgh); Royal and Ancient (St Andrews).

DUNN, James Anthony; MP Kirkdale Division of Liverpool since 1964 (Lab 1964-81, SDP since 1981); *b* 30 Jan. 1926; *s* of James Richard Dunn and Margaret (*née* McDermott); *m* 1954, Dorothy (*née* Larkey); two *s* two *d. Educ:* St Teresa's Sch., Liverpool; London Sch. of Economics and Political Science. Opposition Whip, 1971-74; a Lord Comr, HM Treasury, 1974-76; Parly Under-Sec. of State, Northern Ireland Office, 1976-79. Member: Estimates Cttee; House of Commons Services Cttee; House of Commons Select Cttee on Defence, 1981-. Sec., Anglo-Manx Commonwealth Parly Gp, 1976-. Pres., Merseyside Chinese Community Co-ordinating Cttee, 1977-. *Address:* 45 Lisburn Lane, Liverpool L13 9AF. *T:* 051-226 6054.

DUNN, Brig. Keith Frederick William, CBE 1941; DL; retired; *b* 31 July 1891; *s* of Brig.-Gen. R. H. W. Dunn, DL, Althrey, Wrexham, and Constance, *d* of Maj.-Gen. G. E. Erskine; *m* 1st, 1915, Ava (*d* 1938), *d* of Brig.-Gen. H. F. Kays, CB; one *s* one *d* (and one *s* decd); 2nd, 1946, Joan, *d* of Sir Frank Beauchamp, 1st Bt, CBE and widow of Major Claude de Lisle Bush. *Educ:* Wellington Coll.; RMA 2nd Lieut RA 1911. Served European War, 1914-19 (despatches). Equitation Sch., Weedon, 1922-25; Adjt RMA, 1926-29; Lieut-Col 1938; served in North West Europe, 1939; Brig. 1939; CRA, 1st Cavalry Div., 1939-40; comd 5th Cavalry Bde, MEF, 1940-41; retd 1942; re-employed, comd Glos Sub-District, 1942-45. Chief Training Officer, Min. of Agriculture and Fisheries, 1946-47. Mem., Pony Club Orgn Cttee, 1948-66; Chm., Pony Club Trng Cttee, 1954-66. DL Glos, 1960. *Recreations:* hunting, golf. *Address:* Bencombe House, Uley, Dursley, Glos. *T:* Dursley 860255. *Club:* Army and Navy.

See also Rt Hon. Sir R. H. W. Dunn.

DUNN, Air Marshal Sir Patrick Hunter, KBE 1965 (CBE 1950); CB 1956; DFC 1941; FRAeS; *b* 31 Dec. 1912; *s* of late William Alexander Dunn, Ardentinny, Argyllshire; *m* 1939, Diana Ledward Smith; two *d. Educ:* Glasgow Academy; Loretto; Glasgow Univ. Commissioned, 1933, Pre-war service in flying boats; as flying instructor 500 (County of Kent) Sqdn, AAF; with the Long Range Development Unit and as instructor at the Central Flying Sch. War service included command of 80 and 274 Fighter Squadrons and 71 OTU, all in Middle East (1940-42); at Air Ministry, and in Fighter Command, Sector Commander, 1945-46. Post-war service in Air Ministry,

1947–48; Malaya, 1949–50; NATO Defence Coll., 1950–52; Fighter Command, 1953–56; ADC to the Queen, 1953–58. AOC and Commandant, RAF Flying Coll., 1956–58; Deputy Air Sec., 1959–61; AOC No. 1 Group, Bomber Command, 1961–64; AOC-in-Chief, Flying Training Command, 1964–66; retired from RAF, 1967. Director i/c Management Services, British Steel Corp., 1967–68; resigned to become Dep. Chm., British Eagle Internat. Airlines Ltd; Chm., Eagle Aircraft Services, 1969; Aviation Consultant, British Steel Corporation, 1969–76. Mem. Council, Air League, 1968–73 and 1975–79 (Dep. Chm., 1972–73; Chm., Defence Cttee, 1968–73); Mem., British Atlantic Cttee, 1976–. Dir, Gloucester, Coventry, Cricklewood and Kingston Industrial Trading Estates, 1969–75 and 1977–81. A Trustee and Governor of Loretto, 1959–81; Chairman: Fettesian-Lorettonian Club, 1972–75; Cttee, Assoc. of Governing Bodies of Public Schs, 1976–79. Pres., Lorettonian Soc., 1980–81. *Recreations:* tennis, sailing, shooting. *Address:* Little Hillbark, Cookham Dean, Berks. *Clubs:* Royal Air Force, Hurlingham.
See also Sir John Denton Marsden, Bt.

DUNN, Robert John; MP (C) Dartford, since 1979; *b* July 1946; *s* of Robert and Doris Dunn, Swinton, Lancs; *m* 1976, Janet Elizabeth Wall, BD, *d* of Denis Wall, Dulwich; one *s*. *Educ:* State schs; Univ. of Salford (BA, Politics and History); Post-grad. Dip. Management Studies. Senior Buyer, J. Sainsbury Ltd, 1973–79. Councillor, London Borough of Southwark, 1974–78 (Opposition Minority Gp spokesman on Housing and Finance Matters). Chairman, Eccles Young Conservatives, 1965–67; Vice-Pres., Eccles Conservative Assoc., 1974–; contested (C): Eccles, Gen. Elections, Feb. and Oct. 1974; adopted as Parly Candidate (C) Dartford, 1975. Jt Sec., Conservative backbench Educn Cttee, 1980–81; Mem., Parly Select Cttee on the Environment, 1981–; PPS to Parly Under-Secs of State at DES, 1981–82, to Paymaster General and Chancellor of the Duchy of Lancaster, 1982-. President: Dartford Young Conservatives, 1976–; Kent Gp Young Conservatives, 1982–; SE Area Educn Adv. Cttee, 1982–; Vice-Pres., Dartford branch, Kent Assoc. for the Disabled, 1979–; Chm., Dartford Cttee for the Internat. Year of the Disabled Person, 1981-. Governor: Furness Special School, Hextable, Kent, 1978–; West Hill CP Sch., Dartford, 1980–; NW Kent Coll. of Technol., 1982-. *Recreations:* canvassing; American politics. *Address:* House of Commons, SW1A 0AA. *T:* 01-219 5209. *Clubs:* Carlton; Dartford Rotary (Hon. Mem.).

DUNN, Rt. Hon. Sir Robin Horace Walford, Kt 1969; MC 1944; PC 1980; **Rt. Hon. Lord Justice Dunn;** a Lord Justice of Appeal, since 1980; *b* 16 Jan. 1918; *s* of Brig. K. F. W. Dunn, *qv*, and of Ava, *d* of Brig.-Gen. H. F. Kays, CB; *m* 1941, Judith, *d* of late Sir Gonne Pilcher, MC; one *s* one *d* (and one *d* decd). *Educ:* Wellington; Royal Military Academy, Woolwich (Sword of Honour). First Commissioned, RA, 1938; RHA, 1941; Staff Coll., 1946; retired (hon. Major), 1948. Second World War of 1939–45; France and Belgium, 1939–40; Western Desert and Libya, 1941–42; Normandy and NW Europe, 1944–45 (wounded thrice, despatches twice, MC); Hon. Col Comdt, RA, 1980–. Called to Bar (Inner Temple), 1948; Master of the Bench, Inner Temple, 1969. Western Circuit, Junior Counsel to Registrar of Restrictive Trading Agreements, 1959–62; QC 1962; Judge of the High Court of Justice, Family Division (formerly Probate, Divorce and Admiralty Division), 1969–80; Presiding Judge, Western Circuit, 1974–78. Treas., Gen. Council of the Bar, 1967–69 (Mem., 1959–63); Chm. Betting Levy Appeal Tribunal, 1964–69; Dep. Chm., Somerset QS, 1965–71; Mem., Lord Chancellor's Cttee on Legal Educn, 1968–69. *Recreation:* hunting. *Address:* 42 Roland Way, SW7. *T:* 01-373 1319; Lynch, Allerford, Somerset. *T:* Porlock 862509.

DUNN, Prof. Thomas Alexander; Professor of Literature and Head of Department of English Studies, University of Stirling, since 1966; *b* 6 March 1923; *s* of James Symington Dunn and Elizabeth Taylor; *m* 1947, Joyce Mary Armstrong; two *s* one *d*. *Educ:* Dumfries Academy; Edinburgh Univ. (MA, PhD). Served War, Pilot, Fleet Air Arm, Sub-Lt (A) RNVR, 1942–45. Univ. of Ghana, 1953, Prof., 1960; Prof., Univ. of Lagos, 1964–65; Visiting Prof., Univ. of Western Ontario, 1965–66; University of Stirling: Mem., Academic Council, 1966–, Univ. Court, 1968–72; Chm., Board of Studies for Arts, 1975–81; Chm., MacRobert Arts Centre, 1973–82. Member: Inter-Univ. Council for Higher Educn Overseas, 1967–75; Scottish Univs Council on Entrance, 1968–74, 1979–81; Consultative Cttee on the Curriculum, 1968–76. Member: Scottish Arts Council, 1969–76; Arts Council of Gt Britain, 1971–73; Broadcasting Council for Scotland, 1972–76; Films of Scotland, 1972–82; Chairman: Univs Cttee on Scottish Literature, 1970–; Drama Cttee, 1972–76; Grants to Publishers Panel, 1975–78; Pres., Assoc. for Scottish Literary Studies, 1972–76. *Publications:* Philip Massinger: the man and the playwright, 1957; (with D. E. S. Maxwell) Introducing Poetry, 1966; Massinger and Field: The Fatal Dowry, 1969; (ed) Universitas (Ghana), 1955–63; (ed) Fountainwell Drama Texts. *Recreations:* gardening, theatre and arts generally. *Address:* Coney Park, 121 Henderson Street, Bridge of Allan, Stirling FK9 4RQ. *T:* Stirling 833373. *Club:* Stirling and County (Stirling).

DUNN, Sir Vivian; see Dunn, Sir F. V.

DUNN, William Francis N.; see Newton Dunn.

DUNN, William Hubert, QC 1982; a Recorder of the Crown Court, since 1980; *b* 8 July 1933; *s* of William Patrick Millar Dunn and Isabel (*née* Thompson); *m* 1971, Maria Henriqueta Theresa d'Arouje Perestrello de Moser; one *s* one *d*. *Educ:* Rockport, Co. Down, N Ireland; Winchester Coll.; New Coll., Oxford (Hons degree PPE) (Half-Blue fencing 1954–55). 2nd

Lieut, Life Guards, 1956–57; Household Cavalry Reserve of Officers, 1957–64. Cholmondeley Scholar, Lincoln's Inn, 1958, called to Bar, 1958; Local Govt Commissioner, 1963; a Deputy Circuit Judge, 1972. *Recreations:* hunting, travel, literature. *Address:* 19 Clarendon Street, SW1. *T:* 01-834 5578; Tudor Hall, Holywood, Co. Down, N Ireland. *T:* Holywood 3139. *Clubs:* Boodle's; Ulster (Belfast).

DUNNE, Irene, (Mrs F. D. Griffin), Hon. Doctor of Music, Hon. LLD; *b* Louisville, Kentucky, USA, 20 Dec. 1904; *d* of Joseph A. Dunne and Adelaide A. Henry; *m* 1927, Dr Francis D. Griffin (*d* 1965); one *d*. *Educ:* Loretta Academy, St Louis, Mo., USA; Chicago Musical Coll., Chicago. Acted in the original Show Boat, 1929. Entered motion pictures, 1931; first film Cimarron. Films include: Back Street, Awful Truth, Roberta, Anna and the King of Siam, Life with Father, I Remember Mama, The Mudlark (as Queen Victoria), Never a Dull Moment. Laetare Medal, University of Notre Dame. Mem. Defence Advisory Cttee, US, to advise on welfare matters in the women's services, 1951; Mem. US Delegation to United Nations 12th Gen. Assembly. *Recreation:* golf. *Address:* 461 North Faring Road, Moment, Los Angeles, Calif 90024, USA. *T:* Crestview 56226.

DUNNE, Most Rev. Patrick, DD; Auxiliary Bishop of Dublin, (RC) and titular Bishop of Nara since 1946; Parish Priest of St Mary's Haddington Road, Dublin; Dean of the Metropolitan Chapter; Vicar-General; *b* Dublin, 3 June 1891. *Educ:* Holy Cross Coll., Clonliffe, Dublin; Irish Coll., Rome. Ordained in Rome, 1913; Sec. to Archbishops of Dublin, 1919–43; Parish Priest, Church of the Holy Family, Aughrim Street, Dublin, 1943–47; Domestic Prelate, 1943. *Address:* St Mary's, Haddington Road, Dublin.

DUNNE, Thomas Raymond, JP; HM Lord-Lieutenant, County of Hereford and Worcester, since 1977; *b* 24 Oct. 1933; *s* of Philip Dunne, MC, and Margaret Walker; *m* 1957, Henrietta Crawley; two *s* two *d*. *Educ:* Eton; RMA Sandhurst. Served Army, 1951–59: Royal Horse Guards. Herefordshire CC, 1962–68. Pres., 3 Counties Agric. Soc., 1977. Dir, West Regional Bd, Central TV, 1981. Chairman: N Hereford Conservative Assoc., 1968–74; Governors, Lucton Sch., 1970–; Mem. Council, Malvern Coll., 1980. High Sheriff 1970, DL 1973, Herefordshire; JP Hereford and Worcester, 1977. KStJ 1978. *Address:* Gatley Park, Leinthall Earls, Leominster, Herefordshire HR6 9TT. *T:* Wigmore 227. *Clubs:* White's; Mid Ocean (Bermuda).

DUNNET, Prof. George Mackenzie, PhD; Regius Professor of Natural History, University of Aberdeen, since 1974; *b* 19 April 1928; *s* of John George and Christina I. Dunnet; *m* 1953, Margaret Henderson Thomson; one *s* two *d*. *Educ:* Peterhead Academy; Aberdeen Univ. BSc (1st cl. hons) 1949; PhD 1952. Research Officer, CSIRO, Australia, 1953–58; Lectr in Ecology, Dir Culterty Field Stn, Univ. of Aberdeen, 1958–66, Sen. Lectr 1966–71; Sen. Research Fellow, DSIR, NZ, 1968–69; Prof. of Zoology, Univ. of Aberdeen, 1971–74. Member: Red Deer Commn, 1975–80; Scottish Adv. Cttee of Nature Conservancy Council, 1979–; Chairman: Shetland Oil Terminal Environment Adv. Gp, 1977–; Adv. Cttees on Protection of Birds, 1979–81. Pres., British Ecological Soc., 1980–81. FRSE 1970; FInstBiol 1974; FRSA 1981. *Publications:* contrib. Ibis, Jl Applied Ecol., Aust. Jl Zool., CSIRO Wildl. Res. *Recreations:* hill walking, photography. *Address:* Culterty House, Newburgh, Ellon, Aberdeenshire AB4 0AA. *T:* Newburgh (Aberdeen) 633. *Club:* Royal Commonwealth Society.

DUNNETT, Alastair MacTavish; Director: Thomson Scottish Petroleum Ltd (Chairman, 1972–79); Scottish Television, 1975–79; Member Executive Board, The Thomson Organisation Ltd, 1973–78; *b* 26 Dec. 1908; *s* of David Sinclair Dunnett and Isabella Crawford MacTavish; *m* 1946, Dorothy Halliday; two *s*. *Educ:* Overnewton Sch.; Hillhead High Sch., Glasgow. Commercial Bank of Scotland, Ltd, 1925; Co-founder of The Claymore Press, 1933–34; Glasgow Weekly Herald, 1935–36; The Bulletin, 1936–37; Daily Record, 1937–40; Chief Press Officer, Sec. of State for Scotland, 1940–46; Editor, Daily Record, 1946–55; Editor, The Scotsman, 1956–72; Man. Dir, The Scotsman Publications Ltd, 1962–70, Chm., 1970–74. Smith-Mundt Scholarship to USA, 1951. Governor, Pitlochry Festival Theatre. Member: Scottish Tourist Board, 1956–69; Press Council, 1959–62; Council of Nat. Trust for Scotland, 1962–69; Council of Commonwealth Press Union, 1964–78; Edinburgh Univ. Court, 1964–66; Edinburgh Festival Council, 1967–80. Hon. LLD Strathclyde, 1978. *Publications:* Treasure at Sonnach, 1935; Heard Tell, 1946; Quest by Canoe, 1950, repr. 1967, as It's Too Late in the Year; Highlands and Islands of Scotland, 1951; The Donaldson Line, 1952; The Land of Scotch, 1953; (as Alec Tavis) The Duke's Day, 1970; (ed) Alistair Maclean Introduces Scotland, 1972; No Thanks to the Duke, 1978; *plays:* The Original John Mackay, Glasgow Citizens, 1956; Fit to Print, Duke of York's, 1962. *Recreations:* sailing, riding, walking. *Address:* 87 Colinton Road, Edinburgh EH10 5DF. *T:* 031-337 2107. *Clubs:* Caledonian; Scottish Arts, New (Edinburgh).

DUNNETT, Denzil Inglis, CMG 1967; OBE 1962; HM Diplomatic Service, retired; London Representative, Scottish Development Agency, since 1978; *b* 21 Oct. 1917; *s* of late Sir James Dunnett, KCIE and late Annie (*née* Sangster); *m* 1946, Ruth Rawcliffe (*d* 1974); two *s* one *d*. *Educ:* Edinburgh Acad.; Corpus Christi Coll., Oxford. Served with RA, 1939–45. Diplomatic Service: Foreign Office, 1947–48; Sofia, 1948–50; Foreign Office, 1950–53; UK Delegn to OEEC, Paris, 1953–56; Commercial Sec., Buenos Aires, 1956–60; Consul, Elisabethville, 1961–62; Commercial Counsellor, Madrid, 1962–67; seconded to BoT, 1967–70; Counsellor, Mexico City, 1970–73; Ambassador to Senegal, Mauritania, Mali and Guinea, 1973–76, and to Guinea-Bissau, 1975–76;

Diplomatic Service Chm., CS Selection Bd, 1976-77. *Recreations:* golf, music. *Address:* 11 Victoria Grove, W8 5RW. *T:* 01-584 7523. *Club:* Oxford & Cambridge University.

DUNNETT, Sir George Sangster, KBE 1952; CB 1950; *b* 12 May 1907; *e s* of late Sir James Dunnett, KCIE; *m* 1938, Margaret Rosalind (*d* 1977), *er d* of David Davies, MD, Tunbridge Wells; one *s* three *d. Educ:* Edinburgh Academy; Corpus Christi Coll., Oxford. Bd of Educn, 1930; Treasury, 1931; Min. of Civil Aviation, 1946; Dep. Sec., Min. of Agriculture and Fisheries, 1947-56; Chm., Sugar Board, 1956-70. *Recreations:* golf, philosophy. *Address:* Basings Cottage, Cowden, Kent. *T:* Cowden 398. *Club:* Athenæum.

DUNNETT, Jack; MP (Lab) Nottingham East, since 1974 (Central Nottingham, 1964-74); *b* 24 June 1922; *m* 1951; two *s* three *d. Educ:* Whitgift Middle Sch., Croydon; Downing Coll., Cambridge (MA, LLB). Served with Cheshire Regt, 1941-46 (Capt.). Admitted Solicitor, 1949. Middlesex CC, 1958-61; Councillor, Enfield Borough Council, 1958-61; Alderman, Enfield Borough Council, 1961-63; Councillor, Greater London Council, 1964-67. Former PPS to: Minister of State, FCO; Minister of Transport. Chm., FA, 1981- (Vice-Pres., 1981; Mem. Council, 1977-); Mem., Football League Management Cttee, 1977-; Pres., Football League, 1981-; Chm., Notts County FC, 1968-. *Recreation:* watching professional football. *Address:* Whitehall Court, SW1A 2EP. *T:* 01-839 6962.

DUNNETT, Sir (Ludovic) James, GCB 1969 (KCB 1960; CB 1957); CMG 1948; Permanent Under-Secretary of State, Ministry of Defence, 1966-74; *b* 12 Feb. 1914; *s* of late Sir James Dunnett, KCIE; *m* 1944, Olga Adair (*d* 1980); no *c. Educ:* Edinburgh Acad.; University Coll., Oxford. Entered Air Ministry, 1936; Private Sec. to Permanent Sec., 1937-44; transferred to Ministry of Civil Aviation, 1945; Under Sec., 1948; Under Sec., Min. of Supply, 1951, Deputy Sec., 1953; Deputy Sec., Min. of Transport, 1958; Permanent Secretary: Min. of Transport, 1959-62; Min. of Labour, 1962-66. Mem., SSRC, 1977-. Visiting Fellow, Nuffield Coll., Oxford, 1964-72. Chm., Internat. Maritime Industries Forum, 1976-79; Pres., Inst. of Manpower Studies, 1977-80; Trustee, Charities Aid Foundn. *Recreation:* golf. *Address:* 2 Warwick Square, SW1. *T:* 01-834 5144. *Club:* Reform.

DUNNING, John Ernest Patrick, CBE 1973; retired; Director, Rocket Propulsion Establishment, Westcott, 1955-72; *b* 19 Sept. 1912; *s* of late Rev. E. M. Dunning, MA, sometime Rector of Cumberworth and Denby Dale, Yorks; *m* 1939, Mary Meikle Robertson. *Educ:* Wheelwright Gram. Sch., Dewsbury; Downing Coll., Cambridge (Exhibr, MA). 1st cl. hons Mech. Scis Tripos, 1935. Blackstone Ltd, Stamford, 1935-37; Bristol Aeroplane Co. Ltd (Engines), 1937-38; Armstrong Whitworth Securities Ltd (Kadenacy Dept), 1938-40; RAE, 1940-50; Asst Dir, Min. of Supply, 1950-55; Dir, Engine Research, Min. of Supply, 1955. FRAeS, FIMechE; FRSA. *Publications:* scientific and technical papers. *Address:* 24 Coombe Hill Crescent, Thame, Oxon. *T:* Thame 3893. *Club:* North Oxford Golf.

DUNNING, Prof. John Harry, PhD; Professor of International Investment and Business Studies, since 1974 and Head of Department of Economics since 1964, University of Reading; *b* 26 June 1927; *m* 1st, 1948, Ida Teresa Bellamy (marr. diss. 1975); one *s* ; 2nd, 1975, Christine Mary Brown. *Educ:* Lower Sch. of John Lyon, Harrow; University Coll. London (BSc (Econ); PhD). Research Asst, University Coll. London, 1951-52; Lectr and Sen. Lectr, Univ. of Southampton, 1952-64; Prof. of Economics, Univ. of Reading, 1964-74. Visiting Prof.: Univ. of Western Ontario, Canada; Univ. of California (Berkeley), 1968-69; Boston Univ., USA, 1976; Stockholm Sch. of Economics, 1978; HEC, Univ. of Montreal, Canada, 1980; Walker-Ames Prof., Univ. of Washington, Seattle, 1981. Consultant to UN, 1974- and OECD, 1975-. Member: SE Economic Planning Council, 1966-68; Chemicals EDC, 1968-77; UN Study Gp on Multinational Corps, 1973-74. Dir of Economists Advisory Gp Ltd. Fellow, Acad. of Internat. Business. Hon. PhD Uppsala, 1975. *Publications:* American Investment in British Manufacturing Industry, 1958; British Industry (with C. J. Thomas), 1963; Economic Planning and Town Expansion, 1963; Studies in International Investment, 1970; (ed) The Multinational Enterprise, 1971; An Economic Study of the City of London (with E. V. Morgan), 1971; (ed) International Investment, 1972; (ed) Economic Analysis and the Multinational Enterprise, 1974; US Industry in Britain, 1976; (with T. Houston) UK Industry Abroad, 1976; (with R. D. Pearce) The World's Largest Industrial Companies, 1981; International Production and the Multinational Enterprise, 1981; (ed jtly) International Capital Movements, 1982; numerous articles in learned and professional jls. *Address:* University of Reading, Whiteknights Park, Reading, Berks. *T:* Reading 875123.

DUNNING, Joseph, CBE 1977; retired; Principal, Napier College of Commerce and Technology, Edinburgh, 1963-81; *b* 9 Oct. 1920; *s* of Joseph and Elizabeth Ellen Dunning; *m* 1948, Edith Mary Barlow (*d* 1972); one *s* one *d. Educ:* London University (BSc Hons); Durham University (MEd); Manchester College of Technology (AMCT). Metallurgical Industry and lecturing, 1936-56; Principal, Cleveland Technical College, 1956-63. MA Open Univ.; FEIS. *Recreations:* silversmithing, photography. *Address:* 50 Frogston Terrace, Edinburgh EH10 7AE. *Club:* New (Edinburgh).

DUNNING, Sir Simon (William Patrick), 3rd Bt, *cr* 1930; *b* 14 Dec. 1939; *s* of Sir William Leonard Dunning, 2nd Bt, and of Kathleen Lawrie, *d* of J. P. Cuthbert, MC; *S* father, 1961; *m* 1975, Frances Deirdre Morton, *d* of Major

Patrick Lancaster; one *d. Educ:* Eton. *Recreation:* shooting. *Address:* Low Auchengillan, Blanefield, by Glasgow. *T:* Blanefield 70323. *Clubs:* Turf; Western (Glasgow).

DUNNINGTON-JEFFERSON, Sir Mervyn (Stewart), 2nd Bt *cr* 1958; Company Director, since 1968; *b* 5 Aug. 1943; *s* of Sir John Alexander Dunnington-Jefferson, 1st Bt, DSO, and of Frances Isobel, *d* of Col H. A. Cape, DSO; *S* father, 1979; *m* 1971, Caroline Anna, *o d* of J. M. Bayley; one *s* two *d. Educ:* Eton College. Joined Charrington & Co. Ltd (Brewers), 1961; left in 1968 to become joint founder and director of Hatton Builders Ltd, specialising in building contracting and property development. *Recreations:* sport—cricket, skiing, golf, etc. *Heir:* s John Alexander Dunnington-Jefferson, *b* 23 March 1980. *Address:* 7 Bolingbroke Grove, SW11 6ES. *T:* 01-675 3395.

DUNPARK, Hon. Lord; Alastair McPherson Johnston, TD; BA, LLB; FSAScot; a Senator of the College of Justice in Scotland and Lord of Session, since 1971; *b* 15 Dec. 1915; *s* of late Rev. A. M. Johnston, BD, Stirling; *m* 1939, Katharine Margaret (Bunty), *d* of Charles Mitchell, Chislehurst; three *s. Educ:* Merchiston Castle Sch.; Jesus Coll., Cambridge; Edinburgh Univ. RA (TA), 1939-46 (despatches); Staff Coll., Haifa, 1943; Major 1943. Mem. of Faculty of Advocates, 1946; QC (Scotland), 1958. Sheriff of Dumfries and Galloway, 1966-68; Mem., Scottish Law Commn, 1968-71. Chairman: The Cockburn Assoc. (Edinburgh Civic Trust), 1969-74; Royal Artillery Assoc., E of Scotland District, 1946-60, Scottish Region, 1962-78; Edinburgh Marriage Guidance Council, 1969-72 (Pres., 1973-); Council, St George's Sch. for Girls, Edinburgh, 1973-; Edinburgh Legal Dispensary, 1961-. Hon. Fellow, Dept of Law, Edinburgh Univ., 1969. *Publications:* Jt Editor, 3rd edn of Walton's Law of Husband and Wife, 1951; Jt Editor, 7th edn of Gloag and Henderson's Introduction to Law of Scotland, 1968. *Recreations:* formerly fishing, golf; now walking and gardening. *Address:* 8 Heriot Row, Edinburgh EH3 6HU. *T:* 031-556 4663; Parkend, Stichill, Roxburghshire. *T:* Stichill 256. *Club:* New (Edinburgh).

DUNPHIE, Maj.-Gen. Sir Charles (Anderson Lane), Kt 1959; CB 1948; CBE 1942; DSO 1943; *b* 20 April 1902; *s* of late Sir Alfred Dunphie, KCVO, Rotherfield Greys, Oxon; *m* 1st, 1931, Eileen (*d* 1978), *d* of late Lieut-Gen. Sir Walter Campbell, KCB, KCMG, DSO; one *s* one *d* ; 2nd, 1981, Susan, widow of Col P. L. M. Wright. *Educ:* RN Colls Osborne and Dartmouth; RMA Woolwich. Commissioned into RA, 1921; served War of 1939-45 (wounded, despatches); Brig. RAC, 1941; Comdr 26 Armoured Bde, 1942-43; Dep. Dir RAC, War Office, 1943-45; Temp. Maj.-Gen., Dir Gen. Armoured Fighting Vehicles 1945-48; retired 1948. Joined Vickers Ltd, 1948; Chm., 1962-67. One of HM's Honourable Corps of Gentlemen-at-Arms, 1952-62. US Legion of Merit (Commander); US Silver Star. *Address:* Roundhill, Wincanton, Somerset. *Club:* Army and Navy.

DUNPHY, Rev. Thomas Patrick, SJ; Parish Priest, Corpus Christi, Boscombe, since 1980; *b* Donnybrook, Dublin, 17 Aug. 1913; *o s* of Thomas Joseph Dunphy and Agnes Mary (née Rogers), Dublin. *Educ:* Wimbledon Coll. Joined Soc. of Jesus, 1932; Priest, 1946. Headmaster of St John's (preparatory sch. of Beaumont Coll.), 1949-64; Rector, Beaumont Coll., 1964-67; Socius to the Provincial of the Society of Jesus, 1967-71; Rector, Stonyhurst Coll., 1971-77; Vicar for Religious Sisters in Devon and Dorset, 1977-79; Spiritual Father, St Mary's Hall, Stonyhurst, 1979-80. *Address:* Corpus Christi, 757 Christchurch Road, Boscombe, Bournemouth BH7 6AN. *T:* Bournemouth 425286.

DUNRAVEN and MOUNT-EARL, 7th Earl of, *cr* 1822; **Thady Windham Thomas Wyndham-Quin;** Baron Adare, 1800; Viscount Mountearl, 1816; Viscount Adare, 1822; Bt 1871; *b* 27 Oct. 1939; *s* of 6th Earl of Dunraven and Mount-Earl, CB, CBE, MC, and Nancy, *d* of Thomas B. Yuille, Halifax County, Va; *S* father 1965; *m* 1969, Geraldine, *d* of Air Commodore Gerard W. McAleer, CBE, MB, BCh, DTM&H, Wokingham; one *d. Educ:* Ludgrove; Le Rosey. *Address:* Kilcurley House, Adare, Co. Limerick, Ireland. *T:* Limerick 94201. *Club:* Kildare Street and University (Dublin).

DUNROSSIL, 2nd Viscount, *cr* 1959; **John William Morrison,** CMG 1981; HM Diplomatic Service; High Commissioner in Bridgetown, Barbados, since 1982, and High Commissioner (non-resident) to Antigua and Barbuda, Dominica, St Vincent and the Grenadines, and Grenada, and concurrently British Government Representative to West Indies Associated States; *b* 22 May 1926; *e s* of William Shepherd Morrison, 1st Viscount Dunrossil, PC, GCMG, MC, QC; *S* father, 1961; *m* 1st, 1951, Mavis (marr. diss. 1969), *d* of A. Ll. Spencer-Payne, LRCP, MRCS, LDS; three *s* one *d* ; 2nd, 1969, Diana Mary Cunliffe, *d* of C. M. Vise; two *d. Educ:* Fettes; Oxford. Royal Air Force, 1945-48, Flt-Lieut (Pilot). Joined Commonwealth Relations Office, 1951; Asst Private Sec. to Sec. of State, 1952-54; Second Sec., Canberra, 1954-56; CRO, 1956-58; First Sec. and Acting Deputy High Commissioner, Dacca, East Pakistan, 1958-60; First Sec., Pretoria/Capetown, 1961-64; FO, 1964-68; seconded to Intergovernmental Maritime Consultative Org., 1968-70; Counsellor and Head of Chancery, Ottawa, 1970-74; Counsellor, Brussels, 1975-78; High Comr in Fiji, and High Comr (non-resident) to Republic of Nauru and to Tuvalu, 1978-82. *Heir:* s Hon. Andrew William Reginald Morrison, *b* 15 Dec. 1953. *Address:* c/o Foreign and Commonwealth Office, SW1. *Clubs:* Royal Air Force, Royal Commonwealth Society; Cercle Royal Gaulois (Brussels).

DUNSANY, 19th Baron of, *cr* 1439; **Randal Arthur Henry Plunkett;** Lieut-Col (retd) Indian Cavalry (Guides); *b* 25 Aug. 1906; *o s* of 18th Baron Dunsany, DL, LittD, and Rt Hon. Beatrice, Lady Dunsany (*d* 1970); *S* father, 1957; *m* 1st, 1938, Mrs Vera Bryce (from whom he obtained a divorce, 1947), *d* of Señor G. De Sà Sottomaior, São Paulo, Brazil; one *s*; 2nd, 1947, Sheila Victoria Katrin, widow of Major John Frederick Foley, Baron de Rutzen, DL, JP, CC, Welsh Guards (killed in action, 1944), *o d* of Sir Henry Philipps, 2nd Bt; one *d. Educ:* Eton. Joined the 16th/5th Lancers (SR), 1926; transferred to the Indian Army, 1928, Guides Cavalry, Indian Armoured Corps, retired, 1947. *Heir: s* Hon. Edward John Carlos Plunkett [*b* 10 Sept. 1939. *Educ:* Eton; Slade Sch. of Fine Art]. *Address:* (Seat) Dunsany Castle, Co. Meath, Ireland. *T:* 046-25198. *Clubs:* Beefsteak, Cavalry and Guards; Kildare Street and University (Dublin).

DUNSTAN, (Andrew Harold) Bernard, RA 1968 (ARA 1959); PRWA; painter; President, Royal West of England Academy, since 1980; *b* 19 Jan. 1920; *s* of late Dr A. E. Dunstan; *m* 1949, Diana Maxwell Armfield; three *s. Educ:* St Paul's; Byam Shaw Sch.; Slade Sch. Has exhibited at RA since 1945. Many one-man exhibitions; now exhibits regularly at Agnews, Bond St. Pictures in public collections include London Museum, Bristol Art Gall., Nat. Gall. of NZ, Arts Council, Nat. Portrait Gall., and many in private collections. Member: New English Art Club; Council, Artists' General Benevolent Instn. *Publications:* Learning to Paint, 1970; Painting in Progress, 1976; Painting Methods of the Impressionists, 1976. *Recreations:* music, walking in London. *Address:* 10 High Park Road, Kew, Richmond, Surrey. *T:* 01-876 6633.

DUNSTAN, Hon. Donald Allan, AC 1979; QC 1965; Premier of South Australia, 1967, and 1970-79; MP (Labor), 1953-79; *b* 21 Sept. 1926; of S Australian parents; *m* 1st, 1949, Gretel Ellis (marr. diss.); two *s* one *d*; 2nd, 1976, Adele Koh (*d* 1978). *Educ:* St Peter's Coll. and Univ. of Adelaide, S Australia. Attorney-Gen. of S Australia, 1965; Premier, Treasurer, Attorney-Gen. and Minister of Housing, 1967-68; Leader of Opposition, 1968-70; Premier, Treasurer, 1970-79. Freeman of City of Georgetown, Penang, 1973. *Address:* 15 Clara Street, Norwood, SA 5067, Australia.

DUNSTAN, Lt-Gen. Sir Donald (Beaumont), KBE 1980 (CBE 1969; MBE 1954); CB 1972; Governor of South Australia, since 1982; *b* 18 Feb. 1923; *s* of late Oscar Reginald Dunstan and of Eileen Dunstan; *m* 1947, Beryl June Dunningham; two *s. Educ:* Prince Alfred Coll., South Australia; RMC, Duntroon. Served War of 1939-45: Regimental and Staff appts in SW Pacific Area, 1942-45. Served in Korea, 1954; Instructor: RMC Duntroon, 1955-56, 1963; Staff Coll., Queenscliff, 1958; Staff Coll., Camberley, 1959-60; Dep. Comdr 1 Task Force, Vietnam, 1968-69; Comdr, 10th Task Force, Holsworthy, NSW, 1969; idc 1970; Commander Aust. Force, Vietnam, 1971; Chief of Material, 1972-74; GOC Field Force Comd, 1974-77; CGS, 1977-82. *Recreations:* golf, fishing. *Address:* Government House, Adelaide, SA 5000, Australia. *Clubs:* Commonwealth (Canberra); Royal Canberra Golf.

DUNSTAN, Rev. Prof. Gordon Reginald; F. D. Maurice Professor of Moral and Social Theology, King's College, London, 1967-82, now Emeritus; Chaplain to the Queen, since 1976; *b* 25 April 1917; *yr s* of late Frederick John Menhennet and Winifred Amy Dunstan (*née* Orchard); *m* 1949, Ruby Maud (*née* Fitzer); two *s* one *d. Educ:* Plymouth Corp. Gram. Sch.; University of Leeds; College of the Resurrection, Mirfield. BA, 1st cl. Hist., 1938, Rutson Post-Grad. Schol. 1938, MA w dist. 1939, Leeds Univ.; FSA 1957; Hon. DD Exeter 1973; Fellow, King's College London, 1974. Deacon 1941, priest 1942; Curate, King Cross, Halifax, 1941-45; Huddersfield, 1945-46; Sub Warden, St Deiniol's Library, Hawarden, 1945-49; Vicar of Sutton Courtney with Appleford, 1949-55; Lecturer, Wm Temple Coll., 1947-49; Ripon Hall, Oxford, 1953-55; Minor Canon, St George's Chapel, Windsor Castle, 1955-59; Westminster Abbey, 1959-67; Canon Theologian, Leicester Cathedral, 1966-82, Canon Emeritus, 1982-. Sec., C of E Council for Social Work, 1955-63; Sec., Church Assembly Jt Bd of Studies, 1965-66; Editor of Crucible, 1962-66; Editor of Theology, 1965-75; Dep. Priest in Ordinary to the Queen, 1959-64, Priest in Ordinary, 1964-76; Select Preacher: University of Cambridge 1960, 1977; Leeds, 1970; Hulsean Preacher, 1977. Lectures: Prideaux, Univ. of Exeter, 1968; Moorhouse, Melbourne, 1973; Stephenson, Sheffield, 1980. Gresham's Prof. in Divinity, City Univ., 1969-71. Mem. Council, Canterbury and York Secs., 1950-. Mem. or Sec. cttees on social and ethical problems; Vice-Pres., 1965-66, and Chm. Brit. Cttee of Internat. Union of Family Organizations, 1964-66; Member: London Medical Gp and Soc. for Study of Medical Ethics, 1967-; Adv. Gp on Transplant Policy, Dept of Health, 1969; Council of Tavistock Inst. of Human Relations (Vice-Pres., 1977-82), and Inst. of Marital Studies, 1969-; Adv. Gp on Arms Control and Disarmament, FCO, 1970-74; Adv. Cttee on Animal Experiments, Home Office, 1975-; Council, Advertising Standards Auth., 1981-. Pres., Open Section, RSM, 1976-78. Vice Pres., Devon and Cornwall Record Soc., 1976-. *Publications:* The Family Is Not Broken, 1962; The Register of Edmund Lacy, Bishop of Exeter 1420-1455, 5 vols, 1963-72; A Digger Still, 1968; Not Yet the Epitaph, 1968; The Sacred Ministry, 1970; The Artifice of Ethics, 1974; A Moralist in the City, 1974; (ed) Duty and Discernment, 1975. *Recreations:* local history, music. *Address:* Mayfield Avenue, Exeter EX4 6JN. *T:* Exeter 214691.

DUNSTAN, Ivan, PhD; CChem, FRIC; Director, Building Research Establishment, Department of the Environment, since 1979; *b* 27 Aug. 1930; *s* of Edward Ernest and Sarah Kathleen Dunstan; *m* 1955, Monica Jane (*née* Phillips); two *s* one *d. Educ:* Falmouth Grammar Sch.; Bristol Univ. (BSc).

Joined Scientific Civil Service, working at Explosives Research and Development Estabt, Waltham Abbey, 1954; became Supt of Gen. Chemistry Div., 1967; Warren Spring Laboratory (DTI) as Dep. Dir (Resources), 1972-74; Dir, Materials Quality Assurance, MoD (PE), 1974-79. *Publications:* research papers on analytical and synthetic chem.; contribs to Annual Reports on Progress of Applied Chem., and to encyclopaedia, etc. *Recreations:* sailing, tennis, badminton, gardening. *Address:* 5 Aldock, Welwyn Garden City, Herts AL7 4QF. *T:* Welwyn Garden 22272.

DUNSTER, (Herbert) John, CB 1979; Director, National Radiological Protection Board, since 1982; *b* 27 July 1922; *s* of Herbert and Olive Grace Dunster; *m* 1945, Rosemary Elizabeth, *d* of P. J. Gallacher; one *s* three *d. Educ:* University Coll. Sch.; Imperial College of Science and Technology (ARCS, BSc). Scientist, UK Atomic Energy Authority, 1946-71; Asst Dir, Nat. Radiological Protection Bd, 1971-76; Dep. Dir Gen., HSE, 1976-82. Member: Internat. Commn on Radiological Protection, 1977-; Sci. and Tech. Cttee, Euratom, 1982-. *Publications:* numerous papers in technical jls. *Recreations:* music, photography. *Address:* 25 Dale Close, St Ebbs, Oxford. *T:* Oxford 48764. *Club:* East India, Devonshire, Sports and Public Schools.

DUNTZE, Sir George (Edwin Douglas), 6th Bt, *cr* 1774; CMG 1960; *b* 1 June 1913; *o s* of Sir George Puxley Duntze, 5th Baronet, and Violet May, *d* of late Henry M. Sanderson; *S* father, 1947; *m* 1st, 1941, Joan, *d* of late Major F. E. Bradstock, DSO, MC (marr. diss. 1966); one *d*; 2nd, 1966, Nesta, *e d* of late Thomas R. P. Herbert, Newport, Mon. *Educ:* Shrewsbury Sch.; Trinity Coll., Oxford. (MA). Entered Colonial Administrative Service, 1936. Provincial Comr, Uganda, 1952-61. *Heir:* kinsman, John Alexander Duntze [*b* 13 Nov. 1909; *m* 1935, Emily Ellsworth, *d* of Elmer E. Harlow, USA]. *Address:* 25 Ennismore Gardens, SW7. *Clubs:* Hurlingham; Leander.

DUNWICH, Bishop Suffragan of, since 1980; **Rt. Rev. Eric Nash Devenport;** *b* 3 May 1926; *s* of Joseph and Emma Devenport; *m* 1954, Jean Margaret Richardson; two *d. Educ:* Kelham Theological Coll. BA (Open Univ.). Curate, St Mark, Leicester, 1951-54; St Matthew, Barrow-in-Furness, 1954-56; Succentor, Leicester Cathedral, 1956-59; Vicar of Shepshed, 1959-64; Oadby, 1964-73; Proctor in Convocation, 1964-80; Hon. Canon of Leicester Cathedral, 1973-80; Leader of Mission, Diocese of Leicester, 1973-80. Chaplain, Worshipful Company of Framework Knitters, 1964-80. *Recreation:* theatre. *Address:* 94 Henley Road, Ipswich, Suffolk IP1 4NJ. *T:* Ipswich 58394.

DUNWOODY, Gwyneth (Patricia); MP (Lab) Crewe, since Feb. 1974; *b* 12 Dec. 1930; *d* of late Morgan Phillips and of Baroness Phillips, *qv*; *m* 1954, Dr John Elliott Orr Dunwoody, *qv* (marr. diss. 1975); two *s* one *d.* MP (Lab) Exeter, 1966-70; Parly Sec. to BoT, 1967-70; Mem., European Parlt, 1975-79; Front Bench Spokesman on Foreign Affairs, 1980, on Health Service, 1980-. Mem., Labour Party NEC, 1981-. Dir, Film Production Assoc. of GB, 1970-74. *Address:* 113 Cromwell Tower, Beech Street, EC2Y 6DD.

DUNWOODY, Dr John (Elliott Orr); general practitioner; Chairman, Bloomsbury District Health Authority, since 1982; *b* 3 June 1929; *s* of Dr W. O. and late Mrs F. J. Dunwoody; *m* 1st, 1954, Gwyneth Patricia (*née* Phillips), *qv* (marr. diss. 1975); two *s* one *d*; 2nd, 1979, Evelyn Louise (*née* Borner). *Educ:* St Paul's Sch.; King's Coll., London Univ.; Westminster Hosp. Med. Sch. MB, BS London; MRCS, LRCP 1954. House Surgeon, Westminster (Gordon) Hosp., 1954; House Physician, Royal Berks Hosp., 1954-55; Sen. House Physician, Newton Abbot Hosp., 1955-56; Family Doctor and Medical Officer, Totnes District Hosp, 1956-66; MO, Staff Health Service, St George's Hosp., 1976-77. MP (Lab) Falmouth and Camborne, 1966-70; Parly Under-Sec., Dept of Health and Social Security, 1969-70. Vice-Chm., 1974-77, Chm., 1977-82, Kensington, Chelsea and Westminster AHA (T). Member: Exec. Cttee, British Council, 1967-69; Council, Westminster Med. Sch., 1974-; (co-opted) Social Services Cttee, Westminster City Council, 1975-78; Nat. Exec. Council, FPA, 1979-, Dep. Chm., 1980, Chm., 1981-. Hon. Dir, Action on Smoking and Health, 1971-73. Governor, Pimlico Sch., 1972-75. *Publication:* (jtly) A Birth Control Plan for Britain, 1972. *Address:* 9 Cautley Avenue, SW4. *T:* 01-673 7471.

DUNWORTH, John Vernon, CB 1969; CBE 1955; President, International Committee of Weights and Measures, Sèvres, France, since 1975; *b* 24 Feb. 1917; *o c* of late John Dunworth and Susan Ida (*née* Warburton); *m* 1967, Patricia Noel Boston; one *d. Educ:* Manchester Grammar Sch.; Clare Coll., Cambridge; Denman Baynes Research Studentship, 1937, Robins Prize, 1937; MA, PhD; Twisden Studentship and Fellowship, Trinity Coll., 1941. War Service: Ministry of Supply on Radar Development, 1939-44; National Research Council of Canada, on Atomic Energy Development, 1944-45. Univ. Demonstrator in Physics, Cambridge, 1945. Joined Atomic Energy Research Establishment, Harwell, 1947; Dir, NPL, 1964-76. Alternate United Kingdom Member on Organising Cttee of UN Atoms for Peace Confs in Geneva, 1955 and 1958. Pres., Internat. Cttee of Weights and Measures, 1975- (Vice-Pres., 1968-75). Fellow Amer. Nuclear Soc. 1960. Chm., British Nuclear Energy Soc., 1964-70; Vice-President, Institute of Physics: Physical Soc., 1966-70. CEng 1966. Comdr (with Star), Order of Alfonso X el Sabio, Spain, 1960. *Address:* The Warbuck, Kirk Michael, Isle of Man. *T:* Kirk Michael 359. *Club:* Athenæum.

du PLESSIS, Prof. Daniel Jacob, FRCS; Vice-Chancellor and Principal, University of the Witwatersrand, since 1978; *b* 17 May 1918; *s* of D. J. du Plessis and L. du Plessis (*née* Carstens); *m* 1946, Louisa Susanna Wicht; two *s*. *Educ:* Univ. of Cape Town (MB ChB); Univ. of the Witwatersrand (ChM). Served, SA Medical Corps, 1942-46. Postgraduate study, 1947-48; Surgeon and Lectr, Univ. of Cape Town, 1949-58; Prof. of Surgery, Univ. of the Witwatersrand, 1958-77. Hon. FACS 1974; Hon. Fellow: Assoc. of Surgeons of GB and Ireland, 1979; Amer. Surgical Assoc., 1981. *Publications:* Principles of Surgery, 1968, 2nd edn 1976; Synopsis of Surgical Anatomy, 10th edn (with A. Lee McGregor), 1969, 11th edn 1975; numerous articles in learned jls on surgical topics, espec. on diseases of parotid salivary gland and gastric ulcers. *Address:* University of the Witwatersrand, 1 Jan Smuts Avenue, Johannesburg 2001, S Africa. *T:* 716-1111; (home) 13 Jubilee Road, Parktown, Johannesburg 2193. *T:* 642-4969.

DUPONT-SOMMER, André; Member of the Institut de France (Secrétaire Perpétuel de l'Académie des Inscriptions et Belles-Lettres) since 1961; Hon. Professor: the Collège de France; the Sorbonne; Director of Studies, Ecole des Hautes Etudes, since 1938; *b* 23 Dec. 1900. Gen. Sec., Collège de France, 1934; Pres., Institut d'Etudes Sémitiques, University of Paris, 1952. Member: Accademia dei Lincei, 1972; Österreichische Akademie der Wissenschaften, 1974. Officier de la Légion d'Honneur; Comdr des Palmes académiques. *Publications:* Le Quatrième Livre des Machabées, 1939; La Doctrine gnostique de la lettre "Wâw", 1946; Les Araméens, 1949; Aperçus préliminaires sur les manuscrits de la mer Morte, 1950 (publ. Eng. The Dead Sea Scrolls, a Preliminary Survey, 1952); Nouveaux Aperçus sur les manuscrits de la mer Morte, 1953 (publ. Eng. The Jewish sect of Qumran and the Essenes, 1954); Le Livre des Hymnes découvert près de la mer Morte, 1957; Les inscriptions araméennes de Sfiré, 1958; Les écrits esséniens découverts près de la mer Morte, 1959 (Eng. trans., The Essene Writings from Qumran); articles in Revue d'Assyriologie, Revue d'Histoire des Religions, Semitica, Syria, Jl of Semitic Studies, Vetus Testamentum, etc. *Address:* 25 Quai de Conti, 75006 Paris, France. *T:* 329.55.10.

DUPPA-MILLER, John Bryan Peter; *see* Miller, J. B. P. D.

DUPPLIN, Viscount; Charles William Harley Hay; *b* 20 Dec. 1962; *s* and *heir* of 15th Earl of Kinnoull, *qv. Educ:* Summer Fields; Eton. *Recreation:* philately. *Club:* Lansdowne.

du PRÉ, Jacqueline, OBE 1976; British violoncellist; *b* 1945; *m* 1967, Daniel Barenboim, *qv. Educ:* studied with William Pleeth both privately and at Guildhall Sch. of Music, with Paul Tortelier in Paris, and with Rostropovich in Moscow. Concert début at Wigmore Hall at age of sixteen, followed by appearances on the continent and with principal English orchestras and conductors. Soloist in London and at Bath and Edinburgh Festivals. N American début, 1965. Continued studies in Moscow with Rostropovitch, 1966, returning later to USSR as soloist with BBC Symphony Orchestra. Toured N America, and appeared New York and at World Fair, Montreal; subseq. concerts, major musical centres, 1967. Awarded Suggia Gift at age of ten; Gold medal, Guildhall Sch. of Music, and Queen's Prize, 1960; City of London Midsummer Prize, 1975; Musician of the Year Award, Incorporated Soc. of Musicians, 1980; FGSM, 1975; FRCM; Hon. RAM. Hon. MusD: London; Open; Sheffield; Hon. DLit Salford, 1980. *Address:* c/o Harold Holt Ltd, 31 Sinclair Road, W14 0NS.

DUPREE, Sir Peter, 5th Bt *cr* 1921; *b* 20 Feb. 1924; *s* of Sir Victor Dupree, 4th Bt and of Margaret Cross; S father, 1976; *m* 1947, Joan, *d* of late Captain James Desborough Hunt. *Heir: cousin* Thomas William James David Dupree, *b* 5 Feb. 1930. *Address:* Great Seabrights, Galley Wood, near Chelmsford, Essex.

DUPUCH, Hon. Sir (Alfred) Etienne (Jerome), Kt 1965; OBE 1949; KCSG, OTL, CHM; Editor, 1919-72, Contributing Editor since 1972, The Tribune, Nassau, Bahamas; *b* Nassau, 16 Feb. 1899; *s* of Leon Edward Hartman Dupuch, Founder of The Tribune, and Elizabeth Harriet Saunders; *m* 1928, Marie Plouse, USA; three *s* three *d. Educ:* Boys' Central Sch., Nassau; St John's Univ., Collegeville, Minn, USA. Served War, 1914-18, Eastern and Western Fronts, BWI Regt; Rep. for Inagua and Mayaguana, House of Assembly, Bahamas, 1925-42; Eastern District, New Providence, 1949-56; MLC, 1960-64; Mem. Senate, 1964-68. Mem., US Nat. Adv. Bd, Amer. Security Council, 1981. Board Member: ES-U, Miami; United World Colls, NY. Hon. Member: East Nassau Rotary Club; Coral Gables Rotary Club; Lions Club, Pennsylvania. Hon. LittD, Hon. LLD. IAPA Award for breaking down racial discrimination in Bahamas, 1956; IAPA Award for successful defence of Freedom of Press, 1969; Citation from Associated Press N American Editors' Assoc. for outstanding coverage of fire on SS Yarmouth Castle, 1965; Paul Harris Award for work in social services (Rotary Club of Lucaya, Freeport). Has RSA medal and several decorations from governments of three nations. Kt, SMO Malta, 1977. *Publications:* We Call Him Friend (tribute to Rt Hon. Lord Beaverbrook), 1961; The Tribune Story, 1967; A Salute to Friend and Foe, 1981. *Address:* Camperdown Heights, PO Box N-3207, Nassau, Bahamas; 700 Coral Way, Coral Gables, Florida, USA. *Clubs:* East India, Devonshire, Sports and Public Schools; The Admirals of the Florida Fleet; Country (Coral Gables, Fla).

DURACK, Dame Mary, (Mrs Horrie Miller), DBE 1978 (OBE 1966); novelist and historian; *b* 20 Feb. 1913; *d* of Michael Patrick Durack and Bessie Ida Muriel (*née* Johnstone); *m* 1938, Captain H. C. Miller (decd); two *s* two *d* (and two *d* decd). *Educ:* Loreto Convent, Perth. Formerly: lived at Argyle and Ivanhoe Stns, E Kimberley; mem. staff, West Australian Newspapers Ltd. Member: Aust. Soc. of Authors; National Trust; Royal Western Aust. Hist. Soc.; Kuljak Playwrights Inc. Formerly Exec. Mem., Aboriginal Cultural Foundn. Dir, Aust. Stockman's Hall of Fame. Hon. Life Member: WA Br., Fellowship of Aust. Writers (Pres., 1958-63); Internat. PEN, Australia. Commonwealth Lit. Grant, 1973, 1977 and Australian Research Grants Cttee Grant, 1980. Hon. DLitt Univ. of WA, 1978. *Publications:* (E Kimberley District stories illus. by sister, Elizabeth Durack): All-about, 1935; Chunuma, 1936; Son of Djaro, 1938; The Way of the Whirlwind, 1941, new edn 1979; Piccaninnies, 1943; The Magic Trumpet, 1944; (with Florence Rutter) Child Artists of the Australian Bush, 1952; (novel) Keep Him My Country, 1955; (family documentary) Kings in Grass Castles, 1959; To Ride a Fine Horse, 1963; The Courteous Savage, 1964 (new edn as Yagan of the Bibbulmun, 1976); Kookanoo and Kangaroo, 1963; An Australian Settler, 1964 (pub. Australia, A Pastoral Emigrant); The Rock and the Sand, 1969; (with Ingrid Drysdale) The End of Dreaming, 1974; To Be Heirs Forever, 1976; Tjakamarra—boy between two worlds, 1977; *plays:* The Ship of Dreams, 1968; Swan River Saga, 1972; scripts for ABC drama dept; libretto for opera, Dalgerie (music by James Penberthy), 1966; six dramatised Kookanoo stories on tape and record, 1973. *Address:* 12 Bellevue Avenue, Nedlands, WA 6009, Australia. *T:* 386-1117.

DURAND, Rev. Sir (Henry Mortimer) Dickon (Marion St George), 4th Bt *cr* 1892; Rector, Youghal Union of Parishes, Co. Cork, since 1982; *b* 19 June 1934; *s* of Lt-Comdr Mortimer Henry Marion Durand, RN (*y s* of 1st Bt) (*d* 1969), and Beatrice Garvan-Sheridan, *d* of Judge Sheridan, Sydney, NSW; S uncle, 1971; *m* 1971, Stella Evelyn, *d* of Captain C. C. L'Estrange; two *s* two *d. Educ:* Wellington College; Sydney University; Salisbury Theological College. Curate: All Saints, Fulham, 1969-72; St Leonard's, Heston, 1972-74. Curate-in-Charge, St Benedict's, Ashford, Mddx, 1975-79; Bishop's Curate, Kilbixy Union of Parishes, Co. Westmeath, 1979-82. *Recreations:* heraldry, philately, model railways, printing, militaria, painting, poetry, travel. *Heir: s* Edward Alan Christopher Percy Durand, *b* 21 Feb. 1974. *Address:* The Rectory, Youghal, Co. Cork, Ireland.

DURAND, Victor Albert Charles, QC 1958; *s* of Victor and Blanche Durand; *m* 1935, Betty Joan Kirchner; one *s* one *d. Educ:* Howard High Sch. (Kitchener Scholar). LLB, BSc, AMInstCE. Served War 1939-45 with RE. Called to Bar, Inner Temple, 1939. Dep. Chm., Warwicks QS, 1961. *Address:* Queen Elizabeth Building, Temple, EC4Y 9BS.

DURANT, Rear-Adm. Bryan Cecil, CB 1963; DSO 1953; DSC 1945; *b* 17 June 1910; *o s* of Francis Durant and Dulce, *d* of Fraser Baddeley; *m* 1st, 1939, Pamela (*d* 1963), *yr d* of Brig.-Gen. William Walter Seymour; three *d* (and one *s* decd); 2nd, 1967, Rachel, *d* of late Col Hon. David Bruce, and Hon. Mrs David Bruce. *Educ:* Radley. Entered Royal Navy, 1929; specialised in navigation, 1935. War of 1939-45; actions in HMS Dorsetshire in Atlantic and Indian Oceans including sinking of Bismarck, 1940-42; sunk by Japanese aircraft, 1942 (despatches); actions in HMS Victorious off North Norway, Sabang, Palembang, Okinawa and Japan, 1942-45; suicide Bomber attacks, 1945 (DSC). Comdr 1945; Capt. 1951; Comd 4th Frigate Sqdn in Korean War, 1952-54 (DSO). Dir, Ops Div., Admlty, 1957; Captain of the Fleet, Home Fleet, 1959; Chief of Staff Far East Station, 1961-63; retired list, 1963. Dir-Gen., Navy League, 1964-75. ADC to the Queen, 1960. Liveryman, Fishmongers Co. DL Greater London, 1970-78. Commendador Henriquina (Portuguese), 1960. *Address:* The Old House, Bighton, near Alresford, Hants. *Club:* Army and Navy.

DURANT, Robert Anthony Bevis, (Tony Durant); MP (C) Reading North, since Feb. 1974; *b* 9 Jan. 1928; *s* of Captain Robert Michael Durant and Mrs Violet Dorothy Durant (*née* Bevis); *m* 1958, Audrey Stoddart; two *s* one *d. Educ:* Dane Court Prep. Sch., Pyrford, Woking; Bryanston Sch., Blandford, Dorset. Royal Navy, 1945-47. Coutts Bank, Strand, 1947-52; Cons. Party Organisation, 1952-67 (Young Cons. Organiser, Yorks; Cons. Agent, Clapham; Nat. Organiser, Young Conservatives). Member: Select Cttee Parly Comr (Ombudsman), 1974-; Council of Europe, 1981-; Chairman: All Party Gp on Widows and One Parent Families, 1977-; Cons. Nat. Local Govt Adv. Cttee, 1981-; Vice-Chm., Parly Gp for World Govt, 1979-; Sec., Parly and Scientific Cttee, 1980-. Parliamentary Consultant: The Film Production Association of Great Britain Ltd; Delta Electrical Div. of Delta Metal Co. Ltd; Gambica. Mem., Inland Waterways Adv. Council, 1975-. Dir, British Industrial Scientific Film Assoc., 1967-70; Company Sec., Talking Pictures Ltd, 1972-. *Recreations:* boating, golf. *Address:* Hill House, Surley Row, Caversham, Reading RG4 8ND.

DURBIN, Prof. James; Professor of Statistics, University of London (London School of Economics), since 1961; *b* 30 June 1923; *m* 1958, Anne Dearnley Outhwaite; two *s* one *d. Educ:* St John's Coll., Cambridge. Army Operational Research Group, 1943-45. Boot and Shoe Trade Research Assoc., 1945-47; Dept of Applied Economics, Cambridge, 1948-49; Asst Lectr, then Lecturer, in Statistics, London Sch. of Economics, 1950-53; Reader in Statistics, 1953-61. Visiting Professor: Univ. of North Carolina, 1959-60; Stanford Univ., 1960; Johns Hopkins Univ., 1965-66; Univ. of Washington, 1966; ANU, 1970-71; Univ. of Calif, Berkeley, 1971; Univ. of Cape Town, 1978. Chm., Res. Resources and Methods Cttee, SSRC. Mem., Internat. Statistical Inst., 1955, Pres., 1983-; Fellow, Inst. of Mathematical Statistics, 1958; Fellow,

Amer. Statistical Assoc., 1960; Fellow, Econometric Soc., 1967; Royal Statistical Society: Vice Pres., 1969-70 and 1972-73; Guy Medal in Bronze, 1966, in Silver, 1976. *Publications:* Distribution Theory for Tests based on the Sample Distribution Function, 1973; articles in statistical journals, incl. Biometrika, Jl of Royal Statistical Society, etc. *Recreations:* travel, opera, theatre. *Address:* 31 Southway, NW11. *T:* 01-458 3037.

DURBIN, Leslie, CBE 1976; MVO 1943; silversmith; *b* 21 Feb. 1913; *s* of late Harry Durbin and of Lillian A. Durbin; *m* 1940, Phyllis Ethel Durbin (*see* Phyllis E. Ginger); one *s* one *d. Educ:* Central Sch. of Arts and Crafts, London. Apprenticed to late Omar Ramsden, 1929-39; full-time schol., 1938-39, travelling schol., 1939-40, both awarded by Worshipful Co. of Goldsmiths. Started working on own account in workshop of Francis Adam, 1940-41. RAF, Allied Central Interpretation Unit, 1941-45. Commissioned by Jt Cttee of Assay Offices of GB to design Silver Jubilee Hall Mark. Retrospective exhibn, Leslie Durbin, years of Silversmithing, Goldsmiths' Hall, 1982. Hon. LLD Cambridge, 1963. Council of Industrial Design Awards for Silver for the 70's. *Address:* 298A Kew Road, Richmond TW9 3DU.

DURBRIDGE, Francis (Henry); playwright and author; *b* 25 Nov. 1912; *s* of late Francis and Gertrude Durbridge; *m* 1940, Norah Elizabeth Lawley; two *s. Educ:* Bradford Grammar Sch.; Wylde Green Coll.; Birmingham Univ. After period in stockbroker's office, began to write (as always intended); short stories and plays for BBC; many subseq. radio plays, including Promotion, 1933; created character of Paul Temple. Entered Television with The Broken Horseshoe, 1952 (the first adult television serial); other serials followed; Portrait of Alison, 1954; My Friend Charles, 1955; The Other Man, 1956; The Scarf 1960; The World of Tim Frazer (Exec. Prod.), 1960-61; Melissa, 1962; Bat Out of Hell, 1964; Stupid Like a Fox, 1971; The Doll, 1976; Breakaway, 1980. The television serials have been presented in many languages, and are continuing; novels, based on them, have been published in USA, Europe, etc. The European Broadcasting Union asked for a radio serial for an internat. market (La Boutique, 1967, being broadcast in various countries); German, French and Italian productions, 1971-72. Films include two for Korda and Romulus, 1954-57. Stage plays: Suddenly at Home, 1971; The Gentle Hook, 1974; Murder With Love, 1976; House Guest, 1980. *Publications:* include contribs to newspapers and magazines, at home and abroad. *Recreations:* family, reading, travel. *Address:* 4 Fairacres, Roehampton Lane, SW15 5LX.

DURHAM, 6th Earl of, *cr* 1833; Baron Durham, 1828; Viscount Lambton, 1833 [Disclaimed his Peerages for life, 1970]; *see under* Lambton, A. C. F.

DURHAM, Baron; a subsidiary title of Earldom of Durham (disclaimed 1970), used by Hon. Edward Richard Lambton, *b* 19 Oct. 1961, *heir* to disclaimed Earldom.

DURHAM, Bishop of, since 1973; **Rt. Rev. John Stapylton Habgood,** MA, PhD; *b* 23 June 1927; *s* of Arthur Henry Habgood, DSO, MB, BCh, and Vera (*née* Chetwynd-Stapylton); *m* 1961, Rosalie Mary Anne Boston; two *s* two *d. Educ:* Eton; King's Coll., Cambridge; Cuddesdon Coll., Oxford. Univ. Demonstrator in Pharmacology, Cambridge, 1950-53; Fellow of King's Coll., Cambridge, 1952-55; Curate of St Mary Abbots, Kensington, 1954-56; Vice-Principal of Westcott House, Cambridge, 1956-62; Rector of St John's Church, Jedburgh, 1962-67; Principal of Queen's College, Birmingham, 1967-73. Hon. DD Durham, 1975. *Publications:* Religion and Science, 1964; A Working Faith, 1980. *Recreation:* repairing castles. *Address:* Auckland Castle, Bishop Auckland, Co. Durham. *T:* Bishop Auckland 602576. *Club:* Athenæum.

DURHAM, Dean of; *see* Baelz, Very Rev. P. R.

DURHAM, Archdeacon of; *see* Perry, Ven. M. C.

DURHAM, Kenneth; Chairman, Unilever plc, since 1982; Director, Unilever NV, since 1974; *b* 28 July 1924; *s* of late George Durham and Bertha (*née* Aspin); *m* 1946, Irene Markham; one *s* one *d. Educ:* Queen Elizabeth Grammar Sch., Blackburn; Univ. of Manchester (Hatfield Schol.; BSc Hons, Physics). Flight Lieut, RAF, 1942-46. ARE, Harwell, 1950; Unilever: joined Res. Lab., Port Sunlight, 1950, Head of Lab., 1961; Head, Res. Lab., Colworth, Bedford, 1965; assumed responsibility for animal feed interests, 1970; Chm., BOCM Silcock Ltd, 1971; Dir, Unilever Ltd, 1974, Vice-Chm., 1978. Mem. Bd, British Aerospace, 1980-. Chairman: Food, Drink and Packaging Machinery Sector Wkg Party, NEDO, 1981; Trade Policy Res. Centre, 1982; Industry and Commerce Liaison Cttee, Royal Jubilee Trusts, 1982; Dep. Chm., British Nat. Cttee, ICC, 1981; Member: British-N America Cttee, 1982; British Shippers Council, 1982; Bd, British Exec. Service Overseas, 1982. Attended Harvard Advanced Management Program, 1962; Mem. Council, PSI, 1978. Trustee: Leverhulme Trust, 1974; Civic Trust, 1982. *Publications:* Surface Activity and Detergency, 1960; various scientific papers. *Recreations:* walking, golf. *Address:* c/o Unilever plc, PO Box 68, Blackfriars, EC4P 4BQ. *T:* 01-822 5252.

DURIE, Sir Alexander (Charles), Kt 1977; CBE 1973; Vice-President, The Automobile Association, since 1977 (Director-General, 1964-77); *b* 15 July 1915; *er s* of late Charles and Margaret Durie (*née* Gardner), Shepton Mallet, Somerset; *m* 1941, Joyce, *o c* of late Lionel and Helen Hargreaves (*née* Hirst), Leeds and Bridlington, Yorks; one *s* one *d. Educ:* Queen's Coll., Taunton.

Joined Shell-Mex and BP Ltd, 1933. Served War of 1939-45, Royal Artillery; Gunnery Staff Course (IG), 1941; Lieut-Col 1945. Dir Shell Co. of Australia Ltd, 1954-56; Dir, 1962, Man. Dir, 1963-64, Shell-Mex and BP Ltd; Director: Mercantile Credit Co. Ltd, 1973-80; Thomas Cook Group Ltd, 1974-79; Provident Association for Medical Care Ltd, 1977-; H. Clarkson (Holdings) Ltd, 1978-; Chelsea Building Soc., 1979-. Mem. Council, Motor and Cycle Trades Benevolent Fund, 1959-73; Vice-Pres. British Assoc. of Industrial Editors, 1959-71; Gen. Commissioner of Income Tax, 1960-; Member Govt Inquiries into: Civilianisation of Armed Forces, 1964; Cars for Cities, 1964; Road Haulage Operators' Licensing, 1978. FBIM, 1959, Council Mem., 1962-73, Chm. Exec. Cttee, 1962-65, Vice-Chm. Council, 1962-67, Chm., Bd of Fellows, 1970-73 (Verulam Medal 1973); Member: Nat. Road Safety Adv. Council, 1965-68; Adv. Council on Road Res., 1965-68; Brit. Road Fedn Ltd, 1962- (Vice-Pres., 1978); Council, Internat. Road Fedn Ltd, London, 1962-64; Marketing Cttee, BTA, 1970-77; Adv. Cttee on Traffic and Safety, TRRL, 1973-77; Vice-Pres., Alliance Internationale de Tourisme, 1965-71, Pres., 1971-77; Chm., Indep. Schs Careers Orgn, 1969-73 (Vice-Pres., 1973-); Governor: Ashridge Coll., 1963-78 (Vice Pres., 1978-); Queen's Coll., Taunton, 1969-. Mem. Cttee, Surrey CCC, 1970-80 (Vice-Pres., 1980-) Freeman of City of London and Liveryman, Worshipful Co. of Paviors, 1965. FCIT; Hon. FInstHE 1969. Spanish Order of Touristic Merit Silver Medal, 1977. *Recreations:* cricket, curling, golf, racing. *Address:* The Garden House, Windlesham, Surrey GU20 6AD. *T:* Bagshot 72035. *Clubs:* MCC, Carlton; Royal and Ancient; Berkshire Golf.

DURKIN, Air Marshal Sir Herbert, KBE 1976; CB 1973; CEng, FIEE, FRAeS; CBIM; Controller of Engineering and Supply (RAF), 1976-78; *b* 31 March 1922; *s* of Herbert and Helen Durkin, Burnley, Lancs; *m* 1951, Dorothy Hope, *d* of Walter Taylor Johnson, Burnley; one *s* two *d. Educ:* Burnley Grammar Sch.; Emmanuel Coll., Cambridge (MA). Commissioned into Tech. Br., RAF, Oct. 1941. Served War, with No 60 Gp, until 1945. India, 1945-47, becoming ADC to AOC-in-C India; Central Bomber Estabt, 1947-50; Sqdn Ldr, 1950; Atomic Weapons Research Estabt, 1950-52; RAF Staff Coll., 1953; Chief Signals Officer, AHQ, Iraq, 1954-56; Wing Comdr, Chief Instr of Signals Div. of RAF Tech. Coll., 1956-58; Air Ministry, 1958-60; jssc, 1961; HQ, 2 ATAF, 1961-63; Gp Capt 1962; Sen. Tech. Staff Officer, HQ Signals Command, 1964-65; Comdt, No 2 Sch. of Tech. Trg, Cosford, 1965-67; Air Cdre, 1967; Director of Eng (Policy), MoD, 1967-69; IDC, 1970; AOC No 90 Group, RAF, 1971-73; Dir-Gen. Engineering and Supply Management, 1973-76. Pres., IEE, 1980 (Dep. Pres., 1979). FBIM. *Recreation:* golf. *Address:* Willowbank, Drakes Drive, Northwood, Middlesex HA6 2SL. *T:* Northwood 23167. *Club:* Royal Air Force.

DURLACHER, Adm. Sir Laurence (George), KCB 1961 (CB 1957); OBE 1943; DSC 1945; retired; *b* 24 July 1904; *s* of late Frederick Henry Keeling Durlacher and V. M. Durlacher (*née* Hanson); *m* 1934, Rimma, *d* of late R. V. Sass-Tissovsky; one *s* one *d. Educ:* RNC Osborne and Dartmouth. Lieut 1927; Comdr 1939; Capt. 1945; Cdre 1st Class, 1952; Rear-Adm. 1955; Vice-Adm. 1958; Adm. 1961. On Staff of Adm. of the Fleet Viscount Cunningham of Hyndhope during N Africa, Sicily and Italian Campaigns (despatches); commanded HMS Volage, 1944-45; Admiralty, 1945-47; commanded 3rd Destroyer Flotilla, Mediterranean, 1949-50; commanded Admiralty Signals and Radar Establishments, 1950-52; Chief of Staff to C-in-C Far East Station, 1952-54; Dep. Chief of Naval Personnel (Personal Services), at Admiralty, 1955-57; Flag Officer Commanding Fifth Cruiser Squadron and Flag Officer Second-in-Command, Far East Station, 1957-58; Dep. Chief of Naval Staff and Fifth Sea Lord, 1959-62; retired, 1962. US Legion of Merit, 1945. *Address:* Mas Tournamy, 06250 Mougins, France.

DURNFORD-SLATER, Adm. Sir Robin (Leonard Francis), KCB 1957 (CB 1955); *b* 9 July 1902, *s* of Captain L. Slater, Royal Sussex Regiment (killed in action, 1914), and Constance Dorothy Durnford-Slater; *m* 1936, Mary Alice Hilleary, *d* of late Col E. H. Gregson, CMG, CIE; one *s* one *d. Educ:* Osborne; Dartmouth. Comdr, 1938; Capt., 1944; Rear-Adm., 1953; Vice-Adm., 1956; Adm., 1959. Served War of 1939-45; Executive officer, HMS Hermes, HMS Vernon; Senior Officer, 42nd and subseq. 7th Escort Grp Western Approaches; Trg Capt. Western Approaches; Dir of Underwater Weapons, Admiralty (Bath). Post War: Senior Officer 1st Escort Flotilla, Far East; Commandant Sch. of Amphibious Warfare; Capt. HMS Gambia; Dep. Controller, Admiralty, 1953-56; Flag Officer, 2nd in Command, Mediterranean Fleet, 1956-58; Commander-in-Chief, The Nore, 1958-61; retd. Flag Officer Naval Brigade, Coronation, 1953. Comdr of the Legion of Honour, 1958. *Address:* Four Chiltley Lane, Liphook, Hants.

DURRANDS, Kenneth James, DGS (Birm), MSc, CEng, FIMechE, FIEE, FIProdE; Rector, The Polytechnic, Queensgate, Huddersfield, since 1970; *b* 24 June 1929; *s* of A. I. Durrands, Croxton Kerrial; *m* 1956 (marr. diss. 1971), one *s. Educ:* King's Sch., Grantham; Nottingham Technical Coll.; Birmingham Univ. (DGS). Min. of Supply Engrg Apprentice, ROF, Nottingham, 1947-52; Techn. Engr, UKAEA, Risley, 1954-58; Lecturer in Mechanical and Nuclear Engrg, Univ. of Birmingham, 1958-61; Head of Gen. Engrg Dept, Reactor Engrg Lab., UKAEA, Risley, 1961-67; Mem. Council, IMechE, 1963-66; Visiting Lecturer, Manchester Univ., 1962-68; Technical Dir, Vickers Ltd, Barrow Engrg Works, 1967-70. Member: DoI Educn and Training Cttee, 1973-75 (Chm., 1975-); DoI Garment & Allied Industries Requirements Bd, 1975- (Chm. Computer Cttee, 1975-); BEC Educn Cttee, 1975-; BEC Business Studies Bd, 1976-; Inter-Univ. Council, 1978-; Hon. Sec./Treas., Cttee of Dirs of Polytechnics, 1970-. Member: Council and

Court, Leeds Univ., 1970-; Court, Bradford Univ., 1973-. *Publications:* several technical papers. *Recreations:* motor sport, gardening, squash rackets. *Address:* Church Cottage, Croxton Kerrial, Grantham, Lincolnshire. *Club:* Athenæum.

DURRANT, Albert Arthur Molteno, CBE 1945; CEng; FIMechE; FCIT; FRSA; retired from London Transport Board; *b* 11 Sept. 1898; *s* of late Sir Arthur I. Durrant, CBE, MVO; *m* 1922, Kathleen (*d* 1977), *d* of Arthur J. Wright; no *c. Educ:* Alleyn's Sch., Dulwich. Joined London Gen. Omnibus Co., 1919; Chief Engineer (Buses and Coaches), London Passenger Transport Bd, 1935-40; Director of Tank Design, Ministry of Supply, 1940-45; Chief Mechanical Engineer (Road Services) London Transport, 1945-65. *Address:* c/o Williams and Glyn's Bank, Holts Branch, 22 Whitehall, SW1.

DURRANT, Maj.-Gen. James Thom, CB 1945; DFC 1941; City Councillor, Johannesburg, 1969-77; *b* 1913; *s* of late J. C. Durrant, Hertford and Johannesburg; *m* 1970, Margaret, *d* of late Archie White, Johannesburg. Commanded a group in Air Command, South-East Asia, 1945; Dir-Gen. South African Air Force, 1947-51; retired, 1952. *Address:* 71 First Avenue East, Parktown North, Johannesburg, South Africa.

DURRANT, Sir William Henry Estridge, 7th Bt, *cr* 1784; JP (NSW); *b* 1 April 1901; *s* of Sir William Durrant, 6th Bt; *S* father 1953; *m* 1927, Georgina Beryl Gwendoline (*d* 1968), *d* of Alexander Purse, Kircubbin, Co. Down, N Ireland; one *s* one d. Served War of 1939-45 (Pacific Area). NSW Registrar, Australian Inst. of Company Dirs, 1959. *Heir: s* William Alexander Estridge Durrant [*b* 26 Nov. 1929; *m* 1953, Dorothy (BA), *d* of Ronal Croker, Quirindi, NSW; one *s* one *d*]. *Address:* Woodside Gardens, Yardley Avenue, Waitara, NSW 2077, Australia.

DURRELL, Gerald Malcolm; Zoologist and Writer since 1946; regular contributor to BBC Sound and TV Services; *b* Jamshedpur, India, 7 Jan. 1925; *s* of Lawrence Samuel Durrell, Civil Engineer, and Louisa Florence Dixie; *m* 1st, 1951, Jacqueline Sonia Rasen (marr. diss. 1979); no *c* ; 2nd, 1979, Lee Wilson McGeorge. *Educ:* by Private Tutors, in France, Italy, Switzerland and Greece. Student Keeper, Whipsnade, 1945-46; 1st Animal Collecting Expedition, British Cameroons, 1947-48; 2nd Cameroon Expedition, 1948-49; Collecting trip to British Guiana, 1949-50; began writing, script writing and broadcasting, 1950-53; trip with wife to Argentine and Paraguay, 1953-54; filming in Cyprus, 1955; 3rd Cameroon Expedition with wife, 1957; Trans-Argentine Expedition, 1958-59; Expedition in conjunction with BBC Natural History Unit, Sierra Leone, 1965; collecting trip to Mexico, 1968; Aust. Expedn, 1969-70; expedns to Mauritius, 1976 and 1977, Assam, 1978, Mexico, 1979, Madagascar, 1981. Founder and Hon. Director: Jersey Zoological Park, 1958; Jersey Wildlife Preservation Trust, 1964. Founder Chm. SAFE Internat. USA, 1972. FZS; (Life) FIAL; FRGS; FRSL 1972; MBOU; MIBiol. Hon. LHD Yale, 1977. *Films for TV:* 1st series, 1956; Two in the Bush, 1962; Catch Me a Colobus, 1966; Animal People-Menagerie Manor, 1967; Garden of the Gods, 1967; The Stationary Ark, 1976; The Ark on the Move, 1981. *Publications:* The Overloaded Ark, 1953, Three Singles to Adventure, 1954; The Bafut Beagles, 1954; The New Noah, 1955; The Drunken Forest, 1956; My Family and Other Animals, 1956; Encounters with Animals, 1958; A Zoo in my Luggage, 1960; The Whispering Land, 1961; Island Zoo, 1961; Look at Zoos, 1961; My Favourite Animal Stories, 1962; Menagerie Manor, 1964; Two in the Bush, 1966; Rosy is My Relative, 1968; The Donkey Rustlers, 1968; Birds, Beasts and Relatives, 1969; Fillets of Plaice, 1971; Catch Me a Colobus, 1972; Beasts in My Belfry, 1973; The Talking Parcel, 1974; The Stationary Ark, 1976; Golden Bats and Pink Pigeons, 1977; The Garden of the Gods, 1978; The Picnic & Suchlike Pandemonium, 1979; The Mockery Bird, 1981; The Amateur Naturalist, 1982; contribs to Zoo Life, etc. *Recreations:* reading, riding, filming, photography, drawing, swimming, study of the History and Maintenance of Zoological Gardens. *Address:* Jersey Zoo Park, Les Augres Manor, Trinity, Jersey, Channel Isles. *T:* Central 61949.

See also Lawrence G. Durrell.

DURRELL, Lawrence George, FRSL 1954; lately Director of Public Relations, Government of Cyprus; *b* 27 Feb. 1912; *m* 1937, 1947 and 1960; two *d. Educ:* College of St Joseph, Darjeeling, India; St Edmund's Sch., Canterbury. Formerly: Foreign Service Press Officer, Athens and Cairo; Press Attaché, Alexandria; Dir of Public Relations, Dodecanese Islands; Press Attaché, Belgrade, Yugoslavia; Dir of British Council Institutes of Kalamata, Greece, and Cordoba, Argentina. Mellon Lectr in Humanities, Calif. Inst. of Technology, Pasadena, 1975. *Publications:* (novel, under pseudonym Charles Norden) Panic Spring, 1937; The Black Book, 1938 (France and USA), 1973 (England); Private Country (poetry), 1943; Prospero's Cell, 1945; (trans) Four Greek Poets, 1946; Cities, Plains and People, 1946; Cefalu, 1947 (republished as The Dark Labyrinth, 1958); On Seeming to Presume, 1948; (trans) Pope Joan, 1948; Sappho (verse play), 1950; Reflections on a Marine Venus, 1953; The Tree of Idleness, 1955; Selected Poems, 1956; Bitter Lemons, 1957 (Duff Cooper Memorial Prize); White Eagles Over Serbia (juvenile), 1957; The Alexandria Quartet: Justine, 1957, Balthazar, 1958 (Prix du Meilleur Livre Etranger, Paris), Mountolive, 1958, Clea, 1960; Esprit de Corps, 1957; Stiff Upper Lip, 1958; (ed) The Best of Henry Miller, 1960; Collected Poems, 1960, new edn with additions and revisions, 1968; An Irish Faustus (verse play), 1963; The Ikons, 1966; The Revolt of Aphrodite: Tunc, 1968, Nunquam, 1970; Spirit of Place: letters and essays on travel, 1969; The Red Limbo Lingo: a poetry notebook for 1968-70, 1971; Vega and other poems, 1973; Monsieur,

or the Prince of Darkness, 1974 (James Tait Black Memorial Prize); The Best of Antrobus, 1975; Selected Poems, 1976; Sicilian Carousel, 1976; The Greek Islands, 1978; Livia or Buried Alive, 1978; Collected Poems, 1980; Smile in the Mind's Eye, 1980; Constance or Solitary Practices, 1982. *Recreation:* travel. *Address:* c/o Grindlay's Bank, 13 St James's Square, SW1.

See also Gerald M. Durrell.

DÜRRENMATT, Friedrich; Swiss author and playwright; *b* Konolfingen, Switzerland, 5 Jan. 1921; *s* of Reinhold Dürrenmatt, pastor, and Hulda (née Zimmermann); *m* 1946, Lotti Geissler; one *s* two d. *Educ:* Gymnasium, Bern; University of Bern; University of Zürich. Prix Italia, 1958; Schillerpreis, 1960; Grillparzer-Preis, 1968; Kunstpreis, Bern, 1969. Hon DLitt, Temple Univ. Philadelphia, 1969; Dr (*hc*): Hebrew Univ. of Jerusalem, 1977; Univ. of Nice, 1977; Univ. of Neuchâtel, 1981. Buber-Rosenzweig Medaille, Frankfurt, 1977. *Publications: plays:* Es steht geschrieben, 1947; Der Blinde, 1948; Romulus der Grosse, 1949; Die Ehe des Herrn Mississippi (The Marriage of Mr Mississippi), 1952 (produced New York, Fools Are Passing Through, 1958; filmed, 1961); Nächtliches Gespräch mit einem verachteten Menschen, 1952; Ein Engel kommt nach Babylon (An Angel Comes to Babylon), 1953; Der Besuch der alten Dame, 1956 (The Visit, produced New York, 1958, London, 1960) (Eng. trans., by Patrick Bowles, publ. 1962); Frank V-Oper einer Privatbank, 1959; Die Physiker, 1962 (prod. Aldwych Theatre, London as The Physicists, 1963); The Meteor (prod. Aldwych Theatre, London, 1966); Die Wiedertäufer, 1967; Die Panne (The Deadly Game, 1955, prod. Savoy Theatre, 1967); König Johann, nach Shakespeare, 1968; Play Strindberg, 1969; Titus Andronicus, nach Shakespeare, 1970; Porträt eines Planeten, 1970 (Portrait of a Planet, prod London, 1973); Komödien, I, II, III, 1972; Der Mitmacher, 1973; Die Frist, 1977; Die Punne Komödie, 1979; *plays for radio:* Der Doppelgänger; Der Prozess um des Esels Schatten; Nächtliches Gespräch; Stranitzki und der Nationalheld; Herkules und der Stall des Augias; Das Unternehmen der Wega; Die Panne; Abendstunde im Spätherbst; *essays and criticism:* Theater-Schriften und Reden I, II (Eng. trans., Writings on Theatre and Drama, 1977); Theater-probleme; Gerechtigkeit und Recht; Friedrich Schiller, Rede; Sätze aus Amerika, 1970; Gespräch mit Heinz Ludwig Arnold, 1976; Zusammenhänge: Essay über Israel, 1976; Der Mitmacher: ein Komplex, 1976; Frankfurter Rede, 1977; Friederich Dürrenmatt, Lesebuch, 1978; Einstein-Vortrag, 1979; *novels:* Pilatus, 1949; Der Nihilist, 1950; Die Stadt (short stories), 1952; Der Richter und sein Henker, 1952 (Eng. trans. by Therese Pol, The Judge and His Hangman, 1955); Der Verdacht, 1953 (Eng. trans. as The Quarry, by Eva H. Morreale), 1962; Grieche sucht Griechin, 1955; Die Panne, 1956 (Eng. trans. by R. and C. Winston, The Dangerous Game, 1960); Das Versprechen, 1958 (Eng. trans. by R. and C. Winston, The Pledge, 1959); Der Sturz, 1971. *Recreations:* painting and astronomy. *Address:* Pertuis du Sault 34, Neuchâtel, Switzerland.

du SAUTOY, Peter Francis, CBE 1971 (OBE 1964); *b* 19 Feb. 1912; *s* of late Col E. F. du Sautoy, OBE, TD, DL; *m* 1937, Phyllis Mary (Mollie), *d* of late Sir Francis Floud, KCB, KCSI, KCMG; two *s. Educ:* Uppingham (Foundn Schol.); Wadham Coll., Oxford (Sen. Class. Schol.). MA, 1st cl. Lit. Hum. Dept of Printed Books, British Museum, 1935-36; Asst Educn Officer, City of Oxford, 1937-40; RAF, 1940-45; joined Faber & Faber Ltd, 1946; Dir, Dec. 1946; Vice-Chm., 1960-71; Chm., 1971-76, editorial consultant, 1977-; Chm., Faber and Faber (Publishers) Ltd, 1971-76; Mem. Bd, Faber Music Ltd, 1966- (Chm., 1971-76, Vice Chm., 1977-81); Mem. Bd, Yale Univ. Press Ltd, London, 1977-. Mem. Council, Publishers Assoc., 1957-63, 1965-77 (Pres., 1967-69); Mem. Exec. Cttee, Internat. Publishers Assoc., 1972-76; Pres., Groupe des Editeurs de Livres de la CEE, 1973-75. Official visits on behalf of Publishers Assoc. and British Council to Australia, USSR, Finland, Hungary, Nigeria, China. Mem. Council, Aldeburgh Festival-Snape Maltings Foundn Ltd, 1976- (Vice-Chm., 1977-80; Dep. Chm., 1982-). *Publications:* various articles on publishing. *Address:* 31 Lee Road, Aldeburgh, Suffolk. *T:* Aldeburgh 2838. *Club:* Garrick.

DUTHIE, Prof. Herbert Livingston, MD; FRCS, FRCSEd; Provost of the Welsh National School of Medicine, University of Wales, since 1979; *b* 9 Oct. 1929; *s* of Herbert William Duthie and Margaret McFarlane Livingston; *m* 1959, Maureen McCann; three *s* one d. *Educ:* Whitehill Sch., Glasgow; Univ. of Glasgow (MB, ChB 1952; MD Hons 1962; ChM Hons 1959). FRCSEd 1956; FRCS 1957. Served RAMC, 1954-56. Sen. House Officer, Registrar, and Lectr in Surgery, Western Infirmary, Glasgow, 1956-59; Rockefeller Travelling Fellow, Mayo Clinic, Rochester, Minn, USA, 1959-60; Lectr in Surg., Univ. of Glasgow, 1960-61; Sen. Lectr in Surg., Univ. of Leeds, 1961-63, Reader, 1964; Prof. of Surg., Univ. of Sheffield, 1964-79 (Dean, Faculty of Medicine, 1976-78). Pres., Surgical Res. Soc., 1978-80; Mem., GMC, 1976-. *Publications:* articles on gastroenterological topics. *Address:* 86 Dan-y-Bryn Avenue, Radyr, Cardiff CF4 8DQ. *T:* Cardiff 843472. *Clubs:* Army and Navy; Cardiff and County (Cardiff).

DUTHIE, Prof. Robert Buchan, MA Oxon, MB, ChM; FRCSE, FRCS; Nuffield Professor of Orthopædic Surgery, Oxford University; Professorial Fellow, Worcester College, Oxford; Surgeon, Nuffield Orthopædic Centre, Oxford; Civilian Consultant Adviser in Orthopaedic Surgery to Royal Navy, since 1978; *b* 4 May 1925; 2nd *s* of late James Andrew Duthie and late Elizabeth Jean Duthie, Edinburgh; *m* 1956, Alison Ann Macpherson Kittermaster, MA; two *s* two d. *Educ:* Aberdeen Grammar Sch.; King Edward VI Gram. Sch., Chelmsford; Heriot-Watt Coll., Edinburgh; University of Edinburgh Med. Sch. Robert Jones Prize 1947, MB, ChB 1948, ChM (with dist.) (Gold Medal for Thesis) 1956, University of Edinburgh; FRCSE 1953.

Ho. Surg. Royal Infirmary, 1948-49; Ho. Phys., Western Gen. Hosp., Edinburgh, 1949. Active service in Malaya, RAMC, 1949-51. Registrar, Royal Infirmary, Edinburgh, 1951-53; David Wilkie Res. Schol. of University of Edinburgh, 1953-; Res. Fellow of Scottish Hosps Endowment Research Trust, Edinburgh, 1953-56; Res. Fellow, Nat. Cancer Inst., Bethesda, USA, 1956-57; Extern. Mem. of MRC in Inst. of Orthopædics, London and Sen. Registrar, 1957-58; Prof. of Orthopædic Surg., University of Rochester Sch. of Medicine and Dentistry and Orthopædic Surg.-in-Chief, University of Rochester Med. Centre, 1958-66. Consultant Adviser in Orthopaedics and Accident Surgery to DHSS, 1971-80. Mem., Royal Commn on Civil Liability and Compensation for Personal Injury, 1973-78; Chairman: Adv. Cttee of Res. in Artificial Limbs and Appliances, DHSS, 1975; Working Party on Orthopaedic Services to Sec. of State for Social Services, 1980-81. Governor: St Edward's Sch., Oxford; Oxford Sch. for Boys. Fellow Brit. Orthopædic Assoc.; Member: Internat. Soc. for Orthopædic Surgery and Traumatology; Orthopædic Research Soc.; Inter-urban Orthopædic Club: Internat. Orthopædic Club. Amer. Rheumatism Assoc.; Hon. Member: Portuguese Soc. of Orthopaedic Surgery and Traumatology; Japanese Orthopaedic Assoc.; Corresp. Mem., Assoc. of Orthopaedic Surgery and Traumatology, Yugoslavia. President's Prize, Soc. Internat. de Chirurgie, 1957. Commander, SMO, Malta. *Publications:* (co-author) Textbook of Orthopædic Surgery, 7th edn, 1982; contribs to med. and surg. jls relating to genetics, histochemistry, transplantation, pathology, neoplasia of musculo-skeletal tissues, and clinical subjects. *Recreations:* family, tennis. *Address:* Nuffield Orthopædic Centre, Headington, Oxford; Barna Brow, Harberton Mead, Headington, Oxford. *T:* 62745.

DUTHIE, Robert Grieve, CBE 1978; CA; Chairman, Black & Edgington Ltd, since 1972; Chairman, Scottish Development Agency, since 1979; Director: British Assets Trust, since 1977; Edinburgh American Assets Trust, since 1977; Royal Bank of Scotland Ltd, since 1978; *b* 2 Oct. 1928; *s* of George Duthie and Mary (*née* Lyle); *m* 1955, Violetta Noel Maclean; two *s* one *d*. *Educ:* Greenock Academy. Apprentice Chartered Accountant with Thomson Jackson Gourlay & Taylor, CA, 1946-51; joined Blacks of Greenock, 1952, Man. Dir, 1962. Chm., Clyde Port Authority, 1977-79. FBIM 1976. *Recreations:* curling, golf. *Address:* Fairhaven, Finnart Street, Greenock PA16 8JA. *T:* Greenock 22642. *Club:* Greenock (Greenock).

DUTTON, family name of **Baron Sherborne.**

DUTTON, James Macfarlane; HM Diplomatic Service, retired; *b* 3 June 1922; *s* of late H. St J. Dutton and Mrs E. B. Dutton; *m* 1958, Jean Mary McAvoy; one *s*. *Educ:* Winchester Coll.; Balliol Coll., Oxford. Dominions Office, 1944-46; Private Sec. to Permanent Under Sec., 1945; Dublin, 1946-48; CRO, 1948-50; Asst Private Sec. to Sec. of State, 1948; 2nd Sec., New Delhi, 1950-53; CRO, 1953-55; 1st Sec., Dacca and Karachi, 1955-58, Canberra, 1958-62; Head of Constitutional and Protocol Dept, CRO, 1963-65; Canadian Nat. Defence Coll., 1965-66; Dep. High Comr and Counsellor (Commercial), Colombo, 1966-70; Head of Rhodesia Econ. Dept, FCO, 1970-72; attached CSD, 1972-73; seconded to: British Electrical & Allied Manufacturers Assoc. (Dir, Overseas Affairs), 1973-74; Wilton Park and European Discussion Centre, 1974-75; Consul-Gen., Gothenburg, 1975-78. *Recreations:* golf, trout-fishing. *Address:* Cockerhurst, Tyrrells Wood, Leatherhead, Surrey KT22 8QH.

DUTTON, Ralph Stawell, FSA; *b* 25 Aug. 1898; *s* of late Henry John Dutton, Hinton Ampner House, Hants; *heir pres.* to 7th Baron Sherborne, qv. *Educ:* Eton; Christ Church, Oxford. Employed in the Foreign Office, 1939-45. High Sheriff of Hants, 1944. A Trustee of the Wallace Collection, 1948-69. Member: Cttees of Nat. Trust, 1955-73; Historic Buildings Council, 1963-72. *Publications:* The English Country House, 1935; The English Garden, 1937; The Land of France (with Lord Holden), 1939; The English Interior, 1948; Wessex, 1950; The Age of Wren, 1951; London Homes, 1952; Normandy and Brittany, 1953; The Victorian Home, 1954; The Châteaux of France, 1957; English Court Life, 1963; Hinton Ampner; A Hampshire Manor, 1968; Hampshire, 1970. *Address:* Hinton Ampner House, Alresford, Hants. *T:* Bramdean 222; 95N Eaton Square, SW1. *T:* 01-235 2950. *Club:* Brooks's.

DUTTON, Reginald David Ley; *b* 20 Aug. 1916; *m* 1951, Pamela Jean (*née* Harrison); two *s* one *d*. *Educ:* Magdalen Coll. Sch., Oxford. Joined OUP; subseq. joined leading British advertising agency, London Press Exchange (now Lopex Ltd), 1937. During War of 1939-45 served in Royal Navy. Returned to agency after his service; there, he worked on many of major accounts; Dir, 1954; Man. Dir and Chief Exec., 1964; Chm., 1971-76; retired 1976. Pres. Inst. Practitioners in Advertising, 1969-71; Chm., Jt Ind. Council for TV Advertising Research, 1973-75; Mem. Council, BIM, 1970-74; FIPA 1960. Councillor, Canterbury CC, 1976-77. *Recreation:* deep sea fishing. *Address:* 55 Stalham Road, Hoveton, Norwich. *T:* Wroxham 3145.

DUVAL, Sir (Charles) Gaetan, Kt 1981; QC 1975; barrister; Lord Mayor of Port-Louis, Mauritius, 1971 (Mayor, 1969-71); *b* 9 Oct. 1930. *Educ:* Royal Coll., Curepipe; Faculty of Law, Univ. of Paris. Called to the Bar, Lincoln's Inn. Entered politics, 1956; Mem., Town Council, Curepipe, 1960-62 (Chm., 1960-61); re-elected 1963; Mem., Legislative Council; Minister of Housing, 1964-65; Minister of External Affairs, Tourism and Emigration, 1969. *Address:* Place Foch, Port-Louis, Mauritius.

DUVAL, Sir Francis (John), Kt 1977; CBE 1970; Chairman: Arafura Mining Co. Pty Ltd; Duval Pastoral Co. Pty Ltd; Dover Fisheries Pty Ltd; Duval and Co. (Japan); *b* Narrandera, NSW, Australia, 31 Aug. 1909; *s* of late Francis William Duval; *m* 1960, Chieko, *d* of late Isakichi Hanada. *Educ:* Chatswood High, NSW. Served War, 1939-45: Major AIF, ME, Ceylon, New Guinea and Japan. *Recreations:* golf, deep sea game fishing. *Address:* Churinga House, 1 Old Beach Road, Old Beach, Tasmania 7402, Australia. *T:* Hobart 49-1155. *Clubs:* Royal Automobile, Imperial Service, Australian Jockey (Sydney); Commonwealth (Canberra); Tokyo (Tokyo, Japan).

DUVAL, Sir Gaetan; see Duval, Sir C. G.

DWIGHT, Reginald Kenneth; see John, E. H.

DWORKIN, Paul David, FSS; Assistant Director, Central Statistical Office, since 1982; *b* 7 April 1937; *s* of Louis and Rose Dworkin; *m* 1959, Carole Barbara Burke; two *s*. *Educ:* Hackney Downs Grammar Sch., London; LSE (BScEcon 1958). FSS 1969. E Africa High Commn, Dar es Salaam, Tanganyika, 1959; E African Common Services Org., Nairobi, Kenya, 1961; Asst Statistician, BoT, 1962, Stat. 1965; Chief Statistician: DTI, 1972; Dept of Employment, 1977; Under Sec., Depts of Trade and Industry, 1977-81. *Recreations:* golf, skiing, theatre, reading. *Address:* 17 Cornbury Road, Edgware, Mddx. *T:* 01-952 2673. *Clubs:* Civil Service; Stanmore Golf.

DWORKIN, Prof. Ronald Myles, FBA 1979; Professor of Jurisprudence, Oxford University, since 1969; Fellow of University College, Oxford, since 1969; *b* 11 Dec. 1931; *s* of David Dworkin and Madeline Talamo; *m* 1958, Betsy Celia Ross; one *s* one *d*. *Educ:* Harvard Coll.; Oxford Univ.; Harvard Law Sch. Legal Sec. to Judge Learned Hand, 1957-58; Associate, Sullivan & Cromwell, New York, 1958-62; Yale Law School: Associate Prof. of Law, 1962-65; Prof. of Law, 1965-68; Wesley N. Hohfeld Prof. of Jurisprudence, 1968-69. Rosenthal Lectr, Northwestern Univ., 1975; Academic Freedom Lectr, Univ. of Witwatersrand, 1976; Roscoe Pound Lectr, Univ. of Nebraska, 1979. Vis. Prof. of Philosophy, Princeton Univ., 1974-75; Prof. of Law, NY Univ. Law Sch., 1975-; Prof.-at-Large, Cornell Univ., 1976-; Vis. Prof. of Philosophy and Law, Harvard Univ., 1977, Vis. Prof. of Philosophy, 1979. Co-Chm., US Democratic Party Abroad, 1972-76. Fellow, Amer. Acad. of Arts and Scis, 1979. Hon. LLD Williams Coll., 1981. *Publications:* Taking Rights Seriously, 1977; (ed) The Philosophy of Law, 1977; several articles in legal and philosophical jls. *Address:* University College, Oxford. *Clubs:* Garrick; Oxford American Democrats (Oxford).

DWYER, Most Rev. George Patrick, MA, DD, PhD; former Archbishop of Birmingham; *b* 25 Sept. 1908; *s* of John William and Ima Dwyer. *Educ:* St Bede's Coll., Manchester; Ven. English Coll., Rome; Christ's Coll., Cambridge. PhD 1929, DD 1934, Gregorian Univ., Rome; ordained Priest, 1932; BA Mod. and Med. Lang. Trip. Cambridge (Lady Margaret Scholar, Christ's Coll.). Teaching, St Bede's, Manchester, 1937-47; Catholic Missionary Society, 1947; Editor of Catholic Gazette, 1947-51; Superior, Catholic Missionary Society, 1951-57; Bishop of Leeds, 1957-65; Archbishop of Birmingham, 1965-81; Apostolic Administrator, 1981-82. Pres., RC Bishops' Conference of England and Wales, 1976-79. Hon. Fellow, St Edmund's House, Univ. of Cambridge, 1980. Hon. DLitt: Keele, 1979; Warwick, 1980. *Publications:* The Catholic Faith, 1954; Mary-Doctrine for Everyman (with Rev. T. Holland, DD), 1956. *Address:* St Paul's Convent, Selly Park, Birmingham B29 7LL.

DWYER, Air Vice-Marshal Michael Harington, CB 1961; CBE 1955; retired; *b* 18 Sept. 1912; *s* of late M. H. Dwyer, Royal Garrison Artillery; *m* 1936, Barbara, *d* of late S. B. Freeman, CBE; one *s* one *d*. *Educ:* Oundle Sch. Entered RAF, 1931; served India, 1933-36; UK and NW Europe, 1939-45; Middle East, 1949-51; Air Officer Commanding No 62 Group, 1954-56; SASO No 3 Group, RAF, 1956-57; Student at Imperial Defence Coll., 1958; Air Officer Commanding No 3 Group, 1959-61; AOA, HQ Bomber Command, 1961-65; Regional Dir of Civil Defence, North-West Region, 1966-68. Chm., Harington Carpets, 1973-74. *Address:* Island House, Rambledown Lane, West Chiltington, Sussex.

DYALL, Valentine; actor; *b* 7 May 1908; *s* of late Franklin Dyall; *m* 1936, Marjorie Stonor (decd), *d* of Hon. Maurice Stonor; *m* 1940, Babette Holder (decd), adopted *d* of N. F. Holder; two *s*; *m* Kay Woodman; one *d*. *Educ:* Harrow; Christ Church, Oxford. Began acting career at the Old Vic, 1930 and continued regularly on the West End stage until 1938; subsequently mainly in films and broadcasting. First appeared in films, 1941, and has acted in numerous pictures. Took the role of The Man in Black in a radio series. *Publications:* Unsolved Mysteries, 1954; Famous Sea Tragedies, 1955; Flood of Mutiny, 1957. *Recreations:* fishing, golf. *Address:* c/o Essanay Ltd, 75 Hammersmith Road, W14 8UZ.

DYBALL, Maj.-Gen. (Hon.) Antony John, CBE 1970 (OBE 1966); MC 1945; TD; Director, Printers' Charitable Corporation, since 1979; *b* 10 July 1919; *s* of John Francis Dyball; *m* 1941, Elizabeth Margaret Siddle; one *d*. *Educ:* Downsend; Epsom College. London Irish Rifles (TA); joined Depot RUR, Armagh, 1939; 1st Bn RUR, part of 6th Airborne Div., NW Europe, 1945 (MC); Trng Major, RUR Depot at Ballymena, 1954-56; comd Queen's Univ. OTC, Belfast, 1956-58; Bde Major, 124 Inf. Bde (TA), 1958-60; CO, London Irish Rifles (TA), 1960-62; AAG, Middle East Comd, 1963-65; Bde Comdr, 107 Independent Inf. Bde (TA), 1965-67; Chief of Staff, HQ

Northern Ireland, 1967-69, and Dep. Dir Ops, 1969-70 (acting Maj.-Gen.); Dep. Comdr, Northumberland District, 1970-73, retired; Hon. Maj.-Gen., 1973. *Recreations:* golf, racing. *Address:* 49 Palewell Park, East Sheen, SW14. *T:* 01-878 0394.

DYDE, John Horsfall, CBE 1970 (OBE 1957); Chairman, Eastern Gas Board, 1959-69; *b* 4 June 1905; *m* 1930, Ethel May Hewitt; two *s. Educ:* Scarborough High Sch.; University of Leeds (MSc). Engineer and Manager, North Middlesex Gas Co., 1937-42; prior to nationalisation was Engineer and Gen. Manager of Uxbridge, Maidenhead, Wycombe & District Gas Co. and Slough Gas & Coke Co.; also Technical Director of group of undertakings of the South Eastern Gas Corp. Ltd; Dep.-Chm., Eastern Gas Board, 1949. President: Western Junior Gas Assoc., 1935-36; Southern Assoc. of Gas Engineers and Managers, 1949-50; Institution of Gas Engineers, 1951-52; British Road Tar Association. CEng, FIChemE; Hon. FIGasE. *Recreations:* golf, fishing. *Address:* Stable End, Thellusson Lodge, Aldeburgh, Suffolk. *T:* Aldeburgh 3148.

DYE, Maj.-Gen. Jack Bertie, CBE 1968 (OBE 1965); MC; DL; Director, Volunteers, Territorials and Cadets, 1971-74; Major-General late Royal Norfolk Regiment; *b* 1919. Served War of 1939-45 (MC). Brigadier, 1966; psc. Commanded South Arabian Army, 1966-68; GOC Eastern District, 1969-71. Col Comdt, The Queen's Division, 1970-; Col, Royal Anglian Regt, 1976-82 (Dep. Col, 1974-76). DL Suffolk, 1979.

DYER, Charles; playwright and novelist; actor-director (as Raymond Dyer); *b* 7 July 1928; *s* of James Sidney Dyer and Florence (*née* Stretton); *m* 1959, Fiona Thomson, actress; three *s. Educ:* Queen Elizabeth's Sch., Barnet. *Plays:* Clubs Are Sometimes Trumps, 1948; Who On Earth!, 1951; Turtle in the Soup, 1953; The Jovial Parasite, 1954; Single Ticket Mars, 1955; Time, Murderer, Please, and Poison In Jest, 1956; Wanted—One Body!, 1958; Prelude to Fury, 1959 (also wrote theme music); Rattle of A Simple Man, 1962 (also in Berlin, Paris, NY, Rome and London); Staircase, 1966 (for RSC; also in NY, Paris, Amsterdam, Berlin, Rome); Mother Adam, Paris, Berlin, 1970, London, 1971, 1973, NY, 1974; The Loving Allelujah, 1974; Circling Dancers, 1979; Lovers Dancing, 1981; Futility Rites, 1981; as R. Kraselchik: Red Cabbage and Kings, 1960 (also wrote theme music); *screenplays:* Rattle, 1964; Insurance Italian Style, 1967; Staircase, 1968; Brother Sun and Sister Moon, 1970. Also directed plays for the stage and television. Acted in: *plays:* Worm's Eye View, 1948; Room For Two, 1955; Dry Rot, 1958; *films:* Cuptie Honeymoon, 1947; Britannia Mews, 1949; Road Sense, 1950; Off The Record, 1952; Pickwick Papers, 1952; Dockland Case, 1953; Strange Case of Blondie, 1953; Naval Patrol, 1959; Loneliness of the Long Distance Runner, 1962; Mouse On The Moon, 1962; Knack, 1964; Rattle of A Simple Man, 1964; How I Won The War, 1967; Staircase, 1968; *television series:* Hugh and I, 1964. *Publications:* (as Charles Dyer): plays: Wanted—One Body!, 1961; Time, Murderer, Please, 1962; Rattle Of A Simple Man, (Fr.) 1963; Staircase, 1966; Mother Adam, 1970; The Loneliness Trilogy, 1972; Hot Godly Wind, 1973; novels: Rattle Of A Simple Man, 1964; Charlie Always Told Harry Almost Everything, 1969 (USA and Europe, 1970); The Rising of our Herbert, 1972. *Recreations:* amateur music and carpentry. *Address:* Old Wob, Gerrards Cross, Bucks.

DYER, Sir Henry Peter Francis S.; *see* Swinnerton-Dyer.

DYER, Lois Edith, MCSP; (First) Adviser in Physiotherapy, Department of Health and Social Security, since 1976; *b* 18 March 1925; *d* of Richard Morgan Dyer and Emmeline Agnes (*née* Wells). *Educ:* Middlesex Hospital. Variety of posts as physiotherapist in Britain, Southern, Central and North Africa, 1948-71; extensive travel world wide, visiting and lecturing at national and internat. conferences. First Physiotherapist Member, NHS Health Adv. Service, 1971; first non-medical Chm., Chartered Society of Physiotherapy, 1972-75; Hon. Life Vice-Pres., S African Soc. of Physiotherapy. *Publications:* Care of the Orthopaedic Patient (jtly), 1977; numerous papers in professional jls. *Recreations:* music, country pursuits, bird watching, bridge. *Address:* Garden Flat, 6 Belsize Grove, NW3 4UN. *T:* (home) 01-722 1794; (office) 01-703 6380, ext. 3519.

DYER, Mark; His Honour Judge Dyer; a Circuit Judge, since 1977; *b* 20 Nov. 1928; *er s* of late Maj.-Gen. G. M. Dyer, CBE, DSO, and of Evelyn Mary (*née* List); *m* 1953, Diana, *d* of Sir Percy Lancelot Orde, CIE; two *d. Educ:* Ampleforth Coll.; Christ Church, Oxford (MA). 2nd Lieut: Royal Scots Greys, 1948-49; The Westminster Dragoons (2nd CLY) TA, 1950. Called to the Bar, Middle Temple, 1953; Mem., Gen. Council of the Bar, 1965-69. Dep. Chm., Isle of Wight QS, 1971. A Recorder of the Crown Court, 1972-77. *Address:* Furbelow House, 17 King Street, The Green, Richmond, Surrey. *Club:* Cavalry and Guards.

DYER-SMITH, Rear-Adm. John Edward, CBE 1972; Director-General Aircraft (Naval), Ministry of Defence, 1970-72, retired; *b* 17 Aug. 1918; *s* of Harold E. Dyer-Smith and Emily Sutton; *m* 1940, Kathleen Powell; four *s* one *d. Educ:* Devonport High Sch.; RN Engineering Coll.; Imperial Coll. of Science. Served War of 1939-45: Engineer Officer, HMS Prince of Wales, 1940-41; Asst Fleet Engr Officer, Eastern Fleet, 1942-43; HMS Illustrious, 1943. Various MAP and Min. of Aviation appts, 1946-54; Head of Naval Air Dept, RAE, 1957-61; Dir of RN Aircraft/Helicopters, Min. of Aviation, 1961-64; Defence and Naval Attaché, Tokyo, 1965-67; Superintendent, RN

Aircraft Yard, Belfast, 1968-70. *Recreations:* painting, golf. *Address:* Casa Gomila, Alcaufar, Menorca. *Club:* Royal Automobile.

DYKE, Sir Derek William H.; *see* Hart Dyke.

DYKES, Hugh John; MP (C) Harrow (East) since 1970; Associate Member, Quilter, Hilton, Goodison, Stockbrokers, since 1978; *b* 17 May 1939; *s* of Richard Dykes and Doreen Ismay Maxwell Dykes; *m* 1965, Susan Margaret Dykes (*née* Smith); three *s. Educ:* Weston super Mare Grammar Sch.; Pembroke Coll. Cambridge. Partner, Simon & Coates, Stockbrokers, 1968-78. Contested (C) Tottenham, Gen. Elec., 1966. PPS: to three Parly Under-Secs of State for Defence, 1970; to Parly Under-Sec. of State in Civil Service Dept attached to Cabinet Office, 1973; Mem., European Parlt, Strasbourg, 1974. Chm., Cons. Parly European Cttee, 1979-80 (Vice-Chm., 1974-79); Vice-Pres., Cons. Gp for EEC, 1982- (Chm., 1978-81). Mem., Wider Share Ownership Council; Research Sec., Bow Gp, 1965; Chm., Coningsby Club, 1969. Governor, Royal Nat. Orthopaedic Hosp., 1975-82. *Publications:* (ed) Westropp's "Invest £100", 1964, and Westropp's "Start Your Own Business", 1965; many articles and pamphlets on political and financial subjects. *Recreations:* music, theatre, swimming, travel. *Address:* House of Commons, SW1. *T:* 01-219 3000. *Clubs:* Garrick, Carlton, Beefsteak.

DYKES BOWER, S(tephen) E(rnest), MA; FRIBA; FSA; Surveyor of the Fabric of Westminster Abbey, 1951-73, now Emeritus; Consulting Architect, Carlisle Cathedral, 1947-75; *b* 18 April 1903; 2nd *s* of Ernest Dykes Bower, MD; unmarried. *Educ:* Cheltenham Coll.; Merton Coll., Oxford (Organ Schol.); Architectural Assoc. Sch. of Architecture. Private practice as architect since 1931, work chiefly domestic and ecclesiastical. Architect for: New High Altar, Baldachino and American Memorial Chapel, St Paul's Cathedral (with W. Godfrey Allen); enlargement of Bury St Edmunds Cathedral; Cathedral Library and Bishop's Palace, Exeter; completion of Lancing Coll. Chapel; re-building of Gt Yarmouth Parish Church; St Vedast, Foster Lane, EC; and other churches in London and country; work in Canterbury, Winchester, Norwich, Ely, Gloucester, Wells, Oxford, Carlisle, Peterborough and other cathedrals, Oxford and Cambridge Colls, Public Schs, Halls of City Livery Cos, etc. Lay Canon of St Edmundsbury Cathedral, 1979-. *Publications:* papers and addresses on architectural subjects. *Address:* Quendon Court, Quendon, near Saffron Walden, Essex. *T:* Rickling 242. *Clubs:* Athenæum, United Oxford & Cambridge University.

DYMOKE, Rear-Adm. Lionel Dorian, CB 1974; *b* 18 March 1921; *s* of Henry Lionel Dymoke and Dorothy (*née* Briscoe); *m* 1st, 1952, Patricia Pimlott (*d* 1968); one *s*; 2nd, 1970, Iris Hemsted (*née* Lamplough). *Educ:* Nautical Coll., Pangbourne. Entered Royal Navy, 1938; Comdr 1953; Captain 1961; Rear-Adm. 1971; retired 1976. *Address:* 3 Woodland Place, Bath, Avon. *T:* Bath 64228.

DYMOND, Charles Edward, CBE 1967; JP; HM Diplomatic Service, retired; *b* 15 Oct. 1916; *s* of Charles George Dymond and Dora Kate Dymond (*née* Gillingham); *m* 1945, Dorothy Jean Peaker; two *s* two *d. Educ:* Tiverton Grammar Sch.; Exeter Univ. BSc (Econ) London. Royal Artillery, 1939-46; BoT Regional Div., 1946; Trade Commn Service, 1951; Trade Comr, Johannesburg, 1951; Cape Town, 1955; Nairobi, 1957; Sen. Trade Comr, Lagos, 1963-64; Counsellor (Commercial), Lagos, 1965-66; Counsellor i/c, British High Commn, Auckland, 1967-73; Comr for Pitcairn Island, 1970-72; Consul-General, Perth, 1973-76. JP Western Australia, 1980. *Address:* PO Box 15, Sawyers Valley, WA 6074, Australia.

DYNEVOR, 9th Baron *cr* 1780; **Richard Charles Uryan Rhys;** *b* 19 June 1935; *s* of 8th Baron Dynevor, CBE, MC; *S* father, 1962; *m* 1959, Lucy (marr. diss. 1978), *d* of Sir John Rothenstein, *qv*; one *s* three *d. Educ:* Eton; Magdalene Coll., Cambridge. *Heir: s* Hon. Hugo Griffith Uryan Rhys, *b* 19 Nov. 1966. *Address:* Flat 2, 17 Sheffield Terrace, W8. *T:* 01-727 7439.

DYSART, Countess of (11th in line), *cr* 1643; **Rosamund Agnes Greaves;** Baroness Huntingtower, 1643; *b* 15 Feb. 1914; *d* of Major Owain Greaves (*d* 1941), RHG, and Wenefryde Agatha, Countess of Dysart (10th in line); *S* mother, 1975. *Heir: sister* Lady Katherine Grant of Rothiemurchus [*b* 1 June 1918; *m* 1941, Colonel John Peter Grant of Rothiemurchus, MBE; one *s* one *d*]. *Address:* Bryn Garth, Grosmont, Abergavenny, Gwent.

DYSON, Rev. Anthony Oakley, BD, MA, DPhil; Samuel Ferguson Professor of Social and Pastoral Theology, Manchester University, since 1980; *b* 6 Oct. 1935; *s* of Henry Oakley Leslie Dyson and Lilian Dyson; *m* 1960, Edwina Anne Hammett; two *s. Educ:* William Hulme's Grammar Sch., Manchester; Univs of Cambridge and Oxford. 2nd Lieut, West Yorks Regt, 1954-56; Emmanuel Coll., Cambridge, 1956-59; Exeter Coll., Oxford and Ripon Hall, Oxford, 1959-61; Curate of Putney, Dio. Southwark, 1961-63; Chaplain of Ripon Hall, Oxford, 1963-69; Principal of Ripon Hall, 1969-74; Canon of St George's Chapel, Windsor Castle, 1974-77; Custodian, 1975-77; Lectr in Theology, Univ. of Kent, 1977-80. Licensed to Officiate Dio. Oxford, 1965-75, Dio. Canterbury, 1978-80, Dio. Chester, 1980-, Dio. Manchester, 1980-. Examng Chaplain to Bishop of Carlisle; Select Preacher, Univ. of Oxford, 1971; Hensley Henson Lectr, Univ. of Oxford, 1972-73; Pollock Lectr, Halifax, NS, 1973. Associate Dir, Centre for the Study of Religion and Society, Canterbury, 1978-80. Editor: The Teilhard Review, 1966-72; The Modern Churchman, 1982-. *Publications:* Existentialism, 1965; Who is Jesus Christ?, 1969; The Immortality of the Past, 1974; We Believe, 1977; contribs to Evolution Marxism and Christianity, 1967; What Kind of Revolution?, 1968; A Dictionary of Christian Theology, 1969; The Christian Marxist Dialogue, 1969; Teilhard Reassessed, 1970; Oxford Dictionary of the Christian Church, 2nd edn, 1974; Education and Social Action, 1975; Ernst Troeltsch and the Future of Theology, 1976; The Language of the Church in Higher and Further Education, 1977; The Nature of Religious Man, 1982; Theology, The Modern Churchman, Study Encounter, The Month, TLS, etc. *Recreations:* literature, sport. *Address:* Department of Social and Pastoral Theology, Faculty of Theology, University of Manchester, Manchester M13 9PL. *T:* 061-273 3333 (ext. 3545); 43 Hill Top Avenue, Cheadle Hulme, Cheshire SK8 7HZ. *T:* 061-485 3162.

DYSON, Edith Mary Beatrice, OBE 1946; RRC 1948, Bar to RRC 1952; *b* 18 June 1900. *Educ:* Greenhead, Huddersfield. Student Nurse, Royal Free Hospital, London, 1919-24; joined Army Nursing Service, 1924, Germany (with the Army of Occupation, 1926), also India, Burma; served War of 1939-45, i/c nursing units Hong Kong; Prisoner of War, 1941-45; War Office, 1946-48; Col, Queen Alexandra's Royal Army Nursing Corps and Deputy Dir Army Nursing Services, 1951-52; retired 1952. *Address:* Vine Cottage, Higher Trevilla, Feock, Cornwall.

DYSON, Fred; General Secretary, National Union of Dyers, Bleachers and Textile Workers, 1973-79; *b* 28 Sept. 1916; *s* of James Dyson and Jane Anne Dyson (*née* Ashwood); *m* 1948, Beatrice Lilian (*née* Goepel); one *d. Educ:* Nields Council School. MIWP. Served with RAFVR, 1940-46. Woollen Spinner, 1934-39 and 1946-53; National Union of Dyers, Bleachers and Textile Workers: Organiser, 1953; Work Study Officer, 1958; No 4 District Sec., Manchester Area, 1970; Asst Gen. Sec., 1972. Mem. TUC General Council, 1975-79. Member: Garment and Allied Industries Requirements Bd, 1976-79; Industrial Injuries Adv. Council, 1977-81; Central Arbitration Cttee, 1976-79; Industrial Disputes Tribunals, 1974-; Council, British Textile Confedn, 1973-79; co-opted Mem., Northumberland Co. Highways and Transport Cttee, 1981-; Governor: Tweedmouth First Sch., 1981-; Tweedmouth Middle Sch., 1981-. *Recreations:* landscape painting, swimming. *Address:* 6 Lindisfarne Gardens, Berwick-upon-Tweed, Northumberland TD15 2YA. *T:* Berwick 2176. *Clubs:* Slaithwaite Working Men's (Slaithwaite); Shipley Trades Hall (Shipley); Lidgett Green Working Men's (Bradford).

DYSON, Prof. Freeman John, FRS 1952; Professor, School of Natural Sciences, Institute for Advanced Study, Princeton, New Jersey, since 1953; *b* 15 Dec. 1923; *s* of late Sir George Dyson, KCVO; *m* 1st, 1950, Verena Esther (*née* Huber) (marr. diss. 1958); one *s* one *d* ; 2nd, 1958, Imme (*née* Jung); four *d. Educ:* Winchester; Cambridge; Cornell University. Operational research for RAF Bomber Command, 1943-45. Fellow of Trinity Coll., Cambridge, 1946-50; Commonwealth Fund Fellow at Cornell and Princeton, USA, 1947-49; Mem. of Institute for Advanced Study, Princeton, USA, 1949-50; Professor of Physics, Cornell Univ., Ithaca, NY, USA, 1951-53. Mem. of National Academy of Sciences (USA), 1964. Lorentz Medal, Royal Netherlands Acad. of Sciences, 1966; Hughes Medal, Royal Soc., 1968; Max Planck Medal, German Physical Soc., 1969. *Publications:* Disturbing the Universe, 1979; contrib. to The Physical Review, Annals of Mathematics, etc. *Address:* School of Natural Sciences, Institute for Advanced Study, Olden Lane, Princeton, NJ 08540, USA.

DYSON, Dr James, FRS 1968; Deputy Chief Scientific Officer, National Physical Laboratory, 1975-76; retired 1976; *b* 10 Dec. 1914; *s* of George Dyson and Mary Grace (*née* Bateson); *m* 1st, Ena Lillian Turner (marr. diss. 1948); one *d* ; 2nd, 1948, Marie Florence Chant (*d* 1967); 3rd 1975, Rosamund Pearl Greville Shuter. *Educ:* Queen Elizabeth Sch., Kirkby Lonsdale; Christ's Coll., Cambridge. BA 1936; MA 1960; ScD 1960. Student Apprentice, BT-H Co., Rugby, 1936-39; Research Engr, BT-H Co., Rugby, 1939-46; Consultant (Optics), AEI Research Lab., Aldermaston, 1946-63; Supt, Div. of Mech. and Optical Metrology, NPL, 1963-74. FInstP 1960; Hon. Fellow Royal Microscopical Soc., 1969. *Publications:* Interferometry, 1969; papers on applied optics in learned jls. *Recreations:* astronomy, mechanical occupations, music, people, deploring the motor-car and Women's Lib. *Address:* 6 Rectory Close, Tadley, Basingstoke, Hants RG26 6PH.

DYSON, John Anthony, QC 1982; *b* 31 July 1943; *s* of Richard and Gisella Dyson; *m* 1970, Jacqueline Carmel Levy; one *s* one *d. Educ:* Leeds Grammar Sch.; Wadham Coll., Oxford (Open Classics Scholar; MA). Harmsworth Law Scholar, 1968, called to Bar, Middle Temple, 1968. *Recreations:* piano playing, gardening, walking. *Address:* 11 King's Bench Walk, Temple, EC4. *T:* 01-353 9281.

DYSON, John Michael; Master of the Supreme Court of Judicature (Chancery Division) since 1973; *b* 9 Feb. 1929; *s* of late Eric Dyson, Gainsborough and Hope Patison (*née* Kirkland). *Educ:* Bradfield Coll.; Corpus Christi Coll., Oxford. 2nd Lieut, Royal Tank Regt, 1948. Admitted Solicitor, 1956; Partner, Field Roscoe & Co., 1957 (subseq. Field Fisher & Co. and Field Fisher & Martineau). *Address:* 10 Barnsbury Square, N1 1JL. *T:* 01-607 4360. *Club:* United Oxford & Cambridge University.

DYSON, Richard George; Director, Commonwealth Development Finance Co. Ltd, 1968-81; *b* 17 July 1909; 2nd *s* of late Charles Dyson and late Ellen Gwendoline Dyson (*née* Barrington-Ward), Huddersfield, Yorks; *m* 1940, Lorna Marion, *d* of late H. H. Elkin, Alexandria, Egypt, and Port Lincoln,

Australia; four *s* (two *d* decd). *Educ:* Charterhouse (Sen. Schol.); Christ Church, Oxford (Open Classical Exhibn). MA 1st cl. Hons in Hon. Mods and Greats. Joined Barclays Bank Ltd, 1933; transf. to Barclays Bank DCO, 1936; served overseas in Egypt, Sudan and E Africa until 1945; apptd an Asst Gen. Manager, 1951, a Gen. Manager, 1959, a Vice-Chm., 1967, and the Dep. Chm., 1968-76 (Bank renamed Barclays Bank International Ltd, 1971); Dir, Barclays Bank Ltd, 1972-80; Dep. Chm., Antony Gibbs Holdings Ltd, 1976-80; Chm., Lombard Assoc., 1962-63. Vice-Pres. Council, Inst. of Bankers, 1974- (Mem. 1963-74, Dep. Chm. 1970, Pres. 1972-74); Governor: Sutton's Hosp. in Charterhouse; Charterhouse Sch., Godalming. FIB 1960. *Recreations:* cricket, gardening. *Address:* Brickfields, Chobham, Surrey. *T:* Chobham 8150. *Clubs:* MCC; Free Foresters.

DYSON, Prof. Roger Franklin, PhD; Professor and Director of Adult Education, University of Keele, since 1976; *b* 30 Jan. 1940; *s* of John Franklin Dyson and Edith Mary Jobson; *m* 1964, Anne Greaves; one *s* one *d. Educ:* Counthill Grammar Sch., Oldham; Keele Univ. (BA Hons 1st cl. Hist. and Econs, 1962); Leeds Univ. (PhD 1971). Asst Lectr, 1963, Lectr, 1966, Adult Educn Dept, Leeds Univ.; Dep. Dir and Sen. Lectr in Ind. Relations, Adult Educn Dept, Keele Univ., 1974. Consultant Advr on Ind. Relations to Sec. of State, DHSS, 1979-81. Chm., N Staffs HA, 1982-. Mem., RSocMed; FRSA 1980. Editor, Health Services Manpower Review, 1975-. *Publications:* contribs to BMJ. *Recreations:* gardening, gastronomy. *Address:* Elendil, Newcastle Road, Ashley Heath, Market Drayton TF9 4PH. *T:* Ashley 2906. *Club:* Carlton.

E

EABORN, Prof. Colin, PhD, DSc (Wales); FRS 1970; FRSC; Professor of Chemistry, University of Sussex, since 1962; *b* 15 March 1923; *s* of Tom Stanley and Caroline Eaborn; *m* 1949, Joyce Thomas. *Educ:* Ruabon Grammar Sch., Denbighshire; Univ. Coll. of N Wales, Bangor. Asst Lecturer, 1947, Lecturer, 1950, and Reader 1954, in Chemistry, Univ. of Leicester. Research Associate, Univ. of California at Los Angeles, 1950-51; Robert A. Welch Visiting Scholar, Rice Univ., Texas, 1961-62; Erskine Fellow, Univ. of Canterbury (NZ), 1965; Pro-Vice Chancellor (Science), Univ. of Sussex, 1968-72; Dist. Prof., New Mexico State Univ., 1973; Canadian Commonwealth Fellow, Univ. of Victoria, BC, 1976. Hon. Sec., Chemical Society, 1964-71, Vice-Pres., Dalton Div., 1971-75; Mem. Council, Royal Soc., 1978-80; Chm., British Cttee on Chemical Educn, 1967-69; Mem., Italy/UK Mixed Commn, 1972-. F. S. Kipping Award, Amer. Chem. Soc., 1964; Organometallic Award, Chem. Soc., 1975; Ingold Lectureship and Medal, Chem. Soc., 1976. *Publications:* Organosilicon Compounds, 1960; Organometallic Compounds of the Group IV Elements, Vol 1, Part 1, 1968; numerous publications, mainly in Jl of Chem. Soc. and Jl of Organometallic Chemistry (Regional Editor). *Address:* School of Chemistry and Molecular Sciences, University of Sussex, Brighton BN1 9QJ. *T:* Brighton 606755.

EADEN, Maurice Bryan; HM Diplomatic Service; Consul General, Amsterdam, 1980-83; *b* 9 Feb. 1923; *s* of William Eaden and Florence Ada Eaden (*née* Hudson); *m* 1947, Nelly Margaretha Dorgelo; three *s. Educ:* Bemrose Sch., Derby. Served Army, 1942-47. Foreign Office, 1947; Vice-Consul, Leopoldville, 1955; First Secretary (Commercial): Addis Ababa, 1958; Beirut, 1963; FO, 1967; First Sec. (Commercial), Bombay, 1970; Counsellor (Administration), Brussels, 1972-75; Consul-Gen., Karachi, 1975-79. *Recreations:* walking in Derbyshire; languages. *Address:* New Houses, Cressbrook, Buxton, Derbyshire. *T:* Tideswell 871404. *Clubs:* Royal Commonwealth Society, Royal Over-Seas League.

EADIE, Alexander, BEM 1960; JP; MP (Lab) Midlothian since 1966; *b* 23 June 1920; *m* 1941; one *s. Educ:* Buckhaven Senior Secondary Sch. Coal-miner from 1934. Chm., Fife County Housing Cttee, 9 yrs; Chm., Fife County Educn Cttee, 18 mths; Governor, Moray House Teachers' Training Coll., Edinburgh, 5 years; Exec. Committee: Scottish Council of Labour Party, 9 yrs; NUM Scottish Area, 2 yrs; Mem., Eastern Regional Hosp. Bd (Scotland), 14 yrs. Contested Ayr, 1959 and 1964; Former PPS to Miss M. Herbison, MP, Minister of Social Security, and Mem. of Parly Select Cttee on Scottish Affairs; Opposition Front Bench Spokesman on Energy (incl. N Sea Oil), 1973-74; Parly Under-Sec. of State, Dept of Energy, 1974-79; No 2 Shadow Front Bench Spokesman on Energy, 1979-80, 1980-81, 1981-82; Chairman: Parly Labour Party Power and Steel Gp; Miners' Parly Gp; Vice-Chm., Parly Trade Union Group. JP Fife, 1951. *Recreations:* bowling, gardening. *Address:* Balkerack, The Haugh, East Wemyss, Fife. *T:* Buckhaven 3636.

EADIE, Mrs Ellice (Aylmer), CBE 1966; Standing Counsel to General Synod of Church of England, 1972-80; *b* 30 June 1912; *d* of late Rt Rev. R. T. Hearn, LLD, sometime Bishop of Cork, and of late Dr M. E. T. Hearn, MD, FRCPI; *m* 1946, John Harold Ward Eadie. *Educ:* Cheltenham Ladies' Coll.; St Hugh's Coll., Oxford. Called to Bar, Gray's Inn, 1936. Flt Officer, WAAF, 1941-46. Parliamentary Counsel Office, 1949-72, Parly Counsel, 1968-72. *Address:* 74 Roebuck House, Palace Street, SW1E 5BD. *T:* 01-828 6158.

EADY, family name of **Baron Swinfen.**

EAGERS, Derek; Under-Secretary, Department of Trade, since 1975; *b* 13 Sept. 1924; *s* of late Horace Eagers and Florence (*née* Green); *m* 1953, Hazel Maureen Henson; two *s. Educ:* King Edward VII Sch., Sheffield; Brasenose Coll., Oxford. RNVR, 1943-47. Min. of Fuel and Power, 1949; UK Atomic Energy Authority, 1955-57; British Embassy, Washington, 1958-60; Principal Private Sec. to successive Ministers of Power, 1963-65; Petroleum Counsellor, Washington, 1966-68; Min. of Power (subseq. Min. of Technology, Dept of Trade and Industry), 1969; Dept of Industry, 1974. *Recreation:* concealing his true ignorance of cricket, gardening and railway history. *Address:* Gurneys, Town Hill, Lingfield, Surrey RH7 6AG. *T:* Lingfield 832737.

EAGGER, Brig. Arthur Austin, CBE 1944 (OBE 1940), TD 1945; *b* 14 March 1898; *s* of Edward and Elsie Eagger; *m* 1st, 1935, Kate Mortimer Hare (*d* 1946); three *s* ; 2nd, 1948, Barbara Noel Hare. *Educ:* Aberdeen Univ. (MB ChB 1922). Lieut 6th Bn Gordon Hldrs. Commissioned RAMC (TA), 1928; late DDMS 1 Airborne Corps. Medical Dir, Slough Industrial Health Service, retired 1963, Consultant 1963-79. Bronze Star (USA), 1945. *Publications:* Industrial Resettlement (Proc. RSM), 1952; Health in the Factory (Jl Royal Institute of Public Health and Hygiene), 1953; Venture in Industry, 1965. *Address:* 1 Underwood Close, Dawlish, Devon EX7 9RY. *T:* Dawlish 864597.

EAGLES, Lt-Col Charles Edward James; Member, HM Bodyguard of the Honourable Corps of Gentlemen at Arms, since 1967, Harbinger since 1981; *b* 14 May 1918; *o s* of late Major C. E. C. Eagles, DSO, RMLI and Esmé Field; *m* 1941, Priscilla May Nicolette, *d* of late Brig. A. F. B. Cottrell, DSO, OBE; one *s* three *d. Educ:* Marlborough Coll. 2nd Lieut RM, 1936; served: HMS Sussex, Mediterranean and S Atlantic, 1938-40; Mobile Naval Base Def. Orgn, UK, ME, Ceylon and India, 1940-43; 1 HAA Regt RM, India, UK and NW Europe, 1943-45; Asst Mil. Sec., 1945; Amphibious Trng Wing, 1945-47; Staff of Maj.-Gen. RM, Portsmouth, 1947-50; HMS Devonshire, 1951-52; RN Staff Course, 1952; DS, Amphibious Warfare Sch., 1952-55; HMS Afrikander, SO (Intell.), S Atlantic, 1955-57; Dep. Dir, PRORM, 1957-59; CSO, Plymouth Gp, 1960; AAG, Staff of CGRM, 1960-62; Dir, PRORM, 1962-65; retd 1965; Civil Service, MoD, 1965-83. *Recreations:* shooting, genealogy. *Address:* Fallowfield, Westwell, Ashford, Kent TN25 4LQ. *T:* Charing 2552. *Club:* Army and Navy.

EAGLESHAM, Eric John Ross, MA, BEd, LLB; Professor of Education, Durham University, 1947-66, retired; Professor Emeritus, 1966; *b* 29 Oct. 1905; 3rd *s* of late Reverend David Eaglesham, Chapelknowe, Canonbie, Dumfriesshire; *m* 1957, Nancy, *yr d* of late J. F. Rintoul; three *s* one *d. Educ:* Dumfries Acad.; Edinburgh Univ., 1923-27, 1930-31. Asst Teacher, Gretna Sch., 1927-30; Asst Teacher, Lockerbie Academy, 1931-35; Lecturer, Education Dept, Manchester Univ., 1936-38; Master of Method, Jordanhill Training Centre, Glasgow, 1938-40; RAF, rank Flight Lieut, on planning staff of Air Ministry dealing with questions of International Law, 1941-42; Principal Master of Method, Jordanhill Training Centre, Glasgow, 1942-43; Depute Dir of Studies, Jordanhill Training Centre, 1944-46. *Publications:* From School Board to Local Authority, 1956; Morant on the March (Yearbook of Education), 1957; The Foundations of Twentieth Century Education in England, 1967; articles in various learned journals. *Address:* The Croft, Park Road, Scotby, Cumbria.

EAGLETON, Guy Tryon; *b* 1 July 1894; *s* of late John Eagleton and of Violet Marion Eagleton; *m* 1947, Amy Rubina Gothard; no *c. Educ:* Aldenham Sch. Solicitor, 1919; Asst Clerk Haberdashers' Company, 1925; Clerk of the Haberdashers' Company, 1931-50, retired. *Address:* 31 Hillydeal Road, Otford, Sevenoaks, Kent TN14 5RT. *T:* Otford 3220. *Club:* Royal Blackheath Golf (Captain General, Sen. Past Captain).

EAKER, Lt-Gen. Ira Clarence, Hon. KCB 1945; Hon. KBE 1943; DSM, US Army (2 Oak Leaf Clusters), US Navy; DFC (Oak Leaf Cluster); Silver Star; Legion of Merit; Wright Brothers Trophy, 1977; Special Congressional Gold Medal, 1979; *b* Field Creek, Texas, 13 April 1896; *s* of Y. Y. Eaker and Dona Lee; *m* Ruth Huff Apperson; no *c. Educ:* South Eastern State Teachers' Coll., Durant, Okla; University of Southern California; Columbia Univ., 2nd Lieut of Infantry, Regular Army, 1917; Capt. 1920; Major, 1935; Lieut-Col (temp.) 1937; Lieut-Col 1940; Col (temp.), 1941; Brig.-Gen. (temp.) Jan. 1942; Maj.-Gen. (temp.) Sept. 1942; Lieut-Gen. (temp.) 1943; permanent Brig.-Gen. RA 1944. Served in Philippines, 1919-22; pilot of one of planes of Pan-American Flight round South America, 1926-27 (DFC); chief pilot of Airplane Question Mark on refuelling endurance flight, 1929, establishing a new world flight endurance record (Oak Leaf Cluster for DFC). In command of VIII Bomber Command in European Theatre of Operations, 1942; commanded Eighth Air Force, 1942-44 and also US Army Air Forces in UK, 1943-44; comd. Mediterranean Allied Air Forces in Italy, 1944; Dep. Comdg Gen. Army Air Forces and Chief of Air Staff, US, 1945-47; retired 1947. Vice-President: Hughes Tool Co., 1947-57; Douglas Aircraft, 1957-61. Author, syndicated weekly column on subjects in nat. security area, 1962-. DSM 1981, awarded by USAF for exceptionally meritorious service, 1957-81. French Legion of Honour (Grand Officer) and many other foreign decorations. *Publications:* (with Gen. Arnold); Army Flyer, This Flying Game, Winged Warfare. *Address:* 2202 Decatur Place, Washington, DC 20008, USA.

EALES, Victor Henry James, CEng, MIMechE; Director of Weapons Production and Quality (Naval), 1980-81, and Head of Naval Weapons Professional and Technical Group, 1979-81, Ministry of Defence; *b* 11 Dec. 1922; *s* of William Henry and Frances Jean Eales; *m* 1949, Elizabeth Gabrielle Irene James; two *s* one *d. Educ:* Wimbledon Central Sch.; Guildford Technical Coll.; Portsmouth Polytechnic. Ministry of Defence: Asst Director, Weapons Production (Naval), 1970; Dep. Director, Surface Weapons Projects (Naval), 1975; Director, Weapons Production (Naval), 1979. *Recreation:* golf. *Address:* 11 Penrhyn Avenue, East Cosham, Portsmouth, Hants PO6 2AX.

EAMES, Eric James, JP; Lord Mayor of Birmingham, 1974-75, Deputy Lord Mayor, 1975-76; *b* Highley, Shropshire, 13 April 1917; *s* of George Eames; *m* (marr. diss.); one *s. Educ:* Highley Sch., Highley, Shropshire. Mem., Governing Board, Internat. Center for Information Co-operation and Relationship among World's Major Cities; Governor, Harper Adams Agric. Coll. *Recreations:* gardening, do-it-yourself enthusiast. *Address:* 78 Westley Road, Acocks Green, Birmingham B27 7UH. *T:* 021-706 7629.

EAMES, Rt. Rev. Robert Henry Alexander; *see* Down and Dromore, Bishop of.

EARDLEY-WILMOT, Sir John (Assheton), 5th Bt *cr* 1821; MVO 1956; DSC 1943; Staff of Monopolies Commission since 1967; *b* 2 Jan. 1917; *s* of Commander Frederick Neville Eardley-Wilmot (*d* 1956) (*s* of 3rd Bt) and Dorothy Little (*d* 1959), formerly of Brooksby, Double Bay, Sydney; *S* uncle, 1970; *m* 1939, Diana Elizabeth, *d* of Commander Aubrey Moore, RN, and Mrs O. Bassett; one *s* one *d. Educ:* Stubbington; RNC, Dartmouth. Motor Torpedo Boats, 1939-43; served HMS Apollo, 1944; HMS Fencer, 1945-46; RN Staff Course, 1950; Commander 1950; HMS Opossum, 1951-53; Cabinet Office, 1954-57; Admiralty, 1958-67; retired 1967, as Deputy Director Naval Administrative Planning. MBIM 1978; FRSA 1970. Freeman, City of London (by Redemption). *Recreation:* fishing. *Heir: s* Michael John Assheton Eardley-Wilmot [*b* 13 Jan. 1941; *m* 1971, Wendy, *y d* of A. J. Wolstenholme; two *s* one *d*]. *Address:* 41 Margravine Gardens, W6. *T:* 01-748 3723.

EARL, Christopher Joseph, MD, FRCP; Physician to: Neurological Department, Middlesex Hospital, since 1971; National Hospital, Queen Square, since 1958; Moorfields Eye Hospital, since 1959; Consultant Neurologist, King Edward VII Hospital for Officers, since 1966 and Hospital of St John and St Elizabeth, since 1967; Civil Consultant in Neurology, Royal Air Force, since 1976; *b* 20 Nov. 1925; *s* of Christopher and Winifred Earl, Ashbourne, Derbyshire; *m* 1951, Alma Patience Hopkins, Reading; two *s* three *d. Educ:* Cotton Coll.; Guy's Hosp. House phys. and house surg., Guy's Hosp., and MO, RAF, 1948-50. Lecturer in Chemical Pathology, Guy's Hosp., 1950-52; Research Fellow, Harvard Med. Sch., and Neurological Unit, Boston City Hosp., 1952-54; Resident MO, Nat. Hosp., Queen Square, 1954-56; Chief Asst, Neurological Dept, Guy's Hosp., 1956-58; Physician, Neurological Dept, London Hosp., 1961-71. Hon. Dir of Photography, Royal Society of Medicine, 1967-73. Hon. Sec., Assoc. British Neurologists, 1968-74. Vice-Pres., Med. Defence Union; Chm., Cttee on Neurology, RCP. Corresp. Mem., Amer. Neurological Assoc. *Publications:* Papers in learned jls on Biochemistry and Neurology. *Recreation:* reading history. *Address:* 23 Audley Road, Ealing, W5. *T:* 01-997 0380. *Club:* Garrick.

EARL, Eric Stafford, Clerk to the Worshipful Company of Fishmongers, since 1974; *b* 8 July 1928; *s* of late Alfred Henry Earl and Mary Elizabeth Earl; *m* 1951, Clara Alice Alston. *Educ:* SE Essex Technical Coll.; City of London Coll. Served with RA, 1946-48. Joined Fishmongers' Co. 1948: Accountant, 1961-68; Asst Clerk, 1969-73; Actg Clerk, 1973-74; Liveryman, 1977. Clerk to Governors of Gresham's Sch., 1974-; Hon. Sec., Shellfish Assoc. of Great Britain; Secretary: Atlantic Salmon Research Trust Ltd; City and Guilds of London Art School Ltd; Jt Hon. Sec., Central Council for Rivers Protection; Hon. Asst River Keeper of River Thames; Mem., Nat. Anglers' Council; Mem. Council, Anglers' Co-operative Assoc. Director: Hulbert Property Co. Ltd; Hulbert Property Holdings Ltd. *Recreations:* fishing, gardening, tennis, cricket. *Address:* Dolphins, Watling Lane, Thaxted, Essex CM6 2RA. *T:* Thaxted 758. *Club:* Flyfishers'.

EARLE, Air Chief Marshal Sir Alfred, GBE 1966 (KBE 1961; CBE 1946); CB 1956; *b* 1907; *s* of late Henry Henwood Earle, and Mary Winifred Earle, Beaworthy, Devon; *m* 1st, 1934, Phyllis Beatrice (*d* 1960), *o d* of W. J. Rice, Watford; one *s* one *d* ; 2nd, 1961, Rosemary (*d* 1978), *widow* of Air Vice-Marshal F. J. St G. Braithwaite, and *d* of late G. Grinling Harris, Clifford's Inn; 3rd, 1979, Mrs Clare Newell, *widow* of Rev. Gp Captain Ivor Newell and *d* of Dr Thomas Yates, DD. *Educ:* Shebbear Coll., Beaworthy, Devon. Graduated from Royal Air Force Coll., Cranwell, 1929. Served in Bomber Squadrons in United Kingdom and Iraq and as instructor at RAF Sch. of Photography, 1930-38; pea 1939; Training Command, 1940; Air Ministry, in Directorate of Plans, 1941-42; Comd No 428 RCAF Sqdn and stations in Bomber Comd, 1942-43; Offices of War Cabinet and Minister of Defence (attended Cairo and Yalta Confs), 1943-45; AOC No 300 Transport Grp (Austr.) and No 232 Transport Grp (Far East), 1945-46; Directing Staff, RAF Staff Coll., 1946-49; idc 1950; Comd RAAF Staff Coll., 1951-53; Air Ministry, Dir of Policy (Air Staff), 1954; Asst Chief of Air Staff (Policy), 1955-57; AOC No 13 Group, 1957-59; Deputy Chief of Defence Staff, 1960-62; AOC-in-C, Technical Training Command, 1962-64; Vice-Chief of Defence Staff, 1964-66; retd 1966; Dir Gen. of Intelligence, Min. of Defence,

1966-68. Chm., Waveney DC, 1974-76. *Recreation:* gardening. *Address:* 3 Buttermere Gardens, Alresford, Hants. *Club:* Royal Air Force.

EARLE, Arthur Frederick; President, Boyden Consulting Group Ltd, since 1974; Vice-President, Boyden Associates, since 1975 (Associate, since 1974); *b* Toronto, 13 Sept. 1921; *s* of Frederick C. Earle and Hilda M. Earle (*née* Brown); *m* 1946, Vera Domini Lithgow; two *s* one *d. Educ:* Toronto; London Sch. of Economics (BSc (Econ.), PhD; Hon. Fellow 1980). Royal Canadian Navy (Rating to Lieut Comdr), 1939-46. Canada Packers Ltd, 1946-48; Aluminium Ltd cos in British Guiana, West Indies and Canada, 1948-53; Treas., Alumina Jamaica Ltd, 1953-55; Aluminium Union, London, 1955-58; Vice-Pres., Aluminium Ltd Sales Inc., New York, 1958-61; Dir, 1961-74, Dep. Chm., 1961-65, Man. Dir, 1963-65, Hoover Ltd; Pres., Internat. Investment Corp. for Yugoslavia, 1972-74. Principal, The London Graduate School of Business Studies, 1965-72. Member: Commn of Enquiry, Jamaican Match Industry, 1953; Consumer Council, 1963-68; NEDC Cttee on Management Educn, Training and Develt, 1967-69; NEDC for Electrical Engineering Industry. Chm., Canadian Assoc. of Friends of LSE, 1975-. Governor: Ashridge Management Coll., 1962-65; LSE, 1968; NIESR, 1968-74; Governor and Mem. Council, Ditchley Foundn, 1967. Fellow, London Business Sch., 1973. Thomas Hawksley Lecture, IMechE, 1968. *Publications:* numerous, on economics and management. *Recreations:* hill climbing, model ship building. *Address:* Suite 2701 Commerce Court North, PO Box 389, Toronto, Ont. M5L 1G3, Canada. *T:* (416) 869-3848; Suite 1905, 50 Quebec Avenue, Toronto, Ont. M6P 4B4, Canada. *T:* (416) 767-7221; 144 Regent Street, Niagara-on-the-Lake, Ont. L0S 1J0. *T:* (416) 468-3119. *Clubs:* Travellers'; National (Toronto).

EARLE, Lt-Col Charles, DSO 1945; OBE 1943; jssc; psc; *b* 23 Nov. 1913; *s* of late Col Maxwell Earle, CB, CMG, DSO; *m* 1st, 1939, Marguerite (marr. diss., 1956), 2nd *d* of Herbert Carver; one *s* two *d*; 2nd, 1957, Fenella, *o d* of late H. C. Whitehouse. *Educ:* Wellington; RMC. Grenadier Guards, 1933; Lt-Col 1953, Retired 1958. Sec.-Gen., Internat. Cargo Handling Assoc., 1961-72. Served War of 1939-45 in NW Europe, Africa and Italy. Adjt RMA Sandhurst, 1948. Croix de Guerre with palm, France, 1943. *Address:* 3 The Tithe Barn, Queen Camel, Yeovil, Somerset BA22 7NE. *T:* Marston Magna 850937.

EARLE, Ven. E(dward) E(rnest) Maples; Archdeacon of Tonbridge, 1953-76, Archdeacon Emeritus since 1977; Vicar of Shipbourne, Kent, since Nov. 1959; *b* 22 Dec. 1900; 2nd *s* of Ernest William Earle and Lilian Geraldine Earle (*née* Hudson); *m* 1966, Mrs Jocelyn Mary Offer, widow of Canon C. J. Offer. *Educ:* London Coll. of Divinity; St John's Coll., Durham University (LTh, MA). Vicar of: St John, Bexley, 1936-39; Rainham (Kent), 1939-44; Secretary Rochester Diocesan Reorganisation Cttee, 1944-52, Great Appeal Cttee, etc., 1944-49; Hon. Canon, Rochester Cathedral, 1949; Rector of Chatham, 1950-52; Proctor in Convocation, 1950-53. Rector of Wrotham 1952-59. *Recreations:* artistic and architectural interests. *Address:* The Vicarage, Shipbourne, Kent. *T:* Plaxtol 810478.

EARLE, Sir George; see Earle, Sir H. G. A.

EARLE, Very Rev. George Hughes, SJ; MA; Superior of the English Province of the Society of Jesus, since 1981; *b* 20 Sept. 1925; *s* of late Lieut-Col F. W. Earle, DSO, JP, Morestead House, Winchester, and late Marie Blanche Lyne-Stivens. *Educ:* Pilgrims' Sch., Winchester; Westminster Sch.; Peter Symonds' Sch., Winchester; Balliol Coll., Oxford. Served with RAF, 1943-47. Joined Soc. of Jesus, 1950. Taught at Beaumont Coll., 1955-57, and Stonyhurst Coll., 1962-63; Headmaster, Stonyhurst Coll., 1963-72; Superior of Southwell House, 1972-75; Educnl Asst to Provincial, 1972-75; Co-editor, The Way, 1974-78; Rector of St Aloysius, Glasgow, 1978-81. *Recreations:* none; wasting time. *Address:* 114 Mount Street, W1Y 6AH.

EARLE, Sir (Hardman) George (Algernon), 6th Bt *cr* 1869; *S* father, 1979; *m*; one *s* one *d. Heir: s.*

EARLE, Ion, TD 1946; Assistant to the Directors, Clive Discount Co., 1973-81, retired; *b* 12 April 1916; *s* of late Stephen Earle and of E. Beatrice Earle (*née* Blair White); *m* 1946, Elizabeth Stevens, US citizen; one *s* one *d. Educ:* Stowe Sch.; University Coll., Oxford; Université de Grenoble. Federation of British Industries, Birmingham, 1938-51, London, 1951-60; Chief Executive, Export Council for Europe, 1960-64; Dep. Dir-Gen., BNEC, 1965-71 (Dir, 1964-65); Head of Personnel, Kleinwort Benson Ltd, 1972. Royal Artillery, TA, 1939-46 (Major). *Recreations:* golf, tennis, gardening. *Address:* 69 Sea Avenue, Rustington, West Sussex BN16 2DP. *T:* Rustington 73550. *Club:* Royal Wimbledon Golf.

EARLE, Rev. John Nicholas Francis, (Rev. Nick Earle); Headmaster, Bromsgrove School, since 1971; *b* 14 Nov. 1926; *s* of John William Arthur Earle and Vivien Constance Fenton (*née* Davies); *m* 1959, Ann Veronica Lester; one *s* two *d. Educ:* Winchester Coll.; Trinity Coll., Cambridge. 1st cl. Maths Tripos pt 2, 1st cl. Theol. Tripos pt 1; MA. Deacon, 1952; Priest, 1953. Curate, St Matthew, Moorfields, 1952-57; PARS Fellow, Union Theol Seminary, New York, 1957-58; Lectr, St Botolph, Aldgate, 1958-61; Asst Master, Dulwich Coll., 1961-71. *Publications:* What's Wrong With the Church?, 1961; Culture and Creed, 1967; Logic, 1973. *Recreations:* travel, gardening. *Address:* Headmaster's House, Bromsgrove School, Worcs B61 7DU. *T:* Bromsgrove 32774.

EARLES, Prof. Stanley William Edward, PhD, DScEng; CEng, FIMechE; Professor of Mechanical Engineering and Head of Department of Mechanical Engineering, King's College, University of London, since 1976; *b* 18 Jan. 1929; *s* of William Edward Earles and late Winnifred Anne Cook; *m* 1955, Margaret Isabella Brown; two *d. Educ:* King's Coll., Univ. of London (BScEng, PhD, DScEng, AKC). CEng, FIMechE 1976. Nuffield Apprentice, Birmingham, 1944-50; King's Coll., Univ. of London, 1950-53; Scientific Officer, Royal Naval Scientific Service, 1953-55; Queen Mary Coll., Univ. of London: Lectr in Mech. Eng, 1955-69; Reader in Mech. Eng, 1969-75; Prof. of Mech. Eng, 1975-76. James Clayton Fund prize, IMechE, 1967; Engineering Applied to Agriculture Award, IMechE, 1980. *Publications:* papers and articles in Proc. IMechE, Jl of Mech. Eng Science, Jl of Sound and Vibration, Wear, Proc. ASME and ASLE, and Eng. *Recreations:* squash rackets, real tennis, gardening. *Address:* Woodbury, Church Lane, Wormley, Broxbourne, Herts EN10 7QF. *T:* Hoddesdon 64616.

EARNSHAW, (Thomas) Roy, CBE 1978 (OBE 1971); Adviser on Export United to British Overseas Trade Board, since 1978; *b* 27 Feb. 1917; *s* of Godfrey Earnshaw and Edith Annie (*née* Perry); *m* 1953, Edith Rushworth; two *d. Educ:* Marlborough Coll., Liverpool. MIEx; AICS. Served War, Army, 1940-46: Major Lancs Fusiliers. Shipbroking, Liverpool, 1933-39; appts with subsid. cos of Turner & Newall Ltd: Turner Brothers Asbestos Co. Ltd, Rochdale (mainly Export Sales Manager), 1939-40 and 1946-53; Dir, AM&FM Ltd, Bombay, 1954-59; Export Dir, Ferodo Ltd, Chapel-en-le-Frith, 1959-66; Dir and Gen. Man. of Div., TBA Industrial Products Ltd, Rochdale, 1966-76; British Overseas Trade Board: Export Year Adviser, 1976-77; Mem. Adv. Council, 1975-. Director: Actair Holdings Ltd, 1979-; Actair Internat. Ltd, 1979-; Unico Finance Ltd, 1979-81. Formerly: Pres., Rochdale Chamber of Commerce; Chm., NW Region Chambers of Commerce; UK Delegate to European Chambers of Commerce. London Economic Adviser to Merseyside CC, 1980-82. Vis. Fellow, ASC, 1981-. FRSA. *Recreations:* gardening, oil painting, hill walking. *Address:* 89 St Andrews Road, Henley-on-Thames, Oxon RG9 1PN. *T:* Henley-on-Thames 6620. *Clubs:* Rotarian, Leander (Henley-on-Thames); Athenæum (Liverpool).

EASON, Henry, CBE 1967; JP; a Vice-President of the Institute of Bankers, 1969-75, and Consultant with special reference to overseas relationships, 1971-74 (Secretary-General, 1959-71); *b* 12 April 1910; *s* of late H. Eason and F. J. Eason; *m* 1939 (at Hexham Abbey), Isobel, *d* of Wm Stevenson; one *s* two *d. Educ:* Yarm (Schol.); King's Coll., University of Durham. Graduated (with distinction) in economics and history. Barrister-at-law, Gray's Inn. Served Lloyds Bank until 1939; Asst Sec., Institute of Bankers, 1939. Served War of 1939-45 and until 1946, with Royal Air Force (Wing Commander, despatches twice). Asst Dir, Military Gov. (Banking), NW Europe, 1944-46; United Nations Adviser (Banking) to Pakistan Govt, 1952; Deputy Sec., Institute of Bankers, 1956; Governor, City of London Coll., 1958-69; Mem., British National Cttee, Internat. Chamber Commerce, 1959-74. Director: Internat. Banking Summer Sch., 1961, 1964, 1970; Cambridge Banking Seminar, 1968 and 1969. Editor, Jl Inst. of Bankers, 1959-71. Hon. FIB 1971. JP Bromley 1967. Gen. Comr of Income Tax, Bromley, 1973-76. *Publications:* contributions to professional journals. *Recreations:* golf, walking, gardening, world travel. *Address:* 12 Redgate Drive, Bromley BR2 7BT. *T:* 01-462 1900. *Clubs:* Gresham; Overseas Bankers; Langley Park Golf.

EASON, His Honour Robert Kinley; HM's First Deemster, Clerk of the Rolls and Deputy Governor of the Isle of Man, 1974-80; *b* 12 April 1908; 2nd *s* of Henry Alexander Eason and Eleanor Jane Eason (*née* Kinley); *m* 1937, Nora Muriel, *d* of Robert Raisbeck Coffey, Douglas, IOM. *Educ:* Douglas High Sch.; King William's Coll., IOM; University Coll. London. LLB (Hons). Called to Bar, Gray's Inn, 1929; Advocate, Manx Bar, 1930. High Bailiff and Chief Magistrate, Isle of Man, 1961-69; HM's Second Deemster, IOM, 1969-74. Chairman: Criminal Injuries Compensation Tribunal, IOM, 1969-74; IOM Income Tax Appeal Comrs, 1974-80; IOM Unit Trust Tribunal, 1968-74; Tourist (IOM) Appeal Tribunal, 1969-74; Tynwald Arrangements Cttee, 1974-80; Chm. of Trustees: Cunningham House Scout and Guide Headquarters, 1964-; Ellan Vannin Home, 1971-; Trustee, Manx Marine Soc., 1974-. President: Ellynyn Ny Gael, 1974-; IOM Anti-Cancer Assoc., 1969-; Wireless Telegraphy Appeal Bd for IOM, 1971-80; Legion Players, 1971-; SS&AFA, IOM Br., 1973-; Licensing Appeal Court, 1969-74; King William's College Soc., 1978-80; past Pres., IOM Soc. for Prevention of Cruelty to Animals. Queen's Silver Jubilee Medal, 1977. *Recreation:* organ music. *Address:* Greenacres, Highfield Drive, Baldrine, Lonan, Isle of Man. *T:* Ramsey 781622. *Clubs:* Ellan Vannin, Manx Automobile (Douglas).

EASSON, Rt. Rev. Edward Frederick; *b* 29 July 1905; *s* of Edward Easson and Ada Jessie Easson (*née* Betsworth); *m* 1937, Mary Forbes Macdonald; two *s. Educ:* Morgan Academy, Dundee; St Andrews Univ.; Edinburgh Theological College. Maths and Science Master at Lasswade Secondary School, 1929-31; Assistant Curate of St Peter's, Lutton Place, 1933-36, with charge of St Aidan's, Craigmillar, 1936-39; Rector of St Peter's, Peterhead, and Chaplain to HM Prison, 1940-48; Diocesan Inspector of Schools, 1945-55; Canon of St Andrew's Cathedral, Aberdeen, 1946; Rector of St Devenick's, Bieldside, 1948-56; Dean of Aberdeen and Orkney, 1953-56; Bishop of Aberdeen and Orkney, 1956-72. Hon. DD St Andrews, 1962. *Address:* 25 Corbiehill Avenue, Davidsons Mains, Edinburgh EH4 5DX.

EASSON, Prof. Eric Craig, CBE 1978; FRCPGlas, FRCR; Hon. FFRRCSI; Director of Radiotherapy, Christie Hospital and Holt Radium Institute,

Manchester, 1962-79; Professor of Radiation Therapeutics, University of Manchester, 1973-79, now Emeritus Professor; Consultant Adviser in Radiotherapy to Department of Health, 1974-79; *b* 28 Jan. 1915; *s* of William Easson and Helen (*née* Whitton); *m* 1938, Moira McKechnie Greig; two *s* one *d. Educ:* Glasgow Univ. (MB ChB 1938; MD 1958); MSc Manchester 1977. Served War, RAF, UK and SE Asia, 1939-45. Christie Hospital, 1946-79; Regional Advsr in Radiotherapy, NW RHA, 1962-79; Chm., Regional Adv. Cttee on Oncological Services, 1973-79. Past Mem. Council and Radiobiol. Sub-cttee, British Inst. of Radiology; Vice-Pres., Hon. Treas., Examiner and Mem. Council, Faculty of Radiologists, 1957-70; Knox Lectr, 1967; Pres., RCR, 1975-77; Mem., MRC Leukaemia Working Party, 1960-70; Mem./Chm. various WHO Expert Cttees on Cancer, 1962-74; Mem. Council and Exec. Cttee, Internat. Union Against Cancer and Chm., Cancer Control Commn, 1966-74; Mem. Council, Nat. Soc. for Cancer Relief; Hon. FFRRCSI 1976; Fellow: RSM; Manchester Med. Soc.; Hon. Fellow, Manchester Polytechnic, 1979. *Publications:* co-author, The Curability of Cancer in Various Sites, 1968; ed and co-author, Cancer of the Uterine Cervix, 1973; many papers, leading articles and chapters in learned jls and books in UK and abroad, all on various aspects of cancer. *Recreations:* bee-keeping, fly fishing, current affairs. *Address:* Sheriffmuir, 105 Buxton Old Road, Disley, via Stockport, Cheshire SK12 2BX. *T:* Disley 2541.

EAST, David Albert, QPM 1982; Chief Constable, Devon and Cornwall Constabulary, since 1982; *b* 5 June 1936; *s* of Albert East and Florence Emily East; *m* 1957, Gloria (*née* Swinden); one *d. Educ:* King Alfred Grammar Sch., Wantage, Berks; University Coll. London (LLB Hons). Berks Constabulary, 1958-65 (constable to sergeant); First Special Course, Police Coll., Bramshill, 1962 (Johnson Prize and Cert. of Distinction); Inspector, York City Police, 1965-68; UCL, 1965-68; Metropol. Police Chief Inspector to Chief Supt, 1968-75; Eight Sen. Comd Course, Bramshill, 1971; Asst Chief Constable, Avon and Somerset Constab., 1975-78; RCDS, 1978; Dep. Chief Constable, Devon and Cornwall Constab., 1978-82; seconded to Cyprus, 1981 and to Singapore, 1982. Police Long Service and Good Conduct Medal, 1980. *Recreations:* Rugby, cricket. *Address:* Chief Constable's Office, Devon and Cornwall Constabulary, Middlemoor, Exeter EX2 7HQ. *T:* Exeter 52101.

EAST, Frederick Henry, CB 1976; MInstP, CEng, FIEE, FRAeS; consulting engineer and company director; Deputy Secretary, and Chief Weapon System Engineer (Polaris), Ministry of Defence, 1976-80, retired; *b* 15 Sept. 1919; *s* of Frederick Richard East; *m* 1942, Pauline Isabel Veale Horne (*d* 1972). *Educ:* Skinners' Company's Sch., Tunbridge Wells; University Coll., Exeter (Visc. St Cyres Schol., Tucker and Franklin Prize, 1939). BSc London 1940. Joined Research Dept, Min. of Aircraft Production, 1940; various appts in RAE, 1942-57; Asst Dir of Air Armament Research and Develt, Min. of Supply/Aviation, 1957-62; Head of Weapon Project Gp, RAE, 1962-67; Student, IDC, 1968; Asst Chief Scientific Adviser (Projects), MoD, 1969-70; Dir, Royal Armament Res. and Develt Establishment, 1971-75. Reader, C of E, 1969-; Mem., Candidates Cttee, ACCM, 1981-. *Publications:* contrib. to: Application of Critical Path Techniques, 1968; official reports, and articles in jls. *Address:* 2 Beacon Rise, Sevenoaks, Kent. *T:* Sevenoaks 453942. *Club:* Athenæum.

EAST, Gerald Reginald Ricketts; Chairman, Incorporated Froebel Educational Institute, since 1979; *b* 17 Feb. 1917; *s* of late R. B. East and Dora East (*née* Ricketts); *m* 1944, Anna Elder Smyth; one *s* two *d. Educ:* Peter Symonds' Sch.; St Edmund Hall, Oxford. Goldsmiths' Company's Exhibnr; MA 1945. Royal Artillery, 1939-46; Control Commn for Germany, 1946-47; Asst Principal, War Office, Oct. 1947; Private Sec. to Under-Sec. of State for War, 1949; Directing Staff Imperial Defence Coll., 1952-54; Private Sec. to Sec. of State for War, 1954-55; Asst Sec. (Inspector of Establishments), 1958; Comd Sec., BAOR, 1961-64; Asst Sec. (Establishments), MoD, 1965-70; Asst Under-Sec. of State, MoD, 1970-74; a Civil Service Comr, 1974-78. *Address:* 43 Manor Road North, Esher, Surrey. *T:* 01-398 2446. *Club:* Royal Commonwealth Society.

EAST, Grahame Richard, CMG 1961; Special Commissioner of Income Tax, 1962-73; *b* 1908; 2nd *s* of William Robert and Eleanor East; *m* 1937, Cynthia Mildred, *d* of Adam Louis Beck, OBE; two *s* two *d. Educ:* Bristol Grammar Sch.; Corpus Christi Coll., Oxford. Asst Master, Royal Belfast Academical Institution, Belfast, 1929; Inland Revenue Dept, Secretaries Office, 1930, Asst Sec., 1941. *Address:* 44 Devonshire Road, Sutton, Surrey. *T:* 01-642 0638.

EAST, Kenneth Arthur, CMG 1971; HM Diplomatic Service, retired; Ambassador to Iceland, 1975-81; *b* 9 May 1921; *s* of H. F. East; *m* 1946, Katherine Blackley; two *s* three *d. Educ:* Taunton's Sch; Southampton Univ. Served HM Forces, 1942-46. India Office/Commonwealth Relations Office, 1946-50; Asst Private Sec. to Sec. of State; First Secretary: Ottawa, 1950-53; Colombo, 1956-60; Head of East and General Africa Dept, CRO, 1961-63; Head of Personnel Dept, CRO, 1963-64; Counsellor, Diplomatic Service Administration, 1965; Counsellor and Head of Chancery, Oslo, 1965-70; Minister, Lagos, 1970-74. *Club:* Royal Commonwealth Society.

EAST, Sir (Lewis) Ronald, Kt 1966; CBE 1951; retired as Chairman, State Rivers and Water Supply Commission, Victoria (1936-65) and as Commissioner, River Murray Commission, Australia (1936-65); *b* 17 June 1899; *s* of Lewis Findlay East, ISO, Evansford, Vic., Australia and Annie Eleanor (*née* Burchett) Brunswick, Vic.; *m* 1927, Constance Lilias Keil, MA, Kilwinning, Ayrshire; three *d. Educ:* Scotch Coll., Melbourne; Melbourne

Univ. BCE (Melbourne) 1922; MCE (Melbourne) 1924. Mem., Snowy Mountains Coun., until 1965; Pres., Instn of Engrs, Austr., 1952-53; Mem. Coun., Instn of Civil Engrs, 1960-62; Vice-Pres., Internat. Commn on Irrigation and Drainage, 1959-62. Hon. Fellow, Instn of Engineers, Australia, 1969. Kernot Memorial Medal, University of Melbourne, 1949; Peter Nicol Russell Memorial Medal, Instn of Engineers, Australia, 1957. Hon. DEng Melbourne, 1981. *Publications:* River Improvement, Land Drainage and Flood Protection, 1952; A South Australian Colonist of 1836 and his Descendants, 1972; The Kiel Family and related Scottish Pioneers, 1974; More Australian Pioneers: the Burchetts and related families, 1976; (ed) The Gallipoli Diary of Sergeant Lawrence, 1981; many technical papers on water conservation and associated subjects in Proc. Instn Engs, Austr., Proc. Instn Civil Engrs, Amer. Soc. Civil Engrs and other jls. *Recreation:* handicrafts (model engineering). *Address:* 57 Waimarie Drive, Mt Waverley, Victoria 3149, Australia. *T:* Melbourne 277-4315.

EAST, Sir Ronald; see East, Sir L. R.

EAST, Ronald Joseph; Chairman, Wettern Brothers plc; Director, Amstrad Consumer Electronics plc; *b* 17 Dec. 1931; *s* of Joseph William and Marion Elizabeth Emma East; *m* 1955, Iris Joyce Beckwith; two *d. Educ:* Clare Coll., Cambridge Univ. (MA). Engineering Apprenticeship, Ford Trade Sch., Ford Motor Co. Ltd, 1945-52. Troop Comdr, RA (Lieut), 1953-55. Managerial posts in economics, product planning, finance, and engineering areas of Ford Motor Co. Ltd, 1959-65; Guest, Keen & Nettlefolds Ltd: Corporation Staff Dir of Planning, 1965-70; Planning Exec., Automotive and Allied Products Sector, 1972-73; Chairman: GKN Castings Ltd, 1974-77; GKN Kent Alloys Ltd, 1974-77; GKN Shotton Ltd, 1974-77. Dir, GKN (UK) Ltd, 1974-77; Corporate Staff Dir, Group Supplies, GKN Ltd, 1976-77. Dir, Programme Analysis and Review (PAR) and Special Advisor to Chief Sec. to the Treasury, 1971-72. *Recreations:* walking, ski-ing, ethnology, dramatic art. *Address:* The Waldrons, Feckenham, Worcs. *T:* Astwood Bank 2486.

EAST, William Gordon; Professor of Geography in the University of London at Birkbeck College, 1947-70, now Emeritus Professor; *b* 10 Nov. 1902; *s* of George Richard East and Jemima (*née* Nicoll); *m* 1934, Dorothea Small; two *s* two *d. Educ:* Sloane Sch., Chelsea; Peterhouse, Cambridge. Open scholarship in History, 1921, and research studentship, 1924, at Peterhouse. BA (Hons), Cambridge Univ. (History), 1924. MA 1928; Thirlwall Prizeman of Cambridge Univ., 1927. Asst in historical geography, London Sch. of Economics, 1927; temp. administrative officer in Ministry of Economic Warfare and Foreign Office, 1941-45; Reader in Geography in University of London, 1946. Visiting Professor: Univ. of Minnesota, 1952; Univ. of California, Los Angeles, 1959-60; Univ. of Michigan, 1966-67; Univ. of Wisconsin, 1969-70; Univ. of Saskatchewan, 1971. Myres Memorial Lectr, Oxford Univ., 1970-71. Mem., RGS Council, 1956-59; Pres., Inst. of British Geographers, 1959. Murchison Award, RGS, 1972. *Publications:* The Union of Moldavia and Wallachia, 1859, 1929, repr. 1973; An Historical Geography of Europe, 1935; The Geography Behind History, 1938; Mediterranean Problems, 1940; (ed jtly) The Changing Map of Asia, 1950, 1971; (Jt) The Spirit and Purpose of Geography, 1951; (ed jtly) The Changing World, 1956; (ed) The Caxton Atlas, 1960; (ed) Regions of The British Isles, 1960-; The Soviet Union, 1963, 2nd edn 1976; (jt) Our Fragmented World, 1975; contributions to journals of geography, history and foreign affairs. *Address:* Wildwood, Danes Way, Oxshott, Surrey. *T:* Oxshott 2351.

EAST AFRICA, Archdiocese of; divided into two archdioceses of Kenya and Tanzania.

EAST ANGLIA, Bishop of, (RC), since 1976; **Rt. Rev. Alan Charles Clark;** *b* 9 Aug. 1919; *s* of William Thomas Durham Clark and Ellen Mary Clark (*née* Compton). *Educ:* Westminster Cathedral Choir Sch.; Ven. English Coll., Rome, Italy. Priest, 1945; Curate, St Philip's, Arundel, 1945-46; postgrad. studies, Rome, 1946-48; Doctorate in Theol., Gregorian Univ., Rome, 1948; Tutor in Philosophy, English Coll., Rome, 1948-53, Vice-Rector, 1954-64; Parish Priest, St Mary's, Blackheath, SE3, 1965-69; Auxiliary Bishop of Northampton, 1969-76; Titular Bishop of Elmham, 1969-76. *Peritus* at Vatican Council, 1962-65; Jt Chm., The Anglican/Roman Catholic Internat. Commn, 1969-81 (Lambeth Cross). Freeman, City of London, 1969. *Recreation:* music. *Address:* The White House, 21 Upgate, Poringland, Norwich NR14 7SH. *T:* Framingham Earl 2202.

EASTAUGH, Rt. Rev. Cyril, MC 1917; MA (Oxon); Principal of the Society of the Faith, since 1972; *b* 22 Dec. 1897; *y s* of late Robert Wilgress Eastaugh; *m* 1948, Lady Laura Mary Palmer, *d* of 3rd Earl of Selborne, PC, CH; one *s* two *d. Educ:* Christ Church, Oxford; Cuddesdon College. Served European War, 1914-18, S Staffs Regt. Chaplain, Cuddesdon Coll., 1930-34; Vice-Principal, 1934-35; Vicar of St John the Divine, Kennington, 1935-49; Suffragan Bishop of Kensington, 1949-61; Bishop of Peterborough, 1961-72. Hon. Canon of Southwark, 1947; Proctor in Convocation, 1943. Chaplain and Sub-Prelate of the Order of St John of Jerusalem, 1961-. *Address:* Blackmoor House, Liss, Hants. *T:* Bordon 3777.

EASTAUGH, Rt. Rev. John (Richard Gordon); see Hereford, Bishop of.

EASTCOTT, Harry Hubert Grayson, MS; FRCS; FRCOG; Consultant Surgeon, St Mary's Hospital, and Lecturer in Surgery, St Mary's Hospital

Medical School since 1955; Consultant in Surgery and Vascular Surgery to the Royal Navy since 1957; Consultant Surgeon, King Edward VII Hospital for Officers, since 1965; *b* 17 Oct. 1917; *s* of Harry George and Gladys Eastcott; *m* 1941, Doreen Joy, *e d* of Brenchley Ernest and late Muriel Mittell; four *d. Educ:* Latymer Sch.; St Mary's Hosp. Medical School and Middlesex Hospital Medical Sch., University of London; Harvard Med. Sch. War of 1939-45, Junior surgical appts and service as Surgeon Lieut, RNVR up till 1946. Surg. Lieut Comdr RNVR, London Div., until 1957. MRCS; LRCP; MB, BS (Hons), 1941; FRCS 1946; MS (London), 1951. Sen. Registrar, 1950 as Hon. Cons. to St Mary's and Asst Dir Surgical Unit; Research Fellow in Surgery, Harvard Med. Sch., and Peter Bent Brigham Hosp., Boston, Mass, 1949-50; recognised teacher, 1953, and Examr, 1959, in surgery, University of London; Surgeon, Royal Masonic Hosp., 1964-80; Hon. Surg., RADA, 1959-; External Examr in Surgery: Queen's Univ., Belfast, 1964-67; Cambridge Univ., 1968; Univ. of Lagos, Nigeria, 1970-71. Editorial Sec., British Jl of Surgery, 1972-78. Royal College of Surgeons: Hunterian Prof., 1953; Mem. Court of Examrs, 1964-70; Mem. Council, 1971-; Bradshaw Lectr, 1980; Vice-Pres., 1981-; RCS Visitor to RCOG Council, 1972-80. FRSocMed (Hon. Sec., Section of Surgery, 1963-65, Vice-President, 1966, Pres., 1977; Pres., United Services Section, 1981-83). Fellow Medical Soc. of London (Hon. Sec., 1962-64, Vice-Pres. 1964, Pres., 1976, Fothergill Gold Medal, 1974). Pres., Assoc. of Surgeons of GB and Ireland, 1982-83. Mem., Soc. Apothecaries, 1967. Hon. FACS, 1977; Hon. FRACS, 1978; Hon. Fellow Amer. Surgical Assoc., 1981; Hon. Fellow Amer. Heart Assoc., 1981. Editor, Brit. Jl of Surg., 1973-79. *Publications:* Arterial Surgery, 1969, 2nd edn 1973; various articles on gen. and arterial surgery, and on tissue transplantation and preservation, Lancet, Brit. Jl of Surg., etc; contrib. chap. of peripheral vascular disease, Med. Annual, 1961-80; various chaps in textbooks on these subjects. *Recreations:* music, languages, travel, ski-ing, and a lifelong interest in aeronautics. *Address:* 4 Upper Harley Street, NW1 4PN. *T:* 01-935 2020. *Club:* Garrick.

EASTER, Bertie Harry, CMG 1944; CBE 1936 (MBE 1927); BA; retired as Resident Tutor, Windward Islands, for University College of the West Indies (Extra-Mural Studies); *b* 4 June 1893; *s* of Samuel and Lucy Elizabeth Easter; *m* 1930, Hazel Marie Swabey; one *s. Educ:* Christ's Coll., Finchley. Head Master, St Mary's Coll., St Lucia and Secondary Sch., Grenada; Dir of Education, Grenada; Acting Colonial Sec. (or Administrator), Grenada, Jamaica; Dir of Education, Jamaica, 1932-48; Information Officer and Officer i/c Broadcasting, 1939; served European War, Royal Naval Div. and Scots Guards (Lieut). Emeritus Pres., St Lucia Archæol and Hist. Soc. *Address:* Castries, St Lucia, West Indies.

EASTERBROOK, Prof. William Thomas James, FRSC 1957; Professor of Economics, University of Toronto, Canada, 1956-77, now Professor Emeritus; Chairman, Department of Political Economy, University of Toronto, 1961-70; *b* 4 Dec. 1907; *s* of W. J. Easterbrook and Emily McKerr; *m* 1937, Dorothy Mary Walker; two *s* one *d. Educ:* Universities of Manitoba, Toronto, and Harvard. BA (Hon.) Manitoba, 1933; University of Toronto Sch. of Grad. Studies, 1933-36; MA 1935; Harvard Univ., 1936-37; PhD, University of Toronto, 1937. Dept Economics, Univ. of Manitoba, 1938-40 and 1942-47; Guggenheim Fellow, 1940-41; Research Associate, Research Center in Entrepreneurial History, Harvard Univ., 1949 (leave of absence from Toronto). Vice-Pres. Economic History Assoc. (US), 1959-61; Trustee, Business History Inc., 1959-; Mem. Research Cttee on Culture and Communications (Ford Foundation), 1953-55. Pitt Prof. of American History and Institutions, Cambridge Univ., 1955-56; Marshall Lecturer, University of Cambridge, 1956; Professorial Fellow of Jesus Coll. Cambridge, 1955-56; MA Cantab. 1956. Economic Adviser, Ministry of Economic Affairs and Devel Planning, Tanzania, 1966-67. LLD Manitoba, 1963. *Publications:* Agricultural Credit in Canada, 1937; Canadian Economic History (with H. Aitken), 1955; Approaches to Canadian Economic History (with M. H. Watkins), 1968; articles contrib. to Canadian Jl of Economics and Political Science, Jl of Economic History, American Economic Review, etc.; also to Canada (ed George Brown) UN Series, and The Progress of Underdeveloped Countries (ed B. Hoselitz). *Address:* 50 Prince Arthur Avenue, Apt 1901, Toronto 5, Canada. *Club:* University Faculty (Toronto).

EASTHAM, Kenneth; MP (Lab) Manchester, Blackley, since 1979; *b* 11 Aug. 1927; *s* of late James Eastham; *m* 1951, Doris, *d* of Albert Howarth. Planning engr, GEC, Trafford Park. Mem., Manchester CC, 1962-80 (Dep. Leader 1975-79; Chairman: Planning Cttee, 1971-74; Educn Cttee, 1978-79); Mem., NW Econ. Planning Council, 1975-79. *Address:* House of Commons, SW1; 12 Nan Nook Road, Manchester M23 9BZ.

EASTHAM, Hon. Sir (Thomas) Michael, Kt 1978; **Hon. Mr Justice Eastham;** a Judge of the High Court of Justice, Family Division, since 1978; *b* 26 June 1920; *y s* of late His Hon. Sir Tom Eastham, QC; *m* 1942, Mary Pamela, *o d* of late Dr H. C. Billings; two *d. Educ:* Harrow; Trinity Hall, Cambridge. Served with Queen's Royal Regiment, 1940-46 (Capt.). Called to the Bar, Lincoln's Inn, 1947, Bencher, 1972. QC 1964. Recorder: of Deal, 1968-71; of Cambridge, 1971; Hon. Recorder of Cambridge, 1972; a Recorder of the Crown Court, 1972-78. Inspector, Vehicle and General Insurance Company, 1971. *Address:* 7a Porchester Terrace, W2. *T:* 01-723 0770. *Club:* Garrick.

EASTICK, Brig. Sir Thomas (Charles), Kt 1970; CMG 1953; DSO 1942; ED 1939; CStJ 1946; KCSA 1975; JP (for the State of South Australia);

Chairman Standing Committee "Call to the People of Australia", 1951-54; President, El Alamein Group (SA), 1946-60; Chairman of Trustees, Poppy Day Fund (Inc.), 1950-77; President of Australia Day Council, S Australian Branch (Federal), 1962-65 and since 1976; Chairman of Trustees Services Cemeteries Trust; Deputy Chairman, World War II Fund; *b* 3 May 1900; *s* of Charles William Lone and Agnes Ann Eastick; *m* 1925, Ruby Sybil Bruce; five *s. Educ:* Goodwood Sch., Australia. Senior Cadets, 1914-18; Citizen Forces, 1918 (Artillery); Lieut 1922, Capt. 1926, Major 1930, Lieut-Col 1939. Served War of 1939-45 (despatches, ED, DSO); raised and commanded 2/7 Aust. Fd Regt 1940-43; Middle East, Alamein; Brig., CRA 7 Aust. Div., 1943; CRA 9 Aust. Div., 1944; Comdr Kuching Force, 1945; took Japanese surrender and relieved Kuching Prisoner Compound; administered comd 9 Aust. Div., Dec. 1945-Feb. 1946, when Div. disbanded. Hon. ADC to Governor-Gen. of Australia, 1950-53; Mem., Betting Control Board, 1954-65; State Pres. Returned Sailors, Soldiers and Airmen's Imperial League of Australia, S Australia, 1950-54-61-72; Comdr HQ Group Central Command, 1950-54. Pres., SA Womens Meml Playing Fields, 1954-. Col Comdt, Royal Australian Artillery, 1955-60. Pres. Engine Reconditioners Assoc. of Austr., 1958-61. FAIM. Rotary Club of Adelaide Service Award, 1969-70. *Recreation:* photography. *Address:* Astana, Cameron Avenue, Kingston Park, S Australia 5049, Australia. *Club:* Naval, Military and Air Force of SA (Adelaide).

EASTMAN, Rev. Canon Derek Ian Tennent, MC 1945; Canon of St George's Chapel, Windsor, since 1977; *b* 22 Jan. 1919; *s* of Archibald Tennent Eastman and Gertrude Towler Eastman (*née* Gambling); *m* 1949, Judith Mary, *e d* of Canon Philip David Bevington Miller; three *s* one *d. Educ:* Winchester; Christ Church, Oxford; Cuddesdon Theol. Coll. BA 1941; MA 1946. Coldstream Guards, 1940-46: Guards Armoured Div., Temp. Major. Cuddesdon Theol. Coll., 1946-48; Deacon 1948; Priest 1949; Asst Curate, Brighouse, 1948-51; Priest-in-Charge, St Andrew's, Caversham, 1951-56; Vicar: Headington, Oxford, 1956-64; Banbury, 1964-70; Archdeacon of Buckingham, and Vicar of Chilton and Dorton, 1970-77. Proctor in Convocation for Dio. of Oxford, 1964-70. Mem., General Synod, 1975-77. *Recreations:* sea fishing, painting. *Address:* 4 The Cloisters, Windsor Castle, Berks SL4 1NJ. *T:* Windsor 64142.

EASTON, Admiral Sir Ian, KCB 1975; DSC 1946; Commandant, Royal College of Defence Studies, 1976-77; retired 1978; *b* 27 Nov. 1917; *s* of Walter Easton and Janet Elizabeth Rickard; *m* 1st, 1943, Shirley Townend White (marr. diss.); one *s* one *d*; 2nd, 1962, Margharetta Elizabeth Martinette Van Duyn de Sparwoude; one *d. Educ:* The Grange, Crowborough; RNC, Dartmouth. Entered Royal Navy, 1931, and, as an actg Sub-Lt, qualified as a pilot, 1939. During War of 1939-45 served as pilot in HM Ships Glorious, Ark Royal and Formidable and as Direction Officer HMS Indefatigable; Comdr, 1952; Naval Staff Coll., 1953; on staff of BJSM, Washington, 1955-57; Staff Direction Officer, on Staff of Flag Officer Aircraft Carriers, 1957-59; JSSC, 1959; Captain, 1960; Asst Dir of Tactical and Weapons Policy Div., 1960-62; two years exchange service with RAN, in command of HMAS Watson, 1962-64; Naval Asst to Naval Member of Templer Cttee, 1965; Dir of Naval Tactical and Weapons Policy Div., 1966-68; Comdg Officer of HMS Triumph, Far East, 1968-69; Asst Chief of the Naval Staff (Policy), 1969-71; Flag Officer, Admiralty Interview Bd, 1971-73; Head of British Defence Staff and Defence Attaché, Washington, 1973-75. *Recreations:* boats, books, gardening. *Address:* Causeway Cottage, Freshwater, Isle of Wight. *T:* Freshwater 2775. *Club:* Royal Solent Yacht (Yarmouth, IoW).

EASTON, Air Cdre Sir James (Alfred), KCMG 1956; CB 1952; CBE 1945; RAF retired; Associate Member, Overseas Advisory Associates Inc., Detroit, since 1975; *b* 11 Feb. 1908; *s* of late W. C. Easton, Winchester; *m* 1st, 1939, Anna Mary (*d* 1977), *d* of Lieut-Col J. A. McKenna, Ottawa; one *s* one *d*; 2nd, 1980, Jane Walker, *d* of late Dr J. S. Leszynski and *widow* of Mr William M. Walker Jr, both of Detroit. *Educ:* Peter Symonds' Sch., Winchester; RAF Coll., Cranwell. Joined RAF 1928; served NWF India, 1929-32, Egypt, 1935-36, and Canada, 1937-39, as Air Armament Adviser to Dept of National Defence; despatches, 1940; Group Capt., 1941; Air Cdre, 1943; Dir in Air Staff Branch, Air Ministry, 1943-45, and then in RAF Delegation, Washington; retired, 1949; attached Foreign Office, 1945-58; HM Consul-Gen., Detroit, 1958-68. Res. Consultant on Trade Develt of Great Lakes Area, USA, 1968-71; Dep. Chm., Host Cttee for 1974 World Energy Conf., 1972-75. Officer Legion of Merit (US). *Publication:* The Transportation of Freight in the Year 2000, 1970. *Recreations:* travel and travel literature, gardening, golf. *Address:* 390 Chalfonte Avenue, Grosse Pointe Farms, Mich 48236, USA; 71 Cornwall Gardens, SW7. *T:* 01-937 0430. *Clubs:* Royal Air Force; Country, Detroit, Grosse Pointe (Detroit).

EASTON, John Francis; Under-Secretary (Legal), Solicitor's Office, Inland Revenue, since 1980; *b* 20 Aug. 1928; *s* of Rev. Cecil Gordon Easton and Nora Gladys Easton (*née* Hall); *m* 1960, Hon. Caroline Ina Maud, *e d* of Baron Hawke, *qv*; one *s* one *d. Educ:* City of London Sch.; Keble Coll., Oxford (MA). Called to Bar, Middle Temple, 1951. National Service, RASC, 1951-53. Joined Inland Revenue Solicitor's Office, 1955. Member, General Synod of Church of England, 1970-75; Licensed Diocesan Reader, dio. of St Albans, 1969-. *Recreation:* Church affairs. *Address:* The Old Hall, Barley, Royston, Herts SG8 8JA. *T:* Barkway 368.

EASTWOOD, Christopher Gilbert, CMG 1947; Assistant Under-Secretary of State, Colonial Office, 1947-52, and 1954-66; *b* 21 April 1905; *s* of late

W. Seymour Eastwood, West Stoke House, Chichester, and Cecil Emma Eastwood; *m* 1934, Catherine Emma, *d* of late John Douglas Peel, Stonesfield Manor, near Oxford; one *s* three *d*. *Educ*: Eton (Schol.); Trinity Coll., Oxford. Entered Home Civil Service, 1927; appointed to Colonial Office; Private Sec. to High Commissioner for Palestine, 1932-34; Sec. of International Rubber Regulation Cttee, 1934; Private Sec. to Lord Lloyd and Lord Moyne when Secs of State for Colonies, 1940-41. Prin. Asst Sec. Cabinet Office, 1945-47; Commissioner of Crown Lands, 1952-54. *Address*: Stonesfield Manor, Oxford OX7 2PT. *T*: Stonesfield 222.

EASTWOOD, Major Sir Geoffrey (Hugh), KCVO 1965 (CVO 1956); CBE 1945; *b* 17 May 1895; *s* of late John Edmund Eastwood. Served 1914-19, 3rd King's Own Hussars. Hon. Attaché, Brit. Emb., Paris, 1919-21; Clerk and Prin. Clerk, House of Lords, 1924-58. Comptroller to Gov.-Gen. of Canada, 1941-46; Comptroller to the Princess Royal, 1959-65; Extra Equerry to the Queen, 1965; Chief Steward, Hampton Court Palace, 1970-75. *Address*: Wilderness House, Hampton Court Palace, Surrey. *T*: 01-977 5550. *Clubs*: Brooks's, MCC.

EASTWOOD, (George) Granville, OBE 1973; General Secretary, Printing and Kindred Trades Federation, 1958-73; *b* 1906; *s* of George and Anne Eastwood; *m* 1st, 1934, Margaret Lambert (*d* 1967); no *c* ; 2nd, 1971, Elizabeth Gore Underwood (*d* 1981). *Educ*: Burnley Council. Compositor, Burnley, 1927; Asst Sec., Printing and Kindred Trades Fedn, 1943-58. Workpeople's Sec., HMSO Deptl Whitley Council, 1958-73; Jt Secretary: Printing and Allied Trades Jt Industrial Council, 1958-66; Jt Bd for Nat. Newspaper Industry, 1965-67. Member: Council, Printing Industry's Research Assoc., 1958-73; City and Guilds of London Inst., 1958-73; Council, Inst. of Printing, 1961-; ILO Printing Conf., Geneva, 1963; Econ. Develt Cttee for Printing and Publishing, 1966-72; Printing and Publishing Industry Trng Bd, 1968-74; Industrial Arbitration Bd, 1973-76; Editorial Adv. Bd, Ind. Relns Digest, 1973-; DHSS Community Health Council, 1974-76; Advisory, Conciliation and Arbitration Service Panel, 1976-; toured USA and Europe with EDC Jt Mission, 1968. Governor: Chelsea Sch. of Art, 1963-; Nat. Heart Hosp., Brompton Hosp. and London Chest Hosp., 1969-76. *Publications*: George Isaacs, 1952; Harold Laski, 1977. *Recreations*: reading, gardening. *Address*: 16 The Vineries, Enfield, Mddx. *T*: 01-363 2502.

EASTWOOD, Gerald; General Secretary, Association of Patternmakers and Allied Craftsmen, since 1970; *b* 14 May 1929; *s* of William and Emily Eastwood; *m* 1952, Beryl; three *d*. *Educ*: St Hubert's Secondary Modern, Gt Harwood; Blackburn Technical Coll. Pres., CSEU, 1981-82. Mem., Design Council, 1979-. *Recreations*: gardening, fell walking, reading, community service work. *Address*: 11 Honister Gardens, Stanmore, Mddx. *T*: 01-907 2364.

EASTWOOD, Sir John (Bealby), Kt 1975; DL; Chairman, Adam Eastwood & Sons Ltd, Builders, since 1946; *b* 9 Jan. 1909; *s* of William Eastwood and Elizabeth Townroe Eastwood (*née* Bealby); *m* 1929, Constance Mary (*née* Tilley) (*d* 1981); two *d*. *Educ*: Queen Elizabeth's Grammar Sch., Mansfield. Civil Engr and Contractor, 1925; founded W. & J. B. Eastwood Ltd, 1945. DL Notts, 1981. OStJ 1972. *Recreations*: shooting, horse-racing, golf, cricket. *Address*: Hexgreave Hall, Farnsfield, Newark, Notts. *Club*: Farmers'.

EASTWOOD, Dr Wilfred, FEng; Senior Partner, Eastwood and Partners, Consulting Engineers, since 1972; *b* 15 Aug. 1923; *s* of Wilfred Andrew Eastwood and Annice Gertrude Eastwood; *m* 1947, Dorothy Jean Gover; one *s* one *d*. Road Research Laboratory, 1945-46; University of Manchester, 1946-47; University of Aberdeen, 1947-53; University of Sheffield, 1954-70: Head, Dept of Civil Engrg, 1964-70; Dean, Faculty of Engrg, 1967-70. Pres., IStructE, 1976-77; Mem. Bd and Exec., CEI, 1979- (Vice-Chm., 1982-83). *Publications*: papers in Proc. ICE and Jl IStructE, etc. *Address*: 242 Abbeydale Road South, Sheffield S17 3LL. *T*: 364645. *Club*: Yorks County Cricket.

EATES, Edward Caston, CMG 1968; MVO 1961; QPM 1961; CPM 1956; Commissioner, The Royal Hong Kong Police, 1967-69, retired; re-employed at Foreign and Commonwealth Office, 1971-76; *b* London, 8 April 1916; *o s* of late Edward Eates and Elizabeth Lavinia Issac Eates (*née* Caston); *m* 1941, Maureen Teresa McGee; no *c*. *Educ*: Highgate Sch.; King's Coll., London (LLB). Asst Examr, Estate Duty Office, 1935. Army, 1939-46: 22nd (Cheshire) Regt, later Royal Tanks; served with 2nd Derbs Yeomanry, Western Desert and NW Europe, 1941-44; Adjt 1943; Sqdn Ldr 1944; Staff Coll., Quetta (sc), 1945; DAAG Nagpur District. Apptd to Colonial Police Service, Nigeria, 1946; Sen. Supt, Sierra Leone, 1954; Comr, The Gambia, 1957; Asst Comr, 1963, Dep. Comr, 1966, Hong Kong. *Recreations*: cricket and association football (inactive); travel, motoring. *Address*: Banjul, Toadpit Lane, Ottery St Mary, Devon. *T*: Ottery St Mary 2838. *Clubs*: Royal Commonwealth Society, East India, Devonshire, Sports and Public Schools; Surrey County Cricket.

EATHER, Maj.-Gen. Kenneth William, CB 1947; CBE 1943; DSO 1941; Executive Director, Water Research Foundation of Australia, 1958-79; *b* 1901; *m* 1st, 1924, Adeline Mabel, *d* of Gustavus Lewis; one *s* one *d* ; 2nd, 1968, Kathleen, *d* of M. F. Carroll. Served War of 1939-45; AMF, Middle East and SW Pacific (despatches, DSO, CBE). *Address*: 6 Edensor Road, Epping, NSW 2121, Australia. *T*: 8691131. *Club*: Imperial Service (Sydney).

EATON, Air Vice-Marshal Brian Alexander, CB 1969; CBE 1959; DSO and Bar, DFC, American Silver Star; Regional Executive, Canberra Rolls-Royce Ltd, since 1974; *b* Launceston, Tas, 15 Dec. 1916; *s* of S. A. Eaton; *m* 1952, Josephine Rumbles; one *s* two *d*. *Educ*: Carey Grammar Sch., Melbourne; RAAF Coll., Pt Cook. Served war of 1939-45: Co 3 Sqdn N Africa-Medit., 1943, CO 239 Wing RAF Italy, 1944-45. UK, 1945-46; OC 81 Fighter Wing, Japan, 1948; OC BCAIR, 1948-49; OC 78 Wing Malta, 1952-54; Dir of Ops, RAAF HQ, 1955; OC Williamtown RAAF and Comdt Sch. of Land-Air Warfare, 1957-58; Dir Joint Service Plans, 1959-60; Imp. Defence Coll., 1961; Dir-Gen. of Operational Requirements, 1962; Deputy Chief of Air Staff, 1966-67; AOC HQ 224 Mobile Group (RAF) Far East Air Force, Singapore, 1967-68; Chief of Staff HQFEAF, 1968-69; Air Mem. for Personnel, Dept of Air, Canberra, 1969-73; AOC Operational Comd, RAAF, 1973-74. *Recreations*: shooting, fishing. *Address*: 125 Mugga Way, Red Hill, ACT 2603, Australia. *Club*: Commonwealth (Canberra).

EATON, Peter; owner of the largest antiquarian bookstore in England; *b* 24 Jan. 1914; *m* 1st, Ann Wilkinson; 2nd, Valerie Carruthers; two *s* ; 3rd, Margaret Taylor; two *d*. *Educ*: elementary sch.; Municipal Sch. (later Coll.) of Technology, Manchester Univ. (expelled). Born in London at 8 York Gate, Regent's Park; advertised for adoption in Nursing Times, Feb. 1914; brought up in Rochdale, where became apprentice printer; became a tramp; in London, later helped found now defunct Domestic Workers Union; advised on start of Tribune newspaper; mem. of Labour Party for 40 yrs; Conscientious Objector, tried at Royal Courts of Justice, 1939; voluntarily joined London Rescue Squad for duration of War and helped Bomb Disposal Squad; started bookselling in Portobello Road when it was predominantly a fruit and vegetable market, 1945; bought Queen Victoria's books from Kensington Palace (now in Victoria State Library, Australia); bought part or all of libraries of Bernard Shaw, H. G. Wells, Marie Stopes and R. H. Tawney; formed many important collections of books, incl. world's largest collection of books on the atom (now in Texas Univ.). Travelled in many parts of the world, incl. Alaska, India and African jungles; FRGS 1950. *Publications*: Marie Stopes: a bibliographical list of her books, 1977; History of Lilies, 1982; articles in trade jls. *Recreations*: taking the dog for a walk, watching my wife play tennis. *Address*: Lilies, Weedon, Aylesbury, Bucks HP22 4NS. *T*: Aylesbury 641393.

EAYRS, Prof. John Thomas, PhD, DSc; Sands Cox Professor of Anatomy, University of Birmingham, 1968-77; *b* 23 Jan. 1913; *e s* of late Thomas William Eayrs, AMICE, and late Florence May (*née* Clough); *m* 1941, Frances Marjorie Sharp; one *s* two *d*. *Educ*: King Edward's, Birmingham; University of Birmingham. In industry until 1938. War service: Pte Royal Warwicks Regt, 1939-40; 2nd Lieut Manchester Regt, 1940; Lieut 1940; Capt. 1941; Major 1942; Worcester Regt, 1943; sc Staff Coll., Camberley, 1944. University of Birmingham: Peter Thompson Prize, 1947; John Barritt Melson Memorial Gold Medal, 1947; Lectr in Anatomy, 1948; Bertram Windle Prize, 1950; Sen. Lectr 1955; Research Fellow, Calif. Inst. of Technology, 1956-57; Reader in Comparative Neurology, Birmingham, 1958; Henry Head Research Fellow, Royal Society, London, 1957-62; Prof. of Neuroendocrinology, Birmingham, 1961; Fitzmary Prof. of Physiology, London Univ., 1963-68. Governor, King Edward's Foundn, Birmingham, 1968-77. *Publications*: Scientific Papers dealing with developmental neuroendocrinology and behaviour in Jl Endocrin., Jl Anat. (London), Anim. Behav., etc. *Recreations*: cruising, foreign travel and languages. *Address*: 51 Old Street, Upton upon Severn, Worcs; Penllyn Dyfi, Aberangell, Powys.

EBAN, Abba; a Member of the Knesset, since 1959; Minister for Foreign Affairs, Israel, 1966-74; *b* 2 Feb. 1915, Cape Town, SA; *s* of Avram and Alida Solomon; *m* 1945, Susan Ambache; one *s* one *d*. *Educ*: Cambridge Univ. (MA). Res. Fellow and Tutor for Oriental Languages, Pembroke Coll., Cambridge, 1938. Liaison officer of Allied HQ with Jewish population in Jerusalem, 1942-44; Chief Instructor, Middle East Arab Centre, Jerusalem, 1944-46; Jewish Agency, 1946-47; Liaison Officer with UN Special Commn on Palestine, 1947; UN: Representative of provisional govt of Israel, 1948; Permanent rep., 1949-59; Vice-Pres., General Assembly, 1953; Ambassador to USA, 1950-59; Minister without Portfolio, 1959-60; Minister of Educn and Culture, 1960-63; Dep. Prime Minister, 1963-66. Pres., Weizmann Inst. of Science, 1958-66; Vice-Pres., UN Conf. on Science and Technology in Advancement of New States, 1963; Mem., UN Adv. Cttee on Science and Technology for Develt. Fellow: World Acad. of Arts and Sciences; Amer. Acad. of Arts and Sciences. Hon. Doctorates include: New York; Boston; Maryland; Cincinnati; Temple; Brandeis; Yeshiva. *Publications*: The Modern Literary Movement in Egypt, 1944; Maze of Justice, 1946; Social and Cultural Problems in the Middle East, 1947; The Toynbee Heresy, 1955; Voice of Israel, 1957; Tide of Nationalism, 1959; Chaim Weizmann: a collective biography, 1962; Reality and Vision in the Middle East (Foreign Affairs), 1965; Israel in the World, 1966; My People, 1968; My Country, 1972; An Autobiography, 1978; articles in English, French, Hebrew and Arabic. *Address*: The Knesset, Jerusalem, Israel.

EBBISHAM, 2nd Baron, *cr* 1928, of Cobham, Surrey; **Rowland Roberts Blades,** Bt, *cr* 1922; TD; MA; *b* 3 Sept. 1912; *o s* of 1st Baron Ebbisham, GBE, and Margaret (MBE 1943, Officer Legion of Honour, OStJ) (*d* 1965), *d* of Arthur Reiner, Sutton, Surrey; *S* father, 1953; *m* 1949, Flavia Mary, *y d* of Charles Meade, Pen y lan, Meifod, Montgomeryshire; three *d*. *Educ*: Winchester; Christ Church, Oxford (MA). Served War of 1939-45; Lieut 98th (Surrey and Sussex Yeo.) Field Regt, RA. Master, Mercers' Co., 1963;

Common Councilman, City of London, 1947-; Chm., City Lands Cttee, and Chief Commoner, Corp. of London, 1967-68; one of HM Lieutenants, City of London, 1966-. President: London Chamber of Commerce, 1958-61; Assoc. of British Chambers of Commerce, 1968-70; British Importers' Confedn, 1978-81; Mem., European Trade Cttee, BOTB, 1973-; Hon. Treasurer, BPIF, 1971-81; Director: Williams, Lea Ltd; Zürich Life Assurance Co. Ltd; Private Patients Plan Ltd; Chm., Anglo-Dal Ltd. Vice-Pres. The London Record Society. Captain, Surrey II XI, 1946-54; Order of Yugoslav Flag with gold wreath, 1976. *Address:* The Old Rectory, Blechingley, Surrey. *T:* Godstone 843388. *Club:* MCC.

EBERHART, Richard (Ghormley); Professor Emeritus of English and Poet in Residence, Dartmouth College, USA; *b* Austin, Minn, 5 April 1904; *s* of late Alpha La Rue Eberhart and late Lena Eberhart (*née* Lowenstein); *m* 1941, Helen Elizabeth Butcher, Christ Church, Cambridge, Mass; one *s* one *d*. *Educ:* Dartmouth Coll., USA (AB); St John's Coll., Cambridge Univ., England (BA, MA); Harvard Univ. Grad. Sch. of Arts and Sciences. Taught English, 1933-41, also tutor to son of King Prajadhipok of Siam for a year. Served War in USN Reserve finishing as Lieut-Comdr, 1946; subseq. entered Butcher Polish Co., Boston, Mass, as Asst Man., finishing as Vice-Pres. (now Hon. Vice-Pres. and Mem. Bd of Directors). Founder (and first Pres.) Poets' Theatre Inc., Cambridge, Mass, 1950. Called back to teaching, 1952, and has served as Poet in Residence, Prof., or Lecturer at University of Washington, University of Conn., Wheaton Coll., Princeton, and in 1956 was apptd Prof. of English and Poet in Residence at Dartmouth Coll. Class of 1925 Chair, 1968 (being absent as Consultant in Poetry to the Library of Congress, 1959-61). Visiting Professor: Univ. of Washington, 1967, Jan.-June 1972; Columbia Univ., 1975; Distinguished Vis. Prof., Florida Univ., 1974-82 (President's Residency, 1977); Regents Prof., Univ. of California, Davis, 1975; First Wallace Stevens Fellow, Timothy Dwight Coll., Yale, 1976. Shelley Memorial Prize; Bollingen Prize, 1962; Pulitzer Prize, 1966; Fellow, Acad. of Amer. Poets, 1969 (Nat. Book Award, 1977). Advisory Cttee on the Arts, for the National Cultural Center (later John F. Kennedy Memorial Center), Washington, 1959; Member: Amer. Acad. and Inst. of Arts and Letters, 1960; Nat. Acad. of Arts and Sciences, 1967; Elliston Lecturer on Poetry, University of Cincinnati, 1961. Poet Laureate of New Hampshire, 1979. Apptd Hon. Consultant in American Letters, The Library of Congress, 1963-66, reapptd, 1966-69. Hon. Pres., Poetry Soc. of America, 1972. Participant, Poetry International, London, 1973. Hon. LittD: Dartmouth Coll., 1954; Skidmore Coll., 1966; Coll. of Wooster, 1969; Colgate Univ., 1974; Hon. DHL, Franklin Pierce, 1978. Phi Beta Kappa poem, Harvard, 1967; Hon. Mem., Alpha Chapter, Mass, 1967; New York Qly Poetry Day Award, 1980. Diploma, World Acad. of Arts and Culture, China, 1981. *Publications:* (concurrently in England and America): A Bravery of Earth, 1930; Reading the Spirit, 1936; Selected Poems, 1951; Undercliff, Poems, 1946-53, also Great Praises, 1957; Collected Poems, 1930-60, 1960; Collected Verse Plays, 1962 (USA); The Quarry, 1964; Selected Poems, 1930-65, New Directions, 1965; Thirty One Sonnets, 1967 (USA); Shifts of Being, 1968; Fields of Grace, 1972 (Nat. Book Award nominee, 1973); Poems to Poets, 1975; Collected Poems 1930-1976, 1976; To Eberhart from Ginsberg: a letter about 'Howl', 1956, 1976; Of Poetry and Poets (criticism), 1979; Ways of Light, 1980 (USA); Survivors, 1980 (USA); Four Poems, 1980; New Hampshire/Nine Poems, 1980; Chocorua, 1981 (USA); Florida Poems, 1981 (USA); Recorded Readings of his Poetry, 1961, 1968; two documentary films, 1972, 1975; *Festschrift:* (in New England Review, 1980) Richard Eberhart: A Celebration. *Recreations:* swimming, cruising, tennis, flying 7-ft kites. *Address:* 5 Webster Terrace, Hanover, New Hampshire 03755, USA. *Clubs:* Century (New York); Buck's Harbor Yacht (S Brooksville, Maine); Signet (Harvard).

EBERLE, Adm. Sir James (Henry Fuller), GCB 1981 (KCB 1979); Commander-in-Chief, Naval Home Command, since 1981; Flag ADC to the Queen, since 1981; *b* 31 May 1927; *s* of late Victor Fuller Eberle and of Joyce Mary Eberle, Bristol; *m* 1950, Ann Patricia Thompson, Hong Kong; one *s* two *d*. *Educ:* Clifton Coll.; RNC Dartmouth and Greenwich. Served War of 1939-45 in MTBs, HMS Renown, HMS Belfast; subseq. in Far East; qual. Gunnery Specialist 1951; Guided Missile Develt and trials in UK and USA, 1953-57; Naval Staff, 1960-62; Exec. Officer, HMS Eagle, 1963-65; comd HMS Intrepid, 1968-70; Asst Chief of Fleet Support, MoD (RN), 1971-74; Flag Officer Sea Training, 1974-75; Flag Officer Carriers and Amphibious Ships, 1975-77; Chief of Fleet Support, 1977-79; C-in-C, Fleet, and Allied C-in-C, Channel and Eastern Atlantic, 1979-81. Vice-Pres., RUSI, 1979. Freeman, London and Bristol. *Recreations:* hunting (Master of Britannia Beagles), tennis (Pres., RN Lawn Tennis Assoc.), squash (Pres. RN Squash Racquets Assoc.). *Address:* Admiralty House, Portsmouth, PO1 3LR. *Clubs:* Farmers'; Society of Merchant Venturers (Bristol).

EBERT, Peter; Producer; *b* 6 April 1918; *s* of Carl Ebert, CBE, and Lucie Oppenheim; *m* 1st, 1944, Kathleen Havinden; two *d*; 2nd, 1951, Silvia Ashmole; five *s* three *d*. *Educ:* Salem Sch., Germany; Gordonstoun, Scotland. BBC Producer, 1948-51; 1st opera production, Mefistofele, Glasgow, 1951; Mozart and Rossini guest productions: Rome, Naples, Venice, 1951, 1952, 1954, 1955: Wexford Festival: 12 prods, 1952-65; 1st Glyndebourne Fest. prod., Ariecchino, 1954, followed by Seraglio, Don Giovanni, etc.; 1st Edinburgh Fest. prod., Forza del Destino, 1955; Chief producer: Hannover State Opera, 1954-60; Düsseldorf Opera, 1960-62; directed opera class, Hannover State Conservatory, 1954-60; Head of Opera studio, Düsseldorf, 1960-62. Guest productions in Europe, USA, Canada. TV productions of Glyndebourne operas, 1955-64; 1st TV studio prod., 1963; Opera Adviser to BBC TV, 1964-65; Dir of Productions, 1965-77, Gen. Administrator, 1977-80, Scottish Opera Co. First drama prod., The Devils, Johannesburg, 1966; first musical, Houdini, London, 1966. Dir, Opera Sch., University of Toronto, 1967-68; Intendant: Stadttheater, Augsburg, 1968-73; Stadttheater Bielefeld, 1973-75; Staatstheater Wiesbaden, 1975-77. Hon. DMus St Andrews, 1979. *Recreation:* raising a family. *Address:* Ades House, Chailey, East Sussex. *T:* Newick 2441.

EBOO PIRBHAI, Count Sir; Kt 1952; OBE 1946; Director of Companies; *b* 25 July 1905; *m* 1925, Kulsambai; two *s* three *d* (and one *s* decd). *Educ:* Duke of Gloucester Sch., Nairobi. Representative of HH The Aga Khan. Member, Nairobi City Council, 1938-43. MLC Kenya, 1952-60; Member of various other official bodies; Past President Central Muslim Association; President Aga Khan Supreme Council, Africa, Europe, Canada and USA. Given title of Count, created by HH The Aga Khan, 1954. Brilliant Star of Zanzibar, 1956; Order of Crescent Cross of the Comores, 1966. *Address:* PO Box 40898, Nairobi, Kenya. *T:* 65049. *Clubs:* Reform, Lansdowne, Royal Commonwealth Society; Nairobi, Muthaiga (Kenya).

EBRAHIM, Sir (Mahomed) Currimbhoy, 4th Bt, *cr* 1910; BA, LLB, Advocate, Pakistan; Member, Standing Council of the Baronetage, 1961; *b* 24 June 1935; *o s* of Sir (Huseinali) Currimbhoy Ebrahim, 3rd Bt, and Alhaja Lady Amina Khanum, *d* of Alhaj Cassumali Jairajbhoy; *S* father 1952; *m* 1958, Dur-e-Mariam, *d* of Minuchehir Ahmud Ghulamaly Nana; three *s* one *d*. *Recreations:* tennis (Karachi University No 1, 1957, No 2, 1958), cricket, table-tennis, squash, reading (literary), art, poetry writing, debate, quotation writing. *Heir:* *s* Zulfiqar Ali Currimbhoy Ebrahim, *b* 5 Aug. 1960. *Address:* Bait-ul-Aman, 33 Mirza Kalig Beg Road, Jamshed Quarters, Karachi, Pakistan.

EBRINGTON, Viscount; Charles Hugh Richard Fortescue; *b* 10 May 1951; *s* and *heir* of 7th Earl Fortescue, *qv*; *m* 1974, Julia, *er d* of Air Commodore J. A. Sowrey; two *d*. *Address:* Ebrington Manor, Chipping Campden, Glos.

EBSWORTH, Ann Marian; a Recorder of the Crown Court, since 1978; barrister-at-law; *b* 19 May 1937; *d* of Arthur E. Ebsworth, OBE, BEM, RM (retd) and late Hilda Mary Ebsworth. *Educ:* Notre Dame Convent, Worth, Sussex; Portsmouth High Sch., GPDST; London Univ. BA Hons (History). Called to Bar, Gray's Inn, 1962. *Recreations:* Italian travel, medieval history, needlework. *Address:* 33 Warren Drive, Wallasey, Cheshire. *T:* 051-639 1579; (chambers) 3rd Floor, 27 Dale Street, Liverpool. *T:* 051-227 1081. *Club:* Royal Commonwealth Society.

EBURNE, Sidney Alfred William, MC 1944; Senior Crown Agent and Chairman of the Crown Agents for Oversea Governments and Administrations, since 1978; *b* 26 Nov. 1918; *s* of Alfred Edmund Eburne and Ellen Francis Eburne; *m* 1942, Phoebe Freda (*née* Beeton Dilley); one *s* one *d*. *Educ:* Downhills School. Served War, 1939-46; Captain, RA. Joined Morgan Grenfell & Co. Ltd, 1946; Director: Morgan Grenfell & Co. Ltd, 1968-75; Morgan Grenfell Holdings Ltd, 1971-75; Crown Agents: Dir of Finance, 1975; Man. Dir, 1976. *Recreations:* golf, travelling. *Address:* Marchurst Barn, Shipbourne, near Tonbridge, Kent. *Club:* Carlton.

EBURY, 6th Baron, *cr* 1857; **Francis Egerton Grosvenor;** *b* 8 Feb. 1934; *s* of 5th Baron Ebury, DSO and Ann Acland-Troyte; *heir-pres.* to 7th Earl of Wilton, *qv*; *S* father 1957; *m* 1st, 1957, Gillian Elfrida (Elfin) (marr. diss. 1962), *d* of Martin Soames, London; one *s*; 2nd, 1963, Kyra (marr. diss. 1973), *d* of late L. L. Aslin; 3rd, 1974, Suzanne Jean, *d* of Graham Suckling, Christchurch, NZ; one *d*. *Educ:* Eton. *Recreation:* golf. *Heir:* *s* Hon. Julian Francis Martin Grosvenor, *b* 8 June 1959. *Address:* 5 Landale Road, Toorak, Vic. 3142, Australia. *Club:* Savage (Melbourne).

ECCLES, family name of Viscount Eccles.

ECCLES, 1st Viscount, *cr* 1964; 1st Baron, *cr* 1962; **David McAdam Eccles,** PC 1951; KCVO 1953; MA Oxon; Chairman, British Library Board, 1973-78; *b* 18 Sept. 1904; *s* of late W. McAdam Eccles, FRCS and Anna Coralie, *d* of E. B. Anstie, JP; *m* 1928, Sybil (*d* 1977), *e d* of Viscount Dawson of Penn, PC, GCVO, KCB, KCMG; two *s* one *d*. *Educ:* Winchester, New Coll., Oxford. Joined Ministry of Economic Warfare, Sept. 1939; Economic Adviser to HM Ambassadors at Madrid and Lisbon, 1940-42; Ministry of Production, 1942-43. MP (C) Chippenham Div. of Wilts, 1943-62; Minister of Works, 1951-54; Minister of Education, 1954-57; Pres. of the Board of Trade, 1957-59; Minister of Education, Oct. 1959-July 1962; Paymaster-General, with responsibility for the arts, 1970-73. Trustee, British Museum, 1963-, Chm. of Trustees, 1968-70; Dir, Courtaulds, 1962-70. Chm., Anglo-Hellenic League, 1967-70. Pres., World Crafts Council, 1974-78. Hon. Fellow, RIBA. *Publications:* Half-Way to Faith, 1966; Life and Politics: A Moral Diagnosis, 1967; On Collecting, 1968. *Heir:* *s* Hon. John Dawson Eccles, *qv*. *Address:* Dean Farm, Chute, near Andover, Hants; 6 Barton Street, SW1. *T:* Chute Standen 210. *Clubs:* Brooks's, Roxburghe.

ECCLES, Sir John Carew, Kt 1958; FRS 1941; FRSNZ; FAA; *b* 27 Jan. 1903; *s* of William James and Mary Eccles; *m* 1st, 1928, Irene Frances Miller (marr. diss. 1968); four *s* five *d*; 2nd, 1968, Helena Táboříková. *Educ:* Melbourne Univ.; Magdalen Coll., Oxford. Melbourne University: 1st class Hons MB,

BS 1925; Victoria Rhodes Scholar, 1925. Univ. of Oxford: Christopher Welch Scholar; 1st class Hons Natural Science (Physiology), 1927; MA 1929; DPhil 1929; Gotch Memorial Prize, 1927; Rolleston Memorial Prize, 1932. Junior Res. Fellow, Exeter Coll., Oxford, 1927-32; Staines Med. Fellow, Exeter Coll., 1932-34; Fellow and Tutor of Magdalen Coll., and Univ. Lectr in Physiology, 1934-37; Dir, Kanematsu Memorial Inst. of Pathology, Sydney, 1937-44; Prof. of Physiology: Univ. of Otago, Dunedin, NZ, 1944-51; ANU, Canberra, 1951-66; Mem., Inst. for Biomedical Res., Chicago, 1966-68; Dist. Prof. and Head of Res. Unit of Neurobiology, Health Sci. Faculty, State Univ. of NY at Buffalo, 1968-75, now Dist. Prof. Emeritus. Lectures: Waynflete, Magdalen Coll., Oxford, 1952; Herter, Johns Hopkins Univ., 1955; Ferrier, Royal Soc., 1959; Sherrington, Liverpool Univ., 1966; Patten, Indiana Univ., 1972; Pahlavi, Iran, 1976; Gifford, Edinburgh, 1978, 1979. Pres., Australian Acad. of Science, 1957-61. Member: Pontifical Acad. of Science; Deutsche Akademie der Naturforscher Leopoldina. Foreign Hon. Member: Amer. Acad. of Arts and Sciences; Amer. Philosophical Soc.; Amer. Neurological Soc.; Accademia Nazionale dei Lincei. Hon. Life Mem., New York Acad. of Sciences, 1965; Foreign Associate, Nat. Acad. of Sciences; For. Mem., Max-Planck Soc. Hon. Fellow: Exeter Coll., Oxford, 1961; Magdalen Coll., Oxford, 1964; Amer. Coll. of Physicians, 1967. Hon. ScD Cantab; Hon. DSc: Oxon; Tasmania; British Columbia; Gustavus Adolphus Coll., Minnesota; Marquette Univ., Wisconsin; Loyola, Chicago; Yeshiva, NY; Fribourg; Hon. LLD Melbourne; Hon. MD Charles Univ., Prague. (Jointly) Nobel Prize for Medicine, 1963; Baly Medal, RCP, 1961; Royal Medal, Royal Soc., 1962; Cothenius Medal, Deutsche Akademie der Naturforscher Leopoldina, 1963. *Publications:* (jt author) Reflex Activity of Spinal Cord, 1932; Neuro-physiological Basis of Mind, 1953; Physiology of Nerve Cells, 1957; Physiology of Synapses, 1964; (jt author) The Cerebellum as a Neuronal Machine, 1967; The Inhibitory Pathways of the Central Nervous System, 1969; Facing Reality, 1970; The Understanding of the Brain, 1973; (jt author) The Self and Its Brain, 1977; The Human Mystery, 1979; (jt author) Sherrington, his Life and Thought, 1979; The Human Psyche, 1980; papers in Proc. Royal Soc., Jl of Physiology, Jl of Neurophysiology, Experimental Brain Research. *Recreations:* walking, European travel. *Address:* Ca' a la Gra', CH 6611 Contra (Locarno), Ticino, Switzerland. *T:* 093-672931.

ECCLES, Hon. John Dawson; *b* 20 April 1931; *er s* and *heir* of 1st Viscount Eccles, *qv*; *m* 1955, Diana Catherine, *d* of Raymond Sturge, *qv*; one *s* three *d*. *Educ:* Winchester Coll.; Magdalen Coll., Oxford (BA). Director: Glynwed Ltd; Finance for Industry. Mem., Monopolies and Mergers Commn, 1976-, Dep. Chm., 1981-. *Address:* Moulton Hall, Richmond, N Yorks. *T:* Barton 227. *Club:* Brooks's.

ECCLES-WILLIAMS, Hilary a'Beckett, CBE 1970; non-executive Director, Rabone Petersen, since 1982; *b* 5 Oct. 1917; *s* of late Rev. Cyril Eccles-Williams and Hermione (*née* Terrell); *m* 1941, Jeanne, *d* of W. J. Goodwin; two *s* four *d*. *Educ:* Eton; Brasenose Coll., Oxford (MA). Served War of 1939-45, Major RA (anti-tank). Consul: for Nicaragua, 1951-59; for Cuba, 1952-60; for Costa Rica, 1964-; for Bolivia, 1965-82. Chairman of companies; has travelled 900,000 miles on export business. Chairman: Brit. Export Houses Assoc., 1958-59; Asian Christian Colls Assoc., 1960-66; President: Birmingham Chamber of Commerce, 1965-66; Assoc. of Brit. Ch. of Commerce (93 Chambers), 1970-72. Comr of Income Tax, 1966-70. Chairman: Birmingham Dist Cons. Assoc., 1976-79 (Pres., 1979); European Parlt constituency of Birmingham South Cons. Assoc., 1978-82 (Pres., 1982); W Midlands Metropolitan Co. Co-ordinating Cttee, Cons. Party, 1980-; Guardians of Birmingham Assay Office, 1979- (Guardian, 1970-). Mem., Brit. Hallmarking Council, 1976-; Pres., Birmingham Consular Assoc., 1973-74; Chm., Brit. Heart Foundn, Midland Counties, 1973-74; Governor, Birmingham Univ., 1966-; Liveryman, Worshipful Co. of Glaziers, 1974; Hon. Captain, Bolivian Navy, 1969. Numerous TV appearances. *Recreations:* lawn tennis, squash, sailing. *Address:* 36 St Bernard's Road, Solihull, West Midlands B92 7BB. *T:* 021-706 0354. *Clubs:* Edgbaston Priory (Birmingham); Olton Mere Sailing.

ECCLESHARE, Colin Forster; formerly London Manager and Director Group Projects, Cambridge University Press; *b* 2 May 1916; *yr s* of Albert and Mary Alice Eccleshare, Derby; *m* 1942, Elizabeth, *e d* of late H. S. Bennett, FBA, and of Joan Bennett, *qv*; one *s* two *d* (and one *d* decd). *Educ:* Bemrose Sch., Derby; St Catharine's Coll., Cambridge (MA). Joined Cambridge Univ. Press, 1939. War Service, 1940-46; commissioned RE; Captain Survey Directorate, War Office, 1944; Major, HQ, ALFSEA, 1945. Rejoined Cambridge Univ. Press, 1946; Asst London Manager, 1948; London Manager, 1963-72; Dir Group Projects, 1972-77. Publishing Consultant, British Library, 1977. Acting Sec., Athlone Press, Univ. of London, 1978-79. Director: Educational Associates Ltd (Hong Kong); John Wiley & Sons Ltd. Mem. Council, Publishers Assoc., 1965-71; Treasurer, 1971-73; Pres., 1973-75; Vice-Pres., 1975-77. Board Mem., Book Development Council, 1968-70 and 1975-79 (Chm., 1975-77); Member: Books Advisory Panel, British Council; Exec. and Internat. Cttees, Internat. Publishers' Assoc., 1975-77; Groupe des Editeurs du Livre de la CEE; Adv. Cttee, British Library Bibliographical Services Div., 1975-78; British Nat. Bibliography Res. Fund Cttee, 1978-; UK Nat. Commn UNESCO, 1978-; Chairman: Other-Media Cttee of Internat. Scientific, Technical and Medical Publishers Gp; Soc. of Bookmen, 1977-80. Missions (for Publishers Assoc., BDC, Brit. Council) to: Hungary, USSR, 1964; Philippines, Japan, 1968; Pakistan, 1971; USSR, Australia, 1974; Saudi Arabia, 1976; Israel, 1977. *Publications:* contributor to The Bookseller,

1950-62. *Address:* 4 Branch Hill, NW3. *T:* 01-794 3496; Tyddyn Pandy, Barmouth. *T:* Barmouth 280315. *Club:* Garrick.

ECCLESTON, Harry Norman, OBE 1979; PRE 1975 (RE 1961; ARE 1948); RWS 1975 (ARWS 1964); Artist Designer at the Bank of England Printing Works since 1958; *b* 21 Jan. 1923; *s* of Harry Norman Eccleston and Kate Pritchard, Coseley, Staffs; *m* 1948, Betty Doreen Gripton; two *d*. *Educ:* Sch. of Art, Bilston; Coll. of Art, Birmingham; Royal College of Art. ATD 1947; ARCA (1st Class) 1950. Studied painting until 1942. Served in Royal Navy, 1942-46; Temp. Commn, RNVR, 1943. Engraving Sch., Royal College of Art, 1947-51; engraving, teaching, free-lance graphic design, 1951-58. Pres., Royal Soc. of Painter-Etchers and Engravers, 1975-. *Recreation:* reading. *Address:* 110 Priory Road, Harold Hill, Romford, Essex. *T:* Ingrebourne 40275. *Club:* Arts.

ECCLESTONE, Jacob Andrew; Deputy General Secretary, National Union of Journalists, since 1981; *b* 10 April 1939; *s* of Alan Ecclestone and late Delia Reynolds Abraham; *m* 1966, Margaret Joan Bassett; two *s* one *d*. *Educ:* High Storrs Grammar Sch., Sheffield; Open Univ. (BA). Journalism: South Yorkshire Times, 1957-61; Yorkshire Evening News, 1961-62; The Times, 1962-66, 1967-81. Member: Nat. Exec., NUJ, 1977 (Vice-Pres. 1978, Pres., 1979); Press Council, 1977-80; Exec., Nat. Council for Civil Liberties, 1982-. *Recreations:* gardening, climbing, music. *Address:* 40 Chatsworth Way, SE27 9HN. *T:* 01-670 8503.

ECHLIN, Sir Norman David Fenton, 10th Bt, *cr* 1721; Captain 14/1st Punjab Regiment, Indian Army; *b* 1 Dec. 1925; *s* of Sir John Frederick Echlin, 9th Bt, and Ellen Patricia (*d* 1971), *d* of David Jones, JP, Dublin; *S* father, 1932; *m* 1953, Mary Christine, *d* of John Arthur, Oswestry, Salop. *Educ:* Masonic Boys' School, Dublin. *Heir:* none. *Address:* Nartopa, 36 Marina Avenue, Appley, Ryde, IoW.

ECKERSLEY, Sir Donald (Payze), Kt 1981; OBE 1977; farmer, since 1946; Inaugural President, National Farmers' Federation of Australia, 1979-81; *b* 1 Nov. 1922; *s* of Walter Roland Eckersley and Ada Gladys Moss; *m* 1949, Marjorie Rae Clarke; one *s* two *d*. *Educ:* Muresk Agricl Coll. (Muresk Diploma in Agriculture). Aircrew, RAAF, 1940-45. Pres., Milk Producers' Assoc., 1947-50; Farmers' Union of WA: Executive, 1962-67; Pres., Milk Sect., 1965-70; Vice-Pres., 1969-72; Gen. Pres., 1972-75; Pres., Australian Farmers' Fedn, 1975-79; Austr. Rep., Internat. Fedn of Agric., 1979-81. Pres., Harvey Shire Council, 1970-79; Dir, Chamberlain John Deere. Chairman: Leschenault Inlet Authority, 1977-81; Artificial Breeding Bd of WA, 1981-; Member: WA Waterways Commn, 1977-81; Nat. Energy Adv. Cttee, 1979-81; Senate, Univ. of WA, 1981-. Mem., Harvey Rotary Club. WA Citizen of Year award, 1976; Man of Year, Austr. Agriculture, 1979. *Publication:* (contrib.) Farm Focus: the '80s, 1981. *Recreations:* golf, fishing. *Address:* Korijedale, Harvey, WA 6220, Australia. *T:* 097-291472. *Clubs:* Weld (Perth); Harvey Golf.

ECKERSLEY, Thomas, OBE 1948; RDI 1963; AGI; graphic designer; Head of Department of Design, London College of Printing, 1958-76; *b* Sept. 1914; *s* of John Eckersley and Eunice Hilton; *m* Daisy Eckersley; three *s*; *m* 1966, Mary Kessell, painter. *Educ:* Salford Sch. of Art. Free-lance Graphic Designer for London Transport, Shell Mex, BBC, GPO, MOI, Unicef, CoID and other leading concerns since 1936. Work exhibited in Sweden, USA, Paris, Hamburg, Lausanne, Milan, Amsterdam; permanent collection of work in V&A Museum, Imperial War Museum and Nat. Gall. of Australia. One-man exhibitions: Soc. of Artists and Designers, 1976; Camden Arts Centre, British Arts Centre, Yale, 1980; Peel Park Gall., Salford, Edinburgh, 1981. Mem. of Alliance Graphique Internationale; Hon. Fellow, Manchester Coll. of Art and Design; FSTD. *Publications:* contribs to Graphis, Gebrauchsgraphik, Form und Technik, Art and Industry, Print Design and Production, Penrose Annual. *Recreation:* cricket. *Address:* 53 Belsize Park Gardens, NW3. *T:* 01-586 3586.

ECKERSLEY-MASLIN, Rear Adm. David Michael; Assistant Chief of Defence Staff (CIS), since 1982; *b* Karachi, 27 Sept. 1929; *e s* of Comdr E. Eckersley-Maslin, OBE, RN, Hillwood, Tasmania, and Mrs L. M. Lightfoot, Bedford; *m* 1955, Shirley Ann, *d* of Captain and Mrs H. A. Martin; one *s* one *d*. *Educ:* Britannia Royal Naval Coll. Qual. Navigation Direction Officer, 1954; rcds 1977. Far East Malayan Campaign, 1950-53; Australian Navy, 1954-56; BRNC Dartmouth, 1959-61; commanded HM Ships Eastbourne, Euryalus, Fife and Blake, 1966-76; Captain RN Presentation Team, 1974; Dir, Naval Operational Requirements, 1977-80; Flag Officer Sea Training, 1980-82. Naval Gen. Service Decoration, Palestine, 1948, and Malaya, 1951. *Recreations:* tennis, squash, cricket. *Address:* Dunningwell, Hall Court, Shedfield, near Southampton SO3 2HL. *T:* Wickham 832350. *Clubs:* MCC, Royal Commonwealth Society.

EDDEN, Alan John, CMG 1957; HM Diplomatic Service, retired; *b* 2 Dec. 1912; *s* of late Thomas Frederick Edden and Nellie Shipway; *m* 1939, Pauline Klay; one *s*. *Educ:* Latymer Sch., Edmonton; Gonville and Caius Coll., Cambridge (Exhibitioner). Served at HM Legation, Bangkok, 1935; Batavia, 1938; Foreign Office, 1939; HM Legation, Bangkok, 1940; HM Legation, Tehran, 1942; Kermanshah, 1944; with SHAEF, May 1945; Actg Consul-Gen. Amsterdam, June 1945; Foreign Office, Oct. 1945; HM Embassy, Warsaw, 1948; Brit. Information Services, New York, 1951; FO, 1953; Counsellor, Foreign Office, 1954-58; Counsellor, HM Embassy, Beirut, 1958-62; HM

Consul-Gen., Durban, 1962-66; HM Ambassador to: Cameroon, Central African Republic, Gabon and Chad, 1966-70; Equatorial Guinea, 1969-70; Lebanon, 1970-71. *Recreation:* music. *Address:* 77 Hosking Road, Pietermaritzburg, South Africa. *Club:* Victoria (Pietermaritzburg).

EDDEN, Vice-Adm. Sir (William) Kaye, KBE 1960 (OBE 1944); CB 1956; DL; *b* 27 Feb. 1905; *s* of late Major H. W. Edden, The Cameronians, and late Mrs H. W. Edden (*née* Neilson); *m* 1936, Isobel Sybil Pitman (*d* 1970), Bath, *g d* of Sir Isaac Pitman; one *s*. *Educ:* Royal Naval Colls, Osborne and Dartmouth. Comdr, 1938; Admiralty, 1938-40; served War of 1939-45: HMS London, 1941-42; Staff C-in-C, Eastern Fleet, 1942-44 (OBE); Capt. 1944, Admty, 1944-47; RNAS Yeovilton, 1947-49; Capt. (D) 6th Destroyer Sqdn, and HMS Battleaxe, 1949-51; Admiralty, 1951-53; Rear-Adm. 1954; Commandant, Jt-Services Staff Coll., Latimer, 1953-56; Flag Officer Commanding Fifth Cruiser Sqdn and Flag Officer Second-in-Command, Far East Station, 1956-57; Vice-Adm. 1957; Admiral Commanding Reserves, 1958-60, retd 1960. DL West Sussex, 1977. *Address:* Littlecroft, Old Bosham, West Sussex PO18 8LR. *T:* Bosham 573119. *Clubs:* Army and Navy; Royal Naval Sailing Association; Bosham Sailing.

EDDERY, Patrick James John; jockey (retained by M. V. O'Brien and J. Tree); *b* 18 March 1952; *s* of Jimmy and Josephine Eddery; *m* 1978, Carolyn Jane (*née* Mercer). Rode for Peter Walwyn, 1972-80; Champion Jockey, 1974, 1975, 1976, 1977; won the Oaks, 1974, 1979, the Derby, on Grundy, 1975; Prix de l'Arc de Triomphe, 1980. *Recreations:* swimming, golf, snooker. *Address:* Musk Hill Farm, Lower Winchendon, Aylesbury, Bucks HP18 0DT. *T:* Haddenham 290282. *Club:* The Subscription Rooms (Newmarket).

EDDEY, Prof. Howard Hadfield, CMG 1974; FRCS, FRACS, FACS; Foundation Professor of Surgery, University of Melbourne, at Austin Hospital and Repatriation General Hospital, 1967-75, now Emeritus; also Dean of Austin Hospital and Repatriation General Hospital Clinical School, 1971-75; *b* Melbourne, 3 Sept. 1910; *s* of Charles Howard and Rachel Beatrice Eddey; *m* 1940, Alice Paul; two *s* one *d*. *Educ:* Melbourne Univ.; St Bartholomew's Hosp. Med. Sch. BSc, MB BS, 1934; FRCS 1938; FRACS 1941; FACS 1964; Hallet Prize of RCS of Eng., 1938. Served War, 1941-45: AAMC, Major and Surgical Specialist; served in PoW camps: Changi (Singapore); Sandakan and Kuching (Borneo). Hon. Surgeon, Royal Melbourne Hosp., 1947-67; Cons. Surg., 1967, Royal Melbourne and Royal Women's Hosps; Peter MacCallum Clinic. Mem. AMA, 1935; Mem., Faculty of Med., Univ. of Melbourne, 1950-75 (Mem. Convocation, 1965-67); Indep. Lectr in Surgical Anatomy, Univ. of Melb., 1950-65; Dean, Royal Melb. Hosp. Clin. Sch., 1965-67; Colombo Plan Visitor to India, 1960-65; Cons. in Surg., Papuan Med. Coll., 1965-68; Mem. Cancer Inst. Bd, 1958-67; Mem. Med. and Sci. Cttee, Anti-Cancer Council of Vic., 1958-67; Chm., Melb. Med. Postgrad. Cttee, 1963-71; Vice-Pres., Aust. Postgrad. Fedn in Med., 1965-71 (Life Governor, 1972). Mem. Council, RACS, 1967-75 (Mem. Bd of Examrs, 1958-75, Chm. Bd, 1968-73; Hon. Librarian, 1968-75). Mem. Med. Bd of Vic., 1968-77; Mem. Austin Hosp. Bd of Management, 1971-77 (Vice-Pres., 1975-77; Life Governor, 1977). Hunterian Prof., RCS, 1960; Vis. Prof. of Surg., 1962, External Examr in Surg., 1970, Univ. of Singapore; Leverhulme Fellow, Univ. of Melb., 1974; Vis. Prof. of Surg., Univ. of Hong Kong, 1974. Howard Eddey Medal, named in 1972 by RACS and awarded to most successful cand., Part I exam (surgery) for FRACS in SE Asia, in recognition of dist. service to RACS. Hon. Surgeon to HRH Prince Charles on his visit to Victoria, 1974. Melbourne and Australian Universities Lacrosse Blue. *Publications:* many, in sci. jls, particularly in relation to diseases of salivary glands and cancer of mouth. *Recreations:* travel, gardening. *Address:* c/o National Bank of Australasia, Melbourne Office, Melbourne, Australia. *Clubs:* Naval and Military (Melbourne), Melbourne Cricket.

EDDINGTON, Paul (Clark); actor; *b* 1 June 1927; *s* of Albert Clark Eddington and Frances Mary (*née* Roberts); *m* 1952, Patricia Scott; three *s* one *d*. *Educ:* Holy Child Convent, Cavendish Sq., W1; Friends (Quaker) Sch., Sibford Ferris, Banbury, Oxon; RADA. First appearance on stage with ENSA, 1944; joined Birmingham Repertory Th., 1945; has played with several other rep. theatres during subseq. 30 years; first appearance in West End in The 10th Man, Comedy Th., 1961; first (and only, so far) appearance in New York in A Severed Head, 1964; joined National Theatre to play in revival of Who's Afraid of Virginia Woolf?, 1981; Noises Off, Savoy, 1982. Many TV appearances, including series, The Good Life and Yes Minister. Mem. Council, Equity, 1972-75; Governor, Bristol Old Vic Theatre Trust, 1975-. *Recreations:* listening to music, reading, washing up. *Address:* c/o ICM Ltd, 22 Grafton Street, W1. *T:* 01-629 8080. *Club:* Garrick.

EDDISON, Rear-Adm. Talbot Leadam, CB 1961; DSC 1945; *b* 10 June 1908; *e s* (yr twin) of late Edwin and Mrs Eddison (*née* Leadam); *m* 1932, Doris (*née* Mavrogordato); one *s* one *d*. *Educ:* Royal Naval Coll., Dartmouth. Entered Dartmouth 1922. Commodore, Royal Naval Barracks, Devonport, 1958-59; Rear-Adm. 1959; served as Vice-Naval Dep. to Supreme Allied Comdr Europe, 1959-62; retired, 1962. *Address:* 4 Halton Close, Bransgore, Christchurch, Dorset BH23 8HZ. *T:* Bransgore 72593. *Club:* Royal Commonwealth Society.

EDDLEMAN, Gen. Clyde Davis; DSM with oak leaf cluster (US); Silver Star; Legion of Merit; Bronze Star; Philippines Distinguished Service Star; Vice-Chief of Staff, US Army, 1960-62; *b* 17 Jan. 1902; *s* of Rev. W. H. Eddleman and Janie Eddleman (*née* Tureman); *m* 1926, Lorraine Heath; one

s (and one *s* decd). *Educ:* US Military Academy, West Point, New York. Commissioned 2nd Lieut of Infantry upon graduation from US Military Academy, 1924. Advanced, through the ranks, and reached grade of Gen. 1959. Comdr, Central Army Group (NATO), and C-in-C, US Army, Europe, at Heidelberg, Germany, 1959-60. Knight Commander's Cross, Order of Merit (Germany); Kt Grand Cross of the Sword (Sweden). *Recreations:* hunting, fishing. *Address:* 1101 S Arlington Ridge Road 802, Arlington, Va 22202, USA.

EDDY, Prof. Alfred Alan; Professor of Biochemistry, University of Manchester Institute of Science and Technology since 1959; *b* 4 Nov. 1926; Cornish parentage; *s* of late Alfred and Ellen Eddy; *m* 1954, Susan Ruth Slade-Jones; two *s*. *Educ:* Devonport High Sch.; Open scholarship Exeter Coll., Oxford, 1944; BA 1st Class Hons, 1949. ICI Research Fellow, 1950; DPhil 1951. Joined Brewing Industry Research Foundation, Nutfield, 1953. *Publications:* various scientific papers. *Address:* Larchfield, Buxton Road, Disley, Cheshire.

EDE, Jeffery Raymond, CB 1978; Keeper of Public Records, 1970-78; *b* 10 March 1918; *e s* of late Richard Arthur Ede; *m* 1944, Mercy, *d* of Arthur Radford Sholl; one *s* one *d*. *Educ:* Plymouth Coll.; King's Coll., Cambridge (MA). Served War of 1939-45, Intell. Corps (despatches); GSO2 HQ 8 Corps District, BAOR, 1945-46. Asst Keeper, Public Record Office, 1947-59; Principal Asst Keeper, 1959-66; Dep. Keeper, 1966-69. Lectr in Archive Admin., Sch. of Librarianship and Archives, University Coll., London, 1956-61; Unesco expert in Tanzania, 1963-64. Chm., British Acad. Cttee on Oriental Documents, 1972-78; Vice Pres., Internat. Council on Archives, 1976-78. Pres., Soc. of Archivists, 1974-77. FRHistS 1969. Hon. Mem., L'Institut Grand-Ducal de Luxembourg, 1977. Freeman: Goldsmiths' Company, 1979; City of London, 1979. *Publications:* Guide to the Contents of the Public Record Office, Vol. II (major contributor), 1963; articles in archival and other professional jls. *Recreations:* theatre, countryside. *Address:* Palfreys, East Street, Drayton, Langport, Som TA10 0JZ. *T:* Langport 251314.

EDEL, (Joseph) Leon; Citizens Professor of English, University of Hawaii, 1970-78, now Emeritus; *b* 9 Sept. 1907; *e s* of Simon Edel and Fanny (*née* Malamud), Pittsburgh, Pa; *m* 1st, 1935, Bertha Cohen (marr. diss. 1950); 2nd, 1950, Roberta Roberts (marr. diss. 1979); 3rd, 1980, Marjorie Sinclair; no *c*. *Educ:* McGill Univ., Montreal (BA 1927, MA 1928); Univ. of Paris (Docteur-ès-Lettres 1932). Served with US Army in France and Germany, 1943-47: Bronze Star Medal (US), 1945; Chief of Information Control, News Agency, US Zone, 1946-47. Asst Prof., Sir George Williams Coll., Montreal, 1932-34; miscellaneous writing and journalism, 1934-43; Christian Gauss Seminar in Criticism, Princeton Univ., 1951-52; New York University: Vis. Prof., 1952-53; Associate Prof., 1953-55; Prof. of English, 1955-66; Henry James Prof. of English and American Letters, 1966-72. Guggenheim Fellow, 1936-38, 1965-66; Alexander Lectures, Toronto, 1956; Vis. Professor: Indiana, 1954; Hawaii, 1955, 1969, 1970; Harvard, 1959-60; Purdue, 1970; Centenary Vis. Prof., Toronto, 1967; Vernon Vis. Prof. in Biography, Dartmouth, 1977. Pres., US Center of PEN, 1957-59. Pres., Hawaii Literary Arts Council, 1978-79. Fellow, Amer. Acad. of Arts and Sciences, 1959; Bollingen Fellow, 1959-61. Member: Nat. Inst. of Arts and Letters, 1964- (Sec., 1965-67); Amer. Acad. of Arts and Letters, 1972; Council, Authors' Guild, 1965-68 (Pres., 1969-70). FRSL 1970. Hon. Member: W. A. White Psychiatric Inst., 1966; Amer. Acad. Psychoanalysis, 1975. Hon. DLitt: McGill, 1963; Union Coll., Schenectady, 1963. Nat. Inst. of Arts and Letters Award, 1959; US Nat. Book Award for non-fiction, 1963; Pulitzer Prize for biography, 1963; AAAL Gold Medal for biography, 1976; Hawaii Literary Arts Award, 1978; Nat. Arts Club Medal for Literature, 1981. *Publications:* James Joyce: The Last Journey, 1947; (ed) The Complete Plays of Henry James, 1949; (with E. K. Brown) Willa Cather, 1953; The Life of Henry James: The Untried Years, 1953, The Conquest of London, 1962, The Middle Years, 1963, The Treacherous Years, 1969, The Master, 1972, rev. edn in 2 vols, 1978; The Psychological Novel, 1955; (ed) Selected Letters of Henry James, 1956; Literary Biography, 1957; (ed) The Complete Tales of Henry James, 12 vols, 1962-65; (ed) The Diary of Alice James, 1964; (ed) Literary History and Literary Criticism, 1965; Thoreau, 1970; (ed) Henry James: Stories of the Supernatural, 1971; (ed) Harold Goddard Alphabet of the Imagination, 1975; (ed) Henry James Letters: vol. I, 1843-1875, 1975; vol. II, 1875-1883, 1980; vol. III, 1883-1895, 1981; (ed) Edmund Wilson: The Twenties, 1975; Bloomsbury: A House of Lions, 1979; (ed) Edmund Wilson: The Thirties, 1980. *Recreations:* music, swimming. *Address:* c/o William Morris Agency, 1350 Avenue of the Americas, New York 10019, USA. *Clubs:* Athenæum; Century (New York).

EDELL, Stephen Bristow; Law Commissioner since 1975; *b* 1 Dec. 1932; *s* of late Ivan James Edell and late Hilda Pamela Edell; *m* 1958, Shirley Ross Collins; two *s* one *d*. *Educ:* St Andrew's Sch., Eastbourne; Uppingham. LLB London. Legal Mem., RTPI. Commnd RA, 1951. Articled to father, 1953; qual. Solicitor 1958; Partner, Knapp-Fishers (Westminster), 1959-75. Mem. Cttee, 1973-, and a Vice-Pres., 1980-, City of Westminster Law Soc. Makers of Playing Cards' Company: Liveryman, 1955-; Mem., Ct of Assts, 1978-; Sen. Warden, 1980-81; Master, 1981-82. *Publications:* Inside Information on the Family and the Law, 1969; The Family's Guide to the Law, 1974. *Recreations:* family life; music, opera, theatre; early astronomical instruments; avoiding gardening; interested in problems of developing countries. *Address:* The Old

Farmhouse, Twineham, Haywards Heath, Sussex. *T:* Hurstpierpoint 832058.

EDELMAN, Prof. Gerald Maurice, MD, PhD; Vincent Astor Distinguished Professor of Biochemistry, The Rockefeller University, New York, since 1974; *b* NYC, 1 July 1929; *s* of Edward Edelman and Anna Freedman; *m* 1950, Maxine Morrison; two *s* one *d. Educ:* Ursinus Coll. (BS); University of Pennsylvania (MD); The Rockefeller University (PhD). Med. Hse Officer, Massachusetts Gen. Hosp., 1954–55; Asst Physician, Hosp. of The Rockefeller Univ., 1957–60; The Rockefeller University: Asst Prof. and Asst Dean of Grad. Studies, 1960–63; Associate Prof. and Associate Dean of Grad. Studies, 1963–66; Prof., 1966–74. Trustee, Rockefeller Brothers Fund, 1972–, Associate, Neurosciences Res. Program, 1965– (Scientific Chm., 1980; Dir, Neurosciences Inst., 1981). Mem., Adv. Bd, Basel Inst. Immunology, 1970–77 (Chm., 1975–77); Chm., Bd Governors, Weizmann Inst. of Science, 1971–; non-resident Fellow and Mem. Bd Trustees, Salk Inst. for Biol. Studies; Member: Biophysics and Biophys. Chem. Study Section, Nat. Insts of Health, 1964–67; Sci. Council, Center for Theoretical Studies, 1970–72; Bd of Overseers, Faculty Arts and Scis, Univ. of Pa; Board of Trustees, Carnegie Inst. of Washington (Mem., Adv. Cttee). Member: Nat. Acad. Scis; Amer. Acad. Arts Scis; Amer. Philosophical Soc., 1977; Fellow, NY Acad. Scis; Member: Amer. Soc. Biol Chemists; Amer. Assoc. Immunologists; Genetics Soc. of America; Harvey Soc. (Pres., 1975–76); Amer. Chem. Soc.; Amer. Soc. Cell Biol.; Soc. for Developmental Biol.; Sigma XI; Alpha Omega Alpha; Amer. Assoc. for the Advancement of Sci.; Council of Foreign Relations. Hon. Member: Pharmaceutical Soc. of Japan; Japanese Biochem. Soc.; Foreign Mem., Academie des Sciences, Institut de France. Spencer Morris Award, Univ. of Pennsylvania, 1954; Eli Lilly Award in Biol Chem., Amer. Chem. Soc., 1965; Annual Alumni Award, Ursinus College, 1969; (jtly) Nobel Prize in Physiology or Medicine, 1972; Albert Einstein Commemorative Award, Yeshiva Univ., 1974; Buchman Meml Award, Caltech, 1975; Rabbi Shai Shacknai Meml Prize in Immunology and Cancer Res., Hebrew Univ. Hadassah Med. Sch., 1977. Hon. DSc: Pennsylvania, 1973; Gustavus Adolphus Coll., Minn., 1975; Hon. ScD: Ursinus Coll., 1974; Williams Coll., 1976; Hon. MD Univ. Siena, Italy, 1974. *Recreation:* music. *Address:* Department of Developmental and Molecular Biology, The Rockefeller University, 1230 York Avenue, New York, NY 10021, USA.

EDEN, family name of **Earl of Avon** and of **Barons Auckland** and **Henley.**

EDEN, Conrad W., TD; DMus Lambeth 1973; BMus Oxon; Hon. FRCO; retired 1974; *m* 1943, Barbara L., *d* of late Rev. R. L. Jones, Shepton Mallet. *Educ:* Wells Cath. Sch.; Rugby; RCM; St John's Coll., Oxford. Organist, Wells Cathedral, 1933–36; Durham Cathedral, 1936–74. *Address:* The Vale, Highmore Road, Sherborne, Dorset. *T:* Sherborne 3488.

EDEN, Edward Norman, CB 1980; Consultant; Under Secretary, Metrology, Quality Assurance, Safety and Standards Division, Department of Trade, retired 1982; *b* 5 Nov. 1921; *o s* of late Edward Eden and late Eva Eunice Eden; *m* 1st, 1967, Madge Nina Savory (*d* 1969); 2nd, 1974, Norma Veronica Berringer. *Educ:* Bancroft's Sch.; University Coll. London (BSc(Eng), PhD). Served RN, 1941–46. Senior Scientific Officer, Min. of Fuel and Power, 1953, Senior Principal Scientific Officer 1965, DCSO 1967–71; Head, Fuel Policy Planning Unit, Min. of Technology, later DTI, 1969–71; Under Sec., Metrology, Quality Assurance, Safety and Standards Div., DTI, later Dept of Prices and Consumer Protection, later Dept of Trade, 1971–81. Chm., Working Party on Metrological Control Systems. *Publications:* Report, Metrological Control Systems, 1977; articles in learned jls. *Recreations:* walking, bird watching, odd-jobbing. *Address:* 13 Allison Grove, Dulwich, SE21 7ER. *T:* 01-693 7267.

EDEN, Rt. Hon. Sir John (Benedict), 9th Bt *cr* 1672 and 7th Bt *cr* 1776; PC 1972; MP (C) Bournemouth West since Feb. 1954; Director: Chesham Amalgamations & Investments; Central & Sheerwood Ltd; Associated Book Publishers Ltd; Lady Eden's Schools Ltd; *b* 15 Sept. 1925; *s* of Sir Timothy Calvert Eden, 8th and 6th Bt and Patricia, *d* of Arthur Prendergast; *S* father, 1963; *m* 1st, 1958, Belinda Jane (marr. diss. 1974), *o d* of late Sir John Pascoe; two *s* two *d* ; 2nd, 1977, Margaret Ann, Viscountess Strathallan. Lieut Rifle Bde, seconded to 2nd KEO Goorkha Rifles and Gilgit Scouts, 1943–47. Contested (C) Paddington North, 1953. Mem. House of Commons Select Cttee on Estimates, 1962–64; Vice-Chm., Conservative Parly Defence Cttee, 1963–66; Chm., Defence Air Sub-Cttee; Hon. Sec., Space Sub-Cttee; Vice-Chm., Aviation Cttee, 1963–64; Additional Opposition Front Bench Spokesman for Defence, 1964–66; Jt Vice-Chm., Cons. Parly Trade and Power Cttee, 1966–68; Opposition Front Bench Spokesman for Power, 1968–70; Minister of State, Min. of Technology, June-Oct. 1970; Minister for Industry, DTI, 1970–72; Minister of Posts and Telecommunications, 1972–74; Mem., Expenditure Cttee, 1974–76; Chairman: House of Commons Select Cttee on European Legislation, 1976–79; Home Affairs Cttee, 1981–. Vice-Chm., Assoc. of Conservative Clubs Ltd, 1964–67, Vice-Pres., 1970–; President: Wessex Area Council, Nat. Union of Conservative and Unionist Assocs, 1974–77; Wessex Area Young Conservatives, 1978–80. UK Deleg. to Council of Europe and to Western European Union, 1960–62; Mem., NATO Parliamentarians' Conf., 1962–66. Pres., Independent Schs Assoc., 1969–71; a Vice-Pres., Nat. Chamber of Trade, 1974–. Hon. Vice-Pres., Nat. Assoc. of Master Bakers, Confectioners & Caterers, 1978–82. *Heir: s* Robert Frederick

Calvert Eden, *b* 30 April 1964. *Address:* 41 Victoria Road, W8; Knoyle Place, East Knoyle, Salisbury, Wilts. *Clubs:* Boodle's, Pratt's, Royal Automobile.

EDEN, Dr Richard John, OBE 1978; Reader in Theoretical Physics, since 1964, and Head of Energy Research Group, since 1974, Cavendish Laboratory, University of Cambridge; Fellow of Clare Hall, Cambridge, since 1966; *b* 2 July 1922; *s* of James A. Eden and Dora M. Eden; *m* 1949, Elsie Jane Greaves; one *s* one *d* and one step *d. Educ:* Hertford Grammar Sch.; Peterhouse, Cambridge. BA 1943, MA 1948, PhD 1951. War service, 1942–46, Captain REME, Airborne Forces. Cambridge Univ.: Bye-Fellow, Peterhouse, 1949–50; Stokes Student, Pembroke Coll., 1950–51; Clare Coll.: Research Fellow, 1951–55; Official Fellow, 1957–66; Dir of Studies in Maths, 1951-53, 1957-62; Royal Soc. Smithson Res. Fellow, 1952-55; Mem., Princeton Inst. for Advanced Study, 1954, 1959, 1973; Sen. Lectr in Physics, Univ. of Manchester, 1955-57; Lectr in Maths, Univ. of Cambridge, 1957-64 (Stokes Lectr, 1962); Head of High Energy Theoretical Physics Gp, Cavendish Lab., Cambridge, 1964–74; Vis. Scientist: Indiana Univ., 1954-55; Univ. of California, Berkeley, 1960, 1967; Vis. Professor: Univ. of Maryland, 1961, 1965; Columbia Univ., 1962; Scuola Normale Superiore, Pisa, 1964; Univ. of Marseilles, 1968; Univ. of California, 1969. Mem., UK Adv. Council on Energy Conservation, 1974–; Energy Adviser to UK NEDO, 1974–. Smiths Prize, Univ. of Cambridge, 1949; Maxwell Prize and Medal, Inst. of Physics, 1970. *Publications:* (jtly) The Analytic S Matrix, 1966; High Energy Collisions of Elementary Particles, 1967; Energy Conservation in the United Kingdom (NEDO report), 1975; Energy Prospects (Dept of Energy report), 1976; World Energy Demand to 2020 (World Energy Conf. report), 1977; (jtly) Energy Economics, 1981; papers and review articles on nuclear physics and theory of elementary particles. *Recreations:* painting, reading, gardening, travel. *Address:* Cavendish Laboratory, Cambridge. *T:* Cambridge 66477; 6 Wootton Way, Cambridge. *T:* Cambridge 355591.

EDES, (John) Michael, CMG 1981; HM Diplomatic Service; Ambassador to Libya, since 1980; *b* 19 April 1930; *s* of late Lt-Col N. H. Edes and Mrs Louise Edes; *m* 1978, Angela Mermagen; one *s. Educ:* Blundell's Sch.; Clare Coll., Cambridge (Scholar; BA); Yale Univ. (MA). HM Forces, 1948-49; Mellon Fellow, Yale Univ., 1952-54; FO, 1954; MECAS, 1955; Dubai, 1956-57; FO, 1957-59 (Moscow, 1959); Rome, 1959-61; FO, 1961-62; UK Deleg to Conf. on Disarmament, Geneva, 1962-65 (UK Mission to UN, NY, 1963); FO, 1965-68; Cabinet Office, 1968-69; FCO, 1969-71; Ambassador to Yemen Arab Republic, 1971-73; Mem., UK Deleg to CSCE, Geneva, 1973-74; FCO, 1974-77; RIIA, 1977-78; Paris, 1978-79. *Recreations:* listening to music, gardening. *Address:* c/o Foreign and Commonwealth Office, SW1. *Clubs:* Athenæum; Hawks (Cambridge).

EDEY, Prof. Harold Cecil, BCom (London), FCA; Professor of Accounting, London School of Economics, University of London, 1962-80, now Emeritus; *b* 23 Feb. 1913; *s* of Cecil Edey and Elsie (*née* Walmsley); *m* 1944, Dilys Mary Pakeman Jones; one *s* one *d. Educ:* Croydon High Sch. for Boys; LSE. Chartered Accountant, 1935. Commnd in RNVR, 1940-46. Lectr in Accounting and Finance, LSE, 1949-55; Reader in Accounting, Univ. of London, 1955-62; Pro-Dir, LSE, 1967-70. Mem., UK Adv. Coun. on Educn for Management, 1961-65; Mem., Academic Planning Bd for London Grad. Sch. of Business Studies, and Governor, 1965-71; Chm., Arts and Social Studies Cttee, CNAA, 1965-71, and Mem. Council, 1965-73; Chm., Bd of Studies in Econs, 1966-71, Mem. Senate, 1975-80, University of London; Mem. Council, Inst. of Chartered Accountants in England and Wales, 1969-80. Hon. Freeman, Co. of Chartered Accountants in England and Wales, 1981. Hon. Professorial Fellow, UCW, Aberystwyth, 1980-. Hon. LLD CNAA, 1972. *Publications:* (with A. T. Peacock) National Income and Social Accounting, 1954; Business Budgets and Accounts, 1959; Introduction to Accounting, 1963; (with B. S. Yamey and H. Thomson) Accounting in England and Scotland 1543-1800, 1963; (with B. V. Carsberg) Modern Financial Management, 1969; (with B. S. Yamey) Debits, Credits, Finance and Profits, 1974; (with L. H. Leigh) The Companies Act 1981, 1981; articles in various jls. *Address:* 10 The Green, Southwick, Brighton BN4 4DA.

EDGCUMBE, family name of **Earl of Mount Edgcumbe.**

EDGE, Geoffrey; Senior Research Fellow, North East London Polytechnic, since 1982; *b* 26 May 1943; single. *Educ:* London Sch. of Econs (BA); Birmingham Univ. Asst Lectr in Geography, Univ. of Leicester, 1967-70; Lectr in Geog., Open Univ., 1970-74. Bletchley UDC, 1972-74 (Chm. Planning Sub-cttee 1973-74); Milton Keynes District Councillor, 1973-76 (Vice-Chm. Planning Cttee, 1973-75); Mem. Bucks Water Bd, 1973-74. MP (Lab) Aldridge-Brownhills, Feb. 1974-1979; PPS to Minister of State for Educn, Feb.-Oct. 1974, 1976-79, to Minister of State, Privy Council Office, Oct. 1974-76. Research Fellow, Dept of Planning Landscape, Birmingham Polytechnic, 1979-80; Sen. Res. Fellow, Preston Polytechnic, 1980-81. Hon Res. Fellow, Birmingham Polytechnic, 1980-81. Chm., W Midlands Enterprise Bd; Mem., W Midlands CC, 1981- (Chm., Econ. Develt Cttee). *Publications:* (ed jtly) Regional Analysis and Development, 1973; Open Univ. booklets on industrial location and urban development. *Recreations:* music, reading, touring. *Address:* 18 Harringworth Court, Lichfield Road, Shelfield, Walsall, W Midlands; 31 Dudley Road West, Tividale, Warley, Worcs. *T:* 021-557 3858. *Clubs:* Castle, Walsall Wood Labour (Walsall).

EDGE, Sir Knowles, 2nd Bt *cr* 1937; JP; *b* 31 Dec. 1905; *s* of Capt. Sir William Edge, 1st Bt, and Ada (*d* 1973), *d* of I. Ickringill, Keighley; *S* father, 1948;

m 1932, Dorothea Eunice (*d* 1976) *y d* of Robert Walker, Newhaven, Conn, USA; two *s. Educ:* Bolton Sch.; Trinity Hall, Cambridge. Formerly Chm. and Man. Dir William Edge & Sons Ltd and assoc. cos. Contested Hillsborough Div. of Sheffield, 1950. Mem. of Bolton Town Council, 1931-58. Chm., British Federation of Music Festivals, 1951-76. Mem. Cttee of Management, Royal National Lifeboat Institution. JP Lancs 1955. *Recreation:* yacht cruising. *Heir: s* William Edge [*b* 5 Oct. 1936; *m* 1959, Avril Elizabeth Denson; two *s* two *d*]. *Address:* Fair Lawn, Fair Lawn Road, Lytham, Lancs. *Club:* Athenæum.

EDGE, Maj.-Gen. Raymond Cyril Alexander, CB 1968; MBE 1945; FRICS 1949; Director General, Ordnance Survey, 1965-69, retired; *b* 21 July 1912; *s* of Raymond Clive Edge and Mary (*née* Masters); *m* 1939, Margaret Patricia (*d* 1982), *d* of William Wallace McKee, Tyrone, N Ireland; one *s* one *d. Educ:* Cheltenham Coll.; RMA; Caius Coll., Cambridge (BA). Commissioned in RE, 1932. Served in India, Royal Bombay Sappers and Miners and Survey of India, 1936-39. War Service in India, Burma (despatches), and Malaya. Lt-Col 1951; Col 1954; Dir (Brig.) Ordnance Survey, 1961; Maj.-Gen. 1965. Col Comdt, RE, 1970-75 (Representative Col Comdt, 1974). Mem., Sec. of State for the Environment's Panel of Independent Inspectors, 1971-. Chairman: Assoc. British Geodesists, 1963-65; Geodesy Sub-Ctte Royal Soc., 1968-75; Field Survey Assoc., 1968-70. Pres., Section E, British Assoc., 1969. Member: Council, RGS, 1966-69; Council, RICS, 1966-72 (Vice-Pres. 1970-72); Land Surveyors Council (Chm. 1970-72). *Publications:* contrib. A History of the Ordnance Survey, 1980; various papers on geodetic subjects in Bulletin Géodesique and other publications. *Recreation:* music. *Address:* Greenway House, North Curry, near Taunton, Som. *T:* North Curry 490358.

EDGEWORTH-JOHNSTONE, Maj.-Gen. Ralph, CBE 1947; *b* 23 Nov. 1893; *s* of Ralph William Johnstone; *m* 1933, Cecily Margaret Thorp. *Educ:* France and Germany. Enlisted Fort Garry Horse, 1914; served European War, 1914-18 (wounded twice); commissioned Royal North'd Fusiliers, 1915. Retired, 1938, to join Public Relations Directorate War Office; Asst Dir, Lieut-Col, 1940; Dep. Dir, Brig., 1944; Dir, Maj.-Gen., 1946-52. *Address:* c/o Lloyds Bank, 6 Pall Mall, SW1.

EDGEWORTH JOHNSTONE, Prof. Robert; *see* Johnston.

EDIE, Thomas Ker; His Honour Judge Edie; a Circuit Judge, South Eastern Circuit, since 1972; *b* 3 Oct. 1916; *s* of H. S. Ker Edie, Kinloss, Morayshire; *m* 1945, Margaret, *d* of Rev. A. E. Shooter, TD; four *s* one *d. Educ:* Clifton; London Univ. Called to Bar, Gray's Inn, 1941. Metropolitan Magistrate, 1961-70; Dep. Chm. Middlesex QS, 1970-71. *Address:* Worfield Lodge, Pennington Road, Southborough, Kent.

EDINBURGH, Bishop of, since 1975; **Most Rev. Alastair Iain Macdonald Haggart;** Primus of the Episcopal Church in Scotland, since 1977; *b* 10 Oct. 1915; *s* of Alexander Macdonald Haggart and Jessie Mackay; *m* 1945, Margaret Agnes Trundle (*d* 1979); two *d. Educ:* Hatfield Coll. (Exhibnr); Durham Univ. (Exhibnr); Edinburgh Theol College. LTh 1941; BA 1942; MA 1945. Deacon, 1941, Priest 1942. Curate: St Mary's Cath., Glasgow, 1941-45; St Mary's, Hendon, 1945-48; Precentor, St Ninian's Cath., Perth, 1948-51; Rector, St Oswald's, King's Park, Glasgow, 1951, and Acting Priest-in-Charge, St Martin's, Glasgow, 1953-58; Synod Clerk of Glasgow Dio. and Canon of St Mary's Cath., Glasgow, 1958-59; Provost, St Paul's Cathedral, Dundee, 1959-71; Principal and Pantonian Prof., Episcopal Theological Coll., Edinburgh, 1971-75; Canon, St Mary's Cathedral, Edinburgh, 1971-75. Exam. Chap. to Bp of Brechin, 1964. Hon LLD Dundee, 1970. *Recreations:* walking, reading, listening to music, asking questions. *Address:* 19 Eglinton Crescent, Edinburgh EH12 5BY. *T:* 031-337 8948.

EDINBURGH, Provost of (St Mary's Cathedral); *see* Crosfield, Very Rev. G. P. C.

EDMENSON, Sir Walter Alexander, Kt 1958; CBE 1944; DL; shipowner; *b* 1892; 2nd *s* of late Robert Robson Edmenson; *m* 1918, Doris Davidson (*d* 1975); one *d* (and one *s* killed in action, 1940). Served European War, 1914-18, RFA (despatches). Min. of War Transport Rep., N Ireland, 1939-45. President: The Ulster Steamship Co. Ltd; G. Heyn & Sons Ltd; Clyde Shipping Co.; Director: The Belfast Banking Co. Ltd, 1946-70; The North Continental Shipping Co. Ltd, 1946-70; The Belfast Bank Executor & Trustee Co. Ltd, 1946-70; Commercial Insurance Co. of Ireland Ltd, 1964-72; Member Board: BEA, 1946-63; Gallaher Ltd, 1946-66. Chm., N Ireland Civil Aviation Adv. Council, 1946-61; Member: Bd, Ulster Transport Authority, 1948-64; Council, Chamber of Shipping, 1943-73; Lloyd's Register of Shipping, 1949-74; Belfast Harbour Comr, 1940-61; Irish Lights Comr. DL Belfast, 1951. Amer. Medal of Freedom with Palms, 1945. *Address:* 101 Bryansford Road, Newcastle, Co. Down. *T:* Newcastle (Co. Down) 22769. *Clubs:* Ulster (Belfast); Kildare Street and University (Dublin).

EDMONDS, Charles; *see* Carrington, C. E.

EDMONDS, John Christopher, CMG 1978; CVO 1971; HM Diplomatic Service, retired; *b* 23 June 1921; *s* of late Captain A. C. M. Edmonds, OBE, RN, and late Mrs. Edmonds; *m* 1st, 1948, Elena Tornow (marr. diss., 1965); two *s*; 2nd, 1966, Armine Williams. *Educ:* Kelly College. Entered Royal Navy, 1939; psc, 1946. Staff: of NATO Defence Coll., Paris, 1953-55; of

ww—22

C-in-C Home Fleet, 1956-57 (Comdr, 1957); of Chief of Defence Staff, 1958-59. Entered Diplomatic Service, 1959; Foreign Office, 1959-60; 1st Secretary (Commercial), Tokyo, 1960-62; FO, 1963-67; 1st Secretary and Head of Chancery, Ankara, 1967-68; Counsellor: Ankara, 1968-71; Paris, 1972-74; Head of Arms Control and Disarmament Dept, FCO, 1974-77; Leader, UK Delegn to Comprehensive Test Ban Treaty Negotiations, Geneva, with personal rank of Ambassador, 1978-81. Vis. Fellow in Internat. Relations, Reading Univ., 1981-. *Recreations:* golf, gardening, travel. *Address:* North Lodge, Sonning, Berks RG4 0ST. *Club:* Army and Navy.

EDMONDS, John Walter; National Industrial Officer, General and Municipal Workers' Union, since 1972; *b* 28 Jan. 1944; *s* of Walter and Rose Edmonds; *m* 1967, Linden (*née* Callaby); two *d. Educ:* Brunswick Park Primary; Christ's Hosp.; Oriel Coll., Oxford (BA 1965, MA 1968). General and Municipal Workers' Union: Res. Asst, 1966; Dep. Res. Officer, 1967; Reg. Officer, 1968. Dir, National Building Agency, 1978-. Mem., Royal Commn on Environmental Pollution, 1979-. *Recreations:* carpentry, cabinet making. *Address:* 50 Graham Road, Mitcham, Surrey. *T:* 01-648 9991.

EDMONDS, Robert Humphrey Gordon, CMG 1969; MBE 1944; HM Diplomatic Service, retired; Adviser, Kleinwort Benson, since 1978; *b* 5 Oct. 1920; *s* of late Air Vice-Marshal C. H. K. Edmonds, CBE, DSO; *m* 1st, 1951, Georgina Combe (marr. diss.); four *s*; 2nd, 1976, Mrs Enid Balint, widow of Dr Michael Balint. *Educ:* Ampleforth; Brasenose Coll., Oxford. Pres., Oxford Union, 1940. Served Army, 1940-46; attached to Political Div., Allied Commn for Austria, 1945-46. Entered Foreign Service, Dec. 1946; served Cairo, 1947; FO, 1949; Rome, 1953; Warsaw, 1957; FO, 1959; Caracas, 1962; FO, CO and FCO, 1966-69; Minister, Moscow, 1969-71; High Comr, Nicosia, 1971-72; Vis. Fellow, Glasgow Univ., 1973-74; Asst Under Sec. of State, FCO, 1974-77. Fellow, Woodrow Wilson Internat. Centre for Scholars, Washington, 1977. *Publication:* Soviet Foreign Policy 1962-1973: the paradox of super-power, 1975. *Address:* Ashburton Cottage, 43 North Road, Highgate Village, N6; Orchard Cottage, Street, Som. *Club:* Turf.

EDMONDS, Sheila May, MA, PhD; Fellow, and Lecturer in Mathematics, Newnham College, Cambridge, 1945-82 (Vice-Principal, 1960-81); Fellow Emeritus, Newnham College, 1982; *b* 1 April 1916; *d* of Harold Montagu Edmonds and Florence Myra Edmonds. *Educ:* Wimbledon High Sch.; Newnham Coll., Cambridge. Research Student of Westfield Coll., 1939-40, and of Newnham Coll., 1940-41; Research Fellow of Newnham Coll., 1941-43; Asst Lecturer, Newnham Coll., 1943-45. *Publications:* papers in mathematical journals. *Recreations:* travel, photography. *Address:* 5 Cross Lane Close, Orwell, Royston, Herts SG8 5QW. *T:* Cambridge 207789.

EDMONDS, Winston Godward, CBE 1966; ERD 1945; Managing Director, Manchester Ship Canal Co., 1961-70; *b* 27 Nov. 1912; *s* of Wilfred Bell Edmonds and Nina (*née* Godward); *m* 1940, Sheila Mary (*née* Armitage); one *s. Educ:* Merchant Taylors'. Joined LNER, first as traffic apprentice and then in various positions, 1930-46; Manchester Ship Canal Co.: Commercial Manager, 1947-58; Manager, 1959-61. *Recreations:* golf, philately. *Address:* Herons Wood, 22 Castlegate, Prestbury, Cheshire SK10 4AZ. *T:* Prestbury 828966. *Club:* St James's (Manchester).

EDMONDSON, family name of **Baron Sandford.**

EDMONDSON, Anthony Arnold; His Honour Judge Edmondson; a Circuit Judge (formerly County Court Judge and Commissioner, Liverpool and Manchester Crown Courts), since 1971; *b* 6 July 1920; *s* of late Arnold Edmondson; *m* 1947, Dorothy Amelia Wilson, Gateshead-on-Tyne; three *s* one *d. Educ:* Liverpool Univ. (LLB Hons); Lincoln Coll., Oxford (BCL Hons). Served RA (Adjutant), 1940-44; RAF (Pilot), 1944-46; thereafter RA (TA) and TARO. Called to the Bar, Gray's Inn, 1947; William Shaw Schol. 1948; practised on Northern Circuit, 1948-71; Chairman, Liverpool Dock Labour Bd Appeal Tribunal, 1955-66; Mem. Court of Liverpool Univ., 1960-. Dep. Chm., Lancashire QS, 1970-71; Pres., S Cumbria Magistrates' Assoc., 1977-; JP Lancs, 1970. *Recreations:* walking, fishing. *Address:* County Sessions House, Preston, Lancs.

EDMONDSON, Leonard Firby; Executive Council Member, Amalgamated Union of Engineering Workers, 1966-77; *b* 16 Dec. 1912; *s* of Arthur William Edmondson and Elizabeth Edmondson; unmarried. *Educ:* Gateshead Central Sch. Served apprenticeship as engr, Liner Concrete Machinery Co. Ltd, Newcastle upon Tyne, 1929-34; worked in a number of engrg, ship-bldg and ship-repairing firms; shop steward and convener of shop stewards in several firms. AUEW: Mem., Tyne Dist Cttee, 1943-53; Tyne Dist Sec., 1953-66. CSEU: Mem., Exec. Council, 1966; Pres., 1976-77. Member: Shipbldg Industry Trng Bd, 1966-79; Council, ACAS, 1976-78; Royal Commn on Legal Services, 1976-79; Council on Tribunals, 1978-; Cttee of Inquiry into Prison Services, 1978-79; Gen. Council of TUC, 1970-78. Mem., Birtley Canine Soc. *Recreation:* exhibiting Shetland sheep dogs. *Address:* 6 Kenwood Gardens, Low Fell, Gateshead, Tyne and Wear NE9 6PN. *T:* Low Fell 879167. *Clubs:* Northern Counties Shetland Sheep Dog; Manors Social (Newcastle-upon-Tyne).

EDMONSTONE, Sir Archibald (Bruce Charles), 7th Bt *cr* 1774; *b* 3 Aug. 1934; *o* surv. *s* of Sir Charles Edmonstone, 6th Bt, and Gwendolyn Mary, *d* of late Marshall Field and Mrs Maldwin Drummond; *S* father, 1954; *m* 1st, 1957, Jane (marr. diss. 1967), *er d* of Maj.-Gen. E. C. Colville, CB, DSO; two

s one *d*; 2nd, 1969, Juliet Elizabeth, *d* of Maj.-Gen. C. M. F. Deakin, *qv*; one *s* one *d. Educ:* St Peter's Court; Stowe Sch. *Heir: s* Archibald Edward Charles Edmonstone, *b* 4 Feb. 1961. *Address:* Duntreath Castle, Blanefield, Stirlingshire.
See also Sir A. R. J. B. Jardine, Captain Sir C. E. McGrigor.

EDMONTON (Alberta), Archbishop of, (RC), since 1973; **Most Rev. Joseph Neil MacNeil;** *b* 15 April 1924; *s* of John Martin MacNeil and Kate MacNeil (*née* MacLean). *Educ:* St Francis Xavier Univ., Antigonish, NS (BA 1944); Holy Heart Seminary, Halifax, NS; Univs of Perugia, Chicago and St Thomas Aquinas, Rome (JCD 1958). Priest, 1948; pastor, parishes in NS, 1948-55; Chancery Office, Antigonish, 1958-59; admin. dio. Antigonish, 1959-60; Rector, Antigonish Cathedral, 1961; Dir of Extension Dept, St Francis Xavier Univ., Antigonish, 1961-69; Vice-Pres., 1962-69; Bishop of St John, NB, 1969-73. Pres., Canadian Conf. of Catholic Bishops, 1979 (Vice-Pres., 1977-79). Chancellor, Univ. of St Thomas, Fredericton, NB, 1969. Founding Mem., Inst. for Res. on Public Policy, 1968-80. *Address:* 10044 113th Street, Edmonton, Alberta T5K 1N8, Canada.

EDMONTON, Area Bishop of; Rt. Rev. William John Westwood; appointed Bishop Suffragan of Edmonton, 1975; *b* 28 Dec. 1925; *s* of Ernest and Charlotte Westwood; *m* 1954, Shirley Ann, *yr d* of Dr Norman Jennings; one *s* one *d. Educ:* Grove Park Gram. Sch., Wrexham; Emmanuel Coll. and Westcott House, Cambridge. MA Cantab. Soldier, 1944-47. Curate of Hull, 1952-57; Rector of Lowestoft, 1957-65; Vicar of S Peter Mancroft, Norwich, 1965-75; Hon. Canon, Norwich Cathedral, 1969-75; Rural Dean of Norwich, 1966-70, City Dean, 1970-73. Member: General Synod, 1970-75 and 1977-; Archbishop's Commission on Church and State, 1966-70; Press Council, 1975-81; Church Commissioner, 1973-78; Chm., Church Information Cttee, 1979-. Chm. Governors, Coll. of All Saints, Tottenham, 1976-78. Formerly Chm. of three Housing Assocs. *Recreation:* modern poetry. *Address:* 6 Gower Street, WC1E 6DP. *T:* 01-636 5572.

EDMUND-DAVIES, family name of **Baron Edmund-Davies**.

EDMUND-DAVIES, Baron *cr* 1974 (Life Peer), of Aberpennar, Mid Glamorgan; **Herbert Edmund Edmund-Davies,** PC 1966; Kt 1958; a Lord of Appeal in Ordinary, 1974-81; Life Governor and Fellow, King's College, London University; Hon. Fellow, Exeter College, Oxford; *b* 15 July 1906; 3rd *s* of Morgan John Davies and Elizabeth Maud Edmunds; *m* 1935, Eurwen Williams-James; three *d. Educ:* Mountain Ash Grammar Sch.; King's Coll., London; Exeter Coll., Oxford. LLB (London) and Postgraduate Research Scholar, 1926; LLD London, 1928; BCL (Oxon) and Vinerian Scholar, 1929; called to Bar, Gray's Inn, 1929; QC 1943; Bencher, 1948; Treasurer, 1965; Lecturer and Examiner, London School of Economics, 1930-31; Army Officers' Emergency Reserve, 1938; Infantry OCTU; commissioned in Royal Welch Fusiliers, 1940; Lt-Col; later seconded to JAG's Dept; Asst Judge Advocate-General, 1944-45; Recorder of Merthyr Tydfil, 1942-44; of Swansea, 1944-53; of Cardiff, 1953-58; Chm., QS for Denbighshire, 1953-64; Judge of High Court of Justice, Queen's Bench Division, 1958-66; a Lord Justice of Appeal, 1966-74. Foreign Office Observer, Cairo espionage trials, 1957. Chairman: Transport Users' Consultative Cttee for Wales, 1959-61; Lord Chancellor's Cttee on Limitation of Actions, 1961; Tribunal of Inquiry into Aberfan Disaster, 1966; Council of Law Reporting 1967-72; Home Secretary's Criminal Law Revision Cttee, 1969-77; Home Sec's Police Inquiry Cttee, 1977-79. President: London Welsh Trust/London Welsh Assoc., 1982-; University College of Swansea, 1965-75; Pro-Chancellor, Univ. of Wales, 1974-. Hon. Life Member, Canadian Bar Assoc.; CIBA Foundn Trustee; Hon. Life Member, Royal Soc. of Medicine. Hon. LLD Wales, 1959. *Publications:* Law of Distress for Rent and Rates, 1931; miscellaneous legal writings. *Address:* House of Lords, SW1; 5 Gray's Inn Square, WC1. *Clubs:* Reform; Cardiff and County (Cardiff); City (Chester); Bristol Channel Yacht.

EDMUNDS, Christopher Montague, MusD; *b* 26 Nov. 1899; 2nd *s* of Charles Edmunds; *m* 1923, Kathleen, *d* of Arthur Vaughan-Jones; one *s* one *d. Educ:* King Edward VI Sch., Camp Hill, Birmingham; Birmingham Univ.; Manchester Univ.; Birmingham Sch. of Music. 1st Cl. Hons BMus Birmingham, 1922; MusD, Manchester, 1936. Theory Teacher and Dir of opera class, Birmingham Sch. of Music, 1928-45; Principal, Birmingham Sch. of Music, 1945-56; Fellow Birmingham Sch. of Music; Fellow Trinity Coll. of Music (Mem. Corp. and Examiner, 1940-78). *Publications:* compositions include: the Blue Harlequin (opera); chamber and orchestral music; vocal and instrumental music; Romance, 1946 (pianoforte and orchestral work, commissioned by BBC). *Recreation:* gardening. *Address:* 247 Mereside Way, Solihull, West Midlands B92 7AY. *T:* 021-706 8055.

EDNAM, Viscount; William Humble David Jeremy Ward; *b* 27 March 1947; *s* and *heir* of Earl of Dudley, *qv* and of Stella Viscountess Ednam, *d* of M. A. Carcano, KCMG, KBE; *m* 1st, 1972, Sarah (marr. diss. 1976), *o d* of Sir Alastair Coats, Bt, *qv*; 2nd, 1976, Debra Louise (marr. diss. 1980), *d* of George Robert and Marjorie Elvera Pinney; one *d. Educ:* Eton; Christ Church, Oxford. *Address:* Rowlandson Ground, near Coniston, Cumbria. *T:* Coniston 397.

EDWARD, David Alexander Ogilvy, CMG 1981; QC (Scotland) 1974; *b* 14 Nov. 1934; *s* of J. O. C. Edward, Travel Agent, Perth; *m* 1962, Elizabeth Young McSherry; two *s* two *d. Educ:* Sedbergh Sch.; University Coll., Oxford; Edinburgh Univ. Sub-Lt RNVR (Nat. Service); HMS Hornet,

1956-57. Admitted Advocate, 1962; Clerk of Faculty of Advocates, 1967-70; Treasurer, 1970-77; Trustee, Nat. Library of Scotland, 1966-; Leader, UK Delegn to Consultative Cttee of Bars and Law Societies, EEC, 1976-77, Pres. Consultative Cttee, 1978-80; Mem. Law Adv. Panel, British Council. Distinguished Cross, First Class, Order of St Raymond of Penafort, Spain, 1979. *Publications:* The Professional Secret, Confidentiality and Legal Professional Privilege in the EEC, 1976; articles in legal jls. *Address:* 32 Heriot Row, Edinburgh EH3 6ES; Ardargie Cottage, Forgandenny, Perthshire. *Club:* New (Edinburgh).

EDWARDES, family name of **Baron Kensington**.

EDWARDES, Sir Michael (Owen), Kt 1979; Non-Executive Chairman, Chloride Group PLC, since 1982; Chairman, Mercury Communications Ltd, since 1982; Chairman and Chief Executive, BL Ltd (formerly British Leyland), 1977-82; *b* 11 Oct. 1930; *s* of Denys Owen Edwardes and Rydney Noel (*née* Copeland); *m* 1958, Mary Margaret (*née* Finlay); three *d. Educ:* St Andrew's Coll., Grahamstown, S Africa; Rhodes Univ., Grahamstown (BA; Hon. LLD). Employed Chloride Group Ltd, 1951-81; Chm., 1974-77; non-exec. Dep. Chm., 1977-82; Non-Exec. Director: Hill Samuel Group PLC, 1980-; Internat. Management Develt Inst., Washington, 1978-. Member: CBI Council, 1974-81; CBI President's Cttee, 1981-; Nat. Enterprise Bd, 1975-77; Queen's Award for Industry Review Cttee, 1975. CBIM (a Vice-Chm., 1977-80); Pres., Comité des Constructeurs d'Automobiles du Marché Commun (CCMC), 1979-80. Hon. FIMechE, 1981. *Recreations:* sailing, squash, water ski-ing, tennis. *Address:* Chloride Group PLC, 52 Grosvenor Gardens, SW1W 0AU. *T:* 01-730 0866. *Clubs:* Royal Automobile; Jesters; Rand (Johannesburg).

EDWARDES JONES, Air Marshal (Retd) Sir (John) Humphrey, KCB 1957 (CB 1954); CBE 1943; DFC 1940; AFC 1941; retired 1961; *b* 15 Aug. 1905; *s* of late G. M. Edwardes Jones, KC and G. R. Johnston; *m* 1935, Margaret Rose Graham; one *s* one *d. Educ:* Brighton Coll.; Pembroke Coll., Cambridge. Entered RAF, Sept. 1926; served in Egypt, 4 Flying Training Sch. and 208 Sqdn, 1930-35; Commanded: No 213 Fighter Sqdn, 1937-40; No 56 Op. Trg Unit, 1940; Nos 60 and 58 OTU's, 1941; Exeter Fighter Sector, 1942; No 323 Fighter Wing, Algiers, Nov. 1942; AOC, No 210 Group, Algiers, 1943; idc 1950; Dir of Plans, Air Ministry, 1951. Commandant, Sch. of Land/Air Warfare, RAF, Old Sarum, Wilts, 1955-57; Comdr-in-Chief, 2nd Tactical Air Force, and Comdr, 2nd Allied Tactical Air Force, 1957-61. Legion of Honour (French), 1946. *Recreation:* golf. *Address:* Old Marks, Holtye, Sussex. *T:* Cowden 317. *Club:* Royal Air Force.

EDWARDS, family name of **Baron Chelmer**.

EDWARDS, (Alfred) Kenneth, MBE 1963; Deputy Director-General, Confederation of British Industry, since 1982; *b* 24 March 1926; *s* of late Ernest Edwards and Florence Edwards (*née* Branch); *m* 1949, Jeannette Lilian, *d* of David Speeks, MBE; one *s* two *d. Educ:* Latymer Upper Sch.; Magdalene Coll., Cambridge; University Coll. London (BScEcon). Served RAF, 1944-47; RAF Coll., Cranwell, 1945, FO (Pilot). Entered HMOCS, Nigeria, 1952; Provincial Administration, Warri and Benin, 1952-54; Lagos Secretariat, 1954; Sen. Asst Sec., Nigerian Min. of Communications and Aviation, 1959; retired, 1962. Secretary, British Radio Equipment Manufrs' Assoc., 1962; Gp Marketing Manager, Thorn Elec. Industries Ltd, 1965; Internat. Dir, Brookhirst Igranic Ltd (Thorn Gp), 1967; Gp Marketing Dir, Cutler Hammer Europa, 1972; Dep. Chm., BEAMA Overseas Trade Cttee, 1973; Chief Exec., British Friesian Cattle Soc., 1975-76; Chief Exec., BEAMA, 1976-82. CBI: Member: Council, 1974, 1976-82; Finance and Gen. Purposes Cttee, 1977-82; Vice-Chm., Eastern Reg. Council, 1974; Chm., Working Party on Liability for Defective Products, 1978-82; Mem., President's Cttee, 1979-82. Member: Elec. Engrg EDC, 1976; Council, Elec. Res. Assoc. Ltd, 1976-82; Exec. Cttee, Organisme de Liaison des Industries Metalliques Européennes (ORGALIME), 1976-82; Exec. Bd, BSI, 1978- (Chm., British Electrotechnical Cttee and Electrotechnical Divisional Council, 1981-); BOTB, 1982-; Salvation Army Adv. Bd (London); President: Eur. Cttee for Electrotechnical Standardisation (CENELEC), 1977-79; Liaison Cttee for Electrical and Electronic Industries, ORGALIME, 1979-82 (Chm., 1980-82). Mem. Court, Cranfield Inst. of Technol., 1970-75. *Publications:* contrib. technical jls; lectures and broadcasts on industrial subjects. *Recreations:* music, books, walking. *Address:* Confederation of British Industry, Centre Point, 103 New Oxford Street, WC1. *Clubs:* East India, Devonshire, Sports and Public Schools, Royal Air Force, Royal Commonwealth Society.

EDWARDS, Brig. Arthur Bertie Duncan, CBE 1943; MC; *b* 29 April 1898; *s* of Joseph Arthur Edwards, Portsmouth, and Rosa May Duncan, Isle of Wight; *m* 1925, Clara Elizabeth, 3rd *c* of late Edmund Barkworth, JP, Seaton, Devon; three *s. Educ:* RMA Woolwich. 2nd Lieut RE 1916; Capt. 1926; Major 1935; Lt-Col 1942; Temp. Col 1943, Temp. Brig. 1943; Col 1945; Brig. 1949. Served France, 1917-18 (BWM and VM); India, 1918-19; Iraq, 1919-20 (MC, BGS with Iraq clasp); India, 1920-22; England, 1922-35; Malta, 1935-39; England, 1939-40; France, 1940 (despatches); Greece, 1940-41; Libya, 1941; CRE Eighth Army Troops Engineers, Libya and Egypt, 1941-42 (despatches twice, OBE, North African Star); Dep. Chief Engineer, N Delta Defences, Egypt, 1942; Chief Engineer, Malta, 1942-43 (CBE); Chief Engineer, British Troops in Egypt, 1943; No 13 CE Works (Construction), Middle East, 1943-44; Engineer Adviser, AA Command, England, 1944; Dep. Dir Works 21 Army Group BLA and BAOR, 1944-48 (despatches; Kt Comdr of Orange-Nassau with swords); Chief Engineer, Eastern Command, United Kingdom, 1948-51; retired, 1951. *Address:* c/o Lloyds Bank Ltd, 6 Pall Mall, SW1.

EDWARDS, Arthur Frank George; Vice-Chairman, Thames Water Authority, since 1973; *b* 27 March 1920; *o s* of Arthur Edwards and Mabel (Elsie) Edwards; *m* 1946, Joyce May Simmons; one *s* one *d. Educ:* West Ham Grammar Sch.; Garnett Coll., London; West Ham Coll. of Technology. CEng, FIChemE, MSE; Hon. FIWM. Various posts with Ever Ready (GB) Ltd, 1936-50; Prodn Man., J. Burns & Co. Ltd, 1950-53; various lectrg posts, 1954-65; Organiser for science and techn. subjects, London Boroughs of Barking and Redbridge, 1965-. Member: West Ham Co. Borough Council, 1964-65; Newham Council, 1964- (Mayor, 1967-68); GLC, 1964- (Dep. Chm., 1970-71; Chm., Public Services Cttee, 1973-77); Chm. of Governors, NE London Polytechnic, 1972-. Mem., Fabian Soc. *Recreations:* reading, Association football (watching West Ham United). *Address:* 18 Wanstead Park Avenue, E12 5EN. *T:* 01-633 5086; County Hall, SE1 7PB. *T:* 01-633 5000. *Club:* West Ham Supporters'.

EDWARDS, Brian; Regional Administrator, Trent Regional Health Authority, since 1981; *b* 19 Feb. 1942; *s* of John Albert Edwards and Ethel Edwards; *m* 1964, Jean (*née* Cannon); two *s* two *d. Educ:* Wirral Grammar Sch. Jun. Administrator, Clatterbridge Hosp., 1958-62; Dep. Hosp. Sec., Cleaver Hosp., 1962-64; National Trainee, Nuffield Centre, Leeds, 1964-66; Administrator, Gen. Infirmary, Leeds, 1966-67; Hosp. Sec., Keighley Victoria Hosp., 1967-68; Administrator, Mansfield HMC, 1969-70; Lectr, Univ. of Leeds, 1970-72; Dep. Gp Sec., Hull A HMC, 1972-74; Dist Administrator, Leeds AHA(T), 1974-76; Area Administrator, Cheshire AHA, 1976-81. Inst. of Health Service Administrators: Mem., 1964-; Pres., 1982-83; Mem. Editorial Cttee, Health Care in the UK: its organisation and management, 1982-. Jt Editor, Health Services Manpower Review, 1970-. *Publications:* Si Vis Pacem-preparations for change in the NHS, 1973; Profile for Change, 1973; Bridging in Health, Planning the Child Health Services, 1975; Industrial Relations in the NHS: managers and industrial relations, 1979; conf. papers presented in UK, Norway, Germany and USA; contrib. prof. jls. *Recreations:* golf, stage management. *Address:* 3 Royal Croft Drive, Baslow, Derbyshire DE4 1SN. *T:* Baslow 3459.

EDWARDS, Carl Johannes; stained glass artist; *b* 15 Feb. 1914; *m* 1941, Kathleen Margaret Selina Morgan; two *d. Educ:* studied Art under James Hogan, RDI, and at various London Art Schs. Chief Designer Whitefriars Glass Works, 1948; resigned 1952. Governor Harrow Sch. of Art, 1949; Liveryman, Worshipful Company of Glaziers, 1949. Chief works in: Cairo Cathedral; Liverpool Cathedral; House of Lords; Lambeth Palace Chapel; Temple Church; Royal Air Force Church, St Clement Dane's; Portsmouth Cathedral; St David's Cathedral, Wales; Auckland Cathedral, NZ; Westminster Sch., and several works in concrete and glass for England and abroad. *Recreations:* golf and music. *Address:* The Glasshouse, 11 Lettice Street, Fulham, SW6 4EH. *T:* 01-736 3113; 36 Denman Drive South, NW11. *Clubs:* Challoner; Highgate Golf.

EDWARDS, Charles Harold, FRCP; Dean of St Mary's Hospital, Paddington, 1973-79; *b* 1913; *m* 1959; one *s* two *d. Educ:* Guy's Hosp. Med. Sch. MRCS 1937; LRCP 1937; MRCP 1946; FRCP 1961. Formerly: Resident Medical Appts, Guy's Hosp.; Resident Med. Officer, Nat. Hosp., Queen Square; Neurological Registrar, St Mary's Hosp., Paddington; Consultant Physician, Dept Nervous Diseases, St Mary's Hosp., 1954-78; Consultant Neurologist: Royal Nat. Throat, Nose and Ear Hosp., 1955-78; King Edward VII Hosp., Windsor, 1952-78; Canadian Red Cross Meml Hosp., Taplow, 1952-78; Maidenhead Hosp., 1952-78. Mem., British Assoc. of Neurologists; FRSocMed. *Publications:* Neurology of Ear, Nose and Throat, 1973; Neurological Section: Synopsis of Otolaryngology, 1967; Scott-Brown, Diseases of Ear, Nose and Throat, 1971; contrib. Qly Jl Medicine, Lancet, etc. *Recreations:* words, gardening. *Address:* Cardinal House, The Green, Hampton Court, Surrey. *T:* 01-979 6922. *Club:* Garrick.

EDWARDS, Sir Christopher (John Churchill), 5th Bt *cr* 1866; *b* 16 Aug. 1941; *s* of Sir (Henry) Charles (Serrell Priestley) Edwards, 4th Bt and of Lady (Daphne) Edwards (*née* Birt); *S* father, 1963; *m* 1972, Gladys Irene Vogelgesang; two *s. Educ:* Frensham Heights, Surrey; Loughborough, Leics. Managing Dir, Kelsar Corp., California. *Heir: s* David Charles Priestley Edwards, *b* 22 Feb. 1974. *Address:* 5110 Glen Verde Drive, Bonita, California 92002, USA. *T:* 714-267-3873.

EDWARDS, Sir Clive; *see* Edwards, Sir J. C. L.

EDWARDS, David; Secretary, Legal Aid, The Law Society, since 1976, and Deputy Secretary-General since 1982; *b* 27 Oct. 1929; *s* of Col Cyril Edwards, DSO, MC, DL and Jessie Edwards; *m* 1966, Gay Clothier; two *s* one *d. Educ:* Felsted Sch.; Trinity Hall, Cambridge (MA, LLB). Called to the Bar, Middle Temple, 1952; Harmsworth Scholar, Middle Temple, 1955; admitted Solicitor, 1958. Partner, E. Edwards Son & Noice, 1959-75. Chm., Offshore Racing Council, 1970-78; Dep. Chm., Royal Yachting Assoc., 1976-81. *Recreation:* sailing. *Address:* Olivers, Colchester, Essex CO2 0HJ. *Clubs:* Royal Ocean Racing; Royal Yacht Squadron (Cowes).

See also Baron Chelmer, J. T. Edwards.

EDWARDS, Very Rev. David Lawrence; Provost of Southwark Cathedral since 1983; *b* 20 Jan. 1929; *s* of Lawrence Wright and Phyllis Boardman Edwards; *m* 1960, Hilary Mary (*née* Phillips); one *s* three *d. Educ:* King's Sch., Canterbury; Magdalen Coll., Oxford. Lothian Prize, 1951; 1st cl. hons Mod. Hist., BA 1952; MA 1956. Fellow, All Souls Coll., Oxford, 1952-59. Deacon, 1954; Priest, 1955. On HQ staff of Student Christian Movement of Gt Brit. and Ireland, 1955-66; Editor and Man. Dir, SCM Press Ltd, 1959-66; Gen. Sec. of Movt, 1965-66. Curate of: St John's, Hampstead, 1955-58; St Martin-in-the-Fields, 1958-66; Fellow and Dean of King's College, Cambridge, 1966-70; Asst Lectr in Divinity, Univ. of Cambridge, 1967-70; Rector of St Margaret's, Westminster, 1970-78; Canon of Westminster, 1970-78; Sub-Dean, 1974-78; Speaker's Chaplain, 1972-78; Dean of Norwich, 1978-82. Exam. Chaplain: to Bp of Manchester, 1965-73; to Bp of Durham, 1968-72; to Bp of Bradford, 1972-78; to Bp of London, 1974-78; to Archbishop of Canterbury, 1975-78. Hulsean Lectr, 1967; Six Preacher, Canterbury Cathedral, 1969-76. Chairman: Churches' Council on Gambling, 1970-78; Christian Aid, 1971-78. *Publications:* A History of the King's School, Canterbury, 1957; Not Angels But Anglicans, 1958; This Church of England, 1962; God's Cross in Our World, 1963; Religion and Change, 1969; F. J. Shirley: An Extraordinary Headmaster, 1969; The Last Things Now, 1969; Leaders of the Church of England, 1971; What is Real in Christianity?, 1972; St Margaret's, Westminster, 1972; The British Churches Turn to the Future, 1973; Ian Ramsey, Bishop of Durham, 1973; Good News in Acts, 1974; What Anglicans Believe, 1974; Jesus for Modern Man, 1975; A Key to the Old Testament, 1976; Today's Story of Jesus, 1976; The State of the Nation, 1976; A Reason to Hope, 1978; Christian England: its story to the Reformation, 1981; Catholic, Protestant, English: from the Reformation to the Eighteenth Century, 1982; (ed) The Honest to God Debate, 1963; (ed) Collins Children's Bible, 1978. *Address:* Provost's Lodging, 51 Bankside, SE1.

EDWARDS, David Michael; HM Diplomatic Service; Legal Counsellor, Foreign and Commonwealth Office, since 1979; *b* 28 Feb. 1940; *s* of Ernest William Edwards and Thelma Irene Edwards; *m* 1966, Veronica Margaret Postgate; one *s* one *d. Educ:* The King's Sch., Canterbury; Univ. of Bristol. LLB Hons. Admitted to Roll of Solicitors, 1964. Solicitor of Supreme Court, 1964-67; Asst Legal Adviser, Foreign Office, 1967; Legal Adviser: British Military Govt, Berlin, 1972; British Embassy, Bonn, 1974; Legal Counsellor, 1977; Dir, Legal Div., IAEA, Vienna (on secondment), 1977-79; Agent of the UK Govt in cases before EEC and Court of Human Rights, 1979-82. *Recreations:* reading, walking, gardening. *Address:* c/o Foreign and Commonwealth Office, SW1.

EDWARDS, Donald Isaac, CBE 1965 (OBE 1958); Managing Director, Independent Television News, 1968-71; *b* 27 Sept. 1904; *s* of late Isaac Edwards, Bolton, Lancs; *m* 1930, Enid Bent; two *s. Educ:* Bolton Sch.; Emmanuel Coll., Cambridge (MA). Tillotsons Newspapers, 1926-28; Daily News, 1928-30; Allied Newspapers, 1930-33; Daily Telegraph, 1933-39; BBC: Asst European News Editor, 1940-42; European News Editor, 1942-45; Correspondent in India, 1946; Dir, European News, 1946-48; Head of External Services, News Dept, 1948-58; Editor, News, 1958-60; News and Current Affairs, 1960-67; Gen. Man., Local Radio Development, 1967-68. *Publications:* The Two Worlds of Donald Edwards (autobiography), 1970; contrib to various books on journalism and broadcasting. *Recreations:* gardening, music, golf, walking. *Address:* Spindles, Miles Lane, Cobham, Surrey. *T:* Cobham 2257.

EDWARDS, Douglas John; Consultant, Argyll Foods Ltd (formerly Louis C. Edwards & Sons (Manchester) Ltd), since 1979 (Joint Chairman and Managing Director 1966-79); Chairman and Managing Director, Imexport Meats Ltd, since 1979; *b* 18 March 1916; *s* of Louis Edwards; *m* 1st, 1941, Emmeline H. Haslam (*d* 1964); two *s*; 2nd, 1973, Valerie Barlow-Hitchen. *Educ:* De La Salle Coll., Salford. Member of Lloyd's, 1965-. Joined Manchester Conservative Party, 1947; Mem. Manchester City Council, 1951-74; Alderman, 1967-74; Lord Mayor of City of Manchester, 1971-72; Greater Manchester Metropolitan CC, 1974-78 (High Sheriff, 1975). President: Manchester Cttee, Grenadier Guards Assoc., 1968-81; Greater Manchester Youth Assoc., 1973-80. Chm., Northern Cttee, Hotel and Catering Benev. Assoc., 1976-81. Governor: De La Salle Teacher Training Coll., Greater Manchester, 1972-81; De La Salle Coll., Salford, 1972-81. DL Greater Manchester, 1979-81. Freeman and Liveryman, Co. of Playing Cards Makers, 1974. Polonia Restituta, 1972. *Recreations:* golf, sailing. *Address:* Apt 10A, The Marbella, 250 South Ocean Boulevard, Boca Raton, Florida 33432, USA. *T:* (305) 392-8203. *Clubs:* Carlton; Royal Thames Yacht; Lloyd's Yacht; Lancs County Cricket (Life Mem.); Cheshire Polo; Altrincham Rifle; Antibes Yacht.

EDWARDS, Prof. Edward George, PhD, BSc, FRSC; Vice-Chancellor and Principal, University of Bradford, 1966-78, Hon. Professor, since 1978; Principal of Bradford Institute of Technology, 1957-66; *b* 18 Feb. 1914; *m* 1940, Kathleen Hewitt; two *s* two *d. Educ:* Cardiff High Sch.; University of South Wales; Cardiff Coll. of Technology. Lecturer in Chemistry, University of Nottingham, 1938-40; Research Chemist (ICI Ltd), 1940-45; Head of Dept of Chemistry and Applied Chemistry, Royal Technical Coll., Salford, 1945-54; Principal, Coll. of Technology, Liverpool, 1954-57. Hon. DTech Bradford, 1980. *Publications:* various research papers in chemical jls; articles and papers on higher educn, technological innovation, university planning. *Recreations:* philosophy, music, walking, travel. *Address:* Corner Cottage, Westwood Drive, Ilkley, West Yorks. *T:* Ilkley 607112.

EDWARDS, Frederick Edward, RD 1968 and Clasp, 1977; Director of Social Work, Strathclyde Region, since 1976; *b* 9 April 1931; *s* of Reginal Thomas Edwards and Jessie Howard Simpson; *m* 1957, Edith Jocelyn Price; two *s* one *d*. *Educ*: St Edward's Coll., Liverpool; Univ. of Glasgow (Dip. Applied Soc. Studies 1965). BA Open Univ., 1973. FBIM; FISW. Merchant Navy Deck Officer, 1948-58; Perm. Commn, RNR, 1953, Lt-Comdr 1963; sailed Barque Mayflower to USA, 1957. Morgan Refractories, 1958-60; Probation Service, Liverpool, 1960-69; Dir of Social Work: Moray and Nairn, 1969-74; Grampian, 1974-76. Member: Scottish Marriage Guidance Council, 1970- (Chm., 1980-); Scottish Council on Crime, 1972-75; Adv. Council on Social Work, 1976-81. *Publications*: articles in social work jls. *Recreations*: sailing, natural history, reading. *Address*: Tigh na Bealach, Empress Road, Rhu, Dunbartonshire G84 8LT. *T*: Rhu 820365.

EDWARDS, Gareth Owen; a Recorder of the Crown Court, since 1978; *b* 26 Feb. 1940; *s* of Arthur Wyn Edwards and Mair Eluned Edwards; *m* 1967, Katharine Pek Har Goh; two *s* one *d*. *Educ*: Herbert Strutt Grammar Sch., Belper; Trinity Coll., Oxford (BA,BCL). Called to the Bar, Inner Temple, 1963; Army Legal Service, 1963-65; Commonwealth Office, 1965-67. Practised, Wales and Chester Circuit, 1967-. *Recreations*: climbing, chess. *Address*: 58 Lache Lane, Chester CH4 7LS. *T*: Chester 677795. *Club*: Army and Navy.

EDWARDS, Gareth Owen, MBE 1975; Welsh Rugby footballer; Director of Engineering Company in S Wales; *b* 12 July 1947; *s* of Granville and Anne Edwards; *m* 1972, Maureen Edwards; two *s*. *Educ*: Pontardawe Tech. Sch.; Millfield Sch.; Cardiff College of Educn. Rugby Football: 1st cap for Wales, 1967 (*v* France); Captain of Wales on 13 occasions; youngest Captain of Wales (at 20 years), 1968; British Lions Tours: 1968, 1971, 1974; Barbarians, 1967-78. Member of Cardiff RFC, 1966-; a record 53 consecutive caps, to 1978; retired, 1978. *Publications*: Gareth: an autobiography, 1978; (jtly) Rugby Skills, 1979; Rugby Skills for Forwards, 1980. *Recreations*: fishing, golf. *Address*: 211 West Road, Nottage, Porthcawl, Mid-Glamorgan CF36 3RT. *T*: Porthcawl 5669.

EDWARDS, Geoffrey, CEng, FICE, FRICS, FCIArb, MConsE, FASCE; Chairman: Thames Water Authority, since 1978; GEP Consulting Group, since 1966; Westfield Trust Ltd, since 1966; Principal, Edwards Newstead, since 1967; *b* 28 April 1917; *s* of Frank Edwards, boot and shoe manufr, and Gladys Evelyn, *d* of Joseph Downes, mining engr; *m* 1st, 1943, Barbara Henrietta Edwards (*d* 1959); no *c*; 2nd, 1960, Pauline Nancy, *d* of Walter James Edwards, boot and shoe manufr, and Anne Evelyn Gully; two *d*. *Educ*: private prep. sch.; St Brendan's Coll., Clifton, Bristol; Merchant Venturers/Bristol Univ. FRICS 1951; CEng, FICE 1956; FCIArb 1976. Defence works, 1939-43; Civil Engr, BOAC, W Africa, 1943-45; various appts, BOAC, 1945-66, incl. Gen. Man. Properties and Services, and Mem. of Exec. Management. Dir and Dep. Chm., N Surrey Water Co., 1962-78; Dir and Dep. Chm., Sutton Dist Water Co., 1970-73; Chm., Surveyors Holdings Ltd; Mem., National Water Council, 1978. Chm., Westminster Chamber of Commerce, 1982- (former Chm. Bldg Gp); formerly Member: Council, RICS; Airport Engrg Bd, ICE; Council, Nat. Fedn of Housing Assocs. Freeman and Liveryman, City of London; Asst to Court, Worshipful Co. of Plumbers. Founder and Chm., first five World Airports Confs; broadcaster on airport subjects. Mem., Lloyds. Steward, Henley Royal Regatta. *Publications*: contrib. to technical and other jls. *Recreations*: swimming, shooting, farming. *Address*: 402 Drake House, Dolphin Square, SW1. *T*: 01-834 9929; Coldharbour Farm, Wick, near Bristol BS15 5RJ. *T*: Abson 2212. *Clubs*: City Livery, Hurlingham, Farmers'.

EDWARDS, Geoffrey Francis, CBE 1975 (OBE 1968; MBE 1956); TD; HM Diplomatic Service, retired; *b* 28 Sept. 1917; *s* of late Oliver and Frances Margaret Edwards, Langley, Bucks; *m* 1st, 1949, Joyce Black (*d* 1953); one *d*; 2nd, 1961, Johanna Elisabeth Franziska Taeger. *Educ*: Brighton Coll. Joined Pixley & Abell, Bullion Brokers, 1936. Commissioned RA (TA), June 1939; served with 117 Fd Regt and 59 (Newfoundland) Heavy Regt RA in NW Europe, 1939-45; joined Control Commn for Germany, 1945; joined British Military Govt, Berlin, 1949; Economic Adviser, 1956; Consul-General, Berlin, 1966-75. Ernst Reuter Silver Plaque, Berlin, 1975. *Recreations*: gardening, fishing, golf. *Address*: Whitegates, Mathon Road, Colwall, near Malvern, Worcs WR13 6ER.

EDWARDS, George, FFARCS; Consulting Anæsthetist: St George's, General Lying-in (St Thomas'), Samaritan (St Mary's) and Queen Charlotte's Hospitals; *b* 14 Jan. 1901; *m* 1934, Jean Lilian Smith, MD; one *s*. *Educ*: Royal Grammar Sch., Worcester; St George's Hospital (Johnson Anatomy Prize). MRCS, LRCP 1926; DA, RCP and S 1936; FFARCS 1948. RAMC, 1941-44; Lt-Col. Adviser in Anæsthetics, BNAF and CMF. Hon. Mem. (Pres. 1945-46), Sect. Anæsthetics, RSocMed. Mem. of Bd of Faculty of Anæsthetists, RCS, 1948-54; first Hewitt Lectr, RCS, 1950; first Snow Memorial Lectr, Assoc. of Anæsthetists, 1958. *Publications*: articles in medical journals. *Address*: Davenham, Graham Road, Malvern, Worcester WR14 2HY. *T*: Malvern 64338.

EDWARDS, Sir George (Robert), OM 1971; Kt 1957; CBE 1952 (MBE 1945); FRS 1968; DL; now retired; Chairman, British Aircraft Corporation Ltd, 1963-75; Pro-Chancellor, University of Surrey, 1964-79, now Pro-Chancellor Emeritus; *b* 9 July 1908; *m* 1935, Marjorie Annie (*née* Thurgood); one *d*. *Educ*: S West Essex Tech. Coll.; London Univ. (BScEng). Gen.

engineering, 1928-35; joined Design Staff, Vickers-Aviation Ltd, Weybridge, 1935; Experimental Manager, Vickers-Armstrongs Ltd, Weybridge Works, 1940. Chief Designer, Weybridge Works, 1945; Dir, Vickers Ltd, 1955-67. Pres., Royal Aeronautical Soc., 1957-58; Vice-Pres., Royal Society of Arts, 1958-61. Mem., Royal Instn, 1971-. Pres., Surrey CCC, 1979 (Vice-Pres., 1974). DL Surrey, 1981. FEng; Hon. Fellow: RAeS 1960; IMechE; Manchester Coll. of Science and Technology; Hon. FAIAA. Hon. DSc: Southampton, 1962; Salford, 1967; Cranfield Inst. of Technology, 1970; City Univ., 1975; Stirling, 1979; Surrey, 1979; Hon. DSc(Eng) London, 1970; Hon. LLD Bristol, 1973. George Taylor Gold Medal, 1948; British Gold Medal for Aeronautics, 1952; Daniel Guggenheim Medal, 1959; Air League Founders Medal, 1969; Albert Gold Medal (RSA), 1972; Royal Medal, Royal Soc., 1974. *Publications*: various papers and lectures in JI RAeS, Amer. Inst. of Aeronautical Sciences and Amer. Soc. of Automotive Engrs. *Recreations*: golf, sailing, painting. *Address*: Albury Heights, White Lane, Guildford, Surrey. *T*: Guildford 504488. *Clubs*: Athenæum; Royal Air Force Yacht.

EDWARDS, Harold Clifford, CBE 1945; MS, FRCS, FRCOG, FACS (Hon.); Honorary Colonel RAMC; Consulting Surgeon to King's College Hospital; Emeritus Lecturer, and Director, Department of Surgery, King's College Hospital Medical School, 1956-70; Surgeon to Royal Masonic Hospital, 1956-70; Consulting Surgeon to King Edward VII Hospital for Officers, 1956-70; St Saviour's Hospital; Consultant Adviser in Surgery to the Minister of Health, 1956-70; Surgeon Emeritus to the Evelina Hospital for Children; *b* 15 Aug. 1899; *s* of William Evans Edwards and Mary Selina Jones; *m* 1926, Ida Margaret Atkinson Phillips (*d* 1981); two *s*. *Educ*: University Coll., Cardiff; King's College Hospital, London. Served in Royal Engineers, 1917-19; entered University Coll., Cardiff, 1919; MRCS, LRCP, MB, BS 1923; FRCS 1926; MS London Univ., 1928; Hon. Surgeon to King's Coll. Hosp., 1928, and to Evelina Hosp. for Children, 1931; Robert Jones Gold Medal for an Essay upon Injuries to Muscles and Tendons, 1930, and Jacksonian Prize of RCS for a Dissertation on Diverticula of the Intestine, 1932; Hunterian Prof., RCS, 1934; Consulting Surg. Southern Comd, England, 1942-44; Consulting Surg., Central Mediterranean Forces, 1944-46; late Dean of King's College Hosp. Medical Sch. Past Master, Worshipful Soc. of Apothecaries. Mem. Court of Examiners, 1931-60, and Mem. Council, 1955-71, RCS (past Vice-Pres.). Examiner in Surgery, Univs of London, Cambridge, Wales, Birmingham, Dublin and Bristol. Chm., Armed Forces Adv. Cttee on Postgraduate Med. and Dental Officers, 1971-75; President: British Soc. of Gastroenterology, 1961; Assoc. of Surgeons of Gt Brit. and Ireland, 1962; FRCOG 1971; Hon. Fellow: American Surgical Assoc.; Assoc. of Surgeons of W Africa; Assoc. of Surgeons of West Indies; Mem. Académie de Chirurgie. Former Editor of GUT the British Jl of Gastro-enterology. Hon. Gold Medal, RCS, 1972; Eric Farquharson Award, RCSE, 1978. *Publications*: Surgical Emergencies in Children, 1935; Diverticula and Diverticulitis of the Intestine, 1939; Recent Advances in Surgery, 1954; papers in BMJ, Lancet, etc. *Recreation*: gardening. *Address*: Nickersons, Barton, Cambridge. *T*: Comberton 2367. *Club*: Athenæum.
See also Prof. J. H. Edwards.

EDWARDS, Iorwerth Eiddon Stephen, CMG 1973; CBE 1968; MA, LittD; FBA 1962; Keeper of Egyptian Antiquities, British Museum, 1955-74; *b* 21 July 1909; *s* of late Edward Edwards and Ellen Jane (née Higgs); *m* 1938, Elizabeth, *y d* of late Charles Edwards Lisle; one *d* (one *s* decd). *Educ*: Merchant Taylors'; Gonville and Caius Coll., Cambridge (Major Scholar). Merchant Taylors' Sch. Exhibitioner and John Stewart of Rannoch Univ. Scholar, Cambridge, 1928; 1st Cl. Oriental Languages Tripos, Parts I and II, 1930-31; Mason Prize, Tyrwhitt Scholarship and Wright Studentship, 1932. Entered Dept of Egyptian and Assyrian Antiquities, British Museum, 1934; seconded to Foreign Office; attached to British Embassies, Cairo and Baghdad, and to Secretariat, Jerusalem, 1942-45. T. E. Peet Prize, Liverpool Univ., 1947. Visiting Prof., Brown Univ., Providence, RI, USA, 1953-54. Glanville Mem. Lectr, Cambridge Univ., 1980. Pioneered and chose objects for Tutankhamun Exhibition, London, 1972. Mem., Unesco-Egyptian Min. of Culture Archaeol. Cttee for saving monuments of Philae, 1973-80. Vice-Pres. Egypt Exploration Soc.; Mem. of German Archæological Inst.; Associate Mem., Inst. of Egypt; Mem., Cttee of Visitors of Metropolitan Museum of Art, NY; Corres. Mem., Fondation Egyptologique Reine Elisabeth. *Publications*: Hieroglyphic Texts in the British Museum, Vol. VIII, 1939; The Pyramids of Egypt, 1947, 2nd edn 1961; Hieratic Papyri in the British Museum, 4th Series (Oracular Amuletic Decrees of the Late New Kingdom), 1960; The Early Dynastic Period in Egypt, 1964; Joint Editor of The Cambridge Ancient History (3rd edn), 1970; Treasures of Tutankhamun (Catalogue of London exhibn), 1972; Treasures of Tutankhamun (Catalogue of US exhibn), 1976; Tutankhamun's Jewelry, 1976; Tutankhamun: his tomb and its treasures, 1976; articles in Journal of Egyptian Archæology and other scientific periodicals. *Recreations*: golf, gardening. *Address*: Dragon House, The Bullring, Deddington, Oxon OX5 4TT. *T*: Deddington 38481. *Club*: Athenæum.

EDWARDS, Jack Trevor, CEng, FICE; FCIT; Senior Partner, Freeman Fox & Partners, since 1979; *b* 23 June 1920; *s* of late Col Cyril Ernest Edwards, DSO, MC, JP, and Jessie Boyd; *m* 1959, Josephine, (Sally), *d* of late S. W. Williams; one *d*. *Educ*: Felsted Sch.; City and Guilds Coll., Imperial Coll. London (BScEng, ACGI). RAF Armament and Airfield Construction Branches, Sqdn Ldr, 1941-46. Civil Engr on hydro-electric and power station stations, James Williamson and Partners, 1946-50; Freeman Fox & Partners, Engineer, 1951-64; Partner, 1965-79; special field: civil engrg and building works associated with thermal power stations and railways at home and overseas; major project: Hong Kong Mass Transit Railway, opened 1980; Engineer to Dean and Chapter of St Paul's Cathedral. Mem. Council, British Consultants Bureau, 1979-. Liveryman, Worshipful Co. of Painter-Stainers, 1969-. *Publications:* contrib. Proc. Instn of Civil Engrs. *Recreation:* sailing. *Address:* Keepers, 77 Brentwood Road, Ingrave, Brentwood, Essex CM13 3NU. *T:* Brentwood 810285. *Clubs:* St Stephen's Constitutional, Royal Cruising.

EDWARDS, Prof. James Griffith, DM, FRCP, FRCPsych; Professor of Addiction Behaviour, Institute of Psychiatry, University of London, since 1979; Hon. Director, Addiction Research Unit, since 1970; Hon. Consultant, Bethlem and Maudsley Hospitals, since 1967; Medical Director, Alcohol Education Centre, since 1980; *b* 3 Oct. 1928; *s* of late Dr J. T. Edwards and Constance Amy (*née* McFadyean); *m* 1st, 1969, Evelyn Humphries Morrison (marr. diss. 1981); one *s* one *d* (and one *d* decd); 2nd, 1981, Frances Susan Stables. *Educ:* Andover Grammar Sch.; Balliol Coll., Oxford (MA); St Bartholomew's Hosp. DM Oxford, 1966; DPM London, 1962; FRCP 1976; FRCPsych 1976. Served RA, 1948-49 (2nd Lieut). Jun. hosp. appts, King George, Ilford, St Bartholomew's, Hammersmith and Maudsley Hosps, 1956-62; Inst. of Psychiatry: res. worker, 1962; Lectr, 1966; Sen. Lectr, 1967; Reader, 1973. Chm., Royal Coll. of Psych. Special Cttee on Alcohol and Alcoholism, 1975-78; Member: Home Office Working Party on Drunkenness Offenders, 1967-70; DoE Cttee on Drinking and Driving, 1974-75; Home Office Adv. Council on Misuse of Drugs, 1972-; DHSS Adv. Cttee on Alcoholism, 1975-78; SSRC, 1981-; WHO Expert Adv. Cttee on Drug Dependence, 1969-; Internat. Adv. Bd, Addiction Res. Foundn, Toronto, 1971-; Adv. Bd, Nat. Alcohol Res. Center, Rutgers, USA, 1977-. Trustee, Community Drug Proj., 1967-. Steven's Lectr and Gold Medallist, RSM, 1971; Dent Lectr, King's Coll., 1980; Roche Vis. Prof., Aust. and NZ, 1982. Jellinek Meml Award, 1980. Editor, British Jl of Addiction, 1978-. *Publications:* Unreason in an Age of Reason, 1971; (jtly) Alcohol Control Policies, 1975; (ed jtly) Drugs and Drug Dependence, 1976; (ed jtly) Alcohol Dependence and Smoking Behaviour, 1976; (jtly) Alcoholism, 1977; (ed jtly) Alcohol-Related Disabilities, 1977; (ed jtly) Drugs in Socio-Cultural Perspective, 1980; (ed jtly) Treatment in Transition, 1980; (jtly) Opium and the People, 1981; Treatment of Drinking Problems, 1982; articles in jls on scientific and policy aspects of alcohol and drug dependence. *Address:* 42 Crooms Hill, SE10 8HD. *T:* 01-858 5631.

See also J. M. McF. Edwards.

EDWARDS, James Keith O'Neill; (Jimmy Edwards), DFC 1945; MA (Cantab); MFH; *b* 23 March 1920; *s* of late Prof. R. W. K. Edwards and late Mrs P. K. Edwards; *m* 1958, Valerie Seymour (marr. diss. 1969). *Educ:* St Paul's Cathedral Choir Sch.; King's Coll. Sch., Wimbledon; St John's Coll., Cambridge. Served War of 1939-45, in RAF, 1940-46. Windmill Theatre, London, 1946; Adelphi Theatre, 1950-51, 1952-54, 1954-55 and 1960-61; *Radio and Television:* Take It From Here, BBC, 1948-59; Does The Team Think?, BBC, 1957-77; Whack-O!, BBC Television, 1957-61 and 1971-72; Seven Faces of Jim, 1961-62; Six More Faces of Jim, 1962-63; Bold as Brass, 1964; John Jorrocks, Esq., BBC-2, 1966; Fosset Saga, ATV, 1969; The Glums, LWT, 1979. *Films:* Three Men in a Boat, 1957; Bottoms Up, 1960; Nearly a Nasty Accident, 1961; The Plank, 1979; Rhubarb, 1980. *Stage:* Big Bad Mouse, Shaftesbury, 1966-68; Prince of Wales, 1971; Halfway up the Tree, Queen's, 1968; Maid of the Mountains, Palace, 1972; Hulla Baloo, Criterion, 1972; Doctor in the House, 1978; Oh Sir James, 1979. Lord Rector of Aberdeen Univ., 1951-54. *Publications:* Take It From Me, 1952; Oh Sir James (play), 1979. *Recreations:* foxhunting, polo, flying, squash, brass bands. *Address:* c/o O'Neill Productions Ltd, Atheralls Farm, Fletching, Uckfield, East Sussex TN22 3TD. *T:* Newick 2258. *Club:* Savile.

EDWARDS, James Valentine, CVO 1978; MA; Headmaster of Heatherdown School, 1959-82; *b* 4 Feb. 1925; *s* of Captain Alfred Harold Edwards, OBE, and Mrs Eleanor Edwards; *m* Barbara, *d* of late Sir John Hanbury-Williams, CVO, and Lady Hanbury-Williams; two *d*, and one step *s* one step *d*. *Educ:* St Edmund's, Hindhead; Radley; Magdalen Coll., Oxford (MA). Served RN, 1943-47. Oxford, 1943 and 1947-49; Heatherdown Sch., 1952-82. *Address:* Long Sutton House, Long Sutton, near Langport, Som. *T:* Long Sutton 284. *Clubs:* MCC, Free Foresters.

EDWARDS, John; Editor, Yorkshire Post, since 1969; *b* 2 Jan. 1932; *s* of late Arthur Leonard Edwards; *m* 1st, 1954, Nancy Woodcock (*d* 1978); one *s* one *d*; 2nd, 1979, Brenda Rankin; one *d*. *Educ:* Wolverhampton Municipal Grammar School. Entered journalism, Wolverhampton Chronicle; subseq. worked on newspapers and magazines in Fleet Street and provinces; from 1961, Yorkshire Post: Dep. Night Editor, Business Editor, Asst Editor and Dep. Editor. Director: Yorkshire Post and Evening Post Ltd; East Yorkshire Printers Ltd. *Address:* 1 Edgerton Road, West Park, Leeds LS16 5JD.

EDWARDS, Sir John (Arthur), Kt 1970; CBE 1953; President, London Rent Assessment Panel, 1968-73 (Vice-President, 1965-68); *b* 1 June 1901; *s* of late John Edwards, JP, and Mary Elizabeth Cromar, Rossett; *m* 1932, Dorothy Margaret, *y d* of late Sir Richard Williams, OBE, DL, JP, Bangor, North Wales; two *s*. *Educ:* Grove Park Sch., Wrexham. FRICS. Chartered Surveyor. Articles and various appointments as a Chartered Surveyor and Land Agent, 1919-28; joined Valuation Office, 1929; Dep. Chief Valuer, Valuation Office, Bd of Inland Revenue, 1950-65. *Recreation:* fishing. *Address:* 29 High Firs, Gills Hill, Radlett, Herts. *T:* 6550.

EDWARDS, John Basil, CBE 1972; JP; Chairman, Magistrates Association, 1976-79; *b* 15 Jan. 1909; *s* of Charles and Susan Edwards; *m* 1935, Molly Patricia Philips (*d* 1979); one *s* two *d*. *Educ:* King's Sch., Worcester; Wadham Coll., Oxford (BA Hons Jurisprudence, MA). Commnd Royal Warwickshire Regt (RE) TA, 1938. Admitted Solicitor, 1933. Worcester CC, 1936; Mayor of Worcester, 1947-49; Alderman, City of Worcester, 1948. Magistrates Association: Mem. Council, 1960; Chm., Worcestershire Br., 1960-66; Hon. Treasurer, 1968-70; Dep. Chm., 1970-76. Mem., James Cttee on Distribution of Criminal Business, 1973-75. Chm., Worcester Three Choirs Festival, 1947-72. Freeman, City of London. Liveryman: Haberdashers Company; Distillers Company. JP Worcs 1940; Chm., Worcester City Justices, 1951-79. *Recreation:* gardening. *Address:* 21 Britannia Square, Worcester. *T:* Worcester 29933. *Club:* Royal Over-Seas League.

EDWARDS, John Braham Scott, MA (Oxon); His Honour Judge Edwards; a Circuit Judge, since 1977; *b* Bristol, 29 March 1928; *s* of late Lewis Edwards and late Hilda Edwards (*née* Scott); *m* 1963, Veronica Mary, *d* of late Lt-Col Howard Dunbar (killed in action, 1942), and of Mrs Brodie Good; one *s* two *d*. *Educ:* Royal Masonic Schools, Bushey; Merton Coll., Oxford. National service, 1946-48. Teaching Fellow, Univ. of Chicago Law Sch., 1952-53. Called to the Bar, Middle Temple, 1954; Bencher 1973. A Recorder of the Crown Court, 1972-77. Hon. Secretary-Gen. of Internat. Law Assoc., 1960-. Churchwarden, St Anne's, Kew. *Recreations:* golf, gardening. *Address:* 17 Ennerdale Road, Kew TW9 3PG. *T:* 01-940 8734. *Club:* Roehampton.

EDWARDS, John Charles, JP; Lord Mayor of Cardiff, 1980-81; *b* 3 April 1925; *s* of John Robert Edwards and Elsie Florence Edwards; *m* 1946, Cynthia Lorraine Bushell; one *s* two *d*. *Educ:* Lansdowne Road Sch., Cardiff. Served War of 1939-45, RM (1939-45 Star, France and Germany Star, War Medal 1939-45); TA, 1948-62, RASC (TEM). Postal Exec. Officer, GPO. Mem., S Glam CC, 1974-78; Dep. Lord Mayor, Cardiff, 1978-79. Freeman of City of London, 1981. JP S Glam, 1979. Mem., St John's Council for S Glam; OStJ 1980. *Recreations:* athletics, football. *Address:* 61 Cosmeston Street, Cathays, Cardiff CF2 4LQ. *T:* Cardiff 21506. *Clubs:* Civil Service; United Services Mess; Cardiff Athletic.

EDWARDS, Sir (John) Clive (Leighton), 2nd Bt *cr* 1921; *b* 1916; *s* of 1st Bt and Kathleen Ermyntrude (*d* 1975) *d* of late John Corfield, JP; *S* father, 1922. *Educ:* Winchester Coll. Volunteered and served in the Army, 1940-46. *Recreations:* motoring, gardening. *Heir:* none. *Address:* Milntown, Lezayre, near Ramsey, Isle of Man.

EDWARDS, John Coates; Head of West Indian and Atlantic Department, Foreign and Commonwealth Office, since 1981; *b* 25 Nov. 1934; *s* of Herbert John Edwards and late Doris May Edwards; *m* 1959, Mary Harris; one *s* one *d*. *Educ:* Skinners' Co. Sch., Tunbridge Wells, Kent; Brasenose Coll., Oxford (MA). Military Service, 1953-55: Lieut, RA. Asst Principal: Min. of Supply, 1958; Colonial Office, 1960; Private Sec. to Parly Under Sec. of State for the Colonies, 1961; Principal: Nature Conservancy, 1962; Min. of Overseas Develt, 1965; First Sec. (Develt), and UK Perm. Rep. to ECAFE, Bangkok, Thailand, 1968; Asst Sec., Min. of Overseas Develt, 1971; Head of E Africa Develt Div., Nairobi, Kenya, 1972; Asst Sec., Min. of Overseas Develt, 1976; Head of British Develt Div. in the Caribbean, Barbados, and UK Dir, Caribbean Develt Bank, 1978. *Address:* Fairways, Ightham, Sevenoaks, Kent. *T:* Borough Green 883556. *Club:* Royal Commonwealth Society.

EDWARDS, Prof. John Hilton, FRCP; FRS 1979; Professor of Genetics, University of Oxford, since 1979; *b* 26 March 1928; *s* of H. C. Edwards, *qv* ; *m* 1953, Felicity Clare, *d* of Dr C. H. C. Toussaint; two *s* two *d*. *Educ:* Univ. of Cambridge (MB, BChir). FRCP 1972. Mem., MRC Unit on Population Genetics, Oxford, 1956-60; Geneticist, Children's Hosp. of Philadelphia, 1960-61; Lectr, Sen. Lectr, and Reader, Birmingham Univ., 1961-67; Hon. Consultant Paediatrician, Birmingham Regional Bd, 1967; Vis. Prof. of Pediatrics, Cornell Univ., and Sen. Investigator, New York Blood Center, 1967-68; Consultant, Human Genetics, Univ. of Iceland, 1967-; Prof. of Human Genetics, Birmingham Univ., 1969-79. *Publications:* Human Genetics, 1978; scientific papers. *Recreations:* gliding, skiing. *Address:* 78 Old Road, Headington, Oxford. *Club:* Athenæum.

EDWARDS, John Lionel; retired civil servant; *b* 29 Aug. 1915; *s* of Rev. Arthur Edwards and Constance Edwards; *m* 1948, Cecily Miller; one *s* two *d*. *Educ:* Marlborough; Corpus Christi Coll., Oxford. Entered Scottish Office, 1938. Served War, (Army), 1940-45. Min. of Labour, 1945: Principal Private Sec. to Minister of Labour, 1956; Asst Sec., 1956; Sec., NEDC, 1968-71; Under-Sec., Dept of Employment, 1971-75; Certification Officer for Trade Unions and Employers' Assocs, 1976-81. *Address:* Little Bedwyn, The Ridgway, Pyrford, Surrey. *T:* Byfleet 43459. *Club:* United Oxford & Cambridge University.

EDWARDS, (John) Michael (McFadyean); QC 1981; Provost, City of London Polytechnic, since 1981; *b* 16 Oct. 1925; *s* of Dr James Thomas Edwards and Constance Amy Edwards, *yr d* of Sir John McFadyean; *m* 1st, 1952, Morna Joyce Piper (marr. diss.); one *s* one *d* ; 2nd, 1964, Rosemary Ann Moore; two *s*. *Educ:* Andover Grammar Sch. (schol.); University Coll., Oxford (BCL, MA). Called to the Bar, Middle Temple, 1949; Asst Parly Counsel, HM Treasury, 1955-60; Dep. Legal Advr and Dir of certain subsid. cos, Courtaulds Ltd, 1960-67; British Steel Corporation: Dir, Legal Services, 1967-71; Man. Dir, BSC (Internat.) Ltd, 1971-81; Chm. and Man. Dir, BSC

(Overseas Services) Ltd, 1975-81; Dir, Associated Communications Corp., 1982-. Member: Overseas Projects Bd, 1973-81; E European Trade Council, 1973-81; Accounting Educn Cons. Bd, 1982-; Student Educn Adv. Gp, ICA; Member: Bar Council, 1971-79, 1980-; Senate of Inns of Court and Bar, 1974-79, 1980-; Vice-Pres., Bar Assoc. for Commerce, Finance and Industry, 1980- (Chm., 1972-74). Governor, Eastman Dental Hosp., 1981-. Dir, Regional Opera Trust, 1981-; Mem. Council of Management, Kent Opera, 1981-. FBIM (Mem. Council and Court, 1978-81), Fellow, Inst. of Dirs; FRSA. Freeman, City of London; Liveryman, Ironmongers' Co. (Mem., Finance Cttee). *Publications:* sections on money and on statutes, Halsbury's Laws of England, 3rd edn 1955. *Recreations:* dinghy sailing, listening to music, vernacular architecture, local history. *Address:* City of London Polytechnic, 117-119 Houndsditch, EC3A 7BU. *T:* 01-283 1030. *Clubs:* Garrick; Bewl Valley Sailing (Lamberhurst).

See also J. G. Edwards.

EDWARDS, Rear Adm. John Phillip, MVO 1972; Director General, Fleet Support Policy and Services, since 1980; *b* 13 Feb. 1927; *s* of Robert Edwards and Dilys (*née* Phillips); *m* 1951, Gwen Lloyd Bonner; three *d. Educ:* Brynhyfryd Sch., Ruthin, Clwyd; HMS Conway; Royal Naval Engrg Colls, Keyham and Manadon. CEng, MIMechE 1963; FBIM 1980. Served, 1948-72: HMS Vengeance, Mauritius, Caledonia, Torquay, Lion, Diamond, Defender, HMCS Stadacona, and HMY Britannia; Mechanical Trng Estab., Portsmouth; Personnel Panel; Staff of C-in-C Fleet; sowc; Dep. Dir, RN Staff Coll., 1972-74; Asst Dir, Dir Gen. Ships, 1974-76; RCDS, 1977; Captain of Portland Naval Base, 1978-80. Comdr 1964, Captain 1971, Rear Adm. 1980. Hon. FISTC 1976. *Recreations:* golf, tennis. *Address:* Ministry of Defence, Whitehall, SW1A 2HB. *T:* 01-218 6450. *Club:* Royal Commonwealth Society.

EDWARDS, Joseph Robert, CBE 1963; JP; Chairman, Penta Motors Ltd, Reading, since 1978; Deputy Chairman, Martin Electrical Equipment (Theale) Ltd, since 1979; Director, CSE Aviation Ltd, since 1973; *b* 5 July 1908; *y s* of late Walter Smith Edwards and Annie Edwards, Gt Yarmouth; *m* 1st, 1936, Frances Mabel Haddon Bourne (*d* 1975); three *s* one *d* ; 2nd, 1976, Joan Constance Mary Tattersall. *Educ:* High Sch., Great Yarmouth. Joined Austin Motor Co., Birmingham, 1928; Hercules factory, 1939; rejoined Austin Motor Co., 1941; Gen. Works Manager, 1951; Local Dir, 1953; Works Dir, 1954; Dir of Manufacturing, British Motor Corp., 1955; Managing Director: British Motor Corp., 1966-68; Pressed Steel/Fisher Ltd, 1956-67; Dep. Chm., Harland & Wolff Ltd, 1968-70, Chm. 1970; Dep. Chm., Associated Engrg, 1969-78; Dir, BPC Ltd, 1973-81; Vice-Chm., Lucas (Industries) Ltd, 1976-79. Pres., Motor Industry Research Assoc. Mem., Commn on Industrial Relations to 1974. JP Oxford, 1964. Hon. MA Oxon, 1968. *Recreation:* golf. *Address:* Flat 16, Shoreacres, Banks Road, Sandbanks, Poole, Dorset BH13 7QH. *T:* Canford Cliffs 709315. *Clubs:* Royal Motor Yacht; Parkstone Golf.

EDWARDS, Julie Andrews; see Andrews, J.

EDWARDS, Kenneth; see Edwards, A. K.

EDWARDS, Rt. Rev. Lewis Mervyn Charles-; see Charles-Edwards.

EDWARDS, Sir Martin Llewellyn, Kt 1974; DL; Solicitor; Consultant with Edwards, Geldard & Shepherd, Cardiff; *b* 21 May 1909; *s* of Charles Ernest Edwards, Solicitor, and Annie Matilda Edwards (*née* Llewellyn); *m* 1936, Dorothy Ward Harrap; one *s* two *d* (and one *d* decd). *Educ:* Marlborough Coll.; Lincoln Coll., Oxford (MA). Admitted Solicitor, 1934. Commnd in RAuxAF, 1937; served 614 (Glamorgan Sqdn RAuxAF, UK, 1937-41; 24 Sqdn, 1941-42; RAF Staff Coll., 1942; Wing Comdr Desert Air Force, HQ Iraq, Persia, and Air Defences Eastern Med., 1942-43; Mem. Directing Staff, ME Jt Staff Coll., Haifa, 1944; Station Comdr, RAF Amman, 1944-45. Mem. Council and Gen. Purposes and Finance Cttees, Glamorgan T&AFA, 1946-68 (Vice-Chm., Air, 1961-68). Mem. Council, Law Society, 1957 (Vice-Pres. 1972-73, Pres., 1973-74; Chm., Educn and Trng Cttee, 1966-69). Pres., Associated Law Socs of Wales, 1960-62; Pres., Incorporated Law Soc. for Cardiff and District, 1969-70. Member: Lord Chancellor's Cttee on Legal Educn, 1967-71. Council, UWIST, 1969-78; Drinking and Driving Cttee, DoE, 1974-76; part-time Chm., Industrial Tribunals, 1975-78. Governor, Coll. of Law, 1967-80 (Chm. of Governors, 1969-72). DL Glamorgan, 1961. *Recreations:* walking, gardening, photography. *Address:* Pentwyn Farm, Graig Llwyn Road, Lisvane, Cardiff CF4 5RP. *T:* Cardiff 751813. *Clubs:* Army and Navy; Cardiff and County (Cardiff).

EDWARDS, Michael; see Edwards, J. M. McF.

EDWARDS, Rt. Hon. Nicholas; see Edwards, Rt Hon. R. N.

EDWARDS, Owen; Director, Sianel 4 Cymru, (Welsh Fourth Channel Authority), since 1981; *b* 26 Dec. 1933; *m* 1958, Shàn Emlyn; two *d. Educ:* Leighton Park, Reading; Lincoln Coll., Oxford (MA). Cataloguer, Nat. Library of Wales, 1958-60; BBC Wales: Compère, TV Programme Heddiw, 1961-66; Programme Organiser, 1967-70; Head of Programmes, 1970-74; Controller, 1974-81. *Recreations:* swimming, walking. *Address:* (office) Sianel 4 Cymru, Sophia Close, Cardiff CF1 9XY. *T:* Cardiff 43421; (home) Coed-y-Pry, 3 Llandennis Avenue, Cyncoed, Cardiff. *T:* Cardiff 751469.

EDWARDS, Prof. Philip Walter, PhD; King Alfred Professor of English Literature, University of Liverpool, since 1974; *b* 7 Feb. 1923; *er s* of late R. H. Edwards, MC, and late Mrs B. Edwards; *m* 1st, 1947, Hazel Margaret (*d* 1950), *d* of late Prof. C. W. and Mrs E. R. Valentine; 2nd, 1952, Sheila Mary, *d* of R. S. and Mrs A. M. Wilkes, Bloxwich, Staffs; three *s* one *d. Educ:* King Edward's High Sch., Birmingham; Univ. of Birmingham. MA, PhD Birmingham; MA Dublin. Royal Navy, 1942-45 (Sub-Lieut RNVR). Lectr in English, Univ. of Birmingham, 1946-60; Commonwealth Fund Fellow, Harvard Univ., 1954-55; Prof. of English Lit., TCD, 1960-66; Fellow of TCD, 1962-66; Vis. Prof., Univ. of Michigan, 1964-65; Prof. of Lit., Univ. of Essex, 1966-74; Vis. Prof., Williams Coll., Mass, 1969; Vis. Fellow, All Souls Coll., Oxford, 1970-71; Visiting Prof., Univ. of Otago, NZ, 1980. Pro-Vice-Chancellor, Univ. of Liverpool, 1980-83. *Publications:* Sir Walter Ralegh, 1953; (ed) Kyd: The Spanish Tragedy, 1959; Shakespeare and the Confines of Art, 1968; (ed) Pericles Prince of Tyre, 1976; (ed with C. Gibson) Massinger, Plays and Poems, 1976; Threshold of a Nation, 1979; (ed jtly) Shakespeare's Styles, 1980; numerous articles on Shakespeare and literature of his time in Shakespeare Survey, Proc. British Acad., etc. *Recreation:* hill walking. *Address:* 12 South Bank, Oxton, Birkenhead L43 5UP. *T:* 051-652 6089.

EDWARDS, Quentin Tytler, QC 1975; **His Honour Judge Quentin Edwards;** a Circuit Judge, since 1982; Chancellor, Diocese of Blackburn, since 1977, Diocese of Chichester, since 1978; *b* 16 Jan. 1925; *s* of Herbert Jackson Edwards and Juliet Hester Edwards; *m* 1948, Barbara Marian Guthrie; two *s* one *d. Educ:* Bradfield Coll.; Council of Legal Educn. Royal Navy, 1943-46. Called to Bar, Middle Temple, 1948; Bencher, 1972. A Recorder of the Crown Court, 1974-82. Licensed Reader, Dio. of London, 1967; Member: Legal Adv. Commn of General Synod of Church of England, 1973; Dioceses Commn, 1978-. Hon. MA (Archbp of Canterbury), 1961. *Publications:* (with Peter Dow) Public Rights of Way and Access to the Countryside, 1951; (with K. Macmorran, et al) Ecclesiastical Law, 3rd edn, Halsbury's Law of England, 1955; What is Unlawful?, 1959; (with J. N. D. Anderson, et al) Putting Asunder, 1966. *Recreations:* the open air; the table; architecture. *Address:* c/o The Treasury, Middle Temple, EC4.

EDWARDS, Richard Lionel, QC 1952; *b* 1 Aug. 1907; *s* of late Lionel T. Edwards, BA, JP, Weston Underwood, Olney, Bucks; *m* 1944, Eleanor Middleton, *d* of late Sir Henry Japp, KBE; no *c. Educ:* Rugby Sch.; Oriel Coll., Oxford. Called to English Bar, 1930; Bencher of Lincoln's Inn, 1957. *Recreations:* gardening, Italian painting and fishing. *Address:* Weston Underwood, Olney, Bucks. *T:* Bedford 711312.

EDWARDS, Robert; MP (Lab and Co-op) Wolverhampton South East, since 1974 (Bilston, 1955-74); National Officer of Transport and General Workers' Union, 1971-76; *b* 16 Jan. 1905; *m* 1933, Edith May Sandham (*d* 1970); one *s. Educ:* Council Schs and Technical Coll. Served with Republicans in Spain during Spanish civil war. Chm. delegns to Russia, 1926 and 1934. Mem. Liverpool City Council, 1929-32; Nat. Chm., ILP, 1943-48; Founder Pres., Socialist Movement for United States of Europe. Contested (ILP) Chorley 1935, Stretford 1939 and Newport 1945. Gen. Sec., Chemical Workers' Union, 1947-71; Chm., Chem. Section, ICF, 1971-. Vice-President: British Section European League for Economic Co-operation; Economic Research Council; Council of Europe, 1969-70; Dep. Leader, British Delgn to Council of Europe, and Chm., Defence Cttee, WEU Assembly, 1968-; Leader, British Delegn, N Atlantic Assembly, 1968-69. Chm., Parly Gp for Industrial Common Ownership, 1976-; Mem., European Parlt, 1977-79. Editor, The Chemical Worker. Trustee, Scott Bader Commonwealth, 1969. *Publications:* Chemicals—Servant or Master, 1947; Study of a Master Spy, 1962; Multinationals and the Trade Unions, 1978; One Year in the European Parliament, 1979. *Address:* House of Commons, SW1.

EDWARDS, Robert Geoffrey; Reader in Physiology, Cambridge University; Fellow, Churchill College, Cambridge; Scientific Director, Bourn Hall Clinic, Cambridgeshire; *b* 27 Sept. 1925; *s* of Samuel and Margaret Edwards; *m* 1956, Ruth Eileen Fowler; five *d. Educ:* Manchester Central High Sch.; Univs of Wales and Edinburgh. PhD (Edin); DSc (Wales). Service in British Army, 1944-48; commnd 1946. UC North Wales, Bangor, 1948-51; Univ. of Edinburgh, 1951-57; Res. Fellow at California Inst. of Tech., 1957-58; Scientist at Nat. Inst. of Medical Research, Mill Hill, NW7, 1958-62; Glasgow Univ. 1962-63; in Dept of Physiology, Cambridge Univ. 1963-; apptd Ford Foundation Reader in Physiology, 1969. Vis. Scientist: in Johns Hopkins Hosp., Baltimore, 1965; Univ. of N Carolina, 1966. *Publications:* A Matter of Life (with P. C. Steptoe), 1980; Conception in the Human Female, 1980; (with C. R. Austin) Mechanisms of Sex Differentiation in Animals and Man; editor of several scientific textbooks on reproduction; numerous articles in scientific and medical jls, organiser of conferences, etc. *Recreations:* farming, politics, music. *Address:* Duck End Farm, Dry Drayton, Cambridge. *T:* Crafts Hill 80602.

EDWARDS, Robert John; Editor, Sunday Mirror, since 1972; *b* 26 Oct. 1925; *m* 1st, 1952, Laura Ellwood (marr. diss. 1972); two *s* two *d* ; 2nd, 1977, Brigid Segrave. *Educ:* Ranelagh Sch., Bracknell. Editor, Tribune, 1951-54; Dep. Editor, Sunday Express, 1957-59; Man. Editor, Daily Express, 1959-61; Editor: Daily Express, 1961, 1963-65; Evening Citizen, Glasgow, 1962-63; The Sunday People, 1966-72; Dir, Mirror Group Newspapers, 1976-. Broadcaster. *Address:* Sunday Mirror, 33 Holborn, EC1P 1DQ. *Clubs:*

Reform, Kennel, Variety Club of Great Britain, Burkes; Royal Southern Yacht.

EDWARDS, Robert Septimus Friar, CVO 1964; CBE 1963; *b* 21 Oct. 1910; *y s* of late Augustus C. Edwards and of Amy Edwards; *m* 1946, Janet Mabel Wrigley; one *s* two *d. Educ:* Hereford Cathedral Sch. Chief Engineering Asst, Hereford, until 1936; Min. of Transport, Highway Engineering, 1936-43; Principal, Min. of War Transport, 1943; Mem. British Merchant Shipping Mission, Washington, DC, 1944-46. Sec. Gen. Internat. Conf. on Safety of Life at Sea, 1948; Principal Private Sec. to Minister of Transport, 1949-51; Shipping Attaché, British Embassy, Washington, DC, 1951-54; Dir of Sea Transport, 1954-57; Gen. Manager, London Airports, 1957-63; Gen. Manager, 1967-69, Dir-Gen., 1969-71, Mersey Docks and Harbour Board. Chm., Morris & David Jones Ltd, 1973-74. Called to the Bar, Middle Temple, 1941. *Recreation:* golf. *Address:* Bryn-y-Groes, Nannerch, Clwyd CH7 5QS. *T:* Mold 740018.

EDWARDS, Robin Anthony, CBE 1981; Partner with Dundas & Wilson, CS (formerly Davidson & Syme, WS), since 1965; *b* 7 April 1939; *s* of Alfred Walton Edwards and Ena Annie Ruffell; *m* 1963, Elizabeth Alexandra Mackay; one *s* one *d. Educ:* Daniel Stewart's Coll., Edinburgh; Edinburgh Univ. (MA, LLB (distinction), Cl. Medallist). Former Lectr in Conveyancing, Edinburgh Univ.; Admitted Member, WS Society, 1964; Mem. Council, Law Society of Scotland, 1969-, Vice-Pres., 1978-79, Pres., 1979-80 (youngest Pres. ever, at that time). *Recreations:* golf, travel. *Address:* 12 Barnton Gardens, Edinburgh EH4 6AF. *T:* 031-336 3272.

EDWARDS, Rt. Hon. (Roger) Nicholas; PC 1979; MP (C) Pembroke since 1970; Secretary of State for Wales, since 1979; *b* 25 Feb. 1934; *s* of late (H. C.) Ralph Edwards, CBE, FSA, and of Marjorie Ingham Brooke; *m* 1963, Ankaret Healing; one *s* two *d. Educ:* Westminster Sch.; Trinity Coll., Cambridge, 1954-57; read History: BA 1957, MA, 1968. Member of Lloyds, 1965-. Opposition spokesman on Welsh affairs, 1975-79. *Publications:* articles and reviews in The Connoisseur and other jls. *Recreations:* fishing, gardening, collecting English drawings. *Address:* Pontesgob Mill, Fforest Coalpit, near Abergavenny, Gwent; 20 Chester Row, SW1; Peach House, Rhos, Haverfordwest, Dyfed. *Clubs:* Carlton; Cardiff and County.

EDWARDS, Dr Roger Snowden, CBE 1964; JP; Chairman, Gas Industry Training Board, 1965-74, retired; *b* 19 Dec. 1904; *s* of late Herbert George Edwards and late Margaret Alice Edwards; *m* 1935, Eveline Brunton, MBE; two *s* one *d. Educ:* Enfield Grammar Sch.; Imperial Coll. of Science. Junior Staff, Imperial Coll. of Science, 1925-28; Physicist, British Xylonite Co., 1928-29; Physicist, Boot Trade Research Association, 1929-39; Dir, Co-operative Wholesale Soc., 1939-49. Chairman: Council of Industrial Design, 1947-52 (Mem., 1944-47); NE Gas Board, 1949-66; Mem., Gas Council, 1966-70. JP Harrogate, 1960; Surrey, 1966. *Recreation:* golf. *Address:* 23 Manor Way, Letchworth, Herts SG6 3NL.

EDWARDS, Prof. Sir Samuel Frederick, (Sir Sam Edwards), Kt 1975; FRS 1966; John Humphrey Plummer Professor of Physics, Cambridge University, since 1972; Fellow, Caius College, since 1972; *b* 1 Feb. 1928; *s* of Richard and Mary Jane Edwards, Manselton, Swansea; *m* 1953, Merriell E. M. Bland; one *s* three *d. Educ:* Swansea Grammar Sch.; Caius Coll., Cambridge (MA, PhD); Harvard University. Inst. for Advanced Study, Princeton, 1952; Univ. of Birmingham, 1953; Univ. of Manchester, 1958, Prof. of Theoretical Physics, 1963-72. Chm., SRC, 1973-77. UK Deleg. to NATO Science Cttee, 1974-79; Mem., Planning Cttee, Max-Planck Gesellschaft, 1974-77. Vice-Pres., Institute of Physics, 1970-73 (Mem. Council, 1967-73); Mem. Council, Inst. of Mathematics and its Applications, 1976- (Vice-Pres., 1979, Pres., 1980-81). Member: Physics Cttee, SRC, 1968-73 (Chm. 1970-73); Polymer Cttee, SRC, 1968-73; Science Bd, SRC, 1970-73; Council, European Physical Soc., 1969-71 (Chm., Condensed Matter Div., 1969-71); UGC, 1971-73; Defence Scientific Adv. Council, 1973- (Chm., 1977-80); Metrology and Standards Req. Bd, Dept of Industry, 1974-77; Adv. Council on R&D, Dept of Energy, 1974-77; Member Council: European R&D (EEC), 1976-80; Royal Soc., 1982-; Chm., Council, BAAS, 1977-. Non-exec. Dir, Lucas Industries, 1981-; Mem., Sci. Adv. Cttee, Allied Corp., NJ, 1980-. FInstP; FIMA. Hon. DTech Loughborough, 1975; Hon. DSc: Salford, Edinburgh, 1976; Bath, 1978. Maxwell Medal and Prize, Inst. of Physics, 1974; High Polymer Physics Prize, Amer. Phys. Soc., 1982. *Publications:* Technological Risk, 1980; contribs to learned jls. *Address:* 7 Penarth Place, Cambridge CB3 9LU. *T:* Cambridge 66610. *Club:* Athenæum.

EDWARDS, Stewart Leslie, CMG 1967; Under-Secretary, Department of Trade, retired; *b* 6 Nov. 1914; *s* of late Walter James and Lilian Emma Edwards; *m* 1940, Dominica Jeanne Lavie, *d* of Joseph Lavie and Jeanne Jauréguiberry; two *s. Educ:* King's Sch., Canterbury; Corpus Christi Coll., Cambridge (Foundn Scholar). BA 1936; MA 1943. Appointed to War Office, 1937. Military service, 1942-44. Called to the Bar, Inner Temple, 1947. Seconded from War Office to OEEC, 1948-51; Board of Trade, 1951-65; Minister (Economic), Bonn, 1965-70; Under-Sec., DTI later Dept of Trade, 1970-74. *Recreations:* music, reading, hill-walking, wine. *Address:* Wildshaw House, West Heath, Limpsfield, Surrey. *T:* Oxted 4753.

EDWARDS, Vero C. W.; *see* Wynne-Edwards.

EDWARDS, William (Henry); solicitor; *b* 6 Jan. 1938; *s* of Owen Henry Edwards and S. Edwards; *m* 1961, Ann Eleri Rogers; one *s* three *d. Educ:* Sir Thomas Jones' Comprehensive Sch.; Liverpool Univ. LLB. MP (Lab) Merioneth, 1966-Feb. 1974; contested (Lab) Merioneth, Oct. 1974; Prospective Parly Cand. (Lab), Anglesey, 1981-. Mem., Historic Building Council for Wales, 1971-76. Editor, Solicitors Diary. *Recreations:* golf, Association football (from the terraces). *Address:* Bryniau Golau, Bala, Gwynedd.

EDWARDS, William Philip Neville, CBE 1949; *b* 5 Aug. 1904; *s* of late Neville P. Edwards, Orford, Littlehampton, Sussex; *m* 1st, 1931, Hon. Sheila Cary (*d* 1976), 2nd *d* of 13th Viscount Falkland; two *s*; 2nd, 1976, Joan, *widow* of Norman Mullins. *Educ:* Rugby Sch.; Corpus Christi Coll., Cambridge; Princeton Univ., USA (Davison Scholar). Joined Underground Electric group of companies, 1927; shortly afterwards appointed Sec. to Lord Ashfield, Chm. of Board; First Sec. of Standing Jt Cttee of Main Line Railway Companies and of LPTB, 1933; Officer of Board as Personal Asst to Gen. Manager of Railways, 1937; Outdoor Supt of Railways, 1938; Public Relations Officer of Board, 1939; Asst to Chm. of Supply Council of Min. of Supply, 1941-42; Head of Industrial Information Div. of Min. of Production and Alternate Dir of Information of British Supply Council in N America, 1943-45; Dir of Overseas Information Div. of BoT, 1945-46; Head of British Information Services in USA, 1946-49. A Dir, Confedn of British Industry (previously FBI), 1949-66; Man. Dir, British Overseas Fairs Ltd, 1959-66, Chm., 1966-68. UK Associate Dir, Business International SA, 1968-75; Chm., Public Relations (Industrial) Ltd, 1970-75. Chevalier (1st class) of Order of Dannebrog (Denmark), 1955; Commander of Order of Vasa (Sweden), 1962. *Recreations:* golf, gardening. *Address:* Four Winds, Kithurst Lane, Storrington, Sussex RH20 4LP. *Club:* Carlton.

EDWARDS-JONES, Ian, QC 1967; a Social Security (formerly National Insurance) Commissioner, since 1979; *b* 17 April 1923; *o s* of late Col H. V. Edwards-Jones, MC, DL, Swansea, Glam; *m* 1950, Susan Vera Catharine McClintock, *o d* of E. S. McClintock and of Mrs A. MacRossie; three *s. Educ:* Rugby Sch.; Trinity Coll., Cambridge (BA). Capt., RA, N Africa, Italy, Palestine, 1942-47. Called to Bar, Middle Temple, Lincoln's Inn, 1948, Bencher, Lincoln's Inn, 1975. *Recreations:* fishing, shooting, photography. *Address:* 7 Stone Buildings, Lincoln's Inn, WC2A 3SZ. *T:* 01-405 3886/7. *Clubs:* United Oxford & Cambridge University; Bar Yacht.

EDWARDS-MOSS, Sir John (Herbert Theodore), 4th Bt *cr* 1868; *b* 24 June 1913; *s* of late Major John Edwards-Moss and Dorothy Kate Gwyllyam, *e d* of late Ven. Henry William Watkins, DD; *S* uncle, Sir Thomas Edwards-Moss, 3rd Bt, 1960; *m* 1951, Jane Rebie, *d* of Carteret John Kempson; five *s* one *d. Educ:* Downhouse, Rottingdean. *Heir: s* David John Edwards-Moss, *b* 2 Feb. 1955. *Address:* Ruffold Farm, Cranleigh, Surrey.

EELES, Air Cdre Henry, CB 1956; CBE 1943; retired as Director of Administrative Plans, Air Ministry, 1959; *b* 12 May 1910; *yr s* of Henry Eeles, Newcastle upon Tyne; *m* 1st, 1940, Janet (*d* 1960), *d* of Major J. H. Norton; two *s* one *d*; 2nd, 1963, Pamela Clarice, *d* of Comdr G. A. Matthew, Royal Navy. *Educ:* Harrow. Entered RAF Coll., 1929; Commnd Dec. 1930; Sqdn Ldr 1938; Group Capt. 1949; Air Cdre 1955. Comdt RAF Coll. and AOC RAF Cranwell, 1952-56. *Address:* The Cottage, Sutton Veny, Warminster, Wilts.

EFFINGHAM, 6th Earl of, *cr* 1837; **Mowbray Henry Gordon Howard;** 16th Baron Howard, of Effingham, *cr* 1554; *b* 29 Nov. 1905; *er s* of 5th Earl and Rosamond Margaret, *d* of late E. H. Hudson; *S* father, 1946; *m* 1st, 1938, Manci Maria Malvina Gertler (marr. diss. 1946); 2nd, 1952, Gladys Irene Kerry (marr. diss. 1971); 3rd, 1972, (Mabel) Suzanne Mingay Cragg, *d* of late Maurice Jules-Marie Le Pen, Paris, and *widow* of Wing Comdr Francis Talbot Cragg. *Educ:* Lancing. Served War 1939-45, RA and 3rd Maritime Reg. *Recreations:* shooting, fishing, philately. *Heir: n* Lt-Comdr David Peter Mowbray Algernon Howard, RN [*b* 29 April 1939; *m* 1964, Anne Mary Sayer (marr. diss. 1975); one *s*]. *Address:* House of Lords, SW1.

EGAN, Dr Harold; Government Chemist, 1970-81; *b* 23 Dec. 1922; *o s* of late Silas Henry Egan and Jenny Egan (*née* Vanner); *m* 1948, Daphne Marian Downing Cleeland; one *s. Educ:* Chiswick County Sch.; Acton Technical Coll.; Imperial Coll. London. BSc, PhD, DIC. St George's Hosp., London (Biochemical Dept), 1940-43; Dept (later Laboratory) of the Government Chemist, 1943-. Visiting Professor: Food Science, Queen Elizabeth Coll., Univ. of London, 1973-77; Chem. Scis, UEA, 1980-; Chem. of the Environment, KCL, 1980-. Member: British Hallmarking Council; ICSU Scientific Cttee on Problems of the Envt, 1979-; Sec., CHEMRAWN (chemical research applied to world needs) Cttee, Internat. Union of Pure and Applied Chemistry, 1979-; Pres., Internat. Acad. of Environmental Safety, 1980-81. FRSC, FRSH, FIFST, FRNS. *Publications:* various papers on trace analysis, particularly pesticide residues and other environmental contaminants. *Recreations:* maps, books on London, Home Counties. *Address:* 49 Medway Gardens, Wembley, Mddx HA0 2RJ. *T:* 01-904 6229. *Club:* Athenæum.

EGDELL, Dr John Duncan; Regional Medical Officer, Mersey Regional Health Authority, since 1977; *b* 5 March 1938; *s* of John William Egdell and Nellie (*née* Thompson); *m* 1963, Dr Linda Mary Flint; two *s* one *d. Educ:* Clifton Coll.; Univ. of Bristol. MB, ChB (Bristol) 1961; DipSocMed (Edin.) 1967; FFCM 1979 (MFCM 1973). Ho. Phys. and Ho. Surg., Bristol Gen.

Hosp., 1961-62; gen. practice, 1962-65; Med. Administration: with Newcastle Regional Hosp. Bd, 1966-69; with South Western Regional Hosp. Bd, 1969-74; Regional Specialist in Community Med., South Western Regional Health Authority, 1974-76; Regional Medical Postgrad. Co-ordinator, Univ. of Bristol, 1973-76. *Recreations:* delving into the past; investigating the obscure. *Address:* 8 Kingsmead Road North, Oxton, Birkenhead, Merseyside L43 6TB. *T:* 051-653 7810.

EGELAND, Leif; *b* 19 Jan. 1903; *s* of late J. J. Egeland, Consul for Norway in Natal, and Ragnhild Konsmo; *m* 1942, Marguerite Doreen, *d* of late W. J. de Zwann, Waterkloof, Pretoria; one *d. Educ:* Durban High Sch.; Natal University Coll.; Oxford Univ. MA English Lang. and Literature, Natal Univ. Coll.; MA, Hons BA, Jurisprudence, BCL Oxon; Rhodes Scholar (Natal), Trinity Coll., Oxford, 1924-27; official Fellow in Law and Classics, Brasenose Coll., 1927-30; Harmsworth Scholar, Middle Temple, 1927-30; Barrister, Middle Temple, 1930, bencher, 1948; Hon. LLD Cambridge, 1948. Admitted as Advocate of Supreme Court of S Africa, 1931; Vice-Consul for Norway, Natal, 1931-44; MP (House of Assembly) for Durban (Berea), 1933-38, for Zululand, 1940-43; SA Minister to Sweden, 1943, to Holland and Belgium, 1946. Served War of 1939-45, as AJAG, in UDF, 1940-43; Middle East with 6th Armoured Div. of UDF, 1943. SA Delegate to San Francisco Conf., 1945, to 1st Gen. Assembly of UN, London, 1946, to Final Assembly of League of Nations, 1946; SA delegate and Pres. of Commn on Italian Political and Territorial Questions at Peace Conf., Paris, 1946. High Comr in London for the Union of South Africa, 1948-50; Chm., Standard Insurance Co. Ltd. Hon. Pres., South Africa Inst. of Internat. Affairs; Chm., Smuts Memorial Trust; Life Trustee, South Africa Foundn. Hon. Pres., SA Guide-dogs Assoc. for the Blind. FRSA 1948. *Recreation:* tennis. *Address:* 11 Fricker Road, Illovo, Johannesburg, S Africa. *Clubs:* Rand, Inanda (S Africa).

EGERTON, family name of **Duke of Sutherland** and **Earl of Wilton.**

EGERTON, Maj.-Gen. David Boswell, CB 1968; OBE 1956; MC 1940; *b* 24 July 1914; *s* of Vice-Admiral W. de M. Egerton, DSO, and late Anita Adolphine (*née* David); *m* 1946, Margaret Gillian, *d* of Canon C. C. Inge; one *s* two *d. Educ:* Stowe; RMA Woolwich. Commissioned Royal Artillery, Aug. 1934; served in India, 1935-39; ops in Waziristan, 1937; France and Belgium, 1940 (MC); Egypt 1942, Italy 1944 (wounded). Technical Staff course, RMCS, 1946; BJSM, Washington, DC, 1950-52; Asst Chief Engineer in charge of ammunition development, Royal Armament R&D Estabt, 1955-58; idc 1959; Army Mem., Defence Research Policy Staff, 1959-62; Comdt, Trials Estabt Guided Weapons, RA, 1962-63; Army Mem., Air Defence Working Party, 1963-64; Dir-Gen. of Artillery, Army Dept, 1964-67; Vice-Pres., Ordnance Board, 1967-69, President, 1969-70; retired 1970. Col Comdt, RA, 1970-74. Gen. Sec., Assoc. of Recognised Eng. Lang. Schs, 1971-79. *Recreations:* gardening, travel. *Address:* Campion Cottage, Cheselbourne, Dorchester. *T:* Milborne St Andrew 641. *Club:* Army and Navy.

EGERTON, Sir John Alfred Roy, (Jack Egerton), Kt 1976; former President, Queensland Trades and Labor Council; Member, Federal Executive of ALP, 1970 (Senior Vice-President, 1972); *b* Rockhampton, 11 March 1918; *s* of J. G. Egerton, Rockhampton; *m* 1940, Moya, *d* of W. Jones; one *s. Educ:* Rockhampton High Sch.; Mt Morgan High Sch.; Australian Admin. Staff Coll. A Union Exec. Officer, 1941-76; Federal Officer of Boilermakers' Union, 1951-66 (Vice-Pres. Fed. Council; rep. Union in China, 1956); Official, Metal Trades Fedn, 1951-67. Aust. Rep. ILO Congresses, Geneva: 1960, 1966, 1968, 1974; Qld Rep. to ACTU Congress and ALP Fed. Conf.; Pres., ALP Qld Exec., 1968-76 (Mem. Qld Central Exec., 1958); Mem., ACTU Interstate Exec., 1969. Director: Qantas Airways Ltd, 1973-; Mary Kathleen Uranium; SGIO Building Soc. Member: Duke of Edinburgh Study Conf. Cttee, 1967-74; Griffith Univ. Council. *Recreations:* reading, Rugby League (Vice-Pres. and Dir, Qld), golf, trotting. *Clubs:* NSW and Queensland League, Virginia Golf, Albion Park Trotting.

EGERTON, Sir Philip John Caledon G.; *see* Grey Egerton.

EGERTON, Sir Seymour (John Louis), GCVO 1977 (KCVO 1970); Director, Coutts & Co., Bankers, since 1947 (Chairman, 1951-76); *b* 24 Sept. 1915; *s* of late Louis Egerton and Jane, *e d* of Rev. Lord Victor Seymour; unmarried. *Educ:* Eton. Served War of 1939-45, in Grenadier Guards. Governor, St George's Hosp., 1958-73. Treasurer, Boy Scouts' Assoc., 1953-64; Vice-Pres., Corporation of the Church House, 1954-48. Sheriff of Greater London, 1968. *Address:* Flat A, 51 Eaton Square, SW1. *T:* 01-235 2164. *Clubs:* Boodle's, Beefsteak, Pratt's.

EGERTON, Stephen Loftus, CMG 1978; HM Diplomatic Service; Assistant Under-Secretary of State, Foreign and Commonwealth Office, since 1982; *b* 21 July 1932; *o s* of late William le Belward Egerton, ICS, and late Angela Doreen Loftus Bland; *m* 1958, Caroline, *er d* of Major and Mrs E. T. E. Cary-Elwes, Laurel House, Bergh Apton, Norfolk; one *s* one *d. Educ:* Summer Fields; Eton (King's Scholar 1946, Newcastle Scholar 1951); Trinity Coll., Cambridge (Major Scholar). BA 1956, MA 1960. 2nd Lieut, 6th Rifles (KRRC), 1952-53. Entered Foreign Service, 1956; Middle East Centre for Arab Studies, Lebanon, 1956-57; Political Officer and Court Registrar, Kuwait, 1958-61; Private Sec. to Parliamentary Under-Secretary, FO, 1961-62; Northern Dept, FO, 1962-63; Oriental Sec. and later also Head of

Chancery, Baghdad, 1963-67; First Sec., UK Mission to the UN, New York, 1967-70; Asst Head of Arabian and Near Eastern Depts, FCO, 1970-72; Counsellor and Head of Chancery, Tripoli, 1972-73; Head of Energy Dept, FCO, 1973-77; Consul-Gen., Rio de Janeiro, 1977-80; Ambassador to Iraq, 1980-82. *Recreations:* conversation, coins and medals. *Address:* c/o Foreign and Commonwealth Office, SW1; 31 Crescent Wood Road, Dulwich, SE26. *Clubs:* Brooks's; Greenjackets.

EGGAR, Timothy John Crommelin, (Tim); MP (C) Enfield North, since 1979; *b* 19 Dec. 1951; *s* of John Drennan Eggar and Pamela Rosemary Eggar; *m* 1977, Charmian Diana Minoprio; one *s* one *d. Educ:* Winchester Coll.; Magdalene Coll., Cambridge (MA); Coll. of Law, London. Called to the Bar, Inner Temple, 1976. Hambros Bank, 1974-75; European Banking Co., 1975-. Chm., Cambridge Univ. Cons. Assoc., 1972; Vice-Chairman: Fedn of Cons. Students, 1973-74; Islington S and Finsbury Cons. Assoc., 1975. PA to Rt Hon. William Whitelaw, 1974; Prospective Parly Candidate, Enfield N, 1975-79. *Recreations:* skiing, village cricket, simple gardening. *Address:* House of Commons, SW1A 0AA. *T:* 01-219 3544. *Clubs:* Bush Hill Park Conservative, Enfield Highway Conservative, Ponders End Conservative, North Enfield Conservative.

EGGINTON, Anthony Joseph; Director of Science and Engineering Divisions, Science Research Council, since 1978; *b* 18 July 1930; *s* of Arthur Reginald Egginton and Margaret Anne (*née* Emslie); *m* 1957, Janet Leta, *d* of late Albert and Florence Herring; two *d. Educ:* Selhurst Grammar Sch., Croydon; University Coll., London. BSc 1951. Res. Assoc., UCL, 1951-56; AERE Harwell (Gen. Physics Div.), 1956-61; Head of Beams Physics Gp, NIRNS Rutherford High Energy Lab., 1961-65; Head of Machine Gp, SRC Daresbury Nuclear Physics Lab., 1965-72; Head of Engrg Div., 1972-74, Dir of Engineering and Nuclear Physics, 1974-78, SRC. *Publications:* papers and articles in jls and conf. proceedings on particle accelerators and beams. *Recreations:* sport, reading, music. *Address:* The Close, Boar's Hill, Oxford. *T:* Oxford 739077.

EGGLESTON, Anthony Francis, OBE 1968; Headmaster, Campion School, Athens, since 1983; *b* 26 Jan. 1928; *s* of late J. F. Eggleston and late Mrs J. M. Barnard, Harrow, Middx; *m* 1957, Jane Morison Buxton, JP, *d* of late W. L. Buxton, MBE and Mrs F. M. M. Buxton, Stanmore, Middx; one *s* two *d. Educ:* Merchant Taylors' Sch., Northwood (Schol.); St John's Coll., Oxford (Sir Thomas White Schol.). BA 1949, MA 1953; 2nd cl. hons Chemistry. National Service, 1950-52; 2nd Lieut, RA, Suez Canal Zone. Asst Master, Cheltenham Coll., 1952-54; Sen. Science Master, English High Sch., Istanbul, 1954-56; Asst Master, Merchant Taylors' Sch., Northwood, 1956-62; Principal, English Sch., Nicosia, 1962-68; Headmaster, Felsted Sch., 1968-82. Governor, British School of Brussels, 1970-. *Recreation:* looking at buildings. *Address:* PO Box 9, Psychico, Athens, Greece. *T:* Athens 8133883; Garden House, Chester Place, Norwich NR2 3DG. *T:* Norwich 616025.

EGGLESTON, Prof. Harold Gordon; Professor of Pure Mathematics in London University and Head of Department of Mathematics, at Royal Holloway College, 1966-81; *b* 27 Nov. 1921; 2nd *s* of H. T. and E. M. Eggleston, Bents Green, Sheffield; *m* 1955, Elizabeth, *o d* of F. R. and C. A. W. Daglish, Beamish, County Durham; two *s* one *d. Educ:* High Storrs Grammar Sch., Sheffield; Trinity Coll., Cambridge. Lecturer and Senior Lecturer, University Coll. of Swansea, 1948-53; Lecturer, University of Cambridge, 1953-58; Prof. of Mathematics, University of London at Bedford Coll., 1958-66. *Publications:* Problems in Euclidean Space, 1957; Convexity, 1958; Elementary Real Analysis, 1962. *Address:* 14 Spring Avenue, Egham, Surrey TW20 9PL.

EGGLESTON, Prof. James Frederick; Professor of Education, University of Nottingham, since 1972; *b* 30 July 1927; *s* of Frederick James and Anne Margaret Eggleston; *m* 1956, Margaret Snowden; three *s* two *d. Educ:* Appleby Grammar Sch.; Durham Univ. (King's Coll., Newcastle upon Tyne). BSc Hons Zoology; DipEd; FIBiol 1975. School teacher, 1953-64, Head of Biol., later Head of Sci., Hinckley Grammar Sch.; Res. Fellow, Res. Unit for Assessment and Curriculum Studies, Leicester Univ. Sch. of Educn, 1964; team leader, later consultant, Nuffield Sci. Teaching Project, 1964-68; Lectr in Educn, Leicester Univ. Sch. of Educn, 1966; apptd to Colls and Curriculum Chair of Educn, Nottingham Univ., 1973, Dean of Educn, 1975-81. *Publications:* A Critical Review of Assessment Procedures in Secondary School Science, 1965; Problems in Quantitative Biology, 1968; (with J. F. Kerr) Studies in Assessment, 1970; (jtly) A Science Teaching Observation Schedule, 1975; (jtly) Processes and Products of Science Teaching, 1976; contributions to: The Disciplines of the Curriculum, 1971; The Art of the Science Teacher, 1974; Frontiers of Classroom Research, 1975; Techniques and Problems of Assessment, 1976; articles in professional jls. *Recreations:* fell walking, golf, photography. *Address:* The Mount, Bown's Hill, Crich, near Matlock, Derbys DE4 5DE. *T:* Ambergate 2870.

EGGLESTON, Hon. Sir Richard (Moulton), Kt 1971; Consultant, Faculty of Law, Monash University, since 1974 (Chancellor, 1975-83); *b* Hampton, Vic, Australia, 8 Aug. 1909; *s* of late John Bakewell Eggleston and Elizabeth Bothwell Eggleston (*née* McCutcheon); *m* 1934, Marjorie, *d* of late F. E. Thom; one *s* three *d. Educ:* Wesley Coll., Melbourne; Univ. of Melbourne (LLB). Barrister, 1932-41 and 1945-60. Staff of Defence Dept, 1942-45; Indep. Lectr in Equity, Melbourne Univ., 1940-49; KC 1950. Judge: Supreme Ct of Norfolk Is, 1960-69; Supreme Ct of ACT, 1960-74; Commonwealth

Industrial Ct, 1960-74; Pres., Trade Practices Tribunal, 1966-74. Dir, Barclays Australia Ltd, 1974-80. Hon. Treas., Victorian Bar Council, 1953-56 (Chm., 1956-58); Mem., Bd of Aust. Elizabethan Theatre Trust, 1961-67; Fellow, Queen's Coll., Univ. of Melbourne, 1964-; Pro-Chancellor, ANU, 1968-72. Chm., Company Law Adv. Cttee, 1967-73. FASSA 1981; Hon. FIArbA, 1977. Hon. LLD Melbourne, 1973. *Publication:* Evidence, Proof and Probability, 1978. *Recreations:* painting, golf, billiards, music. *Address:* 3 Willow Street, Malvern, Vic 3144, Australia. *Clubs:* Australian (Melbourne); Commonwealth (Canberra).

EGGLESTON, Prof. Samuel John, BScEcon, MA, DLitt; FCP; Professor of Education, and Head of the Department of Education, University of Keele, since 1967; *b* 11 Nov. 1926; *s* of Edmund and Josephine Eggleston, Dorchester; *m* 1957, Greta, *d* of James and Alice Patrick, Hereford; two *s* two *d*. *Educ:* Chippenham Grammar Sch.; LSE (BScEcon 1957); Univ. of London Inst. of Educn (MA 1965). Univ. of Keele, DLitt 1977. Teacher, Suffolk and Worcs, 1950-54; Leverhulme Scholarship, LSE, 1954-57; Teacher, Beds, and Headteacher, Oxfordshire, 1957-60; Lectr, Loughborough Coll. of Educn, 1960-63; Lectr, later Sen. Lectr, Leicester Univ., 1963-67; Chm., Bd of Soc. Scis, Keele Univ., 1976-79. Vis. Commonwealth Fellow, Canada, 1973-74. Director: DES Res. Project, Structure and Function of Youth Service, 1968-74; Schs Council Project, Design and Craft Educn, 1968-74; DES Research Projects: Training for Multi-Racial Educn, 1978-80; Minority Gp Adolescence, 1981-. Schs Council Working Party, Whole Curriculum, 1970-74; Council of Europe Working Party, Diversif. of Tertiary Educn, 1972-; Exec. Cttee, Standing Conf. of Studies in Educn, 1972-79; Educnl Res. Bd, SSRC, 1973-77; Panel on Public Disorder and Sporting Events, SSRC, 1976-77; Educn Bd and Arts Design Bd, CNAA, 1977-; Assessment of Performance Unit, DES, Co-ord. Cttee, 1975-80, Consultative Cttee, 1980-; Res. Consultancy Cttee, DES, 1981-; Arts Council Cttee on Trng for the Arts, 1982-. Editor, Studies in Design Education and Craft, 1968-; Chm. Editorial Board: Sociological Rev., 1970-; Paedagogica Europaea, Educnl Yearbook of Council of Europe, 1976- (Editor in Chief, 1968-76); *Publications:* The Social Context of the School, 1967; (with G. N. Brown) Towards an Education for the 21st Century, 1969; (ed with A. R. Pemberton) International Perspectives of Design Education, 1973; (ed) Contemporary Research in the Sociology of Education, 1974; Adolescence and Community, 1976; New Developments in Design Education, 1976; The Sociology of the School Curriculum, 1977; The Ecology of the School, 1977; (ed) Experimental Education in Europe, 1978; Teacher Decision Making in the Classroom, 1979; School Based Curriculum Development, 1980; Work Experience in Secondary Education, 1982; articles in books and jls, incl. Sociol., Brit. Jl of Sociol., New Soc., Educnl Res., Brit. Jl of In-Service Educn, Brit. Jl of Teacher Educn, Res. Intelligence. *Recreations:* work in design and craft, skiing, riding, travel, gardening. *Address:* Hallaton House, Whitmore Heath, Newcastle under Lyme, Staffs ST5 5JA. *T:* Whitmore 680483.

EGGLETON, Anthony, CVO 1970; Federal Director, Liberal Party of Australia, since 1975; *b* 30 April 1932; *s* of Tom and Winifred Eggleton; *m* 1953, Mary Walker, Melbourne; two *s* one *d*. *Educ:* King Alfred's Sch., Wantage. Journalist, Westminster Press Group, 1948-50; Editorial Staff, Bendigo Advertiser, Vic, 1950-51; Australian Broadcasting Commn, 1951-60 (Dir of ABC-TV News Coverage, 1956-60); Dir of Public Relations, Royal Australian Navy, 1960-65; Press Sec. to Prime Ministers of Australia, 1965-71 (Prime Ministers Menzies, Holt, Gorton, McMahon); Commonwealth Dir of Information, London, 1971-74; Special Advr to Leader of Opposition, and Dir of Communications, Federal Liberal Party, 1974-75; Govt Campaign Dir, Federal Elections, 1975, 1977, 1980. Australian Public Relations Inst.'s 1st Award of Honour, 1968. *Address:* c/o Parliament House, Canberra, ACT 2600, Australia. *T:* 732564. *Clubs:* (Foundn Pres.) National Press (Canberra), Commonwealth (Canberra).

EGLINGTON, Charles Richard John; Deputy Chairman, Stock Exchange, since 1981; Director, Akroyd & Smithers plc, since 1978; *b* 12 Aug. 1938; *s* of Richard Eglington and Treena Margaret Joyce Eglington. *Educ:* Sherborne. Mem. Council, Stock Exchange, 1975-. Governor, Sherborne Sch., 1980-. *Recreations:* golf, cricket. *Address:* Austin Friars House, EC2N 2EE. *T:* 01-588 4535. *Clubs:* MCC; Walton Heath Golf; Rye Golf.

EGLINTON and WINTON, 18th Earl of, *cr* 1507; **Archibald George Montgomerie;** Lord Montgomerie, 1448; Baron Seton and Tranent, 1859; Baron Kilwinning, 1615; Baron Ardrossan (UK), 1806; Earl of Winton (UK), 1859; Hereditary Sheriff of Renfrewshire; Managing Director, since 1972, a Deputy Chairman, since 1980, Gerrard & National plc (formerly Gerrard & National Discount Co. Ltd); *b* 27 Aug. 1939; *s* of 17th Earl of Eglinton and Winton and Ursula, *er d* of Hon. Ronald Watson, Edinburgh; *S* father, 1966; *m* 1964, Marion Carolina, *o d* of John Dunn-Yarker; four *s*. *Educ:* Eton. *Heir:* *s* Lord Montgomerie, *qv*. *Address:* The Dutch House, West Green, Hartley Wintney, Hants.

EGLINTON, Prof. Geoffrey, PhD, DSc; FRS 1976; Professor of Organic Geochemistry, University of Bristol, since 1973; *b* 1 Nov. 1927; *s* of Alfred Edward Eglinton and Lilian Blackham; *m* 1955, Pamela Joan Coupland; two *s* one *d*. *Educ:* Sale Grammar Sch.; Manchester Univ. (BSc, PhD, DSc). Post-Doctoral Fellow, Ohio State Univ., 1951-52; ICI Fellow, Liverpool Univ., 1952-54; Lectr, subseq. Sen. Lectr and Reader, Glasgow Univ., 1954-67; Sen. Lectr, subseq. Reader, Bristol Univ., 1967-73. Hon. Fellow, Plymouth Polytechnic, 1981. Gold Medal for Exceptional Scientific

Achievement, NASA, 1973; Hugo Müller Silver Medal, Chemical Soc., 1974; Alfred Treibs Gold Medal, Geochem. Soc., 1981. *Publications:* Applications of Spectroscopy to Organic Chemistry, 1965; Organic Geochemistry: methods and results, 1969; 'Chemsyn', 1972 (2nd edn 1975); contrib. Nature, Geochim. Cosmochim. Acta, Phytochem., Chem. Geol., Sci. American. *Recreations:* gardening, walking, sailing. *Address:* Oldwell, 7 Redhouse Lane, Bristol BS9 3RY. *T:* Bristol 683833. *Club:* Rucksack (Manchester).

EGMONT, 11th Earl of, *cr* 1733; **Frederick George Moore Perceval;** Bt 1661; Baron Perceval, 1715; Viscount Perceval, 1722; Baron Lovell and Holland (Great Britain), 1762; Baron Arden, 1770; Baron Arden (United Kingdom), 1802; *b* 14 April 1914; *o s* of 10th Earl and Cecilia (*d* 1916), *d* of James Burns Moore, Montreal; *S* father, 1932; *m* 1932, Ann Geraldine, *d* of D. G. Moodie; one *s* one *d* (and two *s* decd). *Heir:* *s* Viscount Perceval, *qv*. *Address:* Two-dot Ranch, Nanton, Alberta, Canada.

EGREMONT, 2nd Baron *cr* 1963, **AND LECONFIELD,** 7th Baron *cr* 1859; **John Max Henry Scawen Wyndham;** *b* 21 April 1948; *s* of John Edward Reginald Wyndham, MBE, 1st Baron Egremont and 6th Baron Leconfield, and of Pamela, *d* of Captain the Hon. Valentine Wyndham-Quin, *qv*; *S* father, 1972; *m* 1978, Caroline, *er d* of A. R. Nelson, Muckairn, Taynuilt, Argyll, and Hon. Lady Musker; two *d*. *Educ:* Eton; Christ Church, Oxford (MA Modern History). *Publications:* The Cousins, 1977 (Yorkshire Post First Book Award); Balfour: a life of Arthur James Balfour, 1980. *Heir:* *b* Hon. Harry Hugh Patrick Wyndham, *b* 28 Sept 1957. *Address:* Petworth House, Petworth, West Sussex. *T:* Petworth 42447.

EHRMAN, John Patrick William, FBA 1970; historian; *b* 17 March 1920; *o s* of late Albert and Rina Ehrman; *m* 1948, Elizabeth Susan Anne, *d* of late Vice-Adm. Sir Geoffrey Blake, KCB, DSO; four *s*. *Educ:* Charterhouse; Trinity Coll., Cambridge (MA). Served Royal Navy, 1940-45. Fellow of Trinity Coll., Cambridge, 1947-52; Historian, Cabinet Office, 1948-56; Lees Knowles Lectr, Cambridge, 1957-58; James Ford Special Lectr, Oxford, 1976-77. Hon. Treas., Friends of the National Libraries, 1960-77; Trustee of the Nat. Portrait Gall., 1971-; Member: Reviewing Cttee on Export of Works of Art, 1970-76; Royal Commn on Historical Manuscripts, 1973-; Chm., Adv. Cttee to British Library Reference Div., 1975-; Vice-Pres., Navy Records Soc., 1968-70, 1974-76. FSA 1958; FRHistS. *Publications:* The Navy in the War of William III, 1953; Grand Strategy, 1943-5 (2 vols, UK Official Military Histories of the Second World War), 1956; Cabinet Government and War, 1890-1940, 1958; The British Government and Commercial Negotiations with Europe, 1783-1793, 1962; The Younger Pitt: the years of acclaim, 1969. *Address:* The Mead Barns, Taynton, near Burford, Oxfordshire. *Clubs:* Army and Navy, Beefsteak, Garrick.

EIGEN, Manfred; Director at Max-Planck-Institut für biophysikalische Chemie, Göttingen, since 1964; *b* 9 May 1927; *s* of Ernst and Hedwig Eigen; *m* 1952, Elfriede Müller; one *s* one *d*. *Educ:* Göttingen Univ. Dr rer. nat. (Phys. Chem.) 1951. Research Asst, Inst. für physikal. Chemie, Göttingen Univ., 1951-53; Asst, Max-Planck-Institut für physikal. Chemie, 1953; Research Fellow, Max-Planck-Gesellschaft, 1958; Head of separate dept of biochemical kinetics, Max-Planck-Inst., 1962. Andrew D. White Prof. at Large, Cornell Univ., 1965; Hon. Prof., Technische Hochschule Braunschweig, 1965. For. Hon. Mem., Amer. Acad. of Arts and Sciences, 1964; Mem. Leopoldina, Deutsche Akad. der Naturforscher, Halle, 1964; Mem., Akad. der Wissenschaften, Göttingen, 1965; Hon. Mem., Amer. Assoc. Biol Chemists, 1966; For. Assoc., Nat. Acad. of Scis, Washington, 1966; For. Mem., Royal Soc., 1973. Dr of Science *hc*, Washington, Harvard and Chicago Univs, 1966. Has won prizes, medals and awards including Nobel Prize for Chemistry (jointly), 1967. *Publications:* numerous papers in Z. Elektrochem., Jl Phys. Chem., Trans Faraday Soc., Proc. Royal Soc., Canad. Jl Chem., ICSU Rev., and other learned jls. *Address:* Max-Planck-Institut für biophysikalische Chemie, Karl-Friedrich Bonhoeffer Institut, Postfach 2841, D3400 Göttingen-Nikolausberg, Germany.

EILON, Prof. Samuel; Professor and Head of Department of Management Science (formerly Management Engineering Section), Imperial College of Science and Technology, University of London, since 1963; Director, Amey Roadstone Corporation, since 1974; *b* 13 Oct. 1923; *s* of Abraham and Rachel Eilon; *m* 1946, Hannah Ruth (née Samuel); two *s* two *d*. *Educ:* Reali Sch., Haifa; Technion, Israel Inst. of Technology, Haifa; Imperial Coll., London. PhD 1955, DSc(Eng) 1963, London. Founder FEng, FIMechE, FIProdE. Engr, Palestine Electric Co. Ltd, Haifa, 1946-48; Officer, Israel Defence Forces, 1948-52; CO of an Ordnance and workshop base depot (Major); Res. Asst, Imperial Coll., 1952-55; Lectr in Production Engrg, Imperial Coll., 1955-57; Associate Prof. in Industrial Engrg, Technion, Haifa, 1957-59; Reader, and Head of Section, Imperial Coll., 1959-63; Consultant and Lectr, EPA, Paris, 1960-62. Professorial Research Fellow, Case-Western-Reserve Univ., Cleveland, Ohio, 1967-68. Vis. Fellow, University Coll., Cambridge, 1970-71. Dir, Campari International, 1978-80. Past Mem. of several cttees of IProdE and DES. Member Council: Operational Res. Soc., 1965-67; Inst. of Management Scis, 1970-72, 1980-. Adviser, P-E Consulting Gp, 1961-71; Principal and Dir, Spencer Stuart and Associates, 1971-74. Chief Editor, OMEGA, Internat. Jl of Management Science, 1972-; Deptl Editor, Management Science, 1969-77. CBIM; Hon. FCGI 1978. Two Joseph Whitworth Prizes for papers, IMechE, 1960; Silver Medal, ORS, 1982. *Publications:* Elements of Production Planning and Control, 1962; Industrial Engineering Tables, 1962; (jtly) Exercises in Industrial Management, 1966;

(jtly) Industrial Scheduling Abstracts, 1967; (jtly) Inventory Control Abstracts, 1968; (jtly) Distribution Management, 1971; Management Control, 1971, 2nd edn 1979; (jtly) Applications of Management Science in Banking and Finance, 1972; (jtly) Applied Productivity Analysis for Industry, 1976; Aspects of Management, 1977, 2nd edn 1979; numerous scientific papers. *Recreations:* theatre, tennis, walking. *Address:* Imperial College, Exhibition Road, SW7 2BX. *T:* 01-589 5111. *Club:* Athenæum.

EISENHOWER, Milton Stover; President, The Johns Hopkins University, 1956-67, 1971-72, now President Emeritus; *b* 15 Sept. 1899; *s* of David Jacob and Ida Stover Eisenhower; *m* 1927, Helen Elsie Eakin (decd); one *s* one *d*. *Educ:* Kansas State Univ. (BS); Univ. of Edinburgh. City Ed., Abilene (Kan.) Daily Reflector, 1918 and 1920-21; Asst Prof. Journalism, Kansas State Univ., 1924; Amer. Vice-Consul, Edinburgh, 1924-26; Asst to Sec. of Agric., 1926-28; Dir Inf., US Dept of Agric., 1928-41, Land Use Co-ordinator, 1937-42; Dir, War Relocation Authority, 1942; Assoc. Dir, Office of War Inf., 1942-43; Pres., Kansas State Univ., 1943-50; Pres., Pennsylvania State Univ., 1950-56. Mem. Fact-finding Board in Gen. Motors labor-management dispute, 1945; Famine Emergency Relief Ctee, 1946; Exec. Bd Unesco, 1946; President's Cttee on Government Organisation, 1953-60; Nat. Advisory Cttee on Inter-American Affairs, 1960; Special Ambassador and Personal Rep. of US Pres., on Latin Amer. Affairs, 1953, 1957, 1958, 1959, 1960; Chm., US Nat. Commn for Unesco, 1946-48; Deleg., Unesco Confs, 1946-47-48-49. Mem., President's Commn on Higher Educn, 1946; Problems and Policies Cttee, Amer. Council on Educn, 1950-53; Exec. Cttee, Assoc. Land-Grant Colls and Univs, 1944-47, 1950-53, Chm., 1946-47, 1952-53; Pres. Assoc., 1951-52. Chm. Nat. Cttee for The People Act, 1951-53; Director: Fund for Adult Educn, 1953-61; Freedoms Foundn Inc., 1951-; The Geisinger Memorial Hosp., 1952-; Mem., Atlantic-Pacific Interoceanic Canal Study Commn, 1965-70; Chairman, President's Commn on: Causes and Prevention of Violence, 1968-69; Internat. Radio Broadcasting, 1972-73. Also trusteeships, etc both past and present. Holds numerous hon. degrees (including LLD Johns Hopkins), foreign orders, etc. *Publications:* The Wine is Bitter, 1963; The President is Calling, 1974; ed many publications for US Dept of Agric.; articles for Scholar, Sat. Evening Post, Colliers, Country Gentlemen, etc. *Address:* Evergreen House, 4545 North Charles Street, Baltimore, Md 21210, USA. *T:* 338-7670. *Clubs:* Johns Hopkins, Elkridge (Baltimore).

EKIN, Maj.-Gen. Roger Gillies, CIE 1946; IA, retired; *b* 18 Nov. 1895; *yr s* of T. C. Ekin, MInstCE; *m* 1st, 1923, Phyllis Marian (*d* 1967), *er d* of Maj.-Gen. Sir Henry Croker, KCB, CMG; one *s* two *d*; 2nd, 1972, Mona de Hamel (*d* 1979), *widow* of Etienne Bruno de Hamel. *Educ:* Westminster; RMC Sandhurst. First Commissioned, 1914; Palestine campaign, 1916-19; on Operations in Waziristan, 1920-21; Operations NWFP, 1932; Brevet Lt-Col 1936; Comdt 5th Bn FF Rifles, 1937-40; Comd Kohat Bde Ahmedzal Ops, 1940; Col 1939; Comdt Tactical Sch., India, 1940-41; Comd 46 Inf. Bde, Burma campaign, 1941-42; Nowshera Bde, 1942-45; Kohat (Independent) Bde, 1945-46. Despatches five times. GOC Bihar and Orissa Area, India, 1946-47; retired, 1947; Sec., Hereford Diocesan Board of Finance, 1947-61. *Address:* Waverley Abbey House, near Farnham, Surrey. *Club:* Lansdowne.

EKLUND, Dr (Arne) Sigvard; Director General (now Emeritus), International Atomic Energy Agency, Vienna, 1961-81; *b* Kiruna, Sweden, 1911; *m* 1941, Anna-Greta Johansson; one *s* two *d*. *Educ:* Uppsala Univ., Sweden (DSc). Assoc. Prof. in Nuclear Physics, Royal Inst. of Technology, Stockholm, 1946-56; Dir of Research, later Reactor development Div., AB Atomenergi, 1950-61. Conference Sec.-Gen., 2nd Internat. UN Conf. on Peaceful Uses of Atomic Energy, 1958. Fellow, Amer. Nuclear Soc., 1961; Member: Royal Swedish Acad. of Engineering Sciences, 1953; Royal Swedish Acad. of Sciences, 1972; Hon. Member: British Nuclear Energy Soc., 1963; European Nuclear Soc., 1982. For. Associate, Nat. Acad. of Engineering, USA, 1979. Dr *hc* : Univ. of Graz, 1968; Acad. of Mining and Metallurgy, Cracow, 1971; Univ. of Bucarest, 1971; Chalmers Inst. of Technol., Gothenberg, 1974; Buenos Aires, Budapest, Columbia and Moscow Univs, 1977; Dresden Technical and Yon-sei, Seoul Univs, 1978; Nat. Agrarian Univ. of La Molina, Peru, 1979; Royal Inst. of Technol., Stockholm, 1980. (Jointly) Atoms for Peace Award, 1968; Golden Medal of Honour, Vienna, 1971; Henry DeWolf Smyth Nuclear Statesman Award, 1976; Exceptional Service Award, Amer. Nuclear Soc., 1980. Hon. Senator, Univ. of Vienna, 1977. Kt Comdr, Order of North Star, Sweden, 1971; Das Grosse Goldene Ehrenzeichen am Bande für Verdienste, Austria, 1981; Das Grosse Verdienstkreuz mit Stern und Schulterband, FRG, 1981; Aquila Azteca en el Grado de Banda, Mexico, 1981. *Publications:* Studies in Nuclear Physics, 1946 (Sweden); articles on peaceful uses of nuclear energy. *Address:* Krapfenwaldgasse 48, 1190-Vienna, Austria.

ELAM, His Honour Henry; a Circuit Judge (formerly Deputy Chairman of the Court of Quarter Sessions, Inner London), 1954-76; barrister-at-law; *b* 29 Nov. 1903; *o s* of Thomas Henry Elam, 33 Sackville Street, W1; *m* 1st, 1930, Eunice (*d* 1975), *yr d* of J. G. Matthews, 41 Reddington Road, NW3; one *d*; 2nd, 1975, Doris A. Horsford. *Educ:* Charterhouse; Lincoln Coll., Oxford (MA). Called to Bar, Inner Temple, 1927; Western Circuit; Junior Prosecuting Counsel to the Treasury, Central Criminal Court, 1937; late Dep. Judge Advocate, RAF; Recorder of Poole, 1941-46; 2nd Junior Prosecuting Counsel, 1942-45; 1st Junior, 1945-50; 3rd Senior, Jan.-March 1950; 2nd Senior, 1950-53; Recorder of Exeter, 1946-53; Dep. Chm., West Kent QS,

1947-53. Mem. of Tin Plate Workers' Co. *Recreation:* flyfishing. *Address:* Clymshurst, Burwash Common, East Sussex. *T:* West Burwash 335.

ELAM, (John) Nicholas; Deputy High Commissioner and Counsellor (Economic and Commercial), Salisbury, since 1980; *b* 2 July 1939; *s* of John Frederick Elam, OBE and Joan Barrington Elam (*née* Lloyd); *m* 1967, Florence Helen, *d* of P. Lentz; two *s* one *d*. *Educ:* Colchester Royal Grammar Sch.; New Coll., Oxford (schol.). Frank Knox Fellow, Harvard Univ., 1961-62. Entered HM Diplomatic Service, 1962; FO, 1962-64; Pretoria and Cape Town, 1964-68; Treasury Centre for Admin. Studies, 1968-69; FCO, 1969-71; First Sec., Bahrain, 1971; Commercial Sec., Brussels, 1972-76; FCO, 1976-79, Dep. Head of News Dept, 1978-79; Counsellor and Dep. British Govt Rep., Salisbury, 1979. Zimbabwe Govt Independence Medal, 1980. *Recreations:* fine arts, travel. *Address:* c/o Foreign and Commonwealth Office, SW1A 2AH.

ELATH, Eliahu, PhD; President Emeritus, Hebrew University, Jerusalem; Israeli diplomatist; Chairman, Board of Governors, Israel Afro-Asian Institute; *b* 30 July 1903; *s* of Menachem and Rivka Epstein (Elath); *m* 1931, Zehava Zalel, *Educ:* Hebrew Univ., Jerusalem; American Univ., Beirut, Lebanon. Reuter's Corresp. in Syria and Lebanon, 1931-34. Mem. Political Dept of Jewish Agency for Palestine in Jerusalem, 1934-45; Dir Political Office of Jewish Agency for Palestine in Washington, 1945-48; Special Representative of Provisional Govt of Israel in USA, 1948; Ambassador of Israel to USA, 1948-50; Minister of Israel, 1950-52, Ambassador, 1952-59, to the Court of St James's. Pres., Israel Oriental Soc. Vice-Pres., Jewish Colonization Assoc. (ICA). Hon. PhD: Brandeis; Wayn; Hebrew Union Coll.; Dropsie Coll., USA. *Publications:* The Bedouin, Their Customs and Manners, 1933; Trans-Jordan, 1934; Israel and her Neighbours, 1960; The Political Struggle for Inclusion of Elath in the Jewish State, 1967; San Francisco Diary, 1971; British Routes to India, 1971; Zionism and the Arabs, 1974; Zionism and the UN, 1977; contribs to Quarterly of Palestine Exploration Fund, Jl of Royal Central Asian Society, Encyclopædia Britannica. *Address:* 17 Bialik Street, Beth Hakerem, Jerusalem, Israel. *T:* 524615.

ELBORNE, Sydney Lipscomb, MBE 1918; Chairman of Hunts Quarter Sessions, 1947-63; *b* 6 July 1890; *e s* of late William Elborne, MA, Wootton House, Peterborough; *m* 1925, Cavil Grace Mary, *d* of late George E. Monckton, Fineshade Abbey, Northants; one *s* one *d*. *Educ:* King's Sch., Peterborough; Trinity Coll. Cambridge (MA). Asst Inspector of High Explosives (Technical), The Royal Arsenal, Woolwich, 1914-18; called to Bar, Inner Temple, 1919; Mem. Midland Circuit; Mem. Gen. Council of the Bar, 1940-47; Asst Recorder of Birmingham, 1953. Mem. Hunts CC, 1930-45; JP Hunts, 1932. Pres. Soc. of Chairmen and Dep. Chm. of Quarter Sessions, 1955. Mem. Mr Justice Austen Jones's Cttee on County Court procedure, 1947; a Trustee and Mem. Council, Northants Record Soc.; formerly Trustee of Peterborough Museum Soc. and Maxwell Art Gallery; Mem. Area Cttee (No 11) Legal Aid, 1950-69. Contested (C) Leicester (Bosworth Div.), 1929 and Manchester (Ardwick), by-election, 1931. Formerly FGS, ARIC. *Address:* Water Newton, Peterborough. *T:* Peterborough 233223; 2 Hare Court, Temple, EC4. *Club:* Carlton.

ELDER, David Renwick, MC 1940; CA; *b* 4 Jan. 1920; *s* of John Kidd Elder and Mary Kinnear Swanley; *m* 1947, Kathleen Frances Duncan; two *s* two *d*. *Educ:* Dundee High School. Served 1939-46, The Black Watch (RHR) and Sea Reconnaissance Unit (Major). Royal Dutch Shell Group, 1948-71; Ocean Transport & Trading Ltd, 1971-80 (Dep. Chm., 1975-80; Chm., Ocean Inchcape, 1974-80); Director: Letraset International Ltd, 1975; Capital & Counties Property Ltd, 1979; Whessoe Ltd, 1980. *Recreation:* golf. *Address:* Green Hedges, Lake Roan, Virginia Water, Surrey. *T:* Wentworth 2134. *Clubs:* Wentworth Golf (Virginia Water); Panmure Golf (Carnoustie).

ELDER, Hugh, MA; *b* 1905; *s* of late Rev. Hugh Elder, MA, Edinburgh; *m* 1939, Winifred Mary, *o d* of late Col M. Stagg, OBE, RE; one *s* (and one *s* decd). *Educ:* Edinburgh Academy; Edinburgh Univ. (Scholar); Corpus Christi Coll., Oxford. MA Hons Classics, Edinburgh, 1927; BA, Lit. Hum. 1929, MA 1934, Oxford. Asst Master at Sherborne Sch., 1929-35; Asst Master at Fettes Coll., 1935-38; Headmaster of Dean Close Sch., Cheltenham, 1938-46; Headmaster of Merchant Taylors' Sch., 1946-65. *Recreations:* music, golf. *Address:* Millbrook, Huish Episcopi, Langport, Somerset.

ELDER, Mark Philip; Music Director, English National Opera, since 1979; Principal Guest Conductor: London Mozart Players, since 1980; BBC Symphony Orchestra, since 1982; *b* 2 June 1947; *s* of John and Helen Elder; *m* 1980, Amanda Jane Stein. *Educ:* Bryanston Sch.; Corpus Christi Coll., Cambridge (Music Scholar, Choral Scholar; BA, MA). Music staff, Wexford Festival, 1969-70; Chorus Master and Asst Conductor, Glyndebourne, 1970-71; music staff, Covent Garden, 1970-72; Staff Conductor, Australian Opera, 1972-74; Staff Conductor, ENO, 1974, Associate Conductor, 1977. *Recreations:* theatre, tennis, 'Treasures of Britain'. *Address:* 4 Wolsey Road, Islington, N1 4UH.

ELDER-JONES, His Honour Thomas; retired Circuit Judge (formerly Judge of County Courts), 1953-76; *b* 4 Oct. 1904; *o s* of late David Jones, JP, Foxcote Grange, Andoversford, shipowner, and late Anne Amelia (Roberts); *m* 1948, Hon. Diana Katherine Taylor (*née* Russell) (*d* 1978), *o d* of 25th Baron de Clifford; one adopted *d* one step *s*. *Educ:* Shrewsbury; Trinity Coll., Oxford (MA). Barrister-at-law, Inner Temple, 1927. Served

1939-43, 2nd Royal Gloucestershire Hussars, retired, rank of Hon. Major. Sec. National Reference Tribunal for Coal Mining Industry, 1943-53; Judge of County Courts Circuit 34 (Brentford and Uxbridge), 1953-57, Circuit 52 (Bath-Swindon), 1957-76. At Bar practised in Common Law and Coal Mining matters. *Recreation:* fox-hunting. *Address:* The Dower House, Somerford Keynes, Cirencester, Glos. *T:* Cirencester 861296.

ELDERFIELD, Maurice; Chairman: Throgmorton Trusts, since 1972; Throgmorton Investment Management Ltd, since 1981; Sheldon Freud, since 1981; Saga Ltd, since 1979; Chairman and Chief Executive, Berfield Associates Ltd, since 1980; *b* 10 April 1926; *s* of Henry Elderfield and Kathleen Maud Elderfield; *m* 1953, Audrey June (*née* Knight); one *s* three *d. Educ:* Southgate Grammar Sch. FCA. Fleet Air Arm, 1944-47. Thomson, Kingdom & Co., Chartered Accountants (qual. 1949), 1947-49; Personal Asst to Man. Dir, Forrestell, Land, Timber & Railway Co., 1949-57; Group Chief Accountant, Stephens Group, 1957-60; various posts, Segas, culminating in Board Mem. and Dir for Finance, 1960-73; Dir of Finance, Southern Water Authority, 1973-75; PO Board Mem. for Finance and Corporate Planning, 1975-76; Dir of Finance, Ferranti Ltd, 1977; Finance Mem., British Shipbuilders, 1977-80. *Recreations:* golf, tennis, squash. *Address:* Overton Grange, Rystwood Road, Forest Row, Sussex; (office) 55 Lincoln's Inn Fields, WC2A 3LX. *Club:* Graveye Manor Country.

ELDIN-TAYLOR, Kenneth Roy, CVO 1955; *b* 27 Sept. 1902; *s* of late Thomas Taylor, Welbourn, Lincoln; *m* 1926, Katharine Mary, *er d* of late Frederick Ernest Taylor, FRCS, LRCP, Brancaster, Norfolk; three *s. Educ:* Lincoln School; Selwyn College, Cambridge (BA, LLM, Exhibitioner and Univ. Squire Law Schol.). Called to the Bar, Lincoln's Inn, 1970. Solicitor for Affairs of HM Duchy of Lancaster, 1942-67; Chm., Industrial Appeals Tribunals, 1967-74; Sec., Diocesan Conf., 1966-68; former Member of Council, British Records Association; Chairman: Portsmouth Diocesan Parsonages Bd; Clergy Sustentation Fund. *Recreations:* literature, rowing. *Address:* 4 King Charles Street, Old Portsmouth, Hants. *T:* 826293. *Clubs:* Leander; Royal Naval and Royal Albert Yacht (Portsmouth).

ELDON, 5th Earl of, *cr* 1821; **John Joseph Nicholas Scott;** Baron Eldon 1799; Viscount Encombe 1821; *b* 24 April 1937; *s* of 4th Earl of Eldon, GCVO, and Hon. Magdalen Fraser, OBE (*d* 1969), *d* of 16th Baron Lovat; *S* father, 1976; *m* 1961, Comtesse Claudine de Montjoye-Vaufrey et de la Roche, Vienna; one *s* two *d. Educ:* Ampleforth; Trinity Coll., Oxford. 2nd Lieut Scots Guards (National Service). Lieut AER. *Heir: s* Viscount Encombe, *qv. Address:* 2 Coach House Lane, Wimbledon, SW19.

ELDRIDGE, Eric William, CB 1965; OBE 1948; Consultant with Lee and Pembertons, solicitors, since 1971; *b* 15 April 1906; *o s* of late William Eldridge; *m* 1936, Doris Margaret Kerr; one *s* one *d. Educ:* Millfields Central Sch.; City of London Coll. Admitted Solicitor (Hons), 1934. Chief Administrative Officer, Public Trustee Office, 1955-60; Asst Public Trustee, 1960-63; Public Trustee, 1963-71. *Address:* Old Stocks, Gorelands Lane, Chalfont St Giles, Bucks. *T:* Chalfont St Giles 2159.

ELDRIDGE, John Barron; Chairman, Matthews Wrightson Holdings Ltd, 1971-77; *b* 28 May 1919; *s* of William John Eldridge and Jessie Winifred (*née* Bowditch); *m* 1940, Marjorie Potier; one *s* two *d. Educ:* Lancing Coll. FIA 1950. Dir, Matthews Wrightson Holdings Ltd, 1964. Croix de Guerre 1944. *Address:* Castleton, Warwicks Bench Road, Guildford, Surrey. *T:* Guildford 62687.

ELDRIDGE, Lt.-Gen. Sir (William) John, KBE 1954 (CBE 1941); CB 1944; DSO 1919; MC; Chairman, Kearney and Trecker, CVA Ltd, 1957-68; *b* 2 March 1898; *s* of late William Henry Eldridge; *m* 1954, Violet Elizabeth (*d* 1956), *e d* of John Cane, Wrexham. 2nd Lieut RA 1915; served European War, France and Belgium, 1916-18 (wounded, despatches twice, DSO, MC); Iraq Operations, 1919-20; War of 1939-45 (despatches, CBE, Bar to DSO). Dir-Gen. of Artillery, Ministry of Supply, 1945-48; Comdt Mil. Coll. of Science, 1948-51; GOC Aldershot District, 1951-53; Controller of Munitions, Min. of Supply, 1953-57, retired. Col Comdt: RA, 1951-61; Glider Pilot Regt, Glider Pilot and Parachute Corps, 1951-57. *Address:* Mais House, 18 Hastings Road, Bexhill-on-Sea, Sussex. *Club:* Royal Air Force.

ELEK, Prof. Stephen Dyonis, MD, DSc; FRCP; Professor of Medical Microbiology in the University of London, 1957-74, now Emeritus; Consultant Bacteriologist, St George's Hospital, SW1, 1948-73; *b* 24 March 1914; *s* of Dezso and Anna Elek; *m* Sarah Joanna Hall; three *d. Educ:* Lutheran High Sch., Budapest, Hungary; St George's Hosp. Med. Sch., Univ. of London. MB, BS 1940; MD 1943; PhD 1948; DPH 1943; DSc 1958; MRCP 1960; FRCPath 1964. Clinical Pathologist, Maida Vale Hosp. for Nervous Diseases, 1946-47; Laking-Dakin Fellow, 1942-43; Fulbright Fellow, Harvard Medical Sch., 1956. Member: Pathological Soc. of Great Britain; American Society for Microbiology; New York Academy of Sciences; Soc. of Gen. Microbiology, etc. Editor, Jl of Medical Microbiology, 1972-74. Introduced immuno-diffusion as a new analytical tool in serology, 1948. *Publications:* Staphylococcus pyogenes and its Relation to Disease, 1959; scientific papers relating to diphtheria, leprosy, vaccination against mental retardation due to CM Virus infection during pregnancy, etc, in Lancet, BMJ, Jl Path. and Bact., Brit. Jl Exper. Path. *Recreations:* sculpting, walking. *Address:* Avenue de Cour 155, 1007 Lausanne, Switzerland. *T:* 26.58.14. *Club:* Athenæum.

ELEY, Prof. Daniel Douglas, OBE 1961; ScD, PhD Cantab; MSc, PhD Manchester; FRS 1964; Professor of Physical Chemistry, University of Nottingham, 1954-80, now Emeritus; Dean of Faculty of Pure Science, 1959-62; *b* 1 Oct. 1914; *s* of Daniel Eley and Fanny Allen Eley, *née* Ross; *m* 1942, Brenda May Williams, MA, MB, BChir (Cantab), 2nd *d* of Benjamin and Sarah Williams, Skewen, Glam; one *s. Educ:* Christ's Coll., Finchley; Manchester Univ.; St John's Coll., Cambridge. Manchester Univ.: Woodiwiss Schol. 1933, Mercer Schol. 1934, Darbishire Fellow 1936, PhD 1937; PhD, 1940, ScD 1954, Cambridge. Bristol Univ.: Lectr in Colloid Chemistry, 1945; Reader in Biophysical Chemistry, 1951. Leverhulme Emeritus Fellow, 1981. Lectures: Reilly, Univ. of Notre Dame (USA), 1950; Sir Jesse Boot Foundn, Nottingham Univ., 1955, 1981; Sir Eric Rideal, Soc. of Chem. Industry, 1975. Mem. Council of Faraday Soc., 1951-54, 1960-63; Vice-Pres., 1963-66. Corresp. Mem., Bavarian Acad. of Sciences, 1971. Meetings Sec., British Biophysical Soc., 1961-63, Hon. Sec., 1963-65. Scientific Assessor to Sub-Cttee on Coastal Pollutions, House of Commons Select Cttee on Science and Technology, 1967-68. Medal of Liège Univ., 1950. *Publications:* (ed) Adhesion, 1961; papers in Trans Faraday Soc., Proc. Royal Soc., Jl Chem. Soc., Biochem. Jl, etc. *Recreations:* hill walking, gardening, ski-ing. *Address:* Chemistry Department, Nottingham University, University Park, Nottingham.

ELEY, Sir Geoffrey (Cecil Ryves), Kt 1964; CBE 1947; Member Committee, Royal United Kingdom Benevolent Association, since 1957; Vice-President, Middle East Association, since 1962; Member: Council, Friends of Tate Gallery, since 1977; Court, University of Essex, since 1967; *b* 18 July 1904; *s* of late Charles Cuthbert Eley, JP, VMH, East Bergholt Place, Suffolk, and of Ethel Maxwell Eley (*née* Ryves); *m* 1937, Penelope Hughes, *d* of late Adm. Sir Frederick Wake-Walker, KCB, CBE; two *s* two *d. Educ:* Eton; Trinity Coll., Cambridge (BA 1925; MA 1933); Harvard Univ. (Davison Scholar), 1925-26. On Editorial Staff of Financial News, 1926-28; banking, finance and brokerage in England, France, Switzerland and the USA, 1928-32; London Manager of Post and Flagg, members of New York Stock Exchange, 1932-39; Naval Intelligence Div., Admiralty, 1939-40; Capital Issues Cttee, 1940-41; Min. of Supply as Dir of Contracts in charge of Capital Assistance to Industry, 1941-46; Min. of Supply as Dir of Overseas Disposals, 1946-47. Mem., London Electricity Bd, 1949-59. Chm., British Drug Houses Ltd, 1948-65; Dep. Chm. and Chm., Brush Group, 1953-58; Chairman: Richard Thomas & Baldwin's Ltd, 1959-64; Richard Crittall Holdings Ltd, 1948-68; Thomas Tilling Ltd, 1965-76 (Dir, 1950-76); Heinemann Group of Publishers Ltd, 1965-76; Dep. Chm., British Bank of the Middle East, 1952-77 (Dir, 1950-77); Vice-Chm., BOC International Ltd, 1964-76 (Dir, 1959-76); Director: Equity & Law Life Assurance Soc., 1948-80; Bank of England, 1949-66. Leader, UK Trade Mission to Egypt, Sudan and Ethiopia, 1955. High Sheriff, Co. of London, 1954-55; High Sheriff of Greater London, 1966. *Recreations:* gardening, the arts, foreign travel. *Address:* 27 Wynnstay Gardens, Allen Street, W8 6UR. *T:* 01-937 0797; The Change House, Great Yeldham, Essex CO9 4PT. *T:* Great Yeldham 237260. *Clubs:* Brooks's, Beefsteak.

ELEY, John L.; see Lloyd-Eley.

ELFER, David Francis, QC 1981; a Recorder of the Crown Court, since 1978; *b* 15 July 1941; *s* of George and Joy Elfer; *m* 1958, Karin Ursula Strub; two *s. Educ:* St Bede's Coll., Manchester; Emmanuel Coll., Cambridge (MA). Called to the Bar, Inner Temple, 1964; Western Circuit. *Recreation:* music. *Address:* (home) Monks Park, Luddington Avenue, Virginia Water, Surrey. *T:* Wentworth 3168; (chambers) 1 Paper Building, Temple, EC4Y 7EP.

ELGIN, 11th Earl of, *cr* 1633, **AND KINCARDINE,** 15th Earl of, *cr* 1647; **Andrew Douglas Alexander Thomas Bruce,** KT 1981; DL; JP; Baron Bruce of Kinloss, 1604, Baron Bruce of Torry, 1647; Baron Elgin (UK), 1849; 37th Chief of the Name of Bruce; late Scots Guards; Brigadier of Royal Company of Archers, HM Body Guard for Scotland; Hon. Colonel, Elgin Regiment, Canada; *b* 17 Feb. 1924; *e s* of 10th Earl of Elgin, KT, CMG, TD and Hon. Katherine Elizabeth Cochrane (DBE 1938), *er d* of 1st Baron Cochrane of Cults; *S* father, 1968; *m* 1959, Victoria, *o d* of Dudley Usher, MBE and Mrs Usher of Larach Bhan, Kilchrennan, Argyll; three *s* two *d. Educ:* Eton; Balliol College, Oxford (BA Hons, MA Hons). Served War of 1939-45 (wounded). Director: Dominion Ins. Co.; Gurr, Johns & Co.; Nationwide Building Soc. (Scottish Bd); Royal Highland and Agricultural Soc., 1973-75; Pres., Scottish Amicable Life Assurance Soc., 1975-. Chm., Nat. Savings Cttee for Scotland, 1972-78; Mem., Scottish Postal Bd, 1980-. Lord High Comr, Gen. Assembly of Church of Scotland, 1980-81. County Cadet Commandant, Fife, 1952-65. Hon. Col, 153(H) Regt RCT(V), TAVR, 1976-. JP 1951, DL 1955, Fife. Grand Master Mason of Scotland, 1961-65. Brigade Pres. of the Boys' Brigade; Pres., Royal Caledonian Curling Club, 1968-69. Hon. LLD Dundee, 1977; Hon. DLitt St Mary's, Halifax, NS. Freeman: Bridgetown, Barbados; Regina; Port Elgin; Winnipeg; St Thomas, Ont; Moose Jaw. *Heir: s* Lord Bruce, *qv. Address:* Broomhall, Dunfermline KY11 3DU. *T:* Limekilns 872222. *Clubs:* Beefsteak, Caledonian, Pratt's; New (Edinburgh); Royal Scottish Automobile (Pres.) (Glasgow).

ELGOOD, Captain Leonard Alsager, OBE 1919; MC 1915; DL; JP; FRSE; Director, The Distillers Co. Ltd, 1943-60; Chairman, United Glass Ltd, 1951-61; Director, Royal Bank of Scotland, 1946-66, Extraordinary Director, 1966-68; Chairman of Committee on Natural Resources of Scotland (Scottish Council for Development and Industry), 1958-62; *b* 13 Dec. 1892; *s* of late

William Alsager Elgood, Dundee, and late Mrs Elgood; *m* 1917, Jenny Coventry Wood, *d* of late R. A. Harper Wood and late Mrs Wood, Perth; two *s. Educ:* Dundee High Sch. Served with the Black Watch (Capt.), 1914-19 (despatches thrice); retd, 1919. Chartered Accountant, 1919; Sec., John Dewar & Sons Ltd, Perth, 1936; Sec., The Distillers Co. Ltd, 1939. DL 1948, JP 1943, County of the City of Edinburgh. *Address:* 16 Cumlodden Avenue, Edinburgh EH12 6DR. *T:* 031-337 6919.

ELIAS, Dr Taslim Olawale, CFR 1963; QC 1961; President, International Court of Justice, since 1982; *b* Lagos, 11 Nov. 1914; *s* of Momolesho Elias Frowoshere; *m* 1959, Ganiat Yetunde Elias; three *s* two *d. Educ:* Igbobi Coll., Lagos; University Coll. London (BA, LLM, PhD); Inst. of Advanced Legal Studies, London. Called to the Bar, Inner Temple, 1947 (Hon. Bencher 1982). Simon Res. Fellow, Manchester Univ., 1951-53; Oppenheim Res. Fellow, Oxford, 1954-60. Federal Attorney-Gen. and Minister of Justice, Nigeria, 1960-66; Attorney-Gen., 1966-71; Mem., Fed. Exec. Council, 1966-71; Comr for Justice, 1967-71; Chief Justice of Supreme Court, 1972-75; Mem., Internat. Ct of Justice, 1976- (Vice-Pres., 1979-82; Pres., 1982-); Prof. and Dean of Faculty of Law, Univ. of Lagos, 1966-73. Vis. Prof., Delhi Univ., 1956. Sen. Gen. Editor, Nigerian Law Jl, 1967-73. Member: Internat. Law Commn, UN, 1961-76 (Chm. 1970); Executive: Inst. of Human Rights, Strasbourg, 1969; Internat. Commn of Jurists, 1975-. Mem., Delegn to Nigerian Constitutional Conf., London, 1958; Chm., UN Cttee of Constitnl Experts to draft Congo Constitution, 1961-62; Mem., Expert Cttee drafting OAU Charter, 1963. President: World Assoc. of Judges, 1975; Nigerian Soc. of Internat. Law; Chm., African Inst. of Internat. Law. Chm., Governing Council, Nigerian Inst. of Internat. Affairs, 1972-; Governor, SOAS, 1958-61; Mem., Governing Council, Univ. of Nigeria, 1959-66. Hon. Fellow, Nigerian Inst. of Advanced Legal Studies, 1981; Hon. Member: Amer. Soc. of Internat. Law, 1973; Soc. of Public Teachers of Law, 1981. World Jurist Award, 1973; Nigerian Nat. Merit Award, 1979. *Publications:* Nigerian Land Law and Custom, 1951; Nigerian Legal System, 1954; Makers of Nigerian Law, 1956; Nature of African Customary Law, 1956, 2nd edn 1962; (jtly) British Legal Papers, 1958; The Impact of English Law upon Nigerian Customary Law, 1960; Government and Politics in Africa, 1961, 2nd edn 1963; Ghana and Sierra Leone: development of their laws and constitutions, 1962; British Colonial Law: a comparative study, 1962; (jtly) International Law in a Changing World, 1963; Nigeria: development of its laws and constitution, 1965; (jtly) Sovereignty within the Law, 1965; (jtly) African Law: adaptation and development, 1965; (jtly) Law, Justice and Equity, 1967; (jtly) Nigerian Prison System, 1968; (jtly) Nigerian Press Law, 1969; Problems concerning the Validity of Treaties, 1971; Nigerian Magistrate and the Offender, 1972; Law and Social Change in Nigeria, 1972; Africa and the Development of International Law, 1972; Law in a Developing Society, 1973; Modern Law of Treaties, 1974; Judicial Process in Commonwealth Africa, 1977; New Horizons in International Law, 1979; Africa before the World Court, 1981; contribs to legal jls. *Address:* c/o International Court of Justice, Peace Palace, The Hague, Netherlands; (home) 20 Ozumba Mbadiwe Street, Victoria Island, Lagos, Nigeria. *T:* 612389.

ELIBANK, 14th Lord *cr* 1643 (Scotland); **Alan D'Ardis Erskine-Murray;** Bt (Nova Scotia) 1628; personnel consultant; Deminex UK Oil and Gas, since 1981; *b* 31 Dec. 1923; *s* of Robert Alan Erskine-Murray (*d* 1939) and Eileen Mary (*d* 1970), *d* of late John Percy MacManus; *S* cousin, 1973; *m* 1962, Valerie Sylvia, *d* of late Herbert William Dennis; two *s. Educ:* Bedford Sch.; Peterhouse, Cambridge (MA Law). Barrister-at-Law. RE, 1942-47; Cambridge Univ., 1947-49; Practising Barrister, 1949-55; Shell International Petroleum Co., 1955-80. *Recreations:* golf, tennis. *Heir: s* Master of Elibank, *qv. Address:* The Coach House, Charters Road, Sunningdale, Ascot, Berks SL5 9QB. *T:* Ascot 22099. *Club:* MCC.

ELIBANK, Master of; Hon. Robert Francis Alan Erskine-Murray; *b* 10 Oct. 1964; *s* and *heir* of 14th Lord Elibank, *qv. Educ:* The Grove, Harrow School. *Recreations:* judo, soccer, rugby and karate.

ELIOT, family name of **Earl of St Germans.**

ELIOT, Lord; Peregrine Nicholas Eliot; *b* 2 Jan. 1941; *o s* of 9th Earl of St Germans, *qv,* and of late Helen Mary, *d* of late Lieut-Col Charles Walter Villiers, CBE, DSO, and Lady Kathleen Villiers; *m* 1964, Hon. Jacquetta Jean Frederika Lampson, *d* of 1st Baron Killearn and Jacqueline Aldine Lesley (*née* Castellani); three *s. Educ:* Eton. *Recreation:* mucking about. *Heir: s* Hon. Jago Nicholas Aldo Eliot, *b* 24 March 1966. *Address:* Port Eliot, St Germans, Cornwall. *Clubs:* Pratt's; Cornish.

ELIOT, Ven. Canon Peter Charles, MBE 1945; TD 1945; Archdeacon of Worcester, 1961-75; now Archdeacon Emeritus; Residentiary Canon, Worcester Cathedral, 1965-75; now Canon Emeritus; *b* 30 Oct. 1910; *s* of late Hon. Edward Granville Eliot and late Mrs Eliot; *m* 1934, Lady Alethea Constance Dorothy Sydney Buxton, *d* of 1st and last Earl Buxton, PC, GCMG, and late Countess Buxton; no *c. Educ:* Wellington Coll.; Magdalene Coll., Cambridge. Commissioned in Kent Yeomanry (Lt-Col Comdg, 1949-52), 1933. Admitted Solicitor, 1934; Partner in City firm until 1953. Studied at Westcott House, Cambridge, 1953-54; made Deacon to serve in Parish of St Martin-in-the-Fields, London, 1954; Priest, 1955; Vicar of Cockermouth, 1957-61; Rural Dean of Cockermouth and Workington, 1960-61; Vicar of Cropthorne with Charlton, 1961-65. *Recreations:* amateur acting (Canterbury

Old Stagers); sketching; sight-seeing. *Address:* The Old House, Kingsland, Leominster, Herefordshire HR6 9QS. *T:* Kingsland 285. *Club:* Travellers'.

ELIOTT OF STOBS, Sir Arthur Francis Augustus Boswell, 11th Bt *cr* 1666; Chief of the Clan Elliot; *b* 2 Jan. 1915; *s* of Sir Gilbert Alexander Boswell Eliott, 10th Bt, and Dora Flournoy Adams Hopkins (*d* 1978), Atlanta, Georgia, USA; *S* father, 1958; *m* 1947, Frances Aileen, *e d* of late Sir Francis McClean, AFC; one *d. Educ:* Harrow; King's Coll., Cambridge. BA 1936, MA 1949. 2nd Lieut, King's Own Scottish Borderers (TA), 1939, Major, 1944. Served in East Africa and Burma with King's African Rifles, 1941-45. Member of Queen's Body Guard for Scotland, Royal Company of Archers. *Publication:* The Elliots, the story of a Border Clan, 1974. *Address:* Redheugh, Newcastleton, Roxburghshire. *T:* Liddesdale 213. *Clubs:* New, Puffin's (Edinburgh); Leander.

ELKAN, Prof. Walter; Professor, and Head of Department, of Economics, Brunel University, since 1978; *b* Hamburg, 1 March 1923; *s* of Hans Septimus Elkan and Maud Emily (*née* Barden); *m* Susan Dorothea (*née* Jacobs); one *s* two *d. Educ:* Frensham Heights; London Sch. of Economics. BSc (Econ), PhD. Army, 1942-47; Research Asst, LSE, 1950-53; Sen. Res. Fellow, E African Inst. of Social Research, 1954-58; Vis. Res. Assoc., MIT and Lectr, N Western Univ., 1958; Lectr in Econs, Makerere UC, 1958-60; Lectr in Econs, Durham Univ., 1960; Prof. of Econs, 1966-78, and rotating Head of Dept, 1968-78, Durham Univ. Vis. Res. Prof., Nairobi Univ., 1972-73. Mem. Council, Overseas Develt Inst.; Associate, Inst. of Development Studies. Former Pres., African Studies Assoc.; former Member: Northern Economic Planning Council; R.EconS. Sometime consultant to Govts of Basutoland, Mauritius, Solomon Is, Fiji, Kenya and others. *Publications:* An African Labour Force, 1956; Migrants and Proletarians, 1960; Economic Development of Uganda, 1961; Introduction to Development Economics, 1973; articles on contemp. African econ. history in econ. and other social science jls; ILO, UNESCO, IBRD and British Govt reports. *Recreation:* music. *Address:* Economics Department, Brunel University, Uxbridge, Mddx UB8 3PH. *T:* Uxbridge 37188.

ELKES, Prof. Joel, MD, ChB; FACP, FAPA; Distinguished Service Professor, The Johns Hopkins University, since 1974; Professor of Psychiatry, University of Louisville, since 1980; *b* 12 Nov. 1913; *s* of Dr Elkanan Elkes and Miriam (*née* Malbin); *m* 1943, Dr Charmian Bourne; one *d* ; *m* 1975, Josephine Rhodes, MA. *Educ:* private schools; Lithuania and Switzerland; St Mary's Hosp., London; Univ. of Birmingham Med. Sch. (MB, ChB 1947; MD Hons 1949). MRCS, LRCP 1941. University of Birmingham: Sir Halley Stewart Research Fellow, 1942-45; Lectr, Dept of Pharmacology, 1945-48; Senior Lectr and Actg Head of Dept, 1948-50; Prof. and Chm., Dept of Experimental Psychiatry, 1951-57; Clinical Professor of Psychiatry, George Washington Univ. Med. Sch., Washington, 1957-63; Chief of Clinical Neuropharmacology Research Center, Nat. Inst of Mental Health, Washington, 1957-63; Dir, Behavioral and Clinical Studies Center St Elizabeth's Hosp., Washington, 1957-63; Henry Phipps Prof. and Dir, Dept of Psychiatry and Behavioural Scis, Johns Hopkins Univ. Sch. of Medicine, and Psychiatrist-in-Chief, Johns Hopkins Hosp., 1963-73; Samuel McLaughlin Prof.-in-residence, McMaster Univ., 1975; Prof. of Psychiatry, McMaster Univ., 1976-80. Dir, Foundns Fund for Research in Psychiatry, 1964-68; Consultant, WHO, 1957. Vis. Fellow, New York Univ. and New England Med. Center, Boston, 1950; Benjamin Franklin Fellow, RSA, 1974. Lectures: Harvey, 1962; Salmon, 1963; Jacob Bronowski Meml, 1978. President: (first) Amer. Coll. of Neuropsychopharmacology, 1962; Amer. Psychopathological Assoc., 1968 (Chm., Foundns Fund Prize Bd for Res. in Psychiatry, 1977-81). Formerly Member: Council, Internat. Collegium N Psychopharm; Central Council, Internat. Brain Research Organisation, UNESCO (Chm., Sub-Cttee on Educn); RSM. Fellow: Amer. Acad. of Arts and Scis; Amer. Psych. Assoc.; Amer. Coll. of Psychiatry; RCPsych, GB; Amer. Coll. of Neuropsychopharmacol. Member: Physiological Soc., GB; Pharmacological Soc., GB; Amer. Soc. for Pharmacology and Experimental Therapeutics; Soc. of Biological Psychiatry; New York Acad. of Science; Sigma Xi; Scientific Assoc.; Acad. of Psychoanalysis. *Publications:* papers to various jls and symposia. *Recreation:* painting. *Address:* Department of Psychiatry, University of Louisville, Louisville, Ky 40292, USA. *Clubs:* Cosmos (Washington); West Hamilton (Baltimore).

ELKIN, Adolphus Peter, CMG 1966; DLitt; retired as Professor of Anthropology, University of Sydney (1933-56), now Emeritus Professor; *b* 27 March 1891; *s* of Reuben and Ellen Elkin; *m* 1922, Sara Thompson; two *s. Educ:* East Maitland High Sch.; St Paul's Coll., Sydney; University of Sydney (MA); University of London (PhD). C of E Clergyman (Parishes), 1915-25; Australian Nat. Research Council Fellow, 1927-31; St Paul's College: Fellow, 1935-66; Chm., 1960, 1963-66. Editor (Hon.) of Oceania (Internat. Jl of Anthropology), 1933-; Founder (1966) and Editor (hon.), Jl of Archæology and Physical Anthropology in Oceania; Founder, Jl of Human Biology in Oceania, 1971. Pres., Royal Soc. of New South Wales, 1941; Vice-Chm., Aborigines' Welfare Board of New South Wales, 1941-69; Chm., Aust. Nat. Research Council, 1953-55. Crown Trustee, 1946-72, and Pres. 1961-68, the Australian Museum; Fellow of Senate, Univ. of Sydney, 1959-69; Chm., Council Internat. House (Univ. of Sydney), 1972-77 (Chm., Finance Cttee, 1966-). Macrossan Memorial Lectr, Univ. of Queensland, 1944; David Lectr (Aust. and NZ Assoc. for the Advancement of Science), 1949; Centenary Oration, Royal Soc. of NSW, 1966. Hon. Life Fellow, Pacific Science Assoc., 1961. Hon. DLitt Sydney, 1970. Medal of Royal Society of NSW, 1949;

James Cook Medal, 1955; Mueller Medal, 1957; H. E. Gregory Medal, 1961. *Publications:* The Australian Aborigines: How to Understand Them, 1938 (5th edn 1974); Our Opinions and the National Effort, 1941; Society, the Individual and Change, 1941; Wanted-a Charter for the Peoples of the South-West Pacific, 1943; Citizenship for the Aborigines, 1944; Social Anthropology in Melanesia, 1953; The Diocese of Newcastle: A History, 1955; Aboriginal Men of High Degree, 1946, 2nd edn 1977; Pacific Science Association: Its History and Role in International Cooperation, 1961; contribs to Oceania, American Anthropologist, etc. *Recreations:* music; formerly cricket and tennis. *Address:* 115 Warrina Village, Castle Hill, NSW 2154, Australia. *T:* 680.1718.

ELKIN, Alexander, CMG 1976; international law consultant; *b* Leningrad (St Petersburg), 2 Aug. 1909; *o c* of Boris and Anna Elkin; *m* 1937, Muriel Solomons, Dublin. *Educ:* Grunewald Gymnasium and Russian Academic Sch., Berlin; Univs of Berlin, Kiel and London. DrJur Kiel 1932, LLM London 1935. Called to the Bar, Middle Temple, 1937; practised at English Bar, 1937-39; BBC Monitoring Service, 1939-42; war-time govt service, 1942-45; Associate Chief, Legal Service, UN Interim Secretariat, London, 1945-46; Asst Dir, UN European Office, Geneva, 1946-48; Legal Adviser to UNSCOB, Salonica, 1948; Dep. Legal Adviser, later Legal Adviser, OEEC (OECD 1960-), Paris, 1949-61; UNECA Legal Consultant, formation of African Develt Bank and Econ. Council for Africa, 1962-64; Actg Gen. Counsel of ADB, 1964-65; UNDP Legal Consultant, formation of Caribbean Develt Bank, 1967-68; Special Adviser on European Communities Law, FCO, 1970-79. Legal consultancies for: WHO, 1948; IBRD, 1966; W Afr. Regional Gp, 1968; OECD, 1975. Lectured: on Europ. payments system and OEEC/OECD activs, Univ. of the Saar, 1957-60, and Univ. Inst. of Europ. Studies, Turin, 1957-65; on drafting of treaties, UNITAR Seminars, The Hague, Geneva and NY, for legal advisers and diplomats, 1967-, and at UN Disarmament Centre, NY, and Geneva Graduate Inst. of Internat. Studies, 1979; on language and law, Univs of Bath and Bradford, 1979-. Hon. Vis. Prof., Bradford Univ., 1982-83. Mem., RIIA. Ford Foundn Leadership Grant, 1960. *Publications:* contrib. European Yearbook, Jl du Droit Internat., Revue Générale de Droit Internat. Public, Survey of Internat. Affairs 1939-1946, Travaux pratiques de L'Institut de Droit Comparé de la Faculté de Droit de Paris, etc. *Recreations:* reading, visiting art collections, travel. *Address:* 140 Hamilton Terrace, NW8; 22 Old Buildings, Lincoln's Inn, WC2. *Club:* Travellers'.

ELKIN, Sonia Irene Linda, OBE 1981 (MBE 1966); Director for Smaller Firms, Confederation of British Industry, since 1979; *b* 15 May 1932; *d* of Godfrey Albert Elkin and Irene Jessamine Archibald. *Educ:* Beresford House Sch., Eastbourne. Association of British Chambers of Commerce, 1950-66: Overseas Director, 1956-66; Lloyds Bank Overseas Dept, 1966-67; Confederation of British Industry, 1967-: Head of West European Dept, 1967-72; Head of Regional and Smaller Firms Dept, 1972-73; Dep. Director, Regions and Smaller Firms, 1973-79. Commissioner, Manpower Services Commission, 1982-. *Publications:* What about Europe?, 1967; What about Europe Now?, 1971. *Address:* Confederation of British Industry, Centre Point, 103 New Oxford Street, WC1A 1DU. *Club:* United Oxford & Cambridge University (Lady Associate).

ELKINGTON, Reginald Geoffrey, CB 1962; *b* 24 Dec. 1907; *s* of Harold and Millicent Elkington; *m* 1935, Bertha Phyllis, *d* of William and Bertha Dyason; one adopted *s* one adopted *d*. *Educ:* Battersea Grammar Sch.; Fitzwilliam Coll., Cambridge. Inland Revenue, 1929-42; Min. of Supply, 1942-57 (Under-Sec., 1954); DSIR, 1957-65; Principal Establishment Officer, Min. of Technology, 1964-67; retired from Civil Service, 1967; Estabt Officer (part-time), Monopolies Commn, 1968-73. Sec., AERE Harwell, 1948-51. *Recreations:* gardening, crossword solving. *Address:* Maranwood, Highfield Road, West Byfleet, Surrey. *T:* Byfleet 43766.

ELKINS, Vice-Adm. Sir Robert (Francis), KCB 1958 (CB 1954); CVO 1952; OBE 1942; *b* 12 Jan. 1903; *er s* of Dr F. A. Elkins, Leavesden, Kings Langley; *m* 1940, Gwendolen Hurst Flint. *Educ:* RNC, Osborne and Dartmouth. Qualified as Interpreter (German), 1928; specialised in Gunnery, 1929; Commander, 1937; in comd HMS Bideford, 1939-40 (despatches, 1940); Prisoner of War, 1940; Comdr, HMS Renown, 1940; Capt. Dec. 1942; in comd HMS Dido, 1944-45; ide 1949; in comd HMS Ocean, 1949-50; in comd HMS Excellent, 1950-52; ADC to King George VI, 1952; ADC to the Queen until July 1952; Rear-Adm. 1952; Vice-Adm. 1955; Flag Officer, 2nd in Comd, Far East Station, 1955-56; Admiral, British Joint Staff Mission, Washington, 1956-58, retired 1959. *Recreations:* all outdoor sports. *Address:* Branlea, Foreland Road, Bembridge, IoW. *T:* Bembridge 2522.

ELLACOMBE, Air Cdre John Lawrence Wemyss, CB 1970; DFC 1942 (Bar 1944); MBIM; Administrator to the Special Trustees for St Thomas' Hospital, since 1980; *b* Livingstone, N Rhodesia, 28 Feb. 1920; *s* of Dr Gilbert H. W. Ellacombe; *m* 1951, Wing Officer Mary Hibbert, OBE, WRAF; one *s* two *d*. *Educ:* Diocesan Coll., Rondebosch, Cape. War of 1939-45: RAF, 1939; Fighter Comd and Two ATA Force, 1940-45 (Pilot, Battle of Britain). Aden, 1946-48; RAF Staff Coll., 1948-49; Fighter Command, 1949-57; BJSM, Washington, 1959. JSSC, 1959-60; Gp Captain, CO RAF Linton on Ouse, to Nov 1962; CFE, to Aug. 1965; Defence Operational Analysis Estabt, West Byfleet, 1965-68; Air Cdre, Commander Air Forces Gulf, 1968-70; Dir of Ops (Air Defence and Overseas), MoD (Air), 1970-73; Dir, Scientific Services, St

Thomas' Hosp., 1973-80. *Recreations:* photography, golf, cricket. *Address:* 33 The Drive, Northwood, Middlesex HA6 1HW. *Club:* Royal Air Force.

ELLEN, Eric Frank, QPM 1980; LLB; CBIM; Director, International Chamber of Commerce International Maritime Bureau, since 1981; *b* 30 Aug. 1930; *s* of late Robert Frank Ellen and of Jane Lydia Ellen; *m* 1949, Gwendoline Dorothy Perkins; one *s* one *d*. *Educ:* Wakefield Central Sch.; East Ham; Holborn Coll. of Law, Univ. of London (LLB Hons, London Univ. Certificate in Criminology). CBIM (FBIM 1978). Joined PLA Police, 1951; Sgt 1956; Inspector 1961; Chief Insp. 1972; Supt and Chief Supt 1973; attended 11th Sen. Comd Course, Bramshill Police Coll., 1974; Dep. Chief Constable 1975; Chief Constable, 1975-80. Adviser on security to Ports Div. of Dept of Environment. Sec., Internat. Assoc. of Airport and Seaport Police, 1980- (Pres., 1977-78 and 1978-79); Pres., PLA Section, Internat. Police Assoc., 1975-79. Chm., EEC Assoc. of Airport and Seaport Police, 1975-78. Member: Internat. Assoc. of Ports and Harbours Standing Cttee on Legal Protection of Port Interests, 1977-79 (Chm., Sub-Cttee on Protection of Ports against Sabotage and Terrorism, 1977-79); British Acad. of Forensic Sciences; Hon. Soc. of Middle Temple. Police Long Service and Good Conduct Medal, 1974. Freeman of the City of London, 1978. Police Medal, Republic of China, 1979. *Publications:* International Maritime Fraud, 1981; professional articles on marine fraud and port policing. *Recreations:* golf, swimming. *Address:* Maritime House, 1 Linton Road, Barking, Essex IG11 8HG. *T:* 01-591 3000. *Club:* Wig and Pen.

ELLEN, Patricia Mae H.; *see* Hayward Ellen.

ELLENBOROUGH, 8th Baron *cr* 1802; **Richard Edward Cecil Law;** Director, Towry Law & Co.; *b* 14 Jan. 1926; *s* of 7th Baron and Helen Dorothy, *o d* of late H. W. Lovatt; *S* father, 1945; *m* 1953, Rachel Mary, *o d* of late Major Ivor Hedley; three *s*. *Educ:* Eton Coll.; Magdalene Coll., Cambridge. *Heir: s* Captain the Hon. Rupert Edward Henry Law, Coldstream Guards [*b* 28 March 1955; *m* 1981, Hon. Grania, *d* of Baron Boardman, *qv*]. *Address:* Springhill House, Groombridge, East Sussex. *T:* Groombridge 456. *Clubs:* Gresham, Turf.

ELLERTON, Geoffrey James, CMG 1963; MBE 1956; Director, Globe Investment Trust plc; Chairman, Globe Management Ltd, since 1980; *b* 25 April 1920; *er s* of late Sir Cecil Ellerton; *m* 1946, Peggy Eleanor, *d* of late F. G. Watson; three *s*. *Educ:* Highgate Sch.; Hertford Coll., Oxford (MA). Military Service, 1940-45. Apptd Colonial Administrative Service as District Officer, Kenya, 1945. Acted as Minister for Internal Security and Defence, 1960 and 1962. Retired as Permanent Sec., Prime Minister's Office and Sec. to the Cabinet, at time of Kenya's Independence, Dec. 1963. Sec. to the Maud and Mallaby Cttees on Management and Staffing in Local Government, 1964. Joined Elder Dempster Lines, 1965, Chm., 1972-74; an Exec. Dir, Ocean Transport & Trading Ltd, 1972-80; Dir, Overseas Containers Ltd, 1975-80. Mem. Council, Liverpool Univ., 1974-78. *Recreations:* music, reading. *Address:* Briar Hill House, Broad Campden, Chipping Campden, Glos. *T:* Evesham 841003. *Clubs:* Brooks's, MCC; Nairobi.

ELLES, family name of **Baroness Elles.**

ELLES, Baroness *cr* 1972 (Life Peer), of the City of Westminster; **Diana Louie Elles;** Member (C) Thames Valley, European Parliament, since 1979; Bureau Member, European Democratic Group, since 1979, and Vice President, since 1982, European Parliament; *b* 19 July 1921; *d* of Col Stewart Francis Newcombe, DSO and Elisabeth Chaki; *m* 1945, Neil Patrick Moncrieff Elles, *qv* ; one *s* one *d*. *Educ:* private Schs, England, France and Italy; London University (BA Hons). Served WAAF, 1941-45. Barrister-at-law. Care Cttee worker in S London, 1956-72. UK Deleg. to UN Gen. Assembly, 1972; Mem., UN Sub-Commn on Prevention of Discrimination and Protection of Minorities, 1973-75; UN special rapporteur on Human Rights, 1973-75; Mem., British delegn to European Parlt, 1973-75. Mem., Cripps Cttee on legal discrimination against women; Chm., Sub-cttee of Women's Nat. Adv. Cttee (Conservative Party) on one-parent families (report publ. as Unhappy Families); Internat. Chm., European Union of Women, 1973-79; Chm., Cons. Party Internat. Office, 1973-78; Opposition front bench spokesman, 1975-79. *Publications:* The Housewife and the Common Market (pamphlet), 1971; Human Rights of Aliens, 1980. *Address:* 75 Ashley Gardens, SW1; Villa Fontana, Ponte del Giglio, Lucca, Italy.

ELLES, Neil Patrick Moncrieff; Chairman, Value Added Tax Appeals Tribunal, since 1972; *b* 8 July 1919; *s* of Edmund Hardie Elles, OBE and Ina Katharine Hilda Skene; *m* 1945, Diana Louie Newcombe (*see* Baroness Elles); one *s* one *d*. *Educ:* Eton; Christ Church, Oxford (MA). War Service, RAF, 1939-45. Called to the Bar, Inner Temple, 1947; Tutor, Company Law and Conveyancing, Council of Legal Educn, 1950-57; Sec., Inns of Court Conservative and Unionist Taxation Cttee, 1957-71; Mem., Special Study Gp, Commn on Law of Competition, Brussels, 1962-67. *Publications:* The Law of Restrictive Trade Practices and Monopolies (with Lord Wilberforce and Alan Campbell), 1966; Community Law through the Cases, 1973. *Recreations:* fishing, listening to music, the cultivation of vines. *Address:* 75 Ashley Gardens, SW1. *T:* 01-828 0175; Villa Fontana, Ponte del Giglio, Lucca, Italy. *Clubs:* Flyfishers', MCC.

ELLES, Robin Jamieson, CBE 1974 (OBE 1945; MBE 1942); JP; County Director, Dunbartonshire British Red Cross Society, 1968-80; *b* 4 Jan. 1907;

er s of late Bertram Walter Elles, Malayan Civil Service, and late Jean Challoner Elles; *m* 1932, Eva Lyon Scott Elliot, *d* of Lt-Col William Scott Elliot; one *s*. *Educ*: Marlborough Coll.; Trinity Hall, Cambridge. BA 1928, MA 1950. Sudan Political Service, 1929-34; J. & P. Coats Ltd, India and China, 1935-40; Army, 1940-45: OETA Abyssinia, 1941; Sudan Defence Force, 1942-45, Libya and Tripolitania, Temp. Lt-Col Comdg 10 SDF Inf. Bn, 1944-45; J. & P. Coats Ltd, Personnel, 1946-66, retd 1966. Chm. of Governors, Paisley Coll. of Technology, 1966-76 (Governor, 1950-76); Chairman: Scottish Adv. Cttee, Nat. Youth Employment Council, 1962-71; Nat. Youth Employment Council, 1971-74. JP Dunbartonshire, 1952. *Publications*: various papers. *Recreations*: fishing, rowing (Cambridge Blue, 1927 and 1929; rowed for Leander, 1929). *Address*: Rogart, Garelochhead, Dunbartonshire. *T*: Garelochhead 810304. *Club*: Leander (Henley-on-Thames).

ELLINGWORTH, Richard Henry; HM Diplomatic Service, retired; Course Director (European Training), Civil Service College, since 1978; *b* 9 March 1926; *s* of Vincent Ellingworth; *m* 1952, Joan Mary Waterfield; one *s* three *d*. *Educ*: Uppingham; Aberdeen Univ.; Magdalen Coll., Oxford (Demy). Served War of 1939-45: RA, and Intelligence Corps, 1944-47. Oxford, 1947-50 (first Lit. Hum.); HM Embassy, Japan, 1951-55; FO, 1955-59; HM Embassy: Belgrade, 1959-63; Japan, 1963-68 (Olympic Attaché, 1964); Head of Oil Dept., FCO, 1969-71; Research Associate, Internat. Inst. for Strategic Studies, 1971-72; Counsellor, Tehran, 1972-75; seconded to Dept of Energy, 1975-77. Mem., Farningham Parish Council, 1979. *Publications*: (with A. N. Gilkes) An Anthology of Oratory, 1946; Japanese Economic Policy and Security, 1972. *Recreations*: gardening, music. *Address*: The Mount, Sparepenny Lane, Farningham, Kent. *T*: Farningham 863709.

ELLIOT; *see* Elliot-Murray-Kynynmound, family name of Earl of Minto.

ELLIOT; *see* Scott-Elliot.

ELLIOT, family name of **Baroness Elliot of Harwood**.

ELLIOT OF HARWOOD, Baroness *cr* 1958 (Life Peer); **Katharine Elliot,** DBE 1958 (CBE 1946); JP; *b* 15 Jan. 1903; *d* of Sir Charles Tennant, 1st Bt, Innerleithen, Peeblesshire, and late Mrs Geoffrey Lubbock; *m* 1934, Rt Hon. Walter Elliot, PC, CH, MC, FRS, LLD, MP (*d* 1958); no *c*. *Educ*: Abbot's Hill, Hemel Hempstead; Paris. Chairman: Nat. Assoc. of Mixed Clubs and Girls' Clubs, 1939-49; Adv. Cttee on Child Care for Scotland, 1956-65; Women's Nat. Adv. Cttee of Conservative Party, 1954-57; Nat. Union of Conservative and Unionist Assocs, 1956-67; Carnegie UK Trust, 1965- (Trustee, 1940-); Consumer Council, 1963-68. Chm., Lawrie & Symington Ltd, Lanark. Member: Women's Consultative Cttee, Dept of Employment and Productivity (formerly Min. of Labour), 1941-51, 1958-70; Home Office Adv. Cttee on Treatment of Offenders, 1946-62; King George V Jubilee Trust, 1936-68; NFU. UK Delegate to Gen. Assembly of UN, New York, 1954, 1956 and 1957. Contested (C) Kelvingrove Div. of Glasgow, March 1958. Roxburghshire: CC 1946-75 (Vice-Convener, 1974); JP 1968-. Farms in Roxburghshire. FRSA 1964. Hon. LLD Glasgow, 1959. Grand Silver Cross, Austrian Order of Merit, 1963. *Publication*: Tennants Stalk, 1973. *Recreations*: foxhunting, golf, music. *Address*: Harwood, Bonchester Bridge, Hawick, Roxburghshire TD9 9TL; 17 Lord North Street, Westminster, SW1P 3LD. *T*: 01-222 3230.

ELLIOT, Gerald Henry, FRSE; Chairman, Christian Salvesen Ltd, since 1981; *b* 24 Dec. 1923; *s* of Surg. Captain J. S. Elliot, RN, and Magda Salvesen; *m* 1950, Margaret Ruth Whale; two *s* one *d*. *Educ*: Marlborough Coll.; New Coll., Oxford (BA PPE 1948). FRSE 1978. Captain FF Rifles, Indian Army, 1942-46. Christian Salvesen Ltd, 1948-, Dep. Chm. and Man. Dir, 1973-81. Dir, Scottish Provident Instn, 1971-, Dep. Chm., 1982-; Chairman: Chambers and Fargus, 1975-79; Scottish Br., RIIA, 1973-77 (Sec., 1963-73); Scottish Arts Council, 1980-; FAO Fishery Industries Develt Gp, 1971-76; Forth Ports Authority, 1973-79. Sec., National Whaling Bd, 1953-62; Mem., Nat. Ports Council, 1978-81. Consul for Finland in Edinburgh, 1957-. Kt 1st Cl., Order of White Rose of Finland, 1975. *Publications*: papers on national and internat. control of whaling and fishing. *Address*: 9 Easter Belmont Road, Edinburgh EH12 6EX.

ELLIOT, Prof. Harry, CBE 1976; FRS 1973; Senior Research Fellow at Imperial College, London; Emeritus Professor of Physics, University of London; Professor of Physics at Imperial College, London, 1960-80 (Assistant Director of Physics Department, 1963-71); *b* 28 June 1920; *s* of Thomas Elliot and Hannah Elizabeth (*née* Littleton), Weary Hall, Cumberland; *m* 1943, Betty Leyman; one *s* one *d*. *Educ*: Nelson Sch., Wigton; Manchester Univ. MSc, PhD. Served War, Signals Branch, RAF, incl. liaison duties with USN, 1941-46. Manchester Univ.: Asst Lectr in Physics, 1948-49; Lectr in Physics, 1949-54; Imperial Coll.: Lectr in Physics, 1954-56; Sen. Lectr in Physics, 1956-57; Reader in Physics, 1957-60. Member: Science Research Council, 1971-77; Council, Royal Soc., 1978-79; Science Adv. Cttee, ESA, 1979-. Hon. Prof., Universitad Mayor de San Andres, 1957; Mem., Internat. Academy of Astronautics, 1963; Hon. ARCS, 1965. Fellow, World Acad. of Arts and Scis, 1978. Holweck Prize and Medal, Inst. of Physics and Société Française de Physique, 1976. *Publications*: papers on cosmic rays, solar physics and magnetospheric physics in scientific jls; contrib. scientific reviews and magazine articles. *Recreation*: painting. *Address*: The Blackett Laboratory, Imperial College, SW7 2BZ. *T*: 01-589 5111 (ext. 2301).

ELLIOT, Sir John, Kt 1954; High Sheriff of Greater London, 1970-71; *b* London, 6 May 1898; *m* 1924, Elizabeth, *e d* of late Dr A. S. Cobbledick; one *s* one *d*. *Educ*: Marlborough; Sandhurst. European War in 3rd Hussars; after four years in journalism joined former Southern Rly, 1925, in charge public relations (first in UK). Visited USA, Canada, frequently; Deputy General Manager, Southern Rly, 1937, Gen. Manager, 1947; Chief Regional Officer, Southern Region, British Railways, 1948-49. London Midland Region, Euston, 1950-51; Chairman: Railway Exec., 1951-53; London Transport, 1953-59; Pullman Car Co., 1959-63; Thos. Cook & Son Ltd, 1959-67; Willing & Co. Ltd, 1959-70; London and Provincial Poster Group Ltd, 1965-71. Director: Commonwealth Development Corp., 1959-66; Railway Air Services, Channel Islands Airways, 1933-48; Thomas Tilling Ltd, 1959-70; British Airports Authority, 1965-69; Cie Internationale des Wagons-Lits, 1960-71. Vice-Pres., Internat. Union of Railways (UIC), 1947 and 1951-53. Formerly Col. (Comdg) Engineer and Railway Staff Corps, Royal Engineers, 1956-63. Visited Australia, at invitation of Govt of Victoria, to report on rail and road transport, 1949, 1966, 1970, and E Africa, 1969, on transport study (World Bank). FInstT (Pres., 1953-54). Mem. Société de l'histoire de Paris, 1958-74. Officier, Légion d'Honneur; American Medal of Freedom. *Publications*: The Way of the Tumbrils (Paris during the Revolution), 1958; Where our Fathers Died (Western Front 50 years after), 1964; On and Off the Rails, 1982; regular newspaper feature, Speaking of That . . .; book reviews on military history in Daily Telegraph and Sunday Times; many papers on transport. *Recreations*: gardening, shooting, fishing, cricket (Vice-Pres. Essex CCC). *Address*: Stonyfield, Great Easton, Dunmow, Essex. *Clubs*: Cavalry and Guards, MCC.

ELLIOT, Captain Walter, DSC 1944; RN Retd; *b* 17 Feb. 1910; *s* of John White Elliot and Frances Hampson; *m* 1936, Thelma Pirie Thomson; four *d*. *Educ*: HMS Conway; Royal Naval Coll. Joined RN, 1929; specialised in Naval Aviation. Served War of 1939-45 (DSC, despatches); retired, 1958. Took Economics Degree, London Univ., 1958 (BSc Econ). In business, 1958-60. MP (C) Carshalton and Banstead, 1960-Feb. 1974. *Recreations*: fencing, fishing, tennis.

ELLIOT-MURRAY-KYNYNMOUND, family name of **Earl of Minto**.

ELLIOT-SMITH, Alan Guy, CBE 1957; *b* 30 June 1904; *s* of late F. Elliot-Smith; *m* 1939, Ruth Kittermaster; no *c*. *Educ*: Charterhouse; Oriel Coll., Oxford. Hons Mod. Lang. Sch., 1925; Asst Master, Harrow Sch., 1925-40; Headmaster, Cheltenham Coll., 1940-51; Mem., Harrow UDC, 1933-36; Deleg. to Inst. of Pacific Relations Conf., Calif., 1936; lectured to German teachers on Education, 1947 and 1948; lectured to Service units in the Middle East, 1949; Head-master of Victoria Coll., Cairo, 1952-56; Representative in Nigeria of the West Africa Cttee, 1957-58; Headmaster, Markham Coll., Lima, Peru, 1960-63. *Recreations*: travel, reading. *Address*: Bevois Mount, Rowsley Road, Eastbourne, Sussex.

ELLIOTT, Hon. Lord; Walter Archibald Elliott, MC 1943; Chairman, Scottish Land Court, since 1978; President, Lands Tribunal for Scotland, since 1971; *b* 6 Sept. 1922; 2nd *s* of late Prof. T. R. Elliott, CBE, DSO, FRS, Broughton Place, Broughton, Peeblesshire; *m* 1954, Susan Isobel Mackenzie Ross, Kaimend, North Berwick; two *s*. *Educ*: Eton; Trinity Coll., Cambridge; Edinburgh Univ. Active service in Italy and North West Europe with 2nd Bn Scots Guards, 1943-45; captured and escaped, Salerno landings (MC); demobilised, Staff Capt., 1947. Barrister-at-law, Inner Temple, 1950; Advocate at Scottish Bar, 1950; QC (Scotland) 1963. Standing Junior Counsel to Accountant of Court and later to Minister of Aviation. Mem., Legal Aid Central Cttee, 1966-70; Mem., Royal Company of Archers (Queen's Body Guard for Scotland). *Publications*: articles in legal periodicals. *Recreations*: gardening, ski-ing, shooting. *Address*: Morton House, Fairmilehead, Edinburgh. *T*: 031-445 2548. *Clubs*: New, Arts (Edinburgh).

ELLIOTT, Alan Fraser, MA; Headmaster, Mill Hill School, 1974-78; *b* 12 March 1929; *s* of Rev. Norman and Mrs Winifred Elliott; *m* 1955, Sheila (*née* West); three *d*. *Educ*: Bristol Grammar Sch.; New College, Oxford (MA). Asst Master and Housemaster, Marlborough Coll., 1954-74; Lectr, Univ. of Toronto, 1961-62. *Publication*: (ed) Euripides, Medea, 1969. *Recreation*: cottaging.

ELLIOTT, Dr Charles Kennedy; Physician to the Queen, since 1980; *b* 1919; *e s* of late Charles Harper Elliott and Martha Elliott; *m* 1949, Elizabeth Margaret Kyle. *Educ*: Campbell Coll., Belfast; Trinity Coll., Dublin (MB, BCh 1942). MRCGP, MLCO, MFHom; AFOM. Sir Patrick Dun's Hosp., Dublin, 1943; Captain, RAMC, attached SEAC, 1944; General practitioner, Wisbech, 1949-69; Editor, Rural Medicine, 1969-72; Homoeopathic practitioner, S Kensington, 1973-80; Clinical Asst, Royal London Homoeopathic Hosp., 1973-81; Sub Dean, Faculty of Homoeopathy, 1976-79; Area Surgeon, Cambridgeshire St John Ambulance, 1974-81; Chm., Organizing Cttee, VI Internat. Congress Rural Medicine, Cambridge, 1975; Pres., Internat. Assoc. of Agricl Medicine and Rural Health, 1972-78; Trustee, Rehabilitation Trust of Gt Britain, 1977-; SBStJ 1970; Chevalier de l'Ordre Militaire et Hospitalier de St Lazare de Jerusalem, 1975. *Publications*: articles on homeopathy and agricl medicine in internat. med. pubns and nat. jls. *Recreations*: heraldry, silent cinema, travel. *Address*: West Walton, Wisbech, Cambridgeshire PE14 7EU. *T*: Wisbech 780269. *Club*: Royal Society of Medicine.

ELLIOTT, Rev. Dr Charles Middleton; Director, Christian Aid, since 1982; Assistant General Secretary, British Council of Churches, since 1982; *b* 9 Jan. 1939; *s* of Joseph William Elliott and Mary Evelyn Elliott; *m* 1962, Hilary Margaret Hambling; three *s* (one *d* decd). *Educ:* Repton; Lincoln and Nuffield Colls, Oxford (MA, DPhil). Deacon, 1964; priest, 1965. Lectr in Econs, Univ. of Nottingham, 1963-65; Reader in Econs, Univ. of Zambia, 1965-69; Asst Sec., Cttee on Society, Develt and Peace, Vatican and World Council of Churches, 1969-72; Sen. Lectr in Develt Econs, Univ. of E Anglia, 1972-73; Dir, Overseas Develt Gp, UEA, 1973-77; Minor Canon, Norwich Cathedral, 1974-77; Prof. of Develt Policy and Planning, and Dir, Centre of Develt Studies, Univ. of Wales, 1977-82. *Publications:* The Development of Debate, 1972; Inflation and the Compromised Church, 1973; Patterns of Poverty in the Third World, 1975; articles in Jl of Develt Studies, Econ. Hist. Rev., Theology, World Health Forum and in Proc. Royal Soc. *Recreations:* sailing, fly-fishing, walking, chatting to rural craftsmen. *Address:* 119 Fentiman Road, Kennington, SW8.

ELLIOTT, David Murray; Minister and Deputy UK Permanent Representative to the European Communities, Brussels, since 1982; *b* 8 Feb. 1930; *s* of Alfred Elliott and Mabel Kathleen Emily Elliott (*née* Murray); *m* 1956, Ruth Marjorie Ingram; one *d* (one *s* decd). *Educ:* Bishopshalt Grammar Sch.; London Sch. of Economics and Political Science (BScEcon); Kitchener Scholar. National Service, RAF, 1951-54; Gen. Post Office, 1954-57; seconded to Federal Ministry of Communications, Nigeria, 1958-62; GPO, 1962-69; Asst Secretary: Min. of Posts and Telecommunications, 1969-74; Dept of Industry, 1974-75; Counsellor at UK Representation to the European Communities, Brussels, 1975-78; Under Sec., Cabinet Office, 1978-82. *Recreation:* reading The Times. *Address:* c/o Foreign and Commonwealth Office, SW1; 31 Ailsa Road, St Margaret's, Twickenham, Mddx TW1 1QJ. *T:* 01-892 8961.

ELLIOTT, Denholm Mitchell; actor, stage and films; *b* 31 May 1922; *m* 1954, Virginia McKenna (marr. diss. 1957; she *m* 1957, Bill Travers); *m* 1962, Susan Darby Robinson; one *s* one *d. Educ:* Malvern. *Plays:* The Guinea-Pig, Criterion, 1946; Venus Observed, St James's, 1949; Ring Round the Moon, Martin Beck, New York, 1950; Sleep of Prisoners, St Thomas's, Regent Street, 1950; Third Person, Criterion, 1951; Confidential Clerk, Lyric, 1954; South, Arts, 1955; Who Cares, Fortune, 1956; Camino Real, Phœnix, 1957; Traveller Without Luggage, Arts, 1958; The Ark, Westminster, 1959; Stratford-on-Avon Season, 1960; Write Me a Murder, Belasco Theatre, New York, 1961; The Seagull, The Crucible, Ring Round the Moon, Nat. Repertory Co., New York, 1963-64; Come as You Are, New, 1970; Chez Nous, Globe, 1974; The Return of A. J. Raffles, Aldwych, 1975; Heaven and Hell, Greenwich, 1976; The Father, Open Space, 1979; TV plays. *Films:* Sound Barrier, 1949; The Cruel Sea, 1952; They Who Dare, 1953; Pacific Destiny, 1955; Scent of Mystery, 1959; Station Six Sahara, 1962; Nothing But the Best, 1963; King Rat, 1964; The High Bright Sun, 1964; You Must Be Joking, 1965; Alfie, 1966; Here we go round the Mulberry Bush, 1967; The Seagull, 1968; Too Late the Hero, 1969; Madame Sin, 1972; A Doll's House, 1973; The Apprenticeship of Duddy Kravitz, 1974; Russian Roulette, 1976; Sweeney II, Saint Jack, The Hound of the Baskervilles, Zulu Dawn, A Game for Vultures, Cuba, 1978; Bad Timing, Sunday Lovers, 1980; Brimstone and Treacle, 1982. Has awards, London and New York, incl. BAFTA Best TV Actor, and New Standard Best Film Actor, 1981. *Recreations:* ski-ing, golf. *Address:* 86 Neville Court, Abbey Road, NW8. *Club:* Garrick.

ELLIOTT, Frank Abercrombie, MD, FRCP; Emeritus Professor of Neurology, University of Pennsylvania, since 1979; Director, Elliott Neurology Centre, Pennsylvania Hospital, Philadelphia, since 1975; *b* 18 Dec. 1910; *s* of Arthur Abercrombie Elliott and Kathleen Gosselin; *m* 1st, 1940, Betty Kathleen Elkington; two *d*; 2nd, 1970, Mrs Josiah Marvel (*née* Hopkins). *Educ:* Rondebosch; Univ. of Cape Town. Univ. entrance schol., 1928; Lewis Memorial schol., 1930-34; MB, ChB Cape Town, with Hons and Gold Medal; Hiddingh Travelling Fellowship, 1936-39. House Surg. and House Phys. to professorial units, Cape Town; House Physician, British Postgrad. Sch. of Medicine and Nat. Hosp. for Nervous Diseases, London; Resident MO, Nat. Heart Hosp. RAMC, 1943-48, Lt-Col; Adviser in Neurology, India and War Office. FRCP 1948; FACP 1973. Physician to Charing Cross Hosp., 1947-58; to Moorfields Eye Hospital, 1949-58; Prof. of Neurology, Univ. of Pennsylvania, 1963-78. Lecturer and Examiner, London Univ. Member: Assoc. of British Neurologists; Assoc. of British Physicians; Internat. Soc. of Internal Medicine; Am. Acad. of Neurology; Philadelphia Neurological Soc. *Publications:* (ed) Clinical Neurology, 1952; Clinical Neurology, 1964 (2nd edn, 1971); papers on neurological subjects and the origins of aggressive behaviour. *Address:* Pennsylvania Hospital, Philadelphia, Pa 19107, USA. *Club:* Philadelphia.

ELLIOTT, Frank Alan; Under Secretary, Department of Health and Social Services, Northern Ireland, since 1981; *b* 28 March 1937; *s* of Frank Elliott and Doreen Allen; *m* 1964, Olive Lucy O'Brien; one *s* two *d. Educ:* Royal Belfast Academical Inst.; Trinity Coll., Dublin (BA (Mod.) 1st cl.). Entered NI Civil Service, 1959; Principal, Min. of Health, 1966, Asst Sec., 1971; Sen. Asst Sec., Dept of Health and Social Services, 1975. *Recreations:* music and the arts, motoring. *Address:* Department of Health and Social Services, Dundonald House, Upper Newtownards Road, Belfast, Northern Ireland. *T:* Belfast 650111.

ELLIOTT, George, FRICS; Senior Partner, Edmond Shipway and Partners; *b* 20 Aug. 1932; *s* of Harry Elliott and Nellie Elizabeth Elliott; *m* 1958, Winifred Joan; one *s* one *d. Educ:* Sir George Monoux Grammar Sch.; SW Essex Technical Coll. FRICS 1966. Chief Exec., British Urban Develt Services Unit, 1975-78. *Recreation:* travel. *Address:* Flat 8.6, Stirling Court, Marshall Street, W1V 1LQ. *T:* 01-437 3133.

ELLIOTT, Harold William, CBE 1967; *b* 24 Nov. 1905; *s* of late W. J. Elliott and Ellen Elliott; *m* 1st, 1929, Mary Molyneux (marr. diss. 1935); one *s* one *d*; 2nd, 1937, Betty (*d* 1976), *d* of late C. J. Thumling and Mrs V. A. Thumling; one *s*; 3rd, 1978, Helen Bridget, *y d* of Sir Lionel Faudel-Phillips, 3rd Bt, and *widow* of 5th Earl of Kilmorey. *Educ:* Brighton Coll. Apprenticed to Adolf Saurer, AG Arbon, Switz., 1924; joined Pickfords Ltd, 1926. Mem., Road and Rail Central Conf., 1938; Transport Adv. Cttee, Food Defence Plans Dept, BoT, 1939; Asst Divisional Food Officer (Transport), London, 1940; Controller of Road Transport, Min. of Supply, 1941; Mem., Salvage Bd; Dir of Transport, Middle East Supply Centre, Cairo, 1943; Mem., Road Haulage Central Wages Bd and Vice-Chm., Meat Transport Organisation Ltd, 1945; Gen. Man., Hay's Wharf Cartage Co. Ltd, Pickfords Ltd and Carter Paterson & Co. Ltd, 1947; Chief Officer (Freight), Road Transport Exec.; Mem., Coastal Shipping Adv. Cttee, 1948; Mem. Bd of Management, Brit. Road Services, and Dir, Atlantic Steam Navigation Co. Ltd, 1959; Man. Dir, Pickfords Ltd, 1963-70, Chm., 1970; Life Mem., Road Haulage Assoc. Trustee, Sutton Housing Trust, 1971-79; Chm., Holmwood Common Management Cttee, 1971-79; Governor, Brighton Coll., 1955 (Chm. Governors, 1974-78; a Vice Patron, 1980). Liveryman, Worshipful Co. of Carmen. FCIT (a Vice-Pres., 1970-71). *Address:* Omla, Moushill Lane, Milford, Godalming, Surrey GU8 5BH. *T:* Godalming 20723.

ELLIOTT, Sir Hugh (Francis Ivo), 3rd Bt *cr* 1917; OBE 1953; Editor, Technical Publications, and Research Consultant, International Union for Conservation of Nature, 1970-80, retired; *b* 10 March 1913; *er s* of Sir Ivo Elliott, 2nd Bt; *S* father, 1961; *m* 1939, Elizabeth Margaret, *er d* of A. G. Phillipson; one *s* two *d. Educ:* Dragon Sch.; Eastbourne Coll.; University Coll., Oxford. Tanganyika Administration, 1937; Administrator, Tristan da Cunha, 1950-52; Permanent Sec., Min. of Natural Resources, Tanganyika, 1958; retired, 1961. Commonwealth Liaison Officer for International Union for Conservation of Nature, 1961-66; acting Sec.-Gen., 1962-64, Sec.-Gen., 1964-66, Sec. Ecology Commn, 1966-70. Trustee, British Museum (Natural History), 1971-81; Hon. Sec., British Ornithologists' Union, 1962-66, Vice-Pres. 1970-73, Pres., 1975-79; Chm., British Nat. Sect., Internat. Council for Bird Preservation, 1980-81. Comdr, Order of Golden Ark (Netherlands), 1980. *Publications:* (ed) Proc. 2nd World Conf. on Nat. Parks, Yellowstone, 1972; (jtly) Herons of the World, 1978; contributor to Ibis and various ornithological and conservation jls. *Recreations:* ornithology, travel. *Heir: s* Clive Christopher Hugh Elliott, PhD [*b* 12 Aug. 1945; *m* 1975, Marie-Thérèse, *d* of H. Ruttimann; two *s*]. *Address:* 173 Woodstock Road, Oxford OX2 7NB. *T:* Oxford 55469.

ELLIOTT, Hugh Percival, CMG 1959; retired, 1967; *b* 29 May 1911; *s* of late Major P. W. Elliott, IA; *m* 1951, Bridget Rosalie (*d* 1981), *d* of late Rev. A. F. Peterson. *Educ:* St Lawrence Coll., Ramsgate; Hertford Coll., Oxford. Joined Colonial Administrative Service, Nigeria, 1934; seconded Colonial Office, 1946; Supervisor, Colonial Service Courses, London, 1948-50; Senior District Officer, Nigeria, 1962-67. Many visits to Ethiopia, Kenya, Rhodesia etc, to support the initiatives for Moral Re-Armament by African friends, 1968-78. CON, 1964 (Comdr, Order of the Niger, Nigeria). *Publications:* Darkness and Dawn in Zimbabwe, 1978; Dawn in Zimbabwe, 1980. *Address:* 14 Eldon Avenue, Shirley, Croydon, Surrey.

ELLIOTT, Maj.-Gen. James Gordon, CIE 1947; retd; *b* 6 April 1898; *s* of late Dr William Elliott, Welshpool, Montgomeryshire; *m* 1931, Barbara Eleanor (*d* 1979), *y d* of William Douglas, Malvern; one *s* one *d. Educ:* Blundell's Sch. Commissioned, Indian Army, 1916; 1st Punjab Regt, 1922; GSO2 Staff Coll., Quetta, 1935-37; Dir Military Training, India, 1942-43; Bde Comdr, 1943-44; Dep. Welfare Gen., India, 1945-46; Dep. Sec. (Mil.), Defence Cttee, 1947-48; retired 1948. *Publications:* Administrative Aspect of Tactics and Training, 1938; The Story of the Indian Army, 1939-45, 1965; The Frontier 1839-1947, 1968; Field Sports in India 1800-1947, 1973; India, 1976. *Recreations:* gardening, fishing. *Address:* 13 Barnfield Avenue, Exmouth, Devon. *Club:* Naval and Military.

ELLIOTT, Prof. James Philip, PhD, FRS 1980; Professor of Theoretical Physics, University of Sussex, since 1969; *b* 27 July 1929; *s* of James Elliott and Dora Kate Smith; *m* 1955, Mavis Rosetta Avery; one *s* two *d. Educ:* University College, Southampton; London External degrees: BSc 1949, PhD 1952. Senior Scientific Officer, AERE Harwell, 1951-58; Vis. Associate Prof., Univ. of Rochester, USA, 1958-59; Lecturer in Mathematics, Univ. of Southampton, 1959-62; Reader in Theoretical Physics, Univ. of Sussex, 1962-69. Fellow of former Physical Soc. *Publications:* Symmetry in Physics, 1979; contribs include: The Nuclear Shell Model, Handbuch der Physik, vol 39, 1957; many papers, mostly published in Proc. Roy. Soc. and Nuclear Phys. *Recreations:* gardening, sport and music. *Address:* 36 Montacute Road, Lewes, Sussex BN7 1EP. *T:* Lewes 4783.

ELLIOTT, Prof. John Huxtable, FBA 1972; Professor of History, Institute for Advanced Study, Princeton, NJ, since 1973; *b* 23 June 1930; *s* of Thomas

Charles Elliott and Janet Mary Payne; *m* 1958, Oonah Sophia Butler. *Educ:* Eton College; Trinity College, Cambridge (MA, PhD). Fellow of Trinity Coll., Cambridge, 1954-67; Asst Lectr in History, Cambridge Univ., 1957-62; Lectr in History, Cambridge Univ., 1962-67; Prof. of History, KCL, 1968-73. Wiles Lectr, QUB, 1969; Trevelyan Lectr, Cambridge Univ., 1982-83. Corresp. Fellow, Real Academia de la Historia, Madrid, 1965; Fellow, Amer. Acad. Arts and Scis, 1977. Mem., Amer. Philosophical Soc., 1982; Corresponding Member: Hispanic Soc. of America, 1975; Real Academia Sevillana de Buenas Letras, 1976. *Publications:* The Revolt of the Catalans, 1963; Imperial Spain, 1469-1716, 1963; Europe Divided, 1559-1598, 1968; The Old World and the New, 1492-1650, 1970; ed (with H. G. Koenigsberger) The Diversity of History, 1970; (with J. F. de la Peña) Memoriales y Cartas del Conde Duque de Olivares, 2 vols, 1978-80; (with Jonathan Brown) A Palace for a King, 1980. *Address:* The Institute for Advanced Study, Princeton, NJ 08540, USA; 73 Long Road, Cambridge CB2 2HE. *T:* Cambridge 841332.

ELLIOTT, Mark; HM Diplomatic Service; Head of Far Eastern Department, Foreign and Commonwealth Office, since 1981; *b* 16 May 1939; *s* of William Rowcliffe Elliott, *qv*, and Karin Tess Elliott, (*née* Classen); *m* 1964, Julian Richardson; two *s*. *Educ:* Eton Coll. (King's Scholar); New Coll., Oxford. HM Forces (Intell. Corps), 1957-59. FO, 1963; Tokyo, 1965; FCO, 1970; Private Sec. to Perm. Under-Sec. of State, 1973-74; First Sec. and Head of Chancery, Nicosia, 1975-77; Counsellor, 1977-81, Head of Chancery, 1978-81, Tokyo. *Recreations:* photography, walking and camping, music. *Address:* c/o Foreign and Commonwealth Office, SW1.

ELLIOTT, Dr Michael, CBE 1982; FRS 1979; Deputy Chief Scientific Officer; Head of Department of Insecticides and Fungicides, since 1979, Deputy Director, since 1980, Rothamsted Experimental Station; *b* 30 Sept. 1924; *s* of Thomas William Elliott and Isobel Constance (*née* Burnell); *m* 1950, Margaret Olwen James; two *d*. *Educ:* Skinners Co.'s Sch., Tunbridge Wells, Kent; The Univ., Southampton (BSc, PhD); King's Coll., Univ. of London (DSc). Postgrad. res., University Coll., Southampton, 1945-46, and King's Coll., Univ. of London, 1946-48; Organic Chemist, Dept of Insecticides and Fungicides, Rothamsted Exptl Stn, 1948-, SPSO 1971-79. Vis. Lectr, Div. of Entomology, Univ. of Calif at Berkeley, 1969 and 1974. Burdick and Jackson Internat. Award for Res. in Pesticide Chemistry, 1975; Holroyd Medal and Lectureship, Soc. of Chem. Ind., 1977; John Jeyes Medal and Lectureship, Chem. Soc., 1978; Mullard Medal, Royal Soc., 1981. *Publications:* Synthetic Pyrethroids, 1977; papers on chemistry of insecticides and relation of chemical structure with biological activity; chapters in books on insecticides. *Recreations:* photography, designing insecticides. *Address:* 9 Long Ridge, Aston, Stevenage, Herts SG2 7EW. *T:* Shephall 328. *Club:* Camera.

ELLIOTT, Michael Alwyn; General Administrator, National Theatre, since 1979; *b* 15 July 1936; *s* of W. A. Edwards and Mrs J. B. Elliott (assumed stepfather's name); *m* Caroline Margaret McCarthy; two *s* one *d*. *Educ:* Raynes Park Grammar School. Journalist, 1955-59; Public Relations, Avon Rubber Co. Ltd, 1959-63; Marketing Executive, then Assistant Corporate Planning Manager, CPC International, 1963-68; Kimberly-Clark Ltd: Product Manager, 1968; Marketing Manager, 1969; Marketing and Development Manager, 1975; General Manager, 1976; Director, 1977. Member, Executive Council, Soc. of West End Theatre, 1980-. *Recreations:* golf, squash, theatre. *Address:* 149 Forest Road, Tunbridge Wells, Kent TN2 5EX. *T:* Tunbridge Wells 30615.

ELLIOTT, Michael Paul, OBE 1980; Resident Artistic Director, Royal Exchange Theatre Company, Manchester, since 1973; *b* 26 June 1931; *s* of Canon W. H. Elliott and Edith Elliott; *m* 1959, Rosalind Marie Knight; two *d*. *Educ:* Radley Coll.; Keble Coll., Oxford (BA Hons). Staff producer, BBC TV Drama (over 50 TV plays), 1956-60; freelance, theatre, TV and films, 1960; Associate Dir, RSC, As You Like It, with Vanessa Redgrave, Stratford and London, 1961; John Mortimer's Two Stars for Comfort, with Trevor Howard, Garrick, 1962; last Dir, Old Vic Th., Peer Gynt, with Leo McKern, 1962-63; freelance, 1963-68; Miss Julie, with Albert Finney and Maggie Smith, National Th., 1965; formed 69 Theatre Co., Manchester Univ. Th., 1968; productions incl.: When We Dead Awaken, with Wendy Hiller (also Edin. Fest. and BBC TV); Daniel Deronda, with Vanessa Redgrave; Peer Gynt, with Tom Courtenay; co-producer: She Stoops to Conquer, Garrick; Catch My Soul, Princes; became first Resid. Artistic Dir of 69 Theatre Co. (now called Royal Exchange Th. Co.), 1973; opened new Royal Exch. Th., 1976; productions include: Uncle Vanya, with Albert Finney and Leo McKern; The Ordeal of Gilbert Pinfold, with Michael Hordern; Twelfth Night, Crime and Punishment, with Tom Courtenay; Family Reunion, with Edward Fox; Lady From the Sea, with Vanessa Redgrave; Dir, all 3 plays in Roundhouse season, 1979, The Family Reunion, transf. to Vaudeville, London; The Dresser, 1980, transf. to Queen's, London and NY, 1981; Philoctetes, 1982. Member: Arts Council, 1972-75 (Mem. Panels, and Chm., 1963-70); NT, Bldg Cttee, 1963-66; BBC Adv. Council, 1963-66. Interviewer and broadcaster on BBC Sound and TV; 3 TV Prodns for Norwegian TV; CBS Special Prodn for coast-to-coast Amer. TV, 1964. Hon. Fellow, Manchester Polytechnic, 1977; Hon. MA Manchester, 1980. *Recreations:* photography, painting. *Club:* Savile.

ELLIOTT, Sir Norman (Randall), Kt 1967; CBE 1957 (OBE 1946); MA; Chairman of the Electricity Council, 1968-72; Chairman, Howden Group,

since 1973; Director: Newarthill & McAlpine Group, since 1972; Slumberger Ltd, since 1977; *b* 19 July 1903; *s* of William Randall Elliott and Catherine Dunsmore; *m* 1963, Phyllis Clarke. *Educ:* privately; St Catharine's Coll., Cambridge. Called to the Bar, Middle Temple, 1932 (J. J. Powell Prizeman, A. J. Powell Exhibitioner). London Passenger Transport Board; London and Home Counties Joint Electricity Authority; Yorkshire Electric Power Co.; 21 Army Group: first as CRE (Royal Engineers) then, as Col, Deputy Dir of Works, 21 Army Group (OBE); Chief Engineer and Manager, Wimbledon Borough Council; Gen. Manager and Chief Engineer, London and Home Counties Joint Electricity Authority and sometime Chm. and Dir, Isle of Thanet Electric Supply Co., and Dir, James Howden & Co. Ltd; Chairman: S-E Electricity Bd, 1948-62; S of Scotland Electricity Bd, 1962-67; Member: Brit. Electricity Authority, 1950 and 1951; Central Electricity Authority, 1956 and 1957; Electricity Council, 1958-62; N of Scotland Hydro-Electric Bd, 1965-69. *Publication:* Electricity Statutes, Orders and Regulations, 1947, rev. edn 1951. *Recreations:* ball games and the theatre. *Address:* 3 Herbrand Walk, Cooden, East Sussex. *Clubs:* Athenæum; Western (Glasgow); Royal Northern Yacht.

ELLIOTT, Oliver Douglas; British Council Representative in Yugoslavia, since 1979; *b* 13 Oct. 1925; *y s* of late Walter Elliott and Margherita Elliott, Bedford; *m* 1954, Patience Rosalie Joan Orpen; one *s*. *Educ:* Bedford Modern Sch.; Wadham Coll., Oxford (MA); Fitzwilliam House, Cambridge. Served RNVR (Sub-Lt), 1944-47. Colonial Educn Service, Cyprus, 1953-59; joined British Council, 1959; served Lebanon, 1960-63; Dep. Rep., Ghana, 1963; Dir, Commonwealth I Dept, 1966; Dir, Service Conditions Dept, 1970; Dep. Educn Advr, India, 1973; Representative in Nigeria, 1976-79. *Recreations:* golf, gardening. *Address:* c/o Personnel Records, British Council, 10 Spring Gardens, SW1.

ELLIOTT, Sir Randal (Forbes), KBE 1977 (OBE 1976); President, New Zealand Medical Association, since 1976; *b* 12 Oct. 1922; *s* of Sir James Elliott and Lady (Ann) Elliott (*née* Forbes), MBE; *m* 1949, Pauline June Young; one *s* six *d*. *Educ:* Wanganui Collegiate Sch.; Otago Univ. MB, ChB (NZ), 1947; DO, 1953; FRCS, FRACS. Group Captain, RNZAF. Ophthalmic Surgeon, Wellington Hospital, 1953-. Chm. Council, NZ Med. Assoc. KStJ 1978. *Publications:* various papers in medical jls. *Recreations:* sailing, skiing, mountaineering. *Address:* 88 The Terrace, Wellington, New Zealand. *T:* 721-375. *Club:* Wellington (NZ).

ELLIOTT, Air Vice-Marshal Robert D.; *see* Deacon Elliott.

ELLIOTT, Sir (Robert) William, Kt 1974; MP (C) Newcastle upon Tyne North since March 1957; Vice-Chairman, Conservative Party Organisation, 1970-74; *b* 11 Dec. 1920; *s* of Richard Elliott; *m* 1956, Jane Morpeth; one *s* four *d* (of whom two are twin *d*). *Educ:* Morpeth Grammar Sch. Farmer, 1939-, at Low Heighley, Morpeth, Northumberland. Parliamentary Private Secretary: to joint Parliamentary Secs, Ministry of Transport and Civil Aviation, April 1958-Oct. 1959; to Under-Sec., Home Office, Nov. 1959-60; to Minister of State, Home Office, Nov. 1960-61; to Sec. for Technical Co-operation, 1961-63; Asst Govt Whip (unpaid), 1963-64; Opposition Whip, 1964-70; Comptroller of the Household, June-Sept. 1970. Chm., Select Cttee on Agric., Fisheries and Food, 1980-. *Address:* Lipwood Hall, Haydon Bridge, Northumberland. *T:* Haydon Bridge 777. *Clubs:* Carlton; Northern Counties (Newcastle upon Tyne).

ELLIOTT, Prof. Roger James, FRS 1976; Wykeham Professor of Physics, Oxford University, since 1974; Fellow of New College, Oxford, since 1974; *b* Chesterfield, 8 Dec. 1928; *s* of James Elliott and Gladys Elliott (*née* Hill); *m* 1952, Olga Lucy Atkinson; one *s* two *d*. *Educ:* Swanwick Hall Sch., Derbyshire; New Coll., Oxford (MA, DPhil). Research Fellow, Univ. of California, Berkeley, 1952-53; Research Fellow, UKAEA, Harwell, 1953-55; Lectr, Reading Univ., 1955-57. Fellow of St John's College, Oxford, 1957-74; University Reader, Oxford, 1964-74; Senior Proctor, 1969; Delegate, Oxford Univ. Press, 1971-. Visiting Prof., Univ. of California, Berkeley, 1961; Miller Vis. Prof., Univ. of Illinois, Urbana, 1966; Loeb Lectr, Harvard Univ., 1967; Seaver Lectr, USC, 1972. Maxwell Medal, Inst. of Physics, 1968. *Publications:* Magnetic Properties of Rare Earth Metals, 1973; Solid State Physics and its Applications (with A. F. Gibson), 1973; papers in Proc. Royal Soc., Jl Phys., Phys. Rev., etc. *Recreations:* tennis, squash. *Address:* 11 Crick Road, Oxford. *T:* Oxford 53281. *Club:* Athenæum.

ELLIOTT, Sir Ronald (Stuart), Kt 1981; Director: Brambles Industries Ltd, since 1981; Australian Board, International Commodities Clearing House Ltd, since 1981; *b* 29 Jan. 1918; *s* of Harold J. W. Elliott and Mercedes E. Manning; *m* 1944, Isabella Mansbridge Boyd; one *s* one *d*. *Educ:* C of E Grammar Sch., Ballarat, Victoria. ABIA; FAIM. Commonwealth Banking Corporation: Sec., 1960-61; Dep. Manager for Queensland, 1961-63; Chief Manager, Foreign Div., 1963-64; Chief Manager, Queensland, 1964-65; Gen. Manager, Commonwealth Develt Bank of Australia, 1966-75; Dep. Man. Dir, 1975-76, Man. Dir, 1976-81, Commonwealth Banking Corp.; Chm., Australian European Finance Corp. Ltd, 1976-81. Mem., Sci. and Industry Forum, Australian Acad. of Sci., 1978-81. Dep. Chm., Australian Opera, 1980-; Mem., Australian Film Develt Corp., 1970-75. *Recreations:* golf, reading, music, particularly opera. *Address:* 56 Milray Avenue, Wollstonecraft, NSW 2065, Australia. *T:* 432734. *Clubs:* Union, Australian Golf (Sydney).

ELLIOTT, Sydney Robert; Editor of the Daily Herald, 1953–57; *b* 31 Aug. 1902; *o surv. s* of Robert Scott Elliott and Helen Golden; *m* 1927, Janet Robb Johnston; two *s* one *d* (one *s* decd). *Educ:* Govan High Sch., Glasgow. Managing Editor, Reynolds News, 1929; Editor, Evening Standard, 1943; Political Adviser, Daily Mirror, 1945; Managing Dir, The Argus and Australian Post, Melbourne, 1949; Gen. Manager, Daily Herald, 1952. Collaborated with author of George Wigg by Lord Wigg, 1972. *Publications:* Life of Sir William Maxwell, 1922; Co-operative Storekeeping; Eighty Years of Constructive Revolution, 1925; England, Cradle of Co-operation, 1937. *Address:* 5 Frognal Close, Hampstead, NW3. *T:* 01-435 4149.

ELLIOTT, Walter Archibald; *see* Elliott, Hon. Lord.

ELLIOTT, Sir William; *see* Elliott, Sir R. W.

ELLIOTT, William Rowcliffe, CB 1969; Senior Chief Inspector, Department of Education and Science, 1968–72, retired; *b* 10 April 1910; *s* of Thomas Herbert Elliott and Ada Elliott (*née* Rowcliffe); *m* 1937, Karin Tess, *d* of Ernest and Lilly Classen; one *s. Educ:* St Paul's Sch.; The Queen's Coll., Oxford. Schoolmaster, 1933–36; HM Inspector of Schools: in Leeds, 1936–39; in Leicestershire, 1940–44; in Liverpool, 1944–48; Staff Inspector: for Adult Education, 1948–55; for Secondary Modern Education, 1955–57; Chief Inspector for Educational Developments, 1957–59; for Secondary Educn, 1959–66; Dep. Sen. Chief Insp., 1966–67. Pres., Section L, British Assoc., 1969; Mem., Oxfam Governing Council, 1974–80. Chm. of Governors, Friends' Sch., Saffron Walden, 1982–. *Publication:* Monemvasia, The Gibraltar of Greece, 1971. *Recreations:* village life; photography; writing, cyclamen-growing. *Address:* Astwick House, Farthinghoe, Brackley, Northants. *T:* Banbury 710388. *Club:* Royal Over-Seas League.
   See also Mark Elliott.

ELLIOTT-BINNS, Edward Ussher Elliott, CB 1977; Under-Secretary, Scottish Home and Health Department, 1966–78; *b* 24 Aug. 1918; *e s* of Leonard and Anna Elliott-Binns; *m* 1942, Katharine Mary McLeod, *d* of late Dr J. M. Caie; one *d. Educ:* Harrow; King's Coll., Cambridge. Served in Army, 1939–46; Leics Regt and Special Forces (Major). Asst Principal, Scottish Home Dept, 1946; Principal, 1948; Asst Sec., Royal Commn on Capital Punishment, 1949–53; Private Sec. to Minister of State, Scottish Office, 1956–57; Asst Sec., 1957. *Address:* 22 Wilton Road, Edinburgh EH16 5NX. *T:* 031-667 2464. *Club:* Special Forces.
   See also P. J. Harrop.

ELLIOTT-BLAKE, Henry, TD 1955, and Bar; MA; FRCS, FRCSE; Hon. Plastic Surgeon, St George's Hospital; Emeritus Consultant Plastic Surgeon, St Helier Hospital, Carshalton; *b* 25 Dec. 1902; *s* of Henry Thomas Blake, MIWE, CC, JP, of Herefordshire, and Maud Blake; *m* 1945, Mary, Baroness Swaythling, *d* of Hon. Mrs Ionides. *Educ:* Dean Close, Cheltenham; Queens' Coll., Cambridge (hockey Blue 1931); St Thomas's Hospital, London. MRCS; LRCP 1929; MA, MB, BChir (Cambridge) 1931; FRCS 1941; FRCSE 1941; late Major (surg. specialist), RAMC (TA); served France (Dunkirk) and India; invalided. Founder Mem. British Assoc. Plastic Surgeons; FRSocMed (late Pres., Section of Plastic Surgery). Sometime Consultant Plastic Surgeon: Victoria Hosp. for Children, Tite Street; Royal Alexandra Hosp. for Sick Children, Brighton, Royal Sussex County Hosp., Brighton, Westminster Hosp. Gp (Queen Mary's Hosp., Roehampton, and Carshalton), and Senior Surgeon to the Ministry of Pensions (Roehampton and Stoke Mandeville). Founder Mem. Medical Art Soc. Exhibited: Royal Soc. of Portrait Painters; Royal Academy of Arts; ROI; Armed Forces Art Soc. Founder Mem., Cambridge Senior Soc. *Publications:* four chapters in: Operative Surgery (ed Prof. Charles Rob and Rodney Smith); Butterworths Operative Surgery-Service Vol. 3(b), The Reconstruction of the Penile Urethra in Hypospadias; articles in medical journals. *Recreation:* golf. *Address:* 17 Cadogan Square, SW1X 0HT. *Clubs:* Boodle's; Hawks (Cambridge); Dunkirk Veterans' Assoc.; Royal St George's Golf (Sandwich); Royal Ashdown Forest Golf (Life mem.); Berks Golf (Ascot); Senior Golfing Society.

ELLIS; *see* Scott-Ellis.

ELLIS, Amabel W.; *see* Williams-Ellis.

ELLIS, Arthur Robert Malcolm, DL; **His Honour Judge Ellis;** a Circuit Judge (formerly Judge of County Courts), since 1971; *b* 27 June 1912; *s* of David and Anne Amelia Ellis, Nottingham; *m* 1938, Brenda Sewell; one *d. Educ:* Nottingham High Sch. Admitted Solicitor, 1934; called to the Bar, Inner Temple, 1953. Chm., Nottingham Council of Social Service, 1950–55; Dep. Chm., E Midland Traffic Area, 1955–; Chm., Ministry of Pensions and National Insurance Tribunal, Sutton-in-Ashfield, Notts, 1961–64, resigned; Chm., Min. of Pensions and Nat. Insce Tribunal, Notts, 1964–. Chm., Notts QS, 1963–71 (Dep.-Chm., 1962–63); Chm., Derbyshire QS, 1966–71 (Dep.-Chm., 1965–66). DL Notts, 1973. *Recreations:* golf, bridge. *Address:* Overfields, 104 Cropwell Road, Radcliffe-on-Trent, Notts. *T:* Radcliffe-on-Trent 664. *Clubs:* Borough (Nottingham); Royal Overseas League (Nottingham Branch).

ELLIS, Bryan James; Under-Secretary, Department of Health and Social Security, since 1977; *b* 11 June 1934; *s* of late Frank and Renée Ellis; *m* 1960, Barbara Muriel Whiteley; one *s* one *d. Educ:* Merchant Taylors' Sch.; St John's

Coll., Oxford (MA). Sec., Oxford Union Soc., 1956. Joined Civil Service, entering Min. of Pensions and National Insurance (subseq. Min. of Social Security and DHSS) as Asst Principal, 1958; Principal 1963; Asst Sec. 1971. *Recreations:* theatre and cinema, bridge. *Address:* 6 Crutchfield Lane, Walton-on-Thames, Surrey. *T:* Walton 28664. *Club:* MCC.

ELLIS, Carol Jacqueline, (Mrs Ralph Gilmore), QC 1980 (practises as Miss Ellis); JP (sits as Mrs Gilmore); Editor, The Law Reports and Weekly Law Reports, since 1976; *b* 6 May 1929; *d* of Ellis W. Ellis and Flora Bernstein; *m* 1957, Ralph Gilmore; two *s. Educ:* Abbey Sch., Reading; La Ramée, Lausanne; Univ. of Lausanne; University Coll. London (LLB). Called to the Bar, Gray's Inn, 1951; supernumerary law reporter for The Times, other law reports and legal jls, 1952; law reporter to The Law Reports and Weekly Law Reports, 1954; Asst Editor, Weekly Law Reports, 1969; Managing Editor, The Law Reports and Weekly Law Reports, 1970. JP W Central Div. Inner London, 1972–. *Recreations:* travel, music, theatre. *Address:* 11 Old Square, Lincoln's Inn, WC2. *T:* 01-405 5243/3930.

ELLIS, Rear-Adm. Edward William, CB 1974; CBE 1968; Private Secretary to the Lord Mayor of London, 1974–82; *b* 6 Sept. 1918; *s* of Harry L. and Winifred Ellis; *m* 1945, Dilys (*née* Little); two *s. Joined RN, 1940; War service afloat in HM Ships Broadwater and Eclipse, and liaison duties in USS Wichita and US Navy destroyer sqdn; psc 1952; Staff of Flag Officer Flotillas, Mediterranean, 1954–55; Sec. to 4th Sea Lord, 1956–58; Sec. to C-in-C South Atlantic and South America, 1959–60; HM Ships Bermuda and Belfast, 1960–62; Head of C-in-C Far East Secretariat, 1963–65; Sec. to C-in-C Portsmouth and Allied C-in-C Channel, 1965–66; Sec. to Chief of Naval Staff and 1st Sea Lord, 1966–68; Cdre RN Barracks Portsmouth, 1968–71; Adm. Pres., RNC Greenwich, 1972–74. Comdr 1953; Captain 1963; Rear-Adm. 1972. Freeman of the City of London, 1974; Liveryman, Shipwrights' Co., 1980. OStJ 1981. Commander, Royal Order of Danebrog, 1974. *Recreations:* golf, gardening. *Address:* South Lodge, Minstead, Lyndhurst, Hants. *Clubs:* Army and Navy; Brockenhurst Manor Golf.

ELLIS, Prof. Harold, MA, MCh, DM, FRCS; Professor of Surgery, University of London; Hon. Consultant Surgeon, Westminster Hospital, since 1962; *b* 13 Jan. 1926; *s* of Samuel and Ada Ellis; *m* 1958, Wendy Mae Levine; one *s* one *d. Educ:* Queen's Coll. (State Scholar and Open Scholar in Natural Sciences), Oxford; Radcliffe Infirmary, Oxford. BM, BCh, 1948; FRCS, MA, 1951; MCh 1956; DM 1962. House Surgeon, Radcliffe Infirmary, 1948–49; Hallett Prize, RCS, 1949. RAMC, 1949–51. Res. Surgical Officer, Sheffield Royal Infirm., 1952–54; Registrar, Westminster Hosp., 1955; Sen. Registrar and Surgical Tutor, Radcliffe Infirm., Oxford, 1956–61; Sen. Lectr in Surgery, Westminster Hosp., 1961–62. Hon. Consultant Surgeon to the Army, 1978–. Mem. Council, RCS, 1974–. Member: Association of Surgeons; British Soc. of Gastroenterol.; Surgical Research Soc.; Council: RSocMed; British Assoc. of Surgical Oncology. *Publications:* Clinical Anatomy, 1960; Anatomy for Anaesthetists, 1963; Lecture Notes on General Surgery, 1965; Principles of Resuscitation, 1967; History of the Bladder Stone, 1970; General Surgery for Nurses, 1976; Intestinal Obstruction, 1982; numerous articles on surgical topics in medical journals. *Recreation:* medical history. *Address:* 16 Bancroft Avenue, N2. *T:* 01-348 2720.

ELLIS, Herbert; *see* Ellis, W. H. B.

ELLIS, Humphry Francis, MBE 1945; MA; writer; *b* 1907; 2nd *s* of late Dr John Constable Ellis, Metheringham, Lincs and Alice Marion Raven; *m* 1933, Barbara Pauline Hasseldine; one *s* one *d. Educ:* Tonbridge Sch.; Magdalen Coll., Oxford (Demy). 1st cl. Hon. Mods, 1928; 1st cl. Lit. Hum., 1930. Asst Master, Marlborough Coll., 1930–31. Contributor to Punch, 1931–68; Editorial staff, 1933; Literary and Dep. Ed., 1949–53. Privilege Mem., RFU, 1952–. Served War of 1939–45 in RA (AA Command). *Publications:* So This is Science, 1932; The Papers of A. J. Wentworth, 1949; Why the Whistle Went (on the laws of Rugby Football), 1947; Co-Editor, The Royal Artillery Commemoration Book, 1950; Editor, Manual of Rugby Union Football, 1952; Twenty Five Years Hard, 1960; Mediatrics, 1961; A. J. Wentworth, BA (Retd), 1962; The World of A. J. Wentworth, 1964 (re-issued as A. J. Wentworth, BA, 1980); Swansong of A. J. Wentworth, 1982; contribs to The New Yorker. *Recreation:* fishing. *Address:* Hill Croft, Kingston St Mary, Taunton, Somerset. *T:* Kingston St Mary 264. *Clubs:* Garrick, MCC.

ELLIS, John; *b* Hexthorpe, Doncaster, 22 Oct. 1930; *s* of George and Hilda Ellis; *m* 1953, Rita Butters; two *s* two *d. Educ:* Rastrick Gram. Sch., Brighouse. Laboratory technician, Meteorological Office, 1947–63; Vice-Chm., Staff side, Air Min. Whitley Council, 1961–63; Member Relations Offr, Co-op. Retail Services, Bristol/Bath Region, 1971–74. Mem., Easthampstead RDC, 1962–66; Mem., Bristol City Council, 1971–74. Contested (Lab) Wokingham, 1964; MP (Lab) Bristol North-West, 1966–70, Brigg and Scunthorpe, Feb. 1974–1979; PPS to Minister of State for Transport, 1968–70; an Asst Govt Whip, 1974–76. JP, North Riding Yorks, 1960–61. *Recreations:* gardening, cricket. *Address:* 102 Glover Road, Scunthorpe, South Humberside.

ELLIS, John; Director, Military Vehicles and Engineering Establishment, Chertsey, since 1978; *b* 9 Jan. 1925; *s* of Frank William and Alice Ellis; *m* 1958, Susan Doris (*née* Puttock). *Educ:* Leeds Univ. BSc, 1st cl. hons. Mech. Eng; CEng, MIMechE. Hydro-Ballistic Research Estabt, Admty, 1945–47; David Brown & Sons Ltd, Huddersfield, 1948; RAE, Min. of Supply

(Structures Dept, Armament Dept, Weapons Dept), 1948-68; MVEE (formerly FVRDE), MoD, 1968-. *Recreations:* mountaineering, motoring, golf. *Address:* Well Diggers, 1 and 2 New Cottages, New Pond Road, Compton, Guildford, Surrey. *T:* Godalming 7788.

ELLIS, Sir John (Rogers), Kt 1980; MBE 1943; MA, MD, FRCP; Physician to the London Hospital since 1951; Dean, London Hospital Medical College, since 1968; *b* 15 June 1916; 3rd *s* of late Frederick William Ellis, MD, FRCS; *m* 1942, Joan, *d* of late C. J. C. Davenport; two *s* two *d*. *Educ:* Oundle Sch.; Trinity Hall, Cambridge; London Hosp. Served RNVR, 1942-46, Mediterranean and Far East, Surg-Lieut. Gen. Practice, Plymouth, 1946; Sen. Lectr, Med. Unit, London Hosp., 1948-51; Sub-Dean, London Hosp. Med. Coll., 1948-58, Vice-Dean, 1967-68; Asst Registrar, RCP, 1957-61, Mem. Council 1969-72, Streatfeild Schol., 1957; Physician to Prince of Wales Gen. Hosp., 1958-68; PMO (part-time), Min. of Health, 1964-68. Member: UGC's Med. Sub-cttee, 1959-69; WHO Expert Adv. Panel on Health Manpower, 1963-; Jt Bd of Clinical Nursing Studies, 1969-74; formerly Member: Porritt (Med. Services) Cttee; Royal Commn on Med. Educn; UK Educn Cttee, RCN. Sec., Assoc. for Study of Med. Educn, 1956-71, Vice-Pres., 1971-. Lectures: Goulstonian, RCP, 1956; Wood-Jones, Univ. of Manchester, 1960; Porter, Univ. of Kansas, 1960; Sir Charles Hastings, BMA, 1964; Anders, Coll. of Physicians, Pa, 1965; Adams, RCSI, 1965; Shattuck, Massachusetts Med. Soc., 1969; Shorstein and Sprawson, London Hosp. Med. Coll., 1979; Visiting Lecturer: Assoc. of Amer. Med. Colls, 1957, 1960 and 1963; Ghana Acad. of Sciences, 1967. Corr. Mem., Royal Flemish Acad. of Medicine; Hon. Member: Royal Swedish Med. Soc.; AOA Honor Med. Soc., USA; Sect. of Med. Educn, RSocMed (former Pres.). Member Bd of Governors: Queen Mary Coll.; Atlantic Coll.; Court, Univ. of Essex; City of London AHA (Teaching); Acad. Adv. Bd, Coll. of Occupational Therapists. Formerly Member Bd of Governors: Inst. of Psychiatry; Bethlem Royal and Maudsley Hosps; London Hosp.; British Postgrad. Med. Fedn; CARE for Mentally Handicapped. Former examr in Med., Univs of Birmingham, Bristol, Cambridge, E Africa, London, Nairobi, Ireland, Newcastle upon Tyne, St Andrews. Editor, British Jl of Medical Education, 1966-75. Hon. MD Uppsala, 1977. *Publications:* articles on medical education in medical and scientific journals. *Recreations:* painting, gardening. *Address:* Little Monkhams, Monkhams Lane, Woodford Green, Essex. *T:* 01-504 2292.

ELLIS, Prof. John Romaine; Professor of Automobile Engineering, since 1960, Director, 1960-76, School of Automotive Studies, Cranfield; *b* 30 Sept. 1922; *m* 1947, Madelaine Della Blaker; one *s* one *d*. *Educ:* Tiffin Sch., Kingston-on-Thames. Royal Aircraft Establishment, 1944-56; Fairey Aviation Company, 1946-48; Royal Military Coll. of Science, Shrivenham, near Swindon, Wilts, 1949-60. *Recreations:* golf, tennis, music. *Address:* School of Automotive Studies, Cranfield Institute of Technology, Cranfield, Bedford. *T:* Bedford 750111.

ELLIS, Joseph Stanley, CMG 1967; OBE 1962; Head of News Department, Commonwealth Office, 1967; retired; *b* 29 Nov. 1907; *m* 1933, Gladys Harcombe; one *s*. *Educ:* Woodhouse Grove, Bradford; University Coll., University of London. Journalist, Manchester Evening News, 1930-40; Publications Div., Min. of Inf., 1941-45; Seconded to Dominions Office for service in Australia until 1949. Central Office of Information, 1949-51; Regional Information Officer, Karachi, 1952; Dir, British Information Services: Pakistan, 1953-55; Canberra, Australia, 1955-58; Kuala Lumpur, Malaya, 1958-62; Head, Information Services Dept, Commonwealth Office, 1962-66. *Recreation:* cricket. *Address:* Downview Close, Hindhead, Surrey.

ELLIS, Laurence Edward, MA; Rector, The Edinburgh Academy, since 1977; *b* 21 April 1932; *s* of Dr and Mrs E. A. Ellis; *m* 1961, Elizabeth Ogilvie; two *s* one *d*. *Educ:* Winchester Coll.; Trinity Coll., Cambridge (MA). AFIMA. 2/Lieut Rifle Bde, 1950-52. Marlborough Coll., 1955-77 (Housemaster, 1968). *Publications:* (part-author) texts on school maths, statistics, computing, and calculating; articles in jls. *Recreations:* Lay Reader; writing, music, woodwork. *Address:* 50 Inverleith Place, Edinburgh EH3 5QB. *T:* (office) 031-556 4603.

ELLIS, Mary; actress; singer; *b* New York City, 15 June 1901; *m* 1st, L. A. Bernheimer (decd); 2nd (marr. diss.); 3rd, Basil Sydney (marr. diss.); 4th, J. Muir Stewart Roberts (decd). *Educ:* New York. Studied art for three years; studied singing with Madame Ashforth. First Stage appearance, Metropolitan Opera House, New York, in Sœur Angelica, 1918; with Metropolitan Opera House, 1918-22; first appearance dramatic stage, as Nerissa in Merchant of Venice, Lyceum, New York, 1922; was the original Rose Marie (in the musical play, Rose Marie), Imperial, 1924; The Dybbuk, New York, 1925-26; Taming of the Shrew, 1927, and many New York leads followed; first appearance on London stage, as Laetitia in Knave and Quean, Ambassadors', 1930; in following years alternated between London and US. From 1932-39: London: Strange Interlude, 1932; Double Harness, 1933; Music in the Air, 1934; Glamorous Night, Drury Lane, 1935; Innocent Party, St James's, 1937; 2 years, Hollywood, 1936-37; Dancing Years, Drury Lane, 1939. From 1939-43: doing hospital welfare work and giving concerts for troops. Re-appeared on stage as Marie Foret in Arc de Triomphe, Phœnix, London, 1943; Old Vic (at Liverpool Playhouse), 1944 (Ella Rentheim in John Gabriel Borkman; Linda Valaine in Point Valaine; Lady Teazle in The School for Scandal); Maria Fitzherbert in The Gay Pavilion, Piccadilly, 1945; Season at Embassy: Mrs Dane's Defence, also tour and première of Ian Hay's Hattie

Stowe, 1946-47; post-war successes include: Playbill, Phœnix, 1949; Man in the Raincoat, Edinburgh, 1949; If this be Error, Hammersmith, 1950. Stratford-on-Avon Season, 1952: Volumnia in Coriolanus. London: After the Ball (Oscar Wilde-Noel Coward), Globe, 1954-55; Mourning Becomes Electra, Arts, 1955-56; Dark Halo, Arts, 1959; Look Homeward Angel, Pembroke Theatre, Croydon, 1960; Phœnix, 1962. First appeared in films, in Bella Donna, 1934; films, 1935-38; (Hollywood) Paris in the Spring: The King's Horses; Fatal Lady; Glamorous Night; Gulliver's Travels, 1961; Silver Cord (revival), Yvonne Arnaud, Guildford, 1971; Mrs Warren's Profession, Yvonne Arnaud, Guildford, 1972. Has made several major television appearances; Television plays, 1956-: Shaw's Great Catherine, Van Druten's Distaff Side and numerous others. Theatre lectures in USA, 1977. Has small hideaway in Swiss mountains, where she writes, paints and gets fresh air. *Publication:* Those Dancing Years (autobiog.), 1982. *Recreations:* painting, travel, writing. *Address:* c/o Chase Manhattan Bank, Woolgate House, Coleman Street, EC2.

ELLIS, Dr Mary Jenny Lake, FRCPsych; DPM; Senior Medical Officer, HM Borstal Institution, Feltham, since 1965; *b* 1 Jan. 1921; *d* of John Reginald Taylor and Beatrice Violet Lake Taylor; *m* 1947, Norman William Warr Ellis; two *s* one *d*. *Educ:* The Hall Sch. (now at Bratton Seymour); London Sch. of Medicine for Women, Royal Free Hosp. MB BS 1946; MRCS LRCP 1944; FRCPsych 1977 (MRCPsych 1972); DPM 1964. Neurosurgical and gen. surgical, Ho. Surgs, Enfield and Royal Free Hosp., 1944-45; Res. Surgical Officer, EMS Neurosurgery Unit of SW, 1945-48; Family Planning Clinics, Southend and Basildon New Town, 1951-61; Divl Surg., SJAB, Droitwich, 1961-63; Jun. Dr, then Registrar, Powick Hosp., Worcs, 1961-64; Locum Registrar, Horton Hosp., 1964; Locum Consultant, Runwell Hosp., Wickford, 1965; SMO, HM Borstal, Feltham, 1965- (seniority merit award, 1973); Consultant to Windsor Probation Hostel, 1975-82; Cropwood Fellow, Inst. of Criminology, Cambridge, 1974. Editor, Prison Med. Jl, 1970-76, 1978-82. Mem. Exec., Assoc. of Psychiatric Study of Adolescents, 1973-, Chm., 1978-81; Organiser, APSA Conf., Adolescent and the Law, 1977; Mem., NACRO working party, Children in Prison, 1976-77. *Publications:* articles in New Society, New Behaviour, Prison Med. Jl. *Recreations:* propagating plants and ideas, working with problems of triangular relationships, them, us and those, the management of crisis, watching birds when there is time from watching human behaviour. *Address:* HM Borstal, Bedfont Road, Feltham, Mddx TW13 4ND. *T:* 01-890 0061.

See also Baron Taylor of Harlow.

ELLIS, Maxwell (Philip), MD, MS, FRCS; Dean of the Institute of Laryngology and Otology, University of London, 1965-71; Consulting Surgeon, Royal National Throat, Nose and Ear Hospital; Consulting Ear, Nose and Throat Surgeon, Central Middlesex Hospital; *b* 28 Feb. 1906; *s* of Louis Ellis; *m* 1st, 1935, Barbara Gertrude Chapman (*d* 1977); 2nd, 1979, Mrs Clarice Adler. *Educ:* University Coll., London (Exhibitioner), Fellow 1975; University Coll. Hosp. (Bucknill Exhbnr). Liston and Alexander Bruce Gold Medals, Surgery and Pathology, UCH, 1927-29. MB, BS (London), Hons Medicine, 1930; MD 1931; FRCS 1932; MS 1937; Geoffrey Duveen Trav. Student, Univ. of London, 1934-36; Leslie Pearce Gould Trav. Schol., 1934, Perceval Alleyn Schol. (Surg. research), 1936, UCH; Hunterian Prof., RCS, 1938. RAFVR, 1940-45 (Wing-Comdr). FRSM, also Mem. Council; Past Pres., Section of Otology; Hon. Treasurer and Mem. Council, Med. Soc. London (Hon. Sec. 1961-63; Pres., 1970-71); Hon. Member: Assoc. of Otolaryngologists of India; Salonika Soc. of Otolaryngology; Athens Soc. of Otolaryngology; Corresp. Mem., Société Française d'Oto-Rhino-Laryngologie; Hon. Corresp. Mem., Argentine Soc. of Otolaryngology. Lectr on Diseases of Ear, Nose and Throat, Univ. of London, 1952-. *Publications:* Modern Trends in Diseases of the Ear, Nose and Throat (Ed. and part author), 1954, 2nd edn 1971; Operative Surgery (Rob and Smith), Vol. 8 on Diseases of the Ear, Nose and Throat (Ed. and part author), 1958; 2nd edn 1969; Clinical Surgery (Rob and Smith), Vol. 11, Diseases of the Ear, Nose and Throat (Ed. and part author), 1966; Sections in Diseases of the Ear, Nose and Throat (Ed. Scott-Brown), 1952, new edns 1965, 1971; Sections in Cancer, Vol. 4 (Ed. Raven), 1958; Section in Modern Trends in Surgical Materials (Ed. Gillis), 1958; papers in various medical and scientific jls. *Recreations:* golf, gardening; formerly bridge and squash rackets. *Address:* 48 Townshend Road, NW8. *T:* 01-722 2252. *Clubs:* Royal Automobile; Sunningdale Golf; Royal Mid-Surrey Golf.

ELLIS, Norman David; Under Secretary, British Medical Association, since 1980 (Senior Industrial Relations Officer, 1978-82); *b* 23 Nov. 1943; *s* of late George Edward Ellis and late Annie Elsie Scarfe; *m* 1966, Valerie Ann Fenn; one *s*. *Educ:* Minchenden Sch.; Univ. of Leeds (BA); MA (Oxon), PhD. Research Officer, Dept of Employment, 1969-71; Leverhulme Fellowship in Industrial Relations, Nuffield Coll., Oxford, 1971-74; Gen. Sec., Assoc. of First Division Civil Servants, 1974-78. *Publications:* (with W. E. J. McCarthy) Management by Agreement, 1973; various contribs to industrial relations literature; regular contributor to BMJ. *Recreations:* reading, railways. *Address:* 33 Foxes Dale, SE3 9BH. *T:* 01-852 6244.

ELLIS, Osian Gwynn, CBE 1971; harpist; Professor of Harp, Royal Academy of Music, London, since 1959; *b* Ffynnongroew, Flints, 8 Feb. 1928; *s* of Rev. T. G. Ellis, Methodist Minister; *m* 1951, Rene Ellis Jones, Pwllheli; two *s*. *Educ:* Denbigh Grammar Sch.; Royal Academy of Music. Has broadcast and televised extensively. Has given recitals/concertos all over the world; shared poetry and music recitals with Dame Peggy Ashcroft, Paul Robeson, Burton,

C. Day-Lewis, etc. Mem., Melos Ensemble; solo harpist with LSO. Former Mem., Music and Welsh Adv. Cttees, British Council. Works written for him include Harp Concertos by Hoddinott, 1957 and by Mathias, 1970; Jersild, 1972; Gian Carlo Menotti, 1977; William Schuman, 1978; from 1960 worked with Benjamin Britten who wrote for him Harp Suite in C (Op. 83) and (for perf. with Sir Peter Pears) Canticle V, Birthday Hansel, and folk songs; accompanies Sir Peter Pears on recital tours, Europe and USA, 1974–; records concertos, recitals, folk songs, etc. Film, The Harp, won a Paris award; other awards include Grand Prix du Disque and French Radio Critics' Award. FRAM 1960. Hon. DMus Wales, 1970. *Address:* 90 Chandos Avenue, N20. *T:* 01-445 7896.

ELLIS, Raymond Joseph; MP (Lab) Derbyshire North East, since 1979; *b* 17 Dec. 1923; *s* of Harold and Ellen Ellis; *m* 1946, Cynthia (*née* Lax); four *c. Educ:* elementary school; Sheffield Univ.; Ruskin Coll., Oxford. Coal miner, 1938-79. National Union of Mineworkers: Branch Secretary, Highmoor, 1959-79; Pres., Derbyshire Area, 1972-79. Councillor, South Yorkshire CC, 1976-79. *Address:* 34 Cornwall Drive, Brimington, Chesterfield S43 1EF. *T:* Chesterfield 71613.

ELLIS, (Robert) Thomas; MP Wrexham since 1970 (Lab, 1970-81, SDP, since 1981); *b* 15 March 1924; *s* of Robert and Edith Ann Ellis; *m* 1949, Nona Harcourt Williams; three *s* one *d. Educ:* Universities of Wales and Nottingham. Works Chemist, ICI, 1944-47; Coal Miner, 1947-55; Mining Engineer, 1955-70; Manager, Bersham Colliery, N Wales, 1957-70. Mem., European Parlt, 1975-79. *Publication:* Mines and Men, 1971. *Recreations:* golf, reading, music. *Address:* Whitehurst House, Whitehurst, Chirk, Wrexham. *T:* Chirk 773462.

ELLIS, Ven. Robin Gareth; Archdeacon of Plymouth, since 1982; Vicar of Yelverton, since 1982; *b* 8 Dec. 1929; *s* of Walter and Morva Ellis; *m* 1964, Anne Ellis (*née* Landers); three *s. Educ:* Worksop Coll., Notts; Pembroke Coll., Oxford (BCL, MA). Curate of Swinton, 1960-63; Asst Chaplain, Worksop Coll., 1963-66; Vicar of Swaffham Prior and Reach, and Asst Director of Religious Education, Diocese of Ely, 1966-74; Vicar of S Augustine, Wisbech, 1974-82. *Recreations:* cricket, theatre, prison reform. *Address:* S Paul's Vicarage, Yelverton, Devon. *T:* Yelverton 852362.

ELLIS, Roger Henry, MA; FSA; FRHistS; Secretary, Royal Commission on Historical Manuscripts, 1957-72; *b* 9 June 1910; *e s* of late Francis Henry Ellis, Debdale Hall, Mansfield; *m* 1939, Audrey Honor, *o d* of late H. Arthur Baker, DL; two *d. Educ:* Sedbergh (scholar); King's College, Cambridge (scholar, Augustus Austen Leigh Student). 1st Cl. Class. Tripos, 1933. Asst Keeper, Public Record Office, 1934; Principal Asst Keeper, 1956. Served War of 1939-45: Private, 1939; Major, 5th Fusiliers, 1944; Monuments, Fine Arts and Archives Officer in Italy and Germany, 1944-45. Lectr in Archive Admin, Sch. of Librarianship and Archives, University Coll. London, 1947-57. Mem. London Council, British Inst. in Florence, 1947-55; Hon. Editor, British Records Assoc., and (first) Editor of Archives, 1947-57, Chm. Council, 1967-73, Vice-Pres., 1971–. Vice-Pres., Business Archives Council, 1958–; Member: Adv. Council on Export of Works of Art, 1964-72; Jt Records Cttee of Royal Soc. and Historical MSS Commn, 1968-76; ICA Cttee on Sigillography, 1962-77; Pres., Soc. of Archivists, 1964-73. A Manager, 1973-76, a Vice-Pres., 1975-76, Royal Instn. Corresp. Mem., Indian Historical Records Commn. *Publications:* Catalogue of Seals in the Public Record Office: Personal Seals, vol. I, 1978, vol. II, 1981; Ode on St Crispin's Day, 1979; opuscula and articles in British and foreign jls on care and use of archives and MSS. *Recreations:* poetry, travel, the arts, gardening (unskilled). *Address:* Cloth Hill, 6 The Mount, Hampstead, NW3. *Club:* Athenæum.

ELLIS, Roger Wykeham; Master of Marlborough College, since 1972; *b* 3 Oct. 1929; *s* of Cecil Ellis, solicitor, and Pamela Unwin; *m* 1964, Margaret Jean Stevenson; one *s* two *d. Educ:* St Peter's Sch., Seaford; Winchester Coll.; Trinity Coll., Oxford (Schol., MA). Royal Navy, 1947-49. Asst Master, Harrow Sch., 1952-67, and Housemaster of the Head Master's House, 1961-67; Headmaster of Rossall Sch., 1967-72. Member: Harrow Borough Educn Cttee, 1956-60; Wilts County Educn Cttee, 1975–. *Recreations:* golf, fishing. *Address:* Marlborough College, Wilts.

ELLIS, Sir Ronald, Kt 1978; FEng, FIMechE; FCIT; President and Managing Director, Industrial Division, Allegheny International, since 1982; *b* 12 Aug. 1925; *s* of William Ellis and Besse Brownbill; *m* 1st, 1956, Cherry Hazel Brown (*d* 1978); one *s* one *d*; 2nd, 1979, Myra Ann Royle. *Educ:* Preston Grammar Sch.; Manchester Univ. (BScTech Hons 1949). FIMechE 1949; FCIT 1975; FEng 1981. Gen. Man., BUT Ltd, 1954; Gen. Sales and Service Man., 1962, Gen. Man., 1966, Leyland Motors Ltd; Man. Dir, British Leyland Truck and Bus, 1968; Dir, British Leyland Motor Corp. Ltd, 1970. Head of Defence Sales, MoD, 1976-81. Chm., Bus Manufacturers Hldg Co., 1972-76. Dir of corp. develt, Wilkinson Sword Gp, 1981-82; Director: Yarrow & Co., 1981–; Redman Heenan Internat., 1981–. Vice-Pres., SMMT, 1972-73; Dir, ROFs, 1976-81. Governor, UMIST, 1970–. Hon. Fellow, 1981. FRSA. *Recreations:* fishing, sailing. *Address:* Galloway House, High Street, Old Amersham, Bucks HP7 0ED. *Clubs:* Royal Thames Yacht; Royal Naval Sailing Assoc., Poole Harbour Yacht.

ELLIS, Tom; *see* Ellis, R. T.

ELLIS, Vivian; Lt-Comdr RNVR; composer; author; Deputy President, Performing Right Society, since 1975; *s* of Harry Ellis and Maud Isaacson. *Educ:* Cheltenham Coll. (Musical Exhibition). Commenced his career as concert pianist after studying under Myra Hess; studied composition at the Royal Academy of Music; first song published when fifteen; his first work for the theatre was the composition of additional numbers for The Curate's Egg, 1922; contributed to The Little Revue and The Punch Bowl Revue, 1924; to Yoicks, Still Dancing, and Mercenary Mary, and composer of By the Way, 1925; to Just a Kiss, Kid Boots, Cochran's Revue, My Son John, Merely Molly and composer of Palladium Pleasures, 1926; to Blue Skies, The Girl Friend, and Clowns in Clover, 1927; to Charlot, 1928; and composer of Peg o' Mine, Will o' The Whispers, Vogues and Vanities, 1928; to A Yankee at the Court of King Arthur, The House that Jack Built, and (with Richard Myers) composer of Mister Cinders, 1929; part-composer of Cochran's 1930 Revue, and composer of Follow a Star and Little Tommy Tucker, 1930; part-composer of Stand Up and Sing, and Song of the Drum (with Herman Finck), and composer of Folly to be Wise, and Blue Roses, 1931; part-composer of Out of the Bottle, 1932; composer of Cochran's revue Streamline, 1934; Jill Darling, 1935; music and lyrics of Charlot Revue, The Town Talks, 1936; Hide and Seek, 1937; The Fleet's Lit Up, Running Riot, Under Your Hat, 1938; composer (to Sir A. P. Herbert's libretto) Cochran light operas: Big Ben, 1946; Bless the Bride, 1947; Tough at the Top, 1949; Water Gipsies, 1955; music and lyrics of And So To Bed, 1951; music for The Sleeping Prince, 1953; music and lyrics of Listen to the Wind, 1954; Half in Earnest (musical adaptation of The Importance of Being Earnest), 1958; composer of popular songs; many dance items; Coronation Scot; also music for the films Jack's the Boy, Water Gipsies, 1932; Falling for You, 1933; Public Nuisance No 1, 1935; Piccadilly Incident, 1946, etc. Ivor Novello Award for outstanding services to British music, 1973. *Publications: novels:* Zelma; Faint Harmony; Day Out; Chicanery; *travel:* Ellis in Wonderland; *autobiography:* I'm on a See-Saw; *humour:* How to Make your Fortune on the Stock Exchange; How to Enjoy Your Operation; How to Bury Yourself in the Country; How to be a Man-about-Town; Good-Bye, Dollie; contrib: The Rise and Fall of the Matinée Idol; Top Hat and Tails: biography of Jack Buchanan; The Story and the Song; *for children:* Hilary's Tune; Hilary's Holidays; The Magic Baton; *song book:* Vivian Ellis: a composer's jubilee, 1982. *Recreations:* gardening, painting, operations. *Club:* Garrick.

ELLIS, Wilfred Desmond, OBE 1952; TD; Customer Service and Conversion Manager, Gas Council, 1968-73; Lay Member, Press Council, 1969-76; *b* 7 Nov. 1914; 2nd *s* of late Bertram V. C. W. Ellis and late Winifred Dora Ellis; *m* 1947, Effie Douglas, JP, *d* of late Dr A. Barr, Canonbie, Scotland; one *s* two *d. Educ:* Temple Grove; Canford. Commissioned as 2nd Lt, Middlesex Regt, 1937. Served War of 1939-45 at home and NW Europe with Middlesex Regt (despatches, 1944). Rejoined TA, 1947, retiring as Dep. Comdt 47 (L) Inf. Bde, 1962; County Comdt, Mddx Army Cadet Force, 1958-62; ADC to the Queen, 1966-69. Joined Gas Industry, 1932; Uxbridge, Maidenhead, Wycombe & Dist. Gas Co. until War of 1939-45; returned to Company until nationalisation; served with North Thames Gas Bd in various appts until joining Gas Council Research Station, Watson House, 1963, as Asst, and then Dep. Dir; transf. to Gas Council, 1966, as Manager, Conversion Executive. DL (Greater London), 1964-79. Fellow, Inst. of Marketing. *Recreations:* shooting, local affairs. *Address:* Lea Barn, Winter Hill, Cookham Dean, Berkshire SL6 9TW. *T:* Maidenhead 4230.

ELLIS, Dr (William) Herbert (Baxter), AFC 1954; Industrial Medical Consultant: Plessey Co.; T. M. C.; Wellworthy; Medical Adviser, Department of Health and Social Security; County Surgeon, Gloucestershire, St John Ambulance Brigade, since 1979; Underwriting Member of Lloyd's; *b* 2 July 1921; *er s* of William Baxter Ellis and Georgina Isabella Ellis (*née* Waller); *m* 1st, 1948, Margaret Mary Limb (marr. diss.); one *s* one *d*; 2nd, 1977, Mollie Marguerite Clarke. *Educ:* Oundle Sch.; Durham Univ. (MD, BS). Royal Navy, 1945-59: Surg. Comdr, Fleet Air Arm Pilot. Motor industry, 1960-71; research into human aspects of road traffic accidents, 1960-71; Dir-Gen., Dr Barnardo's, 1971-73; dir of various companies. Part-time Mem., Employment Medical Adv. Service, 1973-81. OStJ 1981. Gilbert Blane Medal, RCP, 1954. *Publications:* Physiological and Psychological Aspects of Deck Landings, 1954; various on the human factor in industrial management. *Recreations:* walking, observing humanity. *Address:* The Manor House, Compton Abdale, near Cheltenham, Glos GL54 4DR. *T:* Withington 247. *Clubs:* Army and Navy, Naval and Military.

ELLIS-REES, Hugh Francis; Regional Director, East and West Midlands Regional Offices, Departments of the Environment and Transport, since 1981; *b* 5 March 1929; *s* of late Sir Hugh Ellis-Rees, KCMG, CB and Lady (Eileen Frances Anne) Ellis-Rees; *m* 1956, Elisabeth de Mestre Gray; three *s* one *d. Educ:* Ampleforth Coll.; Balliol Coll., Oxford. Served Grenadier Guards, 1948-49. Asst Principal, War Office, 1954; Principal 1958; Asst Private Sec. to Sec. of State, 1955-58 and 1961-62; Private Sec. to Minister of Defence (Army), 1965-68; Asst Sec. 1968; DoE, 1970; Cabinet Office, 1972-74; Under Sec., DoE, 1974. *Recreation:* squash. *Address:* The Gabled House, Burford, Oxon.

ELLISON, Prof. Arthur James, DSc(Eng); CEng, FIMechE, FIEE; Professor of Electrical and Electronic Engineering, and Head of Department, The City University, London, since 1972; *b* 15 Jan. 1920; *s* of late Lawrence Joseph and Elsie Beatrice Ellison, Birmingham; *m* 1st, 1952, Marjorie Cresswell (*d* 1955); 2nd, 1963, Marian Elizabeth Gumbrell; one *s* one *d. Educ:* Solihull Sch.,

Warwicks; Birmingham Central Tech. Coll. (now Univ. of Aston); Northampton Polytechnic (now City Univ.), as ext. student of Univ. of London BSc(Eng) (1st Cl. Hons); DSc(Eng). Sen. MIEEE. Design Engr, Higgs Motors, Birmingham, 1938–43; Tech. Asst, RAE, 1943–46; Graduate apprentice with British Thomson-Houston Co., Rugby, 1946, Design Engr, 1947–58; Lectr, Queen Mary Coll. (Univ. of London), 1958–65, Sen. Lectr, 1965–72. Visiting Prof., MIT, USA, 1959; lecture tour of Latin Amer. for Brit. Council, 1968; Hon. Prof., Nat. Univ. of Engrg, Lima, Peru, 1968; numerous overseas lectures and conf. contribs. Ext. Examiner to many UK and overseas univs and polytechnics; Founder and Chm., biennial Internat. Conf. on Elec. Machines, 1974–. Consultant to industrial cos and nationalised industry on elec. machines, noise and vibration problems; Director: Landspeed, 1975–; Landspeed University Consultants, 1975–82; Landspeed International, 1975–. Pres., Soc. for Psychical Research, 1976–79, 1981–; Chm., Theosophical Res. Centre, 1976–. Mem. Council, IEE, 1981–. *Publications:* Electromechanical Energy Conversion, 1965, 2nd edn 1970; Generalized Electric Machines, 1967; Generalized Electric Machine Set Instruction Book (AEI), 1963, 2nd edn 1968; ed, Proc. Queen Mary Coll. Conf., The Teaching of Electric Machinery Theory, 1961; jt ed, Proc. Queen Mary Coll. Conf., Design of Electric Machines by Computer, 1969; contrib. Psychism and the Unconscious Mind, 1968; contrib. Intelligence Came First, 1975; numerous papers in engrg and sci. jls on elec. machines, noise and vibration, future guided land transport (IEE premium, 1964); also papers in Jl Soc. for Psych. Res. *Recreations:* reading, meditation, psychical research, travel. *Address:* 10 Foxgrove Avenue, Beckenham, Kent BR3 2BA. *T:* 01-650 3801; Department of Electrical Engineering, The City University, EC1V 0HB. *T:* 01-253 4399.

ELLISON, Rt. Rev. and Rt. Hon. Gerald Alexander, KCVO 1981; PC 1973; *b* 19 Aug. 1910; *s* of late Preb. John Henry Joshua Ellison, CVO, Chaplain in Ordinary to the King, Rector of St Michael's, Cornhill, and of Sara Dorothy Graham Ellison (*née* Crum); *m* 1947, Jane Elizabeth, *d* of late Brig. John Houghton Gibbon, DSO; one *s* two *d*. *Educ:* St George's, Windsor; Westminster Sch.; New Coll., Oxford (Hon. Fellow, 1974); Westcott House, Cambridge. Curate, Sherborne Abbey, 1935–37; Domestic Chaplain to the Bishop of Winchester, 1937–39; Chaplain RNVR, 1940–43 (despatches); Domestic Chaplain to Archbishop of York, 1943–46; Vicar, St Mark's Portsea, 1946–50; Hon. Chaplain to Archbishop of York, 1946–50; Canon of Portsmouth, 1950; Examining Chaplain to Bishop of Portsmouth, 1949–50; Bishop Suffragan of Willesden, 1950–55; Bishop of Chester, 1955–73; Bishop of London, 1973–81; Dean of the Chapels Royal, 1973–81; Prelate, Order of the British Empire, 1973–81; Prelate, Imperial Soc. of Knights Bachelor, 1973–; Episcopal Canon of Jerusalem, 1973–81. Select Preacher: Oxford Univ., 1940, 1961, 1972; Cambridge Univ., 1957. Chaplain, Master Mariners' Company, 1946–73; Chaplain, Glass Sellers' Company, 1951–73; Chaplain and Sub-Prelate, Order of St John, 1973–. Hon. Chaplain, RNR. Mem. Wolfenden Cttee on Sport, 1960; Chairman: Bd of Governors, Westfield Coll., Univ. of London, 1953–67; Council of King's Coll., London, 1973–80 (FKC 1968; Vice-Chm. newly constituted Council, 1980–); Governor, Sherborne Sch., 1982–. Chm., Archbishop's Commn on Women and Holy Orders, 1963–66; Mem., Archbishop's Commn on Church and State, 1967; President: Actors' Church Union, 1973–81; Pedestrians Assoc. for Road Safety, 1964–75; Nat. Fedn of Housing Assocs, 1981–. Hon. Bencher Middle Temple, 1976. Freeman, Drapers' Co.; Hon. Liveryman: Merchant Taylors' Co.; Glass Sellers' Co.; Painter Stainers' Co.; Mem., Master Mariners' Co. Chm., Oxford Soc. A Steward of Henley Regatta. *Publications:* The Churchman's Duty, 1957; The Anglican Communion, 1960. *Recreations:* oarsmanship, walking. *Address:* Billeys House, 16 Long Street, Cerne Abbas, Dorset. *T:* Cerne Abbas 247. *Clubs:* Army and Navy, Grillions; Leander.

ELLISON, John Harold, VRD 1948; **His Honour Judge Ellison;** a Circuit Judge, since 1972; Chancellor of the Dioceses of Salisbury and Norwich, since 1955; *b* 20 March 1916; *s* of late Harold Thomas Ellison, MIMechE, and late Mrs Frances Amy Swithinbank, both of Woodspeen Grange, Newbury; *m* 1952, Margaret Dorothy Maud, *d* of Maynard D. McFarlane, Pasadena, Calif; three *s* one *d*. *Educ:* Uppingham Sch.; King's Coll., Cambridge (MA). Res. Physicist, then Engr, Thos Firth & John Brown Ltd, Sheffield; Lieut, RE, TA (49th WR) Div., 1937–39; Officer in RNVR, 1939–51 (retd as Lt-Comdr): Gunnery Specialist, HMS Excellent, 1940; Sqdn Gunnery Officer, 8 Cruiser Sqdn, 1940–42; Naval Staff, Admty, 1942–44; Staff Officer (Ops) to Flag Officer, Western Mediterranean, 1944–45. Called to Bar, Lincoln's Inn, 1948; practised at Common Law Bar, 1948–71. Pres., SW London Br., Magistrates' Assoc. Governor, Forres Sch. Trust, Swanage. FRAS. *Publications:* (ed) titles Allotments and Smallholdings, and Courts, in Halsbury's Law of England, 3rd edn, and Allotments and Smallholdings, 4th edn. *Recreations:* organs and music, sailing, ski-ing, shooting. *Address:* Goose Green House, Egham, Surrey TW20 8PE. *Club:* Bar Yacht.

ELLISON, Sir Ralph Henry C.; *see* Carr-Ellison, Sir R. H.

ELLISON, Randall Erskine, CMG 1960; ED 1946; *b* 6 March 1904; 2nd *s* of late Rev. Preb. J. H. J. Ellison, CVO, Rector of St Michael's, Cornhill, EC, and Mrs Ellison; unmarried. *Educ:* Repton Sch.; New Coll., Oxford (MA). Superintendent of Education, Northern Provinces, Nigeria, 1928; seconded to British Somaliland as Dir of Education, 1938–43; Military Service with British Somaliland and Nigerian Forces, 1940–43; Asst Dir of Education, Tanganyika, 1945; Deputy Dir, 1946; Deputy Dir of Education, Northern Region, Nigeria, 1955; Dir of Education, 1956; Adviser on Education, 1957. Chm., Public Service Commission, Northern Region, Nigeria, 1958, retired 1961. Asst Sec., Church Assembly, Dean's Yard, SW1, 1962–63. Chm., Africa Cttee of CMS, 1969–73; Mem. Council, Westfield Coll., London Univ., 1964–78 (Chm., 1967–68; Hon. Treasurer, 1969–76; Hon. Fellow, 1978). Hon. Steward, Westminster Abbey, 1964. *Publication:* An English-Kanuri Sentence Book, 1937. *Recreations:* choral singing, chamber music. *Address:* 32 Oppidans Road, Hampstead, NW3 3AG. *Clubs:* United Oxford & Cambridge University, Royal Commonwealth Society.

ELLMAN-BROWN, Hon. Geoffrey, CMG 1959; OBE 1945; FCA 1950 (ACA 1934); *b* 20 Dec. 1910; *s* of John and Violet Ellman-Brown; *m* 1936, Hilda Rosamond Fairbrother; two *s* one *d*. *Educ:* Plumtree Sch., S Rhodesia. Articled to firm of Chartered Accountants in London, 1929–34; final Chartered Accountant exam. and admitted as Mem. Inst. of Chartered Accountants of England and Wales, 1934. In Rhodesia Air Force (rising to rank of Group Capt.), 1939–46. Resumed practice as Chartered Accountant, 1946–53. Entered S Rhodesia Parliament holding ministerial office (Portfolios of Roads, Irrigation, Local Government and Housing), 1953–58; re-entered Parliament, 1962, Minister of Finance; re-elected, 1962–65, in Opposition Party. Pres. Rhodesia Cricket Union, 1950–52; Mem. S African Cricket Board of Control, 1951–52. Chairman: Rothmans of Pall Mall (Zimbabwe) Ltd; The Zimbabwe Sugar Assoc.; Sugar Sales (Private) Ltd; Discount Co. of Zimbabwe Ltd; Industrial Promotion Corp. Central Africa Ltd; C. T. Bowring and Associates (Pvt) Ltd; Bowmakers (CA) (Pvt) Ltd; Barclays Bank in Zimbabwe; Director: RAL Merchant Bank Ltd; Hippo Valley Estates Ltd; Colonial Mutual Life Assurance Soc. Ltd; Freight Services Ltd. *Recreations:* cricket, golf, shooting, fishing. *Address:* PO Box 8426, Harare, Zimbabwe. *T:* 706381. *Clubs:* Salisbury, Royal Salisbury Golf (Harare, Zimbabwe); Ruwa Country.

ELLMANN, Richard, MA Oxon; PhD Yale; FBA 1979; Goldsmiths' Professor of English Literature, Oxford University, since 1970; *b* Highland Park, Michigan, 15 March 1918; *s* of James Isaac Ellmann and Jeanette (*née* Barsook); *m* 1949, Mary Donahue; one *s* two *d*. *Educ:* Highland Park High Sch.; Yale Univ. (MA, PhD); Trinity Coll., Dublin (LittB). Served War of 1939–45, Office of Strategic Services, USNR, 1943–46. Instructor at Harvard, 1942–43, 1947–48; Briggs-Copeland Asst Prof. of Eng. Composition, Harvard, 1948–51; Prof. of English, Northwestern Univ., 1951, Franklin Bliss Snyder Prof., 1963–68; Prof. of English, Yale, 1968–70. Rockefeller Fellow, 1946–47; Guggenheim Fellow, 1950, 1957, 1970; Kenyon Review Fellow Criticism, 1955–56; Fellow, Sch. of Letters, Indiana Univ., 1956, 1960; Senior Fellow, 1966–72; Frederick Ives Carpenter Vis. Prof., Univ. of Chicago, 1959, 1968, 1975, 1976, 1977; Grantee, Nat. Endowment for the Humanities, 1977–78. Mem., US-UK Educnl Commn, 1970–. Mem. Editorial Committee: Publications of the Modern Language Assoc., 1968–73; American Scholar, 1968–74. FRSL; Fellow, Amer. Acad. and Inst. National Book Award, 1960. Hon. DLitt: NUI, 1976; Boston Coll., 1979; Emory Univ., 1979; Northwestern, 1980; Hon. PhD Gothenburg, 1978; Hon. DHL Rochester, 1981. *Publications:* Yeats: The Man and the Masks, 1948; The Identity of Yeats, 1954; James Joyce: a biography, 1959, revd edn 1982; Eminent Domain, 1967; Ulysses on the Liffey, 1972; Golden Codgers, 1973; The Consciousness of Joyce, 1977; Edited: Selected Writings of Henri Michaux (trans.), 1951; My Brother's Keeper, by Stanislaus Joyce, 1958; (with others) Masters of British Literature, 1958; Arthur Symons: The Symbolist Movement in Literature, 1958; (with Ellsworth Mason) The Critical Writings of James Joyce, 1959; Edwardians and late Victorians, 1959; (with Charles Feidelson, Jr) The Modern Tradition, 1965; Letters of James Joyce (Vols II and III), 1966; James Joyce: Giacomo Joyce, 1968; The Artist as Critic: Oscar Wilde, 1970; Oscar Wilde: twentieth century views, 1970; (with Robert O'Clair) Norton Anthology of Modern Poetry, 1973; Selected Letters of James Joyce, 1975; New Oxford Book of American Verse, 1976; (with Robert O'Clair) Modern Poems, 1976; Selected Writings of Oscar Wilde, 1982. *Address:* New College, Oxford. *Clubs:* The Signet (Harvard); Elizabethan (Yale).

ELLSWORTH, Robert; President, Robert Ellsworth & Co. Inc., since 1977; Deputy Secretary of Defense, 1976–77; *b* 11 June 1926; *s* of Willoughby Fred Ellsworth and Lucille Rarig Ellsworth; *m* 1956, Vivian Esther Sies; one *s* one *d*. *Educ:* Univs of Kansas (BSME) and Michigan (JD). Active service, US Navy, 1944–46, 1950–53 (Lt-Comdr). Mem. United States Congress, 1961–67; Asst to President of US, 1969; Ambassador and Permanent Representative of US on N Atlantic Council, 1969–71; Asst Sec. of Defense (Internat. Security Affairs), 1974–75. Mem. Council, IISS, 1973- (Vice-Chm.). Licensed Lay Reader, Episcopal Dio. of Washington. Hon. LLD: Ottawa, 1969; Boston, 1970. *Recreations:* tennis, ski-ing, swimming. *Address:* 24020 Old Hundred Road, Dickerson, Md 20842, USA. *Clubs:* Brook (New York); Cosmos, Army and Navy (Washington).

ELLWOOD, Air Marshal Sir Aubrey (Beauclerk), KCB 1949 (CB 1944); DSC; DL; *b* 3 July 1897; *s* of late Rev. C. E. Ellwood, Rector of Cottesmore, Rutland, 1888–1926; *m* 1920, Lesley Mary Joan Matthews (*d* 1982); one *s* one *d* (and one *s* decd). *Educ:* Cheam Sch.; Marlborough Coll. Joined Royal Naval Air Service, 1916; permanent commission RAF 1919. Served India 1919–23 and 1931–36 in RAF; RAF Staff Coll., Air Min., Army Co-operation Comd variously, 1938–42; AOC No. 18 Group RAF, 1943–44; Temp. Air Vice-Marshal, 1943; SASO HQ Coastal Comd RAF, 1944–45; Actg Air Marshal, 1947; a Dir-Gen. of Personnel, Air Ministry, 1945–47. Air Marshal, 1949; AOC-in-C, Bomber Command, 1947–50; AOC-in-C, Transport Command, 1950–52; retired, 1952. Governor and Commandant, The Church Lads' Brigade, 1954–70. DL Somerset, 1960. *Recreations:* riding, fishing, music.

Address: The Old House, North Perrott, Crewkerne, Somerset.
See also M. O. D. Ellwood.

ELLWOOD, Captain Michael Oliver Dundas, DSO 1940; *b* 13 July 1894; *s* of late Rev. C. E. Ellwood, Cottesmore, Rutland. *Educ:* Cheam Sch., Surrey; RN Colls, Osborne and Dartmouth. Entered Royal Navy, 1907; retired as Comdr, 1934; rejoined as Capt. on retired list, 1939; reverted to retired list, Sept. 1946. *Club:* Army and Navy.
See also Sir Aubrey Ellwood.

ELMES, Dr Peter Cardwell; Director, Medical Research Council Pneumoconiosis Unit, Llandough Hospital, Penarth, 1976–81, retired 1982; *b* 12 Oct. 1921; *s* of Florence Romaine Elmes and Lilian Bryham (*née* Cardwell); *m* 1957, Margaret Elizabeth (*née* Staley); two *s* one *d*. *Educ:* Rugby; Oxford Univ. (BM, BCh 1945); Western Reserve Univ., Cleveland, Ohio (MD 1943). MRCP 1951. Mil. Service, RAMC, 1946–48. Trng posts, Taunton and Oxford, 1948–50; Registrar, then Sen. Registrar in Medicine, Hammersmith Hosp., 1950–58; Dept of Therapeutics, Queen's Univ., Belfast: Sen. Lectr, 1959–63; Reader, 1963–67; Prof. of Therapeutic Sciences, 1967–71; Whitla Prof. of Therapeutics and Pharmacology, 1971–76. Mem., Medicines Commn, 1976–79. *Publications:* contrib. med. jls on chronic chest disease, treatment and control of infection, occupational lung disease asbestosis, and mesothelioma. *Recreation:* working on house and garden. *Address:* Dawros House, St Andrews Road, Dinas Powys, South Glamorgan CF6 4HB. *T:* Dinas Powys 512102.

ELMHIRST, Air Marshal Sir Thomas (Walker), KBE 1946 (CBE 1943); CB 1945; AFC 1918; RAF retired; Lieutenant-Governor and Commander-in-Chief of Guernsey, 1953–Oct. 1958; *b* 15 Dec. 1895; 4th *s* of late Rev. W. H. Elmhirst, Elmhirst, near Barnsley, Yorks; *m* 1st, 1930, Katharine Gordon (*d* 1965), 4th *d* of William Black, Chapel, Fife; one *s* one *d*; 2nd, 1968, Marian Louisa, *widow* of Col Andrew Ferguson and *d* of late Lt-Col Lord Herbert Montagu-Douglas-Scott. *Educ:* RN Colls, Osborne and Dartmouth. RN, 1908–15, Dardanelles and Dogger Bank in HMS Indomitable; RN Air Service, 1915–18; RAF as Major, Comdg Naval Airship Patrol Station, Anglesey, 1918 (AFC); RAF Staff Coll., 1925; commanded No. 15 Bomber Squadron and Abingdon Wing, 1935–37; 1st British Air Attaché to HM Embassy, Ankara, 1937–39; Dep. Dir Intelligence Air Ministry and Air Cdre HQ Fighter Comd, 1940 (Battle of Britain); RAF mem. of British Mission for Staff conversations with Turkish Gen. Staff, Ankara, 1941; AOC RAF Egypt, 1941 (despatches twice); 2nd in Comd Desert Air Force (Alamein campaigns), 1942 (CBE); Air Officer i/c Administration NW Africa, TAF, 1943 (despatches, CB, Tunis and Sicily campaigns); 2nd in Comd British Air Forces in NW Europe, Normandy-Germany campaign (KBE, despatches), 1944–45; Asst Chief of Air Staff (Intelligence), 1945–47; Chief of Inter-Service Administration in India, 1947; first C-in-C Indian Air Force, 1947–50; retd, 1950. Hon. Air Marshal in the Indian Air Force, 1950. Fife County Councillor, 1950; Civil Defence Controller Eastern Zone, Scotland, 1952–53. DL, County of Fife, 1960–70. Comdr, US Legion of Merit; Grand Officer, Crown of Belgium and Croix de Guerre; Comdr, Legion of Honour and French Croix de Guerre. KStJ 1954. *Recreations:* grandchildren and fishing. *Address:* The Cottage, Dummer, Basingstoke, Hants. *Club:* Royal Air Force.

ELMSLIE, Maj.-Gen. Alexander Frederic Joseph, CB 1959; CBE 1955; psc; *b* 31 Oct. 1905. Commissioned in Royal Army Service Corps, 29 Jan. 1925, and subsequently served in Shanghai, Ceylon, E. Africa and Singapore; Lieutenant 1927; Captain 1935; served War of 1939–45 (despatches); Major, 1942; Lt-Col 1948; Temp. Brig. 1944; Brig. 1953; Maj.-Gen. 1958. Dep. Dir of Supplies and Transport, War Office, 1953–55; Dir of Supplies and Transport, GHQ Far East Land Forces, 1956–57; Inspector, RASC, War Office, 1957–60, retired. Chairman Traffic Commissioners: NW Traffic Area, 1962–64; SE Traffic Area, 1965–75. Hon. Col 43 (Wessex) Inf. Div. Coln, RASC, TA, 1960–64; Col Comdt, RASC, 1964–65; Col Comdt, Royal Corps of Transport, 1965–69. CEng; FIMechE; FCIT; Fellow, Royal Commonwealth Soc. *Address:* c/o Barclays Bank Ltd, Station Parade, Eastbourne, Sussex.

ELPHIN, Bishop of, (RC), since 1971; **Most Rev. Dominic Joseph Conway;** *b* 1 Jan. 1918; *s* of Dominic Conway and Mary Hoare. *Educ:* Coll. of the Immaculate Conception, Sligo; Pontifical Irish Coll., Pontifical Lateran Univ., Pontifical Angelicum Univ., Gregorian Univ. (all in Rome); National Univ. of Ireland. BPh, STL, DEcclHist, Higher Diploma Educn. Missionary, Calabar Dio., Nigeria, 1943–48; Professor: All Hallows Coll., Dublin, 1948–49; Summerhill Coll., Sligo, 1949–51; Spiritual Dir, 1951–65, Rector, 1965–68, Irish Coll., Rome; Sec.-Gen., Superior Council of the Propagation of the Faith, Rome, 1968–70; Auxiliary Bishop of Elphin, 1970–71. *Address:* St Mary's, Sligo, Ireland. *T:* 2670.

ELPHINSTONE, family name of **Lord Elphinstone.**

ELPHINSTONE, 18th Lord *cr* 1509; **James Alexander Elphinstone;** Baron (UK) 1885; *b* 22 April 1953; *s* of Rev. Hon. Andrew Charles Victor Elphinstone (*d* 1975) (2nd *s* of 16th Lord) and of Hon. Mrs Andrew Elphinstone (*née* Jean Mary Woodroffe); *S* uncle, 1975; *m* 1978, Willa, 4th *d* of Major David Chetwode, Upper Slaughter, Cheltenham; two *s*. *Educ:* Eton Coll.; Royal Agricultural Coll., Cirencester ARICS 1979. *Heir: s* Master of Elphinstone, *qv*. *Address:* Drumkilbo, Meigle, Blairgowrie, Perthshire. *T:* Meigle 216. *Clubs:* Turf, White's.

ELPHINSTONE, Master of; Hon. Alexander Mountstuart Elphinstone; *b* 15 April 1980; *s* and *heir* of 18th Lord Elphinstone, *qv*.

ELPHINSTONE, Sir Douglas; *see* Elphinstone, Sir M. D. W.

ELPHINSTONE of Glack, Sir John, 11th Bt *cr* 1701, of Logie Elphinstone and Nova Scotia; Land Agent with Imperial Chemical Industries Ltd, since 1956; *b* 12 Aug. 1924; *s* of Thomas George Elphinston (*d* 1967), and of Gladys Mary Elphinston, *d* of late Ernest Charles Lambert Congdon; *S* uncle, 1970; *m* 1953, Margaret Doreen, *d* of Edric Tasker; four *s*. *Educ:* Eagle House, Sandhurst, Berks; Repton; Emmanuel College, Cambridge (BA). Lieut, Royal Marines, 1942–48. Chartered Surveyor. Past Pres., Cheshire Agricultural Valuers' Assoc.; Past Chm., Land Agency and Agric. Div., Lancs, Cheshire and IoM Branch, RICS; Mem., Lancs River Authority, 1970–74. *Recreations:* shooting, ornithology, cricket. *Heir: s* Alexander Elphinston, *b* 6 June 1955. *Address:* Pilgrims, Churchfields, Sandiway, Northwich, Cheshire. *T:* Sandiway 883327.

ELPHINSTONE, Sir (Maurice) Douglas (Warburton), 5th Bt *cr* 1816; TD 1946; retired, 1973; *b* 13 April 1909; *s* of Rev. Canon Maurice Curteis Elphinstone (4th *s* of 3rd Bt) (*d* 1969), and Christiana Georgiana (*née* Almond); *S* cousin, 1975; *m* 1943, Helen Barbara, *d* of late George Ramsay Main; one *s* one *d*. *Educ:* Loretto School, Musselburgh; Jesus Coll., Cambridge (MA). FFA; FRSE. Actuary engaged in Life Assurance companies until 1956 (with the exception of the war); Member of Stock Exchange, London, 1957–74. War service with London Scottish and Sierra Leone Regt, RWAFF, mainly in W Africa and India. *Publications:* technical papers mainly in Trans Faculty of Actuaries and Jl Inst. of Actuaries. *Recreation:* gardening. *Heir: s* John Howard Main Elphinstone, *b* 25 Feb. 1949. *Address:* Wetheral Crook, Scotby, Carlisle CA4 8EE. *T:* Scotby 280.

ELRINGTON, Christopher Robin, FSA, FRHistS; Editor, Victoria History of the Counties of England, since 1977; *b* 20 Jan. 1930; *s* of Brig. Maxwell Elrington, DSO, OBE, and Beryl Joan (*née* Ommaney); *m* 1951, Jean Margaret (*née* Buchanan), RIBA; one *s* one *d*. *Educ:* Wellington Coll., Berks; University Coll., Oxford (MA); Bedford Coll., London (MA). FSA 1964; FRHistS 1969. Asst to Editor, Victoria County History, 1954; Editor for Glos, 1960; Dep. Editor, 1968. British Acad. Overseas Vis. Fellow, Folger Shakespeare Library, Washington DC, 1976. Mem., Adv. Bd for Redundant Churches, 1982–. Hon. Gen. Editor, Wilts Record Soc., 1962–72. *Publications:* Divers Letters of Roger de Martival, Bishop of Salisbury, 2 vols, 1963, 1972; Wiltshire Feet of Fines, Edward III, 1974; articles in Victoria County History and in learned jls. *Address:* 34 Lloyd Baker Street, WC1X 9AB. *T:* 01-837 4971.

EL SAWI, Amir; Ambassador of the Democratic Republic of the Sudan to the Court of St James's, 1976–82; *b* 1921; *m* 1946, El Sura Mohamed Bella; three *s* six *d*. *Educ:* University Coll., Khartoum; Univ. of Bristol. Min. of Interior, 1944–49; Admin. Officer, Merowi Dist, Northern Province, 1950–51; Asst Dist Comr, Kosti Dist, Blue Nile Prov., 1951–53; Asst Sudan Agent, Cairo, 1953–55; Dist Comr, Gadaraf Dist, Kassala Prov., 1955–56; Asst Permanent Sec., Min. of Foreign Affairs, 1956–58, Min. of Interior, 1958–59; Dep. Governor, Northern Prov., 1959–60; Dep. Perm. Sec., Min. of Interior, 1960–64, Perm. Sec., 1964–70; Perm. Sec., Min. of Civil Service and Admin. Reform, 1971–73; Dep. Minister and Doyen of Sudan Civil Service, 1973–76. *Recreations:* swimming, tennis. *Address:* c/o Ministry of Foreign Affairs, Khartoum, Sudan.

ELSDEN, Sidney Reuben, BA, PhD (Cambridge); Professor of Biology, University of East Anglia, since 1965; *b* 13 April 1915; *s* of late Reuben Charles Elsden, Cambridge; *m* 1st, 1942, Frances Scott Wilson (*d* 1943); 2nd, 1948, Erica Barbara Scott, *er d* of late Grahame Scott Gardiner, Wisbech, Cambs; twin *s*. *Educ:* Cambridge and County High Sch. for Boys; Fitzwilliam House, Cambridge. Lecturer, Biochemistry, University of Edinburgh, 1937–42; Mem. Scientific Staff of ARC Unit for Animal Physiology, 1943–48; Sen. Lectr in Microbiology, 1948–59, West Riding Prof. of Microbiology, 1959–65, Sheffield Univ.; Hon. Dir, ARC Unit for Microbiology, Univ. of Sheffield, 1952–65; Dir, ARC Food Research Inst., 1965–77. Visiting Prof. of Microbiology, Univ. of Illinois, Urbana, Ill, USA, 1956. Pres., Soc. for General Microbiology, 1969–72, Hon. Mem. 1977. *Publications:* contribs to scientific jls on metabolism of micro-organisms. *Recreations:* gardening, angling. *Address:* 26a The Street, Costessey, Norwich NR8 5DB.

ELSE, John, MBE 1946; TD 1946; Regional Chairman of Industrial Tribunals, Eastern Region, Bury St Edmunds, since 1980; *b* 9 Aug. 1911; *s* of late Mr and Mrs A. G. Else; *m* 1937, Eileen Dobson; one *d*. *Educ:* Cowley Sch., St Helens; Liverpool Univ. (LLB 1930). Admitted as solicitor, 1932. Commnd TA, 1932; served War: UK and BEF, 1939–41 (despatches, 1940); Iraq, 1942; India, 1942–45 (ADS GHQ, 1944–45). Practised in St Helens, London and Birmingham, 1932–39; Partner, Beale & Co., London and Birmingham, 1946–61; Mem., Mental Health Review Tribunal, 1960–61; Chm., Traffic Comrs and Licensing Authority for Goods Vehicles, W Midlands Traffic Area, 1961–72; Indust. Tribunals Chm., Birmingham, 1972–76, Cambridge, 1976–80. *Recreations:* photography, gardening. *Address:* The Cottage, Long Lane, Fowlmere, Royston, Herts SG8 7TA. *T:* Fowlmere 367.

ELSMORE, Geoffrey William; Chief Inspector, HM Inspectorate of Schools, since 1981; *b* 29 Oct. 1925; *s* of George Frederick Elsmore and Edith Elsmore;

m 1953, Diana Gwynneth Allen; three *s* three *d. Educ:* City of Worcester Coll. of Educn (qualified teacher). Served RAF, 1943–47. Schoolmaster, Kidlington Jun. Sch., 1950–56; Headmaster, West Kidlington Primary Sch., 1956–63 (also occasional Tutor and Lectr, Oxford Univ. Dept and Inst. of Educn); HM Inspector of Schs, NW Div., 1963–73; HM Staff Inspector, Primary Educn, 1973–81. *Recreations:* sailing, painting, music. *Address:* Department of Education and Science, Elizabeth House, York Road, SE1 7PH. *T:* 01-928 9222.

ELSMORE, Sir Lloyd, Kt 1982; OBE 1977; JP; Mayor of Manukau City, since 1968; *b* 16 Jan. 1913; *s* of George and Minnie Elsmore; *m* 1935, Marie Kirk; two *s* two *d. Educ:* Greymouth High Sch. Commenced grocery business on own account, 1933; President: Grocers' Assoc., 1949, 1950, 1952, Life Member, 1954; NZ Grocers' Federation, 1955, Life Member, 1959. Local Body involvement, 1953–; Mayor of Ellerslie Borough Council, 1956–62. *Recreations:* boating, fishing, gardening. *Address:* 18 Sanctuary Point, Pakuranga, New Zealand. *T:* 567-025. *Club:* Rotary (Pakuranga).

ELSOM, Cecil Harry, CBE 1976; Senior Partner, Elsom Pack & Roberts, Architects, since 1947; *b* 17 Jan. 1912; *s* of Julius Israelson and Leah Lazarus; name changed by deed poll to Elsom, 1930; *m* 1940, Gwyneth Mary Buxton Hopkin; two *s. Educ:* Upton Cross Elem. Sch.; West Ham Polytechnic; Northern Polytechnic Architectural School. FRIBA. Started practice by winning competition for town hall, Welwyn Garden City, 1933; partner in Lyons Israel & Elsom, 1936; won two more competitions, Town Hall, Consett, Co. Durham and Health Clinic in Bilston, Staffs. Served with Ordnance Corps, RE, 1940–46, ending war as Captain. Began new practice, 1947. Works include housing, schools and old people's homes for GLC, Lambeth BC and Westminster CC; office buildings and flats for Church Commissioners, Crown Estate Commissioners, BSC, LWT (Eternit Prize for offices, Victoria St, 1977); stores in Wolverhampton, Guildford and London for Army & Navy Stores; town centres in Slough, Chesterfield, Derby and Tamworth (three Civic Trust Awards, four Commendations). Adviser to DoE on Lyceum Club, Liverpool; Assessor for Civic Trust Awards, 1980. Pres., Nightingale House Old People's Home, 1973–. Liveryman, Worshipful Co. of Painter-Stainers, 1965, of Clockmakers, 1979. FSA 1979; FFOB 1969. *Recreations:* horology, model yacht racing. *Address:* 21 Douglas Street, SW1P 4PE. *T:* 01-834 4411. *Clubs:* Arts, Royal Automobile.

ELSTOB, Peter (Frederick Egerton); Vice-President: International PEN, since 1981 (Secretary-General, 1974–81); English PEN, since 1978; Managing Director: Archive Press Ltd, since 1964 (co-founder 1963); Yeast-Pac Co. Ltd, since 1970 (co-founder and Director, 1938–70); writer and entrepreneur; *b* London, 22 Dec. 1915; *e s* of Frederick Charles Elstob, chartered accountant, RFC, and Lillian Page, London; *m* 1st, 1937, Medora Leigh-Smith (marr. diss. 1953); three *s* one *d* (and one *d* decd); 2nd, 1953, Barbara Zacheisz; one *s* one *d. Educ:* private schs, London, Paris, Calcutta; state schs, NY and NJ; Univ. of Michigan. Reporter, salesman, tourist guide, 1931–36; volunteer, Spanish Civil War, 1936 (imprisoned and expelled); RTR, 1940–46 (despatches); with A. B. Eiloart: bought Arts Theatre Club, London, 1941; founded Peter Arnold Studios (artists' and writers' colony, Mexico), 1951–52, and Archives Designs Ltd, 1954–62; Director: MEEC Prodns (Theatre), 1946–54; Peter Arnold Properties, 1947–61; City & Suffolk Property Ltd, 1962–70; ABC Expedns, 1957–61; Manager, Small World Trans-Atlantic Balloon Crossing, 1958–59. Chm., Dorking Divl Lab. Party, 1949–50. *Publications:* (autobiog.) Spanish Prisoner, 1939; (with A. B. Eiloart) The Flight of the Small World, 1959; novels: Warriors for the Working Day, 1960; The Armed Rehearsal, 1964; military history: Bastogne the Road Block, 1968; The Battle of the Reichswald, 1970; Hitler's Last Offensive, 1971; Condor Legion, 1973; (ed) The Survival of Literature, 1979; (ed series) PEN International Books; PEN Broadsheet, 1977–82. *Recreations:* playing the Stock Exchange unsuccessfully, travelling. *Address:* 22 Belsize Park Gardens, NW3 4LH. *T:* 01-722 6263; Coolderry, Massey's Lane, East Boldre, Hants. *T:* Beaulieu 612428. *Clubs:* Savage, Garrick, PEN, Society of Authors; Authors Guild (New York).

ELSTON, Christopher David; Counsellor (Financial), British Embassy, Tokyo, since 1979; *b* 1 Aug. 1938; *s* of Herbert Cecil Elston and Ada Louisa (*née* Paige); *m* 1964, Jennifer Isabel, *e d* of Dr and Mrs A. E. Rampling, Hale, Cheshire; one *s* two *d. Educ:* University Coll. Sch., Hampstead; King's Coll., Cambridge (BA Classics, 1960, MA 1980); Yale Univ. (MA Econs, 1967). Bank of England, 1960–; seconded to Bank for Internat. Settlements, Basle, Switzerland, 1969–71; Private Sec. to Governor of Bank of England, 1974–76; Asst to Chief Cashier, 1976–79; seconded to HM Diplomatic Service, 1979–. *Recreations:* serious music, photography, walking, cricket, squash. *Address:* c/o British Embassy, 1 Ichiban-cho, Chiyoda-ku, Tokyo, Japan. *T:* (03) 265-5511.

ELSTUB, Sir St John (de Holt), Kt 1970; CBE 1954; BSc, FEng, FIMechE, FInstP; Deputy Chairman, Tube Investments Ltd, since 1979; Director: Rolls-Royce Ltd, since 1971; British Engine Insurance Ltd; Hill Samuel Group Ltd; *b* 16 June 1915; *s* of Ernest Elstub and Mary Gertrude (*née* Whitaker); *m* 1939, Patricia Arnold; two *d. Educ:* Rugby Sch.; Manchester Univ. Joined ICI, Billingham, 1936. Served War of 1939–45 as RAF Bomber Pilot; Supt, Rocket Propulsion Dept, Ministry of Supply, 1945. Joined ICI Metals Div., 1947, Prod. Dir, 1950, Man. Dir, 1957, Chm., 1961; Man. Dir, 1962–74, Chm., 1972–74, Imperial Metal Industries Ltd; Director: Royal Insurance Co., 1970–76; The London & Lancashire Insurance Co., 1970–76; The Liverpool, London & Globe Insurance Co., 1970–76; Averys Ltd,

1974–79; Regional Dir, W Midlands and Wales, Nat. Westminster Bank Ltd, 1974–79. Past Pres., British Non-Ferrous Metals Federation. Chm., Jt Government/Industry Cttee on Aircraft Industry, 1967–69; Member: Plowden Cttee on Aircraft Industry, 1964–65; Engrg Industry Trng Bd, 1964–72; Midlands Electricity Bd, 1966–75; Review Bd for Govt contracts, 1969–75; Pres., IMechE, 1974–75. A Guardian, Birmingham Assay Office; Governor, Administrative Staff Coll., Henley, 1962–74; Mem. Council, Univ. of Aston in Birmingham, 1966–72 (Vice-Chm. 1968–72); Life Governor, Univ. of Birmingham. Hon. DSc Univ. of Aston in Birmingham, 1971. *Recreations:* landscape gardening, travel, motor sport. *Address:* Perry House, Hartlebury, Worcs DY10 4HY. *T:* Hartlebury 250327. *Club:* Army and Navy.

ELTON, family name of **Baron Elton.**

ELTON, 2nd Baron *cr* 1934, of Headington; **Rodney Elton,** TD 1970; Parliamentary Under Secretary of State, Home Office, since 1982; *b* 2 March 1930; *s* of 1st Baron Elton and of Dedi (*d* 1977), *d* of Gustav Hartmann, Oslo; *S* father, 1973; *m* 1958, Anne Frances (divorced, 1979), *e d* of late Brig. R. A. G. Tilney, CBE, DSO, TD; one *s* three *d; m* 1979, S. Richenda Gurney, *y d* of late Sir Hugh Gurney, KCMG, MVO, and Lady Gurney. *Educ:* Eton; New Coll., Oxford (MA). Farming, 1954–74. Assistant Master, Loughborough Grammar Sch., 1962–67; Assistant Master, Fairham Comprehensive School for Boys, Nottingham, 1967–69; Lectr, Bishop Lonsdale College of Education, 1969–72. Cons. Whip, House of Lords, Feb. 1974–76, an Opposition spokesman, 1976–79; Parly Under Sec. of State, NI Office, 1979–81, DHSS, 1981–82. Formerly Director: Andry Montgomery Ltd; Overseas Exhibition Services Ltd; Building Trades Exhibition Ltd. Dep. Sec., Cttee on Internat. Affairs, Synod of C of E, 1976–78. Mem. Boyd Commn to evaluate elections in Rhodesia, 1979. Late Captain, Queen's Own Warwickshire and Worcs Yeo.; late Major, Leics and Derbys (PAO) Yeo. Lord of the Manor of Adderbury, Oxon. *Heir:* s Hon. Edward Paget Elton, *b* 28 May 1966. *Address:* House of Lords, SW1. *Clubs:* Athenæum, Beefsteak, Cavalry and Guards.

ELTON, Arnold, CBE 1982; MS; FRCS; Consultant Surgeon, Northwick Park Hospital and Clinical Research Centre, since 1970; *b* 14 Feb. 1920; *s* of late Max Elton and of Ada Elton; *m* 1952, Billie Pamela Briggs; one *s. Educ:* University Coll. London (exhibnr; MB BS 1943); UCH Med. Sch. (MS 1951); Jun. and Sen. Gold Medal in Surgery. LRCP 1943; MRCS 1943, FRCS 1946. House Surg., House Physician and Casualty Officer, UCH, 1943–45; Sen. Surgical Registrar, Charing Cross Hosp., 1947–51 (Gosse Res. Schol.); Consultant Surgeon: Harrow Hosp., 1951–70; Mount Vernon Hosp., 1960–70. First Chm., Med. Staff Cttee, Chm., Surgical Div. and Theatre Cttee, Mem., Ethical Cttee, Northwick Park Hosp. Examiner: GNC; RCS, 1971–83; Surgical Tutor, RCS, 1970–82. Nat. Chm., Cons. Med. Soc., 1973–; Mem., Cons. Central Council and Nat. Exec. Cttee, 1976–. Mem., Professional Cttee, RADAR, 1976–; Founder Mem., British Assoc. of Surgical Oncology. Fellow: Assoc. of Surgeons of GB; Hunterian Soc.; FRSocMed; FICS; Associate Fellow, British Assoc. of Urological Surgeons. Liveryman: Apothecaries' Soc.; Carmen's Co. Jubilee Medal, 1977. *Publications:* contribs to med. jls. *Recreations:* tennis, music. *Address:* 22 St Stephen's Close, Avenue Road, NW8 6DB. *T:* 01-722 4222; 101 Harley Street, W1N 1DF. *Clubs:* Carlton, Royal Automobile.

ELTON, Sir Charles (Abraham Grierson), 11th Bt *cr* 1717; *b* 23 May 1953; *s* of Sir Arthur Hallam Rice Elton, 10th Bt, and of Lady Elton; *S* father, 1973. *Address:* Clevedon Court, Somerset BS21 6QU.

ELTON, Charles Sutherland, FRS 1953; Director, Bureau of Animal Population, Department of Zoological Field Studies, 1932–67, and Reader in Animal Ecology, Oxford University, 1936–67; Senior Research Fellow, Corpus Christi College, Oxford, 1936–67, Hon. Fellow since Oct. 1967; *b* 29 March 1900; *s* of late Oliver Elton; *m* 1st, 1928, Rose Montague; no *c;* 2nd, 1937, Edith Joy, *d* of Rev. Canon F. G. Scovell; one *s* one *d. Educ:* Liverpool Coll.; New Coll., Oxford. First Class Hons Zoology, Oxford, 1922; served as Ecologist on Oxford Univ. Expedition to Spitsbergen, 1921, Merton Coll. Arctic Expedition, 1923, Oxford Univ. Arctic Expedition, 1924 and Oxford Univ. Lapland Expedition, 1930. Mem. Nature Conservancy, 1949–56. Foreign Hon. Mem., Amer. Acad. of Arts and Sciences, 1968. Linnean Soc. Gold Medal, 1967; Darwin Medal, Royal Soc., 1970; John and Alice Tyler Ecology Award, 1976; Edward W. Browning Achievement Award, for Conserving the Environment, 1977. *Publications:* Animal Ecology, 1927; Animal Ecology and Evolution, 1930; The Ecology of Animals, 1933; Exploring the Animal World, 1933; Voles, Mice and Lemmings, 1942; The Ecology of Invasions by Animals and Plants, 1958; The Pattern of Animal Communities, 1966. *Recreations:* natural history, gardening, reading. *Address:* 61 Park Town, Oxford OX2 6SL. *T:* Oxford 57644.

ELTON, Prof. Geoffrey Rudolph, LittD; PhD; FBA 1967; Professor of English Constitutional History, Cambridge, since 1967; Fellow of Clare College, Cambridge, since 1954; *b* 17 Aug. 1921; changed name to Elton under Army Council Instruction, 1944; *er s* of late Prof. Victor Ehrenberg, PhD; *m* 1952, Sheila Lambert; no *c. Educ:* Prague; Rydal Sch. London External BA (1st Cl. Hons) 1943; Derby Student, University Coll. London, 1946–48; PhD 1949; LittD Cantab 1960. Asst Master, Rydal Sch., 1940–43. Service in E Surrey Regt and Int. Corps (Sgt), 1944–46. Asst in History, Glasgow Univ., 1948–49; Univ. Asst Lectr, Cambridge, 1949–53, Lectr, 1953–63, Reader in Tudor Studies, 1963–67. Visiting Amundson Prof., Univ.

of Pittsburgh, Sept.-Dec. 1963; Vis. Hill Prof., Univ. of Minnesota, 1976. Lectures: Ford's, Oxford, 1972; Wiles, Belfast, 1972; Hagey, Waterloo, 1974. Publications Sec., British Acad., 1981-. Mem., Adv. Council on Public Records, 1977-. FRHistS 1954 (Pres., 1972-76); Founder and Pres., List & Index Soc., 1965-. Fellow, UCL, 1978. Hon. DLitt: Glasgow, 1979; Newcastle, 1981; Bristol, 1981. For. Mem., Amer. Acad. Arts and Scis, 1975. *Publications:* The Tudor Revolution in Government, 1953; England under the Tudors, 1955; (ed) New Cambridge Modern History, vol. 2, 1958, new edn 1975; Star Chamber Stories, 1958; The Tudor Constitution, 1960; Henry VIII: an essay in revision, 1962; Renaissance and Reformation (Ideas and Institutions in Western Civilization), 1963; Reformation Europe, 1963; The Practice of History, 1967; The Future of the Past, 1968; The Sources of History: England 1200-1640, 1969; Political History: Principles and Practice, 1970; Modern Historians on British History 1485-1945: a critical bibliography 1945-1969, 1970; Policy and Police: the enforcement of the Reformation in the age of Thomas Cromwell, 1972; Reform and Renewal, 1973; Studies in Tudor and Stuart Politics and Government: papers and reviews, 1946-1972, 2 vols, 1974; Reform and Reformation: England 1509-1558, 1977; contribs to English Hist. Review, Econ. Hist. Rev., History, Hist. Jl, Times Lit. Supplement, Listener, etc. *Recreations:* squash rackets, joinery, gardening, and beer. *Address:* Clare College, Cambridge; Faculty of History, West Road, Cambridge. *T:* Cambridge 61661.
See also L. R. B. Elton.

ELTON, George Alfred Hugh; Chief Scientist (Fisheries and Food), Ministry of Agriculture, Fisheries and Food, since 1981; *b* 25 Feb. 1925; *s* of Horace and Violet Elton, *m* 1951, Theodora Rose Edith Kingham; two *d. Educ:* Sutton County Sch.; London Univ. (evening student). BSc 1944, PhD 1948, DSc 1956; CChem 1974, FRSC (FRIC 1951); FIFST 1968; FIBiol 1976. Mem. Faculty of Science, and Univ. Examnr in Chemistry, Univ. of London, 1951-58; Dir, Fog Res. Unit, Min. of Supply, 1954-58; Reader in Applied Phys. Chemistry, Battersea Polytechnic, 1956-58; Dir, British Baking Industries Res. Assoc., 1958-66; Dir, Flour Milling and Baking Res. Assoc., 1967-70; Ministry of Agriculture, Fisheries and Food: Chief Sci. Adviser (Food), 1971-81; Head of Food Science Div., 1972-73; Dep. Chief Scientist, 1972; Under-Sec. 1974. Vis. Prof., Surrey Univ. Chairman: National Food Survey Cttee; Consultative Cttee of Dirs of Food Res. Orgs; Scientific Governor, British Nutrition Foundn; Member: Cttee on Medical Aspects of Food Policy; Fisheries Res. and Develt Bd; Cttee on Medical Aspects of Chemicals in Food and the Environment; ARC; MRC/ARC Cttee on Nutrition Res.; ARC Wkg Party on Food Research; NERC; Adv. Bd for Research Councils; UK Delegn, Tripartite Meetings on Food and Drugs, Council, Chemical Soc., 1972-75. Co-inventor, Chorleywood Bread Process (Queen's Award to Industry 1966); Silver Medallist, Royal Soc. of Arts, 1969. *Publications:* research papers in jls of various learned societies. *Recreation:* golf. *Address:* Green Nook, Bridle Lane, Loudwater, Rickmansworth, Herts. *Clubs:* Athenæum, Savage, MCC.

ELTON, John; *see* Elton, P. J.

ELTON, John Bullen; Senior Master of the Supreme Court, Queen's Bench Division, and Queen's Remembrancer, since 1982 (Master since 1966); *b* 18 Jan. 1916; *s* of Percy Maden Elton, company director; *m* 1939, Sonia; three *d. Educ:* Bishop's Stortford Coll.; Brasenose Coll., Oxford. Called to the Bar, Inner Temple, 1938. RNVR, 1943-46. *Recreation:* sailing. *Address:* 3 Ailsa Road, St Margaret's, Twickenham, Middx. *Club:* Royal Victoria Yacht.

ELTON, Air Vice-Marshal John Goodenough, CB 1955; CBE 1945; DFC 1940; AFC 1935; *b* 5 May 1905; *s* of late Rev. George G. Elton, MA Oxon; *m* 1st, 1927, Helen Whitfield (marr. diss.); one *s*; 2nd, 1949, Francesca Cavallero. *Educ:* St John's, Leatherhead. Entered RAF, 1926; service in UK, 1926-31; Singapore, 1932-35 (AFC); Irak, 1939. Served War of 1939-45 (despatches twice, DFC, CBE); CO 47 Sqdn, Sudan, 1940; HQ, ME, Cairo, 1941; comd in succession Nos 242, 238 and 248 Wings, N Africa, 1942; CO RAF Turnberry, Scotland, 1943; CO RAF Silloth, Cumberland, 1944; AOA, HQ Mediterranean Allied Coastal Air Force, 1945-46; idc 1947; Dep. Dir, Air Min., 1948; RAF Mem., UK Delegn, Western Union Military Cttee, 1949-50; Comdt, Sch. of Tech. Training, Halton, 1951; Air Attaché, Paris, 1952; Air Officer i/c Administration, HQ Bomber Comd, 1953-56; Chief of Staff to the Head of British Jt Services Mission, Washington, DC, 1956-59; retired, 1959. *Address:* 64 Lexham Gardens, W8. *Club:* Royal Air Force.

ELTON, Prof. Lewis Richard Benjamin, MA, DSc; FInstP, FIMA, FRSA; Head of Institute for Educational Development (formerly Educational Technology), since 1967, and Professor of Science Education, since 1971, University of Surrey; *b* 25 March 1923; *yr s* of late Prof. Victor Leopold Ehrenberg, PhD, and Eva Dorothea (*née* Sommer); *m* 1950, Mary, *d* of late Harold William Foster and of Kathleen (*née* Meakin); three *s* one *d. Educ:* Stepanska Gymnasium, Prague; Rydal Sch., Colwyn Bay; Christ's Coll., Cambridge (Exhibr); Univ. Correspondence Coll., Cambridge, and Regent Street Polytechnic; University Coll. London (Univ. Research Studentship). BA 1945, Certif.Ed 1945, MA 1948, Cantab; BSc (External) 1st Cl. Hons Maths 1947, PhD 1950, London. Asst Master, St Bees Sch., 1944-46; Asst Lectr, then Lectr, King's Coll., London, 1950-57; Head of Physics Dept: Battersea Coll. of Technology, 1958-66; Univ. of Surrey, 1966-69; Prof. of Physics, Surrey, 1964-71. Research Associate: MIT, 1955; Stanford Univ., 1956; Niels Bohr Inst., Copenhagen, 1962; Vis. Professor: Univ. of Washington, Seattle, 1965; UCL, 1970-77; Univ. of Sydney, 1971; Univ. of Sao Paulo, 1975; Univ.

of Science, Malaysia, 1978, 1979. Member: Governing Body, Battersea Coll. of Technology, 1962-66; Council, Univ. of Surrey, 1966-67, 1981-; Council for Educational Technology of UK, 1975-81; Army Educn Adv. Bd, 1976-80; Convener, Standing Conf. of Physics Profs, 1971-74; Chairman: Governing Council, Soc. for Research into Higher Educn, 1976-78. Vice-Pres., Assoc. for Programmed Learning and Educnl Technology, 1976-. Fellow, Amer. Physical Soc., 1978. *Publications:* Introductory Nuclear Theory, 1959, 2nd edn 1965, Spanish edn 1964; Nuclear Sizes, 1961, Russian edn 1962; Concepts in Classical Mechanics, 1971; (with H. Messel) Time and Man, 1978; contribs to sci. jls on nuclear physics, science educn and educnl technology. *Recreation:* words. *Address:* 107 Farnham Road, Guildford, Surrey GU2 5PF. *T:* Guildford 60285.
See also G. R. Elton.
                                                                                 •
ELTON, (Peter) John, MC 1944; Director: Hill Samuel Group Ltd, since 1976; Alcan Aluminium (UK) Ltd; Consolidated Goldfields; *b* 14 March 1924; 2nd *s* of Sydney George Elton; *m* 1948, Patricia Ann Stephens; two *d. Educ:* Eastbourne Coll.; Clare Coll., Cambridge. Indian Army: 14th Punjab Regt, 1942-45 (twice wounded). Home Degree, Econs and Law, Cambridge. Man. Dir, Alcan Aluminium (UK) Ltd, 1967-74, Exec. Chm. 1974-76, non-Exec. Chm., 1976-78; Chairman: Alcan Booth Industries Ltd, 1968-76; Alcan (UK) Ltd, 1967-76; Director: Alcan Aluminium Ltd, 1972-77; Spillers, 1978-80. *Recreations:* sailing, shooting. *Address:* Salternshill Farm, Buckler's Hard, Beaulieu, Hants. *T:* Buckler's Hard 206. *Clubs:* Bucks; Royal Yacht Squadron (Cowes).

ELVEDEN, Viscount; Arthur Edward Rory Guinness; *b* 10 Aug. 1969; *s* and *heir* of Earl of Iveagh, *qv.*

ELVIN, Herbert Lionel; Emeritus Professor of Education; Director of the University of London Institute of Education, 1958-73 (Professor of Education in Tropical Areas, 1956-58); Director, Department of Education, UNESCO, Paris, 1950-56; *b* 7 Aug. 1905; *e s* of late Herbert Henry Elvin; *m* 1934, Mona Bedortha, *d* of Dr C. S. S. Dutton, San Francisco; one *s. Educ:* elementary schs; Southend High Sch.; Trinity Hall, Cambridge (1st Class Hons, History and English; Hon. Fellow, 1980). Commonwealth Fellow, Yale Univ., USA, Fellow of Trinity Hall, Cambridge, 1930-44; Temporary Civil Servant (Air Min., 1940-42, MOI, 1943-45); Principal, Ruskin Coll., Oxford, 1944-50. Parliamentary candidate (Lab), Cambridge Univ., 1935; Formerly: Pres., English New Education Fellowship; Pres., Council for Education in World Citizenship; Chm., Commonwealth Educn Liaison Cttee. Member: Cttee on Higher Education; Govt of India Educn Commn; University Grants Cttee, 1946-50; Central Advisory Council for Education (England) and Secondary School Examinations Council. *Publications:* Men of America (Pelican Books), 1941; An Introduction to the Study of Literature (Poetry), 1949; Education and Contemporary Society, 1965; The Place of Commonsense in Educational Thought, 1977. *Recreations:* most games indifferently; formerly athletics (half-mile, Cambridge *v* Oxford, 1927). *Address:* 4 Bulstrode Gardens, Cambridge. *T:* Cambridge 358309.

ELVIN, Violetta, (Violetta Prokhorova), (Signora Fernando Savarese); ballerina; a prima ballerina of Sadler's Wells Ballet, Royal Opera House, London (now The Royal Ballet), 1951-56; *b* Moscow, 3 Nov. 1925; *d* of Vassilie Prokhorov, engineer, and Irena Grimouzinskaya, former actress; *m* 1st, 1944, Harold Elvin (divorced 1952), of British Embassy, Moscow; 2nd, 1953, Siegbert J. Weinberger, New York; 3rd, 1959, Fernando Savarese, lawyer; one *s. Educ:* Bolshoi Theatre Sch., Moscow. Trained for ballet since age of 8 by: E. P. Gerdt, A. Vaganova, M. A. Kojuchova. Grad, 1942, as soloist; made mem. Bolshoi Theatre Ballet; evacuated to Tashkent, 1943; ballerina Tashkent State Theatre; rejoined Bolshoi Theatre at Kuibishev again as soloist, 1944; left for London, 1945. Joined Sadler's Wells Ballet at Covent Garden as guest-soloist, 1946; later became regular mem. Has danced all principal rôles, notably, Le Lac des Cygnes, Sleeping Beauty, Giselle, Cinderella, Sylvia, Ballet Imperial, etc. Danced four-act Le Lac des Cygnes, first time, 1943; guest-artist Stanislavsky Theatre, Moscow, 1944, Sadler's Wells Theatre, 1947; guest-prima ballerina, La Scala, Milan, Nov. 1952-Feb. 1953 (Macbeth, La Gioconda, Swan Lake, Petrouchka); guest artist, Cannes, July 1954; Copenhagen, Dec. 1954; Teatro Municipal, Rio de Janeiro, May 1955 (Giselle, Swan Lake, Les Sylphides, Nutcracker, Don Quixote and The Dying Swan); Festival Ballet, Festival Hall, 1955; guest-prima ballerina in Giselle, Royal Opera House, Stockholm (Anna Pavlova Memorial), 1956; concluded stage career when appeared in Sleeping Beauty, Royal Opera House, Covent Garden, June 1956. *Appeared in films:* The Queen of Spades, Twice Upon a Time, Melba. Television appearances in Russia and England. Has toured with Sadler's Wells Ballet, France, Italy, Portugal, United States and Canada. *Recreations:* reading, painting, swimming. *Address:* Marina di Equa, 80066 Seiano, Bay of Naples, Italy. *T:* 081-879 8520.

ELWORTHY, family name of **Baron Elworthy.**

ELWORTHY, Baron *cr* 1972 (Life Peer); **Marshal of the Royal Air Force Samuel Charles Elworthy,** KG 1977; GCB 1962 (KCB 1961; CB 1960); CBE 1946; DSO 1941; MVO 1953; DFC 1941; AFC 1941; Director, Australian Mutual Provident Society (New Zealand), since 1978; *b* 23 March 1911; *e s* of late P. A. Elworthy, Gordon's Valley, Timaru, New Zealand; *m* 1936, Audrey, *o d* of late A. J. Hutchinson, OBE; three *s* one *d. Educ:* Marlborough; Trinity Coll., Cambridge (MA). Commissioned in RAFO 1933, transferred to Auxiliary Air Force (600 Sqdn), 1934; called to Bar,

Lincoln's Inn, 1935, Hon. Bencher 1970; permanent commission in RAF, 1936; War Service in Bomber Comd; Acting Air Cdre, 1944; Air Vice-Marshal, 1957; Air Marshal, 1960; Air Chief Marshal, 1962; Marshal of the RAF, 1967. Comdt RAF Staff Coll., Bracknell, 1957-59; Deputy Chief of Air Staff, 1959-60; C-in-C, Unified Command, Middle East, 1960-63; Chief of Air Staff, 1963-67; Chief of the Defence Staff, 1967-71. Constable and Governor, Windsor Castle, 1971-78; Lord-Lieutenant of Greater London, 1973-78. Director, 1971-78: British Petroleum; Plessey; Nat. Bank of NZ. Chairman: Royal Commn for the Exhibition of 1851, 1971-78; King Edward VII Hospital for Officers, 1971-78; Royal Over-Seas League, 1971-76. Sometime Governor: Bradfield Coll.; Wellington Coll.; Marlborough Coll. Hon. Freeman, Skinners' Co., 1968-, Master 1973-74. KStJ 1976. Retired to live in NZ, 1978. *Address:* Gordon's Valley, RD2, Timaru, South Canterbury, New Zealand. *Clubs:* Royal Air Force; Leander; South Canterbury (NZ); Christchurch (NZ).

ELWYN-JONES, family name of **Baron Elwyn-Jones.**

ELWYN-JONES, Baron *cr* 1974 (Life Peer), of Llanelli and Newham; **Frederick Elwyn-Jones,** PC 1964; CH 1976; Kt 1964; Lord High Chancellor of Great Britain, 1974-79; a Lord of Appeal, since 1979; *b* 24 Oct. 1909; *s* of Frederick and Elizabeth Jones, Llanelli, Carmarthenshire; *m* 1937, Pearl Binder; one *s* two *d. Educ:* Llanelli Grammar Sch.; University of Wales, Aberystwyth; Gonville and Caius Coll., Cambridge (Scholar, MA, Pres. Cambridge Union); Hon. Fellow, 1976. Called to Bar, Gray's Inn, 1935, Bencher, 1960, Treasurer, 1980; QC 1953; QC (N Ireland) 1958; Hon. Bencher, Inn of Court of N Ireland, 1981. Major RA (TA); Dep. Judge Advocate, 1943-45. MP (Lab) Plaistow Div. of West Ham, 1945-50, West Ham South, 1950-74, Newham South 1974; PPS to Attorney-Gen., 1946-51; Attorney General, 1964-70. Recorder: of Merthyr Tydfil, 1949-53; of Swansea, 1953-60; of Cardiff, 1960-64; of Kingston-upon-Thames, 1968-74. Member of British War Crimes Executive, Nuremberg, 1945. UK Observer, Malta Referendum, 1964. Mem., Inter-Departmental Cttee on the Court of Criminal Appeal, 1964. Mem. of Bar Council, 1956-59. Pres., University Coll., Cardiff, 1971-. FKC, 1970. Hon. LLD: University of Wales, 1968; Ottawa Univ., 1975; Columbia Univ., NY, 1976; Warsaw, 1977; Univ. of Philippines, 1979; Law Soc. of Upper Canada, 1982. Hon. Freeman: Llanelli; London. *Publications:* Hitler's Drive to the East, 1937; The Battle for Peace, 1938; The Attack from Within, 1939. *Recreation:* travelling. *Address:* House of Lords, SW1.

ELY, 8th Marquess of, *cr* 1801; **Charles John Tottenham;** Bt 1780; Baron Loftus, 1785; Viscount Loftus, 1789; Earl of Ely, 1794; Baron Loftus (UK), 1801; Headmaster, Boulden House, Trinity College School, Port Hope, Ontario, since 1941; *b* 30 May 1913; *s* of G. L. Tottenham, BA (Oxon), and Cécile Elizabeth, *d* of J. S. Burra, Bockhanger, Kennington, Kent; *g s* of C. R. W. Tottenham, MA (Oxon), Woodstock, Newtown Mount Kennedy, Co. Wicklow, and Plâs Berwyn, Llangollen, N Wales; *S* cousin, 1969; *m* 1st, 1938, Katherine Elizabeth (*d* 1975), *d* of Col W. H. Craig, Kingston, Ont; three *s* one *d*; 2nd, 1978, Elspeth Ann, *o d* of late P. T. Hay, Highgate. *Educ:* Collège de Genève, Internat. Sch., Geneva; Queen's Univ., Kingston, Ont (BA). Career as Schoolmaster. *Recreation:* fishing. *Heir: e s* Viscount Loftus, *qv. Address:* Trinity College School, Port Hope, Ontario, Canada. *T:* 885 5209; 20 Arundel Court, Jubilee Place, SW3. *T:* 01-352 9172. *Club:* University (Toronto).

ELY, Bishop of, since 1977; **Rt. Rev. Peter Knight Walker,** DD; *b* 6 Dec. 1919; *s* of late George Walker and Eva Muriel (*née* Knight); *m* 1973, Mary Jean, JP 1976, *yr d* of Lt-Col J. A. Ferguson, OBE. *Educ:* Leeds Grammar Sch. (Schol.); The Queen's Coll., Oxford (Hastings schol.; Cl. 2 Classical Hon. Mods. 1940, Cl. 1 Lit. Hum. 1947; MA Oxon 1947; Hon. Fellow, 1981); Westcott House, Cambridge. MA Cantab by incorporation, 1958; Hon. DD Cantab, 1978. Served in RN (Lieut, RNVR), 1940-45. Asst Master: King's Sch., Peterborough, 1947-50; Merchant Taylors' Sch., 1950-56. Ordained, 1954; Curate of Hemel Hempstead, 1956-58; Fellow, Dean of Chapel and Lectr in Theology, Corpus Christi Coll., Cambridge, 1958-62 (Asst Tutor, 1959-62), Hon. Fellow, 1978; Principal of Westcott House, Cambridge, 1962-72; Commissary to Bishop of Delhi, 1962-66; Hon. Canon of Ely Cathedral, 1966-72; Bishop Suffragan of Dorchester, and Canon of Christ Church, Oxford, 1972-77. Select Preacher: Univ. of Cambridge, 1962, 1967 (Hulsean); Univ. of Oxford, 1975, 1980; Examining Chaplain to Bishop of Portsmouth, 1962-72. A Governor: St Edward's Sch., Oxford. *Publications:* contrib. to: Classical Quarterly; Theology. *Address:* The Bishop's House, Ely, Cambs CB7 4DW. *T:* Ely 2749. *Clubs:* Cambridge County, Naval.

ELY, Dean of; *see* Shaw, Very Rev. C. A.

ELY, Archdeacon of; *see* Walser, Ven. David.

ELYAN, Prof. Sir (Isadore) Victor, Kt 1970; Professor of Law, and Dean of the Faculty of Law, Durban-Westville University, 1973-77, retired; Chief Justice of Swaziland, 1965-70, retired; *b* 5 Sept. 1909; *s* of Jacob Elyan, PC, JP and Olga Elyan; *m* 1939, Ivy Ethel Mabel Stuart-Weir (*d* 1965); no *c*; *m* 1966, Rosaleen Jeanette O'Shea. *Educ:* St Stephen's Green Sch., Dublin; Trinity Coll., Dublin Univ. BA 1929, LLB 1931, MA 1932, TCD. Admitted a Solicitor of Supreme Court of Judicature, Ireland, 1930; Barrister-at-Law, King's Inns 1949, Middle Temple, 1952. Resident Magistrate, HM Colonial Legal Service, Gold Coast, 1946-54; Senior Magistrate, 1954-55; Judge of

Appeal of the Court of Appeal for Basutoland, the Bechuanaland Protectorate and Swaziland, 1955-66; Judge, High Courts of Basutoland and the Bechuanaland Protectorate, 1955-65; on occasions acted as Judge between 1953 and 1955, Gold Coast; as Justice of Appeal, West African Court of Appeal; and as Chief Justice of Basutoland, the Bechuanaland Protectorate and Swaziland, also Pres. Court of Appeal, during 1956, 1961 and 1964; Judge of Appeal: Court of Appeal for Botswana, 1966-70; Court of Appeal for Swaziland, 1967-70; Court of Appeal, Lesotho, 1968-70. Served War, 1942-46; attached to Indian Army, 1944-46; GSO2 Military Secretary's Branch (DAMS), 1945-46 in rank of Major. Mem., Internat. Adv. Bd, The African Law Reports, 1969. *Publications:* Editor, High Commission Territories Law Reports, 1956, 1957, 1958, 1959, 1960. *Recreation:* sailing. *Address:* PO Box 3052, Durban, Natal, South Africa.

ELYSTAN-MORGAN, family name of Baron Elystan-Morgan.

ELYSTAN-MORGAN, Baron *cr* 1981 (Life Peer), of Aberteifi in the County of Dyfed; **Dafydd Elystan Elystan-Morgan;** Barrister-at-Law; *b* 7 Dec. 1932; *s* of late Dewi Morgan and late Mrs Olwen Morgan; *m* 1959, Alwen, *d* of William E. Roberts; one *s* one *d. Educ:* Ardwyn Grammar Sch., Aberystwyth; UCW, Aberystwyth. LLB Hons Aberystwyth, 1953. Research at Aberystwyth and Solicitor's Articles, 1953-57; admitted a Solicitor, 1957; Partner in N Wales (Wrexham) Firm of Solicitors, 1958-68; Barrister-at-law, Gray's Inn, 1971. MP (Lab) Cardiganshire, 1966-Feb. 1974; Chm., Welsh Parly Party, 1967-68, 1971-74; Parly Under-Secretary of State, Home Office, 1968-70; front-bench spokesman on Home Affairs, 1970-72, on Welsh Affairs, 1972-74. Contested (Lab): Cardigan, Oct. 1974; Anglesey, 1979. Pres., Welsh Local Authorities Assoc., 1967-73. *Address:* Carreg Afon, Dolau, Bow Street, Dyfed.

ELYTIS, Odysseus; Order of the Phoenix 1965; poet; *b* Crete, 2 Nov. 1911; *y c* of Panayiotis and Maria Alepoudelis. *Educ:* Athens Univ. (Law); Sorbonne (Lettres). First publication, 1940; Broadcasting and Program Director, National Broadcasting Inst., 1945-47 and 1953-54; Administrative Board, Greek National Theatre, 1974-76. President, Admin. Board, Greek Broadcasting and Television, 1974. Hon. DLitt: Salonica, 1976; Sorbonne, 1980; Hon. DLit London, 1981. First National Prize in Poetry, 1960; Nobel Prize for Literature, 1979; Benson Silver Medal, RSL, 1981. *Publications:* Orientations, 1940; Sun the First, 1943; The Axion Esti, 1959; Six, but one remorses for the Sky, 1960; The Light Tree, 1971; The Monogram, 1972; Villa Natacha, 1973; The Painter Theophilos, 1973; The Open Book, 1974; The Second Writing, 1976; Maria Nefeli, 1978; Selected Poems, 1981. *Address:* Skoufa Street 23, Athens, Greece. *T:* 3626458.

EMANUEL, Aaron, CMG 1957; Consultant to OECD; *b* 11 Feb. 1912; *s* of Jack Emanuel and Jane (*née* Schaverien); *m* 1936, Ursula Pagel; two *s* one *d. Educ:* Henry Thornton Sch., Clapham; London Sch. of Economics (BSc Econ.). Economist at International Institute of Agriculture, Rome, 1935-38; Board of Trade, 1938; Ministry of Food, 1940; Colonial Office, 1943; Ministry of Health, 1961; Dept. of Economic Affairs, 1965; Min. of Housing and Local Govt, 1969; Under-Sec., Dept of the Environment, 1970-72; Chm., West Midlands Econ. Planning Bd, 1968-72; Vis. Sen. Lectr, Univ. of Aston in Birmingham, 1972-75. *Publication:* Issues of Regional Policies, 1973. *Address:* 119 Salisbury Road, Moseley, Birmingham B13 8LA. *T:* 021-449 5553.

EMANUEL, Richard Wolff, MA, DM Oxon, FRCP; Physician to Department of Cardiology, Middlesex Hospital, since 1963; Lecturer in Cardiology, Middlesex Hospital Medical School since 1963; Physician to National Heart Hospital since 1963; Lecturer to Institute of Cardiology since 1963; Civil Consultant in Cardiology, Royal Air Force, since 1979; *b* 13 Jan. 1923; *s* of Prof. and Mrs J. G. Emanuel, Birmingham; *m* 1950, Lavinia Hoffmann; three *s. Educ:* Bradfield Coll.; Oriel Coll., Oxford; Middlesex Hospital. House Appts at Middx Hospital, 1948 and 1950. Captain RAMC, 1948-50; Med. Registrar, Middx Hosp., 1951-52; Sen. Med. Registrar, Middx Hosp., 1953-55; Sen. Med. Registrar, Nat. Heart Hosp., 1956-58; Fellow in Med., Vanderbilt Univ., 1956-57; Sen. Med. Registrar, Dept of Cardiology, Brompton Hosp., 1958-61; Asst Dir, Inst. of Cardiology and Hon. Asst Physician to Nat. Heart Hosp., 1961-63. Advr in Cardiovascular Disease to Sudan Govt, 1969-. Vis. Lecturer: Univ. of Med. Sciences and Chulalongkorn Univ., Thailand; Univ. of the Philippines; Univ. of Singapore; Univ. of Malaya; Khartoum Univ.; St Cyre's Lectr, London, 1968; Ricardo Molina Lectr, Philippines, 1969. Has addressed numerous Heart Socs in SE Asia. Member Council: British Cardiac Soc., 1981- (Asst Sec., 1966-68; Sec., 1968-70); Chest, Heart and Stroke Assoc., 1978-. FACC; Hon. Fellow, Philippine Coll. of Cardiology; Hon. Mem., Heart Assoc. of Thailand. Member: Brit. Acad. of Forensic Sciences (Med.); Cardiological Cttee, RCP; Assoc. of Physicians of GB and Ireland. Asst Editor, British Heart Journal. *Publications:* various articles on diseases of the heart in British and American jls. *Recreations:* XVIIIth century glass, fishing, sailing. *Address:* 6 Upper Wimpole Street, W1M 7TD. *T:* 01-935 3243; 6 Lansdowne Walk, W11. *T:* 01-727 6688; Canute Cottage, Old Bosham, near Chichester, West Sussex. *T:* Bosham 3318. *Clubs:* Naval and Military, Oriental.

EMBLING, John Francis, CB 1967; Deputy Under-Secretary of State, Department of Education and Science, 1966-71; *b* 16 July 1909; *m* 1940, Margaret Gillespie Anderson; one *s. Educ:* University of Bristol. Teaching: Dean Close, 1930; Frensham Heights, 1931; Lecturer: Leipzig Univ., 1936; SW

Essex Technical Coll., 1938 (Head of Dept, 1942); Administrative Asst, Essex LEA, 1944; Ministry of Education: Principal, 1946; Asst Secretary, 1949; Under-Secretary of State for Finance and Accountant-General, Dept of Education and Science, 1960-66. Research Fellow in Higher Educn, LSE, 1972-73, Univ. of Lancaster, 1974-76. Mem. Council, Klagenfurt Univ., 1972-. Grand Cross, Republic of Austria, 1976. *Address:* The Old Rectory, Wixoe, Suffolk. *T:* Ridgewell 241. *Clubs:* Athenæum, English-Speaking Union.

EMBREY, Prof. Derek Morris, CEng, FIEE, FIERE, MIGasE; Group Technical Director, AB Electronic Products Group PLC, since 1973; *b* 11 March 1928; *s* of Frederick and Ethel Embrey; *m* 1951, Frances Margaret Stephens; one *s* one *d*. *Educ:* Wolverhampton Polytechnic. Chief Designer (Electronics), Electric Construction Co. Ltd, 1960-65, Asst Manager Static Plant, 1965-69; Chief Engineer, Abergas Ltd, 1969-73. Member: Engineering Council, 1982-; Welsh Industrial Develt Adv. Bd, 1982-. Visiting Industrial Professor, Univ. of Technology, Loughborough, 1978-; Lectr, 'State of the Art' conferences. *Publications:* contribs to various jls. *Recreations:* power flying, gliding, music, archaeology. *Address:* 9 Heol Cefn Onn, Lisvane, Cardiff. *T:* Cardiff 758473. *Clubs:* Royal Air Force; Birmingham Electric.

EMECHETA, Buchi; writer and lecturer, since 1972; *b* 21 July 1944; *d* of Alice and Jeremy Emecheta; *m* 1960, Sylvester Onwordi; two *s* three *d*. *Educ:* Methodist Girls' High Sch., Lagos, Nigeria; London Univ. (BSc Hons Sociol.). Librarian, 1960-69; Student, 1970-74; Youth Worker and Res. Student, Race, 1974-76; Community Worker, Camden, 1976-78. Sen. Res. Fellow and Vis. Prof. of English, Univ. of Calabar, Nigeria, 1980-81. Member: Arts Council of GB, 1982-; Home Sec.'s Adv. Council on Race, 1979-. *Publications:* In the Ditch, 1972; Second Class Citizen, 1975; The Bride Price, 1976; The Slave Girl, 1977; The Joys of Motherhood, 1979; Destination Biafra, 1982; Naira Power, 1982; Double Yoke, 1982; *for children:* Titch the Cat, 1979; Nowhere to Play, 1980; The Moonlight Bride, 1981; The Wrestling Match, 1981; contribs to New Statesman, TLS, The Guardian, etc. *Recreations:* gardening, going to the theatre, listening to music, reading. *Address:* 7 Briston Grove, Crouch End, N8 9EX. *T:* 01-340 3762. *Club:* Africa Centre.

EMELEUS, Prof. Harry Julius, CBE 1958; FRS 1946; MA, DSc; Professor of Inorganic Chemistry, University of Cambridge, 1945-70; now Professor Emeritus; Fellow of Sidney Sussex College, Cambridge; Fellow of Imperial College, London; *b* 22 June 1903; *s* of Karl Henry Emeleus and Ellen Biggs; *m* 1931, Mary Catherine Horton; two *s* two *d*. *Educ:* Hastings Grammar Sch.; Imperial Coll., London. 1851 Exhibition Senior Student, Imperial Coll. and Technische Hochschule, Karlsruhe, 1926-29; Commonwealth Fund Fellow, Princeton Univ., 1929-31; Member of Staff of Imperial Coll., 1931-45. President: Chemical Society, 1958; Royal Institute of Chemistry, 1963-65. Trustee, British Museum, 1963-72. Hon. Fellow, Manchester Institute of Science and Technology. Hon. Member: Austrian, Finnish, Indian, Bangladesh and French Chemical Societies; Finnish Scientific Academy; Royal Academy of Belgium; Akad. Naturf. Halle; Akad. Wiss. Göttingen; Spanish Royal Society for Physics and Chemistry. Hon. Doctor: Ghent; Kiel; Lille; Paris; Tech. Hoch. Aachen; Marquette; Kent. Lavoisier Medal, French Chem. Society; Stock Medal, Gesellschaft Deutsche Chemiker; Davy Medal, Royal Society, 1962. *Publications:* scientific papers in chemical journals. *Recreation:* fishing. *Address:* 149 Shelford Road, Trumpington, Cambridge CB2 2ND. *T:* Cambridge 840374.

EMELEUS, Karl George, CBE 1965; MA, PhD; MRIA; Professor of Physics, Queen's University, Belfast, 1933-66, now Emeritus; *b* 4 Aug. 1901; *s* of Karl Henry Emeleus and Ellen Biggs; *m* 1928, Florence Mary Chambers; three *s* one *d*. *Educ:* Hastings Grammar Sch.; St John's Coll., Cambridge. Hon. ScD Dublin; Hon. DSc NUI. *Address:* c/o Queen's University of Belfast, Belfast BT7 1NN.

EMERSON, Michael Ronald, MA; FCA; Director for Macroeconomic Analyses and Policies, Directorate-General II, Commission of the European Communities, Brussels, since 1981; *b* 12 May 1940; *s* of James and Priscilla Emerson; *m* 1966, Barbara Brierley; one *s* two *d*. *Educ:* Hurstpierpoint Coll.; Balliol Coll., Oxford (MA (PPE)). Price Waterhouse & Co., London, 1962-65; Organisation for Economic Cooperation and Development, Paris: several posts in Develt and Economics Depts, finally as Head of General Economics Div., 1966-73; EEC, Brussels: Head of Division for Budgetary Policy, Directorate-General II, 1973-76; Economic Adviser to President of the Commission, 1977; Dir for Nat. Economies and Economic Trends, EEC, 1978-81. *Publications:* contribs to various economic jls and edited volumes on internat. and European economics. *Address:* 50 rue Clement Delpierre, 1310 La Hulpe, Belgium. *T:* 02.354.3730.

EMERSON, Dr Peter Albert, FRCP; Dean, Westminster Medical School, London, since 1981; Consultant Physician, Westminster Hospital, since 1959; *b* 7 Feb. 1923; *s* of Albert Emerson and Gwendoline (*née* Davy); *m* 1947, Ceris Hood Price; one *s* one *d*. *Educ:* The Leys Sch., Cambridge; Clare Coll., Univ. of Cambridge (MA); St George's Hosp., Univ. of London (MB, BChir 1947; MD 1954). FRCP 1964; Hon. FACP 1975. House Physician, St George's Hosp., 1947; RAF Med. Bd, 1948-52 (Sqdn Leader); Registrar, later Sen. Registrar, St George's Hosp. and Brompton Hosp., London, 1952-57; Asst Prof. of Medicine, Coll. of Medicine, State Univ. of New York, Brooklyn, USA, 1957-58; Civilian Consultant Physician in Chest Diseases to RN, 1974-;

Hon. Consultant Phys., King Edward VII Hosp., Midhurst, 1969-. Royal Coll. of Physicians: Asst Registrar, 1965-71; Procensor and Censor, 1978-80; Mitchell Lectr, 1969. FRSocMed. *Publications:* Thoracic Medicine, 1981; articles in med. jls and chapters in books on thoracic medicine and the application of decision theory to clinical medicine. *Recreations:* tennis, restoring old buildings. *Address:* 3 Halkin Street, Belgrave Square, SW1 7DJ. *T:* 01-235 8529. *Club:* Royal Air Force.

EMERTON, Audrey C., CStJ; SRN, SCM, RNT; Regional Nursing Officer, South East Thames Regional Health Authority, since 1973. Formerly: Chief Nursing Officer, Tunbridge Wells and Leybourne HMC; Principal Nursing Officer, Education, Bromley HMC; Senior Tutor, Experimental 2 year and 1 year Course, St George's Hosp., SW1. Kent County Nursing Officer, St John Ambulance Brigade. Pres., Assoc. of Nurse Administrators, 1979-82. *Address:* SE Thames Regional Health Authority, Randolph House, 46-48 Wellesley Road, Croydon CR9 3QA. *T:* 01-686 8877.

EMERTON, Rev. Prof. John Adney, FBA 1979; Regius Professor of Hebrew, Cambridge, since 1968; Fellow of St John's College, since 1970; *b* 5 June 1928; *s* of Adney Spencer Emerton and Helena Mary Emerton; *m* 1954, Norma Elizabeth Bennington; one *s* two *d*. *Educ:* Minchenden Grammar Sch., Southgate; Corpus Christi Coll., Oxford; Wycliffe Hall, Oxford. BA (1st class hons Theology), 1950; 1st class hons Oriental Studies, 1952; MA 1954. Canon Hall Jun. Greek Testament Prize, 1950; Hall-Houghton Jun. Septuagint Prize, 1951, Senior Prize, 1954; Houghton Syriac Prize, 1953; Liddon Student, 1950; Kennicott Hebrew Fellow, 1952. Corpus Christi Coll., Cambridge, MA (by incorporation), 1955; BD 1960; DD 1973. Deacon, 1952; Priest, 1953. Curate of Birmingham Cathedral, 1952-53; Asst Lecturer in Theology, Birmingham Univ., 1952-53; Lecturer in Hebrew and Aramaic, Durham Univ., 1953-55; Lecturer in Divinity, Cambridge Univ., 1955-62; Reader in Semitic Philology and Fellow of St Peter's Coll., Oxford, 1962-68. Visiting Prof. of Old Testament and Near Eastern Studies, Trinity Coll., Toronto Univ., 1960. Select Preacher before Univ. of Cambridge, 1962, 1971. Sec., Internat. Orgn for the Study of the Old Testament, 1971-; Pres., Soc. for OT Study, 1979. Mem. Editorial Bd, Vetus Testamentum, 1971-. Hon. DD Edinburgh, 1977. *Publications:* The Peshitta of the Wisdom of Solomon, 1959; The Old Testament in Syriac: Song of Songs, 1966; (ed) Studies in the Historical Books of the Old Testament, 1979; (ed) Prophecy: essays presented to Georg Fohrer, 1980; Editor, Congress Volumes (International Organization for Study of the Old Testament): Edinburgh 1973, 1974; Göttingen 1977, 1978; Vienna 1980, 1981; articles in Journal of Semitic Studies, Journal of Theological Studies, Theology, Vetus Testamentum, Zeitschrift für die Alttestamentliche Wissenschaft. *Address:* 34 Gough Way, Cambridge CB3 9LN.

EMERY, Rt. Rev. Anthony Joseph; *see* Portsmouth, Bishop of, (RC).

EMERY, Eleanor Jean, CMG 1975; HM Diplomatic Service, retired; *b* 23 Dec. 1918; *d* of Robert Paton Emery and Nellie Nicol Wilson. *Educ:* Western Canada High Sch., Calgary, Alberta; Glasgow Univ. MA Hons in History, 1941. Dominions Office, 1941-45; Asst Private Sec. to Sec. of State, 1942-45; British High Commn, Ottawa, 1945-48; CRO, 1948-52; Principal Private Sec. to Sec. of State, 1950-52; First Sec., British High Commn, New Delhi, 1952-55; CRO, 1955-58; First Sec., British High Commn, Pretoria/Cape Town, 1958-62; Head of South Asia Dept, CRO, 1962-64; Counsellor, British High Commn, Ottawa, 1964-68; Head of Pacific Dependent Territories Dept, FCO, 1969-73; High Comr, Botswana, 1973-77. Jt Vice-Chm., SOS Children's Villages, UK, 1981-. Governor, Commonwealth Inst., 1980-. *Recreations:* walking, gardening. *Address:* 17 Winchmore Drive, Cambridge CB2 2LW. *Club:* Royal Commonwealth Society (Mem. Central Council).
See also J. M. Zachariah.

EMERY, Fred; Presenter, Panorama, BBC TV, 1978-80 and since 1982; *b* 19 Oct. 1933; *s* of Frederick G. L. Emery and Alice May (*née* Wright); *m* 1958, E. Marianne Nyberg; two *s*. *Educ:* Bancroft's Sch.; St John's Coll., Cantab (MA). RAF fighter pilot, 266 & 234 Squadrons, National Service, 1953. Radio Bremen, 1955-56; joined The Times, 1958, Foreign Correspondent, 1961; served in Paris, Algeria, Tokyo, Indonesia, Vietnam, Cambodia, Malaysia and Singapore until 1970; Chief Washington Corresp., 1970-77; Political Editor, 1977-81; Home Editor, 1981-82; Exec. Editor (News), 1982. *Recreations:* skiing, hill walking, tennis. *Address:* 5 Woodsyre, SE26 6SS. *T:* 01-761 0076.

EMERY, George Edward, CB 1980; Director General of Defence Accounts, Ministry of Defence, 1973-80, retired; *b* 2 March 1920; *s* of late Frederick and Florence Emery; *m* 1946, Margaret (*née* Rice); two *d*. *Educ:* Bemrose Sch., Derby. Admiralty, 1938; Min. of Fuel and Power, 1946; Min. of Supply, 1951; Min. of Aviation, 1959; Min. of Technology, 1967; Principal Exec. Officer, 1967; Asst Sec., Min. of Aviation Supply, 1970; Ministry of Defence: Asst Sec., 1971; Exec. Dir, 1973; Under-Sec., 1973. *Recreations:* amateur dramatics, gardening. *Address:* 3 The Orchard, Freshford, Bath BA3 6EW. *T:* Limpley Stoke 3561.

EMERY, Sir (James) Frederick, Kt 1957; JP; Company Director; *b* 17 Dec. 1886; *s* of William Joseph and Ruth Emery; *m* 1912, Florence Beatrice Gradwell; one *d*. *Educ:* Manchester Univ. MP (U) West Salford, 1935-45; Member of Salford City Council, 1921-35 (Councillor 1921-33, Alderman,

1933-35); Pres. North Fylde Conservative Association; Mayor of Salford, 1932-33. JP Salford 1927. *Address:* Rathmines, 189 Victoria Road West, Cleveleys, near Blackpool, Lancs. *T:* Cleveleys 3090.

EMERY, Joan Dawson, (Mrs Jack Emery); *see* Bakewell, J. D.

EMERY, Joyce Margaret; *see* Zachariah, J. M.

EMERY, Sir Peter (Frank Hannibal), Kt 1982; MA; FInstPS; MP (C) Honiton, since 1967 (Reading, 1959-66); *b* 27 Feb. 1926; *s* of late F. G. Emery, Highgate; *m* 1st, 1954 (marr. diss.); one *s* one *d* ; 2nd, 1972, Elizabeth, *y d* of late G. J. R. Monnington; one *s* one *d*. *Educ:* Scotch Plains, New Jersey, USA; Oriel Coll., Oxford. Joint Founder and First Secretary of the Bow Group. Parliamentary Private Secretary: to Rt Hon. David Ormsby-Gore, Minister of State for Foreign Affairs, 1960-61; to Rt Hon. Joseph Godber, when Minister of State for Foreign Affairs, 1961-63, when Secretary of State for War, 1963, and when Minister of Labour, 1963-64; Jt Hon. Secretary, 1922 Cttee, 1964-65; Opposition Front Bench Spokesman for Treasury, Economics and Trade, 1964-66; Parliamentary Under-Secretary of State: DTI, 1972-74; Dept of Energy, 1974; Mem., Select Cttee on Industry and Trade, 1979-. Jt Vice-Chm., Conservative Finance Cttee, 1970-72; Chm., Cons. Housing and Construction Cttee, 1974-75. Member, Delegation to CPA Conference, Westminster, 1961; Member CPA Delegation to Canada, 1962, and Leader, Delegn to Kenya, 1977; Delegate, Council of Europe and WEU, 1962-64, 1970-72. Chm., Shenley Trust Services Ltd; Director: Property Growth Insurance, 1966-72; Phillips Petroleum-UK Ltd, 1963-72; Institute of Purchasing and Supply, 1961-72; Secretary-General, European Federation of Purchasing, 1962-72; Chairman, Consultative Council of Professional Management Organisations, 1968-72. *Recreations:* sliding down mountains, tennis, cricket and golf. *Address:* Tytherleigh Manor, near Axminster, Devon. *T:* South Chard 309; 15 Tufton Court, Tufton Street, SW1. *T:* 01-222 6666. *Clubs:* Carlton, Portland.

EMERY-WALLIS, Frederick Alfred John, FSA; Leader, Hampshire County Council, since 1975 (County Councillor, since 1973; Vice-Chairman, 1975-76); Chairman, Southern Tourist Board, since 1976; *b* 11 May 1927; *o s* of Frederick Henry Wallis and Lillian Grace Emery Coles; *m* 1960, Solange, *o d* of William Victor Randall, London, and Albertine Beaupère, La Guerche-sur-l'Aubois; two *d*. *Educ:* Blake's Academy, Portsmouth. Royal Signals SCU4 (Middle East Radio Security), 1945-48. Portsmouth City Council, 1961-74; Lord Mayor, 1968-69; Alderman, 1969-74. Vice-Chm., Recreation Cttee, ACC, 1977-. Chairman: Portsmouth Develt and Estates Cttee, 1965-74; Portsmouth Papers Editorial Bd, 1966-; S Hampshire Plan Adv. Cttee, 1969-74; South Portsmouth Conservative Assoc., 1971-79; Member: Economic Planning Council for the South East, 1969-74; British Library Adv. Council, 1979-; Council, British Records Assoc., 1979-; Library Council for England, 1980-; Mary Rose Develt Trust, 1980-; Vice-Chm., Standing Adv. Cttee on Local Authorities and Theatre, 1980-. Vice-Chm., Portsmouth Polytechnic, 1967-75; Pres., Hampshire Field Club, 1971-74. Vice-Pres., Mottisfont Soc., 1978-. Pres., Portsmouth YMCA, 1978-. Hon. Fellow, Portsmouth Polytechnic, 1972. FSA 1980. *Publications:* various publications concerning history and develt of Portsmouth and Hampshire. *Recreations:* reading, music. *Address:* Froddington, Craneswater Park, Portsmouth. *T:* Portsmouth 731409.

EMETT, Rowland, OBE 1978; FSIAD; artist and inventor; *b* 1906; *m* 1941, Mary; one *d*. Contributor to Punch for many years. In 1951 The Far Twittering to Oyster Creek Railway forsook the pages of Punch and appeared full-blown and passenger-carrying at The Festival Gardens, for The Festival of Britain. The impact of this led to a succession of large three-dimensional, Gothick-Kinetic, fully-working inventions of ever-increasing complexity, which have been exhibited all over the world. Constructed the Edwardian inventions for the film Chitty Chitty Bang Bang, 1968. Built his first permanent construction The Rhythmical Time Fountain, for the City of Nottingham Victoria Centre, 1974. The fully-working three-dimensional inventions include: the Exploratory Moon-probe Lunacycle "Maud"; the Borg Warner Vintage Car of the Future, permanently in the Museum of Science and Industry, Chicago; SS Pussiewillow II, personal air-and-space vehicle, commnd by and housed in Nat. Mus. of Air and Space, Smithsonian Instn, Washington DC. The Featherstone Kite Openwork Basket-weave Gentleman's Flying Machine, together with seven other inventions, have been acquired by Ontario Science Centre, Toronto. Pussiewillow III, a celestial cats'-cradle, commnd by Basildon New Town. *Publications:* collections from Punch incl. Home Rails Preferred, Engines Aunties and Others, and Saturday Slow; The Early Morning Milk Train, 1978; Alarms and Excursions, 1978; two signed limited-edn prints, 1978. *Address:* Wild Goose Cottage, 113 East End Lane, Ditchling, Hassocks, West Sussex BN6 8UR. *T:* Hassocks 2459; Nell Gwynn House, Sloane Avenue, SW3 3AX.

EMLYN, Viscount; Colin Robert Vaughan Campbell; *b* 30 June 1962; *s* and *heir* of Earl Cawdor, *qv*. *Educ:* Eton; St Peter's College, Oxford. Member, James Bridal Meml Soc., London.

EMLYN JONES, John Hubert, MBE 1941; FRICS; JP; Member of the Lands Tribunal, since 1968; *b* 6 Aug. 1915; *s* of late Ernest Pearson Jones and Katharine Cole Jones (*née* Nicholas); *m* 1954, Louise Anne Montague, *d* of late Raymond Ralph Horwood Hazell; two *s* one *d*. *Educ:* Dulwich. FRICS 1939. Served War, RE, 1939-46: Major 1943. Partner, Rees-Reynolds and

Hunt, and Alfred Savill & Sons, Chartered Surveyors, 1950-68. President: Rating Surveyors Assoc., 1965-66 (Hon. Mem. 1968); Climbers' Club, 1966-69 (Hon. Mem. 1970). Mem. Council, RICS, 1964-69. Mem. Bureau, 1964-72, Treasurer 1967-69, Fédération Internationale des Géomètres; Mem. Council, Rainer Foundn, 1965- (Chm. 1968-71). Mem., expedns to Himalayas: Annapurna, 1950; Ama Dablam, 1959 (Leader). High Sheriff, Bucks, 1967-68, JP 1968. *Publications:* articles and revs in mountaineering jls. *Recreations:* mountaineering, music. *Address:* Ivinghoe Manor, Leighton Buzzard, Beds. *T:* Cheddington 668202. *Clubs:* Garrick, Alpine (Hon. Sec., 1955-62; Pres., 1980-82).

EMMERSON, Sir Harold Corti, GCB 1956 (KCB 1947; CB 1942); KCVO 1953; *b* 1896; *m* 1931, Lucy Kathleen Humphreys; two *s* three *d*. *Educ:* Warrington Secondary Sch. Served War of 1914-18 in Royal Marine Artillery. Ministry of Labour, 1920; Secretary Government Mission on Industrial Conditions in Canada and United States, 1926-27; Secretary Royal Commn on Unemployment Insurance, 1930-32; Principal Private Secretary to Ministers of Labour, 1933-35; Secretary Department of Commissioner for Special Areas, 1938-39; Principal Officer, Civil Defence, Northern Region, 1939-40; Under-Secretary Ministry of Home Security, 1940-42; Chief Industrial Commissioner, Ministry of Labour, 1942-44; Deputy-Secretary and Director General of Man Power, 1944-46; Permanent Secretary: Ministry of Works, 1946-56; Ministry of Labour, 1956-59. Member: Security Inquiry Cttee, 1961; Council on Prices, Productivity and Incomes, 1960-62; War Works Commission, 1960-64; Council on Tribunals, 1961-64. Chairman, London Government Staff Commn, 1963-65. Hon. MA Liverpool. *Publication:* The Ministry of Works, 1956. *Address:* 26 Millfield, Berkhamsted, Herts. *Club:* Arts.

EMMERSON, Rt. Rev. Ralph; an Assistant Bishop, Diocese of Wakefield, since 1980; *b* 7 June 1913; *s* of Thomas and Alys Mary Emmerson; *m* 1942, Ann Hawthorn Bygate (*d* 1982); no *c*. *Educ:* Leeds Grammar Sch.; King's Coll., London (BD, AKC); Westcott House, Cambridge. Leeds Educn Authority Youth Employment Dept, 1930-35; Curate, St George's, Leeds, 1938-41; Priest-in-Charge, Seacroft Estate, 1941-48; Rector of Methley and Vicar of Mickletown, 1949-56; Vicar of Headingley, 1956-66; Hon. Canon of Ripon Cath., 1964; Residentiary Canon and Canon Missioner for Dio. Ripon, 1966-72; Bishop Suffragan of Knaresborough, 1972-79. *Address:* 24 Laburnum Road, Wakefield WF1 3QS. *T:* Wakefield 369455.

EMMET, Dorothy Mary, MA Oxon and Manchester; *b* 1904; *d* of late Rev. C. W. Emmet, Fellow of University Coll., Oxford, and late Gertrude Julia Emmet (*née* Weir). *Educ:* St Mary's Hall, Brighton; Lady Margaret Hall, Oxford. Classical Exhibitioner, Lady Margaret Hall, Oxford, 1923; Hon. Mods Class I, 1925; Lit. Hum. Class I, 1927. Tutor, Maesyrhaf Settlement, Rhondda Valley, 1927-28 and 1931-32; Commonwealth Fellow, Radcliffe Coll., Cambridge, Mass, USA, 1928-30; Research Fellow, Somerville Coll., Oxford, 1930-31; lecturer in Philosophy, Armstrong Coll., Newcastle upon Tyne, 1932-38 (now Newcastle Univ.); lecturer in Philosophy of Religion, University of Manchester, 1938-45; Reader in Philosophy, 1945-46; Prof. of Philosophy, University of Manchester, 1946-66; Prof. Emeritus, 1966. Stanton Lecturer in Philosophy of Religion, University of Cambridge, 1950-53. Visiting Professor: Barnard Coll., Columbia Univ., New York, 1960-61; Univ. of Ibadan, Nigeria, 1974. President Aristotelian Society, 1953-54. Dean of the Faculty of Arts, University of Manchester, 1962-64. Hon. Fellow, Lady Margaret Hall, Oxford. Fellow, Lucy Cavendish Coll., Cambridge, 1967, Emeritus Fellow, 1981. Hon. DLitt: Glasgow, 1974; Leicester, 1976. *Publications:* Whitehead's Philosophy of Organism, 1932, 2nd edn 1982; Philosophy and Faith, 1936; The Nature of Metaphysical Thinking, 1945; Function, Purpose and Powers, 1958, 2nd edn 1972; Rules, Roles and Relations, 1966; (ed with Alasdair MacIntyre) Sociological Theory and Philosophical Analysis, 1970; The Moral Prism, 1979; contributions to philosophical journals. *Recreations:* gardening, reading. *Address:* 11 Millington Road, Cambridge.
See also Prof. R. C. Wilson.

EMMETT, Bryan David; Chief Executive, Employment Service Division, Manpower Services Commission, since 1982; *b* 15 Feb. 1941; *m* 1960, Moira (*née* Miller); one *s*. *Educ:* Tadcaster Grammar Sch. Clerical Officer, Min. of Labour, and National Service, 1958-59; Exec. Officer, War Dept, 1959-64; Asst Principal, MOP, 1965-69 (Asst Private Sec. to Ministers of Power, 1968-69); Principal, Electricity Div., DTI, 1969-74; Department of Energy: Principal, and Private Sec. to Minister of State, 1974-75; Asst Sec., and Principal Private Sec. to Sec. of State for Energy, 1975-76; Asst Sec., Petroleum Engrg Div., 1977-80; Under Sec., and Principal Estab. Officer, 1980-81; Principal Estab. and Finance Officer, 1981-82. *Recreations:* National Hunt racing, hacking, driving a Scimitar. *Address:* Manpower Services Commission, 1 Moorfoot, Sheffield S1 4PQ.

EMMETT, Harold Leslie; Assistant Under-Secretary of State, Ministry of Defence, 1972-79; *b* 20 Sept. 1919; 4th *s* of Alfred and Charlotte Emmett (*née* Frith); *m* 1943, Phyllis Mabel (*née* Tranah); three *s* one *d*. *Educ:* Gillingham Grammar Sch., Kent. Joined Civil Service (Admiralty), 1938; transf. to War Office, 1948; Principal, 1951; Asst Sec., 1960; Command Sec., HQ BAOR, 1964-67; Imperial Defence College, 1968; seconded to Home Office for service with New Scotland Yard, 1969-70. *Recreation:* golf. *Address:* 9 Oakdale Road, Tunbridge Wells, Kent. *T:* Tunbridge Wells 22658.

EMMINGER, Otmar, Dr oec. publ.; Chairman, Deutsche Pfandbriefanstalt, since 1980; Governor, Deutsche Bundesbank (Federal Bank), 1977-79; *b* Augsburg, 2 March 1911; *s* of Erich Emminger, Senatspräsident (Reichsminister der Justiz, 1923-24) and Maria Scharff; *m* 1966, Dr *rer. pol.* Gisela Boden; two *s. Educ:* in Law and Economics, at Univs of Berlin, Munich, Edinburgh, and London Sch. of Economics. Mem. and Div. Chief, Inst. for Business Research (Institut für Konjunkturforschung), Berlin, 1935-39. Served War of 1939-45. Div. Chief, Bavarian Min. of Economics, 1947-50; Mem. German Delegn to OEEC, Paris, 1949-50; Dir, Research and Statistics Dept, Bank deutscher Länder, 1951-53; Mem. Bd of Governors, Deutsche Bundesbank (Federal Bank), 1953-69, Dep. Governor, 1970-77; Exec. Dir, IMF, Washington, 1953-59, a Governor, 1977-80. Dep. Chm., Monetary Cttee, EEC, 1958-77; Chm., Monetary Cttee of OECD, 1969-77; Chm., Deputies of Group of Ten, 1964-67. *Publications:* Die englischen Währungsexperimente der Nachkriegszeit, 1934; Deutschlands Stellung in der Weltwirtschaft, 1953; Währungspolitik im Wandel der Zeit, 1966; Zwanzig Jahre deutsche Geldpolitik, 1968; Verteidigung der D Mark, 1980. *Recreations:* ski-ing, hiking. *Address:* Frankfurt am Main, Hasselhorstweg 36, West Germany. *T:* 684354.

EMMS, David Acfield, MA; Master, Dulwich College, since 1975; *b* 16 Feb. 1925; *s* of late Archibald George Emms and Winifred Gladys (*née* Richards); *m* 1950, Pamela Baker Speed; three *s* one *d. Educ:* Tonbridge Sch.; Brasenose Coll., Oxford. BA Hons Mod. Langs Oxford, 1950, Diploma in Education, 1951; MA 1954. Rugby football, Oxford *v* Cambridge, 1949, 1950. Served War of 1939-45, RA, 1943-47. Undergraduate, 1947-51; Asst Master, Uppingham Sch. (Head of Mod. Languages Dept, CO, CCF Contingent), 1951-60; Headmaster of: Cranleigh School, 1960-70; Sherborne School, 1970-74. Vice-Pres., Independent Schs Careers Organisation, 1973–; Hon. Treasurer, HMC, 1981–. Governor: E-SU; St Felix Sch., Southwold; Feltonfleet Sch., Cobham. Freeman, City of London; Extra Mem., Ct, Skinners' Co. *Publication:* HMC Schools and British Industry, 1981. *Recreations:* radical gardening, sailing. *Address:* Elm Lawn, Dulwich Common, SE21; Seaforth, Spinney Lane, Itchenor, W Sussex. *Clubs:* Athenæum, East India, Devonshire, Sports and Public Schools; Vincent's (Oxford).

EMMS, John Frederick George, FIA; a Vice-Chairman, Commercial Union Assurance Company Ltd, since 1979; *b* 2 Sept. 1920; *s* of late John Stanley Emms and Alice Maud Emms (*née* Davies); *m* 1942, Margaret Alison Hay; one *s* one *d* (and one *s* decd). *Educ:* Harrow County Sch.; Latymer Upper Sch. FIA. Served War RA/RCS, 1939-46. Joined Commercial Union Assurance Co. Ltd, 1938; Investment Manager, 1968-70; Chief Investment Manager, 1970-72; Dir, 1972; Exec. Dir, 1974; Chief General Manager, 1977-82. Dir, Barclays Bank UK, 1981–. Mem., NEB, 1979–. Member: (and past Chm.) Spastics Soc.; Finance Sub-Cttee, British Red Cross. Mem. Adv. Panel, NCB Superannuation and Pension Schemes. *Recreations:* sport, reading. *Address:* 7 Eastglade, Pinner, Middlesex HA5 3AN. *T:* 01-868 6151.

EMPSON, Sir Charles, KCMG 1956 (CMG 1943); Foreign Service, retired; *b* 24 April 1898; *s* of late Arthur Reginald Empson, Yokefleet, East Yorks; *m* 1931, Monica, *d* of late Canon J. W. S. Tomlin; one *s* one *d. Educ:* Harrow; Magdalene Coll., Cambridge. War Service, 1917-19 (Mesopotamia); joined staff of Civil Commissioner, Bagdad, 1920, and remained on staff of High Commissioner, Bagdad, until 1934 (Consul, 1924-32, Commercial Secretary, 1932-34); Commercial Agent for Palestine, 1934-38; Commercial Secretary HM Embassy, Rome, 1938-39; Commercial Counsellor, HM Embassy, Cairo, 1939-46; Minister (Economic), Special Commission in SE Asia, 1946-47; Minister (Commercial) HM Embassy, Rome, 1947-50; Minister (Commercial) HM Embassy, Washington, 1950-55; Ambassador to Chile, 1955-58. Rural District Councillor, Bridge-Blean, 1960-74. *Address:* Seatonden, Ickham, Canterbury, Kent. *Club:* English-Speaking Union.

EMPSON, Adm. Sir (Leslie) Derek, GBE 1975; KCB 1973 (CB 1969); Consultant, THORN EMI (formerly EMI) Ltd, since 1976; Commander-in-Chief Naval Home Command and Flag Officer Portsmouth Area, 1974-75; Flag ADC to The Queen, 1974-75; *b* 29 Oct. 1918; *s* of Frank Harold Empson and Madeleine Norah Empson (*née* Burge); *m* 1958, Diana Elizabeth Kelly; one *s* one *d. Educ:* Eastbourne Coll.; Clare Coll., Cambridge (Class. Exhibn). Athletics Blue, 1939; BA 1940. Joined Royal Navy for pilot duties, 1940; commd as Sub-Lieut (A) RNVR, 1940; flew as Fleet Air Arm pilot, 1940-45; perm. commn in RN, 1944; Naval Asst to First Sea Lord, 1957-59; Comd HMS Eagle, 1963-65; Imp. Def. Coll., 1966; Flag Officer, Aircraft Carriers, 1967-68; Asst Chief of Naval Staff (Operations and Air), 1968-69; Comdr, Far East Fleet, 1969-71; Second Sea Lord and Chief of Naval Personnel, 1971-74. Comdr 1952; Captain 1957; Rear-Adm. 1967; Vice-Adm. 1970; Adm. 1972. Chm. of Governors, Eastbourne Coll., 1972–. *Address:* Deepdale, Hambledon, Hants. *T:* Hambledon 451. *Clubs:* MCC, Naval; Hawks (Cambridge), Achilles.

EMPSON, Sir William, Kt 1979; FBA 1976; Professor of English Literature, Sheffield University, 1953-71, now Emeritus; *b* 27 Sept. 1906; *s* of late A. R. Empson, Yokefleet Hall, Howden, Yorks, and Laura (*née* Micklethwait); *m* 1941, Hester Henrietta Crouse; two *s. Educ:* Winchester; Magdalene Coll., Cambridge. Chair of English Literature, Bunrika Daigaku, Tokyo, 1931-34; Professorship in English Literature, Peking National University, then part of the South-Western Combined Universities, in Hunan and Yunnan, 1937-39;

BBC Chinese Editor, 1941-46, after a year in BBC Monitoring Dept; returned to Peking National Univ., 1947, Prof., Western Languages Department. Hon. LittD East Anglia, 1968; Hon. DLitt Bristol, 1971; Hon. LittD: Sheffield, 1974; Cambridge, 1977. *Publications:* Seven Types of Ambiguity, 1930; Poems, 1935; Some Versions of Pastoral, 1935; The Gathering Storm (verse), 1940; The Structure of Complex Words, 1951; Collected Poems, 1955; Milton's God, 1961; (ed with D. Pirie) Selected Poems of Coleridge, 1972. *Address:* Studio House, 1 Hampstead Hill Gardens, NW3.

EMSLIE, family name of **Baron Emslie.**

EMSLIE, Baron *cr* 1980 (Life Peer), of Potterton in the District of Gordon; **George Carlyle Emslie,** PC 1972; MBE 1946; Lord Justice-General of Scotland and Lord President of the Court of Session, since 1972; *b* 6 Dec. 1919; *s* of late Alexander and Jessie Blair Emslie; *m* Lilias Ann Mailer Hannington; three *s. Educ:* The High School of Glasgow; The University of Glasgow (MA, LLB). Commissioned A&SH, 1940; served War of 1939-45 (despatches): North Africa, Italy, Greece, Austria, 1942-46; psc Haifa, 1944; Brigade Major (Infantry), 1944-46. Advocate, 1948; Advocate Depute (Sheriff Courts), 1955; QC (Scotland) 1957; Sheriff of Perth and Angus, 1963-66; Dean of Faculty of Advocates, 1965-70; Senator of Coll. of Justice in Scotland and Lord of Session, 1970-72. Chm., Scottish Agricultural Wages Bd, 1969-73; Mem., Council on Tribunals (Scottish Cttee), 1962-70. Hon. Bencher: Inner Temple, 1974; Inn of Court of N Ireland, 1981. Hon. LLD Glasgow, 1973. *Recreation:* golf. *Address:* 47 Heriot Row, Edinburgh EH3 6EX. *T:* 031-225 3657. *Clubs:* Caledonian; New (Edinburgh); The Honourable Company of Edinburgh Golfers.

EMSLIE, Prof. Ronald Douglas, FDSRCS; Dean of Dental Studies, Guy's Hospital Medical and Dental Schools, 1968-80, retired; Professor of Periodontology and Preventive Dentistry, University of London, 1970-80, now Emeritus; *b* 9 March 1915; *s* of late Alexander G. H. Emslie and Elizabeth Spence; *m* 1951, Dorothy, *d* of William A. Dennis, Paris, Ill, USA; four *s. Educ:* Felsted Sch.; Guy's Hosp. Dental Sch., London (BDS); Univ. of Illinois, Chicago (MSc). FDSRCS Eng., 1950; DRD (Edin), 1978. Served War: Surg. Lt (D) RNVR, 1943-46; Surg. Lt Comdr (D) RNVR, 1946. Half-time Asst in Dept of Preventive Dentistry, Guy's Hosp., 1946-48, also in private practice with Mr E. B. Dowsett; Research Fellow, Univ. of Illinois, Chicago, 1948-49; Head of Dept of Preventive Dentistry, Guy's Hosp., 1949-55; Reader in Preventive Dentistry, Univ. of London (Guy's Hosp. Dental Sch.), 1956-62; Prof. of Preventive Dentistry, Univ. of London (Guy's Hosp. Dental Sch.), 1963-70. Pres., Brit. Soc. of Periodontology, 1959-60; Chm., Dental Health Cttee of BDA, 1963-69; Member: Internat. Dental Fedn; Internat. Assoc. for Dental Research; Dental Educn Adv. Council (Chm., 1978-80); Bd of Faculty of Dental Surgery, RCS, 1966-81 (Vice-Dean, 1976-77); Fluoridation Soc. (Chm. 1970-80); Bd of Studies in Dentistry, Univ. of London (Chm., 1975-77). Past Pres., Odontological Section, RSM; Vis. Lectr, Univ. of Illinois, 1956; Nuffield Grant to study dental aspects of facial gangrene, in Nigeria, Sept.-Dec. 1961; Sci. Advr, Brit. Dental Jl, 1961-80 (Sci. Asst Ed., 1951-61); WHO expert adv. panel on dental health; Consultant in Periodontology to RN, 1971-80. Fellow, BDA. *Publications:* various contribs to dental literature. *Recreations:* tennis, sailing, old motor cars. *Address:* Little Hale, Woodland Way, Kingswood, Surrey. *T:* Mogador 832662.

EMSON, Air Marshal Sir Reginald (Herbert Embleton), KBE 1966 (CBE 1946); CB 1959; AFC 1941; Inspector-General of the Royal Air Force, 1967-69; *b* 11 Jan. 1912; *s* of Francis Reginald Emson, Hitcham, Buckinghamshire; *m* 1934, Doreen Marjory, *d* of Hugh Duke, Holyport, Maidenhead, Berkshire; two *s* two *d. Educ:* Christ's Hospital; RAF Coll., Cranwell. Joined RAF, 1931; served War of 1939-45 in Aeroplane Armament Establishment Gunnery Research Unit, Exeter; Fighter Command Headquarters and Central Fighter Establishment. Director, Armament Research and Development (Air), Ministry of Supply, 1950-59; Commander RAF Staff and Air Attaché, British Defence Staffs, Washington, 1961-63; Asst Chief of Air Staff (Operational Requirements), 1963-66; Dep. Chief Air Staff, 1966-67. Group Captain, 1943; Air Commodore, 1958; Air Vice-Marshal, 1962; Air Marshal (Acting), 1966. *Address:* Vor Cottage, Holyport, Maidenhead, Berks. *T:* Maidenhead 21992. *Club:* Royal Air Force.

ENCOMBE, Viscount; John Francis Thomas Marie Joseph Columba Fidelis Scott; *b* 9 July 1962; *s* and *heir* of 5th Earl of Eldon, *qv.*

ENDERBY, Prof. John Edwin; Professor of Physics, since 1976, Head of Department of Physics, since 1981 and Director, H. H. Wills Physics Laboratory, since 1981, University of Bristol; *b* 16 Jan. 1931; *s* of Thomas Edwin Enderby and Rheita Rebecca Hollinshead (*née* Stather); *m* 1957, Jennifer Mary (*née* Henson); one *s* one *d. Educ:* Chester Grammar Sch.; London Univ. (BSc, PhD). Lecturer in Physics: Coll. of Technology, Huddersfield, 1957-60; Univ. of Sheffield, 1960-67; Reader in Physics, Univ. of Sheffield, 1967-69; Prof. in Physics and Head of the Dept, Univ. of Leicester, 1969-76. Visiting Fellow, Battelle Inst., 1968-69; Vis. Prof., Univ. of Guelph, Ont., 1978. Member: Physics Cttee, SRC, 1974-77; Neutron Beam Res. Cttee, SRC, 1974-80 (Chm., 1977-80). Mem. Council, Institut Laue-Langevin, Grenoble, 1973-80. FInstP 1970 (Chm., SW Br., 1979-). Associate Editor, Philosophical Magazine, 1975-81. *Publications:* (jointly): Physics of Simple Liquids, 1968; Amorphous and Liquid Semiconductors, 1974; many publications on the structure and properties of liquids in: Phil. Mag. Adv. Phys, Jl Phys, Proc. Royal Soc., etc. *Recreations:* gardening, watching

Association football. *Address:* H. H. Wills Physics Laboratory, Tyndall Avenue, Bristol BS8 1TL. *T:* Bristol 24161.

ENDERBY, Kenneth Albert; General Manager, Runcorn Development Corporation, 1978-81; *b* 7 Aug. 1920; *s* of Albert William Enderby and Frances Enderby; *m* 1946, Mary Florence; one *s* two *d*. *Educ:* Nottingham High Sch.; London Univ. (BSc Econs). IPFA. Served War, Royal Corps of Signals (TA), 1939-46: BEF, MEF, CMF (mentioned in despatches, 1944); Captain. Local Govt Finance: Nottingham, 1936-51; Buckingham, 1951-53; Chief Auditor, City of Sheffield, 1953-56; Dep. City Treasurer, Coventry, 1956-64; Chief Finance Officer, Runcorn Develt Corp., 1964-78. *Recreations:* gardening, camping, fresh air, zymology. *Address:* Four Winds, 2 Helmeth Road, Church Stretton, Salop SY6 7AS. *T:* Church Stretton 722328.

ENDERBY, Col Samuel, CVO 1977; DSO 1943; MC 1939; JP; *b* 15 Sept. 1907; *s* of Col Samuel Enderby and Mary Cuninghame; *m* 1936, Pamela, *e d* of Major Charles Beck Hornby, DSO; two *s* one *d*. *Educ:* Uppingham Sch.; RMC Sandhurst. Regular soldier, commissioned 5th Fusiliers, 1928. Served War, 1939-46: MEF, CMF, comd 2/4th KOYLI and 2/5 Leicester Regt; Commandant, Sch. of Infantry: ACRE, 1945-46; Netheravon, 1947-48; comd 7th Bn Royal Northumberland Fusiliers, 1949; retd 1949. JP 1956; High Sheriff of Northumberland, 1968. Mem., Hon. Corps of Gentlemen at Arms, 1954-77, Standard Bearer, 1976-77. *Address:* The Riding, Hexham, Northumberland. *T:* Hexham 2250. *Club:* Army and Navy.

ENDERL, Dr Kurt H.; Ambassador of Austria to the Court of St James's, 1975-78, retired 1979; *b* 12 April 1913; *s* of Hugo Enderl and Karoline Enderl; *m* 1967, Adele Leigh. *Educ:* Vienna Univ. (Dr of Law). 3rd Sec., Austrian Legation, London, 1946-47; Chargé d'Affaires, Aust. Legation, New Delhi, 1950-53; Austrian Minister in Israel, 1955-58; Head of Multilateral Economic Dept, Min. of Foreign Affairs, Vienna, 1958-61; Austrian Ambassador: in Poland, 1962-67; in Hungary, 1967-72; Chief of Protocol, Vienna, 1972-74. *Recreations:* tennis, ski-ing. *Address:* Linke Wienzeile 12, 1060 Vienna, Austria.

ENDERS, Dr John Franklin; Chief, Virus Unit, Division of Infectious Diseases, Children's Medical Center, Boston, Mass, since 1972 (Chief of Research Division, 1947-72); University Professor Emeritus, Harvard University, since 1967; *b* 10 Feb. 1897; *s* of John Ostrom Enders and Harriet Goulden Whitmore; *m* 1927, Sarah Frances Bennett (*d* 1943); one *s* one *d* ; 1951, Carolyn Bernice Keane; one step *s*. *Educ:* St Paul's Sch., Concord, NH; Yale Univ. (BA 1919); Harvard Univ. (MA 1922, PhD 1930). USNR Flying Corps, 1917-20. Teaching and research in field of infectious diseases of man, 1927-. Member Faculty Harvard Medical Sch., 1929-67; Civ. Cons. to Secretary of War on Epidemic Diseases in Army, 1942-46; Member Commn on Virus Dis, US Army, 1949-68; Member WHO Expert Advisory Panel on Virus Diseases, 1958. Passano Award, 1953; Lasker Award, 1954; Nobel Laureate, 1954, in Physiology or Medicine; Cameron Prize, 1960; Ricketts Award, 1962; Robert Koch Medal, 1963; Galen Award, Soc. of Apothecaries, 1981. US Presidential Medal of Freedom, 1963; Commander of the Republic of Upper Volta, 1965. Member: National Academy of Sciences (US); American Philosophical Society; Academie Nat. de Med. (France); Deut. Akad. d. Naturforsch. (Leopoldina); Hon. Member: RSM (England); Acad. Roy. de Med. (Belgium); Foreign Mem., Royal Soc. (England); Associé honoraire étranger, Académie des Sciences, Inscriptions et Belles-Lettres de Toulouse; Associé étranger, Académie des Sciences de l'Institut de France. Fellow American Academy of Arts and Sciences. Hon. FACS. Holds several honorary degrees. *Publications:* (joint) Immunity: Principles and Application in Medicine and Public Health, 1939; papers in scientific journals. *Recreations:* fishing, sailing. *Address:* 64 Colbourne Crescent, Brookline, Mass 02147, USA. *T:* Longwood 6-3539. *Clubs:* Country (Brookline); Harvard, Saturday (Boston, Mass).

ENERGLYN, Baron *cr* 1968 (Life Peer), of Caerphilly; **William David Evans,** MSc, DSc, PhD; DL; Professor of Geology, University of Nottingham, 1949-78; formerly Dean of the Faculty of Pure Science; *b* 25 Dec. 1912; *s* of Councillor D. G. Evans; *m* 1941, Jean Thompson Miller; no *c*. *Educ:* Caerphilly Grammar Sch.; University Coll., Cardiff. Geologist to HM Geological Survey of Great Britain, 1939; Member of Regional Survey Board of Ministry of Fuel and Power for South Wales Coalfield, 1945; Senior Lecturer in Geology, University College of South Wales and Monmouthshire, 1947. FGS 1939; FRGS 1944; FLS 1945; MIME 1952; MIMM 1949. MSc Wales, 1938; PhD London, 1940. DL Notts, 1974. Hon. Fellow, Mark Twain Soc. of America, 1976. *Publications:* Through the Crust of the Earth, 1974; research papers in Trans and Proc. of Geol Society of London, Royal Geog. Society, Institute of Mining and Metallurgy, etc, on geology of older rocks of Wales, and Cornwall, and cause of dust diseases among coalminers and metalliferous miners at home and abroad. *Address:* 7 The Dentons, Denton Road, Eastbourne, E Sussex BN20 7SW. *Club:* Royal Automobile.

ENFIELD, Viscount; Thomas Edmund Byng; *b* 26 Sept. 1936; *s* and *heir* of 9th Earl of Strafford, *qv* ; *m* 1963, Jennifer Mary (marr. diss.), *er d* of late Rt Hon. W. M. May, PC, FCA, MP, and of Mrs May, Mertoun Hall, Holywood, Co. Down; two *s* two *d* ; *m* 1981, Mrs Judy M. Howard. *Educ:* Eton; Clare Coll., Cambridge. Lieut, Royal Sussex Regt (National Service). *Recreation:* gardening. *Heir: s* Hon. William Robert Byng, *b* 10 May 1964. *Address:* Abbots Worthy House, Abbots Worthy, Winchester, Hants. *T:* Winchester 881333.

ENGHOLM, Sir Basil Charles, KCB 1968 (CB 1964); Director, Comfin Ltd, since 1973; *b* 2 Aug. 1912; *o s* of late C. F. G. Engholm; *m* 1936, Nancy, *er d* of Lifford Hewitt, St Anthony, Rye; one *d*. *Educ:* Tonbridge Sch.; Sorbonne, Paris; Sidney Sussex Coll., Cambridge (Law Tripos, MA). Member of Gray's Inn; Metal business, New York, 1933-34; entered Ministry of Agriculture and Fisheries, 1935; War of 1939-45: part-time NFS; Principal Private Secretary to Minister of Agriculture and Fisheries, 1943-45; Asst Secretary, 1945; Under-Secretary, 1954; Fisheries Secretary, 1960-62; Dep. Secretary, 1964-67; Permanent Sec., MAFF, 1968-72. Governor: Sadler's Wells Theatre, 1975-; BFI, 1978-81 (Chm., 1978-81); Trustee, Theatre Trust, 1977-. *Recreations:* reading, theatre, opera, ballet, films, looking at pictures. *Address:* 93 Meadway, NW11. *T:* 01-455 3975. *Club:* United Oxford & Cambridge University.

ENGLAND, Frank Raymond Wilton; *b* 24 Aug. 1911; *s* of Joseph and Florence England; *m* ; one *d*. *Educ:* Christ Coll., Finchley. Served War, Pilot, RAF, 1941-45. Apprenticeship with Daimler Co. Ltd, Hendon, 1927-32; Racing Mechanic to: Sir Henry Birkin, Whitney Straight, ERA Ltd, Richard Seaman, B. Bira, 1932-38; Service Engr, Service Dept Supt, Alvis Limited, 1938-40. Service Manager, Jaguar Cars Ltd, 1946-56; Service Dir, 1956-61; Asst Man. Dir, 1961-66; Dep. Man. Dir, 1966-67; Jt Man. Dir, 1967; Dep. Chm., 1968; Chm. and Chief Executive, 1972; retd as Chm., Jan. 1974. *Recreation:* motor sport. *Address:* 196 Gmundnerberg, 4813 Altmünster, Austria. *T:* 07612 88316. *Clubs:* Royal Air Force, British Racing Drivers'.

ENGLAND, Glyn, BSc(Eng); FEng, FIEE, FIMechE, FBIM; Chairman, Central Electricity Generating Board, 1977-82 (part-time member, 1975-77); *b* 19 April 1921; *m* 1942, Tania Reichenbach; two *d*. *Educ:* Penarth County Sch.; Queen Mary Coll., London Univ. (BSc (Eng)); London School of Economics. Department of Scientific and Industrial Research, 1939. War service, 1942-47. Electricity Supply Industry 1947-; Chief Ops Engr, CEGB, 1966-71; Dir-Gen., SW Region, 1971-73; Chm., SW Electricity Bd, 1973-77. Mem., British Nat. Cttee, World Energy Conf., 1977; Vice-Pres., Internat. Union of Producers and Distributors of Electrical Energy, 1981-. Sometime Labour Mem., Herts CC; Mem. Council, Magistrates' Assoc. JP Welwyn, Herts, 1962-71. Hon. DSc Bath, 1981. *Publications:* papers on: Clean Air, Conservation of Water Resources, Economic Growth and the Electricity Supply Industry, Security of Electricity Supplies, Planning for Uncertainty, Landscape in the Making. *Recreation:* actively enjoying the countryside. *Address:* Woodbridge Farm, Ubley, Bristol BS18 6PX. *T:* Blagdon 62479.

ENGLE, George Lawrence Jose, CB 1976; First Parliamentary Counsel, since 1981; *b* 13 Sept. 1926; *o s* of late Lawrence Engle; *m* 1956, Irene, *d* of late Heinz Lachmann; three *d*. *Educ:* Charterhouse (scholar); Christ Church, Oxford (Marjoribanks and Dixon schols, MA). Served RA, 1945-48 (2nd Lt, 1947). Firsts in Mods and Greats; Cholmeley Schol., Lincoln's Inn, 1952; called to Bar, Lincoln's Inn, 1953. Joined parly counsel office, 1957; seconded as First Parly Counsel, Fedn of Nigeria, 1965-67; Parly Counsel, 1970-80; Second Parly Counsel, 1980-81; with Law Commn, 1971-73. *Publications:* Law for Landladies, 1955; contributor to: Ideas, 1954, and O Rare Hoffnung, 1960. *Recreations:* book-hunting, oriental and Islamic pots, bricolage. *Address:* 32 Wood Lane, Highgate, N6. *T:* 01-340 9750.

ENGLEDOW, Sir Frank Leonard, Kt 1944; CMG 1935; FRS 1946; MA, BSc; Fellow of St John's College, Cambridge; Drapers' Professor of Agriculture, Cambridge University, 1930-57; *b* 1890; *m* Mildred (*d* 1956); four *d*. *Educ:* St John's Coll., Cambridge. The Queen's Own (Royal West Kent Regt), 1914-18; Adjutant, 5th Batt. Mesopotamian Expeditionary Force; retiring rank Lt-Col; asst Director of Agriculture, Mesopotamia, 1918-19. *Publication:* (ed) Britain's Future in Farming. *Address:* The Hope Nursing Home, Brooklands Avenue, Cambridge CB2 2BQ. *T:* Cambridge 59087.

ENGLISH, Cyril; Director since 1978, and Chief General Manager since 1981, Nationwide Building Society; *b* 18 Feb. 1923; *s* of Joseph and Mary Hannah English; *m* 1945, Mary Brockbank; two *d*. *Educ:* Ashton-under-Lyne Grammar School. ALCM; CBIM. Joined Nationwide Building Society, 1939; Asst Secretary, 1961; Asst General Manager, 1967; General Manager, 1971; Deputy Chief General Manager, 1974. *Recreations:* golf, music. *Address:* Ashton Grange, Cedar Drive, Pangbourne, Berks. *T:* Pangbourne 3841. *Club:* Calcot Park Golf (Reading).

ENGLISH, Sir Cyril (Rupert), Kt 1972; retired; Director-General, City and Guilds of London Institute, 1968-76; *b* 19 April 1913; *m* ; two *s*. *Educ:* Northgate Sch., Ipswich. BScEng Ext. London, 1934. Technical teacher, 1935-39. Served Royal Navy, 1939-46, Lieut-Commander (E). HM Inspector of Schools, 1946-55; Staff Inspector (Engineering), 1955-58; Chief Inspector of Further Education, in connection with Industry and Commerce, 1958-65; Senior Chief Inspector, Dept of Education and Science, 1965-67. Member, Anglo-American Productivity Team, 1951; attended Commonwealth Education Conferences, Delhi, 1962, Ottawa, 1964. Chairman: British Assoc. for Commercial and Industrial Educn, 1970-71, 1971-72; RAF Educn Adv. Cttee; Member: Services Colleges Cttee, 1965-66; Adv. Bd, RAF Coll., Cranwell; Academic Adv. Council, Royal Defence Acad.; Bd of Dirs, Industrial Training Service; Central Training Council; CTC Gen. Policy Cttee; Nat. Adv. Council for Educn in Industry and Commerce; Council for Tech. Educn and Training for Overseas Countries (Bd Mem., Chm. Educn Cttee); Reg. Adv. Council for Technol. Educn (London and Home Counties); Schools Science and Technology Cttee; Educn Cttee, IMechE; Associated

Examining Bd; Cttee of Inquiry into Training of Teachers (James Cttee); Standing Conf. on Schs' Science and Technology; Cttee on Regular Officer training (Army). Vice-Pres., Soc. Electronic and Radio Technicians, 1972-74, Pres., 1975. Governor, Imperial Coll. FIMechE; FIProdE; FIMarE. Hon. Fellow, Inst. of Road Transport Engrs, 1971. Hon. Fellow, Manchester Polytechnic, 1976. Hon. DTech Brunel, 1970; Hon. DSc Loughborough, 1973; DUniv Open, 1974. *Address:* 12 Pineheath Road, High Kelling, Holt, Norfolk.

ENGLISH, Sir David, Kt 1982; Editor: Daily Mail, since 1971; Mail on Sunday, since 1982; *b* 26 May 1931; *m* 1954, Irene Mainwood; one *s* two *d*. *Educ:* Bournemouth Sch. Daily Mirror, 1951-53; Feature Editor, Daily Sketch, 1956; Foreign Correspondent: Sunday Dispatch, 1959; Daily Express, 1960; Washington Correspdt, Express, 1961-63; Chief American Correspdt, Express, 1963-65; Foreign Editor, Express, 1965-67; Associate Editor, Express, 1967-69; Editor, Daily Sketch, 1969-71. *Publication:* Divided They Stand (a British view of the 1968 American Presidential Election), 1969. *Recreations:* reading, ski-ing, boating. *Address:* Daily Mail, EC4Y 0JA. *T:* 01-353 6000. *Clubs:* Press; Royal Temple Yacht.

ENGLISH, Rev. Donald; General Secretary, Methodist Church Division of Home Mission, since 1982; President of the Methodist Conference, 1978-79; *b* 20 July 1930; *s* of Robert and Ena Forster English; *m* 1962, Bertha Forster Ludlow; two *s*. *Educ:* Consett Grammar Sch.; University Coll., Leicester; Wesley House, Cambridge. BA London; DipEd Leicester; MA Cantab. Education Officer, RAF, 1953-55; Travelling Sec., Inter-Varsity Fellowship, 1955-58; Asst Tutor, Wesley Coll., Headingley, 1960-62; ordained into Methodist Ministry, 1962; New Testament Tutor, Trinity Coll., Umuahia, E Nigeria, 1962-66; Circuit Minister, Cullercoats, Northumberland, 1966-72; Tutor in Historical Theology, Hartley Victoria Coll., Manchester (Lord Rank Chair), 1972-73; Tutor in Practical Theol. and Methodism, Wesley Coll., Bristol (Lord Rank Chair), 1973-82. Member: World Methodist Exec., 1976-; Presidium, World Methodist Council, 1981-; Chm., Nationwide Initiative in Evangelism, 1978-. Chm. Governors, Southlands Coll., 1979-. Hon. DD Asbury, USA, 1979. *Publications:* Evangelism and Worship, 1971; God in the Gallery, 1975; Christian Discipleship, 1977; Windows on the Passion, 1978; From Wesley's Chair: Presidential Addresses, 1979; contrib. Expository Times, Epworth Rev., Themelios, Proc. World Methodist Council. *Recreations:* gardening, reading. *Address:* 44 Anne Boleyn's Walk, Cheam, Surrey. *T:* 01-643 3679.

ENGLISH, Gerald; Director, Opera Studio, Victorian College for the Arts, Melbourne, since 1977; *b* 6 Nov. 1925; *m* 1954, Jennifer Ryan; two *s* two *d*; *m* 1974, Linda Jacoby; one *s*. *Educ:* King's Sch., Rochester. After War service studied at Royal College of Music and then began career as lyric tenor; subsequently travelled in USA and Europe, appeared at Sadler's Wells, Covent Garden and Glyndebourne and recorded for major gramophone companies; Professor, Royal Coll. of Music, 1960-77. *Address:* c/o Victorian College for the Arts, 234 St Kilda Road, Melbourne, Vic 3003, Australia.

ENGLISH, Michael; MP (Lab) Nottingham (West) since 1964; *b* 24 Dec. 1930; *s* of late William Agnew English; *m* 1976, Carol Christine Owen; one *s* one *d*. *Educ:* King George V Grammar Sch., Southport; Liverpool Univ. (LLB). Joined Labour Party, 1949; Rochdale County Borough Council, 1953-65 (Chairman Finance Cttee until 1964); contested (Lab) Shipley Div., WR Yorks, 1959. Member, official parliamentary panel NUGMW. Employed until 1964 as Asst Manager of department concerned with organisation and methods in subsidiary of large public company. Parliamentary Private Secretary, Board of Trade, 1966-67; Chairman: Parly Affairs Gp of Parly Lab. Party, 1970-76; Gen. Sub-Cttee of House of Commons Expenditure Cttee, 1974-79; Chm., E Midlands Gp, PLP, 1978-78; Mem., Chairmen's Panel, Treasury and Civil Service, and Procedure (Finance) Cttees, House of Commons. Chm., E Midlands Regional Lab. Party, 1979-80. *Recreation:* reading history. *Address:* House of Commons, SW1. *T:* 01-219 3552/3524.

ENGLISH, Terence Alexander Hawthorne, FRCS; Consultant Cardiothoracic Surgeon, Papworth and Addenbrooke's Hospitals, Cambridge, since 1973; Director, Papworth Heart Transplant Research Unit, since 1980; *b* 3 Oct. 1932; *s* of late Arthur Alexander English and Mavis Eleanor (née Lund); *m* 1963, Ann Margaret, *e d* of late Frederick Mordaunt Dicey and Ann Gwendoline (née Smartt); two *s* two *d*. *Educ:* Hilton Coll., Natal; Witwatersrand Univ. (BSc(Eng) 1954); Guy's Hosp. Med. Sch. (MB, BS 1962). FRCSE 1967, FRCS 1967. House appointments, Guy's Hosp., 1962-63; Demonstrator, Anatomy Dept, Guy's Hosp., 1964-65; Surgical Registrar: Bolingbroke Hosp., 1966; Brompton Hosp., 1967-68; Res. Fellow, Dept of Surgery, Univ. of Alabama, 1969; Sen. Registrar, Brompton, National Heart and London Chest Hosps, 1968-72. Mem., Specialists Adv. Cttee in Cardiothoracic Surgery, 1980-. Member: British Cardiac Soc., 1973-; British Transplantation Soc., 1980-; Soc. of Thoracic and Cardiovascular Surgeons, 1972- (Exec. Council, 1975-77); Thoracic Soc., 1971- (Exec. Council, 1978-81). Mem. Council, RCS, 1981-. Capt., Guy's Hosp. RFC, 1959-60. Hon. MA Cantab, 1977. *Publications:* chapter on Surgery of the Thorax and Heart in Bailey and Love's Short Practice of Thoracic Surgery, 1980; numerous articles in medical jls on matters relating to the practice of cardiac and thoracic surgery. *Recreations:* reading, music, walking, tennis. *Address:* 19 Adams Road, Cambridge CB3 9AD. *T:* Cambridge 68744.

ENNALS, Rt. Hon. David Hedley, PC 1970; MP (Lab) Norwich North, since Feb. 1974; *b* 19 Aug. 1922; *s* of A. F. Ennals, 8 Victoria Terrace, Walsall, Staffs; *m* 1st, 1950, Eleanor Maud Caddick (marr. diss. 1977); three *s* one *d*; 2nd, 1977, Mrs Katherine Tranoy. *Educ:* Queen Mary's Grammar School, Walsall; Loomis Inst., Windsor, Conn, USA. Served with HM Forces, 1941-46: Captain, RAC. Secretary, Council for Education in World Citizenship, 1947-52; Secretary, United Nations Association, 1952-57; Overseas Sec., Labour Party, 1957-64. MP (Lab) Dover, 1964-70; PPS to: Minister of Overseas Development, 1964; Minister of Transport, 1966; Parly Under-Sec. of State, Army, 1966-67; Parly Under-Sec., Home Office, 1967-68; Minister of State: DHSS, 1968-70; FCO, 1974-76; Sec. of State for Social Services, 1976-79. Campaign Dir, Nat. Assoc. for Mental Health, 1970-73; Chairman: Peter Bedford Housing Association, 1972-74; Campaign for Homeless and Rootless, 1972-74; Council, Ockenden Venture, 1972-76, 1979- (Dep. Chm. 1968-72). Chm., John Bellers Ltd, 1972-74. *Publications:* Strengthening the United Nations, 1957; Middle East Issues, 1958; United Nations Peace Force, 1960; United Nations on Trial, 1962; Out of Mind, 1973. *Recreation:* camping. *Address:* 8 St Anne's Close, N6.
See also J. A. F. Ennals, M. Ennals.

ENNALS, John Arthur Ford; Director, United Kingdom Immigrants Advisory Service, since 1970; *b* Walsall, 21 July 1918; *e s* of Arthur Ford Ennals, MC, and Jessie Edith Ennals (née Taylor); one *s* one *d*. *Educ:* Queen Mary's Grammar Sch., Walsall; St John's Coll., Cambridge. MA (History and Psychology). Rotary Travelling Schol. to USA, 1935. Pres., British Univs League of Nations Soc., and Cttee, Cambridge Union, 1938-39. Lectr for British Council, Roumania and Yugoslavia, 1939-40; War Corresp., Greece, Yugoslavia, Albania, 1941; on staff of British Embassy, Madrid, 1941-42, and Foreign Office, 1942-43. Served War: Egypt, Italy and Yugoslavia, 1943-45. Contested (Lab): Walsall South, 1955, 1959; Thames Valley, European Parly elecns, 1979. Secretary-Gen., World Fedn of UN Assocs, 1946-56; Gen.-Sec. and Tutor in Internat. Relations, Ruskin Coll., Oxford, 1956-66; Dir-Gen., UN Assoc., 1966-70 (Vice-Pres., 1978-); Hon. Pres., World Fedn of UN Assocs, 1977-; Member: OXFAM Exec., 1965-75; Exec. Council, Assoc. of Supervisory Staffs, Executives and Technicians, 1960-69. Trustee, Assoc. of Scientific Technical and Managerial Staffs, 1969-; Chm., Anti-Apartheid Movement, 1968-76; Member: Community Relations Cttee, Baptist Union, 1971-; Community and Race Relations Unit, British Council of Churches, 1971-79; Exec. Cttee, British Refugee Council, 1981-. Chm., British-Yugoslav Soc., 1982-. Parish Councillor: Kidlington, 1961-67; Hedgerley, 1976-. *Recreations:* travelling in Europe, Asia, Africa and the Americas; walking in Wales; tennis, cricket. *Address:* 3 Village Lane, Hedgerley, Bucks. *T:* (home) Farnham Common 4302; (office) 01-240 5176. *Club:* India.
See also Rt Hon. D. H. Ennals, M. Ennals.

ENNALS, Kenneth Frederick John; Deputy Secretary, Departments of the Environment and of Transport, since 1980; Director General of Organisation and Establishment; *b* 10 Jan. 1932; *s* of Ernest Ennals and Elsie Dorothy Ennals; *m* 1958, Mavis Euphemia; one *s* two *d*. *Educ:* Alleyn's Sch., Dulwich; LSE (part-time). Joined Export Credits Guarantee Dept, 1952; Principal, DEA, 1965-69; Min. of Housing and Local Govt, later DoE, 1969; Asst Sec., 1970, Under Sec., 1976-80, DoE. *Recreations:* reading, architecture, dog-walking. *Address:* St Anthony's, Tuesley Lane, Godalming, Surrey. *T:* Godalming 7239. *Club:* Royal Commonwealth Society.

ENNALS, Martin; international human rights consultant; Head of the Police Committee Support Unit, Greater London Council, since 1982; Chairman, Human Rights International Documentation System (HURIDOCS); *b* 27 July 1927; *s* of A. Ford Ennals and Jessie E. Ennals (née Taylor); *m* 1951, Jacqueline B. Ennals (née Morris); one *s* one *d*. *Educ:* Queen Mary's Sch., Walsall; London Sch. of Economics. BScEcon (Internat. Relations). UNESCO, 1951-59; Gen. Sec., National Council for Civil Liberties, 1960-66; Information Officer, Nat. Cttee for Commonwealth Immigrants, 1966-68 (resigned in protest at Govt's Commonwealth Immigration Act, 1968); Sec. Gen., Amnesty International (Nobel Peace Prize, 1977), 1968-80. Chm., Human Rights Cttee, UNA; a Vice-Pres., Campaign for Homosexual Equality. *Recreations:* escapist television and ski-ing. *Address:* 157 Southwood Lane, N6. *T:* 01-340 8629.
See also Rt Hon. D. H. Ennals, J. A. F. Ennals.

ENNISKILLEN, 6th Earl of, *cr* 1789; **David Lowry Cole,** MBE 1955; Baron Mountflorence, 1760; Viscount Enniskillen, 1776; Baron Grinstead (UK), 1815; farmer, Kenya and N Ireland; *b* 10 Sept. 1918; *er s* of Hon. Galbraith Lowry Egerton Cole (*d* 1929) (3rd *s* of 4th Earl of Enniskillen) and Lady Eleanor Cole (*d* 1979), *d* of 2nd Earl of Balfour; *S* uncle, 1963; *m* 1st, 1940, Sonia Mary Syers (from whom he obtained a divorce, 1955; she *d* 1982); one *s* one *d*; 2nd, 1955, Nancy Henderson MacLennan, former American Vice Consul. *Educ:* Eton; Trinity Coll., Cambridge. BA Agric. 1940. Served War of 1939-45, Captain Irish Guards: Kenya Emergency, 1953-55, Provincial Comdt, Kenya Police Reserve (MBE). MLC for North Kenya, 1961-63. Formerly: Member Kenya Meat Commn; Member Exec., Kenya National Farmers Union; Vice-Chairman Kenya Stockowners Council; Member Exec., Kenya Board of Agriculture; Member Board: Land and Agric. Bank of Kenya; East African Diatomite Syndicate Ltd. Captain, Ulster Defence Regt, 1971-73. Mem., Fermanagh CC, 1963-69; DL 1963-78, JP 1972-78, Co. Fermanagh. *Recreations:* shooting, golf, fishing. *Heir:* s Viscount Cole, *qv*. *Address:* Florence Court, Enniskillen, N Ireland. *T:* Florencecourt 229; PO Box 30100, Nairobi, Kenya. *Clubs:* Carlton, Turf; Muthaiga Country (Nairobi);

Mombasa (Kenya).
See also Sir J. H. Muir, Bt.

ENNISMORE, Viscount; Francis Michael Hare; *b* 28 June 1964; *s* and *heir* of 5th Earl of Listowel, *qv. Address:* 7 Constable Close, Wildwood Road, NW11.

ENRICI, Most Rev. Domenico, JCD; former Apostolic Nuncio; *b* 9 April 1909; *s* of late Domenico Enrici and Maria Dalmasso Enrici. *Educ:* Diocesan Seminary, Cuneo; Pontifical Gregorian Univ. and Pontifical Ecclesiastical Academy, Rome. Ordained, 1933; parochial work in Dio. Cuneo, 1933-35. Served at various Apostolic Nunciatures and Delegations: Ireland, 1938-45; Egypt, 1946-48; Palestine and Jordan, 1948-53; Formosa, Free China, 1953-55; apptd Titular Archbp of Ancusa, 1955; Apostolic Internuncio to Indonesia, 1955-58; Apostolic Nuncio to Haiti and Apostolic Delegate to West Indies, 1958-60; Apostolic Internuncio to Japan, 1960-62; Apostolic Delegate to Australia, New Zealand and Oceania, 1962-69; Apostolic Delegate to GB and Gibraltar, 1969-73; Pro-Pres., Pontifical Ecclesiastical Acad., 1975-76; Delegate for Pontifical Representations, 1973-79; retired, 1979. Commander, Order of the Nile (Egypt), 1948; Order of the Sacred Treasure, 1st class (Japan), 1962; Assistant to the Pontifical Throne, Vatican City, 1979. *Address:* Via Senatore Toselli, 8, 12100 Cuneo, Italy.

ENRIGHT, Dennis Joseph; freelance writer and teacher; *b* 11 March 1920; *s* of late George Enright; *m* 1949, Madeleine Harders; one *d. Educ:* Leamington Coll.; Downing Coll., Cambridge. MA Cantab; DLitt Alexandria. Lecturer in English, University of Alexandria, 1947-50; Organising Tutor, University of Birmingham Extra-Mural Dept, 1950-53; Vis. Prof., Kōnan Univ., Japan, 1953-56; Vis. Lecturer, Free University of Berlin, 1956-57; British Council Professor, Chulalongkorn Univ., Bangkok, 1957-59; Prof. of English, Univ. of Singapore, 1960-70; Hon. Prof. of English, Univ. of Warwick, 1975-80. Dir, Chatto and Windus, 1974-82. Co-Editor, *Encounter*, 1970-72. FRSL 1961. Cholmondeley Poetry Award, 1974; Queen's Gold Medal for Poetry, 1981. *Publications: poetry:* The Laughing Hyena, 1953; Bread Rather Than Blossoms, 1956; Some Men Are Brothers, 1960; Addictions, 1962; The Old Adam, 1965; Unlawful Assembly, 1968; Selected Poems, 1969; Daughters of Earth, 1972; The Terrible Shears, 1973; Rhyme Times Rhyme (for children), 1974; Sad Ires, 1975; Paradise Illustrated, 1978; A Faust Book, 1979; Collected Poems, 1981; *novels:* Academic Year, 1955; Heaven Knows Where, 1957; Insufficient Poppy, 1960; Figures of Speech, 1965; *novels for children:* The Joke Shop, 1976; Wild Ghost Chase, 1978; Beyond Land's End, 1979; *criticism:* The Apothecary's Shop, 1957; English Critical Texts (co-editor), 1962; Conspirators and Poets, 1966; Shakespeare and the Students, 1970; Man is an Onion, 1972; (ed) A Choice of Milton's Verse, 1975; Samuel Johnson: Rasselas, 1976; (ed) The Oxford Book of Contemporary Verse 1945-1980, 1980; *travel:* The World of Dew: Japan, 1955; Memoirs of a Mendicant Professor, 1969; *translation:* The Poetry of Living Japan (co-editor), 1957; contributor to: Scrutiny, Encounter, Listener, TLS, etc. *Recreations:* reading, writing, television, listening to music. *Address:* c/o Chatto & Windus, 40-42 William IV Street, WC2.

ENRIGHT, Derek Anthony; Member (Lab) Leeds, European Parliament, since 1979; *b* 2 Aug. 1935; *s* of Lawrence and Helen Enright; *m* 1963, Jane Maureen (*née* Simmons); two *s* two *d. Educ:* St Michael's Coll., Leeds; Wadham Coll., Oxford (BA, DipEd). Head of Classics, John Fisher Sch., Purley, Surrey, 1959-67; Dep. Head of St Wilfrid's, North Featherstone, W Yorks, 1967-79. *Recreations:* reading The Guardian, entertaining the family, walking the dogs. *Address:* The Hollies, 112 Carleton Road, Pontefract, W Yorks. *T:* Pontefract 702096. *Clubs:* Irish Centre (Leeds); Labour, Vulcan (Pontefract).

ENSOR, (Alick Charles) David; solicitor, journalist and author; *b* 27 Nov. 1906; *s* of Charles William Ensor, MRCS, LRCP, and Helen Margaret Creighton Ensor; *m* 1st, 1932, Norah Russell (marr. diss.); one *s* two *d* ; 2nd, 1944, Frances Vivienne Mason. *Educ:* Westminster Sch. Solicitor, 1928; Prosecuting Solicitor, Newcastle upon Tyne, 1932; Prosecuting Solicitor, Metropolitan Police, 1935; Law Lecturer, Police Coll., Hendon, 1935; Deputy Clerk of Peace, Middlesex, 1937; Clerk of Peace, London, 1938. War service with Army in France, Africa, Far East, 1939-44. Practised as Solicitor in Brussels, 1945-47. Retired from Law and farmed in Dorset, 1948. MP (Lab) Bury and Radcliffe, 1964-70; Mem., Select Cttee on Estimates, 1964-69; Chairman: Private Bill Cttee, 1967-70; House of Commons Catering Cttee, 1969-70. Mem., SDP, 1981-. Has broadcast regularly for radio and television since 1957. Films include: The Trials of Oscar Wilde; The Pot Carriers; Death and the Sky Above. TV Series, The Verdict is Yours. Vice-Pres., Mark Twain Soc. of America, 1977-. Has travelled extensively in Eastern Europe, Middle and Far East. *Publications:* Thirty Acres and a Cow, 1955; I was a Public Prosecutor, 1958; Verdict Afterwards, 1960; With Lord Roberts through the Khyber Pass, 1963; contributions to Local Government Law in England and Wales, Journal of Criminal Law. *Recreations:* reading, history. *Address:* L'Etoile d'Or, 66701 Argelès-sur-Mer, France.

ENSOR, David; *see* Ensor, A. C. D.

ENSOR, David; Managing Director, Croydon Advertiser Ltd, since 1979; *b* 2 April 1924; *s* of Rev. William Walters and Constance Eva Ensor; *m* 1947, Gertrude Kathleen Brown; two *s. Educ:* Kingswood Sch., Bath; London Coll. of Printing. Served Royal Signals, 1942-46, Captain; ADC to GOC Bengal

Dist. Managing Director: George Reveirs, 1947-59; Charles Skipper & East, 1959-69; Knapp Drewett & Sons, 1969-79; Chairman: Methodist Newspaper Co., 1975-; Methodist Publishing House, 1981-. Member: Council, Newspaper Soc., 1979-; Press Council, 1982-. Pres., London Printing Industries Assoc., 1976. Vice-Pres., Methodist Conf., 1981. *Address:* Milborne Lodge, Beech Close, Cobham, Surrey KT11 2EN. *T:* Cobham 3147.

ENSOR, Michael de Normann, CMG 1980; OBE 1958; *b* 11 June 1919; *s* of Robert Weld Ensor and Dr Beatrice Ensor; *m* 1945, Mona Irene Blackburn; two *s. Educ:* Bryanston School; St. John's Coll., Oxford. Military service, 1940; Colonial Service, Gold Coast/Ghana Civil Service, 1940-58; Secretary, Foundation for Mutual Assistance in Africa South of the Sahara, 1958-64; Dept of Technical Cooperation/Min. of Overseas Development/Overseas Development Administration, 1964-80; Head, East Africa Development Division, 1975-80. *Address:* Flat 1, 12 The Paragon, Blackheath, SE3 0NZ. *T:* 01-852 5345. *Clubs:* Travellers', Royal Blackheath Golf; Karen (Kenya).

ENSOR WALTERS, P. H. B.; *see* Walters.

ENTERS, Angna; mime; dancer; painter; sculptor; author; dramatist; composer; choreographer; scene and costume designer for the theatre; *b* NYC, US, 28 April 1907; *o c* of Edward Enters and Henriette Gasseur-Styleau; *m* Louis Kalonyme. *Educ:* privately and self-educated in US; Europe; Egypt; Greece. Theatre début New York, 1924, presenting in solo performance a new theatre form in which she combined for the first time the arts of mime, dance, music, costume, scenic design; originated phrase dance-mime now in Amer. dictionaries; first performer to be presented in a theatrical performance, 1943, by Metropolitan Museum of Art, NYC; presented for her 25th Broadway (NY) season, 1959; a nationwide television broadcast, in US, presented a composite portrait of her work in theatre, painting, writing, 1959. London début, St Martin's Theatre, 1928; many subseq. British seasons including television. Paris début, 1929; Am. Rep. in Internat. Theatre Season presented by C. B. Cochran, Queen's Theatre, 1931. Rep. Am. Nat. Theatre and Acad., at Internat. Arts Festival, Berlin, and tour of W Germany. Guggenheim Foundation Fellowships, 1934 and 1935 (research in Greece, Egypt, Near East). Début exhibn of painting, NY, 1933, many subseq. Début exhibn of paintings in London, Eng., 1934 and subseq. Début exhibn of sculpture, New York, 1945; subseq. one-woman shows of painting and sculpture in US and Canada. Works are in Metropolitan Museum of Art, New York, etc. Painted mural, modern Penthouse Theatre of University of Washington, Seattle, 1950. Rep. in Exhibns, NY Museum of Modern Art, 1953. First work in Ceramics exhibited in New York and Los Angeles, 1953. Lecture tours US, 1954-. Prof. of Acting, Baylor Univ., Waco, Texas, and Director of plays, Dallas Theatre Center, Dallas, Texas, 1961-62. Fellow: Center for Advanced Studies, Wesleyan Univ., Middletown, Conn, 1962-; Pennsylvania State Univ., 1970. Films based on her original stories: Lost Angel, Tenth Avenue Angel, Silly Girl, 1944-47; You Belong to Me, 1950. Created and staged Commedia dell' Arte (play within play seq.) in film Scaramouche, 1951; Dir, also designer of stage settings and costumes, for play, Yerma, by G. Lorca (Broadway, NY, etc.), 1958. Plays produced: Love Possessed Juana, 1946; The Unknown Lover-A Modern Psyche, 1947. *Publications:* First Person Plural (self-illustr.), 1937, new edn 1978; Love Possessed Juana (self-scored and illustr. play), 1939; Silly Girl (self-illustr. autobiog.), 1944; Among the Daughters (novel), 1955 (publ. London, 1956, as A Thing of Beauty); Artist's Life (self-illustrated), 1957; Artist's Life (publ. London, 1959); (trans. with L. Kalonyme) Chantecler, by E. Rostand, 1960; Angna Enters on Mime, 1965; also illustrated Best American Short Stories of 1945; article on Pantomime, Encyclopædia Britannica.

ENTHOVEN, Roderick Eustace, FRIBA; FSA; architect in private practice; Consultant, Enthoven & Mock, since 1978; *b* 30 May 1900; *o surv. s* of late Ernest James Enthoven, Great Ote Hall, Wivelsfield, Sussex, and Rosaline Mary Eustace Smith; *m* 1933, Cecilia Mary Le Mesurier; three *s. Educ:* Clifton College. Received architectural education at Architectural Association Sch., 1919-24, qualifying with SADG Medal, Architectural Association Diploma. Partner in Enthoven & Mock; Partner in Pakington & Enthoven until war of 1939-45. Civil Camouflage Officer to Air Ministry, 1940-44; served in Italy as Monuments, Fine Arts and Archives Officer, 1944-45. Pres. Architectural Association, 1948-49; Vice-Pres. RIBA, 1951-53. Master of the Art Workers' Guild, 1976; Liveryman, Goldsmiths' Co. Commissions include: Khartoum Univ.; Goldsmiths' Coll.; City of London Polytechnic; Royal Foundn of St Katharine; Queen Elizabeth House, Oxford. *Publications:* contributor to various architectural journals. *Recreations:* theatre, foreign travel. *Address:* 3 Berkeley Gardens, Kensington Church Street, W8 4AP. *T:* 01-229 1482; 4 Raymond Buildings, Gray's Inn, WC1R 5BP. *Club:* Athenæum.

ENTWISTLE, Sir (John Nuttall) Maxwell, Kt 1963; Consultant Solicitor and Notary; Director of companies; Under-writing Member of Lloyd's since 1964; *b* 8 Jan. 1910; *s* of Isaac and Hannah Entwistle; *m* 1940, Jean Cunliffe McAlpine, *d* of late Dr John and Amy Margaret Penman; two *s. Educ:* Merchant Taylors' Sch., Great Crosby. Solicitor, 1931; Notary Public, 1955. Liverpool City: Councillor, 1938; Alderman, 1960; Leader of Liverpool City Council, when initiated preparation of develt plan for City centre. Councillor, Cumbria County, 1979-. Chairman: Merseyside Development Cttee; Mersey Tunnel Cttee, 1961-63; Abbeyfield Liverpool Soc. Ltd, 1970-75; Council of Management, League of Welldoers, 1972-74. Mem., Liverpool Univ. Court and Council, 1955-64. President: Edge Hill Liverpool Conservative Assoc., 1963-71; Liverpool Clerks Assoc., 1964-78. Merchant Taylors' School: Chm., Appeal Cttee, 1969-74; Pres., Old Boys' Assoc., 1969-70; Governor, 1969-75. *Recreations:* gardening, shooting. *Address:* Stone Hall, Sedbergh, Cumbria. *T:* Sedbergh 20700. *Club:* Atlantic (Liverpool).

EPHRAUMS, Maj.-Gen. Roderick Jarvis, CB 1977; OBE 1965; Major-General Royal Marines, Commando Forces, 1976-78, retired; *b* 12 May 1927; *s* of Hugh Cyril Ephraums and Elsie Caroline (*née* Rowden); *m* 1955, Adela Mary (*née* Forster); two *s* one *d. Educ:* Tonbridge. Commnd 2nd Lieut, RM, 1945; HMS Mauritius, 1946-48; 3 Commando Bde, RM, 1952-54; Staff Coll., Camberley, 1960; Bde Major, 3 Commando Bde, 1962-64; CO, 45 Commando RM, 1969-71; Royal Coll. of Defence Studies, 1972; Comdr, 3 Commando Bde, 1973-74; NATO Defense Coll., Rome, 1975. FBIM 1979. *Recreations:* shooting, fishing, sailing. *Club:* Army and Navy.

EPSTEIN, Prof. (Michael) Anthony, FRS 1979; Professor of Pathology, since 1968, and Head of Department, 1968-82, University of Bristol; also Hon. Consultant Pathologist, Bristol Health District (Teaching), since 1968; *b* 18 May 1921; *yr s* of Mortimer and Olga Epstein; *m* 1950, Lisbeth Knight; two *s* one *d. Educ:* St Paul's Sch., London; Trinity Coll., Cambridge (Perry Exhibr, 1940); Middlesex Hosp. Medical Sch. MA, MD, DSc, PhD; FRCPath. Ho. Surg., Middlesex Hosp., London, and Addenbrooke's Hosp., Cambridge, 1944; Lieut and Captain, RAMC, 1945-47; Asst Pathologist, Bland Sutton Inst., Mddx Hosp. Med. Sch., 1948-65, with leave as: Berkeley Travelling Fellow, 1952-53; French Govt Exchange Scholar at Institut Pasteur, Paris, 1952-53; Vis. Investigator, Rockefeller Inst., NY, 1956. Reader in Experimental Pathology, Mddx Hosp. Med. Sch., 1965-68; Hon. Consultant in Experimental Virology, Mddx Hosp., 1965-68. Major lectures: Edgar Allen Meml, Yale Univ., 1960; Kettle Meml, Royal Coll. of Pathologists, 1971; Distinguished Scientist Series, Tulane Univ., 1972; Sydney Watson Smith, RCPE, 1973; Collège de France, Paris, 1975; Long Fox Meml, Bristol, 1976; Chinese Acad. of Medical Scis, Peking, 1977; A. B. Pearson Oration, NZ Soc. of Pathologists, 1978; Korner Meml, Sussex Univ., 1980; Nat. Sci. Res. Foundn, Athens, 1981; Senate Guest, Welsh Nat. Sch. of Medicine, Cardiff, 1981; Wade Foundn, Southampton Univ., 1982. Member: Cttee, Pathological Soc. of GB and Ire., 1969-72; Council, and Vice-Pres., Pathology Section of RSM, 1966-72; Study Gp on Classification of Herpes Viruses, of Internat. Commn for Nomenclature of Viruses, 1971-; Scientific Adv. Bd, Harvard Med. Sch.'s New England Regional Primate Center, 1972-; MRC and Cancer Research Campaign Jt Cttee, 1973-77; Cttee, British Soc. for Cell Biology, 1974-77; MRC, 1982- (Mem. 1979-, Chm. 1982-, Cell Bd). Discovered in 1964 a new human herpes virus, now known as Epstein-Barr virus, which causes infectious mononucleosis and is also causally implicated in some forms of human cancer (Burkitt's lymphoma and nasopharyngeal carcinoma). Paul Ehrlich and Ludwig Darmstaedter Prize and Medal of W German Paul Ehrlich Foundn, 1973; Markham Skerrit Prize, 1977; (jtly) Bristol-Myers Award, NY, 1982. Mem. d'honneur, Belgian Soc. for Cancer Res., 1979. Hon. Prof., Chungshan Med. Coll., Kwangchow, 1980. *Publications:* over 148 scientific papers in internat. jls on tumour cell structure, viruses, tumour viruses, Burkitt's lymphoma, and the EB virus. Jt Founder Editor, The Internat. Review of Experimental Pathology (vols 1-24, 1962-82); (ed jtly) The Epstein-Barr Virus, 1979. *Address:* Department of Pathology, University of Bristol Medical School, University Walk, Bristol BS8 1TD. *T:* Bristol 24161 (ext. 602).

EREAUT, Sir (Herbert) Frank (Cobbold), Kt 1976; Bailiff of Jersey, since 1975; Judge of the Court of Appeal in Guernsey, since 1976; *b* 6 May 1919; *s* of Herbert Parker Ereaut and May Julia Cobbold; *m* 1942, Kathleen FitzGibbon; one *d. Educ:* Tormore Sch., Upper Deal, Kent; Cranleigh Sch., Surrey; Exeter Coll., Oxford. BA 1946, MA 1966. RASC, 1940-46: N Africa, Italy and NW Europe; 2nd Lieut 1940; Lieut 1941; Captain 1943. Called to Bar, Inner Temple, 1947; Solicitor-General, Jersey, 1958-62, Attorney-General, 1962-69; Dep. Bailiff of Jersey, 1969-74. CStJ 1978. *Recreations:* music, gardening. *Address:* Les Cypres, St John, Jersey, Channel Islands. *T:* Jersey 22317.

ERICKSON, Prof. Charlotte Joanne, (Mrs G. L. Watt); Paul Mellon Professor of American History, University of Cambridge, since 1983; Fellow of Corpus Christi College, Cambridge; *b* 22 Oct. 1923; *d* of Knut Eric Erickson and Lael A. R. Johnson; *m* 1952, G. L. Watt; two *s. Educ:* Augustana Coll., Rock Island, Ill (BA 1945); Cornell Univ., Ithaca, NY (MA 1947; PhD 1951). Instructor in History, Vassar Coll., Poughkeepsie, NY, 1950-52; Research Fellow, NIESR, 1952-55; Lillian Gilmore Fellow, Cornell Univ., April-Sept. 1954; Asst Lectr, 1955, Lectr, 1958, Sen. Lectr, 1966, Reader, 1975, Prof., 1979-82, in Economic History, London School of Economics. Guggenheim Fellow, Washington, DC, 1966-67; Sherman Fairchild Distinguished Scholar, Calif Inst. of Technology, 1976-77. Hon. DHumLet Augustana College, 1977. *Publications:* British Industrialists, Steel and Hosiery 1850-1950, 1958; American Industry and the European Immigrant 1860-1885, 1969; Invisible Immigrants, The Adaptation of English and Scottish Immigrants in Nineteenth Century America, 1972; articles in professional jls and collective works. *Recreations:* music, gardening. *Address:* 30 Hartham Road, N7. *T:* 01-607 6220; Corpus Christi College, Cambridge CB2 1RH.

ERICKSON, Prof. John, FRSE 1982; Professor of Politics, University of Edinburgh, since 1969; *b* 17 April 1929; *s* of Henry Erickson and Jessie (*née* Heys); *m* 1957, Ljubica (*née* Petrović); one *s* one *d. Educ:* South Shields High Sch.; St John's Coll., Cambridge (MA). Research Fellow, St Anthony's Coll., Oxford, 1956-58; Lectr, Dept of History, St Andrews Univ., 1958-62; Lectr, Sen. Lectr and Reader, Dept of Government, Univ. of Manchester, 1962-67; Visiting Prof., Russian Research Center, Univ. of Indiana, 1967; Reader, Lectr in Higher Defence Studies, Univ. of Edinburgh, 1967. Vis. Prof., Texas A&M Univ., 1981. Pres., Assoc. of Civil Defence and Emergency Planning Officers, 1981. *Publications:* The Soviet High Command 1918-1941, 1962; Storia dello Stato Maggiore Sovietico, 1963; ed, The Military-Technical Revolution, 1966; ed, The Armed Services and Society, 1970; Soviet Military Power, 1971; The Road to Stalingrad, 1975; (ed) Soviet Military Power and Performance, 1979. *Recreations:* military models and music. *Address:* 13 Ravelston House Road, Edinburgh EH4 3LP. *T:* 031-332 1787. *Club:* Edinburgh University Staff.

ERKIN, Feridun Cemal, Hon. GBE 1967; Minister of Foreign Affairs, Turkey, 1962-65; *b* 1899; *m* Madame Mukaddes Feridun Erkin (*d* 1955). *Educ:* Galatasaray Lyceum, Istanbul; Faculty of Law, University of Paris. First Sec., London, 1928-29; Chief of Section, Ankara, 1930-33; Counsellor and Chargé d'Affaires, Berlin, 1934-35; Consul-Gen., Beirut, 1935-37; Dir-Gen., Econ. Dept, Min. of Foreign Affairs, 1937; Dir-Gen., Polit. Dept, 1939; Asst Sec.-Gen., 1942; Delegate, UN Conf. San Francisco, 1945; Sec.-Gen. of Min., 1945; Chm. Turkish Delegn, final session of League of Nations, 1946; Ambassador to Italy, 1947-48; to USA, 1948-55; to Spain, 1955-57; to France, 1957-60; to the Court of St James's, 1960-62. Lately Senator. Turkish Governor to Internat. Banks, 1954; Mem. Internat. Diplomatic Academy, 1949-; Mem. Inst. of France, 1959-. Holds Grand Cross of several foreign Orders, including Grand Cross of the Legion of Honour of France. *Publications:* The Turkish-Soviet relations and the Problem of the Straits, 1968 (French and Turkish edns); articles in daily papers and journals. *Recreation:* classical music. *Address:* Ayaspaşa, Sarayarkasi Sok 24/9, Istanbul, Turkey.

ERNE, 6th Earl of, *cr* 1789; **Henry George Victor John Crichton,** DL, JP; Baron Erne 1768; Viscount Erne (Ireland), 1781; Baron Fermanagh (UK), 1876; *b* 9 July 1937; *s* of 5th Earl and Lady Katharine Cynthia Mary Millicent (Davina) Lytton (who *m* 1945, Hon. C. M. Woodhouse, *qv*), *yr d* of 2nd Earl of Lytton, KG, PC, GCSI, GCIE; *S* father, 1940; *m* 1958, Camilla Marguerite (marr. diss. 1980), *er d* of late Wing-Comdr Owen G. E. Roberts, and of Mrs Roberts, 30 Groom Place, Belgrave Square, SW1; one *s* four *d* ; *m* 1980, Mrs Anna Carin Hitchcock (*née* Bjork). *Educ:* Eton. Page of Honour to the Queen, 1952-54 (to King George VI, 1952). Joined RN as Ord. Seaman, 1956; Lieut, North Irish Horse, 1959-66. Member: Royal Ulster Agricultural Society; Royal Forestry Society. DL, JP Co. Fermanagh. *Recreations:* sailing, shooting. *Heir: s* Viscount Crichton, *qv. Address:* Crom Castle, Newtown Butler, Co. Fermanagh. *T:* Newton-butler 208; 10 Kylestrome House, Cundy Street Flats, Ebury Street, SW1. *Clubs:* White's; Lough Erne Yacht.

ERRINGTON, Viscount; Evelyn Rowland Esmond Baring; Manager, China Trading Division, Inchcape Far East Ltd, since 1979; *b* 3 June 1946; *e s* of 3rd Earl of Cromer, *qv* ; *m* 1971, Plern Isarangkun Na Ayudhya, *e d* of late Dr Charanphat Isarangkun Na Ayudhya, Thailand. *Educ:* Eton. Director: Moray Petroleum & Development Co. Ltd; Lai Tong Trading Co. Ltd; The Motor Transport Co. of Guangdong & Hong Kong Ltd (China); Alternate Dir, Cluff Oil (Hong Kong) Ltd. Mem. Council, St John Ambulance Assoc., Hong Kong. *Address:* GPO Box 56, Hong Kong; 7B Bowen Road, Hong Kong. *T:* 5-236426, (office) 5-7901233. *Clubs:* Turf, Oriental; Siam Society; Hong Kong, Royal Hong Kong Yacht (Hong Kong).

ERRINGTON, Col Sir Geoffrey (Frederick), 2nd Bt *cr* 1963; Colonel, The King's Regiment, since 1975; Chairman: Executive Appointments Ltd, since 1982 (Director, since 1979); Guy Redmayne & Partners Ltd, since 1982 (Director, since 1979); Moore, Wingate, since 1982; *b* 15 Feb. 1926; *er s* of Sir Eric Errington, 1st Bt, JP, and Marjorie (*d* 1973), *d* of A. Grant Bennett; *S* father, 1973; *m* 1955, Diana Kathleen Forbes, *o d* of late E. Barry Davenport, Edgbaston, Birmingham; three *s. Educ:* Rugby Sch.; New Coll., Oxford. psc 1958; AMBIM 1969. GSO 3 (Int.), HQ 11 Armd Div., 1950-52; GSO 3, MI3 (b), War Office, 1955-57; Bde Major 146 Inf. Bde, 1959-61; Coy Comdr, RMA Sandhurst, 1963-65; Military Assistant to Adjutant-General, 1965-67; CO 1st Bn, The King's Regt, 1967-69; GSO 1, HQ 1st British Corps, 1969-71; Col. GS, HQ NW District, 1971-74. Chm., The King's and Manchester Regts Assoc., 1971-; AAG MI (Army) MoD, 1974-75; retired 1975. Dir, Personnel Services, British Shipbuilders, 1977-78; Employer Bd Mem., Shipbuilding ITB, 1977-78. Freeman, City of London, 1980. Liveryman, Coachmakers' and Coach Harness Makers' Co. *Recreations:* sailing, skiing. *Heir: s* Robin Davenport Errington, *b* 1 July 1957. *Address:* Stone Hill Farm, Sellindge, Ashford, Kent TN25 6AJ. *T:* Sellindge 3191; 203A Gloucester Place, NW1 6BU. *Club:* Army and Navy.

ERRINGTON, Sir Lancelot, KCB 1976 (CB 1962); Second Permanent Secretary, Department of Health and Social Security, 1973-76; *b* 14 Jan. 1917; *e s* of late Major L. Errington; *m* 1939, Katharine Reine, *o d* of late T. C. Macaulay; two *s* two *d. Educ:* Wellington Coll.; Trinity Coll., Cambridge. Entered Home Office, 1939. Served RNVR, 1939-45. Transferred to Ministry of National Insurance, 1945; Principal Private Sec. to Minister of National Insurance, 1951; Asst Sec., 1953; Under-Sec., 1957-65; Cabinet Office, 1965-68; Min. of Social Security, 1968; Asst Under-Sec. of State,

DHSS, 1968-71, Dep. Under-Sec. of State, 1971-73. *Recreation:* sailing. *Address:* St Mary's, Fasnacloich, Appin, Argyll. *T:* Appin 331.

ERRINGTON, Richard Percy, CMG 1955; Chartered Accountant (FCA), retired; *b* 17 May 1904; 2nd *s* of Robert George Errington and Edna Mary Errington (*née* Warr); *m* 1935, Ursula, *d* of Henry Joseph Laws Curtis and Grace Barton Curtis (*née* Macgregor); one *d*. *Educ:* Sidcot Sch. Asst Treasurer, Nigeria Government, 1929-37; Colonial Administrative Service: Nigeria, 1937-46; Nyasaland, 1946-48; Financial Sec. to Govt of Aden Colony (also Mem. Bd of Trustees of Port of Aden), 1948-51; Chm., Aden Port Trust, 1951-60. Mem. Governor's Exec. Council, Aden, 1948-58. Unofficial Mem. Aden Colony Legislative Council, 1951-60 (Official Mem., 1948-51). Chairman: Aden Soc. for the Blind, 1951-60; Aden Lab. Advisory Bd, 1951-57. Area Comr, St John Amb. Bde, 1964-71. SBStJ, 1965. *Recreations:* golf, swimming, walking. *Address:* Whitecliffs, Wodehouse Road, Old Hunstanton, Norfolk PE36 6JD. *T:* Hunstanton 2356.

ERRITT, Michael John Mackey; Assistant Under Secretary of State (Statistics), Ministry of Defence, since 1981; *b* 15 Feb. 1931; *s* of William Albert Erritt, MBE, and Anna Erritt; *m* 1957, Marian Elizabeth Hillock; two *s*. *Educ:* St Andrews Coll., Dublin; Prince of Wales Sch., Nairobi; Queen's Univ., Belfast. BSc(Econ). Research Officer, Science and Industry Cttee, 1953; Asst Statistician, Central Statistical Office, 1955; Statistician: Board of Trade, 1960; Treasury, 1964; Board of Trade, 1967; Chief Statistician: Inland Revenue, 1968; Central Statistical Office, 1973; Depts of Industry, Trade and Prices and Consumer Protection, 1975; MoD, 1979. *Publications:* articles in official, academic and trade jls. *Address:* Shandon, 14 Bluntswood Road, Haywards Heath, Sussex RH16 1NB. *T:* Haywards Heath 413391.

ERROLL, 24th Earl of, *cr* 1452; **Merlin Sereld Victor Gilbert Hay;** Lord Hay, 1429; Baron of Slains, 1452; 28th Hereditary Lord High Constable of Scotland, *cr* 1314; Celtic title, Mac Garadh Mor; 33rd Chief of the Hays (from 1171); Senior Great Officer, Royal Household in Scotland; *b* 20 April 1948; *er s* of 23rd Countess of Erroll and of Sir Iain Moncreiffe of that Ilk, 11th Bt, *qv*; *S* mother, 1978; *m* 1982, Isabelle Astell Hohler, *o d* of T. S. Astell Hohler, *qv*. *Educ:* Eton; Trinity College, Cambridge. Page to the Lord Lyon, 1956. Lieut, Atholl Highlanders, 1974. OStJ 1977. Member, Queen's Body Guard for Scotland, Royal Company of Archers, 1978. *Recreations:* skiing, climbing, TAVR. *Heir: b* Hon. Peregrine David Euan Malcolm Moncreiffe, *b* 16 Feb. 1951. *Address:* Easter Moncreiffe, Perthshire PH2 8QA. *T:* Bridge of Earn 2338. *Clubs:* Turf, White's, Pratt's; Puffin's (Edinburgh).

ERROLL OF HALE, 1st Baron, *cr* 1964; **Frederick James Erroll,** PC 1960; MA, FIEE; FIMechE; Chairman, Bowater Corporation, since 1973; *b* 27 May 1914; *s* of George Murison Erroll, engineer, and Kathleen Donovan Edington, both of Glasgow and London; *m* 1950, Elizabeth, *o d* of R. Sowton Barrow, Exmouth, Devon. *Educ:* Oundle Sch.; Trinity Coll., Cambridge. Engineering Apprenticeship, 1931-32; Cambridge Univ., 1932-35; Engineer at Metropolitan-Vickers Electrical Co. Ltd, Manchester, 1936-38; Commissioned into 4th County of London Yeomanry (Sharpshooters), TA, 1939; technical appointments in connection with Tank Construction and Testing, 1940-43; service in India and Burma, 1944-45; Col 1945. MP (C) Altrincham and Sale, 1945-64. A Dir of Engineering and Mining Companies until April 1955; Parly Sec., Min. of Supply, April 1955-Nov. 1956; Parly Sec., BoT, 1956-58; Economic Sec. to the Treasury, Oct. 1958-59; Minister of State, BoT, 1959-61; Pres., BoT, 1961-63; Minister of Power, 1963-64. Pres., Consolidated Gold Fields, 1982- (Chm., 1976-82); Chairman: ASEA Ltd; Bowater Corporation Ltd; Fläkt Ltd; Whessoe Ltd. Member: Council Inst. Directors, 1949-55, and 1965- (Chm. Council, 1973-76, Pres., 1976-); NEDC, 1962-63. President: London Chamber of Commerce, 1966-69; Hispanic and Luso-Brazilian Councils, 1969-73; British Export Houses Assoc., 1969-72; UK South Africa Trade Assoc., 1979-. Dep. Chm., Decimal Currency Board, 1966-71; Chm., Cttee on Liquor Licensing, 1971-72; Pres., Electrical Research Assoc., 1971-74; Chm., AA, 1974-. FRSA 1971. *Heir:* none. *Address:* House of Lords, SW1. *Club:* Carlton.

ERSKINE; *see* St Clair-Erskine.

ERSKINE, family name of **Earls of Buchan** and **Mar and Kellie,** and of **Baron Erskine of Rerrick.**

ERSKINE OF RERRICK, 2nd Baron *cr* 1964; **Iain Maxwell Erskine;** Bt 1961; a consultant with Marples Ridgway Building and Civil Engineering, since 1979; a director of various small companies; *b* 22 Jan. 1926; *o s* of 1st Baron Erskine of Rerrick, GBE, and of Henrietta, *d* of late William Dunnett; *S* father, 1980; *m* 1st, Marie Elisabeth (later Countess of Caledon) (marr. diss. 1964), *d* of Major Burton Allen, Benvhier House, Ballachulish; no *c* ; 2nd, 1974, Maria Josephine, *d* of late Dr Josef Klupt and of Mona Lilias Klupt, Richmond, Surrey; one *d*. *Educ:* Harrow. Served War of 1939-45: 2nd Lieut Grenadier Guards, 1945. ADC, RMA, 1951-52; Comptroller to Governor-Gen. of New Zealand, 1960-61; retd as Major, 1963. PRO to Household Bde, 1964-66. Associate Dir, Saward Baker & Co. Ltd (Advertising), 1967-. Chm., Guards Flying Club. Mem. Cttee and Dir, De Haviland Mus., Salisbury Hall, Herts. MInstM, MIPR, Mem., Inst. of Dirs. Chevalier, Legion of Honour. OStJ. Chevalier, Chaîne des Rôtisseurs. *Recreations:* fishing, flying, food, photography. *Heir:* none. *Address:* 10 Chesham Place, SW1. *T:* 01-235 3489. *Clubs:* Cavalry and Guards, Caledonian, Special Forces.

ERSKINE, Lord; James Thorne Erskine; Flying Officer, Royal Auxiliary Air Force, since 1982; *b* 10 March 1949; *s* and *heir* of 13th Earl of Mar and 15th Earl of Kellie, *qv*; *m* 1974, Mrs Mary Mooney, *yr d* of Dougal McD. Kirk. *Educ:* Eton; Moray House Coll. of Education, 1968-71. Page of Honour to the Queen, 1962, 1963. Community Service Volunteer, York, 1967-68; Community Worker, Richmond-Craigmillar Parish Church, Edinburgh, 1971-73; Sen. Social Worker, Family and Community Services, Sheffield District Council, 1973-76; Social Worker: Grampian Regional Council, Elgin, 1976-77, Forres, 1977-78; Highland Regional Council, Aviemore, 1979; HM Prison, Inverness, 1979-81; Inverness, Aug.-Dec. 1981; Community Worker, Merkinch Centre, Inverness, Jan.-July 1982. Pilot Officer, RAuxAF, 1979, attached to 2622 Highland Sqdn, RAuxAF Regt. *Recreations:* hill walking, railways, gardening, cycling. *Address:* Claremont House, Alloa, Clackmannanshire. *T:* Alloa 212020; Dumyat, Drummond Crescent, Inverness. *T:* Inverness 220280.

ERSKINE, Sir David; *see* Erskine, Sir T. D.

ERSKINE, Sir George; *see* Erskine, Sir R. G.

ERSKINE, Ralph, CBE 1978; architect; own practice (in Sweden since 1939; also at Byker, Newcastle upon Tyne); *b* 24 Feb. 1914; *s* of late George and Mildred Erskine; *m* 1939, Ruth Monica Francis; one *s* two *d*. *Educ:* Friends' Sch., Saffron Walden, Essex; Regent Street Polytechnic (architecture). ARIBA 1936; AMTPI 1938; SAR 1965. Won number of prizes in arch. comps in Sweden; one year's study at Academy for Fine Arts, Sweden, 1945. *Work executed:* town plans; workers' houses; co-operative housing and industrial housing; flats; hostels; factories; ski-hotel; shopping centre; school; town hall; hall of residence at Clare Coll., Cambridge; churches; housing estates at Newmarket and Killingworth; Allhuset and Sports hall; clearance scheme, Byker, Newcastle upon Tyne; design of new town, Resolute Bay, Canada; University Library, Stockholm. Lecturing: in America, Canada, Japan and many countries in Europe. Hon. Dr, Lund Univ., Sweden, 1975; Hon. DLitt, Heriot-Watt Univ., 1982. For. Mem., Royal Acad. of Arts, Sweden, 1972. Hon Fellow of AIA, 1966; SAR's Kasper Sahlin prize for 1971 and 1981; Ytong Prize, 1974; Guld medal, Litteris et Artibus, 1980; Canadian Gold Medal, RAIC, 1982. *Publications:* for several arch. magazines, on building in northern climates, etc. *Relevant publication:* Ralph Erskine, by Mats Egelius, 1978. *Recreations:* ski-ing, skating, swimming, yachting, ice yachting. *Address:* Gustav III's väg, Drottningholm, Sweden. *T:* 7590352.

ERSKINE, Sir (Robert) George, Kt 1948; CBE 1945; Adviser to and former Director of Morgan Grenfell & Co. Limited; former Director, London & Provincial Trust Ltd (Chairman 1954-71); Member of London Advisory Committee, Scottish Council (Development and Industry); Former Member Council, RAF Benevolent Fund; *b* 5 Nov. 1896; *s* of late John Erskine, Kirkcudbright; unmarried. *Educ:* Kirkcudbright Academy; Edinburgh Univ. (BL). On staff of National Bank of Scotland, 1913-29, when joined Morgan Grenfell; Director, 1945-67; former Director: GKN Ltd; British-Commonwealth Shipping Co. Ltd, etc. Served European War, 1914-18. Dep. Chm. NAAFI, 1941-52; Vice-Pres. Institute of Bankers (Pres., 1954-56); Master of Glaziers' Company, 1960-61; Mem. Jenkins Cttee on Company Law, 1959-62. High Sheriff of Surrey, 1963-64. Mem., Law Soc. of Scotland. Fellow, Inst. of Directors; FRGS. Freeman, City of London; Past Grand Senior Deacon, United Grand Lodge of England. *Address:* Busbridge Wood, Godalming, Surrey. *T:* Hascombe 378.

ERSKINE, Sir (Thomas) David, 5th Bt, *cr* 1821; JP; Vice Lord-Lieutenant, Fife Region, since 1981; Convener, Fife County Council, 1970-73; *b* 31 July 1912; *o surv. s* of Sir Thomas Wilfred Hargreaves John Erskine, 4th Bt, and late Magdalen Janet, *d* of Sir Ralph Anstruther, 6th Bt of Balcaskie; *S* father, 1944; *m* 1947, Ann, *er d* of late Lt-Col Neil Fraser-Tytler, DSO, MC, and of Christian Helen Fraser-Tytler, CBE, *qv* ; two *s* (and one *d* decd). *Educ:* Eton; Magdalene Coll., Cambridge. Employed by Butterfield & Swire, London and China, in 1934 and served with them in China, 1935-41. Joined HM Forces in India and commissioned into Indian Corps of Engineers. Served with them in Mid-East, India and Malaya, being demobilised in 1945 with rank of Major. JP Fife, 1951; DL Fife, 1955-81. *Heir: s* Thomas Peter Neil Erskine [*b* 28 March 1950; *m* 1972, Catherine, *d* of Col G. H. K. Hewlett; two *s*]. *Address:* West Newhall House, Kingsbarns, Fife. *T:* Crail 228. *Club:* New (Edinburgh).

ERSKINE, Thomas Ralph; First Legislative Draftsman, Northern Ireland, since 1979; *b* 14 Oct. 1933; *m* 1966, Patricia Joan Palmer; one *s* one *d*. *Educ:* Campbell College; Queen's University, Belfast. Called to the Bar, Gray's Inn, 1962. *Address:* Office of the Legislative Draftsmen, Parliament Buildings, Belfast BT4 3SW. *T:* Belfast 63210.

ERSKINE-HILL, Sir Robert, 2nd Bt, *cr* 1945; Member of the Royal Company of Archers, Queen's Body Guard for Scotland; Chartered Accountant; Chairman, Life Association of Scotland, since 1960 (Director, since 1951); *b* 6 Feb. 1917; *er s* of Sir Alexander Galloway Erskine-Hill, 1st Bt, KC, DL, and Christian Hendrie, MBE (*d* 1947), *o d* of John Colville, MP, Cleland, Lanarkshire; *S* father, 1947; *m* 1942, Christine Alison, *o d* of late Capt. (A) Henry James Johnstone of Alva, RN; two *s* two *d*. *Educ:* Eton; Trinity Coll., Cambridge (BA). Served War of 1939-45, in RNVR. Partner, Chiene & Tait, CA, Edinburgh, 1946-80. Chm., Merchant Investors Assurance, 1978- (Dir, 1976-). *Heir: s* Alexander Roger Erskine-Hill, *b* 15

Aug. 1949. *Address:* Quothquhan Lodge, Biggar, Lanarkshire. *T:* Tinto 332.

ERSKINE-LINDOP, Audrey Beatrice Noël; novelist; *b* London; *d* of late Lt-Col A. H. Erskine-Lindop, MC, and Ivy Monck-Mason; *m* 1945, Dudley Gordon Leslie, scriptwriter and playwright. *Educ:* Convent of Our Lady of Lourdes, Hatch End, Middx; Blackdown Sch., Wellington, Somerset. Started career in Worthing Repertory Company; became scriptwriter (England and Hollywood). Books have been published in numerous countries. Freeman of City of London, 1954. *Plays:* Beware of Angels (in collaboration with Dudley Leslie), prod Westminster Theatre, 1959; Let's Talk Turkey, prod 1955. *Publications:* In Me My Enemy, 1948; Soldiers' Daughters Never Cry, 1949; The Tall Headlines, 1950; Out of the Whirlwind, 1951; The Singer Not the Song, 1953 (Book Society choice; filmed, 1961); Details of Jeremy Stretton, 1955; The Judas Figures, 1956; I Thank a Fool, 1958; The Way to the Lantern, 1961; Nicola, 1966; I Start Counting, 1966 (Prix Roman Policier, France, 1968); Sight Unseen, 1969; Journey into Stone, 1973; The Self-Appointed Saint, 1975. *Recreations:* history (particularly collecting relics of favourite historical characters); anything to do with birds and cats; very fond of the wilder type of countryside. *Address:* Gray Tiles, Niton Undercliff, IoW PO38 2NA. *T:* Niton 730291.

ERSKINE-MURRAY, family name of **Lord Elibank.**

ERTZ, Susan, (Mrs J. R. McCrindle), FRSL; writer; *d* of Charles Edward Ertz and Mary Gertrude Le Viness of New York; *m* 1932, Major J. Ronald McCrindle, CMG, OBE, MC (*d* 1977). *Publications:* Novels: Madam Claire; Nina; Afternoon; Now East, Now West; The Galaxy; Julian Probert, Face to Face (short stories); The Proselyte, 1933; Now We Set Out, 1934; Woman Alive, 1935; No Hearts to Break, 1937; Big Frogs and Little Frogs (short stories), 1938; Black, White, and Caroline (for children), 1938; One Fight More, 1940; Anger in the Sky, 1943; Two Names upon the Shore, 1947; The Prodigal Heart, 1950; The Undefended Gate, 1953; Charmed Circle, 1956; In the Cool of the Day, 1961; Devices and Desires, 1972; The Philosopher's Daughter, 1976; contributions to various periodicals. *Recreations:* painting, gardening, travel. *Address:* Fir Tree Cottage, Newenden, Hawkhurst, Kent. *T:* Northiam 2196.

ERVINE-ANDREWS, Lieut-Col Harold Marcus, VC 1940; East Lancashire Regiment, retired; *b* 29 July 1911; *s* of late C. C. Ervine-Andrews, New Ross, Wexford, Southern Ireland; *m* 1939, Betty (decd), *er d* of R. I. Torrie; one *s* one *d*; *m* 1981, Margaret Gregory. *Educ:* Stonyhurst Coll.; Royal Military Coll., Sandhurst. 2nd Lieut East Lancs Regt, 1932; Captain 1940; Temp. Major, 1940; War Subst. Major, 1942; Temp. Lieut-Col 1942; served with RAF during North-West Frontier of India Operations, 1936-37 (medal and two clasps, despatches) and NW Frontier, 1938-39; served in France with BEF (VC); attached to RAF in UK, 1940; on loan to Australian Military Forces, 1941; attached RAAF, 1942; GSO 1 Air HQ Allied Land Forces in South-West Pacific Area, 1943; commanding No. 61 Carrier-Borne Army Liaison Section, 1944; SALO in 21st Aircraft Carrier Squadron (East Indies), 1945; Lieut-Col Commanding No. 18 Infantry Holding Bn, 1946; attached to The Army Mobile Information Unit, 1948; Asst Dir of Public Relations to BAOR, 1951, as a Lieut-Col; retired pay, 1952. *Address:* The Old Barn, St Neot, Liskeard, Cornwall. *T:* Dobwalls 20799.

ESAKI, Leo; IBM Fellow since 1967; Manager, Device Physics, IBM T. J. Watson Research Center, since 1962; *b* 12 March 1925; *s* of Soichiro Esaki and Niyoko Ito; *m* 1959, Masako Araki; one *s* two *d*. *Educ:* Univ. of Tokyo. MS 1947, PhD 1959. Sony Corp., Japan, 1956-60; IBM Research, 1960-. Director: IBM-Japan, 1976-; Yamada Science Foundn, 1976-. Research in tunnelling in semiconductor junctions which led to the discovery of the tunnel diode, now working on man-made semiconductor superlattice in search of predicted quantum mechanical effect. Sir John Cass sen. vis. res. fellow, London Poly, 1982. Councillor-at-Large, Amer. Phys. Soc., 1971; Dir, Amer. Vacuum Soc., 1972; Mem., Japan Academy, 1975; For. Associate, Nat. Acad. of Sciences, USA, 1976; For. Associate, Nat. Acad. of Engineering, USA, 1977; Corresp. Mem., Academia Nacional De Ingenieria, Mexico, 1978. Nishina Meml Award, 1959; Asahi Press Award, 1960; Toyo Rayon Foundn Award, 1961; Morris N. Liebmann Meml Prize, 1961; Stuart Ballantine Medal, Franklin Inst., 1961; Japan Academy Award, 1965; Nobel Prize for Physics (jtly), 1973. Order of Culture, Japan, 1974. *Publications:* numerous papers in learned jls. *Address:* IBM Thomas J. Watson Research Center, PO Box 218, Yorktown Heights, New York 10598, USA. *T:* (914) 945-2342.

ESCRITT, (Charles) Ewart, OBE 1970; MA; Secretary, Oxford University Appointments Committee, 1947-70; Fellow, Keble College, Oxford, 1965-70; *b* 26 Aug. 1905; *s* of late Rev. Charles Escritt; *m* 1939, Ruth Mary, *d* of late T. C. Metcalf; two *s* one *d*. *Educ:* Christ's Hospital; Keble Coll., Oxford. Asst Master, Bromsgrove Sch., 1928; Staff of Tootal Broadhurst Lee Co. Ltd, 1933-46. Served War of 1939-45: 42 Div. RASC (TA), 1939; 18 Div. RASC, Capt. 1940; POW, Singapore and Thailand, 1942-45. *Recreation:* Japanese studies. *Address:* 32 Portland Road, Oxford. *T:* Oxford 57072.

ESCRITT, Maj.-Gen. Frederick Knowles, CB 1953; OBE 1943; MRCS; late RAMC, retired Nov. 1953; *b* 29 Nov. 1893; *s* of Harold Teal Escritt; *m* 1931, Elsa Alfrida, *d* of Director Larssen, Stockholm; one *d*. *Educ:* Dulwich Coll.; Guy's Hosp. MRCS, LRCP, 1918. Joined RAMC, Nov. 1918 (1914-15 Star, British War and Victory Medals). Served War of 1939-45 (Gen. Service Iraq,

1939-45 Star, Burma Star, Defence and War Medals, 1939-45). ADMS Eastern and 14 Armies, 1942-45; DDMS 1 Corps Dist, BAOR, 1945-47; Inspector of Training, AMS, 1950-51; DDMS, Eastern Command, 1951-53. QHS, 1952-53. Order of St John (Officer Brother), 1952.

ESDAILE, Philippa Chichele, DSc, FLS; Reader in Biology, University of London, and Head of Biology Department, King's College of Household and Social Science, 1921-51; *b* 1888; *y d* of late George Esdaile, Manchester and late Georgina, *d* of George Doswell, Somerset. *Educ:* Manchester High Sch. for Girls. Graduated Univ. of Manchester, 1910; Research Fellow of University of Manchester and University Coll., Reading; Acting Head of Zoology Dept, Bedford Coll., University of London, 1915-20; Senior Lecturer in Zoology, Birkbeck Coll., University of London, 1920-21; Vice-Pres. of Linnean Soc. of London, 1932-33; Member: Makerere-Khartoum Education Commission, 1937; Advisory Committee on Education, Colonial Office, 1933-38; Committee on Nutrition in the Colonial Empire, Econ. Adv. Coun., 1933; Federation of Univ. Women; Crosby Hall. Formerly Member: Coun. of Girls' Public Day Sch. Trust, Ltd; Governing Body of Hatfield Sch., Herts. *Publications:* Economic Biology for Students of Social Science, Parts 1 and 2; various scientific papers. *Address:* St Audrey's, Church Street, Old Hatfield, Herts. *T:* Hatfield 61990.

ESDALE, Mrs G. P. R.; *see* Lindop, Patricia J.

ESHER, 4th Viscount, *cr* 1897; Baron *cr* 1885; **Lionel Gordon Baliol Brett,** CBE 1970; MA; PPRIBA; DistTP; Rector and Vice-Provost, Royal College of Art, 1971-78; *b* 18 July 1913; *o s* of 3rd Viscount Esher, GBE; *S* father, 1963; *m* 1935, Christian, *e d* of late Col Ebenezer Pike, CBE, MC; five *s* one *d*. *Educ:* Eton (Scholar); New Coll., Oxford (Scholar); BA (1st Class), 1935; Hon. Fellow, 1980; RIBA Ashpitel Prizeman, 1939. Served War in RA, 1940-45; France and Germany, 1944-45 (despatches); Major. Architect Planner, Hatfield New Town, 1949-59; major housing projects: Hatfield, Stevenage, Basildon; consultant architect: Downside Abbey; Maidenhead Town Centre; Abingdon Town Centre; Portsmouth City Centre; York City Centre; Santiago, Chile and Caracas, Venezuela (both for UNDP); principal buildings include: (with Francis Pollen): High Comr's House, Lagos; 82 and 190 Sloane St, London; Pall Mall Ct, Manchester; Downside Sch. extensions; Exeter Coll., and Oxenford Hall, Oxford; (with Teggin & Taylor) Civic Offices, Portsmouth. Lecture tours: USA 1963; India, 1954; Australia, 1959; S America, 1970. Governor, Museum of London, 1970-77; Member: Royal Fine Art Commn, 1951-69; Adv. Bd for Redundant Churches (Chm., 1977-); Advisory Council, Victoria and Albert Museum, 1967-72; Arts Council of GB, 1972-77 (Chm., Art Panel); Environment Panel, British Rail, 1977-; National Trust (Chm., Thames and Chilterns Reg., 1979-); Vice-Pres., RIBA, 1958-59, 1962-63, 1964-65; Pres., 1965-67; Trustee, Soane Museum, 1976-. Hon. DLitt Strathclyde Univ., 1967; Hon. DUniv York, 1970; Hon. DSc Edinburgh, 1981. Hon. Fellow, Amer. Inst. of Architects; Hon. FSIAD, 1975. *Publications:* Houses, 1947; The World of Architecture, 1963; Landscape in Distress, 1965; York: a study in conservation, 1969; Parameters and Images, 1970; (with Elisabeth Beazley) Shell Guide to North Wales, 1971; A Broken Wave, 1981; The Continuing Heritage, 1982. *Recreation:* landscapes. *Heir: s* Hon. Christopher Lionel Baliol Brett [*b* 23 Dec. 1936; *m* 1st, 1962, Camilla Charlotte (marr. diss. 1970), *d* of Sir (Horace) Anthony Rumbold, 10th Bt, *qv* ; one *s* two *d* ; 2nd, 1971, Valerie Harrington; two *s* twin *d*]. *Address:* Christmas Common Tower, Watlington, Oxford. *Clubs:* Athenæum, Arts.
See also Sir Martyn G. Beckett, Sir Evelyn Shuckburgh.

ESMONDE, Sir John Henry Grattan, 16th Bt *cr* 1629; **His Honour Judge Esmonde,** SC; Circuit Court Judge, Western Circuit, since 1977; *b* 27 June 1928; *s* of Sir Anthony Charles Esmonde, 15th Bt, and of Eithne Moira Grattan, *y d* of Sir Thomas Grattan Esmonde, 11th Bt; *S* father, 1981; *m* 1957, Pamela Mary, *d* of late Francis Stephen Bourke, FRCPI; three *s* two *d*. *Educ:* Blackrock College, Dublin; University Coll., Dublin; King's Inns, Dublin. BComm, NUI. Member of the Irish Bar, 1949; Senior Counsel, 1971. TD (Fine Gael) Wexford, 1973-77. *Heir: s* Thomas Francis Grattan Esmonde, *b* 14 Oct. 1960. *Address:* 6 Nutley Avenue, Dublin 4. *T:* Dublin 693040. *Club:* Galway County.

ESPIE, Sir Frank (Fletcher), Kt 1979; OBE 1971; FTS, FIMM, MAIMM, MAIME; Non-executive Director, CRA Ltd, since 1979 (Director, 1968; Deputy Chairman, 1974-79); *b* 8 May 1917; *s* of late Frank Fancett Espie and of Laura Jean Espie; *m* 1941, Madeline Elizabeth Robertson; one *s* three *d*. *Educ:* St Peter's Coll., Adelaide; Univ. of Adelaide (BEng). FTS; FIMM 1958. Bougainville Copper Ltd: Gen. Man., 1965; Man. Dir, 1969; Chm., 1971-79; Dir, 1979-. Director: ICI Aust. Ltd, 1979-; Tubemakers of Australia, 1980-; Bank of New South Wales, 1981-; Woodside Petroleum, 1981-. Member: Exec. Cttee, Aust. Mining Industry Council, 1973-81 (Pres., 1978-80); Council: Australasian Inst. of Mining and Metallurgy (Pres., 1975; Inst. Medal, 1980); Aust. Acad. of Technological Scis. *Recreations:* swimming, golf. *Address:* 31 The Righi, South Yarra, Vic 3141, Australia. *T:* (03) 26.2062. *Clubs:* Melbourne, Athenæum, Royal Melbourne Golf (Melbourne); Union (Sydney); Adelaide (Adelaide).

ESPLEN, Sir William Graham, 2nd Bt, *cr* 1921; Shipowner; *b* 29 Dec. 1899; *s* of 1st Bt and Laura Louise (*d* 1936), *d* of late John Dickinson, Sunderland; *S* father, 1930; *m* 1928, Aline Octavia (marr. diss. 1951), *y d* of late A. Octavius Hedley; one *s*. *Educ:* Harrow; Cambridge. Joined Royal Naval College, Keyham, 1918; retired, 1922. *Recreation:* fishing. *Heir: s* John

Graham Esplen [b 4 Aug. 1932; m 1956, Valerie Joan, yr d of Maj.-Gen. A. P. Lambooy, CB, OBE, and late Doris Lambooy; one s three d]. Address: Heron Bridge, Newsham, Richmond, Yorks. Club: Royal Automobile.

ESPLIN, Air Vice-Marshal Ian (George), CB 1963; OBE 1946; DFC 1943; retired (voluntarily) 1965; b 26 Feb. 1914; s of late Donald Thomas Esplin and Emily Freame Esplin; m 1944, Patricia Kaleen Barlow; one s one d. Educ: Sydney Univ.; Oxford Univ. BEc 1936; MA 1939. Rowing Blue, 1934 and 1935. NSW Rhodes Schol., 1937. Entered RAF from Oxford, 1939. Served War of 1939-45, as Pilot in Night-Fighters; destroyed three enemy aircraft at night; also served at CFS and in HQ, SEAC; Air Min. (Policy), 1945; Comd Desford, 1947; Dep. Senior Personnel Staff Officer, HQ Reserve Comd, 1948; Directing Staff, RAF Staff Coll., 1950-51; Comd first Jet All Weather Wing, Germany (No 148), 1952-54; Flying Coll. Course, 1954; Dep. Dir of Operational Requirements, Air Min., 1955-58; Comd RAF Wartling, 1958-60; Dir of Operational Reqts, 1960-62; Comdr, RAF Staff and Air Attaché, Washington, DC, 1963-65; Dean, Air Attaché Corps, 1964-65. Recreations: golf, tennis, swimming, ski-ing. Address: c/o National Westminster Bank Ltd, West End Office, 1 St James's Square, SW1. Clubs: Vincent's (Oxford); Leander (Henley-on-Thames).

ESSAAFI, M'hamed, Grand Officier, Order of Tunisian Republic, 1963; Chef de Cabinet at the United Nations, since 1982; b 26 May 1930; m 1956, Hedwige Klat; one s one d. Educ: Sadiki Coll., Tunis; Sorbonne, Paris. Secretariat of State for For. Affairs, 1956; 1st Sec., Tunisian Embassy, London, 1956; 1st Sec., Tunisian Embassy, Washington, 1957; Secretariat of State for For. Affairs, Tunis: Dir of Amer. Dept, 1960; America and Internat. Confs Dept, 1962; Ambassador to London, 1964-69; Ambassador to Moscow, 1970-74; Ambassador to Bonn, 1974-76; Sec.-Gen., Ministry of Foreign Affairs, Tunis, 1969-70 and 1976-78; Ambassador to Belgium and EEC, 1978-79; Permanent Rep. of Tunisia to the UN, and Special Rep. of the Sec.-Gen., 1980-81. Recreation: shooting. Address: United Nations, Room 3800E, New York, NY 10017, USA; 1725 York Avenue, New York, NY 10028, USA.

ESSAME, Enid Mary, MA Cantab; Headmistress of Queenswood School, 1943-71; 2nd d of Oliver Essame. Educ: Wyggeston Gram. Sch., Leicester; Girls' High Sch., Newark; Newnham Coll., Cambridge (Hist. Tripos, 1928); King's Coll., University of London (Certificate of Education, 1929). Mary Ewart Travelling Scholar, Newnham Coll., 1934-35; AM in Education, American Univ., Washington, DC, USA, 1935. Asst Headmistress Queenswood Sch., 1935-43. British Council lecturer, India and Pakistan, 1953, Nigeria, 1961. Governor, Chorleywood Coll. for Girls with Little or No Sight, 1962. Hon. Sec. Assoc. of Headmistresses of Boarding Schools, Pres. 1962-64. Chm., Assoc. of Ind. and Direct Grant Schools. Bd Mem., Schoolmistresses and Governesses Benevolent Instn, 1974-; Hon. Adviser, Nat. Assoc. for Gifted Children, 1974-. Governor: St Helen's Sch., Northwood; Channing Sch., Highgate; Trustee, Stormont Sch., Potters Bar. Overseas Grants Cttee, Help the Aged, 1981. JP Herts 1952-76. Address: 4 Elmroyd Avenue, Potters Bar, Herts. T: Potters Bar 53255. Clubs: Royal Over-Seas League, Arts Theatre.

ESSAYAN, Michael, QC 1976; b 7 May 1927; s of late Kevork Loris Essayan and Rita Sirvarte (née Gulbenkian); m 1956, Geraldine St Lawrence Lee Guinness, d of K. E. L. Guinness, MBE; one s one d. Educ: France; Harrow; Balliol Coll., Oxford (1st Cl. Class. Hon. Mods 1949, 1st Cl. Lit. Hum. 1951, MA). Served with RA, 1945-48 (Palestine, 1947-48). Iraq Petroleum Co., London and ME, 1951-56. Called to the Bar, Middle Temple 1957, joined Lincoln's Inn ad eundem 1958. Mem., Bd of Administration, Calouste Gulbenkian Foundn, Lisbon, 1981-. Publications: The New Supreme Court Costs (with M. J. Albery, QC), 1960; (ed with Hon. Mr Justice Walton) Adkin's Landlord and Tenant, 15th, 16th and 17th edns. Recreations: wine and wife. Address: 6 Chelsea Square, SW3. T: 01-352 6786; 9 Old Square, Lincoln's Inn, WC2. T: 01-405 0846. Club: Brooks's.

ESSEN, Louis, OBE 1959; FRS 1960; DSc, PhD; retired; b 6 Sept. 1908; s of Fred Essen and Ada (née Edson); m 1937, Joan Margery Greenhalgh; four d. Educ: High Pavement Sch., Nottingham; London Univ. (Ext.). BSc 1928, PhD 1941, DSc 1948, London. Joined the National Physical Laboratory, 1929; Senior Principal Scientific Officer, 1956-60; Deputy Chief Scientific Officer, 1960-72. Charles Vernon Boys Prize, Phys. Soc. 1957; Tompion Gold Medal, Clockmakers' Company, 1957; Wolfe Award, 1959; A. S. Popov Gold Medal, USSR Acad. of Sciences, 1959. Hon. FUMIST, 1971. Publications: Velocity of Light and Radio Waves, 1969; The Special Theory of Relativity, 1971; scientific papers. Recreations: walking, gardening, music. Address: High Hallgarth, 41 Durleston Park Drive, Great Bookham, Surrey KT23 4AJ. T: Bookham 54103.

ESSEX, 10th Earl of, cr 1661; **Robert Edward de Vere Capell;** Baron Capell, 1641; Viscount Malden, 1661; b 13 Jan. 1920; s of Arthur Algernon de Vere Capell (d 1924) and Alice Mabel (d 1951), d of James Currie, Wimbledon; S kinsman, 1981; m 1942, Doris Margaret, d of George Frederick Tomlinson, Morecambe; one s. Heir: s Viscount Malden, qv. Address: 2 Novak Place, Torrisholme, Morecambe, Lancs.

ESSEX, Francis; author, producer and composer; b 24 March 1929; s of Harold and Beatrice Essex-Lopresti; m 1956, Jeanne Shires; two s. Educ: Cotton Coll., N Staffs. Light Entertainment Producer, BBC Television, 1954-60; Sen. Prod.,

ATV Network Ltd, 1960-65; Controller of Progs, Scottish Television, 1965-69; ATV Network Ltd: Prodn Controller, 1969-76; Mem., Bd of Dirs, 1974; Dir of Production, 1976-81. Wrote and presented, The Bells of St Martins, St Martin's Theatre, 1953; devised and directed, Six of One, Adelphi, 1964; television film scripts include: Shillingbury Tales; Silent Scream; Percy French—the Man from Cavan; The Elizabethan Suite; Cuffy series; scores: Luke's Kingdom; The Seas Must Live; The Lightning Tree; Maddie With Love, etc; writer of plays and songs. Fellow, Royal Television Soc., 1974. British Acad. Light Entertainment Award, 1964, and Leonard Brett Award, 1964, 1981. Recreations: blue-water sailing, gardening. Address: Punta Vista, Aldea de las Cuevas, Benidoleig, Prov. de Alicante, Spain.

ESSEX, Francis William, CMG 1959; retired from HMOCS; b 29 June 1916; s of Frank Essex; m 1947, Marjorie Muriel Joyce Lewis; two s. Educ: Royal Grammar Sch., High Wycombe; Reading Univ.; Exeter Coll., Oxford. Joined Colonial Administrative Service, Sierra Leone, 1939; Asst District Commissioner, 1942; District Commissioner, 1948; Principal, HM Treasury, 1951; Dep. Financial Sec., Sierra Leone, 1953; Financial Sec., British Guiana, 1956-60; Financial Sec. to High Comr for Basutoland, Bechuanaland and Swaziland, 1960-64; Counsellor, British Embassy, South Africa, 1964-65; Sec. for Finance and Development, later Permanent Sec., Min. of Finance, Commerce and Industry, Swaziland, 1965-68; Principal, ODM, 1968-76. Mem., Pearce Commn on Rhodesian opinion, 1971-72. Short term British Technical Co-operation assignments, British Virgin Is, 1977, Tuvalu, 1978 and 1979, Antigua and Barbuda, 1981. Address: Undermoor, Broomhill, Chagford, Devon.

ESSEX, Mary; see Bloom, Ursula.

ESSEX, Rosamund Sibyl, MA; free-lance journalist, since 1979; b 26 July 1900; d of late Rev. Herbert J. Essex and late Rachel Watson; unmarried; one adopted s. Educ: Bournemouth High Sch. for Girls; St Hilda's Coll., Oxford. Editorial staff of the Church Times, 1929-47; Asst Ed., 1947-50; Editor, 1950-60; Member of Staff, Christian Aid, British Council of Churches, 1960-78. Chm. Religious Press Group, 1952-53 and 1957-58. Commissioned and licensed a Reader in the Church of England, dio. St Albans, 12 July 1969. Publications: (with Sidney Dark) The War Against God, 1937; Into the Forest, 1963; Woman in a Man's World (autobiog.), 1977. Recreation: photography. Address: 32 Holywell Hill, St Albans, Herts AL1 1BZ. T: St Albans 53424. Club: Royal Commonwealth Society.

ESSEX-CATER, Dr Antony John, LRCP, MRCS; FFCM; FRAI; Medical Officer of Health, States of Jersey, Channel Islands, since 1974; Venerologist, General Hospital, Jersey, since 1974; Chairman, National Association for Maternal and Child Welfare, since 1975; b 28 Sept. 1923; s of Herbert Stanley Cater and Helen Marjorie Essex; m 1947, Jane Mary Binning; three s one d. Educ: Solihull Sch.; King's Coll., Univ. of London; Charing Cross Hosp.; School of Hyg. and Trop. Med., Univ. of London. Bygott Postgrad. Schol., Univ. of London, 1952-53. DPH, DIH, DCH; FRSH. Medical Br., RAF, 1948-50. Dep. MOH, Swansea, 1953-58; Admin. MOH, Birmingham, 1958-61; Dep. MOH, Manchester, 1961-68; County MOH, Monmouthshire, 1968-74. Part-time Lectr in Child Health, Univ. of Birmingham, 1958-61; Council of Europe Medical Fellow, 1968. Mem. Exec. Cttee 1958, Vice-Chm. 1969, Nat. Assoc. for Maternal and Child Welfare; Member: Public Health Lab. Services Bd, 1969-75; Steering Cttee, Nat. Health Service Reorganization (Wales), 1971-72; Founder Fellow and Mem. First Bd, Fac. of Community Med., Royal Colls of Physicians of UK, 1972-73. Member: BMA; Med. Soc. for Study of Venereal Diseases. Publications: Synopsis of Public Health and Social Medicine, 1960, 2nd edn 1967; Manual of Public Health and Community Medicine, 3rd edn 1979; numerous papers on medical and allied subjects. Recreations: literary, music, sport. Address: Honfleur, La Vallette, Mont Cambrai, St Lawrence, Jersey, CI. T: Jersey 72438. Club: Society of Authors.

ESSLEMONT, Mary, CBE 1955; MA, BSc, MB, ChB, DPH, LLD, JP; d of late George Birnie Esslemont, MP for South Aberdeen. Educ: Aberdeen High Sch. for Girls; Aberdeen Univ. Asst, Botany Dept, University of Aberdeen, 1915-17; Science Lecturer, Stockwell Training Coll., London, 1917-19; Asst MOH, Keighley, Yorks, 1924-29; Gen. Practitioner, Aberdeen, 1929, now retired. Fellow: BMA, 1959; RCGP, 1969. Mem., Aberdeen Univ. Court, 1947-74. Hon. LLD, University of Aberdeen, 1954. JP for District Council of Aberdeen. Freedom, City of Aberdeen, 1981. Recreation: travel. Address: Mile End House, 30 Beechgrove Terrace, Aberdeen AB2 4ED. T: 633601. Club: Soroptimist Headquarters.

ESSLIN, Martin Julius, OBE 1972; Professor of Drama, Stanford University, California (for two quarters annually), since 1977; b 8 June 1918; s of Paul Pereszlenyi and Charlotte Pereszlenyi (née Schiffer); m 1947, Renate Gerstenberg; one d. Educ: Gymnasium, Vienna; Vienna Univ.; Reinhardt Seminar of Dramatic Art, Vienna. Joined BBC, 1940; Producer and Scriptwriter, BBC European Services, 1941-55; Asst Head, BBC European Productions Dept, 1955; Asst Head, Drama (Sound), BBC, 1961; Head of Drama (Radio), BBC, 1963-77. Awarded title Professor by Pres. of Austria, 1967; Vis. Prof. of Theatre, Florida State Univ., 1969-76. Hon. DLitt Kenyon Coll., Ohio, 1978. Publications: Brecht, A Choice of Evils, 1959; The Theatre of the Absurd, 1962; (ed) Beckett (anthology of critical essays), 1965; Harold Pinter, 1967; The Genius of the German Theatre, 1968; Reflections, Essays on Modern Theatre (NY), 1969 (UK, as Brief Chronicles, 1970); The Peopled

Wound: the plays of Harold Pinter, 1970, rev. edn as Pinter: a study of his plays, 1973; (ed) The New Theatre of Europe, 1970; Artaud, 1976; An Anatomy of Drama, 1976; (ed) Illustrated Encyclopaedia of World Theatre, 1977; Mediations, Essays on Brecht, Beckett and the Media, 1981; The Age of Television, 1982. *Recreations:* reading, book collecting. *Address:* 64 Loudoun Road, NW8. *T:* 01-722 4243; Ballader's Plat, Winchelsea, Sussex. *T:* Winchelsea 392; c/o Department of Drama, Stanford University, Stanford, Calif. 94305, USA. *Club:* Garrick.

ESSWOOD, Paul Lawrence Vincent; singer (counter-tenor); Professor, Royal College of Music, since 1973; *b* West Bridgford, Nottingham, 6 June 1942; *s* of Alfred Walter Esswood and Freda Garratt; *m* 1966, Mary Lillian Cantrill, ARCM; two *s.* *Educ:* West Bridgford Grammar Sch.; Royal Coll. of Music (ARCM). Lay-Vicar, Westminster Abbey, 1964-71. Specialist in baroque performance; has made recordings of Bach, Handel, Purcell, Monteverdi, Cavalli, etc; first broadcast, BBC, 1965; co-founder: Pro Cantione Antiqua; A Cappella Male Voice Ensemble for Performance of Old Music, 1967; operatic debut in Cavalli's L'Erismena, Univ. of California, Berkeley, 1968; debut at La Scala, Milan with Zurich Opera in L'Incoronazione di Poppea and Il Ritorno d'Ulisse, 1978; Scottish Opera debut in Dido and Aeneas, 1978; world premiere, Penderecki's Paradise Lost, Chicago Lyric Opera, 1979; performed in major festivals: Edinburgh, Leeds Triennial, English Bach, Vienna, Salzburg, Zurich, Hamburg, Berlin, Naples, Israel, Lucerne, Flanders, Wexford, Holland. *Recreations:* philately, sports, aquariology. *Address:* 6 Gowan Avenue, SW6 6RF. *T:* 01-736 3141.

ESTES, Elliott M.; retired as President and Chief Operating Officer, General Motors Corporation, Detroit, USA; *b* Mendon, Mich. Joined Gen. Motors Corp., 1956; Exec. Vice-Pres., Ops and Staff Dir, 1972-74; Pres. and Chief Operating Officer, 1974-80. Director: Kellogg Co. Inc.; Owens-Illinois Inc.; Communications Satellite Corp. *Address:* c/o General Motors Corporation, 3044 West Grand Boulevard, Detroit, Mich 48202, USA.

ESTEY, Willard Zebedee; Hon. Mr Justice Estey; Justice of the Supreme Court of Canada, since 1977; *b* 10 Oct. 1919; *s* of James Wilfred Estey and Muriel Baldwin Estey; *m* 1946, Marian Ruth McKinnon; three *s* one *d.* *Educ:* Univ. of Saskatchewan (BA, LLB); Harvard Law Sch. (LLM). Mem., Bar of Sask., 1942 and of Ont, 1947; QC Ont 1960. Prof., Coll. of Law, Univ. of Sask., 1946-47; Lectr, Osgoode Hall Law Sch., 1947-51. Practised law, Toronto, 1947-72. Pres., Canadian Bar Assoc., Ont, 1972. Mem. Court of Appeal, 1973, and Chief Justice of High Court, Supreme Court of Ont, 1975; Chief Justice of Ontario, 1976. Commissioner: Steel Profits Inquiry, Royal Commn of Inquiry, 1974; Air Canada Inquiry, 1975. Hon. LLD: Wilfrid Laurier Univ., Waterloo, Ont, 1977; Univ. of Toronto, 1979; Univ. of W Ont, 1980; Law Soc. of Upper Canada, 1981. *Address:* Supreme Court of Canada, Ottawa, Ont K1A 0J1, Canada.

ESTYN EVANS, Emyr; *see* Evans, E. E.

ETCHELLS, (Dorothea) Ruth, MA, BD; Principal, St John's College with Cranmer Hall, University of Durham, since 1979; *b* 17 April 1931; *d* of late Walter and Ada Etchells. *Educ:* Merchant Taylor's School for Girls, Crosby, Liverpool; Universities of Liverpool (MA) and London (BD). Head of English Dept, Aigburth Vale High Sch., Liverpool, 1959; Lectr in English, 1963, Sen. Lectr in English and Resident Tutor, 1965, Chester College of Education; Trevelyan College, Univ. of Durham: Resident Tutor and part-time Lectr in English, 1968; Vice Principal, 1972; Sen. Lectr, 1973. Member: Bishop's Council and Standing Cttee of Diocesan Synod; Cttee, Gen. Synod Bd of Educn; Ecumenical Affairs Div., BCC; Standing Cttee and Gen. Council Church Missionary Soc.; Panel of Reference, Assoc. of Christian Teachers; Panel of Reference, Christians in The Arts; Edit. Bd, The Churchman; Governing Bodies, Dame Allan's Schools and Monkton Combe School. *Publications:* Unafraid To Be, 1969; The Man with the Trumpet, 1970; A Model of Making, 1982. *Recreations:* friends, quiet, country walking, London. *Address:* Principal's Lodging, 7 South Bailey, Durham City. *T:* Durham 69113.

ETHERINGTON-SMITH, (Raymond) Gordon (Antony), CMG 1962; HM Diplomatic Service, retired; *b* 1 Feb. 1914; *o s* of late T. B. Etherington-Smith and Henriette de Pitner; *m* 1950, Mary Elizabeth Besly; one *s* three *d.* *Educ:* Downside; Magdalen Coll., Oxford. Entered FO, 1936. Served at: Berlin, 1939; Copenhagen, 1939-40; Washington, 1940-42; Chungking, 1943-45; Kashgar, 1945-46; Moscow, 1947; Foreign Office, 1947-52; Holy See, 1952-54; Counsellor, Saigon, 1954-57; The Hague, 1958-61; Office of UK Commissioner-Gen. for South-East Asia, Singapore, 1961-63; Ambassador to Vietnam, 1963-66; Minister, and Dep. Commandant, Berlin, 1966-70; Ambassador to Sudan, 1970-74. *Recreations:* fishing, squash rackets, travel. *Address:* The Old Rectory, Melbury Abbas, Shaftesbury, Dorset SP7 0DZ. *T:* Shaftesbury 3105. *Club:* Oriental.

ETHERTON, Ralph, MA; Barrister-at-Law; *b* 11 Feb. 1904; *o s* of late Louis Etherton and Bertha Mary, *d* of late John Bagge; *m* 1944, Johanne Patricia, *y d* of late Gerald Cloherty, Galway, Ireland; one *s* one *d.* *Educ:* Charterhouse; Trinity Hall, Cambridge. Called to Bar, Inner Temple, 1926, and joined Northern Circuit, practised at Common Law Bar until 1939; Municipal Reform Candidate LCC election, N Camberwell 1931, and W. Fulham 1937; served in RAFVR (Special Duties), Flt Lt, 1940-42; MP (Nat. C) for Stretford div. of Lancs, 1939-45; contested (Nat. C) Liverpool (Everton div.),

1935, Stretford div. of Lancs, 1945; engaged in commerce, 1945-73. Chm. of Coningsby Club, 1933-34; Mem. of Parliamentary Delegation to Australia and New Zealand, 1944. *Recreations:* travel, riding. *Address:* Greentree Hall, Balcombe, Sussex RH17 6JZ. *T:* Balcombe 319. *Clubs:* Carlton, Pratt's.

ETIANG, Paul Orono, BA London; an Assistant Secretary-General, Organisation of African Unity. Addis Ababa, since 1978; *b* 15 Aug. 1938; *s* of late Kezironi Orono and Adacat Ilera Orono; *m* 1967, Zahra Ali Foum; two *s* two *d.* *Educ:* Makerere Univ. Coll. Uganda Admin. Officer, 1962-64; Asst Sec., Foreign Affairs, 1964-65; 3rd Sec., 1965-66, 2nd Sec., 1966-67, Uganda Embassy, Moscow; 1st Sec., Uganda Mission to UN, New York, 1968; Counsellor, 1968-69, High Commissioner, 1969-71, Uganda High Commission, London; Chief of Protocol and Marshal of the Diplomatic Corps, Uganda, 1971; Permanent Sec., Uganda Min. of Foreign Affairs, 1971-73; Minister of State for Foreign Affairs, 1973; Minister of State in the President's office, 1974; Minister of Transport and Communications, July 1976, of Transport, Communications and Works, Mar. 1977, of Transport and Works, 1978. *Recreations:* chess, classical music, billiards. *Address:* Organisation of African Unity, PO Box 3243, Addis Ababa, Ethiopia.

ETON, Robert; *see* Meynell, L. W.

ETTLINGER, Prof. Leopold David; Professor of History of Art, University of California, Berkeley, since 1970; *b* 20 April 1913; *s* of Dr Emil Ettlinger, University Librarian, and Dora (*née* Beer); *m* 1st, 1939, Amrei (*née* Jacoby); she *d* 1955; 2nd, 1959, Madeline (*née* Noirot); 3rd, 1973, Helen (*née* Shahrokh). *Educ:* Stadtgymnasium Halle; Universities of Halle and Marburg. Social Worker for Refugee Children from Germany, 1938-41; Asst Master, King Edward VI Grammar Sch., Five Ways, Birmingham, 1941-48; Asst Curator, Photographic Collection, Warburg Institute, University of London, 1948-51; Curator of Photographic Collection, 1951-56; Lectr, Warburg Inst., 1956-59; Durning Lawrence Prof. of History of Art, Univ. of London, 1959-70. Fellowship, Inst. for Advanced Study, Princeton, 1956; Vis. Professor: Yale Univ., 1963-64; Univ. of Calif, Berkeley, 1969; Univ. of Bonn, 1975-76, 1981-82; Univ. of Victoria, BC, 1980; Kress Prof., Nat. Gall. of Art, Washington DC, 1980-81. FSA 1962-. British Academy award, 1963. *Publications:* (with R. G. Holloway) Compliments of the Season, 1947; The Art of the Renaissance in Northern Europe, in New Cambridge Modern History, Vol. I, 1957; Kandinsky's "At Rest", 1961; Art History Today, 1961; The Sistine Chapel before Michelangelo: Religious Imagery and Papal Politics, 1965; (with Helen S. Ettlinger) Botticelli, 1976; Antonio and Piero Pollaiuolo, 1978; contribs to Journal of Warburg and Courtauld Insts, Burlington Magazine, Architectural Review, Connoisseur, Italian Studies and other jls. *Address:* Department of History of Art, University of California, Berkeley, Calif 94720, USA.

ETZDORF, Hasso von; *b* 2 March 1900; *s* of Rüdiger von Etzdorf-Neumark and Agnes Maria Lorentz; *m* Katharina Otto-Margonin. *Educ:* Universities of Berlin, Göttingen, Halle (LLD). German Foreign Office, 1928; served in Berlin, Tokyo, Rome, Genoa (Consul-Gen.); Dep. Head, German Office for Peace Questions, Stuttgart, 1947-50; FO, Bonn, 1950-53; Head of German Delegn at Interim Cttee for Eur. Def. Community in Paris, rank of Minister, 1953; Dep. Sec.-Gen., WEU, London, 1955; Ambassador of German Federal Republic to Canada, 1956-58; Dep. Under-Sec. and Head of Western Dept, FO, Bonn, 1958-61; Ambassador of German Fed. Rep. to Court of St James's, 1961-65. GCVO (Hon.) 1964; Order of Merit with Star, Federal Republic of Germany, 1957. *Address:* Eichtling, D-8018 Grafing bei München, Germany. *T:* Glonn (08093) 1402. *Clubs:* Travellers', White's.

EUGSTER, General Sir Basil, KCB 1970 (CB 1966); KCVO 1968; CBE 1962; DSO 1945; MC 1938, and Bar, 1940; DL; *b* 15 Aug. 1914; *er s* of late Oscar Louis Eugster, DSO, Kempston Hoo, near Bedford; *m* 1939, Marcia Elaine, *er d* of late Air Commodore Sir Percy Smyth-Osbourne, CMG, CBE; two *s.* *Educ:* Beaumont; Christ Church, Oxford (MA). 2nd Lieut Irish Guards, 1935. Served War of 1939-45 in Narvik, Italy and NW Europe; Bde Maj., HQ 140 Inf. Bde, 1943-44; GSO 2 (Ops); HQ 5 Corps CMF, Oct-Nov., 1944; OC 3rd Bn IG, Jan.-Feb., 1945; GSO 1, Guards Div., Dec. 1945-Jan. 1947; OC 2nd Bn, Irish Guards, 1947; JSSC, 1950; OC 1st Bn, Irish Guards, 1951-54; AAG War Office, 1954-56; Comdt, Eaton Hall Officer Cadet Sch., 1956-58; Comdt Mons Officer Cadet Sch., 1958; IDC 1959; Comd, 3rd Inf. Bde Gp, and Dhekelia Area, Cyprus, 1959-62; Comdt Sch. of Infantry, Warminster, 1962-63; GOC 4 Div., BAOR, 1963-65; GOC London Dist, and Maj.-Gen. Comdg Household Bde, 1965-68; Commander, British Forces, Hong Kong, 1968-70; GOC-in-C, Southern Comd, 1971-72; C-in-C, UKLF, 1972-74. ADC (Gen.), 1973-74; retired 1974; Col, Irish Guards, 1969, Hon. Col 1974-80, London Irish Co., N Irish Mil. (V). DL Devon, 1977. *Address:* Holmedown, Exbourne, N Devon. *T:* Exbourne 241. *Clubs:* White's, Buck's.

EURICH, Richard Ernst, RA 1953 (ARA 1942); Artist (Painter); *b* Bradford, 14 March 1903; *s* of late Professor Wm Eurich; *m* 1934, Mavis Llewellyn Pope; two *d* (one *s* decd). *Educ:* St George's Sch., Harpenden; Bradford Grammar Sch. Studied art at Bradford Sch. of Arts and Crafts, and Slade Sch., London; held One Man Show of drawings at Goupil Gallery in 1929, and several exhibitions of paintings at Redfern Gallery; exhibited at Royal Academy, New English Art Club and London Group; works purchased by Contemporary Art Soc. and Chantrey Bequest; Painting, Dunkirk Beach 1940, purchased for Canadian Government; Official War Artist, 1941-45;

representative works in various public galleries. *Recreations:* music and gardening. *Address:* Appletreewick, Dibden Purlieu, Southampton. *T:* Hythe (Hants) 842291.

EUSTON, Earl of; James Oliver Charles FitzRoy, MA, FCA; *b* 13 Dec. 1947; *s* and *heir* of 11th Duke of Grafton, *qv*; *m* 1972, Lady Clare Kerr, BA, *d* of Marquess of Lothian, *qv*; one *s* two *d. Educ:* Eton; Magdalene Coll., Cambridge (MA). Dir, Smith St Aubyn & Co. (Holdings) Limited, 1980-. *Heir: s* Viscount Ipswich, *qv. Address:* 6 Vicarage Gardens, W8; The Racing Stables, Euston, Thetford, Norfolk.

EVAN-COOK, John Edward, JP; *b* 25 Oct. 1902; 2nd *s* of late Evan Cook, JP, of London; *m* 1928, Winifred Elizabeth, *d* of Joseph Samuel Pointon; no *c. Educ:* Westminster City Sch. Served War, 1940-46, Major, RAOC. Adviser on Packaging, War Office, 1940-46. Vice-Chm. London District Rotary, 1950-52; Pres. Rotary Club of Camberwell, 1948. Chairman: Bd of Visitors, HM Prison, Brixton, 1967-73; Evan-Cook Group (retd); Inst. of Packaging (Nat. Chm., 1954, President, 1954-57); Min. of Labour & Nat. Service Local Disablement Cttee, 1959-67. Estates Governor, Dulwich, 1973-. Chief Scouts' Medal of Merit, 1962; Silver Acorn, 1968. Past Master, Worshipful Company of Paviors; Liveryman: Worshipful Co. of Carmen; Worshipful Co. of Farmers. Sheriff of London, 1958-59; Common Councilman, City of London, 1960-66 and 1972-77. JP City of London, 1950. Order of Homayoun, 3rd Class (Iran); Grand Cross of Merit, Order of Merit (Federal Republic of Germany). *Address:* Slough Green House, Slough Green, Cuckfield, Sussex. *T:* Haywards Heath 413220. *Clubs:* City Livery (Pres., 1964-65), United Wards, Royal Automobile, Bentley Drivers', Institute of Advanced Motorists.

EVANS; *see* Parry-Evans and Parry Evans.

EVANS, family name of **Barons Energlyn, Evans of Claughton** and **Mountevans.**

EVANS OF CLAUGHTON, Baron *cr* 1978 (Life Peer), of Claughton in the County of Merseyside; **(David Thomas) Gruffydd Evans;** JP; President of the Liberal Party, 1977-78; Liberal Party Spokesman in House of Lords on Local Government and Housing; *b* 9 Feb. 1928; *s* of John Cynlais Evans and Nellie Euronwy Evans; *m* 1957, Moira Elizabeth (*née* Rankin); one *s* three *d. Educ:* Birkenhead Prep. Sch.; Birkenhead Sch.; Friars Sch., Bangor; Univ. of Liverpool (LLB 1949). Solicitors' final exam., 1952. Pilot Officer, RAF, 1952-54. Hon. Sec., Lancs, Cheshire and N West Liberal Fedn, 1956-60; Chm., Nat. League of Young Liberals, 1960-61. Councillor: Birkenhead CBC, 1957-74; Wirral BC, 1973-78 (Leader Lib. Gp, 1973-77); Merseyside CC, 1973-81 (Leader Lib. Gp, 1977-81). Chairman: Nat. Exec. 1965-68, Assembly Cttee 1971-74, Gen. Election Cttee 1977-79, of the Liberal Party; Vice-Pres., Welsh Liberal Party, 1979-. Mem. Court, Liverpool Univ., 1977-; Governor Birkenhead Sch., 1974-78; Chairman: Birkenhead Council of Voluntary Service, 1964-73; Abbeyfield Soc. (Birkenhead), 1970-74; Liverpool Luncheon Club, 1980-81; Marcher Sound Radio, 1980-. JP Wirral, 1960. *Recreations:* golf; Welsh Rugby; Liverpool FC. *Address:* Sunridge, 69 Bidston Road, Claughton, Birkenhead, Merseyside L43 6TR. *T:* 051-652 3425. *Clubs:* National Liberal; Bluecoat, Lyceum (Liverpool); Oxton Cricket, Birkenhead Squash Racquets, Wirral Ladies' Golf (Birkenhead).

EVANS, A. Briant; Hon. Consulting Gynæcological Surgeon, Westminster Hospital and Chelsea Hospital for Women; Hon. Consulting Obstetric Surgeon, Queen Charlotte's Maternity Hospital; *b* 26 June 1909; *e s* of late Arthur Evans, OBE, MD, MS, FRCS; *m* 1939, Audrey Marie, *er d* of late Roland Eveleigh Holloway; three *s. Educ:* Westminster Sch.; Gonville and Caius Coll., Cambridge; Westminster Hosp. MA, MB, BCh Cantab; FRCS; FRCOG. Sometime Examiner in Obstetrics to Univs of Cambridge and London and to Royal College of Obstetricians and Gynæcologists. Temp. Lieut-Col RAMC, served in Egypt, Italy and Austria; OC No. 9 Field Surgical Unit. *Address:* Studs, Radnage, near High Wycombe, Bucks HP14 4DW. *T:* Radnage 3460. *Club:* Army and Navy.

EVANS, Albert; *b* 10 June 1903; *s* of Moses Richard Evans; *m* 1929, Beatrice Joan, *d* of F. W. Galton. *Educ:* LCC Sch.; WEA. MP (Lab) West Islington, Sept. 1947-Feb. 1950, South-West Islington, 1950-70; retired; Member: Islington Borough Council, 1937-47; LCC, 1946-49. *Address:* Abbey Lodge, 3 Hooks Hill Road, Sheringham, Norfolk.

EVANS, Alfred Thomas, (Fred Evans); BA; *b* 24 Feb. 1914; *s* of Alfred Evans, Miner, and Sarah Jane Evans; *m* 1939, Mary (*née* O'Marah); one *s* two *d. Educ:* Primary and Grammar Schs; University of Wales. Head of Dept, Grammar Sch., Bargoed, Glam, 1937-49; Headmaster, Bedlinog Secondary Sch., Glam, 1949-66; Headmaster, Lewis Boys Grammar Sch., Pengam, Mon, 1966-68. Contested (Lab) Leominster, 1955, Stroud, 1959; MP (Lab) Caerphilly, July 1968-1979. Organising Agent, Caerphilly Constituency Labour Party, 1962-66. Chm., Welsh Parly Lab. Party, 1977; a Chm., Private Bills Cttee, 1975. *Address:* 8 Dilwyn Avenue, Hengoed, Mid Glam CF8 7AG. *Clubs:* Aneurin Labour (Caerphilly); Labour (Bargoed).

EVANS, Alun; *see* Evans, T. A.

EVANS, Alun S.; *see* Sylvester-Evans.

EVANS, Sir Anthony (Adney), 2nd Bt, *cr* 1920; *b* 5 Aug. 1922; *s* of Sir Walter Harry Evans, 1st Bt, and Margaret Mary, *y d* of late Thomas Adney Dickens; *S* father 1954; married; two *s* one *d. Educ:* Shrewsbury; Merton Coll., Oxford. *Club:* Leander (Henley).

EVANS, Anthony Howell Meurig, RD 1968; QC 1971; a Recorder of the Crown Court, since 1972; *b* 11 June 1934; *s* of David Meurig Evans, *qv*; *m* 1963, Caroline Mary Fyffe Mackie, *d* of late Edwin Gordon Mackie; one *s* two *d. Educ:* Bassaleg Sec. Grammar Sch., Mon; Shrewsbury Sch.; St John's Coll., Cambridge. Nat. Service, RNVR, 1952-54 (Lt-Comdr RNR). BA 1957, LLB 1958, Cantab. Called to Bar, Gray's Inn, 1958 (Arden Scholar and Birkenhead Scholar); Bencher, 1979. Fellow, Internat. Acad. of Trial Lawyers, NY, 1975. Mem. Melbourne, Vic, Bar, 1975. *Publication:* (Jt Editor) The Law of the Air (Lord McNair), 1964. *Recreations:* sailing, music. *Address:* 4 Essex Court, Temple, EC4. *T:* 01-583 9191; Milan House, Overton, near Swansea, West Glamorgan. *Clubs:* Cardiff & County; Royal Wimbledon Golf.

EVANS, (Arthur) Mostyn; General Secretary, Transport and General Workers Union, since 1978; Member, TUC General Council, since 1977; *b* 13 July 1925; *m* 1947, Laura Bigglestone; two *s* three *d* (and one *s* decd). *Educ:* Cefn Coed Primary Sch., S Wales; Church Road Secondary Modern Sch., Birmingham. District Officer, Birmingham, Chem. and Eng. Industries, 1956; Regional Officer, Midlands, 1960; Nat. Officer, Eng., 1966; National Secretary: Chem., Rubber, and Oil Industries, 1969; Engineering Industries, 1969; (Automotive Section), TGWU, 1969-73; Nat. Organiser, TGWU, 1973-78. Part-time Mem., Nat. Bus Co., 1976-78; Member: BOTB, 1978-79; NEDC, 1978-; Exec., ITF, 1980-; Vice-Pres., ICEF, 1980-. *Recreation:* music. *Address:* 6 Highland Drive, Hemel Hempstead, Herts. *T:* 57503.

EVANS, Sir Arthur Trevor, Kt 1954; Controller of Death Duties, 1951-57; *b* 7 Nov. 1895; *er s* of Benjamin Evans; *m* 1925, Mary Dagmar (*d* 1977), *d* of J. H. Powell, JP, Aberdare, Glam; one *s* one *d. Educ:* Stationers' Company's Sch.; King's Coll., London. LLB. Asst Controller of Death Duties, 1944. Dep. Controller, 1947. *Address:* Flat 1, Cliff Court, Rottingdean, Brighton BN2 7JD.

EVANS, Sir Athol (Donald), KBE 1963 (CBE 1954; MBE 1939); retired as Secretary for Home Affairs, Government of the Federation of Rhodesia and Nyasaland (Sept. 1953-Dec. 1963); *b* 16 Dec. 1904; *s* of Henry Evans; *m* 1931, Catherine Muriel Greig; one *s* two *d. Educ:* Graeme Coll. and Rhodes Univ., Grahamstown, S Africa (BA, LLB). Joined S Rhodesia Public Service, 1928: consecutively Law Officer, Legal Adviser, Mem. of Public Services Board, and Sec. for Internal Affairs. Chairman of: Board of Trustees Rhodes National Gallery; Rhodesia National Trust; Nat. Council for Care of Aged. Past District Governor, Rotary International. Gold Cross of St Mark (Greece), 1962. *Recreations:* tennis, shooting. *Address:* 8 Harvey Brown Avenue, Harare, Zimbabwe. *T:* 25164. *Club:* Salisbury (Zimbabwe).

EVANS, Briant; *see* Evans, A. B.

EVANS, Rt. Rev. Bruce Read; *see* Port Elizabeth, Bishop of.

EVANS, Carey; *see* Evans, D. C. R. J.

EVANS, Sir Charles; *see* Evans, Sir R. C.

EVANS, Charles; *see* Evans, W. C.

EVANS, Rev. Prof. Christopher Francis, MA; Professor of New Testament Studies, King's College, London, 1962-77, now Emeritus Professor, University of London; *b* 7 Nov. 1909; 2nd *s* of Frank and Beatrice Evans; *m* 1941, Elna Mary (*d* 1980), *d* of Walter and Elizabeth Burt; one *s. Educ:* King Edward's Sch., Birmingham; Corpus Christi Coll., Cambridge. Asst Curate, St Barnabas, Southampton, 1934-38; Tutor Schol. Canc. Linc., 1938-44; Chaplain and Divinity Lecturer, Lincoln Training Coll., 1944-48; Chaplain, Fellow and Lecturer in Divinity, Corpus Christi Coll., Oxford, 1948-58. Emeritus Fellow, 1977; Lightfoot Prof. of Divinity in the University of Durham and Canon of Durham Cathedral, 1959-62. Select Preacher, University of Oxford, 1955-57; Proctor in Convocation for University of Oxford, 1955-58; Exam. Chaplain: to Bishop of Bristol, 1948-58; to Bishop of Durham, 1958-62; to Archbishop of Canterbury, 1962-74; to Bishop of Lichfield, 1969-75. FKC, 1970. Hon. DLitt Southampton, 1977. *Publications:* Christology and Theology, 1961; The Lord's Prayer, 1963; The Beginning of the Gospel, 1968; Resurrection and the New Testament, 1970; (ed jtly) The Cambridge History of the Bible: vol. I, From the Beginnings to Jerome, 1970; Is 'Holy Scripture' Christian?, 1971; Explorations in Theology 2, 1977; contribs to Journal of Theological Studies, Theology and Religious Studies, to Studies in the Gospels and to Christian Faith and Communist Faith. *Recreation:* fishing. *Address:* 4 Church Close, Cuddesdon, Oxford. *T:* Wheatley 4406; 5 The Square, Clun, Craven Arms, Salop.

EVANS, Collis William, CB 1958; CBE 1949; Under Secretary, Ministry of Civil Aviation, 1948-59; *b* 27 May 1895; *s* of late W. J. Evans, Folkestone; *m* 1st, 1938, Annie Urquhart (*d* 1957); 2nd, 1970, Hilda Stewart. Served European War, 1914-18, Yeomanry and RFA, Middle East, Macedonia and France. Exchequer and Audit Dept, 1914; Principal, Air Ministry, 1938; Financial Adviser to HQ RAF, Middle East and North Africa, 1938-43; Adviser on Administration and Finance, Transport Command, 1943; Asst Sec.,

Dept of Civil Aviation, 1944. *Address:* Ringle Crouch, Nash, near Bletchley, Bucks MK17 0EP. *T:* Whaddon 285.

EVANS, David; Chief Economic and Policy Adviser, National Farmers' Union, since 1981; *b* 7 Dec. 1935; *yr s* of William Price Evans and Ella Mary Evans; *m* 1960, Susan Carter Connal, *yr d* of late Dr John Connal and Antoinette Connal; one *s* one *d. Educ:* Welwyn Garden City Grammar Sch.; University Coll. London (BScEcon). Joined Min. of Agriculture, Fisheries and Food, 1959; Private Sec. to Parliamentary Sec. (Lords), 1962-64; Principal, 1964; Principal Private Sec. to Ministers, 1970-71; Asst Sec., 1971; seconded to Cabinet Office, 1972-74; Under-Sec., MAFF, 1976-80. *Address:* 6 Orchard Rise, Kingston upon Thames, Surrey KT2 7EY. *T:* 01-942 7701.

EVANS, Prof. David Alan Price, FRCP; Chairman, Department of Medicine, and Director of Nuffield Unit Medical Genetics, University of Liverpool, since 1972; Consultant Physician, Royal Liverpool Infirmary and Broadgreen Hospital, Liverpool, since 1965; *b* 6 March 1927; *s* of Owen Evans and Ellen (*née* Jones). *Educ:* Univ. of Liverpool (MD, PhD, DSc); Johns Hopkins Univ. House Physician, House Surg. and Med. Registrar, United Liverpool Hosps; Fellow, Dept of Medicine, Johns Hopkins Hosp., 1958-59; Lectr 1960-62, Sen. Lectr 1962-68, Personal Chair, 1968-72, Dept of Medicine, Univ. of Liverpool. Life Mem., Johns Hopkins Soc. of Scholars, 1972. *Publications:* medical and scientific, principally concerned with genetic factors determining responses to drugs. *Recreation:* country pursuits. *Address:* 28 Montclair Drive, Liverpool L18 0HA. *T:* 051-722 3112; Pen-yr-Allt, Paradwys, Llangristiolus, Bodorgan, Gwynedd LL62 5PD. *T:* Bodorgan 346.

EVANS, David Anthony; a Recorder of the Crown Court, since 1980; *b* 15 March 1939; *s* of Thomas John Evans, MD and May Evans; *m* 1974, Angela Bewley, *d* of John Clive Bewley, JP and Cynthia Bewley; two *d. Educ:* Clifton Coll., Bristol; Corpus Christi Coll., Cambridge (BA). Called to the Bar, Gray's Inn, 1965; practised at the Bar, Swansea, 1965-. *Recreations:* sport of all kinds. *Address:* Carey Hall, Neath, W Glamorgan. *T:* Neath 3859. *Clubs:* Turf, MCC; Cardiff and County (Cardiff).

EVANS, His Honour David Carey Rees Jones, MA, BCL Oxon; Judge of County Courts, 1946-71; Deputy Chairman, Quarter Sessions, Norfolk, retired; *b* 3 March 1899; *s* of late Sir David W. Evans; *m* 1937, Margaret Willoughby Gale; one *d. Educ:* Sherborne Preparatory Sch.; Sherborne Sch.; Jesus Coll., Oxford (Scholar); Gray's Inn (Holt Scholar). Called to Bar, 1923; S Wales and Chester Circuit, practising at Cardiff; formerly part-time Lecturer in Law at University Coll. of S Wales and Mon, Cardiff. Chm. of Ministry of Labour Tribunals for Breconshire and Merthyr, 1937-46; Recorder of Merthyr Tydfil, 1945-46. 2nd Lieut RGA 1918-19. *Address:* 16 Cross Street, Hoxne, Diss, Norfolk.

EVANS, Ven. David Eifion; Archdeacon of Cardigan, 1967-79; *b* 22 Jan, 1911; *e s* of John Morris Evans, Borth, Cards; *m* 1st, 1941, Iris Elizabeth Gravelle; one *s* ; 2nd, 1979, Madeleine Kirby. *Educ:* Ardwyn, Aberystwyth; UCW, Aberystwyth; St Michael's Coll., Llandaff. BA 1932; MA 1951. Deacon, 1934; Priest, 1935. Curate: Llanfihangel-ar-Arth, 1934-36; Llanbadarn Fawr, 1936-40; Chaplain to the Forces, 1940-45; Vicar, Llandeloy with Llanrheithan, 1945-48; Penrhyncoch, 1948, with Elerch, 1952-57; St Michael, Aberystwyth, 1957-67; Rural Dean, Llanbadarn Fawr, 1957-67; Chaplain, Anglican Students, 1966-67; Canon of St David's Cathedral (Caerfai), 1963-67; Chaplain, Earl of Lisburne, 1967-69; Vicar: Llanafan with Llanwnnws, 1967-69; Newcastle Emlyn, 1969-. Mem. Governing Body of Church in Wales, 1956-; Mem. Court of Governors, and Mem. Council, UCW, Aberystwyth, 1958-; Sub-Visitor, St David's Univ. Coll., Lampeter, 1972. *Publications:* contributions to: Llên Cymru Yn Y Bedwaredd Ganrif Ar Bymtheg, 1968; Jl of Hist. Soc. of Church in Wales and other Welsh Church periodicals. *Recreation:* reading. *Address:* 31 Bryncastell, Bow Street, Dyfed. *T:* Aberystwyth 828747.

EVANS, His Honour David Eifion Puleston, QC 1954; Member Foreign Compensation Commission, 1963-75; *b* 8 Dec. 1902; *s* of late John Owain Evans, CBE and Margaret Anne Evans; *m* 1933, Roberta (*d* 1966), *y d* of Sir Robert McAlpine, 1st Bt. *Educ:* Towyn Sch.; University Coll. of Wales, Aberystwyth; Downing Coll., Cambridge (Foundation Schol., MA, LLB). Barrister, Gray's Inn, 1926, practised London, Wales and Chester Circuit; commissioned RASC 1940; Office of Judge Advocate Gen., 1941-45, Major; resumed practice, 1945; Mem. General Council of the Bar, 1955-56; Chm.; Radnorshire Quarter Sessions, 1959-62; Deputy Chm., Brecknock Quarter Sessions, 1960-62; County Court Judge, Circuit No 28 (Mid-Wales and Shropshire), 1956-62. *Address:* 104 Westhill, Putney, SW15 2UQ. *Club:* Reform.

EVANS, Prof. (David) Ellis, DPhil; Jesus Professor of Celtic, University of Oxford, and Fellow of Jesus College, since 1978; *b* Llanfynydd, 23 Sept. 1930; *yr s* of David Evans and Sarah Jane (*née* Lewis); *m* 1957, Sheila Mary, *er d* of David and Evelyn Jeremy; two *d. Educ:* Llandeilo Grammar Sch.; University Coll. of Wales, Aberystwyth, and University Coll., Swansea (BA Wales, 1st cl. Hons Greek, Latin and Welsh, 1952; MA Wales, 1954); Jesus Coll., Oxford (Meyricke Grad. Scholar, 1952-54; DPhil 1962, MA 1978). University Coll. of Swansea: Asst Lectr in Welsh, 1957; Lectr, 1960; Reader, 1968; Actg Head, Dept of Welsh, 1973; Prof. of Welsh Lang. and Lit. and Head of Dept of Welsh, 1974. Curator, Taylor Instn, Oxford, 1979-. Sir John

Rhys Meml Lectr, British Acad., 1977; Rudolf Thurneysen Meml Lectr, Univ. of Bonn, 1979; O'Donnell Lectr, Univ. of Wales, 1980. Pres. and Organizing Sec., Seventh Internat. Congress of Celtic Studies, Oxford, 1983. Chairman: Welsh Dialect Studies Group, 1977-80; Council for Name Studies of GB and Ireland, 1980- (Mem. Council, 1962-); Member: Bd of Celtic Studies, Univ. of Wales, 1968-; Court and Council, National Library of Wales, 1974-; Internat. Cttee of Onomastic Sciences, 1975-; Council, Irish Texts Soc., 1978-; Welsh Arts Council, 1981-; Court, University of Wales, 1978-; Court, UC Swansea, 1980-; Court and Council, University Coll. of Wales, Aberystwyth, 1981-. Governor, Christ's Coll., Brecon, 1979-. Hon. Mem., Druidic Order of Gorsedd of Bards, 1976-; Correspondent étranger, Etudes celtiques, 1982. Editor, Lang. and Lit. Section, Bull. of Bd of Celtic Studies, 1972-; Mem. Editorial Bd: Geiriadur Prifysgol Cymru/A Dictionary of the Welsh Language, 1973-; Nomina, 1980-; Welsh Acad. English-Welsh Dictionary, 1981-; Mem. Adv. Bd, Jl of Celtic Studies, 1978-. *Publications:* Gaulish Personal Names: a study of some continental Celtic formations, 1967; (contrib.) Swansea and its Region, ed W. G. V. Balchin, 1971; (contrib.) Homenaje a Antonio Tovar, 1972; (contrib.) The Anatomy of Wales, ed R. Brinley Jones, 1972; Gorchest y Celtiaid yn yr Hen Fyd, 1975; Cofiant Agricola, Rheolwr Prydain, 1975; Termau Gwleidyddiaeth, 1976; (contrib.) Indogermanisch und Keltisch, ed K. H. Schmidt, 1977; (contrib.) Aufstieg und Niedergang der römischen Welt, ed H. Temporini and W. Haase, 1983; contrib. colloquia; articles and revs in Bull. Bd of Celtic Studies, Class. Rev., Etudes celtiques, History, Jl of Welsh Bibliog. Soc., Llên Cymru, Onoma, Proc. of British Acad., Studia Celtica, Y Traethodydd, Trans Hon. Soc. Cymmrodorion, Trivium, Welsh Hist. Rev., Year's Work in Mod. Lang. Studies, and Zeitschrift celt. Phil. *Recreations:* music, walking. *Address:* Jesus College, Oxford. *T:* Oxford 49511.

EVANS, Air Chief Marshal Sir David (George), GCB 1979 (KCB 1977); CBE 1967 (OBE 1962); Vice-Chief of Defence Staff (Personnel and Logistics), since 1981; *b* Windsor, Ont, Canada, 14 July 1924; *s* of William Stanley Evans, Clive Vale, Hastings, Sussex; *m* 1949, Denise Marson Williamson-Noble, *d* of late Gordon Till, Hampstead, London; two *d* (and two step *s*). *Educ:* Hodgson Sch., Toronto, Canada; North Toronto Collegiate. Served War, as Pilot, in Italy and NW Europe, 1944-45. Sqdn Pilot, Tactics Officer, Instructor, 1946-52; Sqdn Comdr, Central Flying Sch., 1953-55; RAF Staff Coll. course, 1955; OC No 11 (F) Sqdn, in Germany, 1956-57; Personal Staff Officer to C-in-C, 2nd Allied TAF, 1958-59; OC Flying, RAF, Coltishall, 1959-61; Coll. of Air Warfare course, 1961; Air Plans Staff Officer, Min. of Defence (Air), 1962-63; OC, RAF Station, Gutersloh, Germany, 1964-66; IDC, 1967; AOC, RAF Central Tactics and Trials Organisation, 1968-70; ACAS (Ops), 1970-73; AOC No 1 (Bomber) Group, RAF, 1973-76; Vice-Chief of Air Staff, 1976-77; C-in-C, RAF Strike Command, and UK NATO Air Forces, 1977-80. Queen's Commendation for Valuable Service in the Air (QCVSA), 1955. CBIM 1978. *Recreations:* rep. RAF at Rugby football and winter sports (President: RAF Winter Sports Assoc.; Combined Services Winter Sports Assoc.); has rep. Gt Brit. at Bobsleigh in World Championships, Commonwealth Games and, in 1964, Olympic Games. *Address:* Royal Bank of Canada, 2 Cockspur Street, SW1. *Club:* Royal Air Force.

EVANS, Prof. Sir David (Gwynne), Kt 1977; CBE 1969; FRS 1960; Demonstrator, Sir William Dunn School of Pathology, University of Oxford, 1976-79, retired; *b* 6 Sept. 1909; *s* of Frederick George Evans, Atherton, Manchester; *m* 1937, Mary (*née* Darby); one *s* one *d. Educ:* Leigh Grammar Sch.; University of Manchester. BSc, 1933; MSc, 1934; PhD, 1938; DSc, 1948. Demonstrator and Asst Lecturer in Chemistry, Dept of Bacteriology, University of Manchester, 1934; Mem. of Scientific Staff, Dept of Biological Standards, Nat. Inst. for Medical Research, London, 1940; Reader in Chemical Bacteriology, Dept of Bacteriology, University of Manchester, 1947; Head of Biological Standards Control Laboratory, Nat. Inst. for Medical Research, London, 1955-58; Dir, Dept of Biological Standards, 1958-61; Prof. of Bacteriology and Immunology, 1961-71, now Emeritus, London Sch. of Hygiene and Tropical Medicine; Dir, Lister Inst. of Preventive Medicine, 1971-72; Dir, Nat. Inst. for Biological Standards and Control, 1972-76. Member: WHO Expert Panel on Biological Standardization, 1956-77; Governing Body, Animal Virus Res. Inst., Pirbright, 1964-75; MRC, 1965-69; Northumberland Cttee on Foot-and-Mouth Disease, 1968-69; Cttee on Safety of Medicines, 1973-77; British Pharmacopœia Commn, 1973-77; Investigation into the Birmingham Smallpox Occurrence, 1978-79. Chm., Veterinary Adv. Cttee, Horserace Betting Levy Bd, 1973-79. Pres., Soc. for General Microbiology, 1972-75. FRCPath, 1965. BMA Stewart Prize Award, 1968; Buchanan Medal, Royal Soc., 1977. *Publications:* numerous scientific papers, mainly on bacteriology and immunology. *Recreation:* listening to opera. *Address:* 4 Craig Wen, Rhos-on-Sea, Colwyn Bay, Clwyd LL28 4TS. *T:* Colwyn Bay 46662. *Club:* Athenæum.

EVANS, Sir David (Lewis), Kt 1958; OBE 1947; BA, BLitt, Hon. DLitt Wales; Keeper of Public Records, Jan. 1959-Oct. 1960, retired (Deputy Keeper of the Records, 1954-58); Commissioner, Historical MSS Commission, 1954-80; *b* 14 Aug. 1893; *s* of Rev. David Evans and Margaret Lewis; *m* 1923, Marie Christine (*d* 1966), *d* of Edwin Austin, JP; two *d. Educ:* Bridgend County Sch.; University Coll. of Wales, Aberystwyth; Jesus Coll., Oxford. Lieut, Duke of Wellington's Regt, 1915-19, France and Belgium (despatches). Entered Public Record Office, 1921; Principal Asst Keeper, 1947. Lectr, Administrative History and Archive Administration, Sch. of Librarianship and Archives, University Coll. London, 1947-54. FRHistS

(Vice-Pres. 1956-60); Council, Hon. Soc. of Cymmrodorion; Member: Advisory Council on Public Records, 1959-65; History and Law Cttee, Bd of Celtic Studies; Exec Committee: Internat. Council on Archives, 1953-68 (Vice-Pres. 1956-60); Pres. 4th Internat. Congress of Archivists, Stockholm, 1960; Governor: British Film Institute, 1961-64; Nat. Library of Wales, 1961- (Council, 1962-80); Nat. Museum of Wales, 1965-. *Publications:* Flintshire Ministers' Accounts, 1328-1352, 1929; History of Carmarthenshire: Chapter on Later Middle Ages, 1935; (part author) Notebook of John Smibert, Painter, Mass Hist. Soc., 1969; articles, reviews, in Cymmrodorion Transactions, Eng. Hist. Review, Nat. Lib. of Wales Jl, Virginia Hist. Soc. Trans, etc. *Address:* 2 Bay Court, Doctors Commons Road, Berkhamsted, Herts. *T:* Berkhamsted 3636. *Club:* National Liberal.

EVANS, David Marshall, QC 1981; *b* 21 July 1937; *s* of Robert Trevor and Bessie Estelle Evans; *m* 1961, Alice Joyce Rogers; two *s. Educ:* Liverpool Coll.; Trinity Hall, Cambridge (MA, LLB); Law Sch., Univ. of Chicago (JD). Called to the Bar, Gray's Inn, 1964. Teaching Fellow, Stanford University Law Sch., 1961-62; Asst Professor, Univ. of Chicago Law Sch., 1962-63; Lectr in Law, University Coll. of Wales, Aberystwyth, 1963-65; joined Northern Circuit, 1965. *Recreations:* walking, photography, visual arts, bird-watching, motorsport. *Address:* 5 Essex Court, Temple, EC4Y 9AH. *T:* 01-353 4363. *Club:* Athenæum (Liverpool).

EVANS, His Honour (David) Meurig; a Circuit Judge (formerly County Court Judge), 1957-79, retired; *b* 9 Sept. 1906; *s* of H. T. Evans, Aberayron, Cards; *m* 1933, Joyce Diedericke Sander (decd), St Albans; two *s* two *d* ; *m* 1969, Mrs Anne Blackmore. *Educ:* Cardiff High Sch.; Aberayron County Sch.; Cardiff Technical Coll. Journalist on staff of Western Mail and The Economist, 1925-31. Called to Bar, Gray's Inn, 1931; practised on Wales and Chester Circuit, 1932-57; Chairman, Cardigan QS, Denbigh QS, Dep. Chm., Anglesey and Caenarvon QS, 1958-71. Served 1940-45, Lieut-Comdr RNVR. Chm., Medical Appeal Tribunal for Wales, 1952-57; Jt Pres., Council of HM Circuit Judges, 1974-75. *Recreations:* golf and yachting. *Address:* Rivendell, Menai Bridge, Gwynedd. *T:* Menai Bridge 712253. *Clubs:* Royal Welsh, Royal Anglesey, etc.
See also A. H. M. Evans.

EVANS, David Milne; Cabinet Office, 1977-81; *b* 8 Aug. 1917; *s* of Walter Herbert Evans, MSc and Florence Mary Evans (*née* Milne); *m* 1946, Gwynneth May (*née* Griffiths), BA. *Educ:* Charterhouse (Scholar); Gonville and Caius Coll., Cambridge (Schol.; Wrangler, Math. Tripos). Administrative Class, Home Civil Service (War Office), 1939. Served in Army (Major, RA), 1940-45. Asst Sec., 1954; Imp. Def. Coll., 1954; Asst Under-Sec. of State, MoD, 1967-77 (Under-Sec., CS Dept, 1972). Coronation Medal, 1953; Silver Jubilee Medal, 1977. *Address:* 1 Church Rise, Walston Road, Wenvoe, Cardiff, South Glamorgan CF5 6DE. *T:* Cardiff 597129.

EVANS, David M.; see Moule-Evans.

EVANS, David Philip, CBE 1968; MSc, PhD, FRSC; Principal, Glamorgan Polytechnic, Treforest, Pontypridd, Glam, 1970-72; *b* 28 Feb. 1908; *s* of D. C. and J. Evans, Port Talbot, Glam; *m* 1938, Vura Helena (*née* Harcombe); one *s. Educ:* Port Talbot County Grammar Sch.; University Coll., Cardiff. Lectr in Chemistry, Cardiff Technical Coll., 1934-44; Principal: Bridgend Technical Coll., Glam, 1944-52; Glamorgan Coll. of Technology, Treforest, 1952-70. *Publications:* numerous papers in various chemical jls. *Recreations:* fishing, gardening, music. *Address:* Tree Tops, St Bride's Road, Ewenny Cross, Ewenny, Bridgend, Mid Glam. *T:* Bridgend 61354.

EVANS, Rt. Rev. David Richard John; see Peru, Bishop of.

EVANS, Prof. Dennis Frederick, FRS 1981; Professor in Inorganic Chemistry, Imperial College, London, since 1981; *b* 27 March 1928; *s* of George Frederick Evans and Gladys Martha Taylor. *Educ:* Nottingham High Sch.; Lincoln Coll., Oxford (open scholar); Gibbs Univ. Scholar, 1949; MA, DPhil. ICI Res. Fellow, 1952-53 and 1954-56; Res. Associate, Univ. of Chicago, 1953-54; Lectr in Inorganic Chemistry, Imperial Coll., London, 1956-63, Sen. Lectr, 1963-64, Reader, 1964-81. *Publications:* articles in various scientific jls. *Recreations:* wine, travel. *Address:* 64A Cathcart Road, SW10. *T:* 01-352 6540.

EVANS, Eben, OBE 1976; Controller, Books Division, British Council, 1976-80; *b* 1 Nov. 1920; *s* of John Evans and Mary Evans; *m* 1946, Joan Margaret Howells; two *s* two *d. Educ:* Llandovery Grammar Sch.; University Coll. of Wales, Aberystwyth (BA 1948). Served War, 1941-46 (Army, Captain). Appointed to British Council, 1948; Cardiff, 1948-55; Thailand, 1955-59; Gambia, 1959-62; Ghana, 1962-64; Personnel Dept, London, 1964-68; Representative: Algeria, 1968-73; Yugoslavia, 1973-76. *Recreations:* walking, music. *Address:* Goroldinog Isaf, Llanfairfechan, Gwynedd.

EVANS, Rt. Rev. Edward Lewis, BD, MTh; *b* 11 Dec. 1904; *s* of Edward Foley Evans and Mary (*née* Walker). *Educ:* St Anselm's, Croydon; Tonbridge Sch.; Bishops' Coll., Cheshunt. BD London 1935, MTh 1938. Deacon, 1937; priest 1938; Curate of St Mary's, Prittlewell, Essex, 1937-39; Warden of St Peter's, Theological Coll., Jamaica, 1940-49; Rector, Kingston Parish Church, Jamaica, 1949-52; Rector of Woodford and Craigton, 1952-57; Archdeacon of Surrey, Jamaica, 1950-57; Bishop Suffragan of Kingston, 1957-60; Bishop of Barbados, 1960-71. *Publication:* A History of the Diocese of Jamaica, 1977.

Address: Bungalow 1, Terry's Cross, Woodmancote, Henfield, Sussex BN5 9SX.

EVANS, Edward Stanley Price, FRTPI; City Planning Officer, Liverpool, since 1974; *b* 13 April 1925; *s* of late Bernard James Reuben Evans and of Nellie Evans; *m* 1948, Eva Magdalena Emma Fry; one *s* (and one *s* decd). *Educ:* Wolverhampton Grammar Sch.; Nottingham Coll. of Art and Crafts (DipTP). FRTPI 1966 (MTPI 1954). Chief Town Planning Officer, Norwich, 1957; City Planning Officer, Nottingham, 1966. Mem., DoE Environmental Bd, 1977-79. Mem., Liverpool Architectural Soc. FRSA. *Recreations:* travel, gardening, bridge (social). *Address:* Willow Cottage, The Ridgeway, Heswall, Wirral, Merseyside L60 8NB. *T:* 051-342 4546. *Club:* Athenæum (Liverpool).

EVANS, Edward Walter, CMG 1931; *b* 1890; 2nd *s* of late Arthur Evans; *m* 1923, Margaret, *d* of late J. K. Young, Barrister-at-Law; two *s* one *d. Educ:* Marlborough Coll.; Corpus Christi Coll., Oxford (Classical Scholar). 1st Class Classical Mods, 1st Class Lit. Hum.; appointed to Colonial service, 1914; served in various dependencies in East Africa and Caribbean area before retiring from post of Colonial Sec., Mauritius, in 1939, after administering the Government of Mauritius on various occasions; during 1939-45 War served in Gibraltar and on Overseas Services of BBC; served on Control Commission for Germany, 1945-46; employed in History Dept Bristol Univ., 1946-55. *Publications:* contrib. Mind, vol LXXX. *Address:* Medway Farm, Askerswell, Dorchester, Dorset.
See also R. M. Evans.

EVANS, Ven. Eifion; see Evans, Ven. D. E.

EVANS, Ellis; see Evans, D. E.

EVANS, Emrys; see Evans, W. E.

EVANS, Prof. Emyr Estyn, CBE 1970; Emeritus Professor of Geography, and Hon. Fellow, Institute of Irish Studies, Queen's University of Belfast; Leverhulme Emeritus Fellow, 1970-72; *b* 29 May 1905; 4th *s* of Rev. G. O. and Elizabeth Evans, Shrewsbury; *m* 1931, Gwyneth Lyon, *e d* of Prof. Abel Jones, Aberystwyth; four *s. Educ:* Welshpool County Sch.; University Coll. of Wales, Aberystwyth. BA Geography and Anthropology, 1925, MA 1931, DSc 1939. Independent Lecturer in Geography, QUB, 1928-44; Reader, 1944-45; Prof., 1945-68; Dir, Inst. of Irish Studies, 1965-70; Dean of the Faculty of Arts, 1951-54; Mem. of Senate. Tallman Visiting Professor: Bowdoin Coll., Maine, 1948-49; Visiting Professor: Indiana Univ., 1964; Louisiana State Univ., 1969. Mem., Historic Monuments Council (NI) (former Chm.); former Mem. Adv. Council, Republic of Ireland; first President: Ulster Folk Life Soc. and Ulster Archæological Soc.; Ulster Architectural Heritage Soc.; former Chm. of Trustees, Ulster Folk and Transport Museum and Trustee, Ulster Museum; Hon. Mem. and former Vice-Pres., Prehistoric Soc. Former Member: Executive Cttee, NI Council of Social Service; NI Tourist Bd; Pres. Sect. E 1958 and Sect. H 1960, Brit. Assoc. for the Advancement of Science (first Chm. NI Area Cttee); Sir James Frazer Memorial Lectr, 1961; Sir Everard im Thurn Memorial Lectr, 1966; Wiles Lectr, 1971. Chm., Northern Ireland Government Cttee on Itinerants; Vice-Chm., Cttee on Nature Conservation. FSA; MRIA; Hon. MRTPI; Hon. Life Mem., Royal Dublin Soc., 1981. Hon. ScD Bowdoin, 1949; Hon. LittD Dublin, 1970; Hon. LLD QUB, 1973; Hon. DLitt: NUI, 1975; Wales, 1977; Hon. DSc NUU 1980. Victoria Medal, RGS, 1973. Hons Award, Assoc. of Amer. Geographers, Pa, 1979. *Publications:* France, A Geographical Introduction, 1937; (joint) Preliminary Survey of the Ancient Monuments of Northern Ireland, 1940; Irish Heritage, 1942; A Portrait of Northern Ireland (Festival of Britain) 1951; Mourne Country, 1951, rev. edn 1967; Lyles Hill: A Late Neolithic Site in County Antrim, 1953; Irish Folk Ways, 1957; Prehistoric and Early Christian Ireland, 1966; (ed) Facts from Gweedore, 1971; The Personality of Wales (Wiles Lectures), 1973, revd edn 1981; The Personality of Wales (BBC Wales Annual Lecture), 1973; (ed) Harvest Home: the last sheaf, 1975; (ed) Ireland's Eye, the photographs of R. J. Welch, 1977; papers in scientific journals. *Address:* 100 Malone Road, Belfast. *T:* 668510. *Club:* Ulster Arts (Hon. Member) (Belfast).

EVANS, Ena Winifred; Headmistress, King Edward VI High School for Girls, Birmingham, since 1977; *b* 19 June 1938; *d* of Frank and Leonora Evans. *Educ:* The Queen's Sch., Chester; Royal Holloway Coll., Univ. of London (BSc); Hughes Hall, Cambridge (CertEd). Asst Mistress, Bolton Sch. (Girls' Div.), 1961-65; Bath High School (GPDST): Head of Mathematics Dept, 1965-72; Second Mistress, 1970-72; Dep. Head, Friends' Sch., Saffron Walden, 1972-77. *Recreation:* music. *Address:* King Edward VI High School for Girls, Edgbaston Park Road, Birmingham B15 2UB. *T:* 021-472 1834.

EVANS, Ven. Eric; see Evans, Ven. T. E.

EVANS, Sir Francis (Edward), GBE 1957; KCMG 1946 (CMG 1944); DL; Agent for the Government of N Ireland in Great Britain, 1962-66; *b* 4 April 1897; *s* of late Thomas Edward Evans, Belfast; *m* 1920, Mary (*d* 1976), *d* of late Rev. Prof. James Dick, MA, DD, Belfast; no *c. Educ:* Royal Academy, Belfast; London Sch. of Economics. Served European War, Lieut Royal Irish Rifles, 1915-19; Consular Service, 1920; Vice-Consul in New York, 1920-26, Boston, 1926-29, Colon, Panama, 1929-32, and Boston, 1932-34; Consul at Los Angeles, 1934-39; in Foreign Office, 1939-43; Consul at New York, 1943;

Consul-Gen., 1944-50; Asst Under-Sec. of State, FO, 1951; British Ambassador to Israel, 1952-54 (Minister, 1951-52); British Ambassador to the Argentine, 1954-57. Dep. Chm. Northern Ireland Development Coun., 1957-65. Pres., Central Council, Ulster 71 Festival. Hon. Col, 6th (T) Bn Royal Ulster Rifles, 1961-67, (T&AVR), 1967-71. Hon. LLD Queen's Univ., Belfast; Hon. DCL Ripon Coll., Wisconsin; Hon. DLitt New University of Ulster. DL Belfast, 1959. KStJ. *Address:* 180 Upper Malone Road, Dunmurry, Belfast BT17 9JZ. *Clubs:* Travellers'; Ulster (Belfast).

EVANS, Fred; *see* Evans, Alfred T.

EVANS, Frederick Anthony, CVO 1973; Adviser for The Handicapped, The Duke of Edinburgh's Award Scheme (General Secretary, 1959-72); *b* 17 Nov. 1907; *s* of Herbert Anthony Evans, mining engineer, and Pauline (*née* Allen); *m* 1934, Nancy (*née* Meakin); two *s* one *d. Educ:* Charterhouse; Corpus Christi, Cambridge. Manager Doondu Coffee Plantation, Kenya, 1927-31; Colonial Service, 1934; Asst District Officer, Nigeria, 1935-39; Provincial Commissioner and Asst Colonial Sec., Gambia, 1940-47; Colonial Sec., Nassau, Bahamas, 1947-51; Acting Governor, 1950; Permanent Sec., Gold Coast (later Ghana), 1951-57. Dir, Anglo-Gambian Archæological Expedition, 1965-66. *Recreations:* golf, ski-ing. *Address:* Bamber Cottage, Saintbury Hill, Froyle, Hants. *Club:* Royal Commonwealth Society.

EVANS, Lt-Gen. Sir Geoffrey (Charles), KBE 1954 (CBE 1945); CB 1946; DSO 1941 (bars 1942, 1944); retired, 1957; *b* 13 March 1901; *s* of late Col C. R. Evans, DSO; *m* 1928, Ida Louise, *d* of late H. R. Sidney; no *c. Educ:* Aldenham Sch.; Royal Military Coll., Sandhurst. 2nd Lieut The Royal Warwickshire Regt, 1920; Adjutant: 1st Bn, 1926-29; 7th Bn (TA), 1934-35; Staff Coll., 1936-37. Served War of 1939-45 (despatches five times): Bde Major, N Africa and Eritrea, 1940-41; OC 1st Bn Royal Sussex Regt, N Africa, 1941-42; Comdt Staff Coll., Quetta, 1942; Brig. Comd., India, 1943; Brig., Gen. Staff 4 Corps, Burma, 1943-44; Bde Commander, Burma, 1944; GOC 5 and 7 Indian Divs, Burma, 1944-45; GOC Allied Land Forces, Siam, 1945-46; GOC 42 (Lancs) Div. and North-West District, 1947-48; Dir of Military Training War Office, 1948-49; GOC 40 Div., Hong Kong, 1949-51; Temp. Comd. (Lt-Gen.), British Forces, Hong Kong, 1951-52; Asst Chief of Staff (Org. and Trng), Supreme HQ, Allied Powers, Europe, 1952-53; GOC-in-C, Northern Command, 1953-57; retired. Hon. Col 7th Bn The Royal Warwickshire Regt, 1959-64. A Vice-Pres., Nat. Playing Fields Assoc.; Chairman: London and Middlesex Playing Fields Association, 1959-70; Anglo-Thai Soc., 1967-71. Comr, Royal Hosp., Chelsea, 1968-76. DL Greater London, 1970-76. *Publications:* The Desert and the Jungle, 1959; (with A. Brett-James) Imphal, 1962; The Johnnies, 1964; Slim as Military Commander, 1969; Tannenberg 1410:1914, 1971; Kensington, 1975; contrib. chapters: The Decisive Battles of the 20th Century, 1975; War Lords, 1976; articles and reviews. *Recreation:* fishing. *Address:* 11 Wellington Square, SW3. *Club:* Naval and Military.

EVANS, George Ewart; author, lecturer, and broadcaster, since 1948; *b* 1 April 1909; *s* of William and Janet Evans, Abercynon, Glamorgan; *m* 1938, Florence Ellen Knappett; one *s* three *d. Educ:* Abertaf Sch.; Mountain Ash Grammar Sch.; UC Cardiff. BA Hons Classics Wales, 1930; DipEd 1931. Writer of short stories, verse, radio and film scripts; specialized in history and folk life of the village. Univ. of Essex: Major Burrows Lectr, 1972; Vis. Fellow, 1973-78; Hon. DU 1982. Pres., Section H (Anthropology), British Assoc. for Advancement of Science, Swansea, 1971. *Publications:* The Voices of the Children, 1947; Ask the Fellows who Cut the Hay, 1956; (ed) Welsh Short Stories, 1959; The Horse in the Furrow, 1960; The Pattern Under the Plough, 1966; The Farm and the Village, 1969; Where Beards Wag All, 1970; (with David Thomson) The Leaping Hare, 1972; Acky, 1973; The Days That We Have Seen, 1975; Let Dogs Delight, 1975; From Mouths of Men, 1976; Horse Power and Magic, 1979. *Recreations:* walking, gardening, watching Rugby football. *Address:* 19 The Street, Brooke, Norwich NR15 1JW. *T:* Brooke 50518.

See also Matthew Evans, David Gentleman.

EVANS, Sir Geraint Llewellyn, Kt 1969; CBE 1959; Opera Singer, retired 1982; formerly Principal Baritone, Royal Opera House, Covent Garden; *b* 16 Feb. 1922; *m* 1948, Brenda Evans Davies; two *s. Educ:* Guildhall Sch. of Music. Has sung at: Royal Opera House, Covent Garden (since 1948); Glyndebourne Festival Opera; Vienna State Opera; La Scala, Milan; Metropolitan Opera, New York; San Francisco Opera; Lyric Opera, Chicago; Salzburg Festival Opera; Edinburgh Festival Opera; Paris Opera; Teatro Colon, Buenos Aires; Mexico City Opera; Welsh Nat. Opera; Scottish Opera; Berlin Opera; Teatr Wielki, Warsaw. Dir, Harlech Television Ltd. President: Guild for Promotion of Welsh Music; Friends of the WNO; Vice-Pres., Kidney Research Unit for Wales Foundn. Mem., Gorsedd of Bards, Royal Nat. Eisteddfod of Wales; Patron, Churchill Theatre, Bromley; Governor, University Coll. of Wales, Aberystwyth. FGSM 1960; FRNCM 1978; FRCM 1981; Fellow: University Coll., Cardiff, 1976; Jesus Coll., Oxford, 1979. Hon. DMus: Wales, 1965; Leicester, 1969; CNAA 1980. Hon. RAM 1969. Worshipful Company of Musicians Sir Charles Santley Meml Award, 1963; Harriet Cohen Internat. Music Award (Opera Medal), 1967; Fidelio Medal, Internat. Assoc. of Opera Dirs, 1980; San Francisco Opera Medal, 1981. *Recreations:* rugby, sailing. *Address:* 17 Highcliffe, 32 Albemarle Road, Beckenham, Kent.

EVANS, Godfrey; *see* Evans, T. G.

EVANS, Gwyneth, OBE 1975; Member of Development Commission, 1969-75; *b* 29 Feb. 1912; *d* of Griffith and Ellen Roberts; *m* 1936, Daniel Marcus Evans; three *s* one *d. Educ:* Grammar Sch. for Girls, Brecon. Did voluntary work with Red Cross and WVS (now WRVS) during War of 1939-45. Member: Merioneth CC, 1949-74 (Alderman, 1969-74 (1st woman Alderman), Chm., Social Services Cttee); Gwynedd CC, 1974-79; Formerly: Member: Children's Regional Planning Cttee for Wales (Chm., 1972-74); North Wales Police Authority; Lord Wolfenden's Cttee on Voluntary Orgns, 1974-; Chm., N Wales Jt Educn Cttee. Mem., Court of Univ. of Wales. *Recreation:* reading. *Address:* Cartre, Ffestiniog, Gwynedd. *T:* Ffestiniog 2709.

EVANS, Gwynfor; President, Plaid Cymru, 1945-81 (Vice-Pres. 1943-45); *b* 1 Sept. 1912; *s* of Dan Evans and Catherine Mary Richard; *m* 1941, Rhiannon Prys Thomas; four *s* three *d. Educ:* Gladstone Road Elementary Sch.; County Sch., Barry; University of Wales, Aberystwyth; St John's Coll., Oxford. Qual. Solicitor, 1939. Hon. Sec. Heddychwyr Cymru (Welsh Pacifist movement), 1939-45; Chm. Union of Welsh Independents, 1954. MP (Plaid Cymru) Carmarthen, July 1966-1970 and Oct. 1974-1979. Member: Carmarthen CC, 1949-74; Ct of Govs, University of Wales and UC, Aberystwyth; Council Univ. of Wales, and UC Aberystwyth. Past Mem. Welsh Broadcasting Council. Hon. LLD Wales, 1973. *Publications:* Plaid Cymru and Wales, 1950; Rhagom i Ryddid, 1964; Aros Mae, 1971; Wales can Win, 1973; Land of My Fathers, 1974; A National Future for Wales, 1975; Diwedd Prydeindod, 1981. *Address:* Talar Wen, Llangadog, Sir Gaerfyrddin, Dyfed. *T:* Llangadog 567.

EVANS, Sir Harold, 1st Bt, *cr* 1963; CMG 1957; OBE 1945; *b* 29 April 1911; *s* of Sidney Evans and Gladys Mary Lythgoe; *m* 1945, Elizabeth Jaffray; one *d* (one *s* decd). *Educ:* King Edward's Sch., Stourbridge. Editorial staff of newspapers in Worcs and Sheffield, 1930-39; Freelance Journalism, 1939-40; British Volunteers in Finland, 1940; Staff of British Legation, Helsinki, 1940-42; Min. of Information Rep. in W Africa (Staff of Resident Minister), 1942-45; Dep. Public Relations Officer, Colonial Office, 1945-53; Chief Information Officer, Colonial Office, 1953-57; Public Relations Adviser to the Prime Minister, 1957-64; Head of Information and Research, Independent Television Authority, 1964-66; Adviser on Public Relations to Bd, Vickers Ltd, 1966-76; Chm., Health Educn Council, 1973-76. *Publications:* Men in the Tropics, Anthology, 1949; Vickers: against the odds 1956-77, 1978; Downing Street Diary, 1981; various contributions. *Address:* 3 Challoners Close, Rottingdean, East Sussex. *T:* Brighton 33397.

EVANS, Harold Matthew; Director, Goldcrest Films and Television, since 1982; *b* 28 June 1928; *s* of late Frederick and late Mary Evans; *m* 1st, 1953, Enid (marr. diss. 1978), *d* of late John Parker and Susan Parker; one *s* two *d* ; 2nd, 1981, Christina Hamley Brown, *d* of George H. Brown, San Pedro de Alcantara, Spain. *Educ:* St Mary's Road Central Sch., Manchester; Durham Univ. BA 1952, MA Durham 1966. Ashton-under-Lyne, Lancs, Reporter Newspapers, 1944-46 and 1949; RAF, 1946-49; Durham Univ., 1949-52; Manchester Evening News, 1952; Commonwealth Fund Fellow in Journalism, Chicago and Stanford Univs, USA, 1956-57; Asst Ed, Manchester Evening News, 1958-61; Ed., Northern Echo, 1961-66; Editor-in-Chief, North of England Newspaper Co., 1963-66; Sunday Times: Chief Asst to Editor, 1966; Managing Editor, 1966; Editor, 1967-81; Editor, The Times, 1981-82. Member, Executive Board: Times Newspapers Ltd, 1968-82 (Mem. Main Bd, 1978); International Press Inst., 1974-80; Director: The Sunday Times Ltd, 1968-82; Times Newspapers Ltd, 1978-82. Writer and Presenter, Evans on Newspapers, BBC TV, 1981. Hon. Vis. Prof. of Journalism, City Univ., 1978-. Internat. Editor of the Year, 1975; Gold Medal Award, Inst. of Journalists, 1979; Editor of the Year, 1982. *Publications:* The Active Newsroom, 1961; Editing and Design (five volumes): vol. 1, Newsman's English, 1972; vol. 5, Newspaper Design, 1973; vol. 2, Newspaper Text, 1974; vol. 3, Newspaper Headlines, 1974; vol. 4, Pictures on a Page, 1977; (jointly): We Learned To Ski, 1974; The Story of Thalidomide, 1978; (ed) Eye Witness, 1981. *Recreations:* music, table-tennis, chess, ski-ing. *Address:* 25 Ponsonby Terrace, SW1. *Clubs:* Garrick, Royal Automobile.

EVANS, (Harry) Lindley, CMG 1963; Pianist; Composer; retired as Professor of Pianoforte, NSW State Conservatorium of Music, Sydney, Australia, 1928-66, a Governor, 1966-73; *b* 18 Nov. 1895; British; *m* 1926, Marie Florence Stewart. *Educ:* St George's Grammar Sch., Capetown, South Africa. Pianist with Dame Nellie Melba, 1922-31. Celebrated a 40-year partnership in giving two-piano recitals, 1964. Melody Man in Children's Hour (ABC) since its inception, 1940. Pres., Musical Assoc. of NSW (life Mem.); Past Pres., Fellowship of Australian Composers (Life Mem.). *Publications:* many musical compositions. *Recreations:* bowls, yachting. *Address:* 47/84 St George's Crescent, Drummoyne, NSW, Australia. *T:* 81-3896. *Club:* Savage (Sydney) (Life Mem.; Pres. 13 yrs).

EVANS, Sir Haydn T.; *see* Tudor Evans.

EVANS, Maj.-Gen. Henry Holland, CB 1972; *b* Harrogate, 18 Nov. 1914; *o s* of Major H. Evans; *m* 1939, Norah Mary, *d* of F. R. Lawson, Wolstanton, Staffs; one *s* one *d. Educ:* King James Grammar Sch., Almondbury, near Huddersfield; Manchester Univ. Commissioned Duke of Wellington's Regt (TA), 1936; Regular Army Commission in AEC, 1939; Officer Instructor, Duke of York's Royal Mil. Sch., 1939-41; Staff Officer: 43 (Wessex) Div., 1942-45; War Office, 1945-48; Chief Educn Officer, Malta and Libya,

1948-51; various RAEC appts, incl. Headmaster DYRMS and Chief Inspector of Army children's schools, to 1963; CEO, Northern Comd, 1963-65; CEO, BAOR, 1965-68; Dir of Army Educn, 1969-72. Sec., Council for Accreditation of Corresp. Colls, 1973-75. Mem., Sevenoaks Town Council, 1973-77. Governor, Sevenoaks Sch., 1974-79. *Address:* c/o Williams & Glyn's Bank Ltd, Whitehall, SW1.

EVANS, Prof. (Henry) John; Director, Medical Research Council Clinical and Population Cytogenetics Unit, Edinburgh, since 1969; *b* 24 Dec. 1930; *s* of David Evans and Gwladys Evans (*née* Jones); *m* 1st, 1957, Gwenda Rosalind (*née* Thomas) (*d* 1974); 2nd, 1976, Roslyn Rose (*née* Angell); four *s. Educ:* Llanelli Boys Grammar Sch.; UCW, Aberystwyth (BSc, PhD 1955). Res. Scientist, MRC Radiobiology Unit, Harwell, 1955-65, Head of Cell Biology Section, 1962-65; Vis. Fellow, Brookhaven Nat. Laboratory, Brookhaven, NY, USA, 1960-61; Prof. of Genetics, Univ. of Aberdeen, 1965-69. Chm., Assoc. Radiation Research, 1970-72; Mem., MRC Biological Res. Bd, 1968-72; Council Mem., MRC, 1978-82. FRSE. Hon. Prof., Univ. of Edinburgh; Vis. Prof., Kyoto Univ., Japan, 1981. *Publications:* papers on radiation cytology, mutagenesis, chromosome structure and human cytogenetics in various internat. jls; editor of various books and jls in the field of genetics and radiobiology. *Recreations:* rugby, golf, music, fishing. *Address:* 45 Lauder Road, Edinburgh EH9 1UE. *T:* 031-667 2437. *Club:* Royal Commonwealth Society.

EVANS, Hubert John Filmer, CMG 1958; LLD; HM Diplomatic Service, retired; Central Asian Research Centre, 1965-70; *b* 21 Nov. 1904; *y s* of late Harry Evans and late Edith Gwendoline Rees; *m* 1948, Marjory Maureen Filmer (*née* Carrick), *widow* of Col R. A. M. Tweedy. *Educ:* City of London Sch.; Jesus Coll., Oxford (Classical Scholar); Montpellier. Studied oriental languages with Ross, Minorsky, and in the East. Entered Indian Civil Service, 1928; served as Magistrate in various districts of United Provinces, 1929-37; Deputy Commissioner of Delhi, and Pres., Delhi Municipal Council, 1938-42; Sec. Delhi Administration, 1942-45; Collector of Agra, 1945-47; appointed to Foreign Service, 1947; at the Foreign Office, 1948-50; Financial Adviser to Persian Gulf Residency, 1950-51; Consul-Gen. at Meshed, 1951; in Latin America, 1952-54; Consul-Gen., Rotterdam, 1955-56; HM Ambassador to Korea, 1957-61. Hon. Sec., Royal Central Asian Soc. and Chm. Ed. Board 1965-70. Hon. MRAS; Hon. LLD Korea, 1960; Freedom of Seoul, 1960. *Publications:* various in oriental jls. *Recreations:* the Persian Poets, and travel. *Address:* Manoir d'Arlette, Fatouville, 27210 Beuzeville, France; Le Vert Feuillage, Honfleur, France. *Club:* Athenæum.

EVANS, Huw Prideaux; Under Secretary, HM Treasury, since 1980; *b* 21 Aug. 1941; *s* of late Richard Hubert Evans and of Kathleen Annie Evans; *m* 1966, Anne (*née* Bray); two *s. Educ:* Cardiff High Sch.; King's Coll., Cambridge (BA); London Sch. of Econs and Polit. Science (MSc). Economist: HM Treasury, 1964-72; European Commn, 1972-73; Asst Econ. Sec., Hong Kong Govt, 1973-75; Sen. Econ. Adviser (Econ. Forecasting), HM Treasury, 1976-79. *Address:* 141 Rosendale Road, SE21 8HE. *T:* 01-670 0982.

EVANS, Hywel Eifion, CB 1974; Welsh Secretary, Ministry of Agriculture, Fisheries and Food, 1968-75; *b* 24 Jan. 1910; *s* of late Gruffydd Thomas and Winnifred Evans, Felin Rhydhir, Pwllheli, Caernarvonshire; *m* 1939, Mary Elizabeth, *d* of late Richard and Hannah Jones, Gilfach, Glanywydden, Llandudno; one *s* one *d. Educ:* Pwllheli Grammar Sch.; University Coll. of North Wales, Bangor. BSc (Hons) (Agric.). Research Asst, Dept of Agricultural Economics, UCW, Aberystwyth, 1934-40; Dist and Dep. Exec. Officer, Leicester WAEC, 1940-46; County Advisory Officer: Radnor AEC, 1946-47; Carmarthen AEC, 1947-57; Dep. Regional Dir, Nat. Agricl Advisory Service for Wales, 1957-59, Regional Dir, 1959-66; Dep. Dir, Nat. Agricl Adv. Service (London), 1967-68. FRAgSs, 1972. *Publications:* articles on agricultural, economic and sociological topics in Welsh Jl of Agriculture, Agriculture, and other jls. *Recreations:* idling, fishing, shooting. *Address:* Llawryglyn, Lan Tyllyd, Llanfarian, Aberystwyth, Wales. *Club:* Farmers'.

EVANS, Sir Hywel (Wynn), KCB 1976 (CB 1972); Chairman, Welsh Arts Council, since 1981; Permanent Secretary, Welsh Office, 1971-80; *b* 30 May 1920; *s* of late Dr T. Hopkin Evans, MusDoc and Adelina Evans; *m* 1949, Jessie Margaret Templeton; one *d. Educ:* Liverpool Collegiate Sch.; Liverpool Univ. RA and Intell. Corps, 1940-46 (despatches). Joined Min. of Labour, as Asst Principal, 1947; seconded to FO, 1952-54; Commonwealth Fellow, 1957-58; Private Sec. to Ministers of Labour, 1959-60; Sec., NEDC, 1964-68; Asst Under-Sec. of State, Welsh Office, 1968-71. Mem., Arts Council of GB, 1981-. Member: Court of Governors: Univ. College of Wales; Nat. Mus. of Wales, 1981-; Prince of Wales Cttee, 1981-; Gorsedd of Bards of Wales. US Bronze Star, 1945. *Publication:* Governmental Regulation of Industrial Relations, 1960 (USA). *Recreations:* opera, watching rugby. *Address:* Coed-yr-Iarll, St Fagans, Cardiff, S Wales CF5 6DU. *T:* Cardiff 565214.

EVANS, Sir Ian William G.; *see* Gwynne-Evans.

EVANS, Ioan (Lyonel); JP; MP (Lab and Co-op) Aberdare, since Feb. 1974; *b* 1927; *m* 1949, Maria Evans, JP (*née* Griffiths); one *s* one *d. Educ:* Llanelly Grammar Sch.; University Coll., Swansea. Has held various Co-op. (incl. Sec. Birm. and Dist Co-op. Party) and Labour Party offices. MP (Lab and Co-op) Birmingham Yardley, 1964-70; Subseq. PPS to Postmaster-Gen.; Asst Govt Whip, 1966-68; Comptroller of HM Household, 1968-70. Formerly Vice-Chm. West Midlands Parly Labour Group of MP's; Chairman: PLP Trade Gp,

1974-; PLP For. Affairs Gp, 1981-; Vice-Chairman: PLP Disabled Gp, 1974-; PLP Prices and Consumer Protection Gp, 1974-; Co-op. Parly Gp, 1974-; Hon. Secretary: Welsh Lab. MPs Gp; Welsh Parly Party. Formerly Vice-Chm., UK Parly delegn to Consultative Assembly of Council of Europe; formerly Mem., UK Delegn to Assembly of WEU; Vice-Chairman: Parly Assoc. for World Govt; Parliamentarians for World Order, 1980-; Mem. Exec. Cttee, British Branch, IPU. Co-opted Mem., W Bromwich Educn Cttee; Governor, W Bromwich Grammar Sch.; Lectr for WEA and NCLC; Dir, Internat. Defence and Aid Fund, 1970-74; Member: Exec. Cttee, Wales Council of Labour; Exec. Cttee, Christian Action Council. Chm., Justice for Rhodesia, 1973-. JP: Birmingham, 1960-70; Middlesex, 1970-. *Address:* 169 Eastcote Road, Ruislip, Mddx. *T:* Ruislip 75251.

EVANS, James Donald; Editor and Editor-in-Chief, The Northern Echo, Darlington, since 1966; Director, North of England Newspapers, since 1971; *b* 12 Nov. 1926; *yr s* of Arthur Evans and Isabella McKinnon Evans; *m* 1946, Freda Bristow; two *s* three *d. Educ:* Royal Grammar Sch., High Wycombe. Jun. Reporter, Bucks Free Press, 1943-45; Army, 1945-48; Chief Reporter, Maidenhead Advertiser, 1948-50; Northern Echo: District Chief Reporter, 1950-60; Industrial Corresp., 1961-65; Industrial Editor, 1965-66. *Recreations:* driving, reading. *Address:* 4 Harewood Hill, Darlington, Co. Durham. *T:* Darlington 68710. *Club:* National Liberal.

EVANS, Col J(ames) Ellis, CBE 1973 (OBE 1952); TD 1947; JP; Lord-Lieutenant of Clwyd, since 1979; *b* 6 Aug. 1910; *s* of James William Evans and Eleanor Evans, MBE, JP; unmarried. *Educ:* Epworth Coll., Rhyl. Chartered Accountant (FCA). Joined TA, 1937; served War of 1939-45, RA: France, 1940; N Africa, 1941-44; Italy, 1944-45; comd 384 Light Regt RA (RWF), TA, 1947-52; Dep. CRA, 53 (Welsh) Div., 1953-57; Chm. Denbigh and Flint TA Assoc., 1961-68; Chm., Wales and Mon TA&VRA, 1971-74 (Vice-Chm., 1968-71); Pres., Wales TA&VRA, 1981-. Mem., Prestatyn UDC, 1939-74 (Chm. 1947); Mayor, Prestatyn Town Council, 1974-75. Clwyd, formerly Flintshire: JP 1951; DL 1953; High Sheriff, 1970-71; Vice-Lieut, 1970-74, Vice Lord-Lieut, 1977-79. Chm., North Wales Police Authority, 1976-78. *Recreations:* lawn tennis (played for Wales and Lancashire, 1936-48), gardening. *Address:* Trafford Mount, Gronant Road, Prestatyn, Clwyd. *T:* Prestatyn 4119. *Clubs:* East India, Devonshire, Sports and Public Schools; City (Chester).

EVANS, Jeremy David Agard; Director, Corporate Development, Britoil Ltd, since 1982; *b* 20 June 1936; *s* of Arthur Burke Agard Evans and Dorothy (*née* Osborne); *m* 1964, Alison Mary (*née* White); one *s* two *d. Educ:* Whitgift Sch.; Christ's Coll., Cambridge (BA Hons). Ministry of Power: Asst Principal, 1960-64 (Private Sec. to Parly Sec., 1963-64); Principal, 1964-69; Sloan Fellow, London Business Sch., 1969-70; Principal, and Private Sec. to Minister for Industry, DTI, 1970-71; Asst Sec., DTI, 1973, Dept of Energy, 1974 (first Dep. Dir of Offshore Supplies Office, 1973); seconded as Sec. to BNOC on its foundn, 1976-78; a Man. Dir, 1978; Man. Dir Corporate Develt, and Sec., 1980-82, Mem. Bd 1981-82. *Recreations:* opera, skiing, tennis, walking. *Address:* Dormans House West, Dormans Park, East Grinstead, West Sussex RH19 2LY. *T:* Dormans Park 518.

EVANS, John; MP (Lab) Newton, since Feb. 1974; Member, National Executive Committee of the Labour Party, since 1982; *b* 19 Oct. 1930; *s* of late James Evans, miner and Margaret (*née* Robson); *m* 1959, Joan Slater; two *s* one *d. Educ:* Jarrow Central School. Apprentice Marine Fitter, 1946-49 and 1950-52; Nat. Service, Royal Engrs, 1949-50; Engr, Merchant Navy, 1952-55; joined AUEW, 1952; joined Labour Party, 1955; worked in various industries as fitter, ship-building and repairing, steel, engineering, 1955-65. Mem. Hebburn UDC, 1962, Leader 1969, Chm. 1972; Sec./Agent Jarrow CLP, 1965-68, resigned. An Asst Govt Whip, 1978-79; Opposition Whip, 1979-80; PPS to Leader of Labour Party, 1980-. Mem., European Parlt, 1975-78; Chm., Regional Policy, Planning and Transport Cttee, European Parlt, 1976-78. Hon. Vice-Pres., Nat. Union of Labour and Socialist Clubs. *Recreations:* watching football, reading, gardening. *Address:* 6 Kirkby Road, Culcheth, Warrington, Cheshire WA3 4BS. *T:* Culcheth 766322. *Clubs:* Labour (Earlestown and Cadishead); Daten (Culcheth).

EVANS, Prof. John; *see* Evans, Prof. H. J.

EVANS, Dr John; *see* Evans, Dr N. J. B.

EVANS, Prof. John Davies, FBA 1973; Director, University of London Institute of Archæology, and Professor of Archæology in the University of London, since 1973; *b* 22 Jan. 1925; *o s* of Harry Evans and Edith Haycocks; *m* 1957, Evelyn Sladdin. *Educ:* Liverpool Institute High Sch. (open schol. in English to Pemb. Coll.); Pembroke Coll., Cambridge. War Service, 1943-47. BA 1948, MA 1950, PhD 1956, LittD 1979. Fellow of British Institute of Archæology at Ankara, 1951-52; Research Fellow of Pembroke Coll., Cambridge, 1953-56; Prof. of Prehistoric Archæology, University of London, 1956-73. President: Prehistoric Soc., 1974-78; Council for British Archæology, 1979-; Mem., Permanent Council, Internat. Union of Prehistoric and Protohistoric Scis, 1975- (Pres., 1982-); Chm., Area Archaeol Adv. Cttee for SE England, 1975-79. FSA 1955 (Dir, 1975-80); Mem., German Archaeological Inst., 1979- (Corr. Mem., 1968-79). *Publications:* Malta (Ancient Peoples and Places Series), 1959; (with Dr A. C. Renfrew) Excavations at Saliagos, near Antiparos, 1968; The Prehistoric Antiquities of the Maltese Islands, 1971; papers and reports in archæological journals.

Recreations: walking, listening to music. *Address:* Institute of Archæology, Gordon Square, WC1H 0PY.

EVANS, John Field, QC 1972; **His Honour Judge Evans;** a Circuit Judge, since 1978; *b* 27 Sept. 1928; 2nd *s* of late John David Evans, Llandaff, and Lucy May Evans (*née* Field). *Educ.* Cardiff High Sch.; Exeter Coll., Oxford (MA). Pilot Officer, RAF, 1948-49. Called to Bar, Inner Temple, 1953; Dep. Chm., Worcestershire QS, 1964-71; a Recorder of the Crown Court, 1972-78. *Recreation:* golf. *Address:* 1 Fountain Court, Birmingham B4 6DR.

EVANS, John Isaac Glyn; Director of Weapons Production (Naval), Ministry of Defence, 1970-79; *b* 1 April 1919; *s* of William Evans; *m* 1943, Hilda Garratt Evans (*née* Lee); two *s* one *d. Educ.* Ystalyfera Grammar Sch.; University Coll., Swansea (BSc Physics, BSc Elec. Engineering). Engineer, GEC, 1940-41. Served War, Captain REME, 1941-46. Development Engineer, GEC, 1946-50; Works Group Engineer, Admiralty, 1950-53; main grade, 1953-59; senior grade, 1959-64; superintending grade, 1964-67; Dep. Dir., 1967-70. FIEE. *Recreations:* tennis, badminton, cricket. *Address:* 16 Woodland Grove, Claverton Down, Bath, Avon.

EVANS, John Kerr Q.; *see* Quarren Evans.

EVANS, John Marten Llewellyn, CBE 1956 (MBE 1945); JP; Official Solicitor to the Supreme Court of Judicature, 1950-70; *b* 9 June 1909; *s* of late Marten Llewellyn Evans, Solicitor, and Edith Helena (*née* Lile); *m* 1943, Winifred Emily, *y d* of late Austin Reed; one *s* one *d. Educ.* Rugby Sch.; Trinity Coll., Oxford. Admitted Solicitor, 1935; Legal Asst to the Official Solicitor, 1937. Served War of 1939-45, Major RA. Senior Legal Asst to the Official Solicitor, 1947; Asst Master in Lunacy, 1950. Vice-Chm., Austin Reed Group Ltd, 1969-77. Master of Worshipful Company of Cutlers, 1967-68. JP City of London, 1969. *Recreations:* the theatre, cricket, golf, tennis. *Address:* The Paddock, Waltham St Lawrence, Reading, Berks. *Clubs:* Garrick, MCC.

EVANS, Rev. Canon John Mascal; Member of the Ridgeway Team Ministry, Diocese of Salisbury, since 1980; *b* 17 May 1915; *s* of Rev. Edward Foley Evans and Mary Evans; *m* 1941, Mary Elizabeth (*née* Rathbone); three *s* two *d. Educ.* St John's Sch., Leatherhead; Brasenose Coll., Oxford; Wells Theological Coll. Asst Curate, St Martin's, Epsom, 1938; Perpetual Curate, Stoneleigh, Epsom, 1942, All Saints, Fleet, 1952; Vicar, St Mary, Walton-on-Thames, 1960-68; Archdeacon of Surrey, 1968-80; Hon. Canon of Guildford, 1963-80, Canon Emeritus, 1980-. Member: General Synod of C of E, 1977-80; C of E Pensions Bd, 1977-; Council of Cremation Soc., 1969-80. *Recreations:* outdoor sports, fishing. *Address:* The Vicarage, Ogbourne St George, Marlborough SN8 1SU.

EVANS, John Robert, CC 1978; MD, DPhil, FRCP, FRCP (C), FACP; Director, Department of Population, Health and Nutrition, International Bank for Reconstruction and Development, Washington DC, since 1979; *b* 1 Oct. 1929; *s* of William Watson Evans and Mary Thompson; *m* 1954, Gay Glassco; four *s* two *d. Educ.* Univ. of Toronto (MD); Oxford Univ. (Rhodes Schol.) (DPhil). FRCP 1980. Jr interne, Toronto Gen. Hosp., 1952-53; Hon. Registrar, Nat. Heart Hosp., London, 1955; Asst Res.: Sunnybrook Hosp., Toronto, 1956; Toronto Gen. Hosp., 1957; Ontario Heart Foundn Fellow, Hosp. for Sick Children, Toronto, 1958; Chief Res. Physician, Toronto Gen. Hosp., 1959; Research Fellow, Baker Clinic Research Lab., Harvard Med. Sch., 1960; Markle Schol. in Acad. Med., Univ. of Toronto, 1960-65; Associate, Dept of Med., Faculty of Med., Univ. of Toronto, 1961-65; Asst Prof., 1965-66; Dean, Faculty of Med., McMaster Univ., 1965-72, Vice-Pres., Health Sciences, 1967-72; Pres., Univ. of Toronto, 1972-78. Member: Council RCP (Can.), 1972-; Inst. of Medicine, Nat. Acad. Sci., USA, 1972- (Mem. Council, 1976-); Adv. Commn Med. Res., WHO, 1976-80. Director: Dominion Foundries and Steel Ltd; Crown Life Insurance Co. Ltd. Hon. LLD: McGill, 1972; Dalhousie, 1972; McMaster, 1972; Queen's, 1974; Wilfrid Laurier, 1975; York, 1977; Yale, 1978; Toronto, 1980; Hon. DSc: Meml Univ. of Newfoundland, 1973; Montreal, 1977; Hon. DU Ottawa, 1978; Hon. DHL Johns Hopkins, 1978. *Recreations:* ski-ing, fishing, farming. *Address:* 58 Highland Avenue, Toronto, Ontario M4W 2A3, Canada.

EVANS, John Roger W.; *see* Warren Evans.

EVANS, John Yorath Gwynne; Deputy Director (Air), Royal Aircraft Establishment, 1972-76, retired; *b* 10 Feb. 1922; *s* of Randell and Florence Evans, Carms; *m* 1948, Paula Lewis, *d* of late Roland Ford Lewis; two *s* one *d. Educ.* UCW Aberystwyth. Royal Aircraft Estabt, 1942; attached to RAF, Germany, 1945-46; Supt Wind Tunnels, RAE Bedford, 1958; Head of Aerodynamics Dept, RAE, 1971. *Publications:* contrib. various sci. and techn. jls. *Recreations:* sailing, travel, reading. *Address:* Rushmoor Cottage, Tilford, Farnham, Surrey. *T:* Frensham 2275.

EVANS, Rt. Rev. Kenneth Dawson; *see* Dorking, Suffragan Bishop of.

EVANS, Laurence James, CBE 1977; HM Diplomatic Service, retired; *b* 16 Dec. 1917; *s* of Albert Victor and Margaret Evans; *m* 1940, Clare Mary (*née* Kolb); one *d. Educ.* Alsop High Sch., Liverpool; Univ. of Liverpool (BA Hons, French); Univ. of Rennes (Diploma). Reader in the Faculté des Lettres, Univ. of Rennes, 1938-39. HM Forces (Intell. Corps), 1939-45. Foreign Office, Asst Principal, 1946-47; Bd of Inland Revenue (HM Inspector of

Taxes), 1947-49; rejoined Foreign Service and apptd to Brussels, 1950-51; HM Vice-Consul, Khorramshahr, 1951-52; FO, 1952-54; Second Sec. and Vice-Consul, Ciudad Trujillo, Dominican Republic, 1954-57 (Chargé d'Affaires, 1955 and 1957); FO, 1957-63 (Asst Head of Communications, 1959); HM Consul, New York, 1963-66; Asst Head of Personnel Dept (Ops), DSAO, 1966-69; HM Consul-Gen., Geneva, 1969-73; HM Consul-General at Barcelona and Andorra, 1973-77; Doyen, Barcelona Consular Corps, 1974-76, Hon. Doyen, 1976-77; Staff Assessor, FCO, 1978-82. *Recreation:* music. *Address:* 16 Oakhurst Rise, Carshalton Beeches, Surrey SM5 4AG. *T:* 01-643 3023. *Clubs:* Royal Commonwealth Society, Civil Service.

EVANS, Lindley; *see* Evans, (Harry) Lindley.

EVANS, Lloyd Thomas; AO 1979; DSc, DPhil; FRS 1976; FAA; Chief Research Scientist, Commonwealth Scientific and Industrial Research Organization Division of Plant Industry, Canberra, Australia; *b* 6 Aug. 1927; *s* of C. D. Evans and G. M. Fraser; *m* 1954, Margaret Honor Newell; two *s* one *d* (and one *d* decd). *Educ.* Wanganui Collegiate Sch., NZ; Univ. of NZ (BSc, MAgrSc, DSc); Univ. of Oxford (DPhil). FAA 1971. Rhodes Scholar, Brasenose Coll., Oxford, 1950-54; Commonwealth Fund Fellow, Calif Inst. of Technol., 1954-56; res. scientist, CSIRO Div. of Plant Industry, Canberra, 1956-. National Acad. of Sciences Pioneer Fellow, 1963; Overseas Fellow, Churchill Coll., Cambridge, 1969-70; Vis. Fellow, Wolfson Coll., Cambridge, 1978. President: ANZAAS, 1976-77; Aust. Acad. of Science, 1978-82. Hon. LLD Canterbury, 1978. *Publications:* Environmental Control of Plant Growth, 1963; The Induction of Flowering, 1969; Crop Physiology, 1975; Daylength and the Flowering of Plants, 1976; Wheat Science: today and tomorrow, 1981; more than 100 scientific papers in jls. *Address:* 3 Elliott Street, Canberra, ACT 2601, Australia. *T:* Canberra 477815.

EVANS, Matthew; Managing Director since 1972 and Chairman since 1981, Faber & Faber Ltd; *b* 7 Aug. 1941; *s* of George Ewart Evans, *qv*; *m* 1966, Elizabeth Amanda (*née* Mead); two *s. Educ.* Friends' Sch., Saffron Walden; London Sch. of Econs and Polit. Science (BScEcon). Bookselling, 1963-64; Faber & Faber, 1964-. Chm., National Book League, 1982; Member: Council, Publishers Assoc., 1978-; Franco-British Soc., 1981-. *Recreation:* cricket. *Address:* 3 Canonbury Place, N1 2NQ. *T:* 01-226 0320.

EVANS, Maurice; Legion of Merit (US) 1945; Actor-manager; *s* of Alfred Herbert Evans, JP (Dorset). *Educ.* Grocers' Company Sch. Commenced theatrical career at Festival Theatre, Cambridge; later in a series of plays at Wyndham's, London; made his first successes in John van Druten's Diversion and R. C. Sherriff's Journey's End; following several years of appearances in West End became leading man at the Old Vic, where he was seen as Hamlet, Richard II, Petruchio, Benedick, etc.; went to America, 1936, to play Romeo to Katharine Cornell's Juliet; also appeared as the Dauphin in St Joan, Napoleon in St Helena. Produced and played title role Richard II, New York City, 1937; uncut Hamlet, 1938-39; produced and played Falstaff in Henry IV (Part 1), 1939; appeared as Malvolio in Twelfth Night with Helen Hayes, 1940-41; produced and played title role in Macbeth, New York City, 1941-42; in each play toured provinces extensively. Went on a lecture tour in aid of British War Relief, 1941. Captain US Army, 1942; disch. with rank of Major, 1945. Played Hamlet in own GI version, 1945-46, New York; 1946-47, in provinces (acting version published Doubleday & Co., 1947). Produced and starred in Man and Superman, New York, 1947-48, establishing record New York run for play of Bernard Shaw; toured provinces, 1948-49; produced, and co-starred with Edna Best in Terence Rattigan's Browning Version, 1949; starred in Shaw's The Devil's Disciple, New York, and toured provinces, 1950; revived Richard II at NY City Center, 1951; starred in Dial 'M' for Murder, New York, 1952-54, and toured provinces, 1954; starred in Shaw's The Apple Cart, New York and provinces, 1956-57; produced and starred in Shaw's Heartbreak House, New York, 1959-60; starred in Tenderloin (musical), New York, 1960-61; The Aspern Papers, New York; 1961-62; with Helen Hayes in Shakespeare Revisited, A Program For Two Players, at Stratford (USA) and on tour, 1962-63; Holiday, Los Angeles, 1980; On Golden Pond, Florida, 1981; produced The Teahouse of the August Moon (Pulitzer-Critics' prize), 1953; No Time for Sergeants, 1955; Artistic Supervisor, New York City Center Theatre Company, 1949-51. Made first American picture 1950, co-starring with Ethel Barrymore in Kind Lady; also made Androcles and the Lion, Warlord, Jack of Diamonds, Planet of the Apes, Rosemary's Baby, Thin Air, Planet of the Apes Revisited, and, in England, Gilbert and Sullivan, 1952 and Macbeth, 1960. Became United States citizen, 1941. Hon. doctorates: Univ. of Hawaii; Lafayette Coll., Penn.; Brandeis Univ. *Address:* c/o Charles H. Renthal & Co., 20 East 46th Street, New York, NY 10017, USA. *Clubs:* Oriental; Players (New York).

EVANS, Meurig; *see* Evans, D. M.

EVANS, Michael; *see* Evans, T. M.

EVANS, Michael Nordon, CMG 1964; Permanent Secretary, Ministry of Health and Housing, Kenya, 1960-64, retired; *b* 27 April 1915; *s* of late Christmas and Lilian Margaret Louise Evans, Tunbridge Wells; *m* 1st, 1939, Mary Stockwood; one *d* ; 2nd, 1951, Mary Josephine Suzette van Vloten; one *d. Educ.* Eastbourne Coll.; Queens' Coll., Cambridge. Apptd District Officer in Colonial Administrative Service, Kenya, 1939; African Courts Officer, Kenya, 1953; Dep. Commissioner for Local Government, 1954; Permanent Sec., 1958. *Recreation:* tennis. *Address:* Glengariff, Stellenbosch Road,

Somerset West, Cape Province, South Africa. *Clubs:* Hawks (Cambridge); Nairobi (Kenya).

EVANS, Mostyn; *see* Evans, Arthur M.

EVANS, Dr (Noel) John (Bebbington), CB 1980; Deputy Chief Medical Officer (Deputy Secretary), Department of Health and Social Security, since 1977; *b* 26 Dec. 1933; *s* of William John Evans and Gladys Ellen (*née* Bebbington); *m* 1st, 1960, Elizabeth Mary Garbutt (marr. diss.); two *s* one *d* ; 2nd, 1974, Eileen Jane McMullan. *Educ:* Hymers Coll., Hull; Christ's Coll., Cambridge (scholar; 1st cl., Nat. Sci. Tripos); Westminster Medical Sch., London; London Sch. of Hygiene and Tropical Med. (Newsholme prize, Chadwick Trust medal and prize). MA, MB, BChir; FRCP, DPH (Dist.). FFCM. Called to Bar, Gray's Inn, 1965. House officer posts at: Westminster, Westminster Children's, Hammersmith, Central Middlesex and Brompton Hosps, 1958–60; Medical Registrar and Tutor, Westminster Hosp., 1960–61; Asst MoH, Warwickshire CC, 1961–65; Dept of Health and Social Security (formerly Min. of Health), 1965–; Sir Wilson Jameson Travelling Fellowship, 1966. *Publications:* The Organisation and Planning of Health Services in Yugoslavia, 1967; contribs to med. jls. *Recreations:* canals, photography. *Address:* 2 Meadow Way, Rickmansworth, Herts. *T:* Rickmansworth 73840.

EVANS, Lady Olwen Elizabeth C.; *see* Carey Evans.

EVANS, Prof. Peter Angus, DMus; FRCO; Professor of Music, University of Southampton, since 1961; *b* 7 Nov. 1929; *y s* of Rev. James Mackie Evans and Elizabeth Mary Fraser; *m* 1953, June Margaret Vickery. *Educ:* West Hartlepool Grammar Sch.; St Cuthbert's Soc., University of Durham. BA (1st cl. hons Music), 1950; BMus, MA 1953; DMus 1958; FRCO 1952. Music Master, Bishop Wordsworth's Sch., Salisbury, 1951–52. Lecturer in Music, University of Durham, 1953–61. Conductor, Palatine Opera Group, 1956–61; Conductor, Southampton Philharmonic Soc., 1965–. *Publications:* Sonata for Oboe and Piano, 1953; Three Preludes for Organ, 1955; Edns of 17th Century Chamber Music, 1956–58; The Music of Benjamin Britten, 1979; contributor to Die Musik, in Geschichte und Gegenwart, since 1955, to A Concise Encyclopædia of Music, 1958, and to the New Oxford History of Music, 1974; writer and reviewer, especially on 17th century and contemporary music. *Address:* 9 Bassett Close, Southampton. *T:* Southampton 768125.

EVANS, Dr Philip Rainsford, CBE 1968; Physician-Paediatrician to the Queen, 1972–76; Physician, The Hospital for Sick Children, Great Ormond Street, 1946–75; *b* 14 April 1910; 2nd *s* of Charles Irwin Evans, headmaster of Leighton Park Sch., and Katharine Evans; *m* 1935, Dr Barbara Dorothy Fordyce Hay-Cooper; three *s* one *d*. *Educ:* Sidcot Sch., Winscombe, Som; Leighton Park Sch., Reading; Manchester University. BSc 1930, MSc 1941, MB, ChB 1933, MD 1941, Manchester; MRCP 1935, FRCP 1945, London. Rockefeller Travelling Research Fellow, 1937–38; Asst Pædiatrician, Johns Hopkins Hosp., Baltimore, 1938–39; Asst Physician to Children's Dept, King's Coll. Hosp., London, 1939–46; Dir, Dept of Paediatrics, Guy's Hosp., 1946–71; Dir, British Tay-Sachs Foundn, 1971–74. Served War of 1939–45, RAMC, N Africa and Italy, 1942–46 (despatches); Hon. Col AMS. Editor, Archives of Disease in Childhood, 1947–54. Hon. Mem., British, French and American Pædiatric Socs. Member, Cttee on Milk Composition, 1957–59, Ministry of Agriculture, Fisheries and Food. FRSM (Pres., Section of Pædiatrics, 1968–69, Section of Comparative Medicine, 1982–); Hon. Sec. British Pædiatric Assoc., 1954–59; Hon. Consultant to the Army in Pædiatrics, 1962–66; formerly Visiting Prof., Makerere, Saigon, Sheffield, Beirut; late Examr Universities of Bristol, Leeds, Birmingham, Cambridge, Jordan, and RCP; Mem. Council, RCP, 1962–65; Censor, RCP, 1972–74. (Jointly) Dawson Williams Prize, BMA, 1969. *Publications:* (joint) Infant Feeding and Feeding Difficulties, 1954; Jt Editor, Garrod, Batten and Thursfield's Diseases of Children, 1953; original papers in med. journals. *Address:* 24 Abbey Road, NW8 9AX. *T:* 01-624 1668.

EVANS, Phyllis Mary Carlyon, MA; Headmistress, St Swithun's School, Winchester, 1952–73; *b* 17 April 1913; *d* of L. L. C. Evans, late Headmaster of Swanbourne House Sch., Bletchley, Bucks, and of Mrs M. Evans (*née* Gore-Browne). *Educ:* Wycombe Abbey Sch., Bucks; St Hugh's Coll., Oxford. Lit Hum, 1935. Classics mistress, St Mary's, Calne, 1935–39; Yates Theology Scholar St Hugh's Coll., Oxford, 1939–40; Degree in Theology, 1940; MA 1940. Senior Classics mistress, The Alice Ottley Sch., Worcester, 1940–45; Head Mistress, Wellington Diocesan Sch. for Girls, Marton, New Zealand, 1946–51. Representative of Winchester Diocese in Church Assembly, 1957–70; Member: Winchester Dio. Bd of Finance; Winchester Dio. Bishop's Council. Lay Reader. Fellow of Woodard Corp. Governor, St Michael's Sch., Petworth. *Address:* April Cottage, 13 St Swithun's Street, Winchester.

EVANS, Very Rev. Raymond Ellis; Dean of Monmouth and Vicar of St Woolos, Newport, Gwent, 1953–75; *m* 1944, Alice Craigie, *d* of John and Alice Logan, Stirling, Scotland; two *c. Educ:* St David's Coll., Lampeter; St John's Coll., Oxford (MA). Deacon, 1934; Priest, 1935; Curate of Penmaen, 1934–36, of St John the Evangelist, Newport, 1936–44; Vicar of St Andrew's, Newport, 1944–47; Examining Chaplain to Bishop of Monmouth, 1946; Vicar of Blackwood, 1947–52; Sec. Monmouth Diocesan Conf., 1951; Vicar of St Mark, Newport, 1952–53. *Address:* 23 Stelvio Park Drive, Newport, Gwent NPT 3EL.

EVANS, Raymond John Morda, MA, PhD; JP; Headmaster, Silcoates School, 1960–78; *b* 1 Oct. 1917; 2nd *s* of late Rev. J. Morda Evans, Congregational Minister; *m* 1942, Catherine Mair Gernos Davies, *er d* of late Rev. J. Gernos Davies, Congregational Minister; one *s* two *d* (and one *s* decd). *Educ:* Silcoates Sch., near Wakefield; (Casberd Schol) St John's Coll., Oxford. BA Oxon (Mod. Langs), 1939, MA 1942; MA, PhD London (Russian Lang. and Lit.), 1959. Dauntsey's Sch., 1939–40; Intelligence Corps (Captain), 1940–46; Leeds Grammar School, 1946–52; Head of Dept of Modern Languages, Royal Naval Coll., Greenwich, 1952–60. *Publications:* contrib. to Slavonic and Eastern European Review, and to Mariners' Mirror. *Recreation:* swimming. *Address:* 16 Kepstorn Road, West Park, Leeds LS16 5HL.

EVANS, Prof. Rhydwyn Harding, CBE 1958; MSc, DSc Manchester, PhD Leeds; FICE, FIMechE, FIStructE, MSocCE France, Hon. MIPlantE; Professor of Civil Engineering and Administrative Head of Engineering Departments, University of Leeds, 1946–68, Emeritus Professor, 1968; *b* 9 Oct. 1900; *s* of late David Evans, Tygwyn, Pontardulais, Glam; *m* 1929, Dilys Elizabeth, *o c* of late George Rees, Welsh Poet and Hymnologist, and Kate Ann Rees, London; one *s. Educ:* Llanelly Grammar Sch.; University of Manchester. Mercantile Marine, 1918–20. BSc top 1st class Graduate Prizeman, 1923; MSc 1928; PhD 1932; DSc 1943. Demonstrator, Asst Lecturer, Lecturer, Senior Lecturer and later Reader in Civil Engineering, University of Leeds, 1926–46; Dean, Faculty of Tech. University of Leeds, 1948–51; Pro-Vice-Chancellor, University of Leeds, 1961–65. Lectures: Unwin Meml ICE, 1960; first George Hondros Meml, WA, 1970. IStructE: Vice-Pres., 1948–49; Chm., Yorks Br., 1940–41, 1955–56 and 1958–59 (Yorkshire Br. Prize, 1946–47 and 1950–51); ICE: Chm. Yorks Assoc., 1942–43 and 1952–53; Mem. Council, 1949–52; Mem., Joint Matriculation Bd, Manchester, 1949–68; Chm., Leeds Univ. Min. of Labour and NS Bd, 1949–60; first Chm., Trng Consultative Cttee, Cement and Concrete Assoc., 1966–73. Consulting Editor in Civil Engineering: McGraw-Hill Book Co. (UK) Ltd, 1975–; Pitman Ltd, 1978–. Hon. Mem., Concrete Soc., 1970. Hon. DeSc Ghent, 1953; Hon. DTech Bradford, 1971. Rugby Engrg Soc. Student's Prize, 1925; Telford Premiums, 1942–43–44; Medal, Ghent Univ., 1949, 1953; George Stephenson Gold Medal, 1956; Institution of Water Engineers, Instn Premium, 1953; Reinforced Concrete Assoc. Medal, 1961; Instn of Struct. Engrs: Research Diploma, 1965; Certif. of Commendation, 1970; Henry Adams Award, 1971. *Publications:* Prestressed Concrete (with E. W. Bennett), 1962; Concrete Plain, Reinforced Prestressed, Shell (with C. B. Wilby), 1963; Reinforced and Prestressed Concrete (with F. K. Kong), 1975 (2nd edn. 1980); papers on elasticity and plasticity of concrete and other building materials; strain and stress distribution in reinforced concrete beams and arches; pre-stressed concrete; extensibility, cracking and tensile stress-strain of concrete; bond stresses; shear stresses; combined bending and shear stresses; torsional stresses; preflexed pre-stressed concrete beams; lightweight aggregate concrete; vibration and pressure moulding of concrete in Journals of Institutions of Civil, Struct. and Water Engineers, Concrete Soc., Philosophical Magazine, Engineer, Engineering, Civil Engineering and Public Works. *Recreations:* motoring, travel, gardening. *Address:* 23 Christopher Rise, Pontlliw, Swansea, West Glamorgan SA4 1EN. *T:* Gorseinon 891961.

EVANS, Richard Mark, CMG 1978; HM Diplomatic Service; Deputy Under-Secretary of State, Foreign and Commonwealth Office, since 1982; *b* 15 April 1928; *s* of Edward Walter Evans, *qv* ; *m* 1973, Rosemary Grania Glen Birkett; two *s. Educ:* Dragon Sch., Oxford; Repton Sch.; Magdalen Coll., Oxford. BA (Oxon) 1949. Joined HM Foreign (now Diplomatic) Service: Third Sec., London, 1952–55; Third Sec., Peking, 1955–57; Second Sec., London, 1957–62; First Sec.: Peking, 1962–64; Berne, 1964–68; London, 1968–70; Counsellor, 1970; Head of Near Eastern Dept, FCO, 1970–72, Head of Far Eastern Dept, 1972–74; Fellow, Centre for Internat. Affairs, Harvard Univ., 1974–75; Commercial Counsellor, Stockholm, 1975–77; Minister (Economic), Paris, 1977–79; Asst Under-Sec. of State, FCO, 1979–82. *Recreations:* travel, reading, music. *Address:* Briar House, Briar Road, Twickenham TW2 6RE. *Club:* United Oxford & Cambridge University.

EVANS, Robert; Chairman, East Midlands Gas Region, since 1977; *b* 28 May 1927; *s* of Gwilym Evans and Florence May Evans; *m* 1950, Lilian May (*née* Ward); one *s* one *d. Educ:* Old Swan Coll.; Blackburn Coll.; City of Liverpool Coll. (Tech.); Liverpool Univ. D. Napier & Son Ltd, 1943–49; North Western Gas Bd, 1950–56; Burmah Oil Co. (Pakistan), 1956–62; Dir of Engrg, Southern Gas Bd, 1962–72; Dep. Dir (Ops), Gas Council, 1972; Dir of Operations, British Gas, 1972–75; Dep. Chm., North Thames Gas, 1975–77. Pres., Instn of Gas Engrs, 1981–82. *Recreations:* motoring, reading, golf. *Address:* East Midlands Gas, PO Box 145, De Montfort Street, Leicester LE1 9DB.

EVANS, Sir (Robert) Charles, Kt 1969; MA, FRCS; Principal, University College of North Wales, since 1958; Vice-Chancellor, University of Wales, 1965–67, and 1971–73; *b* 19 Oct. 1918; *o s* of late R. C. Evans and Mrs Charles Evans; *m* 1957, Denise Nea Morin; three *s. Educ:* Shrewsbury Sch.; University Coll., Oxford. BM, BCh Oxon 1943; MA Oxon 1947; FRCS 1949. RAMC, 1943–46 (despatches). Surgical Registrar, United Liverpool Hosps, and Liverpool Regional Hosps, 1947–57. Hunterian Prof., Royal College Surg. Eng., 1953. Dep. Leader, Mt Everest Expedition, 1953; Leader, Kangchenjunga Expedition, 1955; Pres., Alpine Club, 1967–70; Mem. Council, Royal Geog. Society, 1960–61. Hon. DSc Wales, 1956. Cullum Medal, American Geog. Soc., 1954; Livingstone Medal, Scottish Geog. Soc., 1955; Founder's Medal, Royal Geog. Society, 1956. *Publications:* Eye on

Everest, 1955; On Climbing, 1956; Kangchenjunga-The Untrodden Peak, 1956; articles in Alpine Journal, Geographical Journal, etc. *Address:* Bryn Haul, Bangor, N Wales. *T:* Bangor 2144. *Club:* Alpine.

EVANS, Maj.-Gen. Robert Noel, CB 1981; QHP 1976; Postgraduate Dean and Commandant, Royal Army Medical College, 1979-81; *b* 22 Dec. 1922; *s* of William Evans and Norah Moynihan; *m* 1950, Mary Elizabeth O'Brien; four *s* one *d*. *Educ:* Christian Brothers Sch., Tralee, Co. Kerry; National University of Ireland (MB, BCh, BAO 1947). DTM&H 1961; FFARCS 1963. Commnd RAMC 1951; Consultant Anaesthetist, 1963; CO BMH Rinteln, 1969-71; ADMS 4th Div., 1971-73; DDMS HQ BAOR, 1973-75; Comdt, RAMC Trng Centre, 1975-77; DMS, HQ BAOR, 1977-79. Col Comdt, RAMC, 1981-. MFCM 1978. OStJ 1978. *Recreations:* gardening, walking, music. *Address:* 32 Folly Hill, Farnham, Surrey. *T:* Farnham 726938.

EVANS, Roger W.; *see* Warren Evans.

EVANS, Russell Wilmot, MC 1945; Chairman, The Rank Organisation, since 1982; *b* 4 Nov. 1922; *s* of William Henry Evans and Ethel Williams Wilmot; *m* 1956, Pamela Muriel Hayward; two *s* one *d*. *Educ:* King Edward's Sch., Birmingham; Birmingham Univ. LLB Hons. Served HM Forces, 1942-47; commnd Durham LI, 1942, Major, 1945. Admitted Solicitor, Birmingham, 1949; Solicitor with Shakespeare & Vernon, Birmingham, 1949-50; Asst Sec., Harry Ferguson, 1951; Sec., Massey-Ferguson (Hldgs) and UK subsids, 1955-62; Dir, gp of private cos in construction industry, 1962-67; joined Rank Organisation, 1967: Dep. Sec., 1967-68; Sec., 1968-72; Dir, 1972-; Man. Dir, 1975-82; Dep. Chm., 1981; Dir, principal subsid. and associated cos incl. Rank Xerox, 1975-; Fuji Xerox, 1976-; Chm., Rank City Wall, 1976-; Dir, Eagle Star Insce Co., 1982-. *Recreations:* tennis, squash, photography. *Address:* Walnut Tree, Roehampton Gate, SW15 5JR. *T:* (office) 01-629 7454. *Clubs:* English-Speaking Union, Roehampton (Dir 1971-).

EVANS, Very Rev. Seiriol John Arthur, CBE 1969; Dean of Gloucester, 1953-72; *b* 22 Nov. 1894; *er s* of Rev. John Arthur Evans, DD, Sible Hedingham, Essex, and Amelia Annie Price; *m* 1928, Selina Georgiana, *d* of Rev. Charles Francis Townley, CBE, Fulbourn Manor, Cambridge; no *c*. *Educ:* King's Sch., Worcester; King's Coll., Cambridge; Salisbury Theological Coll. Asst Master at Felsted Sch., 1917-19; Deacon, 1920; Priest, 1921; Curate of St Mary and All Saints, Kidderminster, 1920-22; Minor Canon and Sacrist of Gloucester Cathedral and Assistant Master at King's Sch., Gloucester, 1922-23; Precentor of Ely Cathedral and Headmaster of the Choir Sch., 1923-29; Rector of Upwell-Christchurch 1929-47; Chaplain RNVR, 1940-45; Proctor in Convocation for Diocese of Ely, 1940-47; Archdeacon of Wisbech, 1945-53; Rector of Upwell-St Peter, 1947-53. Chairman: Council for the Care of Churches, 1954-71; Ely Diocesan Adv. Cttee, 1974-. Mem. of the Royal Commission on Historical Manuscripts, 1957; Church Commissioner, 1958-68; Mem., Cttee of Inquiry into Sale of Works of Art, 1963-65; Trustee, National Portrait Gallery, 1963-70. FSA 1935; FRHistS 1940; Fellow, St Michael's Coll., Tenbury, 1958. *Publications:* A Short History of Ely Cathedral, 1925; The Mortification of the Manor of Mepal (EHR vol. 51 no 201), 1936; Ely Chapter Ordinances (Camden Misc.: Vol. XVII), 1940; The Medieval Estate of Ely Cathedral Priory: a preliminary survey, 1973. *Address:* The Old Manor, Fulbourn, near Cambridge. *Club:* Athenæum.

EVANS, Sir Sidney Harold; *see* Evans, Sir Harold.

EVANS, Very Rev. Sydney Hall, CBE 1976; Dean of Salisbury, since 1977; *b* 23 July 1915; *s* of William and Winifred Evans; *m* 1941, Eileen Mary (*née* Evans); two *s* one *d*. *Educ:* Bristol Grammar Sch.; St Chad's Coll., Durham. MA 1940, BD 1945, Durham. Deacon 1939, priest 1940; Curate of Bishop Auckland, Co. Durham, 1939-41; Curate of Ferryhill, Co. Durham, 1941-43. Chaplain RAFVR, 1943-45. Chaplain and Lecturer, King's Coll., London, 1945-48; Warden of King's Coll. post-graduate coll. at Warminster, 1948-56; Dean of King's Coll., London, 1956-77; Hon. Canon of Southwark, 1959-77; Preacher of Gray's Inn, 1960-77; Exam. Chaplain to Bishops of Southwark, Chelmsford, Truro, Durham, London. Public Orator, Univ. of London, 1972-74. FKC 1955. Hon. Bencher, Gray's Inn, 1977. Hon. DD: Lambeth, 1978; London, 1978. *Recreations:* walking and bird-watching. *Address:* The Deanery, Salisbury, Wilts.

EVANS, (Thomas) Alun; HM Diplomatic Service; Counsellor, British Embassy, Pretoria, since 1979; *b* 8 June 1937; *s* of late Thomas Evans and Mabel Elizabeth (*née* Griffiths); *m* 1964, Bridget Elisabeth, *d* of Peter Lloyd, *qv* and Nora Kathleen Williams (*née* Patten); three *s*. *Educ:* Shrewsbury Sch.; University Coll., Oxford (MA). Army, 1956-58. Entered HM Foreign Service, 1961; Third Sec., Rangoon, 1962-64; Second Sec., Singapore, 1964-66; FO, 1966-70; First Sec., Geneva, 1970-74; FCO, 1974-79. *Recreations:* music, fishing. *Address:* c/o Foreign and Commonwealth Office, SW1A 2AH. *Clubs:* Royal Commonwealth Society; Pretoria.

EVANS, Ven. (Thomas) Eric; Archdeacon of Cheltenham, since 1975; Residentiary Canon of Gloucester Cathedral, since 1969; *b* 1928; *s* of late Eric John Rhys Evans and Florence May Rogers; *m* 1957, Linda Kathleen Budge; two *d*. *Educ:* St David's Coll., Lampeter (BA); St Catherine's Coll., Oxford (MA); St Stephen's House, Oxford. Ordained, 1954; Curate, Margate Parish

Church, 1954-58; Sen. Curate, St Peter's, Bournemouth, 1958-62; first Dir, Bournemouth Samaritans; Diocesan Youth Chaplain, dio. Gloucester, 1962-69; Wing Chaplain, ATC, 1963-69; Hon. Chaplain: Gloucester Coll. of Educn, 1968-75; Gloucestershire Constabulary, 1977-. Chm., Glos Trng Cttee, 1967-69; Proctor in Convocation and Mem. Gen. Synod of C of E, 1970-; a Church Comr, 1978- (Mem., Bd of Governors, 1978-). Canon Missioner, dio. Gloucester, 1969-75; Chm., House of Clergy, dio. Gloucester, 1979-. Mem. Exec. Cttee, 1975-, Chm., 1981-, Council for the Care of Churches (formerly Council for Places of Worship). Dir, Ecclesiastical Insurance Office Ltd, 1979-. Vice-Chm., Glos Assoc. for Mental Health, 1965-78. *Recreations:* travel, esp. Middle East, biblical archaeology. *Address:* 9 College Green, Gloucester. *T:* Gloucester 20620. *Clubs:* Carlton; Downhill Only (Wengen).

EVANS, (Thomas) Godfrey, CBE 1960; Public Relations Officer, Skew Bridge Ski and Country Club, Rushden, since 1978; *b* Finchley, 1920; *s* of A. G. L. Evans; *m* 1973, Angela Peart; one *d*. *Educ:* Kent Coll., Canterbury. Joined Kent County Staff at age of 16. First kept wicket for England in Test *v* India, 1946; first overseas Test tour, Australia and New Zealand, 1946-47; has also played in Test matches in W Indies and S Africa. Has played in 91 Test matches (world record 1959); dismissed 218 batsmen in Test cricket from behind the stumps, 88 more than Oldfield, the previous record-holder, and retained the record until 1976; the first wicket-keeper to have dismissed more than 200 victims and scored over 2000 runs in Test cricket; holds world record for not conceding a bye while 1,054 runs were scored in a Test series (Australia, 1946); holds record for longest Test innings without scoring (95 minutes *v* Australia, Adelaide, 1947); holds jointly, with Charles Barnett, record for fastest score before lunch in a Test match (98 *v* India, Lord's, 1952); in making 47 in 29 minutes was three runs off the fastest 50 in Test cricket (*v* Australia, Old Trafford, 1956); first Englishman to tour Australia with MCC four times after War of 1939-45. *Publications:* Behind the Stumps, 1951; Action in Cricket, 1956; The Gloves Are Off, 1960. *Recreations:* real tennis, golf, squash. *Address:* Skew Bridge Ski and Country Club, Northampton Road, Rushden, Northants NN10 9AP. *Club:* Petworth Real Tennis.

EVANS, Thomas Henry, CBE 1957; DL; LLM; Clerk of the Peace, Clerk of the County Council, and Clerk to Lieutenancy for Staffordshire, 1942-72; Clerk of Staffordshire Magistrates Courts Committee, 1952-72; Clerk of Staffordshire County and Stoke-on-Trent Police Authority, 1968-72; *b* 1907; *s* of late Henry Evans, Bootle, Lancs. *Educ:* Merchant Taylors' Sch., Crosby, Lancs; University of Liverpool (LLM). Admitted Solicitor, 1930. Asst Solicitor with Surrey County Council, 1930-35; Asst County Solicitor and later Dep. Clerk of Staffs County Council, 1935-42. Member: Cttee on Consolidation of Highway Law, 1958; Interdepartmental Cttee (Streatfeild) on business of Criminal Courts, 1958; Nat. Advisory Coun. on Training of Magistrates, 1964-73. DL Staffs, 1947. *Publication:* contributor to Macmillan's Local Government Law and Administration. *Address:* 108 Holland Road, Hove, East Sussex.

EVANS, (Thomas) Michael, QC 1973; **His Honour Judge Michael Evans;** a Circuit Judge, since 1979; *b* 7 Sept. 1930; *s* of late David Morgan Evans, Barrister, and of Mary Gwynydd Lloyd; *m* 1957, Margaret Valerie Booker; one *s* four *d*. *Educ:* Brightlands Prep. Sch., Newnham, Glos; Marlborough Coll., Wilts; Jesus Coll., Oxford (MA (Juris.)). Called to the Bar, Gray's Inn, 1954; Wales and Chester Circuit, 1955; a Recorder of the Crown Court, 1972-79. Legal Chm., Mental Health Review Tribunal for Wales, 1970. *Recreations:* golf, sailing. *Address:* The Old Rectory, Reynoldston, Gower, Swansea. *T:* Reynoldston 329.

EVANS, Dr Trevor John; General Secretary, Institution of Chemical Engineers, since 1976; *b* 14 Feb. 1947; *o s* of Evan Alban Evans and Margaret Alice Evans (*née* Hilton); *m* 1973, Margaret Elizabeth (one *s* one *d*. *Educ:* King's Sch., Rochester; University Coll., London (BSc (Eng) 1968, PhD 1972); CEng, MIChemE. Res. Officer, CSIR, Pretoria, 1968-69; Ford Motor Co., Aveley, Essex, 1972-73; Institution of Chemical Engineers: Asst Sec., Technical, 1973-75; Dep. Sec., 1975-76. Member: Bd, Council of Science and Technology Institutes, 1976-; Exec. Cttee, Commonwealth Engineers Council, 1976-; Jt Hon. Sec., European Fedn of Chem. Engrs, 1976-. *Publications:* scientific papers and general articles in Chemical Engrg Science, The Chem. Engr, etc. *Recreations:* photography, the theatre, travel. *Address:* The Institution of Chemical Engineers, 12 Gayfere Street, SW1. *T:* 01-222 2681.

EVANS, Sir Vincent; *see* Evans, Sir W. V. J.

EVANS, William, MD, DSc, FRCP; Consulting Physician: to Cardiac Department, London Hospital; to National Heart Hospital; and to Institute of Cardiology; Consulting Cardiologist to Royal Navy, 1946-67; Hon. Cardiologist to Royal Society of Musicians; *b* 24 Nov. 1895; *s* of late Eben Evans, Tregaron, Cardiganshire; *m* 1936, Christina (*d* 1964), *d* of late John Lessels Downie, Kirkcaldy. *Educ:* University Coll. of Wales, Aberystwyth; London Hospital; London Univ., MB, BS (London) 1925, hons in Surgery; MD (London) 1927; FRCP 1937; DSc (London) 1944; K. E. D. Payne Prize in Pathology, 1927; Hutchinson Triennial Prize in Clinical Surgery, 1929; Liddle Triennial Prize in Pathology, 1931; Sydney Body Gold Medal, 1954; Strickland Goodall Lect., 1942; Finlayson Lect., 1947; St Cyres Lect., 1952; Gerrish Milliken Lect., University of Philadelphia, 1954; First Rufus Stolp

Memorial Lect., University of Evanston, Ill., 1954; Carbutt Memorial Lect., 1957; Schorstein Lect., 1961; Wiltshire Lect., 1961. First Leonard Abrahamson Memorial Lecture, Royal College of Surgeons in Ireland, Dublin, 1963; Sir Thomas and Lady Dixon Lecture, Belfast, 1965. Formerly Asst Dir to Medical Unit, Paterson Medical Officer and Chief Asst to Cardiac Dept, London Hosp. Served European War, 1914-18, Combatant Officer, Lancs Fusiliers, and Battalion Education Officer. Hon. DSc (Wales), 1961. Mem. American Heart Assoc.; Hon. Mem. British Cardiac Soc.; Hon. Mem. Soc. of Phys. in Wales; Hon. FRSM. Guest Lecturer at Centenary Meetings of Royal Melbourne Hospital, 1948. High Sheriff of Cardiganshire, 1959. Hon. Mem. Order of Druids, 1960. *Publications:* Student's Handbook of Electrocardiography, 1934; Cardiography (2nd edn, 1954); Cardiology (2nd edn, 1956); Cardioscopy, 1952; Diseases of the Heart and Arteries, 1964; Journey to Harley Street, 1969; Diary of a Welsh Swagman, 1975; various papers on medical and cardiological subjects in Quarterly Jl of Med., Lancet, BMJ and Brit. Heart Jl. *Recreations:* fishing, gardening, farming. *Address:* Bryndomen, Tregaron, Dyfed, West Wales. *T:* Tregaron 404.

EVANS, William Campbell, OBE 1976; General Manager, Redditch Development Corporation, 1976-79; *b* 13 Jan. 1916; *s* of Frank Randolph Evans and Elizabeth Evans; *m* 1939, Sarah A. Duckworth; one *s* one *d. Educ:* Calday Grange Grammar Sch., West Kirby, Cheshire; Bury High Sch., Bury, Lancs. IPFA; FCA. Served RASC and RE, 1939-42. Local Govt Finance: Bury, 1932-38; Newton-le-Willows, Lancs, 1938-39 and 1942-44; Wolverhampton, 1944-53; Dep. Borough Treas., Northampton, 1953-58; Borough Treas., West Bromwich, 1958-64; Chief Finance Officer, Redditch Develt Corp., 1965-76. Mem. Council, IMTA/CIPFA, 1969-79, Vice-Pres., 1976-77, Pres., 1977-78. *Recreations:* gardening, music, watching sport. *Address:* Helmsley, Church Road, Bradley Green, near Redditch, Worcs. *T:* Hanbury 457.

EVANS, Prof. (William) Charles, PhD; FRS 1979; FRSC, FIBiol; Professor and Head, Department of Biochemistry and Soil Science, University College of North Wales, Bangor, 1951-79, now Emeritus; *b* 1 Oct. 1911; *s* of Robert and Elizabeth Evans; *m* 1942, Dr Irene Antice Woods; three *s* one *d. Educ:* Caernarfon Higher Grade and County Schs; University Coll. of N Wales, Bangor (John Hughes Entrance Scholar; 1st Cl. Hons Chemistry, 1932; MSc Org. Chem., 1934); Med. Sch., Univ. of Manchester (Platt Physiol Scholar; PhD Physiol., 1936). FRIC 1948; FIBiol 1955. Demonstr in Biochem., Sch. of Medicine, Univ. of Leeds, 1937, Dir of Blood Transfusion Labs, 1940; res. staff, Inoculation Dept (Wright-Fleming Inst.), St Mary's Hosp. Med. Sch., London, 1944; Special Lectr in Biochem. and Animal Health, University Coll., Aberystwyth, 1946. *Publications:* contrib. to Jl Chem. Soc., Biochem. Jl, Nature, MRC Reports, Brit. Jl Exp. Path., Brit. Vet. Jl, and Bot. Jl Linnean Soc. *Recreations:* cross country and middle distance running (when younger), farming and out-of-door pursuits, Rugby football. *Address:* Penmaen, Meirion Lane, Bangor, Gwynedd, North Wales. *T:* Bangor 2909; Department of Biochemistry and Soil Science, University College of North Wales, Deiniol Road, Bangor. *T:* Bangor 51151, ext. 411.

EVANS, (William) Emrys, CBE 1981; Senior Regional Director, Wales, Midland Bank Ltd, since 1976; *b* 4 April 1924; *s* of late Richard and Mary Elizabeth Evans; *m* 1946, Mair Thomas; one *d. Educ:* Llanfair Caereinion County Sch. FIB. Served War, RN, 1942-46 (despatches 1944). Entered Midland Bank Ltd, 1941; Asst Gen. Manager (Agric.), 1967-72; Reg. Dir, S Wales, 1972-74; Reg. Dir, Wales, 1974-76. Director: Welsh Industrial Develt Adv. Bd, 1975-; Develt Bd for Rural Wales, 1976-; Royal Welsh Agricl Soc., 1973-; Mem. Council, CBI, Wales, 1975- (Chm., 1979-81). Pres., Royal Nat. Eisteddfod of Wales, 1980-. Vice President: Tenovus Cancer Res. Unit, 1980-; Kidney Res. Unit for Wales Foundn, 1980-; Trustee: Catherine and Lady Grace James Foundn, 1973-; John and Rhys Thomas James Foundn, 1973-; Welsh Sports Trust, 1980- (Vice Chm.); Mem., Design Council Wales Adv. Cttee, 1981-. Treasurer: Congregational Church in Wales, 1975-; Mansfield Coll., Oxford, 1977-; Member Council, and Governor: UC Swansea, 1972-; UC Aberystwyth, 1979-; Governor, UC Cardiff, 1981-; Mem., Ct and Council, Univ. of Wales, 1980. *Recreations:* golf, gardening, music. *Address:* Maesglas, Pen-y-turnpike, Dinas Powis, S Glam CF6 4HH. *T:* Cardiff 512985. *Club:* Cardiff and County (Cardiff).

EVANS, William Ewart; Judge of the High Court of Lesotho, 1967-73 (Acting Chief Justice, 1968); Judge of High Court of Northern Rhodesia and of the Rhodesia and Nyasaland Court of Appeal, 1953-62; *b* 24 May 1899; *s* of late John William Evans and Catherine Evans, Swansea, S Wales; *m* 1919, Agnes May Wilson (*d* 1981); one *s* four *d. Educ:* Swansea Grammar Sch. Served European War, 1917-19, in King's Royal Rifle Corps and Royal Army Service Corps. Called to Bar, 1934; practised on South Wales Circuit; Colonial Legal Service, 1938; acted in various judicial capacities; Resident Magistrate, Lusaka, Livingstone, N'Dola, Broken Hill, and Luanshya, 1940. *Recreation:* gardening. *Address:* 1 Van Riebeeck Street, Bedford, Cape Province, South Africa.

EVANS, William John; retired as General Secretary of Associated Society of Locomotive Engineers and Firemen (Oct. 1960-July 1963); Civil Representative, National Association for Employment of Regular Sailors, Soldiers and Airmen, 1963-69; *b* 4 Oct. 1899; *m* 1919, Ellen Tonks (*d* 1980); one *s. Educ:* Bucknell Sch. Joined LNW Railway, 1916. Royal Navy Service, 1916-21. Great War and Victory Medals; Mine Clearance Service Medal. Served as Executive Cttee Mem. of Trade Union, 1934-39; Pres. of Executive

Cttee, 1937-38-39; Organising Sec., 1939-56; Asst Gen. Sec., 1956-60. Mem., Eastern Region Railways Board, 1963-66. Mem., Eccles Town Council, 1932-34. *Recreations:* boxing, bowling, and Association football. *Address:* 29 Gorsefield Road, Shard End, Birmingham, West Midlands B34 7AN.

EVANS, Sir (William) Vincent (John), GCMG 1976 (KCMG 1970; CMG 1959); MBE 1945; QC 1973; Barrister-at-Law; a Judge of the European Court of Human Rights, since 1980; Chairman, Bryant Symons & Co. Ltd, since 1964; *b* 20 Oct. 1915; *s* of Charles Herbert Evans and Elizabeth (*née* Jenkins); *m* 1947, Joan Mary Symons; one *s* two *d. Educ:* Merchant Taylors' Sch., Northwood; Wadham Coll., Oxford (Hon. Fellow 1981). 1st Class Hons, Jurisprudence, 1937; BCL, 1938; MA, 1941; elected Cassel Scholar, Lincoln's Inn, 1937; called to Bar, Lincoln's Inn, 1939. Served in HM Forces, 1939-46. Legal Adviser (Lt-Col) to British Military Administration, Cyrenaica, 1945-46; Asst Legal Adviser, Foreign Office, 1947-54; Legal Counsellor, UK Permanent Mission to the United Nations, 1954-59; Legal Counsellor, FO, 1959-60; Dep. Legal Adviser, FO, 1960-68; Legal Adviser, FCO, 1968-75, retired. Chm., European Cttee on Legal Cooperation, Council of Europe, 1969-71; UK Rep. Council of Europe Steering Cttee on Human Rights, 1976-80 (Chm., 1979-80); Mem., Human Rights Cttee set up under Internat. Covenant on Civil and Political Rights, 1977- (Vice-Chm., 1979-80); Mem., Council of Management, British Inst. of Internat. and Comparative Law. *Recreation:* gardening. *Address:* (home) 4 Bedford Road, Moor Park, Northwood, Mddx. *T:* Northwood 24085; (office) 2 Hare Court, Temple, EC4. *T:* 01-353 0076. *Club:* Athenæum.

EVANS-ANFOM, Emmanuel, FRCSE 1955; Commissioner for Education and Culture, Ghana, since 1978; Member, Council of State, since 1979; *b* 7 Oct. 1919; *m* 1952, Leonora Francetta Evans; three *s* one *d. Educ:* Achimota School; Edinburgh University (MB; ChB; DTM&H). House Surgeon, Dewsbury Infirmary, 1948-49; Medical Officer, Gold Coast Medical Service, 1950-56, Specialist Surgeon, 1956-67; Senior Lecturer, Ghana Medical School, 1966-67; Vice-Chancellor, Univ. of Science and Technology, Kumasi, 1967-74. Mem., WHO Expert Panel on Med. and Paramed. Educn, 1972-; Chm., Nat. Council for Higher Educn, 1974-78; Chm., Med. and Dental Council. Titular Mem., Internat. Assoc. Surgeons; Past President: Ghana Medical Assoc.; Assoc. of Surgeons of W Africa; FICS. Fellow, Ghana Acad. Arts and Sciences, 1971. Chm., Ghana Hockey Assoc. Hon. DSc Salford, 1974. *Publication:* Aetiology and Management of Intestinal Perforations, Ghana Med. Jl, 1963. *Recreations:* hockey, music, art. *Address:* PO Box M135, Accra, Ghana.

EVANS-BEVAN, Sir Martyn Evan, 2nd Bt *cr* 1958; *b* 1 April 1932; *s* of Sir David Martyn Evans-Bevan, 1st Bt, and of Eira Winifred, *d* of late Sidney Archibald Lloyd Glanley; *S* father, 1973; *m* 1957, Jennifer Jane Marion, *d* of Robert Hugh Stevens; four *s. Educ:* Uppingham. Entered family business of Evan Evans Bevan and Evans Bevan Ltd, 1953; Director, Whitbread (Wales) Ltd and local director, Phoenix Assurance Co. High Sheriff of Breconshire, 1967. *Recreations:* shooting and fishing. *Heir: s* David Gawain Evans-Bevan, *b* 16 Sept. 1961. *Address:* Felinnewydd, Llandefalle, Brecon, Powys. *Club:* Carlton.

EVANS-FREKE, family name of **Baron Carbery.**

EVANS-LOMBE, Edward Christopher, QC 1978; a Recorder of the Crown Court, since 1982; *b* 10 April 1937; *s* of Vice-Adm. Sir Edward Evans-Lombe, KCB, and Lady Evans-Lombe; *m* 1964, Frances Marilyn MacKenzie; one *s* three *d. Educ:* Eton; Trinity Coll., Cambridge (MA). National Service, 1955-57: 2nd Lieut Royal Norfolk Regt. Called to the Bar, Inner Temple, 1963. Standing Counsel to Dept of Trade in Bankruptcy matters, 1971. *Recreations:* fishing, falconry, forestry. *Address:* Marlingford Hall, Norwich. *T:* Norwich 880319. *Club:* Norfolk (Norwich).

EVE, family name of **Baron Silsoe.**

EVELEIGH, Rt. Hon. Sir Edward Walter, PC 1977; Kt 1968; ERD; MA; **Rt. Hon. Lord Justice Eveleigh;** a Lord Justice of Appeal, since 1977; *b* 8 Oct. 1917; *s* of Walter William and Daisy Emily Eveleigh; *m* 1940, Vilma Bodnar; *m* 1953, Patricia Helen Margaret Bury; two *s* (and one *s* decd). *Educ:* Peter Symonds; Brasenose Coll., Oxford (Hon. Fellow 1977). Commissioned in the Royal Artillery (Supplementary Reserve), 1936; served War of 1939-45 (despatches, 1940). Called to Bar, Lincoln's Inn, 1945, Bencher 1968; QC 1961. Recorder of Burton-on-Trent, 1961-64, of Gloucester, 1964-68; Chm., QS, County of Oxford, 1968-71 (Dep. Chm., 1963-68); a Judge of the High Court of Justice, Queen's Bench Div., 1968-77; Presiding Judge, SE Circuit, 1971-76. Mem., Royal Commn on Criminal Procedure, 1978-80. President: British-German Jurists' Assoc., 1974-; Bar Musical Soc., 1980-. Hon. Texas Citizen, 1980. *Address:* Royal Courts of Justice, Strand, WC2. *Club:* Garrick.

EVELEIGH, Air Vice-Marshal Geoffrey Charles, CB 1964; OBE 1945; RAF retired; *b* 25 Oct. 1912; *s* of Ernest Charles Eveleigh, Henley-on-Thames; *m* 1939, Anthea Josephine, *d* of F. H. Fraser, Ceylon; one *s* one *d. Educ:* Brighton Coll.; RAF Coll., Cranwell. Joined RAF, 1932; served War of 1939-45 in Bomber Command and No 2 Group; Dep. Chief of Air Staff, Royal New Zealand Air Force, 1955-57; Air Commodore, 1957; Dir-Gen. of Signals, Air Ministry, 1959-61; Air Vice-Marshal, 1961; Air Officer,

Administration, Fighter Command, 1961-64; retd 1965. *Address:* Cán Tirana, PO Box 20, Puerto de Pollensa, Mallorca, Spain. *Club:* Royal Air Force.

EVELEIGH-DE-MOLEYNS, family name of **Baron Ventry.**

EVELING, Walter Raphael Taylor, CBE 1960; Chartered Surveyor, retired, 1968; Dep. Chief Valuer, Inland Revenue, 1965-68 (Asst Chief Valuer, 1951); *b* 8 March 1908; *s* of late Raphael Eveling, Hampstead Garden Suburb; *m* 1935, Annie Ferguson Newman, Belfast; one *s. Educ:* Paradise House Sch., Stoke Newington. Joined the Valuation Office, Inland Revenue, 1935. FRICS. *Address:* 11 Thornhill Close, Ramsey, Isle of Man.

EVELYN, (John) Michael, CB 1976; Assistant Director of Public Prosecutions, 1969-76, retired (Under-Secretary, 1972); *b* 2 June 1916; *s* of Edward Ernest Evelyn and Kate Rosa Underwood. *Educ:* Charterhouse; Christ Church, Oxford (MA). Called to Bar, 1939. Army service, 1939-46. Dept of Dir of Public Prosecutions, 1946-76. *Publications:* (under pseudonym Michael Underwood): Murder on Trial, 1954; Murder Made Absolute, 1955; Death on Remand, 1956; False Witness, 1957; Lawful Pursuit, 1958; Arm of the Law, 1959; Cause of Death, 1960; Death by Misadventure, 1960; Adam's Case, 1961; The Case against Phillip Quest, 1962; Girl Found Dead, 1963; The Crime of Colin Wise, 1964; The Unprofessional Spy, 1965; The Anxious Conspirator, 1965; A Crime Apart, 1966; The Man who Died on Friday, 1967; The Man who Killed Too Soon, 1968; The Shadow Game, 1969; The Silent Liars, 1970; Shem's Demise, 1970; A Trout in the Milk, 1971; Reward for a Defector, 1973; A Pinch of Snuff, 1974; The Juror, 1975; Menaces, Menaces, 1976; Murder with Malice, 1977; The Fatal Trip, 1977; Crooked Wood, 1978; Anything but the Truth, 1978; Smooth Justice, 1979; Victim of Circumstance, 1979; A Clear Case of Suicide, 1980; Crime upon Crime, 1980; Double Jeopardy, 1981; Hand of Fate, 1981; Goddess of Death, 1982. *Recreations:* writing, reading, opera, cinema, travel. *Address:* Riverbank Coach House, Datchet, Slough SL3 9BY. *Clubs:* Garrick, Detection.

EVERALL, John (Harold); Hon. Fellow, Royal Agricultural Society of the Commonwealth (Hon. Treasurer, 1966-75); *b* 12 Oct. 1908; *s* of late William and Annie Heynes Everall, Shrawardine Castle, Shrewsbury; *m* 1935, Breda, *d* of late Gerald J. Sherlock, Ballsbridge, Dublin; one *s* one *d. Educ:* Malvern Coll. FRICS; Chartered Surveyor (Agriculture) and Pedigree Cattle Breeder (retired). War of 1939-45, Intelligence Officer (Captain), 4 Salop Bn, HG. Past President: Hereford Herd Book Soc.; Nat. Cattle Breeders' Assoc.; Shropshire and Montgomeryshire Agric. Valuers' Assoc.; Shropshire Chamber of Agric.; Vice-Pres., Shropshire and W Midland Agric. Soc., 1964-. Vice-Chairman: Hants and Winchester Br. E-SU, 1974-76; Shrewsbury Div. Conservative Assoc., 1946-50; Livestock Cttee of Brit. Agric. Export Council, 1967-70; (rep. BAEC at Santarem, Portugal, Fairs, 1967 and 1969). Former Mem. Exec. Cttee: Farmers' Club; Royal Smithfield Club; former Hon. Sec., Shropshire, Herefordshire and Mid-Wales branch, RICS. Mem. Council, Royal Agric. Soc. of Eng., 1949-70 (resigned). Rep. UK: World Confs of Pedigree Hereford Cattle Breeders, Hereford 1951, Kansas City, USA, 1960 and Dublin 1964; Royal Agric. Soc. of the Commonwealth Confs (as one of three delegs) at Sydney 1963, Toronto 1967, Nairobi 1969, Christchurch (NZ), 1973. Mem., Stapledon Trust Memorial Cttee, 1969-. Internat. Judge of Pedigree Hereford Cattle and owner of Shrine herd (dispersed 1968). Judged: Palermo, Argentina, 1944 and 1963; Sydney, 1963; Nairobi (Borans), 1969; also at Royal of England, Royal Highland, Royal Welsh and Royal Dublin Shows. Director, QMP Ltd, 1958-65. Freeman of Kansas City, USA, and City of London (Liveryman). *Recreations:* fishing, beagling (Chm., Meon Valley Beagles Hunt Cttee, 1972-79); formerly fox-hunting (Mem. S Shropshire Hunt Cttee, 1953-68); shooting. *Address:* Shrine Lodge, Church Stretton, Shropshire SY6 7AS. *T:* Church Stretton 722979. *Club:* Travellers'.

EVERARD, Maj.-Gen. Sir Christopher E. W.; *see* Welby-Everard.

EVERARD, Lt-Col Sir Nugent Henry, 3rd Bt, *cr* 1911; late The Duke of Wellington's Regiment (W Riding); *b* 28 Feb. 1905; *er s* of 2nd Bt and Louisa Cole, *d* of R. H. Metge, MP, Athlumney, Navan; *S* father, 1929; *m* 1933, Frances Audrey (*d* 1975), *y d* of J. C. Jesson; one *s* one *d.* Retired with the hon. rank of Lt-Col, 1958. *Heir: s* Robin Charles Everard [*b* 5 Oct. 1939; *m* 1963, Ariel Ingrid, *e d* of Col Peter Cleasby-Thompson, The Manor House, Cley-next-the-Sea; one *s* two *d*].

EVERARD, Timothy John, CMG 1978; HM Diplomatic Service; Minister, Lagos, since 1981; *b* 22 Oct. 1929; *s* of late Charles M. Everard and late Monica M. Everard (*née* Barford); *m* 1955, Josiane Romano; two *s* two *d. Educ:* Uppingham Sch.; Magdalen Coll., Oxford. BA (Mod. Langs). Banking: Barclays Bank DCO, 1952-62, in Egypt, Sudan, Kenya, Congo (Manager for Congo). Entered Foreign (later Diplomatic) Service: First Sec., FO, 1962-63; First Sec., Commercial, Bangkok, 1964-66; resigned to take up directorship in Ellis & Everard Ltd, 1966-67. Rejoined Foreign and Commonwealth Office, Oct. 1967: First Sec., FO, 1967-68; Bahrain, 1969-72 (First Sec. and Head of Chancery, HM Political Residency); seconded to Northern Ireland Office, FCO, April-Aug. 1972; Consul-Gen., then Chargé d'Affaires, Hanoi, 1972-73; Economic and Commercial Counsellor, Athens, 1974-78; Commercial Counsellor, Paris, 1978-81. *Recreations:* golf, tennis, sailing. *Address:* c/o Foreign and Commonwealth Office, SW1; Leagues, Stonecross, Crowborough, East Sussex. *T:* Crowborough 3278; 15 Carlyle Mansions, Cheyne Walk, SW3. *T:* 01-352 8474. *Club:* Reform.

EVERED, David Charles; Director of the Ciba Foundation, since 1978; *b* 21 Jan. 1940; *s* of late Thomas Charles Evered and Enid Christian Evered; *m* 1964, Anne Elizabeth Massey Lings, (Kit), *d* of John Massey Lings, Manchester; one *s* two *d. Educ:* Cranleigh Sch., Surrey; Middlesex Hosp. Med. Sch. (BSc 1961, MB 1964, MRCP 1967, MD 1971). Junior hospital appointments, London and Leeds, 1964-70; First Asst in Medicine, Wellcome Sen. Res. Fellow and Consultant Physician, Univ. of Newcastle upon Tyne and Royal Victoria Infirmary, 1970-78. Member: British Library Medical Information Review Panel, 1978-80; Cttee, Assoc. of Med. Res. Charities, 1981-. FRCP 1978; FIBiol 1978; FRSM; Scientific Fellow, Zool Soc. of London; Member: Soc. for Endocrinology; Eur. Thyroid Assoc. (Mem. Exec. Cttee, 1977-81); Amer. Thyroid Assoc.; Med. Res. Soc.; Hague Club. *Publications:* Diseases of the Thyroid, 1976; (with R. Hall and R. Greene) Atlas of Clinical Endocrinology, 1979; (with M. O'Connor) Collaboration in Medical Research in Europe, 1981; numerous papers on endocrinology and medicine in medical jls. *Recreations:* reading, history, squash, sailing. *Address:* 41 Portland Place, W1N 4BN. *T:* 01-636 9456; Keswick, 17 Cumberland Road, Kew, Surrey TW9 3HJ. *T:* 01-940 1579.

EVEREST, Arthur Ernest, DSc, PhD, FRSC; Fellow of the Society of Dyers and Colourists; retired; *b* 1888; *m* 1914, Annie Kathleen Broome (*d* 1982); two *d. Educ:* Wrekin Coll.; University of Birmingham and on the Continent. Formerly Managing Director John W. Leitch & Co. Ltd and associated companies; Vice-Pres. of Royal Institute of Chemistry, 1936-39, Mem. of Council, 1933-36 and 1945-48; Mem. of Council of Assoc. of Brit. Chemical Manufacturers, 1934-54; Mem. of Governing Council Wrekin Coll., 1934-74. *Publications:* two books and various memoirs on Chemical and allied subjects. *Address:* 18 Stanton Road, Ludlow, Shropshire SY8 2LR.

EVEREST, David Anthony, PhD; FRSC; Chief Scientist, Environmental Protection Group, Department of the Environment, since 1979; *b* 18 Sept. 1926; *s* of George Charles and Ada Bertha Everest; *m* 1956, Audrey Pauline (*née* Sheldrick); three *s. Educ:* John Lyon Sch., Harrow; University Coll. London (Bsc, PhD). Lecturer in Chemistry, Battersea Polytechnic, 1949-56; Sen. Scientific Officer, 1956-58, PSO, 1958-64, National Chemical Laboratory; SPSO, 1964-70, Dep. Chief Scientific Officer, 1970-77, National Physical Laboratory; DCSO, RTP Div., Dept of Industry, 1977-79. *Publications:* Chemistry of Beryllium, 1962; section on Beryllium in Comprehensive Inorganic Chemistry, 1972; papers in Inorganic Chemistry, Extractive Metallurgy and Material Science. *Recreations:* astronomy, reading, walking. *Address:* Talland, Chorleywood Road, Chorleywood, Herts WD3 4ER. *T:* Rickmansworth 73253.

EVERETT, Christopher Harris Doyle, JP; MA; Headmaster, Tonbridge School, since 1975; *b* 20 June 1933; *s* of Alan Doyle Everett, MS, FRCS, and Annabel Dorothy Joan Everett (*née* Harris); *m* 1955, Hilary (Billy) Anne (*née* Robertson); two *s* two *d. Educ:* Winchester College; New College, Oxford. MA (Class. Mods and Lit. Hum.). Grenadier Guards, Nat. Service, 1951-53. HM Diplomatic Service, 1957-70: posts included Beirut, Washington and Foreign Office; Headmaster, Worksop Coll., 1970-75. JP, Tonbridge and W Malling, 1976. *Recreations:* reading, walking, tennis. *Address:* School House, Tonbridge, Kent. *Club:* Royal Commonwealth Society.

EVERETT, Rear-Adm. Douglas Henry, CB 1950; CBE 1946 (MBE 1919); DSO 1940; *b* 16 June 1900; *s* of Douglas and Blanche Everett, Park House, Broadlands, Romsey; *m* 1932, Margery Annette Yeldham (*d* 1982); three *s* one *d. Educ:* Oakham Sch.; Cadet HMS Conway, 1913; RN Coll., Dartmouth. Served European War, 1916-18; War of 1939-45 (despatches twice); Flag Officer, Ground Training, 1949-51; Pres. Admiralty Interview Board, 1951-52; retired list, 1952. Chilean Order of Merit, 1939. *Address:* Gillinghams, Milford-on-Sea, Lymington, Hants. *T:* Milford-on-Sea 2368.

EVERETT, Douglas Hugh, MBE 1946; FRS 1980; Leverhulme Professor of Physical Chemistry, University of Bristol, 1954-82, now Emeritus; Dean of Faculty of Science, 1966-68; Pro-Vice-Chancellor, 1973-76; *b* 26 Dec. 1916; *e s* of late Charles Everett and Jessie Caroline; *m* 1942, Frances Elizabeth Jessop; two *d. Educ:* Grammar Sch., Hampton-on-Thames; University of Reading; Balliol Coll., Oxford. Wantage Scholar, Reading Univ., 1935-38; Kitchener Scholar, 1936-39; BSc, 1938; Ramsay Fellow, 1939-41; DPhil 1942. Special Scientific Duties, WO, 1942-45. ICI Fellow, Oxford Univ., 1945-47; Chemistry Lecturer, Dundee Univ. Coll., 1947; MA 1947; Fellow, Lecturer and Tutor, Exeter Coll., Oxford, 1947-48; Prof. of Chemistry, Dundee Univ. Coll., University of St Andrews, 1948-54. Chm., Internat. Union of Pure and Applied Chemistry Commn on Colloid and Surface Chemistry, 1969-73. FRSE 1950; DSc 1956. Mem., Building Research Board, DSIR, 1954-61; a Vice-Pres., Faraday Soc., 1958-61, 1963-65, 1968-70, Pres., 1976-78; Mem. Chemical Soc. Council, 1961-64, 1972-74 (Tilden Lectr, 1955; Award in Colloid and Surface Chemistry, 1971); Pres., Section B, BAAS, 1979-80. *Publications:* Introduction to Chemical Thermodynamics, 1959, 2nd edn, 1971; papers on Physical Chemistry in scientific jls. *Address:* School of Chemistry, The University, Bristol BS8 1TS.

EVERETT, Eileen, (Mrs Raymond Everett); *see* Diss, E.

EVERS, Claude Ronald; MA; Headmaster of Sutton Valence School, 1953-67; *b* 17 Jan. 1908; *s* of late C. P. Evers (formerly housemaster at Rugby Sch.); *m* 1935, Marjorie Janet Ironside Bruce; four *s. Educ:* Rugby; Trinity Coll., Oxford. Asst Master, Wellington Coll., 1931-35; Asst Master, Rugby Sch.,

1936-40; Headmaster of Berkhamsted Sch., 1946-53. Warden of Pendley Residential Centre of Adult Education, 1967-73. War service (Royal Warwicks Regt), 1940-45. Old Stager. *Publication:* Rugby (Blackie's Public School Series), 1939. *Address:* 8 Pelham Square, Brighton, East Sussex.

EVERSLEY, David Edward Charles, PhD; social researcher; *b* 22 Nov. 1921; *s* of Dr Otto Eberstadt and Dela Morel; *m* 1945, Edith Wembridge (*d* 1978), one *s* three *d. Educ:* Goethe-Gymnasium, Frankfurt/Main; Leighton Park Sch., Reading; London Sch. of Economics. BSc (Econ) (London), PhD (Birmingham). Asst Lectr, Lectr, then Reader, in Economic (and then Social) Hist., Univ. of Birmingham, 1949-66. Dir, W Midlands Social and Polit. Res. Unit, 1962-65; Reader in Population and Regional Studies, Univ. of Sussex, 1966; Dir, Social Research Unit, Univ. of Sussex, 1967-69; Prof., 1969. Hon. Sec., Midlands New Towns Soc., 1958-62; Chief Planner (Strategy), Greater London Council, 1969-72; Centre for Environmental Studies, 1972-76; Sen. Res. Fellow, PSI, 1976-81; Vivien Stewart Bursar, Dept of Land Economy, Univ. of Cambridge, 1981-82. Visiting Professor: of Demography, Univ. of California at Berkeley, 1965; Bartlett Sch. of Architecture and Planning, University Coll. London, 1976-79. Mem., W Midlands Economic Planning Coun., 1965-66; Corr. Mem., German Acad. for Urban and Regional Planning, 1972-; Pres., Commn sur la Démographie Historique, Internat. Congress of Hist. Sciences, 1965-70. Chm., Regional Studies Assoc., 1972-75, Vice-Chm., 1975-. Chm., Social Responsibility Council, Society of Friends (Quakers), 1972-75; Pres., British Soc. for Population Studies, 1981-. Hon. MRTPI 1978, Mem. Council, 1979-. *Publications:* Rents and Social Policy, 1955; Social Theories of Fertility and the Malthusian Debate, 1959, new US edn 1975; (with D. Keate) The Overspill Problem in the West Midlands, 1958; (ed and contrib. with D. V. Glass) Population in History, 1965; (with Lomas and Jackson) Population Growth and Planning Policy, 1965; (with F. Sukdeo) The Dependants of the Coloured Commonwealth Population of England and Wales, 1969; (ed and contrib. with D. Donnison) London: urban patterns, problems and policies, 1973; The Planner in Society, 1973; A Question of Numbers?, 1973; (ed and contrib. with J. Platts) Public Resources and Private Lives, 1976; (ed and contrib. with Alan Evans) The Inner City, Industry and Employment, 1980; (ed and contrib. with W. Koellmann) Population Change and Social Planning, 1982; numerous chapters in collected vols; contribs to Victoria History of the Counties of England; articles in jls of history, demography and planning. *Recreations:* walking, talking, working. *Address:* Hummerstons, Cottered, Buntingford, Herts. *T:* Cottered 354.

EVERSON, Sir Frederick (Charles), KCMG 1968 (CMG 1956); *b* 6 Sept. 1910; *s* of Frederick Percival Everson; *m* 1937, Linda Mary Clark; three *s* one *d. Educ:* Tottenham County Sch., Middlesex. BSc (Econ.) London. Entered Civil Service, July 1928; Consular Service, Dec. 1934. Chief Administrative Officer, British Embassy, Bonn, Germany, 1953-56; Ambassador to El Salvador, 1956-60; Commercial Counsellor, British Embassy, Stockholm, 1960-63; Minister (Economic), British Embassy, Paris, 1963-68. *Address:* 8 Gainsborough Court, College Road, Dulwich, SE21 7LT. *T:* 01-693 8125.

EVERSON, John Andrew; HM Chief Inspector of Schools, Secondary Education, Department of Education and Science, since 1981; *b* 26 Oct. 1933; *s* of Harold Leslie Everson and Florence Jane Stone; *m* 1961, Gilda Ramsden; two *s. Educ:* Tiffin Boys' Sch., Kingston-upon-Thames; Christ's Coll., Cambridge (MA); King's Coll., London (PGCE). Teacher: Haberdashers' Aske's Sch., Elstree, 1958-65; City of London Sch., 1965-68; Schools Inspectorate, DES, 1968-. *Publications:* (with B. P. FitzGerald) Settlement Patterns, 1968; (with B. P. FitzGerald) Inside the City, 1972. *Recreations:* opera, walking, theatre, chess. *Address:* Department of Education and Science, Elizabeth House, York Road, SE1 7PH. *T:* 01-928 9222.

EVERY, Sir John (Simon), 12th Bt, *cr* 1641; *b* 24 April 1914; *er s* of Sir Edward Oswald Every, 11th Bt and Lady (Ivy Linton) Every (*d* 1976); *S* father, 1959; *m* 1st, 1938, Annette Constance (marr. diss., 1942), *o c* of late Major F. W. M. Drew, Drewscourt, Co. Cork; 2nd, 1943, Janet Marion, *d* of John Page, Blakeney, Norfolk; one *s* two *d. Educ:* Harrow. Served War of 1939-45. Capt., Sherwood Foresters. Business Co. Dir, 1945-60, Dir of private companies. *Recreations:* cricket, tennis, shooting. *Heir: s* Henry John Michael Every [*b* 6 April 1947; *m* 1974, Susan Mary, *er d* of Kenneth Beaton, Hartford, Hunts; two *s*]. *Address:* Egginton, near Derby. *T:* Etwall 2245. *Club:* MCC.

EVETTS, Lt-Gen. Sir John Fullerton, Kt 1951; CB 1939; CBE 1937; MC; *b* 30 June 1891; *s* of late Lieut-Col J. M. Evetts, Tackley Park, Oxon; *m* 1916, Helen Phyllis (*d* 1980), *d* of late Captain C. A. G. Becher, Burghfields, Bourton on the Water, Glos; one *s. Educ:* Temple Grove; Lancing; Royal Military Coll., Sandhurst; Staff Coll., Camberley. Entered Army, 1911; joined The Cameronians (Scottish Rifles); served European War, 1914-18 (MC, despatches); Lieut 1913; Captain 1915; temp. Major Machine Gun Corps, 1916; Bt-Major 1929; Substantive, 1929; Bt Lt-Col 1931; Substantive Lt-Col Royal Ulster Rifles, 1934; Col 1935; Maj.-Gen. 1941; employed with Iraq Army, 1925-28; DAAG War Office, 1932; Commander British Troops in Palestine, 1935; GSO1 Palestine, 1936; Brig. Comd. 16th Inf. Bde, Palestine and Trans-Jordan, 1936-39 (despatches); BGS, HQ, Northern Command, India, 1939-40; Comdr Western (Indept) Dist, India, 1940-41; Divl Comdr, 1941 (despatches); Asst CIGS, 1942; Senior Military Adviser to Minister of Supply, 1944-46; retired pay, 1946; Head of British Ministry of Supply Staff in Australia, 1946-51, and Chief Executive Officer Joint UK-Australian Long Range Weapons, Board of Administration, 1946-49. Managing Dir, 1951-58,

Chm., 1958-60, Rotol Ltd and Brit, Messier. OStJ. Legion of Merit (US), 1943. *Address:* Pepper Cottage, Kemerton, near Tewkesbury, Glos. *Club:* Army and Navy.

EWALD, Paul P., FRS 1958; DrPhil; Professor Emeritus of Physics, Polytechnic Institute of Brooklyn, since 1959; Professor of Physics, 1949-59, and Head of Department, 1949-57, Polytechnic Institute of Brooklyn; *b* Berlin, Germany, 23 Jan. 1888; *s* of Paul Ewald, Historian (Univ. Berlin), and Clara Ewald, Portrait-Painter; *m* 1913, Ella (Elise Berta) (*née* Philippson); two *s* two *d. Educ:* Victoria Gymnasium, Potsdam; Univs of Cambridge, Göttingen and Munich (DrPhil 1912). Lecturer in Theoretical Physics, Univ. of Munich, 1918; Prof. of Theoretical Physics, TH Stuttgart, 1921-37; Lecturer, later Prof. of Mathematical Physics, The Queen's Univ., Belfast, 1939-49. Corresp. Mem. Acad. Göttingen, 1937; Fellow Amer. Acad. Arts and Sci., US, 1954; Membre d'honneur Société Française de Minéralogie et de Cristallographie, 1955; Ehrenmitglied, Deutsche Mineralog. Ges., 1958. Mem. Exec. Cttee, Internat. Union of Crystallography, 1948-66, Pres., 1960-1963. Corresp. Mem. Bavarian Acad. Sci., 1962; Fellow, Deut. Akad. d. Naturforscher (Leopoldina), 1966. Hon. Mem., Cambridge Philosophical Soc., 1968. Dr *hc* ; TH Stuttgart, 1954; Univ. de Paris, 1958; Adelphi Univ., 1966; Univ. Munich, 1968; Polytechnic Inst., Brooklyn, 1972. Max Planck Medal, Deutsche Physikal Gesellschaft, 1978; Gregory Aminoff Medal, Swedish Acad., 1979. *Publications:* Kristalle und Röntgenstrahlen, 1923 (Germany); 50 Years of X-ray Diffraction, 1962 (Oosthoek, Holland). Contrib. Thermodynamics and Physics of Matter, 1955 (USA), etc. Editor: Zeitschrift für Kristallographie, 1923-37; Acta Crystallographica, 1948-59. *Address:* 108 Sheldon Road, Ithaca, NY 14850, USA.

EWANS, Martin Kenneth, CMG 1980; HM Diplomatic Service; Diplomatic Service Chairman, Civil Service Selection Board, since 1982; *b* 14 Nov. 1928; *s* of late John Ewans; *m* 1953, Mary Tooke; one *s* one *d. Educ:* St Paul's; Corpus Christi Coll., Cambridge (major scholar, MA). Royal Artillery, 1947-49, 2nd Lt. Joined Commonwealth Relations Office, 1952; Second Sec., Karachi, 1954-55; First Sec.: Ottawa, 1958-61; Lagos, 1962-64; Kabul, 1967-69. Counsellor, Dar-es-Salaam, 1969-73; Head of East African Dept, FCO, 1973-77; Minister, New Delhi, 1978-82. *Address:* c/o Foreign and Commonwealth Office, SW1. *Club:* Royal Commonwealth Society.

EWART, Gavin Buchanan, FRSL; freelance writer (poet), since 1971; *b* 4 Feb. 1916; *s* of George Arthur Ewart and Dorothy Hannah (*née* Turner); *m* 1956, Margaret Adelaide Bennett; one *s* one *d. Educ:* Wellington Coll.; Christ's Coll., Cambridge (BA Hons 1937, MA 1942). FRSL 1981. Salesman, Contemporary Lithographs, 1938; served War, Royal Artillery, 1940-46; Production Manager, Editions Poetry, London, 1946; British Council, 1946-52; Advertising copywriter in London advertising agencies, 1952-71. Cholmondeley Award for Poetry, 1971. *Publications:* Poems and Songs, 1939; Londoners, 1964; Pleasures of the Flesh, 1966; The Deceptive Grin of the Gravel Porters, 1968; The Gavin Ewart Show, 1971; Be My Guest!, 1975; No Fool Like An Old Fool, 1976; Or Where a Young Penguin Lies Screaming, 1978; All My Little Ones, 1978; The Collected Ewart 1933-1980, 1980, 2nd edn 1982; The New Ewart, 1982; More Little Ones, 1983. *Recreations:* reading, listening to music. *Address:* 57 Kenilworth Court, Lower Richmond Road, SW15 1EN. *T:* 01-788 7071.

EWART, Sir (William) Ivan (Cecil), 6th Bt, *cr* 1887; DSC 1945; JP; East Africa Regional Representative, Royal Commonwealth Society for the Blind, since 1977; *b* 18 July 1919; *s* of late Major William Basil Ewart (*y s* of late Frederick William Ewart, 7th *s* of 1st Bt); *S* kinsman (Sir Talbot Ewart, 5th Bt), 1959; *m* 1948, Pauline Chevallier (*d* 1964), *e d* of late Wing Comdr Raphael Chevallier Preston, OBE, AFC, JP, Abbey Flat, Bellapais, Kyrenia, Cyprus; one *s* two *d. Educ:* Radley. Joined Ulster Div., RNVR, 1938. Served War of 1939-45; Lieut, RNVR; service in Coastal Forces (Motor Torpedo-Boats), 1939-42 (DSC); POW, Germany, 1942-45. Chairman: William Ewart & Son Ltd, Linen Manufacturers, 1968-73 (Dir, 1954-); William Ewart Investments Ltd, Belfast, 1973-77; Ewart New Northern Ltd, Belfast, 1973-77. Pres., NI Chamber of Commerce and Industry, 1974. A Northern Ireland Delegate to the Duke of Edinburgh's Study Conf. on the Human Problems of Industrial Communities within the Commonwealth and Empire, Oxford, 1956; Pres., Church of Ireland's Young Men's Soc., 1951-61 and 1975-77; Chm. Flax Spinners Assoc., 1961-66; Pres., Oldpark Unionist Assoc., 1950-68. Belfast Harbour Comr, 1968-77. High Sheriff for County Antrim, 1976. *Recreations:* travel, gliding. *Heir: s* William Michael Ewart, *b* 10 June 1953. *Address:* Hill House, Hillsborough, Co. Down, Ireland BT26 6AE. *T:* Hillsborough 683000; PO Box 46656, Nairobi, Kenya. *T:* 26010. *Clubs:* Naval; Ulster (Belfast); Nairobi.

EWART-BIGGS, family name of **Baroness Ewart-Biggs.**

EWART-BIGGS, Baroness *cr* 1981 (Life Peer), of Ellis Green in the County of Essex; **(Felicity) Jane Ewart-Biggs;** *d* of Major Basil Randall; *m* 1960, Christopher Ewart-Biggs, CMG, OBE (HM Diplomatic Service) (*d* 1976); one *s* two *d. Educ:* Downe House School, Cold Ash, Newbury, Berks. Lived in Algiers, Brussels, Paris and Dublin, 1960-76, during husband's service overseas. In 1976, established Christopher Ewart-Biggs Memorial Literary Prize, designed to promote better understanding between people of Britain and Ireland and closer co-operation between partners of the European Community. Hon. DLitt, New Univ. of Ulster, 1978. *Recreations:* travel, discussion and international affairs. *Address:* 31 Radnor Walk, SW3 4BP.

EWART EVANS, George; *see* Evans, G. E.

EWART JAMES, William Henry; His Honour Judge Ewart James; a Circuit Judge, since 1974; *b* 15 Dec. 1910; *e s* of Rev. David Ewart James; *m* 1941, Esmé Vivienne, *y d* of Edward Lloyd, Liverpool and Gresford; two *s* one *d. Educ:* Bishop's Stortford Coll.; Worcester Coll., Oxford. MA (Mod. Hist.). Private Sec. to J. H. Morgan, KC, Counsel to the Indian Princes, 1936; Asst. Sec. European Gp, Bengal Legislature, 1937-38; travelled Far East and America, 1936-39. Served War: in Grenadier Guards, Royal Welch Fusiliers and 1st Airborne Div., Sept. 1939-Dec. 1945. Called to the Bar, 1948; Counsel to the Post Office, Western Circuit, 1957-70; Dep. Chm., Devon QS, 1968-71; a Recorder of the Crown Court, 1972-74. Mem., Hants CC, 1952-74; Alderman, 1965; Chm., Local Govt Cttee, 1963-74. *Recreation:* travel. *Address:* Springfield, Greywell, Basingstoke, Hants. *T:* Odiham 2644.

EWBANK, Hon. Sir Anthony (Bruce), Kt 1980; **Hon. Mr Justice Ewbank;** Judge of the High Court of Justice, Family Division, since 1980; *b* 30 July 1925; *s* of late Rev. Harold Ewbank and Gwendolen Ewbank (*née* Bruce); *m* 1958, Moya McGinn; four *s* one *d. Educ:* St John's Sch., Leatherhead; Trinity Coll., Cambridge, Natural Sciences Tripos (MA). RNVR, 1945-47 and 1951-56. Called to Bar, Gray's Inn, 1954; Bencher, 1980. Junior Counsel to Treasury in Probate matters, 1969; QC 1972; a Recorder of the Crown Court, 1975-80. Chm., Family Law Bar Assoc., 1978-80. *Recreations:* walking, sailing, swimming. *Address:* Royal Courts of Justice, Strand, WC2.

EWBANK, Prof. Inga-Stina; Hildred Carlile Professor of English at Bedford College, University of London, since 1974; *b* 13 June 1932; *d* of Gustav and Ingeborg Ekeblad; *m* 1959, Roger Ewbank; one *s* two *d. Educ:* Högre Allänna Läroverket for Flickor, Gothenburg; Univs of Carleton (BA), Gothenburg (Fil.kand.), Sheffield (MA) and Liverpool (PhD). William Noble Fellow, Univ. of Liverpool, 1955-57; Res. Fellow at Shakespeare Inst., Univ. of Birmingham, 1957-60; Univ. of Liverpool: Asst Lectr, 1960-63; Lectr, 1963-70; Sen. Lectr, 1970-72; Reader in English Literature, Bedford Coll., Univ. of London, 1972-74. Vis. Lectr, Univ. of Munich, 1959-60; Vis. Assoc. Prof., Northwestern Univ., 1966; Vis. Prof., Harvard Univ., 1974. *Publications:* Their Proper Sphere: A Study of the Brontë Sisters as Early-Victorian Female Novelists, 1966; Shakespeare, Ibsen and the Unspeakable (Inaugural Lecture), 1975; chapter in, a New Companion to Shakespeare Studies, 1971; (with Peter Hall) Ibsen's John Gabriel Borkman: An English Version, 1975; (ed with Philip Edwards and G. K. Hunter) Shakespeare's Styles, 1980; chapters in other books; contrib. Shakespeare Survey, Ibsen Yearbook, Rev. Eng. Studies, Mod. Lang. Rev., English Studies, etc. *Recreations:* same as work: reading, theatre; children. *Address:* 19 Woodfield Road, Ealing, W5. *T:* 01-997 2895.

EWBANK, Michael Henry, CBE 1980; Chairman, Ewbank and Partners Ltd, since 1969; *b* 5 May 1930; *s* of Charles Henry Preston Ewbank and Doris Minnie Ewbank; *m* 1959, Julia Ann Bartley; three *s* one *d. Educ:* Stowe School; City and Guilds Coll., London Univ. BSc, ACGI, CEng, FIChemE. Royal Navy, 1951-53; S/Lt RNR. Technical Engineer, Ewbank and Partners Ltd, 1953-57; Director, 1957; Dep. Chairman, 1965. Chairman: British Consultants' Bureau, 1974-76; ME Assoc., 1981-82; Pres., European Cttee of Consulting Firms (CEBI), 1976-78. *Recreations:* riding, skiing, golf. *Address:* Oakwood, Clayhill Road, Leigh, Reigate, Surrey. *T:* Dawes Green 354. *Club:* Eccentric.

EWBANK, Ven. Walter Frederick; Archdeacon of Carlisle, since 1977; Administrator of Church House, Carlisle and Chairman, Diocesan Board of Finance and Diocesan Glebe Committee, since 1977; *b* Poona, India, 29 Jan. 1918; *er s* of late Sir Robert Benson Ewbank, CSI, CIE, and Frances Helen, *d* of Rev. W. F. Simpson; *m* 1st, 1941, Ida Margaret, 3rd *d* of late John Haworth Whitworth, DSO, ME Invner Temple; three *d*; 2nd, 1976, Mrs Josephine Alice Williamson, MD, ChB, FRCOG. *Educ:* Shrewsbury Sch.; Balliol Coll., Oxford. Classical Scholar of Balliol, 1936; 1st, Classical Hon. Mods, 1938; 2nd, Hon. Sch. of Theology, 1946; BA and MA 1946; Bishops' Coll., Cheshunt, 1946; BD 1952. Friends' Ambulance Unit, 1939-42; Deacon, 1946; Priest, 1947; Asst Curate, St Martin's, Windermere, 1946-49; Dio. Youth Chaplain and Vicar of Ings, 1949-52; Chap. to Casterton Sch. and Vicar of Casterton, 1952-62; Domestic Chap. to Bp of Carlisle and Vicar of Raughtonhead, 1962-66; Vicar of St Cuthbert's, Carlisle, and Chap. to Corporation, 1966-71; Rural Dean of Carlisle, 1970-71; Archdeacon of Westmorland and Furness and Vicar of Winster, 1971-77; Canon Residentiary of Carlisle Cathedral, 1977-80; Hon. Canon, 1966-77 and 1982-. Proctor in Convocation and Mem. Ch Assembly, 1957-70; Member: Canon Law Standing Commn, 1968-70; Faculty Jurisdiction Commn, 1979-; Diocesan Dir: of Ordinands, 1962-70; of Post Ordination Trng, 1962-66; Vice-Chm., Diocesan Synod, 1970-79. Chm., Carlisle Tithe Barn Restoration Cttee, 1968-70. Winter War Remembrance Medal (Finland), 1940. *Publications:* Salopian Diaries, 1961; Morality without Law, 1969; Charles Euston Nurse—A Memoir, 1982; articles in Church Quarterly Review. *Recreation:* classical studies. *Address:* High Ridge, Castle Sowerby, Hutton Roof, Penrith, Cumbria CA11 0XY. *Club:* Royal Over-Seas League.
See also A. C. Renfrew.

EWEN, Peter; Chartered Accountant; *b* 4 June 1903; *s* of Alexander H. and Elizabeth Ewen, Liverpool; *m* 1932, Janet Howat (*née* Allan) (*d* 1982); *d. Educ:* Merchant Taylors, Crosby, Qualified as Chartered Accountant, 1927;

after 4 years in India joined Allan Charlesworth & Co., 1931; Partner, 1938; Senior Partner, 1953; retired, 1969. Dir of companies; Chm., Westinghouse Brake and Signal Co. Ltd, 1962-74. *Address:* Kestor, Moretonhampstead, Devon. *T:* Moretonhampstead 307. *Club:* Oriental.

EWENS, John Qualtrough, CMG 1971; CBE 1959; First Parliamentary Counsel, Commonwealth of Australia, 1948-72; *b* 18 Nov. 1907; *er s* of L. J. Ewens, Adelaide; *m* 1935, Gwendoline, *e d* of W. A. Wilson, Adelaide; two *s. Educ:* St Peter's Coll., Adelaide; Univ. of Adelaide. LLB 1929. Barrister and Solicitor, S Australia, 1929. Legal Asst, Attorney-General's Dept, Commonwealth of Australia, 1933; Sen. Legal Officer, 1939; Asst Parly Draftsman, 1945; Principal Asst Parly Draftsman, 1948; First Parly Counsel (formerly called Parly Draftsman), 1948-72; Actg Solicitor-Gen. and Actg Sec., Commonwealth of Australia Attorney-Gen.'s Dept, numerous occasions, 1953-70. Mem. Council: Canberra UC, 1945-60; Australian Nat. Univ., 1960-75; Mem., Australian Law Reform Commn, 1978-80. *Publications:* articles in legal periodicals. *Recreations:* reading, music, bowls. *Address:* 57 Franklin Street, Forrest, ACT 2603, Australia. *T:* Canberra 95 9283. *Club:* University House (Canberra).

EWER, Prof. Tom Keightley, OBE 1978; HDA; BVSc; PhD; MRCVS; Professor of Animal Husbandry, Bristol University, 1961-77, now Emeritus; retired; *b* 21 Sept. 1911; *s* of William Edward Frederick Ewer and Maria Louisa Wales; *m* 1st, 1937, Iva Rosalind Biddle; three *s*; 2nd, 1959, Margaret June Fischer; three *d* one step *s* two step *d. Educ:* Fowey Grammar Sch.; Sydney Univ. (BVSc); Cambridge Univ. (PhD). Veterinary research with NZ Govt, 1938-45; Senior Lecturer, Univ. of NZ, 1945-47; Wellcome Research Fellow, University of Cambridge, 1947-50; Prof. of Animal Husbandry, University of Queensland, 1950-61; Prof. of Animal Resources, King Faisal Univ., Saudi Arabia, 1978-80. *Publications:* Practical Animal Husbandry, 1982; contrib. to scientific publications, on animal nutrition and veterinary education. *Recreation:* music. *Address:* Oakridge, Winscombe, Avon BS25 1LZ. *T:* Winscombe 3279.

EWIN, Sir David Ernest Thomas F.; *see* Floyd Ewin.

EWING; *see* Orr-Ewing and Orr Ewing.

EWING, Vice-Adm. Sir Alastair; *see* Ewing, Vice-Adm. Sir R. A.

EWING, Harry; MP (Lab) Stirling, Falkirk and Grangemouth, since 1974 (Stirling and Falkirk, Sept. 1971-1974); *b* 20 Jan. 1931; *s* of Mr and Mrs William Ewing; *m* 1954, Margaret Greenhill; one *s* one *d. Educ:* Fulford Primary Sch., Cowdenbeath; Beath High Sch., Cowdenbeath. Contested (Lab) East Fife, 1970. Parly Under-Sec. of State, Scottish Office, 1974-79. Mem., Union of Post Office Workers. *Recreations:* bowls, gardening. *Address:* 16 Robertson Avenue, Leven, Fife. *T:* Leven 26123.

EWING, Vice-Adm. Sir (Robert) Alastair, KBE 1962; CB 1959; DSC 1942; *b* 10 April 1909; *s* of late Ian Ewing and Muriel Adèle Child; *m* 1940, Diana Smeed (*d* 1980), *d* of Major Harry Archer, DSO; one *s. Educ:* Royal Naval Coll., Dartmouth. In command of Destroyers during War of 1939-45; NATO Standing Group Staff, 1950-51; Imperial Defence Coll., 1952; in command of HMS Vanguard, 1953-54; Dir of Naval Staff Coll., Greenwich, 1954-56; Naval Sec. to First Lord of the Admiralty, 1956-58; Flag Officer Flotillas (Mediterranean), 1958-60; Adm. Commanding Reserves and Inspector of Recruiting, 1960-62; retd list, 1962. *Address:* Old Port Cove, North Palm Beach, Florida 33408, USA. *Clubs:* Royal Yacht Squadron; Old Port Yacht (Florida).

EWING, Mrs Winifred Margaret; Member (SNP) European Parliament, since 1975, elected for Highlands and Islands, 1979; *b* 10 July 1929; *d* of George Woodburn and Christina Bell Anderson; *m* 1956, Stewart Martin Ewing; two *s* one *d. Educ:* Queen's Park Sen. Sec. Sch.; University of Glasgow (MA, LLB). Qual. as Solicitor, 1952. Lectr in Law, Scottish Coll. of Commerce, 1954-56; Solicitor, practising on own account, 1956-. Sec., Glasgow Bar Assoc., 1961-67, Pres., 1970-71. MP (Scottish Nationalist) for Hamilton, Nov. 1967-70; MP (SNP) Moray and Nairn, Feb. 1974-1979. Vice-Pres., Scottish National Party. Mem., European Parlt, 1975-79. Mem., Exec. Cttee, Scottish Council for Develt and Industry, 1972-. Pres., Glasgow Central Soroptimist Club, 1966-67. *Address:* 52 Queen's Drive, Glasgow G42 8BP. *T:* 041-423 1765.

EWUSIE, Joseph Yanney; Secretary-General, Pan African Institute for Development, since 1980; Visiting Professor: University of Nairobi, Kenya, since 1979; Ahmadu Bello University, Nigeria, since 1980; *b* 18 April 1927; *s* of Samuel Mainsa Wilson Ewusie and Elizabeth Dickson; *m* 1959, Stella Turkson; four *s. Educ:* Winneba Anglican Sch.; Mfantsipim Sch.; University Coll. of the Gold Coast; Univ. of Cambridge. BSc (London), PhD (Cantab). Lectr in Botany, Univ. of Ghana, 1957-62; Gen. Sec. (Chief Exec.), Ghana Academy of Sciences (highest learned and res. org. in Ghana), 1963-68; Univ. of Cape Coast: Associate Prof. of Botany, 1969-72, Prof., 1973-79; Head, Dept of Botany, 1969-73; Dean, Faculty of Science, 1971-74; Pro-Vice Chancellor, 1971-73; Vice Chancellor, 1973-78. Mem. Exec. Cttee, ICSU, 1964-67. FWA 1963; Dipl. of Merit, Internat. Acad. of Science, Letters and Arts, Rome, 1968; Dipl. of Honour, Internat. Inst. of Community Service, 1975. Medal (Govt of Hungary) for internat. understanding between Ghana and Hungary, 1964. *Publications:* School Certificate Biology for Tropical Schools, 1964, 4th edn

EXETER, Tropical Biological Drawings, 1973; Elements of Tropical Ecology, 1980. *Address:* Pan African Institute for Development, PO Box 4056, Douala, Cameroun; Case Postale 38, 1211 Geneva 20, Switzerland.

EXETER, 7th Marquess of, *cr* 1801; **William Martin Alleyne Cecil;** Baron Burghley, 1571; Earl of Exeter, 1605; *b* 27 April 1909; 2nd *s* of 5th Marquess of Exeter, KG, CMG and Hon. Myra Rowena Sibell Orde-Powlett, *d* of 4th Baron Bolton; *S* brother, 1981; *m* 1st, 1934, Edith Lilian De Csanady (*d* 1954); one *s*; 2nd, 1954, Lillian Jane Johnson; one *d* (and one *d* decd). *Educ:* Royal Naval Coll., Dartmouth. *Publications:* Being Where You Are, 1974; On Eagles' Wings, 1977. *Heir: s* Lord Burghley, *qv. Address:* 100 Mile House, PO Box 8, British Columbia, Canada. *T:* 604-395-2323.

EXETER, Bishop of, since 1973; **Rt. Rev. Eric Arthur John Mercer;** *b* 6 Dec. 1917; *s* of Ambrose John Mercer, Kent; *m* 1951, Rosemary Wilma, *d* of John William Denby, Lincs; one *s* one *d. Educ:* Dover Gram. Sch.; Kelham Theol. Coll. Enlisted Sherwood Foresters, 1940, commnd 1940; Capt. and Adjt, 14th Foresters, 1943; served Italy (despatches), 1944; Staff Coll., Haifa, 1944; DAA&QMG, 66 Inf. Bde, Palestine, 1945; GSO2 (SD), HQ, MEF, 1945. Returned Kelham Theol. Coll., 1946-47. Ordained, Chester, 1947; Curate, Coppenhall, Crewe, 1947-51; Priest in charge, Heald Green, 1951-53; Rector, St Thomas', Stockport, 1953-59; Chester Diocesan Missioner, 1959-65; Rector, Chester St Bridget, 1959-65; Hon. Canon of Chester Cathedral, 1964; Bishop Suffragan of Birkenhead, 1965-73. Church Commissioners: Dep. Chm., Pastoral Cttee, 1976-; Mem., Bd of Governors, 1980-. Nat. Chm., CEMS, 1974-78. *Publication:* (contrib.) Worship in a Changing Church, 1965. *Address:* The Palace, Exeter EX1 1HY.

EXETER, Dean of; *see* Eyre, Very Rev. R. M. S.

EXETER, Archdeacon of; *see* Richards, Ven. John.

EXHAM, Maj.-Gen. Robert Kenah; CB 1952; CBE 1949 (OBE 1946); MC 1940; Director Land/Air Warfare, War Office, 1957-60, retired; *b* 25 Jan. 1907; *s* of late Col Frank Simeon Exham, DSO; *m* 1940, Avril Mary, *d* of late Major F. Langley Price; two *s. Educ:* Radley Coll. Served North-West Frontier of India, 1935 (despatches twice, medal with clasp); War of 1939-45 (despatches, MC). Maj.-Gen. late Duke of Wellington's Regt (West Riding). *Address:* Tall Trees, Beech Hill, Mayford, Woking, Surrey GU22 0SB. *T:* Woking 62783.

EXMOUTH, 10th Viscount *cr* 1816; **Paul Edward Pellew;** Bt 1796 (Pellew of Treverry); Baron 1814; *b* 8 Oct. 1940; *s* of 9th Viscount Exmouth and Maria Luisa, Marquesa de Olias (Spain, *cr* 1652; *S* 1940), *d* of late Luis de Urquijo, Marques de Amurrio, Madrid; *S* father, 1970; *m* 1st, 1964 (marr. diss. 1974); one *d*; 2nd, 1975, Rosemary Countess of Burford; twin *s. Educ:* Downside. Mem. Cross benches, House of Lords. Mem., Inst. of Dirs. *Heir: et twin s* Hon. Edward Francis Pellew, *b* 30 Oct. 1978. *Address:* Canonteign, near Exeter, Devon.

EXTON, Clive; scriptwriter and playwright; *b* 11 April 1930; *s* of late J. E. M. Brooks and of Marie Brooks (*née* Rolfe); *m* 1951, Patricia Fletcher Ferguson (marr. diss. 1957); two *d*; *m* 1957, Margaret Josephine Reid; one *s* two *d. Educ:* Christ's Hospital. *TV plays:* No Fixed Abode, 1959; The Silk Purse; Where I Live; Some Talk of Alexander; Hold My Hand, Soldier; I'll Have You to Remember; The Big Eat; The Trial of Doctor Fancy; Land of my Dreams; The Close Prisoner; The Bone Yard; Are You Ready for the Music?; The Rainbirds; Killers (series); Stigma; Henry Intervenes; The Crezz (series); Dick Barton—Special Agent (series). *Stage play:* Have You Any Dirty Washing, Mother Dear?. *Films:* Night Must Fall; Isadora; Entertaining Mr Sloane; Ten Rillington Place; Running Scared; Doomwatch; The House in Nightmare Park; The Awakening; Robin Hood. *Publications:* No Fixed Abode (in Six Granada Plays, anthol.), 1960; Have You Any Dirty Washing, Mother Dear? (in Plays of the Year, vol. 37), 1970. *Address:* c/o A. D. Peters & Co., 10 Buckingham Street, WC2.

EXTON-SMITH, Prof. Arthur Norman, CBE 1981; MD; FRCP; Professor of Geriatric Medicine, University College Hospital Medical School, London, since 1973; *b* 7 Jan. 1920; *s* of Arthur and Ethel Exton-Smith; *m* 1951, Jean Barbara Belcher; one *s* one *d. Educ:* Nottingham High Sch.; Pembroke Coll., Cambridge (MA, MD). FRCP 1964. Consultant Physician: Whittington Hosp., London, 1951-65; UCH, 1965-73. *Publications:* Medical Problems of Old Age, 1955; Geriatrics (with P. W. Overstall), 1979; contrib. Lancet, BMJ. *Address:* 6 North Grove, Highgate, N6 4SL. *T:* 01-341 4433.

EYERS, Patrick Howard Caines, MVO 1966; HM Diplomatic Service; Head of Republic of Ireland Department, Foreign and Commonwealth Office, since 1981; *b* 4 Sept. 1933; *s* of late Arthur Leopold Caines Eyers and Nora Lilian Eyers; *m* 1960, Heidi, *d* of Werner Rüsch, Dipl. Ing, and Helene (*née* Feil); two *s* one *d. Educ:* Clifton Coll.; Gonville and Caius Coll., Cambridge (BA Hons 1957); Institut Universitaire de Hautes Etudes Internationales, Geneva. RA, 1952-54. Asst Editor, Grolier Soc. Inc., New York, 1957; HM Foreign (now Diplomatic) Service, 1959; ME Centre for Arabic Studies, 1960; Dubai, 1961; Brussels, 1964; FO, 1966; Aden, 1969; Abidjan, 1970; British Mil. Govt, Berlin, 1971; FCO, 1974; Counsellor, Bonn, 1977-81. Officer, Order of Leopold, Belgium, 1966. *Recreations:* music, skiing, sailing. *Address:* c/o Foreign and Commonwealth Office, SW1. *Clubs:* Ski of GB; Kandahar Ski; Hurlingham.

EYRE, Hon. Dean Jack; New Zealand High Commissioner to Canada, 1968-73 and 1976-79; *b* Westport, NZ, 1914; *m* ; two *s* one *d. Educ:* Hamilton High Sch.; Auckland University Coll. Served War of 1939-45, Lieut in RNVR. Electrical importer and manufacturer. MP (Nat) North Shore, 1949-66; Minister of Customs, Industries and Commerce, 1954-57; Minister of Social Security and Tourist and Health Resorts, 1956-57; Minister of Housing, State Advances and Defence, New Zealand, 1957; Minister in Charge of Police, 1960-63; Minister of Defence, 1960-66; Minister i/c Tourism, 1961-66. *Recreations:* yachting, fishing. *Address:* 74 Somerset Street W, Apt 4, Ottawa, Ontario K2P 0H3, Canada. *Clubs:* Royal New Zealand Yacht Squadron, Northern, Officers (Auckland); Wellington, United Services (Wellington).

EYRE, Graham Newman, QC 1970; a Recorder of the Crown Court, since 1975; *b* 9 Jan. 1931; *s* of Newman Eyre; *m* 1954, Jean Dalrymple Walker; one *s* three *d. Educ:* Marlborough Coll.; Trinity Coll., Cambridge. BA 1953, LLB 1954, MA 1958. Council Prizewinner, 1954. Called to Bar, Middle Temple, 1954, Harmsworth Law Schol., 1955, Bencher, Middle Temple, 1979; Mem., Lincoln's Inn, 1971. Inspector, Third London Airport Inquiries, 1981-. *Publications:* Rating Law and Valuation, 1963; contrib. Jl Planning Law. *Address:* Walberton House, Walberton, West Sussex. *T:* Yapton 551205. *Club:* Athenæum.

EYRE, Maj. Gen. James Ainsworth Campden Gabriel, CVO 1978; CBE 1980 (OBE 1975); General Officer Commanding London District and Major General Commanding Household Division, since 1983; *b* 2 Nov. 1930; *s* of Edward Joseph Eyre and Hon. Dorothy Elizabeth Anne Pelline (*née* Lyon-Dalberg-Acton); *m* 1967, Monica Ruth Esther Smyth; one *s* one *d. Educ:* Harvard Univ. (BA, LLB). Commissioned RHG, 1955; Commanding Officer, The Blues and Royals, 1970-73; GSO 1 HQ London District, 1973-75; Officer Commanding Household Cavalry and Silver Stick, 1975-78; Col GS HQ Northern Ireland, 1978-80; Sec., Chiefs of Staff Cttee, MoD, 1980-83. *Recreations:* racing, shooting. *Address:* Bockhampton Manor, Lambourn, Berkshire RG16 7LX. *T:* Lambourn 71733. *Club:* Turf.

EYRE, Reginald Edwin; MP (C) Birmingham (Hall Green) since May 1965; Parliamentary Under-Secretary of State, Department of Transport, since 1982; *b* 28 May 1924; *s* of late Edwin Eyre; *m* 1978, Anne Clements; one *d. Educ:* King Edward's Camp Hill Sch., Birmingham; Emmanuel Coll., Cambridge (MA). Midshipman and Sub-Lieut, RNVR, War of 1939-45. Admitted a Solicitor, 1950; Senior Partner, Eyre & Co., solicitors, Birmingham. Hon. Consultant, Poor Man's Lawyer, 1948-58. Contested (C) Birmingham (Northfield) 1959; Conservative Political Centre: Chm., W Midlands Area, 1960-63; Chm., National Advisory Cttee, 1964-66; Opposition Whip, 1966-70; a Lord Comr of the Treasury, June-Sept. 1970; Comptroller of HM Household, 1970-72; Parly Under-Sec. of State, DoE, 1972-74, Dept of Trade, 1979-82. A Vice Chm., Cons. Party Organisation, 1975-79. *Publication:* Hope for our Towns and Cities, 1977. *Address:* 45 Aylesford Street, SW1; 1041 Stratford Road, Birmingham B28 8AS. *Clubs:* Carlton; Birmingham (Birmingham).

EYRE, Richard Charles Hastings; theatre and TV director; *b* 28 March 1943; *m* 1973, Susan Elizabeth Birtwistle; one *d. Educ:* Sherborne Sch.; Peterhouse, Cambridge (BA). Asst Dir, Phoenix Theatre, Leicester, 1966; Lyceum Theatre, Edinburgh: Associate Dir, 1967-70; Dir of Productions, 1970-72; freelance director: Liverpool, 7:84 Co., West End; tours for British Council: W Africa, 1971; SE Asia, 1972; Artistic Dir, Nottingham Playhouse, 1973-78; Prod./Dir, Play for Today, BBC TV, 1978-80; Director: Hamlet, Royal Court, 1980; Guys and Dolls, The Beggar's Opera, and Schweyk in the Second World War, Nat. Theatre, 1982. Films for TV: The Imitation Game, Pasmore, 1980; Country, 1981. Directed premières of plays by Trevor Griffiths, David Hare, Howard Brenton, Ken Campbell, John McGrath, Barrie Keeffe, Stephen Lowe, Ann Jellicoe, Charles Wood, Adrian Mitchell, Henry Livings, Ian McEwan. STV Awards for Best Production, 1969, 1970 and 1971. *Address:* c/o Spokesman, 1 Craven Hill, W2 3EP. *T:* 01-262 1011.

EYRE, Very Rev. Richard Montague Stephens; Dean of Exeter, since 1981; *b* 1929; *s* of Montague Henry and Ethel Mary Eyre; *m* 1963, Anne Mary Bentley; two *d. Educ:* Charterhouse; Oriel Coll. and St Stephen's House, Oxford. MA Oxon. Deacon 1956, priest 1957; Curate, St Mark's Church, Portsea, 1956-59; Tutor and Chaplain, Chichester Theological Coll., 1959-62; Chaplain, Eastbourne Coll., 1962-65; Vicar of Arundel, 1965-73; Vicar of Good Shepherd, Brighton, 1973-75; Archdeacon of Chichester, 1975-81; Treasurer of Chichester Cathedral, 1978-81. *Recreations:* golf, music, wine, travel, NT, gardening. *Address:* The Deanery, Exeter, Devon. *T:* Exeter 72697.

EYRE, Ronald; freelance theatre and television director; writer; *b* 13 April 1929; *s* of Christopher Eyre and Mabel Smith. *Educ:* Queen Elizabeth Grammar Sch., Wakefield, Yorks; University Coll., Oxford (MA English Lang. and Lit.). English Master, Queen Elizabeth Grammar Sch., Blackburn, 1952-54; Sen. English Master, Bromsgrove Sch., 1954-56; Producer, BBC Television, 1956-64. Theatre Director: RSC: Much Ado About Nothing, 1971; London Assurance, London, 1972 and New York, 1974; The Marquis of Keith, 1974; Saratoga, 1978; Othello, 1979; The Winter's Tale, 1981; West End: Enjoy; Three Months Gone, 1970 (also Royal Court); Voyage Round My Father, 1971; Habeas Corpus, 1973; The Secret Policeman's Other Ball, 1981; Hobson's Choice, 1982; Theatre Royal, Stratford East: Widower's

Houses, 1965; Hampstead Theatre Club: Events While Guarding the Bofors Gun, 1966; Bakke's Night of Fame, 1968; Royal Court: Veterans, 1972; A Pagan Place, 1972. Opera Producer: Beatrice and Benedict, Buxton, 1980 (also translator); Mussorgsky's Marriage, Nexus Opera, 1981; Falstaff, Los Angeles and Covent Garden, 1982 and Teatro Communale, Florence, 1983. Playwright: theatre: Something's Burning, 1973; television: I'm not Stopping, 1963; A Crack in the Ice, 1964 (theatre, 1966); Bruno, 1965; The Single Passion, 1967; The Glory of Llewellyn Smiley, 1967. Writer and Presenter, The Long Search, BBC, 1977. *Publication:* Ronald Eyre on The Long Search, 1979. *Address:* c/o L. Dalzell, 3 Goodwin's Court, St Martin's Lane, WC2. *T:* 01-240 3086.

EYRES MONSELL, family name of **Viscount Monsell.**

EYSENCK, Prof. Hans Jurgen, PhD, DSc; Professor of Psychology, University of London, Institute of Psychiatry, since 1955; Director, Psychological Department, Maudsley Hospital, since 1946; *b* 4 March 1916; *s* of Eduard Anton and Ruth Eysenck; *m* 1st, 1938, Margaret Malcolm Davies; one *s*; 2nd, 1950, Sybil Bianca Giuletta Rostal; three *s* one *d. Educ:* school in Germany, France and England; Univ. of London. BA 1938, PhD 1940, DSc 1964. Senior Research Psychologist, Mill Hill Emergency Hosp., 1942-46; Reader in Psychology, Univ. of London (Inst. of Psychiatry), 1950-54; Visiting Prof., Univ. of Pennsylvania, 1949-50; Visiting Prof., Univ. of California, Berkeley, 1954. *Publications:* Dimensions of Personality, 1947; The Scientific Study of Personality, 1952; The Structure of Human Personality, 1953; Uses and Abuses of Psychology, 1953; The Psychology of Politics, 1954; Sense and Nonsense in Psychology, 1957; Dynamics of Anxiety and Hysteria, 1957; Perceptual Processes and Mental Illness, 1957; (ed) Handbook of Abnormal Psychology, 1960, 2nd edn, 1972; (ed) Behaviour Therapy and the Neuroses, 1960; (ed) Experiments in Personality, 1960; (ed) Experiments with Drugs, 1963; (ed) Experiments in Behaviour Therapy, 1964; (ed) Experiments in Motivation, 1964; Crime and Personality, 1964; Causes and Cures of Neurosis, 1965; Fact and Fiction in Psychology, 1965; Smoking, Health and Personality, 1965; The Biological Basis of Personality, 1968; Personality Structure and Measurement, 1969; Race, Intelligence and Education, 1971; Psychology is about People, 1972; (ed) Readings in Introversion-Extraversion, 3 vols, 1971; (ed) Lexikon der Psychologie, 3 vols, 1972; The Measurement of Intelligence, 1973; The Inequality of Man, 1973; (ed jtly) The Experimental Study of Freudian Theories, 1973; (ed jtly) Encyclopaedia of Psychology, 1973; (with Glenn Wilson) Know Your Own Personality, 1975; (ed) Case Studies in Behaviour Therapy, 1976; Sex and Personality, 1976; (with S. B. G. Eysenck) Psychoticism as a Dimension of Personality 1976; You and Neurosis, 1977; Die Zukunft der Psychologie, 1977; (with D. K. B. Nias) Sex, Violence and the Media, 1978; The Structure and Measurement of Intelligence, 1979; (with Glenn Wilson) The Psychology of Sex, 1979; The Causes and Effects of Smoking, 1980; (with M. Eysenck) Mindwatching, 1981; (ed) A Model for Personality, 1981; (with J. Kamin) Intelligence: the battle for the mind, 1981 (US as The Intelligence Controversy, 1981); (with D. K. B. Nias) Astrology: Science or Superstition?, 1982; Editor-in-Chief: Behaviour Research and Therapy, 1963-; Personality and Individual Differences, 1980-; (ed) International Monographs of Experimental Psychology; some 600 articles in British, American, German, Spanish and French Jls of Psychology. *Recreations:* walking, tennis, chess, detective stories, squash. *Address:* 10 Dorchester Drive, SE24.

EYTON, Anthony John Plowden, ARA 1976; Part-time Lecturer, Camberwell School of Art, since 1956; Visiting Teacher, Royal Academy Schools, since 1963; *b* 17 May 1923; *s* of late Captain John Seymour Eyton, ICS, author, and of Phyllis Annie Tyser; *m* 1960, Frances Mary Capell; three *d. Educ:* Twyford Sch.; Canford Sch.; Camberwell Sch. of Art (NDD). Served War, 1939-45, Cameronians (Scottish Rifles), Hampshire Regt, and Army Educn Corps. Abbey Major Scholarship in Painting, 1950-51. Elected Mem., London Gp, 1958; Head of Painting Dept, St Lawrence Coll., Kingston, Ont, 1969-71. One Man Exhibitions: St George's Gall., 1955; Galerie de Seine, 1957; New Art Centre, 1959, 1961, 1968; New Grafton Gall., 1973; William Darby Gall., 1975; Newcastle Polytechnic Art Gall., 1978; Browse and Darby, 1981, 1981; Retrospective Exhibn, S London Art Gall., Towner Art Gall., Eastbourne, and Plymouth Art Gall., 1981; work included in British Painting 1945-77, RA. Work in public collections: Tate Gall.; Arts Council; Plymouth Art Gall.; Towner Art Gall., Eastbourne; Carlisle Art Gall.; DoE, RA; BR. Fellowship awarded by Grocers' Co. (for work and travel in Italy), 1974. Prize, John Moore's Exhibn, Liverpool, 1972; First Prize, Second British Internat. Drawing Biennale, Middlesbrough, 1975. *Recreation:* gardening. *Address:* 34 Hanbury Street, E1.

EZARD, Clarence Norbury, CBE 1954 (OBE 1942); Retired as Ambassador to Costa Rica; *b* 6 Oct. 1896; *m* 1936, Olive Lillian Vaneus. *Educ:* Carlisle Grammar Sch.; Emmanuel Coll., Cambridge. Probationer Vice-Consul in General Consular Service, 1924; Acting Vice-Consul, Havana, 1926; Chargé d'Affaires, May-Oct. 1928; Sec. to Special Mission at Inauguration of Pres. of Republic of Cuba, with Temp. rank of 3rd Sec. in Diplomatic Service, 1929; Subst. rank of Vice-Consul, 1929; Vice-Consul at Bogotá, 1930; local rank of 2nd Sec. in Dipl. Service, 1930; in charge of Consulate at Havana, March-June 1931, of Legation April-June 1931. Transferred to New York, 1932, to Piræus, 1934. Acting Consul at Athens, 1935 and 1936; Consul at Beira, 1938; Montevideo, 1945, with rank of Consul and 1st Sec.; Consul-Gen., Gdansk, 1946; Consul-Gen., Haifa, 1949; Minister to Costa Rica, 1953;

Ambassador to Costa Rica, 1956; retired, 1957. *Address:* Three Fields, Mayfield, East Sussex. *Club:* Carlton.

EZEILO, Prof. James Okoye Chukuka, CON 1979; PhD; Professor of Mathematics, University of Nigeria; *b* 17 Jan. 1930; *s* of Josiah Ezeilo and Janet Ezeilo; *m* 1960, Phoebe Uchechuku; two *s* two *d. Educ:* Dennis Memorial Grammar Sch., Onitsha; University Coll., Ibadan (MSc London); Queens' Coll., Cambridge (PhD). University of Ibadan: Lectr in Maths, 1958-62; Sen. Lectr in Maths, 1962-64; Prof. of Maths, 1964-66; University of Nigeria: Prof. of Maths, 1966-75, 1980-; Vice-Chancellor, 1975-78. Vice-Chancellor, Bayero Univ., Nigeria, 1978-79. Benedict Dist. Prof. of Maths, Carleton Coll., 1979; Vis. Prof. of Maths, Howard Univ., 1979-80. Pres., Nigerian Math. Assoc., 1972-74; Mem., Nigerian Council for Science and Technol., 1970-75; Foundation Mem., Nigerian Acad. of Sciences. *Publications:* over 60 papers on differential equations in math. jls. *Recreation:* gardening. *Address:* Department of Mathematics, University of Nigeria, Nsukka, Nigeria. *Club:* Athenæum.

EZRA, Sir Derek, Kt 1974; MBE 1945; Chairman: Associated Heat Services plc, since 1966; Petrolex PLC, since 1982; Industrial Adviser, Morgan Grenfell & Co. Ltd, since 1982; *b* 23 Feb. 1919; *s* of David and Lillie Ezra; *m* 1950, Julia Elizabeth Wilkins. *Educ:* Monmouth Sch.; Magdalene Coll., Cambridge (MA, Hon. Fellow, 1977). Army, 1939-47. Joined NCB, 1947; representative of NCB at Cttees of OEEC and ECE, 1948-52; Mem. of UK Delegn to High Authority of European Coal and Steel Community, 1952-56; Dep. Regional Sales Manager, NCB, 1956-58; Regional Sales Manager, 1958-60; Dir-Gen. of Marketing, NCB, 1960-65; NCB Bd Mem., 1965-67; Dep. Chm., 1967-71; Chm., 1971-82. Chm., J. H. Sankey & Son Ltd, 1977-82; Director: British Fuel Co., 1966-82; Redland PLC, 1982-; Supervisory Bd, Royal Boskalis Westminster NV, 1982-. Chm., NICG, 1972 and 1980-81; President: Nat. Materials Handling Centre, 1979; Coal Industry Soc., 1981- (Chm., 1961); W European Coal Producers' Assoc., 1976-79; Vice-Pres., BIM, 1978 (Chm., 1976-78); Member: BOTB, 1972-82 (Chm., European Trade Cttee); Cons. Cttee, ECSC, 1973-82 (Pres., 1978-79); Adv. Council for Energy Conservation, 1974-79; Energy Commn, 1977-79; Ct of Governors, Administrative Staff Coll., 1971-82; Governor, London Business Sch., 1973-82. Chm., Keep Britain Tidy Gp, 1979-. Grand Officer, Italian Order of Merit, 1979; Comdr, Luxembourg Order of Merit, 1981; Officer of Légion d'Honneur, 1981. *Address:* 2 Salisbury Road, Wimbledon, SW19 4EZ. *T:* 01-946 2122.

F

FABER, Julian Tufnell; Chairman, Willis Faber Ltd, 1972-77; *b* 6 April 1917; *s* of late Alfred and Edith Faber; *m* 1944, Ann Caroline, *e d* of Rt Hon. Harold Macmillan, *qv*, and late Lady Dorothy Macmillan; four *s* one *d. Educ:* Winchester; Trinity Coll., Cambridge. Joined Willis, Faber & Dumas Ltd, 1938. Served Welsh Guards (Major 2nd Bn), 1939-45. Director: Willis, Faber & Dumas Ltd, 1952; Willis, Faber & Dumas (Agencies) Ltd, 1965; Taisho Marine & Fire Insurance Co. (UK) Ltd, 1972; Cornhill Insurance Co., 1972; Willis Faber (Middle East) SAL, 1973; Morgan Grenfell Ltd, 1974-77; Allianz International Insurance Co., 1974. Mem. Bd of Governors, Summer Fields Sch., Oxford. Member: MCC Cttee; Kent CCC Cttee. *Address:* 3 Chester Square, SW1W 9HH. *T:* 01-730 6474; Bay House, Sandwich, Kent. *Clubs:* White's, City of London, MCC.
See also Rt Hon. M. V. Macmillan.

FABER, Sir Richard (Stanley), KCVO 1980; CMG 1977; FRSL; HM Diplomatic Service, retired; Ambassador to Algeria, 1977-81; *b* 6 Dec. 1924; *er s* of late Sir Geoffrey Faber and of Enid, *d* of Sir Henry Erle Richards, KCSI, KC; unmarried. *Educ:* Westminster Sch.; Christ Church, Oxford (MA). RNVR, 1943-46. 1st cl. Lit. Hum. Oxon; Pres., Oxford Union Soc., 1949. Joined HM Foreign (subseq. Diplomatic) Service, 1950; service in FO and in Baghdad, Paris, Abidjan, Washington; Head of Rhodesia Political Dept, FCO, 1967-69; Counsellor: The Hague, 1969-73; Cairo, 1973-75; Asst Under Sec. of State, FCO, 1975-77. *Publications:* Beaconsfield and Bolingbroke, 1961; The Vision and the Need: Late Victorian Imperialist Aims, 1966; Proper Stations: Class in Victorian Fiction, 1971; French and English, 1975; The Brave Courtier (Sir William Temple), 1983. *Address:* 2 Riverside Court, Nine Elms Lane, SW8 5DB. *Club:* Travellers'.
See also T. E. Faber.

FABER, Thomas Erle, PhD; Chairman, Faber & Faber (Publishers) Ltd, since 1977 (Director since 1969); Lecturer in Physics, University of Cambridge, since 1959; Fellow of Corpus Christi College, Cambridge, since 1953; *b* 25 April 1927; *s* of Sir Geoffrey Faber; *m* 1959, Penelope, *d* of Clive Morton, actor; two *s* two *d. Educ:* Oundle Sch.; Trinity Coll., Cambridge (MA, PhD). Univ. of Cambridge: Res. Fellow, Trinity Coll., 1950-53; Univ. Demonstr, 1953-58; Armourers' and Brasiers' Fellow, 1958-59. Treasurer, Corpus Christi Coll., 1963-76. *Publications:* Introduction to the Theory of Liquid Metals, 1972; papers on superconductivity, liquid metals and liquid crystals. *Recreations:* walking, shooting. *Address:* The Old Vicarage, Thompson's

Lane, Cambridge CB5 8AQ. *T:* Cambridge 356685.
See also Sir R. S. Faber.

FACER, Roger Lawrence Lowe; Under Secretary, Cabinet Office, since 1981; *b* 28 June 1933; *s* of John Ernest Facer and Phyllis Facer; *m* 1960, Ruth Margaret, *o d* of Herbert Mostyn Lewis, PhD, Gresford, Clwyd; three *d. Educ:* Rugby; St John's Coll., Oxford (MA). HM Forces, 2nd Lieut, East Surrey Regt, 1951-53. War Office, 1957; Asst Private Sec. to Secretary of State, 1958; Private Sec. to Permanent Under-Sec., 1958; Principal, 1961; Cabinet Office, 1966; Ministry of Defence, 1968–: Private Sec. to Minister of State (Equipment), 1970; Asst Sec., 1970; Internat. Inst. for Strategic Studies, 1972-73; Counsellor, UK Delegn, MBFR Vienna, 1973-75; Private Sec. to Sec. of State for Defence, 1976-79; Asst Under-Sec. of State, 1979-81. *Publications:* Weapons Procurement in Europe—Capabilities and Choices, 1975; articles in Alpine Garden Soc. Bulletin. *Recreations:* Alpine gardening, hill-walking, opera. *Address:* c/o Cabinet Office, 70 Whitehall, SW1A 2AS.

FACK, Robbert; Commander, Order of Orange-Nassau, 1979; Chevalier, Order of Netherlands Lion 1971; Netherlands diplomat, retired; Ambassador of the Netherlands to the Court of St James's, 1976-82; also, concurrently, Ambassador to Iceland, 1976-82; *b* 1 Jan. 1917; *m* 1943, Patricia H. Hawkins; four *s. Educ:* Univ. of Amsterdam. Military service, 1937-45. Min. of Foreign Affairs, The Hague, 1945-46; New York (UN), 1946-48; Min. of Foreign Affairs, 1948-50; Rome, 1950-54; Canberra, 1954-58; Bonn, 1958-63; Min. of Foreign Affairs, 1963-68; Ambassador-at-large, 1968-70; Perm. Rep. to UN, New York, 1970-74. Holds various foreign decorations. *Address:* Widden Hill House, Horton, near Bristol BS17 6QU. *Club:* Dutch.

FAGE, Prof. John Donnelly, MA, PhD; Director of Centre of West African Studies and Professor of African History, since 1963, Pro-Vice-Chancellor, since 1979, and Vice-Principal since 1981, University of Birmingham; *b* 3 June 1921; *s* of late Arthur Fage, CBE, FRS, and Winifred Eliza Donnelly; *m* 1949, Jean, *d* of late Frederick Banister; one *s* one *d. Educ:* Tonbridge Sch.; Magdalene Coll., Cambridge (scholar, MA, PhD). Served War, Pilot with RAFVR (Flt Lt), 1941-45. Bye-Fellow, Magdalene Coll., Cambridge, 1947-49; Lectr and Sen. Lectr, Univ. Coll. of the Gold Coast, 1949-55; Prof. of History, 1955-59, and Dep. Principal, 1957-59; Lectr in African History, SOAS, Univ. of London, 1959-63. Visiting Prof., Univ. of Wisconsin, Madison, 1957, and Smith Coll., Northampton, Mass, 1962; Dep. Dean, Faculty of Arts, Univ. of Birmingham, 1973-75, Dean, 1975-78; Founding Hon. Sec., African Studies Assoc. of the UK, 1963-66 (Vice-Pres. 1967-68, Pres. 1968-69); Council Mem., Internat. African Inst., 1965-75, and Consultative Dir, 1975-80; Mem., UNESCO Scientific Cttee for Gen. History of Africa, 1971-80; Mem. Culture Adv. Cttee of UK Nat. Commn for UNESCO (Chm., 1978-); FRHistS. Hon. Fellow, SOAS, Univ. of London. Editor (with Roland Oliver), The Jl of African History, 1960-73; Gen. Editor (with Roland Oliver), The Cambridge History of Africa, 8 vols, 1975–. *Publications:* An Introduction to the History of West Africa, 1955, 3rd edn 1962; An Atlas of African History, 1958, 2nd edn, 1978; Ghana, a Historical Interpretation, 1959; A Short History of Africa (with Roland Oliver), 1962, 5th edn 1975; A History of West Africa, 1969; (ed) Africa Discovers Her Past, 1970; (ed with Roland Oliver) Papers on African Prehistory, 1970; A History of Africa, 1978; articles in historical and Africanist jls. *Recreations:* doing things to houses and gardens. *Address:* 17 Antringham Gardens, Birmingham B15 3QL. *T:* 021-455 0020. *Club:* Athenæum.

FAGG, Bernard Evelyn Buller, MBE 1962; MA; FSA; FMA; Curator, Pitt Rivers Museum, Oxford, 1963-75; *b* 8 Dec. 1915; *s* of late W. P. Fagg and Mrs L. Fagg; *m* 1942, Mary Catherine, *d* of G. W. Davidson; one *s* two *d* (and two *s* dead). *Educ:* Dulwich Coll.; Downing Coll., Cambridge. Nigerian Admin. Service, 1939-47. War service with West African Engineers, East African Campaign, 1939-43. Dept of Antiquities, Republic of Nigeria, 1947-63 (Dir, 1957-63); Lincoln Coll., Oxford, 1964; Fellow of Linacre Coll., 1965-75, Emeritus Fellow, 1976. *Publications:* Nok terracottas, 1977; contribs to learned jls. *Address:* 45 Woodstock Road, Oxford. *T:* 54875. *Club:* Leander.

FAGG, William Buller, CMG 1967; ethnologist; tribal art historian and consultant; Keeper, Ethnography Department (from 1972 the Museum of Mankind), British Museum, 1969-74 (Deputy Keeper, 1955-69); *b* 28 April 1914; *s* of late William Percy Fagg and late Lilian Fagg. *Educ:* Dulwich Coll.; Magdalene Coll., Cambridge. Sir Wm Browne's Medal for Latin Epigram; Montagu Butler Prize for Latin Hexameters; BA Classics, 1936; Archaeology and Anthropology, 1937; MA 1939. Asst Keeper Dept of Ethnography, BM, 1938; seconded to Bd of Trade, Industries and Manufactures Dept, 1940-45. Royal Anthropological Institute: Hon. Sec., 1939-56; Mem. Council, 1966-69, 1972-75, 1976-79; Vice-Pres., 1969-72; Patron's Medal, 1966; Hon. Editor, Man: A Monthly Record of Anthropological Science, 1947-65, Hon. Librarian, 1976–. Chm., UK Cttee for First World Festival of Negro Arts, Dakar, 1966; Trustee: UK African Festival Trust, 1973-77; Chm., African Fine Art Gallery Trust, 1974–; Consulting Fellow in African Art, Museum of Primitive Art, NY, 1957–. Consultant on Tribal Art to Christies, 1974–. Fieldwork: Nigeria and Congo, 1949-50; Nigeria, 1953, 1958-59, 1971, 1974; Cameroon, 1966; Mali, 1969. Organised and arranged many loan exhibns including: Nigerian Art (Arts Council), London, Manchester, Bristol, 1960, Munich, Basel, 1961; African Art, Berlin Festival, 1964, Musée des Arts Décoratifs, Paris, 1964-65; African Sculpture, Nat. Gall. of Art, Washington,

DC, Kansas City Art Gall., and Brooklyn Museum, 1970. FRSA (Silver-Medallist, 1951). Member: Reindeer Council of UK; Royal African Soc.; RIIA; Internat. African Inst.; Museums Assoc.; African Studies Assoc.; ICA; Assoc. of Art Historians. *Publications:* The Webster Plass Collection of African Art, British Museum, 1953; (with E. Elisofon) The Sculpture of Africa, 1958; Afro-Portuguese Ivories, 1959; Nigerian Images, 1963 (awarded P. A. Talbot Prize, 1964, and grand prize for best work on African art at World Festival of Negro Arts, Dakar, 1966); (with Margaret Plass) African Sculpture: An Anthology, 1964; Tribes and Forms in African Art, 1966; African Tribal Sculptures, 2 vols, 1967; Arts of Western Africa, Arts of Central Africa (UNESCO), 1967; African Tribal Images (The Katherine White Reswick Collection of African Art), 1968; African Sculpture (Washington, DC), 1970; Miniature Wood Carvings of Africa, 1970; The Tribal Image: wooden figure sculpture of the world, 1970; African Sculpture from the Tara Collection, 1971; (ed) The Living Arts of Nigeria, 1971; Eskimo Art in the British Museum, 1972; Yoruba Beadwork, 1980; Masques d'Afrique, 1980; numerous exhibn catalogues, articles in Man, etc. *Recreations:* photography (esp. of art, incl. ancient churches), listening to music, cycling, travel, geopolitics. *Address:* 6 Galata Road, Barnes, SW13 9NQ. *T:* 01-748 6620.

FAGGE, Sir John William Frederick, 11th Bt, *cr* 1660; *b* 28 Sept. 1910; *s* of late William Archibald Theodore Fagge (*b* of 9th Bt) and Nellie (*d* 1924), *d* of H. T. D. Wise; *S* uncle, 1940; *m* 1940, Ivy Gertrude, *d* of William Edward Frier, 15 Church Lane, Newington, Kent; one *s* one *d. Heir: s* John Christopher Fagge, *b* 30 April 1942. *Address:* 26 The Mall, Faversham, Kent.

FAINT, John Anthony Leonard; Head of South East Asia Development Division, Bangkok, since 1980; *b* 24 Nov. 1942; *s* of Thomas Leonard Faint and Josephine Rosey Faint (*née* Dunkerley); *m* 1978, Elizabeth Theresa Winter. *Educ:* Chigwell Sch.; Magdalen Coll., Oxford (BA LitHum 1965); MA Development Economics, Fletcher Sch., Mass, 1969. Ministry of Overseas Development (later Overseas Development Administration), London, 1965-71 (study leave in Cambridge, Mass, 1968-69); First Secretary (Aid), Blantyre, Malawi, 1971-73; ODM/ODA, London, 1974-80. *Recreations:* music, bridge, chess, tennis, squash. *Address:* SEADD, British Embassy, BFPO 5. *T:* Bangkok 252-7161. *Club:* British (Bangkok).

FAIR, Donald Robert Russell, OBE (mil.) 1945; Board Member, Central Electricity Generating Board, 1975-77; *b* 26 Dec. 1916; *s* of Robert Sidney Fair and Mary Louie Fair; *m* 1941, Patricia Laurie Rudland; one *s. Educ:* Roan Sch., Blackheath; King's Coll., London Univ. (BSc, AKC). CEng, FInstP, FInstE. Served War of 1939-45, RAF (Wing Comdr; despatches 1944; USAAF Commendation 1944). Lectr, RMA Sandhurst, 1948-50; UK AEA, 1950-62; Central Electricity Generating Bd, 1962-77. *Recreations:* sailing, cricket. *Address:* Rozelle, St James' Close, Birdham, Chichester, Sussex PO20 7HE. *T:* Birdham 512711. *Club:* Island Sailing.

FAIRBAIRN, Sir Brooke; *see* Fairbairn, Sir J. B.

FAIRBAIRN, David; Metropolitan Stipendiary Magistrate since 1971; Deputy Circuit Judge, since 1972; *b* 9 Aug. 1924; *s* of Ernest Hulford Fairbairn and late Iva May Fairbairn; *m* 1946, Helen Merriel de la Cour Collingwood, *d* of Harold Lewis Collingwood; two *s* two *d. Educ:* Haileybury Coll.; Trinity Hall, Cambridge (MA). Served War of 1939-45, Lieut, RNVR, in Mediterranean. Called to Bar, Middle Temple, 1949; Central Criminal Court Bar Mess; South Eastern Circuit; Herts and Essex QS; Dep. Chm., Surrey QS, 1969-71. Liveryman, Gold and Silver Wyre Drawers' Company, 1957–. *Recreations:* golf, tennis, country life. *Address:* Wollards Farm, Mayes Green, Ockley, Dorking, Surrey.

FAIRBAIRN, Hon. Sir David Eric, KBE 1977; DFC 1944; Australian Ambassador to the Netherlands, 1977-80; *b* 3 March 1917; *s* of Clive Prell Fairbairn and Marjorie Rose (*née* Jowett); *m* 1945, Ruth Antill (*née* Robertson); three *d. Educ:* Geelong Grammar Sch.; Cambridge Univ. (MA). MP (L) Commonwealth of Australia, 1949-75; Minister: for Air, 1962-64; for Nat. Develt, 1964-69; for Educn and Science, March-Aug. 1971; for Defence, 1971-72. *Recreations:* golf, tennis. *Address:* 2/3 Tasmania Circle, Forrest, ACT 2603, Australia. *T:* 951229. *Clubs:* Leander (Henley); Hawks (Cambridge); Melbourne (Melbourne); Commonwealth (Canberra); Albury (Albury).

FAIRBAIRN, David Ritchie; Director, National Computing Centre, since 1980; *b* 4 July 1934; *s* of G. F. Fairbairn; *m* 1958, Hon. Susan Hill, *d* of Baron Hill of Luton, *qv* ; one *s* two *d. Educ:* Mill Hill Sch.; Gonville and Caius Coll., Cambridge (BAEcon). FBCS; MIDPM. President, Cambridge Union Soc. Overseas Marketing Manager, Arthur Guinness Son & Co. Ltd, 1960; President, Guinness-Harp Corp., New York, 1964; Marketing Dir, Guinness Overseas Ltd, 1969; Man. Dir, Dataset Ltd (ICL), 1970; Manager, Retail and Distribution Sector, International Computers Ltd, 1975; Dir of Marketing, EMI Medical Ltd, 1976. Vice-Pres., Inst. of Data Processing Management, 1980–. *Recreations:* sailing, water-skiing. *Address:* 11 Oak Way, West Common, Harpenden, Herts AL5 2RU. *T:* Harpenden 5820. *Club:* Royal Commonwealth Society.

FAIRBAIRN, Douglas Chisholm, CIE 1945; CBE 1956; MA; retired; formerly Director, Thomas Hamling & Co. Ltd, St Andrew's Dock, Hull; *b*

1904; s of late Rev. R. T. and Mrs Fairbairn; m 1938, Agnes, d of late Rev. William amd Mrs Arnott; two s. Educ: George Heriot's, Edinburgh; Edinburgh Univ. (MA). Formerly: Secretary Bengal Chamber of Commerce and Industry, Calcutta, 1938-56, also in that capacity Sec. Associated Chambers of Commerce of India; Chm., Hull Fishing Vessel Owners and Hull Fishing Industry Associations, 1957-62. JP, City and County of Kingston-upon-Hull, 1966-71. Recreations: golf, gardening. Address: Wildwood, Inchmarlo Road, Banchory, Kincardineshire AB3 4AH. T: Banchory 2926.

FAIRBAIRN, Douglas Foakes, CBE 1971; Co-ordinator of Operations, Commonwealth Development Corporation, since 1971; b 9 Oct. 1919; s of William and Florence Fairbairn; m 1947, Gertrude Betty Buswell; two s. Educ: John Lyon Sch., Harrow; Royal School of Mines, Imperial Coll., London Univ. BSc (Hons), ARSM. Served War, RAF (Sqdn Ldr), 1940-46. Commonwealth Development Corp., 1949-; Regional Controller: Central Africa, 1959-66; West Africa, 1966-71. Dir, Bank of Rhodesia and Nyasaland, 1961-63; Chm., Central African Airways, 1964-68; Mem., Central African Power Corp., 1961-77. Recreation: golf. Address: 11 Portland Terrace, The Green, Richmond, Surrey TW9 1QQ. T: 01-948 1921. Club: Northwood Golf (Mddx).

FAIRBAIRN, Sir (James) Brooke, 6th Bt cr 1869, of Ardwick; b 10 Dec. 1930; s of Sir William Albert Fairbairn, 5th Bt, and of Christine Renée Cotton, d of late Rev. Canon Robert William Croft; S father, 1972; m 1960, Mary Russell, d of late William Russell Scott, MB, ChB, FFARCS; two s one d. Educ: Stowe. Proprietor of J. Brooke Fairbairn & Co., textile converters and wholesalers dealing in furnishing fabrics. Heir: s Robert William Fairbairn, b 10 April 1965. Address: Barkway House, Bury Road, Newmarket, Suffolk CB8 7BT. T: Newmarket 2733; J. Brooke Fairbairn & Co., The Railway Station, Newmarket CB8 9BA. T: Newmarket 5766. Club: City Livery.

FAIRBAIRN of Fordell, Nicholas Hardwick, QC(Scot.) 1972; MP (C) Kinross and Perthshire West, since Oct. 1974; Baron of Fordell; b 24 Dec. 1933; s of William Ronald Dodds Fairbairn, DPsych, and Mary Ann More-Gordon of Charleton and Kinnaber; m 1962, Hon. Elizabeth Mary Mackay (marr. diss. 1979), e d of 13th Baron Reay; three d (and one s one d decd). Educ: Loretto; Edinburgh Univ.; MA, LLB. Author, farmer, painter, poet, TV and radio broadcaster, journalist, dress-designer, landscape gardener, bon viveur and wit. Called to Scots Bar 1957. Cons. Candidate, Central Edinburgh, 1964, 1966. HM Solicitor Gen. for Scotland, 1979-82. Comr of Northern Lighthouses, 1979-82. Mem., Council of World Population Crisis, 1968-70; Vice-Pres., Scottish Minorities Group. Founder and Hon. Pres., Soc. for Preservation of Duddingston Village; Mem., Edinburgh Festival Council, 1971-. Chairman: Traverse Theatre, 1964-72; Edinburgh Brook Adv. Centre, 1968-75; Waverley Broadcasting Co., 1973-74; Dir, Ledlanet Nights, 1960-73. Chm., Scottish Soc. for Defence of Literature and the Arts. Pres., Dysart and Dundonald Pipe Band. Private exhibns Edinburgh, 1960, 1962, 1968-74, and in public exhibns. Publication: contrib., Alistair Maclean Introduces Scotland, 1972. Recreation: being blunt and sharp at the same time. Address: Fordell Castle, By Dunfermline, Fife. T: Dalgety Bay 823311. Clubs: Puffins, Beefsteak, Chatham Dining; New (Edinburgh).

FAIRBAIRN, Sir Robert, Kt 1975; JP; Chairman, Clydesdale Bank Ltd, since 1975 (Director, since 1967; General Manager, 1958-71; Vice-Chairman, 1971-75); b 25 Sept. 1910; s of late Robert Fairbairn and Christina Fairbairn; m 1939, Sylvia Lucinda, d of late Rev. Henry Coulter; two s one d. Educ: Perth Academy. Joined service of The Clydesdale Bank at Perth, 1927; Beckett & Whitehead Prizeman, Inst. of Bankers, 1934; Midland Bank, 1934. Lt-Comdr (S) RNVR, 1939-46. Asst Gen. Manager, Clydesdale & North of Scotland Bank, 1951. Chm., Clydesdale Bank Industrial Finance Ltd, 1981-; Director: Commercial Union Assurance Group (Local Board); Midland Bank Finance Corp. Ltd, 1967-74; Clydesdale Bank Finance Corp. Ltd, 1967-; Clydesdale Bank Insurance Services Ltd, 1970-; Newarthill Ltd; Midland Bank Ltd, 1975-; Chairman: Scottish Computer Services Ltd; Scottish Amicable Life Assce Soc., 1976-78 (Dir to 1981); A Dir, British Nat. Oil Corp., 1976-79. Glasgow Chamber of Commerce (Vice-Pres., 1970-76). Pres., Inst. of Bankers in Scotland, 1961-63; Vice-Pres., Scottish Economic Soc. (Pres. 1966-69); Chairman: Scottish Industrial Develt Advisory Bd, 1972-; Cttee of Scottish Bank General Managers, 1963-66; Vice-Chm., Inst. of Fiscal Studies (Scotland), 1976-; Vice-Pres., British Bankers Assoc., 1966-68; Member: Scottish Council (Develt and Industry), Vice-Pres., 1967-68; Scottish Council of CBI. Chm., Cystic Fibrosis Research Investment Trust plc, 1981-. FIB, FIB (Scot); FRSA; CBIM; Hon. FSIAD. JP Glasgow, 1962. Recreations: golf, fishing. Address: The Grange, Hazelwood Road, Bridge of Weir, Renfrewshire. T: Bridge of Weir 2102. Clubs: Caledonian, MCC; Western (Glasgow); Corinthian Casuals; Royal and Ancient (St Andrews).

FAIRBANKS, Douglas (Elton), (Jr), KBE 1949; DSC 1944; Captain, USNR, retired; company director, producer, actor; Chairman: Douglas Fairbanks Ltd; Fairtel, Inc. (US); Boltons Trading Corp. Inc., etc., and of associated companies, in US and UK, since 1946; Formerly Director or Special Consultant: Scripto Pens Ltd (US and UK), 1952-73; Golden Cycle and subsidiaries, 1965-73; Rambagh Palace Hotel, Ltd (Jaipur, India); Cavalcade Film Co. Ltd (UK), etc; b New York City, 9 Dec. 1909; s of Douglas Elton Fairbanks, Denver, Colorado, and Anna Beth Sully, Providence, RI; m 1939, Mary Lee Epling, Keystone, W Virginia; three d. Educ: Bovée Sch.,

Knickerbocker Greys, Collegiate Mil. Sch., NY; Pasadena Polytechnic, Harvard Mil. Sch., Los Angeles; tutored privately in London and Paris. Began career as film actor, 1923, on stage 1927. Organised own producing company, UK, 1935. Studied painting and sculpture, Paris, 1922-24; began writing, professionally, 1928; articles, fiction and essays on public affairs, etc., 1936-. Vice-Pres. Franco-British War Relief and National Vice-Pres. Cttee "Defend America by Aiding the Allies", 1939-40; Presidential Envoy, Special Mission to Latin America, 1940-41; one-time Consultant to Office of the Presidency (Washington, DC); Lieut (jg), USNR, 1941; promoted through grades to Capt., 1954. National Chm., CARE Cttee, 1947-50; Nat. Vice-Pres. Amer. Assoc. for the UN, 1946-60; Pres. Brit.-Amer. Alumni Assoc. 1950; Bd Gov., English-Speaking Union of the US, 1949-60; Nat. Chm., Amer. Relief for Korea, 1950-54; Trustee, Edwina Mountbatten Trust; Mem. Council, American Museum in Brit.; a Governor and Exec. Cllr, Royal Shakespeare Theatre; Governor, Ditchley Foundations; Trustee, Wellington Museum Trust; Co-Chm., US Capitol Bicentenary 1776-1976; Guild of St Bride's Church, Fleet Street, EC; Mem., Council on Foreign Relations (NY); Vis. Fellow, St Cross Coll., Oxford; MA Oxon; Senior Churchill Fellow, Westminster Coll., Fulton, Mo; Hon. DFA Westminster Coll., Fulton, Mo, USA; Hon. LLD Univ. of Denver, Colo; Silver Star Medal (US); Legion of Merit ("Valor" clasp) (US), Special Naval Commendation (US), KJStJ 1950, etc; Officer Legion of Honour (Fr.), Croix de Guerre with Palm (Fr.); Knight Comdr Order of George I (Greece); Knight Grand Officer, Order del Merito (Chile); Grand Officer, Order of Merit (Italy); Comdr Order of Orange Nassau (Neth.); Officer of: Orders of Crown (Belg.), of Star of Italy, Cross of Mil. Valour (Italy), Southern Cross (Brazil), Hon. Citizen and National Medal of Korea, etc. Films include: Stella Dallas; Little Caesar; Outward Bound; Morning Glory; Catherine the Great; The Amateur Gentleman; The Prisoner of Zenda; Gunga Din; The Corsican Brothers; Sinbad the Sailor; The Exile; The Fighting O'Flynn; State Secret. Plays include: Young Woodley; Romeo and Juliet; The Jest; Man in Possession; Moonlight is Silver; My Fair Lady; The Pleasure of his Company; The Secretary Bird; Present Laughter. Publications: short stories, poems, articles, to periodicals. Relevant publications: Knight Errant, by Brian Connell; The Fairbanks Album, by Richard Schickel. Recreations: swimming, tennis, golf, travel. Address: The Beekman, 575 Park Avenue, New York, NY 10021, USA; The Vicarage, 448 North Lake Way, Palm Beach, Florida 33480, USA; (office) Inverness Corporation, 380 Madison Avenue, New York, NY 10017, USA. Clubs: White's, Buck's, Naval and Military, Garrick; Puffin's (Edinburgh); Brook, Knickerbocker, Century (NY); Metropolitan (Washington, DC); Raquet (Chicago); Myopia Hunt (Hamilton, Mass); Travellers' (Paris).

FAIRCLOUGH, Anthony John; Director for the Environment, Commission of the European Communities, since 1981; b 30 Aug. 1924; m 1957, Patricia Monks; two s. Educ: St Philip's Grammar Sch., Birmingham; St Catharine's Coll., Cambridge. Scholar 1944, BA Cantab 1945, MA 1950. Ministry of Aircraft Production and Ministry of Supply, 1944-48; Colonial Office, 1948; Secretary, Nyasaland Commn of Inquiry, 1959; Private Secretary to Minister of State for Commonwealth Relations and for the Colonies, 1963-64; Assistant Secretary, 1964; Head of Pacific and Indian Ocean Dept, Commonwealth Office (formerly Colonial Office), 1964-68; Head of W Indian Dept, FCO, 1968-70; Head of New Towns 1 Div., DoE, 1970-72; Under-Sec., 1973; Head of Planning, Minerals and Countryside Directorate, 1973, of Planning, Sport and Countryside Directorate, 1973-74; Dir, Central Unit on Environmental Pollution, 1974-78; Dir, Internat. Transport, Dept of Transport, 1978-81. Senior UK Commissioner at Sessions of South Pacific Commn, 1965-67; Minister's Deputy, European Conf. of Mins of Transport, 1978-81; Chm., Environment Cttee, OECD, 1976-79; British Channel Tunnel Co., 1978-81; British Co-Chm., Jt UK/USSR Cttee established under UK/USSR Agreement on cooperation in field of Environmental Protection, 1974-78; Member: Royal Soc.'s British Nat. Cttee on Problems of Environment, 1974-78; EDC for Internat. Freight Movement, 1978-80; Governing Body, Chiswick Sch., 1973-79. FRSA. Address: 6 Cumberland Road, Kew, Richmond, Surrey TW9 3HQ; 12 Résidence Balderic, 30-34 Quai aux Briques, 1000 Brussels, Belgium. Club: Civil Service.

FAIRCLOUGH, Hon. Ellen Louks, OC 1979; PC (Can.) 1957; FCA 1965; Chairman, Hamilton Hydro Electric Commission, since 1978; Member of Progressive Conservative Party, Canada; b Hamilton, Ont, 28 Jan. 1905; d of Norman Ellsworth Cook and Nellie Bell Louks; m 1931, David Henry Gordon Fairclough; one s. Educ: Hamilton Public and Secondary Schs. Certified Public Accountant, public practice, 1935-57. Hamilton City Council, Alderman, 1946-49; Controller, 1950. Elected to House of Commons as Progressive Conservative mem. for Hamilton West, 1950; re-elected at gen. elections, 1953, 1957, 1958, 1962, defeated in 1963 election. Sec. of State for Canada, 1957-58; Minister of Citizenship and Immigration, 1958-62; Postmaster-Gen., 1962-63. Patron, Huguenot Soc. of Canada, 1969-; Chancellor, Royal Hamilton College of Music, 1978-80. LLD (hc), McMaster Univ., 1975. Recreations: music, reading and photography. Address: 25 Stanley Avenue, Hamilton, Ont, Canada. T: Hamilton 522-5248.

FAIRCLOUGH, Wilfred, RE; RWS; ARCA (London); Assistant Director, Kingston Polytechnic, and Head of the Division of Design, 1970-72, retired; Principal of Kingston College of Art, Surrey, 1962-70; b 13 June 1907; s of Herbert Fairclough and Edith Amy Milton; m 1936, Joan Cryer; one s one d. Educ: Royal College of Art, London, 1931-34 (Diploma 1933); British Sch. at Rome, Italy, 1934-37; Rome Scholar in Engraving, 1934-37. Army and

Royal Air Force, 1942-46. Rome Scholarships, Faculty of Engraving, 1951 (Chm., 1964-73); Leverhulme Research Award, 1961. RE 1946 (ARE 1934); RWS 1968 (ARWS 1961). Chairman: Assoc. of Art Instns, 1965-66; Assessors, Vocational Courses of Surrey CC. *Work in public and private collections: paintings:* Min. of Supply; Min. of Works; Surrey CC; Scottish Modern Art Assoc.; Beaumont Coll.; *drawings:* British Museum; V&A Museum; Arts Council; Contemporary Art Soc.; Wye Coll., London Univ.; English Electric Co.; Art Galls at Blackburn, Kingston-upon-Thames, Worthing; Graves Art Gall., Sheffield; Atkinson Art Gall., Southport; *prints:* British Museum, V&A Museum; Ashmolean Museum, Oxford; Contemporary Art Soc.; British Sch. at Rome; South London Art Gall.; Stoke Educn Authority; Wye Coll., London Univ.; Gottenburg Museum; Print Collectors Club. *Publications:* work reproduced: Recording Britain; Londoners' England; Royal Academy Illustrated; Studio; Fine Prints of the Year; Print Collectors Quarterly; illustrated article, Leisure Painter, 1969; paintings, drawings and prints. *Address:* 12 Manorgate Road, Kingston-upon-Thames, Surrey. *Club:* Arts.

FAIREY, Michael John; Regional Administrator, North East Thames Regional Health Authority, since 1973; *b* 20 Sept. 1933; *s* of Ernest John Saunder Fairey and late Lily Emily (*née* Pateman); *m* 1958, Audrey Edwina Kermode; two *s* one *d. Educ:* Queen Elizabeth's Sch., Barnet; Jesus Coll., Cambridge (MA). Deputy House Governor, The London Hosp., 1962, House Governor 1972. *Publications:* various articles in med. and computing jls. *Recreations:* church music, history of medieval exploration, Rugby football. *Address:* 42B Oakleigh Park South, N20 9JN. *Club:* Athenæum.

FAIRFAX, family name of Lord Fairfax of Cameron.

FAIRFAX OF CAMERON, 14th Lord *cr* 1627; **Nicholas John Albert Fairfax;** *b* 4 Jan. 1956; *e s* of 13th Lord and of Sonia, *yr d* of late Capt. Cecil Gunston, MC; *S* father, 1964; *m* 1982, Annabel, *er d* of late Nicholas and of Sarah Gilham Morriss. *Educ:* Eton; Downing Coll., Cambridge (LLB in international law subjects, 1981). Called to the Bar, Gray's Inn, 1977. *Recreations:* sailing, skiing, tennis. *Heir: b* Hon. Hugh Nigel Thomas Fairfax, *b* 29 March 1958. *Address:* 14 Sondan Road, SW11. *T:* 01-622 1650. *Club:* Queen's.

FAIRFAX, Sir Vincent Charles, Kt 1971; CMG 1960; Company Director and Pastoralist, Australia; *b* 26 Dec. 1909; *s* of late J. H. F. Fairfax; *m* 1939, Nancy, *d* late Dr C. B. Heald, CBE, FRCP; two *s* two *d. Educ:* Geelong Church of England Grammar Sch., Australia; Brasenose Coll., Oxford Univ. (BA). Staff, John Fairfax & Sons Pty Ltd, 1933; Advertising Manager, 1937-38. Major, Australian Imperial Forces, 1940-46. Director: John Fairfax & Sons Pty Ltd, 1946-53; John Fairfax Ltd (Publishers, Sydney Morning Herald), 1956; Chm. Australian Sectn, Commonwealth Press Union, 1950-73; Chm., Stanbroke Pastoral Co. Pty Ltd, 1964-82; Director: Bank of NSW, 1953-82; Australian Mutual Provident Soc., 1956-82 (Chm. 1966-82); Chief Comr Scout Assoc., for NSW, 1958-68, for Australia, 1969-73; Pres., Nat. Council, Scout Assoc. of Australia, 1977; Dep. Pres., Royal Agric. Society of Commonwealth, 1966; Mem. C of E Property Trust, 1950-71; Trustee, Walter and Eliza Hall Trust, 1953-; Mem. Council: Art Gall. Soc. of NSW, 1953-69; Royal Flying Doctor Service, 1954-71; Royal Agric. Society of NSW, 1956 (Pres., 1970-79, Vice-Patron, 1979); Mem., Glebe Administration Bd, 1962-73; Rector's Warden, St Mark's, Darling Point, 1948-71. *Recreations:* tennis, golf, trout fishing. *Address:* Elaine, 550 New South Head Road, Double Bay, Sydney, NSW 2000, Australia. *T:* 36 1416. *Clubs:* Leander; Commonwealth (Canberra); Melbourne (Melbourne); Union, Royal Sydney Golf (Sydney); Queensland (Brisbane).

FAIRFAX, Sir Warwick (Oswald), Kt 1967; MA; Director: John Fairfax & Sons Ltd (The Sydney Morning Herald, The Sun Herald, The Sun, The Australian Financial Review, The National Times, and other publications); Vice President, Australian Elizabethan Theatre Trust; Chairman, Australian Opera Auditions Council; owns Harrington Park; *b* 1901; *o s* of Sir James Oswald Fairfax, a Proprietor and Dir of John Fairfax and Sons, Ltd, and Mabel, *d* of Capt. Francis Hixson, RN; *m* 1928, Marcie Elizabeth, *o d* of David Wilson, Barrister of Sydney; one *s* one *d*; *m* 1948, Hanné Anderson, 2nd *d* of Emil Bendixsen, Copenhagen; one *d*; *m* 1959, Mary, *o d* of Kevin Wein; one *s. Educ:* Geelong Grammar Sch., St Paul's Coll., Sydney Univ.; Balliol Coll., Oxford. 2nd Class Hons in Sch. of Philosophy, Politics and Economics; joined staff of John Fairfax and Sons, Ltd, 1925; Dir, 1927; Managing Dir 1930; Cttee of One with admin. and management powers, 1970-76; Chairman of Dirs, 1956-76. Plays: A Victorian Marriage, Vintage for Heroes, The Bishop's Wife, performed Sydney, 1951, 1952, 1956. *Publications:* Men, Parties, and Policies, 1943; The Triple Abyss: towards a modern synthesis, 1965; ed, A Century of Journalism (The Sydney Morning Herald), 1931. *Recreations:* the arts, philosophy, motoring and vintage cars. *Address:* John Fairfax & Sons Ltd, Box 506, GPO Sydney, Australia; Fairwater, 560 New South Head Road, Double Bay, Sydney, NSW 2028, Australia; Harrington Park, Narellan, NSW 2567. *Clubs:* Carlton, Oriental, Australian, Union, Pioneers, Royal Sydney Yacht Squadron (Sydney).

FAIRFAX-CHOLMELEY, Francis William Alfred, CBE 1960; Director: Barclays Bank Ltd, 1957-73; Barclays Bank SA, France, 1968-75 (Chairman, 1968-70); *b* 20 Sept. 1904; *e s* of Hugh Charles Fairfax-Cholmeley, JP of Brandsby, York, and of Alice Jane (*née* Moverley); *m* 1940, Janet Meta, *e d* of Sir John Ogilvy-Wedderburn, 11th and 5th Bt; two *d* (one *s* decd). *Educ:*

Eton; Magdalene Coll., Cambridge (MA). Joined Barclays Bank Ltd, 1926; Local Dir, 54 Lombard Street, 1939-48; Resident Dir in Paris, Barclays Bank (France) Ltd, 1948-64, Chm., 1964-68; Local Dir, Foreign Branches, 1964-66, and Pall Mall East, 1966-68; Hon. Dir, Banque de Bruxelles SA. Served RA, 1939-45 (Major). *Address:* Struie, Forfar Road, Kirriemuir, Angus.

FAIRFAX-LUCY, Sir Edmund (John William Hugh Cameron-Ramsay-), 6th Bt *cr* 1836; painter; *b* 4 May 1945; *s* of Sir Brian Fulke Cameron-Ramsay-Fairfax-Lucy, 5th Bt and of Hon. Alice Caroline Helen Buchan, *o d* of 1st Baron Tweedsmuir, PC, GCMG, GCVO, CH; *S* father, 1974. *Educ:* City and Guilds of London Art Sch.; Royal Academy Schs of Art. *Heir: cousin* Duncan Cameron Cameron-Ramsay-Fairfax-Lucy, FCA [*b* 18 Sept. 1932; *m* 1964, Janet Barclay, *o d* of P. A. B. Niven; one *s* one *d*]. *Address:* Charlecote Park, Warwick.

FAIRGRIEVE, Sir (Thomas) Russell, Kt 1981; CBE 1974; TD 1959; JP; MP (C) Aberdeenshire West, since Feb. 1974; *b* 3 May 1924; *s* of late Alexander Fairgrieve, OBE, MC, JP, and Myrna Margaret Fairgrieve; *m* 1954, Millie Mitchell; one *s* three *d. Educ:* St Mary's Sch., Melrose; Sedbergh School. Major 8th Gurkha Rifles (Indian Army), 1946. Major, KOSB, 1956. Man. Dir, Laidlaw & Fairgrieve Ltd, 1958; Director: Joseph Dawson (Holdings) Ltd, 1961; William Baird and Co. Ltd, 1975-79. Selkirk County and Galashiels Town Councillor, 1949; Pres., Scottish Conservative Assoc., 1965, Vice-Chm., 1971; Chm., Conservative Party in Scotland, 1975-80. Parly Under Sec. of State, Scottish Office, 1979-81. JP Selkirkshire, 1962. *Recreation:* golf. *Address:* Pankalan, Boleside, Galashiels, Selkirk TD1 3NX. *T:* Galashiels 2278. *Clubs:* Carlton; New (Edinburgh); Royal and Ancient (St Andrews).

FAIRHALL, Hon. Sir Allen, KBE 1970; FRSA; Member, House of Representatives, 1949-69; *b* 24 Nov. 1909; *s* of Charles Edward and Maude Fairhall; *m* 1936, Monica Clelland, *d* of James and Ellen Ballantyne; one *s. Educ:* East Maitland Primary and High Sch.; Newcastle Tech. Inst. Founded commercial broadcasting stn 2KO, 1931; Supervising Engr, Radio and Signals Supplies Div., Min. of Munitions, 1942-45; Pres., Austr. Fedn of Commercial Broadcasting Stns, 1942-43. Mem. Australian Delegn to UN Gen. Assembly, 1954; Minister for Interior and Works, 1956-58; Minister for Supply, 1961-66; Minister for Defence, 1966-69. Mem. Newcastle CC, 1941. Hon. DSc Univ. of Newcastle, 1968. *Recreations:* amateur radio; deep sea fishing. *Address:* 7 Parkway Avenue, Newcastle, NSW 2300, Australia. *T:* 2.2295. *Clubs:* Tattersall's, National (Sydney); Newcastle (Newcastle).

FAIRHAVEN, 3rd Baron *cr* 1929 and 1961 (new creation); **Ailwyn Henry George Broughton;** JP; Vice Lord-Lieutenant, Cambridgeshire, since 1977; *b* 16 Nov. 1936; *s* of 2nd Baron Fairhaven and Hon. Diana Rosamond (*d* 1937), *o d* of late Captain Hon. Coulson Fellowes; *S* father, 1973; *m* 1960, Kathleen Patricia, *d* of Col James Henry Magill, OBE; four *s* two *d. Educ:* Eton; RMA, Sandhurst. Royal Horse Guards, 1957-71. Mem., Jockey Club, 1977- (Steward, 1981-82). DL Cambridgeshire and Isle of Ely, 1973; JP South Cambridgeshire, 1975. *Recreation:* shooting. *Heir: s* Hon. James Henry Ailwyn Broughton, *b* 25 May 1963. *Address:* Anglesey Abbey, Cambridge. *T:* Cambridge 811746. *Club:* Turf.

FAIRLEY, Alan Brand; Deputy Chairman of Grand Metropolitan Hotels Ltd, 1970-73; First President of Mecca Ltd since 1972; *b* Edinburgh, *s* of James Fairley and Jane Alexander; *m* 1942, Roma Josephine Haddow; one *d. Educ:* George Watson's Coll., Edinburgh. Joined family catering business (Fairleys of Edinburgh) from college, 1919; opened Dunedin dance hall where broadcast bands and cabaret artists, 1923; opened Piccadilly Club (first night club in Glasgow), internat. stars and bands, 1926; formed a number of Scottish cos to run dance halls, 1934-37; partnership with Carl Heimann to run dance halls all over UK, 1936 (until his death, 1968). Served War of 1939-45, Army Catering Corps, 1940-45, Major. Acquired lease of Café de Paris, London, 1943, and re-opened it, 1948, presenting Noel Coward, Marlene Dietrich, Maurice Chevalier and many others. Created Mecca Ltd, now notable for its promotion of Miss World, TV Come Dancing and Carl-Alan award for outstanding contributions to ballroom dancing, after the Christian names of its founders; Jt Chm. with Carl Heimann, Mecca Ltd, 1952, Chm. Mecca Ltd 1968; Mecca Ltd merged with Grand Metropolitan Hotels Ltd, 1970. Member: Variety Club of Great Britain and Réunion des Gastronômes (both in London). *Recreations:* swimming, golf. *Address:* The Field House, Cronkbourne Village, Tromode, Isle of Man. *Club:* Saints and Sinners.

FAIRLEY, Prof. Barker, OC 1979; MA Leeds, PhD Jena; Hon. LittD: Leeds; Waterloo (Canada); Toronto; Carleton; York (Canada); Western; Hon. LLD Alberta; RCA 1980; FRSC; Emeritus Professor of German in University College, University of Toronto; *b* Barnsley, Yorks, 21 May 1887; *s* of Barker and Charlotte Fairley; *m* 1914, Margaret Adele Keeling (*d* 1968), Bradford, Yorks; one *d. Educ:* Universities of Leeds and Jena. Lektor in English at University of Jena, 1907-10; Lecturer in German at University of Alberta, 1910; Henry Simon Prof. of German Language and Literature, Manchester Univ., 1932-36. Corresp. Fellow, British Acad., 1971. *Publications:* Charles M. Doughty, 1927; Goethe as revealed in his Poetry, 1932; A Study of Goethe, 1947; Goethe's Faust, 1953; Heinrich Heine, An Interpretation, 1954; Wilhelm Raabe, an Introduction to his Novels, 1961; (trans.) Goethe, Faust, 1970; Poems of 1922, 1972. *Address:* 90 Willcocks Street, Toronto, Canada. *Club:* Arts and Letters (Toronto).

FAIRLIE, Professor Alison (Anna Bowie); Professor of French, University of Cambridge, and Professorial Fellow, Girton College, since 1972; *b* 23 May 1917; *e d* of Rev. Robert Paul Fairlie, MA, Minister of the Church of Scotland, and of Florence A. A. Wilson. *Educ:* Ardrossan Acad.; Dumfries Acad.; Penrhos Coll.; St Hugh's Coll. Oxford; Sorbonne. BA 1st Cl. in Final Hons Sch. of Medieval and Mod. Langs, Oxon; MA, DPhil (Oxon). Doctoral Research: in Paris, 1938-40 (interruptions for voluntary war-work); in Oxford, 1940-42; Temp. Admin. Officer, Foreign Office, 1942-44; Lectr in French, Girton Coll., 1944-67; Staff Fellow and Dir of Studies in Mod. Langs, Girton Coll., 1946-67; Univ. Lectr in French, Cambridge, 1948-67, Reader in French, 1967-72. Vice-Pres., Soc. for French Studies, 1965-66 and 1968-69, Pres., 1966-68; Mem. Council, Assoc. Internationale des Etudes françaises, 1969-; Editorial Bd of French Studies, 1972-. Hon. Fellow, St Hugh's Coll., Oxford, 1972. *Publications:* Leconte de Lisle's Poems on the Barbarian Races, 1947; Baudelaire: Les Fleurs du Mal, 1960 (repr. 1975); Flaubert: Madame Bovary, 1962 (repr. 1976); contrib.: to Acta of colloquia, on Baudelaire, Constant, Flaubert, Nerval, etc.; to presentation vols; to learned jls in France, England, Italy, Australia, etc. *Recreations:* reading, travel. *Address:* 11 Parker Street, Cambridge CB1 1JL. *T:* Cambridge 58465.

FAIRLIE, Hugh, MA, MEd; Lecturer, Jordanhill College of Education, since 1975; *b* 14 Dec. 1917; *s* of Thomas and Joanna Fairlie; *m* 1947, Jemima Peden; two *s. Educ:* Univ. of Edinburgh. MA (Hons Maths and NatPhil); MEd (Dist.). Teacher, Maybole Carrick Academy, 1947-49; Asst Director of Education: Morayshire, 1949-52; Fife, 1952-57; Depute Dir of Educn, 1957-64, Dir of Educn, 1964-75, Renfrewshire. Chairman, Scottish Council for Research in Education, 1978-. FEIS 1975. *Recreations:* golf, gardens. *Address:* 26 Thornly Park Avenue, Paisley, Scotland PA2 7SE. *T:* 041-884 2494. *Clubs:* Paisley Burns; Western Gailes Golf.

FAIRLIE-CUNINGHAME, Sir William Alan, 15th Bt *cr* 1630; MC; BE (Sydney); retired as Research Officer, National Standards Laboratory, Sydney; *b* 31 Jan. 1893; *s* of 13th Bt and Georgiana Maud, *d* of late Edward Hardman Macartney; *S* brother, 1939; *m* 1929, Irene Alice (*d* 1970), *d* of late Henry Margrave Terry; one *s. Educ:* Sydney Univ. Served European War, 1915-19 (MC). Res. Officer, Metrology Div., Commonwealth Scientific and Industrial Res. Orgn, 1943-58. *Heir: s* William Henry Fairlie-Cuninghame [*b* 1 Oct. 1930; *m* 1972, Janet Menzies, *d* of late Roy Menzies Saddington; one *s*]. *Address:* 62 Farrer Brown Court, Nuffield Village, Castle Hill, NSW 2154, Australia.

FAIRMAN, Prof. Herbert Walter; Emeritus Professor of Egyptology, University of Liverpool (Brunner Professor of Egyptology, 1948-74); Special Lecturer in Egyptology, University of Manchester, 1948-69; *b* 9 March, 1907; *s* of Rev. W. T. Fairman, DD; *m* 1937, Olive Winnifred Nicholls; one *s* one *d. Educ:* Goudhurst Sch. for Boys, Goudhurst, Kent; University of Liverpool. Excavations of the Egypt Exploration Soc. at Armant and Tell el Amarna (Egypt), 1929-36, and Sesebi and Amarah West (Sudan), 1936-48. Field Dir, Egypt Exploration Society's Nubian Expedition, 1937-48. *Publications:* The Triumph of Horus, 1974; chapters on the inscriptions in: Mond and Myers, The Bucheum, 1934; Frankfort and Pendlebury, The City of Akhenaten II, 1933; (also editor) Pendlebury, The City of Akhenaten III, 1950; articles in Journal of Egyptian Archaeology, Annales du Service des Antiquités de l'Egypte and Bulletin de l'Institut français d'archéologie orientale. *Recreations:* swimming, walking. *Address:* 6 Garth Drive, Mossley Hill, Liverpool L18 6HW. *T:* 051-724 2875.

FAIRN, (Richard) Duncan; Assistant Under-Secretary of State, Home Office, 1964-67; *b* 1 June 1906; *s* of Percy Frederick and Mary Fairn; *m* 1930, Marion Cristina, *d* of James M. Sturrock; one *s* decd. *Educ:* Elementary Sch.; Battersea County (now Henry Thornton) Sch.; failed Bank of England entrance; London Sch. of Economics, BSc (Econ). Voluntary prison teacher and visitor, 1926-30. Education Officer, Pettit Farm Settlement, Dagenham, 1929-30; Joint Warden, The Settlement, York, 1930-38; Dep. Governor, Manchester Prison, 1938-39; Dep. Governor, Wakefield Prison, 1939-42; Governor, Rochester Borstal, 1942-45; First Principal, Prison Service Staff Coll., Wakefield, 1945-48; Asst Comr of Prisons, 1948-55; a Comr of Prisons, 1955-63, when Prison Commn was dissolved; Dir of Prison Administration, 1952-60; Chief Dir, Prison Dept, Home Office, 1960-64; Training Officer, Lord Chancellor's Office, 1967-72. Visited various parts of the world to advise on prison administration, 1955-69; Chm. Cttee on Detention Camps in Kenya, 1959. Swarthmore Lectr, Society of Friends, 1951; Vis. Lectr, UN Inst. at Fuchū, Tokyo, 1967; visited Nigeria to advise on prison admin, 1973. Pres., Pinner Branch of UNA, 1970-; Vice-Pres., Nat. Assoc. of Prison Visitors, 1970-; Member: Council of National Book League, 1951-77; European Cttee on Crime Problems (Strasbourg), 1964-67; Internat. Penal and Penitentiary Foundn, 1965-67; UK deleg. to UN Social Develt Commn, 1967-71; Parole Bd, 1967-71; UN Adv. Cttee of Experts on Prevention of Crime and Treatment of Offenders, 1970-72; Peter Bedford Project, 1974-76. Governor, Leighton Park Sch., 1961-76. Chairman: Management Cttee, E London Family Service Unit, 1958-78; Bd of Governors, Bedales Sch., 1963-65; John Bellers Ltd, 1974-82; Peter Bedford Trust, 1977-; Civil Service Selection Bds, 1972-76. Associate Mem., BFI. *Publications:* Quakerism, a faith for ordinary men, 1951; The Disinherited Prisoner (Eleanor Rathbone Memorial Lecture), 1962; contrib.: Changing Concepts of Crime and its Treatment, 1966; various criminological jls; DNB Supplement, 1961-70. *Recreations:* reading, walking, log-splitting, music and people. *Address:* Lavender Cottage, 82 Paines Lane, Pinner, Mddx HA5 3BL. *T:* 01-866 9650. *Club:* Authors'.

FAIRWEATHER, Brig. Claude Cyril, CB 1967; CBE 1965 (OBE 1944); TD 1944; JP; Vice Lord-Lieutenant, County of Cleveland, since 1977; Chairman, North of England TA&VRA, 1968-71; *b* 17 March 1906; *s* of Nicholas Fairweather, Middlesborough; *m* 1930, Alice Mary, *e d* of late Sir William Crosthwaite; one *s* one *d. Educ:* St Peter's Sch., York. 2nd Lieut, Royal Corps of Signals, 1928; Lt-Col 1941; Col 1943; Brig. 1945. Chm., North Riding T&AFA, 1950-53 and 1962-68; Member: TA Advisory Cttee and TA Exec. Cttee, 1968-71. Chm., St John Council, N Yorks (Vice-Pres., N Yorks St John Amb. Bde); Hon. Col, 34 (N) Signal Regt (V), 1967-75; Chairman: N Riding Co. Cadet Cttee, 1947-52; St Luke's Hosp. Man. Cttee, Middlesborough, 1959-74; Cleveland AHA, 1973-76. Retd Company Dir. Hon. Trust Representative for Cleveland, Royal Jubilee Trusts, 1977-81. DL 1949, JP 1963, NR Yorks. KStJ 1978. *Recreations:* golf, cricket, Rugby football. *Address:* The White Lodge, Hutton Rudby, Yarm, Cleveland TS15 0HY. *T:* Hutton Rudby 700598. *Clubs:* Army and Navy; Cleveland (Middlesborough); Royal and Ancient (St Andrews).

FAIRWEATHER, Dr Frank Arthur; Environmental Safety Officer, Research Division, Unilever House, since 1982; *b* 2 May 1928; *s* of Frank and Maud Harriet Fairweather; *m* 1953, Christine Winifred Hobbs; two *s. Educ:* City of Norwich Sch.; Middlesex Hospital. MB, BS 1954; MRCPath 1963, FRCPath 1975; FIBiol 1972. Clinical house appts, Ipswich Gp of Hosps, 1955-56; Pathologist, Bland Sutton Inst. of Pathology, and Courtauld Inst. of Biochem., Middlesex Hosp., Soho Hosp. for Women, 1956-60; Jt Sen. Registrar in Histopathology, Middlesex and West Middlesex Hosps, 1961-62; Chief Med. Adviser and Cons. Pathologist, Benger Labs, 1962-63; Chief Pathologist, British Industrial Biological Res. Assoc., Carshalton, and Hon. Sen. Lectr, RCS, 1963-65; Associate Res. Dir, Wyeth Labs, Taplow, 1965-69; Sen. Med. Officer, DHSS, and Principal Med. Officer, Cttee on Safety of Medicines, 1969-72; SPMO, DHSS, 1972-82. Member: Expert Panels on Environmental Pollution, Food Toxicology, and Safety, to WHO; EEC Scientific Cttee for Food, 1976- (Chm., Sci. Cttee for Cosmetology); Consultant Adviser in Toxicology to DHSS, 1978-82; Dir, DHSS Toxicological Lab., St Bartholomew's Hosp., 1978-82, now Hon. Dir; Hon. Lectr in Path., Middlesex Hosp., 1972-; Hon. Prof. of Toxicology, Dept of Biochemistry, Univ. of Surrey, 1978. QHP, 1977-80. *Publications:* various toxicological and medical papers. *Recreations:* angling, gardening, painting. *Address:* 394 London Road, Langley, Slough, Berks SL3 7HX.

FAIRWEATHER, Patrick Stanislaus; HM Diplomatic Service; Counsellor (Economic and Commercial), Athens, 1978-83; *b* 17 June 1936; *s* of John George Fairweather and Dorothy Jane (*née* Boanus); *m* 1962, Maria (*née* Merica); two *d. Educ:* Ottershaw Sch., Surrey; Trinity Coll., Cambridge (Hons History). National Service in Royal Marines and Parachute Regt, 1955-57. Entered FCO, 1965; 2nd Secretary, Rome, 1966-69; FCO, 1969-70; 1st Secretary (Economic), Paris, 1970-73; FCO, 1973-75; 1st Sec. and Head of Chancery, Vientiane, 1975-76; 1st Sec., UK Representation to EEC, Brussels, 1976-78. *Recreations:* travel, gardening, photography, dinghy sailing. *Address:* c/o Foreign and Commonwealth Office, SW1.

FAITH, (Irene) Sheila; JP; LDS; MP (C) Belper, since 1979; Dental Surgeon; *b* 3 June 1928; *yr d* of late I. Book; *m* 1950, Dennis Faith. *Educ:* Central High School, Newcastle upon Tyne; Durham Univ. LDS 1950. Member: Northumberland CC, 1970-74; Newcastle City Council, 1975-77. Vice-Chm., Jt Consultative Cttee on Educn for District of Newcastle during local govt reorganisation, 1973-74. Contested (C) Newcastle Central, Oct. 1974. Member: Select Cttee on Health and Social Services, 1979-; Cttee on Unopposed Bills, 1980-; Sec., Conservative back-bench Health and Social Services Cttee, 1982-. Has served as Chm. or Mem. several school governing bodies and Manager of Community Homes. JP: Northumberland County, 1972-74; Newcastle upon Tyne, 1974-78; Inner London, 1978-. *Recreations:* reading, music. *Address:* 2 North Wood Lodge, Oak Hill Park, NW3. *T:* 01-435 3365.

FAITHFULL, family name of **Baroness Faithfull.**

FAITHFULL, Baroness *cr* 1975 (Life Peer), of Wolvercote, Oxfordshire; **Lucy Faithfull,** OBE 1972; *b* 26 Dec. 1910; *d* of Lt Sydney Leigh Faithfull, RE (killed 1916) and late Elizabeth Adie Faithfull (*née* Algie); unmarried. *Educ:* Talbot Heath Sch. (formerly Bournemouth High Sch.). Social Science Dipl., Birmingham Univ., 1933; Family case work training (Charity Welfare Organisation, now Family Welfare Assoc.), 1936, and Cert. in Child Care, 1969. Club Leader and Sub-Warden, Birmingham Settlement, 1932-35; Asst Organiser, Child Care, LCC Education Dept, 1935-40; Regional Welfare Officer (Evacuation Scheme), Min. of Health, 1940-48; Inspector in Children's Br., Home Office, 1948-58; Oxford City Council: Children's Officer, 1958-70; Director of Social Services, 1970-74; retired, 1974. Chm., Adoption Resource Exchange; Mem. Council and Exec. Finance Cttee, Dr Barnardo's; Trustee and Mem. Cttee: Bessel Leigh Sch. for Maladjusted Children; Bridgehead Trust (hostel for adolescent boys). Hon. MA Oxford, 1974; Hon. DLitt Warwick, 1978. *Recreations:* friends, travel, garden. *Address:* 303 Woodstock Road, Oxford OX2 7NY. *T:* Oxford 55389.

FAKLEY, Dennis Charles, OBE 1973; Assistant Chief Scientific Adviser (Nuclear), Ministry of Defence, since 1979; *b* 20 Nov. 1924; *s* of Charles Frederick and Ethel May Fakley; *m* 1976, Louise Grace Swindell. *Educ:* Chatham House Grammar Sch., Ramsgate; Queen Mary Coll., Univ. of London (BSc Special Physics). Royal Naval Scientific Service, 1944-63; Min.

of Defence, 1963-. *Recreations:* reading, cricket. *Address:* 14 Coval Gardens, SW14 7DG. *T:* (home) 01-876 6856; (office) 01-218 7126.

FALCON, Michael Gascoigne, CBE 1979; JP, DL; Chairman: Pauls & Whites Ltd, since 1976 (Director since 1973); Eastern Counties Regional Board, Lloyds Bank Ltd, since 1979 (Director, since 1972); Norwich Union Insurance Group, since 1981 (Director, since 1963; Vice Chairman, 1979-81); *b* 28 Jan. 1928; *s* of Michael Falcon and Kathleen Isabel Frances Gascoigne; *m* 1954, April Daphne Claire Lambert; two *s* one *d. Educ:* Stowe Sch., Bucks; Heriot-Watt Coll., Edinburgh. National Service, Grenadier Gds and Royal Norfolk Regt, 1946-48. Head Brewer and Jt Man. Dir, E. Lacon & Co. Ltd, Great Yarmouth, 1952-68; Exec. Dir, Edgar Watts, Willow Merchants, 1968-73; Chm., National Seed Develt Orgn Ltd, 1972-82; Director: Securicor (East) Ltd, 1969-72; Lloyds Bank UK Management Ltd, 1979-; Matthew Brown plc, 1981-. Trustee, E Anglian Trustee Savings Bank, 1963-75. Mem., Norwich Prison Bd of Visitors, 1969-. JP 1967, High Sheriff 1979, DL 1981, Co. of Norfolk. OStJ 1968. *Recreation:* country pursuits. *Address:* Keswick Old Hall, Norwich, Norfolk NR4 6TZ. *T:* Norwich 54348; Kirkgate, Loweswater, Cockermouth, Cumbria. *Clubs:* Farmers', MCC; Norfolk (Norwich); Royal Norfolk and Suffolk Yacht (Lowestoft).

FALCON, Norman Leslie, FRS 1960; *b* 29 May 1904; 2nd *s* of late Thomas Adolphus Falcon, MA, RBA; *m* 1938, Dorothy Muriel, 2nd *d* of late F. G. Freeman, HM Consular Service; two *s* one *d. Educ:* Exeter Sch.; Trinity Coll., Cambridge. MA Cantab. Joined Anglo-Persian Oil Company as geologist, 1927; FGS, FRGS, 1927; Geological Exploration in Persia, UK and elsewhere, 1927-40. Served War of 1939-45, Intelligence Corps, 1940-45. Rejoined Anglo-Iranian Oil Company as Geologist on Head Office staff, 1945; Chief Geologist, 1955-65, Geological Adviser, 1965-72, British Petroleum Co Ltd. FInstPet, 1959; Geological Soc. of London: Mem. Council, 1954-58, 1967-71; Foreign Sec. 1967-70; Murchison Medal, 1963; Royal Geographical Society: Mem. Council, 1966-69; Vice-Pres. 1973; Founder's Medal, 1973. Mem., NERC, 1968-71. Hon. Mem., American Assoc. Petroleum Geologists, 1973. Bronze Star Medal (USA), 1945. *Publications:* geological papers. *Recreations:* outdoor pursuits. *Address:* The Downs, Chiddingfold, Surrey. *T:* Wormley 3101.

FALCONER, Prof. Alexander Frederick, VRD; BLitt, MA; FRSL; Professor of English in the University of St Andrews, 1955-78; *s* of Alexander W. Falconer and Emily Henrietta Carlow Falconer. *Educ:* Universities of Glasgow, St Andrews and Oxford (Magdalen Coll.). Lecturer, St Salvator's Coll., St Andrews, 1935-39. Served in Home and Eastern Fleets, rank of Lieut, and Lt-Comdr RNVR, 1940-45. Senior Lecturer in Univ. of St Andrews, 1946. Mem. of group of editors for Boswell's correspondence at Yale, 1952-. Folger Fellow, 1958. Jt Gen. Editor, Percy Letters Series, 1964. Naval Officer i/c, St Andrews Univ. Unit, RNR. Trustee, Nat. Library of Scotland, 1956-. Mem., Royal Inst. of Navigation. *Publications:* A. Spir, Right and Wrong (trans.), 1954; The Percy Letters, Vol. IV, 1954, Vol. VI, 1960; Shakespeare and the Sea, 1964; A Glossary of Shakespeare's Sea and Naval Terms, 1965; articles and reviews. *Address:* 6 Alexandra Place, St Andrews. *T:* St Andrews 73457. *Clubs:* Naval, Mayfair.

See also Peter S. Falconer.

FALCONER, Prof. Douglas Scott, FRS 1973; FRSE 1972; *b* 10 March 1913; *s* of Gerald Scott Falconer and Lillias Harriet Gordon Douglas; *m* 1942, Margaret Duke; two *s. Educ:* Edinburgh Academy; Univ. of St Andrews (BSc); Univ. of Cambridge (PhD. ScD). Scientific Staff of Agricultural Research Council, 1947-68; Prof. of Genetics, Univ. of Edinburgh, and Dir, ARC Unit of Animal Genetics, 1968-80. *Publications:* Introduction to Quantitative Genetics, 1960; papers in scientific jls. *Recreations:* music, walking, sailing. *Address:* Institute of Animal Genetics, West Mains Road, Edinburgh EH9 3JN. *T:* 031-667 1081.

FALCONER, Hon. Sir Douglas (William), Kt 1981; MBE 1946; **Hon. Mr Justice Falconer;** a Judge of the High Court of Justice, Chancery Division, since 1981; *b* 20 Sept. 1914; *s* of late William Falconer, S Shields; *m* 1941, Joan Beryl Argent, *d* of late A. S. Bishop, Hagley, Worcs; one *s* one *d. Educ:* South Shields; King's Coll., Durham Univ.; BSc (Hons) Physics, 1935. Served War of 1939-45 (Hon. Major): commissioned E Yorks Regt, 1939. Called to Bar, Middle Temple, 1950, Bencher 1972; QC 1967. Apptd to exercise appellate jurisdiction of BoT, later DoT, under Trade Marks Act, 1970-81; Member: of Departmental Cttee to review British trade mark law and practice, 1972-73; Standing Adv. Cttee on Patents, 1975-79; Standing Adv. Cttee on Trade Marks, 1975-79; Senate of Four Inns of Court, 1973-74; Senate of Four Inns of Court and the Bar, 1974-77; Chm., Patent Bar Assoc., 1971-80. *Publications:* (Jt Editor) Terrell on the Law of Patents (11th and 12th edns), 1965 and 1971. *Recreations:* music, theatre. *Address:* Royal Courts of Justice, Strand, WC2; Ridgewell House, West Street, Reigate, Surrey. *T:* Reigate 44374.

FALCONER, Sir James Fyfe, Kt 1973; MBE 1944; JP; Town Clerk of Glasgow, 1965-75; *b* 18 Nov. 1911; *m* 1938, Jessie Elizabeth Paterson; two *s* two *d. Educ:* Queen's Park Secondary Sch.; Glasgow University. Law Apprentice, 1926-32; Solicitor, 1932-48; Town Clerk Deput, 1948-59; Senior Town Clerk Depute, 1959-65. JP Glasgow, 1962. *Recreations:* gardening, golf, bowling. *Address:* 101 St Andrew's Drive, Glasgow G41 4RA. *T:* 041-423 0681.

FALCONER, Peter Serrell, FRIBA, FRSA; Senior Partner, The Falconer Partnership, Architects and Consultants, since 1959; *b* 7 March 1916; *s* of Thomas Falconer, FRIBA, and Florence Edith Falconer; presumed heir to the Barony (1206) and Lordship (1646) of Halkerton, vacant since 1966; *m* 1941, Mary Hodson; three *s* one *d. Educ:* Bloxham Sch., Banbury. Commenced practice in Stroud, as partner in Ellery Anderson Roiser & Falconer, 1944; became Sen. Partner of Peter Falconer and Partners, 1959 (with br. office in Adelaide, SA, 1970). Specialist in materials handling and industrial architecture; Mem., Materials Handling Inst. *Publications:* Building and Planning for Industrial Storage and Distribution, 1975; contributor to: Architectural Review; Architects' Jl; Material Handling magazines. *Recreations:* restoring historic buildings, garden planning, motor sport. *Address:* St Francis, Lammas Park, Minchinhampton, Stroud, Glos. *T:* Brimscombe 2188.

FALETAU, 'Inoke Fotu; High Commissioner for Tonga in London since Oct. 1972; Ambassador for Tonga to: France, since 1972; Federal Republic of Germany, since 1976; Belgium, Luxembourg, Netherlands and European Economic Community, since 1977; USA, since 1979; USSR, since 1980; Denmark, since 1981; *b* 24 June 1937; 2nd *s* of 'Akau'ola Sateki Faletau and Celia Lyden; *m* 'Evelini Ma'ata Hurrell; three *s* three *d. Educ:* St Peter's, Cambridge, NZ; Tonga High Sch.; Auckland Grammar Sch.; UC Swansea; Manchester Univ. Joined Tonga Civil Service, 1958; Asst Sec., Prime Minister's Office, 1965; Sec. to Govt, 1969; seconded to Univ. of South Pacific, 1971; Sec. to Govt, 1972. *Recreations:* Rugby, tennis, reading, bridge, fishing. *Address:* Greenbanks, Lyndale, NW2. *Clubs:* Royal Commonwealth Society, Travellers' (Hon.), Hurlingham (Hon.); Nuku'alofa Yacht and Motor Boat.

FALK, Sir Roger (Salis), Kt 1969; OBE 1945; CBIM; Chairman, Sadler's Wells Foundation, since 1976; *b* 22 June 1910; *s* of Lionel David Falk; *m* 1938, Margaret Helen (*née* Stroud) (*d* 1958); one *s* two *d. Educ:* Haileybury (Life Governor, 1971-; Council Mem., 1978-); Geneva Univ. Gen. Manager's Office, Rhodesia Railways, Bulawayo, 1931; D. J. Keymer & Co: Manager in Bombay and Calcutta, 1932-35; Dir, 1935-49; Managing Dir, 1945-49; Vice-Chm., 1950; formerly: Dir, P-E International Ltd (Chm., 1973-76); Chm., London Bd, Provincial Insurance Co. Ltd. Shoreditch Borough Council, 1937-45. Dir-Gen. British Export Trade Research Organisation (BETRO) from 1949 until disbandment. Chairman: Furniture Development Council, 1963-82; Central Council for Agric. and Hort. Cooperation, 1967-75; British European Associated Publishers, 1976-79; Action for Dysphasic Adults (ADA), 1982; Dep. Chm., Gaming Bd, 1978-81; Member: Council of Industrial Design, 1958-67; Monopolies and Mergers Commn, 1965-80; Council, RSA, 1968-74; Council, Imp. Soc. of Knights Bachelor, 1979-; Pres., Design and Industries Assoc., 1971-72. Served War of 1939-45, RAFVR; Wing-Comdr, 1942. *Publication:* The Business of Management, 1961, 5th rev. edn 1976. *Recreations:* writing, music, reading, theatre. *Address:* 603 Beatty House, Dolphin Square, SW1. *T:* 01-828 3752. *Clubs:* Garrick, MCC.

FALKENDER, Baroness *cr* 1974 (Life Peer), of West Haddon, Northants; **Marcia Matilda Falkender,** CBE 1970; Personal and Political Secretary to Rt Hon. Sir Harold Wilson, since 1956; *b* March 1932; *d* of Harry Field; *m* 1955, George Edmund Charles Williams (marr. diss. 1960). *Educ:* Northampton High School; Queen Mary Coll., Univ. of London. BA Hons Hist. Secretary to Gen. Sec., Labour Party, 1955-56. Member: Prime Minister's Film Industry Working Party, 1975-76; Interim Cttee on Film Industry, 1977-82. *Publication:* Inside Number 10, 1972. *Address:* 3 Wyndham Mews, Upper Montagu Street, W1.

FALKINER, Lt-Col Sir Terence (Edmond Patrick), 8th Bt of Annmount, Cork, *cr* 1778; DL; late Coldstream Guards; retired 1956; *b* 17 March 1903; *s* of 7th Bt and Kathleen (*d* 1948), *e d* of Hon. Henry Robert Orde-Powlett, 2nd *s* of 3rd Baron Bolton; *S* father, 1917; *m* 1925, Mildred, *y d* of Sir John Cotterell, 4th Bt; two *s* three *d. Educ:* St Anthony's, Eastbourne; The Oratory Sch., Edgbaston. DL Herefordshire, 1965. KStJ. *Heir:* *s* Edmond Charles Falkiner [*b* 24 June 1938; *m* 1960, Janet Iris, *d* of Arthur E. B. Darby, Bromyard, Herefordshire; two *s*]. *Address:* c/o Edmond Falkiner, 111 Wood Street, Barnet, Herts EN5 4BX. *T:* 01-440 2426.

FALKINGHAM, Ven. John Norman; Warden, Community of the Holy Name, since 1969; *b* 9 Feb. 1917; 2nd *s* of Alfred Richard Falkingham and Amy Grant (*née* Macallister); *m* 1947, Jean Dorothy Thoren; two *d. Educ:* Geelong Gram. Sch., Corio, Vic.; Trinity Coll., Univ. of Melbourne. BA (Hons) Melbourne 1940; ThL (1st Cl. Hons), ThD 1978, Australian Coll. of Theol.; prizes for Divinity and Biblical Greek. Deacon, 1941; Priest, 1942. Curate of Holy Trinity, Surrey Hills, Vic., 1941-44; Chaplain, Trinity Coll., Univ. of Melbourne, 1944-50; Incumbent, St Paul's, Caulfield, Vic., 1950-61. Exam. Chaplain to Archbishop of Melbourne, 1947-61; Lectr in Theol. Faculty, Trinity Coll., Melbourne, 1950-60; Canon of St Paul's Cath., Melbourne, 1959-61; Dean of Newcastle, Mar. 1961-75; Rector of St Paul's, Manuka, ACT, 1975-82; Canon of St Saviour's Cath., Goulburn, 1976-81; Archdeacon of Canberra, 1981-82. Sec., Liturgical Commn of Gen. Synod, 1966-78; Mem. Bd of Delegates, Aust. Coll. of Theology, 1962-; Lecturer: Canberra Coll. of Ministry, 1975-; St Mark's Library, Canberra, 1982. *Publications:* articles in various jls. *Recreation:* walking. *Address:* 4 Serra Place, Stirling, ACT 2611, Australia. *Club:* Newcastle.

FALKLAND, 14th Viscount cr 1620; **Lucius Henry Charles Plantagenet Cary; Lord Cary, 1620;** b 25 Jan. 1905; e s of 13th Viscount Falkland and Ella Louise (d 1954), e d of E. W. Catford; S father, 1961; m 1st, 1926, Joan Sylvia (who obtained a divorce, 1933), d of Capt. Charles Bonham Southey, of Frinton-on-Sea; two d ; 2nd, 1933, Constance Mary, d of late Capt. Edward Berry; one s ; 3rd, 1958, Charlotte Anne (marr. diss. 1974), e d of late Bevil Granville, Chadley, Wellesbourne, Warwick. Educ: Eton. Flying Officer RAFVR, 1941-45 (invalided). Heir: s Master of Falkland, qv. Address: 18 Tower Park, Fowey, Cornwall. T: Fowey 3211. Clubs: Carlton, Royal Commonwealth Society.
See also Sir W. V. H. Nelson, Bt.

FALKLAND, Master of; Hon. Lucius Edward William Plantagenet Cary; b 8 May 1935; s and heir of 14th Viscount Falkland, qv ; m 1962, Caroline Anne, o d of late Lt-Comdr Gerald Butler, DSC, RN, and late Mrs Patrick Parish; one s two d (and one d decd). Educ: Wellington Coll.; Alliance Française, Paris. Late 2nd Lieut 8th Hussars. Recreations: golf, cinema, racing. Address: Court House, Winchfield, near Basingstoke, Hants. T: Hartley Wintney 3273. Clubs: Brooks's, Turf; Berkshire Golf.

FALKNER, Sir (Donald) Keith, Kt 1967; Hon. DMus Oxon, 1969; FRCM; Hon. RAM; Hon. GSM; Hon. FTCL; Hon. FLCM; Director, Royal College of Music, 1960-74; professional singer; b Sawston, Cambs, 1900; y s of late John Charles Falkner; m 1930, Christabel Margaret, o d of Thomas Fletcher Fullard, MA; two d. Educ: New Coll. Sch.; Perse Sch.; Royal College of Music; Berlin, Vienna, Paris. Has sung at all principal festivals in England, and many European cities; toured USA eight times, including concerts with Boston Symphony, New York Philharmonic, Cincinnati, St Louis, and Philadelphia Orchestras; toured South Africa, 1935, 1939, 1955, 1962, 1974; Canada in 1953; New Zealand in 1956. British Council Music Officer for Italy, 1946-50. Prof. of the Dept of Music at Cornell Univ., USA, 1950-60. An Artistic Dir, King's Lynn Fest., 1981-. FRSA 1979. Hon. Mem., Assoc. Européene des Conservatoires de Musique, Académies, et Musikhochschulen, 1976. Served European War, 1914-18, in RNAS, 1917-19; War of 1939-45, RAFVR, 1940-45. Recreations: cricket, golf, lawn tennis, squash rackets, walking. Address: Low Cottages, Ilketshall St Margaret, Bungay, Suffolk. T: Bungay 2573. Clubs: Athenæum, Royal Automobile, MCC; Norfolk (Norwich).

FALKUS, Hugh Edward Lance; naturalist, independent writer, film director, broadcaster; b 15 May 1917; s of James Everest Falkus and Alice Musgrove. Educ: The East Anglian Sch. (Culford Sch.). Served War of 1939-45 (Fighter Pilot). TV films include: Salmo-the Leaper; (with Niko Tinbergen) Signals for Survival (Italia Prize, 1969; Amer. Blue Ribbon, New York Film Fest., 1971); Highland Story; The Gull Watchers; The Signreaders; The Beachcombers; The Riddle of the Rook (Venice Film Festival, 1972); Tender Trap; Self-Portrait of a Happy Man. Publications: Sea Trout Fishing, 1962, 2nd edn 1975, revised 2nd edn 1981; The Stolen Years, 1965, 2nd edn 1979; (with Niko Tinbergen) Signals for Survival, 1970; (with Fred Buller) Freshwater Fishing, 1975, new edn 1978; Nature Detective, 1978. Recreations: fishing, shooting, sailing. Address: Cragg Cottage, near Ravenglass, Cumbria CA18 1RT. T: Ravenglass 247. Club: Flyfishers'.

FALL, Brian James Proetel; HM Diplomatic Service; Principal Private Secretary to Secretary of State for Foreign and Commonwealth Affairs, since 1981; b 13 Dec. 1937; s of John William Fall, Hull, Yorkshire, and Edith Juliette (née Proetel); m 1962, Delmar Alexandra Roos; three d. Educ: St Paul's Sch.; Magdalen Coll., Oxford; Univ. of Michigan Law Sch. Joined HM Foreign (now Diplomatic) Service, 1962; served in Foreign Office UN Dept, 1963; Moscow, 1965; Geneva, 1968; Civil Service Coll., 1970; FO Eastern European and Soviet Dept and Western Organisations Dept, 1971; New York, 1975; Harvard Univ. Center for Internat. Affairs, 1976; Counsellor, Moscow, 1977-79; Head of Energy, Science and Space Dept, FCO, 1979-80; Head of Eastern European and Soviet Dept, FCO, 1980-81. Address: c/o Foreign and Commonwealth Office, King Charles Street, SW1A 2AH; 2 St Helena Terrace, Richmond, Surrey. T: 01-940 7683. Club: Travellers'.

FALLA, Paul Stephen; b 25 Oct. 1913; s of Norris Stephen Falla and Audrey Frances Stock, Dunedin, New Zealand; m 1958, Elizabeth Shearer; one d. Educ: Wellington and Christ's Colls, NZ; Balliol Coll., Oxford (Scholar). Appointed to Foreign Office, 1936; served HM Embassies, Warsaw, 1938-39, Ankara, 1939-43, Tehran, 1943; Foreign Office, 1943-46; UK Delegation to UN, New York, 1946-49; Foreign Office, 1949-67 (Dep. Dir of Research, 1958-67). Member: Exec. Cttee, Translators' Assoc., Soc. of Authors, 1971-73 (Vice-Chm., 1973); Council, Inst. Linguists, 1975-81; Cttee, Translators' Guild, 1975-81. Scott Moncrieff prize, 1972 and 1981. Publications: about 45 book translations from various languages, 1967-. Recreations: reading (history, philosophy, poetry, language matters). Address: 63 Freelands Road, Bromley, Kent BR1 3HZ. T: 01-460 4995. Club: Travellers'.

FALLE, Sir Sam, KCMG 1979 (CMG 1964); KCVO 1972; DSC 1945; HM Diplomatic Service, retired; b 19 Feb. 1919; s of Theodore and Hilda Falle; m 1945, Merete Rosen; one s three d. Educ: Victoria Coll., Jersey, CI. Served Royal Navy, 1937-48; joined Foreign (subseq. Diplomatic) Service, 1948; British Consulate, Shiraz, Iran, 1949-51; British Embassy, Tehran, 1952; British Embassy, Beirut, 1952-55; FO, 1955-57; British Embassy, Baghdad, 1957-61; Consul-Gen., Gothenburg, 1961-63; Head of UN Dept, FO, 1963-67; with Lord Shackleton's mission to Aden 1967; Deputy High Comr, Kuala

Lumpur, 1967-69; Ambassador to Kuwait, 1969-70; High Comr, Singapore, 1970-74; Ambassador to Sweden, 1974-77; High Comr in Nigeria, 1977-78; Delegate, Commn of the European Communities, Algiers, 1979-82. Kt Grand Cross, Order of Polar Star, Sweden, 1975. Recreation: swimming. Address: Slättna, 57030 Mariannelund, Sweden.

FALLON, Martin; see Patterson, Harry.

FALLON, Peter, QC 1971; **His Honour Judge Fallon;** a Circuit Judge, since 1979; b 1 March 1931; s of Frederick and Mary Fallon; m 1955, Zina Mary (née Judd); one s two d. Educ: Leigh Grammar Sch.; St Joseph's Coll., Blackpool; Bristol Univ. (LLB Hons). Called to Bar, Gray's Inn, 1953. Commissioned in RAF for three years; commenced law practice as pupil, 1956. A Recorder of the Crown Court, 1972-79. Publications: Crown Court Practice: Sentencing, 1974; Crown Court Practice: Trial, 1978; contrib. Proc. RSM. Recreations: golf, fishing, painting. Address: The Guildhall, Bristol BS1 2HL.

FALMOUTH, 9th Viscount, cr 1720; **George Hugh Boscawen;** 26th Baron Le Despencer, 1264; Baron Boscawen-Rose, 1720; Lord-Lieutenant of Cornwall, since 1977; b 31 Oct. 1919; 2nd but e surv. s of 8th Viscount; S father, 1962; m 1953, Elizabeth Price Browne; four s. Educ: Eton Coll.; Trinity Coll., Cambridge. Served War, 1939-46, Italy. Capt., Coldstream Guards. DL Cornwall, 1968. Heir: s Hon. Evelyn Arthur Hugh Boscawen [b 13 May 1955; m 1977, Lucia Vivian-Neal, e d of R. W. Vivian-Neal; one s]. Address: Tregothnan, Truro, Cornwall; Buston, Hunton, Kent. Clubs: Athenæum, Army and Navy.
See also Hon. R. T. Boscawen.

FALSHAW, Sir Donald, Kt 1967; retired; b 22 Jan. 1905; s of James and Martha Falshaw; m 1937, Jessie Louise Taylor; no c. Educ: Lancaster Royal Gram. Sch.; Sidney Sussex Coll., Cambridge. Indian Civil Service (Punjab), 1928-66: District and Sessions Judge, 1932-46; Judge, Lahore High Court, 1946-47; Judge, Punjab High Court, India, after partition, 1947-66, Chief Justice, Dec. 1961-May 1966. Recreations: cricket, racing. Address: 125 Kenilworth Court, Lower Richmond Road, Putney, SW15. T: 01-788 8058. Club: East India, Devonshire, Sports and Public Schools.

FALVEY, Sir John (Neil), KBE 1976; QC 1970; barrister, Fiji; b 16 Jan. 1918; s of John Falvey and Adela Falvey; m 1943, Margaret Katherine, d of Stanley Weatherby; three s two d (and one d decd). Educ: Eltham and New Plymouth Convent Schs; Whangarei High Sch.; Otago Univ. (BA); Auckland Univ. (LLB). Colonial Admin. Service (incl. mil. service, Fiji and Gilbert and Ellice Is), 1940-48; private legal practice, 1949-70. Mem., Legislative Council, 1953-72; Attorney-General, 1970-77; Senator and Leader of Govt Business, 1972-79. Hon. Danish Consul, 1950-70. Chevalier (First Cl.), Royal Order of Dannebrog, 1968. Recreation: golf. Address: PO Box 1056, Suva, Fiji. T: 312-934. Clubs: Fiji, Defence, Fiji Golf.

FANE, family name of **Earl of Westmorland.**

FANE, Harry Frank Brien, CMG 1967; OBE 1957 (MBE 1945); Department of Employment and Productivity, retired 1968; b 21 Aug. 1915; s of late Harry Lawson Fane and Edith (née Stovold); m 1947, Stella, yr d of John Hopwood; two d. Educ: William Ellis Sch.; Birkbeck Coll., London. Joined Ministry of Labour, 1933. HM Forces, 1940-45: Major, Royal Corps of Signals (despatches); served in N Africa, Italy and Austria. British Embassy, Washington: First Sec. (Labour), 1950-56; Counsellor (Labour), 1960-66. Regional Controller, Dept of Employment and Productivity (formerly Min. of Labour), Birmingham, 1966-68. Address: 40 Winterbourne Road, Solihull, West Midlands B91 1LU.

FANE TREFUSIS, family name of **Baron Clinton.**

FANNER, Peter Duncan; Metropolitan Stipendiary Magistrate since 1972; a Recorder of the Crown Court, since 1980; b 27 May 1926; s of late Robert William Hodges Fanner, solicitor, and Doris Kitty Fanner; m 1949, Sheila Eveline England; one s one d. Educ: Pangbourne Coll. Admitted Solicitor of the Supreme Court, 1951 (holder Justices' Clerks' Society's prize). Served War of 1939-45, Pilot in Fleet Air Arm, Lieut (A) RNVR, 1944-47. Asst Clerk to Bromley Justices, 1947-51; Dep. Clerk to Gore Justices, 1951-56; Clerk to Bath Justices, 1956-72; a Dep. Circuit Judge, 1974-80. Mem. Council of Justices' Clerks' Society, 1966-72; Assessor Mem. of Departmental Cttee on Liquor Licensing, 1971-72. Chairman: Bath Round Table, 1963-64; No Fixed Abode, 1973-75. Publications: Stone's Justices' Manual; contrib. to Justice of the Peace, The Magisterial Officer, The Lawyer's Remembrancer. Recreations: motoring, caravanning, sailing. Address: Marylebone Magistrates Court, Marylebone Road, NW1. T: 01-725 4372.

FANSHAWE, Maj.-Gen. George Drew, CB 1954; DSO 1944; OBE 1944; b 27 Sept. 1901; s of Lt-Col Edward Cardwell Fanshawe; m 1934, Dorothy Elizabeth Norman-Walker; one s one d. Educ: Tonbridge. 2nd Lieut, RFA, 1922, Lieut 1924. RHA 1928; Capt. 1935; Adjt Herts Yeomanry, 1935; Brigade-Maj., RA, 1939, CO 1942; CRA, 3 Div., 1945; 5th Anti-Aircraft Bde, 1949; Comdr 1st Anti-Aircraft Group, 1952-55; retired 1955. BRA Southern Comd, 1950. Col. Comdt, Royal Artillery, 1956-66 (Representative Col Comdt, 1961-62). High Sheriff, Wilts, 1961-62; Alderman, Wilts CC.

CStJ. Order of Merit (US). *Address:* Farley Farm, Farley, Wilts. *T:* Farley 202. *Club:* Army and Navy.

FANSHAWE, Captain Thomas Evelyn, CBE 1971; DSC 1943; RN retd; Captain of the Sea Cadet Corps, 1972-81; Nautical Assessor to House of Lords; *b* 29 Sept. 1918; *s* of Rev. Richard Evelyn Fanshawe and Mrs Isobel Fanshawe (*née* Prosser Hale); *m* 1944, Joan Margaret Moxon; one *s* two *d. Educ:* Dover Coll.; Nautical Coll., Pangbourne. FRHS. Served 1939-45 in destroyers and frigates and comdg HMS Clover (DSC, despatches 1943 and 1944); HM Ships Ocean, Constance and Phoenix, 1945-51; comd HM Ships: Zest and Obedient, 1951-54; Loch Insh, 1955-57; Temeraire, 1957-59; Tyne, 1959-61; NATO Defence Coll. and Liaison Officer with C-in-C Southern Europe, 1961-64; comd HMS Plymouth and Captain (D) 29th Escort Sqdn, 1964-66; Sen. Naval Officer Persian Gulf and Comdr Naval Forces Gulf, 1966-68 (Cdre); SBNO and Naval Attaché, S Africa (Cdre), 1969-71; ADC to the Queen, 1970-71; retd 1971. Cmdr 1955; Captain 1961. *Recreations:* gardening, golf, general interest in sport. *Address:* Freshwater House, Stroud, Petersfield, Hants. *T:* Petersfield 2430. *Clubs:* Naval, MCC; Royal Naval (Portsmouth).

FANTONI, Barry Ernest; novelist, broadcaster, cartoonist, jazz musician; Member of editorial staff of Private Eye, since 1963; *b* 28 Feb. 1940; *s* of Peter Nello Secondo Fantoni and Sarah Catherine Fantoni; *m* 1972, Teresa Frances Reidy. *Educ:* Archbishop Temple Sch.; Camberwell Sch. of Arts and Crafts (Wedgwood Scholar). Cartoonist of The Listener, 1968-; contrib. art criticism to The Times, 1973-77; record reviewer, Punch, 1976-77; designer of film and theatre posters and illustrator of book jackets; film and television actor. One-man shows: Woodstock Gall., London, 1963; Comara Gall., LA, 1964; Brunel Univ., 1974; two-man shows (with Peter Fantoni): Langton Gall., London, 1977; Annexe Gall., London, 1978; work exhibited: AIA Gall., London, 1958, 1961 and 1964; D and AD Annual Exhibn, London, 1964; Royal Acad. Summer Exhibn, 1963 (as Stuart Harris, with William Rushton), 1964, 1975 and 1978 (with Richard Napper); Tate Gall., 1973; Bradford Print Biennale, 1974; National Theatre, 1977; Browse and Darby, 1977. Musical compositions include: popular songs (also popular songs with Marianne Faithfull and with Stanley Myers); The Cantors Crucifixion (musical improvisation for 13 instruments), 1977; (with John Wells) Lionel (musical), 1977. Male TV Personality of the Year, 1966. Editor, St Martin's Review, 1969-74. *Publications:* (with Richard Ingrams) Private Pop Eye, 1968; (as Old Jowett, with Richard Ingrams) The Bible for Motorists, 1970; Tomorrow's Nicodemus, 1974; (as Sylvie Krin, with Richard Ingrams) Love in the Saddle, 1974; Private Eye Cartoon Library 5, 1975; (as E. J. Thribb, with Richard Ingrams) So Farewell Then – – – and Other Poems, 1978; Mike Dime, 1980; (as Sylvie Krin, with Richard Ingrams) Born to be Queen, 1981; Stickman, 1982; (ed) Colemanballs, 1982; *illustrations for:* How To Be a Jewish Mother, 1966; The BP Festivals and Events in Britain, 1966; (with George Melly) The Media Mob, 1980. *Recreations:* snooker, road running, animal welfare. *Address:* c/o Anthony Sheil Associates Ltd, 2/3 Morwell Street, W1B 3AR. *Club:* Chelsea Arts (Chm., 1978-80).

FAREED, Sir Razik, Kt 1951; OBE 1948; Sri Lanka Moor by race and Muslim by religion; Member of Ceylonese Parliament, from 1952; Member of Senate, Ceylon, 1947-52; Member, State Council of Ceylon until Ceylon Independence Act, 1947; Member, Colombo Municipal Council, 1930-; Founder, only Muslim Ladies' College in Ceylon; Founder and President, Moors' Islamic Cultural Home (Inc.); Life Pres., All Ceylon Moors Assoc. Patron: Sri Lanka Moor Youth League; Orchid Circle of Sri Lanka; President: Islamia Home for Needy and Orphan Children; Sri Lanka Sufi Study Circle; Sri Lanka Kennel Club. *Address:* Hajara Villa, 27/1 Fareed Place, Colombo 4, Sri Lanka. *T:* 88357 and 28928. *Clubs:* Ceylon Turf (Vice-Pres.), Ceylon Poultry.

FARIDKOT, Col HH Farzand-i-Saadat Nishan Hazrrat-i-Kaisar-i-Hind, Raja Sir Har Indar Singh Brar Bans Bahadur, Ruler of, KCSI 1941; *b* 29 Jan. 1915; *S* father as Raja, 1919; *m* 1933. *Educ:* Aitchison Chiefs Coll., Lahore. Full Ruling Powers, 1934; is one of Ruling Princes of India; Hon. Col Sikh LI; Hon. Col Bengal Engineer Group; MLA Pepsu LA. Salute, 11 guns. Formerly Mem. National Defence Council of India and of Standing Cttee of Chamber of Princes. Past Grand Master (Hon.), 1974, OSM 1971, Grand Lodge of India; Dist. Grand Master for N India, 1977, United Grand Lodge of England. *Address:* Faridkot, Punjab, India.

FARINGDON, 3rd Baron *cr* 1916; **Charles Michael Henderson;** Bt 1902; *b* 3 July 1937; *s* of Hon. Michael Thomas Henderson (*d* 1953) (2nd *s* of Col Hon. Harold Greenwood Henderson, CVO, and *g s* of 1st Baron) and Oonagh Evelyn Henderson, *er d* of late Lt-Col Harold Ernest Brassey; *S* uncle, 1977; *m* 1959, Sarah Caroline, *d* of J. M. E. Askew, *qv* ; three *s* one *d. Educ:* Eton College; Trinity College, Cambridge (BA). Chm., Witan Investment Co. plc, 1981-. Chm. Bd of Governors, Royal Marsden Hosp., 1980-. *Heir:* s Hon. James Harold Henderson, *b* 14 July 1961. *Address:* Buscot Park, Faringdon, Oxon; Barnsley Park, Cirencester, Glos.

FARLEY, Dr Francis James Macdonald, FRS 1972; Leverhulme Fellow, University of Reading, since 1982; *b* 13 Oct. 1920; *er s* of late Brig. Edward Lionel Farley, CBE, MC; *m* 1945, Josephine Maisie Hayden; three *s* one *d* ; *m* 1977, Margaret Ann Pearce. *Educ:* Clifton Coll.; Clare Coll., Cambridge. MA 1945; PhD 1950; ScD Cantab 1967. Air Defence Research and Development Establishment, 1941-45 (first 3cm ground radar, Doppler radar); Chalk River Laboratories, 1945-46; Research Student, Cavendish Lab.,

Cambridge, 1946-49; Auckland Univ. Coll., NZ, 1950-57; attached AERE, 1955; CERN, Geneva, 1957-67 (muon g-2 experiment); Dean, RMCS, Shrivenham, 1967-82. Vis. Lectr, Univ. of Bristol, 1965-66; Vis. Scientist, CERN, 1967- (muon storage ring, tests of relativity); Vis. Prof., Swiss Inst. of Nuclear Research, 1976-77. Rep. NZ at UN Conf. on Atomic Energy for Peaceful Purposes, 1955. Governor: Clifton Coll.; Welbeck Coll.; Mem. Court, Univ. of Bath. Hon. Mem., Instn of Royal Engineers. FInstP. Hughes Medal, Royal Soc., 1980. *Publications:* Elements of Pulse Circuits, 1955; Progress in Nuclear Techniques and Instrumentation, Vol. I, 1966, Vol. II, 1967, Vol. III 1968; scientific papers on nuclear physics, electronics, high energy particle physics, wave energy. *Recreations:* gliding (FAI gold and diamond); ski-ing, windsurfing, gardening. *Address:* Carswell Barn, Carswell Marsh, near Faringdon, Oxon SN7 8JN. *T:* Buckland 238.

FARLEY, Prof. Martyn Graham, CEng, FRAeS, FIMechE, FIProdE; CBIM; Professor and Head of Management Sciences Department, Royal Military College of Science, Shrivenham, since 1975; *b* 27 Oct. 1924; *s* of Herbert Booth Farley and Hilda Gertrude (*née* Hendey); *m* 1948, Freda Laugharne; two *s* one *d. Educ:* Merchant Venturers Tech. Coll., Bristol; Bristol Aeroplane Co. Tech. Coll. CEng, FRAeS 1968; FIMechE 1969; FIProdE 1975; CBIM 1980. Engine Div., Bristol Aeroplane Co.: Design Apprentice, 1939-45; Engine Design, 1945-46; Develt Engr, 1946-51; Bristol Aero Engines Ltd: Sen. Designer, Gas Turbine Office, 1951-55; Asst Chief Develt Engr, 1955-59; Bristol Siddeley Engines: Asst Chief Mech. Engr, 1959-62; Chief Develt Engr, Small Engines Div., 1962-65, Chief Engr, 1965-67; Small Engines Div., Rolls-Royce: Chief Engr, 1967-68; Gen. Works Manager, 1968-72; Manufg and Prodn Dir, 1972-74; HQ Exec. to Vice-Chm. of Rolls-Royce (1971) Ltd, 1974-75. Chm., British Management Data Foundn, 1978-. Royal Aeronautical Society: Mem. Council, 1972-; Vice Pres., 1980-; Pres. Elect 1982; Dir, Aeronautical Trusts, 1975-. Vice President: Instn of Indust. Engrs, 1981; IProdE, 1982-83 (Mem. Council, 1973-, Chm. Council, 1978-80); Chm., Alliance of Manufg and Management Orgns, 1981-; Member: Chartered Engr Bd, CEI, 1977-; Sen. Awards Cttee, CGLI; Court, Brunel Univ., 1977-80, Loughborough Univ., 1977-, and Cranfield Inst. of Technol., 1977-. Hon. CGIA, 1981; Hon. Fellow, Indian IProdE, 1979; Hon. Member: Amer. Inst. of Indust. Managers, 1979; Australian Inst. of Indust. Engrs, 1981. Mem., Co. of Coachmakers and Coach Harness Makers. Internat. Archimedes Award, Amer. Soc. of Prof. Engrs, 1979; Internat. Award, LA Council of Engrs and Scientists, 1981. *Publications:* various articles and technical pubns; proc. conferences. *Address:* Royal Military College of Science, Shrivenham, Swindon, Wilts SN6 8LA. *T:* Shrivenham 782551, ext. 592. *Club:* Athenæum.

FARMAR, Hugh William, MVO 1973; Clerk to the Drapers' Company, 1952-73; Member of the Court of the Company since 1974; Governor (Treasurer 1952-73), Queen Mary College, University of London, Hon. Fellow, 1967; *b* 6 June 1908; *o s* of late Col H. M. Farmar, CMG, DSO, and Violet, *y d* of late Sir William Dalby and Hyacinthe Wellesley; *m* 1944, Constantia, *o d* of late Rt Hon. Sir Horace Rumbold, 9th Bt, GCB, and late Etheldred, Lady Rumbold, CBE; two *s. Educ:* Eton; Balliol Coll., Oxford. 2nd class clerk, Charity Commn, 1937; RAFVR, 1939-46 (on staff, Resident Minister, Accra, 1942-43; Asst Private Sec. to Sec. of State for Air 1945-46). Principal clerk, Charity Commn, 1946. Hon. LLD William and Mary Coll., Virginia, 1968. *Publications:* The Cottage in the Forest, 1949; A Regency Elopement, 1969; articles and broadcasts on travel and country subjects. *Recreations:* country pursuits. *Address:* Wasing Old Rectory, Aldermaston, Reading, Berks. *T:* Tadley 4873. *Clubs:* Brooks's, Pratt's.

See also Sir H. Anthony Rumbold, Bt, Lord Swinfen.

FARMBROUGH, Rt. Rev. David John; see Bedford, Bishop Suffragan of.

FARMER, Prof. Edward Desmond; Louis Cohen Professor of Dental Surgery, since 1957, Director of Post-Graduate Dental Studies, 1972-77, Dean of the Faculty of Medicine, since 1977 and Pro-Vice-Chancellor, 1967-70, University of Liverpool; *b* 15 April 1917; *s* of late S. R. and L. M. Farmer; *m* 1942, Mary Elwood Little; one *s* two *d. Educ:* Newcastle-under-Lyme High Sch.; Univ. of Liverpool (1936-41); Queens' Coll., Cambridge (1948-50). MA Cantab, 1955; MDS Liverpool, 1951; FDSRCS 1952; MRCPath 1967, FRCPath 1968; Hon. FRCR 1981. RNVR, Surgeon Lieut (D), 1942-45; Lectr in Parodontal Diseases, Univ. of Liverpool, 1950-57; Nuffield Fellow, 1948-50. Hon. Cons. Dent. Surg. to Bd of Govs of United Liverpool Hosps and Liverpool AHA (Teaching), formerly Liverpool Regional Hosp. Bd. Member Council: Brit. Soc. of Periodontology, 1954-59 (Pres. 1957-58); RSM, Odonto. Sect., 1965-68. Member: Central Cttee and Exec., Hosp. Dental Service, 1964-76; Negotiating Cttee of Central Cttee for Hosp. Medical Services, 1968-76; Bd of Govs, United Liverpool Hosps, 1968-71; UGC Dental Sect., 1968-77; Conf. and Exec., Dental Post-Grad. Deans, 1972-77; Cttee of Dental Teachers and Res. Workers Gp, BDA, 1974-79; Liverpool AHA(T) (and Chm., Regional Dental Cttee), 1975-77; RHA, 1977; Faculty of Dental Surgery, RCS, 1974-; Dental Cttee of Medical Defence Union; Council, Medical Insurance Agency; Exec., Teaching Hospitals Assoc.; Chm., Commn of Dental Educn, Fedn Dentaire Internat., 1977-79 (Vice-Chm., 1974-77); Alternate, Dental Adv. Cttee to EEC, 1980-; President: NW Br. BDA, 1967-68; Hospitals' Gp, BDA, 1972-73; Assoc. for Dental Educn in Europe, 1976-78; British Soc. of Oral Medicine, 1982-83; Pres.-elect, Odontological Section, RSM, 1982-83. *Publications:* (with F. E. Lawton) Stones' Oral and Dental Diseases, 5th edn, 1966; papers in

Proceedings Royal Society Med., Jl of Gen. Microbiology, Brit. Med. Jl, Dental Practitioner; Internat. Dental Jl. *Recreations:* golf, gardening, painting and enjoyment of the countryside. *Address:* Heath Moor, Beacon Lane, Heswall, Merseyside L60 0DG. *T:* 051-342 3179.

FARMER, Frank Reginald, OBE 1967; FRS 1981; *b* 18 Dec. 1914; *s* of Frank Henry Farmer and Minnie Godson; *m* 1939, Betty Smart; one *s* two *d. Educ:* St John's Coll., Cambridge (BA). Kestner Evaporator & Engineering Co., 1936-46; Director, Safety Reliability Directorate, Atomic Energy Authority (formerly Dept of Atomic Energy), 1947-79, retired. Editor, Reliability Engineering, 1980-. FInstP 1965; Hon. FSE 1974; Foreign Associate, Nat. Acad. of Engineers, USA, 1980. Churchill Gold Medal, 1974. *Publication:* Nuclear Reactor Safety, 1977. *Recreations:* golf, books. *Address:* The Long Wood, Lyons Lane, Appleton, Warrington WA4 5ND. *T:* Warrington 62503.

FARMER, Sir George; *see* Farmer, Sir L. G. T.

FARMER, Hugh Robert Macdonald, CB 1967; *b* 3 Dec. 1907; *s* of late Charles Edward Farmer and late Emily (*née* Randolph); *m* 1st, 1934, Penelope Frances (*d* 1963), *d* of late Capt. Evelyn Boothby, RN; one *s* three *d* ; 2nd, 1966, Jean, widow of Peter Bluett Winch. *Educ:* Cheam Sch.; Eton Coll.; New Coll., Oxford. House of Commons: Asst Clerk, 1931; Sen. Clerk, 1943; Clerk of Private Bills and Taxing Officer, and Examr of Petitions for Private Bills, 1958-60; Clerk of Cttees, 1960-65; Clerk/Administrator, 1965-72, retired 1972. *Recreations:* golf, gardening. *Address:* Grayswood Cottage, Haslemere, Surrey. *T:* Haslemere 3129. *Club:* MCC.

FARMER, Sir (Lovedin) George (Thomas), Kt 1968; LLD, MA, FCA, JDipMA; Coordinator, Rover and Triumph, 1972-73; Chairman: Rover Co. Ltd, 1963-73; Zenith Carburettor Co. Ltd, 1973-77; *b* 13 May 1908; *m* 1st, 1938, Editha Mary Fisher (*d* 1980); no *c* ; 2nd, 1980, Muriel Gwendoline Mercer Pinfold. *Educ:* Oxford High Sch. 2nd Vice-Chm. and Mem. Adv. Cttee, Metalurgica de Santa Ana, Madrid, 1963-74; Dep. Chm., British Leyland Motor Corp., 1972-73; Director: Empresa Nacional de Automcamiones, 1968-73; ATV Network Ltd, 1968-75; Rea Brothers (Isle of Man) Ltd, 1976-. President: Birmingham Chamber of Commerce, 1960-61; Soc. of Motor Manufrs and Traders, 1962-64 (Dep. Pres., 1964-65; Chm., Exec. Cttee, 1968-72); Past Member: Advisory Council, ECGD (Board of Trade); UK Committee of Federation of Commonwealth and British Chambers of Commerce; Past Vice-Pres., West Midlands Engineering Employers' Assoc.; Governor, Chm. Finance Cttee, Dep. Chm. Executive Council (Chm., 1966-75), Royal Shakespeare Theatre; Pres., Loft Theatre, Leamington Spa. Pro-Chancellor, Birmingham Univ., 1966-75; Hon. LLD Birmingham, 1975. Past Pres., Automobile Golfing Soc. Mem., Worshipful Co. of Coach and Coach Harness Makers. *Recreations:* theatre, golf, fishing. *Address:* Longridge, The Chase, Ballakillowey, Colby, Isle of Man. *T:* Port St Mary 832603. *Club:* Royal and Ancient (St Andrews).

FARMER, Robert Frederick; General Secretary, Institute of Journalists, since 1962; Member of Council, Media Society, since 1982 (Secretary, 1973-82); *b* 19 Aug. 1922; *s* of Frederick Leonard Farmer and Gladys Farmer (*née* Winney); *m* 1958, Anne Walton. *Educ:* Saltley Grammar Sch., Birmingham. FCIS. Served War of 1939-45, Royal Armoured Corps, 1941-52 (commissioned 3rd Carabiniers, despatches, Burma campaign). Secretariat: Instn of Plant Engineers, 1952-59; Instn of Civil Engineers, 1959-62. Consultative Mem., Press Council, 1962-; Mem., Cttee on Defamation, 1971-75. *Recreations:* cookery, walking, archaeology. *Address:* Institute of Journalists, Bedford Chambers, Covent Garden, WC2E 8HA. *T:* 01-836 6541. *Club:* National Liberal.

FARNCOMBE, Charles Frederick, CBE 1977; FRAM; Musical Director: Handel Opera Society, since 1955; Royal Court Theatre, Drottningholm, Sweden, since 1970; *b* 29 July 1919; *o s* of Harold and Eleanor Farncombe, both of London; *m* 1963, Sally Mae (*née* Felps), Riverside, Calif, USA; one *d. Educ:* London Univ., 1936-40 (Archibald Dawnay Scholarship in Civil Engrg, 1936) (BSc Hons (Eng) 1940); Royal Sch. of Church Music, 1947-48; Royal Academy of Music, 1948-51 (RAM, Mann Prize). Civil Engr to John Mowlem & Co, 1940-42. Served War, 1942-47, as Captain in REME, in 21st Army Gp. Free Lance Conductor; formed Handel Opera Soc. (with encouragement of late Prof. Dent), 1955; Chief Conductor, Royal Court Theatre, Drottningholm, Sweden, 1970-. AMICE, 1945 (resigned later); FRAM 1963 (ARAM 1962). Hon DMus Columbus Univ., Ohio, USA, 1959. Gold Medal of the Friends of Drottningholm, 1971; Hon. Fellow Royal Swedish Academy of Music, 1972. *Recreations:* cajoling singers, swimming, cottage on Offa's Dyke. *Address:* Box 153, 17011 Drottningholm, Sweden.

FARNDALE, Lt-Gen. Martin Baker, CB 1980; Commander 1st (British) Corps, BAOR, since April 1983; *b* Alberta, Canada, 6 Jan. 1929; *s* of Alfred Farndale and Margaret Louise Baker; *m* 1955, Margaret Anne Buckingham; one *s. Educ:* Yorebridge Grammar Sch., Yorks. Joined Indian Army, 1946; RMA, Sandhurst, 1947; commnd RA, 1948; Egypt, 1949; 1st RHA, 1950-54 (Germany from 1952); HQ 7 Armoured Div., 1954-57; Staff College, 1959; HQ 17 Gurkha Div., Malaya, 1960-62; MoD, 1962-64; comd Chestnut Troop 1st RHA, Germany and Aden, 1964-66; Instructor, Staff Coll., 1966-69; comd 1st RHA, UK, N Ire., Germany, 1969-71; MoD, 1971-73; comd 7th Armoured Bde, 1973-75. Dir, Public Relations (Army), 1976-78; Dir of Mil.

Ops, MoD (Army), 1978-80; Comdr 2nd Armoured Div., BAOR, 1980-83. Colonel Commandant; Army Air Corps, 1980-; RA, 1982-. *Publications:* Story of Royal Artillery 1914-18, 1976; articles for British Army Rev. and Jl RA. *Recreations:* military history, gardening. *Address:* c/o Lloyds Bank, Cox's and King's Branch, 6 Pall Mall, SW1. *Club:* East India, Devonshire, Sports and Public Schools.

FARNHAM, 12th Baron, *cr* 1756; **Barry Owen Somerset Maxwell;** Bt (Nova Scotia) 1627; Director, Brown, Shipley & Co. Ltd (Merchant Bankers), since 1959; Chairman: Brown, Shipley Holdings Ltd, since 1976; Avon Rubber Co., since 1978; *b* 7 July 1931; *s* of Hon. Somerset Arthur Maxwell, MP (died of wounds received in action, 1942), and Angela Susan (*d* 1953), *o d* of late Capt. Marshall Owen Roberts; *S* grandfather 1957; *m* 1959, Diana Marion, *er d* of Nigel Gunnis; two adopted *d. Educ:* Eton; Harvard Univ. *Heir: b* Hon. Simon Kenlis Maxwell [*b* 12 Dec. 1933; *m* 1964, Karol Anne, *d* of Maj.-Gen. G. E. Prior-Palmer, CB, DSO, and Katherine Edith Bibby; two *s* one *d* (of whom one *s* one *d* are twins)]. *Address:* 11 Earl's Court Gardens, SW5; Farnham, Co. Cavan. *Clubs:* Boodle's; Kildare Street and University (Dublin).

FARNHILL, Rear-Adm. Kenneth Haydn, CB 1968; OBE 1945; Secretary, Defence, Press and Broadcasting Committee, 1973-80; *b* 13 April 1913; *s* of late H. Haydn Farnhill, Bedford; *m* 1938, Helen May, *d* of late W. Houghton, Southsea; one *s* one *d. Educ:* Bedford. Joined RN, 1930. Served 1939-45: Home Fleet, Admty, Eastern Fleet. Sec. to Controller of Navy, 1953-56; Captain, RN Supply Sch., 1958-59; IDC 1960; Dir of Management and Support of Intelligence, MoD, 1966-69. Comdr 1948; Captain 1957; Rear-Adm. 1966; retd 1969. *Address:* 1 Christchurch Gardens, Widley, Portsmouth, Hants. *T:* Cosham 377187.

FARNINGHAM, Alexander Ian, DSC; Managing Director, Industrial Relations and Personnel, British Shipbuilders, 1977-80; *b* 3 Nov. 1923; *s* of Alexander Farningham and Janet Leask Broadley; *m* 1949, Lois Elizabeth Halse (marr. diss. 1981); one *s* two *d* ; *m* 1981, Susan Wyllie. *Educ:* Glebelands Primary Sch., Dundee; Morgan Academy, Dundee; St Andrews Univ. (MA). *Recreations:* walking, birdwatching, photography, sailing. *Address:* South Lodge, Whitehouse, near Tarbert, Argyll PA29 6XR. *T:* Whitehouse (Argyll) 221. *Club:* Royal Northern and Clyde Yacht (Rhu).

FARNSWORTH, John Windsor; Chairman, East Midlands Economic Planning Board, 1965-72; *b* 5 May 1912; *yr s* of late Arthur Claude and Annie Farnsworth, Derby; *m* 1938, Betty Mary Bristow; two *s. Educ:* Hanley High Sch.; Balliol Coll., Oxford; Univ. of Birmingham. Asst Comr, Nat. Savings Cttee, 1935; transf. to Min. of Nat. Insurance, 1948; Regional Controller, N Midland Region, Min. of Pensions and Nat. Insurance, 1961; transf. to Dept of Economic Affairs, 1965; Min. of Housing and Local Govt, later Dept of the Environment, 1969. Pres., Nottingham and E Mids Group, Royal Inst. of Public Administration, 1966-68. *Recreations:* painting, foreign travel. *Address:* 143 Melton Road, West Bridgford, Nottingham. *T:* Nottingham 231937.

FARQUHAR, Charles Don Petrie, JP; DL; Area Manager, Community Industry, since 1972; engineer; *b* 4 Aug. 1937; *s* of late William Sandeman Farquhar and Annie Preston Young Farquhar; *m* ; two *d. Educ:* Liff Road and St Michael's Primary Schs, Dundee; Stobswell Secondary Sch., Dundee. Served with Royal Engineers (Trng NCO); subseq. supervisory staff, plant engrg. Mem., Labour Party Parly Panel; City Councillor, Dundee, 1965-75 (ex-Convener, Museums, Works and Housing Cttees). JP Dundee, 1974; Lord Provost and Lord Lieutenant of City of Dundee, 1975-77; DL Dundee, 1977. *Recreations:* fresh-water angling, gardening, caravanning, numismatics, do-it-yourself. *Address:* 68 Foggyley Gardens, Dundee DD2 3LU. *T:* Dundee 610707.

FARQUHAR, Lt-Col Sir Peter (Walter), 6th Bt, *cr* 1796; DSO 1943 (and Bar 1944); OBE 1982; JP; 16th/5th Lancers; RAC Reserve of Officers, retired; *b* 8 Oct. 1904; *s* of 5th Bt and Violet (*d* 1959), *d* of Col Charles Seymour Corkran, late Grenadier Guards; *S* father, 1918; *m* 1937, Elizabeth Evelyn, *d* of late Francis Cecil Albert Hurt; three *s. Educ:* Eton; RMC, Sandhurst. Served War of 1939-45, France, Middle East and Italy (wounded twice, DSO and Bar). Pres., Swindon Council of Boys' Clubs; Vice-Pres., Nat. Assoc. of Boys' Clubs. Joint-Master of Portman Hounds, 1947-59. JP Dorset, 1955. *Heir: s* Michael Fitzroy Henry Farquhar [*b* 29 June 1938; *m* 1963, Veronica Geraldine, *e d* of Patrick Hornidge, Newton Ferrers, and of Mrs M. F. L. Beebee, Walton, Radnorshire; two *s*]. *Address:* West Kington House, Chippenham, Wiltshire SN14 7JE. *T:* Castle Combe 782331. *See also* Baron Dulverton.

FARQUHARSON of Invercauld, Captain Alwyne Arthur Compton, MC 1944; JP; Head of Clan Farquharson; *b* 1 May 1919; *er s* of late Major Edward Robert Francis Compton, JP, DL, Newby Hall, Ripon, and Isle of Mull, and Sylvia, *y d* of A. H. Farquharson; recognised by Lord Lyon King of Arms as Laird of Invercauld (16th Baron of Invercauld; *S* aunt 1941), also as Chief of name of Farquharson and Head of Clan, since 1949; assumed (surname) Compton as a third fore-name and assumed surname of Farquharson of Invercauld, by warrant granted in Lyon Court, Edinburgh, 1949; *m* 1949, Frances Strickland Lovell, *d* of Robert Pollard Oldham, Seattle, Washington, USA. *Educ:* Eton; Magdalen Coll., Oxford. Joined Royal Scots Greys, 1940. Served War, 1940-45, Palestine, N Africa, Italy, France (wounded); Captain

1943. County Councillor, Aberdeenshire, 1949-75, JP 1951. *Address:* Invercauld, Braemar, Aberdeenshire. *T:* Braemar 213. *Club:* Naval and Military.
See also R. E. J. Compton.

FARQUHARSON, Hon. Sir Donald (Henry), Kt 1981; **Hon. Mr Justice Farquharson;** Judge of the High Court of Justice, Queen's Bench Division, since 1981; *b* 1928; *yr s* of Charles Anderson Farquharson, Logie Coldstone, Aberdeenshire, and Florence Ellen Fox; *m* 1960, Helen Mary, *er d* of Comdr H. M. Simpson, RN (retd), Abbots Brow, Kirkby Lonsdale, Westmorland; three *s* (one *d* decd). *Educ:* Royal Commercial Travellers Sch.; Keble Coll., Oxford (MA). Called to Bar, Inner Temple, 1952; Bencher, 1979. QC 1972. A Recorder of the Crown Court, 1972-81. Dep. Chm., Essex QS, 1970. A Legal Assessor to GMC and GDC, 1978-81. *Recreations:* opera, walking. *Address:* (home) Kumra Lodge, Kelvedon Hatch, Brentwood, Essex. *T:* Coxtie Green 72213; Royal Courts of Justice, Strand, WC2A 2LL.

FARQUHARSON, Sir James (Robbie), KBE 1960 (CBE 1948; OBE 1944); retired, and is now farming; *b* 1 Nov. 1903; *s* of Frank Farquharson, Cortachy, Angus, Scotland, and Agnes Jane Robbie; *m* 1933, Agnes Binny Graham; two *s. Educ:* Royal Technical College, Glasgow; Glasgow Univ. BSc Glasgow 1923. Asst Engineer, LMS Railway, 1923-25; Asst Engineer, Kenya and Uganda Railway, 1925-33; Senior Asst Engineer, Kenya and Uganda Railway, 1933-37; Asst to Gen. Manager, Tanganyika Railways, 1937-41; Chief Engineer, Tanganyika Railways, 1941-45; General Manager, Tanganyika Railways, 1945-48; Deputy General Manager, East African Railways, 1948-52; Gen. Manager, Sudan Railways, 1952-57; Gen. Manager, East African Railways and Harbours, 1957-61; Asst Crown Agent and Engineer-in-Chief of Crown Agents for Overseas Governments and Administrations, 1961-65. Chm., Millbank Technical Services Ordnance Ltd, 1973-75; Mem., Exec. Cttee, Scottish Council for Develt and Industry. *Publication:* Tanganyika Transport, 1944. *Recreation:* cricket. *Address:* Kinclune, by Kirriemuir, Angus, Scotland. *T:* Kingoldrum 210. *Club:* Nairobi (Kenya).

FARQUHARSON, Robert Alexander, CMG 1975; HM Diplomatic Service, retired; *b* 26 May 1925; *s* of late Captain J. P. Farquharson, DSO, OBE, RN, and late Mrs Farquharson (*née* Prescott-Decie); *m* 1955, Joan Elizabeth, *o d* of Sir (William) Ivo Mallet, *qv* ; three *s* one *d. Educ:* Harrow; King's Coll., Cambridge. Served with RNVR, 1943-46. Joined Foreign (now Diplomatic) Service, 1949; 3rd Sec., Moscow, 1950; FO, 1952; 2nd Sec., Bonn, 1955; 1st Sec., Panama, 1958; Paris, 1960; FO, 1964; Counsellor, Dir of British Trade Develt, S Africa, 1967; Minister, Madrid, 1971; Consul-Gen., San Francisco, 1973; Ambassador to Yugoslavia, 1977-80. *Address:* The Old Rectory, Tollard Royal, Wilts. *Clubs:* Naval and Military, Flyfishers'.

FARQUHARSON-LANG, William Marshall, CBE 1970; Member, National Health Service (Scotland) Staff Commission, 1972-77; *b* 2 July 1908; *s* of late Very Rev. Marshall B. Lang, DD, sometime Moderator, Gen. Assembly of Church of Scotland, and Mary Eleanor Farquharson Lang; *m* 1937, Sheila Clive Parker; one *d. Educ:* Edinburgh Acad.; Edinburgh Univ. (MA); London Univ. Sudan Political Service (Educn), 1931-55; Dep. Dir of Educn (Sudan Govt), 1950-55. Mem., 1959, Chm., 1965-72, NE Regional Hosp. Board; Vice-Chm., Scottish Health Services Council, 1964-66; Chm., Cttee on Admin. Practice of Hosp. Bds in Scotland, 1966; Rector's Assessor and Mem., Aberdeen Univ. Court, 1965-76. Mem., Kincardine CC, 1956-59. Laird of Finzean, Aberdeenshire, 1938-61. Hon. LLD Aberdeen 1972. Coronation Medal, 1953. Sudan Republic Medal, 1977. *Recreations:* fishing, country activities. *Address:* Balnahard House, Finzean, Aberdeenshire. *T:* Feughside 270. *Clubs:* Royal Northern (Aberdeen); New (Edinburgh).

FARR, Dennis Larry Ashwell, Hon. DLitt; FRSA, FMA; Director, Courtauld Institute Galleries, since 1980; *b* 3 April 1929; *s* of late Arthur William Farr and late Helen Eva Farr (*née* Ashwell); *m* 1959, Diana Pullein-Thompson (writer), *d* of Captain H. J. Pullein-Thompson, MC, and Joanna (*née* Cannan); one *s* one *d. Educ:* Luton Grammar Sch.; Courtauld Inst. of Art, London Univ. (BA, MA). Asst Witt Librarian, Courtauld Inst. of Art, 1952-54; Asst Keeper, Tate Gallery, 1954-64; Curator, Paul Mellon Collection, Washington, DC, 1965-66; Sen. Lectr in Fine Art, and Dep. Keeper, University Art Collections, Univ. of Glasgow, 1967-69; Dir, City Museums and Art Gallery, Birmingham, 1969-80. Fred Cook Meml Lecture, RSA, 1974. Hon. Art Adviser, Calouste Gulbenkian Foundation, 1969-73; Member: British Council Fine Arts Adv. Cttee, 1971-80; Wright Cttee on Provincial Museums and Galleries, 1971-73; Museums Assoc. Council, 1971-74 (Vice-Pres., 1978-79, 1980-81; Pres., 1979-80); Art Panel, Arts Council, 1972-77; ICOM(UK) Exec. Bd, 1976-; Cttee, Victorian Soc., 1980; Exec. Cttee, Assoc. of Art Historians, 1981- (Chm. of Assoc., 1983-); History of Art and Design and Complementary Studies Bd, CNAA, 1981-; Trustee, Birmingham Mus. and Art Gall. Appeal Fund, 1980- (Chm. Trustees, 1978-80). FRSA 1970; FMA 1972. Hon. DLitt Birmingham, 1981. JP Birmingham, 1977-80. *Publications:* William Etty, 1958; Catalogue of the Modern British School Collection, Tate Gallery (with M. Chamot and M. Butlin), 1964; British Sculpture since 1945, 1965; New Painting in Glasgow, 1968; Pittura Inglese 1660-1840, 1975; English Art 1870-1940, 1978; (contrib.) British Sculpture in the Twentieth Century, 1981; articles in: Apollo, Burlington Magazine, TLS, etc. *Recreations:* riding, reading, foreign travel. *Address:* 12 Blandford Road, Bedford Park, W4 1DU. *T:* 01-995 6400; The Cottage, Longborough, Moreton-in-Marsh, Glos GL56 0QD. *Clubs:*

Athenæum, Institute of Contemporary Arts.
See also Denis Cannan.

FARR, John Arnold; MP (C) Harborough Division of Leicestershire since 1959; Member of Lloyd's; *b* 25 Sept. 1922; *er s* of late Capt. John Farr, JP, and Mrs M. A. Farr, JP; *m* 1960, Susan Ann, *d* of Sir Leonard Milburn, 3rd Bt, and of Joan Lady Milburn, Guyzance Hall, Acklington, Northumberland; two *s. Educ:* Harrow. RN, 1940-46 serving in Mediterranean and S Atlantic; Lieut-Comdr RNVR. Executive Dir, Home Brewery and Apollo Productions Ltd, 1950-55. Contested Ilkeston, General Election, 1955. Secretary: Cons. Parly Agric. Cttee, 1970-74; Parly Conservation Cttee, 1972-. Member: Exec. Cttee, UK Branch CPA, 1972-74; UK Delegn to WEU and Council of Europe, 1973-78 (Vice-Chm., Cttee on Agric.); Chairman: Anglo-Irish Parly Gp, 1977-80; Parly Knitwear Ind. Gp, 1980-; British-Zimbabwe Parly Gp, 1980-. Vice-Pres., Shooting Sports Trust, 1972-; Chm., British Shooting Sports Council, 1977-. *Recreations:* cricket and shooting. *Address:* Shortwood House, Lamport, Northants. *T:* Maidwell 260; 11 Vincent Square, Westminster, SW1; Tanrago, Beltra, Co. Sligo. *T:* Sligo 72106. *Clubs:* Boodle's, MCC.

FARR, Air Vice-Marshal Peter Gerald Desmond, CB 1968; OBE 1952; DFC 1942; retired; Director, Brain Research Trust, since 1973; *b* 26 Sept. 1917; *s* of late Gerald Farr and Mrs Farr (*née* Miers); *m* 1949, Rosemarie, *d* of late R. S. Haward; two *s* one *d. Educ:* Tonbridge Sch. Commnd in RAF, 1937; served War of 1939-45, Middle East, India and Burma; OC, No. 358 Sqdn, 1944-45; OC, RAF Pegu, 1945-46; OC, 120 Sqdn, 1950-51; Dep. Dir, Jt Anti-Submarine sch., 1952-54; OC, RAF Idris, 1954-55; Directing Staff, Jt Services Staff Coll., 1959; SASO, Malta, 1960-63; OC, RAF Kinloss, 1963-64; Air Officer Administration: RAF Germany, 1964-68; Strike Comd, 1969-72. *Recreations:* golf, fishing, music. *Address:* c/o Lloyds Bank, Great Missenden, Bucks. *Club:* Royal Air Force.

FARRANCE, Roger Arthur; Member, Electricity Council, since 1979; *b* 10 Nov. 1933; *s* of Ernest Thomas Farrance and Alexandra Hilda May (*née* Finch); *m* 1956, Kathleen Sheila (*née* Owen); one *d. Educ:* Trinity School of John Whitgift, Croydon; London School of Economics (BScEcon). FIPM; MBIM. HM Inspector of Factories, Manchester, Doncaster and Walsall, 1956-64; Asst Sec., West of England Engineering Employers' Assoc., Bristol, 1964-67; Industrial Relations and Personnel Manager, Foster Wheeler John Brown Boilers Ltd, 1967-68; Dep. Director, Coventry and District Engineering Employers' Assoc., also Coventry Management Trng Centre, 1968-75; Dep. Industrial Relations Adviser (Negotiating), Electricity Council, 1975-76; Industrial Relations Adviser, Electricity Council, 1976-79. *Recreations:* photography, music. *Address:* 126 Somerset Road, Wimbledon, SW19 5HP. *T:* 01-946 9650. *Club:* Royal Automobile.

FARRANDS, Dr John Law, CB 1982; FTS, CEng; FInstP, FAIP; Director, Interscan Australia, since 1980; Chairman, Australian Institute of Marine Science, since 1982; Councillor, National Energy Research Council, since 1978; consultant to companies, since 1982; *b* 11 March 1921; *s* of Harold Rawlings Farrands and Hilda Elizabeth (*née* Bray); *m* 1946; three *s* one *d* (and one *s* decd). *Educ:* Melbourne Univ. (BSc); London Univ. (PhD); Imperial Coll. of Science and Technol. (DIC, CEng). FTS 1976; FInstP 1957; FAIP 1962. Served RAEME, AIF, 1941 (Captain). Scientific Adviser to Mil. Bd, 1957; Chief Supt, Aeronautical Res. Labs, 1967; Chief Def. Scientist, 1971; Permanent Head, Dept of Science and Environment, later Dept of Science and Technol., 1977-82. Leader, Aust. Delegn to UNCSTD, 1980. *Publications:* (jtly) Changing Disease Patterns and Human Behaviour, 1981; articles in scientific and engrg jls. *Recreations:* fishing, music. *Address:* 20 The Boulevard, Glen Waverley, Vic 3150, Australia. *T:* (03) 232-8195. *Clubs:* Commonwealth, Canberra (Canberra).

FARRANT, Maj.-Gen. Ralph Henry, CB 1964; retd; Chairman, Royal National Lifeboat Institution, 1975-79; *b* 2 Feb. 1909; *s* of late Henry Farrant, MICE, Rye, Sussex; *m* 1932, Laura Bonella, *d* of late Lieut-Col G. Clifford M. Hall, CMG, DSO; two *d. Educ:* Rugby; RMA, Woolwich. 2nd Lieut, RA 1929; Field and Mountain Artillery till 1938. War of 1939-45: Tech. Appts in Min. of Defence (1) and HQ, MEF, 3rd British Inf. Div., 1944. Lieut-Col 1950, Min. of Supply; Col 1954; Brig. 1957; Dir of Munitions, Brit. Jt Services Mission, Washington, 1955-58; Sen. Mil. Officer, Armament R&D Estabt, 1958-61; Maj.-Gen. 1961; Vice-Pres., Ordnance Board, 1961-63; Pres. of Ordnance Bd, War Office, 1963-64. Yachtsman's Award, RYA, 1973. *Recreation:* sailing. *Address:* King's Acre, Grange Road, Wareham, Dorset. *Clubs:* Army and Navy, Royal Yacht Squadron, Royal Ocean Racing, Royal Artillery Yacht.

FARRAR, Rex Gordon, MVO 1975; HM Diplomatic Service; Consul-General and Director of Trade Promotion, Osaka, Japan, since 1980; *b* 22 Aug. 1925; *s* of late John Percival Farrar and Ethel Florence Farrar (*née* Leader); *m* 1978, Masako (*née* Ikeda); one *d. Educ:* Latymer's Sch., Edmonton; London Univ. (BA Hons History). Served Royal Navy, 1944-47. Joined HM Diplomatic Service, 1947; served, New Orleans, 1953-57; Jakarta, 1960-63; Caracas, 1964-68; San Salvador, 1968-71; Tokyo, 1971-75; Rangoon, 1978-80. *Recreations:* golf, tennis, studying Japanese. *Address:* c/o Foreign and Commonwealth Office, SW1; 2 Lexham Garden Mews, Kensington W8. *T:* 01-370 7405; British Consulate-General, Hongkong Bank Building, 45 Awaji-machi, 4-chome, Higashi-ku, Osaka, Japan. *Club:* Kobe (Japan).

FARRAR-HOCKLEY, Gen. Sir Anthony Heritage, GBE 1982 (MBE 1957); KCB 1977; DSO 1953 and bar 1964; MC 1944; author (military history); Commander-in-Chief Allied Forces Northern Europe, 1979-82; ADC General to the Queen, 1981-83; *b* 8 April 1924; *s* of late Arthur Farrar-Hockley; *m* 1945, Margaret Bernadette Wells (*d* 1981); two *s* (and one *s* decd). *Educ:* Exeter Sch. War of 1939-45 (despatches, MC): enlisted under-age in ranks of The Gloucestershire Regt and served until Nov. 1942; commissioned into newly forming 1st Airborne Div., campaigning in Greece, Italy, S France, to 1945. Palestine, 1945-46; Korea, 1950-53; despatches, 1954; Cyprus and Port Said, 1956; Jordan, 1958; College Chief Instructor, RMA Sandhurst, 1959-61; commanded parachute bn in Persian Gulf and Radfan campaign, 1962-65; Principal Staff Officer to Dir of Borneo Ops, 1965-66; Comdr, 16 Parachute Bde, 1966-68; Defence Fellowship, Exeter Coll., Oxford, 1968-70 (BLitt); DPR (Army), 1970; Comdr, Land Forces, N Ireland, 1970-71; GOC 4th Div., 1971-73; Dir, Combat Development (Army), 1974-77; GOC SE District, 1977-79. Colonel Commandant: Prince of Wales's Div., 1974-80; Parachute Regt, 1977-; Col, The Gloucestershire Regt, 1978-. *Publications:* The Edge of the Sword, 1954; (ed) The Commander, 1957; The Somme, 1964; Death of an Army, 1968; Airborne Carpet, 1969; War in the Desert, 1969; General Student, 1973; Goughie: the Life of General Sir Hubert Gough, GCB, GCMG, KCVO, 1975. *Recreations:* cricket, badminton, sailing, walking. *Address:* Pye Barn, Moulsford, Oxon. *Club:* Savage.

FARRELL, Arthur Acheson, CB 1962; *b* Portadown, 29 July 1898; *s* of late Arthur T. Farrell, Portadown, solicitor, and of Ellen Moorcroft, *d* of late Hugh Anderson, Belfast; *m* 1st, 1925, Margaret Kerr (*d* 1945), *d* of Archibald Irwin, JP, Belfast; three *s* ; 2nd, 1954, Wilhelmina (*d* 1973) (*sister* of 1st wife). *Educ:* Campbell Coll., Belfast; Trinity Coll., Dublin. Royal Artillery, 1917-19. Chartered Accountant, 1922; Registrar of Claims Tribunal, 1923; Civil Service, Northern Ireland: Ministry of: Finance, Asst Principal, 1924; Home Affairs, Dep. Principal, 1928, Principal, 1935, Asst Sec., 1939; Public Security, 1940; Commerce, 1945-58. Comptroller and Auditor-Gen. for Northern Ireland, 1959-63, retired. *Recreations:* photography, bowls, carpentry.

FARRELL, Arthur Denis, CMG 1970; *b* 27 Jan. 1906; *s* of Joseph Jessop Farrell, CBE; *m* 1953, Margaret Madeline (*née* Cox); one *s.* *Educ:* St Paul's Sch.; Balliol Coll., Oxford. Sixth Form (Classical) Master, Sedbergh Sch., 1929-30, Bradford Grammar Sch., 1930-36; called to the Bar, Middle Temple, 1937; Sixth Form (Classical) Master, Bedford Sch., 1939-41; served RAF, 1941-46. Squadron-Leader; Crown Counsel, Singapore, 1947-51: Legal Draftsman, Fedn of Malaya, 1951-56; Solicitor-Gen., Fedn of Malaya, 1956-58; QC 1957; Puisne Judge, Kenya, 1958-69 (Acting Chief Justice, 1968). Coronation Medal, 1953. *Recreations:* golf, photography, music. *Address:* 64 East Avenue, Bournemouth, Dorset. *T:* Bournemouth 761878.

FARRELL, James; Procurator Fiscal, South Strathclyde, Dumfries and Galloway (formerly Lanarkshire) at Airdrie, 1955-75; Solicitor; *s* of Thomas Farrell and Margaret Farrell (*née* Quigley); *m* 1952, Margaret Clare O'Brien; one *s* three *d. Educ:* Our Lady's High Sch., Motherwell; St Patrick's Coll., Armagh, N Ireland; Glasgow Univ. (BL). In private practice as a solicitor, prior to joining Procurator Fiscal Service of the Crown. In latter (and present) capacity, Prosecutor for the Crown in the Sheriff Court, leading evidence at inquiries, there, into circumstances of death, particularly in suspicious, sudden and unexplained circumstances, fatal accidents, and where the public interest generally is involved; precognition and preparation of cases for High Court of Justiciary, and investigation relating to estates where the Crown may have to intervene as Ultimus Haeres, etc. *Recreations:* golf, bridge, gardening, photography, motoring, walking. *Address:* Clairville, Belleisle Avenue, Uddingston, Glasgow G71 7AP. *T:* Uddingston 3385. *Club:* St Mungo's Academy FP Centenary (Glasgow).

FARRELL, M. J.; *see* Keane, M. N.

FARRELL, Timothy Robert Warwick; Organist, Liberal Jewish Synagogue, St John's Wood, since 1975; *b* 5 Oct. 1943; *m* 1975, Penelope Walmsley-Clark; one *s. Educ:* Diocesan Coll., Cape Town; Royal Coll. of Music, London, etc. FRCO, ARCM (piano and organ). Asst Organist, St Paul's, Knightsbridge, 1962-66; Asst Organist St Paul's Cath., 1966-67; Sub-organist, Westminster Abbey, 1967-74; Organ Tutor at Addington Palace, RSCM, 1966-73; Organist, Choirmaster and Composer, HM Chapels Royal, 1974-79. Broadcaster, gramophone records, etc. *Recreations:* golf, walking, sailing. *Address:* Didcroft, Toat, Pulborough, W Sussex RH20 1BZ.

FARRER, Brian Ainsworth; QC 1978; a Recorder of the Crown Court (Midland/Oxford Circuit) since 1974; *b* 7 April 1930; *s* of A. E. V. A. Farrer and Gertrude (*née* Hall); *m* 1960, Gwendoline Valerie (*née* Waddoup), JP; two *s* one *d. Educ:* King's Coll., Taunton; University Coll., London (LLB). Called to the Bar, Gray's Inn, 1957. Mem. Cttee, Normid Housing Assoc., 1977-. *Recreations:* golf, music, chess, bridge. *Address:* Shutt Cross House, Aldridge, West Midlands; Ardudwy Cottage, Ty Ardudwy, Aberdovey, Gwynedd. *Club:* Aberdovey Golf.

FARRER, Charles Matthew, CVO 1973; Private Solicitor to the Queen, since 1965; Partner in Messrs Farrer & Co, Solicitors, since 1959; *b* 3 Dec. 1929; *s* of Sir (Walter) Leslie Farrer, *qv*, and Hon. Lady Farrer; *m* 1962, Johanna Creszentia Maria Dorothea Bennhold; one *s* one *d. Educ:* Bryanston Sch.; Balliol Coll., Oxford (MA). Hon. Treasurer, British Inst. of Archaeology, Ankara. *Recreations:* travel, reading. *Address:* 6 Priory Avenue, Bedford Park, W4. *T:* 01-994 6052. *Club:* United Oxford & Cambridge University.

FARRER, Sir Leslie; *see* Farrer, Sir W. L.

FARRER, Margaret Irene, OBE 1970; Chairman of Central Midwives Board, 1973-79; *b* 23 Feb. 1914; *e d* of Alfred and Emblyn Farrer. *Educ:* Poltimore Coll., Exeter; UCH London. SRN, SCM, DN (London), MTD, RST. Midwifery Tutor, General Lying-in Hosp., 1942-49; Matron: St Mary's Hosp., Croydon, 1949-56; Forest Gate Hosp., 1956-71; Chief Nursing Officer, Thames Gp, 1971-74. Member: Central Midwives Bd, 1952-; Central Health Services Council, 1963-74; NE Metropolitan Regional Hosp. Bd, 1969-74; NE Thames Regional Health Authority, 1973-76; Editorial Bd, Midwife and Health Visitor; Hon. Treas., Royal Coll. of Midwives, 1967-76. *Recreations:* gardening, walking. *Address:* Coombe Brook, Dawlish, South Devon. *T:* Dawlish 863323.

FARRER, Sir (Walter) Leslie, KCVO 1948; solicitor (retired); *b* 30 Jan. 1900; 2nd *s* of late Bryan Farrer, Binnegar Hall, Wareham, Dorset; *m* 1926, Hon. Marjorie Laura Pollock (*d* 1981), *d* of 1st Viscount Hanworth; one *s* one *d. Educ:* Rugby; Balliol. Admitted a Solicitor, 1926; Partner Messrs Farrer & Co., 1927-64; Mem. Council of Law Soc., 1945-52; Mem. Disciplinary Cttee under Solicitors Acts, 1953-63. Private Solicitor to King George VI and to the Queen, 1937-64. Director, London Life Assoc. Ltd, 1942-80 (Pres., 1966-73). Pres. Selden Soc., 1955. Prime Warden, Fishmongers' Co., 1968-69. *Recreations:* reading and sight-seeing. *Address:* Charlwood Place Farm, Charlwood, Surrey. *T:* Norwood Hill 862413. *Club:* Travellers'.
    See also C. M. Farrer.

FARRER-BROWN, Leslie, CBE 1960; Consultant; Director: Nuffield Foundation, 1944-64; Alliance Building Society, since 1969 (Chairman, 1975-81); *b* 2 April 1904; *er s* of late Sydney and Annie Brown; *m* 1928, Doris Evelyn, *o d* of late Herbert Jamieson; two *s. Educ:* LSE (BSc Econ.), Hon. Fellow 1975; Gray's Inn (Barrister-at-Law, 1932). Asst Registrar, LSE, 1927-28; on Administrative Staff, Univ. of London, 1928-36; Sec., Central Midwives Bd, 1936-45; seconded to Min. of Health, 1941-44. Pres., Surrey and Sussex Rent Assessment Panel, 1965-76. Vice-President, Inst. of Race Relations, 1968-72; Royal Commonwealth Soc., 1969-. Sec., Interdepartmental Cttee on Med. Schs, 1942-44. Chairman: Malta Med. Services Commn, 1956; Highgate Juvenile Court, 1952-61; Highgate Court, 1961-65; Nat. Council of Social Service, 1960-73; Centre for Educational Television Overseas, 1962-70; Overseas Visual Aid Centre, 1958-70; Voluntary Cttee on Overseas Aid and Develt, 1965-76; Centre for Information on Language Teaching, 1966-72; Cttee for Res. and Develt in Modern Languages, 1964-70; Rhodesia Med. Sch. Cttee; Univ. of London Inst. of Child Health, 1966-76. Member: Colonial Adv. Med. Cttee, 1946-61; Colonial Social Science Res. Council, 1954-61; Med. Educn Cttee of UGC, 1945-52; Rating of Charities Cttee, 1958-59; Adv. Council, BBC, 1956-65; Court of Governors, LSE; Chm. Council and Sen. Pro-Chancellor, Univ. of Sussex, 1976-80. Trustee, Nuffield Provincial Hospitals Trust, 1955-67; UK Trustee, Commonwealth Foundn, 1966-. JP: Middx, 1947-65; East Sussex, 1966-81. Hon. FDSRCS. Hon. LLD: Birmingham; Witwatersrand; Sussex; Hon. DSc Keele. *Publication:* (jt) A Short Textbook on Public Health and Social Services. *Recreations:* travel, painting. *Address:* Dale House, Keere Street, Lewes, East Sussex. *Clubs:* Athenæum, Royal Commonwealth Society.

FARRIMOND, Herbert Leonard, CBE 1977; part time Member, British Waterways Board, since 1980; Chairman, H. L. Farrimond & Associates Ltd, since 1978; *b* 4 Oct. 1924; *s* of late George and Jane Farrimond, Newcastle upon Tyne; *m* 1951, Patricia Sara (*née* McGrath); one *s. Educ:* St Cuthbert's Grammar Sch., Newcastle upon Tyne; Durham Univ. BA (Hons) Politics and Economics. Australian Dept of Labour and Nat. Service, 1948-50; Imperial Chemical Industries Ltd, and Imperial Metal Industries Ltd, 1950-68; Upper Clyde Shipbuilders Ltd, 1968-69; Dir of Personnel, Dunlop Ltd, 1969-72; Mem., British Railways Bd, 1972-77. Director: British Rail Engineering Ltd; British Rail Shipping and Internat. Services Div.; Transmark Ltd (Chm.); Portsmouth and Sunderland Newspapers Ltd, 1978-80; Chm., British Transport Hotels, 1976-78. Adviser to industrial and commercial cos, 1978-. Mem. Council, Advisory, Conciliation and Arbitration Service, 1974-78. Mem., British Waterways Bd, 1980-. Governor, British Transport Staff Coll. Ltd, 1972-77. FCIT; FIPM. *Recreations:* golf, gardening, music. *Address:* 9 Ardgare, Shandon, Helensburgh, Dunbartonshire. *T:* Helensburgh 820803.

FARRINGTON, Sir Henry Francis Colden, 7th Bt, *cr* 1818; RA retired; *b* 25 April 1914; *s* of Sir Henry Anthony Farrington, 6th Bt, and Dorothy Maria (*d* 1969), *o d* of Frank Farrington; *S* father, 1944; *m* 1947, Anne, *e d* of late Major W. A. Gillam, DSO; one *s* one *d. Educ:* Haileybury. Retired from Army, 1960 (Major; now Hon. Col). *Heir: s* Henry William Farrington, ARICS [*b* 27 March 1951; *m* 1979, Diana Donn Broughton, *yr d* of Geoffrey Broughton, Somerset]. *Address:* Higher Ford Farm, Wiveliscombe, Taunton, Somerset TA4 2RL. *T:* Wiveliscombe 23219.

FARRIS, Hon. John Lauchlan; Chief Justice of British Columbia and Administrator of Province of British Columbia, 1973-79; *b* 5 Sept. 1911; *s* of late Senator John Wallace de Beque Farris, QC and late Dr Evlyn Fenwick

Farris; *m* 1933, Dorothy Colledge; one *s* two *d. Educ:* Univ. of British Columbia (BA); Harvard Law Sch. (LLB). Lectured on commercial law, Univ. of British Columbia, 1945-55. KC (Canada) 1950. Past Pres., Vancouver Bar Assoc.; Past Chm. of Bd of Governors, Crofton House Sch.; Past Pres., Harvard Club of Vancouver; Pres., Canadian Bar Assoc., 1971-72 (Past Vice-Pres. for BC); Fellow, Amer. Coll. of Trial Lawyers. Hon. Member: Amer. Bar Assoc.; Manitoba Bar Assoc.; Law Soc. of Saskatchewan. Senior Partner, Farris Farris Vaughan Wills & Murphy, until 1973. *Recreations:* boating, woodworking. *Address:* 1403 Angus Drive, Vancouver, BC V6H 1V2, Canada. *T:* (604) 738-1264. *Clubs:* Vancouver (Vancouver); Union (Victoria); Royal Vancouver Yacht, West Vancouver Yacht.

FARROW, Christopher John; Under-Secretary, Department of Industry, since 1981, seconded to Kleinwort Benson, since 1982; *b* 29 July 1937; *s* of late Thomas and Evangeline Dorothea Farrow; *m* 1961, Alison Brown; one *s* one *d. Educ:* Cranleigh Sch.; King's Coll., Cambridge (BA). Board of Trade, 1961; Harkness Fellowship and visiting scholar, Stanford Univ., USA, 1968-69; Private Sec. to Pres. of BoT and Minister for Trade, 1970-72; Air Div., DTI, 1972-74; Industrial Planning Div., Dept of Industry, 1974-75; Cabinet Office, 1975-77; Shipbuilding Policy Div., DoI, 1977-78, Air Div., 1978-81. *Recreation:* gardening. *Address:* 14 Hitherwood Drive, SE19 1XB. *T:* 01-670 6758.

FARROW, Mia (Villiers); actress; *b* 9 Feb. 1945; *d* of John Villiers Farrow and Maureen O'Sullivan; *m* 1970, André Previn (marr. diss. 1979), *qv* ; three *s* two *d. TV series:* Peyton Place, 1965; *films:* Secret Ceremony, 1968; Rosemary's Baby, 1969; John and Mary, 1970; The Public Eye, 1972; The Great Gatsby, 1974; Full Circle, Death on the Nile, A Wedding, 1978; Hurricane, 1980; A Midsummer Night's Sex Comedy, 1982; *stage:* The Importance of Being Earnest, NY, 1963; Mary Rose, Shaw, 1973; The Three Sisters, Greenwich, 1974; The House of Bernarda Alba, Greenwich, 1974; Peter Pan, 1975; The Marrying of Ann Leete, RSC, 1975; The Zykovs, Ivanov, RSC, 1976; A Midsummer Night's Dream, Leicester, 1976; Romantic Comedy, NY, 1979. David Donatello Award, Italy, 1969; Best Actress awards: French Academy, 1969; San Sebastian, 1969; Rio de Janeiro, 1970. *Address:* Bridgewater, Conn, USA.

FARTHING, Richard Bruce Crosby; Deputy Director-General, General Council of British Shipping, since 1980; *b* 9 Feb. 1926; *s* of late Col Herbert Hadfield Farthing and late Marjorie Cora (*née* Fisher); *m* 1959, Anne Brenda (*née* Williams), LLB, barrister, *d* of late Thomas Williams, solicitor; one *s* one *d. Educ:* Alleyns Sch., (Dulwich and Rossall) St Catharine's Coll., Cambridge (MA). Commissioned RA and RHA, 1944-48. Called to Bar, Inner Temple, 1954; Govt Legal Service, 1954-59; joined Chamber of Shipping of the United Kingdom, 1959; Asst General Manager, 1966; Secretary, Cttee of European Shipowners and Cttee of European National Shipowners' Assocs, 1967-74; Secretary-General, Council of European and Japanese National Shipowners' Assocs (CENSA), 1974-76; Director, General Council of British Shipping, 1976-80. Rapporteur, Commn on Sea Transport, Internat. Chamber of Commerce, 1976-. Mem. Court of Common Council (Aldgate Ward), 1982. *Publication:* ed, Vol. 20, Aspinalls Maritime Law Cases, 1961. *Recreations:* sailing, music, golf. *Address:* 18 Woodsford Square, Addison Road, Kensington, W14 8DP. *T:* 01-603 6680. *Clubs:* MCC, Incogniti Cricket, Royal Ocean Racing.

FARVIS, Prof. William Ewart John, CBE 1978 (OBE 1972); BSc, BSc (Eng), CEng, FIEE, FRSE; engineering consultant, since 1977; Professor of Electrical Engineering, University of Edinburgh, 1961-77, now Emeritus Professor; *b* 12 Dec. 1911; *o s* of late William Henry Farvis and Gertrude Anne Farvis; *m* 1939, Margaret May Edmonstone Martin; one *s* one *d. Educ:* Queen Elizabeth's Hosp., Bristol; Bristol and London Univs. Lectr, University Coll., Swansea, 1937-40 and 1945-48; Air Ministry, Telecommunications Res. Estab., 1940-45; Lectr/Sen. Lectr, Edinburgh Univ., 1948-61, Prof. and Head of Dept of Electrical Eng., 1961-77, Chairman, Sch. of Engineering Sci. 1972-75. Mem., British Nat. Cttee for Radio Science, 1960-66; Science Research Council: Mem., Electrical and Systems Cttee, 1968-72; Engineering Board, 1972-75 and 1976-81; Polytechnics Cttee, 1975-78; Chm., Solid-state Devices Panel, 1972-75; Electrical and Systems Cttee 1972-75; Advanced Ground Transport Panel 1975-80; Mem. Council, 1976-81. Mem. Council, IEE, 1972-75 and 1976-79; Editor, Microelectronics Journal 1976-78. *Recreation:* music. *Address:* 14 Cluny Terrace, Edinburgh EH10 4SW. *T:* 031-447 4939. *Club:* Athenæum.

FARWELL, Rt. Rev. Gerard Victor; Abbot of Worth, since 1965; Abbot President of English Benedictine Congregation, since 1967; *b* 15 Oct. 1913; 3rd *s* of late Frederick Arthur Farwell and Monica Mary Quin. *Educ:* St Benedict's, Ealing. Entered Downside Abbey, 1932; Housemaster at Downside Sch., 1946-48; Bursar at Worth, 1950-57; Prior of Worth, 1957-65. *Address:* Worth Abbey, Crawley, West Sussex RH10 4SB.

FATEH, Abul Fazal Muhammad Abul; Ambassador of Bangladesh at Algiers, since 1977; *b* 28 Feb. 1926; *s* of Abdul Gafur and Zohra Khatun; *m* 1956, Mahfuza Banu; two *s. Educ:* Dacca, Bangladesh. MA (English Lit.); special course, LSE, 1949-50. Carnegie Fellow in Internat. Peace, 1962-63. Entered Pakistan Foreign Service, 1949; 3rd Secretary: Paris, 1951-53; Calcutta, 1953-56; 2nd Sec., Washington, DC, 1956-60; Dir, Min. of Foreign Affairs, Karachi, 1961-65; 1st Sec., Prague, 1965-66; Counsellor, New Delhi, 1966-67; Dep. High Comr for Pakistan, Calcutta, 1968-70; Ambassador of

Pakistan, Baghdad, 1971; Adviser to Actg President of Bangladesh, July, 1971; Foreign Sec., Bangladesh, Jan. 1972; Ambassador of Bangladesh to France and Spain, 1972-75; Permanent Deleg. to UNESCO, 1972-76; High Comr for Bangladesh in London, 1976-77. Leader, Bangladesh Delegation: Commonwealth Youth Ministers' Conf., Lusaka, 1973; Meeting of UN Council on Namibia, Algiers, 1980; Ministerial Meeting of Non-aligned Countries Co-ordination Bureau on Namibia, Algiers, 1981. Chm., Commonwealth Human Ecology Council Symposium, 1977. *Address:* Bangladesh Embassy, 141 Boulevard Salah Bouakouir, 5th Floor, Algiers, Algeria.

FATT, Prof. Paul, FRS 1969; Professor of Biophysics, University College, London, since 1976 (Reader, 1956-76), Fellow 1973. *Publications:* papers in: Jl of Physiology, Proc. Royal Soc., etc. *Address:* Department of Biophysics, University College, Gower Street, WC1.

FAULDS, Andrew Matthew William; MP (Lab) Warley East, since 1974 (Smethwick, 1966-74); *b* 1 March 1923; *s* of late Rev. Matthew Faulds, MA, and of Doris Faulds; *m* 1945, Bunty Whitfield; one *d. Educ:* George Watson's, Edinburgh; King Edward VI Grammar Sch., Louth; Daniel Stewart's, Edinburgh; High Sch., Stirling; Glasgow Univ. Three seasons with Shakespeare Memorial Co., Stratford-upon-Avon; BBC Repertory Co.: Jet Morgan in Journey into Space (BBC). Has appeared in over 35 films and many TV and radio performances. Parliamentary Private Secretary: to Minister of State for Aviation, Min. of Technology, 1967-68; to Postmaster General, 1968-69; Opposition spokesman for the Arts, 1970-73, 1979-82; Chairman: British br., Parly Assoc. for Euro-Arab Cooperation, 1974-; All-Party Parly Heritage Gp; Member: UK Nat. Commn for Unesco Culture Adv. Cttee; British Delegn to Council of Europe and WEU, 1975-80; Exec. Cttee, GB China Centre; Exec. Cttee, Franco-British Council; Exec. Cttee, Labour Middle East Council. *Recreation:* cosseting his constituents. *Address:* 14 Albemarle Street, W1. *T:* 01-499 7589.

FAULKNER OF DOWNPATRICK, Lady; Lucy (Barbara Ethel) **Faulkner;** National Governor for Northern Ireland, British Broadcasting Corporation, since 1978; Chairman, Broadcasting Council for Northern Ireland, since 1981; *b* 1 July 1925; *d* of William John Forsythe and Jane Ethel Sewell; *m* 1951, Arthur Brian Deane Faulkner (MP (NI) 1949-73; PC 1959; *cr* Baron Faulkner of Downpatrick, 1977) (killed in a hunting accident, 1977); two *s* one *d. Educ:* Aubrey House; Bangor Collegiate Sch.; Trinity College Dublin. BA (Hons History). Journalist, Belfast Telegraph, 1947; Personal Secretary to Sir Basil Brooke, Prime Minister of N Ireland, 1949. Researcher, Ulster Historical Foundation, 1977. *Recreations:* hunting and dressage, oil painting, genealogy. *Address:* Highlands, Farranfad, Downpatrick, Co. Down. *T:* Seaforde 663.

FAULKNER, Hon. Arthur James; MP (Labour) for Roskill, NZ, since 1957; President, New Zealand Labour Party, since 1976; *b* Auckland, NZ, 1921; *m* 1945, May Cox; two *s* three *d. Educ:* Otahuhu District High Sch., NZ. Served War of 1939-45 with RAF as Spitfire pilot in UK, N Africa and Europe. Formerly a credit manager. Labour Party organiser for North Island, 1952-57. Contested (Lab) Franklin, 1951; North Shore, 1954. Parliamentary experience on Select Cttees on Defence, Foreign Affairs, Statutes Revision, Local Govt Convener of Labour Caucus Cttees on Defence and Foreign Affairs. Fact-finding missions to South-East Asia, 1963 and 1967; travelled to Europe and UK to discuss EEC matters, 1969. Minister of Defence, Minister i/c War Pensions and Rehabilitation, 1972-74; Minister of Labour and State Services, 1974-75. *Recreations:* fishing, boating, aviation. *Address:* 1 Inverness Avenue, Mt Roskill, Auckland, New Zealand.

FAULKNER, David Ewart Riley; Deputy Under-Secretary of State, Home Office, since 1982; *b* 23 Oct. 1934; *s* of Harold Ewart and Mabel Faulkner; *m* 1961, Sheila Jean Stevenson; one *s* one *d. Educ:* Manchester Grammar Sch.; Merchant Taylors' Sch., Northwood; St John's Coll., Oxford (MA Lit Hum). Home Office: Asst Principal, 1959; Private Sec. to Parly Under-Sec. of State, 1961-63; Principal, 1963; Jt Sec. to Inter-Party Conf. on House of Lords Reform, 1968; Private Sec. to Home Sec., 1969-70; Asst Sec., Prison Dept, 1970, Establishment Dept, 1974, Police Dept, 1976; Asst Under-Sec. of State, 1976; Under Sec., Cabinet Office, 1978-80; Asst Under-Sec. of State, Dir of Operational Policy, Prison Dept, Home Office, 1980-82. *Recreations:* railways, birds. *Address:* Home Office, 50 Queen Anne's Gate, SW1.

FAULKNER, Dennis; *see* Faulkner, J. D. C.

FAULKNER, Prof. Douglas, WhSch, BSc, PhD; FEng, FRINA, FIStructE, MSNAME; RCNC; Head of Department of Naval Architecture and Ocean Engineering, University of Glasgow, since 1973; *b* 29 Dec. 1929; *s* of Vincent and Florence Faulkner; *m* 1954, Jenifer Ann Cole-Adams; three *d. Educ:* Sutton High Sch., Plymouth; HM Dockyard Technical Coll., Devonport; RNC, Greenwich. Aircraft Carrier Design, 1955-57; Production Engrg, 1957-59; Structural Research at NCRE, Dunfermline, 1959-63; Asst Prof. of Naval Construction, RNC, Greenwich, 1963-66; Structural Adviser to Ship Dept, Bath, 1966-68; Naval Construction Officer att. to British Embassy, Washington DC, 1968-70, and Mem. Ship Research Cttee, Nat. Acad. of Scis, 1968-71; Res. Associate and Defence Fellow, MIT, 1970-71; Structural Adviser to Ship Dept, Bath, and to the Merrison Box Girder Bridge Cttee, 1971-73. UK Rep., Standing Cttee, Internat. Ship Structures Congress, 1973-. *Publications:* chapters in Ship Structural Design Concepts (Cornell Maritime

Press), 1975; papers related to structural design of ships, in Trans RINA, Jl of Ship Res., Internat. Shipbuilding Progress, etc. *Recreations:* hill walking, swimming, music, chess. *Address:* Woodstock, 52 Buchanan Street, Milngavie, Glasgow G62 8AP. *T:* 041-956 4773.

FAULKNER, Sir Eric (Odin), Kt 1974; MBE 1945; Director, Lloyds Bank Ltd (Chairman, 1969-77); Advisory Director, Unilever, since 1978; *b* 21 April 1914; *s* of late Sir Alfred Faulkner, CB, CBE; *m* 1939, Joan Mary, *d* of Lt-Col F. A. M. Webster; one *s* one *d. Educ:* Bradfield; Corpus Christi Coll., Cambridge (Hon. Fellow, 1975). Joined Glyn, Mills & Co., 1936. Served War of 1939-45, Royal Artillery and Leics Yeomanry; Staff Coll.; Bde Major RA, GSO2; commanded 91 Field Regt RA. Rejoined Glyn, Mills & Co., 1946; Local Dir, 1947-50; Exec. Dir, 1950-68; Dep. Chm., 1959-63; Chm., 1963-68. Chm., Cttee of London Clearing Bankers, 1972-74. Pres., British Bankers' Assoc., 1972-73, 1980-; Chairman: Industrial Soc., 1973-76; City Communications Organisation, 1976-79. Warden of Bradfield Coll., 1965-. *Recreations:* fishing and walking; formerly cricket and Association football (CUAFC XI 1935]. *Address:* Chart Cottage, Seal Chart, Kent.

FAULKNER, Captain George Haines, CB 1947; DSC 1916; Royal Navy; *b* 27 April 1893; *s* of Rev. Thomas George Faulkner and Kate Nicholls; *m* 1st, 1924, Kathleen (*d* 1947), *d* of Dr Henry Wilson, Cheadle, Cheshire; no *c* ; 2nd, 1959, Marjorie Lucy Rowland (*d* 1974), Lustleigh, Devon; 3rd, 1977, Marjorie Charteris Lewin. *Educ:* Lickey Hills Sch., Worcs; RN Colleges, Osborne and Dartmouth. Osborne, 1906; Midshipman, 1910. Served European War, 1914-18, in destroyers (despatches) Battle of Heligoland Bight, special promotion to Lieut; commanded HMS Mystic, Thruster and Patriot, 1918-19; psc 1922-23; served in HMS Hood on Special Service Squadron World Cruise, 1923-24; commanded HMS Voyager, 1926-28; Comdr 1928; Capt. 1935; commanded HMS Bideford, 1937-38; Chief of Staff and Capt. on Staff of C-in-C the Nore, 1939-41; in command of HMS Berwick, 1941-43; Chief of Staff to C-in-C South Atlantic, with rank of Commodore 2nd class and stationed at Capetown, 1943-45; retired list, 1945; re-appointed. First Naval Mem. of New Zealand Naval Board and Chief of Naval Staff, NZ, with rank of Commodore 2nd Class, 1945-47; reverted to retired list, 1947. *Address:* Grove Cottage, Lustleigh, Devon. *T:* 232.

FAULKNER, Hugh (Branston), OBE 1980; Director: Help the Aged, since 1978 (previously Hon. Director from its formation in 1961); Help the Aged Housing Appeal Ltd; Helpage International Ltd; Director of several business companies; *b* Lutterworth, 8 June 1916; *s* of Frank and Ethel Faulkner; *m* 1954, Anne Carlton Milner; one *s* one *d. Educ:* Lutterworth Grammar Sch. ACIS. Educn Administration, City of Leicester, 1936-46; Organising Sec., Fellowship of Reconciliation, 1946-54; business and charity career from 1954. Hon. Dir and later Dir, Voluntary and Christian Service, 1954-79. Christian peace delegate to USSR, 1952, followed by lecture tour in USA, 1953, on internat. relations. Trustee: Phyllis Trust; Lester Trust; Voluntary and Christian Service; Help the Aged Housing Trust. *Recreations:* music, gardening. *Address:* Longfield, 4 One Tree Lane, Beaconsfield, Bucks. *T:* Beaconsfield 4769. *Club:* National Liberal.

FAULKNER, Dr Hugh Charles, FRCGP; Consultant to Regional Health Authority, Tuscany and to Unità Locale del Chianti; Editorial Board, Salute e Territorio; Hon. Lecturer in Social Medicine, Bedford College, University of London, since 1976; Medical Secretary, Medical Practitioners' Union (ASTMS), and Medical Editor of Medical World, 1971-76; *b* 22 Sept. 1912; *s* of Frank Whitehead Faulkner and Emily Maud Knibb; *m* ; one *s* two *d. Educ:* Oundle Sch.; London Hosp. MRCS, LRCP, FRCGP 1979. Boys' Club Manager, 1932-35; qual. MRCS, LRCP, 1943. Served War, RAMC, 1944-46. Gen. Practitioner, 1948-76. Mem. Council of Medical Practitioners' Union, 1948-76. Mem., Ordine dei Medici (Firenze), 1981. *Publications:* Medicina di Base in due paesi, Gran Bretagna e l'URSS, 1977; articles in Medical World, Lancet, etc. *Recreation:* attacking the Establishment. *Address:* La Galera, Passo del Sugame, Greve-in-Chianti, Firenze, Italy.

FAULKNER, (James) Dennis (Compton), CBE 1980; VRD 1960; Chairman, Ladybird (NI) Ltd, since 1963; *b* 22 Oct. 1926; *s* of James and Nora Faulkner; *m* 1952, Janet Cunningham; three *d. Educ:* College of St Columba, Co. Dublin. Served RNVR, 1946-71. Chairman: Belfast Collar Co. Ltd, 1957-63; Belfast Savings Bank, 1960-61; NI Develt Agency, 1978-82; Board Member, Gallaher NI, 1980-. Farming, 1946-; commercial fishing, 1970-. *Recreations:* sailing, hunting, shooting, ocean racing. *Address:* Ringhaddy House, Killinchy, Co. Down, Northern Ireland. *T:* Killinchy 541114. *Clubs:* Royal Ocean Racing, Royal Cruising; Cruising Club of America (New York); Ulster (Belfast).

FAULKNER, John Richard Hayward; Drama Director, Arts Council of Great Britain, since 1977; *b* 29 May 1941; *s* of Richard Hayward Ollerton and Lilian Elizabeth (*née* Carrigan); *m* 1970, Janet Gill (*née* Cummings); one *d* two step *d. Educ:* Archbishop Holgate's Sch., York; Keble Coll., Oxford (BA). Worked with a number of theatre companies, Prospect Productions, Meadow Players, Century Theatre, Sixty-Nine Theatre Co., Cambridge Theatre Co., toured extensively, UK, Europe, Indian Sub-Continent, Australia, 1960-72; Drama Dir, Scottish Arts Council, 1972-77. *Recreations:* intricacies and wilderness. *Address:* 33 Hadley Gardens, Chiswick W4 4NU. *T:* 01-995 3041.

FAULKNER, Most Rev. Leonard Anthony; *see* Townsville, Bishop of, (RC).

FAULKNER, Sir Percy, KBE 1964; CB 1950; Controller of HM Stationery Office and Queen's Printer of Acts of Parliament, 1961-67; *b* 11 May 1907; *s* of Thomas Faulkner and Margaret A. Faulkner (*née* Hood); *m* 1933, Joyce Rosemary Lois MacDonogh; one *s* one *d. Educ:* Royal Academical Institution, Belfast; Trinity Coll., Dublin. Entered Ministry of Transport, 1930; Dep. Sec. (Inland Transport), 1957; Dep. Sec. (Shipping), 1958-61; Chm. British Cttee on Prevention of Pollution of the Sea by Oil, 1953-57; rep. UK at various international conferences on shipping matters, 1947-60. *Address:* Armathwaite, Motherby, Penrith, Cumbria CA11 0RL. *T:* Greystoke 438. *Club:* Athenæum.

FAULKS, Hon. Sir Neville (Major Ginner), Kt 1963; MBE 1944; TD 1946; Judge of the High Court of Justice, Family Division (formerly Probate, Divorce and Admiralty Division), 1963-77; *b* 27 Jan. 1908; *s* of M. J. Faulks, MA and Ada Mabel Faulks; *m* 1st, 1940, Bridget Marigold Bodley (*d* 1963); two *s* one *d* ; 2nd, 1967, Elizabeth, widow of Rt Rev. A. G. Parham, MC; one step *s* four step *d. Educ:* Uppingham Sch. (scholar); Sidney Sussex Coll., Cambridge (Exhibitioner). Called to the Bar, LLB, 1930; QC 1959; Bencher, Inner Temple, 1963. Joined TA; served War of 1939-45 (despatches twice), Alamein. Prosecuting Counsel to Bd of Trade and other ministries at Central Criminal Court, etc., 1946-59. Recorder of Deal, 1957-59; Recorder of Norwich, 1959-63. Chm., Cttee to review Defamation Act, 1952, 1971-74. *Publications:* Fraser on Libel (ed, with late Mr Justice Slade); Investigation into the Affairs of H. Jasper and Company Limited, 1961; No Mitigating Circumstances (autobiog.), 1977; A Law Unto Myself (autobiog.), 1978. *Recreations:* the company of his wife, The Times crossword puzzle. *Address:* Wallis's Cottage, Bowden, Dartmouth, South Devon. *T:* Stoke Fleming 597.

See also P. R. Faulks.

FAULKS, Peter Ronald, MC 1943; **His Honour Judge Faulks;** a Circuit Judge, since 1980; *b* 24 Dec. 1917; *s* of late M. J. Faulks and A. M. Faulks (*née* Ginner); *m* 1949, Pamela Brenda, *d* of Peter Lawless; two *s. Educ:* Tonbridge; Sidney Sussex Coll., Cambridge (MA). Served War of 1939-45, Duke of Wellington's Regt, Dunkirk, N Africa, Anzio, etc; Major 1943; wounded 3 times. Admitted a solicitor, 1949. A Recorder of the Crown Court, 1972-80. Dep. Chm., Agricultural Land Tribunal (SE England), 1972-80; Pres., Berks, Bucks and Oxon Law Soc., 1976-77. *Recreation:* country life. *Address:* Downs Cottage, Westbrook, Boxford, Newbury, Berks. *T:* Boxford 382. *Clubs:* MCC, Farmers'.

See also Sir Neville Faulks.

FAURE, Edgar (Jean); de l'Académie Française; President, National Assembly, France, 1973-78; Member, European Parliament, since 1979; *b* Béziers, 18 Aug. 1908; *s* of Jean-Baptiste Faure and Claire Faure (*née* Lavit); *m* 1931, Lucie Meyer (*d* 1977); two *d* ; *m* 1980, Marie Jeanne Vuez. *Educ:* Ecole de Langues Orientales, Paris. Advocate, Paris Court of Appeal, 1929; Dir of Legislative Services to the Presidency, Council of French Cttee of Nat. Liberation, 1943-44; Asst Deleg. to War Crimes Trials, Nuremberg, 1945; Deputy for the Jura (Radical-Socialist), 1946-58; Mayor of Port-Lesney (Jura), 1947-70; Pres., General Council of the Jura, 1949-67; Secretary of Finance, 1949-50; Minister of Budget, 1950-51; Minister of Justice, 1951-52; Prime Minister, Jan.-Feb. 1952; Pres, Commn of Foreign Affairs of Nat. Assembly, 1952-53; Minister of Finance and Economic Affairs, 1953-54; Minister of Foreign Affairs, Jan.-Feb. 1955; Prime Minister, Feb. 1955-Jan. 1956; Minister of Finance, May-June 1958; Senator for the Jura, 1959-66; Deputy for Doubs, 1966-72, 1973-; Prof. of Law, Univ. of Dijon, 1962-66; Minister of Agriculture, 1966-68; Minister of Education, 1968-69; Dir of Research, Faculty of Law, Besançon, 1970-72; Pres., Internat. Commn of Develt of Educn, 1971-72; Mayor of Pontarlier, 1971; Minister of State for Social Affairs, 1972-73; Pres., Regional Council, Franche-Comté, 1974-; Senator from Doubs, 1980. *Publications:* La politique française du pétrole, 1939; M Langois n'est pas toujours égal à lui-meme (novel), 1950; Le serpent et la tortue (study of China), 1957; La disgrace du Turgot, 1961; Etude sur la capitation de Dioclétian d'après le panégyrique VIII, Prévoir le present, 1966; Philosophie d'une réforme, 1969; L'âme du combat (essay), 1970; Ce que je crois, 1971; Apprendre à être (Rapport de la Commission internationale sur le développement de l'éducation, Unesco), 1972; Pour un nouveau contrat social, 1973; La Banqueroute de Law, 1978. *Address:* 134 rue de Grenelle, 75007 Paris, France; Ermitage de Beaulieu, 77350 France.

FAUVELLE, Major Michael Henry; barrister-at-law; a Recorder of the Crown Court, since 1979; *b* 12 Aug. 1920; *s* of Victor Edmond Fauvelle and Brigid Mary Fauvelle (*née* Westermann); *m* 1964, Marie-Caroline, *e d* of Count and Countess Stanislas d'Orsetti, Château de la Grènerie, 49140 Jarzé, France; one *s* one *d. Educ:* Stonyhurst Coll.; Royal Military Coll., Sandhurst. Commissioned, 2/Lieut The South Lancashire Regt, 1939, T/Major 1944; active service in N Africa, Italy and Palestine (wounded three times, arguably five); Staff employment as GSO 3 (Ops), Gibraltar, 1947; Staff Captain Q HQ Palestine, 1947-48; Staff Captain A HQ BMM to Greece and HQ 3 Inf. Bde, 1948-50; Adjt 1st Bn, 1951; Major 1952; retired, 1953. Called to the Bar, Lincoln's Inn, 1955; Dep. Recorder, Oxford, Bournemouth and Reading, 1971. *Address:* Tadley Cottage, Wherwell, Hampshire SP11 7JU. *T:* Chilbolton 217; 17 Carlton Crescent, Southampton SO9 5AL. *T:* Southampton 36036. *Clubs:* Hampshire (Winchester); Home Guard (Wherwell, Hants).

FAWCETT, Colin, QC 1970; *b* 22 Nov. 1923; *s* of late Frank Fawcett, Penrith; *m* 1952, Elizabeth Anne Dickson; one *s* one *d. Educ:* Sedbergh. Commnd Border Regt, 1943. Called to Bar, Inner Temple, 1952, Bencher, 1978. *Recreations:* fishing, music. *Address:* Fairings, Valley Way, Gerrards Cross, Bucks. *T:* Gerrards Cross 83999.

FAWCETT, James Edmund Sandford, DSC 1942; President, European Commission of Human Rights, 1972-81 (Member, since 1962); *b* 16 April 1913; *s* of Rev. Joseph Fawcett and Edith Fawcett; *m* 1937, Frances Beatrice, 2nd *d* of late Dr E. A. Lowe; one *s* four *d. Educ:* Rugby Sch.; New Coll., Oxford. Practised at the Bar, 1937-39 and 1950-55. Fellow of All Souls Coll., Oxford, 1938. Served War of 1939-45, Royal Navy. Asst Legal Adviser to FO, 1945-50 (to UK Delegn to UN and British Embassy, Washington, 1948-50); Gen. Counsel, IMF, 1955-60; Fellow of All Souls Coll., Oxford, 1960-69; Dir of Studies, RIIA, 1969-73; Prof. of Internat. Law, King's Coll., London, 1976-80. Vis. Fellow, Southampton Univ., 1974-. Mem., Inst. of Internat. Law, 1973-; Chm., British Inst. of Human Rights, 1977-81. Mem., Legislative Cttee of Internat. Union for the Conservation of Nature, 1969. *Publications:* British Commonwealth in International Law, 1963; International Law and the Uses of Outer Space, 1968; The Law of Nations (Penguin), 1968; The Application of the European Convention on Human Rights, 1969; International Economic Conflicts, 1977; Law and Power in International Relations, 1981; numerous articles. *Recreations:* astronomy, piano. *Address:* Field House, Combe, Newbury, Berks.

FAWCETT, John Harold; HM Diplomatic Service; Deputy High Commissioner and Counsellor (Commercial and Economic), Wellington, since 1978; *b* 4 May 1929; *yr s* of late Comdr Harold William Fawcett, OBE, RN, and of late Una Isobel Dalrymple Fawcett (*née* Gairdner); *m* 1961, Elizabeth Shaw; one *s. Educ:* Radley (Scholar); University Coll., Oxford (Scholar). 1st cl. Hon. Mods 1951, 2nd cl. Lit. Hum. 1953. Nat. Service, RN (Radio Electrician's Mate), 1947-49. British Oxygen Co., 1954-63 (S Africa, 1955-57). Entered Foreign Service, 1963; FO, 1963-66; 1st Sec. (Commercial), Bombay, 1966-69; 1st Sec. and Head of Chancery, Port-of-Spain, 1969-70; Asst, Caribbean Dept, FCO, 1971-72; Head of Icelandic Fisheries Unit, Western European Dept, FCO, 1973; Amb. to Democratic Republic of Vietnam, 1974; Head of Chancery, Warsaw, 1975-78. *Recreations:* walking, gardening. *Address:* c/o Foreign and Commonwealth Office, SW1. *Clubs:* Brooks's, Savile; Royal Bombay Yacht.

FAWCUS, Sir (Robert) Peter, KBE 1964 (OBE 1957); CMG 1960; Overseas Civil Service, retd; *b* 30 Sept. 1915; *s* of late A. F. Fawcus, OBE; *m* 1943, Isabel Constance (*née* Ethelston); one *s* one *d. Educ:* Charterhouse; Clare Coll., Cambridge. Served RNVR, 1939-46. Joined Colonial Service (District Officer, Basutoland), 1946; Bechuanaland Protectorate: Govt Sec., 1954; Resident Commissioner, 1959; HM Commissioner, 1963-65; retd 1965. *Address:* Dochart House, Killin, Perthshire.

FAWCUS, Simon James David; a Recorder of the Crown Court, since 1980; *b* 12 July 1938; *s* of late Ernest Augustus Fawcus and of Jill Shaw; *m* 1966, Joan Mary (*née* Oliphant); one *s* four *d. Educ:* Aldenham Sch.; Trinity Hall, Cambridge (MA). Called to the Bar, Gray's Inn, 1961; in practice on Northern Circuit, 1962-. *Recreations:* real tennis and other lesser sporting activities, music (listening). *Address:* 601 Royal Exchange, Manchester M2 7EB. *T:* 061-834 9560. *Clubs:* MCC; Manchester Tennis and Racket, Big Four (Manchester); Wilmslow Golf.

FAWKES, Sir Randol (Francis), Kt 1977; Attorney-at-Law, since 1948; *b* 20 March 1924; *s* of Edward Ronald Fawkes and Mildred Fawkes (*née* McKinney); *m* 1951, Jacqueline Fawkes (*née* Bethel); three *s* one *d. Educ:* public schools in the Bahamas. Called to the Bar, Bahamas, 1948. A founder Citizen Cttee, 1949; People's Penny Savings Bank, 1951. Elected Mem. (Progressive Liberal Party), House of Assembly, 1956; promoted law establishing Labour Day as Public Holiday, 1961. Founder, and Pres. 1955-, Bahamas Fedn of Labour (led 19 day general strike which resulted in major labour and political reforms, 1958). Represented Labour Party at constitutional confs in London, 1963 and 1968; addressed UN Cttee of 24 on preparation of Bahamas for independence, 1966. *Publications:* You Should Know Your Government, 1949; The Bahamas Government, 1962; The New Bahamas, 1966; The Faith That Moved The Fountain: a memoir of a life and the times, 1977. *Recreations:* swimming, music, Bible tract writing. *Address:* PO Box N-7625, John F. Kennedy Drive, Nassau, NP, Bahamas. *T:* (office) 809-32-34053; (home) 809-32-34855.

FAWKES, Wally; cartoonist, since 1945; *b* 21 June 1924; *m* 1st, 1949, Sandra Boyce-Carmichelle; one *s* two *d*; 2nd, 1965, Susan Clifford; one *s* one *d. Educ:* Sidcup Central Sch.; Sidcup Sch. of Art; Camberwell Sch. of Art. Came from Vancouver, BC, to England, 1931. Joined Daily Mail, 1945; started Flook strip, 1949. Political cartoons for: Spectator, 1959-; Private Eye, and New Statesman, 1965-; Observer, and Punch, 1971-. Co-Founder, Humphrey Lyttelton Band, 1948. *Publications:* World of Trog, 1977; collections of Flook strips. *Recreations:* playing jazz (clarinet and soprano saxophone), cooking, cricket. *Address:* 44 Laurier Road, NW5 1SG. *T:* 01-267 2979. *Club:* Middlesex County Cricket.

FAY, His Honour Edgar Stewart, QC 1956; FCIArb; a Circuit Judge (formerly an Official Referee of the Supreme Court of Judicature), 1971-80; *b* 8 Oct. 1908; *s* of late Sir Sam Fay; *m* 1st, Kathleen Margaret, *e d* of late

C. H. Buell, Montreal, PQ, and Brockville, Ont; three *s*; 2nd, Jenny Julie Henriette, *yr d* of late Dr Willem Roosegaarde Bisschop, Lincoln's Inn; one *s. Educ:* Courtenay Lodge Sch.; McGill Univ.; Pembroke Coll., Cambridge (MA). Called to Bar, Inner Temple, 1932; Master of the Bench, 1962. FCIArb 1981. Recorder: of Andover, 1954-61; of Bournemouth, 1961-64; of Plymouth, 1964-71; Dep. Chm., Hants QS, 1960-71. Member: Bar Council, 1955-59, 1966-70; Senate of Four Inns of Court, 1970-72. Chm., Inquiry into Crown Agents, 1975-77. *Publications:* Why Piccadilly?, 1935; Londoner's New York, 1936; Discoveries in the Statute Book, 1937; The Life of Mr Justice Swift, 1939. *Address:* Knox End, Ashdon, Saffron Walden, Essex. *T:* Ashdon 275; 13 Egbert Street, NW1. *T:* 01-586 0725. *Club:* Reform.

FAY, John David; Director for Publications Policy, Organisation for Economic Co-operation and Development, Paris, since 1980; *b* 5 July 1919; *s* of late Stanley John Fay and Muriel Etrenne (*née* Nicholson); *m* 1949, Valerie Joyce Stroud; one *s* two *d. Educ:* Stowe Sch.; King's Coll., Cambridge (Minor Scholar; BA 1941, 1st Cl. both parts Historical Tripos). BoT, London, 1941-46 (Asst Private Sec. to Pres., 1944-46); Washington, 1946-48; Internat. Secretariat of OECD (formerly OEEC), Paris, 1949-: Head of Country Studies Div., 1952; Dir, Econs Br., 1957; Dep. Head of Econs and Statistics Dept, 1958, Head of Dept, 1975. *Publications:* extensive unsigned contribs to OEEC and OECD econ. pubns. *Recreations:* gardening, gastronomy, helping economists to write English. *Address:* 31 avenue du Cardinal de Retz, 78600 Maisons-Laffitte, France. *T:* 962 27 28. *Club:* Athenæum.

FAYRER, Sir John (Lang Macpherson), 4th Bt *cr* 1896; clerical officer; *b* 18 Oct. 1944; *s* of Sir Joseph Herbert Spens Fayrer, 3rd Bt, DSC, and Helen Diana Scott (*d* 1961), *d* of late John Lang; *S* father, 1976. *Educ:* Edinburgh Academy; Scottish Hotel School, Univ. of Strathclyde. *Heir: cousin* Colin Robert Fayrer [*b* 28 Feb. 1907; *m* 1946, Evelyn Elinor May, *d* of late T. A. Carey; two *d*]. *Address:* Overhailes, Haddington, East Lothian.

FEA, William Wallace; Director, Guest, Keen & Nettlefolds Ltd, 1958-72 (Deputy Chairman, 1968-72); *b* Cordova, Argentina, 3 Feb. 1907; *s* of Herbert Reginald Fea and Hilda Florence Fea (*née* Norton); *m* 1935, Norah Anne, *d* of Richard Festing; one *s* (and one *s* decd). *Educ:* Cheltenham Coll. (scholar); Brasenose Coll., Oxford (scholar); BA. ACA 1932; FCA. Mem., Council, Inst. of Chartered Accountants, 1953-71; Mem. Council, BIM, 1969-73; Management Cttee, AA, 1971-77. *Recreations:* (now geriatric) squash racquets, ski-ing, shooting, lawn tennis, interest in music. *Address:* The Lowe, Worfield, near Bridgnorth, Salop. *T:* Worfield 241. *Clubs:* Lansdowne; Edgbaston Priory (Birmingham).

FEARN, John Martin, CB 1976; Secretary, Scottish Education Department, 1973-76, retired; *b* 24 June 1916; *s* of William Laing Fearn and Margaret Kerr Fearn; *m* 1947, Isobel Mary Begbie, MA, MB, ChB; one *d. Educ:* High Sch. of Dundee; Univ. of St Andrews (MA); Worcester Coll., Oxford. Indian Civil Service, Punjab, 1940-47; District Magistrate, Lahore, 1946; Scottish Home Dept, 1947; Asst Sec., 1956; Under-Sec., 1966; Under-Sec., Scottish Educn Dept, 1968. *Recreation:* golf. *Address:* 31 Midmar Gardens, Edinburgh EH10 6DY. *T:* 031-447 5301. *Club:* New (Edinburgh).

FEARN, Patrick Robin; HM Diplomatic Service; Head of South America Department, Foreign and Commonwealth Office, since 1979; *b* 5 Sept. 1934; *s* of Albert Cyprian Fearn and Hilary (*née* Harrison); *m* 1961, Sorrel Mary Lynne Thomas; three *s* one *d. Educ:* Ratcliffe Coll.; University Coll., Oxford (BA Hons, Mod. Langs). Nat. Service, Intelligence Corps, 1952-54. Overseas marketing, Dunlop Rubber Co. Ltd, 1957-61; entered Foreign Service, 1961; FO, 1961-62; Third, later Second Sec., Caracas, 1962-64; Havana, 1965; First Sec., Budapest, 1966-68; FCO, 1969-72; Head of Chancery, Vientiane, 1972-75; Asst Head of Science and Technol. Dept, FCO, 1975-76; Counsellor, Head of Chancery and Consul Gen., Islamabad, 1977-79. *Recreations:* tennis, golf, reading, family life. *Address:* c/o Foreign and Commonwealth Office, SW1; 17 Durham Terrace, W2. *T:* 01-229 1541; 14 Gastard, Corsham, Wilts. *T:* Corsham 713067.

FEARNLEY, John Thorn; HM Diplomatic Service, retired; *b* 9 Feb. 1921; *o s* of Tom Fearnley and Grace Gertrude (*née* Thorn); *m* 1947, Margaret Ann Davies (marr. diss. 1974); two *s* three *d. Educ:* Manchester Gram. Sch.; Caius Coll., Cambridge (Scholar). Served with RN, 1942-46 (Submarine Branch). Joined Foreign Service, 1947; FO, 1947-48; New York (UN), 1948-50; Tehran, 1950-52; FO, Civil Service Selection Bd, 1953; Tehran, 1953-56; Berlin, 1956-58; FO, 1958-60; Lagos, 1960-62; Paris, 1962-65. Head of Oil Dept, FO, 1965-69; Senior Officers' War Course, RN Coll., Greenwich, 1969; Consul-Gen., Frankfurt, 1969-75; Consul-Gen., Sydney, 1975-76. Founder Mem., Foreign (now Diplomatic) Service Assoc. *Recreation:* Monmouth. *Address:* 4 Saint James Street, Monmouth, Gwent NP5 3DL. *T:* Monmouth 3493.

FEARNLEY SCARR, J. G.; see Scarr.

FEATHERSTONE, Hugh Robert, OBE 1974; FCIS, FCIT; Director-General, Freight Transport Association, since 1969; *b* 31 March 1926; *s* of Alexander Brown Featherstone and Doris Olive Martin; *m* 1948, Beryl Joan Sly; one *s* one *d. Educ:* Minchenden Sch., Southgate, London. FCIS 1956; FCIT 1970. Served War, RNVR, 1943-46 (Sub-Lt). Assistant Secretary: Nat. Assoc. of Funeral Dirs, 1946-48; Brit. Rubber Develt Bd, 1948-58; Asst Sec. 1958-60, Sec. 1960-68, Traders Road Transport Assoc. *Publications:* contrib.

to jls concerned with transport and admin. *Recreations:* golf, gardening, wine-making. *Address:* 5 Rossdale, Tunbridge Wells, Kent. *T:* Tunbridge Wells 30063.

FEATHERSTONE, Col (William) Patrick Davies, MC 1944; TD 1960; Vice Lord-Lieutenant of Staffordshire, since 1976; farmer; *b* 17 Sept. 1919; *s* of late Henry Walter Featherstone, OBE, MD, Hon. LLD, JP, and of Margery Eveline (*née* Harston); *m* Joan Llewellyn, *d* of Lt-Col R. H. Waddy, DSO; *two s* one *d. Educ:* Rugby Sch.; Trinity Coll., Cambridge (BA). Served War, 1939-46: RA, France, Belgium, Holland and Germany. Staffs Yeomanry, 1948-62; Lt-Col Comdg, 1959-62; Hon. Col 1972. Member: W Midlands TAVR Assoc.; Lichfield Diocesan Synod and Bd of Finance, 1976-. DL 1963, JP 1967, Staffs; High Sheriff of Staffs, 1969. *Recreations:* shooting, nature conservation. *Address:* Yoxall Lodge, Newchurch, near Burton-on-Trent, Staffs. *T:* Hoar Cross 237.

FEAVER, Rt. Rev. Douglas Russell; *see* Peterborough, Bishop of.

FEDIDA, Sam, OBE 1980; independent consultant, information systems; inventor of Prestel, viewdata system (first public electronic information service); *b* 1918; *m* 1942, Joan Iris Druce. Served Royal Air Force, Radar Officer, 1940-46. Became Asst Dir of Research, The English Electric Company; started research for the Post Office, 1970; Prestel first in use 1979, as public service; MacRobert Award, Council of Engineering Instns, 1979; Prestel sold in Europe, USA, Far East. *Address:* Constable Cottage, Brook Lane, Felixstowe, Suffolk.

FEENY, Max Howard; barrister; *b* 5 Nov. 1928; *s* of late Howard Raymond John Feeny and of Frances Kate Feeny (*née* Muspratt); *m* 1952, June Elizabeth (*née* Camplin); *three s* four *d. Educ:* Stonyhurst Coll.; Oratory Sch.; Univ. of Birmingham (LLB). Called to Bar, Inner Temple, 1953. A Recorder of the Crown Court, 1972-78. *Recreation:* gardening. *Address:* Urlee, Lisselton, near Listowel, Co. Kerry, Eire.

FEHILY, Rt. Rev. Mgr Thomas Francis; Principal RC Chaplain (Army), 1973-77; *b* 16 Nov. 1917; *s* of late Patrick and Mary Fehily, Ballineen, Co. Cork. *Educ:* Capuchin Franciscan Coll., Rochestown, Co. Cork; St Kieran's Coll., Kilkenny. Ordained, 1942; Motherwell Dio., 1943-53. Commissioned Army Chaplain, 1953; served: Germany, 1953-56; Malaya, 1956-59; Germany and Berlin, 1959-63; RMA, Sandhurst, 1963-66. Senior Chaplain: NI, 1966-67; Singapore, 1967-69; HQ 1 Br. Corps, 1969-71; Western Command, 1971; Northern Command, 1972-73. *Recreations:* fishing, golf. *Address:* St John's, Blackwood, Kirkmuirhill, Lanarkshire ML11 9RZ.

FEHR, Basil Henry Frank, CBE 1979; Chairman and Managing Director, Frank Fehr & Co. Ltd London and group of companies, since 1957; Chairman, Fehr Bros Inc. New York and group of companies, since 1970; *b* 11 July 1912; *s* of Frank E. Fehr, CBE and Jane (*née* Poulter); *m* 1st, 1936, Jane Marner (*née* Tallent) (marr. diss. 1951); *two s* one *d*; 2nd, 1951, Greta Constance (*née* Bremner) (marr. diss. 1971); *one d* one step *d*; 3rd, 1974, Anne Norma (*née* Cadman); *one d. Educ:* Rugby Sch.; Neûchatel Ecole de Commerce, Switzerland. Served War, 1939-45: HAC, later Instr, Gunnery Sch. of Anti-Aircraft, RA; retd Major. Joined father in family firm, Frank Fehr & Co., 1934; Partner, 1936; Governing Dir, Frank Fehr & Co. London, 1948; Pres., Fehr Bros (Manufactures) Inc. New York, 1949. Chairman: Cocoa Assoc. of London, 1952; London Commodity Exchange, 1954; London Oil and Tallow Trades Assoc., 1955; Copra Assoc. of London, 1957; Inc. Oilseed Assoc., 1958; United Assocs Ltd, 1959. Elected to Baltic Exchange, 1936; Dir, Baltic Mercantile and Shipping Exchange, 1963-69 and 1970-, Vice Chm. 1973-75, Chm. 1975-77. Jurat of Liberty of Romney Marsh, 1979. *Recreations:* sports generally, farming. *Address:* Slodden Farm, Dymchurch, Romney Marsh, Kent. *T:* Dymchurch 2241; 64 Queen Street, EC4R 1ER. *T:* 01-248 5066. *Clubs:* City Livery, Aldgate Ward, MCC, Royal Automobile; West Kent Cricket; Littlestone Golf.

FEIBUSCH, Hans; painter, mural painter, lithographer, sculptor, writer; *b* 15 Aug. 1898; *s* of Dr Carl Feibusch and Marianne Ickelheimer; *m* 1935, Sidonie (*d* 1963), *e d* of D. Gestetner. *Educ:* Frankfurt a/M and Munich Univs. Studied at the Berlin Academy, at Paris Art Schs, in Florence and Rome; received German State award and grant in 1931; pictures in German Public Galleries; work banned and destroyed by Nazis in 1933; since then in London; large mural paintings in churches: St Wilfred's, Brighton; St Elizabeth's, Eastbourne; St Martin's, Dagenham; St John's, Waterloo Road, SE1; St Ethelburga's, Bishopsgate; St Alban's, Holborn; Town Hall, Dudley; Civic Centre, Newport, Mon; Chichester Cathedral; Chichester Palace; Parish Churches, Egham, Goring, Wellingborough, Welling, Preston, Plumstead, Eltham, Portsmouth, Bexley Heath, Wembley, Merton, Southwark, Harrow, Exeter, Battersea, Rotherhithe, Plymouth, Coventry, Christchurch Priory, Bournemouth, Christ Church, St Laurence, Sydney, Portmeirion, Bath; West London Synagogue; statue, St John the Baptist, St John's Wood Church; statue, Christ, Ely Cathedral; 80th birthday exhibn by GLC, Holland Park, 1978. 6 one-man exhibns, incl. Berlin 1980. Much portrait and figure sculpture, 1975-. German Cross of Merit, 1967. *Publications:* Mural Painting, 1946; The Revelation of Saint John, 1946. *Recreations:* music and poetry. *Address:* 30 Wadham Gardens, NW3. *Club:* Athenæum.

FEILDEN, Bernard Melchior, CBE 1976 (OBE 1969); FRIBA 1968 (ARIBA 1949); Consultant, Feilden and Mawson, Chartered Architects (Partner, 1956-77); Director, International Centre for the Preservation and Restoration of Cultural Property, Rome, since 1977; Member, Cathedrals Advisory Commission for England, since 1981; *b* 11 Sept. 1919; *s* of Robert Humphrey Feilden, MC, and Olive Feilden (*née* Binyon); *m* 1949, Ruth Mildred Bainbridge; *two s* two *d. Educ:* Bedford Sch. Exhibr, Bartlett Sch. of Architecture, 1938. Served War of 1939-45: Bengal Sappers and Miners. AA Diploma (Hons), 1949; Bratt Colbran Schol., 1949. Architect, Norwich Cathedral, 1963-77; Surveyor to the Fabric: York Minster, 1965-77; St Paul's Cathedral, 1969-77. Hoffman Wood Prof. of Architecture, Leeds Univ., 1973-74. Mem., Ancient Monuments Bd (England), 1964-77; Mem. Council, RIBA, 1972-77; President: Ecclesiastical Architects' and Surveyors' Assoc., 1975-77; Guild of Surveyors, 1976-77. FSA 1969; FRSA 1973. Corresp. Mem., Architectes en Chef, France. DUniv York, 1973. *Publications:* The Wonder of York Minster, 1976; Introduction to Conservation, 1979; Conservation of Historic Buildings, 1982; articles in Architectural Review, Chartered Surveyor, AA Quarterly. *Recreations:* painting, sailing, fishing, photography. *Address:* Stiffkey Old Hall, Stiffkey, near Wells-on-Sea, Norfolk NR23 1QJ. *T:* Bingham (Norfolk) 585. *Club:* Athenæum.

See also G. B. R. *Feilden.*

FEILDEN, Geoffrey Bertram Robert, CBE 1966; MA Cantab; FRS 1959; Founder FEng 1976, FIMechE; Principal Consultant, Feilden Associates Ltd, since 1981; *b* 20 Feb. 1917; *s* of Robert Humphrey Feilden, MC, and Olive Feilden (*née* Binyon); *m* 1st, Elizabeth Ann Gorton; one *s* two *d*; 2nd, Elizabeth Diana Angier (*née* Lloyd). *Educ:* Bedford Sch.; King's Coll., Cambridge. Lever Bros. and Unilever Ltd, 1939-40; Power Jets Ltd, 1940-46; Ruston and Hornsby Ltd, 1946-59; Chief Engineer, Turbine Dept, 1949; Engineering Dir, 1954; Man. Dir, Hawker Siddeley Brush Turbines Ltd, and Dir of Hawker Siddeley Industries Ltd, 1959-61; Gp Technical Dir, Davy-Ashmore Ltd, 1961-68; Dep. Dir Gen., British Standards Instn, 1968-70, Dir Gen. 1970-81. Member: Cttees and Sub-Cttees of Aeronautical Research Council, 1947-62; BTC Res. Adv. Council, 1956-61; Council for Sci. and Indust. Res. of DSIR, 1961-65; Design Council (formerly CoID), 1966-78 (Dep. Chm., 1977-78); Central Adv. Council for Science and Technology, 1970-71; Vis. Cttee to RCA, 1968- (Chm., 1977-); Pres., European Cttee for Standardisation, 1977-79. Member, Royal Society Delegation: to USSR, 1965; Latin America, 1968; People's Republic of China, 1975; Leader, BSI Delegn to People's Republic of China, 1980. Technical Adviser to Govt of India, 1968. DSIR Visitor to Prod. Engineering Res. Assoc. of Gt Brit., 1957-65, and to Machine Tool Industry Res. Assoc., 1961-65. Member Council: Royal Society (a Vice-Pres., 1967-69); IMechE, 1955-61, 1969-80; Univ. of Surrey, 1977-78. Dir, Averys Ltd, 1974-79. Hon. DTech Loughborough, 1970; Hon. DSc QUB, 1971; Hon. FIStructE 1976. *Publications:* Gas Turbine Principles and Practice (contributor), 1955; First Bulleid Memorial Lecture (Nottingham Univ.), 1959; Report, Engineering Design, 1963 (Chm. of Cttee); numerous papers and articles on engineering subjects. *Recreations:* sailing, ski-ing, driving kitchen and garden machines. *Address:* Greys End, Rotherfield Greys, Henley-on-Thames, Oxon. *T:* Rotherfield Greys 211. *Club:* Athenæum.

See also B. M. *Feilden.*

FEILDEN, Sir Henry (Wemyss), 6th Bt *cr* 1846; *b* 1 Dec. 1916; *s* of Col Wemyss Gawne Cunningham Feilden, CMG (*d* 1943) (3rd *s* of 3rd Bt) and Winifred Mary Christian (*d* 1980), *d* of Rev. William Cosens, DD; *S* cousin, Sir William Morton Buller Feilden, 5th Bt, 1976; *m* 1943, Ethel May, 2nd *d* of John Atkinson, Annfield Plain, Co. Durham; one *s* two *d. Educ:* Canford Sch.; King's Coll., London. Served War, RE, 1940-46. Clerical Civil Service, 1960-79. *Recreations:* watching cricket, reading. *Heir: s* Henry Rudyard Feilden, BVetSc, MRCVS [*b* 26 Sept. 1951; *m* 1982, Anne Shepperd]. *Address:* Little Dene, Heathfield Road, Burwash, Etchingham, East Sussex TN19 7HN. *T:* Burwash 882205. *Club:* MCC.

FEILDING, family name of **Earl of Denbigh.**

FEILDING, Viscount; Alexander Stephen Rudolph Feilding; *b* 4 Nov. 1970; *s* and *heir* of Earl of Denbigh and Desmond, *qv.*

FEINSTEIN, Prof. Charles Hilliard, PhD; Professor of Economic and Social History, since 1978, and Head of Department of Economic and Related Studies, since 1981, University of York; Managing Editor, The Economic Journal, since 1980; *b* 18 March 1932; *s* of Louis and Rose Feinstein; *m* 1st, 1958, Ruth Loshak; one *s* three *d*; 2nd, 1980, Anne Digby. *Educ:* Parktown Boys' High Sch., Johannesburg; Univ. of Witwatersrand (BCom 1950); Fitzwilliam Coll., Cambridge (PhD 1958). CA (SA) 1954. Research Officer, Dept of Applied Econs, Univ. of Cambridge, 1958-63; Univ. Lectr in Faculty of Econs, Cambridge, 1963-78; Fellow of Clare Coll., Cambridge, 1963-78; Sen. Tutor, Clare Coll. 1969-78. Vis. Res. Fellow, Russian Res. Centre, Harvard Univ., 1967-68; Vis. Lectr, Univ. of Delhi, 1972. Mem. Council: Royal Economic Soc., 1980-; Economic History Soc., 1980-. *Publications:* Domestic Capital Formation in the United Kingdom 1920-1938, 1965; (ed) Socialism, Capitalism and Economic Growth, Essays presented to Maurice Dobb, 1967; National Income, Expenditure and Output of the United Kingdom 1855-1965, 1972; (ed) York 1831-1981, 1981; (jtly) British Economic Growth 1856-1973, 1982; (ed) The Managed Economy: Essays in British Economic Policy and Performance since 1929, 1982. *Recreations:* walking, reading, going to the theatre. *Address:* 48 Marygate, York YO3 7BH.

FELDBERG, Wilhelm Siegmund, CBE 1963; MD Berlin; MA Cantab; FRS 1947; FRCP 1978; Professor Emeritus; Personal Grant Holder, National Institute for Medical Research, London, since 1967; Hon. Lecturer, University of London, since 1950; *b* 19 Nov. 1900; *m* 1925, Katherine (*d* 1976), *d* of late Karl Scheffler; one *d* (and one *s* decd); *m* 1977, Kim O'Rourke (*d* 1981). Reader in Physiology, Cambridge Univ., until 1949; Head of Physiology and Pharmacology Division, National Institute for Medical Research, London, 1949–65 (Hon. Head of Division, 1965–66); Head, Lab. of Neuropharmacology, Nat. Inst. for Med. Res., 1966–74. Lectures: Dunham, Harvard, 1953; Evarts Graham Meml, Washington Univ., St Louis, USA, 1961; Aschoff Meml, Freiburg Univ., 1961; Dixon Meml, RSM, 1964; William Withering, 1966; Nat. Research Council of Canada/Nuffield Foundn, 1970–71; Ferrier, Royal Soc., 1974; Sherrington, 1980. Hon. Member: Br. Pharmacol. Soc.; RSM; Physiol. Soc.; Soc. française d'allergie; Deutsche Phys. Gesell.; Deutsche Pharm. Gesell.; Berliner Medizinische Gesell.; Berliner Phys. Gesell. Hon. MD: Freiburg, Berlin, Cologne, Liège; Hon. DSc: Bradford, 1973; London, 1979; Hon. LLD: Glasgow, 1976; Aberdeen, 1977. Grand Cross, Order of Merit of German Federal Republic, 1961. Baly Medal, 1963; Schmiedeberg Plakette, 1969; Stöhr Medal, 1970. *Publications:* Histamin (with E. Schilf); A Pharmacological Approach to the Brain from its Inner and Outer Surface, 1963; articles in med. and scientific jls. *Recreations:* antique furniture, women's fashions. *Address:* National Institute for Medical Research, Mill Hill, NW7 1AA. *T:* 01-959 3666; Lavenham, 74 Marsh Lane, Mill Hill, NW7 4NT. *T:* 01-959 5545.

FELDMAN, Sir Basil, Kt 1982; Chairman, Solport Ltd, since 1980; *b* 23 Sept. 1926; *s* of Philip and late Tilly Feldman; *m* 1952, Gita Julius; two *s* one *d*. *Educ:* Grocers' School. National Union of Conservative and Unionist Associations, Greater London area: Dep. Chm., 1975–78; Chm., 1978–81; Pres., 1981–; Mem. Nat. Union Exec. Cttee, 1975–, Vice Chm., Nat. Union of Cons. Party, 1982–; Jt Nat. Chm., Cons. Party's Impact 80s Campaign, 1982–; Chm., Environment and Leisure Study Group, 1975–77; Member: Policy Gp for London, 1975–81; Nat. Campaign Cttee, 1976 and 1978; European Direct Elections Steering Cttee, 1977–; Adv. Cttee on Policy, 1981–; Vice-Pres., Greater London Young Conservatives, 1975–77; Mem., Hampstead Cons. Assoc., 1965– (Patron 1981); Pres., Richmond and Barnes Cons. Assoc., 1976–; Pres., Hornsey Cons. Assoc., 1978–82. Contested GLC Elections, Richmond, 1973; Member: GLC Housing Management Cttee, 1973–77; GLC Arts Cttee, 1976–81. Chm., Martlet Services Gp Ltd, 1973–81; Mem., Free Enterprise Loan Soc., 1977–. Underwriting Mem. of Lloyds, 1979–. Membre Consultatif, Institut Internat. de Promotion et de Prestige, Geneva (affiliated to Unesco), 1978–. Mem., Post Office Users National Council, 1978–81 (Mem., Tariffs Sub-Cttee, 1980–81); Chm., Clothing Econ. Develt Cttee (NEDO), 1978–. *Publications:* Constituency Campaigning: a guide for Conservative Party workers; several other Party booklets and pamphlets. *Recreations:* golf, tennis, theatre, opera. *Clubs:* Carlton, St Stephen's Constitutional.

FELL, Sir Anthony, Kt 1982; MP (C) Yarmouth Division of Norfolk, 1951–66 and since 1970; *b* 18 May 1914; *s* of Comdr David Mark Fell, RN; *m* 1938; one *s* one *d*. *Educ:* Bedford Grammar School; New Zealand. Contested (C) Brigg, 1948, South Hammersmith, 1949 and 1950. *Address:* 11 Denny Street, SE11 4UX.

FELL, Charles Percival, LLD; Hon. Director and Member Toronto Advisory Board, Royal Trustco Ltd; Hon. Governor, McMaster University (Chancellor, 1960–65); *b* Toronto, 1894; *s* of I. C. Fell and Sarah (Branton) Fell, both of Toronto, Ont.; *m* 1st, Grace E. Matthews; three *s* one *d*; 2nd, 1976, Marjorie Jane Montgomery. *Educ:* University of Toronto Schs; McMaster Univ. Associated with Dillon, Read & Co., NY, 1921–24; Dominion Securities Corp., Toronto, 1925–29; Chm. Canadian group, Investment Bankers Assoc. of America, 1928. Dir, Canadian Surety Co., 1947–72; Pres., Empire Life Assurance Co., 1934–68. Mem. Bd of Referees (Excess Profits Tax Act, Canada), Ottawa, 1940–45. Pres., Art Gall. of Toronto, 1950–53; Chm., Bd of Trustees, Nat. Gall. of Canada, Ottawa, 1953–59. Coronation Medal, Canada, 1953. Hon. LLD McMaster Univ., 1957. *Address:* 52 Park Lane Circle, Don Mills, Ont. M3C 2N2, Canada. *T:* 447-7523. *Clubs:* York; Toronto.

FELL, Dame Honor Bridget, DBE 1963; FRS 1952; medical research worker, Strangeways Research Laboratory, Cambridge, since 1979 (Director, 1929–70); Foulerton Research Fellow, Royal Society, 1941–67; Fellow of Girton College, Cambridge, 1955; *b* 22 May 1900; *d* of Col William Edwin Fell and Alice Fell (*née* Pickersgill-Cunliffe). *Educ:* Wychwood Sch., Oxford; Madras Coll., St Andrews; Edinburgh Univ. BSc (Edinburgh) 1922; PhD (Edinburgh) 1924; DSc (Edinburgh) 1930; MA (Cantab) 1955. Research Student, DSIR, 1922; Research Asst, MRC, 1923; Junior Beit Fellow, 1924; 4th Year Beit Fellow, 1927; Senior Beit Fellow, 1928; Messel Research Fellow, Royal Society, 1931; Royal Society Research Professor, 1963–67; med. res. worker, Dept of Immunology, Univ. of Cambridge, 1970–79. Hon. LLD: Edinburgh, 1959; Glasgow, 1970; Hon. DSc: Oxon, 1964; London, 1967; Hon. ScD: Smith Coll., USA, 1962; Harvard, 1964; Cambridge, 1969; Hon. MD Leiden 1976; Foreign Member: Royal Netherlands Academy, 1964; Serbian Acad. Sci. and Arts, 1975; Hon. Fellow, Somerville Coll., Oxford, 1964; Fellow, King's Coll., London, 1967. Prix Charles-Leopold Mayer, French Academy of Science, 1965. *Publications:* various communications to biological and medical journals. *Recreation:* travel. *Address:* 42b Queen Edith's Way, Cambridge. *T:* Cambridge 247022.

FELL, Robert, CB 1972; CBE 1966; Commissioner for Securities and Commodities, Hong Kong, since 1981; *b* 6 May 1921; *s* of Robert and Mary Ann Fell, Cumberland; *m* 1946, Eileen Wicks; two *s* one *d*. *Educ:* Whitehaven Grammar School. War Office, 1939; military service, 1940–46 (despatches); BoT, 1947; Trade Comr, Qld, 1954–59; Asst Sec., Tariff Div., 1961; Commercial Counsellor, Delhi, 1961–66; Under-Sec. i/c export promotion, 1967–71; Sec., ECGD, 1971–74; Chief Exec., The Stock Exchange, 1975–82. Mem., British Overseas Trade Board, 1972–75; Pres., City Branch, BIM, 1976–82. FBIM; FRSA. *Recreations:* Rugby football (watching), gardening. *Address:* Dalegarth, Guildown Avenue, Guildford, Surrey. *T:* Guildford 72204. *Club:* Travellers'.

FELLINI, Federico; film director since 1950; *b* 20 Jan. 1920; *s* of late Urbano Fellini and Ida Barbiani; *m* 1943, Giulietta Masina. *Educ:* Bologna, Italy. Journalist, 1937–39; radio-author, scenario writer, etc, 1939–42. Has gained many prizes and awards in every part of the world including four "Oscars" (1957, 1958, 1964, 1975) for films La Strada, Le Notti di Cabiria, 8½ and Amarcord. Films include: (as Assistant Director and writer) Quarta Pagina, 1942; Roma Città Aperta, 1944–45; Paisà, 1946; Il Delitto di Giovanni Episcopo, 1947; In Nome della Legge, 1948–49; La Città si Defende, 1951; Il Brigante di Tacca di Lupo, 1953; San Francesco Giullare di Dio, 1954; Fortunella, 1956; (as Director) Luci del Varietà, 1950; Lo Sceicco Bianco, 1952; I Vitelloni, 1953; Agenzia Matrimoniale, 1953; La Strada, 1954; Il Bidone, 1955; Cabiria, 1957; La Dolce Vita, 1960; The Temptation of Dr Antonio, 1962; 8½, 1963 (foreign awards); Giulietta Degli Spiriti, 1965; Never Bet the Devil Your Head, 1968; Director's Blocknotes, 1969; Satyricon, 1969; The Clowns, 1970; Fellini's Roma, 1972; Amarcord, 1974; Casanova, 1976; Orchestra Rehearsal, 1979; La citta delle donne, 1980. *Publications:* Amarcord (trans. Nina Rootes), 1974; Quattro film, 1975. *Address:* 110 Via Margutta, Rome.

FELLOWES, family name of **Barons Ailwyn** and **De Ramsey.**

FELLOWES, Maj.-Gen. Halford David, CB 1957; DSO 1945; *b* 2 Aug. 1906; *er s* of late Major Halford Le M. Fellowes, 47th Sikhs (retd), Tenterden; *m* 1st, 1932, Angela Mary (marr. diss. 1941), *d* of P. E. Cammiade, ICS (retd); one *d*; 2nd, 1942, Rosemary, *er d* of late Brig.-Gen. Sir Terence Keyes, KCIE, CSI, CMG. *Educ:* St Paul's Sch., London. Royal Marines: 2nd Lieut 1924; Lieut 1927; Capt. 1936; A/Maj. 1940; A/Lt-Col 1940; Bt Major 1941; A/Col 1945; T/Brig. 1945; Major 1946; A/Lieut-Col 1947; Lieut-Col 1948; A/Col 1952; Col 1952; Maj.-Gen. 1954. Served HM Ships Berwick, Resolution, Sheffield, Base Defences Mediterranean, 1935–36; RM Siege Regt, 1940–42; GSO1, Special Service Group, 1943–44; 42 Commando RM (SE Asia), 1944–45 (wounded in Arakan, 1945); HQ 3 Commando Bde, 1945–46; GSO1 (Trg), RM office, 1947–49; Commando Sch., RM, 1949–52; Depot, RM Deal, 1952–54; psc 1943; jssc 1947. Commander Plymouth Group, Royal Marines, 1954–57, retired. *Address:* Cedar Cottage, Brede, Rye, East Sussex TN31 6EH. *T:* Brede 882743. *Club:* Rye Golf.

FELLOWES, Robert; Assistant Private Secretary to the Queen, since 1977; *b* 11 Dec. 1941; *s* of Sir William Fellowes, *qv*; *m* 1978, Lady Jane Spencer, *d* of Earl Spencer, *qv*; one *d*. *Educ:* Eton. Scots Guards (short service commission), 1960–63. Director, Allen Harvey & Ross Ltd, Discount Brokers and Bankers, 1968–77. *Recreations:* cricket, golf, shooting. *Address:* 5A The Old Barracks, Kensington Palace, W8. *T:* 01-937 2979. *Clubs:* White's, Pratt's, MCC.

FELLOWES, Sir William (Albemarle), KCVO 1964 (CVO 1952); Agent to the Queen, Sandringham Estate, 1936–64, retired; Member of firm, Savills (formerly Alfred Savill, Curtis & Henson, before that Alfred Savill & Sons) (Land Agents and Valuers), 1964–77; *b* 10 Sept. 1899; 2nd *surv. s* of Charles Arthur Fellowes and Mary Fellowes; *m* 1934, Jane Charlotte, *d* of Brig.-Gen. A. F. H. Ferguson; two *s* two *d*. *Educ:* Winchester Coll.; Oriel Coll., Oxford. Agent to: Major W. S. Gosling, Hassobury Estate, Essex, 1925–30; Old Warden Estates, Beds, 1930–36. Became Agent to King George VI, 1936. Served with Scots Guards, 1940–45. DL Norfolk, 1965–81. FLAS 1927; Associate of the Chartered Surveyors, 1923. FRICS 1964. *Recreations:* shooting and fishing. *Address:* Flitcham House, Flitcham, King's Lynn, Norfolk. *T:* Hillington 600346.
See also R. Fellowes.

FELLOWS, Derek Edward, FIA; Chief Actuary, Prudential Assurance Co. Ltd, since 1981; *b* 23 Oct. 1927; *s* of Edward Frederick Fellows and Gladys Fellows; *m* 1948, Mary Watkins; two *d*. *Educ:* Mercers' Sch. FIA 1956. Entered Prudential Assurance Co. Ltd, 1943; Gp Pensions Manager, 1973–81. Mem., Occupational Pensions Bd, 1974–78. FPMI 1976; Vice Pres., Inst. of Actuaries, 1980–. *Publications:* contrib. Jl of Inst. of Actuaries. *Recreations:* music, gardening. *Address:* 20 Fairbourne, Cobham, Surrey KT11 2BT. *T:* Cobham 5488.

FENBY, Eric William, OBE 1962; Professor of Harmony, Royal Academy of Music, 1964–77; *b* 22 April 1906; *s* of late Herbert Henry and Ada Fenby; *m* 1944, Rowena Clara Teresa Marshall; one *s* one *d*. *Educ:* Municipal Sch., Scarborough; privately. Amanuensis to Frederick Delius, 1928–34; Mus. Adv. Boosey & Hawkes, 1936–39; début as composer, BBC Promenade Concerts, 1942. Captain, RAEC Sch. of Educn, Cuerdon Hall, 1942–45. Mus. Dir, N Riding Coll. of Educn, 1948–62; Artistic Dir, Delius Centenary Festival, 1962; Pres. Delius Soc., 1964–; Chm., Composers' Guild of Great Britain, 1968,

Mem. Council, 1970. Visiting Prof. of Music and Composer in Residence, Jacksonville Univ., Fla, USA, 1968. Mem. Cttee of Management, Royal Philharmonic Soc., 1972. Hon. Mem., RAM, 1965; Hon. DMus Jacksonville, 1978; Hon. DLitt Warwick, 1978; Hon. DLitt Bradford, 1978. *Publications:* Delius as I Knew Him, 1936, rev. edn 1966; a further rev. edn, 1981, packaged with own recordings of all works dictated to him by Delius, known as The Fenby Legacy; Menuhin's House of Music, 1969; Delius, 1971. *Recreations:* walking, chess. *Address:* 35 Brookfield, Highgate West Hill, N6. *T:* 01-340 5122. *Club:* Royal Academy of Music.

FENDALL, Prof. Neville Rex Edwards, MD; Professor of International Community Health, School of Tropical Medicine, University of Liverpool, 1971-81, now Emeritus Professor; *b* 9 July 1917; *s* of Francis Alan Fendall and Ruby Inez Matthews; *m* 1942, Margaret Doreen (*née* Beynon). *Educ:* University College Hosp. (MD, BSc); London Sch. of Hygiene and Tropical Med. (DPH); FFCM. Colonial Medical Service, 1944-64, incl of Health Services, Kenya; Staff Mem., Rockefeller Foundn, 1964-66; Regional Dir, Population Council Inc., New York, 1966-71. Mem., Panel of Experts, WHO, 1960-82; Consultant: World Bank; UN Fund for Population Activities; ODM; Cento; Internat. Develt Res. Centre, Canada; APHA; USAID; Overseas govts. Visiting Lecturer: Harvard, 1966-82; Inst. of Tropical Medicine, Marseilles; Univ. of Glasgow; Univ. of Bradford; Vis. Consultant, Univ. of Hawaii; Commonwealth Foundn Travelling Lectr, 1976. *Publication:* Auxiliaries in Health Care, 1972 (English, French, Spanish edns); contribs on primary health care, epidemiology, in various jls. *Recreation:* gardening. *Address:* Berwyn, North Close, Bromborough, Wirral L62 2BU. *T:* 051-334 2193. *Clubs:* Royal Commonwealth Society; Athenæum (Liverpool).

FENDER, Percy George Herbert; Chairman and Managing Director, London Wine Exchange, since 1968; *b* Balham, 22 Aug. 1892; *e s* of Percy Robert Fender and Lily Herbert; *m* 1st, 1924, Ruth Marian Clapham (*d* 1937); one *s* one *d*; 2nd, 1962, Susan Victoria Gordon (*née* Kyffin) (*d* 1968). *Educ:* St George's Coll., Weybridge; St Paul's Sch. Cricket for Sussex, 1910-13, for Surrey, 1914-35 (Captain, 1921-32); toured Australia for MCC, 1920-21; also South Africa, 1922-23; toured Australia for London Star as First Special Cricket Correspondent for any newspaper, 1928-29. Fastest hundred ever made in first class cricket (35 mins) for Surrey v Northants (world record, 1920); fastest five wickets in first class cricket (in seven consecutive deliveries) for Surrey v Middlesex at Lords (world record, 1927); first cricketer to achieve cricketer's treble: 1,000 runs, 100 wickets and 50 catches in one season (world record, 1921). Contributor to Field, Sporting and Dramatic, Telegraph, etc. Football for Casuals, Corinthians and Fulham. Training in Vale Paper Mills, Lancs, then Papeterie Belge Droogenbosch, Belgium and Bureau Concours Hippique Brussels; joined Crescens Robinson Co. Ltd, 1912, Dir, 1922, Chm., 1943-68, resigned 1973; created Herbert Fender & Co., 1922, retired as Chm. and Man. Dir, 1977. Served War: England, India and Burma, Royal Fusiliers, 1914-15, Royal Flying Corps, 1915 and Royal Air Force, 1915-18; Special Constable, 1926-40; rejoined RAF as Pilot Officer, 1940-46; Sen. Movement Officer, 2nd TAF, Invasion of Europe (despatches), S Africa, New Zealand, Australia, Phillipines, New Guinea, retired as Wing Comdr, 1945. Mem. LCC for Norwood Div. of Lambeth, 1952-55 and 1955-58. DL County of London, 1958; Greater London, 1965-75. Grant of Arms, 1966. Freeman, City of London, 1960. *Publications:* Defending the Ashes, 1921; Turn of the Wheel, 1929; The Tests of 1930, 1930; Kissing the Rod, 1934; Lonsdale Library on Cricket; ABC of Cricket, 1937, BBC and Television Cricket, etc. *Recreations:* bridge, golf, billiards, snooker, real tennis. *Address:* (home) 6 Cotswold Court, Burford Road, Horsham, Sussex RH13 5SS; (office) West Street, Horsham, Sussex. *Clubs:* Royal Air Force, MCC (Life Mem. 1981); Surrey County Cricket (Life Mem.; Vice-Pres., 1979).

FENECH-ADAMI, Dr Edward; MP Malta, since 1969; Leader of Opposition and Leader of Nationalist Party, since 1977; *b* 7 Feb. 1934; *s* of late Luigi Fenech-Adami and Josephine (*née* Pace); *m* 1965, Mary (*née* Sciberras); four *s* one *d*. *Educ:* St Aloysius Coll., Malta; Royal Univ. of Malta (BA 1955, LLD 1958). Shadow Minister for Labour and Social Services, 1971-77. Editor, Il-Poplu, 1962-69. *Address:* (home) 176 Main Street, Birkirkara, Malta. *T:* 42231; (office) 171 Old Bakery Street, Valletta. *T:* 622096.

FENN, Nicholas Maxted, CMG 1980; HM Diplomatic Service; Ambassador in Rangoon, since 1982; *b* 19 Feb. 1936; *s* of Rev. Prof. J. Eric Fenn and Kathleen (*née* Harrison); *m* 1959, Susan Clare (*née* Russell); two *s* one *d*. *Educ:* Kingswood Sch., Bath; Peterhouse, Cambridge (MA). Third Sec., British Embassy, Rangoon, 1959-63; Asst Private Sec. to Sec. of State for Foreign and Commonwealth Affairs, 1963-67; First Secretary: British Interests Sect., Swiss Embassy, Algiers, 1967-69; Public Relations, UK Mission to UN, NY, 1969-72; Dep. Head, Energy Dept, FCO, 1972-75; Counsellor, Peking, 1975-77; RCDS 1978; Head of News Dept and FCO Spokesman, 1979-82; Spokesman to last Governor of Rhodesia, 1979-80. *Recreation:* sailing. *Address:* c/o Foreign and Commonwealth Office, SW1; Applecroft, Chainhurst, Marden, Tonbridge, Kent TN12 9SS. *T:* Hunton 438. *Club:* United Oxford & Cambridge University.

FENNELL, John Desmond Augustine, OBE 1982; QC; *b* 17 Sept. 1933; *s* of late Dr A. J. Fennell, Lincoln; *m* 1966, Susan Primrose, *d* of late J. M. Trusted; one *s* two *d*. *Educ:* Ampleforth; Corpus Christi Coll., Cambridge. Served with Grenadier Guards, 1956-58. Called to the Bar, Inner Temple, 1959; Dep. Chm., Bedfordshire QS, 1971; a Recorder of the Crown Court,

1972-; QC 1974. Chm., Buckingham Div. Cons. Assoc., 1976-79. *Address:* 2 Crown Office Row, Temple, EC4Y 7HJ. *T:* 01-353 1365; Lawn House, Winslow, Buckingham MK18 3AJ. *T:* Winslow 2464. *Club:* Cavalry and Guards.

FENNELL, Prof. John Lister Illingworth, MA, PhD Cantab; FRSL; Professor of Russian, Oxford University, since 1967; Fellow of New College, Oxford; *b* 30 May 1918; *s* of Dr C. H. Fennell and Sylvia Mitchell; *m* 1947, Marina Lopukhin; one *s* one *d*. *Educ:* Radley Coll.; Trinity Coll., Cambridge. FRSL 1980. Served with Army, 1939-45. Asst Lectr, Dept of Slavonic Studies, Cambridge Univ., 1947-52; Reader in Russian and Head of Dept of Slavonic Languages, Nottingham Univ., 1952-56; Lectr in Russian, Oxford Univ., 1956-67, Fellow and Praelector in Russian, University Coll., Oxford, 1964-67. Vis. Lectr, Harvard Univ., 1963-64; Visiting Professor: Univ. of Calif at Berkeley, 1971, 1977; Virginia Univ., 1974. Organiser, 3rd Internat. Conf. of Historians of Muscovy, Oxford, 1975. Joint Editor: Oxford Slavonic Papers; Russia Mediaevalis. *Publications:* The Correspondence between Prince A. M. Kurbsky and Ivan IV, 1955; Ivan the Great of Moscow, 1961; The Penguin Russian Course, 1961; Pushkin, 1964; Kurbsky's History of Ivan IV, 1965; The Emergence of Moscow, 1968; (ed jtly) Historical Russian Reader, 1969; (ed) Nineteenth Century Russian Literature, 1973; (with A. Stokes) Early Russian Literature, 1974; (ed jtly) The Cambridge Encyclopaedia of Russia and the Soviet Union, 1982; Cambridge Modern History, Vol. II, Chap. 19; articles in Slavonic and East European Review, Jahrbücher für Geschichte Osteuropas, etc. *Recreation:* music. *Address:* 8 Canterbury Road, Oxford. *T:* Oxford 56149.

FENNER, Mrs Bernard; see Fenner, Mrs Peggy.

FENNER, Prof. Frank John, CMG 1976; MBE 1944; FRS 1958; FAA 1954; FRCP 1967; University Fellow, Australian National University, since 1980; Professor of Environmental Studies and Director, Centre for Resource and Environmental Studies, Australian National University, 1973-79; *b* 21 Dec. 1914; *s* of Charles and Emma L. Fenner; *m* 1944, Ellen Margaret Bobbie Roberts; one *d* (and one *d* decd). *Educ:* Thebarton Technical High Sch.; Adelaide High Sch.; Univ. of Adelaide. MB, BS (Adelaide) 1938; MD (Adelaide) 1942; DTM (Sydney) 1940. Served as Medical Officer, Hospital Pathologist, and Malariologist, AIF, 1940-46; Francis Haley Research Fellow, Walter and Eliza Hall Inst. for Medical Research, Melbourne, 1946-48; Rockefeller Foundation Travelling Fellow, 1948-49; Prof. of Microbiology, 1949-73, and Dir, John Curtin Sch. of Med. Research, 1967-73, ANU; Overseas Fellow, Churchill Coll., Cambridge, 1962-63. Fogarty Schol., Nat. Insts of Health, USA, 1973-74. Chm., Global Commn for he Certification of Smallpox Eradication, WHO, 1978-80. For. Associate, Nat. Acad. of Scis, USA, 1977; David Syme Prize, Univ. of Melbourne, 1949; Harvey Lecture, Harvey Soc. of New York, 1957; Leeuwenhoek Lecture, Royal Society, 1961; Matthew Flinders Lecture, Australian Acad. of Science, 1967; Mueller Medal, Australian and New Zealand Assoc. for the Advancement of Science, 1964. Hon. MD Monash, 1966. Britannica Australia Award for Medicine, 1967; ANZAC Peace Award, 1980; ANZAAS Medal, 1980. *Publications:* The Production of Antibodies (with F. M. Burnet), 1949; Myxomatosis (with F. N. Ratcliffe), 1965; The Biology of Animal Viruses, 1968, 2nd edn 1974; Medical Virology (with D. O. White), 1970, 2nd edn 1976; Classification and Nomenclature of Viruses, 1976; (with A. L. G. Rees) The Australian Academy of Science: the First Twenty-five Years, 1980; numerous scientific papers, dealing with virology, epidemiology, bacteriology, and environmental problems. *Recreations:* gardening, tennis, fishing. *Address:* 8 Monaro Crescent, Red Hill, Canberra, ACT 2603, Australia. *T:* 95-9176.

FENNER, Mrs Peggy, (Mrs B. Fenner); MP (C) Rochester and Chatham, 1970-Sept. 1974 and since 1979; Parliamentary Secretary, Ministry of Agriculture, Fisheries and Food, since 1981; *b* 12 Nov. 1922; *m* 1940, Bernard Fenner; one *d*. *Educ:* LCC School, Brockley; Ide Hill, Sevenoaks. Councillor (C) Newcastle-under-Lyme, 1966; Parly Sec., MAFF, 1972-74; Mem., British Delegn to European Parlt, Strasbourg, 1974. Member: West Kent Divisional Exec. Educn Cttee, 1963-72; Sevenoaks Urban District Council, 1957-71 (Chairman, 1962 and 1963); Exec. of Kent Borough and Urban District Councils Assoc., 1967-71; a Vice-Pres, Urban District Councils Assoc., 1971. *Recreations:* reading, travel, theatre, gardening. *Address:* 12 Star Hill, Rochester, Kent. *T:* Medway 42124.

FENNESSY, Sir Edward, Kt 1975; CBE 1957 (OBE 1944); BSc; FIEE, FRIN; Chairman: Biochrom, since 1978; IMA Microwave Products Ltd, since 1979; British Medical Data Systems, since 1981; Deputy Chairman, L.B.K. Instruments Ltd, since 1978; *b* 17 Jan. 1912; *m* 1937, Marion Banks; one *s* one *d*. *Educ:* Univ. of London. Telecommunications Research, Standard Telephones and Cables, 1934-38; Radar Research, Air Min. Research Station, Bawdsey Manor, 1938. War of 1939-45: commissioned RAFVR, 1940; Group Captain, 1945; staff No 60 Group, RAF, 1940-45; resp. for planning and construction radar systems for defence of UK, and Bomber Ops. Joined Bd of The Decca Navigator Co., 1946; Managing Director: Decca Radar Ltd, 1950-65; The Plessey Electronics Group, 1965-69. Chairman: British Telecommunications Research Ltd, 1966-69; Electronic Engineering Assoc., 1967-68; Man. Dir, Telecommunications, 1969-77, and Dep. Chm., 1975-77, Post Office Corp. Pres., Royal Institute of Navigation, 1975-78. DUniv Surrey, 1971. *Recreations:* sailing, golf. *Address:* Northbrook, Littleford Lane, Shamley Green, Surrey. *T:* Guildford 892444. *Clubs:* Royal Air Force; Island Sailing.

FENNEY, Roger Johnson, CBE 1973 (MBE (mil.) 1945); Chairman, Special Trustees, Charing Cross Hospital, since 1980; *b* 11 Sept. 1916; *s* of James Henry Fenney and Annie Sarah Fenney; *m* 1942, Dorothy Porteus; two *d*. *Educ*: Cowley Sch., St Helens; Univ. of Manchester (BA Admin 1939). Served War, 1939-46: Gunner to Major, Field Artillery; served N Africa and Italy (mentioned in despatches). Secretary, Central Midwives Board, 1947-82; Governor, Charing Cross Hosp., 1958-74 (Chm., Clinical Res. Cttee, 1970-80; Mem. Council, Med. Sch., 1970-80); Governor, Hammersmith Hosp., 1956-74; Chm., W London Hosp., 1957-68; First Nuffield Fellow for Health Affairs, USA, 1968; Dep. Chm., Kennedy Inst. of Rheumatol., 1970-77. Member: Exec., Arthritis and Rheumatism Council, 1978-; Ealing, Hammersmith and Hounslow AHA, 1974-79; Field Dir, Jt Study Gp (FIGO/ICM), Accra, Yaounde, Nairobi, Dakar, San José and Bogotá, 1972-76. *Address:* 11 Gilray House, Gloucester Terrace, W2 3DF. *T:* 01-262 8313; Chiltern Cottage, Lower Assendon, Henley-on-Thames, Oxon.

FENNING, Frederick William; Director of Atomic Energy Technical Unit of United Kingdom Atomic Energy Authority, since 1977; *b* 14 Dec. 1919; *s* of Thomas and Lilian Fenning; *m* 1949, Eileen Mary Lyttle; one *s* two *d*. *Educ*: Clacton; Cambridge Univ. BA (Hons). Min. of Aircraft Production, 1940; Min. of Supply, Tube Alloys Project, Cambridge, 1942; Montreal, 1943; Chalk River, Ontario, 1945; AERE, Harwell, 1946-58; Chief Physicist, Risley, 1958; Dir, Reactor Technology, Risley, 1960-66; Dep. Dir, Harwell, 1966-77. *Recreations:* gardening, general DIY. *Address:* 21 St Peter's Hill, Caversham, Reading, Berks RG4 7AX. *T:* Reading 472302.

FENTON, Alexander; Director, National Museum of Antiquities of Scotland, since 1978; *b* 26 June 1929; *s* of Alexander Fenton and Annie Stirling Stronach; *m* 1956, Evelyn Elizabeth Hunter; two *d*. *Educ*: Turriff Academy; Aberdeen Univ. (MA); Cambridge Univ. (BA); Edinburgh Univ. (DLitt). Senior Asst Editor, Scottish National Dictionary, 1955-59; Asst Keeper, Nat. Museum of Antiquities of Scotland, 1959-75; Dep. Keeper, 1975-78. Mem., Ancient Monuments Bd for Scotland, 1979-. Member: Royal Gustav Adolf Acad., Uppsala, Sweden, 1978; Royal Danish Acad. of Scis and Letters, 1979. Co-editor, Tools and Tillage (Copenhagen), 1968-. *Publications:* The Various Names of Shetland, 1973, 2nd edn 1977; Scottish Country Life, 1976, 2nd edn 1978; (trans.) S. Steensen Blicher, En Landsbydegns Dagbog (The Diary of a Parish Clerk, 1976); The Island Blackhouse, 1978; The Northern Isles: Orkney and Shetland, 1978; (with B. Walker) The Rural Architecture of Scotland, 1981; numerous articles in learned jls. *Address:* 132 Blackford Avenue, Edinburgh EH9 3HH. *T:* 031-667 5456. *Club:* New (Edinburgh).

FENTON, Air Cdre Harold Arthur, CBE 1946; DSO 1943; DFC 1942; BA; AFRAeS; *b* Gallegos, Patagonia, Argentine, 9 Feb. 1909; *s* of Dr E. G. Fenton, FRCSI, DPH, Co. Sligo and J. Ormsby, Glen Lodge, Ballina, Co. Mayo; *m* 1935, H. de Carteret; no *c*. *Educ*: Sandford Park Sch.; Trinity Coll., Dublin (BA 1927). Joined RAF 1928. Served India, 1930-33. Flying Instructor at Air Service Training Ltd, Hamble, until outbreak of war. During war commanded: Fighter Sqdn, Battle of Britain; Fighter Wing, and Fighter Group, Western Desert and Libya; Fighter Sector, London Area. Finished war as Senior Staff Officer, Germany (83 Group) (despatches thrice). Managing Dir, Deccan Airways Ltd, Hyderabad, Deccan, until 1947; Gen. Manager of Airways Training Ltd, 1947-48; Operations Manager, BOAC, 1949-52; Managing Dir, Peter Jones, 1952-58. *Recreation:* gardening. *Address:* Le Vallon, St Brelade, Jersey, Channel Islands. *T:* 41172.

FENTON, Rev. Canon John Charles; Canon of Christ Church, Oxford, since 1978; *b* 5 June 1921; *s* of Cornelius O'Connor Fenton and Agnes Claudine Fenton. *Educ*: S Edward's Sch., Oxford; Queen's Coll., Oxford (BA 1943, MA 1947, BD 1953); Lincoln Theol Coll. Deacon 1944, priest 1945. Asst Curate, All Saints, Hindley, Wigan, 1944-47; Chaplain, Lincoln Theol Coll., 1947-51, Sub-Warden, 1951-54; Vicar of Wentworth, Yorks, 1954-58; Principal: Lichfield Theol Coll., 1958-65; S Chad's Coll., Durham, 1965-78. *Publications:* Preaching the Cross, 1958; The Passion according to John, 1961; Crucified with Christ, 1961; Saint Matthew, 1963; Saint John (New Clarendon Bible), 1970; What was Jesus' Message?, 1971; (with M. Hare Duke) Good News, 1976; contrib. Theol., and Jl of Theol Studies. *Recreations:* walking, camping, gardening. *Address:* Christ Church, Oxford. *T:* Oxford 43887.

FENTON, Wilfrid David Drysdale, CBE 1963; FRSE; BSc, FIEE; Director: Project Development Group (Europe), since 1978; Inter G Ltd, since 1978; *b* 27 March 1908; *s* of late David Fenton, Edinburgh; *m* 1st, 1955, Isobel Stewart (marr. diss. 1974); no *c*; 2nd, 1974, Elaine Herman, *d* of late Louis Surut, New York; two step *c*. *Educ*: George Watson's Coll., Edinburgh; Edinburgh Univ. Called to Bar, Middle Temple, 1937. Kennedy and Donkin, Cons. Engrs, London, 1931-33; Central Electricity Bd, London, 1933-38; Personal Asst to Gen. Manager, Midland Counties Electric Supply Co., 1938-44; Commercial Engr, 1944-48, Sec. and Commercial Engr, 1948-55, N of Scotland Hydro-Electric Bd; Chm., 1955-62, Uganda Electricity Bd; Chm., S Wales Electricity Bd, 1962-68; Chm., London Electricity Bd, 1968-72; Dep. Chm., CEGB, 1972-75; Man. Dir, Overseas Consultancy Services, Electricity Council 1975-76 (Dir, 1970-75); Man. Dir, British Electricity International, 1976-77. Dir, Uganda Development Corp., 1955-57; Hon. Treas., 1956-57, Vice-Chm., 1957-62, Makerere Univ. Coll.; Chm. Mulago Hosp. (Kampala) Autonomy Cttee, 1961. *Recreation:* golf. *Address:* 31 Cadogan Lane, SW1X 9DR. *Clubs:* Caledonian, Royal Commonwealth Society.

FENWICK, John James; Chairman, Fenwick Ltd, since 1979 (Deputy Chairman, 1972-79; Managing Director, 1972-82); *b* 9 Aug. 1932; *e s* of James Frederick Trevor Fenwick; *m* 1957, Muriel Gillian Hodnett; three *s*. *Educ*: Rugby Sch.; Pembroke Coll., Cambridge (MA). Chairman: Northumberland Assoc. of Youth Clubs, 1966-71; Retail Distributors Assoc., 1977-79; Vice Chm., National Assoc. of Citizens Advice Bureaux, 1971-79. Member: Newcastle Diocesan Bd of Finance, 1964-69; Retail Consortium Council, 1976-79; Post Office Users' Nat. Council, 1980-. Governor: Royal Grammar Sch., Newcastle upon Tyne, 1975-; Moorfields Eye Hosp., 1981-. *Recreations:* travel, shooting, theatre. *Address:* Heighley Rigg, Morpeth, Northumberland; 99 Chesterfield House, W1Y 5TD. *Clubs:* Garrick, MCC; Northern Counties (Newcastle upon Tyne).

FENWICK, Robert George, CBE 1975; QPM 1969; HM Inspector of Constabulary, 1967-77; *b* 1913; *s* of late George R. F. Fenwick, Horton Grange, Northumberland; *m* 1943, Eileen Winifreda, *d* of late James Carstairs Dodds, Buenos Aires. *Educ*: Dame Allan's Sch. Barrister-at-Law, Gray's Inn, 1951. Metropolitan Police, 1934-59; seconded to Foreign Office for duties in São Paulo, Brazil, 1957-58; Directing Staff, Police Coll., 1959-60; Asst Chief Constable, Glos, 1960-62; Chief Constable, Shropshire, 1962-67. Adviser to Qatar State Police, 1972-77. *Address:* Ebor House, Kingsland, Shrewsbury, Shropshire. *T:* Shrewsbury 4158. *Club:* East India, Devonshire, Sports and Public Schools.

FERENS, Sir Thomas (Robinson), Kt 1957; CBE 1952; *b* 4 Jan. 1903; *e s* of late J. J. T. Ferens, Hull; *m* 1934, Jessie (*d* 1982), *d* of P. G. Sanderson, Hull and Scarborough; two *d*. *Educ*: Rydal; Leeds Univ. (BSc Eng). *Recreation:* fly-fishing. *Address:* Sunderlandwick, Driffield, North Humberside. *T:* Driffield 42323.

FERGUS, Most Rev. James, DD; *b* Louisburgh, Co. Mayo, 23 Dec. 1895. *Educ*: St Jarlath's College, Tuam; and at Maynooth. Ordained priest, 1920; studied Dunboyne; Curate, Glenamaddy, 1921, Tuam, 1924; Archbishop's secretary, 1926; Administrator, Westport, 1943; Parish Priest, Ballinrobe, 1944; Bishop of Achonry, 1947-76, retired 1977. *Address:* Ballaghaderreen, Co. Roscommon, Eire.

FERGUSON, Ernest Alexander; Deputy Chairman, Central Arbitration Committee, since 1977; *b* 26 July 1917; *s* of William Henry and Lilian Ferguson; *m* 1940, Mary Josephine Wadsworth; two *s*. *Educ*: Priory Sch., Shrewsbury; Pembroke Coll., Cambridge. Scholar, Pembroke Coll., 1935-39; MA 1944. Served War, RA (Captain), 1940-45. Entered Ministry of Labour, 1945; Principal, 1948; Asst Sec., 1962; Under-Sec. and Accountant-Gen., Dept of Employment, 1973-77. Chm., Central Youth Employment Executive, 1967-69; Sec. to NEDC, 1971-73. *Recreations:* sport, mountaineering, reading. *Address:* 164 Balcombe Road, Horley, Surrey. *T:* Horley 5254. *Club:* Civil Service.

FERGUSON, John, FIAL; President, The Selly Oak Colleges, Birmingham, since 1979; *b* 2 March 1921; *s* of Prof. Allan and Dr Nesta Ferguson; *m* 1950, Elnora Dixon; no *c*. *Educ*: Bishop's Stortford Coll.; St John's Coll., Cambridge. BD 1st cl. hons London, 1944; BA 1st cl. hons with double distinction Class. Tripos Cantab, 1947; Henry Carrington and Bentham Dumont Koe Studentship, 1947; Denny Studentship, 1947; Kaye Prize, 1951 (for essay in early Church History). Civil Defence, 1941-45; Master at Bishop's Stortford Coll., 1945-46; Lectr in Classics, King's Coll., Newcastle upon Tyne, 1948-53; Sen. Lectr in Classics, Queen Mary Coll., London, 1953-56; Prof. of Classics, Univ. of Ibadan, 1956-66 (Dean, Faculty of Arts, 1958-59, 1960-61); Hill Vis. Prof. 1966-68, Prof. 1968-69, Univ. of Minnesota; Old Dominion Vis. Prof. Humanities, Hampton Inst., Va, 1968-69. Dean and Dir of Studies in Arts, Open Univ., 1969-79 (Dep. Chm. of Senate, 1969-74). Vis. Prof., Univ. of Florida, 1977; Ohio Wesleyan Univ., 1978. Lectures: Emily Hobhouse Meml, 1961; Alex Wood Meml, 1971; Kinchin Smith Meml, 1972; Herbert Collins Meml, 1976; Lady Ardilaun, 1976; Rodes-Helm, 1977; Montgomery, 1977-79; Carpenter, 1978. Chm. 1953-56, Vice-Chm. 1969-78, Fellowship of Reconciliation; Chm., UNA, 1980- (Vice-Chm., 1978-80); British Council of Churches: Chm., Educn Dept, 1971-74; Community Affairs Div., 1974-78; Chairman: British and Foreign Schools Soc.; Birmingham Jt Cttee for Adult Educn Inf. and Advice Services; Mem. Council, Prospect Hall; Governor, Queen's Coll., Birmingham; Vice-Chm., Christian Social and Economic Res. Foundn; President: Friends' Guild of Teachers, 1978-79; London Soc. for Study of Religion, 1978-80; Vice-President: Orbilian Soc., 1973- (Pres., 1972); Nat. Peace Council; Hon. Life Vice-Pres., Assoc. for Reform of Latin Teaching. Hon. Mem., Mark Twain Soc., and Kt of Mark Twain. *Publications:* The Enthronement of Love, 1950; (ed) Studies in Christian Social Commitment, 1954; Pelagius, 1956; (jtly) Letters on Pacifism, 1956; Christian Faith for Today, 1956; The UN and the World's Needs, 1957; (ed) Plato Republic X, 1957; Moral Values in the Ancient World, 1958; (jtly) The Emergent University, 1960; (ed) Studies in Cicero, 1962; Foundations of the Modern World, 1963; (jtly) The Enduring Past, 1965; (jtly) Nigeria under the Cross, 1965; Ibadan Verses, 1966; (ed) Ibadan Versions, 1967; The Wit of the Greeks and Romans, 1968; Christian Byways, 1968; (jtly) Africa in Classical Antiquity, 1969; Socrates: A Source-Book, 1970; Religions of the Roman Empire, 1970; American Verses, 1971; Some Nigerian Church Founders, 1971; Sermons of a Layman, 1972; The Place of Suffering, 1972; A Companion to Greek Tragedy, 1972; Aristotle, 1972; The Heritage of Hellenism, 1973; The Politics of Love, 1973; (ed) War and the Creative Arts, 1973; (rapporteur)

Non-violent Action: a Christian appraisal, 1973; Clement of Alexandria, 1974; Utopias of the Classical World, 1975; The Open University from Within, 1975; Danilo Dolci, 1975; An Illustrated Encyclopaedia of Mysticism and the Mystery Religions, 1976; O My People, 1977; War and Peace in the World's Religions, 1977; Religions of the World, 1978; (jtly) Political and Social Life in the Great Age of Athens, 1978; (ed) Juvenal The Satires, 1979; Greek and Roman Religion: a source book, 1980; Jesus in the Tide of Time, 1980; The Arts in Britain in World War I, 1980; Callimachus, 1980; (ed) Christianity, Society and Education, 1981; Gods Many and Lords Many, 1981; (jtly) Rome: the Augustan Age, 1981; Disarmament: The Unanswerable Case, 1982; some 25 course-unit books for the Open Univ.; *plays*: The Camp, 1956; The Trial, 1957; The Road to Heaven, 1958; Job, 1961; Editor, Nigeria and the Classics, Vols I-IX; Jt Editor, Reconciliation Quarterly; numerous articles on classical subjects, theology, internat. affairs and literature; also some hymns (words editor Hymns for Worship). *Recreations*: cricket, fell-walking, book-hunting, church architecture, drama, opera, conducting madrigals, travelling in the Graeco-Roman world. *Address*: The President's House, Selly Oak Colleges, Birmingham B29 6LQ. *T*: (home) 021-472 2462; (office) 021-472 4231. *Clubs*: Penn; MCC; Union (Cambridge).

FERGUSON, John Alexander; HM Senior Chief Inspector of Schools in Scotland, since 1981; *b* 16 Oct. 1927; *s* of George Ferguson and Martha Crichton Dykes; *m* 1953, Jean Stewart; two *s* one *d. Educ*: Royal Coll. of Science and Technology, Univ. of Glasgow (BSc Hons, Diploma). Teacher, Airdrie Central Sch., 1950-51; Lectr, 1951-55, Head of Dept of Engrg, 1955-61, Coatbridge Technical Coll.; HM Inspector of Schs, 1961-72, Asst Sec., 1972-75, Scottish Educn Dept; HM Depute Sen. Chief Inspector of Schs, 1975-81. *Recreations*: tennis, badminton, bridge. *Address*: 28 Esslemont Road, Edinburgh EH16 5PY. *T*: 031-667 5881. *Clubs*: Craigmillar Park Lawn Tennis, Carlton Bridge (Edinburgh).

FERGUSON, John McIntyre, CBE 1976; FEng 1978, FIEE, FIMechE, FITE; engineering consultant, since 1973; *b* 16 May 1915; *s* of Frank Ferguson and Lilian (*née* Bowen); *m* 1941, Margaret Frances Tayler; three *s. Educ*: Armstrong Coll., Durham Univ. BScEng (1st Cl. Hons). English Electric Co., Stafford: Research, 1936; Chief Engr, 1953; Dir Engrg, Heavy Electric Products, 1965; Dir of Engrg, GEC Power Engrg Co., 1969. Member: Metrication Bd, 1969-76; Science Res. Council, 1972-76; UGC, 1977-. President: IEE, 1977-78; IEETE, 1979-81. *Recreations*: golf, sailing. *Address*: Leacroft, 19 St John's Road, Stafford ST17 9AS. *T*: Stafford 3516. *Club*: Royal Commonwealth Society.

FERGUSON, Sir Neil Edward J.; *see* Johnson-Ferguson.

FERGUSON DAVIE, Rev. Sir (Arthur) Patrick, 5th Bt *cr* 1641 and *re-created* 1847 for General Henry Ferguson, husband of Juliana, *d* of Sir John Davie, 8th Bt of Creedy; TD 1954; Liturgical Adviser to the Anglican Province of Jerusalem and the Middle East, since 1976; *b* 17 March 1909; *s* of late Lt-Col Arthur Francis Ferguson Davie, CIE, DSO (3rd *s* of 3rd Bt), and late Eleanor Blanche Daphne, *d* of late C. T. Naylor (she *m* 1918, Major J. H. W. Knight-Bruce, who *d* 1951; she *d* 1964); *S* uncle, 1947; *m* 1949, Iris Dawn Cable-Buller, *o d* of Capt. and Hon. Mrs Buller, Downes, Crediton; one *s. Educ*: Wellington Coll.; Lincoln Coll., Oxford (MA). Ely Theological Coll., 1932-34; Deacon, 1934, Priest, 1935. Asst Curate, Littleham-cum-Exmouth, 1934-37; St Augustine's, Kilburn, NW6, 1938-39; CF (TA), 1937-45; Hon. CF 1945; served with 4th Bn Devonshire Regt in UK and Gibraltar, 1939-43; CMF, N Africa and Italy, 1943-45; Vicar of St John's Torquay, 1945-48; Rural Dean of Cadbury, 1966-68; Hon. Chaplain to Bishop of Exeter, 1949-73. *Publication*: The Bishop in Church, 1961. *Heir*: *s* Antony Francis Ferguson Davie, *b* 23 March 1952. *Address*: Skalatos House, PO Box 129, Arapköy, Girne, Mersin 10, Turkey. *Club*: Naval and Military.

FERGUSSON, Adam (Dugdale); Member (C) West Strathclyde, European Parliament, since 1979; author and journalist; *b* 10 July 1932; *yr s* of Sir James Fergusson of Kilkerran, 8th Bt, LLD, FRSE, and of Frances Dugdale; *m* 1965, Penelope, *e d* of Peter Hughes, Furneaux Pelham Hall; two *s* two *d. Educ*: Eton; Trinity Coll., Cambridge (BA History, 1955). Glasgow Herald, 1956-61: Leader-writer, 1957-58; Diplomatic Corresp., 1959-61; Statist, 1961-67: Foreign Editor, 1964-67; Feature-writer for The Times on political, economic and environmental matters, 1967-77. Mem., Scotland Says No Referendum Campaign Cttee, 1978-79. *Publications*: Roman Go Home, 1969; The Lost Embassy, 1972; The Sack of Bath, 1973; When Money Dies, 1975; various pamphlets; articles in national and internat. jls and magazines. *Address*: 9 Addison Crescent, W14 8JP. *T*: 01-603 7900; Ladyburn, Maybole, Ayrshire. *T*: Crosshill 206. *Club*: Travellers'.

FERGUSSON of Kilkerran, Sir Charles, 9th Bt *cr* 1703; *b* 10 May 1931; *s* of Sir James Fergusson of Kilkerran, 8th Bt, and Frances, *d* of Edgar Dugdale; *S* father, 1973; *m* 1961, Hon. Amanda Mary Noel-Paton, *d* of Lord Ferrier, *qv*; two *s. Educ*: Eton; Edinburgh and East of Scotland Coll. of Agriculture (Scottish Diploma in Agric.). *Heir*: *s* Adam Fergusson, *b* 29 Dec. 1962. *Address*: Kilkerran, Maybole, Ayrshire KA19 7SJ. *T*: Crosshill 207.

FERGUSSON, Ewen Alastair John; HM Diplomatic Service; Ambassador to South Africa, since 1982; *b* 28 Oct. 1932; *er s* of late Sir Ewen MacGregor Field Fergusson; *m* 1959, Sara Carolyn, *d* of late Brig-Gen. Lord Esmé Gordon Lennox, KCVO, CMG, DSO and *widow* of Sir William Andrew

Montgomery-Cuninghame, 11th Bt; one *s* two *d. Educ*: Rugby; Oriel Coll., Oxford (MA). 2nd Lieut, 60th Rifles (KRRC), 1954-56. Joined Foreign (now Diplomatic) Service, 1956; Asst Private Sec. to Minister of Defence, 1957-59; British Embassy, Addis Ababa, 1960; FO, 1963; British Trade Development Office, New York, 1967; Counsellor and Head of Chancery, Office of UK Permanent Rep. to European Communities, 1972-75; Private Sec. to Foreign and Commonwealth Sec., 1975-78; Asst Under Sec. of State, FCO, 1978-82. *Address*: c/o Foreign and Commonwealth Office, SW1. *Club*: Royal Automobile.

FERGUSSON, Ian Victor Lyon; *b* 22 Jan. 1901; *y s* of late Rev. Dr John Moore Fergusson; *m* 1927, Hannah Grace (*née* Gourlay) (*d* 1978); three *s* one *d. Educ*: Berkhamsted Sch. Joined Evans Medical Ltd. (then Evans Sons Lescher & Webb Ltd), 1919; Dir, 1927; Man. Dir, 1941; Chm. and Man. Dir, Evans Medical Ltd, 1943-62; Dir, Glaxo Group Ltd, 1961-62; Dir, Carless Capel & Leonard Ltd, 1964-72. Pres., Chemists Federation, 1940-41; Chm., Assoc. British Pharmaceutical Industry, 1946-47. Mem., Liverpool Regional Hospital Board, 1958-61. *Recreations*: fishing, gardening. *Address*: Orchard Lodge, Avon Dassett, Leamington Spa, Warwickshire CV33 0AY. *T*: Farnborough 228.

FERGUSSON, James David, CB 1982; Assistant Comptroller, Patent Office, since 1969; *b* 14 Jan. 1923; *s* of James Thomson Fergusson and Agnes Eva Fergusson; *m* 1946, Jean Barbara Debnam; two *s* one *d. Educ*: Montrose Acad.; St Andrews Univ. (BSc). Temp. Experimental Officer, Admiralty, 1943-47; Patent Office Examining Staff, 1947-. *Address*: 42 Cedar Avenue, Chelmsford, Essex CM1 2QH. *T*: Chelmsford 355774.

FERGUSSON, Sir James H. H.; *see* Colyer-Fergusson.

FERMAN, James Alan; Secretary, British Board of Film Censors, since 1975; *b* New York, 11 April 1930; *m* 1956, Monica Sophie (*née* Robinson); one *s* one *d. Educ*: Great Neck High Sch., NY; Cornell Univ. (BA Hons); King's Coll., Cambridge (MA Hons). Actor and univ. lectr until 1957; author/adaptor, Zuleika (musical comedy), Saville Theatre, 1957; Television Director: ABC, 1957-59; ATV, 1959-65; freelance, chiefly at BBC, 1965-75; drama series incl.: The Planemakers, Probation Officer, Emergency Ward 10; plays incl.: The Pistol, Who's A Good Boy Then? I Am, Kafka's Amerika, Death of a Private, Before the Party, Chariot of Fire, When the Bough Breaks, Terrible Jim Fitch; documentaries incl.: Decisions of Our Time, The Four Freedoms, CURE; stage productions incl.: Three Sisters, Mooney and His Caravans, This Space Is Mine; wrote and dir., Drugs and Schoolchildren, film series for teachers and social workers. Lectr in Community Studies, Polytechnic of Central London, 1973-76 (Dir and Chm., Community Mental Health Prog. in assoc. with MIND); Educn Adviser, Standing Conf. on Drug Abuse; Vice-Pres., Assoc. for Prevention of Addiction. *Recreations*: reading and hill-walking. *Address*: The Fairhazel Co-operative, Canfield Gardens, NW6; British Board of Film Censors, 3 Soho Square, W1. *T*: 01-437 2677.

FERMOR, Patrick Michael Leigh, DSO 1944; OBE 1943; author: Hon. Citizen of Herakleion, Crete, 1947, Gytheion, Laconia, 1966, and of Kardamyli, Messenia, 1967; *b* 11 Feb. 1915; *s* of late Sir Lewis Leigh Fermor, OBE, FRS, DSc, and Eileen, *d* of Charles Taaffe Ambler; *m* 1968, Hon. Joan Eyres-Monsell, *d* of 1st Viscount Monsell, PC, GBE. *Educ*: King's Sch., Canterbury. After travelling for four years in Central Europe, Balkans and Greece, enlisted in Irish Guards, 1939; 2nd Lieut, "I" Corps, 1940; Lieut, British Mil. Mission, Greece, 1940; Liaison Officer, Greek GHQ, Albania; campaigns of Greece and Crete; 2 years in German occupied Crete with Cretan Resistance, commanded some minor guerilla operations; Major 1943; team-commander in Special Allied Airborne Reconnaissance Force, N Germany, 1945. Dep.-Dir British Institute, Athens, till middle 1946; travelled in Caribbean and Central American republics, 1947-48. Corres. Mem., Athens Acad., 1980. *Publications*: The Traveller's Tree (Heinemann Foundation Prize for Literature, 1950, and Kemsley Prize, 1951); trans. Colette, Chance Acquaintances, 1952; A Time to Keep Silence, 1953; The Violins of Saint Jacques, 1953; Mani, 1958 (Duff Cooper Meml Prize; Book Society's Choice); (trans.) The Cretan Runner (George Psychoundakis), 1955; Roumeli, 1966; A Time of Gifts, 1977 (W. H. Smith & Son Literary Award, 1978). *Recreation*: travel. *Address*: c/o Messrs John Murray, 50 Albemarle Street, W1. *Clubs*: White's, Travellers', Pratt's, Beefsteak, Special Forces, Puffins.

FERMOR-HESKETH, family name of **Baron Hesketh.**

FERMOY, 5th Baron *cr* 1856; **Edmund James Burke Roche;** Chairman, Eddington Bindery Ltd; Director, Kennetco Estates Co. Ltd; *b* 20 March 1939; *s* of 4th Baron Fermoy and Ruth Sylvia (*see* Dowager Lady Fermoy); *S* father, 1955; *m* 1964, Lavinia Frances Elizabeth, *o d* of late Capt. John Pitman and of Mrs Pitman, Foxley House, Malmesbury, Wilts; two *s* one *d. Educ*: Eton; Sandhurst; RAC, Cirencester. Capt., Royal Horse Guards (The Blues), retd 1967. Trustee, Pheasant Trust. District Councillor (Hungerford), Newbury DC, 1976-79. *Recreation*: steeplechasing. *Heir*: *s* Hon. Patrick Maurice Burke Roche, *b* 11 Oct. 1967. *Address*: Eddington House, Hungerford, Berks. *T*: Hungerford 2540. *Clubs*: White's, Turf, 1,001.

FERMOY, Dowager Lady; Ruth Sylvia; (Rt. Hon. Ruth Lady Fermoy), DCVO 1979 (CVO 1966); OBE 1952; JP; Woman of the Bedchamber to Queen Elizabeth the Queen Mother since 1960 (an extra Woman of the

Bedchamber, 1956-60); *b* 2 Oct. 1908; *y d* of late W. S. Gill, CB, Dalhebity, Bieldside, Aberdeenshire; *m* 1931, Edmund Maurice Burke Roche, 4th Baron Fermoy (*d* 1955); one *s* (*see* 5th Baron Fermoy) two *d*. JP Norfolk, 1944. Freedom of King's Lynn, 1963. Hon. RAM 1968; Hon. MusD Univ. of East Anglia, 1975. *Address:* 36 Eaton Square, SW1.

FERNALD, John Bailey; *b* 21 Nov. 1905; *s* of C. B. Fernald and Josephine Harker; *m* 1942, Jenny Laird; one *d. Educ:* Marlborough Coll.; Trinity Coll., Oxford. Pres., OUDS, 1927; Dramatic Editor, The Pall Mall Magazine, 1929; first professional production, Arts Theatre, 1929; subsequently produced plays continuously in London till 1936, when became Associate Producer for Associated British Pictures Corporation; returned to theatre, 1938; on teaching staff of Royal Academy of Dramatic Art, 1934-40. Joined RNVR, 1940 and served almost continuously at sea until 1945; left service with rank of Lieut-Comdr. Dir of Productions, Reunion Theatre, 1946; Dir of the Liverpool Playhouse, 1946-49; subsequently produced: The Love of Four Colonels, Wyndham's; The White Sheep of the Family, Piccadilly; The First Born, Winter Garden; Nightmare Abbey and Dial M for Murder, Westminster; Escapade, Strand; The Devil's General, Savoy; Crime and Punishment (Television); Saint Joan, St Martin's; The Remarkable Mr Pennypacker, New; The House by the Lake, Duke of York's; Jubilee Production of Peter Pan; Tea and Sympathy, Comedy; Hedda Gabler, Nye Teater, Oslo; The Love of Four Colonels, Kansanteatteri, Helsinki; Ghosts, Old Vic; The Tchekov Centenary Production of The Seagull, Edinburgh Festival and Old Vic; The Affair, Henry Miller Theatre, New York; The Schoolmistress, Savoy; The Enchanted, Arts Theatre; Ivanov, Uncle Vanya, The Seagull, and various plays at Arts Theatre and elsewhere; 1st production in England of Bertolt Brecht's The Caucasian Chalk Circle, Vanbrugh Theatre, RADA, Anton Tchekov's The Cherry Orchard at the National Theatre, Pretoria and Johannesburg; Private Lives, Bristol Old Vic. Shute Lectr on the Art of the Theatre, Liverpool Univ., 1948. Principal, Royal Academy of Dramatic Art, 1955-65; Dir, John Fernald Co., Meadowbrook Theatre, Rochester, Mich, and Prof. of Dramatic Art, Oakland Univ., Rochester, Mich, 1966-70; Prof., Dept of Theatre, NY State Univ., 1970-71; returned from USA, 1972, now largely concerned with teaching of acting at drama schs and directing classical revivals at repertory theatres. Mem., Nat. Council for Drama Trng (Vice-Chm., Accreditation Cttee). Awarded Silver Medal of Royal Soc. of Arts, 1966. *Publications:* The Play Produced: a Manual of Stage Production, 1933; Destroyer from America, 1942; Sense of Direction, 1968; contrib. to Encyclopaedia Britannica, 1972. *Recreations:* music, travelling, looking at cats, and producing the plays of Anton Tchekov. *Address:* 2 Daleham Mews, NW3. *T:* 01-435 2992.

FERNANDES, Most Rev. Angelo; *see* Delhi, Archbishop of, (RC).

FERNANDO, Most Rev. Nicholas Marcus; *see* Colombo, Archbishop of, (RC).

FERNS, Prof. Henry Stanley, MA, PhD Cantab; Professor of Political Science, University of Birmingham, 1961-81, now Emeritus Professor; *b* Calgary, Alberta, 16 Dec. 1913; *er s* of Stanley and Janie Ferns; *m* 1940, Helen Maureen, *d* of John and Eleanor Jack; three *s* one *d. Educ:* St John's High Sch., Winnipeg; Univ. of Manitoba; Trinity Coll., Cambridge. Research Scholar, Trinity Coll., Cambridge, 1938. Secretarial staff of Prime Minister of Canada, 1940; Asst Prof. of History and Government, Univ. of Manitoba, 1945; Fellow, Canadian Social Science Research Council, 1949; Lectr in Modern History and Government, Univ. of Birmingham, 1950; successively Sen. Lectr, Head of Dept and Prof. of Political Science, Dean, Faculty of Commerce and Social Sci., 1961-65. Pres., Bd of Dirs, Winnipeg Citizens' Cooperative Publishing Co. Ltd, 1946-48; Member of various Conciliation Boards appointed by Minister of Labour of Govt of Manitoba, 1947-49. Past Pres., British Assoc. of Canadian Studies. Hon. Fellow, University College, Buckingham. *Publications:* (with B. Ostry) The Age of McKenzie King: The Rise of the Leader, 1955 (Toronto and London), 2nd edn 1976; Britain and Argentina in the Nineteenth Century, 1960 (Oxford); Towards an Independent University, 1969; Argentina, 1969; The Argentine Republic 1516-1971, 1973; The Disease of Government, 1978; articles in learned jls. *Recreations:* journalism, idling and pottering about. *Address:* 1 Kesteven Close, Sir Harry's Road, Birmingham B15 2UT. *T:* 021-440 1016.

FERNYHOUGH, Ven. Bernard; Archdeacon of Oakham, since 1977; Canon Residentiary of Peterborough Cathedral, since 1977; *b* 2 Sept. 1932; *s* of Edward and Edith Fernyhough; *m* 1957, Freda Malkin; one *s* one *d. Educ:* Wolstanton Grammar Sch.; Saint David's Coll., Lampeter (BA 1953). Precentor, Trinidad Cathedral, 1955-61; Rector of Stoke Bruerne with Grafton Regis and Alderton, 1961-67; Vicar of Ravensthorpe with East Haddon and Holdenby, 1967-77; Rural Dean: Preston, 1965-67; Haddon, 1968-70; Brixworth, 1971-77; Non-Residentiary Canon, Peterborough Cathedral, 1974-77. *Address:* 18 Minster Precincts, Peterborough. *T:* Peterborough 62762.

FERNYHOUGH, Rt. Hon. Ernest, PC 1970; *b* 24 Dec. 1908; British; *m* 1934, Ethel Edwards; one *s* one *d* (and one *s* decd). *Educ:* Wood Lane Council Sch. Full-time official, Union of Shop, Distributive and Allied Workers, 1936-47. MP (Lab) Jarrow, May 1947-1979; PPS to the Prime Minister, 1964-67; Jt Parly Under-Sec. of State, Dept of Employment and Productivity (formerly Min. of Labour), 1967-69. Freeman, Borough of Jarrow, 1972. *Address:* 35 Edwards Road, Lache Park, Chester.

FERNYHOUGH, Brigadier Hugh Edward, CBE 1956; DSO 1945; retired; *b* 15 April 1904; *s* of late Col Hugh Clifford Fernyhough and Mrs Beatrice Fernyhough; *m* 1943, Mary, *d* of late T. D. and Mrs Moore, Mill Down, Clyst St Mary, Exeter; one *s. Educ:* Wellington Coll., Berks; RMA Woolwich. 2nd Lieut 1924; Lieut 1927; Capt. 1937; grad. Staff Coll., Camberley, 1939; GSO2, 12 Corps, 1940; GSO2, Instr, Staff Coll., Camberley, 1941; Comdt (Col) NZ Staff Coll., 1942-43; OC 53 (London) Medium Regt, 1944-45; Comdt (Col) RA, OCTU, 1945-46; CRA (Col) HQ, E Africa, 1947-48; Col i/c Admin., E Africa, 1948-49; AAG, RA, War Office, 1949-52; CRA 40 Inf. Div. (Hong Kong), 1952-53; Dep. Dir, RA, 1954-56; retd 1956. Col Comdt, Royal Artillery. *Address:* Mill Down, Clyst St Mary, Exeter. *T:* Topsham 4568. *Club:* Army and Navy.

FEROZE, Rustam Moolan, FRCS, FRCOG; Consultant Obstetrician and Gynæcologist, King's College Hospital; Consulting Obstetrician and Gynæcologist: Queen Charlotte's Maternity Hospital; Chelsea Hospital for Women; President, Royal College of Obstetricians and Gynaecologists, since 1981; *b* 4 Aug. 1920; *s* of Dr J. Moolan-Feroze; *m* 1947, Margaret Dowsett. *Educ:* Sutton Valence Sch.; King's Coll. Hospital, London. MRCS, LRCP 1943; MB, BS 1946; MRCOG 1948; MD (Obst. & Dis. Wom.) London 1952; FRCS 1952; FRCOG 1962. Dean, Inst. of Obstetrics and Gynæcology, Univ. of London, 1954-67. Senr Registrar: Chelsea Hosp. for Women, and Queen Charlotte's Maternity Hosp., London, 1953-54; Hosp. for Women, Soho Square, and Middlesex Hosp., 1950-53; Resident Medical Officer, Samaritan Hosp. for Women, 1948. *Publications:* contribs to medical jls and to Integrated Obstetrics and Gynaecology for Postgraduates, 1976. *Recreation:* Bonsai. *Address:* 127 Harley Street, W1. *T:* 01-935 8157. *Clubs:* Royal Automobile, Rugby.

FERRALL, Sir Raymond (Alfred), Kt 1982; CBE 1969; director, various public and private companies; *b* 27 May 1906; *s* of Alfred C. Ferrall and Edith M. Ferrall; *m* 1931, Lorna, *d* of P. M. Findlay; two *s* two *d. Educ:* Launceston C of E Grammar Sch. Chairman: Launceston Bank for Savings, 1976-82; Tasmanian Colls of Advanced Educn, 1977-81; Launceston C of E Grammar Sch. Bd, 1956-73; Master Warden, Port of Launceston Authority, 1960-80. Captain, Tasmanian Cricket team, 1934; Vice Captain, Tasmanian Amateur Football team, 1932. Freeman, City of Launceston, 1981. Queen's Silver Jubilee Medal, 1977. *Publications:* Partly Personal, 1976; Idylls of the Mayor, 1978; Notable Tasmanians, 1980; The Age of Chiselry, 1981. *Recreations:* writing, print collecting, sailing. *Address:* 135 High Street, Launceston, Tas 7250, Australia. *T:* 31 6081. *Clubs:* Launceston, Northern, Tamar Yacht (Tasmania).

FERRANTI; *see* de Ferranti.

FERRAR, William Leonard; Principal, Hertford College, Oxford, 1959-64; *b* 21 Oct. 1893; *s* of George William Parsons and Maria Susannah Ferrar; *m* 1923, Edna O'Hara; one *s. Educ:* Queen Elizabeth's Hospital, Bristol; Bristol Grammar Sch.; Queen's Coll., Oxford. Open Mathematical Schol., Queen's, 1912; Univ. Junior Math. Schol., 1914; Sen. Schol., 1922; MA Oxon 1920; DSc Oxon 1947. Served European War, 1914-18, in ranks, Artillery and Intelligence, 1914-19. Lecturer, University Coll. of N Wales, Bangor, 1920-24; Sen. Lecturer, Edinburgh, 1924-25; Fellow, Hertford Coll., Oxford, 1925-59, Bursar, 1937-59. Formerly mem. Hebdomadal Council, Gen. Board and the Chest, Oxford Univ.; Sec., London Math. Soc., 1933-38. *Publications:* Convergence, 1938; Algebra, 1941; Higher Algebra for Schools, 1945, Part II, 1948; Finite Matrices, 1951; Differential Calculus, 1956; Integral Calculus, 1958; Mathematics for Science, 1965; Calculus for Beginners, 1967; Advanced Mathematics for Science, 1969; various research papers, 1924-37. *Recreations:* gardening; a little music. *Address:* 21 Sunderland Avenue, Oxford OX2 8DT.

FERRARI, Enzo; President and Managing Director of Ferrari Automobili SpA Sefac, 1940-77; *b* Modena, 20 Feb. 1898; *s* of Alfredo Ferrari and Adalgisa Bisbini; *m* 1923, Laura Garello; one *s* decd. *Educ:* State sch.; Professional Institute of Technology. Started as tester, Turin, 1918; later with CMN, Milan; tester, driver, sales executive, Alfa Romeo, 1920-39; subsequently Dir, Alfa Corse; Pres. and Managing Dir of Scuderia Ferrari, later of Auto Avio Construzione Ferrari, 1940-60. Builder of racing, sports and gran turismo cars in factory built at Maranello in 1943 and reconstructed in 1946. Commendatore, 1928; Cavaliere del Lavoro, 1952. Hon. doctorate in engineering, Bologna, 1960. *Publication:* Le mie gioie terribili (autobiog.). *Address:* viale Trento Trieste 31, Modena, Italy. *T:* 24081-24082; (office) Maranello, Modena, Italy. *T:* 91161-91162.

FERRER, José Vicente; actor, director and producer, USA; *b* 8 Jan. 1912; *s* of Rafael Ferrer and Maria Providencia (née Cintron); *m* 1st, 1938, Uta Hagen (marr. diss. 1948); one *d*; 2nd, 1948, Phyllis Hill (marr. diss. 1953); 3rd, 1953, Rosemary Clooney (marr. diss. 1967); three *s* two *d*; 4th, Stella Daphne Magee. *Educ:* Princeton Univ. AB (architecture), 1933. First appearance, The Periwinkle, Long Island show-boat, 1934; Asst Stage Manager Summer Theatre Stock Co., NY, 1935; first appearance NY stage, 1935; A Slight Case of Murder, 1935; Boy Meets Girl, 1935; Spring Dance, Brother Rat, 1936; In Clover, 1937; Dir Princeton Univ. Triangle Club's Fol-de-Rol, 1937; How To Get Tough About It, Missouri Legend, 1938; Mamba's Daughters, Key Largo, 1939; first star rôle, Lord Fancourt Babberley, Charley's Aunt, 1940; producer and dir, The Admiral Had A Wife, 1941; staged and co-starred, Vickie, 1942; Let's Face It, 1943; played Iago to Paul Robeson's Othello,

Theatre Guild, 1943, 1944, 1945; producer and dir Strange Fruit, 1945; Play's The Thing, Richard III, Green Goddess, 1946; producer and star, Cyrano, 1946; Design For Living, Goodbye Again, 1947; Gen. dir to NY Theatre Co., City Centre, 1948; Silver Whistle, Theatre Guild, 1948; produced, directed and appeared in Twentieth Century, 1950; produced, directed, Stalag 17; The Fourposter, 1951; producer, dir and appeared in The Shrike, 1952; The Chase, 1952; staged My 3 Angels, 1953; dir and co-author, Oh Captain, 1958; producer, dir, and starred in, Edwin Booth, 1959; dir, The Andersonville Trial, 1960; starred in, The Girl Who Came to Supper, 1963-64; Man of La Mancha, 1966; dir, Cyrano de Bergerac, Chichester, 1975; Films include: Joan of Arc, 1947; Whirlpool, 1949; Crisis, Cyrano, 1950; Anything Can Happen, 1951; Moulin Rouge, 1952; Miss Sadie Thompson (Rain), Caine Mutiny, 1953; Deep in My Heart, 1955; Cockleshell Heroes, The Great Man, 1957; The High Cost of Loving, I Accuse, The Shrike (Dir, starred), 1958; Return to Peyton Place (Dir), 1962; State Fair (Dir), 1963; Nine Hours to Rama, Lawrence of Arabia, 1963; Cyrano et D'Artagnan, Train 349 From Berlin, The Greatest Story Ever Told, 1964; Ship of Fools, Enter Laughing, 1966; The Fifth Musketeer, 1976; Fedora, 1977; The Amazing Captain Nemo, 1979; The Big Brawl, 1980. Holds hon. degrees. Various awards for acting, etc, since 1944, include American Academy of Arts and Letters Gold Medal, 1949; Academy Award, 1950 (Best Actor, Cyrano). *Recreations:* tennis, golf. *Address:* 2 Penn Plaza, New York, NY10001, USA.

FERRERS, 13th Earl *cr* 1711; **Robert Washington Shirley;** Viscount Tamworth 1711; Bt 1611; PC 1982; Minister of State, Ministry of Agriculture, Fisheries and Food, and Deputy Leader of the House of Lords, since 1979; High Steward of Norwich Cathedral, since 1979; *b* 8 June 1929; *o s* of 12th Earl Ferrers and Hermione Morley (*d* 1969); *S* father, 1954; *m* 1951, Annabel Mary, *d* of late Brig. W. G. Carr, CVO, DSO; two *s* three *d. Educ:* Winchester Coll.; Magdalene Coll., Cambridge. MA (Agric.). Lieut Coldstream Guards, 1949 (as National Service). A Lord-in-Waiting, 1962-64, 1971-74; Parly Sec., MAFF, 1974; Jt Dep. Leader of the Opposition, House of Lords, 1976-79. Mem., Armitage Cttee on political activities of civil servants, 1976-. Vice-Chm., East Anglian Trustee Savings Bank, 1971-75; Chm., TSB of Eastern England, 1977-79; Mem., TSB Central Bd, 1977-79; Director: Central TSB, 1978-79; TSB Trustcard Ltd, 1978-79; Norwich Union Insurance Group, 1975-79. Mem. of Council, Hurstpierpoint Coll., 1959-68. Pres., East of England Agric. Soc., 1979. *Heir: s* Viscount Tamworth, *qv. Address:* Hedenham Hall, Norfolk. *T:* Woodton 250. *Club:* Beefsteak.

FERRIE, Maj.-Gen. Alexander Martin, CBE 1971; QHS 1978; Commandant, RAMC Training Group and Principal Medical Officer, United Kingdom Land Forces, since 1982; *b* 30 Nov. 1923; *s* of late Archibald Ferrie and Elizabeth Ferrie (*née* Martin). *Educ:* Glasgow Academy; Univ. of Glasgow (MB ChB). Commissioned RAMC, 1947; Commanding RAMC, 1947; Commanding Officer, Queen Alexandra Military Hospital, Millbank, 1973-75; Director of Medical Supply, Min. of Defence, 1975-77; Dep. Dir of Medical Services, UKLF, and Inspector of Trng, TA Medical Services, 1977-81; DMS, UKLF, 1981-82. *Recreation:* gardening. *Address:* c/o Barclays Bank Ltd, 31b Western Road, Hove, Sussex BN3 1AD.

FERRIER, Baron *cr* 1958, of Culter (Life Peer); **Victor Ferrier Noel-Paton,** ED; DL; *b* Edinburgh, 1900; *s* of late F. Noel-Paton, Dir-Gen. of Commercial Intelligence to the Govt of India; *m* 1932, Joane Mary, *d* of late Sir Gilbert Wiles, KCIE, CSI; one *s* three *d. Educ:* Cargilfield and The Edinburgh Academy. Served RE, 1918-19, Indian Auxiliary Force (Major, ED), 1920-46, and IARO. Commercial and Industrial Management, Bombay, 1920-51; one time Dir and Chm. of a number of Cos in India and UK; Pres., Bombay Chamber of Commerce. Mem., Legislative Council, Bombay, 1936 and Hon. ADC to Governor of Bombay. A Dep. Speaker and Chm. of Cttees, House of Lords, 1970-73. Mem. of Royal Company of Archers. DL, Lanarks, 1960. *Recreations:* field sports. *Address:* Kilkerran, Maybole, Ayrshire KA19 7SJ. *T:* Crosshill 515. *Clubs:* Cavalry and Guards, Beefsteak; New (Edinburgh).

See also Sir Charles Fergusson, Bt.

FERRIER, Prof. Robert Patton, FRSE 1977; Professor of Natural Philosophy, University of Glasgow, since 1973; *b* 4 Jan. 1934; *s* of William McFarlane Ferrier and Gwendoline Melita Edwards; *m* 1961, Valerie Jane Duncan; two *s* one *d. Educ:* Glebelands Sch. and Morgan Academy, Dundee; Univ. of St Andrews (BSc, PhD). MA Cantab, FInstP. Scientific Officer, AERE Harwell, 1959-61; Res. Assoc., MIT, 1961-62; Sen. Asst in Res., Cavendish Lab., Cambridge, 1962-66; Fellow of Fitzwilliam Coll., Cambridge, 1965-73; Asst Dir of Res., Cavendish Lab. 1966-71; Lectr in Physics, Univ. of Cambridge, 1971-73; Guest Scientist, IBM Res. Labs San José, Calif, 1972-73. Chm., SERC Semiconductor and Surface Physics Sub-Cttee, 1979-. *Publications:* numerous papers in Phil. Mag., Jl Appl. Physics, Jl Physics, etc. *Recreations:* do-it-yourself, golf, reading crime novels. *Address:* Glencoe, 31 Thorn Road, Bearsden, Dunbartonshire G61 4BS. *T:* (office) 041-339 8855 ext. 7388.

FERRIS, see Grant-Ferris, family name of Baron Harvington.

FERRIS, Francis Mursell, TD 1965; QC 1980; barrister; *b* 19 Aug. 1932; *s* of Francis William Ferris and Elsie Lilian May Ferris (*née* Mursell); *m* 1957, Sheila Elizabeth Hester Falloon Bedford; three *s* one *d. Educ:* Bryanston Sch.; Oriel Coll., Oxford. BA (Modern History) 1955, MA 1979. Served RA, 1951-52; 299 Field Regt (RBY QOOH and Berks) RA, TA 1952-67, Major 1964. Called to the Bar, Lincoln's Inn, 1956; Practice at Chancery Bar, 1958-.

Member: Bar Council, 1966-70; Senate of Inns of Court and the Bar, 1979-; Standing Counsel to Dir Gen. of Fair Trading, 1966-80. *Recreation:* gardening. *Address:* White Gables, Shiplake, Oxfordshire; 13 Old Square, Lincoln's Inn, WC2A 3UA. *T:* 01-242 6105. *Club:* Marlow Rowing.

FERRIS, Paul Frederick; author and journalist; *b* 15 Feb. 1929; *o c* of late Frederick Morgan Ferris and of Olga Ferris; *m* 1953, Gloria Moreton; one *s* one *d. Educ:* Swansea Gram. Sch. Staff of South Wales Evening Post, 1949-52; Womans Own, 1953; Observer Foreign News Service, 1953-54. *Publications: novels:* A Changed Man, 1958; Then We Fall, 1960; A Family Affair, 1963; The Destroyer, 1965; The Dam, 1967; Very Personal Problems, 1973; The Cure, 1974; The Detective, 1976; Talk to Me About England, 1979; *non-fiction:* The City, 1960; The Church of England, 1962; The Doctors, 1965; The Nameless: abortion in Britain today, 1966; Men and Money: financial Europe today, 1968; The House of Northcliffe, 1971; The New Militants, 1972; Dylan Thomas, 1977; Richard Burton, 1981; *television plays:* The Revivalist, 1975; Dylan, 1978; Nye: The Extremist, 1982; contribs to The Observer. *Address:* c/o Curtis Brown Ltd, 1 Craven Hill, W2. *T:* 01-262 1011.

FERRIS, Rt. Rev. Ronald Curry; see Yukon, Bishop of.

FERRY, Alexander, MBE 1977; General Secretary, Confederation of Shipbuilding and Engineering Unions, since 1978; *b* 14 Feb. 1931; *s* of Alexander and Susan Ferry; *m* 1958, Mary O'Kane McAlaney; one *s* two *d* (and one *s* decd). *Educ:* St Patrick's High, Senior Secondary, Dunbartonshire. Apprentice Engineer, 1947-52; served Royal Air Force, 1952-54; Engineer, 1954-64; full-time officer, AUEW, 1964-78. *Publication:* The Red Paper on Scotland (co-author), 1975. *Recreation:* golf. *Address:* 190 Brampton Road, Bexley Heath, Kent. *T:* 01-303 5338.

FESSEY, Mereth Cecil, CB 1977; Director, Business Statistics Office, 1969-77, retired; *b* Windsor, Berks, 19 May 1917; *s* of late Morton Fessey and Ethel Fessey (*née* Blake), Bristol; *m* 1945, Grace Lilian, *d* of late William Bray, Earlsfield, London; one *s* two *d. Educ:* Westminster City Sch.; LSE, Univ. of London. London Transport, 1934; Army, 1940; Min. of Transport, 1947; Board of Trade, 1948; Statistician, 1956; Chief Statistician, 1965. Statistical Adviser to Syrian and Mexican Govts, 1979. Chm. of Council, Inst. of Statisticians, 1970-73; Vice Pres. and Mem., Council, Royal Statistical Soc., 1974-78. *Publications:* articles and papers in: Economic Trends; Statistical News; Jl of Royal Statistical Soc.; The Statistician; Annales de Sciences Economiques Appliquées, Louvain; etc. *Recreations:* chess, walking. *Address:* Undy House, Undy, Gwent NP6 3BX. *T:* Magor 880478.

FETHERSTON-DILKE, Mary Stella, CBE 1968; RRC 1966; Organiser, Citizens' Advice Bureau, since 1971; *b* 21 Sept. 1918; *d* of late B. A. Fetherston-Dilke, MBE. *Educ:* Kingsley Sch., Leamington Spa; St George's Hospital, London (SRN). Joined QARNNS, 1942; Matron-in-Chief, QARNNS, 1966-70, retired. OStJ 1966. *Recreation:* antiques. *Address:* 12 Clareville Court, Clareville Grove, SW7.

FEUILLÈRE, Edwige; Officier de la Légion d'Honneur; Commandeur des Arts et Lettres; French actress; *b* 29 Oct.; *m* (divorced). *Educ:* Lycée de Dijon; Conservatoire National de Paris. *Plays include:* La Dame aux camélias, 1940-42, 1952-53; Sodome et Gomorrhe, 1943; L'Aigle a deux têtes, 1946; Partage de midi, Pour Lucrèce, La Parisienne, Phèdre, Lucy Crown, Constance, Rodogune, 1964; La Folle de Chaillot, 1965-66; Delicate Balance; Sweet Bird of Youth, 1971. *Films include:* L'Idiot, 1946; L'Aigle a deux têtes, 1947; Olivia, 1950; Le Blé en herbe, 1952; En cas de malheur, 1958; La vie à deux, 1958; Les amours célèbres, 1961; Le crime ne paye pas, 1962; La chair de l'orchidée, 1975; Le bâteau pour Lipaïa. *Publication:* Les Feux de la Mémoire, 1977. *Address:* 19 rue Eugène Manuel, 75016 Paris, France.

FEVERSHAM, 6th Baron *cr* 1826; **Charles Antony Peter Duncombe;** free-lance journalist; *b* 3 Jan. 1945; *s* of Col Antony John Duncombe-Anderson and G. G. V. McNalty; *S* (to barony of) *kinsman,* 3rd Earl of Feversham (the earldom having become extinct), 1963; *m* 1st, 1966, Shannon (*d* 1976), *d* of late Sir Thomas Foy, CSI, CIE; two *s* one *d*; 2nd, 1979, Pauline, *d* of John Aldridge, Newark, Notts; one *s. Educ:* Eton; Middle Temple. Chairman: Yorkshire Arts Assoc., 1969-80; Standing Conf. of Regional Arts Assocs, 1969-76; Trustees, Yorkshire Sculpture Park, 1981-. Governor, Leeds Polytechnic, 1969-76. Pres., Soc. of Yorkshiremen in London, 1974; Co-Pres. (with Ted Hughes) The Arvon Foundn, 1976-. Pres., Yorks and Cleveland Local Councils Assoc., 1977-. *Publications:* A Wolf in Tooth (novel), 1967; Great Yachts, 1970. *Heir: s* Hon. Jasper Orlando Slingsby Duncombe, *b* 14 March 1968. *Address:* Beckdale House, Helmsley, York.

FEYNMAN, Prof. Richard (Phillips); Professor of Physics, California Institute of Technology, Pasadena, Calif, since 1951; *b* 11 May 1918; *s* of Melville Feynman and Lucille (*née* Phillips); *m* 1960, Gweneth Howarth, Ripponden, Yorks; one *s* one *d. Educ:* MIT; Princeton Univ. Los Alamos, N Mex. Atomic Bomb Project, 1943-46; Cornell Univ., 1946-51. Nobel Prize for Physics (jointly), 1965. Mem. Brazilian Acad. of Sciences; Fellow (Foreign), Royal Soc., London. *Publications:* The Feynman Lectures in Physics, 1963; The Character of Physical Law, 1965; Statistical Mechanics, 1972; Photon-Hadron Interactions, 1972; papers in Physical Review on quantum electro-dynamics, liquid helium, theory of beta-decay. *Recreations:* Mayan Hieroglyphics, opening safes, playing bongo drums, drawing, biology experiments (none done well). *Address:* 2475 Boulder Road, Altadena, Calif 91001, USA. *T:* 213-797-1262.

FFITCH, George Norman; Managing Director, London Broadcasting Company and Independent Radio News, since 1979; *b* 23 Jan. 1929; *s* of late Robert George Ffitch; *m* 1958, Pamela Mary Lyle; one *s* one *d. Educ:* state schools and London Univ. Industrial Correspondent, Political Correspondent and Output Editor, Independent Television News, 1955-62; interviewer and presenter, ITV, 1962-67; Political Editor and an Asst Editor, The Economist, 1967-74; Associate Editor, Daily Express, 1974-76; columnist and broadcaster, 1976-79. *Recreation:* playing at playing golf. *Address:* 7 St Mary Abbots Terrace, W14 8NX. *T:* 01-602 3494. *Club:* Reform.

ffolkes, Michael, (Brian Davis), FSIAD 1966; freelance artist; *b* 6 June 1925; *s* of late Walter Lawrence Davis, MSIAD, and of Elaine Rachel Bostock; *m* 1st, 1952, Miriam Boxer (marr. diss. 1971); two *s* ; 2nd, 1972, Irene Ogilvy Kemp (marr. diss. 1978); one *d. Educ:* Leigh Hall Coll., Essex; St Martin's School of Art, 1941-43; Chelsea School of Art, 1946-49 (ND Painting 1948). Served Royal Navy, 1943-46. First drawing in Punch, 1943, and regular contributor, 1946-; Illustrator: Daily Telegraph's Way of the World, 1955-; Punch film column, 1961-72, 1978-; Member, Punch Table, 1978-. Drawings appear in The New Yorker, Playboy, Private Eye, Reader's Digest, Pardon, The Saturday Review; exhibitor: Royal Academy, Leicester Galls, Arthur Jeffress Gall., The Workshop; drawings in V&A and BM; has illustrated over fifty books. *Publications:* ffanfare, 1953; How to Draw Cartoons, 1963; Mini Art, 1968; Private Eye Cartoon Library, 1976; ffolkes' ffauna, 1977; ffolkes' Companion to Mythology, 1978. *Recreations:* walking, cinema, music, collecting illustrated books. *Address:* 186 Shaftesbury Avenue, WC2 8BA. *T:* 01-240 1841. *Clubs:* Savage, Chelsea Arts, Toby, Omar Khayyam.

FFOLKES, Sir Robert (Francis Alexander), 7th Bt *cr* 1774; *b* 2 Dec. 1943; *o s* of Captain Sir (Edward John) Patrick (Boschetti) ffolkes, 6th Bt, and Geraldine (*d* 1978), *d* of late William Roffey, Writtle, Essex; *S* father, 1960. *Educ:* Stowe Sch.; Christ Church, Oxford. *Address:* 18 Chiddingstone Street, SW6. *Club:* Turf.

FFORDE, Sir Arthur (Frederic Brownlow), GBE 1964; Kt 1946; MA Oxon; *b* 23 Aug. 1900; *s* of late Arthur Brownlow fforde, Indian Civil Service, and Mary Alice Storer Branson; *m* 1926, Mary Alison, *yr d* of late James MacLehose, printer to University of Glasgow; two *s* one *d. Educ:* Rugby Sch.; Trinity Coll., Oxford. Admitted Solicitor, 1925; Partner in firm of Linklaters & Paines, London, 1928-48; Mem. of Council of Law Soc., London, 1937-48; Deputy Dir-Gen., Ministry of Supply, (Finance) 1940, (Contracts) 1941; Under-Sec., Contracts Finance, Ministry of Supply, 1943; Under-Sec., HM Treasury, 1944-45; Head Master of Rugby Sch., 1948-57; Chm., the British Broadcasting Corporation, 1957-64; Mem., Central Board of Finance of Church of England, 1957-70 (Vice-Chm., 1957-60, Chm., 1960-65); Director, 1957-70: Equity & Law Life Assurance Society Ltd; National Westminster Bank Ltd, and other cos. Hon. LLD University of Wales. *Address:* Wall's End, Wonersh, near Guildford, Surrey.

See also M. W. McCrum.

FFORDE, John Standish; an Adviser to the Governors, Bank of England, since 1982; *b* 16 Nov. 1921; 4th *s* of late Francis Creswell Fforde and late Cicely Creswell; *m* 1951, Marya, *d* of late Joseph Retinger; three *s* one *d. Educ:* Rossall Sch.; Christ Church, Oxford (1st cl. Hons PPE). Served RAF, 1940-46. Prime Minister's Statistical Branch, 1951-53; Fellow, Nuffield Coll., Oxford, 1953-56; entered Bank of England, 1957; Dep. Chief, Central Banking Information Dept, 1959-64; Adviser to the Governors, 1964-66; Chief Cashier, 1966-70; Exec. Dir (Home Finance), 1970-82. *Publications:* The Federal Reserve System, 1945-49, 1953; An International Trade in Managerial Skills, 1957. *Recreations:* travel, walking.

FFOWCS WILLIAMS, Prof. John Eirwyn; Rank Professor of Engineering (Acoustics), University of Cambridge, and Professorial Fellow, Emmanuel College, Cambridge, since 1972; *b* 25 May 1935; *m* 1959, Anne Beatrice Mason; two *s* one *d. Educ:* Friends Sch., Great Ayton; Derby Techn. Coll.; Univ. of Southampton. BSc, MA Cantab, PhD. CEng, FRAeS, FInstP, FIMA, FInstAcoust, Fellow Acoustical Soc. of America. Engrg Apprentice, Rolls-Royce Ltd, 1951-55; Spitfire Mitchell Meml Schol. to Southampton Univ., 1955-60; Aerodynamics Div., NPL, 1960-62; Bolt, Beranek & Newman Inc., 1962-64; Reader in Applied Maths, Imperial Coll. of Science and Technology, 1964-69; Rolls Royce Prof. of Theoretical Acoustics, Imperial Coll., 1969-72. Exec. Consultant, Rolls Royce Ltd, 1969-; Chm., Topexpress Ltd, 1979-; Chm., Noise Research Cttee, ARC, 1969-76. AIAA Aero-Acoustics Medal, 1977. *Publications:* articles in Philosophical Trans Royal Soc., Jl of Fluid Mechanics, Jl IMA, Jl of Sound Vibration, Annual Reviews of Fluid Mechanics, Random Vibration, Financial Times; (jtly) film on Aerodynamic Sound. *Recreations:* friends and cigars. *Address:* 298 Hills Road, Cambridge CB2 2QG. *T:* Cambridge 248275. *Clubs:* Athenæum, Danish.

FFRANGCON-DAVIES, Gwen; Actress; *b* 25 Jan. 1891; *d* of David Ffrangcon-Davies, the famous singer, and Annie Frances Rayner. *Educ:* South Hampstead High Sch.; abroad. First London success The Immortal Hour, 1922; created the part of Eve in Shaw's Back to Methuselah; principal successes, Tess, in Tess of the D'Urbervilles, Elizabeth Barrett, in The Barretts of Wimpole Street, Anne of Bohemia, in Richard of Bordeaux. Played Lady Macbeth to Macbeth of John Gielgud, Piccadilly, 1942. Appeared, in association with

Marda Vanne, in leading parts in various plays in S Africa, 1943-46. Returned to England, 1949; played in Adventure Story, St James's, 1949; Stratford Festival, 1950, as Katherine in King Henry VIII; Portia in Julius Cæsar, Regan in King Lear (again Katherine, Old Vic. 1953); Madame Ranevsky in The Cherry Orchard, Lyric, 1954; Aunt Cleofe in Summertime, Apollo, 1955; Rose Padley in The Mulberry Bush, Royal Court, 1956; Agatha in The Family Reunion, Phoenix, 1956; Miss Madrigal in The Chalk Garden, Haymarket, 1957; Mrs Callifer in The Potting Shed, Globe Theatre, 1958; Mary Tyrone in Long Day's Journey into Night, Edinburgh Fest. and Globe, 1958; Queen Isolde in Ondine, Aldwych, 1961; Queen Mother in Becket, Aldwych, 1961; Hester Bellboys in A Penny for a Song, Aldwych, 1962; Beatrice in Season of Goodwill, Queen's, 1964; Amanda in The Glass Menagerie, Haymarket, 1965; Uncle Vanya, Royal Court, 1970; *Films:* The Burning, 1967; Leo the Last, 1969. Numerous radio and TV plays. *Recreation:* gardening. *Address:* c/o Larry Dalzell, 3 Goodwins Court, WC2.

FFRENCH, family name of Baron ffrench.

FFRENCH, 7th Baron, *cr* 1798; **Peter Martin Joseph Charles John Mary ffrench;** Bt 1779; *b* 2 May 1926; *s* of Capt. Hon. John Martin Valentine ffrench (*d* 1946), *s* of 5th Baron, and of Sophia, *d* of late Signor Giovanni Brambilla, Villa Sucota, Como, Italy; *S* uncle 1955; *m* 1954, Sonia Katherine, *d* of Major Digby Cayley; one *s* two *d. Heir: s* Hon. Robuck John Peter Charles Mario ffrench, *b* 14 March 1956. *Address:* Castle ffrench, Ballinasloe, Co. Galway, Ireland.

FFRENCH-BEYTAGH, Canon Gonville Aubie; Rector of St Vedast-alias-Foster, London, since 1974; Hon. Canon of Johannesburg, since 1972 and of Canterbury, since 1973; *b* 26 Jan. 1912; *s* of Leo Michael and Edith ffrench-Beytagh; unmarried. *Educ:* Monkton Combe Sch., Bath; Bristol Grammar Sch.; St Paul's Theol Coll., Grahamstown (LTh). Priest 1939. Tramp and casual labourer, New Zealand, 1929-33; clerk in Johannesburg, 1933-36; Parish Priest and Diocesan Missioner, Johannesburg Dio., 1939-54; Dean of Salisbury, Rhodesia, 1955-65; Dean of Johannesburg, 1965-72; detained, tried, convicted and sentenced to 5 yrs imprisonment under SA Terrorism Act, 1971-72; conviction and sentence quashed by Appellate Div. and returned to England, 1972. *Publications:* Encountering Darkness, 1973; Encountering Light, 1975; Facing Depression, 1978. *Recreations:* drink, companionship and science fiction. *Address:* St Vedast's Rectory, Foster Lane, EC2. *T:* 01-606 3998.

FICKLING, Benjamin William, CBE 1973; FRCS, FDS RCS; Honorary Consultant Dental Surgeon, since 1974, formerly Dental Surgeon: St George's Hospital, SW1, 1936-74; Royal Dental Hospital of London, 1935-74; Mount Vernon Centre for Plastic and Jaw Surgery (formerly Hill End), 1941-74; *b* 14 July 1909; *s* of Robert Marshall Fickling, LDS RCS, and Florence (*née* Newson); *m* 1943, Shirley Dona, *d* of Albert Latimer Walker, FRCS; two *s* one *d. Educ:* Framlingham; St George's Hosp. Royal Dental Hospital. William Brown Senior Exhibition, St George's Hosp., 1929; LDS RCS, 1932; MRCS, LRCP, 1934; FRCS 1938; FDS, RCS 1947, MGDS RCS 1979. Lectures: Charles Tomes, RCS, 1956; Everett Magnus, Melbourne, 1971; Webb-Johnson, RCS, 1978. Examiner (Chm.), Membership in Gen. Dental Surgery, 1979-. Formerly Examiner: in Dental Surgery, RCS; Univ. of London and Univ. of Edinburgh. Dean of Faculty of Dental Surgery, 1968-71, and Mem. Council, Royal College of Surgeons, 1968-71 (Vice-Dean, 1965; Colyer Gold Medal, 1979); Fellow Royal Society of Medicine (Pres. Odontological Section, 1964-65); Pres., British Assoc. of Oral Surgeons, 1967-68; Mem. GDC, 1971-74. Director: Med. Sickness Annuity and Life Assurance Soc. Ltd; Permanent Insurance Co. Ltd; Medical Sickness Finance Corp. Ltd. Civilian Dental Consultant to RN, 1954-76. *Publications:* (joint) Injuries of the Jaws and Face, 1940; (joint) Chapter on Faciomaxillary Injuries and Deformities in British Surgical Practice, 1951. *Address:* 129 Harley Street, W1. *T:* 01-935 1882; Linksview, Linksway, Northwood, Mddx. *T:* Northwood 22035. *Club:* Ski Club of Great Britain.

FIDDES, James Raffan, QC (Scot.) 1965; Sheriff of South Strathclyde, Dumfries and Galloway at Hamilton, since 1977; *b* 1 Feb. 1919; *er s* of late Sir James Raffan Fiddes, CBE; *m* 1954, Edith Margaret (*d* 1979), 2nd *d* of late Charles E. Lippe, KC. *Educ:* Aberdeen Gram. Sch.; Glasgow Univ. (MA 1942; LLB 1948); Balliol Coll., Oxford, (BA 1944). Advocate, 1948. *Address:* 23 South Learmonth Gardens, Edinburgh EH4 1EZ. *T:* 031-332 1431. *Club:* Scottish Arts (Edinburgh).

FIDLER, Alwyn G. Sheppard, CBE 1963; MA, BArch, DipCD, FRIBA, FRTPI; architect and town planning consultant (Atkins Sheppard Fidler and Associates), since 1964; *b* 8 May 1909; *e s* of late W. E. Sheppard Fidler and Phoebe M. Williams; *m* 1936, Margaret (*d* 1977), *d* of Capt. J. R. Kidner, Newcastle upon Tyne; one *s. Educ:* Holywell Gram. Sch.; University of Liverpool; British Sch. at Rome. Tite Finalist, 1930; studied in USA, 1931; Victory Schol., 1933; Rome Schol. in Architecture, 1933-35. Chief Architect: Land Settlement Assoc., 1937; Barclays Bank Ltd, 1938; Sen. Tech. Intelligence Officer, Min. of Home Security, 1940-46; Chief Archt, Crawley New Town, 1947-52 (Housing Medals of Min. of Housing and Local Govt in 1951, 1952 and 1954); City Archt of Birmingham, 1952-64 (Distinction in Town Planning, 1955, for work at Crawley and Birmingham Redevelopment Areas); private practice, 1964-74. Council Mem., 1953-62, 1963-75, Vice-Pres., 1958-60, Chm. Practice Cttee, 1958-62, Treasurer, 1974-75, External Examr in Architecture, 1958-, RIBA. Pres. City and Borough Architects Soc.,

1956-58; Chm. Exec. Cttee, British Sch. at Rome, 1972- (Chm., Fac. of Architecture, 1958-72). Mem., Royal Commn for the Exhibn of 1851. Chm. ARC of UK, 1960-63; Mem. Jt Consultative Cttee of Architects, Quantity Surveyors and Builders, 1958-61; Mem. Birmingham and Five Counties Architectural Assoc. (Mem. Council, 1956-, Vice-Pres., 1960-62, Pres., 1962-64); Chm. Assoc. of Building Centres, 1964-72; Member Council: Building Centre Gp, 1971-81; Royal Albert Hall, 1974-; Gov., Coll. of Estate Management, 1965-72; Mem. SE Regional Adv. Cttee to Land Commn, 1967-70. Mem. or past Mem., of many other councils and cttees. *Publications:* Contrib. to professional jls. *Recreations:* travel and gardening. *Address:* 1 Burnham Drive, Reigate, Surrey RH2 9HD. *T:* Reigate 43849.

FIDLER, Michael M., JP; President, General Zionist Organisation of Great Britain, since 1973; Founder and National Director, Conservative Friends of Israel, since 1974; Chairman, International Organisation Commission, World Jewish Congress, since 1975; business consultant; Managing Director, Wibye Ltd, since 1968; *b* 10 Feb. 1916; *s* of Louis Fidler and Golda Fidler (*née* Sherr); *m* 1939, Maidie (*née* Davis); one *s* one *d. Educ:* Salford Grammar Sch.; Salford Royal Tech Coll. Cllr, Borough of Prestwich, 1951-63; Mayor, 1957-58; Alderman, 1963-74. Pres., Middleton, Prestwich and Whitfield Div. Cons. Assoc., 1965-69; Chm., Divl Educn Exec. (Prestwich, Whitfield and Radcliffe), Lancs CC, 1967-69. MP (C) Bury and Radcliffe, June 1970-Oct. 1974; Sec., Canadian Gp of Cons. Commonwealth Overseas Cttee, 1970-71; Treasurer, Parly Migraine Gp, 1970-74. Lectr, Extra Mural Dept, Manchester Univ., 1966-. Man. Director: H. & L. Fidler Ltd, 1941-70; Michael Lewis Ltd, 1942-70. Member: Grand Council, CBI, 1965-67; Nat. Exec., Nat. Assoc. of British Manufacturers, 1953-65. President: Fedn of Jewish Youth Socs of Gt Britain and Ireland, 1951-; Manchester Union of Jewish Socs, 1964-; Council of Manchester and Salford Jews, 1966-68 (Hon. Sec., 1950-53); Hon. Treasurer, 1953-55; Vice-Pres., 1954-60); Holy Law Congregation, Manchester, 1967-70 (Life Vice-Pres., 1977-); Bd of Deputies of British Jews, 1967-73; Cons. Friends of Israel, Redbridge Area Council; Dir, Friendship with Israel Group, all party, European Parlt, 1979-; Vice-President: Children and Youth Aliyah Cttee for Gt Britain, 1968-81; Mizrachi, Hapoel-Hamizrachi Fedn of Gt Britain and Ireland, 1968-78; Hillel Foundn of Gt Britain, 1968-; Life Vice-President: Manchester Jewish Bd of Guardians, 1967-; Manchester Jewish Social Services, 1967-; Vice-Chairman: World Conf. on Jewish Educn, 1968-75; World Conf. of Jewish Organisations, 1967-73; Member Exec. Cttee: Council of Christians and Jews, Manchester Branch, 1966-; World Meml Foundn for Jewish Culture and World Conf. on Jewish Material Claims against Germany, 1968-80. Patron, All Party Cttee for release of Soviet Jewry, 1971-. Governor: Stand Grammar Schools, 1955-74; Inst. of Contemporary Jewry, Hebrew Univ. of Jerusalem, 1967-73; St Peter's RC Grammar Sch., 1968-80; Bury Grammar Schools, 1970-74. President: British Parks Lawn Tennis Assoc., 1952-59; SE Lancs Amateur Football League, 1966-67; Prestwich Heys Amateur Football Club, 1965-; Member: House of Commons Motor Club, 1970-74; Parly Flying Club, 1971-74. JP Co. Lancs, 1958. FRGS, FRAS, FREconS, FIAI. *Publications:* One Hundred Years of the Holy Law Congregation, 1964; articles. *Recreations:* politics, travel, reading, filming, foreign affairs, education. *Address:* 51 Tavistock Court, Tavistock Square, WC1H 9HG. *T:* 01-387 4925; 1 Woodcliffe Lodge, Sedgley Park Road, Prestwich, Manchester M25 8JX. *T:* 061-773 1471; Lower Ground Floor, 45 Westbourne Terrace, W2 3UR. *T:* 01-262 2493. *Clubs:* Embassy; Milverton Lodge (Manchester).

FIDLER-SIMPSON, John Cody; *see* Simpson.

FIELD, Brig. Anne, CB 1980; Director, Women's Royal Army Corps, 1977-82; Hon. ADC to the Queen, 1977-82; *b* 4 April 1926; *d* of Captain Harold Derwent and Annie Helena Hodgson. *Educ:* Keswick Sch.; St George's, Harpenden; London Sch. of Economics. Joined ATS, 1947; commissioned: ATS, 1948; WRAC, 1949; Lt-Col, 1968; Col, 1971. Freeman, City of London, 1981. CBIM (FBIM 1978). *Address:* c/o Barclays Bank Ltd, Keswick, Cumbria. *Club:* Lansdowne.

FIELD, Arnold, OBE 1965; Air Traffic Services Adviser; Joint Field Commander, National Air Traffic Services, 1974-77; *b* 19 May 1917; *m* 1943, Kathleen Dulcie Bennett; one *s* one *d. Educ:* King Edward's Grammar Sch., Birmingham. RAF, 1940-46 (Sqdn Ldr). Civil Air Traffic Control Officer, 1946; Centre Supt, Scottish Air Traffic Control Centre, 1954; Centre Supt, London Air Traffic Control Centre, 1957; Divisional Air Traffic Control Officer, Southern Div., 1963; Dir, Civil Air Traffic Ops, 1969. Master, Guild of Air Traffic Control Officers, 1958; Pres., Internat. Fedn of Air Traffic Control Officers, 1970. *Publications:* The Control of Air Traffic, 1981; articles in Intervaia, Times Supplement, Flight, Controller. *Recreations:* vintage cars, boating. *Address:* Footprints, Stoke Wood, Stoke Poges, Bucks. *T:* Farnham Common 2710. *Club:* Bentley Drivers (Long Crendon).

FIELD, Edward John; HM Diplomatic Service; Counsellor (Commercial), Seoul, since 1980; *b* 11 June 1936; *s* of Arthur Field, OBE, MC, TD, and late Dorothy Agnes Field; *m* 1960, Irene Sophie du Pont Darden; one *s* one *d. Educ:* Highgate Sch.; Corpus Christi Coll., Oxford (Open Scholar; MA); Univ. of Virginia. Courtaulds Ltd, 1960-62; FCO, 1963-: 2nd, later 1st Sec., Tokyo, 1963-68; Amer. Dept, FCO, 1968-70; Cultural Attaché, Moscow, 1970-72; 1st Sec. (Commercial), Tokyo, 1973-76; Asst Head, S Asian Dept, FCO, 1976-77; Dept of Trade, 1977-79 (Head, Exports to Japan Unit).

Recreations: tennis, squash, riding, listening to music. *Address:* c/o Foreign and Commonwealth Office, SW1. *Club:* Seoul (Seoul, Republic of Korea).

FIELD, Frank; MP (Lab) Birkenhead, since 1979; *b* 16 July 1942; *s* of Walter and Annie Field. *Educ:* St Clement Danes Grammar Sch.; Univ. of Hull (BSc (Econ)). Teacher: at Southwark Coll. for Further Education, 1964-68; at Hammersmith Coll. for Further Education, 1968-69. Director: Child Poverty Action Gp, 1969-79; Low Pay Unit, 1974-80. Mem., Hounslow BC, 1964-68. Contested (Lab) Buckingham S, 1966. *Publications:* (ed, jtly) Twentieth Century State Education, 1971; (ed, jtly) Black Britons, 1971; (ed) Low Pay, 1973; Unequal Britain, 1974; (ed) Are Low Wages Inevitable?, 1976; (ed) Education and the Urban Crisis, 1976; (ed) The Conscript Army: a study of Britain's unemployed, 1976; (jtly) To Him Who Hath: a study of poverty and taxation, 1976; (with Ruth Lister) Wasted Labour, 1978 (Social Concern Book Award); (ed) The Wealth Report, 1979; Inequality in Britain: freedom, welfare and the state, 1981; Poverty and Politics, 1982. *Recreation:* book collecting. *Address:* House of Commons, SW1. *T:* 01-219 5193.

FIELD, Dr Ian Trevor; Chief Medical and Health Services Adviser, since 1978 and Head, Health and Population Division, since 1980, Overseas Development Administration of Foreign and Commonwealth Office, and Head, International Health Division, Department of Health and Social Security, since 1978; *b* 31 Oct. 1933; *s* of Major George Edward Field, MBE, IA, and Bertha Cecilia Field; *m* 1960, Christine Mary Osman, JP; three *s. Educ:* Shri Shivaji School, Poona; Bournemouth School; Guy's Hosp. Med. School. MB, BS, FFCM. Royal Engineers, 1952-54; Med. Sch., 1954-60; house posts, 1960-62; general practice, 1962-64; Asst Sec., later Under Sec., BMA, 1964-75; DHSS, 1975-. Member: Council, Liverpool Sch. of Trop. Med., 1979-; Bd of Management, London Sch. of Hygiene and Trop. Med., 1979-; WHO Global Adv. Cttee on Malaria Control, 1979-82 (Chm., 1981). *Publications:* contribs to medical jls. *Recreations:* military history, cricket, rugby. *Address:* 10 Rockwells Gardens, Dulwich Wood Park, SE19 1HW. *T:* 01-670 5877.

FIELD, John, CBE 1967; ARAD; Director, London Festival Ballet, since 1982; *b* 22 Oct. 1921; *m* 1958, Anne Heaton. *Educ:* Wheatley Boys' Sch., Doncaster. Sadler's Wells Ballet Co., 1939; RAF, 1942-46; Principal, Sadler's Wells Ballet Co., 1947-56; Resident Dir, Sadler's Wells Theatre Ballet, 1956-57; Asst Dir, 1957-70, Co-Dir, July-Dec. 1970, Royal Ballet Co.; Dir of Ballet, La Scala, Milan, 1971-74; Artistic Dir, 1975-76, Dir, 1976-79, Royal Acad. of Dancing; Artistic Dir, London Festival Ballet, 1979-81. *Address:* 39 Jay Mews, SW7 2ES. *Club:* Garrick.

FIELD, Sir John (Osbaldiston), KBE 1967; Kt 1962; CMG 1959; first Governor, Gilbert and Ellice Islands Colony, 1972-73 (Resident Commissioner, 1970-71); *b* 30 Oct. 1913; *s* of late Frank Osbaldiston Field; *m* 1951, Irene Margaret, 2nd *d* of late Harold Godfrey Judd, CBE. *Educ:* Stellenbosch Boys' High Sch. S Africa; Magdalene Coll., Cambridge (MA). Colonial Administrative Service, Nigeria, 1936; Senior District Officer, 1951; Resident, 1954; Commissioner of the Cameroons, 1956; UK Special Representative for British Cameroons at UN Trusteeship Council, 1956-61; Commissioner of Southern Cameroons, 1960-61; Governor and C-in-C of St Helena, 1962-68; Staff Liaison Officer, HM Overseas Civil Service, 1968-69; acting Administrator, Montserrat, 1969. *Recreation:* fishing. *Address:* Little Park, PO Box 35, Himeville 4585, Natal, South Africa. *Clubs:* United Oxford & Cambridge University; Victoria (Pietermaritzburg).

FIELD, Stanley Alfred, CBE 1982; JP; President, William Baird PLC, since 1981 (Chairman, 1961-81); Chairman: Winterbottom Energy Trust PLC; Expanded Metal Co. PLC; Director: Automobile Association Ltd; Merchants Trust PLC; *b* 1913; *m* 1950, Doreen Plunkett; one *s* two *d.* Senior Partner, W. N. Middleton & Co., 1946-53; Man. Dir, Prestige Group Ltd, 1953-58; Dir, Venesta Ltd, 1956-64 (Chm., 1958-64). Liveryman, Glass Sellers Company. JP City of London, 1969. *Address:* (office) Moorgate Hall, 153 Moorgate, EC2M 6XH; (home) Glasses, Graffham, Petworth, West Sussex GU28 0PU. *Clubs:* Carlton, City Livery, Caledonian.

FIELD, William James; *b* 22 May 1909; *s* of late Frederick William Field, Solicitor; unmarried. *Educ:* Richmond County Sch.; London Univ; abroad. Joined Labour Party, 1935; Parliamentary Private Sec. to Sec. of State for War, May-Oct. 1951 (to Under-Sec. for War, 1950-51); Chm. South Hammersmith Divisional Labour Party, 1945-46; contested Hampstead Div., General Election, 1945; MP (Lab) North Paddington, Nov. 1946-Oct. 1953. Mem. Hammersmith Borough Council, 1945-53, and Leader of that Council, 1946-49; a Vice-Pres. of Assoc. of Municipal Corporations, 1952-53; for several years, mem. Metropolitan Boroughs' Standing Joint Cttee and of many local govt bodies. Volunteered for Army, Sept. 1939 and served in ranks and as officer in Intelligence Corps and RASC.

FIELD-FISHER, Thomas Gilbert, TD 1950; QC 1969; a Recorder of the Crown Court, since 1972; *b* 16 May 1915; *s* of Caryl Field-Fisher, Torquay; *m* 1945, Ebba, *d* of Max Larsen, Linwood, USA. *Educ:* King's Sch., Bruton; Peterhouse, Cambridge. BA 1937, MA 1942. Called to Bar, Middle Temple, 1942, Bencher, 1976. Served Queen Victoria's Rifles, KRRC, 1939-47 (despatches). Judge Advocate Gen.'s Dept, 1945-47; joined Western Circuit, 1947. Mem., Bar Council, 1962-66; Deputy Chairman: SW Agricultural Land Tribunal, 1967-82; Cornwall QS, 1968-71; Chm., Maria Colwell Inquiry, 1973-74. Vice-Chm., London Council of Social Service, 1966-79; Vice-Pres.,

London Voluntary Service Council, 1979-. Mem., Home Secretary's Adv. Cttee on Animal Experimentation, 1980. Chm., Dogs' Home, Battersea, 1982. *Publications:* Animals and the Law, 1964; Rent Regulation and Control, 1967; contribs to Halsbury's Laws of England, 3rd and 4th edns, Law Jl, and other legal publications. *Recreations:* tennis, dogs, collecting watercolours, social welfare. *Address:* 38 Hurlingham Court, SW6. *T:* 01-736 4627; 2 King's Bench Walk, Temple, EC4. *T:* 01-353 1746. *Clubs:* Hurlingham, International Lawn Tennis of Great Britain.

FIELDEN, Frank, MA (Dunelm); Secretary, Royal Fine Art Commission, 1969-79; *b* 3 Oct. 1915; *s* of Ernest and Emma Fielden, Greenfield, Yorks; *m* 1939, Margery Keeler; two *d. Educ:* University of Manchester. Graduated, 1938. Served 1939-45 with Royal Engineers (Special Forces), France, N Africa, Italy, Germany. Town Planning Officer to Nigerian Government, 1945-46; Lecturer and Sen. Lectr, University of Durham, 1946-59; Prof. of Architecture, Univ. of Strathclyde, 1959-69. Mem., Royal Fine Art Commn for Scotland, 1965-69. RIBA Athens Bursar, 1950, Bronze Medallist 1960. Chairman: Soc. of Architectural Historians of Great Britain, 1965-67; Richmond Soc., 1971-74. *Publications:* articles in professional journals and national press. *Recreations:* music, gardening, travel, food and wine. *Address:* 28 Caledonian Road, Chichester, W Sussex PO19 2LQ; Les Glycines, Change, Côte d'Or, France. *Club:* Athenæum.

FIELDGATE, Alan Frederic Edmond, CMG 1945; *b* 20 Nov. 1889; *m* 1915, Dorothy Alice Thomas. *Educ:* Worcester Coll., Oxford (BA). Asst District Commissioner, Gold Coast Colony, 1915; District Commissioner, 1922; Provincial Commissioner, 1934-46. *Address:* Olde Court, Higher Lincombe Road, Torquay, Devon.

FIELDHOUSE, Arnold; *see* Fieldhouse, R. A.

FIELDHOUSE, Bill; *see* Fieldhouse, W.

FIELDHOUSE, Prof. David Kenneth; Vere Harmsworth Professor of Imperial and Naval History, Cambridge University, since 1981; Fellow, Jesus College, Cambridge, since 1981; *b* 7 June 1925; *s* of Rev. Ernest Fieldhouse and Clara Hilda Beatrice Fieldhouse; *m* 1952, Sheila Elizabeth Lyon; one *s* two *d. Educ:* Dean Close Sch., Cheltenham; Queen's Coll., Oxford (MA, DLitt). War Service: RN, Sub-Lt (A), 1943-47. History master, Haileybury Coll., 1950-52; Lectr in Modern History, Univ. of Canterbury, NZ, 1953-57; Beit Lectr in Commonwealth History, Oxford Univ., 1958-81; Fellow, Nuffield Coll., Oxford, 1966-81. *Publications:* The Colonial Empires, 1966, 2nd edn, 1982; The Theory of Capitalist Imperialism, 1967, 2nd edn 1969; Economics and Empire, 1973; Unilever Overseas, 1978; Colonialism 1870-1945, 1981. *Recreations:* music, farming, golf, writing fiction. *Address:* Jesus College, Cambridge. *T:* Cambridge 68611.

FIELDHOUSE, Sir Harold, KBE 1949 (OBE 1934); CB 1947; Secretary, National Assistance Board, 1946-59, retired; Member of Letchworth Garden City, Welwyn Garden City and Hatfield Corporations, retired; *b* Leeds, Yorks; *e s* of Frank and Mary Ellen Fieldhouse; *m* 1922, Mabel Elaine Elliott, Conisborough, Yorks; two *s. Educ:* Armley Higher Grade Sch., Leeds. Asst Clerk, Leeds Board of Guardians, 1909-30; Public Assistance Officer, City of Leeds, 1930-34; Regional Officer, Asst Sec. and Under-Sec. Assistance Board, 1934-46. Liveryman, Clockmakers' Co., 1959. *Recreations:* golf, bridge, music, reading. *Address:* 5 Gayton Court, Harrow, Mddx. *T:* 01-427 0918. *Clubs:* City Livery; Grim's Dyke Golf, West Hill Golf.
    See also Sir J. D. E. Fieldhouse.

FIELDHOUSE, Adm. Sir John (David Elliott), GCB 1982 (KCB 1980); GBE 1982; Chief of Naval Staff and First Sea Lord, since 1982; *b* 12 Feb. 1928; *s* of Sir Harold Fieldhouse, *qv* ; *m* 1953, Margaret Ellen Cull; one *s* two *d. Educ:* RNC Dartmouth. MINucE. Midshipman, E Indies Fleet, 1945-46; entered Submarine Service, 1948; comd HMS Acheron, 1955; CO HMS Dreadnought, 1964-66; Exec. Officer, HMS Hermes, 1967; Captain SM10 (Polaris Sqdn), 1968-70; Captain HMS Diomede, 1971; Comdr, Standing Naval Force Atlantic, 1972-73; Dir, Naval Warfare, 1973-74; Flag Officer, Second Flotilla, 1974-76; Flag Officer, Submarines, and Comdr Submarine Force, E Atlantic Area, 1976-78; Controller of the Navy, 1979-81; C-in-C Fleet, and Allied C-in-C, Channel and Eastern Atlantic, 1981-82. *Recreations:* home, family and friends. *Address:* Pippins, 16 Ryde Place, Lee-on-Solent, Hants. *T:* Lee-on-Solent 550892.

FIELDHOUSE, (Richard) Arnold; building contractor; *b* 1 Aug. 1916; *m* 1952. *Educ:* elem. sch. Elected to Manchester City Council for Levenshulme Ward, 1946: served as Leader of City Council, Chm. Policy Cttee, and Chm. Finance Cttee. Elected to Greater Manchester County Council for Levenshulme Elect. Div., 1973: Leader of Conservative Opposition, 1973-77; Mem., Policy Cttee; Leader of Council, 1977-81. *Recreations:* gardening, sailing. *Address:* Slade Hall, Slade Lane, Manchester M13 0QP. *T:* 061-224 5454.

FIELDHOUSE, William, (Bill Fieldhouse), CBE 1978; Chairman, Carrington Viyella, since 1980 (Director, since 1972); *b* 1 Jan. 1932; *o c* of Joseph Fieldhouse and Elsie Broadbent; *m* 1st, 1953, Joan Lomax; one *s* one *d* ; 2nd, 1978, Torunn Hassel; two *d. Educ:* Wallsend Grammar Sch.; Rutherford Coll., Newcastle upon Tyne. CEng; MIMechE 1967. Parsons Marine, 1949-53; Cunard, 1953-56; Allis-Chalmers, 1956-65; Tarmac, 1965-

67; Peter Dixon, 1967-69; Letraset, 1969-81 (Chm., 1973-81); Director: UBM, 1978-80; Dalgety, 1980-. FRSA 1975. *Recreations:* hunting, skiing, tennis, golf. *Address:* 28 Saville Row, W1X 1AD. *T:* 01-734 5321. *Club:* Royal Automobile.

FIELDING, Colin Cunningham, CB 1981; Controller of Research and Development Establishments, Research and Nuclear Programmes, Ministry of Defence, since 1982; *b* 23 Dec. 1926; *s* of Richard Cunningham and Sadie Fielding; *m* 1953, Gillian Aerona (*née* Thomas); one *d. Educ:* Heaton Grammar Sch., Newcastle upon Tyne; Durham Univ. BSc Hons Physics. British Scientific Instruments Research Assoc., 1948-49; RRE Malvern, 1949-65; Asst Dir of Electronics R&D, Min. of Technology, 1965-68; Head of Electronics Dept, RRE Malvern, 1968-73; RCDS, 1973-74; Dir of Scientific and Technical Intelligence, MoD, 1975-77; Dir, Admiralty Surface Weapons Estabt, 1977-78; Dep. Controller, R&D Estabts and Res. A, and Chief Scientist (RN), MoD, 1978-80; Dep. Chief of Defence Procurement (Nuclear), and Dir, AWRE, MoD, 1980-82. *Publications:* papers in Proc. IEE, Proc. IERE, Nature. *Recreations:* yachting, tennis, music. *Address:* Cheviots, Rosemount Drive, Bickley, Kent. *Club:* Athenæum.

FIELDING, Fenella Marion; actress; *b* London, 17 Nov. 1934. *Educ:* North London Collegiate School. Began acting career in 1954; *plays include:* Jubilee Girl, Victoria Palace, 1956; Valmouth, Lyric, Hammersmith, 1958, Saville, 1959, and Chichester Fest., 1982; Pieces of Eight, Apollo, 1959; Five Plus One, Edinburgh Fest., 1961; Twists, Arts, 1962 (Best Revue Performance of the Year in Variety); Doctors of Philosophy, New Arts, 1962; Luv, New Arts, 1963; So Much to Remember—The Life Story of a Great Lady, Vaudeville, 1963; Let's Get a Divorce, Mermaid, 1966; The Beaux Stratagem and The Italian Straw Hat, Chichester Fest., 1967; The High Bid, Mermaid, 1967; Façade, Queen Elizabeth Hall, 1970; Colette, Ellen Stewart, NY, 1970 (first appearance in NY); Fish Out of Water, Greenwich, 1971; The Old Man's Comforts, Open Space, 1972; The Provok'd Wife, Greenwich, 1973; Absurd Person Singular, Criterion, 1974; Fielding Convertible, Edinburgh Fest., 1976; Jubilee Jeunesse, Royal Opera House, 1977; Look After Lulu, Haymarket, 1978; A personal Choice, Edinburgh Fest., 1978; Fenella on Broadway, W6, Studio, Lyric, Hammersmith, 1979; *films:* Drop Dead, Darling; Lock Up Your Daughters; *television:* A Touch of Venus (series); Ooh La La (series); numerous appearances in UK and USA. *Recreation:* reading. *Address:* c/o Crouch Associates, 59 Frith Street, W1V 5TA.

FIELDING, Frank Stanley, OBE 1966; HM Diplomatic Service, retired; Deputy Consul-General, Toronto, 1975-78; *b* 21 Dec. 1918; *s* of John Edgar Fielding and Anne; *m* 1944, Lela Coombs; one *s. Educ:* St Albans Sch.; UCL; King's Coll., London. Diploma in Journalism. HM Forces, 1940-46. Control Commn for Germany, 1946-48; Third Sec., Brit. Embassy, Vienna, 1948-50; Second Sec., Brit. Embassy, Beirut, 1950-55; Vice Consul, Cleveland, 1955-56; First Secretary: Brit. Embassy, Djakarta, 1956-60; FO, 1960-62; Consul (Commercial), Cape Town, 1962-65; First Sec., Brit. Embassy, Pretoria, 1965-68; Consul, NY, 1968-69; Dep. High Comr, Brisbane, 1969-72; Counsellor (Commercial), Singapore, 1972-75. *Recreations:* golf, fishing. *Address:* 28 Berkeley Square, Havant, Hants. *T:* Havant 48254.

FIELDING, Gabriel, (Alan Gabriel Barnsley); Professor of English, Washington State University, 1967-81, now Professor Emeritus; *b* 25 March 1916; *s* of late George Barnsley, Clerk in Holy Orders, and Katherine Mary (*née* Fielding-Smith), a descendant of Henry Fielding, the novelist; *m* 1943, Edwina Eleanora Cook, Storrington, Sussex; three *s* two *d. Educ:* St Edward's Sch., Oxford; Trinity Coll., Dublin; St George's Hospital, London. BA, TCD, 1939. MRCS (Eng.), LRCP (London) 1942. Served with RAMC, 1943-46 (Capt.). Dep. Medical Officer, HM Training Establishment, Maidstone, Kent, 1954-64. Appointed Author in Residence (Prof. of English) to Washington State Univ., USA, 1966-67. Hon. DLitt Gonzaga Univ., Spokane, Washington, 1967. *Publications: poetry:* The Frog Prince and Other Poems, 1952; Twenty-Eight Poems, 1955; Songs without Music, 1979; *novels:* Brotherly Love, 1954; In the Time of Greenbloom, 1956; Eight Days, 1958; Through Streets Broad and Narrow, 1960; The Birthday King (W. H. Smith Prize for Literature, 1964), 1963; Gentlemen in Their Season, 1966; Pretty Doll-Houses, 1979; *short stories:* New Queens for Old (a novella and nine stories), 1972 (Governor's Literary Award, Washington State, 1972). *Recreations:* televised news, painting, space, theology, walking. *Address:* 945 Monroe Street, Pullman, Washington 99163, USA.

FIELDING, Ven. Harold Ormandy; Archdeacon of Rochdale, 1972-82; Archdeacon Emeritus since 1982; Vicar of St Peter, Bolton, 1965-82; *b* 13 Nov. 1912; *s* of Harold Wolstencroft and Florence Ann Fielding; *m* 1939, Elsie Whillance; three *s* one *d. Educ:* Farnworth Grammar Sch.; Magdalene Coll., Cambridge (MA); Ripon Hall, Oxford. Curate: St Mary, Leigh, 1936-40; St Paul, Walkden, 1940-44; Vicar of St James, New Bury, 1944-65; Hon. Canon of Manchester, 1965-72; Rural Dean of Bolton, 1965-72. *Address:* 6 High Meadows, Bromley Cross, Bolton BL7 9AR. *T:* Bolton 52468.

FIELDING, Leslie; Director-General for External Affairs, Commission of the European Communities, since 1982; *b* 29 July 1932; *o s* of late Percy Archer Fielding and of Margaret (*née* Calder Horry); *m* 1978, Dr Sally P. J. Harvey, MA, FRHistS, Fellow of St Hilda's Coll., Oxford; one *d. Educ:* Queen Elizabeth's Sch., Barnet; Emmanuel Coll., Cambridge (1st Cl. Hons, historical tripos pt II; hon. bac. scholar; MA); School of Oriental and African Studies,

London. Served with Royal Regt of Artillery, 1951-53. Entered HM Diplomatic Service, 1956; served in: Tehran, 1957-60; Foreign Office, 1960-64; Phnom Penh (Chargé d'Affaires), 1964-66; Paris, 1967-70; FCO, 1970-73; Counsellor and Dep. Head of Planning Staff, 1973. Seconded for service with European Commn in Brussels, 1973; Dir (External Relns Directorate Gen.), 1973-77; permanent transfer 1979; Head of Delegn of Commn to Japan, 1978-82. Vis. Fellow, St Antony's Coll., Oxford, 1977-78 (MA). *Recreation:* life in the country. *Address:* 200 rue de la Loi, 1049 Brussels, Belgium. *Club:* Travellers'.

FIELDSEND, John Charles Rowell; Hon. Mr Justice Fieldsend; Chief Justice of Zimbabwe, since 1980; *b* 13 Sept. 1921; *s* of C. E. Fieldsend, MC, and Phyllis (*née* Brucesmith); *m* 1945, Muriel Gedling; one *s* one *d. Educ:* Michaelhouse, Natal; Rhodes University Coll., Grahamstown, SA (BA 1942, LLB 1947). Served RA, 1943-45. Called to the Bar, S Rhodesia, 1947; advocate in private practice, 1947-63; QC S Rhodesia, 1959; Pres., Special Income Tax Court for Fedn of Rhodesia and Nyasaland, 1958-63; High Court Judge, S Rhodesia, 1963, resigned 1968; Asst Solicitor, Law Commn, 1968-78, Sec., 1978-80. *Recreations:* home-making, travel. *Address:* 6 Chancellor Avenue, Harare, Zimbabwe.

FIENNES; *see* Twisleton-Wykeham-Fiennes.

FIENNES, family name of **Baron Saye and Sele.**

FIENNES, Sir Maurice (Alberic Twisleton-Wykeham-), Kt 1965; CEng; FIMechE; Engineering and Industrial Consultant; Chairman and Managing Director of Davy-Ashmore Ltd, 1961-69; Associate Consultant, L. H. Manderstam & Partners Ltd, 1977-80; *b* 1 March 1907; *s* of Alberic Arthur Twisleton-Wykeham-Fiennes and Gertrude Theodosia Pomeroy Colley; *m* 1st, 1932, Sylvia Mabel Joan (marr. diss., 1964), *d* of late Major David Finlay, 7th Dragoon Guards. two *s* three *d* ; 2nd, 1967, Erika Hueller von Huellenried, *d* of late Dr Herbert Hueller, Vienna. *Educ:* Repton; Armstrong Coll., Newcastle upon Tyne. Apprenticeship with Ransomes and Rapier Ltd, Ipswich; joined Sir W. G. Armstrong, Whitworth & Co Ltd (Engineers), Newcastle-upon-Tyne, 1930; with The United Steel Companies Ltd, 1937, first as Commercial Asst to Managing Dir, then in charge Gun Forgings and Gun Dept at Steel Peech & Tozer; Gen. Works Dir, Brush Electrical Engineering Co. Ltd, 1942; Managing Dir, Davy and United Engineering Co. Ltd, 1945; Managing Dir, Davy-Ashmore Ltd, 1960. Steel Industry Advr for UN Industrial Develt Orgn to Govt of Peru, 1974-75; Engineering Advisor for World Bank to Venezuelan Investment Fund, 1976-77. Mem. Economic Develt Cttee for Mech. Eng, 1964-67; Pres. of Iron and Steel Institute, 1962-63; Chairman: Athlone Fellowships Cttee, 1966-71; Overseas Scholarships Bd, CBI, 1970-76; Mem., Reserve Pension Bd, 1974-75. Governor, Yehudi Menuhin School, 1969. *Recreations:* music, grandchildren. *Address:* 11 Heath Rise, Kersfield Road, Putney Hill, SW15 3HF. *T:* 01-785 7489. *Clubs:* Carlton, Naval and Military.

FIENNES, Very Rev. Hon. Oliver William Twisleton-Wykeham-; Dean of Lincoln, since 1969; *b* 17 May 1926; *yr s* of 20th Baron Saye and Sele, OBE, MC, and Hersey Cecilia Hester, *d* of late Captain Sir Thomas Dacres Butler, KCVO; *m* 1956, Juliet, *d* of late Dr Trevor Braby Heaton, OBE; two *s* two *d. Educ:* Eton; New College, Oxford; Cuddesdon College. Asst Curate, New Milton, Hants, 1954; Chaplain, Clifton College, Bristol, 1958; Rector of Lambeth, 1963. ChStJ 1971. *Address:* The Deanery, Lincoln. *T:* Lincoln 23608.

FIENNES, Sir Ranulph Twisleton-Wykeham-, 3rd Bt, *cr* 1916; *b* 7 March 1944; *s* of Lieut-Col Sir Ranulph Twisleton-Wykeham-Fiennes, DSO, 2nd Bt (died of wounds, 1943) and Audrey Joan, *yr d* of Sir Percy Newson, 1st Bt; *S* father 1944; *m* 1970, Virginia Pepper. *Educ:* Eton. Liveryman, Vintners' Company, 1960. French Parachutist Wings, 1965. Lieut, Royal Scots Greys, 1966, Captain 1968 (retd 1970). Attached 22 SAS Regt, 1966, Sultan of Muscat's Armed Forces, 1968 (Dhofar Campaign Medal, 1969; Sultan's Bravery Medal, 1970). T&AVR 1971, Captain RAC. Leader of British expeditions: White Nile, 1969; Jostedalsbre Glacier, 1970; Headless Valley, BC, 1971; (Towards) North Pole, 1977; Transglobe (around the world by Polar route), 1979-82, reached South Pole, 15 Dec. 1980, reached North Pole, 11 April 1982. *Publications:* A Talent for Trouble, 1970; Ice Fall in Norway, 1972; The Headless Valley, 1973; Where Soldiers Fear To Tread, 1975; Hell on Ice, 1979. *Recreations:* alpinism, langlauf, photography. *Heir:* none. *Address:* Robins, Lodsworth, Petworth, West Sussex. *T:* Lodsworth 363.

FIFE, 3rd Duke of, *cr* 1900; **James George Alexander Bannerman Carnegie;** Master of Southesk; *b* 23 Sept. 1929; *o s* of 11th Earl of Southesk, *qv,* and Princess Maud (*d* 1945); *S aunt,* Princess Arthur of Connaught (Dukedom of Fife), 1959; *m* 1956, Hon. Caroline Cicely Dewar (marr. diss. 1966; she *m* 1980, Gen. Sir Richard Worsley), *er d* of 3rd Baron Forteviot, *qv* ; one *s* one *d. Educ:* Gordonstoun. Nat. Service, Scots Guards (Malayan Campaign), 1948-50. Royal Agricultural College. Clothworkers' Company, and Freeman City of London. Pres. of ABA, 1959-73, Vice-Patron, 1973; a Vice-Patron, Braemar Royal Highland Soc.; a Vice-Pres., British Olympic Assoc. *Heir:* s Earl of Macduff, *qv. Address:* Elsick House, Stonehaven, Kincardineshire AB3 2NT. *Club:* Turf.

FIFE, Ian Braham, MC 1945; TD (2 bars) 1946; **His Honour Judge Fife;** a Circuit Judge (formerly County Court Judge), since 1965; *b* 10 July 1911;

o s of late Donald Fulford Fife and Muriel Alice Fife (*née* Pitt); *m* 1947, Pauline, *e d* of late T. R. Parsons and Mrs Winifred Parsons, CBE, Cambridge; two *s* two *d. Educ:* Monkton Combe Sch. Served, Royal Fusiliers, 1939-47. Called to Bar, Inner Temple, 1948; Mem. Bar Council, 1960-64. *Publications:* ed (with E. A. Machin): Redgrave's Factories Acts (edns 20-22); Redgrave's Offices and Shops (edns 1-2); (with E. A. Machin): Redgrave's Health and Safety in Factories (edns 1-2); Health and Safety at Work, 1st edn; contrib. Halsbury's Laws of England, 3rd and 4th edns. *Address:* 2 Castello Avenue, Putney, SW15. *T:* 01-788 6475.

FIFOOT, Erik Richard Sidney, MC 1945; MA; ALA; Bodley's Librarian, and Professorial Fellow of Exeter College, Oxford, 1979-81; *b* 14 June 1925; *s* of Cecil Herbert Stuart Fifoot and Hjordis (*née* Eriksen); *m* 1949, Jean, *o d* of Lt-Col J. S. Thain; two *d. Educ:* Berkhamsted Sch.; Oxford Univ. (MA); London Univ. (DipLibr). HM Coldstream Guards, 1943-46. Leeds University Library: Asst Librarian, 1950-52; Sub-Librarian, 1952-58; Dep. Librarian, Nottingham Univ., 1958-60; Librarian, Univ. of Edinburgh, 1960-79. Chm., Standing Conf. of Nat. and Univ. Libraries, 1979-81; Mem., Exec. Bd, Internat. Fedn of Library Assocs and Instns, 1979-. *Publications:* A Bibliography of Edith, Osbert and Sacheverell Sitwell, 1963, 2nd edn 1971; articles and reviews in library and educnl jls, symposia, and encycl. *Address:* Mill Green, Bampton, Oxon OX8 2HF.

FIFOOT, Paul Ronald Ninnes, CMG 1978; HM Diplomatic Service; Legal Counsellor, Foreign and Commonwealth Office, since 1979; *b* 1 April 1928; *o s* of late Ronald Fifoot, Cardiff; *m* 1952, Erica, *er d* of late Richard Alford, DMD; no *c. Educ:* Monkton House Sch., Cardiff; Queens' Coll., Cambridge. BA 1948, MA 1952. Military Service, 1948-50, RASC (2nd Lieut 1949). Called to Bar, Gray's Inn, 1953; Crown Counsel, Tanganyika, 1953; Asst to the Law Officers, 1960; Legal Draftsman (later Chief Parliamentary Draftsman), 1961; retd from Tanzania Govt Service, 1966; Asst Legal Adviser, Commonwealth Office, 1966; Legislative Counsel, Province of British Columbia, 1967; Asst Legal Adviser, Commonwealth (later Foreign and Commonwealth) Office, 1968; Legal Counsellor, 1971; Agent of the UK Govt in cases before the European Commn and Court of Human Rights, 1971-76; Counsellor (Legal Advr), UK Mission to UN, NY, 1976-79. *Address:* c/o Foreign and Commonwealth Office, SW1.

FIGG, Sir Leonard (Clifford William), KCMG 1981 (CMG 1974); HM Diplomatic Service; Ambassador to Ireland, since 1980; *b* 17 Aug. 1923; *s* of late Sir Clifford Figg and late Lady (Eileen) Figg (*née* Crabb); *m* 1955, Jane Brown; three *s. Educ:* Charterhouse; Trinity Coll., Oxford. RAF, 1942-46 (Flt-Lt). HM Diplomatic Service, 1947; served in: Addis Ababa, 1949-52; FO, 1952-58; Amman, 1958-61; FO, 1961-67; Counsellor, 1965; Deputy Consul-General, Chicago, 1967-69; DTI, 1973; Consul General and Minister, Milan, 1973-77; Asst Under Sec. of State, FCO, 1977-80. *Recreations:* field sports. *Address:* c/o Foreign and Commonwealth Office, SW1. *Clubs:* Brooks's, Pratt's.

FIGGESS, Sir John (George), KBE 1969 (OBE 1949); CMG 1960; a director of Christie, Manson and Woods Ltd, since 1973; *b* 15 Nov. 1909; *e s* of Percival Watts Figgess and Leonora (*née* McCanlis); *m* 1948, Alette, *d* of Dr P. J. A. Idenburg, The Hague; two *d. Educ:* Whitgift Sch. In business in Japan, 1933-38. Commissioned, Intelligence Corps, 1939; Staff Coll., 1941; served with Intelligence Corps, India/Burma Theatre, 1942-45. Attached to UK Liaison Mission, Japan, 1945; Asst Mil. Adviser (Lt-Col), UKLM, Tokyo, 1947-52; GSO1, War Office (MI Directorate), 1953-56; Military Attaché, Tokyo, 1956-61; Information Counsellor, British Embassy, Tokyo, 1961-68; Comr Gen. for Britain, World Exposition, Osaka, Japan, 1968-70. *Publications:* (with Fujio Koyama) Two Thousand Years of Oriental Ceramics, 1960; The Heritage of Japanese Ceramics, 1973; contrib. to Oriental Art, Far Eastern Ceramic Bulletin, etc. *Address:* The Manor House, Burghfield, Berks. *Club:* Army and Navy.

FIGGIS, Anthony St John Howard; HM Diplomatic Service; Counsellor, Belgrade, since 1982; *b* 12 Oct. 1940; *s* of Roberts Richmond Figgis and Philippa Maria Young; *m* 1964, Miriam Ellen Hardt; two *s* one *d. Educ:* Rugby Sch.; King's Coll., Cambridge (Mod Langs). Joined HM Foreign (later Diplomatic) Service, 1962; Third Sec., Belgrade, 1963-65; Commonwealth Office, 1965-68; Second Sec., Polit. Residency, Bahrain, 1968-70; FCO, 1970-71; First Sec. (Commercial), Madrid, 1971-74; FCO, 1974-79; CSCE delegn, Geneva, 1974-75; Asst Head, E European and Soviet Dept, 1976-78; Asst Head, Def. Dept, 1978-79; Madrid: Head of Chancery, 1979-80; Commercial Counsellor, 1980-82. *Recreations:* fly-fishing, tennis, music (piano). *Address:* c/o Foreign and Commonwealth Office, SW1A 2AH; 24 The Crescent, SW13 0NN.

FIGGIS, Arthur Lenox; His Honour Judge Figgis; a Circuit Judge (formerly Judge of County Courts), since 1971; *b* 12 Sept. 1918; *s* of late Frank Fernesley Figgis and late Frances Annie Figgis; *m* 1953, Alison, *d* of late Sidney Bocher Ganthony and late Doris Ganthony; two *s* three *d. Educ:* Tonbridge; Peterhouse, Cambridge (MA). Served War, 1939-46, Royal Artillery. Barrister-at-Law, Inner Temple, 1947. *Recreations:* walking (with dog); rifle shooting half-blue, 1939, and shot for Ireland (Elcho Shield), 1935-39. *Address:* Walliswood Farm, Walliswood Ockley, Surrey. *T:* Oakwood Hill 268. *Club:* United Oxford & Cambridge University.

FIGGURES, Sir Frank (Edward), KCB 1970 (CB 1966); CMG 1959; Director, Julius Baer Bank International Ltd, since 1975; *b* 5 March 1910; *s* of Frank and Alice Figgures; *m* 1st, 1941, Aline (*d* 1975), *d* of Prof. Hugo Frey; one *s* one *d* ; 2nd, 1975, Ismea, *d* of George Napier Magill and *widow* of Jack Barker. *Educ:* Rutlish Sch.; New Coll., Oxford. Harmsworth Senior Scholar, Merton Coll., Oxford, 1931; Henry Fellow, Yale Law Sch., 1933; Called to Bar, Lincoln's Inn, 1936; Military Service (RA), 1940-46; Joined HM Treasury, 1946; Dir of Trade and Finance, OEEC, 1948-51; Under-Sec., HM Treasury, 1955-60; Sec.-Gen. to EFTA, 1960-65; Third Secretary, Treasury, 1965-68; Second Permanent Secretary, 1968-71; Dir-Gen., NEDO, 1971-73; Chm., Pay Bd, 1973-74. Chairman: Central Wagon Co. Ltd, 1976; BBC Gen. Adv. Council, 1978-82. Hon. DSc Aston 1975. *Address:* 9 Main Street, Barrowden, Oakham, Rutland. *Club:* Reform.

FIGURES, Colin Frederick, CMG 1978; OBE 1969; HM Diplomatic Service; *b* 1 July 1925; *s* of late Frederick Joseph Figures and of Muriel Nellie (*née* Hadwell); *m* 1956, Pamela Ann Timmis; one *s* two *d. Educ:* King Edward's Sch., Birmingham; Pembroke Coll., Cambridge (MA). Served Worcestershire Regt, 1943-48. Joined Foreign Office, 1951; attached Control Commn, Germany, 1953-56; Amman, 1956-58; FCO, 1958-59; Warsaw, 1959-62; FCO, 1962-66; Vienna, 1966-69; FCO, 1969-. *Recreations:* watching sport, gardening, beachcombing. *Address:* c/o Foreign and Commonwealth Office, SW1. *Clubs:* United Oxford & Cambridge University; Old Edwardians (Birmingham).

FILER, Albert Jack, CB 1954; Past President, Brick Development Association Ltd; *b* 14 Aug. 1898; 2nd *s* of Albert James Shephard Filer and Jessie (*née* Marrison); *m* 1923, Violet D., *o d* of late Edward T. Booth, Bexhill, Sussex; one *d. Educ:* County Secondary Sch., Holloway, N. Entered Civil Service, 1914, Office of Works. Served European War of 1914-18 in Civil Service Rifles. Principal, 1940, Min. of Works, Asst Sec., 1943, Under Sec., 1948; Gen. Manager, Directorate Gen. of Works, 1958-60, retired from Civil Service, 1960. *Address:* 1 Heatherwood, Midhurst, West Sussex. *T:* Midhurst 2816.

FILLEUL, Peter Amy, MA; Head Master, William Hulme's Grammar School, Manchester, since Sept. 1974; *b* 7 Aug. 1929; *s* of J. C. Filleul and L. A. Mundy; *m* 1963, Elizabeth Ann Talbot; one *s* one *d. Educ:* Victoria Coll., Jersey; Bedford Sch.; (Exhibnr) Exeter Coll., Oxford (MA, DipEd). Royal Air Force, 1952-55. Portsmouth GS, 1955-65; Stationers' Company's Sch., 1965-68; Cardiff High Sch. (Head Master), 1969-74. *Recreations:* rifle shooting, fishing. *Address:* 254 Wilbraham Road, Manchester M16 8PR. *T:* 061-226 2058.

FILON, Sidney Philip Lawrence, TD; Librarian and Secretary to the Trustees, National Central Library, 1958-71, retired; *b* 20 Sept. 1905; *s* of late Prof. L. N. G. Filon, FRS and late Anne Godet; *m* 1st, 1939, Doris Schelling; one *d* ; 2nd, 1959, Liselotte Florstedt; one *d. Educ:* Whitgift Sch.; University Coll., London (BSc). Sch. of Librarianship, University Coll., London, 1929-30; FLA 1931. National Central Library, 1930-39. Military service, 1939-45. Dep. Librarian, National Central Library, 1946-58. Mem., Library Advisory Council (England), 1966-71. *Publication:* The National Central Library: an experiment in library cooperation, 1977. *Address:* 107 Littleheath Road, Selsdon, Surrey.

FILSON, Alexander Warnock; consultant in film industry; *b* 23 Aug. 1913; *s* of late J. T. W. Filson, Indian Police; *m* 1941, Judith Henrietta, *d* of late Major R. H. Greig, DSO, and late Mrs Rokeling; one *s* two *d. Educ:* Clifton Coll., (Schol.); The Queen's Coll., Oxford (Schol.) (MA). Served War of 1939-45 in Army; Asst Sec., Parliamentary Labour Party, 1945-47; Sec. Fabian Soc., 1947-49; Mem. of Kensington Borough Council, 1937-49. Contested (Lab) Brentford and Chiswick, 1955. Director: Fedn of British Film Makers, 1957-66; Film Production Assoc. of GB, 1967-70; Israel Film Industry, London Office, 1971-76. *Publications:* (asst to Prof. G. D. H. Cole) British Trade Unionism Today, 1939; ed (with Prof. G. D. H. Cole) British Working Class Movements, 1789-1875: Select Documents, 1951; Distribution of Films produced in the Countries of the Community (for EEC Commn), 1980; Production and Distribution of Short Films in the Countries of the Community (for EEC Commn), 1981. *Recreations:* reading and sightseeing. *Address:* 6 Grosvenor Road, Richmond, Surrey. *T:* 01-940 2072.

FINCASTLE, Viscount; Malcolm Kenneth Murray; *b* 17 Sept. 1946; *er s* and *heir* of Earl of Dunmore, *qv* ; *m* 1970, Joy Anne, *d* of A. Partridge; one *s* one *d* (both adopted). *Educ:* Launceston Technical High School (Board A Certificate). Electrical Technical Officer, Dept of Aviation. *Recreation:* flying (Tow Master for Soaring Club of Tasmania). *Address:* PO Box 100E, East Devonport, Tasmania 7310, Australia. *T:* (004) 284071. *Club:* Soaring Club of Tasmania.

FINCH; *see* Finch-Knightley.

FINCH, Ven. Geoffrey Grenville; Vicar of Romsey and Archdeacon Emeritus, since 1982; Archdeacon of Basingstoke, 1971-82; *b* 7 Oct. 1923; *yr s* of late R. A. and E. M. Finch; *m* 1951, Margaret Ann Denniston; one *s* three *d. Educ:* Quarry Bank High Sch., Liverpool; St Peter's Hall, Oxford; Wycliffe Hall; Wells Theological Coll. Hon. Sch. of Nat. Sci. and Theology (2nd cl), Oxford, 1942-43; MA 1947. Foreign Office and Allied Commission for Austria, 1944-46; Oxford and Wells, 1947-50; ordained, 1950; Curate, Wigan Parish Church, 1950-54; Vicar, S Peter's, Westleigh, Lancs 1954-59;

Rector, Milton Parish Church, Hants, 1960-71; Vicar of Preston Candover and Bradley, Hants, 1971-76. Proctor in Convocation, 1965-70; Rural Dean of Christchurch, Hants, 1966-71. Member: Gen. Synod, 1973-80; Central Bd of Finance, CofE, 1975-80. *Recreations:* sailing, photography, painting, natural history, pottering. *Address:* The Vicarage, Romsey, Hants SO5 8EP. *T:* Romsey 513125.

FINCH, Maj.-Gen. Lionel Hugh Knightley, CB 1941; DSO 1916, Bar 1917; OBE; FLS; *b* 18 July 1888; *o s* of late Capt. E. H. Franklyn Finch, 30th Regt; *m* 1919, Hildegard, *d* of late Dr Gustav Schild, Herford, Germany and late Mrs J. C. A. Sepp-Clésius, Nijmegen, Holland; one *d. Educ:* Cheltenham Coll.; Birmingham Univ.; London Univ. Served European War, 1914-18 (DSO and bar, OBE, despatches, Bt Major); Staff Coll., Camberley, 1924-25; GSO3 at HQ, Northern Command, 1926-27; DAA and QMG at HQ Northumbrian Area, 1928-29; Bt Lt-Col, 1929; commanded Depot, Cheshire Regt, 1930-33; Comdr, Landi Kotal Bde, 1934; DAQMG at Army HQ India, 1934; comd 1st Bn Lancs Fusiliers, 1934-36; Asst Adjutant-Gen., War Office, 1936-39; Dep. Dir of Recruiting and Organisation, War Office, 1939; Dir of Recruiting and Organisation, War Office, 1939-40; Dep. Adjutant-Gen., War Office, 1940; Divisional Comdr, 1940; Chm., War Office Committees, 1940-41; District Comdr, Home Forces, 1941-42; retired, 1943; late The Lancs Fusiliers, The Cheshire Regt, and The Royal Sussex Regt. *Address:* National Westminster Bank, Petworth, West Sussex.

FINCH HATTON, family name of **Earl of Winchilsea and Nottingham.**

FINCH-KNIGHTLEY, family name of **Earl of Aylesford.**

FINCHAM, Prof. John Robert Stanley, FRS 1969; FRSE 1978; Buchanan Professor of Genetics, University of Edinburgh, since 1976; *b* 11 Aug. 1926; *s* of Robert Fincham and Winifred Emily Fincham (*née* Western); *m* 1950, Ann Katherine Emerson; one *s* three *d. Educ:* Hertford Grammar Sch.; Peterhouse, Cambridge. BA 1946, PhD 1950, ScD 1964. Bye-Fellow of Peterhouse, 1949-50; Lectr in Botany, University Coll., Leicester, 1950-54; Reader in Genetics, Univ. of Leicester, 1954-60; Head of Dept of Genetics, John Innes Inst., 1960-66; Prof. of Genetics, Leeds Univ., 1966-76; Vis. Associate Prof. of Genetics, Massachusetts Inst. of Technology, 1960-61. Pres., Genetical Soc., 1978-81. Editor, Heredity, 1971-78. *Publications:* Fungal Genetics (with P. R. Day), 1963, 4th edn, 1979; Microbial and Molecular Genetics, 1965; Genetic Complementation, 1966; papers in Biochemical Jl, Jl Gen. Microbiol., Jl Biol. Chem., Heredity, Jl Molecular Biol., Genet. Res. *Recreations:* listening to music, mountain walking. *Address:* 93A Mayfield Road, Edinburgh.

FINDLATER, Richard, (Kenneth Bruce Findlater Bain); Assistant Editor, The Observer, since 1963; Editor, The Author, since 1961; *b* 23 Dec. 1921; *s* of Thomas Bain and Elizabeth Bruce; *m* 1st, 1948, Romany Evens (marr. diss. 1961); three *s* one *d* ; 2nd, 1979, Angela Colbert. *Educ:* Archbishop Tenison's Grammar School. Theatre Critic, Tribune, 1948-57; Literary Editor, Tribune, 1950-57; Editor, Books and Art, 1957-58; Literary Editor and Theatre Critic, Sunday Dispatch, 1958-59; Theatre Critic, Time and Tide, 1960-62; Editor, Twentieth Century, 1961-65. Member: BBC Critics, 1953-69; Arts Council Drama Panel, 1953-62 and 1970-74; Housing the Arts Cttee of Inquiry, 1956-61; Theatre Inquiry, 1967-70; Council, English Stage Co., 1978-; Soc. of Authors, 1978-. *Publications:* The Unholy Trade, 1952; Grimaldi, 1955; Michael Redgrave: Actor, 1956; Emlyn Williams, 1957; Six Great Actors, 1957; Banned, 1967; (ed) Memoirs of Grimaldi, 1968; (ed) Comic Cuts, 1970; The Player Kings, 1971; (ed) Public Lending Right, 1971; Lilian Baylis, 1975; The Player Queens, 1976; Joe Grimaldi: his life and theatre, 1978; (with Mary Relph Powell) Little Tich, 1979; (ed) At the Royal Court, 1981; *pamphlets:* The Future of the Theatre, 1959; What are Writers Worth?, 1963; The Book Writers: Who are They?, 1966. *Address:* Foxholes, Kingham, Oxon. *Club:* Garrick.

FINDLAY, Ian Herbert Fyfe; Chairman, Lloyd's, 1978 and 1979 (Deputy Chairman, 1977); *b* 5 Feb. 1918; *s* of Prof. Alexander Findlay, Aberdeen, and Alice Mary (*née* de Rougement); *m* 1950, Alison Mary Ashby; two *s* one *d. Educ:* Fettes Coll., Edinburgh. Served War, Royal Artillery, 1939-46. Chm., Price Forbes (Holdings) Ltd, 1967; Dep. Chm., Sedgwick Forbes Holdings Ltd, 1972, Chm., 1974-77. Mem. Cttee, Lloyd's Insurance Brokers Assoc., 1961-65 and 1966-69; Chm., Non-Marine Cttee, 1967-68; Chm. of Assoc., 1969-70; Chm., British Insurance Brokers Assoc., 1980-82. Mem., Cttee of Lloyd's, 1971-74, 1976-79. Trustee, St George's English Sch., Rome, 1980-; Chm., Guide Dogs for the Blind, 1981-; Governor, Brighton Coll., 1981-. *Recreation:* golf. *Address:* 24 Forest Ridge, Keston Park, Kent BR2 6EQ. *T:* Farnborough (Kent) 52993. *Clubs:* City of London; Royal and Ancient Golf (St Andrews); Royal St George's (Sandwich); Addington (Surrey).

FINDLAY, Comdr James Buchanan, CBE 1957; RN (Retd); Director, Bank of Scotland, 1933-71; *b* 7 Jan. 1895; *m* 1923, Mary Sancroft Findlay-Hamilton; three *s* one *d. Educ:* Royal Naval Colls, Osborne and Dartmouth. Retired from RN after European War of 1914-18; served in War of 1939-45. *Recreations:* shooting, golf, gardening. *Address:* The Garden House, Carnell, Kilmarnock, Ayrshire. *Club:* Lansdowne.

FINDLAY, Prof. John Niemeyer, FBA 1956; Borden Parker Bowne Professor of Philosophy, Boston University, since 1978 (University Professor of Philosophy, since 1972); *b* 25 Nov. 1903; 2nd *s* of J. H. L. Findlay, Pretoria, South Africa; *m* 1941, Aileen May, *d* of G. S. Davidson, Wellington, NZ; one *s* one *d* (and one *d* decd). *Educ:* Boys' High Sch., Pretoria; Transvaal Univ. Coll.; Balliol Coll., Oxford (Rhodes Scholar, 1st Lit. hum.); University of Graz. Lecturer in Philosophy, Transvaal University Coll., 1927-33; Prof. of Philosophy, University of Otago, NZ, 1934-44; Prof. of Philosophy, Rhodes University Coll., Grahamstown, S Africa, 1945; Prof. of Philosophy, Natal University Coll., 1946-48; Prof. of Philosophy, King's Coll., Newcastle upon Tyne, Univ. of Durham, 1948-51; University Prof. of Philosophy, King's Coll., Univ. of London, 1951-66. Gifford Lecturer, Univ. of St Andrews, 1964-66. Prof. of Philosophy, Univ. of Texas, 1966-67; Clark Prof. of Moral Philosophy and Metaphysics, Yale Univ., 1967-72. Fellow, Amer. Acad. of Arts and Scis, 1978. FKC 1970. *Publications:* Meinong's Theory of Objects and Values, 1933, new edn, 1963; Hegel: A Re-Examination, 1958; Values and Intentions, 1961; Language, Mind and Value, 1963; The Discipline of the Cave, 1965; The Transcendence of The Cave, 1967; trans. Husserl, Logische Untersuchungen, 1969; Axiological Ethics, 1970; Ascent to the Absolute: metaphysical papers and lectures, 1970; Plato's Written and Unwritten Doctrines, 1974; Plato and Platonism, 1978; Kant and the Transcendental Object, 1981; articles in Mind, Philosophy, Philosophy and Phenomenological Research, Proc. of the Aristotelian Soc., etc. *Address:* 14 Lambolle Road, NW3; 96 Bay State Road, Boston, Mass 02215, USA. *Club:* Royal Commonwealth Society.

FINER, Prof. Samuel Edward, FBA 1982; Gladstone Professor of Government and Public Administration, University of Oxford, 1974-82; *b* 22 Sept. 1915; *y s* of Max and Fanny Finer, 210a Green Lanes, N4; *m* 1st, 1949, Margaret Ann (marr. diss. 1975), 2nd *d* of Sir Andrew McFadyean; two *s* one *d* ; 2nd, 1977, Dr Catherine J. Jones, 2nd *d* of T. P. Jones, Prestatyn. *Educ:* Holloway Sch., London; Trinity Coll., Oxford. BA (Oxon) 1st Class Hons Mod. Greats, 1937; 1st Cl. Hons Mod. Hist., 1938; MA (Oxon) 1946, DLitt 1979; Sen. George Webb-Medley Schol., 1938-40. Served War, 1940-46; Capt. Royal Signals, 1945. Lecturer in Politics, Balliol Coll., Oxford, 1946-49; Junior Research Fellow, Balliol Coll., Oxford, 1949-50; Prof. of Political Institutions, University of Keele, 1950-66; Prof. of Government, Univ. of Manchester, 1966-74; Dep. Vice-Chancellor, University of Keele, 1962-64. Visiting Prof. and Faculty Mem., Institute of Social Studies, The Hague, Netherlands, 1957-59. Visiting Prof. in Government: Cornell Univ., 1962; Hebrew Univ., Jerusalem, 1969; Simon Fraser Univ., BC, 1976; Europ. Univ. Inst., Florence, 1977; Stanford Univ., 1979; Hong Kong Univ., 1980; Vis. Schweitzer Prof., Columbia Univ., 1982. Chm. Political Studies Assoc. of UK, 1965-69; FRHistSoc. DU Essex, 1982. *Publications:* A Primer of Public Administration, 1950; The Life and Times of Sir Edwin Chadwick, 1952; (with Sir John Maud) Local Government in England and Wales, 1953; Anonymous Empire—a Study of the Lobby in Britain, 1958, 2nd edn 1966; Private Industry and Political Power, 1958; (with D. J. Bartholomew and H. B. Berrington) Backbench Opinion in the House of Commons, 1955-59, 1961; The Man on Horseback: The Rôle of The Military in Politics, 1962, 2nd edn 1976; Great Britain, in Modern Political Systems: Europe, ed Macridis and Ward, 1963, 1968, 1972, 1980; (ed) Siéyès: What is the Third Estate, 1963; Pareto: Sociological Writings, 1966; Comparative Government, 1970; Adversary Government and Electoral Reform, 1975; Five Constitutions, 1979; Britain's Changing Party System, 1980. *Recreation:* oil-painting. *Address:* All Souls College, Oxford; 48 Lonsdale Road, Oxford. *T:* Oxford 58060.

FINESTEIN, Israel, MA; QC 1970; **His Honour Judge Finestein;** a Circuit Judge, since 1972; *b* 29 April 1921; *y c* of late Jeremiah Finestein, Hull; *m* 1946, Marion Phyllis, *er d* of Simon Oster, Hendon, Mddx. *Educ:* Kingston High School, Hull; Trinity Coll., Cambridge (Major Scholar and Prizeman). MA 1946. Called to the Bar, Lincoln's Inn, 1953. Pres., Jewish Hist. Soc. of England. *Publications:* Short History of the Jews of England, 1956; Sir George Jessel, 1959, etc. *Recreation:* reading history. *Address:* 18 Buttermere Court, Boundary Road, NW8.

FINGALL, 12th Earl of *cr* 1628; **Oliver James Horace Plunkett,** MC; Baron Killeen, 1436; Baron Fingall (UK) 1831; Major, late 17th/21st Lancers; *b* 17 June 1896; *er s* of 11th Earl and Elizabeth Mary Margaret (*d* 1944), *e d* of George Burke, JP, Danesfield, Co. Galway; *S* father, 1929; *m* 1926, Jessica (*d* 1965), *yr d* of late Allan Hughes, Lynch, Allerford, Somerset; *m* 1966, Mrs Clair Richardson, widow of Frank Richardson, Geelong, Vic., Aust. *Educ:* Downside. Served European War (MC); retired pay, 1931; in army again, 1939-45. Roman Catholic. *Recreations:* racing and travelling. *Heir:* (to barony of Killeen only) *kinsman,* Baron Dunsany, *qv. Address:* The Commons, Dunsany, Co. Meath, Ireland. *TA:* Fingall, Dunsany. *T:* Navan 25193. *Clubs:* Cavalry and Guards; Kildare Street and University (Dublin).

FINGERHUT, John Hyman; Consultant to the Pharmaceutical and Allied Industries; *b* 2 Nov. 1910; *s* of late Abraham Fingerhut and Emily (*née* Rowe); *m* 1950, Beatrice Leigh, FCA; two *s* two *d. Educ:* Manchester Grammar Sch.; Manchester Univ. FBOA 1931; FPS 1971. Pharmaceutical Chemist, 1932. Served with RAC and Infantry, France, Mauritius and E Africa, 1942-46; commnd Royal Pioneer Corps, transf. to Queen's Royal Regt (seconded King's African Rifles); demobilised as Captain. Merck Sharp & Dohme Ltd: medical rep., 1937-42; Sales Man., 1946; Dep. Man. Dir, 1957; Man. Dir, 1963; Chm., 1967-72; Consultant, 1972-77; Regional Dir, Merck Sharp & Dohme International, 1967-72, Consultant, 1972; Chm., Thomas Morson & Son Ltd, 1967-72; Mem., ABPI Working Party on Resale Price Maintenance, 1970;

Associate: Bracken Kelner and Associates Ltd, 1976; Key Pharmaceutical Appointments, 1978. Admin. Staff Coll., Henley, 1960. Mem., New Southgate Group Hosp. Management Cttee, 1972-74. Associate Mem., Faculty of Homœopathy, 1974. *Recreations:* music, reading, gardening, washing up. *Address:* 76 Green Lane, Edgware, Mddx HA8 7QA. *T:* 01-958 6163.

FINGLAND, Sir Stanley (James Gunn), KCMG 1979 (CMG 1966); HM Diplomatic Service, retired; High Commissioner to Kenya, 1975-79; UK Permanent Representative to the UN Environment Programme 1975-79, and to UN Centre for Human Settlements, 1979; *b* 19 Dec. 1919; *s* of late Samuel Gunn Fingland and late Agnes Christina (*née* Watson); *m* 1946, Nellie (*née* Lister); one *s* one *d. Educ:* Royal High Sch., Edinburgh. TA 1938. War service, 1939-46 as Major, Royal Signals; served N Africa, Sicily, Italy, Egypt. Commonwealth Relations Office, 1948-; British High Commission, India, 1948-51; Australia, 1953-56; Adviser on Commonwealth and External Affairs to Governor-Gen., Nigeria, 1958-60; British High Commission, Nigeria, 1960; Adviser on Commonwealth and External Affairs to Governor-Gen., Fedn of The W Indies, 1960-61, and to the Governor of Trinidad and Tobago, 1962; British Dep. High Commissioner: Trinidad and Tobago, 1962-63; Rhodesia, 1964-66; High Comr, Sierra Leone, 1966-69; Asst Under-Sec. of State, FCO, 1969-72; Ambassador to Cuba, 1972-75. *Recreations:* fishing, golf. *Address:* 34 Ashdown, Eaton Road, Hove, Sussex. *Club:* Royal Overseas League.

FINGLETON, David Melvin; Metropolitan Stipendiary Magistrate, since 1980; *b* 2 Sept. 1941; *s* of Laurence Fingleton and Norma Phillips (*née* Spiro); *m* 1975, Clare, *yr d* of late Ian Colvin. *Educ:* Aldwickbury Sch., Harpenden; Stowe Sch. (Schol.); University Coll., Oxford (Exhibnr; BA Hons Modern History, MA). Called to Bar, Middle Temple, 1965; South Eastern Circuit. Music Correspondent, Contemporary Review, 1969-; Opera and Ballet Critic, Tatler and Bystander, 1970-78; Stage Design Corresp., Arts Review, 1976-; Associate Editor, Music and Musicians, 1977-80; Music Critic: Evening News, 1979-80; The Weekender, 1981-; Daily Express, 1982-. *Publications:* Kiri, 1982; articles in Contemp. Rev., Tatler and Bystander, Music and Musicians, Arts Rev., Evening News, The Weekender. *Recreation:* listening to and writing about music. *Address:* Highbury Corner Magistrates' Court, 51 Holloway Road, N7 8JA. *T:* 01-607 6757. *Clubs:* Garrick, MCC.

FINKELSTEIN, Prof. Ludwik, MSc, CEng, FIEE, MInstP, FInstMC; Professor of Measurement and Instrumentation and Head of Department of Physics, The City University, since 1980; *b* 6 Dec. 1929; *s* of Adolf and Amalia Finkelstein; *m* 1957, Mirjam Emma, *d* of Dr Alfred and Dr Margarethe Wiener; two *s* one *d. Educ:* Univ. of London (MSc). Physicist, Technical Staff, Electronic Tubes Ltd, 1951-52; Scientist, Instrument Br., NCB Mining Res. Estabt, 1952-59; Northampton Coll., London, and City University, London: Lectr, 1959-61; Sen. Lectr, 1961-63; Principal Lectr, 1963-67; Reader, 1967-70; Prof. of Instrument and Control Engineering, 1970-80; Head of Dept of Systems Science, 1974-79. Visiting Prof., Delft Univ. of Technology, 1973-74. Pres., Inst. of Measurement and Control, 1980 (Vice-Pres., 1972-75, 1977-79). Hartley Silver Medal, 1980. *Publications:* papers in learned jls and conference proc. *Recreations:* books, conversation, Jewish studies. *Address:* The City University, Northampton Square, EC1V 0HB. *T:* 01-253 4399; 9 Cheyne Walk, Hendon NW4 3QH. *T:* 01-202 6966.

FINLAISON, Brig. (retd) Alexander Montagu, CBE 1957; DSO 1944; *b* 14 March 1904; *s* of Maj.-Gen. J. B. Finlaison, CMG, late Royal Marines, Dedham, Essex; *m* 1935, Monica Mary Louisa, *d* of T. W. Donald, Grendon, Stirling; two *d. Educ:* RN Colls Osborne and Dartmouth; RMC Sandhurst. Commissioned Cameronians (Scottish Rifles), 1924; seconded Sudan Defence Force, 1932-38; served War of 1939-45; Greece, Crete, Sicily, Italy; commanded 2nd Wiltshires, 2nd Cameronians, 17 Infantry Brigade, Italy, 1943-44; BGS, HQ Scottish Command, 1954-57; ADC to the Queen, 1955-57; retired, 1957; Commandant, Queen Victoria Sch., Dunblane, 1957-64. *Address:* Gledenholm, Ae, Dumfries DG1 1RF. *T:* Parkgate 242. *Club:* Naval and Military.

FINLAY, Alexander William; Past-Chairman, Society for Long Range Planning, (Chairman, 1978-79); *b* 28 Nov. 1921; *s* of late Robert Gaskin Finlay and late Alice Finlay; *m* 1949, Ona Margaret Lewis; no *c. Educ:* Tottenham County School. Flt-Lt RAF, 1941-47; various posts, BOAC, 1947-74; Gen. Man., Fleet Planning, 1967-71; Planning Dir, 1971-74; Planning Dir, British Airways, 1974-78, retired. FCIT. *Recreations:* gardening, photography, conservation. *Address:* 12 Hunters Way, Chichester, West Sussex PO19 4RB. *Club:* Royal Air Force.

FINLAY, Maj.-Gen. Charles Hector, CB 1966; CBE 1958 (OBE 1942); retired; Hon. National Treasurer, Returned Services League of Australia, since 1969; *b* 6 Oct. 1910; 3rd *s* of Frank J. Finlay and Margaret A. Stephenson; *m* 1935, Helen M., *d* of Arthur P. and Edith M. Adams; two *s. Educ:* Sydney; RMC Duntroon, Australia. Graduated RMC, 1931; Light Horse and Cavalry service, 1931-39; ADC to Gov.-Gen., 1932-35; with 14th/20th Hussars, India, 1935-36. Served War of 1939-45; Western Desert, Syria, New Guinea, Philippines, Borneo; Comd 2/24 Inf. Bn, 1942-43. Exchange duty, Canada, 1946-49; DMI, 1950-53; Comd Aust. Component BCFK, 1953-54; attended Imperial Def. Coll., 1955; Aust. Army Rep., London, 1956-57; Quartermaster Gen. AMF, 1957-62; Commandant Royal Military Coll., Duntroon, Australia, 1962-67. Hon. Col, Australian Intelligence Corps, 1973-77. *Recreation:* cricket. *Address:* c/o National HQ, Returned Services League of

Australia, Canberra, ACT, Australia. *Clubs:* Naval and Military (Melbourne); Commonwealth (Canberra).

FINLAY, Frank; actor; *b* Farnworth, Lancs, 6 Aug. 1926; *s* of Josiah Finlay; *m* 1954, Doreen Shepherd; two *s* one *d*. *Educ:* St Gregory the Great, Farnworth; RADA (Sir James Knott Schol.). *Stage:* repertory, 1950-52 and 1954-57; Belgrade, Coventry, 1958; Epitaph for George Dillon, NY, 1958; Royal Court, 1958, 1959-62: Sugar in the Morning; Sergeant Musgrave's Dance; Chicken Soup with Barley, Roots, I'm Talking About Jerusalem; The Happy Haven; Platonov; Chips with Everything, Royal Court, transf. to Vaudeville Theatre, 1962 (Clarence Derwent Best Actor Award); Chichester Festival, 1963: St Joan; The Workhouse Donkey; with National Theatre Co. 1963-70: St Joan, 1963; Willie Mossop in Hobson's Choice, and Iago in Othello (both also Chichester Fest., 1964, Berlin and Moscow, 1965), The Dutch Courtesan (also Chichester Fest.), 1964; Giles Corey in The Crucible, Dogberry in Much Ado About Nothing, Mother Courage, 1965; Joxer Daly in Juno and the Paycock, Dikoy in The Storm, 1966; Bernard in After Haggerty, Aldwych, Criterion, Jesus Christ in Son of Man, Leicester Theatre and Round House (first actor ever to play Jesus Christ on stage in English theatre), 1970; Kings and Clowns (musical), Phoenix, 1978; Filumena, Lyric, 1978, US tour, 1979-80, and NY, 1980; The Girl in Melanie Klein, 1980; *with National Theatre Co.:* Peppino in Saturday, Sunday, Monday, 1973; Sloman in The Party, 1973; Freddy Malone in Plunder, Ben Prosser in Watch It Come Down, Josef Frank in Weapons of Happiness, 1976; Amadeus, 1982; *films include,* 1962-: The Longest Day, Private Potter, The Informers, A Life for Ruth, Loneliness of the Long Distance Runner, Hot Enough for June, The Comedy Man, The Sandwich Man, A Study in Terror, Othello (nominated for Amer. Acad. award; best actor award, San Sebastian, 1966), The Jokers, I'll Never Forget What's 'Is Name, The Shoes of the Fisherman, Deadly Bees, Robbery, Inspector Clouseau, Twisted Nerve, Cromwell, The Molly Maguires (in Hollywood), Assault, Victory for Danny Jones, Gumshoe, Shaft in Africa, Van Der Valk and the Girl, Van Der Valk and the Rich; Van Der Valk and the Dead; The Three Musketeers; The Ring of Darkness, The Wild Geese, The Thief of Baghdad, Sherlock Holmes—Murder by Decree; Enigma; Return of the Soldier; *TV appearances include:* Julius Caesar, Les Misérables, This Happy Breed, The Lie (SFTA Award), Casanova (series), The Death of Adolf Hitler, Don Quixote (SFTA Award), Voltaire, Merchant of Venice, Bouquet of Barbed Wire (series) (Best Actor Award), 84 Charing Cross Road, Saturday Sunday Monday, Count Dracula, The Last Campaign, Napoleon in Betzi, Dear Brutus, Tales of the Unexpected, Tales from 1001 Nights, Aspects of Love—Mona. *Address:* Granstar Ltd, 50 Mount Street, W1. *Club:* Garrick.

FINLAY, Sir Graeme Bell, 1st Bt, *cr* 1964; ERD; Barrister-at-Law; Sous Juge d'Instruction and Assistant Judge of Petty Debts Court for Jersey, 1972-77; *b* 29 Oct. 1917; *yr s* of late James Bell Pettigrew Finlay and late Margaret Helena, *d* of John Euston Davies, JP, Portskewett House, nr Chepstow, Mon.; *m* 1953, June Evangeline, *y d* of Col Francis Collingwood Drake, OBE, MC, DL, late 10th Royal Hussars, Harlow, Essex; one *s* one *d*. *Educ:* Marlborough; University College, London. Served War of 1939-45, 2nd Lieut S Wales Borderers (suppl. res.), 1939; 7th (Croix de Guerre) Bn, 24th Regt (Beach Divs), 1940-41; seconded to 5th Royal Gurkha Rifles (Frontier Force), 1942-45; Martial Law Officer, Upper Sind Force (Hur Rebellion), 1943; Acting Major and DAAG, HQ, NW Army, 1945. Hon. Captain, The Royal Regt of Wales. Called to Bar, Gray's Inn, 1946 (Lord Justice Holker Sen. Exhibr); pupil of Lord Hailsham of St Marylebone; President of Hardwicke Society, 1950-51. Presided over first televised joint debate between Oxford and Cambridge Union Societies, 1950. Contested (C) Ebbw Vale, General Election, 1950; MP (C) Epping Division of Essex, 1951-64; Parliamentary Private Secretary to Rt Hon. Iain Macleod, Minister of Health, 1952-55; Asst Whip, 1957-59; Lord Commissioner of the Treasury, 1959-60; Vice-Chamberlain of the Household, 1960-64; Mem., Parly Delegn to Russia, 1960; a Deputy Judge of County Courts, later Circuit Judge, 1967-72; a Dep. Chm., Agricultural Land Tribunal (SE Region), 1971-72. *Publications:* (jt author) Proposals for an Administrative Court, 1970; frequent contributor to Justice of the Peace and Local Government Review. *Recreations:* reading history and painting. *Heir: s* David Ronald James Bell Finlay, *b* 16 Nov. 1963. *Address:* La Campagne, Rozel, Jersey, CI. *T:* Central 51194; 4 Paper Buildings, Temple, EC4. *T:* 01-353 3366. *Club:* Travellers'.
   See also J. E. B. Finlay.

FINLAY, Ian; see Finlay, W. I. R.

FINLAY, Jane Little, (Sheena), JP; Deputy Chairman, Equal Opportunities Commission, since 1980; *b* 29 Sept. 1917; *e d* of James Whyte Hepburn and Jean Brown, Langside, Glasgow; *m* 1941, John A. R. Finlay, *qv*; one *s* two *d* (and one *d* decd). *Educ:* Spier's Sch., Beith; Hutcheson's Girls' Grammar Sch., Glasgow; Glasgow Univ. (MA Hons English and Philosophy, 1940); Jordanhill Coll., Glasgow (Teacher's Trng Cert., 1941). Asst Principal, Bd of Inland Revenue, 1941-45 (Private Office, 1943-45). Teaching: Mayfield County Sch., Putney, 1946; Cooper's Sch., Chislehurst (part-time), 1962-73. Part-time Mem. Value Added Tax Tribunals, 1973-; Mem (Vice-Chm.), Bromley Community Health Council, 1974-76, Chm., 1976-78; Co-Chm., Women's Nat. Commn, 1975-77; Vice-Pres., 1971-74, Pres., 1975-78, British Fedn of University Women. UK Deleg., Unesco Conf., Bonn, 1975; Mem., UK delegn to UN European Regional Seminar, Groningen, 1977. JP Bromley, 1966 (Mem. 1967, Chm. 1980, Juvenile Panel). *Recreations:*

cooking, reading, gardening, sailing. *Address:* Thornhill, Golf Road, Bickley, Bromley, Kent BR1 2JA. *T:* 01-467 3637.

FINLAY, John Alexander Robertson, QC 1973; **His Honour Judge Finlay;** a Circuit Judge, since 1976; *b* 9 Nov. 1917; *o s* of late Rev. John Adamson Finlay, MA and Mary Hain Miller; *m* 1941, Jane Little Hepburn (Sheena) (*see* J. L. Finlay); one *s* two *d* (and one *d* decd). *Educ:* High Sch. of Glasgow; Glasgow Univ. (Foulis Schol., John Clerk Schol.); Queen's Coll., Oxford (Schol.). Caird Medal, Melville Medal, MA 1st cl. Philosophy Glasgow, 1939; BA 2nd cl. Jurisprudence 1946, MA 1959, Oxon. Served in RN, 1940-46: Seaman 1940; commnd 1941; Lieut RNVR 1942. Called to Bar, Middle Temple, 1946 (Harmsworth Schol.); Bencher, Middle Temple, 1971; Mem. Bar Council, 1970-74. Recorder of the Crown Court, 1975-76. Acting Deemster, IoM Court of Appeal, 1975. Chm., Crosby Hall, 1975-76. Member: Law Guardian Editorial Adv. Cttee, 1971-72; Renton Cttee on Preparation of Legislation, 1973-75. *Recreations:* music, sailing. *Address:* Thornhill, Golf Road, Bickley, Bromley, Kent. *T:* 01-467 3637; 16 Old Buildings, Lincoln's Inn, WC2. *T:* 01-405 1325. *Club:* Medway Yacht.

FINLAY, John Euston Bell, CB 1959; OBE 1946; TD 1947; consultant on indirect taxation, since 1968; *b* 11 Sept. 1908; *e s* of late James Bell Pettigrew Finlay and late Margaret Helena Finlay, Douro Court, Cheltenham; *m* 1941, Zoë Josephine, *d* of late Brigadier Edward Lees, DSO, Whyte Cottage, Selsey, Sussex; one *s* one *d*. *Educ:* Marlborough; Geneva Univ. Junior Legal Asst, Board of Customs, 1933; Senior Legal Asst, 1945. Principal, 1948, Asst Secretary, 1949; Under-Sec., 1954-68; Commissioner and Director of Estab. and Org., 1954-65; Comr i/c Internat. and Tariff Divs, Bd of Customs and Excise, 1965-68; retired, 1968. Chairman, Finance Cttee, Customs Co-operation Council, Brussels, 1967-68. Governor St Dunstan's Educational Foundation, 1964-73. Member Management Cttee, CS Benevolent Fund, 1958-68; Trustee, CS Retirement Fellowship, 1968-. Mem., Chichester DC, 1976-79. Commnd from Trooper Inns of Court Regt to 1st (Rifle) Bn The Mon. Regt TA, 1934. Served, 1939-42, with 38 Div., 53 Div. and at Western Command (ADC to GOC-in-C and GSO2) (ops); psc Staff Coll., Camberley, 1942; seconded 1943-45, AIF; served New Guinea, Moluccas, Philippines and Borneo as GSO2 and GSO1, Anglo-Australian Special Airborne Forces (OBE). Hon. Lieut-Colonel. FRGS. *Recreations:* gardening, racing. *Address:* Bernards Gate House, 22 Lavant Road, Chichester, Sussex. *T:* Chichester 527369; 38 Sloane Court West, SW3. *T:* 01-730 5955. *Clubs:* Travellers', Special Forces.

FINLAY, (William) Ian (Robertson), CBE 1965; MA; HRSA; Director of the Royal Scottish Museum, 1961-71 (Keeper of the Department of Art and Ethnography, 1955-61); Professor of Antiquities to the Royal Scottish Academy, since 1971; *b* Auckland, New Zealand, 2 Dec. 1906; *s* of William R. Finlay and Annie M. Somerville; *m* 1933, Mary Scott, *d* of late W. Henderson Pringle, barrister-at-law; two *s* one *d*. *Educ:* Edinburgh Academy; Edinburgh Univ. Joined staff of Royal Scottish Museum, 1932; Deputy Regional Officer for Scotland, Ministry of Information, 1942-44; Vice-Chairman, Scottish Arts Council, 1967; Secretary, Royal Fine Art Commission for Scotland, 1953-61. Guest of State Department in US, 1960. Freeman of City of London; Member of Livery, Worshipful Company of Goldsmiths, London; Mem., Edinburgh Festival Council, 1968-71. FRSA 1971. Mem., Conseil de Direction, Gazette des Beaux Arts. *Publications:* Scotland, World To-Day Series, 1945; Scottish Art (for British Council), 1945; Art in Scotland, 1948; Scottish Crafts, 1948; The Scottish Tradition in Silver (Saltire booklet), 1948; Scottish Architecture (for schools), 1951; Treasures in Edinburgh, 1951; Scotland, Young Traveller Series, 1953; A History of Scottish Gold and Silver Work, 1956; Scotland, 1957; The Lothians, 1960; The Highlands, 1963; The Young Robert Louis Stevenson, 1965; The Lowlands, 1967; Celtic Art: an introduction, 1973; The Central Highlands, 1976; Priceless Heritage: the future of museums, 1977; Columba, 1979; articles, reviews and broadcast talks on art and general subjects. *Address:* Currie Riggs, Balerno, Midlothian. *T:* Balerno 3249.

FINLAY-MAXWELL, David Campbell, CEng, MIEE, FTI; Chairman and Managing Director, John Gladstone & Co. (Engineering) Ltd, and John Gladstone & Co. Ltd, since 1948; *b* 2 March 1923; *s* of Luke Greenwood Maxwell and of Lillias Maule Finlay; *m* 1954, Constance Shirley Hood; one *s* one *d*. *Educ:* St Paul's; Heriot-Watt/Edinburgh Univ. (CEng, Electronic and Control Engrg). MIEE; FTI. Major Royal Signals, 1945. Harvard Univ. Advanced Management Programme, 1968. Councillor (Dir), British Textile Council, 1977-. Chairman: Manpower Working Party, NEDO, 1970-73; Wool Industries Res. Assoc., 1974-77; Textile Res. Council, 1977-82; Wool Textile EDC, 1977-79, UK Rep., Consultative Cttee for R&D, Brussels, 1979-. Member: Council, Textile Inst., 1972-74; Textile Industry and Dyeing Adv. Cttee, Leeds Univ. Council, 1974-; Soc. of Dyers and Colourists, 1950-. Pres., Comitextil Sci. Res. Cttee, Brussels. Hon. Lectr, Leeds Univ. Dir/Vice-Chm., Sound Recording Bd of Dirs, RNIB (also Mem., Scientific Develt Sub Cttee); Hon. Organiser for UK, Technical Volunteer Helpers for Blind. FRSA 1977. *Recreations:* radio propagation, satellite tracking. *Address:* John Gladstone & Co. Ltd, Wellington Mills, Huddersfield HD3 3HJ. *T:* Huddersfield 653437; Folly Hall House, Cross Lane, Kirkburton, Huddersfield HD8 0ST. *T:* Huddersfield 604546. *Clubs:* Special Forces; Royal Scottish Automobile (Glasgow).

FINLAYSON; see Gordon-Finlayson.

FINLAYSON, Maj.-Gen. Forbes; *see* Finlayson, Maj.-Gen. W. F.

FINLAYSON, George Ferguson, CMG 1979; HM Diplomatic Service; Consul-General, Los Angeles, since 1981; *b* 28 Nov. 1924; *s* of late G. B. Finlayson; *m* 1951, Rosslyn Evelyn (*d* 1972), *d* of late E. N. James; one *d*; *m* 1982, Anthea Perry. *Educ:* North Berwick High Sch. Royal Air Force, 1943–47. Apptd HM Foreign (later Diplomatic) Service, 1949; 2nd Sec. (Inf.), HM Embassy, Rangoon, 1952–54; FO, 1955–59; First Sec., 1959; HM Consul, Algiers, 1959–61; First Sec., HM Embassy, Bamako, 1961–63; HM Consul (Commercial), New York, 1964–68; Counsellor, 1968; Counsellor (Commercial), British High Commn, Singapore, 1969–72; Head of Trade Relations and Exports Dept, FCO, 1972–73; Counsellor (Commercial) Paris, 1973–78; Consul-Gen., Toronto, 1978–81. *Recreations:* travel, walking, tennis, swimming. *Address:* c/o Foreign and Commonwealth Office, SW1; 141b Ashley Gardens, SW1. T: 01-834 6227; 49 Westgate, North Berwick, East Lothian. *T:* North Berwick 2522. *Club:* Oriental.

FINLAYSON, Maj.-Gen. (William) Forbes, OBE 1955; Director, Army Dental Service, 1966–70; *b* 12 Oct. 1911; *s* of late Lieut-Colonel W. T. Finlayson, OBE, Army Dental Corps, Edinburgh; *m* Anne McEwen, *d* of Walter Stables Smith, Peebles; one *s* one *d*. *Educ:* George Heriot's Sch., Edinburgh; Royal College of Surgeons, Edinburgh; FDSRCSE 1970. LDS 1933. Lieut, Army Dental Corps, 1935; Captain 1936; Major 1945; Lieut-Colonel 1952; Colonel 1959; Maj.-General 1966. Served in: UK, 1935–39, 1945–50, 1955–59, 1963–70; Far East, 1939–45 (POW); BAOR, 1950–52, 1959–63; MELF, 1952–55. QHDS, 1966–70. CStJ 1970. *Recreations:* Rugby football, golf, tennis, walking. *Address:* 9 Oldlands Hall, Heron's Ghyll, near Uckfield, Sussex TN22 3DA.

FINLEY, Michael John; Director and General Manager, Kent Messenger Group, since 1979; *b* 22 Sept. 1932; *s* of late Walter Finley and of Grace Marie Butler; *m* 1955, Sheila Elizabeth Cole; four *s*. *Educ:* King Edward VII Sch., Sheffield. Reporter and Sub-Editor, 1951–56, News Editor, 1960–63, Asst Editor, 1963–64, Editor, 1964–69, Sheffield Morning Telegraph (formerly Sheffield Telegraph); Chief Editorial Exec., Kent Messenger Gp, 1969–72, Editorial Dir, 1972–79. Hon. Mem. and Past Chm., Parly and Legal Cttee, Guild of British Newspaper Editors. Chm., Inst. of Dirs (Kent branch), 1980–83. Member: BBC Region Adv. Council, 1967–69; BBC Gen. Adv. Council, 1971–77. *Publication:* contrib. Advertising and the Community, 1968. *Recreations:* tennis, rugby (spectator), snooker. *Address:* Golford Place, Cranbrook, Kent.

FINLEY, Sir Moses, Kt 1979; FBA 1971; Master of Darwin College, Cambridge, 1976–82, Emeritus Fellow, since 1982; *b* 20 May 1912; became British subject, 1962; *m* 1932, Mary F. Thiers; no *c*. *Educ:* Syracuse Univ., USA; Columbia Univ., USA. BA Syracuse 1927 (*magna cum laude*) (Phi Beta Kappa); MA Columbia, 1929 and PhD 1950. Held various teaching, research, editorial and consulting posts with: Encyclopaedia of the Social Sciences, 1930–33; Inst. of Social Research (then affiliated with Columbia Univ.), 1937–39; City Coll. of New York, 1934–42; Columbia Univ., 1933–34, 1948–54; exec. posts with war relief agencies, 1942–47. Fellow in History, Columbia Univ., 1934–35; Fellow, Amer. Council of Learned Socs, 1948; Lectr, then Asst Prof. of History, Newark Colls of Rutgers Univ., 1948–52; Faculty Fellow, Fund for the Advancement of Educn, 1951–52. Lectr in Classics, Cambridge Univ., 1955–64; Fellow, Jesus Coll., 1957–76, Hon. Fellow, 1977; Reader in Ancient Social and Economic History, Cambridge Univ., 1964–70, Prof. of Ancient History, Cambridge Univ., 1970–79; Librarian, Jesus Coll., 1960–64; Chm., Faculty Bd of Classics, Cambridge Univ. 1967–69; Chm., Social and Political Sciences Cttee, Cambridge Univ., 1973–74. Sather Prof. of Classical Literature, Univ. of California, Berkeley, 1972; Lectures: First Mason Welch Gross, Rutgers Univ., 1972; Jane Harrison Meml, Newnham Coll., Cambridge, 1972; Mortimer Wheeler Archaeol, British Acad., 1974; Collège de France, 1978; British Museum Soc., 1979 (at Nat. Theatre); Wiles, QUB, 1980; J. C. Jacobsen Meml, Danish Acad., 1981. Sec., Cambridge Philological Soc., 1959–65, Pres., 1974–76; Convener of Ancient Hist. section, Internat. Economic Hist. Conf., Aix-en-Provence, 1962, Munich, 1965; Edinburgh, 1978; Pres., Jt Assoc. of Classical Teachers, 1981- (Chm., sub-cttee on Ancient Hist., 1964–71); Pres., Classical Assoc., 1973–74. A Trustee, British Museum, 1977–. Editor: Views and Controversies in Classical Antiquity, 1960–73; Ancient Culture and Society, 1969–. FRHistS, 1970; FRSA, 1971. For. Member: Royal Danish Acad. of Scis and Letters, 1975; Accademia Nazionale dei Lincei, 1982; Hon. For. Mem., Amer. Acad. of Arts and Sciences, 1979. Hon. DLitt: Leicester, 1972; Saskatchewan, 1979; Sheffield, 1979; Hon. DHumLitt City Coll. of NY, 1982. Wolfson Literary Award in History, 1974. *Publications:* Studies in Land and Credit in Ancient Athens, 1952; The World of Odysseus, 1954, 2nd edn 1977; (ed) The Greek Historians, 1958; (ed) Slavery in Classical Antiquity, 1960; The Ancient Greeks, 1963; (ed) Josephus, 1965; Aspects of Antiquity, 1968; Ancient Sicily, 1968, 2nd edn, 1979; Early Greece: the Bronze and Archaic Ages, 1970, 2nd edn, 1981; The Ancestral Constitution (inaugural lecture), 1971; (ed) Thucydides, 1972; Knowledge for what? (Encyclopaedia Britannica Lecture), 1973; Democracy Ancient and Modern, 1973; (ed) Problèmes de la terre en Grèce ancienne, 1973; The Ancient Economy, 1973; (ed) Studies in Ancient Society, 1974; The Use and Abuse of History, 1975; (with H. W. Pleket) The Olympic Games: the first thousand years, 1976; (ed) Studies in Roman Property, 1976; (ed) Atlas of Classical Archaeology, 1977; The Idea of a Theatre: the Greek experience, 1980; Ancient Slavery and Modern Ideology, 1980; (ed) The Legacy of Greece: a new appraisal, 1981; Economy and Society in Ancient Greece, 1981; articles and reviews in classical, historical and legal jls, and in literary weeklies and monthlies in Britain and the US. *Recreations:* conversation, listening to music, travel. *Address:* 12 Adams Road, Cambridge CB3 9AD. *T:* Cambridge 357784.

FINLEY, Sir Peter (Hamilton), Kt 1981; OBE 1974; DFC 1944; FCA; Chairman: Boral Ltd, since 1976; Email Ltd, since 1974; Hygienic Lily Ltd, since 1971; Avery Aust. Ltd, since 1972; Custom Credit Corporation Ltd, since 1973; Deputy Chairman, Cadbury Schweppes Aust. Ltd, since 1971; Director, National Bank of Australasia Ltd, since 1970; *b* 6 Dec. 1919; *s* of Cecil Aubert Finley and Evelyn Finley (*née* Daniels); *m* 1947, Berenice Mitchell Finley (*née* Armstrong); one *s* one *d*. *Educ:* The King's Sch., Parramatta. Served RAAF with RAF Bomber Command and RAAF SW Pacific Area, 1941–45. With W. V. Armstrong & Co., Chartered Accountants, 1946–48, Peat, Marwick, Mitchell & Co. (formerly Smith Johnson & Co.), 1949–55, P. H. Finley & Co., 1955–72, when virtually ceased practice. Chm., Nat. Bank of Australasia's Sydney Bd of Advice, 1970–81; Director: Allied Mills Ltd, 1970–; Amalgamated Wireless Australasia Ltd, 1974– (Dep. Chm., 1978–); Burns Philp & Co. Ltd, 1980–; Sir Robert Menzies Meml Trust, 1979–. *Recreations:* cricket, tennis, gardening. *Address:* (business) 2 O'Connell Street, Sydney, NSW 2000, Australia. *T:* 233 6190; (home) 50 Treatts Road, Lindfield, NSW 2070. *T:* 46 5319. *Clubs:* Australian (Sydney); Melbourne (Melbourne).

FINN, Donovan Bartley, CMG 1946; FRSC, FCIC; Director of Fisheries, Food and Agriculture Organization of the United Nations, 1946–64, retired; *b* Hendon, 1 March 1900; *s* of Edwin Bartley Finn and Eleanor Penton; *m* 1946, Florence Stewart Daly. *Educ:* University of Manitoba (BSc, MSc); Cambridge Univ. (PhD). Director Fisheries Expt. Station, Prince Rupert, BC, of the Fisheries Research Board of Canada, 1925; Director Fisheries Expt. Station, Halifax, NS, of Fisheries Research Board of Canada, 1934; Chairman Salt Fish Board of Canada, 1939; Deputy Minister of Fisheries, Dominion of Canada, 1940–46; Member Economic Advisory Cttee, Dominion of Canada, 1941; Chairman Food Requirements Cttee, 1943–46. Represented Canada as delegate and adviser at various international bodies and conferences during war with respect to fisheries and food matters. *Publications:* scientific journals, on physics and chemistry of food proteins. *Recreations:* mountaineering, music. *Address:* Castello di Sterpeto, Sterpeto d'Assisi, Perugia, Italy. *Clubs:* Rideau, University (Ottawa).

FINNEY, Albert; actor, stage and film; film director; Associate Artistic Director, English Stage Company, since 1972; *m* 1957, Jane Wenham, actress (marr. diss.); one *s*; *m* 1970, Anouk Aimée (marr. diss.). *Stage:* London appearance in The Party, New, 1958; Cassio in Othello, and Lysander, Stratford-on-Avon, 1959; subsequently in: The Lily White Boys, Royal Court, 1960; Billy Liar, Cambridge Theatre, 1960; Luther, in Luther: Royal Court Theatre and Phoenix Theatre, 1961–62; New York, 1963; Armstrong in Armstrong's Last Goodnight, Miss Julie and Black Comedy, Chichester, 1965, Old Vic, 1966; A Day in the Death of Joe Egg, NY, 1968; Alpha Beta, Royal Court and Apollo, 1972; Krapp's Last Tape, Royal Court, 1973; Cromwell, Royal Court, 1973; Chez Nous, Globe, 1974; Uncle Vanya, and Present Laughter, Royal Exchange, Manchester, 1977; *National Theatre:* Love for Love, 1965; Much Ado About Nothing, 1965; A Flea in Her Ear, 1966; Hamlet, 1975; Tamburlaine, 1976; The Country Wife, 1977; The Cherry Orchard, Macbeth, Has "Washington" Legs?, 1978; *Directed for stage:* The Freedom of the City, Royal Court, 1973; Loot, Royal Court, 1975; *Films include:* Saturday Night and Sunday Morning; Tom Jones; Night Must Fall; Two for the Road; Charlie Bubbles (also Director); Scrooge; Gumshoe; Alpha Beta; Murder on the Orient Express; Wolfen; Loophole; Looker; Shoot the Moon; Annie. Hon. LittD: Sussex, 1965; Salford, 1979. *Address:* c/o ICM, 388/396 Oxford Street, W1N 9HE.

FINNEY, Prof. David John, CBE 1978; FRS 1955; FRSE; MA, ScD (Cantab); Professor of Statistics, University of Edinburgh, since 1966; Director, Agricultural Research Council Unit of Statistics; *b* Latchford, Warrington, 3 Jan. 1917; *e s* of late Robert G. S. Finney and late Bessie E. Whitlow; *m* 1950, Mary Elizabeth Connolly; one *s* two *d*. *Educ:* Lymm and Manchester Grammar Schools; Clare Coll., Cambridge; Galton Laboratory, Univ. of London. Asst Statistician, Rothamsted Experimental Station, 1939–45; Lecturer in the Design and Analysis of Scientific Experiment, University of Oxford, 1945–54; Reader in Statistics, University of Aberdeen, 1954–63, Professor, 1963–66. United Nations FAO expert attached to Indian Council of Agricultural Research, 1952–73. Scientific Consultant, Cotton Research Corporation, 1959–75. Chm., Computer Bd for Univs and Research Councils, 1970–74 (Mem., 1966–74); Member: Adverse Reactions Sub-Cttee, Cttee on Safety of Medicines, 1963–81; BBC General Adv. Council, 1969–76; Visiting Prof. of Biomathematics, Harvard Univ., 1962–63; President of Biometric Society, 1964–65 (Vice-President, 1963, 1966); Fellow: Royal Statistical Soc. (Pres., 1973–74); American Statistical Assoc.; Mem., Internat. Statistical Inst.; Hon. Fellow Eugenics Society; Hon. Mem., Société Adolphe Quetelet. Weldon Memorial Prize, 1956. Dr *hc*, Faculté des Sciences Agronomiques de l'Etat à Gembloux, Belgium, 1967; Hon. DSc: City, 1976; Heriot-Watt, 1981. *Publications:* Probit Analysis, 1947 (3rd edn 1971); Biological Standardization (with J. H. Burn, L. G. Goodwin), 1950; Statistical Method in Biological Assay, 1952 (3rd edn 1978); An Introduction to Statistical Science in Agriculture, 1953 (4th edn 1972); Experimental Design and its Statistical Basis, 1955; Tecnica y Teoria en el diseño de Experimentos, 1957; An Introduction to the Theory of Experimental Design, 1960; Statistics for Mathematicians: An Introduction, 1968; Statistics for Biologists, 1980.

Numerous papers in statistical and biological journals. *Recreations:* travel (active), music (passive), and the 3 R's. *Address:* Statistics Department, University of Edinburgh, James Clerk Maxwell Building, The King's Buildings, Mayfield Road, Edinburgh EH9 3JZ. *T:* 031-667 1081; 43 Cluny Drive, Edinburgh EH10 6DU. *T:* 031-447 2332.

FINNEY, James; Chairman, Staff Commission for Education and Library Boards, since 1981; Permanent Secretary, Department of Manpower Services for Northern Ireland, 1976-80, retired; *b* 21 Jan. 1920; *s* of James and Ellen Finney, Co. Armagh; *m* 1956, Barbara Ann Bennett, Wargrave, Berks; one *s* three *d. Educ:* Royal Belfast Academical Instn; Trinity Coll., Dublin Univ. BA 1st cl. Mods 1942. Royal Engrs, 1943-46. Min. of Educn for N Ireland, 1946-76. *Recreation:* gardening. *Address:* Honeypots, Ballyhanwood Road, Dundonald, Belfast, N Ireland. *T:* Dundonald 3428.

FINNEY, Jarlath John; a Recorder of the Crown Court, since 1980; *b* Hale, Cheshire, 1 July 1930; *s* of late Victor Harold Finney, MA, and Aileen Rose Finney (*née* Gallagher), Dorking, Surrey; *m* 1957, Daisy Emöke, *y d* of late Dr Matyas Veszy, formerly of Budapest; two *s* two *d. Educ:* Wimbledon College; Gray's Inn. Served, 2nd Lieut, 8 RTR, 1953-55 (Lieut 1955). Called to Bar, Gray's Inn, 1953; Member, SE Circuit, 1955-. Member, Panel of Counsel for HM Customs and Excise before VAT Tribunals, 1973-. *Recreations:* wild flowers, books, walking in the country. *Address:* (chambers) 1 Essex Court, Temple, EC4Y 9AR. *T:* 01-353 5362. *Club:* Wig and Pen.

FINNISTON, Sir (Harold) Montague, Kt 1975; BSc, PhD; FRS 1969; FRSE 1978; Chairman: Anderson Strathclyde PLC, since 1980; Drake and Scull Holdings PLC, since 1980 (Joint Deputy Chairman, 1980); Branon PLC, since 1980; Future Technology Systems PLC, since 1981; Deputy Chairman, Butterfield Harvey, since 1982 (Director, since 1981); Director: Bodycote International Ltd, since 1980; Cluff Oil PLC, since 1976; GKN PLC, since 1976; Barmel Associates Ltd, since 1981; Building Trust Management Co., since 1981; Chairman of Council, Scottish Business School, since 1976; *b* 15 Aug. 1912; *s* of late Robert and Esther Finniston; *m* 1936, Miriam Singer; one *s* one *d. Educ:* Allan Glen's Sch., Glasgow; Glasgow Univ.; Royal College of Science and Technology, Glasgow. Lecturer in Metallurgy, Royal College of Science and Technology, 1933-35; Metallurgist, Stewart & Lloyds, 1935-37; Chief Research Officer, Scottish Coke Research Cttee, 1937-40; Metallurgist, RN Scientific Service, 1940-46; seconded to Ministry of Supply, Chalk River, Canada, 1946-47; Chief Metallurgist, UKAEA, Harwell, 1948-58; Man. Director, International Research and Development Co. (Chm. 1968-77), and Technical Director, C. A. Parsons & Co. Ltd, 1959-67; Chairman: Cryosystems Ltd; System Computors Ltd; Electronics Association of the North-East; Director, C. A. Parsons & Co. Ltd; Mem. Board of Thorn-Parsons Co. Ltd and Northern Economic Planning Council, 1963-67; Dep. Chm. (Technical), BSC, 1967-71; Dep. Chm. and Chief Executive, BSC, 1971-73; Chm., BSC, 1973-76; Dir, Sears Holdings Ltd, 1976-79; Chm., Sears Engrg Ltd, 1976-79. Member: Council British Non-Ferrous Metals Research Assoc., 1965-72 (Vice-Chm. 1969-72; Chm. Research Board, 1965-70); NRDC, 1963-73; NEDC, 1973-76; Advisory Council, R&D (Fuel and Power), Dept of Trade and Industry (formerly Ministry of Power), 1965-74; SRC University Science and Technology Board, 1965-67; NPL Steering Cttee, 1966-68; Iron and Steel Adv. Cttee, 1969-73; Academic Adv. Cttee, Cranfield Inst. of Technology, 1970-75; BBC Science Consultative Group, 1971-74; Chairman: Policy Studies Inst. (formerly PEP), 1975- (Exec. Cttee, 1968-74); Govt Cttee of Inquiry into engineering profession, 1977-79; Building EDC, 1980-; Prison Reform Trust, 1981-; Pres., Ironbridge Gorge Mus. Develt Trust, 1977-. President: Inst. of Metals, 1967-68; Metals Soc., 1974-75 (Hon. Mem., 1980); Inst. Metallurgists, 1975-76; ASLIB, 1976-78 (Vice-Pres., 1974-76); Inst. of Management Services, 1977-82; Design and Industries Assoc., 1978-; ABCC, 1980; BISFA, 1980; Vice-Pres., Iron and Steel Inst., 1968-73; Gen. Sec., BAAS, 1970-73 (Life Mem.); Mem., Soc. of Chem. Industry, 1974. A Vice- Pres., Royal Soc., 1971-72. Mem., Court of Assts, Worshipful Co. of Tinplate Workers, 1974-. Lectures: Dunn Meml, 1968; 19th Hatfield Meml, 1968; 18th Coal Science, BCURA, 1969; Edward Williams, 1970; Andrew Laing, 1970; Cockcroft, UMIST, 1975; Thomas Graham, Harold Moore, R. W. Mann, Marlow (Scotland), Colquhoun, 1976; Edwards Meml, 1977; ASM-TMS/AIME Distinguished, Chicago, 1977; 3rd Cantor, RSA, 1978; John Simmons, 1978; Lillian Gilbreth, 1978; Mason, 1979; Thomson, 1979; Lubbock Meml, 1979; Wilfrid Fish, 1980; Willis Jackson, 1980; Alfred Herbert, 1980; Massey Ferguson Meml, 1981; Barnett Shine, 1981; Conn Meml, 1981. Governor, Carmel Coll., 1973- (Chm., 1980-). Vis. Fellow, Univ. of Lancaster, 1970-. Pro-Chancellor, Surrey Univ., 1978-; Chancellor, Stirling Univ., 1978-. ARTC; FIM; FInstP; FIChemE; FBIM; life FRSA; MRI 1978. Hon. Member: American Iron and Steel Inst., 1974; Japan Iron and Steel Inst., 1975 (Tawara Gold Medal, 1975); Indian Inst. of Metals, 1976; Smeatonian Soc. of Civil Engrs, 1977. Hon. Fellow: UMIST, 1973; Sunderland Polytech., 1975; Imp. Coll. of Science and Technology, 1979; St Cross Coll., Oxford, 1981. Hon. DSc: Strathclyde, 1968; Aston, 1971; City, 1974; Cranfield, 1976; Bath, 1977; Sussex, 1981; Open, 1982; DUniv: Surrey, 1969; Stirling, 1979; Hon. DCL Newcastle, 1976; Hon. DEng Liverpool, 1978; Hon. LLD: Glasgow, 1978; Hull, 1980; Hon. DMet Sheffield, 1979. Bessemer Medal, Metals Soc., 1974; Silver Medal, Inst. Sheet Metal Engrg, 1975; Eichner Medal, Soc. Française de Metallurgie, 1976; A. A. Griffiths Silver Medal, Material Sci. Club, 1976; Glazebrook Medal, Inst. of Physics, 1976. *Publications:* Editor: Metallurgy of the Rarer Metals, 1954-; Progress in Nuclear Energy, 1954-; Structural Characteristics of Materials, 1971;

various scientific papers. *Recreations:* reading, writing and spectator interest in sport. *Address:* (office) 6 Manchester Square, W1. *T:* 01-486 3658; Flat 72, Prince Albert Court, 33 Prince Albert Road, NW8. *T:* 01-722 8197. *Club:* Athenæum.

FINSBERG, Geoffrey, MBE 1959; JP; MP (C) Hampstead, since 1970; Parliamentary Under Secretary of State, Department of Health and Social Security, since 1981; *b* 13 June 1926; *o s* of late Montefiore Finsberg, MC, and May Finsberg (*née* Grossman); *m* 1969, Pamela Benbow Hill. *Educ:* City of London Sch. National Chm., Young Conservatives, 1954-57; Mem., Exec. Cttee, Nat. Union of Cons. and Unionist Assocs, 1953-79 (Mem. Exec. Cttee, Greater London Area, 1949-79); a Vice-Chm., Conservative Party Organisation, 1975-79. Borough Councillor: Hampstead, 1949-65; Camden, 1964-74 (Leader, 1968-70). Chairman: Gtr London Area Cons. Local Govt Cttee, 1972-75. Opposition spokesman on Greater London, 1974-79; Mem. Exec., 1922 Cttee, 1974-75; Member, Select Cttee on Expenditure, 1970-79; Parly Under Sec. of State, Dept of the Environment, 1979-81. Controller of Personnel and Chief Industrial Relations Adviser, Great Universal Stores, 1968-79; Director, London & South Eastern Trustee Savings Bank, 1963-75. Vice-Pres., Assoc. of Municipal Corporations, 1971-74 (Dep. Chm., 1969-71); Member: Post Office Users Nat. Council, 1970-77; Council, CBI, 1968-79 (Chm., Post Office Panel). Patron, Maccabi Assoc. of GB. Governor, Univ. Coll. Sch. JP Inner London, 1962. *Recreations:* bridge, reading. *Address:* House of Commons, SW1A 0AA. *T:* (home) 01-435 5320. *Club:* St Stephen's Constitutional.

FINTRIE, Lord; James Alexander Norman Graham; *b* 16 Aug. 1973; *s* and *heir* of Marquis of Graham, *qv.*

FIRBANK, Maj.-Gen. Cecil Llewellyn, CB 1953; CBE 1951; DSO 1944 and Bar 1945; DL; *b* 18 March 1903; *m* 1st, 1934, Audrey Hobhouse (marr. diss. 1952); one *s* ; 2nd, 1952, Marye Brenda Fleetwood-Wilson. *Educ:* Cheltenham Coll.; RMC Sandhurst. Gazetted to 1st Somerset LI, 1924; served Egypt, 1926-29; seconded to Royal West African Frontier Force, 1929-34; served with Somerset LI, 1934-42; on active service, North West Europe, 1944-45, Comd 2nd Lincolns; Comd 71 Infantry Bde, 1945-46; Staff Coll., 1947-48; Commandant School of Infantry, Warminster, 1948-51; GOC SW District and 43rd Wessex Division (TA), 1951-54; Director of Infantry, War Office, 1955-58; retired pay, 1959. Colonel Commandant, Aden Protectorate Levies, 1958-62; Colonel, Somerset and Cornwall Light Infantry, 1963-68; Dep. Colonel, The Light Infantry (Somerset and Cornwall), 1968-70. Hon. Colonel: 4/5th Somerset LI (TA), 1955-60; North Somerset Yeomanry (44th Royal Tank Regt), 1959-64. Dir, Civil Defence for Wales, 1960-65. DL Somerset, 1959. *Recreations:* cricket, field sports. *Address:* The Owls, Charlton Horethorne, near Sherborne, Dorset. *T:* Corton Denham 279. *Club:* Army and Navy.

FIRMSTON-WILLIAMS, Peter, OBE 1979; Chairman, Covent Garden Market Authority, since 1982; Chairman, Ukay Furniture Stores Ltd, since 1981; Director, BAT Stores Ltd, since 1982; *b* 30 Aug. 1918; *s* of Geoffrey and Muriel Firmston-Williams; *m* Margaret Beaulah; one *s* one *d. Educ:* Harrow. Served War, Infantry, Green Howards Regt, 1939-45 (Captain). J. Lyons & Co. Ltd, 1945-53; Marketing Director, United Canners Ltd, 1953-55; Associated British Foods Ltd, Director, Store Operations, Fine Fare, 1958-61; Fitch Lovell Ltd, Man. Dir, Key Markets Ltd, 1961-71; Associated Dairies Group Ltd, Man. Dir, ASDA Stores, and Dir, Associated Dairies, 1971-81, retired. *Recreations:* golf, water skiing, gardening. *Address:* Oak House, 12 Pembroke Road, Moor Park, Northwood, Mddx. *T:* Northwood 23052; 30 Rowland Place, Northwood, Mddx. *T:* Northwood 24535.

FIRNBERG, David; Managing Director, Eosys Ltd (formerly Urwick Nexos Ltd), since 1980; *b* 1 May 1930; *s* of L. B. Firnberg and K. L. E. Firnberg; *m* 1957, Sylvia Elizabeth du Cros; one *s* three *d. Educ:* Merchant Taylors' Sch., Northwood. FBCS. Went West, 1953-56; Television Audience Measurement Ltd, 1956-59; ICT/ICL, 1959-72; David Firnberg Associates Ltd, 1972-74; Dir, Nat. Computing Centre Ltd, 1974-79. Pres., UK Assoc. of Project Managers, 1978; Dep. Pres., British Computer Soc., 1981-. *Publications:* Computers Management and Information, 1973; Cassell's New Spelling Dictionary, 1976. *Address:* The Great House, Buckland Common, Tring, Herts HP23 6NX. *T:* Cholesbury 448. *Clubs:* English-Speaking Union, Wig and Pen.

FIRTH, Arthur Percival; Assistant Editor, Daily Mail, since 1982; *b* 13 Aug. 1928; *s* of Arthur and Florence Firth; *m* 1957, Joyce Mary (*née* Fairclough); two *d. Educ:* Arnold Sch., Blackpool. Reporter, Lancashire Evening Post, 1950-58; Sub-Editor, Daily Herald, 1959; Daily Express: Sub-Editor, 1960; Night Editor, 1969-72; Northern Editor, 1972-78; Dep. Editor, 1978-80; Editor, 1980-81. *Recreations:* golf, fishing, cricket. *Address:* Greshams, Layters Way, Gerrards Cross, Bucks SL9 7QY. *T:* (office) 01-353 8000.

FIRTH, Maj.-Gen. Charles Edward Anson, CB 1951; CBE 1945; DSO 1943; *b* 9 Oct. 1902; *s* of late Major E. W. A. Firth, Indian Army; *m* 1933, Mary Kathleen (*d* 1977), *d* of late Commander W. St J. Fraser, RN; two *s. Educ:* Wellington Coll., Berks; RMC Sandhurst. 2nd Lieut The Gloucestershire Regt, 1923; Lieut, 1925; Captain, 1935; Staff Coll., 1936-37; War Office, 1938-40; Major, 1940; Middle East: Temp. Lieut-Colonel; AA and QMG 50 Div., 1941-42; OC 1st Royal Sussex Regt in Middle East, 1942-43; Temp. Brigadier, 7th Indian Infantry Bde, 1943; Comd 167 Infantry Bde, 1943-44

(Italy); Comd 21 Tank Bde, 1944 (N. Africa); Comd 2 Infantry Bde, 1944 (Italy); Comdr and Dep. Comdr British Military Mission to Greece, 1944-45. Colonel 1946; War Office, 1946-48; Comd Area Troops, Berlin (British Sector), 1948-50; Maj.-General, 1950; Comd East Anglian Dist, 1950; GOC Salisbury Plain Dist, 1951-53; Director of Personal Services, War Office, 1953-56. Colonel The Gloucestershire Regt, 1954-64; first Colonel Comdt, Military Provost Staff Corps, 1956-61. Governor, Dauntsey's Sch., 1961-77 (Vice-Chairman, 1965-77). Grand Commander Order of the Phoenix (Greek), 1946. *Recreations:* gardening, writing, fishing. *Address:* Crofton Lodge, Crofton, Marlborough, Wilts SN8 3DW. *T:* Marlborough 870270. *Club:* Army and Navy.

FIRTH, David Colin; Headmaster, Cheadle Hulme School, since 1977; *b* 29 Jan. 1930; *s* of Jack and Muriel Firth; *m* 1954, Edith Scanlan; three *s* one *d*. *Educ:* Rothwell Grammar Sch.; Sheffield Univ. (BSc, DipEd). Royal Signals, 1952-54; Stand Grammar Sch., 1954-57; East Barnet Grammar Sch., 1957-61; Bristol Grammar Sch., 1961-73; The Gilberd Sch., 1973-77. *Publications:* A Practical Organic Chemistry, 1966; Elementary Thermodynamics, 1969; (jtly) Introductory Physical Science, 1971. *Recreations:* cricket, fell walking, talking about gardening. *Address:* Cheadle Hulme School, Claremont Road, Cheadle Hulme, Cheadle, Cheshire SK8 6EF.

FIRTH, Edward Michael Tyndall, CB 1951; *b* 17 Feb. 1903; *s* of Edward H. Firth, Sheffield; *m* 1929, Eileen Marie (*d* 1982), *d* of Edward Newman, Hove; two *s*. *Educ:* King Edward VII Sch., Sheffield; University College, Oxford. Classical Scholar, 1922-26. Inland Revenue, 1926; Ministry of Health, 1945; Under Secretary, 1947-58; Registrar General, 1958-63. *Address:* 65 Middle Way, Oxford.

FIRTH, Mrs Joan Margaret, PhD; Under-Secretary, Children's Division, Department of Health and Social Security, since 1981; *b* 25 March 1935; *d* of Ernest Wilson and Ann (*née* Crowther); *m* 1952, Kenneth Firth. *Educ:* Lawnswood High Sch., Leeds; Univ. of Leeds (1st Cl. BSc Colour Chemistry; PhD Dyeing of Wool). Research Asst, Leeds Univ., 1958-60; Head of Science, Selby High Sch., 1960-62; Sen. Lecturer in General Science, Elizabeth Gaskell Coll., Manchester, 1962-66; Lectr in Organic Chemistry, Salford Univ., 1966-67; joined Civil Service as Direct Entry Principal, 1967; Asst Sec., 1974. *Publications:* contrib. Jl Textile Inst., 1958. *Recreations:* eating, dieting, Open University. *Address:* 2 Stratton Court, Devonshire Road, Hatch End, Mddx HA5 4NA. *T:* 01-428 7204.

FIRTH, Prof. Sir Raymond (William), Kt 1973; MA; PhD; FBA 1949; Professor of Anthropology, University of London, 1944-68, now Emeritus; *b* 25 March 1901; *s* of late Wesley Hugh Bourne Firth and Marie Elizabeth Jane Cartmill; *m* 1936, Rosemary, *d* of late Sir Gilbert Upcott, KCB; one *s*. *Educ:* Auckland Grammar Sch.; Auckland University College; London School of Economics (Hon. Fellow, 1970). Anthropological research in British Solomon Islands, including one year on Tikopia, 1928-29; Lecturer in Anthropology, University of Sydney, 1930-31; Acting Professor of Anthropology, University of Sydney, 1931-32; Lecturer in Anthropology, London School of Economics, 1932-35; Reader, 1935-44; Hon. Secretary Royal Anthropological Institute, 1936-39 (President 1953-55); Research in peasant economics and anthropology in Malaya, as Leverhulme Research Fellow, 1939-40; served with Naval Intelligence Division, Admiralty, 1941-44; Secretary of Colonial Social Science Research Council, Colonial Office, 1944-45; Fellow, Center for Advanced Study in the Behavioral Sciences, Stanford, 1958-59; Prof. of Pacific Anthropology, Univ. of Hawaii, 1968-69. Visiting Professor: British Columbia, 1969; Cornell, 1970; Chicago, 1971; Graduate Center, City Univ. of New York, 1971; Univ. of California, Davis 1974, Berkeley 1977; Auckland, 1978. Life Pres., Assoc. of Social Anthropologists, 1975. Foreign Hon. Member American Academy of Arts and Sciences, 1963; Hon. Member Royal Society, NZ, 1964; Foreign Member: American Philosophical Society, 1965; Royal Soc., NSW; Royal Danish Academy of Sciences and Letters, 1966. Social research surveys: W Africa, 1945; Malaya, 1947; New Guinea, 1951; Tikopia, 1952, 1966; Malaya, 1963. Hon. degrees: DPh Oslo, 1965; LLD Michigan, 1967; LittD East Anglia, 1968; Dr Letters ANU, 1969; DHumLett Chicago, 1968; DSc British Columbia, 1970; DLitt Exeter, 1972; DLit Auckland, 1978. *Publications:* The Kauri Gum Industry, 1924; Primitive Economics of the New Zealand Maori, 1929 (new edn, 1959); Art and Life In New Guinea, 1936; We, The Tikopia: A Sociological Study of Kinship in Primitive Polynesia, 1936; Human Types, 1938 (new edn, 1975); Primitive Polynesian Economy, 1939 (new edn, 1964); The Work of the Gods in Tikopia, 1940 (new edn, 1967); Malay Fishermen: Their Peasant Economy, 1946 (enlarged edn, 1966); Elements of Social Organization, 1951 (new edn 1971); Two Studies of Kinship in London (ed.), 1956; Man and Culture: An Evaluation of the Work of Malinowski (ed.), 1957; Social Change in Tikopia, 1959; History and Traditions of Tikopia, 1961; Essays on Social Organization and Values, 1964; (with B. S. Yamey) Capital Saving and Credit in Peasant Societies, 1964; Tikopia Ritual and Belief, 1967; Rank and Religion in Tikopia, 1970; (with J. Hubert and A. Forge) Families and Their Relatives, 1970; Symbols Public and Private, 1973. *Recreations:* Romanesque art, early music. *Address:* 33 Southwood Avenue, N6 5SA. *Club:* Athenæum.

FIRTH, Tazeena Mary; designer; *b* 1 Nov. 1935; *d* of Denis Gordon Firth and Irene (*née* Morris). *Educ:* St Mary's, Wantage; Chatelard Sch. Theatre Royal, Windsor, 1954-57; English Stage Co., Royal Court, 1957-60; partnership in stage design with Timothy O'Brien estabd 1961; output incl.: The Bartered

Bride, The Girl of the Golden West, 1962; West End prodns of new plays, 1963-64; London scene of Shakespeare Exhibn, 1964; Tango, Days in the Trees, Staircase, RSC, and Trafalgar at Madame Tussaud's, 1966; All's Well that Ends Well, As You Like It, Romeo and Juliet, RSC, 1967; The Merry Wives of Windsor, Troilus and Cressida (also Nat. Theatre, 1976), The Latent Heterosexual, RSC, 1968; Pericles (also Comédie Française, 1974), Women Beware Women, Bartholomew Fair, RSC, 1969; 1970: Measure for Measure, RSC; Madame Tussaud's in Amsterdam; The Knot Garden, Royal Opera; 1971: Enemies, Man of Mode, RSC; 1972: La Cenerentola, Oslo; Lower Depths, The Island of the Mighty, RSC; As You Like It, OCSC; 1973: Richard II, Love's Labour's Lost, RSC; 1974: Next of Kin, NT; Summerfolk, RSC; The Bassarids, ENO; 1975: John Gabriel Borkman, NT; Peter Grimes, Royal Opera (later in Paris); The Marrying of Ann Leete, RSC; 1976: Wozzeck, Adelaide Fest.; The Zykovs, RSC; The Force of Habit, NT; 1977: Tales from the Vienna Woods, Bedroom Farce, NT; Falstaff, Berlin Opera; 1978: The Cunning Little Vixen, Göteborg; Evita, London (later in USA, Australia, Vienna); A Midsummer Night's Dream, Sydney Opera House; 1979: Peter Grimes, Göteborg; The Rake's Progress, Royal Opera. Designed independently: The Two Gentlemen of Verona, RSC, 1969; Occupations, RSC, 1971; The Rape of Lucretia, Karlstad, 1982. (Jtly) Gold Medal for Set Design, Prague Quadriennale, 1975. *Recreation:* sailing. *Address:* 33 Lansdowne Gardens, SW8 2EQ. *T:* 01-622 5384.

FISCHER, Annie; Hungarian Pianist; *b* Budapest, 1914; *m* Aladár Toth (decd). *Educ:* Franz Liszt Landemusikhochschule, Budapest. Studied under Arnold Szekule and Ernst von Dohnanyi. Concert Début, Budapest, at age of eight (performed Beethoven's C Major Concerto), 1922; began international career as a concert pianist, Zurich, 1926; toured and played in most European Music centres, 1926-39. Concert pianist, Sweden, during War of 1939-45. Returned to Hungary after War and has made concert tours to all parts of the world. Hon. Prof., Acad. of Music, Budapest, 1965. Awarded 1st prize, Internat. Liszt Competition, Budapest, 1933; Kossuth Prizes 1949, 1955, 1965. Eminent Artist; Red Banner, Order of Labour, 1974. *Address:* Szent Istvan Park 14, H-1137 Budapest XIII, Hungary.

FISCHER, Prof. Ernst Otto; Professor of Inorganic Chemistry, Munich University (Techn); *b* Munich, 10 Nov. 1918; *s* of Prof. Karl T. Fischer and Valentine (*née* Danzer); unmarried. *Educ:* Tech. Univ., Munich. Dip. Chem., 1949; Dr rer. nat., 1952, Habilitation 1954. Associate Prof. of Inorganic Chem., Univ. of Munich, 1957, Prof. 1959, Prof. and Dir, Inorganic Chem. Inst., Tech. Univ., Munich, 1964. Member: Bavarian Acad. of Sciences; Akad. deutscher Naturforscher Leopoldina, 1969; Austrian Acad. of Scis, 1976; Accad. dei Lincei, Italy, 1976; Göttingen Akad. der Wissenschaften, 1977; Soc. of German Chemists, etc; Centennial For. Fellow, Amer. Chem. Soc., 1976. Hon. Dr rer. nat. Munich, 1972; Hon. DSc Strathclyde, 1975; Hon. Dr rer. nat. Erlangen, 1977. Has received many prizes and awards including the Nobel Prize for Chemistry, 1973 (jointly with Prof. Geoffrey Wilkinson) for their pioneering work, performed independently, on the chem. of organometallic "sandwich compounds". *Publications:* (with H. Werner) Metall-pi-Komplexe mit di- und oligoolefischen Liganden, 1963 (trans. as Metal pi-Complexes Vol. 1, Complexes with di- and oligo-olefinic Ligands, 1966-); numerous contribs to learned jls on organometallic chem., etc. *Recreations:* art, history, travel. *Address:* 16 Sohnckestrasse, 8 Munich-Solln, West Germany.

FISCHER-DIESKAU, Dietrich; baritone; *b* Berlin, 28 May 1925; *s* of Dr Albert Fischer-Dieskau; *m* 1949, Irmgard Poppen (*d* 1963); three *s*. *Educ:* High Sch., Berlin; Music Academy, Berlin. First Baritone, Städtische Oper, Berlin, 1948-78, Hon. Mem., 1978-; Mem., Vienna State Opera, 1957-63. Extensive Concert Tours of Europe and USA; soloist in Festivals at Edinburgh, Salzburg, Bayreuth, Vienna, Berlin, Munich, Holland, Luzern, Prades, etc. Opera roles include: Wolfram, Jochanaan, Almaviva, Marquis Posa, Don Giovanni, Falstaff, Mandryka, Wozzeck, Danton, Macbeth, Hans Sachs. Many recordings. Member: Acad. of Arts, Berlin; Acad. of Fine Arts, Munich; Hon. RAM, 1972; Honorary Member: Wiener Konzerthausgesellschaft, 1962; Königlich-Schwedische Akad., 1972; Acad. Santa Cecilia, Rome. Hon. DMus Oxford, 1978; Dr *hc* : Sorbonne, 1980; Yale, 1980. Kunstpreis der Stadt Berlin, 1950; Internationaler Schallplattenpreis, since 1955 nearly every year; Orfeo d'oro, 1955 and 1966; Bayerischer Kammersänger, 1959; Edison Prize, 1961, 1964, 1966, 1970; Naras Award, USA, 1962; Mozart-Medaille, Wien, 1962; Berliner Klammersänger, 1963; Electrola Award, 1970; Léonie Sonning Music Prize, Copenhagen, 1975; Golden Gramophone Award, Germany, 1975; Ruckert-Preis, Schweinfurth, 1979; President's Prize, Charles Gros Acad., Paris, 1980; Ernst Von Siemen Prize, 1980; Artist of the Year, Phonoakademie, Germany, 1980. Bundesverdienstkreuz (1st class), 1958; Grosses Verdienstkreuz, 1974. *Publications:* Texte Deutscher Lieder, 1968 (The Fischer-Dieskau Book of Lieder, 1976); Auf den Spuren der Schubert-Lieder, 1971; Wagner und Nietzsche, 1974; Robert Schumann—Wort und Musik, 1981.

FISH, Francis, BPharm, PhD; FPS; Dean, School of Pharmacy, University of London, since 1978; *b* 20 April 1924; *s* of William Fish and Phyllis (*née* Griffiths); *m* 1949, Hilda Mary Brown; two *s*. *Educ:* Houghton-le-Spring Grammar Sch.; Technical Coll., Sunderland (now Sunderland Polytechnic). BPharm (London) 1946; PhD (Glasgow) 1955. FPS 1946. Asst Lectr, 1946-48, Lectr, 1948-62, Royal Coll. of Science and Technology, Glasgow; University of Strathclyde: Sen. Lectr, 1962-69; Reader in Pharmacognosy and Forensic Science, 1969-76; Personal Prof., 1976-78; Dean, Sch. of Pharmaceutical Sciences, 1977-78; Supervisor, MSc course in Forensic Science, 1966-78. Mem.

Editorial Bd, Jl Pharm. Pharmacol., 1964-70 and 1975-78. Member: Pharm. Soc. Cttee on Pharmacognosy, 1963-74; British Pharm. Codex Pharmacognosy Sub-Cttee A, 1968-73; Brit. Pharm. Conf. Sci. Cttee, 1973-78; Brit. Pharmacopoeia Pharmacognosy Panel, 1974-77; Council, Forensic Science Soc., 1974-77 (Vice-Pres., 1981-82); Professional and Gen. Services Cttee, Scottish Council on Alcoholism, 1976-78; Herbal Sub-Cttee, Cttee on Safety of Medicines, 1978-80; British Pharmacopoeia Commn, 1980-; Cttee on Safety of Medicines, 1980-; Univ. of London Senate, 1981-; DHSS Standing Pharmaceutical Adv. Cttee, 1982-; UGC Panel on Studies Allied to Medicine, 1982-. *Publications*: (with J. Owen Dawson) Surgical Dressings, Ligatures and Sutures, 1967; research pubns and review articles in Pharmaceut., Phytochem. and Forensic Sci. jls. *Recreations*: theatre, winemaking. *Address*: School of Pharmacy, University of London, 29-39 Brunswick Square, WC1N 1AX. *T*: 01-837 7651.

FISH, Hugh, OBE 1971; Chief Executive, Thames Water Authority, since 1978; *b* 6 Jan. 1923; *s* of Leonard Mark and Millicent Fish; *m* 1943, Nancy, *o d* of William and Louise Asquith; two *s* one *d*. *Educ*: Rothwell Grammar Sch.; Leeds Univ. (BSc). War Service, 1942-46, RNVR (Lieut). Chemist, W Riding Rivers Bd, 1949-52; Pollution and Fisheries Inspector, Essex River Bd, 1952-65; River Conservator, Essex River Authy, 1965-69; Chief Purification Officer, Thames Conservancy, 1969-74; Dir of Scientific Services, Thames Water Authy, 1974-78. Member of Council: IWES, 1975-; Freshwater Biol Assoc., 1972-74; Mem., NERC, 1972-. FRIC, FIPHE, FInstWPC, FIWES. *Publications*: Principles of Water Quality Management, 1973; contribs to various jls on natural science of water. *Recreations*: gardening, water sports, inventions, theatre. *Address*: 38 Coleherne Court, SW5 0DN.

FISH, John; formerly Under-Secretary, Head of Establishment General Services Division, Department of Industry, 1973-80; *b* 16 July 1920; *m* 1948, Frances; two *s*. *Educ*: Lincoln School. Entered Customs and Excise, 1937; Exchequer and Audit Dept, 1939; War service, Pilot in RAF, 1940-46; Exchequer and Audit Dept, 1946; BoT, 1949; Principal, 1950; Min. of Materials, 1951; Volta River Preparatory Commn, Accra, 1953; BoT, 1956; Asst Sec., 1960; Min. of Health, 1962; BoT, 1965; DTI, 1970; Under-Sec., 1973; Dept of Industry, 1974. *Recreations*: walking, amateur operatics, carpentry. *Address*: The Green, Stockton, near Rugby, Warwicks CV23 8JF. *T*: Southam 2833. *Club*: Civil Service.

FISHER, family name of **Baron Fisher** and **Baroness Fisher of Rednal.**

FISHER, 3rd Baron, *cr* 1909, of Kilverstone; **John Vavasseur Fisher,** DSC 1944; JP; Director, Kilverstone Latin-American Zoo and Wild Life Park, since 1973; *b* 24 July 1921; *s* of 2nd Baron and Jane (*d* 1955), *d* of Randal Morgan, Philadelphia, USA; *S* father, 1955; *m* 1st, 1949, Elizabeth Ann Penelope (marr. diss. 1969), *yr d* of late Herbert P. Holt, MC; two *s* two *d*; 2nd, 1970, Hon. Mrs Rosamund Anne Fairbairn. *Educ*: Stowe; Trinity Coll., Cambridge. Member: Eastern Gas Bd, 1962-71; East Anglia Economic Planning Council, 1971-77. DL Norfolk, 1968-82; JP Norfolk, 1970. *Heir*: *s* Hon. Patrick Vavasseur Fisher [*b* 14 June 1953; *m* 1977, Lady Karen Carnegie, *d* of Earl of Northesk, *qv*; one *s* one *d*]. *Address*: Kilverstone Hall, Thetford, Norfolk. *T*: Thetford 2222. *Club*: Naval.

See also Baron Clifford of Chudleigh.

FISHER OF REDNAL, Baroness *cr* 1974 (Life Peer), of Rednal, Birmingham; **Doris Mary Gertrude Fisher,** JP; Member of the European Parliament, 1975-79; Member, Warrington and Runcorn (formerly Warrington) Development Corporation, since 1974; *b* 13 Sept. 1919; *d* of late Frederick J. Satchwell, BEM; *m* 1939, Joseph Fisher (*d* 1978); two *d*. *Educ*: Tinker's Farm Girls Sch.; Fircroft Coll.; Bournville Day Continuation Coll. Member: Birmingham City Council, 1952-74; Labour Party, 1945-; UNESCO study group; Nat. Pres. Co-operative Women's Guild, 1961-62. Contested Ladywood, Birmingham, 1969 by-election; MP (Lab) Birmingham, Ladywood, 1970-Feb. 1974. Member: Gen. Medical Council, 1974-79; New Towns Staff Commn, 1976-79; Birmingham Civic Housing Assoc. Ltd, 1982-; Vice-Pres., Assoc. of Municipal Authorities. Warden Guardian, Birmingham Assay Office, 1981- (Guardian, 1979-81); Chm. Governors, Baskerville Special Sch., 1981-. JP Birmingham 1961. Hon. Alderman, 1974, Birmingham District Council. *Recreations*: swimming, walking. *Address*: 60 Jacoby Place, Priory Road, Birmingham B5 7UW. *T*: 021-471 2003.

FISHER, Alan Wainwright; General Secretary, National Union of Public Employees, 1968-82; Member, British Airways Board, since 1972; *b* 20 June 1922; *s* of Thomas Wainwright Fisher and Ethel Agnes Fisher; *m* 1958, Joyce Tinniswood (marr. diss. 1976); two *s* one *d*; *m* 1978, Ruth Woollerton. *Educ*: Primary and Secondary Schools in Birmingham. National Union of Public Employees: Junior Clerk, 1939; Midlands Divisional Officer, 1953; Asst General Secretary, 1962. Mem., TUC Gen. Council, 1968-82; Chm., TUC, 1980-81. Member: Nat. Jt Council for Local Authorities, Services, 1956- (Chm., 1971-72); Ancillary Staffs Council (Sec. 1965-79) and Gen. Council (Chm. 1966-69) of Whitley Councils for Health Services; Potato Marketing Bd, 1969-70; Bd, Centre for Educnl Develt Overseas (Governor 1970-); Bd, BOAC, 1970-72; London Electricity Bd, 1970-80; Nat. Radiological Protection Bd, 1971; Med. Adv. Cttee, Health and Safety Commn, 1977-; Governor, Henley Administrative Staff Coll., 1977-. *Recreation*: seismography. *Address*: 114 Riefield Road, Eltham, SE9. *T*: 01-850 4363.

FISHER, Anne; *see* Fisher, Phyllis Anne.

FISHER, Arthur J.; *see* Jeddere-Fisher.

FISHER, Major (Hon.) Charles Howard Kerridge, MC 1918; JP; Director of property companies, since 1960; *b* 21 Dec. 1895; *s* of late Charles Henry Fisher, Westbury, Wilts.; *m* 1923, Ethel Mary (*d* 1958), *d* of Sidney Redcliffe Chope, JP, Bideford, Devon; one *s* one *d*; *m* 1967, Gertrude Elizabeth, JP, *widow* of William Walter Symper, Harrow. *Educ*: Trowbridge High Sch., Wiltshire. Served European War, 1914-18 (MC); with Hon. Artillery Company and RA in Belgium and France; War of 1939-45: Home Guard and Army Welfare Officer; Hon. Major 1958. Manufacturer ladies' clothing, 1923-59, when retired (Company Dir). Member Acton Borough Council, 1940-45 (Educn Cttee, 1945-65). JP 1947, DL 1961-79, Middlesex (now London). First High Sheriff of Greater London, 1965. Lord Lieutenant's Representative for Acton, 1958-70 (now London Borough of Ealing, 1965-71); Dep. Chairman, Willesden Petty Sessional Division, 1962-69. General Comr of Income Tax, 1965-69. Freeman, City of London, 1947; Liveryman, Haberdashers' Company, 1948; Patron, Local Cadets; President: Boy Scouts Assoc.; Harlesden Branch, British Legion, Vice-President: Acton Branch, British Legion; NW County Met. Area British Legion. Member, War Pension Cttee, Ealing, 1940 (Vice-Chairman 1960). Queen's Jubilee Medal. *Recreations*: local social activities. *Address*: 36 Baronsmede, Ealing, W5 4LT. *T*: 01-567 8281. *Clubs*: City Livery.

FISHER, Desmond (Michael); Director of Broadcasting Development, Radio Telefis Eireann, Dublin, since 1975; *b* 9 Sept. 1920; *e s* of Michael Louis Fisher and Evelyn Kate Shier; *m* 1948, Margaret Elizabeth Smyth; three *s* one *d*. *Educ*: St Columb's Coll., Derry; Good Counsel Coll., New Ross, Co. Wexford; University Coll., Dublin (BA (NUI)). Asst Editor, Nationalist and Leinster Times, Carlow, 1945-48; Foreign Editor, Irish Press, Dublin, 1948-51; Economic Correspondent, Irish News Agency, Dublin, 1951-54; London Editor, Irish Press, 1954-62; Editor, Catholic Herald, 1962-66; Dep. Head of News, 1967-73, Head of Current Affairs, 1973-75, Radio Telefis Eireann. *Publications*: The Church in Transition, 1967; Broadcasting in Ireland, 1978; contributor to The Economist, The Furrow, Irish Digest and to various Irish, US and foreign magazines. *Address*: Louvain 22, Dublin. *T*: 884608.

FISHER, Doris G.; *b* 1907; *d* of Gathorne John Fisher, Pontypool. *Educ*: Farringtons, Chislehurst; Royal Holloway Coll., University of London (BA Hons (English) 1929, (French) 1931); Sorbonne. Senior English Mistress, Maidenhead County Gram. Sch. 1934-39; Second Mistress, Dover County Grammar Sch., 1945; Headmistress of Farringtons, Chislehurst, Kent, 1946-57, retired. Lecturer at Westminster Training Coll., 1957-59; Lecturer at Avery Hill Training Coll., 1959-62. *Address*: 245 Latymer Court, W6.

FISHER, Dudley Henry, IPFA; Chairman, Wales Region, British Gas Corporation, since 1974; *b* 22 Aug. 1922; *s* of Arthur and Mary Fisher; *m* 1946, Barbara Lilian Sexton; one *s* two *d*. *Educ*: City of Norwich Sch. Various accountancy positions in Local Govt and Eastern Electricity Bd, 1938-53. War service, RAF, 1942-46 (Flt Lt). Northern Gas Bd, 1953; Wales Gas Board: Asst Chief Accountant, Dep. Chief Accountant, Chief Accountant, Dir of Finance, 1956-69; Dep. Chm., 1970. Mem., Adv. Cttee on Local Govt Audit, 1979-82. *Recreations*: golf, gardening, reading. *Address*: Norwood Edge, 8 Cyncoed Avenue, Cardiff CF2 6SU. *Club*: Cardiff and County (Cardiff).

FISHER, Rt. Rev. and Ven. Edward George; *see* Knapp-Fisher.

FISHER, Hon. Francis Forman, CBE 1980; MC 1944; Principal, Wolsey Hall, Oxford, since 1980; Master of Wellington College, 1966-80; *b* 25 Sept. 1919; 2nd *s* of late Most Rev. and Rt Hon. Lord Fisher of Lambeth, GCVO; unmarried. *Educ*: Repton; Clare Coll., Cambridge (MA). Commissioned, The Sherwood Foresters, 1940; served War of 1939-45, Middle East, and Western Desert (POW Tobruk, 1942); escaped from Italy and returned to England, 1943; demobilised, rank of Capt., 1946 (MC); returned to Cambridge, 1946; Asst Master, Repton Sch., 1947-54; Housemaster, 1948-54; Warden of St Edward's Sch., Oxford, 1954-66. Incorporated MA Oxford Univ. through Christ Church, 1955. Chm., Headmaster's Conf., 1973. Governor: Rossall Sch.; Repton Sch.; Dragon Sch.; Caldicott and Horris Hill Prep. Schs; Chairman of Governors: Mount House Sch.; Greycotes Sch. Dir, Ecclesiastical Insurance Office Ltd. *Recreations*: cricket, hockey (rep. CUHC *v* Oxford, 1947), and other games. *Address*: New Barn, Cassington Road, Yarnton, Oxford. *T*: Kidlington 6717. *Clubs*: East India, Devonshire, Sports and Public Schools; Hawks (Cambridge).

See also Hon. Sir Henry A. P. Fisher.

FISHER, Francis George Robson, MA Oxon; Deputy Secretary, Headmasters' Conference and Secondary Heads' Association, since 1982; *b* 9 April 1921; *s* of late John Henry Fisher and Hannah Clayton Fisher; *m* 1965, Sheila Vernon, *o d* of late D. Dunsire and Mrs H. E. Butt; one *s*. *Educ*: Liverpool Coll. (Schol.); Worcester Coll., Oxford (Classical Exhibitioner). Served War of 1939-45; Capt. in Ayrshire Yeomanry, North Africa and Italy, 1942-45. Housemaster and Senior English Master, Kingswood Sch., Bath, 1950-59; Headmaster, Bryanston Sch., 1959-74; Chief Master, King Edward's Sch., Birmingham, and Head Master, Sch. of King Edward VI in Birmingham, 1974-82. Chairman: HMC Direct Grant Sub-Cttee, 1979-80; HMC Assisted Places Sub-Cttee, 1981. Governor, Harrow Sch., 1982-. *Recreations*: music, lawn tennis, sailing. *Address:* 4 Putney Common, SW15 1HL. *T:* 01-788 3879.

FISHER, Prof. Frederick Jack, MA; Professor of Economic History, London School of Economics, University of London, 1954-75; *b* 22 July 1908; *s* of A. H. Fisher, Southend-on-Sea; *m* 1943, Barbara Vivienne, *d* of J. E. Whisstock, Southend-on-Sea; one *s* one *d. Educ:* Southend High Sch.; London Sch. of Economics. MA. Served RAF, 1941-46. Asst Lecturer and Lecturer in Economic History, London Sch. of Economics, 1935-47; Reader in Economic History, 1947-54. FRHistS. Wiles' Lectr, QUB, 1973. *Publications:* (ed) Essays in the Economic and Social History of Tudor and Stuart England, 1961; (ed) Calendar of Manuscripts of Lord Sackville of Knole, vol II, 1966; contrib. Economica, Economic History Review. *Address:* 22 Lyndale Avenue, NW2.

FISHER, Fredy; *see* Fisher, M. H.

FISHER, Sir George Read, Kt 1967; CMG 1961; Mining Engineer; President, MIM Holdings Ltd, 1970-75; *b* 23 March 1903; *s* of George Alexander and Ellen Harriett Fisher; *m* 1st, 1927, Eileen Elaine Triggs (*d* 1966); one *s* three *d* ; 2nd, 1973, Marie C. Gilbey. *Educ:* Prince Alfred Coll., Adelaide; Adelaide Univ. (BE). Formerly Gen. Manager of Operations for Zinc Corporation Ltd, Broken Hill, NSW; Chm., Mount Isa Mines Ltd, 1953-70. *Recreations:* shooting and bowling. *Address:* GPO Box 2236, Brisbane, Qld 4001, Australia. *Clubs:* Queensland, Brisbane (Brisbane).

FISHER, Harold Wallace; Director, 1959-69, and Vice-President, 1962-69, Exxon Corporation, formerly Standard Oil Company (New Jersey) New York, retired; *b* 27 Oct. 1904; *s* of Dean Wallace Fisher and Grace Cheney Fisher; *m* 1930, Hope Elisabeth Case; one *s. Educ:* Massachusetts Institute of Technology (BSc). Joined Standard Oil Company (NJ), 1927; Dir Esso Standard Oil Co. and Pres. Enjay Co. Inc., 1945. Resided in London, 1954-59. UK Rep. for Standard Oil Co. (NJ) and Chm. of its Coordination Cttee for Europe, 1954-57; Joint Managing Dir, Iraq Petroleum Co. Ltd and Associated Companies, 1957-59. Mem., Marine Bd, Nat. Acad. of Engineering, 1971-74; Vice-Chm., Sloan-Kettering Inst. for Cancer Research, 1974-75 (Chm., 1970-74); Mem., MIT Corp. Develt Cttee, 1975-; Vice-Chm., and Chm. Exec. Cttee, Community Blood Council of Greater New York, 1969-71. Hon. DSc 1960, Clarkson Coll. of Technology, Nat. Acad. of Engrg. *Publications:* various patents and technical articles relating to the Petroleum Industry. *Recreations:* golf, photography, horology. *Address:* 68 Goose Point Lane, PO Box 1792, Duxbury, Mass 02332, USA. *Clubs:* Pilgrims, American; University (New York); Duxbury Yacht.

FISHER, Hon. Sir Henry (Arthur Pears), Kt 1968; President, Wolfson College, Oxford, since March 1975; *b* 20 Jan. 1918; *e s* of late Lord Fisher of Lambeth, PC, GCVO; *m* 1948, Felicity, *d* of late Eric Sutton; one *s* three *d. Educ:* Marlborough; Christ Church, Oxford (Schol.); Gaisford Greek Prose Prize, 1937; 1st Cl. Hon. Mods 1938; BA 1942; MA 1943. Served Leics Regt, 1940-46; Staff Coll., Quetta, 1943; GSO2, 1943-44. GSO1 HQ 14th Army, 1945. Hon. Lieut-Col 1946 (despatches). Fellow of All Souls Coll., 1946-73, Emeritus, 1976-, Estates Bursar, 1961-66, Sub-Warden, 1965-67. Barrister, Inner Temple, 1947, Bencher, 1966; QC 1960; Recorder of Canterbury, 1962-68; a Judge of the High Court of Justice, Queen's Bench Div., 1968-70; Director: J. Henry Schroder Wagg & Co. Ltd, 1970-75; Schroder International Ltd, 1973-75; Thomas Tilling Ltd, 1970-; Equity and Law Life Assurance Soc. Ltd, 1975-. Mem., Gen. Council of the Bar, 1959-63, 1964-68, Vice-Chm., 1965-66, Chm., 1966-68; Vice-Pres., Senate of the Four Inns of Court, 1966-68; Vice-Pres., Bar Assoc. for Commerce, Finance and Industry, 1973-. Chairman: Cttee of Inquiry into Abuse of the Social Security System, 1971; City Cttee on Company Law, 1974-76; Cttee of Inquiry into self-regulation at Lloyd's, 1979-80; Appeal Cttee, Panel on Take-overs and Mergers, 1981-; Jt Commn on the Constitution (set up by Social Democratic and Liberal Parties), 1981-. Conducted inquiry into Confait case, 1976-77. Member: Private Internat. Law Cttee, 1961-63; Coun. on Tribunals, 1962-65; Law Reform Cttee, 1963-66; Council, Marlborough Coll., 1967- (Chm., 1977-82); BBC Programmes Complaints Commn, 1972-79; Governing Body, Imperial Coll., 1973- (Chm., 1975-); Trustee, Pilgrim Trust, 1965- (Chm., 1979-). Hon. LLD Hull, 1979. *Recreations:* music, walking. *Address:* Wolfson College, Oxford OX2 6UD. *T:* Oxford 56711. *Club:* Travellers'.
See also Hon. F. F. Fisher.

FISHER, Rev. James Atherton; *b* 1 May 1909; *s* of Rev. Legh Atherton Fisher and Beatrice Edith Fisher; *m* 1938, Joan Gardiner Budden; two *s* one *d. Educ:* Haileybury; Sidney Sussex Coll., Cambridge (Scholar); 1st cl. Theological Tripos Pts I and II (Senior Scofield Prize); Cuddesdon Theological Coll; BA 1932, MA 1945; Deacon 1933; Priest, 1934; Asst Curate: St Matthew's, Oxhey, 1933-36; The Priory Church, Dunstable, 1936-39; Chaplain of Bedford Sch., 1939-43; Vicar of St Paul's, Peterborough, 1943-53; Religious Broadcasting Asst, BBC, 1953-58; Chaplain of St Christopher's Coll., Blackheath, 1954-58; Chaplain of Heathfield Sch., Ascot, 1959-64. Canon of St George's, Windsor, 1958-78; Treasurer, 1962-77; Founder Mem., Council of St George's House, Windsor Castle, 1966-78 (resp. for Clergy trng, 1966-74). *Address:* 32 High Lawn, Devizes, Wilts. *T:* Devizes 4254.
See also P. A. Fisher.

FISHER, James Neil; Senior Partner, Theodore Goddard & Co., Solicitors, since 1980 (Partner, 1951); *b* 27 May 1917; *s* of Henry John Fisher and Ethel

Marie Fisher; *m* 1953, Elizabeth Mary Preston; one *s* two *d. Educ:* Harrow Sch.; Balliol Coll., Oxford (MA). Served War, Royal Signals, 1940-46 (Major 1945). Admitted solicitor, 1949. *Recreations:* the piano, walking, reading. *Address:* Ridge Lea, Oak Avenue, Sevenoaks, Kent TN13 1PR. *Club:* City University.

FISHER, Sir John, Kt 1942; Shipowner; *b* 1892; *s* of James Fisher, Barrow-in-Furness; *m* 1947, Maria, *d* of Richard Elsner, Vienna, Austria. *Educ:* Sedbergh; Malvern. President, James Fisher and Sons Limited (Chairman, 1915-76); Chm., Barrow Housing Company Ltd. Mem. Council, Chamber of Shipping of UK, 1935-74; Chm., Coasting & Home Trade Tramp Section, Chamber of Shipping of UK, 1935-39; Mem., Transport Adv. Council, 1934-39; Chm., Coastal Shipping Adv. Cttee, 1957-62; Dir Coasting and Short Sea Shipping, Min. of War Transport, 1939-46; Chm. United Maritime Authority, European Area, 1945-46; Pres. Baltic and International Maritime Conf., 1951-53. FICS. Freeman: Shipwrights' Co.; Borough of Barrow-in-Furness. Served European War, 1914-18, with King's Own Royal Lancaster Regt (Staff Capt. 154 Inf. Brigade, 51st Div., 1915-16). Comdr, Order of Orange Nassau (Netherlands); Officer, Order of Merite Maritime (France); Kt Comdr, Order of Isabel la Católica (Spain); Comdr, Order of Infante Dom Henrique (Portugal). *Address:* Blakeholme Wray, Newby Bridge, Cumbria. *T:* 345. *Club:* Windermere Royal Yacht (Windermere).

FISHER, John Mortimer, CMG 1962; HM Diplomatic Service, retired; part-time Course Director (European Training), Civil Service College, since 1971; *b* 20 May 1915; *yr s* of late Capt. Mortimer Fisher (W Yorks Regt) and Mrs M. S. Fisher (*née* Bailey); *m* 1949, Helen Bridget Emily Caillard; two *s. Educ:* Wellington; Trinity Coll., Cambridge. Entered Consular (subseq. Diplomatic) Service, 1937; Probationer Vice-Consul, Bangkok, 1938. Served at Casablanca, 1942, Naples, 1943; 1st Sec. in Foreign Office, 1946, Mexico City, 1949; Detroit, Mich., USA, 1952; Counsellor in charge of British Information Services, Bonn, 1955; an Inspector in HM Foreign Service, 1959; Counsellor and Consul-Gen. at Bangkok, 1962; Consul-General, Düsseldorf, 1966-70. *Address:* The North Garden, Treyford, Midhurst, West Sussex. *T:* Harting 448.

FISHER, Ven. Leslie Gravatt; Archdeacon of Chester and Canon Residentiary of Chester Cathedral, 1965-75; Vice-Dean, 1973-75; Archdeacon Emeritus since 1975; *b* 18 Aug. 1906; *m* 1935, Dorothy Minnie, (*née* Nash); two *d. Educ:* Hertford Grammar Sch.; London Coll. of Divinity. ALCD 1933. Deacon, 1933; Priest 1934. Curate of Emmanuel, Northwood, 1933-36; Vicar of St Michael and All Angels, Blackheath Park, 1936-39; Rector of Bermondsey, 1939-47; Curate-in-charge, Christ Church, Bermondsey, 1942-47; Chap., Bermondsey Med. Mission Hosp., 1946-47; Home Sec., CMS, and Licensed Preacher, Diocese of Southwark, 1947-; License to Officiate, Bromley, Dio. of Rochester, 1948-. Chm., Church Information Cttee, 1966-75. *Recreations:* music and photography. *Address:* 14 Lamb Park, Chagford, Newton Abbot, Devon. *T:* Chagford 3308.

FISHER, Mrs Margery Lilian Edith; free-lance writer, editor of review journal; *b* 21 March 1913; *d* of late Sir Henry Turner, and late Edith Rose; *m* 1936, James Maxwell McConnell Fisher (*d* 1970); three *s* three *d. Educ:* Rangi Ruru Sch., Christchurch, NZ; Amberley House Sch., NZ; Somerville Coll., Oxford (MA, BLitt). 1st Cl. Hons English, Oxford. Taught English at Queen Anne's Sch., Caversham, and Oundle Sch., 1939-45; coach for university scholarships and entrance exams; some broadcasting (BBC) of book reviews, free-lance lectr; Editor and proprietor of Growing Point (private jl reviewing children's books); Children's Books Editor, Sunday Times. Eleanor Farjeon Award, 1966; May Arbuthnot Award, USA, 1970. *Publications:* (with James Fisher) Shackleton, a biography, 1957; Intent upon Reading (criticism), 1961, rev. edn 1964; Field Day (novel), 1951; Matters of Fact, 1972; Who's Who in Children's Books, 1975; articles in Review of English Studies. *Recreations:* music, gardening. *Address:* Ashton Manor, Northampton NN7 2JL. *T:* Roade 862277.

FISHER, Maurice, CEng, FRINA, FIIM; RCNC; General Manager, HM Dockyard, Rosyth, since 1979; *b* 8 Feb. 1924; *s* of William Ernest Fisher and Lily Edith (*née* Hatch); *m* 1955, Stella Leslie Sumsion; one *d. Educ:* St Luke's Sch., Portsmouth; Royal Dockyard Sch., Portsmouth; Royal Naval Coll., Greenwich. Constructor-in-Charge, HM Dockyard, Simonstown, 1956-60; Staff of Director of Naval Construction, 1960-63; Staff of C-in-C Western Fleet, 1963-65; Dep. Supt, Admiralty Experiment Works, Haslar, 1965-68; Dep. Prodn Manager, HM Dockyard, Devonport, 1968-72; Personnel Manager, HM Dockyard, Portsmouth, 1972-74; Planning Manager, 1974-77, Prodn Manager, 1977-79, HM Dockyard, Devonport. *Recreation:* game fishing. *Address:* 5a Main Street, Crossford, by Dunfermline, Fife KY12 8NJ. *T:* Dunfermline 36446.

FISHER, Max Henry, (Fredy Fisher); Director, S. G. Warburg & Co. Ltd, since 1981; *b* 30 May 1922; *s* of Fritz and Sophia Fischer; *m* 1952, Rosemary Margaret Maxwell; two *s* one *d. Educ:* Fichte-Gymnasium, Berlin; Rendcomb Coll.; Lincoln Coll., Oxford. FO Library, working on German War Documents project, 1949-56; Vis. Lectr, Melbourne Univ., 1956; Financial Times, 1957-80, Editor, 1973-80. Director: Pearson Longman, 1979-; Commercial Union Assurance Co., 1981-; Booker McConnell, 1981-. Governor, LSE. Mem. Council, Policy Studies Inst. *Publication:* (ed with N. R. Rich) The Holstein Papers. *Recreations:* reading, listening to music.

Address: 16 Somerset Square, Addison Road, W14 8EE. *T:* 01-603 9841. *Club:* Reform.

FISHER, Rt. Rev. Brother Michael, SSF, (Reginald Lindsay Fisher); *see* St Germans, Bishop Suffragan of.

FISHER, Prof. Michael Ellis, FRS 1971; Horace White Professor of Chemistry, Physics and Mathematics, since 1973, Chairman, Department of Chemistry, 1975–78, Cornell University; *b* 3 Sept. 1931; *s* of Harold Wolf Fisher and Jeanne Marie Fisher (*née* Halter); *m* 1954, Sorrel Castillejo; three *s* one *d. Educ:* King's Coll., London. BSc 1951, PhD 1957, FKC 1981. Flying Officer (Educn), RAF, 1951–53; London Univ. Postgraduate Studentship, 1953–56; DSIR Sen. Research Fellow, 1956–58. King's Coll., London: Lectr in Theoretical Physics, 1958–62; Reader in Physics, 1962–64; Prof. of Physics, 1965–66; Prof. of Chemistry and Maths, Cornell Univ., 1966–73. Guest Investigator, Rockefeller Inst., New York, 1963–64; Visiting Prof. in Applied Physics, Stanford Univ., 1970–71; Lectures: Buhl, Carnegie-Mellon, 1971; 32nd Richtmyer Meml, 1973; 17th Fritz London Meml, 1975; Morris Loeb, Harvard, 1979; H. L. Welsh, Toronto, 1979; Bakerian, Royal Soc., 1979; Welch Foundn, Texas, 1979; Alpheas Smith, Ohio State Univ., 1982; Walter Ames Prof., Univ. of Washington, 1977; Vis. Prof. of Physics, MIT, 1979. John Simon Guggenheim Memorial Fellow, 1970–71, 1978–79; Fellow, Amer. Acad. of Arts and Scis, 1979; Irving Langmuir Prize in Chemical Physics, 1970; Award in Phys. and Math. Scis, NY Acad. of Scis, 1978; Guthrie Medal, Inst. of Physics, 1980; Wolf Prize in Physics, 1980; FKC 1981; Michelson-Morely Award, Case-Western Reserve Univ., 1982. *Publications:* Analogue Computing at Ultra-High Speed (with D. M. MacKay), 1962; The Nature of Critical Points, (Univ. of Colorado) 1964, (Moscow) 1968; contribs to Proc. Roy. Soc., Phys. Rev., Jl Sci. Insts, Jl Math. Phys., Arch. Rational Mech. Anal., Jl Chem. Phys., Rept Prog. Phys., Rev. Mod. Phys., Physica, etc. *Recreations:* Flamenco guitar, travel. *Address:* Baker Laboratory, Cornell University, Ithaca, New York 14853, USA. *T:* (607) 256 4205.

FISHER, Nancy Kathleen; *see* Trenaman, N. K.

FISHER, Sir Nigel (Thomas Loveridge), Kt 1974; MC 1945; MA (Cambridge); MP (C) Kingston-upon-Thames, Surbiton, since 1974 (Herts, Hitchin, 1950–55, Surbiton, 1955–74); *b* 14 July 1913; *s* of late Comdr Sir Thomas Fisher, KBE, Royal Navy and of late Lady Shakespeare; step *s* of Rt Hon. Sir Geoffrey Shakespeare, 1st Bt; *m* 1935, Lady Gloria Vaughan (marr. diss. 1952), *e d* of 7th Earl of Lisburne; one *s* one *d* ; *m* 1956, Patricia, *o d* of late Lieut-Col Sir Walter Smiles, CIE, DSO, DL, MP (*see* Lady Fisher). *Educ:* Eton; Trinity Coll., Cambridge. Hons Degree, Law, Cambridge, 1934. Served War of 1939–45; volunteered Welsh Guards and commissioned as 2nd Lieut 1939; Hook of Holland, Boulogne, 1940 (despatches); Capt., 1940; Major, 1944; N West Europe, 1945 (wounded, MC). Mem., National Executive Cttee of Conservative Party, 1945–47 and 1973–; contested Chislehurst (N Kent), Gen. Election, 1945. Mem. British Parl. Deleg. to Sweden, 1950, W Indies 1955, Malta 1966, Canada 1966, Uganda 1967, special mission to St Kitts, Anguilla, 1967. Parly Private Sec. to Minister of Food, 1951–54, to Home Sec., 1954–57; Parly Under-Sec. of State for the Colonies, July 1962–Oct. 1963; Parly Under-Sec. of State for Commonwealth Relations and for the Colonies, 1963–64; Opposition Spokesman for Commonwealth Affairs, 1964–66. Treasurer, CPA, 1966–68 (Vice-Chm., 1975–76; Treasurer, 1977–79, Dep. Chm., 1979–, UK Branch). Mem. Exec., 1922 Cttee, 1960–62, 1969–. Vice-Pres., Building Socs Assoc. Pres., British Caribbean Assoc. Member: Executive Committee and Council, Save the Children Fund; Churchill Meml Trust; Heritage of London Trust; Commonwealth Soc. for the Blind. *Publications:* Iain Macleod, 1973; The Tory Leaders, 1977; Harold Macmillan, 1982. *Recreations:* tennis, riding, walking. *Address:* 16 North Court, Great Peter Street, Westminster, SW1. *T:* 01-222 3532; Portavo Point, Donaghadee, Co. Down, N Ireland. *T:* 882435; St George's Court, St George's Bay, Malta, GC. *Club:* MCC.

FISHER, Mrs O. H.; *see* Anderson, Marian.

FISHER, Patricia, (Lady Fisher); Founder and Co-Chairman, Women Caring Trust; *b* 5 April 1921; *d* of late Lieut-Col Sir W. D. Smiles, CIE, DSO, DL, MP for N Down; *m* 1st, 1941, Capt. Neville M. Ford (marr. diss., 1956), 2nd *s* of late Dr Lionel Ford, Headmaster of Harrow and Dean of York; two *d* ; 2nd, 1956, Sir Nigel Fisher, *qv. Educ:* privately and abroad. MP (UU) North Down (unopposed return), April 1953-55 (as Mrs Patricia Ford). *Recreations:* sailing, travel. *Address:* 16 North Court, Great Peter Street, SW1; Portavo Point, Donaghadee, Co. Down, N Ireland. *T:* 882435. *See also W. M. J. Grylls.*

FISHER, (Phyllis) Anne; Headmistress, Wycombe Abbey School, 1962–74; *b* 8 March 1913; *d* of Rev. L. A. Fisher, Rector of Higham on the Hill, Nuneaton, and Beatrice Fisher (*née* Eustace). *Educ:* Sch. of St Mary and St Anne, Abbots Bromley; Bristol Univ. BA History Hons, 1938. Senior History Mistress: St Helen's, Northwood, 1938–41; St Anne's Coll., Natal, SA, 1941–44; Headmistress, St Winifred's Sch., George, SA, 1944–45; Joint Headmistress, St George's, Ascot, 1946–49; Headmistress, Limuru Girls' Sch., Limuru, Kenya, 1949–57; Headmistress, Arundel Sch., Salisbury, Rhodesia, 1957–61. *Recreations:* study of old churches, the history of painting. *Address:* 7 Selwyn House, Selwyn Road, Eastbourne BN21 2LF. *Clubs:* Royal Commonwealth Society, Landsdowne.

See also J. A. Fisher.

FISHER, Rear-Adm. Ralph Lindsay, CB 1957; DSO 1940; OBE 1941; DSC 1943; *b* 18 June 1903; *s* of F. Lindsay Fisher, CBE, one-time Pres. Inst. of Chartered Accountants, and late Owen Pugh, Caernarvon; *m* 1934, Ursula Carver, Torquay; five *d. Educ:* Osborne and Dartmouth. First went to sea, 1920; Commanded: HMS Wakeful, 1940 (Dunkirk, DSO); Musketeer, 1943–45 (sinking of Scharnhorst, DSC); Solebay, 1947–48; Indefatigable, 1952–54. Naval Staff Course, 1934; Jt Services Staff Coll., 1949; Flag Officer Ground Trng (Home Air Comd), 1954–57. Retd, 1957. *Recreation:* sailing. *Address:* Scotnish Farm, by Lochgilphead, Argyll. *T:* Tayvallich 260. *Clubs:* Naval and Military, Royal Cruising.

FISHER, Prof. Reginald Brettauer, CBE 1966; Professor of Biochemistry, University of Edinburgh, 1959–76, Dean of Faculty of Medicine, 1972–75; engaged in research, Medical Research Council, 1976–79, and postgraduate teaching, since 1976; *b* 13 Feb. 1907; *s* of late Joseph Sudbury and Louie Fisher; *m* 1929, Mary, *d* of late C. W. Saleeby; one *s* three *d. Educ:* King Edward VII Sch., Sheffield; St John's Coll., Oxford. MA, DPhil (Oxon), 1933. University Demonstrator in Biochemistry, Oxford, 1933–59; Rockefeller Travelling Fellow, 1939; Research Officer (on secondment), Min. of Home Security, 1942; Air Ministry, 1943–45; Consultant, US War Dept, 1945. Member: Physiological Soc.; Royal Society of Medicine. *Publications:* Protein Metabolism, 1954; contributions to: Biochem. Jl; Jl Physiol.; Jl Biol. Chem.; Am. Jl Physiol., etc. *Address:* University Laboratory of Physiology, Parks Road, Oxford.

FISHER, Richard Colomb; HM Diplomatic Service, retired; *b* Hankow, 11 Nov. 1923; *s* of Comdr Richard Fisher, RN and late Phillipa (*née* Colomb), Lee-on-Solent; *m* 1946, Edwine Kempers; two *s. Educ:* RNC Dartmouth. Joined Navy, 1937; to sea as Midshipman, 1941; War Service in submarines, 1943–45, Far East; flying trng, 1946–47; specialised in navigation/direction, 1948; Comdr 1958; retd from RN and joined Diplomatic Service, 1969; 1st Sec., Bonn, 1970–73; Commercial Counsellor, Warsaw, 1973–76, Rome, 1976–79. *Recreations:* history, languages. *Address:* c/o Natwest Bank, Osborne Road, Southsea, Hants. *Club:* Army and Navy.

FISHER, Sylvia Gwendoline Victoria; (Signora U. Gardini); Principal Soprano, Royal Opera House, London; *d* of John Fisher and Margaret Fisher (*née* Frawley); *m* 1954, Ubaldo Gardini. *Educ:* St Joseph's Coll., Kilmore, Australia; Conservatorium of Music, Melbourne. Won "Sun" Aria Competition, Melbourne, 1936; International Celebrity Concert in Australia, 1947; tour of Australia, 1955. Operatic Debut in Cadmus and Hermione, 1932; Covent Garden Debut in Fidelio (Leonora), 1948. Appeared in: Rome (Sieglinde), 1952; Cagliari (Isolde), 1954; Bologna (Gutrune), 1955; Covent Garden (Brunnhilde), 1956; Frankfurt Opera House (in Der Rosenkavalier), 1957, etc. *Recreations:* gardening and rare books on singing. *Address:* 24 Dawson Place, W2. *T:* 01-229 0175.

FISHER, Thomas Gilbert F.; *see* Field-Fisher.

FISHER, Prof. William Bayne, DUP; Professor of Geography, University of Durham, 1956–81, now Emeritus; first Principal of the Graduate Society, Durham University, 1965–81; *b* 24 Sept. 1916; unmarried. *Educ:* Darwen Gram. Sch.; Universities of Manchester, Louvain, Paris. Research Scholar, Univ. of Manchester, 1937; RAF 1940; Liaison Officer to French in Syria and Lebanon, 1944; Asst Lectr, Univ. of Manchester, 1946; Lectr, Univ. of Aberdeen, 1947; Carnegie Fellow, 1951; Reader, Univ. of Durham, 1954; Dir, Centre of Middle Eastern and Islamic Studies, Durham Univ., 1963–65; Vis. Prof., Leuven Univ., 1978–79. Murchison Award, RGS, 1973. *Publications:* Les Mouvements de population en Normandie, 1940; The Middle East, a Physical Social and Regional Geography, 1951; (with H. Bowen-Jones) Spain, a geographical background; (with H. Bowen-Jones and J. C. Dewdney) Malta, 1961; (Ed) The Cambridge History of Iran, Vol. I (The Land of Iran), 1968; (with J. I. Clarke) Populations of the Middle East and North Africa, 1972; (with P. W. Kent) Resources, Environment and the Future, 1982; various articles in periodicals and works of reference. *Recreations:* music, travel, geographical gastronomy. *Address:* Abbey View, 42 South Street, Durham. *T:* Durham 64291. *Club:* Athenæum.

FISKE, Dudley Astley; Education Officer, Association of Metropolitan Authorities, since 1982; *b* 16 June 1929; *s* of Tom Fiske and late Barbara Fiske; *m* 1958, Patricia Elizabeth, *d* of late Donald MacIver and of Helen MacIver, Weybridge; two *s* one *d. Educ:* Berkhamsted Sch.; Merton Coll., Oxford (MA). Asst Master, Barnard Castle Sch., 1953–56; Asst Tutor, Oxford Univ. Dept of Educn, 1956–58; Admin. Asst, East Sussex, 1959–60; Asst Educn Officer, Berkshire, 1961–65; Dep. Educn Officer, Leeds, 1965–68; Chief Educn Officer, Manchester, 1968–82. Mem. Adv. Council on Penal System, 1970–73; Mem., Clothing and Allied Products ITB, 1969–72; Pres., Educnl Develt Assoc., 1969–74; Mem., Business Educn Council, 1974–80; Mem., Adv. Cttee on Supply and Trng of Teachers, 1974–; President: British Educnl Equipment Assoc., 1973–74; Soc. of Educn Officers, 1978; Commonwealth Educn Fellow in Australia, 1974. *Publications:* articles and reviews in educnl jls. *Recreations:* foreign travel, theatre and cinema-going, reading. *Address:* c/o Association of Metropolitan Authorities, 36 Old Queen Street, SW1H 9JE. *Club:* Royal Commonwealth Society.

FISON, Sir (Frank Guy) Clavering, Kt 1957; JP; DL; Chairman, Fisons Ltd, 1929–62; *b* 1892; *er* surv. *s* of late J. O. Fison, of Stutton Hall, Ipswich; *m* 1922, Evelyn Alice (OBE 1964), *er d* of late F. L. Bland Rookwood,

Copdock, Ipswich; two *d. Educ:* Charterhouse; Christ Church, Oxford. Joined Fisons, 1919; retired 1962. MP (U) Woodbridge Div. of Suffolk, 1929-31. Hon. Life Pres., Fisons Ltd. JP East Suffolk, 1942; High Sheriff 1942, DL 1958, Suffolk. *Address:* Crepping Hall, Stutton, Ipswich, Suffolk IP9 2SZ.

FISON, Sir Guy; *see* Fison, Sir R. G.

FISON, Sir (Richard) Guy, 4th Bt *cr* 1905; DSC 1944; Director: Saccone & Speed Ltd since 1952 (Chairman, 1979-82); Whitehead Mann Ltd, since 1982; Chairman, Percy Fox & Co. Ltd; *b* 9 Jan. 1917; *er s* of Sir William Guy Fison, 3rd Bt; *S* father, 1964; *m* 1952, Elyn Hartmann; one *s* one *d. Educ:* Eton; New Coll., Oxford. Served RNVR, 1939-45. Entered Wine Trade, 1948. Master of Wine, 1954; Pres., Wine and Spirit Assoc., 1977-78; Chm., Wine Develt Bd, 1982-. Hon. Freeman, 1976, Renter Warden, 1981-82, Upper Warden, 1982-83, Vintners' Co. *Heir: s* Charles William Fison, *b* 6 Feb. 1954. *Address:* Wingate, Long Sutton, Basingstoke, Hants. *T:* Long Sutton 576.

FISTOULARI, Anatole; Principal Conductor of London Philharmonic Orchestra, 1943, now guest conductor; *b* Kiev, Russia, 20 Aug. 1907; obtained British nationality, 1948; *s* of Gregor and late Sophie Fistoulari; *m* 1942, Anna Mahler (marr. diss., 1956); one *d* ; 1957, Mary Elizabeth, *y d* of late James Lockhart, Edinburgh. *Educ:* Kiev, Berlin, and Paris. Conducted first concert at age of 7 at Opera House in Kiev and later all over Russia; at 13 gave concerts in Germany and Holland; at 24 conducted Grand Opera Russe in Paris at the Châtelet Theatre with Colonne Orchestra and Chaliapine with whom he then toured France and Spain; then conducted the Ballet de Monte-Carlo with Massine in Drury Lane and Covent Garden before the War; toured with same company all over America, France, and Italy; in England in 1941 started opera production of Sorotchinsky Fair by Moussorgsky; March 1942 gave first Symphony Concert with London Symphony Orchestra and later conducted it regularly at Cambridge Theatre; first concert with London Philharmonic Orchestra in Bristol, Jan. 1943; concert engagements in numerous countries, from 1949. Founder, 1946, and Principal Conductor, London Internat. Orch. Guest conductor for Sadler's Wells Ballet, Royal Opera House, Covent Garden and NY Metropolitan Opera House, 1955; on tour with London Philharmonic Orchestra, to Moscow, Leningrad, Paris, 1956. Has made recordings for several firms. *Recreation:* listening to good concerts. *Address:* 65 Redington Road, NW3. *Club:* Savage.

FITCH, Alan; *see* Fitch, E. A.

FITCH, Douglas Bernard Stocker, FRICS; Chief Surveyor, Agricultural Development and Advisory Service, Ministry of Agriculture, Fisheries and Food, since 1980; *b* 16 April 1927; *s* of William Kenneth Fitch and Hilda Barrington; *m* 1952, Joyce Vera Griffiths; three *s. Educ:* St Albans Sch.; Royal Agricl Coll. (Dip. 1951). FRICS 1977. Served Army, RE, 1944-48. Joined Land Service, MAFF, 1951; Divl Surveyor, Guildford, 1971; Regional Surveyor, SE Reg., 1979. Member: Gen. Council, and Land Agency and Agric. Divl Council, RICS, 1980-; Bd of Governors, Royal Agricl Coll., 1981-. *Recreations:* golf, re-building old cars, allotmenteering. *Address:* Ministry of Agriculture, Fisheries and Food, Great Westminster House, Horseferry Road, SW1P 2AE. *T:* 01-216 6281. *Clubs:* Farmers', Civil Service.

FITCH, (Ernest) Alan, JP; MP (Lab) Wigan Division, since June 1958; *b* 10 March 1915; *e s* of late Rev. and of Mrs E. W. Fitch; *m* 1950, Nancy Maude, *y d* of late R. Kennard Davis; one *s* one *d. Educ:* Kingswood Sch., Bath. Was formerly Mineworker. Asst Whip (paid), 1964-66; a Lord Comr of the Treasury, 1966-69; Vice-Chamberlain, HM Household, Oct. 1969-June 1970; Opposition Whip, 1970-71. Mem., Chairmen's Panel, 1971-78; Mem., European Parlt, 1978-79. Chm., North West Regional Council of the Labour Party. JP Lancs, 1958. Hon. Freeman, Co. Borough of Wigan, 1974. *Recreations:* reading, walking. *Address:* 117 The Avenue, Leigh, Lancs. *T:* Leigh 673992.

FITCH, Rear-Adm. Richard George Alison; Naval Secretary, since 1980; *b* 2 June 1929; *s* of Edward William Fitch and Agnes Jamieson Fitch; *m* 1969, Kathleen Marie-Louise Igert; one *s. Educ:* Royal Naval College, Dartmouth. Seagoing appointments, 1946-66; HMS Berwick in Command, 1966-67; Staff of Flag Officer, Second in Command, Far East Fleet, 1967-69; Directorate of Naval Plans, MoD, 1969-71; RCDS 1972; HMS Apollo in Command, 1973-74; Naval Asst to First Sea Lord, 1974-76; HMS Hermes in Command, 1976-78; Dir of Naval Warfare, 1978-80. Liveryman, Coachmakers' and Coach Harness Makers' Co. FBIM. *Recreations:* gardening, philately, following sport. *Address:* West Hay, 32 Sea Lane, Middleton-on-Sea, West Sussex PO22 7RT. *T:* Middleton-on-Sea 2361. *Clubs:* Royal Commonwealth Society; Middleton Sports.

FITCH, Rodney Arthur, FSIAD 1976; design consultant; Founder, 1971, major shareholder, Deputy Chairman and Creative Director, Fitch and Company (Design Consultants) Ltd; *b* 19 Aug. 1938; *s* of Arthur and Ivy Fitch; *m* 1965, Janet Elizabeth, *d* of Sir Walter Stansfield, *qv* ; one *s* four *d. Educ:* Willesden Polytechnic, Sch. of Building and Architecture; Central School of Arts and Crafts (Theatre, TV Design); Hornsey School of Art (Interior and Furniture Design). Trainee designer, Hickman Ltd, 1956-58; National Service, RAPC, 1958-60; Charles Kenrick Associates, 1960-62;

Conran Design Gp Ltd, 1962-69; C.D.G. (Design Consultants) Ltd, 1969-71; thereafter, Fitch and Company, a multi-discipline design practice engaged on a wide range of UK and overseas projects embracing environmental design, airports, shops, stores, etc, with offices in London, Paris, Dubai and Abu Dhabi. Governor, St Martin's College of Art, 1976-. Vice-Pres., SIAD, 1982. FRSA 1976. *Publications:* regular contributor to design publications. *Recreations:* horse riding, tennis, music, theatre, his family. *Address:* Flat 2, 24 Palace Court, Bayswater, W2. *T:* 01-229 7954.

FITCHEW, Geoffrey Edward; Assistant Secretary, HM Treasury, since 1980; *b* 22 Dec. 1939; *s* of Stanley Edward Fitchew and Elizabeth Scott; *m* 1966, Mary Theresa Spillane; two *s. Educ:* Uppingham School; Magdalen Coll., Oxford (MA); London Sch. of Economics (MScEcon). Asst Principal, HM Treasury, 1964; Private Sec. to Minister of State, 1968-69; Principal, 1969; Gwilym Gibbon Research Fellow, Nuffield Coll., Oxford, 1973-74; Asst Sec., Internat. Finance Div., HM Treasury, 1975-77; Counsellor (Economics and Finance), UK Perm. Rep. to EEC, 1977-80. *Recreations:* gardening, tennis, squash. *Address:* c/o HM Treasury, SW1.

FITT, Gerard; MP (Socialist) Belfast West; *b* 9 April 1926; *s* of George Patrick and Mary Ann Fitt; *m* 1947, Susan Gertrude Doherty; five *d* (and one *d* decd). *Educ:* Christian Brothers' Sch., Belfast. Merchant Seaman, 1941-53; various positions, 1953-. Councillor, later Alderman, Belfast Corp., 1958-81; MP (Eire Lab), Parlt of N Ireland, Dock Div. of Belfast, 1962-72; Mem. (SDLP), N Belfast, NI Assembly, 1973-75, NI Constitutional Convention, 1975-76; Dep. Chief Exec., NI Exec., 1974; elected MP (Repub. Lab) 1966, a founder and Leader, Social Democratic and Labour Party, and MP (SDLP), 1970-79, when resigned Leadership, now sitting as a Socialist. *Recreation:* full-time politics. *Address:* 85 Antrim Road, Belfast, N Ireland BT15 2BJ. *T:* 743226.

FITT, Robert Louis, CMG 1975; *b* 9 Aug. 1905; *s* of late R. F. Fitt; *m* 1936, Elsie Ockleshaw, *d* of late William Ockleshaw, Liverpool; one *s. Educ:* Launceston and Barnstaple Grammar Schs; City and Guilds Coll., London. BSc; FCGI. Engineer with Sudan Govt, 1927-31; with Mott Hay & Anderson, on Mersey Tunnel and London Underground Extensions, 1931-39. Joined Sir Alexander Gibb & Partners, 1939; Partner, 1946; retired, 1978; responsible for industrial develts, irrigation works, water supplies, thermal and hydro-electric power projects, airports, and economic develt surveys, in countries incl. UK, Iran, Iraq, Sudan, Argentina, Kenya, Tanzania, Swaziland, Rhodesia, Australia and Jamaica. Chm., Assoc. of Consulting Engineers, 1961-62; Vice-Pres., Middle East Assoc., 1972, Pres., Internat. Fedn of Consulting Engrs (FIDIC), 1972-74. FEng, FICE (Vice-Pres., 1976-78). Order of Homayoun, Iran, Third Class, 1955. *Recreations:* gardening, golf. *Address:* 27 Longdown Lane North, Ewell, Surrey KT17 3HY. *T:* 01-393 1727. *Club:* East India, Devonshire, Sports and Public Schools.

FITTER, Richard Sidney Richmond; author and naturalist; *b* 1 March 1913; *o s* of Sidney and Dorothy Fitter; *m* 1938, Alice Mary (Maisie) Stewart, *e d* of Dr R. S. Park, Huddersfield; two *s* one *d. Educ:* Eastbourne Coll.; LSE. BSc(Econ). Research staff: PEP, 1936-40; Mass-Observation, 1940-42; Operational Research Section, Coastal Command, 1942-45; Sec., Wild Life Cons. Special Cttee of Hobhouse Cttee on Nat. Parks, 1945-46; Asst Editor, The Countryman, 1946-59; Open Air Corresp., The Observer, 1958-66; Dir, Intelligence Unit, Council for Nature, 1959-63; Editor, Kingfisher, 1965-72. Vice-Chm., Flora and Fauna Preservation Soc., 1981- (Hon. Secretary, 1964-81); Member: Survival Service Commn, Internat. Union for Cons. of Nature, 1963- (Chm., Steering Cttee, 1975-); Conservation Adv. Cttee, World Wildlife Fund Internat., 1977-79; Scientific Authority for Animals, DoE, 1965-81; Trustee, World Wildlife Fund, UK, 1977-; Past Pres., Berks, Bucks and Oxfordshire Naturalists' Trust; Chm., Council for Nature, 1979; Hon. Sec., Falkland Is Foundn, 1980-82; Minister's Representative, Southern Council for Sport and Recreation, 1980-; formerly Hon. Treasurer and Hon. Sec., British Trust for Ornithology; Chm., Gen. Purposes Cttee, Royal Soc. for Protection of Birds; Editor, The London Naturalist; and council or cttee mem. of numerous nat. history and conservation bodies. Scientific FZS. *Publications:* London's Natural History, 1945; London's Birds, 1949; Pocket Guide to British Birds, 1952; Pocket Guide to Nests and Eggs, 1954; (with David McClintock) Pocket Guide to Wild Flowers, 1956; The Ark in Our Midst, 1959; Six Great Naturalists, 1959; Guide to Bird Watching, 1963; Wildlife in Britain, 1963; Britain's Wildlife: rarities and introductions, 1966; (with Maisie Fitter) Penguin Dictionary of Natural History, 1967; Vanishing Wild Animals of the World, 1968; Finding Wild Flowers, 1972; Birds of Britain and Europe, with North Africa and the Middle East, 1972; (with A. Fitter and M. Blamey) Flowers of Britain and Northern Europe, 1974; The Penitent Butchers, 1979; (with M. Blamey) Handguide to the Wild Flowers of Britain and Northern Europe, 1979; (with M. Blamey) Gem Guide to Wild Flowers, 1980; (with N. Arlott and A. Fitter) The Complete Guide to British Wildlife, 1981; (ed with Eric Robinson) John Clare's Birds. *Recreations:* botanising, observing wild and human life, exploring new habitats, reading. *Address:* Drifts, Chinnor Hill, Oxford. *T:* Kingston Blount 51223. *Club:* Athenæum.

FITTS, Sir Clive (Hamilton), Kt 1963; MD Melbourne, FRCP, FRACP, DTM Sydney; retired 1978; formerly Consulting Physician to: Royal Melbourne Hospital; Royal Women's Hospital; Austin Hospital for Chronic Diseases; Victorian Tuberculosis Service; *b* 14 July 1900; *s* of Hamilton Fitts and Katherine Fitts (*née* Pardey); *m* 1939, Yrsa E., *d* of Prof. W. A. Osborne;

two s three d. *Educ:* Scotch Coll. and Melbourne Church of England Gram. Sch., Melbourne; Trinity Coll., University of Melbourne. Post-Graduate: England, Switzerland, USA; Carnegie Scholarship, 1948. Tudor Edwards Meml Lecture, RCP, 1967. Member: Brit. Cardiac Soc.; Brit. Thoracic Soc.; Med. Soc., London; Pres. Cardiac Soc. of Aust. and NZ, 1960; Vice-Pres. RACP, 1958; Hon. Life Mem., Nat. Heart Foundn of Australia, 1980 (Vice-Pres. and Mem. Exec. Cttee, 1960-65); formerly Mem. Council: University of Melbourne; Melbourne C of E Gram. Sch.; Chm. Felton Bequest Cttee; First Pres., Nat. Gall. Soc.; Hon. Life Mem., Friends of the Baillieu Library, Univ. of Melbourne, 1979; Fellow, Trinity Coll., Univ. of Melbourne, 1980. Formerly Mem. Commonwealth Drug Evaluation Cttee. Major AAMC Reserve. *Publications:* various papers on diseases of heart and lungs in medical journals. *Recreations:* mountaineering, tennis (represented University of Melbourne, and Victoria), fly fishing. *Address:* Tucks Road, Main Ridge, Victoria 3928, Australia. *T:* (059) 89.6003. *Clubs:* Beefsteak; Melbourne, Beefsteak (Melbourne).

FITZALAN-HOWARD, family name of **Lady Herries** and of **Duke of Norfolk.**

FITZALAN-HOWARD, Maj.-Gen. Lord Michael, GCVO 1981 (KCVO 1971; MVO 1952); CB 1968; CBE 1962; MC 1944; DL; Her Majesty's Marshal of the Diplomatic Corps, 1972-81; *b* 22 Oct. 1916; 2nd s of 3rd Baron Howard of Glossop, MBE, and Baroness Beaumont (11th in line), OBE; *b* of 17th Duke of Norfolk, *qv* ; granted title and precedence of a Duke's son, 1975; *m* 1st, 1946, Jean (*d* 1947), *d* of Sir Hew Hamilton-Dalrymple, 9th Bt; one *d* ; 2nd, 1950, Margaret, *d* of Capt. W. P. Meade-Newman; four *s* one *d. Educ:* Ampleforth Coll.; Trinity Coll., Cambridge. Joined Scots Guards, 1938. Served in: North West Europe, 1944-45; Palestine, 1945-46; Malaya, 1948-49; Egypt, 1952-53; Germany, 1956-57 and 1961-66; Commander Allied Command Europe Mobile Forces (Land), 1964-66; Chief of Staff, Southern Command, 1967-68; GOC London Dist, and Maj.-Gen. comdg The Household Division, 1968-71. Col: The Lancs Regt (Prince of Wales's Volunteers), 1966-70; The Queen's Lancashire Regiment, 1970-78; Colonel of The Life Guards, 1979-; Gold Stick to the Queen, 1979-; Joint Hon. Col, Cambridge Univ. OTC, 1968-71. Chm. Council, TAVR Assocs, 1973-81, Pres., 1981-. DL Wilts. 1974. *Address:* Fovant House, Fovant, Salisbury, Wilts. *T:* Fovant 617. *Clubs:* Turf, Buck's.

FITZCLARENCE, family name of **Earl of Munster.**

FitzCLARENCE, Viscount; Anthony Charles FitzClarence; stained glass conservator for Burrell collection, since 1979; *b* 21 March 1926; *s* and *heir* of 6th Earl of Munster, *qv* ; *m* 1st, 1949, Diane Delvigne (marr. diss. 1966); two *d* ; 2nd, 1966, Pamela Hyde (marr. diss. 1979); one *d* ; 3rd, 1979, Alexa Maxwell. *Educ:* St Edward's School, Oxford. Served RN, 1942-46, Mediterranean, Far East, Pacific. Graphic Designer, 1946-76. *Recreations:* carpentry, design of stained glass. *Address:* 17 Lowndes Street, Barrhead, Glasgow. *Club:* Chelsea Arts.

FITZER, Herbert Clyde, CB 1971; OBE 1958; Head of Royal Naval Engineering Service, 1970-71, Director of Engineering (Ships), Navy Department, Ministry of Defence, 1968-71, retired; *b* 3 Nov. 1910; *s* of Herbert John Fitzer; *m* 1938, Queenie Stent; one *d. Educ:* Portsmouth Royal Dockyard Sch.; RNC Greenwich; London Univ. 1st cl. hons BSc (Eng) London, 1932; Greenwich Professional Certif. in Electrical Engrg, 1933. CEng, FIEE 1959. Asst Elec. Engr, Admty, 1936; Sheerness Dockyard, 1938; Elec. Engr, Submarine Design, Admty, 1939; Shore Estabs, 1945; Suptg Elec. Engr, Submarine Design, 1950; Asst Dir of Elec. Engrg, Ships Power Systems, 1961; Polaris Project, 1963; Dep. Dir of Elec. Engrg, 1966. Licensed Lay Reader, Dio. Bath and Wells. *Publication:* Christian Flarepath, 1956. *Address:* Rosefield, Sway Road, Lymington SO4 8LR. *T:* Lymington 73238.

FitzGEORGE-BALFOUR, Gen. Sir (Robert George) Victor, KCB 1968 (CB 1965); CBE 1945; DSO 1950; MC 1939; DL; Chairman, National Fund for Research into Crippling Diseases, since 1975; *b* 15 Sept. 1913; *s* of Robert S. Balfour and Iris (*née* FitzGeorge), 47 Wilton Crescent, SW1; *m* 1943, Mary (Diana), *er d* of Rear-Adm. Arthur Christian, 3 Sloane Gardens, SW3; one *s* one *d. Educ:* King's Coll., Cambridge (BA). Commissioned 2nd Lieut Coldstream Guards, 1934; Palestine, 1936; Middle East, 1937-43; France and NW Germany, 1944-46; commanded 2nd Bn Coldstream Guards, Malaya, 1948-52; idc 1955; Chief of Staff to Governor of Cyprus, 1956; Commanded 1st Guards Brigade, 1957; Chief of Staff, HQ Southern Comd, 1962-63; Dir of Military Operations, Ministry of Defence, 1964-66; Senior Army Instructor, IDC, 1966-68; Vice-Chief of the General Staff, 1968-70; UK Mil. Representative, NATO, 1971-73. ADC (Gen.), 1972-73. Col Comdt, HAC, 1976-. DL West Sussex, 1977. Knight Commander of the Order of Orange Nassau with swords (Netherlands), 1946. *Address:* The Old Rectory, West Chiltington, West Sussex. *T:* West Chiltington 2255. *Club:* Army and Navy.

FITZGERALD, family name of **Duke of Leinster.**

FITZGERALD, Charles Patrick; Professor of Far Eastern History, Australian National University, 1953-67, now Emeritus; Visiting Fellow, Department International Relations, Australian National University, 1968-69; *b* 5 March 1902; *s* of Dr H. Sauer; *m* 1941, Pamela Knollys; three *d. Educ:* Clifton. China, 1923-27, 1930-32, 1936-38, 1946-50. Leverhulme Fellowship for

Anthropological Research in South-West China. DLitt ANU 1968. *Publications:* Son of Heaven, 1932; China, a Cultural History, 1935; The Tower of Five Glories, 1941; (with George Yeh) Introducing China, 1948; Revolution in China, 1951 (revised version (Penguin) as The Birth of Communist China, 1965); The Empress Wu, 1955; Flood Tide in China, 1958; Barbarian Beds: the origin of the chair in China, 1965; A Concise History of Eastern Asia, 1965; The Third China, Chinese Communities in SE Asia, 1965; Des Mantchous à Mao Tse-tong, 1968; History of China, 1969; Communism Takes China, 1970; The Southern Expansion of the Chinese People: Southern Fields and Southern Ocean, 1972; Mao Tsetung and China, 1976; Ancient China, 1978. *Address:* 82 Gloucester Terrace, W2; Odalengo Piccolo, 15020, Alessandria, Italy. *Club:* Savile.

FITZ-GERALD, Desmond John Villiers, (29th Knight of Glin); Irish Agent, Christie, Manson & Woods Ltd, since 1975; *b* 13 July 1937; *s* of Desmond Windham Otho Fitz-Gerald, 28th Knight of Glin (*d* 1949), and Veronica (who *m* 2nd, 1954, Ray Milner, CC (Canada), QC, Edmonton, Alta, and Qualicum Beach, Vancouver Island, BC), 2nd *d* of late Ernest Amherst Villiers, MP, and of Hon. Elaine Augusta Guest, *d* of 1st Baron Wimborne; *m* 1st, 1966, Louise Vava Lucia Henriette (marr. diss. 1970), *d* of the Marquis de la Falaise, Paris; 2nd, 1970, Olda Ann, *o d* of T. V. W. Willes, 39 Brompton Sq., SW3; three *d. Educ:* Stowe Sch.; University of British Columbia (BA 1959); Harvard Univ. (MA 1961). FSA 1970. Asst Keeper, 1965-72, Dep. Keeper, 1972-75, Dept of Furniture and Woodwork, V&A. Director: Irish Architectural Archive (Dublin), 1976-; Historic Irish Tourist Houses Assoc., 1977-; Castletown Foundn, 1979-. Vice-Pres., Irish Georgian Soc. Mem., Heritage Gardens Cttee, An Taisce (Irish National Trust), 1978-; Mem. Steering Cttee, Internat. Union of Historic Houses Assocs, 1981-. *Publications:* (ed) Georgian Furniture, 1969; (with Maurice Craig) Ireland Observed, a handbook to the buildings and antiquities, 1970; The Music Room from Norfolk House, 1972; (with Edward Malins) Lost Demesnes: Irish Landscape Gardening 1660-1845, 1976; (with Anne Crookshank) The Painters of Ireland, 1978; Irish Furniture, 1978; Catalogues: Irish Houses and Landscapes (jointly), 1963; Irish Architectural Drawings (jointly), 1965; Irish Portraits 1660-1860 (jointly), 1969; (jtly) Mildred Anne Butler, 1981; articles and reviews on architecture and the decorative arts in many Art periodicals. *Address:* Glin Castle, Glin, Co. Limerick, Ireland. *TA:* Knight Glin. *T:* Listowel 34173 and 34112; 52 Waterloo Road, Dublin 4. *T:* Dublin 680585. *Clubs:* Beefsteak, White's; Kildare Street and University (Dublin).

FITZGERALD, Rev. (Sir) Edward Thomas, 3rd Bt *cr* 1903; a Roman Catholic priest; *b* 7 March 1912; *S* father, Sir John Joseph Fitzgerald, 2nd Bt, 1957, but does not use title. *Heir: b* Rev. Daniel Patrick Fitzgerald, *b* 28 June 1916.

FITZGERALD, Garret, PhD; Barrister-at-Law; Member of the Dáil (TD) (Fine Gael Party) for Dublin South East, since 1969; Leader of the Opposition, since 1982; *b* Dublin, 9 Feb. 1926; *s* of late Desmond FitzGerald (Minister for External Affairs, Irish Free State, 1922-27, and Minister for Defence, 1927-32) and Mabel FitzGerald (*née* McConnell); *m* 1947, Joan, *d* of late Charles O'Farrell; two *s* one *d. Educ:* St Brigid's Sch., Bray; Coláiste na Rinne, Waterford; Belvedere Coll., University Coll., and King's Inns, Dublin. Aer Lingus (Irish Air Lines), 1947-58; Rockefeller Research Asst, Trinity Coll., Dublin, 1958-59; College Lectr, Dept of Political Economy, University Coll., Dublin, 1959-73 (currently on secondment, 1973-). Minister for Foreign Affairs, Ireland, 1973-77; Leader, Fine Gael Party, 1977-; Taoiseach (Prime Minister of Ireland), 1981-82. Member: Seanad Eireann (Irish Senate), 1965-69; Oireachtas Library Cttee, 1965-69; Dáil Cttee on Public Accounts, 1969-73; Internat. Exec. Cttee of European Movement, 1972-73, 1977-; President: Fine Gael Party; Irish Council of European Movement; Electoral Reform Soc., London. Governor, Atlantic Inst. of Internat. Relations, Paris, 1972-73, 1977-; Mem., Senate of National Univ. of Ireland. Formerly: Irish Correspondent of BBC, Financial Times, Economist and other overseas papers; Economic Correspondent, Irish Times; also Past Managing Dir, Economist Intelligence Unit of Ireland; Economic Consultant to Fedn of Irish Industries and Construction Industry Fedn, and Rep. Body for Guards; Past Member: Exec. Cttee and Council, Inst. of Public Admin; Council, Statistical and Social Inquiry, Soc. of Ireland; Senate Electoral Law Commn; Workmen's Compensation Commn; Transport Advisory Cttee for Second Programme; Cttee on Industrial Organisation; Gen. Purposes Cttee of Nat. Industrial Economic Council. Lectures: Radcliffe, Warwick Univ., 1979; Richard Dimbleby, BBC, 1982. Hon. LLD: New York, 1974; St Louis, 1974. *Publications:* State-sponsored Bodies, 1959; Planning in Ireland, 1968; Towards a New Ireland, 1972; Unequal Partners, 1979. *Address:* Leinster House, Kildare Street, Dublin 2, Ireland. *Clubs:* Stephen's Green (Dublin); Royal Irish Yacht (Dun Laoghaire).

FitzGERALD, Sir George (Peter Maurice), 5th Bt *cr* 1880; 23rd Knight of Kerry; MC 1944; Major, Army, retired; *b* 27 Feb. 1917; *s* of Sir Arthur Henry Brinsley FitzGerald, 4th Bt, and Mary Eleanor (*d* 1967), *d* of late Capt. Francis Forester; *S* father 1967; *m* 1939, Angela Dora Mitchell; one *s* one *d. Educ:* Harrow; RMC, Sandhurst. Commnd into Irish Guards, 1937; 2nd in comd, 1st Bn, 1944; 2nd in comd, 2nd Bn, 1946; retired, 1948. *Heir: s* Adrian James Andrew Denis FitzGerald, *b* 24 June 1940. *Address:* Cedar Court, Alderton, near Woodbridge, Suffolk. *T:* Shottisham 411331. *Clubs:* Army and Navy, Pratt's.

FitzGERALD, Brig. (retd) Gerald Loftus, CBE 1956; DSO 1945; *b* 5 May 1907; *s* of late Col D. C. V. FitzGerald, MC, Nairobi Kenya; *m* 1937, Mary Stuart, *d* of late Charles E. Mills, Holbrook, Suffolk; one *s* one *d*. *Educ:* Wellington Coll.; Royal Military Academy, Woolwich. Commissioned 2nd Lieut RA, 1926; Regimental duty UK and overseas, 1926–39; staff and regimental duty in UK and NW Europe during War of 1939–45. Brit. Mil. Mission to Greece, 1946–48; Chief Instructor, Officer Cadet Sch., 1949–50; Brit. Joint Services Mission, Washington, USA, 1951–52; Comdr Trg Bde, RA, 1953–55; Dep. Dir, War Office, 1956–58; retired pay, 1959. Order of Leopold (with Palm), Belgium, 1945; Croix de Guerre (with Palm), 1945. *Recreations:* field sports, travel. *Club:* Army and Navy.

FitzGERALD, Michael Frederick Clive, QC 1980; *b* 9 June 1936; *s* of Sir William James FitzGerald, *qv*, and Mrs E. J. Critchley; *m* 1966, Virginia Grace Cave; one *s* three *d*. *Educ:* Downside; Christ's Coll., Cambridge, 1956–59 (MA). 2nd Lieut 9th Queen's Royal Lancers, 1954–56. Called to the Bar, Middle Temple, 1961. *Recreations:* fishing, shooting. *Address:* Udiam Farm, Bodiam, Sussex TN32 5XD; 49 Cheval Place, SW7. *Clubs:* Athenæum, Special Forces.

FITZGERALD, Prof. Patrick John; Professor of Law, Carleton University, Ottawa, since 1971; *b* 30 Sept. 1928; *s* of Dr Thomas Walter and Norah Josephine Fitzgerald; *m* 1959, Brigid Aileen Judge; two *s* one *d*. *Educ:* Queen Mary's Grammar Sch., Walsall; University Coll., Oxford. Called to the Bar, Lincoln's Inn, 1951; Fellow, Trinity Coll., Oxford, 1956–60. Professor of Law: Leeds Univ., 1960–66; Univ. of Kent at Canterbury, 1966–71. Visiting Prof., University of Louisville, 1962–63. Consultant, Law Reform Commn of Canada, 1973–. *Publications:* Criminal Law and Punishment, 1962; Salmond on Jurisprudence (12th edn), 1966; This Law of Ours, 1977; Looking at Law, 1979. *Recreations:* music, golf, bridge. *Address:* 207 Belmont Avenue, Ottawa, Canada.

FITZGERALD, Penelope Mary, (Mrs Desmond Fitzgerald); writer; *b* 1916; *d* of E. V. Knox and Christina Hicks; *m* 1941, Desmond Fitzgerald, MC; one *s* two *d*. *Educ:* Wycombe Abbey; Somerville Coll., Oxford (BA). *Publications:* Edward Burne-Jones, 1975; The Knox Brothers, 1977; The Golden Child, 1977; The Bookshop, 1978; Offshore, 1979 (Booker Prize); Human Voices, 1980; At Freddie's, 1982; (ed) William Morris's unpublished Novel on Blue Paper, 1982. *Recreations:* listening, talking, growing orange and lemon trees. *Address:* c/o Wm Collins, 14 St James's Place, SW1A 1PS.

FITZGERALD, Terence; Chief Charity Commissioner, 1975–82; *b* 20 March 1919. *Educ:* Allhallows Sch.; Exeter Coll., Oxford; Middle Temple. Royal Artillery, 1940–46; attached Royal Indian Artillery, 1941–45. Home Office, 1948; Imperial Defence Coll., 1962; HM Treasury, 1963–64; Asst Under-Sec. of State, Home Office, 1964–75. *Address:* 9 Roselands, Sidmouth, Devon.

FitzGERALD, Sir William James, Kt 1944; MC; QC 1936; *b* Cappawhite, Co. Tipperary, May 1894; *s* of late Joseph FitzGerald, MB, Cappawhite; *m* 1st, 1933, Erica (marr. diss. 1946), *d* of F. J. Clarke, Chikupi Ranch, Northern Rhodesia; one *s*; 2nd, Cynthia Mary Mangnall, *d* of late W. Foster, OBE, Jerusalem; one step *s*. *Educ:* Blackrock Coll.; Trinity Coll., Dublin (Hon. LLD 1960). Served European War, Durham Light Infantry and XV Corps Mounted Troops (MC and Croix de Guerre); BA 1919; Barrister-at-Law, King's Inns, Dublin, 1922, and Middle Temple; Nigerian Administrative Service, 1920; Police Magistrate, Lagos, 1921; Crown Counsel, Nigeria, 1924; Solicitor-Gen., N Rhodesia, 1932; Attorney-Gen., N Rhodesia, 1933; Palestine, 1937–43; Chief of Justice of Palestine, 1944–48. Pres. Lands Tribunal, 1950–65. *Address:* 47 Sussex Square, Brighton, Sussex. *Club:* Athenæum.
See also M. F. C. FitzGerald.

FITZGERALD, William Knight, CBE 1981; JP; DL; Convener, Tayside Regional Council, since 1978; *b* 19 March 1909; *e s* of John Alexander Fitzgerald and Janet Fitzgerald; *m* 1938, Elizabeth (*d* 1980), *d* of Alexander Grant; three *s*. *Educ:* Robertson Grammar Sch., S Africa. Assessor, Dundee Repertory Theatre, 1967–77; Member: Tayside Economic Consultative Group, 1970–77; Dundee Harbour Trust, 1970–73; University Court, Dundee, 1970–; Dundee Town Council, 1956; City Treasurer, 1967–70; Lord Provost of Dundee, and Lord Lieutenant of County of the City of Dundee, 1970–73; Chairman: Tay Road Bridge Joint Board, 1970–73 and 1975–; Dundee High Sch. Directors, 1970–73; Vice-Chairman: Dundee Coll. of Art and Technology, 1970–75; Scottish Council on Alcoholism, 1972–; E Scotland Water Bd, 1973–75. President: Convention of Scottish Local Authorities, 1979–82; Dundee Bn, Boys' Brigade, Dundee: JP 1948; DL 1974. Hon. LLD Dundee, 1981. *Recreations:* gardening, reading. *Address:* Morven, Roxburgh Terrace, Dundee DD2 1NZ. *T:* 68475. *Club:* University (Dundee).

FitzGIBBON, Constantine; see FitzGibbon, R. L. C. L.-D.

FitzGIBBON, Louis Theobald Dillon; writer and company director; *b* 6 Jan. 1925; *s* of Comdr Francis Lee-Dillon FitzGibbon, RN, and Kathleen Clare (*née* Atchison), widow of Hon. Harry Lee-Dillon; *m* 1st, 1950, Josephine Miriam Maud (*née* Webb) (marr. diss.); 2nd, 1962, Madeleine Sally (*née* Hayward-Surry) (*d* 1980); one *s* two *d*; 3rd, 1980, Joan Elizabeth Jevons. *Educ:* St Augustine's Abbey Sch.; Royal Naval Coll., Dartmouth. Royal Navy, 1942–54 (incl. War of 1939–45); Polish interpreter's course, 1950–52. Dir, De Leon Properties Ltd, 1954–72. Solicitor's articled clerk, 1960–63;

Anglo-Polish Conf., Warsaw, 1963. Personal Asst to the then Rt Hon. Duncan Sandys, MP (later Lord Duncan-Sandys), 1967–68; Gen. Sec., British Council for Aid to Refugees, 1968–72; United Nations (UNHCR) Mission to South Sudan, 1972–73; Dir of a medical charity, 1974–76; Nat. Assoc. for Freedom, 1977–78; Gen. Sec. of a trade assoc., 1978–80; missions to: Somalia, 1978, 1980–81; Sudan and Egypt, 1982. Mem., RIIA, 1982. Won first Airey Neave Meml Scholarship (proj. on Somalia), 1981. Hon. Sec., Katyn Memorial Fund, 1971–77; Area Pres., St John Amb. Brigade (Hants East), 1974–76. Holds Sov. Mil. Order of Malta (Kt of Honour and Devotion), and other religious orders, inc. Knight Grand Cross of the Holy Sepulchre, Order of the Rose and Cross of Jerusalem (Pres., British Assoc., 1982). Polish Gold Cross of Merit, 1969; Order of Polonia Restituta (Polish Govt in Exile) (Officer, 1971; Comdr, 1972; Kt Comdr, 1976); Katyn Meml Medal Bronze, USA, 1977; Leavreate van de Arbeid, Netherlands, 1982. *Publications:* Katyn—A Crime without Parallel, 1971; The Katyn Cover-up, 1972; Unpitied and Unknown, 1975; Katyn—Triumph of Evil (Ireland), 1975; The Katyn Memorial, 1976; Katyn Massacre (paper) 1977, 2nd edn 1979; Katyn (USA), 1979; Katyn Horror (in German), 1979; The Betrayal of the Somalis, 1982; contrib. to internat. and nat. jls and publications. *Recreations:* travelling, politics, writing, reading, history, languages, refugee problems, Horn of Africa affairs, Islamic matters, *pro deo*. *Address:* Langstone Towers, Langstone High Street, Havant, Hants PO9 1RY. *T:* Havant 475355. *Club:* Beefsteak.
See also R. L. C. FitzGibbon.

FitzGIBBON, (Robert Louis) Constantine (Lee-Dillon); writer; *b* 8 June 1919; *s* of Comdr Francis Lee-Dillon FitzGibbon, RN, and Georgette Folsom, Lenox, Mass, USA; *m* 1967, Marjorie (*née* Steele); one *d*; (by a previous marr. to Marion (*née* Gutmann) one *s*, *b* 1961). *Educ:* Wellington Coll.; Munich Univ.; Sorbonne; Exeter Coll., Oxford. Served War of 1939–45, British Army (Oxford and Bucks Light Infantry), 1939–42; US Army, 1942–46. Schoolmaster, Saltus Gram. Sch., Bermuda, 1946–47; now independent writer. Mem. Irish Acad. of Letters. FRSL; Fellow, Guggenheim Memorial Foundn, 1966. *Publications:* The Arabian Bird, 1949; The Iron Hoop, 1950; Dear Emily 1952: Miss Finnigan's Fault, Norman Douglas, The Holiday, 1953; The Little Tour, 1954; The Shirt of Nessus, 1955; In Love and War, 1956; The Blitz, 1957; Paradise Lost and More, 1959; When the Kissing had to Stop, 1960; Going to the River, 1963; Random Thoughts of a Fascist Hyena, 1963; The Life of Dylan Thomas, 1965; (ed) Selected Letters of Dylan Thomas, 1966; Through the Minefield, 1967; Denazification, 1969; High Heroic, 1969; Out of the Lion's Paw, 1969; Red Hand: The Ulster Colony, 1971; The Devil at Work (play), 1971; A Concise History of Germany, 1972; In the Bunker, 1973; The Life and Times of Eamon de Valera, 1973; The Golden Age, 1976; Secret Intelligence, 1976; Man in Aspic, 1977; Teddy in the Tree, 1977; Drink, 1979; The Rat Report, 1980; The Irish in Ireland, 1982; and trans from French, German and Italian. Contributor to Encyc. Brit., newspapers and periodicals in Britain, America and elsewhere. *Address:* Newbridge Mews, Sandymount, Dublin 4, Ireland. *Club:* Beefsteak
See also L. T. D. FitzGibbon.

FitzHARRIS, Viscount; James Carleton Harris; *b* 19 June 1946; *o s* and *heir* of 6th Earl of Malmesbury, *qv*; *m* 1969, Sally Ann, *yr d* of Sir Richard Newton Rycroft, *qv*; three *s* two *d*. *Educ:* Eton; Queen's Coll., St Andrews (MA). *Heir:* *s* Hon. James Hugh Carleton Harris, *b* 29 April 1970. *Address:* Heather Row Farm House, Nately Scures, Basingstoke, Hants RG27 9JP. *T:* Hook 3138. *Club:* Royal Yacht Squadron.

FITZHERBERT, family name of **Baron Stafford.**

FITZHERBERT, Cuthbert; *b* 24 May 1899; British; 4th *s* of William Joseph Fitzherbert-Brockholes, CBE, and Blanche Winifred Mary, 2nd *d* of late Maj.-Gen. Hon. Sir Henry Hugh Clifford, VC, KCMG, CB; *m* 1930, Barbara (*d* 1975), *e d* of Henry Scrope, Danby; three *s* three *d* (and one *s* decd). *Educ:* Oratory Sch.; New Coll., Oxford (BA). Commissioned Coldstream Guards, 1917; served European War, 1914–18, in 1st Bn Coldstream Guards (wounded). Joined Barclays Bank Ltd, 1922; Union Bank of Manchester, 1923–26; Local Dir, Barclays Bank Ltd, Darlington, 1926; Local Dir, Barclays Bank Ltd, Birmingham, 1939. Served War of 1939–45, with Coldstream Guards, 1940–44. Returned as Gen. Man. (Staff), Barclays Bank Ltd, 1944; a Director: Barclays Bank Ltd (Vice-Chm., 1948–64), 1948–72; Barclays Bank DCO, retd 1971; formerly Dir, London Montrose Investment Trust, retd 1972. *Publications:* Henry Clifford VC, his letters and sketches from the Crimea (ed), 1953; The Prince and the Pedlar (stalking memories), 1977. *Recreations:* shooting, stalking. *Address:* 1 Lochmore House, Ebury Street, SW1W 9JX. *T:* 01-730 8710. *Club:* Cavalry and Guards.
See also S. P. E. C. W. Towneley.

FitzHERBERT, Giles Eden; HM Diplomatic Service; *b* Dublin, 8 March 1935; *e s* of late Captain H. C. FitzHerbert, Irish Guards, and Sheelah, *d* of J. X. Murphy; *m* 1962, Margaret Waugh; two *s* three *d*. *Educ:* Ampleforth Coll.; Christ Church Oxford; Harvard Business Sch. 2nd Lieut, 8th King's Royal Irish Hussars, 1957–58. Vickers da Costa & Co., 1962–66. First Secretary: Foreign Office, 1966; Rome, 1968–71; FCO, 1972–75; Counsellor: Kuwait, 1975–77; Nicosia, 1977–78; Head of Eur. Community Dept (Ext.), FCO, 1978–82; on sabbatical leave, LSE 1982. Contested (L) Fermanagh and South Tyrone, Gen. Elect., 1964. *Address:* Cove House, Cove, Tiverton, Devon. *Clubs:* Beefsteak; Kildare Street and University (Dublin).

FitzHERBERT, Sir John (Richard Frederick), 8th Bt, *cr* 1784; TD; *b* 15 Sept. 1913; *s* of Ven. Henry E. FitzHerbert, sometime Archdeacon of Derby, and Hon. Margaret Elinor (*d* 1957), *d* of 3rd Baron Heytesbury; *S* uncle, Sir William FitzHerbert, 7th Bt, 1963; *m* 1957, Kathleen Anna Rees; no *c. Educ:* Charterhouse; Royal Agricultural Coll., Cirencester. Served War of 1939-45, Sherwood Foresters (TA). FLAS 1950; FRICS 1970. *Heir: nephew* Richard Ranulph FitzHerbert, *b* 2 Nov. 1963. *Address:* Tissington Hall, Ashbourne, Derbyshire. *T:* Parwich 246. *Club:* Derby County (Derby).

FITZHERBERT-BROCKHOLES, Michael John, JP; Vice Lord-Lieutenant of Lancashire, since 1977; *b* 12 June 1920; *s* of John William Fitzherbert-Brockholes and Eileen Agnes; *m* 1950, Mary Edith Moore; four *s. Educ:* The Oratory Sch.; New Coll., Oxford. Scots Guards, 1940-46. Mem., Lancs CC, 1968-; Chm., Educn Cttee, 1977-81. JP 1960, DL 1975, Lancs. KSG 1978. *Recreation:* gardening. *Address:* Claughton Hall, Garstang, near Preston, Lancs. *T:* Brock 40286.

FitzHUGH, James, QC 1973; **His Honour Judge FitzHugh**; a Circuit Judge, since 1976; *b* 2 April 1917; *s* of T. J. FitzHugh and S. FitzHugh (formerly Jocelyn); *m* 1955, Shelagh (*née* Bury), *d* of R. W. and B. Bury, Lytham St Annes. *Educ:* St Bede's Coll., Manchester; Manchester Univ. (BA (Admin)); London Univ. (LLB). Commissioned in Supplementary Reserve of Officers, RA, 1938; War of 1939-45: Captain, GSO. Called to Bar, Gray's Inn, and became a Member of Northern Circuit, 1948. *Recreations:* travel, golf. *Address:* 186 St Leonard's Road East, St Annes on the Sea, Lytham St Annes, Lancs. *T:* St Annes 723068. *Clubs:* St James's (Manchester); Royal Lytham and St Annes Golf.

FITZ-MAURICE, family name of **Earl of Orkney.**

FITZMAURICE; *see* Petty-Fitzmaurice.

FITZMAURICE, Lt-Col Sir Desmond FitzJohn, Kt 1946; CIE 1941; late RE; *b* 17 Aug. 1893; *s* of John Day Stokes Fitzmaurice, ICS, Tralee, Co. Kerry; *m* 1926, Nancy (*d* 1975), *d* of Rev. John Sherlock Leake, Grayswood, Surrey; one *s* three *d. Educ:* Bradfield; RMA, Woolwich; Cambridge Univ. Joined RE, 1914. Served in France, Belgium and Italy, European War, 1914-18 (despatches); Instructor, RMA Woolwich, 1918-20; Cambridge Univ., 1920-22; Instructor, Sch. of Military Engineering, Chatham, 1923, 1924; hp list, 1925; Deputy Mint Master, Bombay, 1929-30; Calcutta, 1931-32; Deputy Master, Security Printing, India, 1932; Master Security Printing and Controller of Stamps, India, 1934; retired. *Address:* Mount Rivers, Killorglin, Co. Kerry.

FitzPATRICK, Air Cdre David Beatty, CB 1970; OBE 1953; AFC 1949 and Bar, 1958; *b* 31 Jan. 1920; *s* of late Comdr D. T. FitzPatrick, RN and Beatrice Anne Ward; *m* 1941, Kathleen Mary Miles; one *d. Educ:* Kenilworth Coll., Exeter; Midhurst. Commnd RAF, 1938; served War of 1939-45, Atlantic, Mediterranean and Far East theatres; comd No 209 Sqdn (Far East), 1944; (GD Pilot) Sqdn flying duty, 1945-52; cfs, pfc and GW Specialist, RAF Henlow, 1952-57; GW (Trials) Project Officer, Min. of Supply, 1957-59; Base Comdr Christmas Island, 1959-60 (British Nuclear Trials); NATO Def. Coll., and jssc, 1960-61; Dep. Dir (Ops) Air Staff, 1961-64; comd RAF Akrotiri and Nicosia, 1964-66; Dir of (Q) RAF, MoD, 1966-69; attached NBPI for special duty, 1969; Dir, Guided Weapons (Trials and Ranges), Min. of Technology, 1969-72; Dir, Guided Weapons Trials, MoD (PE), 1972-74. Retired 1975. FBIM 1980; MRAeS. *Recreations:* swimming (Life Vice-Pres., Royal Air Force Swimming Assoc.), deep-sea fishing, cricket. *Address:* Whistledown, 38 Courts Mount Road, Haslemere, Surrey. *T:* Haslemere 4589. *Clubs:* Royal Air Force; Naval, Military and Air Force (Adelaide).

FITZPATRICK, Gen. Sir (Geoffrey Richard) Desmond, GCB 1971 (KCB 1965; CB 1961); DSO 1945; MBE 1943; MC 1939; *b* 14 Dec. 1912; *o s* of late Brig.-Gen. Sir Richard Fitzpatrick, CBE, DSO, and Lady (G. E.) Fitzpatrick; *m* 1944, Mary Sara, *o d* of Sir Charles Campbell, 12th Bt; one *s* one *d. Educ:* Eton; RMC Sandhurst. Commissioned The Royal Dragoons, 1932. Served in Palestine, 1938-39 (MC); War of 1939-45 (despatches, MBE, DSO); in Middle East, Italy, NW Europe. Bt. Lieut-Col 1951; Col 1953; ADC to the Queen, 1959; Maj.-Gen. 1959; Asst Chief of Defence Staff, Ministry of Defence, 1959-61; Dir Mil. Ops, War Office, 1962-64; Chief of Staff, BAOR, 1964-65; Lt-Gen. 1965; GOC-in-C, N Ire., 1965-66; Vice-Chief of Gen. Staff, 1966-68; Gen. 1968; C-in-C, BAOR, and Commander N Army Gp 1968-70; Dep. Supreme Allied Comdr, Europe, 1970-73; ADC (General) to the Queen, 1970-73. Lieutenant-Governor and C-in-C, Jersey, 1974-79. Col, The Royal Dragoons, 1964-69; Dep. Col, 1969-74, Col, 1979-, The Blues and Royals, and Gold Stick to the Queen, 1979-; Col Comdt, RAC, 1971-74. *Address:* Belmont, Otley, Suffolk IP6 9PF. *Clubs:* Cavalry and Guards; Royal Yacht Squadron.

FITZPATRICK, James Bernard, JP; Managing Director and Chief Executive, Mersey Docks and Harbour Company, since 1977; *b* 21 April 1930; *s* of late B. A. Fitzpatrick and Mrs J. E. Fitzpatrick; *m* 1965, Rosemary, *d* of late Clement E. B. Clark, RD and bar, RNR (Croix de Guerre avec Palme, Polish Golden Cross of Merit with Swords), and late Mrs K. E. Clark, Claughton; one *s* one *d. Educ:* Bootle Grammar Sch.; London Univ. (LLB). Admitted Solicitor, 1962; FCIT 1973 (AMInstT 1954, by examination). Joined Mersey Docks and Harbour Bd, 1951: various management posts from 1965; Personnel and Industrial Relns Dir, 1971, on formation of Mersey Docks

and Harbour Co.; Jt Man. Dir, 1974; Dep. Chief Exec., 1975. Chairman: Nat. Assoc. of Port Employers, 1979-82 (Vice-Chm., 1973-79); Employers' Assoc. of Port of Liverpool, 1974-; Member: Liverpool Dock Labour Bd, 1974-76 (Chm., 1976); Exec. Council, British Ports Assoc., 1976-; Nat. Dock Labour Bd, 1978-; Vice Pres., Inst. of Materials Handling, 1978. FIMH. JP Liverpool 1977. *Recreations:* fell walking, gardening, music, reading. *Address:* 30 Abbey Road, West Kirby, Merseyside. *T:* 051-625 9612; Pierhead, Liverpool L3 1BZ. *T:* 051-200 2003. *Clubs:* Oriental; West Kirby Sailing.

FITZPATRICK, Air Vice-Marshal John Bernard, CB 1982; Director General of Organisation, RAF, since 1982; *b* 15 Dec. 1929; *s* of Joseph FitzPatrick and Bridget FitzPatrick; *m* 1954, Gwendoline Mary Abbott; two *s* one *d. Educ:* St Patrick's Academy, Dungannon, N Ireland; Royal Air Force College, Cranwell. Officer Commanding: No 81 PR Sqdn, 1966-68; No 35 Sqdn, 1971-72; Group Captain Plans, HQ COMAIREASTLANT COMAIRCHAN, 1973; OC, Royal Air Force Scampton, 1974-75; RCDS, 1976; Director of Operations (Strike), RAF, 1977-79; SASO, HQ Strike Command, 1980-82. *Recreations:* Rugby, housebuilding. *Address:* c/o Lloyds Bank Ltd, 1-2 Market Place, Reading, Berks RG1 2EQ. *Club:* Royal Air Force.

FITZPATRICK, John Ronald; Solicitor and Parliamentary Officer, Greater London Council, since 1977; *b* 22 Sept. 1923; *s* of Henry Fitzpatrick and Mary Lister; *m* 1952, Beryl Mary Newton; two *s* one *d. Educ:* St Bede's Coll., Manchester; Univ. of Manchester (LLB). Admitted Solicitor, 1947; LMRTPI 1951. Asst Solicitor: Burnley, 1947; Stockport, 1948-51; Asst/Principal Asst Solicitor, Mddx CC, 1951-65; Asst Clerk/Asst Dir-Gen., GLC, 1965-69; Asst Dir, 1969-72, Dir, 1972-77, Planning and Transportation, GLC. *Recreations:* golf, bridge. *Address:* Courtlands, 2 Langley Grove, New Malden, Surrey. *T:* 01-942 8652.

FITZ ROY, family name of **Viscount Daventry.**

FitzROY, family name of **Duke of Grafton** and of **Southampton Barony.**

FitzROY, Charles; late 2nd Lieutenant Royal Horse Guards and Pioneer Corps; *b* 3 Jan. 1904; *o s* of 4th Baron Southampton, OBE, and late Lady Hilda Mary Dundas, *d* of 1st Marquess of Zetland; *S* father, 1958, as 5th Baron Southampton, but disclaimed his title for life, 16 March 1964; *m* 1st, 1927, Margaret (*d* 1931), *d* of Prebendary H. Mackworth Drake, Vicar of Paignton; one *s* ; 2nd, 1940, Mrs Joan Leslie (marr. diss., 1944); 3rd, 1951, Rachel Christine, *d* of Charles Zaman, Lille, France. *Educ:* Harrow. Served Royal Horse Guards, 1923-25; re-employed, 1940, with RA, Pioneer Corps, 1941. Joint-master, Grove Fox-hounds, 1930-32. *Heir:* (to disclaimed barony): *s* Hon. Charles James FitzRoy [*b* 12 Aug. 1928; *m* 1951, Pamela Anne, *d* of E. Henniker, Maidenhead, Berks; one *s* one *d* (and one *s* decd)]. *Address:* Preluna Hotel, Sliema, Malta.

FitzROY NEWDEGATE, Francis Humphrey Maurice, DL; *b* 17 Dec. 1921; *s* of late Comdr Hon. John Maurice FitzRoy Newdegate and *nephew* of Viscount Daventry, *qv* ; *m* 1959, Hon. Rosemary, *e d* of 1st Baron Norrie, GCMG, GCVO, CB, DSO, MC; two *s* one *d. Educ:* Eton. Served War of 1939-45 with Coldstream Guards, N Africa and Italy; Captain 1943. ADC to Viceroy of India, 1946-48. JP 1960, DL 1970, High Sheriff 1970, Warwickshire; Vice-Lieut 1974. *Address:* Temple House, Arbury, Nuneaton, Warwickshire. *T:* Nuneaton 383514. *Club:* Boodle's.

FITZSIMMONS, Rt. Hon. William Kennedy, PC (N Ireland) 1965; JP; *b* 31 Jan. 1909; *m* 1935, May Elizabeth Lynd; two *d. Educ:* Skegoniell National Sch.; Belfast Jun. Techn. Sch. Mem., Belfast City and Dist Water Comrs, 1948-57 (Chm. 1954-55); Pres., Duncairn Unionist Assoc.; N Ireland Parliament: MP, Duncairn Div. of Belfast, 1956-72; Dep. Govt Whip, 1961-63; Parl. Secretary: Min. of Commerce, 1961-65; Min. of Home Affairs, 1963-64; Min. of Develt, 1964-65; Min. of Education, 1965-66 and 1968-69; Minister of Development, 1966-68; Minister of Health and Social Services, 1969-72. MRSH; JP Belfast, 1951. *Address:* 4 Tudor Oaks, Holywood, Co. Down, Northern Ireland BT18 0PA.

FITZWALTER, 21st Baron, *cr* 1295; **(Fitzwalter) Brook Plumptre**, JP; Hon. Captain, The Buffs; *b* 15 Jan. 1914; *s* of late George Beresford Plumptre, Goodnestone, Canterbury, Kent; *S* uncle, 1943 (FitzWalter Barony called out of abeyance in his favour, 1953); *m* 1951, Margaret Melesina, *yr d* of (Herbert) William Deedes, JP, Galt, Hythe, Kent; five *s. Educ:* Diocesan Coll., Rondebosch, Cape; Jesus Coll., Cambridge. Served War of 1939-45, with the Buffs (Royal East Kent Regt) in France, Belgium, UK and India; attached RIASC, as Capt. JP Kent, 1949. Landowner and farmer; succeeded to family estate, 1943. *Heir: s* Hon. Julian Brook Plumptre, *b* 18 Oct. 1952. *Address:* Goodnestone Park, Canterbury, Kent. *T:* Nonington 840218.

FLACK, Bertram Anthony, CMG 1979; HM Diplomatic Service, retired; *b* 3 Feb. 1924; *y s* of Dr F. H. Flack and Alice Cockshut, Nelson, Lancs; *m* 1948, Jean W. Mellor; two *s* two *d. Educ:* Epsom Coll.; Liverpool Univ. (LLB Hons). Enlisted Gren. Gds, 1942; commissioned E Lancashire Regt, 1943; served in NW Europe (Captain). Joined Foreign Service, 1948; served Karachi, 1948-50; Alexandria, 1950-52; Stockholm, 1955-58; Accra, 1958-61; Johannesburg, 1964-67; Dep. High Comr, E Pakistan, 1967-68; Inspector, Diplomatic Service, 1968-70; Head of Communications Dept, FCO, 1971-73;

Commercial Counsellor, Stockholm, 1973-75; Canadian Nat. Defence Coll., 1975-76; Dep. High Comr, Ottawa, 1976-79; High Comr, Repub. of Uganda, 1979-80. *Recreations:* cricket, golf. *Address:* Ripple Cottage, Douglas Street, Castletown, Isle of Man.

FLAGG, Rt. Rev. John William Hawkins; Assistant Bishop, Diocese of Liverpool, and Vicar of St Cyprian's with Christ Church, Edge Hill, since 1978; *b* 16 April 1929; *s* of Wilfred John and Emily Flagg; *m* 1954, Marjorie Lund; two *s* four *d*. *Educ:* All Nations Christian Coll.; Clifton Theological Coll. Agricultural missionary, Chile, 1951; Chaplain and Missionary Superintendent, St Andrew's, Asunción, Paraguay, 1959-64; Archdeacon, N Argentine, 1964-69; Diocesan Bishop of Paraguay and N Argentine, 1969-73; Bishop of Peru and Bolivia, 1973; Bishop, Diocese of Peru, 1977. Member of Anglican Consultative Council, 1974-79; Presiding Bishop of Anglican Council of South America (CASA), 1974-77. *Address:* St Cyprian's Vicarage, 52 Deane Road, Liverpool L7 0ET. *T:* 051-263 4170.

FLAHIFF, His Eminence Cardinal George Bernard; *see* Winnipeg, Archbishop of, (RC).

FLANDERS, Dennis, RWS 1976 (ARWS 1970); RBA 1970; artist: townscapes and landscapes in pencil and water-colour; *b* 2 July 1915; *s* of late Bernard C. Flanders, ARAM (pianist), and Jessie Marguarite Flanders, ARMS (artist); *m* 1952, Dalma J. Darnley, *o d* of late J. Darnley Taylor and of Mrs Joan Darnley Taylor; one *s* one *d*. *Educ:* Merchant Taylors' Sch.; Regent Street Polytechnic; St Martin's Art Sch.; Central Sch. of Arts and Crafts, Princess Louise Gold Medal at age of 7. Mem. of St Paul's Watch, 1940-42; Royal Engineers, 1942-46. Occasional drawings for Daily Telegraph and other journals; series of drawings for Yorkshire Post, 1949; Birmingham Post, 1950-51; "Famous Streets," Sunday Times, 1952-53; Special artist to the Illustrated London News, 1956-64. Water-colours (reproduced as prints) of: RMA Sandhurst; Police Coll., Bramshill; St Edward's Sch., Oxford; Glencorse Barracks, Midlothian. Drawings in private collections and Nat. War Collection (1939-45), Guildhall Library, Bank of England, Nat. Library of Wales, and Museums at Exeter, York, Lincoln, Kensington, St Marylebone, Walthamstow, Wolverhampton, and Bury, Lancs. Exhibitor: RA and in provinces: one-man shows: London, 1947, 1951, 1953, 1955, 1964, 1967; Bedford, 1965, 1966; Boston (Lincs), 1966; Southport, 1969; Buxton-Lammas, Norfolk, 1972; Worthing, 1972; Cambridge, 1980; York, 1981. Member: Art Workers Guild (Master 1975); Soc. for Protection of Ancient Buildings. Freeman: City of London, 1970; Painter Stainers' Co., 1970. Lord Mayor's Art Award, 1966. *Publications:* illustrations: Bolton Abbey, 1947; Chelsea by Richard Edmonds, 1956; Soho for East Anglia by Michael Brander, 1963; A Westminster Childhood by John Raynor, 1973; The Twelve Great Livery Companies of London, 1973. *Recreations:* walking, riding, reading Who's Who. *Address:* 51 Great Ormond Street, WC1. *T:* 01-405 9317; Baker's Cross House, Cranbrook, Kent. *T:* Cranbrook 712018.

FLANNERY, Martin Henry; MP (Lab) Hillsborough, Sheffield, since Feb. 1974; *b* 2 March 1918; *m* 1949; one *s* two *d*. *Educ:* Sheffield Grammar Sch.; Sheffield Teachers' Trng College. Served with Royal Scots, 1940-46. Teacher, 1946-74 (Head Teacher, 1969-74). Chm., Tribune Group, 1980-. *Recreations:* music, rambling. *Address:* 53 Linaker Road, Sheffield S6 5DS.

FLATHER, Mrs Shreela, JP; Member: Commission for Racial Equality, since 1980; Police Complaints Board, since 1982; Councillor, Royal Borough of Windsor and Maidenhead, since 1976 (first ethnic minority woman Councillor in UK); *b* India; *m* Gary Flather; two *s*. *Educ:* University Coll. London (LLB). Called to the Bar, Inner Temple, 1962. Infant Teacher, ILEA, 1965-67; Teacher of English as a second lang., Altwood Comp. Sch., Maidenhead, 1968-74, Broadmoor Hosp., 1974-78. Member: Cttee of Inquiry (Rampton, now Swann Cttee) into Educn of Children from Ethnic Minority Gps, 1979-; Cons. Women's Nat. Adv. Cttee, 1978-; Exec. Cttee, Anglo-Asian Cons. Soc., 1979-; Bd of Visitors, Holloway Prison, 1981-; Vice-Chm., Maidenhead CAB. Governor, Altwood Comp. Sch. Formerly: Vice-Chm. and Founder Mem., Maidenhead Community Relns Council; Mem., W Metrop. Conciliation Cttee, Race Relns Bd, 1973-78; Sec./Organiser, Maidenhead Ladies Asian Club, 1968-78; started New Star Boys' Club for Asian Boys and Summer Sch. Project for Asian children, Maidenhead; prepared English Teaching Scheme for Asian adults 'Stepping Stones'. JP Maidenhead, 1971 (first Asian woman magistrate). *Recreations:* travel, cinema. *Address:* Triveni, Ascot Road, Maidenhead, Berks. *T:* Maidenhead 25408. *Club:* Oriental.

FLATLEY, Derek Comedy, FJI; Public Affairs Correspondent, Southend Evening Echo, since 1970; *b* 16 Oct. 1920; *m* 1959, Valerie Eve Stevens; one *d*. *Educ:* Grammar sch. Trained West Essex Gazette, 1936. Served War of 1939-45: Household Cavalry, 1945. Army newspaper unit, Southend Standard, 1947; Chief Reporter, 1949. Mem., Press Council, 1968-72; Mem. Council (rep. Essex), Inst. of Journalists, 1957- (Pres. 1966-67); also Chairman: Salaries and Conditions Bd of the Inst., 1958-67; Estabt Cttee, 1963-65; Exec., 1967-70. Fellow, Inst. of Journalists, 1962-. *Recreations:* football, cricket, tennis. *Address:* Windyridge House, 22 Earls Hall Avenue, Southend-on-Sea, Essex. *T:* Southend-on-Sea 43485.

FLAVELL, Geoffrey, FRCS; FRCP; Hon. Consulting Thoracic Surgeon to: The London Hospital; Chelmsford and Harlow Districts Health Authorities; Whipps Cross Hospital; *b* 23 Feb. 1913; *o* surviving *s* of late W. A. Flavell, JP, of Wellington, NZ; *m* 1943, Joan Margaret, *o d* of S. Ewart Adams,

Hawkwell, Essex; no *c*. *Educ:* Waitaki; Otago; University of New Zealand; St Bartholomew's Hospital, London. Qualified in medicine, 1937; House appts, St Bartholomew's Hosp., 1937-39; Resident Surgical Officer, Brompton Hosp., 1940-41. Surgeon Specialist, RAF, 1942, O/C Surgical Divs RAF Gen. Hosps, Carthage and Algiers, 1943; RAF Gen. Hosp., Cairo; Adviser in Surgery RAF Med. and Middle East Command, 1944; retired rank of Wing Comdr, 1958. Consultant Thoracic Surgeon, British Legion Hosp., and to LCC, 1946; Senior Registrar to London Hosp., 1947; Sen. Surgeon, Dept of Cardiovascular and Thoracic Surgery, London Hosp., 1950-78 (Chm., Surgical Div., 1974-77); Mem., Faculty of Med., Univ. of London, 1953-; Consultant Thoracic Surgeon, Royal Masonic Hosp., 1957-78; Sen. Thoracic Surgeon, Broomfield Hosp., 1947-78. Visiting Thoracic Surgeon to: Whipps Cross Hosp.; St Margaret's Hosp., Epping; Harold Wood Hosp.; Harts Hosp.; Oldchurch Hosp., Romford. Consultant, Qatar Govt, 1969-. Chm., Adv. Cttee on Cardiothoracic Surgery to NE Thames RHA, 1970-78; Senior Member: Soc. of Thoracic Surgeons of GB and Ireland; Thoracic Soc. Ivor Lewis Lectr, 1978. Liveryman, Hon. Soc. of Apothecaries; Freeman, City of London. *Publications:* Introduction to Chest Surgery, 1957; Basic Surgery (Thoracic section), 1958; The Oesophagus, 1963; many contribs to surgical textbooks and med. jls; various articles on travel, wine and food, in lay periodicals. *Recreations:* history; architecture; literature and art; indulging the senses. *Address:* Belfield House, Weymouth, Dorset DT4 9RD. *T:* Weymouth 784013. *Club:* Royal Air Force.

FLAVELLE, Sir (Joseph) David (Ellsworth), 3rd Bt *cr* 1917; *b* 9 Nov. 1921; *s* of Sir (Joseph) Ellsworth Flavelle, 2nd Bt, and of Muriel, *d* of William Norman McEachren; *S* father, 1977; *m* 1942, Muriel Barbara, *d* of Reginald Morton; three *d*. *Address:* Waterlot, 1420 Watersedge Road, Clarkson, Ontario L5J 1A4, Canada.

FLEET, Kenneth George; City Editor, The Sunday Express, since 1979; *b* 12 Sept. 1929; *s* of Fred Major Fleet and late Elizabeth Doris Fleet; *m* 1953, (Alice) Brenda, *d* of late Captain H. R. Wilkinson, RD, RNR and Mrs Kathleen Mary Wilkinson; three *s* one *d*. *Educ:* Calday Grange Grammar Sch., Cheshire; LSE (BScEcons). Jl of Commerce, Liverpool, 1950-52; Sunday Times, 1955-56; Dep. City Editor, Birmingham Post, 1956-58; Dep. Financial Editor, Guardian, 1958-63; Dep. City Editor, Daily Telegraph, 1963; City Editor, Sunday Telegraph, 1963-66; City Editor, Daily Telegraph, 1966-77; Editor, Business News, Sunday Times, 1977-78. Dir, Young Vic, 1976-. Wincott Award, 1974. *Recreations:* theatre, books, sport. *Address:* c/o Sunday Express, Fleet Street, EC4Y 2NJ. *Clubs:* MCC, Lord's Taverners; Chigwell Golf.

FLEETWOOD-HESKETH, Charles Peter F.; *see* Hesketh.

FLEMING, Sir Charles (Alexander), KBE 1977 (OBE 1964); FRS 1967; Honorary Lecturer in Geology, Victoria University of Wellington, since 1974; Chief Palæontologist, New Zealand Geological Survey, Department of Scientific and Industrial Research, 1953-77; *b* 9 Sept. 1916; *s* of Geo. H. Fleming, Auckland, NZ; *m* 1941, Margaret Alison, *d* of S. G. Chambers, Auckland; three *d*. *Educ:* King's Coll., Auckland; University of Auckland. Boyhood interest in birds and shell-collecting led to participation in Auckland Mus. expedns, 1933-35; student fieldwork on birds of NZ and Chatham Is (basis of papers publ. 1939); Asst Geologist, NZ Geol Survey, 1940; subseq. Palæontologist and Sen. Palæontologist. Overseas service as coastwatcher, Auckland Is, 1942-43. Pres., Ornithol. Soc. NZ, 1948-49; NZ Delegate: Internat. Geol Congresses, 1948, 1960; British Commonwealth Conf. on Geology and Mineral Resources, 1948; Mem. Bd of Trustees: Nat. Art Gall. and National (formerly Dominion) Mus., 1954-76 (Chm., Mus. Council, 1972-75); Nat. Library, 1971-72; NZ Fauna Protection Adv. Council; NZ Nat. Commn for Unesco, 1966-70; Nat. Parks Authority, 1970-81; Environmental Council, 1970-73. President: Internat. Paleont. Union (Oceania Filial), 1964-68; Aust. and NZ Assoc. for Advancement of Science, 1968-70. FRSNZ 1952 (Pres. 1962-66); Fellow, Art Galls and Museums Assoc. of NZ, 1956; Corresp. Fellow, American Ornithologists' Union, 1962; Commonwealth and Foreign Fellow, Geol. Soc. London, 1967; For. Mem., Amer. Philosophical Soc., 1973; Hon. FZS 1979; Sen. ANZAC Fellow, 1979. Several scientific prizes and awards. *Publications:* (ed) Checklist of New Zealand Birds, 1953; trans. Hochstetter's Geology of New Zealand, 1959; Marwick's Illustrations of New Zealand Shells, 1966; The Geological History of New Zealand and its Life, 1979; Geo. E. Lodge's Paintings of New Zealand Birds, 1982; geol and palæontol bulletins; about 300 research papers on mollusca, cicadas, birds, geology, palæontology, biogeography. *Recreations:* recorded music, natural history. *Address:* Balivean, 42 Wadestown Road, Wellington, NZ. *T:* Wellington 737-288.

FLEMING, Prof. Charles Mann, CBE 1964; Emeritus Professor of Administrative Medicine, since 1971 (Professor 1960-71), Dean of the Faculty of Medicine, 1959-70, and Dean of Postgraduate Medicine, 1970-72, in University of Glasgow; *b* 1 March 1904; *y s* of John Somerville Fleming and Christina Taylor Gerard, Glasgow; *m* 1930, Margaret Hamilton Barrie, *er d* of George Simpson, Newfoundland; one *d*. *Educ:* Hillhead High Sch; Glasgow Univ. MA 1924, MB, ChB 1929, MD 1933 (Glasgow); MRCPEd 1945, FRCPEd 1952, FRFPS (G.) 1959, FRCP (Glasgow) 1962. Hon. FRCGP 1964. Regional MO, 1937-39, Hospital Officer (Eastern Dist, Scotland), 1939-46, Principal MO, 1946-59, Dept of Health for Scotland. Convener Post-Grad. Med. Board, University of Glasgow, 1959-72; Chm., Western Regional Cttee for Postgrad. Medical Educn, 1970-72; Member:

General Medical Council, 1961-73; WHO Expert Advisory Panel on Organisation of Medical Care, 1959-76; Royal Commission on Med. Educn, 1966-68; Central Cttee on Postgraduate Med. Educn (GB), 1967-71; Scottish Council for Postgraduate Med. Educn, 1970-72. Addtl Mem. Gen. Dental Council, 1965-73. *Publications:* contributions to medical journals. *Recreation:* golf. *Address:* 8 Thorn Road, Bearsden, Glasgow. *T:* Bearsden 2810.

FLEMING, Hon. Donald Methuen, PC (Canada) 1957; QC (Ontario) 1944; *b* Exeter, Ont., 23 May 1905; *s* of Louis Charles and Maud Margaret Wright Fleming; *m* 1933, Alice Mildred Watson, Toronto; two *s* one *d*. *Educ:* public schools and Collegiate Inst., Galt; Univ. of Toronto (BA, LLB); Osgoode Hall Law Sch. Called to Bar, Ontario, 1928; subsequently practised in Toronto, 1928-57; Counsel to Blake, Cassels and Graydon, Barristers and Solicitors, Toronto, 1963-67. MP for Toronto-Eglinton, 1945-63; Minister of Finance and Receiver-General, 1957-62; Minister of Justice and Attorney-General of Canada, 1962-63. A Governor, Internat. Bank and IMF, 1957-63; Chairman: Commonwealth Finance Ministers' Conf., Mont Tremblant, Province of Quebec, 1957; Commonwealth Trade and Economic Conf., Montreal, 1958; OECD, 1961, 1962; Leader: delegn of Canadian Ministers to meetings of US-Canada Jt Trade and Economic Cttee, Washington, 1957, 1960, 1961 (Chm. Ottawa meeting, 1959, 1962), and meeting of Canada-Japan Jt Cttee of Ministers, Tokyo, 1963; Canadian delegn to OEEC Confs, Paris, 1960; Canadian delegate: NATO Conf. of Heads of Govt, Paris, 1957; NATO Ministerial Confs, 1958, 1959, 1961; Commonwealth Parly Confs, London, 1948, Ottawa, 1952, Nairobi, 1954. Has taken part in numerous parly, political, municipal and civic welfare activities and in church affairs. Man. Dir, Bank of Nova Scotia Trust Cos; General Counsel to Bank of Nova Scotia in Bahamas, 1968-80; Chm., M&G (Cayman) Ltd; Director: Gore Mutual Insurance Co., and numerous other companies. Mem. Senate, 1944-48, Bd of Governors, 1964-68, Univ. of Toronto. Past Pres., Toronto YMCA. Hon. Mem., Canadian Legion; Hon. Life Mem., Canadian Bar Assoc. DCL hc Bishop's Univ., 1960; LLD hc Waterloo Lutheran Univ., 1967. *Publications:* numerous works and articles on legal subjects; contribs to legal periodicals including Canadian Encyclopedic Digest, Canadian Bar Review, Canadian Abridgement, etc. *Recreations:* all branches of sport. *Address:* Bayview, PO Box N 3016, Nassau, Bahamas. *Clubs:* Canadian (Pres., 1964), Empire, Granite, National, Queen's, Rosedale Golf, Toronto Cricket (Toronto); Rideau, Country (Ottawa); Lyford Cay (Bahamas).

FLEMING, Ian, RSA 1956 (ARSA 1947); RSW 1947; RWA 1975; Head, Gray's School of Art, Aberdeen, 1954-71, retired; *b* 19 Nov. 1906; *s* of John and Catherine Fleming; *m* 1943, Catherine Margaret Weetch; one *s* two *d*. *Educ:* Hyndland Sch., Glasgow; Glasgow Sch. of Art. Lectr, Glasgow Sch. of Art, 1931-48; Warden, Patrick Allen-Fraser Art Coll., Hospitalfield, Arbroath, 1948-54. Chm., Peacock Printmakers Workshop (Aberdeen), 1973-. *Recreation:* anything Scottish. *Address:* 15 Fonthill Road, Aberdeen. *T:* 20680. *Club:* Rotary (Aberdeen).

FLEMING, Rear-Adm. Sir John, KBE 1960; DSC 1944; Director of the Naval Education Service, 1956-60; *b* 2 May 1904; *s* of late James Fleming; *m* 1930, Jean Law, *d* of late James Stuart Gillitt, South Shields; no *c*. *Educ:* Jarrow Grammar Sch.; St John's Coll., Cambridge. BA 1925, MA 1957. Entered RN as Instructor Lieut, 1925; Instr Lieut-Comdr, 1937; Instr Comdr, 1939; Instr Capt., 1950; Instr Rear-Adm., 1956. Asst Dir Naval Weather Service, 1945, Dep. Dir, 1947; Fleet Instructor Officer and Fleet Meteorological Officer, Home Fleet, 1950; Command Instructor Officer, The Nore, 1951; Education Dept, Admiralty, 1952. *Recreation:* gardening. *Address:* Mullion Cottage, Tanners Lane, Haslemere, Surrey. *T:* Haselmere 2412.

FLEMING, John, FRSL; writer; *b* 12 June 1919; *s* of Joseph Fleming and Elizabeth Stawart. *Educ:* Rugby Sch.; Trinity Coll., Cambridge (BA). FRSL 1963. Editor of Style & Civilisation, Art in Context, and, Architect and Society, for Penguin Books, 1964-. *Publications:* Robert Adam and his Circle in Edinburgh and Rome, 1962; (with Sir Nikolaus Pevsner and Hugh Honour) The Penguin Dictionary of Architecture, 1966 (rev. edn 1972); (with Hugh Honour) The Penguin Dictionary of Decorative Arts, 1977; (with Hugh Honour) A World History of Art, 1982. *Recreation:* gardening. *Club:* Travellers'.

FLEMING, John Bryden; Secretary, Scottish Special Housing Association, since 1978; *b* 23 June 1918; *s* of W. A. Fleming, advocate, and Maria MacLeod Bryden; *m* 1942, Janet Louise Guthrie (*d* 1981); one *s* three *d*. *Educ:* Edinburgh Academy; Univs of Edinburgh and London. MA 1st Cl. Hons Geog. Edinburgh, BScEcon London. Army, 1940-46, RASC and REME (Major). Planning Officer, Dept of Health for Scotland, 1946; Principal, 1956; Asst Sec., Scottish Develt Dept, 1963, Under Sec., 1974-78. *Recreation:* gardening. *Address:* 28 Mortonhall Road, Edinburgh EH9 2HN. *T:* 031-667 0453. *Clubs:* Royal Commonwealth Society; Scottish Arts (Edinburgh).

FLEMING, Rt. Rev. Launcelot; *see* Fleming, Rt Rev. W. L. S.

FLEMING, Prof. Marston Greig, BSc; PhD; FEng; FIMM; Senior Research Fellow, Imperial College of Science and Technology; Professor of Mineral Technology in the University of London (Imperial College), 1961-80, Emeritus 1980; Consultant; *b* 10 Jan. 1913; *s* of late Alexander Greig Fleming, Montreal; *m* 1951, E. Box, painter; two *s* one *d* (by a previous marriage). *Educ:* Westmount High Sch.; Queen's Univ., Canada. Metallurgist with

Canadian goldmining companies, 1936-41. RCAF navigator, 1941-46; Flight Lieut, 1943. Imperial Coll., Royal Sch. of Mines: Lecturer, 1946-51, Senior Lecturer, 1951-58, Reader, 1958-61; Head of Dept of Mining and Mineral Technology, 1967-74; Dean, 1968-71. Pro-Rector, Imperial Coll., 1974-79; Head of Dept of Mineral Resources Engrg, 1979-80. Mineral processing consultant to governments, mining companies and to HM Govt, at various times, 1946-. Chm., Mineral Processing Cttee, DSIR and Min. of Technology, 1959-66; Member: Cttee on Overseas Geology and Mining, DTC, 1962-63; Steering Cttee, Warren Spring Lab., 1966-68. Chm. Advisory Panel, BCURA, 1961-66; IMM Council, 1962-83, Vice-Pres., 1968-71, Pres., 1971-72; Member: Cttee on Mineral Planning Control, DoE, 1972-75; Chemicals and Minerals Requirements Bd, Dept of Industry, 1972-75. British rep., Scientific Cttee, Internat. Mineral Processing Congress, France, 1963, USA, 1964, USSR, 1968, Czechoslovakia, 1970, London 1973 (Chm., 1973-75), Italy 1975, Poland 1979; Canada 1982; Council of Mining and Metall. Instns, 1969- (Vice-Chm., 1971-76; Chm., 1976-). Dir, UNESCO Regional Course, Benares, 1964; Chm., Brighton Conf. on the Technologist in the Mineral Ind. of the Future, 1969. Member: Governing Body, Imperial Coll., 1968-80 (Fellow, 1982); Ct of Governors, Camborne Sch. of Mines, 1971-82. Hon. ARSM, 1966. 10th Julius Werner Lectr, 1973. IMM Gold Medal, 1981. *Publications:* Identification of Mineral Grains (with M. P. Jones), 1965; papers in a number of scientific and technical journals, etc. *Address:* Zoffany House, 65 Strand-on-the-Green, W4. *Club:* Garrick.

FLEMING, Patrick Lyons; retired Director of Companies; *b* Aberdeen, 3 April 1905; *er s* of late Col Frank Fleming, DSO; *m* 1929, Eleanor (*d* 1970), *d* of late H. G. Tapper; two *d*. *Educ:* Shrewsbury; Lincoln Coll., Oxford (Schol., MA). Dir of numerous companies, mainly connected with what became the Drayton Gp, 1934-78; Council Member: Inst. of Directors, 1948-75 (Treasurer 1974-75); Aims of Industry, 1952-75; Chm. of Epsom Division Conservative Assoc., 1949-50. *Publications:* sundry contribs to financial jls. *Recreations:* reading, formerly rowing and field sports. *Address:* Baltic House, The Common, Cranleigh, Surrey. *T:* Cranleigh 3676.

FLEMING, Raylton Arthur; Director of Information, United Nations University, on loan from COI, since 1978; *b* 1925; *s* of Arthur and Evelyn Fleming; *m* 1967, Leila el Doweini; one *s*. *Educ:* Worksop Coll. Associate Producer, World Wide Pictures Ltd, 1952; Head of Overseas Television Production, Central Office of Information, 1957; Dep. Dir, Films/Television Div., COI, 1961; Asst Controller (Overseas) COI, 1968; Actg Controller (Overseas), 1969; Dir, Exhibns Div. COI, 1971; Controller (Home), COI, 1972-76; Controller (Overseas), COI, 1976-78. *Recreations:* music, opera. *Address:* c/o United Nations University, 29th Floor, Toho Seimei Building, 15-1, Shibuya 2-chome, Shibuya-ku, Tokyo 150, Japan.

FLEMING, Rt. Rev. (William) Launcelot (Scott), KCVO 1976; DD (Lambeth); MA (Cambridge), MS (Yale); FRSE; *b* 7 Aug. 1906; *y s* of late Robert Alexander Fleming, MD, LLD; *m* 1965, Jane, widow of Anthony Agutter. *Educ:* Rugby Sch.; Trinity Hall and Westcott House, Cambridge; Yale Univ. Commonwealth Fund Fellow, Yale Univ., 1929-31; Deacon, 1933; Priest, 1934; Expeditions to Iceland and Spitzbergen, 1932 and 1933; Chaplain and Geologist, British Graham Land Expedition to the Antarctic, 1934-37; Polar Medal, 1935-37; Examining Chaplain to Bishop of Southwark, 1937-49, to Bishop of St Albans, 1940-43, to Bishop of Hereford, 1942-49; Fellow and Chaplain, Trinity Hall, Cambridge, 1933-49, Dean, 1937-49; Director of Scott Polar Research Institute, Cambridge, 1947-49; Bishop of Portsmouth, 1949-59; Bishop of Norwich, 1959-71; Dean of Windsor, 1971-76; Register, Order of the Garter, 1971-76; Domestic Chaplain to the Queen, 1971-76. Chaplain RNVR, HMS King Alfred, 1940; HMS Queen Elizabeth, 1940-43; HMS Ganges, 1943-44; Director of Service Ordination Candidates, 1944-46. Chairman: Church of England Youth Council, 1950-61; Archbishops' Advisers for Needs and Resources, 1963-73. Parly Gp for World Govt: Vice-Chm., 1969-71; Chm., Associate Members, 1971-76. Member: Council, Univ. of E Anglia, 1964-71; Royal Commn on Environmental Pollution, 1970-73; Chairman of Governors, Portsmouth Grammar Sch., 1950-59; Canford Sch., 1954-60; Mem., Governing Body, United World Coll. of the Atlantic; a Governor, Bryanston Sch.; Pres., Young Explorers Trust, 1976-79; Trustee, Prince's Trust. Hon. Chaplain, RNR (RNVR 1950). Hon. Fellow, Trinity Hall, Cambridge, 1956; Hon. Vice-President, Royal Geographical Society, 1961. Hon. DCL Univ. of East Anglia, 1976. *Address:* Tithe Barn, Poyntington, near Sherborne, Dorset DT9 4LF. *T:* Corton Denham 479.

FLEMINGTON, Rev. William Frederick, MA Oxon, BD Cantab; Principal of Wesley House, Cambridge, 1955-67; held Greenhalgh Chair of New Testament Language and Literature, Wesley House, Cambridge, 1937-67, retired; *b* 24 May 1901; *er s* of Rev. William Frederick Flemington and Annie Mary Geden Bate; *m* 1930, Ethel Phyllis Goodenough, *er d* of Rev. John Henry Doddrell; one *s* one *d*. *Educ:* Liverpool Coll.; Jesus Coll., Oxford (Exhibitioner, 2nd Cl. Classical Hon. Mods, 2nd Cl. Lit. Hum.); Jesus Coll., Fitzwilliam Coll. and Wesley House, Cambridge (Carus Greek Testament Prize; 1st Cl. Theological Tripos, Pt II, Sect. 2, New Testament). Entered Wesleyan Methodist Ministry, 1925; Asst Tutor, Handsworth Coll., Birmingham, 1926-30; Minister in Stourbridge Circuit (Cradley), 1930-33; West Bromwich Circuit, 1933-37; Tutor, Wesley House, 1937-55. Select Preacher, Cambridge Univ., 1944, 1950, 1954. Pres. of Cambridge Theological Soc., 1963-65. *Publications:* The New Testament Doctrine of Baptism, 1948; contributor to Prayer and Worship, 1945; articles and reviews in Expository Times and Jl of Theological Studies. *Recreations:* walking, reading. *Address:* 204 Chesterton Road, Cambridge.

FLEMMING, John Stanton; Chief Adviser, Bank of England, since 1980; *b* 6 Feb. 1941; *s* of Sir Gilbert Nicolson Flemming, KCB, and of Virginia Coit; *m* 1963, Jean Elizabeth (*née* Briggs); three *s* one *d. Educ:* Rugby Sch.; Trinity and Nuffield Colls, Oxon. BA Oxon 1962, MA 1966. Lecturer and Fellow, Oriel Coll., Oxford, 1963-65; Official Fellow in Economics, 1965-80, Emeritus Fellow, 1980, and Bursar, 1970-79, Nuffield Coll., Oxford. Member: Nat. Freight Corp., 1978-80; Council, Royal Economic Soc., 1980-; Chm., Economics Cttee, SSRC, 1981-. Associate Editor: Oxford Economic Papers, 1970-73; Review of Economic Studies, 1973-76; Editor, Economic Jl, 1976-80. *Publications:* Inflation, 1976; contrib. economic jls. *Address:* Bank of England, Threadneedle Street, EC4. *T:* 01-601 4963.

FLETCHER, family name of **Baron Fletcher.**

FLETCHER, Baron *cr* 1970 (Life Peer), of Islington; **Eric George Molyneux Fletcher,** PC 1967; Kt 1964; LLD London; Solicitor, Consultant to Denton, Hall & Burgin, Gray's Inn and Paris; *b* 26 March 1903; *s* of late Clarence George Eugene Fletcher, Town Clerk of Islington; *m* 1929, Bessie Winifred, *d* of late James Butt, Enfield; two *s* one *d. Educ:* Radley; University of London, LLB London, 1923; Admitted Solicitor, 1924; BA London, 1926; LLD London, 1932; FSA 1954; FRHistS. MP (Lab) East Islington, 1945-70; Minister without Portfolio, 1964-66; Chairman of Ways and Means and Deputy Speaker, House of Commons, 1966-68. Mem. LCC for South Islington, 1934-49 (Chm. Finance Cttee); formerly Mem. Exec. Cttee Fabian Soc.; Dep. Chm., Associated British Picture Corp., 1946-64; Commissioner for Public Works Loans, 1946-55; Senator of London Univ., 1946-50 and 1956-74; Mem. Exec. Cttee Grotius Soc.; Pres. of Seldon Soc., 1967-70; Chm., Management Cttee, Inst. of Archaeology, 1968-73; Governor: Birkbeck Coll., 1934-62; London Sch. of Economics; Member: Evershed Cttee on Practice and Procedure of Supreme Court; Church Assembly, 1962; Commission on Church and State, 1951; Advisory Council on Public Records, 1959-64; Royal Commission on Historical Manuscripts, 1966-; Statute Law Cttee, 1951-76. A Trustee of the British Museum, 1968-77. Chm., Advisory Bd for Redundant Churches, 1969-74. Pres. British Archæological Assoc., 1960-63. *Publications:* The Students' Conflict of Laws, 1928 (with late E. Leslie Burgin); The Carrier's Liability, 1932; miscellaneous articles on legal historical, and archæological subjects. *Recreations:* golf, swimming. *Address:* 90 Chancery Lane, WC2. *T:* 01-242 1212. The Barn, The Green, Sarratt, Rickmansworth, Herts WD3 6BP. *T:* King's Langley 63385. *Club:* Athenæum.

FLETCHER, Alan Gerard, RDI 1972; FSIAD; designer; Partner, Pentagram Design; *b* Nairobi, Kenya, 27 Sept. 1931; *s* of Bernard Fletcher and Dorothy Murphy; *m* 1956, Paola Biagi; one *d. Educ:* Christ's Hosp. Sch.; Central Sch. of Arts and Crafts; Royal Coll. of Art (ARCA); Sch. of Architecture and Design, Yale Univ. (Master of Fine Arts). FSIAD 1964. Designer, Fortune Magazine, New York, 1958-59; freelance practice, London, 1959-62; Partner: Fletcher Forbes Gill, 1962-65; Crosby Fletcher Forbes, 1965-72; Partner, Pentagram, 1972-. Pres., Designers and Art Dirs Assoc., 1973; Mem., Alliance Graphique Internat. Served on design competition juries for: Designers and Art Dirs Assoc. Exhibns, London; Internat. poster Biennale, Warsaw; Annual Awards for Newspaper Design, London; Art Dirs Club, Toronto; European Illustration, London; Common Market EEC symbol, Brussels; Amer. Inst. of Graphic Arts. Designers and Art Dirs Assoc. Gold Award for Design, 1974, and President's Award for Outstanding Contribn to Design, 1977; One Show Gold Award for Design, New York, 1974. *Publications:* (jtly) Graphic Design: a visual comparison, 1963; (jtly) A Sign Systems Manual, 1970; (jtly) Identity Kits, 1971; (jtly) Living by Design, 1978; (also illus.) Was Ich Sah, 1967. *Address:* Pentagram, 61 North Wharf Road, W2 1LA. *T:* 01-402 5511.

FLETCHER, Hon. Sir Alan (Roy), Kt 1972; Minister for Education and Cultural Activities, Queensland, 1968-74, retired 1975; MLA (Country Party) for Cunningham, Queensland, 1953-74; *b* Pittsworth, 26 Jan. 1907; *s* of Alexander Roy Fletcher, Pittsworth, and Rosina Wilhemina (*née* McIntyre); *m* 1934, Enid Phair, *d* of James Thompson, Ashburton, NZ; two *s* two *d. Educ:* Irongate State Sch.; Scots Coll., Warwick, Qld. Pittsworth Shire: Councillor, 1945-57, Chm., 1949-57. Speaker, Legislative Assembly, Qld, 1957-60; Minister for Lands, 1960-68. Dir, Queensland Co-op. Milling Assoc., 1951-65. Member: Presbyterian Schs Council, Warwick, 1951-, (Chm., 1958-61); Council, Darling Downs Inst. of Advanced Educn, 1975-. Pres., Old Boys' Assoc., Scots Coll., Warwick, 1948-. *Recreations:* shooting, croquet. *Address:* Te Mata, Mount Tyson, Queensland 4356, Australia. *T:* Irongate 938184.

FLETCHER, Alexander MacPherson; MP (C) Edinburgh North since Nov. 1973; Parliamentary Under Secretary of State, Scottish Office, since 1979; *b* 26 Aug. 1929; *s* of Alexander Fletcher and Margaret Muirhead; *m* 1950, Christine Ann Buchanan; two *s* one *d. Educ:* Greenock High School. Chartered Accountant, 1956. Marketing Exec., internat. co., 1956-64; Man. Dir, 1964-71; private practice as Chartered Accountant, 1971-. Mem. East Kilbride Develt Corp., 1971-73. Opposition front bench spokesman on Scottish Affairs, 1977-79. Mem., European Parlt, 1976-77. Contested (C) West Renfrewshire, 1970. Elder, Cramond Kirk. *Recreations:* golf, music. *Address:* House of Commons, SW1. *Clubs:* Caledonian; New (Edinburgh).

FLETCHER, Ann Elizabeth Mary, (Mrs Michael Fletcher); *see* Leslie, A. E. M.

FLETCHER, Dr Archibald Peter; Research Physician, Upjohn International Inc., Brussels, since 1979; *b* 24 Dec. 1930; *s* of Walter Archibald Fletcher and Dorothy Mabel Fletcher; *m* 1972, Patricia Elizabeth (*née* Marr); three *s* two *d. Educ:* Kingswood Sch.; London Hosp. Med. Coll.; St Mary's Hosp. Med. Sch., London Univ. MB, BS; PhD (Biochemistry). Sen. Lectr in Chemical Pathology, St Mary's Hosp., London, 1961-69; Head of Biochemistry, American Nat. Red Cross, USA, 1970-73; Med. Dir, Upjohn, Scandinavia; PMO, Medicines Div., DHSS, 1977; Med. Assessor to Cttee on Safety of Medicines; Chief Sci. Officer and SPMO, DHSS, 1978-79. *Publications:* numerous papers in scientific and medical journals on glycoproteins, physical chemistry and metabolism of blood cells. *Recreations:* gardening, golf. *Address:* Hall Corner Cottage, Little Maplestead, Halstead, Essex. *T:* Halstead 5465.

FLETCHER, Augustus James Voisey, OBE 1977; GM 1957; HM Diplomatic Service; Foreign and Commonwealth Office, since 1982; *b* 23 Dec. 1928; *s* of James Fletcher and Naomi Fletcher (*née* Dudden); *m* 1956, Enyd Gwynne Harries; one *s* one *d. Educ:* Weston-super-Mare Grammar Sch.; Oriental Language Institute, Malaya. Colonial Service, Palestine, 1946-48, Malaya, 1948-58; Min. of Defence, 1958-64; FCO, 1964-: Hong Kong (seconded HQ Land Forces), 1966-70; FCO, 1970-73; Hong Kong, 1973-76; FCO, 1976-79; Counsellor, New Delhi, 1979-82. *Recreations:* trout fishing, walking, food/wine, theatre. *Address:* c/o Foreign and Commonwealth Office, SW1; 14 Hermitage Close, E18 2BW. *T:* 01-989 0766. *Clubs:* Travellers', Royal Commonwealth Society.

FLETCHER, Prof. Basil Alais, MA, BSc; Emeritus Professor, University of Leeds; Research Fellow, Bristol University, 1971; *b* 10 April 1900; *s* of Walter Henry and Julia Fletcher; *m* 1928, Gerrardine Mary, *d* of William Daly; one *s* one *d. Educ:* Ilford Sch., Essex; University Coll., London. Physics Master, Gresham's Sch., Holt, Norfolk, 1922-26; Fellow Commoner, Sidney Sussex Coll., Cambridge, 1926-27; Senior Science Master, Gresham's Sch., Holt, 1927-30; Albert Kahn Fellow for Great Britain, 1930-31; Headmaster, Chippenham Sch., Wilts, 1932-35; Prof. of Education, Dalhousie Univ., Halifax, Canada, 1935-39; Prof. of Education, University Coll., Southampton, 1939-41; Prof. of Education, Bristol Univ., 1941-55; Vice-Principal of the University Coll. of Rhodesia and Nyasaland, Salisbury, 1956-60. *Publications:* Laboratory Physics (with H. W. Heckstall-Smith), 1926; Youth Looks at the World, 1932; Education and Colonial Policy, 1936; Child Psychology for Parents, 1938; The Next Step in Canadian Education, 1939; Education and Crisis, 1946; A Philosophy for the Teacher, 1961; Universities in the Modern World, 1968; The Challenge of the Outward Bound, 1971. *Address:* 4 Belmont, Lansdown, Bath BA1 5DZ.

FLETCHER, Charles Montague, CBE 1952; MD, FRCP; Physician to Hammersmith Hospital, 1952-76; Professor of Clinical Epidemiology, University of London at Royal Postgraduate Medical School, 1973-76 (Reader, 1952-73), now Professor Emeritus; *b* 5 June 1911; *s* of late Sir Walter Morley Fletcher, FRS and Mary Frances Fletcher (*née* Cropper); *m* Louisa Mary Sylvia Seely, *d* of 1st Baron Mottistone; one *s* two *d. Educ:* Eton Coll.; Trinity Coll., Cambridge (Sen. Schol.; rowed in Univ. Boat, 1933); St Bartholomew's Hospital. MA 1936, MD 1945, Cantab; MRCP 1942; FRCP 1947; FFCM 1974. Michael Foster Research Student, Trinity Coll., 1934-36; Nuffield Res. Student, Oxford, 1940-42. Asst Phys., EMS, 1943-44; Dir, MRC Pneumoconiosis Res. Unit, 1945-52. Sec., MRC Cttee on Bronchitis Res., 1954-76; Sec., RCP Cttee on Smoking and Health, 1961-71; WHO Consultant: Pulmonary Heart Disease, 1960; Chronic Bronchitis, 1962; Smoking and Health, 1970. Mem., Central Health Services Cttee and Standing Med. Adv. Cttee, 1966-76; Vice-Chm., Health Educn Council, 1967; Chairman, Action on Smoking and Health (ASH), 1971-78, Pres., 1979. Introd. many TV med. programmes incl. Hurt Mind, 1955, Your Life in Their Hands, 1958-65, Television Doctor, 1969-70. Goulstonian Lectr, RCP, 1947; Mem. Council, RCP, 1959-62; Bissett Hawkins Gold Medal, RCP, 1969. *Publications:* Communication in Medicine, 1973; Natural History of Chronic Bronchitis and Emphysema, 1976; many papers on: first use of penicillin, 1941; dust disease of lungs, 1946-55; bronchitis and emphysema, 1952-76. *Recreations:* music, gardening, beekeeping. *Address:* 20 Drayton Gardens, SW10 9SA. *T:* 01-373 2827; 2 Coastguard Cottages, Newtown, IoW PO30 4PA. *T:* Calbourne 321. *Club:* Brooks's.

FLETCHER, Edward Joseph; MP (Lab) Darlington since 1964; *b* 25 Feb. 1911; *m* Constance Murial, *d* of George Lee, Whickham, Hants; two *d. Educ:* St Mary's Sch., Handsworth; Fircroft Coll., Bourneville, Birmingham. Joined Labour Party, 1926; has held many offices; Chm., Tribune Group, 1977-78. Member: AEU, 1932 (Mem. Birmingham Dist Cttee); Clerical and Admin. Workers' Union, 1950 (Northern Area Sec., 1949-64); Newcastle City Council, 1952-64 (Chm. Finance Cttee, Dep. Ldr Labour Gp). Chm. N Eastern Assoc. for the Arts, 1961-65. *Address:* House of Commons, SW1.

FLETCHER, Geoffrey Bernard Abbott, MA Cantab; *b* Hampstead, 28 Nov. 1903; *s* of J. Alexander Fletcher and Ursula Constance, *d* of William Richard Rickett and *cousin* of Rt Honourable Sir Joseph Compton-Rickett, MP. *Educ:* Rugby Sch.; King's Coll., Cambridge (Senior Scholar), First Class, Classical Tripos, Part I, 1924; First Class Classical Tripos, Part 2, 1926; Prendergast Student, 1926; Asst Lectr in Classics, University of Leeds, 1927-28;

Lectr in Greek, University of Liverpool, 1928-36; Prof. of Classics in the University of Durham, King's Coll., Newcastle upon Tyne, 1937-46, Prof. of Latin, 1946-63; Prof. of Latin, University of Newcastle upon Tyne, 1963-69, now Emeritus Prof. Examiner in Greek, University of Leeds, 1940-42; Examiner in Latin, Queen's Univ., Belfast, 1949-51, University of Wales, 1954-56, Bristol, 1961-63; Dean of Faculty of Arts, University of Durham, 1945-47; Public Orator, University of Durham, 1956-58. *Publications:* an appendix on Housman's Poetry in Housman, 1897-1936, by Grant Richards, 1941; Annotations on Tacitus, 1964; many contributions to classical and other periodicals, British and foreign, and to co-operative works. *Recreations:* music, reading, art-galleries, walking, travel. *Address:* Thirlmere Lodge, Elmfield Road, Gosforth, Newcastle upon Tyne NE3 4BB. *T:* Gosforth 852873. *Club:* Athenæum.

FLETCHER, Geoffrey Scowcroft; artist and author; *o s* of Herbert Fletcher and Annie Talence Fletcher; *m* 1953, Mary Jean Timothy. *Educ:* University Coll., London Univ. (Dip. in Fine Art). Abbey Major Schol., British Sch. at Rome, 1948. Drawings appeared in Manchester Guardian, 1950; London drawings and articles featured in The Daily Telegraph, 1958-. Author of television features on unusual aspects of London; has been instrumental in saving a number of metropolitan buildings from demolition. Drawings and paintings in various public and private collections in England and abroad, incl. exhibn of paintings and drawings in possession of Islington Council, 1972, 1978; Geoffrey Fletcher Room, decorated with the artist's drawings, opened Selfridge Hotel, London, 1973. Designed enamel box for St Paul's Cathedral Appeal, 1972; exhibn of drawings, Miles Gall., St James's, 1980. *Publications:* The London Nobody Knows (filmed, 1968), 1962; Down Among the Meths Men, 1966; Geoffrey Fletcher's London, 1968; City Sights, 1963; Pearly Kingdom, 1965; London's River, 1966; Elements of Sketching, 1966 (Amer. edn, 1968); London's Pavement Pounders, 1967; London After Dark, 1969; Changing London (Drawings from The Daily Telegraph), 1969; The London Dickens Knew, 1970; London Souvenirs, 1973; Paint It In Water Colour, 1974; Italian Impressions, 1974; Sketch It In Black and White, 1975; Daily Telegraph Series: London Prints, 1975, London Colour Prints, 1978, London Portraits, 1978, London at My Feet, 1979; London Alleys, 1980. *Address:* c/o The Daily Telegraph, Fleet Street, EC4.

FLETCHER, Sir James Muir Cameron, Kt 1980; FCA; President, Fletcher Challenge Ltd, Wellington, New Zealand; Chairman: BP New Zealand Ltd; Forest Investments Ltd; Hikurangi Forest Farms Ltd; Lusteroid Holdings (NZ) Ltd; Marac Holdings Ltd; Nylex New Zealand Ltd; Pacific Steel Ltd; Director, Alcan New Zealand Ltd; *b* Dunedin, NZ, 25 Dec. 1914; *s* of Sir James Fletcher; *m* 1942, Margery Vaughan, *d* of H. H. Gunthorp; three *s. Educ:* Waitaki Boys' High School; Auckland Grammar School. South British Insurance Co., 1931-37; then Fletcher Construction Co. and Fletcher Holdings. Member, Lloyd's Register of Shipping NZ Cttee. *Address:* Fletcher Challenge Ltd, Private Bag, Auckland, New Zealand; 2 Crescent Road, Parnell, Auckland, NZ.

FLETCHER, James Thomas, CBE 1967; Chairman, North Yorkshire County Council, 1973-77 (formerly North Riding of Yorkshire County Council, 1957-73); *b* 3 Dec. 1898; *s* of Thomas Fletcher; *m* 1933, A. Walburn; two *s* one *d. Educ:* St John's Sch., Whitby. Mayor of Borough of Redcar, 1944; Chm., S Tees-side Hosp. Man. Cttee, 1958-74; Mem., N Riding Yorks. CC, 1934. *Address:* Fordbridge, 12 Whin Green, Sleights, Whitby, N Yorks. *T:* Sleights 620.

FLETCHER, Sir John Henry Lancelot A.; *see* Aubrey-Fletcher.

FLETCHER, (Leopold) Raymond; MP (Lab) Ilkeston since 1964; Journalist; *b* 3 Dec. 1921; *s* of Leopold Raymond Fletcher, Ruddington, Notts; *m* 1st, 1947, Johanna Klara Elisabeth (*d* 1973), *d* of Karl Ising, Berlin; 2nd, 1977, Dr Catherine Elliott. *Educ:* abroad. Served 1941-48 with Indian Army Ordnance Corps. Columnist on The Times and contributor to other journals at home and abroad. Vice-Pres., Assembly of Council of Europe, 1974-76; Leader, UK Delegn to Council of Europe and WEU, 1974-76; Leader, Socialist Gp in Council of Europe, 1974-76. Mem., T&GWU. Founder and Council Mem., Airship Assoc. *Publication:* Sixty Pounds a Second on Defence, 1963. *Recreation:* theatre. *Address:* 304 Frobisher House, Dolphin Square, SW1V 3LX.

FLETCHER, Leslie; General Manager (Chief Executive Officer) Williams Deacon's Bank Ltd, 1964-70, Director, 1966-70, retired; *b* 30 Jan. 1906; *s* of late Edward Henry and Edith Howard Fletcher; *m* 1934, Helen, *d* of Frank Turton; one *s* one *d. Educ:* City Gram. Sch., Chester; Manchester Univ. (BA Com). Entered Williams Deacon's Bank Ltd 1922; Asst Gen. Man., 1957; Dep. Gen. Man., 1961. Fellow and Mem. Council, Inst. of Bankers. *Recreations:* lawn tennis, golf. *Address:* Mote Cottage, Burley, near Ringwood, Hants. *T:* Burley 2291.

FLETCHER, Sir Norman Seymour, Kt 1977; agriculturalist and pastoralist, Western Australia; *b* Sydney, 20 Sept. 1905; *s* of Thomas Fletcher, Nottingham and Ivy Jeffrey, Goulburn, NSW. Established the Dirk Brook Stud at Keysbrook in 1948 and pioneered the introduction to WA of the Hereford cattle breed. AASA. Past Pres., Western Australia Royal Agricultural Soc.; has given outstanding service to the agricultural and pastoral industries in WA for 30 years; worked hard for advancement and development of cattle and meat industry, both in the southern areas of WA

and in the Kimberleys. *Address:* 6 The Esplanade, Perth, Western Australia. *Clubs:* Weld, Western Australian (Perth).

FLETCHER, Paul Thomas, CBE 1959; Deputy Chairman, Atomic Power Constructions Ltd (Managing Director, 1971); Director, Nuclear Power Co. Ltd; *b* 30 Sept. 1912; *s* of Stephen Baldwin Fletcher and Jessie Carrie; *m* 1941, Mary Elizabeth King; three *s. Educ:* Nicholson Inst., Stornaway, Isle of Lewis; Maidstone Grammar Sch.; Medway Techn. Coll. BSc(Eng); FEng, FICE, FIMechE, FIEE. Served 3-year apprenticeship with E. A. Gardner & Sons Ltd, Maidstone, remaining for 7 years; joined Min. of Works, 1939, initially in Test Br. of Engrg Div., later with responsibility for variety of engrg services in public bldgs and Govt factories and for plant and equipment for Govt civilian and service res. estabts; Chief Mech. and Elec. Engr, 1951. On formation of UKAEA in 1954, became Dep. Dir of Engrg in Industrial Gp, later Engrg Dir and Dep. Man. Dir; Dir, United Power Co., 1961; Man. Dir, GEC (Process Engrg) Ltd, 1965. Chairman: BSI, 1979; Pressure Vessels Quality Assurance Bd, 1977-. Pres., IMechE, 1975-76. *Publications:* papers to IMechE. *Recreations:* photography, motoring. *Address:* 26 Foxgrove Avenue, Beckenham, Kent BR3 2BA. *T:* 01-650 5563.

FLETCHER, Air Chief Marshal Sir Peter Carteret, KCB 1968 (CB 1965); OBE 1945; DFC 1943; AFC 1952; Director, Corporate Strategy and Planning, British Aerospace, 1977-82; Director, Airbus Industry Supervisory Board, 1979-82; *b* 7 Oct. 1916; *s* of F. T. W. Fletcher, Oxford (sometime tobacco farmer, Southern Rhodesia), and Dora Clulee, New Zealand; *m* 1940, Marjorie Isobel Kotze; two *d. Educ:* St George's Coll., Southern Rhodesia; Rhodes Univ., S Africa. SR Law Dept, 1937. Served War of 1939-45: SR Air Force, 1939; trans. to RAF, 1941; commanded 135 and 258 Fighter Sqdns and RAF Station Belvedere. Directing Staffs at: RAF Staff Coll., 1945-46; Jt Services Staff Coll., 1946-48; Imp. Defence Coll., 1956-58; Mem. Jt Planning Staff, 1951-53; comdg RAF Abingdon, 1958-60; Dep. Dir Jt Planning Staff, 1960-61; Dir of Opl Requirements (B), Air Min., 1961-63; Asst Chief of Air Staff (Policy and Plans), 1964-66; AOC, No 38 Group, Transport Command, 1966-67; VCAS, 1967-70; Controller of Aircraft, Min. of Aviation Supply (formerly Min. of Technology), 1970-71; Air Systems Controller, Defence Procurement Executive, MoD, 1971-73; Dir, Hawker Siddeley Aviation Ltd, 1974-77. *Recreations:* books, travel. *Address:* Woodlands, Sandy Lane, Tilford, Surrey GU10 2ET. *T:* Frensham 2897.

FLETCHER, Raymond; *see* Fletcher, L. R.

FLETCHER, Richard Cawthorne, OBE 1981; MA; JP; Headmaster, Worcester College for the Blind, 1959-80; *b* 30 Aug. 1916; *s* of late Philip C. Fletcher, MC, and of Edith Maud (*née* Okell); *m* 1946, Joan Fairlie Woodcock; one *s* one *d. Educ:* Marlborough; University Coll., Oxford. Served Army (Emergency Commn), 1939-46. Asst Master, Charterhouse, 1946-Aug. 1959. *Publication:* (ed) The Teaching of Science and Mathematics to the Blind, 1973. *Recreation:* music. *Address:* Yew Tree Cottage, Wick, near Pershore, Worcestershire.
See also R. A. Fletcher.

FLETCHER, Robin Anthony, DSC 1944; DPhil; Warden of Rhodes House Oxford, since 1980; Professorial Fellow, Trinity College, Oxford, since 1980; *b* 30 May 1922; *s* of Philip Cawthorne Fletcher, MC, and Edith Maud Fletcher (*née* Okell); *m* 1950, Jinny May (*née* Cornish); two *s. Educ:* Marlborough Coll.; Trinity Coll., Oxford (MA, DPhil). Served Royal Navy (Lieut RNVR), 1941-46. University Lecturer in Modern Greek, 1949-79; Domestic Bursar, Trinity Coll., Oxford, 1950-74; Senior Proctor, 1966-67; Member, Hebdomedal Council, 1967-74. President, Hockey Assoc., 1972-. *Publications:* various articles. *Recreations:* sport, music. *Address:* Rhodes House, Oxford. *T:* Oxford 55745. *Clubs:* Naval; Vincent's (Oxford).
See also Richard Cawthorne Fletcher.

FLETCHER-COOKE, Sir Charles (Fletcher), Kt 1981; QC 1958; MP (C) Darwen Division of Lancashire since 1951; *b* 5 May 1914; *yr s* of late Capt. C. A. and Gwendolen May Fletcher-Cooke; *m* 1959, Diana Lady Avebury (whom he divorced, 1967), *d* of late Capt. Edward King and of Mrs J. St Vincent Hand; no surv. *c. Educ:* Malvern Coll. (Scholar); Peterhouse, Cambridge (Schol., MA 1940). Pres., Cambridge Union, 1936; Editor, The Granta, 1936. Called to Bar through Lincoln's Inn, 1938 (1st Class Hons, Bar Final Examination; Studentship and Certificate of Honour); Bencher 1969. Mem. Senate, Four Inns of Court, 1970-74. Served War of 1939-45, in Naval Intelligence Div. and on Joint Intelligence Staff, with rank of Lieut-Comdr, RNVR. Contested (Lab) East Dorset Div., 1945, re-adopted, 1946, but resigned from Labour Party shortly afterwards. Legal Adviser to British Delegation, Danube Conf., Belgrade, 1948; Deleg. to Consultative Assembly of Council of Europe, 1954-55; Mem., European Parlt, 1977-79. Mem., Statute Law Cttee, 1955-61, 1970-; Chm., Select Cttee on Parliamentary Commissioner for Administration, 1974-77. Joint Parliamentary Under-Sec. of State, Home Office, 1961-63. Dato SPMB, Brunei, 1978. *Publications:* (with others) The Rule of Law; (with M. J. Albery) Monopolies and Restrictive Trade Practices. *Recreations:* tennis, fishing. *Address:* 4 North Court, Great Peter Street, SW1. *T:* 01-799 5859; 2 Paper Buildings, Temple, EC4. *T:* 01-353 1853. *Clubs:* Garrick, Pratt's.
See also Sir John Fletcher-Cooke.

FLETCHER-COOKE, Sir John, Kt 1962; CMG 1952; MA Oxon; *b* 8 Aug. 1911; *er s* of late Charles Arthur and Gwendolen May Fletcher-Cooke; *m* 1st,

1949, Alice (marr. diss. 1971), *d* of Dr Egner, Washington, DC; two *s* one *d* ; 2nd, 1977, Marie-Louise, *widow* of Louis Vicomte Fournier de la Barre. *Educ:* Malvern Coll. (Barham Schol.); University of Paris (Diplomé, degré supérieur); Oxford Univ. (Kitchener Scholar, Senior Exhibitioner, St Edmund Hall). First Cl. Hons Politics, Philosophy and Economics; economic research, Oxford Univ., 1933; Asst Principal, Colonial Office, 1934; Private Sec. to successive Permanent Under-Secs of State for the Colonies, 1937; Officer Malayan CS, 1937; Asst Sec., FMS, 1938; special duty, FMS, 1939; Magistrate, Singapore, 1939; Sec., Foreign Exchange Control, Malaya, 1939; Dist Officer, FMS, 1940. Served with RAF as intelligence officer, FO, 1942-46; Prisoner of War in Japan, 1942-45. Attached to Colonial Office for special duty and accompanied Constitutional Comr to Malta, 1946; Under-Sec. to Govt of Palestine, 1946-48; Mem. Exec. Council, Palestine, 1947; Special Rep. for Palestine at UN discussions on Palestine, 1948; UK rep. on Special Cttee and later on Trusteeship Council UN, Geneva and Lake Success, 1948-50; Counsellor (Colonial Affairs), Perm. UK Deleg. to UN, New York, 1949-51; Colonial Adviser to UK Deleg. to UN Gen. Assembly, 1948-50 and alternate UK deleg. to UN Gen. Assembly 1949; Colonial Sec., Cyprus, 1951-55. Acted as Governor of Cyprus for various periods, 1951-55. Attached Colonial Office for Special Duty (temp.), 1956; Minister for Constitutional Affairs, Tanganyika, 1956-59; Chief Sec. to the Govt of Tanganyika, 1959-60. Special Rep. of Tanganyika at Ghana Independence Celebrations, 1957, at Economic Commission for Africa, Addis Ababa, 1959, and at Trusteeship Council, UN, New York, 1957, 1958, 1959, 1960 and 1961. Acted as Governor of Tanganyika for various periods, 1959-61; Dep. Governor, Tanganyika, 1960-61. Visiting Prof. (African Affairs) University of Colorado, Boulder, USA, 1961-62, 1966, and 1973-74; Fellow, African Studies Assoc., NY, 1961-. Mem. Constituencies Delimitation Commn for Kenya, 1962; Mem. Exec. Cttee, Overseas Employers' Federation, 1963-67. Contested (C) Luton, Nov. 1963. MP (C) Test Div. of Southampton, 1964-66. Mem. Councils of Royal Commonwealth Society and of United Society for Propagation of the Gospel, 1964-67. Vice-Chm., Internat. Team to review structure and organisation of FAO, Rome, 1967. Dir, Programmes in Diplomacy, Carnegie Endowment for International Peace, New York, 1967-69. Mission for British Govt to Anglo-French Condominium of New Hebrides, 1969. Chm., various Civil Service Commn Selection Boards, 1971-. *Publications:* The Emperor's Guest, 1942-45, 1971, 3rd edn 1982 (also issued as Talking Book for the Blind, 1982); contrib. to Parliament as an Export, 1966, and to many periodicals. *Recreation:* building dry Cotswold stone walls. *Address:* c/o Lloyds Bank, Stock Exchange Branch, 111 Old Broad Street, EC2N 1AU. *Clubs:* Travellers', Royal Commonwealth Society.
See also Sir Charles Fletcher-Cooke.

FLETCHER-VANE, family name of **Baron Inglewood.**

FLEW, Prof. Antony Garrard Newton; Professor of Philosophy, University of Reading, since 1973; *b* 11 Feb. 1923; *o s* of Rev. Dr R. N. Flew; *m* 1952, Annis Ruth Harty; two *d. Educ:* St Faiths Sch., Cambridge; Kingswood Sch., Bath; Sch. of Oriental and African Studies, London; St John's Coll., Oxford (John Locke Schol., MA); DLitt Keele, 1974. Lectr: Christ Church, Oxford, 1949-50; Univ. of Aberdeen, 1950-54; Prof. of Philosophy: Univ. of Keele, 1954-71; Univ. of Calgary, 1972-73. Many temp. vis. appts. Gavin David Young Lectr, Adelaide, 1963. A Vice-Pres., Rationalist Press Assoc., 1973-; Chm., Voluntary Euthanasia Soc., 1976-79. *Publications:* A New Approach to Psychical Research, 1953; Hume's Philosophy of Belief, 1961; God and Philosophy, 1966; Evolutionary Ethics, 1967; An Introduction to Western Philosophy, 1971; Crime or Disease?, 1973; Thinking About Thinking, 1975; The Presumption of Atheism, 1976; Sociology, Equality and Education, 1976; A Rational Animal, 1978; Philosophy: an introduction, 1979; The Politics of Procrustes, 1981; articles in philosophical and other jls. *Recreations:* walking, climbing, house maintenance. *Address:* 26 Alexandra Road, Reading, Berks RG1 5PD. *T:* Reading 61848. *Club:* Union Society (Oxford).

FLINT, Prof. David, TD, MA, BL, CA; Professor of Accountancy, since 1964 (Johnstone Smith Chair, 1964-75), and Vice-Principal, since 1981, University of Glasgow; *b* 24 Feb. 1919; *s* of David Flint, JP, and Agnes Strang Lambie; *m* 1953, Dorothy Mary Maclachlan Jardine; two *s* one *d. Educ:* Glasgow High Sch.; University of Glasgow. Served with Royal Signals, 1939-46, Major (despatches). Awarded distinction final examination of Institute of Chartered Accountants of Scotland, 1948. Lecturer, University of Glasgow, 1950-60; Dean of Faculty of Law, 1971-73. Partner, Mann Judd Gordon & Co. Chartered Accountants, Glasgow, 1951-71. Hon. Pres. Glasgow Chartered Accountants Students Soc., 1959-60; Chm., Assoc. of Univ. Teachers of Accounting, 1969. Mem. Council, Scottish Business Sch., 1971-77; Vice-Pres., Scottish Economic Soc.; Vice-Pres., Inst. of Chartered Accountants of Scotland, 1973-75, Pres., 1975-76; Pres.-elect, European Accounting Assoc., 1982-83; Member: Management and Ind. Rel. Cttee, SSRC, 1970-72 and 1978-80; Commn for Local Authy Accounts in Scotland, 1978-80. *Recreation:* golf. *Address:* 3 Merrylee Road, Newlands, Glasgow G43 2SH. *T:* 041-637 3060.

FLINT, Rachael H.; *see* Heyhoe Flint, R.

FLORY, Prof. Paul John; J. G. Jackson—C. J. Wood Professor in Chemistry, Stanford University, 1965-75, now Emeritus; *b* 19 June 1910; *s* of Ezra Flory and Martha Brumbaugh Flory; *m* 1936, Emily Catherine Tabor; one *s* two *d. Educ:* Manchester Coll., Ind; Ohio State Univ. BSc Manchester Coll. 1931; PhD (Phys Chem.) Ohio 1934. Research Chemist, E. I. DuPont de Nemours & Co., 1934-38; Res. Associate, Cincinnati Univ., 1938-40; Res. Chemist, Esso Lab., Standard Oil Co., 1940-43; Section Head, Res. Lab., Goodyear Tire & Rubber Co., 1943-48; Prof., Cornell Univ., 1948-56; Exec. Dir of Res., Mellon Inst., 1956-61; Prof., Stanford Univ., 1961-; Chm., Dept of Chem., Stanford Univ., 1969-71. FAAAS; Fellow, Amer. Phys. Soc.; Member: Amer. Chem. Soc.; Amer. Acad. Arts and Scis; Nat. Acad. Scis; Amer. Philos. Soc.; Nat. Res. Council: Chm., Cttee on Macromolecular Chemistry, 1955-59; Chm., Div. of Chem. and Chem. Technology, 1966-68. Holds numerous medals and awards, including: Priestley Medal (Amer. Chem. Soc.) 1974; Nobel Prize for Chemistry, 1974; US Nat. Medal of Science, 1974; Perkin Medal, Soc. of Chem. Industry, 1977; Carl-Dietrich-Harries Medal, German Rubber Soc., 1977; Eringen Medal, Soc. of Engineering Sci., 1978. Hon. ScD: Manchester Coll., 1950; Ohio State, 1970; Hon. DSc Manchester, 1969; Hon. PhD: Weizmann Inst. of Sci., Israel, 1976; Clarkson Coll., 1978. *Publications:* Principles of Polymer Chemistry, 1953 (trans. Japanese, 1955); Statistical Mechanics of Chain Molecules, 1969 (trans. Japanese, 1971, Russian, 1971); numerous papers on phys. chem. of polymers and macromolecules. *Recreations:* swimming, cycling, hiking. *Address:* Department of Chemistry, Stanford University, Stanford, Calif 94305, USA. *T:* 415-497-4574.

FLOUD, Mrs Jean Esther, CBE 1976; MA, BSc(Econ); Principal, Newnham College, Cambridge, since 1972; *b* 3 Nov. 1915; *d* of Annie Louisa and Ernest Walter McDonald; *m* 1938, Peter Castle Floud, CBE (*d* 1960; *s* of late Sir Francis Floud, KCB, KCSI, KCMG; formerly Keeper of Circulation, Victoria and Albert Museum); one *s* two *d. Educ:* public elementary and selective secondary schools; London School of Economics (BScEcon), Hon. Fellow, 1972. Asst Dir of Educn, City of Oxford, 1940-46; Teacher of Sociology in the University of London (London School of Economics and Inst. of Educn), 1947-62; Official Fellow of Nuffield College, Oxford, 1963-72. Member: Franks Commission of Inquiry into the University of Oxford, 1964-66; University Grants Cttee, 1969-74; Social Science Research Council, 1970-73; Exec. Cttee, PEP, 1975-77; Adv. Bd for the Res. Councils, 1976-; Council, Policy Studies Inst., 1979-. Hon. LittD: Leeds, 1973; City, 1978. *Publications:* Social Class and Educational Opportunity (with A. H. Halsey and F. M. Martin), 1956; papers and reviews in sociological jls. *Recreations:* books, music. *Address:* Newnham College, Cambridge. *T:* Cambridge 62273.

FLOWER, family name of **Viscount Ashbrook.**

FLOWER, Group Capt. Arthur Hyde, CBE 1939; *b* Bemboka, NSW, 13 Dec. 1892; *s* of late Thomas Flower; *m* 1924, Nina Joan Castleden Whitby (*d* 1976); no *c*; *m* 1977, Margaret June, *d* of late Cecil Vernon Wickens, Adelaide, SA. *Educ:* Tilba, NSW. Served with AIF, Egypt and France, 1915-16; Transferred to Royal Flying Corps, 1917; served in No. 42 Squadron, France and Italy, 1917-1918 (French Croix de Guerre with palm); Egypt and Turkey, 1920-23; Egypt, 1926-31 and 1934-36; Palestine, 1937-38 (CBE, despatches); France, Sept. 1939-May 1940; England, 1940-42; SWP Area, Aug. 1942-Nov. 1944; retired May 1945; returned to Australia, 1948. Comdr Order of Leopold (Belgium). *Recreations:* shooting, golf. *Address:* Garden Cottage, Longwood Road, Heathfield, SA 5153, Australia.

FLOWER, Desmond John Newman, MC 1944; Editorial Consultant, Sheldon Press, since 1973; Chairman, Cassell & Co. Ltd, 1958-71; President, Cassell Australia Ltd, 1965-71; *b* London, 25 Aug. 1907; *o s* of late Sir Newman Flower; *m* 1st, 1931, Margaret Cameron Coss (marr. diss., 1952); one *s* ; 2nd, 1952, Anne Elizabeth Smith (marr. diss. 1972); one *s* two *d. Educ:* Lancing; King's Coll., Cambridge. Entered Cassell & Co. 1930; Dir, 1931; Literary Dir, 1938; Dep.-Chm., 1952; Chm. Cassell & Co. (Holdings) Ltd, 1958-70. Served War of 1939-45 (despatches, MC); commissioned 1941, 5 Bn Argyll and Sutherland Highlanders later 91 (A&SH) A/T-Regt. Chm., the Folio Society, 1960-71; Liveryman, Stationers' Co.; Freeman, City of London. President des Comités d'Alliance Française en Grande Bretagne, 1963-72. Officier de la légion d'honneur, 1972 (Chevalier 1950). DLitt (*hc*) University of Caen, 1957. *Publications:* founder and editor (with A. J. A. Symons) Book Collector's quarterly, 1930-34; ed, Complete Poetical Works of Ernest Christopher Dowson, 1934; compiled (with Francis Meynell and A. J. A. Symons) The Nonesuch Century, 1936; The Pursuit of Poetry, 1939; (with A. N. L. Munby) English Poetical Autographs, 1938; Voltaire's England, 1950; History of 5 Bn Argyll and Sutherland Highlanders, 1950; (with James Reeves) The War, 1939-1945, 1960. *Recreations:* golf, book collecting. *Address:* 187 Clarence Gate Gardens, NW1 6AR. *T:* 01-262 4690. *Club:* Royal and Ancient (St Andrews).

FLOWER, Rear-Adm. Edward James William, CB 1980; Director, Post-Design (Ships), Ministry of Defence (Navy), 1977-80, retired; *b* 1923; *m* ; three *d.* Joined RN, 1941; served in HM Ships Norfolk, Duke of York, Liverpool, Whitby, Urchin and Tenby; Canadian Nat. Defence Coll., 1966; Fleet Marine Engineering Officer, Western Fleet, 1967-69; commanded RN Nuclear Propulsion Test and Trng Estab., 1970-71; MoD (Navy), 1971-75; Flag Officer Portsmouth, and Port Admiral, Portsmouth, 1975-76; Dir of Engrg (Ships), MoD, 1976-77. *Address:* Fairmount, Hinton Charterhouse, Bath.

FLOWERS, family name of **Baron Flowers.**

FLOWERS, Baron *cr* 1979 (Life Peer), of Queen's Gate in the City of Westminster; **Brian Hilton Flowers,** Kt 1969; FRS 1961; Rector of The Imperial College of Science and Technology, since 1973; *b* 13 Sept. 1924; *o* s of late Rev. Harold J. Flowers, Swansea; m 1951, Mary Frances, er d of late Sir Leonard Behrens, CBE; two step s. Educ: Bishop Gore Grammar Sch., Swansea; Gonville and Caius Coll. (Exhibitioner), Cambridge (MA); Hon. Fellow, 1974; University of Birmingham (DSc). Anglo-Canadian Atomic Energy Project (Tube Alloys), Montreal and Chalk River, Ont., Canada, 1944-46; Research work in nuclear physics and atomic energy at Atomic Energy Research Establishment, Harwell, 1946-50; Dept of Mathematical Physics, University of Birmingham, 1950-52; Visiting Prof., Mass. Institute of Technology and University of Calif., 1955. Head of Theoretical Physics Div., AERE, Harwell, 1952-58, and Chief Research Scientist, 1958; Prof. of Theoretical Physics, 1958-61, Langworthy Prof. of Physics, 1961-72, Univ. of Manchester. Chairman: Science Research Council, 1967-73; Royal Commn on Environmental Pollution, 1973-76; Standing Commn on Energy and the Environment, 1978-81; Univ. of London Working Party on future of med. and dent. teaching resources, 1979-80; Member: Council, Physical Society, 1956-60; Council, Inst of Physics and Physical Soc., 1960, and Vice-Pres. 1962-66; Cttee of Managers, Royal Institution, 1976-79; President: Inst. of Physics, 1972-74; European Science Foundn, 1974-80; Nat. Soc. for Clean Air, 1977-79. Nuffield Vis. Professorship at Universities of British Columbia and Alberta, July-Aug., 1960; Visiting Prof., Cairo Univ., Jan., 1963. Member: Advisory Council on Scientific Policy, 1962-64; Council for Scientific Policy, 1965-67; Adv. Bd for the Res. Council, 1972-73; Computer Agency Council, 1973-75; Adv. Council, Science Policy Foundn, 1975-; Governing Board, National Institute for Research in Nuclear Science, 1962-65; Bd of Governors, Weizmann Inst. of Science, Israel, 1969-; UKAEA, 1971-81; Energy Commn, 1977-79. Chairman: joint working group on computers for research, 1965; Computer Bd for Univs and Research Councils, 1966-70; Member: Bd of Directors, Fulmer Research Inst., 1972-75; Senatsausschusses für Forschungspolitik und Forschungsplanung der Max-Planck-Gesellschaft, 1973-75. Trustee, Radcliffe Trust, 1980-; a Managing Trustee, Nuffield Foundn, 1982-. Founder Mem., SDP, 1981. 1st Leverhulme Meml Lectr, Liverpool, 1971; The Queen's Lecture, Berlin, 1973. Editor: Advances in Physics, 1959-63; Cambridge Monographs, 1962-66. Rutherford Medal and Prize, IPPS, 1968; Chalmers Medal, Chalmers Univ. of Technol., Sweden, 1980. FInstP 1961. Hon. FCGI, 1975; Hon. MRIA (Science Section), 1976; Hon. FIEE, 1975. MA Oxon, 1956; Hon. DSc: Sussex, 1968; Wales 1972; Manchester, 1973; Leicester, 1973; Liverpool, 1974; Bristol, 1982. Officier de la Légion d'Honneur, 1981 (Chevalier, 1975). Publications: (with E. Mendoza) Properties of Matter, 1970; various contribs to scientific periodicals, on the structure of the atomic nucleus, on nuclear reactions, on science policy, on energy and the environment. Recreations: music, walking, painting. Address: Imperial College, SW7 2AZ. T: 01-589 5111.

FLOYD, Sir Giles (Henry Charles), 7th Bt cr 1816; Director, Burghley Estate Farms, since 1958; b 27 Feb. 1932; s of Sir John Duckett Floyd, 6th Bt, TD, and of Jocelin Evadne (d 1976), d of late Sir Edmund Wyldbore Smith; S father, 1975; m 1954, Lady Gillian Moyra Katherine Cecil (marr. diss. 1978), 2nd d of 6th Marquess of Exeter, KCMG; two s. Educ: Eton College. High Sheriff of Rutland, 1968. Heir: er s David Henry Cecil Floyd [b 2 April 1956; m 1981, Caroline, d of John Beckly, Manor Farm, Bowerchalke, Salisbury, Wilts]. Address: Tinwell Manor, Stamford, Lincs. T: Stamford 2676. Clubs: Turf, Farmers'.

FLOYD, John Anthony; Chairman: Christie Manson & Woods Ltd, since 1974; Christies International Ltd, since 1976; b 12 May 1923; s of Lt-Col Arthur Bowen Floyd, DSO, OBE; m 1948, Margaret Louise Rosselli; two d. Educ: Eton. Served King's Royal Rifle Corps, 1941-46. Address: 26 Park Village East, NW1 7PZ. T: 01-387 6311. Clubs: Boodle's, White's, MCC.

FLOYD EWIN, Sir David Ernest Thomas, Kt 1974; MVO (4th class) 1954; OBE 1965; MA; Lay Administrator, 1939-44, Registrar and Receiver, 1944-78, Consultant to the Dean and Chapter, since 1978, St Paul's Cathedral; Notary Public; Chairman: Tubular Barriers Ltd, since 1978; Grandstand Tribunes Ltd, since 1981; Grandstand Tribunes Inc., since 1981; b 17 Feb. 1911; 7th s of late Frederick P. Ewin and Ellen Floyd; m 1948, Marion Irene, d of William R. Lewis; one d. Educ: Eltham. MA (Lambeth) 1962. Freeman, City of London, 1948; Member of Court of Common Council for Ward of Castle Baynard (Dep., 1972-); Vice-Pres., Castle Baynard Ward Club (Chm. 1962); Chm., Corp. of London Gresham Cttee, 1975-76; Member: Lord Mayor and Sheriffs Cttee, 1976, 1978; Court of Assts, Hon. Irish Soc., 1976-79; Surrogate for Province of Canterbury; Trustee: City Parochial Foundn, 1967- (Chm., Pensions Cttee, 1978-); St Paul's Cathedral Trust, 1978-; Temple Bar Trust, 1979-; Dep. Chm., City of London's Endowment Trust for St Paul's Cathedral, 1982-. Hon. Dir, British Humane Assoc.; Governor and Member of Court: Sons of the Clergy Corp.; St Gabriel's Coll., Camberwell, 1946-72. Past Master: Scriveners Co.; Guild of Freemen of the City of London; Liveryman, Wax Chandlers Co.; Gold Staff Officer at Coronation of HM Queen Elizabeth, 1953. KStJ 1970 (OStJ 1965). Publications: A Pictorial History of St Paul's Cathedral, 1970; The Splendour of St Paul's, 1973; numerous papers and articles. Recreations: tennis, gardening, fishing. Address: 359 Ben Jonson House, Barbican, EC2. T: 01-638 5928; Chapter House, St Paul's Churchyard, EC4. T: 01-248 2705; Silver Springs, Stoke Gabriel, South Devon. T: Stoke Gabriel 264. Clubs: City Livery, Guildhall.

FLYNN, Prof. Frederick Valentine, MD (Lond), FRCP, FRCPath; Professor of Chemical Pathology in University of London at University College School of Medicine, since 1970, and Consultant Chemical Pathologist to University College Hospital, London, since 1960; Civil Consultant in Chemical Pathology to Royal Navy, since 1978; b 6 Oct. 1924; e s of Frederick Walter Flynn and Jane Laing Flynn (née Valentine); m 1955, Catherine Ann, o d of Dr Robert Walter Warrick and Dorothy Ann Warrick (née Dimock); one s one d. Educ: University Coll. London; University Coll. Hosp. Med. Sch. (Fellow, UCL, 1974). Obstetric Ho. Surg. and various posts, incl. Research Asst and Registrar, Dept of Clin. Pathology, UCH, 1947-60; Associate in Clin. Path., Pepper Laboratory of Clin. Medicine, Univ. of Pennsylvania, and British Postgrad. Med. Fedn Travelling Fellow, 1954-55; Member, MRC Working Party on Hypogammaglobulinaemia, 1959-70; Chairman, Assoc. of Clin. Pathologists Working Party on Data Processing in Laboratories, 1964-67; Member: Min. of Health Lab. Equipment and Methods Adv. Gp, 1966-71; Min. of Technol. Working Party on Lab. Instrumentation, 1966-67; BMA Working Party on Computers in Medicine, 1968-69; Dept of Health's Adv. Cttee on Med. Computing, 1969-76, Scientific and Clin. Applications of Computers Adv. Gp, 1971-76 (Chairman), and Laboratory Develts Adv. Gp, 1972-75. Chairman, Panel of Examiners in Chem. Path., RCPath, 1972-; Member: MRC Adv. Panel on Applications for Computing Facilities, 1973-; NW Thames RHA Sci. Cttee, 1973-74; Chairman, Sci. and Technical Cttee, Assoc. of Clin. Biochemists, 1968-70. Member Council, 1968-72, Vice-Pres., 1971-72, Section of Path., RSM; Member Council, 1973-, Vice-Pres., 1975-78, Treas., 1978-, RCPath. Publications: numerous contribs to med. and sci. books and jls. Recreations: photography, carpentry, gardening. Address: 20 Oakleigh Avenue, Whetstone, N20 9JH. T: 01-445 0882.

FLYNN, John Gerrard; HM Diplomatic Service; Counsellor, Madrid, since 1982; b 23 April 1937; s of Thomas Flynn and late Mary Chisholm; m 1973, Drina Anne Coates. Educ: St Columba's High Sch., Greenock; St Joseph's High Sch., Kilmarnock; Glasgow Univ. (MA). Foreign Office, 1965; Second Sec., Lusaka, 1966; First Sec., FCO, 1968; seconded to Canning House as Asst Dir-Gen., 1970; First Sec. (Commercial) and Consul, Montevideo, 1971; FCO, 1976; Chargé d'Affaires, Luanda, 1978; Counsellor and Consul-Gen., Brasilia, 1979. Recreations: walking, golf. Address: c/o Foreign and Commonwealth Office, SW1. Clubs: Travellers'; Golf (Montevideo).

FLYNN, Most Rev. Thomas; see Achonry, Bishop of, (R.C.).

FOAKES, Prof. Reginald Anthony; Professor of English, University of California at Los Angeles, since 1983; b 18 Oct. 1923; 2nd s of William Warren Foakes and Frances (née Poate); m 1951, Barbara, d of Harry Garratt, OBE; two s two d. Educ: West Bromwich Grammar Sch.; Birmingham Univ. (MA, PhD). Fellow of the Shakespeare Inst., 1951-54; Lectr in English, Durham Univ., 1954-62; Sen. Lectr, 1963-64; Prof. of English Lit., Univ. of Kent at Canterbury, 1964-82 (Dean, Faculty of Humanities, 1974-77). Commonwealth Fund (Harkness) Fellow, Yale Univ., 1955-56; Visiting Professor: University Coll., Toronto, 1960-62; Univ. of California, Santa Barbara, 1968-69; UCLA, 1981. Publications: (ed) Shakespeare's King Henry VIII, 1957; The Romantic Assertion, 1958; (ed with R. T. Rickert) Henslowe's Diary, 1961; (ed) The Comedy of Errors, 1962; (ed) The Revenger's Tragedy, 1966; (ed) Macbeth and Much Ado About Nothing, 1968; Romantic Criticism, 1968; Coleridge on Shakespeare, 1971; Shakespeare, the Dark Comedies to the Last Plays, 1971; (ed) The Henslowe Papers, 2 vols, 1977; Marston and Tourneur, 1978. Address: Department of English, University of California at Los Angeles, 405 Hilgard Avenue, Los Angeles, Calif 90024, USA.

FOALE, Air Cdre Colin Henry; Pilot to the Committee for Aerial Photography, University of Cambridge; b 10 June 1930; s of late William Henry Foale and Frances M. (née Muse); m 1954, Mary Katherine Harding, Minneapolis, USA; two s one d. Educ: Wolverton Grammar Sch.; RAF Coll., Cranwell. 1951-74: 13 Sqdn Pilot, Egypt; 32 Sqdn Flt Comdr; Fighter Flt, RAF Flying Coll. Manby; Officer and Aircrew Selection, Hornchurch; OC 73 Sqdn, Cyprus (Sqdn Ldr); Staff Coll., Bracknell; Air Staff, HQ RAF Germany (Wing Comdr); Jt Services Staff Coll., Latimer; OC 39 Sqdn, Malta; SO Flying, MoD (PE) (Gp Captain); Stn Comdr, Luqa, Malta, 1974-76; RCDS, 1977 (Air Cdre); Dir of Public Relations (RAF), 1977-79; retired at own request, for business and writing, 1979. Trng Advr to Chm., Conservative Party, 1980. FBIM, FIIM. Recreations: sailing, swimming, flying, canoeing, music, drama, writing. Address: St Catharine's College, Cambridge; 37 Pretoria Road, Cambridge. Club: Royal Air Force.

FOCKE, Paul Everard Justus, QC 1982; b 14 May 1937; s of Frederick Justus Focke and Muriel Focke; m 1973, Lady Tana Marie Alexander, er d of 6th Earl of Caledon; two d. Educ: Downside; Exeter Coll., Oxford; Trinity Coll., Dublin. National Service, 1955-57; Cheshire Yeomanry, 1957-66 (Captain). Called to Bar, Gray's Inn, 1964. Recreations: travelling, aeroplanes. Address: (chambers) 1 Mitre Court Buildings, Temple, EC4. T: 01-353 0434; (home) 7 Cheyne Walk, SW3. T: 01-351 0299. Clubs: Cavalry and Guards, Turf.

FODEN, Air Vice-Marshal Arthur, CB 1964; CBE 1960; BSc; CEng; FIEE; Director, Racal Datacom, since 1975; b 19 April 1914; s of Henry Foden, Macclesfield, Cheshire; m 1938, Constance Muriel Foden (née Corkill); one s one d. Educ: Manchester Univ. Electronic Engineer, 1935-37; Education Officer, Royal Air Force, 1937-39; Signals Officer, Royal Air Force, 1939; Dep. Dir, Signals Staff, Min. of Def., 1964-67; Asst Chief of Defence Staff (Signals), 1967-69, retired; Dir (C), Govt Communications HQ, 1969-75. Recreations: gardening, music. Address: Ravenglass, Wargrave, Berks. T: Wargrave 2589.

FODEN-PATTINSON, Peter Lawrence; a Deputy Chairman of Lloyd's, 1976; *b* 14 June 1925; *s* of late Hubert Foden-Pattinson; *m* 1956, Joana Pryor (*née* Henderson); one *s. Educ:* Downside. Irish Guards, 1943-47. Lloyd's, 1942-: Underwriting Mem., 1956; Mem., Cttee of Lloyd's, 1973-76; Mem., Cttee of Lloyd's Non-Marine Assoc., 1965, Chm. 1971, Dep. Chm. 1970 and 1972. *Recreations:* boating, music. *Address:* 24A Shawfield Street, SW3 4BD. *T:* 01-352 3843. *Club:* Royal Yacht Squadron.

FOGARTY, Christopher Winthrop, CB 1973; Deputy Secretary, Overseas Development Administration, Foreign and Commonwealth Office, (formerly Ministry of Overseas Development), 1976-81; *b* 18 Sept. 1921; *s* of late Philip Christopher Fogarty, ICS, and late Hilda Spenser Fogarty; *m* 1961, Elizabeth Margaret Ince (*d* 1972). *Educ:* Ampleforth Coll.; Christ Church, Oxford. War Service (Lieut RA), 1942-45. Asst Principal, 1946, Principal, 1949, HM Treasury; Permanent Sec., Min. of Finance of Eastern Nigeria, 1956; Asst Sec., HM Treasury, 1959, Under-Sec., 1966; Treasury Rep., S Asia and FE, 1967-72; Dep. Sec., HM Treasury, and Dir, European Investment Bank, 1972-76. *Address:* 7 Hurlingham Court, Ranelagh Gardens, SW6 3SH. *Clubs:* Royal Commonwealth Society, Travellers'; Royal Selangor Golf.

See also M. P. Fogarty, S. W. Fogarty.

FOGARTY, Michael Patrick; Director, Institute for Family and Environmental Research, since 1981; *b* 3 Oct. 1916; *s* of late Philip Christopher Fogarty, ICS, and Mary Belle Pye, Galway; *m* 1939, Phyllis Clark; two *s* two *d. Educ:* Ampleforth Coll.; Christ Church, Oxford. Lieut RA, 1940 (wounded, Dunkirk). Nuffield Coll., 1941-51 (Fellow, 1944); Montague Burton Prof. of Industrial Relations, University Coll. of S Wales and Mon, 1951-66; Dir and Prof., Econ. and Social Res. Inst., Dublin, 1968-72; Centre for Studies in Social Policy: Sen. Fellow, 1973; Dep. Dir, 1977-78; Dep. Dir, PSI, 1978-82. Also held posts in Administrative Staff Coll., Oxford Institute of Statistics, Nat. Institute of Economic and Social Research, Ministry of Town and Country Planning, and as Asst Editor, The Economist. Chairman: Cttee on Industrial Relations in the Electricity Supply Bd (Ireland), 1968-69; Banks Inquiry, 1970-71; Member: Commn on the Status of Women (Ireland), 1970-72; Commn on Insurance Industry (Ireland), 1970-72; Cttee on Aid to Political Parties, 1975-76. Pres., Newman Assoc., 1957-59; Chm., Catholic Social Guild, 1959-63; Mem., Social Welfare Commn, RC Bishops' Conf. (E&W); Vice-Pres. Assoc. of University Teachers, 1964-66. Prospective Parly candidate (Lab) Tamworth, 1938-44; Parliamentary Candidate (L): Devizes, 1964 and 1966; Abingdon, Feb. and Oct. 1974. Vice-Pres. of the Liberal Party, 1964-66. Contested (L) Thames Valley, European Parlt, 1979. District Councillor, Vale of White Horse, 1973-; CC Oxfordshire, 1981-. Hon. Dr of Political and Social Science, Louvain, 1963. *Publications:* Prospects of the Industrial Areas of Great Britain, 1945; Plan Your Own Industries, 1947; (ed) Further Studies in Industrial Organisation, 1948; Town and Country Planning, 1948; Economic Control, 1955; Personality and Group Relations in Industry, 1956; Christian Democracy in Western Europe, 1820-1953, 1957; The Just Wage, 1961; Under-Governed and Over-Governed, 1962; The Rules of Work, 1963; Company and Corporation—One Law?, 1965; Companies Beyond Jenkins, 1965; Wider Business Objectives, 1966; A Companies Act 1970?, 1967; (with Allen, Allen and Walters) Women in Top Jobs, 1971; (with Rapoport and Rapoport) Sex, Career and Family, 1971; Women and Top Jobs: the next move, 1972; Irish Entrepreneurs Speak For Themselves, 1974; Forty to Sixty, 1975; Company Responsibility and Participation—A New Agenda, 1975; Pensions—where next?, 1976; (with Eileen Reid) Differentials for Managers and Skilled Manual Workers in the UK, 1980; Retirement Age and Retirement Costs, 1980; (with Allen and Walters) Women in Top Jobs 1968-79, 1981. *Recreations:* swimming, walking. *Address:* Red Copse, Boars Hill, Oxford.

See also C. W. Fogarty, S. W. Fogarty.

FOGARTY, Susan Winthrop; Under-Secretary, Highways, Department of Transport, since 1978; *b* 16 April 1930; *d* of late Philip Christopher Fogarty and late Hilda Spenser Fogarty. *Educ:* Badminton Sch., Bristol; King's Coll., Newcastle. BA Dunelm. Joined Min. of Defence, 1951; joined Scottish Educn Dept, 1955; Private Sec. to Jt Parly Under-Sec. for Scotland, 1957-59; Principal, Scottish Educn Dept, 1959; Min. of Transport, 1960; Asst Sec. 1966; Cabinet Office, 1968; Dept of Environment, 1971; Under Sec., DoE, 1973 (Regional Dir, W Midlands, 1975-78). *Recreations:* reading history and thrillers, swimming, walking. *Address:* 401 Howard House, Dolphin Square, SW1V 3PF. *T:* 01-821 0666. *Club:* Royal Commonwealth Society.

See also C. W. Fogarty, M. P. Fogarty.

FOGEL, Prof. Robert W.; Charles R. Walgreen Professor of American Institutions, Chicago University, since 1981; *b* 1 July 1926; *s* of Harry G. Fogel and Elizabeth (*née* Mitnik); two *s. Educ:* Cornell, Columbia and Johns Hopkins Univs. AB Cornell 1948; AM Columbia 1960; PhD Johns Hopkins 1963. Instructor, Johns Hopkins Univ., 1958-59; Asst Prof., Univ. of Rochester, 1960-64; Assoc. Prof., Univ. of Chicago, 1964-65; Prof., Econs and History, Univ. of Chicago, 1965-75, Univ. of Rochester, 1968-75. Taussig Research Prof., Harvard Univ., 1973-74; Pitt Prof. of Amer. History and Instns, Cambridge Univ., 1975-76; Harold Hitchings Burbank Prof. of Econs and Prof. of History, Harvard Univ., 1975-81. President: Economic History Assoc., 1977-78; Soc. Sci. Hist. Assoc., 1980-81. FRHistS 1975. Phi Beta Kappa, 1963; Arthur H. Cole Prize, 1968; Schumpeter Prize, 1971; Bancroft Prize, 1975; Fellow: Econometric Soc., 1971; Amer. Acad. of Arts and Sciences, 1972; Nat. Acad. of Sciences, 1973; Amer. Assoc. for the

Advancement of Science, 1978; FRHistS 1974. *Publications:* The Union Pacific Railroad: a case in premature enterprise, 1960; Railroads and American Economic Growth: essays in econometric history, 1964 (Spanish edn 1972); (jtly) The Reinterpretation of American Economic History, 1971 (Italian edn 1975); (jtly) The Dimension of Quantitative Research in History, 1972; (jtly) Time on the Cross: The Economics of American Negro Slavery, 1974 (Japanese edn 1977, Spanish edn 1981); Ten Lectures on the New Economic History, 1977; numerous papers in learned jls. *Address:* (home) 5321 S University Avenue, Chicago, Illinois 60615, USA; (office) 1101 E 58th Street, Chicago, Illinois 60637, USA.

FOGG, Alan; former Director, PA International; *b* 19 Sept. 1921; *o s* of John Fogg, Dulwich; *m* 1948, Mary Marsh; two *s* one *d. Educ:* Repton; Exeter Coll., Oxford (MA, BSc). Served with RN, 1944-47. *Publications:* (with Barnes, Stephens and Titman) Company Organisation: theory and practice, 1970; various papers on management subjects. *Recreations:* travel, gardening. *Address:* Albury Edge, Merstham, Surrey. *T:* Merstham 2023. *Club:* United Oxford & Cambridge University.

FOGG, Albert, CBE 1972; DSc, CEng; *b* 25 Feb. 1909; *o s* of late James Fogg, Bolton. *Educ:* Manchester University. Scientific staff, National Physical Laboratory, 1930-46; first Dir, Motor Industry Research Assoc., 1946-64; Director: Leyland Motor Corporation, 1964-68; British Leyland Motor Corporation Ltd, 1968-74; ENASA (Spain), 1965-74; retired. Hon. DSc Southampton, 1979. Inst. of Mechanical Engineers: T. Bernard Hall Prize, 1945 and 1955; Starley Premium, 1956; James Clayton Prize, 1962; Viva Shield and Gold Medal, Worshipful Company of Carmen, 1962. *Publications:* numerous papers in jls of scientific socs and professional instns. *Recreations:* sport and travel. *Address:* 5 Carisbrooke, Canford Cliffs Road, Poole, Dorset. *T:* Canford Cliffs 709862.

FOGG, Cyril Percival, CB 1973; Director, Admiralty Surface Weapons Establishment, Ministry of Defence (Procurement Executive), 1973-75, retired; *b* 28 Nov. 1914; *s* of Henry Fogg and Mabel Mary (*née* Orton); *m* 1939, Margaret Amie Millican (*d* 1982); two *d. Educ:* Herbert Strutt Sch., Belper; Gonville and Caius Coll., Cambridge (MA, 1st cl. Mechanical Sciences Tripos). Research Staff, General Electric Co., 1936-37; various positions in Scientific Civil Service from 1937 with Air Ministry, Ministries of Aircraft Production, Supply, Aviation and Technology. Head of Ground Radar Dept, RRE Malvern, 1956-58; Dir Electronics R&D (Ground), 1959-63; Imperial Defence Coll., 1961; Dir of Guided Weapons Research, 1963-64; Dir-Gen. of Electronics R&D, Min. of Aviation, 1964-67; Dep. Controller of Electronics, Min. of Technology, later MoD (Procurement Executive), 1967-72. *Address:* 1 Fairfield Close, Old Bosham, Chichester, West Sussex PO18 8JQ.

FOGG, Prof. Gordon Elliott, FRS 1965; Professor and Head of the Department of Marine Biology, University College of North Wales, Bangor, since 1971; *b* 26 April 1919; *s* of Rev. L. C. Fogg; *m* 1945, Elizabeth Beryl Llechid-Jones; one *s* one *d. Educ:* Dulwich Coll.; Queen Mary Coll., London; St John's Coll., Cambridge. BSc (London), 1939; PhD (Cambridge), 1943; ScD (Cambridge), 1966. Sea-weed Survey of British Isles, 1942; Plant Physiologist, Pest Control Ltd, 1943-45; successively Asst Lectr, Lectr and Reader in Botany, University Coll., London, 1945-60; Rockefeller Fellow, 1954; Prof. of Botany, Westfield Coll., Univ. of London, 1960-71. Trustee, BM (Natural Hist.), 1976-. Member: Royal Commn on Environmental Pollution, 1979-; NERC, 1981-82. Royal Soc. Leverhulme Vis. Prof., Kerala, 1969-70. Botanical Sec., Soc. for Experimental Biology, 1957-60; President: British Phycological Soc., 1961-62; International Phycological Soc., 1964; Inst. of Biology, 1976-77; Chm. Council, Freshwater Biol Assoc., 1974-; Joint Organizing Sec., X International Botanical Congress. Visiting research worker, British Antarctic Survey, 1966, 1974, 1979; Biological Gen. Sec., British Assoc., 1967-72, Pres., Section K, 1973. Fellow, QMC, 1976. Hon. LLD Dundee, 1974. *Publications:* The Metabolism of Algae, 1953; The Growth of Plants, 1963; Algal Cultures and Phytoplankton Ecology, 1965; Photosynthesis, 1968; (jointly) The Blue-green Algae, 1973; papers in learned jls. *Recreations:* water colour painting, walking. *Address:* Marine Science Laboratories, Menai Bridge, Gwynedd; Bodolben, Llandegfan, Menai Bridge, Gwynedd. *T:* Menai Bridge 712 641. *Club:* Athenæum.

FOGGIN, (Wilhelm) Myers, CBE 1974; Principal, Trinity College of Music, London, 1965-79; *b* 23 Dec. 1908; *m* 1952, Lotte Breitmeyer; one *s* one *d. Educ:* Dr Erlich's Sch., Newcastle upon Tyne; Royal Academy of Music. Concert Pianist; Prof. of Piano, RAM, 1936; Conductor, People's Palace Choral and Orchestral Soc., 1936-49. Intelligence Officer, RAF, 1940-45. Guest Conductor, Carl Rosa Opera, Sadler's Wells Opera and BBC; Dir of Opera, RAM, 1948-65; Conductor, Croydon Philharmonic Soc., 1957-73; Warden, RAM, 1949-65. Dir of Music, Queenswood Sch., 1966-82; Pres., Nat. Fedn of Music Socs, 1967-72; Chm., Royal Philharmonic Soc., 1968-81. Hon. FTCL, FRAM, FRCM, Hon. GSM, FRNCM. *Address:* 43 Northway, NW11. *T:* 01-455 7527. *Club:* Athenæum.

FOGGON, George, CMG 1961; OBE 1949 (MBE 1945); Director, London Office, International Labour Organisation, 1976-82; *b* 13 Sept. 1913; *s* of Thomas Foggon, Newcastle upon Tyne; *m* 1st, 1938, Agnes McIntosh (*d* 1968); one *s* ; 2nd, 1969, Audrey Blanch. Joined Min. of Labour, 1930. Served War of 1939-45 (MBE), Wing-Comdr, RAFVR, 1941-46. Seconded to FO, 1946; on staff of Mil. Gov., Berlin, 1946-49; Principal, CO, 1949; Asst Sec.,

W African Inter-Territorial Secretariat, Gold Coast (now Ghana), 1951-53; Comr of Labour, Nigeria, 1954-58; Labour Adviser: to Sec. of State for Colonies, 1958-61; to Sec. for Techn. Co-op., 1962-64; to Min. of Overseas Development, 1965-66; Overseas Labour Advr, FO later FCO, 1966-76. *Recreations:* walking, photography. *Address:* 8 Churton Place, SW1. *T:* 01-828 1492. *Clubs:* Athenæum, Oriental.

FOLDES, Andor; international concert pianist since 1933; Head of Piano Master Class, Conservatory, Saarbrücken, 1957-65; *b* Budapest, Hungary, 21 Dec. 1913; *s* of Emil Foldes and Valerie Foldes (*née* Ipolyi); *m* 1940, Lili Rendy (writer); no *c*. *Educ:* Franz Liszt Academy of Music, Budapest. Started piano playing at 5; first appeared with Budapest Philh. Orch. at 8; studied with Ernest von Dohnanyi, received Master Diploma (Fr. Liszt Acad. of Music, Budapest), 1932. Concerts all over Europe, 1933-39; US debut (NBC Orch.), 1940; toured US extensively, 1940-48. US citizen since 1948. Concerts, since, all over the world, incl. three recitals in Peking, 1978. Grand Prix du Disque, Paris, for Bartok Complete Works (piano solo), 1957. Beethoven concerts, Bonn Festival and throughout Europe. Recordings of all Beethoven Sonatas, and works of Mozart and Schubert. Order of Merit, First Class, 1956, Gr. Cross, 1964 (Germany); Commandeur, Mérite Culturel et Artistique (City of Paris), 1968; Medaille d'Argent de la Ville de Paris, 1971. *Publications:* Keys to the Keyboard, 1950; Cadenzas to Mozart Piano Concertos (W Germany); Is there a Contemporary Style of Beethoven-playing?, 1963; various piano compositions. *Relevant publication:* Wolf-Eberhard von Lewinski, Andor Foldes, 1970. *Recreations:* collecting art, reading, writing on musical subjects; swimming, hiking. *Address:* 8704 Herrliberg, Zürich, Switzerland.

FOLDES, Prof. Lucien Paul; Professor of Economics, University of London, at London School of Economics and Political Science, since 1979; *b* 19 Nov. 1930; *s* of Egon and Marta Foldes. *Educ:* Bunce Court Sch.; Monkton Wyld Sch.; London School of Economics (BCom, MScEcon, DBA). National Service, 1952-54. LSE: Asst Lecturer in Economics, 1954-55; Lectr, 1955-61; Reader, 1961-79. Rockefeller Travelling Fellow, 1961-62. *Publications:* articles in Rev. of Economic Studies, Economica, Jl of Mathematical Economics, and others. *Recreation:* mathematical analysis. *Address:* London School of Economics, Houghton Street, WC2A 2AE. *T:* 01-405 7686.

FOLEY, family name of **Baron Foley.**

FOLEY, 8th Baron *cr* 1776; **Adrian Gerald Foley;** *b* 9 Aug. 1923; *s* of 7th Baron and Minoru (*d* 1968), *d* of late H. Greenstone, South Africa; *S* father, 1927; *m* 1st, 1958, Patricia Meek (marr. diss. 1971); one *s* one *d*; 2nd, 1972, Ghislaine Lady Ashcombe. *Heir: s* Hon. Thomas Henry Foley, *b* 1 April 1961. *Address:* c/o Marbella Club, Marbella, Malaga, Spain. *Clubs:* White's, Turf.

FOLEY, Rt. Rev. Brian C.; *see* Lancaster, Bishop of, (RC).

FOLEY, Maurice (Anthony); Deputy Director General, Directorate General for Development, Commission of the European Communities, since 1973; *b* 9 Oct. 1925; *s* of Jeremiah and Agnes Foley; *m* 1952, Catherine, *d* of Patrick and Nora O'Riordan; three *s* one *d*. *Educ:* St Mary's Coll., Middlesbrough. Formerly: electrical fitter, youth organiser, social worker. Member: ETU, 1941-46; Transport and General Workers Union, 1948-; Royal Arsenal Co-operative Soc. MP (Lab), West Bromwich, 1963-73; Joint Parliamentary Under-Sec. of State, Dept of Economic Affairs, 1964-66; Parly Under-Secretary: Home Office, 1966-67; Royal Navy, MoD, 1967-68; FCO, 1968-70. *Address:* Commission of the European Communities, 200 rue de la Loi, 1049 Brussels, Belgium.

FOLEY, Sir Noel; *see* Foley, Sir T. J. N.

FOLEY, Rt. Rev. Ronald Graham Gregory; *see* Reading, Bishop Suffragan of.

FOLEY, Sir (Thomas John) Noel, Kt 1978; CBE 1967; Chairman of the Board, Bank of New South Wales, since 1978; Chairman: CSR Ltd, since 1980; Allied Manufacturing and Trading Industries (AMATIL) Ltd, 1955-79 (retired); Founding President, World Wildlife Fund, Australia, 1978-80; *b* 1914; *s* of late Benjamin Foley, Brisbane. *Educ:* Brisbane Grammar Sch., Queensland; Queensland Univ. (BA, BCom). *Address:* c/o Bank of New South Wales, 60 Martin Place, Sydney, NSW 2000, Australia.

FOLEY-BERKELEY, family name of **Baroness Berkeley.**

FOLJAMBE, family name of **Earl of Liverpool.**

FOLKESTONE, Viscount; William Pleydell-Bouverie; *b* 5 Jan. 1955; *s* and *heir* of 8th Earl of Radnor, *qv*. *Educ:* Harrow; Royal Agricultural Coll., Cirencester. *Address:* Longford Castle, Salisbury, Wilts. *T:* Salisbury 29732.

FOLLETT, Prof. Brian Keith, PhD, DSc; Professor of Zoology, University of Bristol, since 1978; *b* 22 Feb. 1939; *s* of Albert James Follett and Edith Annie Follett; *m* 1961, Deb (*née* Booth); one *s* one *d*. *Educ:* Bournemouth Sch.; Univ. of Bristol (BSc 1960, PhD 1964); Univ. of Wales (DSc 1975). Res. Fellow, Washington State Univ., 1964-65; Lectr in Zool., Univ. of Leeds, 1965-69; Lectr, subseq. Reader and Prof. of Zool., University Coll. of

N Wales, Bangor, 1969-78. Scientific Medal, Zool Soc. of London, 1976. *Publications:* papers in physiol, endocrinol, and zool jls. *Address:* Department of Zoology, The University, Bristol.

FOLLETT, Samuel Frank, CMG 1959; BSc, CEng, FIEE, FRAeS; *b* 21 March 1904; *o s* of Samuel Charles Follett and Kate Bell; *m* 1932, Kathleen Matilda Tupper. *Educ:* Farnham Gram. Sch.; Univ. of London. Electrical Research Assoc., 1924-27; Electrical Engineering Dept, RAE Farnborough, 1927-45; Asst Dir of Instrument R&D (Electrics), Min. of Supply, 1946-50; Dir of Instrument R&D, 1950-54; Dep. Dir-Gen. Aircraft, Equipment, R&D, 1954-56; Dir.-Gen., Min. of Supply Staff, Brit. Jt Services Mission, Washington, DC, 1956-59; Dep. Dir, RAE Farnborough, 1959-63; Dep. Controller of Guided Weapons, Min. of Aviation, 1963-66; Scientific Adviser to BoT, 1966-69. *Address:* Darby Cottage, St Johns Road, Farnham, Surrey. *T:* Farnham 716610.

FOLLOWS, Sir (Charles) Geoffry (Shield), Kt 1951; CMG 1945; Northern Rhodesia representative on Federal Interim Public Service Commission, 1953-59; *b* 4 July 1896; *m* 1922, Claire Camille, *d* of late Julien Lemarchand. *Educ:* Wellington Sch., Som. 2nd Lieut The King's (Liverpool) Regt 1914; served in France, 1915-18, and in various Staff appts until 1920; Colonial Service, Seychelles, 1920-24; attached Colonial Office, 1925; Gibraltar, 1925-36; N Rhodesia, 1936-45; Chief Financial Adviser to Mil. Admin, Hong Kong, 1945-46; Fin. Sec., Hong Kong, 1946-52; Chm. N Rhodesia Salaries Commn, 1952; Mem. Preparatory Commn on Federation of Rhodesias and Nyasaland, 1952. Mem., Order of the Legion of Merit (Rhodesia), 1979. *Address:* 12 Lanark Road, Harare, Zimbabwe.

FOLLOWS, Sir Denis, Kt 1978; CBE 1967 (MBE 1950); Chairman, British Olympic Association, since 1977; *b* 13 April 1908; *s* of Amos Follows; *m* 1938, Mary Elizabeth Milner; two *d*. *Educ:* City Sch., Lincoln; Nottingham Univ. (BA). Pres., National Union of Students, 1930-32; Pres., Internat. Confedn of Students, 1932-34; Vice-Pres., 1933, Chm., 1948, Pres., 1972-, Universities Athletic Union. Asst Master, Chiswick Grammar Sch. for Boys, 1932-40. Royal Air Force, Flight Lieut, 1940-46. Sec., British Airline Pilots Assoc., 1946-62. Chm., Nat. Jt Council for Civil Air Transport, 1951-52; Secretary of the FA, 1962-73. Hon. Treasurer, CCPR, 1977-; Chairman: Major Spectator Sports Div. CCPR, 1973-; Sports Adv. Cttee, Nat. Assoc. of Youth Clubs, 1975-; Member: Council, Assoc. of Nat. Olympic Cttees, 1979-; Exec. Cttee, Assoc. of European Nat. Olympic Cttees, 1980-. Silver Medal of the Olympic Order, 1980; Manning Award for non-competitive Sportsman of the Year, Sports Writers' Assoc., 1980. *Recreation:* gardening. *Address:* 70 Barrowgate Road, Chiswick, W4. *T:* 01-994 5782.

FONTAINE, André Lucien Georges; Chief Editor, le Monde, Paris, since 1969; *b* 30 March 1921; *s* of Georges Fontaine and Blanche Rochon Duvigneaud; *m* 1943, Belita Cavaillé; two *s* one *d*. *Educ:* Paris Univ. (diplomes études supérieures droit public et économie politique, lic.lettres). Joined Temps Present, 1946; with le Monde from 1947; Foreign Editor, 1951. Mem. Bd, French Inst. of Internat. Relns, 1980-. Comdr, Italian Merit; Officer, Orders of Vasa (Sweden), Leopold (Belgium) and Lion (Finland); Kt, Danebrog (Denmark) and Crown of Belgium; Order of Tudor Vladimirescu (Romania). Atlas' Internat. Editor of the Year, 1976. *Publications:* L'Alliance atlantique à l'heure du dégel, 1960; Histoire de la guerre froide, vol. 1 1965, vol. 2 1966 (English trans., History of the Cold War, 1966 and 1967); La Guerre civile froide, 1969; Le dernier quart du siècle, 1976; La France au bois dormant, 1978; Un seul lit pour deux rêves, 1981; contrib. Foreign Affairs, Affari Esteri, Europa Archiv, BBC, etc. *Address:* 5 rue des Italiens, 75427 Paris, Cedex 09, France. *T:* 246-72-23.

FONTANE, Lynn; actress; *m* Alfred Lunt (*d* 1977), actor. Began as child in pantomime in Drury Lane; walked on in various London companies with Lewis Waller, Beerbohm Tree, Lena Ashwell; played in touring company with Weedon Grossmith for few seasons, playing name part in Young Lady of 17 and other small parts in various curtain raisers; on tour in Milestones, then revival in London; small parts in My Lady's Dress; then America; many plays with Laurette Taylor; name part in Dulcy, followed by many leads including Goat Song, Strange Interlude, Second Man, Caprice, At Mrs Beams, Pygmalion, The Guardsman, Meteor, Design for Living, Point Valaine, Taming of the Shrew, Idiot's Delight; Amphytrion 38 (NY and London), 1938; There Shall Be No Night (NY and London), 1943; Love in Idleness (O Mistress Mine, in New York); Quadrille (London), 1952; The Great Sebastians (NY), 1956; The Visit (London), 1960; The Sea Gull. Presidential Medal of Freedom, 1964; Antoinette Perry Award; Emmy Award. Holds hon. degrees from 12 universities and colleges.

FONTEYN, Dame Margot; *see* Arias, Dame Margot Fonteyn de.

FOOKES, Janet Evelyn; MP (C) Plymouth, Drake, since 1974 (Merton and Morden, 1970-74); *b* 21 Feb. 1936; *d* of late Lewis Aylmer Fookes and of Evelyn Margery Fookes (*née* Holmes). *Educ:* Hastings and St Leonards Ladies' Coll.; High Sch. for Girls, Hastings; Royal Holloway Coll., Univ. of London (BA Hons). Teacher, 1958-70. Councillor for County Borough of Hastings, 1960-61 and 1963-70 (Chm. Educn Cttee, 1967-70). Mem., Speaker's Panel of Chairmen, 1976-. Secretary: Cons. Parly Educn Cttee, 1971-75; Parly Animal Welfare Gp., 1974-; Chm. Educn, Arts and Home Affairs Sub-Cttee of the Expenditure Cttee, 1975-79; Member: Unopposed Bills Cttee, 1973-75; Services Cttee, 1974-76; Chm., Cons. West Country Mems Cttee, 1976-77,

Vice-Chm., 1977. Mem. Council, RSPCA, 1975- (Chm., 1979-81); Member: Nat. Art Collections Fund; Council, SSAFA, 1980-; Council, Stonham Housing Assoc., 1980-. *Recreations:* swimming, gymnasium exercises. *Address:* House of Commons, SW1A 0AA; 51 Tavistock Road, Plymouth PL5 3AF. *T:* Plymouth 778769. *Club:* Royal Over-Seas League.

FOOT, family name of **Baron Caradon** and **Baron Foot.**

FOOT, Baron *cr* 1967 (Life Peer), of Buckland Monachorum; **John Mackintosh Foot;** Senior Partner, Foot & Bowden, Solicitors, Plymouth; Chairman, United Kingdom Immigrants Advisory Service, 1970-78; *b* 17 Feb. 1909; 3rd *s* of late Rt Hon. Isaac Foot, PC and Eva Mackintosh; *m* 1936, Anne, *d* of Dr Clifford Bailey Farr, Bryn Mawr, Pa; one *s* one *d. Educ:* Forres Sch., Swanage; Bembridge Sch., IoW; Balliol Coll., Oxford. Pres., Oxford Union, 1931; Pres., OU Liberal Club, 1931; BA Oxon (2nd cl. hons Jurisprudence), 1931. Admitted Solicitor, 1934. Served in Army, 1939-45 (Hon. Major); jsc 1944. Contested (L); Basingstoke, 1934 and 1935; Bodmin, 1945 and 1950. Member: Dartmoor National Park Cttee, 1963-74; Commn on the Constitution, 1969-73; President: Dartmoor Preservation Assoc., 1976-; Commons, Open Spaces and Footpaths Preservation Soc., 1976-; UK Immigrants Adv. Service, 1978-. *Recreations:* chess, crosswords, defending Dartmoor. *Address:* Yew Tree, Crapstone, Yelverton, Devon. *T:* Yelverton 853417. *Club:* Royal Western Yacht.
See also Baron Caradon, Rt Hon. Michael Foot.

FOOT, Rt. Hon. Michael, PC 1974; MP (Lab) Ebbw Vale, since Nov. 1960; Leader of the Labour Party, since 1980 (Deputy Leader, 1976-80); Leader of the Opposition, since 1980; *b* 23 July 1913; *s* of late Rt Hon. Isaac Foot, PC; *m* 1949, Jill Craigie. *Educ:* Forres Sch., Swanage; Leighton Park Sch., Reading; Wadham Coll., Oxford (Exhibitioner). Pres. Oxford Union, 1933; contested (Lab) Mon, 1935; MP (Lab) Devonport Div. of Plymouth, 1945-55. Sec. of State for Employment, 1974-76; Lord President of the Council and Leader of the House of Commons, 1976-79. Mem., Labour Party Nat. Exec. Cttee, 1971-. Asst Editor, Tribune, 1937-38; Acting Editor, Evening Standard, 1942; Man. Dir, Tribune, 1945-74, Editor, 1948-52, 1955-60; political columnist on the Daily Herald, 1944-64; former Book Critic, Evening Standard. Hon. Fellow, Wadham Coll. 1969. *Publications:* Guilty Men (with Frank Owen and Peter Howard), 1940; Armistice 1918-39, 1940; Trial of Mussolini, 1943; Brendan and Beverley, 1944; Still at Large, 1950; Full Speed Ahead, 1950; Guilty Men (with Mervyn Jones), 1957; The Pen and the Sword, 1957; Parliament in Danger, 1959; Aneurin Bevan: Vol. I, 1897-1945, 1962; Vol. II, 1945-60, 1973; Debts of Honour, 1980. *Recreations:* Plymouth Argyle supporter, chess, reading, walking. *Address:* House of Commons, SW1.
See also Baron Caradon, Baron Foot.

FOOT, Michael Richard Daniell; historian; *b* 14 Dec. 1919; *s* of late R. C. Foot and Nina (*née* Raymond); *m* twice; one *s* one *d* ; 3rd, 1972, Mirjam Michaela, *y d* of late Prof. C. P. M. Romme, Oisterwijk. *Educ:* Winchester (scholar); New Coll., Oxford (scholar). Served in Army, 1939-45 (Major RA, parachutist, wounded). Taught at Oxford, 1947-59; research, 1959-67; Prof of Modern Hist., Manchester, 1967-73; Dir of Studies, European Discussion Centre, 1973-74. French Croix de Guerre, 1945. *Publications:* Gladstone and Liberalism (with J. L. Hammond), 1952; British Foreign Policy since 1898, 1956; Men in Uniform, 1961; SOE in France, 1966; (ed) The Gladstone Diaries: vols I and II, 1825-1839, 1968; (ed) War and Society, 1973; (ed with Dr H. C. G. Matthew) The Gladstone Diaries: vols III and IV, 1840-1854, 1975; Resistance, 1976; Six Faces of Courage, 1978; (with J. M. Langley) MI9, 1979. *Recreations:* reading, talking. *Address:* 88 Heath View, N2 0QB. *Clubs:* Savile, Special Forces.

FOOT, Paul Mackintosh; writer; journalist; with The Daily Mirror, since 1979; *b* 8 Nov. 1937; *m* ; two *s.* Editor of Isis, 1961; President of the Oxford Union, 1961. TUC delegate from Nat. Union of Journalists, 1967 and 1971. Contested (Socialist Workers Party) Birmingham, Stechford, March 1977. Editor, Socialist Worker, 1974-75. *Publications:* Immigration and Race in British Politics, 1965; The Politics of Harold Wilson, 1968; The Rise of Enoch Powell, 1969; Who Killed Hanratty?, 1971; Why You Should Be a Socialist, 1977; Red Shelley, 1981. *Address:* c/o The Daily Mirror, Holborn Circus, EC1.

FOOT, Mrs Philippa Ruth, FBA 1976; Senior Research Fellow, Somerville College, Oxford, since 1970; Professor of Philosophy, University of California at Los Angeles, since 1974; *b* 3 Oct. 1920; *d* of William Sydney Bence Bosanquet, DSO, and Esther Cleveland Bosanquet, *d* of Grover Cleveland, Pres. of USA; *m* 1945, M. R. D. Foot (marr. diss. 1960), *qv* ; no *c. Educ:* St George's Sch., Ascot; privately; Somerville Coll., Oxford (BA 1942, MA 1946). Somerville Coll., Oxford: Lectr in philosophy, 1947; Fellow and Tutor, 1950-69; Vice-Principal, 1967-69. Formerly Vis. Prof., Cornell Univ., MIT, Univ. of California at Berkeley, Princeton Univ., City Univ. of NY; Fellow, Center for Advanced Studies in Behavioral Scis, Stanford, 1981-82. *Publications:* Theories of Ethics (ed), 1967; Virtues and Vices, 1978; articles in Mind, Aristotelian Soc. Proc., Philos. Rev., New York Rev., Philosophy and Public Affairs. *Address:* 15 Walton Street, Oxford. *T:* Oxford 57130.

FOOTE, Maj.-Gen. Henry Robert Bowreman, VC 1944; CB 1952; DSO 1942; *b* 5 Dec. 1904; *s* of Lieut-Col H. B. Foote, late RA; *m* 1st, 1944, Anita Flint Howard (*d* 1970); 2nd, 1981, Mrs Audrey Mary Ashwell. *Educ:* Bedford

Sch. Royal Tank Corps; 2nd Lieut, 1925; Lieut, 1927; Capt., 1936; Staff Coll., 1939; GSO3, WO, 1939; GSO2, WO, 1940; GSO2, Staff Coll., 1940-41; GSO1, 10th Armd Div., 1941-42; OC 7th Royal Tank Regt, 1942; Subst. Major, 1942; GSO1, AFHQ, Italy, 1944; 2i/c, 9th Armd Bde, 1945; Brig. RAC, MELF, 1945-47; Subst. Lieut-Col, 1946; Subst. Col, 1948; OC 2nd Royal Tank Regt, 1947-48; OC Automotive Wing, Fighting Vehicles Proving Establishment, Ministry of Supply, 1948-49; Comd 7th Armd Bde, 1949-50; Maj.-Gen. 1951; Comd 11th Armoured Div., 1950-53; Dir-Gen. of Fighting Vehicles, Min. of Supply, 1953-55; Dir, Royal Armoured Corps, at the War Office, 1955-58; retd. *Address:* Furzefield, West Chiltington Common, Pulborough, West Sussex. *Club:* Army and Navy.

FOOTE, Rev. John Weir, VC 1946; DD, LLD University of Western Ontario, 1947; Minister of Reform Institutions, Government of Ontario, 1950-57; *b* 5 May 1904; *s* of Gordon Foote, Madoc, Ontario; *m* 1929. *Educ:* University of Western Ontario, London, Ont; Presbyterian Coll. (McGill). Served War of 1939-45; Regimental Chaplain with Royal Hamilton Light Infantry (VC). Minister St Paul's Presbyterian Church, Port Hope, Ont. Canadian Army from 1939, Asst Principal Chaplain (P). *Recreations:* golf, fishing. *Address:* Front Road East, Coburg, Ontario, Canada.

FOOTE, Prof. Peter Godfrey; Professor of Scandinavian Studies, University College London, since 1963; *b* 26 May 1924; 4th *s* of late T. Foote and Ellen Foote, Swanage, Dorset; *m* 1951, Eleanor Jessie McCaig, *d* of late J. M. McCaig and of Margaret H. McCaig; one *s* two *d. Educ:* Grammar Sch., Swanage; University Coll., Exeter; Univ. of Oslo; University Coll., London. BA London 1948; MA London 1951; Fil. dr hc Uppsala, 1972. Served with RNVR, 1943-46. Asst Lectr, Lectr and Reader in Old Scandinavian, University Coll., London, 1950-63. Jt Sec., Viking Soc., 1956-, Pres., 1974-76. Member: Royal Gustav Adolfs Academy, Uppsala, 1967; Kungl. Humanistiska Vetenskapssamfundet, Uppsala, 1968; Vísindafélag Íslands, 1969; Vetenskapssocieteten, Lund, 1973; Kungl. Vetenskaps-samhället, Göteborg; Det kongelige Norske Videnskabers Selskab, 1977; Societas Scientiarum Fennica, 1979; Hon. Member: Isl. Bókmenntafélag, 1965; Thjóðvinafélag Isl. íí Vesturheimi, 1975; Corresp. Mem., Kungl. Vitterhets Hist. och Antikvitets Akad., Stockholm, 1971. Crabtree Orator, 1968. Commander, Icelandic Order of the Falcon, 1973; Knight, Order of Dannebrog (Denmark); Comdr, Royal Order of North Star (Sweden), 1977. *Publications:* Gunnlaugs saga ormstungu, 1957; Pseudo-Turpin Chronicle in Iceland, 1959; Laing's Heimskringla, 1961; Lives of Saints: Icelandic manuscripts in fascimile IV, 1962; (with G. Johnston) The Saga of Gisli, 1963; (with D. M. Wilson) The Viking Achievement, 1970, 2nd edn 1980; Jt Editor, Mediæval Scandinavia; Mem. of Ed. Board, Arv, Scandinavica; papers in Saga-Book, Arv, Studia Islandica, Islenzk Tunga, etc. *Recreations:* bell-ringing, walking. *Address:* 18 Talbot Road, N6. *T:* 01-340 1860. *Club:* Athenæum.

FOOTMAN, Charles Worthington Fowden, CMG 1952; *b* 3 Sept. 1905; *s* of Rev. William Llewellyn and Mary Elizabeth Footman; *m* 1947, Joyce Marcelle Law; one *s* two *d. Educ:* Rossall Sch.; Keble Coll., Oxford. Colonial Administrative Service, Zanzibar, 1930; seconded to East African Governors' Conference, 1942; seconded to Colonial Office, 1943-46; Financial Sec., Nyasaland, 1947; Chief Sec., Nyasaland, 1951-60. Retired from HM Overseas Civil Service, 1960. Chm., Public Service Commissions, Tanganyika and Zanzibar, 1960-61; Commonwealth Relations Office, 1962-64; Min. of Overseas Development, 1964-70. *Recreations:* golf and tennis. *Address:* c/o National Westminster Bank, Worthing, West Sussex.

FOOTMAN, David John, CMG 1950; MC 1916; MA 1953; *b* 17 Sept. 1895; *s* of Rev. John Footman and Ella Mary (*née* Kennard); *m* 1927, Joan Isabel (marr. diss. 1936; she *d* 1960), *d* of Edmund Footman; no *c. Educ:* Marlborough; New Coll., Oxford. European War, 1914-19, Royal Berks Regt. Levant Consular Service, 1919-29; Foreign Office, 1935-53; Fellow of St Antony's Coll., Oxford, 1953-63, Emeritus Fellow, 1963-. *Publications:* Half-way East, 1935; Pig and Pepper, 1936; Pemberton, 1943; Red Prelude, 1944; The Primrose Path, 1946; Civil War in Russia, 1961; The Russian Revolutions, 1962; Dead Yesterday, 1974. *Address:* 11a Collingham Gardens, SW5. *Club:* Naval and Military.

FOOTS, Sir James (William), Kt 1975; mining engineer; Chairman, MIM Holdings Ltd, Queensland, since 1970; Director, Bank of New South Wales; *b* 1916; *m* 1939, Thora H. Thomas; one *s* two *d. Educ:* Melbourne Univ. (BME). Mem., Federal Govt's Economic Adv. Gp. Pres., Austr. Inst. Mining and Metallurgy, 1974; Pres., Austr. Mining Industry Council, 1974 and 1975. Fellow, Australian Acad. of Technol Scis. Mem. Senate, Univ. of Queensland, 1970-. Hon. DEng 1982. *Address:* GPO Box 2236, Brisbane, Qld 4001, Australia.

FORBES, family name of **Lord Forbes** and of **Earl of Granard.**

FORBES, 22nd Lord *cr* 1442 or before; **Nigel Ivan Forbes,** KBE 1960; JP, DL. Premier Lord of Scotland; Representative Peer of Scotland, 1955-63; Major (retired) Grenadier Guards; Director: Grampian Television Ltd; Blenheim Travel Ltd, since 1981; Chairman: Rolawn Ltd; Integrated Landscape Services Ltd; President, Scottish Scout Association, since 1970; *b* 19 Feb. 1918; *o s* of 21st Lord and Lady Mabel Anson (*d* 1972), *d* of 3rd Earl of Lichfield; *S* father, 1953; *m* 1942, Hon. Rosemary Katharine Hamilton-Russell, *o d* of 9th Viscount Boyne; two *s* one *d. Educ:* Harrow; RMC

Sandhurst. Served War of 1939-45 (wounded); Adjt, Grenadier Guards, Staff Coll. Military Asst to High Comr for Palestine, 1947-48. Minister of State, Scottish Office, 1958-59. Member: Inter-Parly Union Delegn to Denmark, 1956; Commonwealth Parly Assoc. Delegn to Canada, 1961; Parly Delegn to Pakistan, 1962; Inter-Parly Union Delegn to Hungary, 1965; Inter-Parly Union Delegn to Ethiopia, 1971. Mem., Aberdeen and District Milk Marketing Bd, 1962-72; Mem. Alford District Council, 1955-58; Chm., River Don District Bd, 1962-73. Pres., Royal Highland and Agricultural Society of Scotland, 1958-59; Member: Sports Council for Scotland, 1966-71; Scottish Cttee, Nature Conservancy, 1961-67; Chm., Scottish Br., Nat. Playing Fields Assoc., 1965-80. Dep. Chm., Tennant Caledonian Breweries Ltd, 1964-74. DL Aberdeenshire, 1958. *Heir: s* Master of Forbes, *qv. Address:* Balforbes, Alford, Aberdeenshire. *T:* Whitehouse (Aberdeen) 216. *Club:* Army and Navy.

FORBES, Master of; Hon. Malcolm Nigel Forbes; Financial Director; *b* 6 May 1946; *s* and *heir* of 22nd Lord Forbes, *qv* ; *m* 1969, Carole Jennifer Andrée, *d* of N. S. Whitehead, Aberdeen; one *s* one *d. Educ:* Eton; Aberdeen Univ. Director, Instock Disposables Ltd, 1974-. *Address:* Castle Forbes, Alford, Aberdeenshire. *T:* Whitehouse 209. *Clubs:* Royal Northern, University (Aberdeen).

FORBES, Hon. Sir Alastair (Granville), Kt 1960; President, Courts of Appeal for St Helena, Falkland Islands and British Antarctic Territories, since 1965, and Gibraltar, since 1970; *b* 3 Jan. 1908; *s* of Granville Forbes and Constance Margaret (*née* Davis); *m* 1936, Constance Irene Mary Hughes-White; two *d. Educ:* Blundell's Sch.; Clare Coll., Cambridge. Called to the Bar, Gray's Inn, 1932; Magistrate and Govt Officer, Dominica, BWI, 1936; Crown Attorney, Dominica, 1939; Resident Magistrate, Fiji, 1940; Crown Counsel, Fiji, 1942; Solicitor-Gen., Fiji, and Asst Legal Adviser, Western Pacific High Commission, 1945; Legal Draftsman, Federation of Malaya, 1947; Solicitor-Gen., Northern Rhodesia, 1950; Permanent Sec., Ministry of Justice, and Solicitor-Gen., Gold Coast, 1951; Puisne Judge, Kenya, 1956; Justice of Appeal, Court of Appeal for Eastern Africa, 1957; Vice-Pres., Court of Appeal for Eastern Africa, 1958; Federal Justice, Federal Supreme Court of Rhodesia and Nyasaland, 1963-64; Pres., Ct of Appeal for Seychelles, 1965-76. Mem., Panel of Chairmen of Industrial Tribunals (England and Wales), 1965-73; Pres., Pensions Appeal Tribunals for England and Wales, 1973-80 (Chm., 1965-73); Chairman: Constituencies Delimitation Commissions, N Rhodesia, 1962 and 1963, and Bechuanaland, 1964; Gibraltar Riot Inquiry, 1968. *Publications:* Index of the Laws, Dominica, 1940; Revised Edition of Laws of Fiji, 1944. *Recreations:* fishing, shooting. *Address:* Beeches, Marnhull, Sturminster Newton, Dorset. *T:* Marnhull 820458. *Club:* Royal Commonwealth Society.

FORBES, Sir Archibald (Finlayson), GBE 1957; Kt 1943; Chartered Accountant; President, Midland Bank Ltd, since 1975 (Chairman, 1964-75); *b* 6 March 1903; *s* of late Charles Forbes, Johnstone, Renfrewshire; *m* 1943, Angela Gertrude (*d* 1969), *o d* of late Horace Ely, Arlington House, SW1; one *s* two *d. Educ:* Paisley; Glasgow Univ. Formerly Mem. of firm of Thomson McLintock & Co., Chartered Accountants. Joined Spillers Ltd as Executive Dir, 1935; Chm., 1965-68, Pres., 1969-80. Mem. of various Reorganisation Commns and Cttees appointed by Minister of Agriculture, 1932-39; Chm., Nat. Mark Trade Cttees for Eggs and Poultry, 1936-39; Dir of Capital Finance, Air Min., 1940; Deputy Sec., Min. of Aircraft Production, 1940-43; Controller of Repair, Equipment and Overseas Supplies, 1943-45 (incl. Operational Control, nos 41 and 43 Gps, RAF and Dir, Gen. Repair and Maintenance, RAF); Mem. of Aircraft Supply Council, 1943-45; Chairman: First Iron and Steel Board from its formation, 1946, to dissolution 1949; Iron and Steel Board from its inception under the Iron and Steel Act, 1953, until 1959; British Millers' Mutual Pool Ltd, 1952-62 (Dep. Chm. 1940-52); Central Mining and Investment Corp., 1959-64; Debenture Corp. Ltd, 1949-79; Midland and International Banks Ltd, 1964-76; Director: Shell Transport & Trading Co. Ltd, 1954-73; English Electric Co. Ltd, 1958-76; Dunlop Holdings Ltd, 1958-76. Pres., FBI, 1951-53; Chm., Cttee of London Clearing Bankers, 1970-72 (Dep. Chm., 1968-70); President: British Bankers' Assoc., 1970-71, 1971-72 (Vice-Pres. 1969-70); FBI, 1951-53; Dir, 1950-53, Dep. Chm., 1961-64, Finance Corp. for Industry. Member: Cttee to enquire into Financial Structure of Colonial Develt Corp., 1959; Review Body on Doctors' and Dentists' Remuneration, 1962-65; Governing Body, Imp. Coll. of Science and Technology, 1959-75. Pres., Epsom Coll., 1964-. Hon. JDipMA. *Recreations:* golf and fishing. *Address:* 40 Orchard Court, Portman Square, W1. *T:* 01-935 9304; Mattingley Green Cottage, Mattingley, Hants. *T:* Heckfield 247. *Clubs:* Brooks's, Pratt's, Beefsteak.

FORBES, Bryan; *b* 22 July 1926; *m* 1958, Nanette Newman, *qv;* two *d. Educ:* West Ham Secondary Sch. Studied at RADA, 1941; entered acting profession, 1942, and (apart from war service) was on West End stage, then in films here and in Hollywood, 1948-60. Formed Beaver Films with Richard Attenborough, 1959; wrote and co-produced The Angry Silence, 1960. Subseq. wrote, dir. and prod. numerous films; *films include:* The League of Gentlemen, Only Two Can Play, Whistle Down the Wind, 1961; The L-Shaped Room, 1962; Séance on a Wet Afternoon, 1963; King Rat (in Hollywood), 1964; The Wrong Box, 1965; The Whisperers, 1966; Deadfall, 1967; The Madwoman of Chaillot, 1968; The Raging Moon, 1970; The Tales of Beatrix Potter, 1971; The Stepford Wives, 1974 (USA); The Slipper and the Rose, 1975 (Royal Film Perf., 1976); International Velvet, 1978; (British segment) The Sunday Lovers, 1980; Ménage à Trois, 1981; (narrator) I am a Dancer. *Stage:* Directed Macbeth, Old Vic, 1980. *Television:* produced and

directed: Edith Evans, I Caught Acting Like the Measles, Yorkshire TV, 1973; Elton John, Goodbye Norma Jean and Other Things, ATV 1973; Jessie, BBC, 1980. Man. Dir and Head of Production, ABPC Studios, 1969-71; Man. Dir and Chief Exec., EMI-MGM, Elstree Studios, 1970-71; Dir, Capital Radio Ltd, 1973-. Won British Academy Award, 1960; Writers' Guild Award (twice); numerous internat. awards. Member: BBC Gen. Adv. Council, 1966-69; BBC Schs Council, 1971-73; Trustee, Writers' Guild of GB. *Publications:* Truth Lies Sleeping, 1950 (paperback, 1961); The Distant Laughter, 1972 (paperback, 1973); Notes for a Life, 1974 (paperback, 1977); The Slipper and the Rose, 1976; Ned's Girl: biography of Dame Edith Evans, 1977; International Velvet, 1978; Familiar Strangers, 1979; That Despicable Race, 1980; contribs to: The Spectator, New Statesman, Queen, and other periodicals. *Recreations:* running a bookshop, reading, landscape gardening, photography. *Address:* The Bookshop, Virginia Water, Surrey.

FORBES of Pitsligo, Sir Charles Edward Stuart-, 12th Bt *cr* 1626; Building contractor, retired; *b* 6 Aug. 1903; *s* of Sir Charles Hay Hepburn Stuart-Forbes, 10th Bt, and Ellen, *d* of Capt. Huntley; *S* brother, 1937; *m* 1966, Ijah Leah MacCabe (*d* 1974), Wellington, NZ. *Educ:* Ocean Bay Coll. *Recreations:* motoring, football, cricket, hockey, swimming, deep sea fishing, hunting, rowing, launching, tennis. *Heir: n* William Daniel Stuart-Forbes [*b* 21 Aug. 1935; *m* 1956, Jannette MacDonald; three *s* two *d*]. *Address:* 33 Dillons Point Road, Blenheim, South Island, NZ.

FORBES, Charles Harington Gordon, CBE 1965 (OBE 1941); Registrar, Principal Probate Registry, Somerset House, 1946-64; *b* 20 Feb. 1896; *s* of Harington G. Forbes, OBE; *m* 1927, Jean J. Beith; one *d. Educ:* Malvern Coll. Entered service of Principal Probate Registry, 1914. Served European War, 1914-18, with The Honourable Artillery Company. *Address:* Chetwynd, Watermill Lane, Bexhill-on-Sea, East Sussex.

FORBES, Colin, RDI 1974; Partner, Pentagram Design, since 1972; *b* 6 March 1928; *s* of Kathleen and John Forbes; *m* 1961, Wendy Schneider; one *s* two *d. Educ:* Sir Anthony Browne's, Brentwood; LCC Central Sch. of Arts and Crafts. Design Asst, Herbert Spencer, 1952; freelance practice and Lectr, LCC Central Sch. of Arts and Crafts, 1953-57; Art Dir, Stuart Advertising, London, 1957-58; Head of Graphic Design Dept, LCC Central Sch. of Arts and Crafts, 1958-61; freelance practice, London, 1961-62; Partner: Fletcher/Forbes/Gill, 1962-65; Crosby/Fletcher/Forbes, 1965-72. Mem., Alliance Graphique Internationale, 1965- (Internat. Pres. 1976-79); Vice Pres., Amer. Inst. Graphic Arts, 1981-. *Publications:* Graphic Design: visual comparisons, 1963; A Sign Systems Manual, 1970; Creativity and Communication, 1971; New Alphabets A to Z, 1973; Living by Design, 1978. *Address:* 40 Firth Avenue, Apartment 14E, New York, NY 10011, USA. *T:* 212 460 5146. *Club:* Savile.

FORBES, Donald James, MA; Headmaster, Merchiston Castle School, 1969-81; *b* 6 Feb. 1921; *s* of Andrew Forbes; *m* 1945, Patricia Muriel Yeo; two *s* one *d. Educ:* Oundle; Clare Coll., Cambridge (Mod. Lang. Tripos). Capt. Scots Guards, 1941-46; 1st Bn Scots Guards, 1942-46, N Africa, Italy. Asst Master, Dulwich Coll., 1946-55; Master i/c cricket, 1951-55; Headmaster, Dauntsey's Sch., 1956-69. Diploma in Spanish, Univ. of Santander, 1954; Lectr in Spanish, West Norwood Tech. Coll., 1954-55. *Recreations:* cricket, Rugby football, tennis, Rugby fives; history, literature; instrumental and choral music. *Address:* 33 Coates Gardens, Edinburgh EH12 5LG. Breachacha Castle, Isle of Coll. *Clubs:* Hawks (Cambridge); New (Edinburgh); HCEG (Muirfield).

FORBES of Brux, Hon. Sir Ewan, 11th Bt *cr* 1630, of Craigievar; JP; landowner and farmer; *b* 6 Sept. 1912; 2nd *s* of Sir John Forbes-Sempill, 9th Bt (Forbes) of Craigievar, 18th Lord Sempill; *S* (to Btcy) brother, 1965; *m* 1952, Isabella, *d* of A. Mitchell, Glenrinnes, Banffshire. *Educ:* Dresden; Univ. of Munich; Univ. of Aberdeen. MB, ChB 1944. Senior Casualty Officer, Aberdeen Royal Infirmary, 1944-45; Medical Practitioner, Alford, Aberdeenshire, 1945-55. JP Aberdeenshire, 1969. *Recreations:* shooting, fishing, ski-ing and skating. *Heir: kinsman* John Alexander Cumnock Forbes-Sempill [*b* 29 Aug. 1927; *m* 1st, 1958, Penelope Margaret Ann (marr. diss. 1964), *d* of A. G. Grey-Pennington; 2nd, 1966, Jane Carolyn, *o d* of C. Gordon Evans]. *Address:* Brux Lodge, Alford, Aberdeenshire. *T:* Kildrummy 223.

See also Lady Sempill.

FORBES, Dr Gilbert; Regius Professor of Forensic Medicine, University of Glasgow, 1964-74; *b* 5 Aug. 1908; *s* of late George and Jane Gilbert Forbes; *m* 1938, Marian Margaret Macrae Guthrie, Springfield, Fife; one *d. Educ:* Hillhead High Sch., Glasgow; Glasgow Univ. (BSc). MB, ChB Glasgow, 1933; Brunton Memorial Prize, 1933; FRFPSG 1935; FRCSE 1935; MD 1945. House posts at Western Infirmary, Glasgow, 1933-34; Demonstrator in Anatomy, University of Glasgow, 1934-36; Lecturer in Anatomy, University of Aberdeen, 1936-37; Police Surgeon to City of Sheffield and Lecturer in Forensic Medicine, University of Sheffield, 1937-48; Senior Lectr in Forensic Medicine, Univ. of Sheffield, 1948-56; Reader in Forensic Medicine, Univ. of Sheffield, 1956-64. Asst Deputy Coroner to City of Sheffield, 1945-59. At various times external examiner in forensic medicine in Univs of Manchester, Birmingham, Leeds, Glasgow, Aberdeen and Edinburgh. *Publications:* original papers on medico-legal subjects in medical and scientific journals. *Recreation:* motoring. *Address:* 18 The Glen, Endcliffe Vale Road, Sheffield S10 3FN.

FORBES, Very Rev. Graham John Thomson; Provost, St Ninian's Cathedral, Perth, since 1982; *b* 10 June 1951; *s* of J. T. and D. D. Forbes; *m* 1973, Jane T. Miller; three *s. Educ:* George Heriot's School, Edinburgh; Univ. of Aberdeen (MA); Univ. of Edinburgh (BD). Curate, Old St Paul's Church, Edinburgh, 1976-82. *Recreations:* climbing, running, squash. *Address:* St Ninian's House, 47 Balhousie Street, Perth PH1 5HJ. *T:* Perth 26874/27982.

FORBES, Hon. Sir Hugh (Harry Valentine), Kt 1970; **Hon. Mr Justice Forbes;** a Judge of the High Court, Queen's Bench Division, since 1970; an Additional Judge of the Employment Appeal Tribunal, since 1976; *b* 14 Feb. 1917; *e s* of late Rev. H. N. Forbes, sometime Rector of Castle Bromwich; *m* 1st, 1940, Julia Margaret (marr. diss. 1970), *yr d* of Frank Gilbert Weller; one *s* two *d* ; 2nd, 1970, Janet Moir, *o d* of Campbell Andrews, MD, Harrow. *Educ:* Rossall; Trinity Hall, Cambridge (1st cl. Law). Served War of 1939-45: Major, Gordon Highlanders; GSO2 War Office and GHQ India. Called to Bar, Middle Temple, 1946; QC 1966; Bencher, 1970. Chm., Lincs (Kesteven) QS, 1967-71 (Dep. Chm., 1961-67); Dep. Chm., Hunts and Peterborough QS, 1965-70; Mem., Parole Bd, 1977-79 (Vice-Chm., 1978-79). Chancellor: Dio. of Ely, 1965-69; Dio. of Chelmsford, 1969. Chm. Council, Royal Yachting Assoc., 1971-76. *Publication:* Real Property Law, 1950. *Recreations:* sailing, listening to music. *Address:* Royal Courts of Justice, WC2. *Clubs:* Royal Cruising; Royal Yacht Squadron (Cowes).

FORBES, Ian, QPM 1966; Deputy Assistant Commissioner, Metropolitan Police and National Co-ordinator, Regional Crime Squads (England and Wales), 1970-72; *b* 30 March 1914; *y s* of John and Betsy Forbes, Auchlossan, Lumphanan, Aberdeenshire; *m* 1941, Lilian Edith Miller, Edgware, Mddx; two *s. Educ:* Lumphanan School, Aberdeenshire. Joined Metropolitan Police, 1939; served in East End, Central London Flying Squad, New Scotland Yard; Detective Superintendent, 1964; served on New Scotland Yard Murder Squad, 1966-69; Commander, No 9 Regional Crime Squad (London area), 1969. *Publication:* Squadman (autobiog.), 1973. *Recreations:* gardening, motoring, reading. *Address:* 13 Richmond Avenue, Compton, Wolverhampton WV3 9JB.

FORBES, Vice-Adm. Sir John Morrison, KCB 1978; a Chairman, Civil Service Commissioners interview panel, since 1980; Naval Vice President, Combined Cadet Force, since 1980; Governor of various naval charities; *b* 16 Aug. 1925; *s* of late Lt-Col R. H. Forbes, OBE, and late Gladys M. Forbes (*née* Pollock); *m* 1950, Joyce Newenham Hadden; two *s* two *d. Educ:* RNC, Dartmouth. Served War: HMS Mauritius, Verulam and Nelson, 1943-46. HMS Aisne, 1946-49; Gunnery course and staff of HMS Excellent, 1950-51; served in RAN, 1952-54; Staff of HMS Excellent, 1954-56; HMS Ceylon, 1956-58; Staff of Dir of Naval Ordnance, 1958-60; Comdr (G) HMS Excellent, 1960-61; Staff of Dir of Seaman Officers' Appts, 1962-64; Exec. Officer, Britannia RN Coll., 1964-66; Operational Comdr and 2nd in Comd, Royal Malaysian Navy, 1966-68; Asst Dir, Naval Plans, 1969-70; comd HMS Triumph, 1971-72; comd Britannia RN Coll., Dartmouth, 1972-74; Naval Secretary, 1974-76; Flag Officer, Plymouth, Port Adm., Devonport, Comdr, Central Sub Area, Eastern Atlantic, and Comdr, Plymouth Sub Area, Channel, 1977-79. Naval ADC to the Queen, 1974. Kesatria Manku Negara (Malaysia), 1968. *Recreations:* country pursuits. *Address:* c/o National Westminster Bank Ltd, Waterlooville, Portsmouth, Hants. *Clubs:* Army and Navy, RN Sailing Association.

FORBES, Col Sir John Stewart, 6th Bt of Newe *cr* 1823; DSO; JP; Vice-Lieutenant of Aberdeenshire, since 1973; *b* 8 Jan. 1901; *o* surv. *s* of 5th Bt and late Emma Theodora, *d* of Robert Maxwell; *S* father, 1927; *m* 1933, Agnes Jessie, *er d* of late Lt-Col D. L. Wilson-Farquharson, DSO; five *d. Educ:* Wellington Coll.; RMA, Woolwich. 2nd Lieut RE, 1920; Temp. Brig. 1948; Col 1949; served Norway Campaign, 1940 (DSO, despatches); Burma, 1944-45 (despatches); Comdt, Indian Coll. of Military Engrg, 1947-48; retired 1953. Hon. Col 51st (H) Div. Engineers, TA, 1960-67. DL 1953, JP 1955, Aberdeenshire. *Heir: cousin* Major Hamish Stewart Forbes, MBE, MC [*b* 15 Feb. 1916; *m* 1945, Jacynthe Elizabeth Mary, *o d* of late Eric Gordon Underwood; one *s* three *d*]. *Address:* Allargue, Corgarff, Aberdeenshire AB3 8YP. *Clubs:* Brooks's; Royal Northern (Aberdeen).

FORBES, John Stuart; Sheriff of Tayside, Central and Fife at Dunfermline, since 1980; *b* 31 Jan. 1936; *s* of John Forbes and late Dr A. R. S. Forbes; *m* 1963, Marion Alcock; one *s* two *d. Educ:* Glasgow High Sch.; Glasgow Univ. (MA, LLB). Solicitor, 1959-61; Advocate, Scottish Bar, 1962-76; Sheriff of Lothian and Borders, 1976-80. *Recreations:* squash, tennis, golf. *Address:* 8 Park Avenue, Dunfermline KY12 7HX. *T:* Dunfermline 22206. *Club:* Edinburgh Sports.

FORBES, Mrs Muriel Rose, CBE 1963; JP; Alderman, London Borough of Brent, 1972-74; *b* 20 April 1894; *yr d* of John Henry Cheeseright; *m* 1923, Charles Gilbert Forbes (*d* 1957); two *d. Educ:* Gateshead Grammar Sch.; Southlands Teacher Training Coll. Member: Willesden Borough Council, 1936-47; Middlesex CC, 1934-65 (Chm., 1960-61); GLC, 1964-67 (Vice-Chm., 1964-66). Chairman: St Charles's Gp Hosp. Management Cttee, 1968-69; Paddington Gp Hosp. Management Cttee, 1963-68; Mem., Central Middx Hosp. Management Cttee, 1948-63 (Vice-Chm., 1952-63). JP County of Middx, 1946. Hon. DTech Brunel Univ., 1966. *Address:* 9 Rosemary Road, Halesowen, West Midlands B63 1BN.

FORBES, Nanette; *see* Newman, N.

FORBES, Robert Brown; Director of Education, Edinburgh, 1972-75; *b* 14 Oct. 1912; *s* of Robert James Forbes and Elizabeth Jane Brown; *m* 1939, Nellie Shepley; one *s* one *d. Educ:* Edinburgh Univ. (MA, MEd). Asst Dir of Educn, Edinburgh, 1946, Depute Dir, 1952. Chm., Scottish Council for Research in Educn, 1972. *Address:* 7 Wilton Road, Edinburgh EH16 5NX. *T:* 031-667 1323.

FORBES-LEITH of Fyvie, Sir Andrew (George), 3rd Bt *cr* 1923; landed proprietor; *b* 20 Oct. 1929; *s* of Sir R. Ian A. Forbes-Leith of Fyvie, 2nd Bt, KT, MBE, and Ruth Avis (*d* 1973), *d* of Edward George Barnett; *S* father, 1973; *m* 1962, Jane Kate (*d* 1969), *d* of late David McCall-McCowan; two *s* two *d. Heir: s* George Ian David Forbes-Leith, *b* 26 May 1967. *Address:* Dunachton, Kingussie, Inverness-shire. *T:* Kincraig 226. *Clubs:* Royal Northern (Aberdeen); Highland (Inverness).

FORBES-SEMPILL; *see* Sempill.

FORD; *see* St Clair-Ford.

FORD, Benjamin Thomas; MP (Lab) Bradford North since 1964; *b* 1 April 1925; *s* of Benjamin Charles Ford and May Ethel (*née* Moorton); *m* 1950, Vera Ada (*née* Fawcett-Fancet); two *s* one *d. Educ:* Rowan Road Central Sch., Surrey. Apprenticed as compositor, 1941. War Service, 1943-47, Fleet Air Arm (Petty Officer). Electronic Fitter/Wireman, 1951-64; Convener of Shop Stewards, 1955-64. Pres., Harwich Constituency Labour Party, 1955-63; Clacton UDC, 1959-62; Alderman Essex CC, 1959-65; JP Essex, 1962-67. Chairman: British-Portuguese Parly Gp; British-Malaysian Parly Gp; British-Venezuelan Parly Gp; All-Party Wool Textile Parly Gp; Accom. and Admin Sub-Cttee, H of C Select Cttee (Services); Vice-Chairman: British-Latin American Parly Gp; British-Brazilian Parly Gp; PLP Defence Cttee; Treasurer, IPU British Gp, 1979- (Chm., 1977-79); Sec., British-Namibian Parly Gp. Chm. Jt Select Cttee on Sound Broadcasting, 1976-77. *Publication:* Piecework, 1960. *Recreations:* music, shooting, family. *Address:* House of Commons, SW1. *Clubs:* Royal Automobile, House of Commons Motor (Vice-Chm.); Idle Working Men's.

FORD, Prof. Boris, MA; Professor of Education, School of Education, University of Bristol, 1973-82; *b* 1 July 1917; *s* of late Brig. G. N. Ford, CB, DSO; *m* 1st, 1950, Noreen; one *s* three *d* ; 2nd, 1977, Inge. *Educ:* Gresham's Sch., Holt, Norfolk; Downing Coll., Cambridge. Army Education, finally OC Middle East School of Artistic Studies, 1940-46. Chief Ed. and finally Dir, Bureau of Current Affairs, 1946-51; Information Officer, Technical Assistance Bd, UN (NY and Geneva), 1951-53; Sec., Nat. Enquiry into Liberalising Technical Educn, 1953-55; Editor, Journal of Education, 1955-58; first Head of Sch. Broadcasting, Associated-Rediffusion, 1957-58; Educn Sec., Cambridge Univ. Press, 1958-60; Prof. of Education and Dir of the Inst. of Education, Univ. of Sheffield, 1960-63; Prof. of Education, Univ. of Sussex, 1963-73, Dean, Sch. of Cultural and Community Studies (Educnl Studies), 1963-71, Chm., Educn Area, and Dir, Sch. of Educn, 1971-73. Chairman: Nat. Assoc. for the Teaching of English, 1963-65; Educational Dir, Pictorial Knowledge, 1968-71. Gen. Editor, Pelican Guide to English Literature, 1954-66, New Pelican Guide to English Literature, 1982-83; Editor, Universities Qly, subseq. New Universities Qly, 1955-. *Publications:* Discussion Method, 1949; Teachers' Handbook to Human Rights, 1950; Liberal Education in a Technical Age, 1955; Young Readers: Young Writers, 1960; Changing Relationships between Universities and Teachers' Colleges, 1975. *Recreation:* music. *Address:* 35 Alma Vale Road, Clifton, Bristol.

FORD, Brinsley, CBE 1978; FSA; Member of National Art-Collections Fund since 1927, of Executive Committee since 1960; Vice-Chairman, 1974-75, Chairman 1975-80; Chairman of Trustees, Watts Gallery, Compton (Trustee, since 1955); Secretary, Society of Dilettanti, since 1972; *b* 10 June 1908; *e s* of late Capt. Richard Ford, Rifle Brigade, and Rosamund, *d* of Sir John Ramsden, 5th Bt; *m* 1937, Joan, *d* of late Capt. Geoffrey Vyvyan; two *s* one *d. Educ:* Eton; Trinity Coll., Oxford. Joined TA 1939; served for one year as Troop Sergeant Major, RA; commissioned 1941, and transferred to Intelligence Corps (Major 1945). Selected works for Arts Council Festival of Britain and Coronation Exhibitions; a Trustee of the National Gallery, 1954-61; great-grandson of Richard Ford (1796-1858) who wrote the Handbook for Spain; owner of the Ford Collection of Richard Wilsons. Dir, Burlington Magazine, 1952-. Member: Council, Byam Shaw Sch., 1957-73; Exec. Cttee, City and Guilds of London Art Sch., 1976-. Pres., St Marylebone Soc., 1974-77. Hon. Adviser on Paintings to Nat. Trust, 1980; Hon. Fellow, Royal Acad., 1981. Corres. Mem., Royal Acad. of San Fernando, Madrid. Officer, Belgian Order of Leopold II; US Bronze Star; Médaille d'Argent de la Reconnaissance Française. *Publications:* The Drawings of Richard Wilson, 1951; contributor to the Burlington Magazine and Apollo. *Address:* 14 Wyndham Place, Bryanston Square, W1. *T:* 01-723 0826. *Club:* Brooks's.

FORD, Charles Edmund, FRS 1965; DSc London, FLS, FZS, FIBiol; Member of Medical Research Council's External Staff, Sir William Dunn School of Pathology, Oxford, 1971-78; *b* 24 Oct. 1912; *s* of late Charles Ford and late Ethel Eubornia Ford (*née* Fawcett); *m* 1940, Jean Ella Dowling; four *s. Educ:* Slough Grammar Sch.; King's Coll., University of London. Demonstrator, Dept of Botany, King's Coll., University of London, 1936-38; Geneticist, Rubber Research Scheme, Ceylon, 1938-41 and 1944-45. Lieut

Royal Artillery, 1942-43. PSO Dept of Atomic Energy, Min. of Supply, at Chalk River Laboratories, Ont, Canada, 1946-49. Head of Cytogenetics Section, MRC, Radiobiology Unit, Harwell, 1949-71. *Publications:* papers on cytogenetics in scientific journals. *Recreations:* travel, friends. *Address:* 156 Oxford Road, Abingdon, Oxon. *T:* Abingdon 20001.

FORD, Colin John; Keeper, National Museum of Photography, Film and Television, since 1982; lecturer, writer and broadcaster on films, theatre and photography; exhibition organiser; *b* 13 May 1934; *s* of John William and Hélène Martha Ford; *m* 1961, Margaret Elizabeth Cordwell (marr. diss.); one *s* one *d. Educ:* Enfield Grammar Sch.; University Coll., Oxford (MA). Manager and Producer, Kidderminster Playhouse, 1958-60; Gen. Man., Western Theatre Ballet, 1960-62; Vis. Lectr in English and Drama, California State Univ. at Long Beach and UCLA (Univ. Extension), 1962-64; Dep. Curator, Nat. Film Archive, 1965-72. Organiser, 30th Anniv. Congress of Internat. Fedn of Film Archives, London, 1968; Dir, Cinema City Exhibn, 1970; Programme Dir, London Shakespeare Film Festival, 1972; Keeper of Film and Photography, Nat. Portrait Gall., 1972-81. *Film:* Masks and Faces, 1966 (BBC TV version, Omnibus, 1968). *Publications:* (with Roy Strong) An Early Victorian Album, 1974, 2nd edn 1977; The Cameron Collection, 1975; (ed) Happy and Glorious: Six Reigns of Royal Photography, 1977; Rediscovering Mrs Cameron, 1979; People in Camera, 1979; (with Brian Harrison) A Hundred Years Ago (Britain in the 1880s), 1982; (principal contrib.) Oxford Companion to Film; articles in many jls. *Recreations:* travel, music, small boats. *Address:* National Museum of Photography, Film and Television, c/o Science Museum, SW7 2DD.

FORD, David Robert, MVO 1975; OBE 1976; *b* 22 Feb. 1935; *s* of William Ewart and Edna Ford; *m* 1958, Elspeth Anne (*née* Muckart); two *s* two *d. Educ:* Tauntons School. National Service, 1953-55; regular commn, RA, 1955; regimental duty, Malta, 1953-58; Lieut, UK, 1958-62; Captain, Commando Regt, 1962-66; active service: Borneo, 1964, Aden, 1966; Staff Coll., Quetta, 1967; seconded to Hong Kong Govt, 1967; retired from Army (Major), 1972. Dep. Dir, Hong Kong Govt Information Service, 1972-74, Dir, 1974-76; Dep. Sec., Govt Secretariat, Hong Kong, 1976; Under Sec., NI Office, 1977-79; Sec. for Information, Hong Kong Govt, 1979-80; Hong Kong Commissioner in London, 1980-81; RCDS, 1982. *Recreations:* tennis, fishing, photography, theatre. *Address:* The Old Malthouse, Marnhull, Dorset.

FORD, Rt. Rev. Douglas Albert; Incumbent of All Saints', Cochrane, Diocese of Calgary, since 1981; Assistant Bishop of Calgary, since 1981; *b* 16 July 1917; *s* of Thomas George Ford and Elizabeth Eleanor (Taylor), both English; *m* 1944, Doris Ada (Elborne); two *s* one *d. Educ:* primary and secondary schs, Vancouver; Univ. of British Columbia (BA); Anglican Theological Coll. of BC (LTh); General Synod (BD). Deacon, 1941; Priest, 1942; Curate, St Mary's, Kerrisdale, 1941-42; St George's, Vancouver, 1942-44; Vicar of Strathmore, 1944-49; Rector of: Okotoks, 1949-52; Vermilion, 1952-55; St Michael and All Angels, Calgary, 1955-62; St Augustine, Lethbridge, 1962-66; Dean and Rector, St John's Cath., Saskatoon, 1966-70. Hon. DD: Coll. of Emmanuel and St Chad, Saskatoon, 1970; Anglican Theological coll. of BC, Vancouver, 1971. *Address:* PO Box 1043, Cochrane, Alberta T0L 0W0, Canada.

FORD, Rev. Preb. Douglas William C.; *see* Cleverley Ford.

FORD, Edmund Brisco, FRS 1946; MA, DSc Oxon, Hon. DSc Liverpool; Senior Dean, and Fellow, 1958-71, Fellow Emeritus, 1976-77, and Fellow and Senior Dean, since 1977, All Souls College, Oxford; Professor of Ecological Genetics, 1963-69, and Director of Genetics Laboratory, Zoology Department, 1952-69, Oxford; Emeritus Professor, since 1969; *b* 23 April 1901; unmarried; *s* of Harold Dodsworth Ford and Gertrude Emma Bennett. *Educ:* Wadham Coll., Oxford (Hon. Fellow, 1974). Research worker, Univ. Lectr and Demonstrator in Zoology and Comparative Anatomy, Univ. Reader in Genetics, Oxford; Pres., Genetical Soc. of Great Britain, 1946-49; Mem. of Nature Conservancy, 1949-59; Mem. various scientific (chiefly zoological) societies. Wild Life Conservation Cttee of Ministry of Town and Country Planning, 1945-47 (Cmd Rept 7122). Formerly represented British Empire on Permanent Internat. Cttee of Genetics. Has travelled in USA, NZ, Australia, Near and Far East. Initiated Science of Ecological Genetics. Darwin Medallist, Royal Society, 1954. Delivered Galton Lecture of London Univ., 1939; Woodhall Lectr of the Royal Institution, 1957; Woodward Lectr, Yale Univ., 1959 and 1973. Hon. FRCP 1974; Hon. FRES. Weldon Memorial Prize, Oxford Univ., 1959. Medallist of Helsinki Univ., 1967. Foreign Mem., Finnish Acad. Pres. Somerset Archæological Soc., 1960-61. *Publications:* Mendelism and Evolution, 1931, 8th edn 1965; (with G. D. Hale Carpenter) Mimicry, 1933; The Study of Heredity (Home University Library), 1938, 2nd edn 1950; Genetics for Medical Students, 1942, 7th edn 1973; Butterflies (Vol. I of New Naturalist Series), 1945, 2nd repr. of 4th edn, 1972, pbk 1975, rev. edn 1977; British Butterflies (King Penguin Series), 1951; Moths (New Naturalist Series), 1955, 4th edn 1976; Ecological Genetics, 1964, 4th edn 1975 (trans: Polish 1967, French 1972, Italian 1978); Genetic Polymorphism (All Souls Monographs), 1965; Evolution Studied by Observation and Experiment, 1973; Genetics and Adaptation, 1976; Understanding Genetics, 1979; Taking Genetics into the Countryside, 1981; numerous contribs to scientific jls, on genetical and zoological subjects. Festschrift: Ecological Genetics and Evolution, ed E. R. Creed, 1971. *Recreations:* archæology, literature, travel. *Address:* 5 Apsley Road, Oxford; All Souls College, Oxford.

TA: and *T:* Oxford 58147; Zoology Department, South Parks Road, Oxford. *Club:* Travellers'.

FORD, Sir Edward, Kt 1960; OBE 1945; Professor of Preventive Medicine and Director of the School of Public Health and Tropical Medicine, University of Sydney, 1947-68, now Emeritus; *b* 15 April 1902; *s* of Edward John and Mary Ford, South Yarra, Victoria. *Educ:* Univ. of Melbourne, Sydney and London. RMO, Melbourne Hosp., 1930; Lectr in Anatomy, Melbourne Univ., 1933; Sen. Lectr in Anatomy and Histology, Melbourne Univ., 1934-36; Lectr, Sch. of Public Health and Tropical Medicine, Sydney, 1937-39. Served War of 1939-45: in Australian Army Middle East, New Guinea, Burma; Senior Malariologist, AIF, and late Dir of Hygiene and Pathology, Aust. Army; Col AAMC, 1940-45. Rockefeller Fellow, 1946; Dean of Faculty of Medicine and Fellow of Senate, Sydney Univ., 1953-57. Vice-Pres., RACP, 1970-73. *Publication:* Bibliography of Australian Medicine 1790-1900, 1976. *Address:* Cahors, Macleay Street, Potts Point, NSW 2011, Australia. *Club:* Australian (Sydney).

FORD, Sir Edward (William Spencer), KCB 1967 (CB 1952); KCVO 1957 (MVO 1949); OStJ 1976; MA; FRSA; DL; Secretary and Registrar of the Order of Merit, since 1975; Secretary to the Pilgrim Trust, 1967-75; *b* 24 July 1910; 4th (twin) *s* of late Very Rev. Lionel G. B. J. Ford, Headmaster of Repton and Harrow and Dean of York, and of Mary Catherine, *d* of Rt Rev. E. S. Talbot, Bishop of Winchester and Hon. Mrs Talbot; *m* 1949, Virginia, *er d* of 1st and last Baron Brand, CMG, and *widow* of John Metcalfe Polk, NY; two *s. Educ:* Eton (King's Schol.); New Coll., Oxford (Open Scholar). 1st Class Hon. Mods; 2nd Class Lit. Hum. (Greats). Law Student (Harmsworth Scholar) Middle Temple, 1934-35. Called to Bar, Middle Temple, 1937 and practised 1937-39; 2nd Lieut (Supplementary Reserve of Officers) Grenadier Guards, 1936; Lieut 1939; served in France and Belgium, 1939-40 (despatches), and in Tunisia and Italy, 1943-44 (despatches), Brigade Major 10th Infantry and 24th Guards Brigades; Instructor at Staff Coll., Haifa, 1944-45. psc†. Asst Private Secretary to King George VI, 1946-52, and to the Queen, 1952-67; Extra Equerry to the Queen, 1955. Dir, London Life Assoc. Member: Central Appeals Adv. Cttee, BBC and IBA, 1969-72, 1976-78; York Glaziers' Trust; Chairman: UK/USA Bicentennial Fellowships Cttee, 1975-80; St John Council for Northamptonshire, 1976-82; Grants Cttee, Historic Churches Preservation Trust, 1977-; Mem. Ct of Assts, Goldsmiths' Co., 1970-, Prime Warden, 1979. High Sheriff Northants 1970, DL 1972. *Address:* 18 Hale House, 34 De Vere Gardens, W8 5AQ. *T:* 01-937 2818. *Clubs:* White's, Beefsteak, MCC.

FORD, Elbur; *see* Hibbert, Eleanor.

FORD, Air Marshal Sir Geoffrey (Harold), KBE 1979; CB 1974; Director, The Metals Society, since 1981; *b* 6 Aug. 1923; *s* of late Harold Alfred Ford, Lewes, Sussex; *m* 1951, Valerie, *d* of late Douglas Hart Finn, Salisbury; two *s. Educ:* Lewes Grammar Sch.; Bristol Univ. (BSc). Served War of 1939-45: commissioned, 1942; 60 Gp, 1943; Italy and Middle East, 1944-46. 90 (Signals) Gp, 1946-49; Bomber Development, 1954-57; Air Ministry, 1958-61; RAF Technical Coll., 1961-62; Min. of Aviation, 1963-64; Chief Signals Officer, RAF Germany, 1965-68; MoD, 1968-72; RCDS, 1972; AO Engineering, Strike Command, 1973-76; Dir-Gen. Engineering and Supply Management, RAF, 1976-78; Chief Engr (RAF), 1978-81. CEng, FIEE (Council, 1977-). *Address:* c/o Barclays Bank Ltd, Lewes, East Sussex. *Club:* Royal Air Force.

FORD, George Johnson, DL; Chairman, Cheshire County Council, since 1976 (Member, since 1962); *b* 13 March 1916; *s* of James and Esther Ford; *m* 1941, Nora Helen Brocklehurst; three *s* one *d. Educ:* Chester Coll. Qualified estate agent, 1938. FAI 1938. **Member,** Runcorn RDC, 1953 (Chm., 1962); Mem. Bd, Warrington and Runcorn Develt Corp., 1981- (Runcorn Develt Corp., 1964-81). Pres., Frodsham Conservative Assoc., 1962-. DL Cheshire, 1979. *Recreations:* horse racing, music and drama. *Address:* Manley Old Hall, Manley, via Warrington, Cheshire WA6 9EA. *T:* Manley 254. *Club:* City (Chester).

FORD, Gerald Rudolph; President of the United States of America, Aug. 1974-Jan. 1977; lawyer; *b* Omaha, Nebraska, 14 July 1913; (adopted) *s* of Gerald R. Ford and Dorothy Gardner; *m* 1948, Elizabeth (*née* Bloomer); three *s* one *d. Educ:* South High Sch., Grand Rapids; Univ. of Michigan (BA); Law Sch., Yale Univ. (LLB). Served War: US Navy (Carriers), 1942-46. Partner in law firm of Ford and Buchen, 1941-42; Member, law firm of Butterfield, Keeney and Amberg, 1947-49; subseq. with Amberg, Law and Buchen. Member US House of Representatives for Michigan 5th District, 1948-73; Member: Appropriations Cttee, 1951; Dept of Defense Sub-Cttee, etc; House Minority Leader, Republican Party, 1965-73; Vice President of the United States, Dec. 1973-Aug. 1974. Attended Interparly Union meetings in Europe; Mem. US-Canadian Interparly Gp. Pres., Eisenhower Exchange Fellowship, 1977-; Chm., Acad. of Educational Develt, 1977-. Holds Amer. Pol. Sci. Assoc.'s Distinguished Congressional Service Award, 1961; several hon. degrees. Delta Kappa Epsilon, Phi Delta Phi. *Publication:* (with John R. Stiles) Portrait of an Assassin, 1965. *Recreations:* outdoor sports (formerly football), ski-ing, tennis, golf. *Address:* PO Box 927, Rancho Mirage, Calif 92270, USA.

FORD, Dr Gillian Rachel, CB 1981; Deputy Chief Medical Officer (Deputy Secretary), Department of Health and Social Security, since 1977; *b* 18 March

1934; d of Cecil Ford and Grace Ford. *Educ:* Clarendon Sch., Abergele; St Hugh's Coll., Oxford; St Thomas' Hosp., London. MA, BM, BCh; FFCM; MRCP. Junior hospital posts, St Thomas', Oxford, Reading, 1959-64; Medical Officer, Min. of Health, 1965, Sen. Med. Officer, 1968; Sen. Principal Med. Officer, DHSS, 1974-77. *Publications:* papers on health services research, terminal care and other health subjects in Portfolio for Health, Vol. 1 (Nuffield Provincial Hospitals Trust) and other med. jls. *Recreations:* music, ski-ing, tennis, children's literature. *Address:* 9 Ryecotes Mead, Dulwich Common, SE21. *T:* 01-693 6576.

FORD, Harold Frank; Sheriff at Perth, 1971-80 (Sheriff Substitute at Forfar and Arbroath, 1951-71); *b* 17 May 1915; *s* of Sir Patrick Ford, 1st Bt, and *b* of Sir Henry Ford, *qv*; *m* 1948, Lucy Mary, *d* of late Sheriff J. R. Wardlaw Burnet, KC; one *s* three *d. Educ:* Winchester Coll.; University Coll., Oxford; Edinburgh Univ. War service with Lothians and Border Yeomanry (Prisoner of War, 1940-45): Hon. Capt. Scottish Bar, 1945; Legal Adviser to UNRRA and IRO in British Zone of Germany, 1947. *Recreations:* golf, gardening, shooting. *Address:* Broomhill, by Stanley, Perth, Scotland. *T:* Meikleour 288. *Clubs:* New (Edinburgh); Honourable Company of Edinburgh Golfers, Royal Perth Golfing Society.

FORD, Henry, II; Member of the Board and Chairman, Finance Committee, Ford Motor Company, Dearborn, Michigan; *b* Detroit, 4 Sept. 1917; *s* of Edsel B. and Eleanor (Clay) Ford; *m* 1st, 1940, Anne McDonnell (marr. diss.); one *s* two *d*; 2nd, 1965, Maria Cristina Vettore Austin (marr. diss. 1980); 3rd, 1980, Kathleen DuRoss. *Educ:* Hotchkiss Sch., Lakeville, Conn; Yale Univ. Dir, Ford Motor Co., 1938-; with company from 1940: Vice-Pres., 1943; Executive Vice-Pres., 1944; Pres., 1945; Chief Executive Officer, 1945-79, and Chm., 1960-80. Trustee: The Ford Foundation, 1943-76; Edison Inst.; Chm., Detroit/Wayne Port Authority; Co-chm., Detroit Renaissance, 1970-; Graduate Mem., Business Council (Mem. 1947-); formerly Mem. Bd of Governors, United Nations Assoc. (USA). *Address:* (home) Grosse Pointe Farms, Michigan, USA; (office) Renaissance Center, Detroit, Michigan, USA.

FORD, Sir Henry Russell, 2nd Bt *cr* 1929; TD; JP; *b* 30 April 1911; *s* of Sir Patrick Ford, 1st Bt, and Jessie Hamilton (*d* 1962), *d* of Henry Field, WS, Moreland, Kinross-shire, and Middlebluf, Manitoba; *S* father, 1945; *m* 1936, Mary Elizabeth, *y d* of late Godfrey F. Wright, Whiddon, Bovey Tracy; one *s* three *d. Educ:* Winchester; New Coll., Oxford. War of 1939-45 served in UK, North Africa and Italy (despatches). Chm., Berwick and E Lothian Unionist Assoc., 1948-50, 1958-60. JP 1951. TD 1960. *Recreations:* golf, gardening. *Heir:* s Andrew Russell Ford [*b* 29 June 1943; *m* 1968, Penelope Anne, *d* of Harry Relph; one *s* one *d*]. *Address:* Seaforth, Gullane, East Lothian. *T:* Gullane 842214. *Club:* Hon. Company of Edinburgh Golfers (Muirfield).

See also Harold Frank Ford.

FORD, Air Vice-Marshal Howard, CB 1959; CBE 1954; AFC 1944; RAF (retd); *b* 18 Dec. 1905; *s* of late Lewis Ford and Beatrice Leal; *m* 1936, Marie (*d* 1974), *d* of late Daniel O'Reilly, Cork, and Agnes Mayne, New York. *Educ:* Blundell's Sch.; Pembroke Coll., Cambridge (BA). Represented Cambridge at ski-ing and athletics, also England and Great Britain at athletics; British Olympic Athletic Team, 1928. Joined Royal Air Force, 1930; served War of 1939-45 (AFC). Transferred to Technical Branch, 1951; Dir, Air Armament R&D, Min. of Supply, 1952-55; Senior Technical Staff Officer, Flying Training Command, 1956-59; Vice-Pres. Ordnance Board, 1960-61, Pres., 1962; retired from RAF, 1963. Group Capt., 1947; Air Cdre, 1953; Air Vice-Marshal, 1960. *Club:* Royal Automobile.

FORD, Prof. Sir Hugh, Kt 1975; FRS 1967; FEng; Professor of Mechanical Engineering, since 1969, Pro-Rector, 1978-80, University of London (Imperial College of Science and Technology); Chairman, Ford and Dain Partners Ltd (Director since 1972); Director: Ricardo Consulting Engineers Ltd, since 1980; Air Liquide UK Ltd, since 1979; Prutec Ltd, since 1981; RD Projects Ltd, since 1982; *b* 16 July 1913; *s* of Arthur and Constance Ford; *m* 1942, Wynyard, *d* of Major F. B. Scholfield; two *d. Educ:* Northampton Sch.; City and Guilds Coll., Univ. of London. DSc (Eng); PhD. Practical trng at GWR Locomotive Works, 1931-36; researches into heat transfer, 1936-39; R and Eng, Imperial Chemical Industries, Northwich, 1939-42; Chief Engr, Technical Dept, British Iron and Steel Fedn, 1942-45, then Head of Mechanical Working Div., British Iron and Steel Research Assoc., 1945-47; Reader in Applied Mechanics, Univ. of London (Imp. Coll. of Science and Technology), 1948-51, Prof., 1951-69; Head of Dept of Mech. Engineering, 1965-78. Technical Dir, Davy-Ashmore Group, 1968-71; Dir, Herbert Ltd, 1972-79. John Player Lectr, IMechE, 1973. President: Inst. of Metals, 1963; Section 6, British Assoc., 1975-76; Fellow, 1977, Vice-Pres., 1981-, Fellowship of Engineering; Member: Council, IMechE (Vice-Pres., 1972, 1975, Sen. Vice-Pres., 1976, Pres., 1977-78); SRC, 1968-72 (Chm. Engineering Bd); Council, Royal Soc., 1973-74; ARC, 1976-81. FIMechE; FICE; Whitworth Schol.; FCGI. Hon. DSc: Salford, 1976; QUB, 1977; Aston, 1978; Bath, 1978. Thomas Hawksley Gold Medallist, IMechE, 1948, for researches into rolling of metals; Robertson Medal, Inst. of Metals; Hon. MASME, 1980. *Publications:* Advanced Mechanics of Materials, 1963; papers to Royal Soc., IMechE, Iron and Steel Inst., Inst. of Metals, foreign societies, etc. *Recreations:* gardening, music. *Address:* 18 Shrewsbury House, Cheyne Walk, SW3; Shamley Cottage, Stroud Lane, Shamley Green, Surrey. *Club:* Athenæum.

FORD, James Allan, CB 1978; MC 1946; *b* 10 June 1920; 2nd *s* of Douglas Ford and Margaret Duncan (*née* Allan); *m* 1948, Isobel Dunnett; one *s* one *d. Educ:* Royal High School, Edinburgh; University of Edinburgh. Served 1940-46, Capt. Royal Scots. Entered Civil Service, 1938; Asst Sec., Dept of Agriculture and Fisheries for Scotland, 1958; Registrar Gen. for Scotland, 1966-69; Principal Establishment Officer, Scottish Office, 1969-79. A Trustee, Nat. Lib. of Scotland, 1981-. *Publications:* The Brave White Flag, 1961; Season of Escape, 1963; A Statue for a Public Place, 1965; A Judge of Men, 1968; The Mouth of Truth, 1972. *Address:* 29 Lady Road, Edinburgh EH16 5PA. *T:* 031-667 4489. *Clubs:* Royal Scots, Scottish Arts (Edinburgh).

FORD, Sir John (Archibald), KCMG 1977 (CMG 1967); MC 1945; HM Diplomatic Service, retired; Lay Administrator, Guildford Cathedral, since 1982; *b* 19 Feb. 1922; *s* of Ronald Mylne Ford and Margaret Jesse Coghill, Newcastle-under-Lyme, Staffs; *m* 1956, Emaline Burnett, Leesville, Virginia; two *d. Educ:* St Michael's Coll., Tenbury; Sedbergh Sch., Yorks; Oriel Coll., Oxford. Served in Royal Artillery, 1942-46 (temp. Major); demobilised, 1947. Joined Foreign (subseq. Diplomatic) Service, 1947. Third Sec., British Legation, Budapest, 1947-49; Third Sec. and a Resident Clerk, FO, 1949-52; Private Sec. to Permanent Under-Sec. of State, FO, 1952-54; HM Consul, San Francisco, 1954-56; seconded to HM Treasury, 1956-59; attended Course at Administrative Staff Coll., 1959; First Sec. and Head of Chancery, British Residency, Bahrain, 1959-61; Asst, FO Personnel Dept, 1961-63; Asst, FO Establishment and Organisation Dept, 1963; Head of Diplomatic Service Establishment and Organisation Dept, 1964-66; Counsellor (Commercial), Rome, 1966-70; Asst Under-Sec., FCO, 1970-71; Consul-Gen., USA, and Dir-Gen., British Trade Develt in USA, 1971-75; Ambassador to Indonesia, 1975-78; British High Comr in Canada, 1978-81. Mem. Current Affairs Cttee, E-SU, 1982. *Recreations:* walking, gardening, sailing. *Address:* Loquats, Guildown, Guildford, Surrey. *Clubs:* Farmers'; Yvonne Arnaud Theatre (Guildford).

FORD, (John) Peter, CBE 1969; Chairman and Managing Director, International Joint Ventures Ltd; *b* 20 Feb. 1912; *s* of Ernest and Muriel Ford; *m* 1939, Phoebe Seys, *d* of Herbert McGregor Wood, FRIBA; one *s* two *d. Educ:* Wrekin Coll.; Gonville and Caius Coll., Cambridge. BA (Hons Nat. Sci. Tripos) 1934; MA Cantab 1937. Cambridge Univ. Air Sqdn, 1932-35 (Pilot's A Licence, 1933-). Air Ministry (subsequently FO, RAFVR), 1939-40; Coventry Gauge and Tool Co. Ltd (Asst to Chm.), 1941-45; Gen. Man., Brit. Engineers Small Tools and Equipment Co. Ltd, and Gen. Man. Scientific Exports (Gt Brit.) Ltd, 1945-48; Man. Dir, Brush Export Ltd, Associated British Oil Engines (Export) Ltd and National Oil Engines (Export) Ltd, and Dir of other associated cos of The Brush Group, 1949-55; Dir, Associated British Engineering Ltd and subsidiaries, 1957-58; Man. Dir, Coventry Climax International Ltd, 1958-63; Director: Plessey Overseas Ltd, 1963-70; Bryant & May (Latin America) Ltd, 1970-73. Chm. Institute of Export, 1954-56, 1965-67; President: Soc. of Commercial Accountants, 1970-74 (Vice-Pres., 1956-70); Soc. of Company and Commercial Accountants, 1974-75; Member: Council, London Chamber of Commerce, 1951-72 (Dep. Chm., 1970-72; Vice-Pres., 1972); London Ct of Arbitration, 1970-73; FBI, Overseas Trade Policy Cttee, 1952-63; Council, British Internal Combustion Engine Manufacturers Assoc., 1953-55; BNEC Cttee for Exports to Latin America, 1964-71 (Chm. 1968-71); NEDO Cttee for Movement of Exports, 1972-75; British Overseas Trade Adv. Council, 1975-82. Chm., British Shippers' Council, 1972-75 (Dep. Chm., 1971-72). Chm., British Mexican Soc., 1973-77; Vice-Pres., Hispanic and Luso Brazilian Council, 1980-. Freeman of City of London, 1945; Mem. Ct of Assistants, Ironmongers' Co. Master, 1981); Governor: Wrekin Coll., 1953-57; Oversea Service Coll., 1966-. CEng, CIMechE, CIMarE, MIEE, FIPE. Order of Rio Branco (Brazil), 1977. *Publications:* contributor to technical press and broadcaster on international trade subjects. *Recreations:* Athletics (Cambridge Univ. and Internat. Teams, 1932-35; held various county championships, 1932-37); Hon. Treas. Achilles Club, 1947-58; Pres., London Athletic Club, 1964-66). *Address:* 40 Fairacres, Roehampton Lane, SW15. *T:* 01-876 2146. *Clubs:* United Oxford & Cambridge University, City Livery, MCC; Hawks (Cambridge); Royal Wimbledon Golf.

FORD, Joseph Francis, CMG 1960; OBE 1949; HM Diplomatic Service, retired 1970; *b* 11 Oct. 1912; *s* of J. W. Ford, Chesterfield, Derbs; *m* 1938, Mary Margaret Ford (*née* Taylor); two *s. Educ:* Chesterfield Grammar Sch.; Emmanuel Coll., Cambridge (BA). BA (Hons) Modern Chinese, London, 1958. Appointed probationer Vice-Consul to Peking, Nov. 1935; served at Shanghai, Chungking, Washington, Peking, Hanoi, New Orleans and Saigon; Dir, Res. Dept, FCO (formerly Jt Res. Dept, FO/CO), 1967-70; Director: Univs Service Centre, Hong Kong, 1970-72; Great Britain-China Centre, London, 1974-78. *Address:* 10 Raymond Road, Wimbledon, SW19; Great Britain-China Centre, 22a Queen Anne's Gate, SW1. *Club:* Royal Automobile.

FORD, Percy; Professor Emeritus, The University of Southampton; *b* 19 Feb. 1894; 4th *s* of George Horace Ford, Brighton; *m* 1921, Grace Lister (*d* 1981), Long Eaton; one *s* one *d. Educ:* Varndean Sch.; London Sch. of Economics, University of London (Gerstenberg Scholar). Resident Lecturer, Ruskin Coll.; Lecturer, Amherst Coll., Mass, USA; Lecturer in Dept of Economics, and Sec. of University Extension Board and Tutorial Classes Joint Cttee, King's Coll., Univ. of Durham, 1923-26; Head of Dept and Prof. of Economics, University of Southampton, 1926-59; Sen. Research Fellow, 1959-61. National Service, Ministry of Supply, 1939-46. Hon. LLD

Southampton, 1974 (Hon. degrees of LLD conferred on Prof. P. and Mrs G. Ford at the same time). *Publications:* Economics and Modern Industry, 1930; Work and Wealth in a Modern Port, 1934; Incomes, Means Tests and Personal Responsibility, 1939; Economics of Collective Bargaining, 1958; Social Theory and Social Practice, 1969; Parliamentary Papers Series, 1951-62 (with G. Ford): Breviate of Parliamentary Papers, Vol. I, 1900-16; Vol. II, 1917-39, Vol. III, 1940-54; Select List of British Parliamentary Papers, 1833-1899; Hansard's and Catalogue and Breviate of Parliamentary Papers, 1696-1834; editorial work connected with, and selection of, nineteenth century British Parliamentary Papers for 1,000 vol. reprint (complete set presented to Parliament); Select List of Reports of Irish Dail and Senate, 1922-72; Select List of Reports and Other Papers in House of Commons's Journals, 1688-1800; Guide to Parliamentary Papers; Luke Graves Hansard's Diary, 1814-41; (with J. Bound) Coastwise Shipping and the Small Ports, 1951; (with G. Ford and D. Marshallsay) Select List of Parliamentary Papers 1955-64, 1970; (with C. J. Thomas) Industrial Prospects of Southampton, 1951, Shops and Planning, 1953, Housing, 1953, Problem Families, 1955; Ed., Southampton Civic Survey, 1931; Contributor, Britain in Depression, 1935; articles in journals of economics. *Address:* Lane End, Sandgate Lane, Storrington, Pulborough, West Sussex RH20 3HJ; Little Haven, Debden Purlieu, Hants.

FORD, Peter; *see* Ford, J. P.

FORD, Raymond Eustace, CBE 1963; MD, MRCP; retired as Principal Medical Officer i/c Regional Medical Service, Ministry of Health (1946-63); *b* 24 April 1898; *s* of Rev. George Ford; *m* 1924, Elsie (*née* Tipping); two *s* one *d. Educ:* Sheffield Univ. *Recreations:* golf, gardening. *Address:* St John's Road, Hythe, Kent.

FORD, Gen. Sir Robert (Cyril), GCB 1981 (KCB 1977; CB 1973); CBE 1971 (MBE 1958); Governor, Royal Hospital, Chelsea, since 1981; *b* 29 Dec. 1923; *s* of late John Stranger Ford and Gladys Ford, Yealmpton, Devon; *m* 1949, Jean Claudia Pendlebury, MA (Oxon), *d* of late Gp Capt. Claude Pendlebury, MC, TD, FLAS, FRICS, and late Muriel Pendlebury, Yelverton, Devon; one *s. Educ:* Musgrave's. War of 1939-45: commissioned into 4th/7th Royal Dragoon Guards, from Sandhurst, 1943; served with Regt throughout NW European campaign, 1944-45 (despatches) and in Egypt and Palestine, 1947-48 (despatches). Instructor, Mons OCS, 1949-50; Training Officer, Scottish Horse (TA), 1952-54; Staff Coll., Camberley, 1955; GSO 2 Mil. Ops, War Office, 1956-57; Sqdn Ldr 4/7 RDG, 1958-59; Bde Major, 20th Armoured Bde, 1960-61; Brevet Lt-Col, 1962; Sqdn Ldr, 4/7 RDG, 1962-63; GSO1 to Chief of Defence Staff, 1964-65; commanded 4/7 RDG in S Arabia and N Ireland, 1966-67; Comdr, 7th Armd Bde, 1968-69; Principal Staff Officer to Chief of Defence Staff, 1970-71; Cmdr Land Forces, N Ireland, 1971-73; Comdt, RMA Sandhurst, 1973-76; Military Secretary, 1976-78; Adjutant-General, 1978-81; ADC General to the Queen, 1980-81. Colonel Commandant: RAC, 1980-82; SAS Regt, 1980-. President: Services Kinema Corp., 1978-81; Army Boxing Assoc., 1978-81. Mem., Commonwealth War Graves Commn, 1981-; Chairman: Army Benevolent Fund, 1981-; Royal Cambridge Home for Soldiers' Widows, 1981-; Nat. Pres., Forces Help Soc. and Lord Roberts Workshops, 1981-. Governor, Corps of Commissionaires, 1981-. Freeman, City of London, 1981. CBIM. *Recreations:* cricket, tennis, war studies. *Address:* Royal Hospital, Chelsea, SW3 4SR. *Clubs:* Cavalry and Guards, MCC.

FORD, Robert Webster, CBE 1982; HM Diplomatic Service; Consul-General, Geneva, since 1980; *b* 27 March 1923; *s* of late Robert Ford; *m* 1956, Monica Florence Tebbett; two *s. Educ:* Alleyne's Sch. Served RAF, 1939-45. Served with British Mission, Lhasa, Tibet and Political Agency in Sikkim and Bhutan, 1945-47; joined Tibetan Govt Service, 1947; advised on and installed Tibet's first radio communication system and broadcasting stn; travelled extensively in Northern and Eastern Tibet, 1947-50; taken prisoner during Chinese Occupation of Tibet, 1950; imprisoned in China, 1950-55; free-lance writer and broadcaster on Chinese and Tibetan affairs, 1955; entered Foreign Service, 1956; 2nd Sec., Saigon, 1957-58; 1st Sec. (Information), Djakarta, 1959; Washington, 1960-62; FO, 1962-67; Consul-Gen., Tangier, 1967-70; Counsellor, 1970; Consul-General: Luanda, 1970-74; Bordeaux, 1974-78; Gothenburg, 1978-80. *Publication:* Captured in Tibet, 1956. *Recreations:* ski-ing on snow and water, gardening, travelling. *Address:* c/o Foreign and Commonwealth Office, SW1. *Clubs:* Royal Commonwealth Society, Royal Geographical Society.

FORD, Roy Arthur, MA; Headmaster, King's School, Rochester, since 1975; *b* 10 May 1925; *s* of Arthur Ford and Minnie Elizabeth Ford; *m* 1965, Christine Margaret Moore; two *s. Educ:* Collyer's Sch., Horsham; Corpus Christi Coll., Cambridge (Scholar; 1st Cl. Pts I and II, History Tripos; BA 1949, MA 1971). Asst Master: Uppingham Sch., 1951-54; Tonbridge Sch., 1954-66; Uppingham Sch., (also Head of History and Sixth Form Master), 1966-71; Headmaster, Southwell Minster Grammar Sch., 1971-75. *Recreations:* walking, travel, music. *Address:* Oriel House, Rochester, Kent. *T:* Medway 44259.

FORD, Sir Sidney (William George), Kt 1967; MBE 1944; President, National Union of Mineworkers, 1960-71; *b* 29 Aug. 1909; *s* of George and Harriet Ford; *m* 1st, 1936, Ivy Elizabeth Lewis (*d* 1964); one *s* two *d*; 2nd, 1965, Sheila Simon. *Educ:* Silver Street Elementary Sch. Joined Staff of Miners' Federation of Great Britain (later NUM), 1925. Mem., Central

Transport Consultative Cttee for GB, 1970-71. *Address:* 18 Woodland Way, Winchmore Hill, N21. *T:* 01-886 8837.

FORD, Rev. Wilfred Franklin, CMG 1974; *b* 9 Jan. 1920; *s* of Harold Franklin Ford and Sarah Elizabeth Ford; *m* 1942, Joan Mary Holland (*d* 1981); three *d*; *m* 1982, Hilda Mary Astley. *Educ:* Auckland Univ., NZ (BA); Trinity Theological Coll., NZ. Served War, NZ Army, 1942-44. Entered Methodist Ministry, 1945; Dir, Christian Educn, Methodist Church of NZ, 1956-68; President: Methodist Church of NZ, 1971; NZ Marriage Guidance Council; Life Mem., Wellington Marriage Guidance Council. *Publications:* contribs to NZ and internat. jls, on Christian educn. *Recreations:* gardening, reading. *Address:* 104 Beerescourt Road, Hamilton, New Zealand.

FORD ROBERTSON, Francis Calder, OBE 1959; *b* 19 March 1901; 3rd *s* of Dr W. Ford Robertson, MD, and Marion Elam; *m* 1928, Cynthia Mary de Courcy Ireland (*d* 1977); two *s*; *m* 1977, Nora Aline de Courcy Chapman (*née* Ireland). *Educ:* Edinburgh Academy; Edinburgh Univ. Appointed to Indian Forest Service as probationer, 1923; IFS, 1924-47; Director: Commonwealth Forestry Bureau, Oxford, 1947-64; Dir-Editor, Multilingual Forestry Terminology Project, at Commonwealth Forestry Inst., Oxford and Washington, DC, USA, 1964-70. Hon. Mem., Soc. of American Foresters, 1970. Hon. MA Oxford, 1952. *Publications:* Our Forests, 1934; (ed) The Terminology of Forest Science, Technology, Practice and Products (English lang. version), 1971; also sundry scientific, mainly bibliographical, articles. *Recreations:* choral singing, gardening, local history and archaeology. *Address:* 54 Staunton Road, Headington, Oxford. *T:* Oxford 62073.

FORDE, Rt. Hon. Francis Michael, PC 1944; Australian High Commissioner in Canada, 1946-53; Dean of the Diplomatic Corps, Ottawa, Canada, 1952-53; *m* 1925, Veronica Catherine O'Reilly; three *d* (one *s* decd). *Educ:* Christian Brothers Coll., Toowoomba, Qld, Aust. School teacher; electrical engineer; Mem. of Qld State Parliament, 1917-22; elected to House of Representatives for Capricornia, Qld Gen. Elections, 1922, 1925, 1928, 1929, 1931, 1934, 1937, 1940, 1943; Mem. Jt Select Cttee on Motion Picture Industry in Australia, 1927, and of Royal Commission on same, 1927-28; Mem. of Joint Cttee on Public Accounts, 1929; Acting Minister for Trade and Customs, Australia, 1929-30; Acting Minister for Markets and Transport, 1930-31; Minister for Trade and Customs, 1930-31, 1932; Dep. Leader Federal Parliamentary Labour Party, 1932-46, and Dep. Leader of the Opposition, 1932-41; Dep. Prime Minister, Minister for Army, Mem. and Vice-Chm. of War Cabinet, Australia, 1941-46; Minister for Defence, 1946; Acting Prime Minister, April-July 1944 and Oct. 1944-Jan. 1945; Prime Minister for short period, 1945; Actg Prime Minister (about two months), 1946. Leader of Australian Delegn to UN Conf., San Francisco, April 25 1945. Mem. for Flinders, Qld Parliament, By-Election, March 1955; re-elected, Gen. Election, May 1956. Represented Australia at Gen. Douglas MacArthur's funeral in USA, 1964. LLD (Hon.): Ottawa Univ., 1950; Montreal Univ., 1952; Laval Univ., 1952; Univ. of Qld, Brisbane, 1972. *Recreations:* tennis, golf, bowls. *Address:* 44 Highland Terrace, St Lucia, Brisbane, Queensland 4067, Australia. *T:* Brisbane 370 9447.

FORDER, Ven. Charles Robert; Archdeacon Emeritus, Diocese of York, since 1974; *b* 6 Jan. 1907; *s* of late Henry Forder, Worstead, Norfolk; *m* 1933, Myra, *d* of late Harry Peat, Leeds; no *c. Educ:* Paston Sch., North Walsham; Christ's Coll. and Ridley Hall, Cambridge. Exhibitioner of Christ's Coll. and Prizeman, 1926; 1st Cl. Math. Trip. Part I, 1926, BA (Sen. Opt. Part II) 1928, MA 1932; Ridley Hall, 1928. Curate: St Peter's, Hunslet Moor, 1930-33; Burley, 1933-34; Vicar: Holy Trinity, Wibsey, 1934-40; St Clement's, Bradford, 1940-47; Organising Sec., Bradford Church Forward Movement Appeal, 1945-47; Vicar of Drypool, 1947-55; Rector of Routh and Vicar of Wawne, 1955-57; Canon, and Prebendary of Fenton, York Minster, 1957-76; Rector of Sutton-on-Derwent, 1957-63; Rector of Holy Trinity, Micklegate, York, 1963-66; Archdeacon of York, 1957-72. Chaplain to HM Prison, Hull, 1950-53; Proctor in Convocation, 1954-72; Organising Sec., Diocesan Appeal, 1955-76; Church Comr, 1958-73. *Publications:* A History of the Paston Grammar School, 1934, 2nd edn 1975; The Parish Priest at Work, 1947; Synods in Action, 1970; Churchwardens in Church and Parish, 1976; contrib. to Encyclopædia Britannica. *Recreations:* reading and writing. *Address:* Dulverton Hall, St Martin's Square, Scarborough YO11 2DQ. *T:* Scarborough 73082.

FORDER, Kenneth John; Registrar of the Architects Registration Council of the United Kingdom, since 1977; *b* 11 June 1925; *s* of late James A. Forder and Elizabeth Forder (*née* Hammond); *m* 1948, Dorothy Margôt Burles; two *d. Educ:* Westcliff Sch.; Hertford Coll., Oxford (MA); Queen's Coll., Cambridge. Called to Bar, Gray's Inn, 1963. RAF, Flt Lieut, Aircrew Navigator, 1943-47. District Officer, N Rhodesia, 1951-61; District Commissioner, N Rhodesia, 1962-64; General Secretary, National Federation of Meat Traders, 1964-73; Bar Practice, 1973-77; Registrar, Architects Registration Council of UK (established under Architects Registration Acts 1931 to 1969), 1977-. Freeman of the City of London, 1966. *Recreations:* tennis, bridge, chess. *Address:* 55 Hurlingham Court, SW6 3UP. *T:* 01-736 3958. *Club:* Hurlingham.

FORDHAM, John Jeremy; Metropolitan Stipendiary Magistrate, since 1978; *b* 18 April 1933; *s* of John Hampden Fordham, CBE and Rowena Langran; *m* 1962, Rose Anita (*née* Brandon), *d* of Philip Brandon, Wellington, New Zealand; one *s* one *d. Educ:* Gresham's Sch.; Univ. of New Zealand. LLB

(NZ). Merchant Navy, 1950-55 (2nd Mate (Foreign Going) Cert.); labourer, fireman etc, 1955-60; Barrister and Solicitor, New Zealand, 1960-64; called to Bar, Inner Temple, 1965; practised 1965-71, 1976-78; Sen. Magistrate, Gilbert and Ellice Islands, 1971-75. *Recreations:* boats, games. *Address:* 9 King's Bench Walk, Temple, EC4. *T:* 01-353 5638. *Club:* Garrick.

FORDHAM, Wilfrid Gurney, QC 1967; *s* of Edward Wilfrid Fordham and Sybil Harriet (*née* Langdon-Davies); *m* 1930, Peta Marshall Freeman; one *s*. *Educ:* St George's, Harpenden; Magdalene Coll., Cambridge. Called to Bar, Inner Temple, 1929 (Bencher 1981); Dep. Circuit Judge, 1972-74; a Recorder of the Crown Court, 1974-76. Contested: (L) Bromley, Kent, 1929, 1930; (Lab) Wycombe, Bucks, 1959. *Publications:* various legal books. *Recreation:* travel. *Address:* 4 Paper Buildings, Temple, EC4. *T:* 01-353 2739. *Club:* Garrick.

FORDYCE, Catherine Mary, MA (London and Oxford); *b* Wareham, Dorset, 18 Dec. 1898; *d* of Ernest Chilcott, MA, Vicar of Elberton, Glos; *m* 1929, Prof. Christian James Fordyce (*d* 1974). *Educ:* St Mary's Hall, Brighton; Bedford Coll. for Women. London BA Classical Hons Cl. I, 1920; Gilchrist Studentship, 1921; MA (with distinction), 1922; Fellow and Classical Tutor of Lady Margaret Hall, Oxford, 1922-29. *Publications:* articles in Classical Quarterly, 1923; Essay, Myth and Reality, in Adventure, 1927. *Address:* Baxter House, Lowther Terrace, Kirklee, Glasgow G12 0RN.

FORECAST, Kenneth George; Assistant Director, Central Statistical Office, Cabinet Office, since 1979; *b* 21 Aug. 1925; *s* of late George Albert Forecast and Alice Matilda Forecast (*née* Davies); unmarried. *Educ:* William Morris Sch., Walthamstow; SW Essex Techn. Coll. BSc (Econ) London. Statistical Officer, MAP, 1945-48; Economist/Statistician with de Zoete & Gorton, Stock Exchange, London, 1948-51; Statistician: Central Statistics Office, Dublin, 1951-58; BoT, London, 1958-66; Chief Statistician, MoT, 1966-70; Dir of Statistics, DES, 1970-79. *Publications:* contribs to Review of Internat. Statistical Inst. and to Jl of Statistical and Social Inquiry Soc. of Ireland. *Address:* 51 Richmond Avenue, Highams Park, E4 9RR. *T:* 01-527 3023. *Club:* Civil Service.

FOREMAN, Carl, CBE (Hon.) 1970; FRSA; screen writer; producer; director; former Managing Director and Executive Producer of Open Road Films Ltd; *b* Chicago, USA, 23 July 1914. *Educ:* Crane Coll.; Univ. of Illinois; Northwestern Univ., USA. *Film scripts:* So This is New York; Champion (Academy Award nomination); Home of the Brave; The Men (Academy Award nomination); Cyrano de Bergerac; (writer-prod.) High Noon (Academy Award nomination); The Bridge on the River Kwai; (writer-prod.) The Key; (writer-prod.) The Guns of Navarone (Academy Award nomination); (writer-prod.-dir) The Victors; (writer-prod.) Mackenna's Gold; (writer-prod.) Young Winston (Variety Club of GB Show-business Writer Award, 1972; Best Screenplay Award, Writers' Guild of GB, 1972; Academy Award nomination); Executive Producer, films: The Mouse that Roared; Born Free; Otley; The Virgin Soldiers; Living Free. Mem. Bd of Governors: British Film Inst., 1966-71; National Film Sch., 1971-75; Mem. Exec. Council, Film Production Assoc., 1967-75; Pres., Writers' Guild of GB, 1968-75 (Dist. Service Award, 1968); Writers' Guild of Amer. Laurel Award, 1969; Valentine Davies Award, 1977. Comdr, Order of the Phoenix (Greece), 1962. *Publications:* A Cast of Lions, 1966; Young Winston, 1972. *Address:* 1370 Avenue of the Americas, New York, NY 10019, USA. *Clubs:* Savile, Garrick.

FOREMAN, Michael; AGI; FSIAD; writer and illustrator; *b* 21 March 1938; *s* of Walter and Gladys Mary Foreman; *m* 1st, 1959, Janet Charters (marr. diss. 1966); one *s*; 2nd, 1980, Louise Phillips. *Educ:* Notley Road Secondary Modern Sch., Lowestoft; Royal College of Art, London (ARCA 1st Cl. Hons and Silver Medal). Freelance, 1963-; six animated films produced, 1967-68. Awarded Aigle d'Argent, Festival International du Livre, Nice, 1972. *Publications:* author and illustrator: The Perfect Present, 1966; The Two Giants, 1966; The Great Sleigh Robbery, 1968; Horatio, 1969; Moose, 1971; Dinosaurs and all that Rubbish, 1972 (Francis Williams Prize, 1972); War and Peas, 1974; All The King's Horses, 1976; Panda and his Voyage of Discovery, 1977 (Francis Williams Prize, 1977); Trick a Tracker, 1980; Panda and the Odd Lion, 1981; Land of Dreams, 1982; illustrator of many books by other authors. *Recreations:* football, travelling. *Address:* 1 Stratford Studios, Stratford Road, W8 6RQ. *T:* 01-937 5528. *Club:* Zanzibar.

FOREMAN, Sir Philip (Frank), Kt 1981; CBE 1972; DLC; FEng, FRAeS, FIMechE, FIProdE, CBIM; DL; Managing Director, Short Bros Ltd, since 1967; *b* 16 March 1923; *s* of late Frank and Mary Foreman; *m* 1971, Margaret Cooke; one *s*. *Educ:* Soham Grammar Sch., Cambs; Loughborough Coll., Leics. Royal Naval Scientific Service, 1943-58. Short Bros Ltd, 1958-. Hon. DSc QUB, 1976. DL Belfast, 1975. *Publications:* papers to: Royal Aeronautical Soc.; Instn of Mechanical Engineers. *Recreation:* golf.

FORESTER; *see* Weld Forester, family name of Baron Forester.

FORESTER, 8th Baron *cr* 1821; **George Cecil Brooke Weld Forester;** *b* 20 Feb. 1938; *s* of 7th Baron Forester and of Marie Louise Priscilla, *d* of Col Sir Herbert Perrott, 6th Bt, CH, CB; *S* father, 1977; *m* 1967, Hon. Elizabeth Catherine Lyttelton, 2nd *d* of 10th Viscount Cobham, KG, PC, GCMG, GCVO, TD; one *s* three *d*. *Educ:* Eton; Royal Agricultural College, Cirencester (MRAC). *Heir: s* Hon. Charles Richard George Weld Forester,

b 8 July 1975. *Address:* Willey Park, Broseley, Salop TF12 5JJ. *T:* Telford 882146.

FORESTIER-WALKER, Sir Clive Radzivill F.; *see* Walker.

FORFAR, Prof. John Oldroyd, MC; Professor of Child Life and Health, University of Edinburgh, since 1964; *b* 16 Nov. 1916; *s* of Rev. David Forfar, MA and Elizabeth Edith Campbell; *m* 1942, Isobel Mary Langlands Fernback, MB, ChB, DPH, AFOM; two *s* one *d*. *Educ:* Perth Acad.; St Andrews Univ. BSc 1938, MB, ChB 1941, St Andrews; MRCP 1947; MRCPE 1948; DCH (London) 1948; FRCPE 1953; MD (Commendation) St Andrews, 1958; FRCP 1964; FRSE 1975. House Officer, Perth Royal Infirmary, 1941; RAMC, 1942-46: Med. Off., 47 Royal Marine Commando, 1943-45 (MC 1944; despatches, 1945); Registrar and Sen. Registrar, Dundee Royal Infirmary, 1946-48; Sen. Lectr in Child Health, St Andrews Univ., 1948-50; Sen. Paediatric Phys., Edinburgh Northern Gp of Hosps, and Sen. Lectr in Child Life and Health, Edinburgh Univ., 1950-64. Chm., Jt Paediatric Cttee of Royal Colls of Physicians and British Paediatric Assoc., 1979-; Pres., Assoc. of Clinical Professors and Heads of Departments of Paediatrics, 1980-; Pres., Scottish Paediatric Soc., 1972-74; Chm., Medical Gp of Assoc. of British Adoption Agencies, 1966-76. Fellow, Amer. Coll. of Nutrition, 1977. *Publications:* (ed) Textbook of Paediatrics 1973, 2nd edn 1978; contribs to general medical and to paediatric jls and books. *Recreations:* walking, travelling, gardening. *Address:* 110 Ravelston Dykes, Edinburgh EH12 6HB. *T:* 031-337 7081.

FORGAN, Elizabeth Anne Lucy; Senior Commissioning Editor, Channel Four Television, since 1981; *b* 31 Aug. 1944; *d* of Thomas Moinet Forgan and Jean Margaret Forgan. *Educ:* Benenden Sch.; St Hugh's Coll., Oxford (BA). Journalist: Teheran Journal, 1967-68; Hampstead and Highgate Express, 1969-74; Chief Leader Writer, Evening Standard, 1974-78; Woman's Editor, Asst Features Editor, The Guardian, 1978-81. *Recreations:* church music, cheap novels, Scottish Islands. *Address:* 6 Quadrant Grove, NW5 4JN. *T:* 01-267 0818.

FORGE, Andrew Murray; artist, writer; Dean of School of Art, University of Yale, Conn, USA; *b* Hastingleigh, Kent, 10 Nov. 1923; *s* of Sidney Wallace Forge and Joanna Ruth Forge (*née* Bliss); *m* 1950, Sheila Deane (marr. diss.); three *d*; *m* 1974, Ruth Miller. *Educ:* Downs Sch.; Leighton Park; Camberwell Sch. of Art (NDD). Sen. Lectr, Slade Sch., UCL, 1950-64; Head of Dept of Fine Art, Goldsmith's Coll., 1964-70. Trustee: Tate Gallery, 1964-71 and 1972-74; National Gallery, 1966-72; Member: Nat. Council for Diplomas in Art and Design, 1964-72; Jt NCDAD/NACEA Cttee, 1968-70; Calouste Gulbenkian Foundn Cttee to report on future of conservation studies in UK, 1970-72; Pres., London Group, 1964-71. *Publications:* Klee, 1953; Vermeer, 1954; Soutine, 1965; Rauschenberg, 1972; (with C. Joyes) Monet at Giverny, 1975; (ed) The Townsend Journals, 1976. *Recreation:* travel. *Address:* Malthouse, Elmsted, near Ashford, Kent.

FORMAN, Sir Denis, Kt 1976; OBE 1956; Chairman: Granada Television Ltd, since 1974 (Joint Managing Director, 1965-81); Novello & Co., since 1971; Director, Granada Group; *b* 13 Oct. 1917; *s* of late Rev. Adam Forman, CBE, and Flora Smith; *m* 1948, Helen de Mouilpied; two *s*. *Educ:* at home; Loretto; Pembroke Coll., Cambridge. Served War, 1940-45: Argyll and Sutherland Highlanders; Commandant, Orkney and Shetland Defences Battle Sch., 1942 (wounded, Cassino, 1944). Chief Production Officer, Central Office of Information Films, 1947; Dir, British Film Inst., 1948-55; Chm., Bd of Governors, British Film Inst., 1971-73. Fellow, British Acad. of Film and Television Arts, 1976; Dir, Royal Opera Hse, Covent Gdn, 1981-; Mem. Council, RNCM, 1975- (Hon. Mem., RNCM, 1981). DUniv Stirling, 1982. Ufficiale dell'ordine Al Merito della Repubblica Italiana. *Publication:* Mozart's Piano Concertos, 1971. *Recreations:* music, shooting. *Address:* The Mill House, Howe Street, Great Waltham, Chelmsford, Essex. *Club:* Savile.

See also M. B. Forman.

FORMAN, (Francis) Nigel, MP (C) Carshalton, since March 1976; *b* 25 March 1943; *s* of late Brig. J. F. R. Forman and of Mrs P. J. M. Forman; *m*. *Educ:* Dragon Sch., Oxford; Shrewsbury Sch.; New Coll., Oxford; College of Europe, Bruges; Kennedy Sch. of Govt, Harvard; Sussex Univ. Information Officer, CBI, 1970-71; Conservative Research Dept, 1971-76. Secretary: Cons. Education Cttee, 1976-79; Cons. Energy Cttee, 1977-79; Mem., Select Cttee on Science and Technology, 1976-79. PPS to Lord Privy Seal, 1979-81 and to Minister of State, FCO, 1979-. *Publications:* Towards a More Conservative Energy Policy, 1977; Another Britain, 1979. *Address:* House of Commons, SW1.

FORMAN, Air Vice-Marshal Graham Neil; Director of Legal Services, Royal Air Force, since 1982; *b* 29 Nov. 1930; *s* of late Stanley M. Forman and of Eva Forman (*née* Barrett); *m* 1957, Valerie Fay (*née* Shaw); one *s* two *d*. *Educ:* Boston Grammar School; Nottingham Univ. Law School; Law Society's School of Law; admitted solicitor 1953. Commissioned RAF Legal Branch, 1957; served HQ Far East Air Force, Singapore, 1960-63 and 1965-68; Dep. Dir, RAF Legal Services, HQ Near East Air Force, Cyprus, 1971-72 and 1973-76; Dep. Dir, RAF Legal Services, HQ RAF Germany, 1978; Dep. Dir, Legal Services (RAF), 1978-82. *Recreations:* cricket, tennis, reading, philately, traditional jazz music. *Address:* c/o Lloyds Bank Ltd, High Street, Berkhamsted, Herts. *Clubs:* Royal Air Force; MCC.

FORMAN, Sir John Denis; see Forman, Sir Denis.

FORMAN, Louis, MD London; FRCP; Consultant Dermatologist Emeritus, Guy's Hospital and St John's Hospital for Diseases of the Skin; Hon. Consultant, London Jewish Hospital. *Educ:* Guy's Hosp., Univ. of London. MRCS, LRCP 1923; MB, BS 1924; MRCP 1925; FRCP 1939. Formerly Dermatologist SE Group, London CC; Medical Registrar, Guy's Hosp. Past President: British Assoc. Dermatology; Section of Dermatology, RSM. *Publications:* various articles in med. jls. *Address:* 22 Harley House, Regent's Park, NW1 5HE. *T:* 01-487 3834.

FORMAN, Michael Bertram, TD 1945; Director of Personnel and Organisation, Tube Investments Ltd, since 1973; *b* 28 March 1921; *s* of late Rev. A. Forman, CBE, and Flora Smith; *m* 1947, Mary Railston-Brown, *d* of Rev. W. R. Railston-Brown; four *d. Educ:* Loretto Sch., Musselburgh; Manchester Coll. of Technology. TA commn, 7th KOSB, 1939. War Service in Inf. and Airborne Forces, 1939-46: UK, Holland, Germany (POW), India. Labour Management, Courtaulds Ltd, 1946-53; Dir, Inst. of Personnel Management, 1953-56; Head of Staff Planning, NCB, 1956-59; Chief Staff Officer, SW Div., NCB, 1959-62; Personnel Relations Adviser and Dep. Dir of Personnel, Tube Investments Ltd, 1962-68, Personnel Dir, Steel Tube Div., 1968-73. Mem. NBPI, 1968-70. CIPM. *Recreations:* reading, gardening, fishing, shooting. *Address:* The Priory, Stoke Prior, Bromsgrove, Worcs. *T:* Bromsgrove 32196. *Club:* Savile.
See also Sir D. Forman.

FORMAN, Miloš; film director; *b* Čáslav, 18 Feb. 1932. *Educ:* Acad. of Music and Dramatic Art, Prague. Director: Film Presentations, Czechoslovak Television, 1954-56; Laterna Magika, Prague, 1958-62. Films directed include: Talent Competition; Peter and Pavla, 1963 (Czech. Film Critics' Award; Grand Prix, Locarno, 1964; Prize, Venice Festival, 1965); A Blonde in Love (Grand Prix, French Film Acad., 1966); The Fireman's Ball, 1967; Taking Off, 1971; (co-dir) Visions of Eight, 1973; One Flew Over the Cuckoo's Nest, 1975 (Academy Award, 1976; BAFTA Award, 1977); Hair, 1979; Ragtime, 1982. *Address:* c/o Robert Lantz, The Lantz Office Inc., 114 East 55th Street, New York, NY 10022, USA.

FORMAN, Nigel; see Forman, F. N.

FORMBY, Myles Landseer, CBE 1962; TD 1946; Consulting Otolaryngologist, retired: Consultant Emeritus to the Army, since 1971; University College Hospital, 1933-66, now Hon. Consulting Surgeon; Royal Masonic Hospital, 1948-66; *b* 13 March 1901; *s* of Arthur Formby, South Australia; *m* 1st, 1931, Dorothy Hussey Essex (marr. diss. 1952); one *s* one *d*; 2nd, 1974, Phyllis Mary Helps, *d* of late Engr-Comdr G. S. Holgate, RN. *Educ:* St Peter's Coll., Adelaide, South Australia; Univ. of Adelaide; Magdalen Coll., Oxford. Elder Scholarship, Univ. of Adelaide, 1920 and 1921, Everard Scholarship, 1924; MB, BS, Adelaide, 1924; Rhodes Scholar for S Australia, 1925; BA Oxford, 1927; BSc Oxford, 1928; FRCS 1930; MA Oxford, 1953. Hon. Asst Surg., Ear, Nose and Throat Hosp., Golden Square, 1931; Hon. Surg., Ear, Nose and Throat, Miller Gen. Hosp., 1932; Hon. Asst Surg., Ear, Nose and Throat Dept, University Coll. Hosp., 1933; Hon. Surg., 1940; Hon. Surg., Ear, Nose and Throat Dept, Royal Masonic Hosp., 1948. RAMC TA, Lieut, 1932; Capt., 1933; Major, 1939; Lieut-Col, 1941; Brig. Consulting Oto-Rhino-Laryngologist to the Army, 1943; served in the Middle East, Italy, North West Europe and India, in War of 1939-45. Hon. Civilian Consultant to War Office, 1946. Mem. Court of Examiners, Royal College of Surgeons, 1947-53, Mem. Council, 1952-57; Royal Society of Medicine: Hon. Dir of Photography, 1958-61; Pres., Section of Laryngology, 1959-60; Hon. Treas., 1962-68; Hon. Fellow, 1970; Hon. Laryngologist to Royal Academy of Music; Pres., British Assoc. of Otolaryngologists. Bronze Star, USA, 1945. *Publications:* Dental Infection in the Aetiology of Maxillary Sinusitis, 1934; Treatment of Otitis Media, 1938; Nasal Allergy, 1943; chapters in Diseases of the Ear, Nose and Throat, 1952; The Maxillary Sinus, 1960; Ultrasonic Destruction of the Labyrinth, 1963. *Recreations:* rowing, lacrosse, golf. *Address:* Thorndene, Kithurst Lane, Storrington, West Sussex RH20 4LP. *T:* Storrington 2564. *Clubs:* Royal Automobile; Leander.

FORMSTON, Prof. Clifford; Professor of Veterinary Surgery in the University of London, 1943-74, now Emeritus; former Vice-Principal, Royal Veterinary College (1963); *b* 15 Jan. 1907; *s* of Alfred and Annie Formston; *m* 1934, Irene Pembleton (*d* 1973), *d* of Capt. Roland Wood; one *s* one *d. Educ:* Chester City Grammar Sch.; Royal Veterinary College, London. MRCVS 1928; FRCVS 1944. Mem. of Royal Veterinary Coll. staff, 1928-74, Fellow, 1974. Mem. of Council, RCVS, 1954-62; John Jeyes' Travel Scholarship, 1937; Visiting Professor: Univ. of Cairo, 1960; Univ. of Thessaloniki, 1966; Pahlavi Univ., Iran, 1975; Alfateh Univ., Libya, 1977, 1981; Sir Frederick Hobday Meml Lectr, 1971. Examiner in Veterinary Surgery, Nairobi Univ., 1977. Past President: Royal Counties Veterinary Assoc.; Central Veterinary Soc.; British Equine Veterinary Assoc. Examiner in veterinary surgery to Univs of Bristol, Cambridge, Dublin, Glasgow, Liverpool, London, Edinburgh and Khartoum; Hon. Res. Fellow, Inst. of Ophthalmology; Hon. Cons. Veterinary Surg. to Childe-Beale Trust. Pres., Vet. Benevolent Fund; Life Vice-Pres., Riding for the Disabled Assoc.; Veterinary Patron, Diamond Riding Centre for the Handicapped. Blaine Award, 1971; John Henry Steel Meml Medallist, 1973; Simon Award, 1974; Victory Medal, Central Vet. Soc., 1975. *Publications:* contrib. scientific jls on

general surgery and ophthalmology. *Recreations:* golf, gardening, reading. *Address:* 4 Marlow Court, Chase Side, Southgate, N14 5HR.

FORRES, 4th Baron *cr* 1922; **Alastair Stephen Grant Williamson;** Bt 1909; Director: Agriscot Pty Ltd; Jaga Trading Pty Ltd; *b* 16 May 1946; *s* of 3rd Baron Forres and of Gillian Ann Maclean, *d* of Major John Maclean Grant, RA; *S* father, 1978; *m* 1969, Margaret, *d* of late G. J. Mallam, Mullumbimby, NSW; two *s. Educ:* Eton. *Heir: s* Hon. George Archibald Mallam Williamson, *b* 16 Aug. 1972. *Address:* Myee Estates, Grenfell, NSW 2810, Australia. *Clubs:* Union, Australian Jockey, Sydney Turf (Sydney).

FORREST, Prof. (Andrew) Patrick (McEwen); Regius Professor of Clinical Surgery, University of Edinburgh, since 1970; part-time Chief Scientist, Scottish Home and Health Department, since 1981; Honorary Consultant Surgeon: Royal Infirmary of Edinburgh; Royal Prince Alfred Hospital, Sydney; Civilian Consultant to the Royal Navy; *b* 25 March 1923; *s* of Rev. Andrew James Forrest, BD, and Isabella Pearson; *m* 1955, Margaret Beryl Hall (*d* 1961); one *s* one *d*; *m* 1964, Margaret Anne Steward; one *d. Educ:* Dundee High Sch.; Univ. of St Andrews. BSc 1942; MB, ChB 1945; ChM hons, University Gold Medal, 1954; MD hons, Rutherford Gold Medal, 1958; FRCSE 1950; FRCS 1952; FRCSGlas 1962; FRSE 1976. Surg.-Lt RNVR, 1946-48. Mayo Foundation Fellow, 1952-53; Lectr and Sen. Lectr, Univ. of Glasgow, 1955-62; Prof. of Surgery, Welsh Nat. Sch. of Medicine, 1962-70. McIlrath Vis. Prof., Royal Prince Alfred Hosp., Sydney, 1969; Nimmo Vis. Prof., Royal Adelaide Hosp., 1973; McLauchlin-Gallie Prof., RCP of Canada, 1974; numerous other visiting professorships; Eponymous lectures include: Lister Meml, Canadian Med. Assoc., 1970; Inaugural Bruce Wellesley Hosp., Toronto, 1970; Inaugural Peter Lowe, RCP Glas., 1980. Member: Medical sub-cttee, UGC, 1967-76; MRC, 1974-79; Scientific Adv. Cttee, Cancer Res. Campaign, 1974-; ABRC, 1982-. Asst Editor and Editor, Scottish Med. Jl, 1957-61; Hon. Secretary: Scottish Soc. for Experimental Medicine, 1959-62; Surgical Research Soc., 1963-66, Pres., 1974-76; Chm., British Breast Gp, 1974-77. Member Council: Assoc. of Surgeons of GB and Ireland, 1971-74; RCSE, 1976-; Member: Internat. Surgical Gp, 1963; British Soc. of Gastroenterology, 1960; British Assoc. for Cancer Research, 1961; British Assoc. of Surgical Oncology, 1974; Hon. Fellow, Amer. Surgical Assoc., 1981; Hon. FACS, 1978. Hon. DSc Wales, 1981. *Publications:* (ed jtly) Prognostic Factors in Breast Cancer, 1968; (jtly) Principles and Practice of Surgery, 1982; various papers in surgical jls, mainly on gastro-intestinal disease and breast cancer. *Address:* Department of Clinical Surgery, University of Edinburgh, Royal Infirmary, Edinburgh EH3 9YW. *T:* 031-229 2477.

FORREST, Geoffrey; Consultant Chartered Surveyor; *b* 31 Oct. 1909; *er s* of late George Forrest, CA, Rossie Lodge, Inverness; *m* 1st, 1951, Marjorie Ridehalgh; two *s*; 2nd, 1974, Joyce Grey. *Educ:* Marlborough Coll. Chartered Surveyor. Served War of 1939-45, in Lovat Scouts. Joined Forestry Commn, 1946; Chief Land Agent for Forestry Commn in Wales, 1958-64; Chief Land Agent for Forestry Commn in Scotland, 1964-65; Sen. Officer of Forestry Commn in Scotland, 1965-69. Scottish Partner, Knight, Frank & Rutley, 1973-76. *Publications:* papers on land use and estate management in professional jls. *Recreations:* fishing, shooting, lawn tennis. *Address:* Leadervale House, Earlston, Berwickshire TD4 6AJ. *Club:* New (Edinburgh).

FORREST, Cdre (Retd) Geoffrey Cornish; Master of P & O vessel Arcadia from her completion in Jan. 1954 until Oct. 1956; Commodore P & O Fleet, 1955-56; *b* 1898. *Educ:* Thames Nautical Training Coll. (the Worcester). *Recreations:* photography, chess, bridge. *Address:* 44 Shirlow Avenue, Faulconbridge, NSW 2776, Australia.

FORREST, Sir James (Alexander), Kt 1967; FAA; Chairman: Chase NBA Group Ltd, 1969-80; Alcoa of Australia Ltd, 1970-78; Director, National Bank of Australasia Ltd, 1950-78 (Chairman, 1959-78); Director, Australian Consolidated Industries Ltd, 1950-77 (Chairman, 1953-77); *b* 10 March 1905; *s* of John and Mary Gray Forrest; *m* 1939, Mary Christina Forrest (*née* Armit); three *s. Educ:* Caulfield Grammar Sch.; Melbourne Univ. RAAF and Dept Aircraft Production, 1942-45. Partner, Hedderwick Fookes & Alston, Solicitors, 1933-70, Consultant, 1970-73; Dir, Australian Mutual Provident Society, 1961-77 (Dir, 1945-, Chm., 1955-77, Victoria Branch Bd); Dir, Western Mining Corp. Ltd, 1970-77. Member: Victoria Law Foundn, 1969-75; Council, Royal Children's Hosp. Research Foundn, 1960-78; Scotch Coll. Council, 1959-71; Council, Monash Univ., 1961-71; Council, Boy Scouts Assoc. of Aust., 1949-73; Aust. Scout Educn and Trng Foundn, 1976-; Board, Art Foundn of Victoria, 1977-. FAA (by Special Election) 1977. Hon. LLD Monash, 1979. *Recreations:* golf, reading. *Address:* 11 Russell Street, Toorak, Victoria 3142, Australia. *T:* 20-5227. *Clubs:* Melbourne, Australian (Melbourne); Union (Sydney).

FORREST, John Samuel, MA, DSc; FRS 1966; FInstP, FEng; Visiting Professor of Electrical Engineering, University of Strathclyde, since 1964; *b* 20 Aug. 1907; *m* 1940, Ivy May Olding (*d* 1976); one *s. Educ:* Hamilton Acad.; Glasgow Univ. Physicist, Central Electricity Board: Glasgow, 1930; London, 1931; i/c of CEB Research Lab., 1934-40; Founder, 1940, Central Electricity Research Labs, Leatherhead, Dir, 1940-73; Sec., Electricity Supply Research Council, 1949-72. Hunter Memorial Lectr, 1961; Baird Memorial Lectr, 1963, 1975, 1979; Faraday Lectures, 1963-64; Kelvin Lecture, Royal Philosophical Soc. of Glasgow, 1971; Maurice Lubbock Meml Lecture, 1975. Mem. Bd, Inst. of Physics, 1945-49; Chm., London Br. Inst. of Physics,

1954-58; Chm., Supply Sect. of IEE, 1961-62; Chm., British Nat. Cttee, Conference Internationale des Grands Réseaux Electriques, 1972-76; Pres., Sect. A, Brit. Assoc., 1963; Member Council: IEE; Royal Meteorological Society, 1945-47; Research Associations; Vice-Pres., Royal Soc., 1972-75. Hon. FIEE. Foreign Associate, Nat. Acad. of Engrg of USA, 1979. Hon. DSc: Strathclyde, 1969; Heriot-Watt, 1972. Coopers Hill War Memorial Prize and Medal, 1941; Willans Medal, 1958. *Publications:* papers on electrical power transmission and insulation. *Address:* Arbores, Portsmouth Road, Thames Ditton, Surrey KT7 0EG. *T:* 01-398 4389.

FORREST, Prof. Patrick; *see* Forrest, Prof. A. P. M.

FORREST, Rear-Adm. Sir Ronald (Stephen), KCVO 1975; JP; Commander, St John Ambulance, Devon, since 1980; *b* 11 Jan. 1923; *s* of late Stephen Forrest, MD, and Maud M. McKinstry; *m* 1st, 1947, Patricia (*d* 1966), *e d* of Dr and Mrs E. N. Russell; two *s* one *d* ; 2nd, 1967, June (*née* Weaver), widow of late Lieut G. Perks, RN; one step *s* one step *d. Educ:* Belhaven Hill; RNC, Dartmouth. War Service at Sea, Lieut 1943 (despatches 1944); Comdr 1955; CO HMS Teazer, 1956; on loan to Pakistan Navy, 1958-60; Captain 1963; jssc 1963; Chief Staff Officer to Adm. Comdg Reserves, 1964; comd Dartmouth Trng Sqdn, 1966; Dir, Seaman Officers Appointments, 1968; CO, HMS London, 1970; Rear-Adm. 1972; Defence Services Secretary, 1972-75. Naval Gen. Service Medal, 1949. OStJ 1977. JP Honiton, 1978. *Recreations:* gardening, golf. *Address:* Higher Seavington, Millhayes, Stockland, near Honiton, Devon. *Clubs:* Naval, Army and Navy.

FORREST, Prof. William George Grieve; Wykeham Professor of Ancient History, Oxford University, since 1977; Fellow of New College, Oxford, since 1977; *b* 24 Sept. 1925; *s* of William and Ina Forrest; *m* 1956, Margaret Elizabeth Mary Hall; two *d. Educ:* University College Sch., Hampstead; New Coll., Oxford (MA). Served RAF, 1943-47; New Coll., Oxford, 1947-51; Fellow, Wadham Coll., Oxford, 1951-76. Visiting Professor: Trinity and University Colls, Toronto, 1961; Yale, 1968. *Publications:* Emergence of Greek Democracy, 1966; History of Sparta, 1968, 2nd edn 1980; articles in classical and archaeological periodicals. *Address:* 9 Fyfield Road, Oxford. *T:* Oxford 56187; New College, Oxford. *T:* Oxford 48451.

FORREST, Surgeon Rear-Adm. (D) William Ivon Norman, CB 1970; Director of Naval Dental Services, Ministry of Defence, 1968-71; *b* 8 June 1914; *m* 1942, Mary Margaret McMordie Black; three *s. Educ:* Christ's Hospital. Guy's Hospital, 1931-36. LDS, RCS. Dental House Surgeon, Guy's Hosp., 1936-37. Royal Navy: Surg. Lieut (D), 1937; Surg. Lt-Comdr (D), 1943; Surg. Comdr (D), 1950; Surg. Capt. (D), 1960; Surg. Rear-Adm. (D), 1968. Consultant in Dental Surgery, 1963. *Recreations:* golf, gardening, photography. *Address:* 16 Queen's Road, Waterlooville, Hants. *T:* Waterlooville 3139.

FORRESTER, John Stuart; MP (Lab) Stoke-on-Trent, North, since 1966; *b* 17 June 1924; *s* of Harry and Nellie Forrester; *m* 1945, Gertrude H. Weaver. *Educ:* Eastwood Council Sch.; City Sch. of Commerce, Stoke-on-Trent; Alsager Teachers' Training Coll. Teacher, 1946-66. Sec., Constituency Labour Party, 1961. Councillor, Stoke-on-Trent, 1970-. *Address:* House of Commons, SW1.

FORRESTER, Maj.-Gen. Michael, CB 1969; CBE 1963 (OBE 1960); DSO 1943 and Bar, 1944; MC 1939 and Bar, 1941; retired 1970; *b* 31 Aug. 1917; 2nd *s* of late James Forrester, Chilworth, Hants, and Elsie (*née* Mathwin); *m* 1947, Pauline Margaret Clara (marr. diss. 1960), *d* of late James Fisher, Crossmichael; two *s. Educ:* Haileybury. 2nd Lieut, Queen's Royal Regt, 1938; served in Palestine (Arab Rebellion), 1938-39; served War of 1939-45 in Palestine, Egypt, Greece, Crete, Western Desert, Syria, N Africa, Italy and France; GSO3 (Ops) British Military Mission, Greece, 1940-41; GSO3 (Ops), HQ Western Desert Force and HQ 13 Corps, 1941-42; Staff Coll., Haifa, 1942; Bde Major, 132 Inf. Bde, 1942 (despatches); GSO2 (Ops), HQ 13 Corps and HQ 18 Army Gp, 1943; Comdr, 1st/6th Bn, Queen's Royal Regt, 1943-44; wounded, Normandy; GSO1 (Ops), HQ 13 Corps, 1945-46; Mil. Asst to Supreme Allied Comdr Mediterranean, 1947; Mil. Asst to Comdr Brit. Army Staff and Army Mem., Brit. Jt Services Mission, Washington, DC, 1947-50; Co. Comdr, 2nd Bn Parachute Regt, Cyprus and Canal Zone, 1951-52; Dirg Staff, Staff Coll., Camberley, 1953-55; GSO1 (Ops), GHQ East Africa, 1955-57; transf. to Parachute Regt, 1957; Comdr, 3rd Bn Parachute Regt, 1957-60; Col., Military Operations (4), War Office, 1960-61; Comdr, 16 Parachute Bde Gp, 1961-63; Imp. Def. Coll., 1964; GOC 4th Div., BAOR, 1965-67; Dir of Infantry, MoD, 1968-70. Col Comdt, The Queen's Division, 1968-70. *Address:* Pullens, West Worldham, near Alton, Hants. *T:* Alton 84470.

FORRESTER, Prof. Peter Garnett, CBE 1981; Director, Cranfield School of Management, since 1967, Dean of Faculty, 1972; Pro-Vice-Chancellor, Cranfield Institute of Technology, since 1976; *b* 7 June 1917; *s* of Arthur Forrester and Emma (*née* Garnett); *m* 1942, Marjorie Hewitt, Berks; two *d. Educ:* Manchester Grammar Sch.; Manchester Univ. (BSc, MSc). Metallurgist, Thomas Bolton & Son Ltd, 1938-40; Research Officer, later Chief Metallurgist, Tin Research Inst., 1940-48; Chief Metallurgist and Research Man., Glacier Metal Co. Ltd, 1948-63; Dep. Principal, Glacier Inst. of Management, 1963-64; Consultant, John Tyzack & Partners, 1964-66; Prof. of Industrial Management, Coll. of Aeronautics, Cranfield, 1966. Chm., Conf. of Univ. Management Schs, 1976-77. Mem., Bd of Trustees, European

Foundation for Management Develt, 1976-82. FIM, CBIM, FRSA. Burnham Medal, BIM, 1979. *Publications:* numerous scientific and technological papers on metallurgy, bearing materials, tribology. *Recreations:* sailing, walking. *Address:* 5 West Road, Cranfield, Bedford. *T:* Bedford 752717. *Club:* Helford River Sailing.

FORRESTER, Rev. William Roxburgh, MC; Professor of Practical Theology and Christian Ethics, St Mary's College, St Andrews University, 1934-58; Emeritus Professor; *b* 19 Feb. 1892; *s* of Rev. David Marshall Forrester, DD, and Annie Roxburgh; *m* 1922, Isobel Margaret Stewart McColl (*d* 1976); three *s* two *d. Educ:* Glasgow Acad.; Glasgow and Edinburgh Univs. MA (Hons) Edinburgh, 1914; European War: France, Mesopotamia, Persia and India in RFA, 1914-19 (MC 1917); studies at New Coll., Edinburgh; France and Germany, 1919-22; BD, 1924; Minister at Roslin, 1922-28; Minister at Cairns Memorial Church, Edinburgh, 1928-34; Interim Gen. Sec. Scottish National YMCA, 1940-44; DD (Edinburgh) 1939. Cunningham Lecturer, New Coll., Edinburgh, 1947-48-49; LLD St Andrews, 1959. Associate Minister, St Andrew's Presbyterian Church, Nairobi, Nov. 1961-Nov. 1962. *Publications:* Christian Vocation, Studies in Faith and its Relation to Work, 1951; Conversion, 1937, Concern, 1963; The Pen and the Panga, two Addresses on Education and Religion (East Africa), 1965; Your Life and Mine, 1967. *Recreations:* fishing, gardening. *Address:* 7 Newbattle Terrace, Edinburgh EH10 4RU. *T:* 031-447 2870.
See also Bishop of Manchester.

FORRESTER-PATON, Douglas Shaw, QC 1965; **His Honour Judge Forrester-Paton;** a Circuit Judge (formerly a Judge of County Courts), since 1970; *b* 1921; 3rd *s* of late Alexander Forrester-Paton, JP; *m* 1948, Agnete, *d* of Holger Tuxen; one *s* two *d. Educ:* Gresham's Sch., Holt; Queen's Coll., Oxford (BA). Called to Bar, Middle Temple, 1947; North East Circuit. Served RAF, 1941-45. Recorder: Middlesbrough, 1963-68; Teesside, 1968-70. *Address:* 24 Kirkby Lane, Great Broughton, Middlesbrough, Cleveland TS9 7HG. *T:* Stokesley 712301; 5 King's Bench Walk, Temple, EC4.

FORSBERG, (Charles) Gerald, OBE 1955; Comdr RN (Retd); author; Assistant Director of Marine Services, Ministry of Defence (Navy Department), 1972-75 (Deputy Director, 1958-72); *b* Vancouver, 18 June 1912; *s* of Charles G. Forsberg and Nellie (*née* Wallman); *m* 1952, Joyce Whewell Hogarth, *d* of Dr F. W. Hogarth; one *s* one *d. Educ:* Polytechnic School; Training Ship Mercury; Sir John Cass Coll. Merchant Navy: Cadet to Chief Officer, 1928-38; qual. Master Mariner; transf. RN, 1938. Norwegian campaign, 1940; Malta Convoys, Matapan, Tobruk, Crete, etc, 1940-42; comd HMS Vega as Convoy Escort Comdr, 1943-45 (despatches). Comd HMS Mameluke and HMS Chaplet, 1945-49; comd Salvage Sqdn off Elba in recovery of crashed Comet aircraft in 100 fathoms, 1954. Swam Channel (England-France) in record time, 1957; first person to swim Lough Neagh and Loch Lomond, 1959; British long-distance champion, 1957-58-59; swam Bristol Channel in record time, 1964; many long-distance championships and records, 1951-. Younger Brother of Trinity House, 1958; Civil Service, 1962. President: Channel Swimming Assoc., 1963-; British Long Distance Swimming Assoc., 1982-83. Master of Navy Lodge, 1966; Liveryman, Hon. Co. of Master Mariners. Freeman, City of London, 1968. Elected to Internat. Marathon Swimming Hall of Fame, 1971. *Publications:* Long Distance Swimming, 1957; First Strokes in Swimming, 1961; Modern Long Distance Swimming, 1963; Salvage from the Sea, 1977; Pocket Book for Seamen, 1981; many short stories, articles, papers, and book reviews for general periodicals, technical jls and encyclopædia; regular monthly contribs to Swimming Times. *Recreations:* motoring, Association football refereeing, books. *Address:* c/o Barclays Bank International, Oceanic House, 1 Cockspur Street, SW1Y 5BG. *Clubs:* Victory Services; Otter Swimming.

FORSTER, Archibald William, CEng, MIChemE, FInstPet; Chairman and Chief Executive, Esso Petroleum Co. Ltd, since 1980; Chairman, Esso UK Ltd, since 1982; Executive Board Member, Lloyd's Register of Shipping, since 1981; *b* 11 Feb. 1928; *s* of William Henry and Matilda Forster; *m* 1954, Betty Margaret Channing; three *d. Educ:* Tottenham Grammar Sch.; Univ. of Birmingham (BSc (Hons) ChemEng 1949, Cadman Medalist). Served Royal Air Force, Pilot (FO), 1949-51. Joined Esso Petroleum Co. Ltd, 1951; Refinery Manager, Milford Haven, 1962-63; Supply Manager, London, 1963-64; Refinery Manager, Fawley, 1964-69; Manager, Refining Dept, Esso Europe Inc., 1969-71; Exec. Director, Esso Petroleum Co. Ltd, 1971-73; Exec. Asst to Chm., Exxon Corp., 1973-74; Manager, Corporate Planning Co-ordination, Exxon Corp., 1974-75; Vice-Pres., Esso Europe Inc., 1975-78; Director, Exxon Research & Engineering Co., 1975-78; Man. Dir, Esso Petroleum Co. Ltd, 1979-80; Chairman: Esso Teoranta, 1979-80; Irish Refining Co. Ltd, 1979-80; Chairman, Exxon Ltd, 1980; Director: Esso Europe Inc., 1980-; Esso Africa Inc., 1980-. Chm., Esso Pension Trust, 1980- (Dir, 1979-80). Pres., Oil Industries Club, 1982-. Governor, E-SU, 1981-. Hon. DSc Birmingham, 1981. *Recreation:* sailing. *Address:* Esso House, Victoria Street, SW1E 5JW. *T:* 01-834 6677. *Club:* Royal Southampton Yacht.

FORSTER, Charles Ian Kennerley, CBE 1964; Consultant; *b* 18 July 1911; *s* of Douglas Wakefield Forster; *m* 1942, Thelma Primrose Horton (marr. diss. 1974); one *s* one *d* ; *m* 1975, Mrs Loraine Huxtable. *Educ:* Rossall Sch. FIA 1936. With Sun Life Assurance Soc., 1928-39, and 1946. Served R.A, 1939-45. Statistics Branch, Admty, 1946-54; Ministry of Power, 1954 (Chief Statistician, 1955-65, Dir of Statistics, 1965-69); Min. of Technology, 1969;

Under-Sec., Dept of Trade and Industry, 1970-72, retd. *Publications*: contribs to Jls of Inst. of Actuaries and Inst. of Actuaries Students Soc., Trans VII World Power Conf., Trans Manchester Statistical Soc., Statistical News. *Recreations*: bridge, stamps. *Address*: 140 Watchfield Court, Chiswick, W4. *T*: 01-994 3128.

FORSTER, Donald; Chairman, Warrington and Runcorn Development Corporation, since 1982; *b* 18 Dec. 1920; *s* of Bernard and Rose Forster; *m* 1942, Muriel Steinman; one *s* two *d*. *Educ*: N Manchester Grammar School. Served War, RAF pilot (Flt Lieut), 1940-45. Managing Director, 1945-81, Chairman, 1981-, B. Forster & Co. Ltd, Leigh, Textile Manufacturing Company. *Recreations*: golf, music, paintings. *Address*: Melilia, Mereside Road, Mere, Knutsford, Cheshire WA16 6QW. *T*: Bucklow Hill 830374. *Clubs*: Whitefield Golf; Dunham Forest Country; Warrington.

FORSTER, Donald Murray; a Recorder of the Crown Court, since 1978; barrister-at-law; *b* 18 June 1929; *s* of John Cameron Forster and Maisie Constance Forster. *Educ*: Hollylea Sch., Liverpool; Merton House Sch., Penmaenmawr; Wrekin Coll., Wellington, Shropshire; St Edmund Hall, Oxford. Honour Sch. of Jurisprudence (2nd Cl. Hons). Called to Bar, Gray's Inn, 1953; Head of Chambers, 1968. *Recreation*: sport. *Address*: 54 Castle Street, Liverpool L2 7LQ. *T*: 051-236 4421. *Clubs*: Liverpool Ramblers Association Football (Vice-Pres.); Liverpool Racquet; Mersey Bowmen Lawn Tennis (Liverpool).

FORSTER, Brig. Eric Brown, MBE 1952; General Manager, Potato Marketing Board, 1970-82; *b* 19 May 1917; *s* of late Frank and Agnes Forster; *m* 1943, Margaret Bessie Letitia, *d* of late Lt-Col Arthur Wood, MBE and late Edith Wood; one *s* two *d*. *Educ*: Queen Elizabeth Grammar Sch., Hexham. Commnd from RASC ranks into RAPC, 1941. Dir of Cost and Management Accounting (Army Dept), 1967-68. *Recreations*: golf, gardening. *Address*: Littledene, Guildown Avenue, Guildford, Surrey GU2 5HB. *T*: Guildford 62313. *Clubs*: MCC; Worplesdon Golf.

FORSTER, Prof. Leonard Wilson, FBA 1976; Schröder Professor of German, University of Cambridge, 1961-79; *b* 30 March 1913; *o s* of Edward James Forster, merchant, and Linda Charlotte (née Rogers), St John's Wood, NW8; *m* 1939, Jeanne Marie Louise, *e d* of Dr Charles Otto Billeter, Basel; one *s* two *d*. *Educ*: Marlborough Coll.; Trinity Hall, Cambridge. LittD Cantab, 1976. Thomas Carlyle Student, 1934-35; English Lektor: Univ. of Leipzig, 1934; Univ. of Königsberg, 1935-36; Univ. of Basel, 1936-38; study at Univ. of Bonn, 1935. Fellow and Lectr, Selwyn Coll., Cambridge, 1937; Faculty Asst Lectr, Univ. of Cambridge, 1937; Dr phil., Basel, 1938. Naval Staff Admiralty, 1939-41; Foreign Office, 1941-45; Lt-Comdr RNVR (Sp.), 1945-46. Univ. Lectr in German, Cambridge, 1947-50; Dean and Asst Tutor, Selwyn Coll., 1946-50; Prof. of German, UCL, 1950-61. Pres., Internat. Assoc. for Germanic Studies (IVG), 1970-75. Corresponding Member: Deutsche Akademie für Sprache und Dichtung, 1957; Royal Belgian Academy of Dutch Language and Literature, 1973; Member: Maatschappij der Nederlandse Letterkunde, Leiden, 1966; Royal Netherlands Acad. of Sciences and Letters, 1968. Visiting Professor: Univ. of Toronto, 1957; Univ. of Heidelberg, 1964, 1980; McGill Univ., 1967-68; Univ. of Otago, 1968; Univ. of Utrecht, 1976; Univ. of Kiel, 1980-81. Sen. Consultant, Folger Shakespeare Lib., Washington, 1975. Hon. DLitt: Leiden, 1975; Bath, 1979; Strasbourg, 1980. Gold Medal, Goethe-Institut, Munich, 1966; Friedrich Gundolf-Preis für Germanistik im Ausland, 1981. Grosses Verdienstkreuz (Germany), 1976. *Publications*: G. R. Weckherlin, zur Kenntnis seines Lebens in England, 1944; Conrad Celtis, 1948; German Poetry, 1944-48, 1949; The Temper of Seventeenth Century German Literature, 1952; Penguin Book of German Verse, 1957; Poetry of Significant Nonsense, 1962; Lipsius, Von der Bestendigkeit, 1965; Die Niederlande und die Anfänge der deutschen Barocklyrik, 1967; Janus Gruter's English Years, 1967; The Icy Fire, 1969; The Poet's Tongues: multilingualism in Literature, 1971; Kleine Schriften zur deutschen Literatur im 17 Jahrhundert, 1977; Iter Bohemicum, 1980; The Man Who Wanted to Know Everything, 1981; German Life and Letters (co-ed); articles in British and foreign jls. *Recreation*: foreign travel. *Address*: 49 Maids Causeway, Cambridge. *T*: 357513; Selwyn College, Cambridge. *Club*: Athenæum.

FORSTER, Margaret; author; *b* 25 May 1938; *d* of Arthur Gordon Forster and Lilian (née Hind); *m* 1960, Edward Hunter Davies, *qv*; one *s* two *d*. *Educ*: Carlisle and County High Sch. for Girls; Somerville Coll., Oxford (BA). FRSL. Teacher, Barnsbury Girls' Sch., Islington, 1961-63. Member: BBC Adv. Cttee on Social Effects of Television, 1975-77; Arts Council Literary Panel, 1978-81. Chief non-fiction reviewer, Evening Standard, 1977-80. *Publications*: biography: The Rash Adventurer: the rise and fall of Charles Edward Stuart, 1973; William Makepeace Thackeray: memoirs of a Victorian gentleman, 1978; *novels*: Dame's Delight, 1964; Georgy Girl, 1965 (filmscript with Peter Nichols, 1966); The Bogeyman, 1965; The Travels of Maudie Tipstaff, 1967; The Park, 1968; Miss Owen-Owen is At Home, 1969; Fenella Phizackerley, 1970; Mr Bone's Retreat, 1971; The Seduction of Mrs Pendlebury, 1974; Mother, can you hear me?, 1979; The Bride of Lowther Fell, 1980; Marital Rites, 1981. *Recreations*: walking on Hampstead Heath, reading contemporary fiction. *Address*: 11 Boscastle Road, NW5. *T*: 01-485 3785.

FORSTER, Norvela; Member (C) Birmingham South, European Parliament, since 1979; Founder Chairman and Managing Director of small consultancy

company (plastics, packaging, chemical and allied process industries; researches into marketing and management problems in Europe and overseas); *b* 1931; *m* 1981, Michael, *s* of Norman and Margaret Jones. *Educ*: South Wilts Grammar School, Salisbury; London Univ. BSc Hons. Pres., Bedford Coll. Union Soc. Past Member: Hampstead Borough Council; Council, Bow Group. Member: Council, Management Consultants Assoc.; W European Cttee, London Chamber of Commerce. *Address*: IAL-Industrial Aids Ltd, 14 Buckingham Palace Road, SW1W 0QP. *T*: 01-828 5036; 6 Regency House, Regency Street, SW1. *T*: 01-821 5749; Conservative Association, 16 Greenfield Crescent, Birmingham B15 3AU. *T*: 021-454 1404. *Clubs*: Royal Ocean Racing; Royal Mid-Surrey Golf.

FORSTER, Oliver Grantham, CMG 1976; MVO 1961; HM Diplomatic Service; Ambassador to Pakistan, since 1979; *b* 2 Sept. 1925; 2nd *s* of Norman Milward Forster and Olive Christina Forster (née Cockrell); *m* 1953, Beryl Myfanwy Evans; two *d*. *Educ*: Hurstpierpoint; King's Coll., Cambridge. Served in RAF, 1944-48. Joined Commonwealth Relations Office, 1951. Private Sec. to Parly Under-Sec., 1953-54; Second Sec., Karachi, 1954-56; Principal, CRO, 1956-59; First Sec., Madras, 1959-62; First Sec., Washington, 1962-65; Private Sec. to Sec. of State for Commonwealth Relations, 1965-67; Counsellor, Manila, 1967-70; Counsellor, New Delhi, 1970-75, Minister, 1975; Asst Under-Sec. of State and Dep. Chief Clerk, FCO, 1975-79. *Address*: c/o Foreign and Commonwealth Office, SW1. *Clubs*: United Oxford & Cambridge University, Royal Commonwealth Society.

FORSTER, Walter Leslie, CBE 1942; Legion of Merit (USA), 1944; BSc; FInstPet; Director, various cos; *b* 30 June 1903; *s* of John Mark Forster, Leeds; *m* 1936, Lorna, *d* of T. L. Bonstow, Coulsdon, Surrey; one *s*. *Educ*: Leeds Univ. *Address*: 61 Summit Crescent, Westmount, Montreal, Canada. *Clubs*: St James's, Mount Royal (Montreal).

FORSTER, Sir William (Edward Stanley), Kt 1982; **Hon. Mr Justice Forster;** Chief Justice, Supreme Court of the Northern Territory, since 1979 (Senior Judge 1971, Chief Judge 1977); Judge of the Federal Court of Australia, since 1977; Chancellor, Diocese of the Northern Territory, since 1975; *b* 15 June 1921; *s* of F. B. Forster; *m* 1950, Johanna B., *d* of Brig. A. M. Forbes; one *s* two *d*. *Educ*: St Peter's Coll., Adelaide; Adelaide Univ. (Stowe Prize; David Murray Scholar; LLB). Served RAAF, 1940-46. Private legal practice, 1950-59; Magistrate, Adelaide Police Court, 1959-61; Master, Supreme Court of SA, and Dist Registrar, High Court of Aust., 1966-71 (Dep. Master, and Dep. Dist Registrar, 1961-66). Adelaide University: Lectr in Criminal Law, 1957-58; Lectr in Law of Procedure, 1967-71; Mem., Standing Cttee of Senate, 1967-71. President: NT Div., Australian Red Cross, 1973-; Aboriginal Theatre Foundn, 1972-75; Chairman: Museum and Art Galls Bd, NT, 1974-; NT Parole Bd, 1976-. Air Efficiency Award, 1953. *Address*: Judges' Chambers, Supreme Court, Darwin, NT 5790, Australia. *Clubs*: Adelaide (Adelaide); Darwin Golf.

FORSYTH OF THAT ILK, Alistair Charles William, JP; FSCA, FSAScot; FInstPet; Baron of Ethie; Chief of the Name and Clan of Forsyth; chairman and director of companies; *b* 7 Dec. 1929; *s* of Charles Forsyth of Strathendry, FCA, and Ella Millicent Hopkins; *m* 1958, Ann, *d* of Col P. A. Hughes, IA; four *s*. *Educ*: St Paul's Sch.; Queen Mary Coll., London. FInstPet 1973; FSCA 1976; FSAScot 1979. National Service, 2nd Lieut The Queen's Bays, 1948-50; Lieut The Parachute Regt, TA, 1950-54. Chairman: Caledonian Oil Co. Ltd, 1969-; Farmers' Supply Assoc. of Scotland Ltd, 1969-; Melroses Ltd, 1976-; Hargreaves Reiss and Quinn Ltd, 1982-; Seatainers Services Ltd, 1982-; Pentleton and Hare Ltd, 1982-; Director: Carritt Moran & Co. Ltd, Calcutta, 1961-63; Caledonian Produce (Holdings) Ltd, 1969-; Tuckfield Teas Ltd, Melbourne, 1978-; Miles & Kitson Ltd, 1981-. Member: Co. of Merchants of City of Edinburgh, 1970-; Standing Council of Scottish Chiefs, 1978-; Council, 1977-81, Chapter, 1982-, Priory of Scotland of Most Ven. Order of St John of Jerusalem. CStJ 1982 (OStJ 1974). JP NSW, 1965. *Recreations*: hill walking, Scottish antiquities. *Heir: e s* Charles Alistair Forsyth of that Ilk, younger, Esquire StJ. *Address*: Ethie Castle, by Arbroath, Angus DD11 5SP. *T*: Inverkeilor 280. *Clubs*: Cavalry and Guards; New (Edinburgh).

FORSYTH, Bruce; *see* Forsyth-Johnson, B. J.

FORSYTH, Jennifer Mary; Under-Secretary, Department of Transport, since 1980; *b* 7 Oct. 1924; *o d* of late Matthew Forsyth, theatrical director, and late Marjorie Forsyth. *Educ*: Frensham Heights; London Sch. of Economics and Political Science (Pres. of Students' Union, 1944-45) (BScEcon). Joined Home Finance Div., Treasury, 1945; Economic Asst, UN Economic Commn for Europe, 1949-51; Information Div., Treasury, 1951-53; Principal, Estabts, Overseas Finance and Planning Divs, 1954-62; UK Treasury Delegn, Washington, 1962-64; Assistant Secretary: DEA, 1965-69; Social Services Div., Treasury, 1969-75; Under Sec., Treasury, 1975-80. Governor, Frensham Heights, 1965-76. *Recreations*: going to the theatre and to the Mediterranean. *Address*: 51 Abingdon Road, W8 6AN.

FORSYTH, William Douglass, OBE 1955; Australian Ambassador, retired 1969; *b* Casterton, Australia, 5 Jan. 1909; of Australian parents; *m* 1935, Thelma Joyce (née Sherry); one *s* two *d*. *Educ*: Ballarat High Sch.; Melbourne Univ. (MA, DipEd); Balliol Coll., Oxford (BLitt). Teacher of History, 1931-35; Rockefeller Fellow, Social Studies, Europe, 1936-37 and 1939; Research Fellow, Melbourne Univ., 1940; Editor Austral-Asiatic Bulletin, Melbourne, 1940; Research Sec., Aust. Inst. International Affairs, 1940-41;

Australian Dept of Information, 1941-42; Australian Dept of External Affairs, 1942-69: First Sec., 1946; Counsellor, Aust. Embassy, Washington, 1947-48; Aust. rep. Trusteeship Council, 1948 and 1952-55; Sec.-Gen., South Pacific Commission, 1948-51. Australian Member UN Population Commission, 1946-47; Mem., Australian Delegns to UN General Assembly, 1946-48 and 1951-58; San Francisco UN Confs, 1945 and 1955; Minister, Australian Mission to UN, 1951-55; Asst-Sec., Dept of External Affairs, Canberra, 1956-59, 1961-63; Australian Minister to Laos, 1959-60; Australian Ambassador to Viet-Nam, 1959-61; Sec.-Gen., South Pacific Commn, Nouméa, 1963-66; Australian Ambassador to Lebanon, 1967-68. *Publications:* Governor Arthur's Convict System, 1935, reprinted 1970; The Myth of Open Spaces, 1942; Captain Cook's Australian Landfalls, 1970; articles in Economic Record, etc. *Address:* 88 Banks Street, Yarralumla, Canberra, ACT 2600, Australia.

FORSYTH-JOHNSON, Bruce Joseph, (Bruce Forsyth); entertainer and comedian; *b* 22 Feb. 1928; *m* 1st, 1953, Penny Calvert; three *d* ; 2nd, 1973, Anthea Redfern (marr. diss. 1982); two *d. Educ:* Higher Latimer Sch., Edmonton. Started stage career as Boy Prince—The Mighty Atom, 1942; after the war, appeared in various double acts and did a 2 yr spell at Windmill Theatre; first television appearance, Music Hall, 1954; resident compère, Sunday Night at the London Palladium, 1958-60; own revue, London Palladium, 1962; leading role, Little Me, Cambridge Theatre, 1964; début at Talk of the Town (played there 7 times); compèred Royal Variety Show, 1971, and on subseq. occasions; London Palladium Show, 1973 (also Ottawa and Toronto) and 1980; commenced Generation Game, BBC TV series, 1971 (completed 7 series); compèred Royal Windsor to mark BBC Jubilee Celebrations, 1977; One Man Show, Theatre Royal, Windsor, and Lakeside, 1977; Bruce Forsyth's Big Night, ITV, 1978; Play Your Cards Right, ITV, 1980-. Films include: Star; Can Hieronymous Merkin Ever Forget Mary Humppe and Find True Happiness?; Bedknobs and Broomsticks; The Magnificent 7 Deadly Sins. Numerous records. Show Business Personality of the Year, Variety Club of GB, 1975; TV Personality of the Year, Sun Newspaper, 1976 and 1977; Male TV Personality of the Year, TV Times, 1975, 1976, 1977 and 1978. *Recreation:* golf (handicap 10, Wentworth Golf Club). *Address:* Straidarran, Wentworth Drive, Virginia Water, Surrey. *Clubs:* White Elephant, Crockfords, Empress, Tramp.

FORSYTHE, Air Cdre James Roy, CBE 1966; DFC; Director of Development, Look Ahead Housing Association Ltd; *b* 10 July 1920; *s* of W. R. and A. M. Forsythe; *m* 1946, Barbara Mary Churchman; two *s* two *d. Educ:* Methodist Coll., Belfast; Queen's Univ., Belfast. Bomber Comd, 1944-45; OC, Aberdeen Univ. Air Sqdn, 1952-54; psa 1955; Principal Staff Officer to Dir-Gen. Orgn (RAF), 1956-58; OC, 16 Sqdn, 1958-60; Dirg Staff, Coll. of Air Warfare, Manby, 1960-62; Head of RAF Aid Mission to India, 1963; Stn Comdr, RAF Acklington, 1963-65; Dep. Dir Air Staff Policy, MoD, 1965-68; Dir Public Relations, Far East, 1968-70; Dir Recruiting, RAF, 1971-73; Dir, Public Relations, RAF, 1973-75. Mem., Inst. of Public Relations. *Recreations:* Rugby, golf. *Address:* 104 Earls Court Road, W8 6EG. *T:* 01-937 5291. *Club:* Royal Air Force.

FORSYTHE, (John) Malcolm; Regional Medical Officer, South East Thames Regional Health Authority, since 1978; *b* 11 July 1936; *s* of Dr John Walter Joseph Forsythe and late Dr Charlotte Constance Forsythe (*née* Beatty); *m* 1961, Delia Kathleen Moore, *d* of late Dr J. K. Moore and Mrs Cecilia Moore; one *s* three *d. Educ:* Repton Sch., Derby; Guy's Hosp. Med. Sch., London Univ. BSc(Hons), MB, BS, MSc; DObstRCOG, MRCS, LRCP, FFCM. Area Medical Officer, Kent AHA, 1974-78. Hon. Consultant, Univ. of Kent Services Res. Unit, 1977. Head, UK Deleg., Hospital Cttee, EEC, 1980-; Member: NHS Computer Policy Cttee, 1981; Standing Med. Adv. Cttee, 1982. Mem., Bd of Governors, Guy's Hosp. Med. and Dental Schs, 1978-; Member Council: King's Coll. Hosp. Med. and Dental Schs, 1978-; St Thomas's Hosp. Med. Sch., 1980-. Silver Core Award, IFIP, 1977. *Publications:* (ed jtly) Information Processing of Medical Records, 1969; Proceedings of First World Conference on Medical Informatics, 1975. *Recreations:* squash, music. *Address:* North Downs, 22 Church Lane, Oxted, Surrey RH8 9LB. *T:* Oxted 2483. *Clubs:* Royal Society of Medicine; Chasers.

FORT, Mrs Jean; Headmistress of Roedean School, Brighton, 1961-70; *b* 1915; *d* of G. B. Rae; *m* 1943, Richard Fort (*d* 1959), MP Clitheroe Division of Lancs; four *s* one *d. Educ:* Benenden Sch.; Lady Margaret Hall, Oxford (MA, DipEd). Asst Mistress, Dartford County Sch. for Girls, 1937-39; WVS Headquarters staff, 1939-40; Junior Civil Asst, War Office, 1940-41; Personal Asst to Sir Ernest Gowers, Sen. Regional Comr for Civil Def., London, 1941-44. *Address:* 6 King's Close, Henley-on-Thames, Oxon.

FORTE, family name of **Baron Forte.**

FORTE, Baron *cr* 1982 (Life Peer), of Ripley in the county of Surrey; **Charles Forte;** Kt 1970; FRSA; Chairman, Trusthouse Forte Limited, since 1982 (Executive Chairman, 1978-81, Deputy Chairman, 1970-78, and Chief Executive, 1971-78); *b* 26 Nov. 1908; *m* 1943, Irene Mary Chierico; one *s* five *d. Educ:* Alloa Academy; Dumfries Coll.; Mamiani, Rome. Fellow and Mem. Exec. Cttee, Catering Inst., 1949; Member, Small Consultative Advisory Cttee to Min. of Food, 1946; London Tourist Board. Hon. Consul Gen. for Republic of San Marino. FBIM 1971. Mem. AA. Grand Officier, Ordine al Merito della Repubblica Italiana; Cavaliere di Gran Croce della Repubblica Italiana. *Publications:* articles for catering trade papers. *Recreations:* golf, fishing, shooting, fencing, music. *Address:* 86 Park Lane, W1. *Clubs:* Carlton, Caledonian, Royal Thames Yacht; National Sporting (President).

FORTER, Alexis, CMG 1982; OBE 1963; HM Diplomatic Service, retired; Counsellor, Paris, 1977-82; *b* 6 Sept. 1925; *s* of Sqdn Ldr Michael Forter and Suzanne Forter; *m* 1971, Barbara Wood. *Educ:* St Paul's Sch.; Magdalen Coll., Oxford (First Cl. Hons Oriental Studies). Commissioned RAF, 1944; served Middle East, 1945-47. Joined Foreign (later Diplomatic) Service, 1950; 3rd Sec., Tehran, 1951; Vice-Consul, Basra, 1952; Port Said, 1954; FO, 1955; 1st Sec., Baghdad, 1957; FO, 1958; Tehran, 1959; FO, 1964; Saigon, 1966; FCO, 1969; Nairobi, 1971; FCO, 1973. *Recreations:* beagling, music, shooting. *Address:* c/o Williams & Glyn's Bank, Holt's Branch, Kirkland House, Whitehall, SW1A 2EB. *Club:* Travellers'.

FORTES, Prof. Meyer, MA, PhD; FBA 1967; William Wyse Professor of Social Anthropology, University of Cambridge, 1950-73; Fellow of King's College, Cambridge, 1950-78, Honorary Fellow, since 1980; *b* Britstown, Cape, 25 April 1906; *e s* of late Nathan and late Mrs Bertha Fortes, Cape Town, S Africa; *m* 1928, Sonia (*d* 1956), *d* of late N. Donen, Worcester, Cape, SA; one *d* ; *m* 1960, Doris Y. Mayer, MD, *d* of late D. S. Yankauer, NY. *Educ:* South African Coll. High Sch., Cape Town; University of Cape Town; University of London. Univ. of Cape Town: Roderick Noble Schol., 1926, Willem Hiddingh Schol., 1927-30; London Sch. of Economics: Ratan Tata Student, 1930-31, Rockefeller Fellow, 1933-34; Fellow, International African Institute, 1934-38; Lectr, LSE, 1938-39; Research Lectr, University of Oxford, 1939-41; National Service, West Africa, 1942-44; Head of Sociological Dept, West African Institute, Accra, Gold Coast, 1944-46; Reader in Social Anthropology, Oxford, 1946-50. President: Section H, Brit. Assoc. for the Advancement of Science, 1953; Section 25, ANZAAS, 1975. Lectures: Josiah Mason, Univ. of Birmingham, 1949; Frazer, Glasgow, 1956; Henry Myers, Royal Anthrop. Inst., 1960; Lewis Henry Morgan, Univ. of Rochester, USA, 1963; Munro, Univ. of Edinburgh, 1964, 1973; Emanuel Miller Meml, Assoc. Child Psychol. and Psychiatry, 1972; Ernest Jones Meml, Brit. Psychoanalytical Soc., 1973; Marett, Oxford, 1974; Huxley Meml, Royal Anthrop. Inst., 1977. Chm., Assoc. Social Anthropologists, 1970-73. For. Mem., American Philosophical Soc., 1972; Foreign Hon. Mem. Amer. Acad. of Arts and Sciences, 1964. Field Research: Northern Territories, Gold Coast, 1934-37; Nigeria, 1941-42; Ashanti Gold Coast, 1945-46; Bechuanaland, 1948. Pres., Royal Anthropological Institute; Hon. Editor, Jl Royal Anthropological Inst., 1947-53; Mem. Exec. Council, International African Institute; Mem. Exec. Cttee, British Sociological Assoc., 1952-55. Visiting Professor: Chicago Univ., 1954, 1973; Univ. of Ghana, 1971 (Leverhulme); Australian Nat. Univ., 1975; Univ. of California, Santa Cruz, 1977; Northwestern Univ., 1978 (M. J. Herskovits); Univ. of Manchester, 1980. Fellow: Center for Advanced Study in Behavioral Science, Stanford, 1958-59, and 1967-68; University Coll., London, 1975. Hon. Fellow, LSE, 1979. Rivers Medal, Royal Anthropological Inst., 1946. Hon. DHL Chicago, 1973; Hon. DLitt Belfast, 1975. *Publications:* The Dynamics of Clanship among the Tallensi, 1945; The Web of Kinship among the Tallensi, 1949; Social Anthropology at Cambridge since 1900, 1953; Oedipus and Job in West African Religion, 1959; Kinship and the Social Order, 1969; Time and Social Structure, 1970; (ed) Marriage in Tribal Societies, 1972; (ed with S. Patterson) Studies in African Social Anthropology, 1975; (ed with M. Bourdillon) Sacrifice, 1980; various papers in psychological and anthropological journals. *Address:* 113 Grantchester Meadows, Cambridge CB3 9JN.

FORTESCUE, family name of **Earl Fortescue.**

FORTESCUE, 7th Earl *cr* 1789; **Richard Archibald Fortescue,** JP; Baron Fortescue 1746; Viscount Ebrington 1789; *b* 14 April 1922; *s* of 6th Earl Fortescue, MC, TD, and Marjorie (*d* 1964), OBE, *d* of late Col C. W. Trotter, CB, TD; *S* father, 1977; *m* 1st, 1949, Penelope Jane (*d* 1959), *d* of late Robert Evelyn Henderson; one *s* one *d* ; 2nd, 1961, Margaret Anne, *d* of Michael Stratton; two *d. Educ:* Eton; Christ Church, Oxford. Captain Coldstream Guards (Reserve). JP Oxon, 1964. *Heir: s* Viscount Ebrington, *qv. Address:* The Old Farm, Swinbrook, Burford, Oxon. *T:* Burford 3135. *Club:* White's.

FORTESCUE, Trevor Victor Norman, (Tim); Secretary-General, Food and Drink Industries Council, since 1973; *b* 28 Aug. 1916; *s* of Frank Fortescue; *m* 1st, 1939, Margery Stratford (marr. diss. 1975), *d* of Dr G. H. Hunt; two *s* one *d* ; 2nd, 1975, Anthea Maureen, *d* of Robert M. Higgins. *Educ:* Uppingham Sch.; King's Coll., Cambridge. BA 1938; MA 1945. Colonial Administrative Service, Hong Kong, 1939-47 and Kenya, 1949-51 (interned, 1941-45); FAO, UN, Washington, DC, 1947-49 and Rome, 1951-54; Chief Marketing Officer, Milk Marketing Bd of England and Wales, 1954-59; Manager, Nestlé Gp of Cos, Vevey, Switz., 1959-63 and London, 1963-66. MP (C) Liverpool, Garston, 1966-Feb. 1974; an Asst Govt Whip, 1970-71; a Lord Comr of HM Treasury, 1971-73. Chairman: Conference Associates Ltd, 1978-; Standing Cttee, Confed. of Food and Drink Industries of European Community (CIAA), 1983-. Mem. Council, British Industrial Biol. Res. Assoc., 1980-. Trustee, Uppingham Sch., 1957-63; Patron and Trustee, The Quest Community, Birmingham, 1971-. *Recreations:* marriage to Anthea; Napoleon. *Address:* 34 Stanford Road, W8 5PZ. *T:* 01-937 2125.

FORTEVIOT, 3rd Baron cr 1916; **Henry Evelyn Alexander Dewar**, Bt, cr 1907; MBE 1943; DL; Chairman, John Dewar & Sons Ltd, 1954-76; former Director, Distillers Co. Ltd; b 23 Feb. 1906; 2nd s of 1st Baron Forteviot and Margaret Elizabeth, d of late Henry Holland; S half-brother 1947; m 1933, Cynthia Monica, e d of late Cecil Starkie, Hethe Place, Cowden, Kent; two s two d. Educ: Eton; St John's Coll., Oxford (BA). Served War of 1939-45, with Black Watch (RHR) (MBE). DL Perth, 1961. Heir: s Hon. John James Evelyn Dewar [b 5 April 1938; m 1963, Lady Elisabeth Waldegrave, 3rd d of 12th Earl Waldegrave, qv ; one s three d]. Address: Dupplin Castle, Perth, Perthshire. Club: Brooks's; Royal (Perth).
  See also Duke of Fife, Gen. Sir Richard Worsley.

FORTH, Eric; Member (C) North Birmingham, European Parliament, since 1979; b 9 Sept. 1944; s of William and Aileen Forth; m 1967, Linda St Clair; two d. Educ: Jordanhill Coll. Sch., Glasgow; Glasgow Univ. (MA Hons Politics and Econs). Chm., Young Conservatives', Constituency CPC, 1970-73; Member: Glasgow Univ. Cons. Club, 1962-66; Brentwood UDC, 1968-72. Parly Candidate, Barking, Feb. and Oct. 1974. Chm., Backbench Cttee, European Democ. Gp, European Parlt, 1979-. Recreation: discussion and argument. Address: 40A Goldieslie Road, Sutton Coldfield, West Midlands. Club: Carlton.

FORTIER, Most Rev. Jean-Marie; see Sherbrooke, Archbishop of, (RC).

FORTY, Francis John, OBE 1952; BSc, FICE, FSA, FRSH, FIMunE; City Engineer, Corporation of London, 1938-64; b Hull, Yorks, 11 Nov. 1900; s of J. E. Forty, MA Oxon, headmaster, Hull Grammar Sch., and Maud C. Forty; m 1st, 1926, Doris Marcon Francis (d 1958), d of Dr A. G. Francis, BA Cantab, FRCS; one s two d ; 2nd, 1965, Elizabeth Joyce Tofield. Educ: Hymers Coll., Hull; Glasgow Univ. (BSc 1923). RNAS, RAF, 1918-19 (Commnd Pilot). Engineering Asst, Hull; Engineering Asst, York; Chief Engineering Asst, Willesden. Deputy Borough Surveyor, Ealing; Borough Engineer and Surveyor, Ealing, 1934-38. War duties, 1939-45, included i/c City of London Heavy Rescue Service (Civil Defence Long Service Medal). Works include: (with Sir Albert Richardson) St Paul's Garden, 1951; (in consultation with Prof. W. F. Grimes) exposure and preservation of section of Town Wall of London, 1951-53; London Wall new route between Moorgate and Aldersgate Street, with car park underneath, 1959; Blackfriars Bridgehead Improvement with underpass, 1962-; multi-storey car park, Upper Thames Street, 1962; (with Sir Hugh Casson) Walbrook Wharf Public Cleansing Depot and Wharf 1963. Formerly Member: London Regional Bldg Cttee; Nat. Soc. for Clean Air; Roman and Mediaeval London Excavation Council; Festival of Britain Council for Architecture, Town Planning and Bldg Research; Minister of Transport's Parking Survey Cttee for Inner London; Minister of Housing and Local Govt's Thames Flooding Technical Panel; Sussex Archaeological Trust. Liveryman of the Worshipful Company of Painter-Stainers, of the City of London. Publications: Bituminous Emulsions for Use in Road Works (with F. Wilkinson), 1932; Swimming Bath Water Purification from a Public Health Point of View (with F. W. Wilkinson), various contribs technical and other jls; notably contrib. on exposure and preservation of Roman and mediæval work in the Town Wall of London. Address: Flat 8, Emanuel House, 18 Rochester Row, SW1P 1BS. T: 01-834 4376. Clubs: Athenæum, Royal Air Force.

FORWELL, Dr George Dick, PhD; FRCPE, FRCPGlas; Chief Administrative Officer, Greater Glasgow Health Board, and Hon. Lecturer, Department of Administrative Medicine, Glasgow University, since 1973; b 6 July 1928; s of Harold C. Forwell and Isabella L. Christie; m 1957, Catherine F. C. Cousland; two d. Educ: George Watson's Coll., Edinburgh; Edinburgh Univ. (MB, ChB 1950; PhD 1955). MRCPE 1957, DIH 1957, DPH 1959, FRCPE 1967, FFCM 1972, FRCPGlas 1974. House Officer and Univ. Clin. Asst, Edinburgh Royal Infirm., 1950-52; RAF Inst. of Aviation Med., 1952-54; MRC and RCPE grants, 1954-56; pneumoconiosis field res., 1956-57; Grad. Res. Fellow and Lectr, Edinburgh Univ. Dept of Public Health and Social Med., 1957-60; Asst Dean, Faculty of Med., Edinburgh Univ., 1960-63; Dep. Sen. and Sen. Admin. MO, Eastern Reg. Hosp. Bd, Dundee, 1963-67; PMO, Scottish Home and Health Dept, 1967-73; QHP, 1980-. Publications: papers on clin. res. and on health planning and services, in med. and other jls. Address: 60 Whittingehame Drive, Glasgow G12 0YQ. T: 041-334 7122.

FORWOOD, Sir Dudley (Richard), 3rd Bt cr 1895; Member of Lloyd's; b 6 June 1912; s of Sir Dudley Baines Forwood, 2nd Bt, CMG, and Norah Isabella (née Lockett) (d 1962); S father, 1961; m 1952, Mary Gwendoline (who m 1st, Viscount Ratendone, later 2nd Marquis of Willingdon; 2nd, Robert Cullingford), d of Basil S. Foster. Educ: Stowe Sch. Attaché, British Legation, Vienna, 1934-37; Equerry to the Duke of Windsor, 1937-39. Served War of 1939-45, Scots Guards (Major). Master, New Forest Buckhounds, 1956-65; Official Verderer of the New Forest, 1974-82; Chairman: New Forest Consultative Panel, 1970-; Crufts, 1973-. Recreation: hunting. Heir: cousin Peter Noel Forwood [b 1925; m 1950, Roy Murphy; six d]. Address: 43 Addison Road, W14. T: 01-603 3620; The Old House, Burley, near Ringwood, Hants. T: Burley 2345.

FOSKETT, Douglas John, OBE 1978; FLA; Director of Central Library Services and Goldsmiths' Librarian, University of London, since 1978; b 27 June 1918; s of John Henry Foskett and Amy Florence Foskett; m 1948, Joy Ada (née McCann); one s two d. Educ: Bancroft's Sch.; Queen Mary Coll., Univ. of London (BA 1939); Birkbeck Coll., Univ. of London (MA 1954). Ilford Municipal Libraries, 1940-48; RAMC and Intell. Corps, 1940-46; Metal Box Co. Ltd, 1948-57; Librarian, Univ. of London Inst. of Educn, 1957-78. Chairman of Council, Library Assoc., 1962-63, Vice-Pres., 1966-73, Pres., 1976; Hon. Library Adviser, RNID, 1965-; Mem., Adv. Cttee on Sci. and Techn. Information, 1969-73; Mem. and Rapporteur, Internat. Adv. Cttee on Documentation, Libraries and Archives, UNESCO, 1968-73; Cons. on Documentation to ILO and to European Packaging Fedn; Cttee Mem., UNISIST/UNESCO and EUDISED/Council of Europe Projects; Member: Army Educn Adv. Bd, 1968-73; Library Adv. Council, 1975-77. Visiting Professor: Univ. of Michigan, 1964; Univ. of Ghana, 1967; Univ. of Ibadan, 1967; Brazilian Inst. for Bibliography and Documentation, 1971; Univ. of Iceland, 1974. FLA 1949, Hon. FLA, 1975; Hon. Fellow, Polytechnic of North London, 1981. Publications: Assistance to Readers in Lending Libraries, 1952; (with E. A. Baker) Bibliography of Food, 1958; Information Service in Libraries, 1958, 2nd edn 1967; Classification and Indexing in the Social Sciences, 1963, 2nd edn 1974; Science, Humanism and Libraries, 1964; Reader in Comparative Librarianship, 1977; contrib. to many professional jls. Recreations: books, travel, writing, cricket. Address: 1 Daleside, Gerrard's Cross, Bucks SL9 7JF. T: Gerrard's Cross 82835. Clubs: MCC; Sussex CCC.

FOSS, Kathleen, (Kate); Member, National Consumer Council, since 1980; b 17 May 1925; d of George Arden and May Elizabeth Arden; m 1951, Robert Foss; one s. Educ: Northampton High Sch.; Whitelands Coll. (Teaching Dip.). Teacher: Northants, 1945-47; Mddx, 1947-53 (Dep. Head); Westmorland, 1953-60 (History specialist). Chm., Consumers in European Community Gp (UK), 1979-; Mem., Consumers' Consultative Cttee, Brussels, 1981-; Vice Chm., Keep Britain Tidy Gp, 1979-; Mem. Exec., National Fedn of Women's Insts, 1969-81 (National Treasurer, 1974-78); Chm., Bd of Dirs, WI Books Ltd, 1981-. Recreations: golf, bridge. Address: Merston, Natland, Kendal, Cumbria LA9 7QH. T: Kendal 20855. Club: Ebury Court.

FOSTER; see Hylton-Foster.

FOSTER, Prof. Allan (Bentham); Professor of Chemistry, University of London, since 1966; Head of Division of Chemistry, Chester Beatty Research Institute, Institute of Cancer Research: Royal Cancer Hospital, since 1966; b 21 July 1926; s of late Herbert and Martha Alice Foster; m 1949, Monica Binns; two s. Educ: Nelson Grammar Sch., Lancs; University of Birmingham. Frankland Medal and Prize, 1947; PhD, 1950; DSc, 1957. University Res. Fellow, University of Birmingham, 1950-53; Fellow of Rockefeller Foundn, Ohio State Univ., 1953-54; University of Birmingham: ICI Res. Fellow, 1954-55; Lectr, 1955-62; Sen. Lectr, 1962-64; Reader in Organic Chemistry, 1964-66. FChemSoc (Mem. Coun., 1962-65, 1967-70); Corresp. Mem., Argentinian Chem. Soc. Regional Editor, Carbohydrate Research. Publications: numerous scientific papers mainly in Jl Chem. Soc. and Carbohydrate Research. Recreations: golf, gardening, foreign travel. Address: Chester Beatty Research Institute, Institute of Cancer Research: Royal Cancer Hospital, Fulham Road, SW3. T: 01-352 8133. Clubs: Athenæum; Banstead Downs.

FOSTER, Brendan, MBE 1976; Joint Managing Director, Nike International, since 1981; b 12 Jan. 1948; s of Francis and Margaret Foster; m 1972; one s one d. Educ: St Joseph's Grammar Sch., Hebburn, Co. Durham; Sussex Univ. (BSc); Carnegie Coll., Leeds (DipEd). School Teacher, St Joseph's Grammar Sch., Hebburn, 1970-74; Sports and Recreation Manager, Gateshead Metropolitan Bor. Council, 1974-81. Commonwealth Games: Bronze medal: 1500 metres, 1970; 5000 m, 1978; Silver medal, 5000 m, 1974; Gold medal, 10,000 m, 1978; European Games: Bronze medal, 1500 m, 1971; Gold medal, 5000 m, 1974; Olympic Games: Bronze medal, 10,000 m, 1976; World Records: 2 miles, 1973; 3000 metres, 1974. Hon. Fellow, Sunderland Polytechnic, 1977; Hon. MEd, Newcastle, 1978; Hon. DLitt, Sussex, 1982. Publication: Brendan Foster, 1978. Recreations: running (now only a recreation), sport (as spectator). Address: 3 Ivy Lane, Low Fell, Gateshead, Tyne and Wear NE9 6QD.

FOSTER, Prof. Christopher David, MA; a Director, and Head of Economics and Public Policy Division, Coopers & Lybrand Associates, since 1978; Visiting Professor, London School of Economics, since 1978; b 30 Oct. 1930; s of George Cecil Foster; m 1958, Kay Sheridan Bullock; two s three d. Educ: Merchant Taylors' Sch.; King's Coll., Cambridge (Scholar). Economics Tripos 1954; MA 1959. Hallsworth Research Fellow, Manchester Univ., 1957-59; Senior Research Fellow, Jesus Coll., Oxford, 1959-64; Official Fellow and Tutor, Jesus Coll., 1964-66; Dir-Gen. of Economic Planning, MoT, 1966-70; Head of Unit for Res. in Urban Economics, LSE, 1970-76; Prof. of Urban Studies and Economics, LSE, 1976-78. Governor, 1967-70, Dir, 1976-78, Centre for Environmental Studies. Vis. Prof. of Economics, MIT, 1970. Special Economic Adviser (part time) DoE, 1974-77; Mem. (part time), PO Bd, 1975-77. Chm., Cttee of Inquiry into Road Haulage Licensing, 1977-78; Mem., Cttee of Inquiry into Civil Service Pay, 1981-82. Publications: The Transport Problem, 1963; Politics, Finance and the Role of Economics: an essay on the control of public enterprise, 1972; (with R. Jackman and M. Perlman) Local Government Finance, 1980; papers in various economic and other journals. Address: 6 Holland Park Avenue, W11. T: 01-727 4757. Club: Reform.

FOSTER, Derek; MP (Lab) Bishop Auckland, since 1979; *b* 25 June 1937; *s* of Joseph and Ethel Maud Foster; *m* 1972, Florence Anne Bulmer. *Educ:* Bede Grammar Sch., Sunderland; Oxford Univ. (BA Hons PPE). In industry and commerce, 1960-70; Youth and Community Worker, 1970-73; Further Educn Organiser, Durham, 1973-74; Asst Dir of Educn, Sunderland Borough Council, 1974-79. Councillor: Sunderland Co. Borough, 1972-74; Tyne and Wear County Council, 1973-77 (Chm. Econ. Develt Cttee, 1973-76). Chm., North of England Develt Council, 1974-76. Mem., Select Cttee on Trade and Industry. Vice Chm., Youthaid. *Recreations:* brass bands, choirs, uniformed member Salvation Army. *Address:* 3 Linburn, Rickleton, Washington, Tyne and Wear. *T:* Washington 471580.

FOSTER, George Arthur C.; *see* Carey-Foster.

FOSTER, Sir Idris (Llewelyn), Kt 1977; MA Wales and Oxon; FSA; Jesus Professor of Celtic in the University of Oxford, 1947-78, now Emeritus; Fellow of Jesus College, 1947-78, Honorary Fellow, 1978; Member: Royal Commission on Ancient Monuments in Wales and Monmouthshire; Museums and Galleries Commission (formerly Standing Commission on Museums and Galleries), since 1964; Governing Body, Church in Wales; Vice-President, National Library of Wales; Chairman, Ancient Monuments Board for Wales; *b* 23 July 1911; *e s* of late Harold L. Foster and Ann J. (Roberts), Carneddi, Bethesda, Bangor, Caerns; unmarried. *Educ:* County Sch., Bethesda; University Coll. of North Wales, Bangor (Hon. Professorial Fellow, 1978); National Univ. of Ireland, Dublin. BA (Wales) with First Class Hons, 1932; University Research Student, 1933-35; MA (Wales) with distinction, 1935; Fellow of University of Wales, 1935; Head of Dept of Celtic, University of Liverpool, 1936-47; Warden of Derby Hall, University of Liverpool, 1946-47; served in Intelligence Div., Naval Staff, Admiralty, 1942-45; Sir John Rhys Memorial Lectr, Br. Acad., 1950; O'Donnell Lectr, Univ. of Edinburgh, 1960, Univ. of Wales, 1971-72; G. J. Williams Lectr, University Coll., Cardiff, 1973; University of Oxford: Select Preacher, 1973-74; James Ford Special Lectr, 1979; President: Soc. for Study of Mediæval Languages and Literature, 1953-58; Cambrian Archaeological Assoc., 1968-69; Court of Nat. Eisteddfod of Wales, 1973-77 (Chm. Council, 1970-73); Irish Texts Soc., 1973-; Chm., Gwynedd Archaeol Trust, 1974-79; formerly Chm., Modern Langs Bd, and Anthropol. and Geography Bd, Oxford; Mem., Council for Welsh Language, 1973-78; Hon. Editor, Trans. and publications, Cymmrodorion Soc., 1953-78. *Publications:* (ed with L. Alcock) Culture and Environment, 1963; (ed with Glyn Daniel) Prehistoric and Early Wales, 1965; papers and reviews. *Recreation:* music. *Address:* Cae'ronnen, Carneddi, Bangor, Gwynedd. *Club:* Athenæum.

FOSTER, Joan Mary; Under Secretary, Department of Transport, Highways Planning and Management, 1978-80, retired; *b* 20 January 1923; *d* of John Whitfield Foster and Edith Foster (*née* Levett). *Educ:* Northampton School for Girls. Entered Civil Service (HM Office of Works), Oct. 1939; Ministry of Transport, 1955; Asst Secretary, 1970. *Recreations:* gardening, cooking, good wine. *Address:* Saddlers, Water End, Hemel Hempstead, Herts HP1 3BH. *T:* Hemel Hempstead 47374.

FOSTER, Sir John (Gregory), 3rd Bt *cr* 1930; Consultant Physician, George, Cape Province; *b* 26 Feb. 1927; *s* of Sir Thomas Saxby Gregory Foster, 2nd Bt, and Beryl, *d* of late Dr Alfred Ireland; *S* father, 1957; *m* 1956, Jean Millicent Watts; one *s* three *d*. *Educ:* Michaelhouse Coll., Natal. South African Artillery, 1944-46; Witwatersrand Univ., 1946-51; MB, BCh 1951; Post-graduate course, MRCPE 1955; Medical Registrar, 1955-56; Medical Officer, Cape Town, 1957. DIH London, 1962. *Recreation:* outdoor sport. *Heir: s* Saxby Gregory Foster, *b* 3 Sept. 1957. *Address:* 7 Caledon Street, PO Box 325, George, Cape Province, South Africa. *T:* George 3251. *Club:* Johannesburg Country (S Africa).

FOSTER, (John) Peter; Surveyor of the Fabric of Westminster Abbey since 1973; *b* 2 May 1919; *s* of Francis Edward Foster and Evelyn Marjorie, *e d* of Sir Charles Stewart Forbes, 5th Bt of Newe; *m* 1944, Margaret Elizabeth Skipper; one *s* one *d*. *Educ:* Eton; Trinity Hall, Cambridge. BA 1940, MA 1946; ARIBA 1949. Commnd RE 1941; served Norfolk Div.; joined Guards Armd Div. 1943, served France and Germany; Captain SORE(2) 30 Corps 1945; discharged 1946. Marshall Sisson, Architect: Asst 1948, later Partner; Sole Principal 1971. Surveyor of Royal Academy of Arts, 1965; Partner with John Peters of Vine Press, Hemingford Grey, 1957-63. Master, Art Workers' Guild, 1980 (Mem., 1971). Pres., Surveyors Club, 1980. Member: Churches Cttee for Historic Building Council for England, 1977-; Adv. Bd for Redundant Churches, 1979-. FSA 1973. *Recreations:* painting, books, travel, shooting. *Address:* Harcourt, Hemingford Grey, Huntingdon, Cambs PE18 9BJ. *T:* St Ives 62200; 2a Little Cloister, Westminster Abbey, SW1P 3PA. *Club:* Athenæum.

FOSTER, John Robert; National Organiser, Amalgamated Union of Engineering Workers, 1962-81, retired; *b* 30 Jan. 1916; *s* of George Foster and Amelia Ann (*née* Elkington); *m* 1938, Catherine Georgina (*née* Webb); one *s* one *d*. *Educ:* London County Council. Apprentice toolmaker, 1931-36; toolmaker, 1936-47; Amalgamated Engineering Union: Kingston District Sec. (full-time official), 1947-62. In Guyana for ILO, 1982. Lectr on industrial relns and trade union educn, WEA. Mem., Engrg Industry Trng Bd, 1974-80; Vice-Chm. Electricity Supply Industry Trng Cttee, 1967-81; Mem., Adv. Council on Energy Conservation, 1978-82. Mem., Soc. of Industrial Tutors. MRI 1978. *Recreations:* music, photography, angling, 17th Century English

Revolution. *Address:* 10 Grosvenor Gardens, Kingston-upon-Thames KT2 5BE.

FOSTER, Very Rev. John William, BEM 1946; Dean of Guernsey, since 1978; Rector of St Peter Port, Guernsey, since 1978; *b* 5 Aug. 1921; *m* 1943, Nancy Margaret Allen; one *s*. *Educ:* St Aidan's Coll., Birkenhead. Served Leicestershire Yeomanry, 1939-46; Chaplain, Hong Kong Defence Force, 1958-. Reserve of Officers, Hong Kong Defence Force, 1967-73. Priest 1955; Curate of Loughborough, 1954-57; Chaplain, St John's Cathedral, Hong Kong, 1957-60, Precentor, 1960-63; Dean of Hong Kong, 1963-73; Hon. Canon, St John's Cathedral, Hong Kong, 1973; Vicar of Lythe, dio. York, 1973-78; Hon. Canon of Winchester, 1979. *Address:* The Deanery, Guernsey.

FOSTER, Lawrence; conductor; Chief Conductor, Orchestre National de Monte Carlo, since 1978; *b* Los Angeles, 23 Oct. 1941; *s* of Thomas Foster and Martha Wurmbrandt. *Educ:* Univ. of California, LA; studied under Fritz Zweig, Bruno Walter and Karl Böhm. Asst Conductor, Los Angeles Philharmonic, 1965-68; British début, Royal Festival Hall, 1968; Covent Garden début, Troilus and Cressida, 1976; Chief Guest Conductor, Royal Philharmonic Orchestra, 1969-74; Music Dir and Chief Conductor, Houston Symphony Orchestra, 1971-78. *Recreations:* water skiing, table tennis. *Address:* c/o Harrison/Parrott Ltd, 12 Penzance Place, W11 4PE.

FOSTER, Maj.-Gen. Norman Leslie, CB 1961; DSO 1945; *b* 26 Aug. 1909; *s* of late Col A. L. Foster, Wimbledon; *m* 1937, Joan Constance, *d* of late Canon T. W. E. Drury; two *s*. *Educ:* Westminster; RMA Woolwich. 2nd Lieut, RA, 1929; Served War of 1939-45 in Egypt and Italy; CRA 11th Armoured Division, 1955-56; Deputy Military Sec., War Office, 1958-59; Maj.-Gen., 1959; GOC Royal Nigerian Army, 1959-62; Pres., Regular Commissions Board, 1962-65; retired, 1965. Dir of Security (Army), MoD, 1965-73. Security Advr, CSD, 1974-79. Col Comdt, Royal Regt of Artillery, 1966-74. Chm., Truman and Knightley Educnl Trust Ltd, 1976-80. *Address:* Besborough, Heath End, Farnham, Surrey. *Club:* Army and Navy.

FOSTER, Norman Robert, RIBA, FSIA, FAIA; architect; Principal, Foster Associates London and Oslo; Director, Foster Associates Hong Kong; *b* 1 June 1935; *s* of late Robert Foster and Lilian Smith; *m* 1964, Wendy Ann Cheesman; two *s*. *Educ:* Burnage Grammar Sch., Manchester; Manchester Coll. of Commerce; Univ. of Manchester Sch. of Architecture (RIBA Silver Medal, Heywood Medal, Builders' Assoc. Travelling Schol., MSA Bronze Medal, DipArch 1961, CertTP); Yale Univ. Sch. of Architecture (Henry Fellow, Jonathan Edwards Coll., MArch 1962). Manchester City Treasurer's Dept, 1951-53; worked in offices of Casson & Conder, 1960 and Paul Rudolph, 1962; consultancy works on city planning and urban renewal, USA, 1962-63; private practice in London, 1963-; in collab. with Dr Buckminster Fuller, 1968-; Cons. Architect to Univ. of E Anglia, 1978-. Mem. Council: AA, 1969-70, 1970-71 (Vice Pres., 1974); RCA, 1982-. Taught at: Univ. of Pennsylvania; AA, London; Bath Acad. of Arts; London Polytechnic. External Examr and Mem. Visiting Bd of Educn, RIBA. Projects include: Fred. Olsen Centre and Terminal, Port of London, 1968; IBM Pilot Head Office, Hampshire, 1970; Central redevelopment, Oslo and Offices in Forest Vestby for Fred. Olsen A/S, 1974; Head Office for Willis Faber & Dumas, Ipswich, 1975; Sainsbury Centre for Visual Arts, Univ. of E Anglia, Norwich, 1977; Technical Park for IBM, Greenford, Mddx, Stage one, 1977; Hammersmith Centre, London, 1977; UK headquarters for Renault, 1977; New Generation Furniture System, 1977; Open House Community Centre, 1978; Experimental Dwelling System, 1978; Whitney Gallery develt, NY, 1979; winning design, internat. competition for new headquarters, Hongkong and Shanghai Banking Corp., Hong Kong, 1979; feasibility studies, Third London Airport, for British Airports Authority, 1981-; winning design, internat. competition for Nat. German Indoor Athletic Stadium, Frankfurt, 1981; limited competition headquarters for Humana, Kentucky, USA, 1981. Work exhibited: Mus. of Mod. Art, New York, 1979 and Permanent Exhibn, 1982; Parma, 1979; Copenhagen, 1979; Singapore, 1971. Exhibitions: Foster Associates, Barcelona, 1976; Foster Associates–Original Drawings, RIBA, 1979. BBC2 TV Documentary for Omnibus by John Read, 1981. Guest Editor Special Issues Architectural Review, 1968. IBM Fellow, Aspen Conference, 1980; Hon. FAIA. Hon. DLitt East Anglia, 1980. Awards include: R. S. Reynolds Internat. Awards, USA, 1976, 1979; RIBA Awards and Commendations, 1969, 1972, 1977, 1978, 1981; Financial Times Awards for outstanding Industrial Architecture and Commendations, 1967, 1970, 1971, 1974; Structural Steel Awards, 1972, 1978; Internat. Design Award, 1976, 1980; RSA Award, 1976; Ambrose Congreve Award, 1980. *Publications:* contribs to various books and technical publications. *Recreations:* flying sailplanes, helicopters and light aircraft; running. *Address:* (office) 172-182 Great Portland Street, W1N 5TB. *T:* 01-637 5431. *Club:* Royal Automobile.

FOSTER, Peter; *see* Foster, J. P.

FOSTER, Maj.-Gen. Peter Beaufoy, MC 1944; Major-General Royal Artillery, British Army of the Rhine, 1973-76; retired June 1976; *b* 1 Sept. 1921; *s* of F. K. Foster, OBE, JP, Allt Dinas, Cheltenham; *m* 1947, Margaret Geraldine, *d* of W. F. Henn, sometime Chief Constable of Glos; two *s* one *d* (and one *s* decd). *Educ:* Uppingham School. Commnd RA, 1941; psc 1950; jssc 1958; OC Para. Light Battery, 1958-60; DAMS MS5, WO, 1960-63; Mil. Assistant to C-in-C BAOR, 1963-64; CO 34 Light Air Defence Regt RA, 1964-66; GSO1, ASD5, MoD, 1966-68; BRA Northern Comd, 1968-71;

Comdt Royal Sch. of Artillery, 1971-73. Col Comdt, RA, 1977-82. Chapter Clerk, Salisbury Cathedral, 1978-. *Recreations:* shooting, gardening. *Address:* Braybrooke House, 57 The Close, Salisbury, Wilts. *Club:* Naval and Military.

FOSTER, Hon. Sir Peter Harry Batson Woodroffe, Kt 1969; MBE 1943; TD 1946; **Hon. Mr Justice Foster;** a Judge of the Chancery Division of the High Court of Justice since 1969; *b* 5 Dec. 1912; *s* of late Frank Foster; *m* 1937, Jane Hillcoat Easdale, *d* of late James Easdale; one *s* three *d*. *Educ:* Rugby Sch.; Corpus Christi Coll., Cambridge (BA, LLB). Called to the Bar, Inner Temple, 1936; Bencher, Lincoln's Inn, 1963. Fife and Forfar Yeomanry, 1939; War of 1939-45: Dunkirk, 8th Armd Div., Alamein, 18 Army Gp, Tripoli, Col, 21 Army Group, North Western Europe (despatches thrice, MBE). Resumed practice, 1945; QC 1957. Mem., Gen. Council of the Bar, 1956-60; Mem., Senate, 1966-69, 1976-79. Chm., Chancery Bar Assoc., 1963-68; formerly Member Council: Officers' Assoc.; Royal Albert Hall; Steward British Boxing Board of Control. Church Commissioner for England, 1965-69. Reserve Chm., Conscientious Objectors Tribunal, 1965-69; Chm., Performing Right Tribunal, 1969. *Recreations:* golf, travelling. *Address:* 7 Cadogan House, 93 Sloane Street, SW1. *T:* 01-730 1984. *Clubs:* White's; Royal and Ancient Golf (St Andrews); Hawks (Cambridge).

FOSTER, Peter Martin, CMG 1975; HM Diplomatic Service, retired; Ambassador to German Democratic Republic, 1978-81; *b* 25 May 1924; *s* of Frederick Arthur Peace Foster and Marjorie Kathleen Sandford; *m* 1947, Angela Hope Cross; one *s* one *d*. *Educ:* Sherborne; Corpus Christi Coll., Cambridge. Army (Horse Guards), 1943-47; joined Foreign (now Diplomatic) Service, 1948; served in Vienna, Warsaw, Pretoria/Cape Town, Bonn, Kampala, Tel Aviv; Head of Central and Southern Africa Dept, FCO, 1972-74; Ambassador and UK Rep. to Council of Europe, 1974-78. *Address:* Rew Cottage, Abinger Lane, Abinger Common, Surrey. *T:* Dorking 730114.

FOSTER, Robert, CBE 1963 (OBE 1955; MBE 1949); FCIS; FIB; President, Savings Banks Institute, 1970-75; *b* 4 March 1898; *s* of Robert Foster; *m* 1927, Edith Kathleen (*née* Blackburn); two *d*. *Educ:* Rutherford Coll., Newcastle upon Tyne. RNVR, 1915-19. London Trustee Savings Banks, 1924-63 (Gen. Manager, 1943-63), retired. Mem. Nat. Savings Cttee, 1957-62. Dir, City & Metropolitan Building Soc. Mem. Court, Worshipful Company of Plumbers, 1959- (Master, 1965). *Recreations:* golf, gardening. *Address:* Larchfield, Highercombe Road, Haslemere, Surrey. *T:* Haslemere 4353. *Club:* City Livery.

FOSTER, Sir Robert (Sidney), GCMG 1970 (KCMG 1964; CMG 1961); KCVO 1970; Governor-General and Commander-in-Chief of Fiji, 1970-73 (Governor and C-in-C, 1968-70); retired 1973; *b* 11 Aug. 1913; *s* of late Sidney Charles Foster and late Jessie Edith (*née* Fry); *m* 1947, Margaret (*née* Walker); no *c*. *Educ:* Eastbourne Coll.; Peterhouse, Cambridge. Appointed Cadet, Administrative Service, Northern Rhodesia, 1936; District Officer, N Rhodesia, 1938. War Service, 2nd Bn Northern Rhodesia Regt, 1940-43, Major. Provincial Commissioner, N Rhodesia, 1957; Sec., Ministry of Native Affairs, N Rhodesia, 1960; Chief Sec., Nyasaland, 1961-63; Dep. Governor, Nyasaland, 1963-64; High Comr for W Pacific, 1964-68. Trustee: Beit Trust; Cambridge-Livingstone Trust. KStJ 1968. Officer of the Legion of Honour, 1966. *Recreation:* self-help. *Address:* Kenwood, 16 Ardnave Crescent, Southampton SO1 7FJ. *Clubs:* Royal Over-Seas League; Leander (Henley).

FOSTER-BROWN, Rear-Adm. Roy Stephenson, CB 1958; RN Retired; *b* 16 Jan. 1904; *s* of Robert Allen Brown and Agnes Wilfreda Stephenson; *m* 1933, Joan Wentworth Foster; two *s*. *Educ:* RNC, Osborne and Dartmouth. Specialised in Submarines, 1924-28; specialised in Signals, 1930. Fleet Signal Officer, Home Fleet, 1939-40; Staff Signal Officer, Western Approaches, 1940-44; Comdr HMS Ajax, 1944-46; Capt., 1946; Capt. Sixth Frigate Sqdn, 1951; Dir Signal Div., Admiralty, 1952-53; Capt. HMS Ceylon, 1954; Rear-Adm. 1955; Flag Officer, Gibraltar, 1956-59; retd 1959. Hon. Comdt, Girls Nautical Trng Corps, 1961-. Master, Armourers and Braziers Co., 1964-65, 1974-75. *Recreations:* sailing, shooting, golf, tennis. *Address:* Lee Farm House, Hurley, Berks. *Club:* Army and Navy.

FOSTER-SUTTON, Sir Stafford William Powell, KBE 1957 (OBE (mil.) 1945); Kt 1951; CMG 1948; QC (Jamaica, 1938, Fedn Malaya, 1948); *b* 24 Dec. 1898; *s* of late G. Foster Sutton and Mrs Foster Sutton; *m* 1919, Linda Dorothy, *d* of late John Humber Allwood, OBE, and of Mrs Allwood, Enfield, St Ann, Jamaica; one *d* (one *s* decd). *Educ:* St Mary Magdalen Sch.; private tutor. HM Army, 1914-26; served European War, 1914-18, Infantry, RFC and RAF, active service. Called to the Bar, Gray's Inn, 1926; private practice, 1926-36; Solicitor Gen., Jamaica, 1936; Attorney-Gen., Cyprus, 1940; Col Comdg Cyprus Volunteer Force and Inspector Cyprus Forces, 1941-44; Mem. for Law and Order and Attorney-Gen., Kenya, 1944-48; actg Governor, Aug. and Sept. 1947; Attorney-Gen., Malaya, 1948-50; Officer Administering Govt, Malaya, Sept., Dec. 1950; Chief Justice, Fedn of Malaya, 1950-51; Dir of Man-Power, Kenya, 1944-45; Chm. Labour Advisory Board, Kenya, and Kenya European Service Advisory Board, 1944-48; Pres. of the West African Court of Appeal, 1951-55; Chief Justice, Fedn of Nigeria, 1955-58; Actg Governor-Gen., Nigeria, May-June 1957. Pres., Pensions Appeal Tribunals for England and Wales, 1958-73. Chairman: Zanzibar Commn of Inquiry, 1961; Kenya Regional and Electorial Commns, 1962-; Referendum Observers,

Malta, 1964; Pres., Britain-Nigeria Assoc. Mem. Court, Tallow Chandlers' Co. (Master, 1981). *Address:* 7 London Road, Saffron Walden, Essex.

FOTHERGILL, Dorothy Joan; Director, Postal Pay and Grading, since 1974; *b* 31 Dec. 1923; *d* of Samuel John Rimington Fothergill and Dorothy May Patterson. *Educ:* Haberdashers' Aske's Sch., Acton; University Coll. London. BA (Hons) History. Entered Civil Service as Asst Principal, 1948; Principal, Overseas Mails branch, GPO, 1953; UPU Congress, Ottawa, 1957; Establishments work, 1958-62; HM Treasury, 1963-65; Asst Sec., Pay and Organisation, GPO, 1965; Director: Postal Personnel, 1970; London Postal Region, 1971. *Recreations:* gardening, walking, theatre. *Address:* 38 Andrewes House, Barbican, EC2Y 8AX.

FOTHERGILL, Richard Humphrey Maclean; Director, Microelectronics Education Programme, Department of Education and Science, since 1980; *b* 21 March 1937; *s* of late Col C. G. Fothergill, RM, and of Mrs E. G. Fothergill; *m* 1962, Angela Cheshire Martin; three *d*. *Educ:* Sandle Manor, Fordingbridge; Clifton Coll., Bristol; Emmanuel Coll., Cambridge (BA Hons Nat. Sci. Tripos, 1958). Commnd RASC, National Service, 1959-61. Contemporary Films Ltd, 1961; Head of Biology, SW Ham Technical Sch., 1961-69; Res. Fellow, Nat. Council for Educnl Technol., 1970-72; Founder and Head of PETRAS (Educnl Develt Unit), Newcastle upon Tyne Polytechnic, 1972-80. Co-founder, Sec. and Treasurer, Standing Conf. on Educnl Develt Services in Polytechnics, 1974-80; Member: London GCE Bd and Schools Council Science Cttee, 1968-72; Standards and Specifications Cttee, CET, 1972-80. *Publications:* A Challenge for Librarians, 1971; Resource Centres in Colleges of Education, 1973; (with B. Williams) Microforms in Education, 1977; Child Abuse: a teaching package, 1978; (with I. Butchart) Non-book Materials in Libraries: a practical guide, 1978, 2nd edn 1982; articles in Visual Educn, Educn Libraries Bull., Educnl Media Internat., and Educnl Broadcasting Internat. *Recreations:* reading, television, films, walking. *Address:* 17 Grenville Drive, Brunton Park, Newcastle upon Tyne NE3 5PA. *T:* Newcastle 363380. *Club:* National Film Theatre.

FOU TS'ONG; concert pianist; *b* 10 March 1934; *m* 1st, 1960, Zamira Menuhin (marr. diss. 1970); one *s*; 2nd, 1973, Hijong Hyun. *Educ:* Shanghai and Warsaw. Debut, Shanghai, 1953. Concerts all over Eastern Europe including USSR up to 1958. Arrived in Great Britain, Dec. 1958; London debut, Feb. 1959, followed by concerts in England, Scotland and Ireland; subsequently has toured all five Continents. *Recreations:* many different ones. *Address:* c/o Margaret Pacy, 58 Stanthorpe Road, SW16 2DY. *T:* 01-769 6953, 01-769 1155.

FOULDS, Hugh Jon; Director, since 1976, and Group General Manager, Finance for Industry Ltd; *b* 2 May 1932; *s* of Dr E. J. Foulds and Helen Shirley (*née* Smith); *m* 1st, 1960, Berry Cusack-Smith (marr. diss. 1970); two *s*; 2nd, 1977, Hélène Senn, *d* of Edouard Senn, Paris. *Educ:* Bootham Sch., York. Joined Industrial & Commercial Finance Corp. Ltd, 1959, Dir 1974; Director: Finance Corp. for Industry Ltd, 1975-; Finance for Shipping Ltd, 1977-; Technical Development Capital Ltd, 1977-; Estate Duties Investment Trust, 1979-; Dep. Chm., H. Brammer & Co. Ltd, 1980-. Mem. Council, Bedford Coll., 1981. *Recreations:* tennis, ski-ing, pictures, occasionally gardening. *Address:* 72 Loudoun Road, St John's Wood, NW8 0NA. *T:* 01-722 4464. *Clubs:* Garrick, Hurlingham.

FOULGER, Keith, BSc(Eng); CEng, MIMechE; FRINA, RCNC; Deputy Director, Submarines, Ship Department, Ministry of Defence, since 1981; *b* 14 May 1925; *s* of Percy and Kate Foulger; *m* 1951, Joyce Mary Hart; one *s* one *d*. *Educ:* Southgate County Sch., London; Univ. of London (Mech. Eng.); Royal Naval Coll., Greenwich. Asst Constructor, 1950; Constructor, 1955; Constructor Commander: Dreadnought Project, 1959; C-in-C Western Fleet, 1965; Chief Constructor, 1967; Asst Director, Submarines, 1973; Deputy Director: Naval Construction, 1979; Naval Ship Production, 1979-81. *Recreations:* travel, cars, gardening. *Address:* Wyndles, Entry Hill Drive, Bath, Avon BA2 5NL. *Club:* Civil Service.

FOULIS, Sir Ian P. L.; *see* Liston-Foulis.

FOULKES, George, JP; MP (Lab Co-op) South Ayrshire, since 1979; *b* 21 Jan. 1942; *s* of George and Jessie M. A. W. Foulkes; *m* 1970, Elizabeth Anna Hope; two *s* one *d*. *Educ:* Keith Grammar Sch., Keith, Banffshire; Haberdashers' Aske's Sch.; Edinburgh Univ. (BSc 1964). President: Edinburgh Univ. SRC, 1963-64; Scottish Union of Students, 1965-67; Manager, Fund for Internat. Student Cooperation, 1967-68. Scottish Organiser, European Movement, 1968-69; Director: European League for Econ. Cooperation, 1969-70; Enterprise Youth, 1970-73; Age Concern, Scotland, 1973-79. Councillor: Edinburgh Corp., 1970-75; Lothian Regional Council, 1974-79; Chairman: Lothian Region Educn Cttee, 1974-79; Educn Cttee, Convention of Scottish Local Authorities, 1975-78. Sec./Treas., All Party Pensioners Cttee, 1979-; Mem., H of C Select Cttee on Foreign Affairs, 1981-. UK Delegate to Parly Assembly of Council of Europe, 1979-81. Mem., Scottish Exec. Cttee, Labour Party, 1981-. Rector's Assessor, Edinburgh Univ. Court, 1968-70, Local Authority Assessor, 1971-79. Chm., Scottish Adult Literacy Agency, 1976-79. Dir, St Cuthbert's Co-op. Assoc., 1975-79. JP Edinburgh, 1975. *Publication:* Eighty Years On: history of Edinburgh University SRC, 1964. *Recreations:* boating, fishing. *Address:* 31 Monument Road, Ayr. *T:* Ayr 265776. *Clubs:* Traverse Theatre, Edinburgh University Staff (Edinburgh).

FOULKES, Sir Nigel (Gordon), Kt 1980; Chairman, Equity Capital for Industry, 1983 (Deputy Chairman, 1982); Director: Charterhouse Group Ltd, since 1972; Bekaert Group (Belgium), since 1973; *b* 29 Aug. 1919; *s* of Louis Augustine and Winifred Foulkes; *m* 1948, Elisabeth Walker, *d* of Ewart B. Walker, Toronto; one *s* one *d* of former marr. *Educ:* Gresham's Sch., Holt; Balliol Coll., Oxford (Schol., MA). RAF, 1940-45. Subsequently executive, consulting and boardroom posts with: H. P. Bulmer; P. E. Consulting Gp; Birfield; Greaves & Thomas; International Nickel; Rank Xerox (Asst Man. Dir 1964-67, Man. Dir 1967-70); Chairman: British Airports Authority, 1972-77; Civil Aviation Authority, 1977-82; Ct, Brunel Univ. CBIM; FRSA. *Address:* ECI Ltd, Leith House, 47/57 Gresham Street, EC2V 7EH. *Club:* Royal Air Force.

FOULKES, Maj.-Gen. Thomas Herbert Fischer, CB 1962; OBE 1945; *b* 29 May 1908; *e s* of late Maj.-Gen. C. H. Foulkes, CB, CMG, DSO; *m* 1947, Delphine Elizabeth Smith; two *s. Educ:* Clifton Coll., Bristol (Pres., Old Cliftonian Soc., 1963-65); RMA Woolwich; St Catharine's Coll., Cambridge. BA 1930, MA Cantab 1954. Commissioned into RE, 1928; served in India and Burma, 1931-46 (CRE 39 Indian Div., also CRE 17 Indian Div. during Burma campaign); Comdr Corps RE (Brig.) 1 Br. Corps in BAOR, 1956-57; Chief Engr (Brig.) Middle East, 1957-58; Chief Engr (Brig.) Southern Command, UK, 1958-60; Engineer-in-Chief (Maj.-Gen.), War Office, 1960-63. Col Comdt, Royal Engineers, 1963-73. Hon. Col, RE Resources Units, AER, 1964-67; Hon. Col, RE Volunteers (Sponsored Units), T&AVR, 1967-72. Governor: Clifton Coll., 1964; Handcross Park Sch., 1968-. Pres., Aldershot and N Hants Cons. Assoc., 1978-. Liveryman, Worshipful Co. of Plumbers of City of London, 1960, Master, 1973. Pres., Instn of Royal Engrs, 1965-70; CEng, FICE. *Recreations:* shooting, travel, fishing, photography. *Address:* The Warren, Fitzroy Road, Fleet, Hants GU13 8JW. *T:* Fleet (Hants) 6650. *Club:* Army and Navy.

FOURCADE, Jean-Pierre; Officier de l'ordre national du Mérite; Senator, French Republic, from Hauts-de-Seine, since 1977; *b* 18 Oct. 1929; *s* of Raymond Fourcade (Médecin) and Mme Fourcade (*née* Germaine Raynal); *m* 1958, Odile Mion; one *s* two *d. Educ:* Collège de Sorèze; Faculté de droit de Bordeaux; Institut d'études politiques de Bordeaux (Dip.); Ecole nationale d'administration; higher studies in Law (Dip.). Inspecteur des Finances, 1954. Cabinet of M. Valéry Giscard d'Estaing: Chargé de Mission, 1959-61; Conseiller technique, 1962, then Dir Adjoint to chef de service, Inspection gén. des Finances, 1962; Chef de service du commerce, at Direction-Gén. du Commerce intérieur et des Prix, 1968-70; Dir-gén. adjoint du Crédit industriel et commercial, 1970; Dir-gén., 1972, and Administrateur Dir-gén., 1973; Ministre de l'Economie et des Finances, 1974-76; Ministre de l'Equipement et de l'Aménagement du Territoire, 1976-77. Mayor of Saint-Cloud, 1971-; Conseiller général of canton of Saint-Cloud, 1973-; Conseiller régional d'Ile de France, 1976- (Vice-Président, 1982). Pres., Clubs Perspective et Realités, 1975-. Vice-Pres., Union pour la Démocratie Française, 1978-. *Address:* 8 Parc de Béarn, 92210 Saint-Cloud, France.

FOURNIER, Jean, CD 1972; Director: The Royal Trust Company, since 1979; The Royal Trust Company Mortgage Corporation, since 1981; Chairman, Board of Canadian Human Rights Foundation, since 1982; Commissioner of the Metric Commission, Canada, since 1981; *b* Montreal, 18 July 1914; *s* of Arthur Fournier and Emilie Roy; *m* 1942, May Coote; five *s. Educ:* High Sch. of Québec; Laval Univ. (BA 1935, LLB 1938). Admitted to Bar of Province of Quebec, 1939. Royal Canadian Artillery (NPAM) (Lieut), 1935; Canadian Active Service Force Sept. 1939; served in Canada and overseas; discharged 1944, Actg Lt-Col. Joined Canadian Foreign Service, 1944; Third Sec., Canadian Dept of External Affairs, 1944; Second Sec., Canadian Embassy, Buenos Aires, 1945; Nat. Defence Coll., Kingston, 1948 (ndc); Seconded: to Privy Council Office, 1948-50; to Prime Minister's Office, Oct. 1950-Feb. 1951; First Sec., Canadian Embassy, Paris, 1951; Counsellor, 1953; Consul Gen., Boston, 1954; Privy Council Office (Asst Sec. to Cabinet), 1957-61; Head of European Division (Political Affairs), Dept of External Affairs, 1961-64; Chm., Quebec Civil Service Commn, 1964-71; Agent Gen. for the Province of Quebec in London, 1971-78. Pres., Inst. of Public Administration of Canada, 1966-67; Member: Canadian Inst. of Strategic Studies; Canadian Inst. of Internat. Affairs. Freedom, City of London, 1976. Pres., Canadian Veterans Assoc. of the UK, 1976-77. *Address:* 201 Metcalfe Avenue, Apt 903, Westmount, Québec, Canada H3Z 2H7. *T:* 932-8633. *Clubs:* Oriental, Canada; Quebec Garrison.

FOURNIER, Pierre; 'cellist; Officier Légion d'Honneur; *b* 24 June 1906; *m* 1980, Junko Taguchi; one *s* by former *m. Educ:* University and Conservatoire, Paris. Formerly teacher at the National Conservatoire, Paris. Concert soloist every season in the European Capitals as well as in USA, South America and Far East; also soloist playing with chief orchestras. Commander, Ordre national du Mérite (France); Commander, Ordre Léopold II (Belgium); Officer, Arts and Letters (Paris); Chevalier with Crown (Luxembourg). *Address:* 14 Parc Château Banquet, Geneva, Switzerland.

FOUYAS, Archbishop Methodios; Archbishop of Thyateira and Great Britain; Greek Orthodox Archbishop of Great Britain, since 1979; *b* 14 Sept. 1925. BD (Athens); PhD (Manchester), 1965. Vicar of Greek Church in Munich, 1951-54; Secretary-General, Greek Patriarchate of Alexandria, 1954-56; Vicar of Greek Church in Manchester, 1960-66; Secretary, Holy Synod of Church of Greece, 1966-68; Archbishop of Aksum (Ethiopia), 1968-79. Member, Academy of Religious Sciences, Brussels, 1974-. Estabd Foundn for

Hellenism in GB; Editor, Texts and Studies: a review of the Foundn for Hellenism in GB; Founder-Editor, Abba Salama Review of Ethio-Hellenic Studies, 10 Volumes; Editor: Ekklesiastikos Pharos (Prize of Academy of Athens), 11 Volumes; Ecclesia et Theologia, vols 11, 13, 1982. Hon. DD Edinburgh, 1970. Grand Cordon: Order of Phoenix (Greece); of Sellassie (Ethiopia). *Publications:* Orthodoxy, Roman Catholicism and Anglicanism, 1972; The Person of Jesus Christ in the Decisions of the Ecumenical Councils, 1976; History of the Church in Corinth, 1968; Christianity and Judaism in Ethiopia, Nubia and Meroe, 1st Vol., 1979; contrib. to Theological and Historical Studies Vol. 1, and many other books and treatises. *Recreation:* gardening. *Address:* Thyateira House, 5 Craven Hill, W2. *T:* 01-723 4787.

FOWDEN, Sir Leslie, Kt 1982; FRS 1964; Director, Rothamsted Experimental Station, since 1973; *b* Rochdale, Lancs, 13 Oct. 1925; *s* of Herbert and Amy D. Fowden; *m* 1949, Margaret Oakes; one *s* one *d. Educ:* University Coll., London. PhD Univ. of London, 1948. Scientific Staff of Human Nutrition Research Unit of the MRC, 1947-50; Lecturer in Plant Chemistry, University Coll. London, 1950-55, Reader, 1956-64, Prof. of Plant Chemistry, 1964-73; Dean of Faculty of Science, UCL, 1970-73. Rockefeller Fellow at Cornell Univ., 1955; Visiting Prof. at Univ. of California, 1963; Royal Society Visiting Prof., Univ. of Hong Kong, 1967. Member: Advisory Board, Tropical Product Inst., 1966-70; Council, Royal Society, 1970-72. Consultant Dir, Commonwealth Bureau of Soils, 1973-; Mem., Scientific Adv. Panel, Royal Botanic Gardens, 1977-. Foreign Member: Deutsche Akademie der Naturforscher Leopoldina, 1971; Lenin All-Union Acad. of Agricultural Sciences of USSR, 1978; Corresponding Mem., Amer. Soc. Plant Physiologists, 1981. *Publications:* contribs to scientific journals on topics in plant biochemistry. *Address:* 1 West Common, Harpenden, Herts AL5 2JQ. *T:* Harpenden 64628.

FOWELLS, Joseph Dunthorne Briggs, CMG 1975; DSC 1940; Deputy Director General, British Council, 1976-77, retired; *b* 17 Feb. 1916; *s* of late Joseph Fowells and Maud Dunthorne, Middlesbrough; *m* 1st, 1940, Edith Agnes McKerracher (marr. diss. 1966); two *s* one *d*; 2nd, 1969, Thelma Howes (*d* 1974). *Educ:* Sedbergh Sch.; Clare Coll., Cambridge (MA). School teaching, 1938; service with Royal Navy (Lt-Comdr), 1939-46; Blackie & Son Ltd, Educnl Publishers, 1946; British Council, 1947: Argentina, 1954; Representative Sierra Leone, 1956; Scotland, 1957; Dir Latin America and Africa (Foreign) Dept, 1958; Controller Overseas B Division (foreign countries excluding Europe), 1966; Controller Planning, 1968; Controller European Div., 1970; Asst Dir Gen. (Functional), 1972; Asst Dir Gen. (Regional), 1973-76. *Recreations:* golf, sailing. *Address:* 5/57 Palmeira Avenue, Hove, East Sussex. *T:* Brighton 70349.

FOWKE, Sir Frederick (Woollaston Rawdon), 4th Bt *cr* 1814; *b* 14 Dec. 1910; *e s* of Sir Frederick Ferrers Conant Fowke, 3rd Bt, and Edith Frances Daubeney (*d* 1958), *d* of late Canon J. H. Rawdon; *S* father, 1948; *m* 1948, Barbara, *d* of late E. Townsend; two *d. Educ:* Uppingham. Served War of 1939-45, in Derbs Yeomanry, 1939-43 (wounded). *Recreation:* shooting. *Heir:* n David Frederick Gustavus Fowke, *b* 28 Aug. 1950. *Address:* Lower Woolstone Farm, Bishops Tawton, Barnstaple, N Devon.

FOWLER, Prof. Alastair David Shaw, FBA 1974; Regius Professor of Rhetoric and English Literature, University of Edinburgh, since 1972; *b* 17 Aug. 1930; *s* of David Fowler and Maggie Shaw; *m* 1950, Jenny Catherine Simpson; one *s* one *d. Educ:* Queen's Park Sch., Glasgow; Univ. of Glasgow; Univ. of Edinburgh; Pembroke Coll., Oxford. MA Edin. 1952 and Oxon 1955; DPhil Oxon 1957; DLitt Oxon 1972. Junior Res. Fellow, Queen's Coll., Oxford, 1955-59; Instructor, Indiana Univ., 1957; Lectr, UC Swansea, 1959; Fellow and Tutor in English Lit., Brasenose Coll., Oxford, 1962-71; Visiting Professor: Columbia Univ., 1964; Univ. of Virginia, 1969, 1979; Mem. Inst. for Advanced Study, Princeton, 1966, 1980; Visiting Fellow: Council of the Humanities, Princeton Univ., 1974; Humanities Research Centre, Canberra, 1980. Mem., Scottish Arts Council, 1976-77. Adv. Editor, New Literary History, 1972-; Gen. Editor, Longman Annotated Anthologies of English Verse, 1977-; Mem. Editorial Bd, English Literary Renaissance, 1978-. *Publications:* (trans. and ed) Richard Wills, De re poetica, 1958; Spenser and the Numbers of Time, 1964; (ed) C. S. Lewis, Spenser's Images of Life, 1967; (ed with John Carey) The Poems of John Milton, 1968; Triumphal Forms, 1970; (ed) Silent Poetry, 1970; (ed with Christopher Butler) Topics in Criticism, 1971; Seventeen, 1971; Conceitful Thought, 1975; Catacomb Suburb, 1976; Edmund Spenser, 1977; From the Domain of Arnheim, 1982; contribs to jls and books. *Address:* Department of English, David Hume Tower, George Square, Edinburgh EH8 9JX.

FOWLER, Christopher B.; *see* Brocklebank-Fowler.

FOWLER, Dennis Houston, OBE 1979 (MBE 1963); HM Diplomatic Service; Counsellor and Head of Claims Department, Foreign and Commonwealth Office, since 1980; *b* 15 March 1924; *s* of Joseph Fowler and Daisy Lilian Wraith Fowler (*née* Houston); *m* 1944, Lilias Wright Nairn Burnett; two *s* one *d. Educ:* Alleyn's Sch., Dulwich. Colonial Office, 1940; RAF, 1942-46; India Office (subseq. CRO), 1947; Colombo, 1951; Second Secretary, Karachi, 1955; CRO, 1959; First Secretary, Dar es Salaam, 1961; Diplomatic Service Administration (subseq. FCO), 1965; First Sec. and Head of Chancery, Reykjavik, 1969; FCO, 1973; First Sec., Head of Chancery and Consul, Kathmandu, 1977. *Recreations:* golf, music, do-it-yourself. *Address:* c/o Foreign and Commonwealth Office, SW1; 25 Dartnell Park Road, West

Byfleet, Surrey KT14 6PN. *T:* Byfleet 41583. *Clubs:* West Byfleet Golf; Royal Nepal Golf (Kathmandu).

FOWLER, Derek, CBE 1979; a Vice-Chairman, since 1981, and Member for Finance and Planning, since 1978, British Railways Board (Finance Member, 1975-78); Chairman, British Transport Advertising Ltd, since 1981; *b* 26 Feb. 1929; *s* of late George Edward Fowler and of Kathleen Fowler; *m* 1953, Ruth Fox; one *d*. *Educ:* Grantham, Lincs. Financial appointments with: Grantham Borough Council, 1944-50; Spalding UDC, 1950-52; Nairobi City Council, 1952-62; Southend-on-Sea CBC, 1962-64. British Railways Board: Internal Audit Manager, 1964-67, and Management Acct, 1967-69, W Region; Sen. Finance Officer, 1969-71; Corporate Budgets Manager, 1971-73; Controller of Corporate Finance, 1973-75. FCCA; IPFA (Mem. Council, 1974-); JDipMA; FCIT (Mem. Council, 1980-); CBIM. *Recreation:* cartophily. *Address:* 30 Sutton Avenue, Slough, Berks SL3 7AW. *T:* Slough 34200. *Club:* City Livery.

FOWLER, Sir (Edward) Michael (Coulson), Kt 1981; FNZIA; Mayor of Wellington, New Zealand, since 1974; Partner, Calder Fowler Styles and Turner, since 1960; *b* 19 Dec. 1929; *s* of William Coulson Fowler and Faith Agnes Netherclift; *m* 1953, Barbara Hamilton Hall; two *s* one *d*. *Educ:* Christ's Coll., Christchurch, NZ; Auckland Univ. (MArch). ARIBA 1953; FNZIA 1970. Architect, London office, Ove Arup & Partners, 1954-56; own practice, Wellington, 1957-59. Wellington City Councillor, 1968-74. *Publications:* Wellington Sketches: Folio I, 1971, Folio II, 1974; Country Houses of New Zealand, 1972, 2nd edn 1977; Eating Houses in Wellington, 1980; Wellington Wellington, 1981. *Recreations:* sketching, reading, writing, history, politics. *Address:* 31 Hobson Crescent, Thorndon, Wellington, New Zealand. *T:* Wellington 721.117. *Club:* Wellington (Wellington, NZ).

FOWLER, Prof. Gerald Teasdale; Director, North East London Polytechnic, since 1982; *b* 1 Jan. 1935; *s* of James A. Fowler, Long Buckby, Northants, and Alfreda (*née* Teasdale); *m* 1982, Lorna, *d* of William Lloyd, Preston. *Educ:* Northampton Grammar Sch.; Lincoln Coll., Oxford; University of Frankfurt-am-Main. Craven Fellowship, Oxford Univ., 1957-59; part-time Lectr, Pembroke Coll., Oxford, 1958-59; Lectr, Hertford and Lincoln Colls, Oxford, 1959-65; Lectr, Univ. of Lancaster, 1965-66; Asst Dir, The Polytechnic, Huddersfield, 1970-72; Prof. of Educnl Studies, Open Univ., 1972-74; Prof. Associate, Dept of Government, Brunel Univ., 1977-80; Dep. Dir, Preston Polytechnic, 1980-81. Vis. Prof., Dept of Admin, Strathclyde Univ., 1970-74. Oxford City Councillor, 1960-64; Councillor, The Wrekin DC, 1973-76, Leader, 1973-74; Councillor, Shropshire CC, 1979-. Contested (Lab) Banbury, 1964; MP (Lab) The Wrekin, 1966-70, Feb. 1974-1979; Jt Parly Sec., Min. of Technology, 1967-69; Minister of State: Dept of Educn and Science, Oct. 1969-June 1970, March-Oct. 1974 and Jan.-Sept. 1976; Privy Council Office, 1974-76. President: Assoc. for Teaching of Social Science, 1976-79; Assoc. for Recurrent Educn, 1976-78, 1981-82; Assoc. for Liberal Educn, 1977-79; Chm., Youthaid, 1977-80; Vice Chm., Nat. Parly Youth Lobby, 1978-79. Trustee, Community Projects Foundn, 1978-80. Pres., Comparative Educn in European Soc. (British Section), 1980. Pres., Assoc. of Business Executives, 1979-81. *Address:* North East London Polytechnic, Romford Road, Stratford, E15 4LZ. *T:* 01-590 7722.

FOWLER, Henry Hamill; investment banker; Chairman, Goldman Sachs International Corporation, New York, since 1969; *b* 5 Sept. 1908; *s* of Mack Johnson Fowler and Bertha Browning Fowler; *m* 1938, Trudye Pamela Hathcote; two *d* (one *s* decd). *Educ:* Roanoke Coll., Salem, Va; Yale Law Sch. Counsel, Tennessee Valley Authority, 1934-38, Asst Gen. Counsel, 1939; Special Asst to Attorney-Gen. as Chief Counsel to Sub-Cttee, Senate Cttee, Educn and Labor, 1939-40; Special Counsel, Fed. Power Commn, 1941; Asst Gen. Counsel, Office of Production Management, 1941, War Production Board, 1942-44; Econ. Adviser, US Mission Econ. Affairs, London, 1944; Special Asst to Administrator, For. Econ. Administration, 1945; Dep. Administrator, National Production Authority, 1951, Administrator, 1952; Administrator, Defense Prodn Administration, 1952-53; Dir Office of Defense Mobilization, Mem. Nat. Security Coun., 1952-53; Under-Sec. of the Treasury, 1961-64; Secretary of the US Treasury, 1965-68. Sen. Mem. of Fowler, Leva, Hawes & Symington, Washington, 1946-51, 1953-61, 1964-65. Chairman: Roanoke Coll.; US Adv. Cttee on Reform of Internat. Monetary System, 1973-; Director: Corning Glass Works; US Industries Inc.; US and Foreign Securities Corp.; Atlantic Inst.; Atlantic Council of the US; Foreign Policy Assoc. Trustee: Alfred P. Sloan Foundn; Inst. of Internat. Educn; Lyndon B. Johnson Foundn. Hon. Degrees: Roanoke Coll., 1961; Wesleyan Univ., 1966; Univ. of William and Mary, 1966. *Recreation:* tennis. *Address:* 55 Broad Street, New York, NY, USA. *Clubs:* Links, Recess, River (NYC); Metropolitan (Washington).

FOWLER, Ian; Principal Chief Clerk and Clerk to the Committee of Magistrates for the Inner London area, since 1979; *b* 20 Sept. 1932; *s* of Norman William Frederick Fowler, OBE, QPM, and late Alice May (*née* Wakelin); *m* 1961, Gillian Cecily Allchin; two *s* one *d*. *Educ:* Maidstone Grammar Sch.; Skinners Sch., Tunbridge Wells; King's Sch., Canterbury; St Edmund Hall, Oxford (MA). National Service, commnd 2nd Bn The Green Howards, 1951-53. Called to Bar, Gray's Inn, 1957; entered Inner London Magistrates Courts Service, 1959. Councillor: Herne Bay UDC and Canterbury CC, 1961- (Mayor, 1976-77). *Address:* 3rd Floor, North West Wing, Bush House, Aldwych, WC2B 4PJ. *T:* 01-836 9331; 6 Dence Park, Herne Bay, Kent.

FOWLER, John Francis, DSc, PhD; FInstP; Director of Cancer Research Campaign's Gray Laboratory, at Mount Vernon Hospital, Northwood, since 1970; *b* 3 Feb. 1925; *er s* of Norman V. Fowler, Bridport, Dorset; *m* 1953, Kathleen Hardcastle Sutton, MB, BS; two *s* five *d*. *Educ:* Bridport Grammar Sch.; University Coll. of the South-West, Exeter. BSc 1st class Hons (London) 1944; MSc (London) 1946; PhD (London) 1955; DSc (London) 1974; FInstP 1957. Research Physicist: Newalls Insulation Co. Ltd, 1944; Metropolitan Vickers Electrical Co. Ltd, 1947; Newcastle upon Tyne Regional Hosp. Board (Radiotherapy service), 1950; Principal Physicist at King's Coll. Hosp., SE5, 1956; Head of Physics Section in Medical Research Council Radiotherapeutic Res. Unit, Hammersmith Hosp., 1959 (later the Cyclotron Unit); Reader in Physics, London Univ. at Med. Coll. of St Bartholomew's Hosp., 1962; Prof. of Med. Physics, Royal Postgraduate Med. Sch., London Univ., Hammersmith Hosp., 1963-70, Vice-Dean, 1967-70. Vis. Prof. in Oncology, Mddx Hosp. Med. Sch. President: Hosp. Physicists Assoc., 1966-67; Europ. Soc. Radiat. Biol., 1974-76; British Inst. Radiol., 1977-78. Roentgen Award of the British Inst. of Radiology, 1965; Röntgen Plakette, Deutsches Röntgen Museum, 1978. Hon. MD. *Publications:* contributor: Current Topics in Radiation Research, 1966; Radiation Dosimetry, 1967; Cancer: a comprehensive treatise, 1977; papers on radiation dosimetry, radio-biology, radioisotopes, in Brit. Jl Radiology, Brit. Jl Cancer, Physics in Medicine and Biology, Radiology, etc. *Recreations:* theatre; getting into the countryside. *Address:* Gray Laboratory, Mount Vernon Hospital, Northwood, Mddx. *T:* Northwood 28611.

FOWLER, Sir Michael; *see* Fowler, Sir E. M. C.

FOWLER, Rt. Hon. Norman; *see* Fowler, Rt Hon. P. N.

FOWLER, Peter Howard, FRS 1964; DSc; Royal Society Research Professor, Physics Department, University of Bristol, since 1964; *b* 27 Feb. 1923; *s* of Sir Ralph Howard Fowler, FRS, and Eileen, *o c* of 1st and last Baron Rutherford; *m* 1949, Rosemary Hempson (*née* Brown); three *d*. *Educ:* Winchester Coll.; Bristol Univ. BSc 1948, DSc 1958. Flying Officer in RAF, 1942-46 as a Radar Technical Officer. Asst Lectr in Physics, 1948, Lectr, 1951, Reader, 1961, Bristol Univ. Visiting Prof., Univ. of Minnesota, 1956-57. Hughes Medal, Royal Soc., 1974. *Publication:* (with Prof. C. F. Powell and Dr D. H. Perkins) The Study of Elementary Particles by the Photographic Method, 1959. *Recreations:* gardening, meteorology. *Address:* 320 Canford Lane, Westbury on Trym, Bristol.

FOWLER, Peter James; HM Diplomatic Service; Counsellor, Bonn, since 1981; *b* 26 Aug. 1936; *s* of James and Gladys Fowler; *m* 1962, Audrey June Smith; one *s* three *d*. *Educ:* Nunthorpe Grammar Sch., York; Trinity Coll., Oxford (BA). FCO, 1962-64; Budapest, 1964; Lisbon, 1965-68; Calcutta, 1968-72; FCO, 1972-75; East Berlin, 1975-78; Counsellor, Cabinet Office, 1978-80; Comprehensive Test Ban Delegn, Geneva, 1980. *Recreations:* reading, opera. *Address:* c/o Foreign and Commonwealth Office, King Charles Street, SW1.

FOWLER, Peter Jon, PhD; Secretary, Royal Commission on Historical Monuments (England), since 1979; *b* 14 June 1936; *s* of W. J. Fowler and P. A. Fowler; *m* 1959, Elizabeth (*née* Burley); three *d*. *Educ:* King Edward VI Grammar Sch., Morpeth, Northumberland; Lincoln Coll., Oxford (MA 1961); Univ. of Bristol (PhD 1977). Investigator on staff of RCHM (England), Salisbury office, 1959-65; Staff Tutor in Archaeology, Dept of Extra-Mural Studies, 1965-79, and Reader in Arch., 1972-79, Univ. of Bristol. Mem., Ancient Monuments Bd, 1979-; Pres., Council for British Archaeol., 1981- (Vice-Pres., 1979-81). *Publications:* Regional Archaeologies: Wessex, 1967; (ed) Archaeology and the Landscape, 1972; (ed) Recent Work in Rural Archaeology, 1975; (ed with K. Branigan) The Roman West Country, 1976; Approaches to Archaeology, 1977; (ed with H. C. Bowen) Early Land Allotment in the British Isles, 1978; (with S. Piggott and M. L. Ryder) Agrarian History of England and Wales, I i, 1981; contrib. to Antiquity, and Antiquaries Jl. *Recreations:* reading, writing, sport (esp. cricket). *Address:* Fortress House, 23 Savile Row, W1X 1AB. *T:* 01-734 6010.

FOWLER, Rt. Hon. (Peter) Norman, PC 1979; MP (C) Sutton Coldfield, since Feb. 1974 (Nottingham South, 1970-74); Secretary of State for Social Services, since 1981; *b* 2 Feb. 1938; *s* of late N. F. Fowler and Katherine Fowler; *m* 1979, Fiona Poole, *d* of John Donald; one *d*. *Educ:* King Edward VI Sch., Chelmsford; Trinity Hall, Cambridge (MA). Nat. Service commn, Essex Regt, 1956-58; Cambridge, 1958-61; Chm., Cambridge Univ. Conservative Assoc., 1960. Joined staff of The Times, 1961; Special Corresp., 1962-66; Home Affairs Corresp., 1966-70; reported Middle East War, 1967. Mem. Council, Bow Group, 1967-69; Editorial Board, Crossbow, 1962-69; Vice-Chm., North Kensington Cons. Assoc., 1967-68; Chm., E Midlands Area, Cons. Political Centre, 1970-73. Mem., Parly Select Cttee on Race Relations and Immigration, 1970-74; Jt Sec., Cons. Parly Home Affairs Cttee, 1971-72, 1974 (Vice-Chm., 1974); Chief Opposition spokesman: Social Services, 1975-76; Transport, 1976-79; Opposition spokesman, Home Affairs, 1974-75; PPS, NI Office, 1972-74; Sec. of State for Transport, 1981 (Minister of Transport, 1979-81). *Publications:* After the Riots: the police in Europe, 1979; political pamphlets including: The Cost of Crime, 1973; The Right Track, 1977. *Recreation:* travel. *Address:* House of Commons, SW1A 0AA.

FOWLER, Robert Asa; Vice President for International Marketing, Conoco Inc.; *b* 5 Aug. 1928; *s* of Mr and Mrs William Henry Fowler; *m* 1951, Grace Ohmer Grasselli; three *s* one *d*. *Educ*: Princeton Univ. (BA Econs); Harvard Business Sch. (MBA). Lieut USNR, 1950-53. Various appts with Continental Oil, 1955-75; Area Manager, Northwest Europe, Continental Oil Co., 1975-78; Chm. and Man. Dir, Conoco Ltd, 1979-81. *Recreations:* tennis, skiing. *Address:* 154 Glynn Way, Houston, Texas 77056, USA. *T:* 713-965 1523. *Clubs:* Hurlingham; River, Knickerbocker (NY); Allegheny Country (Pa); Chagrin Valley Hunt (Ohio).

FOWLER, Sir Robert (William Doughty), KCMG 1966 (CMG 1962); HM Diplomatic Service, retired; *b* 6 March 1914; *s* of William and Martha Louise Fowler; *m* Margaret MacFarquhar (*née* MacLeod); one *s* one *d* (twins). *Educ:* Queen Elizabeth's Grammar Sch., Mansfield; Emmanuel Coll., Cambridge. Burma CS, 1937-48; Burma Army (Military Administration), 1944-46; Additional Sec. to Governor of Burma, 1947; Commonwealth Relations Office from 1948; seconded to Foreign Service for UK Delegn to UN, 1950-53; Fedn of Rhodesia and Nyasaland and High Commn Territories Dept, CRO, 1954-56; Dep. High Comr: Pakistan, 1956-58; Canada, 1960-62; Nigeria, 1963-64. Attended IDC, 1959. British High Comr to Tanzania, Aug. 1964, until diplomatic relations broken off in Dec. 1965; Ambassador to Sudan from 1966 until break in relations in 1967; reappointed Ambassador, 1968-70 (during the break, Administrator of Gibraltar Referendum and Under-Sec. of State, Commonwealth Office). *Recreations:* gardening, painting, photography. *Address:* 7 Leicester Close, Henley-on-Thames, Oxon. *T:* Henley 2404. *Clubs:* Royal Commonwealth Society; Leander (Henley).

FOWLER, Ronald Frederick, CBE 1950; *b* 21 April 1910; *e s* of late Charles Frederick Fowler; *m* 1937, Brenda Kathleen Smith. *Educ:* Bancroft's Sch.; LSE, University of London; Universities of Lille and Brussels. BCom (hons) London, 1931. Sir Ernest Cassel Travelling Scholar, 1929-30; Asst, later Lectr in Commerce, LSE, 1932-40; Central Statistical Office, 1940-50; Dir of Statistics, Min. of Labour, 1950-68; Dir of Statistical Res., Dept of Employment, 1968-72. *Publications:* The Depreciation of Capital, 1934; The Duration of Unemployment, 1968; Some Problems of Index Number Construction, 1970; Further Problems of Index Number Construction, 1973; articles in British and US economic and statistical jls. *Address:* 10 Silverdale Road, Petts Wood, Kent. *Club:* Reform.

FOWLER, Prof. William Alfred, PhD; Medal for Merit, USA, 1948; Institute Professor of Physics, California Institute of Technology, since 1970; *b* Pittsburgh, Pa, 9 Aug. 1911; *s* of late John McLeod Fowler and Jennie Summers (*née* Watson); *m* 1940, Ardiane Foy Olmsted, Pasadena, Calif.; two *d*. *Educ:* Ohio State Univ. (B.Eng. Phys); California Inst. of Technology (PhD Phys). Member: Tau Kappa Epsilon; Tau Beta Pi; Sigma Xi. California Inst. of Technology: Research Fellow in Nuclear Physics, 1936-39; Asst Prof. of Physics, 1939-42; Associate Prof. of Physics, 1942-46; Prof. of Physics, 1946-70. Defense record: Research and develt proximity fuses, rocket ordnance, and atomic weapons; Research staff mem.: Sect. T, NDRC, and Div. 4, NDRC, 1941; Asst Dir of Research, Sect. L. Div. 3, NDRC, 1941-45; Techn. Observer, Office of Field Services and New Develts Div., War Dept, in South and Southwestern Pacific Theatres, 1944; Actg Supervisor, Ord. Div., R&D, NOTS, 1945; Sci. Dir, Project VISTA, Dept Defense, 1951-52. Guggenheim Fellow and Fulbright Lectr, Cavendish Laboratory, Univ. of Cambridge, Eng., 1954-55; Guggenheim Fellow, St John's Coll., and Dept Applied Math. and Theor. Phys., Univ. of Cambridge, Eng., 1961-62; Walker-Ames Prof. of Physics, Univ. of Washington, 1963; Visitor, The Observatories, Univ. of Cambridge, Summer 1964; Vis. Prof. of Physics, Mass. Inst. of Technology, 1966; Vis. Fellow, Inst. of Theoretical Astronomy, Univ. of Cambridge, Summers 1967-72. Numerous lectureships in USA, 1957-; those given abroad include: Lectr, Internat. Sch. of Physics "Enrico Fermi", Varenna, 1965. Lectr, Advanced Sch. on Cosmic Physics, Erice, Italy, 1969, in addition to past lectures at Cavendish Laboratory, Cambridge; also Lectr at Research Sch. of Physical Sciences, Australian National Univ., Canberra, 1965; Jubilee Lectr, 50th Aniversary, Niels Bohr Inst., Copenhagen, 1970; Scott Lectr, Cavendish Laboratory, Cambridge Univ., Eng., 1971; George Darwin Lectr, RAS, 1973; 22nd Liège Internat. Astrophysical Symposium, 1978; Vis. Scholar, Phi Beta Kappa, 1980-81. Member: Nat. Science Bd, Nat. Science Foundation, USA, 1968-74; Space Science Bd, Nat. Academy of Sciences, 1970-73 and 1977-80; Space Program Adv. Council, NASA, 1971-74; Bd of Directors, American Friends of Cambridge Univ., 1970-78; Governing Bd, Amer. Inst. of Physics, 1974-80; Cttee Chm., Nuclear Science Adv. Cttee, Nat. Science Foundn/Dept of Energy, USA, 1977-79; Chm., Off. Phys. Sci., Nat. Acad. Sci., 1981-. Has attended numerous conferences, congresses and assemblies. Various awards and medals for science etc, both at home and abroad, including Vetlesen Prize, 1973, Nat. Medal of Sci., 1974; Eddington Medal, RAS, 1978; Bruce Gold Medal, Astron. Soc. Pacific, 1979. Member: Internat. Astro. Union; Amer. Assoc. for Advancement of Science; Amer. Assoc. of Univ. Professors; Nat. Acad. of Sciences; Mem. corres., Soc. Royale des Sciences de Liège; Fellow: Amer. Physical Soc. (Pres., 1976); Amer. Acad. of Arts and Sciences; British Assoc. for Advancement of Science; Benjamin Franklin Fellow, RSA; ARAS. Hon. Mem., Mark Twain Soc. Hon. DSc: Chicago, 1976; Ohio State, 1978; Denison, 1982; Dr *hc*: Liège, 1981; Inst. d'Astrophysique, Paris, 1981. *Publications:* contributor to: Physical Review, Astrophysical Jl, Proc. Nat. Acad. of Sciences, Amer. Jl of Physics, Geophysical Jl, Nature, Royal Astronomical Soc., etc. *Address:* Kellogg Radiation Laboratory 106-38, California Institute of Technology, Pasadena,

California 91125, USA. *Clubs:* Cosmos (Washington, DC); Athenæum (Pasadena, Calif); Cambridge and District Model Engineering Society.

FOWLER HOWITT, William; *see* Howitt, W. F.

FOWLES, John; writer; *b* 31 March 1926; *s* of Robert John Fowles and Gladys May Richards; *m* 1956, Elizabeth Whitton. *Educ:* Bedford Sch.; New Coll., Oxford. English Centre PEN Silver Pen Award, 1969; W. H. Smith Award, 1970. *Publications:* The Collector, 1963; The Aristos, 1965; The Magus, 1966, rev. edn 1977; The French Lieutenant's Woman, 1969; Poems, 1973; The Ebony Tower, 1974; Shipwreck, 1975; Daniel Martin, 1977; Islands, 1978; (with Frank Horvat) The Tree, 1979; (ed) John Aubrey's Monumenta Britannica, parts 1 and 2, 1980, part 3 and Index, 1982; The Enigma of Stonehenge, 1980; Mantissa, 1982. *Recreations:* mainly Sabine. *Address:* c/o Anthony Sheil Associates, 2/3 Morwell Street, WC1.

FOX; *see* Lane Fox.

FOX, Sir David S.; *see* Scott Fox.

FOX, Edward; actor; *b* 13 April 1937; *s* of Robin and Angela Muriel Darita Fox; *m* Tracy (*née* Pelissier); one *d*; and one *d* by Joanna Fox. *Educ:* Ashfold Sch.; Harrow Sch. RADA training, following National Service, 1956-58; entry into provincial repertory theatre, 1958, since when, films, TV films and plays, and plays in the theatre, have made up the sum of his working life. *Plays include:* The Family Reunion, Vaudeville, 1979; Anyone for Denis, Whitehall, 1981; Quartermaine's Terms, Queen's, 1981; Hamlet, Young Vic, 1982. *Films include:* The Go-Between, 1971 (Soc. of Film and Television Arts Award for Best Supporting Actor, 1971); The Day of the Jackal, A Doll's House, 1973; Galileo, 1976; The Squeeze, A Bridge Too Far (BAFTA Award for Best Supporting Actor, 1977), The Duellists, The Cat and the Canary, 1977; Force Ten from Navarone, 1978; The Mirror Crack'd, 1980. *Television Series include:* Hard Times, 1977; Edward and Mrs Simpson, 1978 (BAFTA Award for Best Actor, 1978; TV Times Top Ten Award for Best Actor, 1978-79; British Broadcasting Press Guild TV Award for Best Actor, 1978; Royal TV Soc. Performance Award, 1978-79). *Recreations:* music, reading, walking. *Clubs:* Garrick, Savile.

FOX, Sir (Henry) Murray, GBE 1974; MA, FRICS; *b* 7 June 1912; *s* of late S. J. Fox and Molly Button; *m* 1941, Helen Isabella Margaret, *d* of late J. B. Crichton; one *s* two *d*. *Educ:* Malvern; Emmanuel Coll., Cambridge. Chairman: Trehaven Trust Group, 1963-; City & Metropolitan Building Society, 1976- (Dir, 1972-); Managing Trustee, Municipal Mutual Insurance Ltd, 1977-. Dir, Toye, Kenning & Spencer Ltd, 1976-. Governor: Christ's Hosp., 1966; Bridewell Royal Hosp., 1966 (Vice-Pres. 1976-); Trustee, Morden Coll., 1976-. Court of Common Council, 1963; Past Master: Wheelwrights' Co.; Coopers' Co.; Alderman, Ward of Bread Street, 1966-82; Sheriff, City of London, 1971-72; Lord Mayor of London, 1974-75; one of HM Lieutenants, City of London, 1976-. Order of Rising Sun and Sacred Treasure (Japan), 1971; Order of Stor (Afghanistan), 1971; Order of Orange Nassau (Netherlands), 1972. *Recreations:* golf, reading. *Address:* Flat 2, 45 Beech Street, EC2. *T:* 01-606 3631; (office) 5 Plough Place, New Fetter Lane, EC4. *T:* 01-583 0222. *Clubs:* City of London, City Livery (Pres. 1966-67).

FOX, (John) Marcus, MBE 1963; MP (C) Shipley, since 1970; Parliamentary Under Secretary of State, Department of the Environment, 1979-81; *b* 11 June 1927; *s* of late Alfred Hirst Fox; *m* 1954, Ann, *d* of F. W. J. Tindall; one *s* one *d*. *Educ:* Wheelright Grammar Sch., Dewsbury. Mem. Dewsbury County Borough Council, 1957-65; contested (C): Dewsbury, 1959; Huddersfield West, 1966. An Asst Govt Whip, 1972-73; a Lord Comr, HM Treasury, 1973-74; Opposition Spokesman on Transport, 1975-76; Mem., Parly Select Cttee on Race Relations and Immigration, 1970-79; Sec., Cons. Party's Transport Industries Cttee, 1970-72; a Vice-Chm., Cons. Party Orgn, 1976-79. *Recreations:* reading, tennis, squash. *Address:* House of Commons, SW1.

FOX, Kenneth Lambert; Director of Supplies, Greater London Council, since 1975; *b* 8 Nov. 1927; *s* of J. H. Fox, Grimsby, Lincolnshire; *m* 1959, P. E. Byrne; one *d*. *Educ:* City of London Coll.; Univ. of London. BSc (Hons); FInstPS, MIWM. Plant Man., Rowntree Gp, 1950-63; Supply Man., Ford Motor Co. (UK), 1963-67; Sen. Management Conslt, Cooper & Lybrand Ltd, 1967-70; Man. of Conslts (Europe), US Science Management Corpn, 1971-72; Supply Management, British Gas Corpn, 1972-75. *Recreations:* tennis, painting, bird watching, DIY. *Address:* 39 Parkland Avenue, Upminster. *T:* Upminster 28927.

FOX, Rt. Rev. Langton Douglas, DD; retired Bishop of Menevia; *b* 21 Feb. 1917; *s* of Claude Douglas Fox and Ethel Helen (*née* Cox). *Educ:* Mark Cross, Wonersh and Maynooth. BA 1938; DD 1945. Priest 1942. Lectr, St John's Seminary, Wonersh, 1942-55; Mem., Catholic Missionary Soc., 1955-59; Parish Priest, Chichester, 1959-65; Auxiliary Bishop of Menevia, 1965-72; Bishop of Menevia, 1972-81. *Address:* Bishop's House, Pantasaph, Holywell, Clwyd CH8 8PB.

FOX, Leslie, DSc Oxon; Professor of Numerical Analysis, Oxford University, and Professorial Fellow, Balliol College, since 1963; Director, Oxford University Computing Laboratory, since 1957; *b* 30 Sept. 1918; *m* 1st, 1943, Paulene Dennis; 2nd, 1973, Mrs Clemency Clements, *er d* of Thomas Fox.

Educ: Wheelwright Grammar Sch., Dewsbury; Christ Church, Oxford. Admiralty Computing Service, 1943-45; Mathematics Div., Nat. Physical Laboratory, 1945-56; Associate Prof., Univ. of California, Berkeley, 1956-57; Research Prof., Univ. of Illinois, 1961-62; Vis. Prof., Open Univ., 1970-71. Pres., Math./Phys. Section, BAAS, 1975. *Publications:* Numerical Solution of Boundary-value Problems in Ordinary Differential Equations, 1957; (ed) Numerical Solution of Ordinary and Partial Differential Equations, 1962; An Introduction to Numerical Linear Algebra, 1964; (ed) Advances in Programming and Non-Numerical Computation, 1966; Chebyshev Polynomials in Numerical Analysis (with I. J. Parker), 1968; Computing Methods for Scientists and Engineers (with D. F. Mayers), 1968; numerous papers in learned journals. *Recreations:* sport, music, literature. *Address:* 2 Elsfield Road, Marston, Oxford. *T:* Oxford 722668; University Computing Laboratory, 19 Parks Road, Oxford. *T:* Oxford 54409.

FOX, Marcus; *see* Fox, J. M.

FOX, Rt. Hon. Sir Michael John, Kt 1975; PC 1981; **Rt. Hon. Lord Justice Fox;** a Lord Justice of Appeal, since 1981; *b* 8 Oct. 1921; *s* of late Michael Fox; *m* 1954, Hazel Mary Stuart; three *s* one *d. Educ:* Drayton Manor Sch., Hanwell; Magdalen Coll., Oxford (BCL, MA). Admiralty, 1942-45. Called to the Bar, Lincoln's Inn, 1949, Bencher, 1975; QC 1968. Judge of the High Court of Justice, Chancery Div., 1975-81. *Address:* Royal Courts of Justice, Strand, WC2. *T:* 01-405 7641.

FOX, Sir Murray; *see* Fox, Sir H. M.

FOX, Paul Leonard; Managing Director, since 1977 and Director of Programmes, since 1973, Yorkshire Television; Director: Independent Television News, since 1977; Independent Television Publications Ltd, since 1981; *b* 27 Oct. 1925; *o s* of late Dr Walter Fox and Mrs Hilda Fox; *m* 1948, Betty Ruth (*née* Nathan); two *s. Educ:* Bournemouth Grammar Sch. Parachute Regt, 1943. Reporter: Kentish Times, 1946; The People, 1947; Scriptwriter, Pathé News, 1947; BBC Television: Scriptwriter, 1950; Editor, Sportsview, 1953, Panorama, 1961; Head, Public Affairs Dept, 1963; Head, Current Affairs Group, 1965. Controller, BBC1, 1967-73. Dir, Trident Television Ltd, 1973-81; Chairman: ITV Network Programme Cttee, 1978-80 Council, ITCA, 1982-. Mem., Royal Commn on Criminal Procedure, 1978-80. *Recreations:* television, attending race meetings. *Address:* Yorkshire Television, The Television Centre, Leeds. *T:* Leeds 38283.

FOX, Sir (Robert) David (John) S.; *see* Scott Fox.

FOX, Roy, CMG 1980; OBE 1967; HM Diplomatic Service, retired; Board Member, British Shipbuilders; Director, British Shipbuilders (Offshore Division), since 1981; consultant with various companies; *b* 1 Sept. 1920; *s* of J. S. and A. Fox; *m* 1st, 1943, Sybil Verity; two *s* one *d* ; 2nd, 1975, Susan Rogers Turner. *Educ:* Wheelwright Grammar Sch., Dewsbury; Bradford Technical Coll. Served in RNVR, 1940-46. Bd of Trade, 1947-58; British Trade Commissioner: Nairobi, 1958-60; Montreal, 1960-62; Winnipeg, 1962-64; Dep. Controller, Bd of Trade Office for Scotland, 1964-65. First Sec. Commercial, Karachi, 1965-68; Deputy High Comr, E Pakistan, 1968-70; Consul-Gen. and Comm. Counsellor, Helsinki, 1970-74; promoted to Minister, 1977; Consul-Gen., Houston, 1974-80. *Recreations:* golf, reading, tennis. *Address:* Beechcroft, Forest Drive, Kingswood, Surrey. *Club:* Oriental.

FOX, Ruth W.; *see* Winston-Fox.

FOX, Sir Theodore, Kt 1962; MA, MD Cambridge, LLD Glasgow, DLitt Birmingham; FRCP; *b* 1899; 3rd *s* of late R. Fortescue Fox; *m* Margaret (*d* 1970), *e d* of late W. S. McDougall, Wallington, Surrey; four *s. Educ:* Leighton Park Sch.; Pembroke Coll., Cambridge (scholar); London Hosp. (house physician). Mem. of Friends' Ambulance Unit, BEF, 1918; Ship Surg., 1925; joined staff of The Lancet, 1925; served in RAMC, 1939-42 (late temp. Major); Ed., The Lancet, 1944-64. Dir, Family Planning Assoc., 1965-67. Croonian Lectr, RCP, 1951; Heath Clark Lectr, Univ. of London, 1963; Harveian Orator, RCP, 1965; Maurice Bloch Lectr, Univ. of Glasgow, 1966. Hon. Fellow, Royal Australian Coll. of Gen. Practitioners. *Publication:* Crisis in Communication, 1965. *Address:* Green House, Rotherfield, East Sussex. *T:* Rotherfield 2870. *Club:* Athenæum.

FOX, Prof. Wallace, CMG 1973; MD, FRCP, FFCM; Professor of Community Therapeutics, Cardiothoracic Institute, Brompton Hospital, since 1979; Director, Medical Research Council Tuberculosis and Chest Diseases Unit, Brompton Hospital, since 1965; Hon. Consultant Physician, Brompton Hospital, since 1969; WHO Consultant, since 1961; Member of WHO Expert Advisory Panel on Tuberculosis, since 1965; *b* 7 Nov. 1920; *s* of Samuel and Esther Fox; *m* 1956, Gaye Judith Akker; three *s. Educ:* Cotham Grammar Sch., Bristol; Guy's Hosp. MB, BS (London) 1943; MRCS, LRCP, 1943; MRCP 1950; MD (Dist.) (London) 1951; FRCP 1962; FFCM 1976. Ho. Phys., Guy's USA Hosp., 1945-46; Resident Phys., Preston Hall Sanatorium, 1946-50; Registrar, Guy's Hosp., 1950-51; Asst Chest Physician, Hammersmith Chest Clinic, 1951-52; Mem. Scientific Staff of MRC Tuberculosis and Chest Diseases Unit, 1952-56, 1961-65; seconded to WHO, to establish and direct Tuberculosis Chemotherapy Centre, Madras, 1956-61; Dir, WHO Collaborating Centre for Tuberculosis Chemotherapy and its Application, 1976-. Lectures: Marc Daniels, RCP, 1962; First John Barnwell Meml, US

Veterans Admin, 1968; Philip Ellman, RSocMed, 1976; Martyrs Meml, Bangladesh Med. Assoc., 1977; first Quezon Meml, Philippine Coll. of Chest Physicians, 1977; Morriston Davies Meml, BTA, 1981; Mitchell, RCP, 1982. Waring Vis. Prof. in Medicine, Univ. of Colorado and Stanford Univ., 1974. Mem. Tropical Med. Research Bd, 1968-72; Mem., several MRC Cttees; Mem., BCG Vaccination Sub-Cttee, Min. of Health, 1968-; Mem. Council, Chest, Heart & Stroke Assoc., 1974-; International Union Against Tuberculosis: Mem., later Chm., Cttee of Therapy, 1964-71; Associate Mem., Scientific Cttees, 1973; Mem., Exec. Cttee, 1973- (Chm., 1973-77). Chm., Acid Fast Club, 1971-72. Editor, Advances in Tuberculosis Research. Elected Corresp. Mem., Amer. Thoracic Soc., 1962; Mem., Mexican Acad. of Medicine, 1976; Hon. Life Mem., Canadian Thoracic Soc., 1976; Corresp. Mem., Argentine Nat. Acad. of Medicine, 1977; Corresp. For. Member: Argentine Soc. of Phtisiol. and Thoracic Pathol., 1977; Coll. of Univ. Med. Phtisiologists of Argentine, 1978; Hon. Member: Argentine Med. Assoc., 1977; Singapore Thoracic Soc., 1978. Sir Robert Philip Medal, Chest and Heart Assoc., 1969; Weber Parkes Prize, RCP, 1973; Carlo Forlanini Gold Medal, Fedn Ital. contra la Tuberculosi e le Malattie Polmonari Sociali, 1976; Hon. Medal, Czech. Med. Soc., 1980; Robert Koch Centenary Medal, Internat. Union against Tuberculosis, 1982; Presidential Citation Award, Amer. Coll. of Chest Physicians, 1982. *Publications:* Reports on tuberculosis services in Hong Kong to Hong Kong Government: Heaf/Fox, 1962; Scadding/Fox, 1975; contribs to med. jls: on methodology of controlled clinical trials, on epidemiology and on chemotherapy, particularly in tuberculosis, asthma and carcinoma of the bronchus and other respiratory diseases. *Address:* 2 The Orchard, Bedford Park, W4 1JX. *T:* 01-994 0974.

FOX, Winifred Marjorie, (Mrs E. Gray Debros); Under-Secretary, Department of the Environment, 1970-76; *d* of Frederick Charles Fox and Charlotte Marion Ogborn; *m* 1953, Eustachy Gray Debros (*d* 1954); one *d. Educ:* Streatham County Sch.; St Hugh's Coll., Oxford. Unemployment Assistance Board, 1937; Cabinet Office, 1942; Ministry of Town and Country Planning, 1944; Ministry of Housing and Local Govt, 1952 (Under-Sec., 1963); Dept of the Environment, 1970; seconded to CSD as Chm., CS Selection Bd, 1971-72. *Address:* The Coach House, Hinton in the Hedges, S Northants. *T:* Brackley 702100.

FOX-ANDREWS, James Roland Blake, QC 1968; a Recorder, and Honorary Recorder of Winchester, since 1972; *b* 24 March 1922; step *s* of late Norman Roy Fox-Andrews, QC; *m* 1950, Angela Bridget Swift; two *s. Educ:* Stowe; Pembroke Coll., Cambridge. Called to the Bar, Gray's Inn, 1949, Bencher, 1974. Dep. Chm., Devon QS, 1970-71; Recorder of Winchester, 1971. Leader, Western Circuit, 1982-. Member: Gen. Council of the Bar, 1968-72; Senate of Inns of Court and the Bar, 1976-79. *Publications:* (jtly) Leasehold Property (Temporary Provisions) Act, 1951; contrib. Halsbury's Laws of England, 3rd edn, building contracts, architects and engineers; (jtly) Landlord and Tenant Act, 1954; Business Tenancies, 1970, 3rd edn 1978. *Address:* 20 Cheyne Gardens, SW3. *T:* 01-352 9484; Lepe House, Exbury, Hants. *Club:* Hampshire (Winchester).

FOX-PITT, Maj.-Gen. William Augustus Fitzgerald Lane, CVO 1966 (MVO 1936); DSO 1940; MC 1916; retired; DL; Member of HM Bodyguard of Hon. Corps of Gentlemen-at-Arms, 1947-66; Lieutenant, 1963-66; (Standard Bearer, 1961-63); *b* 28 Jan. 1896; *s* of late Lieut-Col W. A. Fox-Pitt, Presaddfed, Anglesey; *m* 1931, Mary Stewart, *d* of A. H. H. Sinclair, MD, FRCSE; two *s* one *d. Educ:* Charterhouse. ADC to the King, 1945-47; joined Cheshire Regt 1914; served with Welsh Gds, 1915-39; Comd, 1st Bn, 1934-37; OC Welsh Guards Regt, 1937-40; Comd Gds Bde BEF, 1940, Armd Bde, 1941-43; Comdr, East Kent Dist as Maj.-Gen., 1943; retired with hon. rank of Maj.-Gen. 1947. Mem. Dorset CC 1952; DL Dorset, 1957. *Recreations:* shooting, golf. *Address:* Marsh Court, Sherborne, Dorset. *T:* Bishops Caundle 230. *Clubs:* Pratt's, Cavalry and Guards.

FOX-STRANGWAYS, family name of **Earl of Ilchester.**

FOXELL, Clive Arthur Peirson; Senior Director of Development and Procurement, British Telecom, since 1981; *b* 27 Feb. 1930; *s* of Arthur Turner Foxell and Lillian Ellerman; *m* 1956, Shirley Ann Patey Morris; one *d. Educ:* Harrow High Sch.; Univ. of London. BSc; CEng, FIEE, FInstP. GEC Res. Labs, 1947; Man., GEC Semiconductor Labs, 1968; Man. Dir, GEC Semiconductors Ltd, 1971; Dep. Dir of Research, PO, 1975; Dep. Dir, PO Procurement Exec., 1978-79; Dir of Purchasing, PO, 1980; Dir of Procurement, British Telecom, 1981. Member: Council, IEE, 1975-78 (Vice-Chm., Electronics Div., 1980-); SRC Engrg Bd, 1977-80 (Chm., Silicon Working Party, 1980-); Chm., ACARD Working Party on Inf. Tech., 1981. *Publications:* Low Noise Microwave Amplifiers, 1968; articles and papers on electronics. *Recreations:* photography, railways. *Address:* 4 Meades Lane, Chesham, Bucks. *T:* Chesham 5737.

FOXLEE, James Brazier; company director; *b* 20 Nov. 1921; *s* of late Arthur Brazier Foxlee and late Mary Foxlee (*née* Fisher); *m* 1952, Vera June (*née* Guiver); one *s* two *d. Educ:* Brentwood Sch. Entered Min. of Agric. and Fisheries (later MAFF) as Clerical Officer, 1938. Served War, RNVR, Ordinary Seaman, 1941; commissioned, 1942; Lieut, in comd Light Coastal Forces craft and mine-sweepers. MAFF: Exec. Officer, 1946; HEO, 1948; SEO, 1950; Principal, 1955 (Welsh Dept, 1955-57; Treas., 1961-62); Asst Sec., 1965 (Regional Controller, Leeds, 1965-69); Under Sec., 1971-81.

Recreations: watching cricket, camping, oenology. *Address:* Arran, 43 Foxley Lane, Purley, Surrey CR2 3EH. *T:* 01-660 1085.

FOXLEY-NORRIS, Air Chief Marshal Sir Christopher (Neil), GCB 1973 (KCB 1969; CB 1966); DSO 1945; OBE 1956; FRSA; Chairman: Cheshire Foundation, 1974-82, now Chairman Emeritus (Vice-Chairman, 1972-74); Battle of Britain Fighter Association, since 1978; Director, Brookdale Hutton & Associates, since 1974; Chairman, General Portfolio Life Assurance, since 1974; *b* 16 March 1917; *s* of Major J. P. Foxley-Norris and Dorothy Brabant Smith; *m* 1948, Joan Lovell Hughes; no *c. Educ:* Winchester; Trinity Coll., Oxford (Hon. Fellow, 1973); Middle Temple. Commissioned RAFO, 1936; France, 1940; Battle of Britain, 1940; various operational tours of duty in wartime. MA 1946. ACDS, 1963; AOC No 224 Gp, FEAF, 1964-67; Dir-Gen., RAF Organization, MoD, 1967-68; C-in-C, RAF Germany and Comdr, NATO 2nd Tactical Air Force, 1968-70; Chief of Personnel and Logistics, MoD, 1971-74; retd. Vice Pres., RUSI, 1979. Chm. Gardening for the Disabled, 1980-. CBIM. *Publications:* A Lighter Shade of Blue, 1978; various in RUSI and other service jls. *Recreations:* golf, sailing. *Address:* Tumble Wood, Northend Common, Henley-on-Thames. *T:* Turville Heath 457. *Clubs:* Royal Air Force; Huntercombe (Oxon).

FOXON, David Fairweather, FBA 1978; Reader in Textual Criticism and Fellow of Wadham College, Oxford, since 1968; *b* 9 Jan. 1923; *s* of late Rev. Walter Foxon and Susan Mary (*née* Fairweather); *m* 1947, Dorothy June (marr. diss. 1963), *d* of late Sir Arthur Jarratt, KCVO; one *d. Educ:* Kingswood Sch., Bath; Magdalen Coll., Oxford. BA 1948, MA 1953. Foreign Office, 1942-45; Asst Keeper, Dept of Printed Books, British Museum, 1950-65; Harkness Fellow, 1959-61; Professor of English, Queen's Univ., Kingston, Ontario, 1965-67; Guggenheim Fellow, 1967-68. Sen. Res. Fellow, Clark Library, UCLA, 1974-75; Lyell Reader in Bibliography, Oxford, 1975-76; Sandars Reader in Bibliography, Cambridge, 1977-78. Pres., Bibliographical Soc., 1980-81. John H. Jenkins Award for Bibliography, 1977. *Publications:* T. J. Wise and the Pre-Restoration Drama, 1959; Libertine Literature in England, 1660-1745, 1964; (ed) English Bibliographical Sources, 1964-67; English Verse 1701-1750: a catalogue, 1975; contribs to bibliographical jls. *Recreation:* music. *Address:* 7 Fane Road, Marston, Oxford OX3 0RZ. *T:* Oxford 48350.

FOXON, Prof. George Eric Howard, MA, MSc; Professor of Biology, University of London, 1955-72, now Emeritus Professor; Head of Biology Department, Guy's Hospital Medical School, 1948-72; *b* 1908; *s* of George Thomas Foxon, OBE, and Edith Maud (*née* Lewis); *m* 1932, Joan Burlinson; one *s* one *d* (and one *s* decd). *Educ:* King's Coll. Sch., Wimbledon; Queens' Coll., Cambridge. BA 1930, 1st Cl. Hons Nat. Sci. Tripos Pt II, 1931; MA 1934; MSc (Wales) 1943. Asst in Zoology, University of Glasgow, 1932-37; Asst Lectr and Lectr in Zoology, University Coll., Cardiff, 1937-48; Reader in Biology, University of London, 1948-55. Chm. of the British Univs Film Council, 1959-63, 1967-69. Fellow Cambridge Philosophical Soc., FLS; FIBiol; FZS. *Publications:* various scientific papers, mainly dealing with the comparative study of the heart and blood system of vertebrate animals. *Address:* Thorpe Cloud, Woodfield Lane, Ashtead, Surrey KT21 2BE. *T:* Ashtead 72306.

FOXON, Harold Peter, OBE 1976; Group Managing Director, Inchcape plc, since 1981 (Director, since 1971; a Managing Director, since 1978); *b* 7 April 1919; *s* of William Henry Foxon and Kathleen Avis (*née* Perry); *m* 1948, Elizabeth Mary Butterfield; one *s* three *d. Educ:* Bancroft's. Served War, 1939-46, Royal Signals, Captain. Insurance, 1935-39; Smith Mackenzie & Co. Ltd (East Africa), 1946-69; Chm., Mackenzie Dalgety Ltd, 1966-69; Man. Dir, Gilman & Co. Ltd, Hong Kong, and Chm., Inchcape Hong Kong Ltd, 1969-77. Director: Dodwell & Co., Ltd, 1978-81; Anglo-Thai Corpn, 1978-82; Berry Trust Ltd, 1977-; Member: Hong Kong Trade Adv. Gp, 1978-; South East Asia Trade Adv. Gp, 1978-82. *Recreation:* golf. *Address:* Inchcape plc, 40 St Mary Axe, EC3; 48 Abingdon Villas, W8 6BT. *T:* 01-937 8713; Thurso, Ashlyns Road, Frinton-on-Sea, Essex. *T:* Frinton 2208. *Clubs:* City of London, Oriental; Muthaiga (Kenya); Hong Kong (Hong Kong).

FOXTON, Maj.-Gen. Edwin Frederick, CB 1969; OBE 1959; MA; Fellow and Domestic Bursar, Emmanuel College, Cambridge, 1969-79; *b* 28 Feb. 1914; *y s* of F. Foxton and T. Wilson; unmarried. *Educ:* Worksop Coll.; St Edmund Hall, Oxford. Commissioned from General List TA, 1937; served: India, 1939-42; Middle East, 1942-45; India, 1945-47 (Chief Educn Officer, Southern Comd, India); War Office, 1948-52; Chief Instructor, Army Sch. of Educn, 1952-55; Dist Educn Officer, HQ Northumbrian District, 1955-57; War Office, 1957-60; Commandant, Army Sch. of Educn, 1961-63; War Office, 1963-65; Chief Educn Officer, FARELF, 1965; Dir of Army Educn, 1965-69. *Address:* 7 Tamar House, Kennington Lane, SE11. *Club:* United Oxford & Cambridge University.

FOYLE, Christina Agnes Lilian, (Mrs Ronald Batty); Managing Director, W. & G. Foyle Ltd; *d* of late William Alfred Foyle; *m* 1938, Ronald Batty. *Educ:* Aux Villas Unspunnen, Wilderswil, Switzerland. Began Foyle's Literary Luncheons, 1930, where book lovers have been able to see and hear great personalities. Member: Ct, Univ. of Essex; Council, RSA, 1963-69; Chm. East Anglian Region, RSA, 1978; Pres. Chelmsford District, Nat. Trust, 1979. DUniv Essex, 1975. *Recreations:* bird-watching, gardening, playing the piano. *Address:* Beeleigh Abbey, Maldon, Essex.

FOZARD, John William, OBE 1981; CEng, FIMechE; FRAeS, FAIAA; Marketing Director, Kingston-Brough Division, British Aerospace Corporation, Kingston upon Thames, since 1978; *b* 16 Jan. 1928; *s* of John Fozard and Eleanor Paulkit; *m* 1951, Mary, *d* of Regtl Sgt-Major C. B. Ward, VC, KOYLI; two *s. Educ:* Univ. of London (1st Cl. Hons BScEng 1948); Coll. of Aeronautics, Cranfield (DCAe with distinction 1950). CEng, FIMechE 1971; FRAeS 1964; FAIAA 1981. Hawker Aircraft Ltd: Design Engr, 1950; Head of Proj. Office, 1960; Hawker Siddeley Aviation: Chief Designer, Harrier, 1963; Exec. Dir, 1971. Vice Pres., RAeS, 1980-. *Publications:* papers in aeronautical jls and in specialist press, 1954-. *Recreations:* music, engineering history. *Address:* Wychbury Cottage, Warreners Lane, St George's Hill, Weybridge, Surrey KT13 0LH. *T:* Weybridge 45204.

FRAENKEL, Heinrich; freelance author; *b* 28 Sept. 1897; *s* of Benno Fraenkel and Alwina (*née* Taendler); *m* 1936, Gretel Levy-Ries; two *s. Educ:* German schools and universities. Began career in film trade journalism, Berlin; as screen-writer, went to Hollywood for two years but returned to Germany; continued to write screen plays but increasingly interested in politics; emigrated to avoid arrest in night of Reichstag fire, 1933; went to Paris, then London; still made living writing screen-plays but wrote political books, lectured on German history, the roots of Nazism, etc. At war's end, determined to return to Germany; disillusioned by many long trips made for the New Statesman; sought British nationality, 1949. Has written chess column in New Statesman (as Assiac), 1949-76. Order of Merit (1st class) of Fed. Rep. of Germany, 1967. *Publications:* The German People Versus Hitler, 1940; Help Us Germans to Beat the Nazis, 1941; The Winning of the Peace, 1942; The Other Germany, 1943; A Nation Divided, 1949; The Boy Between, 1956; Farewell to Germany, 1958; with Roger Manvell: Dr Goebbels, 1959; Hermann Goering, 1962; The July Plot, 1964; Heinrich Himmler, 1965; The Incomparable Crime, 1967; The Canaris Conspiracy, 1969; History of the German Cinema, 1971; Rudolf Hess, 1971; Inside Hitler, 1973; Seizure of Power, 1974; Adolf Hitler: the man and the myth, 1977, English enlgd edn, 1978, repr. 1982. As Assiac: Adventure in Chess, 1950; Delights of Chess, 1960, US, French, Dutch, Spanish and German edns substantially enlgd and revised; (with Kevin O'Connell) Prepared Variations, 1981; More Delights of Chess, 1982. *Address:* Christopher Cottage, Thaxted (Dunmow), Essex. *T:* Thaxted 830293. *Club:* Authors'.

FRAENKEL, Peter Maurice, CEng, FICE, FIStructE; Founder and Senior Partner, Peter Fraenkel & Partners, since 1972; *b* 5 July 1915; *s* of Ernest Fraenkel and Luise (*née* Tessmann); *m* 1946, Hilda Muriel, *d* of William Norman; two *d. Educ:* Battersea Polytechnic; Imperial Coll., London. BSc (Eng). FICE 1954, FIStructE 1954, MConsE 1962. Asst Engr with London firm of contractors, engaged on design and construction of marine and industrial structures, 1937-40; served in Army, 1941-42; Works Services Br., War Dept, 1942-45; Rendel, Palmer & Tritton, Cons. Engineers: Civil Engr, 1945; Sen. Engr, 1953; Partner, 1961-72; seconded to Tyne Improvement Commn as Resident Engr on construction of Ore Unloading Terminal at Tyne Dock, 1951-53. Has been responsible for, or closely associated with, technical and management aspects of many feasibility and planning studies, and planning, design and supervision of construction of large civil engrg projects, incl. ports, docks, offshore terminals, inland waterways, highways, power stations and tunnels in Gt Britain, Middle East, India, Far East and Australia, including: new Oil port at Sullom Voe, Shetland; new Naval Dockyard, Bangkok; Shatin to Tai Po coastal Trunk Road, Hong Kong; comprehensive study for DoE, of maintenance and operational needs of canals controlled by Brit. Waterways Bd (Fraenkel Report); new ore port at Port Talbot, UK, and new commercial port at Limassol, Cyprus; off-shore coal loading terminal at MacKay, Qld, and power stations at Aberthaw, Eggborough and Ironbridge, UK. James Watt Medal, 1963, Telford Gold Medal, 1971, ICE. *Publications:* (jtly) papers to Instn of Civil Engrs: Special Features of the Civil Engineering Works at Aberthaw Power Station, 1962; Planning and Design of Port Talbot Harbour, 1970. *Address:* Little Paddock, Oxted, Surrey RH8 0EL. *T:* Oxted 2927. *Club:* Athenæum.

FRAGA-IRIBARNE, Manuel; Founder-Member, Popular Alliance, Spain, 1976, Leader, since 1979; elected to the Cortes, 1977 and 1979; *b* 23 Nov. 1922; *m* 1948, María del Carmen Estévez; two *s* three *d. Educ:* Insts of Coruña, Villalba and Lugo; Univs of Santiago de Compostela and Madrid. Prof. of Polit. Law, Univ. of Valencia, 1945; Prof. of Polit. Sci. and Constit. Law, Univ. of Madrid, 1953; Legal Adviser to the Cortes, 1945; entered Diplomatic Service, 1945; Sec.-Gen., Instituto de Cultura Hispánica, 1951; Sec.-Gen. in Min. of Educn, 1953; Head, Inst. of Polit. Studies, 1961; Minister of Information and Tourism, 1961-69; Ambassador to UK, 1973-75; Interior Minister, Spain, 1975-76. Holds numerous foreign orders. *Publications:* various books on law, polit. sci., history and sociology, incl. one on British Parlt. *Recreations:* shooting, fishing. *Address:* Joaquín María López 72, Madrid (15), Spain. *T:* 244 4980. *Clubs:* Athenæum, Travellers'.

FRAME, Sir Alistair (Gilchrist), Kt 1981; MA, BSc, FEng; Joint Deputy Chairman and Chief Executive, Rio Tinto-Zinc Corporation Ltd, since 1978; Director: Plessey Company Ltd, since 1978; Toronto Dominion Bank, since 1981; Vickers Ltd, since 1981; *b* Dalmuir, Dunbartonshire, 3 April 1929; *s* of Alexander Frame and Mary (*née* Fraser); *m* 1953, Sheila (*née* Mathieson); one *d. Educ:* Glasgow and Cambridge Univs. Director, Reactor and Research Groups, UK Atomic Energy Authority, 1964-68; joined Rio Tinto-Zinc Corp., 1968; appointed to main Board, 1973. Member: NEB, 1978-79;

Engineering Council, 1982-. *Recreations:* tennis, gardening, walking. *Address:* Flat L, 19 Hyde Park Gardens, W2; Pine Cottage, Holmbury St Mary, Dorking, Surrey.

FRAME, Rt. Rev. John Timothy, DD; Dean of Columbia and Rector of Christ Church Cathedral, Victoria, BC, since 1980; *b* 8 Dec. 1930; *m* ; three *d. Educ:* Univ. of Toronto. Burns Lake Mission, Dio. Caledonia, 1957; Hon. Canon of Caledonia, 1965; Bishop of Yukon, 1968-80. *Address:* c/o Christ Church Cathedral, 912 Vancouver Street, Victoria, BC V8V 3V7, Canada.

FRAMPTON, Meredith, RA 1942 (ARA 1934); Honorary Retired Academician; *b* 1894; *s* of Sir George Frampton, RA; *m* 1951, Hilda Norman, *d* of late James B. Dunn, RSA, FRIBA, and of Mrs Dunn, Edinburgh. *Educ:* Westminster. Retrospective exhibition, Tate Gall., 1982. *Address:* Hill Barn, Monkton Deverill, Warminster, Wilts. *Club:* Athenæum.

FRANCE, Sir Arnold William, GCB 1972 (KCB 1965; CB 1957); Director, Rank Organisation; *b* 20 April 1911; *s* of late W. E. France; *m* 1940, Frances Margaret Linton, *d* of late Dr C. J. L. Palmer; four *d. Educ:* Bishop's Stortford Coll. District Bank, Ltd, 1929-40. Served War of 1939-45, Army, 1940-43; Deputy Economic and Financial Adviser to Minister of State in Middle East, 1943; HM Treasury, 1945; Asst Sec., 1948; Under Sec., 1952; Third Sec., 1960; Ministry of Health: Dep. Sec., 1963-64; Permanent Sec., 1964-68; Chm., Bd of Inland Revenue, 1968-73. Director: Pilkington Bros, 1973-81; Tube Investments, 1973-81. Chm., Central Bd of Finance, C of E, 1973-78. Chm., Bd of Management, Lingfield Hosp. Sch., 1973-81. *Address:* Thornton Cottage, Lingfield, Surrey. *T:* Lingfield 832278. *Club:* Reform.
See also J. N. B. Penny.

FRANCE, Christopher Walter; Deputy Under Secretary of State (Personnel and Logistics), Ministry of Defence, since 1981 (on secondment from HM Treasury); *b* 2 April 1934; *s* of W. J. and E. M. France; *m* 1961, Valerie (*née* Larman); one *s* one *d. Educ:* East Ham Grammar Sch.; New College, Oxford (BA (PPE), DipEd). CDipAF. HM Treasury, 1959-: Assistant Secretary, 1971; Principal Private Secretary to the Chancellor of the Exchequer, 1973-76; Under Secretary, 1976; Principal Establishment Officer, 1977-80; on secondment to Electricity Council, 1980-81; Dep. Sec., 1981. *Recreations:* keeping the house up and the garden down. *Address:* Brooks Grove, Halstead, Sevenoaks, Kent TN14 7EU.

FRANCIS, (Alan) David, CBE 1959; MVO 1957; *b* 2 Dec. 1900; *m* 1932, Norah Turpin; two *s. Educ:* Winchester; Magdalen Coll., Oxford (MA); Corpus Christi Coll., Cambridge (BA). Passed into General Consular Service, 1923; after course in Economics at Cambridge, appointed Vice-Consul, Antwerp, 1925; served as Vice-Consul at Rotterdam, Panama, Bogota and Prague; was also Lloyds Agent at Prague; served in FO, 1936, appointed Vice-Consul, Brussels, and Consul there, 1937. Attached to Costarican Delegation to Coronation of King George VI. Seconded as Principal in Aliens Dept, Home Office, 1940; Consul at Lisbon, 1941; Barcelona, 1942; First Sec. and Consul, Caracas, 1944; Chargé d'Affaires there, 1946; served in FO, 1947; Consul-Gen. at Danzig, 1949, New Orleans, 1951; Consul-Gen., Oporto, 1955-58; retired, 1958. Mem., Lord Chancellor's Advisory Council on Public Records, 1962-67. FRHistS. *Publications:* The Methuens and Portugal, 1966; The Wine Trade, 1972; The First Peninsular War, 1975; articles in learned periodicals. *Recreation:* walking. *Address:* 21 Cadogan Street, SW3. *Club:* Travellers'.

FRANCIS, Alfred Edwin, OBE 1952; Consultant to major theatre companies in London, Cardiff and Bristol; *b* 27 March 1909; *er s* of Reginald Thomas Francis and Ellen Sophia Francis, Liverpool; *m* 1941, Joan Quayle Stocker (*d* 1979), Cheshire; one *s. Educ:* Liverpool Coll.; Liverpool Sch. of Architecture. Song writer and stage designer, 1932-39; Hon. Organising Secretary: Liverpool Ballet Club; ENSA, W Command, 1941-45. Overture commnd by Liverpool Philharmonic Soc., 1943. Dir of Liverpool 1951 Festival, 1950; Admin. Dir (later Chm.), London Old Vic, 1952; Man. Dir (later Vice-Chm.), Television Wales and West, 1959; Exec. Chm. Welsh National Opera (and later Drama) Co., 1968-75. Board Member: London Festival Ballet; D'Oyly Carte Trust; London Old Vic Trust; Cardiff New Theatre Trust; former member: Nat. Theatre Bd; Bristol Old Vic Trust; various Arts Council and Welsh Arts Council cttees; Member: British Council Adv. Panel for Drama (former Chm.); Grand Council, Royal Acad. of Dancing. Pres., Vic-Wells Assoc.; Hon. Vice-Pres., UK Cttee for UNICEF (former Chm.). *Recreation:* making a fourth at bridge. *Address:* 20 Selwyn Court, Church Road, Richmond, Surrey TW10 6LR. *T:* 01-940 6612. *Clubs:* Garrick, Saints and Sinners, Green Room, Arts Theatre; Artists (Liverpool) (Hon. Member and former Pres.).

FRANCIS, Clare Mary, (Mrs J. R. Redon), MBE 1978; *b* 17 April 1946; *d* of Owen Francis, *qv* ; *m* 1977, Jacques Robert Redon; one *s. Educ:* Royal Ballet Sch.; University Coll. London (BScEcon). Crossed Atlantic singlehanded, Falmouth to Newport, in 37 days, 1973; placed 3rd in Round Britain Race with Eve Bonham, 1974; Azores and back, Singlehanded Race, 1975; L'Aurore Singlehanded Race, 1975; Observer Transatlantic Singlehanded Race: placed 14th, women's transatlantic singlehanded record (29 days), 1976; L'Aurore Singlehanded Race, 1976; Whitbread Round the World Race, first woman skipper, placed 5th, 1977-78. Hon. Fellow, UMIST, 1981. *Television series:* The Commanding Sea (BBC), 1981 (co-writer and presenter). *Publications:* Come Hell or High Water, 1977; Come Wind or

Weather, 1978; The Commanding Sea, 1981. *Recreations:* reading, music, opera, gardening. *Clubs:* Sea View Yacht, Royal Cruising, Royal Lymington Yacht, Royal Western Yacht, Ocean Cruising, Chichester Yacht, Dartmouth Yacht and others.

FRANCIS, David; *see* Francis, A. D.

FRANCIS, Dick; author; Racing Correspondent, Sunday Express, 1957-73; *b* 31 Oct. 1920; *s* of George Vincent Francis and Catherine Mary Francis; *m* 1947, Mary Margaret Brenchley; two *s. Educ:* Maidenhead County Boys' School. Pilot, RAF, 1940-45 (Flying Officer). Amateur National Hunt jockey, 1946-48, Professional, 1948-57; Champion Jockey, season 1953-54. *Publications:* Sport of Queens (autobiog.), 1957, 3rd updated edn, 1982; Dead Cert, 1962; Nerve, 1964; For Kicks, 1965; Odds Against, 1965; Flying Finish, 1966; Blood Sport, 1967; Forfeit, 1968 (Edgar Allan Poe Award, 1970); Enquiry, 1969; Rat Race, 1970; Bonecrack, 1971; Smoke Screen, 1972; Slay-Ride, 1973; Knock Down, 1974; High Stakes, 1975; In the Frame, 1976; Risk, 1977; Trial Run, 1978; Whip Hand, 1979 (Golden Dagger Award, Crime Writers' Assoc., 1980); Reflex, 1980; Twice Shy, 1981; Banker, 1982. *Recreations:* boating, tennis. *Address:* Penny Chase, Blewbury, Oxon. *T:* Blewbury 850369. *Clubs:* Detection, Crime Writers Association, Sportsman's, Press.

FRANCIS, Prof. Edward Howel, DSc; FRSE, FGS; Professor of Earth Sciences, University of Leeds, since 1977; *b* 31 May 1924; *s* of Thomas Howel Francis and Gwendoline Amelia (*née* Richards); *m* 1952, Cynthia Mary (*née* Williams); one *d. Educ:* Port Talbot County Sch.; Univ. of Wales, Swansea (BSc, DSc). FGS 1948; FRSE 1962. Served Army, 1944-47. Geological Survey of Great Britain (now incorporated in Inst. of Geol. Sciences): Field Geologist, Scotland, 1949-62; Dist Geologist, NE England, 1962-67, N Wales, 1967-70; Asst Dir, Northern England and Wales, 1971-77. Geological Society of London: Murchison Fund, 1963; Mem. Council, 1972-74; Pres., 1980-82; Pres., Section C (Geol.), BAAS, 1976; Mem., Inst. of Geol., 1978. *Publications:* memoirs, book chapters and papers on coalfields, palaeovolcanic rocks and general stratigraphy, mainly of Britain. *Recreations:* opera, golf. *Address:* Michaelston, 11 Millbeck Green, Collingham, near Wetherby, W Yorks LS22 5AJ. *Club:* Sand Moor Golf.

FRANCIS, Ven. Edward Reginald; Archdeacon of Bromley, since 1979; *b* 31 Jan. 1929; *s* of Alfred John and Elsie Hilda Francis; *m* 1950, Joyce Noreen Atkins; three *s. Educ:* Maidstone and Dover Grammar Schools; Rochester Theological College. National Service, RAF, 1947-49. Insurance, including period at Chartered Insurance Inst. (ACII), 1950-59. Ordained, 1961; Chaplain, Training Ship Arethusa, and Curate of All Saints, Frindsbury, 1961-64; Vicar of St William's, Chatham, 1964-73; Vicar and Rural Dean of Rochester, 1973-78. Mem., General Synod of C of E, 1981-. *Recreations:* ornithology, walking, music. *Address:* 6 Horton Way, Farningham, Kent DA4 0DQ. *T:* Farningham 864522.

FRANCIS, Sir Frank (Chalton), KCB 1960 (CB 1958); FSA; FMA; Director and Principal Librarian, British Museum, 1959-68; *b* Liverpool, 5 Oct. 1901; *o s* of late F. W. Francis and Elizabeth Chalton; *m* 1927, Katrina McClennon, Liverpool; two *s* one *d. Educ:* Liverpool Inst.; Liverpool Univ.; Emmanuel Coll., Cambridge. Asst Master, Holyhead Co. Sch., 1925-26; British Museum: entered Library, 1926; Sec., 1946-47; Keeper, Dept of Printed Books, 1948-59. Lectr in Bibliography, Sch. of Librarianship and Archives, University Coll., London, 1945-59. David Murray Lectr, Univ. of Glasgow, 1957. Editor, The Library, 1936-53; Jt Editor, Jl of Documentation, 1947-68. Museums Association: Mem. Council, 1960-; Vice-Pres., 1964-65; Pres., 1965-66. Bibliographical Society: Jt Hon. Sec. (with late R. B. McKerrow), 1938-40; Hon. Sec. 1940-64; Pres., 1964-66. Library Association: Council, 1948-59; Chm. Exec. Cttee, 1954-57; Pres., 1965. President: ASLIB, 1957-58; Internat. Fedn of Library Assocs, 1963-69; Chm. Trustees, Nat. Central Library. Vice-Pres., Unesco Internat. Adv. Cttee on Bibliography, 1954-60. Chairman: Circle of State Librarians, 1947-50; Internat. Cttee of Library Experts, UN, 1948; Council, British Nat. Bibliography, 1949-59; Unesco Provisional Internat. Cttee on Bibliography, 1952; Academic Libraries Section, Internat. Fedn of Library Assocs; Anglo-Swedish Soc., 1964-68. Consultant, Council on Library Resources, Washington, DC, 1959-. Trustee, Imp. War Museum; Governor, Birkbeck Coll. Correspondant, Institut de France; Mem., Bibliographical Soc. of America, and other bibliographical socs; Corresp. Mem., Massachusetts Historical Soc.; Hon. Mem., Kungl. Gustav Adolfs Akademien; Foreign Hon. Mem., Amer. Acad. of Arts and Sciences. Master, Clockmakers' Co., 1974. Hon. Fellow: Emmanuel Coll., Cambridge; Pierpont Morgan Library, NY; Hon. FLA. Hon. LittD: Liverpool; TCD; Cambridge; Hon. DLitt: British Columbia; Exeter; Leeds; Oxford; New Brunswick; Wales. *Publications:* Historical Bibliography in Year's Work in Librarianship, 1929-38; (ed) The Bibliographical Society, 1892-1942: Studies in Retrospect, 1945; (ed) Facsimile of The Compleat Catalogue 1680, 1956; Robert Copland: Sixteenth Century Printer and Translator, 1961; (ed) Treasures of the British Museum, 1971; translations from German, including W. Cohn, Chinese Art, 1930; articles and reviews in The Library, TLS, etc. *Recreations:* golf, walking, bibliography. *Address:* The Vine, Nether Winchendon, Aylesbury, Bucks. *Clubs:* Athenæum, Royal Commonwealth Society; Grolier (New York).

FRANCIS, Horace William Alexander, CBE 1976; Director, Trafalgar House Ltd, since 1978; Joint Deputy Chairman: Cementation Civil and International Construction Holdings; Cementation Specialist Holdings;

Cleveland Engineering Holdings; *b* 31 Aug. 1926; *s* of Horace Fairie Francis and Jane McMinn Murray; *m* 1949, Gwendoline Maud Dorricott; two *s* two *d*. *Educ*: Royal Technical Coll., Glasgow. FEng, FICE. Director, Tarmac Civil Engineering Ltd, 1960; Man. Dir, Tarmac Construction Ltd, 1963; Dir, Tarmac Ltd, 1964, Vice-Chm., 1974-77. Member: Export Guarantees Adv. Council, 1974-80; British Overseas Trade Bd, 1977-80; Chm., Overseas Projects Bd, 1977-80. *Recreations*: golf, shooting, fishing, construction. *Address*: The Firs, Cruckton, near Shrewsbury, Shropshire. *T*: Shrewsbury 860796. *Club*: Livery.

FRANCIS, Hugh Elvet, QC 1960; practising at Chancery Bar, 1932-39, and 1945-79; *b* 28 March 1907; *s* of Maurice Evan Francis, JP, Cemmes, Montgomeryshire and Ellen Francis (*née* Jones); *m* 1932, Emma Frances Wienholt, *d* of J. G. W. Bowen, Tyddyn, Llanidloes; three *s* one *d* (and one *s* decd). *Educ*: Machynlleth County Sch.; UCW Aberystwyth; St John's Coll., Cambridge. LLB Wales 1st Cl. Hons, 1929; Schol. St John's Coll., Cambridge, 1930; LLB Cantab 1st Cl. Hons, Macmahon Law studentship, 1931; Arden Schol. and Lord Justice Holker Sen. Schol., Gray's Inn, Certificate of Honour, Bar Final Exams, 1931; Barrister, Gray's Inn, 1932, Bencher, 1956, Treas., 1974; Chancellor of the County Palatine of Durham, 1969-71. Served War of 1939-45 in RA and JAG Dept (despatches). Pres., Iron and Steel Arbitration Tribunal, 1967-74; Chairman: Performing Right Tribunal, 1969-80; Cttee on Rent Acts, 1969-71; Chancery Bar Assoc., 1972-77. Hon. Treas., Bar Council, 1961-64. *Publication*: Jt Ed. Lindley on Partnership, 1950. *Recreations*: fishing, gardening and country pursuits. *Address*: 2 Gray's Inn Square, Gray's Inn, WC1R 5AA. *T*: 01-242 4181; Tyddyn, Llandinam, Powys. *T*: Llanidloes 2448. *Club*: Athenæum.

FRANCIS, Sir Laurie (Justice), Kt 1982; New Zealand High Commissioner to Australia, since 1976; *b* 30 Aug. 1918; *m* 1942, Heather Margaret McFarlane; three *d*. *Educ*: Otago Boys High Sch.; Victoria University of Wellington; Univ. of Otago (LLB). Practised law as Barrister and Solicitor, Winton, Southland, until 1964; Senior Partner in Dunedin firm of Gilbert, Francis, Jackson and Co., Barristers and Solicitors, 1964-76. *Recreations*: golf occasionally, lover of jazz and classical music, follower of Rugby and cricket. *Address*: 21 Mugga Way, Red Hill, ACT 2603, Australia. *T*: 958-909. *Clubs*: Canberra, National Press (Canberra); Melbourne (Melbourne); Tattersalls, Sydney and Union (Sydney).

FRANCIS, Norman; *see* Francis, W. N.

FRANCIS, Owen, CB 1960; Chairman, London Electricity Board, 1972-76; *b* 4 Oct. 1912; *yr s* of Sidney and Margaret Francis, The White House, Austwick, Yorks; *m* 1938, Joan St Leger (*née* Norman); two *d*. *Educ*: Giggleswick Sch., Yorks. Entered Civil Service as Asst Auditor, Exchequer and Audit Dept, 1931; Asst Principal, Mines Dept, 1937; Principal, 1940; Asst Sec., Ministry of Fuel and Power, 1943; Under-Sec., Ministry of Power, 1954-61; Mem., 1962-64, Dep. Chm., 1965-72, CEGB. *Address*: Meadow Cottage, Stanford Dingley, Berks RG7 6LT. *T*: Bradfield 744394. *Clubs*: Royal Yacht Squadron; Seaview Yacht; St Moritz Tobogganing (Vice-Pres.).

See also C. M. Redon.

FRANCIS, Richard Trevor Langford; Managing Director, BBC Radio, since 1982; *b* 10 March 1934; *s* of Eric Roland Francis and Esther Joy (*née* Todd); *m* 1st, 1958, Beate Ohlhagen (marr. diss.); two *s*; 2nd, 1974, Elizabeth Penelope Anne Fairfax Crone; one *s*. *Educ*: Uppingham Sch.; University Coll., Oxford. BA 1956, MA 1960. Commissioned in RA, 1957. BBC Trainee, 1958-60; TV: Prodn Asst, 1960-62; Producer: Afternoon Programmes, 1962-63; Panorama, 1963-65; Asst Editor: Panorama, 1965-66; 24 Hours, 1966-67; Projects Editor, Current Affairs, TV, 1967-70; Head, EBU Operations for US Elections and Apollo, 1968-69; Head of Special Projects, Current Affairs, TV, 1970-71; Asst Head, Current Affairs Group, TV 1971-73; Head, EBU Operations for US Elections, 1972; Controller, BBC NI, 1973-77; Dir, News and Current Affairs, BBC, 1977-82. Visnews: Dir, 1978; Dep. Chm., 1979-82. Mem. British Exec., IPI, 1978-. *Recreations*: offshore sailing, photography, bridge. *Address*: BBC, Broadcasting House, Portland Place, W1A 1AA.

FRANCIS, William Lancelot, CBE 1961; *b* 16 Sept. 1906; *s* of G. J. Francis and Ethel, *d* of L. G. Reed, Durham; *m* 1st, 1937, Ursula Mary Matthew (*d* 1966); two *s* three *d*; 2nd, 1968, Margaret Morris (*d* 1978). *Educ*: Latymer Upper Sch., Hammersmith; King's Coll., Cambridge. MA, PhD. DSIR Sen. Research Award, Cambridge, 1931-33; Rockefeller Foundn Fellowship in Experimental Zoology, Rockefeller Institute, New York, 1933-34; Science Master, Repton Sch., 1935-40; Radar research and administration in Ministries of Supply and Aircraft Production (TRE Malvern), 1940-45; DSIR Headquarters, 1945-65; Secretary, Science Research Council, 1965-72; Consultant, CSD, 1972-75. Member: Nat. Electronics Council, 1965-72; CERN, 1966-70; Advisory Councils: R&D, Fuel and Power, 1966-72; Iron and Steel, 1966-72. Mem. Council, Oxfam, 1975-. *Publications*: papers on physical chemistry and experimental zoology in scientific jls, 1931-37. *Recreations*: gardening, travel. *Address*: 269 Sheen Lane, SW14. *T*: 01-876 3029. *Club*: Athenæum.

FRANCIS, (William) Norman; His Honour Judge Francis; a Circuit Judge (formerly Judge of County Courts), since 1969; *b* 19 March 1921; *s* of Llewellyn Francis; *m* 1951, Anthea Constance (*née* Kerry); one *s* one *d*. *Educ*:

Bradfield; Lincoln Coll., Oxford (BCL, MA). Served War of 1939-45, RA. Called to Bar, Gray's Inn, 1946. Dep. Chm., Brecknock QS, 1962-71. Member: Criminal Law Revision Cttee, 1977-; Policy Adv. Cttee on Sexual Offences, 1977-. Trustee, Cardiff Athletic Club. Chancellor, dio. of Llandaff, 1979-. Mem. Representative Body and Governing Body, Church in Wales. *Recreations*: hockey, walking, golf. *Address*: 2 The Woodlands, Lisvane, near Cardiff. *T*: Cardiff 753070.

FRANCKENSTEIN, Baroness Joseph von; *see* Boyle, Kay.

FRANCKLIN, Comdr (Mavourn Baldwin) Philip, DSC 1940; RN; JP; Lord-Lieutenant of Nottinghamshire, since 1972 (Vice-Lieutenant, 1968-72); *b* 15 Jan. 1913; *s* of Capt. Philip Francklin, MVO, RN (killed in action, 1914); *m* 1949, Xenia Alexandra, *d* of Alex. Davidson, Co. Wicklow; two *s* one *d* (and one *s* decd). *Educ*: RNC Dartmouth. Joined RN, 1926. Served War of 1939-45: Norway, N and S Atlantic, Indian Ocean (despatches twice); Asst to 5th Sea Lord, 1947-49; Comdr 1950; Asst Naval Attaché, Paris, 1952-53. DL, 1963, JP 1958, Notts; High Sheriff of Notts, 1965. KStJ 1973. Croix de Guerre (France). *Address*: Gonalston Hall, Nottingham. *T*: Lowdham 3635. *Club*: Boodle's.

FRANÇOIS-PONCET, Jean André; Director, FMC Corporation, since 1982; *b* 8 Dec. 1928; *s* of André François-Poncet, Grand'Croix de la Légion d'Honneur, and Jacqueline (*née* Dillais); *m* 1959, Marie-Thérèse de Mitry; two *s* one *d*. *Educ*: Paris Law Sch.; Ecole Nationale d'Administration; Wesleyan Univ.; Fletcher Sch. of Law and Diplomacy. Joined Ministry of Foreign Affairs, 1955; Office of Sec. of State, 1956-58; Sec. Gen. of French delegn to Treaty negotiations for EEC and Euratom, 1956-58; Dep. Head, European Orgns, Ministry of Foreign Affairs, 1958-60; Head of Assistance Mission, Morocco, 1961-63; Dep. Head, African Affairs, 1963-65; Counsellor, Tehran, 1969-71. Chm. 1971, Vice-Pres. 1972, Pres. and Chief Exec. 1973-75, Carnaud SA. Sec. of State for Foreign Affairs, Jan.-July 1976; Sec.-Gen. to Presidency of France, 1976-78; Minister for Foreign Affairs, 1978-81. *Publication*: The Economic Policy of Western Germany, 1970. *Address*: 6 boulevard Suchet, 75116 Paris, France.

FRANK, Air Vice-Marshal Alan Donald, CB 1967; CBE 1962; DSO 1943; DFC 1941; Bursar, St Antony's College, Oxford, 1970-74; *b* 1917; *s* of late Major N. G. Frank and late M. H. Frank (*née* Donald); *m* 1941, Jessica Ann Tyrrell; two *s* two *d*. *Educ*: Eton; Magdalen Coll., Oxford. Commanded 51 Squadron Bomber Command, 1943; RAF Staff Coll., 1944; OC 83 Sqdn, 1957; OC RAF Honington, 1958-60; Group Captain Ops, Bomber Comd, 1960-62; Dir Operational Requirements, MoD, 1962-65; Air Attaché and OC, RAF Staff, Washington, 1965-68; SASO, RAF Air Support Command, 1968-70. *Recreations*: ski-ing, squash, tennis. *Address*: Roundway House, Devizes, Wilts.

FRANK, Sir Charles; *see* Frank, Sir F. C.

FRANK, Sir Douglas (George Horace), Kt 1976; QC 1964; President of the Lands Tribunal, since 1974; Deputy Judge of the High Court, since 1975; *b* 16 April 1916; *s* of late George Maurice Frank and late Agnes Winifred Frank; *m* 1979, Audrey, BA (Cantab), *yr d* of Charles Leslie Thomas, Neath, Glam; one *s* four *d* by a former marriage. War service in Royal Artillery. Called to the Bar, Gray's Inn, 1946 (Master of the Bench, 1970). One time Asst Commissioner, Boundary Commission for England. Mem., Cttee Public Participation in Planning (Min. Housing and Local Govt), 1968. Pres., Anglo-American Real Property Inst., 1980-. *Publications*: various legal. *Recreations*: theatre, music, walking. *Address*: 1 Verulam Buildings, WC1. *T*: 01-242 5949; Lands Tribunal, 5 Chancery Lane, WC2. *T*: 01-831 6611.

FRANK, Sir (Frederick) Charles, Kt 1977; OBE 1946; FRS 1954; DPhil; Henry Overton Wills Professor of Physics and Director of the H. H. Wills Physics Laboratory, University of Bristol, 1969-76 (Professor in Physics, 1954-69); now Emeritus Professor; *b* 6 March 1911; *e s* of Frederick and Medora Frank; *m* 1940, Maia Maita Asché, *y d* of late Prof. B. M. Asché; no *c*. *Educ*: Thetford Grammar Sch.; Ipswich Sch.; Lincoln Coll., Oxford. BA, BSc, Oxon. 1933; DPhil Oxon. 1937; Hon. Fellow, Lincoln Coll., 1968. Research: Dyson Perrins Laboratory and Engineering Laboratory, Oxford, 1933-36; Kaiser Wilhelm Institut für Physik, Berlin, 1936-38; Colloid Science Laboratory, Cambridge, 1939-40; Scientific Civil Service (temp.), 1940-46; Chemical Defence Research Establishment, 1940, Air Ministry, 1940-46; Research, H. H. Wills Physical Laboratory, Bristol Univ., 1946-; Research Fellow in Theoretical Physics, 1948; Reader in Physics, 1951-54; a Vice-Pres., Royal Society, 1967-69. Foreign Associate, US Nat. Acad. of Engineering, 1980. Hon. FIP 1978. Hon. DSc: Ghent, 1955; Bath, 1974; TCD, 1978; Warwick, 1981; DUniv Surrey, 1977. Royal Medal, Royal Soc., 1979; Gregory Aminoff Gold Medal, Royal Swedish Acad. of Sciences, 1981; Guthrie Medal and Prize, Inst. of Physics, 1982. *Publications*: articles in various learned journals, mostly dealing either with dielectrics or the physics of solids, in particular crystal dislocations, crystal growth, mechanical properties of polymers and mechanics of the earth's crust. *Address*: Orchard Cottage, Grove Road, Coombe Dingle, Bristol BS9 2RL. *T*: Bristol 68-1708. *Club*: Athenæum.

FRANK, Ilya Mikhailovich; Professor, Moscow University, since 1940; Director, Laboratory of Neutron Physics, Joint Institute for Nuclear Research, Dubna, since 1957; *b* Leningrad, 23 Oct. 1908; *yr s* of Mikhail Lyudvigovich

Frank, Prof. of Mathematics, and Dr Yelizaveta Mikhailovna Gratsianova; *m* 1937, Ella Abramovna Beilikhis, historian; one *s. Educ:* Moscow University (under S. I. Vavilov's guidance). Engaged by State Optical Inst. in Leningrad after graduation, 1931-34 (DSc 1935), and by P. N. Lebedev Physical Inst., USSR Acad. of Scis, Moscow, 1934, Head of Laboratory of Atomic Nucleus (from 1971 part of Inst. for Nuclear Res.), 1947-. Elected Corr. Mem. USSR Acad. of Sciences, 1946, Mem., 1968. Main works in field of optics and nuclear physics. Has participated from beginning in investigations dealing with Vavilov-Cerenkov radiation; carried out many theoretical investigations into Vavilov-Cerenkov effects and in related problems (The Doppler effect in a refractive medium, transition, radiation, etc.) and continues this research. Under his leadership research pulsed reactors of IBR type, IBR-30 with injector and IBR-2 are being developed as well as res. programmes for these pulsed neutron sources, 1957-. Awarded Nobel Prize for Physics (jointly with P. A. Cerenkov and I. E. Tamm) for discovery and interpretation of Cerenkov effect, 1958. USSR State Prize, 1946, 1954, 1971. Decorated with 3 orders of Lenin and 3 other orders. *Address:* Joint Institute for Nuclear Research, Dubna, near Moscow, USSR.

FRANK, Phyllis Margaret Duncan, (Mrs Alan Frank); *see* Tate, P. M. D.

FRANK, Sir Robert John, 3rd Bt, *cr* 1920; FRICS, FAI; late Flying Officer, RAFVR; Director, Ashdale Land and Property Co. Ltd, since 1963; *b* 16 March 1925; *s* of Sir Howard Frank, 1st Bt, GBE, KCB, and Nancy Muriel (she *m* 2nd, 1932, Air-Marshal Sir Arthur Coningham, KCB, KBE, DSO), *e d* of John Brooks; *S* brother, killed in action, 1944; *m* 1st, 1950, Angela Elizabeth (marr. diss. 1959), *e d* of Sir Kenelm Cayley, 10th Bt; two *d*; 2nd, 1960, Margaret Joyce Truesdale; one *s. Heir: s* Robert Andrew Frank, *b* 16 May 1964. *Address:* Ruscombe End, Waltham St Lawrence, near Reading, Berks.

FRANKEL, Dan; *b* 18 Aug. 1900; *s* of Harris Frankel, Mile End; *m* 1921, Lily, *d* of Joseph Marks, Stepney; one *s.* Mem. LCC for Mile End Division of Stepney, 1931-46; MP (Lab) Mile End Division of Stepney, 1935-45.

FRANKEL, Prof. Joseph; Professor of Politics, University of Southampton, 1963-78, now Emeritus; *b* 30 May 1913; *s* of Dr I. and Mrs R. Frankel; *m* 1944, Elizabeth A. Kyle; one *d. Educ:* Univ. of Lwow, Poland (Master of Laws, 1935); Univ. of Western Australia (LLM 1948); Univ. of London (PhD Econ (Internat. Rel.) 1950). Legal Practice, Solicitor, in Poland, 1935-38. Farming in Western Australia, 1938-47; Temp. Asst Lectr, University Coll. London, 1950-51; Lectr and Sen. Lectr, Univ. of Aberdeen, 1951-62. Head of Dept of Politics, 1963-73, Dean, Faculty of Social Sciences, 1964-67, Univ. of Southampton. Res. Associate, RIAA, 1972-73. Vis. Prof., International Christian Univ., Tokyo, 1977. Hon. Professorial Fellow, Univ. of Wales, 1980-. *Publications:* The Making of Foreign Policy, 1962, 2nd edn 1967; International Relations, 1963, 2nd edn 1969; International Politics: conflict and harmony, 1969; National Interest, 1970; Contemporary International Theory and the Behaviour of States, 1973; British Foreign Policy 1945-1973, 1975; International Relations in a Changing World, 1979; contribs to International Affairs, Brit. Jl Internat. Studies, etc. *Recreations:* gardening, travel, classical and contemporary literature, art and music. *Address:* The Old Rectory, Avington, Winchester, Hants SO21 1DD. *T:* Itchen Abbas 275.

FRANKEL, Sir Otto (Herzberg), Kt 1966; FRS 1953; DSc; DAgr; FRSNZ; FAA; Honorary Research Fellow, Division of Plant Industry, CSIRO, Canberra, Australia, since 1966; *b* 4 Nov. 1900; *m* 1939, Margaret Anderson. *Educ:* Vienna; Berlin; Cambridge. Plant Geneticist, 1929-42, and Chief Executive Officer, 1942-49, Wheat Research Institute, NZ; Dir, Crop Research Division, Dept of Scientific and Industrial Research, New Zealand, 1949-51; Chief, Division of Plant Industry, CSIRO, Australia, 1951-62; Member of Executive, Commonwealth Scientific and Industrial Research Organization, Melbourne, Aust, 1962-66. *Publications:* (ed jtly) Genetic Resources in Plants: their exploration and conservation, 1970; (ed jtly) Crop Genetic Resources for Today and Tomorrow, 1975; (with M. E. Soulé) Conservation and Evolution, 1981; numerous articles in British, NZ and Australian scientific journals. *Recreations:* ski-ing, gardening, angling. *Address:* 4 Cobby Street, Campbell, Canberra, ACT 2601, Australia. *T:* 479460.
   See also P. H. Frankel.

FRANKEL, Dr Paul Herzberg, CBE 1981; FInstPet; President, Petroleum Economics Ltd, since 1980 (Chairman, 1955-80); *b* 1 Nov. 1903; *s* of Ludwig and Teresa Herzberg-Frankel; *m* 1931, Helen Spitzer; one *s* four *d. Educ:* Vienna Univ. (Dr of Polit. Econ.). FInstPet 1941. Actively engaged in oil industry, mainly in oil refining and marketing, first on Continent and then in UK, mid 1930s-; Dir of Manchester Oil Refinery Ltd and associated cos in UK and on Continent until 1955; founded Petroleum Economics Ltd, the London internat. consulting firm, 1955. Chevalier de la Légion d'Honneur, 1976; Grosses Verdienstkreuz des Verdienstordens, Bundesrepublik Deutschland, 1977; Grosses Ehrenzeichen für Verdienste, Republik Osterreich, 1978. Cadman Medal, Institute of Petroleum, 1973. *Publications:* Essentials of Petroleum, 1946; Oil: the facts of life, 1962; Mattei: oil and power politics, 1966. *Recreations:* walking, music. *Address:* 30 Dunstall Road, SW20 0HR. *T:* 01-946 5805. *Club:* Reform.
   See also Sir O. H. Frankel.

FRANKEL, Prof. Sally Herbert, MA Rand, PhD London, DScEcon London, MA Oxon; Emeritus Professor in the Economics of Underdeveloped Countries, University of Oxford, and Emeritus Fellow, Nuffield College, Oxford (Professor, and Professorial Fellow, 1946-71); *b* 22 Nov. 1903; *e s* of Jacob Frankel; *m* 1928, Ilse Jeanette Frankel; one *s* one *d. Educ:* St John's Coll., Johannesburg; University of the Witwatersrand; London Sch. of Economics. Prof. of Economics, University of Witwatersrand, Johannesburg, 1931-46; responsible for calculations of National Income of S Africa for the Treasury, 1941-48; Jt Editor of South African Journal of Economics from its inception to 1946; Mem. of Union of South Africa Treasury Advisory Council on Economic and Financial Policy, 1941-45; Mem. of Union of South Africa Miners' Phthisis Commission, 1941-42; Commissioner appointed by Govts of Southern and Northern Rhodesia and the Bechuanaland Protectorate to report upon Rhodesia Railways Ltd, 1942-43; Chm. Commission of Enquiry into Mining Industry of Southern Rhodesia, 1945; Mem. East Africa Royal Commission, 1953-55; Consultant Adviser, Urban African Affairs Commn, Govt of S Rhodesia, 1957-58. Vis. Prof. of Econs, Univ. of Virginia, until 1974. *Publications:* Co-operation and Competition in the Marketing of Maize in South Africa, 1926; The Railway Policy of South Africa, 1928; Coming of Age: Studies in South African Citizenship and Politics (with Mr J. H. Hofmeyr and others), 1930; Capital Investment in Africa: Its Course and Effects, 1938; The Economic Impact on Underdeveloped Societies: Essays on International Investment and Social Change, 1953; Investment and the Return to Equity Capital in the South African Gold Mining Industry 1887-1965: An International Comparison, 1967; Gold and International Equity Investment (Hobart Paper 45), 1969; Money: two philosophies, the conflict of trust and authority, 1977. *Recreation:* gardening. *Address:* The Knoll House, Hinksey Hill, Oxford. *T:* Oxford 35345. *Club:* Reform.

FRANKEL, William, CBE 1970; Editor, Jewish Chronicle, 1958-77; *b* 3 Feb. 1917; *s* of Isaac and Anna Frankel, London; *m* 1st, 1939, Gertrude Freda Reed (marr. diss.); one *s* one *d*; 2nd, 1973, Mrs Claire Neuman. *Educ:* elementary and secondary schs in London; London Univ. (LLB Hons). Called to Bar, Middle Temple, 1944; practised on South-Eastern circuit, 1944-55. General Manager, Jewish Chronicle, 1955-58. Special Adviser to The Times, 1977-81. Director: Jewish Chronicle Ltd; Jewish Gazette Ltd. Chairman: Mental Health Review Appeal Tribunal, 1978-; Supplementary Benefits Appeal Tribunal, 1979-. Vis. Prof., Jewish Theological Seminary of America, 1968-69. JP Co. of London, 1963-69. *Publications:* (ed) Friday Nights, 1973; Israel Observed, 1980. *Address:* 5 Pump Court, Temple, EC4. *T:* 01-353 2628. *Clubs:* Athenæum, MCC.

FRANKEN, Rose (Dorothy); Novelist; Playwright; *b* Texas, 28 Dec. 1895; *d* of Michael Lewin and Hannah (*née* Younker); *m* 1st, 1914, Dr S. W. A. Franken (*d* 1932); three *s*; 2nd, 1937, William Brown Melony (*d* 1970). *Educ:* Ethical Culture Sch., NYC. *Publications: novels:* Pattern, 1925; Twice Born, 1935, new edn 1970; Call Back Love, 1937; Of Great Riches, 1937 (as Gold Pennies, UK, 1938); Strange Victory, 1939; Claudia: the story of a marriage, 1939; Claudia and David, 1940; American Bred, 1941; Another Claudia, 1943; Women in White, 1945; Young Claudia, 1946; The Marriage of Claudia, 1948; From Claudia to David, 1949; The Fragile Years, The Antic Years (as The Return of Claudia, UK), 1952; Rendezvous (as The Quiet Heart, UK), 1954; (autobiography) When All is Said and Done, 1963; You're Well Out of Hospital, 1966; Swan Song, 1976; *plays:* Another Language, 1932; Mr Dooley, Jr: a comedy for children, 1932; Claudia, 1941; Outrageous Fortune, 1944; When Doctors Disagree, 1944; Soldier's Wife, 1945; Hallams, 1948; The Wing, 1971; also short stories in Colliers, Liberty, Cosmopolitan, Harper's Bazaar and anthologies.

FRANKHAM, Very Rev. Harold Edward; Provost of Southwark, 1970-82; *b* 6 April 1911; *s* of Edward and Minnie Frankham; *m* 1942, Margaret Jean Annear; one *s* two *d* (and one *s* decd). *Educ:* London Coll. of Divinity (LCD). Ordained, 1941; Curate: Luton, 1941-44; Holy Trinity, Brompton, 1944-46; Vicar of Addiscombe, 1946-52; Rector of Middleton, Lancs, 1952-61; Vicar of Luton, 1961-70. Hon. Canon of St Albans, 1967-70. Exec. Sec., Archbishops' Council on Evangelism, 1965-73. *Recreations:* music, painting, sailing, travel. *Address:* Montague House, Lambridge, Bath, Avon.

FRANKL, Peter; pianist; *b* 2 Oct 1935; *s* of Laura and Tibor Frankl; *m* 1958, Annie Feiner; one *s* one *d. Educ:* Liszt Ferenc Acad. of Music, Budapest. Regular concert tours with leading orchestras and conductors throughout the world; numerous festival appearances, including Edinburgh, Cheltenham, Lucerne, Flanders, Aldeburgh, Adelaide, Windsor. Winner of internat. competitions: Paris, 1957; Munich, 1957; Rio de Janeiro, 1959. Franz Liszt Award, Budapest, 1958. Hon. Citizen, Rio de Janeiro, 1960. Numerous recordings include: complete works for piano by Schumann and Debussy; orchestral and chamber pieces. *Recreations:* football, opera, theatre. *Address:* 5 Gresham Gardens, NW11 8NX. *T:* 01-455 5228.

FRANKLAND, family name of **Baron Zouche.**

FRANKLAND, (Anthony) Noble, CBE 1976; DFC 1944; MA, DPhil; historian and biographer; Director of Imperial War Museum (at the Main Building, Southwark, London, 1960-82 and at Duxford Airfield, near Cambridge, 1976-82, and the Imperial War Museum Ship, HMS Belfast, the Pool of London, 1978-82); *b* 4 July 1922; *s* of late Edward Frankland, Ravenstonedale, Westmorland; *m* 1st, 1944, Diana Madeline Fovargue (*d* 1981), *d* of late G. V. Tavernor, of Madras and Southern Mahratta Rly, India;

one *s* one *d*; 2nd, 1982, Sarah Katharine, *d* of His Honour the late Sir David Davies, QC and late Lady Davies (Margaret Kennedy). *Educ:* Sedbergh; Trinity Coll., Oxford. Served Royal Air Force, 1941-45 (Bomber Command, 1943-45). Air Historical Branch Air Ministry, 1948-51; Official Military Historian, Cabinet Office, 1951-58. Rockefeller Fellow, 1953. Deputy Dir of Studies, Royal Institute of International Affairs, 1956-60. Lees Knowles Lecturer, Trinity Coll., Cambridge, 1963. Historical advisor, Thames Television series, The World At War, 1971-74. Vice-Chm., British Nat. Cttee, Internat. Cttee for Study of Second World War, 1976-82. Biographer of His late Royal Highness The Duke of Gloucester. Mem., Council, Morley Coll., 1962-66; Trustee: Military Archives Centre, KCL, 1963-82; HMS Belfast Trust, 1971-78 (Vice-Chm., 1972-78); HMS Belfast Bd, 1978-82. *Publications:* Documents on International Affairs: for 1955, 1958; for 1956, 1959; for 1957, 1960; Crown of Tragedy, Nicholas II, 1960; The Strategic Air Offensive Against Germany, 1939-1945 (4 vols) jointly with Sir Charles Webster, 1961; The Bombing Offensive against Germany, Outlines and Perspectives, 1961; Bomber Offensive: the Devastation of Europe, 1970; (ed jtly) The Politics and Strategy of the Second World War (series), 1974-; (ed jtly) Decisive Battles of the Twentieth Century: Land, Sea, Air, 1976; Prince Henry, Duke of Gloucester, 1980; Historical Chapter in Manual of Air Force Law, 1956; other articles and reviews; broadcasts on radio and TV. *Address:* Thames House, Eynsham, Oxford. *T:* Oxford 881327.

FRANKLAND, Noble; *see* Frankland, A. N.

FRANKLIN, Albert Andrew Ernst, CVO 1965; CBE 1961 (OBE 1950); HM Diplomatic Service, retired; *b* 28 Nov. 1914; *s* of Albert John Henry Franklin; *m* 1944, Henrietta Irene Barry; two *d*. *Educ:* Merchant Taylors' Sch.; St John's Coll., Oxford. Joined HM Consular Service, 1937; served in Peking, Kunming, Chungking, Calcutta, Algiers, Marseilles, Kabul, Basle, Tientsin, Formosa, Düsseldorf and in the FO; HM Consul-General, Los Angeles, USA, 1966-74. Member of Kitchener Association. FRSA 1971. *Recreation:* chinese ceramics and paintings. *Address:* 5 Dulwich Wood Avenue, SE19. *T:* 01-670 2769.

FRANKLIN, Alfred White, FRCP; Hon. Consulting Physician, Department of Child Health, Saint Bartholomew's Hospital; Hon. Consulting Pædiatrician, Queen Charlotte's Maternity Hospital; *b* 1905; *yr s* of Philip Franklin, FRCS; *m* 1943, Ann Grizel, *er d* of late Rev. Francis Dent Vaisey; two *s* two *d*. *Educ:* Epsom Coll.; Clare Coll., Cambridge (scholar); St Bartholomew's Hospital. MB, BCh, 1933, FRCP, 1942. Lawrence Scholarship and Gold Medal, 1933 and 1934, St Bartholomew's Hosp.; Temple Cross Research Fellow, Johns Hopkins Hosp., 1934-35. Pædiatrician to Sector III, EMS. Dep. Chm., Attendance Allowance Bd, DHSS, 1970-78; Formerly Chm., Invalid Children's Aid Assoc.; Co-founder, The Osler Club, London. Past Pres., British Pædiatric Assoc.; President: British Soc. for Medical History, 1974-76; Internat. Soc. for Prevention of Child Abuse and Neglect, 1981-. *Publications:* ed, Selected Writings of Sir D'Arcy Power, 1931, and of Sir William Osler, 1951; ed, The Care of Invalid and Crippled Children, 1960; ed, Concerning Child Abuse, 1975; Pastoral Paediatrics, 1976; Widening Horizons of Child Health, 1976; (ed) The Challenge of Child Abuse, 1977; (ed) Child Abuse: Prediction, Prevention and Follow-Up, 1977; contrib. to books and jls on medical, historical and bibliographical subjects. *Address:* 149 Harley Street, W1N 2DE. *T:* 01-935 4444; The Cottage, Northaw, Herts. *T:* Potters Bar 52184. *Club:* Athenæum.

FRANKLIN, Sir Eric (Alexander), Kt 1954; CBE 1952; *b* 3 July 1910; *s* of late William John Franklin; *m* 1936, Joy Stella, *d* of late George Oakes Lucas, Cambridge. *Educ:* The English Sch., Maymyo; Emmanuel Coll., Cambridge. Appointed to ICS in 1935 and posted to Burma; Subdivisional Officer, 1936-39. Deputy Registrar, High Court of Judicature at Rangoon, 1939-40; District and Sessions Judge, Arakan, 1941-42; Deputy Sec. to Government of Burma at Simla, 1942-45; Registrar, High Court of Judicature at Rangoon, 1946-47; retired prematurely from ICS, 1948. Appointed on contract as Deputy Sec. to Government of Pakistan. Cabinet Secretariat, 1949; Joint Sec., Cabinet Secretariat, 1952; Establishment Officer and Head of Central Organisation and Methods Office, 1953; Establishment Sec. to Government of Pakistan, 1956-58; Chm. Sudan Government Commission on terms of service, 1958-59; Civil Service Adviser to Government of Hashemite Kingdom of Jordan, 1960-63; acting Resident Representative, UN Technical Assistance Board, Jordan, 1961; Senior UN Administrative Adviser to Government of Nepal, 1964-66. Chm., Cambridgeshire Soc. for the Blind, 1969-74, Vice-Pres., 1974. FRSA 1971. El Kawkab el Urdoni (Star of Jordan), 1963. *Recreations:* walking, gardening, music. *Address:* The Birches, 16 Cavendish Avenue, Cambridge.

FRANKLIN, George Frederic; formerly Headmaster, Lincoln School, retired Dec. 1957; *b* Greenwich, 28 Dec. 1897; *s* of John and Alice Franklin; *m* 1926, Edith Kate Young; one *s* one *d*. *Educ:* Roan Sch.; King's Coll., Cambridge. Asst Master, Merchant Taylors' Sch., Crosby; Senior Mod. Langs Master, Christ's Hosp. *Publications:* French and German school texts. *Address:* 30 Station Road, Condover, Shrewsbury, Salop SY5 7BQ.

FRANKLIN, George Henry, RIBA, FRTPI; Physical (Land Use) Planning Adviser, Overseas Development Administration, Foreign and Commonwealth Office (formerly Ministry of Overseas Development), since 1966; *b* 15 June 1923; *s* of late George Edward Franklin, RN, and Annie Franklin; *m* 1950, Sylvia D. Franklin; three *s* one *d*. *Educ:* Hastings Grammar Sch.; Hastings Sch.

of Art; Architectural Assoc. Sch. of Arch. (AADipl); Sch. of Planning and Research for Regional Develt, London (SPDip). Served War of 1939-45: Parachute Sqdn; RE, Europe; Bengal Sappers and Miners, SE Asia. Finchley Bor. Council, 1952-54; Architect, Christian Med. Coll., Ludhiana, Punjab, India, 1954-57; Physical Planning Adviser (Colombo Plan) to Republic of Indonesia, 1958-62, and Govt of Malaysia, 1963-64; Physical Planning Adviser, ODM, later ODA, 1966- (Overseas Div., Building Research Station, 1966-73, ODM, later ODA, 1973-). Activities in Commonwealth Assoc. of Planners (Pres., 1980-), Commonwealth Human Ecology Council, United Bible Socs. *Publications:* papers to internat. confs and professional jls concerning planning, building and housing in the Third World. *Recreations:* work, promotion of physical planning in countries of the Third World; fly-fishing. *Address:* 24 Oakleigh Park North, N20 9AR. *T:* 01-445 0336.

FRANKLIN, Henry William Fernehough; Headmaster Epsom College, 1940-1962; *b* 30 June 1901; *s* of Henry Franklin, Schoolmaster; *m* 1931, Phyllis Denham; one *d*. *Educ:* Christ's Hosp.; Christ Church, Oxford. Asst Master, Radley Coll., 1924-27; Asst Master, Rugby Sch., 1927-39. Chm. of Home Office Departmental Cttee on Punishments in Prisons, Borstals, etc., 1948. Mem., Advertising Standards Authority, 1962-67. *Publications:* Fifty Latin Lyrics, 1955; (with J. A. G. Bruce) Latin Prose Composition, 1937; Latin Reader, 1939. *Recreations:* formerly various games: cricket (OU XI 1924; Essex County XI); Rugby football (OU XV 1923; Barbarian FC), hockey, fives, etc.; also music and change-ringing; nowadays mostly teaching and change-ringing. *Address:* The Cottage, Westward Lane, West Chiltington, Pulborough, West Sussex. *T:* W Chiltington 2282.

FRANKLIN, John; *see* Franklin, W. J.

FRANKLIN, Michael David Milroy, CB 1979; CMG 1972; Permanent Secretary, Department of Trade, since 1982; *b* 24 Aug. 1927; *o s* of late Milroy Franklin; *m* 1951, Dorothy Joan Fraser; two *s* one *d*. *Educ:* Taunton Sch.; Peterhouse, Cambridge (1st cl. hons Economics). Served with 4th RHA, BAOR. Asst Principal, Min. of Agric. and Fisheries, 1950; Economic Section, Cabinet Office (subseq. Treasury), 1952-55; Principal, Min. of Agric., Fisheries and Food, 1956; UK Delegn to OEEC (subseq. OECD), 1959-61; Private Sec. to Minister of Agric., Fisheries and Food, 1961-64; Asst Sec., Head of Sugar and Tropical Foodstuffs Div., 1965-68; Under-Sec. (EEC Gp), MAFF, 1968-73; a Dep. Dir Gen., Directorate Gen. for Agric., EC, 1973-77; Dep. Sec., Head of the European Secretariat, Cabinet Office, 1977-81. *Address:* 15 Galley Lane, Barnet, Herts. *Club:* United Oxford & Cambridge University.

FRANKLIN, Norman Laurence, CBE 1975 (OBE 1963); MSc, PhD; FRS 1981; FEng; Managing Director, National Nuclear Corporation Ltd, since 1980; part-time Member, UKAEA, since 1971; part-time Director, British Nuclear Fuels Ltd; *b* 1 Sept. 1924; *s* of William Alexander and Beatrice Franklin; *m* 1949, Bessie Coupland; one *s* one *d*. *Educ:* Batley Grammar School; University of Leeds. British Coke Res. Assoc., 1945-48; Lecturer in Chemical Engineering, Univ. of Leeds, 1948-55; joined UKAEA, 1955; Mem. for Production, 1969-71. Man. Dir, Chief Executive and Dir, British Nuclear Fuels Ltd, 1971-75; Chm. and Man. Dir, Nuclear Power Co. Ltd, 1975-80; Dir, National Nuclear Corporation Ltd, 1974-. FEng, FIChemE (Pres. 1979). Hon. DSc Leeds, 1976. *Publications:* Statistical Analysis in Chemistry and the Chemical Industry, 1954; The Transport Properties of Fluids, Vol. 4, Chemical Engineering Practice, 1957; Heat Transfer by Conduction, Vol. 7, Chemical Engineering Practice, 1963; papers in Trans Instn of Chemical Engineers, 1953-66. *Recreation:* walking. *Address:* The Evergreens, Greenacre Close, Knutsford, Cheshire WA16 8NL. *T:* Knutsford 3045. *Club:* East India, Devonshire, Sports and Public Schools.

FRANKLIN, Olga Heather, CBE 1950 (MBE 1919); RRC 1946 (ARRC 1942); *b* 20 Sept. 1895; *e c* of late Robert Francis Franklin, OBE. *Educ:* St Michael's Lodge, Stoke, Devonport, VAD, 1915-17; WRNS, 1917-19; King's Coll. Hosp., 1923; Queen Alexandra's Royal Naval Nursing Service, 1927-50; Matron-in-Chief, 1947-50; King's Hon. Nursing Sister (the first appointed), 1947-50; retired, 1950. Prisoner of war, Hongkong, 1941-45. *Address:* 57 Dean Court Road, Rottingdean, Brighton BN2 7DL. *T:* Brighton 32202.

FRANKLIN, Dr Raoul Norman, FInstP, FIMA; Vice Chancellor, The City University, London, since 1978; Fellow, Keble College, Oxford, since 1963; *b* 3 June 1935; *s* of Norman George Franklin and Thelma Brinley Davis; *m* 1961, Faith, *d* of Lt-Col H. T. C. Ivens and Eva Gray; two *s*. *Educ:* Howick District High Sch.; Auckland Grammar Sch., NZ; Univ. of Auckland (ME, DSc); Christ Church, Oxford (MA, DPhil, DSc). FInstP 1968; FIMA 1970. Officer, NZ Defence Scientific Corps, 1957-75. Sen. Res. Fellow, RMCS, Shrivenham, 1961-63; Univ. of Oxford: Tutorial Fellow, 1963-78, Dean, 1966-71, Hon. Fellow, 1980, Keble Coll.; Univ. Lectr in Engrg Science, 1966-78; Mem., Gen. Bd, 1967-74 (Vice Chm., 1971-74); Mem., Hebdomadal Council, 1971-74, 1976-78. Consultant, UKAEA Culham, 1968-. Member: UGC Equipment Sub Cttee, 1975-78; Plasma Physics Commn, IUPAP, 1971-; Science Bd, SERC, 1982-. Chairman: Internat. Science Cttee, Phenomena in Ionized Gases, 1976-77; City Techology Ltd, 1978-. Trustee, Ruskin School of Drawing, 1975-78; Mem. Council, Gresham Coll., 1981-. Freeman, City of London, 1981. *Publications:* Plasma Phenomena in Ionized Gases, 1976; papers on plasmas, gas discharges and granular materials. *Recreations:* tennis, walking, gardening. *Address:* The City University, Northampton Square, EC1V 0HB. *T:* 01-253 4399.

FRANKLIN, Richard Harrington, CBE 1973; Consultant Emeritus to the Royal Navy (Consulting Surgeon, 1961-81); Hon. Consulting Surgeon, Star and Garter Home, Richmond, since 1957, Governor, since 1969; Hon. Visiting Surgeon, Royal Postgraduate Medical School (Surgeon, 1945-71); Emeritus Consultant Surgeon to Kingston and Long Grove Group of Hospitals (Surgeon, Kingston, 1946-71); *b* 3 April 1906; *s* of late P. C. Franklin; *m* 1933, Helen Margaret Kimber, *d* of Sir Henry D. Kimber, Bt; two *s. Educ:* Merchant Taylors' Sch.; St Thomas's Hosp., London Univ. MRCS, LRCP 1930; MB, BS 1930; FRCS 1934. First Asst, Brit. Postgrad. Med. Sch., 1936; Surgeon EMS, 1940-45; Hunterian Prof., RCS, 1947; Bradshaw Lectr, 1973; Grey-Turner Lectr, Internat. Soc. Surg., 1973; Hunterian Orator, RCS, 1977. Vis. Prof., Univ. of California, 1972. Fellow, Med. Soc. of London. Mem. Ct of Examrs, RCS, 1956-66; Examr in Surgery, Cambridge Univ., 1958-69. Vice-Pres. 1960, Pres. 1969-70, Sect. of Surgery, RSM; Mem. Coun., RCS, 1965-77, Vice-Pres., 1974-76; Mem. Coun., Imperial Cancer Research Fund, 1967-82 (Vice-Chm., 1975-79), Life Governor, 1975. Hon. Mem., Hellenic Surgical Soc. *Publications:* Surgery of the Oesophagus, 1952; articles in various med. jls and text books. *Recreation:* sailing. *Address:* The Stern Walk, Crespigny Road, Aldeburgh, Suffolk IP15 5EZ. *T:* Aldeburgh 2600. *Clubs:* Ranelagh Sailing, Aldeburgh Yacht.

FRANKLIN, Rt. Rev. William Alfred, OBE 1964; Assistant Bishop (full time), Diocese of Peterborough, and Hon. Canon of the Cathedral, since 1978; *b* 16 July 1916; *s* of George Amos and Mary Anne Catherine Franklin; *m* 1945, Winifred Agnes Franklin (*née* Jarvis); one *s* one *d. Educ:* schools in London; Kelham Theol Coll. Deacon 1940, priest 1941, London; Curate, St John on Bethnal Green, Chaplain ATC and Univ. Settlements, 1941-43; Curate of St John's, Palmers Green, and Chm. for area Interdenominational Youth Activities, 1943-45; Asst Chaplain, St Saviour's, Belgrano, Buenos Aires, Argentina and teaching duties at Green's School, Buenos Aires, 1945-48; Rector of Holy Trinity, Lomas de Zamora, Buenos Aires, Domestic Chaplain to Bishop in Argentina, Sec. Dio. Bd of Missions, and Chaplain St Alban's Coll., Lomas, 1948-58; Rector, Canon and Sub-Dean of Anglican Cathedral, Santiago, Chaplain Grange School and Founder and Chm. Ecumenical Gp in Chile, 1958-65; Rector of St Alban's, Bogotá, Colombia, 1965-71; Archdeacon of Diocese, 1966-71; elected Bishop of Diocese, 1971; resigned, 1978, allowing a national to be elected. Founder and Editor of Revista Anglicana, official magazine of Arensa (Assoc. of Anglican Dioceses in North of S America). *Recreations:* fishing, tennis and cricket. *Address:* 4 Penfold Drive, Great Billing, Northampton. *T:* Northampton 407839. *Clubs:* Royal Commonwealth Society; Anglo-American (Bogotá, Colombia).

FRANKLIN, (William) John, FCA; Managing Director and Chief Executive, Powell Duffryn, since 1976; *b* 8 March 1927; *s* of late William Thomas Franklin and Edith Hannah Franklin; *m* 1951, Sally (*née* Davies); one *d. Educ:* Monkton House Sch., Cardiff. W. R. Gresty, Chartered Accountants, 1947-50; Peat Marwick Mitchell, Chartered Accountants, 1950-55; Powell Duffryn, 1956-: Director, Cory Brothers, 1964; Man. Dir, Powell Duffryn Timber, 1967-70; Dir, Powell Duffryn, 1970-. *Recreation:* golf. *Address:* 2 Kilcorral Close, Epsom, Surrey KT17 4HX. *T:* Epsom 21849. *Clubs:* English-Speaking Union; Cuddington Golf (Banstead).

FRANKLYN, Charles Aubrey Hamilton, MD Lausanne, MB, BS London, MA *hc* Malaya 1951; MRCS, LRCP 1923; FLS; FSA(Scot); Physician and Genealogical-historian; *b* Brentwood, Co. Essex, 25 Aug. 1896; *er s* of late Major Aubrey Hamilton Franklyn and Ethel Mary, *d* of late Walter Gray. *Educ:* Tonbridge Sch.; St Thomas's Hosp.; Universities of London, Lausanne, Oxford (Exeter Coll.), France, 1916-19. Lieut RA (SR), 1915-20; in practice as physician from 1925; temp. MO, P & O Line, 1933; MO (part-time) HM Prison, Lincoln, 1934-37; in EMS (Grade III) from 1939. Mem. of Standing Cttee, University of London, 1927-61 (Senior mem., 1954-61); Bedell of Convocation, University of London, from 1932; a Provincial Supervisor in Charge of Final Degree Examns (June) 1941-56. Mem. BMA, 1923-48; Life Mem. Oxford Soc.; Fellow Philosophical Soc. of England; Mem. Amer. Institute for Philosophical Studies. Hon. Asst to Editor Burke's Landed Gentry, Centenary (15th) edn, 1937, and to Editor Armorial Families, 7th edn, 1929-30 (2 vols). Authority on Academical Dress, University Degrees and Ceremonies, Modern Heraldry and Genealogy, etc. Designer of Official Robes and Academical Dress for Universities: Malaya, Australian National, Southampton, Hull, and New Univ. of Ulster, Coleraine, Co. Londonderry; designed: armorial ensigns and 3 badges, British Transport Commn, 1956; Arms of Borough of Bridgnorth, 1959; Arms of St Peter's Hall (now College), Oxford. MA Malaya 1951, by diploma, *hc*, in absentia; Hon. DLitt: Geneva Theolog. Coll, Vincennes, Ind, 1972; Central Sch. of Religion, Ind. and Redhill, Surrey, 1972. *Publications:* The Bearing of Coat-Armour by Ladies, 1923, repr. with supp. 1973; English and Scottish Heraldry compared and contrasted (Scots. Mag. Jan. 1925); University Hoods and Robes (25 cards), 1926; The Genealogy of the Chavasse Family, 1929; A Genealogical History of The Family of Tiarks of Foxbury, 1929, 2nd edition, rev. and enlarged 1969 (priv. printed); A Genealogical and Heraldic History of Four Families (privately printed), 1932; A Genealogical History of the families of Paulet (or Pawlett), Berewe (or Barrow), Lawrence, and Parker (privately printed), 1964, Supplement, incl. Morgan of Llanfabon, Turner of Oldland in Keymer, Vavasour of Hazlewood, Walwyn of Longford, etc, 1969; A Genealogical History of the Families of Montgomerie of Garboldisham, Hunter of Knap, and Montgomerie of Fittleworth (privately printed), 1967; Academical Dress from the Middle Ages to the Present Day, including Lambeth Degrees (privately printed), 1970; (ed jtly) Haycraft's Degrees and Hoods of the

World's Universities and Colleges, 5th edn, 1972; The Genealogy of Anne the Quene (Anne Bullen) and other English Families, 1977; Cuckfield Rural Dist, Official Local Guide (new edn), 1947; A Dedication Service for the Parish Church of St John the Baptist, Mexborough, 1967; contribs to: Enc. Brit.; 5th edn of Grove's Dic. of Music and Musicians; Pears Cyclopædia; Chambers's Enc.; Internat. Enc. of Higher Educn, etc. *Recreations:* music, cats, motoring, travelling, lecturing, and writing, etc. *Address:* 44 Sackville Gardens, New Church Road, Hove, Sussex BN3 4GH. *T:* Brighton 733071; *c/o* National Westminster Bank Ltd, 1 Lee Road, Blackheath, SE3 9RH; Exeter College, Oxford.

FRANKS, family name of **Baron Franks.**

FRANKS, Baron *cr* 1962, of Headington (Life Peer); **Oliver Shewell Franks,** OM 1977; GCMG 1952; KCB 1946; CBE 1942; PC 1949; DL; FBA 1960; Provost of Worcester College, Oxford, 1962-76; Chancellor of East Anglia University since 1965; *b* 16 Feb. 1905; *s* of late Rev. R. S. Franks; *m* 1931, Barbara Mary Tanner; two *d. Educ:* Bristol Grammar Sch.; Queen's Coll., Oxford (MA). Fellow and Praelector in Philosophy, Queen's College, Oxford, 1927-37; University Lecturer in Philosophy, 1935-37; Visiting Prof., Univ. of Chicago, 1935; Prof. of Moral Philosophy, University of Glasgow, 1937-45; temp. Civil Servant, Ministry of Supply, 1939-46; Permanent Sec. Ministry of Supply, 1945-46; Provost of Queen's Coll., Oxford, 1946-48; British Ambassador at Washington, 1948-52; Director: Lloyds Bank Ltd, 1953-75 (Chm., 1954-62); Schroders; Chm., Friends' Provident & Century Life Office, 1955-62; Cttee of London Clearing Bankers, 1960-62. Mem. of Rhodes Trust 1957-73; Chairman: Bd of Governors, United Oxford Hosps, 1958-64; Wellcome Trust, 1965-82 (Trustee, 1963-65); Commission of Inquiry into Oxford Univ., 1964-66; Cttee on Official Secrets Act, Section 2, 1971-72; Cttee on Ministerial Members, 1976; Political Honours Scrutiny Cttee, 1976-. Mem., National Economic Development Council, 1962-64. Mem. Council, Duchy of Cornwall, 1966-. Pres., Kennedy Memorial Cttee, 1963; Trustee: Pilgrim Trust, 1947-79; Rockefeller Foundn, 1961-70. Hon. Fellow: Queen's Coll., Oxford, 1948; St Catharine's Coll., Cambridge, 1966; Wolfson Coll., Oxford, 1967; Worcester Coll., Oxford, 1976; Lady Margaret Hall, Oxford, 1978; Visiting Fellow, Nuffield Coll., 1959. Hon. DCL, Oxford, and other Honorary Doctorates. DL Oxfordshire, 1978. *Address:* Blackhall Farm, Garford Road, Oxford OX2 6UY. *T:* Oxford 511286. *Club:* Athenæum.

FRANKS, Sir Arthur Temple, (Sir Dick Franks), KCMG 1979 (CMG 1967); HM Diplomatic Service, retired; *b* 13 July 1920; *s* of late Arthur Franks, Hove; *m* 1945, Rachel Marianne, *d* of late Rev. A. E. S. Ward, DD; one *s* two *d. Educ:* Rugby; Queen's Coll., Oxford. HM Forces, 1940-46 (despatches). Entered Foreign Service, 1949; British Middle East Office, 1952; Tehran, 1953; Bonn, 1962; FCO, 1966-81. *Address:* *c/o* Foreign and Commonwealth Office, King Charles Street, SW1A 2AH. *Clubs:* Travellers'; Sunningdale Golf.

FRANKS, Desmond Gerald Fergus; His Honour Judge Franks; a Circuit Judge, since 1972; *b* 24 Jan. 1928; *s* of F. Franks, MC, late Lancs Fus., and E. R. Franks; *m* 1952, Margaret Leigh (*née* Daniel); one *d. Educ:* Cathedral Choir Sch., Canterbury; Manchester Grammar Sch.; University Coll., London (LLB). Called to Bar, Middle Temple, 1952; Northern Circuit; Asst Recorder, Salford, 1966; Deputy Recorder, Salford, 1971; a Recorder of the Crown Court, 1972. *Recreations:* gardening, photography. *Address:* 4 Beathwaite Drive, Bramhall, Cheshire. *T:* 061-485 6065.

FRANKS, Sir Dick; *see* Franks, Sir A. T.

FRANKS, Air Vice-Marshal John Gerald, CB 1954; CBE 1949; RAF retired, 1960; *b* 23 May 1905; *e s* of late James Gordon Franks, and of Margaret, *y d* of Lord Chief Justice Fitz-Gibbon, Dublin; *m* 1936, Jessica Rae West; two *d. Educ:* Cheltenham Coll.; RAF Coll., Cranwell. RAF; commissioned from Cranwell, 1924; No 56 Fighter Sqdn, Biggin Hill, 1925-26; flying duties with FAA HMS Courageous, Mediterranean, 1928-29; India, 1930-35; Middle East, 1936; RAF Staff Coll., 1939; Air Armament Sch., Manby, 1941; Experimental Establishment, Boscombe Down, 1944; Dir Armament Research and Development, 1945-48; idc 1951; Comdt RAF Technical Coll., Henlow, 1952; Air Officer Commanding No 24 Group, Royal Air Force, 1952-55; Pres. of Ordnance Board, 1959-60. Comdr American Legion of Merit, 1948. *Address:* c/o The Bank of Ireland, Bantry, Co. Cork, Irish Republic.

FRASER, family name of **Barons Fraser of Kilmorack, Fraser of Tullybelton,** and **Lovat, Lady Saltoun,** and **Baron Strathalmond.**

FRASER OF ALLANDER; Barony of (*cr* 1964); title disclaimed by 2nd Baron; *see under* Fraser, Sir Hugh, 2nd Bt.

FRASER OF KILMORACK, Baron *cr* 1974 (Life Peer), of Rubislaw, Aberdeen; **Richard Michael Fraser,** Kt 1962; CBE 1955 (MBE 1945); Director: Glaxo Holdings Ltd, since 1975; Whiteaway Laidlaw Co. Ltd, since 1981; *b* 28 Oct. 1915; *yr s* of late Dr Thomas Fraser, CBE, DSO, TD, DL, LLD, Aberdeen; *m* 1944, Elizabeth Chloë, *er d* of late Brig. C. A. F. Drummond, OBE; one *s* (and one *s* decd). *Educ:* Fettes; King's Coll., Cambridge. Begg Exhibition, 1934; James Essay Prize, 1935; BA Hons History, 1937; MA 1945. Served War of 1939-45 (RA); 2nd Lieut 1939; War

Gunnery Staff Course, 1940; Capt. Feb. 1941; Major, June 1941; Lieut-Col (GSO1) 1945. Joined Conservative Research Dept, 1946; Head of Home Affairs Sect., 1950-51, Jt Dir, 1951-59, Dir, 1959-64, Chm., 1970-74; Dep. Chm., Cons. Party Orgn, 1964-75; Dep. Chm., Conservative Party's Adv. Cttee on Policy, 1970-75 (Sec., Aug. 1951-Oct. 1964); Sec. to the Conservative Leader's Consultative Cttee (Shadow Cabinet), Oct. 1964-June 1970 and March 1974-75. Smith-Mundt Fellowship, USA, 1952. Pres., Old Fettesian Assoc., 1977-80. *Recreations:* reading, music, opera, ballet, travel; collecting and recollecting. *Address:* 18 Drayton Court, Drayton Gardens, SW10 9RH. *T:* 01-370 1543. *Clubs:* Brooks's, Carlton, St Stephen's Constitutional (hon. mem.).

FRASER OF TULLYBELTON, Baron *cr* 1974 (Life Peer), of Bankfoot; **Walter Ian Reid Fraser,** PC 1974; a Lord of Appeal in Ordinary, since 1975; Member of the Queen's Body Guard for Scotland (Royal Company of Archers); *b* 3 Feb. 1911; *o s* of late Alexander Reid Fraser, stockbroker, Glasgow; *m* 1943, (Mary Ursula) Cynthia (Gwendolen), *o d* of Col I. H. Macdonell, DSO (late HLI); one *s. Educ:* Repton; Balliol Coll., Oxford (scholar; Hon. Fellow, 1981). BA Oxon 1932; LLB Glasgow 1935; Advocate, 1936; QC Scotland 1953. Lecturer in Constitutional Law, Glasgow Univ., 1936; and at Edinburgh Univ., 1948. Served Army (RA and staff), 1939-45; UK; Burma. Contested (U) East Edinburgh constituency, Gen. Election, 1955. Mem. Royal Commission on Police, 1960. Dean of the Faculty of Advocates, 1959-64; a Senator of HM Coll. of Justice in Scotland, 1964-74. Hon. LLD: Glasgow, 1970; Edinburgh, 1978. Hon. Master of the Bench, Gray's Inn, 1975. *Publication:* Outline of Constitutional Law, 1938 (2nd edn 1948). *Recreations:* shooting, walking. *Address:* 35 Cleaver Square, SE11. *T:* 01-735 3668; Tullybelton House, Bankfoot, Perthshire. *T:* Bankfoot 312. *Clubs:* Garrick; New (Edinburgh).

FRASER, Alexander Macdonald, PhD; FAIM, FTS; Director, Queensland Institute of Technology, since 1966; *b* 11 March 1921; *s* of late John Macdonald Fraser and of Esther Katie Fraser; *m* 1951, Rita Isabel Thomason; one *s. Educ:* Church of England Grammar Sch., Brisbane; Univ. of Queensland (BE); Imperial Coll. of Science and Technology, Univ. of London (DIC, PhD). MIE(Aust.) Military service, 1942-45 (despatches, New Guinea, 1944). Engineer: British Malayan Petroleum Co., 1947-50; Irrigation and Water Supply Commission, Qld, 1951-54 and 1957-65; Research, Imperial Coll. of Science and Technology, 1954-57. *Recreation:* golf. *Address:* 3 Wynard Street, Indooroopilly, Queensland, Australia. *T:* 370.7945. *Club:* Indooroopilly Golf (Brisbane).

FRASER, Angus McKay, CB 1981; TD 1965; Deputy Secretary, Management and Personnel Office (formerly Civil Service Department), since 1980; First Civil Service Commissioner, since 1981; *b* 10 March 1928; *s* of late Thomas Douglas Fraser; *m* 1955, Margaret Neilson (marr. diss. 1968); one *s* one *d. Educ:* Falkirk High Sch.; Glasgow Univ.; Bordeaux Univ. Nat. Service in RA, 1950-52; 44 Parachute Bde (TA), 1953-66. Asst Principal, HM Customs and Excise, 1952; Principal, 1956; HM Treasury, 1961-64; Asst Sec., HM Customs and Excise, 1965; Under-Sec. and Comr of Customs and Excise, 1972; Under-Sec., CSD, 1973; Comr of Customs and Excise, 1976; Dep. Chm., Bd of Customs and Excise, 1978-80. *Recreations:* dinghy sailing, old inns, literary research, book collecting. *Address:* 84 Ennerdale Road, Kew, Richmond, Surrey TW9 2DL. *T:* 01-940 9913. *Clubs:* Reform, City Livery.

FRASER, Air Cdre Anthony Walkinshaw; Director, Society of Motor Manufacturers and Traders, since 1980; *b* 15 March 1934; *s* of late Robert Walkinshaw Fraser and Evelyn Elisabeth Fraser; *m* 1955, Angela Mary Graham Shaw; one *s* three *d. Educ:* Stowe Sch. FBIM, MIL. RAF Pilot and Flying Instructor, 1952-66; sc Camberley, 1967; MA/VCDS, MoD, 1968-70; Chief Instructor Buccaneer OCU, 1971-72; Air Warfare Course, 1973; Directing Staff, National Defence Coll., 1973; Dep. Dir, Operational Requirements, MoD, 1974-76; Comdt, Central Flying Sch., 1977-79. ADC to the Queen, 1977-79. Pres., Comité de Liaison de la Construction Automobile, 1980-; Vice-Pres., Bureau Perm. Internat. des Constructeurs d'Automobiles, 1981-. *Recreations:* shooting, golf, fishing, languages. *Address:* The Society of Motor Manufacturers and Traders Ltd, Forbes House, Halkin Street, SW1X 7DS. *T:* 01-235 7000. *Clubs:* Boodle's, Royal Air Force, Royal Automobile.

FRASER, Antonia; writer; **(Lady Antonia Pinter);** *b* 27 Aug. 1932; *d* of 7th Earl of Longford, *qv,* and Countess of Longford, *qv;* *m* 1st, 1956, Rt Hon. Sir Hugh Charles Patrick Joseph Fraser, *qv* (marr. diss. 1977); three *s* three *d;* 2nd, 1980, Harold Pinter, *qv. Educ:* Dragon School, Oxford; St Mary's Convent, Ascot; Lady Margaret Hall, Oxford. General Editor, Kings and Queens of England series. Member, Arts Council, 1970-72; Chm., Soc. of Authors, 1974-75. *Publications:* (as Antonia Pakenham): King Arthur and the Knights of the Round Table, 1954 (reissued, 1970); Robin Hood, 1955 (reissued, 1971); (as Antonia Fraser): Dolls, 1963; A History of Toys, 1966; Mary Queen of Scots (James Tait Black Memorial Prize, 1969), 1969 (reissued illus. edn, 1978); Cromwell Our Chief of Men, (in USA, Cromwell the Lord Protector), 1973; King James: VI of Scotland, I of England, 1974; (ed) Kings and Queens of England, 1975; (ed) Scottish Love Poems, a personal anthology, 1975; (ed) Love Letters: an anthology, 1976; Quiet as a Nun (mystery), 1977, adapted for TV series, 1978; The Wild Island (mystery), 1978; King Charles II, (in USA, Royal Charles), 1979; (ed) Heroes and Heroines, 1980; A Splash of Red (mystery), 1981; (ed) Mary Queen of Scots: poetry anthology, 1981;

(ed) Oxford and Oxfordshire in Verse: anthology, 1982; Cool Repentance (mystery), 1982; various mystery stories in anthols. *Recreations:* swimming, life in the garden. *Address:* c/o Curtis Brown, 1 Craven Hill, W2. *Club:* PEN.

FRASER, Sir Basil (Malcolm), 2nd Bt, *cr* 1921; *b* 2 Jan. 1920; *s* of Sir (John) Malcolm Fraser, 1st Bt, GBE, and of Irene, *d* of C. E. Brightman of South Kensington; *S* father, 1949. *Educ:* Northaw, Pluckley, Kent; Eton Coll.; Queen's Coll., Cambridge. Served War of 1939-45, RE, 1940-42; Madras Sappers and Miners, 1942-46 (despatches). Mem. AA and RAC. *Recreations:* motoring, music, electronic reproduction of sound. *Heir:* none. *Address:* 175 Beach Street, Deal, Kent CT14 6LE. *Club:* Roadfarers'.

FRASER, Sir Bruce (Donald), KCB 1961 (CB 1956); *b* 18 Nov. 1910; *s* of late Maj.-Gen. Sir Theodore Fraser, KCB and late Constance Ruth Fraser (*née* Stevenson); *m* 1939, Audrey (*d* 1982), *d* of late Lieut-Col E. L. Croslegh; one *s* one *d* decd. *Educ:* Bedford Sch.; Trinity Coll., Cambridge (Scholar); First Class in Classical Tripos Part I, 1930 and in English Tripos Part II, 1932; BA 1932, MA 1964. Ed. the Granta, 1932. Entered Civil Service as Asst Principal, Scottish Office, 1933; transf. to HM Treasury, 1936; Private Sec. to Financial Sec., 1937, and to Permanent Sec., 1941; Asst Sec., 1945; Under Sec., 1951; Third Sec., 1956-60; Dep. Sec., Ministry of Aviation, Jan.-April 1960; Permanent Sec., Ministry of Health, 1960-64; Joint Permanent Under-Sec. of State, Dept of Education and Science, 1964-65; Permanent Sec., Ministry of Land and Natural Resources, 1965-66; Comptroller and Auditor-General, Exchequer and Audit Dept, 1966-71. *Publication:* Sir Ernest Gowers' The Complete Plain Words, rev. edn 1973. *Address:* Jonathan, St Dogmael's, Cardigan SA43 3LF. *T:* Cardigan 612387. *Club:* Athenæum.

FRASER, Sir Campbell; see Fraser, Sir J. C.

FRASER, Charles Annand, MVO 1968; WS; Partner, W. & J. Burness, WS, Edinburgh; *b* 16 Oct. 1928; *o s* of Very Rev. John Annand Fraser, *qv; m* 1957, Ann Scott-Kerr; four *s. Educ:* Hamilton Academy; Edinburgh Univ. (MA, LLB). Purse Bearer to Lord High Commissioner to General Assembly of Church of Scotland, 1969-. Director: United Biscuits (Holdings) Ltd, 1978-; Scottish Widows' Fund, 1978-; British Assets Trust, 1969-; Scottish Television Ltd, 1979-, and other companies; Trustee, Scottish Civic Trust, 1978-; Mem. Council, Law Society of Scotland, 1966-72; Governor of Fettes, 1976-; Mem. Court, Heriot-Watt Univ., 1972-78. WS 1959. *Recreations:* gardening, skiing, squash, piping. *Address:* Shepherd House, Inveresk, Midlothian. *T:* 031-665 2570. *Clubs:* Caledonian; New, Hon. Co. of Edinburgh Golfers (Edinburgh); Royal and Ancient (St Andrews).

FRASER, Maj.-Gen. Colin Angus Ewen, CB 1971; CBE 1968; General Officer Commanding, Southern Command, Australia, 1971-74; retired March 1974; *b* Nairobi, Kenya, 25 Sept. 1918; *s* of A. E. Fraser, Rutherglen, Vic.; *m* 1942, Dorothy, *d* of A. Champion; two *s* one *d. Educ:* Johannesburg; Adelaide High Sch.; RMC, Duntroon (grad. 1938); Melbourne Univ. (BA). Served War of 1939-45: UK, Middle East, Pacific. Staff Coll., Camberley, 1946; Dep. Comdr, Commonwealth Div., Korea, 1955-56; Dir, Military Trng, 1957-58; Services Attaché, Burma, 1960-62; Chief of Staff, Northern Command, Brisbane, 1964-68; Commandant, Royal Military Coll., Duntroon, 1968-69; Commander, Australian Force, Vietnam, 1970-71. *Address:* 364 Orana Road, Ocean Shores, Brunswick Heads, NSW 2483, Australia. *Clubs:* Tasmanian (Hobart); United Services (Qld).

FRASER, Gen. Sir David (William), GCB 1980 (KCB 1973); OBE 1962; DL; retired; *b* 30 Dec. 1920; *s* of Brig. Hon. William Fraser, DSO, MC, *y s* of 18th Lord Saltoun and Pamela, *d* of Cyril Maude and *widow* of Major W. La T. Congreve, VC, DSO, MC; *m* 1st, 1947, Anne Balfour; one *d;* 2nd, 1957, Julia de la Hey; two *s* two *d. Educ:* Eton; Christ Church, Oxford. Commnd into Grenadier Guards, 1941; served NW Europe; comd 1st Bn Grenadier Guards, 1960-62; comd 19th Inf. Bde, 1963-65; Dir, Defence Policy, MoD, 1966-69; GOC 4 Div., 1969-71; Asst Chief of Defence Staff (Policy), MoD, 1971-73; Vice-Chief of the General Staff, 1973-75; UK Mil. Rep. to NATO, 1975-77; Commandant, RCDS, 1978-80; ADC General to the Queen, 1977-80. Col, The Royal Hampshire Regt, 1981-. DL Hants, 1982. *Publication:* Alanbrooke, 1982. *Recreation:* shooting. *Address:* Vallenders, Isington, Alton, Hants. *T:* Bentley 3166. *Clubs:* Turf, Pratt's.

FRASER, Donald Blake, FRCS; FRCOG; Gynæcologist and Obstetrician, St Bartholomew's Hospital, 1946-75; retired 1978; *b* 9 June 1910; *o s* of Dr Thomas B. Fraser, Hatfield Point, NB, Canada; *m* 1939, Betsy, *d* of late Sir James Henderson, KBE; one *s* one *d. Educ:* University of New Brunswick; Christ Church, Oxford. Rhodes Scholar, 1930; BA 1st Cl. Hons, 1932, BM, BCh Oxon 1936; MRCS, LRCP, LMCC, 1936; FRCS, 1939; MRCOG, 1940, FRCOG, 1952. Former Examiner: Central Midwives Bd; Universities of Oxford and London; Conjoint Bd; Royal College of Obstetricians and Gynæcologists. *Publications:* (joint) Midwifery (textbook), 1956. Articles in medical journals. *Recreation:* philately. *Address:* Vine House, 6 Hampstead Square, NW3 1AB.

FRASER, Donald Hamilton, ARA 1975; artist; Tutor, Royal College of Art, since 1958 (Fellow 1970); *b* 30 July 1929; *s* of Donald Fraser and Dorothy Christiana (*née* Lang); *m* 1954, Judith Wentworth-Sheilds; one *d. Educ:* Maidenhead Grammar Sch.; St Martin's Sch. of Art, London; Paris (French Govt Scholarship). Has held 32 one-man exhibitions in Britain, Europe and

N America, 1953-81. Work in public collections includes: Museum of Fine Arts, Boston; Albright-Knox Gall., Buffalo; Carnegie Inst., Pittsburgh; City Art Museum, St Louis; Wadsworth Athenaeum, Hartford, Conn; Hirshhorn Museum, Washington, DC; Yale Univ. Art Museum; Palm Springs Desert Museum; Nat. Gall. of Canada, Ottawa; Nat. Gall. of NSW, Melbourne; many British provincial galleries; Arts Council, DoE, etc. Chm., Artists Gen. Benevolent Inst., 1981-. *Publication:* Gaugin's 'Vision after the Sermon', 1969. *Address:* Bramham Cottage, Remenham Lane, Henley-on-Thames, Oxon RG9 2LR. *T:* Henley-on-Thames 4253. *Club:* Phyllis Court (Henley-on-Thames).

FRASER, Sir Douglas (Were), Kt 1966; ISO 1962; Fellow, Royal Institute of Public Administration (Queensland); Honorary Fellow: Queensland Conservatorium of Music; Institute of Ambulance Officers (Australia); *b* 24 Oct. 1899; *s* of late Robert John Fraser and late Edith Harriet (*née* Shepherd); *m* 1927, Violet Pryke (*d* 1968); three *s. Educ:* State High Sch., Gympie, Qld. Entered Qld State Public Service, 1916; Public Service Board and Public Service Comr's Dept; Sec. to Public Service Comr, 1939; Sen. Public Service Inspector, 1947; Dep. Public Service Comr, 1952; Public Service Comr, 1956; retired 1965; War-time Asst Dir of Civil Defence, Sec., Public Safety Adv. Cttee. Mem. Senate, Univ. of Queensland, 1956-74; Chm. Council, Qld Conservatorium of Music, 1971-79; Pres., Qld Ambulance Transport Brigade Council, 1967-80. *Recreations:* gardening, fishing, music, reading. *Address:* 76 Prince Edward Parade, Redcliffe, Qld 4020, Australia. *T:* 284 5568.

FRASER, Edward; *see* Fraser, J. E.

FRASER, George MacDonald; author and journalist; *b* 2 April 1925; *s* of late William Fraser, MB, ChB and Anne Struth Donaldson; *m* 1949, Kathleen Margarette, *d* of late George Hetherington, Carlisle; two *s* one *d. Educ:* Carlisle Grammar Sch.; Glasgow Academy. Served in British Army, 1943-47: Infantryman XIVth Army, Lieut Gordon Highlanders. Newspaperman in England, Canada and Scotland from 1947; Dep. Editor, Glasgow Herald, 1964-69. *Publications:* Flashman, 1969; Royal Flash, 1970; The General Danced at Dawn, 1970; The Steel Bonnets, 1971; Flash for Freedom!, 1971; Flashman at the Charge, 1973; McAuslan in the Rough, 1974; Flashman in the Great Game, 1975; Flashman's Lady, 1977; Mr American, 1980; Flashman and the Redskins, 1982; film screenplays: The Three Musketeers, 1974; The Four Musketeers, 1975; Royal Flash, 1975; The Prince and the Pauper, 1977. *Recreations:* snooker, backgammon, talking to wife, history, singing. *Address:* Baldrine, Isle of Man.

FRASER, Air Marshal Rev. Sir (Henry) Paterson, KBE 1961 (CBE 1945); CB 1953; AFC 1937; RAF, retired; ordained 1977; Concrete Consultant; *b* 15 July 1907; *s* of late Harry Fraser, Johannesburg, South Africa; *m* 1933, Avis Gertrude Haswell; two *s. Educ:* St Andrews Coll., Grahamstown, South Africa; Pembroke Coll., Cambridge (MA), RAFO, and Pres. University Air Sqdn, Cambridge; joined RAF, 1929; served in India; RAF Engineering Course, Henlow, 1933-34; Aerodynamic Flight, RAE, Farnborough, 1934-38; RAF Staff Coll., 1938; Directorate of War Organization, Air Ministry, 1939-40; commanded Experimental Flying Section, RAE, Farnborough, 1941; Mem. RAF Element, Combined Chiefs of Staff, Washington DC, 1942; Dep. Dir of War Organization, Air Ministry, 1943; Senior Administrative Planner, 2nd Tactical Air Force, 1943-44, and Dep. Air Officer in Charge of Administration, 2nd TAF, 1944-45; commanded Aircraft and Armament Experimental Establishment, Boscombe Down, 1945-46; Dep. Dir (Air Staff) Policy, Air Ministry, 1947-48; Defence Research Policy Staff, Ministry of Defence, 1948-51; idc 1951; Senior Air Staff Officer, Headquarters Fighter Command, 1952-53; Chief of Staff, Headquarters Allied Air Forces, Central Europe, 1954-56; AOC No. 12 Group, Fighter Command, 1956-58; Dir, RAF Exercise Planning, 1959; UK Representative on Permanent Military Deputies Group of Cento, 1959-62; Inspector-Gen., RAF, 1962-64. Taylor Gold Medal of RAeS, 1937; FRAeS. *Address:* 803 King's Court, Ramsey, Isle of Man.

FRASER, Sir Hugh, 2nd Bt *cr* 1961, of Dineiddwg; Chairman, Highland Tourist (Cairngorm Development) Ltd, since 1979; *b* 18 Dec. 1936; *s* of 1st Baron Fraser of Allander, DL, LLD, JP (Bt 1961) and of Kate Hutcheon, *d* of late Sir Andrew Lewis, LLD, JP; *S* to father's Btcy, and disclaimed Barony, 1966; *m* 1st, 1962, Patricia Mary (marr. diss. 1971), *e d* of John Bowie; three *d*; 2nd, 1973, Aileen Ross (marr. diss. 1982). *Educ:* St Mary's, Melrose; Kelvinside Academy. Chairman: House of Fraser Ltd, 1966-81 (Dep. Chm., 1965; Dir, 1958-82); Harrods Ltd, 1966-76 (Dir, 1966-82; Man. Dir, 1970-76); Director: John Barker & Co. Ltd, 1966-81 (Chm. and Man. Dir, 1966-76); Binns Ltd, 1966-81 (Chm. and Man. Dir, 1966-76). *Recreations:* farming, show jumping. *Address:* Strathendrick House, Buchanan Castle Estate, Drymen.

FRASER, Rt. Hon. Sir Hugh (Charles Patrick Joseph), Kt 1980; MBE; PC 1962; MP (C) Stone Div. of Staffs, 1945-50, Stafford and Stone Division of Staffs, since 1950; *b* 23 Jan. 1918; *s* of 16th Baron Lovat; *m* 1956, Lady Antonia Pakenham (*see* Antonia Fraser) (marr. diss. 1977); three *s* three *d. Educ:* Ampleforth Coll.; Balliol Coll., Oxford; The Sorbonne, Paris. Roman Catholic. Ex-Pres. Oxford Union; war service with Lovat Scouts, Phantom and Special Air Service. PPS to Sec. of State for the Colonies, 1951-54; Parly Under-Sec. of State and Financial Sec., War Office 1958-60; Parly Under-Sec. of State for the Colonies, 1960-62; Sec. of State for Air, 1962-64. Pres., West Midlands Conservative and Unionist Assoc., 1967. Director: Sun Alliance; industrial cos. Order of Orange Nassau, Order of Leopold with palm, Belgian

Croix de guerre. *Address:* Eilean Aigas, Beauly, Inverness, Scotland; House of Commons, SW1. *Clubs:* Beefsteak, White's.

FRASER, Col Hugh Vincent, CMG 1957; OBE 1946; TD 1947; retired 1960; *b* 20 Sept. 1908; *yr s* of William Neilson and Maude Fraser; *m* 1941, Noreen, *d* of Col M. O'C. Tandy; one *s* one *d. Educ:* Sherborne Sch. Commissioned into Royal Tank Regt; served War of 1939-45, India and Burma, with 14th Army. Military Attaché, Cairo, 1954-56; NATO, Washington DC, 1957-60. *Recreations:* hunting, shooting; Master Aldershot Command Beagles, 1939. *Address:* Cheyney Holt, Steeple Morden, Cambs. *Club:* Army and Navy.

FRASER, Sir Ian, Kt 1963; DSO 1943; OBE 1940; DL; FRSE, FRCS, FRCSI, FACS; Consulting Surgeon, Belfast; Senior Surgeon: Royal Victoria Hospital, Belfast, 1955-66; Royal Belfast Hospital for Sick Children, 1955-66; Director: Provincial Bank of Ireland; Allied Irish Bank; *b* 9 Feb. 1901; *s* of Robert Moore Fraser, BA, MD, Belfast; *m* 1931, Eleanor Margaret Mitchell; one *s* one *d. Educ:* Royal Academical Institution, Belfast; Queen's Univ., Belfast. MB, BCh 1st Cl. Hons 1923; MD 1932; MCh 1927; FRCSI 1926; FRCS 1927; FRSE 1938; FACS 1945. Coulter Schol.; McQuitty Schol.; 1st place in Ire. as FRCSI. Resident Surgical Officer, St Helen's, Lancs; Surgeon: Royal Belfast Hosp. for Sick Children; Royal Victoria Hosp., Belfast, and former Asst Prof. of Surgery. Served War: (overseas) 1940-45: in W Africa, N. Africa, Sicily, Italy (OBE, DSO, Salerno); invasion of France, India; Officer in charge of Penicillin in Research Team, N Africa; Brig, 1945. Hon. Col (TA): No 204 Gen. Hosp., 1961-71; No 4 Field Amb., 1948-71; Surgeon in Ordinary to the Governor of Northern Ireland; Hon. Cons. Surg. to the Army in NI; Chm., Police Authority, Royal Ulster Constabulary, 1970-76; Mem. Adv. Council, Ulster Defence Regt. Past President: RCSI (1956-57); Assoc. of Surgeons GB and Ireland (1957); BMA (1962-63); Irish Med. Graduates Assoc., London, Queen's Univ. Assoc., London; Services Club, QUB; Ulster Med. Soc. President: Ulster Surgical Club; Queen's Univ. Assoc., Belfast; Chm of Convocation and Mem. Senate QUB. Visiting Lecturer: Leicester, Birmingham, Edinburgh, Bradford, London, Sheffield, Dublin, Cheltenham, Rochester, New York, Copenhagen, Glasgow, Manchester, Middlesex Hosp., Bristol, Barnsley, etc; Delegate to various assocs abroad. John Snow Oration, 1967; Downpatrick Hosp. Bi-Centenary Oration, 1967; Bishop Jeremy Taylor Lecture, 1970; Maj.-Gen. Philip Mitchiner Lecture, 1971; Robert Campbell Orator, 1973; David Torrens Lectr, NUU. Visiting Examiner in Surgery: Liverpool, Cambridge, and Manchester Univs; NUI; Apothecaries' Hall, Dublin; TCD; RCS in Ire.; RCS of Glasgow, Councillor, RCSI; Mem. and Trustee, James IV Assoc. of Surgeons; Mem., Health Educn Cttee, Min. of Health, London; Fellow: BMA; Roy. Soc. Med. Lond.; Roy. Irish Acad. of Med.; Hon. FRCPGlas 1972; Hon. FRCSE; Hon. FRCPI 1977; Hon. Fellow: Brit. Assoc. of Paediatric Surgeons; Ulster Med. Soc., 1977; Foreign Mem., L'Académie de Chirurgie, Paris; Hon. Mem., Danish Assoc. of Surgery, Copenhagen; Mem., Internat. Soc. of Surgeons. Hon. Life Governor, Royal Victoria Hosp., Belfast; Governor for GB, Amer. Coll. Surgeons. Hon. DSc: Oxon, 1963; New Univ. of Ulster, 1977. GCStJ 1974 (KStJ 1940); Mem., Chapter General, London, and Knight Commander of Commandery of Ards, Ulster, Order of St John. DL Belfast, 1955. Gold Medal: Ulster Hosp. for Women and Children; Royal Belfast Hosp. for Sick Children. Commander: Ordre de la Couronne (Belgium) 1963; Order of Orange Nassau, 1969; Ordre des Palmes Académiques, 1970; Chevalier de la Legion d'Honneur, France, 1981. *Publications:* various monographs on surgical subjects. *Recreations:* golf, formerly hockey and rugby. *Address:* (residence) 19 Upper Malone Road, Belfast. *T:* Belfast 668235; (consulting rooms) 35 Wellington Park, Belfast BTQ 6DN. *T:* Belfast 665543. *Clubs:* Ulster, Malone Golf (Belfast).

FRASER, Lt-Comdr Ian Edward, VC 1945; DSC 1943; RD and Bar 1948; JP; Director, Star Offshore Services Ltd, since 1976; Chairman: Nordive (West Africa) Ltd, since 1965; North Sea Diving Services Nederland BV, since 1965; Universal Divers Ltd, since 1965 (Managing Director, 1947-65); *b* 18 Dec., 1920; *s* of S. Fraser, Bourne End, Bucks; *m* 1943, Melba Estelle Hughes; four *s* two *d. Educ:* Royal Grammar Sch., High Wycombe; HMS Conway. Merchant Navy, 1937-39; Royal Navy, 1939-47; Lt-Comdr, RNR, 1951-65; Man. Dir, North Sea Diving Services Ltd, 1965-80. Younger Brother of Trinity House, 1980. JP Wallasey, 1957. Officer, American Legion of Merit. *Publication:* Frogman VC, 1957. *Address:* Innisfallen, 47 Warren Drive, Wallasey, Merseyside. *T:* 051-639 3355.

FRASER, Ian James, CBE 1972; MC 1945; Chairman, Lazard Brothers, since 1980; Deputy Chairman, Vickers Ltd, since 1980; Chairman, Accepting Houses Committee, since 1981; *b* 7 Aug. 1923; 2nd *s* of late Hon. Alastair Thomas Joseph Fraser and Lady Sibyl Fraser (*née* Grimston); *m* 1958, Evelyn Elizabeth Anne Grant; two *s* two *d. Educ:* Ampleforth Coll.; Magdalen Coll., Oxford. Served War of 1939-45: Lieut, Scots Guards, 1942-45 (despatches, MC). Reuter Correspondent, 1946-56; S. G. Warburg & Co. Ltd, 1956-69; Dir-Gen., Panel on Take-overs and Mergers, 1969-72; Part-time Mem., CAA, 1972-74. Chm., City Capital Markets Cttee, 1974-78; Member: Exec. Cttee, City Communications Centre, 1976-; Cttee on Finance for Industry, NEDC, 1976-79; President's Cttee, CBI, 1979-81; Exec. Cttee, Jt Disciplinary Scheme of Accountancy Insts, 1979-81. Director: BOC International Ltd, 1972-; Davy International Ltd, 1972-; Chloride Gp Ltd, 1976-80; S. Pearson & Son Ltd, 1977-; EMI Ltd, 1977-80; Eurafrance SA, 1979-; Pearson-Longman Ltd, 1980-; Chairman: Rolls-Royce Motors, 1971-80; Datastream Ltd, 1976-77. Governor, More House Sch., 1970-75. FRSA 1970; CBIM (FBIM 1974). Kt of Honour and Devotion, SMO of Malta, 1971. *Recreations:* fishing, gardening, Scottish history. *Address:* 70 Limerston Street, SW10. *T:* 01-352 7092; South Haddon Farm, Skilgate, Taunton, Somerset. *T:* Bampton (Devon) 31247. *Club:* White's.

FRASER, Ian Montagu, MC 1945; Secretary, The Buttle Trust, since 1978 (Deputy Secretary, 1971-78); *b* 14 Oct. 1916; *e s* of Col Herbert Cecil Fraser, DSO, OBE, TD, and Sybil Mary Statter; *m* 1st, 1945, Mary Stanley (*d* 1964); one *s* one *d*; 2nd, 1967, Angela Meston, two *s*. *Educ:* Shrewsbury Sch.; Christ Church, Oxford. 1st Cl. Class. Hon. Mods, 1937; 1st Cl. Lit Hum 1939. Regular Commn in Frontier Force Rifles, IA, 1939, and served War of 1939-45, NW Frontier, Iraq, Syria and Western Desert (MC, despatches twice, POW); retired 1948. Executive, Guthrie and Co. Ltd, 1948; Gen. Sec., The John Lewis Partnership, 1956-59, Consultant, 1959-64. RARO, Rifle Bde, 1948-. MP (C) Sutton Div. of Plymouth, 1959-66; PPS to Sec. of State for the Colonies, 1962; Asst Govt Whip, 1962-64; Opposition Whip, 1964-66; Conservative Research Dept, 1966-67. Exec. Dir, GUS Export Corp., 1967-70. *Recreations:* flyfishing, sailing. *Address:* How Hatch, Chipstead, Surrey. *T:* Downland 51944. *Clubs:* Carlton; Royal Western Yacht (Plymouth).

FRASER, Very Rev. Dr Ian Watson, CMG 1973; Chairman, New Zealand Refugee Homes Board, since 1962; retired as Minister of St Stephen's Presbyterian Church, Lower Hutt, Wellington, NZ (1961-73); *b* 23 Oct. 1907; *s* of Malcolm Fraser (*b* Inverness; 1st NZ Govt Statistician) and Caroline (*née* Watson; *b* Napier, NZ); *m* 1932, Alexa Church Stewart; one *s* two *d*. *Educ:* Scots Coll., Wellington, NZ; Victoria Univ. of Wellington (MA (Hons)); Theol Hall, Dunedin; BD (Melb.); Univ. of Edinburgh; Univ. of Bonn, Germany; Union Theol Seminary, NY (STM, ThD). Minister: St Andrew's Presbyterian Church, Levin, 1933-39; Presbyterian Ch., Wyndham, 1939-42; Chaplain, St Andrew's Coll., Christchurch, 1942-48; Minister, St John's Pres. Ch., Papatoetoe, Auckland, 1948-61. Moderator, Presbyterian Church of NZ, 1968-69. Mail clerk for Bank of NSW. Refugee Award of Nat. Council of Churches, 1970. *Publications:* Understandest Thou? (Introd. to NT), 1946; Understanding the OT, 1958; various booklets. *Recreations:* music, reading. *Address:* 19A Bloomfield Terrace, Lower Hutt, Wellington, New Zealand. *T:* Wellington 697-269.

See also T. R. C. Fraser.

FRASER, Sir (James) Campbell, Kt 1978; FRSE 1978; Chairman, Dunlop Holdings Ltd, since 1978; Chairman and Managing Director, Dunlop Ltd, since 1977; Chairman, Dunlop International AG, since 1978; *b* 2 May 1923; *s* of Alexander Ross Fraser and Annie McGregor Fraser; *m* 1950, Maria Harvey (*née* McLaren); two *d*. *Educ:* Glasgow Univ.; McMaster Univ.; Dundee Sch. of Economics. BCom. Served RAF, 1941-45. Raw Cotton Commn, Liverpool, 1950-52; Economist Intelligence Unit, 1952-57; Dunlop Rubber Co. Ltd, 1957-: Public Relations Officer, 1958; Group Marketing Controller, 1962; Man. Dir, Dunlop New Zealand Ltd, 1967; Exec. Dir, 1969; Jt Man. Dir, 1971; Man. Dir, 1972; Chm., Scottish Television Ltd, 1975-; Director: British Petroleum, 1978-; BAT Industries, 1980-; Charterhouse Group, 1982-. Pres., CBI, 1982- (Dep. Pres., 1981-82). Founder Mem., Past Chm. and Pres., Soc. of Business Economists; Mem. Exec. Cttee, SMMT. Trustee, The Economist, 1978-. Vis. Prof., Strathclyde Univ., 1980-. FBIM 1971; FPRI 1978. Hon. LLD Strathclyde, 1979; DUniv Stirling, 1979. *Publications:* many articles and broadcasts. *Recreations:* reading, theatre, cinema, gardening, walking. *Address:* Silver Birches, 4 Silver Lane, Purley, Surrey. *T:* 01-660 1703. *Club:* Caledonian.

FRASER, Prof. Sir James (David), 2nd Bt, *cr* 1943; Postgraduate Dean, Faculty of Medicine, University of Edinburgh, since 1981; *b* 19 July 1924; *o s* of Sir John Fraser, 1st Bt, KCVO, MC, and Agnes Govane Herald, The Manse, Duns, Berwickshire; *S* father 1947; *m* 1950, Maureen, *d* of Rev. John Reay, MC, Bingham Rectory, Nottingham; two *s*. *Educ:* Edinburgh Academy; Magdalen Coll., Oxford (BA); Edinburgh Univ. (MB, ChB); ChM 1961; FRCSE 1953; FRCS 1973. RAMC (Major), 1948-51; Senior Lectr in Clinical Surgery, Univ. of Edinburgh and Hon. Cons. Surgeon, Royal Infirmary, Edinburgh, 1951-70; Prof. of Surgery, Univ. of Southampton, 1970-80, and Hon. Cons. Surgeon, Southampton Univ. Hospital Gp, 1970-80. Pres., RCSEd, 1982. *Recreations:* golf, swimming. *Heir: s* Iain Michael Fraser [*b* 27 June 1951; *m* 1982, Sherylle, *d* of Keith Gillespie, New Zealand]. *Address:* 2 Lennox Street, Edinburgh EH4 1QA.

FRASER, Col James Douglas, CBE 1976; TD 1950 (1st clasp 1951, 2nd clasp 1958); DL; retired Insurance Broker and Consultant; Chairman, Strathclyde Valuation Appeal Panel, since 1975; *b* 12 July 1914; *s* of John Fraser and Jessie Victoria McCallum or Fraser; *m* 1st, 1944, Esme Latta (*d* 1964); one *s* one *d*; 2nd, 1966, Nancy McGregor or Stewart; one step *d*. *Educ:* Glasgow Acad. ACII 1933. Insurance Broker with Stenhouse Holdings Ltd, 1947-69 (Dir, 1954-69); Insurance Consultant, 1969-74. Commnd TA, 1938; War Service, Highland Light Infantry, 1939-46; Comd 5/6th Bn HLI, 1953-56; Dep. Comdr (Colonel), 154 (Highland) Bde, 1956-58; Chm., Lowland TAVRA, 1973-76. DL Dunbartonshire, 1975. OStJ 1980. *Recreations:* golf, reading, music. *Address:* 6B Lennox Court, 22 Stockiemuir Avenue, Bearsden, Glasgow G61 3JN. *T:* 041-942 3020. *Clubs:* Caledonian; Western, Buchanan Castle Golf (Glasgow).

FRASER, (James) Edward; Under Secretary, Scottish Home and Health Department, since 1981; *b* 16 Dec. 1931; *s* of late Dr James F. Fraser, TD, Aberdeen, and late Dr Kathleen Blomfield; *m* 1959, Patricia Louise Stewart;

two *s*. *Educ:* Aberdeen Grammar Sch.; Univ. of Aberdeen (MA); Christ's Coll., Cambridge (BA). RA, 1953; Staff Captain 'Q', Tel-el-Kebir, 1954-55. Asst Principal, Scottish Home Dept, 1957-60; Private Sec. to Permanent Under Sec. of State, 1960-62, and to Parly Under-Sec. of State, 1962; Principal: SHHD, 1962-64; Cabinet Office, 1964-66; HM Treasury, 1966-68; SHHD, 1968-69; Asst Sec., SHHD, 1970-76; Asst Sec., 1976, Under Sec., 1976-81, Scottish Office Finance Div. *Recreations:* reading, music, hill walking. *Address:* 59 Murrayfield Gardens, Edinburgh EH12 6DH. *T:* 031-337 2274. *Club:* Royal Commonwealth Society.

FRASER, Very Rev. John Annand, MBE 1940; TD 1945; DD; Moderator of the General Assembly of the Church of Scotland, May 1958-May 1959; Extra Chaplain to The Queen, in Scotland, since 1964 (Chaplain, 1952-64); *b* 21 June 1894; *er s* of Rev. Charles Fraser, BD, Minister of Croy, Inverness-shire, and Elizabeth Annand; *m* 1925, Leila, *d* of Col Ewen Campbell; one *s* one *d*. *Educ:* Robert Gordon's Coll., Aberdeen; Inverness Royal Academy; Universities of Aberdeen and Edinburgh. MA Aberdeen 1919. Served European War, 1914-18: in ranks 4th Bn Gordon Highlanders, 1915, Commd 7th Bn 1917. CF (TA) 1935; SCF, 52nd (Lowland) Div., 1940; Dep. Asst Chaplain Gen., West Scotland Dist, 1942. Asst Minister, St Matthew's, Edinburgh, 1921; Minister of Humbie, East Lothian, 1923; Minister of Hamilton, Second Charge, 1931, First Charge, 1949; Minister, Aberdalgie and Dupplin, Perth, 1960-70. Convener of Maintenance of Ministry Cttee of Church of Scotland, 1950-54; Convener of Business Cttee, 1962-67; Convener of Gen. Administration Cttee, 1962-66; Chm. of Judicial Commn, 1962-66; Chm. of Church of Scotland Trust, 1962-66; Mem. Broadcasting Council for Scotland, 1963-67. Hon. DD Aberdeen, 1951. *Recreations:* fishing, gardening. *Address:* 133 Glasgow Road, Perth. *T:* Perth 21462. *Club:* Caledonian (Edinburgh).

See also C. A. Fraser.

FRASER, John Denis; MP (Lab) Lambeth, Norwood, since 1974 (Norwood, 1966-74); *b* 30 June 1934; *s* of Archibald and Frances Fraser; *m* 1960, Ann Hathaway; two *s* one *d*. *Educ:* Sloane Grammar Sch., Chelsea; Co-operative Coll., Loughborough; Law Soc. Sch. of Law (John Mackrell Prize). Entered Australia & New Zealand Bank Ltd, 1950; Army service, 1952-54, as Sergt, RAEC (educnl and resettlement work). Solicitor, 1960; practised with Lewis Silkin and Partners. Mem. Lambeth Borough Coun., 1962-68 (Chm. Town Planning Cttee; Chm. Labour Gp). PPS to Rt Hon. Barbara Castle, 1968-70; Opposition front bench spokesman on Home Affairs, 1972-74; Parly Under-Sec. of State, Dept of Employment, 1974-76; Minister of State, Dept of Prices and Consumer Protection, 1976-79; Opposition Spokesman on Trade, 1979-. *Recreations:* athletics, walking. *Address:* House of Commons, SW1.

FRASER, Rt. Hon. (John) Malcolm, CH 1977; PC 1976; MA Oxon; MP; Prime Minister of Australia, since 1975; *b* 21 May 1930; *s* of late J. Neville Fraser, Nareen, Vic, Australia; *m* 1956, Tamara, *d* of S. R. Beggs; two *s* two *d*. *Educ:* Melbourne C of E Grammar Sch.; Magdalen Coll., Oxford (MA 1952). MHR (L) for Wannon, Vic, 1955-; Mem. Jt Party Cttee on Foreign Affairs, 1962-66; Minister: for the Army, 1966-68; for Educn and Science, 1968-69, 1971-72; for Defence, 1969-71; Leader of Parly Liberal Party and Leader of the Opposition, 1975. Mem. Council, Aust. Nat. Univ., 1964-66. *Recreations:* fishing, photography, vintage cars. *Address:* Parliament House, Canberra, ACT 2600, Australia. *Clubs:* Melbourne; Commonwealth (Canberra).

FRASER, Kenneth John Alexander; Head of Marketing Division, Unilever, 1976-79 and since 1981; *b* 22 Sept. 1929; *s* of Jack Sears Fraser and Marjorie Winifred (*née* Savery); *m* 1953, Kathleen Grace Booth; two *s* one *d*. *Educ:* Thames Valley Grammar Sch., Twickenham; London School of Economics (BScEcon Hons). Joined Erwin Wasey & Co. Ltd, 1953, then Lintas Ltd, 1958; Managing Director, Research Bureau Ltd, 1962; Head of Marketing Analysis and Evaluation Group, Unilever, 1965; Head of Marketing Division, Unilever, 1976. Mem., Consumer Protection Adv. Cttee, Dept of Prices and Consumer Protection, 1975; Chairman: CBI Marketing and Consumer Affairs Cttee, 1977; Internat. Chamber of Commerce Marketing Commn, 1978; two-year secondment to NEDO, as Industrial Director, 1979-81. *Recreations:* canoeing, walking, music, reading. *Address:* 14 Coombe Lane West, Kingston, Surrey KT2 7BX. *T:* 01-949 3760. *Clubs:* Royal Commonwealth Society, Wig and Pen.

FRASER, Louis Nathaniel B.; *see* Blache-Fraser.

FRASER, Rt. Hon. Malcolm; *see* Fraser, Rt Hon. J. M.

FRASER, Air Marshal Rev. Sir Paterson; *see* Fraser, Air Marshal Rev. Sir H. P.

FRASER, Peter Lovat, QC (Scot.) 1982; MP (C) South Angus, since 1979; Solicitor General for Scotland, since 1982; advocate; *b* 29 May 1945; *s* of Rev. George Robson Fraser and Helen Jean Meiklejohn or Fraser; *m* 1969, Fiona Macdonald Mair; one *s* two *d*. *Educ:* St Andrews Prep. Sch., Grahamstown, S Africa; Loretto Sch., Musselburgh; Gonville and Caius Coll., Cambridge (BA Hons; LLB Hons); Edinburgh Univ. Legal apprenticeship, Edinburgh, 1968; called to Scottish Bar, 1969. Lectr in Constitutional Law, Heriot-Watt Univ., 1972-74; Standing Jun. Counsel in Scotland to FCO, 1979. Chm., Scottish Conservative Lawyers Law Reform Group, 1976. Contested N Aberdeen, Oct. 1974; adopted Prospective Parly Candidate, S Angus, 1975.

PPS to Sec. of State for Scotland, 1981-82. *Recreations:* skiing, golf, wind-surfing. *Address:* Slade House, Carmyllie by Arbroath, Angus. *T:* Carmyllie 215.

FRASER, Peter Marshall, MC 1944; MA; FBA 1960; Fellow of All Souls College, Oxford, since 1954, Sub-Warden, 1980-82; Lecturer in Hellenistic History, 1948-64, Reader since 1964; *b* 6 April 1918; *y s* of late Archibald Fraser; *m* 1st, 1940, Catharine, *d* of late Prebendary Heaton-Renshaw (marr. diss.); one *s* three *d* ; 2nd, 1955, Ruth Elsbeth, *d* of late F. Renfer, Bern, Switzerland; two *s* ; 3rd, 1973, Barbara Ann Stewart, *d* of late L. E. C. Norbury, FRCS. *Educ:* City of London Sch.; Brasenose Coll., Oxford (Hon. Fellow 1977). Seaforth Highlanders, 1941-45; Military Mission to Greece, 1943-45. Sen. Scholar, Christ Church, Oxford, 1946-47; Junior Proctor, Oxford Univ., 1960-61; Domestic Bursar, All Souls Coll., 1962-65. Dir, British Sch. of Archaeol. at Athens, 1968-71. Vis. Prof. of Classical Studies, Indiana Univ., 1973-74. Chm., Managing Cttee, Soc. of Afghan Studies, 1972-. Ordinary Mem., German Archaeol. Soc., 1979. *Publications:* (with G. E. Bean) The Rhodian Peraea and Islands, 1954; (with T. Rönne) Boeotian and West Greek Tombstones, 1957; Rostovtzeff, Social and Economic History of the Roman Empire, 2nd edn, revised, 1957; Samothrace, The Inscriptions, (Vol. ii, Excavations of Samothrace), 1960; E. Löfstedt, Roman Literary Portraits, trans. from the Swedish (Romare), 1958; The Wares of Autolycus; Selected Literary Essays of Alice Meynell (ed.), 1965; E. Kjellberg and G. Säflund, Greek and Roman Art, trans. from the Swedish (Grekisk och romersk konst), 1968; Ptolemaic Alexandria, 1972; Rhodian Funerary Monuments, 1977; A. J. Butler, Arab Conquest of Egypt, 2nd edn, revised, 1978; articles in learned journals. *Address:* All Souls College, Oxford.

FRASER, Sir Robert; *see* Fraser, Sir W. R.

FRASER, Sir Robert Brown, Kt 1949; OBE 1944; Chairman, Independent Television News, 1971-74; *b* 26 Sept. 1904; *s* of Reginald and Thusnelda Fraser, Adelaide, South Australia; *m* 1931, Betty Harris; one *d.* *Educ:* St Peter's Sch., Adelaide; Trinity Coll., Univ. of Melbourne (BA); Univ. of London (BSc Econ.). Leader Writer Daily Herald, 1930-39; Empire Div., Ministry of Information, 1939-41; Dir, Publications Div., Ministry of Information, 1941-45; Controller of Production, Ministry of Information, 1945-46; Dir-Gen., Central Office of Information, 1946-54; Dir-General, ITA, 1954-70. Hon. Fellow, LSE, 1965. Hon. Life Mem., Royal Inst. of Public Administration, 1975; Editor, New Whitehall Series, for Royal Inst. of Public Administration, 1951-70. Gold Medal, Royal Television Soc., 1970. *Address:* Flat 5M, Portman Mansions, Chiltern Street, W1. *Club:* Athenæum.

FRASER, Ronald Petrie, CB 1972; Secretary, Scottish Home and Health Department, 1972-77; *b* 2 June 1917; *yr s* of late T. Petrie Fraser, Elgin; *m* 1962, Ruth Wright Anderson; one *d.* *Educ:* Daniel Stewart's Coll., Edinburgh; University of Edinburgh; The Queen's Coll., Oxford. Joined Dept of Health for Scotland for work on emergency hosp. service, 1940; Asst Private Sec. to Sec. of State for Scotland, 1944; Cabinet Office, 1947; Sec., Scottish Hosp. Endowments Commn, 1950; Asst Sec., Dept of Health for Scotland, 1954; Asst Sec., Scottish Education Dept, 1961; Under-Sec., 1963; Under-Sec., 1968-71, Dep. Sec., 1971, Min. of Agriculture, Fisheries and Food. Chief Counting Officer for Scotland Act Referendum, 1979. *Recreations:* walking, music. *Address:* 40A Lygon Road, Edinburgh EH16 5QA. *T:* 031-667 8298. *Club:* New (Edinburgh).

FRASER, Russell; *see* Fraser, T. R. C.

FRASER, Rt. Hon. Thomas, PC 1964; retired; *b* 18 Feb. 1911; *s* of Thomas and Mary Fraser, Kirkmuirhill, Lanarks; *m* 1935, Janet M. Scanlon, Lesmahagow, Lanarks; one *s* one *d.* *Educ:* Lesmahagow Higher Grade Sch. Left school 1925 and started work in a coal-mine (underground); worked underground, 1925-43; Miners' Union Branch Official, 1938-43; Sec., Lanark Constituency Labour Party, 1939-43; MP (Lab) Hamilton Div. of Lanarks, 1943-67; Joint Parliamentary Under-Sec. of State, Scottish Office, 1945-51; Minister of Transport, 1964-65. Member: Royal Commn on Local Govt in Scotland, 1966-69; Highlands and Islands Develt Bd, 1967-70; Chm., N of Scotland Hydro-Electric Bd, 1967-73; Mem., S of Scotland Electricity Bd, 1967-73; Chairman: Scottish Local Govt Staff Commn, 1973-77; Scottish Local Govt Property Commn, 1976-77; Commn for Local Authority Accounts in Scotland, 1974-79. Freeman of Hamilton, 1964. *Address:* 15 Broompark Drive, Lesmahagow, Lanarks.

FRASER, Prof. (Thomas) Russell (Cumming), MD, FRCP; Deputy Director, Medical Research Council, New Zealand, 1975-81; *s* of Malcolm Fraser and Caroline (*née* Watson). *Educ:* Otago Univ. Medical School. MB, ChB (distinction) 1932; MRCP 1936; DPM (Eng.) 1937; MD (NZ) 1945; FRCP 1948. Hallett Prize, 1935; NZ University Travel Fellowship, 1935; Rockefeller Travel Fellowship, 1938. Formerly Asst Med. Officer, Maudsley Hosp.; Research Fellow in Medicine, Harvard Univ.; Reader in Medicine, Postgrad. Med. Sch., London; Prof. of Clinical Endocrinology in Univ. of London, RPMS, 1957-74. Member: Assoc. Physicians of Gt Brit.; Med. Research Soc. Hon. DSc, NZ. *Publications:* contribs to medical journals. *Address:* 63 Atkin Avenue, Mission Bay, Auckland 5, New Zealand. *See also* Very Rev. Dr I. W. Fraser.

FRASER, Veronica Mary; Adviser on Schools to the Bishop of Winchester, since 1981; *b* 19 April 1933; *o d* of late Archibald Fraser. *Educ:* Richmond County Sch. for Girls; St Hugh's Coll., Oxford. Head of English Department: The Alice Ottley Sch., Worcester, 1962-65; Guildford County Sch. for Girls, 1965-67 (also Librarian); Headmistress, Godolphin Sch., Salisbury, 1968-80. *Address:* 12 Shepherd's Close, Bartley, Hants S04 2LJ.

FRASER, William, CBE 1969; CEng, FIEE; Chairman, BICC Ltd, 1973-76; *b* 15 July 1911; *e s* of late Alexander Fraser and Elizabeth Williamson Fraser; *m* 1938, Kathleen Mary Moore (*d* 1971), 3rd *d* of late Alderman and Mrs J. W. Moore; two *s* two *d.* *Educ:* Glasgow High Sch.; University Coll. London (BSc Hons). Production Engr, Joseph Lucas Ltd, 1935-37; joined Scottish Cables Ltd, 1937; Dir, 1938; Managing Dir, 1948-62; Chm., 1958-76; Chm., Scottish Cables (S Africa) Ltd, 1950-76; Dir, British Insulated Callender's Cables Ltd, 1959, on entry of Scottish Cables into BICC Group; Exec. Dir (Overseas Cos), 1962-64; Managing Dir (Overseas), 1964-68; Managing Dir (Overseas & Construction Gp), 1968-70; Dep. Chm. and Chief Exec., 1971-73. Vice-Chm., Phillips Cables Ltd (of Canada), 1961-70; Dir and Dep. Chm., Metal Manufactures Ltd (of Australia) and Subsidiaries, 1962-70; Chm., Balfour, Beatty & Co. Ltd, 1969-70; Director: Anglesey Aluminium Ltd, 1971-75; Clydesdale Bank Ltd, 1974-. Chm., Scottish Council of FBI, 1959-61. Pres., Electrical and Electronics Industries Benevolent Assoc., 1974-75. *Recreations:* fishing, shooting, golf. *Address:* Fenwick Lodge, Ewenfield Road, Ayr. *T:* Ayr 265547.

FRASER, William James; JP; Lord Provost of Aberdeen, 1977-80; *b* 31 Dec. 1921; *s* of late William and Jessie Fraser; *m* 1961, Mary Ann; three *s* one *d.* *Educ:* York Street Sch., Aberdeen; Frederick Street Sch., Aberdeen. Mem., Scottish Exec., Labour Party, 1949-74 (Chm., 1962-63). Pres., Aberdeen Trades Council, 1952. JP Aberdeen 1950. *Address:* 79 Salisbury Place, Aberdeen. *T:* Aberdeen 51040.

FRASER, Sir William (Kerr), KCB 1979 (CB 1978); Permanent Under-Secretary of State, Scottish Office, since 1978; *b* 18 March 1929; *s* of A. M. Fraser and Rachel Kerr; *m* 1956, Marion Anne Forbes; three *s* one *d.* *Educ:* Eastwood Sch., Clarkston; Glasgow Univ. (MA, LLB). Joined Scottish Home Dept, 1955; Private Sec. to Parliamentary Under-Sec., 1959, and to Secretary of State for Scotland, 1966-67; Civil Service Fellow, Univ. of Glasgow, 1963-64; Asst Sec., Regional Development Div., 1967-71; Under Sec., Scottish Home and Health Dept, 1971-75; Dep. Sec., Scottish Office, 1975-78. Hon. LLD Glasgow, 1982. *Address:* 14 Braid Avenue, Edinburgh EH10 6EE. *T:* 031-447 3751. *Club:* New (Edinburgh).

FRASER, Sir (William) Robert, KCB 1952 (CB 1939); KBE 1944; MA; *b* Hemingford Abbots, St Ives, Hunts, 9 Oct. 1891; *e s* of Garden William Fraser (W. F. Garden) and Ethel Mary Syson; *g g s* of Francis Fraser, Findrack, Aberdeenshire; *m* 1915, Phyllis (*d* 1970), *d* of William Smith, London; three *s* one *d.* *Educ:* Christ's Hosp.; University Coll., Oxford (MA). First Mods 1912; First Lit. Hum. 1914; entered Treasury, 1914; Principal, 1919; Asst Sec., 1932; Princ. Asst Sec., 1934-39; Sec., Dept of Health for Scotland, 1939-43; Sec. War Damage Commn, 1943, and Central Land Bd, 1947; Dep. Chm. and Permanent Sec., 1949-59; Chm. (part-time), 1959-62. Vice-Pres., Lawn Tennis Assoc. (Chm., 1958, Hon. Treasurer, 1962-70); Vice-Pres. Civil Service Sports Council; Pres., Civil Service Lawn Tennis Assoc. *Recreations:* gardening, crosswords, radio, chess, large print books. *Address:* 33 Hollycroft Avenue, NW3. *T:* 01-435 3566. *Clubs:* United Oxford & Cambridge University, All-England Lawn Tennis.

FRASER McLUSKEY, Rev. James; *see* McLuskey.

FRASER ROBERTS, John Alexander; *see* Roberts.

FRASER-TYTLER, Christian Helen, CBE (mil.) 1941; TD; JP; Senior Controller ATS, retired; *b* 23 Aug. 1897; *d* of John Campbell Shairp, Houstoun; *m* 1919, Col Neil Fraser-Tytler, DSO, Croix de Guerre (*d* 1937); two *d.* *Educ:* Home. Foreign Office, 1917-19; War Office, 1939-43; AA Command until 1945 (TD). *Recreation:* fishing. *Address:* 116 H Market Street, St Andrews. *T:* St Andrews 76826; 43 Sussex Square, W2. *T:* 01-723 2565.
See also Sir Thomas David Erskine, Bt, Sir Patrick Morgan.

FRAYLING, Prof. Christopher John, MA, PhD; Professor and Head of Department of Cultural History, Royal College of Art, London, since 1979; *b* 25 Dec. 1946; *s* of Arthur Frederick Frayling and Barbara Kathleen (*née* Imhof); *m* 1981, Helen Snowdon. *Educ:* Repton Sch.; Churchill Coll., Cambridge (BA, MA, PhD). Churchill Research Studentship, 1968-71; Lectr in Modern History, Univ. of Exeter, 1971-72; Tutor, Dept of General Studies, Royal College of Art, 1972-73, Vis. Lectr, 1973-79; Research Asst, Dept of Information Retrieval, Imperial War Mus., 1973-74; Lectr in the History of Ideas and European Social History, Univ. of Bath, 1974-79; founded Dept of Cultural History (ex General Studies), RCA, 1979. Lectr, critic, contributor to radio and TV. Member: Education Cttee, Crafts Council, 1981-; Crafts Council, 1982-; V&A Mus. Advisory Council, 1981-; Chm. of Trustees, Crafts Study Centre, Bath, 1982-. *Publications:* Napoleon Wrote Fiction, 1972; The Vampyre-Lord Ruthven to Count Dracula, 1978; Spaghetti Westerns-Cowboys and Europeans, from Karl May to Sergio Leone, 1981; contribs to: Reappraisals of Rousseau-studies in honour of R. A. Leigh, 1980; Cinema, Politics and Society in America, 1981; Rousseau et Voltaire en 1978, 1981; Rousseau After Two Hundred Years-Proc. of Cambridge Bicentennial Colloquium, 1982; articles on film, popular culture and the visual arts/crafts in Cambridge Rev., 1970, Cinema, 1971, London Magazine, 1973-74, New Society, 1981, Crafts, 1982, Burlington Magazine, 1982, and various learned jls. *Recreations:* thinking while walking, collecting Victorian and Edwardian popular fiction, photography. *Address:* Department of Cultural History, Royal College of Art, Kensington Gore, SW7 2EU. *T:* 01-584 5020.

FRAYN, Michael; writer; *b* 8 Sept. 1933; *s* of late Thomas Allen Frayn and Violet Alice Lawson; *m* 1960, Gillian Palmer; three *d. Educ:* Kingston Gram. Sch.; Emmanuel Coll., Cambridge. Reporter, Guardian, 1957-59; Columnist, Guardian, 1959-62; Columnist, Observer, 1962-68. TV: Jamie (play), 1968; Birthday (play) 1969; Imagine a City Called Berlin (documentary), 1975; Vienna—The Mask of Gold (documentary), 1977; Three Streets in the Country (documentary), 1979; The Long Straight (documentary), 1980; stage plays: The Two of Us, 1970; The Sandboy, 1971; Alphabetical Order, 1975; Donkeys' Years, 1976; Clouds, 1976; Liberty Hall, 1980; Make and Break, 1980; Noises Off, 1982. Somerset Maugham Award, 1966; Hawthornden Prize, 1967; Nat. Press Award, 1970; Evening Standard Drama Award (Best Comedy), 1975; Soc. of West End Theatre (Best Comedy), 1976; Drama Critics' Awards (Best New Play and Best Comedy), 1980; New Standard Drama Award (Best Comedy), 1980. *Publications:* collections of columns: The Day of the Dog, 1962; The Book of Fub, 1963; On the Outskirts, 1964; At Bay in Gear Street, 1967; *non-fiction:* Constructions, 1974; *novels:* The Tin Men, 1965; The Russian Interpreter, 1966; Towards the End of the Morning, 1967; A Very Private Life, 1968; Sweet Dreams, 1973; *translations:* The Cherry Orchard, 1978 (prod. 1978); The Fruits of Enlightenment, 1979 (prod. 1979). *Address:* c/o Elaine Greene Ltd, 31 Newington Green, N16.

FRAZER, Prof. Malcolm John, PhD, FRSC; Professor of Chemical Education, University of East Anglia, Norwich, since 1972; *b* 7 Feb. 1931; *m* 1957, Gwenyth Ida (*née* Biggs), JP, MA; three *s. Educ:* Univ. of London; BSc 1952, PhD 1955. Royal Military Coll. of Science, 1956-57; Lecturer and Head of Dept of Chemistry, Northern Polytechnic, London, 1965-72. Pro-Vice Chancellor, Univ. of East Anglia, 1976-81. Mem., Soc. for Research into Higher Educn; Gen. Sec./Vice-Pres., British Assoc. for the Advancement of Science. *Publications:* (jointly) Resource Book on Chemical Education in the UK, 1975; contribs to Jl Chem. Soc., etc. *Address:* School of Chemical Sciences, University of East Anglia, Norwich, Norfolk NR4 7TJ.

FREDERICK, Sir Charles Boscawen, 10th Bt *cr* 1723; *b* 11 April 1919; *s* of Sir Edward Boscawen Frederick, 9th Bt, CVO and Edith Katherine (Kathleen) Cortlandt (*d* 1970), *d* of late Col W. H. Mulloy, RE; *S* father, 1956; *m* 1949, Rosemary, *er d* of late Lt-Col R. J. H. Baddeley, MC; two *s* two *d. Educ:* Eton. 2nd Lieut Grenadier Guards, 1942; served N Africa and Italy, 1943-45 (despatches); Capt. 1945; Palestine, 1946-47 (despatches); Malaya, 1948-49; Egypt, 1952-53; Major, 1953. Member: London Stock Exchange, 1954-62; Provincial Brokers Stock Exchange, 1962 (Mem. Council, 1966; Dep. Chm. 1972); Stock Exchange Council, and Chm., Provincial Unit, 1973-75. JP 1960. General Commissioner of Income Tax, 1966. *Recreations:* sailing, fishing. *Heir: s* Christopher St John Frederick, *b* 28 June 1950. *Address:* The Granary, Lerryn, Lostwithiel, Cornwall. *Club:* Royal Fowey Yacht.

FREDERICTON, Archbishop of, since 1980; **Most Rev. Harold Lee Nutter,** DD; Metropolitan of the Ecclesiastical Province of Canada; *b* 29 Dec. 1923; *s* of William L. Nutter and Lillian A. Joyce; *m* 1946, Edith M. Carew; one *s* one *d. Educ:* Mount Allison Univ. (BA 1944); Dalhousie Univ. (MA 1947); Univ. of King's College (MSLitt 1947). Rector: Simonds and Upham, 1947-51; Woodstock, 1951-57; St Mark, Saint John, NB, 1957-60; Dean of Fredericton, 1960-71; Bishop of Fredericton, 1971. Co-Chairman, NB Task Force on Social Development, 1970-71; Mem., Adv. Cttee to Sec. of State for Canada on Multi-culturalism, 1973. Hon. DD: Univ. of King's College, 1960; Montreal Diocesan Coll., 1982; Hon. LLD, Mount Allison Univ., 1972. *Publication:* (jointly) New Brunswick Task Force Report on Social Development, 1971. *Address:* 791 Brunswick Street, Fredericton, NB, Canada. *T:* 4558667.

FREEBODY, Air Vice-Marshal Wilfred Leslie, CB 1951; CBE 1943; AFC; RAF Technical Branch; Director of Work Study, at Air Ministry. Squadron Leader, 1937; Acting Air Commodore commanding 226 Group, Air Cdre, 1949; Actg Air Vice-Marshal, 1956; Air Vice-Marshal, 1957. Has Order of Polonia Restituta 3rd class, of Poland.

FREEDMAN, Charles; Commissioner, Customs and Excise, since 1972; *b* 15 Oct. 1925; *s* of late Solomon Freedman, OBE, and Lilian Freedman; *m* 1949, Sarah Sadie King; one *s* two *d. Educ:* Westcliff High Sch.; Cheltenham Grammar Sch.; Trinity Coll., Cambridge (Sen. Schol., BA). Entered HM Customs and Excise, 1947; Asst Sec., 1963. *Address:* King's Beam House, Mark Lane, EC3R 7HE. *T:* 01-626 1515. *Clubs:* Civil Service; Essex Yacht.

FREEDMAN, Dawn Angela, (Mrs N. J. Shestopal); barrister-at-law; Metropolitan Stipendiary Magistrate, since 1980; *b* 9 Dec. 1942; *d* of Julius and Celia Freedman; *m* 1970, Neil John Shestopal. *Educ:* Westcliff High Sch. for Girls; University Coll., London (LLB Hons). Called to the Bar, Gray's Inn, 1966. Mem., Bd of Deputies of British Jews. *Recreations:* theatre, television, cooking. *Address:* 3 Gray's Inn Square, Gray's Inn, WC1R 5AH. *T:* 01-242 0328.

FREEDMAN, Prof. Lawrence David, DPhil; Professor of War Studies, King's College, London, since 1982; *b* 7 Dec. 1948; *s* of Lt-Comdr Julius Freedman and Myra Freedman; *m* 1974, Judith Anne Hill; one *s. Educ:* Whitley Bay Grammar Sch. BAEcon Manchester; BPhil York; DPhil Oxford. Teaching Asst, York Univ., 1971-72; Research Fellow, Nuffield Coll., Oxford, 1974-75; Research Associate, International Inst. for Strategic Studies, 1975-76; Research Fellow, Royal Inst. of International Affairs, 1976-78; Head of Policy Studies, RIIA, 1978-82. *Publications:* US Intelligence and the Soviet Strategic Threat, 1977; Britain and Nuclear Weapons, 1980; The Evolution of Nuclear Strategy, 1981. *Recreations:* tennis, political caricature. *Address:* c/o Department of War Studies, King's College, Strand, WC2R 2LS. *T:* 01-836 5454, ext. 2193.

FREEDMAN, Louis, CBE 1978; Proprietor, Cliveden Stud; Chairman, City and Hackney District Health Authority, since 1982; *b* 5 Feb. 1917; 4th *s* of Sampson and Leah Freedman; *m* 1st, 1944, Cara Kathlyn Abrahamson (marr. diss.); one *s* one *d* ; 2nd, 1960, Valerie Clarke; one *s. Educ:* University College School. FSVA. TA, RE, 1938; commnd RA, 1943; Devonshire Regt, 1944. Dir, Land Securities Investment Trust, 1958-77. Mem., Race Relations Bd, 1968-77. Chm., Nat. Assoc. Property Owners, 1971-72; Pres., Racehorse Owners Assoc., 1972-74. Vice-Chm., NE Thames RHA, 1975-79; Chm., Camden and Islington AHA, 1979-82. Governor, Royal Hosp. of St Bartholomew the Great, 1971-74; Special Trustee, St Bartholomew's Hosp., 1974-. *Recreation:* gardening. *Address:* Cliveden Stud House, Taplow, Maidenhead, Berks SL6 0HL. *Clubs:* Garrick; Jockey (Newmarket) (Deputy Senior Steward, 1981-).

FREEDMAN, Hon. Samuel; Hon. Chief Justice Freedman; Chief Justice of Manitoba, since 1971; *b* Russia, 1908; *s* of Nathan Freedman and Ada (*née* Foxman); came to Canada, 1911; *m* 1934, Claris Brownie Udow; one *s* two *d. Educ:* Winnipeg schs; Univ. of Manitoba. BA 1929, LLB 1933. Called to Manitoba Bar, 1933; KC (Canada) 1944; Judge, Court of Queen's Bench, Manitoba, 1952, Court of Appeal 1960. Chancellor, Univ. of Manitoba, 1959-68; Pres., Manitoba Bar Assoc., 1951-52; Mem. Bd of Governors, Hebrew Univ., Jerusalem, 1955-; Chm., Rhodes Scholarship Selection Cttee, Manitoba, 1956-66; Pres., Medico-Legal Soc. of Manitoba, 1954-55; Mem. Adv. Bd, Centre of Criminology, Univ. of Toronto; Mem. Bd of Dirs, Confedn Centre of the Arts in Charlottetown; one-man Industrial Inquiry Commn, CNR run-throughs, 1964-65. Holds numerous hon. degrees. *Publications:* Report of Industrial Inquiry Commission on Canadian National Railways Run-Throughs, 1965; (chapter) Admissions and Confessions, in, Studies in Canadian Criminal Evidence, ed Salhany and Carter, 1972; contrib. Canadian Bar Review. *Recreations:* walking, golf, reading. *Address:* 425 Cordova Street, Winnipeg, Manitoba R3N 1A5, Canada. *T:* 489-2922. *Club:* Glendale Country (Winnipeg).

FREELAND, John Redvers, CMG 1973; HM Diplomatic Service; Second Legal Adviser, Foreign and Commonwealth Office, since 1976; *b* 16 July 1927; *o s* of C. Redvers Freeland and Freda Freeland (*née* Walker); *m* 1952, Sarah Mary, *er d* of late S. Pascoe Hayward, QC; one *s* one *d. Educ:* Stowe; Corpus Christi Coll., Cambridge. Royal Navy, 1945 and 1948-51. Called to Bar, Lincoln's Inn, 1952; Mem. *ad eundem,* Middle Temple. Asst Legal Adviser, FO, 1954-63, and 1965-67; Legal Adviser, HM Embassy, Bonn, 1963-65; Legal Counsellor, FCO (formerly FO), 1967-70; Counsellor (Legal Advr), UK Mission to UN, NY, 1970-73; Legal Counsellor, FCO, 1973-76. *Address:* c/o Foreign and Commonwealth Office, SW1. *Club:* Travellers'.

FREELING, Nicolas; writer since 1960; *b* 1927, of English parents; *m* 1954, Cornelia Termes; four *s* one *d. Educ:* primary and secondary schs. Hotel-restaurant cook, throughout Europe, 1945-60; novelist, 1960-. *Publications:* (numerous trans.) Love in Amsterdam, 1961; Because of the Cats, 1962; Gun before Butter, 1962; Valparaiso, 1963; Double Barrel, 1963; Criminal Conversation, 1964; King of the Rainy Country, 1965; Dresden Green, 1966; Strike Out Where Not Applicable, 1967; This is the Castle, 1968; Tsing-Boum, 1969; Kitchen Book, 1970; Over the High Side, 1971; Cook Book, 1971; A Long Silence, 1972; Dressing of Diamond, 1974; What Are the Bugles Blowing For?, 1975; Lake Isle, 1976; Gadget, 1977; The Night Lords, 1978; The Widow, 1979; Castang's City, 1980; One Damn Thing After Another, 1981; Wolfnight, 1982. *Address:* Grandfontaine, 67130 Schirmeck, France.

FREEMAN, Sir Bernard; see Freeman, Sir N. B.

FREEMAN, David John; Senior Partner, and Founder, 1952, D. J. Freeman & Co., Solicitors; *b* 25 Feb. 1928; *s* of Meyer and late Rebecca Freeman; *m* 1950, Iris Margaret Alberge; two *s* one *d. Educ:* Christ's Coll., Finchley. Lieut, Army, 1946-48. Admitted Solicitor, 1952. Dept of Trade Inspector into the affairs of AEG Telefunken (UK) Ltd, and Credit Collections Ltd, 1977. Governor, Royal Shakespeare Theatre, 1979-. *Recreations:* reading, gardening. *Address:* Flat 10, 6 Hyde Park Gardens, W2. *T:* 01-262 0895; Upper Neatham Mill, Holybourne, Hants. *Club:* Reform.

FREEMAN, Dr Ernest Allan, CEng, FIEE, FIMA; Director, Trent Polytechnic, since 1981; *b* 16 Jan. 1932; *s* of William Freeman and Margaret Sinclair; *m* 1954, Mary Jane Peterson; two *d. Educ:* Sunderland Technical Coll.; King's Coll., Univ. of Durham (Mather Scholarship, 1955-57). BSc, PhD, Durham; DSc Newcastle upon Tyne; MA (Oxon) 1972. Sunderland Forge & Engineering Co. Ltd. 1949-55; English Electric Co., 1957-58; Ferranti Ltd (Edinburgh), 1958-59; Sunderland Polytechnic: Dir of Research,

1959-65; Head of Control Engrg Dept, 1965-72; Rector, 1976-80; Tutor and Fellow in Engrg, St Edmund Hall, Oxford Univ., 1972-76. FRSA. *Publications:* contribs mainly in the fields of control engrg, systems theory and computing, to Wireless Engr, Proc. IEE (Heaviside Prize, 1974), Jl of Electronics and Control, Trans AIEE, Electronic Technol., Control, Jl of Optimisation Theory and Application, Trans Soc. of Instrument Technol., Proc. Internat. Fedn for Analogue Computation, Internat. Jl of Control. *Recreations:* swimming, browsing around antique shops. *Address:* Trent Polytechnic, Burton Street, Nottingham NG1 4BU.

FREEMAN, George Vincent; Under-Secretary (Legal), Treasury Solicitor's Department, 1973-76, retired; *b* 30 April 1911; *s* of Harold Vincent Freeman and Alice Freeman; *m* 1945, Margaret Nightingale; one *d. Educ:* Denstone Coll., Rocester. Admitted Solicitor, 1934; in private practice Birmingham until 1940. Served RN, 1940-46, Lieut RNVR. Legal Asst, Treasury Solicitor's Dept, 1946; Sen. Legal Asst 1950; Asst Treasury Solicitor 1964. *Recreations:* gardening, photography. *Address:* 8 Shelley Close, Ashley Heath, Ringwood, Hants. *T:* Ringwood 77102. *Clubs:* Civil Service; Conservative (Ringwood).

FREEMAN, Harold Webber; Author; *b* 1899; *s* of Charles Albert Freeman and Emma Mary Ann Mills; *m* Elizabeth Boedecker. *Educ:* City of London Sch.; Christ Church, Oxford (classical scholar). 1st class Hon. Mods, 2nd class Lit. Hum. Main background was work on the land, mostly organic gardening; travelled in Europe (foot and bicycle); casual work as linguist (translation, monitoring, travel trade). Has lived mostly in Suffolk, but also, for long periods, in Italy. *Publications:* Joseph and His Brethren, 1928; Down in the Valley, 1930; Fathers of Their People, 1932; Pond Hall's Progress, 1933; Hester and Her Family, 1936; Andrew to the Lions, 1938; Chaffinch's, 1941; Blenheim Orange, 1949; The Poor Scholar's Tale, 1954; Round the Island: Sardinia Re-explored, 1956. *Address:* c/o National Westminster Bank Ltd, Princes Street, Ipswich.

FREEMAN, Hugh Lionel, FRCPsych; Consultant Psychiatrist, Salford Health Authority, University of Manchester School of Medicine, since 1961; *b* Salford, 4 Aug. 1929; *s* of late Bernard Freeman, FBOA and Dora Doris Freeman (*née* Kahn); *m* 1957, Sally Joan, MEd, PhD, ABPsS, *er d* of Philip and late Rebecca Casket; three *s* one *d. Educ:* Altrincham Grammar Sch.; St John's Coll., Oxford (open schol.; BM BCh 1954; MA); MSc Salford 1980. DPM 1958; FRCPsych 1971. Captain, RAMC, 1956-58. House Surg., Manchester Royal Inf., 1955; Registrar, Bethlem Royal and Maudsley Hosps, 1958-60; Sen. Registrar, Littlemore Hosp., Oxford, 1960-61; Consltnt Psychiatrist, Salford Royal Hosp., 1961-70; Hon. Consultant Psychiatrist: Salford Health Dept, 1961-74; Salford Social Services Dept, 1974-. Hon. Med. Consultant, and Mem., Public Inf. Cttee, NAMH, 1963-74. Consltnt Psychiatrist, NW Reg., DHSS, 1963-; Med. Advisor, NW Fellowship for Schizophrenia. Chairman: Psychiatric Sub-Cttee, NW Reg. Med. Adv. Cttee, 1978; Area Med. Cttee and Med. Exec. Cttee, Salford AHA, 1974-78. University of Manchester: pt-time Lectr, 1973-; Member: Deptl Bd, Psychiatry; Bd, Faculty of Medicine. Vis. Prof., Univ of WI, 1970; Rockefeller Foundn Vis. Fellow, Italy, 1980. Examiner: Univ. of Manchester; RCPsych. Med. Mem., Mental Health Rev. Tribunal, 1982. Member: Sex Educn Panel, Health Educn Council, 1968-72; Working Party on Behaviour Control, Council for Sci. and Society, 1973-76; Minister of State's Panel on Private Practice, DHSS, 1974-75. WHO Consultant: Grenada, 1970; Chile, 1978; Philippines, 1979; Bangladesh, 1981. Editor, British Jl of Clin. and Social Psych., 1982-; Dep. Editor, Internat. Jl of Social Psych., 1980-; Asst Editor, British Jl of Psych., 1978-; Co-Editor, Bull. of RCPsych, 1983-; Associate Editor, Internat. Jl of Mental Health. Mem. Internat. Res. Seminars, US Nat. Inst. of Mental Health: Washington, 1966; Pisa, 1977; has lectured to and addressed univs, confs and hosps worldwide; advr on and participant in radio and TV progs. Member: Session Steering Cttee, BAAS, 1980; Exec. Cttees, Royal Medico-Psychol Assoc., 1965-69; Exec. Cttee, Soc. of Clin. Psychs. Royal College of Psychiatrists: Foundn Mem., 1971; Vice-Chm., Social and Community Gp; External Assessor; FRSH (Hon. Sec., Mental Health Gp, 1973-76). Corresp. Mem., US Assoc. for Behavioral Therapies; Hon. Member: Chilean Soc. of Psych., Neurol. and Neurosurgery; Egyptian Psychiatric Assoc. Dir, Manchester Heritage Trust. Freeman, City of London; Yeoman, Soc. of Apothecaries, 1979-. Distinguished Service Commendation, US Nat. Council of Community Mental Health Centers, 1982. *Publications:* (ed jtly) Trends in the Mental Health Services, 1963; (ed) Psychiatric Hospital Care, 1965; (ed jtly) New Aspects of the Mental Health Service, 1968; (ed) Progress in Behaviour Therapy, 1969; (ed) Progress in Mental Health, 1970; (ed) Pavlovian Approach to Psychopathology, 1971; (ed jtly) Dangerousness, 1982; contribs to national press and learned jls. *Recreations:* architecture, travel, music. *Address:* Wykeham, Alan Drive, Hale, Cheshire WA15 0LR. *T:* 061-980 4597. *Club:* United Oxford & Cambridge University.

FREEMAN, Ifan Charles Harold, CMG 1964; TD 1961; Registrar, University of Malawi, 1965-72, retired; *b* 11 Sept. 1910; *s* of late C. E. D. W. Freeman; *m* 1937, Enid, *d* of late Edward Hallum; two *d. Educ:* Friars Sch., Bangor; Univ. of Wales (MA). Served with Royal Artillery, 1939-46 (Major; despatches). Colonial Service: Kenya, 1946-58; Nyasaland, 1958-65. *Recreation:* gardening. *Address:* Swn y Wylan, Marianglas, Gwynedd. *Clubs:* Royal Commonwealth; Mombasa (Kenya).

FREEMAN, His Eminence Sir James Darcy, Cardinal; *see* Sydney, Archbishop of, (RC).

FREEMAN, Sir James Robin, 3rd Bt *cr* 1945; *S* father, 1981. *Heir:* none.

FREEMAN, Rt. Hon. John, PC 1966; MBE 1943; Chairman: LWT (Holdings) Ltd, since 1976; London Weekend Television, since 1971; Page & Moy (Holdings) Ltd, since 1979; Director, Hutchinson Ltd, since 1978 (Chairman, 1978-82); *b* 19 Feb. 1915; *e s* of Horace Freeman, barrister-at-law, New Square, Lincoln's Inn; *m* 1st, 1938, Elizabeth Allen Johnston (marr. diss., 1948); 2nd, 1948, Margaret Ista Mabel Kerr (*d* 1957); one adopted *d* ; 3rd, 1962, Catherine Dove (marr. diss. 1976); two *s* one *d* ; 4th, 1976, Judith Mitchell; one *d. Educ:* Westminster Sch.; Brasenose Coll., Oxford (Hon. Fellow, 1968). Advertising Consultant, 1937-40. Active Service, 1940-45. MP (Lab) Watford Div. of Herts, 1945-50, Borough of Watford, 1950-55; PPS to Sec. of State for War, 1945-46; Financial Sec., War Office, 1946; Parliamentary Under Sec. of State for War, April 1947; Leader, UK Defence Mission to Burma, 1947; Parliamentary Sec., Ministry of Supply, 1947-51, resigned. Asst Editor, New Statesman, 1951-58; Deputy Editor, 1958-60; Editor, 1961-65. British High Commissioner in India, 1965-68; British Ambassador in Washington, 1969-71. Chm., ITN, 1976-81; Governor, BFI, 1976-. Vice-Pres., Royal Television Soc., 1975- (Gold Medal, 1981). *Address:* c/o LWT (Holdings) Ltd, South Bank Television Centre, Kent House, SE1.

FREEMAN, John Allen, OBE 1958; PhD; FRES, FIBiol; Director, Ministry of Agriculture, Fisheries and Food's Pest Infestation Control Laboratory, 1977-79; *b* 30 Sept. 1912; *s* of Laurence Freeman and Maggie Rentoul Freeman; *m* 1945, Hilda Mary Jackson; one *s* one *d. Educ:* City of London Sch. (Jun. Corp. Scholar, Travers Scholar); Imperial Coll. of Science and Technol., London Univ. (BSc Special 1st Cl. Hons 1933, PhD 1938). ARCS; FRES 1943; FIBiol 1963. Min. of Agric. Scholar in Entomology, 1934-37: Hull University Coll., 1934-35; Rothamsted Exper. Stn, 1936; Cornell Univ., USA, 1936-37; Vineland Exper. Stn, Ont, Canadian Dept of Agric., 1937. Res. Asst, Imp. Coll., London, 1938-40; Jun. Scientific Officer, Dept of Science and Indust. Res. Pest Infestation Lab., 1940; seconded Min. of Food Infest. Control, 1940-47; Chief Entomologist, 1944; Sen. Sci. Officer, 1946; transf. Min. of Agric., 1947; Principal Sci. Off., 1947; seconded OECD, 1954-55, and CENTO, 1957-58; Sen. Principal Sci. Off., 1958; Dep. Chief Sci. Off., and Dep. Dir Pest Infest. Control Lab., 1971; Chief Sci. Off., 1977. Member: British Ecol Soc.; Assoc. of Applied Biol. Treasurer, Royal Entomol Soc. of London, 1977-; Hon. Treas., Inst. of Biol, 1965-69. Pres., Royal Coll. of Science Union and Imp. Coll. Union, 1934. Has travelled professionally in N and S America, Europe, Africa, ME and Far East. Freeman of City of London, 1947. *Publications:* scientific articles, mainly on pests of stored foods. *Recreations:* gardening, photography, travel, DIY. *Address:* 5 Woodmere Way, Park Langley, Beckenham, Kent BR3 2SJ. *T:* 01-658 6970.

FREEMAN, Joseph William, OBE 1968; Director of Social Service, Leeds, 1970-78; *b* 8 April 1914; *s* of Thomas and Emma Freeman; *m* 1939, Louise King; one *s* one *d. Educ:* Liverpool Univ.; Toynbee Hall. CQSW. Qual. social worker; Probation Service, Birmingham, 1938; served War of 1939-45: Army, 1940, commnd RA, 1941; Probation Service, Liverpool, 1946; Children's Officer: Warrington, 1948; Bolton, 1951; Sheffield, 1955. *Publications:* papers in social work jls. *Recreations:* music, swimming. *Address:* 40 Forest Grove, Eccleston Park, Prescot, Merseyside L34 2RZ. *T:* 051-426 6928.

FREEMAN, Michael Alexander Reykers, MD; FRCS; Consultant Orthopaedic Surgeon, The London Hospital, since 1968; *b* 17 Nov. 1931; *s* of Donald George and Florence Julia Freeman; *m* 1st, 1951, Elisabeth Jean; one *s* one *d* ; 2nd, 1959, Janet Edith; one *s* one *d* ; 3rd, 1968, Patricia; one *d* (and one *s* decd). *Educ:* Stowe Sch.; Corpus Christi Coll., Cambridge (open scholarship and closed exhibn); London Hospital Med. Coll. BA (1st cl. hons), MB BCh, MD (Cantab). FRCS 1959. Trained in medicine and surgery, London Hosp., and in orthopaedic and traumatic surgery, London, Westminster and Middlesex Hosps; co-founder, Biomechanics Unit, Imperial Coll., London, 1964; Cons. Surg. in Orth. and Traum. Surgery, London Hosp., also Res. Fellow, Imperial Coll., 1968; resigned from Imperial Coll., to devote more time to clinical activities, 1979. Special surgical interest in field of reconstructive surgery in lower limb, concentrating on joint replacement; originator of new surgical procedures for reconstruction and replacement of arthritic hip, knee, ankle and joints of foot; has lectured and demonstrated surgery, Canada, USA, Brazil, Japan, China, Australia, S Africa, continental Europe; guest speaker at nat. and internat. profess. congresses. Member: BMA; Brit. Orth. Assoc.; Amer. Acad. Orth. Surgs; Orth. Res. Soc.; Soc. Internat. Chirurg. Orth. and Traum.; RSM; Past Member: MRC; Clin. Res. Bd, London Hosp. Bd of Governors; Brent and Harrow AHA; DHSS working parties. Bacon and Cunning Prizes and Copeman Medal, CCC; Andrew Clark and T. A. M. Ross Prize in Clin. Med., London Hosp. Med. Coll.; Robert Jones Medal, Brit. Orth. Assoc. *Publications:* editor and part-author: Adult Articular Cartilage, 1973, 2nd edn 1979; Scientific Basis of Joint Replacement, 1977; Arthritis of the Knee, 1980; chapters in: Bailey and Love's Short Practice of Surgery; Mason and Currey's Textbook of Rheumatology; papers in Proc. Royal Soc., Proc. RSM, and med. jls. *Recreations:* writing, reading, surgery. *Address:* 79 Albert Street, NW1. *T:* 01-387 0817.

FREEMAN, Sir (Nathaniel) Bernard, Kt 1967; CBE 1956; Chairman, Metro-Goldwyn-Mayer Pty Ltd, 1967, retired; *b* 1 Sept. 1896; *s* of Adolph and Malvina Freeman; *m* 1926, Marjorie Arabel (*née* Bloom); one *s* one *d*. *Educ*: Public Sch. and Xavier Coll., Melbourne. Served European War, 1914–18: 38th Bn, 3rd Div., First AIF, and Austr. Flying Corps; inaugurated free films to Austr. Troops, 1939–45. Founded Metro-Goldwyn-Mayer Austr., NZ and S Pacific, 1925; Man. Dir, Metro-Goldwyn-Mayer, 1925–66. First Mem. Chm., Motion Picture Distributors' Assoc. of Austr., 1939–41, also 1963. Chm. various cttees, appeals and trusts, 1945–; National Chm., UNICEF, 1952; Chm., World Refugee Year, NSW, 1960; Chm. of Trustees and Internat. Houses Appeal, Univs of Sydney and NSW; Chm., NSW and Canberra, ANZAC Memorial and Forest in Israel; Mem. Exec., Sydney Opera House Trust, 1962–69; mem. of many other cttees; Life Mem., RSL State Br., 1945–; Life Governor: Royal NSW Instn for Deaf and Blind Children; Vic. Ear and Eye Hosp.; Vic. Sch. for Deaf Children. Fellow, Sydney University Internat. House. Library of Univ. of NSW now named Sir Bernard Freeman Library. Paul Harris Award, Sydney Rotary Club, 1981. *Recreations*: swimming, bowls. *Address*: 2/c Hopewood Gardens, 13 Thornton Street, Darling Point, NSW 2027, Australia. *Clubs*: American National (Sydney), City Bowling (Sydney).

FREEMAN, Nicholas Hall; barrister; Leader, Kensington and Chelsea Borough Council, since 1977; *b* 25 July 1939; *s* of William Freeman and Grace Freeman, Leicester. *Educ*: Stoneygate Sch., Leicester; King's Sch., Canterbury. Admitted Solicitor, 1962; called to the Bar, Middle Temple, 1968. Chancellor, Diocese of Leicester, 1979–. Kensington and Chelsea Borough Council: Member, 1968; Vice-Chm., Town Planning Cttee, 1973, Chm., 1975. Vice-Chm., General Purposes Cttee, London Boroughs Assoc., 1978–. Mem., Conservative Central Office Policy Gp for London, 1971–. Contested (C) Hartlepool, Feb. and Oct. 1974. Governor, Emmanuel Sch., Clapham, 1974–78. Freeman, City of London, 1981. *Recreations*: reading, particularly biography, holidays in France, theatre. *Address*: 51 Harrington Gardens, SW7 4JU. *T*: 01-370 3197. *Clubs*: Carlton; Leicestershire (Leicester).

FREEMAN, Paul, ARCS, DSc (London), FRES; Keeper of Entomology, British Museum (Natural History), 1968–81; *b* 26 May 1916; *s* of Samuel Mellor Freeman and Kate Burgis; *m* 1942, Audrey Margaret Long; two *d*. *Educ*: Brentwood Sch., Essex; Imperial Coll., London. Demonstrator in Entomology, Imperial Coll., 1938. Captain, RA and Army Operational Research Group, 1940–45. Lecturer in Entomology, Imperial Coll., 1945–47. Asst Keeper, Dept of Entomology, British Museum (Nat. Hist.), 1947–64, Dep. Keeper, 1964–68, Keeper, 1968. Hon. Sec., Royal Entomological Soc. of London, 1958–62 (Vice-Pres., 1956, 1957); Sec., XIIth Internat. Congress of Entomology, London, 1964. *Publications*: Diptera of Patagonia and South Chile, Pt III-Mycetophilidae, 1951; Simuliidae of the Ethiopian Region (with Botha de Meillon), 1953; numerous papers in learned jls, on taxonomy of Hemiptera and Diptera. *Recreations*: gardening, natural history. *Address*: Briardene, 75 Towncourt Crescent, Petts Wood, Orpington, Kent BR5 1PH. *T*: Orpington 27296.

FREEMAN, Paul Illife, PhD; Director, Central Computer and Telecommunications Agency, since 1983; *s* of John Percy Freeman and Hilda Freeman; *m* 1959, Enid Ivy May Freeman; one *s* one *d*. *Educ*: Victoria University of Manchester (BSc (Hons) Chemistry, PhD). Post Doctoral Fellow, Nat. Research Council of Canada, 1959–61; Research Scientist, Dupont De Nemours Co. Ltd, Wilmington, Del, USA, 1961–64; Nat. Physical Laboratory: Sen. Scientific Officer, 1964–70; Principal Scientific Officer, 1970–74; Exec. Officer, Research Requirements Bds, DoI, 1973–77; Director: Computer Aided Design Centre, 1978–83; National Engrg Lab., 1980–83. Vis. Prof. Univ. of Strathclyde, 1981. *Publications*: scientific papers. *Recreations*: reading, walking, gardening. *Address*: 12 Broadway, Wilburton, Ely, Cambridgeshire CB6 3RT. *T*: Ely 740576.

FREEMAN, Sir Ralph, Kt 1970; CVO 1964; CBE 1952 (MBE (mil.) 1945); FEng, FICE, FCIT, FASCE; Consultant, Freeman, Fox & Partners, Consulting Engineers, since 1979 (Senior Partner, 1963–79, Partner, 1947–79); *b* 3 Feb. 1911; *s* of late Sir Ralph Freeman and late Mary (*née* Lines); *m* 1939, Joan Elizabeth, *er d* of late Col J. G. Rose, DSO, VD, FRIC, Wynberg, Cape, S Africa; two *s* one *d*. *Educ*: Uppingham Sch.; Worcester Coll., Oxford (MA; Hon. Fellow, 1980). Construction Engineer: Dorman Long & Co., S Africa, Rhodesia and Denmark, 1932–36 and 1937–39; Braithwaite & Co., 1936–37; on staff of Freeman, Fox & Partners, 1939–46, Admty and other war work; served RE, 1943–45 (Temp. Major) at Exp. Bridging Estab. and later seconded as bridging adviser to CE 21 Army Gp HQ, NW Europe campaign. Consulting Engr to the Queen for Sandringham Estate, 1949–76. Past Pres., Instn of Civil Engrs (Mem. Council, 1951–55 and 1957–61, Vice-Pres., 1962–66; Pres., 1966–67); Member: Governing Body, SE London Techn. Coll. 1952–58; Nat. Cons. Council to Min. of Works, 1952–56; Bd of Governors, Westminster Hosp., 1963–69; Council, Worcester Coll. Soc., 1964–; Adv. Council on Scientific Res. and Develt (MoD), 1966–69; Defence Scientific Adv. Council, 1969–72; Royal Fine Art Commn, 1968–; Council, Assoc. of Consulting Engrs, 1969–72, 1973–77, Chm., 1975–76; Governing Body, Imp. Coll. of Science and Technology, 1975–; Chm., Limpsfield Common Local Management Cttee, Nat. Trust, 1972–82; Pres., Welding Inst., 1975–77. Col, Engr and Rly Staff Corps RE (T&AVR), 1963–76, Col comdg 1970–74. DUniv surrey, 1978. Hon. Mem., Instn Royal Engrs, 1971; Hon. FIMechE, 1971; Hon. Fellow, Zimbabwe (formerly Rhodesian) Instn of Engrs, 1969; FRSA. Kt, Order of Orange Nassau (Netherlands), 1945. *Publications*: several papers in Proc. ICE. *Recreations*: golf, carpentry, sailing. *Address*: Ballards Shaw, Ballards Lane, Limpsfield, Oxted, Surrey RH8 0SN. *T*: Limpsfield

Chart 3284. *Clubs*: Army and Navy; Leander (Henley-on-Thames). See also D. L. Pearson.

FREEMAN, Raymond, MA, DPhil, DSc (Oxon); FRS 1979; Fellow of Magdalen College and Lecturer in Physical Chemistry, Oxford University, since 1973; *b* 6 Jan. 1932; *s* of late Albert and of Hilda Frances Freeman; *m* 1958, Anne-Marie Périnet-Marquet; two *s* three *d*. *Educ*: Nottingham High Sch. (scholar); Lincoln Coll., Oxford (open scholar). Ingénieur, Centre d'Etudes Nucléaires de Saclay, Commissariat à l'Energie Atomique, France, 1957–59; Sen. Scientific Officer, Nat. Phys. Lab., Teddington, Mddx, 1959–63; Man., Nuclear Magnetic Resonance Research, Varian Associates, Palo Alto, Calif, 1963–73. Chem. Soc. Award in Theoretical Chem. and Spectroscopy, 1978. *Publications*: articles on nuclear magnetic resonance spectroscopy in various scientific journals. *Recreations*: swimming, traditional jazz. *Address*: 4 Rolfe Place, Harberton Mead, Headington, Oxford. *T*: Oxford 68362.

FREEMAN, Richard Gavin; His Honour Judge Freeman; a Circuit Judge (formerly County Court Judge), since 1968; *b* 18 Oct. 1910; *s* of John Freeman, MD, and Violet Alice Leslie Hadden; *m* 1937, Marjorie Pear; one *s* two *d*; *m* 1961, Winifred Ann Bell. *Educ*: Charterhouse; Hertford Coll., Oxford. Called to Bar, Gray's Inn, 1947. Deputy Chairman, Warwicks Quarter Sessions, 1963–71. Hon. Major, RA. *Recreations*: cricket, gardening. *Address*: 10 Rees Street, N1. *Club*: Streatley Cricket.

FREEMAN-GRENVILLE, family name of **Lady Kinloss.**

FREER, Charles Edward Jesse, DL; *b* 4 March 1901; *s* of late Canon S. Thorold Winckley, FSA and Elizabeth (*née* Freer); changed name to Freer by Deed Poll, 1922; *m* 1st, 1927, Violet Muriel (*d* 1944), *d* of H. P. Gee, CBE, Leicester; two *s* two *d*; 2nd, 1945, Cynthia Lilian, *d* of Leonard R. Braithwaite, FRCS, Leeds; two *d*. *Educ*: Radley Coll. Solicitor, 1924; served RA (TA) in France, 1940; DJAG in Iceland, 1941–42; at SHAEF, 1943–44, Lt-Col. TA., Leicestershire QS, 1949–71. Chm. Leicester Diocesan Board of Finance, 1946–56; Chm. Mental Health Tribunal, Sheffield Regional Board, 1961–73. A Chm. of Industrial Tribunals, 1966–73. DL 1946, JP 1946–71, Leics. *Recreations*: reading, walking. *Address*: Shoal House, 48 Pearce Avenue, Parkstone, Dorset. *T*: Parkstone 748393. *Clubs*: East India, Devonshire, Sports and Public Schools; Parkstone Yacht.

FREER, Air Chief Marshal Sir Robert (William George), GBE 1981 (CBE 1966); KCB 1977; Commandant, Royal College of Defence Studies, 1980–82, retired; *b* Darjeeling, 1 Sept. 1923; *s* of late William Freer, Stretton, Cirencester, Glos; *m* 1950, Margaret, 2nd *d* of late J. W. Elkington and Mrs M. Elkington, Ruskington Manor, near Sleaford, Lincs; one *s* one *d*. *Educ*: Gosport Grammar Sch. S Africa and UK, 1944–47; RAF Coll., Cranwell, 1947–50; served 54 and 614 Fighter Sqdns, 1950–52; Central Fighter Estabt, 1952–54; commanded 92 Fighter Sqdn, 1955–57 (Queen's Commendation, 1955); Directing Staff, USAF Acad., 1958–60; Staff of Chief of Defence Staff, 1961–63; Station Comdr, RAF Seletar, 1963–66; DD Defence Plans (Air), MoD, 1966–67. Air ADC to the Queen, 1969–71; Dep. Comdt, RAF Staff Coll., 1969–71; SASO, HQ Near East Air Force, 1971–72; AOC 11 Group, 1972–75; Dir-Gen., Organisation (RAF), April-Sept. 1975; AOC No 18 Group, RAF, 1975–78; Dep. C-in-C, Strike Command, 1978–79; psa, 1957; pfc, 1960; IDC, 1968. Pres., RAF LTA, 1975–81; Mem., Sports Council, 1980–. CBIM (FBIM 1977). *Recreations*: golf, tennis. *Address*: c/o Lloyds Bank, 6 Pall Mall, SW1. *Club*: Royal Air Force.

FREESON, Rt. Hon. Reginald, PC 1976; MP (Lab) Brent East, since Feb. 1974 (Willesden East, 1964–74); *b* 24 Feb. 1926; *m*; one *s* one *d*. *Educ*: Jewish Orphanage, West Norwood. Served in Army, 1944–47. Middle East magazines and newspapers, 1946–48. Joined Labour Party on return to United Kingdom, 1948, Co-operative Party, 1958 and Poale Zion, 1964. Journalist, 1948–64: magazines, newspaper agencies and television; Everybody's Weekly, Tribune, News Chronicle, Daily Mirror. Asst Press Officer with Min. of Works, British Railways Board. Some short story writing, research and ghosting of books and pamphlets. Editor of Searchlight, against fascism and racialism, 1964–67. Radio and television: housing, urban planning, race relations and foreign affairs. Elected Willesden Borough Council, 1952; Alderman, 1955; Leader of Council, 1958–65; Chm. of new London Borough of Brent, 1964–65 (Alderman, 1964–68). PPS to Minister of Transport, 1964–67; Parly Secretary: Min. of Power, 1967–69; Min. of Housing and Local Govt, 1969–70; Labour Front-Bench Spokesman on Housing, 1970–74; Minister for Housing and Construction, DoE, 1974–79. Mem., Internat. Voluntary Service and UNA International Service. Sponsor, three Willesden Housing co-operatives, 1958–60. Founder-Chairman: Willesden (now Brent) Coun. of Social Service, 1960–62; Willesden Social Action, 1961–63; Willesden and Brent Friendship Council (now Brent Community Relns Council), 1959–63 (Vice-Pres., 1967); Chm., Warsaw Memorial Cttee, 1964–71; Mem., NCCL; Vice-Pres., Campaign for Democracy in Ulster; Mem., Jewish Welfare Bd, 1971–74 (Mem. Exec., 1973–74). *Recreations*: gardening, music, theatre, reading, country walking. *Address*: 159 Chevening Road, NW6.

FREETH, Andrew; see Freeth, H. A.

FREETH, Denzil Kingson; Member of Stock Exchange; *b* 10 July 1924; *s* of late Walter Kingson and late Vera Freeth. *Educ*: Highfield Sch., Liphook, Hants; Sherborne Sch. (Scholar); Trinity Hall, Cambridge (Scholar). Served

War, 1943-46: RAF (Flying Officer). Pres. Union Soc., Cambridge, 1949; Chm. Cambridge Univ. Conservative Assoc. 1949; debating tour of America, 1949, also debated in Ireland; Mem. Exec. Cttee Nat. Union, 1955. MP (C) Basingstoke Division of Hants, 1955-64. PPS to Minister of State, Bd of Trade, 1956, to Pres. of the Bd of Trade, 1957-59, to Minister of Educn, 1959-60; Parly Sec. for Science, 1961-63. Mem. Parliamentary Cttee of Trustee Savings Bank Assoc., 1956-61. Mem. Select Cttee on Procedure, 1958-59. Employed by and Partner in stockbroking firms, 1950-61 and 1964-; Mem. of Stock Exchange, 1959-61, 1965-. Churchwarden, All Saints' Church, Margaret St, W1, 1977-. *Recreations:* good food, wine and conversation. *Address:* 3 Brasenose House, 35 Kensington High Street, W8 5BA. *T:* 01-937 8685. *Clubs:* Carlton; Pitt (Cambridge).

FREETH, Hon. Sir Gordon, KBE 1978; Chairman, Australian Consolidated Minerals, since 1981; *b* 6 Aug. 1914; *s* of late Rt Rev. Robert Evelyn Freeth, and of Gladys Mary Snashall; *m* 1939, Joan Celia Carew Baker; one *s* two *d. Educ:* Sydney Church of England Grammar Sch.; Guildford Grammar Sch.; Univ. of Western Australia. Rowed for Australia in British Empire Games, Sydney, 1938. Admitted as Barrister and Solicitor, WA, 1938; practised Law at Katanning, WA, 1939-49. Served as Pilot, RAAF, 1942-45. Elected to House of Representatives as Member for Forrest, 1949; MP 1949-69; Minister: for Interior and Works, 1958-63; for Shipping and Transport, 1963-68; Assisting Attorney-Gen., 1962-64; for Air, and Minister Assisting the Treasurer, 1968; for External Affairs, 1969; Ambassador to Japan, 1970-73; practised law in Perth, WA, 1973-77; High Comr for Australia in UK, 1977-80. *Recreations:* squash, golf. *Address:* Tingrith, 25 Owston Street, Mosman Park, WA 6012, Australia. *Club:* Weld (Perth).

FREETH, H. Andrew, RA 1965 (ARA 1955); RE 1946; PPRWS (RWS 1955); RBA 1949; RP 1966; Portrait Painter and Etcher; on staff of Sir John Cass College, Whitechapel; *b* Birmingham, 29 Dec. 1912; *s* of John Stewart Freeth and Charlotte Eleanor Stace, Hastings; *m* 1940, Roseen Marguerite Preston; three *s* one *d. Educ:* College of Art, Birmingham; British School at Rome, 1936-39 (Rome Scholarship in Engraving). ARE 1938. Served in Intelligence Corps (Major), 1940-46, in Mediterranean theatre; loaned to RAF Middle East as Official War Artist, 1943. Drawings and etchings have been purchased by Contemporary Art Society for British Museum, by Fitzwilliam Museum, by British Council, Bristol, Birmingham and Sunderland Art Galleries, by numerous Oxford and Cambridge Colls, etc; by Nat. Portrait Gall., Ashmolean Museum, Imperial War Museum, and Victoria and Albert Museum; reproduced in various publications. Best known works: (Portraits): Sir Alec Douglas-Home, J. Enoch Powell, W. Somerset Maugham, G. E. Moore, Walter de la Mare, Lord Avon, Sir Bernard Lovell, Lord MacDermott, Lord Chief Justice of N Ireland, Bishops of Dover, London, Peterborough, Derby, Gloucester, St Albans, Lord Edmund-Davies, Sir Anthony Wagner. Pres., RWS, 1974-76. Freeman and Liveryman, Painter-Stainers Co., 1977. *Address:* 37 Eastbury Road, Northwood, Mddx. *T:* Northwood 21350.

FREMANTLE, family name of **Baron Cottesloe.**

FRÉMAUX, Louis Joseph Felix; Principal Guest Conductor, Sydney Symphony Orchestra, since 1982 (Musical Director and Principal Conductor, 1979-81); *b* 13 Aug. 1921. *Educ:* Conservatoire National Supérieur de Musique de Paris. Chef d'orchestre permanent et directeur, l'Orchestre National de l'Opéra de Monte Carlo, 1956-66; Principal Conductor, Orchestre de Lyon, 1968-71; Musical Dir and Principal Conductor, City of Birmingham Symphony Orch., 1969-78. Hon. DMus Birmingham, 1978. Hon. Member, Royal Academy of Music, 1978. Légion d'Honneur; Croix de Guerre (twice). *Recreations:* walking, photography. *Address:* Spring Cottage, Box, Stroud, Glos GL6 9HD.

FRENCH, family name of **Baron De Freyne** and **Earl of Ypres.**

FRENCH, Prof. Anthony Philip, PhD; Professor of Physics, Massachusetts Institute of Technology, since 1964; *b* 19 Nov. 1920; *s* of Sydney James French and Elizabeth Margaret (*née* Hart); *m* 1946, Naomi Mary Livesay; one *s* one *d. Educ:* Varndean Sch., Brighton; Sidney Sussex Coll., Cambridge (major schol.; BA Hons 1942, MA 1946, PhD 1948). British atomic bomb project, Tube Alloys, 1942-44; Manhattan Project, Los Alamos, USA, 1944-46; Scientific Officer, AERE, Harwell, 1946-48; Univ. Demonstrator in Physics, Cavendish Laboratory, Cambridge, 1948-51; Lectr 1951-55; Dir of Studies in Natural Sciences, Pembroke Coll., Cambridge, 1949-55, Fellow of Pembroke, 1950-55; Visiting research scholar: California Inst. of Technology, 1951; Univ. of Michigan, 1954; Prof. of Physics, Univ. of S Carolina, 1955-62 (Head of Dept, 1956-62); Guignard Lectr, 1958; Vis. Prof., MIT, 1962-64; Vis. Fellow of Pembroke Coll., Cambridge, 1975. Member, Internat. Commn on Physics Educn, 1972- (Chm., 1975-81). *Publications:* Principles of Modern Physics, 1958; Special Relativity, 1968; Newtonian Mechanics, 1971; Vibrations and Waves, 1971; Introduction to Quantum Physics, 1978; Einstein: a centenary volume, 1979. *Recreations:* music, squash, reading, writing. *Address:* c/o Physics Department, Massachusetts Institute of Technology, Cambridge, Mass 02139, USA.

FRENCH, Hon. Sir Christopher James Saunders, Kt 1979; **Hon. Mr Justice French;** Judge of the High Court of Justice, Queen's Bench Division, since 1982 (Family Division, 1979-82); Presiding Judge, South Eastern Circuit, since 1982; *b* 14 Oct. 1925; 2nd *s* of late Rev. Reginald French, MC,

MA, Hon. Chaplain to the Queen, and Gertrude Emily Mary (*née* Haworth); *m* 1957, Philippa, *d* of Philip Godfrey Price, Abergavenny; one *s* one *d. Educ:* Denstone Coll. (scholar); Brasenose Coll., Oxford (scholar). Coldstream Guards, 1943-48 (Capt.). Called to the Bar, Inner Temple, 1950; QC 1966; Master of the Bench, 1975. Dep. Chm., Bucks QS, 1966-71. Recorder of Coventry, 1971-72; a Recorder, and Hon. Recorder of Coventry, 1972-79. Member: Gen. Council of the Bar, 1963-67; Senate of Inns of Court and Bar, 1978-79; Lord Chancellor's Adv. Cttee on Trng Magistrates, 1974-80. *Recreations:* walking, hunting, music, painting. *Address:* Royal Courts of Justice, Strand, WC2. *Club:* Garrick.

FRENCH, Henry William, CBE 1971; BSc (London); CEng, FIEE, FInstP; FCP; Senior Pro-Chancellor and Chairman of the Council, Loughborough University of Technology, since 1981 (Pro-Chancellor since 1978); Vice-Chairman of Council, Brighton Polytechnic, since 1980; *b* 14 Feb. 1910; *s* of Henry Moxey French and Alice French (*née* Applegate); *m* 1936, Hazel Anne Mary Ainley; two *s. Educ:* Varndean School, Brighton; Woolwich Polytechnic. Engineering Technician, 1925-27; Armed Forces (Royal Corps of Signals, Army Educational Corps), 1927-38; Lecturer, Radar Engineering, Mil. Coll. of Science, 1938-46; Dep. Dir, Educn and Training, Electric and Musical Industries, 1946-48; HM Inspector of Schools (Further Education), 1948-56; Regional Staff Inspector (NW), 1956-59; Staff Inspector (Engineering), 1956-65; Chief Inspector for Further Educn for Industry and Commerce, DES, 1965-72; Sen. Chief Inspector, DES, 1972-74. Hon. DSc Loughborough Univ. of Technology, 1966. *Publications:* Technician Engineering Drawing 1, 1979; Engineering Technicians: some problems of nomenclature and classification, 1980. *Recreations:* polyphonic music, opera, physics of music, travel. *Address:* 26 Crossways, Sutton, Surrey. *T:* 01-642 5277.

FRENCH, Leslie Richard; Actor; *b* Kent, 23 April 1904; *s* of Robert Gilbert French and Jetty Sands Leahy; unmarried. *Educ:* London Coll. of Choristers. Began stage work 1914; early Shakespearean training with Sir Philip Ben Greet; parts include Hansel in Hansel and Gretel, Bert in Derby Day; Shakespearean parts include Puck, Ariel, Feste, Costard, etc; The Spirit in Comus; played Feste in the ballet Twelfth Night with the International Ballet at His Majesty's Theatre. Joined the Royal Corps of Signals, 1942; Lord Fancourt Babberly in Charley's Aunt, Christmas 1943. Produced Much Ado About Nothing and The Tempest for OUDS; Everyman as a ballet for the International Ballet Co., Lyric Theatre, 1943; Comus for the International Ballet, London Coliseum, 1946. Productions include: Charles and Mary, Cheltenham Festival, 1948; The Servant of Two Masters; Aladdin (Widow Twanky); Mother Goose (Mother Goose); She Stoops to Conquer for Edinburgh Festival (Tony Lumpkin), 1949; pantomime, Cinderella, 1950; The Dish Ran Away, Whitehall, 1950; Midsummer Night's Dream (Puck), Open Air Theatre during Cheltenham Festival; Open Air Theatre, Regent's Park, 1951; pantomime, Nottingham, 1951-52; The Ghost Train, Huddersfield, 1952; Pisanio in Cymbeline, Attendant Spirit in Comus, Open Air Theatre, 1952; Dyrkin in Out of the Whirlwind, Westminster Abbey, 1953; Open Air Theatre, Cape Town: The Taming of the Shrew, 1956; Midsummer Night's Dream, 1957; As You Like It (Touchstone), 1958; Johannesburg: The Tempest, 1956; Hamlet, 1957; Shakespearean seasons in Cape Town, 1959, 1960, 1961, 1962, 1963, 1966, 1969; Tempest, E. Oppenheimer Theatre, OFS, 1968; The Tell Tale Heart, 1969; An Evening with Shakespeare (tour), 1969; Twelfth Night, Port Elizabeth, 1970; The Way of the World, S Africa, 1970; Co-dir, Open Air Theatre, Regent's Park, 1958. Prod., Twelfth Night (in Great Hall of Hampton Ct Palace), 1965; Le Streghe (for Visconti), 1966; toured USA, 1969-70 and 1970-71: One Man Shakespearean Recitals, and Shylock in Merchant of Venice; The Chaplain in The Lady's not for Burning, Chichester Festival, 1972; toured USA 1973; recitals and prod Twelfth Night; The Tempest, Cape Town, 1973; As You Like It, Port Elizabeth, 1973; Caroline, Yvonne Arnaud Theatre; Directed: Saturday Sunday Monday, Nat. Arts Council, S Africa, 1976; Romeo and Juliet, Cape Town, 1980; numerous appearances on TV. *Films:* Orders to Kill (M Lafitte), 1957; The Scapegoat (M Lacoste), 1958; The Singer not the Song (Father Gomez); The Leopard (Chevalley), 1963; The Witches, 1966; Happy Ever After, 1966; Joseph of Coppertino, 1966; Death in Venice (Visconti), 1970. Several TV appearances incl. Villette (serial), 1970. First Exhibition of Paintings-oil and water colour, Parsons Gall. Presented with Key to City of Cape Town, Jan. 1963. Gold Medals: Port Elizabeth Shakespeare Society, 1973; 1820 Settlers, 1978; Grahamstown Festival, 1977; Hon. Life Mem., Mark Twain Soc., USA, 1976 (all in recognition of his contribution to art and culture in the theatre in England and overseas). *Recreations:* gardening and painting. *Address:* 39 Lennox Gardens, SW1X 0DF. *T:* 01-584 4797; La Stalla, Dosso, Levanto, La Spezia, Italy. *T:* Levanto 807-403. *Club:* Garrick.

FRENCH, Neville Arthur Irwin, CMG 1976; MVO 1968; HM Diplomatic Service, retired; *b* 28 April 1920; *s* of late Ernest French and Alice Irwin (*née* Powell); *m* 1945, Joyce Ethel, *d* of late Henry Robert Greene, Buenos Aires and Montevideo; one *s* two *d. Educ:* London Sch. of Economics (BSc (Econ)). Fleet Auxiliary and Special Duties, Min. of War Transport, 1939-45. Colonial Admin. Service, Tanganyika, 1948, later HMOCS; District Comr, 1949-61; Principal Asst Sec., (External Affairs), Prime Minister's Office, Dar es Salaam, 1961; retd from HMOCS, 1962; Central African Office, 1963-64; 1st Sec., British High Commn, Salisbury, 1964-66; Head of Chancery, British Embassy, Rio de Janeiro, 1966-69; Asst Head of Western Organisations Dept, FCO, 1970-72; Counsellor, and Chargé d'Affaires, Havana, 1972-75; Governor and C-in-C, Falkland Islands, and High Comr, British Antarctic

Territory, 1975-77; Dep. High Comr, Madras, 1977-80. Mem., Anglo-Spanish Soc. Comdr, Order of Rio Branco (Brazil), 1968. *Recreations:* sailing, books. *Address:* c/o Barclays Bank, 84 High Street, Bideford, Devon. *Clubs:* Royal Commonwealth Society; Madras.

FREND, Rev. Prof. William Hugh Clifford, TD 1959 (Clasp, 1966); DD, FRSE, FSA; Professor of Ecclesiastical History, since 1969, and Dean of Divinity Faculty, 1972-75, Glasgow University; *b* 11 Jan. 1916; 2nd *s* of late Rev. E. G. C. Frend, Shottermill, Surrey and late Edith (*née* Bacon); *m* 1951, Mary Grace, *d* of E. A. Crook, *qv*; one *s* one *d. Educ:* Fernden Sch.; Haileybury Coll. (Schol.); Keble Coll., Oxford (Schol.). 1st cl. hons Mod. Hist., 1937; Craven Fellow, 1937; DPhil 1940; BD Cantab 1964; DD Oxon 1966. Asst Princ., War Office, 1940; seconded Cabinet Office, 1941; FO, 1942; service in N Africa, Italy and Austria, 1943-46; Ed. Bd, German Foreign Min. Documents, 1947-51; Res. Fellow, Nottingham Univ., 1951; S. A. Cook Bye-Fellow, 1952, Fellow, 1956-69, Dir Studies, Archaeology, 1961-69, Gonville and Caius Coll.; University Asst Lectr, 1953, Lectr in Divinity, 1958-69; Birkbeck Lectr in Ecclesiastical History, 1967-68. Chm., AUT (Scotland), 1976-78. Vice-Pres., Internat. Commn for Comparative Study of Ecclesiastical History (CIHEC), 1975-80, Pres., 1980-. Assoc. Dir, Egypt Exploration Soc. excavations at Q'asr Ibrim, Nubia, 1963-64; Guest Scholar at Rhodes Univ., 1964 and Peter Ainslie Mem. Lecturer; Guest Prof., Univ. of S Africa, 1976; Vis. Prof. of Inter-religious Studies (Walter and Mary Tuohy Chair), John Carroll Univ., Cleveland, 1981. Licensed Lay Reader, 1956, Deacon, 1982; serving in Aberfoyle parish. Editor, Modern Churchman, 1963-82. Commission Queen's Royal Regt (TA), 1947-67. FSA 1952; FRHistS 1954; FRSE 1979. Hon. DD Edinburgh, 1974. *Publications:* The Donatist Church, 1952; Martyrdom and Persecution in the Early Church, 1965; The Early Church, 1965; (contrib.) Religion in the Middle East, 1968; The Rise of the Monophysite Movement, 1972; Religion Popular and Unpopular in the Early Christian Centuries, 1976; (contrib.) Cambridge History of Africa, vol. ii, 1978; Town and Country in the Early Christian Centuries, 1980; The Rise of Christianity, 1982; articles in Jl Theol Studies, Jl Roman Studies, Jl Eccles. History, etc. *Recreations:* archæology, occasional golf and tennis, writing, collecting old coins and stamps. *Address:* Marbrae, Balmaha, Stirlingshire. *T:* Balmaha 227. *Club:* Authors'.

FRERE, Alexander Stewart, CBE 1946; MA Cantab; *b* 23 Nov. 1896; *m* 1933, Patricia Marion Caldecott, *d* of late Edgar Wallace; two *s* one *d. Educ:* Christ's Coll., Cambridge. Served Royal East Kent Yeomanry, seconded Royal Flying Corps. European War, 1914-18; edited the Granta, Cambridge, 1920-21; on staff of London Evening News, 1922-23; joined William Heinemann Ltd, Publishers, 1923; Dir, 1926; Man. Dir, 1932-40; Chm., 1945-61; Pres., 1961-62; Mem. of council Publishers Assoc., 1938-39. Assisted organise National Service Campaign, Ministry of Labour and National Service, Jan.-June 1939; Dir of Public Relations, Min. of Labour and National Service, 1940-44. Adviser to HM Govt Delegn to ILO Conf., Columbia Univ., New York, 1941. Chevalier de la Légion d'Honneur, 1953. *Address:* Knoll Hill House, Aldington, Kent. *Clubs:* White's, Garrick, Royal Thames Yacht; Century (NY); Travellers' (Paris).

FRERE, James Arnold, FSA, FRGS; *b* 20 April 1920; *e s* of late John Geoffrey Frere. *Educ:* Eton Coll.; Trinity Coll., Cambridge. Lieut Intelligence Corps, 1944-47. Regular Army R of O, 1949-67. Bluemantle Pursuivant of Arms, 1948-56; Chester Herald of Arms, 1956-60; an Officer of Supreme Court of Judicature, 1966-70. Member: Surrey Archæological Soc. (Council, 1949-53, 1954-58 and 1959-63); American Soc. of Authors; Soc. for the Protection of Ancient Buildings; Council of the Harleian Soc., 1951-66; Hon. Mem. Heraldry Soc. of Southern Africa, 1953-; a Vice-Pres. of Museum of Costume, 1952-60. Press Sec., New Gallery Clinic, 1967-70. Liveryman, Worshipful Co. of Scriveners. KM 1959; Knight Grand Cross, and Clairvaux King of Arms, SMO of Temple of Jerusalem, 1981. *Publications:* The British Monarchy at Home, 1963; (jointly with the Duchess of Bedford) Now . . . The Duchesses, 1964. *Recreations:* walking, painting, archæology. *Address:* c/o Society of Antiquaries, Burlington House, Piccadilly, W1.

FRERE, Prof. Sheppard Sunderland, CBE 1976; FSA 1944; FBA 1971; Professor of the Archæology of the Roman Empire, Oxford University, since 1966; *b* 23 Aug. 1916; *e s* of late N. G. Frere, CMG; *m* 1961, Janet Cecily Hoare; one *s* one *d. Educ:* Lancing Coll.; Magdalene Coll., Cambridge. BA 1938, MA 1944, LittD 1976, DLitt 1977. Master, Epsom Coll., 1938-40. National Fire Service, 1940-45. Master, Lancing Coll., 1945-54; Lecturer in Archæology, Manchester Univ., 1954-55; Reader in Archæology of Roman Provinces, London Univ. Inst. of Archæology, 1955-62; Prof. of the Archæology of the Roman Provinces, London Univ., 1963-66. Dir, Canterbury Excavations, 1946-60; Dir, Verulamium Excavations, 1955-61. Vice-Pres., Soc. of Antiquaries, 1962-66; President: Oxford Architectural and Historical Soc., 1972-80; Royal Archæological Inst., 1978-81. Hon. Corr. Mem. German Archæological Inst., 1964, Fellow, 1967; Member: Royal Commn on Hist. Monuments (England), 1966-; Ancient Monuments Board (England), 1966-82. Hon. LittD Leeds, 1977. Editor, Britannia, 1969-79. *Publications:* (ed) Problems of the Iron Age in Southern Britain, 1961; Britannia, a history of Roman Britain, 1967 (rev. edn 1974); Verulamium Excavations, vol. I, 1972; Excavations on the Roman and Medieval Defences of Canterbury, 1982; papers in learned jls. *Recreation:* gardening. *Address:* All Souls College, Oxford.

FRESHWATER, Prof. Donald Cole; Head of Department of Chemical Engineering, University of Technology, Loughborough, since 1957; Dean of Pure and Applied Science, since 1982; *b* 21 April 1924; *s* of Thomas and Ethel May Freshwater; *m* 1948, Margaret D. Worrall (marr. diss. 1977); one *s* three *d* ; *m* 1980, Eleanor H. Lancashire (*née* Tether). *Educ:* Brewood Grammar Sch.; Birmingham Univ. (BSc, PhD); Sheffield Univ.; Loughborough Coll. (DLC). Fuel Engineer, Min. of Fuel and Power, 1944; Chemical Engr: APV Co. Ltd, 1948; Midland Tar Distillers Co. Ltd, 1950; Lectr, Dept of Chem. Engrg, Univ. of Birmingham, 1952. Visiting Professor: Univ. of Delaware, USA, 1962; Georgia Inst. of Technology, 1980-81. Chm., Chem. Engrg Gp, Soc. of Chemical Industry, 1973-75. *Publications:* Chemical Engineering Data Book, 1959; numerous papers on mass transfer and particle technology in chem. engrg jls. *Recreations:* sailing, collecting watercolours. *Address:* Head of Department of Chemical Engineering, Loughborough University of Technology, Ashby Road, Loughborough, Leics LE11 3TU. *T:* Loughborough 63171. *Club:* Athenæum.

FRETWELL, Elizabeth, OBE 1977; operatic and dramatic soprano; *b* Melbourne, Australia; *m* Robert Simmons; one *s* one *d. Educ:* privately. Joined National Theatre, Melbourne, 1950; came to Britain, 1955; joined Sadler's Wells, 1956; Australia, Elizabethan Opera Co., 1963; tour of W Germany, 1963; USA, Canada and Covent Garden, 1964; tour of Europe, 1965; guest soprano with Cape Town and Durban Opera Cos, South Africa, 1970; joined Australian Opera, 1970. Rôles include Violetta in La Traviata, Leonora in Fidelio, Ariadne in Ariadne auf Naxos, Senta in The Flying Dutchman, Minnie in The Girl of the Golden West, Leonora in Il Trovatore, Aida, Ellen Orford in Peter Grimes, Leonora in Forza del Destino, Alice Ford in Falstaff, Amelia in Masked Ball, Georgetta in Il Tabarro, opening season of Sydney Opera Hse, 1973. Has sung in BBC Promenade Concerts and on TV. *Recreation:* rose-growing. *Address:* c/o Australian Opera, PO Box R223, Royal Exchange, Sydney, NSW 2000, Australia.

FRETWELL, Sir George (Herbert), KBE 1953; CB 1950; Director General of Works, Air Ministry, 1947-59, retired; *b* 21 March 1900; *s* of late Herbert Fretwell, Ripley, Derbyshire; *m* 1930, Constance Mabel, *d* of late George Ratcliffe, Woodford Green, Essex; no *c. Educ:* Heanor Grammar Sch., Derbs. Entered Air Ministry as Asst Civil Engineer, 1928; service in Inland area RAF, Aden, South Arabia and Air Defence Gp; Civil Engineer, 1934; Superintending Engineer, RAF Malaya, 1937; Chief Engineer, Far East Command, 1940; Chief Supt of Design (Works), 1941; Chief Engr ADGB/Fighter Command, 1944; Dep. Dir of Works, 1945, Dir, 1946. *Address:* North Lodge, 2 North Street, Sheringham, Norfolk. *T:* Sheringham 822336.

FRETWELL, Sir (Major) John (Emsley), KCMG 1982 (CMG 1975); HM Diplomatic Service; Ambassador to France, since 1982; *b* 15 June 1930; *s* of F. T. Fretwell; *m* 1959, Mary Ellen Eugenie Dubois; one *s* one *d. Educ:* Chesterfield Grammar Sch.; Lausanne Univ.; King's Coll., Cambridge (MA). HM Forces, 1948-50. Diplomatic Service, 1953; 3rd Sec., Hong Kong, 1954-55; 2nd Sec., Peking, 1955-57; FO, 1957-59; 1st Sec., Moscow, 1959-62; FO, 1962-67; 1st Sec. (Commercial), Washington, 1967-70; Commercial Counsellor, Warsaw, 1971-73; Head of European Integration Dept (Internal), FCO, 1973-76; Asst Under-Sec. of State, FCO, 1976-79; Minister, Washington, 1980-81. *Recreations:* skiing, walking. *Address:* c/o Foreign and Commonwealth Office, SW1A 2AH.

FREUD, Clement Raphael; MP (L) Isle of Ely, since July 1973; writer, broadcaster, caterer; *b* 24 April 1924; *s* of late Ernst and Lucie Freud; *m* 1950, Jill, 2nd *d* of H. W. Flewett, MA; three *s* two *d.* Apprenticed, Dorchester Hotel, London. Served War, Royal Ulster Rifles; Liaison Officer, Nuremberg, 1946. Trained, Martinez Hotel, Cannes. Proprietor, Royal Court Theatre Club, 1952-62. Sports writer, Observer, 1956-64; Cookery Editor: Time and Tide, 1961-63; Observer Magazine, 1964-68; Daily Telegraph Magazine, 1968-. Sports Columnist, Sun, 1964-69; Columnist: Sunday Telegraph, 1963-65; News of the World, 1965; Financial Times, 1964-; Daily Express, 1973-75. Liberal spokesman on: educn and science, 1973-74; educn and the arts, 1974-77; NI, broadcasting and the arts, 1977-79; broadcasting, the arts and sport, 1979-; sponsor, Official Information Bill, 1978-79. Chm., Finance and Admin Bd, Liberal Party. Member: Services Cttee of the House, 1973-76; Broadcasting Sub Cttee; Security Sub Cttee; Catering Sub Cttee, 1973-76. Rector, Univ. of Dundee, 1974-80. Patron, Down's Children Assoc. £5,000 class winner, Daily Mail London-NY air race, 1969. Writer and performer Sweet and Sour (Southern), 1962-64; Freud on Food (Tyne Tees), 1968-71; BBC: Frost Shows; Braden Shows; Jackanory; ITV: (talk shows): Eamon Andrews, Simon Dee; David Jacobs, Late Late Show (Telefis Eireann); Carson Show (NBC, USA), etc. Award winning petfood commercial: San Francisco, Tokyo, Berlin, 1967. BBC (sound) Just a Minute, 1968-. *Publications:* Grimble, 1968; Grimble at Christmas, 1973; Freud on Food, 1978; Clicking Vicky, 1980; The Book of Hangovers, 1981; contributor to: Punch, Queen, Town, Which, New Yorker, etc. *Recreations:* racing, cricket, backgammon, golf. *Address:* 22 Wimpole Street, W1. *T:* 01-580 2222. *Clubs:* MCC, Lord's Taverners'; British Rail Staff Assoc. (March).
See also Lucian Freud.

FREUD, Lucian; painter; *b* 8 Dec. 1922; *s* of late Ernst and Lucie Freud; *m* 1st, 1948, Kathleen Garman Epstein (marr. diss. 1952), *d* of Jacob Epstein; two *d* ; 2nd, 1953, Lady Caroline Maureen Blackwood (marr. diss. 1957), *d* of 4th Marquess of Dufferin and Ava. *Educ:* Central Sch. of Art; East Anglian Sch.

of Painting and Drawing. Worked on merchant ship SS Baltrover as ordinary seaman, 1941. Teacher, Slade Sch. of Art, 1948–58; Vis. Asst, Norwich Sch. of Art, 1964–65. Held his first one-man exhibn in London, 1944, in New York, 1978 and in Tokyo, 1979; other one-man shows, 1946, 1950, 1952, 1958, 1963, 1968, 1972, 1978; first retrospective exhibn, Hayward Gall., 1974, subseq. Bristol, Birmingham and Leeds. Painted mostly in France and Greece, 1946–48. Rep. GB, Venice Biennale, 1954 (with Francis Bacon, Ben Nicholson). Works included in public collections: Tate Gall.; Museum of Modern Art, NY; Nat. Gall., Melbourne, NSW; Arts Council of GB; British Council; Fitzwilliam Mus., Cambridge; Walker Art Gall., Liverpool; Liverpool Univ.; Hartlepool Art Gall.; Southampton Art Gall.; Beaverbrook Foundn, Fredericton, New Brunswick; V&A Museum; Harris Museum and Art Gallery, Preston; Whitworth Gall., Manchester; Nat. Mus. of Wales, Cardiff; Musée d'Art Moderne, Paris; Cleveland Museum of Art, Ohio; Nat. Portrait Gall., etc. *Address:* c/o Anthony d'Offay, 9 Dering Street, W1.
See also C. R. Freud.

FREW, Sir John Lewtas, Kt 1981; OBE 1976; MD; FRCP, FRACP; Hon. Consulting Physician, Royal Melbourne Hospital; *b* 10 Sept. 1912; *s* of Captain J. D. Frew; *m* 1940, Joyce M. E., *d* of A. F. Bell; one *s. Educ:* Camberwell Grammar Sch.; Scotch Coll., Melbourne; Ormond Coll., Melbourne Univ. Served War, 1941–45: Captain 13 AGH (POW). Royal Melbourne Hospital: Med. Supt, 1938–41; Sub-Dean, 1947–54; Pres., Cttee of Management, 1973–79 (Vice-Pres., 1968–73). Vis. Specialist, Heidelberg Repatriation Hosp., 1948–79; Comr, Commonwealth Serum Labs, 1967–70. Royal Australasian College of Physicians: Censor-in-Chief, 1966–70; Vice-Pres., 1970–72; Pres., 1972–74. Hon. FACP. *Address:* 34 Queen's Road, Melbourne, Vic 3004, Australia. *Club:* Melbourne (Melbourne).

FREYBERG, family name of **Baron Freyberg.**

FREYBERG, 2nd Baron, *cr* 1951, of Wellington, New Zealand, and of Munstead in the Co. of Surrey; **Paul Richard Freyberg,** OBE 1965; MC 1945; *b* 27 May 1923; *s* of 1st Baron Freyberg, VC, GCMG, KCB, KBE, DSO (and 3 bars), and Barbara, GBE (*d* 1973), *d* of Sir Herbert Jekyll, KCMG, and Lady Jekyll, DBE; *S* father, 1963; *m* 1960, Ivry Perronelle Katharine Guild, Aspall Hall, Debenham, Suffolk; one *s* three *d. Educ:* Eton Coll. Joined NZ Army, 1940; served with 2nd NZEF: Greece, 1941; Western Desert, 1941–42; transferred to British Army, 1942; Grenadier Guards; North Africa, 1943; Italy, 1943–45 (MC); Palestine, 1947–48; Cyprus, 1956–58; British Cameroons, 1961; Comd HAC Infantry Battalion, 1965–68; Defence Policy Staff, MoD, 1968–71; Dir Volunteers, Territorials and Cadets, 1971–75; Col, Gen. Staff, 1975–78, retired. Staff Coll., 1952; jssc 1958; sowc 1971. *Heir: s* Hon. Valerian Bernard Freyberg, *b* 15 Dec. 1970. *Address:* Munstead House, Godalming, Surrey. *T:* Godalming 6004. *Clubs:* Boodle's, Royal Automobile.

FRICKER, (Anthony) Nigel, QC 1977; a Recorder of the Crown Court, since 1975; *b* 7 July 1937; *s* of late Dr William Shapland Fricker and of Margaret Fricker; *m* 1960, Marilyn Ann, *d* of A. L. Martin, Pa, USA; one *s* two *d. Educ:* King's School, Chester; Liverpool Univ. (LLB 1958). President of Guild of Undergraduates, Liverpool Univ., 1958–59. Called to Bar, Gray's Inn, 1960; Member: Gen. Council of the Bar, 1966–70; Senate of the Inns of Court and the Bar and of Gen. Council of the Bar, 1975–78. Prosecuting Counsel to DHSS, Wales and Chester Circuit, 1975–77. An asst comr of Boundary Commn for Wales, 1981–83. *Address:* 6 Park Square, Leeds LS1 2LW. *T:* Leeds 468862; Farrar's Building, Temple, EC4Y 7BD. *T:* 01-583 9241. *Club:* Yorkshire (York).

FRICKER, Prof. Peter Racine, FRCO, ARCM; Professor of Music, Music Department, University of California, Santa Barbara, since 1964; Director of Music, Morley College, 1952–64; *b* 5 Sept. 1920; *s* of late Edward Racine Fricker; *m* 1943, Audrey Helen Clench. *Educ:* St Paul's Sch. Royal College of Music, 1937–40. Served War, 1940–46, in Royal Air Force, working in Signals and Intelligence. Has worked as Composer, Conductor, and Music Administrator since 1946. Hon Professorial Fellow, Univ. of Wales, Cardiff, 1971. Hon. RAM, 1966. Hon. DMus (Leeds), 1958. Order of Merit, West Germany, 1965. *Publications:* Four Fughettas for Two Pianos, 1946; Wind Quintet, 1947; Three Sonnets of Cecco Angiolieri da Siena, for Tenor and Seven Instruments, 1947; String Quartet in One Movement, 1948; Symphony No 1, 1948–49; Prelude, Elegy and Finale for String Orchestra, 1949; Concerto for Violin and Orchestra, 1949–50; Sonata for Violin and Piano, 1950; Concertante for Cor Anglais and String Orchestra, 1950; Symphony No 2, 1950; Concertante for Three Pianos, Strings and Timpani, 1951; Four Impromptus for Piano; Concerto for Viola and Orchestra, 1951–53; Concerto for Piano and Orchestra, 1952–54; String Quartet No 2, 1952–53; Rapsodia Concertante for Violin and Orchestra, 1953–54; Dance Scene for Orchestra, 1954; Musick's Empire for Chorus and Small Orchestra, 1955; Litany for Double String Orchestra, 1955; 'Cello Sonata, 1956; Oratorio, The Vision of Judgement, 1956–58; Octet, 1958; Toccata for Piano and Orchestra, 1958–59; Serenade No 1, 1959; Serenade No 2, 1959; Symphony No 3, 1960; Studies for Piano, 1961; Cantata for Tenor and Chamber Ensemble, 1962; O Longs Désirs: Song-cycle for Soprano and Orchestra, 1963; Ricercare for Organ, 1965; Four Dialogues for Oboe and Piano, 1965; Four Songs for High Voice and Orchestra, 1965; Fourth Symphony, 1966; Fantasy for Viola and Piano, 1966; Three Scenes for Orchestra, 1966; The Day and the Spirits for Soprano and Harp, 1967; Seven Counterpoints for Orchestra, 1967; Magnificat, 1968; Episodes for Piano, 1968; Concertante No 4, 1968; Toccata for Organ, 1968;

Saxophone Quartet, 1969; Praeludium for Organ, 1969; Paseo for Guitar, 1970; The Roofs for coloratura soprano and percussion, 1970; Sarabande In Memoriam Igor Stravinsky, 1971; Nocturne for chamber orchestra, 1971; Intrada for organ, 1971; A Bourrée for Sir Arthur Bliss for cello, 1971; Concertante no 5 for piano and string quartet, 1971; Introitus for orchestra, 1972; Come Sleep for contralto, alto flute and bass clarinet, 1972; Fanfare for Europe for trumpet, 1972; Ballade for flute and piano, 1972; Seven Little Songs for chorus, 1972; Gigue for cello, 1973; The Groves of Dodona for six flutes, 1973; Spirit Puck, for clarinet and percussion, 1974; Two Petrarch Madrigals, 1974; Trio-Sonata for Organ, 1974; Third String Quartet, 1975; Fifth Symphony, 1975; Seachant for flute and double bass, 1976; Sinfonia for 17 wind instruments, 1976; Anniversary for piano, 1977; Sonata for two pianos, 1977; Serenade for four clarinets, 1977; Laudi Concertati for organ and orchestra, 1979; Serenade No 5, 1979; In Commendation of Music, 1980; Five Short Pieces for organ, 1980; Six Mélodies de Francis Jammes for tenor, violin, cello and piano, 1980; Spells for solo flute, 1980; Bagatelles for clarinet and piano, 1981; For Three, for oboes, 1981; Two Expressions for Piano, 1981; Rondeaux for horn and orchestra, 1982; also music for film, stage and radio. *Recreation:* travel. *Address:* Department of Music, University of California, Santa Barbara, Calif 93106, USA. *Club:* East India, Devonshire, Sports and Public Schools.

FRIEDLANDER, Frederick Gerard, (Friedrich Gerhart), PhD; FRS 1980; Reader Emeritus, University of Cambridge, since 1982; *b* Vienna, 25 Dec. 1917. *Educ:* Univ. of Cambridge (BA, PhD). Fellow of Trinity Coll., Cambridge, 1940; Temporary Experimental Officer, Admiralty, 1943; Faculty Asst Lectr, Cambridge, 1945; Lecturer: Univ. of Manchester, 1946; Univ. of Cambridge, 1954; Fellow of St John's Coll., Cambridge, 1961; Fellow of Wolfson Coll., Cambridge, 1968; Reader in Partial Differential Equation's, Univ. of Cambridge, 1979. *Publications:* Sound Pulses, 1958; The Wave Equation on a Curved Space-Time, 1975; Introduction to the Theory of Distributions, 1982; papers in mathematical jls. *Address:* Department of Applied Mathematics and Theoretical Physics, Silver Street, Cambridge CB3 9EW. *T:* Cambridge 51645.

FRIEDMAN, Prof. Milton, PhD; Economist, USA; Senior Research Fellow, Hoover Institution, Stanford University, since 1976; Professor of Economics, University of Chicago, since 1948; Member of Research Staff, National Bureau of Economic Research, 1948–81; Economic Columnist, Newsweek, since 1967; *b* New York, 31 July 1912; *s* of Jeno Saul and Sarah E. Friedman; *m* 1938, Rose Director; one *s* one *d. Educ:* Rutgers (AB), Chicago (AM), and Columbia (PhD) Univs. Associate Economist, Natural Resources Cttee, Washington, 1935–37; Nat. Bureau of Economic Research, New York, 1937–46 (on leave 1940–45). During 1941–45: Principal Economist, Tax Research Div., US Treasury Dept, 1941–43; Associate Dir, Statistical Research Gp, Div. of War Research, Columbia Univ., 1943–45. Fulbright Lecturer, Cambridge Univ., 1953–54; Vis. Prof., Econs, Columbia Univ., 1964–65, etc. Member: President's Commn on an All-Volunteer Armed Force, 1969–70; Commn on White House Fellows, 1971–73. Mem. Bd of Editors, Econometrica, 1957–65; Pres., Amer. Economic Assoc., 1967; Pres., Mont Pelerin Soc., 1970–72. John Bates Clark Medal, Amer. Econ. Assoc., 1951; Fellowships and awards, in USA. Nobel Memorial Prize for Economics, 1976. Member various societies, etc., incl. Royal Economic Soc. (GB). Holds several Hon. doctorates. *Publications:* Income from Independent Professional Practice (with Simon Kuznets), 1946; Sampling Inspection (with others), 1948; Essays in Positive Economics, 1953; A Theory of the Consumption Function, 1957; A Program for Monetary Stability, 1959; Capitalism and Freedom, 1962; Price Theory: a Provisional Text, 1962; A Monetary History of the United States 1867–1960 (with Anna J. Schwartz), 1963; Inflation: Causes and Consequences, 1963; The Balance of Payments: Free versus Flexible Exchange Rates (with Robert V. Roosa), 1967; Dollars and Deficits, 1968; Optimum Quantity of Money and Other Essays, 1969; Monetary vs Fiscal Policy (with Walter W. Heller), 1969; Monetary Statistics of the United States (with Anna J. Schwartz), 1970; A Theoretical Framework for Monetary Analysis, 1971; Social Security: Universal or Selective? (with Wilbur J. Cohen), 1972; An Economist's Protest, 1972; Money and Economic Development, 1973; There's No Such Thing as a Free Lunch, 1975; Price Theory, 1976; Free to Choose (with Rose Friedman), 1980; Monetary Trends in the United States and the United Kingdom (with Anna J. Schwahtz), 1982. *Recreations:* tennis, carpentry. *Address:* Hoover Institution, Stanford, Calif 94305, USA. *Club:* Quadrangle (Chicago).

FRIEL, Brian; writer; *b* 9 Jan. 1929; *s* of Patrick Friel and Christina Friel (née MacLoone); *m* 1954, Anne Morrison; one *s* four *d. Educ:* St Columb's Coll., Derry; St Patrick's Coll., Maynooth; St Joseph's Trng Coll., Belfast. Taught in various schools, 1950–60; writing full-time from 1960. Lived in Minnesota during first season of Tyrone Guthrie Theater, Minneapolis. *Publications: collected stories:* The Saucer of Larks, 1962; The Gold in the Sea, 1966; *plays:* Philadelphia, Here I Come!, 1965; The Loves of Cass McGuire, 1967; Lovers, 1968; The Mundy Scheme, 1969; Crystal and Fox, 1970; The Gentle Island, 1971; The Freedom of the City, 1973; Volunteers, 1975; Living Quarters, 1976; Aristocrats, 1979; Faith Healer, 1979; Translations, 1981 (Ewart-Biggs Meml Prize, British Theatre Assoc. Award); (trans.) Three Sisters, 1981. *Recreations:* reading, trout-fishing, slow tennis. *Address:* Ardmore, Muff, Lifford, Co. Donegal, Ireland. *T:* Muff 30.

FRIEND, Archibald Gordon; His Honour Judge Friend; a Circuit Judge (formerly Deputy Chairman, Inner London, later Middlesex, Quarter

Sessions), since 1965; *b* 6 July 1912; *m* 1940, Patricia Margaret Smith; no *c.* Called to Bar, Inner Temple, 1933. Dep. Chm., Herts Quarter Sessions, 1963-71. *Recreation:* gardening. *Address:* The Crown Court, 1 Hans Crescent, SW1X OLQ. *T:* 01-589 5400.

FRIEND, Bernard Ernest; Director, British Aerospace, since 1977; *b* 18 May 1924; *s* of Richard Friend and Ada Florence Friend; *m* 1951, Pamela Florence Amor; one *s* two *d. Educ:* Dover Grammar Sch. Chartered Accountant. Flying Officer, RAF, 1943-47. Arthur Young & Co., Chartered Accountants, 1948-55; Comptroller, Esso Petroleum Co. Ltd, 1961-66; Dep. Controller, Esso Europe, 1967-68; Man. Dir, Essoheat, 1968-69; Vice-Pres., Esso Chemicals, Brussels, 1970-73; Chm. and Man. Dir, Esso Chemicals Ltd, 1974-76. Non-Exec. Dir, Iron Trades Insurance Gp, 1980-. *Recreation:* cricket. *Address:* British Aerospace, Brooklands Road, Weybridge, Surrey KT13 0SJ. *Club:* Royal Air Force.

FRIEND, Dame Phyllis (Muriel), DBE 1980 (CBE 1972); Chief Nursing Officer, Department of Health and Social Security, 1972-82; *b* 28 Sept. 1922; *d* of Richard Edward Friend. *Educ:* Herts and Essex High Sch., Bishop's Stortford; The London Hospital (SRN); Royal College of Nursing (RNT). Dep. Matron, St George's Hospital, 1956-59; Dep. Matron, 1959-61, Matron, 1961-68, Chief Nursing Officer 1969-72, The London Hospital. *Address:* Barnmead, Start Hill, Bishop's Stortford, Herts. *T:* Bishop's Stortford 54873.

FRINK, Dame Elisabeth, DBE 1982 (CBE 1969); RA 1977 (ARA 1971); sculptor; *b* 14 Nov. 1930; British; *m* 1st, 1955, Michel Jammet (marr. diss. 1963); one *s*; 2nd, Edward Pool, MC (marr. diss. 1974); 3rd, Alexander Csáky. *Educ:* Convent of The Holy Family, Exmouth. Guildford Sch. of Art, 1947-49; Chelsea Sch. of Art, 1949-53. Exhibitions: Beaux Arts Gallery, 1952; St George's Gallery, 1955; exhibits regularly at Waddington Gallery, now Waddington and Tooth Galleries, London. Represented in collections in USA, Australia, Holland, Sweden, Germany and Tate Gallery, London. Member: Bd Trustees, British Museum, 1975-; Royal Fine Art Commn, 1976-81. *Address:* c/o Waddington and Tooth Galleries, 2 Cork Street, W1.

FRIPP, Alfred Thomas, BM; FRCS; *b* 3 July 1899; *s* of late Sir Alfred Fripp, KCVO, and late Lady M. S. Fripp, *d* of late T. B. Haywood; *m* 1931, Kathleen Kimpton; one *s* two *d. Educ:* Winchester; Christ Church, Oxford. 2nd Lieut 1st Life Guards, 1917-18. Christ Church, Oxford, 1919-21; Guy's Hospital, 1921; Surg., Royal National Orthopædic Hospital, 1934-64. Mem., Pensions Appeal Tribunal, 1966-74. FRCS 1927. Pres. Orthopædic Section, RSocMed, 1950-51. *Recreations:* gardening, rowing. *Address:* Mascalls, London Road, Ardingly, West Sussex RH17 6TG. *T:* Ardingly 892351. *Club:* Leander (Henley-on-Thames).

FRISBY, Audrey Mary; *see* Jennings, A. M.

FRISBY, Roger Harry Kilbourne, QC 1969; *b* 11 Dec. 1921; 2nd *s* of late Herbert Frisby and Hylda Mary Frisby; *m* 1961, Audrey Mary (*née* Jennings), *qv* (marr. diss. 1980); two *s* one *d* (and one *s* one *d* by previous marriage). *Educ:* Bablake Sch.; Christ Church, Oxford; King's Coll., Univ. of London. Called to the Bar, Lincoln's Inn, 1950. A Recorder of the Crown Court, 1972-78. *Address:* 3 King's Bench Walk, Temple, EC4. *T:* 01-353 0431. *Clubs:* United Oxford & Cambridge University; Hurlingham.

FRISBY, Terence; playwright and actor; *b* 28 Nov. 1932; *s* of William and Kathleen Frisby; *m* 1963, Christine Vecchione (marr. diss.); one *s. Educ:* Dobwalls Village Sch.; Dartford Grammar Sch.; Central Sch. of Speech Training and Dramatic Art. Substantial repertory acting experience, also TV, films and musicals, 1957-63; appeared in A Sense of Detachment, Royal Court, 1972-73 and X, Royal Court, 1974. Has written many TV scripts, incl. series Lucky Feller, 1976; film, There's A Girl in My Soup, 1970 (Writers Guild Award, Best British Comedy Screenplay). *Publications: plays:* The Subtopians, 1964; There's a Girl in My Soup, 1966; The Bandwagon, 1970; It's All Right if I Do It, 1977; Seaside Postcard, 1978. *Recreations:* golf, chess, scuba diving. *Address:* c/o Harvey Unna and Stephen Durbridge Ltd, 24 Pottery Lane, Holland Park, W11. *T:* 01-727 1346. *Club:* Wentworth Golf.

FRITH, Anthony Ian Donald; Chairman, South Western Region, British Gas Corporation, since 1973; *b* 11 March 1929; *s* of Ernest and Elizabeth Frith; *m* 1952, Joyce Marcelle Boyce; one *s* one *d. Educ:* various grammar schs and techn. colls. CEng, FIGasE, MInstM. Various appts in North Thames Gas Bd and Gas Light & Coke Co., 1945-65; Sales Man. 1965-67, Dep. Commercial Man. 1967-68, North Thames Gas Bd; Marketing Man., Domestic and Commercial Gas, Gas Council, 1968-72; Sales Dir, British Gas Corp., 1972-73. *Publications:* various techn. and prof. in Gas Engineering and other jls. *Recreations:* fishing, golf. *Address:* Firbank, 32 High Street, Saltford, Avon.

FRITH, Donald Alfred, OBE 1980; MA; Secretary, Headmasters' Conference and General Secretary, Secondary Heads Association, 1979-Aug. 1983; *b* 13 May 1918; *yr s* of late Charles Henry Frith and Mabel (*née* Whiting); *m* 1941, Mary Webster Tyler, *yr d* of late Raymond Tyler and Rosina Mary (*née* Wiles); four *s* one *d. Educ:* Whitgift Sch. (schol.); Christ's Coll., Cambridge (schol.). MA Cantab 1944. Served War, 1940-46; commnd RASC; served in

Middle East, Italy and at WO. Deme Warden, University College Sch., 1946-52; Headmaster, Richmond Sch., Yorks, 1953-59; Headmaster, Archbishop Holgate's Grammar Sch., York, 1959-78. Additional Mem., N Yorks CC Educn Cttee, 1973-77. Chairman: York Community Council, 1971-79; Schools Council Industry Project, 1979-. JP York, 1966-79. *Recreations:* music, gardening, walking. *Address:* (to Aug. 1983) 29 Gordon Square, WC1H 0PS; (from Aug. 1983) Kilburn, York YO6 4AQ. *Clubs:* Athenæum; Yorkshire (York).

FRITH, Air Vice-Marshal Edward Leslie, CB 1973; *b* 18 March 1919; *s* of late Charles Edward Frith, ISO. *Educ:* Haberdashers' Askes School. Gp Captain, 1961; Air Cdre, 1968; Dir of Personal Services (2) RAF, MoD, 1969-71; Air Vice-Marshal, 1971; Air Officer Administration, Maintenance Comd, later Support Comd, 1971-74. *Recreations:* lawn tennis, bridge. *Address:* 27 Chartwell, 80 Parkside, Wimbledon, SW19 5LN. *T:* 01-789 2979. *Clubs:* All England Lawn Tennis and Croquet, International Lawn Tennis of GB.

FRITH, Brig. Sir Eric (Herbert Cokayne), Kt 1973; CBE 1945 (MBE 1926); DL; JP; Chairman, Official Side, Police Council for UK, 1966-74; *b* 10 Sept. 1897; *s* of late Brig.-Gen. Herbert Cokayne Frith, CB, Taunton; *m* 1925, Joan Margaret, *yr d* of late Major R. B. Graves-Knyfton; one *s. Educ:* Marlborough Coll.; RMC Sandhurst. 2nd Lieut Somerset LI, 1915; served European War, 1914-18 (wounded); psc; served War of 1939-45; retd Dec. 1948. Somerset County Council: Mem. 1949 (Chm. 1959-64, Vice-Chm. 1956-59); Alderman 1957. DL 1953, JP 1953, Somerset. Order of Polonia Restituta (Poland), 1945; Medal of Freedom with Silver Palm (US), 1945. *Recreations:* cricket, Rugby football, hunting, shooting, hockey (in the past). *Address:* The Cottage, Mount Street, Taunton TA1 3QE. *T:* Taunton 84180. *Clubs:* Naval and Military; Somerset Stragglers Cricket.

FRITSCH, Elizabeth; potter; *b* Wales, 1940. *Educ:* Royal College of Art, London. Established workshop at Welwyn Garden City. Won Herbert Read Memorial Prize; Royal Copenhagen Jubilee competition, 1972. Member, Crafts Council (Bursary awarded, 1980). Has exhibited: Crafts Advisory Cttee Exhibition, 1972; Copenhagen, 1974; Waterloo Place Gallery, London, 1976; Warwick Gallery, Modern Master Works, 1979. One-woman show, Victoria and Albert Museum, 1979. Work in museums, including Kunst-Industrie Museum, Copenhagen; Leeds Museum and Art Gallery. *Address:* Unit 3, Digswell House, Monks Rise, Welwyn Garden City, Herts.

FRIZZELL, Edward, CBE 1981; QPM 1978; HM Chief Inspector of Constabulary for Scotland, since 1979; *b* 6 Dec. 1918; *s* of late Edward Frizzell and Mary (*née* Cox); *m* 1945, May Russell; one *s* one *d. Educ:* Greenhill Primary Sch.; Coatbridge High Sch. Served War, RAF, 1943-45 (Flying Officer). Det. Sgt, 1953, Det. Chief Inspector, 1961, Paisley Burgh Police; Det. Chief Supt, 1968, Asst Chief Constable, 1968, Renfrew and Bute Constab.; Chief Constable: Stirling and Clackmannan Police, 1970; Central Scotland Police, 1975. OStJ 1971. *Recreations:* shooting, golf. *Address:* 24 Alexander Drive, Bridge of Allan, Stirling FK9 4QB. *T:* Bridge of Allan 3846. *Club:* Stirling and County (Stirling).

FRODSHAM, Anthony Freer, CBE 1978; Vice Chairman, British Export Finance Advisory Council; Independent Chairman, Compressed Air and Allied Machinery Committee, since 1976; Director, F. Pratt Engineering Corporation Ltd, since 1982; Chairman, European Foundation Committee; *b* Peking, China, 8 Sept. 1919; *er s* of late George William Frodsham and Constance Violet Frodsham (*née* Neild); *m* 1953, Patricia Myfanwy, *o c* of late Cmdr A. H. Wynne-Edwards, DSC, RN; two *s. Educ:* Ecole Lacordaire, Paris; Faraday House Engineering Coll., London. DFH, CEng, FIMechE, FIMC, CBIM. Served War, 1940-46: Engineer Officer, RN, Asst Fleet Engr Officer on staff of C-in-C Mediterranean, 1944-46 (despatches, 1945). P-E Consulting Group Ltd, 1947-73: Man. Dir and Gp Chief Exec., 1963-72; Group Specialist Adviser, United Dominions Trust Ltd, 1973-74; Dir-Gen., EEF, 1975-82; Dir, Arthur Young Management Services, 1973-79. Chairman: Management Consultants Assoc., 1968-70; Machine Tools EDC, 1973-79; Pres., Inst. of Management Consultants, 1967-68; Member: CBI Grand Council, 1975-; CBI President's Cttee, 1979-; Engineering Industry Training Bd, 1975-79; W European Metal Working Employers' Assoc., 1975-; a General Commissioner of Tax, 1975-. Underwriting Member of Lloyd's. *Publications:* contrib. to technical jls; lectures and broadcasts on management subjects. *Address:* 1 The Grange, Wimbledon Common, SW19. *T:* 01-946 3413. *Club:* Carlton.

FROGGATT, Sir Leslie (Trevor), Kt 1981; Director, Shell Australia Ltd, since 1969; Chairman and Chief Executive Officer, Shell Group in Australia, 1969-80; *b* 8 April 1920; *s* of Leslie and Mary Helena Froggatt (*née* Brassey); *m* 1945, Jessie Elizabeth Grant; three *s. Educ:* Birkenhead Park Sch., Cheshire. Joined Asiatic Petroleum Co. Ltd, 1937; Shell Singapore, Shell Thailand, Shell Malaya, 1947-54; Shell Egypt, 1955-56; Dir of Finance, Gen. Manager, Kalimantan, Borneo, and Dep. Chief Rep., PT Shell Indonesia, 1958-62; Shell International Petroleum Co. Ltd: Area Co-ordinator, S Asia and Australasia, 1962-63; assignment in various Shell cos in Europe, 1964-66; Shell Oil Co., Atlanta, 1967-69. Director: Moonee Valley Racing Club Nominees Pty Ltd, 1977-; Dunlop Olympic Ltd, 1978- (Vice-Chm., 1981). Dir, Australian Industry Develt Corp., 1978-. Mem., Australian Nat. Airlines Commn (Trans Australia Airlines), 1981-. *Recreations:* reading, music, racing, golf. *Address:* 20 Albany Road, Toorak, Vic 3142, Australia. *T:* (03) 20.1357. *Clubs:*

Melbourne, Australian, Victoria Racing, Victoria Amateur Turf, Moonee Valley Racing, Commonwealth Golf (all Melbourne).

FROGGATT, Peter, MD, FRCPI; President and Vice-Chancellor, Queen's University of Belfast, since 1976. MB BCh, BAO 1952; DPH Belfast 1956; MD Dublin 1958; PhD Belfast 1967; FFCM 1972; FRCPI 1973; MRCP 1974; FFOM 1976; FFCMI 1977. Formerly Consultant, Eastern Area, Health and Social Services Board; Dean of Faculty of Medicine (Social and Preventive Medicine), and Prof. of Epidemiology, Queen's Univ., Belfast. Mem. Soc. Social Med.; FSS. *Publications:* (jtly) Causation of Bus-driver Accidents: Epidemiological Study, 1963; contribs to jls. *Address:* Queen's University of Belfast, Belfast, Northern Ireland BT7 1NN.

FRÖHLICH, Prof. Albrecht, PhD; FRS 1976; Professor of Pure Mathematics, King's College, University of London, 1962–81, now Emeritus Professor; Senior Research Fellow, Imperial College, University of London, since 1982; Fellow, Robinson College, Cambridge, since 1982; *b* 22 May 1916; *s* of Julius Fröhlich and Frida Fröhlich; *m* 1950, Dr Evelyn Ruth Brooks; one *s* one *d. Educ:* Realgymnasium, Munich; Bristol Univ. (BSc 1948, PhD 1951). Asst Lectr in Maths, University Coll., Leicester, 1950–52; Lectr in Maths, University Coll. of N Staffs, 1952–55; King's College, London: Reader in Pure Maths, 1955–62; Hd, Dept of Maths, 1971–81. Vis. Royal Soc.-Israeli Acad. Research Prof., 1978; George A. Miller Prof., Univ. of Illinois, 1981–82. Corres. Mem., Heidelberg Acad. of Scis, 1982. FKC 1977. Senior Berwick Prize, London Math. Soc., 1976. *Publications:* Formal Groups, 1968; papers in math. jls. *Recreations:* cooking, eating, walking, music. *Address:* 63 Drax Avenue, Wimbledon, SW20. *T:* 01-946 6550.

FRÖHLICH, Herbert, FRS 1951; DPhil; Professor of Theoretical Physics, The University of Liverpool, 1948–73, Professor Emeritus, since 1973; *b* 9 Dec. 1905; *m* 1950, Fanchon Aungst. *Educ:* Munich. Studied Theoretical Physics at University of Munich; DPhil 1930; Subsequently Privatdozent at Freiburg Univ. Left Germany in 1933. Research Physicist, Lecturer, and Reader in Theoretical Physics, University of Bristol, 1935–48; Prof. of Solid State Electronics, Univ. of Salford, 1973–76, Vis. Fellow, 1976–81; For. Mem., Max-Planck-Inst., Stuttgart, 1980–. Hon. Dr of Science, Rennes, 1955; Hon. LLD Alberta, 1968; Hon. ScD Dublin, 1969; Dr rer. nat. *hc* Stuttgart, 1980; Hon. DSc Purdue, 1981. Max Planck Medal, 1972. *Publications:* various scientific papers and books. *Address:* Department of Physics, Oliver Lodge Laboratory, The University, Oxford Street, PO Box 147, Liverpool L69 3BX.

FROME, Sir Norman (Frederick), Kt 1947; CIE 1945; DFC 1918; MSc, FIEE; late Consultant, Messrs Preece, Cardew & Rider, Consulting Engineers; formerly Indian Posts and Telegraphs Department; *b* 23 Sept. 1899; *s* of late John Frome, Bristol; *m* 1928, Edith S. Guyan (*d* 1981). *Educ:* Fairfield Grammar Sch.; University of Bristol. Served European War, 1914–18, in RFC and RAF, 1917–18. Joined Indian Posts and Telegraphs Dept, 1923; Dir of Telegraphs, 1937; Postmaster-Gen., 1941; Chief Engineer, 1946. *Publications:* articles on telecommunications, 1928–60. *Recreations:* astronomy, ornithology. *Address:* Elmwood, Gussage All Saints, near Wimborne, Dorset BH21 5ET. *Club:* Royal Commonwealth Society.

FROOD, Alan Campbell, Managing Director, since 1978, Crown Agent, since 1980, Crown Agents for Oversea Governments and Administrations; *b* 15 May 1926; *s* of James Campbell Frood and Margaret Helena Frood; *m* 1960, Patricia Ann Cotterell; two *s* two *d. Educ:* Cranleigh Sch.; Peterhouse, Cambridge (BA Hons). Royal Navy, 1944–47 (Sub-Lt RNVR). Bank of England, 1949; Colonial Admin. Service, 1952; Bankers Trust Co., 1962; Dir, Bankers Trust Internat. Ltd, 1967; Gen. Man., Banking Dept, Crown Agents, 1975; Dir of Financial Services, Crown Agents, 1976–78. *Recreations:* sailing, gardening. *Address:* West Orchard, Holmbush Lane, Henfield, West Sussex. *T:* Poynings 257.

FROSSARD, Charles Keith; Bailiff of Guernsey, since 1982; *b* 18 Feb. 1922; *s* of late Edward Louis Frossard, CBE, MA, Hon. CF, Dean of Guernsey, 1947–67, and Margery Smith Latta; *m* 1950, Elizabeth Marguerite, *d* of late J. E. L. Martel, OBE; two *d. Educ:* Elizabeth Coll., Guernsey; Univ. de Caen (Bachelier en Droit). Enlisted Gordon Highlanders, 1940; commnd 1941, 17 Dogra Regt, Indian Army; seconded to Tochi Scouts and Chitral Scouts; served India and NW Frontier, 1941–46. Called to Bar, Gray's Inn, 1949; Advocate of Royal Court of Guernsey, 1949; People's Deputy, States of Guernsey, 1958–67; Conseiller, States of Guernsey, 1967–69; HM Solicitor General, Guernsey, 1969–73; HM Attorney General, Guernsey, 1973–76; Dep. Bailiff of Guernsey, 1977–82. Member, Church Assembly and General Synod, Church of England, 1960–. *Recreations:* hill walking, fishing. *Address:* Les Lierres, Rohais, St Peter Port, Guernsey. *T:* 22076. *Clubs:* Army and Navy, Naval and Military.

FROST, Abraham Edward Hardy, CBE 1972; Counsellor, Foreign and Commonwealth Office, 1972–78; *b* 4 July 1918; *s* of Abraham William Frost and Margaret Anna Frost; *m* 1972, Gillian (*née* Crossley); two *d. Educ:* Royal Grammar Sch., Colchester; King's Coll., Cambridge (MA); London Univ. (BScEcon). FCIS. RNVR, 1940–46 (Lieut). ILO, Geneva, 1947–48; HM Treasury, 1948–49; Manchester Guardian, City Staff, 1949–51; FO (later FCO), 1951–78. *Publication:* In Dorset Of Course (poems), 1976. *Address:* Hill View, Buckland Newton, Dorset. *T:* Buckland Newton 415.

FROST, Albert Edward; Director: British Steel Corporation, since 1980 (Chairman, Audit Committee); Marks & Spencer Ltd, since 1976; S. G. Warburg & Co. Ltd, since 1976; *b* 7 March 1914; *s* of Charles Albert Frost and Minnie Frost; *m* 1942, Eugénie Maud Barlow. *Educ:* Oulton Sch., Liverpool; London Univ. Called to the Bar, Middle Temple (1st Cl. Hons). HM Inspector of Taxes, Inland Revenue, 1937; Imperial Chemical Industries Ltd: Dep. Head, Taxation Dept, 1949; Dep. Treasurer, 1957; Treasurer, 1960; Finance Dir, 1968; retd 1976. Director: BAC, 1976–80; BL Ltd, 1977–80. Member: Panel on Take-overs and Mergers; Council, St Thomas's Med. Sch., London (Chm., Finance Cttee); Council and Finance Cttee, Morley Coll., London; Adv. Council, Assoc. for Business Sponsorship of the Arts; Org. Cttee, Carl Flesch Internat. Violin Competition, London; Exec. Cttee for Develt Appeal, Royal Opera House, Covent Garden; Arts Council of GB, 1982–; Chm., Robert Mayer Trust for Youth and Music, 1981- (Dir, 1977-). Trustee, Monteverdi Trust; Treas., Loan Fund for Mus. Instruments. FRSA. *Publications:* (contrib.) Simon's Income Tax, 1952; (contrib.) Gunns Australian Income Tax Law and Practice, 1960; articles on financial matters affecting industry and on arts sponsorship. *Recreations:* violinist (chamber music); swimming (silver medallist, Royal Life Saving Assoc.); athletics (county colours, track and cross country); walking; arts generally. *Address:* Michael House, Baker Street, W1A 1DN. *T:* 01-935 4422. *Club:* Royal Automobile.

FROST, David (Paradine), OBE 1970; author, producer, columnist; star of "The Frost Report", "The Frost Programme", "Frost on Friday", "The David Frost Show", "The Frost Interview", etc; Joint Founder, London Weekend Television; Chairman and Chief Executive, David Paradine Ltd, since 1966; Joint Founder and Director, TV-AM; *b* 7 April 1939; *s* of late Rev. W. J. Paradine Frost, Tenterden, Kent. *Educ:* Gillingham Grammar Sch.; Wellingborough Grammar Sch.; Gonville and Caius Coll., Cambridge (MA). Sec., The Footlights; Editor, Granta. LLD, Emerson Coll., USA. BBC Television series: That Was the Week That Was, 1962–63 (in USA, 1963–64); A Degree of Frost, 1963, 1973; Not So Much a Programme, More a Way of Life, 1964–65; The Frost Report, 1966–67; Frost Over England, 1967; Frost Over America, 1970; Frost's Weekly, 1973; The Frost Interview, 1974; We British, 1975–76; Forty Years of Television, 1976; The Frost Programme, 1977. David Frost at the Phonograph (BBC Sound), 1966, 1972. Frost on Thursday (LBC), 1974. ITV series: The Frost Programme, 1966–67, 1967–68; Frost on Friday, 1968–69, 1969–70; The Frost Programme, 1972, 1973; The Sir Harold Wilson Interviews, 1976; A Prime Minister on Prime Ministers, 1977–78; Are We Really Going to be Rich?, 1978; David Frost's Global Village, 1979, 1980, 1982; The 25th Anniversary of ITV, The Begin Interview, and Elvis—He Touched Their Lives, 1980; The BAFTA Awards, and Onward Christian Soldiers 1981; A Night of Knights: a Royal Gala, 1982; The End of the Year Show, 1982; TVam, 1983. Other programmes include: David Frost's Night Out in London, (USA), 1966–67; The Next President, (USA), 1968; Robert Kennedy the Man, (USA), 1968; The David Frost Show, (USA), 1969–70, 1970–71, 1971–72; The David Frost Revue (USA), 1971–72, 1972–73; That Was the Year That Was, (USA), 1973; David Frost Presents the Guinness Book of Records (USA), 1973, 1974, 1975, 1976; Frost over Australia, 1972, 1973, 1974, 1977; Frost over New Zealand, 1973, 1974; The Unspeakable Crime (USA), 1975; Abortion—Merciful or Murder? (USA), 1975; The Beatles—Once Upon a Time (USA), 1975; David Frost Presents the Best (USA), 1975; The Nixon Interviews with David Frost, 1976–77; The Crossroads of Civilization, 1977–78; Headliners with David Frost, 1978; A Gift of Song—MUSIC FOR UNICEF Concert, The Bee Gees Special, and The Kissinger Interview, 1979; The Shah Speaks, and The American Movie Awards, 1980; Show Business, This Is Your Life 30th Anniversary Special, The Royal Wedding (CBS), 1981; David Frost Presents The Internat. Guinness Book of World Records, 1981. Produced films: The Rise and Rise of Michael Rimmer, 1970; Charley One-Eye, 1972; Leadbelly, 1974; The Slipper and the Rose, 1975; James A. Michener's Dynasty, 1975; The Ordeal of Patty Hearst, 1978; The Remarkable Mrs Sanger, 1979. Mem., British/USA Bicentennial Liaison Cttee, 1973–76. Golden Rose, Montreux, for Frost Over England, 1967; Royal Television Society's Silver Medal, 1967; Richard Dimbleby Award, 1967; Emmy Award (USA), 1970, 1971; Religious Heritage of America Award, 1970; Albert Einstein Award, Communication Arts, 1971. *Stage:* An Evening with David Frost (Edinburgh Fest.), 1966. *Publications:* That Was the Week That Was, 1963; How to Live under Labour, 1964; Talking with Frost, 1967; To England With Love, 1967; The Presidential Debate 1968, 1968; The Americans, 1970; Whitlam and Frost, 1974; I Gave Them a Sword, 1978; I Could Have Kicked Myself, (David Frost's Book of the World's Worst Decisions), 1982; Who Wants to be a Millionaire?, 1983. *Address:* 46 Egerton Crescent, SW3.

FROST, Jeffrey Michael Torbet; Associate Director, London & Continental Bankers, since 1982; *b* 11 June 1938; *s* of late Basil Frost and Dorothy Frost. *Educ:* Diocesan Coll., Cape, South Africa; Radley Coll.; Oriel Coll., Oxford; Harvard Univ. Exec. Dir, Cttee on Invisible Exports, 1976–81. Hon. Sec., Anglo-Brazilian Soc. *Address:* 34 Paradise Walk, SW3. *T:* 01-352 8642.

FROST, Maj.-Gen. John Dutton, CB 1964; DSO 1943 and Bar, 1945; MC 1942; farmer; *b* 31 Dec. 1912; *s* of late Brig.-Gen. F. D. Frost, CBE, MC; *m* 1947, Jean MacGregor Lyle; one *s* one *d. Educ:* Wellington Coll.; RMC Sandhurst. Commissioned The Cameronians, Sept. 1932; Capt., Iraq Levies, 1938–41; Major and Lt-Col, Parachute Regt, 1941–45 (Bruneval raid 1942, Oudna 1942, Tunisian campaign, 1942–43, Primosole Bridge, 1943, Italian campaign, 1943, Arnhem Bridge, 1944); Staff Coll., Camberley, 1946; GSO2,

HQ Lowland Dist, 1948-49; GSO2, Senior Officers' Sch., 1949-52; AA and QMG, 17 Gurkha Div., 1952-53; GSO1, 17 Gurkha Div., 1953-55; Comd, Netheravon, 1955-57; Comd, 44 Parachute Bde, 1958-61; Comdr 52nd Lowland Div./District, 1961-64; GOC Troops in Malta and Libya, 1964-66; Comdr Malta Land Force, 1965; retired, 1967. Cross of Grand Officer, SMO, Malta, 1966. *Publication:* A Drop Too Many, 1980. *Recreations:* field sports, polo, golf. *Address:* Northend Farm, Milland, Liphook, Hants. *Club:* Army and Navy.

FROST, Norman, CBE 1959; KPM 1950; *b* 18 March 1899; *s* of William Frost and Maud Frost (*née* Strickland); *m* 1927, Ivy Edna (*née* Bush); two *s*. *Educ:* March, Cambs. Royal Engineers (Signals), 1917-20. Peterborough Police, 1926-44; Boston Police, 1944-47; seconded Home Office; Commandant Police Training Sch., 1945-47; Eastbourne Police, 1947-54; Chief Constable of Bristol, 1954-64. OStJ. *Recreation:* collecting antiques. *Address:* Westovers, Wedmore, Somerset. *T:* Wedmore 712568. *Club:* St John House.

FROST, Dame Phyllis Irene, DBE 1974 (CBE 1963); JP; Chairman, Keep Australia Beautiful Council, since 1971; Member: Victorian Prison Advisory Council, Australia, and State Flood Relief Committee, since 1974; State Relief Committee, since 1964; National Fitness Council, since 1957; Past Chairman and Member many community service organisations; *b* 14 Sept. 1917; *née* Turner; *m* 1941, Glenn Neville Frost, LDS, BDSc, JP; three *d*. *Educ:* Croydon Coll., Vic.; St Duthus Coll.; Presbyterian Ladies' Coll.; Univ. of Melbourne. Dip. of Physiotherapy, 1938; studied Criminology, 1955. Past Member: Adult Parole Bd (Female), 1957-74; Youth Advisory Council, 1957-72 (Vice-Chm.). Past Nat. and State appts also include: Past-Pres., Australian Freedom from Hunger Campaign, and many Exec. memberships and positions. Has attended several internat. confs as accredited Aust. delegate or rep. Internat. Council of Women; notably Chairman: Freedom from Hunger Campaign Conf. (4th Session in Rome), 1969; 3rd Regional Congress of FFHC for Asia and the Far East, at Canberra, 1970, and Rome, 1971. Convenor, Public Questions Cttee, Congregational Union of Victoria (Exec. Council Mem. of Union, 1970-). JP Croydon, Vic., 1957-. *Address:* 296 Dorset Road, Croydon, Victoria 3136, Australia. *Clubs:* Royal Commonwealth Society; Royal Automobile (Vic.).

FROST, Hon. Sir Sydney; *see* Frost, Hon. Sir T. S.

FROST, Terence, (Terry Frost); artist; Professor of Painting, University of Reading, 1977-81 (formerly Reader in Fine Art), Professor Emeritus 1981; *b* Oct. 1915; *m* 1945; five *s* one *d*. *Educ:* Leamington Spa Central Sch. Exhibitions: Leicester Galls, 1952-58; Waddington Galls, 1958-; B. Schaeffer Gallery, New York, 1960-62; Plymouth 1976; Bristol 1976; Serpentine Gall., 1977; Paris, 1978; Norway, 1979. Oil paintings acquired by Tate Gallery, National Gallery of Canada, National Gallery of NSW; also drawing acquired by Victoria and Albert Museum. Other work in public collections; Canada, USA, Germany, Australia, and in Edinburgh, Dublin, Leeds, Hull, Manchester, Birmingham, Liverpool, Bristol, etc. Gregory Fellow in Painting, Univ. of Leeds, 1954-56. Hon. LLD CNAA, 1978. *Address:* Gernick Field Studio, Tredavoe Lane, Newlyn, Penzance. *T:* Penzance 5902.

FROST, Hon. Sir (Thomas) Sydney, Kt 1975; Chief Justice of Papua New Guinea, 1975-78, retired; *b* 13 Feb. 1916; *s* of late Thomas Frost, Redfern, NSW; *m* 1943, Dorothy Gertrude (*née* Kelly); two *s* one *d*. *Educ:* Univ. of Melbourne (LLM). Served 2nd AIF, 1941-45. Barrister, Victoria, 1945-64; QC 1961; Judge of the County Court of Victoria, 1964; Judge of Supreme Court of Papua New Guinea, 1964-75. Chairman: Aust. Govt Inquiry into Whales and Whaling, 1978; Royal Commn of Inquiry into Housing Commn Land Purchases and Valuation Matters, Vic., 1979-81; Bd of Accident Inquiry into causes of crash of Beechcroft Super King Air 200 VH-AAV, Sydney, 21 Feb. 1980, 1982. Pres., Medical Services Review Tribunal, 1979-. *Recreation:* golf. *Address:* Park Tower, 201 Spring Street, Melbourne, Victoria, Australia. *T:* 662 3239. *Clubs:* Australian, Royal Melbourne Golf (Melbourne).

FROY, Prof. Martin; Professor of Fine Art, University of Reading, since 1972; *s* of late William Alan Froy and Helen Elizabeth Spencer. *Educ:* St Paul's Sch.; Magdalene Coll., Cambridge (one year); Slade Sch. of Fine Art. Dipl. in Fine Art (London). Visiting Teacher of Engraving, Slade Sch. of Fine Art, 1952-55; taught at Bath Acad. of Art, latterly as Head of Fine Art, 1954-65; Head of Painting Sch., Chelsea Sch. of Art, 1965-72. Gregory Fellow in Painting, Univ. of Leeds, 1951-54; Leverhulme Research Award, six months study in Italy, 1963; Sabbatical Award, Arts Council, 1965. Mem., Fine Art Panel, 1962-71, Mem. Council, 1969-71, Nat. Council for Diplomas in Art and Design; Trustee: National Gall., 1972-79; Tate Gall., 1975-79. Fellow, UCL, 1978. *One-Man Exhibitions:* Hanover Gall., London, 1952; Wakefield City Art Gall., 1953; Belgrade Theatre, Coventry, 1958; Leicester Galls, London, 1961; Royal West of England Acad., Bristol, 1964; Univ. of Sussex, 1968; Hanover Gall., London, 1969; Park Square Gall., Leeds, 1970; Arnolfini Gall., Bristol, 1970; City Art Gall., Bristol (seven paintings), 1972; Univ. of Reading, 1979; New Ashgate Gall., Surrey, 1979. *Other Exhibitions:* Internat. Abstract Artists, Riverside Mus., NY, 1950; ICA, London, 1950; Ten English Painters, Brit. Council touring exhibn in Scandinavia, 1952; Drawings from Twelve Countries, Art Inst. of Chicago, 1952; Figures in their Setting, Contemp. Art Soc. Exhibn, Tate Gall., 1953; Beaux Arts Gall., London, 1953; British Painting and Sculpture, Whitechapel Art Gall., London, 1954; Le Congrès pour la Liberté de la Culture Exhibn, Rome, Paris, Brussels, 1955; Pittsburgh Internat., 1955; Six Young Painters, Arts Council touring Exhibn, 1956; ICA Gregory Meml Exhibn, Bradford City Art Gall., Leeds, 1958; City Art Gall., Bristol, 1960; Malerei der Gegenwart ans Sudwestengland, Kunstverein, Hanover, 1962; Corsham Painters and Sculptors, Arts Council Touring Exhibn, 1965; Three Painters, Bath Fest. Exhibn, 1970; Park Square Gall., Leeds, 1978; Ruskin Sch., Univ. of Oxford, 1978; Newcastle Connection, Newcastle, 1980. *Commissions, etc:* Artist Consultant for Arts Council to City Architect, Coventry, 1953-58; mosaic decoration, Belgrade Th., Coventry, 1957-58; two mural panels, Concert Hall, Morley Coll., London, 1958-59. *Works in Public Collections:* Tate Gall.; Mus. of Mod. Art, NY; Chicago Art Inst.; Arts Council; Contemp. Art Soc.; Royal W of England Acad.; Leeds Univ.; City Art Galls of Bristol, Carlisle, Leeds, Southampton and Wakefield. *Address:* Department of Fine Art, University of Reading, London Road, Reading, Berks RG1 5AQ.

FRY, Christopher; dramatist; *b* 18 Dec. 1907; *s* of Charles John Harris and Emma Marguerite Hammond, *d* of Emma Louisa Fry; *m* 1936, Phyllis Marjorie Hart; one *s*. *Educ:* Bedford Modern Sch. Actor at Citizen House, Bath, 1927; Schoolmaster at Hazlewood Preparatory Sch., Limpsfield, Surrey, 1928-31; Dir of Tunbridge Wells Repertory Players, 1932-35; life too complicated for tabulation, 1935-39; The Tower, a pageant-play produced at Tewkesbury Fest., 1939; Dir of Oxford Repertory Players, 1940 and 1944-46, directing at Arts Theatre, London, 1945; Staff dramatist, Arts, 1947. FRSL. Queen's Gold Medal (for Poetry), 1962. *Plays:* A Phoenix Too Frequent, Mercury, 1946; The Lady's Not for Burning, Arts, 1948, Globe, 1949, Chichester, 1972; The Firstborn, Edinburgh Festival, 1948; Thor, with Angels, Canterbury Festival, 1949; Venus Observed, St James's, 1950; The Boy with a Cart, Lyric, Hammersmith, 1950; Ring Round the Moon (translated from French of Jean Anouilh), Globe, 1950; A Sleep of Prisoners, produced St Thomas' Church, Regent Street, W1, 1951; The Dark is Light Enough, Aldwych, 1954; The Lark (trans. from French of Jean Anouilh), Lyric, Hammersmith, 1955; Tiger at the Gates (trans. from French of Jean Giraudoux), Apollo, 1955; Duel of Angels (trans. from Pour Lucrèce, of Jean Giraudoux), Apollo, 1958; Curtmantle, Edinburgh Festival, 1962; Judith (trans. from Giraudoux), Her Majesty's, 1962; A Yard of Sun, National, 1970; Peer Gynt (trans.), Chichester, 1970; Cyrano de Bergerac (trans.), Chichester, 1975. *TV:* The Brontës of Haworth, four plays, 1973; Sister Dora, 1977; The Best of Enemies, 1977. *Film Commentary* for The Queen is Crowned (Coronation film, 1953); *Film scripts:* (participation) Ben Hur; Barabbas; The Bible; The Beggar's Opera. *Publications:* The Boy with a Cart, 1939; The Firstborn, 1946; A Phoenix Too Frequent, 1946; The Lady's Not for Burning, 1949; Thor, with Angels, 1949; Venus Observed, 1950; (trans.) Ring Round the Moon, 1950; A Sleep of Prisoners, 1951; The Dark is Light Enough, 1954; (trans.) The Lark, 1955; (trans.) Tiger at The Gates, 1955; (trans.) Duel of Angels, 1958; Curtmantle, 1961 (Heinemann Award of RSL); (trans.) Judith, 1962; A Yard of Sun, 1970; (trans.) Peer Gynt, 1970 (this trans. included in The Oxford Ibsen, vol. III, Brand and Peer Gynt, 1972); Four television plays: The Brontës at Haworth, 1954; (trans.) Cyrano de Bergerac, 1975; Can You Find Me: a family history, 1978; (ed and introd) Charlie Hammond's Sketch Book, 1980. *Address:* The Toft, East Dean, Chichester, West Sussex.

FRY, Prof. Dennis Butler; Emeritus Professor of Experimental Phonetics, University College, London, Professor 1958-75; Hon. Research Fellow, University College London; *b* 3 Nov. 1907; *s* of late F. C. B. Fry and Jane Ann (*née* Butler), Stockbridge, Hants; *m* 1937, Chrystabel, *er d* of late Charles Smith, JP, Brighton; one *s* two *d*. *Educ:* Gosport Grammar Sch.; University of London. Asst Master, Tewkesbury Grammar Sch., 1929-31; Asst Master, Kilburn Grammar Sch., 1931-34; Asst Lecturer in Phonetics, University Coll., London, 1934-37; Lecturer and Superintendent of Phonetics Laboratory, 1937-49. Served as Squadron Leader, RAFVR, 1940-45; in charge of Acoustics Laboratory, Central Medical Establishment, RAF, 1941-45. Reader in Experimental Phonetics, University of London, 1948; Head of Dept of Phonetics, UCL, 1949-71. Editor of Language and Speech, 1958-78. Pres., Permanent Internat. Council for Phonetic Sciences, 1961; Hon. Fellow, College of Speech Therapists, 1964; Fellow, Acoustical Soc. of America, 1966; Governor: Sadler's Wells Foundation, 1966. Trustee, Inst. for Cultural Research. FRSA 1970. *Publications:* The Deaf Child (with E. M. Whetnall), 1963; Learning to Hear (with E. M. Whetnall), 1970; Homo Loquens, 1977; The Physics of Speech, 1979; papers on speech and hearing in scientific and linguistic journals. *Recreation:* music, especially singing. *Address:* 18 Lauriston Road, SW19. *T:* 01-946 3046.

FRY, Donald William, CBE 1970; Director, Atomic Energy Establishment, Winfrith, 1959-73; *b* 30 Nov. 1910; *m* 1934, Jessie Florence (*née* Wright); three *s*. *Educ:* Weymouth Gram. Sch.; King's Coll., London. Research Physicist, GEC Laboratories, 1932; RAE Farnborough (Radio Dept), 1936; Air Min. Research Establishment (later the Telecommunications Research Establishment, TRE) Swanage, 1940; moved with the Estab. to Malvern, 1942; joined staff of AERE (still at Malvern), 1946; demonstrated with other mems of group a new Principle for accelerating particles: the travelling wave linear accelerator, 1947. Awarded Duddell Medal of Physical Soc., 1950; Head of Gen. Physics Div. at AERE Harwell, 1950; Chief Physicist, 1954, Dep. Dir, 1958, AERE Harwell. CEng, FIEE 1946; FIEEE 1960; FInstP 1970; Hon. Freeman of Weymouth, 1958. FKC London, 1959. *Publications:* papers in learned journals. *Address:* Coveway Lodge, Overcombe, near Weymouth, Dorset. *T:* Preston (Weymouth) 833276. *Club:* Royal Dorset Yacht.

FRY, E. Maxwell, CBE 1953; RA 1972 (ARA 1966); BArch; FRIBA, FRTPI; Dist Town Planning; consultant architect and town planner in retirement; active painter; *b* 2 Aug. 1899; *s* of Ambrose Fry and Lydia Thompson; *m* 1927, Ethel Speakman (marr. diss.); one *d*; *m* 1942, Jane B. Drew, *qv*. *Educ:* Liverpool Inst.; Liverpool Univ. Sch. of Architecture. Practised with Walter Gropius as Gropius and Fry, 1934-36; as Maxwell Fry and Jane Drew, 1945-50, as Fry, Drew, Drake, & Lasdun, 1951-58; now as Fry, Drew, Knight & Creamer. Work includes schools, hospitals, working-class and other flats, houses in England and educational buildings in Ghana and Nigeria. Served with Royal Engineers, 1939-44. Town Planning Adviser to Resident Minister for West Africa, 1943-45; Senior Architect to New Capital Chandigarh, Punjab, 1951-54. One-man show, Drian Gall., 1974. Ex-Mem. Royal Fine Art Commission; Corr. Mem. Académie Flamande, 1956; Hon. FAIA 1963; Council Mem. RIBA (Vice-Pres. 1961-62) and RSA; Royal Gold Medal for Architecture, 1964. Hon. LLD Ibadan Univ., 1966. *Publications:* Fine Building, 1944; (jointly with Jane B. Drew) Architecture for Children, 1944; Tropical Architecture, 1964; Art in a Machine Age, 1969; Maxwell Fry: autobiographical sketches, 1975; contribs to architectural and other papers. *Address:* 63 Gloucester Place, W1H 4DJ. *T:* 01-935 3318; The Lake House, Rowfant, Sussex. *T:* Crawley 882182.

FRY, Dr Ian Kelsey, DM, FRCP, FRCR; Dean, Medical College of St Bartholomew's Hospital, since 1981; Consultant Radiologist, St Bartholomew's Hospital, since 1966; *b* 25 Oct. 1923; *s* of Sir William and Lady Kelsey Fry; *m* 1951, Mary Josephine Casey; three *s* (one *d* decd). *Educ:* Radley Coll.; New Coll., Oxford; Guy's Hosp. Medical Sch. BM BCh 1948, DM Oxon 1961; MRCP 1956, FRCP 1972; DMRD 1961; FFR 1963; FRCR 1975. RAF Medical Services, 1949-50 (Sqdn Ldr). Research Fellow, Guy's Hosp., 1956-59; Director, Dept of Radiology, BUPA Medical Centre, 1973-; Mem. Council, Royal College of Radiologists, 1979-82; President, British Institute of Radiology, 1982-83. *Publications:* chapters and articles in books and jls. *Recreations:* golf, walking. *Address:* The Pines, Woodlands Road, Bickley, Bromley, Kent. *T:* 01-467 4150.

FRY, John, OBE 1975; MD, FRCS, FRCGP; general practitioner, since 1947; *b* 16 June 1922; *s* of Ansel and Barbara Fry; *m* 1944, Joan, *d* of James and Catherine Sabel; one *s* one *d*. *Educ:* Whitgift Middle Sch., Croydon; Guy's Hosp., Univ. of London (MD). FRCS 1947, FRCGP 1967. Hon. Consultant in Gen. Practice to the Army, 1968-; Consultant to WHO, 1965-; Trustee, Nuffield Provincial Hosps Trust, 1956-. Mem., GMC, 1970- (Sen. Treasurer, 1975-); Councillor, RCGP, 1960-. *Publications:* The Catarrhal Child, 1961; Profiles of Disease, 1966; Medicine in Three Societies, 1969; Common Diseases, 1974, 2nd edn 1979; Textbook of Medical Practice, 1976; Scientific Foundations of Family Medicine, 1978; A New Approach to Medicine, 1978; Primary Care, 1980. *Recreations:* reading, writing, researching, running. *Address:* 138 Croydon Road, Beckenham, Kent BR3 4DG. *T:* 01-650 0568.

FRY, Sir John (Nicholas Pease), 4th Bt *cr* 1894; *b* 23 Oct. 1897; *s* of Sir John Pease Fry, 2nd Bt and Margaret Theodora (*d* 1941), *d* of Francis Edward Fox, JP; *S* brother, 1971; *m* 1927, Helen Murray (*d* 1981), *d* of late William Gibson Bott, MRCS, JP; one *d* (and one *d* decd). *Educ:* Clifton; Trinity College, Cambridge (BA). Served European War, 1914-18 with Friends Ambulance Unit; War of 1939-45, with Special Constabulary. *Heir:* *b* Francis Wilfrid Fry, OBE [*b* 2 May 1904; *m* 1943, Anne Pease, *e d* of late Kenneth Henry Wilson, OBE, JP]. *Address:* c/o Mrs M. J. Redway, 6 Turners Wood Drive, Chalfont St Giles, Bucks HP8 4NE.

FRY, Maxwell; see Fry, E. Maxwell.

FRY, Peter Derek; MP (C) Wellingborough since Dec. 1969; Insurance Broker since 1963; *b* 26 May 1931; *s* of Harry Walter Fry and late Edith Fry; *m* 1st, 1958, Edna Roberts (marr. diss. 1982); one *s* one *d*; 2nd, 1982, Helen Claire Mitchell. *Educ:* Royal Grammar School, High Wycombe; Worcester College, Oxford (MA). Tillotsons (Liverpool) Ltd, 1954-56; Northern Assurance Co., 1956-61; Political Education Officer, Conservative Central Office, 1961-63. Member Bucks County Council, 1961-67. Contested (C) North Nottingham, 1964, East Willesden, 1966. Vice-Chm., British Yugoslav Parly Gp; Jt Chm., All Party Roads Study Gp; Chairman: All Party Footwear and Leather Gp; Anglo-Bahamian Parly Gp; Mem., Select Cttee on Transport. Played Rugby for Bucks County, 1956-58, Hon. Secretary, 1958-61. *Recreations:* watching Rugby football; reading history and biographies. *Address:* Glebe Farmhouse, 24 Church Lane, Cranford, Kettering, Northants. *Club:* Royal Automobile.

FRY, Peter George Robin Plantagenet S.; see Somerset Fry.

FRY, Richard Henry, CBE 1965; Financial Editor of The Guardian, 1939-65; *b* 23 Sept. 1900; *m* 1929, Katherine (*née* Maritz); no *c*. *Educ:* Berlin and Heidelberg Univs. *Address:* 8 Montagu Mews West, W1. *T:* 01-262 0817. *Club:* Reform.

FRY, Ronald Ernest, FSS; Director of Economics and Statistics, Departments of the Environment and Transport, 1975-80, retired; *b* 21 May 1925; *s* of Ernest Fry and Lilian (*née* Eveling); *m* 1954, Jeanne Ivy Dawson; one *s* one *d*. *Educ:* Wilson's Grammar Sch., Camberwell; Birkbeck Coll., Univ. of London (BSc (Special)). MIS. Telecommunications Technician, Royal Signals, 1944-47; Scientific Asst, CEGB (London Region), 1948-52; Statistician: Glacier Metal Co., London, 1952-54; CEGB HQ, London, 1954-64; Gen. Register Office, 1965-66; Asst Dir of Research and Intelligence,

GLC, 1966-69; Chief Statistician: (Social Statistics) Cabinet Office, 1969-74; (Manpower Statistics) Dept of Employment, 1974-75. *Publications:* various technical publns in statistical and other professional jls. *Recreations:* photography, reading, motoring. *Address:* 39 Claremont Road, Hadley Wood, Barnet, Herts EN4 0HR. *T:* 01-440 1393.

FRY, Hon. Sir William Gordon, Kt 1980; President, Legislative Council of Victoria, Australia, 1976-79; *b* 12 June 1909; *s* of A. G. Fry, Ballarat; *m* 1936, Lilian G., *d* of A. W. Macrae; four *s*. *Educ:* Ballarat High School; Melbourne Univ. Served War of 1939-45, 2nd AIF (Lt-Col, despatches). Education Dept of Victoria for 40 years; Headmaster of various schools, including Cheltenham East, Windsor, Cheltenham Heights. Councillor, City of Moorabbin; Mayor, 1968; MLC (Lib) for Higinbotham, Vic, 1967-79. Past Chm., Parly Select Cttee, Road Safety. Vice-Pres., Victoria League; Mem., RSL. Formerly Dep. Chm., World Bowls. Life Governor: Melbourne and Dist Ambulance Soc.; Royal Women's Hosp.; Royal Melbourne Hosp.; Gen. Management Cttee, Royal Victoria Eye and Ear Hosp.; Management Bd, Cheltenham-Mordialloc Hosp. *Recreations:* lawn bowls, golf, swimming. *Address:* The Point, 405 Beach Road, Beaumaris, Victoria 3193, Australia. *Club:* West Brighton.

FRY, William Norman Hillier-; see Hillier-Fry.

FRYBERG, Sir Abraham, Kt 1968; MBE 1941; retired; *b* 26 May 1901; *s* of Henry and Rose Fryberg; *m* 1939, Vivian Greensil Barnard; one *s*. *Educ:* Wesley Coll., Melbourne; Queen's Coll., University of Melbourne. MB, BS (Melbourne) 1928; DPH, DTM (Sydney) 1936; Hon. MD (Qld); Hon. FACMA. Served with 9 Australian Div. (Tobruk, Alamein), 1940-45. Resident Med. Officer, then Registrar, Brisbane Hosp. and Brisbane Children's Hosp., 1929-33; GP, Hughenden, 1934; Health Officer, Qld Health Dept, 1936-46 (except for war service); Dep. Dir-Gen., 1946, Dir-Gen. of Health and Medical Services, Qld, 1947-67, retired. Hon. Col, RAAMC Northern Comd, 1962-67. SBStJ 1958. *Recreation:* racing. *Address:* 19 Dublin Street, Clayfield, Qld 4011, Australia. *T:* Brisbane 2622549. *Club:* United Service (Brisbane).

FRYER, David Richard; Secretary-General, Royal Town Planning Institute, since 1976; *b* 16 May 1936; *s* of Ernest William Fryer and Gladys Edith Battey; *m* 1961, Carole Elizabeth Hayes; one *s* two *d*. *Educ:* Chesterfield Sch.; New Coll., Oxford (MA, BCL). LMRTPL. Admitted solicitor, 1961. Articled Clerk and Asst Solicitor, Chesterfield Bor. Council, 1958-61; Associate Lawyer, Messrs Jones, Day, Cockley & Reavis, Cleveland, Ohio, 1961-63; Asst Solicitor, N Riding CC, 1963-65; Sen. Asst Solicitor, Bucks CC, 1966-69; Dep. Sec., RICS, 1970-75. Sec., Brit. Chapter, Internat. Real Estate Fedn, 1970-75; Member: Bureau and Council, Internat. Fedn for Housing and Planning, 1976-; Exec. Cttee and Council, Public Works Congress and Exhibn Council Ltd, 1976-; Exec. Cttee, Nat. Council for Social Service, 1976-79 (Chm., Planning and Environment Gp); Council and Standards Cttee, Nat. House-Bldg Council, 1976-. FRSA 1981. *Recreations:* international affairs, history, architecture, travel, music, the countryside, cricket, family activities. *Address:* 8 Willowmead, Hartwell, Aylesbury, Bucks. *T:* Aylesbury 748538. *Clubs:* East India, Devonshire, Sports and Public Schools; Colwyn Bay Cricket (Rhos-on-Sea).

FRYER, Dr Geoffrey, FRS 1972; Deputy Chief Scientific Officer, Windermere Laboratory, Freshwater Biological Association, since 1981; *b* 6 Aug. 1927; *s* of W. and M. Fryer; *m* 1953, Vivien Griffiths Hodgson; one *s* one *d*. *Educ:* Huddersfield College. DSc, PhD London. Royal Navy, 1946-48. Colonial Research Student, 1952-53; HM Overseas Research Service, 1953-60: Malawi, 1953-55; Zambia, 1955-57; Uganda, 1957-60; Sen., then Principal, then Sen. Principal Scientific Officer, Freshwater Biological Assoc., 1960-81. H. R. Macmillan Lectr, Univ. of British Columbia, 1963. Mem. Council, Royal Soc., 1978-80. *Publications:* (with T. D. Iles) The Cichlid Fishes of the Great Lakes of Africa: their biology and evolution, 1972; numerous articles in scientific jls. *Recreations:* natural history, walking, books, photography. *Address:* Elleray Cottage, Windermere, Cumbria LA23 1AW.

FRYER, Maj.-Gen. (retd) Wilfred George, CB 1956; CBE 1951 (OBE 1941); *b* 1 May 1900; *s* of James and Marion Fryer, Kington, Herefordshire; *m* 1931, Jean Eleanore Graham, *d* of Graham Binny, RSW, Edinburgh; two *s* (and one *s* decd). *Educ:* Christ Coll., Brecon; RMA Woolwich. Commissioned 2nd Lieut RE, 1919, Regular Army; served in India, Royal Bombay Sappers and Miners, 1933-38; Major RE, Instructor, Sch. of Mil. Engineering, Chatham, 1938. Served War of 1939-45: Lt-Col RE, ADWE & M, GHQ, Middle East, 1941; SO1 to Chief Engineer, Eighth Army, Western Desert Campaign (OBE), 1941; Col DDWE & M, GHQ, Middle East, 1942; GSO1 to Scientific Adviser to Army Council, 1944; ADWE & M, GHQ and Dep. Chief Engineer, 8 Corps, NW Europe Campaign (despatches), 1944-45; Brig.-Chief Engr, Brit. Army Staff, Washington, DC, 1945; Col E (Equipment), War Office, 1946-48; Brig.-Chief Engr, Singapore Dist, 1948-51; Brig.-Chief Engr, Southern Comd, UK, 1951-53; Maj.-Gen. 1954; Chief Engineer, Middle East Land Forces, 1954-57. "A" Licence air pilot, 1942. MIEE 1952. Chm., Warminster Press Ltd. Nat. Champion, Wayfarer Dinghy, 1960. *Recreations:* ocean racing (Transatlantic Race, 1931), ski-ing (Lauberhorn Cup), tennis. *Address:* 47 Belmore Lane, Lymington, Hants SO4 9NR. *Clubs:* Army and Navy, Royal Ocean Racing, Hurlingham.

FUAD, Kutlu Tekin; Hon. Mr Justice Fuad; Judge of the High Court of Hong Kong, since 1980; *b* 23 April 1926; *s* of Mustafa Fuad Bey, CMG, and Belkis Hilmi; *m* 1952, Inci Izzet; two *s* one *d*. *Educ:* Temple Grove; Marlborough Coll.; St John's Coll., Cambridge (MA). Called to the Bar, Inner Temple, 1952. Mil. Service, Lieut KRRC, 1944-48. Colonial Legal Service, 1953-62: Magistrate, Cyprus; Resident Magistrate, Sen. Crown Counsel, Legal Draftsman, and Dir of Public Prosecutions, Uganda; Judge of the High Court, Uganda, 1963-72 (Pres., Industrial Court; Chm., Law Reform Cttee); Dir, Legal Div., Commonwealth Secretariat, 1972-80. Formerly Chm., Visitation Cttee, Makerere University Coll. *Recreations:* music, Rugby football, tennis. *Address:* Supreme Court, Hong Kong; 51 Earl's Court Road, Kensington, W8. *T:* 01-937 9209. *Club:* Army and Navy.

FUCHS, Sir Vivian (Ernest), Kt 1958; MA, PhD; FRS 1974; Director of the British Antarctic Survey, 1958-73; Leader Commonwealth Trans-Antarctic Expedition, 1955-58; *b* 11 Feb. 1908; *s* of late E. Fuchs, Farnham, Surrey, and late Violet Anne Fuchs (*née* Watson); *m* 1933, Joyce, 2nd *d* of late John Connell; one *s* one *d* (and one *d* decd). *Educ:* Brighton Coll.; St John's Coll., Cambridge. Geologist with: Cambridge East Greenland Expedn, 1929; Cambridge Expdn to E African Lakes, 1930-31; E African Archæological Expdn, 1931-32; Leader Lake Rudolf Rift Valley Expedn, 1933-34; Royal Geog. Society Cuthbert Peek Grant, 1936; Leader Lake Rukwa Expedn, 1937-38. 2nd Lieut Cambs Regt, TA, 1939; served in W Africa, 1942-43; Staff Coll., Camberley, 1943; served NW Europe (despatches), 1944-46; demobilized (Major), 1946. Leader Falkland Islands Dependencies Survey (Antarctica), 1947-50; Dir FIDSc Bureau, 1950-55. President: Internat. Glaciological Soc., 1963-66; British Assoc. for Advancement of Science, 1972; Mem. Council, RGS, 1958-61, Vice-Pres. 1961-64, Pres., 1982. Founder's Gold Medal, Royal Geog. Soc., 1951; Silver Medal RSA, 1952; Polar Medal, 1953, and Clasp, 1958; Special Gold Medal, Royal Geog. Soc., 1958; Gold Medal Royal Scottish Geog. Society 1958; Gold Medal Geog. Society (Paris), 1958; Richthofen Medal (Berlin), 1958; Kirchenpauer Medal (Hamburg), 1958; Plancius Medal (Amsterdam), 1959; Egede Medal (Copenhagen), 1959; Hubbard Medal, Nat. Geog. Soc. (Washington), 1959; Explorers Club Medal (New York), 1959; Geog. Soc. (Chicago) Gold Medal, 1959; Geol. Soc. of London Prestwich Medal, 1960. Hon. Fellow, Wolfson (formerly University Coll.), Cambridge, 1970. Hon. LLD Edinburgh 1958; Hon. DSc Durham 1958; Cantab 1959; Leicester 1972; Hon. ScD Swansea, 1971; Hon. LLD Birmingham, 1974. *Publications:* The Crossing of Antarctica (Fuchs and Hillary), 1958; Antarctic Adventure, 1959; (ed) Forces of Nature, 1977; geographical and geological reports and papers in scientific jls. *Recreations:* squash racquets, swimming. *Address:* 78 Barton Road, Cambridge. *T:* Cambridge 59238. *Club:* Athenæum.

FUGARD, Athol; playwright, director, actor; *b* 11 June 1932; *s* of Harold David Fugard and Elizabeth Magdalene Potgieter; *m* 1956, Sheila Meiring; one *d*. *Educ:* Univ. of Cape Town. Directed earliest plays, Nongogo, No Good Friday, Johannesburg, 1960; acted in The Blood Knot, touring S Africa, 1961; Hello and Goodbye, 1965; directed and acted in The Blood Knot, London, 1966; Boesman and Lena, S Africa, 1969; directed Boesman and Lena, London, 1971; directed Serpent Players in various prodns, Port Elizabeth, from 1963, directed co-authors John Kani and Winston Ntshona in Sizwe Bansi is Dead, SA, 1972, The Island, 1973, and London, 1973-74; acted in film, Boesman and Lena, 1972; directed and acted in Statements after an Arrest under the Immorality Act, in SA, 1972, directed in London, 1973; wrote Dimetos for Edinburgh Fest., 1975; directed and acted in, A Lesson from Aloes, SA, 1978, London, 1980 (staged NY, 1981, winning NY Critics Circle Award for Best Play); staged Master Harold and the Boys, NY, 1982 (Drama Desk Award). Hon. DLitt Natal, 1981. *Films:* Boesman and Lena, 1973; The Guest, 1977; (acted in) Meetings with Remarkable Men (dir, Peter Brook), 1979; (wrote and acted in) Marigolds in August (Silver Bear Award, Berlin), 1980. *Publications:* The Blood Knot, 1962; People Are Living There, Hello and Goodbye, 1973; Boesman and Lena, 1973; (jtly) Three Port Elizabeth Plays: Sizwe Bansi is Dead, The Island, Statements after an Arrest under the Immorality Act, 1974; Tsotsi (novel), 1980 (also USA); A Lesson from Aloes, 1981 (also USA). *Recreations:* angling, skin-diving, bird-watching. *Address:* PO Box 5090, Walmer, Port Elizabeth, South Africa.

FUJIYAMA, Naraichi; Industrial Adviser to Located in Scotland (LIS), in Japan, since 1982; *b* 17 Sept. 1915; *m* 1946, Shizuko Takagi. *Educ:* Faculty of Law, Tokyo Univ.; Univ. of NC, USA. Consul, New York, 1953-54; Counsellor, Austria, 1959, Indonesia, 1963; Chief of Protocol, Min. of Foreign Affairs, Tokyo, 1965; Dir-Gen., Public Inf. Bureau, Min. of For. Affairs, 1968; Ambassador to: Austria, 1971-75; Italy, 1975-79, Great Britain, 1979-82. Chm., Bd of Governors, IAEA, Vienna, 1973-74; Press Sec. to the Emperor of Japan for State Visit to USA, 1975. Grand Cross, Order Al Merito, Peru; Kt Grand Cross, Order Al Merito, Italy; Grand Decoration of Honour for Merit in Gold with Sash, Austria. *Recreation:* golf. *Address:* 7-7-19, Koyama, Shinagawa-ku, Tokyo, Japan.

FUKUI, Prof. Dr Kenichi; Order of Culture, Person of Cultural Merits (Japan), 1981; President, Kyoto University of Industrial Arts and Textile Fibers, since 1982; *b* 4 Oct. 1918; *s* of Ryokichi Fukui and Chie Fukui (*née* Sugizawa); *m* 1947, Tomoe Horie; one *s* one *d*. *Educ:* Kyoto Imperial Univ. (AB Engrg, PhD Engrg). Lecturer, 1943-45, Asst Professor, 1945-51, Professor, 1951-82, Kyoto Imperial University. Nobel Prize in Chemistry (jtly), 1981. *Address:* 23 Kitahirakawahirai-cho, Sakyo-ku, Kyoto-city, Kyoto 606, Japan. *T:* 075-781-5785.

FULBRIGHT, J. William, Hon. KBE 1975; US Senator (Democrat) for Arkansas, 1945-74; *b* Sumner, Mo, 9 April 1905; *s* of Jay Fulbright and Roberta (*née* Waugh); *m* 1932, Elizabeth Kremer Williams; two *d*. *Educ:* public schools of Fayetteville, Arkansas; University of Arkansas (AB); (Rhodes Scholar) Pembroke Coll., Oxford Univ. (BA, MA); George Washington Univ. Sch. of Law (LLB). Special Attorney, Dept. of Justice, 1934-35; Lectr in Law, George Washington Univ., 1935-36; Mem. Law Sch. Faculty, University of Arkansas, 1936-39, and Pres. of University, 1939-41. Elected to Congress for 3rd Dist of Arkansas, 1942; Mem. Foreign Affairs Cttee. Elected to Senate, 1945, and subsequently; Mem. US Delegn to Gen. Assembly, UN, 1954; Chm. Banking and Currency Cttee of Senate, 1955-59, resigning to become Chm. Senate Cttee on Foreign Relations, also Mem. Finance Cttee and Jt Economic Cttee. First McCallum Meml Lectr, Oxford, 1975. Hon. Fellow, Pembroke Coll., Oxford, 1949; Fellow, Amer. Acad. of Arts and Sciences (Boston), 1950; Award by Nat. Inst. of Arts and Letters, 1954. Holds several hon. degrees, including DCL Oxford, 1953, and LLD Cantab, 1971. *Publications:* Old Myths and New Realities, 1964; Prospects for the West, 1965; The Arrogance of Power, 1967. *Address:* 815 Connecticut Avenue, Washington, DC 20006, USA.

FULCHER, Derick Harold, DSC 1944; Interviewer for Civil Service Commission; *b* 4 Nov. 1917; *s* of late Percy Frederick Fulcher and Gertrude Lilian Fulcher; *m* 1943, Florence Ellen May Anderson; one *s* one *d*. *Educ:* St Olave's Grammar School. Served in Royal Navy, 1940-46 (Lieut, RNVR). Entered Civil Service (War Office), 1936; Asst Principal, Ministry of National Insurance, 1947; Principal, 1950; Admin. Staff Coll., Henley, 1952; Asst Sec. 1959. Seconded to HM Treasury, 1957-59; served on an ILO mission in Trinidad and Tobago, 1967-69; Asst Under-Sec. of State, Dept of Health and Social Security, 1969-70. UK Delegate to and Chairman: NATO Management Survey Cttee, 1970-71; Council of Europe Management Survey Cttee, 1971-72. Chm., Supplementary Benefit Appeal Tribunals, 1971-75; Head of UK res. project in W Europe into social security provision for disablement, 1971-72; Res. Consultant, Office of Manpower Econs, 1972-73; Served on technical aid mission to Indonesia, 1973; ILO Res. Consultant on Social Security, 1973-80; Consultant to: EEC Statistical Office, 1974; Govt of Thailand on Social Security, 1978-79 and 1981. Fellow, Inst. for European Health Services Research, Leuven Univ., Belgium, 1974-. *Publications:* Medical Care Systems, 1974; Social Security for the Unemployed, 1976. *Recreations:* walking, photography, travel. *Address:* 100 Downs Road, Coulsdon, Surrey CR3 1AF. *T:* Downland 54231. *Club:* Civil Service.

FULFORD, Robert John; Keeper, Department of Printed Books, British Library (formerly British Museum), since 1967; *b* 16 Aug. 1923; *s* of John Fulford, Southampton; *m* 1950, Alison Margaret Rees; one *s* one *d*. *Educ:* King Edward VI Sch., Southampton; King's Coll., Cambridge (Charls Univ., Prague. Asst Keeper, Dept of Printed Books, British Museum, 1945-65; Dep. Keeper, 1965-67 (Head of Slavonic Div., 1961-67); Keeper, 1967-. *Address:* 5 Fosse Bank Close, Tonbridge, Kent. *T:* Tonbridge 359310.

FULFORD, Sir Roger (Thomas Baldwin), Kt 1980; CVO 1970; *b* 24 Nov. 1902; *o* surv. *s* of late Canon Fulford; *m* 1937, Sibell (*d* 1980), widow of late Rev. Hon. C. F. Lyttelton and *d* of late Charles Adeane, CB. *Educ:* St Ronans; Lancing; Worcester Coll., Oxford. Pres. of Union, 1927; called to Bar, 1931; Liberal Candidate for Woodbridge Div. of Suffolk, 1929; for Holderness Div. of Yorks, 1945; for Rochdale, 1950; joined editorial staff of The Times, 1933; Part-time Lecturer in English, King's Coll., London, 1937-48; Asst Censor, 1939-40; Civil Asst War Office, 1940-42; Asst Private Sec. to Sec. of State for Air, 1942-45. Pres., Liberal Party, 1964-65. *Publications:* Royal Dukes, 1933; George IV, 1935; The Right Honourable Gentleman, 1945; The Prince Consort, 1949; Queen Victoria, 1951; History of Glyn's, 1953; Votes for Women, 1957; The Liberal Case, 1959; Hanover to Windsor, 1960; C. H. Wilkinson, 1965; Samuel Whitbread, 1967; The Trial of Queen Caroline, 1967; ed (with late Lytton Strachey) The Greville Memoirs, 1937; (ed) The Autobiography of Miss Knight, 1960; (ed) Letters Between Queen Victoria and the Princess Royal: Dearest Child, 1964; Dearest Mama, 1968; Your Dear Letter, 1971; Darling Child, 1976; Beloved Mama, 1981. *Address:* Barbon Manor, Carnforth, Lancs. *Club:* Boodle's.

FULHAM, Bishop Suffragan of, since 1982; **Rt. Rev. Brian John Masters;** *b* 17 Oct. 1932; *s* of Stanley William and Grace Hannah Masters; unmarried. *Educ:* Collyers School, Horsham; Queens' Coll., Cambridge (MA 1959); Cuddesdon Theological Coll. Lloyds broker, 1955-62. Asst Curate, S Dunstan and All Saints, Stepney, 1964-69; Vicar, Holy Trinity with S Mary, Hoxton, Nl, 1969-82. *Recreations:* theatre, squash. *Address:* 13 North Audley Street, W1. *T:* 01-626 3891. *Club:* United Oxford & Cambridge University.

FULLER, Buckminster; *see* Fuller, R. B.

FULLER, Geoffrey Herbert, FRINA, FIMarE; RCNC; Director of Dockyard Manpower and Productivity, Ministry of Defence, since 1982; *b* 16 Jan. 1927; *s* of late Major Herbert Thomas Fuller and Clarice Christine Fuller; *m* 1952, Pamela-Maria Quarrell; one *d*. *Educ:* Merchant Taylors', Northwood, Mddx; Royal Naval Engrg Coll., Keyham; Royal Naval Coll., Greenwich. FRINA 1965; FIMarE 1974. Constructor Commander: Staff of Flag Officer (Submarines), 1958; British Navy Staff, Washington, 1960; Chief Constructor, 1967; Sen. Officers War Course, 1969; RCDS, 1973; Head of Ship Material Engrg, 1974; Support Manager Submarines, 1976; Dep. Dir, Submarines/Polaris, Ship Dept, MoD, 1979; Dir of Naval Ship Production,

1981-82. *Address:* Foxhill Grove, Fox Hill, Bath BA2 5AT. *T:* Combe Down 837546. *Club:* Civil Service.

FULLER, Hon. Sir John (Bryan Munro), Kt 1974; MLC, New South Wales, 1961-78; NSW Minister for Planning and Environment, 1973-76; Vice-President of Executive Council, 1968-76; Leader of Government in Legislative Council, 1968-76, Leader of Opposition, 1976-78; *b* 22 Sept. 1917; *s* of late Bryan Fuller, QC; *m* 1940, Eileen, *d* of O. S. Webb; one *s* one *d. Educ:* Knox Grammar Sch., Wahroonga. Chm., Australian Country Party (NSW), 1959-64; Minister for Decentralisation and Development, 1965-73. Vice-Pres., Graziers Assoc. of NSW, 1965; Member: Council, Univ. of NSW, 1967-78; Cttee, United World Colls Trust, NSW, 1978-; Bd, Foundn for Res. and Treatment Alcohol and Drug Addiction, 1980-; Council, Nat. Heart Foundn, NSW, 1980-; Management Cttee, Dr Barnardo's in Australia, 1980-; Council, Aust. Inst. of Export (NSW), 1980-; Pres., Aust. Arthritis and Rheumatism Foundn, 1980-; Leader of various NSW Govt trade missions to various parts of the world. Fellow Australian Inst. of Export 1969. *Recreations:* tennis, bowls. *Address:* 54/8 Fullerton Street, Woollahra, NSW 2025, Australia. *Clubs:* Australian, American National, (Sydney); Coolah Bowling.

FULLER, Major Sir John (William Fleetwood), 3rd Bt *cr* 1910; Major, The Life Guards, retired; *b* 18 Dec. 1936; *s* of Major Sir John Gerard Henry Fleetwood Fuller, 2nd Bt, and of Fiona, Countess of Normanton, *d* of 4th Marquess Camden, GCVO; *S* father, 1981; *m* 1968, Lorna Marian, *o d* of F. R. Kemp-Potter, Findon, Sussex; three *s. Heir: s* James Henry Fleetwood Fuller, *b* 1 Nov. 1970. *Address:* Ganbrook Farm, Broughton Gifford, Melksham, Wilts.

FULLER, Richard Buckminster; American geometer, educator and architect-designer; University Professor Emeritus, Southern Illinois University and University of Pennsylvania; *b* Milton, Mass, 12 July 1895; *s* of Richard Buckminster Fuller and Caroline Wolcott Fuller (*née* Andrews); *m* 1917, Anne Hewlett; one *d* (and one *d* decd). *Educ:* Milton Acad.; Harvard Univ., US Naval Acad. Apprentice machine fitter, Richards, Atkinson & Haserick, 1914; Ensign to Lieut, US Navy, 1917-19; Asst Export Man., Armour & Co., 1919-21; Nat. Accounts Sales Man., Kelly-Springfield Truck Co., 1922; Pres. Stockade Building System, 1922-27; Founder, Pres., 4-D Co., Chicago, 1927-32; Editor and Publisher, Shelter Magazine, Philadelphia, 1930-32; Asst to Dir of Housing Res., Pierce Foundn, NY, and American Radiator & Standard Sanitary Manftg Co., Buffalo, 1930-31; Founder, Dir and Chief Engr, Dymaxion Corp., Bridgeport, 1932-36; Asst to Dir, Res. and Develt, Phelps Dodge Corp., 1936-38; Tech. Consultant, Fortune Mag., 1938-40; Vice-Pres. and Chief Engr, Dymaxion Co. Inc., Delaware, 1940-50; Chief Mech. Engr, US Bd of Econ. Warfare, 1942-44; Special Asst to Dep. Dir, US Foreign Econ. Administration, 1944; Chm. Bd and Chief Engr, Dymaxion Dwelling Machines, 1944-46; Chm. Bd of Trustees, Fuller Research Foundn, Wichita, Kansas, 1946-54; Pres. Geodesics Inc., Forest Hills, 1949-; Pres., Synergetics Inc., Raleigh, NC, 1954-59; Pres. Plydomes Inc., Des Moines, 1957-; Chm. Bd, Tetrahelix Corp., Hamilton, 1959-; Pres., Triton Foundn, Cambridge, Mass, 1967-; Editor-at-large, World Magazine, NY, 1972-75; Internat. Pres., MENSA, Paris, 1975-; Internat. Pres., World Soc. for Ekistics, Athens, 1975-; contrib. Editor, Saturday Review, 1976-; Consultant, Design Science Inst., Philadelphia, 1972-. Charles Eliot Norton Prof. of Poetry, Harvard Univ., 1961-62; Harvey Cushing Orator, Amer. Assoc. of Neuro-Surgeons, 1967; Jahawarlal Nehru Lectr, New Delhi, 1969; Hoyt Fellow, Yale Univ., 1969; World Fellow in Residence, Consortium of Univ. of Pennsylvania, Haverford Coll., Swarthmore Coll., Bryn Mawr Coll., and Univ. City Science Center, 1972-. Holds 26 patents in architecture, transport, cartography (first and only cartography patent awarded in USA) and other fields; *inventions include:* the World Game, Dymaxion house, car, bathroom, map; discovered energetic/synergetic geometry, 1917; geodesic structures, 1947 (over 200,000 geodesic domes erected in 100 countries). *Architect of:* US pavilion for Montreal World Fair, 1967; Samuel Beckett Theatre, St Peter's Coll., Oxford, 1969-; geodesic auditorium, Kfar Menachem Kibutzin, Israel, 1969; Tri-centennial Pavilion of S Carolina, Greenfield, 1970; Religious Center, Southern Illinois Univ., 1971; Chief Architect, internat. airports at New Delhi, Bombay and Madras, 1973; consultant to Architects Team 3, Penang Urban Center, 1974-. Mem. many professional inscns; Hon. Fellow, St Peter's Coll., Oxford, 1970; Hon. FRIBA 1968; FAIA 1975; holds hon. degrees from 43 univs/colleges; awards include Industrial Designers Soc. of Amer. (first) Award of Excellence, 1966; Gold Medal, Architecture, Nat. Inst. of Arts and Letters, 1968; Royal Gold Medal for Architecture, RIBA, 1968; Humanist of the Year Award, Amer. Assoc. of Humanists, 1969; Master Designer Award, McGraw Hill, 1969; Gold Medal, Amer. Inst. Architects, 1970. *Publications:* 4D Timelock, 1927; Nine Chains to the Moon, 1938 (UK 1973); The Dymaxion World of Buckminster Fuller (with Robert Marks), 1960 (rev. edn 1973); No More Second Hand God, 1962; Education Automation, 1963 (UK 1973); Ideas and Integrities (ed Robert Marks), 1963; untitled epic poem on history of industrialization, 1963; World Resources Inventory (6 documents) (with John McHale), 1963-67; Operating Manual for Spaceship Earth, 1969; Utopia or Oblivion, 1969; The Buckminster Fuller Reader (ed James Meller), 1970; I Seem to be a Verb (with Jerome Agel and Quentin Fiore), 1970; Intuition, 1972; Earth Inc., 1973; Synergetics: Explorations in the Geometry of Thinking (with E. J. Applewhite, 1975, Vol. 2, 1979; And It Came to Pass, Not to Stay, 1977; Critical Path, 1981; many contribs to jls etc. *Address:* 3501 Market Street, Philadelphia, Pa 19104, USA. *T:* (215) 387-5400.

FULLER, Roy Broadbent, CBE 1970; MA Oxon (by Decree); FRSL; poet and author; solicitor; Professor of Poetry, University of Oxford, 1968-73; *b* 11 Feb. 1912; *e s* of late Leopold Charles Fuller, Oldham; *m* 1936, Kathleen Smith; one *s. Educ:* Blackpool High Sch. Admitted a solicitor, 1934; served Royal Navy, 1941-46; Lieut, RNVR, 1944; Asst Solicitor to Woolwich Equitable Building Soc., 1938-58, Solicitor, 1958-69, Director, 1969-. Vice-Pres., Bldg Socs Assoc., 1969- (Chm. Legal Adv. Panel, 1958-69). A Governor of the BBC, 1972-79; Mem., Arts Council, 1976-77 (Chm., Literature Panel, 1976-77); Mem., Library Adv. Council for England, 1977-79. Queen's Gold Medal for Poetry, 1970. Cholmondeley Award, Soc. of Authors, 1980. *Publications:* Poems, 1939; The Middle of a War, 1942; A Lost Season, 1944; Savage Gold, 1946; With My Little Eye; Byron for Today, 1948; Questions and Answers in Building Soc. Law and Practice; Epitaphs and Occasions, 1949; The Second Curtain, 1953; Counterparts; Fantasy and Fugue, 1954; Image of a Society, 1956; Brutus's Orchard, 1957; The Ruined Boys, 1959; The Father's Comedy, 1961; Collected Poems, 1962; The Perfect Fool, 1963; Buff, 1965; My Child, My Sister, 1965; Catspaw, 1966; New Poems, 1968 (Duff Cooper Memorial Prize 1968); Off Course, 1969; The Carnal Island, 1970; Owls and Artificers: Oxford lectures on poetry, 1971; Seen Grandpa Lately?, 1972; Tiny Tears, 1973; Professors and Gods: last Oxford lectures on poetry, 1973; From the Joke Shop, 1975; An Ill-Governed Coast, 1976; Poor Roy, 1977; The Other Planet, 1979; The Reign of Sparrows, 1980; Souvenirs (autobiog.), 1980; Fellow Mortals—An Anthology of Animal Verse, 1981; Vamp Till Ready (autobiog.), 1982; The Individual and His Times (selected poems), 1982; (ed) The Building Societies Acts, various dates. *Address:* 37 Langton Way, Blackheath, SE3. *T:* 01-858 2334. *Club:* Athenæum.

FULLER-ACLAND-HOOD, Sir (Alexander) William; *see* Hood, Sir William Acland.

FULLER-GOOD, Air Vice-Marshal James Laurence Fuller, CB 1957; CVO 1953; CBE 1951; RAF retired; Air Officer Commanding, Air Headquarters, Malaya, 1951-52 (CBE); Director of Personal Services (Air), Air Ministry, 1952-53; Air Officer Commanding No 22 Group, Technical Training Command, 1953-57; Commandant-Gen. of the Royal Air Force Regt and Inspector of Ground Combat Trng, 1957-59, retd. Air Vice-Marshal, 1954. *Club:* Royal Air Force.

FULLERTON, Peter George Patrick Downing; Assistant Secretary, Atomic Energy Division, Department of Energy, since 1977; *b* 17 Jan. 1930; *s* of late Major R. A. D. Fullerton and Janet Mary Fullerton (*née* Baird); *m* 1962, Elizabeth Evelyn Newman Stevens, *d* of late George Stevens; two *s* two *d. Educ:* Radley Coll.; Magdalen Coll., Oxford (MA). HMOCS, Kenya, 1953-63, retd as Dist Comr; joined CRO (later FCO), 1963; Private Sec. to Minister of State, 1963-64; Dar-es-Salaam, 1964-65; Lusaka, 1966-69; seconded to British Leyland Motor Corp., 1970; FCO, 1971; Northern Ireland Office, 1972; FCO 1973; Canberra, 1974-77. *Address:* Hydon Heath Corner, Godalming, Surrey GU8 4BB. *T:* Hascombe 326. *Clubs:* United Oxford & Cambridge University; Leander.

FULLERTON, William Hugh; HM Diplomatic Service; Counsellor (Economic and Commercial) since 1980, and Consul General since 1981, Islamabad, Pakistan; *b* 11 Feb. 1939; *s* of late Major Arthur Hugh Theodore Francis Fullerton, RAMC, and of Mary (*née* Parker); *m* 1968, Arlene Jacobowitz; one *d. Educ:* Cheltenham Coll.; Queens' Coll., Cambridge (MA Oriental Langs). Shell Internat. Petroleum Co., Uganda, 1963-65; FO, 1965; MECAS, Shemlan, Lebanon, 1965-66; Information Officer, Jedda, 1966-67; UK Mission to UN, New York, 1967; FCO, 1968-70; Head of Chancery, Kingston, Jamaica, 1970-73, and Ankara, 1973-77; FCO, 1977-80. *Recreations:* travelling in remote areas, sailing, reading, walking. *Address:* c/o Foreign and Commonwealth Office, King Charles Street, SW1. *Club:* Travellers'.

FULTHORPE, Henry Joseph, FRINA; General Manager, HM Dockyard, Portsmouth (Deputy Director of Naval Construction), 1967-75; *b* Portsmouth, 2 July 1916; *s* of Joseph Henry and Clarissa Fulthorpe; *m* 1939, Bette May Forshew; two *s* one *d. Educ:* Royal Naval Coll., Greenwich. Principal (Ship) Overseer, Vickers, Barrow-in-Furness, 1943-46; Dep. Manager, HM Dockyard, Malta, 1946-49; Sec., Radiological Defence Panel, 1949-52; Staff Constr, first British atom bomb, Montebello Is, 1952-53; Constr i/c Minesweeper Design, Admty, Bath, 1953-54; Chief Constr, Maintenance, Bath, 1954-56; Dep. Manager, HM Dockyard, Portsmouth, 1956-58; Chief Constructor: HM Dockyard, Singapore, 1958-61; Dockyard Dept, Bath, 1961-63; Asst Dir of Naval Construction, Bath, 1963-64; Production Manager, HM Dockyard, Chatham, 1964-67; Manager, Constructive Dept, HM Dockyard, Portsmouth, 1967. *Recreations:* travel, winemaking, cooking. *Address:* Gerard House, 60 Granada Road, Southsea. *T:* Portsmouth 734876.

FULTON, family name of **Baron Fulton.**

FULTON, Baron, *cr* 1966, of Falmer (Life Peer); **John Scott Fulton,** Kt 1964; Hon. Fellow, Balliol College, Oxford; *b* 27 May 1902; *y s* of the late Principal A. R. Fulton, Dundee; *m* 1939, Jacqueline, *d* of K. E. T. Wilkinson, York; three *s* one *d. Educ:* Dundee High Sch.; St Andrews Univ.; Balliol Coll., Oxford (Exhibitioner). Asst in Logic and Scientific Method, London Sch. of Economics, 1926-28; Fellow, 1928-47, Balliol Coll. Oxford; Tutor in Philosophy, 1928-35; Tutor in Politics, 1935-47; Jowett Lecturer, 1935-38;

Jowett Fellow, 1945-47; Rockefeller Fellow, 1936-37; Faculty Fellow, Nuffield Coll., 1939-47; Principal, University Coll. of Swansea, 1947-59; Vice-Chancellor: University of Wales, 1952-54 and 1958-59; University of Sussex, 1959-67. Chairman: Inter Univ. Council for Higher Educn Overseas, 1964-68; British Council, 1968-71; Cttee on the Civil Service, 1966-68; a Governor of the BBC, 1965-70 (Vice Chm., 1965-67 and 1968-70). Principal and Asst Sec., Mines Dept, 1940-42; Principal Asst Sec. Min. of Fuel and Power, 1942-44. Dir Wales and Mon Industrial Estates Ltd, 1948-54. Chairman: Board for Mining Qualifications, 1950-62; Universities Council for Adult Educ., 1952-55; Council of Nat. Inst. of Adult Educ., 1952-55; Commn on educational requirements of Sierra Leone, 1954; Selection Cttee for Miners' Welfare Nat. Scholarships, 1949-59; Nat. Adv. Coun. on the Training and Supply of Teachers, 1959-63; Univs Central Coun. on Admissions, 1961-64; Commn on Royal Univ. of Malta, 1962-72; Commn on establishment of a second University in Hong Kong, 1962; BBC Liaison Advisory Cttee on Adult Education Programmes, 1962-65; BBC Further Education Adv. Coun. for the UK, 1965; Institute of Development Studies, 1966-67; ITA Adult Educn Adv. Cttee, 1962-65; Coun. of Inst. of Educn, University of London, 1967-71; Coun. of Tavistock Inst. of Human Relations, 1968-78; Manpower Soc., 1973-76. Member: National Reference Tribunal for Coal Industry of Great Britain, 1957-65; Cttee on University Teaching Methods, 1961-64. Pres., Soc. for Research into Higher Education, 1964-67; Pres., Morley College, 1969-. Hon. LLD: Chinese Univ. of Hong Kong, 1964; California, 1966; Yale, 1967; Sussex, 1967; Wales, 1968; Dundee, 1968; Hon. DLitt; Ife, 1967: Royal Univ. of Malta, 1967; Carleton, 1970; DUniv Keel, 1971. *Publications:* (with C. R. Morris) In Defence of Democracy, 1935; various articles and named lectures. *Recreation:* golf. *Address:* Brook House, Thornton Dale, Pickering, N Yorks. *T:* Pickering 74221. *Club:* Athenæum.

FULTON, Hon. Edmund Davie, PC (Canada) 1957; **Hon. Mr Justice Fulton;** Puisne Judge, Supreme Court of British Columbia, since 1973; *b* 10 March 1916; *s* of Frederick John Fulton, KC, and Winifred M. Davie; *m* 1946, Patricia Mary, *d* of J. M. Macrae and Christine Macrae (*née* Carmichael), Winnipeg; three *d. Educ:* St Michael's Sch., Victoria, BC; Kamloops High Sch.; University of British Columbia; St John's Coll., Oxford. BA (BC), BA Oxon (Rhodes Scholar, elected 1936). Admitted to Bar of British Columbia, 1940. Served in Canadian Army Overseas as Company Comdr with Seaforth Highlanders of Canada and as DAAG 1st Canadian Inf. Div., 1940-45, including both Italian and Northwest Europe campaigns (despatches); transferred to R of O with rank of Major, 1945. Practised law with Fulton, Verchere & Rogers, Kamloops, BC, 1945-68, and with Fulton, Cumming, Richards & Co., Vancouver, 1968-73. QC (BC) 1957. Elected to House of Commons of Canada, 1945; re-elected in 1949, 1953, 1957, 1958, 1962, 1965. Mem. Senate, University of British Columbia, 1948-57, 1969-75. Acting Minister of Citizenship and Immigration, June 1957-May 1958; Minister of Justice and Attorney Gen., Canada, June 1957-Aug. 1962; Minister of Public Works, Aug. 1962-April, 1963. Hon. Col, Rocky Mountain Rangers, 1959. Mem. Bar of Ontario. Hon LLD: Ottawa, 1960; Queen's, 1963. *Address:* (business) Court House, Vancouver; (home) 1632 West 40th Avenue, Vancouver, BC, V6M 1V9. *Clubs:* Vancouver, Shaughnessy Golf and Country (Vancouver); Rideau (Ottawa).

FUNG, Hon. Sir Kenneth Ping-Fan, Kt 1971; CBE 1965 (OBE 1958); JP; Chairman, Fung Ping Fan & Co. Ltd, and Chairman or Director of other companies; Director (and Chief Manager, retd), of The Bank of East Asia Ltd, Hong Kong; *b* 28 May 1911; *yr s* of late Fung Ping Shan, JP; *m* 1933, Ivy (*née* Kan) Shiu-Han, OBE, JP, *d* of late Kan Tong-Po, JP; four *s* one *d. Educ:* Government Vernacular Sch.; Sch. of Chinese Studies, Univ. of Hong Kong. Unofficial Mem., Urban Council, 1951-60; Unofficial MLC, 1959-65, MEC, 1962-72; Life Mem., Court of Univ. of Hong Kong; Council of Chinese Univ. of Hong Kong; Fourth Pan-Pacific Rehabilitation Conf.; Pres., Chm., etc. of numerous social organisations, both present and past. Member: Program for Harvard and East Asia (Mem. Internat. Org. Cttee); Rotary Internat. (Paul Harris Fellow). Comr St John Ambulance Bde (first Chinese to serve), 1953-58; first Chinese Hon. ADC to 4 successive Governors and Officers Admin. Govt (rep. StJAB). JP Hong Kong, 1952; KStJ 1958. Hon. degrees: LLD, Chinese Univ. of Hong Kong, 1968; DSocSc, Univ. of Hong Kong, 1969. Founder Mem., Royal Asiatic Soc.; Mem. other Socs and Assocs. Order of the Sacred Treasure (Japan), 1969. *Recreations:* racing, golf, swimming. *Address:* (home) 14 South Bay Road, Hong Kong. *T:* 92514; (office) Fung Ping Fan & Co. Ltd, 2705-2715 Connaught Centre, Hong Kong. *T:* 220311. *Clubs:* Royal Hongkong Jockey (Steward), Royal Hongkong Golf, Royal Hongkong Yacht, Hongkong Polo Assoc., Sports, Hongkong Country, Hongkong, Shek O Country, Hongkong Squash (Life Mem.), Chinese Recreation (Hon. Pres.), American, Japanese (Pres.), CASAM, Hongkong Automobile Assoc., Rotary, Clear Water Bay Golf and Country (Chm. Organizing Cttee) (all in Hong Kong); Knickerbocker, Sky Explorers', Amer. Photographic Soc., Bohemian (all in New York, USA); Hakone Country, Toride Internat. Golf, Hodogaya (Japan).

FUNSTON, G(eorge) Keith; *b* Waterloo, Iowa, USA, 12 Oct. 1910; *s* of George Edwin and Genevieve (Keith) Funston; *m* 1939, Elizabeth Kennedy; one *s* two *d. Educ:* Trinity Coll., Hartford, Conn; Harvard. AB, Trinity Coll., 1932; MBA (*cum laude*), Harvard, 1934. Mem. Research Staff, Harvard Business Sch., 1934-35; Asst to VP Sales, then Asst to Treas., American Radiator & Standard Sanitary, 1935-40; Dir, Purchases & Supplies, Sylvania

Electronics, 1940-44; Special Asst to Chm., War Production Bd, 1941-44; Lt-Comdr, US Navy, 1944-46; Pres., Trinity Coll., Hartford, 1944-51; Pres. and Governor, New York Stock Exchange, 1951-67. Chm., Olin Corp., 1967-72; Director: IBM; Metropolitan Life; Republic Steel; AVCO Corp.; Illinois Central Industries; Chemical Bank; Putnam Trust; Hartford Steam Boiler & Insurance Co.; Winn-Dixie Stores; Paul Revere Investors. Holds numerous hon. doctorates. *Recreations:* riding, reading, ski-ing, tennis. *Address:* (home) 74 Vineyard Lane, Greenwich, Conn 06830, USA. *T:* Townsend 9-5524. *Clubs:* Round Hill (Greenwich, Conn.); University, The Century Assoc., The Links, (New York).

FÜRER-HAIMENDORF, Prof. Christoph von, DPhil Vienna; Emeritus Professor and Hon. Fellow, School of Oriental and African Studies, University of London, since 1976; *b* 27 July 1909; *s* of Rudolf Fürer von Haimendorf und Wolkersdorf; *m* 1938, Elizabeth Barnardo; one *s. Educ:* Theresianische Akademie, Vienna. Asst Lecturer, Vienna Univ., 1931-34; Rockefeller Foundation Fellowship, 1935-37; Lecturer, Vienna University, 1938; Anthropological Fieldwork in Hyderabad and Orissa, 1939-43; Special Officer Subansiri, External Affairs Dept, Govt of India, 1944-45; Adviser to HEH the Nizam's Govt and Prof. of Anthropology in the Osmania Univ., 1945-49; Reader in Anthropology with special reference to India, University of London, 1949-51; Prof. of Asian Anthropology, School of Oriental and African Studies, 1951-76 (Dean of Sch., 1969-74, acting Director, 1974-75). Anthropological Research: in India and Nepal, 1953; in Nepal, 1957, 1962, 1966, 1972, 1976, 1981; in the Philippines, 1968; in India, 1970, 1976-81. Munro Lectr, Edinburgh Univ., 1959; Visiting Prof., Colegio de Mexico, 1964, 1966. Pres., Royal Anthropological Inst., 1975-77. Corresponding Member: Austrian Academy of Science, 1964; Anthropological Soc. of Vienna, 1970. Rivers Memorial Medal of Royal Anthropological Institute, 1949; S. C. Roy Gold Medal, Asiatic Soc., Calcutta, 1964; Sir Percy Sykes Memorial Medal, Royal Central Asian Soc., 1965; King Birendra Prize, Royal Nepal Acad., 1976; Annandale Medal, Asiatic Soc. of Bengal, 1979. Austrian Order of Merit for Art and Science, 1982. *Publications:* The Naked Nagas, 1939; The Chenchus, 1943; The Reddis of the Bison Hills, 1945; The Raj Gonds of Adilabad, 1948; Himalayan Barbary, 1955; The Apa Tanis, 1962; (joint author) Mount Everest, 1963; The Sherpas of Nepal, 1964; (ed and jt author) Caste and Kin in Nepal, India and Ceylon, 1966; Morals and Merit, 1967; The Konyak Nagas, 1969; (ed and jt author) Peoples of the Earth, vol. 12: The Indian Sub-continent, 1973; (ed and jt author) Contributions to the Anthropology of Nepal, 1974; Himalayan Traders, 1975; Return to the Naked Nagas, 1976; The Gonds of Andhra Pradesh, 1979; A Himalayan Tribe, 1980; (ed and jt author) Asian Highland Societies, 1981; Highlanders of Arunathal Pradesh, 1982; Tribes of India, 1982; articles in Journal of Royal Anthropological Inst., Man, Anthropos, Geographical Jl, Man in India. *Recreation:* music. *Address:* 32 Clarendon Road, W11. *T:* 01-727 4520, 01-637 2388.

FURLONG, Mrs Monica; *b* 17 Jan. 1930; *d* of Alfred Gordon Furlong and Freda Simpson; *m* 1953, William John Knights (marr. diss. 1977); one *s* one *d. Educ:* Harrow County Girls' Sch.; University College London. Truth, Spectator, Guardian, 1956-61; Daily Mail, 1961-68; Producer, BBC, 1974-78. Moderator, Movement for the Ordination of Women, 1982-. *Publications:* Travelling In, 1971; Contemplating Now, 1971; God's A Good Man (poems), 1974; Puritan's Progress, 1975; Christian Uncertainties, 1975; The Cat's Eye (novel), 1976; Merton (biography), 1980. *Recreation:* the telephone. *Address:* c/o Anthony Sheil Associates, 2/3 Morwell Street, WC1. *T:* 01-636 2901. *Club:* Society of Authors.

FURLONG, Hon. Robert Stafford, MBE (mil.) 1945; Chief Justice of Newfoundland, 1959-79; *b* 9 Dec. 1904; *o s* of Martin Williams Furlong, KC, and Mary Furlong (*née* McGrath). *Educ:* St Bonaventure's Coll., St John's, Newfoundland. Called to the Bar, 1926, appointed KC 1944. Temp. Actg Lt-Comdr (S) RNVR. OStJ 1937; Knight of St George Federal 1958. *Recreations:* golf and motoring. *Address:* 8 Winter Avenue, St John's, Newfoundland. *T:* (709) 726-7228. *Clubs:* Naval (London); Bally Haly Golf and Country, Crow's Nest (all in St John's).

FURLONG, Ronald (John), FRCS; Orthopædic Surgeon to St Thomas' Hospital since 1946; Hon. Consulting Orthopædic Surgeon to the Army since 1951; *b* 3 March 1909; *s* of Frank Owen Furlong and Elsie Muriel Taffs, Woolwich; *m* 1st, 1936, Elva Mary Ruth Lefeaux (marr. diss., 1947); one *s* three *d*; 2nd, 1948, Nora Christine Pattinson (marr. diss. 1969); one *d*; 3rd, 1970, Eileen Mary Watford. *Educ:* Eltham Coll.; St Thomas's Hosp. MB, BS London 1931; MRCS, LRCP, 1931; FRCS 1934. Served with Royal Army Medical Corps, 1941-46. Home Commands, North Africa and Italy; Brigadier, Consulting Orthopædic Surgeon to the Army, 1946. *Publications:* Injuries of the Hand, 1957; (trans.) Pauwel's Atlas of the Biomechanics of the Normal and Diseased Hip, 1978; (trans.) Pauwel's Biomechanics of the Locomotor Apparatus, 1980. *Recreations:* reading, history and archæology. *Address:* 149 Harley Street, W1. *T:* 01-935 4444. *Club:* Athenæum.

FURLONGE, Sir Geoffrey (Warren), KBE 1960 (OBE 1942); CMG 1951; *b* 16 Oct. 1903; *s* of Robert Shekleton Furlonge and Agnes Mary (*née* Hatch); *m* 1952, Anne (*d* 1975), *d* of late E. A. Goldsack; *m* 1975, Vera Kathleen, widow of late Major Guy Farquhar. *Educ:* St Paul's Sch.; Emmanuel Coll., Cambridge. Entered Levant Consular Service, 1926; served at Casablanca, 1928-31; Jedda, 1931-34; Beirut, 1934-46; Political Officer with HM Forces in the Levant States, 1941-46. At Imperial Defence Coll., 1947; served in FO,

1948 (Head of Commonwealth Liaison Dept, 1948-50, Head of Eastern Dept, 1950-51); Minister (later Ambassador) to Jordan, 1952-54; Minister to Bulgaria, 1954-56; Ambassador to Ethiopia, 1956-59. *Publications:* The Lands of Barbary, 1966; Palestine is my Country, 1969. *Address:* 7 Heathfield Close, Midhurst, West Sussex GU29 9PS.

FURLONGER, Robert William, CB 1981; retired public servant, Australia; *b* 29 April 1921; *s* of George William Furlonger and Germaine Rose Furlonger; *m* 1944, Verna Hope Lewis; three *s* one *d*. *Educ:* Sydney High Sch.; Sydney Univ. (BA). Served War, AMF, 1941-45. Australian Dept of External (later Foreign) Affairs, 1945-69 and 1972-77 (IDC, 1960; Dir, Jt Intell. Org., Dept of Def., 1960-72); appointments included: High Comr, Nigeria, 1961; Aust. Perm. Rep. to the European Office of the UN, 1961-64; Minister, Aust. Embassy, Washington, 1965-69; Ambassador to Indonesia, 1972-74, and to Austria, Hungary and Czechoslovakia, 1975-77; Dir-Gen., Office of National Assessments, Canberra, 1977-81. *Recreations:* golf, cricket, music. *Address:* 12 Norman Street, Deakin, ACT 2600, Australia. *T:* 813656. *Clubs:* Commonwealth (Canberra); Royal Canberra Golf.

FURMSTON, Bentley Edwin, FRICS; Director of Overseas Surveys and Survey Adviser, Ministry of Overseas Development, since 1980; *b* 7 Oct. 1931; *s* of Rev. Edward Bentley Furmston and Mary Furmston (*née* Bennett); *m* 1957, Margaret (*née* Jackson); two *s* one *d*. *Educ:* The Nelson Sch., Wigton, Cumbria; Victoria Univ., Manchester (BSc Mathematics). Entered Civil Service as Surveyor, Directorate of Overseas Surveys, 1953, with service in Gambia, Swaziland, Basutoland, N Rhodesia; Sen. Surveyor, N Rhodesia, 1960; Sen. Computer, DOS, 1963; seconded to Govt of Malawi as Dep. Commissioner of Surveys, 1965; Principal Survey Officer, DOS, 1968: Overseas Supervisor, Sch. of Military Survey; Regional Survey Officer, W Africa; Asst Director (Survey), 1971; Asst Dir (Cartography), Ordnance Survey, 1973; Dep. Dir, Field Survey, Ordnance Survey, 1974; Dep. Dir (Survey), DOS, 1977. *Publications:* contribs to technical jls. *Recreations:* reading, gardening, hill walking, climbing. *Address:* 7 Wembury Park, Newchapel, Lingfield, Surrey RH7 6HH. *T:* Lingfield 832373.

FURNEAUX, Robin; *see* Birkenhead, 3rd Earl of.

FURNELL, Very Rev. Raymond; Provost, St Edmundsbury Cathedral, since 1981; *b* 18 May 1935; *s* of Albert George Edward and Hetty Violet Jane Furnell; *m* 1967, Sherril Whitcomb; one *s* three *d*. *Educ:* Hinchley Wood School, Surrey; Brasted Place Theological Coll.; Lincoln Theol Coll. Thomas Meadows & Co. Ltd, 1951; RAF, 1953; Lummus Co. Ltd, 1955; Geo. Wimpey & Co. Ltd, 1960; Brasted Place, 1961; Lincoln Theol Coll., 1963; Curate, St Luke's, Cannock, 1965; Vicar, St James the Great, Clayton, 1969; Rector, Hanley Team Ministry and RD, Stoke North, 1975. *Recreations:* music, drama. *Address:* Provost's House, Bury St Edmunds, Suffolk IP33 1RS.

FURNER, Air Vice-Marshal Derek Jack, CBE 1973 (OBE 1963); DFC 1943; AFC 1954; *b* 14 Nov. 1921; *s* of Vivian J. Furner; *m* 1948, Patricia Donnelly; three *s*. *Educ:* Westcliff High Sch., Essex. Joined RAF, 1941; commnd as navigator, 1942; Bomber Comd (2 tours), 1942-44; Transport Comd, Far East, 1945-47; Navigation Instructor, 1948-50; trials flying, Boscombe Down, 1951-53 and Wright-Patterson, Ohio, 1953-56; Air Min., 1957; OC Ops Wing, RAF Waddington, 1958-60; Planning Staff, HQ Bomber Comd, 1961-63 and SHAPE, Paris, 1964-65; Dep. Dir Manning, MoD (Air), 1966-67; OC RAF Scampton, 1968; AOC Central Reconnaissance Estab., 1969-70; Sec., Internat. Mil. Staff, NATO, Brussels, 1970-73; Asst Air Secretary, 1973-75. Dir, 1976, Gen. Manager, 1977-81, Harlequin Wallcoverings. FIPM 1975; MBIM 1975. *Recreations:* mathematical problems, music. *Address:* 2 High Trees, Stock, Essex. *T:* Stock 840753. *Club:* Royal Air Force.

FURNESS, family name of Viscount Furness.

FURNESS, 2nd Viscount, *cr* 1918; **William Anthony Furness;** Baron Furness, *cr* 1910, of Grantley; *b* 31 March 1929; *s* of 1st Viscount and Thelma (*d* 1970), *d* of late Harry Hays Morgan, American Consul-Gen. at Buenos Aires; *S* father, 1940. *Educ:* Downside; USA. Served as Guardsman, Welsh Guards (invalided, 1947). Delegate to Inter-Parliamentary Union Conferences, Washington, 1953, Vienna, 1954, Helsinki, 1955, Warsaw, 1959, Brussels, 1961, Belgrade, 1963. Mem. Council, Hansard Soc. for Parliamentary Govt, 1955-67. Founder Chm., Anglo-Mongolian Soc., 1963. Sovereign Military Order of Malta: joined 1954; Sec., Assoc. of Brit. Members, 1956-65, Sec.-Gen. 1965-78; Mem. Sovereign Council, 1960-62; Mem. Board of Auditors, 1979-80; Grand Officer of Merit, 1965; Kt of Justice, 1977. Grand Officer, Order of Merit, Italy, 1961; KStJ 1971 (CStJ 1964); KCSG 1966. *Heir:* none. *Address:* c/o Midland Bank Ltd, 69 Pall Mall, SW1. *Clubs:* Boodle's, Carlton; Travellers' (Paris).

FURNESS, Alan Edwin; HM Diplomatic Service; Counsellor, Warsaw, since 1982; *b* 6 June 1937; *s* of Edwin Furness and Marion Furness (*née* Senton); *m* 1971, Aline Elizabeth Janine Barrett; two *s*. *Educ:* Eltham Coll.; Jesus Coll., Cambridge (BA, MA). Commonwealth Relations Office, 1961; Private Sec. to Parliamentary Under-Secretary of State, 1961-62; Third, later Second Secretary, British High Commn, New Delhi, 1962-66; First Secretary, DSAO (later FCO), 1966-69; First Sec., UK Delegn to European Communities, Brussels, 1969-72; First Sec. and Head of Chancery, Dakar, 1972-75; First Sec.,

FCO, 1975-78; Counsellor and Head of Chancery, Jakarta, 1978-81. *Recreations:* music, literature, gardening. *Address:* c/o Foreign and Commonwealth Office, SW1. *T:* 01-233 3000. *Club:* United Oxford & Cambridge University.

FURNESS, Robin; *see* Furness, Sir S. R.

FURNESS, Sir Stephen (Roberts), 3rd Bt *cr* 1913; farmer and sporting/landscape artist (as Robin Furness); *b* 10 Oct. 1933; *e s* of Sir Christopher Furness, 2nd Bt, and of Flower, Lady Furness, OBE, *d* of late Col G. C. Roberts; *S* father, 1974; *m* 1961, Mary, *e d* of J. F. Cann, Cullompton, Devon; one *s* one *d*. *Educ:* Charterhouse. Entered RN, 1952; Observer, Fleet Air Arm, 1957; retired list, 1962. NCA, Newton Rigg Farm Inst., 1964. Member: Armed Forces Art Soc.; Darlington Art Soc. Jt MFH, Bedale Hunt, 1979-. *Recreations:* looking at paintings, foxhunting, racing. *Heir: s* Michael Fitzroy Roberts Furness, *b* 12 Oct. 1962. *Address:* Stanhow Farm, Great Langton, near Northallerton, Yorks DL7 0TJ. *T:* Northallerton 748614.

FURNISS, Air Vice-Marshal Peter, DFC 1944; TD 1964; Director of Legal Services, RAF, 1978-82; *b* 16 July 1919; *s* of John and Mary Furniss; *m* 1954, Denise Cotet; one *s* two *d*. *Educ:* Sedbergh School. Commissioned 1st Bn The Liverpool Scottish TA, Queen's Own Cameron Highlanders, 1939; seconded to RAF, 1942; Comd No 73 Fighter Sqdn, 1945-46; demobilised 1946; admitted as Solicitor, 1948; commissioned in Legal Branch, RAF, 1950; Director of Legal Services: HQ Air Forces Middle East, Aden, 1961-63; HQ Far East Air Force, Singapore, 1969-71; HQ RAF Germany, 1973-74; Dep. Dir of Legal Services (RAF), 1975-78. *Recreations:* shooting, gardening, golf. *Address:* 18 Sevington Park, Loose, Maidstone, Kent ME15 9SB. *T:* Maidstone 44620. *Club:* Royal Air Force.

FURNIVAL JONES, Sir (Edward) Martin, Kt 1967; CBE 1957; *b* 7 May 1912; *s* of Edward Furnival Jones, FCA; *m* 1955, Elizabeth Margaret, *d* of Bartholomew Snowball, BSc, AMIEE; one *d*. *Educ:* Highgate Sch.; Gonville and Caius Coll., Cambridge (exhibitioner). MA 1938. Admitted a Solicitor, 1937. Served War of 1939-45: General Staff Officer at Supreme Headquarters, Allied Expeditionary Force, and War Office (despatches, American Bronze Star Medal). Chm. of Bd, Frensham Heights, 1973-76 (Pres. 1977). *Recreation:* birdwatching. *Address:* The Little House, Oakley, Bedford. *T:* Oakley 2181. *Club:* United Oxford & Cambridge University.

FURNIVALL, Barony *cr* 1295; in abeyance. *Co-heiresses:* Hon. Rosamond Mary Dent (Sister Ancilla, OSB); *b* 3 June 1933; Hon. Patricia Mary Dent [*b* 4 April 1935; *m* 1st, 1956, Captain Thomas Hornsby (marr. diss., 1963; he *d* 1967); one *s* one *d*; 2nd, 1970, Roger Thomas John Bence; one *s* one *d*].

FURNIVALL, Maj.-Gen. Lewis Trevor, CB 1964; DSO 1943; Dir of Medical Services, Far East Land Forces, 1965-66; retired 1967; *b* 6 Sept. 1907; *er s* of late Lt-Col C. H. Furnivall, CMG, and late Mrs D. Furnivall (*née* Macbean); *m* 1941, Audrey Elizabeth Furnivall (*née* Gibbins); three *s* one *d*. *Educ:* Blundell's Sch.; St Mary's Hosp., London. MRCS, LRCP 1931; House Surg., Worcester Gen. Infirmary, 1931; Lieut, RAMC 1931; NW Frontier of India (Mohmand), 1933 (medal and clasp); Capt. 1934; Major 1941; Lieut-Col 1947; Col 1953; Brig. 1960; Maj.-Gen. 1961. Service in India, 1932-38; DADMS, 1939-. War Service, 1939-45 (UK, MELF, Italy, France, Germany); ADMS, 1944-48 (despatches, 1946); DDMS, HQ, BAOR, 1949-52; ADMS, HQ, Land Forces, Hong Kong, 1953-54; ADMS, HQ, Northumbrian Dist, 1955-57; Dep. Chief Med. Officer, SHAPE, 1957-60; Inspector of Training, Army Med. Services, 1960; Deputy Dir Medical Services, Eastern Command, 1961-65. QHS 1961-67. La Médaille d'Honneur du Service de Santé, 1960. *Address:* Woodside, 80 Lynch Road, Farnham, Surrey. *T:* Farnham 5771.

FURSDON, Maj.-Gen. Francis William Edward, CB 1980; MBE (Gallantry) 1958; KStJ 1980; Defence and Military Correspondent, The Daily Telegraph, since 1980; Director of Ceremonies, Order of St John, since 1980; *b* 10 May 1925; *s* of late G. E. S. Fursdon and of Mrs Fursdon; *m* 1950, Joan Rosemary (*née* Worssam); one *s* one *d*. *Educ:* Westminster Sch. MLitt (Aberdeen) 1978; DLitt (Leiden) 1979. Passed AMIMechE; FBIM. Enlisted RE, 1942; RE Course, Birmingham Univ., 1943; in ranks until commnd, 1945; 1945-67: Royal W Afr. Frontier Force, India, Burma and Gold Coast; Student RMCS; staff and regtl duty, UK, Singapore, Canal Zone and Cyprus; Staff Coll.; DAA&QMG 19 Inf. Bde, UK and Port Said; GSO2 RE Sch. of Inf.; JSSC; OC 34 Indep. Fd Sqdn, E Africa and Kuwait; Instr, Staff Coll., Camberley; 2 i/c 38 Engr Regt; Admin. Staff Coll., Henley; CO 25 Engr Regt, BAOR, 1967-69; AA&QMG HQ Land Forces, Gulf, 1970-71; Dep. Comd and COS Land Forces, Gulf, 1971; Col Q (Qtg) HQ BAOR, 1972-73; Service Fellow, Aberdeen Univ., 1974; Dir of Def. Policy (Europe and NATO), MoD, 1974-77; Dir, Military Assistance Office, MoD, 1977-80; Mil. Adv. to Governor of Rhodesia, and later Senior British Officer, Zimbabwe, 1980, retired 1980. *Publications:* Grains of Sand, 1971; There are no Frontiers, 1973; The European Defence Community: a History, 1980. *Recreations:* skiing, tennis, photography (IAC Internat. Award, 1967), gardening, travel. *Address:* c/o National Westminster Bank Ltd, 1 St James's Square, SW1Y 4JX. *Clubs:* Army and Navy, St John House, Special Forces.

FURTADO, Robert Audley, CB 1970; Special Commissioner, 1946-77, Presiding Commissioner, 1963-77; *b* 20 August 1912; *yr s* of Montague C.

Furtado; *m* 1945, Marcelle Elizabeth, *d* of W. Randall Whitteridge; one *s* one *d*. *Educ:* Whitgift Sch.; University Coll., London. LLB London Univ., 1933; called to Bar, Gray's Inn, 1934. Served War of 1939-45, in Army in India and Burma (Despatches); demobilised rank of Lieut-Col, 1945. *Recreation:* bricolage. *Address:* Hillfold, Langton Herring, Dorset. *T:* Abbotsbury 502; 39 Strand Court, Topsham, Devon.

See also *J. E. Pater, Prof. David Whitteridge and Sir Gordon Whitteridge.*

FYFE, Prof. William Sefton, FRS 1969; Chairman, Department of Geology, and Professor of Geology, University of Western Ontario, since 1972; *b* 4 June 1927; *s* of Colin and Isabella Fyfe; *m* 1968; two *s* one *d*. *Educ:* Otago Univ., New Zealand. BSc 1948, MSc 1949, PhD 1952; FRSC 1980. Univ. of California, Berkeley, Calif: Lecturer in Chemistry, 1952, Reader, 1958; Prof. of Geology, 1959; Royal Soc. Res. Prof. (Geochemistry), Univ. of Manchester, 1967-72. Hon. Fellow, Geological Soc. Amer.; Corresp. Mem., Brazilian Acad. of Science. Mineralogical Soc. of Amer. Award, 1964. *Publications:* Metamorphic Reactions and Metamorphic Facies, 1958; The Geochemistry of Solids, 1964; Fluids in the Earth's Crust, 1978; also numerous scientific papers. *Address:* Department of Geology, University of Western Ontario, London, Ontario N6A 5B7, Canada.

FYJIS-WALKER, Richard Alwyne, CMG 1980; CVO 1976; HM Diplomatic Service; Ambassador to Sudan, since 1979; *b* 19 June 1927; *s* of Harold and Marion Fyjis-Walker; *m* 1st, 1951, Barbara Graham-Watson (marr. diss.); one *s*; 2nd, 1972, Gabrielle Josefi; one *s*. *Educ:* Bradfield Coll.; Magdalene Coll., Cambridge (BA). Army (KRRC); 1945-48. Joined Foreign (subseq. Diplomatic) Service, 1955; served: Amman, 1956; FO, 1957-61; Paris, 1961-63; Cairo, 1963-65; FCO, 1966-71; Counsellor, 1970; Ankara, 1971-74; Counsellor (Information), Washington, 1974-78; Counsellor, UK Mission to UN, NY, 1978-79. *Address:* c/o Foreign and Commonwealth Office, SW1.

FYNN, Sir Basil Mortimer L.; *see* Lindsay-Fynn.

G

GABB, (William) Harry, CVO 1974 (MVO 1961); DMus (Lambeth), 1974; Organist, Choirmaster and Composer at HM Chapels Royal, 1953-Easter 1974; Sub-Organist, St Paul's Cathedral, London, 1946-Easter 1974; Professor and Examiner of Organ Playing at the Trinity College of Music, London; Special Commissioner for Royal School of Church Music; Member, Council of the Royal College of Organists; Adjudicator and Recitalist; *b* 5 April 1909; *m* 1936, Helen Burnaford Mutton; one *s*. *Educ:* Scholarship at Royal Coll. of Music for Organ and Composition, ARCO 1928; FRCO 1930; ARCM Solo Organ, 1931; Organist, St Jude's, West Norwood, 1925; Organist and Choirmaster, Christ Church, Gypsy Hill, 1928; Sub-Organist, Exeter Cathedral, also Organist, Church of St Leonard's, Exeter and Heavitree Parish Church, 1929-37; Organist and Master of the Choristers, Llandaff Cathedral, 1937; Lectr, St Michael's Theological Coll., Llandaff; Royal Armoured Corps, War of 1939-45. Returned from Army to Llandaff, Jan. 1946. Played organ at the Coronation of Elizabeth II and at many Royal Weddings and Baptisms. Hon. FTCL, 1954. *Address:* St Lawrence Cottage, Bagshot Road, Chobham, Woking, Surrey. *T:* Chobham 7879.

GADD, Maj.-Gen. Alfred Lockwood, (David), CBE 1962 (OBE 1955); *b* 10 July 1912; *s* of late Charles A. Gadd; *m* 1st, 1936, Gwenrudd Eluned (*d* 1965), *d* of late Morgan Edwards; one *s* one *d*; 2nd, 1965, Anna Louisa Margaret (*d* 1977), *d* of late Carl-August Koehler; 3rd, 1980, Agnes Muriel, *widow* of William E. McKenzie-Hill. *Educ:* Harvey Grammar Sch., Folkestone; Peterhouse, Cambridge (Open Scholar, MA). Asst Master: Bedford Sch., 1934-35; King's Sch., Rochester, 1935-39; Marlborough Coll., 1939-40. Commissioned Intelligence Corps, 1941; GSO3 War Office, 1942; Major, 1942; Lt-Col 1944; Chief Instructor 5 Formation Coll., 1945; Comdt No 1 Army Coll., 1946; Chief Education Officer, Far ELF, 1947; various Education Staff appts, 1950-62; Dir of Army Education, WO, 1962-65. *Publications:* (as David Gadd): Georgian Summer: the story of 18th century Bath, 1971; The Loving Friends: a portrait of Bloomsbury, 1974. *Recreations:* reading and writing. *Address:* Flete, Ermington, Ivybridge, Devon PL21 9NZ. *T:* Holbeton 425 and 416.

GADD, David; *see* Gadd, A. L.

GADD, John; Chairman, North Thames Gas, since 1977; *b* 9 June 1925; *s* of late George Gadd and of Winifred Gadd, Dunstable, Bedfordshire; *m* 1959, Nancy Jean, *d* of late Pryce Davies, Henley-on-Thames. *Educ:* Cedars Sch., Leighton Buzzard; Cambridgeshire Technical Coll. Joined Gas Industry, 1941. Served War, RNVR, 1943-46. Numerous engineering appts with Southern Gas Bd; attended Administrative Staff Coll., Henley-on-Thames, 1961; Personnel Manager, Southern Gas Bd, 1962; Dep. Chm., Southern Gas Bd, 1969; Chm., Eastern Region, British Gas Corp., 1973. *Recreation:* gardening.

GADD, (John) Staffan; Chief Executive, since 1980, and Chairman, since 1982, Samuel Montagu & Co. Ltd; *b* 30 Sept. 1934; *s* of John Gadd and Ulla Olivecrona; *m* 1958, Margaretha Löfborg; one *s* one *d*. *Educ:* Stockholm Sch. of Econs. MBA. Sec., Confedn of Swedish Industries, 1958-61; Skandinaviska Banken, Stockholm, 1961-69 (London Rep., 1964-67); Dep. Man. Dir, Scandinavian Bank Ltd, London, 1969-71, Chief Exec. and Man. Dir, 1971-80. Dir, Boliden Intertrade AB, Stockholm, 1977-. *Recreations:* shooting, ski-ing. *Address:* Locks Manor, Hurstpierpoint, West Sussex BN6 9JZ; 8 South Eaton Place, SW1W 9JA.

GADDES, (John) Gordon; Director General, British Electrical and Allied Manufacturers' Association, since 1982; *b* 22 May 1936; *s* of late James Graham Moscrop Gaddes and of Irene Gaddes (*née* Murray; who married E. O. Kine); *m* 1958, Pamela Jean (*née* Marchbank); one *s* one *d*. *Educ:* Carres Grammar Sch., Sleaford; Selwyn Coll., Cambridge (MA Hons Geography); London Univ. (BScEcon Hons). Joint Services Sch. of Languages, Russian Translator in RAF, 1955-57. Asst Lectr in Business Studies, Peterborough Technical Coll., 1960-64; Lectr in Business Studies, later Head of Business Studies, then Vice-Principal, Dacorum Coll. of Further Educn, Hemel Hempstead, 1964-69; Head of Export Services: British Standards Instn, 1969-72; Quality Assurance Dept, 1972-73; Dir, BSI Hemel Hempstead Centre, 1973-77; Commercial Dir, BSI, 1977-81; Dir, Information, Marketing and Resources, BSI, 1981-82. Secretary, BSI Quality Assurance Council, 1976-80; Member: Council, CBI, 1982-; Elec. Engrg EDC; Council, Elec. Res. Assoc. Ltd; Council, British Elec. Approvals Bd. Project Leader for BNEC project in Hong Kong, 1970; BSI Assessor on Council of Agrément Bd, 1972-80; (first) Chm., British Approvals Service for Electric Cables (BASEC), 1973-74; Project Leader for ISO/UNESCO inf. network study, 1974-75; UK Rep., ORGALIME. Formerly: Dir, BASEC, BEAB; Treas., Nat. Council for Quality and Reliability; Member: Adv. Council for Calibration and Measurement; Internat. Standardisation Org. Cttees; consultant to UNIDO. Councillor, Hemel Hempstead Bor. Council, 1968-71; Leader of Council and Labour Gp, 1972-74. Left Labour Party, 1976; Founder Mem., SDP. *Publications:* papers in range of jls and proc., eg Amer. Soc. for Quality Control, Instn of Gas Engrs, BSI News, Business Weekly, Business Educn, Europe Select Rev. *Recreations:* squash, swimming. *Address:* British Electrical and Allied Manufacturers' Association, Leicester House, 8 Leicester Street, WC2H 7BN. *T:* 01-437 0678. *Club:* United Oxford & Cambridge University.

GADSBY, Gordon Neville, CB 1972; *b* 29 Jan. 1914; *s* of William George and Margaret Sarah Gadsby; *m* 1938, Jeanne (*née* Harris); two *s* one *d*. *Educ:* King Edward VI Sch., Stratford-upon-Avon; University of Birmingham. BSc 1935, DipEd 1937, Cadbury Prizeman 1937, Birmingham; FRSC, CChem. Princ. Lectr, RMCS, 1946-51; Supt, Army Operational Research Gp, 1951-55; Dep. Sci. Adviser to Army Coun., 1955-59; idc 1960; Dir of Army Operational Science and Research, 1961; Dir, Army Operational Res. Estab., 1961-64; Dir of Biol. and Chem. Defence, MoD, 1965-67; Dep. Chief Scientist (Army), MoD, 1967-68; Dir, Chemical Defence Estabt, Porton, Wilts, 1968-72; Minister, Defence R&D, British Embassy, Washington, 1972-75, retired. *Publications:* Lubrication, 1949; An Introduction to Plastics, 1950. *Recreations:* oil painting, photography. *Address:* Beech Gate, Hurdle Way, Compton Down, Winchester, Hants SO21 2AN. *T:* Twyford (Hants) 713878.

GADSDEN, Sir Peter (Drury Haggerston) GBE 1979; MA; FEng; Lord Mayor of London for 1979-80; Company Director; Underwriting Member of Lloyd's; Mineral Marketing Consultant since 1969; *b* Canada, 28 June 1929; *er s* of late Basil Claude Gadsden, ACT, ThL, and late Mabel Florence Gadsden (*née* Drury); *m* 1955, Belinda Ann, *e d* of late Captain Sir (Hugh) Carnaby de Marie Haggerston, 11th Bt; four *d*. *Educ:* Rockport, Belfast; The Elms, Colwall; Wrekin Coll., Wellington; Jesus Coll., Cambridge (MA). 2nd Lieut King's Shropshire LI, attached Oxf. and Bucks LI and Durham LI, Germany, 1948-49; Man. Dir, London subsid. of Australian Mineral Sands Producer, 1964-70; Marketing Economist (Mineral Sands) to UN Industrial Development Organisation, 1969; pt-time Mem., Crown Agents for Oversea Govts and Admins, and Crown Agents Hldg and Realisation Bd, 1981-. Chm., Executive Travelair Ltd, 1980-; Director: City of London (Arizona) Corp., 1970-; Guthrie Corp. Ltd, 1964-; Guthrie & Co. (UK) Ltd, 1970-74; Ellingham Estate Ltd, 1974-; LRC Int. plc, 1978-; LRC (Malaysia) Sdn Bhd, 1981-; Inchcape International Trading Ltd, 1981-; Provident Assoc. for Med. Care, (PPP), 1981-; Beam Components, 1981-; Sylvan Ginsbury (UK), 1981-. Dir, Clothworkers' Foundn, 1978-; Hon. Mem. London Metal Exchange. President: Nat. Assoc. of Charcoal Manufacturers, 1970-; Embankment Rifle Club, 1975-; Leukaemia Res. Fund, City of London Br., 1975-; Fishmongers' and Poulterers' Instn, 1979-; Metropolitan Soc. for the Blind; Council, London World Trade Centre Assoc., 1980-; St John Ambulance (Eastern Area). Sheriff London, 1970-71; Common Councilman (Cripplegate Within and Without), 1969-71; Alderman, City of London (Ward of Farringdon Without), 1971-; HM Lieutenant, City of London, 1979-; Liveryman: Clothworkers' Co. (Court), 1965- (Warden 1981-83); Plaisterers' Co. (Hon.), 1975-; Marketors Co. (Hon.), 1978-; Corp. Sons of the Clergy (Court), 1979-; Hon. Freeman, Actuaries' Co., 1981-; Master, Cripplegate Ward Club, 1982-83; Member: Guild of Freemen (Court); Royal Soc. of St George (City of London Br.); Council, Britain Australia Soc. (Chm. Exec. Cttee). Vice-President: Sir Robert Menzies Meml Trust; Shropshire Soc. in London. Governor: Lady Eleanor Holles Sch., 1968-; Imperial College of Science and Technology, 1981-. Fellowship of Engrg Distinction Lectr, 1980. Trustee: Chichester Festival Theatre, 1978-; Mary Rose Develt Trust, 1980-; Pres.,

Ironbridge Forge Museum Devlt Trust, 1981–; Mem., Management Council, Shakespeare Theatre Trust, 1979–; Patron, St Bart's Music Trust, 1978–. JP, City of London, 1971 (Inner London Area of Greater London, 1969–71). Hon. FInstM, 1976; FIMM 1979 (Mem. Council); CEng 1979, FEng 1980. Mem. and Hon. Mem. Court, HAC. KStJ 1980 (OStJ 1977). Officier de l'Etoile Equatoriale de la République Gabonaise, 1970. Hon. DSc 1979. *Publications:* articles in: InstMM Transactions, 1971; RSM Jl, 1979; Textile Institute and Industry, 1980; articles on titanium, zirconium, and hafnium in Mining Jl Annual Reviews. *Recreations:* ski-ing, sailing, walking, photography, farming, forestry. *Address:* Wandylaw House, Chathill, Northumberland NE67 5HG. *T:* Chathill 217; 49 Moorgate, EC2R 6BQ. *T:* 01-638 8346. *Clubs:* City of London (Mem. Cttee), City Livery (Mem. Council), United Wards, Farringdon Ward (patron), Light Infantry (Hon.), Mining (Hon.); Presscala (Hon.), Canada; Royal London Yacht (Hon.); Birdham Yacht (Hon.).

GAEKWAD, Lt-Col Fatesinghrao P.; *b* 2 April 1930; *s* of HH Sir Pratapsingh Gaekwar, GCIE, Maharaja of Baroda; *S* father, 1968; title abolished, 1971. *Educ:* privately; under English tutor; passed Senior Cambridge Examination, 1947. Entered politics, 1956; elected to Lok Sabha 1957, 1962, 1971, 1977 and 1980; Parly Sec. to Defence Minister, 1957–62, Mem. Public Accounts Cttee, 1963–64. MP (Congress), Gujarat, 1967–71; Minister for Health, Gujarat Govt, 1967–71. Chancellor, Maharaja Sayajirao Univ., Baroda, 1951–. Chairman: Baroda Rayon Corp.; Suri & Nayar Ltd. Chm., Bd of Governors, Nat. Inst. of Sports, Patiala, 1962–63; well-known cricketer and sportsman; Manager, Indian Cricket Team to England, 1959 and to Pakistan, 1978; Pres., Bd of Control for Cricket in India, 1963–66; expert commentator for cricket matches both in India and UK, summarises for BBC. Member: CCI, Bombay; MCC, London. FZS London. Internat. Trustee, World Wildlife Fund, for 6 years (Founder Pres., Indian Nat. Appeal); Member: IUCN; Fauna Preservation Soc.; RSPB; Indian Bd for Wildlife; World Poultry Science Assoc. Travelled with four friends by car, India to Europe through Middle East, 1955; also two months safari in Belgian Congo and E Africa, 1955; has visited most countries around Globe. *Publication:* Palaces of India, 1980. *Recreations:* photography, cooking, reading, poetry. *Address:* Laxmi Vilas Palace, Baroda 390 001, (Gujarat), India.

GAFFNEY, Michael Anthony Bowes B.; *see* Burke-Gaffney.

GAGE, family name of **Viscount Gage.**

GAGE, 7th Viscount *cr* 1720; **George John St Clere Gage;** Bt 1622; Baron Gage (Ire.) 1720; Baron Gage (GB), 1790; *b* 8 July 1932; *s* of 6th Viscount Gage, KVCO, and Hon. Alexandra Imogen Clare Grenfell (*d* 1969), *yr d* of 1st Baron Desborough, KG, GCVO; *S* father, 1982; *m* 1971, Valerie Ann (marr. diss. 1975), *yr d* of J. E. Dutch. *Educ:* Eton. *Heir: b* Hon. Henry Nicolas Gage, *b* 9 April 1934. *Address:* White Friars, Alciston, Polegate, East Sussex.

GAGE, Sir Berkeley (Everard Foley), KCMG 1955 (CMG 1949); Retired; *b* 27 Feb. 1904; *s* of late Brig.-Gen. M. F. Gage, DSO; *m* 1931, Maria von Chapuis (marr. diss. 1954), Liegnitz, Silesia; two *s*; *m* 1954, Mrs Lillian Riggs Miller. *Educ:* Eton Coll.; Trinity Coll., Cambridge. 3rd Sec. Foreign Office or Diplomatic Service, 1928; appointed to Rome, 1928; transferred to Foreign Office, 1931; 2nd Sec., 1933; Private Sec. to Parl. Under-Sec. of State, 1934; served Peking, 1935; FO 1938; China, 1941; FO 1944; UK Deleg. Dumbarton Oaks Conf., 1944; UK Deleg., San Francisco Conf., April–June 1945; Foreign Service Officer, Grade 5, 1950; Counsellor, British Embassy, The Hague, 1947–50; Chargé d'Affaires, The Hague, in 1947 and 1948; Consul-Gen., Chicago, 1950–54; Ambassador to Thailand, 1954–57; Ambassador to Peru, 1958–63. Chairman: Latin America Cttee, BNEC, 1964–66; Anglo-Peruvian Soc., 1969–71; Member: Council for Volunteers Overseas, 1964–66; Council of Fauna Preservation Soc., 1969–73. Grand Cross, Order of the Sun (Peru), 1964. *Recreation:* swimming. *Address:* 24 Ovington Gardens, SW3 1LE. *T:* 01-589 0361. *Clubs:* Beefsteak (Life Hon. Mem.), Buck's, Saints and Sinners; Tavern (Chicago).

GAGE, His Honour Conolly Hugh; a Circuit Judge (formerly Judge of County Courts), 1958–78; Barrister-at-law; Fellow Commoner, Sidney Sussex College, Cambridge, 1962; *b* 10 Nov. 1905; *s* of William Charles Gage and May Guerney Holmes, *d* of Rt Hon. Lord Justice Holmes; *m* 1932, Elinor Nancy Martyn; one *s* one *d*. *Educ:* Repton; Sidney Sussex Coll., Cambridge. Called to Bar, Inner Temple, 1930; enlisted as Gunner in RA, TA, April 1939; served with First Canadian Army as ADJAG (Br.) (despatches). MP (UU) S Belfast, 1945–52; Recorder of Maldon and Saffron Walden, 1950–52; Chm., Huntingdonshire and Peterborough QS, 1963–71; Dep. Chm., Essex QS, 1955–71. Chm., County Court Rules Cttee, 1974–78. Chancellor, dio. of Coventry, 1948–76, of Lichfield, 1954–76. Member, British Delegns to: Commonwealth Relations Conf., Canada, 1949; Consultative Assembly, Council of Europe, 1949–52. *Recreations:* fishing, shooting, gardening. *Address:* Manor Lodge, Brill, Bucks. *T:* Brill 238213. *Clubs:* Carlton, Ulster (Belfast).

See also W. M. Gage.

GAGE, William Marcus; QC 1982; *b* 22 April 1938; *s* of His Honour Conolly Gage, *qv*; *m* 1962, Penelope Mary Groves; three *s*. *Educ:* Repton; Sidney Sussex Coll., Cambridge. MA. National Service, Irish Guards, 1956–58. Called to the Bar, Inner Temple, 1963. Chancellor, diocese of Coventry, 1980–.

Recreations: shooting, fishing, smallholding. *Address:* Evershaw House, Biddlesden, Brackley, Northants NN13 5TT.

GAILEY, Thomas William Hamilton, CBE 1968; Member, Economic and Social Committee, EEC, 1973–78; *b* 7 Oct. 1906; *s* of late Thomas Andrew Gailey, ISO, and late Mabel Gailey; *m* 1st, 1937, Beryl (*d* 1972), *er d* of late Harold Kirkconnel; one *d*; 2nd, 1973, Mary Diana (*d* 1981), *y d* of late Frederick Priddle. *Educ:* King's Sch., Rochester; University Coll., Oxford (MA). Served with companies in Tilling Bus Group, 1932–59. Served War of 1939–45, with RAF: Wing Comdr, RAF Transp. Comd and psa, 1943. Vice-Chm., Bristol Wing, Air Trng Corps, 1945–56. Mem., Tilling Gp Management Bd, 1960–64; Chm., Tilling Bus Gp, 1965–68; Dir, Passenger Planning, Transp. Holding Co., 1967–68; Mem., Nat. Bus Company, 1968–74, Chief Executive, 1968–71; Mem., Nat. Council for Omnibus Industry, 1960–69; Dir, Bristol Commercial Vehicles and Eastern Coach Works, 1962–71; Director: Leyland National Co. Ltd; Park Royal Vehicles Ltd, 1969–71. Mem., Scottish Transport Gp, 1968–71. Chm., Public Transp. Assoc., 1967–69. Vice-Chm., Road Operators' Safety Council, 1964–68. Transport Advr, English Tourist Bd, 1972–74. FCIT (Vice-Pres., 1966–68); FRSA. Freeman of City of London; Liveryman, Worshipful Co. of Carmen; Governor, British Transp. Staff Coll., 1969–75. *Publications:* various papers for professional institutes and societies. *Address:* Wheatsheaf Pond Cottage, Liphook, Hants. *T:* Liphook 723467. *Clubs:* Travellers'; Bristol Savages (Bristol).

GAINFORD, 3rd Baron *cr* 1917; **Joseph Edward Pease;** *b* 25 Dec. 1921; *s* of 2nd Baron Gainford, TD, and of Veronica Margaret, *d* of Sir George Noble, 2nd Bt; *S* father, 1971; *m* 1953, Margaret Theophila Radcliffe, *d* of late Henry Edmund Guise Tyndale; two *d*. *Educ:* Eton and Gordonstoun. FRGS; Member, Society of Surveying Technicians. RAFVR, 1941–46. Hunting Aerosurveys Ltd, 1947–49; Directorate of Colonial Surveys, 1951–53; Soil Mechanics Ltd, 1953–58; London County Council, 1958–65; Greater London Council, 1965–78. UK Delegate to UN, 1973. Mem., Coll. of Guardians, Nat. Shrine of Our Lady of Walsingham, 1979–. Mem., Plaisterers' Co., 1976. *Recreations:* golf, music, veteran and vintage aviation. *Heir: b* Hon. George Pease [*b* 20 April 1926; *m* 1958, Flora Daphne, *d* of late Dr N. A. Dyce Sharp; two *s* two *d*]. *Address:* 60 Lansdowne Road, W11 2LR. *T:* 01-229 6279. *Clubs:* MCC, Pathfinder.

GAINHAM, Sarah Rachel, (Mrs Kenneth Ames); Author; *b* 1 Oct. 1922; *d* of Tom Stainer and May Genevieve Gainham; *m* 1964, Kenneth Ames (*d* 1975). *Educ:* Newbury High Sch. for Girls; afterwards largely self educated. From 1947 onwards, travelled extensively in Central and E Europe; Central Europe Correspondent of The Spectator, 1956–66. Mem. PEN, England. *Publications:* Time Right Deadly, 1956; Cold Dark Night, 1957; The Mythmaker, 1957; Stone Roses, 1959; Silent Hostage, 1960; Night Falls on the City, 1967 (Book Soc. Choice and US Book of Month Club); A Place in the Country, 1968; Takeover Bid, 1970; Private Worlds, 1971; Maculan's Daughter, 1973; To the Opera Ball, 1975; The Habsburg Twilight, 1979; contrib. to Encounter, Atlantic Monthly, BBC, etc. *Recreations:* theatre, opera, European history. *Address:* c/o Ed Victor, 162 Wardour Street, W1; altes Forsthaus, Schlosspark, A2404 Petronell, Austria.

GAINSBOROUGH, 5th Earl of, (2nd) *cr* 1841; **Anthony Gerard Edward Noel,** Bt 1781; Baron Barham, 1805; Viscount Campden, Baron Noel, 1841; JP; *b* 24 Oct. 1923; *s* of 4th Earl and Alice Mary (*d* 1970), *e d* of Edward Eyre, Gloucester House, Park Lane, W1; *S* father 1927; *m* 1947, Mary, *er d* of Hon. J. J. Stourton (and of Mrs Kathleen Stourton, Withington, Glos), *qv*; four *s* three *d*. *Educ:* Georgetown, Garrett Park, Maryland, USA. Chairman: Oakham RDC, 1952–67; Executive Council RDC's Association of England and Wales, 1963 (Vice-Chairman 1962, Pres., 1965); Pres., Assoc. of District Councils, 1974–80; Vice-Chm. Rutland CC, 1958–70, Chm., 1970–73; Chm., Rutland Dist Council, 1973–76. Chm., Bd of Management, Hosp. of St John and St Elizabeth, NW8, 1970–80. Mem. Court of Assistants, Worshipful Co. of Gardeners of London, 1960 (Upper Warden, 1966; Master, 1967), Hon. FIMunE 1969. JP Rutland, 1957, Leics 1974. Knight of Malta, 1948; Bailiff Grand Cross Order of Malta, 1958; Pres. Br. Assoc., SMO, Malta, 1968–74. KStJ 1970. *Recreations:* shooting, sailing. *Heir: s* Viscount Campden, *qv*. *Address:* Exton Park, Oakham, Leics LE15 8NN. *T:* Oakham 812209. *Clubs:* Boodle's, Brooks's; Bembridge Sailing.

See also Earl of Liverpool, Hon. G. E. W. Noel.

GAINSBOROUGH, George Fotheringham, CBE 1973; PhD, FIEE; Barrister-at-law; Secretary, Institution of Electrical Engineers, 1962–80; *b* 28 May 1915; *o s* of late Rev. William Anthony Gainsborough and of Alice Edith (*née* Fennell); *m* 1937, Gwendoline (*d* 1976), *e d* of John and Anne Berry; two *s*. *Educ:* Christ's Hospital; King's Coll., London; Gray's Inn. Scientific Staff, Nat. Physical Laboratory, 1938–46; Radio Physicist, British Commonwealth Scientific Office, Washington, DC, USA, 1944–45; Administrative Civil Service (Ministries of Supply and Aviation), 1946–62. Imperial Defence College, 1960. Secretary, Commonwealth Engineering Conf., 1962–69; Sec.-General, World Fedn of Engineering Organizations, 1968–76. *Publications:* papers in Proc. Instn of Electrical Engineers. *Address:* 19 Glenmore House, Richmond Hill, Richmond, Surrey. *T:* 01-940 8515; 46 rue Schaub, 1202 Genève, Switzerland. *T:* (022) 33 76 59. *Club:* Athenæum.

See also Michael Gainsborough.

GAINSBOROUGH, Michael; Assistant Secretary, Ministry of Defence; *b* 13 March 1938; *s* of George Fotheringham Gainsborough, *qv: m* 1962, Sally (*née* Hunter); one *s* two *d. Educ:* St Paul's Sch.; Trinity Coll., Oxford (MA). Air Ministry, 1959-64; Ministry of Defence, 1964-78; Defence Counsellor, UK Delegn to NATO, Brussels, FCO, 1978-81; MoD, 1981-. *Recreations:* boats and birds. *Address:* c/o Ministry of Defence, SW1.

GAINSFORD, Ian Derek, FDSRCS; Dean of Dental Studies and Director of Clinical Dental Services, King's College Hospital, London, since 1977; *b* 24 June 1930; *s* of late Rabbi Morris Ginsberg, MA, PhD, AKC, and Anne Freda; *m* 1957, Carmel Liebster; one *s* two *d. Educ:* Thames Valley Grammar Sch., Twickenham; King's Coll. and King's College Hosp. Med. Sch., London (BDS); Toronto Univ., Canada (DDS Hons). Junior Staff, King's College Hosp., 1955-57; Member staff, Dept of Conservative Dentistry, London Hosp. Med. Sch., 1957-70; Sen. Lectr/Consultant, Dept of Conservative Dentistry, King's College Hosp., 1970-, Dep. Dean of Dental Studies, 1973-77. President, British Soc. for Restorative Dentistry, 1973-74; Member: Internat. Dental Fedn, 1966-; American Dental Soc. of London, 1960- (Pres., 1982); Amer. Dental Soc. of Europe, 1965- (Hon. Treas. 1971-77); Examiner for Membership in General Dental Surgery, RCS, 1979- (Chm., 1982); Fellow, and Mem. Odontological Sect., RSM, 1967-. FICD 1975; MGDS RCS 1979. *Publication:* Silver Amalgam in Clinical Practice, 1965, 2nd edn 1976. *Recreations:* squash, theatre, canal cruising. *Address:* 31 York Terrace East, NW1 4PT. *T:* 01-935 8659. *Clubs:* Athenæum, Carlton.

GAIRDNER, Gen. Sir Charles Henry, GBE 1969 (KBE 1960; CBE 1941); KCMG 1948; KCVO 1954; CB 1946; Governor of Tasmania, 1963-68; *b* 20 March 1898; *e surv s* of late C. A. Gairdner, Lisbeg House, County Galway; *m* 1925, Hon. Evelyn Constance Handcock, CStJ, *o d* of 5th Baron Castlemaine, Moydrum Castle, Co. Westmeath; no *c. Educ:* Repton; RMA, Woolwich. Entered Army in 1916, served in France and Flanders (wounded); Staff Coll., Camberley, 1933-35; commanded 10th Royal Hussars, 1937-40; GSO 1st grade 7 Armoured Division, 1940-41; Deputy Dir of Plans, Middle East, 1941; GOC 6th Armoured Division, 1942; Commandant, Higher Commanders Sch., 1943. GOC 8th Armoured Division, 1943; CGS North Africa, 1943; Maj.-Gen. Armoured Fighting Vehicles, India, 1944; Maj.-Gen., 1941; Lt-Gen., 1944; Head, UK Liaison Mission, Japan, 1945-46. Prime Minister's Special Representative in Far East, 1945-48. Gov., State of W Australia, 1951-63. Col 10th Royal Hussars, 1949-52; Hon. Col 10th Light Horse, 1952-68; Hon. Col Royal Tasmanian Regt, 1964-68. Hon. Air Commodore, RAAF. KStJ 1951; Hon. DLitt W Australia, 1956; Hon. LLD, University of Tasmania, 1967. American Medal of Freedom with Silver Palm, 1948. *Recreations:* hunting, polo, golf, yachting. *Address:* 24 The Esplanade, Peppermint Grove, W Australia. *Clubs:* Cavalry and Guards; Weld, West Australian (Perth), Royal Perth Yacht, Royal Freshwater Bay Yacht.

GAIRY, Rt. Hon. Sir Eric Matthew, PC 1977; Kt 1977; Prime Minister of Grenada, 1974-79; also Minister of External Affairs, Planning and Development Lands and Tourism, Information Service, Public Relations and Natural Resources, 1974-79; *b* 18 Feb. 1922; *m* Cynthia Gairy; two *d.* Member of Legislative Council, 1951-52 and 1954-55; Minister of Trade and Production, 1956-57; Chief Minister and Minister of Finance until 1962; Premier, 1967-74; independence of Grenada, 1974.

GAISFORD, Prof. Wilfrid Fletcher, MD London, MSc Manchester, FRCP; Czechoslovak Military Medal of Merit, 1st class, 1945; First Professor of Child Health and Paediatrics and Director of the Department of Child Health, University of Manchester, 1947-67, now Emeritus; *b* 6 April 1902; *s* of Captain Harold Gaisford, RN, and Anne, *d* of Captain Wm Fletcher, RIN; *m* 1933, Mary, *d* of Captain Wm Guppy; one *s* four *d. Educ:* Bristol Grammar Sch.; St Bartholomew's Hosp., London, MB London, 1925; MD London, 1928; Post-graduate study in St Louis Children's Hosp., University of Washington, USA, 1928-29; FRCP, 1940; MSc Manchester, 1951. Hon. Asst Physician, East London Children's Hosp., 1932; Mem., British Paediatric Assoc., 1933. Physn, Dudley Road Hosp., Birmingham, 1935-42; Cons. Paediatrician, Warwicks CC, 1942-47; Leonard Parsons Memorial Lecturer, University of Birmingham, 1954-55; Catherine Chisholm Memorial Lecturer, 1965. Hon. Physician, Royal Manchester Children's Hosp. and St Mary's Hosp., Manchester; Hon. Cons. Paediatrician, United Manchester Hosp., 1967. Regional Adviser in Child Health, 1948. Hon. Member: Canadian Paediatric Association, 1949; Swedish Paediatric Association, 1960; Finnish Paediatric Association, 1965; Hon. Fellow, American Acad. of Pediatrics, 1962; Pres., British Paediatric Assoc., 1964-65. Extraord. Mem., Swiss Paediatric Soc., 1965; Pres., Paediatric Section, Manchester Med. Soc., 1966-67. *Publications:* contrib. to the Encyclopædia of British Medical Practice, Lancet, BMJ, Practitioner, Archives of Disease in Childhood, Jl Pediatrics, etc. Joint Editor, Paediatrics for the Practitioner (Gaisford and Lightwood). *Recreation:* gardening. *Address:* Treloyhan, Restronguet Point, Feock, Truro TR3 6RB. *T:* Devoran 862620.

GAITSKELL, Baroness, *cr* 1963, of Egremont (Life Peer); **Anna Dora Gaitskell;** *d* of Leon Creditor; *m* 1937, Rt Hon. Hugh Todd Naylor Gaitskell, PC, CBE, MP (*d* 1963), *s* of late Arthur Gaitskell, Indian Civil Service; two *d* (and one *s* by a former marriage). Trustee, Anglo-German Foundn, 1974-. Mem., House of Lords All Party Cttee on Bill of Human Rights, 1977-. *Address:* 18 Frognal Gardens, NW3.
See also Sir Arthur Gaitskell.

GAITSKELL, Sir Arthur, Kt 1970; CMG 1949; Member, Commonwealth (formerly Colonial) Development Corporation, 1954-73, retired; *b* Oct. 1900; *s* of late Arthur Gaitskell, ICS; *m* 1939, Jeanne Stephanie, *d* of Col E. C. Townsend, ICS; one *s* two *d. Educ:* Winchester Coll.; New Coll., Oxford. Manager, Sudan Plantations Syndicate, 1945-50; Chm. and Managing Dir, Sudan Gezira Board, 1950-52. Consultant, 1952-53; Member: Royal Commission on East Africa, 1953-54; Tanganyika Agricultural Corp., 1955. Research Fellow, Nuffield Coll., Oxford, 1955-58; Nominee of International Bank on Food and Agriculture Commn. Pakistan, 1959-60; Consultant: to Mitchell Cotts, Ethiopia, to Kenya African National Union, Kenya, and to Ford Foundation, Nigeria, 1961-62. Lecturer at Economic Development Institute, International Bank, Washington, 1963. Consultant to: Euphrates Project Authority, 1965; Sir Alex Gibb and Partners on Indus Basin Survey, 1965-66; World Food Program, Mexico, 1966; FAO for Philippines, 1967, for Thailand, 1968. Member: Coun., Overseas Develt Inst., 1965; Adv. Bd, Mekong River, 1968; ILO Mission to Colombia, 1970; Mission to Jamaica for Agric. Sector, Jamaican Govt, 1973. *Publication:* Gezira, 1959. *Address:* Bicknoller, Taunton, Somerset.
See also Baroness Gaitskell.

GAJDUSEK, Daniel Carleton, MD; Director of Program for Study of Child Growth and Development and Disease Patterns in Primitive Cultures, and Laboratory of Slow Latent and Temperate Virus Infections, National Institute of Neurological and Communicative Disorders and Stroke, National Institutes of Health, Bethesda, Md, since 1958; Chief, Central Nervous System Studies Laboratory, NINCDS, since 1970; *b* Yonkers, NY, 9 Sept. 1923; *s* of Karol Gajdusek and Ottilia Dobroczki; twenty-two adopted *s* (all from New Guinea and Micronesia). *Educ:* Marine Biological Lab., Woods Hole, Mass; Univ. of Rochester (BS *summa cum laude*); Harvard Medical Sch. (MD); California Inst. of Technology (Post-Doctoral Fellow). Served Medical Corps; appts in various children's hosps; Sen. Fellow, Nat. Research Council, Calif Inst. of Tech., 1948-49; Children's Hosp., Boston, Mass, 1949-51; Research Fellow, Harvard Univ. and Sen. Fellow, Nat. Foundn for Infantile Paralysis, 1949-52; Walter Reed Army Medical Center, 1952-53; Institut Pasteur, Tehran, Iran and Univ. of Maryland, 1954-55; Vis. Investigator, Nat. Foundn for Infantile Paralysis and Walter and Eliza Hall Inst., Australia, 1955-57. Member: Nat. Acad. of Sciences, 1974; Amer. Philos. Soc., 1978; Amer. Acad. of Arts and Scis, 1978; Soc. for Pediatric Research; Amer. Pediatric Soc.; Amer. Epidemiological Soc., Amer. Soc. of Tropical Medicine and Hygiene, and many others. Studied unique forms of virus and brain diseases. E. Meade Johnson Award, Amer. Acad. Pediatrics, 1963; DHEW Superior Service Award, 1970; DHEW Distinguished Service Award, 1975; Lucien Dautrebande Prize, Belgium, 1976; shared with Dr Baruch Blumberg Nobel Prize in Physiology or Medicine, for discoveries concerning new mechanisms for the origin and dissemination of infectious diseases, 1976; George Cotzias Meml Prize, Amer. Acad. of Neurol., 1978. Hon. DSc: Univ. of Rochester, 1977; Med. Coll. of Ohio, 1977; Washington and Jefferson Coll., 1980; Hon. LHD Hamilton Coll., 1977; Docteur *hc* Univ. of Marseille, 1977; Hon. LLD Aberdeen, 1980. *Publications:* Acute Infectious Hemorrhagic Fevers and Mycotoxicoses in the USSR, 1953; ed, with C. S. Gibbs and M. P. Alpers, Slow, Latent and Temperate Virus Infections, 1966; Journals 1957-81, 31 vols, 1963-77; Smadel-Gajdusek Correspondence 1955-1958; (ed with J. Farquhar) Kuru, 1981; over 400 papers in major jls of medicine, microbiology, immunology, molecular biology, anthropology, inc. Nature, Science, etc. *Recreations:* mountaineering, linguistics. *Address:* Laboratory of Central Nervous System Studies, NINCDS, National Institutes of Health, Bethesda, Md 20205, USA. *T:* 301-496-3281.

GAJE GHALE, VC 1943; Subedar 2/5 Royal Gurkha Rifles FF; *b* 1 July 1922; *s* of Bikram Ghale; *m* 1939, Dhansuba; no *c. Educ:* IA 2nd class certificate of education. Enlisted as a Recruit Boy 2nd Bn 5th Royal Gurkha Rifles FF, Feb. 1935; transferred to the ranks, Aug. 1935; Naik, 1941; Acting Havildar, May 1942; War Subst. Havildar, Nov. 1942; Bn Havildar Major June 1943; Jemadar, Aug. 1943. Waziristan operations, 1936-37 (medal with clasp); Burma, 1942-43 (1939-45 Star, VC). *Recreations:* football, basketball, badminton and draughts.

GALBRAITH, family name of **Baron Strathclyde.**

GALBRAITH, James Hunter; Under Secretary, Department of Employment, since 1975; *b* 16 July 1925; *o s* of late Prof. V. H. Galbraith, FBA, and Dr G. R. Galbraith; *m* 1954, Isobel Gibson Graham; two *s. Educ:* Edinburgh Academy; Balliol Coll., Oxford. Fleet Air Arm, 1944-46. Entered Ministry of Labour, 1950; Private Sec. to Permanent Sec., 1953-55; Jun. Civilian Instructor, IDC, 1958-61; Private Sec. to Minister of Labour, 1962-64; Chm. Central Youth Employment Exec., 1964-67; Sen. Simon Research Fellow, Manchester Univ., 1967-68; Asst Under-Sec. of State, Dept of Employment and Productivity (Research and Planning Div.), 1968-71; Dir, Office of Manpower Economics, 1971-73; Under-Sec., Manpower Gen. Div., Dept of Employment, 1973-74; Sec., Manpower Services Commn, 1974-75. *Recreations:* golf, fishing. *Address:* 27 Sandy Lodge Lane, Moor Park, Mddx. *T:* Northwood 22458.
See also G. M. Moore.

GALBRAITH, Prof. John Kenneth; Paul M. Warburg Professor of Economics, Harvard University, 1949-75, now Emeritus Professor; *b* Ontario, Canada, 15 Oct. 1908; *s* of William Archibald and Catherine Galbraith; *m* 1937, Catherine M. Atwater; three *s. Educ:* Univ. of Guelph; California Univ.

BS, MS, PhD. Tutor, Harvard Univ., 1934-39; Social Science Research Fellow, Cambridge Univ., 1937; Asst Prof. of Economics, Princeton Univ., 1939; Asst Administrator, Office of Price Administration, 1941; Deputy Administrator, 1942-43; Dir, State Dept Office of Economic Security Policy, 1945; Mem. Bd of Editors, Fortune Magazine, 1943-48. United States Ambassador to India, 1961-63 (on leave from Professorship). Reith Lecturer, 1966; Vis. Fellow, Trinity Coll., Cambridge, 1970-71. Chm., Americans for Democratic Action, 1967-69; Pres., Amer. Econ. Assoc., 1972. LLD Bard, 1958; Miami Univ., 1959; University of Toronto, 1961; Brandeis Univ., 1963; University of Mass, 1963; University of Saskatchewan, 1965; Rhode Island Coll., 1966; Boston Coll., 1967; Hobart and William Smith Colls, 1967; Univ. of Paris, 1975; and others. TV series, The Age of Uncertainty, 1977. President's Certificate of Merit; Medal of Freedom. *Publications:* American Capitalism, the Concept of Countervailing Power, 1952; The Great Crash, 1929, 1955, new edn 1979; The Affluent Society, 1958, new edn 1976; Journey to Poland and Yugoslavia, 1958; The Liberal Hour, 1960; Made to Last, 1964; The New Industrial State, 1967, rev. edn, 1978; Indian Painting, 1968; Ambassador's Journal, 1969; Economics, Peace and Laughter, 1971; A China Passage, 1973; Economics and the Public Purpose, 1974; Money: whence it came, where it went, 1975; The Age of Uncertainty, 1977; Almost Everyone's Guide to Economics, 1978; Annals of an Abiding Liberal, 1979; The Nature of Mass Poverty, 1979; A Life in Our Times, 1981; contribs to learned jls. *Address:* 207 Littauer Center, Harvard University, Cambridge, Mass 02138, USA; 30 Francis Avenue, Cambridge, Mass 02138, USA. *Clubs:* Century (NY); Federal City (Washington).

GALBRAITH, Neil, CBE 1975; QPM 1959; DL; HM Inspector of Constabulary, 1964-76, retired; *b* 25 May 1911; *s* of late Peter and Isabella Galbraith; *m* 1942, Catherine Margaret Thornton; one *s* one *d. Educ:* Kilmarnock Academy. Constable to Inspector, Lancs Constabulary, 1931-46. Chief Supt, Herts Constabulary, 1946-51; Asst Chief Constable, Monmouthshire Constabulary, 1951-55; Chief Constable, Leicester City Police, 1956; Chief Constable, Monmouthshire Constabulary, 1957-64. DL Gwent (formerly Monmouth), 1973. *Recreation:* reading. *Address:* Neath House, Trostrey, Usk, Gwent. *T:* Usk 2779.

GALBRAITH, William Campbell, QC 1977; *b* 25 Feb. 1935; *s* of William Campbell Galbraith and Margaret Watson or Galbraith; *m* 1959, Mary Janet Waller; three *s* (and one *s* decd). *Educ:* Merchiston Castle Sch.; Pembroke Coll., Cambridge (BA); Edinburgh Univ. (LLB). Teacher, Turkey, 1959-61; Lectr, Meshed Univ., Iran, 1961-62; admitted to Faculty of Advocates, 1962; in practice at Scottish Bar, 1962-67; Sen. State Counsel, Malaŵi, 1967-70; Parly Draftsman, London, 1970-74; Parly Counsel, Canberra, 1974; returned to practice, 1975. *Recreations:* fishing, music, travel.

GALE, Prof. Ernest Frederick, FRS 1953; BSc London; BA, PhD, ScD Cantab; Professor of Chemical Microbiology, University of Cambridge, 1960-81, now Emeritus; Fellow of St John's College, Cambridge, since 1949; *b* 15 July 1914; *s* of Nellie Annie and Ernest Francis Edward Gale; *m* 1937, Eiry Mair Jones; one *s. Educ:* St John's Coll. Cambridge (Scholar). Research in biochemistry, Cambridge, 1936-; Senior Student, Royal Commn for Exhibition of 1851, 1939; Beit Memorial Fellow, 1941; Scientific Staff of Med. Research Council, 1943; Reader in Chemical Microbiology, University of Cambridge, 1948-60; Dir, Medical Research Council Unit for Chemical Microbiology, 1948-62. Herter Lecturer, Johns Hopkins Hosp., Baltimore, USA, 1948; Commonwealth Travelling Fellow, Hanna Lecturer, Western Reserve Univ., 1951; Harvey Lectr, New York, 1955; Leeuwenhoek Lectr, Royal Society, London, 1956; Malcolm Lectr, Syracuse Univ., 1967; M. Stephenson Meml Lectr, 1971; Linacre Lectr, St John's Coll., Cambridge, 1973. Visiting Fellow, ANU, 1964-65. Hon. Mem., Society for General Microbiology, 1978- (Meetings Sec., 1954-58; International Representative, 1963-67; Pres., 1967-69); Mem. Food Investigation Board, 1954-58; Mem. International Union of Biochemistry Commission on Enzymes, 1957-61. *Publications:* Chemical Activities of Bacteria, 1947; The Molecular Basis of Antibiotic Action, 1972, 2nd edn 1981; scientific papers in Biochem. Journal, Journal of General Microbiology, Biochimica et Biophysica Acta, etc. *Recreation:* photography. *Address:* 25 Luard Road, Cambridge. *T:* Cambridge 247585.

GALE, Hon. George Alexander, CC 1977; Chief Justice of Ontario 1967-76; Vice-Chairman, Ontario Law Reform Commission, 1977-81; *b* 24 June 1906; *s* of late Robert Henry and Elma Gertrude Gale; *m* 1934, Hilda Georgina Daly; three *s. Educ:* Prince of Wales High Sch., Vancouver; Toronto Univ. (BA); Osgoode Hall Law Sch., Toronto. Called to Ontario Bar, 1932; Partner, Mason, Foulds, Davidson & Gale, 1944; KC (Can.) 1945; Justice, Supreme Court of Ontario, 1946; Justice, Court of Appeal, Ontario, 1963; Chief Justice of High Court of Justice for Ontario, 1964. Formerly Chm. Judicial Council for Provincial Judges; Chm., Cttee on Rules of Practice for Ontario (Mem. 1941-76); former Mem. Canadian Bar Assoc. (formerly Mem. Council); Hon. Mem., Georgia Bar Assoc.; formerly Hon. Lectr, Osgoode Law Sch.; formerly Mem. Exec. Cttee, Canadian Judicial Council. Mem., Ontario Adv. Cttee on Confederation; formerly Chm., Ontario Rhodes Scholarship Selection Cttee; Hon. Mem., Canadian Corps of Commissionaires, 1977. Mem. Bd of Governors: Wycliffe Coll., Toronto Univ.; Ecumenical Foundn of Canada; formerly, Upper Canada Coll., Toronto; Mem. Delta Kappa Epsilon, Phi Delta Phi (Hon.). Anglican; Warden, St John's, York Mills, for 5 years. Hon. Pres., Ontario Curling Assoc. Hon. LLD: McMaster, 1968; York (Toronto), 1969. *Publication:* (ed with Holmested) Practice and Procedure in Ontario,

6th edn. *Recreations:* golf, photography. *Address:* 2 Brookfield Road, Willowdale, Ontario M2P 1A9, Canada. *Clubs:* University, Lawyers, (Hon. Mem.) York (Toronto); Toronto Curling, Chippewa Golf.

GALE, George Stafford; journalist, author, broadcaster; *b* 22 Oct. 1927; *e s* of George Pyatt Gale and Anne Watson Gale (*née* Wood); *m* 1951, Patricia Marina Holley; four *s. Educ:* Royal Grammar Sch., Newcastle upon Tyne; Peterhouse, Cambridge; Göttingen University. 1st cl. hons Historical Tripos, Cantab, 1948 and 1949. Leader writer, reporter, Labour Corresp., Manchester Guardian, 1951-55; Special and Foreign Corresp., Daily Express, 1955-67; Columnist, Daily Mirror, 1967-69; freelance journalist, 1969-70; Editor, The Spectator, 1970-73; columnist, Daily Express, 1976-. Presenter, phone-in programmes, London Broadcasting, 1973-80; commentator, Thames Television, 1977-79. *Publications:* No Flies in China, 1955; (with P. Johnson) The Highland Jaunt, 1973; (contrib.) Conservative Essays, 1979; countless articles. *Recreations:* looking, brooding, disputing, writing poetry, and roasting beef. *Address:* 3 Great Hyde Hall, Sawbridgeworth, Herts. *T:* Bishop's Stortford 723911; D5, Albany, Piccadilly, W1V 9RG. *T:* 01-734 4282; Tattingstone Place, Tattingstone, Suffolk. *Clubs:* Garrick, Press, Wig and Pen; Wivenhoe Arts (Wivenhoe).

GALE, John; Chairman, Theatres National Committee, since 1979; Director: Lisden Productions Ltd, since 1975; John Gale Productions Ltd, since 1960; Gale Enterprises Ltd, since 1960; West End Managers Ltd, since 1972; Theatres Mutual Ltd, since 1977; *b* 2 Aug. 1929; *s* of Frank Haith Gale and Martha Edith Gale (*née* Evans); *m* 1950, Liselotte Ann (*née* Wratten); two *s. Educ:* Christ's Hosp.; Webber Douglas Acad. of Dramatic Art. Formerly an actor; presented his first production, Inherit the Wind, London, 1960; has since produced or co-produced, in London, British provinces, USA, Australia, New Zealand and S Africa, over 80 plays, including: Candida, 1960; On the Brighter Side, 1961; Boeing-Boeing, 1962; Devil May Care, 1963; Windfall, 1963; Where Angels Fear to Tread, 1963; The Wings of the Dove, 1963; Amber for Anna, 1964; Present Laughter, 1964, 1981; Maigret and the Lady, 1965; The Platinum Cat, 1965; The Sacred Flame, 1966; An Evening with G. B. S., 1966; A Woman of No Importance, 1967; The Secretary Bird, 1968; Dear Charles, 1968; Highly Confidential, 1969; The Young Churchill, 1969; The Lionel Touch, 1969; Abelard and Héloïse, 1970; No Sex, Please—We're British, 1971; Lloyd George Knew My Father, 1972; The Mating Game, 1972; Parents' Day, 1972; At the End of the Day, 1973; Birds of Paradise, 1974; A Touch of Spring, 1975; Separate Tables, 1977; The Kingfisher, 1977; Sextet, 1977; Cause Célèbre, 1977; Shut Your Eyes and Think of England, 1977; Can You Hear Me at the Back?, 1979; Middle Age Spread, 1979; Private Lives, 1980; A Personal Affair, 1982. The Secretary Bird and No Sex, Please—We're British set records for the longest run at the Savoy and Strand Theatres respectively; No Sex, Please—We're British is the longest running comedy in the history of World Theatre and passed 4,600 performances at the Garrick Theatre in June 1982. President, Soc. of West End Theatre Managers, 1972-75; Governor and Almoner, Christ's Hospital, 1976-; Member, Amicable Soc. of Blues, 1981-. Liveryman, Gold and Silver Wyredrawers Company, 1974. *Recreations:* travel, Rugby. *Address:* Strand Theatre, Aldwych, WC2B 5LD. *T:* 01-240 1656. *Clubs:* Garrick, Green Room; London Welsh Rugby Football (Richmond) (Chairman, 1979-81).

GALE, Malcolm, CBE 1964 (MBE 1948); HM Diplomatic Service, retired; *b* 31 Aug. 1909; *s* of late George Alfred Gale and late Agnes Logan Gale (*née* Ruthven); *m* 1st, 1932, Doris Frances Wells; 2nd, 1936, Ilse Strauss; one *s* one *d. Educ:* Sedbergh; Madrid Univ. Market Officer, Santiago, 1945; Third Sec., Dec. 1947; Second Sec. (Commercial), Caracas, 1948; First Sec. (Commercial), 1952; First Sec. (Commercial), Ankara, 1953; Actg Counsellor (Commercial), 1954; First Sec. (Commercial), Bahrein, 1955; Consul (Commercial), Milan, 1958; Acting Consul-Gen., Milan, 1958 and 1959; Counsellor, 1959; Counsellor (Commercial): Washington, 1960-64; Lisbon, 1964-67; Minister (Commercial) Buenos Aires, 1967-69. *Recreations:* golf, photography. *Address:* Apartado 32, Sintra, Portugal. *T:* Lisbon 299-0575.

GALE, Michael, QC 1979; a Recorder of the Crown Court, since 1977; *b* 12 Aug. 1932; *s* of Joseph Gale and Blossom Gale; *m* 1963, Joanna Stephanie Bloom; one *s* two *d. Educ:* Cheltenham Grammar Sch.; Grocers' Sch.; King's Coll., Cambridge (Exhibnr; BA History and Law, 1954, MA 1958). National Service, Royal Fusiliers and Jt Services Sch. for Linguists, 1956-58. Called to the Bar, Middle Temple, 1957; Harmsworth Law Scholar, 1958. *Recreations:* the arts and country pursuits. *Address:* 6 Pump Court, Temple, EC4Y 7AR. *T:* 01-353 7242. *Club:* United Oxford & Cambridge University.

GALE, Michael Sadler, MC 1945; Assistant Under-Secretary of State, Prison Department, Home Office, 1972-79; *b* 5 Feb. 1919; *s* of Rev. John Sadler and Ethel Gale; *m* 1950, Philippa, *d* of Terence and Betty Ennion; three *s* one *d. Educ:* Tonbridge Sch.; Oriel Coll., Oxford (Scholar, MA). Served War of 1939-45: enlisted 1939, Royal Fusiliers; commnd 1940, Queen's Own Royal W Kent Regt, Major 1944; served N Africa and NW Europe. Housemaster, HM Borstal, Rochester, 1946-48; Dep. Governor, HM Prison, Durham, 1948-49; Staff Course Tutor, Imperial Trng Sch., Wakefield, 1949-50; Principal, 1950-52; Governor, HM Prison: The Verne, 1952-57; Camp Hill, 1957-62; Wandsworth, 1962-66; Asst Dir, Prison Dept, Home Office, 1966-69; Controller, Planning and Develt, 1969-75; Controller, Operational Administration, 1975-79; Mem. Prisons Board, 1969-79. *Recreations:* walking, reading, gardening. *Address:* 42 St Cross Road, Winchester, Hants. *T:* Winchester 3836.

GALES, Kathleen Emily, (Mrs Heinz Spitz); Senior Lecturer in Statistics, London School of Economics, since 1966; *b* 1927; *d* of Albert Henry and Sarah Thomson Gales; *m* 1970, Heinz Spitz. *Educ:* Gateshead Grammar Sch.; Newnham Coll., Cambridge (Exhibr); Ohio Univ. (Schol.). BA Cantab 1950, MA Ohio, 1951. Asst Statistician, Foster Wheeler Ltd, 1951-53; Statistician, Municipal Statistical Office, Birmingham, 1953-55; Res. Asst and part-time Lectr, LSE, 1955-58; Asst Lectr in Statistics, LSE, 1958-60, Lectr, 1960-66. Vis. Assoc. Prof. in Statistics, Univ. of California, 1964-65. Statistical Consultant: Royal Commn on Doctors' and Dentists' Remuneration, 1959; WHO, 1960; Turkish Min. of Health, 1963. Mem. Performing Rights Tribunal, 1974-80. *Publications:* (with C. A. Moser and P. Morpurgo) Dental Health and the Dental Services, 1962; (with B. Abel-Smith) British Doctors at Home and Abroad, 1964; (with T. Blackstone et al.) Students in Conflict: LSE in 1967, 1970; articles in Jl RSS. *Recreations:* singing, ski-ing, reading. *Address:* 39 High View Road, E18 2HL. *T:* 01-989 6311.

GALLAGHER, (Francis George) Kenna, CMG 1963; HM Diplomatic Service, retired; *b* 25 May 1917; *er s* of late George and Johanna Gallagher. *Educ:* St Joseph's Coll.; King's Coll., University of London (LLB (Hons)). Clerical officer, Min. of Agric., 1935-38; Asst Examr, Estate Duty Office, 1938-44; served in HM Forces, 1941-45; Examr, Estate Duty Office, 1944-45; apptd a Mem., HM Foreign (subseq. Diplomatic) Service, 1945; Vice-Consul Marseilles, 1946-48; Acting Consul-Gen., there, in 1947; HM Embassy, Paris, 1948-50; FO, 1950-53; First Sec., HM Embassy, Damascus, 1953-55; acted as Chargé d'Affaires, 1953, 1954 and 1955; FO, 1955; appointed Counsellor and Head of European Economic Organisations Dept, 1960; Counsellor (Commercial), HM Embassy, Berne, 1963-65; acted as Chargé d'Affaires (Berne) in 1963 and 1964; Head of Western Economic Dept, CO, 1965-67, of Common Market Dept, 1967-68; Asst Under-Sec. of State, FCO, 1968-71; Ambassador and Head of UK Delegn to OECD, 1971-77. Consultant on Internat. Trade Policy, CBI, 1978-80. *Recreations:* music, chess. *Address:* 29A Lexham Gardens, W8 5JR. *T:* 01-373 5808; The Old Courthouse, Kirkwhelpington, Northumberland NE19 2RS. *T:* Otterburn 40373.

GALLAGHER, Francis Heath, CMG 1957; Hon. Mr Justice Gallagher; Coal Industry Tribunal (Australia), since 1947; *b* 10 Feb. 1905; *s* of James Gallagher; *m* 1938, Heather Elizabeth Clark; no *c*. *Educ:* Sydney Grammar Sch.; University of Sydney. BA 1929, LLB 1933, University of Sydney. Admitted as solicitor, Supreme Court of NSW, 1933. Mem. of Industrial Commn of NSW, 1955-57; Presidential Mem., Commonwealth Arbitration Commn, 1957-71. *Recreations:* reading, gardening, sailing, surfing. *Address:* 2 Foam Crest Avenue, Newport Beach, NSW 2106, Australia. *T:* 99-1724. *Clubs:* Australian Jockey, Turf (Sydney).

GALLAGHER, Kenna; *see* Gallagher, F. G. K.

GALLAGHER, Michael; Member (Lab) Nottingham, European Parliament, since 1979; *b* 1 July 1934; *s* of Michael and Annie Gallagher; *m* 1959, Kathleen Mary Gallagher; two *s* three *d*. *Educ:* Univ. of Nottingham; Univ. of Wales. Dip. General Studies. Branch Official, NUM, 1967-70; day release, Univ. of Nottingham, 1967-69; TUC scholarship, Univ. of Wales, 1970-72; Univ. of Nottingham, 1972-74. Councillor: Mansfield Borough Council, 1970-74; Nottinghamshire CC, 1973-. Contested (Lab) Rushcliffe, general election, Feb. 1974. *Recreations:* leisure, sports. *Address:* The Cliff, 31 Woodhouse Road, Mansfield, Notts. *T:* Mansfield 31659.

GALLAGHER, Dame Monica (Josephine), DBE 1976; State President, New South Wales, and General President, Sydney Archdiocese, Catholic Women's League, Australia, 1972-80 (National President, 1972-74); Member, Executive Board, Mater Misericordiae Hospital, North Sydney; *m* 1946, Dr John Paul Gallagher, KCSG, KM; two *s* two *d*. Mem. Exec. Cttee, Associated Catholic Cttee, 1958-82; has been and remains active member: Adv. Bd, Festival of Light; Australian Church Women; Austcare; Inst. of Public Affairs (NSW); Community Refugee Settlement Cttee; Dr Horace Nowland Travelling Scholarship Settlement Cttee; Queen Elizabeth Silver Jubilee Cttee; Exec. Cttee, Order of British Empire; Chm., Catholic Inst. of Nursing Studies. Former Member: NSW Div., UNA; UN Status of Women Cttee; Nat. Council of Women; NSW Council on the Ageing. Augustae Crucis Insigne pro Ecclesia et Pontifice, 1980. *Address:* 1 Robert Street, Willoughby, NSW 2068, Australia.

GALLAGHER, Patrick Joseph, DFC 1943; Managing Director, Patrick Gallagher Associates, since 1979; Director, Player Promotions International, since 1980; *b* 15 April 1921; *s* of Patrick Gallagher and Mary Bernadine Donnellan; *m* 1950, Veronica Frances Bateman (*d* 1981); one *s*. *Educ:* Prior Park, Bath. Served War, 1941-46: Flt Lieut; Pilot, RAFVR. Principal, HM Treasury, 1948-58: ASC, 1956; Adviser, Raisman Commn, Nigeria, 1957-58; Consultant, Urwick, Orr & Partners Ltd, 1958-60; Dir, Ogilvy, Benson & Mather, 1960-65; Man. Dir, Glendinning Internat. Ltd, 1965-69; Pres., Glendinning Cos Inc., 1970-74; Managing Director: London Broadcasting Co. Ltd, 1975-79; Independent Radio News Ltd, 1975-79; Chm., Radio Sales & Marketing Ltd, 1976-79. *Publications:* The E Factor in Management, 1981; Promoting Profit in Independent Retail Business, 1981; contribs to business, advertising and marketing pubns in UK and USA. *Recreations:* music, travel. *Address:* 6 Kinnerton Yard, Kinnerton Street, SW1. *T:* 01-245 9467. *Club:* Royal Air Force.

GALLAHER, Patrick Edmund, CBE 1975; Chairman, North West Gas, 1974-82; Part-time Member, British Gas Corporation, 1973-81; *b* 17 June 1917; *s* of late Cormac and Agnes Gallaher; *m* 1947, Louise Hatfield (*d* 1965); one *s* two *d*. *Educ:* St Philip's Grammar School and College of Technology, Birmingham. Chemist and Engineer, City of Birmingham Gas Dept, 1934-46; Asst Engineer, Redditch Gas Co., 1946-49. With West Midlands Gas Board: Engineer and Manager, Redditch, 1949-53; Divisional Engineer, 1953-62; Regional Distribution Engineer, 1962-64; Distribution Controller, 1964-66; Area Construction Engineer, 1966-67; Area Distribution Engineer, 1967-68. Wales Gas Board (later Wales Gas Region): Dep Chm., 1968-70; Chm., 1970-74. Pres., IGasE, 1977-78. *Recreations:* sailing, gardening, travel. *Address:* March, Warrington Road, Mere, Knutsford, Cheshire.

GALLEY, Robert Albert Ernest, PhD; FRSC; Director, Shell Research Ltd, Woodstock Agricultural Research Centre, Sittingbourne, Kent, 1960-69; *b* 23 Oct. 1909; *s* of John and Jane A. Galley; *m* 1933, Elsie Marjorie Walton; one *s* two *d*. *Educ:* Colfe's Gram. Sch.; Imperial Coll., London. BSc 1930, PhD 1932, FRIC 1944. Research Chemist, Wool Industries Research Assoc., 1932-34; Chemist, Dept of War Department Chemist, 1934-37; Lectr, Sir John Cass Coll., 1937-39; Prin. Exper. Officer, Min. of Supply, Chemical Inspectorate, 1939-45, Flax Establishment, 1945-46; Sen. Prin. Scientific Officer, Agric. Research Council (Sec. Interdepartmental Insecticides Cttees), 1946-50; seconded to Scientific Secretariat, Office of Lord Pres. of Council, 1950-52; Dir, Tropical Products Institute, Dept of Scientific and Industrial Research (formerly Colonial Products Laboratory), 1953-60. *Publications:* papers in Journal of Chem. Soc., Chemistry and Industry, World Crops, etc. *Recreations:* tennis, gardening, sailing. *Address:* 3 Jackson Close, Elmbridge, Cranleigh, Surrey. *Club:* Farmers'.

GALLIE, Prof. Walter Bryce; Professor of Political Science, and Fellow of Peterhouse, Cambridge University, 1967-78, Professor Emeritus, 1978, Emeritus Fellow 1982; *b* 5 Oct. 1912; 3rd *s* of Walter S. Gallie, structural engineer; *m* 1940, Menna Humphreys; one *s* one *d*. *Educ:* Sedbergh Sch.; Balliol Coll., Oxford (Classical Exhibitioner). BA (1st Cl. PPE), 1934, BLitt 1937, MA Oxon, 1947. University Coll. of Swansea: Asst Lectr, Philosophy, 1935; Lectr, 1938; Sen. Lectr, 1946; Prof. of Philosophy, University Coll. of North Staffordshire 1950; Prof. of Logic and Metaphysics, Queen's Univ., Belfast, 1954-67. Visiting Prof., New York Univ., 1962-63; Lectures: Lewis Fry Meml, Bristol Univ., 1964; Wiles, QUB, 1976; J.R. Jones Meml, UC Swansea, 1983. Pres., Aristotelian Soc., 1970-71. Hon. Professorial Fellow, Univ. of Wales, 1980. Served War, 1940-45, ending with rank of Major, Croix de Guerre, 1945. *Publications:* An English School, 1949; Peirce and Pragmatism, 1952; Free Will and Determinism Yet Again (Inaugural Lecture), 1957; A New University: A. D. Lindsay and the Keele Experiment, 1960; Philosophy and the Historical Understanding, 1964; Philosophers of Peace and War, 1978; articles in Mind, Aristotelian Soc. Proc., Philosophy, Political Studies, etc. *Recreations:* travelling and reading. *Address:* Cilhendre, Upper Saint Mary Street, Newport, Dyfed, Wales. *T:* Newport (Dyfed) 820574.

GALLIERS-PRATT, Anthony Malcolm, CBE 1977; President, F. Pratt Engineering Corporation Ltd, since 1981 (Chairman, 1974-81); *b* 31 Jan. 1926; *s* of George Kenneth and Phyllis Galliers-Pratt; *m* 1950, Angela, *d* of Sir Charles Cayzer, 3rd Bt, and of Lady Cayzer, OBE; three *s*. *Educ:* Eton. Entered F. Pratt Engineering Corp. Ltd, as trainee, 1949; Director, 1951; subseq. Dep. Man. Dir, Man. Dir, Vice-Chm. Underwriting Member of Lloyd's. *Recreations:* yachting, shooting. *Address:* Résidence Europa, Place des Moulins, Monte Carlo. *Clubs:* Brooks's, Bucks.

GALLIFORD, Rt. Rev. David George; *see* Hulme, Bishop Suffragan of.

GALLINER, Peter; Director, International Press Institute, since 1975; Chairman, Peter Galliner Associates, since 1970; *b* 19 Sept. 1920; *s* of Dr Moritz and Hedwig Galliner; *m* 1948, Edith Marguerite Goldschmidt; one *d*. *Educ:* Berlin and London. Reuters, 1944-47; Foreign Manager, Financial Times, 1947-60; Chm. and Man. Dir, Ullstein Publishing Co., Berlin, 1960-64; Vice-Chm. and Man. Dir, British Printing Corporation Publishing Gp, 1965-70. Order of Merit, 1st cl. (German Federal Republic). *Recreations:* reading, music. *Address:* 27 Queen's Grove, NW8 6HL. *T:* 01-722 0361; Längenstrasse 110, 8964 Rudolfstetten, Switzerland. *Club:* Reform.

GALLOWAY, 13th Earl of, *cr* 1623; Randolph Keith Reginald Stewart; Lord Garlies, 1607; Bt 1627, 1687; Baron Stewart of Garlies (GB), 1796; *b* 14 Oct. 1928; *s* of 12th Earl of Galloway, and Philippa Fendall (*d* 1974), *d* of late Jacob Wendell, New York; *S* father, 1978; *m* 1975, Mrs Lily May Budge, DLJ, *y d* of late Andrew Miller, Duns, Berwickshire. *Educ:* Harrow. KLJ. *Heir:* cousin Alexander David Stewart, MBE, TD, formerly Major, City of London Yeomanry [*b* 26 Dec. 1914; *m* 1948, Daphne Marion, *widow of* FO Clyde Euan Miles Graham, RAF, and *o d* of Sir Reginald Bonsor, 2nd Bt; two *s* one *d*]. *Address:* 4 Bernard Terrace, Edinburgh EH8 9NX.

GALLOWAY, Bishop of, (RC), since 1981; Rt. Rev. Maurice Taylor, DD; *b* 5 May 1926; *s* of Maurice Taylor and Lucy Taylor (*née* McLaughlin). *Educ:* St Aloysius Coll., Glasgow; Our Lady's High School, Motherwell; Pontifical Gregorian Univ., Rome (DD). Served RAMC in UK, India, Egypt, 1944-47. Ordained to priesthood, Rome, 1950; lectured in Philosophy, 1955-60, in Theology 1960-65, St Peter's Coll., Cardross; Rector, Royal Scots Coll., Valladolid, Spain, 1965-74; Parish Priest, Our Lady of Lourdes, East Kilbride,

1974-81. *Publication:* The Scots College in Spain, 1971. *Address:* Candida Casa, 8 Corsehill Road, Ayr KA7 2ST. *T:* Ayr 266750.

GALLOWAY, Rev. Prof. Allan Douglas; Professor of Divinity, University of Glasgow, since 1968 and Principal of Trinity College, Glasgow, since 1972; *b* 30 July 1920; *s* of late William Galloway and Mary Wallace Galloway (*née* Junor); *m* 1948, Sara Louise Phillipp; two *s. Educ:* Stirling High Sch.; Univ. of Glasgow; Christ's Coll., Cambridge; Union Theol Seminary, New York. MA, BD, STM, PhD. Ordained, Asst Minister, Clune Park Parish, Port Glasgow, 1948-50; Minister of Auchterhouse, 1950-54; Prof. of Religious Studies, Univ. of Ibadan, Nigeria, 1954-60; Sen. Lectr, Univ. of Glasgow, 1960-66, Reader in Divinity, 1966-68. Hensley Henson Lectr in Theology, Oxford Univ., 1978; Cunningham Lectr, Edinburgh, 1979. *Publications:* The Cosmic Christ, 1951; Basic Readings in Theology, 1964; Faith in a Changing Culture, 1966; Wolfhart Pannenberg, 1973. *Recreation:* sailing. *Address:* 5 Straid Bheag, Clynder, Helensburgh, Dunbartonshire G84 0QX.

GALLOWAY, Lt-Col Arnold Crawshaw, CIE 1946; OBE 1941; *b* 1901; *o s* of late Percy Christopher Galloway; *m* 1946, Mary, *d* of Arthur William Odgers, Oxford; three *s. Educ:* City of London Sch.; RMC. 2/10 Gurkha Rifles, 1921-28. Member, Middle Temple. Entered Indian Political Service, 1928; Under-Sec. Rajputana, 1929-30; Vice-Consul, Ahwaz, Persia, 1930-31; Vice-Consul, Zahidan, Persia, 1932-33; Under-Sec. to Resident, Persian Gulf, 1934; Sec., British Legation, Kabul, Afghanistan, 1935-36; Sec. to Polit. Resident, Persian Gulf, 1937-38; Polit. Agent, Kuwait, Persian Gulf, 1939-41; Polit. Advr to British Forces in Iraq and Persia, 1941-43 (despatches); Consul-Gen., Ahwaz, 1943-44; Polit. Agent, Muscat, 1944-45; Polit. Resident, Persian Gulf, 1945; Polit. Agent, Bahrein, 1945-47; Consul-Gen., Bushire, 1947; Polit. Agent, Kuwait, 1948-49; UK Repres. of Bahrain Petroleum Company Ltd, 1950-68; Chm., Middle East Navigation Aids Service, 1958-68. *Address:* Yeo House, Long Load, near Langport, Somerset TA10 9JX. *T:* Long Sutton 329. *Club:* Flyfishers'.

GALLOWAY, Maj.-Gen. Kenneth Gardiner, CB 1978; OBE 1960; Director Army Dental Service, 1974-March 1978; *b* 3 Nov. 1917; *s* of David and Helen Galloway, Dundee and Oban; *m* 1949, Sheila Frances (*née* Dunsmor); two *d* (one *s* decd). *Educ:* Oban High Sch.; St Andrews Univ. LDS 1939, BDS 1940. Lieut Army Dental Corps, 1940; Captain 1941; Major 1948; Lt-Col 1955; Col 1963; Brig. 1972; Maj.-Gen. 1974. Served in Egypt, Palestine, Syria and Iraq, 1942-46; Chief Instructor and 2nd in comd, Depot and Training Establishment, RADC, 1956-60; Asst Dir Dental Service, MoD, 1967-71; Dep. Dir Dental Service: Southern Comd, 1971-72; BAOR, 1972-74. QHDS 1971-78. Col Comdt, RADC, 1980-82. OStJ 1960. *Recreations:* tennis, golf, gardening. *Address:* Berwyn Court, Avenue Road, Farnborough, Hants. *T:* Farnborough 44948.

GALLWEY, Sir Philip Frankland P.; *see* Payne-Gallwey.

GALPERN, family name of **Baron Galpern.**

GALPERN, Baron *cr* 1979 (Life Peer), of Shettleston in the District of the City of Glasgow; **Myer Galpern,** Kt 1960; DL; JP; *b* 1903. *Educ:* Glasgow Univ. Lord Provost of Glasgow and Lord Lieut for the County of the City of Glasgow, 1958-60. MP (Lab) Glasgow, Shettleston, 1959-79; Second Dep. Chm. of Ways and Means, 1974-76, First Dep. Chm., 1976-79. Mem. of the Court of Glasgow Univ.; Mem., Advisory Cttee on Education in Scotland. Hon. LLD Glasgow, 1961; Hon. FEIS, 1960. DL, Co. of City of Glasgow, 1962; JP Glasgow. *Address:* 42 Kelvin Court, Glasgow.

GALPIN, Sir Albert James, KCVO 1968 (MVO, 4th class 1958; 5th class 1945); CBE 1963 (OBE 1953); Secretary, Lord Chamberlain's Office, 1955-68; Serjeant-at-Arms to the Queen, 1955-68; *b* 1903; *s* of C. A. Galpin; *m* 1930, Vera (*d* 1980); one *s* one *d.* Entered Lord Chamberlain's Office, 1936; Asst Sec., 1941. *Recreation:* scouting. *Address:* Alderman's Cottage, Knowl Hill, Reading, Berks. *T:* Littlewick Green 2637.

GALPIN, Brian John Francis; His Honour Judge Galpin; a Circuit Judge, since 1978; *b* 21 March 1921; *s* of Christopher John Galpin, DSO and Gladys Elizabeth Galpin (*née* Souhami); *m* 1st, 1947, Ailsa McConnel (*d* 1959); one *d* decd; 2nd, 1961, Nancy Cecilia Nichols; two adopted *s. Educ:* Merchant Taylors' Sch.; Hertford Coll., Oxford. MA 1947. RAF Officer, 1940-45. Editor, Isis, 1946. Called to Bar, 1948; a Recorder of the Crown Court, 1972-78. Councillor, Metropolitan Borough of Fulham, 1950-59; Chm., Galpin Soc. for Study of Musical Instruments, 1954-72, Vice-Pres., 1974-; Mem. Cttee, Bach Choir, 1954-61. *Publications:* A Manual of International Law, 1950; Maxwell's Interpretation of Statutes, 10th edn 1953 and 11th edn 1962; Every Man's Own Lawyer, 69th edn 1962, 70th edn 1971, 71st edn 1981; contrib. Halsbury's Laws of England, 3rd and 4th edns, Encycl. of Forms and Precedents, Galpin Soc. Jl. *Recreations:* cricket (retired), music, chess. *Address:* St Bruno House, Charters Road, Sunningdale, Berks. *T:* Ascot 20284. *Clubs:* Travellers', Pratt's; Hampshire (Winchester).

GALSWORTHY, Sir Arthur (Norman), KCMG 1967 (CMG 1953); HM Diplomatic Service; retired; *b* 1 July 1916; *s* of late Captain Arthur Galsworthy and late Violet Gertrude Harrison; *m* 1st, 1940, Margaret Agnes Hiscocks (*d* 1973); two *s* ; 2nd, 1976, Aylmer Jean Martin. *Educ:* Emanuel Sch.; Corpus Christi Coll., Cambridge. Entered Colonial Office as Asst Principal, Administrative Grade, Oct. 1938. On active service, Dec. 1939-Dec.

1945: enlisted Royal Fusiliers, Sept. 1939; commnd in DCLI, 1940; attached Intelligence Corps, 1941; N Africa (First Army), 1942-43; Captain 1942; Sicily and Italy (Eighth Army), 1943-44; Major 1943; GSO1 with HQ, 21 Army Gp, 1944-45. Returned to Colonial Office, Dec. 1945; Asst Sec. in charge of International Relations Dept of Colonial Office, 1947-51; Chief Sec., West African Inter-Territorial Secretariat, Accra, 1951-54; in charge of Colonial Office Finance Dept, 1954-56; Asst Under-Sec. of State, 1956-65; Dep. Under-Sec. of State, Colonial Office, 1965-66, Commonwealth Office, 1966-68, FCO, 1968-69; British High Comr in NZ, 1969-72, in Tonga and W Samoa (non-resident), 1970-73; Governor of Pitcairn, 1970-73; Ambassador to Republic of Ireland, 1973-76. *Recreations:* fishing, bird-watching. *Address:* Bluecoat Farm, Lympsham, near Weston-super-Mare, Somerset. *Club:* United Oxford & Cambridge University.

See also Sir J. E. Galsworthy.

GALSWORTHY, Sir John (Edgar), KCVO 1975; CMG 1968; HM Diplomatic Service, retired; *b* 19 June 1919; *s* of Arthur Galsworthy; *m* 1942, Jennifer Ruth Johnstone; one *s* three *d. Educ:* Emanuel Sch.; Corpus Christi Coll., Cambridge. HM Forces 1939-41; Foreign Office, 1941-46; Third Sec., Madrid, 1946; Second Sec., Vienna, 1949; First Sec., Athens, 1951; Foreign Office, 1954; Bangkok, 1958; Counsellor, Brussels (UK Delegation to EEC) 1962; Counsellor (Economic), Bonn, 1964-67; Counsellor and subsequently Minister (European Econ. Affairs), Paris, 1967-71; Ambassador to Mexico, 1972-77. *Recreation:* fishing. *Address:* Lanzeague, St Just in Roseland, Truro, Cornwall. *Club:* United Oxford & Cambridge University.

See also Sir Arthur Galsworthy.

GALTON, Raymond Percy; author and scriptwriter since 1951 (in collaboration with Alan Simpson, *qv*); *b* 17 July 1930; *s* of Herbert and Christina Galton; *m* 1956, Tonia Phillips; one *s* two *d. Educ:* Garth Sch., Morden. *Television:* Hancock's Half Hour, 1954-61 (adaptation and translation, Fleksnes, Norwegian TV); Comedy Playhouse, 1962-63; Steptoe and Son, 1962- (adaptations and translations: Sanford and Son, US TV; Stiefbeen and Zoon, Dutch TV; Albert and Herbert, Swedish TV); Galton-Simpson Comedy, 1969; Clochemerle, 1971; Dawsons Weekly, 1975; The Galton and Simpson Playhouse, 1977; with Johnny Speight: Tea Ladies, 1979; Spooner's Patch, 1979, 1980, 1981; *films:* The Rebel, 1960; The Bargee, 1963; The Wrong Arm of the Law, 1963; The Spy with a Cold Nose, 1966; Loot, 1969; Steptoe and Son, 1971; Steptoe and Son Ride Again, 1973; The Last Fleksnes (Norway and Sweden), 1974; Die Skraphandlerne, 1975; *theatre:* Way Out in Piccadilly, 1966; The Wind in the Sassafras Trees, 1968; Albert och Herbert (Sweden), 1981. Awards: Scriptwriters of the Year, 1959 (Guild of TV Producers and Directors); Best TV Comedy Series, Steptoe and Son, 1962/3/4/5 (Screenwriters Guild); John Logie Baird Award (for outstanding contribution to Television), 1964; Best Comedy Series (Steptoe and Son, Dutch TV), 1966; Best comedy screenplay, Steptoe and Son, 1972 (Screenwriters Guild). *Publications:* (jointly with Alan Simpson, *qv*): Hancock, 1961; Steptoe and Son, 1963; The Reunion and Other Plays, 1966; Hancock's Half Hour, 1974. *Recreations:* reading, worrying. *Address:* The Ivy House, Hampton Court, Mddx. *T:* 01-977 1236.

GALWAY, 12th Viscount *cr* 1727; **George Rupert Monckton-Arundell;** Baron Killard, 1727; Lieut Comdr RCN, retired; *b* 13 Oct. 1922; *s* of Philip Marmaduke Monckton (*d* 1965) (*g g s* of 5th Viscount) and of Lavender, *d* of W. J. O'Hara; *S* cousin, 1980; *m* 1944, Fiona Margaret, *d* of late Captain P. W. de P. Taylor; one *s* three *d. Heir: s* Hon. John Philip Monckton, *b* 8 April 1952. *Address:* 583 Berkshire Drive, London, Ontario N6J 3S3, Canada.

GALWAY AND KILMACDUAGH, Bishop of, (RC), since 1976; **Most Rev. Eamonn Casey,** DD; also Apostolic Administrator of Kilfenora, since 1976; *b* Firies, Co. Kerry, 23 April 1927; *s* of John Casey and late Helena (*née* Shanahan). *Educ:* St Munchin's Coll., Limerick; St Patrick's Coll., Maynooth. LPh 1946; BA 1947. Priest, 1951. Curate, St John's Cath., Limerick, 1951-60; Chaplain to Irish in Slough; set up social framework to re-establish people into new environment; started social welfare scheme, 1960-63; invited by Cardinal Heenan to place Catholic Housing Aid Soc. on national basis; founded Family Housing Assoc.; Dir, British Council of Churches; Trustee, Housing the Homeless Central Fund; Founder-Trustee of Shelter (Chm. 1968); Mem. Council, Nat. Fedn of Housing Socs; Mem., Commn for Social Welfare; Founder Mem., Marian Employment Agency; Founder Trustee, Shelter Housing Aid Soc., 1963-69; Bishop of Kerry, 1969-76. *Publication:* (with Adam Ferguson) A Home of Your Own. *Recreations:* music, theatre, concerts, films when time, conversation, motoring. *Address:* Mount St Mary's, Galway, Ireland; (office) The Diocesan Office, The Cathedral, Galway. *T:* Galway 63566, 62255, 66553.

GALWAY, James, OBE 1977; fluteplayer; *b* 8 Dec. 1939; *s* of James Galway and Ethel Stewart Clarke; *m* 1972, Anna Christine Renggli; one *s* twin *d* (and one *s* by former *m*). *Educ:* St Paul's Sch., and Mountcollyer Secondary Modern Sch., Belfast; RCM, and Guildhall Sch. of Music, London; Conservatoire National Supérieur de Musique, Paris. Principal Flute, London Symphony Orch., 1966, Royal Philharmonic Orch., 1967-69; Principal Solo Flute, Berlin Philharmonic Orch., 1969-75; now pursuing solo career. Recordings of works by C. P. E. Bach, J. S. Bach, Beethoven, Franck, Mozart, Prokoviev, Reicha, Rodrigo, Stamitz, Telemann and Vivaldi. Hon. MA Open, 1979; Hon. DMus: QUB, 1979; New England Conservatory of Music,

1980. *Publication:* James Galway: an autobiography, 1978. *Recreations:* music, walking, swimming, films, theatre, TV, chess, backgammon, talking to people. *Address:* c/o London Artists, 73 Baker Street, W1M 1AH.

GAMBLE, Sir David, 5th Bt *cr* 1897; *b* 5 June 1933; *s* of Sir David Arthur Josias Gamble, 4th Bt and Elinor Mary (*d* 1961), *d* of Henry E. Cole; *S* father, 1982; *m* 1956, Dawn Adrienne, *d* of late David Hugh Gittins; one *s* two *d*. *Educ:* Shrewsbury. *Heir: s* David Hugh Norman Gamble, *b* 1 July 1966. *Address:* The Roadmaker, Gorsley, Ross-on-Wye, Herefordshire HR9 7SW.

GAMBLE, Sir (Frederick) Herbert, KBE 1964; CMG 1955; HM Diplomatic Service, retired; *b* 21 May 1907; *s* of Frederick West Gamble and Edith (*née* Moore); *m* 1942, Janine Corbisier de Cobreville; two *d*. *Educ:* Portora Royal School, Enniskillen; Trinity Coll., Dublin. Entered Levant Consular Service, Nov. 1930; HM Consul, Suez, 1945-46; Commercial Counsellor, Bagdad, 1948-52; Commercial Counsellor, Athens, 1952-55; Ambassador to Ecuador, 1955-59; HM Consul-Gen., Los Angeles, 1959-64; HM Ambassador to Bolivia, 1964-67. *Recreations:* tennis, golf. *Address:* Santana, Delgany, Co. Wicklow, Ireland.

GAMBLING, Prof. William Alexander, PhD, DSc; FEng, FIEE, FIERE; Professor of Optical Communication, University of Southampton, since 1980; industrial consultant and company director; *b* 11 Oct. 1926; *s* of George Alexander Gambling and Muriel Clara Gambling; *m* 1952, Margaret Pooley; one *s* two *d*. *Educ:* Univ. of Bristol (BSc, DSc); Univ. of Liverpool (PhD). FIERE 1964; CEng, FIEE 1967; FEng 1979. Lectr in Electric Power Engrg, Univ. of Liverpool, 1950-55; National Res. Council Fellow, Univ. of BC, 1955-57; Univ. of Southampton: Lectr, Sen. Lectr, and Reader, 1957-64; Dean of Engrg and Applied Science, 1972-75; Prof. of Electronics, 1964-80, Hd of Dept, 1974-79. Vis. Professor: Univ. of Colo, USA, 1966-67; Bhabha Atomic Res. Centre, India, 1970; Osaka Univ., Japan, 1977; Selby Fellow, Australian Acad. of Science, 1982. Pres., IERE, 1977-78. Member: Electronics Res. Council, 1977-80 (Mem., Optics and Infra-Red Cttee, 1965-69 and 1974-80); Board, Council of Engrg Instns, 1974-79; National Electronics Council, 1977-78; Technol. Sub-Cttee of UGC, 1973-; Adv. Bds, Optical and Quantum Electronics, and Materials Letters; British Nat. Cttee for Radio Science, 1978-; Vice-Chm., Commn D, Internat. Union of Radio Science, 1981-; Nat. Adv. Bd for Local Authority Higher Educn, Engrg Working Gp, 1982-. FRSA. Bulgin Premium, IERE, 1961, Rutherford Premium, IERE, 1964, Electronics Div. Premium, IEE, 1976 and 1978, Oliver Lodge Premium, IEE, 1981, Heinrich Hertz Premium, IERE, 1981, and J. J. Thomson Medal, IEE, 1982, for research papers. Academic Enterprise Award, 1982. *Publications:* papers on electronics and optical fibre communications. *Recreations:* music, reading, walking. *Address:* Department of Electronics, University of Southampton, Southampton SO9 5NH. *T:* Southampton 559122.

GAMES, Abram, OBE 1958; RDI 1959; graphic designer; *b* 29 July 1914; *s* of Joseph and Sarah Games; *m* 1945, Marianne Salfeld; one *s* two *d*. *Educ:* Grocers' Company Sch., Hackney Downs. Studio, 1932-36; freelance designer, 1936-40. Infantry, 1940-41; War Office Poster Designer, 1941-46. Freelance, 1946-; Lecturer Royal College of Art, 1947-53. Postage Stamps for Great Britain and Israel, Festival of Britain, BBC Television, Queen's Award to Industry Emblems. One-man shows of graphic design: London, New York, Chicago, Brussels, Stockholm, Jerusalem, Tel Aviv, São Paulo. Rep. Gt Brit. at Museum of Modern Art, New York; first prizes, Poster Competitions: Helsinki, 1957; Lisbon, 1959; New York, 1960; Stockholm, 1962, Barcelona, 1964; Internat. Philatelic Competition, Italy, 1976; Design Medal, Soc. of Industrial Artists, 1960. Silver Medal, Royal Society of Arts, 1962. Inventor of Imagic Copying Processes. *Publication:* Over my Shoulder, 1960. *Recreations:* painting, carpentry. *Address:* 41 The Vale, NW11. *T:* 01-458 2811.

GAMINARA, Albert William, CMG 1963; HMOCS (retired); *b* 1 Dec. 1913; *s* of late Albert Sidney Gaminara and late Katherine Helen Copeman; *m* 1947, Monica (*née* Watson); one *s* three *d*. *Educ:* City of London Sch.; St John's Coll., Cambridge; Oriel Coll., Oxford. MA Cantab 1943. Appointed to Sierra Leone as Administrative Cadet, 1936; seconded to Colonial Office as Principal, 1947-50; Transferred as Administrative Officer to N Rhodesia, 1950; Mem. of Legislative Council, 1963; Admin. Sec. to Govt of Northern Rhodesia (now Zambia), 1961-63; Sec. to the Cabinet, 1964, Adviser, Cabinet Office, Zambia, 1965. *Recreation:* sailing. *Address:* Stratton House, Over Stratton, South Petherton, Somerset. *Club:* Hawks.

GAMMANS, Lady, (Ann Muriel); FRSA; *d* of late Frank Paul, Warblington, Hants; *m* 1917, David Gammans, 1st and last Bt, *cr* 1955, MP (*d* 1957). *Educ:* Portsmouth High Sch. Travelled widely in the Far East, Europe and North America. Spent many years of her married life in Malaya and Japan. MP (C) Hornsey, 1957-66. Retired March 1966. Order of the Sacred Treasure, 2nd class (Japan), 1971. *Recreation:* travel. *Address:* 34 Ashley Gardens, Ambrosden Avenue, SW1. *T:* 01-834 4558. *Club:* (Assoc. Lady Member) Naval and Military.

GAMMELL, James Gilbert Sydney, MBE 1944; CA; Chairman, Ivory & Sime Ltd, since 1975; Director: Bank of Scotland, since 1969; Standard Life Assurance Company, since 1954; *b* 4 March 1920; *e s* of Lt-Gen. Sir James A. H. Gammell, KCB, DSO, MC; *m* 1944, Susan Patricia Bowring Toms, *d* of late Edward Bowring Toms; five *s* one *d*. *Educ:* Winchester Coll. Chartered Accountant, 1949. Served War, Major Grenadier Guards, 1939-46: France, 1940 and 1944, Russia, 1945. *Recreation:* farming. *Address:* Foxhall, Kirkliston, West Lothian EH29 9ER. *T:* 031-333 3275. *Club:* New (Edinburgh).

See also J. F. Gammell.

GAMMELL, John Frederick, MC 1943; MA; Assistant Secretary, Cambridge University Careers Service, since 1978; *b* 31 Dec. 1921; 2nd *s* of Lieut-Gen. Sir James A. H. Gammell, KCB, DSO, MC; *m* 1947, Margaret Anne, *d* of Ralph Juckes, Fiddington Manor, Tewkesbury; two *s* one *d*. *Educ:* Winchester Coll.; Trinity Coll., Cambridge. MA 1953. Asst Master, Horris Hill, Newbury, 1940-41. War Service with KRRC, 1941-44; wounded, 1943; invalided out, 1944. Trinity Coll., Cambridge, 1946-47 (BA); Asst Master, Winchester Coll., 1944-45 and 1947-68; Exchange with Sen. Classics Master, Geelong Grammar Sch., Australia, 1949-50; Housemaster of Turner's, Winchester Coll., 1958-68; Headmaster, Repton Sch., 1968-78. *Recreation:* friends. *Address:* 15 Hale Street, Cambridge. *T:* Cambridge 354414.

See also J. G. S. Gammell.

GAMMIE, Gordon Edward, CB 1981; Legal Adviser and Solicitor to Ministry of Agriculture, Fisheries and Food, to Forestry Commission and to Intervention Board for Agricultural Produce, since 1979; *b* 9 Feb. 1922; *e s* of Dr Alexander Edward Gammie and Ethel Mary Gammie (*née* Miller); *m* 1949, Joyce Rust; two *s*. *Educ:* St Paul's Sch.; The Queen's Coll., Oxford (MA). War service, 1941-45; Captain, 1st Bn Argyll and Sutherland Highlanders. Called to Bar, Middle Temple, 1948. Entered Govt Legal Service, 1949; Asst Solicitor, Mins of Health and of Housing and Local Govt, 1967; Under-Sec. (Principal Asst Solicitor), Min. of Housing and Local Govt, later DoE, 1969-74; Under-Sec., Cabinet Office, 1975-77; Dep. Treasury Solicitor, 1977-79. Chm., Civil Service Legal Soc., 1970-72. *Recreations:* tennis, listening to music. *Address:* Ty Gwyn, 52 Sutton Lane, Banstead, Surrey. *T:* Burgh Heath 55287.

GAMON, Hugh Wynell, CBE 1979; MC 1944; Senior Partner, Sherwood & Co., since 1972; HM Government Agent, since 1970; *b* 31 March 1921; *s* of Judge Hugh R. P. Gamon and E. Margaret Gamon; *m* 1949, June Elizabeth, *d* of William and Florence Temple; one *s* three *d*. *Educ:* St Edward's Sch., Oxford; Exeter Coll., Oxford, 1946-48. MA 1st Cl. Hons Jurisprudence; Law Society Hons; Edmund Thomas Childe Prize. Served War, 1940-46: Royal Corps of Signals, N Africa, Italy and Palestine, with 1st Division. Articled to Clerk of Cumberland CC, 1949-51; Asst Solicitor, Sherwood & Co., 1951; Parly Agent, 1954; Partner, Sherwood & Co., 1955. *Recreations:* gardening, walking. *Address:* Black Charles, Underriver, Sevenoaks, Kent TN15 0FY. *T:* Hildenborough 833036. *Club:* St Stephen's Constitutional.

GANDAR, Hon. Leslie Walter; JP; High Commissioner for New Zealand in UK, 1979-82; *b* 26 Jan. 1919; *s* of Max Gandar and Doris Harper; *m* 1945, M. Justine, *d* of T. A. Smith and Florence Smith; four *s* one *d* (and one *d* decd). *Educ:* Wellington College; Victoria Univ., Wellington (BSc 1940). FNZIAS, FInstP. Served RNZAF and RAF, 1940-44. Farming, 1945-. MP, Ruahine, 1966-78; Minister of Science, Energy Resources, Mines, Electricity, 1972; Minister of Education, Science and Technology, 1975-78. Chairman, Pohangina County Council, 1954-69. Chancellor, Massey Univ., 1970-76. Hon. DSc Massey, 1977. JP 1958. *Recreations:* music—when not watching cricket; wood-carving; work. *Address:* Flat 14, 213 The Terrace, Wellington, New Zealand. *Clubs:* East India, Devonshire, Sports and Public Schools, Royal Automobile; Feilding, Rangitikei (NZ).

GANDAR DOWER, Eric Leslie, MA (Law); founder of Aberdeen Airport, Allied Airways (Gandar Dower) Ltd, Aberdeen Flying School Ltd, Aberdeen Flying Club Ltd, and Aberdeen Aerodrome Fuel Supplies Ltd; 3rd *s* of late Joseph Wilson Gandar-Dower and late Amelia Frances Germaine. *Educ:* Brighton Coll.; Jesus Coll., Cambridge. Trained for stage at RADA. Toured with Alan Stevenson, Cecil Barth and Harold V. Neilson's Companies in Kick In, Betty at Bay, The Witness for the Defence, and The Marriage of Kitty. Played wide range of parts on tour with Sir Philip Ben Greet's Shakespeare Company, including Horatio in Hamlet, Antonio in Merchant of Venice, Sicinius Velutus in Coriolanus, Don Pedro in Much Ado About Nothing and Oliver in As You Like It, also in London Shakespeare for Schools LCC Educational Scheme. Wrote and produced The Silent Husband. Toured under own management as Lord Stevenage in Young Person in Pink. Competed King's Cup Air Race 5 years. Holder of FAI Aviators Certificate. Built Dyce (Aberdeen) Airport. Founded Allied Airways (Gandar Dower) Ltd, 1934; Mem. Exec. Council Aerodrome Owners Assoc., 1934-45; Founder Mem. Air Registration Bd; Pioneered Scottish Air Lines Aberdeen/Edinburgh, Aberdeen/Glasgow, Aberdeen/Wick/Thurso/Kirkwall/Stromness and Shetland, which operated throughout 1939-45 War. Pioneered first British/Norwegian Air Line, 1937, Newcastle to Stavanger. Founded, May 1939, 102nd Aberdeen Airport Air Training Corps. Served as Flight Lieut RAFVR, 1940-43. First Chm. and Founder, Assoc. of Brit. Aircraft Operators, 1944. MP (C) Caithness and Sutherland, 1945-50. Attached Mau Mau Campaign, Kenya, 1952-53. *Recreations:* ski-ing, squash, tennis, lawn tennis, swimming, poetry, flying, motoring. *Address:* Westerings, Clos des Fosses, St Martin, Guernsey, Channel Islands. *T:* Guernsey 38637. *Clubs:* Royal Automobile; Hawks, Amateur Dramatic, Footlights (Cambridge); Automobile de France (Paris).

GANDEE, John Stephen, CMG 1967; OBE 1958; HM Diplomatic Service, retired; British High Commissioner in Botswana, 1966-69; *b* 8 Dec. 1909; *s* of John Stephen and Constance Garfield Gandee; *m* 1st, May Degenhardt (*d* 1954); one *s* two *d* ; 2nd, Junia Henman (*née* Devine); two *d* (and one step *s* one step *d*). *Educ:* Dorking High Sch. Post Office, Dorking, 1923-30; India Office, 1930-47; Private Sec. to Parly Under-Sec. of State, 1946-47; and 1947-49; Asst Private Sec. to Sec. of State, 1947; First Sec., Ottawa, 1952-54; seconded to Bechuanaland Protectorate, 1958-60 and 1961; seconded to Office of High Comr for Basutoland, Bechuanaland Protectorate and Swaziland, 1960-61; Head of Administration Dept, CRO, 1961-64; Head of Office Services and Supply Dept, Diplomatic Service Administration, 1965-66. *Recreations:* walking, gardening. *Address:* South View, Holmwood, Dorking, Surrey RH5 4LT. *T:* Dorking 6513.

GANDELL, Sir Alan (Thomas), Kt 1978; CBE 1959; FCIT; Member, National Ports Authority, New Zealand, 1969-81; Chancellor, Order of St John, New Zealand, 1972-81; *b* 8 Oct. 1904; *s* of William Gandell and Emma Gandell; *m* 1933, Edna Marion (*née* Wallis); one *s*. *Educ:* Greymouth Dist High Sch. Mem., Inst. of Engineers, NZ, 1940; FCIT 1959. NZ Govt Railways: civil engrg appts, 1920-52; Mem., Bd of Management, 1953-57; Gen. Man., 1955-66, retd. KStJ 1971. *Recreations:* bowling, gardening. *Address:* 43 Donald Street, Karori, Wellington 5, New Zealand. *T:* Wellington 767-313.

GANDELL, Captain Wilfrid Pearse, CBE 1940; Royal Navy; *b* 1 Nov. 1886; *s* of T. Pearse Gandell, 16 Earl's Court Square, SW5; *m* 1923, Lilian Amabel Marian (*d* 1982) (BEM 1970; Diocesan Pres., Mothers' Union, dio. Chichester, 1943-52; WVS-WRVS Centre Organiser, Horsham Urban and Rural Dists, 1946-74; Long Service Medal and bar 1970), *d* of Maj.-Gen. Maxwell Campbell, RE; one *d* (one *s* decd). *Educ:* Stoke House; HMS Britannia. Went to sea as Midshipman in 1902; specialised in torpedo; present at battle of Jutland in HMS St Vincent; ns 1922; retired in 1929; recalled Sept. 1939; served as Principal Sea Transport Officer, French Ports, from declaration of war till fall of France (despatches, CBE), then as PSTO Clyde till 1941, both with rank of Commodore; Chief Staff Officer, Plymouth, 1941-44 (US Legion of Merit); Senior Officer Reserve Fleet, Forth Area, 1944-46; reverted to retired list, April 1946. Member: West Sussex CC, 1958-64; Horsham RDC, 1952-64; Asst Chief Warden CD, Horsham Area, 1952-65. RHS medal, 1918. *Address:* Hayes Warren, Slinfold, Horsham, West Sussex RH13 7RF. *T:* Slinfold 790246. *Clubs:* Naval and Military, MCC.

GANDER, L(eonard) Marsland; journalist, war correspondent, author; Television and Radio Correspondent and Critic of The Daily Telegraph 1946-70; *b* London, 27 June 1902; *s* of James Gander and Ellen Marsland; *m* 1931, Hilda Mabel Ellen Rowley (*d* 1980); two *s*. *Educ:* Higher Elementary Sch., Stratford; City of London Coll. Reporter, Stratford Express, West Ham, 1919-24; Chief Reporter, Times of India, Bombay, 1924-26; Acting Editor, Illustrated Weekly of India, 1925; Radio Correspondent of the Daily Telegraph, 1926, Television Critic and Correspondent, 1935; War Correspondent of The Daily Telegraph, 1941-45; covered campaigns in Burma, Dodecanese, Italy, Southern France, Greece, 1943-44; with 6th Airborne Div. and 1st Canadian Army, Europe, 1945. Chm., Press Club, 1959; Fellow of the Royal Television Soc., 1961 (Mem. Council, 1965). Toured United States for Ford Fund for Advancement of Education, 1963. Special Governor, Crossways Trust Old People's Homes, 1972-75. Collaborated with Asa Briggs on Sound and Vision, final vol. of History of Broadcasting in UK, 1979. *Publications:* Atlantic Battle, 1941; Long Road to Leros, 1945; After These Many Quests, autobiography, 1950; Television for All, 1950. *Recreations:* desultory chess, swimming, gardening, washing-up. *Address:* 8 Paddock Green, Rustington, Sussex BN16 3AU. *T:* Rustington 2966. *Clubs:* Press, Savage, Roehampton, Lord's Taverners'.

GANDHI, Mrs Indira; Prime Minister of India, 1966-77 and since 1980; President of the Indian National Congress, since 1978; *b* 19 Nov. 1917; *d* of late Pandit Jawaharlal Nehru and Kamala Kaul; *m* 1942, Feroze Gandhi (*d* 1960); one *s* (and one *s* decd). *Educ:* Visva-Bharati. Founded Vanar Sena (Congress children's organisation), 1929; joined Indian National Congress, 1938; Mem., Working Cttee, 1955; Pres., Congress Party, 1959-60; Chm., Citizens' Central Council, 1962; Mem., Lok Sabha, 1964-77, 1978, 1980-; Minister of Information and Broadcasting, 1964-66; Minister: for Home Affairs, 1970-73; for Atomic Energy, 1967-77, 1980-; for Defence, 1980-82. Dep. Chm., Internat. Union of Child Welfare; Vice-Pres., Indian Coun. of Child Welfare. Most admired person in world, Gallup Poll, USA, 1971. Hon. DCL Oxon, 1971. *Publications:* India: speeches and reminiscences, 1975; Eternal India, 1980. *Address:* 1 Safdarjang Road, New Delhi, India.

GANDHI, Manmohan Purushottam, MA, FREconS, FSS; Editor, Major Industries of India Annual and Textile Industry Annual; Member, All-India Board of Management Studies; Director: Indian Link Chain Manufacturers Ltd; Zenith Steel Pipes and Industries Ltd; Hon. Metropolitan Magistrate, Bombay; *b* 5 Nov. 1901; *s* of late Purushottam Kahanji Gandhi, of Limbdi (Kathiawad); *m* 1926, Rambhagauri, BA (Indian Women's Univ.), *d* of Sukhlal Chhaganlal Shah of Wadhwan. *Educ:* Bahauddin Coll., Junagad; Gujerat Coll., Ahmedabad; Hindu Univ., Benares. BA (History and Econs), Bombay Univ., 1923; MA (Political Econ. and Political Philosophy), Benares Hindu Univ., 1925; Ashburner Prize of Bombay Univ., 1925. Statistical Asst, Govt of Bombay, Labour Office, 1926; Asst Sec., Indian Currency League, Bombay, 1926; Sec., Indian Chamber of Commerce, Calcutta, 1926-36; Sec.,

Indian Sugar Mills Assoc., 1932-36; Officer-in-Charge, Credit Dept, National City Bank of New York, Calcutta, 1936-37; Chief Commercial Manager, Rohtas Industries Ltd; Dalmia Cement Ltd, 1937-39; Dir, Indian Sugar Syndicate Ltd, 1937-39; Controller of Supplies, Bengal and Bombay, 1941-43; Sec., Indian Nat. Cttee, Internat. Chamber of Commerce, Calcutta, 1929-31; Sec., Fedn of Indian Chambers of Commerce and Industry, 1928-29. Member: East Indian Railway Adv. Cttee, 1939-40; Bihar Labour Enquiry Cttee, 1937-39; UP and Bihar Power Alcohol Cttee, 1938; UP and Bihar Sugar Control Board, 1938; Western Railway Adv. Cttee, Bombay, 1950-52; Small Scale Industries Export Prom. Adv. Cttee; Technical Adviser, Indian Tariff Board, 1947. Hon. Prof., Sydenham Coll. of Commerce, 1943-49. Member: All India Council of Tech. Educn, 1948-73; All India Bd of Studies in Commerce, 1948-70; Senate and Syndicate, Bombay Univ., 1957-69; Dean, Commerce Faculty, Bombay Univ., 1966-67. Director: E India Cotton Assoc., 1953-73; Bombay Oils & Oilseeds Exchange, 1972-74. *Publications:* How to Compete with Foreign Cloth, 1931; The Indian Sugar Industry: Its Past, Present and Future, 1934; The Indian Cotton Textile Industry-Its Past, Present and Future, 1937; The Indian Sugar Industry (annually, 1935-64); The Indian Cotton Textile Industry, (annually, 1936-60); Centenary Volume of the Indian Cotton Textile Industry, 1851-1950; Major Industries of India (Annually, 1951-); Problems of Sugar Industry in India, 1946; Monograph on Handloom Weaving in India, 1953; Some Impressions of Japan, 1955. *Recreations:* tennis, badminton, billiards, bridge, swimming. *Address:* Nanabhay Mansions, Pherozeshah Mehta Road, Fort, Bombay 400001, India. *T:* (home) 828405, (office) 256033 and 250647. *TA:* Gandhi caste Keen, Bombay. *Clubs:* Radio, National Sports, Rotary, Fifty-Five Tennis (Bombay).

GANDY, Christopher Thomas; HM Diplomatic Service, retired; *b* 21 April 1917; *s* of late Dr Thomas H. Gandy and late Mrs Ida Gandy (authoress of A Wiltshire Childhood, Around the Little Steeple, etc); unmarried. *Educ:* Marlborough; King's Coll., Cambridge. On active service with Army and RAF, 1939-45. Entered Foreign Office, Nov. 1945; Tehran, 1948-51; Cairo, 1951-52; FO, 1952-54; Lisbon, 1954-56; Libya, 1956-59; FO, 1960-62; apptd HM Minister to The Yemen, 1962, subsequently Counsellor, Kuwait; Minister (Commercial) Rio de Janeiro, 1966-68. *Publications:* articles in Asian Affairs, Middle East International, The New Middle East and The Annual Register of World Events. *Recreations:* music, photography, gardening. *Address:* 60 Ambleside Drive, Headington, Oxford. *Club:* Travellers'.

GANDY, Ronald Herbert; Treasurer to the Greater London Council, 1972-77, retired; *b* 22 Nov. 1917; *s* of Frederick C. H. Gandy and Olive (*née* Wilson); *m* 1942, Patricia M. Turney; two *s* one *d*. *Educ:* Banister Court Sch. and Taunton's Sch. (now Richard Taunton Coll.), Southampton. Town Clerk's Dept, Civic Centre, Southampton County Borough Council, 1936; LCC: Admin. Officer, Comptroller's (i.e. Treasurer's) Dept, 1937; Asst Comptroller, 1957; Dep. Comptroller, 1964; Dep. Treasurer, GLC, 1965; Dep. Chief Financial Officer, Inner London Educn Authority, 1967. Mem., C of E Central Bd of Finance, 1981-. Hon. Treas., Notting Hill Housing Trust, 1979-. Mem. CIPFA. *Address:* Braemar, 4 Roughwood Close, Watford, Herts. *T:* Watford 24215.

GANE, Michael, DPhil, MA; economic and environmental consultant; *b* 29 July 1927; *s* of late Rudolf E. Gane and Helen Gane; *m* 1954, Madge Stewart Taylor; one *d*. *Educ:* Colyton Grammar Sch., Devon; Edinburgh Univ. (BSc Forestry 1948); London Univ. (BScEcon 1963); Oxford Univ. (DPhil, MA 1967). Asst Conservator of Forests, Tanganyika, 1948-62; Sen. Research Officer, Commonwealth Forestry Inst., Oxford, 1963-69; Dir, Project Planning Centre for Developing Countries, Bradford Univ., 1969-74; Dir, England, Nature Conservancy Council, 1974-81. *Publications:* various contribs to scientific and technical jls. *Recreations:* natural history, gardening. *Address:* 1 Ridgeway Close, Sidbury, near Sidmouth, Devon EX10 0SW.

GANE, Richard Howard; Chairman of the Board of Directors, George Wimpey & Co. Ltd, 1973-76; *b* 5 Nov. 1912; *s* of Richard Howard Gane and Ada (*née* Alford); *m* 1st, 1939, Betty Rosemary Franklin (*d* 1976); two *s* one *d*; 2nd, 1977, Elizabeth Gaymer. *Educ:* Kingston Grammar School. Joined George Wimpey & Co. Ltd, 1934; also Chm. of George Wimpey Canada Ltd, and Dir, Markborough Properties Ltd, Toronto, 1965-73. *Recreations:* golf, shooting. *Address:* Woodlands, Cranley Road, Burwood Park, Walton-on-Thames, Surrey.

GANILAU, Ratu Sir Penaia Kanatabatu, KBE 1974 (OBE 1960); CMG 1968; CVO 1970; DSO 1956; ED 1974; Deputy Prime Minister of Fiji since 1973, and Minister for Home Affairs (conjointly), since 1975; Minister for Fijian Affairs and Rural Development, since 1977; Member of House of Representatives, Fiji; *b* 28 July 1918; Fijian; *m* 1949, Adi Laisa Delaisomosomo Yavaca (decd); five *s* two *d* ; *m* 1975, Adi Lady Davila Ganilau. *Educ:* Provincial Sch. Northern, Queen Victoria Meml Sch., Fiji. Devonshire Course for Admin. Officers, Wadham Coll., Oxford Univ., 1947. Served with FIR, 1940; demobilised, retained rank of Captain, 1946. Colonial Admin. Service, 1947; District Officer, 1948-53; Mem. Commn on Fijian Post Primary Educn in the Colony, 1953. Service with Fiji Mil. Forces, 1953-56; demobilised, retained rank of Temp. Lt-Col, 1956; Hon. Col, 2nd Bn (Territorial), FIR, 1973. Seconded to post of Fijian Acon. Devel Officer and Roko Tui Cakaudrove conjoint, 1956; Tour Manager and Govt Rep., Fiji Rugby football tour of NZ, 1957; Dep. Sec. for Fijian Affairs, 1961; Minister for Fijian Affairs and Local Govt, 1965; Leader of Govt Business and Minister for

Home Affairs, Lands and Mineral Resources, 1970; Minister for Communications, Works and Tourism, 1972. Mem., Council of Ministers; Official Mem., Legislative Council; Chairman: Fijian Affairs Bd; Fijian Develt Fund Bd; Native Land Trust Bd; Great Council of Chiefs. *Recreation:* Rugby football (rep. Fiji against Maori All Black, 1938 and during Rugby tour of NZ, 1939). *Address:* Ministry for Fijian Affairs and Rural Development, Suva, Fiji. *T:* 22971. *Clubs:* Fiji, Defence (Suva, Fiji).

GANZ, Prof. Peter Felix; Professor of German Language and Literature, University of Oxford, since 1972; Fellow of St Edmund Hall, Oxford, since 1972; *b* 3 Nov. 1920; *s* of Dr Hermann and Dr Charlotte Ganz; *m* 1949, Rosemary (*née* Allen); two *s* two *d. Educ:* Realgymnasium, Mainz; King's Coll., London. MA 1950; PhD 1954; MA Oxon 1960. Buchenwald, 1938; Internment Camp, IoM, 1940; Army service, 1940-45. Asst Lectr, Royal Holloway Coll., London Univ., 1948-49; Lectr, Westfield Coll., London Univ., 1949-60; Reader in German, Oxford Univ., 1960-72; Fellow of Hertford Coll., Oxford, 1963-72 (Hon. Fellow, 1977). Vis. Professor: Erlangen-Nürnberg Univ., 1964-65 and 1971; Munich Univ., 1970 and 1974. Comdr, Order of Merit, Germany, 1973. Jt Editor: Beiträge zur Geschichte der deutschen Sprache und Literatur, 1976-; Oxford German Studies, 1978-. *Publications:* Der Einfluss des Englischen auf den deutschen Wortschatz 1740-1815, 1957; Geistliche Dichtung des 12. Jahrhunderts, 1960; Graf Rudolf, 1964; (with F. Norman and W. Schwarz) Dukus Horant, 1964; (with W. Schröder) Probleme mittelalterlicher Uberlieferung und Textkritik, 1967; Jacob Grimm's Conception of German Studies, 1973; Gottfried von Strassburgs 'Tristan', 1978; Jacob Burckhardt, Über das Studium der Geschichte, 1981; articles on German medieval literature and language in jls. *Recreations:* music, walking, travel. *Address:* 516 Banbury Road, Oxford OX2 8LG. *T:* Oxford 59342.

GANZONI, family name of **Baron Belstead.**

GAON, Dr Solomon; Haham (Chief Rabbi) of the Communities affiliated to the World Sephardi Federation in the Diaspora, since 1978; *b* 15 Dec. 1912; *s* of Isaac and Rachael Gaon; *m* 1944, Regina Hassan; one *s* one *d. Educ:* Jesuit Secondary Sch., Travnik, Yugoslavia; Jewish Teachers Seminary, Sarajevo, Yugoslavia; Jews' Coll., London Univ. (BA 1941, PhD 1943; Rabbinic Dip. 1948). Spanish and Portuguese Jews Congregation: Student Minister, 1934-41; Asst Minister, 1941-44; Minister, 1944-46; Sen. Minister, 1946-49; Haham of Spanish and Portuguese Jews Congregation and Associated Sephardi Congregations, 1949-77; Haham (Chief Rabbi), Assoc. of Sephardi Congregations, 1977-80. Pres., Union of Sephardi Communities of England, N America and Canada, 1969-; Vice-Pres., World Sephardi Fedn, 1965-. Prof. of Sephardi Studies, Yeshiva Univ., New York, 1970-, Head of Sephardi Dept, 1977-. Hon. DD Yeshiva Univ., 1974. Alfonso el Sabio (for Cultural Work with and on Spanish Jewry), Spain, 1964. *Publications:* Influence of Alfonso Tostado on Isaac Abravanel, 1944; The Development of Jewish Prayer, 1949; Relations between the Spanish & Portuguese Synagogue in London and its Sister Congregation in New York, 1964; (ed) Book of Prayer of the Spanish & Portuguese Jews' Congregation, London, 1965; Edgar Joshua Nathan, Jr (1891-1965), 1965; Abravanel and the Renaissance, 1974; The Contribution of the English Sephardim to Anglo-Jewry, 1975. *Recreations:* walking, tennis, music. *Address:* 25 Ashworth Road, W9 1JW. *T:* 01-289 1575.

GARBO, Greta, (Greta Lovisa Gustafsson); film actress; *b* Stockholm, 18 Sept. 1905; *d* of Sven and Louvisa Gustafsson. *Educ:* Dramatic Sch. attached to Royal Theatre, Stockholm. Began stage career as dancer in Sweden. First film appearance in The Atonement of Gosta Berling, 1924; went to US, 1925; became an American Citizen, 1951. Films include: The Torrent, 1926; The Temptress, 1926; Flesh and the Devil, 1927; Love, 1927; The Divine Woman, 1928; The Mysterious Lady, 1928; A Woman of Affairs, 1929; Wild Orchids, 1929; The Single Standard, 1929; The Kiss, 1929; Anna Christie, 1930 (first talking rôle); Susan Lenox, Her Fall and Rise, 1931; Mata Hari, 1931; Grand Hotel, 1932; As You Desire Me, 1932; Queen Christina, 1933; Anna Karenina, 1935; Camille, 1936; Conquest, 1937; Ninotchka, 1939; Two-Faced Woman, 1941.

GARCIA, Arthur; Hon. Mr Justice Garcia; Judge of the High Court, Hong Kong, since 1979; *b* 3 July 1924; *s* of late F. M. Garcia and of Maria Fung; *m* 1948, Hilda May; two *s. Educ:* La Salle Coll., Hong Kong; Inns of Court Sch. of Law. Called to the Bar, Middle Temple, 1957. Jun. Clerk, Hong Kong Govt, 1939-41; Staff Mem., British Consulate, Macao, 1942-45; Clerk to Attorney Gen., Hong Kong, 1946-47; Asst Registrar, 1951-54; Colonial Develt and Welfare Scholarship, Inns of Court Sch. of Law, 1954-57; Legal Asst, Hong Kong, 1957-59; Magistrate, 1959; Sen. Magistrate, 1968; Principal Magistrate, 1968; Dist Judge, 1971. *Recreations:* photography, swimming. *Address:* Supreme Court, Hong Kong. *Club:* Royal Hong Kong Jockey (Hong Kong).

GARCIA-PARRA, Jaime; Gran Cruz, Orden de San Carlos, Colombia, 1977; Gran Cruz de Boyaca, Colombia, 1981; Senator, since 1982; *b* 19 Dec. 1931; *s* of Alfredo Garcia-Cadena and Elvira Parra; *m* 1955, Lillian Duperly; three *s. Educ:* Gimnasio Moderno, Bogotá, Colombia; Univ. Javeriana, Bogotá; Univ. la Gran Colombia, Bogotá; Syracuse Univ., USA (MA); LSE, London (MSc). Lawyer. Minister (Colombian Delegn) to Internat. Coffee Org., 1963-66; Finance Vice-Pres., Colombian Nat. Airlines AVIANCA, 1966-69; Consultant in private practice, 1969-74; Actg Labour and Social Security

Minister and Minister of Communications, 1974-75; Minister of Mines and Energy, 1975-77; Ambassador of Colombia to UK, 1977-78; Minister of Finance, Colombia, 1978-81; Exec. Dir, World Bank, 1981-82. Mem., several delegns to UNCTAD and FAO Confs at Geneva, 1964, New Delhi, 1968, Rome, 1970, 1971. Hon. Fellow, LSE, 1980. Gran Cruz, Orden del Baron de Rio Branco, Brasil, 1977. *Publications: essays:* La Inflación y el Desarrollo de América Latina (Inflation and Development in Latin America), 1968; La Estrategia del Desarrollo Colombiano (The Strategy of Colombian Development), 1971; El Problema Inflacionario Colombiano (Colombia's Inflationary Problem), 1972; Petróleo un Problema y una Políitica (Oil—a Problem and a Policy), 1975; El Sector Eléctrico en la Encrucijada (The Electrical Sector at the Cross-Roads), 1975; Una Políitica para el Carbón (A Policy for Coal), 1976; La Cuestión Cafetera (The Coffee Dilemma), 1977; Políitica Agraria (Agrarian Policy), 1977. *Recreations:* walking, reading, poetry, tennis, cooking. *Address:* Calle 111, No 2-10, Apt 201, Bogota, Colombia. *Clubs:* Jockey, Country (Bogotá).

GARDAM, David Hill, QC 1968; *b* 14 Aug. 1922; *s* of late Harry H. Gardam, Hove, Sussex; *m* 1954, Jane Mary Gardam, *qv;* two *s* one *d. Educ:* Oundle Sch.; Christ Church, Oxford. MA 1948. War Service, RNVR, 1941-46 (Temp. Lieut). Called to the Bar, Inner Temple, 1949; Bencher 1977. *Recreation:* painting. *Address:* 22 Old Buildings, Lincoln's Inn, WC2A 3UJ. *T:* 01-405 2072; 53 Ridgway Place, SW19.

GARDAM, Jane Mary; novelist; *b* 11 July 1928; *d* of William Pearson, Coatham Sch., Redcar and Kathleen Mary Pearson (*née* Helm); *m* 1954, David Hill Gardam, *qv;* two *s* one *d. Educ:* Saltburn High Sch. for Girls; Bedford Coll., London Univ. Red Cross Travelling Librarian, Hospital Libraries, 1951; Sub-Editor, Weldon's Ladies Jl, 1952; Asst Literary Editor, Time and Tide, 1952-54. FRSL 1976. *Publications:* A Few Fair Days, 1971; A Long Way From Verona, 1971; The Summer After The Funeral, 1973; Black Faces, White Faces, 1975; Bilgewater, 1977; God on the Rocks, 1978; The Sidmouth Letters, 1980; The Hollow Land (Whitbread Literary Award), 1981; Bridget and William, 1981. *Recreations:* walking, gardening, travelling. *Address:* 53 Ridgway Place, SW19 4SP.

GARDENER, Sir (Alfred) John, KCMG 1954 (CMG 1949); CBE 1944; JP; *b* 6 Feb. 1897; *s* of late G. Northcote Gardener, Exeter; *m* 1st, 1929, Dorothy Caroline (*d* 1967), *d* of late Emile Purgold, Liverpool; no *c;* 2nd, 1968, Marion May (*d* 1977), *d* of Linden E. W. Huish, Exeter; no *c. Educ:* Heles Sch., Exeter; Trinity Hall, Cambridge. Served in Army in France and Belgium, 1916-18. Joined Consular Service, 1920, and served in various posts in S Persia, Morocco, Syria and USA. In June 1941 served as Political Officer during Syrian Campaign with rank of Lieut-Col (subsequently Col). Served in Foreign Office, 1946-49; British Ambassador to Afghanistan, 1949-51, and to Syria, 1953-56; retired, 1957. JP Devon, 1959. *Address:* c/o Barclay's Bank, Exeter, Devon.

GARDHAM, Arthur John, MS, FRCS; formerly Senior Surgeon to University College Hospital and Examiner in Surgery to University of London; *b* Leytonstone, Essex, Nov. 1899; 2nd *s* of Arthur and Elizabeth Gardham; *m* 1936, Audrey Glenton, 3rd *d* of late Francis Carr, CBE; one *s* two *d. Educ:* Bancroft's Sch.; University College and University College Hospital, London. MRCS, LRCP 1921; MB, BS (London), 1923; FRCS 1924; MS (London), 1926. Served RNVR, 1917-18. Qualified 1921; House appts at UCH; Pearce Gould Scholar, 1925; Asst to Prof. Clairmont at Kantonsspital, Zürich, 1925; Surgical Registrar and later Asst Dir of Surgical Unit, UCH. Surgeon to Hampstead Gen. Hosp. (Royal Free Hosp. Group). Served RAMC, 1940-45; Consulting Surgeon to 14th Army and Eastern Comd, India (despatches). Mem. Court of Examiners of RCS, 1945-51; Examiner in Surgery: to Univ. of Cambridge, 1951-57; to Univ. of Edinburgh, 1957-60; to Univ. of London, 1958-62; associated with Emergency Bed Service of King Edward's Hosp. Fund for London since its foundation in 1938; Hunterian Prof., RCS; Fellow: Royal Society of Medicine (Pres. of Surgical Sect., 1963-64); University Coll., London; Assoc. of Surgeons (late Mem. Council). Late Hon. Sec., Devon and Somerset Stag-hounds. *Publications:* (with Davies) The Operations of Surgery, 1963, Vol. 2, 1969; Sections of Grey Turner's Modern Operative Surgery; various papers on surgical subjects. *Recreations:* field sports. *Address:* Castle Green, Oare, Brendon, near Lynton, Devon. *T:* Brendon 205.

GARDHAM, Air Vice-Marshal Marcus Maxwell, CB 1972; CBE 1965; *b* 5 Nov. 1916; *s* of late Arthur Gardham, High Wycombe; *m* 1954, Rosemary Hilda (*née* Wilkins); one *s. Educ:* Royal Grammar Sch., High Wycombe. Commissioned RAF (Accountant Br), 1939; RAF Ferry Command, 1941; HQ AEAF, 1944. BJSM, Washington, 1946 (SOA); RAPO, 1949; psc 1952; No 16 MU, 1953; 2nd TAF (Org. Staff), 1955; Air Ministry (Personnel Staff), 1957; jssc 1957; Technical Trng Command (Org. Staff), 1959; FEAF (Command Accountant), 1965; Dir of Personal Services, MoD (Air), 1966; Head of RAF Secretarial Br., 1971-72; AOA, RAF Trng Comd, 1969-72. Registrar, Ashridge Management Coll., 1972-82. MBIM. *Recreations:* gardening, golf. *Address:* Almond Cottage, Millfield, Berkhamsted. *T:* Berkhamsted 3988. *Club:* Royal Air Force.

GARDINER, family name of **Baron Gardiner.**

GARDINER, Baron *cr* 1963, of Kittisford (Life Peer); **Gerald Austin Gardiner,** PC 1964; CH 1975; Chancellor, The Open University, 1973-78;

b 30 May 1900; *s* of late Sir Robert Gardiner; *m* 1st, 1925, Lesly (*d* 1966), *o d* of Edwin Trounson, JP; one *d* ; 2nd, 1970, Mrs Muriel Box. *Educ:* Harrow Sch.; Magdalen Coll., Oxford (MA). 2nd Lieut Coldstream Guards, 1918; Pres. Oxford Union and OUDS, 1924; called to the Bar, 1925; KC 1948. Friends Ambulance Unit, 1943-45. Mem. Cttee on Supreme Court Practice and Procedure, 1947-53; Mem. of Lord Chancellor's Law Reform Cttee, 1952-63. A Master of the Bench of the Inner Temple, 1955; Chm. Gen. Council of the Bar, 1958 and 1959; former Chm., Council of Justice; Mem., Internat. Cttee of Jurists, 1971-. Chm (JT), National Campaign for Abolition of Capital Punishment. Alderman, London County Council, 1961-63. Lord High Chancellor of Great Britain, 1964-70. BA Open Univ., 1977. Hon. LLD: Southampton, 1965; London, 1969; Manitoba, 1969; Law Soc. of Upper Canada, 1969; Birmingham, 1971; Melbourne, 1973; DUniv York, 1966. *Publications:* Capital Punishment as a Deterrent, 1956; (Jt Ed.) Law Reform Now, 1963. *Recreations:* law reform and the theatre. *Address:* Mote End, Nan Clark's Lane, Mill Hill, NW7 4HH. *Club:* Garrick.

GARDINER, Lt-Col Christopher John, DSO 1940; OBE 1945; TD 1942; DL; RE; late Chairman of Gardiner, Sons and Co. Ltd, Bristol, merchants; *b* 2 June 1907; *s* of Edward John Lucas Gardiner, Clifton, Bristol; *m* 1938, Bridget Mary Taplin; three *s* one *d.* *Educ:* Clifton Coll., Bristol. Commissioned in South Midland RE, TA, in 1926; CRE 48 Div., 59 Div., and 12 Corps Tps RE (despatches thrice). Past Pres., Soc. of Builders Merchants. Governor, Clifton Coll. DL Glos 1953; DL Avon 1974. *Recreations:* Rugby (played for Clifton Coll), fishing. *Address:* 3 Norland Road, Clifton, Bristol BS8 3LP. *T:* 735187.

GARDINER, Duncan; see Gardiner, J. D. B.

GARDINER, Ernest David, CMG 1968; CBE 1967; Head of Science Department, Melbourne Grammar School, 1948-74; Chairman, Commonwealth Government's Advisory Committee on Standards for Science Facilities in Independent Secondary Schools, 1964-76; *b* 14 July 1909; 2nd *s* of Ernest Edward Gardiner and Isabella Gardiner (*née* Notman), Gisborne, Vic.; *m* 1940, Minnie Amanda Neill; one *s* one *d.* *Educ:* Kyneton High Sch.; Melbourne Univ. BSc 1931, BEd 1936, Melbourne; FACE 1968. Secondary Teacher with Educn Dept of Vic., 1932-45; Melbourne Grammar Sch., 1946-74. *Publications:* Practical Physics (2 vols), 1948; Practical Problems in Physics, 1959; Problems in Physics, 1969; Practical Physics, 1972. *Recreations:* music, theatre, swimming, Scottish country dancing. *Address:* 122 Ferguson Street, Williamstown, Vic 3016, Australia. *T:* 397 6132.

GARDINER, Frederick Keith, JP; Past President, Neepsend Steel and Tool Corporation, Ltd; *b* Plumstead, Kent; *s* of Frederick Gardiner and Edith Mann; *m* 1929, Ruth Dixon; two *s.* Various editorial positions with newspaper companies in the South of England and at Darlington, York, Oxford and Sheffield; formerly Ed. and Dir, The Sheffield Telegraph; President: Inst. of Journalists, 1950; Hallam Cons. Assoc. Former Vice-Chm., Sheffield Wednesday FC. FJI. JP Sheffield; Chm., Magistrates' Courts Cttee; former Vice-Chm., Sheffield Bench. *Recreation:* golf. *Address:* 5 Chorley Road, Fulwood, Sheffield S10 3RJ. *Club:* Hallamshire Golf (Past Pres.) (Sheffield).

See also J. D. B. Gardiner.

GARDINER, George Arthur; MP (C) Reigate and Banstead since Feb. 1974; *b* 3 March 1935; *s* of Stanley and Emma Gardiner; *m* 1st, 1961, Juliet Wells (marr. diss. 1980); two *s* one *d* ; 2nd, 1980, Helen Hackett. *Educ:* Harvey Grammar Sch., Folkestone; Balliol Coll., Oxford. 1st cl. hons PPE. Sec., Oxford Univ. Conservative Assoc., 1957. Chief Political Corresp., Thomson Regional Newspapers, 1964-74. Mem. Exec. Cttee, British Council of European Movt, 1971; Mem. Cttee, Conservative Gp for Europe, 1971; Sec., Cons. European Affairs Cttee, 1976-79, Vice-Chm., 1979-80, Chm., 1980-. Editor, Conservative News, 1972-79. Contested (C) Coventry South, 1970. *Publications:* Europe for the Regions, 1971; The Changing Life of London, 1973; Margaret Thatcher: from childhood to leadership, 1975. *Address:* House of Commons, SW1.

GARDINER, Dame Helen (Louisa), DBE 1961 (CBE 1952); MVO 1937; *b* 24 April 1901; *y d* of late Henry Gardiner, Bristol. *Educ:* Clifton High School. Formerly in Private Secretary's Office, Buckingham Palace; Chief Clerk, 1946-61. *Recreations:* reading, gardening. *Address:* Higher Courlands, Lostwithiel, Cornwall.

GARDINER, (John) Duncan (Broderick); author and broadcaster; Editor, Western Mail, 1974-81; *b* 12 Jan. 1937; *s* of Frederick Keith Gardiner, *qv* ; *m* 1965, Geraldine Mallen; one *s* one *d.* *Educ:* St Edward's School, Oxford. Various editorial positions in Sheffield, Newcastle, Sunday Times, London (1963-64, 1966-73) and Cardiff. *Recreations:* travel, all sport, wine and food, crosswords. *Address:* 145 Pencisely Road, Llandaff, Cardiff. *T:* 33022.

GARDINER, John Eliot; conductor; Musical Director, English Baroque Soloists, Monteverdi Choir and Monteverdi Orchestra; Principal Conductor, CBC Vancouver Orchestra, since 1980; Musical Director, Lyons Opera, since 1982; *b* 20 April 1943; *s* of Rolf Gardiner and Marabel Gardiner (*née* Hodgkin); *m* 1981, Elizabeth Suzanne Wilcock. *Educ:* Bryanston Sch.; King's Coll., Cambridge (MA History); King's Coll., London (Certif. of Advanced Studies in Music, 1966). French Govt Scholarship to study in Paris and Fontainebleau with Nadia Boulanger, 1966-68. Founded: Monteverdi Choir,

following performance of Monteverdi's Vespers of 1610, King's Coll., Cambridge, 1964; Monteverdi Orchestra, 1968; English Baroque Soloists (period instruments), 1978. Youngest conductor of Henry Wood Promenade Concert, Royal Albert Hall, 1968; Début with: Sadler's Wells Opera, Coliseum, conducting The Magic Flute, 1969; Royal Opera House, Covent Garden, conducting Iphigénie en Tauride, 1973; concert revivals in London of major dramatic works of Rameau, culminating in world première of Les Boréades, 1975. Artistic Dir, Göttingen Handel Fest., 1981-83. Grand Prix du Disque, 1978, 1979; Gramophone Awards for early music and choral music records, 1978, 1980. *Publications:* (ed) Claude le Jeune Hélas! Mon Dieu, 1971; contrib. to opera handbook on Gluck's Orfeo, 1980. *Recreations:* pedigree sheep-breeding, organic corn-growing (in Dorset); ecological rehabilitation in Central Africa. *Address:* Gore Farm, Ashmore, Salisbury, Wilts. *T:* Fontmell Magna 811295; 7 Pleydell Avenue, W6. *T:* 01-741 0987.

GARDINER, John Ralph, QC 1982; *b* 28 Feb. 1946; *s* of late Cyril Ralph Gardiner and of Mary Gardiner; *m* 1976, Pascal Mary Issard-Davies; one *d.* *Educ:* Bancroft's Sch., Woodford; Fitzwilliam Coll., Cambridge (BA (Law Tripos), LLB, MA). Called to the Bar, Middle Temple, 1968 (Harmsworth Entrance Scholar and Harmsworth Law Scholar); practice at the Bar, 1970-. *Publications:* contributor to Pinson on Revenue Law, 6th to 15th (1982) edns. *Recreations:* tennis, cricket, squash. *Address:* 11 New Square, Lincoln's Inn, WC2. *T:* 01-242 3981; 21 Palace Gardens Terrace, W8. *T:* 01-229 2226. *Club:* Cumberland Lawn Tennis.

GARDINER, Peter Dod Robin; First Deputy Head, Stanborough School, Hertfordshire, since 1979; *b* 23 Dec. 1927; *s* of Brig. R. Gardiner, *qv* ; *m* 1959, Juliet Wright; one *s* one *d.* *Educ:* Radley College; Trinity Coll., Cambridge. Asst Master, Charterhouse, 1952-67, and Housemaster, Charterhouse, 1965-67; Headmaster, St Peter's School, York, 1967-79. *Publications:* (ed) Twentieth-Century Travel, 1963; (with B. W. M. Young) Intelligent Reading, 1964; (with W. A. Gibson) The Design of Prose, 1971. *Recreations:* reading, music, walking, acting. *Address:* Stanborough School, Lemsford Lane, Welwyn Garden City, Herts AL8 6YR.

GARDINER, Brig. Richard, CB 1954; CBE 1946 (OBE 1944); *b* 28 Oct. 1900; *s* of Major Alec Gardiner, RE; *m* 1924, Catherine Dod (*née* Oliver); two *s.* *Educ:* Uppingham Sch.; Royal Military Academy. Commissioned into RFA, 1920; transferred to RE, 1924; Asst Executive Engineer, E Indian Rly, 1927; Sec. to Agent, E Indian Rly, 1930; Exec. Engineer, 1934; Govt Inspector of Rlys, Burma, 1938; reverted to military duty, 1940; Dir of Transportation, India, 1942; reverted to Home Establishment, 1945; Dir of Transportation, War Office, 1948; Dir of Engineer Stores, War Office, 1950; retired Dec. 1953; Man. Dir, Peruvian Corp., Lima, 1954-63. ADC to King George VI, 1951-52, to the Queen, 1952-53. FCIT. *Recreations:* music, gardening. *Address:* Bridgham Farmhouse, Shamley Green, Surrey.

See also P. D. R. Gardiner.

GARDINER, Robert (Kweku Atta); Commissioner for Economic Planning, Ghana, 1975-78; *b* Kumasi, Ghana, 29 Sept. 1914; *s* of Philip H. D. Gardiner and Nancy Torraine Ferguson; *m* 1943, Linda Charlotte Edwards; one *s* two *d.* *Educ:* Adisadel Coll., Cape Coast; Ghana; Fourah Bay Coll., Sierra Leone; Selwyn Coll., Cambridge (BA); New Coll., Oxford. Lectr in Economics at Fourah Bay Coll., 1943-46; UN Trusteeship Dept, 1947-49; Dir, Extra-Mural Studies, University Coll., Ibadan, 1949-53; Dir, Dept of Social Welfare and Community Development, Gold Coast, 1953-55; Perm. Sec., Min. of Housing, 1955-57; Head of Ghana Civil Service, 1957-59; Dep. Exec. Sec., Economic Commn for Africa, 1959-60; Mem. Mission to the Congo, 1961; Dir Public Admin. Div., UN Dept of Economic and Social Affairs, 1961-62; Officer-in-Charge, UN Operation in the Congo, 1962-63; Exec. Sec., UN Economic Commn for Africa, Addis Ababa, 1962-75. Chm., Commonwealth Foundation, 1970-73. Reith Lectures, 1965; David Livingstone Vis. Prof. of Economics, Strathclyde, 1970-75; Vis. Prof. of Economics, 1974-75, and Consultant, Centre for Development Studies, 1977-74, Univ. of Cape Coast. Lectures: Gilbert Murray Meml, 1969; J. B. Danquah Meml, 1970; Aggrey-Fraser-Guggisberg Meml, 1972. Mem Professional Socs, and activities in internat. affairs. Hon. Fellow: Univ. of Ibadan; Selwyn Coll., Cambridge. Hon. DCL: East Anglia, 1966; Sierra Leone, 1969; Tuskegee Inst., 1969; Liberia, 1972; Hon. LLD: Bristol, 1966; Ibadan, 1967; E Africa, 1968; Haile Sellassie I Univ., 1972; Strathclyde, 1973; Hon. PhD Uppsala, 1966; Hon. DSc: Kumasi, 1968; Bradford, 1969. *Publications:* (with Helen Judd) The Development of Social Administration, 1951, 2nd edn 1959; A World of Peoples (BBC Reith Lectures), 1965. *Recreations:* golf, music, reading, walking.

GARDINER, Victor Alec, OBE 1977; Director and General Manager, London Weekend Television, since 1971; Director: London Weekend Television (Holdings) Ltd, since 1976; London Weekend Services Ltd, since 1976; Richard Price Television Associates, since 1981; Chairman: Dynamic Technology Ltd, since 1972; Standard Music Ltd, since 1972; London Weekend Television International, since 1981; *b* 9 Aug. 1929; *m* ; one *s* two *d.* *Educ:* Whitgift Middle Sch., Croydon; City and Guilds (radio and telecommunications). Techn. Asst, GPO Engrg, 1947-49; RAF Nat. Service, 1949-51; BBC Sound Radio Engr, 1951-53; BBC TV Cameraman, 1953-55; Rediffusion TV Sen. Cameraman, 1955-61; Malta TV Trng Man., 1961-62; Head of Studio Prodn, Rediffusion TV, 1962-67; Man. Dir, GPA Productions, 1967-69; Production Controller, London Weekend Television, 1969-71. Mem., Royal Television Soc., 1970- (Vice-Chm. Council, 1974-75;

Chm. Papers Cttee, 1975; Chm. Council, 1976-77; Fellow, 1977). *Recreations:* music, building, gardening. *Address:* c/o London Weekend Television Ltd, Kent House, Upper Ground, SE1 9LT.

GARDINER-SCOTT, Rev. William, OBE 1974; MA; Emeritus Minister of Scots Memorial Church and Hospice, Jerusalem; *b* 23 February 1906; *o s* of late William Gardiner Scott, Portsoy, Banffshire; *m* 1953, Darinka Milo, *d* of late Milo Glogovac, Oakland, Calif; one *d. Educ:* Grange School, Bo'ness, West Lothian; Edinburgh University and New College, Edinburgh. In catering business, 1926-30; graduated in Arts, Edin., 1934; Theological Travel Scholarship to Palestine, 1936; travelled as ship's steward to America and India, 1936; ordained to Ministry of Church of Scotland, 1939; Sub-Warden 1939, Deputy Warden 1940, New College Settlement, Edinburgh; enlisted as Army Chaplain, 1941; served in Egypt, 1942-44 and developed community centre at RA Depot, Cairo and initiated publication of weekly Scots newspaper, The Clachan Crack; founded Montgomery House, Alexandria, as community centre for all ranks of allied troops, 1943; served in Palestine as Church of Scotland Chaplain for Galilee and district, 1944-46; Senior Chaplain at Scottish Command, 1946-47; Warden of Student Movement House, London, 1947-49; Chaplain at Victoria Univ. Coll., Wellington, NZ, 1950-54; locum tenens St John's West Church, Leith, 1955; Minister of Church of Scotland, Jerusalem, 1955-60 and 1966-73; Parish of Abernethy, 1960-66. ChStJ. Distinguished Citizen of Jerusalem. *Recreations:* travel, gardening, cooking, walking. *Address:* Scots Memorial Church and Hospice, PO Box 14216, Jerusalem, Israel.

GARDINI, Signora U.; *see* Fisher, Sylvia.

GARDNER, family name of **Baroness Gardner of Parkes.**

GARDNER OF PARKES, Baroness *cr* 1981 (Life Peer), of Southgate, Greater London, and of Parkes, NSW; **(Rachel) Trixie (Anne) Gardner;** JP; dental surgeon; Member for Havering, 1970-73, for Enfield-Southgate since 1977, Greater London Council; British Chairman, European Union of Women, since 1978; *b* Parkes, NSW, 17 July 1927; eighth *c* of late Hon. J. J. Gregory McGirr and late Rachel McGirr, OBE, LC; *m* 1956, Kevin Anthony Gardner, *o s* of George Waldron and Rita Gardner, Sydney, Australia; three *d. Educ:* Monte Sant Angelo Coll., N Sydney; East Sydney Technical Coll.; Univ. of Sydney (BDS 1954). Cordon Bleu de Paris, Diplôme 1956. Came to UK, 1955. Member Westminster City Council, 1968-78. Contested (C) Blackburn, 1970; N Cornwall, Feb. 1974. Member: Inner London Exec. Council, NHS, 1966-71; Standing Dental Adv. Cttee for England and Wales, 1968-76; Westminster, Kensington and Chelsea Area Health Authority, 1974-82; Industrial Tribunal Panel for London, 1974-; N Thames Gas Consumer Council; Dept of Employment's Adv. Cttee on Women's Employment. UK rep. on UN Status of Women Commn, 1982-; British Chm., European Union of Women, 1978-82. Governor: Eastman Dental Hosp., 1971-80; Nat. Heart Hosp., 1974-. JP North Westminster, 1971. *Recreations:* gardening, cooking, reading, travel, needlework. *Address:* 10 Loudoun Road, St John's Wood, NW8 0LR.

GARDNER, Antony John; Principal Registration Officer, Central Council for Education and Training in Social Work, since 1970; *b* 27 Dec. 1927; *s* of David Gardner, head gardener, and Lillian Gardner; *m* 1956, Eveline A. Burden. *Educ:* Elem. school; Co-operative Coll.; Southampton Univ. Pres. Union, Southampton, 1958-59; BSc (Econ) 1959. Apprentice toolmaker, 1941-45; National Service, RASC, 1946-48; building trade, 1948-53. Tutor Organiser, Co-operative Union, 1959-60; Member Education Officer, Co-operative Union, 1961-66. Contested (Lab): SW Wolverhampton, 1964; Beeston, Feb. and Oct. 1974; MP (Lab) Rushcliffe, 1966-70. *Recreations:* angling, gardening and the countryside generally. *Address:* 30 Brookside Avenue, East Leake, Loughborough, Leics. *T:* East Leake 2454. *Club:* Parkstone Trades and Labour (Poole).

GARDNER, Sir Douglas Bruce B.; *see* Bruce-Gardner.

GARDNER, Edward Lucas, QC 1960; MP (C) South Fylde, since 1970; a Recorder of the Crown Court, since 1972; *b* 10 May 1912; *s* of late Edward Walker Gardner, Fulwood, Preston, Lancs; *m* 1st, 1950, Noreen Margaret (marr. diss. 1962), *d* of late John Collins, Moseley, Birmingham; one *s* one *d;* 2nd, 1963, Joan Elizabeth, *d* of late B. B. Belcher, Bedford; one *s.* one *d. Educ:* Hutton Grammar Sch. Served War of 1939-45: joined RNVR as ordinary seaman, 1940; served in cruisers, Mediterranean; commnd RNVR; Chief of Naval Information, E Indies, 1945. Journalist (free-lance; Lancashire Daily Post, then Daily Mail) prior to 1940; broadcasting and free-lance journalism, 1946-49; called to Bar, Gray's Inn, 1947; Master of the Bench of Gray's Inn, 1968; admitted to Nigerian and British Guianan Bars, 1962; has also appeared in Courts of Goa, High Court of Singapore, and Supreme Court of India. Deputy Chairman of Quarter Sessions: East Kent, 1961-71; County of Kent, 1962-71; Essex, 1968-71. Contested (C) Erith and Crayford, April 1955; MP (C) Billericay Div. of Essex, 1959-66; PPS to Attorney-General, 1962-63; Chairman: Justice Working Party on Bail and Remands in Custody, 1966; Bar Council Cttee on Party Privilege, 1967; Chm., Soc. of Cons. Lawyers, 1975 (Chm. Exec. Cttee, 1969-; Chm., Cttee responsible for pamphlets, Rough Justice, on future of the Law, 1968, Crisis in Crime and Punishment, 1971, The Proper Use of Prisons, 1978, Who Do We Think We Are?, 1980, on need for new nationality law); Exec. Cttee, Justice, 1968. Member: Departmental Cttee on Jury Service, 1963; Cttee on Appeals in

Criminal Cases, 1964; Commonwealth War Graves Commn, 1971-. A Governor: Thomas Coram Foundn for Children, 1962-; Queenswood Sch., 1975. Steward, British Boxing Bd of Control, 1975-. *Publication:* (part author) A Case for Trial (pamphlet recommending procedural reforms for committal proceedings implemented by Criminal Justice Act, 1967). *Recreation:* walking. *Address:* 4 Raymond Buildings, Gray's Inn, WC1. *T:* 01-242 4719; Outlane Head, Chipping, Lancs. *Clubs:* Garrick, United and Cecil (Chm. 1970).

GARDNER, Dame Frances, DBE 1975; FRCP; Consulting Physician: Royal Free Hospital, London, since 1978; Hospital for Women, Soho Square, London; Physician, The Mothers' Hospital, London; *b* 28 Feb. 1913; *d* of late Sir Ernest and Lady Gardner; *m* 1958, George Qvist, FRCS (*d* 1981). *Educ:* Headington Sch., Oxford; Westfield Coll., Univ. of London; Royal Free Hospital School of Medicine. BSc London, 1935; MB, BS London, 1940; MD London, 1943; MRCP 1943, FRCP 1952. Medical Registrar, Royal Free Hosp., 1943; Clinical Asst, Nuffield Dept of Medicine, Oxford, 1945; Fellow in Medicine, Harvard Univ., USA, 1946; Consultant Physician, Royal Free Hosp., 1946-78; Chief Asst, National Hosp. for Diseases of the Heart, 1947; late Physician, Royal National Throat, Nose and Ear Hosp., London; former Dean, Royal Free Hosp. Sch. of Medicine; Visitor, Med. Faculty, Khartoum, 1981. Commonwealth Travelling Fellow, 1962; late Examnr, MB, BS, Univ. of London; Rep. Gen. Med. Schools on Senate of Univ. of London, 1967; Mem., Gen. Med. Council, 1971; Pres., Royal Free Hosp. Sch. of Medicine, 1979. Formerly Chm., London/Riyadh Univs Med. Faculty Cttee. *Publications:* papers on cardiovascular and other medical subjects in BMJ, Lancet, and British Heart Jl. *Address:* 72 Harley Street, W1. *T:* 01-580 9944.

GARDNER, Dame Helen (Louise), DBE 1967 (CBE 1962); FBA 1958; FRSL 1962; DLitt; Emeritus Professor of English Literature, University of Oxford and Hon. Fellow, Lady Margaret Hall and St Hilda's College; *b* 13 Feb. 1908; *d* of late C. H. Gardner and Helen M. R. Gardner. *Educ:* North London Collegiate Sch.; St Hilda's Coll., Oxford. BA Oxford (1st class Hons Sch. of English Lang. and Lit.), 1929; MA 1935; DLitt 1963. Asst Lectr, Royal Holloway Coll., Univ. of London, 1931-34; Lectr, Univ. of Birmingham, 1934-41; Tutor in English Literature, St Hilda's Coll., 1941-54, and Fellow, 1942-66; Reader in Renaissance English Literature, Univ. of Oxford, 1954-66; Merton Prof. of English Literature, Univ. of Oxford and Fellow of Lady Margaret Hall, 1966-75; Vis. Prof., Univ. of California, Los Angeles, 1954; Lectures: Riddell Meml, Univ. of Durham, 1956; Alexander, Univ. of Toronto, 1962; Messenger, Cornell Univ., 1967; T. S. Eliot Meml, Univ. of Kent, 1968; Charles Eliot Norton, Harvard, 1979-80. Delegate, Oxford University Press, 1959-75. Mem., Robbins Cttee on Higher Education, 1961-63; Mem., Council for National Academic Awards, 1964-67; Trustee, National Portrait Gallery, 1967-78. Foreign Hon. Member: Amer. Acad. of Arts and Scis; Amer. Philosophical Soc.; Bavarian Acad. Hon. DLitt: Durham, 1960; East Anglia, 1967; London, 1969; Birmingham, 1970; Harvard, 1971; Yale, 1973; Warwick, 1976; Hon. LittD Cambridge, 1981; Hon. LLD Aberdeen, 1967. R. M. Crawshay Prize, British Acad., 1952, 1980. *Publications:* The Art of T. S. Eliot, 1949; The Divine Poems of John Donne, 1952, 2nd edn 1978; The Metaphysical Poets (Penguin), 1957; (ed with G. M. Story) The Sonnets of William Alabaster, 1960; The Business of Criticism, 1960; The Elegies and Songs and Sonnets of John Donne, 1965; A Reading of Paradise Lost, 1965; John Donne: Selected Prose (co-ed with T. Healey), 1967; (ed) Shakespearian and Other Studies by F. P. Wilson, 1969; Religion and Literature, 1971; (rev. and ed) F. P. Wilson, Shakespeare and the New Bibliography, 1971; (ed) The Faber Book of Religious Verse, 1972; (ed) The New Oxford Book of English Verse 1250-1950, 1972; The Composition of Four Quartets, 1978; In Defence of the Imagination, 1982. *Recreations:* gardening, foreign travel. *Address:* Myrtle House, Eynsham, Oxford. *T:* Oxford 881497.

GARDNER, Rear-Adm. Herbert, CB 1976; Chartered Engineer; *b* 23 Oct. 1921; *s* of Herbert and Constance Gladys Gardner; *m* 1946, Catherine Mary Roe, Perth, WA. *Educ:* Taunton Sch.; Weymouth Coll. War of 1939-45; joined Dartmouth, 1940; RN Engineering Coll., Keyham, 1940; HMS Nigeria, Cumberland, Adamant, and 4th Submarine Sqdn, 1944; HM S/M Totem, 1945. Dept of Engr-in-Chief, 1947; HM S/M Telemachus, 1949; Comdr, 1956; HMS Caledonia, 1956; HMS Blackpool, 1958; Asst to Manager Engrg Dept, Rosyth Dockyard, 1960; HMS Maidstone, 1963; Capt., 1963; Dep. Manager, Engrg Dept, Devonport Dockyard, 1964; Chief Engr and Production Manager, Singapore Dockyard, 1967; Chief Staff Officer (Technical) to Comdr Far East Fleet, 1968; course at Imperial Defence Coll., 1970; Chief of Staff to C-in-C Naval Home Comd, 1971-73; Vice Pres., Ordnance Bd, 1974-76, Pres., 1976-77. *Recreations:* sailing, golf. *Address:* c/o Lloyds Bank Ltd, Weymouth, Dorset.

GARDNER, Hugh, CB 1966; CBE 1953; *b* 28 March 1910; *yr s* of C. H. Gardner; *m* 1934, Margaret Evelyn Carvalho; one *s* two *d. Educ:* University College Sch.; Merton Coll., Oxford (MA). Served Min. of Agriculture, Fisheries and Food (formerly Min. of Agriculture and Fisheries), 1933-70; Under-Sec., 1953-70, retired; Mem., Sec. of State for the Environment's Panel of Independent Inspectors, 1970-80. Chm., Assoc. of First Div. Civil Servants, 1945-48. *Publication:* Tales from the Marble Mountain, 1967. *Recreations:* golf, gardening, writing. *Address:* The Cobb, North Road, Berkhamsted,

Herts. *T:* Berkhamsted 5677. *Club:* United Oxford & Cambridge University.

GARDNER, James, CBE 1959; RDI 1947; Major RE; industrial designer and consultant; *b* 29 Dec. 1907; *s* of Frederic James Gardner; *m* 1935, Mary Williams; two *s. Educ:* Chiswick and Westminster Schools of Art. Jewellery Designer, Cartier Ltd, 1924-31. Served War of 1939-45, Chief Development Officer, Army Camouflage, 1941-46. Designer, Britain Can Make It Exhibition, 1946; Chief Designer, Festival Gardens, Battersea, 1950; British Pavilion, Brussels, 1958; British Pavilion, Expo '67, Montreal; currently designer to Evoluon Museum, Eindhoven, Netherlands, and St Helens Glass Museum, Lancs; responsible for main display Geological Museum, London, 1972; responsible for visual design of QE2 and sternwheeler Riverboat Mississippi Queen, Heritage Centre, York and Mus. of Diaspora, Tel Aviv. *Address:* The Studio, 144 Haverstock Hill, Hampstead, NW3.

GARDNER, James Jesse, DL; Chief Executive, Tyne and Wear County Council, since 1973; *b* 7 April 1932; *s* of James and Elizabeth Rubina Gardner; *m* 1955, Diana Sotheran; three *s* one *d. Educ:* Kirkham Grammar Sch.; Victoria Univ., Manchester (LLB). Nat. Service, 1955-57. Articled to Town Clerk, Preston, 1952-55; Legal Asst, Preston Co. Borough Council, 1955; Crosby Borough Council: Asst Solicitor, 1957-59; Chief Asst Solicitor, 1959-61; Chief Asst Solicitor, Warrington Co. Borough Council, 1961-65; Stockton-on-Tees Borough Council: Dep. Town Clerk, 1966; Town Clerk, 1966-68; Asst Town Clerk, Teesside Co. Borough Council, 1968; Associate Town Clerk and Solicitor, London Borough of Greenwich, 1968-69; Town Clerk and Chief Exec. Officer, Co. Borough of Sunderland, 1970-73. DL Tyne and Wear, 1976. FRSA 1976. *Recreations:* golf, music, theatre, food and drink. *Address:* Wayside, 121 Queen Alexandra Road, Sunderland, Tyne and Wear. *T:* Sunderland 282525.

GARDNER, John Linton, CBE 1976; composer; *b* 2 March 1917; *s* of late Dr Alfred Gardner, Ilfracombe, and Muriel (*née* Pullein-Thompson); *m* 1955, Jane, *d* of N. J. Abercrombie, *qv* ; one *s* two *d. Educ:* Eagle House, Sandhurst; Wellington Coll.; Exeter Coll., Oxford (BMus). Served War of 1939-45: RAF, 1940-46. Chief Music Master, Repton Sch., 1939-40. Staff, Covent Garden Opera, 1946-52; Tutor: Morley Coll., 1952-76 (Dir of Music, 1965-69); Bagot Stack Coll., 1955-62; London Univ. (extra-mural) 1959-60; Dir of Music, St Paul's Girls' Sch., 1962-75; Prof. of Harmony and Composition, Royal Acad. of Music, 1956-. Conductor: Haslemere Musical Soc., 1953-62; Dorian Singers, 1961-62; European Summer Sch. for Young Musicians, 1966-; Bromley YSO, 1970-76. Brit. Council Lecturer: Levant, 1954; Belgium, 1960; Iberia, 1963; Yugoslavia, 1967. Adjudicator, Canadian Festivals, 1974, 1980. Member: Arts Council Music Panel, 1958-62; Council, Composers' Guild, 1961- (Chm., 1963; Delegate to USSR, 1964); Cttee of Management, Royal Philharmonic Soc., 1965-72, 1977-; Brit. Council Music Cttee, 1968. Dir, Performing Right Soc., 1965-. Worshipful Co. of Musicians: Collard Fellow, 1962-64; elected to Freedom and Livery, 1965. Hon. RAM 1959. Bax Society's Prize, 1958. *Works include: orchestral:* Symphony no 1, 1947; Variations on a Waltz of Carl Nielsen, 1952; Piano Concerto no 1, 1957; Sinfonia Piccola (strings), 1960; Occasional Suite, Aldeburgh Festival, 1968; An English Ballad, 1969; Three Ridings, 1970; Sonatina for Strings, 1974; Divertimento, 1977; *chamber:* Concerto da Camera (4 insts), 1968; Partita (solo 'cello), 1968; Chamber Concerto (organ and 11 insts), 1969; English Suite (harpsichord), 1971; Sonata Secolare for organ and brass, 1973; Sonata da Chiesa for two trumpets and organ; String Quartet, 1979; Hebdomade, 1980; *ballet:* Reflection, 1952; *opera:* A Nativity Opera, 1950; The Moon and Sixpence, 1957; The Visitors, 1972; Bel and the Dragon, 1973; The Entertainment of the Senses, 1974; Tobermory, 1976; *musical:* Vile Bodies, 1961; *choral:* Cantiones Sacrae 1973; (sop., chor. and orch.), 1952; Jubilate Deo (unacc. chor.), 1957; The Ballad of the White Horse (bar., chor. and orch.), 1959; Herrick Cantata (ten. solo, chor. and orch.), 1961; A Latter-Day Athenian Speaks, 1962; The Noble Heart (sop., bass, chor. and orch.), Shakespeare Quatercentenary Festival, 1964; Cantor popularis vocis, 18th Schütz Festival Berlin, 1964; Mass in C (unacc. chor.), 1965; Cantata for Christmas (chor. and chamb. orch.), 1966; Proverbs of Hell (unacc. chor.), 1967; Cantata for Easter (soli, chor., organ and percussion), 1970; Open Air (chor. and brass band), 1976; Te Deum for Pigotts, 1981. Many smaller pieces and music for films, Old Vic and Royal Shakespeare Theatres, BBC. Contributor to: Dublin Review, Musical Times, Tempo, Composer, Listener, Music in Education. *Recreation:* bore-watching. *Address:* 10 Lynton Road, New Malden, Surrey. *T:* 01-942 7322. *Club:* Ronnie Scott's.

GARDNER, John William; writer; consultant; *b* 8 Oct. 1912; *s* of William Frederick and Marie (Flora) Gardner; *m* 1934, Aida Marroquin; two *d. Educ:* Stanford Univ. (AB 1935, AM 1936); Univ. of Calif. (PhD 1938). 1st Lt-Captain, US Marine Corps, 1943-46. Teaching Asst in Psychology, Univ. of Calif., 1936-38; Instructor in Psychology, Connecticut Coll., 1938-40; Asst Prof. in Psychology, Mt Holyoke Coll., 1940-42; Head of Latin Amer. Section, Federal Communications Commn, 1942-43. Carnegie Corporation of New York: Staff Mem., 1946-47; Exec. Associate, 1947-49; Vice-Pres., 1949-55; Pres., 1955-67; Pres., Carnegie Foundn for Advancement of Teaching, 1955-67; Sec. of Health, Education and Welfare, 1965-68; Chairman: Urban Coalition, 1968-70; Common Cause, 1970-77; Independent Sector, 1980-. Chairman: US Adv. Commn on Internat. Educational and Cultural Affairs, 1962-64; Pres. Johnson's Task Force on Educn, 1964; White House Conf. on Educn, 1965; President's Commn on White House Fellowships, 1977-81. Dir, Amer. Assoc. for Advancement of Science, 1963-

65. Director: New York Telephone Co., 1962-65; Shell Oil Co., 1962-65; Time Inc., 1968-71; American Airlines, 1968-71; Rockefeller Brothers Fund, 1968-77; New York Foundn, 1970-76. Trustee: Metropolitan Museum of Art, 1957-65; Stanford Univ., 1968-. Benjamin Franklin Fellow, RSA, 1964. Holds hon. degrees from various colleges and univs. USAF Exceptional Service Award, 1956; Presidential Medal of Freedom, 1964; Public Welfare Medal, Nat. Acad. of Science, 1967. *Publications:* Excellence, 1961; (ed) Pres. John F. Kennedy's book, To Turn the Tide, 1961; Self-Renewal, 1964, rev. edn 1980; No Easy Victories, 1968; The Recovery of Confidence, 1970; In Common Cause, 1972; Know or Listen to Those who Know, 1975; Morale, 1978; Quotations of Wit and Wisdom, 1980. *Address:* 2030 M Street NW, Suite 603, Washington, DC 20036, USA.

GARDNER, Kenneth Burslam; Deputy Keeper of Oriental MSS and Printed Books, The British Library, since 1974; *b* 5 June 1924; *s* of D. V. Gardner; *m* 1949, Cleone Winifred Adams; two *s* two *d. Educ:* Alleyne's Grammar Sch., Stevenage; University College, London; School of Oriental and African Studies, Univ. of London (BA Hons Japanese). War service, Intelligence Corps (Captain), 1943-47. Assistant Librarian, School of Oriental and African Studies, 1949-54; Assistant Keeper, Department of Oriental Printed Books and MSS, British Museum, 1955-57, Keeper, 1957-70; Principal Keeper of Printed Books, British Museum (later The British Library), 1970-74. Order of the Sacred Treasure (3rd class), Japan, 1979. *Publications:* Edo jidai no sashie hangaka-tachi (in Japanese, on book illustration in Japan and related topics), 1977; contrib. to jls of oriental studies, art and librarianship. *Address:* 1 Duncombe Road, Bengeo, Hertford.

GARDNER, Norman Keith Ayliffe; Under Secretary, Department of Employment, since 1979; *b* 2 July 1925; *s* of late Charles Ayliffe Gardner and Winifred Gardner; *m* 1951, Margaret Patricia Vinson; one *s* one *d. Educ:* Cardiff High Sch.; University Coll., Cardiff (BScEng); College of Aeronautics, Cranfield; Univ. of London Commerce Degree Bureau (BScEcon Hons). CEng. Flight Test Observer, RAE, 1944; Test Observer, Westland Aircraft Ltd, 1946; Development Engr, Handley Page Ltd, 1950; Engr, Min. of Aviation, 1964; Economic Adviser, Min. of Technology, 1970; Asst Dir (Engrg), DTI, 1973; Sen. Economic Adviser, 1974, Under Sec., 1977, DoI. *Publications:* The Economics of Launching Aid, in The Economics of Industrial Subsidies (HMSO), 1976; papers in Jl Instn Prodn Engrs and other engrg jls. *Recreations:* woodcarving, music. *Address:* 15 Chanctonbury Way, N12 7JB. *T:* 01-445 4162.

GARDNER, Ralph Bennett, MM 1944; Under Secretary (Legal), Treasury Solicitor's Department, 1976-82, retired; *b* 7 May 1919; *s* of late Ralph Wilson Gardner and Elizabeth Emma (*née* Nevitt-Bennett); *m* 1950, Patricia Joan Ward (*née* Bartlett); one *s* one *d. Educ:* Worksop Coll. Served War, 1939-46, RA. Admitted a solicitor, 1947; Solicitor, private practice, Chester, 1947-48; Legal Asst, Treasury Solicitor's Dept, 1948; Sen. Legal Asst, 1957; Asst Treas. Solicitor, 1972. Lord of the Manor of Shotwick, County of Chester (by inheritance, 1964). *Recreations:* gardening and local history. *Address:* Wychen, St Mary's Road, Leatherhead, Surrey. *T:* Leatherhead 73161. *Club:* East India, Devonshire, Sports and Public Schools.

GARDNER, Prof. Richard Lavenham, PhD; FRS 1979; Royal Society Henry Dale Research Professor, since 1978; Student of Christ Church, Oxford, since 1974; *b* 10 June 1943; *s* of Allan Constant and Eileen May Gardner; *m* 1968, Wendy Joy Cresswell. *Educ:* St John's Sch., Leatherhead; North East Surrey Coll. of Technology; St Catharine's Coll., Cambridge (BA 1st Cl. Hons Physiol., 1966; MA; PhD 1971). Res. Asst, Physiological Lab., Cambridge, 1970-73; Lectr in Developmental and Reproductive Biology, Dept of Zoology, Oxford Univ., 1973-77; Res. Student, Christ Church, Oxford, 1974-77. Scientific Medal, Zoological Soc. of London, 1977. *Publications:* contribs to Jl of Embryology and Experimental Morphology, Nature, Jl of Cell Science, and various other jls and symposia. *Recreations:* ornithology, music, sailing, gardening. *Address:* Green Hedges, 20 Ladder Hill, Wheatley, Oxon OX9 1SX.

GARDNER, Robert Dickson Robertson, CBE 1978; FCIS, FHA; Secretary, Greater Glasgow Health Board, since 1974; *b* 9 May 1924; *s* of Robert Gardner and Isabella McAlonan; *m* 1950, Ada Stewart; two *s* one *d.* Dep. Sec., 1962-66, Sec., 1966-74, Western Regional Hospital Board, Scotland. *Recreations:* swimming, Scottish country dancing, reading. *Address:* 5 Linn Drive, Muirend, Glasgow G44 3PT. *T:* 041-637 8070.

GARDNER, W(alter) Frank, CBE 1953; Director, The Prudential Assurance Co. Ltd, 1961-71 (Deputy Chairman, 1965-69); *b* 6 Nov. 1900; *s* of late Walter Gardner and late Emma Mabel Gardner, Streatham Hill, SW2; *m* 1, 1925, Constance Gladys (*d* 1945), *d* of late Ellen Haydon and late Frederick William Haydon, Norwich; one *d* ; 2nd, 1949, Kathleen Lilian, *y d* of late Florence Charlotte and late George William Smith, Hampton Hill, and widow of Dr Frederick Lishman, Bexhill. *Educ:* Dulwich College; Institute of Actuaries. Chief Actuary, Prudential Assurance Co. Ltd, 1945-50; Chief General Manager, 1950-60. Fellow (FIA), 1924; President, 1952-54. FSS 1952. *Publications:* contributions to Journal of Institute of Actuaries. *Recreations:* bowls, cine-photography. *Address:* 8c South Cliff Tower, Eastbourne, East Sussex BN20 7JN. *Clubs:* Carlton; Devonshire (Eastbourne); Eastbourne Bowling.

GARDNER, William Maving; designer and craftsman in private practice; b 25 May 1914; s of Robert Haswell Gardner, MIMarE and Lucy (née Maving); m 1940, Joan Margaret Pollard; two s one d. Trained at Royal College of Art, 1935-39 (ARCA 1938, Design Sch. Trav. Schol., Scandinavia, 1939). Mem., Royal Mint Panel of Artists, 1938-. Vis. lectr, Central Sch. of Arts and Crafts, 1959-62, Cambridgeshire Coll. of Art and Technology, 1959-62, Hampstead Garden Suburb Inst., 1959-73; Examr in craft subjects AEB City and Guilds of London Inst., 1957-60; served Typography Jury of RSA, Ind. Design Bursary Scheme. FRSA 1953, FSIA 1964, Leverhulme Res. Fellow, 1969-70. Vis. Prof. and Fine Art Program Lectr, Colorado State Univ., 1963; Churchill Meml Trav. Fellow, 1966-67 (USA, Polynesia, NZ, Australia, Nepal); Hon. Mem., RNS, NZ, 1966. Work exhib. Fort Collins and Denver, Colo, 1963, Monotype House, London, 1965, Portsmouth Coll. of Art, 1965, Hammond Mus., NY, 1970; (with family) Rye Art Gall., 1977. Awarded the Queen's Silver Jubilee Medal, 1977. *Works include:* HM Privy Council Seal 1955, HM Greater and Lesser Royal Signets 1955, Seal of HM Dependencies, 1955; seals for BMA, 1957, RSA, 1966, Univ. of Aston, Birmingham, 1966; *coinage models:* for Jordan 1950, UK 1953, Cyprus 1955 and 1963, Algeria 1964, Guyana 1967, Dominican Republic 1969, UNFAO (Ceylon 1968, Cyprus 1970, Guyana 1970), Falkland Islands 1974, UK 20p coin 1982; *medallic work:* includes Britannia Commemorative Soc. Shakespeare Medal 1967, Churchill Meml Trust's Foundn Medal 1969, Nat. Commemorative Soc. Audubon Medal 1970, Internat. Iron and Steel Inst. Medal 1971, Inst. of Metals Kroll medal 1972, and thirty-six medallic engravings depicting the history of the Royal Arms, completed 1974; participant in series of Commonwealth Silver Jubilee crown pieces, 1977; *calligraphy:* includes Rolls of Honour for House of Commons 1949, LTE 1964, Household Cavalry and the five regiments of Foot Guards, completed 1956, Warrants of Appointment by Queen Elizabeth the Queen Mother as Lord Warden of the Cinque Ports, 1979, Royal Marines Corps Book of Remembrance MSS for Canterbury Cath. and elsewhere; *work in other media* for Postmaster Gen. (Jersey definitive stamp 1958), Royal Soc. (Tercentenary stained glass window, 1960), King's College, London, 1971, City of London, 1972—and for Univs, schools, presses, libraries, banks, industrial and other authorities, also privately. *Publications:* Chapter VIII of The Calligrapher's Handbook, 1956; Calligraphy for A Wordsworth Treasury, 1978; Alphabet at Work, 1982. *Address:* Chequertree, Wittersham, Tenterden, Kent.

GARDNER, Air Commodore William Steven, CB 1958; OBE 1945; DFC 1940 and bar 1941; AFC 1943; b 16 Dec. 1909; s of late Campbell Gardner, JP, Groomsport, Co. Down, Northern Ireland; m 1937, Theodora, d of W. G. Bradley, Castlerock, Co. Derry; one s one d (and one d decd). *Educ:* Campbell Coll., Belfast. Joined RAF 1935; served in 106, 44 and 144 Squadrons, Bomber Command, 1939-45. Group Capt. 1951; Air Commodore, 1956; Head of Plans and Operations, CENTO, 1957-59; Acting Air Vice-Marshal, 1963; Provost Marshal, 1960-63; Director-General of Personal Services, 1963. *Recreation:* sailing. *Address:* Corner Cottage, Shipton Green, Itchenor, Sussex. *Club:* Royal Ulster Yacht.

GARDNER-MEDWIN, Robert Joseph, RIBA, FRTPI; architect and town planning consultant; Professor Emeritus, Liverpool University, since 1973; b 10 April 1907; s of late Dr and Mrs F. M. Gardner-Medwin; m 1935, Margaret, d of late Mr Justice and Mrs Kilgour, Winnipeg; four s. *Educ:* Rossall Sch., Lancashire; School of Architecture, Liverpool Univ. (BArch, Dipl Civ Des). Commonwealth Fund Fellowship in City Planning and Landscape Design, Harvard Univ., 1933-35; private practice, and architectural teaching at Architectural Association and Regent Street Polytechnic, 1936-40. Served War of 1939-45, with Royal Engineers (Major, RE), 1940-43. Adviser in Town Planning and Housing to Comptroller of Development and Welfare in the British West Indies, 1944-47, Chief Architect and Planning Officer to Department of Health for Scotland, 1947-52; Roscoe Prof. of Architecture, Liverpool Univ., 1952-73. President, Liverpool Architectural Society, 1966; Chm., Merseyside Civic Soc., 1972-76, 1979-80. FRSA. Golden Order of Merit, Poland, 1976. *Publications:* (with H. Myles Wright, MA, FRIBA) Design of Nursery and Elementary Schools, 1938; contributions to Town Planning Review, Architects' Journal, Journals of the RIBA and the RTPI, etc. *Address:* 6 Kirby Mount, West Kirby, Wirral, Merseyside.

GARDNER-THORPE, Col and Alderman Sir Ronald (Laurence), GBE 1980; TD 1948 (3 bars); JP; company director; b 13 May 1917; s of Joseph Gardner and Hannah Coulthurst Thorpe; m 1938, Hazel Mary (née Dass), Dame of Magistral Grace, SMO, 1982; one s. *Educ:* De la Salle Coll. Commnd Hants Heavy Regt, 1938; served War, 1939-45: France, Germany, Italy, British Army Staff Washington; 1945-47: AA&QMG 56 London Div., and XIII Corps; Grade 1 SO XIII Corps; GSO 1 GHQ CMF; comd 5th Bn The Buffs, 1956-60; Col 1960. City of London: Alderman, Ward of Bishopsgate, 1972 (Pres., Bishopsgate Ward Club, 1975); Sheriff, 1978-79; Lord Mayor, 1980-81; HM Lieut, 1980-. Vice-Pres., City of London Red Cross, 1977-. Underwriting Mem. of Lloyds, 1977-. Member: Lord Lieuts Cttee, 1955-; Council, Magistrates' Assoc., 1972-; London Court of Arbitration, 1975-; Public Sch. Governing Body, 1963-; Governor: St John's Coll., Southsea, 1963- (Vice-Chm. Governors, 1976-); St Joseph's, Beulah Hill, 1966-; Christ's Hosp., 1972-; Trustee: United Westminster Schs, 1974-; The Buffs (Royal East Kent Regt) Museum, 1976-; Morden Coll., 1979-; Rowland Hill Benevolent Fund, 1979-; Mental Health Foundn, 1981-; Royal Foundn of Greycoat Hosp., 1981-; President: 25th Anniv. Appeal Fund, The Duke of Edinburgh's Award, 1980-; David Isaacs Fund, 1982- (Vice-Pres., 1973-82). Chancellor, City Univ., 1980-81; Adm., Port of London, 1980-81. Member:

Kent Territorial Assoc., 1954-62 (Mem., Finance Cttee, 1954); City of London T & AVR Assoc., 1977-. JP Inner London, 1965 (Dep. Chm. 1968); JP City of London, 1969 (Dep. Chm. 1970); Hon. Treas., Inner London Magistrates, 1972- (Vice Chm., 1977). Freeman, City of London, 1971; Liveryman and Member of Court: Worshipful Co. of Painter Stainers, 1972-; Worshipful Co. of Builders Merchants, 1979-; Mem. Court, Hon. Artillery Co., 1972. KStJ 1980; Kt of Magistral Grace, SMO, 1982. Kt Comdr, Royal Order of the Dannebrog, 1960; Kt Comdr, Order of Infant Henri, Portugal, 1979; Kt Comdr, Right Hand of the Ghurka, Nepal, 1980; Kt Comdr, Royal Order of King Abdul Aziz, Saudi Arabia, 1981. Hon. DCL City, 1980; Hon. DH Lewis, Chicago, 1981. *Recreations:* interest in Fine Arts and in City of London tradition. *Address:* 8 Cadogan Square, SW1X 0JU. *Clubs:* Belfry, City Livery, United Wards, Bishopsgate Ward.

GARDYNE, John B.; see Bruce-Gardyne.

GAREL-JONES, (William Armand Thomas) Tristan; MP (C) Watford, since 1979; an Assistant Government Whip, since 1982; b 28 Feb. 1941; s of Bernard Garel-Jones and Meriel Garel-Jones (née Williams); m 1966, Catalina (née Garrigues); four s one d. *Educ:* The King's Sch., Canterbury. Principal, Language Sch., Madrid, Spain, 1960-70; Merchant Banker, 1970-74; worked for Cons. Party, 1974-79 (Personal Asst to Party Chm., 1978-79). Contested (C): Caernarvon, Feb. 1974; Watford, Oct. 1974. PPS to Minister of State, CSD, 1981. *Recreation:* collecting books. *Address:* 12 Catherine Place, SW1E 6HF. *T:* 01-828 3348. *Clubs:* Carlton, Royal Automobile; Watford Football; Club de Campo (Madrid).

GARFIELD, Leon; author; b 14 July 1921; s of David Garfield and Rose Garfield; m 1949, Vivien Dolores Alcock; one d. *Educ:* Brighton Grammar Sch. Served War, RAMC, 1941-46: attained and held rank of Private. Worked in NHS (biochemistry), until 1969; full-time author, 1969-. *Publications:* Jack Holborn, 1964; Devil-in-the-Fog, 1966; Smith, 1967; Black Jack, 1968 (filmed 1979); Mister Corbett's Ghost and Other Stories, 1969; The Boy and the Monkey, 1969; The Drummer Boy, 1970; The Strange Affair of Adelaide Harris, 1971; The Ghost Downstairs, 1972; The Captain's Watch, 1972; Lucifer Wilkins, 1973; Baker's Dozen, 1973; The Sound of Coaches, 1974; The Prisoners of September, 1975; The Pleasure Garden, 1976; The Booklovers, 1976; The House of Hanover, 1976; The Lamplighter's Funeral, 1976; Mirror, Mirror, 1976; Moss and Blister, 1976; The Cloak, 1976; The Valentine, 1977; Labour in Vain, 1977; The Fool, 1977; Rosy Starling, 1977; The Dumb Cake, 1977; Tom Titmarsh's Devil, 1977; The Filthy Beast, 1977; The Enemy, 1977; The Confidence Man, 1978; Bostock & Harris, 1978; John Diamond, 1980 (Whitbread Book of the Year Award, 1980); Mystery of Edwin Drood (completion), 1980; Fair's Fair, 1981; The House of Cards, 1982; with Edward Blishen: The God Beneath the Sea, 1970; The Golden Shadow, 1973; with David Proctor: Child O'War, 1972. *Recreations:* snooker, collecting pictures and china; also wine, women and song. *Address:* c/o Winant, Towers Ltd, Clerkenwell House, 45/47 Clerkenwell Green, EC1. *T:* 01-251 4707. *Clubs:* PEN, Puffin.

GARFITT, Alan; His Honour Judge Garfitt; a Circuit Judge, since 1977, and Judge, Cambridge County Court and Wisbech Crown Court, since 1978; b 20 Dec. 1920; s of Rush and Florence Garfitt; m 1st, 1941, Muriel Ada Jaggers; one s one d; 2nd, 1973, Ivie Maud Hudson; 3rd, 1978, Rosemary Lazell; one s one d. *Educ:* King Edward VII Grammar Sch., King's Lynn; Metropolitan Coll. and Inns of Court Sch. of Law. Served War of 1939-45, RAF, 1941-46. LLB London 1947; called to the Bar, Lincoln's Inn, 1948; practising barrister. Hon. Fellow, Faculty of Law, Cambridge, 1978. *Publications:* Law of Contracts in a Nutshell, 4 edns 1949-56; The Book for Police, 5 vols, 1958; jt ed, Roscoe's Criminal Evidence, Practice and Procedure, 16th edn, 1952; contribs to Jl of Planning Law, Solicitors' Jl and other legal pubns. *Recreations:* farming, gardening, DIY activities, horse riding and, as a member since 1961 and President since 1978 of the Association of British Riding Schools, the provision of good teaching and riding facilities for non-horse owners. *Address:* Leap House, Barcham Road, Soham, Ely, Cambs CB7 5TU. *Club:* Wig and Pen.

GARING, Air Commodore William Henry, CBE 1943; DFC 1940; Director, Bryn Mawr Chianina Stud Cattle Company, since 1975; b Corryong, Victoria, 26 July 1910; s of late George Garing, retired grazier, and late Amy Evelyn Garing; m 1st, 1940 (marr. diss. 1951); one s one d; 2nd, 1954, Marjorie Irene Smith, Preston, England; two d. *Educ:* Corryong Higher Elementary School; Melbourne Technical Coll.; Royal Military Coll., Duntroon, ACT. Began career as Electrical and Mechanical Engineer, 1928; entered RMC, Duntroon, 1929, as specially selected RAAF Cadet; Flying Training in Australia, 1931-32, in UK 1934-35; Seaplane Flying Instructor and Chief Navigation Instructor, Point Cook, Victoria, 1936; commanded Seaplane Squadron, Point Cook; conducted first Specialist Air Navigation Course in Australia, 1938; posted to United Kingdom in 1939; served with No 10 Squadron, RAAF, as Flt Commander in Coastal Command, RAF, 1939; operations in N Atlantic, France and Mediterranean (DFC); flew Lord Lloyd to France for discussions with Pétain Government prior to collapse of France, 1940, and subsequently was pilot to the late Duke of Kent and to Mr Eden (later Viscount Avon), and others (despatches). Arrived Australia, 1941; Senior Air Staff Officer, HQ Northern Area (extended from Neth. Indies through New Guinea, British Solomons to New Caledonia), 1941; commanded No 9 (Ops) Group RAAF, New Guinea, 1942; Milne Bay Campaign, 1942; Buna Campaign, 1942-43 (American DSC); 1943 (CBE);

commanded No 1 Operational Training Unit, 1943 (1939–43 star); Director Operational Requirements, 1944; SASO to RAAF Rep., Washington, 1945-46; OC Western Area, 1947; Joint Services Staff Coll., 1948; Commandant School Land/Air Warfare, NSW, 1950; OC Amberley, Qld, 1951; Imperial Defence Coll., London, 1952. AOC Overseas HQ, London, 1953; AOC RAAF, Richmond, NSW, 1953-55; AOC RAAF and Commandant RAAF Staff Coll., Point Cook, Victoria, 1955-60; Air Officer, South Australia, and OC, RAAF, Edinburgh Field, Salisbury, SA, 1960-64, retired. Exec. Dir, Rothmans Nat. Sport Foundn, Sydney, Australia, 1964; Commercial Relations Manager, Alfred Dunhill Ltd, 1971-75. Holds No 1 Air Navigators' Certificate (Australia); Air Master Navigator (RAF); Freeman, GAPAN. FAIM 1964. *Recreations:* Alpine ski-ing, water ski-ing, yachting, golf, shooting, flying (holds commercial pilot's licence). *Address:* Bryn Mawr, 25 Bangalla Street, Warrawee, NSW 2074, Australia. *Clubs:* Imperial Service, Royal Commonwealth (Sydney).

GARLAKE, Maj.-Gen. Storr, CBE 1949; *b* 11 April 1904; *yr s* of John Storr Inglesby and Dorothy Eleanor Garlake, Cradock, CP; *m* 1932, Catherine Ellen, *er d* of James Wightman, Cape Town; one *s* one *d*. *Educ:* St Andrew's Prep. Sch., Grahamstown; RN Colleges, Osborne and Dartmouth. Joined BSAP, 1925; commissioned 1929; transferred to S Rhodesia Staff Corps, 1933; Maj.-Gen. 1953. Served War of 1939-45, ME and India, 1942-45; Commander Military Forces, S Rhodesia, 1947-53; Imp. Defence Coll., 1949; Chief of General Staff, Federation of Rhodesia and Nyasaland, 1953-59. Additional ADC to the Queen, 1952-54; retired 1959. *Address:* Flat 208, Warick House, Montague Avenue, Harare, Zimbabwe. *Club:* Salisbury (Harare, Zimbabwe).

GARLAND, Ailsa Mary, (Mrs John Rollit Mason); broadcaster on TV and radio; *d* of James Francis Garland and Elsie Elizabeth Langley; *m* 1948, John Rollit Mason; one *s*. *Educ:* La Retraite, Clapham Park; St Mary's, Woodford Green, Essex. Fashion Editor, Vogue Export Book, 1947-50; Editor, Shopping Magazine, 1952-53; Woman's Editor, Daily Mirror, 1953-59, Assistant Editor, 1959-60; Editor of Vogue, 1960-63; Director, Condé Nast Publications Ltd, 1961-63; Editor in Chief, Woman's Jl, 1963-68; Editor of Fashion, 1963-68; Dir, Fleetway Publications Ltd, 1963-68; Fashion Coordinator, IPC Magazines Ltd, 1970-72. Governor, London College of Fashion, 1961-68. Mem. Consultative Cttee, Coll. of Fashion and Clothing Technology. Vice-Chm., Suffolk Heritage Trust, 1979; Trustee, Suffolk Historic Churches Trust, 1979. *Publication:* Lion's Share (autobiog.), 1970. *Recreations:* gardening, reading, theatre. *Address:* The Little House, Lady Street, Lavenham, Suffolk.

GARLAND, Basil; Registrar, Family Division of High Court of Justice; *b* 30 May 1920; *o c* of late Herbert George Garland and Grace Alice Mary Martha Garland; *m* 1942, Dora Mary Sudell Hope; one *s*. *Educ:* Dulwich Coll.; Pembroke Coll., Oxford (MA). Served in Royal Artillery, 1940-46: commnd 1941; Staff Officer, HQ RA, Gibraltar, 1943-45; Hon. Major 1946. Called to Bar, Middle Temple, 1948; Treasury Junior Counsel (Probate), 1965; Registrar, Principal Probate Registry, 1969. *Publications:* articles in Law Jl. *Recreations:* sailing, drama. *Address:* Dalethorpe End, Dedham, Essex. *T:* Colchester 322263. *Clubs:* Cruising Association, Bar Yacht, Royal Harwich Yacht.

GARLAND, (Frederick) Peter (Collison), CVO 1969; QPM 1965; *b* 4 Sept. 1912; *s* of late Percy Frederick Garland, Southsea, Hants; *m* 1945, Gwendolen Mary, *d* of late Henry James Powell, Putney; three *d*. *Educ:* Bradfield Coll. Joined Metropolitan Police, 1934. Served in RAF (Air Crew), 1941-45. Asst Chief Constable of Norfolk, 1952-56, Chief Constable, 1956-75. CStJ 1961. *Address:* 2 Eaton Road, Norwich. *T:* Norwich 53043. *Club:* Royal Air Force.

GARLAND, Patrick; director of plays, films, television; writer; *b* 10 April 1935; *s* of Ewart Garland and late Rosalind, *d* of Herbert Granville Fell, editor of The Connoisseur; *m* 1980, Alexandra Bastedo. *Educ:* St Mary's Coll., Southampton; St Edmund Hall, Oxford (BA). Actor, Bristol Old Vic, 1959; Age of Kings, BBC TV, 1961; lived in Montparnasse, 1961-62; writing—two plays for ITV, 1962; Research Asst, Monitor, BBC, 1963; Television interviews with: Stevie Smith, Philip Larkin, Sir Noel Coward, Sir John Gielgud, Sir Ralph Richardson, Dame Ninette de Valois, Claire Bloom, Tito Gobbi, Marcel Marceau, 1964-78. Director and Producer, BBC Arts Dept, 1962-74; Stage Director: 40 Years On, Brief Lives, 1968; Getting On, 1970; Cyrano, 1971; Hair (Israel), 1972; The Doll's House (New York and London), 1975; Under the Greenwood Tree, 1978; Look After Lulu, 1978; Beecham, 1980 (all West End); York Mystery Plays, 1980; My Fair Lady (US), 1980; Artistic Director, Chichester Festival Theatre, 1980-: The Cherry Orchard, 1981; The Mitford Girls, 1981 (also London, 1981); On the Rocks, 1982; Cavell, 1982; Goodbye, Mr Chips, 1982. *Films:* The Snow Goose, 1974; The Doll's House, 1976. *Publications:* Brief Lives, 1967; poetry in: London Magazine, 1954; New Poems, 1956; Poetry West; short stories in: Transatlantic Review, 1976; England Erzählt, Gemini, Light Blue Dark Blue. *Recreations:* reading Victorian novels, walking in Corsica. *Address:* 47 Cadogan Square, SW1. *Club:* Garrick.

GARLAND, Patrick Neville, QC 1972; a Recorder of the Crown Court, since 1972; *b* 22 July 1929; *s* of Frank Neville Garland and Marjorie Garland; *m* 1955, Jane Elizabeth Bird; two *s* one *d*. *Educ:* Uppingham Sch.; Sidney Sussex Coll., Cambridge (MA, LLB). Called to Bar, Middle Temple, 1953,

Bencher, 1979. Asst Recorder, Norwich, 1971. *Publications:* articles in legal and technical jls. *Recreations:* shooting, sailing, gardening, industrial archaeology, *Address:* 9 Ranulf Road, NW2. *T:* 01-435 5877; 11 King's Bench Walk, Temple, EC4Y 7EQ. *Clubs:* Norfolk (Norwich); Cumberland Lawn Tennis, Grafham Water Sailing.

GARLAND, Peter; see Garland, F. P. C.

GARLAND, Peter Bryan, PhD; FRSE; Professor of Biochemistry, Medical Sciences Institute, University of Dundee, since 1970; Member, Medical Research Council. *Educ:* Univ. of Cambridge (BChir 1958, MB 1959, PhD 1964). Formerly Reader in Biochem., Bristol Univ. *Publications:* (ed with A. P. Mathias) Biochemistry of the Cell Nucleus, 1977; (ed with C. N. Hales) Substrate Mobilization and Energy Provision in Man, 1978; (with R. Williamson) Biochemistry of Genetic Engineering, 1979. *Address:* Department of Biochemistry, Medical Sciences Institute, The University, Dundee DD1 4HN.

GARLAND, Hon. Sir (Ransley) Victor, KBE 1982; High Commissioner of Australia, in the UK, since 1981; *b* 5 May 1934; *m* Lynette May Jamieson, MusBach (Melb.); two *s* one *d*. *Educ:* Univ. of Western Australia. BA (Econ); FCA. Member, House of Representatives, for Curtin, W Aust., 1969-81. Minister for Supply, 1971-72; Executive Councillor, 1971-; Minister Asstg Treasurer, 1972; Actg Minister for Customs and Excise, during 1972; Minister: for Post and Telecom., also Minister Asstg Treas., 1975-76; for Veterans' Affairs, 1977-78; for Special Trade Representations, also Minister Asstg Minister for Trade and Resources, 1977-79; periodically, Actg Minister for Trade and Resources, 1978, 1979, 1980; Minister for Business and Consumer Affairs and Minister Asstg Minister for Industry and Commerce, 1979-80; Acting Minister: for Ind. and Commerce, for Productivity, for Special Trade Representations, periods during 1980. Govt Representative Minister: at Commonwealth Ministerial Meeting for Common Fund, London, 1978; at Ministerial Meetings of: ESCAP, New Delhi, 1978; SPEC, Tonga, 1979; Minister representing Treas., at Ministerial Meeting of OECD, Paris, 1978; Leader, Aust. Delegn to UNCTAD V and Chm. Commonwealth Delegns to UNCTAD V, Manila, 1979; attended, with Premier, Commonwealth Heads of Govt meeting, Lusaka, 1979. Parly Adviser, Aust. Mission to UN Gen. Assembly, New York, 1973; Chief Opposition Whip, 1974-75; Chairman: House of Reps Expenditure Cttee, 1976-77; Govt Members' Treasury Cttee, 1977. Freeman, City of London, 1982. *Address:* Australian High Commission, Australia House, Strand, WC2. *T:* 01-438 8000; Richardson Avenue, Claremont, Western Australia; Mugga Way, Canberra, ACT.

GARLICK, Prof. George Frederick John, BSc, PhD, DSc, FInstP; *b* 21 Feb. 1919; *s* of George Robert Henry Garlick and Martha Elizabeth (*née* Davies); *m* 1943, Dorothy Mabel Bowsher; one *d* ; *m* 1977, Harriet Herta Forster. *Educ:* Wednesbury High Sch.; Univ. of Birmingham (BSc 1940, PhD 1943, DSc 1955). War service: Scientific Officer (Radar Research). In Charge Luminescence Laboratory, Birmingham Univ., 1946-56 (Research Physicist, 1946-49, Lecturer in Physics, 1949-56); Prof. of Physics, Univ. of Hull, 1956-78; Research Prof., Univ. of Southern California, LA, 1978-79; private scientific consultant, 1979-82. FInstP 1949. Jubilee Medal, 1977. *Publications:* Luminescent Materials, 1949; numerous papers in learned scientific journals. *Recreation:* music (organ). *Address:* 267 South Beloit Avenue, Los Angeles, California 90049, USA.

GARLICK, Sir John, KCB 1976 (CB 1973); Permanent Secretary, Department of the Environment, 1978-81; *b* 17 May 1921; *m* 1945, Frances Esther Munday; three *d*. *Educ:* Westcliff High Sch., Essex; University of London. Entered Post Office Engineering Dept, 1937; Ministry of Transport, 1948; Private Secretary to Rt Hon. Ernest Marples, 1959-60; Assistant Secretary, 1960; National Economic Development Office, 1962-64; Under-Sec., Min. of Transport, 1966, later DoE; Dep. Sec., DoE, 1972-73; Dir-Gen., Highways, DoE, 1973-74; Second Permanent Sec., Cabinet Office, 1974-77. Mem., London Docklands Develt Corp., 1981-. Dir, Abbey National Bldg Soc., 1981-. *Address:* 16 Astons Road, Moor Park, Northwood, Mddx. *T:* Northwood 24628.

GARLICK, Kenneth John; Keeper of Western Art, Ashmolean Museum, Oxford, since 1968; Fellow of Balliol College, Oxford, since 1968; *b* 1 Oct. 1916; *s* of late D. E. Garlick and Annie Hallifax. *Educ:* Elmhurst Sch., Street; Balliol Coll., Oxford; Courtauld Inst. of Art, London. MA Oxon, PhD Birmingham; FSA, FMA. RAF Signals, 1939-46. Lectr, Bath Academy of Art, 1946-48; Asst Keeper, Dept of Art, City of Birmingham Museum and Art Gallery, 1948-50; Lectr (Sen. Lectr 1960), Barber Inst. of Fine Arts, Univ. of Birmingham, 1951-68. Governor, Royal Shakespeare Theatre, 1978-. *Publications:* Sir Thomas Lawrence, 1954; Walpole Society Vol. XXXIX (Lawrence Catalogue Raisonné), 1964; Walpole Society Vol. XLV (Catalogue of Pictures at Althorp), 1976; (ed with Angus Macintyre) The Diary of Joseph Farington, Vols I-II, 1978, III-VI, 1979; numerous articles and reviews. *Recreations:* travel, music. *Address:* c/o Ashmolean Museum, Oxford. *T:* Oxford 57522. *Club:* Reform.

GARLICK, Rev. Canon Wilfrid; *b* 12 Oct. 1910; *s* of late Arthur and Clemence Garlick; *m* 1936, Edith, *d* of late H. Goddard; one *s*. *Educ:* Oldham Hulme Grammar Sch.; Manchester Univ. (MA *hc* 1968); Egerton Hall Theological Coll. BSc 1931, Manchester. Curate St Andrew, Ancoats, Manchester, 1933-35; Curate St Clement, Chorlton-cum-Hardy, 1935-38;

Rector St Nicholas, Burnage, Manchester, 1938-44; Officiating Chaplain to Forces, 1938-44; Vicar of St George, Sheffield, 1944-48; Vicar of St George, Stockport, 1948-75; Rector of Alderley, 1975-82; Hon. Canon of Chester, 1958-82. Hon. Chaplain to the Queen, 1964-80. *Recreations:* golf, travel. *Address:* 10 Glasfryn Avenue, Meliden, Prestatyn, N Wales.

GARMOYLE, Viscount; Simon Dallas Cairns; *b* 27 May 1939; *er s* and *heir* of 5th Earl Cairns, *qv; m* 1964, Amanda Mary, *d* of late Major E. F. Heathcoat Amory, and of Mrs Roderick Heathcoat Amory, Oswaldkirk Hall, York; three *s. Educ:* Eton; Trinity Coll., Cambridge. Man. Dir, S. G. Warburg & Co. Ltd, 1979-. *Heir: s* Hon. Hugh Sebastian Cairns, *b* 26 March 1965. *Address:* Queen Hoo Hall, Tewin, Herts. *T:* Tewin 7361. *Club:* Turf.

GARNER, family name of **Baron Garner.**

GARNER, Baron *cr* 1969 (Life Peer), of Chiddingly; **(Joseph John) Saville Garner,** GCMG 1965 (KCMG 1954; CMG 1948); Treasurer and Chairman, Board of Governors, Highgate School, since 1976 (Governor since 1962); *b* 14 Feb. 1908; *s* of Joseph and Helena Maria Garner, Highgate, N; *m* 1938, Margaret Beckman, Cedar Lake, Ind, USA; two *s* one *d. Educ:* Highgate Sch.; Jesus Coll., Cambridge. Appointed Dominions Office, 1930; Private Sec. to successive Secretaries of State, 1940-43; Senior Sec., office of UK High Comr Ottawa, 1943-46; Dep. High Comr for the UK, Ottawa, Canada, 1946-48; Asst Under-Sec., Commonwealth Relations Office, 1948-51; Deputy High Commissioner for the UK in India, 1951-53; Deputy Under-Secretary, Commonwealth Relations Office, 1952-56; British High Commissioner in Canada, 1956-61; Permanent Under-Secretary of State, Commonwealth Relations Office, 1962-65, Commonwealth Office, 1965-68; Head of HM Diplomatic Service, 1965-68. Secretary, Order of St Michael and St George, 1966-68 (Registrar, 1962-66). Chairman: Bd of Governors, Commonwealth Inst., 1968-74; Commonwealth Scholarship Commn in the UK, 1968-77; Cttee of Management, Inst. of Commonwealth Studies, 1971-79; Bd of Management, RPMS, 1971-80; London Bd, Bank of Adelaide, 1971-80 (Dir, 1969-80); Jt Commonwealth Societies Council, 1981-. Member: Council, Voluntary Service Overseas, 1969-74; Security Commission, 1968-73. Bd of Governors, SOAS, Univ. of London, 1968-73. Hon. LLD: Univ. of Brit. Columbia, 1958; Univ. of Toronto, 1959; Hon. Fellow, Jesus College, Cambridge, 1967. President, Old Cholmeleian Society, 1964. *Publications:* The Books of the Emperor Wu Ti (transl. from German), 1930; The Commonwealth Office 1925-68, 1978. *Recreations:* gardening, travel. *Address:* Highdown Farmhouse, Horam, Heathfield, E Sussex TN21 0JR. *T:* Chiddingly 432. *Club:* Royal Automobile.

GARNER, Alan; author; *b* 17 Oct. 1934; *s* of Colin and Marjorie Garner; *m* 1st, 1956, Ann Cook; one *s* two *d* ; 2nd, 1972, Griselda Greaves; one *s* one *d. Educ:* Alderley Edge Council Sch.; Manchester Grammar Sch.; Magdalen Coll., Oxford. *Publications:* The Weirdstone of Brisingamen, 1960; The Moon of Gomrath, 1963; Elidor, 1965; Holly from the Bongs, 1966; The Old Man of Mow, 1967; The Owl Service, 1967 (Library Assoc. Carnegie Medal 1967, Guardian Award 1968); The Hamish Hamilton Book of Goblins, 1969; Red Shift, 1973 (with John Mackenzie, filmed 1978); (with Albin Trowski) The Breadhorse, 1975; The Guizer, 1975; The Stone Book, 1976; Tom Fobble's Day, 1977; Granny Reardun, 1977; The Aimer Gate, 1978; Fairy Tales of Gold, 1979; The Lad of the Gad, 1980; *plays:* Lurga Lom, 1980; To Kill a King, 1980; Feel Free, 1980; Strandloper, 1982; Sally Water, 1982; *dance drama:* The Green Mist, 1970; *libretti:* The Bellybag, 1971 (music by Richard Morris); Potter Thompson, 1972 (music by Gordon Crosse). *Recreation:* work. *Address:* Blackden, Cheshire CW4 8BY.

GARNER, Anthony Stuart; Director of Organisation, Conservative Central Office, since 1976; *b* 28 Jan. 1927; *s* of Edward Henry Garner, MC, FIAS, and Dorothy May Garner; *m* 1967, Shirley Doris Taylor; two *s. Educ:* Liverpool Coll. Young Conservative Organiser, 1948-51; Conservative Agent, Halifax, 1951-56; Nat. Organising Sec., Young Conservative Org., 1956-61; Conservative Central Office Agent for: London Area, 1961-64; Western Area, 1964-66; North West Area, 1966-76. Chm., Conservative Agents' Examination Bd, 1976-. Pres., Conservative Agents' Benevolent Assoc., 1976-. Life Governor, Liverpool Coll., 1980-. *Recreations:* sailing, theatre. *Address:* 1 Blomfield Road, W9. *Clubs:* Carlton, St Stephen's Constitutional.

GARNER, Frank Harold; farmer since 1971; *b* 4 Dec. 1904; *m* 1929, Hilda May Sheppard; one *d. Educ:* Swindon Technical Sch.; Universities of Cambridge, Oxford, Reading and Minnesota, USA. MA (Cantab), MA (Oxon), MSc (Minnesota, USA); FRAgsS. Assistant to Director of Cambridge University Farm, 1924; University Demonstrator in Agriculture at Cambridge, 1927; University Lecturer (Animal Husbandry) at Cambridge, 1929; Assistant to Executive Officer, Cambridgeshire War Agriculture Executive Cttee, 1939; County Agricultural Organiser, East Suffolk, 1940; General Manager of Frederick Hiam Ltd, 1944-58; Principal, RAC, Cirencester, Glos, 1958-71. Chm., Bucks NFU, 1978. Liveryman, Farmers' Livery Co., Master, 1971-72. *Publications:* Cattle of Britain, 1943; The Farmers Animals, 1943; British Dairy Farming, 1946; (with E. T. Halnan and A. Eden) Principles and Practice of Feeding Farm Animals, 1940, 5th edn 1966; (ed) Modern British Farming Systems, 1975. *Recreation:* swimming. *Address:* Collins Farm House, Looseley Row, Princes Risborough, Bucks. *Club:* Farmers'.

GARNER, Frederic Francis, CMG 1959; Ambassador to Costa Rica, 1961-67; retired; *b* 9 July 1910; *m* 1946, Muriel (*née* Merrick). *Educ:* Rugby Sch.; Worcester Coll., Oxford. Joined HM Consular Service in China, 1932; served at Peking, Canton, Shanghai, POW in Japan, 1942-45. Consul, Tangier, 1947-50; First Secretary, Bogota, 1950-54; Consul-General, Shanghai, 1954-56; Head of Consular Department, Foreign Office, 1956-58; Ambassador at Phnom Penh, 1958-61. *Address:* 44 Belgrave Mews South, SW1X 8BT. *T:* 01-235 7507.

GARNER, Frederick Leonard; Chairman, Pearl Assurance Company Ltd, since 1977; *b* 7 April 1920; *s* of Leonard Frank Garner and Florence Emily Garner; *m* 1953, Giovanna Maria Anzani, Italy. *Educ:* Sutton County Sch., Surrey. Served War, RA, 1940-46. Joined Pearl Assurance Co., 1936; rejoined, 1946; sole employment, 1946-. Dir of cos. *Address:* 98 Tudor Avenue, Worcester Park, Surrey. *T:* 01-337 3313, (office) 01-405 8441. *Club:* Royal Automobile.

GARNER, Maurice Richard; Visiting Professor, Department of Government, London School of Economics and Political Science, since 1981; student of the structure and governmental control of public enterprises, University of Kent, since 1974; *b* 31 May 1915; *o s* of Jesse H. Garner; *m* 1943, Joyce W. Chapman; one *s* one *d. Educ:* Glendale County Sch.; London Sch. of Economics and Political Science. Royal Armoured Corps, 1942-45 (despatches). Inland Revenue (Tax Inspectorate), 1938-46; BoT, Asst Principal and Principal, 1947; Commercial Sec. and UK Trade Comr in Ottawa, 1948-55; transf. to Min. of Power, 1957; Asst Sec. 1960; Under-Sec., Electricity Div., Min. of Technology, 1969, later DTI, retired 1973. *Recreations:* sailing, reading, oenology. *Address:* Albany Lodge, Staple, Canterbury, Kent CT3 1JX. *T:* Ash 812011.

GARNETT, John; see Garnett, W. J. P. M.

GARNETT, Thomas Ronald, MA; Headmaster of Geelong Church of England Grammar School, Australia, 1961-73; Gardening Editor, The Age, since 1982; *b* 1 Jan. 1915; *s* of E. N. Garnett; *m* 1946, Penelope, *d* of Philip Frere; three *s* two *d. Educ:* Charterhouse (Scholar); Magdalene Coll., Cambridge (Scholar). BA 1936, MA 1946. Assistant master: Westminster School, 1936-38; Charterhouse, 1938-52; Master of Marlborough College, 1952-61. Served War of 1939-45, RAF, India and Burma, 1941-46, Squadron Leader (despatches). Cricket for Somerset, 1939. *Recreations:* gardening, ornithology. *Address:* Simmons Reef, Blackwood, via Trentham, Victoria, Australia. *T:* 053 686514. *Club:* Melbourne (Melbourne).

GARNETT, (William) John (Poulton Maxwell), CBE 1970; MA; Director, Industrial Society, since 1962; Chairman, Spencer Stuart & Associates, Management Consultants, 1979-81; *b* 6 Aug. 1921; *s* of Dr Maxwell Garnett, CBE, and Margaret Lucy Poulton; *m* 1943, Barbara Rutherford-Smith; two *s* two *d. Educ:* Rugby Sch.; Kent Sch., USA; Trinity Coll., Cambridge. Royal Navy, 1941-46 (commnd. 1942). ICI Ltd, 1947-62. Dep. Chm. UNA, 1954-56, Treasurer, 1979-81. Mem., Ct of inquiry into miners' strike, 1972; Arbitrator, Lorry Drivers' Strike, 1979. Mem., Royal Dockyard Policy Bd. Chm., Churches Council on Gambling, 1965-71. DUniv Essex, 1977; Hon. DTech Loughborough, 1978; Hon. LLD, CNAA, 1980. *Publications:* The Manager's Responsibility for Communication, 1964; The Work Challenge, 1973, 1977. *Recreations:* sailing, timber construction. *Address:* 3 Carlton House Terrace, SW1. *Clubs:* Athenæum; Leander (Henley).

See also P. J. Bottomley.

GARNETT-ORME, Ion; Chairman, St Dunstan's, since 1975 (Member of Council, since 1958); Director: Brown Shipley Holdings Limited, 1960-81 (Chairman, 1963-75); United States Debenture Corporation Ltd, since 1951 (Chairman, 1958-78); *b* 23 Jan. 1910; *er s* of George Hunter Garnett-Orme and Alice Richmond (*née* Brown); *m* 1946, Katharine Clifton, *d* of Brig.-Gen. Howard Clifton Brown. *Educ:* Eton; Magdalene Coll., Cambridge. Served War, Welsh Guards, 1939-45. Joined: Brown, Shipley & Co, Merchant Bankers, 1945; Bd of London Scottish American Trust Ltd and United States Debenture Corp. Ltd, 1951; Bd of Avon Rubber Co Ltd, 1956-66; Dir, Ellerman Lines Ltd, 1971-75. *Address:* Cheriton Cottage, Cheriton, near Alresford, Hants SO24 0PR. *Club:* Carlton.

GARNHAM, Prof. Percy Cyril Claude, CMG 1964; FRS 1964; MD; Professor of Medical Protozoology (now Emeritus Professor), London University, and Head of Department of Parasitology, London School of Hygiene and Tropical Medicine, 1952-68, Hon. Fellow, 1976; Senior Research Fellow, Imperial College of Science and Technology, 1968-79, Hon. Fellow, 1979; Visiting Professor, Department of Biology, University of Strathclyde, since 1970; *b* 15 Jan. 1901; *s* of late Lieut P. C. Garnham, RN Division, and late Edith Masham; *m* 1924, Esther Long Price, Talley, Carms; two *s* four *d. Educ:* privately; St Bartholomew's Hospital. MRCS, LRCP, 1923, MB, BS London, 1923, DPH Eng. 1924, MD London, 1928 (University Gold Medal); Dipl. de Méd. Malariol., University of Paris, 1931. Colonial Medical Service, 1925-47; on staff of London School of Hygiene and Tropical Medicine, first as Reader, then as Professor, 1947-68. Heath Clark Lectr, Univ. of London, 1968; Fogarty Internat. Scholar, Nat. Insts of Health, Maryland, 1970, 1972; Manson Orator, 1969, Theobald Smith Orator, 1970; Ross Orator, 1980. Member, Expert Panel of Parasitic Diseases, of WHO; Hon. Pres., European Fedn of Parasitologists; Past President: British Soc. of Parasitologists; Royal

Society of Tropical Medicine and Hygiene; Vice-President: World Federation of Parasitologists; International Association against Filariasis; Corresponding Member: Académie Royale des Sciences d'Outre Mer, Belgium; Accad. Lancisiana, Rome; Soc. de Geografia da Lisboa; Hon. Member: Amer. Soc. Tropical Medicine; Société Belge de Médecine Tropicale; Brazilian Soc. Tropical Medicine; Soc. of Protozoologists; Société de Pathologie Exotique (Médaille d'Or, 1971); Acad. Nationale de Médecine, France (Médaille en Vermeil, 1972); Amer. Soc. of Parasitology; Mexican Soc. of Parasitologists; Polish Soc. of Parasitologists; British Soc. of Parasitologists; Groupement des Protistologues de la Langue Française; Foreign Member: Danish Royal Acad. of Sciences and Letters, 1976; Acad. Royale de Médecine, Belgium, 1979; Royal Entomolog. Soc. of London, 1979. Hon. FRCP Edinburgh, 1966; FRCP 1967; FIBiol, 1962. Freedom, City of London in Farriers Co., 1964. DSc London, 1952; Hon. Dr, Univ. of Bordeaux, 1965; Academician of Pontifical Acad. of Sciences, 1970; Univ. of Montpellier, 1980. KLJ 1979. Darling Medal and Prize, 1951; Bernhard Nocht Medal, 1957; Gaspar Vianna Medal, 1962; Manson Medal, 1965; Emile Brumpt Prize, 1970; Mary Kingsley Medal, 1973; Rudolf Leuckart Medal, 1974. *Publications:* Malaria Parasites, 1966; Progress in Parasitology, 1970; numerous papers on parasitology in medical journals. *Recreations:* chamber music and European travel. *Address:* Southernwood, Farnham Common, Bucks. *T:* 3863. *Club:* Nairobi (Kenya).

GARNOCK, Viscount; David Lindesay-Bethune; *b* 9 Feb. 1926; *er s* of 14th Earl of Lindsay, *qv*; *m* 1st, 1953, Hon. Mary Clare Douglas-Scott-Montagu (marr. diss., 1968), *y d* of 2nd Baron Montagu of Beaulieu; one *s* one *d*; 2nd, 1969, Penelope, *er d* of late Anthony Crossley, MP. *Educ:* Eton; Magdalene Coll., Cambridge. Scots Guards, 1943-45. US and Canadian Railroads, 1948-50. Chairman: Severn Valley Railway (Holdings) Ltd, 1972-76 (Pres., 1976-); Romney, Hythe and Dymchurch Light Rly Co., 1976-, Holdings Co., 1976-; Sallingbury Holdings, 1977-; Sallingbury Ltd, 1977-; Director: Carpets International Group Services Ltd, 1959-; Crossley Karastan Carpet Mills Ltd, Canada, 1961-; Festiniog Railway Co. Ltd, 1960-; Abbey Life Insurance Co. of Canada, 1964-81; Carpets International Georgia Inc., 1972-; Bank of Montreal, 1975-; Manuge Galleries (Nova Scotia), 1976-; International Harvester Co. of GB Ltd, 1976-; Bain Dawes Ltd (Northern), 1978-; Bain Dawes (Canada), 1978-; Jubilee Park (Leisure Projects) Ltd, 1979-; Riverside Plantation Co., Inc., 1982-; Associated Marine Industries Offshore Resources Ltd, 1982-; Mem. International Harvester World Adv. Council, 1980-; Vice-Chm., N American Adv. Gp, BOTB, 1973-; Vice-Pres., Transport Trust, 1973-; Mem., BTA, 1976-. Chm., British Carpets Manufacturers' Assoc. Export Council, 1976-. Mem., Queen's Body Guard for Scotland (Royal Company of Archers), 1960. *Recreation:* catching up. *Heir: s* Master of Garnock, *qv*. *Address:* Combermere Abbey, Whitchurch, Salop. *T:* Burleydam 287; Coates House, Upper Largo, Fife. *T:* Upper Largo 249. *Club:* Carlton.

See also Sir Bourchier Wrey, Bt.

GARNOCK, Master of; Hon. James Randolph Lindesay-Bethune; *b* 19 Nov. 1955; *s* and *heir* of Viscount Garnock, *qv*; *m* 1982, Diana, *er d* of Major Nigel Chamberlayne-Macdonald, Cranbury Park, Winchester. *Educ:* Eton; Univ. of Edinburgh; Univ. of Calif, Davis. *Address:* Pond Farm, Biddenden, Kent.

GARNONS WILLIAMS, Basil Hugh; Headmaster of Berkhamsted School, 1953-72; *b* 1 July 1906; 5th *s* of Rev. A. Garnons Williams, Rector of New Radnor; *m* 1943, Margaret Olive Shearme (*d* 1981); one *s* two *d*. *Educ:* Winchester Coll. (Scholar); Hertford Coll., Oxford (Scholar). 1st Hon. Classical Moderations 1927; 2nd Lit Hum 1929; BA 1929; BLitt 1933; MA 1938; Classical VI Form Master, Sedbergh Sch., 1930-35; Marlborough Coll., 1935-45; Headmaster of Plymouth Coll., 1945-53. *Publications:* A History of Berkhamsted School, 1541-1972, 1980; articles in Classical Quarterly and Greece and Rome; contributor to History of the World (ed by W. N. Weech), 1944. *Address:* 84 High Street, Lavenham, Sudbury, Suffolk CO10 9PT. *T:* Lavenham 247654.

GARNONS WILLIAMS, Captain Nevill Glennie, MBE 1919; Royal Navy (Retired); *b* 1899; *s* of late Rev. Arthur Garnons Williams, Abercamlais, Brecon; *m* 1928, Violet (*d* 1979), *d* of late B. G. Tours, CMG; one *d*. *Educ:* RN Colls, Osborne and Dartmouth; Caius Coll., Cambridge. Joined Royal Navy, 1912; served European War, 1914-18, Jutland (despatches); and War of 1939-45; retired as Captain, 1946. DL 1948, JP 1956, Brecknockshire; Vice-Lieutenant, 1959-64, Lord Lieutenant, 1964-74, Brecknockshire. Croix de Guerre (avec Palmes), 1916. KStJ 1973. *Recreations:* forestry, fishing, cricket, scouting. *Address:* Abercamlais, Brecon, Powys. *T:* Sennybridge 206. *Clubs:* Army and Navy, MCC.

GARNSEY, Rt. Rev. David Arthur; *b* 31 July 1909; *s* of Canon Arthur Henry Garnsey and Bertha Edith Frances Garnsey (*née* Benn); *m* 1934, Evangeline Eleanor Wood; two *s* two *d*. *Educ:* Trinity and Sydney Grammar Schs; St Paul's Coll., University of Sydney; New Coll., Oxford. University of Sydney, BA (1st cl. Latin and Greek) 1930; Travelling Sec. Australian SCM, 1930-31; NSW Rhodes Scholar, 1931, New Coll. Oxford, BA (2nd cl. Lit. Hum.) 1933, 2nd cl. Theol. 1934, MA 1937; Ripon Hall, Oxford, 1933. Deacon, 1934; Priest, 1935; Curate, St Mary the Virgin (University Church), and Inter-Collegiate Sec. of SCM, Oxford, 1934-38; St Saviour's Cathedral, Goulburn, NSW, 1938-41; Rector of Young, NSW, 1941-45; Gen. Sec. Australian SCM, 1945-48; Exam. Chap. to Bp of Goulburn, 1939-45, 1948-58;

Head Master Canberra Grammar Sch., 1948-58; Canon of St Saviour's Cathedral, Goulburn, 1949-58; Bishop of Gippsland, 1959-74. Pres., Australian Council of Churches, 1970-73. Chm., Bd of Delegates, Aust. Coll. of Theology, 1971-77; Hon. ThD, Australian Coll. of Theology, 1955. Coronation Medal, 1953. *Publications:* booklets for study. *Recreation:* walking. *Address:* 33 Dutton Street, Dickson, Canberra 2602, Australia. *T:* 062-474786.

GARNSWORTHY, Most Rev. Lewis Samuel; *see* Toronto, Archbishop of.

GARRAN, Sir (Isham) Peter, KCMG 1961 (CMG 1954); HM Diplomatic Service, retired; Chairman, Quality Assurance Council, British Standards Institution, 1971-82; *b* 15 Jan. 1910; *s* of late Sir Robert Randolph Garran, GCMG, QC; *m* 1935, Mary Elisabeth, *d* of late Sir Richard Rawdon Stawell, KBE, MD; two *s* one *d*. *Educ:* Melbourne Grammar Sch.; Trinity Coll., Melbourne Univ. (BA 1st cl. Hons). Joined Foreign Office, 1934; Foreign posts: Belgrade, 1937-41; Lisbon, 1941-44; Berlin (seconded to CCG as Chief of Political Div.), 1947-50; The Hague, 1950-52; Inspector in HM Foreign Service, 1952-54; Minister (Commercial), Washington, 1955-60; Ambassador to Mexico, 1960-64; Ambassador to the Netherlands, 1964-70. Director: Lend-Lease Corp., NSW, 1970-78; UK Br., Australian Mutual Provident Soc., 1970-82; Chm., Securicor Nederland BV, 1976-82. *Recreation:* gardening. *Address:* Roanoke, Bosham Hoe, Sussex. *T:* Bosham 572347. *Club:* Boodle's.

See also A. L. Coleby.

GARRARD, Henry John; His Honour Judge Garrard; a Circuit Judge (formerly a County Court Judge), since 1965; *b* 15 Jan. 1912; *s* of late C. G. Garrard; *m* 1945, Muriel, *d* of late A. H. S. Draycott, Stratford-on-Avon; one *s* one *d*. *Educ:* Framlingham Coll., Suffolk. Called to the Bar, Middle Temple, Nov. 1937; Mem. of Oxford Circuit. Served 1939-45, Staffs Yeomanry (QORR) and Worcestershire Regt, East and North Africa, rank of Lieut; prisoner-of-war, 1942-45. Mem. of Mental Health Review Tribunal for Birmingham Area, 1963-65; Recorder of Burton-on-Trent, 1964-65. *Recreations:* family, dogs, country life. *Address:* The General's Farmhouse, Chartley, Stafford. *T:* Dapple Heath 268.

GARRARD, Rev. Lancelot Austin, LLD; BD, MA; Professor of Philosophy and Religion, Emerson College, Boston, USA, 1965-71, now Emeritus; *b* 31 May 1904; *s* of late Rev. W. A. Garrard; *m* 1932, Muriel Walsh; two *s*. *Educ:* Felsted (Scholar); Wadham Coll., Oxford (exhibitioner); Manchester Coll., Oxford; Marburg (Hibbert scholar). 2nd Class, Classical Mods; 2nd Class Lit Hum; Abbot Scholar; BD, MA (Oxon). Asst Master: Edinburgh Acad., 1927; St Paul's Sch., 1928; Unitarian Minister, Dover, 1932-33; Tutor and Bursar, Manchester Coll., Oxford, 1933-43; Minister, Lewins Mead Meeting, Bristol, 1941-43; Liverpool, Ancient Chapel of Toxteth, 1943-52; Tutor, Unitarian Coll., Manchester, 1945-51; Manchester Coll., Oxford, 1952-56; Principal of Manchester Coll., Oxford, 1956-65, Pres., 1980-; Editor of The Hibbert Journal, 1951-62. Hon. Chief, Chickasaw Nation. Hon. LLD (Emerson Coll, Boston). *Publications:* Duty and the Will of God, 1935; The Interpreted Bible, 1946; The Gospels To-day, 1953; The Historical Jesus: Schweitzer's Quest and Ours, 1956; Athens or Jerusalem?, 1965. *Recreation:* cycling. *Address:* 13 Holmlea Road, Goring, Reading, Berks. *Club:* Athenæum.

GARRATT, Gerald Reginald Mansel, MA, CEng, FIEE; FRAeS; retired; Keeper, Department of Aeronautics and Marine Transport, Science Museum, South Kensington, 1966-71; *b* 10 Dec. 1906; *s* of Reginald R. and Florence Garratt; *m* 1931, Ellen Georgina Brooks, Antwerp, Belgium; two *d*. *Educ:* Marlborough Coll.; Caius Coll., Cambridge. International Telephone & Telegraph Laboratories, 1929-30; RAE, Farnborough, 1930-34; Asst Keeper: Dept of Textiles and Printing, Science Museum, 1934; Dept of Telecommunications, 1936; Dep. Keeper 1949. Served RAF 1939-46 (Wing Comdr). Founder Mem., Cambridge Univ. Air Squadron, 1926. Commissioned RAF Reserve of Officers, 1928; retired 1966 (Wing Comdr). *Publications:* One Hundred Years of Submarine Cables, 1950; The Origins of Maritime Radio, 1972; numerous articles on history of telecommunications. *Recreations:* sailing, amateur radio. *Address:* Littlefield, 28 Parkwood Avenue, Esher, Surrey KT10 8DG. *T:* 01-398 1582. *Club:* Royal Automobile.

GARRELS, John Carlyle; retired; Chairman: Monsanto Chemicals Ltd, 1965-71; Monsanto Textiles Ltd, 1970-71; formerly Director: Forth Chemicals Ltd; Monsanto Australia Ltd; Monsanto Oil Co. of UK, Inc.; British Saccharin Sales Ltd; *b* 5 March 1914; *s* of John C. and Margaret Ann Garrels; *m* 1st, 1938, Valerie Smith; one *s* two *d*; 2nd, 1980, Isabelle Rogers Kehoe. *Educ:* Univ. of Michigan (BS (Chem. Eng.); Harvard (Advanced Management Programme). Pennsylvania Salt Mfg Co., Production Supervisor, 1936-42; Monsanto Co.: various appts, 1942-54; Asst Gen. Manager, 1955; Monsanto Chemicals Ltd: Dep. Man. Dir, 1960; Man. Dir, 1961; Chm. and Man. Dir, 1965. Pres., British Plastics Fedn, 1970, 1971. Member: National Economic Development Cttee for Chemical Industry, 1971; Council, Chemical Industries Assoc. *Recreations:* golf, shooting, fishing. *Address:* 3111 SE Fairway West, Stuart, Fla 33494, USA. *T:* 305-283-6132. *Clubs:* American; Sunningdale Golf; Yacht and Country (Stuart, Fla).

GARRETT, Alexander Adnett, MBE 1934; *b* London, 1886; *e s* of late Adnett William Garrett and Marion Walker Bruce; *m* 1928, Mildred (*d* 1975), *g d* of L. S. Starrett, Athol, Mass. *Educ:* Owen's Sch., London; London

Sch. of Economics (BSc); King's Coll., London (Gilbart Prizeman); Christ's Coll., Cambridge (Economics Tripos). FCIS; attended the 20th Convention of the American Institute of Accountants, St Louis, USA, 1924; Internat. Congresses on Accounting, Amsterdam, 1926, New York, 1929, and Berlin, 1938; Asst Sec., 4th Internat. Congress on Accounting, London, 1933; sometime Hon. Mem., former Soc. of Incorporated Accountants (Sec. 1919-49, retired 1949; Asst Sec., 1913); visited Accountancy Bodies in Canada, USA, Australia, New Zealand, South Africa, 1947-50. Dept of Applied Economics, Cambridge, 1950-59. Hon. Mem., Australian Soc. of Accountants, 1956. Served Royal Naval Reserve, 1915-31; Comdr (S), RNR (retired). *Publication:* History of the Society of Incorporated Accountants, 1885-1957, 1961. *Address:* 7 King's Bench Walk, Temple, EC4. *T:* 01-353 7880. *Clubs:* Athenæum, Reform.

GARRETT, Maj.-Gen. Henry Edmund Melvill Lennox, CBE 1975; Director of Security (Army), Ministry of Defence, since 1978; *b* 31 Jan. 1924; *s* of John Edmund Garrett and Mary Garrett; *m* 1973, Rachel Ann Beadon; one step *s* one step *d*. *Educ:* Wellington Coll.; Clare Coll., Cambridge (MA). Commnd 1944; psc 1956; DAAG, HQ BAOR, 1957-60; US Armed Forces Staff Coll., 1960; OC 7 Field Sqdn RE, 1961-63; GSO2 WO, 1963-65; CO 35 Engr Regt, 1965-68; Col GS MoD, 1968-69; Comdr 12 Engr Bde, 1969-71; RCDS, 1972; Chief of Staff HQ N Ireland, 1972-75; Maj.-Gen. i/c Administration, HQ UKLF, 1975-76; Vice Adjutant General, MoD, 1976-78. Col Comdt RE, 1982. Chm. Governors, Royal Soldiers' Daughters Sch., 1983. *Recreations:* riding, walking. *Address:* c/o National Westminster Bank Ltd, 1 Market Street, Bradford, Yorkshire BD1 1EQ. *Club:* Army and Navy.

GARRETT, John Laurence; MP (Lab) Norwich South since Feb. 1974; *b* 8 Sept. 1931; *s* of Laurence and Rosina Garrett; *m* 1959, Wendy Ady; two *d*. *Educ:* Selwyn Avenue Primary Sch., London; Sir George Monoux Grammar Sch., London; University Coll., Oxford (MA, BLitt); Grad. Business Sch. of Univ. of California at Los Angeles (King George VI Fellow). Labour Officer, chemical industry, 1958-59; Head of Market Research, motor industry, 1959-63; Management Consultant, Dir of Public Services, management consultancy gp, 1963-74. PPS to Minister for Civil Service, 1974, to Minister for Social Security, 1977-79; Opposition Treasury spokesman, 1979-80; spokesman on Industry, 1980-. *Publications:* Visual Economics, 1966; (with S. D. Walker) Management by Objectives in the Civil Service, 1969; The Management of Government, 1972; Administrative Reform, 1973; Policies Towards People, 1973 (Sir Frederic Hooper Award); Managing the Civil Service, 1980; articles and papers on industry, management and govt. *Recreations:* theatre, walking in Norfolk, family life. *Address:* c/o House of Commons, SW1A 0AA.

GARRETT, Hon. Sir Raymond (William), Kt 1973; AFC, AEA; JP; President, Legislative Council of Victoria, Australia, 1968-76 (Chairman of Committees, 1964-68); Chairman, Parliamentary Library Committee and Vice-Chairman, House Committee, 1968-76; *b* 19 Oct. 1900; *s* of J. J. P. Garrett, Kew, Australia; *m* 1934, Vera H., *d* of C. E. Lugton; one *s* two *d*. *Educ:* Royal Melbourne Technical Coll.; Univ. of Melbourne. Grad. RAAF Flying Sch., Point Cook, 1926; Citizen Air Force, 1927-37; Commercial Air Pilot, 1927-46. Founded Gliding Club of Vic., and Vic. Gliding Assoc., 1928; British Empire Glider Duration Record, 1931. Served War of 1939-45, RAAF; retd as Gp Captain, 1945 (AFC, AEA). Pres., No 2 Squadron RAAF Asoc. Councillor, Shire of Doncaster and Templestone, 1954-60; Pres. and Chief Magistrate, 1955-56. Member Legislative Council: for Southern Province, Vic., 1958-70; for Templestowe Province, 1970-76. Member, Statute Law Revision Cttee, 1963-64; Govt Rep. on Council of Monash Univ., 1967-71. Knighted for services in politics, civic affairs and defence, Victoria; Life Governor, Lady Nell Seeing Eye Dog School. Chairman of Directors: Ilford (Aust.) Pty Ltd, 1965-75; Cine Service Pty Ltd. Pres., Victorian Parly Former Members' Assoc; Pres., Baden Powell Guild, Victoria. FInstD. *Recreations:* photography, sports cars. *Address:* Flat 4, 24 Tintern Avenue, Toorak, Victoria 3142, Australia. *Clubs:* Royal Automobile, No 10 (London); Air Force (Vic.).

GARRETT, Richard Anthony, CBIM; Chairman, National Association of Boys' Clubs, since 1980; *b* 4 July 1918; 3rd *s* of Charles Victor Garrett and Blanche Michell; *m* 1946, Marie Louise Dalglish; one *s* two *d* (and one *d* decd). *Educ:* King's Sch., Worcester. MInstD; CBIM 1979. Served War, 1939-45 (despatches, 1945). Joined W.D. & H.O. Wills, 1936; Chm., ITL, retd 1979; Chm. and Man. Dir, John Player & Sons, 1968-71; Chairman: T.J. & J. Smith Ltd, 1978-; Frederick Muller Ltd, 1978-; Vice-Chm., HTV Gp, 1978- (Dir of HTV and of W of England Bd); Dir, Standard Commercial Tobacco Co. Inc., 1980-. Member: (Founder), Assoc. of Business Sponsorship of the Arts (Dep. Chm., Adv. Council); National Cttee for Electoral Reform; Trustee, Glyndebourne Arts Trust. Liveryman, Worshipful Co. of Tobacco Pipe Makers and Tobacco Blenders. *Recreations:* golf, gardening, music, opera, reading. *Address:* Marlwood Grange, Thornbury, Bristol BS12 2JB. *T:* Thornbury 412630. *Clubs:* Naval and Military, MCC, XL; Bristol and Clifton Golf; Clifton Rugby (Pres.); Clifton Cricket (Vice-Pres.).

GARRETT, Prof. Stephen Denis, FRS 1967; Professor of Mycology, 1971-73, now Professor Emeritus (Reader 1961-71), and Director of Sub-department of Mycology, 1952-73, University of Cambridge; Fellow of Magdalene College, Cambridge, since 1963; *b* 1 Nov. 1906; *s* of Stephen and Mary Garrett, Leiston, Suffolk; *m* 1934, Ruth Jane Perkins; three *d*. *Educ:*

Eastbourne Coll.; Cambridge Univ.; Imperial Coll., London. Asst Plant Pathologist, Waite Agric. Res. Inst., Univ. of Adelaide, 1929-33; Research Student, Imperial Coll., 1934-35; Mycologist, Rothamsted Experimental Stn, 1936-48; Lectr, later Reader, Botany Sch., University of Cambridge, 1949-71. Hon. Mem., British Mycological Soc., 1975. Hon. Fellow, Indian Acad. of Sciences, 1973. *Publications:* Root Disease Fungi, 1944; Biology of Root-infecting Fungi, 1956; Soil Fungi and Soil Fertility, 1963, 2nd edn 1981; Pathogenic Root-infecting Fungi, 1970. *Address:* 179 Hills Road, Cambridge CB2 2RN. *T:* Cambridge 247865.

GARRETT, Terence, CBE 1967; Counsellor (Science and Technology), British Embassy, Bonn, since 1978; *b* 27 Sept. 1929; *e s* of late Percy Herbert Garrett and Gladys Annie Garrett (*née* Budd); *m* 1960, Grace Elizabeth Bridgeman Braund, *yr d* of Rev. Basil Kelly Braund; two *s* three *d*. *Educ:* Alleyn's Sch.; Gonville and Caius Coll., Cambridge (Scholar; 1st Cl. Hons, Mathematics). DipMathStat; FSS. Instructor Lieut RN, 1952-55. Lecturer, Ewell County Technical Coll., 1955-56; Sen. Lectr, RMCS, Shrivenham, 1957-62; Counsellor (Scientific), British Embassy, Moscow, 1962-66 and 1970-74; Programmes Analysis Unit, Min. of Technology, 1967-70; Internat. Technological Collaboration Unit, Dept of Trade, 1974-76; Sec. to Bd of Governors and to Gen. Conf. of Internat. Atomic Energy Agency, Vienna, 1976-78. *Recreations:* squash, travel. *Address:* c/o Foreign and Commonwealth Office, SW1; Lime Tree Farmhouse, Chilton, Didcot, Oxon OX11 0SW. *T:* Abingdon 834521. *Club:* Royal Commonwealth Society.

GARRETT, Thomas John; Principal, Royal Belfast Academical Institution, since 1978; *b* 13 Sept. 1927; *s* of late Thomas John Garrett and of Violet Garrett; *m* 1958, Sheenah Agnew, *o d* of late Mr and Mrs G. Marshall, Drymen, Stirlingshire; one *d*. *Educ:* Royal Belfast Acad. Instn; QUB (BA); Heidelberg Univ. Asst Master: Royal Belfast Acad. Instn, 1951-54; Nottingham High Sch. for Boys, 1954-56; Sen. German Master, Campbell Coll., Belfast, 1956-73, Housemaster, 1968-73; Headmaster, Portora Royal Sch., Enniskillen, 1973-78. *Publications:* Modern German Humour, 1969; Two Hundred Years at the Top—a dramatised history of Portora Royal School, 1977. *Recreations:* writing, broadcasting, amateur dramatics, angling, hill-walking, ornithology. *Address:* Fairy Hill, 6 Osborne Gardens, Belfast BT9 6LE. *T:* Belfast 665635. *Club:* Ulster Arts (Belfast).

GARRETT, William Edward; MP (Lab) Wallsend since 1964; *b* 21 March 1920; *s* of John Garrett, coal miner, and Frances (*née* Barwise); *m* 1st, 1946, Beatrice Kelly (*d* 1978); one *s* ; 2nd, 1980, Noel Stephanie Ann Johnson. *Educ:* Prudhoe Elementary Sch.; London Sch. of Economics. Commenced work in coal mines, 1934; served engineering apprenticeship, 1934-40; employed by ICI, 1946-64; Union Organiser at ICI, 1946-64; Mem. of AEU. Member: Prudhoe UDC, 1946-64; Northumberland County Council, 1955-64. Mem. of Labour Party, 1939-; Labour Candidate for Hexham 1953-55, Doncaster 1957-64. Member: Select Cttee on Agriculture, 1966-69; Expenditure Cttee, 1971-79; Sec., All-Party Group for Chem. Industry. Parliamentary Adviser: Bursen-Marsteller Public Relations; Machine Tools Trades Assoc. *Recreations:* gardening, walking, reading. *Address:* 84 Broomhill Road, Prudhoe-on-Tyne, Northumberland. *T:* Prudhoe 32580. *Club:* Prudhoe Working Men's.

GARRINGTON, Rev. Elsie Dorothea C.; *see* Chamberlain-Garrington.

GARRIOCH, Sir (William) Henry, Kt 1978; Chief Justice, Mauritius, 1977-78, retired; *b* 4 May 1916; *s* of Alfred Garrioch and Jeanne Marie Madeleine Colin; *m* 1964, Jeanne Louise Marie-Thérèse Desvaux de Marigny. *Educ:* Royal Coll., Mauritius. Called to the Bar, Gray's Inn, 1952. Civil Service (clerical), Mauritius, 1936-48; law student, London, 1949-52; Dist Magistrate, Mauritius, 1955; Crown Counsel, 1958; Sen. Crown Counsel, 1960; Solicitor-Gen., 1964; Dir of Public Prosecutions, 1966; Puisne Judge, 1967; Sen. Puisne Judge, 1970; Actg Governor-Gen., 1977-78. *Recreations:* reading, chess, badminton. *Address:* Lees Street, Curepipe, Mauritius. *T:* 862708.

GARROW, Sir Nicholas, Kt 1965; OBE 1956; JP; retired, 1960; Chairman, Northumbria Tourist Board, since 1974; *b* 21 May 1895; *m* 1919; two *s* one *d*. Chm., Northumberland CC, 1952-67 (CC 1925; CA 1937); JP Northumberland, 1936-; Vice-Pres., Royal National Institute for Blind, 1974- (Mem., 1936-); Foundation and Life Mem., Royal Commonwealth Society for the Blind, 1974; Vice-President: North Regional Assoc. for the Deaf, 1975-; Northumberland Playing Fields Assoc., 1975-; Mem., Church of Christ, 1917-, Senior Elder, 1950-. Hon. Alderman, Northumberland CC, 1974. *Address:* Essendene, Kenilworth Road, Ashington, Northumberland.

GARRY, Robert Campbell, OBE 1976; Regius Professor of Physiology, University of Glasgow, 1947-70, retired; *b* April 1900; *s* of Robert Garry and Mary Campbell; *m* 1928, Flora Macdonald, *d* of Archibald and Helen Campbell; one *s*. *Educ:* Glasgow Univ. MB, ChB with Hons, Glasgow Univ., 1922; Brunton Memorial Prize; DSc, Glasgow Univ., 1933; continued studies in Freiburg im B, Germany; University Coll., London; Medical Sch., Leeds; Asst and then Lectr, Institute of Physiology, Glasgow Univ.; Head of Physiology Dept, Rowett Research Institute, Aberdeen, 1933-35; Lectr on the Physiology of Nutrition, University of Aberdeen, 1933-35; Prof. of Physiology, University Coll., Dundee, The University of St Andrews, 1935-47; Member: MRC, 1955-59; Sci. Adv. Cttee on Med. Res. in Scotland, 1948-52, 1955-59; Physiol. Sub-Cttee of Flying Personnel Res. Cttee, 1951-75

(Chm., 1967-75); Bd of Management, Hill Farming Res. Orgn, 1963-72. Hon. Mem. Physiol. Soc., 1925; foundn Mem., Nutrition Soc., 1941, Pres., 1950-53, Hon. Mem., 1981. FRSE 1937; FRCPGlas 1948. *Publications:* Papers in scientific periodicals, dealing especially with gastrointestinal physiology and nutrition. *Recreations:* gardening, reading. *Address:* Laich Dyke, Dalginross, Comrie, Crieff, Perthshire PH6 2HB. *T:* Comrie 474.

GARSIDE, Kenneth; Director of Central Library Services and Goldsmiths' Librarian, University of London, 1974-78; *b* 30 March 1913; *s* of Arthur Garside and Ada (*née* Speight); *m* 1951, Anne Sheila Chapman; one *s. Educ:* Bradford Grammar Sch.; Univ. of Leeds. BA Mod. Langs 1935, DipEd 1936, MA Spanish 1937. War Service, 1941-46: commnd into Intell. Corps; campaign in NW Europe, 1944-45; GSO2 (Intell.) BAOR, 1946. CO, Univ. of London OTC, 1958-63. Asst Librarian, Univ. of Leeds, 1937-45; Dep. Librarian, UCL, 1945-58; Librarian, King's Coll., London, 1958-74 (FKC 1981). Mem., Enemy Wartime Publications (Requirements) Cttee, 1946-48; Jt Hon. Sec., Univ. and Res. Section of Library Assoc., 1948-51; Chm., Assoc. of British Theol and Philos. Libraries, 1961-66; Trustee, Liddell Hart Centre for Military Archives, King's Coll., London, 1963-; Hon. Sec., Council of Mil. Educn Cttees of Univs of UK, 1966-78; Sec., Nat. and Univ. Libraries Sect., Internat. Fedn of Library Assocs, 1967-68, Univ. Libraries Sub-Sect., 1967-73; Mem., Univ. of London Cttee on Library Resources, 1968-71; Mem., CNAA Librarianship Bd, 1971-81; Mem., British Library Adv. Cttee for Reference Division (Bloomsbury), 1975-78; Hon. Keeper, Military Archives, King's Coll., London, 1979-. Vice-Chm., British Theatre Museum Assoc., 1971-77. Editor, LIBER Bull., 1980-. *Publications:* contrib. to literature of librarianship. *Recreations:* travel, wine and food, bird watching. *Address:* Pavilion Cottage, 36 New Road, Esher, Surrey KT10 9NU. *T:* Esher 65157. *Clubs:* Arts, Authors' (Chm. 1969-72).

GARSIDE, Air Vice-Marshal Kenneth Vernon, CB 1962; DFC 1942; RAF, retired; Managing Director of petro-chemical companies, since 1966; *b* 13 Aug. 1913; *s* of late Dyson Garside, Maidenhead, Berks; *m* 1940, Margery June, *d* of late William Henry Miller, Tanworth-in-Arden; one *s* one *d. Educ:* Bradfield Coll.; St John's Coll., Oxford (MA). First commissioned RAF, 1937. Served War of 1939-45 (despatches twice, DFC); Sqdn and War Service in Far East, Mediterranean and Indian Ocean theatres, 1938-44; European theatre, 1944-45. Command and staff appts in UK and USA, 1945-57; Air Cdre 1957; AOC No 16 Group, 1957; Dep. COS, Logistics and Admin., Allied Forces Central Europe, 1958; Dir of Quartering, Air Min., 1959; Air Vice-Marshal 1960; Senior Air Staff Officer, HQ Coastal Command, RAF, 1961-63; AOC No 18 Group, Coastal Command, and Air Officer, Scotland and Northern Ireland, 1963-65. Liveryman, Worshipful Co. of Horners; Freeman of City of London. *Recreations:* rowing (Blue 1936), swimming (Blue 1935). *Address:* The Garden House, 15 High Street, Thame, Oxon. *Clubs:* Royal Air Force; Vincent's (Oxford); Leander (Henley).

GARSON, Greer; Actress; *b* Northern Ireland, 29 Sept. 1908; *d* of George Garson and Nina Sophia Greer; *m* 1st, Edward A. Shelson (marr. diss.); 2nd, 1943, Richard Ney (marr. diss.); 3rd, 1949, Col E. E. Fogelson, Texas. *Educ:* London and Grenoble Univs. BA Hons London. Birmingham Repertory Theatre, 1932 and 1933; London Theatre debut, Whitehall, 1935; lead roles in 13 London plays; entered films in 1939; *films include:* Goodbye Mr Chips, Pride and Prejudice, When Ladies Meet, Blossoms in the Dust, Mrs Miniver (Academy Award), Random Harvest, Madame Curie, Mrs Parkington, Valley of Decision, That Forsyte Woman, Julius Caesar, The Law and the Lady, Her Twelve Men, Sunrise at Campobello (Golden Globe award), Strange Lady in Town, The Singing Nun, The Happiest Millionaire; *stage appearances include:* Auntie Mame, Tonight at 8.30, Captain Brassbound's Conversion. Appeared in pioneer British TV, on American TV. Hon. DHum, Rollins Coll., Florida, 1950; Hon. Dr in Communication Arts, Coll. of Santa Fe, 1970; Hon. DLitt Ulster, 1977; winner of many awards and medals; current interests include The Greer Garson Theater and Fogelson Library Center, Coll. of Santa Fe; Mem. Bd, Dallas Theater Center; adjunct prof. in drama, S.M.U. Univ., Dallas; Mem., State Commn on the arts in Texas and New Mexico; Mem. Nat. Cttee, St John's Coll., Santa Fe. With husband operates Forked Lightning Ranch, Pecos, New Mexico, also breeding and racing thoroughbred horses (stable includes Ack Ack, horse of the year, 1971). *Recreations:* nature study, music, golf, primitive art. *Address:* Republic Bank Building, Dallas, Texas 75201, USA.

GARSON, Cdre Robin William, CBE 1978; RN retd; Director of Leisure Services, London Borough of Hillingdon, since 1975; *b* 13 Nov. 1921; *s* of late Peter Garson and Ada Frances (*née* Newton); *m* 1946, Joy Ligertwood Taylor (*née* Hickman); one *s* one *d. Educ:* School of Oriental and African Studies. Japanese Interpreter. MBIM, AMINucE. Entered Royal Navy, 1937; served War of 1939-45, HM Ships: Resolution, Nigeria, Cyclops, and HM Submarines: Seawolf, H.33, Spark; subsequent principal appointments: In Command HM Submarines: Universal, Usher, Seraph, Saga, Sanguine, Springer, Thule, Astute, 1945-54; Chief Staff Officer Intelligence, Far East, 1966-68; Sen. Polaris UK Rep., Washington, 1969-71; Captain 1st Submarine Sqdn, 1971-73; Commodore, HMS Drake, 1973-75; ADC to the Queen, 1974. Adviser to AMA on Arts and Recreation, 1976; Mem., Library Adv. Council (England), 1977. *Recreations:* golf, ski-ing, tennis. *Address:* Ringwood, 44 Linksway, Northwood, Mddx HA6 2XB. *T:* Northwood 24380. *Club:* Moor Park (Rickmansworth).

GARSTANG, Walter Lucian, BSc, MA; Headmaster of the Roan School, Greenwich, 1959-68, retired 1968; *b* 2 Sept. 1908; *o s* of late Walter Garstang, MA, DSc; *m* 1933, Barbara Mary, *d* of late Dr S. E. Denyer, CMG, MD; one *s* two *d.* (and one *s* decd). *Educ:* Oundle Sch.; Oxford. Scholar of Trinity Coll., Oxford, 1927-31. Research chemist, The Gas Light and Coke Co., 1931-37; asst master, Oundle Sch., 1937-44; asst master, Merchant Taylors' Sch., 1944-46; senior science master, Maidstone Grammar Sch., 1946-48; Headmaster, Owen's Sch., 1949-54; Headmaster, Loughborough Grammar Sch., 1955-58. *Address:* 14 Montpellier Villas, Cheltenham GL50 2XE.

GARTHWAITE, Sir William, 2nd Bt, *cr* 1919; DSC 1941 and Bar, 1942; former Chairman, Sir William Garthwaite (Holdings) Ltd; *b* 3 Jan. 1906; *o s* of Sir William Garthwaite, 1st Bt and Francesca Margherita, *d* of James Parfett; *S* father 1956; *m* 1st, 1931, Hon. Dorothy Duveen (marr. diss., 1937), *d* of 1st Baron Duveen; 2nd, 1945, Patricia Leonard (marr. diss., 1952); one *s* ; 3rd, 1957, Patricia Merriel, *d* of Sir Philip d'Ambrumenil; three *s* (one *d* decd). *Educ:* Bradfield Coll., Berks; Hertford Coll., Oxford. Lloyd's Underwriter and Insur. Broker at Lloyd's, 1926-. Farmer. Contested (C): Hemsworth Div. of W Riding of Yorks, 1931; Isle of Ely, 1935; E Div. of Wolverhampton, 1945. Served War of 1939-45 as pilot, Fleet Air Arm (DSC and bar, despatches thrice, Air Crew Europe Star, Atlantic Star, Africa Star, 1939-45 Star, Defence Medal). Coronation Medal, 1953. *Recreations:* flying, ski-ing, golf and sailing. *Heir: s* William Mark Charles Garthwaite [*b* 4 Nov. 1946; *m* 1979, Mrs Victoria Lisette Hohler, *e d* of Gen. Sir Harry Tuzo, *qv* ; one *s* one *d. Address:* Matfield House, Matfield, Kent TN12 7JT. *T:* Brenchley 2454. *Clubs:* Portland, Naval, Royal Automobile, Royal Thames; Jockey (Paris).

GARTON, George Alan, PhD, DSc; FRSE 1966; FRS 1978; Deputy Director since 1968, and Head of Lipid Biochemistry Department since 1963, Rowett Research Institute, Bucksburn, Aberdeen; *b* 4 June 1922; *o s* of late William Edgar Garton, DCM, and late Frances Mary Elizabeth Garton (*née* Atkinson), Scarborough, N Yorks; *m* 1951, Gladys Frances Davison; two *d. Educ:* Scarborough High Sch.; Univ. of Liverpool (BSc: (War Service) 1944, (Hons Biochem.) 1946; PhD 1949, DSc 1959). Experimental Asst, Chemical Inspection Dept, Min. of Supply, 1942-45; Johnston Research and Teaching Fellow, Dept of Biochem., Univ. of Liverpool, 1949-50; Biochemist, Rowett Research Inst., Bucksburn, 1950-. Hon. Research Associate, Univ. of Aberdeen, 1966-; Sen. Foreign Fellow of Nat. Science Foundn (USA), and Vis. Prof. of Biochem., Univ. of N Carolina, 1967. Chm., British Nat. Cttee for Nutritional Scis, 1982-; Pres., Internat. Confs on Biochem. Lipids, 1982-. *Publications:* papers, mostly on aspects of lipid biochemistry, in scientific jls. *Recreations:* gardening, golf, foreign travel. *Address:* Ellerburn, 1 St Devenick Crescent, Cults, Aberdeen AB1 9LL. *T:* Aberdeen 867012. *Clubs:* Farmers'; Deeside Golf (Aberdeen).

GARTON, John Leslie, CBE 1974 (MBE (mil.) 1946); President: Henley Royal Regatta, since 1978; Leander Club, since 1980; *b* 1 April 1916; *er s* of late C. Leslie Garton and Madeline Laurence; *m* 1939, Elizabeth Frances, *d* of late Sir Walter Erskine Crum, OBE; two *s* (and one *s* decd). *Educ:* Eton; Magdalen Coll., Oxford (MA). Commissioned TA, Royal Berkshire Regt, 1938. Served War, in France, 1940; psc 1943; Gen. Staff Ops Br., First Canadian Army HQ, in Europe, 1944-46; transf. to RARO, Scots Guards, 1951. Chm., Coca-Cola Bottling Co. (Oxford) Ltd, 1951-65, Coca-Cola Western Bottlers Ltd, 1966-71. Henley Royal Regatta: Steward, 1960; Mem. Cttee of Management, 1961-77; Chm., 1966-77. Amateur Rowing Association: Exec. Cttee and Council, 1948-77; Pres., 1969-77; Hon. Life Vice-Pres., 1978. Hon. Sec. and Treas., OUBC Trust Fund, 1959-69; Mem., Finance and Gen. Purposes Cttee, British Olympic Assoc., 1969-77; Thames Conservator, 1970-74; Chm., World Rowing Championships, 1975. Liveryman, Grocers' Company, 1947-. High Sheriff, Bucks, 1977. *Recreations:* supporting the sport of rowing (rowed in Eton VIII, 1934, 1935 (Capt of the Boats, 1935); rowed in the Boat Race for Oxford, 1938, 1939 (Pres. OUBC, 1939), shooting (particularly deer-stalking), fishing. *Address:* Fingest Manor, Henley-on-Thames, Oxfordshire. *T:* Turville Heath 332. *Club:* Leander (elected 1936, Life Mem., 1953, Cttee, 1956, Chm. Executive, 1958-59).

GARTON, Prof. William Reginald Stephen, FRS 1969; Professor of Spectroscopy, University of London, Imperial College, 1964-79, now Professor Emeritus; Associate Head, 1970-79, and Senior Research Fellow, since 1979, Department of Physics, Imperial College; *b* Chelsea, SW3, 7 March 1912; *s* of William and Gertrude Emma Caroline Garton; *m* 1st, 1940, Margarita Fraser Callingham (marr. diss. 1976); four *d* ; 2nd, 1976, Barbara Lloyd (*née* Jones). *Educ:* Sloane Sch., SW10; Chelsea Polytechnic, SW3; Imperial Coll., SW7. BSc, ARCS 1936; DSc 1958. Demonstrator in Physics, Imperial Coll., 1936-39. Served in RAF, 1939-45. Imperial Coll.: Lectr in Physics, 1946-54; Sen. Lectr, 1954-57; Reader, 1957-64. Associate, Harvard Coll. Observatory, 1963-. W. F. Meggers Award, 1976, Fellow, 1979, Optical Soc. of America. Hon DSc, York Univ., Toronto, 1972. *Publications:* contrib. on Spectroscopy in Advances in Atomic and Molecular Physics (ed D. R. Bates), 1966 (New York); numerous papers on Spectroscopy and Atomic Physics. *Recreations:* speliology, Oriental history. *Address:* Blackett Laboratory, Imperial College, SW7. *T:* 01-589 5111; Chart House, Great Chart, Ashford, Kent TN23 3AP. *T:* Ashford 21657; 7 callé Tico Medina, Mojacar (Almeria), Spain.

GARTRELL, Rt. Rev. Frederick Roy; *b* 27 March 1914; *s* of William Frederick Gartrell and Lily Martha Keeble; *m* 1940, Grace Elizabeth Wood; three *s* one *d*. *Educ:* McMaster Univ. (BA); Wycliffe Coll. (LTh, BD). Deacon, 1938; Priest, 1939. Curate, St James the Apostle, Montreal, 1938; Rector, All Saints', Noranda, PQ, 1940; Senior Asst, St Paul's, Bloor Street, Toronto, 1944; Rector, St George's, Winnipeg, Manitoba, 1945; Archdeacon of Winnipeg, 1957; Rector, Christ Church Cathedral, Ottawa, and Dean of Ottawa, 1962-69; Bishop of British Columbia, 1970-80. DD (*hc*): Wycliffe Coll., Toronto, 1962; St John's Coll., Winnipeg, 1965. *Recreation:* golf. *Address:* 1794 Barrie, Victoria V8N 2W7, BC, Canada.

GARVAGH, 5th Baron *cr* 1818; **Alexander Leopold Ivor George Canning;** Accredited Representative, Trade and Industry, The Cayman Islands, since 1981; *b* 6 Oct. 1920; *s* of 4th Baron and Gladys Dora May (*d* 1982), *d* of William Bayley Parker; *S* father 1956; *m* 1st, 1947, Christine Edith (marr. diss. 1974), *d* of Jack Cooper; one *s* two *d* ; 2nd, 1974, Cynthia Valerie Mary, *d* of Eric E. F. Pretty, CMG, Kingswood, Surrey. *Educ:* Eton; Christ Church, Oxford. Commissioned Corps of Guides Cavalry, Indian Army, 1940; served Burma (despatches). Chairman: Garvagh & Partners Ltd; A.O.D.C. (UK) Ltd; Equitable Shipping Ltd; Stonehaven Shipping (Management) Ltd; Langpoint Ltd; Langpoint (Projects) Ltd; Public Transport Vouchers Ltd; Orient TV Ltd (Hong Kong). Chm., Kennedy Trust Homes; Pres., Disaster Relief Assoc. Mem. Court, Painter Stainers Co. MBIM; MIEX; FInstD. *Publications:* contrib. to The Manufacturing Optician, 1949. *Recreations:* travel, motoring, and motor sport; writing articles, short stories, etc. *Heir:* s Hon. Spencer George Stratford de Redcliffe Canning [*b* 12 Feb. 1953; *m* 1979, Julia Margery Morison Bye, *er d* of Col F. C. E. Bye, Twickenham]. *Address:* Lyzzick Gate, Millbeck, Keswick, Cumbria. *Club:* Steering Wheel.

GARVEY, Sir Ronald Herbert, KCMG 1950 (CMG 1947); KCVO 1953; MBE 1941; *b* 4 July 1903; *s* of Rev. H. R. Garvey, MA, and Alice M. Lofthouse; *m* 1934, Patricia Dorothy Edge, *d* of Dr V. W. T. McGusty, *qv* ; one *s* three *d*. *Educ:* Trent Coll.; Emmanuel Coll., Cambridge. MA 1930; appointed to Colonial Service, 1926, and attached to Western Pacific High Commission, Suva, Fiji; District Officer British Solomon Islands, 1927-32; Asst Sec. Western Pacific High Commission, 1932-40; acted on various occasions as Res. Comr, Gilbert and Ellice Islands Colony; Asst to Res. Comr New Hebrides Condominium, 1940-41; acted as British Res. Comr, New Hebrides, on various occasions; Nyasaland Protectorate, District Officer, 1942-44; Administrator, St Vincent, Windward Islands, BWI, 1944-48; acted as Governor of Windward Is, 1946, 1948; Governor and C-in-C, British Honduras, 1948-52; Governor and C-in-C, Fiji, Governor, Pitcairn Is, Consul-Gen. for Western Pacific, and Senior Commissioner for UK on South Pacific Commission, 1952-58; Ambassador Plenipotentiary for Tonga, 1958; Lieutenant-Governor of the Isle of Man, 1959-66; Sec., Soil Assoc., 1967-71. Dir, Garvey (London) SA Ltd, 1966. Hon. Mem., E Anglia Tourist Bd. KStJ. *Recreations:* golf, deep-sea fishing, gardening. *Address:* The Priory, Wrentham, Beccles, Suffolk NR34 7LR.

GARVEY, Sir Terence Willcocks, KCMG 1969 (CMG 1955); HM Diplomatic Service, retired; *b* Dublin, 7 Dec. 1915; *s* of Francis Willcocks Garvey and Ethel Margaret Ray; *m* 1st, 1941, Barbara Hales Tomlinson (marr. diss.); two *s* one *d* ; 2nd, 1957, Rosemary, *d* of late Dr Harold Pritchard. *Educ:* Felsted; University Coll., Oxford (Scholar). BA Oxon (1st Class Philosophy, Politics and Economics), 1938; Laming Fellow of The Queen's Coll., Oxford, 1938. Entered Foreign (subsequently Diplomatic) Service, 1938; has served in USA, Chile, Germany, Egypt and at Foreign Office; Counsellor, HM Embassy, Belgrade, 1958-62; HM Chargé d'Affaires, Peking, 1962-65 and Ambassador to Mongolia, 1963-65; Asst Under-Sec. of State, Foreign Office, 1965-68; Ambassador to Yugoslavia, 1968-71; High Comr in India, 1971-73; Ambassador to the USSR, 1973-75. *Publication:* Bones of Contention, 1978. *Recreation:* fishing. *Address:* 11A Stonefield Street, N1 0HW. *Club:* Travellers'.

GARVIN, Clifton Canter, Jr; Chairman of the Board, Exxon Corporation, since 1975; *b* 22 Dec. 1921; *s* of Clifton C. Garvin, Sr, and Esther Ames; *m* 1943, Thelma Volland; one *s* three *d*. *Educ:* Virginia Polytechnic Inst. BSE (ChemEng). Exxon: Process Engr, subseq. Refining Operating Supt, Baton Rouge, Louisiana Refinery, 1947-61; Manager, Supply and Distribution Dept, Exxon Co., USA, Houston, 1961-62; subseq. Vice-Pres., 1962-64; Exec. Asst to Chm., Exxon Corp., NY, 1964-65; Dir, subseq. Exec. Vice-Pres. and Mem. Exec. Cttee, subseq. Pres., Exxon Corp., 1968-75; Chm. of the Bd, Chief Exec. Officer, Chm. of Management Cttee, 1975–. Chm., American Petroleum Inst.; Director: Citicorp and Citibank, PepsiCo, Inc.; Sperry Corp. Member: ACS, Amer. Inst. of Chem. Engrs, Business Cttee for the Arts, Inc., Business Council, Business Roundtable, Council on Foreign Relns, Nat. Petroleum Council, Sloan-Kettering Inst. for Cancer Res., Soc. of Chem. Ind. (Amer. Section), United Way of Amer.; Trustee: The Conference Bd; Vanderbilt Univ. Bd of Trust. MCLE Virginia Polytechnic Inst. *Recreations:* golf, bird watching. *Address:* 1251 Avenue of the Americas, New York, NY 10020, USA. *T:* (212) 398-5701. *Clubs:* Blind Brook (Port Chester); The Economic Club of New York; Harvard Business School Club of New York; International (Wash., DC); Links (New York); Stanwich (Greenwich); Twenty-Five Year Club of the Petroleum Industry (Chicago); Augusta National Golf (Augusta).

GARY, Lesley; *see* Blanch, L.

GASCH, Pauline Diana, (Mrs F. O. Gasch); *see* Baynes, P. D.

GASCOIGNE, Bamber, FRSL; author, broadcaster and publisher; *b* 24 Jan. 1935; *s* of Derick Gascoigne and Midi (*née* O'Neill); *m* 1965, Christina Ditchburn. *Educ:* Eton (Scholar); Magdalene Coll., Cambridge (Scholar). Commonwealth Fund Fellow, Yale, 1958-59. Theatre Critic, Spectator, 1961-63, and Observer, 1963-64; Co-editor, Theatre Notebook, 1968-74. Founded Saint Helena Press, 1977; Chm., Ackermann Publishing, 1981-. Theatre: Share My Lettuce, London, 1957-58; Leda Had a Little Swan, New York, 1968; The Feydeau Farce Festival of Nineteen Nine, Greenwich, 1972. Television: presenter of: University Challenge, (weekly) 1962-; Cinema, 1964; (also author) The Christians, 1977; author of: The Four Freedoms, 1962; Dig This Rhubarb, 1963; The Auction Game, 1968. FRSL 1976. *Publications:* Twentieth Century Drama, 1962; World Theatre, 1968; The Great Moghuls (with photographs by Christina Gascoigne) 1971; Murgatreud's Empire, 1972; The Heyday, 1973; The Treasures and Dynasties of China (with photographs by Christina Gascoigne) 1973; Ticker Khan, 1974; The Christians (with photographs by Christina Gascoigne) 1977; Images of Richmond, 1978; Images of Twickenham, 1981; (illus. by Christina Gascoigne): Why the Rope went Tight, 1981; Fearless Freddy's Magic Wish, 1982; Fearless Freddy's Sunken Treasure, 1982. *Address:* Saint Helena Terrace, Richmond, Surrey.

GASCOIGNE, Maj.-Gen. Sir Julian (Alvery), KCMG 1962; KCVO 1953; CB 1949; DSO 1943; DL; *b* 25 Oct. 1903; *e s* of late Brig.-Gen. Sir Frederick Gascoigne, KCVO, CMG, DSO, and Lady Gascoigne, Ashtead Lodge, Ashtead, Surrey; *m* 1928, Joyce Alfreda (*d* 1981), *d* of late Robert Lydston Newman and Mrs Newman; one *s* one *d*. *Educ:* Eton; Sandhurst. 2nd Lieut Grenadier Guards, 1923; Staff Coll., Camberley, 1938-39; served War of 1939-45, commanding 1st Bn Grenadier Guards, 1941-42; commanding 201 Guards Brigade, 1942-43; North Africa and Italy, 1943 (wounded). Imperial Defence Coll., 1946; Dep. Comdr British Jt Services Mission (Army Staff), Washington, 1947-49. GOC London District and Maj.-Gen. commanding Household Brigade, 1950-53; retired pay, 1953; Mem. of Stock Exchange and Partner in Grievson Grant & Co., 1955-59; Governor and C-in-C Bermuda, 1959-64; Col Commandant, Hon. Artillery Co., 1954-59. Patron, Union Jack Services Clubs, 1977 (Vice-Pres., 1955-64; Pres., 1964-76); a Comr of the Royal Hospital, Chelsea, 1958-59; Chm. Devon and Cornwall Cttee, The National Trust, 1965-75. JP 1966, DL Devon, 1966. KStJ, 1959. *Address:* Sanders, Stoke Fleming, Dartmouth, S Devon. *Club:* Royal Bermuda Yacht.

GASCOIGNE, Hon. Stanley, CMG 1976; OBE 1972; Secretary to the Cabinet, Bermuda, 1972-76; Vice-President, Senate, since 1980 (Member, since 1976); *b* 11 Dec. 1914; *s* of George William Gascoigne and Hilda Elizabeth Gascoigne; *m* 1st, 1941, Sybil Wellspring Outerbridge (*d* 1980); 2nd, 1980, Sandra Alison Lee; one *s*. *Educ:* Mt Allison Univ., Canada (BA 1937): London Univ., England (DipEd 1938): Boston Univ., USA (MEd 1951). Teacher, 1939-51; Inspector of Schools, 1951-59; Director, Marine and Ports Authority, 1959-69; Permanent Sec., Education, 1969-72. Exec. Dir, Inst. of Chartered Accountants of Bermuda, 1976-. *Recreation:* ornithology. *Address:* Alcyone, Shelly Bay, Hamilton Parish, Bermuda. *T:* 3-1304. *Clubs:* Royal Bermuda Yacht, Royal Hamilton Amateur Dinghy (Bermuda).

GASH, Prof. Norman, FBA 1963; FRSL 1973; FRSE 1977; FRHistS; Professor of History, St Salvator's College, University of St Andrews, 1955-80, now Emeritus; *b* 16 Jan. 1912; *s* of Frederick and Kate Gash; *m* 1935, Ivy Dorothy Whitehorn; two *d*. *Educ:* Reading Sch.; St John's Coll., Oxford. Scholar, St John's Coll.; 1st cl. Hons Mod. Hist., 1933; BLitt, 1934; MA 1938. FRHistS 1953. Temp. Lectr in Modern European History, Edinburgh, 1935-36; Asst Lectr in Modern History, University Coll., London, 1936-40. Served War, 1940-46: Intelligence Corps; Capt. 1942; Major (Gen. Staff) 1945. Lectr in Modern British and American History, St Salvator's Coll., University of St Andrews, 1946-53; Prof. of Modern History, University of Leeds, 1953-55; Vice-Principal, 1967-71, Dean of Faculty of Arts, 1978-80, St Andrews Univ. Hinkley Prof. of English History, Johns Hopkins Univ., 1962; Ford's Lectr in English History, Oxford Univ., 1963-64; Sir John Neale Lectr in English Hist., UCL, 1981. Vice-Pres., Hist. Assoc. of Scotland, 1963-64. *Publications:* Politics in the Age of Peel, 1953; Mr Secretary Peel, 1961; The Age of Peel, 1968; Reaction and Reconstruction in English Politics, 1832-1852, 1966; Sir Robert Peel, 1972; Peel, 1976; (jtly) The Conservatives: a history from their origins to 1965, 1978; Aristocracy and People: England 1815-1865, 1979; articles and reviews in eg. Hist. Review, Trans. Royal Historical Society, and other learned jls. *Recreations:* gardening, swimming. *Address:* Old Gatehouse, Portway, Langport, Som. *T:* Langport 250334.

GASH, Robert Walker; Chief Executive, since 1973, and Clerk to the Liutenancy, since 1972, Royal County of Berkshire; Clerk, Thames Valley Police Authority, since 1974; *b* 8 Jan. 1926; *s* of William Edward Gash and Elsie Hutton (*née* Armstrong); *m* 1951, Rosamond Elizabeth Brown; two *s*. *Educ:* Carlisle Grammar Sch.; Christ Church, Oxford (MA). Solicitor. Asst Solicitor, Cumberland CC, 1955-58; Asst Clerk of Council, Dep. Clerk of Peace, E Suffolk, 1958-68; Dep. Clerk of Council, Dep. Clerk of Peace, Northamptonshire, 1968-72; Clerk of Council, Royal Co. of Berkshire, 1972-74. *Recreations:* Gilbert and Sullivan, crosswords. *Address:* 9 Brocks Way, Shiplake, Henley-on-Thames, Oxon. *T:* Wargrave 3746.

GASK, Daphne Irvine Prideaux, (Mrs John Gask), OBE 1976; JP; Member, Royal Commission on Criminal Procedure, 1978-80; *b* 25 July 1920; *d* of

Roger Prideaux Selby and Elizabeth May (*née* Stirling); *m* 1945, John Gask, MA, BM, BCh; one *s* one *d*. *Educ:* St Trinnean's, Edinburgh; Tolmers Park, Herts; Collège Brillantmont, Lausanne, Switzerland. BA Open Univ., 1979. Member: Shropshire Probation and After-Care Cttee, 1960-80 (Chm., 1978-80); Exec. Cttee, Central Council of Probation and After-Care Cttees, 1964-80 (Vice-Chm., 1977-80); Council, Magistrates Assoc., 1968-80 (Mem. Exec. Cttee, 1976-80); Sports Council Adv. Gp, 1978-80; Inner London Commn of the Peace, 1982-; NACRO, 1982-; Asst Sec., L'Association Internationale des Magistrats de la Jeunesse et de la Famille, 1979- (Mem. Exec. Bd). Served on Salop CC, 1965-77; Chm., Leisure Activities Cttee, 1974-77. Mem., W Midland Reg. Sports Council (Vice-Chm., 1970-77). JP Salop, 1952. *Recreations:* tennis, skiing, photography. *Address:* 5 The Old School House, Garrett Street, Cawsand, near Torpoint, Cornwall PL10 1PD. *T:* Plymouth 822136; Flat 5, 92 Westbourne Terrace, W2.

GASKELL, (John) Philip (Wellesley), MA, PhD, LittD; Fellow and Librarian of Trinity College, Cambridge, since 1967; Tutor, since 1973; *b* 6 Jan. 1926; *s* of John Wellesley Gaskell and Olive Elizabeth, *d* of Philip B. Baker; *m* 1948, Margaret, *d* of late H. S. Bennett, FBA, and of Joan Bennett, *qv* ; two *s* one *d*. *Educ:* Dragon Sch., Oxford; Oundle Sch.; King's Coll., Cambridge. MA, PhD 1956, LittD, 1980. Served War, 1943-47, Lance-Bdr RA: BLA, 1944-45; Radio SEAC, 1946-47. Fellow of King's Coll., Cambridge, 1953-60, Dean, 1954-56, Tutor, 1956-58; Head of English Dept, and Librarian, Oundle Sch., 1960-62; Keeper of Special Collections, Glasgow Univ. Library, 1962-66; Warden of Maclay Hall, 1962-64, of Wolfson Hall, 1964-66, Glasgow Univ.; Sandars Reader in Bibliography, Cambridge Univ., 1978-79. Editor, The Book Collector, 1952-54. *Publications:* The First Editions of William Mason, 1951; John Baskerville, a bibliography, 1959, rev. edn 1973; Caught!, 1960; A Bibliography of the Foulis Press, 1964; Morvern Transformed, 1968, rev. edn 1980; (with R. Robson) The Library of Trinity College, Cambridge, 1971; A New Introduction to Bibliography, 1972, rev. edns 1974, 1979; From Writer to Reader, 1978; Trinity College Library, the first 150 years, 1980; ed and trans (with P. Bradford) The Orthotypographia of Hieronymus Hornschuch, 1972; contrib. The Library, Jl Printing Historical Soc., etc. *Recreations:* music (Humphrey Lyttelton's band, 1948; Paris Jazz Festival, 1949); flying (PPL); photography (jt exhibn with David Inshaw, 1976). *Address:* Trinity College, Cambridge CB2 1TQ. *T:* Cambridge 358201.

GASKILL, William; freelance stage director; Director, Joint Stock Theatre Group, since 1973; *b* 24 June 1930; *s* of Joseph Linnaeus Gaskill and Maggie Simpson. *Educ:* Salt High Sch., Shipley; Hertford Coll., Oxford. Asst Artistic Dir, English Stage Co., 1957-59; freelance Dir with Royal Shakespeare Co., 1961-62; Assoc. Dir, National Theatre, 1963-65, and 1979; Artistic Director, English Stage Company, 1965-72, Mem. Council, 1978-. *Address:* 124A Leighton Road, NW5.

GASKIN, Catherine; author; *b* Co. Louth, Eire, 2 April 1929; *m* 1955, Sol Cornberg. *Educ:* Holy Cross Coll., Sydney, Australia. Brought up in Australia; lived in London, 1948-55, New York, 1955-67, Ireland, 1967-81. *Publications:* This Other Eden, 1946; With Every Year, 1947; Dust In Sunlight, 1950; All Else Is Folly, 1951; Daughter of the House, 1952; Sara Dane, 1955; Blake's Reach, 1958; Corporation Wife, 1960; I Know My Love, 1962; The Tilsit Inheritance, 1963; The File on Devlin, 1965; Edge of Glass, 1967; Fiona, 1970; A Falcon for a Queen, 1972; The Property of a Gentleman, 1974; The Lynmara Legacy, 1975; The Summer of the Spanish Woman, 1977; Family Affairs, 1980; Promises, 1982. *Recreations:* music, reading. *Address:* White Rigg, East Ballaterson, Maughold, Isle of Man.

GASKIN, Prof. Maxwell, DFC 1944 (and Bar 1945); Jaffrey Professor of Political Economy, Aberdeen University, since 1965; *b* 18 Nov. 1921; *s* of late Albert and Beatrice Gaskin; *m* 1952, Brenda Patricia, *yr d* of late Rev. William D. Stewart; one *s* three *d*. *Educ:* Quarry Bank Sch., Liverpool; Liverpool Univ. (MA). Lever Bros Ltd, 1939-41. Served War, RAF Bomber Comd, 1941-46. Economist, Raw Cotton Commn, 1949-50; Asst Lectr, Liverpool Univ., 1950-51; Lectr and Sen. Lectr, Glasgow Univ., 1951-65; Visiting Sen. Lectr, Nairobi Univ., 1964-65. Member, Committee of Inquiry: into Bank Interest Rates (N Ire.), 1965-66; into Trawler Safety, 1967-68; Mem. and Chm., Bd of Management for Foresterhill and Associated Hosps, 1971-74; Independent Member: Scottish Agricl Wages Bd, 1972-; EDC for Civil Engineering, 1978-; Chm., Industry Strategy Cttee for Scotland (Building and Civil Engrg EDCs), 1974-76. Director: Offshore Med. Support Ltd, 1978-; Aberdeen Univ. Research & Industrial Services, 1981-. President: Section F, British Assoc., 1978-79; Scottish Economic Soc., 1981-. *Publications:* The Scottish Banks, 1965; (co-author and ed) North East Scotland: a survey of its development potential, 1969; (jtly) The Economic Impact of North Sea oil on Scotland, 1978; articles in economic and banking jls. *Recreations:* music and country life. *Address:* 6 Westfield Terrace, Aberdeen AB2 4RU. *T:* Aberdeen 51614. *Club:* Royal Commonwealth Society.

GASS, Sir Michael David Irving, KCMG 1969 (CMG 1960); HM Overseas Civil Service, retired; *b* 24 April 1916; *e s* of late George Irving Gass and late Norah Elizabeth Mustard; *m* 1975, Elizabeth Periam, *e d* of late Hon. John Acland-Hood, Wootton House, near Glastonbury. *Educ:* King's Sch., Bruton; Christ Church, Oxford (MA); Queens' Coll., Cambridge (BA). Appointed Colonial Administrative Service, Gold Coast, 1939. Served War of 1939-45 (despatches twice) with The Gold Coast Regt, RWAFF; East Africa, Burma;

Major. District Commissioner, Gold Coast, 1945; Asst Regional Officer, Ashanti, 1953-56; Permanent Sec., Ministry of the Interior, Ghana, 1956-58; Chief Sec. to the Western Pacific High Commission, 1958-65; Acting High Commissioner for the Western Pacific for periods in 1959, 1961, 1963 and 1964; Colonial Secretary, Hong Kong, 1965-69. Actg Governor, Hong Kong, for periods in 1966, 1967, and 1968; High Comr for W Pacific and British High Comr for New Hebrides, 1969-73. Mem., Somerset CC, 1977-81. *Recreation:* ornithology. *Address:* Fairfield, Stogursey, Bridgwater, Som. *T:* Nether Stowey 732251. *Clubs:* East India, Devonshire, Sports and Public Schools; Hong Kong (Hong Kong).

GASSMAN, Lewis, JP; a Recorder of the Crown Court, since 1972; 2nd *s* of late Isaac Gassman and Dora Gassman; *m* 1940, Betty Henrietta, *o c* of late H. Jerrold and Mrs A. F. Annenberg; one *d*. Admitted Solicitor, 1933. Borough of Barnes: Councillor and Chm. of Cttees, 1933-41. Contested (Lab): Richmond, Surrey, 1935; Hastings, 1945. War of 1939-45: Army service, Capt. RAOC. JP Surrey, 1948, also SW London; Chm., Mortlake Magistrates, 1953-56 and 1961-71. Consultant in law firm of Kershaw, Gassman & Matthews. A Dep. Chm. of Surrey Quarter Sessions, 1968-71; Chm. of Magistrates, Richmond-upon-Thames, 1971-74. *Recreations:* music, painting, walking. *Address:* 21 Castelnau, Barnes, SW13 9RP. *T:* 01-748 7172. *Club:* Reform.

GASTAMBIDE, Philippe, FCIArb; QC 1979; avocat honoraire à la Cour de Paris, 1979; *b* 30 Sept. 1905; *s* of Maurice Gastambide and Marthe (*née* Kullmann); *m* 1st, 1931, Pascale Miraband (decd); one *s* two *d* ; 2nd, 1970, Nicole Vingtain. *Educ:* Sorbonne, Paris (Faculty of Law); Christ Church, Oxford. Lic. ès lettres et en droit; MA (Oxon). Avocat à la Cour de Paris, 1933-78, Avocat honoraire 1979; called to the Bar, Lincoln's Inn, 1934. FCIArb 1978. *Recreations:* tennis, bridge, music. *Address:* 4 King's Bench Walk, Temple, EC4Y 7DL. *T:* 01-353 3581; 9 rue d'Anjou, 75008 Paris. *T:* Paris 266 13-44. *Clubs:* United Oxford & Cambridge University; Cercle du Bois de Boulogne (Paris).

GASTON, John, FIEE; Chairman, Northern Ireland Electricity Service, since 1980; *b* 18 July 1925; *s* of Hill Gaston and Elizabeth (*née* McConnell); *m* 1951, Elizabeth Gordon; two *s*. *Educ:* Ballymena Acad.; QUB (BSc Elec. Eng, BScEcon). FIEE 1970. BICC Ltd, 1946-48; Anglo-Portuguese Telephone Co., 1948-49; Electricity Board, Northern Ireland: various positions, 1949-64; Distribution Engr, 1964-68; Asst Chief Engr, 1968-73; NI Electricity Service: Commercial Dir, 1973-77; Dep. Chm., 1977-80. FRSA. *Recreations:* gardening, walking, music. *Address:* 11 Larch Hill Avenue, Craigavad, Holywood, Co. Down BT18 0JW. *T:* Holywood 6453.

GATACRE, Rear-Adm. Galfry George Ormond, CBE 1960; DSO 1952; DSC 1941 (and Bar 1942); Company Director; *b* Wooroolin, Australia, 11 June 1907; *s* of R. H. W. Gatacre, Bath, Somerset, and Wooroolin, and of C. E. Gordon, Banchory, Scotland; *m* 1933, Wendy May, *d* of E. A. Palmer, Sydney, Australia; one *s* one *d*. *Educ:* Brisbane Boys' Coll.; Royal Australian Naval Coll. Service at sea has been in HM and HMA ships around the world. Lieut 1930; Lieut-Comdr 1938; Comdr 1942; Capt. 1948; Rear-Adm. 1958. Australian Naval Attaché in USA, 1953-55; Command of HMAS Melbourne, 1955-56; Dep. Chief of Naval Staff, 1957-58; Flag Officer Comdg HM Australian Fleet, 1959; Head, Australian Joint Services Staff in USA, 1960-61; Flag Officer East Australian Area, 1962-64. Australasian Representative, Marconi Space & Defence Systems, 1968-. *Publication:* Reports of Proceedings: a naval career 1921-1964, 1982. *Recreations:* golf, tennis. *Address:* 76 Newcastle Street, Rose Bay, Sydney, Australia. *Club:* Royal Sydney Golf.

GATEHOUSE, Graham Gould; Director of Social Services, Surrey County Council, since 1981; *b* 17 July 1935; *s* of G. and G. M. Gatehouse; *m* 1960, Gillian M. Newell; two *s* one *d*. *Educ:* Crewkerne Sch., Somerset; Exeter Univ., Devon (DSA); London School of Economics (Dip. Mental Health). Served Royal Artillery, 1954-56. Somerset County Council, 1957-67; Worcestershire CC, 1967-70; Norfolk CC, 1970-73; West Sussex CC, 1973-81. *Recreations:* Rugby football, cricket, theatre. *Address:* Flat 1, 28 St Marys Road, Long Ditton, Surrey.

GATEHOUSE, Robert Alexander, QC 1969; *b* 30 Jan. 1924; *s* of late Major-Gen. A. H. Gatehouse, DSO, MC; *m* 1st, 1951, Henrietta Swann; 2nd, 1966, Pamela Fawcett. *Educ:* Wellington Coll.; Trinity Hall, Cambridge. Served War of 1939-45: commissioned into Royal Dragoons; NW Europe. Called to the Bar, Lincoln's Inn, 1950; Bencher, 1977. Governor, Wellington Coll., 1970-. *Recreation:* golf. *Address:* 1 Brick Court, Temple, EC4. *T:* 01-583 0777.

GATES, Ernest Everard, MA; formerly Company Director, now retired; *b* 29 May 1903; *o c* of Ernest Henry Gates, Old Buckenham Hall, Norfolk, and Eva, *y d* of George Siggs, JP, Streatham; *m* 1931, Stella (*d* 1981), *y d* of Henry Knox Simms. *Educ:* Repton; Corpus Christi Coll., Cambridge. Formerly a director, Manchester Chamber of Commerce (1945-51), and various companies. Gazetted Lieut RA Sept. 1939; Major, 1941. MP (C) Middleton and Prestwick Div. of Lancs, May 1940-Oct. 1951. PPS to Rt Hon. W. S. Morrison, Min. of Town and Country Planning, 1943-45. *Recreations:* shooting, fishing, golf, travel. *Address:* Pride's Crossing, Ascot, Berks. *T:* Ascot 22330. *Club:* Portland.

GATES, Emeritus Prof. Ronald Cecil, AO 1978; FASSA; Vice-Chancellor, University of New England, since 1977; *b* 8 Jan. 1923; *s* of Earle Nelson Gates and Elsie Edith (*née* Tucker); *m* 1953, Barbara Mann; one *s* two *d* (and one *s* decd). *Educ:* East Launceston State Sch., Tas; Launceston C of E Grammar Sch., Tas; Univ. of Tas (BCom Econs and Commercial Law); Oxford Univ. (MA PPE). FASSA 1968. Served War, 1942-45: Private, AIF. Clerk, Aust. Taxation Office, Hobart, 1941-42; Rhodes Scholar (Tas), Oxford, 1946-48; Historian, Aust. Taxation Office, Canberra, 1949-52; Univ. of Sydney: Sen. Lectr in Econs, 1952-64; Associate Prof., 1964-65; Rockefeller Fellow in Social Sciences, 1955; Carnegie Travel Grant, 1960; Prof. of Econs, Univ. of Qld, 1966-77 (Pres., Professorial Bd, 1975-77). Pres., Econ. Soc. of Australia and NZ, 1969-72. Chairman: statutory Consumer Affairs Council of Qld, 1971-73; Aust. Inst. of Urban Studies, 1975-77. Comr, Commonwealth Commn of Inquiry into Poverty, 1973-77. Chairman: Aust. Nat. Commn for Unesco, 1981 (Vice-Chm., 1979); Adv. Council for Inter-govt Relations, 1979-. Hon. FRAPI 1976; Hon. Fellow, Aust. Inst. of Urban Studies, 1979. Hon. DEcon Qld, 1978. *Publications:* (with H. R. Edwards and N. T. Drane) Survey of Consumer Finances, Sydney 1963-65: Vol. 2, 1965; Vols 1, 3 and 4, 1966; Vols 5, 6 and 7, 1967; (jtly) The Price of Land, 1971; (jtly) New Cities for Australia, 1972; (jtly) Land for the Cities, 1973; (with P. A. Cassidy) Simulation, Uncertainty and Public Investment Analysis, 1977; chapters in books and articles in learned jls. *Recreations:* jazz music, beef cattle, tennis. *Address:* Trevenna, University of New England, Armidale, NSW 2351, Australia. *T:* (067) 72 3433. *Club:* University of New England Staff (Armidale).

GATES, Thomas S(overeign), Jr; *b* Philadelphia, 10 April 1906; *s* of Thomas Sovereign Gates and Marie (*née* Rogers); *m* 1928, Millicent Anne Brengle; three *d* (one *s* decd). *Educ:* Chestnut Hill Acad.; University of Pennsylvania (AB). Joined Drexel & Co., Philadelphia, 1928; Partner, 1940-. War Service, 1942-45 (Bronze Star, Gold Star): US Naval Reserve (Capt.). Under-Sec. of Navy, 1953-57; Sec. of the Navy, 1957-59; Dep. Sec. of Defense, 1959; Sec. of Defense, USA, Dec. 1959-Jan. 1961. Director: Morgan Guaranty Trust Co., 1971- (Chm., Exec. Cttee, 1961-62, 1965-68, 1969-71; Pres., 1962-65); Bethlehem Steel Corp.; General Electric Co.; Campbell Soup Co.; Insurance Co. of N America; Philadelphia Contributionship for Insce of Houses from Loss by Fire; Scott Paper Co. Chief of US Liaison Office, Peking, 1976-77. Life Trustee, University of Pennsylvania. Hon. LLD: University of Pa, 1956; Yale Univ. 1961; Columbia Univ. 1961. *Address:* Mill Race Farm, Devon, Pennsylvania, USA. *Clubs:* Philadelphia, Racquet (Philadelphia); The Links (NYC); Metropolitan (Washington, DC); Gulph Mills Golf.

GATES, William Thomas George, CBE 1967; Chairman, West Africa Committee, London, 1961-76; *b* 21 Jan. 1908; *s* of Thomas George and Katherine Gates; *m* 1938, Rhoda (*née* Sellars), *d* of Mrs W. E. Loveless; two *s. Educ:* Ilford County High Sch., London Univ. National Bank of New Zealand, London, 1925-30; John Holt & Co. (Liverpool) Ltd, resident Nigeria, 1930-46; Gen. Manager: Nigeria, 1940; Gold Coast, 1947; Liverpool, 1947; Man. Dir, 1956; Dep. Chm., 1964; retired, 1967. MLC, Nigeria, 1940-46; Director: W African Airways Corp, 1941-46; Campbell, Scott & Co, Louisville, Ky, 1954-67; Edward Bates & Sons (Holdings) Ltd, 1964-70; Edinburgh & Overseas Investment Trust Ltd, Edinburgh, 1964-71. Dist Scout Comr, Northern Nigeria 1940-42; Mem. Liverpool Dist Cttee, Royal National Life-Boat Instn, 1956-73; Mem. Bd of Govs, United Liverpool Hosps, 1958-70; Gen. Comr of Income Tax, 1967-73; Chm., Liverpool Porterage Rates Panel, 1969-74. Chm., Royal African Soc., 1975-77, Vice-Pres., 1978-. *Recreations:* golf, fishing, cricket, gardening. *Address:* Masongill, Long Street, Sherborne, Dorset. *T:* Sherborne 4214. *Clubs:* Travellers', MCC; Royal Liverpool Golf (Hoylake).

GATHORNE-HARDY, family name of **Earl of Cranbrook.**

GATTY, Trevor Thomas, OBE 1974; HM Diplomatic Service: Consul-General, Atlanta, since 1981; *b* 8 June 1930; *s* of Thomas Alfred Gatty and Lillian Gatty (*née* Wood); *m* 1956, Jemima Bowman (marr. diss. 1982); two *s* one *d. Educ:* King Edward's Sch., Birmingham. Served Army, 1948-50, 2/Lieut Royal Warwickshire Regt, later Lieut Royal Fusiliers (TA), 1950-53. Foreign Office, 1950; Vice-Consul, Leopoldville, 1954; FO, 1958-61; Second (later First) Sec., Bangkok, 1961-64; Consul, San Francisco, 1965-66; Commercial Consul, San Francisco, 1967-68; FCO, 1968-73; Commercial Consul, Zürich, 1973-75; FCO, 1975-76; Counsellor (Diplomatic Service Inspector), 1977-80; Head, Migration and Visa Dept, FCO, 1980-81. *Recreations:* reading, walking, photography, dogs, railway history. *Address:* c/o Foreign and Commonwealth Office, SW1; Brookside, Great Stambridge, near Rochford, Essex. *T:* Canewdon 436. *Club:* Travellers'.

GATWARD, (Anthony) James; Managing Director, Television South Ltd, since 1979; *b* 4 March 1938; *s* of George James Gatward and Lillian Georgina (*née* Strutton); *m* 1969, Isobel Anne Stuart Black, actress; three *d. Educ:* George Gascoigne Sch., Walthamstow; South West Essex Technical Coll. and Sch. of Art (drama course). Entered TV industry, 1957; freelance drama producer/director: Canada and USA, 1959-65; BBC and most ITV cos, 1966-70; partner in prodn co., acting as Exec. Prod. and often Dir of many internat. co-prodns in UK, Ceylon, Australia and Germany, 1970-78; Dir, Southstar, Scottish and Global TV, 1971-78. Instigated and led preparation of application for South and SE England television franchise, 1979-80 (awarded Dec. 1980). *Recreations:* farming, sailing, music. *Address:* TVS, Television Centre, Southampton SO9 5HZ. *Club:* Reform.

GAU, John Glen Mackay; independent television producer; Director, John Gau Productions, since 1981; *b* 25 March 1940; *s* of Cullis William Gau and Nan Munro; *m* 1966, Susan Tebbs; two *s. Educ:* Haileybury and ISC; Trinity Hall, Cambridge; Univ. of Wisconsin. BBC TV: Assistant Film Editor, 1963; Current Affairs Producer, 1965-74; Editor, Nationwide, 1975; Head of Current Affairs Programmes, 1978-81. *Address:* 82 Home Park Road, SW19. *T:* 01-946 4686.

GAUDRY, Roger, CC (Canada) 1968; DSc, FRSC; President, International Association of Universities, 1975-80; *b* 15 Dec. 1913; *m* 1941, Madeleine Vallée; two *s* three *d. Educ:* Laval Univ. (BA 1933; BSc 1937; DSc 1940); Rhodes Scholar, Oxford Univ., 1937-39. Organic Chemistry, Laval Univ.: Lectr, 1940; Prof., 1945; Full Prof., 1950. Ayerst Laboratories: Asst Dir of Research, 1954; Dir of Research, 1957; Vice-Pres. and Dir of Research, 1963-65. Chm., Science Council of Canada, 1972-75; Rector, Univ. of Montreal, 1965-75. Chm. Bd, UN Univ., 1974-76. Parizeau Medal from Assoc. Canadienne Française pour l'Avancement des Sciences, 1958. Hon. doctorates: (Laws) Univ. of Toronto, 1966; (Science) RMC of Kingston, 1966; (Science) Univ. of BC, 1967; (Laws) McGill Univ., 1967; Univ. of Clermont-Ferrand, France, 1967; (Laws) St Thomas Univ., 1968; (Laws) Brock Univ., 1969; (Civil Laws) Bishop's Univ., 1969; (Science) Univ. of Saskatchewan, 1970; (Science) Univ. of Western Ontario, 1976; Hon. Fellow, RCPS (Can.) 1971. *Publications:* author and co-author of numerous scientific papers in organic and biological chemistry. *Address:* 445 Beverley Avenue, Town of Mount Royal, Montreal, PQ H3P 1L4, Canada. *Club:* St Denis (Montreal).

GAULD, William Wallace; Under-Secretary, Department of Agriculture and Fisheries for Scotland, 1972-79; *b* 12 Dec. 1919; *e s* of late Rev. W. W. Gauld, DD, of Aberdeen, and Charlotte Jane Gauld (*née* Reid); *m* 1943, Jean Inglis Gray; three *d. Educ:* Fettes; Aberdeen Univ. MA (1st Cl. Hons Classics). Served Pioneer Corps, 1940-46 (Major 1945). Entered Dept of Agriculture for Scotland, 1947; Private Sec. to Secretary of State for Scotland, 1955-57; Asst Sec., 1958; Scottish Development Dept, 1968-72; Mem. Agricultural Research Council, 1972-79. Pres., Botanical Soc., Edinburgh, 1978-80. *Recreations:* natural history, hill walking. *Address:* 1 Banks Crescent, Crieff, Perthshire PH7 3SR.

GAULT, Charles Alexander, CBE 1959 (OBE 1947); retired from HM Foreign Service, 1959; *b* 15 June 1908; *o s* of late Robert Gault, Belfast, and late Sophia Ranken Clark; *m* 1947, Madge, *d* of late William Walter Adams, Blundellsands; no *c. Educ:* Harrow; Magdalene Coll., Cambridge. Entered Levant Consular Service, 1931; served in Egypt, Persia, Saudi Arabia, at Foreign Office, India (on secondment to Commonwealth Relations Office), Libya, Israel, Bahrain (HM Political Agent, 1954-59). *Recreation:* walking. *Address:* 103 Old Bath Road, Cheltenham, Glos. *Club:* Oriental.

GAULT, David Hamilton; Executive Chairman, Gallic Management Co. Ltd, since 1974; *b* 9 April 1928; *s* of Leslie Hamilton Gault and Iris Hilda Gordon Young; *m* 1950, Felicity Jane Gribble; three *s* two *d. Educ:* Fettes Coll., Edinburgh. Nat. Service, commnd in RA, 1946-48; Clerk, C. H. Rugg & Co. Ltd, Shipbrokers, 1948-52; H. Clarkson & Co. Ltd, Shipbrokers: Man. 1952-56; Dir 1956-62; Jt Man. Dir 1962-72; Gp Man. Dir, Shipping Industrial Holdings Ltd, 1972-74; Chm., Jebsen (UK) Ltd, 1962-81; Chm., Seabridge Shipping Ltd, 1965-73. *Recreations:* gardening, walking. *Address:* Telegraph House, North Marden, Chichester, West Sussex. *T:* Harting 206. *Clubs:* Boodle's, City; India House (New York).

GAUNT, Rev. Canon Howard Charles Adie, (Tom Gaunt); Precentor, Winchester Cathedral, 1967-73; Sacrist, 1963 and Hon. Canon, 1966, Canon Emeritus, since 1974; *b* 13 Nov. 1902; *s* of C. F. Gaunt, Edgbaston; *m* 1st, 1927, Mabel Valery (*d* 1978), *d* of A. E. Bond, Wannerton, near Kidderminster; two *s*; 2nd, 1979, Mary de Lande Long. *Educ:* Tonbridge Sch.; King's Coll., Cambridge. Asst Master: King Edward's Sch., Birmingham, 1928-29; Rugby Sch., 1929-37; Headmaster, Malvern Coll., 1937-53; Chaplain, Winchester Coll., 1953-63. Select Preacher, Universities of Oxford and Cambridge. Hymnwriter. *Publications:* Two Exiles: A School in Wartime, 1946; School: A Book for Parents, 1950; contribs to 100 Hymns for Today and More Hymns for Today, also to numerous hymnbooks in USA, Canada and UK. *Address:* 57 Canon Street, Winchester.

GAUNT SUDDARDS, Henry; *see* Suddards.

GAUSDEN, Ronald, CB 1982; nuclear consultant; *b* 15 June 1921; *s* of Jesse Charles William Gausden and Annie Gausden (*née* Durrant); *m* 1943, Florence May (*née* Ayres); two *s. Educ:* Varndean Grammar Sch., Brighton; Brighton Techn. Coll. and Borough Polytechnic. CEng, FIEE. RN Sci. Service, 1943-47; AERE, Harwell, 1947-50; UKAEA Windscale Works, Cumbria: Instrument Engr, 1950-53; Asst Gp Man., 1953-55; Gp Man., 1955-60; Nuclear Installations Inspectorate: Principal Inspector, 1960-63; Asst Chief Inspector, 1963-73; Dep. Chief Inspector, 1973-75; Chief Inspector, 1976-81; Dir, Hazardous Installations Gp, HSE, 1978-81. *Publications:* contrib. Brit. Nuclear Energy Soc. and Inst. Nuclear Engrs. *Recreations:* golf, shooting, fishing. *Address:* Granary Cottage, Itchingfield, near Horsham, Sussex. *T:* Slinfold 790646.

GAUTIER-SMITH, Peter Claudius, FRCP; Physician, National Hospitals for Nervous Diseases, Queen Square and Maida Vale, since 1962; *b* 1 March

1929; s of late Claudius Gautier-Smith and Madeleine (née Ferguson); m 1960, Nesta Mary Wroth; two d. Educ: Cheltenham Coll. (Exhibnr); King's Coll., Cambridge; St Thomas's Hosp. Med. Sch. MA, MD. Casualty Officer, House Physician, St Thomas' Hosp., 1955-56; Medical Registrar, University Coll. Hosp., 1958; Registrar, National Hosp., Queen Square, 1960-62; Consultant Neurologist, St George's Hosp., 1962-75; Dean, Inst. of Neurology, 1975-82. Mem., Bd of Governors, Nat. Hosps for Nervous Diseases, 1975-. *Publications:* Parasagittal and Falx Meningiomas, 1970; papers in learned jls on neurology. *Recreations:* literary (nineteen novels published under a pseudonym); squash (played for Cambridge v Oxford, 1951; Captain, London Univ., 1954); tennis. *Address:* Institute of Neurology, Queen Square, WC1N 3BG. *T:* 01-837 3611. *Clubs:* MCC, Hawks, Jesters.

GAUTREY, Peter, CMG 1972; CVO 1961; DK (Brunei) 1972; HM Diplomatic Service, retired; High Commissioner in Guyana, 1975-78, concurrently Ambassador (non-resident) to Surinam, 1976-78; b 17 Sept. 1918; s of late Robert Harry Gautrey, Hindhead, Surrey, and Hilda Morris; m 1947, Marguerite Etta Uncles; one s one d. Educ: Abbotsholme Sch., Derbys. Joined Home Office, 1936. Served in Royal Artillery, (Capt.), Sept. 1939-March 1946. Re-joined Home Office; Commonwealth Relations Office, 1948; served in British Embassy, Dublin, 1950-53; UK High Commission, New Delhi, 1955-57 and 1960-63; British Deputy High Commissioner, Bombay, 1963-65; Corps of Diplomatic Service Inspectors, 1965-68; High Comr, Swaziland, 1968-71, Brunei, 1972-75. FRSA 1972. *Recreations:* golf, music, art. *Address:* 24 Fort Road, Guildford, Surrey.

GAVIN, Maj.-Gen. James Merricks Lewis, CB 1967; CBE 1963 (OBE 1953); Technical Director, British Standards Institution, 1967-76; b Antofagasta, Chile, 28 July 1911; s of Joseph Merricks Gavin; m 1942, Barbara Anne Elizabeth, d of Group Capt. C. G. Murray, CBE; one s two d. Educ: Uppingham Sch.; Royal Military Academy; Trinity Coll., Cambridge. 2nd Lieut Royal Engineers, 1931. Mem. Mt Everest Expedn, 1936. Instructor, Royal Military Academy, 1938; Capt. 1939; served War of 1939-45 in Far East, Middle East, Italy, France, including special operations; Brit. Jt Services Mission, Washington, 1948-51; Commanding Officer, 1951-53; Col Staff Coll., Camberley, 1953-55; BAOR, 1956-58; Comdt (Brig.) Intelligence Centre, Maresfield, 1958-61; Maj.-Gen. 1964; Asst Chief of Staff (Intelligence), SHAPE, 1964-67. Col Comdt, RE, 1968-73. *Recreations:* mountaineering, sailing, ski-ing. *Address:* Slathurst Farm, Milland, near Liphook, Hants. *Clubs:* Royal Cruising, Royal Ocean Racing, Alpine.

GAVIN, Malcolm Ross, CBE 1966 (MBE 1945); MA, DSc, CEng, FIEE, FInstP; Chairman of Council, Royal Dental Hospital School of Dental Surgery, University of London, 1974-81; b 27 April 1908; 3rd s of James Gavin; m 1935, Jessie Isobel Hutchinson; one s one d. Educ: Hamilton Acad.; Glasgow Univ. Mathematics Teacher, Dalziel High Sch., Motherwell, 1931-36; Physicist, GEC Res. Labs, Wembley, 1936-47; HMI, Scottish Education Dept, 1947-50; Head of Dept of Physics and Mathematics and Vice-Principal, College of Technology, Birmingham, 1950-55; Prof. of Electronic Engrg and Head of Sch. of Engrg Sci, University Coll. of N Wales, 1955-65; Principal, Chelsea Coll., Univ. of London, 1966-73; Dir, Fulmer Res. Inst., 1968-73. Member: Electronics Res. Coun., Min. of Aviation, 1960-64; Res. Grants Cttee of DSIR (Chm., Electrical and Systems Sub-Cttee, 1964-65); SRC (Mem. Univ. Sci. and Tech. Bd and Chm. Electrical Sub-Cttee, 1965-69; Chm. Control Engineering Cttee, 1969-73; Mem. Engineering Bd, 1969-73); Inter-Univ. Council for Higher Education Overseas, 1967-74; UGC, Hong Kong, 1966-76; Council, European Physical Soc., 1968-70; Murray Cttee, Univ. of London, 1970-72; Council, N Wales Naturalist Trust, 1973-77; Council, University Coll. of North Wales, 1974-77; Visitor, Nat. Inst. Industrial Psychology, 1970-74; Pres. Inst. of Physics and Physical Soc., 1968-70 (Vice-Pres., 1964-67). Hon. ACT, Birmingham, 1956; Hon. DSc (Ife), 1970. Hon. Fellow, Chelsea Coll. *Publications:* Principles of Electronics (with Dr J. E. Houldin), 1959. Numerous in Jl of IEE, Brit. Jl of Applied Physics, Wireless Engineer, Jl of Electronics, etc. *Recreations:* gardening, grandchildren. *Address:* Mill Cottage, Pluscarden, Elgin, Morayshire. *T:* Dallas 281. *Clubs:* Athenæum; Varis (Forres).

GAY, Geoffrey Charles Lytton; Consultant, Knight, Frank & Rutley, since 1973; World President, International Real Estate Federation (FIABCI), 1973-75; a General Commissioner for Inland Revenue since 1953; b 14 March 1914; s of late Charles Gay and Ida, d of Sir Henry A. Lytton (famous Savoyard); m 1947, Dorothy Ann, d of Major Eric Rickman; one s two d. Educ: St Paul's School. FRICS. Joined Knight, Frank & Rutley, 1929. Served War of 1939-45: Durham LI, BEF, 1940; two; Lt-Col; Chief of Staff, Sind District, India, 1943. Mem. Westminster City Council, 1962-71. Governor, Benenden Sch.; Mem. Council of St John, London; Liveryman, Broderers' Co. Chevalier de l'Ordre de l'Economie Nationale, 1960. OStJ 1961; KStJ 1979. *Recreations:* photography, fishing, music, theatre. *Address:* Brookmans Old Farm, Iwerne Minster, Blandford Forum, Dorset DT11 8NG. *T:* Fontmell Magna 811621. *Clubs:* Carlton, MCC, Flyfishers'.

GAY, Rear-Adm. George Wilsmore, CB 1969; MBE 1946; DSC 1943; JP; Director-General of Naval Training, 1967-69; retired; b 1913; s of late Engr Comdr G. M. Gay and Mrs O. T. Gay (née Allen); m 1941, Nancy Agnes Clark; two s one d. Educ: Eastman's Sch., Southsea; Nautical Coll., Pangbourne. Entered RN, 1930; Cadet Trng, 1930-32; RNEC, Keyham, 1932-35; HMS Glorious, 1935-37; Engr. Off., HMS Porpoise, 1939-41, HMS Clyde, 1941-43; HMS Dolphin, 1938 and 1943-46; HM Dockyard,

Portsmouth, 1946-47; HMS Euryalus, 1947-49; Sqdn Engr Off., 1st Submarine Sqdn, HMS Forth, 1949-50; Trng Comdr, HMS Raleigh, 1951-53; Admiralty Engr Overseer, Vickers Armstrong Ltd, 1953-55; HMS Dolphin, 1956-58; Senior Officer, War Course, Royal Naval Coll., Greenwich, 1958; HM Dockyard, Malta, 1959-60; CO, HMS Sultan, Gosport 1960-63; Chief Staff Off. Material to Flag Off. Submarines, 1963-66; Admty Interview Bd, 1966. Comdr 1947; Capt. 1958; Rear-Adm. 1967. FIMechE (MIMechE 1958). JP Plymouth 1970. *Recreations:* fishing, sailing, gardening. *Address:* 29 Whiteford Road, Mannamead, Plymouth, Devon. *T:* Plymouth 664486. *Club:* Army and Navy.

GAYDON, Prof. Alfred Gordon, FRS 1953; Warren Research Fellow of Royal Society, 1945-74; Professor of Molecular Spectroscopy, 1961-73, now Emeritus, and Fellow, since 1980, Imperial College of Science and Technology, London; b 26 Sept. 1911; s of Alfred Bert Gaydon and Rosetta Juliet Gordon; m 1940, Phyllis Maude Gaze (d 1981); one s one d. Educ: Kingston Grammar Sch., Kingston-on-Thames; Imperial Coll., London. BSc (Physics) Imperial Coll., 1932; worked on molecular spectra, and on measurement of high temperatures, on spectra and structure of flames, and shock waves, 1939-; DSc (London) 1942; Hon. Dr (University of Dijon), 1957. Rumford Medal, Royal Society, 1960; Bernard Lewis Gold Medal, Combustion Inst., 1960. *Publications:* Identification of Molecular Spectra (with Dr R. W. B. Pearse), 1941, 1950, 1963, 1965, 1976; Spectroscopy and Combustion Theory, 1942, 1948; Dissociation Energies and Spectra of Diatomic Molecules, 1947, 1953, 1968; Flames, their Structure, Radiation and Temperature (with Dr H. G. Wolfhard), 1953, 1960, 1970, 1979; The Spectroscopy of Flames, 1957, 1974; The Shock Tube in High-temperature Chemical Physics (with Dr I. Hurle), 1963. *Recreations:* wild-life photography; formerly rowing. *Address:* Dale Cottage, Shellbridge Road, Slindon Common, Sussex. *T:* Slindon 277.

GAYRE of Gayre and Nigg, Robert, ERD; Lieutenant-Colonel (late Reserve of Officers); ethnologist and armorist; Editor: The Armorial, since 1959; The Mankind Quarterly, 1960-78 (Hon. Editor in Chief, since 1979), etc; Director of several companies; s of Robert Gayre of Gayre and Nigg, and Clara Hull; m 1933, Nina Mary, d of Rev. Louis Thomas Terry, MA and Margaret Nina Hill; one s. Educ: University of Edinburgh (MA); Exeter Coll., Oxford. BEF France, 1939; Staff Officer Airborne HQ, 1942; Educnl Adviser, Allied Mil. Govt, Italy, 1943-44; Dir of Educn, Allied Control Commn for Italy, 1944; Chief of Educn and Religious Affairs, German Planning Unit, SHAEF, 1944; Prof. of Anthropology and head of Dept of Anthropo-geography, University of Saugor, India, 1954-56; Falkland Pursuivant Extraord., 1958; Consultore pro lingua Anglica, Coll. of Heralds, Rome, 1954-; Chamberlain to the Prince of Lippe, 1958-; Grand Bailiff and Comr-Gen. of the English Tongue, Order of St Lazarus of Jerusalem, 1961-69; Grand Referendary, 1969-73; Grand Comdr and Grand Almoner, 1973-; Sec.-Gen., VIth Internat. Congress of Genealogy, Edinburgh, 1962. Chm., The Seventeen Forty-Five Association, 1964-80. President: Scottish Rhodesia Soc., to 1968; Aberdeenshire and Banffshire Friends of Rhodesia Assoc., 1969-; St Andrew Soc. of Malta, 1968; Ethnological Soc. of Malta; Life Pres., Heraldic Soc. of Malta, 1970-; Hon. Pres., Sicilian Anthropological Soc. Sec.-Gen., Internat. Orders' Commn (Chm., 1978-); Mem. Coun. Internat. Inst. of Ethnology and Eugenics, New York. Mem. Cttee of Honour: Inst. Politicos, Madrid; Cercle Internat. Généalogique, Paris, Mem. Nat. Acad. Sci. of India; Fellow: Collegio Araldico, Rome; Nat. Soc., Naples; Peloritana Acad., Messina; Pontaniana Acad., Naples; Royal Academy, Palermo; F Ist Ital di Geneal. e Arald., Rome; FInstD; FRSH; MInstBE. Hon. or corr. mem. of heraldic and other socs of many countries. Grand Cross of Merit, SMO Malta, 1963 (Kt Comdr, 1957). Holds knighthoods in international and foreign orders, hon. Doctorates from Italian Univs, and heraldic societies' medals, etc. Hon. Lt-Col, ADC to Governor, Georgia, USA, 1969-; Hon. Lt-Col, ADC, State Militia, Alabama; Hon. Lt-Col, Canadian Arctic Air Force. Hon. Citizen, Commune of Gurro, Italy. *Publications:* Teuton and Slav on the Polish Frontier, 1944; Italy in Transition, 1946; Wassail! In Mazers of Mead, 1948; The Heraldry of the Knights of St John, 1956; Heraldic Standards and other Ensigns, 1959; The Nature of Arms, 1961; Heraldic Cadency, 1961, Gayre's Booke, 4 vols 1948-59; Who is Who in Clan Gayre, 1962; A Case for Monarchy, 1962; The Armorial Who is Who, 1961-62, 1963-65, 1966-68, 1969-75, 1976-79; Roll of Scottish Arms (Pt I Vol. I, 1964, Pt I Vol. II, 1969, Vol. III, 1980); Ethnological Elements of Africa, 1966; More Ethnological Elements of Africa, 1972; The Zimbabwean Culture of Rhodesia, 1972; Miscellaneous Racial Studies, 2 vols, 1972; The Knightly Twilight, 1974; Aspects of British and Continental Heraldry, 1974; The Lost Clan, 1974; Syro-Mesopotamian Ethnology, 1974; The Mackay of the Rhinns of Islay, 1979; Minard Castle, 1980; contribs Mankind Quarterly, contrib. Encyc. Brit., etc. *Recreations:* yachting, ocean cruising. *Address:* c/o 1-3 Gloucester Lane, Edinburgh EH3 6ED. *T:* 031-225 1896; Lezayre Mount, Ramsey, Isle of Man. *T:* 813854; (owns as feudal baron of Lochoreshyre) Lochore Castle, Fife. *Clubs:* Army and Navy, United Oxford & Cambridge University, Royal Thames Yacht; Caledonian (Edinburgh); Pretoria (Pretoria, SA); Casino Maltese (Valletta); Raven (Ramsey, IoM); Royal Forth Yacht, Royal Highland Yacht, Royal Malta Yacht, etc.

GAZE, Dr Raymond Michael, FRS 1972; FRSE 1964; Head, Division of Developmental Biology, since 1970, and Deputy Director, since 1977, National Institute for Medical Research; b 22 June 1927; s of late William Mercer Gaze and Kathleen Grace Gaze (née Bowhill); m 1957, Robinetta Mary Armfelt; one s two d. Educ: at home; Sch. of Medicine, Royal Colleges,

Edinburgh. LRCPE, LRCSE, LRFPSG; MA, DPhil. House Physician, Chelmsford and Essex Hosp., 1949; National Service, RAMC, 1953-55; Lectr, later Reader, Dept of Physiology, Edinburgh Univ., 1955-70. Alan Johnston, Lawrence and Moseley Research Fellow, Royal Soc., 1962-66; Visiting Professor: of Theoretical Biology, Univ. of Chicago, 1972; of Biology, Middlesex Hosp. Med. Sch., 1972-74. Mem. Physiological Soc. *Publications*: The Formation of Nerve Connections, 1970; Editor, 1975-, and contrib., Jl Embryology and Exper. Morphology, various papers on neurobiology in Jl Physiology, Qly Jl Exper. Physiology, Proc. Royal Soc., etc. *Recreations*: drawing, hill-walking, music. *Address*: 65 Talbot Road, N6 4QX. *T*: 01-340 3870.

GAZZARD, Roy James Albert (Hon. Major); FRIBA; FRTPI; Pro-Director, Centre for Middle Eastern and Islamic Studies, Durham University; *b* 19 July 1923; *s* of James Henry Gazzard, MBE, and Ada Gwendoline Gazzard (*née* Willis); *m* 1947, Muriel Joy Morgan; one *s* two *d* (and one *s* decd). *Educ*: Stationers' Company's Sch.; Architectural Assoc. Sch. of Architecture (Dip.); School of Planning and Research for Reg. Develt (Dip.). Commissioned, Mddx Regt, 1943; active service Palestine and ME. Acting Govt Town Planner, Uganda, 1950; Staff Architect, Barclays Bank Ltd, 1954; Chief Architect, Peterlee Develt Corp., 1960; Dir of Develt, Northumberland CC, 1962; Lectr and supervisor of post grad. studies in Urban Geography and Planning, Univ. of Durham, 1970; Chief Professional Adviser to Sec. of State's Environmental Bd, 1976; Under Sec., DoE, 1976-79. Prepared: Jinja (Uganda) Outline Scheme, 1954; Municipality of Sur (Oman) Develt Plan, 1975. Govt medals for Good Design in Housing; Civic Trust awards for Townscape and Conservation. *Publications*: contribs to HMSO publns on built environment. *Recreations*: travel, writing, broadcasting. *Address*: 51 South Street, Durham DH1 4QP. *T*: Durham 64067. *Club*: Naval and Military.

GEACH, Gertrude Elizabeth Margaret; *see* Anscombe, G. E. M.

GEACH, Prof. Peter Thomas, FBA 1965; Professor of Logic, University of Leeds, 1966-81; *b* 29 March 1916; *o s* of Prof. George Hender Geach, IES, and Eleonora Frederyka Adolfina Sgonina; *m* 1941, Gertrude Elizabeth Margaret Anscombe, *qv*; three *s* four *d*. *Educ*: Balliol Coll., Oxford (Domus Schol.; Hon. Fellow, 1979). 2nd cl. Class, Hon. Mods, 1936; 1st cl. Lit. Hum., 1938. Gladstone Research Student, St Deiniol's Library, Hawarden, 1938-39; philosophical research, Cambridge, 1945-51; University of Birmingham: Asst Lectr in Philosophy, 1951; Lectr, 1952; Sen. Lectr, 1959; Reader in Logic, 1961. Lectures: Stanton, in the Philosophy of Religion, Cambridge, 1971-74; Hägerström, Univ. of Uppsala, 1975; O'Hara, Univ. of Notre Dame, 1978. *Publications*: Mental Acts, 1957; Reference and Generality, 1962, 3rd rev. edn 1980; (with G. E. M. Anscombe) Three Philosophers, 1961; God and the Soul, 1969; Logic Matters, 1972; Reason and Argument, 1976; Providence and Evil, 1977; The Virtues, 1977; Truth, Love, and Immortality: an introduction to McTaggart's philosophy, 1979; articles in Mind, Philosophical Review, Analysis, Ratio, etc. *Recreation*: reading stories of detection, mystery and horror. *Address*: 3 Richmond Road, Cambridge. *T*: 353950. *Club*: Union Society (Oxford).

GEAR, William, DA (Edinburgh) 1936; RBSA 1966; Painter; Head of Department of Fine Art, Birmingham Polytechnic (formerly Birmingham College of Art and Design), 1964-75; Member London Group, 1953; *b* Methil, Fife, 2 Aug. 1915; *s* of Porteous Gordon Gear; *m* 1949, Charlotte Chertok; two *s*. *Educ*: Buckhaven High Sch.; Edinburgh Coll. of Art; Edinburgh Univ.; Moray House Training Coll.; Edinburgh Coll. of Art: Post-grad. schol., 1936-37; Travelling schol., 1937-38; Académie Fernand Leger, Paris, 1937; study in France, Italy, Balkans; Moray House Trg Coll., 1938-39. War Service with Royal Corps of Signals, 1940-46, in Middle East, Italy and Germany. Staff Officer, Monuments, Fine Arts and Archives Br., CCG, 1946-47; worked in Paris, 1947-50; Curator, Towner Art Gallery, Eastbourne, 1958-64. Guest lecturer, Nat. Gall. of Victoria, Melbourne, and University of Western Australia, 1966. Chairman: Fine Art Panel, Nat. Council for Diplomas in Art and Design, 1972; Fine Art Bd, CNAA, 1974; Council Mem., Midlands Arts Centre, 1978. One-man exhibitions since 1944 in various European cities, N and S America, Japan, etc.; London: Gimpel Fils Gall., 1948-; S London Art Gall. (retrospective), 1954; Edinburgh Fest., 1966; (retrospective) Arts Council, N Ireland, 1969; (retrospective) Scottish Arts Council, 1969; Univ. of Sussex, 1964-75; RBSA Birmingham, 1976 (retrospective); Talbot Rice Art Centre, Univ. of Edinburgh, and Ikon Gall., Birmingham (retrospective), 1982. Works shown in many exhibitions of contemporary art, also at Royal Acad., 1960, 1961, 1967, 1968. Awarded £500 Purchase prize, Fest. of Britain, 1951; David Cargill Award, Royal Glasgow Inst., 1967; Lorne Fellowship, 1976. FIAL, 1960; FRSA 1971. *Works in permanent collections*: Tate Gall.; Arts Council; Brit. Council; Contemp. Art Soc.; Scottish National Gall. of Modern Art; Scottish Arts Council; Victoria & Albert Museum; Laing Art Gall., Newcastle; Nat. Gall. of Canada; Bishop Suter Art Gall., NZ; Art Gall., Toronto; City Art Gall., Toledo, Ohio; Museum of Art, Tel Aviv; New Coll., Oxford; Cincinnati Art Gall., Ohio; Nat. Gall. of NSW; Bishop Otter Coll., Chichester; City Art Gall., Manchester; Albright Art Gall., Buffalo, NY; Musée des Beaux Arts, Liège; Inst. of Contemp. Art, Lima, Peru; Towner Art Gall., Eastbourne; Brighton Art Gall.; Pembroke Coll., Cambridge; Chelsea Coll. of Physical Educn; Southampton Art Gall.; Univ. of Glasgow; Arts Council of Northern Ireland, Whitworth Art Gall., Manchester; Univ. of Birmingham; City Museum and Art Gall., Birmingham; Aberdeen, Dundee and Glasgow Art Galleries, and in numerous private collections in Gt Britain, USA, Canada, Italy, France, etc. Furnishing textiles designed for various firms.

Recreations: cricket, music, gardening. *Address*: 46 George Road, Edgbaston, Birmingham B15 1PL.

GEDDES, family name of **Baron Geddes** and of **Baron Geddes of Epsom.**

GEDDES, 3rd Baron *cr* 1942; **Euan Michael Ross Geddes;** Company Director since 1964; *b* 3 Sept. 1937; *s* of 2nd Baron Geddes, KBE, and of Enid Mary, Lady Geddes, *d* of late Clarance H. Butler; *S* father, 1975; *m* 1966, Gillian, *d* of William Arthur Butler; one *s* one *d*. *Educ*: Rugby; Gonville and Caius Coll., Cambridge (MA 1964); Harvard Business School. *Recreations*: golf, bridge, music, gardening. *Heir*: *s* Hon. James George Neil Geddes, *b* 10 Sept. 1969. *Address*: 83 Kingsway, WC2B 6RH. *T*: 01-405 8621. *Club*: Brooks's.

GEDDES OF EPSOM, Baron *cr* 1958, of Epsom (Life Peer); **Charles John Geddes,** Kt 1957; CBE 1950; Chairman, Polyglass Ltd and associated Companies; *b* 1 March 1897; *s* of Thomas Varney Geddes and Florence Louisa Mills. *m* 1920, Julia Burke; one *d*. *Educ*: Blackheath Central Sch. Post Office: boy messenger, telegraph learner, telegraphist. Served European War, 1914-18. RFC. Lieut, 1916-19, Pilot, 1918-19. Formerly: General Sec. of the Union of Post Office Workers; Member of the General Council of the Trades Union Congress (Pres. of the TUC, 1954-55); Retired, 1957. *Recreations*: television, reading, gardening. *Address*: 5 Cleeve Close, Framfield, Sussex TN22 5PQ. *T*: Framfield 562.

GEDDES, Air Cdre Andrew James Wray, CBE 1946 (OBE 1941); DSO 1943; *b* 31 July 1906; *s* of late Major Malcolm Henry Burdett Geddes, Indian Army, and late Mrs Geddes, Seaford, Sussex; *m* 1929, Anstice Wynter, *d* of late Rev. A. W. Leach, Rector of Leasingham, Lincs; one *s* one *d*. *Educ*: Oakley Hall, Cirencester, Glos; Wellington Coll., Berks; Royal Military Academy Woolwich. 2nd Lt Royal Artillery, 1926; seconded Flying Officer RAF 1928-32; Lieut RA 1929; seconded Flight Lieut RAF 1935-38; Capt. RA 1939; served War of 1939-45 (despatches twice, OBE, DSO, CBE, Commander Legion of Merit, USA); seconded Squadron Leader RAF 1939; Acting Wing Commander RAF 1940; Acting Group Capt., 1942; Acting Air Commodore, 1943; War Subst. Group Capt., 1943; Major RA 1943; Air Commodore Operations and Plans, HQ 2nd TAF for the Invasion. Transferred from RA to RAF, 1945; Air Cdre Dir of Organisation (Establishments), Air Ministry, 1945-47; Group Capt. (subst.), 1947; graduated Imperial Defence Coll., London, 1948; Commanding No. 4 Flying Training Sch. and RAF Station, Heany, S Rhodesia, 1949-51; Dep. Dir of Organisation, Plans, Air Ministry, 1951-54, retd with rank of Air Cdre, 1954; Asst County Civil Defence Officer (Plans), East Sussex County Council, 1957-65; Deputy Civil Defence Officer, Brighton County Borough, 1965-66. Mem., British Hang-gliding Assoc., 1975 (believed to be oldest living person who has flown a hang-glider; first solo when aged 68 years 9 months); qualified instructor/examiner, Nat. Cycling Proficiency Scheme, RoSPA, 1977; Founder Mem., Cuckmere Valley Canoeing Club. *Address*: c/o Midland Bank Ltd, Farnham, Surrey.

GEDDES, Sir (Anthony) Reay (Mackay), KBE 1968 (OBE 1943); Hon. President, Dunlop Holdings plc, since 1978 (Chairman, 1968-78); Director, since 1967, and a Deputy Chairman, since 1978, Midland Bank plc; *b* 7 May 1912; *s* of late Rt Hon. Sir Eric Geddes, PC, GCB, GBE; *m* 1938, Imogen, *d* of late Captain Hay Matthey, Brixham; two *s* three *d*. *Educ*: Rugby; Cambridge. Bank of England, 1932-35; Dunlop Rubber Company Ltd, 1935. Pres., Soc. of Motor Manufacturers and Traders, 1958-59; Part-time Mem., UK AEA, 1960-65; Mem. Nat. Economic Devel. Council, 1962-65; Chm., Shipbuilding Inquiry Cttee, 1965-66. Director: Shell Transport and Trading Co., 1968-82; Rank Organisation Ltd, 1975-. Pres., Internat. Chamber of Commerce, 1980. Hon. DSc, Aston, 1967; Hon. LLD Leicester, 1969; Hon. DTech Loughborough, 1970. *Address*: 13 Wilton Crescent, SW1.

GEDDES, Ford Irvine, MBE 1943; *b* 17 Jan. 1913; *e s* of Irvine Campbell Geddes and Dorothy Jefford Geddes (*née* Fowler); *m* 1945, Barbara Gertrude Vere Parry-Okeden; one *s* four *d*. *Educ*: Loretto Sch.; Gonville and Caius Coll., Cambridge (BA). Joined Anderson Green & Co. Ltd, London, 1934. Served War RE, 1939-45 (Major). Director: Bank of NSW (London Adv. Bd), 1950-81; Equitable Life Assce Soc., 1955-76 (Pres. 1963-71); British United Turkeys Ltd, 1962-78 (Chm., 1976-78); Chairman: P&O Steam Navigation Co., 1971-72 (a Dep. Chm., 1968-71; Dir, 1960-72); British Shipping Federation, 1965-68; Pres., Internat. Shipping Fedn, 1967-69. *Address*: The Manor, Berwick St John, Shaftesbury, Dorset SP7 0EX. *T*: Donhead 363. *Clubs*: City of London; Union (Sydney).

GEDDES, Sir Reay; *see* Geddes, Sir A. R. M.

GEDDES, William George Nicholson, CBE 1979; FRSE; FEng, FICE, FIStructE; Senior Partner, Babtie Shaw and Morton, Consulting Engineers, 1976-79, retired, Consultant since 1979 (Partner, 1950-76); *b* 29 July 1913; *s* of William Brydon Geddes and Ina (*née* Nicholson); *m* 1942, Margaret Gilchrist Wilson; one *s* one *d*. *Educ*: Dunbar High Sch.; Univ. of Edinburgh (BSc, 1st Cl. Hons). Engineer: Sir William Arrol & Co., F. A. Macdonald & Partners, Shell Oil Co.; ICI, Babtie Shaw and Morton, 1935-49. President: Instn of Structural Engrs, 1971-72; Instn of Engrs and Shipbuilders in Scotland, 1977-79; Instn of Civil Engrs, 1979-80. Visiting Professor, Univ. of Strathclyde, 1978. Hon. DSc Edinburgh, 1980. *Publications*: numerous papers to engrg instns and learned socs both at home and abroad. *Recreations:* fly-fishing, golf, hill-walking. *Address:* 22 Riverside Road, Eaglesham, Glasgow G76 0DF. *T:* 041-644 3216. *Clubs:* Caledonian; Royal Scottish Automobile (Glasgow).

GEDLING, Raymond, CB 1969; Deputy Secretary, Department of Health and Social Security, 1971-77; *b* 3 Sept. 1917; *s* of late John and late Mary Gedling; *m* 1956, Joan Evelyn Chapple; one *s. Educ:* Grangefield Grammar Sch., Stockton-on-Tees. Entered Civil Service as Executive Officer, Min. of Health, 1936; Asst Principal, 1942, Principal, 1947. Cabinet Office, 1951-52; Principal Private Sec. to Minister of Health, 1952-55; Asst Sec., 1955; Under-Sec., 1961; Asst Under-Sec. of State, Dept of Educn and Science, 1966-68; Dep. Sec., Treasury, 1968-71. *Recreations:* walking, chess. *Address:* 27 Wallace Fields, Epsom, Surrey. *T:* 01-393 9060.

GEE, Prof. Geoffrey, CBE 1958; FRS 1951; Sir Samuel Hall Professor of Chemistry, University of Manchester, 1955-76, now Emeritus Professor; *b* 6 June 1910; *s* of Thomas and Mary Ann Gee; *m* 1934, Marion (*née* Bowden); one *s* two *d. Educ:* New Mills Grammar Sch.; Universities of Manchester and Cambridge, BSc 1931, MSc 1932, Manchester; PhD 1936, ScD 1947, Cambridge. ICI (Dyestuffs Group) Research Chemist, 1933-38; British Rubber Producers' Research Association: Research Chemist, 1938-47; Dir, 1947-53. Prof. of Physical Chemistry, 1953-55, and Pro-Vice Chancellor, 1966-68, 1972-77, Univ. of Manchester. Pres., Faraday Soc., 1969 and 1970. Hon. Fellow, Manchester Polytechnic, 1979. *Publications:* numerous scientific papers in Transactions of the Faraday Soc., and other journals. *Recreation:* gardening. *Address:* 8 Holmfield Drive, Cheadle Hulme, Cheshire. *T:* 061-485 3713.

GEE, Timothy Hugh; HM Diplomatic Service; Consul-General, Istanbul, since 1981; *b* 12 Nov. 1936; *s* of Arthur William Gee and Edith (*née* Ingham); *m* 1964, Gillian Eve St Johnston; two *s* one *d. Educ:* Berkhamsted; Trinity Coll., Oxford. 2 Lieut 3rd Regt RHA, 1959-61. Joined British Council, 1961; New Delhi, 1962-66; entered HM Diplomatic Service, 1966; FO, 1966-68; Brussels, 1968-72; FCO, 1972-74; Kuala Lumpur, 1974-79; Counsellor, on secondment to NI Office, 1979-81. *Address:* c/o Foreign and Commonwealth Office, King Charles Street, SW1. *Club:* Travellers'.

GEFFEN, Dr Terence John; Senior Principal Medical Officer, Department of Health and Social Security, since 1972; *b* 17 Sept. 1921; *s* of late Maximilian W. Geffen and Maia Geffen (later Reid); *m* 1965, Judith Ann Steward; two *s. Educ:* St Paul's Sch.; University Coll., London; UCH. MD, FRCP. House Phys., UCH, 1943; RAMC, 1944-47; hosp. posts, Edgware Gen. Hosp., Hampstead Gen. Hosp., UCH, 1947-55; Min. of Health (later DHSS), 1956-. *Publications:* various in BMJ, Lancet, Clinical Science, etc. *Recreations:* music, reading, bridge. *Address:* 2 Stonehill Close, SW14 8RP. *T:* 01-878 0516.

GELDER, Prof. Michael Graham; W. A. Handley Professor of Psychiatry, University of Oxford, since 1969; Fellow of Merton College, Oxford; *b* 2 July 1929; *s* of Philip Graham Gelder and Margaret Gelder (*née* Graham); *m* 1954, Margaret (*née* Anderson); one *s* two *d. Educ:* Bradford Grammar Sch.; Queen's Coll., Oxford. Scholar, Theodore Williams Prize 1949 and first class Hons, Physiology finals, 1950; MA, DM Oxon, FRCP, FRCPsych; DPM London (with distinction) 1961. Goldsmit Schol., UCH London, 1951; MRC Fellow in Clinical Research, 1962-63; Gold Medallist, Royal Medico-Psychological Assoc., 1962; Sen. Lectr, Inst. of Psychiatry, 1965-67 (Vice-Dean, 1967-68); Physician, Bethlem Royal and Maudsley Hosps, 1967-68. Hon. Consultant Psychiatrist, Oxford DHA. Mem., MRC (Chm., Neurosciences Bd), 1978-79. Chairman: Assoc. of Univ. Teachers of Psychiatry, 1979-82; Jt Cttee on Higher Psychiatric Trng, 1981-. *Publications:* (jtly) Agoraphobia: nature and treatment, 1981; articles in medical jls. *Recreations:* theatre, gardening, real-tennis. *Address:* St Mary's, Jack Straw's Lane, Oxford OX3 0DN.

GELL, Prof. Philip George Houtham, FRS 1969; Professor and Head of Department of Experimental Pathology, Birmingham University, 1968-78; retired; *b* 20 Oct. 1914; *s* of late Major P. F. Gell, DSO, and Mrs E. Lewis Hall; *m* 1941, Albinia Susan Roope Gordon; one *s* one *d. Educ:* Stowe Sch.; Trinity Coll., Cambridge; University Coll. Hosp. MRCS, LRCP, 1939; MB, BCh, 1940; FRCPath, 1969. Ho. Phys. to Med. Unit, UCH, 1939; Emergency Public Health Laboratory Service, 1940-43. On staff of Nat. Inst. for Med. Research, 1943-48; Reader in Dept of Exptl Pathology, Birmingham Univ., 1948-60; Prof. (Personal) of Immunological Pathology, Dept of Exptl Pathology, 1960-68. *Publications:* (ed with R. R. A. Coombs and P. J. Lachmann) Clinical Aspects of Immunology, 3rd edn, 1974; contribs to Jl of Experimental Med., Immunology, 1960-. *Recreations:* gardening, painting, philosophy of science. *Address:* Wychwood, Cranes Lane, Kingston, Cambridge. *T:* Comberton 2714.

GELL-MANN, Murray; Robert Andrews Millikan Professor of Theoretical Physics at the California Institute of Technology since 1967; *b* 15 Sept. 1929; *s* of Arthur and Pauline Gell-Mann; *m* 1955, J. Margaret Dow (*d* 1981); one *s* one *d. Educ:* Yale Univ.; Massachusetts Inst. of Technology. Mem., Inst. for Advanced Study, Princeton, 1951; Instructor, Asst Prof., and Assoc. Prof., Univ. of Chicago, 1952-55; Assoc. Prof. 1955-56, Prof. 1956-66, California Inst. of Technology. Vis. Prof., Collège de France and Univ. of Paris, 1959-60. Overseas Fellow, Churchill Coll., Cambridge, 1966. Mem., President's Science Adv. Cttee, 1969-72. Regent, Smithsonian Inst., 1975-; Chm. of Bd, Aspen Center for Physics, 1973-79; Dir, J. D. and C. T. MacArthur Foundn, 1979-; Vice-Pres. and Chm. of Western Center, Amer. Acad. of Arts and Sciences, 1970-77; Mem., Nat. Acad. of Sciences, 1960-. Foreign Mem., Royal Society, 1978. Dannie Heineman Prize (Amer. Phys. Soc.), 1959; Ernest O. Lawrence Award, 1966; Franklin Medal (Franklin Inst., Philadelphia), 1967; John J. Carty Medal (Nat. Acad. Scis), 1968; Research Corp. Award, 1969; Nobel Prize in Physics, 1969. Hon. ScD: Yale, 1959; Chicago, 1967; Illinois, 1968; Wesleyan, 1968; Utah, 1970; Columbia, 1977; Hon. DSc Cantab, 1980; Hon. Dr, Turin, 1969. *Publications:* (with Yuval Ne'eman) The Eightfold Way, 1964; various articles in learned jls on topics referring to classification and description of elementary particles of physics and their interactions. *Recreations:* walking in wild country, study of natural history, languages. *Address:* 1024 Armada Drive, Pasadena, Calif 91103, USA. *T:* 213-792-4740. *Clubs:* Cosmos (Washington); Athenæum (Pasadena).

GELLHORN, Peter; Conductor and Chorus Master, Glyndebourne Festival Opera, 1954-61, rejoined Glyndebourne Music Staff, 1974 and 1975; Professor, Guildhall School of Music and Drama, since 1981; *b* 24 Oct. 1912; *s* of late Dr Alfred Gellhorn, and late Mrs Else Gellhorn; *m* 1943, Olive Shirley (*née* Layton), 3rd *d* of 1st Baron Layton, CH, CBE; two *s* two *d. Educ:* Schiller Realgymnasium, Charlottenburg; University of Berlin; Berlin Music Acad. After passing final exams (with dist.) as pianist and conductor, left Germany 1935. Musical Dir, Toynbee Hall, London, E1, 1935-39; Asst Conductor, Sadler's Wells Opera, 1941-43. On industrial war service, 1943-45. Conductor, Royal Carl Rosa Opera (115 perfs), 1945-46. Conductor and Head of Music Staff, Royal Opera House, Covent Garden (over 260 perfs), 1946-53; Dir, BBC Chorus, 1961-72; Conductor, Elizabethan Singers, 1976-80. Has also been working at National Sch. of Opera, annually at Summer Sch. of Music at Dartington Hall; broadcasting frequently as conductor or pianist; composes; writes or arranges music for silhouette and puppet films of Lotte Reiniger (at intervals, 1933-). Mem., Music Staff, London Opera Centre, 1973-78; Conductor: Morley Coll. Opera Gp, 1974-79; Barnes Choir; Music Dir, Opera Players Ltd; Mem. Staff, Opera Sch., RCM, 1980-, conducting its opera perfs, 1981. Lectures on Courses arranged by Oxford Univ. Extra-Mural Delegacy, the WEA, and various County Councils. Musical Dir, Opera Barga, Italy, from foundn, 1967-69. *Recreations:* reading, walking and going to plays. *Address:* 33 Leinster Avenue, East Sheen, SW14 7JW. *T:* 01-876 3949. *Club:* BBC.

GELLNER, Prof. Ernest André, FBA 1974; Professor of Philosophy, London School of Economics, since 1962; *b* Paris, 9 Dec. 1925; *s* of Rudolf Gellner and Anna (*née* Fantl), Prague; *m* 1954, Susan Ryan; two *s* two *d. Educ:* Prague English Grammar Sch.; St Albans County Sch.; Balliol Coll., Oxford. MA (Oxon), PhD (Lond). On staff of London School of Economics, 1949-. *Publications:* Words and Things, 1959; Thought and Change, 1964; Saints of the Atlas, 1969; Cause and Meaning in the Social Sciences, 1973; Contemporary Thought and Politics, 1974; The Devil in Modern Philosophy, 1974; Legitimation of Belief, 1975; Spectacles and Predicaments, 1979; Muslim Society, 1981; Nationalism, 1982; numerous contributions to learned jls. *Recreation:* sailing. *Address:* Old Litten Cottage, Froxfield, Petersfield, Hants. *T:* Hawkley 311. *Clubs:* Reform; Chichester Yacht.

GEMMELL, Prof. Alan Robertson, OBE 1981; Professor of Biology, University of Keele, 1950-77, now Emeritus; *b* 10 May 1913; *s* of Alexander Nicol Gemmell and Mary Robertson; *m* 1942, Janet Ada Boyd Duncanson; two *s. Educ:* Ayr Academy; University of Glasgow. BSc (Hons) Glasgow. Commonwealth Fund Fellow, University of Minnesota, 1935-37 (MS); Agricultural Research at West of Scotland Agricultural Coll., 1937-41; PhD Glasgow, 1939. Lecturer in Botany, Glasgow Univ., 1942-44; Biologist at West Midland Forensic Science Laboratory, 1944-45; Lecturer in Botany, Manchester Univ., 1945-50. Regular broadcaster since 1950. Mem., Adv. Council for Horticultural Therapy, 1981-. President: Staffs Assoc. of Village Produce Guilds; British Agricl and Horticultural Plastics Assoc. *Publications:* Science in the Garden, 1963; Gardeners Question Time Books, 1965, 1967; Developmental Plant Anatomy, 1969; The Sunday Gardener, 1974; The Penguin Book of Basic Gardening, 1975; The Practical Gardener's Encyclopedia, 1977; Basics of Gardening, 1978; (Associate Editor) Chronica Botanica, Vol. I, 1935; many contributions to scientific journals. *Recreations:* golf, gardening, popular science, reading. *Address:* Highfield House, Aston, Nantwich, Cheshire. *T:* Crewe 780408. *Club:* Farmers'.

GENDERS, Rt. Rev. Roger Alban Marson, (Father Anselm, CR); *b* 15 Aug. 1919; *yr s* of John Boulton Genders and Florence Alice (*née* Thomas). *Educ:* King Edward VI School, Birmingham; Brasenose College, Oxford (Sen. Scholar 1938, BA Lit. Hum. 1946, MA 1946). Served War, Lieut RNVR, 1940-46. Joined Community of the Resurrection, Mirfield, 1948; professed, 1952; ordained, 1952; Tutor, College of the Resurrection, 1952-55; Vice-Principal 1955, and Principal 1957-65, Codrington Coll., Barbados; Exam. Chaplain to Bishop of Barbados, 1957-65; Treasurer of St Augustine's Mission, Rhodesia, 1966-75; Archdeacon of Manicaland, 1970-75; Asst Bursar, Community of the Resurrection, Mirfield, 1975-77; Bishop of Bermuda, 1977-82; Assistant Bishop of Wakefield, 1983-. *Publications:* contribs to Theology. *Address:* Community of the Resurrection, House of the Resurrection, Mirfield, W Yorks WF14 0BN.

GENGE, Rt. Rev. Mark; *see* Newfoundland, Central, Bishop of.

GENSCHER, Hans-Dietrich; Federal Minister for Foreign Affairs and Deputy Chancellor, Federal Republic of Germany, since May 1974 (in government of Helmut Schmidt, to Oct. 1982, then in government of Helmut Kohl); Chairman of the Free Democratic Party, since Oct. 1974; *b* Reideburg/Saalkreis, 21 March 1927; *m* Barbara; one *d. Educ:* Higher Sch. Certif. (Abitur); studied law and economics in Halle/Saale and Leipzig Univs, 1946-49. Served War, 1943-45. Mem., state-level org. of LDP, 1946. Re-settled in W Germany, 1952: practical legal training in Bremen and Mem. Free Democratic Party (FDP); FDP Asst in Parly Party, 1956; Gen. Sec.: FDP Parly Party, 1959-65; FDP at nat. level, 1962-64. Elected Mem., Bundestag, 1965; a Parly Sec., FDP Parly Party, 1965-69; Dep. Chm., FDP, 1968-74; Federal Minister of the Interior, Oct. 1969 (Brandt-Scheel Cabinet); re-apptd Federal Minister of the Interior, Dec. 1972. He was instrumental in maintaining pure air and water; gave a modern structure to the Federal Police Authority; Federal Border Guard Act passed; revised weapons laws, etc. Mem. Delegn of FDP politicians who met Premier Kosygin in the Kremlin, 1969; campaigned for exchange of declarations of renunciation of force, with all Warsaw Pact countries. *Publications:* Umweltschutz: Das Umweltschutzprogram der Bundesregierung, 1972; Bundestagsreden, 1972. *Recreations:* reading, walking, swimming. *Address:* Auswärtiges Amt, Bonn, Federal Republic of Germany.

GENTLEMAN, David, RDI 1970; graphic designer and painter; *b* 11 March 1930; *s* of Tom Gentleman; *m* ; one *d* ; 2nd, 1968, Susan, *d* of George Ewart Evans, *qv* ; one *s* two *d. Educ:* Hertford Grammar Sch.; St Albans Sch. of Art; Royal College of Art, 1950-53. Tutor, RCA, 1953-55; since then has worked as freelance designer, illustrator and painter. Work includes: edns of lithographs of architecture and landscape, published 1967, 1970, 1972, 1973, 1975, 1976, 1979, 1980; and of screen prints; posters for London Transport and National Trust; mural designs for Charing Cross underground station, 1979; British postage stamps (incl. Shakespeare, Churchill, Charles Darwin, Battle of Hastings, Liverpool and Manchester Railway, Ships, Fire Engines, Social Reformers, etc); illustrations include drawings and engravings for books and book jackets. Exhibitions of watercolours of India, 1970, Covent Garden, 1972 and 1980, South Carolina, 1973, Bath, 1975, East Africa, 1976; Nauru and Samoa, 1981; stamp designs, Nat. Postal Mus., 1970. Member: Design Council, 1974-80; College Court of RCA; Alliance Graphique Internationale. Phillips Gold Medal for Stamp Design, 1969, 1979; Design Council Poster Award, 1973, 1976 and 1977. *Publications:* Fenella in Ireland, in Greece, in Spain, in the South of France, 1967; Design in Miniature, 1972; Everyday Architecture in Towns, in Countryside, at the Seaside, Industrial, 1975 (RIBA wall-charts); A Cross for Queen Eleanor, 1979; David Gentleman's Britain, 1982; *book illustrations include:* Plats du Jour, 1957; Bridges on the Backs, 1961; Swiss Family Robinson, 1963; The Shepherd's Calendar, 1964; Poems of John Keats, 1966; Pattern under the Plough, 1966; The Jungle Book, 1968; covers for New Penguin Shakespeare, 1968-78; Where Beards Wag All, 1970; The Golden Vanity, 1972; St George and the Dragon, 1973; Tales of the Punjab, 1973; Robin Hood, 1977; A Familiar Tree, 1978; The Dancing Tigers, 1979; Shakespeare and his Theatre, 1982. *Address:* 25 Gloucester Crescent, NW1 7DL. *T:* 01-485 8824.

GENTRY, Maj.-Gen. (retd) Sir William George, KBE 1958 (CBE 1950); CB 1954; DSO 1942, and Bar 1945; *b* 20 Feb. 1899; *e s* of late Major F. C. Gentry, MBE and late Mrs F. C. Gentry; *m* 1926, Alexandra Nina Caverhill; one *s* one *d. Educ:* Wellington Coll., NZ; RMC of Australia. Commissioned NZ Army, Dec. 1919; attached Indian Army and served in Waziristan, 1921, and Malabar, 1921. Served War of 1939-45 with 2nd NZ Div. (Middle East and Italy): GSO 2 and AA and QMG, 1940; GSO 1, 1941-42; Comd 6 NZ Inf. Bde, 1942-43; DCGS, Army HQ, NZ, 1943-44; Comd 9 NZ Inf. Bde (Italy), 1945. Adjutant Gen., NZ Army, 1949-52; Chief of the Gen. Staff, NZ Army, 1952; retired, 1955. Mem. Licensing Commn, 1957-67. Hon. Pres. NZ Boy Scouts Assoc., 1957-67. Greek Military Cross, 1941; United States Bronze Star, 1945. *Address:* 52 Kings Crescent, Lower Hutt, New Zealand. *T:* 660208. *Clubs:* Wellington, United Services (Wellington, NZ).

GEOFFREY-LLOYD, family name of **Baron Geoffrey-Lloyd.**

GEOFFREY-LLOYD, Baron *cr* 1974 (Life Peer), of Broomfield, Kent; **Geoffrey William Geoffrey-Lloyd,** PC 1943; *b* 17 Jan. 1902; *e s* of late G. W. A. Lloyd, Andover House, Newbury. *Educ:* Harrow Sch.; Trinity Coll., Cambridge (MA); Pres. of the Cambridge Union, 1924. Contested (C) SE Southwark, 1924, Ladywood, 1929; Private Sec. to Rt Hon. Sir Samuel Hoare (Sec. of State for Air), 1926-29; Private Sec. to Rt Hon. Stanley Baldwin, 1929-31; MP (U) Ladywood Div. of Birmingham, 1931-45; PPS to Rt Hon. Stanley Baldwin (Lord Pres. of the Council), 1931-35, (Prime Minister), 1935; Parly Under-Sec., Home Office, 1935-39; Sec. for Mines, 1939-40; Sec. for Petroleum, 1940-42; Chm. Oil Control Board, 1939-45; Minister in charge of Petroleum Warfare Dept 1940-45, and Parly Sec. (Petroleum), Min. of Fuel and Power, 1942-45; Minister of Information, 1945; a Governor of BBC, 1946-49; MP (C) King's Norton, Birmingham, 1950-55; Minister of Fuel and Power, 1951-55; MP (C) Sutton Coldfield, 1955-Feb. 1974; Minister of Education, 1957-Oct. 1959; President Birmingham Conservative and Unionist Assoc., 1946-76. Chm., Leeds Castle Foundn, 1974-. *Address:* 77 Chester Square, SW1W 9DY. *T:* 01-730 0014. *Clubs:* Carlton, Pratt's, Royal Yacht Squadron.

GEORGALA, Douglas Lindley, PhD; Head of Laboratory, Unilever Colworth Laboratory, since 1977; Member, Unilever Research Division Executive, since 1979; Chairman, Fisheries Research Board, since 1980; *b* 2 Feb. 1934; *s* of late John Michael Georgala and of Izetta Iris Georgala; *m* 1959, Eulalia Catherina Lochner; one *s* one *d. Educ:* South African College Sch., Cape Town; Univ. of Stellenbosch (BScAgric); Univ. of Aberdeen (PhD). Research Officer, Fishing Research Inst., Univ. of Cape Town, 1957-60; Research Microbiologist, 1960-69, Division Manager, 1969-72, Unilever Colworth Laboratory; Technical Member, Unilever Meat Products Co-ordination, 1973-77. Mem., Adv. Council of Applied Research & Development (ACARD), 1980-. *Publications:* papers in jls of general microbiology, applied bacteriology, hygiene, etc. *Recreations:* gardening, cycling, recorded music. *Address:* 8 Crofton Close, Bedford MK41 8AJ. *T:* Bedford 54041.

GEORGE; *see* Lloyd George.

GEORGE, Rev. (Alfred) Raymond, MA, BD; Warden, John Wesley's Chapel, Bristol, since 1982; *b* 26 Nov. 1912; *s* of A. H. and G. M. George. *Educ:* Crypt Sch., Gloucester; Balliol Coll., Oxford (1st cl. Hon. Classical Mods, 1st cl. Lit. Hum., BA 1935, MA 1938, BD 1955); Wesley House, Cambridge (1st cl. Theol Tripos, Pt I Sect. B, BA 1937, MA 1962); Marburg University. Asst Tutor, Handsworth Coll., Birmingham, 1938-40; ordained as Methodist minister, 1940;Asst Tutor, Hartley-Victoria Coll., Manchester, 1940-42; Circuit Minister, Manchester, 1942-46; Tutor, Wesley Coll., Headingley, Leeds, 1946-67, Principal, 1961-67; Associate Lectr, Leeds Univ., 1946-67; Actg Head, Theol. Dept, 1967-68; Principal, Richmond Coll., London Univ., 1968-72; Tutor, Wesley College, Bristol, 1972-81. Select Preacher, Cambridge, 1963; Member, World Council of Churches Commn on Faith and Order, 1961-75; Pres. of Methodist Conf., 1975-76; Moderator, Free Church Federal Council, 1979-80. *Publications:* Communion with God in the New Testament, 1953; chapter in vol. I, A History of the Methodist Church in Great Britain, 1965, ed (jtly), vol. II, 1978, and contrib. chapter; jt Editor of series: Ecumenical Studies in Worship; also articles in jls. *Address:* 40 Knole Lane, Bristol BS10 6SS. *T:* Bristol 503698.

GEORGE, Rear Adm. Anthony Sanderson, FIBM, CEng, FIWM; Director, Dockyard Production and Support, since 1981; *b* 8 Nov. 1928; *s* of Sandys Parker George and Winifred Marie George; *m* 1953, Mary Veronica Frances Bell; two *d. Educ:* Royal Naval Coll., Dartmouth; Royal Naval Engrg Coll., Manadon. MIMechE 1957; FIBM 1977; FIWM 1979. Sea-going appts, 1950-62; warship design, Ship Dept of MoD, 1962-64; RN Staff Coll., 1965; British High Commn, Canberra, 1966-67; MEO, HMS Hampshire, 1968-69; Staff of Flag Officer Sea Trng, 1970-71; Dep. Prodn Manager, HM Dockyard, Portsmouth, 1972-75; RCDS, 1976; CSO (Trng) to C-in-C Naval Home Comd, 1977-78; Prodn Manager, HM Dockyard, Portsmouth, 1979-81. Comdr 1965, Captain 1972, Rear Adm. 1981. *Recreations:* sailing, swimming, walking. *Address:* c/o Dockyard Department, Ministry of Defence, Carpenter House, Bath BA1 5AB. *T:* Bath 28391.

GEORGE, Sir Arthur (Thomas), Kt 1972; solicitor and company director; Chairman and Managing Director, George Investment Pty Ltd Group, since 1943; Chairman: Phillips Australia Holding Ltd; Australia Solenoid Holdings Ltd, since 1967; Director, Thomas Nationwide Transport Ltd, since 1973; *b* 17 Jan. 1915; *s* of late Thomas George; *m* 1939, Renee, *d* of Anthony Freeleagus; one *d. Educ:* Sydney High Sch., NSW. Director: Ansett Transport Industries, 1981-; Bliss Welded Products, 1981-; Hospital Corp. of Australia Pty, 1981-. Chairman: Assoc. for Classical Archæology, of Sydney Univ., 1966-; Australian Soccer Fedn., 1969-. Vice-Pres., Confed. of Aust. Sport, 1977-. Chm. and Founder, The Arthur T. George Foundation Ltd, 1972. Coronation Medal; Silver Jubilee Medal. Grand Commander (Keeper of the Laws), Cross of St Marks, and Gold Cross of Mount Athos, Greek Orthodox Church; Order of Phoenix (Greece). *Recreations:* interested in sport, especially Association football, etc. *Address:* 1 Little Queen's Lane, Vaucluse, NSW 2030, Australia.

GEORGE, Bruce Thomas; MP (Lab) Walsall South since Feb. 1974; *b* 1 June 1942. *Educ:* Mountain Ash Grammar Sch.; UCW Swansea; Univ. of Warwick. BA Politics Wales 1964, MA Warwick 1968. Asst Lectr in Social Studies, Glamorgan Polytechnic, 1964-66; Lectr in Politics, Manchester Polytechnic, 1968-70; Senior Lectr, Birmingham Polytechnic, 1970-74. Member: former Select Cttee on Violence in the Family; Select Cttee on Defence; RIIA; IISS; RUSI. Patron, Nat. Assoc. of Widows; Co-founder, Sec., House of Commons FC; Hon. Consultant, Confed. of Long Distance Pigeon Racing Assocs; Vice-Pres., Psoriasis Assoc. Pres., Walsall and District Gilbert and Sullivan Soc. Fellow, Parliament and Industry Trust, 1977-78. *Recreations:* Association football, snooker, student of American Indians, eating Indian food. *Address:* 42 Wood End Road, Walsall, West Midlands WS5 3BG. *T:* Walsall 27898. *Clubs:* Bentley Labour, Darlaston Labour, Caldmore Liberal; North Walsall, Pleck and Station Street Working Men's Clubs.

GEORGE, Prof. Donald William, AO 1979; Vice-Chancellor and Principal, University of Newcastle, New South Wales, since 1975; Chairman, Australian Atomic Energy Commission, since 1976; *b* 22 Nov. 1926; *s* of late H. W. George, Sydney; *m* 1950, Lorna M. Davey, Parkes, NSW; one *s* one *d. Educ:* Univ. of Sydney. BSc, BE, PhD, FTS, FIEE, FIMechE, FIEAust, FAIP. Lectr, Elec. Engrg, NSW Univ. of Technology, 1949-53; Exper. Officer, UKAEA,

Harwell, 1954–55; Res. Officer, Sen. Res. Officer, AAEC, Harwell and Lucas Heights, 1956–59; Sen. Lectr, Elec. Engrg, Univ. of Sydney, 1960–66; Associate Prof., Elec. Engrg, Univ. of Sydney, 1967–68; P. N. Russell Prof. of Mech. Engrg, Univ. of Sydney, 1969–74. Chm., Australian-American Educational Foundn, 1977–. Trustee, Asian Inst. of Technology, 1978–. *Publications:* numerous sci. papers and techn. reports. *Address:* University of Newcastle, New South Wales 2308, Australia. *T:* 68-0401.

GEORGE, Edward Alan John; Executive Director, Bank of England, since 1982; *b* 11 Sept. 1938; *s* of Alan George and Olive Elizabeth George; *m* 1962, Clarice Vanessa Williams; one *s* two *d*. *Educ:* Dulwich Coll.; Emmanuel Coll., Cambridge (BAEcon 2nd Cl. (i); MA). Joined Bank of England, 1962; worked initially on East European affairs; seconded to Bank for International Settlements, 1966–69, and to International Monetary Fund as Asst to Chairman of Deputies of Committee of Twenty on Internat. Monetary Reform, 1972–74; Adviser on internat. monetary questions, 1974–77; Dep. Chief Cashier, 1977–80; Asst Dir (Gilt Edged Div.), 1980–82. *Recreations:* family, sailing, bridge. *Address:* Bank of England, EC2R 8AH. *T:* 01-601 4444.

GEORGE, Griffith Owen, TD; DL; a Recorder of the Crown Court, 1972–74; *b* 5 Dec. 1902; *s* of late John and Emiah Owen George, Hirwaun, Glam; *m* 1937, Anne Elinor, *e d* of late Charles and Anne Edwards, Llandaff; one *s*. *Educ:* Westminster Sch.; Christ Church, Oxford (MA). Beit Prize Essay, 1923; Barrister, Gray's Inn, 1927, Wales and Chester Circuit. Served War of 1939–45, 2nd Lieut RA, 1939; Capt. 1941; Major 1943; on JAG's staff, N Africa, Italy, Middle East, 1943–45. Contested Llanelly (Nat. Con.), 1945. Commissioner in Wales under the National Insurance Acts, 1950–67. Dep. Chm., Glamorgan Quarter Sessions, 1956–66, Chm., 1966–71. JP Glamorgan, 1952–72; DL Glamorgan, 1970. *Address:* Glanyrafon, Ponterwyd, Aberystwyth SY23 3JS. *T:* Ponterwyd 661.

GEORGE, Henry Ridyard, CBE 1979; FInstPet; oil and gas exploration and production consultant; *b* 14 May 1921; *s* of Charles Herbert George and Mary Ridyard; *m* 1948, Irene May Myers; one *s*. *Educ:* George Dixon's Secondary Sch., Birmingham; Univ. of Birmingham (1st Cl. Hons degree, Oil Engrg and Refining and Petroleum Technol., 1941). Served War, REME/IEME, 1941–46 (2nd Lieut, later Captain). Pet. Engr with Royal Dutch/Shell Gp, 1947–68: service in USA, Holland, Brunei, Nigeria and Venezuela in a variety of positions, incl. Chief Pet. Engr in last 3 countries; Dept of Energy, 1968–81, Dir of Pet. Engrg, 1973–81. FRSA 1979. *Recreations:* gardening, golf. *Address:* 39 Lodge Close, Stoke D'Abernon, Cobham, Surrey KT11 2SG. *T:* Cobham 3878.

GEORGE, Herbert Horace, CB 1944; MC; *b* 1890; *s* of John George, Clapham; *m* 1913, Emily Rose (*d* 1952), *d* of Thomas Eaton, Clapham; no *c*. *Educ:* Westminster City Sch.; Trinity Coll., Cambridge. Entered Civil Service, 1913. Served in RA in European War, 1914–19. Under-Sec. for Finance and Accountant-Gen., Ministry of Health, 1946–50; retired, 1950. *Address:* Fouryews, Telham, Battle, East Sussex. *T:* Battle 2927.

GEORGE, Hywel, CMG 1968; OBE 1963; Bursar, Churchill College, Cambridge, since 1972; *b* 10 May 1924; *s* of Rev. W. M. George and Catherine M. George; *m* 1955, Edith Pirchl; three *d*. *Educ:* Llanelli Gram. Sch.; UCW Aberystwyth; Pembroke Coll., Cambridge. RAF, 1943–46. Cadet, Colonial Admin. Service, N Borneo, 1949–52; District Officer, 1952–58; Secretariat, 1959–62; Resident, Sabah, Malaysia, 1963–66; Administrator, 1967–69, Governor, 1969–70, St Vincent; Administrator, British Virgin Is, 1971. Panglima Darjah Kinabalu (with title of Dato), Sabah, 1964; JMN, Malaysia, 1966. CStJ 1969. *Recreations:* tennis, walking. *Address:* 70 Storey's Way, Cambridge. *T:* Cambridge 61200.

GEORGE, Prof. Kenneth Desmond; Professor and Head of Department of Economics, since 1973, Deputy Principal, since 1980, University College, Cardiff; *b* 11 Jan. 1937; *s* of Horace Avory George and Dorothy Margaret (*née* Hughes); *m* 1959, Elizabeth Vida (*née* Harries); two *s* one *d*. *Educ:* Ystalyfera Grammar Sch.; University Coll. of Wales, Aberstwyth (MA). Res. Asst, then Lectr in Econs, Univ. of Western Australia, 1959–63; Lectr in Econs, University Coll. of N Wales, Bangor, 1963–64; Univ. Asst Lectr, Univ. of Cambridge, 1964–66, Univ. Lectr, 1966–73; Fellow and Dir of Studies in Econs, Sidney Sussex Coll., Cambridge, 1965–73. Vis. Prof., McMaster Univ., 1970–71. Part-time Mem., Monopolies and Mergers Commn, 1978–. Editor, Jl of Industrial Economics, 1970–. *Publications:* Productivity in Distribution, 1966; Productivity and Capital Expenditure in Retailing, 1968; Industrial Organisation, 1971, 3rd edn (with C. Joll), 1981; (with T. S. Ward) The Structure of Industry in the EEC, 1975; (ed with C. Joll) Competition Policy in the UK and EEC, 1975; (with J. Shorey) The Allocation of Resources, 1978; articles in Econ. Jl, Oxford Econ. Papers, Aust. Econ. Papers, Jl Indust. Econs, Rev. of Econs and Stats, Oxford Bull., Scottish Jl Polit. Econ., and British Jl Indust. Relations. *Recreations:* walking, music, cricket. *Address:* Ein-Tŷ-Ni, 39 St Fagans Drive, St Fagans, Cardiff. *T:* Cardiff 562801.

GEORGE, Llewellyn Norman Havard; a Recorder of the Crown Court, since 1980; *b* 13 Nov. 1925; *s* of Benjamin William George, DSO, RNR, and Annie Jane George; *m* 1950, Mary Patricia Morgan (*née* Davies); one *d*. *Educ:* Cardiff High Sch.; Fishguard Grammar Sch. HM Coroner, 1965–80; Recorder, Wales and Chester Circuit, 1980–. President, West Wales Law Society, 1973–74; Chairman, (No 5) South Wales Law Society Legal Aid Cttee, 1979. *Recreations:* golf, reading, chess. *Address:* Four Winds, Tower

Hill, Fishguard, Dyfed SA65 9LA. *T:* Fishguard 873894. *Clubs:* Pembrokeshire County; Newport (Pembs) Golf.

GEORGE, Peter John, OBE 1974; HM Diplomatic Service, retired; Counsellor and Consul General, British Embassy, Manila, 1976–79; Chargé d'Affaires *ai*, 1978; *b* 12 Dec. 1919; *s* of late Cecil John George and Mabel George; *m* 1946, Andrée Louise Pernon; one *d*. *Educ:* Sutton Grammar Sch., Plymouth. Served War, 1939–46: Captain. Home Civil Service, 1936; HM Diplomatic Service, 1966; First Secretary, Commercial: Colombo, 1967–70; Seoul, 1971–73 (Chargé d'Affaires *ai*, 1971 and 1972); Prague, 1973–76. *Recreations:* golf, tennis, ski-ing, bridge. *Address:* St Just, Walton Park, Walton-on-Thames, Surrey.

GEORGE, Rev. Raymond; *see* George, Rev. A. R.

GEORGE, Timothy John Burr; HM Diplomatic Service; Counsellor and Head of Chancery, United Kingdom Permanent Delegation to the OECD, since 1982; *b* 14 July 1937; *s* of Brig. J. B. George, late RAMC, retd; *m* 1962, Richenda Mary, *d* of Alan Reed, architect; one *s* two *d*. *Educ:* Aldenham Sch.; Christ's Coll., Cambridge (BA). National Service, 2nd Lieut RA, 1956–58; Cambridge Univ., 1958. FCO, 1961; 3rd Secretary: Hong Kong, 1962; Peking, 1963; 2nd, later 1st Sec., FCO, 1966; 1st Sec. (Economic), New Delhi, 1969; Asst Political Adviser, Hong Kong, 1972; Asst European Integration Dept (Internal), FCO, 1974; Counsellor and Head of Chancery, Peking, 1978–80; Res. Associate, IISS, 1980–81. *Recreations:* walking, reading, old buildings. *Address:* c/o Foreign and Commonwealth Office, SW1.

GEORGE, Prof. William David, FRCS; Professor of Surgery, University of Glasgow, since 1981; *b* 22 March 1943; *s* of William Abel George and Peggy Eileen George; *m* 1967, Helen Marie (*née* Moran); one *s* three *d*. *Educ:* Reading Bluecoat Sch.; Henley Grammar Sch.; Univ. of London (MB, BS 1966; MS 1977). FRCS 1970. Jun. surgical jobs, 1966–71; Registrar in Surgery, Royal Postgrad. Med. Sch., 1971–73; Lectr in Surg., Univ. of Manchester, 1973–77; Sen. Lectr in Surg., Univ. of Liverpool, 1977–81. *Publications:* articles in BMJ, Lancet, British Jl of Surg. *Recreations:* veteran rowing, fishing, squash. *Address:* 21 Kingsborough Gardens, Glasgow G12 9NH. *T:* 041-339 9546. *Club:* Clyde Amateur Rowing (Glasgow).

GEORGE-BROWN, family name of **Baron George-Brown.**

GEORGE-BROWN, Baron *cr* 1970 (Life Peer), of Jevington, Sussex; **George Alfred George-Brown,** PC 1951; Director: Commercial Credit (Holdings) Ltd, since 1974; Commercial Credit Services (Holdings), since 1980; *b* 2 Sept. 1914; *s* of George Brown; name changed to George-Brown by deed poll, 1970; *m* 1937, Sophie Levene; two *d*. MP (Lab) Belper Div. of Derbyshire, 1945–70; Parliamentary Private Secretary to Minister of Labour and National Service, 1945–47, to Chancellor of the Exchequer, 1947; Joint Parliamentary Secretary, Ministry of Agriculture and Fisheries, 1947–51; Min. of Works, April-Oct. 1951; First Secretary of State and Secretary of State for Economic Affairs, Oct. 1964–Aug. 1966; Secretary of State for Foreign Affairs, 1966–68. Dep. Leader, Labour Party, 1960–70. Pres., Social Democratic Alliance, 1981–. Productivity Counsellor, Courtaulds Ltd, 1968–73; Deputy Chairman: G. C. Turner Group Ltd, 1977–; J. Compton, Sons & Webb (Holdings) Ltd, 1980–; Chm., William Cotton Gp, 1982–; Director: British Northrop Ltd, 1978; GT Japan Investment Trust Ltd, 1980–. Order of Cedar of Lebanon, 1971. Biancamano Prize (Italy), 1972. *Publications:* In My Way (memoirs), 1970; The Voice of History, 1979. *Address:* c/o House of Lords, SW1.
See also R. W. Brown.

GEORGES, (Philip) Telford; barrister; Judge of the Supreme Court of Zimbabwe, since 1981; *b* Dominica, 5 Jan. 1923; *s* of John Georges and Mihitine Cox; *m* Grace Glasgow. *Educ:* Dominica Grammar Sch.; Toronto Univ. (BA). Called to the Bar, 1949; in private practice, Trinidad and Tobago, 1949–62; Judge of the High Court, Trinidad and Tobago, 1962–74; on secondment as Chief Justice of Tanzania, 1965–71; acting Justice of Appeal, Trinidad and Tobago, 1972; Judge of the Courts of Appeal, Belize, Bahamas, Bermuda, Turks and Caicos Is, 1975–. Prof. of Law, 1974–81, and Dean of the Faculty of Law, 1977–79, Univ. of WI at Cave Hill. Vice-Chm., Trinidad and Tobago Constitutional Reform Commn, 1971–74; Chm., Crime Commn, Bermuda, 1977–78. Hon. LLD: Toronto; Dar-es-Salaam. *Recreation:* walking. *Address:* PO Box 8159, Causeway, Harare, Zimbabwe; 27 Prior Park, St James', Barbados. *T:* 04450.

GEORGES-PICOT, Jacques Marie Charles, KBE (Hon.) 1963; Commandeur, Légion d'Honneur; Hon. Chairman of the Board, Suez Finance Company (Chairman, 1957–70); *b* 16 Dec. 1900; *s* of Charles Georges-Picot and Marthe Fouquet; *m* 1925, Angéline Pelle; five *s*. *Educ:* Lycée Janson de Sailly, Paris. Inspector of Finance, 1925; Chef de Cabinet, Minister of Budget, 1931; Dir Min. of Finance, 1934; Agent Supérieur in Egypt, of Suez Canal Co., 1937; Asst Dir-Gen. of Suez Canal Co., 1946; Dir-Gen., 1953; Pres., 1957. Dir, Fondation des Sciences Politiques, Paris. *Publication:* La véritable crise de Suez, 1975. *Recreation:* tennis. *Address:* 2 Square Mignot, 75016 Paris, France. *T:* 727-7968. *Club:* Circle Interallié (Paris).

GERARD, family name of **Baron Gerard.**

GERARD, 4th Baron, *cr* 1876, Bt 1611; **Robert William Frederick Alwyn Gerard;** *b* 23 May 1918; *o s* of 3rd Baron Gerard, MC, and late Mary Frances

Emma, *d* of Sir Martin Le Marchant Hadsley Gosselin, GCVO, KCMG, CB; *S* father, 1953. *Heir: cousin* Rupert Charles Frederick Gerard, MBE [*b* 6 Oct. 1916; *m* 1948, Huguette Reiss-Brian (marr. diss. 1969); two *s*]. *Address:* Blakesware, Ware, Herts. *T:* 3665.

GERARD, Geoffrey; *see* Gerard, W. G.

GERARD, Rt. Rev. George Vincent, CBE 1944; Assistant Bishop of Sheffield, 1947-71; Residentiary Canon of Sheffield Cathedral, 1960-69; Chairman, House of Clergy, Church Assembly, 1965-70; *b* 24 Nov. 1898; *e s* of late George and late Frederikke Marie Gerard, Snowdon, Canterbury, New Zealand; *m* 1920, Elizabeth Mary Buckley; one *s* one *d. Educ:* Waihi Sch., Winchester, NZ; Christ's Coll., Christchurch, NZ; Brasenose Coll., Oxford. Inns of Court, OTC 1917; 2nd Lieut The Buffs, 1918, Lieut 1918 (MC); demobilised, 1919; BA (Oxon), 1921; MA 1925; deacon, 1922; priest, 1923; Vicar of Pahiatua, 1929-32; Petone, 1932-36; St Matthew, Auckland, 1936-38; Bishop of Waiapu, 1938-44; served as Senior Chaplain to the NZ Forces, 1940-41 (prisoner, but repatriated to England, 1943). Senior NZ Chaplain South Pacific, 1944; Hospital Ship, 1945. Vicar and Rural Dean of Rotherham, 1945-60; Hon. Canon of Sheffield, 1947-60. Proctor in Convocation of York, 1950 and 1952-70. *Address:* 18 Barton Court Avenue, New Milton, Hants BH25 7HD.

GERARD, (William) Geoffrey, CMG 1963; Chairman of Directors, Gerard Industries Pty Ltd, S Australia, 1950-80 (Managing Director, 1930-76); *b* 16 June 1907; *s* of late A. E. Gerard; *m* 1932, Elsie Lesetta, *d* of late A. Lowe; one *s* one *d. Educ:* Adelaide Technical High Sch. President: Electrical Manufrs' Assoc. of SA, 1949-52; Electrical Develt Assoc. of SA, 1952; SA Chamber of Manufactures, 1953-54; Associated Chambers of Manufactures of Aust., 1955; SA Metal Industries Assoc., 1952 and 1957; Aust.-Amer. Assoc. in SA Incorp., 1961-63; Aust. Metal Industries Assoc., 1962-64; Vice-Chm., Standards Assoc. of Aust., 1956-79; Chm., Nat. Employers' Assoc., 1964-66; Member: SA Industries Adv. Cttee, 1952-53; Commonwealth Immigration Planning Council, 1956-74; Commonwealth Manufg Industries Advisory Coun., 1958-62; Nat. Employers' Policy Cttee, 1964-66; Commonwealth Electrical Industries Adv. Council, 1977-80. Pres., Prince Alfred Coll. Foundn, 1975-80. Pres., Liberal and Country League, SA Div., 1961-64. Rotary Governor's representative in founding Barossa Valley Club, 1956. FAIM. *Recreations:* golf, tennis. *Address:* 9 Robe Terrace, Medindie, SA 5081, Australia. *T:* 44 2560. *Clubs:* Adelaide, Commonwealth (Adelaide), Kooyonga Golf (SA) (Captain, 1953-55, Pres., 1976-78), Rotary (Prospect) (Pres., 1954).

GERARD-PEARSE, Rear-Adm. John Roger Southey, CB 1979; Group Personnel Manager, Jardine Matheson Co. Ltd, Hong Kong, since 1980; *b* 10 May 1924; *s* of Dr Gerard-Pearse; *m* 1955, Barbara Jean Mercer; two *s* two *d. Educ:* Clifton College. Joined RN, 1943; comd HM Ships Tumult, Grafton, Defender, Fearless and Ark Royal; Flag Officer, Sea Training, 1975-76; Asst Chief, Naval Staff (Ops), 1977-79. *Recreations:* sailing, carpentry. *Address:* Enbrook, 170 Offham Road, West Malling, Kent. *T:* West Malling 842375.

GERE, John Arthur Giles, FBA 1979; Keeper, Department of Prints and Drawings, British Museum, 1973-81; *b* 7 Oct. 1921; *o s* of Harold Gere and Carol Giles; *m* 1958, Charlotte Douie; one *s* one *d. Educ:* Winchester; Balliol College, Oxford. Assistant Keeper, British Museum, 1946; Deputy Keeper, 1966. *Publications:* (with Robin Ironside) Pre-Raphaelite Painters, 1948; (with Philip Pouncey) Italian Drawings in the British Museum, vol. iii: Raphael and his Circle, 1962; Taddeo Zuccaro: his development studied in his drawings, 1969; I disegni dei maestri: il manierismo a Roma, 1971; (ed with John Sparrow) Geoffrey Madan's Notebooks, 1981; (with Philip Pouncey) Italian Drawings in the British Museum, vol. v: Artists Working in Rome c 1550-c 1640, 1982; various exhibition catalogues; contribs to Burlington Magazine, Master Drawings, etc. *Recreation:* retirement. *Address:* 21 Lamont Road, SW10. *T:* 01-352 5107.

GERHARD, Dr Derek James (known as Jeremy); Deputy Master and Comptroller, Royal Mint, since 1977; *b* 16 Dec. 1927; *s* of late F. J. Gerhard, Banstead; *m* 1952, Dr Sheila Cooper, *d* of late Dr G. K. Cooper; three *s* two *d. Educ:* Highgate Sch.; Fitzwilliam Coll., Cambridge (MA); Reading Univ. (PhD). Dept of Scientific Adviser, Air Ministry, 1952-57; transf. to DSIR, 1957; Sec., British Commonwealth Scientific Cttee, 1959-60; Asst Sci. Attaché, British Embassy, Washington, 1961-64; transf. to Admin. CS, 1964; Board of Trade, latterly leader UK Delgn to Internat. Consultative Shipping Gp, 1964-69; Head of Management Services, BoT, 1969-71; loaned to CSD (Personnel Management), 1971-73; Dept of Industry, leader UK Delgn to Internat. Tin Council, 1973-75; Air Div., DoI, 1975-77. Pres., Mint Dir's Conf., 1982-. *Publications:* various scientific papers. *Recreation:* woodwork. *Address:* Royal Mint, 7 Grosvenor Gardens, SW1W 0BH. *T:* 01-828 8724.

GERKEN, Rear-Adm. Robert William Frank, CBE 1975; Flag Officer Second Flotilla, since 1981; *b* 11 June 1932; *s* of Francis Sydney and Gladys Gerken; *m* 1966, Christine Stephenson (*d* 1981); two *d. Educ:* Chigwell Sch.; Royal Naval Coll., Dartmouth. Sea service as Lieut and Lt-Comdr, 1953-66; RN Staff Course, 1967; in command HMS Yarmouth, 1968-69; Commander Sea Training, 1970-71; Naval Staff, 1972-73; in command: Sixth Frigate Sqdn, 1974-75; HMS Raleigh, 1976-77; Captain of the Fleet, 1978-81. Comdr 1966, Captain 1972, Rear-Adm. 1981. *Recreations:* hearth and home maintenance.

Address: c/o Midland Bank Ltd, 7 Palmerston Road, Southsea, Hants. *T:* Portsmouth 753535. *Club:* Army and Navy.

GERMAN, Sir Ronald (Ernest), KCB 1965; Kt 1959; CMG 1953; Director: Securicor Ltd, 1966-80; National Counties Building Society, 1966-80; *b* 19 Oct. 1905; *m* 1931, Dorothy Sparks; no *c. Educ:* HM Dockyard Sch., Devonport. Entered GPO 1925; Asst Dir Posts & Telegraphs Dept, Sudan, 1942; British Post Office, 1945; Postmaster-Gen., East Africa, 1950-58; Dep. Dir Gen. of the Post Office, UK, 1959-60, Dir Gen., 1960-66. Chm. Makerere Coll. Council, 1957-58 (Vice-Chm. 1954). CStJ, 1963. *Address:* Flat 1, 8A Grassington Road, Eastbourne, East Sussex.

GERNSHEIM, Helmut Erich Robert; photo-historian and author; *b* Munich, 1 March 1913; 3rd *s* of Karl Gernsheim, historian of literature at Munich Univ., and Hermine Gernsheim (*née* Scholz); *m* 1942, Alison Eames, London (*d* 1969); no *c*; *m* 1971, Irène Guénin, Geneva. *Educ:* St Anne's Coll., Augsburg; State Sch. of Photography, Munich. Settled in England as free-lance photographer, 1937; became British subject, 1946; during War of 1939-45 made photogr. surveys of historic bldgs and monuments for Warburg Inst. (London Univ.); exhibns of these at Churchill Club and Courtauld Inst., 1945 and 1946, Nat. Gall., 1944; one-man show at Royal Photogr. Society 1948; since 1945 has built up Gernsheim photo-historical collection, since 1964 at University of Texas, Austin; selections were shown at art museums, Europe and America. Re-discovered world's first photograph (taken in 1826), 1952 and Lewis Carroll's chief hobby, 1948. Co-ed. Photography Yearbook, 1953-55; British Representative World Exhibition of Photography, Lucerne, 1952, Biennale and Unesco Conference on Photography, Paris, 1955, etc. Photographic adviser to Granada TV on first British action still films, 1958-62. Editorial Adviser, Encyclopædia Britannica and several Museums and Universities. Chm., History of Photo. Seminar, Rencontres Internat. de la Photo.: Arles, 1978, Venice, 1979; Frankfurt, 1981. Distinguished Visiting Professor: Univ. of Texas at Austin, 1979; Arizona State Univ., 1981. Dir, Photo-Graphic Editions. Trustee, Swiss Foundn for Photography; Hon. Fellow: Club Daguerre; New York Photohist. Soc., 1979. First German cultural prize for photography, 1959; Gold Medal, Accademia Italia, Parma, 1980. Order of Merit, Germany, 1970. *Publications include:* New Photo Vision, 1942; Julia Margaret Cameron, 1948, revd and enlarged edn, 1975; Lewis Carroll-Photographer, 1949, new edn 1969; Beautiful London, 1950; Masterpieces of Victorian Photography, 1951; Those Impossible English, 1952; Churchill, His Life in Photographs, 1955; Creative Photography, 1962, new edn 1975; (with Alison Gernsheim): Roger Fenton, 1954, new edn 1973; The History of Photography, 1955, new and enlarged edns, 1969 and 1982; L. J. M. Daguerre, 1956, new edn 1968; Queen Victoria, a Biography in Word and Picture, 1959; Historic Events, 1960; Edward VII and Queen Alexandra, 1962; Fashion and Reality, 1963, new edn 1981; Concise History of Photography, 1965, new edn 1971; Alvin Langdon Coburn, photographer, 1966, new edn 1978; Bibliography of Early British Photographic Literature, 1981; contrib. Oxford History of Technology, 19th and 20th century; numerous articles in art and photographic journals in many countries. *Recreations:* travelling, classic music, opera. *Address:* Residenza Tamporiva, Via Tamporiva 28, 6976 Castagnola, Ticino, Switzerland. *T:* Lugano 091 515904.

GEROSA, Peter Norman; Under-Secretary, Rural Affairs, Department of the Environment, since 1981; *b* 1 Nov. 1928; *s* of late Enrico Cecil and Olive Doris Gerosa; *m* 1955, Dorothy Eleanor Griffin; two *d. Educ:* Whitgift Sch.; London Univ. (Birkbeck). BA (Hons) 1st Cl., Classics. Clerk, Foreign Office, 1945. Exec. Officer, Home Office, 1949. HM Customs and Excise: Asst Principal, 1953; Principal, 1956; Customs Expert, EFTA, 1961-63. Asst Sec., Min. of Transport, 1966; Dept of the Environment: Asst Sec., 1970; Under-Sec., 1972; Under Sec., Dept of Transport, 1977. *Recreations:* singing, gardening, walking. *Address:* 1 Wray Mill House, Reigate, Surrey. *T:* Redhill 64470.

GERRARD, Prof. Alfred Horace; Professor of Sculpture in University of London at University College Slade School of Fine Art, 1948-68, now Emeritus; *b* 7 May 1899; *m* 1933, Katherine Leigh-Pemberton (*d* 1970); *m* 1972, Nancy Sinclair. *Educ:* Hartford County Council Sch.; Manchester Sch. of Art; Slade Sch. of Fine Art, University Coll., London. Head of Dept of Sculpture, Slade Sch., UCL, 1925-48. Served European War, 1914-18, Cameron Highlanders, 1916-17; RFC, 1917-19; War of 1939-45, Staff Captain, War Office, attached Royal Engineers, 1939-43; war artist, 1944-45; temp. Head, Slade Sch. of Fine Art, 1948-49. RBS Silver Medal, 1960. Fellow, University Coll. London, 1969. *Recreation:* gardening. *Address:* Dairy House, Leyswood, Groombridge, Tunbridge Wells, Kent. *T:* Groombridge 268.

GERRARD, Basil Harding; His Honour Judge Gerrard; a Circuit Judge (formerly a Judge of County Courts), since 1970; *b* 10 July 1919; *s* of late Lawrence Allen Gerrard and Mary (*née* Harding); *m* Sheila Mary Patricia (*née* Coggins), *widow* of Walter Dring, DSO, DFC (killed in action, 1945); one *s* two *d* and one step *d. Educ:* Bryanston Sch.; Caius Coll., Cambridge (BA). Royal Navy, 1940-46. Called to Bar, Gray's Inn, 1947; Recorder of Barrow-in-Furness, 1969-70. Mem., Parole Bd for England and Wales, 1974-76. Chm., Selcare Trust, 1971-78, Vice Pres., 1978-. *Recreations:* golf, gardening. *Address:* Northwood, Toft Road, Knutsford, Cheshire. *Clubs:* Knutsford Golf; Bowdon Croquet.

See also J. J. Rowe.

GERRARD, John Henry, CBE 1981 (OBE 1972); MC 1944; QPM 1975; Assistant Commissioner, Metropolitan Police, 1978-81; *b* 25 Nov. 1920; *s* of Archie Reginald and Evelyn Gerrard; *m* 1943, Gladys Hefford; two *s*. *Educ:* Cordwainers Technical Coll. Served War, Army, 1939-46: Iceland, 1940-42; commissioned 1st Mddx Regt, 1943; NW Europe, 1944-46 (Captain). Constable to Commander, 1946-65; Comdr, West End Central, 1965-68; Comdr 'A' Dept (Public Order/Operations), 1968-70; Deputy Assistant Commissioner: 'A' (Operations), 1970-74; No 1 Area, 1974-78. CStJ 1980 (OStJ 1976); Dep. Comr, London Dist, SJAB, 1979-. *Recreations:* philately, history. *Address:* c/o Edwina Mountbatten House, 63 York Street, W1H 1PS.

GERRARD, Ronald Tilbrook, FEng, FICE, FIWES; Senior Partner, Binnie & Partners, Consulting Engineers, since 1974; *b* 23 April 1918; *s* of Henry Thomas Gerrard and Edith Elizabeth Tilbrook; *m* 1950, Cecilia Margaret Bremner; three *s* one *d*. *Educ:* Imperial Coll. of Science and Technology, Univ. of London. BSc(Eng). FCGI; FEng 1979; FICE 1957; FIWE 1965; MEIC. Served War, RE, 1939-45. Resident Engr, sea defence and hydro-electric works, 1947-50; Asst Engr, design of hydro-power schemes in Scotland and Canada, 1951-54; Binnie & Partners: Sen. Engr, 1954; Partner, 1959; resp. for hydro-power, water supply, river engrg, coast protection and indust. works in UK and overseas. Chm., Assoc. of Cons. Engrs, 1969-70; Mem. Council, ICE, 1974-77. Telford Silver Medal, ICE, 1968. *Publications:* (jtly) 3 papers to ICE. *Address:* 6 Ashdown Road, Epsom, Surrey. *T:* Epsom 24834. *Club:* Athenæum.

GERRARD-WRIGHT, Maj.-Gen. Richard Eustace John, CBE 1977 (OBE 1971; MBE 1965); Director Territorial Army and Cadets, since 1982; *b* 9 May 1930; *s* of Rev. R. L. Gerrard-Wright; *m* 1960, Susan Kathleen Young; two *s* two *d*. *Educ:* Christ's Hospital; RMA, Sandhurst; Defence Services Staff Coll., India (psc); Jt Services Staff Coll. (jssc); Nat. Defence Coll., Canada (ocds Can). Commnd Royal Lincolnshire Regt, 1949; served Egypt, Germany and UK, 1950-55; Malaya, 1955-58 (despatches, 1958); Instructor, RMA, Sandhurst, 1958-62 (2nd E Anglian Regt, 1960); Staff Coll., India, 1962-63; served Kenya, Aden, Malta, Malaya, 1963-70 (Royal Anglian Regt, 1964); Bn Comdr, UK, Germany, NI, 1970-73 (despatches 1973); Comdr, 39 Inf. Bde, Belfast, 1975-77; Nat. Defence Coll., Canada, 1977-78; Chief of Staff, 1 (Br) Corps, 1978-79; GOC Eastern District, 1980-82. Dep. Col, Royal Anglian Regt, 1975-80; Col Comdt, Queen's Div., 1981-. *Address:* c/o Lloyds Bank Ltd, Cox's and King's Branch, 6 Pall Mall, SW1Y 5NH. *Clubs:* Naval and Military, MCC; Free Foresters.

GERSHEVITCH, Dr Ilya, FBA 1967; Reader in Iranian Studies, University of Cambridge, since 1965; *b* Zürich, 24 Oct. 1914; *o s* of Arkadi and Mila Gershevitch, Smolensk, Russia; *m* 1951, Lisbeth, *d* of Josef Syfrig, Lucerne; one *d*. *Educ:* Swiss schools at Locarno and Lugano; Univ. of Rome (classics); Univ. of London (Oriental studies). Dottore in Lettere, Univ. of Rome, 1937; PhD, Univ. of London, 1943. Monitored foreign broadcasts, London, 1942-47; Lecturer in Iranian Studies, Univ. of Cambridge, 1948; MA Cambridge, 1948. First European to penetrate into certain areas of Western Makran (dialect field-work), 1956; Vis. Prof. at Columbia Univ., New York, 1960-61 and 1965-66; Fellow of Jesus Coll., Cambridge, 1962; Univ. Exchange Visitor, USSR, 1965; Ratanbai Katrak Lecturer, Univ. of Oxford, 1968. Pres., Philological Soc., 1980-. Hon. PhD Berne, 1971. *Publications:* A Grammar of Manichean Sogdian, 1954; The Avestan Hymn to Mithra, 1959; articles in specialist jls, encyclopaedias and collective books. *Recreation:* music. *Address:* 54 Owlstone Road, Cambridge CB3 9JH. *T:* Cambridge 57996.

GERSTENBERG, Richard Charles; *b* Little Falls, NY, 24 Nov. 1909; *s* of Richard Paul Gerstenberg and Mary Julia Booth; *m* 1934, Evelyn Josephine Hitchingham; one *s* one *d*. *Educ:* Univ. of Michigan (AB). General Motors Corporation: Asst Comptroller, 1949-55; Treasurer, 1956-60; Vice-Pres., in charge of financial staff, 1960-67; in charge of Finance, 1967-70; Vice-Chm. Bd and Chm. Finance Cttee, 1970-72; Chm., 1972-74; a Director, 1967-. Member of Board: National Detroit Corp.; National Bank of Detroit; Detroit Edison Co.; Marsh McLennan Corp.; Miles Laboratories Inc.; Chm., Alfred Sloan Foundn. *Address:* 80 Cranbrook Road, Bloomfield Hills, Michigan, USA. *Clubs:* University, Links (New York City); Recess, Detroit Athletic (Detroit); Bloomfield Hills Country; Paradise Valley Country (Scottsdale, Arizona).

GERVIS-MEYRICK, Sir George David Eliott Tapps-; *see* Meyrick.

GERY, Robert Lucian W.; *see* Wade-Gery.

GESTETNER, David; Joint Chairman, Gestetner Holdings Ltd, since 1972; *b* 1 June 1937; *s* of Sigmund and Henny Gestetner; *m* 1961, Alice Floretta Sebag-Montefiore; one *s* three *d*. *Educ:* Midhurst Grammar Sch.; Bryanston Sch.; University Coll., Oxford (MA). *Recreation:* sailing. *Address:* 13 Loudoun Road, NW8 0LP. *T:* 01-624 2757.
See also J. Gestetner.

GESTETNER, Jonathan; Joint Chairman, Gestetner Holdings Ltd, since 1972; *b* 11 March 1940; *s* of Sigmund and Henny Gestetner; *m* 1965, Jacqueline Margaret Strasmore; two *s* one *d*. *Educ:* Bryanston Sch.; Massachusetts Institute of Technology (BScMechEngrg). Joined Gestetner Ltd, 1962. Member: Executive Council, Engineering Employers' London Assoc., 1972-77 (Vice-Pres., 1975-77); Maplin Development Authority, 1973-74; Social

Science Research Council, 1979-. *Recreation:* the visual arts. *Address:* 7 Oakhill Avenue, NW3 7RD. *T:* 01-435 0905.
See also David Gestetner.

GETHIN, Lt-Col (Retd) Sir Richard Patrick St Lawrence, 9th Bt, *cr* 1665; late REME; *b* 13 May 1911; *s* of Col Sir Richard Walter St Lawrence Gethin, 8th Bt, and Helen (*d* 1957), *d* of W. B. Thornhill; *S* father 1946; *m* 1946, Fara, *y d* of late J. H. Bartlett; one *s* four *d*. *Educ:* Oundle Sch. Lieut RAOC, 1935; Lieut-Col REME, 1943; Officer Commanding No 11 Vehicle Depot Workshops, until 1957, retired. Restorer of antique furniture. Hon. Research Fellow (Physics), Aston Univ., Birmingham, 1977-. *Publication:* Restoring Antique Furniture, 1974. *Heir: s* Richard Joseph St Lawrence Gethin [*b* 29 Sept. 1949; *m* 1974, Jacqueline, *d* of Comdr David Cox; two *d*]. *Address:* Easter Cottage, Bredon, near Tewkesbury, Glos. *T:* Bredon 72354.

GETHING, Air Commodore Richard Templeton, CB 1960; OBE 1945; AFC 1939; *b* 11 Aug. 1911; *s* of George A. Gething, Wilmslow, Cheshire; *m* 1940, Margaret Helen, *d* of late Sir Herbert Gepp, Melbourne, Australia; one *s* one *d*. *Educ:* Malvern; Sydney Sussex Coll., Cambridge. Joined RAF, 1933. Served War of 1939-45: Canada; UK; India; Burma. Actg Group Capt., 1943; Group Capt., 1950; Actg Air Commodore, 1956; Dir Operations, Maritime Navigation and Air Traffic, Air Ministry, 1956-60, retired. FIN 1956. *Recreation:* gliding. *Address:* Garden Hill, Kangaroo Ground, Victoria 3097, Australia. *Club:* Royal Air Force.

GHALE, Subedar Gaje; *see* Gaje Ghale.

GHURBURRUN, Sir Rabindrah, Kt 1981; Minister of Economic Planning and Development, Mauritius, 1976-82; *b* 27 Sept. 1929; *s* of Mrs Sookmeen Ghurburrun; *m* 1959; one *s* one *d*. *Educ:* Keble Coll., Oxford. Called to the Bar, Middle Temple; practised as Lawyer, 1959-68; High Comr for Mauritius in India, 1968-76; MLA 1976; Minister of Justice, 1976. Member: Central Board; Bar Council. Former President: Mauritius Arya Sabha; Mauritius Sugar Cane Planters' Assoc.; Hindu Educn Authority; Nat. Congress of Young Socialists. *Address:* 18 Dr Lesur Street, Cascadelle, Beau Bassin, Mauritius. *T:* 54-6421.

GIAEVER, Dr Ivar; Staff Member, General Electric Research and Development Center, since 1958; *b* 5 April 1929; *s* of John A. Giaever and Gudrun (*née* Skaarud); *m* 1952, Inger Skramstad; one *s* three *d*. *Educ:* Norwegian Inst. of Tech.; Rensselear Polytechnical Inst. ME 1952; PhD 1964. Norwegian Army, 1952-53; Norwegian Patent Office, 1953-54; Canadian General Electric, 1954-56; General Electric, 1956-58. Fellow, Amer. Phys. Soc.; Member: Nat. Acad. of Sciences; Nat. Acad. of Engineering; Amer. Acad. of Arts and Scis; Norwegian Acad. of Scis; Norwegian Acad. of Technology; Norwegian Profl Engrs. Oliver E. Buckley Prize, 1964; Nobel Prize for Physics, 1973; Zworykin Award, 1974. Hon. DSc: RPI, 1974; Union Coll., 1974; Hon. DEng, Michigan Tech. Univ., 1976; Hon. DPhys, Oslo, 1976. *Publications:* contrib. Physical Review, Jl Immunology. *Recreations:* ski-ing, tennis, camping, hiking. *Address:* General Electric Research and Development Center, PO Box 8, Schenectady, New York 12301, USA. *T:* 518-346-8771.

GIAMATTI, Prof. (Angelo) Bartlett, PhD; President of Yale University, USA, since 1977; *b* Boston, Mass, 4 April 1938; *s* of Prof. Emeritus Valentine Giamatti and Mary Walton; *m* 1960, Toni Smith; two *s* one *d*. *Educ:* South Hadley High Sch.; Internat. Sch. of Rome; Phillips Acad., Andover Mass; Yale Univ. (BA *magna cum laude*); Yale Grad. Sch. (PhD). Instructor in Italian and Comparative Literature, Princeton Univ., 1964; Asst Prof., 1965; Asst Prof. of English, Yale Univ., 1966; Associate Professor of: English, 1968, English and Comparative Literature, 1970; Prof. of English and Comparative Literature, Yale Univ., 1971 (Ford chair, 1976-77, but he relinquished to assume newly founded chair); John Hay Whitney Prof. in the Humanities, Yale Univ., 1977, also (Spring, 1977) Dir of Div. of Humanities, Faculty of Arts and Scis. Master of Ezra Stiles Coll. (a residential coll. of Yale), 1970-72; Dir of Visiting Faculty Program of Yale, 1974-76; Associate Dir of Nat. Humanities Inst., Yale, 1977. Guggenheim Fellow, 1969-70. Mem., Council on For. Relations. Member: Mediaeval Soc. of America; Modern Lang. Assoc.; Nat. Council on the Humanities; Amer. Philosophical Soc., 1982-; Fellow, Amer. Acad. of Arts and Scis. Hon. LLD: Princeton, 1978; Harvard, 1978; Notre Dame, 1982; Hon. LittD: Amer. Internat. Coll., 1979; Jewish Theol Seminary of Amer., 1980; Atlanta Univ., 1981. Comdr, Order of Merit (Italy), 1979. *Publications:* (ed jtly) The Songs of Bernart de Ventadorn, 1962; The Earthly Paradise and the Renaissance Epic, 1966; (ed jtly) Ludovico Ariosto's Orlando Furioso, 1968; (ed jtly) A Variorum Commentary on the Poems of John Milton, vol. 1, 1970; Play of Double Senses: Spenser's Faerie Queene, 1975; The University and the Public Interest, 1981; gen. editor, 3 vol. anthology Western Literature, 1971. *Recreations:* interested in sport and ballet. *Address:* Office of the President, Yale University, New Haven, Conn 06520, USA.

GIBB, Andrew (McArthur); a Recorder of the Crown Court since 1977; *b* 8 Sept. 1927; *s* of William and Ruth Gibb; *m* 1956, Olga Mary (*née* Morris); three *d*. *Educ:* Sedbergh; Queens' Coll., Cambridge (MA). Called to the Bar, Middle Temple, 1952. Chm., Cttee of Public Inquiry into fire at Wensley Lodge, Hessle, Humberside, 1977. *Recreations:* golf, reading, music. *Address:* 7 St Ives Crescent, Brooklands, Cheshire M33 3RU.

GIBB, Bill; see Gibb, W. E.

GIBB, Francis Ross, CBE 1982; FEng; FICE; Chairman and Joint Managing Director, Taylor Woodrow Construction, since 1978; Joint Managing Director, Taylor Woodrow Group, since 1979; Chairman, National Nuclear Corporation, since 1981; b 29 June 1927; s of Robert Gibb and Violet Mary Gibb; m 1950, Wendy Marjorie Fowler; one s two d. Educ: Loughborough Coll. BSc(Eng); CEng. Engineer, Handley Page, 1947–48; Engineer, 1948–57, Manager, 1957–63, Dir, 1963–70, Man. Dir, 1970, Taylor Woodrow Construction; Director: Taylor Woodrow Internat., 1969–; Taylor Woodrow Ltd, 1972–; Chm., Taywood Santa Fe, 1975–. Member: Construction Industry Adv. Cttee, HSE, 1978–81; Gp of Eight, 1979–81; Board, British Nuclear Associates, 1980– (Chm., Agrément Bd, 1980–82). Member: Council, CBI, 1979–80; Industrial Policy Cttee, CBI, 1980–. Dir, Holiday Pay Scheme, 1980– and Trustee, Benefits Scheme, 1980–, Building and Civil Engrg Trustees. Federation of Civil Engineering Contractors: Vice-Chm., 1978–79; Chm., 1979–80; Vice Pres., 1980–. FRSA. Recreations: ornithology, gardening, walking, music. Address: Latchend, 18 Latchmoor Avenue, Gerrards Cross, Bucks SL9 8LJ. Club: Arts.

GIBB, George Dutton, CB 1979; Chief Dental Officer, Department of Health and Social Security and Department of Education and Science, since 1971; b 9 March 1920; s of late Dr William Forsyth Gibb and Margaret Jane Gibb (née Dutton); m 1948, Mary Dupree; two d. Educ: St Helen's Coll., Southsea; University Tutorial Coll., London; Guy's Hospital. LDS RCS 1950, FDS RCS 1979. Enlisted RNVR, 1940; commnd (Exec. Br.) 1941. Gen. Dental Practitioner, High Wycombe, 1950–71. Mem., Bucks Exec. Council, 1957–65; Hon. Sec., Bucks Local Dental Cttee, 1957–65; Mem., Standing Dental Adv. Cttee, 1964–71; Mem., Central Health Services Council, 1967–71; Chm. of Council, British Dental Assoc., 1967–71; Mem., GDC (Crown nominee), 1972–; Mem., Odontological Section, RSocMed, 1972–. Address: Alexander Fleming House, Elephant and Castle, SE1 6BY.

GIBB, Ian Pashley; Director and Keeper, British Library Reference Division, since 1977; b 17 April 1926; s of John Pashley Gibb and Mary (née Owen); m 1953, Patricia Mary Butler; two s. Educ: Latymer Upper Sch.; UCL (BA). ALA. Sen. Library Asst, Univ. of London, 1951–52; Asst Librarian, UCL, 1952–58; Dep. Librarian, National Central Library, 1958–73; British Library: Dep. Dir, Science Reference Library, 1973–75; Head of Divl Office, Reference Div., 1975–77. Part-time Lectr, UCL, 1967–77, Hon. Research Fellow, 1977–. Hon. Treasurer, Bibliographical Soc., 1961–67. Publications: various articles. Recreations: music, watching cricket, bridge. Address: The Old Cottage, 16 Tile Kiln Lane, Leverstock Green, Hemel Hempstead, Herts HP3 8ND. T: Hemel Hempstead 56352.

GIBB, Walter Frame, DSO 1945; DFC 1943; JP; Chairman, since 1980 and Managing Director, since 1978, British Aerospace, Australia, Ltd; b 26 March 1919; British; m 1944, Pauline Sylvia Reed; three d. Educ: Clifton Coll. Apprentice, Bristol Aero Engines, 1937. RAF, 1940–46. Test Pilot, Bristol Aircraft Ltd, 1946; Asst Chief Test Pilot, 1953; Chief Test Pilot, Bristol Aeroplane Co. Ltd, 1956–60; Product Support Manager, BAC Filton, 1960–78. World Altitude Height Record 63,668 feet in Olympus-Canberra, 1953, and second record 65,890 ft in same machine, 1955. MRAeS. JP Bristol, 1974. Recreation: sailing. Address: Bennelong House, 55 Macquarie Street, Sydney, NSW 2000, Australia. Clubs: Royal Air Force; Royal Sydney Yacht Squadron.

GIBB, William Elphinstone, (Bill Gibb); Company Director, Bill Gibb Ltd, since 1972; Chairman, Bill Gibb Fashion Group Ltd, since 1982; b 23 Jan. 1943; s of George and Jessie Gibb. Educ: Fraserburgh Acad.; St Martin's Sch. of Art (DipAD); Royal Coll. of Art (DesRCA). Fellow, Indust. Arts Soc., 1976. First shop, Alice Paul, 1967; Designer at Baccarat, 1967–79; founded Bill Gibb Ltd, 1972. Created first ballet costumes for Remy Charlip's Mad River, 1972; designed costume for Lynn Seymour as Salomé, 1981. Dress in Cecil Beaton Exhibn, V&A, 1971; 10 yrs Retrospective Fashion show for 7,000 people, Royal Albert Hall, 1977. Nominated for Yardley Award, New York, 1967; Vogue Designer of the Year, 1970 (outfit now in Bath Museum); award from Today programme (ITV) for best Fashion show of 1979. Recreations: historical reading, travelling to regenerate inspiration. Address: 38 Drayton Court, Drayton Gardens, SW10. Clubs: Embassy, Legends, The Gardens, Ritz Casino.

GIBB, William Eric, MA, DM Oxon; FRCP; Physician: St Bartholomew's Hospital, 1947–76; The Metropolitan Hospital, 1952–76; b 30 April 1911; s of late James Glenny Gibb, MD, FRCS, and Georgina Henman; m 1952, Mary Edith Gertrude Feetham; three s. Educ: Rugby Sch.; Oriel Coll., Oxford; St Bartholomew's Hosp. BA Oxon 1st Cl. Hons Final Sch. of Nat. Science; Prox. Access. Theodore Williams Scholarship (Anatomy); BM, BCh Oxon 1936; MRCP 1940; DM Oxon 1947; FRCP 1949; George Herbert Hunt Travelling Schol. (University of Oxford), 1938. Res. House appts, St Bart's Hosp. and Brompton Chest Hosp.; Cattlin Research Scholar, 1947. War service with RAFVR Medical Branch, 1941–46; Actg Wing Comdr i/c a Medical Div. Examiner in Medicine, University of Oxford, 1952–59 and Examiner in Medicine, Examg Bd of England. Mem., Pension Appeal Tribunals. Fellow, Royal Soc. Med. Publications: various articles in medical journals. Recreation: gardening. Address: 12 Sheldon Avenue, N6.

GIBBENS, (Edward) Brian, MA Oxon; QC 1962; **His Honour Judge Brian Gibbens;** a Circuit Judge, since 1973; b 26 Sept. 1912; s of Rev. George Percy Gibbens and Dr Fanny Gibbens; m 1939, Kathleen Joan Rosier; two s one d. Educ: Newcastle-under-Lyme High Sch.; St Catherine's Society, Oxford. Called to the Bar, Gray's Inn, 1934; Bencher of Gray's Inn, 1967; practised on Oxford Circuit from 1934. Served in RA and as staff officer, Nov. 1939–45. Major in Army Officers Emergency Reserve, 1946–. Mem. Gen. Council of the Bar, 1947–52, 1964–68, 1969–73; a Recorder of Crown Courts, 1972–73 (Recorder of West Bromwich, 1959–65, of Oxford, 1965–71); Hon. Recorder, City of Oxford, 1972–. Dep. Chm. QS, Oxon., 1964–71; Comr of Assize, Bristol, 1970, Oxford, 1971, Birmingham, 1971; Leader of the Oxford Circuit, 1966–71; Jt Leader, Midland and Oxford Circuit, 1972. Conducted Home Office inquiry into corporal punishments at Court Lees approved sch., 1967; conducted public inquiry into automatic level crossings after railway accident at Hixon, Staffs, 1968; leading counsel for the Army in Widgery Tribunal of Inquiry into shooting of civilians in Londonderry, 1972. Hon. Mem., Midland Inst. of Forensic Medicine. Recreation: gardening. Address: Central Criminal Court, Old Bailey, EC4. T: 01-940 4461.

GIBBENS, Frank Edward Hilary George; His Honour Judge Frank Gibbens; a Circuit Judge, since 1973; b 23 April 1913; s of Frank Edward George and Geraldine Edel Gibbens; m 1940, Margaret Gertrude Wren; three d. Educ: Malvern; Peterhouse, Cambridge (BA). Called to Bar, Inner Temple, 1938. Served War, commission in RAF, 1940–46. Sqdn Leader, rank on demobilisation. On appt as Judge, retired from Bar, 1973. Recreation: golf. Address: Warren Close, Coombe Hill Road, Kingston-upon-Thames.

GIBBENS, Prof. Trevor Charles Noel, CBE 1977 (MBE 1945); MA, MD; FRCP, FRCPsych; Professor of Forensic Psychiatry, Institute of Psychiatry, London University, 1967–78, now Emeritus Professor; Hon. Consultant, Bethlem Royal and Maudsley Hospitals, since 1951; Consultant to London Remand Home for Girls, since 1951; b 28 Dec. 1912; s of George Gibbens and Sarah Jane Hartley; m 1950, Patricia Margaret, d of A. E. and E. Mullis; two s one d. Educ: Westminster Sch.; Emmanuel Coll., Cambridge; St Thomas's Hosp., London. RAMC, 1939; POW, 1940–45. Sen. Lectr, Forensic Psychiatry, 1950–67. Member: Cttee on Business of the Criminal Courts (Streatfield Cttee), 1958; Royal Commn on Penal Reform, 1964–66. President: British Acad. of Forensic Sciences, 1967–68; Internat. Soc. of Criminology, 1967–74. Chm., Inst. for Study and Treatment of Delinquency, 1974–81; Vice-Chm., Howard League, 1975–; Mem., Parole Board, 1972–75. Member: Adv. Gp on Law of Rape (Heilbron Cttee), 1975; Policy Adv. Cttee to Criminal Law Revision Cttee, 1976–. Publications: Shoplifting, 1962; Psychiatric Studies of Borstal Lads, 1963; Cultural Factors in Delinquency, 1966; Medical Remands in Criminal Courts, 1977; articles in scientific jls. Address: c/o Institute of Psychiatry, de Crespigny Park, SE5 8AF. T: 01-703 5411.

GIBBERD, Sir Frederick, Kt 1967; CBE 1954; RA 1969 (ARA 1961); FRIBA, FRTPI, FILA, FSIA; practising as an Architect, Town Planning Consultant and Landscape Architect; b 7 Jan. 1908; e s of late Frederick Gibberd, Kenilworth, Warwicks; m 1st, 1938, Dorothy (d 1970), d of late J. H. Phillips, Hampstead; one s two d; 2nd, 1972, Patricia Fox Edwards. Educ: King Henry VIII Sch., Coventry. Private practice in London since 1930. Principal buildings include: Pullman Court, Streatham; London Airport, Terminal Buildings and Chapel; Bath Technical College; St Neots Bridge; Hinkley Point and Didcot Power Stations; Metropolitan Cathedral, Liverpool (won in open competition); New Monastery, Douai Abbey; Longmans Green Offices, Harlow; Doncaster Law Courts (with L. J. Tucker); Designs for: London Mosque (won in open competition); Arundel Great Court; Coutts Bank, Strand; Inter-Continental Hotel, Hyde Park Corner. Principal town designs, Harlow New Town (Architect-Planner, 1947–80); master plan, Memorial Univ., Newfoundland. Civic Centres for: Doncaster; Harlow; Leamington Spa; Nuneaton and St Albans. Shopping Centres: Lansbury Market; Redcar; Harvey Centre, Harlow; Stratford-upon-Avon. Principal Landscape and Garden Designs: Harlow, overall landscape design and Water Gardens; Queen's Gardens, Hull; Llyn Celyn, Derwent and Kielder Reservoirs; Potash Mine at Boultby; Dinorwic Pump Storage Scheme. Member: Royal Fine Art Commission, 1950–70; Council RIBA, 1959–76; Past President, Building Centre; Past Principal, Architectural Association School of Architecture. Hon. LLD, Liverpool, 1969. RIBA Bronze Medal; Gold Medal, RTPI, 1978; two Festival of Britain Awards; four Housing Medals; five Civic Trust Awards; two European Architectural Heritage Year awards. Publications: The Architecture of England, 1938; Town Design, 1953; Metropolitan Cathedral of Christ the King, Liverpool, 1968; The Design of Harlow, 1980; (jtly) Harlow: the story of a new town, 1980. Recreation: gardening. Address: Marsh Lane, Harlow, Essex CM17 0NA.

GIBBINGS, Peter Walter; Chairman, Guardian and Manchester Evening News plc, since 1973; b 25 March 1929; s of late Walter White Gibbings and Margaret Russell Gibbings (née Torrance); m 1st, Elspeth Felicia Macintosh; two d; 2nd, Hon. Louise Barbara, d of Viscount Lambert, qv; one s. Educ: Rugby; Wadham Coll., Oxford (Scholar). Called to Bar, Middle Temple, 1953 (Garraway Rice Pupillage Prize; Harmsworth Schol.). Served in 9th Queen's Royal Lancers, 1951–52; Dep. Legal Adviser, Trinidad Oil Co. Ltd, 1955–56; Associated Newspapers Ltd, 1956–60; The Observer, 1960–67 (Deputy Manager and Dir, 1965–67); Man. Dir, Guardian Newspapers Ltd, 1967–73; Dir, Manchester Guardian and Evening News Ltd, 1967–73. Director: Anglia Television Gp plc; Press Assoc. Ltd. Mem., Press Council,

1970-74. *Recreations:* lawn mowing, tennis. *Address:* c/o Guardian and Manchester Evening News Ltd, 164 Deansgate, Manchester M60 2RR.

GIBBINS, Elizabeth Mary, BA; Headmistress, St Mary's School, Calne, Wilts, 1946-72; *b* 2 May 1911; *d* of late Kenneth Mayoh Gibbins, MB, BS. *Educ:* Sandecotes Sch., Parkstone; Westfield Coll., University of London; Cambridge Univ. Training Coll. for Women (Postgraduate). History Mistress, St Brandons Clergy Daughters' Sch., Bristol, 1935-38; Headmistress, Diocesan Girls' Sch., Hongkong, 1939-45, Acting Headmistress, Oct. 1972-May 1973. Hon. Sec., Hong Kong Diocesan Assoc., 1974-80. *Address:* 8 Moreton Road, Old Bosham, Chichester, West Sussex. *T:* Bosham 573038.

GIBBINS, Rev. Dr Ronald Charles; Superintendent Minister, Wesley's Chapel, London, since 1978; *s* of Charles and Anne Gibbins; *m* 1949, Olive Ruth (*née* Patchett); one *s* two *d. Educ:* London Univ. (BScSociol); Wesley Theological Coll., Bristol; Eden Theological Seminary, US (DMin). Methodist Minister: Bradford, 1948-49; Spennymoor, 1949-50; Middlesbrough, 1950-57; Basildon, 1957-64; East End Mission, London, 1964-78. *Publications:* Mission for the Secular City, 1976; The Lumpen Proletariat, 1979. *Recreations:* travel, boating, veteran cars. *Address:* 49 City Road, EC1. *T:* 01-253 2262.

GIBBON, Gen. Sir John (Houghton), GCB 1977 (KCB 1972; CB 1970); OBE 1945 (MBE 1944); Master-General of the Ordnance, 1974-77; ADC (General) to the Queen, 1976-77; *b* 21 Sept. 1917; *er s* of Brigadier J. H. Gibbon, The Manor House, Little Stretton, Salop; *m* 1951, Brigid Rosamund, *d* of late Dr D. A. Bannerman, OBE, ScD, FRSE, and Muriel, *d* of T. R. Morgan; one *s. Educ:* Eton; Trinity Coll., Cambridge. Commissioned into Royal Artillery, 1939. Served with 2nd Regt RHA: France, 1939-40; Western Desert, 1940-41; Greece, 1941; on staff of HQ 30 Corps; Western Desert, 1941-43; Sicily, 1943; GSO 1, RA, HQ 21 Army Gp, 1944-45; 6 Airborne Div., Palestine, 1946-47; Instructor and Chief Instructor, RMA Sandhurst, 1947-51; GSO 2, War Office, 1951-53; Battery Comdr, 1953-54; AQMG, War Office, 1955-58; CO Field Regt, BAOR, 1959-61; Bde Comdr, Cyprus, 1962; Dir of Defence Plans, Min. of Def., 1962-64; Sec., Chiefs of Staff Cttee and Dir, Defence Operations Staff, 1966-69; Dir, Army Staff Duties, MoD, 1969-71; Vice-Chief of the Defence Staff, 1972-74. Col Comdt, RA, 1972-82. Chm., Regular Forces Employment Assoc., 1982- (Vice-Chm., 1977-82). *Recreations:* rowing, shooting, fishing. *Address:* Beech House, Northbrook Close, Winchester, Hants SO23 8JR. *T:* Winchester 66155.

GIBBON, Michael, QC 1974; **His Honour Judge Gibbon;** a Circuit Judge, since 1979; *b* 15 Sept. 1930; 2nd *s* of late F. O. Gibbon; *m* 1956, Malveen Elliot Seager; two *s* one *d. Educ:* Brightlands; Charterhouse; Pembroke Coll., Oxford (MA). Commnd in Royal Artillery, 1949. Called to Bar, Lincoln's Inn, 1954. A Recorder of the Crown Court, 1972-79. Chm., Electoral Adv. Cttee to Home Sec., 1972. Chm., Local Govt Boundary Commn for Wales, 1978-79 (Dep. Chm., 1974-78). *Recreations:* music, golf. *Address:* Gellihirion, 3 Cefn-Coed Road, Cardiff CF2 6AN. *T:* Cardiff 751852. *Clubs:* Cardiff and County (Cardiff); Royal Porthcawl Golf, Cardiff Golf.

GIBBON, Monk; *see* Gibbon, W. M.

GIBBON, (William) Monk, PhD (Dublin); FRSL; poet and writer; *b* Dublin, 15 Dec. 1896; *o s* of late Canon William Monk Gibbon, MA, Rural Dean, Taney, Dundrum, Co. Dublin, and Isabel Agnes Pollock (*née* Meredith); *m* 1928, Mabel Winifred, *d* of Rev. Walter Molyneux Dingwall, MA, and Mabel Sophia Spender; two *s* four *d. Educ:* St Columba's Coll., Rathfarnham; Keble Coll., Oxford (Open History Exhibn). Served European War, 1914-18, as Officer, RASC; France, 1916-17; Invalided out, 1918. Taught in Switzerland; master at Oldfeld Sch., Swanage (12 yrs). Silver Medal for Poetry, Tailteann Games, 1928. Tredegar Memorial Lecture, Royal Society of Literature, 1952; Tagore Centenary Lecture, Abbey Theatre, Dublin, 1961. Mem. Irish Acad. of Letters, 1960 (Vice-Pres., 1967). *Publications:* poetry: The Tremulous String, 1926; The Branch of Hawthorn Tree, 1927; For Daws to Peck At, 1929; Seventeen Sonnets, 1932; This Insubstantial Pageant (collected poems), 1951; The Velvet Bow and other poems, 1972; autobiography: The Seals, 1935; Mount Ida, 1948; Inglorious Soldier, 1968; The Brahms Waltz, 1970; The Pupil, 1981; biography: Netta (Hon. Mrs Franklin), 1960; novel: The Climate of Love, 1961; ballet and film criticism: The Red Shoes Ballet, 1948; The Tales of Hoffmann, 1951; An Intruder at The Ballet, 1952; travel: Swiss Enchantment, 1950; Austria, 1953; In Search of Winter Sport, 1953; Western Germany, 1955; The Rhine and its Castles, 1957; Great Houses of Europe, 1962; Great Palaces of Europe, 1964; literary criticism: The Masterpiece and the Man, 1959. The Living Torch (an Æ anthology), 1937. *Recreations:* watching ballet and good films. *Address:* 24 Sandycove Road, Sandycove, Co. Dublin, Eire. *T:* 805120.

GIBBONS, Hon. David; *see* Gibbons, Hon. J. D.

GIBBONS, Brig. Edward John, CMG 1956; CBE 1947 (MBE 1939); *b* 30 Aug. 1906; *s* of Edward Gibbons, Coventry; *m* 1946, Gabrielle Maria (*d* 1982), widow of Capt. P. A. Strakosh; one step *d. Educ:* King Henry VIII Sch., Coventry; Gonville and Caius Coll., Cambridge. Nigerian Administrative Service, 1929. Army Service, 1941-46: Dir of Civil Affairs, South East Asia Command; Brig. Sec. Eastern Provinces, Nigeria, 1948; Commissioner of the Cameroons (under UK Trusteeship), 1949-56; Dept of Technical

Cooperation, 1962-64; Min. of Overseas Develt, 1964-68. *Recreation:* wood engraving. *Address:* 6 Grove House, The Grove, Epsom, Surrey. *T:* Epsom 26657. *Club:* Royal Automobile.

GIBBONS, Hon. (John) David, JP; MP Bermuda, since 1972; Premier of Bermuda, 1977-82; Minister of Finance, since 1975; *b* 15 June 1927; *s* of late Edmund G. Gibbons, CBE, and Winifred G. Gibbons, MBE; *m* 1958, Lully Lorentzen; three *s* (and one *d* by former *m*). *Educ:* Saltus Grammar Sch., Bermuda; Hotchkiss Sch., Lakeville, Conn; Harvard Univ., Cambridge, Mass (BA). FBIM. Mem. Govt Boards: Social Welfare Bd, 1949-58; Bd of Civil Aviation, 1958-60; Bd of Educn, 1956-59 (Chm., 1973-74); Trade Develt Bd, 1960-74. Minister of Health and Welfare, 1974-75. Mem., Law Reform Cttee, 1969-72. Mem. Governing Body, subseq. Chm., Bermuda Technical Inst., 1956-70. Mem., Bermuda Athletic Assoc. JP Bermuda, 1974. *Recreations:* tennis, golf, skiing, swimming. *Address:* Leeward, Point Shares, Pembroke, Bermuda. *T:* 809-29 52396. *Clubs:* Phoenix (Cambridge, Mass); Harvard (New York); Royal Bermuda Yacht, Royal Hamilton Amateur Dinghy, Mid-Ocean, Riddells Bay Golf, Spanish Point Boat (Bermuda).

GIBBONS, Ven. Kenneth Harry; Archdeacon of Lancaster, since 1981; Priest-in-charge of Weeton, since 1981; *b* 24 Dec. 1931; *s* of Harry and Phyllis Gibbons; *m* 1962, Margaret Ann Tomlinson; two *s. Educ:* Blackpool and Chesterfield Grammar Schools; Manchester Univ. (BSc); Cuddesdon Coll., Oxford. RAF, 1952-54. Ordained, 1956; Assistant Curate of Fleetwood, 1956-60; Secretary for Student Christian Movement in Schools, 1960-62; Senior Curate, St Martin-in-the-Fields, Westminster, 1962-65; Vicar of St Edward, New Addington, 1965-70; Vicar of Portsea, 1970-81; RD of Portsmouth, 1973-79; Hon. Canon of Portsmouth, 1974. *Recreations:* gardening, cinema. *Address:* St Michael's Vicarage, Weeton, Preston, Lancs PR4 3WD. *T:* Weeton 249.

GIBBONS, Stella Dorothea, (Mrs A. B. Webb), FRSL; Poet and Novelist; *b* London, 5 Jan. 1902; *d* of C. J. P. T. Gibbons, MD; *m* 1933, Allan Bourne Webb (*d* 1959), actor and singer; one *d. Educ:* N London Collegiate Sch.; University Coll., London. Journalist, 1923-33; BUP, Evening Standard, The Lady. *Publications:* The Mountain Beast (Poems), 1930; Cold Comfort Farm, 1932 (Femina Vie Heureuse Prize, 1933); Bassett, 1934; The Priestess (Poems), 1934; Enbury Heath, 1935; The Untidy Gnome, 1935; Miss Linsey and Pa, 1936; Roaring Tower (Short Stories), 1937; Nightingale Wood, 1938; The Lowland Venus (Poems), 1938; My American, 1939; Christmas at Cold Comfort Farm (Short Stories), 1940; The Rich House, 1941; Ticky, 1943; The Bachelor, 1944; Westwood, 1946; The Matchmaker, 1949; Conference at Cold Comfort Farm, 1949; Collected Poems, 1950; The Swiss Summer, 1951; Fort of the Bear, 1953; Beside the Pearly Water (short stories), 1954; The Shadow of a Sorcerer, 1955; Here Be Dragons, 1956; White Sand and Grey Sand, 1958; A Pink Front Door, 1959; The Weather at Tregulla, 1962; The Wolves were in the Sledge, 1964; The Charmers, 1965; Starlight, 1967; The Snow Woman, 1969; The Woods in Winter, 1970; unpublished works: Verses for Friends; The Yellow Houses; An Alpha. *Recreations:* reading, listening to music.

GIBBONS, Sir William Edward Doran, 9th Bt *cr* 1752; Assistant Shipping and Port Manager, Sealink UK Ltd, Parkeston Quay, since 1979; *b* 13 Jan. 1948; *s* of Sir John Edward Gibbons, 8th Bt, and of Mersa Wentworth, *y d* of late Major Edward Baynton Grove Foster; *S* father, 1982; *m* 1972, Patricia Geraldine Archer, *d* of Roland Archer Howse; one *d. Educ:* Pangbourne; RNC Dartmouth; Bristol Univ. (BSc). MCIT. Parish Councillor, Manningtree. *Address:* Oxford House, Mistley, Manningtree, Essex.

GIBBS, family name of **Barons Aldenham** and **Wraxall.**

GIBBS, Air Vice-Marshal Charles Melvin, CB 1976; CBE 1966; DFC 1943; RAF retd; Recruiting Consultant with Selleck Associates, Colchester, since 1977; *b* 11 June 1921; American father, New Zealand mother; *m* 1947, Emma Pamela Pollard; one *d. Educ:* Taumarunui, New Zealand. MECI 1980. Joined RNZAF, 1941; service in Western Desert and Mediterranean, 1942-44; Coastal Comd, 1945; India, 1946-47; commanded Tropical Experimental Unit, 1950-52; RAF Staff Coll., 1953; commanded No 118 Squadron, 1954-55; Directing Staff, RAF Staff Coll., 1956-58; Pakistan, 1958-61; Chief Instructor, RAF Chivenor, 1961-63; CO, Wattisham, 1963-66; idc 1967; Defence Policy Staff, 1968-69; Dir of Quartering, 1970-72; AOA, Germany, 1972-74; Dir-Gen. Personal Services, RAF, 1974-76. *Recreations:* fishing, golf. *Address:* North View, 6 Parsons Hill, Lexden, Colchester, Essex. *Clubs:* Royal Air Force; Nayland Golf (Nayland).

GIBBS, Dennis Raleigh, CMG 1962; CVO 1966; DSO 1944; Former Managing Director, Hewanorra Enterprises Ltd, Vieux Fort, St Lucia, retired; *b* 3 March 1922; *e s* of late Gerard Yardley Gibbs, Epping, and Carol Gibbs (*née* Francis); *m* 1952, Barbara Erica Batty, MB, ChB; two *s* one *d. Educ:* Bradfield Coll. RAF, 1940-46; CO 82 Sqdn, 1942-44; Wing Comdr Air Staff, Air HQ, Burma, 1945. Seconded FO, 1946; Colonial Admin. Service, 1946-56, then E Nigerian Public Service, 1956-64 (Perm. Sec., Min. of Works, 1958, Adv. to Min. of Economic Planning, 1962-64); Administrator of Montserrat, WI, 1964-71; real estate develt, St Lucia, 1972-77; Man. Dir, Mustique Co., St Vincent, 1977-79. *Recreations:* outdoor activities. *Address:* Box 479, Plymouth, Montserrat, WI. *Club:* Royal Commonwealth Society.

GIBBS, Hon. Eustace Hubert Beilby, CMG 1982; HM Diplomatic Service; Vice Marshal of the Diplomatic Corps, since 1982; *b* 3 July 1929; 2nd surv. *s* of 1st Baron Wraxall, PC; *b* and *heir-pres.* of 2nd Baron Wraxall, *qv* ; *m* 1957, Evelyn Veronica Scott; three *s* two *d. Educ:* Eton College; Christ Church, Oxford (MA). ARCM 1953. Entered HM Diplomatic Service, 1954; served in Bangkok, Rio de Janeiro, Berlin and Vienna; Counsellor, Caracas, 1971-73; Royal College of Defence Studies, 1974; Inspector, 1975-77; Consul-Gen., Paris, 1977-82. *Recreations:* music, golf. *Address:* Coddenham House, Coddenham, Ipswich, Suffolk. *Clubs:* Brooks's, Pratt's, Beefsteak.

GIBBS, Sir Frank Stannard, KBE 1954 (OBE 1939); CMG 1949; *b* 3 July 1895; *m* 1944, Sylvia Madeleine Knight; one *s* one *d.* Probationer Vice-Consul, Genoa, 1920; served Madrid, Rio de Janeiro, Paris, Marseilles, Beira, Milan; Vice-Consul, 1923; transferred to China Consular Service with Consular rank, 1935; Actg Consul-Gen., Canton, 1937, Addis Ababa, 1939; served Rosario and Tunis: Consul-Gen., 1946; Foreign Service Officer, Grade 5, 1947; Consul-Gen., Saigon, 1947-51, with personal rank of Minister, 1950-51; Ambassador to the Republic of the Philippines, 1954-55 (Minister, 1951-54), retired 1955. *Address:* El Rincón, High Street, Old Woking, Surrey. *T:* Woking 70147.

GIBBS, Air Marshal Sir Gerald Ernest, KBE 1954 (CBE 1945); CIE 1946; MC; *b* 3 Sept. 1896; *s* of Ernest William Cecil and Fanny Wilmina Gibbs; *m* 1938, Margaret Jean Bradshaw; one *s* one *d.* Served European War, 1914-18; transferred from Army to RFC 1916, and RAF 1918 (MC and 2 bars, Légion d'Honneur, Croix de Guerre). Served various overseas periods with RAF in Iraq, Palestine, Sudan and Kenya between the two wars; commanded No 47 Sqdn RAF Sudan and RAF Kenya. Senior Air Staff Officer of No 11 Group, Fighter Command, 1940-41 during Battle of Britain; Dir of Overseas Operations, Air Ministry, 1942-43; Senior Air Staff Officer, HQ 3rd Tactical Air Force, South-East Asia, 1943-44; Chief Air Staff Officer, Supreme HQ, SEAC, 1945-46; Senior Air Staff Officer, HQ, RAF Transport Command, 1946-48; Head of Service Advisers to UK Delegation and Chm. UK Members of Military Staff Cttee, UN, 1948-51; Chief of Air Staff and Commander-in-Chief, Indian Air Force, 1951-54, retired 1954. *Publication:* Survivor's Story, 1956. *Recreations:* golf, ski-ing, sailing. *Address:* Lone Oak, 170 Coombe Lane West, Kingston-upon-Thames, Surrey. *Clubs:* Royal Air Force; Royal Wimbledon Golf (Wimbledon); Seaford Golf (East Blatchington); Trevose Golf (Cornwall).

GIBBS, Rt. Hon. Sir Harry (Talbot), GCMG 1981; KBE 1970; PC 1972; **Rt. Hon. Mr Justice Gibbs;** Chief Justice of Australia, since 1981; *b* 7 Feb. 1917; *s* of late H. V. Gibbs, formerly of Ipswich, Qld; *m* 1944, Muriel Ruth (*née* Dunn); one *s* three *d. Educ:* Ipswich Grammar Sch., Qld; Univ. of Queensland (BA, LLM). Served War, Australia and New Guinea, 1939-45, Major (despatches). Admitted as Barrister, Qld, 1939; QC 1957; Judge of Supreme Court of Qld, 1961; Judge of Federal Court of Bankruptcy and of Supreme Court of Australian Capital Territory, 1967; Justice of High Court of Australia, 1970. Hon. Bencher, Lincoln's Inn. Hon. LLD Queensland, 1980. *Address:* 27 Stanhope Road, Killara, NSW 2071, Australia. *T:* 498-6924. *Clubs:* Australian (Sydney); Queensland (Brisbane); Commonwealth (Canberra).

GIBBS, Rt. Hon. Sir Humphrey Vicary, PC 1969; GCVO 1969 (KCVO 1965); KCMG 1960; OBE 1959; Governor of Rhodesia (lately S Rhodesia), 1959-69; *b* 22 Nov. 1902; 3rd *s* of 1st Baron Hunsdon; *m* 1934, Molly Peel Nelson (*see* Molly Peel Gibbs); five *s. Educ:* Eton; Trinity Coll., Cambridge. Started farming near Bulawayo, 1928. Hon. LLD Birmingham, 1969; Hon. DCL East Anglia, 1969. *Address:* Bonisa Farm, Private Bag 5583W, Bulawayo, Zimbabwe. *Clubs:* Athenæum; Bulawayo (Bulawayo, Zimbabwe); Salisbury (Salisbury, Zimbabwe).

GIBBS, Rt. Rev. John; *see* Coventry, Bishop of.

GIBBS, Martin St John Valentine, CB 1958; DSO 1942; TD; JP; Lord-Lieutenant of Gloucestershire, since 1978; *b* 14 Feb. 1917; *er s* of late Major G. M. Gibbs, Parkleaze, Ewen, Cirencester; *m* 1947, Mary Margaret (*widow* of late Captain M. D. H. Wills, MC), *er d* of late Col Philip Mitford; two *d. Educ:* Eton. 2nd Lieut, Royal Wilts Yeomanry, 1937; served War of 1939-45 with Royal Wilts Yeo., Major 1942, Lieut-Col 1951, Brevet-Col 1955, Col 1958; Hon. Col: Royal Wilts Yeomanry Sqdn, T&AVR, 1972-; The Royal Yeomanry, RAC, T&AVR, 1975-; Col Comdt Yeomanry, RAC, 1975-. Gloucestershire: JP 1965; High Sheriff, 1958; DL Wilts 1972. *Recreations:* country pursuits. *Address:* Ewen Manor, Ewen, Cirencester, Glos. *T:* Kemble 206. *Club:* Cavalry and Guards.
See also Field Marshal Sir R. C. Gibbs, Sir G. R. Newman, Bt.

GIBBS, Dame Molly (Peel), DBE 1969; (Hon. Lady Gibbs); *b* 13 July 1912; 2nd *d* of John Peel Nelson; *m* 1934, Rt Hon. Sir Humphrey Vicary Gibbs, *qv* ; five *s. Educ:* Girls' High School, Barnato Park, Johannesburg. *Address:* Bonisa, Private Bag 5583W, Bulawayo, Zimbabwe. *T:* Bulawayo 69002.

GIBBS, Prof. Norman Henry, MA, DPhil; Emeritus Fellow, All Souls College, Oxford, since 1977; Chichele Professor of the History of War in the University of Oxford, 1953-77; *b* 17 April 1910; *m* 1941, Joan Frances Leslie-Melville; two *d* ; *m* 1955, Kathleen Phebe Emmett. Open Exhibitioner, Magdalen Coll., Oxford, 1928; Senior Demy, 1931; Asst Lecturer, University Coll., London, 1934-36; Fellow and Tutor in Modern History, Merton Coll.,

Oxford, 1936. 1st King's Dragoon Guards, 1939; Historical Section, War Cabinet Office, 1943. Former Chm., Naval Education Advisory Cttee; former Member: Internat. Council of Institute for Strategic Studies; Council, Royal United Service Institution; Research Associate, Center for Internat. Studies, Princeton, 1965-66. Visiting Professor: Univ. of New Brunswick, 1975-76; US Military Academy, West Point, 1978-79. US Outstanding Civilian Service Medal, 1979. *Publications:* 2nd edition, Keith, British Cabinet System, 1952; The Origins of the Committee of Imperial Defence, 1955; contribs to: Cambridge Modern History (new edn); L'Europe du XIXme et du XXme siècles, (Milan) 1966; (ed) The Soviet System and Democratic Society, 1967; History of the Second World War, Grand Strategy, Vol. 1, 1976. *Address:* All Souls College, Oxford; Flat No 1, Grange Court, Shore Road, Bonchurch, Isle of Wight.

GIBBS, Oswald Moxley, CMG 1976; consultant in trade, industrial and community development; *b* 15 Oct. 1927; *s* of Michael Gibbs and Emelda Mary (*née* Cobb); *m* 1955, Dearest Agatha Mitchell; two *s* two *d. Educ:* Grenada Boys' Secondary Sch.; Christy Trades Sch., Chicago; City of London Coll. Solicitors' Clerk, 1948-51; Operator at Oil Refinery in Curaçao, 1951-55; Civil Servant, 1955-57; Welfare Officer, Eastern Caribbean Commission, London, 1965-67; Trade Secretary, 1967-72; Deputy Commissioner, 1972-73; Actg Commissioner, 1973-75; High Comr for Grenada in London, 1974-78; Consultant, Centre for Industrial Develt, Lomé Convention, Brussels, 1979-80. *Address:* Woodside Green, SE25.

GIBBS, Richard John Hedley; barrister; a Recorder of the Crown Court, since 1981; *b* 2 Sept. 1941; *s* of Brian Conaway Gibbs and Mabel Joan Gibbs; *m* 1965, Janet (*née* Whittall); one *s* three *d. Educ:* Oundle Sch.; Trinity Hall, Cambridge (MA). Called to the Bar, Inner Temple, 1965. *Address:* 1 Fountain Court, Steelhouse Lane, Birmingham B4 6DR. *T:* 021-236 5721.

GIBBS, Roger Geoffrey; Chairman, Gerrard & National plc, since 1975; *b* 13 Oct. 1934; 4th *s* of Hon. Sir Geoffrey Gibbs, KCMG, and late Hon. Lady Gibbs, CBE. *Educ:* Eton; Millfield. Jessel Toynbee & Co. Ltd, 1954, Dir 1960; de Zoete & Gorton, Stockbrokers, 1964, Partner 1966; Gerrard & National plc, 1971-. *Address:* 23 Tregunter Road, SW10 9LS. *T:* 01-370 3465. *Clubs:* Brooks's, Pratt's.

GIBBS, Field Marshal Sir Roland (Christopher), GCB 1976 (KCB 1972); CBE 1968; DSO 1945; MC 1943; Vice Lord-Lieutenant for Wiltshire, since 1982; Chief of the General Staff, 1976-79; ADC General to the Queen, 1976-79; *b* 22 June 1921; *yr s* of late Maj. G. M. Gibbs, Parkleaze, Ewen, Cirencester; *m* 1955, Davina Jean Merry; two *s* one *d. Educ:* Eton Coll.; RMC Sandhurst. Commnd into 60th Rifles, 1940; served War of 1939-45 in N Africa, Italy and NW Europe. Comd 3rd Bn Parachute Regt, 1960-62; GSO1, Brit. Army Staff, Washington, 1962-63; Comdr 16 Para. Bde, 1963-66; Chief of Staff, HQ Middle East, 1966-67; IDC 1968; Commander, British Forces, Gulf, 1969-71; GOC 1 (British) Corps, 1972-74; C-in-C, UKLF, 1974-76. Colonel Commandant: 2nd Bn The Royal Green Jackets, 1971-78; Parachute Regt, 1972-77. Salisbury Regional Dir, Lloyds Bank, 1979-. DL Wilts, 1980. *Recreation:* out-of-door sports. *Address:* Patney Rectory, Devizes, Wilts. *Club:* Turf.
See also M. St J. V. Gibbs.

GIBBS, Stephen, CBE 1981; Chairman, Turner & Newall Ltd, since 1979; *b* 12 Feb. 1920; *s* of Arthur Edwin Gibbs and Anne Gibbs; *m* 1941, Louise Pattison; one *s* one *d. Educ:* Oldbury Grammar Sch.; Birmingham Univ. (part-time). FPRI. British Industrial Plastics Ltd, Oldbury, Warley, W Midlands, 1936-39. Served RASC, 1939-46. British Industrial Plastics Ltd: Technical Dept, 1946-52; General Sales Manager, 1952-56; Director, and Chm. of subsidiary cos, 1956-68; Turner & Newall Ltd, Manchester: Director, 1968-72; Man. Dir, 1972-76; Dep. Chm., 1976-79. Chm., Energy Policy Cttee, CBI, 1981-. *Address:* Nicholas Green, Pumphouse Lane, Hanbury, near Droitwich, Worcs WR9 7EB. *T:* Hanbury 423.

GIBRALTAR, Bishop of, (RC), since 1973; **Rt. Rev. Edward Rapallo,** DCnL; *b* 19 March 1914; *s* of Edward and Anne Rapallo. *Educ:* Pontifical Univ. of Salamanca, Spain; Lateran Univ., Rome (DCnL). Priest, 1937; Port Chaplain, Gibraltar, 1939-45; Cathedral Choir Master, 1945-54; Diocesan Chancellor, 1955-67; Cathedral Administrator, 1956-72; Vicar General, 1967-72; Vicar Capitular 1973. Chaplain of HH The Pope, 1960; Hon. Prelate of HH The Pope, 1964. *Recreations:* reading, music. *Address:* Bishop's House, 4A Engineer Road, Gibraltar. *T:* 74995 and 4688.

GIBRALTAR, Dean of; *see* Pope, Very Rev. R. W.

GIBRALTAR IN EUROPE, Bishop of, since 1980; **Rt. Rev. John Richard Satterthwaite;** Guild Vicar, St Dunstan-in-the-West, City of London, since 1959; *b* 17 Nov. 1925; *s* of William and Clara Elisabeth Satterthwaite. *Educ:* Millom Grammar Sch.; Leeds Univ. (BA); Coll. of the Resurrection, Mirfield. History Master, St Luke's Sch., Haifa, 1946-48; Curate: St Barnabas, Carlisle, 1950-53; St Aidan, Carlisle, 1953-54; St Michael Paternoster Royal, London, 1955-59, Curate-in-Charge, 1959-65. Gen. Sec., Church of England Council on Foreign Relations, 1959-70 (Asst Gen. Sec., 1955-59); Gen. Sec., Archbp's Commn on Roman Catholic Relations, 1965-70; Bishop Suffragan of Fulham, 1970; Bishop of Gibraltar, 1971; known as Bishop of Fulham and Gibraltar until creation of new diocese, 1980. Hon. Canon of Canterbury, 1963-; ChStJ 1972 (Asst ChStJ 1963); Hon. Canon of Utrecht, Old Catholic

Church of the Netherlands, 1969. Holds decoration from various foreign churches. *Recreations:* fell walking, music. *Address:* 5A Gregory Place, W8 4NG. *T:* 01-937 2796. *Club:* Athenæum.

GIBRALTAR IN EUROPE, Suffragan Bishop of, since 1980; **Rt. Rev. Ambrose Walter Marcus Weekes,** CB 1970; FKC; Dean, Pro-Cathedral of the Holy Trinity, Brussels, since 1980; *b* 25 April 1919; *s* of Lt-Comdr William Charles Tinnoth Weekes, DSO, RNVR, and Ethel Sarah Weekes, JP. *Educ:* Cathedral Choir Sch., Rochester; Sir Joseph Williamson's Sch., Rochester; King's Coll., London; AKC 1941, FKC 1972; Scholae Cancellarii, Lincoln. Asst Curate, St Luke's, Gillingham, Kent, 1942-44; Chaplain, RNVR, 1944-46, RN 1946-72; HMS: Ganges, 1946-48; Ulster, 1948-49; Triumph, 1949-51; Royal Marines, Deal, 1951-53; 3 Commando Bde, RM, 1953-55; HMS: Ganges, 1955-56; St Vincent, 1956-58; Tyne, 1958-60; Ganges, 1960-62; 40 Commando, RM, 1962-63; MoD, 1963-65; HMS: Eagle, 1965-66; Vernon, 1966-67; Terror, and Staff of Comdr Far East Fleet, 1967-68; HMS Mercury, 1968-69; Chaplain of the Fleet and Archdeacon for the Royal Navy, 1969-72; QHC, 1969-72; Chaplain of St Andrew, Tangier, 1972-73; Dean of Gibraltar, 1973-77; Assistant Bishop, Diocese of Gibraltar, 1977, until creation of new diocese, 1980. *Recreations:* yachting, music. *Address:* 11 Lanark Road, Maida Vale, W9 1DD. *Clubs:* Athenæum, Naval and Military.

GIBRALTAR IN EUROPE (Diocese), Auxiliary Bishops of; *see* Capper, Rt Rev. E. M. H.; Isherwood, Rt Rev. H.; Pina-Cabral, Rt Rev. D. P. dos S. de.

GIBSON, family name of **Barons Ashbourne** and **Gibson.**

GIBSON, Baron *cr* 1975 (Life Peer), of Penn's Rocks; **Richard Patrick Tallentyre Gibson;** Chairman: S. Pearson & Son plc, since 1978; National Trust, since 1977; *b* 5 Feb. 1916; *s* of Thornely Carbutt Gibson and Elizabeth Anne Augusta Gibson; *m* 1945, Elisabeth Dione Pearson; four *s*. *Educ:* Eton Coll.; Magdalen Coll., Oxford (Hon. Fellow, 1977). London Stock Exchange, 1937. Served with Mddx Yeo, 1939-46; N Africa, 1940-41; POW, 1941-43; Special Ops Exec., 1943-45; Political Intell. Dept, FO, 1945-46. Westminster Press Ltd, 1947-78 (Dir, 1948); Director: Whitehall Securities Corp. Ltd, 1948-60, 1973-; Financial Times Ltd, 1957-78 (Chm., 1975-77); Economist Newspaper Ltd, 1957-78; S. Pearson & Son Ltd, 1960 (Dep. Chm., 1969); Exec. Dep. Chm., 1975); Royal Exchange Assce, 1961-69; Chm., Pearson Longman Ltd, 1967-79. Hon. Treas. Commonwealth Press Union, 1957-67. Chm., Arts Council, 1972-77. Trustee, Historic Churches Preservation Trust, 1958; Member: Exec. Cttee, National Trust, 1963-72; Council, Nat. Trust, 1966; Adv. Council, V&A Museum, 1968-75 (Chm., 1970); UK Arts Adv. Commn, Calouste Gulbenkian Foundn, 1969-72; Redundant Churches Fund, 1970-71; Exec. Cttee, Nat. Art Collections Fund, 1970; Bd, Royal Opera House, 1977-; Trustee, Glyndebourne Fest. Opera, 1965-72 and 1977-. Hon. DLitt Reading, 1980. *Recreations:* music, gardening, architecture. *Address:* Penn's Rocks, Groombridge, Sussex. *T:* Groombridge 244. *Clubs:* Garrick, Brooks's.

GIBSON, Dr Alan Frank, FRS 1978; FInstP; Head of Laser Division, Rutherford and Appleton Laboratories, since 1977; *b* 30 May 1923; *s* of Hezeltine Gibson and Margaret Wilson; *m* 1945, Judith Cresswell; one *s* two *d*. *Educ:* Rydal Sch., Colwyn Bay; Birmingham Univ. (BSc, PhD). FInstP 1965. Joined TRE, Malvern, 1944; conducted research and later lead res. groups on aspects of solid state physics and devices, notably semiconductor devices; Dep. Chief Scientific Officer (by individual merit), 1961; Univ. of Essex: first Prof. of Physics, 1963; res. on optical properties of semiconductors using lasers; Chm. of Physics Dept, 1963-69 and 1971-76; Dean of Phys. Sciences, 1964-68; Pro-Vice-Chancellor, 1968-69 and 1974-75. FRSA. *Publications:* (General Editor) Progress in Semiconductors: Vol. 1, 1956 to Vol. 9, 1965; An Introduction to Solid State Physics and its Applications, 1974 (repr. with corrections 1976); over 70 res. pubns in learned jls. *Address:* Dunstan Lodge, Letcombe Regis, Wantage, Oxon OX12 9JY. *T:* Wantage 66531.

GIBSON, Sir Alexander (Drummond), Kt 1977; CBE 1967; FRSE 1978; Principal Conductor and Musical Director, Scottish National Orchestra, since 1959; Founder and Artistic Director, Scottish Opera Company, since 1962; Principal Guest Conductor, Houston Symphony Orchestra, since 1981; *b* 11 Feb. 1926; *s* of late James McClure Gibson and of Wilhelmina Gibson (née Williams); *m* 1959, Ann Veronica Waggett; three *s* one *d*. *Educ:* Dalziel; Glasgow Univ.; Royal College of Music; Mozarteum, Salzburg, Austria; Accademia Chigiano, Siena, Italy. Served with Royal Signals, 1944-48. Repetiteur and Asst Conductor, Sadler's Wells Opera, 1951-52; Asst Conductor, BBC Scottish Orchestra, Glasgow, 1952-54; Staff Conductor, Sadler's Wells Opera, 1954-57; Musical Dir, Sadler's Wells Opera, 1957-59. FRSA 1980. Hon. RAM 1969; Hon. FRCM, 1973; Hon. FRSAM, 1973; Hon. RSA, 1975. Hon. LLD Aberdeen, 1968; Hon. DMus Glasgow, 1972; DUniv: Stirling, 1972; Open, 1978. St Mungo Prize, 1970; Musician of the Year award, ISM, 1976; Sibelius Medal, 1978. *Recreations:* motoring, tennis, reading. *Address:* 15 Cleveden Gardens, Glasgow G12 0PU. *T:* 041-339 6668. *Clubs:* Garrick, Oriental.

GIBSON, Sir Christopher (Herbert), 3rd Bt *cr* 1931; Sales Representative, National Homes Ltd, Abbotsford, BC, Canada; *b* 2 Feb. 1921; *s* of Sir Christopher H. Gibson, 2nd Bt, and Lady Dorothy E. O. Gibson (née Bruce); *S* father, 1962; *m* 1941, Lilian Lake Young, *d* of Dr George Byron Young,

Colchester; one *s* three *d*. *Educ:* St Cyprian's, Eastbourne; St George's Coll., Argentina. Served, 1941-45 (5 war medals and stars): 28th Canadian Armd Regt (BCR), Lieut. Sugar Cane Plantation Manager, Leach's Argentine Estates, 1946-51; Manager, Encyclopædia Britannica, 1952-55; Design Draughtsman, Babcock & Wilcox, USA, 1956-57; Tea Plantation Manager, Liebig's, 1958-60; Ranch Manager, Liebig's Extract of Meat Co., 1961-64; Building Inspector, Industrias Kaiser, Argentina, 1964-68; Manager and part-owner, Lakanto Poultry Farms, 1969-76. *Recreations:* shooting, fishing, tennis, cricket. *Heir: s* Rev. Christopher Herbert Gibson, CP, *b* Argentina, 17 July 1948.

GIBSON, Rev. Sir David, 4th Bt *cr* 1926; Catholic Priest; *b* 18 July 1922; *s* of Sir Ackroyd Herbert Gibson, 3rd Bt; *S* father, 1975. Founder of Societas Navigatorum Catholica, 1954. *Address:* The Presbytery, Our Lady and St Neot, West Street, Liskeard, Cornwall PL14 6BW.

GIBSON, Vice-Adm. Sir Donald Cameron Ernest Forbes, KCB 1968 (CB 1965); DSC 1941; JP; *b* 17 March 1916; *s* of late Capt. W. L. D. Gibson, Queen's Own Cameron Highlanders, and of Elizabeth Gibson; *m* 1939, Marjorie Alice, *d* of H. C. Harding, Horley, Surrey; one *s*. *Educ:* Woodbridge Sch., Suffolk. Cadet, Brit. India SN Co. and Midshipman, Royal Naval Reserve, 1933-37; transf. to Royal Navy, 1937; specialised as Pilot, 1938. Served War of 1939-45: HMS Glorious, Ark Royal, Formidable, Audacity; trng Pilots in USA; Empire Central Flying Sch., 1942; Chief Flying Instr, Advanced Flying Sch., 1946-47; HMS Illustrious, 1947-48; Air Gp Comdr, HMS Theseus, 1948-49; Comdr (Air), RNAS Culdrose, 1950-52; RN Staff Course, 1952-53; Comdr (Air) HMS Indomitable and Glory, 1953-54; Capt. RNAS Brawdy, 1954-56, HMS Dainty, 1956-58; Dep. Dir Air Warfare, 1958-60; Canadian Nat. Defence Coll., 1960-61; Capt., HMS Ark Royal, 1961-63; Rear-Adm. 1963; Flag Officer: Aircraft Carriers, 1963-64; Naval Flying Trg, 1964-65; Naval Air Comd, 1965-68; Vice-Adm. 1967. Dir, HMS Belfast Trust, 1971-72; Chm., Man. Cttee, N Devon Cheshire Home, 1977. Mem., N Devon Community Health Council. JP Barnstaple 1973. *Recreations:* fishing, painting. *Address:* Lower Bealy Court, Chulmleigh, North Devon. *T:* Chulmleigh 264.

GIBSON, Sir Donald (Evelyn Edward), Kt 1962; CBE 1951; DCL; MA, FRIBA (Distinction Town Planning), FRTPI; Controller General, Ministry of Public Building and Works, 1967-69, now Consultant; *b* 11 Oct. 1908; *s* of late Prof. Arnold Hartley Gibson; *m* 1st, 1936, Winifred Mary (née McGowan) (decd); three *s* one *d*; 2nd, 1978, Grace Haines. *Educ:* Manchester Gram. Sch.; Manchester Univ. BA Hons Architecture; MA. Work in USA, 1931; private practice, 1933; professional Civil Service (Building Research), 1935; Dep. County Architect, Isle of Ely, 1937; City Architect and Town Planning Officer, County and City of Coventry, 1939; County Architect, Notts, 1955; Dir-Gen. of Works, War Office, 1958-62; Dir-Gen., R&D, MPBW, 1962-67; Hoffmann Wood Prof. of Architecture, University of Leeds, 1967-68. Mem. Central Housing Advisory Cttee, 1951, 1953 and 1954. President: RIBA, 1964-65; Dist Heating Assoc., 1971-. *Publications:* various publications dealing with housing, planning and architecture in RIBA and RTPI Journals. *Recreation:* model railways. *Address:* Bryn Castell, Llanddona, Beaumaris, Gwynedd LL58 8TR. *T:* Beaumaris 810399.

GIBSON, Prof. Frank William Ernest, FRS 1976; FAA; Professor of Biochemistry, Australian National University, since 1967; *b* 22 July 1923; *s* of John William and Alice Ruby Gibson; *m* 1st, 1949, Margaret Isabel Nancy (marr. diss. 1979); two *d*; 2nd, 1980, Robin Margaret; one *s*. *Educ:* Queensland, Melbourne, and Oxford Univs. BSc, DSc (Melb.), DPhil (Oxon). Research Asst, Melbourne and Queensland Univs, 1938-47; Sen. Demonstrator, Melbourne Univ., 1948-49; ANU Scholar, Oxford, 1950-52. Melbourne University: Sen. Lectr, 1953-58; Reader in Chem. Microbiology, 1959-65; Prof. of Chem. Microbiology, 1965-66; Prof. of Biochem. and Head of Biochem. Dept, John Curtin Sch. of Medical Res., ANU, 1967-76; Howard Florey Prof. of Medical Res., and Dir, John Curtin Sch. of Med. Res., ANU, 1977-79. Newton-Abraham Vis. Prof., Oxford Univ., 1982-83. David Syme Research Prize, Univ. of Melb., 1963. FAA 1971. *Publications:* scientific papers on the biochemistry of bacteria, particularly the biosynthesis of aromatic compounds, energy metabolism. *Recreations:* tennis, skiing. *Address:* Biochemistry Department, John Curtin School of Medical Research, PO Box 334, Canberra City, ACT 2601, Australia.

GIBSON, Harold Leslie George, OBE 1978 (MBE 1971); General President, National Union of Hosiery and Knitwear Workers, 1975-82; *b* 15 July 1917; *s* of George Robert and Ellen Millicent Gibson; *m* 1941, Edith Lunt (decd); one *s* one *d*. *Educ:* elementary and grammar schools, Liverpool. Officer of National Union of Hosiery and Knitwear Workers, 1949; General Secretary, 1962-75. Member: Monopolies and Mergers Commn, 1978-; Management Cttee, Gen. Fedn of Trade Unions; TUC Textile Cttee; Exec. Cttee, British Textile Confdn; Knitting, Lace & Net Industry Training Board; Strategy Working Party for the Hosiery Industry. Pres., Internat. Textile, Garment and Leather Workers' Fedn, Brussels. Hon. LLM Leicester, 1982. JP 1949-77. *Recreations:* photography, golf, music. *Address:* 15 Links Road, Kibworth Beauchamp, Leics. *T:* (private) Kibworth 2149; (business) Leicester 556703.

GIBSON, Sir John (Hinshelwood), Kt 1969; CB 1962; TD 1944; QC (Scotland) 1961; *b* 20 May 1907; *y s* of late William John Gibson, Solicitor, Falkirk; *m* 1948, Jane, *o d* of late Captain James Watt; one *s* one *d*. *Educ:*

Fettes Coll. (Scholar); University of Edinburgh. MA 1928; LLB 1931. Admitted to Faculty of Advocates, and called to Bar (Scot.), 1932. Entered Lord Advocate's Dept, 1945; Legal Sec. and First Parly Draftsman for Scotland, 1961-69; Counsel to Scottish Law Commn, 1969-77. Member: Editorial Bd, Statutes in Force, 1968-77; Cttee on Preparation of Legislation, 1973-75. TA (Royal Artillery), 1931-45 (War service, 1939-45); hon. Major. *Address:* 9 Belgrave Crescent, Edinburgh EH4 3AH. *T:* 031-332 2027. *Club:* New (Edinburgh).

GIBSON, John Peter; engineering consultant, since 1976; *b* 21 Aug. 1929; *s* of John Leighton Gibson and Norah Gibson; *m* 1954, Patricia Anne Thomas; two *s* three *d. Educ:* Caterham Sch.; Imperial Coll., London (BSc (Hons Mech. Engrg), ACGI). Post-grad. apprenticeship Rolls Royce Derby, 1953-55; ICI (Billingham and Petrochemicals Div.), 1955-69; Man. Dir, Lummus Co., 1969-73; Dir Gen. Offshore Supplies Office, Dept of Energy, 1973-76. Dep. Chm., Seaforth Maritime, 1978. *Recreations:* work, gardening, handyman. *Address:* Batworthy-on-the-Moor, Kestor, Chagford, Devon TQ13 8EU. *T:* Chagford 3433. *Club:* Royal Scottish Automobile (Glasgow).

GIBSON, John Sibbald; Under Secretary, Department of Agriculture and Fisheries for Scotland, since 1980; Member, Agricultural Research Council, since 1979; *b* 1 May 1923; *s* of John McDonald Frame Gibson and Marion Watson Sibbald; *m* 1948, Moira Helen Gillespie; one *s* one *d. Educ:* Paisley Grammar Sch.; Glasgow Univ. Army, 1942-46, Lieut in No 1 Commando from 1943; Far East. Joined Admin. Grade Home Civil Service, 1947; Asst Principal, Scottish Home Dept, 1947-50; Private Sec. to Parly Under-Sec., 1950-51; Private Sec. to Perm. Under-Sec. of State, Scottish Office, 1952; Principal, Scottish Home Dept, 1953; Asst Sec., Dept of Agriculture and Fisheries for Scotland, 1962; Under-Sec., Scottish Office, 1973-80. *Publications:* Ships of the '45: the rescue of the Young Pretender, 1967; Deacon Brodie: Father to Jekyll and Hyde, 1977. *Recreation:* writing. *Address:* 28 Cumond Gardens, Edinburgh EH4 6PU. *T:* 031-336 2931. *Club:* Scottish Arts (Edinburgh).

GIBSON, John Walter; Under Secretary, Ministry of Defence, since 1977; *b* 15 Jan. 1922; *s* of late Thomas John Gibson and Catherine Gibson (*née* Gregory), Manor of Bingham, Northumberland; *m* 1951, Julia, *d* of George Leslie Butler, Buxton, Derbyshire; two *s* one *d. Educ:* A. J. Dawson Sch., Durham; Sheffield Univ.; University Coll., London. RNVR, 1942-46. Sheffield Univ., 1940-42, 1946-47 (BSc); University Coll., London, 1947-48; Safety-in-Mines Research Estabt, 1948-53; BJSM, Washington, DC, 1953-56; Royal Armament Research and Develt Estabt, 1957-60; Head of Statistics Div., Ordnance Bd, 1961-64; Supt, Assessment Br., Royal Armament Research and Develt Estabt, 1964-66, Prin. Supt, Systems Div., 1966-69; Asst Chief Scientific Adviser (Studies), MoD, 1969-74; Under-Sec., Cabinet Office, 1974-76. FSS 1953. *Address:* 17 Lyndhurst Drive, Sevenoaks, Kent. *T:* Sevenoaks 54589.

GIBSON, Joseph, CBE 1980; PhD; CChem, FRSC; FEng, FInstE; Coal Science Adviser, National Coal Board, since 1981 (Member for Science, 1977-81); *b* 10 May 1916; *m* 1944, Lily McFarlane Brown; one *s* one *d. Educ:* King's Coll. (now Univ. of Newcastle upon Tyne; MSc, PhD). Res., Northern Coke Res. Lab. 1938; Head of Chemistry Dept, Sunderland Technical Coll., and Lectr, Durham Univ., 1946; Chief Scientist, Northern Div., 1958, and Yorks Div., 1964, NCB; Director: Coal Res. Estab., 1968; Coal Utilisation Res., 1975. President: Inst. of Fuel, 1975-76; BCURA, 1977-81 (Chm. 1972-77). Cadman Meml Lectr, 1980; Prof. Moore Meml Lectr, 1981; Coal Science Lecture Medal, 1977; Carbonisation Sci. Medal, 1979. Hon. FIChemE. Hon. DCL Newcastle, 1981. *Publications:* Carbonisation of Coal, 1971; Coal and Modern Coal Processing, 1979; Coal Utilisation: technology, economics and policy, 1981; papers on coal conversion and utilisation. *Recreations:* bridge, gardening, golf. *Address:* 31 Charlton Close, Charlton Kings, Cheltenham, Glos. *T:* Cheltenham 517832.

GIBSON, Joseph David, CBE 1979; High Commissioner for Fiji in New Zealand, since 1981; *b* 26 Jan. 1928; *s* of late Charles Ivan Gibson and Mamao Lavenia Gibson; *m* Emily Susan Bentley; three *s* two *d. Educ:* Levuka Public Sch., Suva, Auckland Univ., NZ (BA); Auckland Teachers' Coll. (Teachers' Cert.). Asst Teacher, Suva Boys' Grammar Sch., 1952-57; Principal, Suva Educnl Inst., 1957; Principal, Queen Victoria School, Fiji, 1961-62 (Asst Teacher, 1958-59; Sen. Master, 1959; 1st Asst, 1960); Sec. Sch. Inspector, Fiji Educn Dept, 1964-65; Asst Dir of Educn, 1966-69; Dep. Dir of Educn, 1970; Dir of Educn and Permanent Sec. for Educn, 1971-74; Dep. High Comr, London, 1974-76, High Comr, 1976-81. Represented Fiji at: Dirs of Educn Conferences, Western Samoa and Pago Pago, 1968, Honolulu, 1970; Commonwealth Ministers of Educn Meeting, Canberra, 1971; Head of Fiji Delegn, Commonwealth Ministers of Educn Meeting, Jamaica, 1974. Member: Fiji Broadcasting Commn, 1971-73; Univ. Council, Univ. of South Pacific, 1971-74. *Recreations:* golf, fishing, represented Auckland and Suva, Fiji, in hockey. *Address:* Fiji High Commission, 2nd Floor, Robert Jones House, Jervois Quay, Wellington, New Zealand; 16 Hurman Street, Wellington, New Zealand.

GIBSON, Col Leonard Young, CBE 1961 (MBE 1940); TD 1947; DL; Master of Newcastle and District Beagles since 1945; *b* 4 Dec. 1911; *s* of late William McLure Gibson and Wilhelmina Mitchell, Gosforth; *m* 1949, Pauline Mary Anthony; one *s* one *d. Educ:* Royal Grammar Sch., Newcastle upon

Tyne; France and Germany. Service in TA, 1932-61: 72nd (N) Fd Regt RA TA, 1932-39; Bde Major RA: 50th (N) Div., rearguard Dunkirk, 1939-40 (MBE, despatches); 43rd (W) Div., 1941-42; GSO2, SE Army, 1942; GSO2 (Dirg Staff), Staff Coll., Camberley, 1942-43 (psc†); GSO1 Ops Eastern Comd, 1943-44; 2nd in Comd 307 Med. Regt S Notts Hussars, RHA TA, France, Belgium, Holland, Germany, 1944-45 (despatches; Croix de Guerre with Gold Star, France, 1944); GSO1 Mil. Govt Germany, 1945; Bty Comd, The Elswich Bty, 1947-51; OC 272 (N) Field Regt RA TA, 1956-58; Dep. Comdr RA 50th Inf. Div. TA, 1959-61; Colonel TA, retd. Mem., Northumberland T&AFA, 1958-68. Pres., Masters of Harriers and Beagles Assoc., 1968-69. DL Northumberland, 1971. *Recreations:* hunting, breeding horses and hounds. *Address:* Simonburn Cottage, Humshaugh, Northumberland. *T:* Humshaugh 402. *Clubs:* Army and Navy; Northern Counties (Newcastle upon Tyne).

GIBSON, Hon. Sir Marcus (George), Kt 1970; *b* 11 Jan. 1898; *e s* of late Clyde Gibson, Oatlands, Tasmania, and Lucy Isabel (*née* Stanfield); *m* 1929, Iris Lavinia, *d* of A. E. Shone, East Risdon, Tas; one *s* one *d. Educ:* Leslie House Sch., Hobart; Univ. of Tasmania. LLB (Tas) 1921; LLM (Tas) 1924. Served European War: Gunner, AIF, 1917-19. Admitted to bar of Supreme Court, Tasmania, 1921; private practice, 1921-29; Solicitor to the Public Trust Office, 1929-38; Police Magistrate, 1939-42; Asst Solicitor-General, 1942-46; KC 1946; Solicitor-General, 1946-51; Puisne Judge, Supreme Court of Tasmania, 1951-68; on several occasions Actg Chief Justice and Administrator, Govt of Tasmania. President: Tasmanian Council on the Ageing, 1964-76; E-SU (Tasmanian Br.). *Recreations:* theatre, gardening. *Address:* 296 Sandy Bay Road, Hobart, Tas. 7005, Australia. *T:* Hobart 235624. *Club:* Tasmanian (Hobart).

GIBSON, Rt. Hon. Sir Maurice White, PC 1975; Kt 1975; **Rt. Hon. Lord Justice Gibson;** Lord Justice of Appeal, Supreme Court of Judicature, Northern Ireland, since 1975; Member, Restrictive Practices Court, since 1971; *b* 1 May 1913; 2nd *s* of late William James Gibson, Montpelier House, Belfast, and of Edith Mary Gibson; *m* 1945, Cecily Winifred, *e d* of late Mr and Mrs Dudley Roy Johnson, Cordova, Bexhill-on-Sea, Sussex; one *s* one *d. Educ:* Royal Belfast Academical Institution; Queen's Univ., Belfast (LLB, BA). English Bar Final Exam. First Cl. and Certif. of Honour, 1937; Called to bar of NI with Special Prize awarded by Inn of Court of NI, 1938; called to Inner Bar, NI, 1956. Puisne Judge, NI High Court of Justice, 1968-75. Apptd Mem. several Govt Cttees on Law Reform in NI; Dep. Chm., Boundary Commn for NI, 1971-75; Mem. Incorp. Council of Law Reporting for NI; Chm., NI Legal Quarterly. Chm., NI Scout Council. *Address:* 13 Broomhill Park, Belfast BT9 5JB. *T:* Belfast 666239. *Clubs:* Ulster (Belfast); Royal Belfast Golf.

GIBSON, Captain Michael Bradford; Managing Director of Racquet Sports International Ltd, since 1975; *b* 20 March 1929; *s* of Lt-Col B. T. Gibson; *m* 1953, Mary Helen Elizabeth Legg; two *s. Educ:* Taunton Sch.; RMA Sandhurst; Sidney Sussex Coll., Cambridge (BA). Commnd into RE, 1948, retd 1961. Official Referee to Lawn Tennis Assoc. and All England Lawn Tennis Club, 1961-75. Dir, Piccadilly Sports, 1980-. Mem., Inst. of Directors. *Recreations:* hunting, boating. *Address:* Olde Denne, Warnham, Horsham, Sussex. *T:* Horsham 65589. *Clubs:* All England Lawn Tennis and Croquet; Cottesmore Golf.

GIBSON, Rear-Adm. Peter Cecil, CB 1968; *b* 31 May 1913; 2nd *s* of Alexander Horace Cecil Gibson and Phyllis Zeline Cecil Gibson (*née* Baume); *m* 1938, Phyllis Anna Mary Hume, *d* of late Major N. H. Hume, IMS, Brecon; two *s* one *d. Educ:* Ealing Priory; RN Engrg Coll., Keyham. RN, 1931; HMS Norfolk, EI, 1936-38; maintenance test pilot, RN Aircraft Yard, Donibristle, 1940-41; Air Engr Officer, RNAS, St Merryn, 1941-42; Staff of RANAS, Indian Ocean, E Africa, 1942-43, Ceylon, 1943-44; Staff Air Engr. Off., British Pacific Fleet, 1945-46; Aircraft Maintenance and Repair Dept, 1946-49; loan service RAN, 1950-52; Trng Off., RNAS, Arbroath, 1952-54; Engr Off., HMS Gambia, 1954-56 and as Fleet Engr. Off, E Indies, 1955-56; Staff Engr. Off., Flag Off. Flying Trng, 1957-60; Dep. Dir Service Conditions, 1960-61; Dir Engr Officers' Appts, 1961-63; Supt RN Aircraft Yard, Fleetlands, 1963-65; Dep. Controller Aircraft (RN), Min. of Aviation, 1966-67, Min. of Technology, 1967-69, retired, 1969. ADC, 1965-66. Comdr 1946; Capt. 1957; Rear-Adm. 1966. Chm. United Services Catholic Assoc., 1966-69. *Recreations:* vintage cars, bridge. *Address:* Pangmere, Hampstead Norreys, Newbury, Berks. *Club:* Army and Navy.

GIBSON, Hon. Sir Peter (Leslie), Kt 1981; **Hon. Mr Justice Peter Gibson;** Judge of the High Court of Justice, Chancery Division, since 1981; *b* 10 June 1934; *s* of late Harold Leslie Gibson and Martha Lucy (*née* Diercking); *m* 1968, Katharine Mary Beatrice Hadow; two *s* one *d. Educ:* Malvern Coll.; Worcester Coll., Oxford (Scholar). 2nd Lieut RA, 1953-55 (National Service). Called to the Bar, Inner Temple, 1960; Bencher, Lincoln's Inn, 1975. 2nd Jun. Counsel to Inland Revenue (Chancery), 1970-72; Jun. Counsel to the Treasury (Chancery), 1972-81. *Address:* Royal Courts of Justice, Strand WC2A 2LL.

GIBSON, Prof. Quentin Howieson, FRS 1969; Professor of Biochemistry and Molecular Biology, Cornell University, Ithaca, NY, since 1966; *b* 9 Dec. 1918; *s* of William Howieson Gibson, OBE, DSc; *m* 1951, Audrey Jane, *yr d* of G. H. S. Pinsent, CB, CMG, and Katharine Kentisbeare, *d* of Sir George Radford, MP; one *s* three *d. Educ:* Repton. MB, ChB, BAO, Belfast, 1941,

MD 1944, PhD 1946, DSc 1951. Demonstrator in Physiology, Belfast, 1941-44; Lecturer in Physiology: Belfast, 1944-46; Sheffield Univ., 1946-55; Professor of Biochem., Sheffield Univ., 1955-63; Prof. of Biophys. Chem., Johnson Research Foundn, University of Pennsylvania, 1963-66. Fellow, Amer. Acad. of Arts and Sciences, 1971; MNAS 1982. *Recreation:* sailing. *Address:* 98 Dodge Road, Ithaca, NY 14850, USA.

GIBSON, Hon. Sir Ralph (Brian), Kt 1977; Hon. Mr Justice Gibson; a Judge of the High Court, Queen's Bench Division, since 1977; Chairman of the Law Commission, since 1981; *b* 17 Oct. 1922; 2nd *s* of Roy and Emily Gibson; *m* 1949, Ann Chapman Ruether, Chicago; one *s* two *d. Educ:* Charterhouse; Brasenose Coll., Oxford. MA Oxon 1948. Army Service, 1941-45: Lieut, 1st KDG; Captain, TJFF. Called to Bar, Middle Temple, 1948, Bencher 1974; QC 1968. A Recorder of the Crown Court, 1972-77. Bigelow Teaching Fellow, University of Chicago, 1948-49. Member: Council of Legal Educn, 1971; Parole Bd, 1979-81. *Address:* 8 Ashley Gardens, SW1. *T:* 01-828 9670.

GIBSON, Prof. Robert Donald Davidson, PhD; Professor of French, University of Kent at Canterbury since 1965; *b* Hackney, London, 21 Aug. 1927; *o s* of Nicol and Ann Gibson, Leyton, London; *m* 1953, Sheila Elaine, *o d* of Bertie and Ada Goldsworthy, Exeter, Devon; three *s. Educ:* Leyton County High Sch. for Boys; King's Coll., London; Magdalene Coll., Cambridge; Ecole Normale Supérieure, Paris. BA (First Class Hons. French) London, 1948; PhD Cantab. 1953. Asst Lecturer, St Salvator's Coll., University of St Andrews, 1954-55; Lecturer, Queen's Coll., Dundee, 1955-58; Lecturer, Aberdeen Univ., 1958-61; Prof., Queen's Univ. of Belfast, 1961-65. *Publications:* The Quest of Alain-Fournier, 1953; Modern French Poets on Poetry, 1961; (ed) Le Bestiaire Inattendu, 1961; Roger Martin du Gard, 1961; La Mésentente Cordiale, 1963; (ed) Brouart et le Désordre, 1964; (ed) Provinciales, 1965; (ed) Le Grand Meaulnes, 1968; The Land Without a Name, 1975; reviews and articles in: French Studies, The London Magazine, Times Literary Supplement, Encyclopædia Britannica, Collier's Encyclopædia. *Recreations:* reading, writing, talking. *Address:* 7 Sunnymead, Tyler Hill, Canterbury, Kent CT2 9LZ.

GIBSON, Sir Ronald (George), Kt 1975; CBE 1970 (OBE 1961); MA Cantab; FRCS, FRCGP; Chairman of Council, British Medical Association, 1966-71; *b* 28 Nov. 1909; *s* of George Edward Gibson and Gladys Muriel, *d* of William George Prince, JP, CC, Romsey, Hants; *m* 1934, Dorothy Elisabeth Alberta, *d* of Thomas Alfred Rainey, Southampton; two *d. Educ:* Mill Hill Sch., St John's Coll., Cambridge; St Bartholomew's Hosp., London. Gen. Practitioner, retired 1977. MO, Winchester Coll. and St Swithun's Sch., Winchester, 1950-77. Lieut-Col RAMC (Emergency Reserve), PMO Italian Somaliland, 1944-45. Mem. Council: BMA, 1950-72 (Chm., Representative Body, 1963-66; Chm. Council, 1966-71); RCS, 1962-67 (FRCS 1968); Mem., GMC, 1974-79. First Provost, SE Eng. Faculty, Royal College of General Practitioners, 1954 (James Mackenzie Lectr, 1967; FRCGP 1967). Member: Central Health Services Council, 1966-76 (Vice-Chm., 1972-76); Personal Social Services Council, DHSS, 1973-76; Standing Med. Adv. Cttee, 1966-76 (Chm., 1972-76); Adv. Council on Misuse of Drugs; Steering Cttee on Barbiturates (Chm.); Council, Med. Insurance Agency (Chm.); Medical Information Rev. Panel, British Library, 1978- (Chm.); VAT Tribunals (part time); Tribunal on Alleged Atrocities, NI, 1971. Governor, Eastleigh Coll. of Further Educn, 1977-. Mem. Ct, Univ. of Southampton, 1979-. Mem., Ct of Assts, Worshipful Soc. of Apothecaries of London, 1971 (Liveryman, 1964; Master, 1981). Gold Medallist, BMA, 1970; BMA Winchester Address, 1979 (And Is There Honey Still For Tea). Hon. LLD Wales, 1965; Hon. DM Southampton, 1980. *Publications:* Care of the Elderly in General Practice (Butterworth Gold Medal), 1956; The Satchel and the Shining Morning Face, 1971; The One with the Elephant, 1976; Adolescence, 1978; The Family Doctor, His Life and History, 1981; contrib. Lancet, BMJ, etc. *Recreations:* medicine, music, cricket, gardening. *Address:* 21 St Thomas' Street, Winchester, Hants SO23 9HJ. *T:* Winchester 4582. *Clubs:* Athenæum, MCC.

GIBSON, Thomas, FRCSE, FRCSGlas, FRSE; Director, Glasgow and West of Scotland Regional Plastic and Maxillofacial Surgery Service, 1970-80; Consultant Plastic Surgeon to Greater Glasgow Health Board (formerly Western Regional Hospital Board), 1947-80; *b* 24 Nov. 1915; *s* of late Thomas Gibson and Mary Munn; *m* 1944, Patricia Muriel McFeat; two *s* two *d. Educ:* Paisley Grammar Sch.; Glasgow Univ. (MB, ChB 1938). FRCSE 1941, FRFPSG 1955, FRCSGlas 1962; FRSE 1974. House Surg. and Phys., Western Infirmary, Glasgow, 1939-40; Asst Lectr in Surg., Glasgow Univ., and Extra Dispensary Surg., Western Infirm., Glasgow, 1941-42; full-time appt with MRC, Burns Unit, Glasgow Royal Infirm., 1942-44; RAMC, 1944-47: Lieut, rank of Major 1945; OC No 1 Indian Maxillofacial Unit, 1945-47. Vis. Prof., Bioengrg Unit, Univ. of Strathclyde, 1966-. Royal Coll. of Physicians and Surgeons of Glasgow: Hon. Librarian, 1963-73; Visitor, 1975-76; Pres., 1977-78. Hon. FRACS 1977. Hon. DSc Strathclyde, 1972. Editor, British Jl of Plastic Surgery, 1968-79. *Publications:* Modern Trends in Plastic Surgery: vol. 1, 1964; vol. 2, 1966; contrib. med. and surg. jls. *Recreations:* history, horticulture, handicrafts. *Address:* Eastbrae, 26 Potterhill Avenue, Paisley PA2 8BA. *T:* 041-884 2181.

GIBSON, Wilford Henry, CBE 1980; QPM 1976; Assistant Commissioner (Administration and Operations), Metropolitan Police, since 1977; *b* 12 Oct. 1924; *s* of late Ernest Gibson and Frances Mary (*née* Kitching); *m* 1949, Betty

Ann Bland; two *d.* Served War, Signaller, RAF, 1943-47. Joined Metropolitan Police as Constable, 1947; Inspector 1960; Supt 1965; Comdr 1971; Dep. Asst Comr, A Dept (Operations), 1974. Chairman: Met. Police Flying Club; Met. Police Modern Pentathlon Club. OStJ 1977. *Recreations:* riding, boxing, swimming, flying. *Address:* New Scotland Yard, Broadway, SW1H 0BG. *T:* 01-230 1212. *Club:* Special Forces.

GIBSON, Major William David; Chairman, W. J. Tatem Ltd, since 1974 (Director, since 1957); *b* 26 Feb. 1925; *s* of G. C. Gibson, OBE, Landwade Hall, Exning, Newmarket, Suffolk; *m* 1st, 1959, Charlotte Henrietta (*d* 1973), *d* of N. S. Pryor; three *s* one *d* ; 2nd, 1975, Jane Marion, *d* of late Col L. L. Hassell, DSO, MC. *Educ:* St Peter's Court; Harrow; Trinity Coll., Cambridge. Commissioned into Welsh Guards, July 1945; retired as Major, 1957. Dir, West of England Ship Owners Mutual Protection & Indemnity Assoc., 1959-; Chm., Internat. Shipowners Investment Co., SA Luxembourg, 1978-. National Hunt Cttee, Oct. 1959- (Sen. Steward, 1966); Jockey Club, 1966- (Dep. Sen. Steward, 1969-71); Tattersalls Cttee, 1963-69 (Chm., 1967-69). Master, Worshipful Co. of Farriers, 1979. *Recreations:* racing (won 4 Grand Military Gold Cups, 1950-52 and 1956); shooting, sailing. *Address:* Edradynate, Aberfeldy, Perthshire PH15 2JX. *T:* Strathtay 215. *Clubs:* Royal Thames Yacht, Royal Yacht Squadron.

GIBSON, Air Vice-Marshal William Norman, CBE 1956; DFC; Royal Australian Air Force, retired; Senior Air Staff Officer, Operational Comd, RAAF, 1963-64 and 1966; *b* 28 April 1915; *s* of late Hamilton Ross Gibson; *m* 1938, Grace Doreen, *d* of John Walter Downton, Sydney; one *d. Educ:* NZ; Parramatta High Sch.; Point Cook. RAN, 1936-39; RAAF: CO, Port Moresby, 1942; SASO, RAAF Command, 1943-44; SASO, 1st Tactical Air Force, 1947-48; CO, RAAF East Sale, 1953-54; Dir of Training, 1955-56; Air Cdre, Plans, 1957; CO, RAAF Amberley, 1959-62; SASO, HQ Far East Air Force, 1964-66. ADC to HM the Queen, 1955-58. Legion of Merit (USA). *Address:* 26 Hillcrest Avenue, Mona Vale, NSW 2103, Australia. *Club:* Imperial Service (Sydney).

GIBSON-CRAIG-CARMICHAEL, Sir David Peter William, 15th Bt *cr* 1702 (Gibson Carmichael) and 8th Bt *cr* 1831; *b* 21 July 1946; *s* of Sir Archibald Henry William Gibson-Craig-Carmichael, 14th Bt and Rosemary Anita (*d* 1979), *d* of George Duncan Crew, Santiago, Chile; *S* father, 1969; *m* 1973, Patricia, *d* of Marcos Skarnic, Santiago, Chile; one *s* one *d. Educ:* Queen's Univ., Canada (BSc, Hons Geology, 1971). *Heir: s* Peter William Gibson-Craig-Carmichael, *b* 29 Dec. 1975. *Address:* Cassilla 2461, Santiago, Chile.

GIBSON-WATT, Baron *cr* 1979 (Life Peer), of the Wye in the District of Radnor; **James David Gibson-Watt,** MC 1943 and 2 Bars; PC 1974; DL; a Forestry Commissioner, since 1976; *b* 11 Sept. 1918; *er s* of late Major James Miller Gibson-Watt, DL, JP; *m* 1942, Diana, 2nd *d* of Sir Charles Hambro; two *s* two *d* (and one *s* decd). *Educ:* Eton; Trinity Coll (BA). Welsh Guards, 1939-46; N African and Italian campaigns. Contested (C) Brecon and Radnor constituency, 1950 and 1951; MP (C) Hereford, Feb. 1956-Sept. 1974; a Lord Commissioner of the Treasury, 1959-61; Minister of State, Welsh Office, 1970-74. FRAgS; Pres., Royal Welsh Agric. Soc., 1976 (Chm. Council, 1976-). Chm., Council on Tribunals, 1980-. Mem., Historic Buildings Council, Wales, 1975-79. DL Powys (formerly Radnorshire), 1968. *Address:* Doldowlod, Llandrindod Wells, Powys. *T:* Newbridge-on-Wye 208. *Club:* Boodle's.

GICK, Rear-Adm. Philip David, CB 1963; OBE 1946; DSC and Bar, 1942; Chairman: Emsworth Shipyard Group; A. R. Savage, Ltd; Emsworth Marine Engineering Ltd; *b* 22 Feb. 1913; *s* of late Sir William John Gick, CB, CBE; *m* 1938, Aylmer Rowntree; one *s* three *d. Educ:* St Lawrence Coll., Ramsgate. Joined RN, 1931; qualified as Pilot, 1936. Capt. 1952; Comd HMS Daring, RNAS, Lossiemouth, HMS Bulwark, 1952-58; Pres., Second Admiralty Interview Board; Rear-Adm. 1961; Flag Officer, Naval Flying Training, 1961-64, retd. *Recreation:* sailing. *Address:* Furzefield, Bosham Hoe, Sussex. *T:* Bosham 572219. *Clubs:* Royal Yacht Squadron, Royal Ocean Racing; Royal Naval Sailing Association; Bosham Sailing.

GIDDEN, Barry Owen Barton, CMG 1962; *b* Southampton, 4 July 1915; *s* of late Harry William Gidden, MA, PhD. *Educ:* King Edward VI Sch., Southampton; Jesus Coll., Cambridge (Scholar; Class. Tripos Pts 1 and 2; BA). Apptd Asst Principal, HM Office of Works, 1939. Served War of 1939-45: BEF, 1939-40, Major 1943. Principal, Min. of Works, 1946; Private Sec. to Minister of Works, 1946-48; Principal, Colonial Office, 1949, Asst Sec 1951; Counsellor, UK Mission to UN, New York, 1954-58; Establishment Officer, Colonial Office, 1958-65; Asst Sec., DHSS, 1965-75. *Recreation:* golf. *Address:* 15 Chesham Street, SW1. *T:* 01-235 4185. *Club:* Walton Heath.

GIDDINGS, Air Marshal Sir (Kenneth Charles) Michael, KCB 1975; OBE 1953; DFC 1945; AFC 1950 and Bar 1955; Independent Panel Inspector, Department of the Environment, since 1979; Director, National Counties Building Society, since 1982; *b* 27 Aug. 1920; *s* of Charles Giddings and Grace Giddings (*née* Gregory); *m* 1946, Elizabeth McConnell; two *s* two *d. Educ:* Ealing Grammar Sch. Conscripted, RAF, 1940; Comd, 129 Sqdn, 1944; Empire Test Pilots Sch., 1946; Test pilot, RAE, 1947-50; HQ Fighter Command, 1950-52; RAF Staff Coll., 1953; OC, Flying Wing, Waterbeach, 1954-56; CFE, 1956-58; OC, 57 Sqdn, 1958-60; Group Captain Ops, Bomber Command, 1960-62; Supt of Flying, A&AEE, 1962-64; Dir Aircraft Projects,

MoD, 1964–66; AOC, Central Reconnaissance Estabt, 1967–68; ACAS (Operational Requirements), 1968–71; Chief of Staff No 18 (M) Group, Strike Command, RAF, 1971–73; Dep. Chief of Defence Staff, Op. Requirements, 1973–76. *Recreations:* golf, gardening, music. *Address:* 159 Long Lane, Tilehurst, Reading, Berks. *T:* Reading 23012.

GIELGUD, Sir (Arthur) John, CH 1977; Kt 1953; Hon. LLD St Andrews 1950; Hon. DLitt Oxon 1953; Hon. DLitt London 1977; Actor; *b* 14 April 1904; *s* of late Frank Gielgud and Kate Terry Lewis; unmarried. *Educ:* Westminster. First appearance on stage at Old Vic, 1921; among parts played are Lewis Dodd in Constant Nymph, Inigo Jollifant in The Good Companions, Richard II in Richard of Bordeaux, Hamlet, and Romeo; Valentine in Love for Love, Ernest Worthing in The Importance of Being Earnest, Macbeth and King Lear. Directed Macbeth, Piccadilly, 1942. Raskolnikoff in Crime and Punishment, Jason in The Medea, New York, 1947. Eustace in The Return of the Prodigal, Globe, 1948; directed The Heiress, Haymarket, 1949; directed and played Thomas Mendip, The Lady's not for Burning, Globe, 1949; Shakespeare Festival, Stratford-on-Avon, 1950; Angelo in Measure for Measure, Cassius in Julius Caesar, Benedick in Much Ado About Nothing, the name part in King Lear; directed Much Ado About Nothing and King Lear; Shakespeare season at Phoenix, 1951–52; Leontes in The Winter's Tale, Phoenix, 1951, directed Much Ado About Nothing and played Benedick, 1952. Season at Lyric, Hammersmith, 1953; directed Richard II and The Way of the World (played Mirabel); played Jaffeir in Venice Preserved; directed A Day by the Sea, and played Julian Anson, Haymarket, Nov. 1953–54; also directed Charley's Aunt, New Theatre, Dec. 1953, and directed The Cherry Orchard, Lyric, May, 1954, and Twelfth Night, Stratford, 1955; played in King Lear and Much Ado About Nothing (also produced Much Ado), for Shakespeare Memorial Theatre Company (London, provinces and continental tour), 1955; directed The Chalk Garden, Haymarket, 1956; produced (with Noel Coward) Nude with Violin, and played Sebastien, Globe, 1956–57; produced The Trojans, Covent Garden, 1957; played Prospero, Stratford, and Drury Lane, 1957; played James Callifer in The Potting Shed, Globe, 1958 and Wolsey in Henry VIII, Old Vic, 1958; directed Variation on A Theme, 1958; produced The Complaisant Lover, Globe, 1959; (Shakespeare's) Ages of Man, Queen's, 1959 (recital, based on Shakespeare anthology of G. Rylands); previous recitals at Edinburgh Fest. and in US, also subseq. in US, at Haymarket, 1960 and tour of Australia and NZ, 1963–64; Gothenburg, Copenhagen, Warsaw, Helsinki, Leningrad, Moscow and Dublin, 1964; produced Much Ado About Nothing, at Cambridge, Mass, Festival, and subseq. in New York, 1959; prod. Five Finger Exercise, Comedy, 1958, NY, 1959; acted in The Last Joke, Phoenix, 1960; prod. Britten's A Midsummer Night's Dream, Royal Opera House, 1961; prod Big Fish Little Fish, New York, 1961; prod Dazzling Prospect, Globe, 1961. Stratford-on-Avon Season, 1961: took part of Othello, also of Gaieff in The Cherry Orchard, Aldwych, 1962; produced The School for Scandal, Haymarket, 1962; prod The School for Scandal, and played Joseph Surface, USA tour, and New York, 1962–63; dir. The Ides of March, and played Julius Caesar, Haymarket, 1963; dir. Hamlet, Canada and USA, 1964; Julian in Tiny Alice, New York, 1965; played Ivanov and directed Ivanov, Phoenix, 1965, United States and Canada, 1966; played Orgon in Tartuffe, Nat. Theatre, 1967; directed Halfway up the Tree, Queen's, 1967; played Oedipus in Oedipus, Nat. Theatre, 1968; produced Don Giovanni, Coliseum, 1968; played Headmaster in 40 Years On, Apollo, 1968; played Sir Gideon in The Battle of Shrivings, Lyric, 1970; Home, Royal Court, 1970, NY 1971 (Evening Standard Best Actor award and Tony award, NY, 1971); dir, All Over, NY, 1971; Caesar and Cleopatra, Chichester Festival, 1971; Veterans, Royal Ct, 1972; dir, Private Lives, Queen's, 1972; dir, The Constant Wife, Albery, 1973; played Prospero, Nat. Theatre, 1974; Bingo, Royal Court, 1974; dir, The Gay Lord Quex, Albery, 1975; No Man's Land, Nat. Theatre, 1975, Toronto, Washington, NY, 1977; Julius Caesar, Volpone, Nat. Theatre, 1977; Half-Life, NT and Duke of York's, 1977; *films include:* (GB and US) The Good Companions, 1932; The Secret Agent, 1937; The Prime Minister (Disraeli), 1940; Julius Caesar (Cassius), 1952; Richard III (Duke of Clarence), 1955; The Barretts of Wimpole Street (Mr Moulton Barrett), 1957; St Joan (Warwick), 1957; Becket (Louis VII), 1964; The Loved One, 1965; Chimes at Midnight, 1966; Mister Sebastian, 1967; The Charge of the Light Brigade, 1968; Shoes of the Fisherman, 1968; Oh What a Lovely War!, 1968; Julius Caesar, 1970; Eagle in a Cage, Lost Horizon, 1973; 11 Harrowhouse, 1974; Gold, 1974; Murder on the Orient Express, 1974; Aces High, 1976; Providence, Joseph Andrews, Portrait of a Young Man, Caligula, 1977; The Human Factor, The Elephant Man, 1979; The Conductor, Murder by Decree, Sphinx, Chariots of Fire, The Formula, Arthur (Oscar, 1982), 1980; Lion of the Desert, 1981; Priest of Love, 1982. President: Shakespeare Reading Soc., 1958–; RADA, 1977–. Has appeared on television, including Great Acting, 1967, The Mayfly and the Frog, Dorian Gray, In Good King Charles's Golden Days, Parson's Pleasure, Inside the Third Reich, Richard Wagner, Marco Polo, and Edward Ryder in Brideshead Revisited, 1981. Hon. degree Brandeis Univ. Companion, Legion of Honour, 1960. *Publications:* Early Stages, 1938; Stage Directions, 1963; Distinguished Company, 1972; (jtly) An Actor and His Time (autobiog.), 1979. *Recreations:* music, painting. *Address:* South Pavilion, Wotton Underwood, Aylesbury, Bucks. *Clubs:* Garrick, Arts; Players' (New York).

GIELGUD, Maina; free-lance ballerina; *b* 14 Jan. 1945; *d* of Lewis Gielgud and Elisabeth Grussner. *Educ:* BEPC (French). Ballet du Marquis de Cuevas, 1962–63; Ballet Classique de France, 1965–67; Ballet du XXème Siècle, Maurice Béjart, 1967–72; London Festival Ballet, 1972–77; Royal Ballet,

1977–78; free-lance, 1978–; rehearsal director, London City Ballet, 1981–. *Address:* Stirling Court, 3 Marshall Street, W1. *T:* 01-734 6612.

GIFFARD, family name of **Earl of Halsbury.**

GIFFARD, Adam Edward; *b* 3 June 1934; *o s* of 3rd Earl of Halsbury, *qv* (but does not use courtesy title Viscount Tiverton); *m* 1st, 1963, Ellen, *d* of late Brynjolf Hovde; 2nd, 1976, Joanna Elizabeth, *d* of Frederick Harry Cole; two *d. Address:* PO Box 13, North Branch, NY 12766, USA.

GIFFARD, (Charles) Sydney (Rycroft), CMG 1976; HM Diplomatic Service; *b* 30 Oct. 1926; *m* 1st, 1951, Wendy Patricia Vidal (marr. diss. 1976); one *s* one *d*; 2nd, 1976, Hazel Beatrice Coleby Roberts, OBE. Served in Japan, 1952; Foreign Office, 1957; Berne, 1961 and Tokyo, 1964–67; Counsellor, FCO, 1968; Royal Coll. of Defence Studies, 1971; Counsellor, Tel Aviv, 1972; Minister in Tokyo, 1975–80; Ambassador to Switzerland, 1980–82. *Address:* c/o Foreign and Commonwealth Office, SW1.

GIFFORD, family name of **Baron Gifford.**

GIFFORD, 6th Baron, *cr* 1824; **Anthony Maurice Gifford;** QC 1982; Barrister at Law, practising since 1966; *b* 1 May 1940; *s* of 5th Baron Gifford and Lady Gifford (*née* Margaret Allen), Sydney, NSW; *S* father 1961; *m* 1965, Katherine Ann, *o d* of Dr Mundy; one *s* one *d. Educ:* Winchester Coll. (scholar); King's Coll., Cambridge (scholar). Student at Middle Temple, 1959–62, called to the Bar, 1962. BA Cantab, 1961. Chm., Cttee for Freedom in Mozambique, Angola and Guiné, 1968–75; Chm., N Kensington Neighbourhood Law Centre, 1974–77 (Hon. Sec., 1970–74); Chm., Legal Action Gp, 1978–. *Heir: s* Hon. Thomas Adam Gifford, *b* 1 Dec. 1967. *Address:* 35 Wellington Street, WC2. *T:* 01-836 5917.

GIFFORD, Prof. Charles Henry; Winterstoke Professor of English, University of Bristol, 1967–75, Professor of English and Comparative Literature, Jan.–July 1976, retired; *b* 17 June 1913; *s* of Walter Stanley Gifford and Constance Lena Gifford (*née* Henry); *m* 1938, Mary Rosamond van Ingen; one *s* one *d. Educ:* Harrow Sch.; Christ Church, Oxford. BA 1936, MA 1946. War Service, 1940–46, Royal Armoured Corps; Univ. of Bristol: Asst Lectr, 1946; Sen. Lectr, 1955; Prof. of Modern English Literature, 1963. Gen. Editor, Cambridge Studies in Russian Literature, 1980–. *Publications:* The Hero of his Time, 1950; (with Charles Tomlinson) Castilian Ilexes: versions from Antonio Machado, 1963; The Novel in Russia, 1964; Comparative Literature, 1969; Tolstoy: a critical anthology, 1971; Pasternak: a critical study, 1977; Tolstoy, 1982; articles and reviews on English and comparative literature. *Address:* 10 Hyland Grove, Bristol BS9 3NR. *T:* Bristol 502504.

GIFFORD, (James) Morris, CBE 1973; FCIT; Director-General, National Ports Council, 1963–78 (Member of Council, 1964–78); *b* 25 March 1922; *y s* of Frederick W. Gifford, Dunfermline; *m* 1943, Margaret Lowe Shaw, MA, Dunfermline; two *s* one *d. Educ:* Dunfermline High Sch. (Dux 1939); Edinburgh Univ. (First Bursar). MA Hons Classics, 1946. Lieut RA, 1942–45. Called to Bar, Middle Temple, 1951. Shipping Fedn, 1946–55: Asst Sec., Mersey, 1948–50 and Thames, 1950–53; Sec., Clyde, 1954–55; Gen. Man., Nat. Assoc. of Port Employers, and Mem. Nat. Dock Labour Bd, 1955–63. Vice-Pres., CIT, 1975, Pres., 1976. *Recreations:* crosswords, reading, gardening. *Address:* 15 Bourne Avenue, Southgate, N14 6PB. *T:* 01-886 1757. *Club:* Oriental (Chm., 1978–79).

GIGGALL, Rt. Rev. George Kenneth, OBE 1961; Assistant Bishop, Diocese of Blackburn, since 1982; *b* 15 April 1914; *s* of Arthur William and Matilda Hannah Giggall; unmarried. *Educ:* Manchester Central High Sch.; Univ. of Manchester; St Chad's Coll., Univ. of Durham. BA, DipTheol. Deacon, 1939; Priest, 1940. Curate of St Alban's Cheetwood, Dio. Manchester, 1939–41, St Elisabeth's Reddish, 1941–45; Chaplain, RN, 1945; HMS Braganza, 1945; 34th Amphibious Support Regt, RM, 1945–46; Chaplain, Sch. of Combined Ops, 1946–47; HMS: Norfolk, 1947–49; Ocean, 1949–50; Flotilla Comd Mediterranean and HMS Phoenicia, 1950–52; HMS Campania for Operation Hurricane, 1952; RNC Dartmouth, 1952–53; HMS: Centaur, 1953–56; Ceylon, 1956–58; Fisgard, 1958–60; Royal Arthur and Lectr RAF Chaplains' Sch., 1960–63; HMS: Eagle, 1963–65; Drake, 1965–69; QHC, 1967–69; Dean of Gibraltar and Officiating Chaplain, HMS Rooke and Flag Officer, Gibraltar, 1969–73; Bishop of St Helena, 1973–79; Chaplain of San Remo with Bordighera, Italy, and Auxiliary Bishop, dio. of Gibraltar, 1979–81. *Recreation:* music. *Address:* Fosbrooke House, 8 Clifton Drive, Lytham, Lancs FY8 5RQ. *T:* Lytham 734100. *Clubs:* Royal Commonwealth Society, Sion College; Exiles (Ascension Island).

GILBERT, Carl Joyce; President, Association of Independent Colleges and Universities in Massachusetts, since 1972; *b* 3 April 1906; *s* of Seymour Parker Gilbert and Carrie Jennings Gilbert (*née* Cooper); *m* 1936, Helen Amory Homans; one *s. Educ:* University of Virginia; Harvard. AB University of Virginia, 1928; LLB Harvard, 1931. Admitted to Mass bar, 1931; Associate Ropes, Gray, Boyden & Perkins, 1931–38; member firm (name changed to Ropes, Gray, Best, Coolidge & Rugg), 1938–49; Treasurer-Vice-Pres., The Gillette Company (formerly Gillette Safety Razor Company), Boston, 1949–56; Pres., 1956–57; Chm. of Board and Chief Exec. Officer, 1957–66; Chm. Exec. Cttee, 1966–68. Special Representative for Trade Negotiations, Washington, DC, in Exec. Office of President, with rank of Ambassador,

1969-71. Hon. LLD Boston Coll., Mass, 1958; Hon. DSc Worcester Polytechnic Inst., 1976; Hon. LHD: Northeastern Univ., 1977; Taft Univ., 1980. *Address:* Strawberry Hill Street, Dover, Mass 02030, USA. *T:* 785 0311. *Clubs:* Somerset, Dedham Country and Polo (Boston).

GILBERT, Frederick; Retired as Special Commissioner of Income Tax; *b* North Cornwall, 15 Nov. 1899; *s* of William Gilbert, farmer, and Jessie Cleave; *m* 1st, Ethel (decd), *d* of William Baily, Launceston; three *d* ; 2nd, Blanche, *d* of William Banyard, Cambridge. *Recreations:* bowls, painting. *Address:* 2 Grinley Court, Cranfield Road, Bexhill-on-Sea, East Sussex TN40 1QD. *T:* Bexhill 211793.

GILBERT, Prof. Geoffrey Alan, FRS 1973; Professor of Biochemistry, University of Birmingham, since 1969; *b* 3 Dec. 1917; *s* of A. C. Gilbert and M. M. Gilbert (*née* Cull); *m* 1948, Lilo M. Gilbert (*née* Czigler de Egerszalok); two *s. Educ:* Kingsbury County Sch., Mddx; Emmanuel Coll., Cambridge; Dept of Colloid Science, Cambridge. MA, PhD, ScD (Cantab). Lectr, Chemistry Dept, Univ. of Birmingham, 1943-46. Research Fellow, Medical Sch., Harvard Univ., 1946-47. Univ. of Birmingham: Sen. Lectr, Chemistry Dept, 1947-61, Reader, 1961-69. Chm., British Biophysical Soc., 1974. *Publications:* articles and papers in scientific jls. *Recreations:* travel, listening to classical music, photography. *Address:* 194 Selly Park Road, Birmingham B29 7HY. *T:* 021-472 0755.

GILBERT, Maj.-Gen. Glyn Charles Anglim, CB 1974; MC 1944; Director, Fitness for Industry Ltd, since 1981; *b* 15 Aug. 1920; *s* of C. G. G. Gilbert, OBE, MC, and H. M. Gilbert, MBE; *m* 1943, Heather Mary Jackson; three *s* one *d. Educ:* Eastbourne Coll.; RMC Sandhurst. Commnd 1939; served with 2nd Lincolns, 1940-47, NW Europe and Palestine; Instructor, Sch. of Infantry, 1948-50; 3rd Bn Para. Regt, 1951; Staff Coll., 1952; staff and regimental appts in MoD, Airborne Forces, Royal Lincolns and Para. Regt, 1952-66, Cyprus, Egypt and Malaya; idc 1966; comd Sch. of Infantry, 1967-70; GOC 3rd Div., 1970-72; Comdt, Joint Warfare Estab., 1972-74, retired. *Recreation:* following the sun. *Address:* c/o Lloyds Bank Ltd, Warminster, Wilts. *Clubs:* Army and Navy; Royal Bermuda Yacht.

GILBERT, Hugh Campbell; Chairman and Chief Executive Officer, Price & Pierce (Holding Co.) Ltd, since 1972; Director, Tozer Kemsley & Millbourn (Holdings) Ltd, since 1971; *b* 25 March 1926; *s* of Hugh Gilbert and Nessie Campbell; *m* 1956, Beti Gwenllian, *d* of Prof. Henry Lewis, CBE. *Educ:* John Neilson High Sch.; Univ. of Glasgow (MA 1st Cl. Hons Pol. Econ.). Mil. Service in Scots Gds, then in Argyll and Sutherland Highlanders, Europe and ME, 1944-48; Territorial Service with 5/6 Argyll and Sutherland Highlanders (Captain), 1948-53. Imperial Chemical Industries, 1951-53; PA Management Consultants Ltd, 1953-62; Dir, Blyth, Greene, Jourdain & Co. Ltd, 1962-81; Man. Dir, Price & Pierce (Holding Co.) Ltd, 1969. Hon. Professorial Fellow, UCNW, Bangor, 1975-79. *Recreations:* racing, opera, travel. *Address:* 59 Wynnstay Gardens, W8 6UU. *T:* 01-937 3134. *Clubs:* City of London, Caledonian.

GILBERT, Ian Grant; Under Secretary, International Relations Division, Department of Health and Social Security, since 1979; *b* Kikuyu, Kenya, 18 June 1925; *s* of Captain Alexander Grant Gilbert, DCM, indust. missionary, Lossiemouth and Kenya, and Marion Patrick Cruickshank; *m* 1960, Heather Margaret Donald, PhD (biographer of Lord Mount Stephen), *y d* of Rev. Francis Cantlie and Mary Donald, Lumphanan, Aberdeenshire. *Educ:* Fordyce Acad., Banffshire; Royal High Sch. of Edinburgh; Univ. of Edinburgh (MA 1950). Served HM Forces (Captain Indian Artillery), 1943-47. Entered Home Civil Service as Asst Principal and joined Min. of National Insurance, 1950; Private Sec. to Perm. Sec., 1954, and to Parly Sec., 1955; Principal, Min. of Pensions and Nat. Ins., 1956; seconded to HM Treasury, 1962-66; Asst Sec., Min. of Social Security (later DHSS), 1967; Head of War and Civilian Disabled Branches, DHSS, 1974-79. Hon. Treasurer, Presbytery of England (Church of Scotland), 1965-77; Session Clerk, Crown Court Ch. of Scotland, Covent Garden, 1975-80. *Recreations:* keeping half-an-acre in good heart, local and natural history, choral singing. France. *Address:* 20B Westwood Park, SE23 3QF. *T:* 01-699 6227. *Club:* Royal Commonwealth Society.
See also C. R. C. Donald.

GILBERT, Prof. John Cannon; Professor of Economics in the University of Sheffield, 1957-73, now Emeritus; Dean of Faculty of Economic and Social Studies, 1959-62; *b* 28 Sept. 1908; *s* of James and Elizabeth Louisa Gilbert; *m* 1938, Elizabeth Hadley Crook; two *s. Educ:* Bancroft's Sch.; The London Sch. of Economics and Political Science, University of London. Student of the Handels-Hochschule, Berlin (Sir Ernest Cassel Travelling Schol.), 1927-28; BCom Hons London, 1929. Asst on teaching staff, LSE, 1929-31; Lecturer in Economics, Sch. of Economics, Dundee, 1931-41. Ministry of Supply, 1941-45. Lecturer in Economics, University of Manchester, 1945-48; Senior Lecturer in Economics, University of Sheffield, 1948-56, Reader, 1956-57. Mem. Editorial Bd Bulletin of Economic Research, 1949-73. *Publications:* A History of Investment Trusts in Dundee, 1873-1938, 1939; Keynes's Impact on Monetary Economics, 1982; articles in Economica, Review of Economic Studies, etc. *Recreations:* walking, hill climbing. *Address:* 81 High Storrs Drive, Ecclesall, Sheffield S11 7LN. *T:* Sheffield 663544.

GILBERT, John Orman, CMG 1958; retired; *b* London, 21 Oct. 1907; *s* of Rev. T. H. Gilbert, late of Chedgrave Manor, Norfolk; *m* 1935, Winifred Mary Harris, Dublin; two *s* two *d. Educ:* Felsted Sch., Essex; Pembroke Coll.,

Oxford. Joined Sarawak Civil Service, 1928; various posts, from Cadet, to District Officer in 1940. During War of 1939-45 served in Bengal Sappers and Miners stationed in India and attained rank of Major. Came back to Sarawak with BM Administration, 1946; Resident, 4th Div., Sarawak, 1946-53; British Resident, Brunei, 1953-58; retd 1959. Coronation Medal, 1953. *Recreations:* sailing, shooting and fishing. *Address:* Moonrising, PO Box 100, Somerset West, Cape, South Africa.

GILBERT, Rt. Hon. Dr John (William); PC 1978; MP (Lab) Dudley East, since Feb. 1974 (Dudley, 1970-74); *b* April 1927; *m* 1963, Jean Olive Ross Skinner; two *d* of previous marriage. *Educ:* Merchant Taylors' Sch.; St John's Coll., Oxford; New York Univ. (PhD in Internat. Economics, Graduate Sch. of Business Administration). Chartered Accountant, Canada. Contested (Lab): Ludlow, 1966; Dudley, March 1968. Opposition front-bench spokesman on Treasury affairs, 1972-74; Financial Secretary to the Treasury, 1974-75; Minister for Transport, DoE, 1975-76; Minister of State, MoD, 1976-79. Chm., PLP Defence Gp, 1981-. Member: Fabian Soc.; Royal Inst. of Internat. Affairs; Nat. Council for Civil Liberties; Internat. Inst. for Strategic Studies; Cooperative Members' Assoc. (Sec., 1967-73); Select Cttee on Defence; NUGMW; Chm., Labour Economic Finance and Taxation Assoc. (Sec., 1970-74). *Address:* House of Commons, SW1. *Club:* Reform.

GILBERT, Air Vice-Marshal Joseph Alfred, CBE 1974; Assistant Chief of Staff (Policy), since 1983; *b* 15 June 1931; *s* of Ernest and Mildred Gilbert; *m* 1955, Betty, *yr d* of late William and Eva Lishman; two *d. Educ:* William Hulme's Sch., Manchester; Univ. of Leeds (BA, Hons Econ. and Pol Science). Commnd into RAF, 1952; Fighter Sqdns, 1953-61; Air Secretary's Dept, 1961-63; RAF Staff Coll., 1964; CO 92 (Lightning) Sqdn, 1965-67; jssc 1968; Sec., Defence Policy Staff, and Asst Dir of Defence Policy, 1968-71; CO, RAF Coltishall, 1971-73; RCDS, 1974; Dir of Forward Policy (RAF), 1975; ACAS (Policy), MoD, 1975-77; AOC 38 Group, 1977-80; ACDS (Policy), 1980-82. *Publications:* articles in defence jls. *Recreations:* hockey, tennis, South of France, strategic affairs. *Address:* Supreme Headquarters Allied Powers Europe, BFPO 26. *Club:* Royal Air Force.

GILBERT, Martin (John), MA; FRSL; historian; Fellow of Merton College, Oxford, since 1962; Official Biographer of Sir Winston Churchill since 1968; of Lord Avon (Anthony Eden), 1977-80; *b* 25 Oct. 1936; *s* of Peter and Miriam Gilbert; *m* 1st, 1963, Helen Constance, *yr d* of late Joseph Robinson, CBE; one *d* ; 2nd, Susan, *d* of Michael Sacher, *qv* ; two *s. Educ:* Highgate Sch.; Magdalen Coll., Oxford. Nat. Service (Army), 1955-57; Sen. Research Scholar, St Antony's Coll., Oxford, 1960-62; Vis. Lectr, Budapest Univ., 1961; Res. Asst (sometime Sen. Res. Asst) to Hon. Randolph S. Churchill, 1962-67; Vis. Prof., Univ. of S Carolina, 1965; Recent Hist. Correspt for Sunday Times, 1967; Res. Asst (Brit. Empire) for BBC, 1968; Historical Adviser (Palestine) for Thames Television, 1977-78. Visiting Professor: Tel-Aviv Univ., 1979; Hebrew Univ. of Jerusalem, 1980- (Vis. Lectr 1975); has lectured on historical subjects at Univs throughout Europe and USA. Script designer and co-author, Genocide (Acad. Award winner, best doc. feature film), 1981; Historical Consultant to Southern Pictures TV series, Winston Churchill: The Wilderness Years, 1980-81; Historical Adviser, BBC TV, for Auschuitz and the Allies, 1981-82; script writer, Yalta 1945, for BBC TV, 1982-83. Governor, Hebrew Univ. of Jerusalem, 1978-. Hon. DLitt Westminster Coll., Fulton, 1981. *Publications:* The Appeasers, 1963 (with Richard Gott) (trans. German, Polish, Rumanian); Britain and Germany Between the Wars, 1964; The European Powers, 1900-1945, 1965 (trans. Italian, Spanish); Plough My Own Furrow: The Life of Lord Allen of Hurtwood, 1965; Servant of India: A Study of Imperial Rule 1905-1910, 1966; The Roots of Appeasement, 1966; Recent History Atlas 1860-1960, 1966; Winston Churchill (Clarendon Biogs for young people), 1966; British History Atlas, 1968; American History Atlas, 1968; Jewish History Atlas, 1969, rev. edn 1976 (trans. Spanish, Dutch, Hebrew); First World War Atlas, 1970; Winston S. Churchill, vol. iii, 1914-1916, 1971, companion volume (in two parts) 1973; Russian History Atlas, 1972; Sir Horace Rumbold: portrait of a diplomat, 1973; Churchill: a photographic portrait, 1974; The Arab-Israeli Conflict: its history in maps, 1974, 3rd edn 1979 (trans. Spanish, Hebrew); Churchill and Zionism (pamphlet), 1974; Winston S. Churchill, vol. iv, 1917-1922, 1975, companion volume (in three parts), 1977; The Jews in Arab Lands: their history in maps, 1975, illustr. edn, 1976 (trans. Hebrew, Arabic, French, German); Winston S. Churchill, vol. v, 1922-1939, 1976, companion volume, part one, The Exchequer Years 1922-1929, 1980, part two, The Wilderness Years 1929-1935, 1981, part three, The Coming of War 1936-1939, 1982; The Jews of Russia: Illustrated History Atlas, 1976 (trans. Spanish); Jerusalem Illustrated History Atlas, 1977 (trans. Hebrew, Spanish); Exile and Return: The Emergence of Jewish Statehood, 1978; Children's Illustrated Bible Atlas, 1979; Final Journey, the Fate of the Jews of Nazi Europe, 1979 (trans. Dutch, German, Hebrew); Auschwitz and the Allies, 1981 (trans. German); Churchill's Political Philosophy, 1981; Atlas of the Holocaust (Macmillan Atlas of the Holocaust, in USA), 1982 (trans. German, Hebrew); Winston S. Churchill, vol. vi, 1939-45, 1983; Editor: A Century of Conflict: Essays Presented to A. J. P. Taylor, 1966; Churchill, 1967, and Lloyd George, 1968 (Spectrum Books); compiled Jackdaws: Winston Churchill, 1970; The Coming of War in 1939, 1973; contribs historical articles and reviews to jls (incl. Purnell's History of the Twentieth Century). *Recreation:* drawing maps. *Address:* Merton College, Oxford. *T:* Oxford 49651. *Club:* Athenæum.

GILBERT, Michael Francis, CBE 1980; TD 1950; Partner, Trower Still & Keeling, Solicitors; crime writer; *b* 17 July 1912; *s* of Bernard Samuel Gilbert and Berwyn Minna Cuthbert; *m* 1947, Roberta Mary, *d* of Col R. M. W. Marsden; two *s* five *d*. *Educ*: Blundell's Sch.; London University. LLB 1937. Served War of 1939-45, Hon. Artillery Co., 12th Regt RHA, N Africa and Italy (despatches 1943). Joined Trower Still & Keeling, 1947. Legal Adviser to Govt of Bahrain, 1960. Member: Arts Council Cttee on Public Lending Right, 1968; Royal Literary Fund, 1969; Council of Soc. of Authors, 1975; (Founder) Crime Writers' Assoc.; Mystery Writers of America. *Publications: novels:* Close Quarters, 1947; They Never Looked Inside, 1948; The Doors Open, 1949; Smallbone Deceased, 1950; Death has Deep Roots, 1951; Death in Captivity, 1952; Fear to Tread, 1953; Sky High, 1955; Be Shot for Sixpence, 1956; The Tichborne Claimant, 1957; Blood and Judgement, 1958; After the Fine Weather, 1963; The Crack in the Tea Cup, 1965; The Dust and the Heat, 1967; The Etruscan Net, 1969; The Body of a Girl, 1972; The Ninety Second Tiger, 1973; Flash Point, 1974; The Night of the Twelfth, 1976; The Empty House, 1978; Death of a Favourite Girl, 1980; *short stories:* Games Without Rules; Stay of Execution; Petrella at Q, 1977; Mr Calder and Mr Behrens, 1982; *plays:* A Clean Kill; The Bargain; Windfall; The Shot in Question; *edited:* Crime in Good Company, 1959; has also written radio and TV scripts. *Recreations:* walking, croquet, contract bridge. *Address:* Luddesdown Old Rectory, Cobham, Kent. *T:* Meopham 814272. *Club:* Garrick.

GILBERT, Patrick Nigel Geoffrey; General Secretary of the Society for Promoting Christian Knowledge, since 1971; *b* 12 May 1934; adopted *s* of late Geoffrey Gilbert and Evelyn (*née* Miller), Devon. *Educ:* Cranleigh Sch.; Merton Coll., Oxford. OUP, 1964-69; Linguaphone Group (Westinghouse), 1969-71 (Man. Dir in Group, 1970). World Assoc. for Christian Communication: Trustee, 1975-; European Vice-Chm., 1975-82; representative to EEC, 1975-82, to Conf. of Eur. Churches, 1976-82, to Council of Europe, 1976-82, and to Central Cttee, 1979-. Member: Bd for Mission and Unity of Gen. Synod, 1971-78; Archbishops' Cttee on RC Relations, 1971-81; Church Inf. Cttee, 1978-81; Church Publishing Cttee, 1980-; Council, Conf. of British Missionary Socs, 1971-78; Council, Christians Abroad, 1974-79; Exec., Anglican Centre, Rome, 1981-; British National Cttee, UNESCO World Bank Congress, 1982. Greater London Arts Association: Mem. Exec., 1968-78; Hon. Life Mem., 1978; Chm., 1980- (Dep. Chm., 1979-80); Initiator, 1972 Festivals of London. Art Workers' Guild: Hon. Brother, 1971; Chm. Trustees and Hon. Treas., 1976- (Trustee, 1975). Chairman: Standing Conf. of London Arts Councils, 1975-78; Embroiderers' Guild, 1977-78 (Hon. Treas., 1974-77); Vice-President: Camden Arts Council, 1974- (Chm., 1970-74); Nat. Assoc. of Local Arts Councils, 1980- (Founder Chm., 1976-80); Mem., Arts Adv. Cttee, CRE, 1979- (Chm., Multicultural Touring Cttee (Concord), 1980-); Steward, Artists' Gen. Benevolent Instn, 1971-. Trustee: Harold Buxton Trust; Overseas Bishoprics Fund, 1973-; All Saints Trust, 1978- (Chm., Investment Cttee); Schulze Trust, 1980-; Vis. Trustee, Seabury Press, NY, 1978-80. Mem. Executive: GBGSA, 1981-; Assoc. of Vol. Colls, 1980-; Mem. Governing Body: SPCK Australia, 1977-; Partners for World Mission, 1979-; Governor: Contemp. Dance Trust, 1981-; All Saints Coll., Tottenham, 1971-78; St Martin's Sch. for Girls, 1971- (Vice Chm., 1978-); Ellesmere Coll., 1978-; St Michael's Sch., Petworth, 1978- (rep. to GBGSA and to ISCO); Roehampton Inst., 1978- (rep. to Assoc. of Vol. Colls); Fellow, Corp. of SS Mary and Nicholas (Woodard Schs), 1972- (Mem. Exec., 1981-; Chm., S Div. Res. Cttee, 1972-). Freeman, City of London, 1966; Liveryman, Worshipful Co. of Woolmen (Mem. Ct, 1981-); Parish Clerk, All Hallows, Bread Street; Mem., Worshipful Co. of Parish Clerks. Lord of the Manor of Cantley Netherhall, Norfolk. FRSA 1978; FBIM 1982; FInstD 1982. Order of St Vladimir, 1977. *Publications:* articles in various jls. *Recreations:* walking, reading, travel (over 100 countries), enjoying the Arts, golf. *Address:* 3 The Mount Square, NW3 6SU. *T:* 01-794 8807. *Clubs:* Athenæum; Walton Heath Golf.

GILBERT, Ronald Stuart J.; *see* Johnson-Gilbert.

GILBERT, Stuart William; Director, Department for National Savings, since 1981 (Deputy Secretary); *b* 2 Aug. 1926; *s* of Rodney Stuart Gilbert and Ella Edith (*née* Esgate); *m* 1955, Marjorie Laws Vallance; one *s* one *d*. *Educ:* Maidstone Grammar Sch.; Emmanuel Coll., Cambridge (Open Exhibnr and State Scholar; BA). Served RAF, 1944-47. Asst Principal, Min. of Health, 1949; Asst Private Sec.: to Minister of Housing and Local Govt, 1952; to Parly Sec., 1954; Principal, 1955; Sec., Parker Morris Cttee on Housing Standards, 1958-61; Rapporteur to ECE Housing Cttee, 1959-61; Reporter to ILO Conf. on Workers' Housing, 1960; Asst Sec., Local Govt Finance Div., 1964; Under-Sec., DoE, 1970-80 (for New Towns, 1970, Business Rents, 1973, Construction Industries, 1974, Housing, 1974, Planning Land Use, 1977); Dep. Dir, Dept for Nat. Savings, 1980-81. *Recreations:* sailing, music, woodwork. *Address:* 3 Westmoat Close, Beckenham, Kent. *T:* 01-650 7213. *Club:* United Oxford & Cambridge University.

GILBERT, Prof. Walter, DPhil; American Cancer Society Professor of Molecular Biology, Harvard University, since 1972; *b* Boston, 21 March 1932; *s* of Richard V. Gilbert and Emma (*née* Cohen); *m* 1953, Celia Stone; one *s* one *d*. *Educ:* Harvard Coll. (AB *summa cum laude* Chem. and Phys., 1953); Harvard Univ. (AM Phys., 1954); Cambridge Univ. (DPhil Maths, 1957). National Science Foundn pre-doctoral Fellow, Harvard Univ. and Cambridge Univ., 1953-57, post-doctoral Fellow in Phys., Harvard, 1957-58; Harvard University: Lectr in Phys., 1958-59; Asst Prof. in Phys., 1959-64; Associate Prof. of Biophys., 1964-68; Prof. of Biochem., 1968-72; Guggenheim Fellow, Paris, 1968-69. Member: Amer. Acad. of Arts and Sciences, 1968; National Acad. of Sciences, 1976; Amer. Phys. Soc.; Amer. Soc. of Biol Chemists.

Lectures: V. D. Mattia, Roche Inst. of Molecular Biol., 1976; Smith, Kline and French, Univ. of Calif, Berkeley, 1977. Hon. DSc: Chicago, 1978; Columbia, 1978; Rochester, 1979. Many prizes and awards, incl. (jtly) Nobel Prize for Chemistry, 1980. *Publications:* chapters, articles and papers on theoretical physics and molecular biology. *Address:* Biological Laboratories, Harvard University, 16 Divinity Avenue, Cambridge, Mass 02138, USA. *T:* (617) 495-4795; 107 Upland Road, Cambridge, Mass 02140. *T:* (617) 864-8778.

GILBERT, Brig. Sir William (Herbert Ellery), KBE 1976 (OBE 1945); DSO 1944; Director, New Zealand Security Intelligence Service, 1956-76, retired; *b* 20 July 1916; *s* of Ellery George Gilbert and Nellie (*née* Hall); *m* 1944, Patricia Caroline Anson Farrer; two *s* one *d*. *Educ:* Wanganui Collegiate Sch., NZ; RMC, Duntroon, Australia. NZ Regular Army, 1937-56; War Service with 2NZEF, ME and Italy, 1940-45; retd, Brig. Bronze Star, USA, 1945. *Recreations:* golf, fishing, gardening. *Address:* 38 Chatsworth Road, Silverstream, New Zealand. *T:* Wellington 286570. *Clubs:* Wellington, Wellington Golf (NZ).

GILBERTSON, Sir Geoffrey, Kt 1981; CBE 1972; *b* 29 May 1918; *s* of A. J. Gilbertson and M. O. Gilbertson; *m* 1940, Dorothy Ness Barkes; four *c*. *Educ:* Durham Sch.; Jesus Coll., Cambridge. Served War, 4th/7th Royal Dragoon Guards, 1940-45, Captain. Imperial Chemical Industries, 1946-74: Director, Agricl Div., 1960-67; Plant Protection Ltd, 1964-67; Group General Manager, 1967-74. Dir, Guildway Ltd. Member, Pay Board, 1973-74. Chairman: NEDC (Ship building), 1974-77; Nat. Adv. Cttee, Employment of Disabled People, 1975-81; Fit for Work Award Scheme, 1980-. FRSA; FIPM. Croix de Guerre (Gold Star), 1944. *Recreation:* fishing. *Address:* Greta Bridge, Barnard Castle, County Durham DL12 9SD. *T:* Teesdale 27276. *Clubs:* Cavalry and Guards, Flyfishers'; Leander (Henley-on-Thames); Hawks (Cambridge).

GILBEY, family name of **Baron Vaux of Harrowden.**

GILBEY, Sir (Walter) Derek, 3rd Bt, *cr* 1893; Lieut 2nd Bn Black Watch; *b* 11 March 1913; *s* of Walter Ewart Gilbey and Dorothy Coysgarne Sim; *S* grandfather, 1945; *m* 1948, Elizabeth Mary, *d* of Col Keith Campbell and Marjorie Syfret; one *s* one *d*. *Educ:* Eton. Served War of 1939-45 (prisoner). *Heir: s* Walter Gavin Gilbey [*b* 14 April 1949; *m* 1980, Mary Pacetti, *d* of late William E. E. Pacetti and of Mrs Mary Greer]. *Address:* Grovelands, Wineham, near Henfield, Sussex. *T:* Bolney 311. *Club:* Portland.

GILCHRIST, Sir Andrew (Graham), KCMG 1964 (CMG 1956); HM Diplomatic Service, retired; formerly Ambassador and administrator; *b* 19 April 1910; *e s* of late James Graham Gilchrist, Kerse, Lesmahagow; *m* 1946, Freda Grace, *d* of late Alfred Slack; two *s* one *d*. *Educ:* Edinburgh Acad.; Exeter Coll., Oxford. Diplomatic career, 1933-70, included junior posts in Bangkok, Paris, Marseilles, Rabat, Stuttgart, Singapore, Chicago, also in FO; subseq. Ambassador at Reykjavik, Djakarta and Dublin, retired. Chm., Highlands and Islands Develt Bd, 1970-76. War Service as Major, Force 136 in SE Asia (despatches). *Publications:* Bangkok Top Secret, 1970; Cod Wars and How to Lose Them, 1978 (Icelandic edn 1977). *Address:* Arthur's Crag, Hazelbank, by Lanark ML11 9XL. *T:* Crossford 263. *Clubs:* Special Forces; New (Edinburgh).

GILCHRIST, (Andrew) Rae, CBE 1961; MD Edinburgh, FRCPE, FRCP, Hon. FRACP, Hon. FRFPS Glasgow; Consulting Physician Royal Infirmary, Edinburgh; *b* 7 July 1899; *o s* of late Rev. Andrew Gilchrist, BA, Edinburgh; *m* 1st, 1931, Emily Faulds (*d* 1967), *yr d* of late W. Work Slater, Edinburgh and Innerleithen, Peeblesshire; one *s* one *d* ; 2nd, 1975, Elspeth, widow of Dr Arthur Wightman. *Educ:* Belfast, Edinburgh, New York. RFA 1917-18; MB, ChB Edinburgh, 1921; Lauder-Brunton Prizeman, Milner-Fothergill Medallist, McCunn Medical Res. Scholar, Edinburgh Univ., 1924; MD (gold medal) 1933; resident hospital appointments at Addenbrooke's Hosp., Cambridge, Princess Elizabeth Hosp. for Children, London, E1, and at Royal Infirmary, Edinburgh, 1922-24; Resident Asst Physician Rockefeller Hosp. for Medical Research, New York, USA, 1926-27; Asst Physician, 1930; Physician, Royal Infirmary, Edinburgh, 1939-64; Gibson Lecturer RCP Edinburgh, 1944; Lecturer: Canadian Heart Assoc., 1955; Litchfield Lecture, Oxford Univ., 1956; Californian Heart Assoc., 1957; St Cyres Lecturer, National Heart Hosp., London, 1957; Hall Overseas Lecturer, Australia and NZ, 1959; Carey Coombs Memorial Lecture, Bristol Univ., 1960; Gwladys and Olwen Williams Lecture in Medicine, Liverpool Univ., 1961; Orford Lectr, College of Physicians of S Africa, 1962. William Cullen Prize, 1962 (shared). Pres. of the Royal College of Physicians of Edinburgh, 1957-60. Examr in Med. in Univs of Edinburgh, Glasgow, Aberdeen, St Andrews, East Africa (Makerere Coll.), and Baghdad. Mem. Assoc. of Physicians of Gt Brit., of Brit. Cardiac Soc. Hon. Mem. Cardiac Soc. of Australia and NZ. *Publications:* numerous contributions on disorders of heart and circulation, in British and American medical journals. *Recreation:* fishing. *Address:* Grovedale, 16 Winton Terrace, Edinburgh EH10 7AP. *T:* 031-445 1119. *Clubs:* Flyfishers'; New (Edinburgh).

GILCHRIST, Archibald; Managing Director, Vosper Private, Singapore, since 1980; *b* 17 Dec. 1929; *m* 1958, Elizabeth Jean Greenlees; two *s* one *d*. *Educ:* Loretto; Pembroke Coll., Cambridge (MA). Barclay Curle & Co. Ltd, Glasgow, 1954-64, various managerial posts; ultimately Dir, Swan Hunter Group; Brown Bros & Co. Ltd, Edinburgh, 1964-72: Dep. Man. Dir, 1964;

Man. Dir, 1969; Man. Dir, Govan Shipbuilders, 1971-79, Chm., 1978-79. Dir, Scottish Opera. Chm. of Governors, Cargilfield Sch. *Recreations:* golf, shooting, fishing, music. *Address:* Inchmaholm, Barnton Avenue, Edinburgh. *T:* 031-336 4288; 19 Victoria Park Road, Singapore 1026. *Clubs:* Western (Glasgow); Hon. Company of Edinburgh Golfers.

GILCHRIST, Sir (James) Finlay (Elder), Kt 1978; OBE 1946; Life President and Director, Harrisons & Crosfield plc (Chairman, 1962-77); *b* 13 Aug. 1903; *s* of late Thomas Dunlop Gilchrist and Agnes Crawford Elder; *m* 1933, Dorothy Joan Narizzano; two *s* one *d*. *Educ:* Glasgow Academy. *Address:* South Cottage, Hapstead Farm, Ardingly, Sussex. *T:* Ardingly 892368. *Club:* East India.

GILCHRIST, John; a Recorder of the Crown Court, since 1980; *b* 28 Nov. 1929; *s* of late John T. Gilchrist and of Dorothy Gilchrist; *m* Margaret Mercedes Summers, MD, FRCPath; one *s*. Schoolmaster, 1958-64. Called to the Bar, Gray's Inn, 1967. *Recreation:* sailing. *Address:* 10 Ridgeway Avenue, Marford, Clwyd. *Clubs:* Cruising Association; Athenæum (Liverpool); Bar Yacht, Royal Anglesey Yacht.

GILCHRIST, Rae; *see* Gilchrist, A. R.

GILDER, Robert Charles, FIA, FSS, FPMI; Directing Actuary, Government Actuary's Department, since 1979; *b* 22 April 1923; *s* of Charles Henry Gilder and Elsie May (*née* Sayer); *m* 1954, Norah Mary Hallas; two *s*. *Educ:* Brentwood School. Liverpool Victoria Friendly Soc., 1940-41 and 1946-48. Served War, RAF, 1941-46. Government Actuary's Dept, 1948-: Actuary, 1959; Principal Actuary, 1973. FIA 1951; FSS 1956; FPMI 1980. *Recreations:* cricket, tennis, playing the clarinet, hill-walking, travel, odd jobs in house and garden. *Address:* Government Actuary's Department, 22 Kingsway, WC2B 6LE. *T:* 01-242 6828, ext. 217.

'GILES'; *see* Giles, Carl Ronald.

GILES, Sir Alexander (Falconer), KBE 1965 (MBE 1946); CMG 1960; HM Colonial Service retired; *b* 1915; *o s* of late A. F. Giles, MA, LLD; *m* 1953, Mrs M. E. Watson, *d* of late Lieut-Col R. F. D. Burnett, MC, and *widow* of Lieut-Col J. L. Watson; two *step s* one *step d*. *Educ:* The Edinburgh Academy; Edinburgh Univ.; Balliol Coll., Oxford (BA). Pres. Oxford Union Soc., 1939. 2nd Lieut the Royal Scots, 1940; attached RWAFF, 1941; 81 (WA) Div., 1943; Lieut-Col comdg 5 GCR, 1945 (MBE, despatches). Cadet Colonial Service, Tanganyika, 1947; Administrator, St Vincent, 1955-62; Resident Commissioner, Basutoland, 1962-65; British Govt Representative, Basutoland, 1965-66. Chairman: Victoria League in Scotland, 1968-70; Scottish Council, Royal Over-Seas League, 1969-70, Central Council, 1972-75. Dir, Toc H, 1968-74. Gen. Sec., Scotland, Royal Over-Seas League, 1976-78. *Publications:* articles in service jls. *Recreation:* the printed word. *Address:* 4 Royal Crescent, Edinburgh EH3 6PZ.

GILES, Carl Ronald, OBE 1959; Cartoonist, Daily and Sunday Express, since 1943; *b* 29 Sept. 1916; *m* 1942, Sylvia Joan Clarke. *Educ:* various schools. Trained as animated cartoonist; Animator for Alexander Korda, 1935; Cartoonist, Reynolds News, 1937-43. Cartoons extensively reproduced in US and syndicated throughout world. Produced and animated Documentary Films for Min. of Information, also War Correspondent-cartoonist in France, Belgium, Holland and Germany, War of 1939-45. *Publications:* "Giles" Annual, 1945-; various overseas collections. *Recreations:* yachting, workshops, farming. *Address:* Hillbrow Farm, Witnesham, Suffolk. *Clubs:* British Racing Drivers', Royal Harwich Yacht, Press.

GILES, Frank Thomas Robertson; Editor, The Sunday Times, since 1981 (Deputy Editor, 1967-81); *b* 31 July 1919; *s* of late Col F. L. N. Giles, DSO, OBE, and Mrs Giles; *m* 1946, Lady Katharine Pamela Sackville, *o d* of 9th Earl De La Warr and Countess De La Warr; one *s* two *d*. *Educ:* Wellington Coll.; Brasenose Coll., Oxford (Open Scholarship in History; MA 1946). ADC to Governor of Bermuda, 1939-42; Directorate of Mil. Ops, WO, 1942-45; temp. mem. of HM Foreign Service, 1945-46 (Private Sec. to Ernest Bevin; Mem. of Sir Archibald Clark Kerr's mission to Java); joined editorial staff of The Times, 1946; Asst Correspondent, Paris, 1947; Chief Corresp., Rome, 1950-53, Paris, 1953-60; Foreign Editor, Sunday Times, 1961-77; Dir, Times Newspapers Ltd, 1981-. Member: Academic Council, Wilton Park; Exec. Cttee, GB-USSR Assoc.; Steering Cttee, Anglo-German Königswinter Conf. Governor: Wellington Coll.; Sevenoaks Sch. *Publication:* A Prince of Journalists: the life and times of de Blowitz, 1962. *Recreations:* going to the opera; collecting, talking about, consuming the vintage wines of Bordeaux and Burgundy. *Address:* 42 Blomfield Road, W9 1AH; Bunns Cottage, Lye Green, Crowborough, East Sussex TN6 1UY. *Clubs:* Brooks's, Beefsteak.

GILES, Sir (Henry) Norman, Kt 1969; OBE 1966; *b* Northam, WA, 3 May 1905; *s* of late J. O. Giles, Claremont, WA; *m* 1929, Eleanor, *d* of late S. J. Barker; one *s* one *d*. *Educ:* Christ Church Grammar Sch., WA. Served War of 1939-45: RAAF, 1941-44; Flt-Lt (Aust. and New Guinea). Joined Elder Smith & Co. Ltd, 1922; Asst Manager for WA, 1944-47; Manager for WA, 1947-48; Asst Gen. Manager, Aust., 1948-52; Gen. Manager, Aust., 1952-55; Man. Dir, 1955-62; name changed, on amalgamation, to Elder, Smith, Goldsbrough Mort Ltd; Gen. Manager, 1962-67, Chm., 1967-76. Chm., Commonwealth Develt Bank Exec. Cttee, 1959-77; Director: Commonwealth Banking Corp., 1959-77 (Dep. Chm. 1959-62, 1967-75);

Babcock Australian Hldgs Ltd, 1959-76; P&O Australia Ltd, 1959-75 (Chm. 1969-75); Elder Smith Goldsbrough Mort Gp Cos, 1962-76; Gove Alumina Ltd, 1969-72; Reyrolle Parsons of Australia Ltd (Gp), 1971-76; Reyrolle Pty Ltd Gp, 1973-76; Chm., Farming Management Services Ltd (WA), 1977-. Member: Commonwealth Export Develt Council, 1965-70 (Mem. Exec. and Dep. Chm., 1966-70); SA Industrial Adv. Council, 1967-70; Australian Wool Industry Adv. Cttee, 1970-71. Member: SA State Cttee, CSIRO, 1962-71; Australia-Japan Business Co-operation Cttee, 1966-75; Council, Duke of Edinburgh's 3rd Commonwealth Study Conf., 1966; Acad. of Science Industry Forum, 1967-72; Pacific Basin Econ. Council, 1968-75. Vice-Pres. and Mem. Exec. Cttee, WA Chamber of Commerce, 1947-50; Mem. Exec., Nat. Council of Wool Selling Brokers of Australia, WA, 1947-53, SA, 1953-62. Mem. Council, Aust. Admin. Staff Coll., 1950-75; Fellow: Council for C of E Schools, WA, 1933-53; Australia Inst., Rotterdam, 1965-76. *Address:* 31 Strathearn, 16 King's Park Avenue, Crawley, WA 6009, Australia.

GILES, Rear-Adm. Morgan Charles M.; *see* Morgan-Giles.

GILES, Sir Norman; *see* Giles, Sir H. N.

GILES, Air Commandant Dame Pauline, DBE 1967; RRC; Matron-in-Chief, Princess Mary's Royal Air Force Nursing Service, 1966-70, retired; *b* 17 Sept. 1912. *Educ:* Sheffield. Joined PMRAFNS, Nov. 1937; later appointments included Principal Matron for Royal Air Force Command in Britain and Western Europe; became Matron-in-Chief, PMRAFNS, Sept. 1966. *Address:* 7 Hever Crescent, Bexhill-on-Sea, East Sussex TN39 4HQ. *Club:* Royal Air Force.

GILES, Robert Frederick; Senior Clerk, House of Commons, since 1979; *b* 27 Dec. 1918; *s* of Robert and Edith Giles; *m* 1948, Mabel Florence Gentry; two *d*. *Educ:* Drayton Manor Sch., Hanwell. Min. of Agriculture, 1936-39. Royal Navy, 1939-45: CO, HMS Tango, 1942-44. Various assignments, MAF, from 1945; Regional Controller, Northern Region MAFF, 1963-68; Head, Food Standards/Food Science Div., 1968-74; Under Sec., MAFF, 1975-78; Food Standards and Food Subsidies Gp, 1975; Food Feedingstuffs and Fertilizer Standards Gp, 1977. *Recreations:* walking, theatre, wine. *Address:* 8 The Ridings, Copthill Lane, Kingswood, Surrey KT20 6HJ. *Club:* Civil Service.

GILES, Roy Curtis, MA; Head Master, Highgate School, since 1974; *b* 6 Dec. 1932; *s* of Herbert Henry Giles and Dorothy Alexandra Potter; *m* 1963, Christine von Alten; two *s* one *d*. *Educ:* Queen Elizabeth's Sch., Barnet; Jesus Coll., Cambridge (Open Scholar). Asst Master, Dean Close Sch., 1956-60; Lektor, Hamburg Univ., 1960-63; Asst Master, Eton Coll., 1963-74, Head of Modern Languages, 1970-74. Mem., Council of Management, Davies's Educn Services, 1975-; Governor, The Hall, Hampstead, 1976-. *Recreations:* music, theatre. *Address:* Head Master's House, 12 Bishopswood Road, N6 4PR. *T:* 01-340 7626.

GILHAM, Harold Sidney, CB 1956; Asst Comptroller of the Patent Office, Board of Trade, 1955-59, retired. Formerly a Superintending Examiner at the Patent Office.

GILKISON, Sir Alan (Fleming), Kt 1980; CBE 1972; Chairman: J. E. Watson & Co. Ltd, Invercargill, New Zealand, 1958-81; Southland Frozen Meat & P.E. Co. Ltd, 1959-82; *b* 4 Nov. 1909; *s* of John Gilkison and Margaret Gilkison (*née* Thomson); *m* 1950, Noeline Cramond; two *s*. *Educ:* Southland Boys' High School; Timaru Boys' High School. Started work with J. E. Watson & Co. Ltd, 1930; became General Manager, 1958. Director and Deputy Chairman, Air New Zealand, 1961-75; Chairman, NZ National Airways Corp., 1967-75. *Address:* PO Box 208, Wanaka, New Zealand. *T:* Wanaka 597. *Clubs:* Invercargill, Wellington (NZ).

GILL, Anthony Keith, CEng, FIMechE, FIProdE; Joint Group Managing Director, Lucas Industries Ltd, since 1980; *b* 1 April 1930; *s* of Frederick William and Ellen Gill; *m* 1953, Phyllis Cook; one *s* two *d*. *Educ:* High Sch., Colchester; Imperial Coll., London (BScEng Hons). National Service officer, REME, 1954-56. Joined Bryce Berger Ltd, 1956, subseq. Director and Gen. Manager until 1972; Lucas CAV Ltd, 1972, subseq. Director and Gen. Manager until 1978; Divisional Managing Director, Joseph Lucas Ltd, 1978. FCGI 1979. *Recreations:* music, tennis, sailing. *Address:* Mockley Close, Gentleman's Lane, Ullenhall, near Henley in Arden, Warwickshire. *T:* Tanworth in Arden 2337.

GILL, Austin, CBE 1955; MA, Licencié-ès-lettres; Marshall Professor of French, University of Glasgow, 1966-71, retired; *b* 3 Sept. 1906; *m* 1939, Madeleine Monier. *Educ:* Bury Municipal Secondary Sch.; Universities of Manchester, Grenoble, Paris. Research Fellow, 1929-30, Faulkner Fellow, 1930-31, and Langton Fellow, 1931-33, Manchester Univ. Asst Lecturer in French, Edinburgh Univ., 1933-34; Lecturer in French, Edinburgh Univ., 1934-43; British Council Representative in French North Africa, 1943-44; British Council Actg Rep. in France, 1944-45; Official Fellow, Tutor in Modern Langs, Magdalen Coll., Oxford, 1945-50 and 1954-66. Dir of Brit. Inst. in Paris, 1950-54. *Publications:* (ed) Les Ramonneurs, 1957; (ed) Life and Letters in France, 1970; The Early Mallarmé, 1980; articles and reviews in literary and philological journals. *Address:* 15 Beaumont Gate, Glasgow G12 9ED.

GILL, Brian; QC (Scot.), 1981; *b* 25 Feb. 1942; *s* of Thomas and Mary Gill, Glasgow; *m* 1969, Catherine Fox; four *s* one *d*. *Educ:* St Aloysius' Coll., Glasgow; Glasgow Univ. (MA 1962, LLB 1964); Edinburgh Univ. (PhD 1975). Lectr, Faculty of Law, Edinburgh Univ., 1964-69 and 1972-77; Advocate 1967; Advocate Depute, 1977-79; Standing Junior Counsel: Foreign and Commonwealth Office (Scotland), 1974-77; Home Office (Scotland), 1979-81; Scottish Education Dept, 1979-81; Chm., Industrial Tribunals, 1981-. *Publications:* The Law of Agricultural Holdings, 1982; articles in legal jls. *Recreation:* church music. *Address:* 5 Strathearn Road, Edinburgh 9. *T:* 031-447 2662. *Club:* Western (Glasgow).

GILL, Cecil Gervase H.; *see* Hope Gill.

GILL, Cyril James, CB 1965; Senior Lecturer in Education, University of Keele, 1968-71, retired (Gulbenkian Lecturer in Education, 1965-68); *b* 29 March 1904; *s* of William Gill, Carnforth, Lancs; *m* 1939, Phyllis Mary, *d* of Joseph Windsor, Ramsey, Isle of Man. *Educ:* Ulverston Grammar Sch.; Liverpool Univ. Sch. Master, Ramsey, IOM and Archbishop Tenison's, London, 1926-42; Head Master, Salford Grammar Sch., 1942-45. HM Inspectorate of Schools, 1945-65; Midland Divisional Inspector, 1954-61; Chief Inspector (Teacher Training), 1961-65. *Publications:* articles on counselling and guidance. *Recreations:* gardening, walking, photography, theatre. *Address:* Grosvenor House, Ballure Road, Ramsey, Isle of Man.

GILL, Cyril James; Telecommunications Management Consultant, 1972-77; *b* 24 Dec. 1907; *s* of William and Alice Gill; *m* 1931, Dae M. (*née* Bingley); one *s* one *d*. *Educ:* Mundella Gram. Sch., Nottingham. Served Army, Royal Signals, 1942-46, to Col GHQI. Engrg Dept, GPO, 1929-48; Telephone Man., Sheffield, 1949; Princ., Post Office HQ, 1950; Princ. Private Sec. to PMG, 1957; Dep. Dir. External Telecommunications Exec., 1958; Controller of Supplies, 1959; Vice-Dir, ETE, 1964; Dir, External Telecomm. Exec., GPO, 1967-69; Dir, Cable and Wireless Ltd, 1967-69; Chm. Commonwealth Telecomm. Council, 1968-69; Chm. Grading Commn, Nigerian Min. of Communications, 1970-71. *Recreations:* gardening, golf, travel. *Address:* 65 Longton Avenue, Upper Sydenham, SE26 6RF. *T:* 01-699 2745.

GILL, Evan W. T.; Canadian Ambassador to Ireland, 1965-68; *b* 2 Nov. 1902; *s* of Robert Gill; *m* 1930, Dorothy Laurie; two *s* one *d*. *Educ:* RMC, Kingston, Ont.; McGill Univ., Montreal, PQ. Began career with industrial and commercial organs; served Canadian Army, 1940-46; Cabinet Secretariat, 1946-50; External Affairs, 1950; Canada House, 1950-51; High Comr for Canada to Union of S Africa, 1954-57; High Comr for Canada to Ghana, 1957-59; Asst Under-Sec. of State for External Affairs, 1959-62; High Commissioner for Canada in Australia, 1962-64. Pres., Internat. Salmon Foundn (Canada) Inc., 1980-. *Recreations:* golf and fishing. *Address:* St Andrews, New Brunswick E0G 2X0, Canada. *Clubs:* Rideau (Ottawa); University (Toronto).

GILL, Frank Maxey; Director, Gill & Duffus Group Ltd, 1957-80; *b* 25 Sept. 1919; fifth *s* of Frederick Gordon Gill, DSO, and Mary Gill; *m* 1st, 1942, Sheila Rosemary Gordon (decd); three *d*; 2nd, 1952, Erica Margaret Fulcher; one *s*. *Educ:* Kingsmead Prep. Sch., Seaford; Marlborough Coll.; De Havilland Aeronautical Technical Sch. Joined Gill & Duffus Ltd, 1940; served RAF (Flt/Lt), 1940-46; rejoined Gill & Duffus Ltd, 1946; Joint Managing Director, 1959; Chm., 1976-79. Hon. Trustee, Confectioners' Benevolent Fund, 1981- (Pres., 1970). *Recreations:* ocean cruising, golf. *Address:* Tile House, Reigate Heath, Reigate, Surrey. *Clubs:* Royal Cruising; Walton Heath Golf (Surrey).

GILL, (George) Malcolm; Head of Foreign Exchange Division, Bank of England, since 1982; *b* 23 May 1934; *s* of Thomas Woodman Gill and late Alice Muriel Gill (*née* Le Grice); *m* 1966, Monica Kennedy Brooks; one *s* one *d*. *Educ:* Cambridgeshire High Sch.; Sidney Sussex Coll., Cambridge (MA). Entered Bank of England, 1957; seconded to UK Treasury Delegation, Washington DC, 1966-68; Private Sec. to Governor of Bank of England, 1970-72; Asst Chief Cashier, 1975; seconded to HM Treasury, 1977-80; Chief Manager, Banking and Credit Markets, Bank of England, 1980-82. *Recreations:* family, music, gardening. *Address:* Bank of England, EC2R 8AH. *T:* 01-601 4444.

GILL, Air Vice-Marshal Harry, CB 1979; OBE 1968; Director-General of Supply, Royal Air Force, 1976-79; *b* 30 Oct. 1922; *s* of John William Gill and Lucy Gill, Newark, Notts; *m* 1951, Diana Patricia, *d* of Colin Wood, Glossop; one *d*. *Educ:* Barnby Road Sch.; Newark Technical Coll. Entered RAF, 1941; pilot trng, 1942; commnd 1943; flying duties, 1943-49; transf. to Equipment Br., 1949; Officer Commanding: Supply Sqdns, RAF Spitalgate and RAF North Coates, 1949-52; HQ Staff No 93 Maintenance Unit Explosives and Fuels Supply Ops, 1952-55; Explosives and Fuels Sch., 1955-58; Staff Officer Logistics Div., HQ Allied Forces Northern Europe, 1958-61; Head of Provision Br., Air Min., 1961-64; Chief Equipment Officer, No 25 Maintenance Unit, RAF Hartlebury, 1964-66; Equipment Staff Officer, HQ Air Forces Middle East, 1966-67; Dep. Dir Supply Systems, MoD Air, 1968-70; RCDS, 1971; Comdt, RAF Supply Control Centre, 1972-73; Dir, Supply Management, MoD Air, 1973-76. *Recreations:* shooting, fishing, squash, tennis, cricket. *Address:* Gretton Brook, South Collingham, Notts. *T:* Newark 892142. *Club:* Royal Air Force.

GILL, Maj.-Gen. Ian Gordon, CB 1972; OBE 1959 (MBE 1949); MC 1940, Bar 1945; idc, psc; Colonel, 4/7 Royal Dragoon Guards, 1973-78; *b* Rochester, 9 Nov. 1919; *s* of late Brig. Gordon Harry Gill, CMG, DSO and Mrs Doris Gill, Rochester, Kent; *m* 1963, Elizabeth Vivian Rohr, MD, MRCP, *o d* of late A. F. Rohr; no *c*. *Educ:* Edinburgh House, Hants; Repton School. Commnd from SRO into 4th/7th Roy. Dragoon Guards, 1938; served with Regt in: BEF, France, 1939-40; BLA, NW Europe, 1944-45 (despatches, 1945); Palestine, 1946-48; Tripolitania, 1951-52; Instructor, Armoured Sch., 1948-50; Staff Coll., Camberley, 1952; Bde Maj., HQ Inf. Bde, 1953-55; comdg 4th/7th RDG, 1957-59; Asst Mil. Sec., HQ, BAOR, 1959-61; Coll. Comdt RMA Sandhurst, 1961-62; Imp. Def. Coll., 1963; Comdr, 7th Armoured Bde, 1964-66; Dep. Mil. Sec. 1, MoD (Army), 1966-68; Head, British Defence Liaison Staff, Dept of Defence, Canberra, 1968-70; Asst Chief of Gen. Staff (Op. Requirements), 1970-72, retired. *Recreations:* equitation, ski-ing, cricket, squash rackets. *Address:* Cheriton House, Thorney, Peterborough PE6 0QD. *Clubs:* Cavalry and Guards, MCC.

GILL, Jack; Deputy Secretary, and Director of Industrial Development Unit, Department of Industry, since 1981; *b* 20 Feb. 1930; *s* of Jack and Elizabeth Gill; *m* 1954, Alma Dorothy; three *d*. *Educ:* Bolton Sch. Export Credits Guarantee Department: Clerical Officer, 1946; Principal, 1962; Asst Sec., 1970; Asst Sec., DTI, 1972-75; Export Credits Guarantee Department: Under Sec., 1975-79; Principal Finance Officer, 1978-79; Sec., Monopolies and Mergers Commn, 1979-81. National Service, REME, 1948-50. *Recreations:* music, chess. *Address:* 9 Ridley Road, Warlingham, Surrey CR3 9LR. *T:* Upper Warlingham 2688.

GILL, James Kenneth; Chairman, Saatchi and Saatchi Company PLC, since 1976; *b* 27 Sept. 1920; *s* of late Alfred Charles and Isabel Gill; *m* 1948, Anne Bridgewater; one *s*. *Educ:* Highgate Sch. Served RAC, 24th Lancers and Intelligence Corps, GSO II, 1939-45. Copywriter, S. T. Garland Advertising Service, 1938-39; Chm., Garland-Compton Ltd, 1970-76. FIPA. *Recreations:* the theatre, the cinema, cricket. *Address:* Davenport House, Duntisbourne Abbots, Cirencester, Glos GL7 7JN. *T:* Miserden 468; 80 Charlotte Street, W1. *T:* 01-636 5060. *Clubs:* Carlton, RAC, MCC.

GILL, Kenneth; General Secretary, Amalgamated Union of Engineering Workers (Technical, Administrative and Supervisory Section) and Member of General Council of TUC, since 1974; *b* 30 Aug. 1927; *s* of Ernest Frank Gill and Mary Ethel Gill; *m* 1967, Sara Teresa Paterson; two *s* one *d*. *Educ:* Chippenham Secondary School. Engrg apprentice, 1943-48; Draughtsman Designer, Project Engr, Sales Engr in various cos, 1948-62; District Organiser, Liverpool and Ireland TASS, 1962-68; Editor, TASS Union Jl, 1968-72; Dep. Gen. Sec., 1972-74. Mem., Commn for Racial Equality, 1981-. *Recreations:* sketching, political caricaturing. *Address:* 164 Ramsden Road, Balham, SW12. *T:* 01-675 1489.

GILL, Air Vice-Marshal Leonard William George, DSO 1945; Consultant in personnel planning, since 1973; Director, Merton Associates (Consultants) Ltd, since 1979; *b* 31 March 1918; *s* of L. W. Gill, Hornchurch, Essex, and Marguerite Gill; *m* 1943, Joan Favill Appleyard (marr. diss. 1982); two *s* two *d*; *m* 1982, Mrs Constance Mary Cull (*née* Button). *Educ:* University Coll. Sch., London. Joined RAF, 1937; served in Far East until 1942; then UK as night fighter pilot; comd No 68 Sqdn for last 6 months of war; subseq. served in various appts incl. comd of Nos 85 and 87 night fighter Sqdns and tour on directing staff at RAF Staff Coll.; Stn Comdr No 1 Flying Trng Sch., Linton-on-Ouse, 1957-60; Dir of Overseas Ops, 1960-62; Nat. Def. Coll. of Canada, 1962-63; Dir of Organisation (Estabs), 1963-66; SASO, RAF Germany, 1966-68; Dir-Gen., Manning (RAF), MoD, 1968-73, retired. Manpower and Planning Advr, P&O Steam Navigation Co., 1973-79. Vice-Pres., RAF Assoc., 1973- (Pres. E Area, 1974). FIPM; FBIM. *Recreations:* shooting, cricket, boats, amateur woodwork. *Address:* March House, 31 Park Street, Windsor, Berks. *T:* Windsor 52516. *Club:* Royal Air Force.

GILL, Malcolm; *see* Gill, G. M.

GILL, Peter, OBE 1980; Associate Director, National Theatre, since 1980; *b* Cardiff, 7 Sept. 1939; *s* of George John Gill and Margaret Mary Browne. *Educ:* St Illtyd's Coll., Cardiff. Associate Dir, Royal Court Theatre, 1970-72; Dir, 1976-80, Associate Dir, 1980, Riverside Studios, Hammersmith. Productions include: Royal Court: A Collier's Friday Night, 1965; The Local Stigmatic, The Ruffian on the Stair, A Provincial Life, 1966; A Soldier's Fortune, The Daughter-in-law, 1967; The Widowing of Mrs Holroyd, 1968; Life Price, Over Gardens Out, The Sleepers' Den, 1969; The Duchess of Malfi, 1971; Crete & Sergeant Pepper, Crimes of Passion, 1972; The Merry-go-round, 1973; Small Change, 1976; Riverside Studios: As You Like It, 1976; Small Change, 1977; The Cherry Orchard, The Changeling, 1978; Measure for Measure, 1979; Julius Caesar, 1980; Scrape off the Black, 1980; National Theatre: A Month in the Country, Don Juan, Scrape off the Black, Much Ado about Nothing, 1981; Danton's Death, The Voysey Inheritance, 1982; other London theatres: O'Flaherty VC, Mermaid, 1966; has also produced plays by Shakespeare and modern writers at Stratford-upon-Avon, Nottingham, Edinburgh and in Canada, Germany, Switzerland and USA. Television productions include: Grace, 1972; Girl, 1973; A Matter of Taste, Fugitive, 1974; Hitting Town, 1976. *Publications:* plays: The Sleepers' Den, 1965; Over

Gardens Out, 1969; Small Change, 1976. *Address:* c/o Margaret Ramsay, 14a Goodwin's Court, St Martin's Lane, WC2N 4LL.

GILL, Stanley Sanderson; His Honour Judge Gill; a Circuit Judge, since 1972; *b* Wakefield, 3 Dec. 1923; *s* of Sanderson Henry Briggs Gill, OBE and Dorothy Margaret Gill (*née* Bennett); *m* 1954, Margaret Mary Patricia Grady; one *s* two *d. Educ:* Queen Elizabeth Grammar Sch., Wakefield; Magdalene Coll., Cambridge (MA). Served in RAF, 1942-46: tour of operations with 514 and 7 (Pathfinder) Sqdn, 1944-45; Flt Lt 1945. Called to Bar, Middle Temple, 1950; Asst Recorder of Bradford, 1966; Dep. Chm., WR Yorks QS, 1968; County Court Judge, 1971. Mem., County Court Rule Cttee, 1980-. Chm., Rent Assessment Cttee, 1966-71. *Recreations:* walking, reading. *Address:* Downe, Baldersby, Thirsk, North Yorks. *T:* Melmerby 283.

GILLAM, Group Captain Denys Edgar, DSO (and 2 bars); DFC (and bar), 1940; RFC 1938; DL; Director, Homfray & Co. Ltd, retired 1981 (Chairman, 1971-81); *b* 18 Nov. 1915; *s* of Maj. T. H. J. and D. Gillam; *m* 1945, Nancye Joan Short; one *s* two *d. Educ:* Bramcote, Scarborough; Wrekin Coll., Salop. Joined RAF, 1935; trained No 1 FTS Netheravon; served 29 Fighter Sqdn, Middle East, 1937-39, Meteorological Flight Aldergrove. Award Air Force Cross, 1938. 616 Sqdn (Fighter), 1939-40 (DFC, after Battle of Britain); 312 Sqdn (F), 1940-41; HQ 9 Group till March 1941, rank Sqdn Ldr; commanded 306 Sqdn (Polish), then 615 Sqdn (F) (bar DFC and DSO for shipping attacks in Channel); RAF Staff Coll.; then commanded first Typhoon Wing (despatches); graduated US Command and Gen. Staff Coll.; commanded Tangmere Wing (Typhoons), Jan.-March 1944 (bar, DSO for attacks on V-weapon sites); promoted Group Capt., commanded 20 Sector 2nd TAF, then 146 Wing 2 TAF (Typhoon) till March 1945 (2nd bar DSO); then Group Capt. Ops 84 Group (Main) 2nd TAF. DL for West Riding of Yorks and the City and County of York, 1959. *Recreations:* fishing, shooting, sailing. *Address:* The Glebe, Brawby, Malton, North Yorks. *T:* Kirbymoorside 31530. *Club:* Royal Ocean Racing.

GILLAM, Patrick John; Managing Director, British Petroleum Company plc, since 1981; Chairman: BP Shipping Ltd, since 1981; BP Minerals International Ltd/Selection Trust Ltd, since 1982; BP Coal Ltd, since 1982; *b* 15 April 1933; *s* of late Cyril B. Gillam and of Mary J. Gillam; *m* 1963, Diana Echlin; one *s* one *d. Educ:* London School of Economics (BA Hons History). Foreign Office, 1956-57; British Petroleum Co. Ltd, 1957-: Vice-Pres., BP North America Inc., 1971-74; General Manager, Supply Dept, 1974-78; Director, BP International Ltd (formerly BP Trading Ltd), 1978-. *Recreation:* gardening. *Address:* British Petroleum Company plc, Britannic House, Moor Lane, EC2Y 9BU. *T:* 01-920 6615.

GILLAM, Stanley George, MA, MLitt; Librarian, The London Library, 1956-80; *b* 11 Aug. 1915; *s* of Harry Cosier Gillam, Oxford; *m* 1950, Pauline, *d* of Henry G. Bennett, Oxford; one *s. Educ:* Southfield Sch.; Saint Catherine's Coll., Oxford. Bodleian Library, Oxford, 1931-40 and 1946-54. Oxfordshire and Bucks Light Infantry (1st Bucks Bn), 1940-46. Asst Sec. and Sub-Librarian, The London Library, 1954-56. *Publications:* The Building Accounts of the Radcliffe Camera, 1958; articles in The Bodleian Library Record and other periodicals. *Address:* 18 Forest Side, Kennington, Oxford OX1 5LQ. *T:* Oxford 730832. *Club:* United Oxford & Cambridge University.

GILLANDERS, Prof. Lewis Alexander; Clinical Professor in Radiology, University of Aberdeen, and Consultant in Charge, Radiology Services (Grampian Health Board), since 1964; *b* 7 Feb. 1925; *s* of Kenneth John Alexander Gillanders and Nellie May Sherris; *m* 1960, Nora Ellen Wild; one *s* one *d. Educ:* Dingwall Academy; Univ. of Glasgow (graduated in medicine, 1947). Commissioned, RAMC, 1948-50; general medical practice, Scottish Highlands, 1950-52; trained in Diagnostic Radiology, Glasgow Royal Infirmary and United Birmingham Hosps, 1953-58; Consultant Radiologist, Aberdeen Teaching Hosps, 1958. Examiner in Radiology for: RCR, 1969-79; Faculty of Radiologists, RCSI, 1975-77; Univ. of Nairobi, 1978-80; Univ. of Wales, 1981-. Member, GMC, 1979-; Vice-Pres., RCR, 1981-83. *Publications:* chapter in Pye's Surgical Handicraft (1st edn 1884), 20th edn 1977; papers in general medical and radiological literature, students' magazines, etc. *Recreations:* derivations and meanings; golf, do-it-yourself. *Address:* Lyndhurst, 41 Deeview Road South, Cults, Aberdeen AB1 9NA. *Clubs:* Victory Services; Royal Northern & University (Aberdeen).

GILLARD, Francis George, CBE 1961 (OBE 1946); public broadcasting interests in USA, since 1970; *b* 1 Dec. 1908; *s* of late Francis Henry Gillard and of late Emily Jane Gillard, Stockleigh Lodge, Exford; unmarried. *Educ:* Wellington Sch., Som.; St Luke's Coll., Exeter (BSc London). Schoolmaster, 1932-41; Freelance broadcaster, 1936-; joined BBC as Talks Producer, 1941; BBC War Correspondent, 1941. BBC Head of West Regional Programmes, 1945-55; Chief Asst to Dir of Sound Broadcasting with Controller rank, 1955-56; Controller, West Region, BBC, 1956-63; Dir of Sound Broadcasting, 1963-68; Man. Dir, Radio, BBC, 1969-70, retired. Distinguished Fellow, Corp. for Public Broadcasting, Washington, 1970-73. Chm., Council, Educational Foundn for Visual Aids, 1977. Mem. Finance Cttee, Exeter Univ., 1968-; Chm. of Governors, Wellington Sch., 1974-80. FRSA 1971. *Address:* Trevor House, Poole, Wellington, Somerset. *T:* Wellington 2890.

GILLARD, Hon. Sir Oliver James, Kt 1975; Judge of the Supreme Court of Victoria, 1962-78; *b* 2 June 1906; *s* of late E. T. V. Gillard, Stawell,

Victoria; *m* 1934, Jean Gillon; three *s. Educ:* Stawell High; Melbourne Univ. BA, LLB. 2nd AIF, 1941-43, Captain. Teacher, Essendon High, 1923-26; Managing Clerk with Vincent Nolan, Solicitor, 1926-31; Barrister, 1930; Legal Office, Commonwealth Dept of Transport, 1943-44; QC 1950; Mem., Victoria Bar Council, 1957-62 (Chm., 1958-61). Chm., Chief Justice's Law Reform Cttee, 1973-78. Director: Murray Valley Coaches Ltd, 1947-50; Barristers' Chambers Ltd, 1959-62; Vary Bros Pty Ltd, 1954-62. Chancellor, Melbourne Univ., 1978-80. Chairman: Churchill Trust (Victoria), 1966-78; Youth Adv. Council, 1967-72; State Youth Council, 1973-78. Pres., Bayside Area Victoria Boy Scouts Assoc., 1963-71. *Recreations:* reading, golf. *Address:* 18 Asling Street, Brighton, Victoria 3186, Australia.

GILLES, Prof. Dennis Cyril; Professor of Computing Science, University of Glasgow, since 1966; *b* 7 April 1925; *s* of George Cyril Gilles and Gladys Alice Gilles (*née* Batchelor); *m* 1955, Valerie Mary Gilles; two *s* two *d. Educ:* Sidcup Gram. Sch.; Imperial Coll., University of London. Demonstrator, Asst Lectr, Imperial Coll., 1945-47; Asst Lectr, University of Liverpool, 1947-49; Mathematician, Scientific Computing Service, 1949-55; Research Asst, University of Manchester, 1955-57; Dir of Computing Lab., University of Glasgow, 1957-66. *Publications:* contribs to Proc. Royal Society and other scientific jls. *Address:* 7 The University, Glasgow G12 8QG. *T:* 041-334 4154.

GILLES, Prof. Chevalier Herbert Michael Joseph, MD; FRCP, FFCM; Alfred Jones and Warrington Yorke Professor of Tropical Medicine, University of Liverpool, since 1972; Dean, Liverpool School of Tropical Medicine, since 1978; *b* 10 Sept. 1921; *s* of Joseph and Clementine Gilles; *m* 1955, Wilhelmina Caruana (*d* 1972); three *s* one *d; m* 1979, Dr Mejra Kačić-Dimitri. *Educ:* St Edward's Coll., Malta; Royal Univ. of Malta (MD). Rhodes Schol. 1942. MSc Oxon; FMCPH (Nig.), DTM&H. Served War of 1939-45 (1939-45 Star, Africa Star, VM). Mem., Scientific Staff, MRC Lab., Gambia, 1954-58; University of Ibadan: Lectr, Tropical Med., 1958-63; Prof. of Preventive and Social Med., 1963-65; Sen. Lectr, Tropical Med., Univ. of Liverpool, 1965-70; Prof. of Tropical Med. (Personal Chair), Univ. of Liverpool, 1970. Vis. Prof., Tropical Medicine, Univ. of Lagos, 1965-68; Royal Society Overseas Vis. Prof., Univ. of Khartoum, Sudan, 1979-80. Consultant Physician in Tropical Medicine, Liverpool AHA(T) and Mersey RHA, 1965-; Consultant in Malariology to the Army, 1974; Consultant in Tropical Medicine to the RAF, 1978. KStJ 1972. Title of Chevalier awarded for medical work in the tropics. Hon. MD Karolinska Inst., 1979. *Publications:* Tropical Medicine for Nurses, 1955, 4th edn 1975; Pathology in the Tropics, 1969, 2nd edn 1976; Management and Treatment of Tropical Diseases, 1971; A Short Textbook of Preventive Medicine for the Tropics, 1973; Atlas of Tropical Medicine and Parasitology, 1976, 2nd edn 1981. *Recreations:* tennis, swimming, music. *Address:* 3 Conyers Avenue, Birkdale, Southport PR8 4SZ. *T:* Southport 66664.

GILLESPIE, Prof. Iain Erskine, MD, MSc, FRCS; Professor of Surgery, since 1970 and Dean of the Medical School, since 1983, University of Manchester; *b* 4 Sept. 1931; *s* of John Gillespie and Flora McQuarie; *m* 1957, Mary Muriel McIntyre; one *s* one *d. Educ:* Hillhead High Sch., Glasgow; Univ. of Glasgow. MB, ChB, 1953; MD (Hons) 1963; MSc Manchester 1974; FRCSE 1959; FRCS 1963; FRCSGlas 1970. Series of progressive surgical appts in Univs of Glasgow, Sheffield, Glasgow (again), 1953-70. Nat. service, RAMC, 1954-56; MRC grantee, 1956-58; US Postdoctoral Research Fellow, Los Angeles, 1961-; Titular Prof. of Surgery, Univ. of Glasgow, 1969. Vis. Prof. in USA, Canada, S America, Kenya, S Africa, Australia and New Zealand. Member: Cttee of Surgical Res. Soc. of GB and Ireland, 1975-; Univ. Grants Cttee, Medical Sub-Cttee, 1975-. *Publications:* jt editor and contributor to several surgical and gastroenterological books; numerous articles in various med. jls of GB, USA, Europe. *Recreations:* none. *Address:* 27 Athol Road, Bramhall, Cheshire. *T:* 061-439 2811.

GILLESPIE, Robert, CBE 1951; *b* 24 Nov. 1897; *s* of late James Gillespie and Ann Wilson Gillespie; *m* 1928, Isabella Brown (*d* 1980), *d* of late Dr Donald Murray, MP; one *s* one *d. Educ:* Queen's Park Sch., Glasgow. Joined Brit. Tanker Co. Ltd, 1922; Asst Manager, 1936; Gen. Manager, 1944; Dir and Gen. Manager, 1946; Managing Dir, 1950-56; a Dir, 1956-67; a Managing Dir of The British Petroleum Co. Ltd, 1956-58, retired; Mem., Council, Chamber of Shipping of UK, 1943-70. Served European War in Army, 1914-19; in ranks with Cameronians (Scottish Rifles) TF in UK; commnd KOSB, served UK, Palestine and France. War of 1939-45, served as Asst Dir, Tanker Div. of Ministry of War Transport, 1942-43. *Recreations:* golf, ornithology, shooting. *Address:* Craigrathan, Kippford, Dalbeattie, Kirkcudbrightshire. *T:* Kippford 653.

GILLESPIE, Prof. Ronald James, PhD, DSc; FRS 1977; FRSC; FRIC; FCIC; Professor of Chemistry, McMaster University, Hamilton, Ont, since 1960; *b* London, England, 21 Aug. 1924; Canadian citizen; *s* of James A. Gillespie and Miriam G. (*née* Kirk); *m* 1950, Madge Ena Garner; two *d. Educ:* London Univ. (BSc 1945, PhD 1949, DSc 1957). FRSC 1965; FCIC 1960; FRIC; Mem., Amer. Chem. Soc. Asst Lectr, Dept of Chemistry, 1948-50, Lectr, 1950-58, UCL; Commonwealth Fund Fellow, Brown Univ., RI, USA, 1953-54; McMaster University: Associate Prof., Dept of Chem., 1958-60; Prof., 1960-62; Chm., Dept of Chem., 1962-65. Professeur Associé, l'Univ. des Sciences et Techniques de Languedoc, Montpellier, 1972-73; Visiting Professor: Univ. of Geneva, 1976; Univ. of Göttingen, 1978. Member: Chem. Soc. (Nyholm Lectr 1979); Faraday Soc. Medals: Ramsay, UCL, 1949;

Harrison Meml, Chem. Soc., 1954; Canadian Centennial, 1967; Chem. Inst. of Canada, 1977; Silver Jubilee, 1978. Awards: Noranda, Chem. Inst. of Canada, 1966 (for inorganic chem.); Amer. Chem. Soc. N-Eastern Reg., 1971 (in phys. chem.); Manufg Chemists Assoc. Coll. Chem. Teacher, 1972; Amer. Chem. Soc., 1973 (for distinguished service in advancement of inorganic chem.), 1980 (for creative work in fluorine chem.); Chem. Inst. of Canada/Union Carbide, 1976 (for chemical educn). *Publications:* Molecular Geometry, 1972 (London; German and Russian trans, 1975); papers in Jl Amer. Chem. Soc., Canadian Jl of Chem., and Inorganic Chem. *Recreations:* skiing, sailing, hiking, Scottish country dancing. *Address:* Department of Chemistry, McMaster University, Hamilton, Ont L8S 4M1, Canada. *T:* (416) 525-9140, ext. 4506.

GILLESPIE, William Hewitt, MD, FRCP; FRCPsych; Emeritus Physician, Maudsley Hospital (Physician, 1936-70); Hon. Member, British Psychoanalytical Society, 1975; *b* 6 Aug. 1905; *s* of Rev. W. H. Gillespie, Manchuria and Co. Down, and of Isabella B. Gillespie (*née* Grills), Co. Down, N Ireland; *m* 1st, 1932, Dr Helen Turover (*d* 1975); one *s* one *d* ; 2nd, 1975, Sadie Mervis. *Educ:* George Watson's Coll.; Universities of Edinburgh and Vienna. University Edinburgh: 1st pl. Open Bursary Exam., 1924, MB, ChB (hons), 1929, Dip. in Psychiatry, 1931, MD 1934; MRCP 1936; FRCP 1962; McCosh Travelling Scholarship, in Vienna, 1930-31. LCC Mental Hosps Service, 1931-36; Lecturer, Inst. of Psychiatry, 1944-70; Dir, London Clinic of Psychoanalysis, 1944-47. Freud Meml Vis. Prof. of Psychoanalysis, Univ. Coll. London, 1976-77. Trng Sec., Inst. of Psychoanalysis, 1947-50; Chm., Inst of Psychoanalysis, 1954-56; President: British Psychoanalytical Soc., 1950-53 and 1971-72; Internat. Psychoanalytic Assoc., 1957-61. FRSocMed. *Publications:* contrib to: Recent Advances in Psychiatry, 1944; Psychiatrie sociale de l'enfant, 1951; Psychoanalysis and the Occult, 1953; The Sexual Perversions, 1956; The Pathology and Treatment of Sexual Deviation, 1964; Foundations of Child Psychiatry, 1968. Various articles in medical, psychiatric and psychoanalytic jls. *Recreations:* music, reading, walking. *Address:* 4 Eton Villas, NW3 4SX.

GILLETT, Eric; Commissioner (Ombudsman) for Local Authority Services in Scotland, since 1982; Chairman, Scottish Association of Citizens' Advice Bureaux, since 1982; Vice-Chairman, Scottish Wildlife Trust, since 1982; *b* 22 July 1920; *m* 1945, Dorothy; one *s*. *Educ:* public primary and secondary schs; Downing Coll., Cambridge. Royal Artillery, 1942; Dept of Health for Scotland, 1946; Under-Sec., Scottish Home and Health Dept, 1969-71; Fisheries Sec., Dept of Agric. and Fisheries for Scotland, 1971-76; Sec., Scottish Develt Dept, 1976-80. *Recreations:* amateur chamber and orchestral music, hill walking, ancient buildings and the modern environment, Citizens' Advice Bureaux. *Address:* 66 Caiystane Terrace, Edinburgh EH10 6SW. *T:* 031-445 1184.

GILLETT, Maj.-Gen. Sir Peter (Bernard), KCVO 1979 (CVO 1973); CB 1966; OBE 1955; Governor, Military Knights of Windsor, since 1980; *b* 8 Dec. 1913; *s* of Bernard George Gillett, OBE, Milford on Sea, Hants; *m* 1952, Pamela Graham, widow of Col R. J. Lloyd Price and *d* of Col Spencer Graham Walker, Winsley, Wilts. *Educ:* Marlborough Coll.; RMA, Woolwich. Commissioned RA, 1934; apptd to RHA, 1945; service in UK and India to 1944; War Office, 1944; BAOR, 1944-45; Instructor, Staff Coll., 1947-49; staff appts in UK and E Africa to 1955; Comd 5 RHA, 1955; SHAPE, 1958; CRA 3 Inf. Div., 1959; IDC, 1962; Chief of Staff, HQ Eastern Comd, 1962-65; GOC, 48th Div. TA, W Midland District, 1965-68. Sec., Central Chancery of the Orders of Knighthood, 1968-79. Col Comdt, Royal Regt of Artillery, 1968-78. *Recreations:* sailing, shooting and travel. *Address:* Mary Tudor Tower, Windsor Castle, Windsor, Berks. *T:* Windsor 68286. *Clubs:* Army and Navy, MCC, Royal Ocean Racing.

GILLETT, Sir Robin (Danvers Penrose), 2nd Bt *cr* 1959; GBE 1976; RD 1965; Director, Wigham Poland Home Ltd; Underwriting Member of Lloyd's; Lord Mayor of London for 1976-77; *b* 9 Nov. 1925; *o s* of Sir (Sydney) Harold Gillett, 1st Bt, MC, and Audrey Isabel Penrose Wardlaw (*d* 1962); *S* father, 1976; *m* 1950, Elizabeth Marion Grace, *e d* of late John Findlay, JP, Busby, Lanarks; two *s*. *Educ:* Nautical Coll., Pangbourne. Served Canadian Pacific Steamships, 1943-60; Master Mariner 1951; Staff Comdr 1957; Hon. Comdr RNR 1971. Elder Brother of Trinity House; Fellow and Founder Mem., Nautical Inst. City of London (Ward of Bassishaw): Common Councilman 1965-69; Alderman 1969; Sheriff 1973; one of HM Lieuts for City of London, 1975; Chm. Civil Defence Cttee, 1967-68; Pres., City of London Civil Defence Instructors Assoc., 1967-78; Chm., City of London Centre, St John Ambulance Assoc.; Pres., Nat. Waterways Transport Assoc.; Dep. Commonwealth Pres., Royal Life Saving Soc. Vice-Chm., PLA, 1979-. Master, Hon. Co. of Master Mariners, 1979-80. Trustee, Nat. Maritime Mus., 1982-. Chm. of Governors, Pangbourne Coll.; Governor, King Edward's Sch., Witley. Chancellor, City Univ., 1976-77. Fellow, Inst. Administrative Management (Pres., 1980-; Gold Medal, 1982). Hon. DSc City, 1976. KStJ 1977 (OStJ 1974). Officer, Order of Leopard, Zaire, 1973; Comdr, Order of Dannebrog, 1974; Order of Johan Sedia Mahkota (Malaysia), 1974; Grand Cross of Municipal Merit (Lima), 1977. *Recreations:* sailing, photography. *Heir:* *s* Nicholas Danvers Penrose Gillett, BSc, ARCS, *b* 24 Sept. 1955. *Address:* 4 Fairholt Street, Knightsbridge, SW7 1EQ. *T:* 01-589 9860; Bevington House, 24/26 Minories, EC3N 1BY. *T:* 01-481 0505. *Clubs:* City Livery, City Livery Yacht (Admiral), Guildhall, Royal Yacht Squadron, Royal London Yacht (Vice Cdre).

GILLIAT, Lt-Col Sir Martin (John), GCVO 1981 (KCVO 1962; CVO 1954); MBE 1946; Vice-Lieutenant of Hertfordshire, since 1971; Private Secretary to Queen Elizabeth the Queen Mother since 1956; *b* 8 Feb. 1913; *s* of late Lieut-Col John Babington Gilliat and Muriel Helen Lycette Gilliat; unmarried. *Educ:* Eton; RMC, Sandhurst. Joined KRRC, 1933. Served War of 1939-45 (despatches, Prisoner of War). Dep. Military Sec. to Viceroy and Governor-Gen. of India, 1947-48; Comptroller to Commissioner-Gen. for UK in South-East Asia, 1948-51; Mil. Sec. to Governor-Gen. of Australia, 1953-55. Hon. Bencher, Middle Temple, 1977. Hon. LLD London, 1977. DL Herts, 1963. *Address:* Appletrees, Welwyn, Herts. *T:* Welwyn 4675. *Clubs:* Travellers', Buck's, Brooks's.

GILLIATT, Penelope Ann Douglass, FRSL; fiction writer for the New Yorker, since 1967; also employed by the Sunday Times; freelance fiction writer of books, plays and films; *d* of late Cyril Conner, and Mary Stephanie Douglass; *m* 1st, 1954, Prof. R. W. Gilliatt, *qv* (marr. diss.); 2nd, 1963, John Osborne, *qv* (marr. diss.); one *d*. *Educ:* Queen's Coll., Harley St, London; Bennington Coll., Vermont. FRSL 1978. Formerly, contributor to New Statesman, Spectator, Guardian, Sight and Sound, Encore; film critic, Observer, 1961-65 and 1966-67; theatre critic, 1965-66; film critic, New Yorker, 1967-79 (six months of each yr). Property, and Nobody's Business (plays), perf. Amer. Place Theatre, New York, 1980; But When All's Said and Done (3 one-act plays), Actor's Studio, 1981; BBC plays incl. Living on the Box, The Flight Fund, 1978, and In the Unlikely Event of an Emergency, 1979; Beach of Aurora (original libretto, with music by Tom Eastwood), ENO, 1982. Oscar nomination for best original screenplay, 1971; awards for best original screenplay, New York Film Critics Circle, National Soc. of Film Critics, USA, and British Soc. of Film Critics, 1971; Grant for creative achievement in fiction, National Inst. of Arts and Letters, 1972. *Publications: novels:* One by One, 1965 (New York 1966); A State of Change, 1967 (New York 1967); The Cutting Edge, 1979 (New York 1979); *short stories collections:* What's It Like Out?, 1968 (Come Back If It Doesn't Get Better, New York 1967); Nobody's Business, 1972 (New York 1972); Splendid Lives, 1978 (New York 1978); Quotations from Other Lives, 1982 (New York 1982); (contrib.) Penguin Modern Stories, 1970; *non-fiction:* Unholy Fools: film and theatre, 1975 (New York 1975); Jean Renoir: essays, conversations, reviews, 1975 (New York 1975); Jacques Tati, 1977; Three-Quarter Face: profiles and reflections (with much additional material), 1980 (New York 1980); *screenplay:* Sunday, Bloody Sunday, 1971 (New York 1971 and 1972); profiles: in New Yorker on Jean Renoir, Woody Allen, Jean-Luc Godard, Jacques Tati, Henri Langlois of the French Cinemathèque, Jeanne Moreau, Diane Keaton, Graham Greene, and Luis Buñuel; in Sunday Telegraph Magazine on John Huston. *Address:* New Yorker Magazine, 25 West 43rd Street, New York, NY 10036, USA; 31 Chester Square, SW1W 9HT.

GILLIATT, Prof. Roger William, MC; DM; FRCP; Professor of Clinical Neurology, University of London, since 1962; Physician, National Hospital, Queen Square, and Middlesex Hospital; only *s* of late Sir William Gilliatt, KCVO; *m* 1963, Mary Elizabeth, *er d* of A. J. W. Green; one *s* two *d*. *Educ:* Rugby; Magdalen Coll., Oxford (BA 1st Cl. Hons Nat. Sci. (MA), BM, BCh Oxon 1949); MRCP 1951, FRCP 1961; DM 1955. Served in KRRC, 1942-45 (MC, despatches). Member: Association of British Neurologists; Physiological Soc.; Corr. Mem., Amer. Neurological Assoc.; Hon. Member: Amer. Acad. of Neurology; Amer. Assoc. of Electromyography and Electrodiagnosis; Société Française de Neurologie; Australian Assoc. of Neurologists; Soc. Suisse de Neurologie; Acad. Royale de Médecine, Belgium. *Publications:* contribs on neurological topics to medical and scientific jls. *Address:* Institute of Neurology, Queen Square, WC1N 3BG. *T:* 01-837 3611.

GILLICK, Rev. John, SJ, MA Oxon; Director, Fons Vitae (Pastoral Institute for Religious), Johannesburg, since 1970; *b* Wallasey, 27 March 1916; 2nd *s* of Laurence Gillick and Catherine Devine. *Educ:* St Francis Xavier's Coll., Liverpool; Heythrop and Campion Hall, Oxford (1st Cl. Hons Mod. History). Asst Master at Mount St Mary's and Beaumont. Two years writing and photography in Italy and Africa. Headmaster, Beaumont Coll., 1964-67; studied psychology at Loyola Univ., Chicago, 1967-68 (MA); Dir, Laboratories for the Training of Religious Superiors in S Africa, 1969. *Publications:* Teaching the Mass, 1961; Baptism, 1962; followed by Teaching the Mass: African, 1963; Teaching the Sacraments: African, 1964; Teaching Confirmation: African, 1964, etc; *illustrations for:* The Breaking of Bread, 1950; The Pilgrim Years, 1956; Our Faith, 1956; The Holy Mass, 1958; Christ Our Life, 1960. *Address:* 493 Marshall Street, Belgravia, Johannesburg, 2094, South Africa; c/o 114 Mount Street, W1Y 6AH.

GILLIE, Dame Annis Calder, (Dame Annis Smith), DBE 1968 (OBE 1961); MB, BS London, FRCP; FRCGP; formerly in general medical practice (1925-63); *b* 3 Aug. 1900; *d* of late Rev. Dr Robert Calder Gillie and Emily Japp; *m* 1930, Peter Chandler Smith, MA, FRIBA; one *s* one *d*. *Educ:* Wycombe Abbey Sch.; University Coll. and University Coll. Hosp., London. MRCP 1927. Member: BMA Council, 1950-64; Council of Medical Protection Soc., 1946-; Medical Practices Cttee, 1948-60; Med. Women's Federation (Pres. London Assoc., 1942-45, Pres. 1954); Foundn Mem., Royal College of General Practitioners (Chm., 1959-62, Pres., 1964-67); Mem., Central Health Services Advisory Council, 1956-70; North West Regional Hosp. Bd, 1958-63; Mem., Oxford Regional Hosp. Bd, 1964-74. Fellow, UCL, 1969. Hon. MD Edinburgh. *Publications:* contributions to medical jls. *Recreations:* reading, listening. *Address:* Bledington, Kingham, Oxford. *T:* Kingham 360.

GILLIES, Sir Alexander, Kt 1959; FRCSEd, FRACS; MChOrth; Consulting Orthopædic Surgeon, Wellington, Nelson and Dannevirke Hospitals, New Zealand; *b* 1891; *s* of Gilbert Gillies; *m* 1920, Effie Lovica, *d* of James Pearson Shaw, Kamloops, BC; two *d* decd; *m* 1978, Joan Mary, *d* of Francis Joseph Kennedy, Wellington, NZ. *Educ:* Otago Boys' High Sch.; Edinburgh Univ. MB, ChB Ed 1923; DMRE Liverpool 1925; FRCSEd 1926; FRACS 1931; MChOrth Liverpool 1936. Asst Orthopædic Surgeon Robert Jones & Agnes Hunt Hosp., Oswestry, Salop, 1924; Fellow, Mayo Clinic, Rochester, Minnesota, 1928. Sen. Orthop. Surg., Wellington Hosp., NZ, 1929-50. President: NZ Red Cross Soc., 1953-61, now Pres. Emeritus (Counsellor of Honour, 1961); NZ Crippled Children Soc., 1968. Emeritus Fellow, Brit. Orthopædic Assoc., 1966. *Publications:* contrib. med. jls. *Recreation:* golf. *Address:* 10C Herbert Gardens, 186 The Terrace, Wellington C1, New Zealand. *T:* Wellington 729-444.

GILLIES, Gordon; *see* Gillies, Maurice G.

GILLIES, (Maurice) Gordon, TD and Bar 1948; QC (Scotland) 1958; Sheriff of South Strathclyde, Dumfries and Galloway (formerly Lanarkshire), at Lanark, since 1958; *b* 17 Oct. 1916; *s* of James Brown Gillies, Advocate in Aberdeen, and Rhoda Ledingham; *m* 1954, Anne Bethea McCall-Smith. *Educ:* Aberdeen Grammar Sch.; Merchiston Castle; Edinburgh Univ. Advocate, 1946; Advocate Depute, 1953-58. *Recreation:* golf. *Address:* Redwalls, Biggar, Lanarkshire. *T:* Biggar 20281. *Clubs:* New (Edinburgh); Hon. Company of Edinburgh Golfers.

GILLILAND, David Jervois Thetford; practising solicitor and farmer; *b* 14 July 1932; *s* of late Major W. H. Gilliland and of Mrs N. H. Gilliland; *m* 1st, 1958, Patricia, *o d* of late J. S. Wilson and late Mrs Wilson (marr. diss. 1976); two *s* three *d*; 2nd, 1976, Jennifer Johnston, *qv*. *Educ:* Rockport Prep. Sch.; Wrekin Coll.; Trinity Coll., Dublin. BA 1954, LLB 1955. Qualified as solicitor, 1957, own practice. Mem. ITA, 1965-70; Chm., N Ireland Adv. Cttee of ITA, 1965-70. Mem. Council, Internat. Dendrology Soc., 1966-75; etc. *Recreations:* gardening, sailing, fishing. *Address:* Brook Hall, Londonderry, Northern Ireland. *T:* Londonderry 51297. *Club:* Northern Counties (Londonderry).

GILLILAND, Jennifer, (Mrs David Gilliland); *see* Johnston, J.

GILLINGHAM, (Francis) John, CBE 1982 (MBE 1944); FRSE 1970; Professor of Neurological Surgery, University of Edinburgh, 1963-80, now Emeritus; at Royal Infirmary of Edinburgh and Western General Hospital, Edinburgh, 1963-80; Consultant Neuro-Surgeon to the Army in Scotland, 1966-80; *b* 15 March 1916; *s* of John H. Gillingham, Upwey, Dorset; *m* 1945, Irene Judy Jude; four *s*. *Educ:* Hardye's Sch., Dorset; St Bartholomew's Hosp. Medical Coll., London. Matthews Duncan Gold Medal, 1939, MRCS, LRCP Oct. 1939; MB, BS (London) Nov. 1939; FRCS 1947; FRCSE 1955; FRCPE 1967; FRCPGlas. Hon. MD Thessaloniki, 1973. Hunterian Prof., RCS, 1957; Morison Lectr, RCP of Edinburgh, 1960; Colles Lectr, College of Surgeons of Ireland, 1962; Elsberg Lectr, College of Physicians and Surgeons, NY, 1967; Penfield Lectr, Middle East Med. Assembly, 1970. Hon. Mem., Soc. de Neurochirurgie de Langue Française, 1964; Hon. Mem., Soc. of Neurol. Surgeons (USA), 1965; Hon. Mem., Royal Academy of Medicine of Valencia, 1967; Hon. and Corresp. Mem. of a number of foreign neuro-surgical societies. President: Medico-Chirurgical Soc. of Edinburgh, 1965-67; European Soc. of Stereostatic and Functional Neurosurgery, 1972-76; Vice-Pres., RCSE, 1974-77, Pres., 1979-82. Jim Clark Foundn Award, 1979. *Publications:* Clinical Surgery: Neurological Surgery, 1969; papers on surgical management of cerebral vascular disease, head and spinal injuries, Parkinsonism and the dyskinesias, epilepsy and other neurosurgical subjects. *Recreations:* sailing, travel, photography. *Address:* Easter Park House, Barnton Avenue, Edinburgh EH4 6JR. *T:* 031-336 3528. *Clubs:* English-Speaking Union; New (Edinburgh).

GILLINGHAM, Rev. Canon Peter Llewellyn, MVO 1955; MA 1940; Chaplain to the Queen, since 1952; Hon. Canon of Chichester Cathedral (Wisborough Prebendary), 1969-77, Canon Emeritus since 1977; *b* 3 May 1914; *s* of late Rev. Canon Frank Hay Gillingham; *m* 1947, Diana, *d* of Lieut-Gen. Sir Alexander Hood; two *s* two *d*. *Educ:* Cheam; Marlborough; Oriel Coll., Oxford. Curate, Tonbridge Parish Church, 1937-40; Curate-in-Charge, St George's Church, Oakdale, Poole, 1940-43. Served War of 1939-45, Chaplain, RNVR, 1943-46; Chaplain, Blundell's Sch., Tiverton, 1946-49; Hon. Chaplain to King George VI, 1949-52; Chaplain to Royal Chapel of All Saints, Windsor Great Park, 1949-55; Vicar of St Mildred's, Addiscombe, 1955; Vicar of St Mary the Virgin, Horsham, 1960-77; Rural Dean of Horsham, 1974-77; Asst Chaplain, Sherborne Girls' Sch., 1977-79, Chaplain and Librarian, 1979-82. *Recreations:* golf, sailing. *Address:* Maplestead Cottage, Leiston Road, Aldeburgh, Suffolk. *T:* 2739.

GILLIS, His Honour Bernard (Benjamin), QC 1954; MA Cantab; a Circuit Judge (Additional Judge, Central Criminal Court), 1964-80; *m* ; one *s*. *Educ:* Downing Coll., Cambridge, Hon. Fellow, 1976. Squadron Leader, RAF, 1940-45. Called to the Bar, Lincoln's Inn, 1927, Bencher 1960, Treasurer 1976; North Eastern Circuit and Central Criminal Court. Commr, Central Criminal Court, 1959; Commissioner of Assize: Lancaster, 1960; Chelmsford, 1961; Bodmin, 1963. Recorder of Bradford, 1958-64. *Address:* 3 Adelaide Crescent, Hove, E Sussex. *Club:* Royal Air Force.

GILLMAN, Bernard Arthur, (Gerry Gillman); General Secretary, Society of Civil and Public Servants, since 1973; *b* 14 April 1927; *s* of Elias Gillman and Gladys Gillman; *m* 1951, Catherine Mary Antonia Harvey. *Educ:* Archbishop Tenison's Grammar Sch. Civil Service, 1946-53; Society of Civil Servants, 1953-. *Recreations:* watching London Welsh Rugby, theatre, music. *Address:* 2 Burnham Street, Kingston-upon-Thames, Surrey KT2 6QR. *T:* 01-546 6905; Society of Civil and Public Servants, 124/126 Southwark Street, SE1 0TU. *Club:* MCC.

GILLMORE, Air Vice-Marshal Alan David, CB 1955; CBE 1944; RAF (retired); *b* 17 Oct. 1905; *s* of late Rev. David Sandeman Gillmore and Allis Emily Widmer; *m* 1931, Kathleen Victoria Morris; three *s*. *Educ:* St Dunstan's Sch., Burnham-on-Sea; King's Sch., Ely. RAF Cadet Coll., Cranwell, Lincs, 1923-25; Commission in RAF, 1925. Commandant RAF Staff Coll., Bracknell, 1951-53; Senior Air Staff Officer, Far East Air Force, 1953-56; Senior Air Staff Officer, Home Command, 1956-59; retired 1959. *Address:* Southpen, 17 Naish Road, Burnham-on-Sea, Som. *Club:* Royal Air Force. *See also D. H. Gilllmore.*

GILLMORE, David Howe, CMG 1982; HM Diplomatic Service; Assistant Under Secretary of State, Foreign and Commonwealth Office, since 1981; *b* 16 Aug. 1934; *s* of Air Vice-Marshal A. D. Gillmore, *qv* ; *m* 1964, Lucile Morin; two *s*. *Educ:* Trent Coll.; King's Coll., Cambridge (MA). Reuters Ltd, 1958-60; Asst to Dir-Gen., Polypapier, SA, Paris, 1960-65; Teacher, ILEA, 1965-69; HM Diplomatic Service, 1970; Foreign and Commonwealth Office, 1970-72; First Sec., Moscow, 1972-75; Counsellor, UK Delegn, Vienna, 1975-78; Head of Defence Dept, FCO, 1979-81. *Publication:* novel A Way From Exile, 1967. *Recreations:* books, music, exercise. *Address:* Foreign and Commonwealth Office, Downing Street, SW1.

GILLSON, Thomas Huntington, OBE 1973; HM Diplomatic Service, retired; *b* 2 July 1917; *s* of Robert and Ellen Gillson; *m* 1st, Margaret Dorothy Mumford (marr. diss.); two *d* ; 2nd, 1969, Elizabeth Anne Fothergill (marr. diss.). *Educ:* Emanuel Sch., London. Bd of Educn, 1935; FO, 1937; served with Royal Corps of Signals, 1940-46; Budapest, 1946; FO, 1947; Milan, 1948; Buenos Aires, 1949; Warsaw, 1952; Vice-Consul, Kirkuk, 1953; FO, 1957; 1st Sec., The Hague, 1959; Pretoria, 1962; FO, 1966; Kabul, 1970; Counsellor, Ankara (Cento), 1973. *Recreation:* painting in watercolours (exhibitor RI, RWA, etc). *Address:* 7 Long Copse Court, Long Copse Lane, Emsworth, Hants PO10 7UW. *T:* Emsworth 6260. *Club:* Royal Commonwealth Society.

GILMARTIN, Hugh, OBE 1981; HM Diplomatic Service; Consul-General, Brisbane, since 1980; *b* 20 Nov. 1923; *s* of late Edward Gilmartin and Catherine Gilmartin (*née* McFadyen); *m* 1962, Olga, *d* of late Nicholas Alexander Plotnikoff; two *s* one *d*. *Educ:* Holy Cross Academy; Edinburgh Univ. Entered HM Diplomatic Service, 1946; Rome, 1945; Vienna, 1945-47; FO, 1947; UN Special Cttee on the Balkans, 1948; Bahrain, 1949-50; FO, 1951-53; Jakarta, 1953-55; Buenos Aires, 1955-57; Second Secretary, Asuncion, 1957-58; Bahrain, 1959-60; Panama, 1961-63; FO, 1963-65; First Sec. and Head of Chancery, Tegucigalpa, 1965-67; Zürich, 1968-73; First Sec., Office of UK Permanent Representative to the European Communities, Brussels, 1973-75; Asst Head of Training Dept, FO, 1975-79; Basle, 1979-80. *Recreations:* walking, swimming, skiing, gardening. *Address:* c/o Foreign and Commonwealth Office, SW1; 12 Gladesville Street, Kenmore, Brisbane, Queensland 4069, Australia. *T:* Brisbane 378 6881. *Clubs:* Challoner; Queensland, United Service, Brisbane, Tattersalls (Brisbane).

GILMORE, Brian Terence; Under Secretary, HM Treasury, since 1981 (Civil Service Department, 1979-81); *b* 25 May 1937; *s* of John Henry Gilmore and Edith Alice Gilmore; *m* 1962, Rosalind Edith Jean Fraser. *Educ:* Wolverhampton Grammar Sch.; Christ Church, Oxford (Passmore-Edwards Prize, 1956; BA Lit. Hum.; MA 1961). CRO and Diplomatic Service Admin Office, 1958-65: Private Sec. to Perm. Sec., 1960-61, to Parly Under Sec., 1961-62; Asst Private Sec. to Sec. of State, 1962-64; British Embassy, Washington, 1965-68; Min. of Technology and DTI, 1968-72: Private Sec. to Minister of State, Industry, 1969-70, and to Lord Privy Seal and Leader of the House of Lords, 1971-72; CSD, 1972-81; Principal, CS Coll., 1979-81. *Recreations:* reading, music, Greece. *Address:* 3 Clarendon Mews, W2 2NR. *T:* 01-262 4459. *Club:* Athenæum.

GILMORE, Carol Jacqueline; *see* Ellis, C. J.

GILMOUR, Dr Alan Breck, FRCGP; Director, National Society for the Prevention of Cruelty to Children, since 1979; *b* 30 Aug. 1928; *er surv. s* of Andrew Gilmour, *qv*; *m* 1957, Elizabeth, *d* of late H. and of L. Heath; two *d*. *Educ:* Clayesmore Sch.; King's Coll., London; King's Coll. Hosp. (Raymond Gooch Schol.). MB BS, LMSSA 1956; FRCGP 1974 (MRCGP 1965). General medical practitioner, 1958-67; during this period served as Member: Standing Med. Adv. Cttee, Min. of Health; Working Party on General Practice; Educn Cttee, RCGP; BMA Council, and others. British Medical Association Secretariat, 1967-79: Asst Sec., 1967; Under Sec., 1972; Dep. Sec., 1977; appts included: Overseas Sec. and Med. Dir, Commonwealth Med. Adv. Bureau, 1967-72; Med. Dir, Career Service, 1967-76; Sec., Bd of Sci. and Educn, 1972-76 (Commonwealth Med. Assoc. meetings, Singapore/Malaysia, Jamaica, Ghana; Observer, Commonwealth Med. Conf., Mauritius, 1971); Jt Sec., Med. Sci. meetings, Vancouver, Jamaica, Dublin; Dep. Sec., Jt Consultants Cttee, 1976-79. Hon. Treas., Assoc. for Study of

Med. Educn, 1975-80; Vice-Pres., Sect. Med. Educn, RSM, 1979-82. Liveryman, Worshipful Soc. of Apothecaries of London, 1973-. *Publications:* various articles, espec. in med. jls, on med. educn, careers in medicine, gen. practice; ed or ed jtly, Care of the Elderly, Primary Health Care Teams, Competence to Practise, and other reports. *Recreations:* gardening, homecare, walking, music. *Address:* NSPCC, 1 Riding House Street, W1P 8AA. *T:* 01-580 8812; 44 Hammersmith Grove, W6. *T:* 01-748 6277.

GILMOUR, Alexander Clement; Consultant, Grieveson Grant, since 1982; *b* 23 Aug. 1931; *s* of Sir John Little Gilmour, 2nd Bt, and of Lady Mary Gilmour; *m* 1954, Barbara M. L. Constance Berry; two *s* one *d*. *Educ:* Eton. National Service, commn in Black Watch, 1950-52. With Joseph Sebag & Co. (subseq. Carr, Sebag), 1954-82; Director: Carr, Sebag & Co., 1972-82; Safeguard Industrial Investments, 1974-. Chm., Nat. Playing Fields Assoc., 1976- (Past-Chm. Appeals Cttee, 10 yrs). Governor, LSE, 1969-. *Recreations:* tennis, skiing, fishing, gardening, golf. *Address:* Denchworth Manor, Wantage, Oxon OX12 0DX. *Clubs:* White's; Hon. Company of Edinburgh Golfers.
See also Rt Hon. Sir Ian Gilmour, Bt.

GILMOUR, Colonel Allan Macdonald, OBE 1961; MC 1942, and Bar 1943; Lord-Lieutenant of Sutherland, since 1972; Chairman, Highland Health Board, since 1981 (Member, since 1973); Member: Sutherland District Council, since 1975; Highland Regional Council, since 1977; *b* 23 Nov. 1916; *o s* of late Captain Allan Gilmour, of Rosehall, Sutherland, and late Mary H. M. Macdonald, of Viewfield, Portree, Skye; *m* 1941, Jean Wood; three *s* one *d*. *Educ:* Winchester Coll. Gazetted, The Seaforth Highlanders, Jan. 1939. Served War, in Middle East, France and Germany (despatches, 1945); DSC (USA) 1945. Staff Coll., 1946; Regimental and Staff Service in: Germany, Middle East, UK, Pakistan and Africa, 1946-67, incl. Instructor, Staff Coll., Quetta, on loan to Pakistan Army, 1952-54. Chief of Gen. Staff, Ghana Armed Forces, 1959-62; service in Congo, 1961-62; retired from Army, 1967. Chairman: Sutherland Council of Social Service, 1973-77; Sutherland District Council, 1975-77. Mem., Sutherland CC, 1970. DL Sutherland, 1971. *Recreations:* fishing, local government. *Address:* Invernauld, Rosehall, Lairg, Sutherland. *T:* Rosehall 204.

GILMOUR, Andrew, CMG 1949; Malayan Civil Service, retired; *b* 18 July 1898; *s* of late James Parlane Gilmour, Solicitor, Burntisland, and late Mima Simpson; *m* Nelle Twigg; two *s* three *d* (and one *s* killed in action). *Educ:* Royal High Sch., Edinburgh; Edinburgh Univ. (MA Hons Classics, 1920). Served European War, 1914-18, Argyll and Sutherland Highlanders, 1915-17. Appointed to Malayan Civil Service, 1921; Asst Controller of Labour, 1923-26; Head of Preventive Service, Singapore, 1927; Resident, Labuan, 1928-29; District Officer, Jasin, 1929-30, Ulu Kelantan, 1930-36; Asst Colonial Sec., SS, 1936-38; Registrar-Gen. of Statistics, SS and FMS, 1938-39; Shipping Controller, Singapore, 1939-41; Defence Intelligence Officer, Hong Kong, Dec. 1941; interned Hong Kong 1942-45; Sec. for Economic Affairs, Singapore, 1946-52; Staff Grade, MCS, 1947; Chm. N Borneo Rubber Commn, 1949; MEC and MLC Singapore (nominated official); acted as Colonial Sec., Singapore, June-Aug. 1948 and March-April 1952; ret. from Colonial Service, 1953; Planning Economist, UN Technical Assistance Mission, Cambodia, 1953-55; Economic Survey Commissioner, British Honduras, 1956. Secretary: British European Assoc., Singapore, 1956-75; Tanglin Trust Ltd, 1961-75; Raeburn Park School Ltd, 1961-75; Editor, BEAM, 1959-75. *Publications:* My Role in the Rehabilitation of Singapore 1946-53, 1973; An Eastern Cadet's Anecdotage, 1974. *Recreations:* cricket (Hon. Life Pres., Singapore Cricket Club); philately (Patron, Singapore Cricket Club). *Address:* Garden Cottage, Gifford, East Lothian EH41 4JE. *T:* Gifford 305. *Clubs:* Royal Over-Seas League; Singapore Cricket (Hon. Life Pres.).
See also A. B. Gilmour.

GILMOUR, Rt. Hon. Sir Ian (Hedworth John Little), 3rd Bt *cr* 1926, of Liberton and Craigmillar; PC 1973; MP (C) Chesham and Amersham, since 1974 (Norfolk Central, Nov. 1962-1974); *b* 8 July 1926; *er s* of Lt-Col Sir John Little Gilmour, 2nd Bt, and of Hon. Victoria Laura, OBE, TD, *d* of late Viscount Chelsea (*e s* of 5th Earl Cadogan); *S* father, 1977; *m* 1951, Lady Caroline Margaret Montagu-Douglas-Scott, *yr d* of 8th Duke of Buccleuch and Queensberry, KT, GCVO, PC; four *s* one *d*. *Educ:* Eton; Balliol Coll., Oxford. Served with Grenadier Guards, 1944-47; 2nd Lieut 1945. Called to the Bar, Inner Temple, 1952. Editor, The Spectator, 1954-59. Parly Under-Sec. of State, MoD, 1970-71; Minister of State: for Defence Procurement, MoD, 1971-72; for Defence, 1972-74; Sec. of State for Defence, 1974; Lord Privy Seal, 1979-81. Chm., Cons. Res. Dept, 1974-75. *Publications:* The Body Politic, 1969; Inside Right: a study of Conservatism, 1977. *Heir: s* David Robert Gilmour [*b* 14 Nov. 1952; *m* 1975, Sarah Anne, *d* of M. H. G. Bradstock; one *s* one *d*]. *Address:* The Ferry House, Old Isleworth, Mddx. *T:* 01-560 6769. *Clubs:* Pratt's, White's.
See also A. C. Gilmour.

GILMOUR, Col Sir John (Edward), 3rd Bt, *cr* 1897; DSO 1945; TD; JP; Lord-Lieutenant of Fife, since 1980 (Vice Lord-Lieutenant, 1979-80); Lord High Commissioner, General Assembly of the Church of Scotland, 1982; *b* 24 Oct. 1912; *o s* of Col Rt Hon. Sir John Gilmour, 2nd Bt, GCVO, DSO, MP, and Mary Louise (*d* 1919), *e d* of late E. T. Lambert, Telham Court, Battle, Sussex; *S* father, 1940; *m* 1941, Ursula Mabyn, *yr d* of late F. O. Wills; two *s*. *Educ:* Eton; Trinity Hall, Cambridge. Served War of 1939-45 (DSO). Bt Col 1950; Captain, Royal Company of Archers (Queen's Body Guard for

Scotland); Hon. Col, The Highland Yeomanry, RAC, T&AVR, 1971-75. MP (C) East Fife, 1961-79. Chm., Cons. and Unionist Party in Scotland, 1965-67. DL Fife, 1953. *Heir: s* John Gilmour [*b* 15 July 1944; *m* 1967, Valerie, *yr d* of late G. W. Russell, and of Mrs William Wilson; two *s* two *d*]. *Address:* Montrave, Leven, Fife. *TA:* Leven. *T:* Leven 26159. *Clubs:* Cavalry and Guards; Leander.
See also Dame Anne Bryans, Viscount Younger.

GILMOUR, John Scott Lennox, MA, FLS; Director, University Botanic Garden, Cambridge, 1951-73, retired; Fellow of Clare College, Cambridge, since 1951; *b* London, 28 Sept. 1906; *s* of late T. L. Gilmour, CBE, and Elizabeth, *o d* of late Sir John S. Keltie; *m* 1935, Molly, *y d* of late Rev. M. Berkley; three *d*. *Educ:* Uppingham Sch.; Clare Coll., Cambridge. Curator of the Herbarium and Botanical Museum, Cambridge, 1930-31; Asst Dir of Royal Botanic Gardens, Kew, 1931-46; seconded to Petroleum Div., Min. of Fuel and Power, as Principal Officer, 1940-45. Dir, Royal Horticultural Society's Garden, Wisley, Surrey, 1946-51. Sec., Systematics Assoc., 1937-46, Chm., 1952-55; Pres., Botanical Soc. of the British Isles, 1947-51; Chm. Internat. Commn on Horticultural Nomenclature, 1952-66, and International Cttee on Nomenclatural Stabilization, 1954; Rapporteur, Internat. Commission on the Nomenclature of Cultivated Plants, 1956-65, Chm., 1965-74; Brit. Rep., Council of Internat. Soc. Hort. Sci., 1960-73. Royal Horticultural Society: Victoria Medal of Honour in Horticulture, 1957; Mem. Council, 1957-61, 1962-66, 1968-73; Chm., Orchid Cttee, 1964-73; Veitch Gold Medal, 1966. Cons., new Botanic Garden at Ramat Hanadiv, Israel, 1964-68; Sec.-Treas. the Classification Society, 1964-68, Vice-Pres., 1968-78; Mem. Adv. Cttee Hunt Bot. Library, Pittsburgh, 1961-; Mem. Council, Bibliogr. Soc., 1963-68. Sandars Reader, Cambridge, 1971. First Chm., Cambridge Humanists, 1955-57, Pres., 1974-; Dir, Rationalist Press Assoc., 1961-74, Hon. Associate, 1976. *Publications:* British Botanists, 1944; Wild Flowers of the Chalk, 1947; Wild Flowers (in New Naturalist Series with S. M. Walters), 1954, pbk edn 1972; (ed) Thomas Johnson: Botanical Journeys in Kent and Hampstead, 1972; Some Verses, 1977; contributions to botanical, bibliographical, and rationalist jls, Jt Editor the New Naturalist, since 1943. *Recreations:* music, book-collecting. *Address:* 5 St Eligius Street, Cambridge. *T:* Cambridge 355776.

GILMOUR, Michael Hugh Barrie; solicitor, retired; Chief Legal Adviser and Solicitor to British Railway Board, 1963-Jan. 1970 (Secretary to Board, Oct. 1965-Jan. 1968); *b* 1 Dec. 1904; *e* surv. *s* of late Thomas Lennox Gilmour, CBE, Barrister, and Elizabeth Hervey, *o c* of late Sir John Scott Keltie, LLD; *m* 1937, Elisabeth, *o d* of late Francis Edward Cuming; one *d*. *Educ:* Leighton Park; abroad. Solicitors Office, Great Western Railway Company, 1929; Solicitor to Company, 1945-47; Solicitor to Railway Executive in Western Region, 1948-49; Chief Solicitor (1949) and Chief Legal Adviser (1951), British Transport Commission, until 1962. Served War of 1939-45, RAFVR, July 1940-Sept. 1941 (Squadron Leader). *Recreations:* walking, reading. *Address:* 55 Strand-on-the-Green, Chiswick, W4 3PD. *Club:* Garrick.

GILPIN, John; *b* 10 Feb. 1930; twin *s* of J. and L. M. Gilpin; *m* 1960, Sally Judd. *Educ:* Cone-Ripman Coll. Michael, in Peter Pan, 1942, 1943; and other rôles (stage, films, and broadcasting) until 1945, when he decided to devote himself exclusively to dancing. Awarded Adeline Genée Gold Medal, 1943. With Ballet Rambert, 1945-48; Roland Petit's Ballets de Paris, 1948-49; Grand Ballet du Marquis de Cuevas, 1949-50; Leading dancer, Festival Ballet, 1950-60; formerly guest dancer, Covent Garden. Produced: Firebird, Tokyo, 1971; Scottish Ballet's revival of Le Spectre de la Rose, 1982. Prix Vaslav Nijinsky, of French Academy of Music and Dance, 1957; Paris International Dance Festival Gold Medal, 1964. *Relevant publication:* John Gilpin by Cyril Swinson. *Recreation:* music. *Address:* 3 Orme Court, W2.

GILPIN, Rt. Rev. William Percy; *b* 26 July 1902; *e s* of late Percy William and Ethel Annie Gilpin. *Educ:* King Edward's, Birmingham; Keble Coll., Oxford. BA 1st class, Theology, 1925; MA 1928. Curate of Solihull, Warwicks, 1925-28; Vice-Principal of St Paul's Coll., Burgh, 1928-30; Chaplain of Chichester Theological Coll., 1930-33; Vicar of Manaccan with St Anthony, 1933-36; Vicar of St Mary, Penzance, 1936-44; Dir of Religious Education, Gloucester, 1944-51; Canon Missioner of Gloucester, 1946-52; Archdeacon of Southwark, 1952-55; Bishop Suffragan of Kingston-upon-Thames, 1952-70. Examining Chaplain to: Bishop of Truro, 1934-44, Bishop of Gloucester, 1945-52. *Recreation:* general railway matters. *Address:* 50 Lower Broad Street, Ludlow, Shropshire SY8 1PH. *T:* Ludlow 3376.

GILROY, John T. Y., ARCA, FRSA; artist; portrait and landscape painter; *b* 30 May 1898; *s* of John William Gilroy, artist; *m* 1924, Gwendoline Peri-Short; one *s*; *m* 1950, Elizabeth Outram Thwaite. *Educ:* King's Coll., Newcastle on Tyne; Hon. MA Univ. of Newcastle upon Tyne, 1975; Royal College of Art, London. Served European War, 1916-18, RFA. British Institute Scholar, 1921; RCA Travelling Scholar, 1922. Exhibition, Upper Grosvenor Galls, 1970. Creator of Guinness posters, 1925-60, also of Royle's publications of humour. Painted many famous portraits throughout Canada and America; also portraits of the Duke of Windsor when King Edward VIII; Queen Elizabeth the Queen Mother; Queen Elizabeth II, The Duke of Edinburgh (for RNEC); Princess Margaret; Prince Charles; Princess Anne; Field Marshal Earl Alexander of Tunis (Nat. Portrait Gall.); Earl Mountbatten of Burma; Rt Hon. Edward Heath; Lord Hailsham of Saint Marylebone; Sir Winston Churchill, 1942; Pope John; Sir Aubrey Smith; Sir John Clements; Sir John Gielgud; Sir Malcolm Sargent. Hon. MA Newcastle upon Tyne,

1976. *Publications:* (illustrated) McGill, The Story of a University, 1960; Rough Island Story (News Reel of Depression), 1931-35. *Recreations:* travelling, conversation. *Address:* 6 Ryecroft Street, Fulham, SW6. *T:* 01-731 3280. *Clubs:* Garrick (Life Mem.; Chm., Works of Art Cttee), Green Room.

GILROY BEVAN, David; *see* Bevan, A. D. G.

GILSON, John Cary, CBE 1967 (OBE 1945); Director, Medical Research Council's Pneumoconiosis Research Unit, 1952-76; *b* 9 Aug. 1912; 2nd *s* of late Robert Cary Gilson, MA and late Marianne C. Gilson, MA (*née* Dunstall); *m* 1945, Margaret Evelyn Worthington, MA, *d* of late Robert A. Worthington, OBE, FRCS; two *s* one *d. Educ:* Haileybury Sch.; Gonville and Caius Coll., Cambridge. MB, BChir Cantab 1937; MRCP 1940; FRCP 1956; FFOM 1979. 1st Asst, London Hosp.; Staff of RAF Inst. of Aviation Medicine, 1940-46; Mem. Scientific Staff of MRC, 1946-76, at Pneumoconiosis Research Unit, Asst Ed., Brit. Jl Industr. Med., 1955-64, and on Ed. Bd of various other jls; Mem., Govt and internat. cttees on Pneumoconiosis and health hazards of asbestos; Pres., British Occupational Hygiene Soc., 1960-61; Pres., Occupational Medicine Section, RSM, 1968-69; Hon. Life Mem., NY Acad. of Sciences, 1966. *Publications:* papers on pulmonary physiology and industrial medicine in scientific jls. *Recreations:* domestic engineering; clouds. *Address:* Hembury Hill Farm, Honiton, Devon EX14 0LA. *T:* Broadhembury 203.

GIMINGHAM, Prof. Charles Henry; FRSE 1961; Regius Professor of Botany, University of Aberdeen, since 1981 (Professor of Botany, since 1969); *b* 28 April 1923; *s* of late Conrad Theodore Gimingham and Muriel Elizabeth (*née* Blake), Harpenden; *m* 1948, Elizabeth Caroline, *o d* of late Rev. J. Wilson Baird, DD, Minister of St Machar's Cathedral, Aberdeen; three *d. Educ:* Gresham's Sch., Holt, Norfolk; Emmanuel Coll., Cambridge (Open scholarship; BA 1944; ScD 1977); PhD Aberdeen 1948. FIBiol 1967. Research Asst, Imperial Coll., Univ. of London, 1944-45; University of Aberdeen: Asst, 1946-48, Lectr, 1948-61, Sen. Lectr, 1961-64, Reader, 1964-69, Dept of Botany. *Publications:* Ecology of Heathlands, 1972; An Introduction to Heathland Ecology, 1975; papers, mainly in botanical and ecological jls. *Recreations:* hill walking, photography, foreign travel, history and culture of Japan. *Address:* 2 Carden Terrace, Aberdeen AB1 1US.

GIMSON, Arthur Clive Stanford, MBE 1944; MC 1945; Head Master, Blundell's School, 1971-80; *b* 28 June 1919; *s* of Harold Gimson, Leicester and Janet Marjorie Stanford, Aldringham, Suffolk; *m* 1957, Fiona Margaret Walton; three *s. Educ:* Uppingham Sch.; Clare Coll., Cambridge (Exhibr, MA). Royal Artillery, 1939-46; Sub-Warden, Mary Ward Settlement, 1947-48; Asst Master: Bradfield Coll., 1948-55; Melbourne Grammar Sch., 1956; Housemaster, Bradfield Coll., 1957-63; Head Master, Sebright Sch., 1963-70. *Recreations:* mountains and monasteries. *Address:* Mansard Cottage, Aldringham, Leiston, Suffolk.

GIMSON, George Stanley, QC (Scotland) 1961; Sheriff Principal of Grampian, Highland and Islands, since 1975; Chairman, Pensions Appeals Tribunals, Scotland, since 1975 (President, 1971-75); *b* 1915. *Educ:* High School of Glasgow; Glasgow Univ. Advocate, 1949; Standing Junior Counsel, Department of Agriculture for Scotland and Forestry Commission, 1956-61; Sheriff Principal of Aberdeen, Kincardine and Banff, 1972-74. Mem., Board of Management: Edinburgh Central Hosps, 1960-70 (Chm., 1964-70); Edinburgh Royal Victoria Hosps, 1970-74 (Vice-Chm.); Dir, Scottish Nat. Orchestra Soc. Ltd, 1962-80; Trustee, Nat. Library of Scotland, 1963-76; Chm., RSSPCC, Edinburgh, 1972-76. Hon. LLD Aberdeen, 1981. *Address:* The Castle, Inverness. *T:* Inverness 30782; 11 Royal Circus, Edinburgh. *T:* 031-225 8055. *Clubs:* University Staff (Edinburgh); Royal Northern and University (Aberdeen).

GINGELL, Air Chief Marshal Sir John, KCB 1978; CBE 1973 (MBE 1962); Deputy Commander-in-Chief, Allied Forces Central Europe, since 1981; *b* 3 Feb. 1925; *e s* of late E. J. Gingell; *m* 1949, Prudence, *d* of late Brig. R. F. Johnson; two *s* one *d. Educ:* St Boniface Coll., Plymouth. Entered RAF, 1943; Fleet Air Arm, 1945-46 as Sub-Lt (A) RNVR; returned to RAF, 1951; served with Nos 58 and 542 Sqdns; CFS 1954; psc 1959; jssc 1965; comd No 27 Sqdn, 1963-65; Staff of Chief of Defence Staff, 1966; Dep. Dir Defence Ops Staff (Central Staff), 1966-67; Mil. Asst to Chm. NATO Mil. Cttee, Brussels, 1968-70; AOA, RAF Germany, 1971-72; AOC 23 Group, RAF Trng Comd, 1973-75; Asst Chief of Defence Staff (Policy), 1975-78; Air Member for Personnnel, 1978-80; AOC-in-C, RAF Support Comd, 1980-81. *Recreations:* ornithology, walking, music. *Address:* c/o Lloyds Bank Ltd, Cox's & King's Branch, 6 Pall Mall, SW1Y 5NH. *Club:* Royal Air Force.

GINGELL, Maj.-Gen. Laurie William Albert, CB 1980; OBE 1966; General Secretary, Officers' Pensions Society, since 1979; *b* 29 Oct. 1925; *s* of late William George Gingell and of Elsie Grace Gingell; *m* 1949, Nancy Margaret Wadsworth; one *s* one *d. Educ:* Farnborough Grammar Sch.; Oriel Coll., Oxford. Commissioned into Royal Gloucestershire Hussars, 1945; transf. Royal Tank Regt, 1947; psc 1956; jssc 1961; Commanded: 1st Royal Tank Regt, 1966-67; 7th Armoured Bde, 1970-71; DQMG, HQ BAOR, 1973-76; Maj.-Gen. Admin, HQ UKLF, 1976-79. ADC to the Queen, 1974-76. FBIM 1979. *Recreations:* golf, tennis, swimming, reading. *Address:* 54 Station Road, Thames Ditton, Surrey KT7 0NS. *T:* 01-398 4521. *Club:* Army and Navy.

GINGER, Phyllis Ethel, (Mrs Leslie Durbin), RWS 1958 (ARWS 1952); Free Lance artist since 1940; *b* 19 Oct. 1907; *m* 1940, Leslie Durbin, *qv* ; one *s* one *d. Educ:* Tiffin's Girls' Sch., Kingston on Thames. LCC three years' scholarship at Central School of Arts and Crafts, 1937-39. Water colours for Pilgrim Trust Recording Britain Scheme, 1941-42; Royal Academy Exhibitor; Drawings and Lithographs purchased by: Washington State Library, 1941; Victoria and Albert Museum, 1952; London Museum, 1954; South London Art Gallery, 1960. *Publications:* Alexander the Circus Pony, 1941; book jacket designs; book illustrations include: London by Mrs Robert Henrey, 1948; The Virgin of Aldemanbury, by Mrs Robert Henrey, 1960. *Address:* 298 Kew Road, Kew, Richmond, Surrey. *T:* 01-940 2221.

GINGOLD, Hermione Ferdinanda; Actress; *b* 9 Dec.; *d* of James and Kate Gingold; *m* 1st, Michael Joseph (marr. diss.); one *s* (and one *s* deed); 2nd, Eric Maschwitz (marr. diss.). *Educ:* privately. Started as child actress at His Majesty's Theatre with Sir Herbert Tree in Pinkie and the Fairies. Played in Shakespeare at Old Vic and Stratford on Avon. Five years in intimate revue. O Dad, Poor Dad, Piccadilly, 1965; Highly Confidential, Cambridge, 1965; A Little Night Music, Majestic, New York, 1973, Adelphi, London, 1975; Side by Side by Sondheim, 1977-78. *Films:* Bell, Book and Candle, 1958; Gigi, 1959; Jules Verne's Rocket to the Moon, 1967; A Little Night Music. Many US television appearances. Has recorded Façade and Lysistrata. *Publications:* The World is Square: my own unaided work, 1945; Sirens should be Seen and Not Heard, 1963; articles and short stories. *Address:* 405 East 54th Street, New York, NY 10022, USA.

GINSBURG, David; MP Dewsbury since 1959 (Lab 1959-81, SDP since 1981); *b* 18 March 1921; *o s* of late N. Ginsburg; *m* 1954, Louise, *er d* of late S. P. Cassy. *Educ:* University Coll. Sch.; Balliol Coll., Oxford. Chm. OU Democratic Socialist Club, 1941; 2nd Cl, Hons Sch. of Politics, Philosophy and Economics, 1941. Commissioned Oxford and Bucks LI, 1942; Capt. Intelligence duties, 1944-45. Senior Research Officer, Govt Social Survey, 1946-52; Sec. of Research Dept of Labour Party and Sec. of Home Policy Sub-Cttee of National Executive Cttee, 1952-59; Chm., Parly and Scientific Cttee, 1968-71; Mem., Select Cttee, Parly Comr for Admin, 1982-. Broadcaster; Market Research and Marketing Consultant. *Publications:* miscellaneous articles and book reviews in contemporary publications. *Recreations:* walking, swimming, opera. *Address:* 3 Bell Moor, East Heath Road, NW3. *Club:* Reform.

GINSBURY, Norman; playwright; *b* Nov. 1902; *s* of late J. S. and Rachel Cecily Ginsbury; *m* 1945, Dorothy Jennings. *Educ:* London University. Plays produced: Viceroy Sarah, Arts Theatre, 1934, Whitehall Theatre, 1935; Walk in the Sun, "Q", and Embassy, 1939; Take Back Your Freedom (with late Winifred Holtby), Neighbourhood, 1940; The Firstcomers, Bradford Civic Playhouse, 1944; The First Gentleman (written, 1935), New and Savoy, 1945; Belasco, New York, 1956; The Gambler (from the story of Dostoievsky), Embassy, 1946; The Happy Man, New, 1948; Portrait by Lawrence (with M. Moiseiwitsch), Theatre Royal, Stratford, 1949; School for Rivals, Bath Assembly and Old Vic, Bristol, 1949. Also following adaptations of plays by Henrik Ibsen: Ghosts, Vaudeville, 1937; Enemy of the People, Old Vic, 1939; Peer Gynt, Old Vic Season at New Theatre, 1944; A Doll's House, Winter Garden, 1946; John Gabriel Borkman, Mermaid, 1961. A new version of Strindberg's Dance of Death at Tyrone Guthrie Theatre, Minneapolis; and at Yvonne Arnaud Theatre, Guildford, 1966; for the Mayflower 350th anniv., The Forefathers, Athenaeum Theatre, Plymouth, 1970; The Wisest Fool, Yvonne Arnaud, 1974. *Publications:* Viceroy Sarah, 1934; Take Back Your Freedom (collab.), 1939; The First Gentleman, 1946; and the following versions of plays by Ibsen: Ghosts, 1938; Enemy of the People, 1939; Peer Gynt, 1945; A Doll's House, 1950; John Gabriel Borkman, 1960; Rosmersholm, 1961; Pillars of Society, 1962. The Old Lags' League (from a story by W. Pett Ridge, in The Best One-Act Plays of 1960-61; The Shoemaker And The Devil (from a story by Tchehov), in The Best Short Plays of 1968 (NY); The Safety Match (from a story by Tchehov), in Best Short Plays of the World Theatre 1968-73 (NY). *Address:* 10 Bramber House, Michel Grove, Eastbourne, East Sussex BN21 1LA. *T:* Eastbourne 29603. *Club:* Dramatists'.

GIOLITTI, Dr Antonio; Member, Commission of the European Communities, since 1977; *b* 12 Feb. 1915; *s* of Giuseppe and Maria Giolitti; *m* 1939, Elena d'Amico; one *s* two *d. Educ:* Rome Univ. (Dr Law); Oxford; München. Mem. Italian Parlt, 1946-77; Minister of Budget and Economic Planning, 1964, 1970-72, 1973-74. Member: Italian Communist Party, 1943-57; Italian Socialist Party, 1958-; Exec., Italian Socialist Party, 1958-. *Publications:* Riforme e rivoluzione, 1957; Il comunismo in Europa, 1960; Un socialismo possibile, 1967. *Recreations:* music, walking. *Address:* 200 rue de la Loi, 1049 Brussels, Belgium.

GIORDANO, Richard Vincent; Group Managing Director and Chief Executive Officer, BOC International Ltd, since 1979; *b* 24 March 1934; *s* of late Vincent Giordano and of Cynthia Giordano; *m* 1956, Barbara Claire Beckett; one *s* two *d. Educ:* Harvard Coll., Cambridge, Mass, USA (BA); Columbia Univ. Law Sch. (LLB). Shearman & Sterling, 1959; Airco, Inc., 1964-74: Gp Vice Pres., 1967; Gp Pres., Chief Operating Officer and Mem. Bd, 1971; Dir, BOC Internat. Ltd, 1974; Chief Exec. Officer, Airco, Inc., 1978. Hon. Dr of Commercial Science, St John's Univ., 1975. *Recreations:* ocean sailing, tennis. *Address:* 24 Chelsea Square, SW3 6LF. *T:* 01-352 0037.

Clubs: The Links, New York Yacht (New York); Duquesne (Pittsburgh, Pa).

GIPPSLAND, Bishop of, since 1980; **Rt. Rev. Neville James Chynoweth,** ED 1966; *b* 3 Oct. 1922; *s* of Percy James and Lilian Chynoweth; *m* 1951, Joan Laurice Wilson; two *s* two *d. Educ:* Manly High School; Sydney Univ. (MA); Melbourne Coll. of Divinity (BD); Moore Theological Coll. (ThL). Assistant, St Michael's, Sydney, 1950; Rector, Kangaroo Valley, 1951-52; Chaplain, Royal Prince Alfred Hospital, 1952-54; Rector: St John's, Deewhy, 1954-63; St Anne's, Strathfield, 1963-66; All Saints, Canberra, 1966-71; St Paul's, Canberra, 1971-74; Archdeacon of Canberra, 1973-74; Assistant Bishop of Canberra and Goulburn, 1974-80. *Recreations:* music, biography. *Address:* Bishopscourt, Sale, Victoria 3850, Australia. *T:* 051-44:2046. *Clubs:* Royal Commonwealth Society; Sale (Sale, Vic.).

GIRDWOOD, Ronald Haxton, MD, PhD, FRCP, FRCPE, FRCPath; FRSE 1978; Professor of Therapeutics, University of Edinburgh, 1962-82; Physician to Royal Infirmary of Edinburgh since 1951; *b* 19 March 1917; *s* of late Thomas Girdwood; *m* 1945, Mary Elizabeth, *d* of late Reginald Williams, Calstock, Cornwall; one *s* one *d. Educ:* Daniel Stewart's Coll., Edinburgh; University of Edinburgh; University of Michigan. MB, ChB (Hons) Edinburgh 1939; Ettles Schol., Leslie Gold Medallist, Royal Victoria Hosp.; Tuberculosis Trust Gold Medallist, Wightman, Beaney and Keith Memorial Prize Winner, 1939; MD (Gold Medal for thesis), 1954. Pres. Edinburgh Univ. Church of Scotland Soc., 1938-39. Served RAMC, 1942-46 (mentioned in Orders); Nutrition Research Officer and Officer i/c Med. Div. in India and Burma. Lectr in Medicine, University of Edinburgh, 1946; Rockefeller Research Fellow, University of Michigan, 1948-49; Cons. Phys., Chalmers Hosp., Edinburgh, 1950-51; Sen. Lectr in Med. and Cons. Phys., Royal Infirmary, 1951; Vis. Lectr, Dept of Pharmacology, Yale Univ., 1956; Reader in Med., University of Edinburgh, 1958; Dean of Faculty of Medicine, Edinburgh Univ., 1975-79. Examiner for RCPE; sometime External Examiner for Universities of London, Sheffield, St Andrews, Dundee, Dublin and Glasgow; Chm., Scottish National Blood Transfusion Assoc.; Member: Council, RCPE, 1966-70, 1978-80 (Vice-Pres., 1981-82); South-Eastern Reg. Hosp. Board (Scotland), 1965-69; Board of Management, Royal Infirmary, Edinburgh, 1958-64; Cttee on Safety of Medicines, 1972-; Exec., Medico-Pharmaceutical Forum, 1972-74; Chairman: Scottish Group of Hæmophilia Soc., 1954-60; Non-Professorial Medical Teachers and Research Workers Gp Cttee (Scot.) of BMA, 1956-62; Scottish Gp of Nutrition Soc., 1961-62; Consultative Council, Edinburgh Medical Gp, 1977-82; Pres. Brit. Soc. for Hæmatology, 1963-64; Member: Coun. Brit. Soc. of Gastroenterology, 1964-68; Council of Nutrition Soc., 1957-60 and 1961-64; numerous Med. Socs; Lay Mem., Scottish Soc. of Artists; former Chm., Bd of Management, Scottish Med. Jl and Mem. of Editorial Bds of Blood and of Brit. Jl of Haematology; Mem. Editorial Bd, Brit. Jl of Nutrition, 1960-65; British Council visitor to W African Hosps, 1963, to Middle East, 1977, to India, 1980; Visiting Prof. and WHO Consultant, India, 1965. Cullen Prize, 1970, Lilly Lectr, 1979, RCPE; Suniti Panja gold medal, Calcutta Sch. Trop. Med., 1980. *Publications:* about 250, particularly in relation to nutrition, hæmatology, gastroenterology and medical history; (ed with A. N. Smith) Malabsorption, 1969; (ed) Blood Disorders due to Drugs and Other Agents, 1973; contrib. Davidson's Principles and Practice of Medicine, 1975; (ed with S. Alstead) Textbook of Medical Treatment, 1978; (ed) Clinical Pharmacology, 1979. *Recreations:* photography, painting. *Address:* 2 Hermitage Drive, Edinburgh EH10 6DD. *T:* (home) 031-447 5137, (hospital) 031-229 2477. *Clubs:* East India, Devonshire, Sports and Public Schools; University Staff (Edinburgh).

GIRLING, Maj.-Gen. Peter Howard, CB 1972; OBE 1961; CEng, FIMechE, FIEE, FIERE; Director of Operations, Open University, 1972-80; *b* 18 May 1915; *m* 1942, Stella Muriel (*née* Hope); two *d.* Commissioned, RAOC, 1939; transferred to REME, 1942; served War of 1939-45; India, 1945-47; Staff Coll., Camberley, 1948; Egypt, 1949-52; JSSC, Latimer, 1953; BAOR, 1953-55; Col, 1961; WO, 1961-65; HQ FARELF 1965-67; Brig., 1965; Comd Berkshire Sub-District, 1967-68; Comdt, REME Training Centre, 1967-69; Maj.-Gen., 1969; Dir of Electrical and Mechanical Engineering (Army), 1969-72; Col Comdt, REME, 1972-77. Hon. MA Open Univ., 1982. *Address:* The Folly, Wicken, Northants. *T:* Wicken 204. *Club:* Army and Navy.

GIROLAMI, Paul, FCA; Chief Executive, Glaxo Holdings, since 1980; *b* 25 Jan. 1926; *m* 1952, Christabel Mary Gwynne Lewis; two *s* one *d. Educ:* London School of Economics (BCom). Chantrey & Button, Chartered Accountants, 1950-54; Coopers & Lybrand, Chartered Accountants, 1954-65; Glaxo Holdings: Financial Controller, 1965; Finance Director, 1968. Director, Inner London Board of National Westminster Bank Ltd, 1974-. *Recreation:* golf. *Address:* 6 Burghley Road, Wimbledon, SW19 5BH.

GIROUARD, Mark, PhD; writer and architectural historian; Slade Professor of Fine Art, University of Oxford, 1975-76; *b* 7 Oct. 1931; *s* of Richard D. Girouard and Lady Blanche Girouard; *m* 1970, Dorothy N. Dorf; one *d. Educ:* Ampleforth; Christ Church, Oxford (MA); Courtauld Inst. of Art (PhD); Bartlett Sch., UCL (BSc, Dip. Arc). Staff of Country Life, 1958-66; studied architecture, Bartlett Sch., UCL, 1966-71; staff of Architectural Review, 1971-75. Member: Council, Victorian Soc., 1979- (Founder Mem. 1958; Mem. Cttee, 1958-66); Royal Fine Art Commn, 1972-; Royal Commn on Historical Monuments (England), 1976-81; Historic Buildings Council (England), 1978-. Chm., Spitalfields Historic Buildings Trust, 1977-. Hon. FRIBA, 1980.

Hon. DLitt Leicester, 1982. *Publications:* Robert Smythson and the Architecture of the Elizabethan Era, 1966; The Victorian Country House, 1971, 2nd edn 1979; Victorian Pubs, 1975; (jtly) Spirit of the Age, 1975 (based on BBC TV series); Sweetness and Light: the 'Queen Anne' movement 1860-1900, 1977; Life in the English Country House, 1978 (Duff Cooper Meml Prize; W. H. Smith Award, 1979); Historic Houses of Britain, 1979; Alfred Waterhouse and the Natural History Museum, 1981; The Return to Camelot: chivalry and the English gentleman, 1981; articles in Country Life, Architect. Rev., Listener. *Address:* 35 Colville Road, W11. *Club:* Beefsteak.

GISBOROUGH, 3rd Baron, *cr* 1917; **Thomas Richard John Long Chaloner;** Lord-Lieutenant of Cleveland, since 1981; *b* 1 July 1927; *s* of 2nd Baron and Esther Isabella Madeleine (*d* 1970), *yr d* of late Charles O. Hall, Eddlethorpe; *S* father 1951; *m* 1960, Shane, *e d* of late Sidney Newton, London, and *g d* of Sir Louis Newton, 1st Bt; two *s. Educ:* Eton. 16th/5th Lancers, 1948-52; Captain Northumberland Hussars, 1955-61; Lt-Col Green Howards (Territorials), 1967-69. CC NR Yorks, 1964-74, Cleveland, 1974-77. DL N Riding of Yorks and Cleveland, 1973. *Heir: s* Hon. Thomas Peregrine Long Chaloner, *b* 17 Jan. 1961. *Address:* Gisborough House, Guisborough, Cleveland. *T:* Guisborough 32002. *Club:* Northern Counties (Newcastle upon Tyne).

GISCARD d'ESTAING, Valéry; Grand Croix de la Légion d'Honneur; Croix de Guerre (1939-45); President of the French Republic, 1974-81; Member from Chamalières, Conseil Général de Puy-de-Dôme, since 1982; *b* Coblence, 2 Feb. 1926; *s* of late Edmond Giscard d'Estaing and May Bardoux; *m* 1952, Anne-Aymone de Brantes; two *s* two *d. Educ:* Lycée Janson-de-Sailly, Paris; Ecole Polytechnique; Ecole Nationale d'Administration. Inspection of Finances: Deputy, 1952; Inspector, 1954; Dep. Dir, Cabinet of Président du Conseil, June-Dec. 1954. Elected Deputy for Puy-de-Dôme, 1956; re-elected for Clermont N and SW, Nov. 1958, Nov.-Dec. 1962, March 1967, June 1968 and March 1973; Sec. of State for Finance, 1959; Minister of Finance, Jan.-April 1962; Minister of Finance and Economic Affairs, April-Nov. 1962 and Dec. 1962-Jan. 1966; Minister of Economy and Finance, 1969-74. Pres., Nat. Fedn of Indep. Republicans, 1966-73 (also a Founder); Pres., comm. des finances de l'économie générale et du plan de l'Assemblée nationale, 1967-68. Mayor of Chamalières, 1967-74. Deleg. to Assembly of UN, 1956, 1957, 1958. Nansen Medal, 1979. *Publication:* Démocratie Française, 1976 (Towards a New Democracy, 1977). *Address:* 11 rue Bénouville, Paris 16e, France. *Club:* Polo (Paris).

GISH, Lillian Diana; Actress; *b* 14 Oct. 1899. *Educ:* privately. Began acting in theatre at five years of age and at twelve entered motion pictures. Katrina in Crime and Punishment (with John Gielgud), 1948, The Curious Savage, 1950, Miss Mabel, 1951 (USA). Acting mainly on television, 1952; in play, The Trip to Bountiful (for the Theatre Guild), 1953-54; The Chalk Garden, 1957; The Family Reunion, 1958; directed, The Beggar's Opera, 1958; All the Way House, 1960-61 (won Drama Critics and Pulitzer prize as best play); A Passage to India, play (Chicago), 1962-63; Too True to be Good (G. B. Shaw's play) (New York), 1963; Romeo and Juliet (Stratford Festival Theatre), 1965; Anya (musical), 1967; I Never Sang for my Father, 1968; Uncle Vanya, NY, 1973; A Musical Jubilee (musical), NY, 1975. Lillian Gish and the Movies: the art of film, 1900-28 (concert programmes), Moscow, Paris, London and USA, 1969-73, QE2 World tour, 1975; lecturing and performing for The Theatre Guild at Sea on the Rotterdam, 1975. *Early films include:* Birth of a Nation; Intolerance; Souls Triumphant; Hearts of the World; The Great Love; Broken Blossoms; Way Down East; The Orphans of the Storm; The White Sister; Romola; *later films include:* The Night of the Hunter, 1954; The Cobweb, 1955; Orders to Kill, 1957; The Unforgiven, 1959; Follow Me Boys, 1966; Warning Shot, 1966; The Comedians, 1967; A Wedding, 1978. *Television:* frequent appearances include three plays, 1962; plays, 1963; Arsenic and Old Lace, 1969; Sparrow, CBS, 1978; Love Boat, and Thin Ice, CBS, 1980. Hon. AFD, Rollins Coll., Fla; Hon. HHD, Holyoke Coll.; Hon. Dr of Performing Arts, Bowling Green State Univ., Ohio, 1976. Hon. Oscar, Acad. Motion Picture Arts and Scis, 1971. Handel Medallion, NYC, 1973. *Publications:* Lillian Gish: an autobiography, 1968; Lillian Gish, The Movies, Mr Griffith and Me, 1969; Dorothy and Lillian Gish, 1973. *Recreation:* travel. *Address:* 430 East 57th Street, New York, NY 10022, USA.

GITTINGS, Robert (William Victor), CBE 1970; LittD Cantab, 1970; poet; biographer; playwright; *b* 1 Feb. 1911; *s* of late Surg.-Capt. Fred Claude Bromley Gittings, RN (retd) and late Dora Mary Brayshaw; *m* 1st, 1934, Katherine Edith Cambell (marr. diss.); two *s*; 2nd, 1949, Joan Grenville Manton; one *d. Educ:* St Edward's Sch., Oxford; Jesus Coll., Cambridge (Scholar). 1st Cl. Historical Tripos, 1933. Research Student, and Research Fellow, 1933-38, Supervisor in History, 1938-40, Hon. Fellow, 1979, Jesus Coll., Cambridge, Leslie Stephen Lectr, 1980; writer and producer for broadcasting, 1940-63; Professor: Vanderbilt University, Tennessee, 1966; Boston Univ., 1970; Univ. of Washington, 1972, 1974 and 1977 (Danz Lectr). Hon. LittD Leeds, 1981. *Publications: poetry and verse-plays:* The Roman Road, 1932; The Story of Psyche, 1936; Wentworth Place, 1950; The Makers of Violence (Canterbury Festival), 1951; Through a Glass Lightly, 1952; Famous Meeting, 1953; Out of This Wood (sequence of plays), 1955; This Tower My Prison, 1961; Matters of Love and Death, 1968; Conflict at Canterbury, 1970; American Journey, 1972; Collected Poems, 1976; *biography and criticism:* John Keats: The Living Year, 1954; The Mask of Keats, 1956; Shakespeare's Rival, 1960; (ed) The Living Shakespeare, 1960; (ed with E.

Hardy) Some Recollections by Emma Hardy, 1961; (with Jo Manton) The Story of John Keats, 1962; The Keats Inheritance, 1964; (ed) Selected Poems and Letters of John Keats, 1966; John Keats, 1968 (W. H. Smith Literary Award, 1969); John Keats: Selected Letters, 1970; The Odes of Keats, 1970; Young Thomas Hardy, 1975 (Christian Gauss Award, Phi Beta Kappa, 1975); The Older Hardy, 1978 (RSL Heinemann Award, 1979, James Tait Black Meml Prize, 1979); The Nature of Biography, 1978; (with Jo Manton) The Second Mrs Hardy, 1979; (ed with J. Reeves) Selected Poems of Thomas Hardy, 1981; contrib. to Keats-Shelley Memorial Bulletin, Keats-Shelley Journal, Harvard Library Bulletin, etc. Recreations: most outdoor pursuits except blood-sports. Address: The Stables, East Dean, Chichester, West Sussex. T: Singleton 328.

GIULINI, Carlo Maria; conductor; Music Director, Los Angeles Philharmonic Orchestra, since 1978; b 9 May 1914; m; three s. Educ: Accademia Santa Cecilia, Rome. Début as conductor, Rome, 1944; formed Orchestra of Milan Radio, 1951; Principal Conductor, La Scala, Milan, 1953-55; début in Great Britain, conducting Verdi's Falstaff, Edinburgh Festival, 1955; closely associated with Philharmonia Orchestra; Principal Guest Conductor, Chicago Symphony Orch., 1969-78; Music Dir, Vienna Symphony Orch., 1973-76; conducted new prodn of Falstaff in Los Angeles and at Covent Garden, 1982, after 14 year hiatus from opera (co-prodn by LA Philharmonic, Covent Garden and Teatro Comunale). Hon. Mem., Gesell. der Musikfreunde, Vienna, 1978; Hon. DHL DePaul Univ., Chicago, 1979. Gold Medal, Bruckner Soc., 1978. Recreation: sailing. Address: c/o Los Angeles Philharmonic Association, 135 N Grand Avenue, Los Angeles, Calif 90012, USA.

GIVEN, Edward Ferguson, CMG 1968; CVO 1979; Director General, Middle East Association, since 1979; b 13 April 1919; o s of James K. Given, West Kilbride, Ayrshire; m 1st, 1946, Philida Naomi Bullwinkle; one s; 2nd, 1954, Kathleen Margaret Helena Kelly. Educ: Sutton County Sch.; University Coll., London. Served RA, 1939-46. Entered HM Foreign Service, 1946; served at Paris, Rangoon, Bahrain, Bordeaux, Office of Political Adviser to C-in-C Far East, Singapore, Moscow, Beirut; Ambassador: United Republic of Cameroon and Republic of Equatorial Guinea, 1972-75; Bahrain, 1975-79, retired, 1979. Recreation: sailing. Address: 24 Bellevue Road, SW13 0BJ. Clubs: Army and Navy, Travellers'.

GIVEN, Rear-Adm. John Garnett Cranston, CB 1955; CBE 1945 (OBE 1943); MIMechE, MIMarE; retired from Royal Navy, June 1955; b 21 Sept. 1902; s of late J. C. M. Given, MD, FRCP, and Mrs May Given, Liverpool; m 1931, Elizabeth Joyce (née Payne), Brenchley, Kent, and Durban, Natal; one s two d. Educ: King William's Coll., IOM; Charterhouse, Godalming. RNEC Keyham, 1922-25; HMS Hood, 1926; RN Coll. Greenwich, 1928; Admiralty, 1930; HMS Berwick, China Station, 1933; HMS Neptune, 1940; Admiralty, 1942; HMS Howe, East Indies, 1944; Fleet Train, British Pacific Fleet, 1945; Asst Engineer-in-Chief, Admiralty, 1947; Commanding Officer Royal Naval Engineering Coll., Plymouth, 1948-51; idc 1952; Staff of Comdr-in-Chief, The Nore, 1953-55; Managing Dir, Parsons Marine Turbine Co., Wallsend, 1955-62. Recreations: fishing and walking. Address: c/o National Westminster Bank, 26 The Haymarket, SW1. Club: Army and Navy.

GLADSTONE, David Arthur Steuart; HM Diplomatic Service; Head of Western European Department, Foreign and Commonwealth Office, since 1979; b 1 April 1935; s of Thomas Steuart Gladstone and Muriel Irene Heron Gladstone; m 1961, April (née Brunner); one s one d. Educ: Eton; Christ Church, Oxford (BA History). National Service, 1954-56; Oxford Univ., 1956-59. Annan, Dexter & Co. (Chartered Accountants), 1959-60; FO, 1960; MECAS, Lebanon, 1960-62; Bahrain, 1962-63; FO, 1963-65; Bonn, 1965-69; FCO, 1969-72; Cairo, 1972-75; British Mil. Govt, Berlin, 1976-79. Recreations: squash, tennis, music, theatre, cinema, dreaming, carpentry, gardening. Address: 2 Mountfort Terrace, N1 1JJ. T: 01-607 8200.

GLADSTONE, Sir (Erskine) William, 7th Bt cr 1846; DL; Chief Scout of United Kingdom and Overseas Branches, 1972-82; Member, World Scout Committee (Chairman, 1979-81); b 29 Oct. 1925; s of Charles Andrew Gladstone, (6th Bt) and Isla Margaret, d of late Sir Walter Erskine Crum; S father, 1968; m 1962, Rosamund Anne, yr d of late Major A. Hambro; two s one d. Educ: Eton; Christ Church, Oxford. Served RNVR, 1943-46. Asst Master at Shrewsbury, 1949-50, and at Eton, 1951-61; Head Master of Lancing Coll., 1961-69. DL Flintshire, 1969, Clwyd, 1974; Alderman, Flintshire CC, 1970-74. Chm., Rep. Body of Church in Wales, 1977-. Publications: various school textbooks. Recreations: reading history, shooting, gardening. Heir: s Charles Angus Gladstone, b 11 April 1964. Address: Hawarden Castle, Deeside, Clwyd. T: Hawarden 532210; Fasque, Laurencekirk, Kincardineshire. T: Fettercairn 341.

GLADSTONE, Sir William; see Gladstone, Sir E. W.

GLADWIN, Derek Oliver, CBE 1979 (OBE 1977); JP; Regional Secretary (Southern Region), General and Municipal Workers' Union, since 1970; Member: Post Office Board (formerly Post Office Corporation), since 1972; British Aerospace, since 1977; b 6 June 1930; s of Albert Victor Gladwin and Ethel Gladwin (née Oliver); m 1956, Ruth Ann Pinion; one s. Educ: Carr Lane Junior Sch., Grimsby; Wintringham Grammar Sch.; Ruskin Coll., Oxford; London Sch. of Economics. British Railways, Grimsby, 1946-52;

fishing industry, Grimsby, 1952-56; Regional Officer 1956-63, Nat. Industrial Officer 1963-70, Gen. and Municipal Workers' Union. Chm., Labour Party's Conf. Arrangements Cttee. Trustee, Duke of Edinburgh's Commonwealth Study Conf. (UK Fund); Chm., Governing Council, Ruskin Coll., Oxford, 1979-. Vis. Fellow, Nuffield Coll., Oxford, 1978. JP Surrey, 1969. Address: 2 Friars Rise, Ashwood Road, Woking, Surrey; (office) Cooper House, 205 Hook Road, Chessington, Surrey KT9 1EP T: 01-397 8881.

GLADWYN, 1st Baron cr 1960; Hubert Miles Gladwyn Jebb, GCMG 1954 (KCMG 1949; CMG 1942); GCVO 1957; CB 1947; Grand Croix de la Légion d'Honneur, 1957; Deputy Leader of Liberal Party in House of Lords, and Liberal Spokesman on foreign affairs and defence, since 1965; b 25 April 1900; s of late Sydney Jebb, Firbeck Hall, Yorks; m 1929, Cynthia, d of Sir Saxton Noble, 3rd Bart; one s two d. Educ: Eton; Magdalen Coll., Oxon. 1st in History, Oxford, 1922. Entered Diplomatic Service, 1924; served in Tehran, Rome, and Foreign Office; Private Sec. to Parliamentary Under-Sec. of State, 1929-31; Private Sec. to Permanent Under-Sec. of State, 1937-40; appointed to Ministry of Economic Warfare with temp. rank of Asst Under-Sec., Aug. 1940; Acting Counsellor in Foreign Office, 1941; Head of Reconstruction Dept, 1942; Counsellor, 1943, in that capacity attended the Conferences of Quebec, Cairo, Tehran, Dunbarton Oaks, Yalta, San Francisco and Potsdam. Executive Sec. of Preparatory Commission of the United Nations (Aug. 1945) with temp. rank of Minister; Acting Sec.-Gen. of UN, Feb. 1946; Deputy to Foreign Sec. on Conference of Foreign Ministers, March 1946; Assistant Under-Sec. of State and United Nations Adviser, 1946-47; UK rep. on Brussels Treaty Permanent Commission with personal rank of Ambassador, April 1948; Dep. Under-Sec., 1949-50; Permanent Representative of the UK to the United Nations, 1950-54; British Ambassador to France, 1954-60, retired. Mem., European Parlt, 1973-76 (Vice Pres., Political Cttee); contested (L) Suffolk, European Parlt, 1979. Vice-Chm., European Movement; former Pres., Atlantic Treaty Assoc.; Chm., Campaign for European Political Community; Mem., Parly Delegns to Council of Europe and WEU Assemblies, 1966-73. Hon. DCL: Oxford; Syracuse, NY 1954; Essex 1974; Hon. Fellow Magdalen Coll. Publications: Is Tension Necessary?, 1959; Peaceful Co-existence, 1962; The European Idea, 1966; Half-way to 1984, 1967; De Gaulle's Europe, or, Why the General says No, 1969; Europe after de Gaulle, 1970; The Memoirs of Lord Gladwyn, 1972. Recreations: gardening, broadcasting, cooking, shooting and most other forms of sport. Heir: s Hon. Miles Alvery Gladwyn Jebb [b 3 March 1930. Educ: Eton and Oxford]. Address: Bramfield Hall, Halesworth, Suffolk. T: Bramfield 241; 62 Whitehall Court, SW1. T: 01-930 3160. Club: Garrick.
See also Baron Thomas of Swynnerton.

GLAMIS, Lord; Michael Fergus Bowes Lyon; b 7 June 1957; s and heir of 17th Earl of Strathmore and Kinghorne, qv. Educ: Univ. of Aberdeen (BLE 1979). Page of Honour to HM Queen Elizabeth The Queen Mother, 1971-73; commissioned, Scots Guards, 1980. Address: Glamis Castle, Forfar, Angus. Club: Turf.

GLANCY, Dr James Edward McAlinney; Senior Principal Medical Officer, Department of Health and Social Security, 1972-76; b 9 Feb. 1914; s of Michael James Glancy and Anne Teresa McAlinney; m 1945, Margaret Mary Redgrove; one s one d. Educ: Blackrock Coll., Dublin; National Univ. of Ireland (MD). FRCP, FRCPsych. Consultant Psychiatrist: Goodmayes Hosp., 1948-; King George Hosp., Ilford, and Barking Hosp., 1970-; Whipps Cross Hosp., 1948-72; Consultant in Clinical Neurophysiology, Oldchurch Hosp., Romford, 1950-60; Physician Supt, Goodmayes Hosp., 1960-72. Recreations: painting, photography, gardening. Address: 129 Goddard Way, Saffron Walden, Essex CB10 2DQ.

GLANDINE, Viscount; Richard James Graham-Toler; b 5 March 1967; s and heir of 6th Earl of Norbury, qv.

GLANUSK, 4th Baron, cr 1899; David Russell Bailey; Bt, cr 1852; Lieutenant-Commander RN (retired); b 19 Nov. 1917; o s of late Hon. Herbert Crawshay Bailey, 4th s of 1st Baron Glanusk and late Kathleen Mary, d of Sir Shirley Harris Salt, 3rd Bt; S cousin 1948; m 1941, Lorna Dorothy, o d of late Capt. E. C. H. N. Andrews, MBE, RA; one s one d. Educ: Orley Farm Sch., Harrow; Eton. RN, 1935-51. Managing Dir, Wandel & Goltermann (UK) Ltd, 1966-81; Chm., W&G Instruments Ltd, 1981-. Heir: s Hon. Christopher Russell Bailey [b 18 March 1942; m 1974, Frances, d of Air Chief Marshal Sir Douglas Lowe, qv; one s one d. Address: Sawmill House, Park Farm Road, High Wycombe, Bucks HP12 4AF.

GLANVILLE, Alec William; Assistant Under-Secretary of State, Home Office, 1975-81, retired; b 20 Jan. 1921; y s of Frank Foster and Alice Glanville; m 1941, Lilian Kathleen Hetherton; one s one d. Educ: Portsmouth Northern Secondary Sch.; Portsmouth Municipal Coll. War service, RAMC, 1939-46. Exchequer and Audit Dept, 1939-47; General, Criminal, Police and Probation and After-care Depts, Home Office, 1947-81 (seconded to Cabinet Office, 1956-58); Private Sec. to Permanent Under Sec. of State, 1949-50; Principal Private Sec. to Sec. of State, 1960-63; Sec., Interdepartmental Cttee on Mentally Abnormal Offenders, 1972-75.

GLANVILLE, Brian Lester; author and journalist since 1949; b 24 Sept. 1931; s of James Arthur Glanville and Florence Glanville (née Manches); m 1959, Elizabeth Pamela de Boer (née Manasse), d of Fritz Manasse and Grace Manasse (née Howden); two s two d. Educ: Newlands Sch.; Charterhouse.

Joined Sunday Times (football correspondent), 1958. *Publications:* The Reluctant Dictator, 1952; Henry Sows the Wind, 1954; Along the Arno, 1956; The Bankrupts, 1958; After Rome, Africa, 1959; A Bad Streak, 1961; Diamond, 1962; The Director's Wife, 1963; The King of Hackney Marshes, 1965; A Second Home, 1965; A Roman Marriage, 1966; The Artist Type, 1967; The Olympian, 1969; A Cry of Crickets, 1970; The Financiers, 1972; The History of the World Cup, 1973; The Thing He Loves, 1973; The Comic, 1974; The Dying of the Light, 1976; Never Look Back, 1980; (jtly) Underneath The Arches (musical), 1981; A Visit to the Villa (play), 1981; *juvenile:* Goalkeepers are Different (novel), 1971; Target Man (novel), 1978; The Puffin Book of Football, 1978; The Puffin Book of Tennis, 1981. *Recreation:* playing football. *Address:* 160 Holland Park Avenue, W11. *T:* 01-603 6908. *Club:* Chelsea Casuals.

GLANVILLE BROWN, W(illiam); *see* Brown, W. G.

GLASER, Prof. Donald Arthur; Professor of Physics and Molecular Biology, University of California, since 1960; *b* 21 Sept. 1926; *s of* William Joseph and Lena Glaser. *Educ:* Case Institute of Technology; California Inst. of Technology. Prof., University of Michigan, 1949–59; National Science Foundation Fellow, 1961; Guggenheim Fellow, 1961–62; Research Biophysicist (Miller Research Professorship, University of Calif, 1962–64). Member: National Academy of Sciences (USA), 1962; NY Acad. of Science; Fellow Amer. Physical Soc.; FAAAS. Henry Russel Award, 1955; Charles Vernon Boys Prize, 1958; Amer. Phys. Soc. Prize, 1959; Nobel Prize, 1960. Hon. ScD Case Inst., 1959. *Publications:* chapters in: Topics in the Biology of Aging, 1965; Biology and the Exploration of Mars, 1966; Frontiers of Pattern Recognition, 1972; New Approaches to the Identification of Microorganisms, 1975; contrib. to Yearbook of the Physical Soc., London, 1958; articles in Physical Review, Bulletin of Amer. Phys. Soc., Nuovo Cimento, Handbuch der Physik, Jl Molecular Biol., Jl of Bacteriol., Cell, Applied and Environmental Microbiol., Annual of NY Acad. of Scis, Pattern Recognition and Image Processing, Somatic Cell Genetics, Cell Tissue Kinetics, Computers and Biomed. Res., Proc. Nat. Acad. of Scis (USA), Cold Spring Harbor Symposium Quant. Biol. 1968, etc. *Address:* 229 Molecular Biology-Virus Laboratory, University of California, Berkeley, Calif 94720, USA.

GLASGOW, 9th Earl of, *cr* 1703; **David William Maurice Boyle,** CB 1963; DSC 1941; Baron Boyle, 1699; Viscount of Kelburn, 1703; Baron Fairlie (UK), 1897; Rear-Admiral, retired; *b* 24 July 1910; *e s of* 8th Earl of Glasgow, DSO; *S* father, 1963; *m* 1st, 1937, Dorothea (marriage dissolved, 1962), *o d* of Sir Archibald Lyle, 2nd Bart; one *s* two *d*; 2nd, 1962, Vanda, the Hon. Lady Wrixon-Becher, 2nd *d* of 4th Baron Vivian. *Educ:* Eton. Served War of 1939–45 in Atlantic, Channel, Arctic and Far East (despatches, DSC). Comdr., 1945; Capt., 1952; Capt. of the Fleet, Home Fleet, 1957–59; Commodore, RN Barracks, Portsmouth, 1959–61; Rear-Adm., 1961; Flag Officer, Malta, 1961–63; retd Sept. 1963. Mem. of the Royal Co. of Archers (Queen's Body Guard for Scotland). *Recreations:* shooting, golf, travel. *Heir:* *s* Viscount of Kelburn, *qv. Address:* Kelburn Castle, Fairlie, Ayrshire. *T:* Fairlie 204.

See also Viscount Caldecote.

GLASGOW, Archbishop of, (RC), since 1974; **Most Rev. Thomas J. Winning,** DCL, STL. Formerly parish priest, St Luke, Braidhurst, Motherwell; Auxiliary Bishop of Glasgow, 1971–74; parish priest, Our Holy Redeemer's, Clydebank, 1972–74. Mem., Sacred Congregation for the Doctrine of the Faith, 1978-. *Address:* 40 Newlands Road, Glasgow G43 2JD.

GLASGOW, Auxiliary Bishops of, (RC); *see* Devine, Rt Rev. J.; Renfrew, Rt Rev. C. McD.

GLASGOW, Provost of (St Mary's Cathedral); *see* Grant, Very Rev. M. E.

GLASGOW AND GALLOWAY, Bishop of, since 1981; **Rt. Rev. Derek Alec Rawcliffe,** OBE 1971; *b* 8 July 1921; *s of* James Alec and Gwendoline Rawcliffe; *m* 1977, Susan Kathryn Speight. *Educ:* Sir Thomas Rich's School, Gloucester; Univ. of Leeds (BA, 1st cl. Hons English); College of the Resurrection, Mirfield. Deacon 1944, priest 1945, Worcester; Assistant Priest, Claines S George, Worcester, 1944–47; Asst Master, All Hallows School, Pawa, Solomon Islands, 1947–53; Headmaster, 1953–56; Headmaster, S Mary's School, Maravovo, Solomon Is, 1956–58; Archdeacon of Southern Melanesia, New Hebrides, 1959–74; Assistant Bishop, Diocese of Melanesia, 1974–75; First Bishop of the New Hebrides, 1975–80. New Hebrides Medal, 1980; Vanuatu Independence Medal, 1980. *Recreation:* music. *Address:* 48 Drymen Road, Bearsden, Glasgow G61 2RH. *T:* 041-943 0612.

GLASGOW AND GALLOWAY, Dean of; *see* Singer, Very Rev. S. S.

GLASGOW, Mary Cecilia, CBE 1949 (MBE 1942); BA; Director (formerly Chairman), Mary Glasgow Holdings Ltd, Educational Publishers (firm founded 1957); *b* 24 May 1905; *d* of late Edwin Glasgow. *Educ:* Lady Margaret Hall, Oxford (Hons Sch. of French Language and Literature). Inspector of Schs, Bd of Education, 1933–39; Sec.-Gen., The Arts Council of Great Britain (formerly CEMA), 1939–51. Dir, The Opera Players. Pres., Institute of Linguists, 1978–81 (Chm., 1975–78; Diamond Jubilee Medal,

1971); Chairman: Inst. of Linguists Educnl Trust Ltd; Mary Glasgow Language Trust Ltd. Officier, l'Ordre National du Mérite, 1977 (Chevalier, 1968). *Address:* 5 Justice Walk, Chelsea, SW3 5DE. *T:* 01-352 7457; Entrechaux, 84340 Malaucène, France. *T:* Entrechaux (90) 36 07 48.

GLASHOW, Prof. Sheldon Lee, PhD; Higgins Professor of Physics, Harvard University, since 1979 (Professor of Physics, since 1966); *b* 5 Dec. 1932; *s of* Lewis and Bella Glashow; *m* 1972, Joan (*née* Alexander); three *s* one *d. Educ:* Cornell Univ. (AB); Harvard Univ. (AM, PhD). National Science Foundn Fellow, Copenhagen and Geneva, 1958–60; Res. Fellow, Calif Inst. of Technol., 1960–61; Asst Prof., Stanford Univ., 1961–62; Associate Prof., Univ. of Calif at Berkeley, 1962–66. Vis. Professor: CERN, 1968; Marseille, 1971; MIT, 1974 and 1980. Consultant, Brookhaven Nat. Lab., 1966-. Pres., Sakharov Internat. Cttee, Washington, 1980-. Hon. DSc: Yeshiva, 1978; Aix-Marseille, 1982. Nobel Prize for Physics (jtly), 1979. *Publications:* articles in learned jls. *Recreations:* scuba diving, tennis. *Address:* 30 Prescott Street, Brookline, Mass 02146, USA. *T:* 617-277-5446.

GLASS, Ven. Edward Brown; Archdeacon of Man, 1964–78, now Emeritus; Rector of Kirk Andreas, Isle of Man, 1964–78; *b* 1 July 1913; *s of* William and Phoebe Harriet Glass; *m* 1940, Frances Katharine Calvert; one *s* two *d. Educ:* King William's Coll., IoM; Durham Univ. (MA). Deacon 1937, priest 1938, dio. Manchester; Curate: St Mary's, Wardleworth, Rochdale, 1937; Gorton Parish Church, Manchester, 1937–42; Vicar: St John's, Hopwood, Heywood, Manchester, 1942–51; St Olave's, Ramsey, IoM, 1951–55; Castletown, IoM, 1955–64. Sec., Diocesan Convocation, 1958–64; Proctor for Clergy, Convocation of York, 1959–64; Member, Church Assembly and General Synod, 1959–78; Warden of Diocesan Readers, 1969–78; Chm., Diocesan Advisory Cttee, 1975–78. *Recreations:* gardening, ornithology, touring in Norway. *Address:* Balholm, Lhen Bridge, Kirk Andreas, Isle of Man. *T:* Kirk Andreas 568.

GLASS, Sir Leslie (Charles), KCMG 1967 (CMG 1958); HM Diplomatic Service, retired; Chairman, Anglo-Romanian Bank, 1973–81; *b* 28 May 1911; *s of* Ernest Leslie and Kate Glass; *m* 1st, 1942, Pamela Mary Gage; two *s* one *d*; 2nd, 1957, Betty Lindsay Hoyer-Millar (*née* Macpherson); two step *d. Educ:* Bradfield Coll.; Trinity Coll., Oxford (Hon. Fellow, 1982); Sch. of Oriental Studies, London Univ. Indian Civil Service, 1934; Asst Warden, Burma Oilfields, 1937; Settlement Officer, Mandalay, 1939; Far Eastern Bureau Min. of Inf., 1942; Lt-Col Head of Burma Section, Psychological Warfare Div., SEAC; Head of Information Div., Burma Mil. Admin, 1943; Sec. Information Dept, Govt of Burma, 1945; Comr of Settlements and Land Records, Govt of Burma, 1946; joined Foreign Office as 1st Sec. (Oriental Sec.), HM Embassy, Rangoon, 1947; Foreign Office, 1949–50; Head of Chancery, HM Legation Budapest (Chargé d'Affaires, 1951–52), 1950–53; Head of Information Div., British Middle East Office, 1953; seconded to Staff of Governor of Cyprus, 1955–56; Counsellor and Consul-Gen., British Embassy, Washington, 1957–58; Dir-Gen. of British Information Services in the US and Information Minister, British Embassy, Washington 1959–61; Minister employed in the Foreign Office, 1961; Asst Under-Sec. of State, Foreign Office, 1962–65; Ambassador to Romania, 1965–67; Ambassador and Dep. Permanent UK Representative to UN, 1967–69; High Comr in Nigeria, 1969–71, retired; re-employed FCO, 1971–72. Governing Council, Bradfield Coll., 1973–81. Trustee, Thomson Foundn, 1974–; Dir, Irvin Great Britain, 1981–. Hon. Fellow, Trinity Coll., Oxford, 1982. *Recreation:* fishing. *Address:* Stone House, Ivington, Leominster, Herefordshire. *T:* Ivington 204. *Club:* East India, Devonshire, Sports and Public Schools.

GLASS, Ruth, MA; Director, Centre for Urban Studies, University College London, since 1958; *d* of Eli and Lilly Lazarus; *m* 1st, 1935, Henry Durant (marr. diss. 1941); 2nd, 1942, David V. Glass, FRS, FBA (*d* 1978); one *s* one *d. Educ:* Geneva and Berlin Univs; London Sch. of Economics; Columbia Univ., NY. Sen. Research Officer, Bureau of Applied Social Research, Columbia Univ., 1940–42; Res. Off., Min. of Town and Country Planning, 1948–50; University College London: Dir, Soc. Res. Unit, Dept of Town Planning, 1951–58; Hon. Res. Associate, 1951–71; Vis. Prof., 1972-; Vis. Prof., Essex Univ., 1980–83. Chm., Urban Sociol. Res. Cttee, Internat. Sociol Assoc., 1958–75. Editorial Adviser: London Jl; Internat. Jl of Urban and Regional Res.; Sage Urban Studies Abstracts. Hon. FRIBA, 1972. Hon. LittD Sheffield, 1982. *Publications:* Watling, A Social Survey, 1939; (ed) The Social Background of a Plan, 1948; Urban Sociology in Great Britain, 1955; Newcomers, The West Indians in London, 1960; London's Housing Needs, 1965; Housing in Camden, 1969; contributor to: Town Planning Review; Architectural Review; Population Studies; Internat. Social Science Jl; Monthly Review; Trans. World Congresses of Sociology, New Society, etc. *Address:* 10 Palace Gardens Terrace, W8; Eastway Cottage, Walberswick, Suffolk.

GLASSE, Thomas Henry, CMG 1961; MVO 1955; MBE 1946; retired as Counsellor in HM Diplomatic Service, and Head of Protocol Department, Foreign Office (1957–61); *b* 14 July 1898; *s of* late Thomas and Harriette Glasse; *m* 1935, Elsie May Dyter (*d* 1965); no *c*; *m* 1966, Ethel Alice Needham. *Educ:* Latymer Foundation Upper Sch., Hammersmith. Entered Civil Service as a Boy Clerk, 1914. Army Service, 1/10th Bn Mx Regt, 1917–19. Joined the Foreign Office, 1921. Delegate of United Kingdom to Vienna Conference on Diplomatic Relations, 1961. *Recreations:* books, music, garden, travel. *Address:* 72 Lynch Road, Farnham, Surrey. *T:* Farnham 716662. *Club:* Travellers'.

GLASSPOLE, Most Hon. Sir Florizel (Augustus), ON 1973; GCMG 1981; CD 1970; Governor-General of Jamaica, since 1973; *b* Kingston, Jamaica, 25 Sept. 1909; *s* of late Rev. Theophilus A. Glasspole (Methodist Minister) and Florence (*née* Baxter); *m* 1934, Ina Josephine Kinlocke; one *d. Educ:* Central British Elementary Sch.; Wolmer's Sch.; Ruskin Coll., Oxford. British TUC Schol., 1946–47. Accountant (practising), 1932–44. Gen. Sec: Jamaica United Clerks Assoc., 1937–48; Jamaica TUC, 1939–52, resigned; Water Commn and Allied Workers Assoc., 1941–48; Municipal and Parochial Gen. Workers Union, 1945–47; First Gen. Sec., Nat. Workers Union, 1952–55; President: Jamaica Printers & Allied Workers Union, 1942–48; Gen. Hosp. and Allied Workers Union, 1944–47; Mental Hosp. Workers Union, 1944–47; Machado Employees Union, 1945–52; etc. Workers rep. on Govt Bds, etc, 1942–. Mem. Bd of Governors Inst. of Jamaica, 1944–57; Mem., Kingston Sch. Bd, 1944–. Founding Mem., PNP, 1938; MHR (PNP) for Kingston Eastern and Port Royal, 1944; Sec., PNP Parly Gp, 1944–73, resigned; Vice-Pres., People's National Party; Minister of Labour, Jamaica, 1955–57; Leader, House of Representatives, 1957–62, 1972–73; Minister of Educn, 1957–62, 1972–73; A Rep. for Jamaica, on Standing Fedn Cttee, West Indies Federation, 1953–58; Mem. House of Reps Cttee which prepared Independence of Jamaica Constitution, 1961; Mem. Delegn to London which completed Constitution document, 1962. Hon. LLD Univ. of the West Indies, 1982. Order of Andres Bello (1st cl.), Venezuela, 1973; Order of the Liberator, Venezuela, 1978. *Recreations:* gardening, sports, reading. *Address:* Kings House, Kingston 10, Jamaica.

GLAUERT, Audrey Marion, JP; ScD; Head of Electron Microscopy Department, since 1956, and Associate Director, since 1979, Strangeways Research Laboratory, Cambridge; Fellow of Clare Hall, Cambridge, since 1966; *b* 21 Dec. 1925; *d* of late Hermann Glauert, FRS and Muriel Glauert (*née* Barker). *Educ:* Perse Sch. for Girls, Cambridge; Bedford Coll., Univ. of London. BSc 1946, MSc 1947, London; MA Cantab 1967, ScD Cantab 1970. Asst Lectr in Physics, Royal Holloway Coll., Univ. of London, 1947–50; Mem. Scientific Staff, Strangeways Res. Lab., Cambridge, Sir Halley Stewart Research Fellow, 1950–. Chairman: British Joint Cttee for Electron Microscopy, 1968–72; Fifth European Congress on Electron Microscopy, 1972; Pres., Royal Microscopical Soc., 1970–72, Hon. Fellow, 1973. JP Cambridge, 1975. *Publications:* Fixation Dehydration and Embedding of Biological Specimens, 1974; papers on cell and molecular biology in scientific jls. *Recreations:* sailing, gardening. *Address:* 29 Cow Lane, Fulbourn, Cambridge. *T:* Cambridge 880463; Strangeways Research Laboratory, Wort's Causeway, Cambridge. *T:* Cambridge 243231.

GLAVES-SMITH, Frank William, CB 1975; Deputy Director-General of Fair Trading, 1973–79, retired; *b* 27 Sept. 1919; *m* 1941, Audrey Glaves; one *s* one *d. Educ:* Malet Lambert High Sch., Hull. Inland Revenue, 1938; served with Army, 1940–46. Called to Bar, Middle Temple, 1947. Board of Trade, 1947; Princ. Private Sec. to Pres. of Bd of Trade, 1952–57; Asst Secretary: HM Treasury, 1957–60; Cabinet Office, 1960–62; Bd of Trade, 1962–65; Under-Sec., BoT, 1965–69, Dept of Employment and Productivity, 1969–70, DTI, 1970–73; Dep. Sec., 1975. Mem., Export Guarantees Adv. Council, 1971–73. *Recreations:* croquet, gardening, fell-walking. *Address:* 8 Grange Park, Keswick, Cumbria.

GLAVIN, William Francis; Executive Vice-President, since 1980, (Reprographics and Operations, since 1982), Xerox Corporation; *b* 29 March 1932; *m* 1955, Cecily McClatchy; three *s* four *d. Educ:* College of the Holy Cross, Worcester, Mass (BS); Wharton Graduate Sch. (MBA). Vice-Pres., Operations, Service Bureau Corp. (subsid. of IBM), 1968–70; Exec. Vice-Pres., Xerox Data Services, 1970; Pres., Xerox Data Systems, 1970–72; Gp Vice-Pres., Xerox Corp., and Pres., Business Development Gp, 1972–74; Rank Xerox Ltd: Man. Dir, 1974–80; Chief Operating Officer, 1974–77; Chief Exec. Officer, 1977–80; Sen. Staff Officer, Xerox Corp., 1980–82. *Recreations:* golf, music, tennis. *Address:* 3 Alden Terrace, Greenwich, Conn 06830, USA.

GLAZE, Michael John Carlisle; HM Diplomatic Service; Consul-General, Bordeaux, since 1980; *b* 15 Jan. 1935; *s* of late Derek Glaze and of Shirley Gardner (formerly Glaze, *née* Ramsay); *m* 1965, Rosemary Potter (*née* Duff); two step-*d. Educ:* Repton; St Catharine's Coll., Cambridge (open Exhibitioner, BA 1958); Worcester Coll., Oxford. Colonial Service, Basutoland, 1959–65; HMOCS, Dep. Permanent Sec., Finance, Lesotho, 1966–70; Dept of Trade (ECGD), 1971–73; FCO, 1973–75; Abu Dhabi, 1975–78; Rabat, 1978–80. *Recreations:* golf, grand opera, the garden. *Address:* c/o Foreign and Commonwealth Office, SW1.

GLAZEBROOK, His Honour Francis Kirkland; a Circuit Judge (formerly a Judge of County Courts), 1950–72; *b* 18 Feb. 1903; 3rd *s* of late William Rimington Glazebrook; *m* 1930, Winifred Mary Elizabeth Davison; one *s* two *d. Educ:* Marlborough Coll.; Trinity Coll., Cambridge; Harvard Univ., USA. Called to the Bar, Inner Temple, 1928; Practised in the Common Law. Served War in Army, 1939–45. Croix de Guerre (France); Bronze Star (USA). *Recreations:* fishing, gardening, golf. *Address:* Rectory Park, Horsmonden, Kent.

GLAZEBROOK, Mark; *see* Glazebrook, R. M.

GLAZEBROOK, Reginald Field; formerly Director: Liverpool & London & Globe Insurance Co. Ltd; Liverpool Warehousing Co. Ltd; Liverpool Grain Storage & Transit Co. Ltd; Gandy Belt Ltd; *b* 23 April 1899; *s* of late William Rimington Glazebrook; *m* 1928, Daisy Isabel Broad; four *s. Educ:* Marlborough. Served European War, Lieut RFC, 1916–18. Cotton Merchant; Past Pres. Liverpool Cotton Assoc. *Recreations:* fishing, shooting, gardening. *Address:* Brynbella, Tremeirchion, St Asaph, Clwyd LL17 0UE.

See also R. M. Glazebrook.

GLAZEBROOK, (Reginald) Mark; Gallery Director, San José State University, since 1977; writer on art and arranger of exhibitions; *b* 25 June 1936; *s* of Reginald Field Glazebrook, *qv* ; *m* 1st, 1965, Elizabeth Lea Claridge (marr. diss., 1969); one *d* ; 2nd, 1974, Wanda Barbara O'Neill (*née* Osińska); one *d. Educ:* Eton; Pembroke Coll., Cambridge (MA); Slade School of Fine Art. Worked at Arts Council, 1961–64; Lectr at Maidstone Coll. of Art, 1965–67; Art Critic, London Magazine, 1967–68; Dir, Whitechapel Art Gall., 1969–71; Head of Modern English Paintings and Drawings, P. and D. Colnaghi & Co. Ltd, 1973–75. FRSA 1971. *Publications:* (comp.) Artists and Architecture of Bedford Park 1875–1900 (catalogue), 1967; (comp.) David Hockney: paintings, prints and drawings 1960–1970 (catalogue), 1970; Edward Wadsworth 1889–1949: paintings, prints and drawings (catalogue), 1974; (introduction) John Armstrong 1893–1973 (catalogue), 1975; (introduction) John Tunnard (catalogue), 1976; articles in: Studio International, London Magazine. *Recreations:* travelling, theatre, tennis, swimming. *Address:* 5 Priory Gardens, Bedford Park, W4. *Clubs:* Lansdowne, Chelsea Arts.

GLEADELL, Maj.-Gen. Paul, CB 1959; CBE 1951; DSO 1945; *b* 23 Feb. 1910; *s* of late Captain William Henry and Katherine Gleadell; *m* 1937, Mary Montgomerie Lind, *d* of late Col Alexander Gordon Lind, DSO, and Mrs Lind; two *s* two *d. Educ:* Downside Sch.; Sandhurst. Commissioned in The Devonshire Regt, 1930 (Adjutant 1936–39); DAAG, Rawalpindi Dist, 1940; Staff Coll. (Quetta), 1941; Brigade Major 80th Indian Bde, 1942; Commanded 12th Bn The Devonshire Regt (6th Airborne Div.), 1944–45; Secretariat, Offices of the Cabinet and Ministry of Defence, 1945–48; Joint Services Staff Coll., 1948; Col (G S Intelligence), GHQ Far East Land Forces, 1949–51; comd 1st Bn The Devonshire Regt (3rd Inf. Div.), 1951–53; Senior Army Instructor, Joint Services Staff Coll., 1953–55; Brigade Comdr, 24th Independent Infantry Brigade, 1955–56; Imperial Defence Coll., 1957; Chief of Staff to Dir of Operations, Cyprus, 1958–59; in command 44th Div. (TA) and Home Counties District, and Dep. Constable of Dover Castle, 1959–62; Dir of Infantry, 1962–65; Clerk to Governors, Rookesbury Park School, 1966–72, Governor, 1973–80. French Croix de Guerre with Palm, 1944. *Address:* Anchorage, 58 Shore Road, Warsash, Hants SO3 6FT. *Clubs:* Naval and Military, Challoner.

GLEAVE, Ruth Marjory; Headmistress, Bradford Girls' Grammar School, since 1976; *b* 29 May 1926; *d* of Harold Gleave and Alice Lillian Dean. *Educ:* Birkenhead High Sch., GPDST; Univ. of Liverpool (BA Hons Geography, DipEd). Head of Geography Dept, Wade Deacon Girls' Grammar Sch., Widnes, 1947–54; Head of Geography Dept and Deputy Head, Withington Girls' Sch., Manchester, 1954–60; Head, Fairfield High Sch., Droylsden, Manchester, 1960–75. *Recreations:* travel, natural history, outdoor activities, the arts—literature and art. *Address:* Bradford Girls' Grammar School, Squire Lane, Bradford BD9 6RB.

GLEDHILL, Alan, MA Cantab, LLD London; Professor Emeritus of Oriental Laws, University of London, Hon. Fellow, School of Oriental and African Studies; *b* 26 Oct. 1895; *s* of late O. Gledhill, Redroofs, Wells Road, Wolverhampton; *m* 1st, 1922, Mercy (*d* 1963), *d* of Victor Harvey, Calcutta; two *s* one *d* ; 2nd, 1967, Marion Glover, *d* of late C. W. Watson, Santa Cruz, Argentine. *Educ:* Rugby; Corpus Christi Coll., Cambridge; Gray's Inn. Served European War, 1914–18, Lieut Monmouthshire Regt 1915–16; joined ICS 1920; District and Sessions Judge, 1927; Special Judge, Tharrawaddy, 1930–33; War of 1939–45; Dep. Comr, Cachar, Assam, 1942–43; Dep. Chief Judicial Officer, British Military Administration, Burma, 1944–45 (despatches); Actg Judge High Court Rangoon, Oct. 1945; Puisne Judge, 1946–48; Lecturer in Indian and Burmese Law, Sch. of Oriental and African Studies, 1948–54; Reader in Oriental Laws, 1954–55; Prof. of Oriental Laws, University of London, 1955–63; Lectr in Hindu Law, Inns of Court Sch. of Law, 1955–67. *Publications:* The British Commonwealth: The Development of its Laws and Constitutions, Vol 6, The Republic of India, 1951 (2nd edn, 1964). Vol. 8, The Islamic Republic of Pakistan, 1957 (2nd edn, 1967); Fundamental Rights in India, 1955; The Penal Codes of Northern Nigeria and the Sudan, 1963. *Recreations:* swimming, walking. *Address:* Springwood Residential Home, Duffield, Derby. *Club:* Royal Commonwealth Society.

GLEDHILL, Anthony John, GC 1967; Detective Sergeant, Metropolitan Police, since 1976; *b* 10 March 1938; *s* of Harold Victor and Marjorie Edith Gledhill; *m* 1958, Marie Lilian Hughes; one *s* one *d. Educ:* Doncaster Technical High Sch., Yorks. Accounts Clerk, Officers' Mess, RAF Bruggen, Germany, 1953–56. Metropolitan Police Cadet, 1956–57; Police Constable, Metropolitan Police, 1957–75. *Recreations:* football, carpentry. *Address:* 98 Pickhurst Lane, Hayes, Bromley, Kent. *T:* 01-462 4033. *Club:* No 4 District Metropolitan Police (Hayes, Kent).

GLEDSTANES, Elsie, RBA 1929 (ARBA 1923); portrait, figure and landscape painter; *d* of late Francis Garner Gledstanes, late mem. Stock Exchange Cttee. *Educ:* Eastbourne; Paris. Studied art at Paris, Slade Sch. and Byam Shaw, and Vicat Cole Sch. of Art; served in WRNS, 1917–18; London Auxiliary Ambulance Driver, 1939–45; WVS Transport, 1941–42; Driver Women's Legion, 1942–45; exhibited works in RA, RBA, RPS, NPS,

International Soc. and in the Provinces; works in Imperial War Museum, etc. Mem. of Pastel Soc. FRSA. *Address:* 61 Campden Street, W8 7EL. *T:* 01-727 8663; Glan-y-Gors, Prenteg, Portmadoc. *T:* Portmadoc 2510.

GLEESON, Most Rev. James William; *see* Adelaide, Archbishop of, (RC).

GLEISSNER, Dr Heinrich; at Federal Ministry for Foreign Affairs, Vienna, since 1982; *b* Linz, Upper Austria, 12 Dec. 1927; *s* of Heinrich and Maria Gleissner. *Educ:* Univ. of Vienna (Dr jur 1950); Univ. of Innsbruck; Bowdoin Coll., Brunswick, Maine, USA; Coll. of Europe, Bruges. Entered Austrian Foreign Service, 1951; Austrian Embassy, Paris, and Office of Austrian Observer at Council of Europe, Strasbourg, 1952-53; Min. for Foreign Affairs, Vienna, 1953-55; Austrian Embassy, London, 1955-57; sabbatical, Univ. of Vienna, 1957-59; Min. for For. Affairs, 1959-61; Austrian National Bank, 1961; Min. for For. Affairs, 1961-62; Mission to Office of UN, Geneva, 1962-65; Consulate-General, New York, 1965-66, Consul-Gen., 1966-73; Min. for For. Affairs, 1973-75 (Head, Western Dept, 1974-75); Dir, Security Council and Polit. Cttees Div., UN, New York, 1975-79; Austrian Ambassador to the Court of St James's, 1979-81. *Recreation:* music. *Address:* Federal Ministry for Foreign Affairs, Ballhausplatz 2, 1010 Vienna, Austria. *Club:* St Johann's (Wien).

GLEN, Sir Alexander (Richard), KBE 1967 (CBE 1964); DSC 1942 (and Bar), 1945; Chairman, British Tourist Authority, 1969-77; Deputy Chairman, British Transport Hotels, since 1978; Group Chairman, Anglo World Travel, since 1977; *b* 18 April 1912; *s* of late R. Bartlett Glen, Glasgow; *m* 1947, Baroness Zora de Collaert. *Educ:* Fettes Coll.; Balliol Coll., Oxford. BA, Hons Geography. Travelled on Arctic Expeditions, 1932-36; Leader, Oxford Univ. Arctic Expedition, 1935-36; Banking, New York and London, 1936-39. RNVR, 1939-59, Capt. 1955. Export Council for Europe; Dep. Chm., 1960-64; Chm., 1964-66. Member: BNEC, 1966-72; Board of BEA, 1964-70; Nat. Ports Council, 1966-70; Horserace Totalisator Bd, 1976-. Dir, BICC, 1964-70. Chm., Adv. Council, V&A Museum, 1978-; Mem., Historic Buildings Council, 1976-80. Awarded Cuthbert Peek Grant by RGS, 1933; Bruce Medal by RSE, 1938; Andrée Plaque by Royal Swedish Soc. for Anthropology and Geography, 1939; Patron's Gold Medal by RGS, 1940. Polar Medal (clasp Arctic 1935-36), 1942; Norwegian War Cross, 1943; Chevalier (1st Class), Order of St Olav, 1944; Czechoslovak War Cross, 1946. *Publications:* Young Men in the Arctic, 1935; Under the Pole Star, 1937; Footholds Against a Whirlwind (autobiog.), 1975. *Recreations:* travel, skiing, sailing. *Address:* Stanton Court, Stanton, Glos. *Clubs:* City of London; Explorers (NY).

GLEN, Archibald; Solicitor; *b* 3 July 1909; *m* 1938, Phyllis Mary; one *s* two *d. Educ:* Melville Coll., Edinburgh. Admitted Solicitor, 1932. Town Clerk: Burnley, Lancs, 1940-45; Southend-on-Sea, 1945-71. President: Soc. of City and Borough Clerks of the Peace, 1960; Soc. of Town Clerks, 1963-64; Assoc. of Town Clerks of British Commonwealth, 1964-, etc. Lay Member, Press Council, 1969-75; Mem., Local Govt Staff Commn for England, 1972-76. Hon. Freeman, Southend-on-Sea, 1971. *Recreations:* golf, swimming. *Address:* Harbour House, 2 Drummochy, Lower Largo, Fife. *T:* Lundin Links 320724.

GLEN HAIG, Mrs Mary Alison, CBE 1977 (MBE 1971); Assistant District Administrator, South Hammersmith Health District; President, British Sports Association for the Disabled, since 1981; *b* 12 July 1918; *e d* of late Captain William James and Mary (*née* Bannochie); *m* 1943, Andrew Glen Haig (decd). *Educ:* Dame Alice Owen's Girls' School. Mem., Sports Council, 1966-; Vice Pres., CCPR, 1982 (Chm., 1975-81); Mem., Internat. Olympic Cttee, 1982-. Hon. Sec., Amateur Fencing Assoc., 1956-64, Pres., 1974-; Pres., Ladies' Amateur Fencing Union, 1964-74. British Ladies' Foil Champion, 1948-50. Olympic Games, 1948, 1952, 1956, 1960; British Commonwealth Games Gold Medal, 1950-54, Bronze Medal, 1958; Captain, Ladies' Foil Team, 1950-57. Administrator (Hospitals), S Hammersmith District, 1974, Asst Dist Administrator 1975. *Recreations:* fencing, gardening. *Address:* 66 North End House, W14 0RX. *T:* 01-602 2504; 2 Old Cottages, Holyport Street, Holyport, near Maidenhead, Berks. *T:* Maidenhead 33421. *Club:* Lansdowne.

GLENAMARA, Baron *cr* 1977 (Life Peer), of Glenridding, Cumbria; **Edward Watson Short,** PC 1964; CH 1976; Chairman, Cable and Wireless Ltd, 1976-80; *b* 17 Dec. 1912; *s* of Charles and Mary Short, Warcop, Westmorland; *m* 1941, Jennie, *d* of Thomas Sewell, Newcastle upon Tyne; one *s* one *d. Educ:* Bede College, Durham. LLB London. Served War of 1939-45 and became Capt. in DLI. Headmaster of Princess Louise County Secondary School, Blyth, Northumberland, 1947; Leader of Labour Group on Newcastle City Council, 1950; MP (Lab) Newcastle upon Tyne Central, 1951-76; Opposition Whip (Northern Area), 1955-62; Dep. Chief Opposition Whip, 1962-64; Parly Sec. to the Treasury and Govt Chief Whip, 1964-66; Postmaster General, 1966-68; Sec. of State for Educn and Science, 1968-70; Lord Pres. of the Council and Leader, House of Commons, 1974-76. Dep. Leader, Labour Party, 1972-76. Hon. FCP, 1965. *Publications:* The Story of The Durham Light Infantry, 1944; The Infantry Instructor, 1946; Education in a Changing World, 1971; Birth to Five, 1974. *Recreation:* painting. *Address:* 21 Priory Gardens, Corbridge, Northumberland. *T:* Corbridge 2880; Glenridding, Cumbria. *T:* Glenridding 273.

GLENAPP, Viscount; (Kenneth) Peter (Lyle) Mackay, AIB; Director, Gray Mackenzie & Co. Ltd, London, since 1980 (Regional Director, Bahrain, 1978-80); *b* 23 Jan. 1943; *er s* and *heir* of 3rd Earl of Inchcape, *qv ; m* 1966, Georgina, *d* of S. C. Nisbet and of Mrs G. R. Sutton; one *s* two *d. Educ:* Eton. Late 2nd Lieut 9/12th Royal Lancers. *Recreations:* shooting, fishing, golf, sailing. *Heir: s* Hon. Fergus James Kenneth Mackay, *b* 9 July 1979. *Address:* Manor Farm, Clyffe Pypard, near Swindon, Wilts SN4 7PY. *Clubs:* White's, Oriental, City.

GLENARTHUR, 4th Baron *cr* 1918; **Simon Mark Arthur;** Bt 1903; a Lord in Waiting (Government Whip), since 1982; *b* 7 Oct. 1944; *s* of 3rd Baron Glenarthur, OBE, and of Margaret, *d* of late Captain H. J. J. Howie; *S* father, 1976; *m* 1969, Susan, *yr d* of Comdr Hubert Wyndham Barry, RN; one *s* one *d. Educ:* Eton. Commissioned 10th Royal Hussars (PWO), 1963; Captain 1970; Major 1973; retired 1975; Royal Hussars (PWO), TA, 1976-80. British Airways Helicopters Captain, 1976-82; Dir, Aberdeen and Texas Corporate Finance Ltd, 1977-82. MCIT 1979. *Recreations:* field sports, flying, gardening. *Heir: s* Hon. Edward Alexander Arthur, *b* 9 April 1973. *Address:* Birch Hill, Torphins, Banchory, Kincardineshire. *T:* Torphins 287. *Club:* Cavalry and Guards.

GLENAVY, 4th Baron *cr* 1921; **Michael Mussen Campbell;** Bt 1916; *b* 25 Oct. 1924; *s* of 2nd Baron Glenavy and Beatrice Moss (*d* 1970), *d* of William Elvery, Rothbury, Foxrock, Co. Dublin; *S* brother, 1980. *Educ:* St Columba's College, Rathfarnham; Trinity College, Dublin. Called to the Bar, King's Inns, Dublin, 1947. *Publications:* Peter Perry, 1956; Oh Mary This London, 1959; Across the Water, 1961; Princess in England, 1964; Lord Dismiss Us, 1967; Nothing Doing, 1970. *Heir:* none. *Address:* 39 Kendal Street, W2.

GLENCONNER, 2nd Baron, *cr* 1911; **Christopher Grey Tennant;** Bt *cr* 1885; *b* 14 June 1899; *s* of 1st Baron and Pamela (*d* 1928), *d* of late Hon. Percy Scawen Wyndham (she *m* 2nd, 1922, 1st Viscount Grey); *S* father, 1920; *m* 1st, 1925, Pamela (who obtained a divorce, 1935), 2nd *d* of Sir Richard Paget, 2nd Bt; two *s ;* 2nd, 1935, Elizabeth Mary, *er d* of late Lieut-Col E. G. H. Powell; one *s* two *d. Heir: s* Hon. Colin Christopher Paget Tennant, *qv. Address:* Rovinia, Liapades, Corfu, Greece. *Club:* White's.

GLENDEVON, 1st Baron, *cr* 1964; **John Adrian Hope;** PC 1959; Director and Deputy Chairman, Ciba-Geigy (UK) Ltd, 1971-78; Director: ITT (UK) Ltd; Colonial Mutual Life Assurance Society Ltd, 1952-54, 1962-67; British Electric Traction Omnibus Services Ltd; *b* 7 April 1912; *yr twin s* of 2nd Marquess of Linlithgow, KG, KT, PC; *m* 1948, Elizabeth Mary, *d* of late (William) Somerset Maugham, CH; two *s. Educ:* Eton; Christ Church, Oxford (MA 1936). psc†; served War of 1939-45 (Scots Guards) at Narvik, Salerno and Anzio (despatches twice). MP (C) Northern Midlothian and Peebles, 1945-50, Pentlands Div. of Edinburgh, 1950-64; (Joint) Parliamentary Under-Sec. of State for Foreign Affairs, Oct. 1954-Nov. 1956; Parliamentary Under-Sec. of State for Commonwealth Relations, Nov. 1956-Jan. 1957; Jt Parly Under-Sec. of State for Scotland, 1957-Oct. 1959; Minister of Works, Oct. 1959-July 1962. Mem., Departmental Cttee to examine operation of Section 2 of Official Secrets Act, 1971. Chairman: Royal Commonwealth Society, 1963-66; Historic Buildings Council for England, 1973-75. Fellow of Eton, 1956-67. FRSA 1962. *Publication:* The Viceroy at Bay, 1971. *Heir: s* Hon. Julian John Somerset Hope, *b* 6 March 1950. *Address:* Mount Lodge, Mount Row, St Peter Port, Guernsey.

GLENDINING, Rev. Canon Alan, MVO 1979; Rector of St Margaret's Lowestoft, and Team Leader of the Lowestoft Group, since 1979; Chaplain to the Queen, since 1979; Hon. Canon of Norwich Cathedral, since 1977; *b* 17 March 1924; *s* of late Vincent Glendining, MS, FRCS and Freda Alice; *m* 1948, Margaret Locke, *d* of Lt-Col C. M. Hawes, DSO and Frances Cooper Richmond; one *s* one *d* (and one *d* decd). *Educ:* Radley; Westcott House, Cambridge. Newspaper publishing, 1945-58. Deacon, 1960; Priest, 1961. Asst Curate, South Ormsby Group of Parishes, 1960-63; Rector of Raveningham Group of Parishes, 1963-70; Rector, Sandringham Group of Parishes, and Domestic Chaplain to the Queen, 1970-79; Rural Dean of Heacham and Rising, 1972-76. *Recreation:* writing. *Address:* 16 Corton Road, Lowestoft, Suffolk.

GLENDINNING, Edward Green; Chief Executive, City of Edinburgh District Council, 1975-80; *b* 3 Dec. 1922; *yr s* of late George M. Glendinning and Isabella Green; *m* 1944, Jane Rollo Dodds Greig; one *s* one *d. Educ:* Boroughmuir Sch., Edinburgh; Edinburgh Univ. (BL). Lieut RNVR (Air Br., Pilot), 1941-46; Edinburgh Univ., 1940-41 and 1946-48; admitted Solicitor, 1948; Edinburgh Corporation, 1949; Depute Town Clerk, 1959; Town Clerk, City and Royal Burgh of Edinburgh, 1972-75. Comdr, Order of Pole Star (Sweden), 1976. *Recreations:* friends, talking, listening to music, walking (but not too far).
See also J. G. Glendinning.

GLENDINNING, James Garland, OBE 1973; Managing Director, Gestam Guinness Peat International Realty Ltd, since 1980; Director: The Fine Art Society Ltd, since 1972; North American Property Unit Trust, since 1975 (Chairman, 1975-80); Masterpack Ltd, since 1981; *b* 27 April 1919; *er s* of late George M. Glendinning and Isabella Green; *m* 1st, 1943, Margaret Donald (*d* 1980); one *d ;* 2nd, 1980, Mrs Anne Ruth Law. *Educ:* Boroughmuir Sch., Edinburgh; Military Coll. of Science. Mil. Service, 1939-46: 2nd Bn London Scottish and REME in UK and NW Europe. HM Inspector of Taxes,

1946–50; various appts with Shell Petroleum Co. Ltd, 1950–58; Dir Anglo Egyptian Oilfields Ltd and Dep. Chief Representative Shell-BP companies in Egypt, 1959–61; Gen. Manager in Borneo and East Java for Shell Indonesia, 1961–64; Head of Industrial Studies (Diversification) in Shell Internat. Petroleum Co. Ltd, 1964–67; various appts in Japan, 1967–72, incl.: Director: Shell Sekiyu KK, 1967–72 (Vice Pres.); Shell Kosan KK, 1969–72 (Vice Pres.); Japan Shell Technology KK, 1970–72 (Man. Dir); Showa Sekiyu KK, 1967–72; Showa Yokkaichi KK, 1967–72; West Japan Oil Exploration KK, 1968–72; Nippon LNG KK, 1970–72; Industrial and Commercial Property Unit Trust, 1977–81. Chm., British Chamber of Commerce in Japan, 1970–72; Mem., London Transport Exec., 1972–80; Chm., London Transport Pension Fund Trustees Ltd, 1974–80. Mem. Council, Japan Soc., London, 1974–78 and 1981–. FCIT 1973; FRSA 1977. *Address:* 20 Albion Street, W2 2AS. *Club:* Caledonian.
  See also E. G. Glendinning.

GLENDYNE, 3rd Baron, *cr* 1922; **Robert Nivison,** Bt 1914; Senior Partner in the firm of R. Nivison & Co., Stockbrokers; *b* 27 Oct. 1926; *o s* of 2nd Baron and late Ivy May Rose; *S* father, 1967; *m* 1953, Elizabeth, *y d* of late Sir Cecil Armitage, CBE; one *s* two *d. Educ:* Harrow. Grenadier Guards, 1944–47. *Heir: s* Hon. John Nivison, *b* 18 Aug. 1960. *Address:* Hurdcott, Barford St Martin, near Salisbury, Wilts. *Club:* City of London.
  See also Maj.-Gen. P. R. Leuchars, Maj.-Gen. D. J. St M. Tabor.

GLENISTER, Prof. Tony William, CBE (mil.) 1979; TD; Professor of Anatomy, University of London, at Charing Cross Hospital Medical School, since 1970; Dean, Charing Cross Hospital Medical School, since 1976; *b* 19 Dec. 1923; *o s* of Dudley Stuart Glenister and Maria (née Leytens); *m* 1948, Monique Marguerite, *o d* of Emile and Marguerite de Wilde; four *s. Educ:* Eastbourne Coll.; St Bartholomew's Hosp. Med. Coll. MRCS, LRCP 1947; MB, BS 1948, PhD 1955, DSc 1963, London. House appts, St Bartholomew's Hosp. and St Andrew's Hosp., Dollis Hill, 1947–48; served in RAMC, 1948–50; Lectr and Reader in Anatomy, Charing Cross Hosp. Med. Sch., 1950–57; Internat. Project Embryological Res., Hubrecht Lab., Utrecht, 1954; Prof. of Embryology, Univ. of London, 1967–70; Vice-Dean, Charing Cross Hosp. Med. Sch., 1966–69 and 1971–76; Hon. Cons. in Clin. Anatomy and Genetics to Charing Cross Gp of Hosps, 1972–; Hon. Brig. late RAMC, TA (TD, TA 1963 and TAVR 1978). Apothecaries' Soc. Lectr in History of Medicine, 1971–; Arnott Demonstrator, RCS, 1972; Pres., Anatomical Soc. GB and Ireland, 1979–81 (Sec., 1974–76). ADMS 44 (Home Counties) Div. TA, 1964–67; CO 217 (London) Gen. Hosp. RAMC(V), 1968–72; QHP 1971–73; Hon. Col 220 (1st Home Counties) Field Amb. RAMC(V), 1973–78; TAVR Advr to DGAMS, 1976–79; Hon. Col 217 (London) Gen. Hosp. RAMC, TAVR, 1981–. Member: Ealing, Hammersmith and Hounslow AHA(T), 1976–82; Hammersmith and Fulham Health Authority, 1982–; GMC, 1979–; sometime examiner: Univs of Cambridge, Liverpool, London, St Andrews, Singapore; NUI; RCS; RCSE. Special Trustee, Charing Cross Hosp.; Trustee, Tablet Trust; Member Governing Bodies: Soc. for Study of Med. Ethics; Linacre Centre for study of Ethics of Health Care. Mem., Ct of Assts, Soc. of Apothecaries of London; Freeman, City of London. OStJ 1967. *Publications:* (with J. R. W. Ross) Anatomy and Physiology for Nurses, 1965, 3rd edn 1980; (contrib.) A Companion to Medical Studies, ed Passmore, 1963, 2nd edn 1976; (contrib.) Methods in Mammalian Embryology, ed Daniel, 1971; (contrib.) Textbook of Human Anatomy, ed Hamilton, 1976; papers and articles mainly on prenatal development. *Recreations:* the countryside, history. *Address:* The Keep, 42 Marlborough Crescent, Riverhead, Sevenoaks, Kent. *T:* Sevenoaks 451775. *Club:* Army and Navy.

GLENKINGLAS, Baron *cr* 1974 (Life Peer), of Cairndow, Argyll; **Michael Antony Cristobal Noble,** PC 1962; *b* 19 March 1913; 3rd *s* of Sir John Henry Brunel Noble, 1st Bt, of Ardkinglas; *m* 1940, Anne, *d* of Sir Neville Pearson, 2nd Bt, *qv*; four *d. Educ:* Eton Coll.; Magdalen Coll., Oxford. Served RAFVR, 1941–45. Argyll County Council, 1949–51. MP (C) Argyllshire, June 1958–Feb. 1974; PPS to Sec. of State for Scotland, 1959; Asst Govt Whip (unpaid), 1960 (Scottish Whip, Nov. 1960); a Lord Comr of the Treasury, 1961–62; Sec. of State for Scotland, 1962–64; President of the Board of Trade, June–Oct. 1970; Minister for Trade, DTI, Oct. 1970–Nov. 1972. Chm., Unionist Party in Scotland, 1962–63. Chairman: Associated Fisheries, 1966–70; Glendevon Farms (Winchburgh), 1969–70; British Agricultural Export Council, 1973–77; Hanover Housing (Scotland) Assoc., 1978–80; Director: John Brown Engineering Ltd, 1973–77; Monteith Holdings Ltd, 1974–. *Recreations:* gardening, fishing, shooting. *Address:* Strone, Cairndow, Argyll. *T:* Cairndow 284. *Club:* Boodle's.

GLENN, Sir Archibald; *see* Glenn, Sir J. R. A.

GLENN, Senator John H(erschel), Jr; US Senator from Ohio (Democrat), since 1975; *b* Cambridge, Ohio, 18 July 1921; *s* of John H. and Clara Glenn; *m* 1943, Anna Castor; one *s* one *d. Educ:* Muskingum Coll., New Concord, Ohio. Joined US Marine Corps, 1943; Served War (2DFC's, 10 Air Medals); Pacific Theater, 1944; home-based, Capt., 1945–46; Far East, 1947–49; Major, 1952; served Korea (5 DFC's, Air Medal with 18 clusters), 1953. First non-stop supersonic flight, Los Angeles–New York (DFC), 1957; Lieut-Col, 1959. In Jan. 1964, declared candidacy for US Senate from Ohio, but withdrew owing to an injury; recovered and promoted Col USMC, Oct. 1964; retired from USMC, Dec. 1964. Became one of 7 volunteer Astronauts, man-in-space program, 1959; made 3-orbit flight in Mercury capsule, Friendship 7, 20 Feb.

1962 (boosted by rocket; time 4 hrs 56 mins; distance 81,000 miles; altitude 160 miles; recovered by destroyer off Puerto Rico in Atlantic). Vice-Pres. (corporate develt) and Dir, Royal Crown Cola Co., 1962–74. Holds hon. doctorates, US and foreign. Awarded DSM (Nat. Aeronautics and Space Admin.), Astronaut Wings (Navy), Astronaut Medal (Marine Corps), etc, 1962; Galabert Internat. Astronautical Prize (jointly with Lieut-Col Yuri Gagarin), 1963; also many other awards and citations from various countries and organizations. *Address:* 204 Rayburn Senate Office Building, Washington, DC 20515, USA; (home) 3996 Old Poste Road, Columbus, Ohio 43220, USA.

GLENN, Sir (Joseph Robert) Archibald, Kt 1966; OBE 1965; BCE; FIChemE, FIE (Aust.); Chairman: Collins Wales Pty Ltd, since 1973; I.C. Insurance Australia Ltd, since 1973; Tioxide Australia Ltd, since 1977; Director: Bank of New South Wales, since 1967; Hill Samuel Australia Ltd, since 1973; Alcoa of Australia Ltd, since 1973; Newmont Pty Ltd, since 1977; Westralian Sands Ltd, since 1977; *b* 24 May 1911; *s* of late J. R. Glenn, Sale, Vic., Aust.; *m* 1939, Elizabeth M. M., *d* of late J. S. Balderstone; one *s* three *d. Educ:* Scotch Coll. (Melbourne); University of Melbourne; Harvard (USA). Joined ICI Australia Ltd, 1935; Design and Construction Engr, 1935–44; Explosives Dept, ICI(UK), 1945–46; Chief Engineer, ICI Australia Ltd, 1947–48; Controller, Nobel Group, 1948–50; General Manager, 1950–52; Managing Director, 1953–73; Chm., 1963–73; Dir, ICI, London, 1970–75; Chairman: Fibremakers Ltd, 1963–73; IMI Australia Ltd, 1970–78. Chancellor, La Trobe Univ., 1967–72 (Hon. DUniv 1981); Chairman: Council of Scotch Coll., 1960–81. Ormond Coll. Council, 1976–81; Member: Manufacturing Industry Advisory Council, 1960–77; Industrial Design Council, 1958–70; Australia/Japan Business Co-operation Cttee, 1965–75; Royal Melbourne Hospital Bd of Management, 1960–70; Melbourne Univ. Appointments Bd; Council, Inst. of Pacific Affairs, 1976–; Governor, Atlantic Inst. of Internat. Affairs. J. N. Kirby Medal, 1970. *Recreations:* golf, tennis, collecting rare books. *Address:* 3 Heyington Place, Toorak, Melbourne, Vic 3142, Australia. *T:* 20 4453. *Clubs:* Australian, Melbourne, Frankston Golf, Victoria Racing, Melbourne Univ. Boat (all in Melbourne); Australian (Sydney).

GLENN, William James, CB 1968; BA, BAI, FICE; Director-General, Water Engineering, Department of the Environment, 1971–72, retired; *b* 26 June 1911; *s* of late John Glenn, Londonderry; *m* 1937, Wilhelmina Jane Gibson, MA, *d* of late John Gibson, Dublin; two *s. Educ:* Trinity Coll., Dublin Univ. Entered Air Min. as Asst Civil Engr, Directorate Gen. of Works, 1937; Sen. Civil Engr, Air HQ, W Africa, 1944–45; service in Airfield Construction Br, RAF, BAFO Germany, 1948–50; Chief Engr Flying Trng Comd, RAF, 1952–54; Dep. Dir of Works, 1956–57; Chief Engr, Far East Air Force, 1957–59; Dir of Works, 1962–65; Chief Civil Engr, MPBW, 1965–68; Chief Engineer, Min. of Housing and Local Govt, 1968–71. Mem. Bd, Maplin Develt Authy, 1973–74. Hon. FIPHE. *Recreation:* golf. *Address:* Bucklers, Hungerford Lane, Shurlock Row, near Reading RG10 0NY. *T:* Twyford 343445. *Clubs:* Royal Air Force; East Berkshire Golf.

GLENNIE, Alan Forbes Bourne, CMG 1956; *b* 11 April 1903; *s* of late Vice-Adm. R. W. Glennie, CMG; *m* 1931, Dorothy Sybil, *d* of late J. A. H. Johnston, DSc; one *s* one *d. Educ:* RN Colls Osborne and Dartmouth; Trinity Coll., Cambridge (MA). Joined Provincial Administration, N Rhodesia, 1924; Provincial Commissioner, 1945; Resident Commissioner, Barotseland Protectorate, Northern Rhodesia, 1953–57, retired; Government Sec., St Helena, 1963–65, retired. *Address:* 85 Gibson Road, Kenilworth 7700, Cape Province, Republic of South Africa. *Club:* Royal Over-Seas League.

GLENNY, Dr Robert Joseph Ervine, CEng, FIM; Group Head of Aerodynamics, Structures and Materials Departments, Royal Aircraft Establishment, since 1979; *b* 14 May 1923; *s* of late Robert and Elizabeth Rachel Glenny; *m* 1947, Joan Phillips Reid; one *s* one *d. Educ:* Methodist Coll., Belfast; QUB (BSc Chemistry); London Univ. (BSc Metallurgy, PhD). CEng, 1979; FIM 1958. Res. Metallurgist, English Electric Co. Ltd, Stafford, 1943–47; National Gas Turbine Establishment, 1947–70; Materials Dept, 1947–66; Head of Materials Dept, 1966–70; Supt, Div. of Materials Applications, National Physical Lab., 1970–73; Head of Materials Dept, RAE, 1973–79. *Publications:* research and review papers on materials science and technology, mainly related to gas turbines, in ARC (R&M series) and in Internat. Metallurgical Rev. *Recreations:* reading, gardening. *Address:* 77 Gally Hill Road, Church Crookham, Aldershot, Hants GU13 0RU. *T:* Fleet 5877.

GLENTORAN, 2nd Baron, *cr* 1939, of Ballyalloly; **Daniel Stewart Thomas Bingham Dixon,** 4th Bt, *cr* 1903; PC (Northern Ireland) 1953; KBE 1973; Lord-Lieutenant, City of Belfast, since 1976 (HM Lieutenant, 1950–76); *b* 19 Jan. 1912; *s* of 1st Baron, PC, OBE and Hon. Emily Ina Florence Bingham (*d* 1957), *d* of 5th Baron Clanmorris; *S* father 1950; *m* 1933, Lady Diana Mary Wellesley, *d* of 3rd Earl Cowley; two *s* one *d. Educ:* Eton; RMC Sandhurst. Reg. Army, Grenadier Guards; served War of 1939–45 (despatches); retired 1946 (with hon. rank of Lieut-Col); psc. MP (U) Bloomfield Division of Belfast, NI Parliament, Oct. 1950–Feb. 1961; Parliamentary Sec., Ministry of Commerce, NI, 1952–53; Minister of Commerce, 1953–61; Minister in Senate, NI, 1961–72, Speaker of Senate, 1964–72. Hon. Col 6th Battalion Royal Ulster Rifles, 1956–61, retd rank of Hon. Col. *Heir: s* Hon. Thomas Robin Valerian Dixon, MBE [*b* 21 April 1935; *m* 1st, 1959, Rona, *d* of Capt. G. C. Colville, Mill House, Bishop's Waltham, Hants; three *s*; 2nd, 1979, Alwyn Mason].

Address: Drumadarragh House, Doagh, Co. Antrim, Northern Ireland. *T:* Doagh 222. *Club:* Ulster (Belfast).

GLENTWORTH, Viscount; Edmund Christopher Pery; *b* 10 Feb. 1963; *s* and *heir* of 6th Earl of Limerick, *qv. Educ:* Eton. *Recreations:* skiing, sword swallowing. *Address:* 30 Victoria Road, W8 5RG. *T:* 01-937 0573; Chiddinglye, West Hoathly, East Grinstead, West Sussex RH19 4QT. *T:* Sharpthorne 810214.

GLIDEWELL, Hon. Sir Iain (Derek Laing), Kt 1980; **Hon. Mr Justice Glidewell;** a Judge of the High Court of Justice, Queen's Bench Division, since 1980; Presiding Judge, North Eastern Circuit, since 1982; *b* 8 June 1924; *s* of late Charles Norman and Nora Glidewell; *m* 1950, Hilary, *d* of late Clinton D. Winant; one *s* two *d. Educ:* Bromsgrove Sch.; Worcester Coll., Oxford. Served RAFVR, 1942-46. Called to the Bar, Gray's Inn, 1949, Bencher 1977. QC 1969; a Recorder of the Crown Court, 1976-80; a Judge of Appeal, Isle of Man, 1979-80. Member: Senate of Inns of Court and the Bar, 1976-79; Supreme Court Rule Cttee, 1980-. Chm., Panels for Examination of Structure Plans: Worcestershire, 1974; W Midlands, 1975; conducted Heathrow Fourth Terminal Inquiry, 1978. Associate, RICS, 1982. *Recreations:* beagling, walking, spasmodic interest in the Arts. *Address:* Royal Courts of Justice, Strand, WC2A 2LL; Oldfield, Knutsford, Cheshire WA16 8NT. *Clubs:* Garrick; Manchester (Manchester).

GLIN, Knight of; *see* Fitz-Gerald, D. J. V.

GLOAK, Graeme Frank, CB 1980; Solicitor for the Customs and Excise, 1978-82; *b* 9 Nov. 1921; *s* of late Frank and of Lilian Gloak; *m* 1944, Mary, *d* of Stanley and Jane Thorne; one *s* one *d* (and one *s* decd). *Educ:* Brentwood School. Royal Navy, 1941-46; Solicitor, 1947; Customs and Excise: Legal Asst, 1947; Sen. Legal Asst, 1953; Asst Solicitor, 1967; Principal Asst Solicitor, 1971. Sec., Civil Service Legal Soc., 1954-62. *Publication:* (with G. Krikorian and R. K. F. Hutchings) Customs and Excise, in Halsbury's Laws of England, 4th edn, 1973. *Recreations:* badminton, walking, watching cricket. *Address:* Northwold, 123 Priests Lane, Shenfield, Essex. *T:* Brentwood 212748. *Clubs:* MCC; Essex County Cricket (Chelmsford).

GLOCK, Sir William (Frederick), Kt 1970; CBE 1964; Chairman, London Orchestral Concerts Board, since 1975; Artistic Director, Bath Festival, since 1975; *b* London, 3 May 1908. *Educ:* Christ's Hospital; Caius Coll., Cambridge. Studied pianoforte under Artur Schnabel. Joined The Observer, 1934; chief music critic, 1939-45. Served in RAF, 1941-46. Dir, Summer Sch. of Music, Bryanston, 1948-52, Dartington Hall, 1953-79. Editor of music magazine The Score, 1949-61; adjudicated at Canadian music festivals, 1951; has lectured on music throughout England and Canada. Music Critic, New Statesman, 1958-59; Controller of Music, BBC, 1959-72. Editor, Eulenburg books on music, 1973-. Member: Bd of Dirs, Royal Opera House, 1968-73; Arts Council, 1972-75. Hon. Mem., Royal Philharmonic Soc., 1971. Hon. DMus Nottingham Univ., 1968; DUniv York, 1972. Albert Medal, RSA, 1971. *Address:* Sudbury House, Faringdon, Oxfordshire. *T:* Faringdon 20381.

GLOSSOP, Peter; Principal Baritone, Royal Opera House, Covent Garden, until 1967, now Guest Artist; *b* 6 July 1928; *s* of Cyril and Violet Elizabeth Glossop; *m* 1st, 1955, Joyce Elizabeth Blackham (marr. diss. 1977); no *c*; 2nd, 1977, Michèle Yvonne Amos. *Educ:* High Storrs Grammar Sch., Sheffield. Began singing professionally in chorus of Sadler's Wells Opera, 1952, previously a bank clerk; promoted to principal after one season; Covent Garden Opera, 1962-67. Début in Italy, 1964; La Scala, Milan, début, Rigoletto, 1965. Sang Otello and Rigoletto with Metropolitan Opera Company at Newport USA Festival, Aug. 1967; Rigoletto and Nabucco with Mexican National Opera Company, Sept. 1967. Guest Artist (Falstaff, Rigoletto, Tosca) with American National Opera Company, Oct. 1967. Has sung in opera houses of Bologna, Parma Catania, Vienna, 1967-68, and Berlin and Buenos Aires. Is a recording artist. Hon. DMus, Sheffield, 1970. Winner of 1st Prize and Gold Medal in First International Competition for Young Opera Singers, Sofia, Bulgaria, 1961; Gold Medal for finest performance (in Macbeth) of 1968-69 season, Barcelona. *Films:* Pagliacci, Otello. *Recreations:* New Orleans jazz music, squash rackets. *Address:* Elmcroft, 91 Cambridge Road, Teddington, Mddx. *Club:* Green Room.

GLOSTER, John, MD; Hon. Consultant, Moorfields Eye Hospital; *b* 23 March 1922; *m* 1947, Margery (*née* Williams); two *s. Educ:* Jesus Coll., Cambridge; St Bartholomew's Hosp. MB, BChir 1946; MRCS, LRCP 1946; DOMS 1950; MD Cantab 1953; PhD London 1959. Registrar, Research Dept, Birmingham and Midland Eye Hosp., 1950-54; Mem. Staff, Ophth. Research Unit, MRC, 1954-63; Prof. of Experimental Ophthalmology, Inst. of Ophth., Univ. of London, 1963; Dean of the Inst. of Ophthalmology, 1975-80. FRSocMed; Mem. Ophth. Soc. UK. *Publications:* Tonometry and Tonography, 1966; (jtly) Physiology of the Eye, System of Ophthalmology IV, ed Duke-Elder, 1968; contribs to jls. *Address:* Institute of Ophthalmology, Judd Street, WC1H 9QS.

GLOUCESTER, Bishop of, since 1975; **Rt. Rev. John Yates;** *b* 17 April 1925; *s* of late Frank and late Edith Ethel Yates; *m* 1954, Jean Kathleen Dover; one *s* two *d. Educ:* Battersea Grammar School; Blackpool Grammar School; Jesus College, Cambridge (MA). RAFVR (Aircrew), 1943-47; University of Cambridge, 1947-49; Lincoln Theological College, 1949-51. Curate, Christ Church, Southgate, 1951-54; Tutor and Chaplain, Lincoln Theological College, 1954-59; Vicar, Bottesford-with-Ashby, 1959-65; Principal, Lichfield Theological College, 1966-72; Bishop Suffragan of Whitby, 1972-75. *Address:* Bishopscourt, Pitt Street, Gloucester GL1 2BQ.

GLOUCESTER, Dean of; *see* Jennings, Very Rev. K. N.

GLOUCESTER, Archdeacon of; *see* Wagstaff, Ven. C. J. H.

GLOVER, Anthony Richard Haysom; Chief Executive Officer, City Council of Norwich, since 1980; *b* 29 May 1934; 2nd *s* of late Arthur Herbert Glover and late Marjorie Florence Glover; *m* 1960, Ann Penelope Scupham, *d* of John Scupham, *qv*; two *s* one *d. Educ:* Culford Sch., Bury St Edmunds; Emmanuel Coll., Cambridge (BA). HM Customs and Excise: Asst Principal, 1957; Principal, 1961; on secondment to HM Treasury, 1965-68; Asst Sec., 1969; Asst Sec., HM Treasury, 1972-76; Dep. Controller, HM Stationery Office, 1976-80. MBIM 1978. *Recreations:* music, reading, writing, alpine gardening. *Address:* 7 Hillside Road, Thorpe St Andrew, Norwich. *T:* Norwich 33508.

GLOVER, Eric; Secretary-General, Institute of Bankers, since 1982; *b* 28 June 1935; *s* of William and Margaret Glover; *m* 1960, Adele Diane Hilliard; three *s. Educ:* Liverpool Institute High Sch.; Oriel Coll., Oxford (MA). Shell International Petroleum (Borneo and Uganda), 1957-63; Institute of Bankers, 1963-. *Publications:* articles on banking education in banking jls. *Recreations:* mainly sport-golf, squash, tennis. *Address:* 12 Manor Park, Tunbridge Wells, Kent TN4 8XP. *T:* Tunbridge Wells 31221; (business) 01-623 3531. *Club:* Overseas Bankers'.

GLOVER, Sir Gerald (Alfred), Kt 1971; Senior Partner, Glover & Co.; President, Edger Investments Ltd, since 1980; *b* 5 June 1908; *m* 1933, Susan Drage (OBE 1982; Chm., Nat. Adoption Soc. for England); two *d. Educ:* City of London School. Solicitor, 1932. King's Messenger, 1938-40; served War of 1939-45, Mil. Intell., at home and abroad; Major. Conservative Party: Mem. 1935-; Mem. 1960-, Chm. 1963-71, Vice-Pres. 1972-74, Patron 1978-, E Midland Area Exec.; Treas. Kettering Div., 1953-67; President: Kettering Cons. Club, 1970-; Kettering Cons. Assoc., 1971-. Patron, London Branch, Red Cross; Trustee: National Adoption Soc. for England; Bankside Arts Centre; Founder: South Bank Arts Centre and Gallery, Southwark; East Kent Arts Centre and Gallery, Folkestone; Pres., Kettering and District Scouts; Past Pres., Northants Agricultural Soc. (Pres., 1970). CC Northants (Vice-Chm., 1972-74; Chm., Police Authority, 1978-). Liveryman, Basketmakers' Co. Freeman, City of London. *Recreations:* bloodstock breeding and racing (bred, raced and owns Privy Councillor, winner of 2000 Guineas, 1962), landscape gardening, visual art. *Address:* Pytchley House, Northants. *T:* Kettering 790258. *Clubs:* White's, Boodle's.
See also Sir James Spooner.

GLOVER, Harold, CB 1977; Coinage Consultant, International Nickel Co. Ltd, since 1977; *b* 29 Jan. 1917; 4th *s* of late George Glover, Wallasey, Ches; *m* 1949, Olive, *d* of late E. B. Robotham, Sawbridgeworth, Herts; two *s. Educ:* Wallasey Gram. Sch. Joined Customs and Excise, 1933; joined Min. of Works, 1949 (now DoE); Controller of Supplies, 1957; Under-Secretary, 1967-70; Dep. Master, Royal Mint, 1970-74; Controller, HMSO, 1974-77. Served RAF, 1940-46 (Flt Lieut Signals). FRSA 1963 (Mem Council, 1974-79; Bicentenary Medal, 1967); Hon. FSIAD 1975. *Recreation:* music. *Address:* 23 Walnut Tree Crescent, Sawbridgeworth, Herts. *T:* Bishops Stortford 223256. *Clubs:* Reform, Royal Air Force.

GLOVER, Lt-Gen. Sir James (Malcolm), KCB 1981; MBE 1964; Deputy Chief of Defence Staff (Intelligence), since 1981; *b* 25 March 1929; *s* of Maj.-Gen. Malcolm Glover, CB, OBE; *m* 1958, Janet Diones De Pree; one *s* one *d. Educ:* Wellington College; RMA, Sandhurst. Commissioned, RA, 1949; RHA, 1950-54; Instructor RMA Sandhurst, 1955-56; transferred to Rifle Brigade, 1956; Brigade Major, 48 Gurkha Bde, 1960-62; Directing Staff, Staff Coll., 1966-68; CO, 3rd Bn Royal Green Jackets, 1970-71; Col General Staff, Min. of Defence, 1972-73; Comdr 19 Airportable Bde, 1974-75; Brigadier General Staff, Min. of Defence, 1977-78; Commander Land Forces N Ireland, 1979-80; has served in W Germany, Malaya, Hong Kong, Cyprus (3 times) and N Ireland. *Recreations:* travel, gardening, shooting, hill walking. *Address:* c/o Lloyds Bank Ltd, Cox's & King's Branch, 6 Pall Mall, SW17 5NH. *Club:* Army and Navy.

GLOVER, Jane Alison, DPhil; conductor; Musical Director, Glyndebourne Touring Opera, since 1982; Senior Research Fellow, St Hugh's College, Oxford, since 1982; *b* 13 May 1949; *d* of Robert Finlay Glover, *qv. Educ:* Monmouth School for Girls; St Hugh's Coll., Oxford (BA, MA, DPhil). Junior Research Fellow, St Hugh's Coll., 1973-75; Lecturer in Music: St Hugh's Coll., 1976-; St Anne's Coll., 1976-80; Pembroke Coll., 1979-; elected to OU Faculty of Music, 1979. Professional conducting début at Wexford Festival, 1975; thereafter, operas and concerts repeatedly for BBC; Musica nel Chiostro, Batignano, Florence, Venice, Paris, London and Manchester; English Bach Fest.; Camden Fest.; National Gallery; Round House; Glyndebourne Festival Opera: joined Music Staff, 1979; Chorus Dir, 1980; Musical Dir of Touring co. and Fest. conductor, 1982; Teatro la Fenice, Venice; London Philharmonic Orch.; Bournemouth Sinfonietta; RTE Symphony Orch., etc. Television documentaries and presentation for BBC and LWT, esp. South Bank Show. *Publications:* Cavalli, 1978; articles in Music and Letters, Proc. of Royal Musical Assoc., Musical Times, The Listener, TLS, Early Music, and others. *Recreations:* The Times crossword puzzle, theatre, tennis. *Address:* 118 Bravington Road, W9 3AL. *T:* 01-960 8291.

GLOVER, John Neville, CMG 1963; *b* 12 July 1913; *s* of John Robert Glover and Sybil Glover (*née* Cureton); *m* 1st, 1940, Margot Burdick; one *s* ; 2nd, 1956, June Patricia Bruce Gaskell. *Educ:* Tonbridge Sch. Commissioned 6th Bn Devonshire Regt (TA), 1933; RAF (Gen. Duties Branch), 1934. Served RAF, 1934-46; RAFRO, 1946-59 (retained rank of Group Capt.). Called to Bar, Gray's Inn, 1949. Appointed to Colonial Legal Service, 1951; served: Ghana (Crown Counsel and Senior Crown Counsel), 1951-57; Western Pacific High Commission (Legal Adviser and Attorney-General, British Solomon Islands Protectorate), 1957-63. QC (Western Pacific), 1962. Retired from HM Overseas Civil Service, 1963. Comr to examine Human Rights Laws in the Bahamas, 1964-65. Legal Draftsman in the Bahamas, 1965-66. Law Revision Comr for certain overseas territories, 1967-. *Recreation:* fishing. *Address:* Clam End, Trebullett, near Launceston, Cornwall. *T:* Coad's Green 347. *Club:* Royal Air Force.

GLOVER, Kenneth Frank; Assistant Under-Secretary of State (Statistics), Ministry of Defence, 1974-81, retired; *b* 16 Dec. 1920; *s* of Frank Glover and Mabel Glover; *m* 1951, Iris Clare Holmes. *Educ:* Bideford Grammar Sch.; UC of South West, Exeter; LSE (MScEcon). Joined Statistics Div., MoT, 1946; Statistician, 1950; Statistical Adviser to Cttee of Inquiry on Major Ports (Rochdale Cttee), 1961-62; Dir of Econs and Statistics at Nat. Ports Council, 1964-68; Chief Statistician, MoT and DoE, 1968-74. *Publications:* various papers; articles in JRSS, Dock and Harbour Authority. *Recreations:* boating, idleness. *Address:* Riverdown, 11 Platway Lane, Shaldon, Teignmouth, South Devon TQ14 0AR. *T:* Shaldon 2700.

GLOVER, Myles Howard; Clerk of the Skinners' Company since 1959; Hon. Secretary, Governing Bodies' Association since 1967; *b* 18 Dec. 1928; *yr s* of Cedric Howard Glover and Winifred Mary (*née* Crewdson); *m* 1969, Wendy Gillian, *er d* of C. M. Coleman; one *s* two *d. Educ:* Rugby; Balliol Coll., Oxford (MA). Called to the Bar, Lincoln's Inn, 1954. Chm., Cttee of Clerks to Twelve Chief Livery Cos of City of London, 1975-81; Member: City & Guilds Art Sch. Cttee, 1960-71; City Univ. Adv. Cttee on the Arts, 1975-. *Recreation:* music. *Address:* Buckhall Farm, Bull Lane, Bethersden, near Ashford, Kent TN26 3HB. *T:* Bethersden 634.

GLOVER, Maj.-Gen. Peter James, CB 1966; OBE 1948; *b* 16 Jan. 1913; *s* of late G. H. Glover, CBE, Sheephatch House, Tilford, Surrey, and late Mrs G. H. Glover; *m* 1946, Wendy Archer; one *s* two *d. Educ:* Uppingham; Cambridge (MA). 2nd Lieut RA, 1934; served War of 1939-45, BEF France and Far East; Lieut-Col 1956; Brig. 1961; Comdt, Sch. of Artillery, Larkhill, 1960-62; Maj.-Gen. 1962; GOC 49 Infantry Division TA and North Midland District, 1962-63; Head of British Defence Supplies Liaison Staff, Delhi, 1963-66; Director, Royal Artillery, 1966-69, retd. Col Comdt, RA, 1970-78. *Address:* Lukesland, Diptford, Totnes, Devon.

GLOVER, Robert Finlay, TD 1954; Deputy Secretary, Headmasters' Conference and Association, 1977-82; *b* 28 June 1917; *yr s* of T. R. Glover, Public Orator in University of Cambridge, and Alice, *d* of H. G. Few; *m* 1941, Jean, *d* of late N. G. Muir, Lincoln; one *s* two *d. Educ:* The Leys Sch.; Corpus Christi Coll., Oxford. Served in Royal Artillery (TA), 1939-46; Staff Coll., Camberley, 1944; Major, 1944. Asst Master, Ampleforth Coll., 1946-50; Head of Classics Dept, King's Sch., Canterbury, 1950-53; Headmaster, Adams' Grammar Sch., Newport, Salop, 1953-59; Headmaster, Monmouth Sch., 1959-76. *Publications:* Notes on Latin, 1954; (with R. W. Harris) Latin for Historians, 1954. *Recreations:* normal. *Address:* Brockhill Lodge, West Malvern Road, The Wyche, Malvern, Worcs WR14 4EJ. *T:* Malvern 64247. *Club:* East India, Devonshire, Sports and Public Schools.
See also J. A. Glover.

GLOVER, William James, QC 1969; a Recorder of the Crown Court, since 1975; *b* 8 May 1924; *s* of late H. P. Glover, KC and Martha Glover; *m* 1956, Rosemary D. Long; two *s. Educ:* Harrow; Pembroke Coll., Cambridge. Served with Royal West African Frontier Force in West Africa and Burma, 1944-47. Called to Bar, Inner Temple, 1950, Bencher, 1977. Second Junior Counsel to Inland Revenue (Rating Valuation), 1963-69. *Recreation:* golf. *Address:* The White House, Well, Hants; Alderney, CI.

GLUBB, Lt.-Gen. Sir John Bagot, KCB 1956; CMG 1946; DSO 1941; OBE 1925; MC; Chief of General Staff, the Arab Legion, Amman, Jordan, 1939-56; *b* 16 April 1897; *s* of late Maj.-Gen. Sir F. M. Glubb, KCMG, CB, DSO; *m* 1938, Muriel Rosemary, *d* of Dr J. G. Forbes; two *s* two *d. Educ:* Cheltenham; Royal Military Academy, Woolwich, Aug. 1914; 2nd Lieut RE, 1915; served in France (wounded thrice, MC); to Iraq as Lieut RE, 1920; resigned commission, 1926, and became Administrative Inspector, Iraq Govt; transferred Transjordan, 1930; Officer Commanding Desert Area, 1932; Officer Commanding Arab Legion, Transjordan, 1939-56. *Publications:* Story of the Arab Legion, 1948; A Soldier with the Arabs, 1957; Britain and the Arabs, 1959; War in the Desert, 1960; The Great Arab Conquests, 1963; The Empire of the Arabs, 1963; The Course of Empire, 1965; The Lost Centuries, 1967; The Middle East Crisis-A Personal Interpretation, 1967; Syria, Lebanon, Jordan, 1967; A Short History of The Arab Peoples, 1969; The Life and Times of Muhammad, 1970; Peace in the Holy Land, 1971; Soldiers of Fortune, 1973; The Way of Love, 1974; Haroon al Rasheed, 1976; Into Battle: a soldier's

diary of the Great War, 1977; Arabian Adventures, 1978; A Purpose for Living, 1979. *Address:* West Wood, Mayfield, Sussex.

GLUE, George Thomas; Director-General of Supplies and Transport (Naval), Ministry of Defence, 1973-77; *b* 3 May 1917; *s* of Percy Albert Glue and Alice Harriet Glue (*née* Stoner); *m* 1947, Eileen Marion Hitchcock; one *d. Educ:* Portsmouth Southern Secondary School. Admiralty: Asst Naval Store Officer, 1937; Dep. Naval Store Officer, Mediterranean, 1940; Naval Store Officer, Mediterranean, 1943; Asst Dir of Stores, 1955; Suptg Naval Store Officer, Devonport, 1960; Dep. Dir of Stores, 1963; Dir of Stores, 1970; Dir, Supplies and Transport (Naval), 1971. *Recreations:* gardening, bridge. *Address:* Pine Court, 77 Victoria Road, Trowbridge, Wilts BA14 7LA. *T:* Trowbridge 61011.

GLYN, family name of **Baron Wolverton.**

GLYN, Dr Alan, ERD; MP (C) Windsor and Maidenhead, since 1974 (Windsor, 1970-74); *b* 26 Sept. 1918; *s* of John Paul Glyn, late Royal Horse Guards (Blues), Barrister-at-Law, Middle Temple, and late Margaret Johnston, Edinburgh; *m* 1962, Lady Rosula Caroline Windsor Clive, *y d* of 2nd Earl of Plymouth, PC, GCStJ (*d* 1943), St Fagan's, Cardiff, S Wales; two *d. Educ:* Westminster; Caius Coll., Cambridge; St Bartholomew's and St George's Hosps. BA (Hons) Cantab 1939. Qualified medical practitioner, 1948. Served War of 1939-45; Far East, 1942-46; psc 1945; Bde Major, 1946; re-employed Captain (Hon. Major) Royal Horse Guards (ER) until 1967; att. French Foreign Legion, 1960. Called to Bar, Middle Temple, 1955. Co-opted Mem. LCC Education Cttee, 1956-58. MP (C) Clapham Div. of Wandsworth, 1959-64. Member: Chelsea Borough Council, 1959-62; No 1 Divisional Health Cttee (London), 1959-61; Inner London Local Med. Cttee, 1967-; Governing Body, Brit. Postgrad. Med. Fedn, 1967-82; Greater London Cent. Valuation Panel, 1967-; Bd of Governors, Nat. Heart and Chest Hosps Special Health Auth., 1982-. Former Governor, Henry Thornton and Aristotle Schs; Manager, Macaulay C. of E. Sch., Richard Atkins, Henry Cavendish, Telfescot, Glenbrook and Boneville Primary Schs in Clapham. One of Earl Marshal's Green Staff Officers at Investiture of HRH Prince of Wales, Caernarvon, 1969. Freeman, Worshipful Soc. of the Art and Mystery of Apothecaries of the City of London, 1961. Pro-Hungaria Medal of SMO Malta, 1959. *Publication:* Witness to Viet Nam (the containment of communism in South East Asia), 1968. *Address:* 17 Cadogan Place, Belgrave Square, SW1. *T:* 01-235 2957. *Club:* Carlton.

GLYN, Sir Anthony (Geoffrey Leo Simon), 2nd Bt, *cr* 1927; author; *b* 13 March 1922; *s* of Sir Edward Davson, 1st Bt, and Margot, OBE (*d* 1966), *er d* of late Clayton Glyn and late Mrs Elinor Glyn; *S* father, Sir Edward Rae Davson, KCMG, 1937; assumed by deed poll, 1957, the surname of Glyn in lieu of his patronymic, and the additional forename of Anthony; *m* 1946, Susan Eleanor, barrister-at-law, 1950, *er d* of Sir Rhys Rhys-Williams, 1st Bt, DSO, QC, and Dame Juliet Rhys-Williams, DBE; one *d* (and one *d* decd). *Educ:* Eton. Jnd Welsh Guards, 1941; served Guards Armoured Div., 1942-45; Staff Capt, 1945. *Publications:* Romanza, 1953; The Jungle of Eden, 1954; Elinor Glyn, a biography, 1955 (Book Society Non-Fiction Choice); The Ram in the Thicket, 1957 (Dollar Book Club Choice); I Can Take it All, 1959 (Book Society Choice); Kick Turn, 1963; The Terminal, 1965; The Seine, 1966; The Dragon Variation, 1969; The Blood of a Britishman, 1970 (US edn, The British; trans. French, Spanish, Japanese). *Recreations:* ski-ing, Aubusson tapestry designing. *Heir:* *b* Christopher Michael Edward Davson, ACA, late Capt. Welsh Guards [*b* 26 May 1927; *m* 1962, Evelyn Mary (marr. diss. 1971), *o d* of late James Wardrop; one *s* ; 2nd, 1975, Kate, *d* of Ludovic Foster, Greatham Manor, Pulborough]. *Address:* 13 Rue le Regrattier, Ile Saint-Louis, 75004 Paris, France. *T:* 633:3475; Friedegg, Westendorf, Tyrol, Austria. *Clubs:* Savile, Pratt's.

GLYN, Hilary B.; *b* 12 Jan. 1916; *s* of Maurice Glyn and Hon. Maud Grosvenor; *m* 1938, Caroline Bull; one *s* two *d. Educ:* Eton; New Coll., Oxford. DipEconPolSc. Joined Gallaher Ltd, 1937. Served, RASC Supp. Reserve, 1939-46 (A/Major). Director, Gallaher Ltd, 1962; Asst. Man. Dir, 1975; retd, 1976. *Recreations:* shooting, horse trials. *Address:* Oakum House, Albury, Ware, Herts SG11 2LW. *T:* Albury 328.
See also J. P. R. Glyn.

GLYN, John Patrick Riversdale, CBE 1974; FIB; Chairman, First National Finance Corporation Ltd, since 1975 (Deputy Chairman, 1974-75); *b* 17 April 1913; *s* of Maurice G. C. Glyn and Hon. Maud Grosvenor; *m* 1937, Audrey Margaret Stubbs; two *s* two *d. Educ:* Eton; New Coll., Oxford. Major, Grenadier Guards. A Man. Dir, Glyn, Mills & Co., 1950-70; Chairman: John Govett & Co Ltd, 1970-75; Govett European Trust Ltd, 1972-75; Alexanders Discount Co. Ltd, 1961-81; Yorkshire Bank Ltd, 1970-81; Agricultural Mortgage Corp. Ltd, 1964-82. Mem., Develt Commn, 1965-81. FIB 1978. *Recreations:* fishing, shooting. *Address:* The Dower House, Chute Standen, near Andover, Hants. *T:* Chute Standen 228. *Clubs:* Boodle's, Pratt's.
See also H. B. Glyn.

GLYN, Sir Richard (Lindsay), 10th Bt *cr* 1759, and 6th Bt *cr* 1800; *b* 3 Aug. 1943; *s* of Sir Richard Hamilton Glyn, 9th and 5th Bt, OBE, TD, and Lyndsay Mary (*d* 1971), *d* of T. H. Baker; *S* father, 1980; *m* 1970, Carolyn Ann Williams (marr. diss. 1979); one *s* one *d. Educ:* Eton. *Recreation:* tennis. *Heir:* *s* Richard Rufus Francis Glyn, *b* 8 Jan. 1971. *Address:* Ashton Farmhouse, Wimborne, Dorset. *T:* Witchampton 840585.

GLYNN, Prof. Alan Anthony, MD; FRCP, FRCPath; Director, Central Public Health Laboratory, Colindale, London, since 1980; Visiting Professor of Bacteriology, St Mary's Hospital Medical School, since 1980; *b* 29 May 1923; *s* of Hyman and Charlotte Glynn; *m* 1962, Nicole Benhamou; two *d.* *Educ:* City of London Sch.; University Coll. London (Fellow, 1982) and UCH Med. Sch., London (MB, BS 1946, MD 1959). MRCP 1954, FRCP 1974; MRCPath 1963, FRCPath 1973. House Physician, UCH, 1946; Asst Lectr in Physiol., Sheffield Univ., 1947-49; National Service, RAMC, 1950-51; Registrar, Canadian Red Cross Meml Hosp., Taplow, 1955-57; St Mary's Hospital Medical School: Lectr in Bacteriology, 1958-61; Sen. Lectr, 1961-67; Reader, 1967-71; Prof., 1971-80; Hon. Consultant Bacteriologist, St Mary's Hosp., 1961-. Examr in Pathol., Univs of Edinburgh, 1974-76, Glasgow, 1975-78, and London, 1979-80. Member: DHSS Jt Cttee on Vaccination and Immunization, 1979-; Adv. Gp, ARC Inst. for Res. in Animal Diseases. Almroth Wright Lectr, Wright-Fleming Inst., 1972; Erasmus Wilson Demonstrator, RCS, 1973. Mem. Editorial Board: Immunology, 1969-79; Parasite Immunity, 1979-. *Publications:* papers on bacterial infection and immunity in jls. *Recreations:* theatre, walking, carpentry. *Address:* 33 Pembridge Square, W2 4DT. *T:* 01-229 2049.
See also Prof. I. M. Glynn.

GLYNN, Prof. Ian Michael, MD, PhD, FRS 1970; Professor of Membrane Physiology, University of Cambridge, since 1975; Fellow, Trinity College, since 1955, Vice-Master, since 1980; *b* 3 June 1928; 2nd *s* of Hyman and Charlotte Glynn; *m* 1959, Jenifer Muriel, 2nd *d* of Ellis and Muriel Franklin; one *s* two *d.* *Educ:* City of London Sch.; Trinity Coll., Cambridge; University Coll. Hosp. 1st cl. in Pts I and II of Nat. Sci. Tripos; BA (Cantab) 1949; MB, BChir, 1952; MD 1970. House Phys., Central Mddx Hosp., 1952-53; MRC Scholar at Physiol. Lab., Cambridge; PhD 1956. Nat. Service in RAF Med. Br., 1956-57; Trin. Coll. Res. Fellow, 1955-59, Staff Fellow and Dir of Med. Studies, 1961-73; Cambridge Univ. Demonstrator in Physiology, 1958-63, Lecturer, 1963-70, Reader, 1970-75. Vis. Prof., Yale Univ., 1969. Member: MRC, 1976-80 (Chm., Physiological Systems and Disorders Bd, 1976-78); Council, Royal Soc., 1979-81; ARC, 1981-. Chm., Editorial Bd, Jl of Physiology, 1968-70. *Publications:* scientific papers dealing with transport of ions across living membranes, mostly in Jl of Physiology. *Address:* Physiological Laboratory, Cambridge; Daylesford, Conduit Head Road, Cambridge. *T:* Cambridge 353079.
See also Prof. A. A. Glynn.

GLYNN, Prudence Loveday, (Lady Windlesham); journalist; editorial staff of The Times, 1966-81 (Fashion Editor, 1966-80); *b* 22 Jan. 1935; *d* of late Lt-Col R. T. W. Glynn, MC, and Evelyn Margaret Vernet Glynn; *m* 1965, 3rd Baron Windlesham, *qv*; one *s* one *d.* Member: Design Council, 1973-79; selection panel, Duke of Edinburgh's Design prize, 1971-73; CNAA, 1977-; CNAA Cttee for Art and Design, 1972-; Crafts Council, 1977-80; Mem. Council, Royal College of Art, 1969-77. Governor, English-Speaking Union, 1972-78; Trustee, Museum of London, 1981-. FRSA 1974. Cavaliere al merito della Repubblica Italiana, 1975. *Publications:* In Fashion, 1978; Skin to Skin, 1982; contribs to numerous jls, BBC, television etc. *Address:* The Manor House, Westhall Hill, Burford, Oxon.

GLYNN GRYLLS, Rosalie; *see* Mander, Lady (Rosalie).

GOAD, Sir (Edward) Colin (Viner), KCMG 1974; Secretary-General, Inter-Governmental Maritime Consultative Organization, 1968-73 (Deputy Secretary-General, 1963-68); Member, Advisory Board, International Bank, Washington DC, since 1974; *b* 21 Dec. 1914; *s* of Maurice George Viner Goad and Caroline (*née* Masters); *m* 1939, Joan Olive Bradley (*d* 1980); one *s.* *Educ:* Cirencester Grammar Sch.; Gonville and Caius Coll., Cambridge (Scholar, BA, First Class Hons). Ministry of Transport: Asst Principal, 1937; Principal, 1942; Asst Sec., 1948; Imperial Defence Coll., 1953; Under-Sec., 1963. *Recreations:* gardening, reading, eighteenth-century furniture. *Address:* The Paddock, Ampney Crucis, Glos. *T:* Poulton 353.

GOADBY, Hector Kenneth, FRCP; retired; Hon. Consulting Physician, St Thomas' Hospital, London; *b* 16 May 1902; *s* of late Sir Kenneth Goadby, KBE; *m* 1937, Margaret Evelyn (*née* Boggon); one *s* two *d.* *Educ:* Winchester; Trinity Coll., Cambridge (MA, MD). MRCS, LRCP 1926; FRCP 1936. Physician at Thomas's Hosp., 1934-67; Cons. Physician, Southern Army and Eastern Comd, India, 1945; Physician, St Peter's Hosp., Chertsey, 1948. *Publications:* contribs to Jl of Physiology, Lancet, Acta Medica Scandinavica. *Recreations:* sailing, golf. *Address:* Four Oaks Cottage, Beckley, Rye, East Sussex. *T:* Beckley 335. *Clubs:* Royal Cruising; Rye Golf.

GOBBI, Tito; opera singer, baritone; *b* 24 Oct. 1915; *s* of Giovanni and Enrica Weiss; *m* 1937, Tilde de Rensis; one *d.* *Educ:* Padua Univ. Scholarship, Scala Opera House, 1936-37. Appeared Rome Opera House, 1939. Repertoire of 100 operas. Has sung in all the major opera houses and concert halls throughout the world. Notably Salzburg Festival: Don Giovanni (under Fürtwangler), 1950; Falstaff (under von Karajan), 1957. Has recorded 27 Complete Operas and made numerous other records; has made many films and appeared on television all over the world. Started as Stage Director, Lyric Opera of Chicago, Oct. 1965; then Royal Opera House, Covent Garden; Master classes in Italy, USA and UK. Mem., The Friends of Covent Garden; Hon. Mem., Univ. of Chicago; Hon. RAM. Dr *hc* Rosary Coll., River Forest, Ill, USA, 1980. Disco d'Oro (Golden Record), 1959; Leopardo d'Oro, 1962.

Hon. Officer, NY Police, 1969. Commendatore al Merito della Repubblica Italiana, 1958; Officer of San Jago, Portugal, 1970; Grand Officer, Order of Merit, Italy, 1976. *Publication:* My Life, 1979. *Recreations:* painting, driving, shooting, moulding. *Address:* via Valle della Muletta 47, 00123 La Storta, Rome, Italy. *T:* 6990996. *Clubs:* Arts (London) (Hon. Mem.); Societa Dante Alighieri; (Patron) Verdi Soc. (Liverpool); Roma Libera (Rome); Lyons (Hon. Mem.).

GOBBO, Hon. Sir James (Augustine), Kt 1982; Hon. Mr Justice Gobbo; Judge of the Supreme Court of Victoria, Australia, since 1978; *b* 22 March 1931; *s* of Antonio Gobbo and Regina Gobbo (*née* Tosetto); *m* 1957, Shirley Lewis; two *s* three *d.* *Educ:* Xavier Coll., Kew, Victoria; Melbourne Univ. (BA Hons); Magdalen Coll., Oxford Univ. (MA). Called to Bar, Gray's Inn, London, 1956; Barrister and Solicitor, Victoria, Aust., 1956; signed Roll of Counsel, Victorian Bar, 1957; QC 1971. Commendatore all'Ordine di Merito, Republic of Italy, 1971. *Publications:* (ed) Cross on Evidence (Australian edn), 1970-1978. *Address:* 6 Florence Avenue, Kew, Victoria 3101, Australia. *T:* (03) 80-1669.

GOBLE, John Frederick; Solicitor, Senior Partner, Herbert Smith & Co., from May 1983 (partner since 1953); *b* 1 April 1925; *o s* of late John and Evileen Goble; *m* 1953, Moira Murphy O'Connor; one *s* three *d.* *Educ:* Highgate Sch.; Brasenose Coll., Oxford (MA). Sub-Lieut, RNVR, 1944-46. Admitted solicitor, 1951. A Crown Agent for Oversea Govts and Admins, 1974-79 (Dep. Chm., 1975-79); Mem. and Dep. Chm., Crown Agents for Oversea Govts and Admins, and Crown Agents Holding and Realisation Bd, 1980-82. Governor, Highgate Sch., 1978; The Friends of Highgate Sch. Soc., 1978-. *Recreations:* music, golf. *Address:* 63 Dovehouse Street, SW3. *T:* 01-352 6169; Watling House, 35-37 Cannon Street, EC4M 5SD. *T:* 01-236 3070. *Clubs:* Garrick, MCC, Hurlingham; New Zealand Golf (West Byfleet).

GODBER, Geoffrey Chapham, CBE 1961; DL; Chief Executive, West Sussex County Council, 1974-75, retired (Clerk of the Peace and Clerk to the Council, 1966-74); Clerk to the Lieutenancy of West Sussex, 1974-76 (Sussex, 1968-74); *b* 22 Sept. 1912; *s* of late Isaac Godber, Willington Manor, near Bedford; *m* 1937, Norah Enid (*née* Finney); three *s.* *Educ:* Bedford Sch. LLB (London) 1935; Solicitor, 1936. Deputy Clerk of the Peace, Northants, 1938-44; Clerk of the Peace, Clerk of the County Council and Clerk of the Lieutenancy, Salop, 1944-66; Hon. Sec., Soc. of Clerks of the Peace of Counties, 1953-61 (Chm., 1961-64); Chm., Assoc. of County Chief Executives, 1974-75. Member: Probation Adv. and Trg Bd, 1949-55; Child Care Adv. Council, 1953-56; Cttee of Inquiry into Inland Waterways, 1956-58; Redevelopment Adv. Cttee, Inland Waterways, 1959-62; Waterways Sub-Commn, Brit. Transport, 1959-62; Central Adv. Water Cttee, 1961-70; Minister of Health's Long Term Study Group, 1965-69; S-E Economic Planning Council, 1969-75; CS Adv. Council, 1971-78; British Waterways Bd, 1975-81; Chichester Harbour Conservancy, 1975-78; Shoreham Port Authority, 1976-82 (Dep. Chm., 1978-82); Chm., Open Air Museum, Weald and Downland, 1975-82. DL W Sussex 1975. *Recreations:* sailing, shooting. *Address:* Pricklows, Singleton, Chichester, West Sussex. *T:* Singleton 238. *Club:* Naval and Military.
See also Sir G. E. Godber.

GODBER, Sir George (Edward), GCB 1971 (KCB 1962; CB 1958); Chairman, Health Education Council, 1977-78 (Member, 1976-78); *b* 4 Aug. 1908; *s* of late I. Godber, Willington Manor, Bedford; *m* 1935, Norma Hathorne Rainey; two *s* one *d* (and two *s* two *d* decd). *Educ:* Bedford Sch.; New Coll., Oxford (Hon. Fellow, 1973); London Hospital; London Sch. of Hygiene. BA Oxon 1930; DM Oxon 1939; FRCP 1947; DPH London 1936. Medical Officer, Min. of Health, 1939; Dep. Chief Medical Officer, Min. of Health, 1950-60; Chief Medical Officer, DHSS, DES and Home Office, 1960-73. QHP, 1953-56. Scholar in Residence, NIH Bethesda, 1975. Vice-Pres., RCN, 1973. Fellow: American Hospital Assoc., and American Public Health Assoc., 1961; British Orthopaedic Assoc.; Mem. Dietetic Assoc., 1961; Hon. Member: Faculty of Radiologists, 1958; British Paediatric Assoc.; Pharmaceut. Soc., 1973. FRCOG ad eundem, 1966; FRCPsych 1973; FFCM 1974; Hon. FRCS, 1973; Hon. FRSM, 1973. Hon. LLD: Manchester, 1964; Hull, 1970; Nottingham, 1973; Hon. DCL: Newcastle 1972; Oxford 1973; Hon. DSc Bath, 1979. Hon. Fellow, London Sch. of Hygiene and Tropical Medicine, 1976. Bisset Hawkins Medal, RCP, 1965; 150th Anniversary Medal, Swedish Med. Soc., 1966; Leon Bernard Foundn Medal, 1972; Ciba Foundn Gold Medal, 1970; Therapeutics Gold Medal, Soc. of Apothecaries, 1973. Lectures: Thomas and Edith Dixon Belfast, 1962; Bartholomew, Rotunda, Dublin, 1963; Woolmer, Bio-Engineering Soc., 1964; Monkton Copeman, Soc. of Apothecaries, 1968; Michael M. Davis, Chicago, 1969; Harold Diehl, Amer. Public Health Assoc., 1969; Rhys Williams, 1969; W. M. Fletcher Shaw, RCOG, 1970; Henry Floyd, Inst. of Orthopaedics, 1970; First Elizabeth Casson Meml, Assoc. of Occ. Therapists, 1973; Cavendish, W London Med.-Chir. Soc., 1973; Heath Clark, London Univ., 1973; Rock Carling, Nuffield Provincial Hosps Trust, 1975; Thom Bequest, RCSE, 1975; Maurice Bloch, Glasgow, 1975; Ira Hiscock, Yale, 1975; John Sullivan, St Louis, 1975; Fordham, Sheffield, 1976; Lloyd Hughes, Liverpool, 1977; Gale Meml, SW England Faculty RCGP, 1978; Gordon, Birmingham, 1979; Samson Gamgee, Birm. Med. Inst., 1979. *Publications:* (with Sir L. Parsons and Clayton Fryers) Survey of Hospitals in the Sheffield Region, 1944; The Health Service: past, present and future (Heath Clark Lectures), 1974; Change in Medicine (Rock Carling monograph), 1975; British National Health

Service: Conversations, 1977; papers in Lancet, BMJ, Public Health. *Recreation:* golf. *Address:* 21 Almoners' Avenue, Cambridge CB1 4NZ. *T:* Cambridge 247491.

See also G. C. Godber.

GODDARD, Ann Felicity, QC 1982; a Recorder of the Crown Court, since 1979; *b* 22 Jan. 1936; *o c* of late Graham Elliott Goddard and Margaret Louise Hambrook Goddard (*née* Clark). *Educ:* Grey Coat Hosp., Westminster; Birmingham Univ. (LLB); Newnham Coll., Cambridge (LLB and Dip. in Comparative Legal Studies). Called to the Bar, Gray's Inn, 1960. *Recreation:* travel. *Address:* 3 Temple Gardens, Temple, EC4Y 9AU. *T:* 01-353 3102.

GODDARD, Lt-Gen. Eric Norman, CB 1947; CIE 1944; CBE 1942 (OBE 1919); MVO 1936; MC; IA, retired; *b* 6 July 1897; 3rd *s* of late Arthur Goddard, Chartered Acct, London; *m* 1939, Elizabeth Lynch, *d* of late Major Lynch Hamilton, and late Frances Prioleau; one *s. Educ:* Dulwich Coll. Commissioned Indian Army, 1915; service in Mesopotamia, Persia and Kurdistan, 1916–19 (despatches twice, OBE, MC); GSO3 AHQ India, 1923–25; 12th Frontier Force Regt, 1928; Staff Coll., Quetta, 1928–29; Bde Major, Nowshera Bde, 1932–34; Chitral relief, 1932 (despatches, bar to MC); Mohmand operations, 1933 (despatches); Bt Major, 1933; GSO2 Eastern Comd, 1934–36; Officer i/c King's Indian Orderly Officers, 1936 (MVO 4th class); Comdt 4th Bn 15 Punjab Regt, 1936; Bt Col 1939 and Col i/c Administration, Burma Army; Brigade Commander, Oct. 1940; Maj.-Gen. i/c Administration Army in Burma, Dec. 1941; served in Burma and on Eastern front, Dec. 1941–Dec. 1944, including Maj.-Gen. i/c Admin 11th Army Group and Allied Land Forces SE Asia, 1943–44 (despatches four times, CIE, CBE); GOC-in-C Southern Comd, India, 1947–48; Subst. Maj.-Gen. 1944; Actg Lieut-Gen. 1947; retired Nov. 1948 with hon. rank of Lieut-Gen. Special appointment CC Germany, 1949–53; Dir of Civil Defence, North-Western Region (Manchester), 1955–63; Pres., East Lancs Br., British Red Cross, 1964–66. *Address:* Muddles Cottage, Sparrows Green, Wadhurst, East Sussex TN5 6TW. *T:* Wadhurst 2364. *Club:* Army and Navy.

GODDARD, Harold Keith; QC 1979; barrister-at-law; a Recorder of the Crown Court, since 1978; *b* 9 July 1936; *s* of Harold and Edith Goddard; *m* 1963, Susan Elizabeth (*née* Stansfield); two *s. Educ:* Manchester Grammar Sch.; Corpus Christi Coll., Cambridge (Scholar; 1st Cl. Law Tripos 1957; MA, LLB). Bacon Scholar, Gray's Inn; called to the Bar, Gray's Inn, 1959. Practised on Northern Circuit, 1959–. Chm., Disciplinary Appeals Cttee, 1974–80, Mem. Council, 1980–, UMIST. *Recreation:* golf. *Address:* 77 Manchester Road, Wilmslow, Cheshire. *T:* Wilmslow 26409. *Clubs:* Manchester Tennis and Racquet; Wilmslow Golf; La Moye Golf (Jersey).

GODDARD, Maj.-Gen. John Desmond, MC 1944; *b* 13 Jan. 1919; *s* of late Major J. Goddard, HAC, Bombay and Gerrards Cross, Bucks; *m* 1948, Sheila Noel Vera, *d* of late C. W. H. P. Waud, Bombay and St John, Jersey; three *s* one *d. Educ:* Sherborne; RMA Woolwich. 2 Lieut, RA, 1939. Served War of 1939–45: France, 1939–40; N Africa, 1943; Italy, 1943–45. Brevet Lt-Col 1957; JSSC 1957; CO, 2 Fd Regt, RA, 1960–62; IDC 1964; CRA, 3 Div., 1965–66; BGS, Directorate Mil. Ops, MoD, 1966–69; Dir, Mil. Assistance Office, MoD, 1969–72, retired. Staff Dir, British Leyland Internat., 1972–78. *Recreations:* yachting, riding, shooting, golf, carpentry, gardening. *Address:* Cranford, Pinewood Hill, Fleet, Hants. *T:* Fleet 4825. *Clubs:* Army and Navy; Royal Lymington Yacht.

GODDARD, Air Marshal (retired) Sir (Robert) Victor, KCB 1947 (CB 1943); CBE 1940; MA Cantab; *b* 1897; *s* of late Charles Ernest Goddard, OBE, TD, MD; *m* 1924, Mildred Catherine Jane (*d* 1979), *d* of Alfred Markham Inglis; two *s* one *d. Educ:* RN Colls Osborne and Dartmouth; Jesus Coll., Cambridge; Imperial Coll. of Science, London. Served European War, 1914–19, with RN, RNAS, RFC and RAF; War of 1939–45 (despatches, American DSM); Dep. Dir of Intelligence, Air Min., 1938–39; AOA, GHQ, BEF, France, 1939, SASO 1940; Dir of Military Co-operation, Air Ministy, 1940–41; Chief of the Air Staff, New Zealand, and Commander Royal NZ Air Forces, South Pacific, 1941–43; AOA, Air Command, South-East Asia, 1943–46; RAF Representative at Washington, USA, 1946–48; Mem. of Air Council for Technical Services, 1948–51; retd 1951. Principal of the Coll. of Aeronautics, 1951–54. Pres., Airship Assoc., 1975–. Governor (Chm. 1948–57), St George's Sch., Harpenden, 1948–64; Governor, Bryanston Sch., 1957–78. Occasional broadcaster, 1934–. *Publications:* The Enigma of Menace, 1959; Flight towards Reality, 1975; Skies to Dunkirk, 1982. *Address:* Meadowgate Lodge, Brasted, Westerham, Kent TN16 1LN.

GODDEN, Charles Henry, CBE 1982; HM Diplomatic Service; Governor (formerly HM Commissioner), Anguilla, since 1978; *b* 19 Nov. 1922; *s* of Charles Edward Godden and late Catherine Alice Godden (*née* Roe); *m* 1943, Florence Louise Williams; two *d. Educ:* Tweeddale Sch., Carshalton; Morley Coll., Westminster. Served Army, 1941–46. Colonial Office, 1950–66 (seconded British Honduras, 1961–64: Perm. Sec., External Affairs; Dep. Chief Sec.; Clerk of Executive Council); FCO, 1966–: First Sec., 1968; Asst Private Sec. to Sec. of State for Colonies; Private Secretary: to Minister of State, FCO, 1967–70; to Parly Under Sec. of State, 1970; First Sec. (Commercial), Helsinki, 1971–75; First Sec., Belize, 1975–76; Dep. High Comr and Head of Chancery, Kingston, 1976–78. *Recreations:* cricket, walking, reading. *Address:* c/o Foreign and Commonwealth Office, SW1; (home) Stoneleigh, Blackboys, Sussex. *T:* Framfield 410. *Clubs:* MCC, Royal Commonwealth Society.

GODDEN, Ven. Max Leon; Archdeacon of Lewes and Hastings, since 1975 (of Lewes, 1972–75); Vicar of Glynde, Firle and Beddingham, since 1962; *b* 25 Nov. 1923; *s* of Richard George Nobel and Lucy Godden; *m* 1945, Anne, *d* of Kenneth and Edith Hucklebridge; four *d. Educ:* Sir Andrew Judd Sch., Tonbridge; Worcester Coll., Oxford (MA 1950). Served RAFVR, 1940–47 (despatches). Deacon, 1952; priest, 1953; Assistant Curate: Cuckfield, 1952–53; Brighton, 1953–57; Vicar of Hangleton, 1957–62. *Recreations:* life in a country parish, the garden. *Address:* Glynde Vicarage, Lewes, East Sussex. *T:* Glynde 234.

GODDEN, Rumer; *see* Haynes Dixon, Margaret Rumer.

GODDEN, Tony Richard Hillier, CB 1975; Secretary, Scottish Development Department, since 1980; *b* 13 Nov. 1927; *o s* of late Richard Godden and of Gladys Eleanor Godden; *m* 1953, Marjorie Florence Snell; one *s* two *d. Educ:* Barnstaple Grammar Sch.; London Sch. of Economics. Commissioned, RAF Education Branch, 1950. Entered Colonial Office as Asst Principal, 1951; Private Sec. to Parly Under-Sec. of State, 1954–55; Principal, 1956; Cabinet Office, 1957–59; transferred to Scottish Home Dept, 1961; Asst Sec., Scottish Development Dept, 1964; Under-Sec., 1969; Sec., Scottish Economic Planning Dept, 1973–80. *Address:* New St Andrew's House, Edinburgh EH1 3SZ. *Club:* New (Edinburgh).

GODFREY, Derrick Edward Reid, MSc, PhD; Director, Thames Polytechnic, 1970–78; *b* 3 May 1918; *s* of Edward Godfrey; *m* 1944, Jessie Mary Richards; three *s* one *d. Educ:* Shooters Hill Grammar Sch.; King's Coll., London. Design and development of aero-engines, with D. Napier & Sons, 1940–45; Lectr and Reader in Applied Mathematics, Battersea Polytechnic, 1945–58; Head of Dept of Mathematics and later Principal, Woolwich Polytechnic, 1958–70. Mem. Council for Nat. Academic Awards, 1964–67. *Publications:* Elasticity and Plasticity for Engineers, 1959; contribs to learned jls, etc, on mathematics and on educational matters. *Recreations:* music, gardening. *Address:* Higher Pitt, Coombelake, Ottery St Mary, Devon. *T:* Ottery St Mary 2551.

GODFREY, Gerald Michael, QC 1971; *b* 30 July 1933; *s* of late Sidney Godfrey and late Esther (*née* Lewin); *m* 1960, Anne Sheila, *er d* of David Goldstein; three *s* two *d. Educ:* Lower Sch. of John Lyon, Harrow; King's Coll., London Univ. LLB 1952, LLM 1954. Called to the Bar: Lincoln's Inn, 1954 (Bencher 1978); Bahamas, 1972; Hong Kong, 1974; Kenya, 1978; Singapore, 1978; Malaysia, 1979; Brunei, 1979; National Service as 2nd Lt, RASC, 1955; Temp. Captain, 1956. In practice at the Chancery Bar, 1957–. Chm., Justice Cttee on Parental Rights and Duties and Custody Suits (Report, 1975); DoT Inspector into Affairs of Saint Piran Ltd (Report, 1981). Member: Senate of Inns of Court and the Bar, 1974–77, 1981– (Chm., Law Reform Cttee); Council of Justice, 1976. *Publication:* Editor, Business Law Review, 1958. *Recreations:* cricket, claret, music. *Address:* 10 Brampton Grove, NW4; 9 Old Square, Lincoln's Inn, WC2A 3SR. *Club:* MCC.

GODFREY, Dr Malcolm Paul Weston, JP; Dean of Royal Postgraduate Medical School, since 1974; *b* 11 Aug. 1926; *s* of late Harry Godfrey and of Rose Godfrey; *m* 1955, Barbara Goldstein; one *s* two *d. Educ:* Hertford Grammar Sch.; King's Coll., London Univ.; KCH Med. Sch. MB, BS (Hons and Univ. Medal) 1950; MRCP 1955, FRCP 1972. Hosp. posts at KCH, Nat. Heart and Brompton Hosps; RAF Med. Br., 1952–54; Fellow in Med. and Asst Physician (Out-patients Dept) Johns Hopkins Hosp., USA, 1957–58; MRC Headquarters Staff, 1960–74: MO, 1960; Sen. MO, 1964; Principal MO, 1970; Sen. Principal MO, 1974. University of London: Member: Senate, 1980–; Court, 1981–; Chm., Jt Med. Adv. Cttee, 1979–; Member: Sci. Adv. Panel CIBA Foundn, 1974–; Ealing, Hammersmith and Hounslow AHA(T), 1975–80; NW Thames RHA, 1980–; Sec. of States Adv. Gp on London Health Services, 1980–81; Council, Charing Cross Hosp. Med. Sch., 1975–80; Governing Body, British Postgrad. Med. Fedn, 1974–; GMC, 1979–81; Court of Assts, Worshipful Soc. of Apothecaries, 1979–. JP Wimbledon, 1972 (Dep. Chm., Juvenile Panel, 1979–). *Publications:* contrib. med. jls on cardiac and respiratory disorders. *Recreations:* theatre, planning holidays (sometimes taking them), walking. *Address:* Flat 7, 21 Hyde Park Square, W2 2JR. *T:* 01-723 2588; Royal Postgraduate Medical School, Hammersmith Hospital, Du Cane Road, W12 0HS. *T:* 01-743 2030. *Club:* Savile.

GODFREY, Norman Eric; Commissioner, HM Customs and Excise, since 1979; *b* 16 Aug. 1927; *s* of Cecil and Beatrice Godfrey. *Educ:* Northampton Grammar Sch.; London Sch. of Econs (BScEcon). HM Customs and Excise: Asst Principal, 1949; Principal, 1954; Asst Sec., 1965; on loan to NEDO, 1967, and to Min. of Transport/DoE, 1968–71; Under Sec. on loan to Price Commn, 1976–79. *Address:* HM Customs and Excise, King's Beam House, Mark Lane, EC3 7HE.

GODFREY, Peter, FCA; Senior Partner, Ernst & Whinney, Chartered Accountants; *b* 23 March 1924; *m* 1951, Heather Taplin; two *s* one *d. Educ:* West Kensington Central Sch.; City of London Coll. Served War, Army, 1942, until released, rank Captain, 1947. Qual. as an Incorporated Accountant, 1949; joined Whinney Smith & Whinney, 1949; admitted to partnership, 1959. Appointed: BoT Inspector into Affairs of Pinnock Finance Co. (GB) Ltd, Aug. 1967; DTI Inspector into Affairs of Rolls-Royce Ltd, April 1971; Mem., ODM Cttee of Inquiry on Crown Agents, April 1975. *Recreations:* family, militaria. *Address:* Oak Tree Cottage, Heathside Park Road, Woking, Surrey. *T:* Woking 60318. *Clubs:* Army and Navy, City of London.

GODLEY, family name of **Baron Kilbracken.**

GODLEY, Prof. Hon. Wynne Alexander Hugh; Director of Department of Applied Economics, since 1970, Professor of Applied Economics, since 1980, University of Cambridge; Fellow of King's College, Cambridge, since 1970; *b* 2 Sept. 1926; *yr s* of Hugh John, 2nd Baron Kilbracken, CB, KC and Elizabeth Helen Monteith, *d* of Vereker Monteith Hamilton; *m* 1955, Kathleen Eleonora, *d* of Sir Jacob Epstein, KBE; one *d*. *Educ:* Rugby; New Coll., Oxford; Conservatoire de Musique, Paris. Professional oboist, 1950. Joined Economic Section, HM Treasury, 1956; Dep. Dir, Economic Sect., HM Treasury, 1967-70. Dir, Investing in Success Equities Ltd, 1970-; a Dir, Royal Opera House, Covent Garden, 1976-. An Economic Consultant, HM Treasury, 1975; Official Advr, Select Cttee on Public Expenditure. *Publications:* (with T. F. Cripps) Local Government Finance and its Reform, 1976; The Planning of Telecommunications in the United Kingdom, 1978; (with K. J. Coutts and W. D. Nordhaus) Pricing in the Trade Cycle, 1978; articles, in National Institute Review, Economic Jl, London and Cambridge Economic Bulletin, Cambridge Economic Policy Review, Economica. *Address:* Eversden House, Great Eversden, Cambs.

GODSELL, Stanley Harry; Regional Director (South West), Departments of Environment and Transport, 1978-80; retired; *b* 19 March 1920; *s* of Thomas Harry Godsell and Gladys Godsell; *m* 1946, Rosemary Blackburn; one *s* (and one *s* decd). *Educ:* Alsop High Sch., Liverpool. Civil Service: PO, 1937-48; Min. of Town and Country Planning, 1948; Asst Sec., Min. of Housing and Local Govt, 1965. Chm., Bristol Citizens Advice Bureau, 1980-. *Recreations:* swimming, photography. *Address:* 6 Pitch and Pay Park, Sneyd Park, Bristol BS9 1NJ. *T:* Bristol 683791.

GODWIN, Dame (Beatrice) Anne, DBE 1962 (OBE 1952); a Governor of the BBC, 1962-68; a full-time Member of the Industrial Court, 1963-69; *b* 1897. Gen. Sec., Clerical and Administrative Workers' Union, 1956-62. Chm. of the TUC, 1961-62. *Recreations:* talking, gardening, reading. *Address:* 25 Fullbrooks Avenue, Worcester Park, Surrey KT4 7PE.

GODWIN, Prof. Sir Harry, Kt 1970; FRS 1945; FLS; MA, ScD; Professor of Botany, University of Cambridge, 1960-68, Emeritus 1968; Fellow of Clare College, Cambridge, since 1925; *b* 9 May 1901; *m* 1927, Margaret Elizabeth Daniels; one *s* decd. University Reader in Quaternary Research, Cambridge, Oct. 1948-60. Croonian Lectr, Royal Soc., London, 1960. Pres., Xth International Botanical Congress, 1964. Foreign Member: Royal Danish Acad. of Science and Letters; Royal Scientific Soc. of Uppsala; German Acad. of Science Leopoldina; Amer. Acad. Arts and Scis; Hon. Mem., Royal Soc. of New Zealand; MRIA. Hon. ScD, Trinity Coll., Dublin, 1960. Hon. DSc: Lancaster, 1968; Durham, 1974. Prestwick Medal, Geol. Soc., London, 1951; Gold Medal, Linnean Soc., London, 1966; Gunnar Erdtman Medal for Palynology, 1980. *Publications:* Plant Biology, 1930; History of the British Flora, 1956, new edn, 1975; Fenland: its ancient past and uncertain future, 1978; The Archives of the Peat Bogs, 1981. *Address:* 30 Barton Road, Cambridge CB3 9LF; Clare College, Cambridge. *T:* Cambridge 350883.

GOEHR, Prof. Alexander; composer; Professor of Music, and Fellow of Trinity Hall, University of Cambridge, since 1976; *b* 10 Aug. 1932; *s* of Walter and Laelia Goehr. *Educ:* Berkhamsted; Royal Manchester Coll. of Music; Paris Conservatoire. Lectr, Morley Coll., 1955-57; Music Asst, BBC, 1960-67; Winston Churchill Trust Fellowship, 1968; Composer-in-residence, New England Conservatory, Boston, Mass, 1968-69; Associate Professor of Music, Yale University, 1969-70; West Riding Prof. of Music, Leeds Univ., 1971-76. Artistic Dir, Leeds Festival, 1975; Vis. Prof., Peking Conservatoire of Music, 1980. Mem., Bd of Dirs, Royal Opera House, 1982-. Hon. FRMCM; Hon. FRAM 1975; Hon. FRNCM 1980; Hon. FRCM 1981. Hon. DMus Southampton, 1973. *Compositions include:* Fantasia Op. 4; Violin Concerto; Little Symphony; Pastorals; Romanza for 'cello; Symphony in one Movement, Op. 29; Piano Concerto, 1970; Concerto for Eleven, 1972; Metamorphosis/Dance, 1973; Lyric Pieces, 1974; Konzertstück, 1974; Kafka Fragments, 1979; Sinfonia, 1980; Deux Etudes, 1981; chamber music; *opera:* Arden must die; *cantatas:* Sutter's Gold; The Deluge; Triptych (Naboth's Vineyard; Shadowplay; Sonata about Jerusalem); Babylon the Great is Fallen. *Address:* Trinity Hall, Cambridge; University Music School, West Road, Cambridge; c/o Schott & Co Ltd, 48 Great Marlborough Street, W1.

GOFF, Martyn, OBE 1977; Director of the National Book League since 1970; *b* 7 June 1923; *s* of Jacob and Janey Goff. *Educ:* Clifton College. Served in Royal Air Force, 1941-46. Film business, 1946-48; Bookseller, 1948-70. Has lectured on: music; English fiction; teenager morality; the book trade, 1946-70; Fiction reviewer, Daily Telegraph, 1975-. Founder and Chm., Bedford Square Bookbang, 1971. Member: Arts Council Literature Panel, 1970-78; Arts Council Trng Cttee, 1973-78; Greater London Arts Assoc. Literature Panel, 1973-81; British Nat. Bibliography Res. Fund, 1976-; British Library Adv. Council, 1977-82; PEN Exec. Cttee, 1978-; Chairman: Paternosters '73 Library Adv. Council, 1972-74; New Fiction Soc., 1975-; School Bookshop Assoc., 1977-; Soc. of Bookmen, 1982-; Trustee: Cadmean Trust, 1981-; Battersea Arts Centre, 1981-. FIAL 1958, FRSA 1979. *Publications:* The Plaster Fabric, 1957; A Short Guide to Long Play, 1957; A Season with Mammon, 1958; A Further Guide to Long Play, 1958; A Sort of Peace, 1960; LP Collecting, 1960; The Youngest Director, 1961; Red on the Door, 1962; The Flint Inheritance, 1965; Indecent Assault, 1967; Why Conform?, 1968; Victorian and Edwardian Surrey, 1972; Record Choice,

1974; Royal Pavilion, 1976; The Liberation of Rupert Bannister, 1978; Organising Book Exhibitions. *Recreations:* travel, collecting paintings and sculptures, music. *Address:* Book House, 45 East Hill, Wandsworth, SW18 2QZ. *T:* 01-870 9055/8. *Clubs:* Athenæum, Savile.

GOFF, Rt. Hon. Sir Robert (Lionel Archibald), Kt 1975; PC 1982; DCL; **Rt. Hon. Lord Justice Goff;** a Lord Justice of Appeal, since 1982; *b* 12 Nov. 1926; *s* of Lt-Col L. T. Goff and Mrs Goff (*née* Denroche-Smith); *m* 1953, Sarah, *er d* of Capt. G. R. Cousins, DSC, RN; one *s* two *d* (and one *s* decd). *Educ:* Eton Coll.; New Coll., Oxford (MA 1953, DCL 1972). Served in Scots Guards, 1945-48 (commnd 1945). 1st cl hons Jurisprudence, Oxon, 1950. Called to the Bar, Inner Temple, 1951; Bencher, 1975; QC 1967. Fellow and Tutor, Lincoln Coll., Oxford, 1951-55; in practice at the Bar, 1956-75; a Recorder, 1974-75; Judge of the High Ct, QBD, 1975-82; Judge i/c Commercial List, and Chm. Commercial Court Cttee, 1979-81. Chairman: Council of Legal Educn, 1976- (Vice-Chm., 1972-76; Chm., Bd of Studies, 1970-76); Common Professional Examination Bd, 1976-78; Hon. Prof. of Legal Ethics, Univ. of Birmingham, 1980-81. Member: Gen. Council of the Bar, 1971-74; Senate of Inns of Court and Bar, 1974- (Chm., Law Reform and Procedure Cttee, 1974-76). Hon. DLitt City, 1977. *Publications:* (with Prof. Gareth Jones) The Law of Restitution, 1966. *Address:* Royal Courts of Justice, Strand, WC2.

GOFF, Sir Robert (William Davis-), 4th Bt *cr* 1905; Director, Cynthia O'Connor & Co. Ltd, Art Dealers, Dublin; *b* 12 Sept. 1955; *s* of Sir Ernest William Davis-Goff, 3rd Bt, and of Alice Cynthia Davis-Goff (*née* Woodhouse); *S* father, 1980; *m* 1978, Nathalie Sheelagh, *d* of Terence Chadwick; one *s*. *Educ:* Cheltenham College, Glos. *Recreation:* shooting. *Heir: s* William Nathaniel Davis-Goff, *b* 20 April 1980. *Address:* 199 Strand Road, Dublin 4, Ireland. *Club:* Kildare Street and University (Dublin).

GOHEEN, Robert Francis; educator; President Emeritus, Princeton University; *b* Venguria, India, 15 Aug. 1919; *s* of Dr Robert H. H. Goheen and Anne Ewing; *m* 1941, Margaret M. Skelly; two *s* four *d*. *Educ:* Princeton Univ. AB 1940; PhD 1948. Princeton University: Instructor, Dept of Classics, 1948-50; Asst Prof., 1950-57; Prof., 1957-72; President, 1957-72. Chm., Council on Foundns, 1972-77; US Ambassador to India, 1977-80. Dir, Mellon Fellowships in the Humanities, 1982-. Sen. Fellow in Classics, Amer. Academy in Rome, 1952-53; Dir Nat. Woodrow Wilson Fellowship Program, 1953-56. Former Member: Bd, Carnegie Foundn for Advancement of Teaching; Bd, Rockefeller Foundation; Bd, Amer. Acad. in Rome; Bd, Equitable Life Assurance Soc.; Bd, Dreyfus Third Century Fund; Bd, Reza Shah Kabir Univ., Iran; Member: Internat. Adv. Bd, Chemical Bank; Adv. Council, Woodrow Wilson Sch., Princeton Univ. (Sen. Fellow, 1981-); American Philological Soc.; American Academy of Arts and Sciences; Phi Beta Kappa; Trustee: Midlantic Banks Inc.; Thomson Newspapers Inc.; Carnegie Endowment for Internat. Peace; Inst. of Internat. Educn; United Bd of Christian Higher Educn in Asia. Hon. degrees: Harvard, Rutgers, Yale, Temple, Brown, Columbia, New York, Madras, Pennsylvania, Hamilton, Middlebury, Saint Mary's (Calif), State of New York, Denver, Notre Dame, N Carolina, Hofstra, Nebraska, Dropsie, Princeton; Tusculum Coll.; Trinity Coll., USA; Coll. of Wooster; Jewish Theological Seminary of America; Ripon Coll.; Rider Coll. *Publications:* The Imagery of Sophocles' Antigone, 1951; The Human Nature of a University, 1969; articles. *Recreations:* tennis and golf. *Address:* 1 Orchard Circle, Princeton, New Jersey 08540, USA. *T:* 452-3000. *Clubs:* Princeton, University, Century Association (New York); Cosmos (Washington); Nassau (Princeton); Gymkhana, Delhi Golf (Delhi).

GOLD, Arthur Abraham, CBE 1974; President, European Athletic Association, since 1976; Chairman, Commonwealth Games Council for England, since 1979; Honorary Secretary, British Amateur Athletic Board, 1965-77 (Life Vice President, 1977); President, Counties Athletic Union, since 1978; Member, Sports Council, since 1980; *b* 10 Jan. 1917; *s* of late Mark and Leah Gold; *m* 1942, Marion Godfrey, *d* of late N. Godfrey; one *s*. *Educ:* Grocers' Company's Sch. Inst. of Motor Industry Wakefield Gold Medallist, 1945. Internat. high jumper, 1937; Past President: London AC; Middlesex County AAA; Athletics Team Leader Olympic Games: Mexico, 1968; Munich, 1972; Montreal, 1976. Council Mem., European Athletic Assoc., 1966-76; Mem. Council and F&GP Cttee, British Olympic Assoc.; Mem. Exec. Cttee, CCPR. *Publications:* Ballet Training Exercises for Athletes, 1960; various contribs to technical books on athletics. *Recreations:* walking, talking, reading, weeding. *Address:* 49 Friern Mount Drive, Whetstone, N20 9DJ. *T:* 01-445 2848. *Clubs:* City Livery; London Athletic.

GOLD, Jack; film director; *b* 28 June 1930; British; *m* 1957, Denyse (*née* Macpherson); two *s* one *d*. *Educ:* London Univ. (BSc (Econs), LLB). Asst Studio Manager, BBC radio, 1954-55; Editor, Film Dept, BBC, 1955-60; Dir, TV and film documentaries and fiction, 1960-. Desmond Davies Award for services to television, BAFTA, 1976. *TV films:* Tonight; Death in the Morning (BAFTA Award, 1964); Modern Millionairess; Famine; Dispute; 90 Days; Dowager in Hot Pants; World of Coppard (BAFTA Award, 1968); Mad Jack (Grand Prix, Monte Carlo, 1971); Stocker's Copper (BAFTA Award, 1972); Arturo Ui; The Lump; Catholics (Peabody Award, 1974); The Naked Civil Servant (Italia Prize, 1976, Internat. Emmy, and Critics Award, 1976); Thank You Comrades; Marya; Charlie Muffin; A Walk in the Forest; Merchant of Venice; Bavarian Night; A Lot of Happiness (Kenneth Macmillan), 1981; Praying Mantis, Macbeth, L'Elegance, 1982; *cinema:* The

Bofors Gun, 1968; The Reckoning, 1969; The National Health, 1973 (Evening News Best Comedy Award); Who?, 1974; Man Friday, 1974; Aces High, 1976 (Evening News Best Film Award); The Medusa Touch, 1977; The Sailor's Return, 1978 (jt winner, Martin Luther King Meml Prize, 1980; Monte Carlo Catholic Award, 1981; Monte Carlo Critics Award, 1981); Little Lord Fauntleroy, 1981 (Christopher Award); *stage play:* The Devil's Disciple, Aldwych, 1976. *Recreations:* music, reading. *Address:* 18 Avenue Road, N6 5DW.

GOLD, John (Joseph Manson); Manager of Public Relations, Hong Kong Mass Transit Railway, 1975-79; *b* 2 Aug. 1925; *m* 1953, Berta Cordeiro; one *d. Educ:* Claysmore Sch., Dorset. Yorkshire Evening News, 1944-47; London Evening News, 1947-52; Australian Associated Press (New York), 1952-55; New York Corresp., London Evening News, 1955-66; Editor, London Evening News, 1967-72; Dir, Harmsworth Publications Ltd, 1967-73. Freelance writer and lectr, Far East, 1973-75. *Address:* 21 Brookside, Cambridge CB2 1JQ.

GOLD, Sir Joseph, Kt 1980; Senior Consultant, International Monetary Fund, since 1979; *b* 12 July 1912; *m* 1939, Ruth Schechter; one *s* two *d. Educ:* Univ. of London (LLB 1935, LLM 1936); Harvard Univ. (SJD). Asst Lectr, University Coll., London, 1937-39; British Mission, Washington, DC, 1942-46; joined IMF, 1946; General Counsel and Dir, Legal Dept, 1960-79. *Publications:* The Fund Agreement in the Courts, vol. I, 1962, vol. II, 1982; The Stand-by Arrangements of the IMF, 1970; Voting and Decisions in the IMF, 1972; Membership and Nonmembership in the IMF, 1974; Los Acuerdos de Derechos de Giro del Fondo Monetario Internacional, 1976; Legal and Institutional Aspects of the International Monetary System, 1979; Aspectos Legales de La Reforma Monetario Internacional, 1979; numerous pamphlets and articles on internat. and nat. monetary law in many countries. *Recreations:* collecting first editions 20th century English and American poetry, assemblages of found objects, gardening, defence of English language. *Address:* 7020 Braeburn Place, Bethesda, Maryland 20817, USA. *T:* 301-229-3278.

GOLD, Stephen Charles, MA, MD, FRCP; Consulting Physician to: the Skin Department, St George's Hospital; St John's Hospital for Diseases of the Skin; King Edward VII Hospital for Officers; Former Hon. Consultant in Dermatology: to the Army; to Royal Hospital, Chelsea; *b* Bishops Stortford, Herts, 10 Aug. 1915; *yr s* of late Philip Gold, Stansted, Essex, and late Amy Frances, *er d* of James and Mary Perry; *m* 1941, Betty Margaret, *o d* of late Dr T. P. Sheedy, OBE; three *s* one *d. Educ:* Radley Coll.; Gonville and Caius Coll., Cambridge; St George's Hosp. (Entrance Exhibnr); Zürich and Philadelphia. BA 1937; MRCS, LRCP 1940; MA, MB, BChir 1941; MRCP 1947; MD 1952; FRCP 1958. Served RAMC, 1941-46. Late Med. First Asst to Out-Patients, St George's Hosp., Senior Registrar, Skin Dept, St George's Hosp., Sen. Registrar, St John's Hosp. for Diseases of the Skin; Lectr in Dermatology, Royal Postgraduate Med. Sch., 1949-69. Sec., Brit. Assoc. of Dermatology, 1965-70 (Pres., 1979). FRSM (late Sec. Dermatological Section, Pres., 1972-73); Fellow St John's Hosp. Dermatological Soc. (Pres., 1965-66). *Address:* 149 Harley Street, W1N 2DE. *T:* 01-935 4444.

GOLD, Prof. Thomas, FRS 1964; Director, Center for Radio-Physics and Space Research, 1959-81, and John L. Wetherill Professor of Astronomy, since 1971, Cornell University; *b* 22 May 1920; *s* of Max and Josefine Gold; *m* 1st, 1947, Merle E. Gold (née Tuberg); three *d* ; 2nd, 1972, Carvel B. Gold (née Beyer); one *d. Educ:* Zuoz Coll., Switzerland; Trinity Coll., Cambridge. BA Mechanical Sciences (Cambridge), 1942; MA Mechanical Sciences, Cambridge, 1946; ScD, Cambridge, 1969. Fellow Trinity Coll., Cambridge, 1947. British Admiralty, 1942-46; Cavendish Laboratory, Cambridge, 1946-47 and 1949-52; Med. Research Council, Zoological Lab., Cambridge, 1947-49; Sen. Principal Scientific Officer (Chief Asst), Royal Greenwich Observatory, 1952-56; Prof. of Astronomy, 1957-58, Robert Wheeler Willson Prof. of Applied Astronomy, 1958-59, Harvard Univ. Hon. MA (Harvard), 1957. Member: Amer. Philosophical Soc.; Nat. Acad. of Sciences; Fellow, Amer. Acad. of Arts and Sciences. *Publications:* contribs to learned journals on astronomy, physics, biophysics. *Recreations:* ski-ing, travelling. *Address:* Center for Radiophysics and Space Research, Space Sciences Building, Cornell University, Ithaca, NY 14853, USA.

GOLD, Prof. Victor, FRS 1972; Professor of Chemistry, since 1964, Head of Department of Chemistry since 1971, and Dean of Faculty of Natural Science, 1978-80, King's College, University of London; *b* 29 June 1922; *yr s* of late Dr Oscar and Mrs Emmy Gold; *m* 1954, Jean (née Sandiford); one *s* one *d. Educ:* King's Coll. and University Coll., London, Fellow UCL, 1973, FKC, 1975. BSc 1942, PhD 1945, DSc 1958; FRSC. Tuffnell Scholar 1942-44, Ramsay Meml Medal 1944, UCL; King's Coll., London: Demonstrator, 1944-46; Asst Lectr, 1946-47; Lectr in Chemistry, 1947-56; Reader in Physical Organic Chemistry, 1956-64. Res. Fellow and Resident Dr, Cornell Univ., 1951-52; Vis. Professor: Cornell Univ., 1962, 1963, 1965; Univ. of California, Irvine, 1970; Case Western Reserve Univ., 1975; Vis. Sen. Scientist, Brookhaven Nat. Lab., NY, 1962, 1966. Chairman: British Cttee on Chemical Educn, 1977-78; British Nat. Cttee for Chemistry, 1978-. Mem. Council: Faraday Soc., 1963-66; Chem. Soc., 1971-74. Editor, Advances in Physical Organic Chemistry, 1963-. *Publications:* pH Measurements: their theory and practice, 1956; (with D. Bethell) Carbonium Ions: an introduction, 1967; (ed, with E. F. Caldin) Proton-Transfer Reactions, 1975; scientific papers, chiefly in Jl Chem. Soc. and Trans Faraday Soc. *Recreations:* music, computing.

Address: Department of Chemistry, King's College, Strand, WC2R 2LS. *T:* 01-836 5454. *Club:* Athenæum.

GOLDBERG, Prof. Abraham; Regius Professor of the Practice of Medicine, University of Glasgow, since 1978 (Regius Professor of Materia Medica, 1970-78); Consultant Physician, Western Infirmary, Glasgow; *b* 7 Dec. 1923; *s* of late Julius Goldberg and Rachel Goldberg (née Varinofsky); *m* 1957, Clarice Cussin; two *s* one *d. Educ:* George Heriot's Sch., Edinburgh; Edinburgh University. MB, ChB 1946, MD (Gold Medal for thesis) 1956, Edinburgh; DSc Glasgow 1966; FRCP, FRCPE, FRCPGlas, FRSE. Nuffield Research Fellow, UCH Med. Sch., London, 1952-54; Eli Lilly Trav. Fellow in Medicine (MRC) in Dept of Medicine, Univ. of Utah; Lectr in Medicine 1956, Titular Prof. 1967, Univ. of Glasgow. Mem., Grants Cttee, Clinical Res. Bd, MRC, 1971-77, Chm., Grants Cttee I, Clinical Res. Bd, MRC, 1973-77. Mem., Chief Scientist Cttee, SHHD, 1977-; Chm., Biomed. Res. Cttee, SHHD Chief Scientist Orgn, 1977-; Chm., Cttee on Safety of Medicines, 1980-. Mem., Editorial Bd, Jt Formulary Cttee, British Nat. Formulary, 1972-78. Editor, Scottish Medical Jl, 1962-63. Lectures: Sydney Watson Smith, RCPE, 1964; Henry Cohen, Hebrew Univ., Jerusalem, 1973. Watson Prize, RCPGlas, 1959; Alexander Fleck Award, Univ. of Glasgow, 1967. *Publications:* (jtly) Diseases of Porphyrin Metabolism, 1962; (ed jtly) Recent Advances in Haematology, 1971; papers on clinical and investigative medicine. *Recreations:* swimming, writing. *Address:* 16 Birnam Crescent, Bearsden, Glasgow G61 2AU.

GOLDBERG, Arthur J(oseph), DJur; lawyer, USA; Ambassador-at-Large, 1977-78; private practice, Washington DC, since 1971; *b* Chicago, Ill, 8 Aug. 1908; *s* of Joseph Goldberg and Rebecca (née Perlstein); *m* 1931, Dorothy Kurgans; one *s* one *d. Educ:* City Coll., Chicago; North-western Univ. (JD). Admitted to Bar of Ill., 1929, US Supreme Ct Bar, 1937. Private practice, 1929-48. Gen. Counsel: Congress of Industrial Workers, 1948-55; United Steel workers, 1948-61; Industrial Union Dept, AFL-CIO, 1955-61; Special Counsel, AFL-CIO, 1955-61. Member firm: Goldberg, Devoe, Shadur & Mikva, Chicago, 1945-61; Goldberg, Feller & Bredhoff, Washington, 1952-61; Paul, Weiss, Goldberg, Rifkind, Wharton & Garrison, NY, 1968-71. Sec. of Labor, 1961-62. Associate Judge, US Supreme Court, Washington, 1962-65; US Ambassador to UN, 1965-68; Chm., UNA of USA, 1968-70, Hon. Chm., 1970-; Chm., US Delegn to Conf. on Security and Co-operation in Europe, Belgrade, 1977-78. Is a Democrat. Charles Evans Hughes Prof., Woodrow Wilson Sch. of Diplomacy, Princeton Univ., 1968-69; Distinguished Prof., Sch. of Internat. Relations, Columbia Univ., 1969-70; Univ. Prof. of Law and Diplomacy, Amer. Univ., 1971-73; Distinguished Prof., Univ. of Calif, SF, 1974-. Assoc. Fellow, Morse Coll., Yale Univ. Member: Chicago Bar Assoc.; Ill. Bar Assoc.; Amer. Bar Assoc.; DC Bar Assoc.; Assoc. Bar City of NY; Amer. Acad. Arts and Scis. Holds numerous awards and Hon. degrees. *Publications:* Civil Rights in Labor-Management Relations: a Labor Viewpoint, 1951; AFL-CIO-Labor United, 1956; Unions and the Anti-Trust Laws, 1956; Management's Reserved Rights, 1956; Ethical Practices, 1958; A Trade Union Point of View, 1959; Suggestions for a New Labor Policy, 1960; The Role of the Labor Union in an Age of Bigness, 1960; The Defenses of Freedom: The Public Papers of Arthur J. Goldberg, 1966; Equal Justice: the Warren era of the Supreme Court, 1972. *Address:* 2801 New Mexico Avenue NW, Washington, DC 20007, USA.

GOLDBLATT, Simon, QC 1972. Called to the Bar, Gray's Inn, 1953. *Address:* 2 Garden Court, Temple, EC4Y 9BL.

GOLDBY, Prof. Frank; Professor of Anatomy, London University, St Mary's Hospital Medical School, 1945-70, now Emeritus; *b* Enfield, Middlesex, 25 May 1903; *s* of Frank and Ellen Maud Goldby; *m* 1932, Helen Rosa Tomlin; five *s* one *d. Educ:* Mercers' School, Holborn; Gonville and Caius College, Cambridge; King's College Hospital; MRCS, LRCP 1926; MRCP 1928; MD (Cambridge), 1936; FRCP, 1963; Resident appointments King's Coll. Hospital, 1926-28; Asst Clinical Pathologist, King's College Hospital, 1929-30; Senior Demonstrator in Anatomy, University College, London, 1931; Lecturer in charge of Anatomy Dept, Hong Kong, 1932-33; Lecturer in Anatomy, University of Cambridge and Fellow of Queens' College, 1934-37; Prof. of Anatomy, Univ. of Adelaide, 1937-45. *Publications:* papers on Embryology and on the Pathology and Comparative Anatomy of the Nervous System. *Address:* 1 St Mark's Court, Barton Road, Cambridge CB3 9LE.

GOLDEN, Grace Lydia, ARCA (London); *d* of H. F. Golden. *Educ:* City of London Sch. for Girls. Art Training at Chelsea Art Sch. and Royal College of Art; further studies at Regent Street Polytechnic; Black and White Illustrator, Posters, Panoramas, watercolour artist and wood-engraver; Exhibitor at Royal Academy, 1936, 1937, 1938 and 1940; watercolour, Summer Evening, Embankment Gardens, and oil-painting, Free Speech, purchased by Chantry Trustees; work also purchased by V&A Mus., Imp. War Mus., Mus. of London, and S London Art Gall. Retrospective exhibn, South London Art Gall., 1979. *Publication:* Old Bankside, 1951. *Recreation:* singing. *Address:* 21 Douglas Waite House, 73-75 Priory Road, NW6 3NJ. *T:* 01-624 3204.

GOLDFINGER, Ernő, RA 1975; FRIBA 1963; private architect; *b* Budapest, 11 Sept. 1902; *s* of Dr Oscar Goldfinger and Regine (née Haiman); *m* 1931, Ursula Ruth Blackwell; two *s* one *d. Educ:* Gymnasium Budapest and Vienna; Le Rosay Rolle, Gstad, Switzerland; Ecole des Beaux Arts, Paris; Inst.

d'Urbanisme, Sorbonne, 1927-28. DPLG 1932; RIBA 1946. Main Buildings: Shop, Helena Rubinstein, London, 1926; Monument, Algiers, 1928; House, Broxted, Essex, 1935; Terraced Houses, Willow Road, Hampstead, 1937 (scheduled as bldg of Architect. Interest, 1974); Houses, Bruxelles, 1951; (competition winner) Alex. Fleming House, Min. of Health, 1960 (Civic Trust Award, 1964); French govt's Tourist Offices, London and Paris; houses, flats, schs, neighbourhood units, newspaper bldg offices, warehouse, factories, farm, shops, old people's home, cinema; also Sunlight Studies, 1931 (designed Heliometer Machine). Exhibitions: Sect. of British Pavilion, Internat. Exhibn, Paris, 1937; ICI, Olympia BIF, 1938; MARS Gp, 1938; Grille CIAM, Aix en Provence, 1955; This is Tomorrow, London, 1956. Drawing and models at RIBA Heinz Gall. collection and RA. Lecture tours: English and Amer. univs; France, Spain, Hungary. Hon. Sec., Brit. Sect., Internat. Reunion of Architects, parent body of Internat. Union of Archs (UIA), 1936; 1st Org. Sec., UIA, 1946 (drafted Statutes); RIBA Deleg., UIA Council, Cuba and Mexico, 1963; Deleg., UIA Sports Bldgs Commission: Oslo, 1964; Krakow, 1967; Mexico City, 1968; Moscow, 1970. Member: French Sect., CIAM, 1928 (deleg. Congress, Athens, 1933); MARS Gp, 1934; Architect. Assoc., 1935 (Mem. Council, 1960-63, 1965-68); For. Relns Cttee, RIBA, 1937-45; Council, ARCUK, 1941-49; Bldg Req. Sub-cttee, Sci. Adv. Cttee to MPBW, 1943-45; Council of Industrial Design, 1961-65; Cercle d'Etudes Architecturals, Paris, 1975. Hon. Member: AASTA (now ABT), 1937; Assoc. of Hungarian Architects, 1963. FRSA. British Corresp., Architecture d'Aujourd'hui, 1934-74. *Publications:* County of London Plan Explained (jtly), 1945; British Furniture Today, 1951; contrib. Arch. Rev., RIBA Jl, Jl Inst. Amer. Architects, Architect. Year Book; *relevant publications:* Goldfinger Ernő, by Prof. M. Major, 1973 (Budapest); special number Architect. Design (Jan. 1963); articles in Architect. Rev., Archs Jl, Architecture d'Aujourd'hui, Arch. & Urbanism, Tokyo, New Yorker 1957, Contemporary Architects, 1980. *Recreations:* travel, architecture. *Address:* 2 Willow Road, Hampstead, NW3 1TH. *T:* 01-435 6166. *Club:* Savile.

GOLDING, Dame (Cecilie) Monica, DBE 1958; RRC 1950 (ARRC 1940); *b* 6 Aug. 1902; *o d* of Ben Johnson and Clara (*née* Beames); *m* 1961, Brig. the Rev. Harry Golding, CBE (*d* 1969). *Educ:* Croydon Secondary Sch. Professional training: Royal Surrey County Hospital, Guildford, 1922-25; Louise Margaret Hosp., Aldershot and Queen Victoria's Institute of District Nursing. Joined Army Nursing Services, 1925; India, 1929-34; France, 1939-40; Middle East, 1940-43 and 1948-49; Southern Comd, 1943-44 and 1950-52; WO, 1945-46; India and SE Asia, 1946-48; Far East, 1952-55; Eastern Comd, 1955-56; Matron-in-Chief and Dir of Army Nursing Services, 1956-60, retired (with rank of Brig.), 1960. QHNS 1956-60; Col Commandant, Queen Alexandra's Royal Army Nursing Corps, 1961-66. OStJ 1955. *Recreations:* motoring; amateur bird watching and nature study. *Address:* 9 Sandford Court, 32 Belle Vue Road, Southbourne, Bournemouth, Dorset BH6 3DR. *T:* 431608. *Club:* United Nursing Services.

GOLDING, Felicity Ann, (Mrs R. M. Golding); see Lott, F. A.

GOLDING, F(rederick) Campbell, MB, ChM, FRCP, DMRE, FFR; retired; Director, X-Ray Diagnostic Department, Middlesex Hospital, 1956-67; Lecturer in Radiology, Middlesex Hospital Medical School; Hon. Consultant Radiologist, Royal National Orthopædic Hospital; Civilian Consultant in Radiology, RN and RAF; Consultant Radiologist, Arthur Stanley Institute for Rheumatic Diseases; Consultant Radiologist, Chelsea Hospital for Women; *b* 4 June 1901; *o s* of late Frederick Golding, Sydney, Australia, and Nell Campbell, Castlemaine, Victoria; *m* 1942, Barbara Hubbard, *d* of late Charles Hubbard, Nassau and of Mrs Hubbard, 15 Grosvenor Square, W1; two *s. Educ:* Scots Coll., Melbourne; St Andrews Coll., University of Sydney. Late Dir, X-Ray Diagnostic Dept, Royal Marsden Hosp.; Examiner in Radiology, Royal College of Physicians, 1954-57. Watson-Jones Lecturer, Royal College of Surgeons, 1964; Mackenzie Davidson Lecturer, British Institute of Radiology, 1961. *Publications:* (contrib.) Textbook of X-Ray Diagnosis by British Authors; (contrib.) Textbook of Rheumatic Diseases; (Jt) Survey of Radiology of the Chest, British Encyclopædia of Medical Practice, 1956; various other medical publications. *Recreation:* fishing in north of Scotland. *Address:* The Barn, Hursley, Winchester, Hants.

GOLDING, John; MP (Lab) Newcastle-under-Lyme since Oct. 1969; *b* Birmingham, 9 March 1931; *m* 1958, Thelma Gwillym; one *s*; *m* 1980, Llinos Lewis (*née* Edwards). *Educ:* Chester Grammar Sch.; London Univ.; Keele Univ. BA History, Politics, Economics, 1956. Asst Res. Officer, 1960-64, Education Officer, 1964-69, Political and Parly Officer, 1969-, Post Office Engineering Union. Mem., Nat. Exec. Cttee, Labour Party, 1978-. PPS to Minister of State, Min. of Technology, Feb.-June 1970; Opposition Whip, July 1970-74; a Lord Comr, HM Treasury, Feb.-Oct. 1974; Parly Under-Sec. of State, Dept of Employment, 1976-79. Chm., Select Cttee on Employment, 1979-; Former Mem. Select Cttee on Nationalised Industries. Governor: University Coll. Hosp., 1970-74; Ruskin Coll., 1970-. *Publications:* co-author Fabian Pamphlets: Productivity Bargaining; Trade Unions—on to 1980. *Address:* House of Commons, SW1.

GOLDING, John, PhD; painter; Senior Tutor in the School of Painting, Royal College of Art, since 1981 (Tutor, 1973); *b* 10 Sept. 1929; *s* of Harold S. Golding and Dorothy Hamer. *Educ:* Ridley Coll. (St Catherine's, Ontario); Univ. of Toronto; Univ. of London. BA; MA; PhD. Lectr, 1962-77, and Reader in History of Art, 1977-81, Courtauld Inst., Univ. of London; Slade

Prof. of Fine Art, Cambridge Univ., 1976-77. *Publications:* Cubism 1907-14, 1959, rev. edn, 1968; (with Christopher Green) Leger & Purist Paris, 1970; Duchamp: The Bride Stripped Bare by her Bachelors, Even, 1972; (ed with Roland Penrose) Picasso, 1881-1973, 1973. *Address:* 24 Ashchurch Park Villas, W12. *T:* 01-749 5221.

GOLDING, John Anthony, CVO 1966; Queen's Messenger, 1967-80; *b* 25 July 1920; *s* of George Golding, Plaxtol, Kent; *m* 1950, Patricia May, *d* of Thomas Archibald Bickel; two *s. Educ:* Bedford Sch.; King's Coll., Auckland. Served with King's African Rifles and Military Administration, Somalia, 1939-46 (Captain). Entered Colonial Service, 1946; Dep. Provincial Comr, Tanganyika, 1961; Administrator, Turks and Caicos Is, 1965-67. *Recreations:* gardening, fishing, shooting. *Address:* Elmore House, Sway, Hants.

GOLDING, Dame Monica; see Golding, Dame C. M.

GOLDING, Terence Edward, FCA; Chief Executive, National Exhibition Centre, Birmingham, since 1978; *b* 7 April 1932; *s* of Sydney Richard Golding and Elsie Golding; *m* 1955, Sheila Jean (*née* Francis); one *s* one *d. Educ:* Harrow County Grammar Sch. FCA 1967. Earls Court Ltd (Exhibition Hall Proprietors): Chief Accountant, 1960; Co. Sec., 1965; Financial Dir, 1972; Financial Dir, Olympia Ltd, and Earls Court & Olympia Ltd, 1973; Commercial Dir, Earls Court & Olympia Group of Cos, 1975; Dep. Chief Exec., National Exhibn Centre, 1978. Chm., Exhibition Liaison Cttee, 1979 and 1980. Director: British Exhibitions Promotion Council, 1981-; Birmingham Convention and Visitor Bureau, 1981-. *Recreations:* following sport, collecting antiques. *Address:* Pinn Cottage, Pinner Hill, Pinner, Mddx. *T:* 01-866 2610.

GOLDING, William (Gerald), CBE 1966; author; *b* 19 Sept. 1911; *s* of Alec A. and Mildred A. Golding; *m* 1939, Ann, *e d* of late E. W. Brookfield, The Homestead, Bedford Place, Maidstone; one *s* one *d. Educ:* Marlborough Grammar Sch.; Brasenose Coll., Oxford. MA Oxon 1961. FRSL 1955. Hon. Fellow, Brasenose Coll., Oxford, 1966. Hon. DLitt, Sussex, 1970. *Publications:* Lord of the Flies, 1954 (filmed 1963); The Inheritors, 1955; Pincher Martin, 1956; Brass Butterfly (play), 1958; Free Fall, 1959; The Spire, 1964; The Hot Gates, 1965; The Pyramid, 1967; The Scorpion God, 1971; Darkness Visible, 1979 (James Tait Black Memorial Prize, 1980); Rites of Passage, 1980 (Booker McConnell Prize); A Moving Target, 1982. *Recreations:* music, Greek. *Address:* Ebble Thatch, Bowerchalke, Wilts. *T:* Broad Chalke 275. *Clubs:* Athenæum, Savile.

GOLDMAN, Peter, CBE 1959; Director of Consumers' Association, since 1964; Patron of International Organisation of Consumers Unions (President, 1970-75); Vice-President, Bureau Européen des Unions de Consommateurs, since 1979; *b* 4 Jan. 1925; *o s* of late Captain Samuel Goldman and late Jessie Goldman (*née* Englander); *m* 1st, 1961, Cicely Ann Magnay (marr. diss. 1969); 2nd, 1970, Stella Maris Joyce. *Educ:* Pembroke Coll., Cambridge; London Univ. BA 1st cl. hons History 1946, MA 1950, Cantab; Pres., Cambridge Union; Hadley Prize, Pembroke Coll., 1946; BA 1st cl. hons History, London, 1948. Smith-Mundt Fellowship, USA, 1955-56. Joined Conservative Research Dept, 1946; Head of Home Affairs Section, 1951-55; Dir of Conservative Political Centre, 1955-64; Mem., LCC Educn Cttee, 1958-59; contested (C) West Ham South, 1959, Orpington, 1962; Chm., Coningsby Club, 1958-59, Treas., 1953-58, 1963-; Sec., Research Inst. for Consumer Affairs, 1964-; Sec., Good Food Club, 1965-; Member: Post Office Users' Nat. Council, 1970-72; Community Relations Commn, 1973-75; Wine Standards Bd, 1973-81; Cttee of Inquiry into the Future of Broadcasting, 1974-77; Royal Commn on Legal Services, 1976-79; Council on Internat. Develt, 1977-79; Consumer Consultative Cttee, EEC, 1979-80; Monopolies and Mergers Commn, 1980-. FRSA 1970 (Silver Medal, 1969). *Publications:* County and Borough, 1952; Some Principles of Conservatism, 1956; The Welfare State, 1964; Consumerism: art or science?, 1969; Multinationals and the Consumer Interest, 1974. *Address:* 34 Campbell Court, Queen's Gate Gardens, SW7. *T:* 01-589 9464. *Club:* Carlton.

GOLDMAN, Sir Samuel, KCB 1969 (CB 1964); Chairman, Henry Ansbacher Holdings Ltd and Henry Ansbacher Ltd, 1976-82; *b* 10 March 1912; *y s* of late Philip and late Sarah Goldman; *m* 1st, 1933, Pearl Marre (*d* 1941); one *s*; 2nd, 1943, Patricia Rosemary Hodges. *Educ:* Davenant Foundation Sch.; Raine's Sch.; London Sch. of Economics, London Univ. Inter-Collegiate Scholar. BSc (Econ.), First Class Hons in Economics and Gladstone Memorial Prize, 1931; MSc (Econ.), 1933. Hutchinson Silver Medallist. Moody's Economist Services, 1934-38; Joseph Sebag & Co., 1938-39; Bank of England, 1940-47. Entered Civil Service, 1947, as Statistician in Central Statistical Office; transferred to Treasury, Sept. 1947; Chief Statistician, 1948; Asst Sec., 1952; Under-Sec., 1960-62; Third Sec., 1962-68; Second Perm. Sec., 1968-72. UK Alternate Executive Dir, International Bank, 1961-62. Exec. Dir, 1972-74, Man. Dir, 1974-76, Orion Bank Ltd. Chm., Covent Garden Market Authority, 1976-81; Mem. Council, Inst. for Fiscal Studies. Hon. Fellow LSE. *Publication:* Public Expenditure Management and Control, 1973. *Recreation:* gardening. *Address:* White Gate, Church Lane, Haslemere, Surrey. *T:* Haslemere 4889. *Club:* Reform.

GOLDREIN, Neville Clive; Senior Partner, Goldrein & Co., Solicitors, since 1953; *b* 28 Aug.; *s* of Saville and Nina Goldrein; *m* 1949, Dr Sonia Sumner, MB, BS Dunelm; one *s* one *d. Educ:* Hymers Coll., Hull; Pembroke Coll., Cambridge (MA). Served Army: commnd E Yorks Regt; served East Africa

Comd. Admitted Solicitor of the Supreme Court, 1949. Mem., Crosby Bor. Council, 1957-71; Mayor of Crosby, 1966-67, Dep. Mayor, 1967-68; Mem., Lancs CC, 1965-74; Merseyside County Council: Mem., 1973-; Dep. Leader, Cons. Gp, 1974-77; Vice-Chm. of Council, 1977-80; Leader, 1980-81; Leader, Cons. Gp, 1981-. Chm., S Sefton Div., St John Ambulance, 1975-; Member: NW Econ. Planning Council, 1966-72; Bd of Deputies of British Jews, 1966-; Council, Liverpool Univ., 1977-81. Dir, Merseyside Economic Develt Co. Ltd, 1981-. Governor, Merchant Taylors' Sch., Crosby, 1965-74. *Recreations:* squash, swimming, cine-photography, music. *Address:* Torreno, St Andrew's Road, Blundellsands, Liverpool L23 7UR. *T:* 051-924 2065. *Club:* Athenæum (Liverpool).

GOLDRING, Mary; freelance economist; Presenter, BBC 'Analysis' programme, since 1977. *Educ:* Our Lady's Priory, Sussex; Lady Margaret Hall, Oxford (PPE). Air and Science correspondent, 1949-74, Business editor, 1966-74, Economist Newspaper; economist and broadcaster, 1974-. Mem. Selection Cttee, Harkness Fellowships, 1980-. Blue Circle Award for industrial journalism, 1979. *Publication:* Economics of Atomic Energy, 1957. *Recreation:* small-scale landscaping. *Address:* c/o BBC, Portland Place, W1.

GOLDS, Anthony Arthur, CMG 1971; MVO 1961; HM Diplomatic Service, retired; Director, British National Committee, International Chamber of Commerce, since 1977; *b* 31 Oct. 1919; *s* of late Arthur Oswald Golds and Florence Golds (*née* Massey); *m* 1944, Suzanne Macdonald Young; one *s* one *d. Educ:* King's Sch., Macclesfield; New Coll., Oxford (Scholar). HM Forces (Royal Armoured Corps), 1939-46; CRO, 1948; 1st Sec., Calcutta and Delhi, 1951-53; Commonwealth Office, 1953-56; Head of Chancery, British Embassy, Ankara, 1957-59; Karachi, 1959-61; Counsellor in Commonwealth Office and Foreign Office, 1962-65; Head of Joint Malaysia/Indonesia Dept, 1964-65; Counsellor, HM Embassy, Rome, 1965-70; Ambassador to the Republic of Cameroon, the Republic of Gabon and the Republic of Equatorial Guinea, 1970-72; High Comr to Bangladesh, 1972-74; Senior Civilian Instructor, RCDS, 1975-76. *Recreations:* music, cricket, golf, literature. *Address:* International Chamber of Commerce, Centre Point, 103 New Oxford Street, WC1A 1QB. *Club:* United Oxford & Cambridge University.

GOLDSMID, Sir James Arthur d'A.; *see* d'Avigdor-Goldsmid.

GOLDSMITH, Edward René David; Publisher and Editor, The Ecologist, since 1970; *b* 8 Nov. 1928; *s* of late Frank B. H. Goldsmith, OBE, TD, MP (C) for Stowmarket, Suffolk, 1910-18, and Marcelle (*née* Mouiller); *m* 1st, 1953, Gillian Marion Pretty; one *s* two *d*; 2nd, 1981, Katherine Victoria James; one *s. Educ:* Magdalen Coll., Oxford (MA Hons). Consultant: Environment Canada, 1975; Atlanta 2000, 1973-76; ECE and UNEP (UN Environment Programme), 1977; Vice-Chm., ECOROPA (Ecological Action for Europe). Adjunct Associate Prof., Univ. of Michigan, 1975. Contested (Ecology Party): Eye, Feb. 1974; Cornwall and Plymouth, European parly election, 1979. *Publications:* Can Britain Survive?, 1971; (jtly) A Blueprint for Survival, 1972; The Future of an Affluent Society: the case of Canada (report for Env. Canada) 1976; The Stable Society, 1977; (jtly, also ed) La Médecine à la Question, 1981. *Address:* Whitehay, Withiel, Bodmin, Cornwall. *T:* Lanivet 237. *Club:* Travellers' (Paris).
See also Sir James Goldsmith.

GOLDSMITH, Sir James (Michael), Kt 1976; Chairman, Générale Occidentale SA Paris; Director, Diamond International (USA); Publisher, L'Express magazine, France; *b* 26 Feb. 1933; *s* of Frank Goldsmith, OBE and Marcelle Mouiller; *m* 1st, Maria Isabel Patino (*d* 1954); one *d*; 2nd, Ginette Lery; one *s* one *d*; 3rd, Lady Annabel Vane Tempest Stewart; two *s* one *d. Educ:* Eton College. *Address:* 65/68 Leadenhall Street, EC3A 2BA. *Clubs:* Buck's, Brooks's; Travellers' (Paris).
See also E. R. D. Goldsmith.

GOLDSMITH, John Herman Thorburn, CBE 1959; a Manager of the Royal Institution, 1964-67 and 1968-71, Vice President 1969; Part-time Member, NW Area Gas Board, 1955-64; *b* 30 May 1903; *m* 1932, Monica, *d* of late Capt. Harry Simon; one *d. Educ:* Marlborough; Magdalen Coll., Oxford. War of 1939-45, Fire Staff Officer, Grade I, National Fire Service. Dep. Chm., Civil Service Selection Bd, 1945; Chm., Civil Service Selection Board, and a Civil Service Commissioner, 1951-63. Haakon Cross, Norway, 1945; Order of Orange Nassau, Netherlands, 1945. *Publications:* Hildebrand (Children's Stories), 1931, 1949; Three's Company, 1932. *Recreation:* fly-fishing. *Address:* Flat 92, Edwin Court, Binsey Lane, Oxford OX2 0QJ. *T:* Oxford 727337.

GOLDSMITH, John Stuart; Director General Defence Accounts, Ministry of Defence, since 1980; *b* 2 Nov. 1924; *o s* of R. W. and S. E. Goldsmith; *m* 1948, Brenda; two *s* one *d. Educ:* Whitgift Middle Sch.; St Catharine's Coll., Cambridge. Royal Signals, 1943-47 (Captain). War Office, 1948; Principal, 1952; Treasury, 1961-64; Asst Sec., MoD, 1964; RCDS 1971; Asst Under-Sec. of State, MoD, 1973; Chm. Civil Service Selection Bd, 1973. *Recreations:* gardening, jazz, travel. *Address:* Cobthorne House, Church Lane, Rode, Somerset. *T:* Frome 830681. *Clubs:* Civil Service, Royal Commonwealth Society.

GOLDSMITH, Mac; retired; *b* 3 July 1902; *s* of David and Klara Goldschmidt; *m* 1936, Ruth (*née* Baum); one *s* one *d. Educ:* Oberealschule, Marburg; Technical Coll., Mannheim. Founded Mecano GmbH Frankfurt/M, 1925; Metallgummi GmbH Frankfurt/M, 1933; Metalastik Ltd, Leicester, 1937; British Bundy Tubing Co., Welwyn Garden City, 1937; acquired Precision Rubbers Ltd for Metalastik Ltd, 1955, and merged Metalastik Ltd with John Bull Gp of Cos (Dep. Chm. and Man. Dir); merged with Dunlop Ltd, 1958; retd from Dunlop Gp, 1970. Farmer, Normanton House and Manor Farms, Thurlaston, Leics. Trustee: Leicester Theatre Trust; Leics Med. Res. Foundn; Life Mem., Ct and Mem., Council, Leicester Univ.; Member: Leicester and District Disablement Adv. Cttee of Dept of Employment; Leicester Museums, Libraries and Publicity Cttee; various cttees, Royal Leicester, Rutland and Wycliffe Soc. for the Blind; Bd of Governors, Jerusalem Coll. of Technology Sch. of Applied Sciences; Life Governor, Hillel House, London; Trustee, Leicester Hebrew Congregation; President: Leicester Maccabi Assoc.; Leicester Symphony Orchestra; Leicester Gramophone Soc.; Friends of Groby Road Hosp.; Vice-Pres., City of Leicester Competitive Festival of Music; Patron, Leics Org. for Relief of Suffering. Hon. LLD Leicester, 1971. Freeman, City of Leicester, 1971. *Recreations:* formerly golf, riding, ski-ing. *Address:* 3 Birkdale Avenue, Knighton Road, Leicester LE2 3HA. *T:* Leicester 708127.

GOLDSMITH, Maj.-Gen. Robert Frederick Kinglake, CB 1955; CBE 1952; retired; *b* 21 June 1907; *s* of late Col Harry Dundas Goldsmith, CBE, DSO; *m* 1935, Brenda, *d* of Frank Bartlett, late Ceylon Civil Service; one *s. Educ:* Wellington Coll., Berks. Commnd Duke of Cornwall's LI, 1927; served War of 1939-45, in N Africa, Italy, NW Europe; Dep. Chief of Staff, First Allied Airborne Army, 1944-45; comd 131 Inf. Bde (TA), 1950-51; Chief of Staff, British Troops in Egypt, 1951-54, and of HQ Western Command, 1956-59; GOC Yorks District, 1959-62; Col, Duke of Cornwall's LI, 1958-59; Col Somerset and Cornwall LI, 1960-63. Editor, The Army Quarterly, 1966-73. Comdr, Legion of Merit (US) 1945. *Address:* 15 Headbourne Worthy House, Winchester, Hants SO23 7JG. *Clubs:* Army and Navy, MCC.

GOLDSMITH, Walter Kenneth, FCA; FRSA; CBIM; Director General, Institute of Directors, since 1979; *b* 19 Jan. 1938; *s* of Lionel and Phoebe Goldsmith; *m* 1961, Rosemary Adele, *d* of Joseph and Hannah Salter; two *s* two *d. Educ:* Merchant Taylors' School. Admitted Inst. of Chartered Accountants, 1960; Manager, Mann Judd & Co., 1964; joined Black & Decker Ltd, 1966: Dir of Investment, Finance and Administration, Europe, 1967; Gen. Man., 1970; Man. Dir, 1974; Chief Executive and European Dir, 1975; Black & Decker USA, 1976-79: Corporate Vice-Pres. and Pres. Pacific Internat. Operations. Director: Bestobell Ltd, 1980-; BUPA Medical Centre, 1980-. Mem. Council, British Exec. Service Overseas, 1979-. Trustee and Chm., Industrial Adv. Council-Stress Syndrome Foundn, 1981-. *Recreations:* boating, music. *Address:* Institute of Directors, 116 Pall Mall, SW1Y 5ED. *T:* 01-839 1233.

GOLDSTEIN, Alfred, CBE 1977; Senior Partner, R. Travers Morgan & Partners, Consulting Engineers, since 1972; *b* 9 Oct. 1926; *s* of late Sigmund and Regina Goldstein; *m* 1959, Anne Milford, *d* of late R. A. M. Tweedy and of Maureen Evans, and step *d* of Hubert Evans; two *s. Educ:* Rotherham Grammar Sch.; Imperial Coll., Univ. of London. BSc (Eng); ACGI 1946; DIC. FICE 1959; FIStructE 1959; FIHE 1959; MConsE 1959; FEng 1979. Partner, R. Travers Morgan & Partners, 1951; responsible for planning, design and supervision of construction of major road and bridge projects and for planning and transport studies, incl. M23, Belfast Transportation Plan, Clifton Bridge, Nottingham, Elizabeth Bridge, Cambridge, Itchen Bridge, Southampton. Transport Consultant to Govt SE Jt Planning Team for SE Regional Plan; in charge London Docklands Redevelopment Study; Cost Benefit Study for 2nd Sydney Airport for Govt of Australia; Review of Railway Finances, 1982. Member: Building Research Bd, subseq. Adv. Cttee on Building Research, 1963-66; Civil Engrg EDC on Contracting in Civil Engrg since Banwell, 1965-67; Baroness Sharp's Adv. Cttee on Urban Transport Manpower Study, 1967-69; Commn of Inquiry on Third London Airport, 1968-70; Urban Motorways Cttee, 1969-72; Genesys Bd, 1969-74; Chairman: DoE and Dept of Transport Planning and Tnspt Res. Adv. Council, 1973-79; DoE Environmental Bd, 1975-78; Mem., TRRL Adv. Cttee on Transport, 1974-80; Mem. Bd, Coll. of Estate Management, Reading Univ. *Publications:* papers and lectures (inc. Criteria for the Siting of Major Airports, 4th World Airports Conf., 1973; Highways and Community Response, 9th Rees Jeffreys Triennial Lecture, RTPI, 1975). *Recreations:* carpentry, music, bridge. *Address:* 136 Long Acre, WC2E 9AE. *T:* 01-836 5474; Kent Edge, Crockham Hill, Edenbridge, Kent TN8 6TA. *T:* Crockham Hill 227. *Club:* Athenæum.

GOLDSTEIN, Joan Delano, (Mrs Julius Goldstein); *see* Aiken, J. D.

GOLDSTEIN, Simon Alfred; a Recorder of the Crown Court, since 1980; *b* 6 June 1935; *s* of Harry and Constance Goldstein; *m* 1973, Zoë Philippa, *yr d* of Basil Gerrard Smith, *qv. Educ:* East Ham Grammar Sch.; Fitzwilliam Coll., Cambridge (BA 1956). Educn Officer, RAF, 1957-60. Called to the Bar, Middle Temple, 1961; Dep. Circuit Judge, 1975. *Recreation:* bridge. *Address:* 13 King's Bench Walk, Temple, EC4. *Club:* London Duplicate Bridge.

GOLDSTEIN, Sydney, FRS 1937; MA; PhD; Gordon McKay Professor of Applied Mathematics, Harvard University, Emeritus; *b* 3 Dec. 1903; *o s* of Joseph and Hilda Goldstein, Hull; *m* 1926, Rosa R. Sass, Johannesburg; one *s* one *d. Educ:* Bede Collegiate Sch., Sunderland; University of Leeds; St John's Coll., Cambridge. Mathematical Tripos, 1925; Smith's Prize, 1927; PhD, 1928; Rockefeller Research Fellow, University of Göttingen, 1928-29; Lectr in Mathematics, Manchester Univ., 1929-31; Lectr in Mathematics in the Univ. of Cambridge, 1931-45; Fellow of St John's Coll., Cambridge, 1929-32, 1933-45; Leverhulme Research Fellow, Calif. Inst. of Technology, 1938-39; Beyer Prof. of Applied Mathematics, Manchester Univ., 1945-50; Prof. of Applied Mathematics, 1950-55; and Chm. Aeronautical Engineering Dept, 1950-54, Technion Institute of Technology, Haifa, Israel, and Vice-Pres. of the Institute, 1951-54. Worked at Aerodynamics Div., National Physical Laboratory, 1939-45; Adams Prize, 1935. Chm., Aeronautical Research Council, 1946-49. Foreign Member: Royal Netherlands Acad. of Sciences and Letters (Section for Sciences), 1950; Finnish Scientific Soc. (Section for maths and phys), 1975. Hon. Fellow: St John's Coll., Cambridge, 1965; Weizmann Inst. of Science, 1971; Hon. FRAeS, 1971; Hon. FIMA, 1972. Hon. DEng Purdue Univ., 1967; Hon. DSc: Case Inst. of Technology, 1967; The Technion, Israel Inst. of Technology, Haifa, Israel, 1969; Leeds Univ., 1973. Timoshenko Medal of Amer. Soc. of Mech. Engrs (for distinguished contribs to Applied Mechanics), 1965; Hon. Mem., ASME, 1981. *Publications:* (ed) Modern Developments in Fluid Dynamics, 1938; Lectures on Fluid Mechanics, 1960; papers on mathematics and mathematical physics, especially hydrodynamics and aerodynamics. *Address:* 28 Elizabeth Road, Belmont, Mass 02178, USA.

GOLDSTEIN-JACKSON, Kevin Grierson; Chief Executive and Programme Controller, TSW-Television South West Ltd, since 1982; *b* 2 Nov. 1946; *s* of H. G. and W. M. E. Jackson; *m* 1975, Jenny Mei Leng, *e d* of Ufong Ng, Malaysia; one *d. Educ:* Reading Univ. (BA Phil. and Sociol.); Southampton Univ. (MPhil Law). Staff Relations Dept, London Transport (Railways), 1966; Scottish Widows Pension & Life Assurance Soc., 1967; Prog. Organizer, Southern TV, 1970-73; Asst Prod., HK-TVB, Hong Kong, 1973; freelance writer/TV prod., 1973-75; Head of Film, Dhofar Region TV Service, Sultanate of Oman, 1975-76; Founder and Dir, Thames Valley Radio, 1974-77; Asst to Head of Drama, Anglia TV, 1977-81; Founder, TSW-Television South West, Jt Man Dir and Programme Controller, 1981. Director: TSW Music Ltd; Independent Television Publications Ltd. Writer of TV scripts. FRSA 1978. FBIM 1982. *Publications:* The Right Joke for the Right Occasion, 1973; Experiments with Everyday Objects, 1976; Joke After Joke, 1977; Things to make with Everyday Objects, 1978; Magic with Everyday Objects, 1979; Activities with Everyday Objects, 1980; contrib. law, sociol and gen. pubns. *Recreations:* writing, TV, films, theatre, reading, music, walking, philosophical and sociological investigation. *Address:* c/o TSW-Television South West Holdings PLC, Derry's Cross, Plymouth, Devon PL1 2SP.

GOLDSTONE, David Israel, CBE 1971; JP; DL; Chairman, Sterling McGregor Ltd Group of Companies; *b* Aug. 1908; *s* of Philip and Bessie Goldstone; *m* 1931, Belle Franks; one *s* two *d.* Pres., Manchester Chamber of Commerce and Industry, 1970-72, Emeritus Dir, 1978; Chm., NW Regions Chambers of Commerce Council, 1970-73; Exec. Mem., Association British Chambers of Commerce Nat. Council, 1970-73; Exec. Mem., British Nat. Council, Internat. Chambers of Commerce; Mem., NW Telecommunications Bd; Vice-Pres., Greater Manchester Youth Assoc.; Trustee and Exec. Mem., Greater Manchester Museum of Science and Industry; Mem. local tribunals, charitable organisations, etc. JP Manchester, 1958; DL Manchester, 1978; High Sheriff of Greater Manchester, 1980-81. Hon. MA Manchester, 1979. *Address:* Dellstar, Elm Road, Didsbury, Manchester, M20 0XD. *T:* 061-445 1868.

GOLDSTONE, Prof. Jeffrey, PhD; FRS 1977; Professor of Physics, Massachusetts Institute of Technology, since 1977; *b* 3 Sept. 1933; *s* of Hyman Goldstone and Sophia Goldstone; *m* 1980, Roberta Gordon. *Educ:* Manchester Grammar Sch.; Trinity Coll., Cambridge (MA 1956, PhD 1958). Trinity Coll., Cambridge: Entrance Scholar, 1951; Res. Fellow, 1956; Staff Fellow, 1962; Cambridge University: Lectr, 1961; Reader in Math. Physics, 1976. Vis. appointments: Institut for Teoretisk Fysik, Copenhagen; CERN, Geneva; Harvard Univ.; MIT; Inst. for Theoretical Physics, Santa Barbara; Stanford Linear Accelerator Center. Smith's Prize, Cambridge Univ., 1955; Dannie Heineman Prize, Amer. Phys. Soc., 1981. *Publications:* articles in learned jls. *Address:* Department of Physics, Massachusetts Institute of Technology, Cambridge, Mass 02139, USA. *T:* (office) 253-6263.

GOLDSTONE, Peter Walter; His Honour Judge Goldstone; a Circuit Judge, since 1978; *b* 1 Nov. 1926; *y s* of late Adolph Lionel Goldstone and Ivy Gwendoline Goldstone; *m* 1955, Patricia (*née* Alexander), JP; one *s* two *d. Educ:* Manchester Grammar Sch.; Manchester Univ. Solicitor, 1951. Fleet Air Arm, 1944-47. Partner in private practice with brother Julian S. Goldstone, 1951-71. Manchester City Councillor (L), 1963-66; Chm., Manchester Rent Assessment Panel, 1967-71; Reserve Chm., Manchester Rent Tribunal, 1969-71; Dep. Chm., Inner London QS, Nov. 1971; a Metropolitan Stipendiary Magistrate, 1971-78; a Recorder of the Crown Court, 1972-78. *Recreations:* walking, gardening, reading. *Address:* 2 Old Forge Close, Stanmore, Mddx. *T:* 01-954 1901.

GOLDSWORTHY, Rt. Rev. Arthur Stanley; *see* Bunbury, Bishop of.

GOLDWATER, Barry M(orris); US Senator from Arizona, 1953-64, and since 1969; *b* Phoenix, Arizona, 1 Jan. 1909; *s* of late Baron Goldwater and Josephine Williams; *m* 1934, Margaret Johnson; two *s* two *d. Educ:* Staunton Mil. Acad., Virginia; University of Arizona. 2nd Lieut, Army Reserve, 1930; transferred to USAAF, 1941; served as ferry-command and fighter pilot instructor, Asia, 1941-45 (Lieut-Col); Chief of Staff, Arizona Nat. Guard, 1945-52 (Col); Maj.-Gen., USAF Reserves. Joined Goldwater's Inc., 1929 (Pres., 1937-53). City Councilman, Phoenix, 1949-52; Republican Candidate for the Presidency of the USA, 1964. Member: Advisory Cttee on Indian Affairs, Dept of Interior, 1948-50; Armed Services Cttee; Commerce, Science and Transportation Cttee; Select Cttee on Intelligence; Heard Museum; Museum of Northern Arizona; St Joseph's Hosp.; Vice-Chairman: Amer. Graduate Sch. of Internat. Management; Bd of Regents, Smithsonian Institution; Member: Veterans of Foreign Wars; American Legion; Royal Photographic Society, etc. US Junior Chamber of Commerce Award, 1937; Man of the Year, Phoenix, 1949. 33° Mason. *Publications:* Arizona Portraits (2 vols), 1940; Journey Down the River of Canyons, 1940; Speeches of Henry Ashurst: The Conscience of a Conservative, 1960; Why Not Victory?, 1962; Where I Stand, 1964; The Face of Arizona, 1964; People and Places, 1967; The Conscience of the Majority, 1970; Delightful Journey, 1970; The Coming Breakpoint, 1976; With No Apologies, 1979. *Address:* PO Box 1601, Scottsdale, Arizona 85252, USA.

GOLIGHER, Prof. John Cedric, ChM, FRCS; Professor and Chairman, Department of Surgery, Leeds University, 1954-77, now Emeritus; Consulting Surgeon, St Mark's Hospital for Diseases of Rectum and Colon, London, since 1954; *b* Londonderry, N Ireland, 13 March 1912; *s* of John Hunter Goligher, Londonderry; *m* 1952, Gwenllian Nancy, *d* of Norman R. Williams, Melbourne, Aust.; one *s* two *d. Educ:* Foyle Coll., Londonderry; Edinburgh Univ. MB, ChB 1934; ChM 1948, Edinburgh; FRCS, FRCSE 1938. Demonstrator of Anatomy, Edinburgh Univ., 1935-36; House Surg., Edinburgh Royal Infirmary; Res. Surg. Officer, St Mark's Hosp., London; served War 1940-46, RAMC, as Surgical Specialist; then Surgical Registrar, St Mary's Hosp., London; Surg., St Mary's Hosp., and St Mark's Hosp. for Diseases of the Rectum and Colon, 1947. Mem. Council, RCS, 1968-80. FRSocMed; Fellow, Assoc. Surgeons of Gt Brit. and Ire. (Past Pres.); Mem. Brit. Soc. of Gastroenterology (Past Pres.). Hon. FACS, 1974; Hon. FRCSI, 1977; Hon. FRACS, 1978; Hon. Fellow: Brasilian Coll. of Surgeons; Amer. Surg. Assoc.; Swiss Surg. Assoc.; Soc. of Colon and Rectal Surgeons; Soc. for Surgery of the Alimentary Tract. Hon. MD: Göteborg, 1976; Belfast, 1981; Hon. DSc Leeds, 1980. *Publications:* Surgery of the Anus, Rectum and Colon, 1961, 4th edn 1980; contribs to books and med. journals, dealing mainly with gastric, colonic and rectal surgery. *Recreations:* reading and travel. *Address:* (professional) 5 Shaw Lane, Leeds LS6 4DH; Ladywood, Linton, Wetherby, West Yorks.

GOLLANCZ, Livia Ruth; Governing Director and Joint Managing Director, Victor Gollancz Ltd, since 1965; *b* 25 May 1920; *d* of Victor Gollancz and Ruth Lowy. *Educ:* St Paul's Girls' Sch.; Royal Coll. of Music (ARCM, solo horn). Horn player: LSO, 1940-43; Hallé Orch., 1943-45; Scottish Orch., 1945-46; BBC Scottish Orch., 1946-47; Covent Garden, 1947; Sadler's Wells, 1950-53. Joined Victor Gollancz Ltd as editorial asst and typographer, 1953; Dir, 1954. *Publication:* (ed and introd) Victor Gollancz, Reminiscences of Affection, 1968 (posthumous). *Recreations:* singing, hill walking. *Address:* 14 Henrietta Street, WC2E 8QJ. *T:* 01-836 2006. *Club:* Alpine.

GOLLIN, Prof. Alfred M., DLitt; Professor of History, University of California, Santa Barbara, since 1967 (Chairman, Department of History, 1976-77); *b* 6 Feb. 1926; 2nd *s* of Max and Sue Gollin; *m* 1st, 1951, Gurli Sørensen (marr. diss.); two *d*; 2nd, 1975, Valerie Watkins (*née* Kilner). *Educ:* New York City Public Schs; State College of New York; Harvard Univ.; New Coll., Oxford (BA); St Antony's Coll., Oxford (MA); DPhil Oxon 1957; DLitt Oxon 1968. Served US Army, 1943-46; taught history at New Coll., Oxford, 1951-54; official historian for The Observer, 1952-59; Lectr, City Coll. of New York, 1959; Univ. of California, Los Angeles: Acting Asst Prof., 1959-60; Research Associate, 1960-61; Associate Prof., Univ. of California, Santa Barbara, 1966-67. Dir, Study Center of Univ. of California, UK and Ire., 1971-73; Mem., US-UK Educnl Commn, 1971-72. Fellow, J. S. Guggenheim Foundn, 1962, 1964, 1971; Fellow, Amer. Council of Learned Socs, 1963, 1975. FRHistS 1976. *Publications:* The Observer and J. L. Garvin, 1960; Proconsul in Politics: a study of Lord Milner, 1964; From Omdurman to V. E. Day: the Life Span of Sir Winston Churchill, 1964; Balfour's Burden, 1965; Asquith, a New View, in A Century of Conflict, Essays for A. J. P. Taylor, 1966; Balfour, in The Conservative Leadership (ed D. Southgate), 1974; articles and reviews in various jls. *Recreation:* swimming. *Address:* Department of History, University of California, Santa Barbara, Calif 93106, USA. *Clubs:* Reform, United Oxford & Cambridge University.

GOLOMBEK, Harry, OBE 1966; Chess Correspondent, The Times, since 1945; writer on chess; *b* London, 1 March 1911; *s* of Barnet and Emma Golombek; unmarried. *Educ:* Wilson's Gram. Sch.; London Univ. Editor British Chess Magazine, 1938, 1939, 1940. Served in RA, 1940-42, Foreign Office, 1942-45. Joint Editor, British Chess Magazine, 1949-67; Chess corresp. for The Observer, 1955-79; Consultant to Computer Games Ltd on Fidelity Chess Challenger machines, 1980-. British Chess Champion, 1947, 1949, and 1955 (prize-winner 14 times); 1st prize in 4 international chess tournaments. Recognized as international master by Federation Internationale des Echecs, 1948. Represented Great Britain in 9 Chess Olympiads and capt. Brit. team,

Helsinki, 1952, Amsterdam, 1954, Munich, 1958, Leipzig, 1960, Varna, 1962. Pres., Zone 1 World Chess Fedn, 1974-78. *Publications:* 50 Great Games of Modern Chess, 1942; Capablanca's 100 Best Games of Chess, 1947; World Chess Championship, 1948, 1949; Pocket Guide to Chess Openings, 1949; Hastings Tournament, 1948-49, 1949; Southsea Tournament, 1949, 1949; Prague, 1946, 1950, Budapest, 1952, 1952; Reti's Best Games of Chess, 1954; World Chess Championship, 1954, 1954; The Game of Chess (Penguin), 1954; 22nd USSR Chess Championship, 1956; World Chess Championship, 1957, 1957; Modern Opening Chess Strategy, 1959; Fischer v Spassky 1972, 1973; A History of Chess, 1976; (with W. Hartston) The Best Games of C. H. O'D. Alexander, 1976; Encyclopedia of Chess, 1977 (new edn 1981 as Penguin Handbook); Beginning Chess, 1981. *Recreations:* music, the Stock Exchange and the theatre. *Address:* Albury, 35 Albion Crescent, Chalfont St Giles, Bucks HP8 4ET. *T:* Chalfont 2808. *Clubs:* Athenæum; Surrey County Cricket.

GOLT, Sidney, CB 1964; Consultant; Adviser on International Trade: International Chamber of Commerce; Malmgren Inc. (Washington DC); Director, Malmgren, Golt, Kingston & Co. Ltd; *b* West Hartlepool, 31 March 1910; *s* of late Wolf and Fanny Golt; *m* 1947, Jean, *d* of Ralph Oliver; two *d. Educ:* Portsmouth Grammar Sch.; Christ Church, Oxford. PPE 1931; James Mew Scholar, Oxford, 1934; Statistician, Tin Producers' Assoc., 1936-40; joined Central Price Regulation Cttee, 1941; Asst Sec., Bd of Trade, 1945-60; Sec., Central Price Regulation Cttee, 1945-46; Under-Sec., Bd of Trade, 1960-68, Adviser on Commercial Policy, 1964-68, Deputy Secretary, 1968-70. UK Mem., Preparatory Cttee for European Free Trade Assoc., Geneva, 1960; Leader, UK Delegns to UN Conf. on Trade and Development, New Delhi, 1968, and to Trade and Development Bd, 1965-68; UK Mem., Commonwealth Gp of Experts on Internat. Economic Policy, 1975-77; Chm., Linked Life Assurance Gp, 1972-81. *Publications:* Ed., Tin, and Tin World Statistics, 1936-40; (jtly) Towards an Open World Economy, 1972; The GATT Negotiations, 1974, 1978; The New Mercantilism, 1974; The Developing Countries in the GATT System, 1978; (jtly) Western Economies in Transition, 1980. *Recreations:* travel, reading, bridge. *Address:* 37 Rowan Road, W6 7DT. *T:* 01-602 1410; The Gore Cottage, Burnham, Bucks. *T:* 4948. *Club:* Reform.

GOMBRICH, Sir Ernst (Hans Josef), Kt 1972; CBE 1966; FBA 1960; FSA 1961; PhD (Vienna); MA Oxon and Cantab; Director of the Warburg Institute and Professor of the History of the Classical Tradition in the University of London, 1959-76, now Emeritus Professor; *b* Vienna, 30 March 1909; *s* of Dr Karl B. Gombrich, Vice-Pres. of Disciplinary Council of Lawyer's Chamber, Vienna, and Prof. Leonie Gombrich (*née* Hock), pianist; *m* 1936, Ilse Heller; one *s. Educ:* Theresianum, Vienna; Vienna Univ. Research Asst, Warburg Inst., 1936-39. Served War of 1939-45 with BBC Monitoring Service. Senior Research Fellow, 1946-48, Lectr, 1948-54, Reader, 1954-56, Special Lectr, 1956-59, Warburg Inst., Univ. of London; Durning-Lawrence Prof. of the History of Art, London Univ., at University Coll., 1956-59; Slade Prof. of Fine Art in the University of Oxford, 1950-53; Visiting Prof. of Fine Art, Harvard Univ., 1959; Slade Prof. of Fine Art, Cambridge Univ., 1961-63; Lethaby Prof., RCA, 1967-68; Andrew D. White Prof.-at-Large, Cornell, 1970-77. A Trustee of the British Museum, 1974-79; Mem., Museums and Galleries Commn (formerly Standing Commn on Museums and Galleries), 1976-. Hon. Fellow, Jesus Coll., Cambridge, 1963; FRSL 1969; Foreign Hon. Mem., American Academy of Arts and Sciences, 1964; For. Mem., Amer. Philosophical Soc., 1968. Corresponding Member: Accademia delle Scienze di Torino, 1962; Royal Acad. of Arts and Sciences, Uppsala, 1970; Koninklijke Nederlandse Akademie van Wetenschapen, 1973; Bayerische Akad. der Wissenschaften, 1979; Royal Swedish Acad. of Sciences, 1981. Hon. FRIBA, 1971. Hon. DLit: Belfast, 1963; London, 1976; Hon. LLD St Andrews, 1965; Hon. LittD: Leeds, 1965; Cambridge, 1970; Manchester, 1974; Hon. DLitt: Oxford, 1969; Harvard, 1976; Hon. Dr Lit. Hum.: Chicago, 1975; Pennsylvania, 1977; DU Essex, 1977; Hon. DHL Brandeis, 1981. W. H. Smith Literary Award, 1964; Erasmus Prize, 1975; Hegel Prize, 1976. Medal of New York Univ. for Distinguished Visitors, 1970; Ehrenkreuz für Wissenschaft und Kunst, 1st cl., Austria, 1975; Medal of Collège de France, 1977; Orden Pour le Mérite für Wissenschaften und Kunst, 1977. *Publications:* Weltgeschichte für Kinder, 1936; (with E. Kris) Caricature, 1940; The Story of Art, 1950, 13th edn 1978; Art and Illusion (The A. W. Mellon Lectures in the Fine Arts, 1956), 1960; Meditations on a Hobby Horse, 1963; Norm and Form, 1966; Aby Warburg, an intellectual biography, 1970; Symbolic Images, 1972; In Search of Cultural History, 1972; (jtly) Art, Perception and Reality, 1973; (ed jtly) Illusion in Nature and Art, 1973; Art History and the Social Sciences (Romanes Lect.), 1975; The Heritage of Apelles, 1976; Means and Ends (W. Neurath Lect.), 1976; The Sense of Order (Wrightsman Lect.), 1979; Ideals and Idols, 1979; The Image and the Eye, 1982; contributions to learned journals. *Address:* 19 Briardale Gardens, NW3 7PN. *T:* 01-435 6639.

See also R. F. Gombrich.

GOMBRICH, Prof. Richard Francis, DPhil; Boden Professor of Sanskrit, Oxford University, since 1976; Fellow of Balliol College, Oxford, since 1976; Emeritus Fellow of Wolfson, 1977; *b* 17 July 1937; *s* of Sir Ernst Gombrich, *qv* ; *m* 1964, Dorothea Amanda Friedrich; one *s* one *d. Educ:* Magdalen Coll., Oxford (MA, DPhil); Harvard Univ. (AM). Univ. Lectr in Sanskrit and Pali, Oxford Univ., 1965-76; Fellow of Wolfson Coll., 1966-76. Hon. Sec., Pali Text Soc., 1982-. *Publications:* Precept and Practice: traditional Buddhism in the rural highlands of Ceylon, 1971; (with Margaret Cone) The Perfect Generosity of Prince Vessantara, 1977; On being Sanskritic, 1978; contribs to

oriental and anthropological journals. *Recreations:* singing, walking, photography. *Address:* Balliol College, Oxford OX1 3BJ.

GOMES, Sir Stanley Eugene, Kt 1959; Retired Chief Justice, West Indies Federation; *b* Georgetown, British Guiana, 24 March 1901; *s* of late Mr and Mrs M. Gomes; *m* 1936, Elaine Vera (*née* Wight). *Educ:* St Joseph's Coll., Dumfries, Scotland; Jesus Coll., Cambridge. BA Cantab, 1923; called to Bar, Gray's Inn, 1924. British Guiana: Magistrate, 1929; Asst Attorney-Gen., 1933; Attorney-Gen., Leeward Islands, 1944; QC 1946; Puisne Judge, Trinidad, 1948. Chief Justice: Barbados, 1957-58; Trinidad, 1958; WI Fedn, 1961. Pres., Brit. Caribbean Court of Appeal, 1962. Retd Dec. 1962. *Recreations:* fishing, golf. *Address:* Wycherley 2, Balmoral Road, Hastings, Barbados.

GOMEZ, Jill; singer; *b* Trinidad, of Spanish and English parents. *Educ:* Royal Academy of Music and Guildhall School of Music, London. Operatic début with Glyndebourne Festival Opera, 1969, where she won the John Christie Award and has subseq. sung leading roles, incl. Mélisande, Calisto, and Anne Truelove in The Rake's Progress; has appeared with The Royal Opera, English Opera Gp and Scottish Opera in roles including Pamina, Ilia, Fiordiligi, The Countess in Figaro, Elizabeth in Elegy for Young Lovers, Tytania, Lauretta in Gianni Schicchi, and the Governess in The Turn of the Screw; created the role of Flora in Tippett's The Knot Garden, at Covent Garden, and of the Countess in Thea Musgrave's Voice of Ariadne, Aldeburgh, 1974; sang title role in Massenet's Thaïs at Wexford, 1974, and Jenifer in The Midsummer Marriage with WNO, 1976; created title role in William Alwyn's Miss Julie for radio, 1977; Tatiana in Eugene Onegin with Kent Opera, 1977; Donna Elvira in Don Giovanni, Ludwigsburg Fest., 1978; title rôle BBC world première, Prokoviev's Maddalena, 1979; Fiordiligi in Cosi fan tutte, Bordeaux, 1979; première of Eighth Book of Madrigals, Monteverdi Fest., Zürich, 1979; Violetta in La Traviata, Kent Opera, Edinburgh Fest., 1979, Sadler's Wells, 1980; Cinna in Mozart's Lucio Silla, Zürich and Vienna, 1981; Governess in Turn of the Screw, Geneva, 1981; Cleopatra in Giulio Cesare, Frankfurt, 1981; Teresa in Benvenuto Cellini, Lyons Berlioz Fest., 1982. Recitalist; Concert repertoire includes Rameau, Bach, Handel (Messiah and cantatas), Haydn's Creation and Seasons, Mozart's Requiem and concert arias, Beethoven's Ninth, Berlioz's Nuits d'Eté, Brahms's Requiem, Fauré's Requiem, Ravel's Shéhérazade, Mahler's Second, Fourth and Eighth Symphonies, Strauss's Four Last Songs, Britten's Les Illuminations, Spring Symphony and War Requiem, Tippett's A Child of Our Time, Messiaen's Poèmes pour Mi, Webern op. 13 and 14 songs, and Schubert songs orch. Webern. Regular engagements in France, Belgium, Holland, Germany, Scandinavia, Switzerland, Italy, Spain, Israel, America; festival appearances include Aix-en-Provence, Spoleto, Bergen, Versailles, Flanders, Holland and Prague. Recent recordings include three solo recitals (French, Spanish, and songs by Mozart), Ravel's Poèmes de Mallarmé with Boulez, Handel's Admeto with Alan Curtis, Acis and Galatea with Neville Marriner, Elvira in Don Giovanni, Fauré's Pelléas et Mélisande with David Zinman, Handel's Ode on St Cecilia's Day with Philip Ledger and King's College Choir, Rameau's La Danse with John Eliot Gardiner, and Britten's Quatre Chansons Françaises with Simon Rattle. *Address:* c/o Lies Askonas, 19a Air Street, Regent Street, W1R 6LQ.

GOMM, Richard Culling C.; *see* Carr-Gomm, R. C.

GOMME, Robert Anthony; Under Secretary, Department of the Environment, since 1981; *b* 19 Nov. 1930; *s* of Harold Kenelm Gomme and Alice Grace (*née* Jacques); *m* 1960, Helen Perris (*née* Moore); one *s* one *d. Educ:* Colfe's Grammar Sch., Lewisham; London School of Economics, Univ. of London (BScEcon 1955). National Service, Korea, with Royal Norfolk Regt, 1951-52; Pirelli Ltd, 1955-66; NEDO, 1966-68; Principal, Min. of Public Building and Works, 1968; Asst Sec., DoE, 1972; RCDS 1975; Cabinet Office, 1976-78; Director of Defence Services I, DoE/Property Services Agency, 1981-. Mem., Print Collectors Club. *Recreations:* reading, listening to music, theatre, talking. *Address:* c/o Department of the Environment, Whitgift Centre, Wellesley Road, Croydon CR9 3LY. *T:* 01-686 8710.

GONZI, Most Rev. Michael, KBE 1946; DD, ICD, BLit; Archbishop Emeritus of Malta; *b* Vittoriosa, Malta, 13 May 1885; *s* of Joseph Gonzi and Margaret Tonna. *Educ:* Malta Seminary; Malta Univ.; Beda Coll., Rome. Priest, 1908; Prof. of Holy Scripture and Hebrew at the Malta Univ., 1915; Sec. to the Archbishop of Malta, 1921; Mem. of the Senate of the Maltese Parliament, 1921; Canon Theologian of the Malta Cathedral, 1923; Bishop of Gozo, 1924; Coadjutor to Bishop of Malta, 1943; Archbishop of Malta, 1943-76; Assistant at the Pontifical Throne, 1949. Bailiff Grand Cross of the Order of Malta, St John of Jerusalem, 1949. *Address:* Archbishop's Palace, Valletta, Malta GC.

GOOCH, Sir (Richard) John (Sherlock), 12th Bt *cr* 1746; JP; *b* 22 March 1930; *s* of Sir Robert Eric Sherlock Gooch, 11th Bt, KCVO, DSO and Katharine Clervaux (*d* 1974), *d* of late Maj.-Gen. Sir Edward Walter Clervaux Chaytor, KCMG, KCVO, CB; *S* father, 1978. *Educ:* Eton. Captain, The Life Guards; retired, 1963. JP Suffolk, 1970. *Heir: b* Major Timothy Robert Sherlock Gooch, MBE [*b* 7 Dec. 1934; *m* 1963, Susan Barbara Christie, *o d* of Maj.-Gen. Kenneth Christie Cooper, *qv* ; two *d*]. *Address:* Benacre Hall, Beccles, Suffolk. *T:* Lowestoft 740333. *Club:* Turf.

GOOCH, Sir Robert Douglas, 4th Bt *cr* 1866; *b* 19 Sept. 1905; *m* ; one *d. Heir: kinsman,* Trevor Sherlock Gooch.

GOOD, Tan Sri Donal Bernard Waters, CMG 1962; JMN (Malaysia), 1965; PSM (Malaysia), 1970; Commissioner of Law Revision, Malaysia, 1963; *b* 13 April 1907; *er s* of William John and Kathleen Mary Good, Dublin; *m* 1930, Kathryn, *er d* of Frank Lucas Stanley and Helena Kathleen Stanley, Dublin; one *s* one *d. Educ:* The High Sch., and Trinity Coll., Dublin. Scholar and Moderator in Classics, TCD, 1927-29; MA 1932; LLB 1933; Barrister, King's Inns, Dublin (Benchers' Prizeman), 1935; Barrister, Gray's Inn, 1948. Resident Magistrate, Kenya, 1940-45; Malayan Planning Unit, 1945; Crown Counsel, Malayan Union, 1946-48; Legal Adviser: Negri Sembilan and Malacca, 1948-49; Johore, 1949-50; Legal Draftsman, Sierra Leone, 1951-52; Legal Adviser, Selangor, 1952; Senior Federal Counsel, Federation of Malaya, 1952-55; Actg Solicitor-Gen., 1953 and 1955; Actg Judge of Supreme Court, 1953; Judge of Supreme Court, 1955-59; Judge of the Court of Appeal, Federation of Malaya, 1959-62. Chm. Detainees Review Commn, 1955-60; Pres. Industrial Court, 1956-57; Chm. Detained Persons Advisory Board, 1960. Coronation Medal, 1953. *Recreations:* orchid-growing, bridge. *Address:* Attorney-General's Chambers, Kuala Lumpur, Malaysia. *T:* 83551. *Clubs:* Kildare Street and University (Dublin); Selangor, Lake and Ipoh (Malaysia).

GOOD, Air Vice-Marshal James Laurence Fuller F.; *see* Fuller-Good.

GOOD, Prof. Ronald D'Oyley, ScD; Head of Department of Botany, University of Hull, 1928-59, Professor Emeritus, 1959; *b* 5 March 1896; 2nd *s* of William Ernest and Mary Gray Good; *m* 1927, Patty Gwynneth Griffith (*d* 1975); one *d. Educ:* Weymouth Coll.; Downing Coll., Cambridge (Senior Scholar). MA, ScD Cantab. Served European War, 1914-18, 4th Bn Dorset Regt, and 2/5th Bn Lincolnshire Regt (France); Staff of Botany Department, British Museum (Nat. Hist.), 1922-28. Trustee, Dorset County Museum. *Publications:* Plants and Human Economics, 1933; The Old Roads of Dorset, 1940, 1966; Weyland, 1945; The Geography of the Flowering Plants, 1947, revd new edn, 1974; A Geographical Handbook of the Dorset Flora, 1948; Features of Evolution in the Flowering Plants, 1956, new edn USA, 1974; The Last Villages of Dorset, 1979; The Philosophy of Evolution, 1981; contribs to scientific journals. *Address:* The Mansion, Albury Park, Albury, Guildford, Surrey GU5 9BB. *T:* Shere 3138.

GOODACRE, Kenneth, TD 1952; DL; Practising as K. Goodacre & Co., Solicitors; Deputy Clerk to GLC, 1964-68; Clerk and Solicitor of Middlesex CC, 1955-65; Clerk of the Peace for Middlesex, 1959-65; *b* 29 Oct. 1910; *s* of Clifford and Florence Goodacre; *m* 1936, Dorothy, *d* of Harold Kendall, Solicitor, Leeds; one *s. Educ:* Doncaster Grammar Sch. Admitted Solicitor, 1934; Asst Solicitor: Doncaster Corp., 1934-35; Barrow-in-Furness Corp., 1935-36; Sen. Solicitor, Blackburn Corp., 1936-39; served War of 1939-45, TA in E Lancs Regt and Staff 53 Div. (Major), and 2nd Army (Lieut-Col); released from Army Service, 1945, and granted hon. rank of Major; Dep. Town Clerk: Blackburn, 1945-49, Leicester, 1949-52; Town Clerk, Leicester, 1952-55. DL, Greater London (DL Middlesex, 1960-65), 1965. *Address:* 4 Chartfield Avenue, Putney, SW15. *T:* 01-789 0794. *Club:* Army and Navy.

GOODALE, Cecil Paul; *b* 29 Dec. 1918; *s* of Cecil Charles Wemyss Goodale and Annie Goodale; *m* 1946, Ethel Margaret (*née* Studer). *Educ:* East Sheen County Sch. War Office, 1936; Min. of Supply, 1939; Min. of Health, later DHSS, 1947-: Sen. Exec. Officer, 1950; Principal, 1953; Principal Regional Officer, 1962; Asst Sec., 1967; Under-Sec., 1976-78. *Recreations:* music, photography. *Address:* 37 Highfield Drive, Kingsbridge, Devon. *T:* Kingsbridge 3511.

GOODALE, Sir Ernest (William), Kt 1952; CBE 1946; MC 1917; Director, 1928, Managing Director, 1930-61, Chairman, 1949-71, and Chairman Emeritus since 1971, Warner & Sons Ltd, textile manufacturers: *b* 6 Dec. 1896; *s* of Wm Thos Goodale, Charter Town Clerk of Barnes, Surrey, and Frances Mary Wheatley; *m* 1st, 1924, Gwendolen Branscombe (*d* 1972); *yr d* of late Sir Frank Warner, KBE; one *s* one *d*; 2nd, 1973; Pamela June, *d* of Stanley A. Bone, Betchworth, Surrey. *Educ:* St Catherine's Coll., Richmond, Surrey; Surrey County Sch., Richmond; King's Coll., London Univ. London Univ. OTC, 1914-15; served European War, 2nd Lieut and Lieut Royal Warwicks Regt, 1916-19, Mesopotamia, Persia, Caucasus, etc. Admitted Solicitor, 1920; Partner, Minet, Pering, Smith & Co., London, retired 1928. Member of: Council for Art and Industry, 1934-39; Council of Industrial Design, 1945-49; Ramsden Cttee on Exhibitions and Fairs, 1945; Bd of Trade Advisory Cttees on Exhibitions and Fairs, 1948-65; Chm. Sub-Cttee on BIF ("Goodale Report"), 1953; Chm. BIF Ltd, 1954-56; Inst. of Export (Vice-Pres., 1956-66); Douglas Cttee on Purchase Tax, 1951; Council, Royal College of Art, 1950-53; Hon. Fellow, Society of Industrial Artists and Designers, 1960; Textile Inst., 1937- (Pres. 1939-40 and 1957-59); Silk and Rayon Controller (Min. of Supply), 1939; Pres., Silk and Man-Made Fibres (formerly Rayon) Users' Assoc. (Inc.), 1945-70; Vice-President: International Silk Assoc., 1949-68; British Man-Made (formerly Rayon and Synthetic) Fibres Federation, 1943-74; Chairman: Furnishing Fabric Fedn, 1945-68; Furnishing Fabrics Export Group, 1940-68; Hon. Pres., Furnishing Fabric Manufacturers' Assoc.; a Vice-Pres. and Mem. Grand Council and Cttees, FBI (Chm. Industrial Art Cttee, 1949-62); Mem. Council, CBI, 1965-74; Mem. Council Royal Society Arts, 1935- (Chm., 1949-52, now a Vice-Pres.); Pres. British Colour Council, 1953-70; Mem. Bd of National Film Finance Corp., 1957-69; Mem. Min. of Educn Adv. Council on Art Educn, 1959-66; Mem. for Dorking (North), Surrey CC, 1961-70, Alderman, 1970-74. Liveryman, Worshipful Co. of

Weavers, 1929- (Court of Assistants, 1946-. Renter Bailiff, 1956-57, Upper Bailiff, 1957-58); Mem. of Law Soc. *Publications:* Weaving and the Warners, 1971; contributions to trade literature. *Address:* Branscombe, Nutcombe Lane, Dorking, Surrey.
See also J.-P. F. E. Warner.

GOODALL, Anthony Charles, MC 1942; **His Honour Judge Goodall;** a Circuit Judge (formerly a Judge of County Courts), since 1968; *b* 23 July 1916; *er s* of late Charles Henry and Mary Helen Goodall, The Manor House, Sutton Veny, Wilts; *m* 1947, Anne Valerie, *yr d* of late John Reginald Chichester and of Audrey Geraldine Chichester, Lurley Manor, Tiverton, Devon; one *s* two *d. Educ:* Eton; King's Coll., Cambridge. Called to Bar, Inner Temple, 1939 (Certif. of Hon.). Served War of 1939-45, 1st Royal Dragoons; taken prisoner (twice), 1944. Practised at Bar, 1946-67. Pres., Plymouth Magistrates' Assoc., 1976-; Mem., County Court Rule Cttee, 1978-. *Publications:* (ed jtly) Faraday on Rating; contrib. to Encycl. Court Forms and Precedents. *Address:* Mardon, Moretonhampstead, Devon. *T:* Moretonhampstead 239.

GOODALL, (Arthur) David (Saunders), CMG 1979; HM Diplomatic Service; Deputy Secretary of the Cabinet, since 1982; *b* 9 Oct. 1931; *o c* of late Arthur William and Maisie Josephine Goodall; *m* 1962, Morwenna, *y d* of late Percival George Beck Peecock; two *s* one *d. Educ:* Ampleforth; Trinity Coll., Oxford. 1st Cl. Hons Lit. Hum., 1954; MA. Served 1st Bn KOYLI (2nd Lieut), 1955-56. Entered HM Foreign (now Diplomatic) Service, 1956; served at: Nicosia, 1956; FO, 1957-58; Djakarta, 1958-60; Private Sec. to HM Ambassador, Bonn, 1961-63; FO, 1963-68; Head of Chancery, Nairobi, 1968-70; FCO, 1970; Dep. Head, Permanent Under-Secretary's Dept, FCO, 1971-73; UK Delegn, MBFR, Vienna, 1973-75; Head of Western European Dept, FCO, 1975-79; Minister, Bonn, 1979-82. *Publications:* contribs to: Ampleforth Jl; Tablet; Irish Genealogist. *Address:* c/o Foreign and Commonwealth Office, SW1. *Club:* United Oxford & Cambridge University.

GOODALL, David William, PhD (London); DSc (Melbourne); ARCS, DIC, FLS; FIBiol; Senior Principal Research Scientist, CSIRO Division of Land Resources Management, 1974-79, Senior Research Fellow, since 1979; *b* 4 April 1914; *s* of Henry William Goodall; *m* 1st, 1940, Audrey Veronica Kirwin (marr. diss. 1949); one *s*; 2nd, 1949, Muriel Grace King (marr. diss. 1974); two *s* one *d*; 3rd, 1976, Ivy Nelms (*née* Palmer). *Educ:* St Paul's Sch.; Imperial Coll. of Science and Technology (BSc). Research under Research Inst. of Plant Physiology, on secondment to Cheshunt and East Malling Research Stns, 1935-46; Plant Physiologist, W African Cacao Research Inst., 1946-48; Sen. Lectr in Botany, University of Melbourne, 1948-52; Reader in Botany, University Coll. of the Gold Coast, 1952-54; Prof. of Agricultural Botany, University of Reading, 1954-56; Dir, CSIRO Tobacco Research Institute, Mareeba, Qld, 1956-61; Senior Principal Research Officer, CSIRO Div. of Mathematical Statistics, Perth, Australia, 1961-67; Hon. Reader in Botany, Univ. of Western Australia, 1965-67; Prof. of Biological Science, Univ. of California Irvine, 1966-68; Dir, US/IBP Desert Biome, 1968-73; Prof. of Systems Ecology, Utah State Univ., 1969-74. *Publications:* Chemical Composition of Plants as an Index of their Nutritional Status (with F. G. Gregory), 1947; ed, Evolution of Desert Biota, 1976; editor-in-chief, Ecosystems of the World (series), 1977-; co-editor: Simulation Modelling of Environmental Problems, 1977; Arid-land Ecosystems: Structure, Functioning and Management, 1979, 1981; Mediterranean-type Shrublands, 1981; numerous papers in scientific journals. *Recreations:* acting, reading, walking. *Address:* CSIRO Division of Land Resources Management, Private Bag, PO Wembley, WA 6014, Australia.

GOODALL, Rev. Dr Norman; Minister of United Reformed Church, retired; *b* 30 Aug. 1896; *s* of Thomas and Amelia Goodall; *m* 1920, Doris Elsie Florence (*née* Stanton); two *s* one *d. Educ:* Council sch., Birmingham; Mansfield Coll., Oxford (MA, DPhil, Hon. Life Fellow 1980). Minister: Trinity Congregational Church, Walthamstow, 1922-28; New Barnet Congregatnl Ch., 1928-36; Foreign Sec., London Missionary Soc., 1936-44; Sec., Internat. Missionary Council, 1944-61; Asst Gen. Sec., World Council of Churches, 1961-63. Chm., Congregatnl Union of England and Wales, 1954-55; Moderator: Internat. Congregatnl Council, 1962-66; Free Ch. Federal Council, 1966-67. Dale Lectr, Mansfield Coll., Oxford, 1965-66; Associate Lectr, Heythrop Coll., 1970-71; Vis. Lecturer: Selly Oak Colls, 1963-66 (Hon. Fellow, 1981); Irish Sch. of Ecumenics, Dublin, 1971-73; Vis. Prof., Pontifical Gregorian Univ., Rome, 1975. *Publications:* With All Thy Mind, 1933; Pacific Pilgrimage, 1941; One Man's Testimony, 1949; History of the London Missionary Society 1895-1945, 1954; The Ecumenical Movement, 1961 (2nd edn 1964); Christian Missions and Social Ferment, 1964; Ecumenical Progress, 1972; Second Fiddle: recollections and reflections, 1979. *Recreations:* friends, music, books. *Address:* Greensleeves, 15 Old London Road, Benson, Oxford OX9 6RR. *T:* Wallingford 38246. *Club:* National Liberal.

GOODCHILD, David Hicks, CBE 1973; Partner of Clifford-Turner, Solicitors, since 1962 (resident in Paris); *b* 3 Sept. 1926; *s* of Harold Hicks Goodchild and Agnes Joyce Wharton Goodchild (*née* Mowbray); *m* 1954, Nicole Marie Jeanne (*née* Delamotte); one *s* one *d. Educ:* Felsted School. Lieut, Royal Artillery, 1944-48; articled clerk, Longmores, Hertford; qual. Solicitor, 1952; HAC, 1952-56. *Recreations:* golf, cricket. *Address:* 53 Avenue

Montaigne, 75008 Paris, France. *T:* 225-49-27. *Clubs:* MCC, HAC; Cercle Interallié, Polo (Paris).

GOODCHILD, Rt. Rev. Ronald Cedric Osbourne; *b* 17 Oct. 1910; *s* of Sydney Osbourne and Dido May Goodchild; *m* 1947, Jean Helen Mary (*née* Ross); one *s* four *d*. *Educ:* St John's School, Leatherhead; Trinity Coll. (Monk Schol.), Cambridge; Bishops' Coll., Cheshunt. 2nd Cl. Hist. Tripos Parts I and II, 1931, Dealtry Exhibn. 1932, 3rd Class Theol. Tripos, 1932, Asst Master, Bickley Hall Sch., Kent, 1932-34; Curate, Ealing Parish Church, 1934-37; Chap. Oakham Sch., 1937-42. Chap. RAFVR, 1942-46 (despatches), Warden St Michael's House, Hamburg, 1946-49; Gen. Sec., SCM in Schools, 1949-53; Rector of St Helen's Bishopgate with St Martin Outwich, 1951-53; Vicar of Horsham, Sussex, 1953-59; Surrogate and Rural Dean of Horsham, 1954-59; Archdeacon of Northampton and Rector of Ecton, 1959-64; Bishop Suffragan of Kensington, 1964-80. Examiner, Religious Knowledge, Southern Univs Jt Bd, 1954-58; Examining Chaplain to Bishop of Peterborough, 1959. Chairman Christian Aid Dept, British Council of Churches, 1964-74. Mem. of General Synod of C of E, 1974-. *Publication:* Daily Prayer at Oakham School, 1938. *Recreations:* tennis, golf, photography. *Address:* Star Cottage, Welcombe, N Devon. *Club:* Royal Air Force.

GOODCHILD, Lt-Col Sidney, MVO 1969; DL; retired; Vice-Lieutenant of Caernarvonshire, 1969-74; *b* 4 Jan. 1903; *s* of late Charles Goodchild; *m* 1934, Elizabeth G. P. Everett; two *s* one *d*. *Educ:* Friars Sch.; Staff Coll., Quetta. Commnd Royal Welch Fusiliers, 1923; 14th Punjab Regt, Indian Army, 1930; Staff Captain, 4th Inf. Bde, 1937; DAQMG (Movements), Army HQ India, 1939; AQMG (Movts), Iraq, 1940; comd 7/14 Punjab Regt, 1942; AQMG, Army HQ India, 1945; comd 1st Sikh LI and 5th Bde, 4th Indian Div., 1946; despatches thrice, 1940-44. Chm., NW Wales War Pensioners' Cttee. Alderman, Caernarvonshire CC, 1972-74. DL Caernarvonshire, 1964; DL Gwynedd, 1974. *Address:* Plas Oerddwr, Beddgelert, Gwynedd, N Wales. *T:* Beddgelert 237.

GOODDEN, Robert Yorke, CBE 1956; RDI 1947; Architect and Designer; Professor, School of Silversmithing and Jewellery, 1948-74, and Pro-Rector, 1967-74, Royal College of Art; *b* 7 May 1909; 2nd *s* of late Lieut-Col R. B. Goodden, OBE and Gwendolen Goodden; *m* 1st, 1936, Kathleen Teresa Burrow; 2nd, 1946, Lesley Macbeth Mitchell; two *s* two *d*. *Educ:* Harrow Sch. Trained AA Sch. of Architecture, 1926-31; AA Diploma 1932; ARIBA 1933; private practice as architect and designer, 1932-39; served RAFVR, 1940-41; RNVR, 1941-45; resumed private practice, 1946. Joint architect and designer: Lion and Unicorn Pavilion, South Bank Exhibition, 1951; Western Sculpture Rooms, Print Room Gall. and Gall. of Oriental Art, British Museum, 1969-71; designer of: domestic pressed glassware for Chance Brothers, 1934-48; Asterisk Wallpapers, 1934; sports section, Britain Can Make It Exhbn, 1946; Coronation hangings for Westminster Abbey, 1953; gold and silver plate in collections: Victoria and Albert Museum, Worshipful Co. of Goldsmiths, Royal Society of Arts, Downing Coll. and Sidney Sussex Coll., Cambridge, Royal Coll. of Art; glass for King's Coll., Cambridge, Grosvenor House, Min. of Works, and others; metal foil mural decorations in SS Canberra, 1961. Consulting Architect to Board of Trade for BIF, Olympia, 1947, Earls Ct, 1949, Olympia, 1950 and 1951. Member: Council of Industrial Design, 1955; National Council for Diplomas in Art and Design, 1961; Adv. Council, V&A Museum, 1977; Chm., Crafts Council, 1977-82. Mem. Council, Essex Univ., 1973. FSIA, 1947; Hon. Fellow, Sheffield Polytechnic, 1971. Hon. DesRCA, 1952; Hon. Dr RCA, 1974; Sen. Fellow, RCA, 1981. SIAD Design Medal, 1972. Master of Faculty, RDI, 1959-61. Liveryman, Worshipful Co. of Goldsmiths, Prime Warden 1976. *Publication:* (with P. Popham) Silversmithing, 1972. *Recreation:* daydreaming. *Address:* 16 Hatfield Buildings, Widcombe Hill, Bath, Avon BA2 6AF.

GOODE, Prof. Royston Miles, OBE 1972; Crowther Professor of Credit and Commercial Law, since 1973, and Director, Centre for Commercial Law Studies, since 1980, Queen Mary College, University of London; *b* 6 April 1933; *s* of Samuel and Bloom Goode; *m* 1964, Catherine Anne Rueff; one *d*. *Educ:* Highgate School. LLB London, 1954; LLD London, 1976. Admitted Solicitor, 1955. Partner, Victor Mishcon & Co., solicitors, 1966-71, Consultant 1971-; Mem. Cttee on Consumer Credit, 1968-71; Prof. of Law, Queen Mary Coll., London, 1971-73, Head of Dept and Dean of Faculty of Laws, 1976-80. Vis. Prof., Melbourne, 1975; Aust. Commonwealth Vis. Fellow, 1975. Chm., Advertising Adv. Cttee, IBA, 1976-80. Mem., Monopolies and Mergers Commn, 1981-. Mem. Council, Justice. *Publications:* Hire-Purchase Law and Practice, 1962, 2nd edn 1970, with Supplement 1975; The Hire-Purchase Act 1964, 1964; (with J. S. Ziegel) Hire-Purchase and Conditional Sale: a Comparative Survey of Commonwealth and American Law, 1965; Introduction to the Consumer Credit Act, 1974; Consumer Credit Legislation, 1977; (ed) Consumer Credit, 1978; Commercial Law, 1982; contrib. Halsbury's Laws of England, 4th edn, Encycl. of Forms and Precedents, 4th edn, and other works; articles and notes in legal jls. *Recreations:* chess, reading, walking, browsing in bookshops. *Address:* 20 Hocroft Road, NW2 2BL. *Club:* Hampstead Chess.

GOODE, Sir William (Allmond Codrington), GCMG 1963 (KCMG 1957; CMG 1952); DL; *b* 8 June 1907; *e s* of late Sir Richard Goode, CMG, CBE; *m* 1st, 1938, Mary Armstrong Harding (*d* 1947); 2nd, 1950, Ena Mary McLaren; one *d*. *Educ:* Oakham Sch.; Worcester Coll., Oxford (Classical exhibitioner). Barrister-at-Law, Gray's Inn, 1936. Joined Malayan Civil Service, 1931; District Officer, Raub, 1936-39; Asst Commissioner for Civil

Defence, Singapore, 1940. Mobilised in 1st Bn Singapore Volunteer Corps as Lance-Corporal, 1941 (prisoner of war, Singapore, 1942; moved to Thailand for work on the Burma Railway; released 1945). Dep. Economic Sec., Federation of Malaya, 1948; Chief Sec., Aden, 1949-53; Acting Governor, Aden, 1950-51; Chief Sec., Singapore, 1953-57; Governor of Singapore, Dec. 1957-2nd June 1959; Yang di-Pertuan Negara of the State of Singapore and UK Commissioner, Singapore, 1959; Governor and C-in-C, North Borneo, 1960-63; Chm., Water Resources Bd, 1964-74. DL Berks 1975. KStJ 1958. *Address:* East Streatley House, Streatley-on-Thames, Berks. *Club:* East India, Devonshire, Sports and Public Schools.

GOODENOUGH, Anthony Michael; HM Diplomatic Service; Head of Chancery, Islamabad, since 1982; *b* 5 July 1941; *s* of late Rear-Adm. M. G. Goodenough, CMG, DSO, and of Nancy Waterfield (*née* Slater); *m* 1967, Veronica Mary, *d* of Col Peter Pender-Cudlip, MVO; two *s* one *d*. *Educ:* Wellington Coll.; New Coll., Oxford. MA 1980. Voluntary Service Overseas, Sarawak, 1963-64; Foreign Office, 1964; Athens, 1967; Private Secretary to Parliamentary Under Secretary, 1971, and Minister of State, FCO, 1972; Paris, 1974; Asst Hd of Maritime Aviation and Environment Dept, 1977 and of European Community Dept (Internal), 1978, FCO; Counsellor on secondment to Cabinet Office, 1980. *Address:* c/o Foreign and Commonwealth Office, SW1.

GOODENOUGH, Cecilia Phyllis, MA; STh; DD; *b* 9 Sept. 1905; *d* of late Adm. Sir William Goodenough, GCB, MVO. *Educ:* Rochester Grammar Sch.; Liverpool Coll., Huyton; St Hugh's Coll., Oxford, LCC Care Cttee Sec., 1927-30; Sunday Sch. and Evangelistic work, Diocese of Caledonia, Fort St John, BC, Canada, 1931-36; Head of Talbot Settlement, 14 Bromley Hill, Bromley, Kent, 1937-45; Asst to Diocesan Missioner, Diocese of Southwark, 1954-72. Examining Chaplain to the Bishop of Southwark, 1973-. *Address:* 115 Camberwell Grove, Camberwell, SE5 8JH. *T:* 01-701 0093.

GOODENOUGH, Frederick Roger, FIB; Director: Barclays Bank PLC, since 1979; Barclays Bank UK Ltd, since 1971; Barclays Bank International Ltd, since 1977; *b* 21 Dec. 1927; *s* of Sir William Macnamara Goodenough, 1st Bt, and Lady (Dorothea Louisa) Goodenough; *m* 1954, Marguerite June Mackintosh; one *s* two *d*. *Educ:* Eton; Magdalene Coll., Cambridge (MA). MA Oxon; FIB 1968. Joined Barclays Bank Ltd, 1950; Local Director: Birmingham, 1958; Reading, 1960; Oxford, 1969-; Mem., London Cttee, Barclays Bank DCO, 1966-71, Barclays Bank Internat. Ltd, 1971-80. Sen. Partner, Broadwell Manor Farm, 1968-; Curator, Oxford Univ. Chest, 1974-; Trustee: Nuffield Med. Trust, 1968-; Nuffield Dominions Trust, 1968-; Nuffield Orthopaedic Trust, 1978- (Chm., 1981-); Oxford and Dist Hosps Improvement and Develt Fund, 1968-; Oxford Preservation Trust, 1980-; Governor: Shiplake Coll., 1963-74 (Chm., 1966-70); Wellington Coll., 1968-74. Fellow of Linnean Soc. (Mem. Council, 1968-75, Treasurer, 1970-75); FRSA. *Recreations:* shooting, fishing, photography, ornithology. *Address:* Broadwell Manor, Lechlade, Glos GL7 3QS. *T:* Filkins 326. *Club:* Brooks's.

GOODENOUGH, Prof. John Bannister; Professor of Inorganic Chemistry, University of Oxford, since 1976; *b* 25 July 1922; *s* of Erwin Ramsdell Goodenough and Helen Lewis Goodenough; *m* 1951, Irene Johnston Wiseman. *Educ:* Yale Univ. (AB, Maths); Univ. of Chicago (MS, PhD, Physics). Meteorologist, US Army Air Force, 1942-48; Research Engr, Westinghouse Corp., 1951-52; Research Physicist (Leader, Electronic Materials Gp), Lincoln Laboratory, MIT, 1952-76. Mem., Nat. Acad. of Engrg, 1976-; Associate Mem., Indian Acad. of Science. Dr *hc*, Bordeaux, 1967. Associate Editor: Materials Research Bulletin, 1966-; Jl Solid State Chemistry, 1969-; Structure and Bonding, 1978-; Solid State Ionics, 1980-; Co-editor, International Series of Monographs on Chemistry, 1979-. *Publications:* Magnetism and the Chemical Bond, 1963; Les oxydes des elements de transition, 1973; numerous research papers in learned jls. *Recreations:* walking, travel. *Address:* Inorganic Chemistry Laboratory, Oxford University, South Parks Road, Oxford OX1 3QR.

GOODENOUGH, Kenneth Mackenzie, CMG 1949; MC 1918; *b* Bristol, 30 Oct. 1891; 3rd *s* of late W. T. Goodenough, Bristol; *m* 1916, Florence Alda Bolwell (*d* 1971); two *s*. *Educ:* Fairfield Sch., Bristol. Entered surveying profession and qualified as a Professional Associate of the Surveyors Institution. Served European War, 1914-18 in Royal Artillery, commissioned 1917 (MC). Took up business appointment in S Rhodesia, 1928. Pres. Bulawayo Chamber of Commerce, 1942 and 1943; Dep. Mayor of Bulawayo, 1944. High Comr for S Rhodesia, 1946-Jan. 1953. Freeman of City of London; Liveryman of Worshipful Co. of Needlemakers. *Address:* 30 North Shore Road, Hayling Island, Hants. *Club:* Bulawayo (Bulawayo).

GOODENOUGH, Sir Richard (Edmund), 2nd Bt *cr* 1943; *b* 9 June 1925; *e s* of Sir William (Macnamara) Goodenough, 1st Bt, and of Dorothea (Louisa), *er d* of late Ven. and Hon. K. F. Gibbs, DD; *S* father 1951; *m* 1951, Jane, *d* of late H. S. P. McLernon and of Mrs McLernon, Gisborne, NZ; one *s* two *d*. *Educ:* Eton Coll.; Christ Church, Oxford. Military service, 1943-45, invalided. Christ Church, Oxford, 1945-47. *Heir:* *s* William McLernon Goodenough [*b* 5 Aug. 1954; *m* 1982, Louise Elizabeth, *d* of Captain Michael Ortmans, MVO, RN and Julia Ortmans].

GOODENOUGH, Samuel Kenneth Henry; Senior Partner, Knight Frank & Rutley, since 1978; KFLH Zimbabwe, since 1980; Chairman, Knight Frank

& Rutley (Nigeria) Agricultural Services Ltd, since 1981; *b* 3 April 1930; 3rd surv. *s* of Sir William Goodenough, 1st Bt, and of Dorothea Lady Goodenough, *d* of late Hon. Kenneth Gibbs, one time Archdeacon of St Albans; *m* 1979, Patricia, *er d* of P. C. Barnett, Prae Wood, St Albans; one step-*s* one step-*d. Educ:* Eton Coll. (Oppidan Schol.); Christ Church, Oxford. MA Oxon. FRICS. Knight, Frank & Rutley: articled, 1952; Partner, 1961. Partner in family farming enterprise, 1965-. Pres., Agricl Section, Internat. Real Estate Fedn, 1975-78. Governor, London House for Overseas Graduates, 1961- (Vice-Chm., 1980-); Chm., Homœpathic Medical Trust, 1970-. Mem. Ct of Assts, Goldsmiths' Co., 1981-. FRSA 1980. *Recreations:* shooting, painting, organ playing, gardening. *Address:* 20 Hanover Square, W1R 0AH. *T:* 01-629 8171; Filkins Hall, Filkins, Lechlade, Glos. *T:* Filkins 413. *Clubs:* Brooks's, Pratt's; New (Edinburgh).

GOODFELLOW, Maj.-Gen. Howard Courtney, CB 1952; CBE 1946 (OBE 1943); retired 1954; *b* 28 July 1898; *yr s* of late Thomas Goodfellow, Plymouth; *m* 1928, Vera St John, *yr d* of late H. St J. Hewitt, Salisbury. *Educ:* Plymouth Coll.; RMC Sandhurst. Commissioned into ASC, 1916; served European War, 1914-18, in France and Italy; seconded to Iraq Army, 1928-32; War of 1939-45, served in Italy and NW Europe, rank of Brig. Order of Rafidain, Class IV (Iraq), 1931. *Address:* Chapel Lodge, Greywell, Hants. *T:* Odiham 2076.

GOODFELLOW, Mrs Rosalind Erica, JP; Moderator of the General Assembly of the United Reformed Church, May 1982-May 1983; *b* 3 April 1927; *d* of late Rev. William Griffith-Jones and Kathleen (*née* Speakman); *m* 1949, Keith Frank Goodfellow, QC (*d* 1977); two *s* one *d. Educ:* Milton Mount Coll. (now Wentworth Milton Mount); Royal Holloway Coll., London Univ. (BA Hons). Member: British Council of Churches Div. of Community Affairs Bd, 1980-; Churches' Council for Covenanting, 1981-. JP Surrey (Esher and Walton PSD), 1960. *Recreations:* chauffeuring the young, attending committee meetings. *Address:* Kilverstone House, Gordon Road, Claygate, Surrey. *T:* Esher 67656. *Club:* University Women's.

GOODHART, Charles Albert Eric, PhD; a Chief Adviser to the Bank of England, since 1980; *b* 23 Oct. 1936; *s* of late Prof. Arthur Goodhart, Hon. KBE, QC, FBA, and of Cecily (*née* Carter); *m* 1960, Margaret (Miffy) Ann Smith; one *s* three *d. Educ:* Eton; Trinity Coll., Cambridge (scholar; 1st Cl. Hons Econs Tripos); Harvard Grad. Sch. of Arts and Sciences (PhD 1963). National Service, 1955-57 (2nd Lieut KRRC). Prize Fellowship in Econs, Trinity Coll., Cambridge, 1963; Asst Lectr in Econs, Cambridge Univ., 1963-64; Econ. Adviser, DEA, 1965-67; Lectr in Monetary Econs, LSE, 1967-69; Adviser in Bank of England, with particular reference to monetary policy, 1969-. *Publications:* The New York Money Market and the Finance of Trade, 1900-13, 1968; The Business of Banking, 1891-1914, 1972; Money, Information and Uncertainty, 1975; articles in econ. jls and papers contrib. to econ. books. *Recreations:* keeping sheep, gardening, tennis, skiing. *Address:* Bank of England, Threadneedle Street, EC2R 8AH. *T:* 01-601 4444.
See also Sir P. C. Goodhart, W. H. Goodhart.

GOODHART, Rear-Adm. Hilary Charles Nicholas, CB 1972; FRAeS; *b* 28 Sept. 1919; *s* of G. C. Goodhart; *m* 1975, Molly Copsey. *Educ:* RNC Dartmouth; RNEC Keyham. Joined RN, 1933; served in Mediterranean in HM Ships Formidable and Dido, 1941-43; trained as pilot, 1944; served as fighter pilot in Burma Campaign, 1945; trained as test pilot, 1946; served on British Naval Staff, Washington, 1953-55; idc 1965; Rear-Adm. 1970; Mil. Dep. to Head of Defence Sales, MoD, 1970-73, retired. British Gliding Champion, 1962, 1967 and 1971. Holder of UK gliding distance record, 360 miles. Freedom of London, 1945; Mem. Ct of Grocers' Co., 1975, Master, 1981. US Legion of Merit, 1958. *Recreations:* design of man-powered aircraft, bee-keeping. *Address:* Lower Farm, Inkpen Common, Newbury, Berks. *T:* Inkpen 297. *Clubs:* Army and Navy, City Livery.

GOODHART, Sir Philip (Carter), Kt 1981; MP (C) Bromley, Beckenham, since March 1957; *b* 3 Nov. 1925; *s* of late Prof. Arthur Goodhart, Hon. KBE, QC, FBA, and of Cecily (*née* Carter); *m* 1950, Valerie Winant; three *s* four *d. Educ:* Hotchkiss Sch., USA; Trinity Coll., Cambridge. Served KRRC and Parachute Regt, 1943-47. Editorial staff, Daily Telegraph, 1950-55; Editorial staff, Sunday Times, 1955-57. Contested (C) Consett, Co. Durham, Gen. Election, 1950; Member: LCC Educn Cttee, 1956-57; British Delegation to Council of Europe and WEU, 1961-63; British Delegation to UN Gen. Assembly, 1963; NATO Parly Assembly, 1964-79 (Chm. Arms Standardization Sub-Cttee, 1966-69). Parly Under-Sec. of State, Northern Ireland Office, and Minister responsible for Dept of the Environment (NI), 1979-81; Parly Under Sec. of State, MoD, Jan.-Sept. 1981. Joint Hon. Sec., 1922 Cttee, 1970-79. Sec., Cons. Parly Defence Cttee, 1967-72, Chm. 1972-74, Vice-Chm., 1974-79; Mem., Cons. Adv. Cttee on Policy, 1973-79; Chm., Parly NI Cttee, 1976-79. Member: Council, Consumers' Assoc., 1959-68, 1970-79; Adv. Council on Public Records, 1970-79; Exec. Council, British Council, 1974-79; Council, RUSI, 1973-76. *Publications:* The Hunt for Kimathi (with Ian Henderson, GM), 1958; In the Shadow of the Sword, 1964; Fifty Ships that Saved the World, 1965; (with Christopher Chataway) War without Weapons, 1968; Referendum, 1970; (with Ursula Branston) The 1922: the history of the 1922 Committee, 1973; Full-Hearted Consent, 1975; various pamphlets. *Recreation:* skiing (Chm., Develt Cttee, Nat. Ski Fedn of GB, 1970-71; Chm., Lords and Commons Ski Club, 1971-73). *Address:* 27 Phillimore Gardens, W8. *T:* 01-937 0822; Whitebarn, Boars Hill, Oxford. *T:*

Oxford 735294. *Clubs:* Beefsteak, Carlton, Garrick.
See also C. A. E. Goodhart, W. H. Goodhart.

GOODHART, Sir Robert (Anthony Gordon), 4th Bt *cr* 1911; Medical Practitioner, Beaminster, Dorset; *b* 15 Dec. 1948; *s* of Sir John Gordon Goodhart, 3rd Bt, FRCGP, and of Margaret Mary Eileen, *d* of late Morgan Morgan; *S* father, 1979; *m* 1972, Kathleen Ellen, *d* of late Rev. A. D. MacRae; two *s* one *d. Educ:* Rugby; Guy's Hospital Medical School, London Univ. MB BS (Lond.), MRCS, LRCP, MRCGP, DObstRCOG. Qualification, 1972; Junior Medical Registrar, Guy's Hosp., 1974; GP, Bromley, 1976-80. *Recreations:* cricket, music, sailing. *Heir: s* Martin Andrew Goodhart, *b* 9 Sept. 1974. *Address:* The Old Rectory, Netherbury, Dorset.

GOODHART, William Howard, QC 1979; *b* 18 Jan. 1933; *s* of late Prof. A. L. Goodhart, Hon. KBE, QC, FBA and of Cecily (*née* Carter); *m* 1966, Hon. Celia McClare Herbert, *d* of 2nd Baron Hemingford; one *s* two *d. Educ:* Eton; Trinity Coll., Cambridge (Scholar, MA); Harvard Law Sch. (Commonwealth Fund Fellow, LLM). Nat. Service, 1951-53 (2nd Lt, Oxford and Bucks Light Infantry). Called to Bar, Lincoln's Inn, 1957. Vice-Chm., Exec. Cttee, Justice (British Section, Internat. Commn of Jurists), 1978-. Trustee, Campden Charities, 1975-. *Publications:* contribs to Halsbury's Laws of England; articles in legal periodicals. *Recreations:* walking, skiing. *Address:* 43 Campden Hill Square, W8 7JR. *T:* 01-221 4830; Youlbury House, Boars Hill, Oxford. *T:* Oxford 735477. *Club:* Athenæum.
See also C. A. E. Goodhart, Sir P. C. Goodhart.

GOODHEW, Sir Victor (Henry), Kt 1982; MP (C) St Albans Division of Herts since Oct. 1959; *b* 30 Nov. 1919; *s* of late Rudolph Goodhew, Mannings Heath, Sussex; *m* 1st, 1940, Sylvia Johnson (marr. diss.); one *s* one *d* ; 2nd, 1951, Suzanne Gordon-Burge (marr. diss. 1972); 3rd, 1972, Eva Rittinghausen (marr. diss. 1981). *Educ:* King's Coll. Sch. Served War of 1939-45: RAF, 1939-46; comd Airborne Radar Unit, attached 6th Airborne Div.; Sqdn Ldr 1945. Mem. Westminster City Council, 1953-59. Contested (C) Paddington North, 1955. Mem. LCC, 1958-61. PPS to Mr C. I. Orr-Ewing, OBE, MP (when Civil Lord of the Admiralty), May 1962-63; PPS to Hon. Thomas Galbraith, MP (Jt Parly Sec., Min. of Transport), 1963-64; Asst Govt Whip, June-Oct. 1970; a Lord Comr, HM Treasury, 1970-73. Member: Speaker's Panel of Chairmen, 1975-; Select Cttee, House of Commons Services, 1978-; House of Commons Commn, 1979-; Jt Sec. 1922 Cttee, 1979-; Vice-Chm., Cons. Defence Cttee, 1974-. *Recreations:* swimming, reading. *Address:* House of Commons, SW1A 0AA. *T:* 01-219 4211.

GOODING, Air Vice-Marshal Keith Horace, CB 1966; OBE 1951; *b* 2 Sept. 1913; *s* of Horace Milford Gooding, Romsey, Hants; *m* 1st, 1943, Peggy Eileen (*d* 1962), *d* of Albert William Gatfield, Guildford, Surrey; one *s* ; 2nd, 1968, Jean, *d* of Maurice Stanley Underwood, Andover, Hants; two *s* one *d* (of whom one *s* one *d* are twins). *Educ:* King Edward VI Sch., Southampton. Joined RAF 1938; served Aden, Fighter Comd, 1939-45; Germany, 1945-47; NATO Defence Coll., 1953-54; NATO, Oslo, 1954-55; Bomber Comd, 1958-61; AOA Maintenance Comd, 1965-68; Dir-Gen. of Equipment, later Supply (RAF), 1968-71, retired. *Recreations:* tennis, bridge. *Address:* c/o Lloyds Bank Ltd, Guildford, Surrey. *Club:* Royal Air Force.

GOODINGS, Alfred Cecil, MBE 1946; MSc, PhD; Director of Textile Research, Ontario Research Foundation, 1930-67; *b* Leith, Scotland, 10 Sept. 1902; *yr s* of late William George Goodings; *m* 1931, *yr d* of late Rev. F. W. Ambery Smith; two *s. Educ:* Leeds Univ. PhD for research in textiles. *Publications:* papers in scientific periodicals relating to textile fibres and technology. *Address:* 101 Collegeview Avenue, Toronto M5P 1K2, Canada.

GOODINGS, Rt. Rev. Allen; *see* Quebec, Bishop of.

GOODISON, Alan Clowes, CMG 1975; CVO 1980; HM Diplomatic Service; Assistant Under-Secretary of State, Foreign and Commonwealth Office, since 1981; *b* 20 Nov. 1926; *o s* of Harold Clowes Goodison and late Winifred Goodison (*née* Ludlam); *m* 1956, Anne Rosemary Fitton; one *s* two *d. Educ:* Colfe's Grammar Sch.; Trinity Coll., Cambridge. Scholar, Mod. and Medieval Langs Tripos, first cl.; MA 1951. Army, Lt, Intell. Corps, 1947-49. Foreign Office, Third Sec., 1949; Middle East Centre for Arab Studies, 1950; Cairo, 1950-51; Tripoli, 1951-53; Khartoum, 1953; FO, 1953-56; Second Sec., later First Sec. (Commercial), Lisbon, 1956-59; Amman, 1960-62; FO, 1962-66; Bonn, 1966-68; Counsellor, Kuwait, 1969-71; Head of Trg Dept and Dir, Diplomatic Service Lang. Centre, FCO, 1971-72; Head of S European Dept, FCO, 1973-76; Minister, Rome, 1976-80. Pres., Beckenham Chorale, 1972-73. Licensed Lay Reader of Anglican Church, 1959-62 and 1966-. Mem. Council: Jerusalem and the East Mission, 1964-65; Anglican Centre, Rome, 1977-80. Grande Ufficiale dell'Ordine al Merito della Repubblica Italiana (Hon.), 1980. *Publications:* trans. numerous articles for Encyclopaedia of Islam. *Recreations:* looking at pictures, singing, reading. *Address:* c/o Foreign and Commonwealth Office, SW1. *Club:* Travellers'.

GOODISON, Sir Nicholas (Proctor), Kt 1982; stockbroker; Senior Partner, Quilter Goodison & Co., since 1975; Chairman of The Stock Exchange, since 1976; *b* 16 May 1934; *s* of Edmund Harold Goodison and Eileen Mary Carrington Proctor; *m* 1960, Judith Abel Smith; one *s* two *d. Educ:* Marlborough Coll.; King's Coll., Cambridge (Scholar; BA Classics 1958, MA; PhD Architecture and History of Art, 1981). H. E. Goodison & Co. (now

Quilter Goodison & Co.), Members of the Stock Exchange, 1958; Partner, 1962; elected to Council of Stock Exchange, 1968 (Chm. various standing cttees, 1971-76). Hon. Treas., Furniture History Soc.; Hon. Keeper of Furniture, Fitzwilliam Museum, Cambridge; Mem., Exec. Cttee, Nat. Art-Collections Fund; Chm., Management Cttee, Courtauld Inst. of Art; Vice-Chm., English Nat. Opera; Dir, City Arts Trust; Editorial Dir, Burlington Magazine. Governor, Marlborough Coll. FSA, FRSA. *Publications:* English Barometers 1680-1860, 1968, 2nd edn 1977; Ormolu: The Work of Matthew Boulton, 1974; many papers and articles on history of furniture, clocks and barometers. *Recreations:* history of furniture and decorative arts, opera, walking, fishing. *Address:* Garrard House, Gresham Street, EC2; Stock Exchange, EC2. *Club:* Beefsteak.

GOODISON, Robin Reynolds, CB 1964; consultant; Deputy Chairman, 1972-77, Acting Chairman, Jan.-March 1972, Civil Aviation Authority; *b* 13 Aug. 1912; *s* of Arthur Leathley Goodison; *m* 1936, Betty Lydia, *d* of Comdr L. Robinson, OBE, Royal Navy (retired); three *d. Educ:* Finchley Grammar Sch.; University Coll., London Univ. (MA). Joined Ministry of Labour, 1935, transferred to Ministry of Transport, 1936; Principal, 1940; Asst Sec., 1946; Imperial Defence Coll., 1950; Under-Sec., Ministry of Transport and Civil Aviation, 1957, Ministry of Aviation, 1959, Board of Trade, 1966; Second Sec., BoT, 1969-70; Dep. Sec., DTI, 1970-72. Assessor, Heathrow Terminal Inquiry, 1978-79; Specialist Adviser, House of Lords Select Cttee, 1979-80. *Recreation:* sailing. *Address:* 37 Coldharbour Lane, Bushey, Herts. *T:* 01-950 1911.

GOODLAD, Alastair Robertson; MP (C) Northwich since Feb. 1974; a Lord Commissioner of HM Treasury, since 1982; *b* 4 July 1943; *y s* of late Dr John Goodlad and late Isabel (*née* Sinclair); *m* 1968, Cecilia Barbara, 2nd *d* of late Col Richard Hurst and Lady Barbara Hurst; two *s. Educ:* Marlborough Coll.; King's Coll., Cambridge (MA, LLB). Contested (C) Crewe Div., 1970. An Asst Govt Whip, 1981-82. Jt Hon. Secretary: Cons. Party Trade Cttee, 1978- (Jt Vice-Chm., 1979-81); Cons. NI Cttee, 1979-81; Hon. Sec., All Party Heritage Gp, 1979-81; Mem., Select Cttee on Agriculture, 1979-81. *Address:* Common Farm, Rhuddal Heath, Tarporley, Cheshire. *T:* Tarporley 2255. *Club:* Brooks's.

GOODMAN, family name of **Baron Goodman.**

GOODMAN, Baron, *cr* 1965, of the City of Westminster (Life Peer); **Arnold Abraham Goodman,** CH 1972; MA, LLM; Master of University College, Oxford, since 1976; Senior Partner, Goodman Derrick and Co., Solicitors; *b* 21 Aug. 1913; *s* of Joseph and Bertha Goodman; unmarried. *Educ:* University Coll., London; Downing Coll., Cambridge (Hon. Fellow, 1968). Enlisted Gunner, RA, TA, Sept. 1939, retd as Major, Nov. 1945. Mem., Royal Commn on Working of Tribunals of Enquiry (Evidence) Act, 1921, 1966-; Chm., Cttee of Inquiry on Charity Law, 1974. Chairman: Housing Corporation, 1973-77; Nat. Building Agency, 1973-78. Chairman: Cttee (on behalf of Arts Council) on London orchestras, 1964, reporting 1965; Arts Council of GB, 1965-72; Theatres' Trust, 1976-; Theatre Investment Fund, 1976-; Motability, 1977-; Jewish Chronicle Trust; Member: British Council, 1967- (Dep. Chm., 1974-); South Bank Theatre Board, 1968-; Life Mem., Royal Phil. Orch., 1976; Director: Royal Opera House, Covent Garden, 1972-; English National Opera Ltd, 1973- (Chm., 1977-); The Observer Ltd, 1976-81; Governor, Royal Shakespeare Theatre, 1972-; President: Nat. Book League, 1972-; Theatres Adv. Council, 1972-; Inst. of Jewish Affairs, 1975-. Chairman: Observer Trust, 1967-76; Newspaper Publishers' Assoc., 1970-75; IRC, 1969-71; British Lion Films Ltd, 1965-72; Charter Film Productions, 1973-; Dir of various companies. Mem., British/USA Bicentennial Liaison Cttee, 1973. Governor, College of Law, 1975-. Fellow UCL; Hon. LLD London and other Univs; Hon. DLitt City, 1975. *Address:* University College, Oxford. *T:* Oxford 41661.

GOODMAN, Geoffrey George; Assistant Editor, since 1976, and Industrial Editor, since 1969, The Daily Mirror; *b* 2 July 1921; *s* of Michael Goodman and Edythe (*née* Bowman); *m* 1947, Margit (*née* Freudenbergova); one *s* one *d. Educ:* elementary schs, Stockport and Manchester; grammar schs, London; LSE (BScEcon). RAF, 1940-46. Manchester Guardian, 1946-47; Daily Mirror, 1947-48; News Chronicle, 1949-59; Daily Herald, 1959-64; The Sun (IPC), 1964-69; Daily Mirror, 1969-. Fellow, Nuffield Coll., Oxford, 1974-76. Head of Govt's Counter-inflation Publicity Unit, 1975-76; Member: Labour Party Cttee on Industrial Democracy, 1966-67; Royal Commn on the Press, 1974-77; TGWU; NUJ. Hon. MA Oxon. *Publications:* General Strike of 1926, 1951; Brother Frank, 1969; The Awkward Warrior, 1979; contrib. London Inst. of World Affairs, 1948. *Recreations:* pottering, poetry, supporting Tottenham Hotspur FC, and climbing—but not social. *Address:* 64 Flower Lane, Mill Hill, NW7. *Club:* Savile.

GOODMAN, Howard; *see* Goodman, R. H.

GOODMAN, Prof. John Francis Bradshaw, PhD; FIPM; Frank Thomas Professor of Industrial Relations, University of Manchester Institute of Science and Technology, since 1975 (Vice-Principal, 1979-81); *b* 2 Aug. 1940; *s* of Edwin and Amy Goodman; *m* 1967, Elizabeth Mary Towns; one *s* one *d. Educ:* Chesterfield Grammar Sch.; London Sch. of Economics (BSc Econ; PhD); MSc Manchester. FIPM. Personnel Officer, Ford Motor Co. Ltd, 1962-64; Lectr in Industrial Econs, Univ. of Nottingham, 1964-69; Industrial Relations Adviser, NBPI, 1969-70; Sen. Lectr in Industrial Relations, Univ.

of Manchester, 1970-74; Chm., Dept of Management Scis, UMIST, 1977-79. Vis. Prof., Univ. of WA, 1981. *Publications:* Shop Stewards in British Industry, 1969; Shop Stewards, 1973; Rulemaking and Industrial Peace, 1977; Ideology and Shop-floor Industrial Relations, 1981; contribs to British Jl of Industrial Relations, ILR, Industrial Relations Jl, Monthly Labor Rev., Jl of Management Studies, Personnel Management, etc. *Recreations:* fell walking, ornithology, squash, football. *Address:* 24 Regent Close, Bramhall, Stockport, Cheshire. *T:* 061-439 7136.

GOODMAN, M(ichael) Bradley; a Recorder of the Crown Court, since 1972; Vicar-General of the Province of Canterbury, since 1977; *b* 3 May 1930; *s* of Marcus Gordon Goodman and Eunice Irene May Goodman (*née* Bradley); *m* 1967, Patricia Mary Gorringe; two *d* (one *s* decd). *Educ:* Aldenham; Sidney Sussex Coll., Cambridge (MA). Called to Bar, Middle Temple, 1953; Western Circuit. Chm., William Temple Assoc., 1963-66; Prosecuting Counsel to DHSS, 1975-; Pres., Wireless Telegraphy Appeals Tribunal, 1977-; Member: Commn on Deployment and Payment of the Clergy, 1965-67; C of E Legal Adv. Commn, 1973-; General Synod, Church of England, 1977-; Chancellor: Dio. Guildford, 1968-; Dio. Lincoln, 1970-; Dio. Rochester, 1971-; Lay Chm., Dulwich Deanery Synod, 1970-73. Governor: Liddon Hse, London, 1964-; Pusey Hse, Oxford, 1965-. *Address:* Francis Taylor Building, Temple, EC4. *T:* 01-353 7768. *Club:* Hurlingham.

GOODMAN, Michael Jack, PhD; Social Security Commissioner (formerly National Insurance Commissioner), since 1979; *b* 3 Oct. 1931; *s* of Vivian Roy Goodman and Muriel Olive Goodman; *m* 1958, Susan Kerkham Wherry; two *s* one *d. Educ:* Sudbury Grammar Sch., Suffolk; Corpus Christi Coll., Oxford (MA). PhD Manchester. Solicitor. Lectr, Gibson & Weldon, 1957; solicitor, Lincoln, 1958-60; Lectr, Law Society's Sch., 1961-63; Lectr, then Sen. Lectr in Law, Manchester Univ., 1964-70; Prof. of Law, Durham Univ., 1971-76; Perm. Chm. of Indust. Tribunals, Newcastle upon Tyne, 1976-79. Gen. Editor, Encyclopedia of Health and Safety at Work, 1974-. *Publications:* Industrial Tribunals' Procedure, 1976, 2nd edn 1979; contrib. Mod. Law Rev., and Conveyancer. *Recreations:* model railways, The Times crossword. *Address:* Office of the Social Security Commissioners, 6 Grosvenor Gardens, SW1W 0DH. *T:* 01-730 0344.

GOODMAN, Rt. Rev. Morse Lamb; *see* Calgary, Bishop of.

GOODMAN, Perry; Deputy Chief Scientific Officer, Department of Industry, since 1981; *b* 26 Nov. 1932; *s* of Cyril Goodman and Anne (*née* Rosen); *m* 1958, Marcia Ann (*née* Morris); one *s* one *d. Educ:* Haberdashers' Aske's Hampstead Sch.; University Coll., London. BSc, AICeram. Royal Corps of Signals, 1955-57; Jt Head, Chemistry Res. Lab., then Project Leader, Morgan Crucible Co. Ltd, 1957-64; Sen. Scientific Officer, DSIR, 1964-65; Principal Scientific Officer, Process Plant Br., Min. of Technology, 1965-67; 1st Sec. (Scientific), 1968-70, Counsellor (Scientific), 1970-74, British Embassy, Paris; Research Gp, DoI, 1974; Hd, Policy and Perspectives Unit, DoI, 1980-81. *Recreations:* travel, walking, conversation. *Address:* 118 Westbourne Terrace Mews, W2 6QG. *T:* 01-262 0925.

GOODMAN, (Robert) Howard, ARIBA; DipArch (Hons); Director of Development, Department of Health and Social Security, since 1978; *b* 29 March 1928; *s* of Robert Barnard Goodman and Phyllis Goodman; *m* 1955, Doris Richardson; two *s. Educ:* St George Grammar Sch., Bristol; Northern Polytechnic, London. Articled pupil, 1944-47; Arch. Asst to City of Bristol, 1947-49; Asst Architect to SW Regional Hosp. Bd, 1949-54. Design of various hosp. projects in SW England; with various private architects, 1954-60; design of several hosps in UK, Africa and India. MOH (now DHSS): Main Grade Arch., 1960; Sen. Grade, 1961; Principal Arch., 1963; Asst Chief Arch., 1966; Chief Arch., 1971-78. Member: Constr. and Housing Res. Adv. Council; Bldg Res. Estab. Adv. Council; Council of Centre on Environment for the Handicapped. Research and develt into health planning, systems building and computer aided design. *Publications:* contribs to: Hospitals Handbook, 1960; Hospital Design, 1963; Hospital Traffic and Supply Problems, 1968; Portfolio for Health, 1971; Technology of the Eighties, 1972; Industrialised Hospital Building, 1972; CAD Systems, 1976; various articles in architectural, medical and general press. *Recreations:* eating, drinking, talking. *Address:* 75 Linkfield Street, Redhill, Surrey.

GOODPASTER, Gen. Andrew Jackson; United States Army, retired; DSC (US); DSM (Def.) (Oak Leaf Cluster); DSM (Army) (3 Oak Leaf Clusters); DSM (Navy); DSM (Air Force); Silver Star; Legion of Merit (Oak Leaf Cluster); Purple Heart (Oak Leaf Cluster); Superintendent, United States Military Academy, West Point, New York (in grade of Lt-Gen.), 1977-81; *b* 12 Feb. 1915; *s* of Andrew Jackson Goodpaster and Teresa Mary Goodpaster (*née* Mrovka); *m* 1939, Dorothy Anderson Goodpaster (*née* Anderson); two *d. Educ:* McKendree Coll., Lebanon, Ill; US Mil. Academy, 1935-39 (BS); Princeton Univ., 1947-50 (MSE, MA, PhD). 11th Eng. Panama, 1939-42; Ex O, 390th Eng. Gen. Svc Regt, Camp Claiborne, La, 1942-43; Comd and Gen. Staff Sch., Ft Leavenworth, Kansas, Feb.-April 1943; CO, 48th Eng. Combat Bn, II Corps, Fifth Army, 1943-44; Ops Div., Gen. Staff, War Dept (incl. Jt War Plans Cttee, JCS, 1945-46), 1944-47; Student, Civil Eng. Course and Polit. Sc. Grad. Sch., Princeton Univ., 1947-50; Army Mem., Jt Advanced Study Cttee, JCS, 1950-51; Special Asst to Chief of Staff, SHAPE, 1951-54; Dist Eng., San Francisco Dist, Calif, July-Oct. 1954; Def. Liaison Officer and Staff Sec. to President of US, 1954-61; Asst Div. Comdr, 3rd Inf. Div., April-Oct. 1961, and CG, 8th Inf. Div., Oct. 1961-Oct. 1962, USAREUR;

Sp. Asst (Policy) to Chm., JCS, Washington, DC, Nov. 1962-Jan. 1964; Asst to Chm., JCS, Washington, DC, Jan. 1964-July 1966; Dir Joint Staff, JCS, Washington, DC, Aug. 1966-Mar. 1967; Dir of Sp. Studies, Office Chief of Staff, USA, Washington, DC, April 1967-July 1967; Senior US Army Mem., Mil. Staff UN, May 1967-July 1968; Comdt. Nat. War Coll., Washington, DC, Aug. 1967-July 1968; Mem. US Delegn for Negotiations with N Vietnam, Paris (addl duty), April 1968-July 1968; Dep. Comdr, US Mil. Assistance Comd, Vietnam, July 1968-April 1969; Supreme Allied Commander Europe, 1969-74; C-in-C, US European Command, 1969-74. Sen. Fellow, Woodrow Wilson Internat. Center for Scholars, Washington DC, 1975-76; Prof. of Govt and Internat. Studies, The Citadel, Charleston, SC, 1976-77. *Publication:* For the Common Defense, 1977. *Recreations:* golf, fishing, ski-ing, music. *Address:* 409 North Fairfax Street, Alexandria, Va 22314, USA.

GOODRICH, Rt. Rev. Philip Harold Ernest; *see* Worcester, Bishop of.

GOODSELL, Sir John William, Kt 1968; CMG 1954; FASA; Company Director, since 1971; Member: State Cancer Council, 1962-78; Council, University of New South Wales, since 1948; Convocation, Macquarie University, since 1965; Chairman: Unisearch Ltd; Winston Churchill Fellowship Trust; *b* 6 July 1906; *s* of late Major S. P. Goodsell, VD, Croix de Guerre (avec Palme), and of late Mrs L. A. Goodsell; *m* 1932, Myrtle Thelma, *d* of late R. H. Austin; three *d. Educ:* Canterbury High Sch., NSW. Member: Public Library Bd, 1948-55; Public Accountants Registration Bd, 1948-55; Under-Sec. and Comptroller of Accounts, New South Wales Treasury, 1948-55; Metropolitan Water Sewerage and Drainage Board, Sydney, April 1955-Sept. 1960; Chm., NSW Public Service Bd, 1960-71; Member: Council, Australian Soc. of Accountants, 1959-61; Sydney Harbour Transport Board, 1951-55; Appointments Bd, Univ. of Sydney, 1963-71; Prince Henry Hospital Bd, 1960-76 (Chm., 1960-61); Prince of Wales Hospital Bd, 1961-76; Eastern Suburbs Hospital Bd, 1968-76; Chm., Tax Agents Board, 1948-55; Custodian Trustee, Legislative Assembly Members Superannuation Fund, 1948-55; Trustee, Kuring-gai Chase Trust, 1962-64. Hon. DSc Univ. of NSW, 1976. Coronation Medal, 1953. *Recreations:* tennis and fishing. *Address:* 22 King Street, Ashbury, NSW 2193, Australia. *T:* 798 4826.

GOODSON, Alan, OBE 1978; QPM 1972; Chief Constable of Leicestershire (sometime Leicester and Rutland), since 1972; *b* 2 June 1927; *s* of Aubrey and Bessie Goodson; *m* 1954, Mary Anne Reilly; one *s* two *d. Educ:* Hitchin Grammar Sch.; King's Coll., London (LLB). Served Royal Navy, 1945-48. Metropolitan Police, 1951-65; Chief Constable of Pembrokeshire, 1965-68; Asst Chief Constable of Dyfed-Powys, 1968; Asst Chief Constable, then Dep. Chief Constable of Essex and Southend-on-Sea, 1968-72; idc 1970. Mem. Adv. Council on Penal System, 1975-78. Pres., Assoc. of Chief Police Officers, 1979-80. *Address:* 420 London Road, Leicester LE2 2PT. *T:* Leicester 700911.

GOODSON, Lt-Col Sir Alfred Lassam, 2nd Bt *cr* 1922; *b* 26 Aug. 1893; *er s* of of 1st Bt; *S* father, 1940; *m* 1920, Joan (*d* 1939), *d* of C. J. Leyland, Haggerston Castle, Beal, Northumberland; *m* 1941, Enid Clayton Leyland, *d* of late Robert Clayton Swan, Barrowby Grange, Grantham. *Educ:* Radley. Served European War, 1914-19, Captain City of London Yeomanry, TF, 1916; commanded No 1 Bn Northumberland Home Guard, 1940-45. Master, College Valley Foxhounds, 1924-81. *Heir: n* Mark Weston Lassam Goodson [*b* 12 Dec. 1925; *m* 1949, Barbara Mary Constantine, *d* of Surg.-Capt. R. J. McAuliffe Andrews, RN; one *s* three *d*]. *Address:* Corbet Tower, Kelso, Roxburghshire. *T:* Morebattle 203.

GOODSTEIN, Prof. Reuben Louis, PhD, DLit (London); ScD (Cantab); Professor of Mathematics, University of Leicester, 1948-77, now Emeritus; *b* 15 Dec. 1912; 2nd *s* of late Alexander and Sophia Goodstein; *m* 1938, Louba, *d* of late Samuel Atkin; one *s* one *d. Educ:* St Paul's Sch. (scholar and sen. scholar); Magdalene Coll., Cambridge (BA, MSc). Scholar and Research Scholar, Magdalene Coll., 1931-35; Lectr in Mathematics, Univ. of Reading, 1935-47; Dean of the Faculty of Science, 1954-57; Pro-Vice-Chancellor, 1966-69, Univ. of Leicester. Hon. Librarian, Mathematical Assoc., 1955-77, Pres., 1975-76; Editor, Mathematical Gazette, 1956-62. Mem. Council, Assoc. for Symbolic Logic, 1965-69. *Publications:* Mathematical Analysis, 1948; Constructive Formalism, 1951, 2nd edn, 1965; The Foundations of Mathematics, 1952; Axiomatic Projective Geometry, 1953, 2nd edn 1962; Mathematical Logic, 1957, 2nd edn 1962 (Russian trans. 1961); Recursive Number Theory, 1957 (Russian trans. 1970); Recursive Analysis, 1961 (Russian trans. 1970); Fundamental Concepts of Mathematics, 1962, 2nd edn 1979; Boolean Algebra, 1963 (Dutch trans. 1965, Japanese trans. 1969); Essays in the Philosophy of Mathematics, 1965; Complex Functions, 1965 (Spanish trans. 1975); Development of Mathematical Logic, 1971 (Japanese trans. 1978); articles in British, continental and American jls. *Address:* Hadfield, Manor Road, Leicester.

GOODWIN, Prof. Albert, MA; Professor of Modern History in the University of Manchester, 1953-69 (Dean of the Faculty of Arts, 1966-68), now Emeritus Professor; *b* 2 Aug. 1906; 3rd *s* of Albert and Edith Ellen Goodwin; *m* 1935, Mary Ethelwyn (*d* 1981), *e d* of late Capt. W. Millner, Tettenhall, Staffs; two *s* one *d. Educ:* King Edward VII School, Sheffield; Jesus Coll., Oxford; Sorbonne. Scholar; Gladstone Memorial Prizeman (Oxford) 1926; 1st Cl. Mod. Hist., 1928; Laming Travelling Fellow, The Queen's Coll.,

Oxford, 1928-29. Asst Lectr in European History, Univ. of Liverpool, 1929-31; Lectr in Mod. Hist. and Economics, 1931, Fellow and Tutor, Jesus Coll., Oxford, 1933; Junior Dean, Librarian and Dean of Degrees, 1931-39; Univ. Lectr in Mod. French Hist., 1938. Staff Officer (Sqdn Ldr) in RAFVR in Air Ministry War Room, 1940-43; Historical Branch, Air Ministry, 1944-45. Senior Tutor, 1947-48, and Vice-Principal of Jesus Coll., Oxford, 1949-51. Examiner in Final Hon. Sch. of Mod. Hist. (Oxford) 1948-49, Chm., 1950; Senior Univ. Lectr in Revolutionary and Napoleonic Period, 1948-53; Vis. Fellow, All Souls Coll., Oxford, 1969-70. Member: Council of Royal Historical Soc. (Vice-Pres.); Royal Commn on Historical MSS, 1966-81; Governor of John Rylands Library, Manchester. Pres., Sherborne Hist. Soc.; Chm., Sherborne Museum Council. *Publications:* The Abbey of St Edmundsbury, 1931; The Battle of Britain (Air Ministry Pamphlet 156), 1943; The French Revolution, 1953; The European Nobility in the Eighteenth Century (contrib. and ed), 1953; A select list of works on Europe and Europe Overseas, 1715-1815 (co-editor contributor), 1956; The Friends of Liberty: the English democratic movement in the age of the French Revolution, 1979; (ed and contrib.) Vol. VIII New Cambridge Modern History; articles in Eng. Hist. Review, History, Encyclopædia Britannica, etc. *Recreations:* golf, antiques. *Address:* 12 Hound Street, Sherborne, Dorset DT9 3AA. *T:* Sherborne 2280.

GOODWIN, Air Vice-Marshal Edwin Spencer, CB 1944; CBE 1941; AFC. Served European War, 1914-19; Flt Sub-Lieut RNAS, 1916; War of 1939-45 (CBE, CB). Group Capt. 1939; Air Commodore, 1941; Air Vice-Marshal, 1948. Air Officer i/c Administration, HQ Bomber Command, 1945; retired, 1948.

GOODWIN, Dr Eric Thomson, CBE 1975; retired; *b* 30 July 1913; *s* of John Edward Goodwin and Florence Goodwin; *m* 1st, 1940, Isobel Philip (*d* 1976); two *s*; 2nd, 1977, Avis Mary (*née* Thomson). *Educ:* King Edward VI Sch., Stafford; Harrow County Sch.; Peterhouse, Cambridge. BA 1934, Rayleigh Prize 1936, MA 1937, PhD 1938. Asst Lectr, Sheffield Univ., 1937-39; war service: Mathematical Lab., Cambridge, 1939-43; Admty Signal Estabt, Witley, 1943-44; Admty Computing Service, Bath, 1945; Maths Div., Nat. Physical Lab., 1945-71 (Supt 1951-71); Dep. Dir, Nat. Phys. Lab., 1971-74, retd. *Publications:* papers in learned jls on theoretical physics and numerical analysis. *Recreations:* music, reading, the countryside, philately. *Address:* 32 Castle Mount Crescent, Bakewell, Derbyshire DE4 1AT. *T:* Bakewell 3647.

GOODWIN, Prof. Geoffrey Lawrence, BSc (Econ.); Montague Burton Professor of International Relations in the University of London (tenable at London School of Economics), 1962-78, now Emeritus; *b* 14 June 1916; *s* of Rev. J. H. Goodwin and Mrs E. M. Goodwin; *m* 1951, Janet Audrey (*née* Sewell); one *s* two *d. Educ:* Marlborough Coll.; RMC, Sandhurst; London Sch. of Economics. Regular Army Officer, 1936-43 (The Suffolk Regt; Army Physical Training Staff; Combined Ops; Major, comdg Indep. Company, Gibraltar). Foreign Office, 1945-48; London Sch. of Economics, 1948-81. Principal, St Catharine's, Windsor Great Park, 1971-72. Comr on Internat. Affairs, World Council of Churches, 1968-76. Mem. Council, RIIA, 1974-77; Hon. Pres., British Internat. Studies Assoc., 1977-80. FRSA 1975. *Publications:* (ed.) The University Teaching of International Relations, 1951; Britain and the United Nations, 1958; (ed) New Dimensions of World Politics, 1975; (ed) A New International Commodity Regime, 1979; (ed) Ethics and Nuclear Deterrence, 1982; articles in International Affairs, International Organization, Political Studies, etc. *Recreations:* painting, sketching, singing. *Address:* Webbs Farm, Church Lane, Headley, Surrey. *T:* Leatherhead 77354.

GOODWIN, Prof. John Forrest, MD, FRCP; Professor of Clinical Cardiology, Royal Postgraduate Medical School, London, since 1963; Consulting Physician, Hammersmith Hospital, since 1949; Hon. Consulting Cardiologist, St Mary's Hospital, Paddington, since 1982; *b* 1 Dec. 1918; *s* of late Col William Richard Power Goodwin, DSO, RAMC, and late Myrtle Dale Goodwin (*née* Forrest); *m* 1943, Barbara Cameron Robertson; one *s* one *d. Educ:* Cheltenham Coll.; St Mary's Hosp. Medical Sch. (Univ. of London). FRSocMed 1943; MD London 1946; FRCP 1957. Med. Registrar, St Mary's Hosp., 1943-44; Physician, Anglo-Iranian Oil Co., Abadan, 1944-45; Med. 1st Asst, Royal Infirmary, Sheffield, 1946-49; Lectr in Medicine and Cons. Physician, Postgraduate Med. Sch., London, 1949-59; Sen. Lecturer, 1959-63. Visiting Professor: Univ. of California at Los Angeles, 1966; Georgetown Univ. Sch. of Med., Washington, 1973; Lumleian Lectr, RCP, 1980. Mem., Expert Cttee on Cardiovascular Diseases, WHO, 1979. Member: Brit. Cardiac Soc., 1950 (Pres., 1972-76); Med. Res. Soc., 1952; Assoc. of Physicians of Great Britain and Ireland, 1953; Council, Brit. Heart Foundation, 1964; Past Pres., Internat. Soc. and Fedn of Cardiology (Pres., 1977-81); 2nd Vice-Pres., RCP, 1979-80. Member: Società Italiana di Cardiologia, 1964; Thoracic Soc., 1967; Assoc. of European Pædiatric Cardiologists, 1967; Cardiac Soc. of Australia and NZ, 1974; Venezuelan Soc. of Cardiology, 1969; Hon. Member: Swiss Cardiol. Soc.; Cardiac Soc., Ecuador; Hellenic Cardiac Soc., 1974; Cardiac Soc. of Mexico, 1977; Fellow Amer. Coll. of Cardiology, 1967; Fellow, Council on Clinical Cardiology, Amer. Heart Assoc., 1970. SPk 1968. Commander, Order of Icelandic Falcon, 1972. *Publications:* (jt ed. with R. Daley and R. E. Steiner) Clinical Disorders of the Pulmonary Circulation, 1960; (with W. Cleland, L. McDonald, D. Ross) Medical and Surgical Cardiology, 1969; (ed with P. Yu) Progress in Cardiology, annually since 1973; papers on diagnosis and treatment of congenital and acquired heart disease in British and foreign cardiac and other journals. *Recreations:*

photography, history, travel. *Address:* 2 Pine Grove, Lake Road, Wimbledon, SW19 7HE. *T:* 01-947 4851. *Clubs:* Athenæum, Royal Society of Medicine.

GOODWIN, Leonard George, CMG 1977; FRCP; FRS 1976; Director, Nuffield Laboratories of Comparative Medicine, Institute of Zoology, The Zoological Society of London, 1964-80; Director of Science, Zoological Society of London, 1966-80; *b* 11 July 1915; *s* of Harry George and Lois Goodwin; *m* 1940, Marie Evelyn Coates; no *c. Educ:* William Ellis Sch., London; University Coll. London (Fellow, 1981); School of Pharmacy, London; University Coll. Hospital. BPharm 1935, BSc 1937, MB, BS 1950, (London). MRCP 1966, FRCP 1972. Demonstrator, Sch. of Pharmacy, London, 1935-39; Head of Wellcome Labs of Tropical Medicine, 1958-63 (Protozoologist, 1939-63). Jt Hon. Sec., Royal Soc. of Tropical Medicine and Hygiene, 1968-74, Pres., 1979-81. Chairman: Trypanosomiasis Panel, ODM, 1974-77; Filariasis Steering Cttee, WHO Special Programme, 1978-. Hon. FPS, 1977. Soc. of Apothecaries Gold Medal, 1975; Harrison Meml Medal, 1978; Schofield Medal, Guelph Univ., 1979; Silver Medal, Zoological Soc., 1980. Chm. Editorial Bd, Parasitology, 1980-. *Publications:* (pt author) Biological Standardization, 1950; (contrib.) Biochemistry and Physiology of Protozoa, 1955; (jointly) A New Tropical Hygiene, 1960, 2nd edn 1972; (contrib.) Recent Advances in Pharmacology, 1962; many contribs to scientific jls, mainly on pharmacology and chemotherapy of tropical diseases, especially malaria, trypanosomiasis and helminth infections. *Recreations:* Dabbling in arts and crafts especially pottery (slipware), gardening and passive participation in music and opera. *Address:* Shepperlands Farm, Park Lane, Finchampstead, Berks RG11 4QF. *T:* Eversley 732153.

GOODWIN, Michael Felix James; Director-General, Institute for the Study of Conflict, since 1979 (formerly Administrative Director); *b* 31 Jan. 1916; *e s* of late F. W. Goodwin; *m* 1944, Alison, *y d* of Capt. Lionel Trower and Ethel Matheson of Achany; one *s* one *d. Educ:* privately. Joined BBC, 1935; North Reg. Drama Dir, 1938; West Reg. Drama Dir, 1939. Served War of 1939-45, in Royal Artillery, 1939-43. Returned to BBC in Features Dept and Overseas News Service, 1943-47. Dramatic critic, The Weekly Review, 1945-46; succeeded Helen Waddell as Asst Editor, The Nineteenth Century and After, 1945-47; Editor, The Twentieth Century (formerly The Nineteenth Century and After), 1947-52; toured US at invitation of State Dept, 1952; Editor, Bellman Books, 1952-55; Dir, Contact Publications, 1955-60; Dir, Newman Neame Ltd, 1960-65. Financial Advr, Internat. Assoc. for Cultural Freedom, Paris, 1967-73. *Publications:* Nineteenth Century Opinion, 1949 (Penguin); Artist and Colourman, 1966; Concise Dictionary of Antique Terms, 1967. *Address:* 16 Cope Place, W8. *T:* 01-937 3802. *Club:* Travellers'.

GOODWIN, Noël; see Goodwin, T. N.

GOODWIN, Peter Austin; Secretary, Public Works Loan Commission, since 1979; Comptroller General, National Debt Office, since 1980; Director, National Investment and Loans Office, since 1980; *b* 12 Feb. 1929; *s* of late Stanley Goodwin and of Louise Goodwin; *m* 1950, Audrey Vera Webb; one *d. Educ:* Harrow County School. Served Royal Air Force, 1947-49. Executive Officer, Public Works Loan Commn, 1950; Principal, Civil Aviation Authority, 1973-76; Asst Secretary and Establishment Officer, Public Works Loan Commn, 1976-79. *Recreations:* theatre, opera, ballet, country dancing, model railways. *Address:* 87 Woodmansterne Road, Carshalton Beeches, Surrey SM5 4JW. *T:* 01-643 3530.

GOODWIN, Sir Reginald (Eustace), Kt 1968; CBE 1960; DL; Leader of the Labour Party, Greater London Council, 1967-80, Leader of the Council, 1973-77, Leader of the Opposition, 1967-73 and 1977-80; *b* 3 July 1908; *s* of late Thomas William Goodwin, Streatham, London; *m* 1943, Penelope Mary, *d* of late Capt. R. T. Thornton, MBE, MC, Chepstow, Mon; two *s* one *d. Educ:* Strand Sch., London. Tea Buyer in City of London, 1928-34; Asst Gen. Sec., Nat. Assoc. of Boys' Clubs, 1934-45. Served War of 1939-45. Mem., Bermondsey Borough Council, 1937-65 (Leader of Council, 1947-65); Hon. Freeman of the Borough, 1963; Mem. LCC, 1946-65; Alderman, 1961 (Chm. Gen. Purposes Cttee, 1954-58; Establishment Cttee, 1958-60; Housing Cttee, 1960-61; Finance Cttee, 1961-65); Mem., GLC, 1964-81 (Chm. Finance Cttee, 1964-67; Chm. ILEA Finance Sub-Cttee, 1964-67, 1970-73). Dep. Chm., Basildon Develt Corp., 1970-78, Chm. 1979-80. Gen. Sec., Nat. Assoc. of Boys' Clubs, 1945-73. Mem. Ct, Univ. of London, 1968-. DL County of London, 1958-. *Recreations:* local government; gardening. *Address:* Twitten Cottage, Marehill, Pulborough, West Sussex. *T:* Pulborough 2202.

GOODWIN, Lt-Gen. Sir Richard (Elton), KCB 1963 (CB 1959); CBE 1954; DSO 1944; Vice Lord-Lieutenant, Suffolk, since 1978; *b* 17 Aug. 1908; *s* of late Col W. R. P. Goodwin, DSO, and Mrs Goodwin; *m* 1940, Anthea Mary Sampson; three *s. Educ:* Cheltenham Coll.; Royal Military Coll., Sandhurst. Commissioned into Suffolk Regt, 1928; served in India, 1930-38; ADC to Governor of Madras, 1935; Adjutant 2nd Suffolk, 1935-38; 2nd i/c 9th Royal Warwickshire, 1941-42; CO 1st Suffolk, 1943-45; College Comdr, RMA Sandhurst, 1947-49; Comdt, Sch. of Infantry, 1951-54; Comdr, 6th Infty Bde, 1954-57; GOC 49th Infty Div. (TA) and N Midland Dist, 1957-60; GOC, E Africa Comd, 1960-63; Comdr 1st (British) Corps, 1963-66; Military Secretary, MoD (Army), 1966-69. Lieutenant, HM Tower of London, 1969-72. Col 1st E Anglian Regt (Royal Norfolk and Suffolk), 1962-64; Dep. Col The Royal Anglian Regt, 1964-66, Col, 1966-71. DL Suffolk 1973.

Recreations: hunting and other field sports. *Address:* Barrow House, Barrow, Bury St Edmunds, Suffolk. *Club:* Army and Navy.

GOODWIN, Prof. Richard Murphey; Professor of Economic Science, Siena University, since 1980; *b* 24 Feb. 1913; *s* of William Murphey Goodwin and Mary Florea Goodwin; *m* 1937, Jacqueline Wynmalen; no *c. Educ:* Harvard Univ. (AB, PhD); Oxford Univ. (BA, BLitt). Harvard Univ.: Instructor in Econs, 1939-42; Instructor in Physics, 1942-45; Asst Prof. of Econs, 1945-51; Lectr in Econs, 1951-69, Reader in Economics, 1969-80, and Fellow of Peterhouse, 1956-80 (Emeritus Fellow, 1982), Univ. of Cambridge. *Publications:* Elementary Economics from the Higher Standpoint, 1970; Essays in Economic Dynamics, 1980; Essays in Linear Economic Structures, 1980; contrib. Econ. Jl, Econometrica, Review of Econs and Statistics. *Recreations:* painting, walking. *Address:* Dorvis's, Ashdon, South Walden, Essex. *T:* Ashdon 302.

GOODWIN, (Trevor) Noël; freelance critic, writer and broadcaster, specialising in music and dance; *b* 25 Dec. 1927; *s* of Arthur Daniel Goodwin and Blanche Goodwin (*née* Stephens); *m* 1st, 1954, Gladys Marshall Clapham (marr. diss. 1960); 2nd, Anne Myers (*née* Mason); one step *s. Educ:* mainly in France. BA (London). Assistant Music Critic: News Chronicle, 1952-54; Manchester Guardian, 1954-55; Music and Dance Critic, Daily Express, 1956-78; regular reviewer for: The Times, 1978-; Internat. Herald Tribune, 1978-; Opera News, 1975-; Ballet News, 1979-; Dance and Dancers, 1957- (Associate Editor, 1972-). Member: Arts Council of GB, 1979-81 (Mem., 1973-81, Chm., 1979-81, Dance Adv. Panel; Mem., 1974-81, Dep. Chm., 1979-81, Music Adv. Panel; Council's rep. on Visiting Arts Unit of GB, 1979-81); Dance Adv. Panel, UK Branch, Calouste Gulbenkian Foundn, 1972-76; Nat. Enquiry into Dance Educn and Trng in Britain, 1975-80; Drama and Dance Adv. Cttee, British Council, 1973-; HRH The Duke of Kent's UK Cttee for European Music Year 1985, 1982- (Chm., sub-cttee for Writers and Critics); Trustee-dir, Internat. Dance Course for Professional Choreographers and Composers, 1975-. Pres., The Critics' Circle, 1977. Planned and presented numerous radio programmes of music and records for BBC Home and World Services during past 25 years, and contributes frequently to music and arts programmes on Radios 3 and 4. *Publications:* London Symphony: portrait of an orchestra, 1954; A Ballet for Scotland, 1979; editor, Royal Opera and Royal Ballet Yearbooks, 1978, 1979, 1980; area editor and writer, New Grove Dictionary of Music and Musicians, 1981; contribs to: Encyclopaedia Britannica, 15th edn, 1974; Encyclopaedia of Opera, 1976; Britannica Books of the Year, 1980, 1981, 1982, 1983; Cambridge Encyclopaedia of Russia and the Soviet Union, 1982; Oxford Companion to Music, 11th edn, 1983. *Recreation:* travel. *Address:* 76 Skeena Hill, SW18 5PN. *T:* 01-788 8794.

GOODWIN, Prof. Trevor Walworth, CBE 1975; FRS 1968; Johnston Professor of Biochemistry, University of Liverpool, since 1966; *b* 22 June 1916; British; *m* 1944, Kathleen Sarah Hill; three *d. Educ:* Birkenhead Inst.; Univ. of Liverpool. Lectr 1944, Sen. Lectr 1949, in Biochemistry, University of Liverpool; Prof. of Biochemistry and Agricultural Biochemistry, UCW, Aberystwyth, 1959. Chairman: Cttee, Biochem. Soc., 1970-73; Brit. Nat. Cttee for Biochem., 1976-82; Member: Council, Royal Society, 1972, 1974; UGC, 1974-81; SRC Science Bd, 1975-78; ARC Grants Bd, 1975-82; Wirral Educn Cttee, 1974-; Lawes Agricl Trust Cttee, 1977-; Exec. Cttee, FEBS, 1975- (Chm., Publication Cttee, 1975-). Corresp. Mem., Amer. Soc. Plant Physiologists. Ciba Medallist, Biochemical Soc., 1970; Prix Roussel, 1982. *Publications:* Comparative Biochemistry of Carotenoids, 1952, 2nd edn 1980; Recent Advances in Biochemistry, 1960; Biosynthesis of Vitamins, 1964; (ed) Chemistry and Biochemistry of Plant Pigments, 1965, 2nd edn, 2 vols, 1976; (with E. I. Mercer) Introduction to Plant Biochemistry, 1972, 2nd edn 1982; numerous articles in Biochem. Jl, Phytochemistry, etc. *Recreation:* gardening. *Address:* Monzar, 9 Woodlands Close, Parkgate, Wirral, Cheshire L64 6RU. *T:* 051-336 4494.

GOODWIN HUDSON, Rt. Rev. Arthur William; see Hudson.

GOODY, Prof. John Rankine, FBA 1976; William Wyse Professor of Social Anthropology, University of Cambridge, since 1973; *b* 27 July 1919; *m* 1956, Esther Robinson Newcomb; one *s* four *d. Educ:* St Albans Sch.; St John's Coll., Cambridge; Balliol Coll., Oxford. BA 1946, Dip. Anthrop. 1947, PhD 1954, ScD 1969, Cantab; BLitt Oxon 1952. HM Forces, 1939-46. Educnl admin, 1947-49; Cambridge Univ.: Asst Lectr, 1954-59; Fellow, St John's Coll., 1960; Lectr, 1959-71; Dir, African Studies Centre, 1966-73; Smuts Reader in Commonwealth Studies, 1972. Foreign Hon. Mem., Amer. Acad. of Arts and Scis, 1980. *Publications:* The Social Organisation of the LoWiili, 1956; (ed) The Developmental Cycle in Domestic Groups, 1958; Death, Property and the Ancestors, 1962; (ed) Succession to High Office, 1966; (with J. A. Braimah) Salaga: the struggle for power, 1967; (ed) Literacy in Traditional Societies, 1968; Comparative Studies in Kinship, 1969; Technology, Tradition and the State in Africa, 1971; The Myth of the Bagre, 1972; (with S. J. Tambiah) Bridewealth and Dowry, 1973; (ed) The Character of Kinship, 1973; (ed) Changing Social Structure in Ghana, 1975; Production and Reproduction, 1977; The Domestication of the Savage Mind, 1977; (with J. W. D. K. Gandah) Une Recitation du Bagré, 1981; Cooking, Cuisine and Class, 1982; contrib. learned jls. *Address:* St John's College, Cambridge. *T:* Cambridge 61621.

GOODY, Most Rev. Launcelot John; *see* Perth (Aust.), Archbishop of, (RC).

GOODYEAR, Prof. Francis Richard David; Hildred Carlile Professor of Latin, University of London, since 1966; Head of Department of Latin, Bedford College, London, since 1966; *b* 2 Feb. 1936; *s* of Francis Goodyear and Gladys Ivy Goodman; *m* 1967, Cynthia Rosalie Attwood; one *s*. *Educ:* Luton Grammar Sch.; St John's Coll., Cambridge. MA, PhD (Cantab). Open schol., St John's Coll., Cambridge, 1953; Craven schol., Hallam Prize, 1956; Classical Tripos, Pts 1 and 2, cl. 1, 1956-57; Chancellor's Medal, H. A. Thomas Studentship, 1957. Research Fellow, St John's Coll., 1959-60; Official Fellow, Queens' Coll., 1960-66; Librarian, Queens' Coll., 1960-64. Dean of Faculty of Arts, Bedford Coll., London, 1971-73; Mem., Adv. Editorial Bd, Cambridge Classical Texts and Commentaries, 1974-; Chm., Bd of Studies in Classics, London Univ., 1977-78. Mem., Virgilian Academy of Mantua, 1975. *Publications:* Incerti auctoris Aetna, 1965; Appendix Vergiliana (jt editor), 1966; Corippi Iohannidos libri viii (jt editor), 1970; Tacitus, a survey, 1970; The Annals of Tacitus, vol. i, 1972, vol. ii, 1981; papers and reviews in learned jls, contribs to works of reference. *Recreations:* light reading, travel. *Address:* 56 The Avenue, Hatch End, Mddx HA5 4HA. *T:* 01-428 2644.

GOOLD, Sir George (Leonard), 7th Bt *cr* 1801; retired engineer; *b* 26 Aug. 1923; *s* of Sir George Ignatius Goold, 6th Bt, and Rhoda Goold; *S* father, 1967; *m* 1945, Joy Cecelia, *d* of William Cutler, Melbourne; one *s* four *d*. *Educ:* Port Pirie, S Australia. *Heir: s* George William Goold [*b* 25 March 1950; *m* 1973, Julie Ann, *d* of Leonard Crack; two *s*]. *Address:* 5 Afford Road, Port Pirie South, SA 5540, Australia. *T:* Pirie 323617.

GOOLD-ADAMS, Richard John Moreton, CBE 1974; MA; Vice-President, SS Great Britain Project, since 1982 (Chairman, 1968-82); *b* Brisbane, Australia, 24 Jan. 1916; *s* of Sir Hamilton Goold-Adams, Governor of Qld, and Elsie Riordon, Montreal; *m* 1939, Deenagh Blennerhassett. *Educ:* Winchester; New Coll., Oxford. Served 1939-46 in Army, Major, in Middle East and Italy. The Economist, latterly as an Asst Editor, 1947-55. Councillor: Internat. Inst. for Strategic Studies, 1958-76 (a Founder and Vice-Chm., 1958-62; Chm., 1963-73); National Inst. of Industrial Psychology, 1956-70; Royal Inst. of Internat. Affairs, 1957-81; Soc. for Nautical Research, 1970-73, 1975-78; Chm., British Atlantic Cttee, 1959-62, Vice-Pres., 1963-. Governor: Atlantic Inst. in Paris, 1962-71; Academic Council, Wilton Park, 1963-. Dep. Chm., Guthrie Estates Agency Ltd, 1962-63, resigned; re-elected to board, 1964; merged into The Guthrie Corp., 1965; Dir, 1965-69. Formerly broadcasting and television on current affairs, and lecturing. *Publications:* South Africa To-day and Tomorrow, 1936; Middle East Journey, 1947; The Time of Power: a reappraisal of John Foster Dulles, 1962; The Return of the Great Britain, 1976. *Recreation:* photography. *Address:* c/o National Westminster Bank, 116 Fenchurch Street, EC3M 5AN. *Club:* Travellers'.

GOOLDEN, Barbara; novelist; *b* 5 June 1900; *d* of Charles and Isabel Goolden (*née* Armit); one adopted s decd. *Educ:* Community of the Holy Family; two private schools. Has appeared on TV and spoken on radio. *Publications:* The Knot of Reluctance, 1926; The Sleeping Sword, 1928; Children of Peace, 1928; The Conquering Star, 1929; The Waking Bird, 1929; The Ancient Wheel, 1930; Toils of Law, 1931; Thin Ice, 1931; Sugared Grief, 1932; Eros, 1933; Separate Paths, 1933; Slings and Arrows, 1934; Victory to the Vanquished, 1935; Wise Generations, 1936; The Primrose Path, 1936; Morning Tells the Day, 1937; The Wind My Posthorse, 1937; Within a Dream, 1938; Young Ambition, 1938; Call the Tune, 1939; The Asses Bridge, 1940; The Best Laid Schemes, 1941; Crown of Life, 1941; Men as Trees, 1942; Swings and Roundabouts, 1943; Community Singing, 1944; Ichabod, 1945; Daughters of Earth, 1947; Jig Saw, 1948; From the Sublime to the Ridiculous, 1949; Strange Strife, 1952; Venetia, 1952; The China Pig, 1953; Truth is Fallen in the Street, 1953; Return Journey, 1954; Who is my Neighbour?, 1954; Bread to the Wise, 1955; The World His Oyster, 1955; At the Foot of the Hills, 1956; To Have and to Hold, 1956; The Singing and the Gold, 1956; The Nettle and the Flower, 1957; Through the Sword Gates, 1957; The Linnet in the Cage, 1958; The Ships of Youth, 1958; Sweet Fields, 1958; A Pilgrim and his Pack, 1959; For Richer, For Poorer, 1959; Falling in Love, 1960; New Wine, 1960; Where Love is, 1960; To Love and to Cherish, 1961; One Autumn Face, 1961; Against the Grain, 1961; The Little City, 1962; The Pebble in the Pond, 1962; Marriages are Made in Heaven, 1963; Love-in-a-Mist, 1963; Battledore and Shuttlecock, 1963; Fools' Paradise, 1964; The Gentle Heart, 1964; The Gift, 1964; Blight on the Blossom, 1965; A Finger in the Pie, 1965; The Lesser Love, 1965; Anvil of Youth, 1966; Nobody's Business, 1966; A Time to Love, 1966; Second Fiddle, 1967; A Time to Build, 1967; All to Love, 1968; The Eleventh Hour, 1968; The Reluctant Wife, 1968; A Marriage of Convenience, 1969; Today Belongs to Us, 1969; The Snare, 1970; A Question of Conscience, 1970; Fortune's Favourite, 1971; No Meeting Place, 1971; Before the Flame is Lit, 1971; A Leap in the Dark, 1972; A Law for Lovers, 1973; Time to Turn Back, 1973; The Broken Arc, 1974; Mirage, 1974; The Crystal and the Dew, 1975; Silver Fountains, 1975; Goodbye to Yesterday, 1976; In the Melting Pot, 1976; Unborn Tomorrow, 1977; The Rags of Time, 1978; *for children:* Minty, 1959; Five Pairs of Hands, 1961; Minty and the Missing Picture, 1963; Minty and the Secret Room, 1964; Trouble for the Tabors, 1966; Top Secret, 1969. *Recreation:* reading. *Address:* Top End, Felcourt, East Grinstead, West Sussex.

GOONERATNE, Tilak Eranga; Ambassador of Sri Lanka to the Commission of the European Communities, and concurrently to Belgium, 1975-78; *b* 27 March 1919; *m* 1948, Pamela J. Rodrigo (*d* 1978); two *d*. *Educ:* BA (London Univ.); Ceylon Law Coll. Advocate, Supreme Ct of Ceylon. Joined Ceylon Civil Service, 1943; Asst Sec., Min. of External Affairs, 1947-51; Govt Agent: Trincomalee, 1951-54; Matara, 1954-56; Registrar Gen., Marriages, Births and Deaths, 1956-58; Dir-Gen. of Broadcasting and Dir of Information, Ceylon, 1958-60; Comr Co-operative Develt, 1960-63; Dir of Economic Affairs, 1963; Dep. Sec. to Treasury, 1963-65; Pres., Colombo Plan Council for Technical Co-operation in S and SE Asia, 1964-65; Ceylon deleg. to UN Gen. Assembly, 1964-65; Dep. Sec.-Gen., Commonwealth Secretariat, London, 1965-70; High Comr in UK, 1970-75. Commonwealth Fund for Technical Co-operation: Chm., Bd of Representatives, 1975-76; Chm., Review Gp of Experts. *Publications:* An Historical Outline of the Development of the Marriage and Divorce Laws of Ceylon; An Historical Outline of the Development of the Marriage and Divorce Laws Applicable to Muslims in Ceylon; Fifty Years of Co-operative Development in Ceylon. *Address:* 17B Warwick Avenue, W9. *T:* 01-286 4675.

GOOSSENS, Léon Jean, CBE 1950; FRCM; Hon. RAM; Solo Oboist; *b* Liverpool, 12 June 1897; *s* of late Eugène Goossens, musician and conductor; *m* 1st, 1926; one *d* ; 2nd, 1933, Leslie, *d* of Brig. A. Burrowes; two *d*. *Educ:* Christian Brothers Catholic Institute, Liverpool; Liverpool Coll. of Music. Started oboe studies at 10 yrs of age with Charles Reynolds; at 14 studied at RCM, London, and at 16 joined London Symphony Orchestra on tour with Nikisch; same year toured Wales with Sir Henry Wood and Queen's Hall Orchestra as principal oboist, the following year accepting post as permanency. Served in European War, 1915-18 (wounded). Principal oboe, London Philharmonic Orchestra, also at Covent Garden Opera House with Sir Thomas Beecham; Prof. at RCM and RAM; after recitals in London and other English cities, toured USA, 1927 and 1928; Rep. British Music in most European capitals, at NY World Fair, with Sir Adrian Boult; also in Washington with Dr Clarence Raybould; recitals for BBC and lectures in schools, music clubs, univs and on TV. Has produced in England a new school of oboe-playing and promoted the oboe to the ranks of other solo instruments, for which leading composers of the day have written and, in many cases, dedicated their works to this artist; *works include:* concerti by Malcolm Arnold, Arnold Cooke, Dr Vaughan Williams, Rutland Boughton, Cyril Scott, Gordon Jacob, Francesco Ticciati, Ralph Nicholson, Sir Eugène Goossens; solo or chamber works by Dr Walter Stanton, Gustav Holst, Sir Edward Elgar, Sir George Henschel, John Addison, Dame Ethel Smyth, Franz Reizenstein, Thomas Pitfield, Somers Cocks, Gerald Finzi, Sir Arthur Bliss, Sir Arnold Bax, William Wordsworth, Lord Britten, Sigtenhurst Meyer, Alec Templeton, Alec Rowley, Alan Richardson, Francis Poulenc, Morgan Nicholas, Thomas Dunhill and Edwin Roxburgh. Toured Australia and New Zealand, also played in Singapore, 1954; visited Persia and Turkey, also Austria, 1955; toured Jugoslavia, 1954; toured USSR with Music Delegation headed by Master of The Queen's Musick, 1956; Coast to Coast Tour Canada, 1957; toured Scandinavia and Portugal, 1959, USA 1965, Munich 1972, St Moritz and Aberdeen (with Internat. Youth Orch.), 1971-73. Recitals in Malta, 1962-77. Pres., Art Soc., Gordonstoun Sch., 1980. Belgrade Jurist, Internat. Wind Competition, 1981. Cobbett Medal for services to Chamber Music, 1954. *Publication:* (jtly with Edwin Roxburgh) The Oboe, 1977. *Relevant publication:* Music in the Wind, by Barry Wynne, 1967. *Recreation:* sailing. *Address:* Park Cottage, 7a Ravenscourt Square, W6 0TW. *T:* 01-748 5112. *Clubs:* Chelsea Arts, London Corinthian Sailing; Malta Union.

GOPAL, Dr Sarvepalli; Professor of Contemporary History, Jawaharlal Nehru University, New Delhi, since 1972; Fellow of St Antony's College, Oxford, since 1966; *b* 23 April 1923; *y c* and *o s* of Sir Sarvepalli Radhakrishnan, Hon. OM, Hon. FBA. *Educ:* Mill Hill School; Madras Univ.; Oxford Univ. MA (Madras and Oxon), BL (Madras), DPhil (Oxon), DLitt (Oxon). Lecturer and Reader in History, Andhra Univ., Waltair, 1948-52; Asst Dir, Nat. Archives of India, 1952-54; Dir, Historical Div., Min. of Extl Affairs, New Delhi, 1954-66; Commonwealth Fellow, Trin. Coll., Cambridge, 1963-64; Reader in S Asian History, Oxford Univ., 1966-71. Chm. Nat. Book Trust, India, 1973-76; Member: Indian UGC, 1973-79; UNESCO Exec. Bd, 1976-80; Vis. Prof., Leeds, 1977. Pres., Indian History Congress, 1978. Corresp. FRHistS. Hon. Prof., Tirupati; Hon. DLitt: Andhra Univ., 1975; Tirupati Univ., 1979. Sahitya Akademi award, 1976. *Publications:* The Permanent Settlement in Bengal, 1949; The Viceroyalty of Lord Ripon, 1953; The Viceroyalty of Lord Irwin, 1957; British Policy in India, 1965; Modern India, 1967; Jawaharlal Nehru, vol. 1, 1975, vol. 2, 1979; general editor, Selected Works of Jawaharlal Nehru; contribs articles to historical jls. *Recreations:* good food and travel. *Address:* St Antony's College, Oxford; 97 Radhakrishna Salai, Mylapore, Madras 4, India. *Club:* United Oxford & Cambridge University.

GORAI, Rt. Rev. Dinesh Chandra; *see* Calcutta, Bishop of.

GORARD, Anthony John; business consultant; *b* 15 July 1927; *s* of William James and Rose Mary Gorard; *m* 1954, Barbara Kathleen Hampton; one *s* three *d*. *Educ:* Ealing Grammar School. Chartered Accountant, 1951; Manufacturing Industry, 1952-58; Anglia Television Ltd, 1959-67, Executive Director and Member of Management Cttee; Managing Director, HTV Ltd, 1967-78; Chief Exec., HTV Gp Ltd, 1976-78; Director: Independent Television Publications Ltd, 1967-78; Independent Television News Ltd, 1973-78; Chief Exec., Cardiff Broadcasting Co. Ltd, 1979-81. Chm., British Regional Television Association, 1970-71. *Recreations:* tennis, rambling.

Address: Chew Hill House, Chew Magna, Somerset. *T:* Chew Magna 2593.

GORAY, Narayan Ganesh; High Commissioner for India in London, 1977-79; *b* 15 June 1907; *s* of Ganesh Govind Gore and Saraswati; *m* 1935, Sumati Kirtani (decd); one *d. Educ:* Fergusson Coll., Poona. BA, LLB. Mem., Congress Socialist Party, 1934; (Mem. Nat. Exec., 1934); Jt Sec., Socialist Party, 1948; Gen. Sec., Praja Socialist Party, 1953-65, Chm., 1965-69; Member: Lok Sabha, 1957-62; Rajya Sabha, 1970-76. Mayor of Pune, 1968. Editor, Janata Weekly, 1971-. *Publications include:* History of the United States of America, 1959. *Recreations:* music, painting, writing. *Address:* 1813 Sadashiv Peth, Poona 30, Maharashtra State, India.

GORDIMER, Nadine; Author; *b* 20 Nov. 1923; *d* of Isidore Gordimer; *m* Reinhold Cassirer; one *s* one *d. Educ:* Convent Sch.; Witwatersrand Univ. Neil Gunn Fellowship, Scottish Arts Council, 1981. Hon. Member: Amer. Acad. of Art and Literature, 1979; Amer. Acad. of Arts and Sciences, 1980. DLit *hc* Leuven, Belgium, 1980. *Publications:* The Soft Voice of the Serpent (stories), 1953; The Lying Days (novel), 1953; Six Feet of the Country (stories), 1956; A World of Strangers (novel), 1958; Friday's Footprint (stories), 1960 (W. H. Smith Lit. Award, 1961); Occasion for Loving (novel), 1963; Not for Publication (stories), 1965; The Late Bourgeois World (novel), 1966; South African Writing Today (jt editor), 1967; A Guest of Honour (novel), 1971 (James Tait Black Meml Prize, 1971); Livingstone's Companions (stories), 1972; The Conservationist (novel), 1974 (jtly, Booker Prize 1974; Grand Aigle d'Or, France, 1975); Selected Stories, 1975; Some Monday for Sure (stories), 1976; Burger's Daughter, 1979; A Soldier's Embrace (stories), 1980; July's People (novel), 1981. *Address:* 7 Frere Road, Parktown West, Johannesburg, South Africa.

GORDINE, Dora, (Hon. Mrs Richard Hare); FRBS; FRSA; sculptor and painter; *b* 1906; *d* of late Mark Gordin, St Petersburg, Russia; *m* 1936, Hon. Richard Hare (*d* 1966). Studied sculpture, Paris. First exhibited in the Salon des Tuileries, Paris, 1932. One-man exhibitions: Leicester Galleries, London, 1928, 1933, 1938, 1945, 1949; Flechtheim Gallery, Berlin, 1929. Commissioned to decorate with bronzes new Town Hall in Singapore, 1930-35; built studio and sculpture gallery in London according to her own designs (1936). Spent a year in America, executing commissions in Hollywood and delivering lectures on art (1947). Also represented by Sculpture in American, Asiatic, African and Australian collections. In England 3 works are in Tate Gallery; other bronzes in: Senate House, London Univ.; RIBA; Westminster Infant Welfare Centre; Maternity Ward in Holloway Prison; Esso Petroleum Refinery, Milford Haven; Royal Marsden Hospital, Surrey; Herron Museum of Art, Indianapolis; schs, institutions and many private collections. *Publications:* articles in Journal of Royal Asiatic Society. *Address:* Dorich House, Kingston Vale, SW15.

GORDON, family name of **Marquess of Aberdeen and Temair** and **Marquess of Huntly.**

GORDON, Lord Adam (Granville), KCVO 1970 (CVO 1961); MBE 1945; Comptroller to Queen Elizabeth the Queen Mother, 1953-73; Extra Equerry to Queen Elizabeth the Queen Mother, since 1974; *b* 1 March 1909; *s* of late Lt-Col Douglas Gordon, CVO, DSO, and *brother* of 12th Marquess of Huntly, *qv*; *m* 1947, Pamela, *d* of Col A. H. Bowhill, CBE, Inchmarlo, Banchory, Kincardineshire; two *s. Educ:* Eton. Asst Sec., Hurlingham Club, 1936-39. Served War of 1939-45 (despatches, MBE); Hants Yeomanry in GB, N Africa and Italy; retired 1945, with rank of Major. Sec., Brooks's Club, 1946-53. Mem. Queen's Body Guard for Scotland (Royal Co. of Archers). *Address:* Hethersett, Littleworth Cross, Seale, Surrey. *Clubs:* Brooks's, Pratt's, MCC.

GORDON, (Alexander) Esmé, RSA, FRIBA, FRIAS; *b* 12 Sept. 1910; *s* of Alexander Shand Gordon, WS and Elizabeth Catherine (*née* Logan); *m* 1937, Betsy, *d* of James and Bessie McCurry, Belfast; two *s* one *d. Educ:* Edinburgh Acad.; School of Arch., Edinburgh Coll. of Art. RIBA. Owen Jones Schol., 1934. War Service with RE in Europe. RSA 1967 (ARSA 1956); Sec., RSA, 1973-78; Pres., Edinburgh AA, 1955-57; Mem. Scottish Cttee, Arts Council of Gt Brit., 1959-65. *Work in Edinburgh includes:* Third Extension and other work for Heriot-Watt Coll.; Head Office for Scottish Life Assce Co. Ltd; Head Office and Showroom for S of Scotland Elec. Bd; for the High Kirk of St Giles: East End treatment for National Service in Coronation year, War Memorial Chapel, and (in Chapel of Order of Thistle) Memorial to HM King George VI, and other work. *Publications:* A Short History of St Giles Cathedral, 1954; The Principles of Church Building, Furnishing, Equipment and Decoration, 1963; The Royal Scottish Academy 1826-1976, 1976. *Address:* 10a Greenhill Park, Edinburgh EH10 4DW. *T:* 031-447 7530.

GORDON, Alexander John, CBE 1974 (OBE 1967); RIBA; architect; Senior Partner, Alex Gordon and Partners, since 1960; *b* 25 Feb. 1917; *s* of John Tullis Gordon and Euphemia Baxter Simpson Gordon. *Educ:* Swansea Grammar Sch.; Welsh Sch. of Architecture (Diploma with Special Distinction). ARIBA 1949; FRIBA 1962; FSIAD 1975. Served RE, 1940-46. Partnership with T. Alwyn Lloyd, 1948-60. Member: Welsh Arts Council, 1959-73 (Vice-Chm. 1969-73); Central Housing Adv. Cttee, 1959-71; MPBW (now DoE) Cttee for Computer Applications in Construction Industry, 1966-71; Exec. Bd, BSI, 1971-74 (Chm., Codes of Practice Cttee for Building, 1965-77); UGC Planning, Architecture and Building Studies Sub-Cttee, 1971-74; UGC

Technology Sub-Cttee, 1974-79; Construction and Housing Res. Adv. Council, 1971-79; ARCUK, 1968-71; Design Council, 1973-77; Council, Architectural Heritage Year (and Welsh Cttee), 1973-76; Royal Fine Art Commn, 1973-; RCA Visiting Cttee, 1973-; Council for Sci. and Soc., 1973-; Bldg Res. Estab. Adv. Council (Chm., 1975-); Adv. Cttee, York Centre for Continuing Educn, 1975-80; Construction Industry Continuing Professional Develt Gp (Chm. 1981-); Standing Cttee on Structural Safety, 1976; British Council Wales Cttee, 1976- (Chm., 1980-, and Mem. Bd British Council); Pres., Comit é de Liaison des Architectes du Marché Commun, 1974-75. Trustee, Civic Trust Board for Wales, 1965-. Pres., Building Centre Trust, 1976. Life Mem., Court, UWIST (Mem. Council, 1980-, Vice-Pres., 1982-); Vis. Prof., Sch. of Environmental Studies, UCL, 1969, Mem. Bd of Studies, 1970-, Governor, Centre for Environmental Studies, 1974-77. RIBA: Chm., Bd of Educn, 1968-70; Pres., 1971-73; Chm., European Affairs Cttee, 1973-80; Chm., Co-ordinating Cttee for Project Inf., 1979-. Reg. Dir, Nationwide Bldg Soc., 1972-; Consultant, ABS Insurance Agency Ltd, 1980- (Dir, 1975-80). Extraord. Hon. Mem., Bund Deutscher Architekten; Hon. Mem., Soc. Mexican Architects; Hon. Corresp. Mem., Fedn of Danish Architects, 1976; Hon. FRAIC; Hon. FAIA, 1974; Hon. FCIBS 1975; Hon. FISE 1980. Hon. LLD Univ. of Wales, 1972. *Publications:* periodic contribs to professional jls. *Recreations:* skiing, the visual arts. *Address:* 6 Cathedral Road, Cardiff CF1 9XW. *T:* Cardiff 372121; 32 Grosvenor Street, W1. *T:* 01-629 7910. *Clubs:* Arts; Cardiff and County.

GORDON, Sir Andrew C. L. D.; *see* Duff Gordon.

GORDON, Rt. Rev. Archibald Ronald McDonald; *see* Portsmouth, Bishop of.

GORDON, Aubrey Abraham; a Recorder of the Crown Court, since 1978; *b* 26 July 1925; *s* of Isaac and Fanny Gordon; *m* 1949, Reeva R. Cohen; one *s* twin *d. Educ:* Bede Collegiate Boys' Sch., Sunderland; King's Coll., Durham Univ., Newcastle upon Tyne (LLB 1945). Admitted solicitor, 1947. President: Houghton le Spring Chamber of Trade, 1955; Hetton le Hole Rotary Club, 1967; Sunderland Law Soc., 1976; Chairman: Houghton Round Table, 1959; Sunderland Victims Support Scheme, 1978-80. *Recreations:* local communal and religious interests, photography. *Address:* 1 Acer Court, Sunderland SR2 7EJ. *T:* Sunderland 58993.

GORDON, Brian William, OBE 1974; HM Diplomatic Service, 1949-81, retired; Commercial Counsellor, Caracas, 1980-81; *b* 24 Oct. 1926; *s* of William and Doris Margaret Gordon; *m* 1951, Sheila Graham Young; two *s* one *d. Educ:* Tynemouth Grammar School. HM Forces (Lieut in IA), 1944-47; joined HM Foreign Service (now Diplomatic Service), 1949; served in: Saigon; Libya; Second Sec. in Ethiopia, 1954-58 and in Peru, 1959-61; HM Consul: Leopoldville, Congo, 1962-64; New York, 1965-67; Puerto Rico, 1967-69; Consul-General, Bilbao, 1969-73; Asst Head, Trade Relations and Export Dept, FCO, 1974-77; Dep. Consul-Gen., Los Angeles, 1977-80. *Recreations:* golf, walking. *Address:* 16 Woodburn Drive, Whitley Bay, Tyne and Wear.

GORDON, Sir Charles (Addison Somerville Snowden), KCB 1981 (CB 1970); Clerk of the House of Commons, since 1979; *b* 25 July 1918; *s* of late C. G. S. Gordon, TD, Liverpool, and of Mrs E. A. Gordon, Rydons, Wimbledon; *m* 1943, Janet Margaret Beattie; one *s* one *d. Educ:* Winchester; Balliol Coll., Oxford. Served in Fleet Air Arm throughout War of 1939-45. Apptd Asst Clerk in House of Commons, 1946; Senior Clerk, 1947; Fourth Clerk at the Table, 1962; Principal Clerk of the Table Office, 1967; Second Clerk Assistant, 1974; Clerk Asst, 1976. Sec., Soc. of Clerks-at-the-Table in Commonwealth Parliaments, and co-Editor of its journal, The Table, 1952-62. *Publications:* Parliament as an Export (jointly), 1966; contribs to: The Table; The Parliamentarian. *Address:* 279 Lonsdale Road, Barnes, SW13 9QB. *T:* 01-748 6735; House of Commons, SW1.

GORDON, Prof. Cyrus H.; Gottesman Professor of Hebrew, since 1973 and Director, Center for Ebla Research, since 1982, New York University; *b* 29 June 1908; *s* of Dr Benj. L. and Dorothy Cohen Gordon; *m* 1946, Joan Elizabeth Kendall; two *s* three *d. Educ:* Univ. of Pennsylvania (AB, MA, PhD). Harrison Schol., Univ. of Pennsylvania 1928-29, and Harrison Fellow, 1929-30; US Army Officer on active duty, 1942-46 (Col, US Air Force Reserve, retired). Instructor of Hebrew and Assyrian, University of Penn., 1930-31; Fellow and Epigrapher, American Schs of Oriental Research in Jerusalem and Baghdad, 1931-35; Fellow, Amer. Coun. of Learned Socs, 1932-33; Teaching Fellow, Oriental Seminary, Johns Hopkins Univ., 1935-38; Lecturer in Hebrew and Ancient History, Smith Coll., 1938-39 and 1940-41; Fellow, Amer.-Scandinavian Foundn, 1939; Mem., Institute for Advanced Study, Princeton, NJ, 1939-40 and 1941-42; Professor of Assyriology and Egyptology, Dropsie Coll., 1946-56; Joseph Foster Prof. of Near Eastern Studies, and Chm., Dept of Mediterranean Studies, Brandeis Univ., 1956-73 (Dean of Graduate Sch. and Associate Dean of Faculty, 1957-58). Mem. Managing Cttee, Amer. Sch. of Classical Studies, Athens, 1958-73; Vis. Fellow in Humanities, Univ. of Colorado, March 1967; Vis. Prof., New York Univ., 1970-73; Vis. Prof. in History and Archaeology, Univ. of New Mexico, 1976; Distinguished Vis. Professor: in Humanities, SW Missouri State Univ., 1977-79; in Archaeology, New Mexico State Univ., 1979; Gay Lectr, Simmons Coll., 1970; Visitor's Fellowship, Japan Foundn, 1974. Fellow: Amer. Acad. of Arts and Sciences, 1968-; Explorers Club, 1968-; Amer. Acad. of Jewish Res., 1981-; Hon. Fellow, Royal Asiatic Soc., 1975-. Member:

Amer. Oriental Soc.; Soc. of Biblical Literature; Archæological Inst. of America; Amer. Historical Assoc.; Amer. Philological Assoc.; Amer. Assoc. of Univ. Professors. Corresp. Mem., Inst. for Antiquity and Christianity, Claremont Graduate Sch. and University Center, 1967-. Trustee: Boston Hebrew Coll., 1965-; Internat. Council for Etruscan Studies, Jerusalem, 1970-; Fenster Gallery of Jewish Art, Tulsa, Oklahoma, 1977-. Hon. Dr of Hebrew Letters, Baltimore Hebrew Coll., 1981. Alumni Award, Gratz Coll., 1961; Directory of Educational Specialists Award, 1970. *Publications:* Nouns in the Nuzi Tablets, 1936; Lands of the Cross and Crescent, 1948; Ugaritic Literature, 1949; Smith College Tablets, 1952; Ugaritic Manual, 1955; Adventures in the Nearest East, 1957; Hammurapi's Code, 1957; World of the Old Testament, 1958 (rev. edn: The Ancient Near East, 1965); Before the Bible, 1962 (rev. edn: The Common Background of Greek and Hebrew Civilizations, 1965); Ugaritic Textbook, 1965, rev. edn 1967; Ugarit and Minoan Crete, 1966; Evidence for the Minoan Language, 1966; Forgotten Scripts: How they were deciphered and their Impact on Contemporary Culture, 1968, rev. edn 1971, 1982; Poetic Legends and Myths from Ugarit, 1977; some works translated other languages; numerous articles in learned jls dealing with Near East, Mediterranean, OT and Egypto-Semitic philology; *relevant publications:* Orient and Occident: essays presented to Cyrus H. Gordon on the occasion of his Sixty-fifth Birthday, 1973; The Bible World: essays in honor of Cyrus H. Gordon, 1980. *Address:* (home) 130 Dean Road, Brookline, Mass 02146, USA. *T:* 617-734-3046.

GORDON, Maj.-Gen. Desmond Spencer, CB 1961; CBE 1952; DSO 1943; JP; DL; Commissioner-in-Chief, St John Ambulance Brigade, 1973-78; *b* 25 Dec. 1911; *s* of late Harold Easty Gordon and Gwendoline (*née* Blackett); *m* 1940, Sybil Mary Thompson; one *s* one *d. Educ:* Haileybury Coll.; RMC Sandhurst. Commissioned into Green Howards, 1932; India, 1933-38: Adjutant, Regimental Depot, 1938-40; War of 1939-45 (despatches 1944): Norway with Green Howards, 1940; Bde Major, 69 Inf. Bde, 1941-42; Student Staff Coll., Quetta, 1942; Comd 1/7 Queens, 1943; Comd 151 (Durham) Inf. Bde, 146 Inf. Bde, 131 Lorried Inf Bde, 1944-46; Col. GSHQ BAOR, 1946-49; Student Joint Service Staff Coll., 1949; GSO1 Inf. Directorate, War Office, 1950; Dep. Dir Inf., War Office, 1951-52; Comd 16 Indep. Para. Bde Gp, 1952-55; Asst Comd RMA Sandhurst, 1956-57; Student, Imperial Defence Coll., 1958; DA & QMG HQ I (BR) Corps, 1959; GOC 4th Division, 1959-61; Chief Army Instructor, Imperial Defence Coll., 1962-64; Asst Chief of Defence Staff (G), 1964-66: Col The Green Howards, 1965-74. JP Hants, 1966; DL Hants, 1980. KStJ 1973 (CStJ 1972). Knight Commander, Order of Orange Nassau with swords (Holland), 1947. *Recreations:* fishing, gardening. *Address:* Southfields, Greywell, Basingstoke, Hants. *Club:* Army and Navy.

GORDON, Donald McDonald, CMG 1970; HM Diplomatic Service, retired; *b* 14 Aug. 1921; *s* of late Donald McDonald Gordon and late Anabella Gordon (*née* Wesley); *m* 1948, Molly Denise, *o d* of Maurice Norman, Paris; three *s. Educ:* Robert Gordon's Coll., Aberdeen; Aberdeen Univ. Served in RA, 1941-47 (despatches). Entered Foreign (later Diplomatic) Service, 1947; FO, 1947; 2nd Sec. (Commercial), Lima, 1950; 2nd, later 1st Sec. (Commercial), Vienna, 1952; FO, 1956; 1st Sec. and Head of Chancery, Rangoon, 1960; 1st Sec., later Counsellor and Head of Chancery, Pretoria/Cape Town, 1962; Imp. Def. Coll., 1966; Counsellor and Consul-Gen., Saigon, 1967-69; Head of SE Asia Dept, FCO, 1969-72; Dep. High Comr, Kuala Lumpur, 1972-75; High Comr, Nicosia, 1975-79; Ambassador to Austria, 1979-81. Hon. LLD Aberdeen, 1982. *Address:* 23 Kew Green, Richmond, Surrey.

GORDON, Rt. Rev. Eric; *see* Gordon, Rt Rev. G. E.

GORDON, Esmé; *see* Gordon, A. E.

GORDON, Rt. Rev. (George) Eric; *b* 29 July 1905; *s* of George Gordon, Dulwich; *m* 1938, Elizabeth St Charaine (*d* 1970), *d* of Lt-Comdr A. J. Parkes, OBE, RN, Squeen, Ballaugh, Isle of Man; one *d* ; *m* 1971, Rose Gwynneth Huxley-Jones, FRBS, *d* of Benjamin Holt, Wednesbury, and widow of Thomas Bayliss Huxley-Jones, FRBS, Broomfield, Essex. *Educ:* St Olave's Sch., London; St Catharine's Coll., Cambridge (MA); Wycliffe Hall, Oxford. Deacon, Leicester, 1929; Priest, Peterborough for Leicester, 1930; Vice-Principal, Bishop Wilson Coll., Isle of Man, 1931, Principal, and Domestic Chaplain to Bishop of Sodor and Man, 1935; Rector of Kersal, and Examining Chaplain to Bishop of Manchester, 1942; Rector and Rural Dean of Middleton, Manchester, 1945; Proctor in Convocation, 1948; Provost of Chelmsford Cathedral and Rector of Chelmsford, 1951-66; Bishop of Sodor and Man, 1966-74. *Recreation:* local history. *Address:* Cobden, Queen Street, Eynsham, Oxford. *T:* Oxford 881378.

GORDON, Gerald Henry, QC (Scot.) 1972; LLD; Sheriff of Glasgow and Strathkelvin, since 1978; *b* 17 June 1929; *er s* of Simon Gordon and Rebecca Gordon (*née* Bulbin), Glasgow; *m* 1957, Marjorie Joseph, *yr d* of Isaac and Aimée Joseph (*née* Strump), Glasgow; one *s* two *d. Educ:* Queen's Park Senior Secondary Sch., Glasgow; Univ. of Glasgow (MA (1st cl. Hons Philosophy with English Literature) 1950; LLB (Distinction) 1953; PhD 1960); LLD Edinburgh 1968. National Service, RASC, 1953-55 (Staff-Sgt, Army Legal Aid, BAOR, 1955). Admitted Scots Bar 1953; practice at Scottish Bar, 1953, 1956-59; Faulds Fellow, Univ. of Glasgow, 1956-59. Procurator Fiscal Depute, Edinburgh, 1960-65. University of Edinburgh: Sen. Lectr, 1965; Personal Prof. of Criminal Law, 1969-72; Head of Dept of Criminal Law and Criminology, 1965-72; Prof. of Scots Law, 1972-76; Dean of Faculty of Law,

1970-73; Sheriff of S Strathclyde, Dumfries and Galloway at Hamilton, 1976-77. Commonwealth Vis. Fellow and Vis. Res. Fellow, Centre of Criminology, Univ. of Toronto, 1974-75. Temporary Sheriff, 1973-76. Mem., Interdepartmental Cttee on Scottish Criminal Procedure, 1970-77. *Publications:* The Criminal Law of Scotland, 1967, 2nd edn 1978; (ed) Renton and Brown's Criminal Procedure (4th edn), 1972; (ed) Scottish Criminal Case Reports, 1981-; various articles. *Recreations:* Jewish studies, coffee conversation. *Address:* 52 Eastwoodmains Road, Giffnock, Glasgow G46 6QD. *T:* 041-638 8614.

GORDON, Dr Hugh Walker, MC 1917; MA; MB; FRCP; Consulting Physician to Department of Skin Diseases, St George's Hospital; Consulting Dermatologist to Royal Marsden Hospital and West London Hospital; Fellow Royal Society Medicine (Past President of Section of Dermatology); Member (Past President) British Association of Dermatology; Member of St John's Dermatological Society; *b* Maxwellton, Kircudbrightshire, 5 Aug. 1897; *er s* of late H. Sharpe Gordon, OBE, JP, Dumfries, Scotland and of late John Ann, *d* of Hugh Gilmour, London; *m* 1929, Jean Helen, *d* of late H. W. Robertson, Butterfield and Swire, London; one *s* one *d. Educ:* Marlborough Coll.; Pembroke Coll., Cambridge (History Exhibitioner); St George's Hospital (entrance scholar); Paris; Vienna, MB, BCh Cambridge, 1926; MRCS 1925; FRCP 1940. Late Vice-Dean, St George's Hosp. Med. Sch., 1946-51, Actg Dean, 1944-46; Dermatologist EMS Sector VII, 1939-46; Med. Officer i/c St George's Hosp., EMS, 1939-45; late Dermatologist to St John's Hosp., Lewisham, Shadwell Children's Hosp. and East Ham Memorial Hosp. Late Resident Med. Officer, St George's Hosp., and House Surg. and House Physician. Served European War, 1914-18, RFA, 1916-18, invalided out of Army. *Publications:* chapters in Modern Practice of Dermatology, 1950; articles on dermatology in med. journals. *Recreations:* country pursuits. *Address:* 3 High Street, Kirkcudbright, SW Scotland. *T:* Kirkcudbright 30740. *Club:* Oriental.

GORDON, Prof. Ian Alistair, CBE 1971; MA, PhD; Professor of English Language and Literature, University of Wellington, NZ, 1936-74, now Emeritus; *b* Edinburgh, 1908; *e s* of Alexander and Ann Gordon; *m* 1936, Mary Ann McLean Fullarton, Ayr; one *s* three *d. Educ:* Royal High Sch., Edinburgh; University of Edinburgh. Bruce of Grangehill Bursar, Sloan Prizeman, Gray Prizeman, Scott Travelling Scholar (Italy), Dickson Travelling Scholar (Germany), Elliot Prizeman in English Literature, Pitt Scholar in Classical and English Literature; MA (Hons Classics) 1930, (Hons English) 1932; PhD 1936. Asst Lecturer in English language and lit., University of Edinburgh, 1932; Sub-Ed., Scot. Nat. Dictionary, 1930-36; Dean: Faculty of Arts, Victoria Univ. Coll., Wellington, 1944-47, 1952, 1957-61; Faculty of Languages, 1965-68; Vice-Chancellor Univ. of New Zealand, 1947-52; Chm., Academic Bd, 1954-61. Visiting Professor: KCL 1954; Univ. of Edinburgh, 1962; Univ. of South Pacific, Fiji, 1972; Research Associate, UCL, 1969; Vis. Fellow, Edinburgh Univ., 1974-75; Vis. Fellow in Commonwealth Literature, Univ. of Leeds, 1975; Vis. Professor: France and Belgium, 1976; Univ of Waikato, 1980. Member: Copyright Cttee and Tribunal, 1958; UGC, 1960-70; Chairman: English Language Institute,, 1961-72; NZ Literary Fund, 1951-73; Exec. Council, Assoc. of Univs of Br. Commonwealth, 1949-50. NZ representative at internat. confs: Utrecht, 1948; Bangkok, 1960; Kampala, 1961; Karachi, 1961. Army Educ. Service, 2 NZEF, Hon. Major. Hon. LLD Bristol, 1948; Hon. DLitt NZ, 1961; DUniv Stirling, 1975. *Publications:* John Skelton, Poet Laureate, 1943; New Zealand New Writing, 1943-45; The Teaching of English, a study in secondary education, 1947; English Prose Technique 1948; Shenstone's Miscellany, 1759-1763, 1952; Katherine Mansfield, 1954; The Movement of English Prose, 1966; John Galt (biog.), 1972; Word (festschrift), 1974; Undiscovered Country, 1974; Katherine Mansfield's Urewera Notebook, 1979; Word Finder, 1979; A Word in Your Ear, 1980; (ed) Collins Concise English Dictionary, NZ edn, 1982; edited the following works of John Galt: The Entail, 1970; The Provost, 1973; The Member, 1975; The Last of the Lairds, 1976; Short Stories, 1978; part-author: Edinburgh Essays in Scottish Literature, 1933; Essays in Literature, 1934; The University and the Community, 1946; John Galt (bicent. vol.), 1980; articles in research journals and other periodicals. *Address:* 91 Messines Road, Wellington, NZ. *Club:* Aorangi Ski, New Zealand (former Pres.).

GORDON, Maj.-Gen. James Leslie, OBE 1944; Deputy Medical Officer of Health, City of Canterbury, 1965-74, retired; *b* 10 Sept. 1909; *s* of Dr James Leslie Gordon and Annie Laycock; *m* 1939, Dorothy Roberson. *Educ:* Epsom Coll.; Middlesex Hosp. MRCS LRCP 1935, DPH London 1948. Commandant, Army Sch. of Health, 1956. Prof. of Army Health, Royal Army Medical Coll., 1958; Dir of Army Health, War Office, 1962-64 (Ministry of Defence, April-May 1964). Mem., Faculty of Community Medicine, RCP, 1972. *Address:* 28 St Stephen's Hill, Canterbury, Kent. *Club:* Naval and Military.

GORDON, Rt. Hon. John Bowie, (Peter), PC 1978; retired politician; company director (banking, meat, transport); *b* 24 July 1921; *s* of Dr W. P. P. Gordon, CBE, and Dr Doris Gordon, OBE; *m* 1943, Dorothy Elizabeth (*née* Morton); two *s* one *d. Educ:* Stratford Primary Sch.; St Andrew's Coll., Christchurch; Lincoln Coll., Canterbury. Served War, RNZAF, 1941-45 (Flt Lt, pilot; mentioned in despatches, 1943). Farming cadet, 1936-39; road transp. industry, 1945-47; farming on own account, 1947-; Nuffield Scholarship, farming, 1954; co. dir, 1950-60; MP Clutha, 1960-78; Minister: Transport, Railways and Aviation, 1966-72; Marine and Fisheries, 1969-71; Labour and

State Services, 1975–78; retd from politics on med. grounds, 1978. Past Pres., Returned Services, Federated Farmers, and A. & P. Show Assoc., Otago. USA Leadership Award, 1964. *Publication:* Some Aspects of Farming in Britain, 1955. *Recreations:* golf, gardening, cooking. *Address:* Tapanui, Otago, New Zealand. *T:* Tapanui 116. *Club:* Tapanui Returned Services Association.

GORDON, Sir John Charles, 9th Bt, *cr* 1706; *b* 4 Jan. 1901; *s* of 8th Bt and Elizabeth, *d* of Rev. John Maitland Ware; *S* father, 1939; *m* 1928, Marion, 3rd *d* of James Wright, Springfield, Sydney; one *s* one *d. Heir: s* Robert James Gordon [*b* 17 Aug. 1932; *m* 1976, Helen, *d* of Margery Perry, Cammeray, Sydney]. *Address:* 61 Farrer-Brown Court, Nuffield Village, Castle Hill, NSW 2154, Australia.

GORDON, John Gunn Drummond, CBE 1964; Director: Grindlays Bank Ltd, 1969–79; Steel Brothers Holdings Ltd, 1974–79; *b* 27 April 1909; *s* of late Rev. J. Drummond Gordon, MA, BD, BSc; *m* 1947, Mary Livingstone Paterson; two *s* one *d. Educ:* Edinburgh Academy. Served War, King's African Rifles, 1940–45. Career: spent 30 years out of 45, overseas, mainly in Eastern Africa, but also in India, with Grindlays Bank Ltd, finishing up as Group Managing Director; retired 1974. Mem., Bd of Crown Agents, 1974–77. *Address:* Ashdown, 17 Kippington Road, Sevenoaks, Kent TN13 2LJ. *T:* Sevenoaks 54188. *Clubs:* Oriental; Wilderness Golf (Sevenoaks); Nairobi (Nairobi).

GORDON, Kathleen Olivia, CBE 1966; Director, The Royal Academy of Dancing, 1948–68, Hon. Fellow, 1976; *b* 15 Jan. 1898; *d* of George R. Gordon, OBE, MD and Alice Maude Gordon. *Educ:* Manchester High Sch. for Girls; King's Coll., London Univ. With Royal Academy of Dancing, 1924–68; Coronation Award, 1964. *Recreations:* reading, theatre, and ballet. *Address:* 23 Addisland Court, W14. *T:* 01-602 0430.

GORDON, Sir Keith Lyndell, Kt 1979; CMG 1971; Chairman, Public Service Board of Appeal, since 1978; Justice of Appeal, West Indies Associated States Supreme Court, 1967–72, retired; *b* 8 April 1906; 3rd *s* of late George S. E. Gordon, Journalist, and Nancy Gordon; *m* 1947, Ethel King; one *d. Educ:* St Mary's Coll., St Lucia, WI; Middle Temple, London. Magistrate, Grenada, 1938; Crown Attorney, Dominica, 1942; Trinidad and Tobago: Magistrate, 1943–46 and 1949–53; Exec. Off., Black Market Board, 1946–48; Puisne Judge, Windward Islands and Leeward Islands, 1954–59; Puisne Judge, British Guiana, 1959–62; Chief Justice, West Cameroon, 1963–67. *Recreation:* gardening. *Address:* Vigie, Castries, St Lucia.

GORDON, Sir Lionel Eldred Peter S.; *see* Smith-Gordon.

GORDON, Nadia, (Mrs Charles Gordon); *see* Nerina, N.

GORDON, Patrick W.; *see* Wolrige-Gordon.

GORDON, Rt. Hon. Peter; *see* Gordon, Rt Hon. J. B.

GORDON, Peter Macie, CMG 1964; *b* 4 June 1919; *o s* of late Herbert and Gladys Gordon (*née* Simpson); *m* 1945, Marianne, *er d* of Dr Paul Meerwein, Basle; two *d. Educ:* Cotham Sch., Bristol; University Coll., Exeter; Merton Coll., Oxford. Served War, 1940–46; commissioned Argyll and Sutherland Highlanders, 1941; Campaign in North-West Europe, 1944–45 (despatches). Entered Colonial Administrative Service as District Officer, 1946; Senior District Commissioner, 1957; Asst Sec., Ministry of Agriculture, 1958; Under-Sec., 1960; Permanent Sec., Ministry of Agriculture and Animal Husbandry, Kenya, 1961; retired, 1964; Asst Sec., Univ. of Exeter, 1964–70. Supervisor, Zimbabwe-Rhodesia Elections, 1980; Mem., Commonwealth Observer Gp, Uganda Elections, 1980. *Address:* The Manor House, Willersey, Broadway, Worcs.

GORDON, Richard, (Dr Gordon Ostlere); formerly: anaesthetist at St Bartholomew's Hospital, and Oxford University; assistant editor, British Medical Jl; ship's surgeon. Author of the "Doctor" series, and other novels.

GORDON, Robert Wilson, MC 1944; Deputy Chairman of the Stock Exchange, London, 1965–68; Partner, Pidgeon de Smitt (Stockbrokers), 1978–80; *b* 3 March 1915; *s* of late Malcolm Gordon and late Blanche Fayerweather Gordon; *m* 1st, 1946, Joan Alison (*d* 1965), *d* of late Brig. A. G. Kenchington, CBE, MC; one *d*; 2nd, 1967, Mrs Dianna E. V. Ansell (*née* Tyrwhitt-Drake) (*d* 1980). *Educ:* Harrow. Served War of 1939–45 (despatches); Royal Ulster Rifles, and Parachute Regt; Instructor, Staff Coll., 1943–44. Elected to the Council, Stock Exchange, London, 1956. Chm., Airborne Forces Security Fund, 1974–. *Recreation:* golf. *Address:* 41 Cadogan Square, SW1. *T:* 01-235 4496.

GORDON, Sir Sidney, Kt 1972; CBE 1968 (OBE 1965); CA; JP; Chairman: Sir Elly Kadoorie Continuation Ltd, since 1971; Rediffusion (Hong Kong) Ltd; The Hong Kong Building & Loan Agency Ltd; Deputy Chairman: China Light & Power Co. Ltd; Hongkong & Shanghai Hotels Ltd; *b* 20 Aug. 1917; *s* of late P. S. Gordon and late Angusina Gordon; *m* 1950, Olive W. F. Eldon, *d* of late T. A. Eldon and late Hannah Eldon; two *d. Educ:* Hyndland Sch., Glasgow; Glasgow Univ. Sen. Partner, Lowe Bingham & Matthews, Chartered Accountants, Hong Kong, 1956–70. MLC, 1962–66, MEC, Hong Kong, 1965–80. Chm., Univ. and Polytechnic Grants Cttee, 1974–76. JP Hong

Kong, 1961. Hon. LLD The Chinese University of Hong Kong, 1970. *Recreation:* golf. *Address:* 7 Headland Road, Hong Kong. *T:* 5-92577. *Clubs:* Oriental; Hong Kong, Royal Hong Kong Jockey (Steward), Royal Hong Kong Golf, Hong Kong Country, Hong Kong Cricket, Shek O Country, etc.

GORDON, Strathearn, CBE 1967 (OBE 1953); Librarian of the House of Commons, 1950–67; *b* 3 Sept. 1902; 2nd *s* of Hon. Huntly D. Gordon, Sheriff-Substitute of Ross and Cromarty, and Violet, *d* of John Gaspard Fanshawe, Parsloes; *m* 1934, Elizabeth, *d* of Lovelace Serjeantson; two *s* one *d. Educ:* Edinburgh Academy; RMC Sandhurst. Joined 2nd Bn Highland Light Infantry, 1923; invalided 1927. Clerk in the House of Commons, 1930. *Publications:* Our Parliament, 1945; (with T. G. B. Cocks) A People's Conscience, 1952. *Address:* Avoch House, Avoch, Ross-shire IV9 8RF. *T:* Fortrose 20432. *Club:* Army and Navy.

GORDON, Lt-Col William Howat Leslie, CBE 1957 (MBE 1941); MC 1944; Adviser on overseas business to firms, to Ministry of Overseas Development, 1971–75, and to International Finance Corporation; *b* 8 April 1914; *o s* of late Frank Leslie Gordon, ISE (retd), FICE; *m* 1944, Margot Lumb; one *s* three *d. Educ:* Rugby; RMA Woolwich. Commnd Royal Signals, 1934; Palestine, Africa, Italy, NW Europe; 1 Armoured, 1 Airborne Divs, 1937–45 (despatches); Instructor, Staff Coll., Camberley, 1947–49. Chief Executive, The Uganda Co. Ltd, 1949–60; John Holt & Co. (Liverpool) Ltd and Lonrho Exports Ltd, 1960–71; MLC Uganda, 1952–57; Director: Gordon Automations Ltd; Rickmansworth & Uxbridge Water Co. Chm., St John Council, Bucks, 1974–82; KStJ. *Recreations:* golf, fishing, shooting. *Address:* Shenstone House, Chalfont St Giles, Bucks. *T:* Little Chalfont 2047. *Clubs:* White's, Institute of Directors, MCC; Rye Golf.

GORDON-BROWN, Alexander Douglas; Receiver for the Metropolitan Police District, since 1980; *b* 5 Dec. 1927; *s* of late Captain and Mrs D. S. Gordon-Brown; *m* 1959, Mary Hilton; three *s. Educ:* Bryanston Sch.; New Coll., Oxford. MA; 1st cl. hons PPE. Entered Home Office, 1951; Asst Private Sec. to Home Sec., 1956; Sec., Franks Cttee on section 2 of Official Secrets Act 1911, 1971; Asst Under-Sec. of State, Home Office, 1972–75, 1978–80; Under Sec., Cabinet Office, 1975–78. *Recreations:* music, golf. *Address:* New Scotland Yard, 10 Broadway, SW1.

GORDON-CUMMING, Alexander Roualeyn, CMG 1978; CVO 1969; Director, Invest in Britain Bureau, Department of Industry, since 1979; *b* 10 Sept. 1924; *s* of late Lt-Comdr R. G. Gordon-Cumming and of Mrs M. V. K. Wilkinson; *m* 1st, 1965, Beryl Joyce Macnaughton Dunn (*d* 1973); one *d*; 2nd, 1974, Elizabeth Patricia Blackley; one *d. Educ:* Eton Coll. RAF, 1943; retd with rank of Gp Captain, 1969. Board of Trade, 1969; Asst Sec., Air Div., Dept of Trade and Industry, 1973; seconded HM Diplomatic Service, 1974–79. *Recreations:* gardening, skiing, fell walking, ballet. *Address:* 33 Amerland Road, SW18. *T:* 01-870 4902; Farinay Cottage, Walderton, Chichester, Sussex. *T:* Compton 393. *Club:* Royal Air Force.

GORDON CUMMING, Sir William Gordon, 6th Bt, *cr* 1804; Royal Scots Greys; *b* 19 June 1928; *s* of Major Sir Alexander Penrose Gordon Cumming, 5th Bt, MC, and Elizabeth Topham, *d* of J. Topham Richardson, Harps Oak, Merstham; *S* father, 1939; *m* 1953, Elisabeth (marr. diss. 1972), *d* of Maj.-Gen. Sir Robert Hinde, KBE, CB, DSO; one *s* three *d. Educ:* Eton; RMC, Sandhurst. Late Royal Scots Greys; retired 1952. *Heir: s* Alexander Penrose Gordon Cumming, *b* 15 April 1954. *Address:* Altyre, Forres, Morayshire.

GORDON DAVIES, Rev. John; *see* Davies, Rev. John G.

GORDON-DUFF, Col Thomas Robert, MC 1945; JP; Lord-Lieutenant of Banffshire since 1964; Convener of County Council, 1962–70; *b* 1911; *er s* of Lachlan Gordon-Duff (killed in action, 1914); *m* 1946, Jean (*d* 1981), *d* of late Leslie G. Moir, Bicester; one *s. Educ:* RMC, Sandhurst. Entered Army, 2nd Lieut, Rifle Brigade, 1932; served War of 1939–45 (MC); retired, 1947. Lt-Col 5/6 Bn Gordon Highlanders (TA), 1947, retiring as Col. DL 1948, JP 1959. Vice-Lieut 1961, Banffshire. *Address:* Drummuir, Keith, Banffshire. *T:* Drummuir 224. *Club:* Army and Navy.

GORDON-FINLAYSON, Air Vice-Marshal James Richmond, DSO 1941; DFC 1940; *b* 19 Aug. 1914; *s* of late Gen. Sir Robert Gordon-Finlayson, KCB, CMG, DSO, and late Lady (Mary) Gordon-Finlayson, OBE; *m* 1953, Margaret Ann (*d* 1965), *d* of Col G. C. Richardson, DSO, MC; one *s* one *d* by a former marriage. *Educ:* Winchester; Pembroke Coll., Cambridge (MA). Mem. Inner Temple, 1935; joined RAF, 1936; ADC to Gov. of Kenya, 1938–39; served in Libya, 1940 and 1941–42, Greece, 1940–41 (despatches), Syria, 1941; Sqdn Ldr 1940; OC 211 Sqdn, 1940–41; RAF Staff Coll., 1942; Air Staff, Air Min., 1942–45; RAF Liaison Offr to HQ, US Army Strategic Air Force, Guam, 1945; Air Staff, Air Comd, SEA, 1945–46; SASO, AHQ, Burma, 1946; OC 48 Sqdn, 1946–47; on directing staff, JSSC, Group Captain 1951; Air Staff, Air Min., 1951–54, OC, RAF Deversoir, 1954; OC, RAF Khormaksar, 1954–56; on staff of HQ Bomber Command, 1956, Asst Comdt, RAF Staff Coll., Bracknell; Air Cdre, 1958; Air Vice-Marshal, 1961; Dir-Gen. of Personal Services, Air Ministry, 1960–63; retired, June 1963. Greek DFC, 1941; Sheikh el Bilharith. *Publications:* Epitaph for a Squadron, 1965; Their Finest Hour, 1976; articles on strategic and air and military affairs in various jls; verse. *Recreations:* fishing, sailing, travel and literary interests. *Address:* Quizas Quizas, Guadarranque, San Roque, Cadiz, Spain. *Clubs:* MCC; RAF

Yacht.
See also Maj.-Gen. R. Gordon-Finlayson.

GORDON-FINLAYSON, Maj.-Gen. Robert, OBE 1957 (MBE 1945); JP; DL; *b* 28 Oct. 1916; *yr s* of late Gen. Sir Robert Gordon-Finlayson, KCB, CMG, DSO, DL; *m* 1945, Alexandra, *d* of late John Bartholomew, Rowde Court, Rowde, Wilts; two *s. Educ:* Winchester Coll.; RMA, Woolwich. 2 Lt RA, 1936; Major, BEF, 1940; Staff Coll., 1941; Middle East, 1942-43; NW Europe, 1944-45; India and Burma, 1945-47; GSO 1 1945; RHA, 1952-53; JSSC, 1953; Bt Lieut-Col, 1955; AA and QMG, 3 Inf. Div., 1955-57; Near East (Suez Ops), 1956; Middle East, 1958; Lieut-Col 1958; Comdr, 26 Field Regt RA, 1958-59; Col 1959; GSO 1, Staff Coll., 1960-62; Brig. CRA, 49 Div. TA, 1962-64; Brig. DQMG, HQ, BAOR, 1964-66. GOC 49 Inf. Div., TA/N Midland Dist, 1966-67; GOC E Midland District, 1967-70; retd, 1970. Hon. Col, 3rd (Volunteer) Bn The Worcestershire and Sherwood Foresters Regt, TAVR, 1971-78; Chm., Notts Co. Army Benevolent Fund, 1970-; Mem., Notts Co. and E Midlands TAVR Assocs, 1971-. Pres., Notts Co. Royal British Legion, 1971-79; Vice-President: Notts Co. SSAFA and PDSA, 1970-; Central Notts Scout Assoc., 1971-. JP 1972, High Sheriff 1974, DL 1974, Notts. *Recreations:* shooting, fishing, ski-ing, gardening, walking. *Address:* South Collingham Manor, near Newark, Notts. *T:* Newark 892204; c/o Lloyds Bank Ltd, Cox's & King's Branch, 6 Pall Mall, SW1.
See also Air Vice-Marshal J. R. Gordon-Finlayson.

GORDON-HALL, Maj.-Gen. Frederick William, CB 1958; CBE 1945; *b* 28 Dec. 1902; *s* of Col Frederick William George Gordon-Hall and Clare Frances (*née* Taylor); *m* 1930, Phyllis Dorothy Miller; one *s* one *d. Educ:* Winchester Coll.; RMC Sandhurst. Gazetted Royal Tank Corps, 1923; Staff Capt., War Office, 1935-39; Ministry of Supply, 1939-43; HQ Allied Armies in Italy, 1943-45; Military Dir of Studies, Mil. Coll. of Science, 1946-49; Dir of Technical Services (Land), British Joint Staff Mission, Washington, 1950-52; Dir of Inspection of Fighting Vehicles, Ministry of Supply, Dec. 1952-June 1955. Dir-Gen. of Fighting Vehicles, Min. of Supply, 1955-58, retd. *Recreations:* model engineering, foreign travel, cabinet making. *Address:* Whitegates, Salisbury Road, Horsham, West Sussex. *T:* Horsham 3304.

GORDON JONES, Air Marshal Sir Edward, KCB 1967 (CB 1960); CBE 1956 (OBE 1945); DSO 1941; DFC 1941; idc; jssc; qs; Air Officer Commanding-in-Chief, Near East Air Force, and Administrator, Sovereign Base Areas, 1966-69; Commander, British Forces Near East, 1967-69; retired 1969; *b* 31 Aug. 1914; *s* of late Lt-Col Dr A. Jones, DSO, MC, MD, DPh; *m* 1938, Margery Thurston Hatfield; two *s.* Served War of 1939-45 (despatches, DFC, DSO, OBE, Greek DFC). ACOS (Intelligence), Allied Air Forces Central Europe, 1960-61; Air Officer Commanding RAF Germany, 1961-63; Senior RAF Directing Staff, Imperial Defence Coll., 1963-65; AOC, RAF, Malta, and Dep. C-in-C (Air), Allied Forces, Mediterranean, 1965-66. Mem., Council, Executive and various cttees, Caravan Club. Comdr Order of Orange Nassau. *Recreations:* sport, photography, travel, music. *Address:* 14 Chaucer Road, Cambridge. *T:* Cambridge 63029. *Club:* Royal Air Force.

GORDON-LENNOX, family name of **Duke of Richmond.**

GORDON LENNOX, Rear-Adm. Sir Alexander (Henry Charles), KCVO 1972; CB 1962; DSO 1942; Serjeant at Arms, House of Commons, 1962-76; *b* 9 April 1911; *s* of Lord Bernard Charles Gordon Lennox and Evelyn (*née* Loch); *m* 1936, Barbara, *d* of Maj.-Gen. Julian Steele; two *s. Educ:* Hetherdown, Ascot; RNC Dartmouth. Served as young officer in small ships in Far East and Home Fleet; communication specialist. Served War of 1939-45 (despatches 1943); in ME, East Coast Convoys, Russian Convoys; subsequently commanded HMS Surprise, HMS Mermaid and 2nd Frigate Sqdn, HMS Mercury and HMS Newcastle. Dep. Chief of Supplies and Transport, 1959-62; President, RNC Greenwich, 1961-62. Liberty Medal (Norway). *Recreations:* shooting, fishing and gardening. *Address:* Quags Corner, Minstead, Midhurst, West Sussex. *T:* Midhurst 3623. *Club:* Naval (Portsmouth).

GORDON LENNOX, Lieut-Gen. Sir George (Charles), KBE 1964; CB 1959; CVO 1952; DSO 1943; King of Arms, Order of British Empire, since 1968; *b* 29 May 1908; *s* of late Lord Bernard Charles Gordon Lennox, 3rd *s* of 7th Duke of Richmond and Gordon and late Evelyn Loch, *d* of 1st Baron Loch; *m* 1931, Nancy Brenda Darell; two *s. Educ:* Eton; Sandhurst. Served Grenadier Guards, 1928-52; served with Regt and on Staff, war of 1939-45, in Europe, Africa and Far East; Lieut-Col Commanding Grenadier Guards, Jan. 1951-July 1952; Comdr 1st Guards Brigade, 1952-54; IDC, 1955; BGS (SD and Trg), HQ, BAOR, 1956-57; GOC 3rd Div., 1957-59; Comdt, RMA Sandhurst, 1960-63; Dir-Gen. of Military Training, 1963-64; GOC-in-C Scottish Comd and Governor of Edinburgh Castle, 1964-66. Col, Gordon Highlanders, 1965-78. *Recreations:* field sports. *Address:* Gordon Castle, Fochabers, Morayshire. *T:* Fochabers 820275. *Club:* Cavalry and Guards.

GORDON LENNOX, Lord Nicholas Charles, CMG 1978; MVO 1957; HM Diplomatic Service; Assistant Under Secretary of State, Foreign and Commonwealth Office, since 1979; *b* 31 Jan. 1931; *yr s* of Duke of Richmond and Gordon, *qv* ; *m* 1958, Mary, *d* of late Brig. H. N. H. Williamson, DSO, MC; one *s* three *d. Educ:* Eton; Worcester Coll., Oxford (Scholar). 2nd Lieut KRRC, 1950-51. Entered HM Foreign Service, 1954; FO, 1954-57; Private Sec. to HM Ambassador to USA, 1957-61; 2nd, later 1st Sec., HM Embassy, Santiago, 1961-63; Private Sec. to Perm. Under-Sec., FO, 1963-66; 1st Sec.

and Head of Chancery, HM Embassy, Madrid, 1966-71; seconded to Cabinet Office, 1971-73; Head of News Dept, FCO, 1973-74, Head of N America Dept, 1974-75; Counsellor and Head of Chancery, Paris, 1975-79. *Address:* c/o Foreign and Commonwealth Office, SW1. *Clubs:* Brooks's, Beefsteak.
See also Earl of March and Kinrara.

GORDON-SMITH, David Gerard; CMG 1971; Director-General in Legal Service, Council of Ministers, European Communities, since 1976; *b* 6 Oct. 1925; *s* of late Frederic Gordon-Smith, QC, and Elsie Gordon-Smith (*née* Foster); *m* 1952, Angela Kirkpatrick Pile; one *d* (and one *s* decd). *Educ:* Rugby Sch.; Trinity Coll., Oxford. Served in RNVR, 1944-46. BA (Oxford) 1948; called to Bar, Inner Temple, 1949; Legal Asst, Colonial Office, 1950; Sen. Legal Asst, 1954; CRO, 1963-65; Asst Legal Adviser, CO, 1965-66; Legal Counsellor, CO, later FCO, 1966-72; Dep. Legal Advr, FCO, 1973-76. *Address:* Kingscote, Westcott, Surrey. *T:* Dorking 5702; 14 Avenue Ptolémée, 1180 Brussels, Belgium.

GORDON-SMITH, Ralph; President, since 1973 (Chairman, 1951-73), Smiths Industries Ltd (formerly Smith and Sons (England) Ltd); *b* 22 May 1905; *s* of late Sir Allan Gordon-Smith, KBE, DL and Hilda Beatrice Cave; *m* 1932, Beryl Mavis Cundy; no *c. Educ:* Bradfield Coll. Joined Smiths Industries, 1927; Dir, 1933. Dir of EMI Ltd, 1951-75. FBHI 1961. *Recreations:* shooting, fishing. *Address:* Brook House, Bosham, West Sussex. *T:* Bosham 573475; 23 Kingston House East, Princes Gate, SW7. *T:* 01-584 9428. *Club:* Bosham Sailing.

GORDON WATSON, Hugh; *see* Watson.

GORE, family name of **Earl of Arran.**

GORE; *see* Ormsby Gore.

GORE, Frederick John Pym, RA 1972 (ARA 1964); Painter; Head of Painting Department, St Martin's School of Art, WC2, 1951-79, and Vice-Principal, 1961-79; *b* 8 Nov. 1913; *s* of Spencer Frederick Gore and Mary Johanna Kerr. *Educ:* Lancing Coll.; Trinity Coll., Oxford; studied art at Ruskin, Westminster and Slade Schs. Taught at: Westminster Sch. of Art, 1937; Chelsea and Epsom, 1947; St Martin's, 1946-79. *One-man exhibitions:* Gall. Borghèse, Paris, 1938; Redfern Gall., 1937, 1949, 1950, 1953, 1956, 1962; Mayor Gall., 1958, 1960; Juster Gall., NY, 1963. *Paintings in public collections include:* Contemporary Art Soc., Leicester County Council, GLC, Southampton, Plymouth, Rutherston Collection and New Brunswick. Served War of 1939-45: Mx Regt and RA (SO Camouflage). *Publications:* Abstract Art, 1956; Painting, Some Principles, 1965. *Recreation:* Russian folk dancing. *Address:* Flat 3, 35 Elm Park Gardens, SW10. *T:* 01-352 4940.

GORE, John Francis, CVO 1941; TD; journalist and author; *b* 15 May 1885; *y s* of late Sir Francis Gore, KCB; *m* 1926, Lady Janet Helena Campbell, *er d* of 4th Earl Cawdor; one *s* two *d. Educ:* Radley Coll.; Trinity Coll., Oxford (MA). Barrister-at-Law, Inner Temple, 1909; served European War, 1914-19 (despatches); Captain Bedfordshire Yeomanry; Sec. Training Grants Cttee, Ministry of Labour, 1920; took up journalism, 1923; pen-name The Old Stager, of the Sphere's Newsletter, 1928-64. JP Sussex, 1932-59, Chm. Midhurst Bench, 1944-58. *Publications:* The Trial Stone, 1919; A Londoner's Calendar, 1925; The Way In, 1927; The Ghosts of Fleet Street, 1929; Charles Gore, father and son, 1932; Creevey's life and times, 1934; Nelson's Hardy and his wife, 1935; Sydney Holland, Lord Knutsford, 1936; Geoffrey Colman; Mary, Duchess of Bedford (privately printed), 1938; King George V, 1941 (awarded J. T. Black Memorial Prize, 1941); Creevey, 1948; Edwardian Scrapbook, 1951; Three Howard Sisters (with another), 1955. *Address:* Littlehay, Burley, Ringwood, Hants. *T:* Burley 3306. *Club:* I Zingari.
See also Sir Charles Cave.

GORE, Paul Annesley, CMG 1964; CVO 1961; JP; *b* 28 Feb. 1921; *o s* of late Charles Henry Gore, OBE and late Hon. Violet Kathleen (*née* Annesley); *m* 1946, Gillian Mary, *d* of T. E. Allen-Stevens; three *s. Educ:* Winchester Coll.; Christ Church, Oxford. Military Service, 1941-46: 16/5 Lancers. Colonial Service, 1948-65; Dep. Governor, The Gambia, 1962-65. JP City of Oxford, 1973-74; JP Suffolk, 1977. *Address:* 1 Burkitt Road, Woodbridge, Suffolk.

GORE, Sir Richard (Ralph St George), 13th Bt *cr* 1621; *b* 19 Nov. 1954; *s* of Sir (St George) Ralph Gore, 12th Bt, and of Shirley, *d* of Clement Tabor; *S* father, 1973. *Educ:* The King's Sch., Parramatta; Univ. of New England; Queensland Coll. of Art. *Heir:* uncle Nigel Hugh St George Gore [*b* 23 Dec. 1922; *m* 1952, Beth Allison (*d* 1976), *d* of R. W. Hooper; one *d*]. *Address:* 14 Brodie Street, Toowoomba, Queensland 4350, Australia.

GORE-BOOTH, family name of **Baron Gore-Booth.**

GORE-BOOTH, Baron *cr* 1969 (Life Peer), of Maltby; **Paul Henry Gore-Booth,** GCMG 1965 (KCMG 1957; CMG 1949); KCVO 1961; HM Diplomatic Service, retired; Director: Grindlays Bank, 1969-79; United Kingdom Provident Institution, 1969-79; Registrar, Order of St Michael and St George, 1966-79; *b* 3 Feb. 1909; *m* 1940, Patricia Mary Ellerton; twin *s* two *d. Educ:* Eton; Balliol Coll., Oxford. Joined Foreign Service, 1933; FO 1933-36; Vienna, 1936-37; Tokyo, 1938-42; Washington, 1942-45; FO, 1945-49; Head of UN (Economic and Social) and Refugees Depts, 1947-48;

Head of European Recovery Dept, Foreign Office, 1948-49; Dir British Information Services in United States, 1949-53; Ambassador to Burma, 1953-56; Dep. Under-Sec. (Economic Affairs), Foreign Office, 1956-60; British High Commissioner in India, 1960-65; Permanent Under-Sec. of State, FO, 1965-69; Head of HM Diplomatic Service, 1968-69. Hot Springs Food Conference, 1943; UNRRA Conference, 1943; Chicago Civil Aviation Conference, 1944; San Francisco Conf., 1945; UN Assembly, 1946 (Sec. of UK Deleg.) Jan. and Oct. and 1947; British Rep., Gp of Four drafting Convention setting up OECD. Chairman: Save the Children Fund, 1970-76; Disasters Emergency Cttee, 1974-77. Chm. Bd of Governors, Sch. of Oriental and African Studies, Univ. of London, 1975-80. Pres., Sherlock Holmes Soc. of London, 1967-79; Chm., Windsor Music Festival, 1971-73. *Publications:* With Great Truth and Respect (autobiog.), 1974; (ed) Satow's Guide to Diplomatic Practice, 5th edn, 1978. *Address:* 70 Ashley Gardens, SW1P 1QG. *Clubs:* Athenæum, Baker Street Irregulars.
   See also Hon. David Gore-Booth.

GORE-BOOTH, Hon. David Alwyn; HM Diplomatic Service; Counsellor (Commercial), Jedda, Saudi Arabia, since 1980; *b* 15 May 1943; twin *s* of Baron Gore-Booth, *qv*; *m* 1st, 1964, Jillian Sarah (*née* Valpy) (marr. diss. 1970); one *s*; 2nd, 1977, Mary Elisabeth Janet (*née* Muirhead). *Educ:* Eton Coll.; Christ Church, Oxford (MA Hons). Entered Foreign Office, 1964; Middle East Centre for Arabic Studies, 1964; Third Secretary, Baghdad, 1966; Third, later Second Sec., Lusaka, 1967; FCO, 1969; Second Sec., Tripoli, 1969; FCO, 1971; First Sec., UK Permanent Representation to European Communities, Brussels, 1974; Asst Head of Financial Relations Dept, FCO, 1978. *Recreations:* tennis, squash, the island of Hydra (Greece). *Address:* c/o Foreign and Commonwealth Office, SW1A 2AH; 31 Lorn Road, SW9 0AB. *T:* 01-733 3229. *Clubs:* MCC; Bill's Bar (Hydra).

GORE-BOOTH, Sir Michael Savile, 7th Bt, *cr* 1760; *b* 24 July 1908; *s* of 6th Bt and Mary (*d* 1968), *d* of Rev. S. L'Estrange-Malone; *S* father, 1944. *Educ:* Rugby; Trinity Coll., Cambridge. *Heir: b* Angus Josslyn Gore-Booth [*b* 25 June 1920; *m* 1948, Hon. Rosemary Vane (marr. diss., 1954), *o d* of 10th Baron Barnard; one *s* one *d*]. *Address:* Lissadell, Sligo.

GORE BROWNE, Sir Thomas (Anthony), Kt 1981; Senior Government Broker, 1973-81; Director, South West Regional Board, National Westminster Bank, since 1981; *b* 20 June 1918; 2nd *s* of Sir Eric Gore Browne, DSO; *m* 1946, Lavinia, *d* of Gen. Sir (Henry) Charles Loyd, GCVO, KCB, DSO, MC; three *s* one *d. Educ:* Eton Coll.; Trinity Coll., Cambridge. Served Grenadier Guards, 1938-48, France, N Africa, Italy. Joined Mullens & Co., 1948, Partner 1949-81. Treasurer, Imperial Cancer Res. Fund, 1980-. *Address:* The Old Rectory, Lydlinch, Sturminster Newton, Dorset DT10 2JA. *T:* Sturminster Newton 72074. *Clubs:* Brooks's, White's, Pratt's.

GORE-LANGTON; *see* Temple-Gore-Langton, family name of Earl Temple of Stowe.

GORELL, 4th Baron *cr* 1909; **Timothy John Radcliffe Barnes;** *b* 2 Aug. 1927; *e s* of 3rd Baron Gorell and Elizabeth Gorell, *d* of Alexander Nelson Radcliffe; *S* father, 1963; *m* 1954, Joan Marion, *y d* of late John Edmund Collins, MC, Sway, Hants; two adopted *d. Educ:* Eton Coll.; New Coll., Oxford. Lieut, Rifle Brigade, 1946-48. Barrister, Inner Temple, 1951. Joined Royal Dutch/Shell Group, 1959. *Heir: b* Hon. Ronald Alexander Henry Barnes [*b* 28 June 1931; *m* 1957, Gillian Picton Hughes-Jones; one *s* one *d*]. *Address:* 4 Roehampton Gate, SW15. *T:* 01-876 6042. *Club:* Roehampton Golf.

GORELL BARNES, Sir William (Lethbridge), KCMG 1961 (CMG 1949); CB 1956; Director: Tarmac Ltd, since 1971; Donald Macpherson Group Ltd, since 1972; *b* 23 Aug. 1909; *y s* of late Sir Frederic Gorell Barnes and Caroline Anne Roper Lethbridge; *m* 1935, Barbara Mary Louise, *e d* of late Brig. A. F. B. Cottrell, DSO, OBE; one *s* three *d. Educ:* Marlborough Coll.; Pembroke Coll., Cambridge, 1st Cl. Classical Tripos Pt 1, 1st Cl. Mod. Langs Tripos Pt 2. Served in HM Diplomatic Service, 1932-39; Offices of War Cabinet, 1939-45; Personal Asst to Lord Pres. of the Council, 1942-45; Asst Sec., HM Treasury, 1945-46; Personal Asst to Prime Minister, Oct. 1946-Feb. 1948; Seconded to Colonial Office, 1948; Asst Under-Sec. of State, 1948-59; Dep. Under-Sec. of State, 1959-63. Mem. UK delegn for negotiations with European Economic Community, 1962, retired 1963. Director: Doulton & Co., 1966-80 (Dep. Chm., 1969-80); Royal Gp of Insurance Cos, 1963-80 (Dep. Chm., 1972-80); Limmer Holdings Ltd, 1966-71 (Chm., 1971); Vice-Chm. and Financial Dir, Harvey's of Bristol, 1963-66; Chm., James Templeton & Co., 1967-69. Chm., Cons. Commonwealth and Overseas Council, 1974-76. Mem. Council, Westfield Coll., London Univ., 1970-77 (Hon. Fellow, 1978). *Publication:* Europe and the Developing World, 1967. *Recreations:* gardening, walking, reading. *Address:* Mattishall Hall, Dereham, Norfolk. *T:* Dereham 858181. *Clubs:* Reform; Norfolk (Norwich).

GORING, Marius; Actor; *b* Newport, IOW, 23 May 1912; *s* of Dr Charles Buckman Goring, MD, BSc, and Katie Winifred Macdonald; *m* 1931, Mary Westwood Steel (marr. diss.); one *d*; *m* 1941, Lucie Mannheim (*d* 1976); *m* 1977, Prudence FitzGerald. *Educ:* Perse Sch., Cambridge; Universities of Frankfurt, Munich, Vienna, and Paris. Studied for stage under Harcourt Williams and at Old Vic dramatic school. First stage appearance in London in one of Jean Sterling Mackinlay's matinées, 1927; toured in France and Germany with English Classical Players, 1931; played two seasons at Old Vic

and Sadler's Wells, 1932-34. First West End appearance as Hugh Voysey in The Voysey Inheritance, Shaftesbury, 1934; toured France, Belgium, and Holland with Compagnie des Quinze (acting in French), 1934-35; appeared London, 1935-39, in: Hamlet, Noah, The Hangman, Sowers of the Hills, Mary Tudor, The Happy Hypocrite, Girl Unknown, The Wild Duck, The Witch of Edmonton, Twelfth Night, Henry V, Hamlet, The Last Straw, Surprise Item, The White Guard; Satyr. In management at Duke of York's, 1939; produced Nora (A Doll's House); played Ariel in, and partly produced, The Tempest, Old Vic, 1940. Served War of 1939-45, Army, 1940-41; Foreign Office, 1941-45; supervisor of productions of BBC broadcasting to Germany, 1941. Toured British zone of Germany, 1947 (playing in German), 1948; Rosmersholm, Too True to be Good, Cherry Orchard, Marriage, The Third Man, at Arts Theatre; Daphne Laureola, Berlin (playing in German), 1949; The Madwoman of Chaillot, St James's, 1951; Richard III, Antony and Cleopatra, Taming of the Shrew, King Lear, Stratford-upon-Avon, 1953; Antony and Cleopatra, Princes, 1953; Marriage, Wuppertal, 1954; has toured France, Holland, Finland, 1957, and India, 1958, with own company of English comedians; Tonight at 8.30 (in German), Berlin Fest., 1960; Measure for Measure, Stratford-upon-Avon, 1962; A Penny for a Song, Aldwych, 1962; Ménage à Trois, Lyric, 1963; The Poker Session, Globe, 1964; The Apple Cart, Cambridge, 1965; The Bells, Vaudeville, 1968; The Demonstration, Nottingham, 1969; Sleuth, 1970-73; Zaïde, Old Vic, 1982. Co-founder, London Theatre Studio. *Films include:* The Case of the Frightened Lady, A Matter of Life and Death, Take my Life, The Red Shoes, Mr Perrin and Mr Traill, Odette, Circle of Danger, Highly Dangerous, So Little Time, Nachts auf den Strassen (Germany), The Man Who Watched the Trains Go By, Rough Shoot, The Barefoot Contessa, Family Doctor, Ill Met by Moonlight, The Inspector, The Crooked Road, Up from the Beach, 25th Hour.. Broadcaster and writer of radio scripts. *Television:* co-prod. and played lead in The Scarlet Pimpernel (series), 1955; The Expert (series), 1968-70; appears on TV in Germany and France. Vice-Pres. British Actors' Equity Assoc., 1963-65 and 1975-82. *Recreations:* skating and riding. *Address:* Middle Court, The Green, Hampton Court, Surrey. *T:* 01-977 4030. *Club:* Garrick.

GORING, Sir William (Burton Nigel), 13th Bt, *cr* 1627; Member of London Stock Exchange since 1963; *b* 21 June 1933; *s* of Major Frederick Yelverton Goring (*d* 1938) (6th *s* of 11th Bt) and Freda Margaret, *o d* of N. V. Ainsworth, 2 Closewalks, Midhurst, Sussex; *S* uncle, Sir Forster Gurney Goring, 12th Bt, 1956; *m* 1960, Hon. Caroline Thellusson, *d* of 8th Baron Rendlesham, *qv*, and of Mrs Patrick Barthropp. *Educ:* Wellington; RMA Sandhurst, Lieut, The Royal Sussex Regt. *Recreation:* bridge. *Heir: b* Edward Yelverton Combe Goring [*b* 20 June 1936; *m* 1969, Daphne Christine Sellar; two *d*]. *Address:* 16 Linver Road, SW6 3RB. *T:* 01-736 6032. *Club:* Hurlingham.

GORING-MORRIS, Rex, OBE 1975; HM Diplomatic Service; Counsellor, Consul-General and Head of Chancery, Stockholm, since 1979; *b* 17 Oct. 1926; *s* of Cecil Goring Morris and Doris Flora Edna (*née* Howell); *m* 1st, 1950, Constance Eularia Heather (*d* 1979), *d* of late Mr and Mrs Cecil Bartram, Oxford; two *s* three *d*; 2nd, 1979, Mrs Mary Poole (*née* King), Aldenham, Herts; one step *s* one step *d. Educ:* Chichester High Sch.; New Coll., Oxford; RAF Coll., Cranwell, 1945-46. No 66 (F) Sqdn, 1947-50; Central Flying Sch., 1950; No 6 FTS, 1950-51; French Air Force, Marrakech and Rabat, 1951-53; RAF Odiham, 1954-56; Flt Cdr No 66 (F) Sqdn, 1956-57; HQ Fighter Comd, 1957; HQ RAF Germany, 1957-59; RAF Staff Coll., 1959; Sqdn Cdr, Central Fighter Estabt, 1959-61; Military Agency for Standardisation, NATO, London, 1962-63; Wing Comdr 1963; Air Attaché, Tel Aviv, 1964-67; jssc 1968; Jt Warfare Estabt, 1969; retired from RAF and joined HM Diplomatic Service, 1969; 1st Sec., FCO, 1969-71; 1st Secretary and Head of Chancery: Tunis, 1971-75; Bangkok, 1975-77; Counsellor, Consul-Gen. and Hd of Chancery, Bangkok, 1978-79. *Recreations:* travel, photography; Oxford blue for Association Football, 1944-45. *Address:* c/o Foreign and Commonwealth Office, SW1; c/o Lloyds Bank Ltd, Cox's & King's Branch, 6 Pall Mall, SW1. *Clubs:* Royal Air Force; British (Bangkok).

GORLEY PUTT, Samuel; *see* Putt.

GORMAN, John Peter, QC 1974; a Recorder of the Crown Court, since 1972; *b* 29 June 1927; *er s* of James S. Gorman, Edinburgh; *m* 1st, 1955, Avril Mary (*née* Penfold) (*d* 1978); one *s* three *d*; 2nd, 1979, Patricia (*née* Myatt). *Educ:* Stonyhurst Coll.; Balliol Coll., Oxford (MA). Called to Bar, Inner Temple, 1953; Midland and Oxford Circuit. Part-time Chm., Industrial Tribunal, 1968-73; Dep. Chm. 1969, Chm. 1972-79, Agricultural Lands Tribunal (E Midlands); Dep. Chm., Northants QS, 1970-71. *Address:* 2 Dr Johnson's Buildings, Temple, EC4.

GORMAN, John Reginald, CVO 1961; CBE 1974 (MBE 1959); MC 1944; DL; Vice-Chairman and Chief Executive, Northern Ireland Housing Executive, since 1979; *b* 1 Feb. 1923; *s* of Major J. K. Gorman, MC; *m* 1948, Heather, *d* of George Caruth, solicitor, Ballymena; two *s* two *d. Educ:* Rockport, Haileybury and ISC Portora; Glasgow Univ.; Harvard Business Sch. FCIT, FIPM; AMIH. Irish Guards, 1941-46, Normandy, France, Belgium, Holland, Germany (Captain, 1944-46). Royal Ulster Constabulary, 1946-60; Chief of Security, BOAC, 1960-63 (incl. Royal Tour of India, 1961); Personnel Dir and Mem. Bd of Management, BOAC, 1964-69; British Airways: Regional Man., Canada, 1969-75; Regional Man., India, Bangladesh, Sri Lanka, 1975-79. Pres., British Canadian Trade Assoc., 1972-74;

Vice-Chm., Federated Appeal of Montreal, 1973-74. Chm., Bd of Airline Representatives, India, 1977-79. DL Co. Down, 1982. *Recreations:* gardening, country pursuits. *Address:* The Red House, Rademon, Crossgar, Co. Down. *Clubs:* Cavalry and Guards; Ulster (Belfast); St James (Montreal); Gymkhana (Delhi).

GORMAN, William Moore, FBA 1978; Official Fellow, Nuffield College, Oxford, since 1979; *b* 17 June 1923; *s* of late Richard Gorman, Lusaka, Northern Rhodesia, and Sarah Crawford Moore, Kesh, Northern Ireland; *m* 1950, Dorinda Scott. *Educ:* Foyle Coll., Derry; Trinity Coll., Dublin. Asst Lectr, 1949, Lectr, 1951, and Sen. Lectr, 1957, in Econometrics and Social Statistics, University of Birmingham; Prof. of Economics, University of Oxford, and Fellow of Nuffield Coll., Oxford, 1962-67; Prof. of Economics, London Univ., at LSE, 1967-79. Vice-Pres. 1970-71, Pres. 1972, Econometric Soc. Hon. DSocSc Birmingham, 1973; Hon. DSc(SocSc) Southampton, 1974. *Publications:* articles in various economic journals. *Address:* Nuffield College, Oxford.

GORMANSTON, 17th Viscount *cr* 1478; **Jenico Nicholas Dudley Preston;** Baron Gormanston (UK), 1868; Premier Viscount of Ireland; *b* 19 Nov. 1939; *s* of 16th Viscount and Pamela (who *m* 2nd, 1943, M. B. O'Connor, Irish Guards; he *d* 1961, she *d* 1975), *o d* of late Capt. Dudley Hanly, and Lady Marjorie Heath (by her 1st marriage); *S* father, who was officially presumed killed in action, France, 9 June 1940; *m* 1974, Eva Antoine Landzianowska; two *s. Educ:* Downside. *Heir: s* Hon. Jenico Francis Tara Preston, *b* 30 April 1974. *Address:* 8 Dalmeny House, Thurloe Place, SW7.

GORMLEY, family name of **Baron Gormley.**

GORMLEY, Baron *cr* 1982 (Life Peer), of Ashton-in-Makerfield in Greater Manchester; **Joseph Gormley,** OBE 1969; President, National Union of Mineworkers, 1971-82; *b* 5 July 1917; *m* 1937, Sarah Ellen Mather; one *s* one *d. Educ:* St Oswald's Roman Catholic Sch., Ashton-in-Makerfield. Entered Mining Industry at age of 14 and was employed in practically every underground job in mining. Served as Councillor in Ashton-in-Makerfield. Elected to Nat. Exec. Cttee of Nat. Union of Mineworkers, 1957; Gen. Sec. of North Western Area, 1961, when he relinquished his appt as a JP, owing to other commitments. Former Mem., Nat. Exec. Cttee, Labour Party; former Chm., Internat. and Organisation Cttee, Labour Party. Member: TUC Gen. Council, 1973-80. Director: British Investment Trust, 1978-; United Racecourses Ltd, 1982-. Hon. Fellow, UMIST, 1980. *Publication:* Battered Cherub (autobiog.), 1982. *Address:* 1 Springfield Grove, Sunbury-on-Thames, Middlesex.

GORRINGE, Christopher John; Secretary, All England Lawn Tennis and Croquet Club, Wimbledon, since 1979 (Assistant Secretary, 1973-79); *b* 13 Dec. 1945; *s* of Maurice Sydney William Gorringe and Hilda Joyce Gorringe; *m* 1976, Jennifer Mary Chamberlain; two *d. Educ:* Bradfield Coll., Berks; Royal Agricl Coll., Cirencester. ARICS. Asst Land Agent, Iveagh Trustees Ltd (Guinness family), 1968-73. *Recreations:* lawn tennis, squash, soccer. *Address:* All England Lawn Tennis Club, Church Road, Wimbledon, SW19 5AE. *T:* 01-946 2244. *Clubs:* East India, Devonshire, Sports and Public Schools; All England Lawn Tennis and Croquet, International Lawn Tennis of GB, Queen's, St George's Hill Lawn Tennis, Jesters.

GORST, John Michael; MP (C) Barnet, Hendon North, since 1974 (Hendon North, 1970-74); *b* 28 June 1928; *s* of Derek Charles Gorst and Tatiana (*née* Kolotinsky); *m* 1954, Noël Harington Walker; five *s. Educ:* Ardingly Coll.; Corpus Christi Coll., Cambridge (MA). Advertising and Public Relations Manager, Pye Ltd, 1953-63; and Trade Union and Public Affairs Consultant, John Gorst & Associates, 1964-. Public relations adviser to: British Lion Films, 1964-65; Fedn of British Film Makers, 1964-67; Film Production Assoc. of GB, 1967-68; BALPA, 1967-69; Guy's Hosp., 1968-74. Dir, Cassius Film Productions Ltd, 1969-. Founder: Telephone Users' Assoc., 1964-80 (Sec. 1964-70); Local Radio Assoc. 1964 (Sec., 1964-71). Contested (C) Chester-le-Street, 1964; Bodmin, 1966. Sec., Cons. Consumer Protection Cttee, 1973-74; Mem., Employment Select Cttee, 1980-. *Recreation:* chess. *Address:* House of Commons, SW1A 0AA. *Club:* Garrick.

GORT, 8th Viscount (Ire.), *cr* 1816; **Colin Leopold Prendergast Vereker,** JP; Baron Kiltarton 1810; company director; *b* 21 June 1916; *s* of Commander Leopold George Prendergast Vereker, RD, RNR (*d* 1937) (*g s* of 4th Viscount) and Helen Marjorie Campbell (*d* 1958); *S* kinsman, 1975; *m* 1946, Bettine Mary Mackenzie, *d* of late Godfrey Greene; two *s* one *d. Educ:* Sevenoaks. Trained at Air Service Training, Hamble, in Aeronautical Engineering, etc., 1937-39; served Fleet Air Arm, 1939-45 (despatches). Member of House of Keys, IOM, 1966-71. JP IOM 1962. *Recreations:* golf, fishing, gardening. *Heir: er s* Hon. Foley Robert Standish Prendergast Vereker [*b* 24 Oct. 1951; *m* 1979, Julie Denise, *o d* of D. W. Jones, Ballasalla, IoM]. *Address:* Westwood, The Crofts, Castletown, Isle of Man. *T:* Castletown 2545. *Club:* Carlton.

GORTON, Rt. Hon. Sir John (Grey), PC 1968; GCMG 1977; CH 1971; MA; retired; *b* 1911; *m* 1935, Bettina, *d* of G. Brown, Bangor, Me, USA; two *s* one *d. Educ:* Geelong Gram. Sch.; Brasenose Coll., Oxford (MA, Hon. Fellow, 1968). Orchardist. Enlisted RAAF, Nov. 1940; served in UK, Singapore, Darwin, Milne Bay; severely wounded in air ops; discharged with rank of Flt-Lt, Dec. 1944. Councillor, Kerang Shire, 1947-52 (Pres. of Shire);

Mem., Lodden Valley Regional Cttee. Senator for State of Victoria, Parlt of Commonwealth of Australia, 1949-68 (Govt Leader in Senate, 1967-68); Minister for Navy, 1958-63; Minister Assisting the Minister for External Affairs, 1960-63 (Actg Minister during periods of absence overseas of Minister); Minister in Charge of CSIRO, 1962-68; Minister for Works and, under Prime Minister, Minister in Charge of Commonwealth Activities in Educn and Research, 1963-66; Minister for Interior, 1963-64; Minister for Works, 1966-67; Minister for Educn and Science, 1966-68; MHR (L) for Higgins, Vic, 1968-75; Prime Minister of Australia, 1968-71; Minister for Defence, and Dep. Leader of Liberal Party, March-Aug. 1971; Mem. Parly Liberal Party Exec., and Liberal Party Spokesman on Environment and Conservation and Urban and Regional Develt, 1973-75; Dep. Chm., Jt Parly Cttee on Prices, 1973-75. Contested Senate election (Ind.), ACT, Dec. 1975. *Address:* Suite 3, 9th Floor, 197 London Circuit, Canberra City, ACT 2601, Australia.

GORTVAI, Rosalinde; *see* Hurley, R.

GOSCHEN, family name of **Viscount Goschen.**

GOSCHEN, 4th Viscount *cr* 1900; **Giles John Harry Goschen;** *b* 16 Nov. 1965; *s* of 3rd Viscount Goschen, KBE, and of Alvin Moyanna Lesley, *yr d* of late Harry England, Durban, Natal; *S* father, 1977. *Address:* Hilton House, Crowthorne, Berks.

GOSCHEN, Sir Edward (Christian), 3rd Bt, *cr* 1916; DSO 1944; Rifle Brigade; *b* 2 Sept. 1913; *er s* of Sir Edward Henry Goschen, 2nd Bt, and Countess Mary, 7th *d* of Count Danneskiold, Samsoe, Denmark; *S* father, 1933; *m* 1946, Cynthia, *d* of late Rt Hon. Sir Alexander Cadogan, PC, OM, GCMG, KCB; one *s* one *d. Educ:* Eton; Trinity Coll., Oxford. Mem., Stock Exchange Council (Dep. Chm., 1968-71). Commonwealth War Graves Comr, 1977-. *Heir: s* Edward Alexander Goschen [*b* 13 March 1949; *m* 1976, Louise Annette, *d* of Lt-Col R. F. L. Chance, MC, and Lady Ava Chance; one *d*]. *Address:* Lower Farm House, Hampstead Norreys, Newbury, Berks RG16 0SG. *T:* Hermitage 201270.

GOSFORD, 7th Earl of, *cr* 1806; **Charles David Nicholas Alexander John Sparrow Acheson;** Bt (NS) 1628; Baron Gosford 1776; Viscount Gosford 1785; Baron Worlingham (UK) 1835; Baron Acheson (UK) 1847; *b* 13 July 1942; *o s* of 6th Earl of Gosford, OBE, and Francesca Augusta, *er d* of Francesco Cagiati, New York; *S* father, 1966. *Educ:* Harrow; Byam Shaw Sch. of drawing and painting; Royal Academy Schs. *Heir: u* Hon. Patrick Bernard Victor Montagu Acheson [*b* 4 Feb. 1915; *m* 1946, Judith, *d* of Mrs F. B. Bate, Virginia, USA; three *s* two *d*].

GOSLING, Sir Donald, Kt 1976; Joint Chairman, National Car Parks Ltd, since 1950; Chairman, Palmer & Harvey Ltd, since 1967; Director, Lovell Holdings Ltd, since 1975; *b* 2 March 1929; *m* 1959, Elizabeth Shauna, *d* of Dr Peter Ingram and Cecily Ingram; three *s.* Joined RN, 1944; served Mediterranean, HMS Leander. Member: Council of Management, White Ensign Assoc. Ltd, 1970- (Chm., 1978-); Council, World of Property Housing Trust, 1976-; Queen's Silver Jubilee Appeal, Gander, 1977; Chm., Selective Employment Scheme, 1976-; Trustee: Fleet Air Arm Museum, Yeovilton, 1974- (Chm., Mountbatten Meml Hall Appeals Cttee, 1980); RYA Seamanship Foundn, 1981-; Patron, Submarine Meml Appeal, 1978-. *Recreations:* swimming, sailing, shooting. *Address:* National Car Parks Ltd, 21 Bryanston Street, Marble Arch, W1A 4NH. *T:* 01-499 7050. *Clubs:* Royal Thames Yacht, Royal London Yacht, Royal Naval Sailing Association, Thames Sailing; Saints and Sinners.

GOSLING, Justin Cyril Bertrand; Principal, St Edmund Hall, Oxford, since 1982; *b* 26 April 1930; *s* of Vincent and Dorothy Gosling; *m* 1958, Margaret Clayton; two *s* two *d. Educ:* Ampleforth Coll.; Wadham Coll., Oxford (BPhil, MA). Univ. of Oxford: Fereday Fellow, St John's Coll., 1955-58; Lectr in Philosophy, Pembroke Coll. and Wadham Coll., 1958-60; Fellow in Philosophy, St Edmund Hall, 1960-82; Sen. Proctor, 1977-78. Barclay Acheson Prof., Macalester Coll., Minnesota, 1964; Vis. Res. Fellow, ANU, Canberra, 1970. *Publications:* Pleasure and Desire, 1969; Plato, 1973; (ed) Plato, Philebus, 1975; (with C. C. W. Taylor) The Greeks on Pleasure, 1982; articles in Mind, Phil Rev. and Proc. Aristotelian Soc. *Recreations:* gardening, intaglio printing, recorder music. *Address:* St Edmund Hall, Oxford OX1 4AR. *T:* Oxford 245511.

GOSLING, Col Richard Bennett, OBE 1957; TD 1947; DL; Chairman, Hearne & Co., 1971-82; *b* 4 Oct. 1914; 2nd *s* of late T. S. Gosling, Dynes Hall, Halstead; *m* 1st, 1950, Marie Terese Ronayne (*d* 1976), Castle Redmond, Co. Cork; one adopted *s* one adopted *d* (one *s* decd); 2nd, 1978, Sybilla Burgers van Oyen, *widow* of Bernard Burgers, 't Kasteel, Nijmegen. *Educ:* Eton; Magdalene Coll., Cambridge (MA). CEng, FIMechE, MIMC. Served with Essex Yeomanry, RHA, 1939-45; CO, 1953-56; Dep. CRA, East Anglian Div., 1956-58. Dir-Gen., British Agricl Export Council, 1971-73. Chm., Constructors, 1965-68; Director: P-E International, 1956-76; Doulton & Co., 1962-72; Revertex Chemicals, 1974-81. DL 1954, High Sheriff 1982, Essex. French Croix de Guerre, 1944. *Recreations:* country pursuits, overseas travel. *Address:* Canterburys Lodge, Margaretting, Essex. *T:* Ingatestone 3073. *Clubs:* Bath, MCC; Beefsteak (Chelmsford).

GOSNAY, Maxwell; His Honour Judge Gosnay; a Circuit Judge, since 1973; *b* 31 July 1923; *o s* of William and Milly Gertrude Gosnay; *m* 1959, Constance Ann, *d* of Ben and Constance Mary Hardy; one *s* one *d. Educ:* Leeds Grammar Sch.; Christ Church, Oxford (MA). Called to Bar, Inner Temple, 1945. Asst Recorder, Leeds, 1965-71; Deputy Licensing Authority, Yorks Traffic Comrs, 1965-72; Dep. Chm., WR Yorks QS, 1967-71; a Recorder, 1972-73. *Recreations:* golf, reading. *Address:* 25 Park Lane, Leeds LS8 2EX. *T:* Leeds 663066.

GOSS, Leonard (Cecil); Joint Chief Executive, Council of Christians and Jews, 1975-81, General Secretary since 1981; *b* London, 19 May 1925; *s* of Jack and Sophie Goss; *m* 1978, Mildred, *d* of Hyman and Rebecca Gershon. *Educ:* Raine's Foundn Sch., Stepney, London. Journalist, latterly News Editor, S Wales Evening Post, Swansea, 1944-70; Inf. Officer, University Coll. of Swansea, 1970-75. British Jun. Chamber of Commerce: Vice-Pres., 1954-57; National Hon. PRO, 1952-54 and 1957-62; Senator, Jun. Chamber Internat., 1963-; Vice-Chm., IFL, 1969-74, Vice-Pres. Brit. Section, 1975-, Hon. Dir, Internat. Assembly, 1981 (Jubilee Year). Member: Exec. Cttee, Jewish Scout Adv. Council, 1975-; Bd of Deputies of British Jews, 1976- (Mem. Central Jewish Lecture and Information Cttee, 1979-, Vice-Chm., 1982-); Exec. Cttee, All-Party and Inter-Faith Cttee for Racial Justice, 1977- (founder mem.); Exec. Cttee, Religious Zionist Movement, 1978-; Gp Relations Cttee, AJEX, 1976-. Hon. Secretary: Golders Green AJEX, 1978-; Religious Weekly Press Gp, 1975-. Hon. Treasurer, Internat. CCJ, 1980-82, Exec. Cttee, 1982-. Leader, Brit. contingent to World Conf. of Jewish Journalists, Jerusalem, 1977. Formerly: Vice-Chm., Swansea Citizens' Advice Bureau; Chm., Swansea Br., Save the Children Fund and Chm., all-Wales SCF Conf.; Mem. Wales Cttee, Internat. Refugee Year, and Freedom from Hunger Campaign; W Glam County Scout Officer. Scout Movement's Thanks Badge, 1943, and Medal of Merit, 1970; IFL Internat. Badge of Honour, 1974. Editor, Common Ground (CCJ qly), 1975-81. *Publications:* contrib. to Jewish Chronicle, Catholic Herald, and Baptist Times. *Recreations:* theatre, reading. *Address:* Council of Christians and Jews, 48 Onslow Gardens, SW7 3PX. *T:* 01-589 8854; 42 Golders Gardens, NW11 9BU. *T:* 01-455 5599.

GOSS, Brig. Leonard George, CB 1946; *b* 30 May 1895; *s* of Alfred Herbert Goss, Wellington, NZ; *m* 1920, Ella May, *d* of John Airth Mace, New Plymouth, NZ; one *d. Educ:* New Plymouth Boys' High Sch. (NZ); RMC of Australia. Commissioned in NZ Staff Corps, Lieut 1916; Captain 1919; Major, 1935; Lt-Col 1939; Temp. Brig. 1942. *Recreations:* Rugby, cricket, swimming, boxing. *Address:* 17 Waitui Crescent, Lower Hutt, NZ. *Club:* United Service (Wellington, NZ).

GOSS, Prof. Richard Oliver, PhD; Professor, Department of Maritime Studies, University of Wales Institute of Science and Technology, since 1980; *b* 4 Oct. 1929; *s* of late Leonard Arthur Goss and Hilda Nellie Goss (*née* Casson); *m* Lesley Elizabeth Thurbon; two *s* one *d. Educ:* Christ's Coll., Finchley; HMS Worcester; King's Coll., Cambridge. Master Mariner 1956; BA 1958; MA 1961; PhD 1979. FCIT 1970; MNI (Founder) 1972; FNI 1977. Merchant Navy (apprentice and executive officer), 1947-55; NZ Shipping Co. Ltd, 1958-63; Economic Consultant (Shipping, Shipbuilding and Ports), MoT, 1963-64; Econ. Adviser, BoT (Shipping), 1964-67; Sen. Econ. Adviser (Shipping, Civil Aviation, etc), 1967-74; Econ. Adviser to Cttee of Inquiry into Shipping (Rochdale Cttee), 1967-70; Under-Sec., Depts of Industry and Trade, 1974-80. Nuffield/Leverhulme Travelling Fellow, 1977-78. Governor, Plymouth Polytechnic, 1973-; Mem. Council: RINA, 1969-; Nautical Inst. (from foundn until 1976); Member: CNAA Nautical Studies Bd, 1971-81; CNAA Transport Bd, 1976-. *Publications:* Studies in Maritime Economics, 1968; (with C. D. Jones) The Economies of Size in Dry Bulk Carriers, 1971; (with M. C. Mann, et al) The Cost of Ships' Time, 1974; Advances in Maritime Economics, 1977; A Comparative Study of Seaport Management and Administration, 1979; papers in various jls, transactions and to conferences. *Recreations:* diving, gliding, bar billiards. *Address:* 8 Dunraven House, Castle Court, Westgate Street, Cardiff. *T:* Cardiff 44338.

GOSS, Very Rev. Thomas Ashworth; Dean of Jersey, since 1971; *b* 27 July 1912; *s* of George Woolnough Goss and Maud M. (*née* Savage); *m* 1946, Frances Violet Patience Frampton; one *s* one *d. Educ:* Shardlow Hall; Aldenham Sch.; St Andrews Univ. (MA). Deacon, 1937; Priest, 1938; Curate of Frodingham, 1937-41. Chaplain, RAFVR, 1941-47 (PoW Japan, 1942-45). Vicar of Sutton-le-Marsh, 1947-51; Chaplain, RAF, 1951-67; QHC, 1966-67. Rector of St Saviour, Jersey, 1967-71. *Recreations:* gardening, theatricals. *Address:* The Deanery, Jersey, CI. *T:* Jersey 20001. *Clubs:* Royal Air Force; Victoria, Commonwealth Parliamentary, Société Jersiaise (Jersey).

GOSTLING, Maj.-Gen. Philip le Marchant Stonhouse S.; *see* Stonhouse-Gostling.

GOTLEY, Roger Alwyn H.; *see* Henniker-Gotley.

GOTTLIEB, Bernard, CB 1970; retired; *b* 1913; *s* of late James Gottlieb and Pauline (*née* Littaur); *m* 1955, Sybil N. Epstein; one *s* one *d. Educ:* Haberdashers' Hampstead Sch.; Queen Mary Coll., London Univ. BSc First Class Maths, 1932. Entered Civil Service as an Executive Officer in Customs and Excise, 1932. Air Ministry, 1938; Asst Private Sec., 1941, and Private Sec., 1944, to Permanent Under-Sec. of State (late Sir Arthur Street), Control Office for Germany and Austria, 1945; Asst Sec., 1946. Seconded to National Coal Board, 1946; Min. of Power, 1950; Under-Sec., 1961, Dir of

Establishments, 1965-69; Under-Sec., Min. of Posts and Telecommunications, 1969-73; Secretariat, Pay Board, 1973-74, Royal Commn for Distribution of Income and Wealth, 1974-78. Gwilym Gibbon Research Fellow, Nuffield Coll., Oxford, 1952-53. *Address:* 49 Gresham Gardens, NW11. *T:* 01-455 6172. *Club:* Reform.

GOTTMANN, Prof. Jean, FRGS; FBA 1977; Professor of Geography, University of Oxford, since 1968; Fellow of Hertford College, Oxford, 1968; *b* 10 Oct. 1915; *s* of Elie Gottmann and Sonia-Fanny Ettinger Gottmann; *m* 1957, Bernice Adelson. *Educ:* Lycée Montaigne; Lycée St Louis; Sorbonne. Research Asst Human Geography, Sorbonne, 1937-40; Mem., Inst. for Advanced Study, Princeton, NJ, several times, 1942-65; Lectr, then Associate Prof. in Geography, Johns Hopkins Univ., Baltimore, 1943-48; Dir of Studies and Research, UN Secretariat, NY, 1946-47; Chargé de Recherches, CNRS, Paris, 1948-51; Lectr, then Prof., Institut d'Etudes Politiques, University of Paris, 1948-56; Research Dir, Twentieth Century Fund, NY, 1956-61; Prof. Ecole des Hautes Etudes, Sorbonne, 1960-. Pres., World Soc. for Ekistics, 1971-73. Governor, Univ. of Haifa, 1972-. Hon. Member: Royal Netherlands Geog. Soc., 1963; Soc. Géographique de Liège, 1977; Società Geografica Italiana, 1981; For. Hon. Mem., Amer. Acad. of Arts and Sciences, 1972. Hon. LLD Wisconsin, 1968; Hon. DSc S Illinois, 1969. Charles Daly Medal of Amer. Geograph. Soc., 1964; Prix Bonaparte-Wyse, 1962; Palmes Académiques, 1968; Victoria Medal, RGS, 1980. Hon. Citizen: Yokohama, 1976; Guadalajara, 1978. Chevalier, Légion d'Honneur, 1974. *Publications:* Relations Commerciales de la France, 1942; L'Amérique, 1949 (3rd edn 1960); A Geography of Europe, 1950 (4th edn 1969); La politique des Etats et leur géographie, 1952; Virginia at Mid-century, 1955; Megalopolis, 1961; Essais sur l'Aménagement de l'Espace habité, 1966; The Significance of Territory, 1973; Centre and Periphery, 1980. *Address:* 19 Belsyre Court, Woodstock Road, Oxford. *T:* Oxford 57076. *Club:* United Oxford & Cambridge University.

GOUDGE, Elizabeth de Beauchamp; FRSL 1945; *b* 24 April 1900; *d* of late Henry Leighton Goudge, Regius Professor of Divinity in the University of Oxford, and late Ida de Beauchamp Collenette; unmarried. *Educ:* Grassendale, Southbourne; Reading Univ. Writer of novels, children's books, short stories and plays. *Publications: novels:* Island Magic, 1932; The Middle Window, 1933; A City of Bells, 1934; Towers in the Mist, 1936; The Bird in the Tree, 1939; The Castle on the Hill, 1942; Green Dolphin Country, 1944; The Herb of Grace, 1948; Gentian Hill, 1950; The Heart of the Family, 1953; The Rosemary Tree, 1956; The White Witch, 1958; The Dean's Watch, 1960; The Scent of Water, 1963; The Child from the Sea, 1970; *collections of short stories:* Make-Believe, 1949; The Reward of Faith, 1950; White Wings, 1952; The Lost Angel, 1971; *plays:* Three Plays, 1937; *Children's books:* Smokey House, 1938; Henrietta's House (in America: The Blue Hills), 1942; The Little White Horse, 1946 (awarded Carnegie Medal for 1947); The Valley of Song, 1951; Linnets and Valerians, 1964; *biography:* God so Loved the World (Life of Christ), 1951; St Francis of Assisi, 1959; *autobiography:* The Joy of the Snow, 1974; Anthology of Verse and Prose: A Book of Comfort, 1964; 2nd Anthology of Verse and Prose: A Book of Peace, 1967; 3rd Anthology of Verse and Prose: A Book of Faith, 1976. *Recreations:* reading and gardening. *Address:* Rose Cottage, Peppard Common, Henley-on-Thames, Oxon.

GOUDIE, Rev. John Carrick, CBE 1972; on staff of Royal Scottish Corporation, London, since 1980; *b* 25 Dec. 1919; *s* of late Rev. John Goudie, MA and late Mrs Janet Goudie, step *s* of late Mrs Evelyn Goudie; unmarried. *Educ:* Glasgow Academy; Glasgow Univ. (MA); Trinity Coll., Glasgow. Served in RN: Hostilities Only Ordinary Seaman and later Lieut RNVR, 1941-45; returned to Trinity Coll., Glasgow to complete studies for the Ministry, 1945; Asst Minister at Crown Court Church of Scotland, London and ordained, 1947-50; Minister, The Union Church, Greenock, 1950-53; entered RN as Chaplain, 1953; Principal Chaplain, Church of Scotland and Free Churches (Naval), 1970-73; on staff of St Columba's Church of Scotland, Pont Street, 1973-77; Minister of Christ Church URC, Wallington, 1977-80. QHC 1970-73. *Recreations:* tennis, the theatre. *Address:* 501 Frobisher House, Dolphin Square, SW1V 3LL. *T:* 01-828 2806. *Club:* Army and Navy.

GOUDIE, Hon. William Henry, MC 1944; Executive Director and Deputy Chairman, Law Reform Commission of Tasmania, since 1974; *b* 21 Aug. 1916; *s* of Henry and Florence Goudie; *m* 1948, Mourilyan Isobel Munro; two *s. Educ:* Bristol Grammar School. Solicitor (England), 1938; called to Bar, Gray's Inn, 1952. War service, 1939-45, London Scottish Regt and Som LI; JAG's Dept, 1945-48; Prosecutor, Dep. JA, Officer i/c branches Italy, Greece, Austria; Officer i/c Legal Section War Crimes Gp, SE Europe; Sen. Resident Magistrate, Acting Judge, Kenya, 1948-63; Puisne Judge, Aden, 1963-66; Puisne Judge, Uganda (Contract), 1967-71; Puisne Judge, Fiji (Contract), 1971-73. Editor, Kenya and Aden Law Reports. *Recreations:* golf, swimming. *Address:* 24 Nimala Street, Rosny, Hobart, Tasmania 7018, Australia. *Club:* Royal Commonwealth Society.

GOUGH, family name of Viscount Gough.

GOUGH, 5th Viscount (of Goojerat, of the Punjaub, and Limerick), *cr* 1849; **Shane Hugh Maryon Gough;** Irish Guards, 1961-67; *b* 26 Aug. 1941; *o s* of 4th Viscount Gough and Margaretta Elizabeth (*d* 1977), *o d* of Sir Spencer Maryon-Wilson, 11th Bt; *S* father 1951. *Educ:* Abberley Hall, Worcs; Winchester Coll. Mem. Queen's Bodyguard for Scotland, Royal Company of Archers. *Heir:* none. *Address:* Keppoch Estate Office, Strathpeffer, Ross-shire, IV14 9AD. *T:* Strathpeffer 224; 17 Stanhope Gardens, SW7 5RQ. *T:* 01-370 3569. *Clubs:* Pratt's, White's; MCC.

GOUGH, Cecil Ernest Freeman, CMG 1956; Director and Secretary, 1974-78, Assistant Director-General, 1978-80, acting Director-General, 1980-81, British Property Federation; *b* 29 Oct. 1911; *s* of Ernest John Gough; *m* 1938, Gwendolen Lily Miriam Longman; one *s* one *d. Educ:* Southend High Sch.; London Sch. of Economics (evening student) (School of Economics Scholar in Law, 1932). LLB 1934. Asst Examiner Estate Duty Office, Board of Inland Revenue, 1930; Air Ministry, 1938; Principal, 1944; Ministry of Defence, 1947; Asst Sec., 1949; on loan to Foreign Office, as Counsellor, United Kingdom Delegation to NATO, Paris, 1952-56; Chairman: NATO Infrastructure Cttee, 1952-53; Standing Armaments Cttee Western European Union, 1956; returned Ministry of Defence, 1956; Under-Sec., 1958; Under-Sec. at the Admiralty, 1962-64; Asst Under-Sec. of State, Min. of Defence, 1964-68. Man. Dir, Airwork (Overseas) Ltd, 1968-71; Dir, Airwork Services Ltd and Air Holdings Ltd, 1968-73; Sec., Associated Owners of City Properties, 1975-77. Medal of Freedom (USA), 1946; Coronation Medal, 1953. *Recreations:* cookery, gardening, reading, travel. *Address:* 23 Howbridge Road, Witham, Essex CM8 1BY. *T:* Witham 518969. *Club:* Naval and Military.

GOUGH, Brig. Guy Francis, DSO; MC; late Royal Irish Fusiliers; *b* 9 Aug. 1893; *e s* of late Hugh George Gough, Hyderabad, Deccan; *m* 1st, 1914, Dorothy (*d* 1953), *d* of late Edwin Paget Palmer, Patcham House, Sussex; one *s* one *d* ; *m* 2nd, 1954, Elizabeth Treharn, *d* of Lewis David Thomas, Newton, near Porthcawl. *Educ:* The Oratory Sch.; RMC Sandhurst. 2nd Lieut, Royal Irish Fusiliers, Aug. 1914; European War, 1914-18. France and Belgium with 1st Royal Irish Fusiliers, and on the Staff (wounded, despatches, MC, 1915 Star); Staff Course, 1916. Commanded 1st Bn Nigeria Regt, 1936-37; War of 1939-45: Commanded ITC Royal Irish Fusiliers, 1st Battalion Royal Irish Fusiliers (in France and Belgium, May 1940), 202nd and 11th Infantry Brigades, Advanced Base I Army (N Africa), North Aldershot Sub-District. DSO, 1939-45 Star, Africa Star (with 1st Army clasp); retd pay, 1946. Control Commission, Germany as a Senior Control Officer, 1947-48. Coronation Medal, 1937. *Address:* Glyn Deri, Talybont-on-Usk, near Brecon, Powys LD3 7YP.

GOUGH, Rt. Rev. Hugh Rowlands, CMG 1965; OBE (mil.) 1945; TD 1950; DD Lambeth; *b* 19 Sept. 1905; *o s* of late Rev. Charles Massey Gough, Rector of St Ebbe's, Oxford; *m* 1929, Hon. Madeline Elizabeth, *d* of 12th Baron Kinnaird, KT, KBE; one *d. Educ:* Weymouth Coll.; Trinity Coll., Cambridge; London Coll. Divinity. BA 1927, MA Cantab 1931. Deacon, 1928; Priest, 1929; Curate of St Mary, Islington, 1928-31; Perpetual Curate of St Paul, Walcot, Bath, 1931-34; Vicar of St James, Carlisle, 1934-39; Chaplain to High Sheriff of Cumberland, 1937; CF (TA), 1937-45; Chaplain to 4th Bn The Border Regt, 1937-39; Vicar of St Matthew, Bayswater 1939-46; Chaplain to 1st Bn London Rifle Bde, 1939-43; served Western Desert and Tunisia (wounded); Senior Chap. to 1st Armd Div., Tunisia, 1943; DACG 10 Corps, Italy, 1943-45 (despatches); DACG, North Midland Dist, 1945. Hon. Chaplain to the Forces (2nd cl.) 1945. Vicar of Islington, Rural Dean of Islington, 1946-48. Preb. St Paul's Cathedral, 1948; Suffragan Bishop of Barking, 1948-59; Archdeacon of West Ham, 1948-58; Archbishop of Sydney and Primate of Australia, also Metropolitan of New South Wales, 1959-66, retired, 1966. Rector of Freshford, dio. of Bath and Wells, 1967-72; Vicar of Limpley Stoke, 1970-72. Chaplain and Sub-Prelate, Order of St John of Jerusalem, 1959-72. Formerly Member Council: London Coll. of Divinity, Clifton Theol. Coll. (Chm.), Haileybury Coll., Monkton Combe Sch., St Lawrence Coll. (Ramsgate), Chigwell Sch., Stowe Sch., Kingham Hill Trust. Golden Lectr Haberdashers' Co., 1953 and 1955. Pres. Conference, Educational Assoc., 1956. Mem., Essex County Education Cttee, 1949-59; DL Essex, 1952-59. Hon. DD Wycliffe Coll., Toronto; Hon. ThD, Aust. *Recreations:* shooting, tennis. *Address:* The Forge, Over Wallop, Stockbridge, Hants. *T:* Wallop 315. *Club:* National.

GOUGH, John, CBE 1972; Director of Administration, and Secretary, Confederation of British Industry, 1965-74; *b* 18 June 1910; *o s* of H. E. and M. Gough; *m* 1939, Joan Renee Cooper; one *s* one *d. Educ:* Repton Sch.; Keble Coll., Oxford. BA 1st cl. hons History. Senior History Tutor, Stowe Sch., 1933; Fedn of British Industries: Personal Asst to Dir, 1934; Asst Sec., 1940; Sec., 1959; Dir of Administration and Sec., CBI, 1965. *Recreations:* walking, reading, music. *Address:* West Yard, North Bovey, Newton Abbot, Devon. *T:* Moretonhampstead 395. *Club:* Reform.

GOUGH-CALTHORPE, family name of **Baron Calthorpe.**

GOULD, Bryan Charles; journalist, in press and television; Presenter/Reporter, TV Eye, Thames Television, since 1979; *b* 11 Feb. 1939; *s* of Charles Terence Gould and Elsie May Driller; *m* 1967, Gillian Anne Harrigan; one *s* one *d. Educ:* Auckland Univ. (BA, LLM); Balliol Coll., Oxford (MA, BCL). HM Diplomatic Service: FO, 1964-66; HM Embassy, Brussels, 1966-68; Fellow and Tutor in Law, Worcester Coll., Oxford, 1968-74. MP (Lab) Southampton Test, Oct. 1974-1979; Prospective Parly Cand. (Lab), Barking, Dagenham, 1982-. *Recreations:* gardening, food, wine. *Address:* Marymead, Russells Water, near Henley, Oxon.

GOULD, Cecil Hilton Monk; Keeper and Deputy Director of the National Gallery, 1973-78; *b* 24 May 1918; *s* of late Lieut Commander R. T. Gould

and Muriel Hilda Estall. *Educ:* Westminster Sch. Served in Royal Air Force: France, 1940; Middle East, 1941-43; Italy, 1943-44; Normandy, Belgium and Germany, 1944-46. National Gallery: Asst Keeper, 1946; Dep. Keeper, 1962. Vis. Lectr, Melbourne Univ., 1978. FRSA 1968. *Publications:* An Introduction to Italian Renaissance Painting, 1957; Trophy of Conquest, 1965; Leonardo da Vinci, 1975; The Paintings of Correggio, 1976; Bernini in France, 1981; various publications for the National Gallery, including 16th-century Italian Schools catalogue; articles in Encyclopædia Britannica, Chambers's Encyclopedia, Dizionario Biografico degli Italiani, and specialist art journals of Europe and USA. *Recreations:* music, ski-ing. *Address:* Jubilee House, Thorncombe, Dorset. *Club:* Reform.

GOULD, Donald (William), BSc (Physiol.), MRCS, DTM&H; writer and broadcaster on medical and scientific affairs; *b* 26 Jan. 1919; *s* of late Rev. Frank J. Gould; *m* 1st, 1940, Edna Forsyth; three *s* four *d* ; 2nd, 1969, Jennifer Goodfellow; one *s* one *d. Educ:* Mill Hill Sch.; St Thomas's Hosp. Med. Sch., London. Orthopædic House Surg., Botley's Park Hosp., 1942; Surg. Lieut, RNVR, 1942-46; Med. Off., Hong Kong Govt Med. Dept, 1946-48; Lectr in Physiol., University of Hong Kong, 1948-51, Sen. Lectr, 1951-57; King Edward VII Prof. of Physiol., University of Malaya (Singapore), 1957-60; Lectr in Physiol., St Bartholomew's Hosp. Med. Coll., London, 1960-61, Sen. Lectr, 1961-63; External Examr in Physiol., University of Durham (Newcastle), 1961-63; Dep. Ed., Medical News, 1963-65; Editor: World Medicine, 1965-66; New Scientist, 1966-69; Med. Correspondent, New Statesman, 1966-78. Chm., Med. Journalists' Assoc., 1967-71; Vice-Chm., Assoc. of British Science Writers, 1970-71. *Publications:* contributions to: Experimentation with Human Subjects, 1972; Ecology, the Shaping Enquiry, 1972; Better Social Services, 1973; scientific papers in physiological jls; numerous articles on medical politics, ethics and science in lay and professional press. *Recreations:* writing poems nobody will publish, listening, talking, and walking. *Address:* 15 Waterbeach Road, Landbeach, Cambs CB4 4EA. *T:* Cambridge 861243.

GOULD, Maj.-Gen. John Charles, CB 1975; Paymaster-in-Chief and Inspector of Army Pay Services, 1972-75, retired; *b* 27 April 1915; *s* of late Alfred George Webb and Hilda Gould; *m* 1941, Mollie Bannister; one *s* one *d. Educ:* Brighton, Hove and Sussex Grammar School. Surrey and Sussex Yeomanry (TA), 1937; Royal Army Pay Corps, 1941; served: N Africa, Sicily, Italy (despatches), Austria, 1941-46; Egypt, Jordan, Eritrea, 1948-51; Singapore, 1957-59; Dep. Paymaster-in-Chief, 1967-72. *Recreations:* golf, bridge. *Address:* Squirrels Wood, Ringles Cross, near Uckfield, East Sussex TN22 1HB. *T:* Uckfield 4592. *Clubs:* Lansdowne, MCC; Piltdown Golf.

GOULD, Joyce Brenda; Assistant National Agent and Chief Women's Officer of the Labour Party, since 1975; *b* 29 Oct. 1932; *d* of Sydney and Fanny Manson; *m* 1952, Kevin Gould (separated); one *d. Educ:* Cowper Street Primary Sch.; Roundhay High Sch. for Girls; Bradford Technical Coll. Dispenser, 1952-65; Asst Regional Organiser, Labour Party, 1969-75. Sec., National Jt Cttee of Working Women's Orgns, 1975-; Vice-Pres., Socialist Internat. Women, 1978-. *Publications:* (ed) Women and Health, 1979; pamphlets on feminism, socialism and sexism, women's right to work, and on violence in society; articles and reports on women's rights and welfare. *Recreations:* relaxing, sport as a spectator, theatre, cinema, reading. *Address:* Flat 1, 31 Dennington Park Road, NW6 1BB. *T:* 01-435 5085.

GOULD, Patricia, CBE 1978; RRC 1972; Matron-in-Chief, Queen Alexandra's Royal Naval Nursing Service, 1976-80; *b* 27 May 1924; *d* of Arthur Wellesley Gould. *Educ:* Marist Convent, Paignton. Lewisham Gen. Hosp., SRN, 1945; Hackney Hosp., CMB Pt I, 1946; entered QARNNS, as Nursing Sister, 1948; accepted for permanent service, 1954; Matron, 1966; Principal Matron, 1970; Principal Matron Naval Hosps, 1975. QHNS 1976-80. OStJ (Comdr Sister), 1977. *Recreations:* gardening, photography. *Address:* 18 Park Road, Denmead, Portsmouth PO7 6NE. *T:* Waterlooville 55499.

GOULD, R(alph) Blair, MB, ChB Sheffield; DA (England); FFARCS; physician, anæsthetist; Fellow Royal Society of Medicine (Member Section of Anæsthetists); Fellow, Internat. College of Anæsthetists, USA; Fellow, Association of Anæsthetists of Great Britain; Hon. Consultant Anæsthetist: St George's Hospital; Royal Throat Nose and Ear Hospital; *b* Edinburgh, 15 May 1904; *o s* of late Maurice Gould, Bournemouth. *Educ:* King Edward VII Sch., Sheffield; Sheffield Univ. Held Senior Resident appointments at Jessop Hospital for Women, Sheffield; Sheffield Royal Hosp., and West London Hosp., Hammersmith; Surg., Canadian Pacific Steamship Co.; lately: Hon. Asst in the Out-patient Dept., Central London Throat, Nose and Ear Hosp.; Clinical Asst, Central London Ophthalmic Hosp.; Clinical Asst, Aural and Children's Depts, West London Hosp.; Specialist in Anæsthetics: Metropolitan Reg. Hosp. Bds, etc; EMS for London; Senior Consultant Anæsthetist: German Hosp.; Brentwood Dist Hosp.; Royal Nat. Throat Hosp.; Sch. of Dental Surgery, Royal Dental Hosp. (also Lectr); Anæsthetist to LCC and Royal Eye Hosp.; Hon. Anæsthetist: St John's Hosp., Lewisham; Romford Victoria Hosp.; Queen Mary's Hosp., Sidcup; Editor, Anæsthesia; *Publications:* various communications to the medical journals. *Recreations:* music, photography. *Address:* 25 Briardale Gardens, NW3. *T:* 01-435 2646.

GOULD, Sir Ronald, Kt 1955; General Secretary, National Union of Teachers, 1947-70; (First) President of World Confederation of Organizations of the Teaching Profession, 1952-70; Member, Community Relations

Commission, 1968-73; *b* 9 Oct. 1904; *s* of late Fred Gould, OBE; *m* 1928, Nellie Denning Fish (*d* 1979); two *s*. *Educ:* Shepton Mallet Grammar Sch.; Westminster Training Coll. Asst Master Radstock Council Sch., 1924-41; Headmaster Welton County Sch., 1941-46. Dep. Chm., ITA, 1967-72. Chm. Norton Radstock UDC, 1936-46; Pres. NUT, 1943-44; Hon. Fellow; Educational Inst. of Scotland; College of Preceptors, 1965. Hon. MA Bristol, 1943; Hon. LLD: British Columbia, 1963; McGill, 1964; St Francis Xavier, NS, 1969; Leeds 1971; DUniv. York 1972. Officier, Ordre des Palmes Académiques, France, 1969; Das Verdienstkreuz (1st Cl.), Germany, 1979. *Publications:* The Changing Pattern of Education, 1965; Chalk Up the Memory (autobiog.), 1976. *Address:* 12 St John's Avenue, Goring by Sea, Worthing, Sussex BN12 4HU.

GOULD, Thomas William, VC 1942; late Lieutenant RNVR; *b* 28 Dec. 1914; *s* of late Mrs C. E. Cheeseman and late Reuben Gould (killed in action, 1916); *m* 1941, Phyllis Eileen Eldridge; one *s*. *Educ:* St James, Dover, Kent. Royal Navy, 1933-37; Submarines, 1937-45 (despatches); invalided Oct. 1945. Business Consultant, 1965-; company director. *Address:* 47 Meadowcroft, St Albans, Herts. *T:* St Albans 61826.

GOULD, Sir Trevor (Jack), Kt 1961; Justice of Appeal, Fiji Court of Appeal, since 1965; *b* 24 June 1906; *s* of Percy Clendon and Elizabeth Margaret Gould; *m* 1934, May Milne; one *s* two *d*. *Educ:* Auckland Gram. Sch.; Auckland Univ. Coll., NZ. Barrister and Solicitor, Supreme Court of New Zealand, 1928; Supreme Court of Fiji, 1934; Crown Counsel, Hong Kong, 1938; served War, 1941-45 (prisoner of war). Actg Puisne Judge, Hong Kong, 1946, Puisne Judge, 1948; Acting Chief Justice, Hong Kong, 1953-55; Senior Puisne Judge, Hong Kong, 1953-58; Justice of Appeal, Court of Appeal for Eastern Africa, 1958-63; Vice-Pres. Court of Appeal for Eastern Africa, 1963-65. *Recreation:* sports. *Address:* 21 Mount St John Avenue, Auckland 3, New Zealand. *Club:* The Northern (Auckland).

GOULDEN, Gontran Iceton, OBE 1963; TD 1946 (and 3 Clasps); FRIBA; *b* 5 April 1912; *s* of late H. G. R. Goulden, Canterbury, and Alice Mildred Iceton; *m* 1937, Phyllis Nancye, *d* of J. W. F. Crawfurd, Dublin; two *s* one *d*. *Educ:* St Edmund's Sch., Canterbury; Paris; London Univ. (Dipl.). Commissioned RA (TA) 1931, Capt. 1936, Major 1939; served UK, Ceylon (GSO2 to C-in-C), India and SEAC (CO 6 Indian HAA Regt I Artillery; Comd 13 AA Bde), 1939-45; T/Lieut-Col 1943; A/Brig. 1945 (despatches twice); Lieut-Col 1947, Bt Col 1953. Col 1954; Deputy Commander, 33 AA Brigade, 1954-58; TARO 1960; Hon. Col 452 HAA Rgt RA (TA), 1960-61; Hon. Col 254 Fd Regt RA (TA) 1964-65; Mem. Mddx TA&AFA, 1947-53. Surveyor to Wellcome Archæol. Exped. to Near East, 1934-35; Asst to Graham Dawbarn, 1935-39. Teaching staff of Architectural Association Sch. of Architecture, 1945-46. Chief Tech. Officer and Dep. Dir, the Building Centre, 1947-61, Dir, 1962-68, Dir-Gen., 1968-74; Dep. Chm., Building Centre Gp, 1974-77; Governor, Building Centre Trust, 1974-. Mem. of Council AA, 1949-58 (Pres., 1956-57). Hon. Sec. Modern Architectural Research (MARS) group, 1950-53. Member: Architects Registration Council of the UK, 1954-56, 1963-64, 1971-72; RIBA Council, 1956-57, 1962-65; ARCUK/RIBA Observer Liaison Cttee of Architects of the Common Market, 1963-72; Dir, VIth Congress Intern Union of Architects, 1961; Chm. UIA and Foreign Relations Cttee, RIBA, 1962-65. Treasurer UIA, 1965-75; Mem., Franco-British Union of Architects; Honorary Corresponding Mem. Danish Architectural Assoc., 1965; Pres. International Union of Building Centres, 1962-63, Sec.-Gen. 1969-77; Mem. Council, Modular Soc., 1955-59. Sec., The Architecture Club, 1958-64; Member: Min. of Transport Advisory Cttee on landscaping of trunk roads, 1963-64; Ministry of Public Building and Works Cttee on the Agrément System, 1964-65; General Council of BSI, 1964-67. Governor: St Edmund's Sch., Canterbury; St Margaret's Sch., Bushey, 1949-59. Lecturer and broadcaster on architectural subjects. Hereditary Freeman of City of Canterbury. *Publications:* Bathrooms, 1966; regular contrib. to architectural papers. *Recreations:* travel, sailing. *Address:* 28 St Peter's Square, Hammersmith, W6 9NW. *T:* 01-748 6621.

GOULDEN, (Peter) John; HM Diplomatic Service; Head of News Department, Foreign and Commonwealth Office, since 1982; *b* 21 Feb. 1941; *s* of George Herbert Goulden and Doris Goulden; *m* 1962, Diana Margaret Elizabeth Waite; one *s* one *d*. *Educ:* King Edward VII Sch., Sheffield; Queen's Coll., Oxford (BA 1st Cl. Hons History, 1962). FCO (formerly FO), 1962-: Ankara, 1963-67; Manila, 1969-70; Dublin, 1976-79; Head of Personnel Services Dept, 1980-82. *Recreations:* early music, bookbinding, squash. *Address:* c/o Foreign and Commonwealth Office, King Charles Street, SW1.

GOULDING, Hon. Sir (Ernest) Irvine, Kt 1971; **Hon. Mr Justice Goulding;** Judge of the High Court of Justice, Chancery Division, since 1971; *b* 1 May 1910; *s* of late Dr Ernest Goulding; *m* 1935, Gladys (*d* 1981), *d* of late Engineer Rear-Adm. Marrack Sennett; one *s* one *d*. *Educ:* Merchant Taylors' Sch., London; St Catharine's Coll., Cambridge, Hon. Fellow, 1971. Served as Instructor Officer, Royal Navy, 1931-36 and 1939-45. Called to Bar, Inner Temple, 1936; QC 1961; Bencher, Lincoln's Inn, 1966. Pres., Internat. Law Assoc., British branch, 1972-81. *Address:* 9 Constitution Hill, Woking, Surrey. *T:* Woking 61012. *Club:* Travellers'.
See also M. I. Goulding.

GOULDING, Sir Lingard; see Goulding, Sir W. L. W.

GOULDING, Marrack Irvine; HM Diplomatic Service; Counsellor and Head of Chancery, UK Mission to United Nations, New York, since 1979; *b* 2 Sept. 1936; *s* of Hon. Sir Irvine Goulding, *qv* ; *m* 1961, Susan Rhoda D'Albiac, *d* of Air Marshal Sir John D'Albiac, KCVO, KBE, CB, DSO, and of Lady D'Albiac; two *s* one *d*. *Educ:* St Paul's Sch.; Magdalen Coll., Oxford (1st cl. hons. Lit. Hum. 1959). Joined HM Foreign (later Diplomatic) Service, 1959; MECAS, 1959-61; Kuwait, 1961-64; Foreign Office, 1964-68; Tripoli (Libya), 1968-70; Cairo, 1970-72; Private Sec., Minister of State for Foreign and Commonwealth Affairs, 1972-75; seconded to Cabinet Office (CPRS), 1975-77; Counsellor, Lisbon, 1977-79. *Recreations:* travel, birdwatching. *Address:* c/o Foreign and Commonwealth Office, SW1A 2AH; Fairway, Rowe Lane, Pirbright, Surrey. *T:* Brookwood 2673.

GOULDING, Lt-Col Terence Leslie Crawford P.; see Pierce-Goulding.

GOULDING, Sir (William) Lingard (Walter), 4th Bt *cr* 1904; Headmaster of Headfort School, since 1977; *b* 11 July 1940; *s* of Sir (William) Basil Goulding, 3rd Bt, and of Valerie Hamilton (Senator, Seanad Eireann), *o d* of 1st Viscount Monckton of Brenchley, PC, GCVO, KCMG, MC, QC; S father, 1982. *Educ:* Ludgrove; Winchester College; Trinity College, Dublin (BA, HDipEd). Computer studies for Zinc Corporation and Sulphide Corporation, Conzinc Rio Tinto of Australia, 1963-66; Systems Analyst, Goulding Fertilisers Ltd, 1966-67; Manager and European Sales Officer for Rionore, modern Irish jewellery company, 1968-69; Racing Driver, formulae 5000, 3 and 2, 1967-71; Assistant Master: Brook House School, 1970-74; Headfort School (IAPS prep. school), 1974-76. *Recreations:* squash, cricket, running, bicycling, tennis, music, reading; computers. *Heir: b* Timothy Adam Goulding, *b* 15 May 1945. *Address:* Headfort School, Kells, Co. Meath. *T:* Kells 65; Dargle Cottage, Enniskerry, Co. Wicklow. *T:* Dublin 862315.

GOURLAY, Gen. Sir (Basil) Ian (Spencer), KCB 1973; OBE 1956 (MBE 1948); MC 1944; Director General, United World Colleges, since 1975; *b* 13 Nov. 1920; *er s* of late Brig. K. I. Gourlay, DSO, OBE, MC; *m* 1948, Natasha Zinovieff; one *s* one *d*. *Educ:* Eastbourne Coll. Commissioned, RM, 1940; HMS Formidable, 1941-44; 43 Commando, 1944-45; 45 Commando, 1946-48; Instructor, RNC Greenwich, 1948-50; Adjt RMFVR, City of London, 1950-52; Instructor, RM Officers' Sch., 1952-54; psc 1954; Bde Major, 3rd Commando Bde, 1955-57 (despatches); OC RM Officers' Trng Wing, Infantry Training Centre RM, 1957-59; 2nd in Comd, 42 Commando, 1959-61; GSO1, HQ Plymouth Gp, 1961-63; CO 42 Commando, 1963-65; Col GS, Dept of CGRM, Min. of Defence, 1965-66; Col 1965; Comdr, 3rd Commando Bde, 1966-68; Maj.-Gen. Royal Marines, Portsmouth, 1968-71; Commandant-General, Royal Marines, 1971-75; Lt-Gen., 1971; Gen., 1973. Admiral, Texas Navy. Vice Patron, RM Museum. *Recreations:* do-it-yourself, watching cricket, playing at golf. *Address:* c/o Lloyds Bank Ltd, 15 Blackheath Village, SE3. *Clubs:* Army and Navy, MCC; Royal Navy Cricket (Vice-Pres.).

GOURLAY, Harry Philp Heggie, JP; DL; MP (Lab) Kirkcaldy, since Feb. 1974 (Kirkcaldy Burghs, 1959-74); *b* 10 July 1916; *s* of William Gourlay; *m* 1942, Margaret McFarlane Ingram; no *c*. *Educ:* Kirkcaldy High Sch. Coachbuilder, 1932; Vehicle Examiner, 1947. Mem. Kirkcaldy Town Council, 1946, Hon. Treasurer, 1953-57; Magistrate, 1957-59; Vice-Chm. Fife Education Cttee, 1958; Mem. Hospital Management Cttee; Sec. Kirkcaldy Burghs Constituency Labour Party, 1945-59; Mem. Estimates Cttee, 1959-64; Chm. Scottish Parly Labour Group, 1963-64 and 1976-77; Government Whip, 1964-66; a Lord Comr of the Treasury, 1966-68; Dep. Speaker and Dep. Chm. of Ways and Means, 1968-70; Mem., Select Cttee on Procedure, 1974-79; Chm., Scottish Grand Cttee, 1979-. DL Fife, 1978. *Recreations:* chess, golf. *Address:* 34 Rosemount Avenue, Kirkcaldy, Fife. *T:* Kirkcaldy 61919.

GOURLAY, Gen. Sir Ian; see Gourlay, Gen. Sir B. I. S.

GOURLAY, Dame Janet; see Vaughan, Dame Janet.

GOW, Ian, TD 1970; MP (C) Eastbourne since Feb. 1974; *b* 11 Feb. 1937; *yr s* of late Dr and Mrs A. E. Gow; *m* 1966, Jane Elizabeth Packe; two *s*. *Educ:* Winchester. Commnd 15th/19th Hussars, 1956. Solicitor 1962. Contested (C): Coventry East, 1964; Clapham, 1966. PPS to the Prime Minister, May 1979-. *Recreations:* tennis, cricket, gardening. *Address:* The Dog House, Hankham, Pevensey, East Sussex. *T:* Eastbourne 763316; 25 Chester Way, Kennington, SE11. *T:* 01-582 6626. *Clubs:* Carlton, Pratt's, Cavalry and Guards, MCC.

GOW, Gen. Sir (James) Michael, KCB 1979; C-in-C BAOR and Commander, Northern Army Group, 1980-July 1983; ADC General to the Queen, since 1981; *b* 3 June 1924; *s* of late J. C. Gow and Mrs Alastair Sanderson; *m* 1946, Jane Emily Scott; one *s* four *d*. *Educ:* Winchester College. Commnd Scots Guards, 1943; served NW Europe, 1944-45; Malayan Emergency, 1949; Equerry to Duke of Gloucester, 1952-53; psc 1954; Bde Major 1955-57; Regimental Adjt Scots Guards, 1957-60; Instructor Army Staff Coll., 1962-64; comd 2nd Bn Scots Guards, Kenya and England, 1964-66; GSO1, HQ London District, 1966-67; comd 4th Guards Bde, 1968-70; idc 1970; BGS (Int) HQ BAOR and ACOS G2 HQ Northag, 1971-73; GOC 4th Div. BAOR, 1973-75; Dir of Army Training, 1975-78; GOC Scotland and Governor of Edinburgh Castle, 1979-80. Colonel Commandant: Intelligence Corps, 1973-; Scottish Division, 1979-80. Brig., Royal Company of Archers, Queen's Body Guard for Scotland. County Comr, British Scouts W Europe, 1980. Freeman, City of London, 1980; Freeman and Liveryman,

Painters' and Stainers' Co., 1980. *Publications:* articles in mil. and hist. jls. *Recreations:* sailing, squash, music, travel, reading. *Address:* c/o Lloyds Bank Ltd (Guards and Cavalry), Cox's & King's Branch, 6 Pall Mall, SW1Y 5NH. *Clubs:* Pratt's; New (Edinburgh).

GOW, Brig. John Wesley Harper, CBE 1958 (OBE 1945); DL; JP; retired Shipowner; *b* 8 April 1898; *s* of late Leonard Gow, DL, LLD, Glasgow, and Mabel A. Harper, *d* of John W. Harper, publisher, Cedar Knoll, Long Island, NY; *m* 1925, Frances Jean, JP (*d* 1975), *d* of James Begg, Westlands, Paisley; three *s. Educ:* Cargilfield; Sedbergh; RMC Sandhurst; Trinity Coll., Oxford. Entered Scots Guards, 1917; severely wounded, France. Late partner, Gow Harrison & Co. Mem. Queen's Body Guard for Scotland (Royal Company of Archers), 1941. MFH, Lanarkshire and Renfrewshire, 1949-54; Pres. Royal Caledonian Curling Club, 1958-60; Chm. West Renfrewshire Unionist Assoc., 1947-60, Pres. 1960-68; Life Vice-Pres., RNLI, 1978 (Chm. Glasgow Branch, 1937-73); Mem. Council, SS&AFA, 1961-73 (Pres., West of Scotland Br.; Pres., Glasgow Branch, 1955-73); Member Council: Erskine Hosp., 1946-78 (Hon. Pres., 1978); Earl Haig Fund Officers Assoc. (Scotland), 1946-75; Mem. Glasgow TA & AFA, 1947-56. Served War of 1939-45: Scots Guards, RARO; Lt-Col attached RA (LAA), NW Europe; commanded 77 AA Bde, RA (TA), 1947-48; Brig. 1948. Hon. Col 483 HAA (Blythswood) Regt RA, TA, 1951-56; Hon. Col 445 LAA Regt RA (Cameronians) TA, 1959-67, later 445 (Lowland) Regt RA (TA). DL Renfrewshire (formerly City of Glasgow), 1948; JP Renfrewshire, 1952. Lord Dean of Guild, Glasgow, 1965-67. OStJ 1969. Chevalier Order of Crown of Belgium and Croix de Guerre (Belgian), 1945. *Recreations:* curling, hunting, shooting. *Address:* The Old School House, Beith Road, Howwood, Renfrewshire PA9 1AW. *T:* Kilbarchan 2503. *Clubs:* Army and Navy; Western (Glasgow); Prestwick Golf.

GOW, Leonard Maxwell H.; *see* Harper Gow.

GOW, Gen. Sir Michael; *see* Gow, Gen. Sir J. M.

GOW, Neil, QC (Scot.) 1970; Sheriff of South Strathclyde, at Ayr, since 1976; *b* 24 April 1932; *s* of Donald Gow, oil merchant, Glasgow; *m* 1959, Joanna, *d* of Comdr S. D. Sutherland, Edinburgh; one *s. Educ:* Merchiston Castle Sch., Edinburgh; Glasgow and Edinburgh Univs. MA, LLB. Formerly Captain, Intelligence Corps (BAOR). Carnegie Scholar in History of Scots Law, 1956. Advocate, 1957-76. Standing Counsel to Min. of Social Security (Scot.), 1964-70. Contested (C: Kirkcaldy Burghs, Gen. Elections of 1964 and 1966; Edinburgh East, 1970; Mem. Regional Council, Scottish Conservative Assoc. An Hon. Sheriff of Lanarkshire, 1971. Pres., Auchinleck Boswell Soc. FSA (Scot.). *Publications:* A History of Scottish Statutes, 1959; Jt Editor, An Outline of Estate Duty in Scotland, 1970; A History of Belmont House School, 1979; numerous articles and broadcasts on legal topics and Scottish affairs. *Recreations:* golf, books, antiquities. *Address:* Old Auchenfail Hall, by Mauchline, Ayrshire. *T:* Mauchline 50822. *Clubs:* Western (Glasgow); Prestwick Golf.

GOW, Dame Wendy; *see* Hiller, Dame Wendy.

GOW, Very Rev. William Connell; Dean of Moray, Ross and Caithness, 1960-77, retired; Canon of St Andrew's Cathedral, Inverness, 1953-77, Hon. Canon, since 1977; Rector of St James', Dingwall, 1940-77; *b* 6 Jan. 1909; *s* of Alexander Gow, Errol, Perthshire; *m* 1938, Edith Mary, *d* of John William Jarvis, Scarborough; two *s. Educ:* Edinburgh Theological Coll.; Durham Univ. (LTh). Deacon, 1936; Priest, 1937; Curate St Mary Magdalene's, Dundee, 1936-39. Awarded Frihetsmedalje (by King Haakon), Norway, 1947. *Recreations:* fishing, bridge. *Address:* 14 Mackenzie Place, Maryburgh, Ross-shire.

GOWANS, Sir Gregory; *see* Gowans, Sir U. G.

GOWANS, Sir James (Learmonth), Kt 1982; CBE 1971; FRCP 1975; FRS 1963; Deputy Chairman, since 1978, Secretary, since 1977, Medical Research Council; *b* 7 May 1924; *s* of John Gowans and Selma Josefina Ljung; *m* 1956, Moyra Leatham; one *s* two *d. Educ:* Trinity Sch., Croydon; King's Coll. Hosp. Med. Sch. (Fellow, 1979); Lincoln Coll., Oxford. MB, BS (London) 1947; MA, DPhil (Oxford) 1953. Medical Research Council Exchange Scholar, Pasteur Institute, Paris, 1953; Staines Medical Research Fellow, Exeter Coll., Oxford, 1955-60. Fellow, St Catherine's Coll., Oxford, 1961-; Henry Dale Res. Prof. of Royal Society, 1962-77; Hon. Dir, MRC Cellular Immunology Unit, 1963-77; Member: MRC, 1965-69; Adv. Bd for Res. Councils, 1977-; Chm. Biological Research Bd, 1967-69. Royal Society: Mem. Council and a Vice-Pres., 1973-75; Assessor to MRC, 1973-75. Lectures: Harvey, NY, 1968; Sharpey-Schafer, Edinburgh, 1969; William Withering, Birmingham, 1970; Foundation, RCPath, 1970; Dunham, Harvard, 1971; Thomas Young, St George's Hosp. Med. Sch., 1971; Bayne-Jones, Johns Hopkins, 1973. Hon. Member: Amer. Assoc. of Immunologists; Amer. Soc. of Anatomists. Hon. ScD Yale, 1966; Hon. DSc: Chicago, 1971; Birmingham, 1978; Hon. MD Edinburgh, 1979. Gairdner Foundn Award, 1968; Paul Ehrlich Award, 1974; Royal Medal, Royal Society, 1976; Feldberg Foundn Award, 1979; Wolf Prize in Medicine, 1980. *Publications:* articles in scientific journals. *Address:* Medical Research Council, 20 Park Crescent, W1N 4AL.

GOWANS, James Palmer, JP; Lord Provost of Dundee and Lord-Lieutenant of the City of Dundee, since 1980; *b* 15 Sept. 1930; *s* of Charles Gowans and Sarah Gowans (*née* Palmer); *m* 1950, Davina Barnett; one *s* four *d* (and one *s* decd). *Educ:* Rockwell Secondary School, Dundee. Joined National Cash Register Co., Dundee, 1956; now employed testing electronic modules. Elected to Dundee DC, May 1974. JP 1977. *Recreations:* golf, motoring. *Address:* 41 Dalmahoy Drive, Dundee DD2 3UT. *T:* Dundee 84918.

GOWANS, Hon. Sir (Urban) Gregory, Kt 1974; Judge of Supreme Court of Victoria, Australia, 1961-76; *b* 9 Sept. 1904; *s* of late James and Hannah Theresa Gowans; *m* 1937, Mona Ann Freeman; one *s* four *d. Educ:* Christian Brothers Coll., Kalgoorlie, WA; Univs of Western Australia and Melbourne. BA (WA) 1924; LLB (Melb.) 1926. Admitted Victorian Bar, 1928; QC 1949; Mem., Overseas Telecommunications Commn (Aust.), 1947-61; Lectr in Industrial Law, Melb. Univ., 1948-56. Constituted Bd of Inquiry into Housing Commn Land Deals, 1977-78. *Publication:* The Victorian Bar: professional conduct practice and etiquette, 1979. *Recreation:* bush walking. *Address:* 68 Studley Park Road, Kew, Melbourne, Australia. *T:* 861-8714. *Club:* Melbourne (Melbourne).

GOWDA, Prof. Deve Javare, (De-Ja-Gou); Vice-Chancellor, University of Mysore, 1969-76; Senior Fellow, International School of Dravidian Linguistics, Trivandrum, Kerala; *b* Chakkare, Bangalore, 6 July 1918; *s* of Deve Gowda; *m* 1943, Savithramma Javare Gowda; one *s* one *d. Educ:* Univ. of Mysore. MA Kannada, 1943. Mysore University: Lectr in Kannada, 1946; Asst Prof. of Kannada and Sec., Univ. Publications, 1955; Controller of Examinations, 1957; Principal, Sahyadri Coll., Shimoga, Mysore Univ., 1960; Prof. of Kannada Studies, 1966. Hon. Dir of Researches, Kuvempu Vidyavardhaka Trust, Mysore. DLit Karnataka, 1975. Soviet Land Award, 1967. *Publications:* (as De-Ja-Gou) numerous books in Kannada; has also edited many works. *Recreations:* writing, gardening. *Address:* Kalanilaya, J. L. Puram, Mysore-12, India. *T:* 21920.

GOWENLOCK, Prof. Brian Glover, PhD, DSc; FRSE; FRSC; Professor of Chemistry, Heriot-Watt University, since 1966; *b* 9 Feb. 1926; *s* of Harry Hadfield Gowenlock and Hilda (*née* Glover); *m* 1953, Margaret L. Davies; one *s* two *d. Educ:* Hulme Grammar Sch., Oldham; Univ. of Manchester (BSc, MSc, PhD). DSc Birmingham. FRIC 1966; FRSE 1969. Asst Lectr in Chemistry 1948, Lectr 1951, University Coll. of Swansea; Lectr 1955, Sen. Lectr 1964, Univ. of Birmingham; Dean, Faculty of Science, Heriot-Watt Univ., 1969-72. Vis. Scientist, National Res. Council, Ottawa, 1963; Erskine Vis. Fellow, Univ. of Canterbury, NZ, 1976. Mem., UGC, 1976- (Chm., Physical Scis and Equipment Sub-cttees, 1982-). *Publications:* Experimental Methods in Gas Reactions (with Sir Harry Melville), 1964; First Year at the University (with James C. Blackie), 1964; contribs to scientific jls. *Recreations:* genealogy, foreign travel. *Address:* 49 Lygon Road, Edinburgh EH16 5QA. *T:* 031-667 8506.

GOWER; *see* Leveson Gower.

GOWER, Most Rev. Godfrey Philip, DD; *b* 5 Dec. 1899; *s* of William and Sarah Ann Gower; *m* 1932, Margaret Ethel Tanton; two *s* one *d. Educ:* Imperial College, University of London; St John's College, Winnipeg, University of Manitoba. Served RAF, 1918-19. Deacon 1930; Priest 1931; Rector and Rural Dean of Camrose, Alta, 1932-35; Rector of Christ Church, Edmonton, Alta, 1935-41; Exam. Chaplain to Bishop of Edmonton, 1938-41; Canon of All Saints' Cathedral, 1940-44. Chaplain, RCAF, 1941-44. Rector of St Paul's, Vancouver, 1944-51; Bishop of New Westminster, 1951-71; Archbishop of New Westminster, and Metropolitan of British Columbia, 1968-71. Holds Hon. doctorates in Divinity. *Address:* 305-1520 Vidal Street, White Rock, BC V4B 3T7, Canada. *T:* 531-7254.

GOWER, Sir (Herbert) Raymond, Kt 1974; MP (C) Barry Division of Glamorganshire since 1951; journalist and broadcaster; *b* 15 Aug. 1916; *s* of late Lawford R. Gower, FRIBA, County Architect for Glamorgan, and Mrs Gower; *m* 1973, Cynthia, *d* of Mr and Mrs James Hobbs. *Educ:* Cardiff High Sch.; Univ. of Wales; Cardiff Sch. of Law. Solicitor, admitted 1944; practised Cardiff, 1948-63; Partner, S. R. Freed & Co., Harewood Place, W1, 1964-. Contested (C) Ogmore Division of Glamorgan, general election, 1950. Political Columnist for Western Mail for Cardiff, 1951-64. Parliamentary Private Secretary: to Mr Gurney Braithwaite, 1951-54, to Mr R. Maudling, 1951-52, to Mr J. Profumo, 1952-57, to Mr Hugh Molson, 1954-57, Min. of Transport and Civil Aviation, and to Minister of Works, 1957-60. Member: Speaker's Conf. on Electoral Law, 1967-69, 1971-74; Select Cttee on Expenditure, 1970-73; Treasurer, Welsh Parly Party, 1966-; Vice Chm., Welsh Cons. Members, 1975- (Chm., 1970-74). Jt Founder and Dir, first Welsh Unit Trust. Governor, University Coll., Cardiff, 1951-; Member Court of Governors: National Museum of Wales, 1952-; National Library of Wales, 1951-; University Coll., Aberystwyth, 1953-; Vice-President: National Chamber of Trade, 1956-; Cardiff Business Club, 1952; South Wales Ramblers, 1958-; Sec., Friends of Wales Soc. (Cultural); Mem., Welsh Advisory Council for Civil Aviation, 1959-62; President: Wales Area Conservative Teachers' Assoc., 1962-; Glamorgan (London) Soc., 1967-69. FInstD 1958. *Recreations:* tennis, squash rackets, and travelling in Italy. *Address:* House of Commons, SW1; 45 Winsford Road, Sully, South Glam. *Clubs:* Carlton, Royal Over-Seas League.

GOWER, John Hugh, QC 1967; **His Honour Judge Gower;** a Circuit Judge, since 1972; *b* 6 Nov. 1925; *s* of Henry John Gower, JP and Edith (*née* Brooks); *m* 1960, Shirley Mameena Darbourne; one *s* one *d. Educ:* Skinners'

Sch., Tunbridge Wells. RASC, 1945-48 (Staff Sgt). Called to Bar, Inner Temple, 1948. Dep. Chm., Kent QS, 1968-71. Pres., Tunbridge Wells Council of Voluntary Service, 1974-. Hon. Vice-Pres., Kent Council of Voluntary Service, 1971-. Freeman, City of London (by purchase), 1960. *Recreations:* fishing, foxhunting, gardening. *Address:* The Coppice, Lye Green, Crowborough, East Sussex. *T:* Crowborough 4395.

GOWER, Laurence Cecil Bartlett, FBA 1965; Solicitor; Research Adviser to Department of Trade on Company Law; Professor Emeritus, Southampton University (Hon. Professor of Law, 1972-79); *b* 29 Dec. 1913; *s* of Henry Lawrence Gower; *m* 1939, Helen Margaret Shepperson, *d* of George Francis Birch; two *s* one *d*. *Educ:* Lindisfarne Coll.; University Coll., London. LLB 1933; LLM 1934. Admitted Solicitor, 1937. Served War of 1939-45, with RA and RAOC. Sir Ernest Cassel Prof. of Commercial Law in University of London, 1948-62, Visiting Prof., Law Sch. of Harvard Univ., 1954-55; Adviser on Legal Educn in Africa to Brit. Inst. of Internat. and Comparative Law and Adviser to Nigerian Council of Legal Educn, 1962-65; Prof. and Dean of Faculty of Law of Univ. of Lagos, 1962-65; Law Comr, 1965-71; Vice-Chancellor, Univ. of Southampton, 1971-79. Holmes Lectr, Harvard Univ., 1966. Fellow of University Coll., London; Comr on Company Law Amendment in Ghana, 1958; Member: Jenkins Cttee on Company Law Amendment, 1959-62; Denning Cttee on Legal Education for Students from Africa, 1960; Ormrod Cttee on Legal Education, 1967-71; Royal Commn on the Press, 1975-77. Trustee, British Museum, 1968-. Dir, Pirelli General, 1978-. Hon. Fellow, LSE, 1970; Hon. LLD: York Univ., Ont; Edinburgh Univ.; Dalhousie Univ.; Warwick Univ.; QUB; Southampton Univ.; Hon. DLitt Hong Kong. *Publications:* Principles of Modern Company Law, 1954, 4th edn 1979; Independent Africa: The Challenge to the Legal Profession, 1967; numerous articles in legal periodicals. *Recreation:* travel. *Address:* Flat 3, 26 Willow Road, Hampstead, NW3. *T:* 01-435 2507. *Club:* Athenæum.

GOWER, Sir Raymond; *see* Gower, Sir H. R.

GOWER ISAAC, Anthony John; *see* Isaac.

GOWER-JONES, Ven. Geoffrey; Archdeacon of Lancaster, 1966-80, Archdeacon Emeritus, since 1981; Vicar of St Stephen-on-the-Cliffs, Blackpool, 1950-80; *b* 30 April 1910; *s* of late Rev. William Gower-Jones; *m* 1938, Margaret, *d* of late John Alexander; one *s* one *d*. *Educ:* Brasenose Coll., Oxford; Wells Theological Coll. Ordained 1934; Curate: St Paul, Royton, 1934-39; Prestwich, 1939-43; Vicar, Belfield, 1943-50. Canon of Blackburn, 1962-66; Rural Dean of Fylde, 1962; Rural Dean of Blackpool, 1963-66. *Address:* 7 Egerton Drive, Hale, Cheshire. *T:* 061-980 3886.

GOWING, Prof. Sir Lawrence (Burnett), Kt 1982; CBE 1952; MA Dunelm 1952; ARA 1978; painter and writer on painting; Slade Professor of Fine Art at University College London, since 1975; *b* 21 April 1918; *s* of late Horace Burnett and Louise Gowing; *m* Jennifer Akam Wallis; three *d*. *Educ:* Leighton Park Sch., and as a pupil of William Coldstream. Exhibitions: 1942, 1946, 1948, 1955, 1965, 1982 (Waddington); works in collections of Contemp. Art Soc., Tate Gallery, National Gallery of Canada, National Gallery of South Australia, British Council, Arts Council, Ashmolean Museum and galleries of Brighton, Bristol, Manchester, Middlesbrough, Newcastle, Nottingham, etc. Prof. of Fine Art, Univ. of Durham, and Principal of King Edward VII Sch. of Art, Newcastle upon Tyne, 1948-58; Principal, Chelsea Sch. of Art, 1958-65; Keeper of the British Collection, and Dep. Dir of the Tate Gallery, 1965-67; Prof. of Fine Art, Leeds Univ., 1967-75. Adjunct Prof. of History of Art, Univ. of Pa, 1977-. Mem. Arts Council, 1970-72, and 1977-81, Art Panel, 1953-58, 1959-65, 1969-72, 1976-81, Dep. Chm., 1970-72, 1977-81, Chm. Art Films Cttee, 1970-72; a Trustee of Tate Gallery, 1953-60 and 1961-64; a Trustee of National Portrait Gallery, 1960-; Trustee, British Museum, 1976-81; a Member of National Council for Diplomas in Art and Design, 1961-65; Chairman: Adv. Cttee on Painting, Gulbenkian Foundation, 1958-64. Hon. DLitt Heriot-Watt, 1980. *Publications:* Renoir, 1947; Vermeer, 1952; Cézanne (catalogue of Edinburgh and London exhibns), 1954; Constable, 1960; Vermeer, 1961; Goya, 1965; Turner: Imagination and Reality, 1966; Matisse (Museum of Modern Art, New York), 1966, (Hayward Gallery), 1968; Hogarth (Tate Gallery exhibition), 1971; Watercolours by Cézanne (Newcastle and London exhibn), 1973; Matisse, 1979; many exhibition catalogues and writings in periodicals. *Address:* 49 Walham Grove, SW6. *T:* 01-385 5941.

GOWING, Prof. Margaret Mary, CBE 1981; FBA 1975; FRHistS; Professor of the History of Science, University of Oxford, and Fellow of Linacre College, since 1973; *b* 26 April 1921; *d* of Ronald and Mabel Elliott; *m* 1944, Donald J. G. Gowing (*d* 1969); two *s*. *Educ:* Christ's Hospital; London Sch. of Economics (BSc(Econ)). Bd of Trade, 1941-45; Historical Section, Cabinet Office, 1945-59; Historian and Archivist, UK Atomic Energy Authority, 1959-66; Reader in Contemporary History, Univ. of Kent, 1966-72. Member: Cttee on Deptl Records (Grigg Cttee), 1952-54; Adv. Council on Public Records, 1974-; BBC Archives Adv. Cttee, 1976-79; Public Records Inquiry (Wilson Cttee), 1978-80; Trustee, Nat. Portrait Gall., 1978-. Dir, Contemporary Scientific Archives Centre. Royal Society Wilkins Lectr, 1976; Enid Muir Lectr, Newcastle, 1976; Bernal Lectr, Birkbeck, 1977; Rede Lectr, Cambridge, 1978. Hon. DLitt: Leeds, 1976; Leicester, 1982. *Publications:* (with Sir K. Hancock) British War Economy, 1949; (with E. L. Hargreaves) Civil Industry and Trade, 1952; Britain and Atomic Energy, 1964; Dossier

Secret des Relations Atomiques, 1965; Independence and Deterrence: vol. I, Policy Making, vol. II, Policy Execution, 1974; Reflections on Atomic Energy History, 1978; (with Lorna Arnold) The Atomic Bomb, 1979; various articles and reviews. *Address:* Linacre College, Oxford.

GOWING, Prof. Noel Frank Collett; Emeritus Professor of Pathology, University of London; Consultant Pathologist and Director of the Department of Histopathology, The Royal Marsden Hospital, SW3, 1957-82; Professor of Tumour Pathology (formerly Senior Lecturer), Institute of Cancer Research: The Royal Cancer Hospital, 1971-82; *b* 3 Jan. 1917; *s* of Edward Charles Gowing and Annie Elizabeth Gowing; *m* 1942, Rela Griffel; one *d*. *Educ:* Ardingly Coll., Sussex; London Univ. MRCS, LRCP 1941; MB, BS, London, 1947; MD London, 1948. Served RAMC (Capt.), 1942-46, 52nd (Lowland) Div. Lectr in Pathology, St George's Hosp. Med. Sch., 1947-52; Sen. Lectr in Pathology and Hon. Cons. Pathologist, St George's Hosp., 1952-57. Sometime Examiner in Pathology to: Univ. of London; RCPath; Univ. of Newcastle-upon-Tyne; Univ. of Malta; Nat. Univ. of Malaysia. Lectures: Kettle Meml, RCPath, 1968; Whittick Meml, Saskatchewan Cancer Soc., 1974; Symeonidis Meml, Thessaloniki Cancer Inst., Greece, 1977. Pres., Assoc. of Clinical Pathologists, 1982-83. FRCPath (Founder Fellow, Coll. of Pathologists, 1964). *Publications:* A Colour Atlas of Tumour Histopathology, 1980; articles on pathology in medical journals. *Recreations:* gardening, astronomy. *Address:* 258 Coombe Lane, West Wimbledon, SW20 0RW.

GOWLAND, Rev. William; Principal, Luton Industrial College; President of the Methodist Conference, 1979-80; *b* 3 Oct. 1911; *s* of George and Jane Gowland; *m* 1939, Helen Margaret Qualtrough; three *s* one *d*. *Educ:* Darlington Technical Coll.; Hartley Victoria Coll. Methodist Minister: Port Erin, IOM, 1935-39; Tilehurst, Reading, 1939-48; Albert Hall, Manchester, 1948-54; Luton, 1954-; founded Luton Industrial Mission and Community Centre, 1954, and Luton Indust. Coll., 1957. Mem., NUAAW. *Publications:* Militant and Triumphant, 1954 (Australia 1957, USA 1959); San Francisco, 1960 (Glide Lecture); Youth in Community, 1967 (King George VI Meml Lecture); Men, Machines and Ministry, 1971 (Beckley Lecture); contrib. to jls; research papers. *Recreations:* gardening, photography. *Address:* Luton Industrial College, Chapel Street, Luton, Beds. *T:* Luton 29374.

GOWON, Gen. Yakubu Danjuma; jssc, psc; postgraduate student, Warwick University, since 1978; Head of the Federal Military Government and C-in-C of Armed Forces of the Federal Republic of Nigeria 1966-75; *b* Pankshin Div., Benue-Plateau State, Nigeria, 19 Oct. 1934; *s* of Yohanna Gowon (of Angas tribe, a Christian evangelist of CMS) and Saraya Gowon; *m* 1969, Victoria Hansatu Zakari; one *s* two *d*. *Educ:* St Bartholomew's Sch. (CMS), Wusasa, and Govt Coll., Zaria, Nigeria; Warwick Univ. (BA Hons 1978). Regular Officer, Special Trng Sch., Teshie, Ghana; Eaton Hall Officer Cadet Sch., Chester, RMA, Sandhurst, Staff Coll., Camberley and Joint Services Staff Coll., Latimer (all in England). Enlisted, 1954; Adjt, 4th Bn Nigerian Army, 1960 (Independence Oct. 1960); UN Peace-Keeping Forces, Congo, Nov. 1960-June 1961 and Jan.-June 1963 (Bde Major). Lt-Col and Adjt-Gen., Nigerian Army, 1963; Comd, 2nd Bn, Nigerian Army, Ikeja, 1966; Chief of Staff, 1966; Head of State and C-in-C after July 1966 coup; Maj.-Gen. 1967. Maintained territorial integrity of his country by fighting, 1967-70, to preserve unity of Nigeria (after failure of peaceful measures) following on Ojukwu rebellion, and declared secession of the Eastern region of Nigeria, July 1967; created 12 equal and autonomous states in Nigeria, 1967; Biafran surrender, 1970. Promoted Gen., 1971. Is a Christian; works for internat. peace and security within the framework of OAU and UNO. Hon. LLD Cambridge, 1975; also hon. doctorates from Univs of Ibadan, Lagos, Abu-Zaria, Nigeria at Nsuka, Benin, Ife, and Shaw Univ., USA, 1973. Holds Grand Cross, etc, of several foreign orders. *Publication:* Faith in Unity, 1970. *Recreations:* squash, lawn tennis, pen-drawing, photography, cinephotography. *Address:* c/o Department of Politics, Warwick University, Coventry CV4 7AL.

GOWRIE, 2nd Earl of, *cr* 1945; **Alexander Patric Greysteil Hore-Ruthven;** Baron Ruthven of Gowrie, 1919; Baron Gowrie, 1935; Viscount Ruthven of Canberra, 1945; Minister of State, Northern Ireland Office, since 1981; *b* 26 Nov. 1939; *er s* of late Capt. Hon. Alexander Hardinge Patrick Hore-Ruthven, Rifle Bde, and Pamela Margaret (as Viscountess Ruthven of Canberra, she *m* 1952, Major Derek Cooper, MC, The Life Guards), 2nd *d* of late Rev. A. H. Fletcher; *S* grandfather, 1955; *m* 1st, 1962, Xandra (marr. diss. 1973), *yr d* of Col R. A. G. Bingley, CVO, DSO, OBE; one *s*; 2nd, 1974, Adelheid Gräfin von der Schulenburg, *y d* of late Fritz-Dietlof, Graf von der Schulenburg. *Educ:* Eton; Balliol Coll., Oxford. Visiting Lectr, State Univ. of New York at Buffalo, 1963-64; Tutor, Harvard Univ., 1965-68; Lectr in English and American Literature, UCL, 1969-72. A Conservative Whip, 1971-72; Parly Rep. to UN, 1971; a Lord in Waiting (Govt Whip), 1972-74; Opposition Spokesman on Economic Affairs, 1974-79; Minister of State, Dept of Employment, 1979-81. *Publications:* A Postcard from Don Giovanni, 1972; (jt) The Genius of British Painting, 1975; (jt) The Conservative Opportunity, 1976. *Recreation:* wine. *Heir:* *s* Viscount Ruthven of Canberra, *qv*. *Address:* House of Lords, SW1.

GOYDER, Daniel George; solicitor; Partner, Birketts, Ipswich, since 1968; *b* 26 Aug. 1938; *s* of George Armin Goyder, *qv*; *m* 1962, Jean Mary Dohoo; two *s* two *d*. *Educ:* Rugby Sch.; Trinity Coll., Cambridge (MA, LLB); Harvard Law Sch. (Harkness Commonwealth Fund Fellow, LLM). Admitted Solicitor, 1962; Asst Solicitor, Messrs Allen & Overy, 1964-67. Pt-time Lectr in Law, Univ. of Essex, 1981-. Chm., St Edmundsbury and Ipswich Diocesan Bd of Finance, 1977-; Mem., Monopolies and Mergers Commn, 1980-. *Publication:* (with Sir Alan Neale) The Antitrust Laws of the USA, 3rd edn 1981. *Recreations:* choral singing, table tennis, sport. *Address:* Manor House, Old London Road, Capel St Mary, Ipswich, Suffolk IP9 2JV. *T:* Great Wenham 310583. *Clubs:* Law Society; Ipswich and Suffolk (Ipswich).

GOYDER, George Armin, CBE 1976; Managing Director, British International Paper Ltd, 1935-71; *b* 22 June 1908; *s* of late William Goyder and Lili Julia Kellersberger, Baden, Switzerland; *m* 1937, Rosemary, 4th *d* of Prof. R. C. Bosanquet, Rock, Northumberland; *five s three d. Educ:* Mill Hill Sch.; London Sch. of Economics; abroad. Gen. Man., Newsprint Supply Co., 1940-47 (responsible for procurement supply and rationing of newsprint to British Press); The Geographical Magazine, 1935-58. Mem., Gen. Synod of C of E (formerly Church Assembly), 1948-75; Chm., Liberal Party Standing Cttee on Industrial Partnership, 1966. Vice-Pres., Centre for Internat. Briefing, Farnham Castle. Founder Trustee, William Blake Trust; Governor: Mill Hill Sch., 1943-69; Monkton Combe Sch.; Trustee and Hon. Fellow, St Peter's Coll., Oxford; Mem. Council, Wycliffe Hall; Founder Mem. and Sec., British-North American Cttee, 1969. *Publications:* The Future of Private Enterprise, 1951, 1954; The Responsible Company, 1961; The People's Church, 1966; The Responsible Worker, 1975. *Recreations:* music, old books, theology. *Address:* Mansel Hall, Long Melford, Sudbury, Suffolk. *Club:* Reform.
See also D. G. Goyder.

GRAAFF, Sir de Villiers, 2nd Bt *cr* 1911; MBE 1946; BA Cape, MA, BCL Oxon; Barrister-at-Law, Inner Temple; Advocate of the Supreme Court of S Africa; MP for Hottentots Holland in Union Parliament 1948-58, for Rondebosch, Cape Town, 1958-77; *b* 8 Dec. 1913; *s* of 1st Bt and Eileen (*d* 1950), *d* of Rev. Dr J. P. Van Heerden, Cape Town; *S* father, 1931; *m* 1939, Helena Le Roux, *d* of F. C. M. Voigt, Provincial Sec. of Cape Province; two *s one d.* Served War of 1939-45 (prisoner, MBE). Leader, United Party, S Africa, 1956-77; formerly Leader of Official Opposition. Hon. LLD, Rhodes. Decoration for Meritorious Service (RSA), 1979. *Heir: s* David de Villiers Graaff [*b* 3 May 1940; *m* Sally Williams; three *s one d*]. *Address:* De Grendel, Private Bag, GPO, Capetown, South Africa. *Club:* Civil Service (Cape Town).

GRABHAM, Anthony Herbert, FRCS; Chairman of Council, British Medical Association, since 1979; *b* 19 July 1930; *s* of John and Lily Grabham; *m* 1960, Eileen Pamela Rudd; two *s two d. Educ:* St Cuthbert's Grammar School, Newcastle upon Tyne. MB, BS Durham. RSO, Royal Victoria Infirmary, Newcastle upon Tyne; Consultant Surgeon, Kettering and District Gen. Hosp., 1965-. Chm., Central Cttee for Hosp. Med. Services, BMA, 1975-79; Member: GMC, 1979-; Council, World Med. Assoc., 1979-; Vice-Pres., Commonwealth Med. Assoc., 1980-. *Recreations:* collects committees, working parties and European porcelain. *Address:* (home) Rothesay House, 56 Headlands, Kettering, Northants. *T:* Kettering 513299; (business) British Medical Association, Tavistock Square, WC1H 9JP. *T:* 01-387 4499. *Club:* Army and Navy.

GRABINER, Anthony Stephen, QC 1981; *b* 21 March 1945; *e s* of Ralph and Freda Grabiner. *Educ:* Central Foundn Boys' Grammar Sch., London, EC2; LSE, Univ. of London (LLB 1st Cl. Hons 1966, LIM with Distinction 1967). Lincoln's Inn: Hardwicke Scholar, 1966; called to the Bar, 1968; Droop Scholar, 1968. Standing Jun. Counsel to Dept of Trade, Export Credits Guarantee Dept, 1976-81; Jun. Counsel to the Crown, 1978-81. *Publication:* (ed jtly) Sutton and Shannon on Contracts, 7th edn 1970. *Recreations:* cricket, theatre, cinema. *Address:* 1 Essex Court, Temple, EC4Y 9AR. *T:* 01-353 5362. *Club:* Garrick.

GRACE, Sir John (Te Herekiekie), KBE 1968; MVO 1953; AEA (RNZAF) 1950; New Zealand High Commissioner in Fiji, 1970-73; sheep and cattle station owner since 1958; *b* 28 July 1905; *s* of John Edward Grace, JP and Rangiamohia Herekiekie; *m* 1st, 1940, Marion Linton McGregor (*d* 1962); no *c* ; 2nd, 1968, Dorothy Kirkcaldie. *Educ:* Wanganui Boys' Coll.; Te Aute Coll., Hawkes Bay. Served War of 1939-45, Royal NZ Air Force (Sqdn-Ldr). NZ Public Service, 1926-58: Private Sec. to Ministers of the Crown incl. three Prime Ministers, 1947-58; Member: NZ Historic Places Trust, 1952-68; NZ Geographic Bd, 1952-68; Maori Purposes Fund Bd, 1961-68; Maori Educn Foundn, 1962-68; Nature Conservation Coun., 1963-68; Nat. Coun. of Adult Educn, 1964-68; Lake Taupo Forest Trust, 1968-; Fiji Leper Trust Bd, 1972; Rotoaira Forest Trust, 1974-; Tuwharetoa Trust Bd, 1974-; Lake Taupo Reserves Bd, 1975-; Vice-Pres. and Dominion Councillor, NZ Nat. Party, 1959-67. JP 1947. *Publication:* Tuwharetoa, a History of the Maori People of the Taupo District, NZ. *Recreations:* golf, trout fishing, gardening. *Address:* 84 Parkes Avenue, St Johns Hill, Wanganui, New Zealand. *T:* Wanganui 55.323. *Clubs:* Wellesley (Wellington); Wanganui (Wanganui).

GRACE, Dr Michael Anthony, FRS 1967; Reader in Nuclear Physics, Oxford University, since 1972; Student and Tutor in Physics, Christ Church, since 1959; *b* 13 May 1920; *er s* of late Claude Saville Grace, Haslemere, Surrey, and Evelyn Doris (*née* Adams); *m* 1948, Philippa Agnes Lois, *o d* of Sir (Vincent) Zachary Cope, MD, MS, FRCS; one *s three d. Educ:* St Paul's; Christ Church, Oxford. MA 1948; DPhil 1950. Mine Design Dept, HMS Vernon, 1940-45. ICI Research Fellowship, Clarendon Laboratory, Oxford, 1951; University Sen. Res. Officer, Dept of Nuclear Physics, 1955-72; Lectr

in Physics, Christ Church, 1958, Censor, 1964-69; Dr Lee's Reader in Physics, 1972. Governor: St Paul's Schools, 1959; Harrow School, 1969. *Publications:* papers in various jls including Phil. Mag., Proc. Royal Soc., Proc. Phys. Soc., Nuclear Physics. *Recreations:* lawn tennis, swimming. *Address:* 13 Blandford Avenue, Oxford, *T:* Oxford 58464. *Club:* Athenæum.

GRACEY, Howard, FIA, FIAA, FPMI; consulting actuary; Partner, R. Watson and Sons, since 1970; *b* 21 Feb. 1935; *s* of late Charles Douglas Gracey and of Margaret Gertrude (*née* Heggie); *m* 1960, Pamela Jean Bradshaw; one *s two d. Educ:* Birkenhead Sch. FIA 1959; FIAA 1982; FPMI 1977; ASA 1978. National Service, 1960-61 (2nd Lieut). Royal Insurance Co., 1953-69. Church Comr, 1978-; Member: Gen. Synod of CofE, 1970-; CofE Pensions Bd, 1970- (Chm., 1980-); Treasurer and Vice Chm., S Amer. Missionary Soc., 1975. *Recreations:* fell-walking, tennis, photography. *Address:* Pipers Croft, Clandon Road, West Clandon, Guildford, Surrey GU4 7UW. *Club:* Army and Navy.

GRACEY, John Halliday; Director General (Management), Board of Inland Revenue, since 1981; Commissioner of Inland Revenue since 1973; *b* 20 May 1925; *s* of Halliday Gracey and Florence Jane (*née* Cudlipp); *m* 1950, Margaret Procter; three *s. Educ:* City of London Sch.; Brasenose Coll., Oxford. Army, 1943-47. Entered Inland Revenue, 1950; HM Treasury, 1970-73. *Address:* 3 Woodberry Down, Epping, Essex. *T:* Epping 72167. *Club:* Reform.
See also T. A. Lloyd Davies.

GRACIE, George H. H.; *see* Heath-Gracie.

GRADE, family name of **Baron Grade.**

GRADE, Baron *cr* 1976 (Life Peer), of Elstree, Herts; **Lew Grade,** Kt 1969; Chairman and Chief Executive, Embassy Communications International Ltd, since 1982; *b* 25 Dec. 1906; *s* of late Isaac Winogradsky and Olga Winogradsky; *m* 1942, Kathleen Sheila Moody; one *s. Educ:* Rochelle Street Sch. Joint Managing Dir of Lew and Leslie Grade Ltd, until Sept. 1955; Chm. and Man. Dir, ITC Entertainment Ltd, 1958-82; Chm. and Chief Exec., Associated Communications Corp. Ltd, 1973-82; Pres., ATV Network Ltd, 1977-82; Chairman: Bentray Investments Ltd, 1979-82; ACC Enterprises Inc., 1973-82; Stoll Moss Theatres Ltd, 1969-82. KCSS 1979. *Address:* Embassy House, 3 Audley Square, W1Y 5DR.
See also Baron Delfont.

GRADE, Michael Ian; President, Tandem Productions Television, since 1982; *b* 8 March 1943; *s* of Leslie Grade and *g s* of Olga Winogradski; *m* 1967, Penelope Jane (*née* Levinson); one *s one d* ; *m* 1982, Hon. Sarah Lawson, *y d* of Baron Burnham, *qv. Educ:* St Dunstan's Coll., London. Daily Mirror: Trainee Journalist, 1960; Sports Columnist, 1964-66; Theatrical Agent, Grade Organisation, 1966; formed London Management and Representation, 1969, Jt Man. Dir until 1973; London Weekend Television: Dep. Controller of Programmes (Entertainment), 1973; Dir of Programmes and Mem. Bd, 1977-81. Mem. Council, LAMDA, 1981-. *Recreation:* entertainment. *Address:* 181 Shakespeare Tower, Barbican, EC2. *T:* 01-261 3434; Tandem Television, 5752 Sunset Boulevard, Los Angeles, Calif 90028, USA. *Club:* Coombe Hill Golf (Surrey).

GRADY, Terence, MBE 1967; HM Diplomatic Service, retired; Ambassador at Libreville, 1980-82; *b* 23 March 1924; *s* of Patrick Grady and Catherine (*née* Fowles); *m* 1960, Jean Fischer; one *s four d. Educ:* St Michael's Coll., Leeds. HM Forces, 1942-47; Foreign Office, 1949; HM Embassy: Baghdad, 1950; Paris, 1951; Asst Private Secretary to Secretary of State for Foreign Affairs, 1952-55; HM Legation, Budapest, 1955-58; HM Embassy, Kabul, 1958-60; FO, 1960-63; Vice Consul, Elisabethville, 1963; Consul, Philadelphia, 1964-69; UK High Commission, Sydney, 1969-72; FCO, 1972-75; Head of Chancery, Dakar, 1975-77; Consul, Istanbul, 1977-80. *Recreations:* tennis, walking. *Address:* c/o Foreign and Commonwealth Office, SW1. *Club:* Royal Commonwealth Society.

GRAEME, Bruce, (Pseudonym of **Graham Montague Jeffries**); Novelist; *s* of late William Henry Jeffries; *m* 1925, Lorna Helene, *d* of Capt. Hay T. Louch; one *s one d. Educ:* Privately. Finish of education interrupted by Great War; volunteered for Queen's Westminster Rifles; after demobilization became free-lance journalist; travelled several times to USA and France on various commissions, published short stories, 1921-25; interested in film work; financed, produced and sold one reel comedy, 1919-20; resumed this lifelong interest in films as script writer, and producer, 1942; entered Gray's Inn, 1930. *Publications:* The Story of Buckingham Palace, 1928; The Story of St James's Palace, 1929; A Century of Buckingham Palace, 1937; The Story of Windsor Castle, 1937; Blackshirt, 1925; The Trail of the White Knight, 1926; The Return of Blackshirt, 1927; Hate Ship, 1928; Trouble, 1929; Blackshirt Again, 1929; Through the Eyes of the Judge, 1930; The Penance of Brother Alaric, 1930; A Murder of Some Importance, 1931; Unsolved, 1931; Gigins Court, 1932; Alias Blackshirt, 1932; The Imperfect Crime, 1932; Impeached, 1933; Epilogue, 1933; An International Affair, 1934; Public Enemy No 1, 1934; Satan's Mistress, 1935; Blackshirt the Audacious, 1936; Not Proven, 1935; Cardyce for the Defence, 1936; Blackshirt the Adventurer, 1936; Mystery on the Queen Mary, 1937; Blackshirt takes a Hand, 1937; Disappearance of Roger Tremayne, 1937; Racing Yacht Mystery, 1938; Blackshirt; Counter-Spy, 1938; The Man from Michigan, 1938; Body Unknown, 1939; Blackshirt Interferes, 1939; Poisoned Sleep, 1939; 13 in a Fog, 1940; Blackshirt Strikes

Back, 1940; The Corporal Died in Bed, 1940; Seven Clues in Search of a Crime, 1941; Son of Blackshirt, 1941; Encore Allain, 1941; House with Crooked Walls, 1942; Lord Blackshirt, 1942; News Travels by Night, 1943; A Case for Solomon, 1943; Calling Lord Blackshirt, 1944; Work for the Hangman, 1944; Ten Trails to Tyburn, 1944; The Coming of Carew, 1945; A Case of Books, 1946; Without Malice, 1946; A Brief for O'Leary, 1947; No Clues for Dexter, 1948; And a Bottle of Rum, 1948; Tigers Have Claws, 1949; Cherchez la Femme; Dead Pigs at Hungry Farm, 1951; Lady in Black, 1952; Mr Whimset Buys a Gun, 1953; Suspense, 1953; The Way Out, 1954; So Sharp the Razor, 1955; Just an Ordinary Case, 1956; The Accidental Clue, 1957; The Long Night, 1958; Boomerang, 1959; Fog for a Killer, 1960; The Undetective, 1962; Almost Without Murder, 1963; Holiday for a Spy, 1964; Always Expect the Unexpected, 1965; The Devil was a Woman, 1966; Much Ado About Something, 1967; Never Mix Business With Pleasure, 1968; Some Geese Lay Golden Eggs, 1968; Blind Date for a Private Eye, 1969; The Quiet Ones, 1970; The Lady doth Protest, 1971; Yesterday's Tomorrow, 1972; Two and Two Make Five, 1973; Danger in the Channel, 1973; The D Notice, 1974; The Snatch, 1976; Two-Faced, 1977; Double Trouble, 1978; Mather Again, 1979; Invitation to Mather, 1979; Mather Investigates, 1981. *Address:* Gorse Field Cottage, Aldington Frith, near Ashford, Kent. *T:* Aldington 383. *Club:* Paternosters.

GRÆME, Maj.-Gen. Ian Rollo, CB 1967; OBE 1955; Secretary, National Ski Federation of Great Britain, 1967-78; *b* 23 May 1913; *s* of late Col J. A. Græme, DSO, late RE; *m* 1941, Elizabeth Jean Dyas; two *d. Educ:* Boxgrove; Stowe; RMA Woolwich. King's Medal and Benson Memorial Prize, RMA, 1933. 2nd Lt RA 1933; pre-war service at regimental duty UK; War Service in Singapore, Java, India, Burma, Siam; psc 1942; Instructor Staff Coll., Quetta, 1944; CO 1st Burma Field Regt, 1945-46; OC, K Battery, RHA, 1949; jssc 1952; GSO1, HQ Northern Army Group, 1953-54; CO 27 Regt RA, 1955-57; Col GS Staff Coll., Camberley, 1957-59; idc 1960; Dep. Mil. Sec., WO, 1961-63; Dep. Dir Personnel Admin, WO, 1963-64; Dir Army Recruiting, 1964-67; Retd 1967. Mem. Royal Yachting Assoc., 1950-; Life Governor, Royal Life Saving Soc., 1956-; Life Mem., British Olympic Assoc., 1958-; Chm., Army Holiday Cttee for ski-ing, 1963-67; Council, Army Ski Assoc., 1958-; Member: Council, Nat. Ski Fedn of GB, 1964-67 (Life Mem. Fedn); Cttee, Sports Aid Foundn, 1976- (Governor, 1982); Vice-President: English Ski Council, 1979-; British Ski Fedn, 1981-. FBIM; MInstD. Gold Medal, Austrian Govt, 1972. *Recreations:* ski-ing, sailing, mountains. *Clubs:* Army and Navy, English-Speaking Union (Life Mem.); Ski Club of Great Britain, Army Ski Association, Alpbach Visitors Ski, White Hare, Garvock Ski (Pres. 1969-), Kandahar Ski; Ranelagh Sailing, Royal Artillery Yacht.

GRAESSER, Col Sir Alastair Stewart Durward, Kt 1973; DSO 1945; OBE 1963; MC 1944; TD; Honorary Vice President, National Union of Conservative and Unionist Associations, since 1976 (Chairman, 1974-76); President, Wales and Monmouth Conservative and Unionist Council, 1972-77; Director, Development Corporation for Wales and Monmouth; Vice Lord-Lieutenant of Clwyd, since 1980; *b* 17 Nov. 1915; *s* of Norman Hugo Graesser and Annette Stewart Durward; *m* 1939, Diana Aline Elms Neale; one *s* three *d. Educ:* Oundle; Gonville and Caius Coll., Cambridge. Director: Grosvenor Hotel Co Ltd; Municipal Life Assurance Ltd; Municipal General Assurance Ltd; Managing Trustee, Municipal Mutual Insurance Ltd; Trustee, TSB of Wales and Border Counties; Mem., CBI Regional Council for Wales (Past Chm.). Pres., Wales and Monmouth Conservative Clubs Council, 1972-76. Vice-Chm., Wales and Monmouth TA&VR Assoc.; Hon. Col, 3rd Bn Royal Welch Fusiliers (TA), 1972-80. High Sheriff of Flintshire, 1962; DL 1960, JP 1956-78, Clwyd (formerly Flints). CStJ 1980. *Recreation:* shooting. *Address:* Sweet Briar, Berghill Lane, Babbinswood, Whittington, Oswestry, Salop SY11 4PF. *T:* Oswestry 62395. *Clubs:* Naval and Military; Hawks (Cambridge); Leander (Henley-on-Thames); Grosvenor (Chester).

GRAFFTEY-SMITH, Sir Laurence Barton, KCMG 1951 (CMG 1944); KBE 1947 (OBE 1932); *b* 16 April 1892; *s* of late Rev. Arthur Grafftey-Smith and late Mabel, *d* of Rev. Charles Barton, Cheselbourne, Dorset; *m* 1930, Vivien (marr. diss., 1937), *d* of G. Alexander Alderson; two *s*; *m* 1946, Evgenia Owen, *d* of late P. H. Coolidge, Berkeley, Calif. *Educ:* Repton; Pembroke Coll., Cambridge. Student Interpreter, Levant Consular Service, 1914. HM Vice Consul, 1920; served at Alexandria, Cairo (Residency), Jeddah, Constantinople; Asst Oriental Sec. at the Residency, Cairo, 1925-35; HM Consul, Mosul, 1935-37; Baghdad, 1937-39; HM Consul-Gen. in Albania, 1939-40; attached British Embassy, Cairo, 1940; Chief Political Adviser, Diego Suarez, May 1942; Chief Political Officer, Madagascar, July 1942; Consul-Gen., Antananarivo, 1943; Minister to Saudi Arabia, 1945-47; High Comr for UK in Pakistan, 1947-51; retired from Govt service on 31 Dec. 1951; UK Rep. on Gov.-Gen.'s Commn, Khartoum, 1953-56. *Publications:* (with Godfrey Haggard) Visa Verses, 1915 (privately printed); Bright Levant, 1970; Hands to Play, 1975. *Address:* Broom Hill House, Coddenham, Suffolk.

GRAFTON, 11th Duke of, *cr* 1675; **Hugh Denis Charles FitzRoy;** KG 1976; DL; Earl of Euston, Viscount Ipswich; Captain Grenadier Guards; *b* 3 April 1919; *e s* of 10th Duke of Grafton, and Lady Doreen Maria Josepha Sydney Buxton (*d* 1923), *d* of 1st Earl Buxton; *S* father, 1970; *m* 1946, Fortune (*see* Duchess of Grafton); two *s* three *d. Educ:* Eton; Magdalene Coll., Cambridge. ADC to the Viceroy of India, 1943-46. Mem. Historic Buildings Council for England, 1953-; Chairman: Soc. for the Protection of Ancient Buildings; Jt Cttee, Soc. for Protection of Ancient Buildings, Georgian Gp, Victorian Soc.,

and Civic Trust; Architectural Heritage Trust; Mem., National Trust Properties Cttee; Pres. UK Cttee, Internat. Council of Monuments and Sites; Nat. President: Nat. Assoc. of Local Councils; Eastern Fedn of Amenity Socs; Council of British Soc. of Master Glass Painters; Pres., International Students Trust. Chm., Cathedrals Advisory Commn for England, 1981-; Chm. of Trustees, Historic Churches Preservation Trust; Pres. Architecture Club; Mem., Royal Fine Art Commn, 1971-; Chm. Trustees, Sir John Soane's Museum; Vice-Chm. Trustees, Nat. Portrait Gallery; Patron, Hereford Herd Book Soc. Hon. Air Cdre, No 2623 R AuxAF Regt Sqdn, 1982-. DL Suffolk, 1973. *Heir: s* Earl of Euston, *qv. Address:* Euston Hall, Thetford, Norfolk IP24 2QW. *T:* Thetford 3282. *Club:* Boodle's.

GRAFTON, Duchess of; (Ann) Fortune FitzRoy, GCVO 1980 (DCVO 1970; CVO 1965); JP; Mistress of The Robes to The Queen since 1967; *o d* of Captain Eric Smith, MC, LLD, Lower Ashfold, Slaugham; *m* 1946, Duke of Grafton, *qv*; two *s* three *d.* Lady of the Bedchamber to the Queen, 1953-66. SRCN Great Ormond Street, 1945; Mem. Bd of Governors, The Hospital for Sick Children, Great Ormond Street, 1952-66. Pres., W Suffolk Mission to the Deaf; Vice-Pres., Suffolk Br., Royal British Legion Women's Section. Governor: Felixstowe Coll.; Riddlesworth Hall. JP County of London, 1949, W Suffolk, 1972. *Address:* Euston Hall, Thetford, Norfolk. *T:* Thetford 3282.

GRAFTON, NSW, Bishop of, since 1973; **Rt. Rev. Donald Norman Shearman,** OBE 1978; *b* 6 Feb. 1926; *s* of late S. F. Shearman, Sydney; *m* 1952, Stuart Fay, *d* of late Chap. F. H. Bashford; three *s* three *d. Educ:* Fort St and Orange High Schools; St John's Theological College, Morpeth, NSW. Served War of 1939-45: air crew, 1944-46. Theological College, 1948-50. Deacon, 1950; Priest, 1951. Curate: of Dubbo, 1950-52; of Forbes, and Warden of St John's Hostel, 1953-56; Rector of Coonabarabran, 1957-59; Director of Promotion and Adult Christian Education 1959-62; Canon, All Saints Cathedral, Bathurst, 1962; Archdeacon of Mildura and Rector of St. Margaret's, 1963; Bishop of Rockhampton, 1963-71; Chairman, Australian Board of Missions, Sydney, 1971-73. *Address:* Bishopsholme, Grafton, NSW 2460, Australia. *T:* Grafton 42 2070.

GRAFTON, Col Martin John, CBE 1976 (OBE 1964, MBE 1944); TD 1958; DL; Director-General, National Federation of Building Trades Employers, 1964-79, retired; *b* 28 June 1919; *o s* of Vincent Charles Grafton and Maud (*née* Brazier); *m* 1948, Jean Margaret, *d* of James Drummond-Smith, OBE, MA, and Edith M. Drummond-Smith, MBE, MA; two *d. Educ:* Bromsgrove Sch. FFB 1968-80. Served War, RE, 1940-46: Captain 1943; Normandy and NW Europe, 1944-46 (MBE 1944, Rhine Crossing); served TA RE, 1947-66 (TD 1958, Bar 1963): Major 1954, Lt-Col 1960, Col 1964; comd 101 Fd Engr Regt, 1960-64; Dep. Chief Engr, E Anglian Dist, 1964-66. Joined John Lewis Partnership, 1948: Gen. Man., Peter Jones, Sloane Square, 1951-52; Dir of Bldg, 1954-60; a Man. Dir, 1960-63. Dir, Alfred Booth & Co. Ltd, 1979-80. Member: Council, CBI, 1964-79; EDC for Building, 1964-75; Nat. Consult. Council for Building and Civil Engrg, 1964-79. Hon. FCIOB 1978; Mem., Co. of Builders, 1977-80. DL Greater London, 1967; Freeman, City of London, 1978. *Recreations:* travel, reading, music. *Address:* 25 Myddelton Square, EC1R 1YE. *T:* 01-278 8705; Chemin des Rouviéres, Bagnols-en-Forêt, 83600 Fréjus, France. *T:* (94) 40.60.55. *Club:* Army and Navy.

GRAFTON, Peter Witheridge, CBE 1972; retired as Senior Partner, G. D. Walford & Partners, Chartered Quantity Surveyors; *b* 19 May 1916; *s* of James Hawkins Grafton and Ethel Marion (*née* Brannan); *m* 1st, 1939, Joan Bleackley (*d* 1969); two *d* (and one *s* one *d* decd); 2nd, 1971, Margaret Ruth Ward; two *s. Educ:* Westminster City Sch.; Sutton Valence Sch.; Coll. of Estate Management. FRICS, FCIArb. Served War of 1939-45, Queen's Westminster Rifles, Dorsetshire Regt and RE, UK and Far East (Captain). Pres., RICS, 1978-79 (Vice-Pres., 1974-78; Past Chm. Policy Review Cttee); Mem. and Past Chm., Quantity Surveyors Council (1st Chm., Building Cost Information Service); Past Mem. Council, Construction Industries Research and Information Assoc.; Past Mem. Research Adv. Council to Minister of Housing and Construction; Past Mem. Nat. Cons. Council for Building and Civil Engrg Industries and Mem., Agrément Bd; former Chm., Nat. Jt Consultative Cttee for Building Industry. Trustee, United Westminster Schs; Chm. of Governors, Sutton Valence Sch.; Past Chm., Old Suttonians Assoc. Contested (L) Bromley, 1959. *Publications:* numerous articles on techn. and other professional subjects. *Recreations:* golf (founder and Chm., Public Schs Old Boys Golf Assoc., Co-donor Grafton Morrish Trophy; past Captain of Chartered Surveyors Golfing Soc.); writing. *Address:* Corner Cottage, 10 Stanhopes, Limpsfield, Oxted, Surrey RH8 0TY. *T:* Oxted 6685. *Clubs:* Reform, Golfers; Addington Golf, Rye Golf, W Sussex Golf, Tandridge Golf.

GRAHAM, family name of Duke of Montrose.

GRAHAM, Marquis of; James Graham; *b* 6 April 1935; *s* of 7th Duke of Montrose, *qv*; *m* 1970, Catherine Elizabeth MacDonell, *d* of late Captain N. A. T. Young, and of Mrs Young, Ottawa; two *s* one *d. Educ:* Loretto. Mem. Royal Company of Archers (Queen's Body Guard for Scotland), 1980-. Area Director, RHAS. Mem. Council, Scottish NFU. *Heir: s* Lord Fintrie, *qv. Address:* Auchmar, Drymen, Glasgow. *T:* 221.

GRAHAM, Prof. Alastair, DSc, FRS 1979; Professor of Zoology, University of Reading, to 1972, now Emeritus Professor; *b* 6 Nov. 1906. *Educ:*

Edinburgh Univ. (MA, BSc); London Univ. (DSc). Fellow, Zoological Soc., 1939 (Frink Medal, 1976). *Publications:* British Prosobranch Molluscs (jtly), 1962; Other Operculate Gastropod Molluscs, 1971. *Address:* 6 Belle Avenue, Reading, Berks. *T:* Reading 62276.

GRAHAM, Alastair Carew; Head Master, Mill Hill School, since 1979; *b* 23 July 1932; *s* of Col J. A. Graham and Mrs Graham (*née* Carew-Hunt); *m* 1969, Penelope Rachel Beaumont; two *d*. *Educ:* Winchester Coll.; Gonville and Caius Coll., Cambridge (1st Cl. Mod. and Med. Langs). Served 1st Bn Argyll and Sutherland Highlanders, 1951-53. Foy, Morgan & Co. (City), 1956-58; Asst Master, Eton, 1958; House Master, 1970-79. *Recreations:* ball games, walking; theatre and opera; music listening, gardening, boys' club. *Address:* The Grove, Mill Hill, NW7. *T:* 01-959 1006. *Clubs:* Athenæum; Hawks (Cambridge).
See also Maj.-Gen. J. D. C. Graham.

GRAHAM, Alistair; *see* Graham, J. A.

GRAHAM, Rt. Rev. Andrew Alexander Kenny; *see* Newcastle, Bishop of.

GRAHAM, Andrew Winston Mawdsley; Fellow, and Tutor in Economics, Balliol College, Oxford, since 1969; *b* 20 June 1942; *s* of Winston Mawdsley Graham, *qv*; *m* 1970, Peggotty Fawssett. *Educ:* Charterhouse; St Edmund Hall, Oxford. MA (PPE). Economic Assistant: NEDO, 1964; Dept of Economic Affairs, 1964-66; Asst to Economic Adviser to the Cabinet, 1966-68; Economic Adviser to Prime Minister, 1968-69; Policy Adviser to Prime Minister (on leave of absence from Balliol), 1974-75. Tutor, Oxford Univ. Business Summer Sch., 1971, 1972, 1973 and 1976. Estates Bursar, Balliol Coll., 1978, Investment Bursar, 1979-. Member: Wilson Cttee to Review the Functioning of Financial Institutions, 1977-80; Economics Cttee, SSRC, 1978-80; British Transport Docks Bd, 1979-82; Chm., St James Gp (Economic Forecasting), 1982-. ILO Mission to Ethiopia, 1982. Founder Mem. Editorial Bd, Oxford Library of Political Economy, 1982-. *Publications:* contribs to books on economics and philosophy. *Recreations:* sailing, surfing, swimming, skiing, sail-boarding, building walls. *Address:* Balliol College, Oxford OX1 3BJ. *T:* Oxford 49601. *Club:* Savile.

GRAHAM, Prof. Angus Charles, FBA 1981; Professor of Classical Chinese, School of Oriental and African Studies (SOAS), London University, since 1971; *b* 8 July 1919; *s* of Charles Harold and Mabelle Graham; *m* 1955, Der Pao (*née* Chang); one *d*. *Educ:* Ellesmere Coll., Salop; Corpus Christi Coll., Oxford (MA Theol.); SOAS, London (BA, PhD Chinese). Lectr in Chinese, SOAS, 1950-71. *Publications:* Two Chinese Philosophers: Ch'eng Ming-tao and Ch'eng Yi-ch'uan, 1958; The Book of Lieh Tzu, 1960; The Problem of Value, 1961; Poems of the Late T'ang, 1965; Later Mohist Logic, Ethics and Science, 1978; Chuang-tzu: the Seven Inner Chapters and other writings from the book *Chuang-tzu*, 1981. *Address:* 33 Barham Avenue, Elstree, Herts. *T:* 01-953 3736.

GRAHAM, Mrs Anne Silvia; Principal Assistant Solicitor, Department of the Environment, since 1978; *b* 1 Aug. 1934; *o d* of late Benjamin Arthur Garcia and Constance Rosa (*née* Journeaux); *m* Peter Graham, *qv*. *Educ:* Francis Holland Sch., SW1; LSE (LLB). Called to the Bar, Inner Temple, 1958; Yarborough-Anderson Scholar, 1959. Joined Min. of Housing and Local Govt as Legal Asst, 1960; Sen. Legal Asst, 1966; Asst Solicitor, 1972. *Recreations:* gardening, cookery. *Address:* Quince Cottage, Hook Heath Road, Woking, Surrey GU22 0QE.

GRAHAM, Antony Richard Malise; Director: Barrow Hepburn Group Ltd; Maroquinerie Le Tanneur et Tanneries du Bugey, SA; *b* 15 Oct. 1928; *s* of late Col Patrick Ludovic Graham, MC, and late Barbara Mary Graham (*née* Jury); *m* 1958, Gillian Margaret, *d* of late L. Bradford Cook and of Mrs W. V. Wrigley; two *s* one *d*. *Educ:* Abberley Hall; Nautical Coll., Pangbourne. Joined Merchant Navy as an apprentice, 1945; left on obtaining Master Mariner's certif., 1955. Stewarts and Lloyds Ltd, 1955-60; PE Consulting Group Ltd, management consultants, 1960-72 (Regional Dir, 1970-72); Regional Industrial Dir (Under-Sec.), Yorks and Humberside, DoI, 1972-76. Contested (C) Leeds East, 1966. *Address:* 34 Sheffield Terrace, W8 7NA. *T:* 01-727 5091.

GRAHAM, Billy; *see* Graham, William F.

GRAHAM, Sir Charles (Spencer Richard), 6th Bt *cr* 1783; DL; *b* 16 July 1919; *s* of Sir (Frederick) Fergus Graham, 5th Bt, KBE, and of Mary Spencer Revell, CBE, *d* of late Maj.-Gen. Raymond Reade, CB, CMG; *S* father, 1978; *m* 1944, Isabel Susan Anne, *d* of late Major R. L. Surtees, OBE; two *s* one *d*. *Educ:* Eton. Served with Scots Guards, 1940-50, NW Europe (despatches) and Malaya. President, Country Landowners' Assoc., 1971-73. Mem., Nat. Water Council, 1973-. High Sheriff 1955, DL 1971, Cumbria (formerly Cumberland). *Heir: s* James Fergus Surtees Graham [*b* 29 July 1946; *m* 1975, Serena Jane, *yr d* of Ronald Frank Kershaw; two *d*]. *Address:* Crofthead, Longtown, Cumbria. *T:* Longtown 231. *Clubs:* Brooks's, Pratt's.

GRAHAM, Dr Christopher Forbes, FRS 1981; Lecturer in the Department of Zoology, University of Oxford, since 1970; *b* 23 Sept. 1940. *Educ:* Oxford Univ. (BA 1963, DPhil 1966). Formerly Junior Beit Memorial Fellow in Med. Research, Sir William Dunn Sch. of Pathology. Member: Brit. Soc. Cell Biology; Brit. Soc. for Developmental Biology; Soc. for Experimental Biology; Genetical Soc. *Publication:* The Developmental Biology of Plants and Animals, 1976. *Address:* Department of Zoology, University of Oxford, South Parks Road, Oxford OX1 3PS.

GRAHAM, Colin; Artistic Director: English Music Theatre, since 1975; Aldeburgh Festival, since 1969; Director of Productions, English National Opera, and Opera Theatre of St Louis, USA, since 1978; stage director, designer, lighting designer, and author; *b* 22 Sept. 1931; *s* of Frederick Eaton Graham-Bonnalie and Alexandra Diana Vivian Findlay. *Educ:* Northaw Prep. Sch.; Stowe Sch.; RADA (Dip.). Dir of Productions, English Opera Gp, 1963-74; Associate Dir of Prodns, Sadler's Wells Opera/English National Opera, 1967-75. Principal productions for: English Music Theatre; Royal Opera, Covent Garden; Scottish Opera; New Opera Co.; Glyndebourne Opera; BBC TV; Brussels National Opera; St Louis Opera Theatre; Santa Fe Opera; Metropolitan Opera, New York; NYC Opera; dir. world premières of all Benjamin Britten's operas since 1954; of other contemp. composers. Theatre productions for: Old Vic Co.; Bristol Old Vic; Royal Shakespeare Co. Orpheus award (Germany) for best opera production, 1973 (War and Peace, ENO). *Publications:* A Penny for a Song (libretto for Richard Rodney Bennett), 1969; The Golden Vanity (libretto for opera by Britten), 1970; King Arthur (libretto for new version of Purcell opera), 1971; production scores for Britten's: Curlew River, 1969; The Burning Fiery Furnace, 1971; The Prodigal Son, 1973; The Postman Always Rings Twice, 1981; contrib. Opera. *Recreations:* motor cycles, movies, weight lifting. *Address:* The Lion House, Orford, Suffolk IP12 2NR.

GRAHAM, David; *see* Graham, S. D.

GRAHAM, David Alec, FCA, FCIT; Director General, Greater Manchester Passenger Transport Executive, since 1976; *b* 18 Jan. 1930; *s* of John Leonard Graham and May Susan (*née* Wymark); *m* 1956, Valerie Monica Dartnall. *Educ:* Sutton High Sch. FCA 1953; FCIT 1970; CIPFA. Accountant/Finance Dir, Threlfalls Chesters Ltd, 1959-69; Dir of Finance and Admin, Greater Manchester Passenger Transp. Exec., 1969-76. *Recreations:* sailing, gardening. *Address:* The Spinney, Rowanside, Castleford Park, Prestbury, Cheshire. *T:* Prestbury 829963.

GRAHAM, Douglas; *see* Graham, M. G. D.

GRAHAM, Rev. Douglas Leslie, MA (Dublin); retired; *b* 4 Oct. 1909; *s* of late Very Rev. G. F. Graham; *m* 1935, Gladys Winifred Ann, *y d* of J. W. Brittain, JP, Kilronan, Donnybrook, Co. Dublin; three *s*. *Educ:* Portora Royal Sch.; Dublin Univ. (BA); Munich Univ. Lectr in Classics, Dublin Univ., 1932-34; MA and Madden Prizeman, 1934; Asst Master, Eton Coll., 1934-41. Ordained, 1937. Served War as Temp. Chaplain, RNVR, 1941-45; HMS Trinidad, 1941; HMS King Alfred, 1942; HMS Daedalus, 1944; HMS Ferret, 1944; Headmaster, Portora Royal School, 1945-53; Headmaster, Dean Close Sch., 1954-68; Asst Master and Chaplain, Williston Acad., Easthampton, Mass, USA, 1968-72. Select Preacher to the Univs of Dublin, 1945, 1961 and 1965, and Oxford, 1956-57. FRSA. *Publications:* Bacchanalia (trans. from Greek Anthology), 1970; occasional articles on classical subjects. *Recreations:* books, birds and boxing. *Address:* Forest Cottage, West Woods, Lockeridge, near Marlborough, Wilts SN8 4EG. *T:* Lockeridge 432.

GRAHAM, Edward; *see* Graham, T. E.

GRAHAM, Euan Douglas; Principal Clerk of Private Bills, House of Lords; *b* 29 July 1924; *yr s* of Brig. Lord D. M. Graham, CB, DSO, MC; RA. *Educ:* Eton; Christ Church, Oxford (MA). Served RAF, 1943-47. Joined Parliament Office, House of Lords, 1950; Clerk, Judicial Office, 1950-60; Principal Clerk of Private Bills, Examiner of Petitions for Private Bills, Taxing Officer, 1961-. *Address:* 122 Beaufort Mansions, Beaufort Street, SW3. *Clubs:* Brooks's, Beefsteak, Pratt's.

GRAHAM, Maj.-Gen. Frederick Clarence Campbell, CB 1960; DSO 1945; Lord-Lieutenant of Stirling and Falkirk (Central Region), since 1979; *b* Ardencaple Castle, Helensburgh, Scotland, 14 Dec. 1908; *s* of Sir Frederick Graham, 2nd Bt, and Lady Irene Graham (*née* Campbell); *m* 1936, Phyllis Mary, *d* of late Maj.-Gen. H. F. E. MacMahon, CB, CSI, CBE, MC; three *s*. *Educ:* Eton Coll.; RMC Sandhurst. Commissioned Argyll and Sutherland Highlanders, 1929; served 1st and 2nd Bn Argyll and Sutherland Highlanders in China, India, UK and Palestine, 1929-39; Adjutant 1st Bn, 1937; War of 1939-45, served Palestine, N Africa, Crete, Syria, India, Italy; commanded 1st Bn Argyll and Sutherland Highlanders, 1944-end of war in Europe. Since 1945: GSO1, Home Counties District and Home Counties Div.; Joint Services Staff Coll.; Staff Coll., Camberley (Col); Comdr 61 Lorried Infantry Brigade (Brig.); Asst Commandant, RMA Sandhurst; Dep. Comdr, Land Forces, Hong Kong and Comd (Brig.) 40 Inf. Div.; Adviser in recruiting, MoD; Comdr Highland District and 51st (Highland) Div., TA, 1959-62; retd from HM Forces, 1962. Col, The Argyll and Sutherland Highlanders, 1958-72. Col Comdt, The Scottish Div., 1968-69; Hon. Col, Argyll and Sutherland Highlanders of Canada, 1972-77. Mem. of Royal Company of Archers, The Queen's Body Guard for Scotland, 1958-. DL Perthshire, 1966. Mem., Stirling DC, 1976- (Vice-Chm., 1977-80). *Address:* Mackeanston House, Doune, Perthshire. *Club:* Caledonian.

GRAHAM, George Boughen, QC 1964; *b* 17 July 1920; *s* of Sydney Boughen and Hannah Graham, Keswick, Cumberland; *m* Mavis, *o d* of late Frederick Worthington, Blackpool. *Educ:* Keswick Sch. Royal Signals, 1940-46. Barrister, Lincoln's Inn, 1950, Bencher, 1972. Chancellor, Diocese of Wakefield, 1959, Dio. of Sheffield, 1971. Member of Lloyd's, 1968. Comdr, Order of Merit (W Germany); Order of Aztec Eagle (Mexico). *Publications:* Covenants, Settlements and Taxation, 1953; Estate Duty Handbook, 1954. *Recreations:* walking and dining. *Address:* Brocklehurst, Keswick, Cumbria. *T:* Keswick 72042. *Clubs:* Athenæum; Derwent (Keswick).

GRAHAM, Gerald Sandford, MA, PhD, FRHistS; Rhodes Professor of Imperial History, London University, 1949-70, now Emeritus; *b* Sudbury, Ontario, 27 April 1903; *s* of Rev. H. S. Graham and Florence Marian Chambers; *m* 1929, Winifred Emily Ware (marr. diss. 1950); one *s*; *m* 1950, Constance Mary Greey, Toronto; one *s* two *d. Educ:* Queen's Univ., Canada; Harvard, 1926-27; Cambridge, 1927-29; Berlin and Freiburg-im-Breisgau, 1929-30; Instructor in History, and Tutor, Harvard Univ., 1930-36; successively Asst, Associate, and Prof. of History, Queen's Univ., 1936-46; Guggenheim Fellowship to US, 1941; RCNVR, 1942-45; Reader in History, Birkbeck Coll., Univ. of London, 1946-48. Mem., Inst. for Advanced Study, Princeton, 1952. Kemper Knapp Vis. Prof., Univ. of Wisconsin, 1961, Univ. of Hong Kong, 1966; Vis. Prof. of Strategic Studies, Univ. of Western Ontario, 1970-72; Vis. Montague Burton Prof. of Internat. Relations, Univ. of Edinburgh, 1974. FKC 1981. Hon. DLitt Univ. of Waterloo, Ont, 1973; Hon. LLD Queen's Univ., Ont, 1976. *Publications:* British Policy and Canada, 1774-1791, 1930; Sea Power and British North America, 1783-1820, 1941; Contributor to Newfoundland, Economic, Diplomatic and Strategic Studies, 1946; Empire of the North Atlantic, 1950 (2nd edn 1958); Canada, A Short History, 1950; The Walker Expedition to Quebec, 1711 (Navy Records Soc., and Champlain Soc.), 1953; The Politics of Naval Supremacy, 1965; contributor to Cambridge History of the British Empire, Vol. III, 1959; (with R. A. Humphreys) The Navy and South America, 1807-1823 (Navy Records Soc.), 1962; Britain in the Indian Ocean, 1810-1850, 1967; A Concise History of Canada, 1968; A Concise History of the British Empire, 1970; Tides of Empire, 1972; The Royal Navy in the American War of Independence, 1976; The China Station: War and Diplomacy 1830-60, 1978. *Address:* Hobbs Cottage, Beckley, Rye, Sussex. *T:* Beckley 308. *Clubs:* Athenæum, Royal Commonwealth Society.

GRAHAM, Gordon, CBE 1980; PPRIBA; Senior Partner, Gordon Graham and Partners (formerly Architects Design Group), since 1958; President of the Royal Institute of British Architects, 1977-79; *b* Carlisle, 4 June 1920; *s* of late Stanley Bouch Graham and Isabel Hetherington; *m* 1946, Enid Pennington; three *d. Educ:* Creighton Sch.; Nottingham Sch. of Architecture. DipArch, RIBA, 1949. Served Royal Artillery, N Africa, Italy and NW Europe, 1940-46. Sen. Lectr, Nottingham Sch. of Architecture, 1949-61; RIBA Arthur Cates Prizeman, 1949; travelling scholar, South and Central America, 1953. Pres., Nottingham, Derby and Lincoln Soc. of Architects, 1965-66; RIBA: Chm., E Midlands Region, 1967-69; Mem. Council, 1967-73 and 1974; Vice-Pres., 1969-71; Hon. Sec., 1971-72 and 1975-76; Sen. Vice-Pres., 1976; Pres., 1977-79. Mem., Building EDC, 1978-. Principal works in the field of industrial architecture; awards and commendations from RIBA, Civic Trust and Financial Times. Hon. FRAIC 1978. Hon. MA Nottingham, 1979. *Recreations:* Rugby football, architecture. *Address:* Lockington Hall, Lockington, Derby DE7 2RH. *Club:* Reform.

GRAHAM, Air Vice-Marshal Henry Rudolph, CB 1958; CBE 1955; DSO 1941; DFC 1942; *b* 28 March 1910; *s* of Major Campbell Frederick Graham, late Cape Mounted Rifles and South African Mounted Rifles, and Frances Elizabeth Cheeseman; *m* 1949, Maisie Frances Butler; two *s. Educ:* Rondebosch; SA Trng Ship General Botha, S Africa. Union Castle Line, 1926-31; RAF, 1931-62. National Trust, 1966-69. Military Cross (Czechoslovakia), 1940. *Recreation:* farming. *Address:* Majoro, PO Box 189, Magaliesburg, 2805, South Africa. *Clubs:* Wanderers', RAF Officers' (Johannesburg).

GRAHAM, Lt-Gen. Howard Douglas, OC 1967; CVO 1973; CBE 1946; DSO 1943 and Bar 1944; ED; CD; QC (Canada); retired as Lieutenant-General Canadian Army; *b* 1898. Served War of 1914-18: Canadian Infantry in France, Germany and Belgium; served War of 1939-45 (DSO and Bar, CBE), UK, France, 1940, Sicily and Italy; Senior Canadian Army Liaison Officer, London, and Army Adviser to the Canadian High Commissioner in London, 1946-48; Vice-Chief of Canadian General Staff, 1948-50; Gen. Officer Commanding Central Command, Canada, 1951-55; Chief of Canadian Gen. Staff, 1955-58; undertook, on behalf of Canadian Govt, during 1958, a comprehensive survey of all aspects of Canada's civil def. policy and programme. Acted as Canadian Sec. to the Queen, 1959 and 1967. Pres. (retd), Toronto Stock Exchange. Officer, US Legion of Merit; Chevalier Legion of Honour (France); Croix de Guerre with palm (France). *Address:* 33 Colonial Crescent, Oakville, Ont., Canada.

GRAHAM, Ian James Alastair, FSA; Assistant Curator, Peabody Museum of Archaeology, Harvard University; *b* 12 Nov. 1923; *s* of Captain Lord Alastair Graham, *y s* of 5th Duke of Montrose, and Lady Meriel Olivia Bathurst (*d* 1936), *d* of 7th Earl Bathurst; unmarried. *Educ:* Winchester Coll.; Trinity Coll., Dublin. RNVR (A), 1942-47; TCD 1947-51; Nuffield Foundn Research Scholar at The National Gallery, 1951-54; independent archaeological explorer in Central America from 1959. Occasional

photographer of architecture. MacArthur Foundn Prize Fellowship, 1981. *Publications:* Splendours of the East, 1965; Great Houses of the Western World, 1968; Archaeological Explorations in El Peten, Guatemala, 1967; Corpus of Maya Hieroglyphic Inscriptions, 8 parts, 1975-; other reports in learned jls. *Address:* Chantry Farm, Campsey Ash, Suffolk; c/o Peabody Museum, Harvard University, Cambridge, Mass, USA.

GRAHAM, Sir James Bellingham, 11th Bt *cr* 1662; *S* father, 1982. *Heir: b* William Reginald Graham.

GRAHAM, John, CB 1976; Fisheries Secretary, Ministry of Agriculture, Fisheries and Food, 1967-76; *b* 17 March 1918; *s* of late John Graham; *m* 1940, Betty Ramage Jarvie; two *s* three *d. Educ:* Fettes Coll., Edinburgh; Trinity Coll., Cambridge (Schol.). Classical Tripos, MA Cantab. Entered Post Office as Asst Principal, 1939; Min. of Food, 1940.

GRAHAM, Sir John (Alexander Noble), 4th Bt *cr* 1906, of Larbert; KCMG 1979 (CMG 1972); HM Diplomatic Service; Ambassador and UK Permanent Representative to NATO, Brussels, since 1982; *b* 15 July 1926; *s* of Sir John Reginald Noble Graham, 3rd Bt, VC, OBE and of Rachel Septima, *d* of Col Sir Alexander Sprot, 1st and last Bt; *S* father, 1980; *m* 1956, Marygold Elinor Gabrielle Austin; two *s* one *d. Educ:* Eton Coll.; Trinity Coll., Cambridge. Army, 1944-47; Cambridge, 1948-50; HM Foreign Service, 1950; Middle East Centre for Arab Studies, 1951; Third Secretary, Bahrain 1951, Kuwait 1952, Amman 1953; Asst Private Sec. to Sec. of State for Foreign Affairs, 1954-57; First Sec., Belgrade, 1957-60, Benghazi, 1960-61; FO 1961-66; Counsellor and Head of Chancery, Kuwait, 1966-69; Principal Private Sec. to Foreign and Commonwealth Sec., 1969-72; Cllr (later Minister) and Head of Chancery, Washington, 1972-74; Ambassador to Iraq, 1974-77; Dep. Under-Sec. of State, FCO, 1977-79; Ambassador to Iran, 1979-80; Deputy Under-Sec. of State, FCO, 1980-82. *Heir: s* Andrew John Noble Graham, *b* 21 Oct. 1956. *Address:* c/o Foreign and Commonwealth Office, SW1. *Club:* Army and Navy.

GRAHAM, (John) Alistair; General Secretary, The Civil and Public Services Association, since 1982; *b* 6 Aug. 1942; *s* of late Robert Graham and of Dorothy Graham; *m* 1968, Dorothy Jean Wallace; one *s* one *d. Educ:* Royal Grammar Sch., Newcastle upon Tyne. Clerical Asst, St George's Hosp., Morpeth, 1961; Admin Trainee, Northern Regional Hosp. Bd, 1963; Higher Clerical Officer, Royal Sussex County Hosp., Brighton, 1964; Legal Dept, TGWU, 1965; The Civil and Public Services Association: Asst Sec., 1966; Asst Gen. Sec., 1975; Dep. Gen. Sec., 1976. Mem., TUC Gen. Council, 1982-. Parly Candidate (Lab), Brighton Pavilion, 1966. *Recreations:* music, theatre. *Address:* The Civil and Public Services Association, 215 Balham High Road, SW17 7BN.

GRAHAM, Maj.-Gen. John David Carew, CB 1978; CBE 1973 (OBE 1966); Secretary to the Administrative Trustees of the Chevening Estate, since 1978; *b* 18 Jan. 1923; *s* of late Col J. A. Graham, late RE, and of Constance Mary Graham (*née* Carew-Hunt); *m* 1956, Rosemary Elaine Adamson; one *s* one *d. Educ:* Cheltenham Coll. psc 1955; jssc 1962. Commissioned into Argyll and Sutherland Highlanders, 1942 (despatches, 1945); served with 5th (Scottish) Bn, The Parachute Regt, 1946-49; British Embassy, Prague, 1949-50; HQ Scottish Comd, 1956-58; Mil. Asst to CINCENT, Fontainebleau, 1960-62; comd 1st Bn, The Parachute Regt, 1964-66; Instr at Staff Coll., Camberley, 1967; Regtl Col, The Parachute Regt, 1968-69; Comdr, Sultan's Armed Forces, Oman, 1970-72; Indian Nat. Defence Coll., New Delhi, 1973; Asst Chief of Staff, HQ AFCENT, 1974-76; GOC Wales, 1976-78. OStJ 1978, and Chm., St John Council for Kent, 1978-; Chm., Kent ACF Cttee, 1979-. Order of Oman, 1972. *Recreations:* photography, gardening. *Address:* Estate Office, Chevening, Sevenoaks, Kent TN14 6HG.

See also A. C. Graham.

GRAHAM, Sir John (Moodie), 2nd Bt *cr* 1964; Director: John Graham (Dromore) Ltd, since 1966 (Chairman); Electrical Supplies Ltd, since 1967; Concrete (NI) Ltd, since 1967; Irish Terrazzo Ltd; Kwik-Mix Ltd; Ulster Quarries Ltd; Graham (Contracts) Ltd; Fieldhouse Plant (NI) Ltd; Fieldtrac Scotland Ltd; Sykes Pumps (NI) Ltd; Kinnegar Inns Ltd, 1981; *b* 3 April 1938; *s* of Sir Clarence Graham, 1st Bt, MICE, and Margaret Christina Moodie (*d* 1954); *S* father, 1966; *m* 1970, Valerie Rosemary, *d* of Frank Gill, Belfast; three *d. Educ:* Trinity Coll., Glenalmond; Queen's Univ., Belfast. BSc, Civil Engineering, 1961. Joined family firm of John Graham (Dromore) Ltd, Building and Civil Engineering Contractors, on graduating from University. Chm., Concrete Soc., NI, 1972-74; Senior Vice-Pres., Concrete Soc., 1980; Pres., Northern Ireland Leukaemia Research Fund, 1967. *Recreations:* sailing, squash, water ski-ing, photography. *Address:* Sketrick Island, Killinchy, Co. Down. *T:* Killinchy 541449. *Clubs:* Strangford Lough Yacht; Kongelig Dansk Yachtclub (Copenhagen).

GRAHAM, Sir (John) Patrick, Kt 1969; Judge of the High Court of Justice, Chancery Division, 1969-81; Senior Patent Judge; *b* 26 Nov. 1906; *s* of Alexander Graham and Mary Adeline Cock; *m* 1931, Annie Elizabeth Newport Willson; four *s. Educ:* Shrewsbury; Caius Coll., Cambridge. Called to Bar, Middle Temple, 1930; read with Sir Lionel Heald, QC, MP; QC 1953; Treasurer, Middle Temple, 1979. Served War of 1939-45: RAF (VR) and with SHAEF, demobilised, 1945, with rank of Group Capt. Dep.-Chm., Salop Quarter Sessions, 1961-69. Mem., Standing Cttee on Structural Safety, 1975-.

Publication: Awards to Inventors, 1946. *Recreations:* golf, tennis, sailing. *Address:* Tall Elms, Radlett, Herts. *T:* Radlett 6307.

GRAHAM, Kathleen Mary, CBE 1958 (MBE 1945); *d* of late Col R. B. Graham, CBE, and Mrs M. G. Graham, London; unmarried. *Educ:* Cheltenham Ladies' Coll.; Univ. of London (Courtauld Inst. of Art). Courtauld Inst., Dept of Technology War-time Laboratory, 1940–41; Political Warfare Executive, 1942–45; entered HM Foreign Service, 1945; served in FO, 1946–49; Consul (Information) at San Francisco, Calif, 1949–53; served in FO, 1953–55; made Counsellor in HM Foreign Service in 1955 and appointed Dep. Consul-Gen. in New York, 1955–59; HM Consul-Gen. at Amsterdam, 1960–63; in FO, 1964–69, retired. Exec. Dir, 1970–73, a Governor, 1973–80, E-SU. *Recreations:* music, history of art. *Address:* 16 Graham Terrace, SW1W 8JH. *T:* 01-730 4611.

GRAHAM, Kenneth, OBE 1971; Assistant General Secretary, Trades Union Congress, since 1977; Member (part-time), Manpower Services Commission, since 1974; *b* 18 July 1922; *er s* of late Ernest Graham and of Ivy Hutchinson, Cleator, Cumbria; *m* 1945, Ann Winifred Muriel Taylor; no *c. Educ:* Workington Techn. Sch.; Leyton Techn. Coll.; Univ. of London (external). Engrg apprentice, 1938–42; Radar Research Unit, 1942–45; Air Trng Sch., qual. licensed engr, Air Registration Bd, 1947; employed in private industry, Mins of Aircraft Prodn and Supply, BOAC, and RN Scientific Service. Joined AEU, 1938: Mem. Final Appeal Court, Nat. Cttee, Divisional Chm., District Pres., etc, 1947–61; Tutor (part-time) in Trade Union Studies, Univ. of Southampton and WEA, 1958–61; joined TUC Organisation Dept, 1961, Head of TUC Organisation and Industrial Relations Dept, 1966–77. Member: Council, Inst. of Manpower Studies, 1975; Bd, European Foundn for Improvement of Living and Working Conditions, 1976; Adv. Cttee, European Social Fund, 1976. Special Award of Merit, AUEW, 1981. *Publications:* contrib. Job Satisfaction: Challenge and Response in Modern Britain, 1976. *Recreations:* music, military history. *Address:* 90 Springfield Drive, Ilford, Essex. *T:* 01-554 0839.

GRAHAM, (Malcolm Gray) Douglas; Deputy Chairman, The Midland News Association Ltd, since 1978; *b* 18 Feb. 1930; *s* of Malcolm Graham and Annie Jeanette Robinson; *m* 1980, Sara Anne Elwell (*née* Anderson). *Educ:* Shrewsbury Sch. National Service, RM, 1948–50. Newspaper trng, UK and Australia, 1950–53; Dir, Express & Star (Wolverhampton) Ltd, 1957. President: Young Newspapermen's Assoc., 1969; W Midlands Newspaper Soc., 1973–74; Chm., Evening Newspaper Advertising Bureau, 1978–79. *Recreation:* shooting. *Address:* Roughton Manor, Bridgnorth, Shropshire. *T:* Worfield 209.

GRAHAM, Martha; dancer; choreographer; director and teacher of dancing at the Martha Graham School of Contemporary Dance in New York; *b* Pittsburgh, Pa; *d* of Dr and Mrs George Graham. *Educ:* privately, and with Ruth St Denis and Ted Shawn. First appeared in Xochitl, New York, 1920; first recital by pupils, 1926; danced lead in Stravinsky's La Sacre du Printemps, 1930; founded Dance Repertory Theatre, 1930; choreographer of 167 solo and ensemble productions inc. three films (A Dancer's World, 1957; Appalachian Spring, 1958; Night Journey, 1960). Foreign tours, 1954, 1955-56, 1958, 1962, 1963, 1967, 1968, 1979; US tours, 1966, 1970, 1978, 1979; performed and lectured in major cities of Europe, Middle East, Iron Curtain countries, and throughout the Orient; has given solo performances with leading orchestras of United States. Three by Martha Graham, TV, 1969. Teacher: Neighbourhood Playhouse; Juilliard Sch. of Music. In the last five years her sch. has taken students from over forty foreign countries. Guggenheim Fellow, 1932, 1939; holds many doctorates and awards, including the Capezio Award, 1959, Aspen Award in the Humanities, 1965, and Distinguished Service to Arts Award, Nat. Inst. of Arts and Letters, 1970; Medal of Freedom (USA), 1976. *Publication:* The Notebooks of Martha Graham, 1973; *relevant publication:* Martha Graham: Portrait of a Lady as an Artist, by LeRoy Leatherman, 1966. *Address:* Martha Graham School of Contemporary Dance, 316 East 63rd Street, New York, NY 10021, USA. *Club:* Cosmopolitan (New York).

GRAHAM, Martin, QC 1976; Barrister; *b* 10 Feb. 1929; *m* 1962, Jane Patricia Anne Filby; one *d. Educ:* Emanuel School; Trinity College, Oxford (Open Scholar). MA, PPE. Called to Bar, Middle Temple, 1952. Served BAOR, 1953-55. *Recreations:* swimming, tennis. *Address:* 7 Oakeshott Avenue, N6; 1 Garden Court, Temple, EC4. *Clubs:* Reform, Royal Automobile, Hurlingham.

GRAHAM, Sir Norman (William), Kt 1971; CB 1961; FRSE; Member, Council on Tribunals, since 1977; Secretary, Scottish Education Department, 1964–73, retired; *b* 11 Oct. 1913; *s* of William and Margaret Graham; *m* 1949, Catherine Mary Strathie; two *s* one *d. Educ:* High Sch. of Glasgow; Glasgow Univ. Dept of Health for Scotland, 1936; Private Sec. to Permanent Under-Sec. of State, 1939–40; Ministry of Aircraft Production, 1940; Principal Private Sec. to Minister, 1944–45; Asst Sec., Dept of Health for Scotland, 1945; Under-Sec., Scottish Home and Health Dept, 1956–63. Hon. DLitt Heriot-Watt, 1971; DUniv Stirling, 1974. *Recreations:* golf, gardening. *Address:* Suilven, Longniddry, East Lothian. *T:* Longniddry 52130. *Club:* New (Edinburgh).

GRAHAM, Hon. Sir Patrick; see Graham, Hon. Sir J. P.

GRAHAM, Peter, CB 1982; Parliamentary Counsel since 1972; *b* 7 Jan. 1934; *o s* of late Alderman Douglas Graham, CBE, Huddersfield, and of Ena May (*née* Jackson); *m* 1st, Judith Mary Dunbar; two *s* ; 2nd, Anne Silvia Garcia (*see* A. S. Graham). *Educ:* St Bees Sch., Cumberland (scholar); St John's Coll., Cambridge (scholar, MA, LLB); McMahan Law Studentship. Served as pilot in Fleet Air Arm, 1952-55. Called to Bar, Grays Inn, 1958 (Holker Exhbn; H. C. Richards Prize, Ecclesiastical Law); joined Parliamentary Counsel Office, 1959. External Examr (Legislation), Univ. of Edinburgh, 1977–81; with Law Commn, 1979–81. *Recreations:* village church organist, gardening, bridge. *Address:* Quince Cottage, Hook Heath Road, Woking, Surrey. *T:* Woking 72214.

GRAHAM, Peter Alfred, OBE 1969; FIB, CBIM; Group Managing Director, 1977–May 1983, Senior Deputy Chairman, from Sept. 1983, Standard Chartered Bank Limited; Chairman, Standard Chartered Merchant Bank Limited, since 1977; *s* of Alfred Graham and Margaret (*née* Winder); *m* 1953, Luned Mary (*née* Kenealy-Jones); two *s* two *d. Educ:* St Joseph's Coll., Beulah Hill. FIB 1975; CBIM 1981. Served War, RNVR: Pilot, FAA. Joined The Chartered Bank of India, Australia and China, 1947; 24 yrs overseas banking career, incl. appts in Japan, India and Hong Kong; i/c The Chartered Bank, Hong Kong, 1962-70; Chm. (1st), Hong Kong Export Credit Insurance Corp., 1965-70; General Manager 1970, Dep. Man. Dir 1975, Standard Chartered Bank, London. Director: Standard Chartered Finance Ltd, Sydney (formerly Mutual Acceptance Corp.), 1974–; First Bank Nigeria, Lagos, 1976–; Union Bank Inc., Los Angeles, 1979–. Pres., Inst. of Bankers, 1981–; Chm., Adv. Cttee, City University Business Sch., 1981–; formerly Chm., Exchange Banks' Assoc., Hong Kong; Mem., Govt cttees connected with trade and industry, Hong Kong. *Recreations:* golf, tennis, skiing. *Address:* 3 Somers Crescent, W2 2PN. *Clubs:* Naval; Hong Kong (Hong Kong); Rye Golf.

GRAHAM, Sir Ralph Wolfe, 13th Bt *cr* 1629; *b* 14 July 1908; *s* of Percival Harris Graham (2nd *s* of 10th Bt) (*d* 1954) and Louise (*d* 1934), *d* of John Wolfe, Brooklyn, USA; *s* cousin, 1975; *m* 1st, 1939, Gertrude (marr. diss. 1949), *d* of Charles Kaminski; 2nd, 1949, Geraldine, *d* of Austin Velour; two *s. Heir: s* Ralph Stuart Graham [*b* 5 Nov. 1950; *m* 1st, 1972, Roxanne (*d* 1978), *d* of Mrs Lovette Gurzan; 2nd, 1979, Deena Vandergrift]. *Address:* 134 Leisureville Boulevard, Boynton Beach, Fla 33435, USA.

GRAHAM, Dr Ronald Cairns; Chief Administrative Medical Officer, Tayside Health Board, since 1973; *b* 8 Oct. 1931; *s* of Thomas Graham and Helen Cairns; *m* 1959, Christine Fraser Osborne; two *s* one *d. Educ:* Airdrie Acad.; Glasgow Univ. MB, ChB Glasgow 1956; DipSocMed Edin. 1968; FFCM 1973; MRCPE 1981. West of Scotland; house jobs, gen. practice and geriatric med., 1956–62; Dep. Med. Supt, Edin. Royal Infirmary, 1962–65; Asst Sen. Admin. MO, SE Regional Hosp. Bd, 1965-69; Dep. and then Sen. Admin. MO, Eastern Regional Hosp. Bd, 1969-73. *Recreation:* fishing. *Address:* 34 Dalgleish Road, Dundee DD4 7JT. *T:* Dundee 43146.

GRAHAM, Samuel Horatio, CMG 1965; OBE 1962; Puisne Judge, Supreme Court of the Commonwealth of the Bahamas, 1973-79; *b* 3 May 1912; *o s* of late Rev. Benjamin Graham, Trinidad; *m* 1943, Oris Gloria (*née* Teka); two *s* four *d. Educ:* Barbados; External Student, London Univ. BA (London) 1945; LLB (London) 1949. Teacher and journalist until called to Bar, Gray's Inn, 1949. Private practice as Barrister in Grenada, 1949-53; Magistrate, St Lucia, 1953-57; Crown Attorney, St Kitts, 1957-59; Attorney-General, St Kitts, 1960-62; Administrator of St Vincent, 1962-66; Puisne Judge, British Honduras, 1966-69; Pres., Industrial Court of Antigua, 1969-70. Mem., Council of Legal Educn, WI, 1971-. Chairman Inquiries into: Income Tax Reliefs; Coconut Industry, St Lucia, 1955; Legislators' Salaries, St Kitts, 1962. Acted Administrator of St Lucia, St Kitts and Dominica on various occasions. Acted Chief Justice, British Honduras, Feb.-May 1968. CStJ 1964. *Recreations:* cricket, bridge, swimming. *Address:* c/o Supreme Court, PO Box N167, Nassau, Bahamas. *Clubs:* St John's House; St Vincent Aquatic; Lyford Cay (Bahamas).

GRAHAM, (Stewart) David, QC 1977; *b* 27 Feb. 1934; *s* of Lewis Graham and Gertrude Graham; *m* 1959, Corinne Carmona; two *d. Educ:* Leeds Grammar Sch.; St Edmund Hall, Oxford (MA, BCL). Called to the Bar, Middle Temple, 1957; Harmsworth Law Scholar, 1958. Mem., Council of Justice, 1976–; Vice-Chm., Law, Parly and Gen. Purposes Cttee, Bd of Deputies of British Jews, 1979-. *Publications:* (ed jtly) Williams and Muir Hunter on Bankruptcy, 18th edn 1968, 19th edn 1979; (ed) legal textbooks. *Recreations:* literature, music, travel. *Address:* (chambers) 3 Paper Buildings, Temple, EC4 7EU. *T:* 01-353 3721; (home) 133 London Road, Stanmore, Mddx. *T:* 01-954 3783.

GRAHAM, Stuart Twentyman, CBE 1981; DFC 1943; FCIS, FIB; Director, Midland Bank plc, since 1974 (Group Chief Executive, 1981-82); *b* 26 Aug. 1921; *s* of late Twentyman Graham; *m* 1948, Betty June Cox; one *s. Educ:* Kilburn Grammar Sch. Served War, 1940-46: commissioned, RAF, 1942. Entered Midland Bank, 1938; Jt Gen. Manager, 1966-70; Asst Chief Gen. Manager, 1970-74; Chief Gen. Manager, 1974-81. Chairman: Northern Bank Ltd, 1982–; Internat. Commodities Clearing House Ltd, 1982–; Dir, Allied Lyons plc, 1981–. *Recreations:* music, reading. *Address:* 27-32 Poultry, EC2 2BX. *T:* 01-606 9911. *Clubs:* Overseas Bankers', St James's.

GRAHAM, (Thomas) Edward; MP (Lab and Co-op) Enfield, Edmonton since Feb. 1974; *b* 26 March 1925; *m* 1950; two *s. Educ:* elementary sch.; WEA

Co-operative College. BA Open Univ., 1976. Newcastle-on-Tyne Co-operative Soc., 1939-52; Organiser, British Fedn of Young Co-operators, 1952-53; Educn Sec., Enfield Highway Co-operative Soc., 1953-62; Sec., Co-operative Union Southern Section, 1962-67; Nat. Sec., Co-operative Party, 1967-74. PPS to Minister of State, Dept of Prices and Consumer Protection, 1974-76; A Lord Comr of HM Treasury, 1976-79; Opposition spokesman on the environment, 1980-. Mem. and Leader, Enfield Council, 1961-68. *Address:* 17a Queen Annes Grove, Bush Hill Park, Enfield, Mddx EN1 2JR.

GRAHAM, Walter Gerald Cloete, CBE 1952; retired 1975; *b* 13 May 1906; *s* of late Lance Graham Cloete Graham, of HBM Consular Service in China; *m* 1937, Nellor Alice Lee Swan; one *s* ; *m* 1949, Cynthia Anne, *d* of late Sir George Clayton East, Bt; one *s* one *d. Educ:* Malvern Coll.; The Queen's Coll., Oxford. Laming Travelling Fellow of Queen's, 1927-29. Entered Consular Service in China, 1928; served in Peking, Nanking, Shanghai, Mukden Chefoo and Tientsin; Consul: Port Said, 1942-44, Chengtu, 1944-45, Urumchi (Chinese Turkestan), 1945-47; Consul-General, Mukden, 1947-49; Chinese Counsellor, Peking, 1949-50; Counsellor, Foreign Office, 1951-52; Minister to Republic of Korea, 1952-54; Ambassador to Libya, 1955-59; Asia Adviser to Defence Intelligence Staff (formerly Jt Intell. Bureau), Min. of Defence, 1959-67; Res. Adviser, FCO Res. Dept, 1967-75. *Recreations:* golf, watching cricket, gardening. *Address:* Knabb's Farmhouse, Fletching, Uckfield, Sussex. *T:* Newick 2198. *Club:* MCC.

GRAHAM, Rear-Adm. Wilfred Jackson, CB 1979; Director and Secretary, Royal National Lifeboat Institution, since 1979; *b* 17 June 1925; *s* of William Bryce Graham and Jean Hill Graham (*née* Jackson); *m* 1951, Gillian Mary Finlayson; three *s* one *d. Educ:* Rossall Sch., Fleetwood, Lancs. Served War of 1939-45, Royal Navy: Cadet, 1943; specialised in gunnery, 1951; Comdr 1960; Captain 1967; IDC, 1970; Captain, HMS Ark Royal, 1975-76; Flag Officer, Portsmouth, 1976-79, retired. MNI. *Recreations:* sailing, walking, skiing. *Address:* Ackland Cottage, Shirley Holms, near Lymington, Hants; RNLI, West Quay Road, Poole, Dorset. *Clubs:* Army and Navy; Royal Naval Sailing Association.

GRAHAM, William Franklin, (Billy Graham); Evangelist; *b* Charlotte, NC, 7 Nov. 1918; *s* of William Franklin Graham and Morrow (*née* Coffey); *m* 1943, Ruth McCue Bell; two *s* three *d. Educ:* Florida Bible Institute, Tampa (ThB); Wheaton Coll., Ill (AB). Ordained to Baptist ministry, 1940; first Vice-Pres., Youth for Christ Internat., 1946-48; Pres., Northwestern Coll., Minneapolis, 1947-52; Evangelistic campaigns, 1946-; world-wide weekly broadcast, 1950-; many evangelistic tours of Great Britain, Europe, the Far East, South America and Australia. Chairman, Board of World Wide Pictures Inc. FRGS. Holds numerous honorary degrees in Divinity, Laws, Literature and the Humanities, from American universities and colleges; also varied awards from organisations, 1954-, inc. Templeton Foundn Prize, 1982. *Publications include:* Peace with God, 1954; World Aflame, 1965; Jesus Generation, 1971; Angels—God's Secret Agents, 1975; How to be Born Again, 1977; The Holy Spirit, 1978; The Armageddon, 1981. *Recreations:* golf, jogging. *Address:* (office) 1300 Harmon Place, Minneapolis, Minnesota 55403, USA. *T:* (612)338-0500.

GRAHAM, Winston Mawdsley, FRSL; *b* Victoria Park, Manchester; *m* 1939, Jean Mary Williamson; one *s* one *d.* Chm., Soc. of Authors, 1967-69. Books trans. into 17 languages. *Publications:* some early novels (designedly) out of print, and: Night Journey, 1941 (rev. edn 1966); The Merciless Ladies, 1944 (rev. edn 1979); The Forgotten Story, 1945 (ITV prodn, 1982); Ross Poldark, 1945; Demelza, 1946; Take My Life, 1947 (filmed 1947); Cordelia, 1949; Night Without Stars, 1950 (filmed 1950); Jeremy Poldark, 1950; Fortune is a Woman, 1953 (filmed 1956); Warleggan, 1953; The Little Walls, 1955; The Sleeping Partner, 1956 (filmed 1958); Greek Fire, 1957; The Tumbled House, 1959; Marnie, 1961 (filmed 1963); The Grove of Eagles, 1963; After the Act, 1965; The Walking Stick, 1967 (filmed 1970); Angell, Pearl and Little God, 1970; The Japanese Girl (short stories), 1971; The Spanish Armadas, 1972; The Black Moon, 1973; Woman in the Mirror, 1975; The Four Swans, 1976; The Angry Tide, 1977; The Stranger from the Sea, 1981; The Miller's Dance, 1982. BBC TV Series Poldark (the first four Poldark novels), 1975-76, second series (the next three Poldark novels), 1977; Circumstantial Evidence (play), 1979. *Recreations:* golf, gardening. *Address:* Abbotswood House, Buxted, East Sussex. *Clubs:* Savile, Beefsteak.
See also A. W. M. Graham.

GRAHAM-BRYCE, Ian James, DPhil; Director, East Malling Research Station, Maidstone, Kent, since Aug. 1979; *b* 20 March 1937; *s* of late Alexander Graham-Bryce, FRCS, and of Dame Isabel Graham Bryce, qv; *m* 1959, Anne Elisabeth Metcalf; one *s* three *d. Educ:* William Hulme's Grammar Sch., Manchester; University Coll., Oxford (Exhibnr). BA, MA, BSc, DPhil (Oxon). Research Asst, Univ. of Oxford, 1958-61; Lectr, Dept of Biochemistry and Soil Sci., UCNW, Bangor, 1961-64; Sen. Scientific Officer, Rothamsted Exper. Station, 1964-70; Sen. Res. Officer, ICI Plant Protection Div., Jealott's Hill Res. Station, Bracknell, Berks, 1970-72; Special Lectr in Pesticide Chemistry, Dept of Zoology and Applied Entomology, Imperial Coll. of Science and Technology, 1970-72 (Vis. Prof., 1976-79); Rothamsted Experimental Station: Head, Dept of Insecticides and Fungicides, 1972-79; Dep. Director, 1975-79. Cons. Dir, Commonwealth Bureau of Horticulture and Plantation Crops, 1979-; Hon. Lectr, Dept of Biology, Univ. of Strathclyde, 1977-80. Society of Chemical Industry, London: Mem. Council,

1969-72 and 1974-; Vice-Pres., 1980-; Hon. Sec., Home Affairs, 1977-80; Chm., Pesticides Gp, 1978-80; Sec., Physico-Chemical and Biophysical Panel, 1968-70, Chm., 1973-75; Member, Editorial Board: Chemico-Biological Interactions, 1973-77; Pesticide Science, 1978-80; Agriculture and Environment, 1978-. *Publications:* Physical Aspects of Pesticide Behaviour, 1980; papers on soil science, plant nutrition and crop protection in sci. jls. *Recreations:* music (espec. opera), squash racquets, fly fishing. *Address:* Great East, East Malling, near Maidstone, Kent ME19 6BJ. *Club:* Athenæum.

GRAHAM BRYCE, Dame Isabel, DBE 1968; Chairman: Oxford Regional Hospital Board, 1963-72; National Nursing Staff Committee, 1967-75; National Staff Committee, 1969-75; Consultant, British Transport Hotels, 1979-81 (Board Member, 1962-79); Vice-President, Princess Christian College, Manchester, since 1953; President, Goring and District Day Centre for the Elderly; *b* 30 April 1902; *d* of late Prof. James Lorrain Smith, FRS; *m* 1934, Alexander Graham Bryce, FRCS (*d* 1968); two *s. Educ:* St Leonards Sch., St Andrews; Edinburgh Univ. (MA). Investigator, Industrial Fatigue Research Board, 1926-27; HM Inspector of Factories, 1928-34; Centre Organiser, WVS, Manchester, 1938-39; Dir of Organization, Ontario Div., Canadian WVS, 1941-42; Tech. Adviser, American WVS, 1942-43; Res. Fellow Fatigue Lab. Harvard Univ., 1943-44; Nat. Council of Women: Chm., Manchester Br., 1947-50; Vice-Chm., Education Cttee, 1950-51. JP and Mem. Juvenile Court Panel, Manchester City, 1949-55; Vice-Chairman: Assoc. of HMC's, 1953-55; Bd of Visitors, Grendon Prison, 1962-67. Member: Nurses and Midwives Whitley Council, 1953-57; General Nursing Council, 1956-61; Bd of Governors, Eastman Dental Hosp., 1957-63; Maternity and Midwifery Standing Cttee, 1957-72; Public Health Insp., Education Bd, 1958-64; Independent Television Authority, 1960-65 (Chm., General Advisory Council, 1964-65); Bd, ATV Network Ltd, 1968-72; Ancillary Dental Workers Cttee, 1956-68; Experimental Scheme for Dental Auxiliaries, 1958-69; Council, Tyringham Foundn Ltd. Life Mem., British Fedn Univ. Women; Mem., Open Section, Royal Soc. of Medicine. Hon. Mem., Oxford Br., Zouta International. *Publications:* (joint) reports on research into industrial psychological problems. *Address:* The Old Bakery, 14 Wood Street, Wallingford OX10 0BD. *T:* Wallingford 35837. *Club:* VAD Ladies'.
See also I. J. Graham-Bryce.

GRAHAM-CAMPBELL, David John, MA Cantab; Liaison Officer to Schools, Aberdeen University, 1972-76; *b* 18 Feb. 1912; *s* of late Sir R. F. Graham-Campbell; *m* 1940, Joan Sybil, *d* of late Major H. F. Maclean; three *s. Educ:* Eton Coll.; Trinity Coll., Cambridge (Exhibitioner). Assistant Master, Eton Coll., 1935-64; Warden, Trinity Coll., Glenalmond, 1964-72. Served with 2nd Bn KRRC and on the staff, 1939-45 (Lt-Col). *Publications:* Writing English, 1953; Portrait of Argyll and the Southern Hebrides, 1978; Portrait of Perth, Angus and Fife, 1979. *Recreations:* fishing, gardening, walking. *Address:* 17 Muirton Bank, Perth, Perthshire.
See also Baron Maclean.

GRAHAM-DIXON, Anthony Philip, QC 1973; *b* 5 Nov. 1929; *s* of Leslie Charles Graham-Dixon, qv ; *m* 1956, Margaret Suzanne Villar; one *s* one *d. Educ:* Westminster School; Christ Church, Oxford. MA (1st Cl. Hon. Mods, 1st Cl. Lit. Hum.). RNVR, 1953-55, Lieut (SP). Called to the Bar, Inner Temple, 1956, Bencher 1982; Member of Gray's Inn, 1965-. Mem. Council, Charing Cross Hosp. Medical School, 1976-. *Publication:* (mem. adv. bd) Competition Law in Western Europe and the USA, 1976. *Recreations:* music (especially opera), gardening, tennis. *Address:* 31 Hereford Square, SW7. *T:* 01-373 1461; Masketts Manor, Nutley, Uckfield, East Sussex. *T:* Nutley 2719.

GRAHAM-DIXON, Leslie Charles, QC 1950; retired 1956; *b* 17 June 1901; *m* 1926, Dorothy Rivett; two *s. Educ:* Merchant Taylors' Sch.; St John's Coll., Oxford. Called to the Bar, 1925, Inner Temple. Western Circuit. Vice-Pres., Council, Royal Albert Hall, 1965-. Chm. Council, Charing Cross Hosp. Med. Sch., 1973-81, Pres., 1981-. *Address:* The Clock Tower, Nutley, E Sussex. *T:* Nutley 2275.
See also A. P. Graham-Dixon.

GRAHAM DOW, Ronald; see Dow.

GRAHAM-GREEN, Major Graham John, CB 1978; TD 1945; Chief Taxing Master of the Supreme Court, 1972-79 (Master, 1953-72); *b* 16 Dec. 1906; *m* 1933, Eirene Mary Baston; one *d. Educ:* Dulwich. Admitted solicitor, 1929; Partner Kingsford, Dorman & Co., 1935-52; and Director of Companies. Served HAC, 1924-33; RA (TA), 1935-45. Freeman of City of London, 1945; Member: Law Soc., 1929 (Hon. Mem., City of Westminster and Eastbourne Law Socs, 1979); Solicitors Company, 1945; London Maritime Arbitrators' Assoc., 1977. Co-Founder of Catholic Marriage Advisory Council, 1946; Founder Chm., Bd of Trustees, Friends of Osborne House Convalescent Home for Officers, 1979. *Publications:* Cordery's Law Relating to Solicitors, 5th edn, 1961, Supplements 1962, 1963, 1965 and 1966, 6th edn 1968, Supplements 1970, 1974, 7th edn, 1981; Criminal Costs and Legal Aid, 1965, 3rd edn 1973, Supplement 1978, etc. *Recreations:* riding, travelling. *Address:* 38 Linkswood, Compton Place Road, Eastbourne, Sussex. *T:* Eastbourne 36320. *Club:* Army and Navy.

GRAHAM HALL, Jean; see Hall, J. G.

GRAHAM-HARRISON, Francis Laurence Theodore, CB 1962; Deputy Under-Secretary of State, Home Office, 1963-74; *b* 30 Oct. 1914; *s* of late Sir William Montagu Graham-Harrison, KCB, KC, and Lady Graham-Harrison, *d* of Sir Cyril Graham, 5th and last Bt, CMG; *m* 1941, Carol Mary St John, 3rd *d* of late Sir Francis Stewart, CIE; one *s* three *d. Educ:* Eton; Magdalen Coll., Oxford. Entered Home Office, 1938. Private Secretary to Parliamentary Under-Secretary of State, 1941-43; Asst Private Secretary to Prime Minister, 1946-49; Secretary, Royal Commission on Capital Punishment, 1949-53; Asst Secretary, Home Office, 1953-57; Asst Under-Secretary of State, Home Office, 1957-63. Trustee: Tate Gallery, 1975-82; Nat. Gallery, 1981-82. Chm., Exec. Finance Cttee, Dr Barnardo's, 1978-81. *Address:* 32 Parliament Hill, NW3. *T:* 01-435 6316.

GRAHAM-MOON, Sir Peter Wilfred Giles; *see* Moon.

GRAHAM SMITH, Stanley, CBE 1949; *b* 18 Jan. 1896; *s* of late George and Minnie Elizabeth Graham Smith; *m* 1929, Mrs Blanche Violet Horne (*d* 1974), *widow* (*née* Venning); one *s. Educ:* Strand Sch., King's Coll., London. Entered Civil Service, 1914 (Admiralty). Served European War as pilot in Royal Naval Air Service, Dec. 1916-Jan. 1919. Rejoined Admiralty, 1919. Private Secretary to Accountant-General of the Navy, 1922-32; Private Secretary to Civil Lord of Admiralty, 1932-35; Head of Air Branch, Admiralty, 1941-49; Under Secretary (Naval Staff), Admiralty, 1950-56; retired from Civil Service, 1956.

GRAHAM-TOLER, family name of the **Earl of Norbury.**

GRAHAME-SMITH, Prof. David Grahame; Professor of Clinical Pharmacology, University of Oxford, since 1972; Hon. Director, Medical Research Council Unit of Clinical Pharmacology, Radcliffe Infirmary, Oxford; Fellow of Corpus Christi College, Oxford, since 1972; *b* 10 May 1933; *s* of George E. and C. A. Smith; *m* 1957, Kathryn Frances, *d* of Dr F. R. Beetham; two *s. Educ:* Wyggeston Grammar Sch., Leicester; St Mary's Hosp. Medical Sch., Univ. of London. MB, BS (London) 1956; MRCS, LRCP 1956; MRCP 1958; PhD (London) 1966; FRCP 1972. House Phys., Paddington Gen. Hosp., London, 1956; House Surg., Battle Hosp., Reading, 1956-57. Captain, RAMC, 1957-60. Registrar and Sen. Registrar in Medicine, St Mary's Hosp., Paddington, 1960-61; H. A. M. Thompson Research Scholar, RCP, 1961-62; Saltwell Research Scholar, RCP, 1962-65; Wellcome Trust Research Fellow, 1965-66; Hon. Med. Registrar to Med. Unit, St Mary's Hosp., 1961-66; MRC Travelling Fellow, Dept of Endocrinology, Vanderbilt Univ., Nashville, Tennessee, USA, 1966-67; Sen. Lectr in Clinical Pharmacology and Therapeutics, St Mary's Hosp. Med. Sch., Univ. of London, 1967-71; Hon. Cons. Physician, St Mary's Hosp., Paddington, 1967-71. Mem., Cttee on Safety of Medicines, 1975. *Publications:* papers on biochemical, therapeutic and med. matters in scientific jls. *Recreations:* horse riding, jazz. *Address:* Romney, Lincombe Lane, Boars Hill, Oxford. *T:* Oxford 735889.

GRAHAMSTOWN, Bishop of, since 1974; **Rt. Rev. Kenneth Cyril Oram;** *b* 3 March 1919; *s* of Alfred Charles Oram and Sophie Oram; *m* 1943, Kathleen Mary Malcolm; three *s* one *d. Educ:* Selhurst Grammar Sch., Croydon; King's Coll., London; Lincoln Theol Coll. BA Hons English, 1st Cl. AKC. Asst Curate: St Dunstan's, Cranbrook, 1942-45; St Mildred's, Croydon, 1945-46; Upington with Prieska, S Africa, 1946-48; Rector of Prieska and Dir of Prieska Mission District, 1949-51; Rector of Mafeking, 1952-59; Dir of Educn, dio. Kimberley and Kuruman, 1953-62; Archdeacon of Bechuanaland, 1953-59; Dean and Archdeacon: of Kimberley, 1960-64; of Grahamstown, 1964-74. *Recreations:* music, walking. *Address:* Bishopsbourne, PO Box 162, Grahamstown, South Africa. *T:* 2500. *Club:* Albany (Grahamstown).

GRAINGER, Leslie, CBE 1976; BSc; FEng; FIM; MInstF; Managing Director, Branon PLC, since 1981; Chairman, Cavendish Petroleum PLC; *b* 8 August 1917. Mem. for Science, NCB, 1966-77; Chairman: NCB (Coal Products) Ltd, 1975-78; NCB (IEA Services) Ltd, 1975-79. *Address:* 11 Catherine Place, SW1. *T:* 01-630 5727.

GRANADO, Donald Casimir, TC 1970; *b* 4 March 1915; *m* 1959, Anne-Marie Faustin Lombard; one *s* two *d. Educ:* Trinidad. Gen. Sec., Union of Commercial and Industrial Workers, 1951-53; Sec./Treas., Fedn of Trade Unions, 1952-53; Elected MP for Laventille, Trinidad, 1956 and 1961; Minister of: Labour and Social Services, 1956-61; Health and Housing, and Dep. Leader House of Representatives, 1961-63. Ambassador to Venezuela, 1963-64; High Comr to Canada, 1964-69; Ambassador to Argentina and to Brazil, 1965-69; High Comr to London, 1969-71, and Ambassador to France, Germany, Belgium, Switzerland, Italy, Holland, Luxembourg and European Common Market, 1969-71. Led Trinidad and Tobago delegn to UN, 1965; led govt delegn and went on govt business to various parts of the World. First Gen. Sec., People's National Movement. Trinidad and Tobago Football Association: Sec. and Treasurer, E Zone; Chm., Youth Cttee; Mem., Gen. Council. Speaks, reads and writes French and Spanish. *Recreations:* cricket, soccer, bridge and golf; music (tape-recording), writing. *Address:* 20 Grove Road, Valsayn Park, Trinidad.

GRANARD, 9th Earl of, *cr* 1684; **Arthur Patrick Hastings Forbes,** AFC, 1941; Bt 1628; Viscount Granard and Baron Clanehugh, 1675; Baron Granard (UK), 1806; Air Commodore late RAFVR; *b* 10 April 1915; *e s* of 8th Earl of Granard, KP, PC, GCVO, and Beatrice (*d* 1972), OBE, *d* of Ogden Mills, Staatsburg, Dutchess County, USA; *S* father, 1948; *m* 1949, Marie-Madeleine Eugènie, *y d* of Jean Maurel, Millau, Aveyron, formerly wife of late Prince Humbert de Faucigny Lucinge; two *d. Educ:* Eton; Trinity Coll., Cambridge. Served War of 1939-45 (despatches, AFC). Commandeur Légion d'Honneur; Croix de Guerre with Palm; Officer Legion of Merit, USA; Croix des Vaillants of Poland; Order of George I of Greece. *Heir: b* Hon. John Forbes, late Flt Lt RAF [*b* 8 Oct. 1920; *m* 1947, Joan, *d* of A. Edward Smith, Algoa, Westminster Road, Foxrock, Co. Dublin; one *s* three *d*]. *Address:* 11 rue Louis de Savoie, Morges, Switzerland. *Club:* White's.

See also Marquess of Bute.

GRANBY, Marquis of; David Charles Robert Manners; *b* 8 May 1959; *s* and *heir* of 10th Duke of Rutland, *qv.* Assistant Antique Arms dealer in Nottingham. *Address:* Belvoir Castle, Grantham. *Clubs:* Turf; Annabel's.

GRAND, Keith Walter Chamberlain; FCIT; Chairman, Railway Benevolent Institute; *b* 3 July 1900; *m* 1st, 1925, Alice M. (*d* 1969), *d* of late Henry Gates, Brockville, Ont., Canada; one *d* (one *s* decd); 2nd, 1971, Enid M. Wheatley. *Educ:* Rugby. Joined GWR 1919; USA 1926-29; General Manager, British Railways, Western Region, 1948-59. Member (full-time) British Transport Commn, 1959-62; Member Coastal Shipping Advisory Cttee, 1959-62; Chm., Coast Lines, 1968-71. *Recreation:* golf. *Address:* Queen Anne Flat, Little Sodbury Manor, Chipping Sodbury, near Bristol. *Clubs:* Carlton, MCC; Royal Mid-Surrey Golf (Richmond).

GRANDI, Count (di Mordano) *cr* 1937, **Dino;** retired; President Chamber of Fasci and Corporazioni, Italy, 1939-43; late Member of the Chamber of Deputies and of the Fascist Grand Council; *b* Mordano (Bologna), 4 June 1895; *m* 1924, Antonietta Brizzi; one *s* one *d.* Graduated in Law at the University of Bologna, 1919; volunteered for the war and was promoted to Captain for merit and decorated with silver medal, bronze medal, and three military crosses for valour; journalist and political organiser, after the war led the Fascist movement in the North of Italy and took part in the March on Rome as Chief of the General Staff of the Quadrunvirato; elected member of the Chamber of Deputies, 1921, 1924, 1929, 1934, and 1939; member of the General Direction of the Fascist Party Organisation, 1921-23-24; Deputy President of the Chamber of Deputies, 1924; Italian Delegate to the IV, V, International Labour Conference, 1922, 1923; Under-Secretary of State for the Interior, 1924; Under Secretary of State for Foreign Affairs, 1925-29; Italian Delegate, Locarno Conference, 1925; to Conferences for Settlement of War Debt, Washington, 1925 and London, 1926; and Hague Conference on War Debts, 1929; Head of Italian Delegation, London Naval Conference, 1930; Italian Delegate, Danubian Conference, London, 1932; Head of Italian Delegation, Geneva Disarmament Conference, 1932; Minister of Foreign Affairs, 1929-32; Permanent Italian Delegate to the Council of the League of Nations, 1925-32; Italian Ambassador in London, 1932-39; Keeper of the Seal and Minister of Justice, Italy, 1939-43; Head of Italian Delegation to London Naval Conference, 1936; Italian Representative to London Session of Council of League of Nations, 1936; at London Meeting of Locarno Powers, 1936; and on the London International Cttee for Non-Intervention in Spain, 1936, 1937, 1938, 1939. *Publications:* Origins of Fascism, 1929; Italian Foreign Policy, 1931; The Spanish War in the London Committee, 1939; The Frontiers of the Law, 1941, etc. *Recreations:* book collecting, riding, gardening, mountaineering. *Address:* I-41030 Albareto Di Modena, Italy.

GRANDY, Marshal of the Royal Air Force Sir John, GCB 1967 (KCB 1964; CB 1956); KBE 1961; DSO 1945; RAF; Constable and Governor of Windsor Castle, since 1978; *b* Northwood, Mddx, 8 Feb. 1913; *s* of late Francis Grandy and late Nellie Grandy (*née* Lines); *m* 1937, Cecile Elizabeth Florence Rankin, CStJ, *yr d* of Sir Robert Rankin, 1st and last Bt; two *s. Educ:* University College Sch., London. Joined RAF 1931. No 54 (Fighter) Sqdn, 1932-35; 604 (Middx) Sqdn., RAuxAF, 1935-36; Adjt and Flying Instructor, London Univ. Air Sqdn, 1937-39; Comd No 249 (Fighter) Sqdn during Battle of Britain; Staff Duties, HQ Fighter Comd, and Wing Comdr Flying RAF Coltishall, 1941; commanded: RAF Duxford, 1942 (First Typhoon Wing); HQ No 210 Group, No 73 Op Training Unit, and Fighter Conversion Unit at Abu Sueir, 1943-44; No 341 Wing (Dakotas), SE Asia Comd, 1944-45; DSO 1945, despatches 1943 and 1945. SASO No 232 Gp, 1945; psc 1946; Dep. Dir Operational Training, Air Min., 1946; Air Attaché, Brussels, 1949; Comd Northern Sector, Fighter Comd, 1950; Air Staff HQ Fighter Comd, 1952-54; Comdt, Central Fighter Estab., 1954-57; idc 1957; Comdr, Task Force Grapple (British Nuclear Weapon Test Force), Christmas Is., 1957-58; Assistant CAS (Ops), 1958-61; Commander-in-Chief, RAF, Germany and Comdr, Second Allied TAF, 1961-63; AOC-in-C, Bomber Command, 1963-65; C-in-C, British Forces, Far East, and UK Mil. Adviser to SEATO, 1965-67; Chief of the Air Staff, 1967-71; Governor and C-in-C, Gibraltar, 1973-78. Dir, Brixton Estate Ltd, 1971-73, 1978-; Chm. Trustees, Imperial War Museum, 1978-; Dep. Chm. Council, RAF Benevolent Fund, 1980-; Trustee: Burma Star Assoc., 1979- (Vice-Pres.); Shuttleworth Remembrance Trust, 1978- (Chm., Aerodrome Cttee, 1980-); RAF Church, St Clement Danes, 1971-; past Pres., Officers' Assoc.; Vice-President: Officers' Pension Soc., 1971-; Nat. Assoc. of Boys' Clubs, 1971-; Pres., Disablement in the City, 1980-; Member: Management Cttee, RNLI, 1971-; Cttee, Royal Humane Soc., 1978-; Patron, Polish Air Force Assoc. in GB, 1979-. PMN 1967. Hon. Liveryman, Haberdashers' Co., 1968. Freeman, City of London, 1968. KStJ 1974. *Address:* Norman Tower, Windsor Castle, Berks. *Clubs:* White's, Pratt's, Royal Air Force; Royal Yacht Squadron (Cowes); Swinley Forest Golf.

GRANGE, Kenneth Henry, RDI, FSIA; industrial designer; in private practice since 1958; Partner, Pentagram Design Partnership, since 1972; *b* 17 July 1929; *s* of Harry Alfred Grange and Hilda Gladys (*née* Long). *Educ:* London. Technical Illustrator, RE, 1948-50; Design Asst, Arcon Chartered Architects, 1948; Bronek Katz & Vaughn, 1950-51; Gordon Bowyer & Partners, 1951-54; Jack Howe & Partners, 1954-58. RDI 1969; FSIA 1959. 8 CoID Awards; Duke of Edinburgh Award for Elegant Design, 1963. *Recreations:* tennis, ski-ing. *Address:* 61 North Wharf Road, W2 1LA; Acrise Cottage, Christchurch Hill, NW3.

GRANGER, Stewart; (James Lablache Stewart); actor (stage and films); *b* London, 6 May 1913; *s* of late Major James Stewart, RE, and Frederica Lablache; *m* 1st, Elspeth March (marr. diss., 1948); two *c*; 2nd, 1950, Jean Simmons, *qv* (marr. diss. 1960); one *c*; 3rd, 1964, Viviane Lecerf (marr. diss. 1969). *Educ:* Epsom Coll. Began training as doctor but decided to become an actor. Studied at Webber-Douglas School of Dramatic Art; played at Little Theatre, Hull, and with Birmingham Repertory Company; appeared at Malvern Festivals, 1936-37; first London appearance as Captain Hamilton in The Sun Never Sets, Drury Lane, 1938; appeared on London stage, 1938-39; joined Old Vic Company, 1939; Dr Fleming in Tony Draws a Horse, Criterion, 1940; George Winthrop in A House in the Square, St Martin's, 1940; toured, 1940; served War of 1939-45, Army, 1940-42 (invalided). Toured, 1942; succeeded Owen Nares as Max de Winter in Rebecca, Lyric, 1942. Began film career in 1938, and has appeared in many films, including: The Man in Grey, The Lamp Still Burns, Fanny by Gaslight, Blue for Waterloo, The Love Story, The Madonna of the Seven Moons, Cæsar and Cleopatra, The Magic Bow, Captain Boycott, Blanche Fury, Saraband for Dead Lovers, Woman Hater, Adam and Evelyne, King Solomon's Mines, Soldiers Three, Light Touch, Wild North, Scaramouche, Young Bess, Salome, Beau Brummell, Footsteps in the Fog, Green Fire, Bhowani Junction, The Little Hut, North to Alaska, Swordsman of Siena, The Secret Invasion, Flaming Frontier, The Trygon Factor, The Wild Geese. *Publication:* Sparks Fly Upward (autobiog.), 1981. *Address:* PO Box 115, Estepona, Málaga, Spain.

GRANIT, Prof. Ragnar Arthur, Commander, Order of Nordstjernan, Sweden, 1964; Professor Emeritus, since 1967, Karolinska Institutet, Stockholm; *b* 30 Oct. 1900; *s* of Arthur W. Granit and Albertina Helena Granit (*née* Malmberg); *m* 1929, Baroness Marguerite (Daisy) Bruun; one *s*. *Educ:* Swedish Normallyceum; Helsingfors University. MagPhil 1923, MD 1927. Prof. of Physiology, Helsingfors, 1937; Prof. of Neurophysiology, Stockholm, 1940; Dir of Dept of Neurophysiology, Medical Nobel Inst., 1945; retired, 1967. President, Royal Swedish Acad, Science, 1963-65. Lectures: Silliman, Yale, 1954; Sherrington, London, 1967; Liverpool, 1971; Murlin, Rochester, NY 1973; Hughlings Jackson, McGill, 1975. Visiting Professor: Rockefeller Univ., NY, 1956-66; St Catherine's Coll., Oxford, 1967; Pacific Medical Center, San Francisco, 1969; Fogarty Internat. Foundn, Nat. Inst. of Health, Bethesda, USA, 1971-72, 1975; Düsseldorf Univ., 1976; Max-Planck Inst., Bad Nauheim, 1977. Hon. MD: Oslo, 1951; Loyola, 1969; Pisa, 1970; Hon. DSc: Oxford, 1956; Hong Kong, 1961; Hon. DPhil Helsingfors, 1982; Catedr. Hon., Lima, Santiago, Bogotá, 1958. Retzius Gold Medal, 1957; Donders Medal, 1957; Jahre Prize (Oslo), 1961; III Internat. St Vincent Prize, 1961; Nobel Prize for Medicine (jointly), 1967; Sherrington Medal, 1967; Purkinje Gold Medal, 1969. For. Mem., Royal Soc., 1960; Nat. Acad. Sci., Washington, 1968; Accad. Naz. dei Lincei, 1978; Hon. Mem., Amer. Acad. of Arts and Sciences. Mem. and Hon. Mem. of several learned societies. Cross of Freedom (Finland), 1918. *Publications:* Sensory Mechanisms of the Retina, (UK) 1947 (US 1963); Receptors and Sensory Perception, (US) 1955; Charles Scott Sherrington: An Appraisal, (UK) 1966; Basis of Motor Control, (UK) 1970; Regulation of the Discharge of Motoneurons (UK), 1971; The Purposive Brain (US), 1977; Ung Mans Väg till Minerva, 1941. *Recreations:* island life, gardening. *Address:* 14 Eriksbergsgatan, S-114 30 Stockholm 4, Sweden.

GRANT, family name of **Baron Strathspey.**

GRANT, Alexander Ludovic, TD 1940; DL; JP; Director, Barclays Bank Ltd, 1945-73 (Chairman, Manchester and Liverpool Local Boards, 1945-73; Local Director, Liverpool, 1930, Manchester, 1940); Director, Barclays Bank (DCO), 1948-72; *b* 26 March 1901; *s* of late John Peter Grant of Rothiemurchus, Aviemore, Inverness-shire, and late Lady Mary Grant, *d* of 3rd Earl Manvers; *m* 1946, Elizabeth Langley, *widow* of Capt. J. G. F. Buxton, Grenadier Guards, and *d* of late Major Robert Barbour, Bolesworth Castle, Tattenhall, Cheshire; two *d. Educ:* Winchester; New Coll., Oxford (MA). Entered Barclays Bank Ltd, 1925; General Manager, Union Bank of Manchester, 1938-39 (Union Bank of Manchester was absorbed by Barclays Bank, 1940). Served Lovat Scouts, 1920-40 (Major 1935), and with Cheshire Home Guard, 1940-45. High Sheriff of Cheshire, 1956; DL Cheshire, 1963. *Recreations:* shooting, fishing, gardening. *Address:* Marbury Hall, Whitchurch, Salop. *T:* Whitchurch 3731. *Clubs:* Pratt's, MCC.

GRANT, Alexander (Marshall), CBE 1965; Artistic Director, National Ballet of Canada, since 1976; *b* Wellington, New Zealand, 22 Feb. 1928; *s* of Alexander and Eleather Grant. *Educ:* Wellington Coll., NZ. Arrived in London, Feb. 1946, to study with Sadler's Wells School on Scholarship given in New Zealand by Royal Academy of Dancing, London; joined Sadler's Wells Ballet (now Royal Ballet Company), Aug. 1946. Dir, Ballet for All (touring ballet company), 1971-76 (Co-director, 1970-71). Danced leading

rôles in following: Mam'zelle Angot, Clock Symphony, Boutique Fantasque, Donald of the Burthens, Rake's Progress, Job, Three Cornered Hat, Ballabile, Cinderella, Sylvia, Madame Chrysanthème, Façade, Daphnis and Chloé, Coppélia, Petrushka, Ondine, La Fille Mal Gardée, Jabez and the Devil, Persephone, The Dream, Jazz Calendar, Enigma Variations, Sleeping Beauty (Carabosse), A Month in the Country; *films:* Tales of Beatrix Potter (Peter Rabbit and Pigling Bland); Steps of the Ballet. *Recreations:* gardening, cinephotography. *Address:* National Ballet of Canada, 157 King Street East, Toronto, Ont M5C 1G9, Canada.

GRANT, Alexander Thomas Kingdom, CB 1965; CMG 1949; MA; Fellow of Pembroke College, Cambridge, 1966-73, now Fellow Emeritus; *b* 29 March 1906; *s* of late Harold Allan Grant and Marie F. C. Grant; *m* 1930, Helen Frances, *d* of late Dr and Mrs H. Newsome, Clifton, Bristol. *Educ:* St Olave's Sch.; University Coll., Oxford (Scholar in Modern History). Research on international financial problems at RIIA, 1932-35. Leverhulme Research Fellow, 1935-37. Lectr in Dept of Polit. Econ., UCL, 1938-39. Joined HM Treasury, 1939; Under-Sec., 1956; Under Sec., ECGD, 1958-66. UK member on Managing Board of European Payments Union, 1952-53; Secretary of Faculty of Economics, Cambridge, 1966-71; Senior Research Officer, Dept of Applied Economics, 1971-73. *Publications:* Society and Enterprise, 1934; A Study of the Capital Market in Post-War Britain, 1937; The Machinery of Finance and the Management of Sterling, 1967; The Strategy of Financial Pressure, 1972; Economic Uncertainty and Financial Structure, 1977; miscellaneous articles. *Address:* 11 Marlowe Road, Newnham, Cambridge CB3 9JW. *T:* Cambridge 63119. *Club:* United Oxford & Cambridge University.

GRANT, Alistair; *see* Grant, D. A. A.

GRANT, Allan Wallace, OBE 1974; MC 1941; TD 1947; President, Ecclesiastical Insurance Office Ltd, since 1981 (Managing Director, 1971-77; Chairman, 1975-81); *b* 2 Feb. 1911; *s* of late Henry Grant and late Rose Margaret Sheppard; *m* 1939, Kathleen Rachel Bamford; one *d. Educ:* Dulwich Coll. LLB Hons (London). FCII. Eccles. Insurance Office, 1929; Chief Officer, 1952; Dir, 1966. Served War of 1939-45: Major, 2 i/c, 3rd Co. of London Yeomanry (Sharpshooters), N Africa, Sicily, Italy, NW Europe. Pres., Sharpshooters Assoc. Called to Bar, Gray's Inn, 1948. President: Insurance Inst. of London, 1966-67; Chartered Insce Inst., 1970-71; Insce Charities, 1973-74; Insce Orchestral Soc., 1973-74; Chairman: Insce Industry Training Council, 1973-75; Clergy Orphan Corp., 1967-80 (Vice-Pres., 1980); Coll. of All Saints, Tottenham, 1967-76; Governor: St Mary's Sch., Wantage, 1967-; St Edmund's Sch., Canterbury, 1967-; St Margaret's Sch., Bushey, 1967-; Mem., Policyholders Protection Bd, 1975-81; Treasurer: Historic Churches Preservation Trust, 1977-; Soc. for Advancing Christian Faith, 1977-. Assistant, Coopers' Co. Hon. DCanL Lexington, 1975. *Recreations:* golf, travel. *Address:* Fulham Palace (EIO Wing), Bishops Avenue, SW6 6EA. *T:* 01-736 0251. *Clubs:* City Livery; Richmond Golf; Parkstone Golf.

GRANT, Andrew Francis Joseph, CB 1971; BSc, CEng, FICE; *b* 25 Feb. 1911; *er s* of Francis Herbert and Clare Grant; *m* 1934, Mary Harrison; two *s* two *d. Educ:* St Joseph's Coll., Beulah Hill; King's Coll., London. Asst Civil Engr with Contractors on London Underground Rlys, 1931; Port of London Authority, 1935; entered Civil Engineer-in-Chief's Dept, Admiralty, and posted to Singapore, 1937; Suptg Civil Engr, Durban, 1942; Civil Engr. Adviser, RN Home Air Comd, 1947; Suptg Civil Engr, Malta, 1951; Asst Dir, Navy Works, 1956; Fleet Navy Works Officer, Mediterranean, 1960; Director for Wales, MPBW, 1963; Regional Director, Far East, 1966; Dir, Home Regional Services, DoE, 1968-71. *Recreations:* painting, golf, travel. *Address:* The Lodge, Herington Grove, Hutton Mount, Shenfield, Essex. *T:* Brentwood 216486. *Club:* Civil Service.

GRANT, Anthony; MP (C) Harrow Central since 1964; Solicitor and Company Director; *b* May 1925; *m* Sonia Isobel; one *s* one *d. Educ:* St Paul's Sch.; Brasenose Coll., Oxford. Admitted a Solicitor, 1952; Liveryman, Worshipful Company of Solicitors; Freeman, City of London; Master, Guild of Freemen, 1979. Army 1943-48, Third Dragoon Guards (Capt.). Opposition Whip, 1966-70; Parly Sec., Board of Trade, June-Oct. 1970; Parliamentary Under-Secretary of State: Trade, DTI, 1970-72; Industrial Develt, DTI, 1972-74; Chm., Cons. back bench Trade Cttee, 1979-; Mem., Foreign Affairs Select Cttee, 1980-; a Vice-Chm., Conservative Party Organisation, 1974-76. Member: Council of Europe (Chm., Econ. Cttee, 1980-); WEU. *Recreations:* watching Rugby and cricket, playing golf; Napoleonic history. *Address:* House of Commons, SW1.

GRANT, Sir Archibald, 13th Bt, *cr* 1705; *b* 2 Sept. 1954; *e s* of Captain Sir Francis Cullen Grant, 12th Bt, and of Lady Grant (Jean Margherita, *d* of Captain Humphrey Douglas Tollemache, RN), who *m* 2nd, Baron Tweedsmuir, *qv*; *S* father, 1966. *Heir: b* Francis Tollemache Grant, *b* 18 Dec. 1955. *Address:* House of Monymusk, Aberdeenshire. *T:* Monymusk 220.

GRANT, Brian; *see* Grant, H. B.

GRANT, Cary; actor; Director: Fabergé Inc.; Metro Goldwyn Mayer Inc.; *b* Bristol, 18 Jan. 1904; *s* of Elias Leach and Elsie Kingdom; became US citizen, 1942; *m* 1st 1934, Virginia Cherill (marr. diss., 1934); 2nd, 1942, Barbara Hutton (marr. diss., 1945); 3rd, 1949, Betsy Drake; 4th, 1965, Dyan Cannon (marr. diss., 1968); one *d* ; 5th, 1981, Barbara Harris. *Educ:* Fairfield Academy, Somerset. Dir Emeritus, Western Airlines. Mem., Board of Governors, United Services Orgn, 1976-. Started acting, New York, 1921; appeared in: Golden Dawn; Polly; Boom Boom; Wonderful Night; Street Singer; Nikki. *Films include:* Arsenic and Old Lace; None but the Lonely Heart; The Bishop's Wife; The Bachelor and the Bobby Soxer; Mr Blandings Builds His Dream House; To Catch a Thief; The Pride and the Passion; An Affair to Remember; Indiscreet; North by North-West; Operation Petticoat; A Touch of Mink; Charade; Father Goose; Walk, Don't Run. Special Academy Award for contributions to motion picture industry, 1969. *Recreation:* riding.

GRANT, Rt. Rev. Charles Alexander, MA; LCL; Bishop of Northampton, (RC), 1967-82, Apostolic Administrator 1982; *b* 25 Oct. 1906; *s* of Frank and Sibylla Christina Grant. *Educ:* Perse Sch., Cambridge; St Edmund's, Ware; Christ's Coll., Cambridge; Oscott Coll., Birmingham; Gregorian Univ., Rome. Curate, Cambridge, 1938; Parish Priest: Ely, 1943; Kettering, 1945. Bishop-Auxiliary of Northampton, 1961-67. *Address:* St John's Convent, Kiln Green, near Reading RG10 9XP.

GRANT, Sir Clifford (Harry), Kt 1977; Chief Stipendiary Magistrate, Western Australia, since 1982; *b* England, 12 April 1929; *m* 1962, Karen Ann Ferguson. *Educ:* Montclair, NJ, USA; Harrison Coll., Barbados; Liverpool Coll.; Liverpool Univ. (LLB (Hons) 1949). Solicitor, Supreme Court of Judicature, 1951; Comr for Oaths, 1958; in private practice, London; apptd to HM Overseas Judiciary, 1958; Magistrate, Kenya, 1958, Sen. Magistrate, 1962; transf. to Hong Kong, Crown Solicitor, 1963, Principal Magistrate, 1965; transf. to Fiji, Sen. Magistrate, 1967; admitted Barrister and Solicitor, Supreme Court of Fiji, 1969; Chief Magistrate, 1971; Judge of Supreme Court, 1972; Chief Justice of Fiji, 1974-80. Pres., Fiji Court of Appeal, and Chm., Judicial and Legal Services Commn; sole Comr, Royal Commn on Crime, 1975 (report published 1976). Sometime Actg Governor-General, 1973-79. Fiji Independence Medal, 1970. *Publications:* articles for legal jls. *Recreations:* photography, literature, music. *Address:* 20 The Crest, Woodvale, WA 6026, Australia.

GRANT, Derek Aldwin, DSO 1944; QC 1962; **His Honour Judge Grant;** a Circuit Judge (formerly an Additional Judge of the Central Criminal Court), since 1969; *b* 22 Jan. 1915; *s* of late Charles Frederick Grant; *m* 1954, Phoebe Louise Wavell-Paxton; one *s* three *d*. *Educ:* Winchester Coll.,; Oriel Coll., Oxford. Called to Bar 1938. Served in RAF, 1940-46 (King's Commendation, DSO). Master of the Bench, Inner Temple, 1969. Deputy Chairman, East Sussex County Sessions, 1962-71; Recorder of Salisbury, 1962-67, of Portsmouth, 1967-69. *Address:* Carters Lodge, Handcross, West Sussex. *Club:* Travellers'.

GRANT, Donald Blane, TD 1964; Partner, Thomson McLintock & Co., CA (formerly Moody Stuart & Robertson), since 1950; *b* 8 Oct. 1921; *s* of Quintin Blane Grant and Euphemia Phyllis Grant; *m* 1944, Lavinia Margaret Ruth Ritchie; three *d*. *Educ:* High Sch. of Dundee. CA 1948. Served War, RA, 1939-46: TA Officer, retd as Major. Director: Dundee & London Investment Trust Ltd, 1969-; HAT Group Ltd, 1969-. Inst. of Chartered Accountants of Scotland: Mem. Council, 1971-76; Vice Pres., 1977-79, Pres., 1979-80. *Recreations:* shooting, fishing, golf, bridge, gardening. *Address:* Summerfield, 24 Albany Road, West Ferry, Dundee. *T:* Dundee 737804. *Clubs:* Institute of Directors; New (Edinburgh); Royal and Ancient Golf (St Andrews); Panmure Golf (Carnoustie).

GRANT, Donald David; Director General, Central Office of Information, since 1982; *b* 1 Aug. 1924; *s* of Donald Herbert Grant and Florence Emily Grant; *m* 1954, Beatrice Mary Varney; two *d*. *Educ:* Wandsworth Sch. Served War, RNVR, Sub-Lt (A), 1942-46. Journalist, Evening Standard, Reuters, 1946-51; Dir, Sidney Barton Ltd, PR Consultants, 1951-61; Chief Information Officer, Min. of Aviation and Technology, 1961-67; Dir, Public Relations, STC Ltd, 1967-70; Director of Information: GLC, 1971-72; DTI, 1972-74; Home Office, 1974-82. *Recreation:* sailing. *Address:* Holly Lodge, 1 Calonne Road, Wimbledon, SW19. *T:* 01-947 2383. *Club:* Reform.

GRANT, Douglas Marr Kelso; Sheriff of South Strathclyde, Dumfries and Galloway (formerly of Ayr and Bute), since 1966; *b* 5 April 1917; *m* 1952, Audrey Stevenson Law; two *s* two *d*. *Educ:* Rugby; Peterhouse, Cambridge. Entered Colonial Admin. Service, Uganda Protectorate, 1939. Army Service, 1940-46. Called to Bar, Gray's Inn, 1945; Judicial and Legal Dept, Malaya, 1946-57. Admitted to Faculty of Advocates and Scottish Bar, 1959. *Address:* Drumellan House, Maybole, Ayrshire. *T:* Maybole 82279.

GRANT, (Duncan) Alistair (Antoine), RBA, ARCA; Head of Printmaking Department, Royal College of Art, since 1970; Chairman, Faculty of Printmaking, British School at Rome, since 1978; *b* London, 3 June 1925; *s* of Duncan and Germaine Grant; *m* 1949, Phyllis Fricker; one *d*. *Educ:* Froebel, Whitehill, Glasgow; Birmingham Sch. of Art; Royal Coll. of Art. Joined staff of RCA, 1955. *One Man Shows* at the following galleries: Zwemmer; Piccadilly; AIA; Ashgate; Bear Lane, Oxford; Midland Group, Nottingham; Balclutha; Ware, London; 46, Edinburgh; Editions Alecto; Redfern. *Works in the collections of:* V&A Museum; Tate Gallery; Min. of Works; LCC (now GLC); Arts Council; Carlisle Art Gall.; Ferens Art Gall., Hull; The King of Sweden; Dallas Museum; Cincinnati; Boston; Museum of Modern Art, New York; Chicago Art Inst.; Lessing J. Rosenwald Collection; Beaverbrook Foundn, Fredericton, NB; Vancouver Art Gall.; Victoria Art Gall. *Group*

Exhibitions in Bahamas, Canada, Europe, S America, USA and UK. Awarded Silver Medal, Internat. Festival of Youth, Moscow, 1957. *Address:* 13 Redcliffe Gardens, SW10 9BG. *T:* 01-352 4312.

GRANT, Edward; Lord Mayor, City of Manchester, May 1972-May 1973; *b* 10 Aug. 1915; *s* of Edward and Ada Grant; *m* 1942, Winifred Mitchell. *Educ:* Moston Lane Sch.; Manchester High Sch. of Commerce. City Councillor, Manchester, 1950- (Alderman, 1970); Hosp. Administrator, Manchester AHA (T) North Dist (formerly NE Manchester HMC), 1948-75, now retired. *Recreations:* swimming, reading, gardening. *Address:* 14 Rainton Walk, New Moston, Manchester M10 0FR. *T:* 061-681 4758.

GRANT, Brig. Eneas Henry George, CBE 1951; DSO 1944 and Bar, 1945; MC 1936; JP; Hon. DL; retired; *b* 14 Aug. 1901; *s* of late Col H. G. Grant, CB, late Seaforth Highlanders and late Mrs Grant, Balnespick, Inverness-shire; *m* 1926, Lilian Marion (*d* 1978), *d* of late S. O'Neill, Cumberstown House, Co. Westmeath; one *s* (and *er s*, Lieut Seaforth Highlanders, killed in action, Korea, 1951). *Educ:* Wellington Coll., Berks; RMC, Sandhurst. 2nd Lieut Seaforth Highlanders, 1920; Adjt Lovat Scouts, 1928-33; served in Palestine, 1936; War of 1939-45; France 1940; France and Germany, 1944-45. Lieut-Colonel 1942 (Subs. 1947); Colonel 1944 (Subs. 1948); Brigadier 1944 (Subs. 1952); Bde Commander, 1944-49; Comdr Gold Coast District, 1949-52. Col Comdt Gold Coast Regt, 1949-52; Deputy Commander, Northumbrian District, 1952-55; retired 1955. JP Inverness-shire, 1957. DL Inverness-shire, 1958-80. Chairman Inverness-shire TA and Air Force Association, 1961-65. *Recreations:* country pursuits. *Address:* Inverbrough Lodge, Tomatin, Inverness-shire. *Club:* Highland (Inverness).

GRANT, Sir Ewan George M.; *see* Macpherson-Grant.

GRANT, Maj.-Gen. Ferris Nelson, CB 1967; Governor, School for Visually Handicapped; *b* 25 Dec. 1916; *s* of late Lieut-Gen. H. G. Grant and of Mrs N. L. B. Grant (*née* Barker); *m* 1940, Patricia Anne (*née* Jameson); one *s* one *d*. *Educ:* Cheltenham Coll. Joined Royal Marines, 1935. Capt., HMS Suffolk, 1940-42; US Marine Corps Staff Coll., Major, 1943; Staff of SACSEA, Lt-Col 1943; Army Staff Coll., Camberley, 1946; 45 Commando, 1947; Chief Instructor, Commando Sch., 1949; CO 41 Commando, Korea, 1950; jssc, 1951; Bde Major, Commando Bde, 1952; Instructor, USMC Staff Coll., 1958; CO Amphibious Trng Unit, 1960; CO Depot RM, 1961; CO Infantry Trng Centre, 1963; Comdr, Plymouth Group, Royal Marines, 1965-68, retired. Lay reader. Legion of Merit (US). *Recreations:* sailing, gardening, painting; Past Pres. RN Boxing Assoc. *Address:* Little Burrow Farmhouse, Broadclyst, Exeter, Devon. *Clubs:* Army and Navy; Royal Yacht Squadron, Royal Naval Sailing Association.

GRANT, Frank, CB 1953; OBE 1939; former Under-Secretary, Ministry of Agriculture and Fisheries; *b* 1890; *s* of late J. F. Grant, Evesham; *m* 1926, Eileen, *d* of late T. H. Carey; one *s* one *d*. *Address:* 9 Harefield Gardens, Middleton-on-Sea, Bognor Regis, West Sussex. *T:* Middleton-on-Sea 3511.

GRANT, George; MP (Lab) Morpeth, since 1970; *b* 11 Oct. 1924; *m* 1948, Adeline (*née* Conroy), Morpeth; one *s* four *d*. *Educ:* Netherton Council Sch. and WEA. Member Bedlingtonshire UDC, 1959-70 (Chm. for two years). Member: Labour Party, 1947-; NUM (Chm., 1963-70). PPS to Minister of Agriculture, 1974-76. *Recreations:* sport, gardening. *Address:* House of Commons, SW1; 4 Ringway, Choppington, Northumberland. *Clubs:* Working Men's, in the Bedlington and Ashington area.

GRANT, (Hubert) Brian; His Honour Judge Brian Grant; a Circuit Judge of Sussex and Kent (formerly Judge of County Courts since 1965); *b* 5 Aug. 1917; *m* 1946, Jeanette Mary Carroll; one *s* three *d*. *Educ:* Trinity Coll., Cambridge (Sen. Schol.). 1st cl. hons, Law Tripos, 1939; MA. War service, 1940-44: Commandos, 1942-44. Called to Bar, Gray's Inn, 1945 (Lord Justice Holker Senior Scholar). Mem., Law Reform Cttee, 1970-73. Vice-Chm., Nat. Marriage Guidance Council, 1970-72; Founder Pres., Parenthood, 1979. *Publications:* Marriage, Separation and Divorce, 1946; Family Law, 1970; Conciliation and Divorce, 1981. *Recreations:* travel and collecting books. *Address:* Cleeves, Roedean Road, Tunbridge Wells, Kent TN2 5JX.

GRANT, Maj.-Gen. Ian Hallam L.; *see* Lyall Grant.

GRANT, Isabel Frances, MBE 1959; LLD (Edinburgh); *b* 21 July 1887; *d* of late Colonel H. G. Grant, CB, late the Seaforth Highlanders; *g d* of late Field Marshal Sir Patrick Grant, KCB, GCMG; unmarried. *Educ:* privately. Founder of the Highland Folk Museum at Kingussie. *Publications:* Everyday Life on an Old Highland Farm, 1922, reprinted 1981; Social and Economic Development of Scotland before 1603, 1929; In the Tracks of Montrose, 1931; Everyday Life in Old Scotland, 1933; Social and Economic History of Scotland, 1934; Lordship of the Isles, 1935; Highland Folk Ways, 1961; Angus Og of the Isles, 1969; Along a Highland Road, 1980. *Recreation:* reading. *Address:* 22 Lennox Row, Edinburgh EH5 3JW.

GRANT, Rt. Rev. James Alexander; Bishop Coadjutor, Diocese of Melbourne, since 1970; *b* 30 Aug. 1931; *s* of late V. G. Grant, Geelong. *Educ:* Trinity College, Univ. of Melbourne (BA Hons); Melbourne College of Divinity (BD). Deacon 1959 (Curate, St Peter's, Murrumbeena), Priest 1960; Curate, West Heidelberg 1960, Broadmeadows 1961; Leader Diocesan Task

Force, Broadmeadows, 1962; Domestic and Examining Chaplain to Archbishop of Melbourne, 1966; Chairman, Brotherhood of St Laurence, 1971- (Director, 1969); Chaplain, Trinity Coll., Univ. of Melbourne, 1970-75, Fellow, 1975-. *Publications:* (with Geoffrey Serle) The Melbourne Scene, 1957; Perspective of a Century-Trinity College, 1872-1972, 1972. *Recreation:* historical research. *Address:* Cathedral Buildings, Flinders Lane, Melbourne, Vic 3000, Australia.

GRANT, James Currie, CBE 1975; Editor, The Press and Journal, Aberdeen, 1960-75, Associate Editor, 1975-76, retired; *b* 5 May 1914; *s* of Alexander Grant, Elgin; *m* 1940, Lillias Isabella Gordon; one *d. Educ:* Elgin Academy. With the Northern Scot, Elgin, 1930-36; joined The Press and Journal, as reporter, 1936; served with Royal Artillery, 1940-46; Sub-editor, The Press and Journal, 1946, Dep. Chief Sub-Editor, 1947-53, Asst Editor, 1953-56, Dep. Editor, 1956-60. Chm., Editorial Cttee, Scottish Daily Newspaper Soc., 1972-75. *Recreations:* voluntary social work, gardening. *Address:* 42 Fonthill Road, Aberdeen AB1 2UJ. *T:* 22090.

GRANT, James Pineo; Executive Director, United Nations Children's Fund (UNICEF), since 1980; *b* 12 May 1922; *s* of John B. and Charlotte Grant; *m* 1943, Ethel Henck; three *s. Educ:* Univ. of California, Berkeley (BA); Harvard Univ. (JD). US Army, 1943-45; UN Relief and Rehabilitation Admin, 1946-47; Acting Exec. Sec. to Sino-American Jt Cttee on Rural Reconstruction, 1948-50; Law Associate, Covington and Burling, Washington, DC, 1951-54; Regional Legal Counsel in New Delhi for US aid programs for S Asia, 1954-56; Dir, US aid mission to Ceylon, 1956-58; Dep. to Dir of Internat. Co-operation Admin, 1959-62; Dep. Asst Sec. of State for Near East and S Asian Affairs, 1962-64; Dir, AID program in Turkey, with rank of Minister, 1964-67; Asst Administrator, Agency for Internat. Develt (AID), 1967-69; Pres., Overseas Develt Council, 1969-80. Hon. LLD: Notre Dame, 1980; Maryville Coll., 1981; Hon. DrSci Hacettepe, Ankara, 1980. *Publications:* articles in Foreign Affairs, Foreign Policy, Annals. *Address:* 866 United Nations Plaza, Room A-6004, New York, NY 10017, USA. *T:* (212) 754-7848. *Clubs:* Metropolitan, Cosmos (Washington, DC).

GRANT, James Shaw, CBE 1968 (OBE 1956); Member, Highlands and Islands Development Board, 1970-82; *b* 22 May 1910; *s* of William Grant and Johanna Morison Grant, Stornoway; *m* 1951, Catherine Mary Stewart; no *c. Educ:* Nicolson Inst.; Glasgow Univ. Editor, Stornoway Gazette, 1932-63; Mem., Crofters' Commn, 1955-63, Chm., 1963-78. Dir, Grampian Television, 1969-80. Mem. Scottish Adv. Cttee, British Council, 1972. Governor, Pitlochry Festival Theatre, 1954-, Chairman, 1971-; Chm., Harris Tweed Assoc. Ltd, 1972-. Mem. Council, Nat. Trust for Scotland, 1979-. FRAgS 1973; FRSE 1982. Hon. LLD Aberdeen, 1979. *Publications:* Highland Villages, 1977; Their Children Will See, 1979; several plays. *Recreations:* golf, photography. *Address:* Ardgrianach, Inshes, Inverness. *T:* Inverness 31476. *Club:* Royal Over-Seas League.

GRANT, Joan, (Mrs Denys Kelsey); *b* 12 April 1907; *d* of John Frederick Marshall, 1st, 1927, Arthur Leslie Grant; one *d* ; 2nd, 1940, Charles Robert Longfield Beatty; 3rd, 1960, Denys Edward Reginald Kelsey, MB, MRCP. Is engaged in psychotherapy as well as in writing. *Publications:* Winged Pharaoh, 1937; Life as Carola, 1939; Eyes of Horus, 1942; The Scarlet Fish and other Stories, 1942; Lord of the Horizon, 1943; Redskin Morning, 1944; Scarlet Feather, 1945; Vague Vacation, 1947; Return to Elysium, 1947; The Laird and the Lady, 1949 (US edn, Castle Cloud); So Moses Was Born, 1952; Time out of Mind (autobiography), 1956 (US edn, Far Memory); A Lot to Remember, 1962; (with Denys Kelsey) Many Lifetimes, 1969; The Collected Works of Joan Grant, 1979. *Address:* c/o A. P. Watt Ltd, 26-28 Bedford Row, WC1R 4HL.

GRANT, Rear-Adm. John, CB 1960; DSO 1942; *b* 13 Oct. 1908; *s* of late Maj.-Gen. Sir Philip Grant, KCB, CMG, and of late Annette, Lady Grant, Park Lodge, East Lulworth, Dorset; *m* 1935, Ruth Hayward Slade; two *s* two *d. Educ:* St Anthony's, Eastbourne; RN Colls, Dartmouth and Greenwich. Midshipman, HMS Queen Elizabeth, 1926; Sub-Lieut, HMS Revenge, 1930; Lieut, HMS Kent, China Station, 1932; specialised in anti-submarine warfare, 1933-39; Staff Officer Convoys, Rosyth, 1940; in comd HMS Beverley, 1941-42 (DSO); Trng Comdr, HMS Osprey, 1942, and subseq. in HMS Western Isles; in comd HMS Philante, 1943; Trng Comdr, HMS Osprey, 1944; in comd HMS Opportune, Fame and Crispin, 1945-47; Joint Staff Coll., 1947; Executive Officer, HMS Vernon; Capt. 1949; Dep. Dir Torpedo Anti-Submarine and Mine Warfare Div., Naval Staff, Admiralty, 1949-51; in comd HMS Cleopatra, 1952-53; Imperial Defence Coll., 1954; in comd HMS Vernon, 1955-57; on staff of Chief of Defence Staff, Min. of Defence, 1957-59; Rear-Adm., 1959; Flag Officer Commanding Reserve Fleet, 1959-60; retired list, 1961. Rank Organisation, 1961-65; Director, Conference of the Electronics Industry, 1965-71. *Address:* 4 Priors Barton, Kingsgate Road, Winchester, Hants.

GRANT, (John) Anthony; see Grant, A.

GRANT, John Douglas; MP Islington Central, since 1974 (Islington East, 1970-74) (Lab, 1970-81, SDP since 1981); *b* 16 Oct. 1932; *m* 1955, Patricia Julia Ann; two *s* one *d. Educ:* Stationers' Company's Sch., Hornsey. Reporter on various provincial newspapers until 1955; Daily Express, 1955-70 (Chief Industrial Correspondent, 1967-70). Contested (Lab) Beckenham, 1966; Chm., Bromley Constituency Labour Party, 1966-70. Chm., Labour and Industrial

Correspondents' Group, 1967. Opposition Front Bench Spokesman for policy on broadcasting and the press, 1973-74, on employment, 1979-81; Parly Sec., CSD, March-Oct. 1974; Parliamentary Under-Secretary of State: ODM, 1974-76; Dept of Employment, 1976-79; SDP employment spokesman, 1981-. *Publications:* Member of Parliament, 1974; articles in national newspapers and periodicals. *Recreations:* tennis, watching soccer. *Address:* 16 Magpie Hall Lane, Bromley, Kent. *T:* 01-467 0227.

GRANT, John James, CBE 1960; Director, University of Durham Institute of Education, 1963-77; *b* 19 Oct. 1914; *s* of John and Mary Grant; *m* 1945, Jean Graham Stewart; two *s. Educ:* Shawlands Academy, Glasgow; Univ. of Glasgow (MA, EdB). Supply teaching, Glasgow, 1939-40. Served War: UK, India, Burma, 1940-46. Mod. Lang. Master, High Sch. of Glasgow, 1946-48; Lectr in Educn, Univ. of Durham, 1948-52; Vice-Principal, Fourah Bay Coll., Sierra Leone, 1953-55, Principal, 1955-60; Principal, St Cuthbert's Soc., Univ. of Durham, 1960-63. Hon. DCL Durham, 1960. *Recreations:* golf, theatre, gardening. *Address:* Tithe Barn, Shincliffe, Durham. *T:* Durham 64728.

GRANT, Captain John Moreau, CBE 1944; Royal Canadian Navy, retired; *b* 22 July 1895; *s* of late Hon. MacCallum Grant and Laura MacNeil Parker; *m* 1923, Jocelyn Clare Weaver-Bridgman; one *d. Educ:* Heidelberg Coll., Germany; RCN Coll., Halifax, NS. *Address:* 601 Transit Road, Victoria, British Columbia, Canada. *T:* 598-2138.

GRANT, Keith Wallace; Director, Design Council, since 1977; *b* 30 June 1934; *s* of Randolph and Sylvia Grant; *m* 1968, Deanne (*née* Bergsma); one *s* one *d. Educ:* Trinity Coll., Glenalmond; Clare Coll., Cambridge (MA). Account Exec., W. S. Crawford Ltd, 1958-62; General Manager: Covent Garden Opera Co., later Royal Opera, 1962-73; English Opera Group, 1962-73; Sec., Royal Soc. of Arts, 1973-77. Mem. Adv. Council, V&A Mus., 1977-; Chm., English Music Theatre Co., 1979-; Governor: Central Sch. of Art and Design, 1974-77; Birmingham Polytechnic, 1981-. *Address:* c/o Design Council, 28 Haymarket, SW1. *Club:* Garrick.

GRANT, Sir (Kenneth) Lindsay, CMT 1969; Kt 1963; OBE 1956; ED 1944; Director, T. Geddes Grant Ltd (Chairman, 1946-64); Chairman, Vice-Chairman, and Director of numerous other companies; *b* Trinidad, 10 Feb. 1899; *s* of T. Geddes Grant (Canadian); *m* 1923, (Edith) Grace Norman; no *c. Educ:* Queen's Royal College, Trinidad; Maritime Business Coll., Halifax, NS. Served European War: (3rd Trinidad Contingent, 1916-17, 5th BWI Regt, 1917, RFC, 1917) 2nd Lieut; (RAF 1917-19) Flying Officer; War of 1939-45: (Trinidad Volunteers) Major, 2nd in Comd, 1944-45. Joined T. Geddes Grant Ltd, 1919; Manager, Office Appliances Dept, 1921; Director, 1927; Chm. and Man. Dir, 1946 (retd as Man. Dir, Sept. 1962; Chm. until 1964; Pres., 1964-68 and 1979-). Pres., 1957-75, Hon. Life Pres., 1975-, Trinidad and Tobago Leprosy Relief Assoc. Past and present activities: Church (Elder, Greyfriars); Boy Scouts; Cadets; Social Service. *Recreations:* none now; played cricket, Association football, tennis, golf. *Address:* (office) T. Geddes Grant Ltd, Box 171, Port of Spain, Trinidad. *T:* 54805; (home) 50 Ellerslie Park, Maraval, Trinidad. *T:* 25202, Port of Spain. *Clubs:* Royal Commonwealth Society, Royal Over-Seas League, (Hon. Life) MCC (all London); Union, Country, Queen's Park Cricket, etc (Trinidad).

GRANT, Sir Lindsay; see Grant, Sir K. L.

GRANT, Very Rev. Malcolm Etheridge; Provost and Rector of St Mary's Cathedral, Glasgow, since 1981; *b* 6 Aug. 1944; *s* of Donald Etheridge Grant and Nellie Florence May Grant (*née* Tuffey). *Educ:* Dunfermline High School; Univ. of Edinburgh (Bruce of Grangehill Bursar, 1962; BSc (Hons Chemistry); BD (Hons New Testament); Divinity Fellowship, 1969); Edinburgh Theological College. Deacon 1969, priest 1970; Assistant Curate: St Mary's Cathedral, Glasgow, 1969; St Wulfram's, Grantham (in charge of Church of the Epiphany, Earlesfield), 1972; Team Vicar of Earlesfield, Grantham, 1972; Priest-in-charge, St Ninian's, Invergordon, 1978; Examining Chaplain to Bishop of Moray, Ross and Caithness, 1979; Member, Highland Regional Council Education Cttee, 1979-81. *Address:* 45 Rowallan Gardens, Glasgow G11 7LH. *T:* 041-339 4956; (office) 10 Holyrood Crescent, Glasgow G20 6HJ. *T:* 041-339 6691.

GRANT, Michael, CBE 1958 (OBE 1946); MA, LittD (Cambridge); *b* 21 Nov. 1914; *s* of late Col Maurice Harold Grant and Muriel, *d* of C. Jorgensen; *m* 1944, Anne Sophie Beskow, Norrköping, Sweden; two *s. Educ:* Harrow Sch.; Trinity Coll., Cambridge. Porson Prizeman, First Chancellor's Classical Medallist, Craven Student; Fellow Trinity Coll., Cambridge, 1938-49. Served War of 1939-45, Army, War Office, 1939-40, Actg Capt.; first British Council Rep. in Turkey, 1940-45; Prof. of Humanity at Edinburgh Univ., 1948-59; first Vice-Chancellor, Univ. of Khartoum, 1956-58; Pres. and Vice-Chancellor of the Queen's Univ. of Belfast, 1959-66; Pres., 1953-56, and Medallist, 1962, Royal Numismatic Soc.; Huntington Medallist, American Numismatic Soc., 1965. J. H. Gray Lectr, Cambridge, 1955; FSA. Chairman, National Council for the Supply of Teachers Overseas, 1963-66. President: Virgil Soc., 1963-66; Classical Assoc., 1977-78. Chm., Commonwealth Conf. on Teaching of English as 2nd Language at Makerere, Uganda, 1961. Hon. LittD Dublin, 1961; Hon. LLD QUB, 1967. Gold Medal for Educn, Sudan, 1977. *Publications:* From Imperium to Auctoritas, 1946; Aspects of the Principate of Tiberius, 1950; Roman Anniversary Issues, 1950; Ancient History, 1952; The Six Main Aes Coinages of Augustus, 1953; Roman Imperial Money, 1954; Roman Literature, 1954; translations of Tacitus and

Cicero; Roman History from Coins, 1958; The World of Rome, 1960; Myths of the Greeks and Romans, 1962; Birth of Western Civilization (ed), 1964; The Civilizations of Europe, 1965; The Gladiators, 1967; The Climax of Rome, 1968; The Ancient Mediterranean, 1969; Julius Caesar, 1969; The Ancient Historians, 1970; The Roman Forum, 1970; Nero, 1970; Cities of Vesuvius, 1971; Herod the Great, 1971; Roman Myths, 1971; Cleopatra, 1972; The Jews in the Roman World, 1973; The Army of the Caesars, 1974; The Twelve Caesars, 1975; (ed) Greek Literature, 1976; The Fall of the Roman Empire, 1976; Saint Paul, 1976; Jesus, 1977; History of Rome, 1978; (ed) Latin Literature, 1978; The Etruscans, 1980; Greek and Latin Authors 800 BC-AD 1000, 1980; The Dawn of the Middle Ages, 1981; From Alexander to Cleopatra, 1982. *Address:* Le Pitturacce, Gattaiola, Lucca, Italy. *Club:* Athenæum.

GRANT, Sir Patrick Alexander Benedict, 14th Bt *cr* 1688; Chieftain of Clan Donnachy; advocate; *b* 5 Feb. 1953; *e s* of Sir Duncan Alexander Grant, 13th Bt, and of Joan Penelope, *o d* of Captain Sir Denzil Cope, 14th Bt; *S* father, 1961; *m* 1981, Carolyn Elizabeth Highet, MB, ChB, DRCOG. *Educ:* St Conleth's Coll., Dublin; The Abbey Sch., Fort Augustus. Called to the Scottish Bar, 1981. Piper; dealer in pipes and Celtic instruments. *Heir: b* Denzil Mohun Bede Grant [*b* 19 April 1935; *m* 1977, Nicola, *d* of A. T. Savill; one *d*]. *Address:* 2 The Crescent, Busby, Lanarkshire.

GRANT, Prof. Peter John, MA, PhD, MIMechE, FInstP; Professor of Nuclear Power, Imperial College of Science and Technology, London, since 1966; *b* London, 2 July 1926; *s* of Herbert James Grant; *m* Audrey, *d* of Joseph Whitham; one *s. Educ:* Merchant Taylors' Sch.; Sidney Sussex Coll., Cambridge. BA 1947, MA, PhD 1951. Research in Nuclear Physics at Cavendish Laboratory, 1947-50; Lectr in Natural Philosophy, Univ. of Glasgow, 1950-55; Chief Physicist, Atomic Energy Div., GEC Ltd, 1956-59; Reader in Engineering Science, Imperial Coll. of Science and Technology, 1959-66. *Publications:* Elementary Reactor Physics, 1966; Nuclear Science, 1971; papers on radioactivity, nuclear reactions, physics of nuclear reactors. *Address:* 49 Manor Road South, Esher, Surrey. *T:* 01-398 2001. *Club:* Athenæum.

GRANT, Ronald Thomson, OBE; FRS 1934; MD, FRCP, DPH; formerly physician on staff of Medical Research Council; Consultant Physician Emeritus, Guy's Hospital; *b* 5 Nov. 1892. *Educ:* Glasgow Univ. *Publications:* articles in scientific journals. *Address:* Farley Green Cottage, Shophouse Lane, Albury, Guildford, Surrey GU5 9EQ. *T:* Shere 2164.

GRANT, Air Vice-Marshal Stanley Bernard, CB 1969; DFC 1942; bar to DFC 1943; RAF; *b* 31 May 1919; *s* of late Harry Alexander Gwatkin Grant and Marjorie Gladys Hoyle; *m* 1948, Barbara Jean Watts (*d* 1963); one *s* one *d* ; *m* 1965, Christiane Marie Py (*née* Bech); one step *s* two step *d. Educ:* Charterhouse; RAF Coll., Cranwell. Joined RAF, 1937; War of 1939-45; service in UK, Malta, Egypt and Italy. Air Ministry, 1946-47; Flying Training Command, 1948-54; Fighter Command, 1955-56; SEATO, Bangkok, 1957-59; Fighter Command, 1960-61; idc course, 1962; NATO, Fontainebleau, 1963-64; Directing Staff, IDC, 1965-68; Comdr, British Forces, Gulf, 1968-69; retired 1970. *Address:* 14 rue des Cordeliers, 83170 Brignoles, France. *Club:* Royal Air Force.

GRANT-FERRIS, family name of Baron Harvington.

GRANT-SUTTIE, Sir (George) Philip; *see* Suttie, Sir G. P. G.

GRANTCHESTER, 2nd Baron *cr* 1953; **Kenneth Bent Suenson-Taylor,** QC 1971; a Recorder of the Crown Court, since 1975; President, Value-added Tax Tribunals, since 1972; Chairman, Licensed Dealers' Tribunal, since 1976; *b* 18 Aug. 1921; *s* of 1st Baron Grantchester, OBE, and of Mara Henriette (Mamie), *d* of late Albert Suenson, Copenhagen; *S* father, 1976; *m* 1947, Betty, *er d* of Sir John Moores, *qv;* three *s* three *d. Educ:* Westminster School; Christ's College, Cambridge (MA, LLM). Lieut RA, 1941-45. Called to the Bar, Middle Temple, 1946; admitted *ad eundem* by Lincoln's Inn, 1947. Lecturer in Company Law, Council of Legal Education, 1951-72. Pres., Aircraft and Shipbuilding Ind. Arbitration Tribunal, 1980-. *Heir: e s* Hon. Christopher John Suenson-Taylor [*b* 8 April 1951; *m* 1972, Jacqueline, *d* of Dr Leo Jaffe; one *s* one *d*]. *Address:* The Gate House, Coombe Wood Road, Kingston Hill, Surrey. *T:* 01-546 9088.

GRANTHAM, Bishop Suffragan of, since 1972; **Rt. Rev. Dennis Gascoyne Hawker;** *b* 8 Feb. 1921; *o s* of late Robert Stephen and Amelia Caroline Hawker; *m* 1944, Margaret Hamilton, *d* of late Robert and Daisy Henderson; one *s* one *d. Educ:* Addey and Stanhope Grammar Sch.; Queens' Coll., Cambridge (MA); Cuddesdon Theological Coll., Oxford. Lloyds Bank, 1939-40. Served War, Commissioned Officer, Royal Marines, 1940-46 (War Substantive Major). Deacon, 1950; Priest, 1951; Asst. Curate, St Mary and St Eanswythe, Folkestone, 1950-55; Vicar, St Mark, South Norwood, 1955-60; St Hugh's Missioner, Dio. Lincoln, 1960-65; Vicar, St Mary and St James, Gt Grimsby, 1965-72; Canon and Prebendary of Clifton, in Lincoln Cath., 1964-; Proctor in Convocation, 1964-74. Hon. Chaplain, RNR, 1979-. *Address:* Fairacre, 243 Barrowby Road, Grantham, Lincs NG31 8NP. *T:* Grantham 4722. *Club:* Army and Navy.

GRANTHAM, Adm. Sir Guy, GCB 1956 (KCB 1952; CB 1942); CBE 1946; DSO 1941; retired; Governor and Commander-in-Chief of Malta, 1959-62;

b 9 Jan. 1900; *s* of late C. F. Grantham, The Hall, Skegness, Lincs; *m* 1934, Beryl Marjorie, *d* of late T. C. B. Mackintosh-Walker, Geddes, Nairn; two *d.* Served War of 1939-45 (despatches, twice, DSO, CB, CBE); Chief of Staff to C-in-C, Mediterranean, 1946-48; Naval ADC to the King, 1947-48; Flag Officer (Submarines), 1948-50; Flag Officer, Second-in-Command, Mediterranean Fleet, 1950-51; Vice-Chief of Naval Staff, 1951-54; Comdr-in-Chief, Mediterranean Station, and Allied Forces, Mediterranean, 1954-57; Comdr-in-Chief, Portsmouth, Allied Comdr-in-Chief, Channel and Southern North Sea, 1957-59; First and Principal Naval ADC to the Queen, 1958-59. Retired list, 1959. Hon. Freeman of Haberdashers' Company. Mem., Commonwealth War Graves Commn 1962-70 (Vice-Chm. 1963-70). Governor, Corps of Commissionaires, 1964-. *Address:* Stanleys, Hatch Lane, Liss, Hants. *T:* Liss 2135.

GRANTHAM, Roy Aubrey; General Secretary, Association of Professional, Executive, Clerical & Computer Staff (APEX), since 1970; *b* 12 Dec. 1926; *m* 1964; two *d. Educ:* King Edward Grammar Sch., Birmingham. APEX: Midland area Organiser, 1949; Midland area Sec., 1959; Asst Sec., 1963. Exec. Member: European Movement; Labour Cttee for Europe; Confedn of Shipbuilding and Engineering Unions. Member: Royal Commn on Environmental Pollution, 1976-79; CNAA, 1976-79. A Dir, Chrysler UK Ltd, 1977-79, Talbot UK Ltd, 1979-81. Henley Management Coll., 1979-; Ditchley Foundn, 1982-. *Publication:* Guide to Grading of Clerical and Administrative Work, 1968. *Recreations:* walking, reading, chess. *Address:* 18 The Grange, Shirley, Croydon CR0 8AP.

GRANTHAM, Mrs Violet Hardisty; Member of Newcastle upon Tyne City Council, 1937-74; Alderman of City, 1951-58; *o d* of Thomas Taylor, BSc, and Sarah Taylor; *m* John Grantham (*d* 1945) (formerly Sheriff of Newcastle upon Tyne, and Lord Mayor, 1936-37). *Educ:* privately. Dir of Private Companies. Lady Mayoress of Newcastle upon Tyne, 1936-37 and 1949-50; Sheriff of Newcastle upon Tyne, 1950-51 (first woman to hold this office); Lord Mayor, 1952-53 and 1957 (first woman to hold this office). Mem. Newcastle upon Tyne HMC, 1948-72; Founder Mem., and Mem. of Cttee, Percy Hedley Home for Spastic Children. Trustee: St Mary the Virgin Hosp. Trust (Chm.); Mary Magdalene and Holy Jesus Hosp. Trust (Vice-Chm.). Formerly Northern Area Chm. of Women's Junior Air Corps; formerly Pres. Newcastle upon Tyne Branch of Royal College of Nursing; active in Townswomen's Guilds and other women's organisations. Freeman, City and Co. of Newcastle upon Tyne, 1968. *Address:* 74 Mary Magdalene Bungalows, Newcastle upon Tyne 2.

GRANTLEY, 7th Baron, *cr* 1782; **John Richard Brinsley Norton,** MC 1944; Baron of Markenfield, 1782; a Member of Lloyd's; Director, Leslie & Godwin Ltd; *b* 30 July 1923; *o s* of 6th Baron and Jean Mary (*d* 1945), *d* of Sir David Alexander Kinloch, CB, MVO, 11th Bt; *S* father 1954; *m* 1955, Deirdre Mary Freda, *e d* of 5th Earl of Listowel, *qv* ; two *s. Educ:* Eton; New Coll., Oxford. Served War of 1939-45, 1942-45, in Italy as Capt. Grenadier Guards (MC). *Heir: s* Hon. Richard William Brinsley Norton, *b* 30 Jan. 1956. *Address:* 53 Lower Belgrave Street, SW1; Markenfield Hall, Ripon, North Yorks. *Clubs:* White's, Pratt's.

GRANVILLE, family name of Baron Granville of Eye.

GRANVILLE, 5th Earl, *cr* 1833; **Granville James Leveson Gower,** MC 1945; Viscount Granville, 1815; Baron Leveson, 1833; Major Coldstream Guards (Supplementary Reserve); Vice-Lord-Lieutenant, Islands Area of the Western Isles, since 1976; *b* 6 Dec. 1918; *s* of 4th Earl Granville, KG, KCVO, CB, DSO, and Countess Granville, GCVO; *S* father, 1953; *m* 1958, Doon Aileen, *d* of late Hon. Brinsley Plunket and of Mrs V. Stux-Rybar, Luttrellstown Castle, Co. Dublin; two *s* one *d. Educ:* Eton. Served throughout War, 1939-45, Tunisia and Italy (twice wounded, despatches, MC). DL Inverness, 1974. *Heir: s* Lord Leveson, *qv. Address:* 49 Lyall Mews, SW1. *T:* 01-235 1026; Callernish, Sollas, North Uist, Outer Hebrides, Inverness-shire. *T:* Bayhead 213.

GRANVILLE OF EYE, Baron *cr* 1967, of Eye (Life Peer); **Edgar Louis Granville;** *s* of Reginald and Margaret Granville; *b* Reading, 12 Feb. 1899; *m* 1943, Elizabeth *d* of late Rev. W. C. Hunter; one *d. Educ:* High Wycombe, London and Australia. Served as officer in AIF, Gallipoli, Egypt and France. Capt. RA, 1939-40. MP (L) Eye Div. of Suffolk, 1929-51; Hon. Sec., Liberal Agricultural Group, House of Commons, 1929-31; Hon. Sec. Foreign Affairs Group, Vice-Pres. National League of Young Liberals; Chm., Young Liberals Manifesto Group; Parliamentary Private Sec. to Sir Herbert Samuel, first National Government, 1931; Parliamentary Private Sec. to Sir John Simon, National Government, 1931-36; Mem. of Inter-Departmental Cttee for the World Economic Conference, 1933. *Recreations:* cricket, football, ski-ing. *Address:* 112 Charlton Lane, Cheltenham, Glos.

GRANVILLE, Sir Keith, Kt 1973; CBE 1958; FCIT; *b* 1 Nov. 1910; *m* 1st, 1933, Patricia Capstick; one *s* one *d* ; 2nd, 1946, Truda Belliss; one *s* four *d. Educ:* Tonbridge Sch. Joined Imperial Airways as Trainee, 1929 and served Italy, Tanganyika, Southern and Northern Rhodesia, Egypt, India. BOAC: Manager African and Middle East Div., 1947; Commercial Dir, 1954; Dep. Managing Dir, 1958-60; Mem. Bd, 1959-72; Dep. Chm., 1964-70; Man. Dir, 1969-70; Chm. and Chief Exec., 1971-72; Mem. Bd, BEA, 1971-72; British Airways Board: Mem., 1971-74; Dep. Chm., 1972-74; Chairman: BOAC Associated Companies Ltd, 1960-64; BOAC Engine Overhaul Ltd, 1971-72;

International Aeradio Ltd, 1965-71 (Dep.-Chm., 1962-65). Mem. Bd, Maplin Development Authority, 1973-74. President: Inst. of Transport, 1963-64; IATA, 1972-73. Chm., British Residents' Assoc. of Switzerland, 1979-81. Hon. FRAeS, 1977. *Address:* Speedbird, 1837 Château d'Oex, Switzerland. *T:* (029) 4 76 03.

GRANVILLE SLACK, George; *see* Slack, G. G.

GRANVILLE-WEST, Baron, *cr* 1958 (Life Peer), of Pontypool, in the County of Monmouthshire; **Daniel Granville West;** formerly Senior Partner in the firm of D. Granville West, Chivers & Morgan, Newbridge and Pontypool; *b* 17 March 1904; *s* of John West, Newbridge, Monmouthshire, and Elizabeth West (*née* Bridges); *m* 1937, Vera (JP Monmouthshire, 1956), *d* of J. Hopkins, Pontypool; one *s* one *d.* Admitted a Solicitor, 1929. Served War of 1939-45: Royal Air Force Volunteer Reserve, Flight Lt. MP (Lab) Pontypool Div. of Monmouthshire, July 1946-58. PPS to Home Sec., 1950-51. Mem. of Abercarn Urban District Council, 1934-38 and of Monmouthshire County Council, 1938-47. *Address:* Brynderwen, Abersychan, Pontypool, Gwent. *T:* Talywain 236.

GRASAR, Rt. Rev. William Eric, DCL, STL; *b* 18 May 1913. *Educ:* Brigg Grammar School; Panton; English College, Rome. Priest 1937; Vice-Rector, English College, Rome, 1942-46; Chancellor, Nottingham Diocese, 1948-52; Rector of St Hugh's College, Tollerton, 1952-56; Vicar-General, Nottingham Diocese, 1956-62; Bishop of Shrewsbury, 1962-80. *Address:* St Vincent's, Bentinck Road, Altrincham, Cheshire WA14 2BP. *T:* 061-928 1689.

GRASS, Günter Wilhelm; German writer and artist; *b* Danzig, 16 Oct. 1927; *m* 1954, Anna Schwarz; three *s* (inc. twin *s*) one *d. Educ:* Volksschule and Gymnasium, Danzig; Düsseldorf Kunstakademie; Hochschule für Bildende Künste. Lecture Tour of US, 1964, and many other foreign tours. Member: Akademie der Künste, Berlin; Deutscher PEN, Zentrum der Bundesrepublik; Verband Deutscher Schriftsteller; Amer. Academy of Arts and Sciences. Prizes: Lyric, Süddeutscher Rundfunk, 1955; Gruppe 47, 1959; Bremen Literary, 1959 (zurückgezogen); Literary, Assoc. of German Critics, 1960; Meilleur livre étranger, 1962; Georg-Büchner, 1965; Theodor-Heuss, 1969. *Publications: novels:* Die Blechtrommel, 1959 (The Tin Drum, 1962; filmed 1979); Katz und Maus, 1961 (Cat and Mouse, 1963); Hundejahre, 1963 (Dog Years, 1965); Örtlich Betäubt, 1969 (Local Anaesthetic, 1970); Der Butt, 1976 (The Flounder, 1978); Das Treffen in Telgte, 1979 (The Meeting at Telgte, 1981); Headbirths, 1982; Kopfgeburten, 1980; *poetry:* Die Vorzüge der Windhühner, 1956; Gleisdreieck, 1960; Ausgefragt, 1967; *poetry in translation:* Selected Poems, 1966; Poems of Günter Grass, 1969; In the Egg and other poems, 1978; *drama:* Hochwasser, 1957 (Flood, 1968); Noch zehn Minuten bis Buffalo, 1958 (Only Ten Minutes to Buffalo, 1968); Onkel, Onkel, 1958 (Onkel, Onkel, 1968); Die bösen Köche, 1961 (The Wicked Cooks, 1968); Die Plebejer proben den Aufstand, 1966 (The Plebeians rehearse the Uprising, 1967); Davor, 1969; *prose:* Über das Selbstverständliche, 1968; (Speak Out!, 1969); Aus dem Tagebuch einer Schnecke, 1972 (From the Diary of a Snail, 1974); Dokumente zur politischen Wirkung, 1972. *Address:* Niedstrasse 13, Berlin 41, Germany.

GRATTAN, Donald Henry; Controller, Educational Broadcasting, BBC, since 1972; *b* St Osyth, Essex, 7 Aug. 1926; *s* of Arthur Henry Grattan and Edith Caroline Saltmarsh; *m* 1950, Valmai Dorothy Morgan; one *s* one *d. Educ:* Harrow Boys Grammar Sch.; King's Coll., Univ. of London. BSc 1st Cl. Hons, Mathematics Dip. in Radio-Physics. Jun. Scientific Officer, TRE, Gt Malvern, 1945-46; Mathematics Teacher, Chiswick Grammar Sch., 1946-50; Sen. Master, Downer Grammar Sch., Mddx, 1950-56. BBC: Sch. Television Producer, 1956-60; Asst Head, Sch. Television, 1960-64; Head of Further Educn, Television, 1964-70; Asst Controller, Educnl Broadcasting, 1970-72. Member: Open Univ. Council, 1972- (and Univ. Delegacy for Continuing Educn, 1978-); Council for Educnl Technology, 1973-; Adv. Council for Adult and Continuing Educn, 1978-; European Broadcasting Union Working Party on Educn, 1972-; Venables' Cttee on Continuing Educn, 1976-78. Chm., Adult Literacy Support Services Fund, 1975-80. Mem., Royal TV Soc., 1982-. Burnham Medal of BIM for services to Management Educn, 1969. *Publications:* Science and the Builder, 1963; Mathematics Miscellany (jt, BBC), 1966; numerous articles. *Recreations:* education (formal and informal), boating, planning and organizing, people. *Address:* Delabole, Gossmore Close, Marlow, Bucks. *T:* Marlow 73571.

GRATTAN-BELLEW, Sir Arthur (John), Kt 1959; CMG 1956; QC (Tanganyika), 1952; *b* 23 May 1903; *s* of Sir Henry (Christopher) Grattan-Bellew, 3rd Bt, and Lady Sophia Forbes, *d* of 7th Earl of Granard, KP; *m* 1931, Freda Mary Mahony (*d* 1979); one *s* one *d. Educ:* Downside Sch.; Christ's Coll., Cambridge (BA). Called to Bar, Lincoln's Inn, 1925; practised in London until 1935, Legal Service, Egyptian Govt, 1936-38; Colonial Legal Service, Malaya, 1938-41. Military Service, 1941-45 (POW 1942-45). Colonial Legal Service; Malaya, 1946-48; Attorney-General: Sarawak, 1948-52; Tanganyika, 1952-56; Chief Sec., Tanganyika, 1956-59; Legal Adviser's Dept, Foreign and Commonwealth Office, retired. Chm., Bellew, Parry and Raven Gp of companies. *Address:* Pledgdon Green, Henham, near Bishop's Stortford, Herts.

GRATTAN-BELLEW, Sir Henry Charles, 5th Bt, *cr* 1838; *b* 12 May 1933; *s* of Lt-Col Sir Charles Christopher Grattan-Bellew, 4th Bt, MC, KRRC and Maureen Peyton, *niece* and adopted *d* of late Sir Thomas Segrave, Shenfield,

Essex; *S* father, 1948; *m* 1st, 1956, Naomi Ellis (marr. diss. 1966); 2nd, 1967, Gillian Hulley (marr. diss. 1973); one *s* one *d* ; 3rd, 1978, Elzabé Amy (*née* Body), *widow* of John Westerveld, Pretoria, Tvl, SA. *Educ:* St Gerard's, Bray, Co. Wicklow; Ampleforth Coll., York. Publisher: Horse and Hound, SA, and Sustagen Supersport, 1977. Sports administrator, leading radio and TV commentator, hotelier, thoroughbred breeder and owner. *Heir: s* Patrick Charles Grattan-Bellew, *b* 7 Dec. 1971. *Address:* Sandford Park, PO Box 7, Bergville, Natal, 3350, South Africa.

GRATTAN-COOPER, Rear Admiral Sidney, CB 1966; OBE 1946; *b* 3 Dec. 1911; *s* of Sidney Cooper; *m* 1940, Felicity Joan Pitt; two *s. Educ:* privately. Entered RN 1936; served in war of 1939-45; Chief of Staff Flag Officer (Air) Home, 1957-59; Staff of Supreme Allied Cdr Atlantic (NATO), 1961-63; Dep. Controller (Aircraft) RN, Min. of Aviation, 1964-66; retired 1966. *Recreations:* golf, swimming. *Address:* Hursley, St James, Cape, S Africa. *Club:* Army and Navy.

GRATWICK, John, OBE 1979; Chairman: Empire Stores (Bradford) Ltd, since 1978; Guild Sound and Vision Ltd, since 1976; Lovat Enterprise Fund Ltd, since 1980; Director: Export Finance Consultant Ltd, since 1972; R. Kelvin Watson Ltd, since 1974; Deputy Chairman, Lake & Elliot Ltd, since 1977; *b* 23 April 1918; *s* of Percival John and Kathleen Mary Gratwick; *m* 1944, Ellen Violet Wright; two *s* two *d. Educ:* Cranbrook Sch., Kent; Imperial Coll., Univ. of London. Asst Production Manager, Armstrong Siddeley, 1941-45; Director, Urwick, Orr & Partners Ltd, 1959, Man. Dir, 1968, Vice-Chm., 1971; Member: Monopolies and Mergers Commn, 1969-76; CAA, 1972-74; EDC for the Clothing Industry, 1967-; Senate of Univ. of London, 1967-; Univ. of London Careers Adv. Bd, 1962-78; Chm., Management Consultants Assoc., 1971-72. Governor, Cranbrook Sch., Kent, 1972; Trustee, Foundn for Business Responsibilities. Liveryman: Worshipful Co. of Farriers; Glovers' Co. *Recreations:* golf, sailing, photography, philately. *Address:* Silver Howe, Nuns Walk, Virginia Water, Surrey. *T:* Wentworth 3121. *Clubs:* Royal Automobile, City Livery; Wentworth (Surrey).
See also Stephen Gratwick.

GRATWICK, Stephen, QC 1968; *b* 19 Aug. 1924; *s* of late Percival John Gratwick, Fawkham, Kent; *m* 1954, Jocelyn Chaplin, Horton Kirby, Kent; four *d. Educ:* Charterhouse, Balliol Coll., Oxford. Oxford 1942-44; Signals Research and Develt Estab., 1944-47. BA (Physics) 1946; MA 1950. Called to Bar, Lincoln's Inn, 1949, Bencher, 1976. *Recreations:* sailing, ski-ing, tennis, swimming, making and mending things. *Address:* 11 South Square, Gray's Inn, WC1R 5EU. *Club:* Little Ship.
See also John Gratwick.

GRAVE, Walter Wyatt, CMG 1958; MA (Cambridge); Hon. LLD (Cambridge and McMaster); Hon. Fellow of Fitzwilliam College, Cambridge; *b* 16 Oct. 1901; *s* of late Walter and Annie Grave; *m* 1932, Kathleen Margaret, *d* of late Stewart Macpherson; two *d. Educ:* King Edward VII Sch., King's Lynn; Emmanuel Coll., Cambridge (Scholar); Fellow of Emmanuel Coll., 1926-66, 1972-; Tutor, 1936-40; University Lecturer in Spanish, 1936-40; Registrary of Cambridge Univ., 1943-52; Principal of the University Coll., of the West Indies, Jamaica, 1953-58; Censor of Fitzwilliam House, Cambridge, 1959-66; Master of Fitzwilliam Coll., Cambridge, 1966-71. Temporary Administrative Officer, Ministry of Labour and National Service, 1940-43. *Address:* 18 Luard Road, Cambridge. *T:* 47415.

GRAVES, family name of **Baron Graves.**

GRAVES, 8th Baron, *cr* 1794; **Peter George Wellesley Graves;** Actor; *b* 21 Oct. 1911; *o s* of 7th Baron Graves; *S* father, 1963; *m* 1960, Vanessa Lee. *Educ:* Harrow. First appeared on London stage in 1934, and has subsequently played many leading parts. Mem. Windsor repertory co., 1941. Has appeared in films since 1940. *Recreation:* lawn tennis. *Heir: kinsman,* Evelyn Paget Graves [*b* 17 May 1926; *m* 1957, Marjorie Ann, *d* of late Dr Sidney Ernest Holder; two *s* two *d*]. *Address: c/o* Messrs Coutts & Co., 440 Strand, WC2. *Club:* All England Lawn Tennis.

GRAVES, Robert Ranke; writer; Hon. Fellow, St John's College, Oxford; *b* London, 1895; *s* of late Alfred Perceval and Amy Graves; *m* 1st, Nancy, *d* of late Sir Wm Nicholson; one *s* two *d* (and one *s* killed in Burma); 2nd, Beryl, *d* of late Sir Harry Pritchard; three *s* one *d. Educ:* Charterhouse; St John's Coll., Oxford (Hon. Fellow, 1971). Served in France with Royal Welch Fusiliers; Prof. of English Literature, Egyptian Univ., 1926. Clarke Lecturer at Trinity Coll., Cambridge, 1954. Arthur Dehon Little Memorial Lecturer, Massachusetts Institute of Technology, 1963. Professor of Poetry, Univ. of Oxford, 1961-66. Books (over 137) and manuscripts, on permanent exhibition, at Lockwood Memorial Library, Buffalo, NY. Bronze Medal for Poetry, Olympic Games, Paris, 1924; Gold Medal for Poetry, Cultural Olympics, Mexico, 1968; Gold Medal of Nat. Poetry Soc. of America, 1960; Queen's Gold Medal for Poetry, 1968. Adoptive son of Deyá village, Mallorca, 1968, where resident since 1929. *Publications:* Goodbye to All That, An Autobiography, 1929 (revised 1957); But it Still Goes on, 1930; The Real David Copperfield, 1933; I, Claudius, 1934 (awarded Hawthornden and James Tait Black Memorial Prizes for 1934); Claudius the God, 1934; Antigua Penny Puce, 1936; T. E. Lawrence to his Biographer, 1938; Count Belisarius, 1938 (awarded Stock Prize, 1939); Sergeant Lamb of the Ninth, 1940; The Long Week End: A Social History (with Alan Hodge), 1940; Proceed, Sergeant

Lamb, 1941; Wife to Mr Milton, 1943; The Reader Over Your Shoulder (with Alan Hodge), 1943; The Golden Fleece, 1944; King Jesus, 1946; The White Goddess, 1947; Collected Poems, 1948; Seven Days in New Crete, 1949; The Common Asphodel (Collected Essays on Poetry), 1949; The Isles of Unwisdom, 1949; Occupation: Writer, 1950; Poems and Satires, 1951; The Nazarene Gospel Restored (with Joshua Podro), 1953; The Greek Myths, 1955 (new edn, Greek Myths and Legends, 1968, illustrated edn, 1982); Homer's Daughter, 1955; The Crowning Privilege, 1955; Adam's Rib, 1955; Catacrok (stories), 1956; Jesus in Rome (with Joshua Podro), 1957; They hanged my saintly Billy, 1957; (ed) English and Scottish Ballads, 1957; Steps, 1958; Collected Poems, 1959; The Penny Fiddle, 1960; More Poems, 1961; Oxford Addresses, 1962; New Poems, 1962; (with Raphael Patai) Hebrew Myths: Genesis, 1964; Collected Short Stories, 1964; Man Does, Woman Is (poems), 1964; Mammon and the Black Goddess, 1964; Hebrew Myths: Genesis (with Rafael Patai), 1965; Ann at High Wood Hall, 1965; Collected Short Stories, 1965; Love Respelt, 1965; Majorca Observed, 1965; Collected Poems, 1965; Seventeen Poems Missing from Love Respelt, 1966; Two Wise Children, 1967; Colophon, 1967; Poetic Craft and Principle, 1967; The Poor Boy who followed his Star, 1968; Poems 1965-68, 1968; The Crane Bag and other disputed subjects, 1968; Beyond Giving, 1969; Poems 1968-1970, 1970; The Song of Songs (with lithographs by Hans Erni), 1971; The Green-Sailed Vessel, 1971; All Things to all Men (play), 1971; Poems: abridged for dolls and princes, 1971; Poems 1970-72, 1972; Difficult Questions: Easy Answers, 1973; Timeless Meeting, 1973; At the Gate, 1974; Collected Poems 1975, 1975; An Ancient Castle (for children), 1980; translations: The Golden Ass, 1949; Alarcón's Infant with the Globe, 1956; Galvan's The Cross and the Sword, 1956; George Sand's Winter in Majorca, 1957; Suetonius's Twelve Cæsars; Lucan's Pharsalia; Homer's Anger of Achilles, 1959; Terence's Comedies, 1962; Rubaiyyat of Omar Khayaam (with Omar Ali-Shah), 1967. Address: c/o A. P. Watt Ltd, 26/28 Bedford Row, WC1.

GRAVESON, Prof. Ronald Harry, CBE 1972; QC 1966; Barrister-at-Law; Professor Emeritus of Private International Law, King's College, University of London, 1978; b 2 Oct. 1911; o s of Harry Graveson, Sheffield; m 1937, Muriel, o d of John Saunders, Sheffield; one s two d. Educ: King Edward VII Sch., Sheffield. LLB 1932, LLM 1933, LLD 1955 Sheffield; SJD Harvard 1936; PhD London 1941; LLD London 1951; Gregory Scholar in International Law of Harvard Univ.; Solicitor (Hons), 1934. Army, 1940-46 (Driver, RE; Lieut-Col RASC, G5 Div. SHAEF). Called to Bar, Gray's Inn, 1945; Bencher, 1965; Vice-Treas., 1982, Treas., 1983. Reader in English Law, University Coll., Univ. of London, 1946-47; Prof. of Law, 1947-74, and of Private Internat. Law, 1974-78, KCL; Dean of the Faculty of Laws, Univ. of London, 1951-54, 1972-74, and KCL, 1951-58, 1959-63, 1966-70. Vis. Prof., Harvard Law Sch., 1958-59. Chm., UK, National Cttee of Comparative Law, 1955-57. Member: Review Body on pay of doctors and dentists, 1971-81; Cttees of Inquiry into Pay of Nurses and Midwives and of Professions supplementary to Medicine, 1974-75; Pres., Harvard Law Sch. Assoc. of the UK, 1959-61, 1977-81. Jt Editor, Internat. and Comparative Law Quarterly, 1955-61; Consultant Editor of the Law Reports and the Weekly Law Reports, 1970-75. Pres. International Association of Legal Science (UNESCO), 1960-62. Mem. Inst. of International Law; Pres., Soc. of Public Teachers of Law, 1972-73. Member: Polish Acad. of Sci., 1977; Council, Univ. Internat. Luxembourg; Council, Luxembourg Soc.; Council, Anglo-Belgian Union; Council, British Inst. of Internat. and Comparative Law; Council, Selden Soc.; Rome Inst. for the Unification of Private Law; Internat. Acad. of Comparative Law. Mem., Clockmakers' Co. Pres., KCL Assoc., 1982-; FKC 1962. LLD (hc) Ghent, 1964; Uppsala, 1977; Leuven, 1978; Dr Juris (hc) Freiburg, 1969. JP St Alban's City, 1961-66. Commandeur de l'Ordre de la Couronne de Chêne, 1964; Comdr, Order of Oranje Nassau, 1970; Order of National Merit, France, 1970; Grand Cross of Order of Merit, German Federal Republic, 1975; Legion of Honour, 1977; Comdr, Order of the Crown (Belgium), 1977. Publications: English Legal System, 1939; Conflict of Laws, 1948 (7th edition 1974); Cases on the Conflict of Laws, 1949; The Comparative Evolution of Principles of the Conflict of Laws in England and the USA 1960; General Principles of Private International Law, 1964; (jtly) The Conflict of Laws and International Contracts, 1951; Status in the Common Law, 1953, reprinted 1983; (jtly) A Century of Family Law, 1957; Law: An Introduction, 1967; (jtly) Unification of the International Law of Sale, 1968; Problems of Private International Law in Non-unified Legal Systems, 1975; Comparative Conflict of Laws, 1976; One Law, 1976; Gen. Editor, Problems in Private International Law, 1977; various articles, notes or reviews since 1936 in English and foreign law reviews. Contributor to various collective volumes including essays in honour of British and foreign colleagues; Apollo; Connoisseur. Recreations: Gray's Inn, works of art, international friendship. Address: 2 Gray's Inn Square, Gray's Inn, WC1R 5AA. T: 01-242 8492; Castle Hill Farm House, Bakewell, Derbys. Clubs: Athenæum, Royal Commonwealth Society.

GRAY, 22nd Lord, cr 1445; **Angus Diarmid Ian Campbell-Gray;** b 3 July 1931; s of Major Hon. Lindsay Stuart Campbell-Gray, Master of Gray, MC (d 1945), and Doreen (d 1948), d of late Cyril Tubbs, Thedden Grange, Alton, Hants; S grandmother 1946; m 1959, Patricia Margaret, o d of late Capt. Philip Alexander, Kilmorna, Lismore, Co. Waterford; one s three d. Heir: s Master of Gray, qv. Address: Airds Bay House, Taynuilt, Argyll. Clubs: Carlton, MCC.

GRAY, Master of; Hon. Andrew Godfrey Diarmid Stuart Campbell-Gray; b 3 Sept. 1964; s and heir of 22nd Lord Gray, qv.

GRAY, Alexander Stuart, FRIBA; Consultant to Watkins, Gray, Woodgate International, 1968-75, retired; b 15 July 1905; s of Alexander and Mary Gray; m 1932, Avis (d 1980), d of John Radmore, Truro; one s two d. Educ: Mill Hill Sch. Articled to R. S. Balgarnie Wyld, ARIBA; studied at Central Sch. of Arts and Crafts; Royal Academy Schools (Bronze Medal, 1928; Silver Medal and Travelling Studentship, 1932; Gold Medal and Edward Stott Trav. Studentship (Italy), 1933); Brit. Instn Schol., 1929. Lectr on Arch. subjects at Central Sch. of Arts and Crafts, Brixton Sch. of Bldg, and Hammersmith Sch. of Bldg, 1936-39; Lectr on Hosp. Planning at King Edward VII Hosp. Fund Colleges, 1950-. In partnership with W. H. Watkins won architectural comp. for new St George's Hosp., Hyde Park Corner, London (partnership 1939-68); before retirement Architect with partners to: Radcliffe Infirmary, Oxford, United Bristol Hospitals, Royal Free Hospital, Guy's Hospital, London Hospital, Eastman Dental Hospital, St Mary's, Manchester, and other hosps in London and the provinces; also in West Indies, where they were responsible for banks, and commercial buildings as well; hospitals for Comptroller of Development and Welfare in BWI, 1941-46; rebuilding of centre of Georgetown, British Guiana, after the fire of 1945, including new GPO, Telecommunications Building, etc. In Nigeria, University Coll. Hosp., Ibadan, and other works, also in Qatar (Persian Gulf), etc. Publications: various papers read at confs on Hosp. Planning with special ref. to designing for the tropics, and contrib. Tech. Jls. Address: 1 Temple Fortune Hill, NW11. T: 01-458 5741. Clubs: Arts, Old Millhillians.

GRAY, Andrew Aitken, MC 1945; Chairman, Wellcome Foundation Ltd, 1971-77; b 11 Jan. 1912; s of John Gray and Margaret Eckford Gray (née Crozier); m 1939, Eileen Mary Haines (d 1980); three s. Educ: Wyggeston School, Leicester; Christ Church, Oxford. Served Royal Engineers, 1939-46 (MC, despatches). Unilever Ltd, 1935-52. Dir, Wellcome Foundation Ltd, 1954, Dep. Chm., 1967; Chm. and Man. Dir, Cooper, McDougall & Robertson, 1963-70. Chm., Herts AHA, 1974-77. Comdr, Orden del Mérito Agricola; Comdr, Order of Merit, Italy. Recreations: fishing, gardening, theatre. Address: Rainhill Spring, Stoney Lane, Bovingdon, Herts. T: Hemel Hempstead 833277. Club: East India, Devonshire, Sports and Public Schools.

GRAY, Sir Anthony; see Gray, Sir F. A.

GRAY, Anthony James; management consultant; Chief Executive, Cogent Ltd; b 12 Feb. 1937; o s of Sir James Gray, CBE, MC, FRS; m 1963, Lady Lana Mary Gabrielle Baring (d 1974), d of Earl of Cromer, qv; one s one d; m 1980, Mrs Maxine Redmayne, er d of Captain and Mrs George Brodrick. Educ: Marlborough Coll.; New Coll., Oxford. C. T. Bowring & Co. (Insurance) Ltd, 1959-64; Sen. Investment Analyst, de Zoete & Gorton, 1965-67; Research Partner, James Capel & Co., 1967-73. Member, London Stock Exchange, 1971-73. Dep. Dir, Industrial Development Unit, Dept of Industry, 1973-75; Adviser, Special Industry Problems, Dept of Industry, 1975-76. Member: Foundries EDC, 1977-79; Hammersmith and Fulham DHA, 1982. Mem. Council, Charing Cross Hosp. Med. Sch., 1982. Recreations: golf, fishing, music. Address: 5 Ranelagh Avenue, SW6. Club: Garrick.

GRAY, Basil, CB 1969; CBE 1957; MA; FBA 1966; Keeper of Oriental Antiquities, British Museum, 1946-69, Acting Director and Principal Librarian, 1968; b 21 July 1904; s of late Surgeon-Major Charles Gray and Florence Elworthy, d of Rev. H. v. H. Cowell; m 1933, Nicolete, d of late Laurence Binyon, CH; two s two d (and one d decd). Educ: Bradfield; New Coll., Oxford. British Academy excavations in Constantinople, 1928; entered British Museum (Printed Books), 1928; transferred to sub-Dept of Oriental Prints and Drawings, 1930; in charge of Oriental Antiquities (including Oriental Prints and Drawings) from 1938; Dep. Keeper, 1940. Mem. of Art Panel of the Arts Council, 1952-57, and 1959-68; President: Oriental Ceramic Soc., 1962-65, 1971-74, 1977-78; 6th Internat. Congress of Iranian Art and Archaeology, Oxford, 1972. Mem., Reviewing Cttee on Export of Works of Art, 1971-79; Chm., Exhibn cttee, The Arts of Islam, Hayward Gallery, 1976. Pres., Soc. for Afghan Studies, 1979-. A Visitor of Ashmolean Museum, Oxford, 1969-79. Sir Percy Sykes Meml Medal, 1978. Publications: Persian Painting, 1930; Persian Miniature Painting (part author), 1933; Chinese Art (with Leigh Ashton), 1935; The English Print, 1937; Persian Painting, New York, 1940; Rajput Painting, 1948; (joint) Commemorative Catalogue of the Exhibition of the Art of India and Pakistan, 1947-48, 1950; Treasures of Indian Miniatures in the Bikanir Palace Collection, 1951; Early Chinese Pottery and Porcelain, 1953; Japanese Screen-paintings, 1955; Buddhist Cave paintings at Tun-huang, 1959; Treasures of Asia; Persian Painting, 1961; (with D. E. Barrett) Painting of India, 1963; An Album of Miniatures and Illuminations from the Bâysonhori Manuscript of the Shâhnâmeh of Ferdowsi, 1971; The World History of Rashid al-Din, a study of the RAS manuscript, 1979; (ed, and jt author) The Arts of the Book in Central Asia 1370-1506, 1979; (ed, and jt author) The Arts of India, 1981; (ed) Faber Gallery of Oriental Art and Arts of the East Series. Address: Dawber's House, Long Wittenham, Oxon OX14 4QQ. Club: Savile.

GRAY, Charles Herbert, FRCS; Hon. Consultant Orthopædic Surgeon, Royal Free Hospital; formerly Consulting Orthopædic Surgeon, British Postgraduate Medical School, Hammersmith Hospital, and Connaught Hospital, Walthamstow. Educ: Victoria University, Manchester. BSc; MB, ChB (hons) 1932; MRCS, LRCP, 1932; FRCS, 1935. Temp. Lt-Col, Royal Army Medical Corps. Hunterian Prof., Royal College of Surgeons, 1946,

1949. Formerly, Fracture and Orthopædic Registrar, Middlesex Hosp.; Surg. Registrar, Royal Nat. Orthopaedic Hospital. Fellow: British Orthopaedic Assoc.; Hunterian Soc.; Membre Société Internationale de Chirurgie, Orthopédie et Traumatologie. *Publications:* various articles in medical jls. *Address:* 8 Upper Wimpole Street, W1. *T:* 01-580 5307; 16 Hamilton Close, NW8.

GRAY, Charles Horace, MD (London), DSc, FRCP, FRIC, FRCPath; Visiting Professor, Division of Clinical Chemistry, MRC Clinical Research Centre, Harrow; Emeritus Professor of Chemical Pathology in the University of London (Professor, at King's College Hospital Medical School, 1948-76); Consulting Chemical Pathologist, King's College Hospital District, 1976-81 (Consultant, 1938-76); *b* 30 June 1911; *s* of Charles H. Gray and Ethel Hider, Erith, Kent; *m* 1938, Florence Jessie Widdup, ARCA, *d* of Frank Widdup, JP, Barnoldswick, Yorks; two *s. Educ:* Imperial Coll. and University Coll., London (Fellow, UCL, 1979); University Coll. Hospital Medical Sch. Demonstrator in Biochemistry, University Coll., London, 1931-36; Bayliss-Starling Scholar in Physiology and Biochemistry, 1932-33; Visiting Teacher in Biochemistry, Chelsea Polytechnic, 1933-36; Demonstrator and Lecturer in Physiology, University Coll., 1935-36; Graham Scholar in Pathology, UCH Medical Sch., 1936-38; Pathologist in Charge Sector Biochemical Laboratory, Sector 9, Emergency Health Service, 1939-44; Hon. Consultant, Miles Laboratories Ltd, 1953-76. Acting Head, Dept of Chem. Pathol., Hosp. for Sick Children, Gt Ormond St, Jan.-Dec. 1979. Member: Chem. Res. Bd of Med. Res. Council, 1964-68; Arthritis and Rheumatism Council Res. Cttee, 1960-68 (Chm., 1963-66); Chairman: MCB Exams Cttee, 1971-73; Steroid Reference Collection and Radioactive Steroid Synthesis Steering Cttee, MRC, 1973-76; Regional Scientific Cttee, SE Thames RHA (Mem. Regional Branch Cttee, 1974-). Sec., Soc. for Endocrinology, 1950-53; Chm. Cttee of Management, Jl of Endocrinology Ltd, 1970-74; Member: Cttee of Management, Inst. of Psychiatry, 1966-73; Council, RCPath (Chm., Specialist Adv. Cttee in Chemical Pathology); Assoc. of Biochemists (Pres. 1969-71). Mem., Worshipful Soc. of Apothecaries of London, 1951-. Mem., Editorial Bd, Biochemical Jl, 1955-60. *Publications:* The Bile Pigments, 1953; Clinical Chemical Pathology, 1953, 1959, 1963, 1965, 1968, 1971, 1974, 1977, 1979; The Bile Pigments in Health and Disease, 1961; (ed) Laboratory Handbook of Toxic Agents; (ed jtly) Hormones in Blood, 1961, 1967, 1978; (ed jtly) High Pressure Liquid Chromatography in Clinical Chemistry, 1976; contributions to medical and scientific journals. *Recreations:* music and travel. *Address:* Barn Cottage, Linden Road, Leatherhead, Surrey KT22 7JF. *T:* Leatherhead 372415; 34 Cleaver Square, SE11 4EA. *T:* 01-735 9652; Owls Mount, Portland, Dorset DT5 1AP. *T:* Portland 820574. *Club:* Athenæum.

GRAY, David, CBE 1977 (OBE 1964); QPM 1960; HM Chief Inspector of Constabulary for Scotland, 1970-79; retired; *b* 18 Nov. 1914; *s* of William Gray and Janet Borland; *m* 1944, Mary Stewart Scott; two *d. Educ:* Preston Grammar Sch. Chief Constable: Greenock, 1955-58; Stirling and Clackmannan, 1958-69. Hon. Sec., Chief Constables' (Scotland) Assoc., 1958-69. English-Speaking Union Thyne Scholar, 1969. *Recreations:* fishing, shooting, golf. *Address:* Kingarth, 42 East Barnton Avenue, Edinburgh EH4 6AQ. *T:* 031-336 6342. *Club:* Bruntsfield (Edinburgh).

GRAY, David; Secretary-General, International Tennis Federation, since Aug. 1976; *b* 31 Dec. 1927; *s* of David Reginald Gray and Beatrice Gladys (*née* Goodyear); *m* 1962, Margaret Clare Emerson; three *s* one *d. Educ:* King Edward VI Grammar Sch., Stourbridge; Birmingham Univ. (BA Hons English). Journalist: Evening Telegraph, Blackburn, 1951-53; News Chronicle, 1953-54. Guardian: Manchester Guardian/Guardian, 1954-76; Midlands Correspondent, 1955-56; Lawn Tennis Correspondent, 1956-76; Sports Editor, 1961-68. Sports Writer of the Year Award, 1975. *Publications:* contrib. to Oxford Companion to Sport and other sports ref. books. *Recreations:* theatre, hill climbing. *Address:* 50 Luttrell Avenue, SW15 6PF. *T:* 01-788 4809. *Clubs:* Queen's, International Lawn Tennis (GB, France, Italy and USA), Players' Theatre.

GRAY, Prof. Douglas; J. R. R. Tolkien Professor of English Literature and Language, University of Oxford, since 1980; *b* 17 Feb. 1930; *s* of Emmerson and Daisy Gray; *m* 1959, Judith Claire Campbell; one *s. Educ:* Wellington College, NZ; Victoria Univ. of Wellington (MA 1952); Merton Coll., Oxford (BA 1954, MA 1960). Asst Lecturer, Victoria Univ. of Wellington, 1952-54; Lectr, Pembroke and Lincoln Colls, Oxford, 1956-61; Fellow, Pembroke Coll., 1961-80, now Emeritus; University Lectr in English Language, 1976-80; Professorial Fellow, Lady Margaret Hall, Oxford, 1980-. Mem. Council, EETS, 1981-; Pres., Soc. for Study of Mediæval Langs and Lit., 1982-. *Publications:* (ed) Spenser, The Faerie Queene, Book 1, 1969; Themes and Images in the Medieval English Religious Lyric, 1972; (ed) A Selection of Religious Lyrics, 1975; (part of) A Chaucer Glossary, 1979; Robert Henryson, 1979; articles on medieval literature. *Address:* Lady Margaret Hall, Oxford.

GRAY, Dulcie; see Denison, D. W. C.

GRAY, Dr Edward George, FRS 1976; Head of the Laboratory of Ultrastructure, National Institute for Medical Research, Mill Hill, since 1977; *b* 11 Jan. 1924; *s* of Will and Charlotte Gray; *m* 1953, May Eine Kyllikki Rautiainen; two *s. Educ:* University Coll. of Wales, Aberystwyth (BSc, PhD). Anatomy Dept, University Coll., London: Lectr, 1958; Reader, 1962; Prof.

(Cytology), 1968-77. *Recreations:* violin playing, water colouring, gardening. *Address:* 58 New Park Road, Newgate Street, Hertford SG13 8RF. *T:* Cuffley 2891.

GRAY, Sir (Francis) Anthony, KCVO 1981; Secretary and Keeper of the Records of the Duchy of Cornwall, 1972-81; *b* 3 Aug. 1917; *s* of late Major F. C. Gray; *m* 1947, Marcia, *d* of late Major Hugh Wyld; one *s* two *d. Educ:* Marlborough; Magdalen Coll., Oxford. Treas., Christ Church, Oxford, 1952-72, Emeritus Student, 1972. Mem., Agricultural Adv. Council, 1963-68; Mem. Council, Royal Coll. of Art, 1967-73. *Recreation:* travel. *Address:* Temple House, Upton Scudamore, Warminster, Wilts. *Club:* Travellers'.

GRAY, Geoffrey Leicester, CMG 1958; OBE 1953; Secretary for Local Government, N Borneo (now Sabah), 1956-61, retired; *b* 26 Aug. 1905; *s* of late Leonard Swainson Gray, Resident Magistrate of Kingston, Jamaica, and of late Marion Scotland, Vale Royal, Kingston, Jamaica; *m* 1932, Penelope Milnes (*d* 1971), MBE 1962, *o c* of late Philip Henry Townsend, OBE and late Gwenyth Gwendoline Roberts. *Educ:* Latymer Upper Sch. Cadet, North Borneo Civil Service, under British North Borneo (Chartered) Co., 1925; after qualifying in Malay and Law, served in various admin. posts, 1925-30; studied Chinese in Canton, 1931; attached Secretariat for Chinese Affairs and Educ. Dept, Hong Kong, 1931; Dist Officer, Jesselton, Supt, Govt Printing Office, and Editor, British North Borneo Herald and Official Gazette, 1932-35; Dist Officer, Kudat, 1935; Under-Sec., 1935-38; Govt Sec. Class 1b and ex-officio MLC, 1938-46; Additional Sessions and High Court Judge, 1938-46; interned by Japanese, 1941-45; Class 1a, 1946; accredited to HQ Brit. Mil. Admin (Brit. Borneo) at Labuan, 1946; assimilated into HM Colonial Admin. Service (later HM Overseas Service) on cession of North Borneo to the Crown, 1946; Actg Dep. Chief Sec., 1946; Protector of Labour and Sec. for Chinese Affairs, 1947; Resident, E Coast, in addition, 1947; Mem. Advisory Council, 1947-50; Comr of Immigration and Labour, 1948-51: Official MLC and MEC, 1950-61; Actg Fin. Sec., 1951-52; Dep. Chief Sec., Staff Class, 1952-56; represented North Borneo at Coronation, 1953; Chm., Bd of Educn and Town and Country Planning Bd, 1956-61; Actg Chief Sec. (intermittently), 1952-60; administered Govt, 1958, 1959; acted as high Comr, Brunei, 1959; retd, 1961. Life Associate, N Borneo and UK Branches, CPA, 1961. Chm., Borneo Mission Assoc., 1961-76; Commissary for Bp of Jesselton (later Sabah), 1961. Elected Incorporated Mem. of SPG (Mem., Standing Cttee, 1964-66; Mem., East Asia and Pacific Sub-Cttees, 1964-69); Mem. USPG Council, 1965, Mem. Gen. Cttee, 1966, Mem. Overseas Cttee, Grants and Budget Groups, 1969, Mem. Programmes Cttee, 1979. *Address:* 36A Osborne Villas, Hove, Sussex BN3 2RB. *T:* Brighton 203478. *Clubs:* Royal Commonwealth Society, Travellers'.

GRAY, Gilbert, QC 1971; a Recorder of the Crown Court, since 1972; *b* 25 April 1928; *s* of late Robert Gray, JP, Scarborough, and of Mrs Elizabeth Gray; *m* 1954, Olga Dilys Gray (*née* Thomas), BA, JP; two *s* two *d. Educ:* Scarborough Boys' High Sch.; Leeds Univ. (LLB). Pres., Leeds Univ. Union. Called to the Bar, Gray's Inn, 1953; Bencher, 1979. *Recreation:* sailing. *Address:* Treasurer's House, York; 2 Park Square, Leeds LS1 2NE; 90 Clifford's Inn, Fetter Lane, EC4. *Clubs:* Leeds (Leeds); Scarborough Sailing.

GRAY, Gordon; Chairman Emeritus, National Trust for Historic Preservation; *b* 30 May 1909; *s* of Bowman and Nathalie Lyons Gray; *m* 1938, Jane Boyden Craige (*d* 1953); four *s* ; *m* 1956, Nancy Maguire Beebe; three step *d. Educ:* Woodberry Forest Sch., Woodberry Forest, Va; University of N Carolina, Chapel Hill, NC; Yale Law Sch., New Haven, Conn. Admitted to NY Bar, 1934, and associated with Carter, Ledyard & Milburn, 1933-35; with Manly, Hendren & Womble, Winston-Salem, NC, 1935-37; admitted to North Carolina Bar, 1936; Pres., Piedmont Publishing Company, 1937-47. N Carolina Senate, 1939, 1941, 1945. Enlisted in US Army as private, 1942; Capt., 1945. Asst Sec. of Army, 1947; Under-Sec. of Army, 1949; Sec. of Army, 1949; Special Asst to the President, USA, April-Nov. 1950; Dir, Psychological Strategy Board, July-Dec. 1951. Pres. of Univ. of N Carolina, Feb. 1950-Nov. 1955; Asst Sec. of Defense, International Sec. Affairs, US, 1955-57; Dir, Office of Defense Mobilization, 1957-58; Special Asst to President, USA, for National Security Affairs, 1958-61; Mem., President's Foreign Intelligence Adv. Bd, 1961-77. Chm., Summit Communications, Inc.; Director Emeritus: American Security Bank; Media General, Inc.; Trustee: Brookings Instn, 1961-75; Federal City Council. Pres., Kensington Orchids Inc. Holds several hon. degrees. *Address:* 1224 30th Street NW, Washington, DC 20007, USA; (Office) 1616 H Street NW, Washington, DC 20006, USA. *Clubs:* Alibi, Burning Tree, Metropolitan (all Washington); The Brook (New York).

GRAY, His Eminence Cardinal Gordon Joseph; see St Andrews and Edinburgh, Archbishop of, (R.C.).

GRAY, Rear-Adm. Gordon Thomas Seccombe, CB 1964; DSC 1940; *b* 20 Dec. 1911; *s* of late Rev. Thomas Seccombe Gray and Edith Gray; *m* 1939, Sonia Moore-Gwyn; one *s* one *d. Educ:* Nautical Coll., Pangbourne. Entered RN, 1929; Sub-Lieut and Lieut, Mediterranean Fleet, 1934-36, ashore Arab revolt in Palestine (despatches); 1st Lieut, HMS Stork, 1939, Norwegian campaign (despatches, DSC); Comd HMS Badsworth, 1942-43 (despatches); Comd HMS Lamerton, 1943-45 (despatches). After the War comd destroyers Consort, Contest and St Kitts; JSSC, 1948; Comdr 1949; Directing Staff, RN Staff Coll., Greenwich, 1950; Exec. Officer, cruiser HMS Glasgow, 1951-53;

Capt. 1953; Naval Deputy to UK Nat. Military Representative, at SHAPE; Capt. of 5th Frigate Sqdn, and Comd HMS Wakeful and HMS Torquay, 1956-59; Asst Chief of Staff to C-in-C Eastern Atlantic Command, 1959-61; in comd of Naval Air Anti-Submarine Sch. at Portland and Chief Staff Officer to Flag Officer Sea Trng, 1961-62; Senior Naval Instructor, Imperial Defence Coll., 1963-65, retd. *Recreation:* yachting. *Address:* Hollies, Wispers, Midhurst, West Sussex.

GRAY, Rt. Hon. Hamish; *see* Gray, Rt Hon. J. H. N.

GRAY, Hanna Holborn, PhD; President, University of Chicago, since 1978; *b* 25 Oct. 1930; *d* of Hajo and Annemarie Holborn; *m* 1954, Charles Montgomery Gray. *Educ:* Bryn Mawr Coll., Pa (BA); Univ. of Oxford (Fulbright Schol.); Univ. of Harvard (PhD). Instructor, Bryn Mawr Coll., 1953-54; Harvard University: Teaching Fellow, 1955-57, Instr, 1957-59, Asst Prof., 1959-60, Vis. Lectr, 1963-64; Asst Prof., Univ. of Chicago, 1961-64, Associate Prof., 1964-72; Dean and Prof., Northwestern, Evanston, Ill, 1972-74; Provost, and Prof. of History, Yale Univ., 1974-78, Acting Pres., 1977-78. Hon. degrees: MA Yale, 1971; LHD: Grinnell Coll. Lawrence, Dennison, 1974; Wheaton Coll., 1976; Marlboro', 1979; Rikkyo, 1979, Roosevelt, 1980; Knox, 1980; Southern California, 1980; Duke, 1982; Clark, 1982; LittD St Lawrence, 1974; HHD St Mary's Coll., 1974; LLD: Union Coll., 1975; Regis Coll., 1976; Dartmouth Coll., 1978; Trinity Coll., 1978; Bridgeport, 1978; Yale, 1978; Dickenson Coll., 1979; Wittenberg, 1979; Brown, 1979; Rochester, 1980; Notre Dame, 1980; Michigan, 1981; DLitt Oxford, 1979. *Publications:* ed (with Charles M. Gray) Jl Modern History, 1965-70; articles in professional jls. *Address:* (office) 5801 South Ellis Avenue, Chicago, Illinois 60637, USA. *T:* (312) 962-8001. *Clubs:* Commercial, Mid-America, Economic, Fortnightly, Quadrangle, Women's Athletic, University, Chicago (Chicago); University, Cosmopolitan (New York City).

GRAY, Harold James, CMG 1956; retired, 1972; *b* 17 Oct. 1907; 2nd *s* of late John William Gray and of Amelia Frances (*née* Miller); *m* 1928, Katherine Gray (*née* Starling); one *d*. *Educ:* Alleyn's Sch.; Dover County Sch.; Queen Mary Coll., London Univ. (MSc, LLB); Gray's Inn; Harvard University, USA (Master of Public Administration). Customs and Excise Dept, 1927; Asst Examiner, Patent Office, 1930, Examiner, 1935; Industries and Manufactures Dept, Board of Trade, 1938; Ministry of Supply, 1939; Asst Sec., Min. of Supply, 1942. transf. to Bd of Trade, 1946; Commercial Relations and Exports Dept, Board of Trade, 1950; Under-Sec., 1954; UK Senior Trade Comr and Economic and Commercial Adviser to High Comr in Australia, 1954-58; UK Senior Trade Comr and Economic Adviser to the High Comr in Union of South Africa, 1958-60; Dir, Nat. Assoc. of British Manufacturers, 1961-65; Dir, Legal Affairs, CBI, 1965-72. FRSA; Mem. Inst. of Physics; Commonwealth Fund Fellowship, 1949-50. Chm., NUMAS (Management Services) Ltd. *Publications:* Electricity in the Service of Man, 1949; Economic Survey of Australia, 1955; Dictionary of Physics, 1958; (jtly) New Dictionary of Physics, 1975. *Recreations:* golf, swimming, riding. *Address:* 27 Byron Road, Penenden Heath, Maidstone, Kent ME14 2HA. *Club:* East India, Devonshire, Sports and Public Schools.

GRAY, Hugh, BSc(Soc), PhD; Lecturer in South Asia Politics, School of Oriental and African Studies, since 1970; *b* 19 April 1916; *s* of William Marshall Kemp Gray; *m* 1954, Edith Esther (*née* Rudinger); no *c*. *Educ:* Battersea Gram. Sch.; London Sch. of Economics. Army Service (Intelligence Corps), 1940-45. UNRRA, 1945-48; Internat. Refugee Organisation, 1948-52; Social Worker, 1952-57; Student on Leverhulme Adult Schol. at LSE, 1957-60; Fellow in S Asian Studies, SOAS, 1960-62; Lectr in Sociology with ref. to S Asia, SOAS, University of London, 1962-66; MP (Lab) Yarmouth, 1966-70; contested (Lab): Cheltenham, Feb. 1974; Norfolk South, Oct. 1974; Norfolk, Eur. Parlt, 1979. *Publications:* various articles on Indian politics in Jl of Commonwealth Studies, Asian Survey, etc. *Recreations:* ski-ing, skating, theatre, ballet. *Address:* 22 Bridstow Place, W2. *Club:* Reform.

GRAY, Ian; MA; Managing Director and Chief Executive, Welsh Development Agency, since 1976; Member: Development Corporation for Wales, since 1976; Design Council Wales Advisory Committee, since 1977; *b* 29 Aug. 1926; *er s* of late Henry Gray and Elizabeth Cowan Gray; *m* 1954, Vaudine Angela Harrison-Ainsworth; one *s* one *d*. *Educ:* Royal High Sch., Edinburgh; Univ. of Edinburgh (MA Econ.). War Service with Royal Scots and Indian Army, 1944-45 (2nd Lieut). Joined BoT, 1948; Private Sec. to successive Parly Secs, 1951-52 and to Pres., 1952-54; British Trade Comr, Wellington, 1954-56; Principal British Trade Comr, Cape Town, 1957-60; BoT, London, 1961-67; BoT Controller for Wales, Cardiff, 1967-69; Dir, Min. of Technology Office for Wales, 1970; Dir for Wales, DTI, 1971; Skelmersdale Develt Corporation: Gen. Manager, 1972-73; Man. Dir, 1973-76. Mem. Bd of Management, Corlan Housing Assoc., 1979-82. Member: Ormskirk District HMC, 1972-74; Lancs AHA, 1973-76. *Recreations:* photography, carpentry, making and drinking wine. *Address:* Welsh Development Agency, Treforest Industrial Estate, Treforest, Mid Glamorgan. *T:* Treforest 2666. *Club:* Cardiff and County.

GRAY, Rt. Hon. James Hector Northey, (Rt. Hon. Hamish Gray), PC 1982; MP (C) Ross and Cromarty since 1970; Minister of State, Department of Energy, since 1979; *b* 28 June 1927; *s* of late J. Northey Gray, Inverness, and of Mrs E. M. Gray; *m* 1953, Judith Waite Brydon, BSc, Helensburgh; two *s* one *d*. *Educ:* Inverness Royal Academy. Served in Queen's Own

Cameron Hldrs, 1945-48. An Asst Govt Whip, 1971-73; a Lord Comr, HM Treasury, 1973-74; an Opposition Whip, 1974-Feb. 1975; Opposition spokesman on Energy, 1975-79. Member, Inverness Town Council, 1965-70. *Recreations:* golf, walking, family life. *Address:* The Cedars, Drummond Road, Inverness. *Club:* Highland (Inverness).

GRAY, John; *see* Gray, R. J.

GRAY, Rev. Prof. John; Professor of Hebrew, University of Aberdeen, 1961-80, now Professor Emeritus; *b* 9 June 1913; *s* of James Telfer Gray; *m* Janet J. Gibson; five *c*. *Educ:* Kelso High Sch.; Edinburgh Univ. (MA, BD, PhD). Colonial Chaplain and Chaplain to Palestine Police, 1939-41; Minister of the Church of Scotland, Kilmory, Isle of Arran, 1942-47; Lectr in Semitic Languages and Literatures, Manchester Univ., 1947-53; Lectr in Hebrew and Biblical Criticism, University of Aberdeen, 1953-61. Mem., Soc. for Old Testament Study. Hon. DD St Andrews, 1977. *Publications:* The Krt Text in the Literature of Ras Shamra, 1955 (2nd edn 1964); The Legacy of Canaan, 1957 (2nd edn 1965); Archæology and the Old Testament World, 1962; The Canaanites, 1964; Kings I and II: a Commentary, 1964, 3rd edn 1977; Joshua, Judges and Ruth, 1967; A History of Jerusalem, 1969; Near Eastern Mythology, 1969; The Biblical Doctrine of the Reign of God, 1979; contribs to various Bible Dictionaries, memorial volumes and learned journals. *Recreations:* beekeeping, gardening, trout-fishing. *Address:* Tanlaw Cottage, Hendersyde Park, Kelso, Roxburgh. *T:* Kelso 24374.

GRAY, Sir John (Archibald Browne), Kt 1973; MA, MB, ScD; FRS 1972; Member, External Scientific Staff, MRC, Marine Biological Association Laboratories, Plymouth, since 1977; *b* 30 March 1918; *s* of late Sir Archibald Gray, KCVO, CBE; *m* 1946, Vera Kathleen Mares; one *s* one *d*. *Educ:* Cheltenham Coll.; Clare Coll., Cambridge (Hon. Fellow, 1976); University Coll. Hospital. BA 1939; MA 1942; MB, BChir 1942; ScD 1962. Service Research for MRC, 1943-45; Surg. Lieut, RNVR, 1945-46; Scientific Staff of MRC at Nat. Inst. for Med. Research, 1946-52; Reader in Physiology, University Coll., London, 1952-58; Prof. of Physiology, University Coll., London, 1959-66; Medical Research Council: Second Sec., 1966-68; Sec., 1968-77; Dep. Chm., 1975-77. QHP 1968-71. FIBiol; FRCP 1974. *Publications:* papers, mostly on sensory receptors and sensory nervous system, in Jl of Physiology, etc. *Recreations:* painting, sailing, tennis. *Address:* Seaways, North Rock, Kingsand, near Plymouth PL10 1NG. *T:* Plymouth 822745.

GRAY, Air Vice-Marshal John Astley, CB 1945; CBE 1943; DFC; GM; retired; *b* 1899. *Educ:* Framlingham Coll. Served European War, 1917-19; War of 1939-45. Air Vice-Marshal 1944; AOC 91 (B) Gp, 1944-46; AOC RAF Mission to Greece, 1947-48; SASO, HQ Transport Comd, 1949-51; AOA, HQ ME Air Force, 1951-54; retired, 1954. *Address:* Bittern, Thorpeness, Suffolk. *Club:* Royal Air Force.

GRAY, John Magnus, CBE 1971 (MBE 1945); ERD 1946; Chairman, Northern Ireland Electricity Service, 1974-80 (Deputy Chairman, 1973-74); *b* 15 Oct. 1915; *o s* of Lewis Campbell Gray, CA and Ingeborg Sanderson Gray (*née* Ross), Glasgow; *m* 1947, Patricia Mary, OBE 1976, *widow of* Major Aubrey D. P. Hodges and *d* of John Norman Eggar and Emma Frances Eggar (*née* Garrett), Epsom and Godalming; one *d*. *Educ:* Horris Hill, Newbury; Winchester College. Served RA, 1939-46 (Major). Joined Wm Ewart & Son Ltd, Linen Manufrs, Belfast, 1934; Dir 1950; Man. Dir 1958-72. Chairman: Irish Linen Guild, 1958-64; Central Council, Irish Linen Industry, 1968-74 (Mem., 1957; Vice-Chm., 1966-68); Linen Industry Standards Cttee of BSI, 1969-74; Belfast Br., RNLI, 1970-76; Member: Council of Belfast T&AFA, 1948-68; Council of Belfast Chamber of Commerce, 1955-59; Gen. Synod of Church of Ireland, 1955–; Councils of FBI and CBI, 1956-74, 1979-80; NI Legal Aid Cttee, 1958-59; Export Council for Europe, 1964-70; Northern Ireland Adv. Council for BBC, 1968-72; Design Council, 1974-80; Asst Comr for Commn on Constitution, 1969-73. Captain, Royal Co. Down Golf Club, 1963. *Recreations:* golf, gardening. *Address:* Blairlodge, Dundrum, Newcastle, Co. Down BT33 0NF. *T:* Dundrum 271. *Clubs:* Army and Navy; Ulster (Belfast).

GRAY, Vice-Adm. Sir John (Michael Dudgeon), KBE 1967 (OBE 1950); CB 1964; *b* Dublin, 13 June 1913; British; *m* 1939, Margaret Helen Purvis; one *s* one *d*. *Educ:* RNC, Dartmouth. HMS Nelson, 1931; Midshipman, HMS Enterprise, 1932-33; Sub-Lieut, HMS Devonshire, 1934; specialised in Gunnery, 1938. Served War of 1939-45; HMS Hermes; HMS Spartan; with US in Anzio; 8th Army in Italy; French Army in France (despatches). HMS Duke of York, 1945, Comdr 1947; Naval Adviser, UK Mission, Japan, 1947-50 (OBE Korean War); HMS Swiftsure, 1950, Capt. 1952; HMS Lynx, 1956; HMS Victorious, 1961; Rear-Adm. 1962; Dir-Gen. of Naval Trng, Min. of Def., 1964-65 (Admiralty, 1962-64); Vice-Adm. 1965; C-in-C, S Atlantic and S America, 1965-67. Sec., Oriental Ceramic Soc., 1974–. *Recreations:* squash, tennis, athletics (represented RN in 220 and 440 yds). *Address:* 55 Elm Park Gardens, SW10. *T:* 01-352 1757. *Club:* Naval and Military.

GRAY, Prof. John Richard; Professor of African History, University of London, since 1972; *b* 7 July 1929; *s* of Captain Alfred William Gray, RN and of Christobel Margaret Gray (*née* Raikes); *m* 1957, Gabriella, *d* of Dr Camillo Cattaneo; one *s* one *d*. *Educ:* Charterhouse; Downing Coll., Cambridge (Richmond Scholar). BA Cantab 1951; PhD London 1957. Lectr, Univ. of Khartoum, 1959-61; Res. Fellow, Sch. of Oriental and African

Studies, London, 1961-63, Reader, 1963-72. Vis. Prof., UCLA, 1967. Editor, Jl African History, 1968-71; Chairman: Africa Centre, Covent Garden, 1967-72; Britain-Zimbabwe Soc., 1981-. Order of St Silvester, 1966. *Publications:* The Two Nations: aspects of the development of race relations in the Rhodesias and Nyasaland, 1960; A History of the Southern Sudan, 1839-1889, 1961; (with D. Chambers) Materials for West African History in Italian Archives, 1965; (ed, with D. Birmingham) Pre-Colonial African Trade, 1970; (ed) The Cambridge History of Africa, vol. 4, 1975 (ed, with E. Fasholé-Luke and others) Christianity in Independent Africa, 1978. *Recreation:* things Italian. *Address:* 39 Rotherwick Road, NW11 7DD. *T:* 01-458 3676.

GRAY, Very Rev. John Rodger, VRD 1956; Minister at Dunblane Cathedral, since 1966; Moderator of the General Assembly of the Church of Scotland, 1977-78; *b* 9 Jan. 1913; *s* of John Charles Gray, Hartlea, Coatbridge, and Jeannie Gilmour Rodger; *m* 1952, Dr Sheila Mary Whiteside; three *s*. *Educ:* High Sch. of Glasgow; Glasgow Univ. (MA 1934); Yale Univ. (BD 1938); Princeton Univ. and Seminary (ThM 1939). Pres., Glasgow Univ. Union, 1934-35. Commonwealth Fund Fellow, Yale, 1937-39; Asst Minister, Barony of Glasgow, 1939-41; Chaplain: RN, 1941-46; RNVR, 1946-63; Minister, St Stephen's, Glasgow, 1946-66. Hastie Lectr in Theol., Glasgow Univ., 1947-50; Lectr in Theol., Glasgow Sch. of Study and Trng, 1948; Lectr, Princeton Inst. of Theol., 1949 and 1968. Convener, Church and Nation Cttee, Gen. Assembly of Church of Scotland; Mem., Religious Adv. Cttees, BBC, IBA, and STV. Select Preacher, Univ. of Oxford, 1977. Hon. DD Tulsa, 1979; Hon. LHD, Presb. Coll., S Carolina, 1980. *Publications:* The Political Theory of John Knox, 1939; Splintering the Gates of Hell (monograph), 1977; (ed and contrib.) The Pulpit Digest, 1979-81; chapter in Ministers for the 1980s, 1979; chapter in Grow or Die, 1981; articles, sermons, and book revs in Expository Times, Gen. Practitioner, and Princeton Sem. Jl. *Address:* The Cathedral Manse of Dunblane, Dunblane, Perthshire FK15 0AQ. *T:* Dunblane 822205. *Club:* New (Edinburgh).

GRAY, John Walton David; HM Diplomatic Service; Head of Maritime, Aviation and Environment Department, Foreign and Commonwealth Office, 1982; *b* Burry Port, Carmarthenshire, 1 Oct. 1936; *s* of Myrddin Gray and Elsie Irene (*née* Jones), Llanelli, Carms; *m* 1957, Anthoula, *e d* of Nicolas Yerasimou, Nicosia, Cyprus; one *s* two *d*. *Educ:* Blundell's Sch.; Christ's Coll., Cambridge (MA; Scholar and Tancred Student); ME Centre, Oxford; Amer. Univ., Cairo. National Service, 1954-56. Joined Foreign Service, 1962; served: Mecas, 1962; Bahrain Agency, 1964; FO, 1967; Geneva, 1970; Sofia, 1974; Counsellor (Commercial), 1978, Counsellor and Hd of Chancery, 1980, Jedda. *Recreations:* most spectator sports, amateur dramatics, light history, things Welsh. *Address:* 35 Royal Avenue, Chelsea, SW3 4QE. *T:* 01-730 3535; Tynewydd, Llanddew, Brecon, Powys. *T:* Brecon 3096. *Clubs:* Travellers', Royal Commonwealth Society.

GRAY, Rt. Rev. Joseph; *see* Shrewsbury, Bishop of, (RC).

GRAY, Kenneth Walter, PhD; Chief Scientific Officer, Ministry of Defence, since 1982; Deputy Director, Royal Signals and Radar Establishment, since 1982; *b* 20 March 1929; *s* of Robert W. Gray and late Ruby M. Gray; *m* 1962, Jill Henderson; two *s* one *d*. *Educ:* Blue Coat Sch.; Univ. of Wales (BSc, PhD). Research on magnetic resonance, as Nat. Res. Council of Canada post-doctoral Fellow, Univ. of British Columbia, Vancouver, 1963-65; research on semiconductor devices and on radiometry, N American Rockwell Science Center, Thousand Oaks, Calif, 1965-70; research on devices and systems at Royal Signals and Radar Estabt, 1971; Supt Solid State Physics and Devices Div., 1976; Head of Physics Group, 1979; RCDS 1981. Visiting Research Fellow: Univ. of Newcastle, 1972-74; Univ. of Leeds, 1976-. *Publications:* over 30 scientific and technical papers in various learned jls. *Recreations:* squash, tennis, bridge. *Address:* 15 Churchdown Road, Poolbrook, Malvern, Worcestershire WR14 3JK. *T:* Malvern 4227.

GRAY, Linda Esther, (Mrs Peter McCrorie); opera singer; *b* 29 May 1948; *d* of James and Esther Gray; *m* 1971, Peter McCrorie; one *d*. *Educ:* Greenock Academy; Royal Scottish Academy of Music and Drama. Cinzano Scholarship, 1969; Goldsmith Schol., 1970; James Caird Schol., 1971; Kathleen Ferrier Award, 1972; Christie Award, 1972. London Opera Centre, 1969-71; Glyndebourne Festival Opera, 1972-75; Scottish Opera, 1974-79; Welsh Opera, 1980-; English National Opera, 1979-; American début, 1981. Record of Tristan und Isolde, 1981. *Recreations:* cooking, swimming. *Address:* 171 Queens Road, SW19. *T:* 01-542 3053.

GRAY, Margaret Caroline, MA Cantab; Headmistress, Godolphin and Latymer School, 1963-Dec. 1973; *b* 25 June 1913; *d* of Rev. A. Herbert Gray, DD, and Mrs Gray (Mary C. Dods, *d* of Principal Marcus Dods of New Coll., Edinburgh). *Educ:* St Mary's Hall, Brighton; Newnham Coll., Cambridge. Post graduate fellowship to Smith Coll., Mass, USA, 1935-36. Asst History mistress, Westcliff High Sch. for Girls, 1937-38; Head of History Dept, Mary Datchelor Girls' Sch., Camberwell, 1939-52; Headmistress, Skinners' Company's Sch., Stamford Hill, 1952-63. Chm., Nat. Advisory Centre on Careers for Women, 1970-. Governor: Francis Holland Schs; Hampton Sch.; West Heath Sch., Sevenoaks; Unicorn Sch., Kew; Chm. of Trustees, Godolphin and Latymer Bursary Fund. *Recreations:* gardening, motoring, walking. *Address:* 15 Fitzwilliam Avenue, Kew, Richmond, Surrey. *T:* 01-940 4439.

GRAY, Mary Elizabeth, CBE 1946 (OBE 1942); WRVS Administrator, Midland Region, 1949-71; resigned as County Commissioner, Gloucestershire Girl Guides (1949-61); *b* 19 May 1903; *d* of late Edward Wilmot Butler and Ethel Margaret Gray. *Educ:* Lanherne House, Dawlish; Switzerland. Joined WVS 1938; WVS Administrator, Eastern Counties Region 4, 1938-44; Deputy Vice-Chm., WVS, 1944; WVS Administrator SEAC and FE, 1944-48. *Address:* Clanmere Nursing Home, Great Malvern, Worcs.

GRAY, Maj.-Gen. Michael Stuart, OBE 1970; General Officer Commanding South West District, since 1981; *b* Beverley, E Yorkshire, 3 May 1932; *e s* of late Lieut Frank Gray, RNVR, and Joan Gray (*née* Gibson); *m* 1958, Juliette Antonia Noon, Northampton; two *s* one *d*. *Educ:* Christ's Hosp., Horsham; RMA, Sandhurst. FBIM. Enlisted RA, 1950; commissioned E Yorkshire Regt, 1952; served Malaya; transf. to Parachute Regt, 1955; served Cyprus, Suez, Jordan, Greece, Bahrein, Aden, N Ireland; sc Camberley, 1963; commanded 1st Bn Parachute Regt, 1969-71; DS Staff Coll., Camberley, 1971-73; Col GS 1 Div. BAOR, 1973-75; RCDS 1976; last Comdr 16 Para Bde, 1977; Comdr 6 Field Force and COMUKMF, 1977-79; Comdr British Army Staff and Mil. Attaché, 1979-81, and Head of British Def. Staff and Def. Attaché, 1981, Washington. Vice-Pres., French Assoc., ASPEG, and Curator of Exhibits at 'Pegasus Bridge' Museum, Normandy, 1972-; Vice-Pres. and Trustee to UK Trust, AAN, to preserve the history of 6 AB Division in Normandy, 1979-. *Recreations:* travelling, DIY, photography, painting; sporting interests: Rugby, cricket, swimming, squash. *Address:* c/o National Westminster Bank, 60 Market Place, Beverley, North Humberside.

GRAY, Milner Connorton, CBE 1963; RDI 1938; FSIAD; AGI; MInstPack; Founder Partner and Senior Consultant, Design Research Unit; Past Master, Faculty of Royal Designers for Industry; Past President, Society of Industrial Artists and Designers; Past Master Art Workers' Guild; *b* 8 Oct. 1899; *s* of late Archibald Campbell Gray and Katherine May Hart, Eynsford, Kent; *m* 1934, Gnade Osborne-Pratt; no *c*. *Educ:* studied painting and design, London Univ., Goldsmiths' Coll. Sch. of Art. Head of Exhibitions Branch, Ministry of Information, 1940-41, and Adviser on Exhibitions, 1941-44; Senior Partner in Industrial Design Partnership, 1934-40; Principal, Sir John Cass Coll. of Art, 1937-40; on Visiting Staff: Goldsmiths' Coll. Sch. of Art, London Univ., 1930-40; Chelsea Sch. of Art, 1934-37; Royal Coll. of Art, 1940; Founder Mem., Soc. of Industrial Artists, 1930, Hon. Sec., 1932-40, Pres., 1943-48 and 1968; Member of Council: Design and Industries Assoc., 1935-38; RSA, 1959-65; Artists Gen. Benevolent Instn, 1959-; Adviser to BBC "Looking at Things" Schs Broadcasts, 1949-55. Member: Min. of Education Nat. Adv. Cttee on Art Examinations, 1949-52; Nat. Adv. Council on Art Education, 1959-69; Royal Mint Adv. Cttee, 1952-. Mem. Council, RCA, 1963-67, Mem. Court 1967-, Senior Fellow, 1971. British Pres., Alliance Graphique Internationale, 1963-71. Consultant Designer: BR Bd for BR Corporate Identity Prog., 1963-67; (jointly) to Orient Line, SS Oriana, 1957-61; Ilford Ltd, 1946-66; Internat. Distillers and Vintners, 1954-; Watney Mann Group, 1956-; British Aluminium Co., 1965-; ICI, 1966-; Min. of Technology, 1970-. Governor: Central Sch. of Art and Design, 1944-46; Hornsey Coll. of Art and Design, 1959-65. Hon. Fellow, Soc. of Typographic Designers, 1979. Hon. Des. RCA, 1963, Hon. Dr RCA, 1979; Hon. DÀ Manchester, 1964. Served in 19th London Regt, and Royal Engineers, attached Camouflage Sch., 1917-19. Gold Medal, Soc. of Ind. Artists and Designers, 1955. *Publications:* The Practice of Design (jointly), 1946; Package Design, 1955; (jtly) Lettering for Architects and Designers, 1962; articles, lectures and broadcasts on various aspects of design. *Address:* 8 Holly Mount, Hampstead, NW3 6SG. *T:* 01-435 4238; Felix Hall, Kelvedon, Essex. *Clubs:* Arts, Garrick.

GRAY, Monique Sylvaine, (Mrs P. F. Gray); *see* Viner, M. S.

GRAY, Nicol; *see* Gray, W. N.

GRAY, Paul Edward, ScD; FIEEE; President, Massachusetts Institute of Technology, since 1980; *b* 7 Feb. 1932; *s* of Kenneth Frank Gray and Florence (*née* Gilleo); *m* 1955, Priscilla Wilson King; one *s* three *d*. *Educ:* Massachusetts Inst. of Technol. (SB 1954, SM 1955, ScD 1960). FIEEE. Served Army, 1955-57 (1st Lieut). Massachusetts Inst. of Technology: Mem., Faculty of Engrg, 1960-71; Prof. of Electrical Engrg, 1968-71; Dean, Sch. of Engrg, 1970-71; Chancellor and Mem. of Corp., 1971-80. Director: Shawmut Bank, Boston; New England Mutual Life Insurance Co., Boston; A. D. Little Inc., Cambridge; Cabot Corp., Boston. Trustee and Mem. of Corporation: Museum of Science, Boston; Woods Hole Oceanographic Inst.; Chm., Bd of Trustees, Wheaton Coll., Mass, 1976-. Fellow, Amer. Acad. of Arts and Sciences; Member: National Acad. of Engrg; Mexican National Acad. of Engrg; AAAS. *Address:* Massachusetts Institute of Technology, 77 Massachusetts Avenue, Cambridge, Mass 02139, USA; 111 Memorial Drive, Cambridge, Mass 02142.

GRAY, Prof. Peter, MA, PhD, ScD (Cantab); FRS 1977; CChem, FRSC; Professor and Head of Department of Physical Chemistry, University of Leeds, since 1965; *b* Newport, 25 Aug. 1926; *er s* of late Ivor Hicks Gray and Rose Ethel Gray; *m* 1952, Barbara Joan Hume, PhD, 2nd *d* of J. B. Hume, London; two *s* two *d*. *Educ:* Newport, High Sch.; Gonville and Caius Coll., Cambridge. Major Schol., 1943; Prizeman, 1944, 1945 and 1946, Gonville and Caius Coll.; BA 1st cl hons Nat. Sci. Tripos, 1946; Dunlop Res. Student, 1946; Ramsay Mem. Fellow, 1949-51; PhD 1949; Fellow, Gonville and Caius Coll., 1949-53; ICI Fellow, 1951; ScD 1963. University Demonstrator in Chem. Engrg, University of Cambridge, 1951-55; Physical Chemistry Dept,

University of Leeds: Lectr, 1955; Reader, 1959; Prof., 1962; Chm., Bd of Combined Faculties of Science and Applied Science, 1972-74. Vis. Prof., Univ. of BC, 1958-59; Univ. of W Ont., 1969; Univ. of Göttingen, 1979; Macquarie Univ., 1980. Mem. Council: Faraday Soc., 1965 (Vice-Pres., 1970; Treasurer, 1973); Chemical Soc., 1969. Meldola Medal, Royal Inst. Chem., 1956; Marlow Medal, Faraday Soc., 1959; Gold Medal, Combustion Inst., 1978. *Publications:* papers on phys. chem. subjects in scientific jls. *Recreation:* hill walking. *Address:* 4 Ancaster Road, Leeds LS16 5HH. *T:* Leeds 752826.

GRAY, Maj.-Gen. (Reginald) John, CB 1973; Director, International Generics Ltd, since 1974; *b* 26 Nov. 1916; *s* of late Dr Cyril Gray and Frances Anne Higgins, Higginsbrook, Co. Meath; *m* 1943, Esme, *d* of late G. R. G. Shipp; one *s* one *d. Educ:* Rossall Sch.; Coll. of Medicine, Univ. of Durham. MB, BS. Commissioned into RAMC, 1939; served War of 1939-45 in India; later Burma, NW Europe, Egypt, Malta, BAOR. Comd of 9 (Br.) CCS, 1945; Asst Dir-Gen., AMS, 1953-60, AMD3, 1954-57; comd of David Bruce Mil. Hosp., Mtarfa, 1957-60; 14 Field Amb., 4 Guards Bde, 1960-63; Brit. Mil. Hosp., Rinteln, 1963-64; The Queen Alexandra Mil. Hosp., Millbank, 1964-67; Asst Dir-Gen., AMS, Min. of Defence AMD1, 1967-69; Dep Dir-Gen., AMS, 1969-71. QHS 1970-73; DMS, UK Land Forces, 1972-73, retired. Col Comdt, RAMC, 1977-81. Chief MO, British Red Cross Soc., 1974-82. Mem., Casualty Surgeons Assoc., 1976-; Chm., RAMC Assoc., 1980-. FRSM; FFCM 1972. CStJ 1971 (OStJ 1957). *Recreations:* gardening, wine making, d-i-y slowly. *Address:* 11 Hampton Close, Wimbledon, SW20 0RY. *T:* 01-946 7429.

GRAY, Robin, (Robert Walker Gray), CB 1977; Deputy Secretary, Department of Trade, since 1975; *b* 29 July 1924; *s* of Robert Walker Gray and Dorothy (*née* Lane); *m* 1955, Shirley Matilda (*née* Taylor); two *s* one *d. Educ:* Headstone Council Sch.; Pinner Park Council Sch.; John Lyon Sch., Harrow; Birkbeck Coll., Univ. of London; London Sch. of Economics. BScEcons 1946; Farr Medal in Statistics. Air Warfare Analysis Section of Air Min., 1940-45; BoT, 1947; UK Delegn to OEEC, 1950-51; BoT, 1952-66; Commercial Counsellor, British High Commn, Ottawa, 1966-70; Under-Secretary: DTI, 1971-74; Dept of Prices and Consumer Protection, 1974-75; Dep. Sec., DoI, 1975. *Recreations:* fishing, growing rhododendrons, target shooting. *Address:* Tansy, Brook Road, Wormley, Godalming, Surrey GU8 5UA. *T:* Wormley 2486.

GRAY, Roger Ibbotson, QC 1967; a Recorder of the Crown Court, since 1972; *b* 16 June 1921; *o s* of late Arthur Gray and of Mary Gray (*née* Ibbotson), Seaford, Sussex; *m* 1952, Anne Valerie, 2nd *d* of late Capt. G. G. P. Hewett, CBE, RN; one *s. Educ:* Wycliffe Coll.; Queen's Coll., Oxford. 1st cl. hons Jurisprudence, Oxon, 1941. Commissioned RA, 1942; served with Ayrshire Yeomanry, 1942-45; Normandy and NW Europe, 1944-45; GSO3 (Mil. Ops), GHQ, India, 1946. Pres. of Oxford Union, 1947. Called to Bar, Gray's Inn, 1947; South-Eastern Circuit. A Legal Assessor, GNC, 1976-. Contested (C) Dagenham, 1955. *Publication:* (with Major I. A. Graham Young) A Short History of the Ayrshire Yeomanry (Earl of Carrick's Own) 151st Field Regiment, RA, 1939-46, 1947. *Recreations:* cricket, reading, talk. *Address:* 34 Halsey Street, SW3. *T:* 01-589 0221. *Clubs:* Carlton, MCC.

GRAY, Simon James Holliday; Lecturer in English, Queen Mary College, University of London, since 1965; *b* 21 Oct. 1936; *s* of Dr James Davidson Gray and Barbara Cecelia Mary Holliday; *m* 1965, Beryl Mary Kevern; one *s* one *d. Educ:* Westminster; Dalhousie Univ.; Trinity Coll., Cambridge (MA). Trinity Coll., Cambridge: Sen. Schol., Research Student and Harper-Wood Trav. Student, 1960; Supervisor in English, 1960-63; Sen. Instructor in English, Univ. of British Columbia, 1963-64. *Publications:* novels: Colmain, 1963; Simple People, 1965; Little Portia, 1967; (as Hamish Reade) A Comeback for Stark, 1968; plays: Wise Child, 1968; Sleeping Dog, 1968; Dutch Uncle, 1969; The Idiot, 1971; Spoiled, 1971; Butley, 1971; Otherwise Engaged, 1975 (voted Best Play, 1976-77, by NY Drama Critics Circle); Plaintiffs and Defendants, 1975; Two Sundays, 1975; Dog Days, 1976; Molly, 1977; The Rear Column, 1978; Close of Play, 1979; Stage Struck, 1979; Quartermaine's Terms, 1981; adap. Tartuffe, 1982. *Recreations:* squash, watching cricket and soccer, tennis, swimming. *Address:* c/o Judy Daish Associates, 122 Wigmore Street, W1H 9FE.

GRAY, Sylvia Mary, CBE 1975 (MBE 1952); *b* 10 July 1909; *d* of Henry Bunting and Mary Elizabeth Gray. *Educ:* Wroxall Abbey. Chm., Bay Tree Hotels Ltd, 1946-. Mem., Witney RDC, 1943-54 (Vice-Chm. 1950-54); Chairman: Oxon Fedn Women's Insts, 1951-54; Nat. Fedn of Women's Insts, 1969-74 (Mem., Exec. Cttee, 1955; Hon. Treas., 1958). Member: Keep Britain Tidy Group Exec., 1967-78, Vice-Chm., 1974; Post Office Users' Nat. Council, 1969-78; National Trust, 1971, Chm., S Midlands Regional Cttee, 1975-81; IBA Advertising Standards Adv. Cttee, 1972; Council for European Architectural Heritage, 1972; Nat. Consumer Council, 1975-77; Redundant Churches Cttee, 1976-. *Recreation:* reading. *Address:* Bay Tree Hotel, Burford, Oxon. *T:* Burford 3137. *Club:* Naval and Military.

GRAY, Prof. Thomas Cecil, CBE 1976; JP; MD, FRCS, FRCP, FFARCS; FFARACS (Hon.); FFARCSI (Hon.); Professor of Anæsthesia, The University of Liverpool, 1959-76, now Emeritus, Dean of Postgraduate Medical Studies, 1966-70, of Faculty of Medicine, 1970-76; *b* 11 March 1913; *s* of Thomas and Ethel Gray; *m* 1st, 1937, Marjorie Kathleen (*née* Hely) (*d* 1978); one *s* one *d*; 2nd, 1979, Pamela Mary (*née* Corning); one *s. Educ:* Ampleforth Coll.; University of Liverpool. General Practice, 1937-39. Hon.

Anaesthetist to various hospitals, 1940-47. Active Service, Royal Army Medical Corps, 1942-44. Demonstrator in Anæsthesia, University of Liverpool, 1942, 1944-46; Reader in Anæsthesia, University of Liverpool, 1947-59; Hon. Cons Anæsthetist: United Liverpool Hosps, Royal Infirmary Branch; Liverpool Thoracic Surgical Centre, Broadgreen Hosp.; Mem. Bd, Faculty of Anæsthetists, RCSEng, 1948-69 (Vice-Dean, 1952-54; Dean, 1964-67). Member Council: RCS, 1964-67; Assoc. of Anæsthetists of Great Brit. and Ire., 1948-67 (Hon. Treas. 1950-56; Pres. 1957-59); ASME, 1972-76; FRSocMed (Mem. Council, 1958-61; Pres. Anæsthetic Section, 1955-56; Mem. Council, Sect. of Med. Educn, 1969-72); Chm. BMA Anæsthetic Group, 1957-62; Mem., Liverpool Regional Hosp. Board, 1968-74 (Chm., Anæsthetic Adv. Cttee, 1948-70; Chm., Med. Adv. Council, 1970-74); Mem., Merseyside RHA, 1974-77; Mem., Bd of Governors, United Liverpool Hosp., 1969-74; Mem. Clinical Res. Bd, Med. Res. Council, 1965-69; Hon. Civilian Consultant in Anæsthetics to the Army at Home, 1964-78 (Guthrie Medal 1977), Emeritus Consultant to the Army, 1979. Hon. Consultant to St John's Ambulance; Member Council, Order of St John for Merseyside; Asst Dir-Gen., St John Ambulance, 1977-; Treas., Med. Defence Union, 1977-; Chm., Bd of Governors, Linacre Center for Study of Ethics of Health Care. Examiner in FFARCS, 1953-70; FFARCSI 1967-70: Dip. Vet. Anæsth., RCVS, 1968-76. Hon. FRSocMed, 1979; Hon. Member: Sheffield and East Midlands Soc. of Anæsthetists; Yorks Soc. of Anæsthetists; Austrian Soc. of Anæsthetists; Soc. Belge d'Anesthesie et de Reanimation; Argentinian and Brazilian Socs of Anesthesiologists; Australian and Malaysian Socs of Anæsthetists; Assoc. of Veterinary Anæsthetists. Hon. Corresp. Member: Sociedade das Ciencias Medical di Lisboa; W African Assoc. of Surgeons. Clover Lectr and Medallist, RCS, 1953; Lectures: Simpson-Smith Meml, W London Sch. of Med., 1956; Jenny Hartmann Meml, Univ. of Basle, 1958; Eastman, Univ. of Rochester, NY, 1958; Sims Commonwealth Travelling Prof., 1961; Sir James Young Simpson Meml, RCSE, 1967; Torsten Gordh, Swedish Soc. of Anaesthetists, 1978; Kirkpatrick, Faculty of Anaesthetists, RCSI, 1981; John Gillies, Scottish Soc. of Anaesthetists, 1982. JP City of Liverpool, 1966. OStJ 1979. Medallist, Univ. of Liège, 1947; Henry Hill Hickman Medal, 1972; Hon. Gold Medal, RCS, 1978; Ralph M. Waters medal and award, Illinois Soc. of Anesthesiologists, 1978. *Publications:* Jt Editor, Modern Trends in Anæsthesia; (ed jtly) General Anæsthesia, 1979; (ed jtly) Paediatric Anæsthesia, 1981; many contribs to gen. med. press and specialist jls. *Recreations:* music, golf, amateur dramatics. *Address:* 6 Raven Meols Lane, Formby, Liverpool L37 4DF. *Club:* West Lancs Golf.

GRAY, Trevor Robert, MBE 1973; JP; Company Secretary, Gwent Hospitals Contributory Fund, since 1948; *b* 27 March 1919; *s* of Walter Augustus Gray and Lilian May Gray; *m* 1941, Tessie Patricia Thomas; two *s. Educ:* Alexandra Road Sch.; Belle Vue Central Sch.; Newport Technical Coll. Chm., Wales Leagues of Friends, 1970-; Vice-Chairman: British Hosps Contrib. Schemes Assoc., 1976 (Mem. Exec. Cttee, 1961-; Vice-Pres., 1981); Nat. Assoc. of Leagues of Hosp. Friends, 1968 (Mem. Council, 1955-); Member: Welsh Hosp. Bd, 1968-74; Central Health Services Council, 1976-79; South Gwent Community Health Council, 1974- (Chm., 1975-78); Welsh Assoc. of Community Health Councils, 1974- (Chm., 1978-80); GMC, 1979-. JP Newport, 1968. *Recreations:* reading, walking. *Address:* The Heights, Forge Lane, Bassaleg, Gwent NP1 9NG. *T:* Rhiwderin 3513.

GRAY, Sir William (Hume), 3rd Bt *cr* 1917; Director, Egglestone Estate Co.; *b* 26 July 1955; *s* of William Talbot Gray (*d* 1971) (*er s* of 2nd Bt), and of Rosemarie Hume Gray, *d* of Air Cdre Charles Hume Elliott-Smith; *S* grandfather, 1978. *Educ:* Aysgarth School, Bedale, Yorks; Eton College. BA (Hons) Architecture. *Recreation:* sport. *Heir:* uncle Nicholas Anthony Gray [*b* 21 June 1934; *m* 1956, Amanda, *o d* of H. W. Edwards, Newbury; two adopted *s* one *d*]. *Address:* Eggleston Hall, Barnard Castle, Co. Durham. *T:* Teesdale 50403.

GRAY, William John, CB 1976; FRCPsych; Member of the Parole Board, Home Office, London, 1976-77, retired; *b* 9 Jan. 1911; *m* 1942, Norma Margaret Morrison; two *d. Educ:* Wishaw High Sch.; Glasgow Univ. (MB, ChB). Dep. Medical Supt, Glengall Hosp., Ayr, 1939-42. Served War: Major, RAMC (Specialist Psychiatrist), 1942-47; Corps Psychiatrist and Staff Officer, Italy, 1943-45. SMO, Wakefield, Maidstone and Liverpool Prisons, 1947-62. Nuffield Travelling Fellowship, in six European countries, 1957. First Medical Supt and Governor, HM Prison, Grendon, 1962-75; Sen. PMO and Asst Under-Sec. of State, Home Office, 1971-75. *Publications:* several articles on med. and psychiatric treatment and med. care and protection of prisoners. *Recreations:* angling, bridge, gardening. *Address:* 88 Crosshill Terrace, Wormit, Newport on Tay, Fife DD6 8PS. *T:* Newport on Tay 541355. *Club:* Civil Service.

GRAY, William Macfarlane, OBE 1961; JP; FCCA; FCIS; FSA (Scotland); Senior Partner Macfarlane Gray & Co., Stirling, 1934-71, Consultant, 1971-75; Hon. Sheriff for Stirling and Clackmannan since 1964; *b* 28 March 1910; *s* of Peter M. Gray and Isabella Bain Macfarlane; *m* 1938, Muriel Agnes Elizabeth Lindsay, *d* of James R. Lindsay, Glasgow; two *d. Educ:* The High Sch. of Stirling. Provost of Royal Burgh of Stirling, 1958-64; Nat. Pres., Assoc. of Certified and Corporate Accountants, 1954-56; Chm. Stirling Festival of the Arts Cttee, 1958-67; Chm. Stirlingshire Savings Cttee, 1959-76; Member: Court, Univ. of Stirling, 1968-72; Executive Cttee, Scottish Council (Development and Industry), 1961-75; Scottish Tourist Board, 1963-64; Council, National Trust for Scotland, 1962-74; Chairman: PO Advisory Cttee for Stirlingshire and Clackmannan; of Trustees, Smith Art Gallery and

Museum, Stirling, 1958-64; Sponsoring Cttee for University of Stirling, 1963-65. Member: South of Scotland Electricity Board, 1961-66; Independent Television Authority (Chm. Scottish Adv. Cttee), 1964-70; Nat. Savings Cttee for Scotland, 1969-78; Exec. Cttee, British Council (Chm. Scottish Adv. Cttee), 1970-76. Hon. Freeman: Royal Burgh of Stirling, 1964; Ville de Saint Valery-en-Caux, 1960. Hon. DUniv. Stirling, 1968. KStJ, Receiver Gen., Priory of Scotland, Order of St John of Jerusalem, 1978-. *Recreations:* golf, bowling. *Address:* 12 Park Avenue, Stirling FK8 2QR. *T:* Stirling 4776. *Club:* Stirling and County.

GRAY, (William) Nicol, CMG 1948; DSO 1944, Bar, 1945; KPM 1951; FRICS; *b* 1 May 1908; *e s* of late Dr W. Gray, Westfield, West Hartlepool; *m* 1st, 1953, Jean Marie Frances Backhouse (marr. diss. 1966), *o c* of Lieut-Col G. R. V. Hume-Gore, MC and Mrs W. Lyne-Stephens, and *widow* of Major Sir John Backhouse, Bt, MC; two *d* ; 2nd, 1967, Margaret Clare Galpin, *widow* of Commander Walter Galpin, RN. *Educ:* Trinity Coll., Glenalmond. Royal Marines, 1939-46; GSO II RM Div., no I (Experimental) WOSB; Mil. Instructor, HMS Dorlin; CO 45 RM Commando; Comdt, RM Octu; Inspector-Gen., Palestine Police, 1946-48; Commissioner of Police, Federation of Malaya, 1948-52. Agent to the Jockey Club, Newmarket, 1953-64. Administrator, MacRobert Trusts, 1970-74. Trustee, Duke of Edinburgh's Award Scheme, 1973-78, Hon. Trustee, 1979-. *Address:* Ettrickshaws, Selkirk TD7 5JP. *T:* Ettrick Bridge 218.

GRAY, Sir William (Stevenson), Kt 1974; JP; Chairman, Scottish Development Agency, 1975-79; *b* 3 May 1928; *o s* of William Stevenson Gray and Mary Johnstone Dickson; *m* 1958, Mary Rodger; one *s* one *d.* *Educ:* Glasgow Univ., BL. Solicitor and Notary Public. Chairman: Scottish Special Housing Assoc., 1966-72; Scotland W Industrial Promotion Gp, 1972-75; Irvine New Town Develt Corp., 1974-76; World of Property Housing Trust Scottish Housing Assoc. Ltd, 1974-; Clyde Tourist Assoc., 1972-75; Third Eye Centre, 1975; Scottish Assoc. for Care and Resettlement of Offenders, 1975-; The Oil Club, 1975-. Member: Bd of Dirs, Glasgow Citizens' Theatre, 1970-75 (Vice-Pres., 1975-); Convention of Royal Burghs, 1971-75; Exec., Scottish Council (Develt and Industry), 1971-75; Lower Clyde Water Bd, 1971-72; Scottish Opera Bd, 1971-72; Nat. Trust for Scotland, 1971-72; Scottish Nat. Orchestra Soc., 1972-75; Court, Glasgow Univ., 1972-75; Clyde Port Authority, 1972-75; Adv. Council for Energy Conservation, 1974-; Scottish Adv. Cttee on JPs, 1975-; Scottish Economic Council, 1975-; Governor, Glasgow School of Art, 1961-75; Patron, Scottish Youth Theatre, 1976-; Vice Pres., Charles Rennie Mackintosh Soc., 1974-. Mem., Glasgow Corporation, 1958-75, Chm., Property Management Cttee, 1964-67; Magistrate, City of Glasgow, 1961-64; Hon. Treasurer, City of Glasgow, 1971-72; Lord Provost, City of Glasgow and Lord Lieutenant, County of the City of Glasgow, 1972-75. JP Co. of City of Glasgow, 1965; DL Co. of City of Glasgow, 1971; DL City of Glasgow, 1976. Hon. LLD Strathclyde, 1974. *Recreations:* sailing, theatre. *Address:* 13 Royal Terrace, Glasgow G3 7NY. *T:* 041-332 8877. *Club:* Glasgow Art.

GRAY DEBROS, Winifred Marjorie, (Mrs E. Gray Debros); *see* Fox, W. M.

GRAYSON, Prof. Cecil, MA; FBA 1979; Serena Professor of Italian Studies in the University of Oxford, and Fellow of Magdalen College, since 1958; *b* 5 Feb. 1920; *s* of John M. Grayson and Dora Hartley; *m* 1947, Margaret Jordan; one *s* three *d. Educ:* Batley Grammar Sch.; St Edmund Hall, Oxford. Army service (UK and India), 1940-46 (Major); First Class Hons (Mod. Langs), 1947; Univ. Lectr in Italian, Oxford, 1948; Lectr at St Edmund Hall, 1948; Lectr at New Coll., 1954. Corresp. Fellow, Commissione per i Testi di Lingua, Bologna, 1957; Mem., Accademia Letteraria Ital. dell' Arcadia, 1958; Corresp. Mem., Accademia della Crusca, 1960; Accademia delle Scienze, Bologna, 1964; Accademia dei Lincei, 1967; Istituto Veneto di Scienze, Lettere ed Arti, 1977; Barlow Lecturer, University Coll., London, 1963; Resident Fellow, Newberry Library, Chicago, 1965; Visiting Professor: Yale Univ., 1966; Berkeley, Calif, 1969, 1973; UCLA, 1980; Perth, WA, 1973, 1980; Cape Town, 1980. An editor of Italian Studies. Premio Internazionale Galileo (storia della lingua italiana), 1974; Serena Medal for Italian Studies, British Academy, 1976. Comdr, Order of Merit, Italy, 1975. *Publications:* Early Italian Texts (with Prof. C. Dionisotti), 1949; Opuscoli inediti di L. B. Alberti, 1954; Alberti and the Tempio Malatestiano, 1957; Vincenzo Calmeta, Prose e Lettere edite e inedite, 1959; A Renaissance Controversy: Latin or Italian?, 1960; L. B. Alberti, Opere volgari, I, 1960, II, 1966, III, 1973; L. B. Alberti e la prima grammatica volgare, 1964; Cinque saggi su Dante, 1972; (trans.) The Lives of Savonarola, Machiavelli and Guicciardini by Roberto Ridolfi, 1959, 1963, 1967; (ed) selected works of Guicciardini, 1964; (ed and trans.) L. B. Alberti, De pictura, De statua, 1972; (ed) The World of Dante, 1980; articles in Bibliofilia, Burlington Mag., English Misc., Giorn. Stor. d. Lett. Ital., Ital. Studies, Lettere Italiane, Lingua Nostra, Rassegna d. Lett. Ital., Rinascimento, The Year's Work in Mod. Languages. *Recreation:* music. *Address:* 11 Norham Road, Oxford. *T:* 57045.

GRAYSON, Sir Ronald Henry Rudyard, 3rd Bt of Ravens Point, *cr* 1922; *b* 15 Nov. 1916; *s* of Sir Denys Henry Harrington Grayson, 2nd Bt, and Elsie May (*d* 1973), *d* of Richard Davies Jones; *S* father 1955; *m* 1st, 1936; 2nd, 1946, Vicki Serell. *Educ:* Harrow Sch. Engineering apprenticeship Grayson, Rollo & Clover Docks Ltd, 1934. Dir, 1940-49; Emigrated to Australia, 1953. Served War of 1939-45, RAF. *Heir: uncle* Rupert Stanley Harrington Grayson, writer [*b* 22 July 1897; *m* 1st, 1919, Ruby Victoria, *d* of Walter

Henry Banks; 2nd, 1950, Vari Colette, *d* of Major Henry O'Shea]. *Recreation:* books. *Address:* PO Box 24, Brooklyn, NSW 2253, Australia.

GRAYSTON, Rev. Prof. Kenneth, MA; Professor of Theology, Bristol University, 1965-79, now Emeritus Professor; Pro-Vice-Chancellor, Bristol University, 1976-July 1979; *b* Sheffield, 8 July 1914; *s* of Ernest Edward and Jessie Grayston; *m* 1942, Elizabeth Alison, *d* of Rev. Walter Mayo and Beatrice Aste, Elsfield, Oxon.; no *c. Educ:* Colfe's Grammar Sch., Lewisham; Universities of Oxford and Cambridge. Ordained Methodist Minister, 1942; Ordnance Factory Chaplain, 1942-44; Asst Head of Religious Broadcasting, BBC, 1944-49; Tutor in New Testament Language and Literature, Didsbury Coll., 1949-64; Special Lecturer in Hellenistic Greek, Bristol Univ., 1950-64; Dean, Faculty of Arts, Bristol Univ., 1972-74. Select Preacher to Univ. of Cambridge, 1952, 1962, to Univ. of Oxford, 1971; Sec. Studiorum Novi Testamenti Societas, 1955-65; Chairman: Theolog. Adv. Gp, British Council of Churches, 1969-72; Christian Aid Scholarships Cttee, 1973-78. *Publications:* The Epistles to the Galatians and to the Philippians, 1957; The Letters of Paul to the Philippians and the Thessalonians, 1967; (contrib. in): A Theological Word Book of the Bible, 1950; The Teacher's Commentary, 1955; The Interpreter's Dictionary of the Bible, 1962, etc. (Contrib. to): Expository Times, New Testament Studies, Theology, London Quarterly and Holborn Review, etc. *Recreation:* travel. *Address:* 11 Rockleaze Avenue, Bristol BS9 1NG. *T:* Bristol 683872.

GREATBATCH, Sir Bruce, KCVO 1972 (CVO 1956); Kt 1969; CMG 1961; MBE 1954; *b* 10 June 1917; *s* of W. T. Greatbatch; unmarried. *Educ:* Malvern Coll.; Brasenose Coll., Oxford. Appointed Colonial Service, 1940, Northern Nigeria. War Service with Royal W African Frontier Force, 1940-45, rank of Major, Burma Campaign (despatches). Resumed Colonial Service, Northern Nigeria, 1945; Resident, 1956; Sec. to Governor and Executive Council, 1957; Senior Resident, Kano, 1958; Sec. to the Premier of Northern Nigeria and Head of Regional Civil Service, 1959; Dep. High Comr, Nairobi, Kenya, 1963; Governor and C-in-C, Seychelles, and Comr for British Indian Ocean Territory, 1969-73; Head of British Development Div., Caribbean, 1974-78; freelance consultant, 1978-. KStJ 1969. *Recreations:* shooting, gardening. *Address:* Greenleaves, Painswick, near Stroud, Glos. *Clubs:* East India, Devonshire, Sports and Public Schools, Royal Commonwealth Society.

GREAVES, Jeffrey; HM Diplomatic Service, retired; Consul General, Alexandria, 1978-81; *b* 10 Dec. 1926; *s* of Willie Greaves and Emily Verity; *m* 1949, Joyce Mary Farrer; one *s* one *d. Educ:* Pudsey Grammar Sch. Served RN, 1945-48. Joined HM Foreign Service, 1948; FO, 1948; Benghazi, 1951; Vice Consul, Tehran, 1953; ME Centre for Arab Studies, 1955; Second Sec. and Vice Consul, Paris, 1960; Vice Consul, Muscat, 1962; Second Sec. and Consul, Athens, 1965; Second Sec. (Commercial), Cairo, 1968; First Sec. and Consul, Muscat, 1970; First Sec. (Com.), Bangkok, 1972; FCO, 1976. *Recreations:* bowls, walking. *Address:* 38 Alexandra Road, Pudsey, West Yorks LS28 8BY. *Club:* Pudsey Bowling.

GREBENIK, Eugene, CB 1976; MSc (Economics); Editor, Population Studies; Consultant, Office of Population Censuses and Surveys, since 1977; *b* 20 July 1919; *s* of S. Grebenik; *m* 1946, Virginia, *d* of James D. Barker; two *s* one *d. Educ:* abroad; London Sch. of Economics. Statistician, Dept of Economics, Univ. of Bristol, 1939-40; London Sch. of Economics: Asst. 1940-44 and Lecturer, 1944-49, in Statistics (on leave, 1944-46; served in RN, 1944; Temp. Statistical Officer, Admiralty, 1944-45; Secretariat, Royal Commn on Population, 1945-46); Reader in Demography, Univ. of London, 1949-54; Research Sec., Population Investigation Cttee, 1947-54; Prof. of Social Studies, Univ. of Leeds, 1954-69. Principal, Civil Service Coll., 1970-76 and Dep. Sec., Civil Service Dept, 1972-76. Mem., Impact of Rates Cttee, Ministry of Housing, 1963-64. Social Science Research Council: Statistics Cttee, 1966-69; Cttee on Social Science and Government, 1968-72; Population Panel, 1971-73; Member: Cttee on Governance of London Univ., 1970-72; Council, Royal Holloway Coll., Univ. of London, 1971-. Pres., British Soc. for Population Studies, 1979-81. Sec.-Treasurer, Internat. Union for Scientific Study of Population, 1963-73. Hon. Fellow, LSE, 1969. *Publications:* (with H. A. Shannon) The Population of Bristol, 1943; (with D. V. Glass) The Trend and Pattern of Fertility in Great Britain; A Report on the Family Census of 1946, 1954; various articles in statistical and economic journals. *Address:* Little Mead, Tite Hill, Egham, Surrey TW20 0NH. *T:* Egham 32994.

GRECH, Herbert F., CVO 1954; *b* 18 May 1899; *m* 1923, Alice Machell (*d* 1969); two *d* (one *s* decd). *Educ:* St Aloysius' Coll., Malta. Served in Army, 1917-20, Lieut King's Own Malta Regt of Militia. Malta Police Force, 1920-54; Commissioner of Police, Malta, 1951-54; retired 1954. *Address:* Flat 1, 27 Creche Street, Sliema, Malta. *T:* Sliema 30086. *Club:* Union (Malta).

GREEN, Alan, CBE 1974; Chairman: Walmsley (Bury) Group since 1970; Beloit Walmsley Ltd; Director: Scapa Group Ltd; Wolstenholme Bronze Powders Ltd (Vice-Chairman); Porritts & Spencer (Asia) Ltd, since 1969; Local Director, Barclays Bank, Manchester District, since 1969; *b* 29 Sept. 1911; *s* of Edward and Emily Green; *m* 1935, Hilda Mary Wolstenholme; three *d. Educ:* Brighton Coll. Schoolmaster, 1931-35; joined Scapa Dryers Ltd, Blackburn, 1935. Army Service, 1940-45. Formerly: Dir of Scapa Dryers Ltd, 1945; Vice-Chm. of Scapa Dryers Ltd, 1956; Dir of Scapa Dryers Inc., 1955;

Dir of companies associated with Walmsley (Bury) Group, 1950; Chm. of Walmsley Operating Companies, 1954. Contested (C): Nelson and Colne, 1950-51; Manchester, Blackley, 1979; MP (C) Preston S, 1955-64, 1970-Feb. 1974; Parly Sec., Min. of Labour, 1961-62; Minister of State, BoT, 1962-63; Financial Sec. to the Treasury, 1963-64. Mem., Australia Cttee, BNEC, 1968-72; frequent business visits to Northern and Western Europe and North America. *Recreations:* cricket, golf, tennis, gardening, history. *Address:* The Stables, Sabden, near Blackburn, Lancs. *T:* Padiham 71528. *Clubs:* Reform, Royal Automobile.
See also D. C. Waddington.

GREEN, Prof. Albert Edward, FRS 1958; MA, PhD, ScD (Cambridge); Sedleian Professor of Natural Philosophy, University of Oxford, 1968-77, now Emeritus Professor; Supernumerary Fellow, The Queen's College, Oxford, since 1977 (Fellow, 1968-77); *m* 1939, Gwendoline May Rudston. *Educ:* Jesus Coll., Cambridge Univ. (Scholar). PhD 1937; MA 1938; ScD 1943. Formerly: Lecturer in Mathematics, Durham Colls, University of Durham; Fellow of Jesus Coll., Cambridge, 1936; Prof. of Applied Mathematics, University of Newcastle upon Tyne, 1948-68. Hon. DSc: Durham, 1969; NUI, 1977; Hon. LLD Glasgow, 1975. Timoshenko Medal, ASME, 1974. *Address:* 20 Lakeside, Oxford.

GREEN, Allan David; a Senior Prosecuting Counsel to the Crown at the Central Criminal Court, since 1979; a Recorder of the Crown Court, since 1979; *b* 1 March 1935; *s* of Lionel and Irene Green; *m* 1967, Eva, *yr d* of Prof. Artur Attman and Elsa Attman, Gothenburg, Sweden; one *s* one *d*. *Educ:* Charterhouse; St Catharine's Coll., Cambridge (Open Exhibnr, MA). Served RN, 1953-55. Called to the Bar, Inner Temple, 1959; Jun. Prosecuting Counsel to the Crown, Central Criminal Court, 1977. *Publications:* trans. with wife several Swedish books. *Recreations:* music, yoga, squash. *Address:* 1 Hare Court, Temple, EC4Y 7BE. *T:* 01-353 5324.

GREEN, Anthony Eric Sandall, RA 1977 (ARA 1971); Member, London Group, 1964; Artist (Painter); *b* 30 Sept. 1939; *s* of late Frederick Sandall Green and Marie Madeleine (*née* Dupont); *m* 1961, Mary Louise Cozens-Walker; two *d*. *Educ:* Highgate Sch., London; Slade Sch. of Fine Art, University Coll. London. Henry Tonks Prize for drawing, Slade Sch., 1960; French Govt Schol., Paris, 1960; Gulbenkian Purchase Award, 1963; Harkness Fellowship, in USA, 1967-69. Has exhibited in: London, New York, Haarlem, Rotterdam, Stuttgart, Hanover, Helsingborg, Malmö, Tokyo. Paintings in various public collections, including: Tate Gallery; Olinda Museum, Brazil; Baltimore Mus. of Art, USA; Nat. Mus. of Wales; Gulbenkian Foundn; Arts Council of Gt Brit.; Contemporary Art Soc.; Frans Hals Mus., Holland; Boymans-van Bevningen Mus., Holland; Ulster Mus., Belfast; Ikeda Mus., Tokyo. Exhibit of the Year award, RA, 1977. *Recreations:* travelling, family life. *Address:* 17 Lissenden Mansions, Highgate Road, NW5. *T:* 01-485 1226.

GREEN, Arthur Eatough, CIE 1946; OBE 1937; MC 1917; MSc (Leeds); FICE; JP; Chief Engineer, Public Works Department, Bihar, India, retired; *b* 16 Dec. 1892; *s* of late William Green; *m* 1929, Frances Margaret, *d* of late Col William Henry Savage, CMG; two *s* one *d*. *Educ:* King's Sch., Pontefract; Leeds Univ. Served European War, 1914-18, in 5th Bn West Yorks Regt and RE. Appointed to PWD, India, 1919; served province of Bihar and Orissa, 1919-47; Chief Engineer and Sec. to Govt of Orissa, in PWD, 1942-44, to Govt of Bihar, 1944-47. JP Co. Antrim, 1964. *Recreation:* fishing. *Address:* Drumawillin House, Ballycastle, Co. Antrim, N Ireland. *T:* Ballycastle 62349

GREEN, Arthur Edward Chase, MBE (mil.) 1955; TD; FRICS; Chartered Surveyor; Property Adviser, J. H. Schroder Wagg & Co., since 1972; Director, Schroder Properties Ltd; *b* 5 Nov. 1911; *s* of Harry Catling and Sarah Jane Green, Winchmore Hill, London; *m* 1941, Margaret Grace, *yr d* of John Lancelot and Winifred Churchill, Wallington, Surrey; one *s* two *d*. *Educ:* Merchant Taylors' Sch.; Coll. of Estate Management. HAC, 1932-: King's Prize (Skill-at-Arms), 1938; commnd, 1939; Adjt 11 (HAC) Regt RHA, 1941-42; Western Desert, ME; PoW 1942; despatches 1945; Territorial Efficiency Medal; Court of Assistants, HAC, 1946-76, Treasurer, 1966-69, Vice-Pres., 1970-72; Metropolitan Special Constabulary, HAC Div., 1937-39 and 1946-74 (Long Service Medal and bar); Hon. Mem., Transvaal Horse Artillery. Surveyor, Legal and General Assce Soc., 1934-46, Chief Estates Surveyor, 1946-71. Mem., Cttee of Management, Pension Fund Property Unit Trust, 1972-82; Advr on Policy, Post Office Staff Superannuation Fund, until 1977, Dir, Mereacre Ltd, and Mereacre Farms Ltd (PO Staff Superann. Fund), 1977-; Member: Chancellor of the Exchequer's Property Adv. Panel, 1975-80; Govt Cttee of Inquiry into Agriculture in GB, 1977-79 (Northfield Cttee). Chm., Elecrent Properties Ltd (Electronic Rentals Gp), 1974-; Director: Marlborough Property Hldgs plc; Studley Farms Ltd. Mem., TA&VR Assocs for City of London, to 1977, and for Greater London, to 1981. President: Camden and Islington Corps, St John Ambulance, 1974-75; No 7 Corps, City of London and Hackney, 1976-77; City of London, 1978-. Governor: Bridewell Royal Hosp.; Corpn of the Sons of the Clergy; City of London Sch., to 1981; former Governor, Queenswood Sch. Vice-Pres., Brunswick Boys' Club Trust, 1978 (formerly Founder-Trustee). City of London Court of Common Council (Bread Street Ward), 1971-81; Liveryman: Merchant Taylors' Co.; Gunmakers' Co. DL Greater London, 1967-82 (Representative DL for London Borough of Islington, to 1981). SBStJ 1980. *Recreations:* shooting, gardening, travel, photography. *Address:* Mariners, The Common,

Southwold, Suffolk. *T:* Southwold 723410; 12 Groveland Court, Bow Lane, EC4. *T:* 01-236 7511. *Clubs:* City Livery, Guildhall, Farmers', Sloane.
See also Very Rev. J. H. Churchill.

GREEN, Arthur Jackson; Fellow, Center for International Affairs, Harvard University, 1982-83; *b* 12 Nov. 1928; *s* of F. Harvey Green and Sylvia Marsh Green, MB; *m* 1957, Rosemary Bradley, MA; two *s*. *Educ:* Friends Sch., Lisburn, Co. Antrim; Leighton Park Sch., Reading; Lincoln Coll., Oxford (BA Mod. Hist.); Haverford Coll., Philadelphia (MA Philosophy). Asst Principal, NICS, 1952; Secretary: Cameron Commn, 1969; Scarman Tribunal, 1969-72; Asst Sec., NI Dept of Finance, 1972-78; Under Sec., NI Office, 1978-79; Dir, NI Court Service (Lord Chancellor's Dept), 1979-82. *Address:* 36 St Patrick's Road, Saul, Downpatrick, N Ireland. *T:* Downpatrick 4360. *Club:* Reform.

GREEN, Barry Spencer, QC 1981; a Recorder of the Crown Court, since 1979; *b* 16 March 1932; *s* of Lionel Maurice Green, FRCS and Juliette Green; *m* 1960, Marilyn Rebecca Braverman; two *s*. *Educ:* Westminster Sch.; Christ Church, Oxford (MA, BCL). Called to the Bar, Inner Temple, 1954. *Recreations:* tennis, squash. *Address:* 4 Paper Buildings, Temple, EC4. *T:* 01-353 8215. *Club:* Roehampton.

GREEN, Father Benedict; *see* Green, Rev. H. C.

GREEN, Benny; free-lance writer; *b* 9 Dec. 1927; *s* of David Green and Fanny Trayer; *m* 1962, Antoinette Kanal; three *s* one *d*. *Educ:* Clipstone Street Junior Mixed; subsequently uneducated at St Marylebone Grammar Sch. Mem., West Central Jewish Lads Club (now extinct). Saxophonist, 1947-60 (Most Promising New Jazz Musician, 1953); Jazz Critic, Observer, 1958-77; Literary Critic, Spectator, 1970-; Film Critic, Punch, 1972-77, TV Critic, 1977-; frequent radio and TV appearances, 1955-. Artistic Dir, New Shakespeare Co., 1973-; Mem., BBC Archives Cttee, 1976. Book and lyrics, Boots with Strawberry Jam, Nottingham Playhouse, 1968; revised libretto, Showboat, Adelphi Theatre, London, 1972; co-deviser: Cole, Mermaid, 1974; Oh, Mr Porter, Mermaid, 1977. *Publications:* The Reluctant Art, 1962; Blame it on my Youth, 1967; 58 Minutes to London, 1969; Drums in my Ears, 1973; I've Lost my little Willie, 1976; Swingtime in Tottenham, 1976; (ed) Cricket Addict's Archive, 1977; Shaw's Champions, 1978; Fred Astaire, 1979; (ed) Wisden Anthology, vol. I 1864-1900, 1979, vol. II 1900-1940, 1980, vol. III 1940-1963, 1982; P. G. Wodehouse: a literary biography, 1981. *Recreation:* cricket. *Address:* c/o BBC, Broadcasting House, Portland Place, W1.

GREEN, Rev. Canon Bryan Stuart Westmacott, BD; DD (*hc*); Canon Emeritus of Birmingham Cathedral since 1970 (Hon. Canon, 1950-70); *b* 14 Jan. 1901; *s* of late Hubert Westmacott Green and late Sarah Kathleen Green (*née* Brockwell); *m* 1926, Winifred Annie Bevan; one *s* one *d*. *Educ:* Merchant Taylors' Sch.; London Univ. BD 1922; Curate, New Malden, 1924-28; Staff of Children's Special Service Mission, 1928-31; Chap., Oxford Pastorate, 1931-34; Vicar of Christ Church, Crouch End, 1934-38; Vicar of Holy Trinity, Brompton, 1938-48; Rector of Birmingham, 1948-70. Conducted evangelistic campaigns: Canada and America, 1936, 1944, and annually, 1947-; Australia and New Zealand, 1951, 1953, 1958, 1974; West Africa, 1953; S Africa, 1953, 1955, 1956, 1957, 1959 and 1960; Ceylon, 1954, 1959. DD Hon. St John's Coll. Winnipeg, 1961. *Publications:* The Practice of Evangelism, 1951; Being and Believing, 1956; Saints Alive, 1959. *Recreation:* golf. *Address:* West Field, Southern Road, Thame, Oxon OX9 2EP. *T:* Thame 2026. *Club:* National.

GREEN, Prof. Dennis Howard; Schröder Professor of German, University of Cambridge, since 1979; Fellow of Trinity College, Cambridge, since 1949; *b* 26 June 1922; *s* of Herbert Maurice Green and Agnes Edith Green (*née* Fleming); *m* 1972, Margaret Parry. *Educ:* Latymer Upper Sch., London; Trinity Coll., Cambridge; Univ. of Basle. Univ. of Cambridge, 1940-41 and 1945-47; Univ. of Basle (Dr Phil.), 1947-49; Military service (RAC), 1941-45; Univ. Lecturer in German, St Andrews, 1949-50; Research Fellowship, Trinity Coll., Cambridge (first year held *in absentia*), 1949-52; Univ. Asst Lectr in German, Cambridge, 1950-54; Teaching Fellowship, Trinity Coll., Cambridge, 1952-66; Head of Dept of Other Languages, 1956-79, and Prof. of Modern Languages, Cambridge, 1966-79; Visiting Professor: Cornell Univ., 1965-66; Auckland Univ., 1966; Yale Univ., 1969; ANU, Canberra, 1971; UCLA, 1975; Univ. of Pennsylvania, 1975; Univ. of WA, 1976; Vis. Fellow, Humanities Res. Centre, Canberra, 1978. *Publications:* The Carolingian Lord, 1965; The Millstätter Exodus: a crusading epic, 1966; (with Dr L. P. Johnson) Approaches to Wolfram von Eschenbach, 1978; Irony in the Medieval Romance, 1979; The Art of Recognition in Wolfram's Parzival; reviews and articles in learned journals. *Recreations:* walking and foreign travel. *Address:* Trinity College, Cambridge; 7 Archway Court, Barton Road, Cambridge. *T:* Cambridge 358070.

GREEN, Rev. Canon (Edward) Michael (Bankes); Rector of St Aldate with Holy Trinity, Oxford, since 1975; Principal, St John's College, Nottingham (until July 1970 The London College of Divinity), 1969-75; Canon Theologian of Coventry, 1970-76, Canon Theologian Emeritus since 1978; *b* 20 Aug. 1930; British; *m* 1957, Rosemary Wake (*née* Storr); two *s* two *d*. *Educ:* Clifton Coll.; Oxford and Cambridge Univs. BD Cantab 1966. Exeter Coll., Oxford, 1949-53 (1st cl. Lit. Hum.); Royal Artillery (Lieut, A/Adjt), 1953-55; Queens' Coll., Cambridge, 1955-57 (1st cl. Theol. Tripos Pt III; Carus Greek Testament Prize; Fencing Blue), and Ridley Hall Theol

Coll., 1955-57; Curate, Holy Trinity, Eastbourne, 1957-60; Lectr, London Coll. of Divinity, 1960-69, Principal, 1969. Member: Doctrine Commission of the Church, 1968-77; Church Unity Commn, 1974-. Leader of missions, overseas and in UK. *Publications:* Called to Serve, 1964; Choose Freedom, 1965; The Meaning of Salvation, 1965; Man Alive, 1967; Runaway World, 1968; Commentary on 2 Peter and Jude, 1968; Evangelism in the Early Church, 1970; Jesus Spells Freedom, 1972; New Life, New Lifestyle, 1973; I Believe in the Holy Spirit, 1975; You Must Be Joking, 1976; (ed) The Truth of God Incarnate, 1977; Why Bother With Jesus?, 1979; Evangelism—Now and Then, 1979; What is Christianity?, 1981; I Believe in Satan's Downfall, 1981; The Day Death Died, 1982; contribs to various jls. *Recreations:* family, countryside pursuits, cricket, squash, fly fishing. *Address:* St Aldate's Rectory, 40 Pembroke Street, Oxford. *T:* Oxford 49423.

GREEN, Sir (Edward) Stephen (Lycett), 4th Bt, *cr* 1886; CBE 1964; DL, JP; Chairman, East Anglian Regional Hospital Board, 1959-74; *b* 18 April 1910; *s* of Sir E. A. Lycett Green, 3rd Bt, and Elizabeth Williams; *S* father, 1941; *m* 1935, Constance Mary, *d* of late Ven. H. S. Radcliffe; one *d. Educ:* Eton; Magdalene Coll., Cambridge. Called to Bar, Lincoln's Inn, 1933. Served War of 1939-45 (Major, RA). CC 1946-49, JP 1946, DL 1961, High Sheriff 1973, Norfolk; Dep. Chairman Norfolk QS, 1948-71. Chairman: King's Lynn Hospital Management Cttee, 1948-59; Assoc. of Hosp. Management Cttees, 1956-58; Cttee of Inquiry into Recruitment, Training and Promotion of Administrative and Clerical Staff in Hospital Service, 1962-63; Docking RDC, 1950-57. *Recreations:* shooting, reading. *Heir: b* Lt-Col Simon Lycett Green, TD, Yorks Dragoons Yeomanry [*b* 11 July 1912; *m* 1st, 1935, Gladys (marr. diss. 1971; she *d* 1980), *d* of late Arthur Ranicar, JP, Springfield, Wigan; one *d*; 2nd, 1971, Mary, *d* of late George Ramsden]. *Address:* Ken Hill, Snettisham, King's Lynn. *TA:* Snettisham, Norfolk. *T:* Heacham 70001; 60 Pont Street, SW1. *T:* 01-589 5958. *Clubs:* White's, Pratt's; Norfolk (Norwich); Allsorts (Norfolk).

GREEN, Dr Frank Alan, CEng; FIM, FBIM; Regional Industrial Adviser, Department of Industry, since 1981; *b* 29 Oct. 1931; *s* of Frank Green and Winifred Hilda (*née* Payne); *m* 1957, Pauline Eleanor Tayler; one *s* two *d. Educ:* Mercers Sch., London; Univ. of London (BScEng, PhD). CEng 1980; FIM 1978; FBIM 1979. UKAEA, 1956-57; various appts, Glacier Metal Co. Ltd (Associated Engrg Gp), 1957-65; Technical Dir, Alta Friccion SA, Mexico City, 1965-68; Manufg Dir, Stewart Warner Corp., 1968-72; Marketing Develt Manager, Calor Gp, 1972-74; Manufg Dir, CWTA-77, Man. Dir, 1977-81, British Twin Disc Ltd, Rochester. Dir, Anglo-Mexican Chamber of Commerce, Mexico City, 1966-68. *Publications:* contrib. technical and managerial jls in UK and Mexico. *Recreations:* photography, military history, rough walking, wine. *Address:* Courtwood, Burleigh Road, Charing, Kent TN27 0JB. *T:* Charing 3152. *Club:* Old Mercers.

GREEN, Geoffrey Hugh, CB 1977; Deputy Under-Secretary of State (Policy), Procurement Executive, Ministry of Defence, 1975-80; *b* 24 Sept. 1920; *o s* of late Duncan M. and Kate Green, Bristol; *m* 1948, Ruth Hazel Mercy; two *d. Educ:* Bristol Grammar Sch.; Worcester Coll., Oxford (Exhibr), 1939-41, 1945-47 (MA). Served with Royal Artillery (Ayrshire Yeomanry): N Africa and Italy, 1942-45 (Captain). Entered Min. of Defence, Oct. 1947; Principal, 1949; Asst Sec., 1960; Asst Under-Sec. of State, 1969; Dep. Under-Sec. of State, 1974. *Recreations:* travel, music, walking. *Address:* 47 Kent Avenue, Ealing, W13 8BE.

GREEN, Sir George (Ernest), Kt 1963; Past Chairman of Eagers Holdings Ltd; *b* 1892; *s* of Jabez Green, Brisbane, and Catherine Genevieve, *d* of T. Cronin; *m* Ailsa Beatrice, *d* of Charles George Rools Crane. *Educ:* Maryborough Grammar Sch. Pres., Royal National Agricultural and Industrial Assoc. of Qld, 1955-61. *Address:* 35 Markwell Street, Hamilton, Brisbane, Qld 4007, Australia.

GREEN, Major George Hugh, MBE; MC 1945; TD and 3 bars; Vice-Lieutenant of Caithness, since 1973; retired; *b* 21 Oct. 1911; *s* of George Green, The Breck, John O'Groats; *m* 1936, Isobel Elizabeth Myron; two *s. Educ:* Wick High Sch.; Edinburgh Univ. (MA). Retired as schoolmaster, 1977. Commnd into Seaforth Highlanders, TA, 1935; served War of 1939-45 with 5th Seaforths in 51st (H) Div., N Africa and NW Europe; retd from TA, 1963. DL Caithness 1965. *Recreations:* gardening, bee-keeping. *Address:* Tjaldur, Halkirk, Caithness. *T:* Halkirk 639. *Club:* Highland Brigade (Inverness).

GREEN, Graham John G.; *see* Graham-Green.

GREEN, Hon. Sir Guy (Stephen Montague), KBE 1982; Chief Justice of Tasmania, since 1973; Lieutenant-Governor of Tasmania, since 1982; Member, Faculty of Law, University of Tasmania, since 1974; *b* 26 July 1937; *s* of Clement Francis Montague Green and Beryl Margaret Jenour Green; *m* 1963, Rosslyn Mary Marshall; two *s* two *d. Educ:* Launceston Church Grammar Sch.; Univ. of Tasmania. Alfred Houston Schol. (Philosophy) 1958; LLB (Hons) 1960. Admitted to Bar of Tasmania, 1960; Partner, Ritchie & Parker Alfred Green & Co (Launceston), 1963; Pres., Tasmanian Bar Assoc., 1968-70 (Vice-Pres., 1966-68); Magistrate 1971-73. Mem.-at-Large, Appellate Court Judges' Section, World Assoc. of Judges, 1976-; Chm., Council of Law Reporting, 1978-. Chairman: Tasmanian Cttee, Duke of Edinburgh's Award Scheme in Australia, 1975-80; Sir Henry Baker Meml Fellowship Cttee, 1973-; Dir, Winston Churchill Meml Trust, 1975- (Dep. Nat. Chm., 1980-; Chm. Tasmanian Regional Cttee, 1975-80). Vice Patron: Art Soc. of Tasmania,

1974-; Royal Agricultural Soc. of Tasmania, 1974-. *Recreations:* walking, tennis, cycling, food and wine. *Address:* Judges' Chambers, Supreme Court, Salamanca Place, Hobart, Tasmania 7000. *Clubs:* Launceston (Launceston, Tas.); Tasmanian, Athenæum (Hobart).

GREEN, Henry Rupert, CBE 1960; MA; Legal Senior Commissioner of Board of Control, 1953-60, later Ministry of Health; retired 1977; *b* 29 Dec. 1900; *o s* of late Henry Green, JP, solicitor, and Margaret Helen Green, Stockport, Cheshire; *m* 1937, Marie Elizabeth Patricia Bailey; three *s* one *d. Educ:* Charterhouse; Hertford Coll., Oxford (Exhibitioner). Barrister, Lincoln's Inn, 1926; practised on Northern Circuit, 1926-36; Commissioner of Board of Control, 1936. War of 1939-45: commissioned RAF, 1940; served as Operations Staff Officer, Malta, 1941-43; released, 1944. Pres. Governors, St Mary's Sch. for Girls, Gerrards Cross. *Publications:* title: Persons Mentally Disordered (Pts 2 and 3), Halsbury's Laws of England, 3rd Edn, 1960; title: Persons of Unsound Mind, Halsbury's Statutes (Burrows Edn), 1950 and similar title: Encyclopædia of Court Forms, 1949. *Recreation:* carpentry. *Address:* The Square House, Latchmoor Grove, Gerrards Cross, Bucks. *T:* Gerrards Cross 82316.

GREEN, Hon. Howard Charles, PC (Canada); QC (BC); LLD (University of British Columbia); *b* Kaslo, BC, 5 Nov. 1895; *s* of Samuel Howard and Flora Isabel Green; *m* 1st, 1923, Marion Jean (decd), *d* of Lewis Mounce, Vancouver; two *s*; 2nd, 1956, Donna Enid, *d* of Dr D. E. Kerr, Duncan, BC. *Educ:* High Sch., Kaslo; University of Toronto (BA); Osgoode Hall Law Sch. Served European War, 1915-19. Called to Bar of British Columbia, 1922; elected to Federal Parliament, 1935; Minister of Public Works and Govt House Leader, 1957-59; Acting Minister of Defence Production, 1957-58; Dep. Prime Minister, 1957-63; Canadian Sec. of State for External Affairs, 1959-63. Is a Progressive Conservative. *Address:* 4160 W 8th Avenue, Vancouver, British Columbia, Canada. *Club:* Terminal City (Vancouver, BC).

GREEN, Rev. Humphrey Christian, (Father Benedict Green, CR); Principal, College of the Resurrection, Mirfield, since 1975; *b* 9 Jan. 1924; *s* of late Rev. Canon Frederick Wastie Green and Marjorie Susan Beltt Green (*née* Gosling). *Educ:* Dragon Sch., Oxford; Eton (King's Scholar); Merton Coll., Oxford (Postmaster). BA 1949, MA 1952. Served War, RNVR, 1943-46. Deacon 1951, priest 1952; Asst Curate of Northolt, 1951-56; Lectr in Theology, King's Coll., London, 1956-60. Professed in Community of the Resurrection (taking additional name of Benedict), 1962; Vice-Principal, Coll. of the Resurrection, 1965-75. Associate Lectr in Dept of Theology and Religious Studies, Univ. of Leeds, 1967-. *Publications:* The Gospel according to Matthew (New Clarendon Bible), 1975; contrib.: Towards a Church Architecture (ed P. Hammond), 1962; The Anglican Synthesis (ed W. R. F. Browning), 1964; theological jls. *Recreations:* walking, synoptic criticism. *Address:* College of the Resurrection, Mirfield, W Yorks WF14 0BW. *T:* Mirfield 493362.

GREEN, (James) Maurice (Spurgeon), MBE, TD, MA; Editor, The Daily Telegraph, 1964-74 (Deputy Editor, 1961-64); *b* 8 Dec. 1906; *s* of Lieut-Col James Edward Green, DSO; *m* 1st 1929, Pearl (*d* 1934), *d* of A. S. Oko, Cincinnati, USA; 2nd, 1936, Janet Grace, *d* of Maj.-Gen. C. E. M. Norie, CB, CMG, DSO; two *s. Educ:* Rugby Sch. (scholar); University Coll., Oxford (scholar, 1st Class, Honour Mods and Lit. Hum.). Editor of The Financial News, 1934-38; Financial and Industrial Editor of The Times, 1938-39 and 1944-53 (served in Royal Artillery, 1939-44); Asst Editor, 1953-61. Pres., Inst. of Journalists, 1976-77. *Recreations:* books, music, fishing. *Address:* The Hermitage, Twyford, near Winchester, Hants. *T:* Twyford 713980. *Club:* Reform.

GREEN, John Dennis Fowler; agriculturalist; Chairman, Gloucestershire Branch, Council for the Protection of Rural England (Member, National Executive, 1967-80); *b* 9 May 1909; *s* of late Capt. Henry and Amy Gertrude Green, Chedworth, Glos; *m* 1946, Diana Judith, JP, *y d* of late Lt-Col H. C. Elwes, DSO, MVO, Colesbourne, Glos. *Educ:* Cheltenham Coll.; Peterhouse, Cambridge. President of the Union. Called to the Bar, Inner Temple, 1933; BBC, 1934-62 (Controller, Talks Div., 1956-61); established agricultural broadcasting, 1935. Special Agric. Mission to Aust. and NZ (MAFF), 1945-47; Pres. National Pig Breeders Assoc., 1955-56; Chm., Agricultural Adv. Council, 1963-68; Exec. Mem., Land Settlement Assoc., 1965-80; a Vice-Pres., and Chm. Educn Cttee, RASE, 1973-. Chm., Cirencester and Tewkesbury Conservative Assoc., 1964-78. Governor, Royal Agricl Coll. *Publications:* Mr Baldwin: A Study in Post War Conservatism, 1933; articles and broadcasts on historical and agricultural subjects. *Recreations:* livestock breeding, forestry, shooting. *Address:* The Manor, Chedworth, Cheltenham. *T:* Fossebridge 233. *Clubs:* Oriental, Farmers', Naval and Military, Buck's.

GREEN, John Michael, CB 1976; Commissioner, since 1971, Deputy Chairman, since 1973, Board of Inland Revenue; *b* 5 Dec. 1924; *s* of late George Green and of Faith Green; *m* 1951, Sylvia (*née* Crabb); one *s* one *d. Educ:* Merchant Taylors' Sch., Rickmansworth; Jesus Coll., Oxford (MA (Hons)). Served War, Army, RAC, 1943-46. Entered Inland Revenue as Asst Principal, 1948; served in HM Treasury, as Principal, 1956-57; Asst Sec., 1962; Under Sec., Bd of Inland Revenue, 1971. *Recreation:* gardening. *Address:* 5 Bylands, White Rose Lane, Woking, Surrey. *T:* Woking 72599. *Club:* Reform.

GREEN, Julian Hartridge; Writer; Member of Académie Française, 1971; *b* Paris, France, 6 Sept. 1900. *Educ:* Lycée Janson, Paris; Univ. of Virginia. Member: Acad. de Bavière, 1950; Royal Acad. of Belgium, 1951; Ravenclub, 1922; Acad. de Mannheim, 1952; Phi Beta Kappa, 1948; Amer. Acad. of Arts and Sciences. Prix Harper, Prix Bookman, Prix de Monaco, 1951; Grand Prix National des Lettres, 1966; Grand Prix, Académie Française, 1970. *Publications: fiction:* L'apprenti psychiâtre, 1921; Le voyageur sur la terre, 1924; Mont-Cinère, 1926; Adrienne Mesurat, 1927; Les clés de la mort, 1928; Léviathan, 1929; L'autre sommeil, 1931; Epaves, 1932; Le visionnaire, 1934; Minuit, 1936; Varouna, 1940; Si j'étais vous ...., 1947; Moira, 1950; Le malfaiteur, 1956, new enl. edn 1974; Chaque homme dans sa nuit, 1960; L'autre, 1971; La nuit des fantômes, 1976; Le Mauvais Lieu, 1977; *plays:* Sud, 1953; L'ennemi, 1954; L'ombre, 1956; Demain n'existe pas, 1979; L'automate, 1980; *autobiography and journals:* Memories of Happy Days, 1942; Partir avant le jour, 1963; Mille chemins ouverts, 1964; Terre lointaine, 1966; Jeunesse, 1974; Liberté, 1974; Ce qu'il faut d'amour a l'homme, 1978; Journal: i, Les années faciles, 1928-34, 1938; ii, Derniers beaux jours, 1935-39, 1939; iii, Devant la porte sombre, 1940-43, 1946; iv, L'œil de l'houragan, 1943-45, 1949; v, Le revenant, 1946-50, 1952; vi, Le retrain intérieur, 1950-54, 1955; vii, Le bel aujourd'hui, 1955-58, 1958; viii, Vers l'invisible, 1958-66, 1967; ix, Ce qui reste de jour, 1967-72, 1972; x, La bouteille à la mer, 1972-76, 1976; Dans la gueule du temps (illust. jl), 1979-; Œuvres complètes (La Pleïade), vol. I, 1972; vols II and III, 1973; vols IV and V, 1974. *Address:* Editions de la Pleïade, 5 rue Sébastien-Bottin, 75007 Paris, France.

GREEN, Kenneth, MA; Director, Manchester Polytechnic, since 1981; *b* 7 March 1934; *s* of James William and Elsie May Green; *m* 1961, Glenda (*née* Williams); one *d. Educ:* Helsby Grammar Sch.; Univ. of Wales, Bangor (BA 1st Cl. Hons); Univ. of London (MA). 2nd Lieut, S Wales Borderers, 1955-57. Management Trainee, Dunlop Rubber Co., 1957-58; Teacher, Liverpool, 1958-60; Lecturer: Widnes Technical Coll., 1961-62; Stockport College of Technology, 1962-64; Sen. Lectr, Bolton College of Education, 1964-68; Head of Educn, City of Birmingham College of Education, 1968-72; Dean of Faculty, Manchester Polytechnic, 1973-81. *Recreations:* Rugby football, beer tasting. *Address:* 22 Royden Avenue, Runcorn, Cheshire WA7 4SP. *T:* Runcorn 73294.

GREEN, Maj.-Gen. Kenneth David, CB 1982; OBE; ED; FICE, FIE(Aust); Secretary, Premier's Department, Government of Victoria, 1972-82; *b* 20 Nov. 1917; *s* of D. W. Green; *m* 1945, Phyl, *d* of J. Roohan; one *s. Educ:* Williamstown High Sch.; Melbourne High Sch.; Melbourne Univ. (BCE). Served 2nd AIF. Joined State Rivers and Water Supply Commn, Vic, 1939; design and exec. engrg appts, 1958-65; Commissioner: State Rivers and Water Supply Commn, Vic, 1965-72; Australian Cities Commn, 1972-75. Fourth Task Force, CMF, 1966-69; Southern Comd Trng Gp, 1969-70; Comdr 3rd Div., CMF, 1970-73; Col Comdt, RAE, Vic, 1976-82. Chairman: State Recreation Council (formerly Nat. Fitness Council), Vic; Duke of Edinburgh's Award Scheme Cttee, Vic, 1971-81; Mem., Film Victoria Bd, 1982-. Pres. Council, Chisholm Inst. of Technology, 1982-. Fellow, Aust. Inst. of Urban Studies; FTS; FASCE. *Publications:* technical papers. *Recreations:* golf, swimming, listening to classical music. *Address:* 226 Were Street, East Brighton, Vic 3187, Australia. *Clubs:* Melbourne, Athenaeum, Naval and Military (Melbourne); Melbourne Cricket, Huntingdale Golf, Frankston Golf.

GREEN, Prof. Leslie Leonard, PhD; FInstP; Professor of Experimental Physics, University of Liverpool, since 1964; Director, Daresbury Laboratory, since 1981; *b* 30 March 1925; *s* of Leonard and Victoria Green; *m* 1952, Dr Helen Therese Morgan; one *s* one *d. Educ:* Alderman Newton's Sch., Leicester; King's Coll., Cambridge (MA, PhD). FInstP 1966. British Atomic Energy Proj., 1944-46; Univ. of Liverpool: Lectr, 1948-57; Sen. Lectr, 1957-62; Reader, 1962-64; Dean, Faculty of Sciences, 1969-72; Pro-Vice-Chancellor, 1978-81. Mem., SRC Nuclear Physics Bd, 1972-75 and 1979-82. *Publications:* articles on nuclear physics in scientific jls. *Address:* Seafield Cottage, De Grouchy Street, West Kirby, Merseyside L48 5DX. *Club:* South Caernarvonshire Yacht.

GREEN, Leslie William, CVO 1974; MBE 1953; *b* 1 July 1912; *y s* of late George Green and of Jane E. Green; *m* 1938, Alice Robertshaw; one *s* one *d. Educ:* Moseley Grammar Sch., Birmingham; City of Birmingham Commercial Coll. Cert AIB; FCIT. Accountant Officer, RAF, 1940-46 (Flt-Lt); Asst Airport Man., Heathrow, 1946-47; Airport Man., Croydon, 1947-50; Dep. Airport Man., Heathrow, 1950-55; Airport Man., Heathrow, 1955-62; Admin. Dir, London Airports, 1962-65; Gen. Man., Gatwick, 1965-71; Gen. Man., Heathrow, 1971-73; Special Projects Dir, British Airports Authority, 1973-75. *Recreations:* golf, gardening, watching cricket. *Clubs:* MCC; (Pres.) Chipstead and Coulsdon Cricket; Chipstead Golf.

GREEN, Lucinda Jane, MBE 1978; Director, Bacon Everitt Morris & Associates Ltd, since 1979; *b* 7 Nov. 1953; *d* of late Maj.-Gen. George Erroll Prior-Palmer, CB, DSO, and of Lady Doreen Hersey Winifred Prior-Palmer; *m* 1981, David, *s* of Barrington Green, Brisbane. *Educ:* St Mary's, Wantage; Idbury Manor, Oxon. Member of winning Junior European Team, 1971; Winner, 3 Day Events: Badminton Horse Trials Championships, 1973, 1976, 1977, 1979; Burghley, 1977, 1981; Individual European Championships, 1975, 1977; World Championship, 1982; Member: (unsuccessful) Olympic Team, Montreal, 1976; winning European Championship Team, Burghley, 1977; World Championship Team, Kentucky, 1978, Luhmühlen, W Germany, 1982; European Team, 1979; Alternative Olympic Team, 1980. *Publications:*

Up, Up and Away, 1978; Four Square, 1980. *Recreations:* driving, skiing, holidays abroad. *Address:* Appleshaw House, Andover, Hants. *T:* Weyhill 2333.

GREEN, Rt. Rev. Mark, MC 1945; Hon. Assistant, Christ Church, St Leonards-on-Sea, since 1982; an Assistant Bishop, Diocese of Chichester, since 1982; *b* 28 March 1917; *s* of late Rev. Ernest William Green, OBE, and Miranda Mary Green; unmarried. *Educ:* Rossall Sch.; Lincoln Coll., Oxford (MA). Curate, St Catherine's Gloucester, 1940; Royal Army Chaplains Dept, 1943-46 (despatches, 1945); Dir of Service Ordination Candidates, 1947-48; Vicar of St John, Newland, Hull, 1948-53; Short Service Commn, Royal Army Chaplains' Dept, 1953-56; Vicar of South Bank, Teesside, 1956-58; Rector of Cottingham, Yorks, 1958-64; Vicar of Bishopthorpe and Acaster Malbis, 1964-72; Hon. Chaplain to Archbp of York, 1964-72; Rural Dean of Ainsty, 1964-68; Canon and Prebendary of York Minster, 1963-72; Bishop Suffragan of Aston, 1972-82; Chm. of Governing Body, Aston Training Scheme, 1977-; Provost, Woodard Schs Southern Div., 1982-. Hon. DSc Aston, 1980. *Publication:* Diary of Doubt and Faith, 1974. *Recreations:* Aston Villa, ballet. *Address:* 13 Archery Court, Archery Road, St Leonards-on-Sea, E Sussex TN38 0HZ. *T:* Hastings 444649; *c/o* Christ Church Rectory, 17 Alfred Street, St Leonards-on-Sea, Sussex.

GREEN, Dame Mary Georgina, DBE 1968; BA; Head Mistress, Kidbrooke School, SE3, 1954-73; Chairman, BBC London Local Radio Council, 1973-78; Chairman, General Optical Council, since 1979 (Member, since 1977); *b* 27 July 1913; *er d* of late Edwin George Green and Rose Margaret Green (*née* Gibbs). *Educ:* Wellingborough High Sch.; Westfield Coll., University of London (Hon. Fellow, 1976). Assistant Mistress: Clapham High Sch., 1936-38; Streatham Hill and Clapham High Sch., 1938-40; William Hulme's Sch., Manchester, 1940-45; Head Mistress, Colston's Girls' Sch., Bristol, 1946-53. Member: Central Advisory Council for Education (Eng.), 1956-63; Church of England Board of Education, 1958-65; Council King George's Jubilee Trust, 1963-68; Court of Governors, London Sch. of Economics and Political Science, 1964-; Royal Commission on Trade Unions and Employers' Assocs, 1965-68; Council, City University, 1969-78; Cttee of Inquiry into Nurses' Pay, 1974; Press Council, 1976-79; Review Body on Doctors' and Dentists' Remuneration, 1976-79; Dep. Chm., E-SU, 1976-. A Governor: BBC, 1968-73; Royal Ballet Sch., 1969-72; Centre for Educnl Develt Overseas, 1970-74; Rachel McMillan Coll. of Educn, 1970-73; E-SU, 1974-; Ditchley Foundn, 1978-. Hon. DSc City, 1981. *Address:* 45 Winn Road, SE12 9EX. *T:* 01-857 1514.

GREEN, Maurice; *see* Green, J. M. S.

GREEN, Rev. Canon Michael; *see* Green, Rev. Canon E. M. B.

GREEN, Dr Michael Frederick; Consultant Physician, Department of Geriatric Medicine, Royal Free Hospital, London, since 1971; Editor, Geriatric Medicine, since 1972; *b* 29 Aug. 1939; *s* of Frederick and Kathleen Green; *m* 1977, Janet Mary; seven *s* one *d. Educ:* Dulwich Coll.; Jesus Coll., Cambridge (MA); St Thomas' Hosp. (MB, BChir). FRCP 1980. Consultant, N Middlesex and St Ann's Hosps, 1969-71. Mem., GMC, 1973-79. Medical Adviser, Royal Life Saving Soc., 1970-; Hon. Sec., Medical Commn Internat. Lifesaving Fedn, 1977-. Member various bodies mainly involved with the elderly, including: British Geriatrics Soc.; Age Concern; Cruse (Nat. Assoc. for Widows); London Medical Gp; British Soc. for Research on Ageing. Governor: Queen Elizabeth Schs, Barnet, 1973-79; Christchurch Sch., Hampstead, 1980-81. *Publications:* Health in Middle Age, 1978; co-author books on medical admin; articles on geriatric medicine, heating, lifesaving, hypothermia, endocrinology, medical records, psychiatry in old age, pressure sores. *Recreations:* family, decorating, swimming and lifesaving, writing, lecturing and teaching. *Address:* 1 Binfield Road, Wokingham, Berkshire.

GREEN, Dr Norman Michael, FRS 1981; Research Staff, Division of Biochemistry, National Institute for Medical Research, since 1964; *b* 6 April 1926; *s* of Ernest Green and Hilda Margaret Carter; *m* 1953, Iro Paulina Moschouti; two *s* one *d. Educ:* Dragon Sch., Oxford; Clifton Coll., Bristol; Magdalen Coll., Oxford (BA; Athletics Blue, Cross Country Blue); UCH Med. Sch., London (PhD). Res. Student, Univ. of Washington, Seattle, 1951-53; Lectr in Biochemistry, Univ. of Sheffield, 1953-55; Res. Fellow and Lectr in Chem. Pathol., St Mary's Hosp. Med. Sch., London, 1956-62; Vis. Scientist, NIH, Maryland, 1962-64. *Publications:* research papers on the structure of proteins and of membranes, in scientific jls. *Recreations:* mountain climbing, pyrotechnics. *Address:* 57 Hale Lane, Mill Hill, NW7 3PS.

GREEN, Brig. Percy William Powlett, CBE 1960 (OBE 1956); DSO 1946; *b* 10 Sept. 1912; *er s* of late Brig.-Gen. W. G. K. Green, CB, CMG, DSO, Indian Army; *m* 1943, Phyllis Margery Fitz Gerald May, *d* of late Lieut-Col A. H. May, OBE; one *s* one *d. Educ:* Wellington Coll.; RMC. Commnd Northamptonshire Regt, 1932; Op. NW Frontier, India, 1936-37; BEF 1939-40; Lt-Col Comdg 2nd W Yorks Regt, 1945-46; Burma, 1944-45; Lt-Col Comdg 1 Malay Regt, 1946-47; Comd 4th King's African Rifles, 1954-56; Op. against Mau Mau; Col, then Staff, War Office, 1956-57; Chief of Staff (Brig.) E Africa Comd, 1957-60; DDMI, War Office, 1961-63; Chief of Staff, N Ireland Command, 1963-65; Dep. Comdr, Aldershot District, 1965-67; retired, 1967. ADC to the Queen, 1965-67. Dep. Colonel, Royal Anglian Regt, 1966-76. *Recreations:* field sports. *Address:* Grudds, South

Warnborough, Basingstoke, Hants. *T:* Long Sutton 472. *Club:* Army and Navy.

GREEN, Sir Peter James Frederick, Kt 1982; Chairman, Janson Green Ltd, since 1966; Chairman, Lloyd's, 1980, 1981, 1982; *b* 28 July 1924; *s* of J. E. Green and M. B. Holford; *m* 1950, A. P. Ryan. *Educ:* Harrow Sch.; Christ Church, Oxford. Lloyd's: Underwriter, 1947; Mem. Cttee, 1974-77; Dep. Chm., 1979. *Recreations:* shooting, fishing, sailing, working. *Address:* Lloyd's, Lime Street, EC3M 7HL. *T:* 01-623 7100. *Clubs:* City of London, Royal Ocean Racing, Pratt's; Royal Yacht Squadron (Cowes).

GREEN, Prof. Peter Morris; author and translator since 1953; Professor of Classics, University of Texas at Austin, since 1972; *b* 22 Dec. 1924; *o c* of late Arthur Green, CBE, MC, LLB, and of Olive Slaughter; *m* 1st, 1951, Lalage Isobel Pulvertaft (marr. diss.); two *s* one *d*; 2nd, 1975, Carin Margreta, *y d* of G. N. Christensen, Saratoga, USA. *Educ:* Charterhouse; Trinity Coll., Cambridge. Served in RAFVR, 1943-47: overseas tour in Burma Comd, 1944-46. 1st Cl. Hons, Pts I and II, Classical Tripos, 1949-50; MA and PhD Cantab 1954; Craven Schol. and Student, 1950; Dir of Studies in Classics, 1951-52; Fiction Critic, London Daily Telegraph, 1953-63; Literary Adviser, The Bodley Head, 1957-58; Cons. Editor, Hodder and Stoughton, 1960-63; Television Critic, The Listener, 1961-63; Film Critic, John o'London's, 1961-63; Mem. Book Soc. Cttee, 1959-63. Former Mem. of selection cttees for literary prizes: Heinemann Award, John Llewellyn Rhys, W. H. Smith £1000 Award for Literature. Translator of numerous works from French and Italian, including books by Simone de Beauvoir, Fosco Maraini, Joseph Kessel. FRSL 1956; Mem. Council, Royal Society of Literature, 1958-63 (resigned on emigration). In 1963 resigned all positions and emigrated to Greece as full-time writer. Vis. Prof. of Classics: Univ. of Texas, 1971-72; UCLA, 1976. *Publications:* The Expanding Eye, 1953; Achilles His Armour, 1955; Cat in Gloves (pseud. Denis Delaney), 1956; The Sword of Pleasure (W. H. Heinemann Award for Literature), 1957; Kenneth Grahame, 1859-1932: A Study of his Life, Work and Times, 1959; Essays in Antiquity, 1960; Habeas Corpus and other stories, 1962; Look at the Romans, 1963; The Laughter of Aphrodite, 1965; Juvenal: The Sixteen Satires (trans.), 1967; Armada from Athens: The Failure of the Sicilian Expedition, 415-413 BC, 1970; Alexander the Great: a biography, 1970; The Year of Salamis, 480-479 BC, 1971; The Shadow of the Parthenon, 1972; The Parthenon, 1973; A Concise History of Ancient Greece, 1973; Alexander of Macedon 356-323 BC: a historical biography, 1974; Ovid: The Erotic Poems (trans.), 1982. *Recreations:* travel, swimming, spear-fishing, lawn tennis, table-tennis, squash racquets, amateur archæology, avoiding urban life. *Address:* c/o Department of Classics, University of Texas, Waggener Hall 123, Austin, Texas 78712, USA. *T:* 512 471-5742. *Club:* Savile.

GREEN, Maj.-Gen. Robert Leslie Stuart; Executive Governor, Care for the Mentally Handicapped, since 1980; *b* 1 July 1925; *s* of Leslie Stuart Green and Eliza Dorothea Andrew; *m* 1942, Nancy Isobel Collier; two *d*. *Educ:* Chorlton Sch. 2nd Bn Black Watch, India, 1944-46; 6 Airborne Div., Palestine, 1946; 2 Parachute Bde, UK and Germany, 1946-47; 1st Bn HLI, UK, ME and Cyprus, 1947-56; ptsc 1959; jssc 1962; 1st Bn Royal Highland Fusiliers, UK, Germany and Gibraltar, 1959-69, Comd 1967-69; staff apptmt 1970; Military Dir of Studies, RMCS, 1970-72; Sen. Military Officer, Royal Armament Res. and Develt Estabt, 1973-75; Vice-Pres., Ordnance Bd, 1976-78, Pres., March-June 1978. Col, The Royal Highland Fusiliers, 1979-. Associate, Henderson Financial Management, 1980-. FBIM. *Recreations:* rough shooting, painting, music and sailing. *Address:* Williams & Glyn's Bank, 43 Curzon Street, Mayfair, W1. *Club:* Naval and Military.

GREEN, Roger (Gilbert) Lancelyn; author; *b* 2 Nov. 1918; *s* of Major G. A. L. Green, MC, RFA, and H. M. P. Sealy; *m* 1948, June, *d* of S. H. Burdett, Northampton; two *s* one *d*. *Educ:* Dane Court Sch., Surrey; Liverpool Coll.; privately; Merton Coll., Oxford (MA, BLitt). Part-time professional actor, 1942-45; Dep. Librarian, Merton Coll., Oxford, 1945-50; William Nobel Research Fellow in Eng. Lit., Liverpool Univ., 1950-52; Mem. Council, Univ. of Liverpool, 1964-70; Andrew Lang Lectr, Univ. of St Andrews, 1968. Editor, Kipling Journal, 1957-79. Mythopoeic Schol. Award (USA), 1975. Hon. DLitt Liverpool, 1981. *Publications:* The Lost July, and other poems, 1945; Tellers of Tales, 1946, rev. edn 1965; The Searching Satyrs, 1946; Andrew Lang: a critical biography, 1946; The Sleeping Beauty, and other tales, 1947; The Singing Rose, and other poems, 1947; From the World's End: a fantasy, 1948, repr. USA 1971; Beauty and the Beast, and other tales, 1948; Poulton-Lancelyn: the story of an ancestral home, 1948; The Story of Lewis Carroll, 1949; The Wonderful Stranger, 1950; The Luck of the Lynns, 1952; A. E. W. Mason: a biography, 1952; The Secret of Rusticoker, 1953; King Arthur and his Knights of the Round Table, 1953, 8th edn 1967; The Diaries of Lewis Carroll, 1953; Fifty Years of Peter Pan, 1954; The Theft of the Golden Cat, 1955; The Adventures of Robin Hood, 1956, 6th edn 1966; Mystery at Mycenae, 1957; Two Satyr Plays (Penguin Classics), 1957; Into Other Worlds: space flight in fiction from Lucian to Lewis, 1957; Old Greek Fairy Tales, 1958; The Land Beyond the North, 1958; The Land of the Lord High Tiger, 1958; Tales of the Greek Heroes, 1958, 8th edn 1973; The Tale of Troy, 1958, 10th edn 1973; Lewis Carroll, 1960; The Saga of Asgard, 1960, 3rd edn as Myths of the Norsemen, 1970; J. M. Barrie, 1960; The True Book About Ancient Greece, 1960; The Luck of Troy, 1961, 4th edn 1973; Mrs Molesworth, 1961; Ancient Greece, 1962; Andrew Lang, 1962; The Lewis Carroll Handbook, 1962; Once, Long Ago, 1962; C. S. Lewis, 1963; Authors and Places, 1963; Ancient Egypt, 1963; Tales of the Greeks and Trojans, 1964;

Tales from Shakespeare, 2 vols, 1964-65; A Book of Myths, 1965; Tales the Muses Told, 1965; Myths from Many Lands, 1965; Kipling and the Children, 1965; Andrew Lang: the greatest bookman of his age (Indiana Bookman), 1965; Folk Tales of the World, 1966; Sir Lancelot of the Lake, 1966; Tales of Ancient Egypt, 1967; Stories of Ancient Greece, 1968; Jason and the Golden Fleece, 1968; The Tale of Ancient Israel, 1969; St Andrew's Church, Bebington: a short history, 1969; The Book of Dragons, 1970; Kipling: the critical heritage, 1971; The Book of Magicians, 1973; (with Walter Hooper) C. S. Lewis: a biography, 1974; Holmes, this is Amazing: essays in unorthodox research, 1975; The Book of Other Worlds, 1976; The Tale of Thebes, 1977; (with M. N. Cohen) The Letters of Lewis Carroll, 2 vols, 1979. *Recreations:* book collecting, Greece Ancient and Modern, Greek and Roman theatre. *Address:* Poulton Hall, Poulton-Lancelyn, Bebington, Wirral, Merseyside L63 9LN. *T:* 051-334 2057. *Clubs:* Arts, Players, National Book League.

GREEN, Roger James N.; *see* Northcote-Green.

GREEN, Sam, CBE 1960; Chairman: Dula (ISMA) Ltd, since 1969; Green & Associates Ltd, since 1970; Spear Bros Ltd, since 1970; Vice Chairman, Royal British Legion Poppy Factory, Richmond (Director since 1964); Director, Royal British Legion Industries, since 1967; *b* Oldham, Lancs, 6 Feb. 1907; *s* of Fred Green; *m* 1942, Dr Lilly (*née* Pollak); one *d*. *Educ:* Manchester Coll. of Technology. Apprentice, Platt Bros, Oldham, 1920-34; Designer and Development Engr, British Northrop Automatic Loom Co., Blackburn, 1934-39 (invented 4-colour loom); Chief Engr, Betts & Co., London, 1939-42; Works Manager, Morphy-Richards Ltd, St Mary Cray, Kent, 1942-44; General Works Manager, Holoplast Ltd, New Hythe, near Maidstone, 1944-47; Industrial Adviser, Industrial and Commercial Finance Corp., London, 1947-52; Managing Dir of Remploy Ltd, 1952-64; Chm. and Man. Dir, Ralli Bros (Industries) Ltd, 1964-69; Chm., Industrial Advisers to the Blind, 1964-74; Director: J. E. Lesser Group Ltd, 1969-74; New Day Holdings Ltd, 1972-74. Chm., Inst. of Patentees and Inventors, 1975 (Vice-Chm., 1961). FRSA 1962. CEng; FIEE; FIProdE. *Recreations:* reading, gardening, cycling, walking, golf. *Address:* Holly Lodge, 39 Westmoreland Road, Bromley, Kent BR2 0TF. *T:* 01-460 3306. *Clubs:* Reform, Directors', Pickwick (oldest Bicycle Club).

GREEN, Sir Stephen; *see* Green, Sir E. S. L.

GREEN, Thomas Charles, CB 1971; Chief Charity Commissioner, 1966-75; *b* 13 Oct. 1915; *s* of late Charles Harold Green and late Hilda Emma Green (*née* Thomas); *m* 1945, Beryl Eva Barber, *widow* of Lieut N. Barber; one *d* (and one step *d*). *Educ:* Eltham Coll.; Oriel Coll., Oxford. Entered Home Office, 1938. Served with RAF, 1940-45. Asst Secretary: Home Office, 1950-64; Charity Commn, 1964-65. UK representative on UN Commn on Narcotic Drugs, 1957-64. Nuffield Travelling Fellowship, 1959-60. *Recreations:* gardening, photography. *Address:* Silver Birch Cottage, Burntwood Road, Sevenoaks, Kent.

GREEN, Rev. Vivian Hubert Howard, DD, FRHistS; Fellow and Tutor in History, Lincoln College, Oxford, since 1951, and Sub-Rector, since 1970 (Senior Tutor 1953-62, 1974-77; Chaplain, 1951-69; acting Rector, 1972-73); *b* 18 Nov. 1915; *s* of Hubert James and Edith Eleanor Playle Green; unmarried. *Educ:* Bradfield Coll., Berks; Trinity Hall, Cambridge (Scholar). Goldsmiths' Exhibnr; 1st Cl. Hist. Tripos, Parts I and II; Lightfoot Schol. in Ecclesiastical Hist.; Thirlwall Medal and Prize, 1941; MA 1941; MA Oxon by incorp., 1951; DD Cambridge, 1958; DD Oxon by incorp., 1958. Gladstone Research Studentship, St Deiniol's Library, Hawarden, 1937-38; Fellow of St Augustine's Coll., Canterbury, 1939-48; Chaplain, Exeter Sch. and St Luke's Training Coll., Exeter, 1940-42; Chaplain and Asst Master, Sherborne Sch., Dorset, 1942-51. Deacon, 1939; Priest, 1940. Select Preacher, Oxford, 1959-60. Vis. Prof. of History, Univ. of S Carolina, 1982. *Publications:* Bishop Reginald Pecock, 1945; The Hanoverians, 1948; From St Augustine to William Temple, 1948; Renaissance and Reformation, 1952; The Later Plantagenets, 1955; Oxford Common Room, 1957; The Young Mr Wesley, 1961; The Swiss Alps, 1961; Martin Luther and the Reformation, 1964; John Wesley, 1964; Religion at Oxford and Cambridge (historical survey), 1964; The Universities, 1969; Medieval Civilization in Western Europe, 1971; A History of Oxford University, 1974; The Commonwealth of Lincoln College 1427-1977, 1979; contributor to: Dictionary of English Church History (ed Ollard, Crosse and Bond); The Oxford Dictionary of the Christian Church (ed Cross). *Address:* Lincoln College, Oxford. *T:* Oxford 43658; Calendars, Burford, Oxford. *T:* Burford 3214.

GREEN-PRICE, Sir Robert (John), 5th Bt, *cr* 1874; *b* 22 Oct. 1940; *o s* of Sir John Green-Price, 4th Bt, and Irene Marion (*d* 1954), *d* of Major Sir (Ernest) Guy Lloyd, 1st Bt, *qv*; *S* father, 1964. *Educ:* Shrewsbury. Army Officer, 1961-69; Captain, RCT, retd. ADC to Governor of Bermuda, 1969-72. *Heir: kinsman* John Chase Green-Price, *b* 27 June 1947. *Address:* Gwernaffel, Knighton, Powys. *T:* Knighton 528580.

GREENALL, family name of **Baron Daresbury.**

GREENAWAY, Alan Pearce, JP; Vice-President, Daniel Greenaway & Sons Ltd, since 1978 (Joint Managing Director, 1951-78; Vice-Chairman, 1965-76; Chairman, 1976-78); *b* 25 Nov. 1913; *yr s* of Sir Percy Walter Greenaway, 1st Bt, and Lydie Amy (*d* 1962), *er d* of James Burdick; *m* 1948, Patricia Frances (*d* 1982), *yr d* of Ald. Sir Frederick Wells, 1st Bt; one *s* one *d*. *Educ:*

Canford. Served in King's Liverpool Regt during War of 1939-45, reaching rank of Captain. Liveryman: Worshipful Co. of Merchant Taylors; Worshipful Co. of Stationers and Newspaper Makers (Under-Warden 1971-72, Upper Warden, 1972-73, Master 1973-74). Mem. Court of Common Council for Ward of Bishopsgate, 1952-65; Sheriff for the City of London, 1962-63; JP, Co. London, 1964; Alderman, Lime Street Ward, City of London, 1965-72; Chm. and Treasurer, City of London Sheriffs' Soc., 1979. Officer, l'Ordre de la Valeur Camerounaise, 1963; Commandeur, l'Ordre de Leopold Class III, 1963; Commander, Royal Order of the Phoenix, 1964. *Recreations:* golf, fishing, swimming. *Address:* The Doone, Byfleet Road, Cobham, Surrey KT11 1EA; Greenaway House, 132 Commercial Street, EC1 6NF. *T:* 01-247 4343. *Clubs:* City Livery (Vice-Pres. 1971-72, Pres., 1972-73), Royal Automobile, United Wards; St George's Hill Golf.

GREENAWAY, Sir Derek (Burdick), 2nd Bt *cr* 1933; CBE 1974; TD; JP; DL; First Life President, Daniel Greenaway & Sons Ltd, 132 Commercial Street, E1, since 1976 (Chairman, 1956-76); *b* 27 May 1910; *er s* of Sir Percy Walter Greenaway, 1st Bt and Lydie Amy (*d* 1962), *er d* of James Burdick; *S* father 1956; *m* 1937, Sheila Beatrice, *d* of late Richard Cyril Lockett, 58 Cadogan Place, SW1; one *s* one *d*. *Educ:* Marlborough. Served in Field Artillery during War of 1939-45; Hon. Col: 44 (HC) Signal Regt (Cinque Ports) TA, 1946; 36th (Eastern) Signal Regt (V), 1967-74. Joint Master, Old Surrey and Burstow Foxhounds, 1958-66. Chm. Sevenoaks Constituency C & U Assoc., 1960-63; Pres. 1963-66; Vice Pres., 1966-. Asst Area Treasurer, SE Area Nat. Union of Cons. Assocs, 1966-69, Area Treasurer, 1969-75, Chm. 1975-79. Master, Stationers' and Newspapermakers Co., 1974-75. JP County of Kent, 1962-; High Sheriff, 1971, DL 1973, Kent. FRSA. Life Mem., Assoc. of Men of Kent and Kentish Men. *Recreations:* hunting, shooting. *Heir: s* John Michael Burdick Greenaway [*b* 9 Aug. 1944; *m* 1982, Susan M., *d* of Henry Birch, Tattenhall, Cheshire. Late Lieut, The Life Guards]. *Address:* Dunmore, Four Elms, Edenbridge, Kent. *T:* Four Elms 275. *Clubs:* Carlton, City of London, MCC.

See also A. P. Greenaway, H. F. R. Sturge.

GREENAWAY, Frank, MA, PhD; CChem, FRSC, FSA, FMA; Keeper, Department of Chemistry, The Science Museum, 1967-80; Reader in the History of Science, Davy-Faraday Research Laboratory of the Royal Institution, since 1970; *b* 9 July 1917; 3rd *s* of late Henry James Greenaway; *m* 1942, Margaret (Miranda), 2nd *d* of late R. G. Heegaard Warner and *widow* of John Raymond Brumfit; two *s* three *d*. *Educ:* Cardiff High Sch.; Jesus Coll., Oxford (Meyricke Exhibitioner); University Coll. London. MA Oxon, PhD London. Served War of 1939-45, RAOC, as Inspecting Ordnance Officer, 1940-41 (invalided). Science Master: Bournemouth Sch., 1941-42; Epsom Gram. Sch., 1942-43; Research Labs, Kodak Ltd, 1944-49; Asst Keeper, Science Museum, 1949; Dep. Keeper, 1959; Keeper, 1967. Mem. Council: Brit. Soc. for the Hist. of Science, 1958-68, 1974-78 (Vice-Pres. 1962-65); Museums Assoc., 1961-70, 1973-76 (Hon. Editor, 1965-70). Chm., Cttee of Visitors, Royal Instn, 1964-65; Mem. Brit. Nat. Cttee of Internat. Council of Museums, 1956-58, 1962-71, 1977-; Membre Correspondant de l'Académie Internationale d'Histoire des Sciences, 1963. Member: Council, Soc. for History of Alchemy and Chemistry, 1967- (Sec., 1967-74); History of Medicine Adv. Panel, The Wellcome Trust, 1968-74; Higher Educn Adv. Cttee, The Open Univ., 1970-73; British Nat. Cttee for Hist. of Sci., 1972-81; British Nat. Cttee, ICSU, 1972-77; Council, Internat. Union of the Hist. and Philos. of Science, 1972-81 (Sec., 1972-77); Council of Management, Royal Philharmonic Soc., 1980-; Pres., Commonwealth Assoc. of Museums, 1979-. Boerhaave Medal, Leyden Univ., 1968. *Publications:* Science Museums in Developing Countries, 1962; John Dalton and the Atom, 1966; (ed) Lavoisier's Essays Physical and Chemical, 1971; Editor, Royal Institution Archives, 1971-; Official Publications of the Science Museum; Papers on history of chemistry and on museology. *Recreations:* music, travel. *Address:* 135 London Road, Ewell, Epsom, Surrey. *T:* 01-393 1330. *Club:* Athenæum.

GREENBOROUGH, Sir John Hedley, KBE 1979 (CBE 1975); Chairman, Newarthill, since 1980; Director: Bowater Corporation, since 1979; Lloyds Bank, since 1980; Hogg Robinson Group, since 1980; *b* 7 July 1922; *s* of William Greenborough and Elizabeth Marie Greenborough (*née* Wilson); *m* 1951, Gerta Ebel; one step *s*. *Educ:* Wandsworth School. War service: Pilot, RAF, later Fleet Air Arm, 1942-45; graduated Pensacola; Naval Aviator, USN, 1944. Joined Asiatic Petroleum Co., London, 1939; served with Shell Oil, Calif, 1946-47; Shell Brazil Ltd, 1948-57; Commercial Dir, later Exec. Vice-Pres., Shell Argentina Ltd, Buenos Aires, 1960-66; Area Coordinator, East and Australasia, Shell Internat., London, 1967-68; Man. Dir (Marketing), Shell-Mex and BP Ltd, 1969-71, Man. Dir and Chief Exec., 1971-75; Chm., UK Oil Pipelines Ltd, 1971-77; Dep. Chm., 1976-80, Man. Dir, 1976-78, Shell UK Ltd. President of Confederation of British Industry, 1978-80 (Mem. Council, 1971-). Chairman: UK Oil Ind. Emergency Cttee, 1971-80; UK Petroleum Ind. Adv. Cttee, 1971-77; Member: British Productivity Council, 1969-72; Clean Air Council, 1971-75; Bd of Fellows, BIM, 1973-78 (Chm., 1976-78); NEDC, 1977-80; Vice-Chairman: British Chamber of Commerce in Argentina, 1962-66; British Road Fedn, 1969-75. President: Nat. Soc. for Clean Air, 1973-75; Incorporated Soc. of British Advertisers (ISBA), 1976-78; Inst. of Petroleum, 1976-78; Nat. Council of Voluntary Orgns, 1980-. Fellow, Inst. Petroleum; FBIM. Governor, Ashridge Management Coll., 1972- (Chm., 1977-); Chm. Governing Council, Utd Med. Schs of Guy's and St Thomas' Hosps, 1982-. Liveryman, Co. of Distillers, 1975-. Freeman, City of London. *Recreations:* golf, travel, music. *Address:* 30 Burghley House, Oakfield,

---

Somerset Road, Wimbledon Common, SW19. *Clubs:* Carlton, MCC; Royal and Ancient Golf; Royal Wimbledon Golf.

GREENBURY, Richard; Joint Managing Director, Marks & Spencer Ltd, since 1978; *b* 31 July 1936; *s* of Richard Oswald Greenbury and Dorothy (*née* Lewis); *m* 1959, Sian Eames Hughes; two *s* two *d*. *Educ:* Ealing County Grammar Sch. Joined Marks & Spencer Ltd as Jun. Management Trainee, 1953; Alternate Dir, 1970; Full Dir, 1972. Part-time Dir, British Gas Corp., 1976-. *Recreation:* tennis (Member Mddx County Team for 12 years, has also played for International Tennis Club of GB). *Address:* 10 Tite Street, SW3. *Club:* International Tennis Club of GB.

GREENE, family name of **Baron Greene of Harrow Weald.**

GREENE OF HARROW WEALD, Baron *cr* 1974 (Life Peer), of Harrow; **Sidney Francis Greene,** Kt 1970; CBE 1966; Director: Trades Union Unit Trust, since 1970; RTZ Corporation, 1975-80; Times Newspapers Holdings Ltd, 1980-82 (Times Newspapers Ltd, 1975-80); *b* 12 Feb. 1910; *s* of Frank James Greene and Alice (*née* Kerrod); *m* 1936, Masel Elizabeth Carter; three *d*. *Educ:* elementary. Joined Railway Service, 1924; appointed Union Organiser, 1944, Asst Gen. Sec., 1954, Gen. Sec., Nat. Union of Railwaymen, 1957-74. Mem., TUC Gen. Council, 1957-75 (Chm., 1969-70); Chm., TUC Economic Cttee, 1968-75. Member: National Economic Development Council, 1962-75; Advisory Council, ECGD, 1967-70; part-time Member: Southern Electricity Board, 1964-77; Nat. Freight Corp., 1973-77; a Dir, Bank of England, 1970-78. JP London, 1941-65. FCIT. *Recreations:* reading, gardening. *Address:* 26 Kynaston Wood, Boxtree Road, Harrow Weald, Mddx HA3 6UA.

GREENE, Edward Reginald, CMG 1953; FRSA; art dealer; *b* Santos, Brazil, 26 Nov. 1904; *s* of late Edward Greene and of Eva Greene; *m* Irmingard Fischges. *Educ:* Bedales Sch.; St John's Coll., Cambridge (BA 1926). After Continental banking experience joined coffee merchant firm E. Johnston & Co. Ltd, 1927; has since travelled and traded in coffee, Brazil, USA, East Africa, Continent, Dir of Coffee, Ministry of Food, 1943, subsequently Dir of Raw Cocoa; resigned 1952. Hon. Vice-Pres., Brazilian Chamber of Commerce, 1968-. Mem., The Cambridge Soc. FRSA 1971. *Recreations:* painting, antiques. *Address:* Orbell House, Castle Hedingham, Essex. *T:* Hedingham 60298. *Clubs:* City of London, Garrick.

GREENE, Felix; freelance writer, broadcaster and film-maker; *b* 21 May 1909; *s* of Edward and Eva Greene; *m* 1945, Elena Lindeman; one *d*. *Educ:* Sidcot Sch.: Clare Coll., Cambridge. Parliamentary candidate (Nat. Lab), 1931; Talks Dept, BBC, 1933; first BBC foreign rep., N America, 1936; seconded to FO to visit all capitals in S America and prepare report for Cabinet on German and Italian propaganda, 1938; at request of Canadian Govt travelled to all radio stations in Canada and wrote basic draft of constitution of CBC, 1938-39; resigned from BBC, 1940; Amer. Friends Service Cttee (Quaker), 1941; with Aldous Huxley, Gerald Heard and Christopher Isherwood, founded Trabuco Coll., Calif, 1943. Active in US movement against the war in Vietnam and continued non-recognition of People's Republic of China; first visit to China, 1957, frequent visits since; returned to reside UK, 1968. Chm., Soc. for Anglo-Chinese Understanding, 1974, Vice-Pres. 1977-. Produced and directed films (most of which widely shown in western countries, some receiving internat. awards): China!, 1963; The Peking Symphony Orchestra, 1963; Inside North Vietnam, 1967; Cuba Va!, 1968; series of 8 films under gen. title One Man's China, 1972; Freedom Railway (The Tanzam Railway), 1974; Tibet, 1977. Filmed interviews with: Premier Chou En-lai, 1960, 1963, 1972; President Ho Chi Minh, 1965; Chairman Hua Guofeng, 1979; Vice-Premier Deng Xiaoping, 1979; unofficial discussions with, *inter alios*, the Dalai Lama, Robert McNamara, U Thant, Nehru, Pres. Roosevelt, Pres. Truman. Has lectured at all senior univs in US. Member: RIIA; PEN. Hon. LitD, USA, 1963. *Publications:* (most of which trans. into other languages): ed, Time to Spare, 1935; What's Really Happening in China?, 1959; The Wall has Two Sides, 1961; Let There be a World, 1963, rev. edn 1982; Vietnam! Vietnam!, 1966; The Enemy: notes on Imperialism and Revolutionism, 1970; Peking, 1978; articles in Sunday Times, Observer, Life, Paris Match, etc. *Address:* 8 York House, Upper Montagu Street, W1. *T:* 01-262 5905; PO Box 272, San Miguel de Allende Gto, Mexico.

See also E. R. Greene.

GREENE, Graham, CH 1966; Hon. LittD, Cambridge, 1962; Hon. Fellow of Balliol, 1963; Hon. DLitt: Edinburgh, 1967; Oxford, 1979; Chevalier de la Légion d'Honneur, 1967; *b* 2 Oct. 1904; *s* of late Charles Henry Greene; *m* 1927, Vivien Dayrell-Browning; one *s* one *d*. *Educ:* Berkhamsted; Balliol Coll., Oxford. On staff of The Times, 1926-30; Literary Editor, The Spectator, 1940-41; department of Foreign Office, 1941-44. Director: Eyre & Spottiswoode Ltd, 1944-48; Bodley Head, 1958-68. Mem., Panamanian delegn to Washington for signing of Canal Treaty, 1977. Shakespeare Prize, Hamburg, 1968; John Dos Passos Prize, 1980; Medal, City of Madrid, 1980; Jerusalem Prize, 1981. Hon. Citizen, Anacapri, 1978. *Publications:* Babbling April, 1925; The Man Within, 1929; The Name of Action, 1930; Rumour at Nightfall, 1931; Stamboul Train, 1932; It's a Battlefield, 1934; The Old School (Editor), 1934; The Bear Fell Free (limited edn), 1935; England Made Me, 1935; The Basement Room (short stories), 1935; Journey without Maps (account of a journey through Liberia), 1936; A Gun for Sale, 1936; Brighton Rock, 1938; The Lawless Roads, 1939; The Confidential Agent, 1939; The Power and the Glory, 1940 (Hawthornden Prize for 1940); British Dramatists,

1942; The Ministry of Fear, 1943; Nineteen Stories, 1947; The Heart of the Matter, 1948; The Third Man, 1950; The End of the Affair, 1951; The Lost Childhood and other essays, 1951; Essais Catholiques, 1953; Twenty one Stories, 1954; Loser Takes All, 1955; The Quiet American, 1955; Our Man in Havana, 1958; A Burnt-Out Case, 1961; In Search of a Character, Two African Journals, 1961; A Sense of Reality, 1963; The Comedians, 1966; May we borrow your Husband? And other Comedies of the Sexual Life (short stories), 1967; Collected Essays, 1969; Travels with my Aunt, 1969; A Sort of Life (autobiog.), 1971; The Pleasure-Dome: the collected film criticism 1935-40, ed John Russell Taylor, 1972; Collected Stories, 1972; The Honorary Consul, 1973; Lord Rochester's Monkey, 1974; (ed) An Impossible Woman: the Memories of Dottoressa Moor of Capri, 1975; The Human Factor, 1978 (filmed, 1979); Dr Fischer of Geneva, 1980; Ways of Escape (autobiog.), 1980; J'Accuse: the dark side of Nice, 1982; Monsignor Quixote, 1982; plays: The Living Room, 1953; The Potting Shed, 1957 (filmed for TV, 1981); The Complaisant Lover, 1959; Carving a Statue, 1964; The Return of A. J. Raffles, 1975; Yes and No, 1980; For Whom the Bell Chimes, 1980; The Great Jowett, 1981; for children: The Little Train, 1947; The Little Fire Engine, 1950; The Little Horse Bus, 1952; The Little Steamroller, 1953; film plays: Brighton Rock, 1948; The Fallen Idol, 1948; The Third Man, 1949; Our Man in Havana, 1960; The Comedians, 1967. Address: c/o The Bodley Head, 9 Bow Street, WC2.
See also R. O. Dennys, Sir Hugh Greene and Raymond Greene.

GREENE, Graham Carleton; Managing Director, Jonathan Cape Ltd, since 1966, and Joint Chairman, Chatto, Bodley Head & Jonathan Cape Ltd, since 1970; b 10 June 1936; s of Sir Hugh Carleton Greene, qv, and Helga Mary Connolly; m 1957, Judith Margaret (marr. diss.), d of Rt Hon. Lord Gordon-Walker, CH, PC; m 1976, Sally Georgina Horton, d of Sidney Wilfred Eaton; one s. Educ: Eton; University Coll., Oxford (MA). Merchant Banking, Dublin, New York and London, 1957-58; Publishing: Secker & Warburg Ltd, 1958-62; Jonathan Cape, 1962- (Dir, 1962). Director: Chatto, Bodley Head & Jonathan Cape Ltd, 1969; Jackdaw Publications Ltd (Chm. 1964); Cape Goliard Press Ltd, 1967; Guinness Mahon Holdings Ltd, 1968-79; Australasian Publishing Co. Pty Ltd, 1969 (Chm., 1978); Sprint Productions Ltd, 1971-80; Book Reps (New Zealand) Ltd, 1971; Chatto, Bodley Head & Cape Services Ltd (Chm. 1972); Guinness Peat Group Ltd, 1973; Grantham Book Storage Ltd (Chm. 1974); Triad Paperbacks Ltd, 1975; Chatto, Bodley Head & Jonathan Cape Australia Pty Ltd (Chm., 1977-); Greene, King & Sons Ltd, 1979; Statesman & Nation Publishing Co. Ltd, 1980 (Chm., 1981-); Statesman Publishing Co., 1980 (Chm., 1981-). Pres., Publishers Assoc., 1977-79 (Mem. Council, 1969-); Member: Book Develt Council, 1970-79 (Dep. Chm., 1972-73); Internat. Cttee. Internat. Publishers Assoc., 1977- (Exec. Cttee, 1981-); Groupe des Editeurs de Livres de la CEE, 1977-; Member: Arts Council Working Party Sub-Cttee on Public Lending Right, 1970; Paymaster General's Working Party on Public Lending Right, 1970-72; Board, British Council, 1977-; Chm., Nat. Book League, 1974-76 (Dep. Chm., 1971-74); Mem. Gen. Cttee, Royal Literary Fund, 1975. Trustee, British Museum, 1978-. Leader, 1st deleg. British publishers to China, 1978, etc. Address: 30 Bedford Square, WC1B 3EL. T: 01-636 5767.

GREENE, Sir Hugh (Carleton), KCMG 1964; OBE 1950; Hon. President, The Bodley Head, since 1981 (Chairman, 1969-81); Chairman, Greene, King & Sons Ltd, Westgate Brewery, Bury St Edmunds, 1971-78; Member, Observer Editorial Trust, 1969-76; b Nov. 1910; s of late Charles Henry Greene; m 1934, Helga Guinness (marr. diss.); two s; m 1951, Elaine Shaplen (marr. diss.); two s; m 1970, Tatjana Sais (d 1981). Educ: Berkhamsted; Merton Coll., Oxford (MA). Daily Telegraph Berlin staff, 1934; Chief Correspondent, 1938; expelled from Germany as reprisal, May 1939; Warsaw correspondent, 1939; after the outbreak of war reported events in Poland, Rumania, Bulgaria, Turkey, Holland, Belgium, and France. Joined BBC as head of German Service, 1940, after service in RAF; Controller of Broadcasting in British Zone of Germany, 1946-48; Head of BBC East European Service, 1949-50; Head of Emergency Information Services, Federation of Malaya, 1950-51; Asst Controller, BBC Overseas Services, 1952-55; Controller, Overseas Services, 1955-56; Chm. Federal Commn of Inquiry into Organisation of Broadcasting in Fed. of Rhodesia and Nyasaland, 1955; Dir of Administration, BBC, 1956-58; Dir, News and Current Affairs, BBC, 1958-59; Director-General, 1960-69; a Governor, BBC, 1969-71. Vice-Pres., European Broadcasting Union, 1963-69; Chm., European-Atlantic Action Cttee on Greece, 1971-74. Reported for Govt of Israel on Israel Broadcasting Authority, 1973; reported for Greek Govt on constitution of Greek broadcasting, 1975. CBIM, 1966. Hon. DCL E Anglia, 1969; DUniv Open Univ., 1973; DUniv York, 1973. Grand Cross, Order of Merit (Germany), 1977. Publications: The Spy's Bedside Book (with Graham Greene), 1957; The Third Floor Front, 1969; The Rivals of Sherlock Holmes, 1970; More Rivals of Sherlock Holmes: cosmopolitan crimes, 1971; The Future of Broadcasting in Britain, 1972; The Crooked Counties, 1973; The American Rivals of Sherlock Holmes, 1976; (ed) The Pirate of the Round Pond and Other Strange Adventure Stories, 1977. Address: Earl's Hall, Cockfield, near Bury St Edmunds, Suffolk.
See also R. O. Dennys, Graham Greene, Graham C. Greene and Raymond Greene.

GREENE, Ian Rawdon; b 3 March 1909; o s of Rawdon Greene and Marie Louise, Rahan, Bray, County Wicklow, Ireland; m 1937, Eileen Theodora Stack; one d. Educ: Cheltenham Coll.; Trinity Coll., Dublin (BA, LLB). Crown Counsel, Tanganyika, 1935; Resident Magistrate, Zanzibar, 1937.

Military Service, Kenya, 1940-41. Sen. Resident Magistrate, Zanzibar, 1950; Actg Asst Judge, Zanzibar, on numerous occasions; Actg Chief Justice, Zanzibar, June 1954, and May-Oct. 1955; Judge-in-charge, Somaliland Protectorate, 1955; Chief Justice, Somaliland Protectorate, 1958-60, retired; Stipendiary Magistrate, North Borneo, 1961-64. Registrar to Dean and Chapter, St Patrick's Cathedral, Dublin, 1973-82. Order of Brilliant Star of Zanzibar (4th Cl.), 1953. Publications: Jt Ed., Vols VI and VII, Zanzibar Law Reports. Recreations: cricket, golf, bridge, chess. Address: Malindi, Kilmacanogue, Co. Wicklow, Ireland. T: Dublin 867322. Clubs: The Victory (Services) Association; English (Zanzibar); Hargeisa (Somaliland).

GREENE, Sir (John) Brian M.; see Massy-Greene.

GREENE, Dame Judith; see Anderson, Dame Judith.

GREENE, Raymond; Chevalier of the Legion of Honour; Hon. Consultant Physician, Royal Northern Hospital, Royal Free Hospital and St Luke's Hospital for Clergy; b 17 April 1901; s of late Charles Henry Greene, MA, FRHistSoc; m 1934, Eleanor Craven, d of late Hamilton Gamble, St Louis, USA; one s one d. Educ: Berkhamsted; Pembroke Coll., Oxford (Theodore Williams Scholar in Medicine and Senior Open Scholar); Westminster Hospital (Scholar in Anatomy and Physiology), BA (Hons) Oxon. 1924, MA 1927, DM 1935; MRCP, 1943; FRCP 1954; held various appointments at Westminster Hospital, Queen Charlotte's Hospital, and Radcliffe Infirmary, Oxford. Mem. Kamet Expedition, 1931; Mem. Everest Expedition, 1933. Schorstein Research Fellow in Medical Science, University of Oxford, 1932-34; Senior Clinical Asst in charge of the Endocrine Clinic, Westminster Hosp., 1938-45; Physician: Metropolitan Hosp., 1945-54; Whittington Hosp., 1948-66. Dir, Heinemann Medical Books, 1960-80, Chm., 1970-80. Formerly Chm., Nuffield Inst. of Comparative Medicine. Hunterian Professor, RCS of England, 1943 and 1956; Sandoz Lectr, Inst. of Neurology, 1972. Mem. British Pharmacopœia Commission, 1948-53; Vice-Pres., Royal Society of Medicine and Pres. Section of Endocrinology, 1953, Hon. Mem. 1973; Chm. Fourth Internat. Goitre Conf., 1960; Vice-Pres., Fifth Internat. Thyroid Conf., 1965; Vice-Pres., European Thyroid Assoc., 1966; Corresp. Mem., Amer. Thyroid Assoc.; Ex-Pres., Thyroid Club; Vice-Pres., Alpine Club, 1948-49; Hon. Mem., Oxford Univ. Exploration Club and Oxford Univ. Mountaineering Club. FZS (formerly Vice-Pres.). Publications: The Practice of Endocrinology, 1948; Myasthenia Gravis, 1969; Human Hormones, 1970; Sick Doctors, 1971; (jtly) Benign Enlargement of the Prostate, 1973; Moments of Being, 1974; (jtly) Colour Atlas of Endocrinology, 1979; many scientific and medical papers on the effects of great altitude and exposure to cold, and on endocrinology. Recreations: formerly mountain climbing and travel. Address: 10 Cheltenham Terrace, Chelsea, SW3 4RD. T: 01-730 1434. Clubs: Athenæum, Alpine.
See also R. O. Dennys, Graham and Sir Hugh Greene.

GREENEWALT, Crawford Hallock; Director and Member of the Finance Committee, E. I. du Pont de Nemours & Co., Inc. (Chairman, 1967-74); b Cummington, Mass, 16 Aug. 1902; s of Frank Lindsay and Mary Hallock Greenewalt; m 1926, Margaretta Lammot du Pont; two s one d. Educ: William Penn Charter Sch.; Mass. Institute of Technology (BS). With E. I. du Pont de Nemours & Co., Inc. from 1922; Asst Dir Exptl Station, Central Research Dept, 1939; Dir Chem. Div., Industrial and Biochemicals Dept, 1942; Technical Dir, Explosives Department, 1943; Asst Dir, Development Dept, 1945; Asst Gen. Man. Pigments Dept, 1945-46; Vice-Pres., 1946; Vice-Pres. and Vice-Chm. Exec. Cttee, 1947; Pres., Chm. Exec. Cttee and Mem. Finance Cttee, 1948-62; Chm. Board, 1962-67; Chm. Finance Cttee, 1967-74; Member Board of Directors of various other organisations. Member: Amer. Acad. of Arts and Sciences, National Academy of Sciences, Amer. Philos. Soc.; Carnegie Inst. of Washington; Trustee Emeritus, Nat. Geographic Soc. Holds hon. degrees in Science, Engineering and Laws, and has various scientific awards and medals. Publications: The Uncommon Man, 1959; Hummingbirds, 1960; Bird Song: acoustics and physiology, 1968. Recreation: photography. Address: Greenville, Delaware 19807, USA; (office) Du Pont Building, Wilmington, Delaware 19898, USA. Clubs: Wilmington, Wilmington Country, Du Pont Country, Greenville Country (USA).

GREENFIELD, Prof. Archibald David Mant, CBE 1977; FRCP; Foundation Dean of the Medical School, 1966-81 and Professor of Physiology, 1966-82 in the University of Nottingham; b 31 May 1917; s of late A. W. M. Greenfield, MA, and Winifred (née Peck), Parkstone, Dorset; m 1943, Margaret (née Duane); one s one d. Educ: Poole Grammar Sch.; St Mary's Hospital Medical Sch. BSc London, 1st class hons Physiology, 1937; MB, BS, 1940, MSc 1947, DSc 1953, London; FRCP, 1973. Dunville Prof. of Physiology in the Queen's Univ. of Belfast, 1948-64; Prof. of Physiology in the Univ. of London, at St Mary's Hosp. Med. Sch., 1964-67. WHO. Visiting Prof., India, 1960; Visiting Prof., Univ. of California, San Francisco Medical Center, 1962-63. Sometime Examnr, Oxford, Cambridge and 21 other Univs, RCS and RCSI. Member: Physiol. Systems Bd, MRC, 1976-77; UGC, 1977-82 (Chm. Med. and Dental Sub-Cttees, Assessor to MRC); GMC and GMC Educn Cttee, 1979-82; Med. Sub-Cttee, UPGC, Hong Kong, 1981-; Med. Acad. Adv. Cttee, Chinese Univ., Hong Kong, 1976-80; Councils for Postgrad. Med. Educn for England and Wales, and Scottish Council, 1977-82; DHSS Adv. Cttee on Artificial Limbs, 1971-75; DHSS Med. Manpower and Educn Liaison Cttee, 1974-78; DHSS Academic Forum, 1980-. Member: Sheffield RHB, 1968-74; Nottingham Univ. HMC, 1969-74; Notts AHA(T), 1974-79. Pres., Sect. of Biomed. Scis, British Assoc. for Advancement of Sci.,

1972; Mem., Physiological, Biochemical and Medical Research Societies. Chm., Editorial Bd, Monographs of the Physiological Soc., 1975-79; Member, Editorial Board: Amer. Heart Jl, 1959-66; Clinical Science, 1960-65; Cardiovascular Research, 1966-79; Circulation Res., 1967-73. OStJ 1978. Hon. LLD Nottingham, 1977; Hon. DSc QUB, 1978. *Publications:* papers on control of circulation of the blood, mainly in Lancet, Journal of Physiology, Clinical Science, and Journal of Applied Physiology. *Recreations:* sketching, bird watching, travel. *Address:* 25 Sutton Passeys Crescent, Nottingham NG8 1BX. *T:* Nottingham 782424.

GREENFIELD, Howard; *see* Greenfield, R. H.

GREENFIELD, Hon. Julius MacDonald, CMG 1954; Judge of the High Court of Rhodesia, 1968-74; *b* Boksburg, Transvaal, 13 July 1907; *s* of late Rev. C. E. Greenfield; *m* 1935, Florence Margaret Couper; two *s* one *d. Educ:* Milton Sch., Bulawayo; Universities of Capetown and Oxford. BA, LLB Cape; Rhodes Scholar, 1929; BA, BCL Oxon. Called to the Bar at Gray's Inn, 1933. QC 1948; practised at Bar in S Rhodesia, 1933-50; elected MP for Hillside, S Rhodesia, 1948, and appointed Minister of Internal Affairs and Justice, 1950; participated in London Conferences on Federation in Central Africa. MP Federal Parliament, in Umguza Constituency, 1953-63; Minister of Law, Federation of Rhodesia and Nyasaland, 1954-63; Minister for Home Affairs, 1962-63. *Publications:* Instant Crime, 1975; Instant Statute Case Law, 1977; Testimony of a Rhodesian Federal, 1978. *Address:* 17 Alder Way, West Cross, Swansea. *Clubs:* Bulawayo, Salisbury (Rhodesia); City and Civil Service (Cape Town).

GREENFIELD, (Robert) Howard, FCA; Chairman, North Eastern Region, British Gas Corporation, since 1982; *b* 4 Feb. 1927; *s* of James Oswald Greenfield and Doris Burt Greenfield; *m* 1951, Joyce Hedley Wells; one *s* one *d. Educ:* Rutherford Coll., Newcastle upon Tyne. FCA 1953. Northern Gas Board: Chief Accountancy Asst, 1956; Dep. Divl Manager, Tees Area, 1961; Divl Manager, Cumberland Div., 1963; Regional Service Manager, 1968; Northern Gas: Dir of Customer Service, 1974; Dir of Marketing, 1976; Dep. Chm., 1977. *Recreations:* salmon fishing, photography. *Address:* British Gas Corporation, North Eastern Region, New York Road, Leeds LS2 7PE. *T:* Leeds 436291.

GREENGROSS, Alan; Managing Director, Indusmond (Diamond Tools) Ltd; Director, Blazy & Clement Ltd and associated companies; Member, Greater London Council, since 1977; *b* 1929; *m*; one *s* three *d. Educ:* University Coll. Sch.; Trinity Coll., Cambridge (MA). Member Council, London Borough of Camden (past Alderman). Leader, Planning and Communications Policy, GLC, 1979-81. Mem., Port of London Authority, 1979-. Mem. Governing Council, Univ. Coll. Sch. *Address:* 9 Dawson Place, W2 4TD; Members' Lobby, GLC, County Hall, SE1 7PB.

GREENHALGH, Jack; Vice-Chairman, Cavenham Ltd, since 1974; *b* 25 July 1926; *s* of Herbert Greenhalgh and Alice May (*née* Clayton); *m* 1951, Kathleen Mary Hammond; two *s* two *d. Educ:* Manchester Grammar Sch.; Trinity Coll., Cambridge (MA Hons). FBIM. Marketing Dept, Procter & Gamble Ltd, Newcastle upon Tyne, 1950-59; Marketing Dir, Eskimo Foods Ltd, Cleethorpes, 1959-64; Dir of Continental Ops, Compton Advertising Inc., NY, 1964-65; Cavenham Ltd, 1965-: Man. Dir, 1968-79. *Recreations:* golf, sailing. *Address:* Garden Cottage, 2 Nags Head Lane, Avening, Tetbury, Glos. *T:* Nailsworth 3615.

GREENHAM, Peter George, CBE 1978; RA 1960 (ARA, 1951); PPRBA; RP; NEAC; Keeper of the Royal Academy Schools, since 1964; *b* 1909; *s* of George Frederick Greenham, MBE, civil servant; *m* 1964, Jane, *d* of late Dr G. B. Dowling, FRCP, and Mary Elizabeth Kelly; one *s* one *d. Educ:* Dulwich Coll.; Magdalen Coll., Oxford (Hist. Demy, BA); Byam Shaw Sch. of Art. Pres., RBA, to 1982. Paintings in permanent collections: Tate Gall.; Arts Council; Carlisle Gall.; Plymouth Gall. *Publication:* Velasquez, 1969. *Address:* c/o Royal Academy, Piccadilly, W1.

GREENHILL, family name of **Barons Greenhill** and **Greenhill of Harrow.**

GREENHILL, 2nd Baron, *cr* 1950, of Townhead; **Stanley E. Greenhill,** MD, DPH; FRCP(C), FACP, FFCM; Professor and Chairman, Department of Community Medicine, University of Alberta, Edmonton, Alberta, since 1959; *b* 17 July 1917; *s* of 1st Baron Greenhill and Ida Goodman; *S* father, 1967; *m* 1944, Margaret Jean, *d* of Thomas Newlands Hamilton, Ontario, Canada; two *d. Educ:* Kelvinside Academy, Glasgow; California and Toronto Univs. MD Toronto, DPH Toronto, FRSM. British Information Services, 1941; RAF, 1944. Prof., Dept of Medicine, University of Alberta, 1952. WHO Consultant, 1973-74. *Publications:* contrib. medical journals. *Recreations:* photography, travel. *Heir:* b Hon. Malcolm Greenhill, *b* 5 May 1924. *Address:* 10223, 137th Street, Edmonton, Alta T5N 2G8, Canada. *T:* 403-452-4650; c/o 28 Gorselands, Newbury, Berks. *Club:* Faculty (Edmonton, Alta).

GREENHILL OF HARROW, Baron *cr* 1974 (Life Peer), of the Royal Borough of Kensington and Chelsea; **Denis Arthur Greenhill,** GCMG 1972 (KCMG 1967; CMG 1960); OBE 1941; HM Government Director, British Petroleum Co. Ltd, 1973-78; Member, Security Commission, since 1973; *b* 7 Nov. 1913; *s* of James and Susie Greenhill, Loughton; *m* 1941, Angela McCulloch; two *s. Educ:* Bishop's Stortford Coll.; Christ Church, Oxford

(Hon. Student 1977). Served War of 1939-45 (despatches thrice): Royal Engineers; in Egypt, N Africa, Italy, India and SE Asia; demobilised with rank of Col. Entered Foreign Service, 1946; served: Sofia, 1947-49; Washington, 1949-52; Foreign Office, 1952-54. Imperial Defence Coll., 1954; UK Delegation to NATO, Paris, 1955-57; Singapore, 1957-59; Counsellor, 1959-62; Minister, 1962-64, Washington DC; Asst Under-Sec. of State, FO, 1964-66; Dep. Under-Sec. of State, FO, 1966-69; Perm. Under-Sec. of State, FCO, and Head of the Diplomatic Service, 1969-73. Director: S. G. Warburg & Co.; Clerical Medical and General Assce; Wellcome Foundn Ltd; BAT Industries Ltd; Hawker Siddeley Group; Leyland International, 1977-; Mem., Internat. Adv. Cttee, First Chicago Ltd, 1976-81. A Governor of the BBC, 1973-78. Governor, BUPA, 1978-. Dep. Chm., 1979-. President: Royal Soc. for Asian Affairs; Anglo-Finnish Soc., 1981-. Chm., KCH Med. Sch. Council; Trustee, Rayne Foundn; Governor, Wellington Coll. *Address:* 25 Hamilton House, Vicarage Gate, W8. *T:* 01-937 8362. *Club:* Travellers'.

GREENHILL, Dr Basil Jack, CB 1981; CMG 1967; FRHistS; FSA; Director, National Maritime Museum, Greenwich, since 1967; *b* 26 Feb. 1920; *o c* of B. J. and Edith Greenhill; *m* 1st, 1950, Gillian (*d* 1959), *e d* of Capt. Ralph Tyacke Stratton, MC; one *s*; 2nd, 1961, Ann, *d* of Walter Ernest Giffard; one *s. Educ:* Bristol Grammar Sch.; Bristol Univ. (T. H. Green Scholar; PhD 1980). Served War of 1939-45: RNVR (Air Br.). Joined Diplomatic Service, 1946; served: Pakistan, 1950-54; UK Delegation, New York, 1954; Tokyo, 1955-58; UK Delegate to Conference on Law of the Sea, Geneva, 1958; British Deputy High Comr in E Pakistan, 1958-59; Ottawa, 1961-64. Member: Cttee of Maritime Trust, 1970- (Mem., Council, 1977-); Ancient Monuments Bd for England, 1972-; Vice President: Soc. for Nautical Res., 1975-; Museums Assoc., 1981-; First Pres., Internat. Congress of Maritime Museums, 1975-81. Trustee, Royal Naval Museum, Portsmouth, 1973-. Governor, Dulwich Coll., 1974-; Chairman: Dulwich Picture Gall. Cttee, 1977-; Nat. Museums' Directors' Conf., 1980-; SS Great Britain Project, 1982-. Principal Advisor: BBC TV series, The Commanding Sea, 1980-81; BBC Radio series, The British Seafarer, 1980-81. Kt Comdr, Order of White Rose, Finland, 1980. *Publications:* The Merchant Schooners, Vol. I, 1951, Vol. II, 1957, rev. edns 1968, 1978; (ed and prefaced) W. J. Slade's Out of Appledore, 1959; Sailing For A Living, 1962; (with Ann Giffard) Westcountrymen in Prince Edward's Isle, 1967 (Amer. Assoc. Award) (filmed 1975); (with Ann Giffard) The Merchant Sailing Ship: A Photographic History, 1970; (with Ann Giffard) Women under Sail, 1970; Captain Cook, 1970; Boats and Boatmen of Pakistan, 1971; (with Ann Giffard) Travelling by Sea in the Nineteenth Century, 1972; (with Rear-Adm. P. W. Brock) Sail and Steam, 1973; (with W. J. Slade) West Country Coasting Ketches, 1974; A Victorian Maritime Album, 1974; A Quayside Camera, 1975; (with L. Willis) The Coastal Trade: Sailing Craft of British Waters 900-1900, 1975; Archaeology of the Boat, 1976; (with Ann Giffard) Victorian and Edwardian Sailing Ships, 1976; (with Ann Giffard) Victorian and Edwardian Ships and Harbours, 1978; (ed and prefaced) Georg Kåhrés The Last Tall Ships, 1978; (with Ann Giffard) Victorian and Edwardian Merchant Steamships, 1979; Schooners, 1980; The Life and Death of the Sailing Ship, 1980; (with Michael Mason) The British Seafarer, 1980; (with Denis Stonham) Seafaring Under Sail, 1981; Karlsson, 1982; numerous articles and reviews on maritime history subjects. *Recreations:* boating, travel, coarse gardening. *Address:* c/o National Maritime Museum, Greenwich, SE10. *Clubs:* Arts; Royal Western Yacht (Plymouth); Karachi Yacht (Karachi).
See also C. S. R. Giffard.

GREENING, Rear-Adm. Paul Woollven; Flag Officer, Royal Yachts, since 1981; *b* 4 June 1928; *s* of late Captain Charles W. Greening, DSO, DSC, RN, and Mrs Molly K. Greening (*née* Flowers); *m* 1951, Monica, *d* of late Mr and Mrs W. E. West, East Farndon, Market Harborough; one *s* one *d. Educ:* Mowden Sch., Brighton; Nautical Coll., Pangbourne. Entered RN, 1946; Midshipman, HMS Theseus, 1947-48; Sub-Lt and Lieut, HM Ships Zodiac, Neptune, Rifleman, Asheldham (CO), and Gamecock, 1950-58; Lt-Comdr, HM Ships Messina (CO), Loch Killisport, Urchin, and Collingwood, 1958-63; Comdr 1963; CO HMS Lewiston, and SO 2nd Minesweeping Sqdn, 1963-64; jssc 1964; Naval Plans, MoD (Navy), 1965-67; CO HMS Jaguar, 1967-68; Fleet Plans Officer, Far East Fleet, 1969; Captain 1969; CO HMS Aurora, 1970-71; Captain Naval Drafting, 1971-74; Sen. Officers War Course, 1974; Dir of Officers Appts (Seamen), MoD (Navy), 1974-76; Captain BRNC Dartmouth, 1976-78; Naval Sec., 1978-80. ADC to the Queen, 1978. *Recreations:* cricket, tennis, gardening. *Address:* HMY Britannia, BFPO Ships. *Club:* Army and Navy.

GREENING, Wilfrid Peter, FRCS; Consultant Surgeon to Royal Marsden Hospital, 1952-79; Consulting Surgeon, Charing Cross Hospital since 1975; Lecturer in Surgery to Charing Cross Hospital Medical School; *s* of Rev. W. Greening and M. M. Waller, Saxlingham, Norfolk; *m* 1st, 1939, Hilary Berryman (marr. diss., 1961); one *d*; 2nd, 1962, Susan Ann Clair Huber (marr. diss. 1977); 3rd, 1978, Touba Ghazinoor. *Educ:* St Edmund's Sch., Canterbury; King's Coll.; Charing Cross Hospital Medical Sch. MRCS 1937; LRCP 1937; FRCS 1939. Houseman and Surgical Registrar, Charing Cross Hosp., 1938. Served War of 1939-45 (despatches); Wing Comdr i/c Surgical Div., RAFVR, 1943. Surgical Registrar, Gordon Hospital, 1946; Consultant Surgeon: Woolwich Hospital, 1948; Bromley and District Hospital, 1947-66. *Publications:* contributions to medical literature. *Recreations:* fishing, golf. *Address:* 38 Harley House, Marylebone Road, NW1. *T:* 01-935 2567. *Club:* Garrick.

GREENLAND, Dennis James, DPhil; FInstBiol; Deputy Director General, International Rice Research Institute, Los Baños, Philippines, since 1979; *b* 13 June 1930; *s* of James John and Lily Florence Greenland; *m* 1955, Edith Mary Johnston; one *s* two *d. Educ:* Portsmouth Grammar Sch.; Christ Church, Oxford (MA, DPhil). Lecturer: Univ. of Ghana, 1955-59; Waite Agricl Res. Inst., Adelaide, 1959-63; Reader and Head of Soil Science, Waite Agricl Res. Inst., 1963-70; Professor and Head of Dept of Soil Science, Univ. of Reading, 1970-79. Director of Research, Internat. Inst. of Tropical Agriculture, Nigeria, 1974-76 (on secondment from Univ. of Reading). FInstBiol 1974. Hon. DrAgSci Ghent, 1982. *Publications:* contributions: (jtly) The Soil Under Shifting Cultivation, 1960; (ed jtly) Soil Conservation and Management in the Humid Tropics, 1977; (ed jtly) Chemistry of Soil Constituents, 1978; (ed jtly) Soil Physical Properties and Crop Production in the Tropics, 1979; (ed) Characterisation of Soils in Relation to Their Classification and Management for Crop Production: some examples from the humid tropics, 1981; (ed jtly) The Chemistry of Soil Processes, 1981; numerous scientific articles in learned jls. *Recreations:* golf, bridge, watching cricket. *Address:* International Rice Research Institute, Box 933, Manila, Philippines. *T:* 88-48-69.

GREENLEES, Ian Gordon, OBE 1963; MA; *b* 10 July 1913; *s* of Samuel Greenlees and Rosalie Stewart. *Educ:* Ampleforth Coll.; Magdalen Coll., Oxford. Reader in English Literature at University of Rome, 1934-36; supervisor of cultural centres of English for the British Council and Acting British Council Representative in Italy, 1939-40; Dir, British Institute, Rome, 1940; commissioned in Army, 1940; served in North African and Italian Campaigns, 1942-45, with rank of Major (despatches). Second Sec. (Asst Press Attaché) at British Embassy, Rome, Jan.-Dec. 1946; Asst British Council Representative, Italy, May 1947-Sept. 1948; Deputy British Council Representative, Italy, 1948-54; Dir, British Inst. of Florence, 1958-81. Medaglia d'Argento ai Benemeriti della Cultura (Italy), 1959; Cavaliere Ufficiale, 1963; Hon. Citizen, Bagni di Lucca, 1972; Commendatore dell' Ordine del Merito della Repubblica Italiana, 1975. *Publication:* Norman Douglas, 1957. *Recreations:* swimming, walking, and talking. *Address:* Casa Mansi, Via del Bagno 20, Bagni di Lucca, Prov. di Lucca, Italy. *T:* 0583 87522. *Clubs:* Athenæum; Union (Florence).

GREENOCK, Lord; Charles Alan Andrew Cathcart; *b* 30 Nov. 1952; *s* and heir of 6th Earl Cathcart, *qv*; *m* 1981, Vivien Clare, *o d* of F. D. McInnes Skinner. *Educ:* Eton. Commnd Scots Guards, 1972-75. *Address:* 108 Alderney Street, SW1. *Club:* Cavalry and Guards.

GREENOUGH, Beverly, (Mrs P. B. Greenough); *see* Sills, B.

GREENSHIELDS, Robert McLaren; HM Diplomatic Service; Counsellor, Nairobi, since 1981; *b* 27 July 1933; *s* of late Brig. James Greenshields, MC, TD, and of Mrs J. J. Greenshields; *m* 1960, Jean Alison Anderson; one *s* two *d. Educ:* Edinburgh Academy; Lincoln Coll., Oxford (MA Hons). National Service, 2nd Lieut Highland Light Infantry, 1952-54. District Officer, Tanganyika, HMOCS, 1958-61; Asst Master and Housemaster, Gordonstoun Sch., 1962-68; HM Diplomatic Service, 1969-. *Recreations:* ornithology, golf. *Address:* c/o Foreign and Commonwealth Office, SW1A 2AH. *Club:* Muthaiga (Nairobi).

GREENSLADE, Brigadier Cyrus, CBE 1940; psc; *b* 13 May 1892; *s* of late William Francis Greenslade and R. B. Greenslade, St Mary Church, Torquay; *m* 1917, Edith Margaret Johnson (*d* 1975); one *d. Educ:* Blundell's Sch., Tiverton. 2nd Lieut Devonshire Regt 1914; Capt. South Staffordshire Regt; Major York and Lancaster Regt; Lieut-Col North Staffordshire Regt; Brevets of Major and Lieut-Col; Instructor at Staff Coll., Camberley, 1932-35; GSO2 Army HQ, India, 1936-37; Col. 1936; Brigadier 1940; served European War, 1914-18, France, Salonica; 1919, The Baltic States (despatches, OBE); War of 1939-45, War Office as AQMG and Dir of Quartering; France, as Dep. QMG (CBE); 2 Corps HQ as DA&QMG. Combined Ops Training Centre as 2nd i/c to Vice-Adm. and Chief Instructor; Middle East, Comdr Eritrea Area and Comdr 2nd Bde Sudan Defence Force, 1942-44 (despatches); Palestine, as Comdr Southern Palestine Area, 1944-46; retd pay, 1946. Dep. Chief, Displaced Persons Operation, UNRRA, Germany and Paris, 1946-47; International Refugee Organisation, Geneva HQ, 1947-48; Chief UK Officer, IRO, 1948-51. Exec. Officer, Royal Commonwealth Society for the Blind, 1953-59. Legion of Merit, USA (Commander). *Address:* Manor Farm House, West Chinnock, near Crewkerne, Somerset. *T:* Chiselborough 395. *Club:* Athenæum.

GREENSMITH, Edward William, OBE 1972; BScEng; FCGI; Deputy President, Executive Board of the British Standards Institution, 1973-79 (Chairman, 1970-73); *b* 20 April 1909; *m* 1937, Edna Marjorie Miskin (*d* 1971); three *s*; *m* 1972, Margaret Boaden Miles. ICI, Engrg Adviser, 1964-71. Dir (non-executive), Peter Brotherhood Ltd, 1970-78. *Publications:* contribs: Chemistry Ind., 1957, 1959. *Recreations:* walking, gardening. *Address:* Battle Hill, Tanners Lane, Burford, Oxford OX8 4NA. *T:* Burford 2304.

GREENSMITH, Edwin Lloydd, CMG 1962; *b* 23 Jan. 1900; *s* of Edwin Greensmith; *m* 1932, Winifred Bryce; two *s* two *d. Educ:* Victoria Univ., Wellington, NZ. MCom (Hons), 1930. Accountant; Solicitor. Chief Accountant, Ministry of Works, New Zealand, to 1935; then Treasury (Secretary, 1955-65). Chm., NZ Wool Commn, 1965-72. *Recreation:* gardening. *Address:* Lowry Bay, Wellington, NZ. *T:* 683240. *Club:* Wellington (Wellington NZ).

GREENWAY, family name of **Baron Greenway.**

GREENWAY, 4th Baron *cr* 1927; **Ambrose Charles Drexel Greenway;** Bt 1919; photographer and author; *b* 21 May 1941; *s* of 3rd Baron Greenway and of Cordelia Mary, *d* of late Major Humfrey Campbell Stephen; *S* father, 1975. *Educ:* Winchester. *Publications:* Soviet Merchant Ships, 1976; Comecon Merchant Ships, 1978; A Century of Cross Channel Passenger Steamers, 1980. *Recreations:* ocean racing and cruising, swimming. *Heir: b* Hon. Mervyn Stephen Kelvynge Greenway, *b* 19 Aug. 1942. *Address:* c/o House of Lords, SW1. *Clubs:* House of Lords Yacht; Royal London Yacht (Cowes).

GREENWAY, Harry; MP (C) Ealing North, since 1979; *b* 4 Oct. 1934; *s* of John Kenneth Greenway and Violet Adelaide (*née* Bell); *m* 1969, Carol Elizabeth Helena, *e d* of late John Robert Thomas Hooper, barrister at law and Metropolitan Stipendiary Magistrate; one *s* two *d. Educ:* Warwick Sch.; College of St Mark and St John, London; Univ. of Caen, Normandy. Assistant Master, Millbank Sch., 1957-60; successively, Head of English Dept, Sen. Housemaster, Sen. Master, Acting Dep. Head, Sir William Collins Sch., 1960-72; Dep. Headmaster, Sedgehill Sch. (Comprehensive for 2,000 plus pupils), 1972-79. Chm., All Party Adult Educn Cttee, 1979-; Mem., Parly Select Cttee on Educn, Science and the Arts, 1979-. Mem. Council, Open Univ., 1982-; Trustee, St Clare's Coll., Oxford, 1982-. British Horse Soc. Award of Merit, 1980. *Publications:* Adventure in the Saddle, 1971; regular contributor to educnl and equestrian jls. *Recreations:* riding, ski-ing, choral music, hockey (Vice-Pres., England Schoolboys' Hockey Assoc.; Founder, Lords and Commons Hockey Club), cricket, parliamentary parachutist. *Address:* House of Commons, SW1. *Clubs:* St Stephen's Constitutional, Ski Club of Gt Britain.

GREENWELL, Sir Edward (Bernard), 4th Bt *cr* 1906; farmer, since 1975; *b* 10 June 1948; *s* of Sir Peter McClintock Greenwell, 3rd Bt, TD, and of Henrietta, 2nd *d* of late Peter and Lady Alexandra Haig-Thomas; *S* father, 1978; *m* 1974, Sarah Louise Gore-Anley; two *d. Educ:* Eton; Nottingham University (BSc); Cranfield Institute of Technology (MBA). *Heir: b* Captain James Peter Greenwell, *b* 27 May 1950. *Address:* Gedgrave Hall, Woodbridge, Suffolk. *T:* Orford 440. *Club:* Turf.

GREENWOOD, family name of **Viscount Greenwood.**

GREENWOOD, 2nd Viscount, *cr* 1937 of Holbourne; **David Henry Hamar Greenwood,** FRGS; Baron, *cr* 1929; Bt, *cr* 1915; *b* 30 Oct. 1914; *e s* of 1st Viscount Greenwood, PC, KC, LLD, BA, and Margery (*d* 1968), 2nd *d* of Rev. Walter Spencer, BA; *S* father 1948; unmarried. *Educ:* privately and at Bowers Gifford. Agriculture and Farming. *Heir: b* Hon. Michael George Hamar Greenwood, *b* 5 May 1923. *Recreations:* shooting and reading.

GREENWOOD, Allen Harold Claude, CBE 1974; JP; Deputy Chairman, British Aerospace, 1977-mid 1983 (Member, Organizing Committee, 1976-77); Chairman, British Aircraft Corporation, 1976 (Deputy Chairman, 1972-75); *b* 4 June 1917; *s* of Lt-Col Thomas Claude Greenwood and Hilda Letitia Greenwood (*née* Knight). *Educ:* Cheltenham Coll.; Coll. of Aeronautical Engineering. Pilot's Licence, 1939. Joined Vickers-Armstrongs Ltd, 1940; served RNVR (Fleet Air Arm), 1942-52 (Lt-Cmdr); rejoined Vickers-Armstrongs Ltd, 1946, Dir, 1960; British Aircraft Corp., 1962, Dep. Man. Dir, 1969; Director: British Aircraft Corp. (Holdings), 1972; SEPECAT SA, 1964; Europlane Ltd, 1974-; Chm., Panavia GmbH, 1969-72. Pres., Assoc. Européenne des Constructeurs de Material Aerospatial, 1974-76. Vice-Chm., 1973, Chm., 1976-79, Remploy Ltd. Pres., 1970-72, Dep. Pres., 1981-, SBAC; Vice-Pres., Engineering Employers' Fedn, 1982-. Chm., St John's Sch., Leatherhead; Pres., Cheltenham Coll. Council, 1980-; Member: Council, Cranfield Inst. of Technology, 1970-79; Council, CBI; Assoc. of Governing Bodies of Public Schools. JP Surrey 1962, Hampshire, 1975. Freeman, City of London. Liveryman, Company of Coachmakers. Guild of Air Pilots. General Comr for Income Tax, 1970-74. *Address:* British Aerospace, Brooklands Road, Weybridge KT13 0RN. *T:* Weybridge 45522. *Clubs:* White's, Royal Automobile; Royal Lymington Yacht.

GREENWOOD, Jack Neville; General Manager, Stevenage Development Corporation, 1976-80, retired; *b* 17 March 1922; *s* of Daniel Greenwood and Elvina Stanworth; *m* 1947, Margaret Jane Fincher; two *s* two *d. Educ:* Harrow County Sch. Mem., Chartered Inst. of Public Finance and Accountancy. RAF, 1941-46. Ruislip Northwood UDC, 1938-49; Southall Borough Council, 1949-50; Stevenage Develt Corp., 1950-, Chief Finance Officer, 1967-76. *Recreation:* gardening. *Address:* Woodfield, Rectory Lane, Stevenage, Herts SG1 4BT. *T:* Stevenage 52851.

GREENWOOD, James Russell, MVO 1975; HM Diplomatic Service, retired; *b* 30 April 1924; *s* of J. and L. Greenwood, Padiham; *m* 1957, Mary Veronica, *d* of late Dr D. W. Griffith and Dr Grace Griffith, Bures; one *s. Educ:* RGS, Clitheroe; Queen's Coll., Oxford. Army Service, 1943-47. BA, MA (Oxon) 1949; Foreign Office, 1949; subseq. service in Bangkok, 1950-52; Tokyo and Osaka, 1952-54; London, 1955-58; Rangoon, 1958-61; Rome, 1961-63; Bangkok, 1964-68; Counsellor (Information), Tokyo, 1968-73; Consul-General, Osaka, 1973-77. Order of Sacred Treasure (3rd cl.) Japan, 1975. *Recreations:* travel, golf, cricket. *Address:* c/o Lloyds Bank Ltd, 6 Pall Mall, SW1. *Clubs:* United Oxford & Cambridge University, MCC.

GREENWOOD, Joan; Actress; Theatre, Films, Radio, Television; *b* 4 March 1921; *d* of late Earnshaw Greenwood, Artist; *m* 1960, André Morell (*d* 1978); one *s*. *Educ:* St Catherine's Sch., Bramley, Surrey. First professional stage appearance in Le Malade Imaginaire, 1938; since then has appeared in: Little Ladyship; The Women; Striplings; Damaged Goods; Heartbreak House; Hamlet; Volpone; A Doll's House; Frenzy; Young Wives' Tale; The Confidential Clerk (New York); Peter Pan 1951; The Moon and the Chimney, 1955; Bell, Book and Candle, 1955; Cards of Identity, 1956; Lysistrata, 1957-58; The Grass is Greener, 1959; Hedda Gabler, 1960, 1964; The Irregular Verb to Love, 1961; Oblomov (later Son of Oblomov), 1964; Fallen Angels, 1967; The Au Pair Man, 1969; The Chalk Garden, 1971; Eden End, 1972; In Praise of Love, 1973; The Understanding, 1982. Acted at Chichester Festival, 1962. *Films include:* They Knew Mr Knight, Latin Quarter, Girl in a Million, Bad Sister, The October Man, Tight Little Island, Bad Lord Byron, Train of Events, Flesh and Blood, Kind Hearts and Coronets, The Man in the White Suit, Young Wives Tale, Mr Peek-a-Boo, The Importance of Being Earnest, Monsieur Ripois, Father Brown, Moonfleet, Stage Struck, Tom Jones, The Moonspinners, The Water Babies, Hound of the Baskervilles, Wagner. *Recreations:* reading, ballet, music, painting. *Address:* c/o National Westminster Bank, 352A King's Road, SW3.

GREENWOOD, John Arnold Charles, OBE 1943; Director, Sun Alliance & London Insurance Group, since 1965 (Chief General Manager, 1971-77); *b* 23 Jan. 1914; *o s* of late Augustus George Greenwood and Adele Ellen O'Neill Arnold; *m* 1940, Dorothy Frederica Pestell; two *d*. *Educ:* King's College Sch., Wimbledon. FCII; FRES. Joined Sun Insce Office Ltd, 1932; posted India, 1937-47; served War of 1939-45, TA, 36th Sikh Regt and AA&QMG 4th Indian Div. (Lt-Col, OBE, despatches); subseq. various appts; a Gen. Man., Sun Alliance & London, 1965; Dep. Chief Gen. Man., 1969. Morgan Owen Medal, 1939. *Publications:* papers on insurance, entomology. *Recreations:* entomology, writing, gardening. *Address:* Hambledon House, Rogate, Petersfield, Hants. *T:* Rogate 744.

GREENWOOD, Prof. Norman Neill, DSc Melbourne; PhD; ScD Cambridge; CChem, FRSC; Professor and Head of Department of Inorganic and Structural Chemistry, University of Leeds, since 1971; *b* Melbourne, Vic., 19 Jan. 1925; *er s* of Prof. J. Neill Greenwood, DSc and Gladys, *d* of late Moritz and Bertha Uhland; *m* 1951, Kirsten Marie Rydland, Bergen, Norway; three *d*. *Educ:* University High School, Melbourne; University of Melbourne; Sidney Sussex Coll., Cambridge. Laboratory Cadet, CSIRO Div. of Tribophysics, Melbourne, 1942-44; BSc Melbourne 1945, MSc Melbourne 1948; DSc Melbourne 1966. Masson Memorial Medal, Royal Australian Chem. Institute, 1945. Resident Tutor and Lecturer in Chemistry, Trinity Coll., Melbourne, 1946-48. Exhibn of 1851, Overseas Student, 1948-51; PhD Cambridge 1951; ScD Cambridge 1961. Senior Harwell Research Fellow, 1951-53; Lectr, 1953-60 Senior Lectr, 1960-61, in Inorganic Chemistry, Univ. of Nottingham; Prof. of Inorganic Chemistry, Univ. of Newcastle upon Tyne, 1961-71. Vis. Professor: Univ. of Melbourne, 1968; Univ. of Western Australia, 1969; Univ. of Western Ontario, 1973; Univ. of Copenhagen, 1979; National Science Foundation Distinguished Vis. Prof., Michigan State Univ., USA, 1967. International Union of Pure and Applied Chemistry: Mem., 1963-; Vice-Pres., 1975-77, Pres., 1977-81, Inorganic Chemistry Div.; Chm., Internat. Commn on Atomic Weights, 1969-75; Chemical Society: Tilden Lectr, 1966-67; Vice Pres., 1979-80; Pres., Dalton Div., 1979-81. Award in Main Group Chemistry, 1975. Dr *hc* de l'Université de Nancy I, 1977. *Publications:* Principles of Atomic Orbitals, 1964 (rev. edns 1968, 1973, 1980); Ionic Crystals, Lattice Defects, and Nonstoichiometry, 1968; (jointly) Spectroscopic Properties of Inorganic and Organometallic Compounds, vols I-IX, 1968-76; (with W. A. Campbell) Contemporary British Chemists, 1971; (with T. C. Gibb) Mössbauer Spectroscopy, 1971; Periodicity and Atomic Structure, 1971; (with B. P. Staughan and E. J. F. Ross) Index of Vibrational Spectra, vol. I, 1972, (with E. J. F. Ross) vol. II, 1975, vol. III, 1977; The Chemistry of Boron, 1973 (rev. edn 1975); numerous original papers and reviews in chemical jls and chapters in scientific monographs. *Recreations:* ski-ing, music. *Address:* Department of Inorganic and Structural Chemistry, The University, Leeds LS2 9JT.

GREENWOOD, Peter Bryan; His Honour Judge Greenwood; a Circuit Judge, since 1972. Called to the Bar, Gray's Inn, 1955. Dep. Chm., Essex QS, 1968-71. *Address:* 6 King's Bench Walk, Temple, EC4Y 7DR.

GREENWOOD, Peter Humphry, DSc; FIBiol; Senior Principal Scientific Officer, Ichthyologist, British Museum (Natural History), since 1967; *b* 21 April 1927; *s* of Percy Ashworth Greenwood and Joyce May Wilton; *m* 1950, Marjorie George; four *d*. *Educ:* St John's Coll., Johannesburg; Krugersdorp High Sch.; Univ. of Witwatersrand. BSc (Hons), DSc. S African Naval forces, seconded to RN, 1944-46. Colonial Office Fishery Res. Student, 1950-51; Res. Officer, E African Fisheries Res. Orgn, Jinja, Uganda, 1951-58; British Museum (Natural History): Sen. Res. Fellow, 1958-59; Sen., later Principal, Scientific Officer and Curator of Fishes, 1959-67. Res. Associate, Amer. Mus. of Natural Hist., 1965; H. B. Bigelow Vis. Prof. of Ichthyology, Harvard Univ., 1979. Mem., British subcttee on productivity of freshwaters, Internat. Biol Prog., 1964-75; Chm., Royal Soc./Internat. Biol Prog. subcttee on res. in Lake George, 1967-74. Pres., Linnean Soc. of London, 1976-79. Hon. For. Mem., Amer. Soc. of Ichthyologists and Herpetologists, 1972. Scientific Medal, Zoological Soc. of London, 1963; Linnean Medal for Zoology, 1982. *Publications:* Fishes of Uganda, 1958, 2nd edn 1966; The Cichlid Fishes of Lake Victoria: the biology and evolution of a species flock, 1974; (ed) J. R.

Norman, A History of Fishes, 1st revd edn 1963, 2nd revd edn 1975; (ed with C. Patterson) Fossil Vertebrates, 1967; (ed with C. Patterson and R. Miles) Interrelationships of Fishes, 1973; The Haplochromine Fishes of the East African Lakes, 1981; numerous papers on taxonomy, anatomy, biology and evolution of fishes. *Recreations:* ballet, art, reading, thinking, model building. *Address:* 20 Cromer Villas Road, SW18 1PN. *T:* 01-874 9588.

GREENWOOD, Ronald, CBE 1981; Manager, England Association Football Team, 1977-82; *b* 11 Nov. 1921; *s* of Sam and Margaret Greenwood; *m* Lucy Joan Greenwood; one *s* one *d*. *Educ:* Alperton School. Apprenticed signwriter, 1937; joined Chelsea FC, 1940; served RAF, 1940-45; Bradford Park Avenue FC, 1945 (Captain); Brentford FC, 1949 (over 300 matches); rejoined Chelsea FC, 1952 (League Champions, 1954-55); Fulham FC, Feb. 1955; coached Oxford Univ. team, 3 years, Walthamstow Avenue FC, 2 years; Manager, Eastbourne United FC and England Youth team; Asst Manager, Arsenal FC, 1958; Team Manager, England Under-23, 1958-61; Manager and Coach, later Gen. Manager, West Ham United FC, 1961-77 (FA Cup, 1964 and 1975; European Cup Winners' Cup, 1965); a FIFA technical advisor, World Cup series, 1966 and 1970. *Address:* 8 Kestrel Close, Upper Drive, Hove, Sussex.

GREENWOOD WILSON, J.; see Wilson, John G.

GREER, Germaine, PhD; author and lecturer; Director, The Tulsa Centre for the Study of Women's Literature, since 1979; *b* 29 Jan. 1939. *Educ:* Melbourne Univ.; Sydney Univ.; Cambridge Univ. (BA, PhD). Lecturer in English, Warwick Univ., 1968-73. *Publications:* The Female Eunuch, 1970; The Obstacle Race, 1979; contribs: articles to Listener, Spectator, Esquire, Harpers Magazine, Playboy, Private Eye (as Rose Blight). *Address:* c/o Gillon Aitken, 17 South Eaton Place, SW1W 9ER.

GREET, Rev. Dr Kenneth Gerald; Secretary of the Methodist Conference since 1971; President of the Methodist Conference, July 1980-July 1981; Moderator, Free Church Federal Council, 1982-83; *b* 17 Nov. 1918; *e s* of Walter and Renée Greet, Bristol; *m* 1947, Mary Eileen Edbrooke; one *s* two *d*. *Educ:* Cotham Grammar Sch., Bristol; Handsworth Coll., Birmingham. Minister: Cwm and Kingstone Methodist Church, 1940-42; Ogmore Vale Methodist Church, 1942-45; Tonypandy Central Hall, 1947-54; Sec. Dept of Christian Citizenship of Methodist Church, 1954-71; Member: Brit. Council of Churches, 1955- (Chm. of Exec., 1977-81); World Methodist Council, 1957- (Chm., Exec. Cttee, 1976-81); Chairman: Exec., Temperance Council of Christian Churches, 1961-71; World Christian Temperance Fedn, 1962-72. Rep. to Central Cttee, World Council of Churches, Addis Ababa, 1971, Nairobi, 1975; Beckly Lectr, 1962; Willson Lectr, Kansas City, 1966; Cato Lectr, Sydney, 1975. Hon. DD Ohio, USA. *Publications:* The Mutual Society, 1962; Man and Wife Together, 1962; Large Petitions, 1964; Guide to Loving, 1965; The Debate about Drink, 1969; The Sunday Question, 1970; The Art of Moral Judgement, 1970; When the Spirit Moves, 1975; A Lion from a Thicket, 1978; The Big Sin: Christianity and the arms race. *Recreations:* tennis, photography. *Address:* (office) 1 Central Buildings, Westminster, SW1H 9NH. *T:* 01-222 8757; (residence) 16 Orchard Avenue, Shirley, Croydon CR0 8UA. *T:* 01-777 5376.

GREETHAM, (George) Colin; Headmaster, Bishop's Stortford College, since 1971; *b* 22 April 1929; *s* of late George Cecil Greetham and of Gertrude Greetham (née Heavyside); *m* 1963, Rosemary (née Gardner); two *s* one *d*. *Educ:* York Minster Song Sch.; St Peter's Sch., York; (Choral Scholar) King's Coll., Cambridge. BA (Hons) History Tripos Cantab, Class II, Div. I, 1952; Certif. of Educn (Cantab) 1953. *Recreations:* hockey, cricket, music, choral training. *Address:* Headmaster's House, Bishop's Stortford College, Bishop's Stortford, Herts. *T:* 54220.

GREEVES, Rev. Derrick Amphlet; Methodist Minister; *b* 29 June 1913; *s* of Edward Greeves, Methodist Minister; *m* 1942, Nancy (née Morgans); one *s* three *d*. *Educ:* Bolton Sch.; Preston Gram. Sch.; Manchester Univ. 1931-34 (BA); Cambridge Univ. (Wesley Hse), 1934-37 (MA). Entered Methodist Ministry, 1935; Barnet, 1937; Bristol, 1939; RAF Chaplain, 1943; S Norwood, 1947; Bowes Park, 1952; Westminster Central Hall, 1955; Guildford, 1964; Worcester, 1969; Salisbury, 1974; Langwathby, Cumbria, 1978. *Publications:* Christ in Me, a study of the Mind of Christ in Paul, 1962; A Word in Your Ear (broadcast talks), 1970; Preaching through St Paul, 1980. *Address:* Red Barn, Langwathby, Penrith, Cumbria CA10 1LW. *T:* Langwathby 707.
See also Rev. F. Greeves.

GREEVES, Rev. Frederic, MA; LLD; Principal, 1949-67, and Randles Chair of Systematic Theology and Philosophy of Religion, 1946-67, Didsbury College, Bristol, retired 1967; President, Methodist Conference, 1963-64; *b* 1 June 1903; *s* of Rev. Edward Greeves and Mabel Barnsley Greeves; *m* 1929, Frances Marion Barratt; one *s* one *d*. *Educ:* Merchant Taylors' Sch., Crosby; Manchester Univ. (BA); Didsbury Coll., Manchester; Cambridge Univ. Asst Tutor, Didsbury Coll., Manchester, 1924-28; Methodist Minister, Cheltenham, 1928-30; BA Cambridge, 1932 (MA 1936); Burney Prize, 1933; Minister, Cambridge, 1930-33; Epsom, 1933-39; Oxford, Chaplain to Methodists in Univ., 1939-46. Chm. West Regional Religious Adv. Council, BBC, 1952-57; Fernley-Hartley Lecture, 1956; Cato Lectr, 1960. Hon. LLD (Bristol), 1963. *Publications:* Jesus the Son of God, 1939; Talking about God, 1949; The Meaning of Sin, 1956; Theology and the Cure of Souls, 1960; The Christian Way, 1963. *Address:* 1 Westmorland House, Durdham Park, Bristol

BS6 6XH. *T:* Bristol 741594.
See also Rev. D. A. Greeves.

GREEVES, John Ernest, CB 1966; Permanent Secretary, Ministry of Home Affairs for Northern Ireland, 1964–70, retired; *b* 9 Oct. 1910; *s* of late R. D. Greeves, Grange, Dungannon, Co. Tyrone; *m* 1942, Hilde Alexandra, *d* of E. Hülbig, Coburg, Bavaria; one *s* one *d. Educ:* Royal School, Dungannon. Entered Min. of Labour, NI, 1928; Asst Sec., 1956–62; Permanent Sec., 1962–64; subseq. Min. of Home Affairs. *Address:* 22 Downshire Road, Belfast BT6 9JL. *T:* 648380.

GREEVES, Maj.-Gen. Sir Stuart, KBE 1955 (CBE 1945; OBE 1940); CB 1948; DSO 1944; MC 1917; (ex-Indian Army) Deputy Adjutant General, India, until 1957, retired; *b* 2 April 1897; *s* of late J. S. Greeves; unmarried. *Educ:* Northampton Sch. Served European War, 1914–18 (MC and Bar); War of 1939–45 (DSO and Bar, CBE). *Recreation:* golf. *Address:* c/o Lloyds Bank, 6 Pall Mall, SW1; Flat 601, Grosvenor Square, College Road, Rondebosch, Cape Town, S Africa. *Club:* Naval and Military.

GREG, Barbara, RE; artist and wood engraver; *b* 30 April 1900; *d* of H. P. and J. E. Greg; *m* 1925, Norman Janes (*d* 1980); one *s* two *d. Educ:* Bedales. Studied at Slade Sch. of Fine Art. Has exhibited wood engravings in London, provincial and foreign exhibitions since 1926. ARE 1940; RE 1946. Books illustrated include A Fisherman's Log by Major Ashley Dodd, Enigmas of Natural History and More Enigmas of Natural History by E. L. Grant Watson, The Poacher's Handbook, Fresh Woods, Pastures New, by Ian Niall. *Address:* 70 Canonbury Park South, N1 2JG. *T:* 01-226 1925.

GREGG, Hubert Robert Harry; actor, composer, lyricist, author, playwright and director; *b* London, 19 July 1916; *s* of Robert Joseph Gregg and Alice Maud (*née* Bessant); *m* 1st, 1943, Zoe Gail (marr. diss. 1950); one *d* ; 2nd, 1956, Pat Kirkwood (marr. diss. 1979); 3rd, 1980, Carmel Lytton; one *d. Educ:* St Dunstan's Coll.; Webber-Douglas Sch. of Singing and Dramatic Art. Served War, 1939–44: private, Lincs Regt, 1939; commnd 60th Rifles, 1940; transf. Intell.; with Polit. Warfare Exec., 1942 (duties included broadcasting in German). *Stage:* 1st London appearance, Julien in Martine, Ambassadors', 1933; Birmingham Rep., 1933–34; Shakespearean roles, Open Air Theatre, Regent's Park and at Old Vic, 1934, 1935; 1st New York appearance, Kit Neilan in French without Tears, 1937 (and London, 1938–39); London appearances include: Pip in The Convict, 1935; roles in classics (Orlando, Henry V, Hamlet), 1935–36; Frederick Hackett in Great Possessions, 1937; Peter Scott-Fowler in After the Dance, 1939; Polly in Men in Shadow, 1942; Michael Caraway in Acacia Avenue, 1944; Earl of Harpenden in While the Sun Shines, 1945, 1946; Tom D'Arcy in Off the Record, 1947; Gabriel Hathaway in Western Wind, 1949; (1st musical), John Blessington-Briggs in Chrysanthemum, 1958; Lionel Toope in Pools Paradise, 1961. *Chichester Festival Theatre:* Alexander MacColgie Gibbs in The Cocktail Party, Antonio in The Tempest, and Announcer in The Skin of our Teeth, 1968; Sir Lucius O'Trigger in The Rivals, Britannus in Caesar and Cleopatra, and Marcellin in Dear Antoine (also London), 1971. *Directed, London:* The Hollow (Agatha Christie's 1st stage success), 1951; re-staged To Dorothy - a Son, 1952 (subseq. toured in play, 1952–53); The Mousetrap (for 7 yrs from 1953); Speaking of Murder, 1958; The Unexpected Guest, 1958; From the French, 1959; Go Back for Murder, 1960; Rule of Three, 1962; re-staged The Secretary Bird, 1969 (subseq. toured in play, 1969–70). 1st solo performance, Leicester, 1970; subseq. performances in Britain and America (subjects include Shakespeare, Shaw, Jerome K. Jerome, the London Theatre, and the 20s, 30s and 40s); solo perf., Words by Elgar, Music by Shaw, Malvern Fest., 1978, Edinburgh Fest., 1979. *Films include:* In Which We Serve; Flying Fortress; Acacia Avenue; Once upon a Dream; Robin Hood (Walt Disney); The Maggie; Svengali; Doctor at Sea; Simon and Laura. *Author of plays:* We Have Company (played in tour, 1953); Cheque Mate (dir. and appeared in); Villa Sleep Four (played in tour, 1965); From the French (written under pseudonym of Jean-Paul Marotte); Who's Been Sleeping . . . ? (also appeared in); The Rumpus (played in tour, 1967); Dear Somebody; (screenplay) After the Ball (adapted from own television biog. of Vesta Tilley). *Songs:* Author of over 100, including: I'm going to get lit up; Maybe it's because I'm a Londoner. BBC broadcasts in drama, revue, poetry, etc, 1935–; weekly radio progs with accent on nostalgia, 1965–; Chm., BBC TV Brains Trust, 1955; 40 week radio series on London theatres, 1974–75; biog. series: I Call it Genius, 1980–81; I Call it Style, 1981–; Hubert Gregg Remembers, ITV solo series, 1982–. Has dir., lectured and adjudicated at Webber-Douglas Sch., Central Sch. of Speech Trng and RADA. President: Northern Boys' Book Club, 1975- (succeeded P. G. Wodehouse); Concert Artists Assoc., 1979–80. Freedom of City of London, 1981. *Publications:* April Gentleman (novel), 1951; We Have Company (play), 1953; A Day's Loving (novel), 1974; Agatha Christie and all that Mousetrap, 1980; music and lyrics. *Recreation:* cinematography. *Address:* c/o Broadcasting House, W1A 1AA. *Club:* Garrick.

GREGOIRE, Most Rev. Paul; *see* Montreal, Archbishop of, (RC).

GREGORY, Clifford; Chief Scientific Officer, Department of Health and Social Security, since 1979; *b* 16 Dec. 1924; *s* of Norman and Grace Gregory; *m* 1948, Wyn Aveyard; one *d* (one *s* decd). *Educ:* Royal Coll. of Science, London Univ. (2nd Cl. Hons Physics; ARCS). Served War, RN, 1943–46. Lectr, Mddx Hosp. Med. Sch., 1949; Sen. Physicist, Mount Vernon Hosp., 1954; Dep. Reg. Physicist, Sheffield, 1960; Sen. Principal Scientific Officer, Min. of Health, 1966; Dep. Chief Scientific Officer, DHSS, 1972.

Publications: scientific papers in med. and scientific jls. *Recreations:* outdoor pursuits, natural history, squash, rugby. *Address:* 53 Roundwood Park, Harpenden, Herts AL5 3AG. *T:* Harpenden 2047.

GREGORY, John Peter, JP; CEng, FIMechE; Chairman, Data Recording Instruments Ltd, since 1982; *b* 5 June 1925; *s* of Mr and Mrs P. Gregory; *m* 1949, Lilian Mary (*née* Jarvis); one *s* one *d. Educ:* Ernest Bailey Sch., Matlock; Trinity Hall, Cambridge (MA). CEng, FIMechE 1970. Served War, RAF Pilot, 1943–47. Joined Cadbury Bros Ltd, 1949, Dir 1962; Vice Chm., Cadbury Ltd, 1969–70, Dir, Cadbury Schweppes, 1971–82 (Chm., Overseas Gp and Internat. Tech. Dir, 1973–80); Director: National Vulcan Engrg Ins. Group Ltd, 1970–79; Amalgamated Power Engrg Ltd, 1973–81. Gen. Comr of Income Tax, 1978–. Chm. Trustees, Middlemore Homes. Liveryman, Worshipful Co. of Needlemakers. JP Birmingham, 1979. *Recreations:* music, bridge, country pursuits, tennis. *Address:* Moorgreen Hall, Weatheroak, Alvechurch, Worcs. *T:* Wythall 822303. *Club:* Carlton.

GREGORY, Leslie Howard James; former National Officer of EETPU; *b* 18 Jan. 1915; *s* of J. F. and R. E. Gregory; *m* 1949, D. M. Reynolds; one *s* one *d. Educ:* Junior Section, Ealing College (formerly Acton Coll.) and state schools. Mem. Exec. Council, ETU, 1938–54; full-time Nat. Officer, 1954–79, retired. Member: CSEU Nat. Sub-Cttees, for Shipbuilding from 1966, for Railway Workshops from 1968; Craft Training Cttees of Shipbuilding ITB and Engineering ITB; EDC for Elec. Engrg, 1967–74; EDC for Shipbuilding, 1974–76; Org. Ctte, British Shipbuilders, 1976–77; Bd, British Shipbuilders (part-time), 1977–80. *Address:* 1 St Margarets, Exeter Road, Honiton, Devon. *T:* Honiton 3594.

GREGORY, Philip Herries, PhD, DSc London, DIC; FRS 1962; Head of Plant Pathology Department, Rothamsted Experimental Station, Harpenden, Hertfordshire, 1958–67; *b* Exmouth, Devon, 24 July 1907; *s* of late Rev. Herries Smith Gregory, MA and late Muriel Edith Gregory (*née* Eldridge), Hove, Sussex; *m* 1932, Margaret Fearn Culverhouse; one *s* one *d. Educ:* Brighton Technical Coll.; Imperial Coll. of Science and Technology, London. Research in medical mycology, Manitoba Med. Coll., 1931-34; Research plant pathologist, Seale-Hayne Agric. Coll., Newton Abbot, Devon, 1935–40; Rothamsted Experimental Station, Harpenden; Agric. Research Council Research Officer, 1940–47 (seconded for penicillin research to ICI, Manchester, 1945–46); Mycologist, Rothamsted Experimental Station, 1948-54; Prof. of Botany, University of London, Imperial Coll. of Science and Technology, 1954–58. Pres. British Mycological Soc., 1951. *Publications:* The Microbiology of the Atmosphere, 1961, 2nd edn, 1973; papers on mycology, plant pathology, and virology. *Address:* 11 Topstreet Way, Harpenden, Herts AL5 5TU.

GREGORY, Prof. Richard Langton, FRSE 1969; Professor of Neuropsychology and Director of Brain and Perception Laboratory, University of Bristol, since 1970; *b* 24 July 1923; *s* of C. C. L. Gregory, astronomer, and Patricia (*née* Gibson); *m* 1st, 1953, Margaret Hope Pattison Muir (marr. diss. 1966); one *s* one *d* ; 2nd, 1967, Freja Mary Balchin (marr. diss. 1976). *Educ:* King Alfred Sch., Hampstead; Downing Coll., Cambridge, 1947-50. Served in RAF (Signals), 1941-46; Research, MRC Applied Psychology Research Unit, Cambridge, 1950-53; Univ. Demonstrator, then Lecturer, Dept of Psychology, Cambridge, 1953-67; Fellow, Corpus Christi Coll., Cambridge, 1962-67; Professor of Bionics, Dept of Machine Intelligence and Perception, Univ. of Edinburgh, 1967-70 (Chm. of Dept, 1968-70). Visiting Prof.: UCLA, 1963; MIT, 1964; New York Univ., 1966. President: Section J, British Assoc. for Advancement of Science, 1975; Experimental Psychol. Soc., 1981-82. Royal Instn Christmas Lectr, 1967-68. CIBA Foundn Research Prize, 1956; Craik Prize for Physiological Psychology, St John's Coll., Cambridge, 1958; Waverley Gold Medal, 1960. FRMS 1961; FZS 1972; FRSA 1973. Manager of Royal Instn, 1971-74. Founder Editor, Perception, 1972. *Publications:* Recovery from Early Blindness (with Jean Wallace), 1963; Eye and Brain, 1966, 3rd edn 1977; The Intelligent Eye, 1970; Concepts and Mechanisms of Perception, 1974; (ed jtly) Illusion in Nature and Art, 1973; Mind in Science, 1981; articles in various scientific jls and patents for optical and recording instruments and a hearing aid; radio and television appearances. *Recreations:* punning and pondering. *Address:* Brain and Perception Laboratory, Department of Anatomy, The Medical School, University Walk, Bristol BS8 1TD. *Club:* Savile.

GREGORY, Roderic Alfred, CBE 1971; FRS 1965; George Holt Professor of Physiology, University of Liverpool, 1948-81, now Emeritus Professor; *b* 29 Dec. 1913; *o c* of Alfred and Alice Gregory, West Ham, London; *m* 1939, Alice, *o c* of J. D. Watts, London; one *d. Educ:* George Green's Sch., London; University Coll. and Hospital, London. BSc Hons Physiology, 1934; MSc Biochemistry, 1938; MRCS, LRCP, 1939, FRCP 1977; PhD Physiology, 1942; DSc Physiology, 1949; Paul Philip Reitlinger Prize, 1938; Schafer Prize, 1939; Bayliss-Starling Scholar, 1935; Sharpey Scholar, 1936-39 and 1941-42; Rockefeller Fellow, 1939-41; Lecturer in Physiology, University Coll., London (Leatherhead), 1942-45; Senior Lecturer in Experimental Physiology, University of Liverpool, 1945-48; Mem. Biolog. Res. Bd, MRC, 1965-71, Chm. 1969; Mem., MRC, 1967-71; a Vice-Pres., Royal Soc., 1971-73. Hon. Member: Amer. Gastroenterological Assoc., 1967; British Soc. of Gastroenterology, 1974; Physiol. Soc., 1982; Amer Physiol. Soc., 1982; For. Mem., Amer. Acad. of Arts and Sciences, 1980. Inaugural Bengt Ihre Lecture and Anniversary Medal, Swedish Med. Soc., 1963; Lectures: Purser, TCD, 1964; Waller, Univ. of London, 1966; Meml Lecture, Amer. Gastroenterolog.

Assoc., 1966; Ravdin, Amer. Coll. of Surgeons, 1967; Harvey, 1968; William Mitchell Banks, Liverpool Univ., 1970; Finlayson, RCPGlas, 1970; Bayliss-Starling, Physiological Soc. of GB, 1973. Baly Medal, RCP, 1965; John Hunter Medal, RCS, 1969; Beaumont Triennial Prize, Amer. Gastroenterological Assoc., 1976; Royal Medal, Royal Soc., 1978. Fellow, University Coll., London, 1965; Feldberg Foundn Prize, 1966; Feltrinelli Internat. Prize for Medicine, Accademia Nazionale dei Lincei, Rome, 1979. Hon. DSc, Univ. of Chicago, 1966. *Publications:* Secretory Mechanisms of the Gastro-intestinal Tract, 1962; various papers in Jl Physiol., Qly Jl exp. Physiol. and elsewhere since 1935. *Recreation:* music. *Address:* University of Liverpool, PO Box 147, Liverpool L69 38X.

GREGORY, Roland Charles Leslie, (Roy Gregory), CBE 1973; QC 1982; *b* 16 Jan. 1916; *s* of Charles James Alfred and Lilian Eugenie Gregory; *m* 1st, 1949, Olive Elizabeth (*d* 1973), *d* of late Andrew Gay; one *s*; 2nd, 1974, Charlotte, *d* of Lt-Col Peter Goddard, Send, Woking, Surrey. *Educ:* Strand Sch.; London Univ. (LLB Hons). Called to Bar, Gray's Inn, 1950. First entered Civil Service, 1933; Head of Civil Procedure Br., Lord Chancellor's Office, 1966-79, retired; Consultant, 1979-82. Secretary: Austin Jones Cttee on County Court Procedure, 1947-49; Evershed Cttee on Supreme Court Practice and Procedure, 1949-53; County Court Rule Cttee, 1962-79; Matrimonial Causes Rule Cttee, 1967-79; Asst Sec., Supreme Court Rule Cttee, 1968-79; Chm., Working Party on Revision of County Court Rules, 1979-81. *Publication:* County Court Manual, 1st edn 1946 to 4th edn 1962; editor, County Court Practice, 1950-. *Recreations:* music, travel. *Address:* 36 Howard Avenue, Ewell, Surrey KT17 2QJ. *T:* 01-393 8933; 16 Ratton Garden, Ratton Drive, Eastbourne, E Sussex.

GREGORY, Ronald, CBE 1980; QPM 1971; DL; Chief Constable of West Yorkshire Metropolitan Police, since 1974; *b* 23 Oct. 1921; *s* of Charles Henry Gregory and Mary Gregory; *m* 1942, Grace Miller Ellison; two *s*. *Educ:* Harris College. Joined Police Service, Preston, 1941. RAF (Pilot), 1942-44; RN (Pilot), 1944-46. Dep. Chief Constable, Blackpool, 1962-65; Chief Constable, Plymouth, 1965-68; Dep. Chief Constable, Devon and Cornwall, 1968-69; Chief Constable, West Yorkshire Constabulary, 1969-74. DL West Yorks, 1977. *Recreations:* golf, sailing. *Address:* Police Headquarters, Laburnum Road, Wakefield, West Yorkshire. *T:* Wakefield 375222.

GREGSON, family name of **Baron Gregson.**

GREGSON, Baron *cr* 1975 (Life Peer), of Stockport in Greater Manchester; **John Gregson,** AMCT, CBIM; DL; Executive Director, Fairey Holdings Ltd; Director: Fairey Automation Ltd; Fairey Engineering Ltd; Fairey Hydraulics Ltd; Fairey Nuclear Ltd; Part-time Member, British Steel Corporation, since 1976; *b* 29 Jan. 1924. Joined Stockport Base Subsidiary, 1939; Fairey R&D team working on science of nuclear power, 1946; held overall responsibility for company's work on Trawsfynydd nuclear power station; appointed to Board, 1966. Mem., Hse of Lords Select Cttee on Sci. & Technol., 1980- (Chm., Sub-Cttee II, 1980-). Chm., Defence Manufacturers Assoc., 1980-. Mem. Council, Univ. of Manchester Inst. of Science and Technology, 1976-. DL Greater Manchester, 1979. *Recreations:* mountaineering, skiing and climbing. *Address:* Fairey Holdings Limited, Cranford Lane, Heston, Hounslow, Middlesex TW5 9NQ; The Hollow, Offerton Road, Stockport, Cheshire SK2 5HL; 407 Hawkins House, Dolphin Square, SW1V 3XL.

GREGSON, Maj.-Gen. Guy Patrick, CB 1958; CBE 1953; DSO 1943 and Bar 1944; MC 1942; retired as General Officer Commanding 1st Division, Salisbury Plain District (1956-59); *b* 8 April 1906; *m*; one *s* one *d*. *Educ:* Gresham's Sch., Holt; RMA. 2nd Lieut RA, 1925. Served War of 1939-45 (despatches twice, MC, DSO and Bar, Croix de Guerre); Lt-Col 1942; Brig. 1950. Korea, 1953 (CBE). Regional Dir of Civil Defence, Eastern Region, 1960-68. *Address:* Bear's Farm, Hundon, Sudbury, Suffolk. *T:* Hundon 205.

GREGSON, Peter Lewis; Deputy Secretary, Cabinet Office, since 1981; *b* 28 June 1936; *s* of late Walter Henry Gregson and of Lillian Margaret Gregson. *Educ:* Nottingham High Sch.; Balliol Coll., Oxford. Classical Hon. Mods, class I; Lit. Hum. class I; BA 1959; MA 1962. Nat Service, 1959-61; 2nd Lieut RAEC, attached to Sherwood Foresters. Board of Trade: Asst Principal, 1961; Private Sec. to Minister of State, 1963-65; Principal, 1965; Resident Observer, CS Selection Bd, 1966; London Business Sch., 1967; Private Sec. to the Prime Minister, 1968-72 (Parly Affairs, 1968-70; Econ. and Home Affairs, 1970-72); Asst Sec., DTI, and Sec., Industrial Development Adv. Bd, 1972-74; Under Sec., DoI, and Sec., NEB, 1975-77; Under Sec., Dept of Trade, 1977-80, Dep. Sec. (Civil Aviation and Shipping), 1980-81. *Recreations:* gardening, listening to music. *Address:* Cabinet Office, 70 Whitehall, SW1A 2AS.

GREGSON, William Derek Hadfield, CBE 1970; Assistant General Manager, Ferranti (Scotland) Ltd, since 1959, and Director, Ferranti EI, New York; Deputy Chairman, British Airports Authority, since 1975; *b* 27 Jan. 1920; *s* of William Gregson; *m* 1944, Rosalind Helen Reeves; three *s* one *d*. *Educ:* King William's Coll., IoM; Alpine Coll., Villars; Faraday House Engrg College. DFH, CEng, FIEE, CBIM, FIIM. Served with RAF, NW Europe, 1941-45 (Sqdn Ldr); Techn. Sales Man., Ferranti Ltd, Edinburgh, 1946-51; London Man., 1951-59. Chairman: BIM Adv. Bd for Scotland, 1970-75; Scottish Gen. Practitioners Res. Support Unit, 1971-81; Mem. Council: Electronic Engrg Assoc. (Pres. 1963-64); Soc. of British Aerospace Companies

(Chm. Equipment Gp Cttee 1967); BEAMA (Chm. Industrial Control and Electronics Bd 1964; Chm., Measurement, Control and Automation Conference Bd); BIM, 1975-; Member: Electronics EDC, 1965-75; Bd of Livingston New Town, 1968-76; Scottish Council (Develt and Industry); Scottish Council (CBI); Scottish Econ. Planning Council, 1965-71; Machine Tool Expert Cttee, 1969-70; Design Council; British Telecom Scotland (formerly Scottish Telecommunications Bd), 1977-; Director: Anderson Strathclyde Ltd; East of Scotland Industrial Investments Ltd; Edinburgh Chamber of Commerce, 1975-78; Scottish Nat. Orchestra (Dep. Chm.). Commissioner, Northern Lighthouse Bd (Chm., 1979). *Recreations:* reading, cabinet-making, automation in the home. *Address:* 15 Barnton Avenue, Edinburgh EH4 6AJ. *T:* 031-336 3896. *Clubs:* Royal Air Force; New (Edinburgh).

GREIG, Henry Louis Carron, CVO 1973; Chairman: H. Clarkson & Co. Ltd, since 1973; H. Clarkson (Holdings) Ltd, since 1976; Director: James Purdey & Sons Ltd, since 1972; Baltic Mercantile and Shipping Exchange, since 1978; Gentleman Usher to the Queen, since 1961; *b* 21 Feb. 1925; *s* of late Group Captain Sir Louis Greig, KBE, CVO, DL; *m* 1955, Monica Kathleen, *d* of Hon. J. J. Stourton, *qv*; three *s* one *d*. *Educ:* Eton. Scots Guards, 1943-47, Captain. Joined H. Clarkson & Co. Ltd, 1948; Dir, 1954; Man. Dir, 1962. Vice-Chm., Not Forgotten Assoc., 1979-. *Address:* Brook House, Fleet, Hants; Binsness, Forres, Moray. *Clubs:* White's; Royal Findhorn Yacht.

GREIG, Prof. James, MSc (London), PhD (Birmingham); William Siemens Professor of Electrical Engineering, University of London, King's College, 1945-70, now Emeritus Professor; *b* 24 April 1903; *s* of James Alexander Greig and Helen Bruce Meldrum, Edinburgh; *m* 1931, Ethel May, *d* of William Archibald, Edinburgh; one *d*. *Educ:* George Watson's Coll. and Heriot-Watt Coll., Edinburgh; University Coll., University of London. Experience in telephone engineering with Bell Telephone Company, Montreal, 1924-26; Mem. research staff, General Electric Company, London, 1928-33; Asst lectr, University Coll., London, 1933-36; Lectr, Univ. of Birmingham, 1936-39; Head of Dept of Electrical Engineering, Northampton Polytechnic, 1939-45. FIEE (Chm. Measurement Section, 1949-50; Mem. Council, 1955-58); Dean of the Faculty of Engineering, Univ. of London, 1958-62, and Mem. Senate, 1958-70; Mem. Court, Univ. of London, 1967-70. MRI; Fellow Heriot-Watt Coll., 1951; FRSE 1956; FKC 1963. Mem., British Assoc. for the Advancement of Science. Chm., Crail Preservation Soc., 1959-74. *Publications:* papers (dealing mainly with subject of electrical and magnetic measurements) to: Jl Inst. Electrical Engineers, The Wireless Engineer, and Engineering. *Address:* Inch of Kinnordy, Kirriemuir, Angus. *T:* Kirriemuir 2350. *Club:* Athenæum.

GREIG of Eccles, James Dennis, CMG 1967; commodity and financial futures trader and company director; *b* 1926; *o s* of late Dennis George Greig of Eccles and Florence Aileen Marjoribanks; *m* 1st, 1952, Pamela Marguerite Stock (marr. diss., 1960); one *s* one *d*; 2nd, 1960 (marr. diss., 1967); one *s*; 3rd, 1968, Paula Mary Sterling. *Educ:* Winchester Coll.; Clare Coll., Cambridge; London Sch. of Economics. Military Service (Lieut, The Black Watch, seconded to Nigeria Regt), 1944-47. HMOCS: Administrative Officer, Northern Nigeria, 1949-55; Fedn of Nigeria, 1955-59; Dep. Financial Sec. (Economics), Mauritius, 1960-64; Financial Secretary, Mauritius, 1964-67; retired voluntarily on Mauritius achieving internal self-government, 1967. With Booker Bros. (Liverpool) Ltd, 1967-68; Head of Africa and Middle East Bureau, IPPF, 1968-76; Dir, Population Bureau, ODA, 1976-80. *Recreations:* rough shooting, bowls, gardening, bridge. *Address:* 6 Beverley Close, Barnes, SW13. *T:* 01-876 5354; The Braw Bothy, Eccles, Kelso, Roxburghshire. *Club:* Hurlingham.

GRENFELL, family name of **Barons Grenfell** and **St Just.**

GRENFELL, 3rd Baron *cr* 1902; **Julian Pascoe Francis St Leger Grenfell;** Special Representative of the World Bank to the United Nations, since 1974; *b* 23 May 1935; *o s* of 2nd Baron Grenfell, CBE, TD, and of Elizabeth Sarah Polk, *o d* of late Captain Hon. Alfred Shaughnessy, Montreal, Canada; *S* father, 1976; *m* 1st, 1961, Loretta Maria (marr. diss. 1970), *e d* of Alfredo Reali, Florence, Italy; one *d*; 2nd, 1970, Gabrielle Katharina, *o d* of late Dr Ernst Raab, Berlin, Germany; two *d*. *Educ:* Eton; King's Coll., Cambridge. BA (Hons), President of the Union, Cambridge, 1959. 2 Lieut, KRRC (60th Rifles), 1954-56; Captain, Queen's Royal Rifles, TA, 1963; Programme Asst, ATV Ltd, 1960-61; frequent appearances and occasional scripts, for ATV religious broadcasting and current affairs series, 1960-64. Film and TV adviser, Encyclopaedia Britannica Ltd, 1961-64. Joined World Bank, Washington, DC, 1965; Chief of Information and Public Affairs for World Bank Group in Europe, 1970; Dep. Dir, European Office of the World Bank, 1973. *Recreations:* tennis, wine tasting. *Heir: cousin* Francis Pascoe John Grenfell [*b* 28 Feb. 1938; *m* 1977, Elizabeth Katharine, *d* of Hugh Kenyon]. *Address:* Room 2435, The United Nations, New York, NY 10017, USA. *T:* (212) 754-6008. *Clubs:* Travellers', Royal Green Jackets.

GRENFELL, Andrée, (Mrs Roy Warden); President, Glemby International, UK and Europe, 1976-80; Senior Vice President, Glemby International, USA, 1976-80; Non-Executive Director, NAAFI, since 1981; *b* 14 Jan. 1940; *d* of Stephen Grenfell (writer) and Sybil Grenfell; *m* 1972, Roy Warden; two step *s*. *Educ:* privately. Man. Dir, Elizabeth Arden Ltd, UK, 1974-76; Director: Harvey Nichols Knightsbridge, 1972-74; Peter Robinson Ltd, 1968-72. Mem. Council, Inst. of Dirs, 1976; FBIM 1977. *Recreations:* riding, dressage, swimming, yoga. *Address:* Crown Cottage, Little Missenden, Amersham, Bucks.

GRENFELL-BAINES, Prof. Sir George, Kt 1978; OBE 1960; DL; FRIBA; FRTPI; Founder and Director, The Design Teaching Practice, Sheffield, since 1974; *b* Preston, 30 April 1908; *s* of Ernest Charles Baines and Sarah Elizabeth (*née* Grenfell); *m* 1st, 1939, Dorothy Hodson (marr. diss. 1952); two *d*; 2nd, 1954, Milena Ruth Fleischman; one *s* one *d. Educ:* Roebuck Street Council Sch.; Harris Coll., Preston; Manchester Univ. (DipTP). FIES; RIBA Dist Town Planning, 1963. Commenced architectural practice, 1937; founded Grenfell Baines Gp, 1940; Founder Partner/Chm., Building Design Partnership, a multi-disciplinary practice covering all aspects of built environment, 1959-74, retired. Prof. and Head of Dept of Architecture, Univ. of Sheffield, 1972-75, Emeritus, 1976. Lectr/Critic, 14 USA and Canadian univs, 1966; initiated own lecture tour USSR, visiting 19 cities, 1971; expert adviser: UNESCO Conf. Bldgs; Higher Educn, Chile, 1968; Conescal, Mexico City, 1973. RIBA: Mem. Council (nationally elected), 1952-70; Vice-Pres., 1967-69; Ext. Examr, 12 Schs of Architecture, 1953-70. Chm. of Cttees on Professional Practice, Town Planning, Gp Practice and Consortia; a Competition Assessor 7 times; several competition awards: first place in 7 (one internat.); 17 premiums (four internat.). Hon. Fellow, Manchester Polytechnic, 1974; Hon. Vice-Pres., N Lancs Soc. Architects, 1977. Hon. Fellow, Amer. Inst. of Architects, 1982. Broadcaster, UK and Canada. Hon. DLitt Sheffield, 1981. DL Lancs, 1982. *Publications:* contribs to techn. jls. *Recreations:* brooding: on economics and alternative medicine; walking: on hills and by sea-shore. *Address:* 60 West Cliff, Preston, Lancs PR1 8HU. *T:* Preston 55824.

GRENSIDE, John Peter, CBE 1974; Senior Partner, Peat, Marwick, Mitchell & Co., Chartered Accountants; Chairman, Peat Marwick International, since 1980; *b* 23 Jan. 1921; *s* of late Harold Cutcliffe Grenside and late Muriel Grenside; *m* 1946, Yvonne Thérèse Grau; one *s* one *d. Educ:* Rugby School. ACA 1948, FCA 1960. War Service, Royal Artillery, 1941-46 (Captain). Joined Peat, Marwick, Mitchell & Co., 1948, Partner, 1960, Senior Partner, 1977. Inst. Chartered Accountants: Mem. Council, 1966; Chm. of Parliamentary and Law Cttee, 1972-73; Vice-Pres., 1973-74; Dep. Pres., 1974-75; Pres., 1975-76; Chm., Overseas Relations Cttee, 1976-78; UK Rep. on Internat. Accounting Standards Cttee, 1976-80. Jt Vice-Pres., Groupe d'Etudes des Experts Comptables de la CEE, 1972-75; Mem. Panel of Judges for Accountants' Award for Company Accounts, 1973-77. *Publications:* various articles for UK and US accountancy jls. *Recreations:* travel, tennis. *Address:* 51 Cadogan Lane, SW1. *T:* 01-235 3722. *Clubs:* Athenæum, MCC, All England Lawn Tennis, Queens', Hurlingham.

GRENVILLE; *see* Freeman-Grenville.

GRENVILLE, Prof. John Ashley Soames; Professor of Modern History, University of Birmingham, since 1969; *b* Berlin, 11 Jan. 1928; *m* 1st, 1960, Betty Anne Rosenberg (*d* 1974), New York; three *s*; 2nd, 1975, Patricia Carnie; one *d* one step *d. Educ:* Mistley Place and Orwell Park Prep. Sch.; Cambridge Techn. Sch.; corresp. courses; Birkbeck Coll.; LSE; Yale Univ. BA, PhD London; FRHistS. Postgrad. Schol., London Univ., 1951-53; Asst Lectr, subseq. Lectr, Nottingham Univ., 1953-64; Commonwealth Fund Fellow, 1958-59; Postdoctoral Fellow, Yale Univ., 1960-63; Reader in Modern History, Nottingham Univ., 1964-65; Prof. of Internat. History, Leeds Univ., 1965-69. Vis. Prof., Queen's Coll., NY City Univ., 1964, etc; Guestprofessor, Univ. of Hamburg, 1980. Chm., British Univs History Film Consortium, 1968-71; Mem. Council: RHistS, 1971-73; List and Index Soc., 1966-71. Consultant, American and European Bibliographical Centre, Oxford and California and Clio Press, 1960-; Editor, Fontana History of War and Society, 1969-78; Dir of Film for the Historical Assoc., 1975-78. *Publications:* (with J. G. Fuller) The Coming of the Europeans, 1962; Lord Salisbury and Foreign Policy, 1964 (2nd edn 1970); (with G. B. Young) Politics, Strategy and American Diplomacy: studies in foreign policy 1873-1917, 1966 (2nd edn 1971); Documentary Films (with N. Pronay), The Munich Crisis, 1968; The End of Illusions: from Munich to Dunkirk, 1970; The Major International Treaties 1914-1973: a history and guide, 1974; Europe Reshaped 1848-78, 1975; Nazi Germany, 1976; World History of the Twentieth Century I, 1900-1945, 1980; contrib. various learned jls. *Recreation:* listening to music. *Address:* University of Birmingham, PO Box 363, Birmingham B15 2TT; 42 Selly Wick Road, Birmingham B29 7JA. *T:* 021-472 1273. *Club:* Athenæum.

GRENYER, Herbert Charles, FRICS; Vice-President, London Rent Assessment Panel, 1973-79; Deputy Chief Valuer, Board of Inland Revenue, 1968-73; *b* 22 Jan. 1913; *s* of Harry John and Daisy Elizabeth Grenyer (*née* De Maid); *m* 1940, Jean Gladwell Francis; one *s* one *d. Recreations:* golf, gardening, listening to music. *Address:* Old Rickford, Worplesdon, Surrey. *T:* Worplesdon 232173.

GRESWELL, Air Cdre Jeaffreson Herbert, CB 1967; CBE 1962 (OBE 1946); DSO 1944; DFC 1942; RAF, retired; *b* 28 July 1916; *s* of William Territt Greswell; *m* 1939, Gwyneth Alice Hayes; one *s* three *d. Educ:* Repton. Joined RAF, 1935, Pilot. Served War of 1939-45, in Coastal Command, Anti-Submarine No. 217 Sqdn, 1937-41; No. 172 Sqdn, 1942; OC No. 179 Sqdn, Gibraltar, 1943-44. Air Liaison Officer, Pacific Fleet, 1946-47; Staff of Joint Anti-Submarine Sch., 1949-52; Staff of Flying Coll., Manby, 1952-54; Planning Staff, Min. of Defence, 1954-57; OC, RAF Station Kinloss, 1957-59;

Plans HQ, Coastal Comd, 1959-61; Standing Group Rep. to NATO Council, Paris, 1961-64; Commandant, Royal Observer Corps, 1964-68. Sqdn Ldr 1941; Wing Comdr 1942; Gp Capt. 1955; Air Cdre 1961. *Recreation:* croquet. *Address:* Picket Lodge, Ringwood, Hants.

GRETTON, family name of **Baron Gretton.**

GRETTON, 3rd Baron *cr* 1944, of Stapleford; **John Henrik Gretton;** farmer; *b* 9 Feb. 1941; *s* of 2nd Baron Gretton and of Margaret, *e d* of Captain Henrik Loeffler; *S* father, 1982; *m* 1970, Jennifer Ann, *o d* of Edmund Moore, York; one *s* one *d. Educ:* Shrewsbury. Career in malting and brewing, 1961-74. *Recreations:* travel, miniature railways, reading, music. *Heir: s* Hon. John Lysander Gretton, *b* 17 April 1975. *Address:* Stapleford Park, Melton Mowbray, Leics. *T:* Wymondham 229.

GRETTON, Vice-Adm. Sir Peter (William), KCB 1963 (CB 1960); DSO 1942; OBE 1941; DSC 1936; MA; *b* 27 Aug. 1912; *s* of Major G. F. Gretton; *m* 1943, D. N. G. Du Vivier; three *s* one *d. Educ:* Roper's Preparatory Sch.; RNC, Dartmouth. Prize for Five First Class Certificates as Sub.-Lieut; Comdr 1942; Capt. 1948; Rear-Adm. 1958; Vice-Adm. 1961. Served War of 1939-45 (despatches, OBE, DSO and two Bars). Senior Naval Mem. of Directing Staff of Imperial Defence Coll., April 1958-60; Flag Officer, Sea Training, 1960-61; a Lord Commissioner of the Admiralty, Dep. Chief of Naval Staff and Fifth Sea Lord, 1962-63, retd. Domestic Bursar, University Coll., Oxford, 1965-71, Senior Research Fellow, 1971-79. Vice-Pres., Royal Humane Soc.; Mem., Cttee of AA. Testimonial of Royal Humane Society, 1940. *Publications:* Convoy Escort Commander, 1964; Maritime Strategy: A Study of British Defence Problems, 1965; Former Naval Person: Churchill and the Navy, 1968; Crisis Convoy, 1974. *Address:* 29 Northmoor Road, Oxford. *Club:* Army and Navy.

GREVE, Prof. John; Professor of Social Policy and Administration, University of Leeds, since 1974; *b* 23 Nov. 1927; *s* of Steffen A. and Ellen C. Greve; *m* Stella (*née* Honeywood); one *s* one *d. Educ:* elementary and secondary Schs in Cardiff; London Sch. of Economics (BSc(Econ)). Various jobs, incl. Merchant Navy, Youth Employment Service, and insurance, 1946-55; student, 1955-58; research work, then Univ. teaching, 1958-. Has worked in Norway at research institutes. Community Programmes Dept, Home Office, 1969-74; Prof. of Social Admin, Univ. of Southampton, 1969-74. Mem., Royal Commn on Distribution of Income and Wealth, 1974-79. *Publications:* The Housing Problem, 1961 (and 1969); London's Homeless, 1964; Private Landlords in England, 1965; (with others) Comparative Social Administration, 1969, 2nd edn 1972; Housing, Planning and Change in Norway, 1970; Voluntary Housing in Scandinavia, 1971; (with others) Homelessness in London, 1971; Low Incomes in Sweden, 1978; various articles and papers, mainly on social problems, policies and administration, a few short stories. *Recreations:* walking, painting, listening to music, writing, good company. *Address:* c/o Department of Social Policy and Administration, University of Leeds, Leeds LS2 9JT.

GREVILLE, family name of **Baron Greville,** and of **Earl of Warwick.**

GREVILLE, 4th Baron, *cr* 1869; **Ronald Charles Fulke Greville;** *b* 11 April 1912; *s* of 3rd Baron and Olive Grace (*d* 1959), *d* of J. W. Grace, Leybourne Grange, Kent, and *widow* of Henry Kerr; *S* father 1952. *Educ:* Eton; Magdalen Coll., Oxford Univ. *Recreations:* music, travel, tennis, gardening. *Heir:* none. *Address:* 75 Swan Court, Chelsea Manor Street, SW3. *T:* 01-352 3444; Cubberley, Ross-on-Wye, Herefordshire. *T:* Ross-on-Wye 3522. *Club:* Hurlingham.

GREVILLE, Brig. Phillip Jamieson, CBE 1972; Defence Writer for Adelaide Advertiser, since 1980; *b* 12 Sept. 1925; *s* of Col S. J. Greville, OBE and Mrs D. M. Greville; *m* 1948, June Patricia Anne Martin; two *s* one *d* (and one *s* one *d* decd). *Educ:* RMC Duntroon; Sydney Univ. (BEng). 2/8 Field Co., 2nd AIF, New Guinea, 1945; 1 RAR Korea (POW), 1951-53; Senior Instructor SME Casula, 1953-55; CRE, RMC Duntroon, 1955-58; Staff Coll., Camberley and Transportation Trng UK, 1959-61; Dir of Transportation AHQ, 1962-65; GSO1 1st Div., 1966; CE Eastern Comd, 1969-71; Comdr 1st Australian Logistic Support Group, Vietnam, 1971; Actg Comdr 1st Australian Task Force, Vietnam, 1971-72 (CBE); Dir of Transport, 1973-74; Dir Gen., Logistics, 1975-76; Comdr, Fourth Mil. District, 1977-80, retired. FIE Aust, FCIT. *Publications:* A Short History of Victoria Barracks Paddington, 1969; The Central Organisation for War and its Application to Movements, 1975, Sapper series (RE Officers in Australia); The Army Portion of the National Estate, 1977. *Recreation:* golf. *Address:* 68 Fourth Avenue, St Peters, SA 5069, Australia. *Clubs:* Adelaide; Naval, Military and Air Force (Adelaide); Royal Sydney Golf.

GREY, family name of **Earl Grey,** and of **Baron Grey of Naunton.**

GREY; *see* De Grey.

GREY, 6th Earl, *cr* 1806; **Richard Fleming George Charles Grey;** Bt 1746; Baron Grey, 1801; Viscount Howick, 1806; *b* 5 March 1939; *s* of late Albert Harry George Campbell Grey (Trooper, Canadian Army Tanks, who *d* on active service, 1942) and Vera Helen Louise Harding; *S* cousin, 1963; *m* 1st, 1966, Margaret Ann (marr. diss. 1974), *e d* of Henry Bradford, Ashburton; 2nd, 1974, Stephanie Caroline, *o d* of Donald Gaskell-Brown and formerly wife of Surg.-Comdr Neil Leicester Denham, RN. *Educ:* Hounslow Coll.; Hammersmith Coll. of Bldg (Quantity Surveying). Pres., Assoc. of Cost and Executive Accountants, 1978. Mem., Liberal Party. *Recreations:* golf, sailing. *Heir: b* Philip Kent Grey [*b* 11 May 1940; *m* 1968, Ann Catherine, *y d* of Cecil Applegate, Kingsbridge, Devon; one *s* one *d*]. *Address:* House of Lords, SW1.

GREY OF NAUNTON, Baron, *cr* 1968 (Life Peer); **Ralph Francis Alnwick Grey,** GCMG 1964 (KCMG 1959, CMG 1955); GCVO 1973 (KCVO 1956); OBE 1951; Chancellor, New University of Ulster, since 1980; *b* 15 April 1910; *o s* of late Francis Arthur Grey and Mary Wilkie Grey (*née* Spence); *m* 1944, Esmé, CStJ, *widow* of Pilot Officer Kenneth Kirkcaldie, RAFVR, and *d* of late A. V. Burcher and of Florence Burcher, Remuera, Auckland, New Zealand; two *s* one *d. Educ:* Wellington Coll., NZ; Auckland Univ. Coll.; Pembroke Coll., Cambridge. LLB (NZ). Barrister and Solicitor of Supreme Court of New Zealand, 1932; Associate to Hon. Mr Justice Smith, 1932-36; Probationer, Colonial Administrative Service, 1936; Administrative Service, Nigeria: Cadet, 1937; Asst Financial Sec., 1949; Administrative Officer, Class I, 1951; Development Sec., 1952; Sec. to Governor-Gen. and Council of Ministers, 1954; Chief Sec. of the Federation, 1955-57; Dep. Gov.-Gen., 1957-59; Gov. and C-in-C, British Guiana, 1959-64; Governor and C-in-C of The Bahamas, 1964-68, and of the Turks and Caicos Islands, 1965-68; Governor of N Ireland, 1968-73. Dep. Chm., Commonwealth Development Corp., 1973-79, Chm. 1979-80. Pres., Chartered Inst. of Secretaries, NI, 1970-. Mem., Bristol Regional Bd, Lloyds Bank Ltd, 1973-81; Chm., Central Council, Royal Over-Seas League, 1976-81, Pres., 1981-. Pres., Scout Council, NI, 1968-. Mem. Council, Cheltenham Ladies' College. Hon. Bencher, Inn of Court of N Ireland. Hon. Freeman: City of Belfast, 1972; Lisburn, 1975; Freeman, City of London, 1980. Hon. LLD QUB, 1971; Hon. DLitt NUU, 1980. GCStJ; Kt Comdr, Commandery of Ards, 1968-76. Bailiff of Egle. *Recreation:* golf. *Address:* Overbrook, Naunton, near Cheltenham, Glos. *T:* Guiting Power 263. *Clubs:* Travellers'; Ulster (Hon.).

GREY, Alan Hartley; HM Diplomatic Service; Ambassador at Libreville, since 1982; *b* 26 June 1925; *s* of William Hartley Grey and Gladys Grey; *m* 1950, Joan Robinson; one *s* one *d. Educ:* Bootle Secondary Sch. for Boys. RAF, 1943-48; Foreign Service (Br. B), 1948; Tel Aviv, 1949; Tabriz and Khorramshahr, 1950-52; 3rd Sec., Belgrade, 1952-54; Vice-Consul, Dakar, 1954-57; Second Sec. (Commercial), Helsinki, 1958-61; FO, 1961-64; Second Sec. (Econ.), Paris, 1964-66; FO (later FCO), 1966-70; Consul (Commercial), Lille, 1970-74; FCO, 1974-82. *Recreations:* gardening, Civil Service trade unionism. *Address:* c/o Foreign and Commonwealth Office, SW1A 2AH.

GREY, Sir Anthony (Dysart), 7th Bt *cr* 1814; *b* 19 Oct. 1949; *s* of Edward Elton Grey (*d* 1962) (*o s* of 6th Bt) and of Nancy, *d* of late Francis John Meagher, Perth, WA; *S* grandfather, 1974; *m* 1970. *Educ:* Guildford Grammar School, WA. *Recreations:* fishing, painting. *Address:* 86 Kingsway Gardens, 38 King's Park Road, West Perth, Western Australia.

GREY, Beryl, (Mrs S. G. Svenson), CBE 1973; Prima Ballerina, Sadler's Wells Ballet, now Royal Ballet, 1942-57; Artistic Director, London Festival Ballet, 1968-79; *b* London, 11 June 1927; *d* of Arthur Ernest Groom; *m* 1950, Dr Sven Gustav Svenson; one *s. Educ:* Dame Alice Owens Girls' Sch., London. Professional training: Madeline Sharp Sch., Sadler's Wells Sch. (Schol.), de Vos Sch. Début Sadler's Wells Co., 1941, with Ballerina rôles following same year in Les Sylphides, The Gods Go A'Begging, Le Lac des Cygnes, Act II, Comus. First full-length ballet, Le Lac des Cygnes on 15th birthday, 1942. Has appeared since in leading rôles of many ballets including: Sleeping Beauty, Giselle, Sylvia, Checkmate, Ballet Imperial, Death of the Burthens, Homage, Birthday Offering, The Lady and the Fool. Film: The Black Swan (3 Dimensional Ballet Film), 1952. Left Royal Ballet, Covent Garden, Spring 1957, to become free-lance ballerina. Regular guest appearances with Royal Ballet at Covent Garden and on European, African, American and Far Eastern Tours. Guest Artist, London's Festival Ballet in London and abroad, 1958-64. First Western ballerina to appear with Bolshoi Ballet: Moscow, Leningrad, Kiev, Tiflis, 1957-58; First Western ballerina to dance with Chinese Ballet Co. in Peking and Shanghai, 1964. Engagements and tours abroad include: Central and S America, Mexico, Rhodesia and S Africa, Canada, NZ, Lebanon, Germany, Norway, Sweden, Denmark, Finland, Belgium, Holland, France, Switzerland, Italy, Portugal, Austria, Czechoslovakia, Poland, Rumania. Regular television and broadcasts in England and abroad. Dir-Gen., Arts Educational Trust, 1966-68; Mem. Council, Imperial Soc. of Teachers of Dancing; Vice-Pres., Royal Acad. of Dancing; Governor: Dame Alice Owens Girls' Sch., London; Frances Mary Buss Foundn. Hon. DMus Leicester, 1970; Hon. DLitt City Univ., 1974. *Publications:* Red Curtain Up, 1958; Through the Bamboo Curtain, 1965; My Favourite Ballet Stories, 1981. *Relevant publications:* biographical studies (by Gordon Anthony), 1952, (by Pigeon Crowle), 1952; Beryl Grey, Dancers of Today (by Hugh Fisher), 1955; Beryl Grey, a biography (by David Gillard), 1977. *Recreations:* music, painting, reading, swimming. *Address:* Fernhill, Priory Road, Forest Row, Sussex. *T:* Forest Row 2539.

GREY, Charles Frederick, CBE 1966; miner; Independent Methodist Minister; *b* 25 March 1903; *m* 1925, Margaret, *d* of James Aspey. Mem. of Divisional Labour Exec. MP (Lab) Durham, 1945-70; Opposition Whip (Northern), 1962-64; Comptroller of HM Household, 1964-66, Treasurer, 1966-69. President: Independent Methodist Connexion, 1971; Sunderland and District Free Church Council; Mem., Univ. of Durham Council. Freeman of

Durham City, 1971. Hon. DCL Durham, 1976. *Address:* 38 Gelt Crescent, Lyons Avenue, Hetton-le-Hole, Tyne and Wear DH5 0HX. *T:* Hetton-le-Hole 2292.

GREY, Col Geoffrey Bridgman, CB 1977; CBE 1960; TD 1954; DL, JP; Partner, Messrs Dawkins & Grey, Solicitors, Birmingham, since 1946; *b* 19 Oct. 1911; *s* of Alderman Samuel John Grey (formerly Lord Mayor of Birmingham) and Mrs Jessie Grey; *m* 1939, Betty Francis Mary (*née* Trimingham); two *d. Educ:* Mill Hill Sch., London; Brasenose Coll., Oxford Univ. (MA, BCL). Admitted solicitor, 1937. Commnd TA, S Staffs Regt, 1938; served War, 1939-45: European campaign with S Staffs, and York and Lancaster Regts; mentioned in despatches; Major 1943; TA, 1945-: Lt-Col 1950, Col 1954; comd 5th Bn S Staffs Regt, 1950-53; Hon. Colonel: 5th Bn S Staffs Regt, 1957-67; 5/6 (Territorial) Bn Staffs Regt (Prince of Wales), 1967-69; 5th Staffs Cadet Regt, 1963-; ADC, 1963-66; Chm., W Midland TA&VRA, 1970-77. Hon. Legal Adviser, W Midlands Baptist (Trust) Assoc. Pres., Birmingham Consular Assoc., 1965-67 (Vice-Pres., 1963-65); Hon. Consul for the Netherlands, 1959-81; Vice-Consul for Belgium, 1965-. DL Staffs, 1954; JP City of Birmingham, 1966. Officer, Order of Orange Nassau, 1975. *Recreation:* photography. *Address:* 215 Bristol Road, Edgbaston, Birmingham B5 7UB. *T:* 021-440 3080. *Clubs:* Naval and Military; Edgbaston Priory (Birmingham).

GREY, John Egerton, CB 1980; Clerk Assistant and Clerk of Public Bills, House of Lords, since 1974; *b* 8 Feb. 1929; *s* of late John Grey and Nancy Grey; *m* 1961, Patricia Hanna; two adopted *s. Educ:* Dragon Sch., Oxford; Blundell's; Brasenose Coll., Oxford. MA, BCL. Called to Bar, Inner Temple, 1954; practised at Chancery Bar, 1954-59. Clerk in Parliament Office, House of Lords, 1959-. *Recreation:* gardening. *Address:* 43 Half Moon Lane, SE24. *T:* 01-274 0468. *Club:* Arts.

GREY, (Patrick) Ronald, QC 1980; a Recorder of the Crown Court, since 1981; *b* 17 March 1927; *s* of Eric Grey and Anna Marie Grey (*née* Baggioli); *m* 1st, 1955, Elisabeth Marguerite Southey (marr. diss. 1971); one *d* ; 2nd, 1974, Annabel Hope, 2nd *d* of late Col Max Freeman, OBE, and of Eileen Freeman; one *s. Educ:* Abingdon Sch.; private tutors. Commissioned in 5th Royal Gurkha Rifles (FF), 1945; served as Lieut, 3rd Bn, Java and Malaya, until 1947. Called to the Bar, Middle Temple, 1950; Crown Prosecuting Counsel, Cyprus, 1955-57; Sen. Crown Prosecuting Counsel, Cyprus, 1957-59; Sen. Magistrate, Bermuda, 1959-62; Deputy Circuit Judge, 1976-81. *Recreations:* listening to music, photography, gardening. *Address:* 3 Middle Temple Lane, Temple, EC4. *T:* 01-583 0659; 214 Cranmer Court, Sloane Avenue, SW3. *Club:* Hurlingham.

GREY, Sir Paul (Francis), KCMG 1963 (CMG 1951); *b* 2 Dec. 1908; *s* of Lt-Col Arthur Grey, CIE, and Teresa (*née* Alleyne); *m* 1936, Agnes Mary, *d* of late Richard Weld-Blundell, Ince-Blundell Hall, Lancs; three *s. Educ:* Charterhouse; Christ Church, Oxford. Entered Diplomatic Service, 1933; served in Rome, 1935; Foreign Office, 1939; Rio de Janeiro, 1944; The Hague, 1945; Counsellor, Lisbon, 1949; Minister, British Embassy, Moscow, 1951-54; Assistant Under Sec., Foreign Office, Sept. 1954-57; HM Ambassador to Czechoslovakia, 1957-60; HM Ambassador to Switzerland, 1960-64. *Recreations:* shooting and fishing. *Address:* Holm Wood, Elstead, Godalming, Surrey.

GREY, Robin Douglas, QC 1979; a Recorder of the Crown Court, since 1979; *b* 23 May 1931; *s* of Dr Francis Temple Grey, MA, MB, and Eglantine Grey; *m* 1972, Berenice Anna Wheatley; one *s* one *d. Educ:* Summer Fields Prep. Sch., Oxford; Eastbourne Coll.; London Univ. (LLB Hons). Called to the Bar, Gray's Inn, 1957. Crown Counsel, Colonial Legal Service, Aden, 1959-63 (Actg Registrar Gen. and Actg Attorney Gen. for short periods); practising barrister, 1963-; Dep. Circuit Judge, 1977. Mem., British Acad. of Forensic Sciences. *Recreations:* tennis, golf, fishing. *Address:* 3 King's Bench Walk, Temple, EC4Y 7DQ. *T:* 01-892 6031. *Club:* Hurlingham.

GREY, Ronald; *see* Grey, P. R.

GREY EGERTON, Sir (Philip) John (Caledon), 15th Bt, *cr* 1617; *b* 19 Oct. 1920; *er s* of Sir Philip Grey Egerton, 14th Bt; *S* father, 1962; *m* 1952, Margaret Voase (*d* 1971) (who *m* 1941, Sqdn Ldr Robert A. Ullman, *d* 1943), *er d* of late Rowland Rank. *Educ:* Eton. Served Welsh Guards, 1939-45. *Recreation:* fishing. *Heir: b* Brian Balguy Le Belward Egerton, *b* 5 Feb. 1925. *Address:* 70 Fort George, St Peter Port, Guernsey, Channel Islands. *Club:* Marylebone Cricket (MCC).

GREY-TURNER, Dr Elston, CBE 1980; MC 1944; TD 1955; Secretary, British Medical Association, 1976-79, Vice-President, since 1982; *b* 16 Aug. 1916; *s* of late Prof. George Grey Turner, LLD, DCh, MS, FRCS, FRCSEd, FRACS, and late Alice Grey Schofield, BSc; *m* 1952, Lilias, *d* of late Col Sterling Charles Tomlinson, Hereford; two *s* one *d. Educ:* Winchester Coll.; Trinity Coll., Cambridge; St Bartholomew's Hosp. BA 1938, MA 1942, Cantab; MRCS, LRCP 1942. Ho. Surg., St Bart's Hosp., 1942. Served War in RAMC (N Af., Italy, Germany), 1942-46. Ho. Phys., Addenbrooke's Hosp., 1946; Asst Principal, Min. of Health, 1947-48; Jt Sec., Interdeptl Cttee on Rating of Site Values (Simes Cttee), 1948; Asst Sec., BMA, 1948, Under-Sec. 1960, Dep. Sec. 1964. Sec., Jt Emergency Cttee of the Professions, 1952; Local Sec., Gen. Assembly of World Med. Assoc., 1949; first World Conf. on Med. Educn, 1953; 19th World Med. Assembly, 1965; Sec.-Gen.,

Standing Cttee of Doctors of the EEC, 1976. Freeman, City of London, 1946; Lt-Col RAMC (TA), 1956; Col RAMC (TA), 1958; QHP, 1960-62; Carmichael Lectr, Royal Coll. of Surgeons in Ireland, 1971; Crookshank Lectr, Faculty of Radiologists, 1973. Grey Turner Lectr, Internat. Soc. of Surgery, 1979. Mem., Court of Assistants, Soc. of Apothecaries of London, 1965– (Master, 1975-76); Hon. Col, 257 (Southern) Gen. Hosp., RAMC(V), 1973-78; Trustee RAMC Historical Museum, 1978–. Dir, Provident Assoc. for Medical Care Ltd, 1976–; Mem. Council, Medical Insurance Agency Ltd, 1977–; Chm. Med. Bd, St John Ambulance, 1982–. Silver Jubilee Medal, 1977. OStJ 1961. Hon. MD Newcastle, 1980. *Publications:* (with F. M. Sutherland) History of the British Medical Association, vol. II, 1932-1981, 1982; articles in British and foreign med. jls. *Recreation:* gardener-handyman. *Address:* The Manor House, Petersham, Surrey TW10 7AG. *Club:* Carlton.

GRIBBLE, Rev. Canon Arthur Stanley, MA; Canon Residentiary and Chancellor of Peterborough Cathedral, 1967-79; Canon Emeritus since 1979; *b* 18 Aug. 1904; *er s* of J. B. Gribble; *m* 1938, Edith Anne, *er d* of late Laurence Bailey; one *s. Educ:* Queens' Coll. and Westcott House, Cambridge (Burney Student, Univ. of Cambridge); Univ. of Heidelberg. Curate: St Mary, Windermere, 1930-33, Almondbury, 1933-36; Chaplain Sarum Theological Coll., 1936-38; Rector of Shepton Mallet, 1938-54. Examining Chaplain to Bp of Bath and Wells, 1947-54; Proctor in Convocation, diocese Bath and Wells, 1947-54; Rural Dean of Shepton Mallet, 1949-54; Prebendary of Wiveliscombe in Wells Cathedral, 1949-54; Principal, Queen's Coll., Birmingham, 1954-67; Recognised Lectr, Univ. of Birmingham, 1954-67. Hon. Canon, Birmingham Cathedral, 1954-67. Commissary for the Bishop of Kimberley and Kuruman, 1964-66. Examng Chaplain to Bishop of Peterborough, 1968–. Visiting Lectr, Graduate Theological Union, Berkeley, USA, 1970. *Recreation:* mountaineering. *Address:* 2 Princes Road, Stamford, Lincs. *T:* Stamford 55838.

GRIBBLE, Leonard Reginald; Author; *b* 1 Feb. 1908; *s* of late Wilfred Browning Gribble and late Ada Mary Sterry; *m* 1932, Nancy Mason; one *d.* In 1928 wrote first detective story; literary adviser various London publishers: inaugurated The Empire Bookshelf series for the BBC; judge in two international novel competitions; has devised and written commercial radio programmes and commercial films; founder mem. Paternosters Club; in Press and Censorship Div. of Ministry of Information, 1940-45; co-founder Crime Writers Assoc., 1953. *Publications:* The Gillespie Suicide Mystery, A Christmas Treasury, 1929; The Jesus of the Poets, The Grand Modena Murder, 1930; Is This Revenge?, 1931; The Stolen Home Secretary, 1932; Famous Feats of Detection and Deduction, The Secret of Tangles, 1933; The Riddle of the Ravens, 1934; All The Year Round Stories (with Nancy Gribble), 1935; Riley of the Special Branch; The Case of the Malverne Diamonds, 1936; The Case-book of Anthony Slade, 1937; Tragedy in E flat, 1938; The Arsenal Stadium Mystery (filmed), 1939 and 1950; Heroes of the Fighting RAF, 1941; Death by Design (a film), 1942; Epics of the Fighting RAF, 1943; Heroes of the Merchant Navy, 1944; Toy Folk and Nursery People (verse), 1945; Best Children's Stories of the Year (editor), 1946-50; Profiles from notable Modern Biographies (editor); Atomic Murder, 1947; Hangman's Moon, 1949; They Kidnapped Stanley Matthews, 1950; The Frightened Chameleon, 1951; Murder Out of Season, 1952; Famous Manhunts, 1953; Adventures in Murder, 1954; Triumphs of Scotland Yard, 1955; Death Pays the Piper, 1956; Famous Judges and their Trials, 1957; Great Detective Exploits, 1958; Don't Argue with Death, 1959; Hands of Terror, 1960; Clues that Spelled Guilty, 1961; When Killers Err, 1962; They Challenged the Yard, 1963; Heads You Die, 1964; Such Women are Deadly, 1965; Great Manhunters of the Yard, 1966; Strip Tease Macabre, 1967; Stories of Famous Conspirators, 1968; Famous Stories of Scientific Detection, 1969; Strange Crimes of Passion, 1970; They Got Away with Murder, 1971; Sisters of Cain, 1972; Programmed for Death, 1973; Such was Their Guilt, 1974; They Conspired to Kill, 1975; You Can't Die Tomorrow, 1976; Compelled to Kill, 1977; They Came to Kill, 1979; Crime Stranger than Fiction, 1981; Dead End in Mayfair, 1981; also writes fiction (some filmed) under several pseudonyms; translations in fourteen languages; contribs to Chambers's Encyclopædia, Encyclopedia Americana, DNB; book-reviews, feature articles, short stories and serials to various publications. *Recreations:* motoring abroad, watching things grow. *Address:* Chandons, Firsdown Close, High Salvington, Worthing, West Sussex. *T:* Worthing 61976.

GRIBBON, Maj.-Gen. Nigel St George, OBE 1960; Managing Director, Sallingbury Ltd, since 1977; Director, Gatewood Engineers Ltd, since 1976; *b* Feb. 1917; *s* of late Brig. W. H. Gribbon, CMG, CBE; *m* 1943, Rowan Mary MacLeish; two *s* one *d. Educ:* Rugby Sch.; Sandhurst. King's Own, 1937-42; GSO3 10th Indian Div., 1942; Staff Coll. Quetta, 1943; Bde Major, 1st.Parachute Bde, 1946; RAF Staff Coll., 1947; OC 5 King's Own, 1958-60; AMS WO, 1960-62; Comdr 161 Bde, 1963-65; Canadian Nat. Defence Coll., 1965-66; DMC MoD, 1966-67; ACOS NORTHAG, 1967-69; ACOS (Intelligence), SHAPE, 1970-72. Man. Dir, Partnerplan Public Affairs Ltd, 1973-75; Chm., Sallingbury Ltd, 1975-77. Chm., European Channel Tunnel Gp Public Affairs Cttee, 1980–; Member Council: British Atlantic Cttee; Mouvement Européen Français (Londres); Canada-UK Chamber of Commerce (Pres. 1981); Wyndham Place Trust; Chm., UK Falkland Islands Trust. Radio commentator on public affairs. Mem., European Atlantic Gp. Freeman, City of London; Liveryman, Worshipful Co. of Shipwrights. *Recreation:* sailing. *Address:* The Pump Cottage, Orford, Suffolk. *T:* Orford 413. *Clubs:* Army and Navy, Canada; Little Ship (Rear Commodore

Training, 1978-80); Royal Yachting Association; Army Sailing Association.

GRIDLEY, family name of **Baron Gridley.**

GRIDLEY, 2nd Baron, *cr* 1955; **Arnold Hudson Gridley;** *b* 26 May 1906; *er surv. s* of 1st Baron Gridley, KBE, Culwood, Lye Green, Chesham, Bucks; *S* father, 1965; *m* 1948, Edna Lesley, *d* of late Richard Wheen of Shanghai, China; one *s* three *d. Educ:* Oundle. Overseas Civil Service, Malaya, 1928-41; served in various Govt appts; interned during Japanese occupation in Changi Gaol, Singapore, 1941-45; returned to duty, 1945; Dep.-Comptroller of Customs and Excise, Malaya, 1956, retired 1957. Mem. Exec. Cttee, Overseas Service Pensioners Assoc., 1957–; Govt Trustee, Far East (POW and Internee) Fund, 1973–; with Parly Delegn to BAOR, 1976; visited and toured Rhodesia during Lancaster House Conf. on Public Service Pensions, 1979. Chm., Centralised Audio Systems Ltd, 1970–; Chm. and Dir, Family Insurance Advisory Services, 1981–. Mem., Somerset CC Rating Appeals Tribunal, 1970-73; Adviser to Peoples' Trust for Endangered Species, 1979–; Chm., Board of Governors, Hall Sch., Bratton Seymour, Som, 1970-76. *Heir: s* Hon. Richard David Arnold Gridley, *b* 22 Aug. 1956. *Address:* Coneygore, Stoke Trister, Wincanton, Somerset. *T:* Wincanton 32209. *Club:* Royal Over-Seas League.

GRIER, Anthony MacGregor, CMG 1963; General Manager, Redditch Development Corporation, 1964-76; Member (C), Hereford and Worcester County Council, since 1977; *b* 12 April 1911; *e s* of late Very Rev. R. M. Grier, St Ninian's House, Perth, Scotland, and late Mrs E. M. Grier; *m* 1946, Hon. Patricia Mary Spens, *er d* of 1st Baron Spens, PC, KBE, QC; two *s* one *d. Educ:* St Edward's Sch.; Exeter Coll., Oxford. Colonial Administrative Service, Sierra Leone, 1935; attached to Colonial Office in London and Delhi, 1943-47; North Borneo, now Sabah, Malaysia, 1947-64; Chm., Sabah Electricity Board, 1956-64. Chm. of Governors, King's School, Worcester, 1976–. *Recreations:* tennis, golf, shooting. *Address:* Mulberry House, Abbots Morton, Worcester WR7 4NA. *T:* Inkberrow 792422. *Club:* East India, Devonshire, Sports and Public Schools.
See also F. J. R. Grier, P. A. Grier.

GRIER, Francis John Roy, FRCO; Organist and Tutor in Music, Christ Church, Oxford, since 1981; *b* 29 July 1955; *s* of Anthony MacGregor Grier, *qv; m* 1976, Shelagh Elizabeth (*née* Banks). *Educ:* Eton; Cambridge Univ. (MA). Assistant Organist, Christ Church, Oxford, 1977. University Lecturer, organ soloist and chamber music pianist. *Recreation:* walking. *Address:* 11 Church Street, Bladon, Oxon OX7 1RS. *T:* Woodstock 811053.

GRIER, Patrick Arthur, OBE 1963; HM Diplomatic Service, retired; *b* 2 Dec. 1918; *s* of late Very Rev. R. M. Grier, Provost of St Ninian's Cath., Perth, and Mrs E. M. Grier; *m* 1946, Anna Fraembs, *y d* of Hüttendirektor H. Fraembs, Rasselstein, Neuwied, Germany; one *d. Educ:* Lancing; King's Coll., Cambridge (MA 1946). Served War of 1939-45 with RA and Indian Mountain Artillery, NW Frontier of India and Burma (Major). Kreis Resident Officer of Mönchen-Gladbach, 1946-47; Colonial Administrative Service, N Nigeria, 1947, later HMOCS; Clerk to Exec. Council, Kaduna, 1953-55; W African Inter-territorial Secretariat, Accra, 1955-57; Principal Asst Sec. to Governor of N Nigeria, 1957-59; Dep. Sec. to Premier, 1959-63; retired from HMOCS, 1963. CRO, 1963-64; First Sec., Canberra, 1964-66; Head of Chancery, Port of Spain, 1966-69; Dep. UK Permanent Rep. to Council of Europe, Strasbourg, 1969-74; Counsellor and Head of Chancery, Berne, 1974-78. *Recreations:* tennis, ski-ing. *Address:* Buffalo Cottage, Wootton, New Milton, Hants. *T:* New Milton 618398. *Club:* Royal Commonwealth Society.
See also A. M. Grier.

GRIERSON, Prof. Philip, MA, LittD; FBA 1958; FSA; Fellow, since 1935, Librarian, 1944-69, and President, 1966-76, Gonville and Caius College, Cambridge; Professor of Numismatics, University of Cambridge, 1971-78, now Emeritus; Professor of Numismatics and the History of Coinage, University of Brussels, 1948-81; Hon. Keeper of the Coins, Fitzwilliam Museum, Cambridge, since 1949; Adviser in Byzantine Numismatics to the Dumbarton Oaks Library and Collections, Harvard University, at Washington, USA, since 1955; *b* 15 Nov. 1910; *s* of Philip Henry Grierson and Roberta Ellen Jane Pope. *Educ:* Marlborough Coll.; Gonville and Caius Coll., Cambridge (MA 1936, LittD 1971). University Lectr in History, Cambridge, 1945-59; Reader in Medieval Numismatics, Cambridge, 1959-71. Literary Dir of Royal Historical Society, 1945-55; Ford's Lectr in History, University of Oxford, 1956-57. Pres. Royal Numismatic Society, 1961-66. Corresp. Fellow, Mediaeval Acad. of America, 1972; Corresp. Mem., Koninklijke Vlaamse Acad., 1955; Assoc. Mem., Acad. Royale de Belgique, 1968. Hon. LittD: Ghent, 1958; Leeds, 1978. *Publications:* Les Annales de Saint-Pierre de Gand, 1937; Books on Soviet Russia, 1917-42, 1943; Sylloge of Coins of the British Isles, Vol. 1 (Fitzwilliam Museum: Early British and Anglo-Saxon Coins), 1958; Bibliographie numismatique, 1966, 2nd edn 1979; English Linear Measures: a study in origins, 1973; (with A. R. Bellinger) Catalogue of the Byzantine Coins in the Dumbarton Oaks Collection and in the Whittemore Collection, vols 1, 2, 3, 1966-73; Numismatics, 1975; Monnaies du Moyen Age, 1976; The Origins of Money, 1977; Les monnaies, 1977; Dark Age Numismatics, 1979; Later Medieval Numismatics, 1979; Byzantine Coins, 1982; trans. F. L. Ganshof, Feudalism, 1952; editor: C. W. Previté-Orton, The Shorter Cambridge Medieval History, 1952; H. E. Ives,

The Venetian Gold Ducat and its Imitations, 1954; Studies in Italian History presented to Miss E. M. Jamison, 1956. *Recreations:* squash racquets, science fiction. *Address:* Gonville and Caius College, Cambridge CB2 1TA. *T:* Cambridge 312211.

GRIERSON, Sir Richard Douglas, 11th Bt *cr* 1685; *b* 25 June 1912; *o s* of Sir Robert Gilbert White Grierson, 10th Bt, and Hilda (*d* 1962), *d* of James Stewart, Surbiton, Surrey; *S* father 1957; unmarried. *Educ:* Imperial Service Coll., Windsor. Journalist. *Heir: cousin* Michael John Bewes Grierson [*b* 24 July 1921; *m* 1971, Valerie Anne, *d* of Russell Wright]. *Address:* 4 Modena Road, Hove BN3 5QG. *T:* Brighton 736355.

GRIERSON, Ronald Hugh; Director, General Electric Co., since 1968; Chairman, GEC Inc.; Director: S. G. Warburg & Co. Ltd, 1958–68 and since 1980; R. J. Reynolds Inc., since 1977; Chrysler Corporation, since 1982; Vice-Chairman, Warburg Paribas Becker Inc., since 1980; *b* Nürnberg, Bavaria, 1921; *s* of E. J. Griessmann (name changed by Deed Poll in 1943); *m* 1966, Elizabeth Heather, Viscountess Bearsted, *er d* of Mrs G. Firmston-Williams; one *s*. *Educ:* Lycée Pasteur, Paris; Highgate Sch., London; Balliol Coll., Oxford. Served War 1939–45 (despatches). Staff Mem., The Economist, 1947–48; S. G. Warburg & Co., 1948–68; Dep. Chm. and Man. Dir, IRC, 1966–67; Chm., Orion Bank, 1971–73; Dir-Gen., Industrial and Technological Affairs, EEC, 1973–74. Board Member: BAC, 1970–71; Internat. Computers, 1974–76; Davy Internat., 1969–73. Mem., Adv. Council, Phillips Collection, Washington. Chairman: Philharmonia Trust; EORTC Foundation. Comdr, Order of Merit of the Republic of Italy, 1980. *Address:* General Electric Company, 1 Stanhope Gate, W1.

GRIEVE, Hon. Lord; William Robertson Grieve, VRD 1958; a Senator of the College of Justice in Scotland, since 1972; *b* 21 Oct. 1917; *o s* of late William Robertson Grieve (killed in action 1917) and of Mrs Grieve, Edinburgh; *m* 1947, Lorna St John, *y d* of late Engineer Rear-Adm. E. P. St J. Benn, CB; one *s* one *d*. *Educ:* Glasgow Academy; Sedbergh; Glasgow Univ. MA 1939, LLB 1946 (Glasgow); Pres. Glasgow Univ. Union, 1938–39. John Clark (Mile-end) Scholar, 1939. RNVR: Sub-Lt 1939; Lieut 1942; Lt-Comdr 1950; served with RN, 1939–46. Admitted Mem. of Faculty of Advocates, 1947; QC (Scot.) 1957. Junior Counsel in Scotland to Bd of Inland Revenue, 1952–57. Advocate-Depute (Home), 1962–64; Sheriff-Principal of Renfrew and Argyll, 1964–72; Procurator of the Church of Scotland, 1969–72; a Judge of the Courts of Appeal of Jersey and Guernsey, 1971. Chm. of Governors, Fettes Trust, 1978–. *Recreations:* golf, painting. *Address:* 20 Belgrave Crescent, Edinburgh EH4 3AJ. *T:* 031-332 7500. *Clubs:* New (Edinburgh); Hon. Company of Edinburgh Golfers.

GRIEVE, Sir (Herbert) Ronald (Robinson), Kt 1958; FAMA 1968; Medical Practitioner; *b* 6 June 1896; 2nd *s* of Lieut Gideon James Grieve (killed in action, 1900) and Julia Australia Grieve (*née* Robinson), Sydney, Australia; *m* 1945, Florence Ross Timpson (*d* 1969), formerly of Cheadle Heath, Cheshire; one *s* two *d*; *m* 1972, Margaret Du Vé. *Educ:* Sydney Gram. Sch.; University of Sydney. Grad. in Medicine and Surgery. Resident Medical Officer, Newcastle Gen. Hosp., NSW, 1920–21; House Physician, Manchester Royal Infirmary, 1922–23; Hon. Clinical Asst in Medicine, Royal Prince Alfred Hospital, Sydney, 1941–47. Pres. BMA (NSW Branch), 1947; Mem. NSW Medical Board, 1938–63; Chm. Medical Benefits Fund of Australia, from inception, 1947–75; Pres. Internat. Fedn of Voluntary Health Service Funds, 1968; Mem. Commonwealth of Australia Advisory Cttee on National Health Act, 1953–. MLC, NSW, 1933–34. *Recreations:* angling, the turf; formerly rowing and cricket (rep. Sydney Univ.). *Address:* 113 Homer Street, Earlwood, Sydney, NSW 2206, Australia. *T:* 55-1514. *Clubs:* University, Old Sydneians, Australian Jockey (Sydney).

GRIEVE, Percy; see Grieve, W. P.

GRIEVE, Prof. Sir Robert, Kt 1969; MA, FRSE, FRTPI, MICE; Professor Emeritus, University of Glasgow; *b* 11 Dec. 1910; *s* of Peter Grieve and Catherine Boyle; *m* 1933, Mary Lavinia Broughton Blackburn; two *s* two *d*. *Educ:* N. Kelvinside Sch., Glasgow; Royal Coll. of Science and Technology (now Univ. of Strathclyde). Trng and qual. as Civil Engr, eventually Planner. Local Govt posts, 1927–44; preparation of Clyde Valley Regional Plan, 1944–46; Civil Service, 1946–54; Chief Planner, Scottish Office, 1960–64. Prof. of Town and Regional Planning, Glasgow Univ., 1964–74; retired from Chair, 1974. Chairman: Highlands and Islands Develt Bd, 1965–70; Highlands and Islands Development Consultative Council, 1978–; Royal Fine Arts Commn for Scotland, 1978–; Mem., North Sea Oil Panel, SSRC, 1975–; Hon. President: Scottish Rights of Way Soc.; New Glasgow Soc.; Inverness Civic Trust; Stewartry Mountaineering Club; Scottish Branch, RTPI; Former President: Scottish Mountaineering Council; Scottish Mountaineering Club; Former Vice-Pres., Internat. Soc. of Town and Regional Planners. Hon. Vice-Pres., Scottish Youth Hostels Assoc. Gold Medal, RTPI, 1974. Hon. DLitt Heriot-Watt; Hon. FRIAS. *Publications:* part-author and collaborator in several major professional reports and books; many papers and articles in professional and technical jls. *Recreations:* mountains, poetry. *Address:* Marchburn House, by Cairnryan, Wigtownshire. *T:* Cairnryan 250; 87 Bruntsfield Place, Edinburgh. *Clubs:* Scottish Arts (Edinburgh); Ours (Glasgow).

GRIEVE, Sir Ronald; see Grieve, Sir H. R. R.

GRIEVE, Thomas Robert, CBE 1968; MC 1944; Director: Viking Resources Trust Ltd, since 1972; Oil and Associated Investment Trust, since 1971; Deputy Chairman, Hunterston Development Company Ltd, since 1973; *b* 11 Sept. 1909; *s* of Robert Grieve and Annie Craig (*née* Stark); *m* 1st, 1946, Doreen Bramley Whitehead; two *d*; 2nd, 1978, Mrs R. K. Dimoline. *Educ:* Cargilfield and Fettes Coll., Edinburgh. Joined Anglo-Saxon Petroleum Co. Ltd, 1930; served in London, 1930–40. Commissioned 9th Highland Lt Inf. (TA), 1928, seconded Movement Control, Royal Engineers, 1943–45; served NW Europe, rank of Major. Vice-Pres. in charge of Operations, Shell Oil Co. of Canada, 1945; Exec. Asst to Regional Vice-Pres. of Shell Oil Co., Houston, Texas, 1949; Manager of Distribution and Supply Dept, Shell Petroleum Co. Ltd, London, 1951; Director: Shell-Mex and BP Ltd, Shell Refining Co. Ltd, Shell Co. UK Ltd, 1959–65; Shell International Petroleum Co. Ltd, 1963–65; Vice-Chm. and Man. Dir, Shell-Mex and BP Ltd, 1965–71; Chm., United Kingdom Oil Pipelines Ltd, 1965–71; Dir, London and Provincial Trust Ltd, 1970–80; Chm., Hogg Robinson (Scotland) Ltd, 1975–78; Chm., Newarthill Ltd, 1977–80. Chm., London Exec. Cttee, Scottish Council, 1971–77. Mem., Management Cttee, AA, 1971–80. Governor, Shiplake Coll., Henley-on-Thames, 1980–. *Recreations:* bridge, travel. *Address:* Gearholm, 84 Bell Street, Henley, Oxon RG9 2BD. *T:* Henley 77901. *Clubs:* Caledonian, MCC.

GRIEVE, William Percival, (W. Percy Grieve), QC 1962; MP (C) Solihull Division of Warwickshire since 1964; a Recorder, since 1972 (Recorder of Northampton, 1965–71); *b* 25 March 1915; *o s* of 2nd Lieut W. P. Grieve, the Middlesex Regt (killed in action, Ypres, Feb. 1915), Rockcliffe, Dalbeattie; *m* 1949, Evelyn Raymonde Louise, *y d* of late Comdt Hubert Mijouain, Paris, and of Liliane, *e d* of late Sir George Roberts, 1st and last Bt; one *s* one *d* (and one *s* decd). *Educ:* privately; Trinity Hall, Cambridge. Exhibitioner, Trinity Hall, 1933; Lord Kitchener Nat. Memorial Schol., 1934; BA 1937, MA 1940. Harmsworth Law Schol., 1937, called to Bar, 1938, Middle Temple; Bencher, 1969. Joined Midland Circuit, 1939. Called to the Hong Kong Bar, 1960. Commissioned the Middlesex Regt, 1939; Liaison Officer, French Mil. Censorship, Paris, 1939–40; Min. of Information, 1940–41; HQ Fighting France, 1941–43; Staff Capt. and Exec. Officer, SHAEF Mission to Luxembourg, 1944; Major and GSO2 Brit. Mil. Mission to Luxembourg, 1945; DAAG, BAOR, 1946. Asst Recorder of Leicester, 1956–65; Dep. Chm., Co. of Lincoln (Parts of Holland) QS, 1962–71. Mem. Mental Health Review Tribunal, Sheffield Region, 1960–64. Has served on Gen. Council of the Bar. Contested (C) Lincoln By-election, 1962. Member: House of Commons Select Cttees on Race Relations and Immigration, 1968–70, on Members' Interests, 1979–; UK Delegn, Council of Europe (Chm., Legal Affairs Cttee) and WEU (Chm. Procedure Cttee), 1969; Hon. Vice-Pres., Franco-British Parly Relations Cttee (Chm., 1970–75); Chairman: Luxembourg Soc., 1975; Parly Anglo Benelux Group. Pres., Fulham Cons. Assoc., 1982–. Member: Council, Officers' Assoc., 1969–; Council of Justice, 1971–; Council, Franco-British Soc., 1970; Council, Alliance Française, 1974. Officier avec Couronne, Order of Adolphe of Nassau; Chevalier, Order of Couronne de Chêne and Croix de Guerre avec Palmes (Luxembourg), 1945–46; Bronze Star (USA), 1945; Chevalier de la Légion d'Honneur, 1974; Commandeur de l'Ordre de Mérite (Luxembourg), 1976; Officer de l'ordre de la Couronne (Belgium), 1980. *Recreations:* swimming, travel, the theatre. *Address:* 1 King's Bench Walk, Temple, EC4. *T:* 01-353 8436. *Clubs:* Carlton, Hurlingham.

GRIEVE, William Robertson; see Grieve, Hon. Lord.

GRIEW, Dr Stephen, PhD; President, Athabasca University, since 1980; *b* 13 Sept. 1928; *e s* of late Harry and Sylvia Griew, London, England; *m* 1st, 1955, Jane le Geyt Johnson (marr. diss.); one *s* two *d* (and one *s* decd); 2nd, 1977, Eva Margareta Ursula, *d* of late Dr Johannes Ramberg and of Fru Betty Ramberg, Stockholm, Sweden; one *d* and one step *s*. *Educ:* Univ. of London (BSc, Dip Psych); Univ. of Bristol (PhD). Vocational Officer, Min. of Labour, 1951–55; Univ. of Bristol: Research Worker, 1955–59; Lectr, 1959–63; Kenneth Craik Research Award, St John's Coll., Cambridge, 1960; Prof. of Psychology: Univ. of Otago, Dunedin, NZ, 1964–68 (Dean, Faculty of Science, 1967–68); Univ. of Dundee, 1968–72; Vice-Chancellor, Murdoch Univ., Perth, WA, 1972–77; Chm., Dept of Behavioural Science, Faculty of Medicine, Univ. of Toronto, 1977–80. Consultant, OECD, Paris, 1963–64; Expert, ILO, 1966–67; Mem., Social Commn of Rehabilitation Internat., 1967–75; Consultant, Dept of Employment, 1970–72; Vis. Prof., Univ. of Western Ont., London, Canada, 1970 and 1971. Vice-Pres., Australian Council on the Ageing, 1975–76. FBPsS 1960; Fellow, Gerontological Soc. (USA), 1969. *Publications:* handbooks and monographs on ageing and vocational rehabilitation, and articles in Jl of Gerontology and various psychological jls. *Recreations:* music, travel. *Address:* Athabasca University, 12352-149 Street, Edmonton, Alberta T5V 1G9, Canada. *Club:* English-Speaking Union.

GRIFFIN, Adm. Sir Anthony (Templer Frederick Griffith), GCB 1975 (KCB 1971; CB 1967); President, Royal Institution of Naval Architects, since 1981; Chairman, British Shipbuilders, 1977–80 (Chairman-designate, Dec. 1975); *b* Peshawar, 24 Nov. 1920; *s* of late Col F. M. G. Griffin, MC, and B. A. B. Griffin (*née* Down); *m* 1943, Rosemary Ann Hickling; two *s* one *d*. *Educ:* RN Coll., Dartmouth. Joined RN, 1934; to sea as Midshipman, 1939; War Service in E Indies, Mediterranean, Atlantic, N Russia and Far East; specialised in navigation, 1944; Staff Coll., 1952; Imp. Defence Coll., 1963; comd HMS Ark Royal, 1964–65; Naval Secretary, 1966; Asst Chief of Naval

Staff (Warfare), 1966-68; Flag Officer, Second-in-Command, Far East Fleet, 1968-69; Flag Officer, Plymouth, Comdr Central Sub Area, Eastern Atlantic, and Comdr Plymouth Sub Area, Channel, 1969-71; Controller of the Navy, 1971-75. Comdr 1951; Capt. 1956; Rear-Adm. 1966; Vice-Adm. 1968; Adm., 1971. Mem. Adv. Council, Science Policy Foundn, 1975-. Vice-Pres., Wellington College, 1980-. CBIM, FIIM; ARINA. *Recreation:* sailing. *Address:* Moat Cottage, The Drive, Bosham, West Sussex PO18 8JG. *T:* Bosham 573373. *Club:* Army and Navy.

GRIFFIN, Sir (Charles) David, Kt 1974; CBE 1972; Chairman: Barclays International Australia Ltd; Barclays Credit Corporation Ltd; Aetna Life of Australia & New Zealand Ltd; Vanguard Insurance Co. Ltd; Robert Bosch (Australia) Pty. Ltd; Korn/Ferry International Pty. Ltd; *b* 8 July 1915; *s* of Eric Furnival Griffin and Nellie Clarendon Griffin (*née* Devenish-Meares); *m* 1941, Jean Falconer Whyte; two *s*. *Educ:* Cranbrook Sch., Sydney; Univ. of Sydney (LLB and Golf Blue). 8th Aust. Div. 2nd AIF, 1940-45; POW Changi, Singapore, 1942-45. Associate to Sir Dudley Williams and Mem. Bar NSW, 1946-49; Solicitor, Sydney, 1949-64. Alderman, Sydney City Council, 1962-74, Chm. Finance Cttee, 1969-72; Lord Mayor of Sydney, 1972-73. Hon. Chm., Nabalco Pty Ltd (Chm., 1964-80); Director: Atlas Copco Aust. Pty Ltd; Davis Consolidated Industries Ltd; John Fairfax Ltd; Oil Search Ltd; Zellweger Aust. Pty Ltd; Comr, Aust. Tertiary Educn Commn, 1977-; Mem. Council, Royal Agricl Soc.; Dir, Australian Elizabethan Theatre Trust; Trustee, Nat. Parks and Wildlife Foundn. *Publications:* The Happiness Box (for children); The Will of the People; sundry speeches and short stories. *Recreations:* golf, fly-fishing. *Address:* 10 Churchill Road, Rose Bay, NSW 2029, Australia. *Clubs:* Union, Elanora Country (Sydney); Royal Sydney Golf, Pine Valley Golf (NJ, USA).

GRIFFIN, Sir David; see Griffin, Sir C. D.

GRIFFIN, Col Edgar Allen, CMG 1965; OBE 1943; ED 1945; Regional Director, Northern Region (Arras, France), Commonwealth War Graves Commission, 1969-72; *b* 18 Jan. 1907; 3rd *s* of Gerald Francis and Isabella Margaret Griffin; *m* 1936, Alethea Mary Byrne; two *s* two *d*. Retired from AMF, 1947; Australian Govt Nominee to Staff of War Graves Commn, 1947; Chief Admin. Officer, Eastern Dist (Cairo), 1947-54; UK Dist (London), 1954-58; Regional Dir, Southern Region (Rome), 1958-69. *Address:* 36 Pytchley Road, Kettering, Northants.

GRIFFIN, Mrs Francis D.; see Dunne, Irene.

GRIFFIN, Sir Francis (Frederick), Kt 1971; retired; Director, Ryland Vehicle Group Ltd, 1941-78; *b* 3 June 1904; *s* of James Cecil and Lucy Griffin; *m* 1936, Kathleen Mary Fitzgerald; one *d* (twin *d* and one adopted *s* decd). *Educ:* St Philip's Grammar Sch., Edgbaston. Nat. Deleg., W Midland Div., Motor Agents' Assoc., 1948-54; Mem., Inst. of Motor Industry. Elected to Birmingham City Council, 1949 (Leader of Council, 1964-72). Chm., W Midland Planning Authority Conf., 1966-69; First Chm., W Midland Passenger Transp. Authority, 1969-72; Dir, Nat. Exhibn Centre, 1970-74, 1976-80. Mem., Cons. Gp Metropolitan CC, 1973-. (Chm., 1973-75). Freeman, City of Birmingham, 1970. *Publications:* Selling Municipal Houses, 1967; Selling More Council Houses, 1970. *Recreation:* politics. *Address:* 101 Metchley Lane, Harborne, Birmingham B17 0JH. *T:* 021-427 4554. *Club:* Conservative (Birmingham).

GRIFFIN, Sir John Bowes, Kt 1955; QC 1938; *b* 19 April 1903; *o s* of late Sir Charles Griffin; *m* Eva Orrell (*d* 1977), 2nd *d* of late John Mellifont Walsh, Wexford; two *d*. *Educ:* Clongowes; Dublin Univ. (MA, LLD, First Cl. Moderatorship, Gold Medallist); Cambridge. Barrister-at-Law, Inner Temple, 1926. Administrative Officer, Uganda, 1927; Asst District Officer, 1929; Registrar, High Court, 1929; Crown Counsel, 1933; Actg Solicitor-Gen. and Attorney-Gen., various periods; Attorney-Gen., Bahamas, 1936 (Acting Governor and Acting Chief Justice, various periods); Solicitor-Gen., Palestine, 1939, Acting Attorney-Gen., various periods; Attorney-Gen., Hong Kong, 1946; Chief Justice of Uganda, 1952-56. Secretary: East Africa Law Officers Conference, 1933; Commission of Enquiry Admin. of Justice, East Africa, 1933; Chm. Prisons Enquiry, Bahamas, 1936; miscellaneous Bds and Cttees; Chairman: Tel Aviv Municipal Commn of Enquiry, Palestine, 1942; Review Cttees, Detainees (Defence and Emergency Regulations), Palestine, 1940-46. Retired, Dec. 1956; Actg Chief Justice, N Rhodesia, 1957; Chm. Commn of Enquiry Gwenbe Valley Disturbances, N Rhodesia, 1958; Speaker, Legislative Council, Uganda, 1958-62; Speaker, Uganda National Assembly, 1962-63, retd. Chairman: Public Service Commission, 1963 and Constitutional Council, 1964, N Rhodesia; retd 1965. CStJ 1960. *Publications:* Revised Edn of Laws (Uganda), 1935; (joint) Hong Kong, 1950. *Address:* c/o Williams & Glyn's Bank Ltd, Holt's Branch, Kirkland House, Whitehall, SW1. *Clubs:* East India, Devonshire, Sports and Public Schools; Union (Malta).
See also A. J. Boase, M. H. M. Reid.

GRIFFIN, Dr John Parry, BSc, PhD, MB, BS; MRCP; Senior Principal Medical Officer and Professional Head of Medicines Division, Department of Health and Social Security, since 1977; Medical Assessor, Medicines Commission, since 1977; Hon. Consultant, Lister Hospital, Stevenage; *b* 21 May 1938; *o s* of David J. Griffin and Phyllis M. Griffin; *m* 1962, Margaret, *o d* of late Frank Cooper and of Catherine Cooper; one *s* two *d*. *Educ:* Howardian High Sch., Cardiff; London Hosp. Medical Coll. Lethby and

Buxton Prizes, 1958; BSc (1st Cl. Hons) 1959; PhD 1961; George Riddoch Prize in Neurology, 1962; MB, BS 1964; LRCP, MRCS 1964; MRCP 1980. Ho. Phys., London Hosp. Med. Unit, and Ho. Surg., London Hosp. Accident and Orthopaedic Dept, 1964-65; Lectr in Physiology, King's Coll., London, 1965-67; Head of Clinical Research, Riker Laboratories, 1967-71; SMO, Medicines Div., 1971-76; PMO, Medicines Div., and Medical Assessor, Cttee on Safety of Medicines, 1976-77. Mem., Jt Formulary Cttee for British Nat. Formulary, 1978-; UK Rep., EEC Cttee on Proprietary Med. Products; Chm., Cttee on Prop. Med. Products Working Party on Safety Requirements, 1977-. FRSM. *Publications:* (jtly) Iatrogenic Diseases, 1972, 2nd edn 1979; (jtly) Manual of Adverse Drug Interactions, 1975, 2nd edn 1979; (jtly) Drug Induced Emergencies, 1980; numerous articles in sci. and med. jls, mainly on aspects of neurophysiology and clinical pharmacology and toxicology. *Recreations:* gardening, local history. *Address:* 20 Mornington, Digswell, Herts AL6 08J. *T:* Welwyn 4592.

GRIFFIN, Keith Broadwell, DPhil; President, Magdalen College, Oxford, since 1979; *b* 6 Nov. 1938; *s* of Marcus Samuel Griffin and Elaine Ann Broadwell; *m* 1956, Dixie Beth Griffin; two *d*. *Educ:* Williams Coll., Williamstown, Mass (BA; Hon DLitt, 1980); Balliol Coll., Oxford (BPhil, DPhil). Fellow and Tutor in Econs, Magdalen Coll., Oxford, 1965-76, Fellow by special election, 1977—79; Warden, Queen Elizabeth House, Oxford, 1978-79 (Actg Warden, 1973 and 1977-78); Dir, Inst. of Commonwealth Studies, Oxford, 1978-79 (Actg Dir, 1973 and 1977-78). Chief, Rural and Urban Employment Policies Br., ILO, 1975-76; Vis. Prof., Inst. of Econs and Planning, Univ. of Chile, 1962-63 and 1964-65. Consultant: ILO, 1974, 1982; Internat. Bank for Reconstruction and Develt, 1973; UN Res. Inst. for Social Develt, 1971-72; FAO, 1963-64, 1967, 1978; Inter-Amer. Cttee for Alliance for Progress, 1968; US Agency for Internat. Develt, 1966. Res. Adviser, Pakistan Inst. of Develt Econs, 1965, 1970; Pres., Develt Studies Assoc., 1978-80. Exec. Editor, World Development, 1978-79; Editor, Oxford Economic Papers, 1979-. *Publications:* (with Ricardo ffrench-Davis) Comercio Internacional y Politicas de Desarrollo Economico, 1967; Underdevelopment in Spanish America, 1969; (with John Enos) Planning Development, 1970; (ed) Financing Development in Latin America, 1971; (ed with Azizur Rahman Khan) Growth and Inequality in Pakistan, 1972; The Political Economy of Agrarian Change, 1974, 2nd edn 1979; (ed with E. A. G. Robinson) The Economic Development of Bangladesh, 1974; Land Concentration and Rural Poverty, 1976, 2nd edn 1981; International Inequality and National Poverty, 1978; (with Ashwani Saith) Growth and Equality in Rural China, 1981; (with Jeffrey James) The Transition to Egalitarian Development, 1981. *Recreation:* travel. *Address:* Magdalen College, Oxford. *T:* Oxford 41781. *Clubs:* Athenæum, United Oxford & Cambridge University.

GRIFFIN, Kenneth James, OBE 1970; a Deputy Chairman, British Shipbuilders, since 1977; *b* 1 Aug. 1928; *s* of late Albert Griffin and late Catherine (*née* Sullivan); *m* 1951, Doreen Cicely Simon; two *s* one *d*. *Educ:* Dynevor Grammar Sch., Swansea; Swansea Technical College. Area Sec., ETU, 1960; Dist Sec., Confedn of Ship Building Engrg Unions, 1961; Sec., Craftsmen Cttee (Steel), 1961; Mem., Welsh Council, 1968; Mem., Crowther Commn on Constitution (Wales), 1969; Joint Sec., No 8 Joint Industrial Council Electrical Supply Industry, 1969; Industrial Adviser, DTI, 1971-72; Co-ordinator of Industrial Advisers, DTI, 1972-74; Special Adviser, Sec. of State for Industry, 1974; part-time Mem., NCB, 1973-; Mem., Suppl. Benefits Commn, 1975-80. *Recreations:* golf, music, reading. *Address:* 214 Cyncoed Road, Cyncoed, Cardiff. *T:* Cardiff 752184.

GRIFFIN, Rear-Adm. Michael Harold, CB 1973; antiquarian horologist; *b* 28 Jan. 1921; *s* of late Henry William Griffin and Blanche Celia Griffin (*née* Michael); *m* 1947, Barbara Mary Brewer; two *d*. *Educ:* Plymouth Junior Techn. Coll. CEng, FIMechE, FIMarE. MBHI. Commnd, 1941; HMS Kent, 1942; HM Submarines Trusty, Tactician, Tally Ho, Alderney, 1944-50; Admty, 1950-52; HMS Eagle, 1952-54; staff C-in-C Portsmouth, 1954-57; HM Dockyard, Rosyth, 1957-60; Third Submarine Sqdn, 1960-62; Captain, 1962; HM Dockyard, Chatham, 1963-65; HMS St Vincent, 1966-69; Cdre Supt, Singapore, 1969-71; Dir of Dockyard Production and Support, MoD, 1972-77, retired. Naval Adviser to Vosper Shiprepairers Ltd, 1977-81. *Recreations:* yachting, cruising and racing; tennis, badminton; horology. *Address:* 48 Little Green, Alverstoke, Gosport, Hants. *T:* Gosport 83348.

GRIFFIN, Paul, MBE 1961; MA Cantab; *b* 2 March 1922; *s* of late John Edwin Herman Griffin; *m* 1946, Felicity Grace, *d* of Canon Howard Dobson; one *s* one *d*. *Educ:* Framlingham Coll.; St Catharine's Coll., Cambridge. Served War in Gurkhas, India, Burma, Malaya, 1940-46; North-West Frontier, 1941-43; Chindits, 1943-44. Asst Master and Senior English Master, Uppingham Sch., 1949-55; Principal, English Sch. in Cyprus, 1956-60; Headmaster, Aldenham Sch., 1962-74; Principal, Anglo-World Language Centre, Cambridge, 1976-82. Treasurer, Corp. of Sons of the Clergy, 1978- (Mem. Court, 1973). *Publications:* numerous articles, poems, and broadcast talks and plays. *Recreations:* sea angling, bridge. *Address:* 1 Strickland Place, Southwold, Suffolk IP18 6HN. *T:* Southwold 723709.

GRIFFIN, Very Rev. Victor Gilbert Benjamin; Dean of St Patrick's Cathedral, Dublin, since 1969; *b* 24 May 1924; *s* of Gilbert B. and Violet M. Griffin, Carnew, Co. Wicklow; *m* 1958, Daphne E. Mitchell; two *s*. *Educ:* Kilkenny Coll.; Mountjoy Sch., and Trinity Coll., Dublin. MA, 1st class Hons in Philosophy. Ordained, 1947; Curacy, St Augustine's, Londonderry, 1947-

51; Curacy, Christ Church, Londonderry, 1951-57; Rector of Christ Church, Londonderry, 1957-69. Lecturer in Philosophy, Magee Univ. Coll., Londonderry, 1950-69. *Publications:* Trends in Theology, 1870-1970, 1970; Anglican and Irish, 1976; contrib. to New Divinity, 1970. *Recreations:* music, golf. *Address:* The Deanery, St Patrick's Cathedral, Dublin 8. *T:* Dublin 752451. *Club:* Friendly Brothers of St Patrick (Dublin).

GRIFFITH, Hon. Sir Arthur Frederick, Kt 1977; MLC; President, Legislative Council, Western Australia, since 1974; *b* Geraldton, 22 April 1913; *m* ; one *c. Educ:* public schs in Australia. Served War of 1939-45, RAAF (commnd from ranks). MLA for Canning, WA, 1950-53; MLC (Lib): Suburban, 1953-65; North Metropolitan, 1965-; Minister: for Mines, Housing and Justice, 1959-65; for Mines and Justice, 1965-71, Legislature of Western Australia; Leader of the Opposition, Legislative Council, 1958-59, 1971-74. *Address:* Office of the President, Legislative Council, Perth, Western Australia; 40 Tilton Terrace, City Beach, WA 6015, Australia.

GRIFFITH, Rev. Arthur Leonard; Minister, St Paul's Anglican Church, Toronto, since 1976; Lecturer in Homiletics, Wycliffe College, Toronto, since 1977; *b* 20 March 1920; *s* of Thomas Griffiths and Sarah Jane Taylor; *m* 1947, Anne Merelie Cayford; two *d. Educ:* Public and High Schs, Brockville, Ont; McGill Univ., Montreal (BA, McGill, 1942); United Theological Coll., Montreal (BD 1945; Hon. DD 1962); Mansfield Coll., Oxford, England, 1957-58. Ordained in The United Church of Canada, 1945; Minister: United Church, Arden, Ont, 1945-47; Trinity United Church, Grimsby, Ont, 1947-50; Chalmers United Church, Ottawa, Ont, 1950-60; The City Temple, London, 1960-66; Deer Park United Church, Toronto, 1966-75; ordained in Anglican Church 1976. *Publications:* The Roman Letter Today, 1959; God and His People, 1960; Beneath The Cross of Jesus, 1961; What is a Christian?, 1962; Barriers to Christian Belief, 1962; A Pilgrimage to the Holy Land, 1962; The Eternal Legacy, 1963; Pathways to Happiness, 1964; God's Time and Ours, 1964; The Crucial Encounter, 1965; This is Living!, 1966; God in Man's Experience, 1968; Illusions of our Culture, 1969; The Need to Preach, 1971; Hang on to the Lord's Prayer, 1973; We Have This Ministry, 1973; Ephesians: a positive affirmation, 1975; Gospel Characters, 1976; Reactions to God, 1979. *Recreations:* music, drama, golf, fishing. *Address:* St Paul's Anglican Church, 227 Bloor Street East, Toronto M4W 1L8, Canada.

GRIFFITH, Edward Michael Wynne; Member of Agricultural Research Council since 1973; Chairman, Clwyd Health Authority, since 1980; *b* 29 Aug. 1933; *e s* of Major H. W. Griffith, MBE; *m* Jill Grange, *d* of Major D. P. G. Moseley, Dorfold Cottage, Nantwich; two *s* (and one *s* decd). *Educ:* Eton; Royal Agricultural College. Regional Dir, National Westminster Bank Ltd, 1974-. High Sheriff of Denbighshire, 1969. Mem., Countryside Commn Cttee for Wales, 1972-78; Mem., Min. of Agriculture Regional Panel, 1972-77. *Address:* Greenfield, Trefnant, Clwyd. *T:* Trefnant 633. *Club:* Boodle's.

GRIFFITH, Guy Thompson, FBA 1952; MA; Laurence Reader in Classics, Cambridge University, 1951- Sept. 1975; Fellow of Gonville and Caius College, since 1931; Lecturer in Classics, 1937-75; *b* 7 Jan. 1908; *m* 1940, Josephine Marjorie Rainey; three *s* one *d. Educ:* The Leys Sch., and Gonville and Caius Coll., Cambridge. Served in RAFVR, 1941-45. Joint Editor Classical Quarterly, 1947-51. *Publications:* The Mercenaries of the Hellenistic World, 1935; (with Michael Oakeshott) A Guide to the Classics, 1936; The Greek Historians, in Fifty Years of Classical Studies (ed M. Platnauer), 1954; (with N. G. L. Hammond) A History of Macedonia, vol. ii, 1979; articles mostly on Greek History in periodicals. *Address:* 1 Springfield Road, Cambridge.

GRIFFITH, Prof. John Aneurin Grey, LLB London, LLM London; FBA 1977; Barrister-at-law; Professor of Public Law, London School of Economics and Political Science, University of London, since 1970; *b* 14 Oct. 1918; *s* of Rev. B. Grey Griffith and Bertha Griffith; *m* 1941, Barbara Eirene Garnet, *d* of W. Garnet Williams; two *s* one *d. Educ:* Taunton Sch.; LSE. British and Indian armies, 1940-46. Lectr in Law, UCW, Aberystwyth, 1946-48; Lectr in Law and Reader, LSE, 1948-59, Prof. of English Law, 1959-70. Mem., Marlow UDC, 1950-55, and Bucks CC, 1955-61. Vis. Prof. of Law, Univ. of California at Berkeley, 1966; Sec., Council for Academic Freedom and Democracy. Hon. LLD York Univ., Toronto. Editor, Public Law, 1956-81. *Publications:* (with H. Street) A Casebook of Administrative Law, 1964; Central Departments and Local Authorities, 1966; (with H. Street) Principles of Administrative Law, 5th edn, 1973; Parliamentary Scrutiny of Government Bills, 1974; (with T. C. Hartley) Government and Law, 1975, 2nd edn 1981; (ed) From Policy to Administration, 1976; The Politics of the Judiciary, 1977, 2nd edn 1981; Public Rights and Private Interests, 1981; articles in English, Commonwealth and American jls of law, public administration and politics. *Recreations:* drinking beer and writing bad verse. *Address:* London School of Economics and Political Science, Houghton Street, WC2. *Club:* Tatty Bogle.

GRIFFITH, John Eaton, CMG 1949; OBE 1941; *b* 1894; *s* of L. J. Griffith, Brondesbury; *m* 1921, Violet Godson (*d* 1958); two *d. Educ:* University Coll. RA., 1914-19, Egypt and France; retd disabled, 1919. 1920-50, UK Civil Service; Air Ministry; Ministry of Aircraft Production; Ministry of Production and Ministry of Fuel and Power; Principal Private Sec. to successive Ministers of Aircraft Production, Lord Beaverbrook and Lord Brabazon; Under-Sec., Ministry of Supply, 1949-50; retired, 1950. Chm.

European Coal Organisation, 1946-47; Organising Cttee XIV Olympiad, 1948; Vice-Pres. International Lawn Tennis Federation; Vice-Pres. The Lawn Tennis Assoc.; Life Pres. Bucks Lawn Tennis Assoc. *Address:* St Martins, Grimm's Hill, Great Missenden, Bucks. *T:* Gt Missenden 2244. *Club:* All England (Wimbledon).

GRIFFITH, Kenneth; actor, writer and documentary film-maker; *b* 12 Oct. 1921; *g s* of Ernest and Emily Griffith; three marriages dissolved; three *s* two *d. Educ:* council and grammar schs, Tenby, Pembrokeshire, SW Wales. Became a professional actor at Festival Theatre, Cambridge, 1937; films and television; served War, RAF; post war, associated with Tyrone Guthrie at Old Vic; unknown number of films, partic. for Boulting brothers; unknown number of television plays; rarely theatre, though much under influence of Bernard Miles and Robin Midgley; made first documentary film at invitation of David Attenborough, 1964; best documentaries include: Life of Cecil Rhodes; Hang Out Your Brightest Colours (life of Michael Collins; suppressed by Lew Grade at behest of IBA); The Public's Right to Know; The Sun's Bright Child (life of Edmund Kean); Black as Hell, Thick as Grass (the 24th Regt in Zulu War); The Most Valuable Englishman Ever (life of Thomas Paine for BBC TV); There's Something Wrong With Our Bloody Ships (Battle of Jutland). *Publications:* Thank God we kept the Flag Flying, 1974; (with Timothy O'Grady) Curious Journey, 1981 (based on unshown TV documentary). *Recreations:* talking; collecting British Empire military postal history (envelopes, post-cards), also ephemera connected with southern Africa. *Address:* 110 Englefield Road, Islington, N1 3LQ. *T:* 01-226 9013.

GRIFFITH, Owen Glyn, CBE 1980 (OBE 1969); MVO 1954; HM Diplomatic Service, retired; High Commissioner in Lesotho, 1978-81; *b* 19 Jan. 1922; *s* of late William Glyn Griffith and Gladys Glyn Griffith (*née* Picton Davies); *m* 1949, Rosemary Elizabeth Cecil Earl; two *s. Educ:* Oundle Sch.; Trinity Hall, Cambridge. Commnd in Welsh Guards (twice wounded in N Africa), 1941-43; Colonial Service (later HMOCS), Uganda, 1944-63: District Officer, 1944-51; Private Sec. to Governor, 1952-54; Dist Comr, 1954-61; Perm. Sec., Min. of Commerce and Industry, 1961-63; Principal, CRO, 1963; 1st Sec. and Head of Chancery, British Embassy, Khartoum, 1965; 1st Sec. (Commercial), British Embassy, Stockholm, 1969; Dep. British High Comr, Malawi, 1973; Inspector, 1976-78. *Recreations:* golf, fishing. *Address:* The Sundial, Marsham Way, Gerrards Cross, Bucks SL9 8AD. *Club:* Royal Commonwealth Society.

GRIFFITH, Stewart Cathie, CBE 1975; DFC 1944; TD 1954; Secretary, MCC, 1962-74; *b* 16 June 1914; *yr s* of H. L. A. Griffith, Middleton, Sussex; *m* 1939, Barbara Reynolds; one *s* one *d. Educ:* Dulwich Coll.; Pembroke Coll., Cambridge (MA). Asst Master, Dulwich Coll., 1937-39. Army, 1939-46. Glider Pilot Regt, Lieut-Col. Sec., Sussex County Cricket Club, 1946-50; Cricket Correspondent, Sunday Times, 1950-52; Asst Sec., MCC, 1952-62; Secretary: Internat. Cricket Conference, 1962-74; Cricket Council, 1969-74; Test and County Cricket Bd, 1969-73; President: Sussex CCC, 1975-77; MCC, 1979-80. *Recreations:* cricket, golf, real tennis, walking. *Address:* 7 Sea Way, Middleton, Sussex PO22 7RZ. *T:* Middleton-on-Sea 3000. *Clubs:* East India, Devonshire, Sports and Public Schools, MCC; Hawks (Cambridge), etc.

GRIFFITH EDWARDS, James; see Edwards, J. G.

GRIFFITH-WILLIAMS, Brig. Eric Llewellyn Griffith, CBE 1945; DSO 1918; MC and Bar; DL; psc; late RA; 5th *s* of late A. L. G. Griffith-Williams, Highfields, Marlow, Bucks; *b* 2 May 1894; *m* 1938, Delia (*d* 1964), *o c* of late Lt-Col H. S. Follett, CBE, Rockbeare Manor, Devon; one *d. Educ:* Tonbridge Sch.; RMA, Woolwich. Served European War, 1914-19; Bt. Lt-Col, 1937; War of 1939-45; Col 1940; Brig. 1940; retired pay, 1946. High Sheriff of Devonshire, 1966; DL Devon 1966. *Address:* Rockbeare Manor, Devon EX5 2LU. *Club:* Army and Navy.

GRIFFITHS, Prof. Allen Phillips; Professor of Philosophy, University of Warwick, since 1964; Director, Royal Institute of Philosophy, since 1979; *b* 11 June 1927; *s* of John Phillips Griffiths and Elsie Maud (*née* Jones); *m* 1948, Margaret Lock (*d* 1974); one *s* one *d. Educ:* University Coll., Cardiff (BA); University Coll., Oxford (BPhil). Sgt, Intell. Corps, 1945-48 (despatches). Asst Lectr, Univ. of Wales, 1955-57; Lectr, Birkbeck Coll., Univ. of London, 1957-64. Pro-Vice-Chancellor, Univ. of Warwick, 1970-77. Vis. Professor: Swarthmore Coll., Pa, 1963; Univ. of Calif, 1967; Univ. of Wisconsin, 1965 and 1970. Silver Jubilee Medal, 1977. *Publications:* (ed) Knowledge & Belief, 1967; articles in learned philosophical jls. *Recreations:* handwriting, poker, clocks. *Address:* Department of Philosophy, University of Warwick, Coventry CV4 7AL. *T:* Coventry 24011. *Club:* Conservative (Kenilworth).

GRIFFITHS, Rt. Rev. Ambrose; see Griffiths, Rt. Rev. M. A.

GRIFFITHS, Air Vice-Marshal Arthur, CB 1972; AFC 1964; Chairman: Cititel Consultancy Ltd, since 1979; Consolidated Safeguards Ltd, since 1981 (Director, since 1980); Director, Secureguard Ltd, since 1980; *b* 22 Aug. 1922; *s* of late Edward and Elizabeth Griffiths; *m* 1950, Nancy Maud Sumpter; one *d. Educ:* Hawarden Grammar School. Joined RAF, 1940; war service with No 26 Fighter Reconnaissance Sqdn; post-war years as Flying Instructor mainly at CFS and Empire Flying Sch.; pfc 1954; comd No 94 Fighter Sqdn Germany, 1955-56; Dirg Staff, RCAF Staff Coll., Toronto, 1956-59; HQ Bomber

Comd, 1959-61; comd No 101 Bomber Sqdn, 1962-64; Gp Captain Ops, Bomber Comd, 1964-67; comd RAF Waddington, 1967-69; AOA and later Chief of Staff, Far East Air Force, 1969-71; Head of British Defence Liaison Staff, Canberra, 1972-74; Dir Gen., Security (RAF), 1976-77, and Comdt-Gen. RAF Regt, 1975-77. *Address*: 47 Murray Road, Northwood, Mddx. *T*: Northwood 27973. *Club*: Royal Air Force.

GRIFFITHS, Prof. Brian; Dean, City University Business School, since 1982, and Professor of Banking and International Finance, The City University, since 1977; *b* 27 Dec. 1941; *s* of Ivor Winston Griffiths and Phyllis Mary Griffiths (*née* Morgan); *m* 1965, Rachel Jane Jones; one *s* two *d. Educ:* Dynevor Grammar School; London School of Economics, Univ. of London. BSc (Econ), MSc (Econ). Assistant Lecturer in Economics, LSE, 1965-68, Lecturer in Economics, 1968-76; Dir, Centre for Banking and Internat. Finance, City Univ., 1977-82. Vis. Prof., Univ. of Rochester, USA, 1972-73. Mem., Bank of England's Panel of Academic Consultants, 1977-. *Publications:* Is Revolution Change? (ed and contrib.), 1972; Mexican Monetary Policy and Economic Development, 1972; Invisible Barriers to Invisible Trade, 1975; Inflation: The Price of Prosperity, 1976; (ed with G. E. Wood) Monetary Targets, 1980. *Recreations:* the family and reading. *Address:* 9 Firs Avenue, Muswell Hill, N10. *T:* 01-883 7891.

GRIFFITHS, Bruce (Fletcher), QC 1970; **His Honour Judge Bruce Griffiths;** a Circuit Judge, since 1972; *b* 28 April 1924; *s* of Edward Griffiths and Nancy Olga (*née* Fuell); *m* 1952, Mary Kirkhouse Jenkins, *y d* of late Judge George Kirkhouse Jenkins, QC; two *s* one *d. Educ:* Whitchurch Grammar Sch., Cardiff; King's Coll., London. RAF, 1942-47. LLB (Hons) London, 1951 (Jelf Medallist). Chm., Local Appeals Tribunal (Cardiff), Min. of Social Security, 1964-70; an Asst Recorder of Cardiff, Swansea and Merthyr Tydfil, 1966-71; Vice-Chm., Mental Health Review Tribunal for Wales, 1968-72; Dep. Chm., Glamorgan QS, 1971; Comr of Assize, Royal Cts of Justice, London, 1971; Chancellor, Dio. of Monmouth, 1977-; President of Provincial Court, and Mem. Governing Body (Panel of Chairmen), Church in Wales. Chm., Welsh Sculpture Trust; former Mem., Welsh Arts Council, and Chm., Art Cttee; Purchaser, Contemp. Art Soc. for Wales, 1975-76 (Vice-Chm., 1977-). *Address:* 34 Park Place, Cardiff. *T:* 22454. *Club:* Cardiff and County (Cardiff).

GRIFFITHS, David Howard, OBE 1982; Chairman, Eastern Region, British Gas Corporation, since 1981; *b* 30 Oct. 1922; *s* of David Griffiths and Margaret (*née* Jones); *m* 1949, Dilys Watford John; two *d. Educ:* Monmouth Sch.; Sidney Sussex Coll., Cambridge (Exhibnr; BA 1941, MA 1946, LLB 1946). Admitted Solicitor of the Supreme Court, 1948. Asst Solicitor, Newport Corp., 1948; Wales Gas Board: Solicitor, 1949; Management Develt Officer, 1965; Dir of Develt, 1967; Wales Gas: Dir of Conversion, 1970; Sec., 1973; Dep. Chm., Eastern Gas, 1977. Vice Pres., Contemporary Arts Soc., Wales, 1977. *Recreations:* reading, golf, music. *Address:* Star House, Potters Bar, Herts EN6 2PD. *T:* Potters Bar 55051.

GRIFFITHS, David John; Principal, D. J. Griffiths & Co., Bromley and Harveys, Lewisham, since 1970; a Recorder of the Crown Court, since 1980; *b* 18 Feb. 1931; *m* Anita; three *s* one *d. Educ:* St Dunstan's Coll., Catford, SE6. Admitted to Roll of Solicitors, 1957; apptd Notary Public, 1969. *Recreations:* riding, squash, music (male voice choir). *Address:* 2 Kinnaird Avenue, Bromley, Kent BR1 4HG. *T:* 01-464 1642.

GRIFFITHS, Rev. David Nigel, FSA; Rector of Windsor, since 1973; Chaplain to The Queen, since 1977; *b* 29 Oct. 1927; *o s* of late William Cross Griffiths, LDS, and Doris May (*née* Rhodes); *m* 1953, Joan Fillingham; two *s* one *d. Educ:* Cranbrook; Worcester Coll., Oxford (MA; Gladstone Meml Prize, Arnold Historical Essay Prize); Lincoln Theol Coll. An economist before ordination; Consultant at FAO, Rome, 1952-53. Curate, St Matthew, Northampton, 1958-61; Headquarters Staff, SPCK, 1961-67; Rector of St Mary Magdalene with St Paul and Vicar of St Michael-on-the-Mount, Lincoln, 1967-73; Vice-Chancellor and Librarian, Lincoln Cathedral, 1967-73; Rural Dean of Maidenhead, 1977-. Served TARO and RMFVR, 1946-50; Chaplain, RNR, 1963-77 (Reserve Decoration, 1977); OCF: Household Cavalry, 1973-; 1st Bn Irish Guards, 1977-80. FSA 1973. *Publications:* articles on bibliography and church history. *Recreations:* walking, bibliomania. *Address:* The Rectory, Park Street, Windsor, Berks SL4 1LU. *T:* Windsor 64572.

GRIFFITHS, Edward; *b* 7 March 1929; Welsh; *m* 1954, Ella Constance Griffiths; one *s* one *d. Educ:* University Coll. of N Wales, Bangor. Industrial Chemist, 1951. Mem., Flintshire CC, 1964. MP (Lab) Brightside Div. of Sheffield, June 1968-Sept. 1974; contested (Ind Lab) Sheffield Brightside, Oct. 1974. *Recreation:* sport. *Address:* 8 Wheel Lane, Grenoside, Sheffield S30 3RN.

GRIFFITHS, Eldon Wylie, MA Cantab, MA Yale; MP (C) Bury St Edmunds, since May 1964; *b* 25 May 1925; *s* of Thomas H. W. Griffiths and Edith May; *m*; one *s* one *d. Educ:* Ashton Grammar Sch.; Emmanuel Coll., Cambridge. Fellow, Saybrook Coll., Yale, 1948-49; Correspondent, Time and Life magazines, 1949-55; Foreign Editor, Newsweek, 1956-63; Columnist, Washington Post, 1962-63; Conservative Research Department, 1963-64. Parly Sec., Min. of Housing and Local Govt, June-Oct. 1970; Parly Under-Sec. of State, DoE, and Minister for Sport, 1970-74; opposition spokesman on Europe, 1975-76. Chairman: Anglo-Iranian Parly Gp; Anglo-Polish Parly

Gp. Chm., Special Olympics (UK). Consultant/Adviser, Nat. Police Federation; Pres., Assoc. of Public Health Inspectors, 1969-70. Director: Redman Heenan Ltd; Barber Greene Ltd; Caparo Gp Ltd. *Recreations:* reading, swimming, cricket. *Address:* Lynton Cottage, Ixworth-thorpe, Bury St Edmunds, Suffolk.

GRIFFITHS, (Ernest) Roy; Deputy Chairman since 1975, and Managing Director since 1979, J. Sainsbury Ltd; *b* 8 July 1926; *s* of Ernest and Florence Griffiths; *m* 1952, Winifred Rigby; one *s* two *d. Educ:* Wolstanton Grammar Sch., N Staffs; Keble Coll., Oxford (MA, BCL). Solicitor; FCIS 1959. Monsanto Cos, 1956-68: Legal Adviser, 1956; Dir, Monsanto Europe, 1964-68; J. Sainsbury Ltd, 1968-: Dir, Personnel, 1969. *Recreations:* cricket, gardening. *Address:* Little Earlylands, Crockham Hill, Edenbridge, Kent TN8 6SN. *T:* Crockham Hill 362.

GRIFFITHS, Harold Morris; Assistant Secretary, HM Treasury, since 1978; *b* 17 March 1926; *s* of Rt Hon. James Griffiths, CH; *m* 1st, 1951, Gwyneth Lethby (*d* 1966); three *s* one *d*; 2nd, 1966, Elaine Burge (*née* Walsh); two *s. Educ:* Llanelly Grammar Sch.; London Sch. of Economics. Editorial Staff: Glasgow Herald, 1949-55; Guardian, 1955-67; Information Division, HM Treasury: Deputy Head, 1967-68, Head, 1968-72; Asst Sec., HM Treasury, 1972-75; Counsellor (Economic), Washington, 1975-78. *Address:* 32 Teddington Park, Teddington, Mddx. *T:* 01-977 2464.

GRIFFITHS, Howard; Counsellor (Defence), UK Delegation, Mutual and Balanced Force Reductions (Negotiations), Vienna, since 1980; *b* 20 Sept. 1938; *s* of Bernard and Olive Griffiths; *m* 1963, Dorothy Foster (*née* Todd); one *s* one *d. Educ:* London School of Economics (BScEcon, MScEcon). Ministry of Defence: Research Officer, 1963-69; Principal, Army Dept, 1970-72; Central Staffs, 1972-76; Asst Secretary, Head of Civilian Faculty, National Defence Coll., 1976-78; Procurement Executive, 1978-80. *Address:* c/o Foreign and Commonwealth Office, Whitehall, SW1; Armbrustergasse 14/1, 1190 Vienna, Austria.

GRIFFITHS, Capt. Hubert Penry, OBE 1953; Assistant Commissioner, City of London Police, 1940-60; *b* 24 April 1894; *yr s* of late Henry Griffiths; *m* 1926, Beryl Rees, *o c* of late I. Newton Rees; one *s* (and one *s* one *d* decd). *Educ:* St Paul's Sch. Gazetted to 5th Special Res. Bn, Middlesex Regt, Oct. 1914; seconded to Nigeria Regt, Royal W African Frontier Force, 1915-20; served German W and E African Campaigns, 1915-18; Second in Command, 2nd Bn, 1918; served Egba Rising, 1918; Asst Comr, Nigeria Police, 1920, Commissioner, 1927; Actg Asst Inspector Gen., Northern Provinces, 1935-36; Police Div., Home Office, 1937; Actg Comr, City of London Police, 1952-53 and again for one year in 1954. Liveryman of Gold and Silver Wyre Drawers Company. OStJ 1952. Commander, Order of North Star (Sweden); Commander Star of Ethiopia. *Address:* 33 Seacliffe Avenue, Takapuna, Auckland 9, NZ. *Club:* City Livery.

GRIFFITHS, Rt. Hon. Sir Hugh; *see* Griffiths, Rt Hon. Sir W. H.

GRIFFITHS, Islwyn Owen, QC 1973; a Recorder of the Crown Court, since 1972; Chief Social Security (formerly National Insurance) Commissioner, since 1981 (Commissioner since 1979); *b* 24 Jan. 1924; *m* 1951, Pamela Norah Blizard. *Educ:* Swansea Grammar Sch.; Christ Church, Oxford (MA, BCL). Army (Royal Artillery), 1942-47; TA (RA), 1947-51; TARO, 1951. Called to Bar, Lincoln's Inn, 1953; Dep. Chm., Bucks QS, 1967-71. *Recreation:* sailing. *Address:* 6 Grosvenor Gardens, SW1. *T:* 01-730 9236. *Club:* Garrick.

GRIFFITHS, John Calvert, QC 1972; Attorney-General of Hong Kong, since 1979; Member, Executive Council and Member, Legislative Council, Hong Kong, since 1979; Chairman, Law Reform Commission; *b* 16 Jan. 1931; *s* of Oswald Hardy Griffiths and Christina Flora Griffiths; *m* 1958, Jessamy, *er d* of Prof. G. P. Crowden and Jean Crowden; three *d. Educ:* St Peter's Sch., York (scholar); Emmanuel Coll., Cambridge (senr exhibnr) (BA 1st Cl. Hons 1955; MA 1960). Called to Bar, Middle Temple, 1956; Recorder of the Crown Court, 1972-. Member, Executive Committee: General Council of the Bar, 1967-71; Senate of Inns of Court and the Bar, 1973-77; Mem., Nat. Council of Social Service, 1974-79; Mem., Greater London CAB Exec. Cttee, 1978-79; co-opted Mem., Develt and Special Projects Cttee, 1977-79. Lieutenant, R.E, 1949 (Nat. Service). *Recreations:* fishing, reading, gardening. *Address:* Attorney-General's Chambers, Central Government Office, Hong Kong. *T:* Hong Kong 95255; 2 Crown Office Row, Temple, EC4Y 7HJ. *T:* 01-353 9337. *Clubs:* Flyfishers', Hurlingham.

GRIFFITHS, John Charles, JP; Chairman: Rodhales Ltd, since 1978; Contact PR (London) Ltd, since 1981; Videoscript Ltd, since 1982; President of the Liberal Party, since 1982; *b* 19 April 1934; *s* of Sir Percival Griffiths, *qv*; *m* 1956, Ann Timms (marr. diss.); four *s. Educ:* Uppingham; Peterhouse, Cambridge (MA). Dep. General Manager, Press Association, 1968-70; PR adviser, British Gas, 1970-74; Chm., MSG Public Relations, 1974-78. Chairman: National League of Young Liberals, 1962-64 (Mem., Nat. Exec., 1964-66); Assoc. of Liberals in Small Business and Self Employed, 1980; Party Candidate, General Elections: 1964, 1966, Feb. 1974, Oct. 1974. JP Cardiff, 1960. *Publications:* The Survivors, 1964; Afghanistan, 1967; Modern Iceland, 1969; Three Tomorrows, 1980; The Science of Winning Squash, 1981; Afghanistan: key to a Continent, 1981; The Queen of Spades, 1983. *Recreations:* squash, conversation, reading, music. *Address:* Llethrgnneuen,

Pontfaen, Brecon, Powys LD3 9RP, Wales. *T:* Brecon 89 306; (office) Merthyr Cynog 23041. *Club:* Royal Automobile.

GRIFFITHS, John Edward Seaton, CMG 1959; MBE 1934; retired; *b* 27 Sept. 1908; *s* of A. E. Griffiths, MA, Cape Town; *m* 1937, Helen Parker, *d* of C. C. Wiles, MA, Grahamstown, SA; two *s* one *d. Educ:* South African Coll. Sch.; Cape Town Univ.; Selwyn Coll., Cambridge. Colonial Service (later HM Oversea Civil Service), Tanganyika, 1931-59; Asst Comr, East African Office, 1960-63; Director of Studies, Royal Inst. Public Administration, 1963-67; Administrative Training Officer, Govt of Botswana, 1967-73. *Publications:* articles in Tanganyika Notes and Records, Botswana Notes and Records and in Journal of Administration Overseas. *Address:* c/o National Westminster Bank Ltd, 249 Banbury Road, Summertown, Oxford. *Clubs:* Royal Commonwealth Society; Mountain Club of South Africa (Cape Town).

GRIFFITHS, Prof. John William Roger; Professor of Electronics, Department of Electronic and Electrical Engineering, Loughborough University of Technology, since 1967; *b* 27 Nov. 1921; *s* of Samuel William Henry Griffiths and Alice Griffiths; *m* 1945, Pauline Edyth Griffiths (*née* Marston); one *s. Educ:* Waterloo Grammar Sch.; Bristol Univ. BSc 1949, PhD 1958. FIEE; FIERE. Served War, HM Forces, 1939-46. Scientific Civil Service, 1949-55; Lectr, then Sen. Lectr, Birmingham Univ., 1955-67; Loughborough Univ. of Technology: Head of Dept, 1968-80; Dean of Engineering, 1972-75; Sen. Pro-Vice-Chancellor, 1978-80. Vis. Prof., Inst. of Radio Physics, Calcutta, 1963-65. *Publications:* Signal Processing in Underwater Acoustics, 1972; many papers in learned jls. *Recreations:* sport, gardening. *Address:* 80 Rectory Road, Wanlip, Leicestershire. *T:* Leicester 676336.

GRIFFITHS, Lawrence; a Recorder of the Crown Court, since 1972; *b* 16 Aug. 1933; *s* of Bernard Griffiths and Olive Emily Griffiths (*née* Stokes); *m* 1959, Josephine Ann (*née* Cook); one *s* two *d. Educ:* Gowerton Grammar Sch.; Christ's Coll., Cambridge (MA). Called to Bar, Inner Temple, 1957; practised Swansea, 1958-; Mem. Wales and Chester Circuit; Prosecuting Counsel to Inland Revenue for Wales and Chester Circuit, 1969. *Address:* Peverell, 26 Hillside Crescent, Ffynone, Swansea. *T:* Swansea 59513; (chambers) Iscoed Chambers, 86 St Helens Road, Swansea. *T:* Swansea 52988. *Club:* Cardiff and County (Cardiff).

GRIFFITHS, Rt. Rev. (Michael) Ambrose, OSB; Abbot of Ampleforth, since 1976; *b* 4 Dec. 1928; *s* of Henry and Hilda Griffiths. *Educ:* Ampleforth Coll.; Balliol Coll., Oxford (MA, BSc Chemistry). Entered monastery at Ampleforth, 1950; theological studies at S Anselmo, Rome, 1953-54; ordained priest, 1957; Prof. of Theology at Ampleforth, 1963; Sen. Science Master, Ampleforth Coll., 1967; Inspector of Accounts for English Benedictine Congregation, 1971; Procurator (Bursar) at Ampleforth, 1972; Mem. Public School Bursars' Assoc. Cttee, 1975. *Recreations:* walking and Scouting. *Address:* Ampleforth Abbey, York YO6 4EN. *T:* Ampleforth 421.

GRIFFITHS, Sir Percival Joseph, KBE 1963; Kt 1947; CIE 1943; ICS (retired); formerly President, India, Pakistan and Burma Association; Director of various companies; *b* 15 Jan. 1899; *s* of late J. T. Griffiths, Ashford, Middx; *m* Kathleen Mary (*d* 1979), *d* of late T. R. Wilkes, Kettering; three *s. Educ:* Peterhouse, Cambridge (MA). BSc London; entered Indian Civil Service, 1922; retired, 1937. Leader, European Group, Indian Central Legislature, 1946; Central Organiser, National War Front, India, and Publicity Adviser to Government of India; Mem. Indian Legislative Assembly, 1937. Hon. Fellow, SOAS, 1971. *Publications:* The British in India, 1947; The British Impact on India, 1952; Modern India, 1957; The Changing Face of Communism, 1961; The Road to Freedom, 1964; History of the Indian Tea Industry, 1967; Empire into Commonwealth, 1969; To Guard My People: the history of the Indian Police, 1971; A Licence to Trade: the history of English Chartered Companies, 1975; A History of the Inchcape Group, 1977; A History of the Joint Steamer Companies, 1979. *Address:* St Christopher, Abbotts Drive, Wentworth, Virginia Water, Surrey. *Club:* Oriental.
See also J. C. Griffiths.

GRIFFITHS, Prof. Peter Denham, MD, FRCPath; Professor of Biochemical Medicine since 1968, and Vice-Principal since 1979, University of Dundee; Hon. Consultant Clinical Chemist, Tayside Health Board, since 1966; *b* 16 June 1927; *s* of Bernard Millar Griffiths and Florence Marion Fletcher; *m* 1949, Joy Burgess; three *s* one *d. Educ:* King Edward VI Sch., Southampton; Guy's Hosp. Med. Sch., Univ. of London (BSc 1st Cl. Hons, MD). LRCP, MRCS; MBCS; FRCPath 1978. Served RN, 1946-49. Jun. Lectr in Physiol., Guy's Hosp. Med. Sch., 1957-58; Registrar, then Sen. Registrar in Clin. Path., Guy's and Lewisham Hosps, London, 1958-64; Consultant Pathologist, Harlow Gp of Hosps, Essex, 1964-66; Sen. Lectr in Clin. Chemistry, Univ. of St Andrews and subseq. Univ. of Dundee, 1966-68. Chm., Council of Assoc. of Clin. Biochemists, UK, 1973-76; Member: Tayside Health Bd, 1977-; various cttees of SHHD and DHSS, 1969-. Dir, Dundee Rep. Theatre, 1977-. Jt Editor-in-Chief, Clinica Chimica Acta, 1979-. *Publications:* contrib. scientific and med. jls (pathology, clin. chemistry, computing). *Recreations:* music, gardening, decorating, walking. *Address:* 52 Albany Road, West Ferry, Dundee, Scotland DD5 1NW. *T:* Dundee 76772. *Club:* Royal Commonwealth Society.

GRIFFITHS, Peter Harry Steve; MP (C) Portsmouth North, since 1979; *b* 24 May 1928; *s* of W. L. Griffiths, West Bromwich; *m* 1962, Jeannette Christine (*née* Rubery); one *s* one *d. Educ:* City of Leeds Training Coll. BSc (Econ.) Hons London, 1956; MEd Birmingham, 1963. Headmaster, Hall Green Road Sch., West Bromwich, 1962-64. Senior Lectr in Economic Hist., The Polytechnic, Portsmouth (formerly Portsmouth Coll. of Technology), 1967-79. Fulbright Exchange Prof. of Economics, Pierce Coll., Los Angeles, Calif, 1968-69. Chm., Smethwick Education Cttee; Leader, Conservative Group of Councillors in Smethwick, 1960-64. MP (C) Smethwick, 1964-66; Contested (C) Portsmouth N, Feb. 1974. *Publication:* A Question of Colour?, 1966. *Recreations:* motoring, writing, camping. *Address:* 1 Gloucester Mews, Southsea, Hants. *Clubs:* Sloane; Conservative (Smethwick and Portsmouth).

GRIFFITHS, Sir Peter N.; *see* Norton-Griffiths.

GRIFFITHS, Sir Reginald (Ernest), Kt 1973; CBE 1965; Secretary, Local Authorities' Advisory Board, 1957-73; *b* 4 April 1910; *s* of Arthur Griffiths; *m* 1935, Jessica Lilian Broad; two *s. Educ:* St Marylebone Grammar Sch.; London Univ. (external). Asst Clerk, LCC, 1948-52; Dir of Estabs, LCC, 1952-57. Jt Sec., Police Council, 1957-72; Jt Sec., Nat. Jt Industrial Councils (Local Authorities), 1957-72; Mem., Nat. Industrial Relations Court, 1972-74. *Recreations:* gardening, golf. *Address:* 10 Woolbrook Park, Sidmouth, Devon. *T:* Sidmouth 4884.

GRIFFITHS, Richard Cerdin, CMG 1978; Director, Inter-University Council for Higher Education Overseas, 1970-80; *b* 21 Oct. 1915; *s* of James Griffiths, MBE, and Gwendolen Griffiths, Swansea; *m* 1944, Pamela de Grave Hetherington; three *s* one *d. Educ:* Swansea Grammar Sch.; Jesus Coll., Oxford (Exhibnr, Hon. Schol.). MA. Entered Admiralty as Asst Principal, 1939; Royal Navy (Ord. Seaman), 1940-41; British Admiralty Delegn, Washington, DC, 1941-43. Transf. to HM Treasury, 1946; Private Sec. to Sec. of Treasury (Sir Edward Bridges), 1948-49; Asst Sec., 1949; Treasury Representative in Australia and New Zealand, 1952-53; Imperial Defence Coll., 1957; Head of Arts and Science Div., 1958-63; Under-Sec., Treasury, 1963; Dep. Sec., UGC, 1963-70. Mem., UPGC, Hong Kong, 1967-80; Mem. Council: S Pacific Univ., 1971-73; Queen Elizabeth Coll., Univ. of London; Univ. of East Asia, Macau; Hon. Treasurer, Inst. of Cancer Research, Univ. of London; Mem., Bd of Governors, Royal Marsden Hosp.; Vice Chm., Hill Homes, 1971-81; Trustee and Vice-Pres., Highgate Literary and Scientific Instn; Chm., Robert Whipple Trust. Mem. Council, Hon. Soc. of Cymmrodorion. Symonds Award, Assoc. of Commonwealth Univs, 1979. Hon. LLD: Malaya, 1980; Hong Kong, 1981; Hon. DSc Ulster, 1980. *Recreations:* cricket, walking. *Address:* 2 St Albans Villas, NW5 1QU. *T:* 01-485 1862. *Clubs:* Athenæum; MCC.

GRIFFITHS, Roger Noel Price, MA Cantab; JP; Headmaster of Hurstpierpoint College, since 1964; *b* 25 Dec. 1931; *er s* of late William Thomas and of Anne Evelyn Griffiths; *m* 1966, Diana, *y d* of Capt. J. F. B. Brown, RN; three *d. Educ:* Lancing Coll.; King's Coll., Cambridge. Asst Master at Charterhouse, 1956-64. MA Oxon, by incorporation, 1960. JP Mid Sussex, 1976. *Recreations:* music, theatre, bowls. *Address:* Hurstpierpoint College, Hassocks, West Sussex BN6 9JS. *T:* Hurstpierpoint 833636. *Club:* East India, Devonshire, Sports and Public Schools.

GRIFFITHS, Roy; *see* Griffiths, (Ernest) Roy.

GRIFFITHS, Trevor, BScEng, CEng, FIMechE, FIEE; registered professional engineer, State of California; Engineer Specialist (retired), Bechtel Power Corporation, Norwalk, California; *b* 17 April 1913; *m* 1939, Evelyn Mary Colborn; one *d. Educ:* Bishop Gore Gram. Sch., Swansea; University Coll., London. Metropolitan Vickers Electrical Co. Ltd, 1934; Air Min., 1938; UKAEA, 1955; Min. of Power, 1960; Min. of Technology, 1969 (Chief Inspector of Nuclear Installations, 1964-71); Dep. Chief Inspector of Nuclear Installations, DTI, 1971-73. *Address:* 4240 SE Knapp Street, Portland, Oregon 97206, USA.

GRIFFITHS, Trevor; playwright; *b* 4 April 1935; *s* of Ernest Griffiths and Anne Connor; *m* 1961, Janice Elaine Stansfield (*d* 1977); one *s* two *d. Educ:* Manchester Univ. BA (Hons) Eng. Lang. and Lit. Teaching, 1957-65; Educn Officer, BBC, 1965-72. Writer's Award, BAFTA, 1981. *Publications:* Occupations, 1972, 3rd edn 1980; Sam Sam, 1972; The Party, 1974, 2nd edn 1978; Comedians, 1976, 2nd edn 1979; All Good Men, and Absolute Beginners, 1977; Through the Night, and Such Impossibilities, 1977; Thermidor and Apricots, 1977; (jtly) Deeds, 1978; (trans.) The Cherry Orchard, 1978; Country, 1981; Oi for England, 1982. *Recreations:* soccer, music, chess. *Address:* c/o A. D. Peters, 10 Buckingham Street, WC2. *Clubs:* Trades Council (Leeds); Bradford Labour (Manchester).

GRIFFITHS, Ward David; Part-time Member Board, British Steel Corporation, 1970-79; *b* 9 Oct. 1915; *s* of David and Maud Griffiths; *m* 1940, Maisie Edith Williams; three *s* two *d. Educ:* elementary and technical schools. Steelworker, 1936-70. Br. Sec. and subseq. Exec. Mem., Iron and Steel Trades Assoc., 1960-68. Deleg., Tinplate Jt Industrial Council, 1965-68; Employee Dir, S Wales Gp and subseq. Strip Mills Div., British Steel Corp., 1968-70; Director: Grundy Auto Products Ltd, 1975-79; Ruthner Continuous Crop Systems Ltd, 1976-78. *Recreations:* motoring, Rugby football. *Address:* 18

Cambridge Gardens, Ebbw Vale, Gwent NP3 5HG. *T:* Ebbw Vale 303716. *Club:* Ernest Lever Works (Ebbw Vale).

GRIFFITHS, Rt. Hon. Sir (William) Hugh, Kt 1971; MC 1944; PC 1980; **Rt. Hon. Lord Justice Griffiths;** a Lord Justice of Appeal, since 1980; *b* 26 Sept. 1923; *s* of late Sir Hugh Griffiths, CBE, MS, FRCS; *m* 1949, Evelyn, *d* of Col K. A. Krefting; one *s* three *d. Educ:* Charterhouse; St John's Coll., Cambridge. Commissioned in Welsh Guards, 1942; demobilised after war service, 1946. Cambridge, 1946-48. BA 1948. Called to the Bar, Inner Temple, 1949, Bencher, 1971; QC 1964; Treasurer of the Bar Council, 1968-69. Recorder of Margate, 1962-64, of Cambridge, 1964-70; a Judge of the High Court of Justice, Queen's Bench Division, 1971-80; a Judge, National Industrial Relations Court, 1973-74. Mem., Adv. Council on Penal Reform, 1967-70; Chm., Tribunal of Inquiry on Ronan Point, 1968; Vice-Chm., Parole Bd, 1976-77; Mem., Chancellor's Law Reform Cttee, 1976-. *Recreations:* golf, fishing. *Address:* c/o The Royal Courts of Justice, WC2. *Clubs:* MCC; Hawks (Cambridge); Worplesdon Golf.

GRIFFITHS, Winston James; Member (Lab) South Wales, European Parliament, since 1979; *b* 11 Feb. 1943; *s* of (Rachel) Elizabeth Griffiths and (Evan) George Griffiths; *m* 1966, (Elizabeth) Ceri Griffiths; one *s* one *d. Educ:* State schools in Brecon; University College of South Wales and Monmouthshire, Cardiff. BA, DipEd. Taught in Tanzania, Birmingham, Barry, Cowbridge. Member: World Development Movement; Christian Socialist Movement; Amnesty International; Campaign for Nuclear Disarmament; Fabian Society. Chm., Parliamentarians for World Order in Eur. Parlt; Vice-Pres., Eur. Parlt delegn to S Africa. *Address:* Tŷ Llon, John Street, Y Graig, Cefn Cribwr, Mid Glamorgan CF32 0AB. *T:* Kenfig Hill 740526.

GRIGG, John (Edward Poynder); writer; *b* 15 April 1924; *s* of late 1st Baron Altrincham and Joan Dickson-Poynder; *m* 1958, Patricia, *d* of late H. E. Campbell and Marion Wheeler; two *s. Educ:* Eton; New Coll., Oxford (Exhibitioner). MA, Modern History; Gladstone Memorial Prize. Grenadier Guards, 1943-45. Editor, National and English Review, 1954-60; Columnist for The Guardian, 1960-70. Contested (C) Oldham West, 1951 and 1955. Pres., Greenwich Cons. Assoc., 1979-82. Joined SDP, 1982. FRSL. *Publications:* Two Anglican Essays, 1958; The Young Lloyd George, 1973; Lloyd George: the People's Champion, 1978 (Whitbread Award); 1943: The Victory That Never Was, 1980; Nancy Astor: Portrait of a Pioneer, 1980; contribs to other books; articles and reviews. *Address:* 32 Dartmouth Row, SE10. *T:* 01-692 4973. *Club:* Beefsteak.

GRIGGS, Norman Edward, CBE 1976; Secretary-General, The Building Societies Association, 1963-81, Vice-President since 1981; Vice-President, Metropolitan Association of Building Societies, since 1981; Member, Southern Regional Board, Midshires Building Society, since 1981; *b* 27 May 1916; *s* of late Archibald Griggs and late Maud Griggs (*née* Hewing); *m* 1947, Livia Lavinia Jandolo; one *s* one step *s. Educ:* Newport Grammar Sch.; London Sch. of Econs and Polit. Science (BScEcon). FCIS. Accountancy Dept, County of London Electric Supply Co. Ltd, 1933-40; service in RE and RAPC, Middle East, 1940-46; Asst Sec., Glass Manufrs' Fedn, 1946-52; Sec., Plastics Inst., 1952-56; Asst Sec., Building Socs Assoc., 1956-61, Dep. Sec. 1961-63; Sec.-Gen., Internat. Union of Building Socs and Savings Assocs, 1972-77; Vice-Pres., Chartered Building Socs Inst., 1981-. *Recreation:* print addict. *Address:* 5 Gledhow Gardens, SW5 0BL. *T:* 01-373 5128.

GRIGOROV, Mitko; Hero of Socialist Labour, 1980; Order of Georgi Dimitrov, 1959, 1970, 1980; Member since 1971, Vice-President, since 1974, State Council of People's Republic of Bulgaria; *b* 9 Sept. 1920; *m* 1956, Stanka Stanoeva; one *d. Educ:* Sofia University. Mem. of Parliament from 1953, Minister without Portfolio, 1962-66; Sec., Central Cttee, Bulgarian Communist Party, 1958-66 (Mem., Politbureau, Central Cttee, 1961-66). Bulgarian Ambassador to the Court of St James's, 1969-71. Mem., Editorial Board of magazine Problems of Peace and Socialism, 1966-69. *Recreation:* mountaineering. *Address:* c/o Durzhaven Suvet (State Council of Bulgaria), Dondoukov 2, Sofia, Bulgaria.

GRIGSON, Geoffrey; poet; *b* 2 March 1905; 7th *s* of late Canon W. S. Grigson, Pelynt, Cornwall and of Mary Beatrice Boldero; *m* 1st, Frances Galt (*d* 1937), St Louis, Missouri; one *d* ; 2nd, Berta Kunert (marr. diss.); one *s* one *d* ; 3rd, Jane Grigson, *qv, d* of G.S. McIntire, CBE; one *d.* Editor of New Verse, 1933-39; formerly on staff of Yorkshire Post, Morning Post (Literary Editor) and BBC. *Publications:* Several Observations, 1939; Under the Cliff and other poems, 1943; Henry Moore, 1943; The Isles of Scilly and other poems, 1946; Samuel Palmer, 1947; The Harp of Aeolus, 1947; Places of the Mind, 1949; The Crest on the Silver, 1950; William Barnes (Muses Library), 1950; John Clare (Muses Library), 1950; Essays from the Air, 1951; A Master of Our Time (Wyndham Lewis), 1951; Gardenage, 1952; Legenda Suecana (poems), 1953; Freedom of the Parish, 1954; The Englishman's Flora, 1955; Gerard Manley Hopkins, 1955; English Drawings, 1955; The Painted Caves, 1957; Art Treasures of the British Museum, 1958; The Three Kings, 1958; A Herbal of All Sorts, 1959; The Cherry Tree, 1959; English Excursions, 1960; Christopher Smart, 1961; The Shell Country Book, 1962; Collected Poems, 1963; Poems of Walter Savage Landor, 1964; (with Jane Grigson) Shapes and Stories, 1964; The Shell Country Alphabet, 1966; A Skull in Salop and Other Poems, 1967; Shapes and Adventures, 1967; Poems and Poets, 1968; A Choice of William Morris's Verse, 1968; Ingestion of Ice-Cream and Other Poems,

1969; Shapes and People, 1969; Notes from an Odd Country, 1970; (ed) Faber Book of Popular Verse, 1971; (ed) A Choice of Southey's Verse, 1971; Discoveries of Bones and Stones and Other Poems, 1971 (Duff Cooper Meml Prize 1972); (ed) Unrespectable Verse, 1971; Rainbows, Fleas and Flowers, 1971; Shapes and Creatures, 1972; Sad Grave of an Imperial Mongoose and Other Poems, 1973; (ed) Faber Book of Love Poems, 1973; (ed) Dictionary of English Plant Names, 1974; Angles and Circles and other Poems, 1974; The Contrary View, 1974; Britain Observed, 1975; (ed) Poet to Poet: Charles Cotton, 1975; (ed) Penguin Book of Ballads, 1975; The Goddess of Love, 1976; Faber Book of Epigrams and Epitaphs, 1977; (ed) Faber Book of Nonsense Verse, 1978; The Fiesta and Other Poems, 1978; (ed) Oxford Book of Satirical Verse, 1980; History of Him and other Poems, 1980; (ed) Faber Book of Poems and Places, 1980; Twists of the Way (poems), 1980; Blessings, Kicks and Curses, 1982; Collected Poems, 1982; The Cornish Dancer (poems), 1982; The Private Art, 1982. *Address:* Broad Town Farm, Broad Town, Swindon, Wilts. *T:* Broad Hinton 259.

GRIGSON, Jane; Cookery Correspondent, Observer Colour Magazine, since 1968; *b* 13 March 1928; *d* of George Shipley McIntire, CBE, and Doris Berkley; *m* Geoffrey Grigson, *qv* ; one *d. Educ:* Casterton Sch., Westmorland; Newnham Coll., Cambridge. Editorial Assistant, Rainbird McLean Ltd, and Thames and Hudson Ltd, 1953-55; translator from Italian, 1956-67; cookery writer, 1967-. *Publications:* Charcuterie and French Pork Cookery, 1967; Good Things, 1971; Fish Cookery, 1973; English Food, 1974 (rev. edn 1979); The Mushroom Feast, 1975; Jane Grigson's Vegetable Book, 1978 (Glenfiddich Writer of the Year; André Simon Meml Prize); Food with the Famous, 1979; Jane Grigson's Fruit Book, 1982; contributing editor, World Atlas of Food, 1974; (translated) Of Crimes and Punishments, by Cesare Beccaria, 1964 (John Florio prize). *Address:* Broad Town Farmhouse, Broad Town, Swindon, Wiltshire. *T:* Broad Hinton 259.

GRILLER, Sidney Aaron, CBE 1951; Leader of Griller String Quartet since 1928; *b* London, 10 Jan. 1911; *s* of Salter Griller and Hannah (*née* Green); *m* 1932, Elizabeth Honor, *y d* of James Linton, JP, Co. Down, N Ireland; one *s* one *d. Educ:* Royal Academy of Music. Toured British Isles, Holland, Germany, Switzerland, France, Italy, 1928-38; first concert tour in USA, 1939. Served RAF, 1940-45. Lecturer in Music, University of California, 1949; world tours, 1951, 1953. Prof. of Music: Royal Irish Acad. of Music, 1963; Royal Academy of Music, 1964. Worshipful Company of Musicians Medal for Chamber Music, 1944; FRAM, 1945; Mem. Royal Society of St George, 1955. DUniv York, 1981. *Address:* 63 Marloes Road, W8. *T:* 01-937 7067.

GRILLET, Alain R.; see Robbe-Grillet.

GRIMA, Andrew Peter; Jeweller by appointment to HM the Queen; Managing Director: H. J. Co. Ltd, since 1951; Andrew Grima Ltd, since 1966; *b* 31 May 1921; *s* of John Grima and Leopolda Farnese; *m* 1st, 1947, Helène Marianne Haller (marr. diss. 1977); one *s* two *d* ; 2nd, 1977, Joanne Jill Maughan-Brown, *d* of late Nigel Maughan-Brown and of Mrs G. Rawdon; one *d. Educ:* St Joseph's Coll., Beulah Hill; Nottingham Univ. Served War of 1939-45, REME, India and Burma, 1942-46 (despatches, 1945); commanded div. workshop. Director and jewellery designer, H. J. Co., 1947-. Exhibitions in numerous cities all over the world; designed and made prestige collection of watches, "About Time", 1970; exhibited at Goldsmiths' Hall. Opened shops in Sydney and New York, 1970; Zürich, 1971; Tokyo, 1973. Has donated annual Andrew Grima award to Sir John Cass Coll. of Art, 1963-. Duke of Edinburgh Prize for Elegant Design, 1966; 11 Diamond Internat. New York Awards, 1963-67. Freeman, City of London, 1964; Liveryman, Worshipful Co. of Goldsmiths, 1968. *Publications:* contribs to: International Diamond Annual, S Africa, 1970; 6 Meister Juweliere unserer Zeit, 1971. *Recreations:* paintings, sculpture, food and wine, campaign to rule out red tape. *Address:* Albany, Piccadilly, W1V 9RR. *Clubs:* Royal Automobile, Institute of Directors.

GRIME, Sir Harold (Riley), Kt 1959; DL; JP; Chairman and Editor-in-Chief of the West Lancashire Evening Gazette and associated newspapers; Editor of the Blackpool Gazette, 1926-62; *b* 12 May 1896; *s* of late Frederick Alexander Grime, JP, and late Fannie Grime (*née* Riley); *m* 1925, Mary (Mollie) Bowman (*d* 1970), *d* of late W. Powell Bowman, Leeds; two *d. Educ:* Arnold Sch., Blackpool; Bonn, Germany. East Lancs Regt, 1915-17; Indian Army, 1917-20. Yorkshire Evening Post and London Evening News, 1920-23. Dir, Press Association, 1942-51 (Chm. 1946-47); Dir, Reuters, 1945-47; Founder Mem., British Cttee, Internat. Press Inst., 1951; Chm., Guild of Editors (NW Region), 1957-58. Hon. Sec., Blackpool Victoria Hosp., 1938-48; Hon. Treas., Blackpool Conservative and Unionist Assoc., 1938-45; Dir, Blackpool Tower and Winter Gardens Cos., 1944-68 (Vice-Chm. 1953-68); Pres., Preston and District Chamber of Commerce, 1962-67. Mem., Gen. Advisory Council, BBC, 1960-64. Hon. Freeman of Blackpool, 1950. DL Lancs, 1968. JP for Blackpool, 1943-. *Publications:* The Silver Trumpet, 1942; Sand in My Shoes, 1950. *Address:* 24 Lowcross Road, Poulton-le-Fylde, Lancs.

GRIMES, Prof. William Francis, CBE 1955; DLitt, FSA; FMA; Director of the Institute of Archæology, and Professor of Archæology, University of London, 1956-73; *b* 31 Oct. 1905; *s* of Thomas George Grimes, Pembroke; *m* 1st, 1928, Barbara Lilian Morgan (marr. diss. 1959); one *s* one *d* ; 2nd, 1959, Audrey Williams (*née* Davies) (*d* 1978). *Educ:* University of Wales (MA); DLitt Wales, 1961. Asst Keeper of Archæology, National Museum of Wales,

Cardiff, 1926-38; Asst Archæology Officer, Ordnance Survey, 1938-45; seconded to Min. of Works to record historic monuments on defence sites, 1939-45; Dir London Museum, 1945-56. Mem. Royal Commn on Ancient Monuments in Wales, 1948-78 (Chm., 1967-78), and of Ancient Monuments Boards, England, 1954-77, Wales, 1959-78; Mem. Royal Commn on Historical Monuments (England), 1964-78. Sec. to Coun. for British Archæology, 1949-54, Pres. 1954-59, Vice-Pres., 1961-65, Treas., 1964-74; Pres. London and Middlesex Archæological Soc., 1950-59, Hon. Vice-Pres., 1976-; Pres. Royal Archæological Institute, 1957-60 (Vice-Pres. 1951-57); Vice-President: Soc. of Antiquaries, 1953-57; Soc. for Medieval Archæology; Prehistoric Soc., 1958-61; Soc. for Roman Studies, 1973-; Hon. Dir of Excavations for the Roman and Mediæval London Excavation Council, 1946-; Chm., London Topographical Soc., 1961-73. Pres., Cambrian Archæological Assoc., 1963-64 (G. T. Clark Prize, 1946); Chm., Faculty of Archæology, History and Letters, British Sch. at Rome, 1963-66; President: Stanmore Archæological Soc., 1962-; Tenby Museum, 1969-; Field Studies Council, 1975- (Chm., 1966-75). Hon. Professorial Fellow, University Coll. Swansea, Univ. of Wales, 1974-. *Publications:* Holt, Denbighshire, Legionary Works Depôt (Y Cymmrodor), 1930; Pre-history of Wales, 1951; (ed) Aspects of Archæology in Britain and Beyond, 1951; (with M. D. Knowles) Charterhouse, 1954; (with others) Brooke House, Hackney (London Survey, Vol. XXVIII), 1960; Excavations in Defence Sites, 1939-1945, I, 1960; The Excavation of Roman and Mediæval London, 1968; many papers in learned jls. *Address:* 29 Bryn Road, Swansea, West Glamorgan.

GRIMOND, Rt. Hon. Joseph; TD; PC 1961; LLD Edinburgh; MP (L) Orkney and Shetland since 1950; Leader of the Parliamentary Liberal Party, 1956-67, and May-July 1976; Trustee, The Manchester Guardian and Evening News Ltd, since 1967; Chancellor of University of Kent at Canterbury, since 1970; *b* 29 July 1913; *s* of Joseph Bowman Grimond and Helen Lydia Richardson; *m* 1938, Hon. Laura Miranda, *d* of late Sir Maurice Bonham Carter, KCB, KCVO, and Baroness Asquith of Yarnbury, DBE; two *s* one *d* (and one *s* decd). *Educ:* Eton; Balliol Coll., Oxford (Brackenbury Scholar). 1st Class Hons (Politics, Philosophy, and Economics). Called to the Bar, Middle Temple (Harmsworth Scholar), 1937. Served War of 1939-45, Fife and Forfar Yeomanry and Staff 53 Div. (Major). Contested Orkney and Shetland (Liberal), 1945. Dir of Personnel, European Office, UNRRA, 1945-47; Sec. of the National Trust for Scotland, 1947-49. Rector: Edinburgh Univ., 1960-63; Aberdeen Univ., 1969-72. Chubb Fellow, Yale; Romanes Lectr, 1980. Hon. LLD: Edinburgh, 1960; Aberdeen, 1972; Birmingham, 1974; Hon. DCL Kent, 1970. *Publications:* The Liberal Future, 1959; The Liberal Challenge, 1963; (with B. Neve) The Referendum, 1975; The Common Welfare, 1978; Memoirs, 1979; contributor: The Prime Ministers, 1976; My Oxford, 1977. *Address:* Old Manse of Firth, Kirkwall, Orkney.

GRIMSBY, Bishop Suffragan of, since 1979; **Rt. Rev. David Tustin;** *b* 12 Jan. 1935; *s* of John Trevelyan Tustin and Janet Reynolds; *m* 1964, Mary Elizabeth (*née* Glover); one *s* one *d. Educ:* Solihull School; Magdalene Coll., Cambridge (MA Hons); Geneva Univ. (Cert. in Ecumenical Studies); Cuddesdon Coll., Oxford. Philip Usher Memorial Scholar (in Greece), 1957-58; Deacon 1960, priest 1961; Curate of Stafford, 1960-63; Asst Gen. Sec., C of E Council on Foreign Relations and Curate of St Dunstan-in-the-West, Fleet St, 1963-67; Vicar of S Paul's, Wednesbury, 1967-71; Vicar of Tettenhall Regis, 1971-79; RD of Trysull, 1977-79. Canon and Prebendary of Lincoln Cathedral, 1979-. *Recreations:* music, family life, languages, travel. *Address:* 43 Abbey Park Road, Grimsby, South Humberside DN32 0HS. *T:* Grimsby 58223.

GRIMSHAW, Maj.-Gen. Ewing Henry Wrigley, CB 1965; CBE 1957 (OBE 1954); DSO 1945; *b* 30 June 1911; *s* of Col E. W. Grimshaw; *m* 1943, Hilda Florence Agnes Allison; two *s* one *d. Educ:* Brighton Coll. Joined Indian Army, 1931. Served War of 1939-45, Western Desert and Burma (despatches twice). Transferred to Royal Inniskilling Fusiliers, 1947; Active Service in Malaya, Kenya and Suez, 1956 and Cyprus, 1958. GOC 44th Div. (TA) and Home Counties Dist, 1962-65. Col, The Royal Inniskilling Fusiliers, 1966-68; Dep. Col, The Royal Irish Rangers, 1968-73. *Address:* The Trellis House, Copford Green, near Colchester, Essex.

GRIMSTON, family name of **Baron Grimston of Westbury** and of **Earl of Verulam.**

GRIMSTON, Viscount; James Walter Grimston; *b* 6 Jan. 1978; *s* and *heir* of Earl of Verulam, *qv.*

GRIMSTON OF WESTBURY, 2nd Baron *cr* 1964; **Robert Walter Sigismund Grimston;** Bt 1952; Chairman, Gray's Inn (Underwriting Agency) Ltd, since 1970; Director, Hinton Hill & Coles Ltd, since 1962; *b* 14 June 1925; *s* of 1st Baron Grimston of Westbury and Sybil Edith Muriel Rose (*d* 1977), *d* of Sir Sigismund Neumann, 1st Bt; *S* father, 1979; *m* 1949, Hon. June Mary Ponsonby, *d* of 5th Baron de Mauley; two *s* one *d. Educ:* Eton. Served as Lt Scots Guards, 1943-47; NW Europe, 1944-45. Oil Industry, 1948-53; Sales Director, Ditchling Press, 1953-61. Freeman, City of London, 1981; Liveryman, Worshipful Co. of Gold and Silver Wyre Drawers, 1981. *Recreations:* tennis and shooting. *Heir: s* Hon. Robert John Sylvester Grimston [*b* 30 April 1951. Commissioned The Royal Hussars (PWO), 1969, Captain 1976, retired 1981]. *Address:* The Old Rectory, Westwell, near Burford, Oxon. *Clubs:* Boodle's, City of London.

GRIMTHORPE, 4th Baron, *cr* 1886; **Christopher John Beckett,** Bt 1813; OBE 1958; DL; Deputy Commander, Malta and Libya, 1964-67; *b* 16 Sept. 1915; *e s* of 3rd Baron Grimthorpe, TD, and Mary Lady Grimthorpe (*d* 1962); *S* father, 1963; *m* 1954, Elizabeth Lumley, 2nd *d* of 11th Earl of Scarbrough, KG, PC, GCSI, GCIE, GCVO; two *s* one *d. Educ:* Eton. 2nd Lieut, 9 Lancers, 1936; Lt-Col, 9 Lancers, 1955-58; AAG, War Office, 1958-61; Brigadier, Royal Armoured Corps, HQ, Western Command, 1961-64. Col, 9/12 Royal Lancers, 1973-77. ADC to the Queen, 1964-67. Director: Standard Broadcasting Corp. of Canada (UK), 1972-; Thirsk Racecourse Ltd, 1972-; Yorkshire Post Newspapers, 1973; Pres., London Metropolitan Region YMCA, 1972-. Mem., Jockey Club. DL North Yorkshire, 1969. *Recreations:* travel, horse sports. *Heir: s* Hon. Edward John Beckett, *b* 20 Nov. 1954. *Address:* 87 Dorset House, Gloucester Place, NW1. *T:* 01-486 4374; Westow Hall, York. *T:* Whitwell-on-the-Hill 225. *Club:* Cavalry and Guards.

GRIMWADE, Sir Andrew (Sheppard), Kt 1980; CBE 1977; Australian industrialist; *b* 26 Nov. 1930; *s* of late Frederick and Gwendolen Grimwade; *m* 1959, Barbara, *d* of J. B. D. Kater; one *s. Educ:* Melbourne C of E Grammar Sch.; Trinity Coll., Melbourne Univ. (Exhib. Eng., BSc); Oriel Coll., Oxford (swimming blue; MA). FRACI, FAIM, FInstD. Chairman: Australian Consolidated Industries Ltd, 1977-; Kemtron Ltd Gp, 1964-; Director: National Bank of Australasia; Commonwealth Ind. Gases; National Mutual Life Assoc.; IBM (Aust.); Sony (Aust.); AHI (NZ); Pilkington ACI Ltd. Mem., Australian Govt Remuneration Tribunal, 1976-. Pres., Walter and Eliza Hall Inst. of Med. Research, 1978-. Dep. Pres., Australiana Fund, 1978-. Chairman: Australian Arts Exhibn Corp., 1976-77; Australian Govt Official Estabts Trust, 1979-; Pres., Nat. Gallery of Vic., 1976-; Trustee, Victorian Arts Centre, 1980-. Member: Council for Order of Australia, 1974-; Felton Bequests' Cttee, 1973-. *Publication:* Involvement: The Portraits of Clifton Pugh and Mark Strizic, 1969. *Recreations:* skiing, Santa Gertrudis cattle breeding, Australiana art and books. *Address:* 320 St Kilda Road, Melbourne, Vic. 3004, Australia. *T:* (03)-699-1433. *Clubs:* Melbourne, Savage (Melbourne).

GRIMWADE, Rev. Canon John Girling; Priest-in-Charge of Stonesfield, and Agenda Secretary of Oxford Diocesan Synod, since 1983; Chaplain to the Queen, since 1980; *b* 13 March 1920; *s* of Herbert Alfred and Edith Grimwade; *m* 1951, Adini Anne Carus-Wilson; one *s* one *d. Educ:* Colet Court; St Paul's Sch.; Keble Coll., Oxford; Cuddesdon Coll. MA Oxon. Friends' Ambulance Unit, 1940-45. Curate of Kingston-upon-Thames, 1950-53; Curate, University Church of St Mary-the-Virgin, Oxford, and Secretary of Oxford Univ. Student Christian Movement, 1953-56; Vicar of St Mark's, Smethwick, 1956-62; Rector of Caversham, 1962-81, and Priest-in-Charge of Mapledurham, 1968-81; Rector of Caversham and Mapledurham, 1981-83. Chm., House of Clergy, Oxford Diocesan Synod, 1976-82. Hon. Canon of Christ Church, Oxford, 1974-. *Recreations:* gardening, walking, swimming in the Thames. *Address:* The Rectory, Stonesfield, Oxford OX7 2PB. *T:* Stonesfield 664.

GRIMWOOD, Frank Southgate, BA; DPhil; ABPsS; *b* 14 July 1904; *s* of late Frank Grimwood, Ipswich and Newbury, and Rose Grimwood (*née* Lake), Bucklebury, Berks; *m* 1935, Mary Habberley Price, MA Oxon; one *s* one *d. Educ:* Isleworth County High Sch.; Reading Univ. (Wantage Hall); The Queen's Coll., Oxford. DPhil Oxon; BA Hons University of Reading. Sub-Warden and Foreign Student Sec., SCM, 1929-30; Lecturer in Philosophy and Psychology, City Literary Institute, 1930-40; Welfare Officer (Oxon, Bucks, and Berks), Min. of Labour and Nat. Service, 1940-48. Advanced Student, The Queen's Coll., Oxford, 1948-56, including one year (1951) at Cuddesdon Theological Coll. (thesis on psychotherapy and religion). Lecturer and Tutor, Oxford Univ. Extra-Mural Delegacy, 1956-61; Warden and Director of Studies, Moor Park College, 1961-72; lecturing and tutoring groups for Nat. Marriage Guidance Council, 1965-70; Exec. Sec., Keble Coll., Oxford, Centenary Appeal, 1972-74. Private Consultant Psychotherapist. *Recreations:* painting, walking, biography. *Address:* 69A Jack Straw's Lane, Oxford OX3 0DW. *T:* Oxford 68535.

GRINDEA, Miron, MBE 1977; Chevalier de la Légion d'Honneur 1974; Editor, ADAM International Review (Anglo-French literary magazine), since 1941; *b* 31 Jan. 1909; *m* 1936, Carola Rabinovici, concert pianist; one *d. Educ:* Bucharest Univ.; Sorbonne. Literary and music critic, 1928-39; settled in England, Sept. 1939; together with Benjamin Britten and Henry Moore founded the International Arts Guild, 1943; war-time work with BBC European Service and Min. of Information; coast to coast lecture tours, USA. Visiting Lecturer: Univs of Paris, Aix-en-Provence, Athens, Karachi, Kyoto, Montreal, Toronto, Rejkiavik, Jerusalem, etc. Prix de l'Académie Française, 1955; Lundquist Literary Prize, Sweden, 1965. *Publications:* Malta Calling, 1943; Henry Wood (a symposium), 1944; Jerusalem, a literary chronicle of 3000 years, 1968, 2nd edn, Jerusalem, the Holy City in literature, preface by Graham Greene, 1982; Natalie Clifford Barney, 1963; The London Library (a symposium), 1978; contrib. The Listener, TLS, Figaro, Les Nouvelles Littéraires, New Statesman, The Times, Books and Bookmen. *Recreations:* Mozart, lazing in the sun. *Address:* 1 Palmeira Square, Brighton, Sussex. *T:* Brighton 735682; (office) 28 Emperor's Gate, SW7. *T:* 01-373 7307.

GRINDLE, Captain John Annesley, CBE 1943; RN; JP; *b* 17 Sept. 1900; *s* of late George Annesley Grindle and late Eveleen Grindle; *m* 1925, Joyce Lilian Alton, *d* of J. W. A. Batchelor, Blackheath; two *s. Educ:* Pembroke Lodge, Southbourne; RN Colleges, Osborne and Dartmouth; Pembroke

Coll., Cambridge; Midshipman, 1917; Comdr 1934; Captain 1941; Commanded HMS Apollo, 1944-55, Glenearn, 1946, Victorious 1949-50; Dep. Chief of Combined Ops (Naval), 1946-48. Retired list, 1950. JP (Hants) 1952. *Recreation:* gardening. *Address:* Anchor House, Wicor Path, Castle Street, Portchester, Hants. *T:* Cosham 376067.

GRINDON, John Evelyn, CVO 1957; DSO 1945; AFC 1948; Group Captain, RAF retired; *b* 30 Sept. 1917; *s* of Thomas Edward Grindon (killed in action, Ypres, Oct. 1917), and Dora (*née* Eastlake). *Educ:* Dulwich College. Cadet at RAF College, Cranwell, 1935-37; served in Advanced Air Striking Force, BEF, France, 1939-40 (No 150 Sqdn) and in No 5 Group Bomber Command (Nos 106, 630 and 617 Sqdns) during War of 1939-45, as Flight and Sqdn Comdr; Chief Instructor, Long Range Transport Force, 1946-49; Commanded The Queen's Flight, 1953-56; V-bomber Captain and Station Comdr, 1956-57; retired at own request 1959. Dir/Gen. Manager in printing/publishing, 1961-71; Metropolitan Police, New Scotland Yard, 1976-81. *Recreations:* music, sailing, racing. *Address:* 1 Ovington Gardens, SW3. *T:* 01-589 8822. *Club:* Royal Air Force.

GRINDROD, Helen Marjorie, QC 1982; a Recorder of the Crown Court, since 1981; *b* 28 Feb. 1936; *d* of late Joseph and Marjorie Pritchard; *m* 1958, Robert Michael Grindrod; one *s*. *Educ:* Liverpool Inst. High Sch. for Girls; St Hilda's Coll., Oxford. MA. Teacher, 1957-59. Called to the Bar, Lincoln's Inn, 1966; Northern Circuit, 1966-. *Address:* Cerin Amroth, Beechfield Road, Alderley Edge, Cheshire SK9 7AU. *T:* Alderley Edge 585464.

GRINDROD, Most Rev. John Basil Rowland; *see* Brisbane, Archbishop of.

GRINKE, Frederick, CBE 1979; FRAM; Solo Violinist; Professor of Violin, Royal Academy of Music, London, retired; *b* Winnipeg, Canada, 8 Aug. 1911; *s* of Arthur Grinke, Winnipeg; *m* 1942, Dorothy Ethel Sirr Sheldon; one *s*. *Educ:* Winnipeg; Royal Academy of Music, London (all prizes for solo and chamber music playing). Studied with Adolf Busch in Switzerland, with Carl Flesch in London and Belgium. Was leader and soloist with the Boyd Neel Orchestra for 10 years. Appeared regularly as Soloist with leading orchestras; has played in many countries in Europe also in America, Australia and New Zealand. Has appeared at Festivals: Edinburgh, Bath, Cheltenham, Three Choirs, Salzburg. Has taken part in many Promenade Concerts. A sonata was dedicated to him by Vaughan Williams; has made numerous recordings, including many works with the composers as pianists (such as Rubbra, Ireland, Berkeley, Benjamin). Has acted as mem. of the Jury for several international violin competitions. FRSA 1979. *Recreations:* music, cooking, wine, reading, the theatre. *Address:* Frog's Hall, Braiseworth, near Eye, Suffolk. *T:* Eye 870483.

GRINLING, Jasper Gibbons, CBE 1978; CBIM; Director of Corporate Affairs, Grand Metropolitan Ltd, since 1981; *b* 29 Jan. 1924; *s* of late Lt-Col Antony Gibbons Grinling, MBE, MC, and Jean Dorothy Turing Grinling; *m* 1950, Gertrude Jane Moulsdale; one *s* two *d*. *Educ:* Harrow (Scholar); King's Coll., Cambridge (Exhibnr, BA). FBIM 1969. Served War, 12th Lancers, 1942-46 (Captain). Joined W. & A. Gilbey Ltd, 1947, Dir 1952; Man. Dir, Gilbeys Ltd, 1964; Man. Dir, International Distillers & Vintners Ltd, 1967; Dir, North British Distillery Co. Ltd, 1968-. Pres., EEC Confedn des Industries Agricoles et Alimentaires, 1976-80; Mem. Council, Scotch Whisky Assoc., 1968-. FRSA. *Recreations:* gardening, jazz drumming, painting, vineyard proprietor. *Address:* The Old Vicarage, Helions Bumpstead, near Haverhill, Suffolk CB9 7AS. *T:* Steeple Bumpstead 316. *Club:* Oriental.

GRINSTEAD, Stanley Gordon, FCA; CBIM; Group Managing Director, since 1980, and Chairman, since 1982, Grand Metropolitan Ltd; *b* 17 June 1924; *s* of Ephraim Grinstead and Lucy Grinstead (*née* Taylor); *m* 1955, Joyce Preston; two *d*. *Educ:* Strodes, Egham. Served Royal Navy, 1943-46. Franklin, Wild & Co., Chartered Accountants, 1946-56; Hotel York Ltd, 1957; Grand Metropolitan Ltd, 1957-62; Union Properties (London) Ltd, 1958-66; Grand Metropolitan Ltd, 1964-; Dep. Chm., 1980-82. Dir, Reed International Ltd, 1981-. *Recreations:* gardening, cricket, racing. *Address:* 11/12 Hanover Square, W1A 1DP. *T:* 01-629 7488. *Clubs:* MCC; Surrey County Cricket.

GRINT, Edmund Thomas Charles, CBE 1960; *b* 14 Feb. 1904; *e s* of Edmund Albert Grint; *m* 1930, Olive Maria, *d* of Albert Cheyne Sherras; one *s* two *d*. *Educ:* London Univ. (Dip. Econs). Joined ICI 1929; Commercial Dir, Nobel Div., 1946; Director: Billingham Div., 1952-61; Alkali Div., 1961-63; Mond Div., 1964. Dep. Chief Labour Officer, 1951; Chief Labour Officer, 1952-63; Gen. Manager Personnel, 1963-65. Chm., Nat. Dock Labour Board, 1966-69; Pres., Midland Iron and Steel Wages Bd, 1971-79. *Recreations:* golf, gardening. *Address:* Old Walls, Seal, Sevenoaks, Kent. *T:* Sevenoaks 61364.

GRISEWOOD, Harman Joseph Gerard, CBE 1960; Chief Assistant to the Director-General, BBC, 1955-64, retired; *b* 8 Feb. 1906; *e s* of late Lieut-Col Harman Grisewood and Lucille Cardozo; *m* 1940, Clotilde Margaret Bailey; one *d*. *Educ:* Ampleforth Coll., York; Worcester Coll., Oxford. BBC Repertory Co., 1929-33; Announcer, 1933-36; Asst to Programme Organiser, 1936-39; Asst Dir Programme Planning, 1939-41; Asst Controller, European Div., 1941-45; Actg Controller, European Div., 1945-46; Dir of Talks, 1946-47; Planner, Third Programme, 1947-48; Controller of the Third

Programme, BBC, 1948-52; Dir of the Spoken Word, BBC, 1952-55. Member: Younger Cttee on Privacy, 1970-72; Lord Chancellor's Cttee on Defamation, 1971; Res. Officer, Royal Commn on Civil Liberty, 1973-75. Vice-Pres., European Broadcasting Union, 1953-54. Chm., The Latin Mass Soc., 1969. King Christian X Freedom Medal, 1946. Mem. Hon. Soc. of Cymmrodorion, 1956. Knight of Grace and Devotion, SMO Malta, 1960. *Publications:* Broadcasting and Society, 1949; The Recess, 1963 (novel); The Last Cab on the Rank, 1964 (novel); David Jones: Welsh National Lecture, 1966; One Thing at a Time (autobiography), 1968; The Painted Kipper, 1970. *Address:* c/o Coutts and Co., 10 Mount Street, W1Y 6DP.

GRIST, Ian; MP (C) Cardiff North since Feb. 1974; *b* 5 Dec. 1938; *s* of Basil William Grist, MBE and late Leila Helen Grist; *m* 1966, Wendy Anne (*née* White); two *s*. *Educ:* Repton Sch.; Jesus Coll., Oxford (Schol.). Plebiscite Officer, Southern Cameroons, 1960-61; Stores Manager, United Africa Co., Nigeria, 1961-63; Wales Information Officer, Conservative Central Office, 1963-74; Conservative Research Dept, 1970-74. Chm., Cons. W African Cttee, 1977-. Vice-Chm., Assoc. of Conservative Clubs, 1978-. PPS to Secretary of State for Wales, 1979-81. *Recreations:* reading, listening to music, politics. *Address:* House of Commons, SW1A 0AA; 126 Penlyan Road, Cardiff.

GRIST, John Frank; Managing Director, Sound and Vision Corporation, since 1982; *b* 10 May 1924; *s* of Austin Grist, OBE, MC, and Ada Mary Grist (*née* Ball); *m* Gilian, *d* of late Roger Cranage and Helen Marjorie Rollett; one *s* two *d*. *Educ:* Ryde Sch., IoW; London Sch. of Economics and Political Science (BSc Econ); Univ. of Chicago. RAF Pilot, 1942-46. BBC External Services, 1951-53; Talks Producer, Programme Organiser, Northern Region; Controller, Nat. Programmes, Nigerian Broadcasting Service, 1953-56; BBC TV Talks and Current Affairs at Lime Grove, 1957-72, producer of political programmes and Editor of Gallery and of Panorama; Hd of Current Affairs Gp, 1967-72; Controller, English Regions BBC, 1972-77; US Rep., BBC, 1978-81. *Address:* Chalfont Grove, Gerrard's Cross, Bucks. *T:* Chalfont St Giles 4461.

GRIST, Prof. Norman Roy, FRCPEd; Professor of Infectious Diseases, University of Glasgow, since 1965; *b* 9 March 1918; *s* of Walter Reginald Grist and Florence Goodwin Grist (*née* Nadin); *m* 1943, Mary Stewart McAlister. *Educ:* Shawlands Acad., Glasgow; University of Glasgow, Postgrad. studies at Dept of Bacteriology, University of Liverpool, 1948-49; Virus Reference Lab., Colindale, London, 1951-52; Dept of Epidemiology, University of Michigan, 1956-57. BSc 1939; MB, ChB (Commendation), 1942; Mem. 1950, Fellow 1968, RCP, Edinburgh. Founder Mem., 1963, FRCPath., 1967. Ho. Phys. Gartloch Hosp., 1942-43; RAMC, GDO 223 Fd Amb. and RMO 2/KSLI, 1943-46; Sen. Reg. Victoria Inf., Glasgow, 1946-47; Res. Phys, Ruchill Hosp., Glasgow, 1947-48; Research Asst, Glasgow Univ. Dept of Infectious Diseases, 1948-52; Lectr in Virus Disease, Glasgow Univ., 1952-62, and Regional Adviser in Virology to Scottish Western Reg. Hosp. Bd, 1960-74; Reader in Viral Epidemiology, Glasgow Univ., 1962-65. Consultant in Virus Diseases to WHO, 1967-. Bronze Medal, Helsinki Univ., 1973; Orden Civil de Sanidad, cat. Encomienda, Spain, 1974. *Publications:* Diagnostic Methods in Clinical Virology, 1966, 3rd edn, 1979; numerous contribs. to British and international med. jls. *Recreations:* lazing, travelling, bird-watching. *Address:* 6A Sydenham Road, Glasgow G12 9NR. *T:* 041-339 5242. *Clubs:* Royal Automobile; Royal Scottish Automobile (Glasgow).

GROBECKER, Ven. Geoffrey Frank, MBE 1959; Archdeacon of Lynn, since 1980; *b* 1922; *s* of Archibald Douglas and Ethel May Grobecker; *m* 1949, Audrey Kathleen Bessell; two *d*. *Educ:* St Paul's School; Queens' Coll., Cambridge (BA 1949, MA 1953); Ridley Hall, Cambridge. Deacon 1950, priest 1951, dio. Southwark; Curate of Morden, 1950-52; CF, 1952; Senior Chaplain, RMA, Sandhurst, 1966-69; DACG, 1969-72; ACG, 1972-77; Hon. Chaplain to the Queen, 1973-77; Vicar of Swaffham, 1977-80. *Recreations:* family, walking, gardening, bird-watching. *Address:* Lynn House, Scarning, Dereham, Norfolk NR19 2PF.

GROBLER, Richard Victor; Deputy Circuit Administrator, South Eastern Circuit, since 1979; *b* Umtali, S Rhodesia, 27 May 1936; *m* 1961, Julienne Nora de la Cour (*née* Sheath); one *s* three *d*. *Educ:* Bishop's, Capetown; Univ. of Cape Town (BA). Called to the Bar, Gray's Inn, 1961; joined staff of Clerk of the Court, Central Criminal Court, 1961; Dep. Clerk of the Court, 1970; Dep. Courts Administrator, 1972; Courts Administrator, Inner London Crown Court, 1974; Sec., Lord Chancellor's Adv. Cttee on Justices of the Peace for Inner London and Jt Hon. Sec., Inner London Br. of Magistrates' Assoc., 1974-77; Courts Administrator, Central Criminal Court, and Co-ordinator, Crown Courts Taxations, SE Circuit, 1977-79. Liveryman, Worshipful Company of Gold and Silver Wyre Drawers. *Recreations:* gardening, swimming, golf. *Address:* The Circuit Office, Thanet House, 232 Strand, WC2R 1DA. *T:* 01-353 8060.

GROCOTT, Bruce Joseph; television journalist; *b* 1 Nov. 1940; *s* of Reginald Grocott and Helen Grocott (*née* Stewart); *m* 1965, Sally Barbara Kay Ridgway; two *s*. *Educ:* Hemel Hempstead Grammar Sch.; Leicester and Manchester Univs. BA(Pol), MA(Econ). Admin. Officer, LCC, 1963-64; Tutor in Govt, Manchester Univ., 1964-65; Lectr and Sen. Lectr, Birmingham Polytechnic, 1965-72; Principal Lectr in Govt, North Staffordshire Polytechnic, 1972-74. Chm., Finance Cttee, Bromsgrove UDC, 1972-74. MP (Lab) Lichfield and Tamworth, Oct. 1974-1979; PPS to: Minister for Local

Govt and Planning, 1975-76; Minister of Agriculture, 1976-78. *Publications:* contribs to govt reports on local govt matters. *Recreations:* cricket, snooker, fiction writing. *Address:* 1 Brookside House, Birch Cross, Uttoxeter, Staffs. *Club:* Chasetown Working Men's.

GROMYKO, Andrei Andreevich, Order of Lenin (four awards); Minister of Foreign Affairs of the USSR, since 1957; Member of the Politburo, since 1973; *b* 18 July 1909; *m* Lydia D. Grinevich; one *s* one *d*. *Educ:* Agricultural Institute and Institute of Economics, Moscow. Scientific worker (senior), Acad. of Sciences USSR, 1936-39, also lecturing in Moscow Universities. Chief of American Division National Council of Foreign Affairs, 1939; Counsellor, USSR Washington Embassy, 1939-43; Ambassador to USA and Minister to Cuba, 1943-46; Soviet Representative on UN Security Council, 1946-48; Deputy Foreign Minister, 1946-49, 1953-54; 1st Deputy Minister of Foreign Affairs, 1949-52; Soviet Ambassador in London, 1952-53; First Deputy Foreign Minister in Moscow, 1954-57. Chm. of Delegates, Conference on Post-War Security, Dumbarton Oaks, USA, 1944. Holds many orders and awards of USSR and other countries. *Publication:* Only for Peace, 1979. *Address:* Ministry of Foreign Affairs, 32-34 Smolenskaya-Sennaya Ploshchad, Moscow, USSR.

GRONHAUG, Arnold Conrad; *b* 26 March 1921; *s* of late James Gronhaug, MBE, and Beatrice May Gronhaug; *m* 1945, Patricia Grace Smith; two *d*. *Educ:* Barry Grammar Sch.; Cardiff Technical Coll. CEng, FIEE. Electrical Officer, RNVR, 1941-46. Air Ministry Works Directorate, 1946-63: Area Mech. and Elec. Engr, AMWD Malaya, 1951-52; Air Min. Headquarters, 1952-60; Dep. Chief Engr, AMWD, RAF Germany, 1960-63; Sen. Mech. and Elec. Engr, Portsmouth Area MPBW, 1963-67; Jt Services Staff Coll., 1964-65; Suptg Engr, MPBW, 1967-71; Dir Defence Works (Overseas), MPBW, 1971-73; Dir of Social and Research Services, DoE, 1973-75; Dir of Engrng Services Develt, 1975-76; Dir of Mechanical and Electrical Engineering Services, 1976-81. Hon. FCIBS. *Recreations:* music, photography, do-it-yourself. *Address:* 6 Pine Hill, Epsom, Surrey KT18 7BG. *T:* Epsom 21888.

GROOM, Maj.-Gen. John Patrick, CBE 1975 (MBE 1963); Head of Army Training Review Team, Ministry of Defence (Army), since 1982; *b* Hagley, Worcs, 9 March 1929; *s* of Samuel Douglas Groom and Gertrude Groom (*née* Clinton); *m* 1951, Jane Mary Miskelly; three *d*. *Educ:* King Charles I Sch., Kidderminster; Royal Military Academy, Sandhurst. Enlisted as Sapper, Dec. 1946; commnd into RE, 1949; regimental service, N Africa, Egypt, Singapore, Malaya, UK, 1949-59; sc Camberley, 1960; War Office, 1961-63; regimental service, UK, Aden, 1963-65 (despatches); Directing Staff, Staff Coll., 1965-68; Regimental Comdr, BAOR, 1968-70; MoD, Military Operations, 1970-71; Dep. Sec., Chiefs of Staff Cttee, 1971-73; HQ Near East Land Forces, Cyprus, 1973-75; RCDS 1976; Comdr, Corps of Royal Engineers, BAOR (Brig.), 1976-79; Chief Engineer, HQ BAOR, 1979-82. FBIM 1979; FIPlantE 1976. Liveryman, Worshipful Co. of Plumbers, 1978. *Recreations:* ocean racing, riding, painting, antiques, ornithology, the environment. *Address:* Horsell Grange, Kettlewell Hill, Woking, Surrey. *T:* Woking 73938. *Clubs:* Army and Navy, Royal Ocean Racing; Royal Engineer Yacht (Commodore); British Kiel Yacht (W Germany) (Life Mem.).

GROOM, Sir (Thomas) Reginald, Kt 1961; Chartered Accountant; Partner, Peat, Marwick, Mitchell & Co, Brisbane, Qld, 1932-77; Commissioner, Australian National Airlines Commission, 1961-75; Director: Woodland Ltd (Chairman), 1969-80; Consolidated Rutile Ltd, 1964-78; Mount Isa Mines Holdings Ltd, 1962-77; P & O Australia Ltd, 1958-78; Elder Smith Goldsbrough Mort Ltd, 1966-78; Member of Commonwealth Banking Corporation Board, 1964-74, and of several private companies; *b* 30 Dec. 1906; *s* of Roy Graeme Groom and May Augusta Groom; *m* 1932, Jessie Mary Grace Butcher; two *s* one *d*. *Educ:* Brisbane Grammar Sch.; University of Qld (BA, BCom). Admitted to Institute of Chartered Accountants in Australia, 1932; in public practice, 1932-77. Alderman, Brisbane City Council, 1943-; Lord Mayor of Brisbane, 1955-61. Commissioner, Qld Local Govt Grants Commn, 1977-79. Dir, Australian Elizabethan Theatre Trust. *Recreations:* farming, fishing, golf. *Address:* 31 Jerdanefield Tower, Jerdanefield Road, St Lucia, Brisbane, Qld 4067, Australia. *T:* (home) 3711-983, (office) 221-9411. *Clubs:* Queensland, Johnsonian (Brisbane).

GROOM, Air Marshal Sir Victor E., KCVO 1953; KBE 1952 (CBE 1945; OBE 1940); CB 1944; DFC 1918, and Bar, 1921; RAF retired; *b* 4 Aug. 1898; *e s* of late William E. Groom; *m* 1st, 1924, Maisie Monica Maule (*d* 1961); one *s* (and one *s* decd); 2nd, 1969, Mrs Muriel Constance Brown. *Educ:* Alleyns, Dulwich. Served European War, 1916-18 (DFC); Egypt, Iraq, 1919-22 (bar to DFC); RAF Staff Coll. (psc 1928); India, 1929-34; Bomber Command, 1936-41 (OBE); Directorate of Plans, Air Min., 1941-42; Head of RAF Staff planning the invasion under Chief of Staff to the Supreme Allied Commander, 1942-43; SASO 2nd Tactical Air Force, 1943-45; AOA Flying Trg Command, 1945-46; Dir-Gen. of Manning, Air Ministry, 1947-49; AOC 205 Group RAF, MEAF, 1949-51; C-in-C, MEAF, 1952; AOC-in-C, Technical Training Command, 1952-55, retired 1955. Officer Legion of Honour (France). *Address:* 8 Somerville House, Manor Fields, SW15 3LX. *T:* 01-788 1290. *Club:* Royal Air Force.

GROSBERG, Prof. Percy, PhD; CEng, MIMechE, FTI; Research Professor of Textile Engineering, since 1961, and Head of Department of Textile Industries, since 1975, University of Leeds; *b* 5 April 1925; *s* of late Rev. G.

Grosberg and of Mrs P. Grosberg, Tel-Aviv; *m* 1951, Queenie Fisch; one *s* one *d* (and one *s* decd). *Educ:* Parktown Boys' High Sch., Johannesburg; Univ. of the Witwatersrand; Univ. of Leeds. BScEng, MScEng, PhD Witwatersrand; CEng, MIMechE 1965; FTI 1966. Sen. Res. Officer S African Wool Textile Res. Assoc., 1949-55; ICI Res. Fellow, 1955, Lectr in Textile Engrg, 1955-61, Univ. of Leeds. Warner Memorial Medal, 1968; Textile Inst. Medal, 1972. *Publications:* An Introduction to Textile Mechanisms, 1968; Structural Mechanics of Fibres, Yarns and Fabrics, 1969; papers on rheology of fibrous assemblies, mechan. processing of fibres, and other res. topics in Jl of Textile Inst., Textile Res. Jl, and other sci. jls. *Recreations:* music, gardening, travel. *Address:* 101 King Lane, Leeds LS17 5AX. *T:* Leeds 687478.

GROSS, Anthony, CBE 1982; RA; Hon. RE; painter, etcher; *b* 19 March 1905; *s* of Alexander Gross and Isabelle Crowley; *m* 1930, Marcelle Florenty; one *s* one *d*. *Educ:* Repton; Slade; Paris; Madrid. Exhibits London, Paris, New York, etc. Has also made films and illustrated books. Lives several months each year in France. *Publication:* The Very Rich Hours of Le Boulvé (limited edn), 1980. *Recreation:* restoring an ancient house. *Address:* 115 King George Street, Greenwich, SE10 8PX.

GROSS, John Jacob; Deputy Chairman, Weidenfeld (Publishers) Ltd, since 1982; *b* 12 March 1935; *s* of late Abraham Gross and Muriel Gross; *m* 1965, Miriam May; one *s* one *d*. *Educ:* City of London Sch.; Wadham Coll., Oxford. Editor, Victor Gollancz Ltd, 1956-58; Asst Lectr, Queen Mary Coll., Univ. of London, 1959-62; Fellow, King's Coll., Cambridge, 1962-65; Literary Editor, New Statesman, 1973; Editor, TLS, 1974-81. A Trustee, National Portrait Gall., 1977-. *Publications:* The Rise and Fall of the Man of Letters (1969 Duff Cooper Memorial Prize), 1969; Joyce, 1971. *Address:* 24A St Petersburgh Place, W2.

GROSS, Solomon Joseph, CMG 1966; industrial consultant; Board Member, British Steel Corporation, since 1978; *b* 3 Sept. 1920; *s* of late Abraham Gross; *m* 1948, Doris Evelyn (*née* Barker); two *d*. *Educ:* Hackney Downs Sch.; University Coll., London. RAF, Burma, India. Ministry of Supply, 1947; OEEC, Paris, 1948-51; British Embassy, Washington, 1951-53; Board of Trade, 1954-57; British Trade Commr, Pretoria, SA, 1958-62; Principal British Trade Commr, Ghana, 1963-66; British Deputy High Commr, Ghana, 1966-67; Board of Trade, 1967-69; Minister, British Embassy, Pretoria, 1969-73; Chargé d'Affaires at various times in Ghana and S Africa; Under-Sec., Dept of Industry, 1974-80, retired. *Recreations:* squash, history, do-it-yourself, gardening. *Address:* 7 Northiam, N12. *T:* 01-445 3539. *Club:* Royal Automobile.

GROSSART, Angus McFarlane McLeod; Managing Director, Noble Grossart Ltd, Merchant Bankers, Edinburgh, since 1969; Director, Royal Bank of Scotland, since 1982; *b* 6 April 1937; 3rd *s* of William John White Grossart and Mary Hay Gardiner; *m* 1978, Mrs Gay Thomson. *Educ:* Glasgow Acad.; Glasgow Univ. (MA 1958, LLB 1960). CA 1962; Mem., Faculty of Advocates, 1963. Practised at Scottish Bar, 1963-69. Chairman: Scottish Investment Trust; Wright Dental Gp; Director: American Trust; Canadian Natural Resources; Heron Motor Group; Reed Stenhouse; North Sea Assets; Pict Petroleum. Mem., Scottish Devlet Agency, 1974-78. Formerly, Scottish Editor, British Tax Encyc., and British Tax Rev. *Recreations:* golfing (runner-up, British Youths' Golf Championship, 1957), the decorative arts, Scottish castle restoration. *Address:* 48 Queen Street, Edinburgh EH2 3NR. *T:* 031-226 7011. *Clubs:* New, Honourable Company of Edinburgh Golfers (Edinburgh); Royal and Ancient (St Andrews).

GROSSCHMID-ZSOGÓD, Prof. Géza (Benjamin), LLD; Professor, since 1955, and Chairman, 1978-81, Division of Economic Sciences, Duquesne University, Pittsburgh, USA; *b* Budapest, Hungary, 29 Oct. 1918; *o s* of late Prof. Lajos de Grosschmid and Jolán, *o d* of Géza de Szitányi; *m* 1946, Leonora Martha Nissler, 2nd *d* of Otto Nissler and Annemarie Dudt; one *d*. *Educ:* Piarist Fathers, Budapest; Royal Hungarian Pázmány Péter Univ., Budapest (LLD 1943). With private industry in Hungary, 1943-44; Royal Hungarian Army, 1944-45; UNRRA, 1946-47; Duquesne University: Asst Prof. of Econs, 1948-52; Associate Prof., 1952-55; Dir, Inst. of African Affairs, 1958-70; Dir, African Language and Area Center, 1960-74; Academic Vice Pres., 1970-75. Ford Foundn Fellow, 1958; Fulbright-Hays Fellow, S Africa, 1965; attended Cambridge Colonial Conf., King's Coll., 1961. Director: World Affairs Council of Pittsburgh, 1974-80; Afuture Fund of Philadelphia, 1976-. Mem., Bd of Visitors, Coll. of Arts and Sciences, Univ. of Pittsburgh; Governor, Battle of Britain Museum Foundn, 1977-. Consultore pro lingua hungarica, Collegio Araldico, Rome. Kt of Malta, 1955 (Kt of Obedience, 1974, Comdr of Merit, 1956); Kt, Sacred Mil. Constantinian Order of St George (Naples), 1959 (Kt of Justice, 1961; Pres., Amer. Assoc., 1978); Kt Comdr of St Gregory, 1968. Order of: Valour, Cameroon, 1967; Zaire, 1970; Equatorial Star, Gabon, 1973; Lion, Senegal, 1977. *Publications:* (jtly) Principles of Economics, 1959; (trans. with P. Colombo) The Spiritual Heritage of the Sovereign Military Order of Malta, 1958; contrib. Encyc. Britannica; articles in learned jls. *Recreations:* walking, golf, heraldry, polo. *Address:* 3115 Ashlyn Street, Pittsburgh, Pa 15204, USA. *T:* (412) 331-7744. *Clubs:* Athenæum; Royal Forth Yacht (Edinburgh); Duquesne (Pittsburgh); Metropolitan, Army & Navy (Washington).

GROSVENOR, family name of **Baron Ebury,** and of **Duke of Westminster.**

GROSVENOR, Mrs Beatrice Elizabeth Katherine, CBE 1952; United Kingdom Representative on the Executive Committee of the Programme of the United Nations High Commissioner for Refugees, 1959-60; *b* 6 Nov. 1915; *d* of late Lord Edward Grosvenor and late Lady Dorothy Charteris; *m* 1944 (marr. annulled, 1945), Major Richard Girouard. *Educ:* Holy Child Convent, Cavendish Square, W1. Served War of 1939-45 (despatches), with St John Ambulance Brigade; Asst Superintendent-in-Chief SJAB, 1946-52; Deputy Superintendent-in-Chief, 1952-59; County Pres. for Co. Cork, Eire, SJAB, 1960. DStJ 1958. *Address:* Kenmare House, Killarney, Co. Kerry. *T:* Killarney 41.

GROTRIAN, Sir John (Appelbe Brent), 2nd Bt, *cr* 1934; *b* 16 Feb. 1904; 2nd and *o* surv. *s* of Sir Herbert Brent Grotrian, 1st Bt, KC, JP, and Mary Lilian (*d* 1971), *d* of late Robert Adams, Barrister-at-law of Hamilton, Ont., Canada; *S* father 1951. *Educ:* Eton Coll.; Trinity Coll., Oxford. Served in War of 1939-45 (despatches). *Heir: nephew* Philip Christian Brent Grotrian [*b* 26 March 1935; *s* of Robert Philip Brent Grotrian (*d* on active service, 1945; *y s* of 1st Bt) and Elizabeth Mary Hardy-Wrigley; *m* 1960, Anne Isabel, *d* of Robert Sieger Whyte, Toronto, Canada; one *s*]. *Address:* Raughmere House, Lavant, Chichester, West Sussex. *T:* Chichester 527120.

GROUES, Henri Antoine; see Pierre, Abbé.

GROUND, (Reginald) Patrick, QC 1981; *b* 9 Aug. 1932; *s* of late Reginald Ground and Ivy Elizabeth Grace Irving; *m* 1964, Caroline Dugdale; three *s* one *d*. *Educ:* Beckenham and Penge County Grammar Sch.; Lycée Gay Lussac, Limoges, France; Selwyn Coll., Cambridge (Open Exhibnr; MA Mod. Langs, French and Spanish); Magdalen Coll., Oxford (MLitt, Mod. History). Inner Temple Studentship and Foster Boulton Prize, 1958; called to the Bar, Inner Temple, 1960. National Service, RN, 1954-56: Sub-Lt RNVR; served in Mediterranean Fleet and on staff of C-in-C Mediterranean; rep. RN at hockey and lawn tennis; Lt-Comdr RNR. Worked for FO on staff of Wilton Park European Conf. Centre, 1958-60. Councillor, London Bor. of Hammersmith, 1968-71 (Chm., Cttees responsible for health and social services, 1969-71); contested (C), Hounslow, Feltham and Heston, Feb. and Oct. 1974, and 1979. Treasurer and Pres., Oxford Univ. Cons. Assoc., 1958; Chm., Fulham Soc., 1975-. *Publications:* articles on housing, security of tenure and the Rent Acts in jls and periodicals. *Recreations:* lawn tennis, sailing, travel. *Address:* 13 Ranelagh Avenue, SW6 3PJ. *T:* 01-736 0131. *Clubs:* Brooks's, Carlton.

GROUNDS, George Ambrose, CBE 1958; DSO 1917 (Bar 1918); TD 1933; DL; retired; *b* 19 Nov. 1886; *s* of Frederick and Elizabeth Grounds; *m* 1950, Kathleen Burton Sale (*d* 1968). *Educ:* St Ives (Hunts) Gram. Sch.; Lowestoft Coll. Banking, 1903-45. Served European War, 1914-18, Royal Tank Corps, France (wounded); served War of 1939-45, RA; Lt-Col 1936. DL Lincs, 1951; Chm. Holland (Lincs) CC, 1963-67; Alderman HCC, 1961-74. *Address:* The Elms, 53 Sleaford Road, Boston, Lincs. *T:* Boston 62772.

GROUNDS, Stanley Paterson, CBE 1968; Charity Commissioner, 1960-69; *b* 25 Oct. 1904; 2nd *s* of late Thomas Grounds and Olivia Henrietta (*née* Anear), Melbourne, Australia; *m* 1932, Freda Mary Gale Ransford; twin *s* and *d*. *Educ:* Melbourne High Sch.; Queen's Coll., Melbourne Univ. (1st Cl. hons, MA). With Melbourne Herald, 1926-28; British Empire Producers' Organisation, London, 1928-33. Called to Bar, Middle Temple, 1933; at Chancery Bar, 1934-40. Served Royal Air Force, 1940-45 (Squadron Leader). Asst Charity Commissioner, 1946-58; Sec., Charity Commission, 1958-60. *Publications:* contrib. Encyclopædia of Forms and Precedents, Encyclopædia of Court Forms (on Charities), Halsbury's Laws of England, 3rd edn (on Charities). Articles in law jls. *Recreation:* other men's flowers. *Address:* St Helena, 19 Bell Road, Haslemere, Surrey GU27 3DQ. *T:* Haslemere 51230. *Club:* Army and Navy.

GROVE, Sir Charles Gerald, 5th Bt *cr* 1874; *b* 10 Dec. 1929; *s* of Walter Peel Grove (*d* 1944) (3rd *s* of 2nd Bt) and Elena Rebecca, *d* of late Felipe Crosthwaite; *S* brother, 1974. *Heir: b* Harold Thomas Grove, *b* 6 Dec. 1930.

GROVE, Rear-Adm. John Scott, OBE 1964; Chief Strategic Systems Executive (formerly Chief Polaris Executive), since 1980; *b* 7 July 1927; *s* of late William George Grove and Frances Margaret Scott Grove; *m* 1950, Betty Anne (*née* Robinson); one *s* (one *d* decd). *Educ:* Dundee High Sch.; St Andrews Univ. University Coll., 1944-47 (BScEng 1st Cl. Hons). National Service, Royal Engineers, 1947-48; Instructor Br., Royal Navy, 1948-50; Electrical Engrg Br., RN, 1950, qualified in Submarines, 1953; post graduate trng in Nuclear Engrg, Imperial Coll., London, 1958-59; sea service in HMS Forth and HM Submarines Tally-Ho, Turpin, Porpoise, Dreadnought; commanded HMS Fisgard, 1977-79. Comdr 1963; Captain 1970; Rear-Adm. 1980. *Recreations:* squash, tennis. *Address:* Maryfield, South Close, Wade Court, Havant, Hants PO9 2TD. *T:* Havant 475116. *Club:* Royal Commonwealth Society.

GROVE-WHITE, Robin Bernard; Director, Council for the Protection of Rural England, since 1981; *b* 17 Feb. 1941; *s* of Charles William Grove-White and Cecile Mary Rabbidge; *m* 1st, 1970, Virginia Harriet Ironside (marr. diss.); one *s*; 2nd, 1979, Helen Elizabeth Smith; one *s* one *d*. *Educ:* Uppingham Sch.; Worcester Coll., Oxford (BA). Freelance writer for TV, radio, press and advertising in UK, Canada and US, 1963-70; McCann-Erickson Ltd, London, 1970; Asst Secretary, CPRE, 1972-80. *Publications:* (contrib.) Politics of

Physical Resources, 1975; (contrib.) Future Landscapes, 1976; (with Michael Flood) Nuclear Prospects, 1976; contribs to New Scientist, Nature, Times, Vole, etc. *Recreations:* walking, cricket. *Address:* 102 Tennyson Road, NW6 7SB. *T:* 01-624 0834.

GROVES, Sir Charles (Barnard), Kt 1973; CBE 1968 (OBE 1958); FRCM, Hon. RAM; conductor; Associate Conductor, Royal Philharmonic Orchestra, since 1967; *b* 10 March 1915; *s* of Frederick Groves and Annie (*née* Whitehead); *m* 1948, Hilary Hermione Barchard; one *s* two *d*. *Educ:* St Paul's Cathedral Choir Sch.; Sutton Valence Sch.; Royal College of Music. Free lance accompanist and organist. Joined BBC, Chorus-Master Music Productions Unit, 1938; Asst Conductor BBC Theatre Orchestra, 1942; Conductor BBC Revue Orchestra, 1943; Conductor BBC Northern Orchestra, 1944-51; Dir of Music, Bournemouth Corporation, and Conductor, Bournemouth Municipal Orchestra, 1951-54; Conductor of Bournemouth Symphony Orchestra, 1954-61; Resident Musical Dir, Welsh National Opera Company, 1961-63; Musical Dir and Resident Conductor, Royal Liverpool Philharmonic Orchestra, 1963-77; Music Dir, ENO, 1978-79. President: Nat. Youth Orchestra of GB, 1977-; Incorporated Soc. of Musicians, 1982-; Life Mem., RPO, 1976. FRCM 1961; Hon. RAM 1967; Hon. FTCL 1974; Hon. GSM 1974; Hon. FRNCM 1974. Conductor of the Year Award, 1968, 1978. Has toured Australia, New Zealand, South Africa, N and S America, Japan and Europe. Hon. DMus Liverpool, 1970; DUniv. Open, 1978. *Recreation:* English literature. *Address:* 12 Camden Square, NW1 9UY. *Club:* Athenæum.

GROVES, John Dudley, CB 1981; OBE 1964; Director-General, Central Office of Information, 1979-82; Head of Profession for Government Information Officer Group, 1981-82; *b* 12 Aug. 1922; *y s* of late Walter Groves; *m* 1943, Pamela Joy Holliday; one *s* two *d*. *Educ:* St Paul's Sch. Reporter, Richmond Herald, 1940-41; Queen's Royal Regt, 1941-42; commnd in 43rd Reconnaissance Regt, 1942; served in NW Europe, 1944-45 (despatches); Observer Officer, Berlin, 1945; Press Association (Press Gallery), 1947-51; Times (Press Gallery and Lobby), 1951-58; Head of Press Sect., Treasury, 1958-62; Dep. Public Relations Adviser to Prime Minister, 1962-64 (Actg Adviser, 1964); Chief Information Officer, DEA, 1964-68; Chief of Public Relations, MoD, 1968-77; Dir of Information, DHSS, 1977-78. *Publication:* (with R. Gill) Club Route, 1945. *Recreations:* walking, painting. *Address:* Mortimers, Manningford Bohune, Pewsey, Wilts.

GROVES, Richard Bebb, TD 1966; RD 1979; Partner in H. J. Smith & Co. and Richard Groves & Co., since 1962; a Recorder of the Crown Court, since 1980; *b* 4 Oct. 1933; *s* of George Thomas Groves and Margaret Anne (*née* Bebb); *m* 1958, Eileen Patricia (*née* Farley); one *s* one *d*. *Educ:* Bancroft's Sch., Woodford Green, Essex. Admitted Solicitor of the Supreme Court, 1960. Dep. Circuit Judge, 1978. Nijmegen Medal, Royal Netherlands League for Physical Culture, 1965 and 1966. *Recreations:* Royal Naval Reserve, tennis, philately, walking, reading. *Address:* Pinemead, Wakes Colne, Colchester, Essex CO6 2BX. *T:* Earls Colne 2644. *Club:* Colchester Garrison Officers (Colchester).

GROVES, Ronald, MA, BSc Oxon; FRSC; Secretary, Sir Richard Stapley Educational Trust, since 1969; Trustee, King's College Hospital; Vice-Chairman Council and Fellow, King's College Hospital Medical School; *b* 19 Aug. 1908; *s* of late John Ackroyd Groves and Annie Groves, Bradford, *m* 1939, Hilary Annot, *yr d* of late George Smith; two *s*. *Educ:* Bradford Grammar Sch.; Christ Church, Oxford. 1st Class Hons Nat. Sci. (Chemistry), 1931. Asst Master, Bradfield Coll., 1931-32; Worksop Coll., 1932-35; Senior Science Master and Housemaster, King's Sch., Canterbury, 1935-43; Bursar, 1937-43; Headmaster, Campbell Coll., Belfast, 1943-54; Master, Dulwich Coll., 1954-66. Adviser, Jt Working Party of Governing Bodies' Assoc. and Headmasters' Conf., 1966-73. Chm., Food Standards Cttee, 1959-62. *Address:* 83 Cumnor Hill, Oxford. *Clubs:* Athenæum, MCC.

GROVES, Ronald Edward, CBE 1972; Chairman, since 1976 and Chief Executive, since 1973, International Timber PLC; *b* 2 March 1920; *s* of Joseph Rupert and Eva Lilian Groves; *m* 1940, Beryl Doris Lydia Collins; two *s* one *d*. *Educ:* Watford Grammar School. Joined J. Gliksten & Son Ltd; served War of 1939-45, Flt-Lt RAF, subseq. Captain with BOAC; re-joined J. Gliksten & Son Ltd, 1946: Gen. Works Man. 1947; Dir 1954; Jt Man. Dir 1964; Vice-Chm. 1967; Dir, Gliksten (West Africa) Ltd, 1949; Vice-Chm., International Timber Corp. Ltd, 1970 (name of J. Gliksten & Son Ltd changed to International Timber Corp. Ltd, 1970 following merger with Horsley Smith & Jewson Ltd). Dir, Nat. Building Agency, 1978-82. President: Timber Trade Fedn of UK, 1969-71; London and District Sawmill Owners Assoc., 1954-56; Chm., Nat. Sawmilling Assoc., 1966-67. Chairman: Rickmansworth UDC, 1957-58, 1964-65 and 1971-72; W Herts Main Drainage Authority, 1970-74; Three Rivers District Council, 1977-78. Chairman of Governors: Watford Grammar Sch. for Girls, 1980-; Watford Grammar Sch. for Boys, 1980-. *Recreations:* visiting theatre and opera; local community work. *Address:* 8 Pembroke Road, Moor Park, Northwood, Mddx. *T:* Northwood 23187.

GRUBB, Violet Margaret, DSc London; retired; *b* Oxton, Notts, 1898; *o d* of Rev. H. Percy Grubb and M. A. Crichton-Stuart. *Educ:* Bournemouth High Sch.; Westfield Coll., University of London. BSc Hons London, 1920; DSc London, 1925; Asst Lecturer in Botany, Westfield Coll., 1923-25; Science teacher in I Fang Sch., Changsha, Central China and Lecturer in Hunan

Provincial Univ., 1925–30; Lecturer in Dept of Botany, Westfield Coll., University of London, 1931–37; Headmistress, Westonbirt Sch., Tetbury, Glos, 1937–55; Principal, The Training Coll., Salisbury, 1955–62. Pres., Assoc. Head Mistresses of Boarding Schs, 1943–45. Chm., Assoc. of Independent and Direct Grant Schs, 1950–53; Member: Central Advisory Council for Education (England), 1956–59; Science Museum Advisory Council, 1957–64. *Publications:* Articles on Ecology and Reproduction of Marine Algæ and on distribution of Far Eastern Algæ, in scientific journals in England and abroad. *Address:* 28 Shady Bower Close, Salisbury, Wilts. *T:* Salisbury 28814. *Club:* Royal Over-Seas League.

GRUENBERG, Prof. Karl Walter; Professor of Pure Mathematics in the University of London, at Queen Mary College, since 1967; *b* 3 June 1928; *s* of late Paul Gruenberg and of Anna Gruenberg; *m* 1973, Margaret Semple; one *s* one *d. Educ:* Shaftesbury Grammar Sch.; Kilburn Grammar Sch.; Cambridge Univ. BA 1950, PhD 1954. Asst Lectr, Queen Mary Coll., 1953–55; Commonwealth Fund Fellowship, 1955–57 (at Harvard Univ., 1955–56; at Inst. for Advanced Studies, Princeton, 1956–57). Queen Mary College: Lectr, 1957–61; Reader, 1961–67; Prof., 1967–. Visiting Professor: Univ. of Michigan, 1961–62, 1978; Cornell Univ., 1966–67; Univ. of Illinois, 1972; Australian Nat. Univ., 1979. *Publications:* Cohomological Topics in Group Theory, 1970; Relation Modules of Finite Groups, 1976; Linear Geometry (jtly with A. J. Weir), 2nd edn 1977; articles on algebra in various learned jls. *Address:* Department of Pure Mathematics, Queen Mary College (University of London), Mile End Road, E1 4NS. *T:* 01-980 4811.

GRUENTHER, Gen. Alfred M(aximilian); (Hon.) CB (UK) 1943; DSM (US) (with 2 Oak Leaf Clusters) 1943, 1945, 1956; US Army, retired; Member: The Business Council; President's Commission on an All-Volunteer Armed Force, since 1969; Editorial Board, Foreign Affairs Magazine, since 1959; *b* Nebraska, 3 March 1899; *s* of Christian M. Gruenther and Mary Shea; *m* 1922, Grace Elizabeth Crum (*d* 1979); two *s. Educ:* Military Academy, West Point (BS). Commissioned, Field Artillery, 1918; routine peacetime assignments, including 8 years as instructor and asst professor chemistry and electricity at West Point; Deputy Chief of Staff, Allied Force Headquarters (London, North African Campaign, Algiers), 1942–43; Chief of Staff, Fifth Army (Italy), 1943–44; Chief of Staff, 15th Army Group (Italian Campaign), 1944–45; Dep. Comdr, US Forces in Austria, 1945; Dep. Comdt, Nat. War Coll. Washington, 1945–47; Dir Jt Staff, Jt Chiefs of Staff, 1947–49; Dep. Chief of Staff for Plans and Operations, Army Gen. Staff, 1949–51; Gen., US Army, 1951; Chief of Staff, SHAPE, 1951–53; Supreme Allied Commander, Europe, 1953–56; retd 1956. Director: Pan American World Airways, 1960–72; New York Life Insurance Co., 1960–73; Dart Industries, 1964–80; Federated Department Stores, 1964–76; Mem., Bd of Trustees, Inst. for Defence Analyses, 1964–78. Member: Presidential Arms Control Gen. Adv. Cttee, 1966–69; Presidential Adv. Cttee on Foreign Assistance, 1965–69. Pres., American Red Cross, 1957–64. Chm., English-Speaking Union of US, 1966–68. Hon. Pres., World Bridge Federation. Several decorations, including Grand Cross of Légion d'Honneur, 1954, and Médaille Militaire, 1956. Hon. degrees from 38 universities including Harvard, Yale, Columbia, Dartmouth and Holy Cross. *Publications:* Famous Hands of the Culbertson-Lenz Match, 1932; Duplicate Contract Complete, 1933. *Address:* Cathedral Apartments, 4101 Cathedral Avenue, NW, Washington, DC 20016, USA.

GRUFFYDD, (Robert) Geraint; Librarian, National Library of Wales, since 1980; *b* 9 June 1928; *s* of Moses and Ceridwen Griffith; *m* 1953, Elizabeth Eluned Roberts; two *s* one *d. Educ:* University Coll. of N Wales, Bangor (BA); Jesus Coll., Oxford (DPhil). Asst Editor, Geiriadur Prifysgol Cymru, 1953–55; Lectr, Dept of Welsh, UCNW, 1955–70; Prof. of Welsh Language and Literature, UCW, Aberystwyth, 1970–79. *Publications:* (ed) Meistri'r Canrifoedd, 1973; (ed) Cerddi '73, 1973; (ed) Bardos, 1982; articles, etc, on Welsh literary and religious history in various collaborative vols and learned jls. *Recreations:* reading (preferably theology), walking (preferably in Wales), learning to fly (in contemplation). *Address:* Hengwrt, Llanbadarn Road, Aberystwyth, Dyfed. *T:* Aberystwyth 3577.

GRUFFYDD JONES, Daniel; *see* Jones, D. G.

GRUGEON, Sir John (Drury), Kt 1980; Director, International Garden Festival '84, Liverpool, since 1982; *b* 20 Sept. 1928; *s* of Drury Grugeon and Sophie (*née* Pratt); *m* 1955, Mary Patricia (*née* Rickards); one *s* one *d. Educ:* Epsom Grammar Sch.; RMA, Sandhurst. Commissioned, The Buffs, Dec. 1948; served 1st Bn in Middle and Far East and Germany; Regimental Adjt, 1953–55; Adjt 5th Bn, 1956–58; left Army, 1960. Joined Save and Prosper Group, 1960. Mem., Kent CC, 1967– (Leader, 1973–82). Chm., Policy Cttee, Assoc. of County Councils, 1978– (Chm., Finance Cttee, 1976–79); Member: SE Economic Planning Council, 1971–74; Cons. Council on Local Govt Finance, 1975–; Medway Ports Authority, 1977–. *Recreations:* cricket, shooting, local govt. *Address:* Sand Pett, Charing, Ashford, Kent TN27 0AT. *T:* Charing 2322. *Clubs:* MCC; Kent County CC.

GRUNDY, Air Marshal Sir Edouard (Michael FitzFrederick), KBE 1963 (OBE 1942); CB 1960; Chairman, Short Brothers and Harland, 1968–76; *b* 29 Sept. 1908; *s* of late Frederick Grundy and Osca Marah Ewart; *m* 1st, 1945, Lucia le Sueur (*née* Corder) (*d* 1973); three *s* (and one *d* decd); 2nd, 1975, Mrs Marie Louise Holder. *Educ:* St Paul's Sch.; RAF Coll., Cranwell. 56 (F) Sqdn 1928; 403 Flight FAA, 1929–31; Signals Specialist Course, 1932; RAF North Weald, 1933–36; RNZAF HQ, 1937–40; OC No 80 (S) Wing,

1941–42; CSO, NW African AF, 1942–43; CSO Mediterranean Allied Tactical Air Forces, 1943–44; CSO, RAF, Middle East, 1944–45; Commandant, Empire Radio Sch., 1945–46; Dep. Dir Air Staff Policy, Air Ministry, 1947–49; Air Adviser, Royal Norwegian AF, 1949–51; Dep. CSO, Supreme HQ Allied Powers Europe, 1951–52; idc 1953; Senior Air Staff Officer, Brit. Jt Services Mission in USA, 1954–55; Chm. NATO Military Agency for Standardisation, 1955–58: Air Officer i/c Administration, FEAF, 1958–61; Commandant-Gen. RAF Regt, 1961–62; Controller, Guided Weapons and Electronics, Ministry of Aviation, 1962–66; retired, 1966. Mem., Engineering Industries Council, 1975–. Pres., SBAC, 1975–76. FRAeS. Chevalier, Royal Norwegian Order of St Olaf, 1953. *Recreations:* usual. *Address:* c/o Lloyds Bank Ltd, 6 Pall Mall, SW1. *Club:* Royal Air Force.

GRUNDY, Fred, MD; MRCP; DPH; Barrister-at-law; Assistant Director-General, World Health Organization, Geneva, 1961–66; retired; *b* 15 May 1905; *s* of Thomas Grundy, Manchester; *m* 1932, Ada Furnell Leppington, Hessle, Yorks; one *s* one *d. Educ:* Leeds and London Univs. MB, ChB (Hons), Leeds; MRCS, LRCP, 1927; DPH, RCPS, 1931; MD Leeds, 1933; MRCP, 1951. Called to the Bar, Inner Temple, 1934. Resident hospital appts and gen. practice, 1927–31; Asst County Medical Officer, E Suffolk, 1931–34; Asst MOH to Borough of Willesden, 1934–35; Deputy MOH to Borough of Luton, 1935–37; MOH to Borough of Luton, 1937–49; Mansel Talbot Prof. of Preventive Medicine, Welsh Nat. Sch. of Medicine, 1949–61. *Publications:* A Note on the Vital Statistics of Luton, 1944; (with R. M. Titmuss) Report on Luton, 1945; Handbook of Social Medicine, 1945; The New Public Health, 1949; Preventive Medicine and Public Health: An Introduction for Students and Practitioners, 1951; papers on public health and scientific subjects. *Recreations:* mountaineering, yachting, golf, etc. *Address:* Galmington, Radyr, near Cardiff. *Club:* Yacht (Penarth).

GRUNDY, (James) Milton; Founder and Chairman of the Warwick Arts Trust, since 1978; *b* 13 June 1926. *Educ:* Sedbergh Sch.; Gonville and Caius Coll., Cambridge (MA). Called to the Bar, Inner Temple, 1954. Founder Mem. and Pres., Internat. Tax Planning Assoc., 1975–; Mem. Cttee, Revenue Bar Assoc., 1978–. Founder and Chm., Gemini Trust for the Arts, 1959–66; Charter Mem., Peggy Guggenheim Collection, 1980–. *Publications:* Tax and the Family Company, 1956, 3rd edn 1966; Tax Havens, 1968, 3rd edn 1974; Venice, 1971, 3rd edn 1980; contrib. British Tax Rev. and Jl of Business Law. *Recreation:* conversation. *Address:* New House, Shipton-under-Wychwood, Oxon OX7 6DD. *T:* Shipton-under-Wychwood 830495. *Club:* Reform.

GRUNDY, John Brownsdon Clowes, TD 1951; Officier d'Académie, 1937; MA, PhD, DLit; *b* 21 April 1902; *m* 1939, Dorothea, *d* of Enid Pennington; two *s* three *d. Educ:* Emanuel Sch.; Fitzwilliam Hall, Cambridge (Exhibitioner); University Coll., London (research). Asst Master, St Paul's Sch., 1923–27; English Lektor, University of Göttingen, 1928; "The Connoisseur", 1928–29; Sen. Mod. Langs Master, Shrewsbury Sch., 1929–39. Served War of 1939–45, The Rangers (KRRC); principally in Gen. Staff (Intell.); Normandy-Germany, 1944; rank at release, temp. Col. First Rep. of Brit. Council in Finland, 1945–49; Dir, Brit. Institute, Cairo, 1949–50; head of mod. langs, Harrow Sch., 1950–53; Headmaster of Emanuel Sch., 1953–63; Head of Dept of Modern Languages, University Coll. of Sierra Leone, 1964–66. *Publications:* Tieck and Runge, 1929; Brush Up Your German, series, 1931–61; French Style, 1937; Life's Five Windows, 1968; various edns and translations of foreign texts. *Recreations:* antiquities, hills, foreign parts. *Address:* Llyn Du, Llansantffraid, Powys.

GRUNDY, Milton; *see* Grundy, J. M.

GRUNDY, R(upert) F(rancis) Brooks; consultant engineer; General Manager, Corby Development Corporation, 1950–68, and Industrial Projects Consultant to the Corporation, 1968–70; *b* 6 Sept. 1903; *s* of J. F. E. Grundy, fine art publisher, London and Emily Grundy (*née* Brownsdon); *m* 1938, Heather Mary, *d* of William and Mabel Thomas, Swansea; one *s* one *d. Educ:* Emanuel Sch., London; University Coll., London (BSc (Eng.)); Open Univ. (BA 1975). FICE, FIMunE. Municipal Engrg, 1922–44, at Croydon, Bournemouth, Swansea, Carlisle and Harrow; Borough Engr and Surveyor: Mansfield, 1944–45; Wallasey, 1945–49; Wandsworth, 1949–50. Mem., BBC Midlands Region Adv. Coun., 1966–68. *Publications:* Builders' Materials, 1930; Essentials of Reinforced Concrete, 1939, 1948; papers presented to ICE and IMunE. *Recreations:* golf, walking, reading. *Address:* The Mill House, Brigstock, Kettering, Northants. *T:* Brigstock 218.

GRUNEBERG, Prof. Hans, FRS 1956; PhD Berlin, MD Bonn, DSc London; Professor of Genetics, University College, London, 1956–74, now Emeritus; *b* 26 May 1907; *o s* of late Dr Levi Grüneberg and late Mrs Else Grüneberg (*née* Steinberg), Wuppertal-Elberfeld, Germany; *m* 1st, 1933, Elsbeth (*d* 1944), *d* of late Hugo Capell; two *s*; 2nd, 1946, Hannah (*d* 1962), *d* of late Albrecht Blumenfeld. *Educ:* Städt. Gymnasium, Wuppertal-Elberfeld, Germany. Hon. Research Asst, University Coll., London, 1933–38; Moseley Research Student of Royal Society, 1938–42. Captain, RAMC, 1942–46. Reader in Genetics, University Coll., London, 1946–55. Hon. Dir, MRC Expmtl Genetics Res. Unit, 1955–72. *Publications:* The Genetics of the Mouse, 1943, 1952; Animal Genetics and Medicine, 1947; The Pathology of Development, 1963. Numerous papers in scientific jls. *Recreation:* foreign travel. *Address:* University College, Wolfson House, 4 Stephenson Way, NW1. *T:* 01-387 7050.

GRUNFELD, Prof. Cyril; Professor of Law, London School of Economics, 1966-82; *b* 26 Sept. 1922; *o s* of Samuel and Sarah Grunfeld; *m* 1945, Phyllis Levin; one *s* two *d. Educ:* Canton High Sch., Cardiff; Trinity Hall, Cambridge (MA, LLB). Called to Bar, Inner Temple. British Army, 1942-45; Trinity Hall (Studentship), 1946-48; LSE: Asst, 1946-47; Asst Lectr, 1947-49; Lectr, 1949-56; Reader in Law, 1956—66; Pro-Dir, 1973-76; Convener, Law Dept, 1976-79; Dean, Faculty of Law, Univ. of London, 1978-80. Vis. Research Fellow, ANU, 1970-71; Legal Adviser to Commn on Industrial Relations, 1971-74. Co-editor, Modern Law Review. *Publications:* Modern Trade Union Law, 1966; The Law of Redundancy, 1971, 2nd edn, 1980; contrib. to books and learned jls. *Recreations:* reading, walking. *Address:* London School of Economics and Political Science, Houghton Street, WC2A 2AE. *T:* 01-405 7686.

GRUNFELD, Henry; President, Mercury Securities Ltd (Chairman 1964-74), and S. G. Warburg & Co. Ltd (Chairman 1969-74), since 1974; *b* 1 June 1904; *s* of Max Grunfeld and Rosa Grunfeld (*née* Haendler); *m* 1931, Berta Lotte Oliven; one *s* one *d.* Manager: New Trading Co. Ltd, 1938; S. G. Warburg & Co. Ltd, 1946; Dir, S. G. Warburg & Co. Ltd, 1951-74; *Address:* 30 Gresham Street, EC2P 2EB. *T:* 01-600 4555.

GRUNSELL, Prof. Charles Stuart Grant, CBE 1976; PhD; Professor of Veterinary Medicine, University of Bristol, 1957-80, now Emeritus; *b* 6 Jan. 1915; *s* of Stuart and Edith Grunsell; *m* 1939, Marjorie Prunella Wright; one *s* two *d. Educ:* Shanghai Public Sch.; Bristol Grammar Sch. Qualified as MRCVS at The Royal (Dick) Veterinary Coll., Edinburgh, 1937; FRCVS 1971. In general practice at Glastonbury, Som., 1939-48. PhD Edinburgh, 1952. Senior Lecturer in Veterinary Hygiene and Preventive Medicine, University of Edinburgh, 1952. Pro-Vice-Chancellor, Univ. of Bristol, 1974-77. Chm., Veterinary Products Cttee. Mem., General Synod of C of E, 1980-; a Diocesan Reader. Editor, Veterinary Annual. Defence Medal 1946. *Publications:* papers on the Erythron of Ruminants, on Vital Statistics in Veterinary Medicine, on Preventive Medicine, and on veterinary education. *Recreations:* squash, gardening. *Address:* Towerhead House, Banwell, near Weston-super-Mare, Avon BS24 6PQ. *T:* Banwell 822461.

GRYLLS, Michael; *see* Grylls, W. M. J.

GRYLLS, Rosalie G.; *see* Mander, Lady (Rosalie).

GRYLLS, (William) Michael (John); MP (C) North West Surrey, since 1974 (Chertsey, 1970-74); *b* 21 Feb. 1934; *s* of Brig. W. E. H. Grylls, OBE; *m* 1965, Sarah Smiles Justice, *d* of Captain N. M. Ford and of Lady (Patricia) Fisher, *qv* ; one *s* one *d. Educ:* RN College, Dartmouth; Univ. of Paris. Lieut, Royal Marines, 1952-55. Mem., St Pancras Borough Council, 1959-62. Contested (C) Fulham, Gen. Elecs, 1964 and 1966; Mem., Select Cttee on Overseas Develt, 1970-78; Vice-Chm., Cons. Industry Cttee, 1975-81, Chm., 1981-. Chm., Small Business Bureau, 1979-. Parly Spokesman, Inst. of Directors, 1979-. Mem. GLC, 1967-70; Dep. Leader, Inner London Educn Authority, 1969-70; Chm., Further and Higher Educn, 1968-70; Mem., Nat. Youth Employment Council, 1968-70. *Recreations:* sailing, riding, gardening. *Address:* c/o House of Commons, SW1.

GUAZZELLI, Rt. Rev. Victor; Auxiliary Bishop of Westminster (Bishop in East London) (RC), and Titular Bishop of Lindisfarne since 1970; *b* 19 March 1920; *s* of Cesare Guazzelli and Maria (*née* Frepoli). *Educ:* Parochial Schools, Tower Hamlets; English Coll., Lisbon. Priest, 1945. Asst St Patrick's, Soho Square, 1945-48; Bursar and Prof. at English Coll., Lisbon, 1948-58; Westminster Cathedral: Chaplain, 1958-64; Hon. Canon, 1964; Sub-Administrator, 1964-67; Parish Priest of St Thomas', Fulham, 1967-70; Vicar General of Westminster, 1970. *Address:* The Lodge, Pope John House, Hale Street, E14. *T:* 01-987 4663.

GUDENIAN, Haig, OBE 1980; Associate Director, Stonehart Publications Ltd, since 1974; *b* 16 April 1918; *s* of Miran and Nevric Gudenian; *m* 1949, Lilian Doreen Leavett. *Educ:* University College Sch., London. Trained as journalist, 1934-40. War service in Army, 1940-46: Middle East, N Africa, Italy, Germany (despatches twice). Chief Sub-Editor and Asst Editor, John Bull Magazine, 1946-52; Asst Editor and Associate Editor, Illustrated, 1952-55; Editor, Ideal Home, 1957-64; Founder-Director, GRM Ltd, Publishing Contractors and Consultants, 1966; joined Stonehart Publications, 1974; Dir, Stonehart & Chantry Ltd, 1978-81; Founder-Editor, Tax & Insurance Letter, 1975-. Vice-Chairman, Muscular Dystrophy Group of Great Britain, 1970- (Chm. Management Cttee, 1961-). *Address:* 48a Netherhall Gardens, NW3 5RG. *T:* 01-794 2612.

GUDERLEY, Mrs C.; *see* Hyams, Daisy Deborah.

GUÐMUNDSSON, Guðmundur I., Comdr with Star, Order of the Falcon, 1957; Ambassador of Iceland to Belgium, 1977-79, and concurrently to Luxembourg, NATO and EEC; *b* 17 July 1909; *m* 1942, Rósa Ingólfsdóttir; four *s. Educ:* Reykjavík Grammar Sch.; Univ. of Iceland. Grad. in Law 1934. Practised as Solicitor and Barrister from 1934; Barrister to Supreme Court, 1939; Sheriff and Magistrate, 1945-56. Mem. Central Cttee, Social Democratic Party, 1940-65, Vice-Chm. of Party, 1954-65; Member of Althing (Parlt), 1942-65; Minister of Foreign Affairs, 1956-65; Minister of Finance, 1958-59; Chm., Icelandic Delegn to UN Conf. on Law of the Sea, Geneva, 1958 and 1960; Mem. and Chm. of Board of Dirs, Fishery Bank in Reykjavík, 1957-65;

Ambassador of Iceland: to UK, 1965-71, and concurrently to the Netherlands, Portugal and Spain; to United States, 1971-73, and concurrently to Argentina, Brazil, Canada, Mexico and Cuba; to Sweden, 1973-77 and concurrently to Finland, Austria and Yugoslavia. Establishment of Republic Medal, 1944. Hon. KBE; Grand Cross, Order of: White Rose (Finland); North Star (Sweden); Orange-Nassau (Netherlands); Chêne (Luxembourg); Southern Cross (Brazil); St Olav (Norway); Phoenix (Greece). *Address:* Solvallagata 8, 101 Reykjavik, Iceland.

GUERISSE, Chevalier Albert Marie Edmond, GC 1946; Hon. KBE 1979; DSO 1942 (under name of Patrick Albert O'Leary); medical officer; Major-General in the Belgian Army; Director-General, Medical Service, Belgian Forces; retired 1970; *b* Brussels, 5 April 1911; *m* 1947, Sylvia Cooper Smith; one *s. Educ:* in Belgium; Louvain; Brussels University. Medical Officer, Lieut, 1940; after Belgian capitulation embarked at Dunkirk and became, in Sept. 1940, Lieut-Comdr, RN; first officer of "Q" ship, HMS Fidelity (under name of P. A. O'Leary). Engaged on secret work in France from April 1941 until arrest by Gestapo in March 1943 (chief of an escape organisation). After 2 years in Concentration Camps returned to England. After demobilisation from RN rejoined Belgian Army (1st Lancers); joined Belgian Volunteer Bn, 1951, as Chief of Medical Service in Korea. Officier Légion d'Honneur, 1947; Medal of Freedom with golden palm, 1947; Officier Ordre Léopold, 1946, Grand Officier, 1970; French Croix de Guerre, 1945; Polish Croix de Guerre, 1944. Hereditary Nobility with personal title of Chevalier granted by King of the Belgians, 1981. *Address:* 8 Avenue de Villequier, 1410 Waterloo, Belgium.

GUERITZ, Rear-Adm. Edward Findlay, CB 1971; OBE 1957; DSC 1942, and Bar, 1944; defence consultant, writer and broadcaster; *b* 8 Sept. 1919; *s* of Elton and Valentine Gueritz; *m* 1947, Pamela Amanda Bernhardina Britton, *d* of Commander L. H. Jeans; one *s* one *d. Educ:* Cheltenham Coll. Entered Navy, 1937; Midshipman, 1938; served War of 1939-45 (wounded; DSC and Bar): HMS Jersey, 5th Flotilla, 1940-41; Combined Ops (Indian Ocean, Normandy), 1941-44; HMS Saumarez (Corfu Channel incident), 1946; Army Staff Coll., Camberley, 1948; Staff of C-in-C S Atlantic and Junior Naval Liaison Officer to UK High Comr, S Africa, 1954-56; Near East Operations, 1956 (OBE); Dep. Dir, RN Staff Coll., 1959-61; Naval Staff, Admty, 1961-63; idc 1964; Captain of Fleet, Far East Fleet, 1965-66; Dir of Defence Plans (Navy), 1967; Dir, Jt Warfare Staff, MoD, 1968; Admiral-President, Royal Naval Coll., 1968-70; Comdt, Jt Warfare Estabt, 1970-72. Lt-Comdr 1949; Comdr 1953; Captain 1959; Rear-Adm. 1969; retd 1973. Dep. Dir and Editor, 1976-79, Dir and Editor-in-Chief, 1979-81, RUSI. Specialist Adviser, House of Commons Select Cttee on Defence, 1975-. Chief Hon. Steward, Westminster Abbey, 1975-. Pres., Soc. for Nautical Res., 1974-; Member Council: Marine Soc.; British Atlantic Cttee; Operation Drake; Victoria League; Mem., Bd of War Studies, Univ. of London, 1969-. *Publications:* (jtly) The Third World War, 1978; (ed jtly) Ten Years of Terrorism; (ed jtly) Will the Wells Run Dry; editor, RUSI Brassey's Defence Year Book, 1977-78, 1978-79, 1980, 1981. *Recreations:* history, reading. *Address:* 56 The Close, Salisbury, Wilts. *Club:* Army and Navy.

GUERNSEY, Lord; Charles Heneage Finch-Knightley; *b* 27 March 1947; *s* and *heir* of 11th Earl of Aylesford, *qv* ; *m* 1971, Penelope Anstice, *y d* of Kenneth A. G. Crawley; four *d* (incl. twin *d*). *Educ:* Oundle, Trinity Coll., Cambridge. *Recreations:* shooting, fishing, Real tennis, cricket. *Address:* Rookwood, Packington Park, Meriden, near Coventry. *T:* Meriden 22573.

GUERNSEY, Dean of; *see* Foster, Very Rev. J. W.

GUEST, family name of Viscount Wimborne.

GUEST; *see* Haden-Guest.

GUEST, Baron (Life Peer), *cr* 1961; **Christopher William Graham Guest,** PC 1961; a Lord of Appeal in Ordinary, 1961-71; *b* 7 Nov. 1901; *s* of Edward Graham and Mary Catherine Guest; *m* 1941, Catharine Geraldine Hotham; four *s* one *d. Educ:* Merchiston Castle; Cambridge (MA, LLB); Edinburgh (LLB). Called to Scots Bar, 1925, Inner Temple, 1929; Bencher, Inner Temple, 1961. 2nd Lieut Royal Artillery, TA, 1939; Major, Judge Advocate General's Branch, War Office, 1942. QC, Scots Bar, 1945. Contested (U) Kirkcaldy Burghs, 1945; Advocate Depute, 1945; Pres. Transport Arbitration Tribunal, Scotland, 1947-55; Sheriff of Ayr and Bute, 1952-54; Trustee National Library of Scotland, 1952-57; Sheriff of Perth and Angus, 1954-55; Chm. Building Legislation Cttee, 1954-57; Chm. Scottish Agricultural Wages Board, 1955-61; Chm. Scottish Licensing Law Cttee, 1959-63. Dean of the Faculty of Advocates, 1955-57; a Senator of the College of Justice in Scotland, 1957-61. Hon. Fellow, Clare Coll., Cambridge, 1971. Hon. LLD Dundee, 1973. *Publication:* Law of Valuation in Scotland, 1930. *Address:* 22 Lennox Street, Edinburgh EH4 1QA. *T:* 031-332 4833. *Club:* Buck's.

GUEST, Prof. Anthony Gordon; Barrister-at-Law; Professor of English Law, King's College, University of London, since 1966; *b* 8 Feb. 1930; *s* of late Gordon Walter Leslie Guest and of Marjorie (*née* Hooper), Maidencombe, Devon; unmarried. *Educ:* Colston's Sch., Bristol; St John's Coll., Oxford (MA). Served Army and TA, 1948-50 (Lieut RA). Exhibr and Casberd Schol., Oxford, 1950-54; 1st cl. Final Hon. Sch. of Jurisprudence, 1954. Bacon Schol., Gray's Inn, 1955; Barstow Law Schol., 1955; called to Bar, Gray's Inn, 1956, Bencher, 1978. University Coll., Oxford: Lectr, 1954-55; Fellow and

Prælector in Jurisprudence, 1955-65; Dean, 1963-64; Reader in Common Law to Council of Legal Educn (Inns of Court), 1967-80. Travelling Fellowship to S Africa, 1957; Mem., Lord Chancellor's Law Reform Cttee, 1963-; Mem., Adv. Cttee on establishment of Law Faculty in University of Hong Kong, 1965; UK Deleg. to UN Commn on Internat. Trade Law, NY, Geneva and Vienna, 1968-81, to UN Conf. on Limitation of Actions, 1974; Mem., Board of Athlone Press, 1968-73; Mem. Governing Body, Rugby Sch., 1968-. FKC 1982. *Publications:* (ed) Anson's Principles of the Law of Contract, 21st to 25th edns, 1959-79; Chitty on Contracts: (Asst Editor) 22nd edn, 1961, (Gen. Editor) 23rd to 25th edns, 1968-82; (ed) Oxford Essays in Jurisprudence, 1961; The Law of Hire-Purchase, 1966; (Gen. Editor) Benjamin's Sale of Goods, 1974, 2nd edn, 1981; (ed jtly) Encyclopedia of Consumer Credit, 1975; (jtly) Introduction to the Law of Credit and Security, 1978; articles in legal jls. *Address:* 16 Trevor Place, SW7. *T:* 01-584 9260. *Club:* Garrick.

GUEST, Douglas Albert, CVO 1975; MA Cantab and CVO; MusB Cantab; MusD Cantuar; FRCM, Hon. RAM, FRCO, FRSCM; Organist Emeritus, Westminster Abbey, since 1981; Examiner to Associated Board of Royal Schools of Music; *b* 9 May 1916; 2nd *s* of late Harold Guest, Henley-on-Thames, Oxon; *m* 1941, Peggie Florentia, *d* of late Thomas Falconer, FRIBA, Amberley, Gloucestershire; two *d. Educ:* Reading Sch.; Royal College of Music, London; King's Coll., Cambridge. Organ Scholar, King's Coll., Cambridge, 1935-39; John Stewart of Rannoch Scholar in Sacred Music, Cambridge Univ., 1936-39. Served War of 1939-45, Major, Royal Artillery (HAC) (despatches). Gazetted Hon. Major, April 1945. Dir of Music, Uppingham Sch., 1945-50; Organist and Master of the Choristers, Salisbury Cathedral, 1950-57; Conductor of Salisbury Musical Soc., 1950-57; Dir of Music St Mary's Sch., Calne, 1950-57; Master of the Choristers and Organist, Worcester Cathedral, 1957-63; Conductor Worcester Festival Chorus and Three Choirs Festival, 1957-63; Organist and Master of the Choristers, Westminster Abbey, 1963-81. Prof., RCM, 1963-81. Chm. Council of National Youth Orchestra of Great Britain, 1953-; Member Council: RCO; Musicians' Benevolent Fund. *Recreations:* fly fishing, golf. *Address:* The Gables, Minchinhampton, Glos GL6 9JE. *T:* Brimscombe 883191. *Club:* Flyfishers'.

GUEST, Eric Ronald; Metropolitan Magistrate (West London), 1946-68; Barrister-at-Law; *b* 7 June 1904; *s* of late William Guest; *m* 1932, Sybil Blakelock; one *d. Educ:* Berkhamsted Sch.; Oriel Coll., Oxford. BA 1925 (1st Class Hons Sch. of Jurisprudence); BCL 1926; called to Bar, 1927; practised in London and on Oxford Circuit. Recorder of Worcester, 1941-46; served as Sqdn Leader with RAFVR, 1940-45.

GUEST, George Howell, MA, MusB (Cantab); MusD (Lambeth), 1977; FRCO 1942; FRSCM 1973; Organist of St John's College, Cambridge, since 1951; Fellow, 1956; Special Commissioner, Royal School of Church Music, since 1953; Examiner to Associated Board of Royal Schools of Music, since 1959; *b* 9 Feb. 1924; *s* of late Ernest Joseph Guest and late Gwendolen (*née* Brown); *m* 1959, Nancy Mary, *o d* of late W. P. Talbot; one *s* one *d. Educ:* Friars Sch., Bangor; King's Sch., Chester; St John's Coll., Cambridge. Chorister: Bangor Cath., 1933-35; Chester Cath., 1935-39. Served in RAF, 1942-46. Sub-Organist, Chester Cath., 1946-47; Organ Student, St John's Coll., Cambridge, 1947-51; John Stewart of Rannoch Scholar in Sacred Music, 1948; University Asst Lectr in Music, Cambridge, 1953-56, Univ. Lectr, 1956-82; Prof. of Harmony and Counterpoint, RAM, London, 1960-61. Dir, Berkshire Boy Choir, USA, 1967, 1970. Concerts with St John's Coll. Choir in USA, Canada, Japan, Aust., most countries in W Europe; concerts and choral seminars in the Philippines and in S Africa. Mem. Council, RCO, 1964- (Pres., 1978-80). Aelod er Anrhydedd, Gorsedd y Beirdd, Eisteddfod Genedlaethol Cymru, 1977. Pres., Cathedral Organists' Conference, 1980-82. *Recreation:* the Welsh language. *Address:* 9 Gurney Way, Cambridge. *T:* Cambridge 354932.

GUEST, Henry Alan; Chairman, Rhodes Foods Ltd, since 1980; *b* 29 Feb. 1920; *m* 1947, Helen Mary Price; one *s* one *d. Educ:* Lindisfarne College. FHCIMA. War Service, 1940-46, France, India, Malaya; Captain RA. Supplies Man., J. Lyons & Co. Ltd, Catering Div., 1955; Rank Organisation, Theatre Div.: Dep. Controller, Catering, 1963; Controller, 1965; Group Catering Adviser, Associated British Foods, 1966; Chief Exec., Civil Service Catering Organisation, 1972-80. Mem. Royal Instn of Great Britain. *Publications:* papers on marketing and organisation in techn. jls and financial press. *Recreation:* swimming. *Address:* 14 Pensford Avenue, Kew, Surrey TW9 4HP.

GUEST, Ivor Forbes; Chairman, since 1969, Member, since 1965, Executive Committee of the Royal Academy of Dancing; Solicitor; *b* 14 April 1920; *s* of Cecil Marmaduke Guest and Christian Forbes Guest (*née* Tweedie); *m* 1962, Ann Hutchinson; no *c. Educ:* Lancing Coll.; Trinity Coll., Cambridge (MA). Admitted a Solicitor, 1949; Partner, A. F. & R. W. Tweedie, 1951-. Organised National Book League exhibn of books on ballet, 1957-58; Mem. Cttee, Soc. for Theatre Research, 1955-72; British Theatre Museum: Mem. Exec. Cttee, 1957-77 (Vice-Chm., 1966-77); Mem., Theatre Museum Adv. Council, 1974-. Editorial Adviser to the Dancing Times, 1963-; Sec., Radcliffe Trust, 1966-; Trustee: Calvert Trust, 1976-; Cecchetti Soc. Trust, 1978-. *Publications:* Napoleon III in England, 1952; The Ballet of the Second Empire, 1953-55; The Romantic Ballet in England, 1954; Fanny Cerrito, 1956; Victorian Ballet Girl, 1957; Adeline Genée, 1958; The Alhambra Ballet, 1959; La Fille mal gardée, 1960; The Dancer's Heritage, 1960; The Empire Ballet, 1962; A Gallery of Romantic Ballet, 1963; The Romantic Ballet in Paris, 1966; Carlotta Zambelli, 1969; Dandies and Dancers, 1969; Two Coppélias, 1970; Fanny Elssler, 1970; The Pas de Quatre, 1970; Le Ballet de l'Opéra, 1976; The Divine Virginia, 1977; Adeline Genée: a pictorial record, 1978; Lettres d'un Maître de ballet, 1978; contrib. to Designing for the Dancer, in Costume and the 19th Century Dancer, 1981; Adventures of a Ballet Historian, 1982. *Address:* 17 Holland Park, W11. *T:* 01-229 3780. *Clubs:* Garrick, MCC.

GUEST, Trevor George; Registrar of the Principal Registry of the Family Division of the High Court of Justice, since 1972; Barrister-at-Law; *b* 30 Jan. 1928; *m* 1951, Patricia Mary (*née* Morrison); two *d. Educ:* Denstone Coll., Uttoxeter, Staffs; Birmingham Univ. (LLB (Hons)). Called to the Bar, Middle Temple, 1953. *Recreations:* dogs, Church affairs. *Address:* The Old Rectory, Purleigh, Essex. *T:* Purleigh 375.

GUILD, Ivor Reginald; Partner in Shepherd and Wedderburn, WS, since 1951; *b* 2 April 1924; 2nd *s* of Col Arthur Marjoribanks Guild, DSO, TD, DL, and Phyllis Eliza Cox. *Educ:* Cargilfield; Rugby; New Coll., Oxford (MA); Edinburgh Univ. (LLB). WS 1950. Procurator Fiscal of the Lyon Court, 1960-; Bailie of Holyrood House, 1980-; Registrar, Episcopal Synod of Episc. Church in Scotland, 1967-. Chairman: Edinburgh Investment Trust Ltd; First Scottish American Trust Co. Ltd; Northern American Trust Co. Ltd; Tay & Thames Investments Services Ltd; Dir, London & Holyrood Trust Ltd. Mem., Council on Tribunals, 1976- (Chm., Scottish Cttee, 1976-); Chm., Nat. Mus. of Antiquities of Scotland, 1981-. Editor, Scottish Genealogist, 1959-. *Recreations:* genealogy, golf. *Club:* New (Edinburgh).

GUILDFORD, Dean of; *see* Bridge, Very Rev. A. C.

GUILFORD, 9th Earl of *cr* 1752; **Edward Francis North;** Baron Guilford, 1683; DL; *b* 22 Sept. 1933; *s* of Major Lord North (*d* 1940) and Joan Louise (she *m* 2nd, 1947, Charles Harman Hunt), *er d* of late Sir Merrik Burrell, 7th Bt, CBE; *S* grandfather, 1949; *m* 1966, Osyth Vere Napier, *d* of Cyril Napier Leeston Smith, Trottiscliffe, near West Malling, Kent; one *s. Educ:* Eton. DL Kent 1976. *Heir: s* Lord North, *qv. Address:* Waldershare Park, Dover, Kent. *T:* Dover 820244.

See also Major Hon. Sir Clive Bossom, Bt.

GUILFOYLE, Dame Margaret (Georgina Constance), DBE 1980; Minister for Finance, Commonwealth of Australia, since 1980; Senator for Victoria, since 1971; *b* 15 May 1926; *d* of William and Elizabeth McCartney; *m* 1952, Stanley M. L. Guilfoyle; one *s* two *d.* Accountant, 1947-. Minister for Education, Commonwealth of Australia, 1975, for Social Security, 1975-80. ACIS; FASA. *Recreations:* reading, gardening. *Address:* Parliament House, Canberra, ACT 2600, Australia. *Club:* Lyceum (Melbourne).

GUILLEMIN, Roger Charles Louis, MD, PhD; Resident Fellow and Research Professor, Salk Institute for Biological Studies, La Jolla, California, since 1970; Adjunct Professor of Medicine, University of California, San Diego, since 1970; *b* Dijon, France, 11 Jan. 1924 (naturalized US Citizen, 1963); *s* of Raymond Guillemin and Blanche (*née* Rigollot); *m* 1951, Lucienne Jeanne Billard; one *s* five *d. Educ:* Univ. of Dijon (BA 1941, BSc 1942); Faculty of Medicine, Lyons (MD 1949); Univ. of Montreal (PhD 1953). Resident intern. hosps, Dijon, 1949-51; Associate Dir, then Asst Prof., Inst. of Exper. Medicine and Surgery, Univ. of Montreal, 1951-53; Associate Dir, Dept of Exper. Endocrinol., Coll. de France, Paris, 1960-63; Prof. of Physiol., Baylor Coll. of Med., Houston, 1953-70; Adjunct Prof. of Physiol., Baylor Coll. of Med., 1970-. Member: Nat. Acad. of Sciences, USA; Amer. Acad. Arts and Scis. Mem. Club of Rome. Hon. DSc: Rochester, NY, 1976; Chicago, 1977; Hon. MD: Ulm, 1978; Montreal, 1979; Univ. Libre de Bruxelles, Belgium, 1979; Hon. LMed Baylor Coll. of Med., 1978. Gairdner Internat. Award, 1974; Lasker Award, USA, 1975; National Medal of Science, USA, 1977; (jtly) Nobel Prize in Physiology or Medicine, 1977; Barren Gold Medal, USA, 1979; Dale Medal (Soc. for Endocrinology), UK, 1980. Légion d'Honneur, France, 1974. *Publications:* scientific pubns in learned jls. *Address:* Salk Institute, Box 85800, San Diego, Calif 92138.

GUILLUM SCOTT, Sir John (Arthur), Kt 1964; TD 1945; *b* 27 Oct. 1910; *e s* of late Guy H. Guillum Scott; *m* 1939, Muriel Elizabeth, *d* of late James Ross; one *d. Educ:* King's Sch., Canterbury. Queen Anne's Bounty, 1929-46; Asst Sec., Church Assembly, 1946-48, Sec., 1948-70; Sec.-Gen., General Synod of C of E, 1970-72; Communar of Chichester Cathedral, 1973-79. Inns of Court Regt TA, 1929-53; war service, 1939-45 (despatches); Lieut-Col commanding Inns of Court Regt, 1950-53; Bt Col, 1953. DCL (Lambeth) 1961. *Recreations:* gardening, field sports. *Address:* 5 North Close, St Martins Square, Chichester, West Sussex.

GUILLY, Rt. Rev. Richard Lester, SJ; OBE 1945; Parish Priest in Barbados, since 1981; *b* 6 July 1905; *s* of late Richard Guilly. *Educ:* Stonyhurst Coll.; Campion Hall, Oxford (Hons Mod. Hist.; BA, MA); Heythrop Coll. Entered Soc. of Jesus, 1924; Asst Master, Beaumont Coll., 1933-35; ordained 1938. Served War of 1939-45, Chaplain to the Forces: BEF (France), 1939-40; CF 3rd Cl. 1940; Senior RC Chaplain, N Ireland, 1 Corps District, AA Cmd, 2nd Army, 1940-45 (OBE, despatches). Superior of Soc. of Jesus in British Guiana and Barbados, 1946-54; Titular Bishop of Adraa and Vicar Apostolic of British Guiana and Barbados, 1954-56; Bishop of Georgetown, 1956-72; Parish Priest in Barbados, 1972-77; Apostolic Administrator, Archdiocese of Castries,

1977-81. *Publications:* various articles on Church History, Christian Social Doctrine and Church in Guyana. *Address:* Villa Maria, St Peter, Barbados, WI.

GUINNESS, family name of **Earl of Iveagh** and **Baron Moyne.**

GUINNESS, Sir Alec, Kt 1959; CBE 1955; Hon. DLitt, Hon. DFA; actor; *b* Marylebone, 2 April 1914; *m* 1938, Merula Salaman; one *s. Educ:* Pembroke Lodge, Southbourne; Roborough, Eastbourne. On leaving school went into Arks Publicity, Advertising Agents, as copywriter. First professional appearance walking on in Libel at King's Theatre, Hammersmith, 1933; played Hamlet in modern dress, Old Vic, 1938; toured the Continent, 1939. Served War of 1939-45; joined Royal Navy as a rating, 1941; commissioned 1942. Rejoined Old Vic, 1946-47. Hon. D Fine Arts Boston Coll., 1962; Hon. DLitt Oxon, 1977. Special Oscar, for contribution to film, 1979. *Films include:* Oliver Twist, Kind Hearts and Coronets, The Lavender Hill Mob, The Bridge on the River Kwai (Oscar for best actor of the year, 1957); The Horse's Mouth; Tunes of Glory; Lawrence of Arabia; Star Wars; Little Lord Fauntleroy; Lovesick. *Plays include:* The Cocktail Party (New York); Hotel Paradiso, Ross, Dylan (New York); A Voyage Round My Father; Habeas Corpus; Yahoo (also devised, in collaboration); The Old Country, 1977; *television:* Tinker, Tailor, Soldier, Spy, 1979 (BAFTA Award, 1980); Smiley's People, 1981-82. *Address:* c/o London Management, 235/241 Regent Street, W1. *Club:* Athenæum.

GUINNESS, Bryan; *see* Moyne, 2nd Baron.

GUINNESS, Hon. Desmond (Walter); writer; President, Irish Georgian Society, since 1958; *b* 8 Sept. 1931; *yr s* of Baron Moyne, *qv* ; *m* 1954, Marie-Gabrielle von Urach; one *s* one *d. Educ:* Gordonstoun; Christ Church, Oxford (MA). Founder, 1958, Irish Georgian Society to work for the study of, and protection of, buildings of architectural merit in Ireland, particularly of the Georgian period. Hon. LLD TCD, 1980. *Publications:* Portrait of Dublin, 1967; Irish Houses and Castles, 1971; Mr Jefferson, Architect, 1973; Georgian Dublin, 1980; The White House: an architectural history, 1981; Newport Preserv'd, 1982. *Clubs:* Chelsea Arts; Kildare Street and University (Dublin).
See also Hon. J. B. Guinness.

GUINNESS, Sir Howard (Christian Sheldon), Kt 1981; VRD 1953; Executive Director, S. G. Warburg & Co. Ltd, since 1970; dairy farmer; *b* 3 June 1932; *s* of Edward Douglas Guinness, CBE and late Martha Letière (*née* Sheldon); *m* 1958, Evadne Jane Gibbs; two *s* one *d. Educ:* King's Mead, Seaford, Sussex; Eton Coll. National Service, RN (midshipman); Lt-Comdr RNR. Union Discount Co. of London Ltd, 1953; Guinness Mahon & Co. Ltd, 1953-55; S. G. Warburg & Co. Ltd, 1955-. Dir, Harris & Sheldon Gp Ltd, 1960-81; Dir and Dep. Chm., Youghal Carpets (Holdings) Ltd, 1972-80. Chm., N Hampshire Conservative Assoc., 1971-74; Vice-Chm. 1974, Chm. 1975-78, and Treasurer 1978-81, Wessex Area, Cons. Assoc. Mem. Council, English Guernsey Cattle Soc., 1963-72. *Recreations:* skiing, tennis. *Address:* Knowl Hill House, Kingsclere, Newbury, Berks RG15 8NY. *T:* Kingsclere 298357. *Club:* White's.
See also J. R. S. Guinness.

GUINNESS, James Edward Alexander Rundell; Deputy Chairman, Guinness Peat Group, since 1977 (Chairman, Guinness Mahon Holdings Ltd, 1968-72, Joint Chairman, Guinness Peat Group, 1973-77); *b* 23 Sept. 1924; *s* of late Sir Arthur Guinness, KCMG and Frances Patience Guinness, MBE (*née* Wright); *m* 1953, Pauline Mander; one *s* four *d. Educ:* Eton; Oxford. Served in RNVR, 1943-46. Joined family banking firm of Guinness Mahon & Co., 1946, Partner 1953. Chm., Public Works Loan Bd, 1979– (Comr, 1960-). *Recreations:* hunting, shooting, fishing. *Address:* Coldpiece Farm, Mattingley, Basingstoke RG27 8LQ. *T:* Heckfield 292. *Clubs:* Brooks's, Pratt's; Royal Yacht Squadron (Cowes).

GUINNESS, John Ralph Sidney; Under-Secretary, Department of Energy, since 1980; *b* 23 Dec. 1935; *s* of Edward Douglas Guinness and late Martha Letière (*née* Sheldon); *m* 1967, Valerie Susan North; one *s* one *d* (and one *s* decd). *Educ:* Rugby Sch.; Trinity Hall, Cambridge (BA Hons History, MA Hons). Union Discount Co. Ltd, 1960-61; Overseas Develt Inst., 1961-62; joined FO, 1962; Econ. Relations Dept, 1962-63; Third Sec., UK Mission to UN, New York, 1963-64; seconded to UN Secretariat as Special Asst to Dep. Under-Sec. and later Under-Sec. for Econ. and Social Affairs, 1964-66; FCO, 1967-69; First Sec. (Econ.), Brit. High Commn, Ottawa, 1969-72; seconded to Central Policy Rev. Staff, Cabinet Office, 1972-75; Counsellor, 1974; Alternate UK Rep. to Law of the Sea Conf., 1975-77; seconded to CPRS, 1977-79; transferred to Home Civil Service, 1980. *Recreation:* iconography. *Address:* 9 Hereford Square, SW7 4TS. *T:* 01-373 8648. *Clubs:* Brooks's, Beefsteak.
See also Sir H. C. S. Guinness.

GUINNESS, Hon. Jonathan Bryan; Director: Leopold Joseph & Sons Ltd; Arthur Guinness Son & Co. Ltd; The Red Bank Manufacturing Co. Ltd; *b* 16 March 1930; *s* and heir of Baron Moyne, *qv*, and of Diana (*née* Mitford, now Lady Mosley); *m* 1st, 1951, Ingrid Wyndham (marr. diss. 1962); two *s* one *d* ; 2nd, 1964, Suzanne Phillips (*née* Lisney); one *s* one *d. Educ:* Eton; Oxford (MA, Mod. Langs). Journalist at Reuters, 1953-56. Merchant Banker: trainee at Erlangers Ltd, 1956-59, and at Philip Hill, 1959-62; Exec. Dir,

1962-64, Non-exec. Dir, 1964–, Leopold Joseph. CC Leicestershire, 1970-74; Chairman, Monday Club, 1972-74. *Address:* Osbaston Hall, Nuneaton, Warwickshire; 18 Hereford Square, SW7. *Clubs:* Carlton, Beefsteak; Ibstock Working Men's.

GUINNESS, Sir Kenelm (Ernest Lee), 4th Bt, *cr* 1867; consultant; *b* 13 Dec. 1928; *s* of late Kenelm Edward Lee Guinness and of Mrs Josephine Lee Guinness; *S* uncle 1954; *m* 1961, Mrs Jane Nevin Dickson; two *s. Educ:* Eton Coll.; Massachusetts Institute of Technology, USA. Late Lieut, Royal Horse Guards. With IBRD, Washington, 1954-75. *Heir: s* Kenelm Edward Lee Guinness, *b* 30 Jan. 1962. *Address:* (home) 2814 35th Street NW, Washington, DC 20007, USA. *T:* FE7-3933. *Club:* Cavalry and Guards.

GUINNESS, Loel; *see* Guinness, T. L. E. B.

GUINNESS, Thomas Loel Evelyn Bulkeley, OBE 1942; late Irish Guards; *b* 9 June 1906; *s* of late Benjamin S. Guinness; *m* 1st, 1927, Hon. Joan Yarde-Buller (from whom he obtained a divorce, 1936); one *s* decd; 2nd, 1936, Lady Isabel Manners (marr. diss., 1951), *yr d* of 9th Duke of Rutland; one *s* one *d* ; 3rd, 1951, Gloria (*d* 1980), *d* of Raphael Rubio, Mexico. *Educ:* Sandhurst. MP (U) City of Bath, 1931-45; Contested Whitechapel, 1929, and By-election, 1930; Group Captain Auxiliary Air Force Reserve. Served War of 1939-45: RAF (despatches five times). Comdr Order of Orange Nassau; Officer Legion of Honour, France; Croix de Guerre. *Address:* Villa Zanroc, Epalinges 1066, Vaud, Switzerland. *Clubs:* White's, Buck's, Turf, Beefsteak; Royal Yacht Squadron (Cowes).
See also Marquess of Dufferin and Ava.

GUISE, Sir John, GCMG 1975; KBE 1975 (CBE 1972); MP (Ind), Parliament of Papua New Guinea, since 1977; *b* Papua, 29 Aug. 1914; *m* ; five *s* four *d.* Served War, Australian New Guinea Administrative Unit. Royal Papuan Constabulary, 1946, Mem. contingent attending Queen Elizabeth's Coronation, London, 1953, Sgt Major, later transferred to Dept of Native Affairs for local govt and welfare duties, Port Moresby. Mem., 1st Select Cttee Political Develt, 1961-63, which drew up 1st House of Assembly, 1964; Chm., House of Assembly Select Cttee on Political and Constitutional Develt which drew up 1st Ministerial Govt for 2nd House of Assembly, 1968. Mem. for E Papua, Legislative Council, 1961-63; MHA, Milne Bay District, 1964-67; Speaker, Papua New Guinea House of Assembly, Minister for Interior, and later Deputy Chief Minister and Minister for Agriculture, Papua New Guinea, to 1975; unofficial leader of elected Members, Papua New Guinea House of Assembly, 1964-68. Governor-General, Papua New Guinea, 1975-77. Delegate, S Pacific Conf., Pago Pago, 1962; Mem., Australian delegn to UN, 1962 and 1963; attended UNESCO Conf., Paris, Geneva, London, 1963. Prominent layman in Anglican Church affairs. Hon. LLD. KStJ 1976. *Address:* National Parliament, Port Moresby, Papua New Guinea; Lalaura Village, Cape Rodney, Central Province, Papua New Guinea.

GUISE, Sir John (Grant), 7th Bt *cr* 1783; Jockey Club Official since 1968; *b* 15 Dec. 1927; *s* of Sir Anselm William Edward Guise, 6th Bt and of Lady Guise (Nina Margaret Sophie, *d* of Sir James Augustus Grant, 1st Bt); *S* father, 1970. *Educ:* Winchester; RMA, Sandhurst. Regular officer, 3rd The King's Own Hussars, 1948-61. *Recreations:* hunting, shooting. *Heir: b* Christopher James Guise [*b* 10 July 1930; *m* 1969, Mrs Carole Hoskins Benson, *e d* of Jack Master; one *s* one *d*]. *Address:* Elmore Court, Gloucester. *T:* Gloucester 720293.

GUJADHUR, Hon. Sir Radhamohun, Kt 1976; CMG 1973; MLA Mauritius; Deputy Speaker, Legislative Assembly, Mauritius, since 1974 (and 1968-69); solicitor; Chairman, Consortium Cinematographique Maurice Ltée; Director, Trianon Estates Ltd; Managing Director of Companies; *b* Curepipe Road, Mauritius, 1909; *m* ; eight *c. Educ:* Church of England Aided Sch., Curepipe; Curepipe De la Salle Sch., Port Louis; Royal Coll., Curepipe; St Xavier Coll., Calcutta. Mem. Municipal Council, 1943-47; Dep. Mayor, Port Louis, 1947; Mem. (nominated) Town Council, Curepipe, 1957-60 (Chm., 1963). Elected Mem. for constituency of Bon-Accord/Flacq, 1967. *Address:* Port Louis, Mauritius. *Club:* Mauritius Turf (Steward, 1970; Chm. 1974).

GULL, Sir Michael Swinnerton Cameron, 4th Bt, *cr* 1872; *b* 24 Jan. 1919; *o s* of 3rd Bt and Dona Eva Swinnerton (*d* 1973), *e d* of late Sir Thomas Swinnerton Dyer, 11th Bt; *S* father 1960; *m* 1950, Mrs Yvonne Bawtree, *o d* of Dr Albert Oliver Macarius Heslop, Cape Town; one *s* one *d. Educ:* Eton. Late 2nd Lieut, Scots Guards (SRO). *Heir: s* Rupert William Cameron Gull, *b* 14 July 1954. *Address:* 2 Harcourt Road, Claremont, Cape Town, S Africa.

GULLIVER, James Gerald; Chairman: James Gulliver Associates Ltd, since 1977; Alpine Holdings Ltd, since 1977; Gulliver Foods Ltd, since 1978; Gulliver Hotels Ltd, since 1978; Argyll Foods Ltd (previously Louis C. Edwards (Manchester) Ltd), since 1980; Allied Suppliers, since 1982; Director, Manchester United Football Club Ltd, since 1979; *b* 17 Aug. 1930; *s* of William Frederick and Mary Gulliver; *m* 1st, 1958, Margaret Joan (*née* Cormack); three *s* two *d* ; 2nd, 1977, Joanne (*née* Sims). *Educ:* Campbeltown Grammar Sch.; Univs of Glasgow and Harvard. Royal Navy (Short Service Commn), 1956-59; Dir, Concrete (Scotland) Ltd, 1960-61; Management Consultant, Urwick, Orr & Partners Ltd, 1961-65; Man. Dir, 1965-72, Chm., 1967-72, Fine Fare (Holdings) Ltd; Dir, Associated British Foods Ltd, 1967-72; Chm. and Chief Exec., Oriel Foods Ltd, 1973-76. FBIM; Fellow and

Mem. Council, Inst. of Directors; Vice-Pres., Marketing Soc. Mem., Prime Minister's Enquiry into Beef Prices, 1973. FRSA. Freedom and Livery, Worshipful Co. of Gardeners. Guardian Young Businessman of the Year, 1972. *Recreations:* ski-ing, sailing, music, motoring. *Address:* 49 Pont Street, SW1X 0BD. *Clubs:* Carlton; Royal Thames Yacht.

GULLY, family name of **Viscount Selby.**

GUMLEY, Frances Jane, MA; Roman Catholic Assistant to Head of Religious Broadcasting, BBC, since 1981; *b* 28 Jan. 1955; *o d* of late Franc Stewart Gumley and of Helen Teresa (Eileen) (*née* McNicholas). *Educ:* St Augustine's Priory, Ealing; St Benedict's Sch., Ealing (part-time for Greek); Newnham Coll., Cambridge (MA). Braille transcriber, 1975; Catholic Herald: Editorial Assistant and Assistant Literary Editor, Dec. 1975; Literary Editor and Staff Reporter, 1976-79; Editor, 1979-81. *Recreations:* tending her garden, family and friends. *Address:* 2 Rathgar Avenue, Ealing, W13 9PL.

GUMMER, Ellis Norman, CBE 1974 (OBE 1960); Assistant Director-General (Administration), British Council, 1972-75; *b* 18 June 1915; *o s* of late Robert Henry Gummer, engr, and of Mabel Thorpe, Beckenham, Kent; *m* 1949, Dorothy Paton Shepherd; one *s* (and one *s* decd). *Educ:* St Dunstan's Coll.; St Catherine's Society, Oxford. BLitt, MA. Library service: Nottingham Univ., 1939; Queen's Coll., Oxford, 1940-42; served War of 1939-45, Admty, 1942-45; British Council: East Europe Dept, 1945-50; Personnel Dept, 1950-52; Student Welfare Dept, 1952-59; Literature Group, 1959-61; Controller, Arts and Science Div., 1961-66; Controller, Finance Div., 1966-71. *Publication:* Dickens' Works in Germany, 1940. *Recreations:* books, topography, archaeology. *Address:* 9 Campden Street, W8 7EP. *T:* 01-727 4823.

GUMMER, John Selwyn; MP (C) Eye, Suffolk, since 1979; a Lord Commissioner of HM Treasury, since 1981; *b* 26 Nov. 1939; *s* of Canon Selwyn Gummer and Sybille (*née* Mason); *m* 1977, Penelope Jane, *yr d* of John P. Gardner; two *s* one *d*. *Educ:* King's Sch., Rochester; Selwyn Coll., Cambridge (Exhibr). BA Hons History 1961; MA 1971; Chm., Cambridge Univ. Conservative Assoc., 1961; Pres., Cambridge Union, 1962; Chm., Fedn of Conservative Students, 1962. Editor, Business Publications, 1962-64; Editor-in-Chief, Max Parrish & Oldbourne Press, 1964-66; BPC Publishing: Special Asst to Chm., 1967; Publisher, Special Projects, 1967-69; Editorial Coordinator, 1969-70. Mem., ILEA Educn Cttee, 1967-70; Dir, Shandwick Publishing Co., 1966-81; Man. Dir, EP Gp of Cos, 1975-81; Chairman: Selwyn Shandwick Internat., 1976-81, Siemssen Hunter Ltd, 1979-80 (Dir, 1973-80). Contested (C) Greenwich, 1964 and 1966; MP (C) Lewisham W, 1970-Feb. 1974; PPS to Minister of Agriculture, 1972; an additional Vice-Chm., Conservative Party, 1972-74; an Asst Govt Whip, 1981. *Publications:* (Jtly) When the Coloured People Come, 1966; The Permissive Society, 1971; (with L. W. Cowie) The Christian Calendar, 1974; (contrib.) To Church with Enthusiasm, 1969. *Address:* House of Commons, SW1; Clarence House, Fressingfield, Eye, Suffolk. *T:* Fressingfield 347.

GÜMRÜKÇÜOGLU, Rahmi Kamil; Turkish Ambassador to the Court of St James's, since 1981; *b* 18 May 1927; *m* Elçin; one *s* one *d*. *Educ:* Haydar Pasha Lycée, Istanbul; Faculty of Political Sciences, Ankara Univ. Master's degree in Pol. Economy and Govt, Harvard Univ. Second Secretary, 1952-55, First Sec., 1955, Turkish Embassy, London; Head of Section dealing with Internat. Economic Affairs, Min. of Foreign Affairs, Ankara, 1958-60; Counsellor, Turkish Embassy, Cairo, 1960-63; Dep. Director General, Dept of Internat. Economic Affairs, Ankara, 1963-65; Head of Special Bureau dealing with Economic Co-operation between Turkey and the Soviet Union, 1965-67; Dir Gen., Dept of Internat. Economic Affairs, 1967-71; Turkish Ambassador: to Council of Europe, Strasbourg, 1971-75; to Iran, 1975-78; Sen. Adviser to Min. of Foreign Affairs, and Pres., Defence Industry Co-ordination Board, Ankara, 1978-79; Dep. Sec. Gen. for Economic Affairs, Min. of Foreign Affairs, 1979-81. *Address:* Turkish Embassy, 43 Belgrave Square, SW1. *T:* 01-235 5252.

GUN-MUNRO, Sir Sydney Douglas, GCMG 1979; Kt 1977; MBE 1957; Governor-General of St Vincent, West Indies, since Oct. 1979 (Governor, 1977-79); *b* 29 Nov. 1916; *s* of Barclay Justin Gun-Munro and Marie Josephine Gun-Munro; *m* 1943, Joan Estelle Benjamin; two *s* one *d*. *Educ:* Grenada Boys' Secondary Sch.; King's Coll. Hosp., London (MB, BS Hons 1943); Moorfields Hosp., London (DO 1952). MRCS, LRCP 1943. House Surg., EMS Hosp., Horton, 1943; MO, Lewisham Hosp., 1943-46; Dist MO, Grenada, 1946-49; Surg., Gen. Hosp., St Vincent, 1949-71; Dist MO, Bequia, St Vincent, 1972-76. *Recreations:* tennis, boating. *Address:* Government House, St Vincent, West Indies. *T:* St Vincent 71917.

GUNDRY, Rev. Canon Dudley William, MTh; Canon Residentiary and Chancellor of Leicester since 1963; Church Affairs Consultant and Correspondent to Daily Telegraph, since 1978; *b* 4 June 1916; *e s* of late Cecil Wood Gundry and Lucy Gundry; unmarried. *Educ:* Sir Walter St John's Sch.; King's Coll., London. BD (1st cl. Hons) 1939, AKC (1st cl. Hons Theology) 1939, MTh 1941. Deacon, 1939; Priest 1940. Curate of St Matthew, Surbiton, 1939-44; Lectr in History of Religions, University Coll. of North Wales, Bangor, 1944-60; Mem. Senate and Warden of Neuadd Reichel, 1947-60; Dean of Faculty of Theology, 1956-60; Hon. Sec., British Section, Internat. Assoc. for History of Religions, 1954-60; Select Preacher, Trinity Coll., Dublin, 1957; Prof. and Head of Dept of Religious Studies, and Mem. of

Senate, University Coll., Ibadan, 1960-63; Commissary to Bishop of Northern Nigeria, 1963-69; Rural Dean of Christianity, Leicester, 1966-74; Proctor in Convocation, 1970-80. Sometime Examining Chaplain to Bishops of Bangor, St Davids and Leicester; Examiner to Universities of Leeds, London, Keele, St David's Coll., Lampeter, Gen. Ordination Examination. *Publications:* Religions: An Historical and Theological Study, 1958; Israel's Neighbours (in Neil's Bible Companion), 1959; The Teacher and the World Religions, 1968; many articles and signed reviews in theological and kindred journals; Editor, Leicester Cathedral Qly, 1963-79. *Recreations:* motoring, ecclesiology. *Address:* 3 Morland Avenue, Leicester LE2 2PF. *T:* Leicester 704133. *Clubs:* Athenæum, Press; Leicestershire (Leicester).

GUNLAKE, John Henry, CBE 1946; FIA; FSS; FIS; consulting actuary; *b* 23 May 1905; *s* of late John Gunlake, MRCS, LRCP, and late Alice Emma Gunlake; unmarried. *Educ:* Epsom Coll. Institute of Actuaries: Fellow, 1933; Hon. Sec., 1952-54; Vice-Pres., 1956-59; Pres., 1960-62. A Statistical Adviser, Min. of Shipping, 1940-47. Member: Cttee on Econ. and Financial Problems of Provision for Old Age, 1953-54; Royal Commn on Doctors' and Dentists' Remuneration, 1957-60; Permanent Advisory Cttee on Doctors' and Dentists' Remuneration, 1962-70. *Publications:* Premiums for Life Assurances and Annuities, 1939. Contrib. to Jl of Inst. of Actuaries. *Recreations:* reading, music, walking. *Address:* 120 Clapham Common North Side, SW4 9SP. *T:* 01-228 3008. *Club:* Reform.

GUNN, Mrs Bunty Moffat, OBE 1981; JP; Chairman, Lanarkshire Health Board, since 1981; *b* 4 Sept. 1923; *d* of William M. and Dolina Johnston; *m* 1946, Hugh McVane Houston Gunn; three *s* one *d*. *Educ:* Grange School for Girls; Grangemouth High School. DSCHE 1980. Councillor: Lanark CC, 1970-73; Strathclyde Regional Council, 1973-; Chairman, Scottish Council for Health Education, 1974-80; Member, Lanarkshire Health Board, 1973-81. Vice-Pres., Royal British Legion, CS&W Branch, 1978-. JP City of Glasgow 1972. *Recreations:* golf, theatre, music. *Address:* Kinnoul, 1 Beech Avenue, High Burnside, Rutherglen, Strathclyde. *T:* 041-634 4510. *Club:* Cathkin Braes Golf (Strathclyde).

GUNN, John Angus Livingston; Under-Secretary, Department of the Environment, since 1976; *b* 20 Nov. 1934; *s* of late Alistair L. Gunn, FRCOG, and Alderman Mrs Sybil Gunn, JP, Chislehurst, Kent; *m* 1959, Jane, *d* of Robert Cameron; one *s* one *d*. *Educ:* Fettes Coll., Edinburgh (Foundationer); Christ Church, Oxford (Scholar). MA Oxford, 1st Cl. Hons in Classical Hon. Mod., 1955, and in final sch. of Psychology, Philosophy and Physiology, 1957; Passmore-Edwards Prizeman, 1956. National Service, commnd in S Wales Borderers (24th Regt), 1957-59. Entered Min. of Transport, 1959; Principal Private Sec. to successive Ministers of Transport (Rt Hon. Barbara Castle and Rt Hon. Richard Marsh), 1967-68; Asst Sec., MoT, DoE and Civil Service Dept, 1969-74; Under-Sec., Civil Service Dept, 1975. *Address:* Department of the Environment, 2 Marsham Street, SW1P 3EB.

GUNN, Prof. Sir John (Currie), Kt 1982; CBE 1976; MA (Glasgow and Cambridge); FRSE, FIMA; FInstP; Cargill Professor of Natural Philosophy, 1949-82 and Head of Department, 1973-82, University of Glasgow; *b* 13 Sept. 1916; *s* of Richard Robertson Gunn and Jane Blair Currie; *m* 1944, Betty Russum; one *s*. *Educ:* Glasgow Acad.; Glasgow Univ.; St John's Coll., Cambridge. Engaged in Admiralty scientific service, first at Admiralty Research Laboratory, later at Mine Design Dept, 1939-45; Research Fellow of St John's Coll., Cambridge, 1944; Lecturer in Applied Mathematics: Manchester Univ., 1945-46; University Coll., London, 1946-49. Member: SRC, 1968-72; UGC, 1974-81. Hon. DSc Heriot-Watt, 1981. *Publications:* papers on mathematical physics in various scientific journals. *Recreations:* golf, music, chess. *Address:* 13 The University, Glasgow G12 8QG. *T:* 041-334 3042.

GUNN, Peter Nicholson; author; *b* 15 Aug. 1914; 2nd *s* of Frank Lindsay Gunn, CBE, and Adèle Margaret (*née* Dunphy); *m* 1953, Diana Maureen James; one *s*. *Educ:* Melbourne; Trinity Coll., Cambridge (MA). Served War 1939-45: Rifle Bde; POW 1942-45, Sandhurst, 1949-54. *Publications:* Naples: a Palimpsest, 1961 (German trans. 1964, Italian trans. 1971); Vernon Lee: a Study, 1964; The Companion Guide to Southern Italy, 1969; My Dearest Augusta: a Biography of Augusta Leigh, Byron's half-sister, 1969; A Concise History of Italy, 1971; (ed) Byron's Prose, 1972; Normandy: Landscape with figures, 1975; Burgundy: Landscape with figures, 1976; The Actons, 1978; Napoleon's Little Pest: The Duchess of Abrantès, 1979; (with R. Beny) Churches of Rome, 1981 (trans. German and Italian, 1982). *Address:* Hunt House, Whitaside, near Richmond, North Yorkshire. *T:* Richmond 86386. *Club:* University Pitt (Cambridge).

GUNN, Thomson William, (Thom Gunn); *b* 29 Aug. 1929; *s* of Herbert Smith Gunn, and Ann Charlotte Gunn (*née* Thomson); unmarried. *Educ:* University Coll. Sch., Hampstead; Trinity Coll., Cambridge. British Army (National Service), 1948-50; lived in Paris six months, 1950; Cambridge, 1950-53; lived in Rome, 1953-54; has lived in California since 1954. Formerly Associate Prof., English Dept, University of Calif (Berkeley). *Publications:* Poetry from Cambridge, 1953; Fighting Terms, 1954; The Sense of Movement, 1957; My Sad Captains, 1961; Selected Poems (with Ted Hughes), 1962; Five American Poets (ed with Ted Hughes), 1962; Positives (with Ander Gunn), 1966; Touch (poems), 1967; Poems 1950-1966: a selection, 1969; Moly (poems), 1971; Jack Straw's Castle and other poems, 1976; Selected Poems, 1979; The Passages of Joy, 1982; The Occasions of Poetry (ed Clive Wilmer),

1982. *Recreations:* cheap thrills. *Address:* 1216 Cole Street, San Francisco, Calif 94117, USA.

GUNN, Sir William (Archer), KBE 1961; CMG 1955; JP; Australian grazier and company director; Chairman, International Wool Secretariat, 1961–73; *b* Goodiwindi, Qld, 1 Feb. 1914; *s* of late Walter and Doris Isabel Gunn, Goodiwindi; *m* 1939, Mary (Phillipa), *d* of F. B. Haydon, Murrurundi, NSW; one *s* two *d. Educ:* The King's Sch., Parramatta, NSW. Director: Rothmans of Pall Mall (Australia) Ltd; Grazcos Co-op. Ltd; Clausen Steamship Co. (Australia) Pty Ltd; Walter Reid and Co. Ltd; Gunn Rural Management Pty Ltd; Chairman and Managing Director: Moline Pastoral Co. Pty Ltd; Roper Valley Pty Ltd; Coolibah Pty Ltd; Mataranba Pty Ltd; Unibeef Australia Pty Ltd; Gunn Development Pty Ltd; Chairman: Australian Wool Bd, 1963–72; Qld Adv. Bd, Develt Finance Corp., 1962–72; Member: Commonwealth Bank Bd, 1952–59; Qld Bd, Nat. Mutual Life Assoc., 1955–67; Reserve Bank Bd, 1959–; Aust. Meat Bd, 1953–66; Aust. Wool Bureau, 1951–63 (Chm. 1958–63); Aust. Wool Growers Council, 1947–60 (Chm. 1955–58); Graziers Federal Council of Aust., 1950–60 (Pres. 1951–54); Aust. Wool Growers and Graziers Council, 1960–65; Export Develt Council, 1962–65; Australian Wool Corp., 1973; Faculty of Veterinary Science, University of Qld, 1953–; Exec. Council, United Graziers Assoc. of Qld, 1944–69 (Pres., 1951–59; Vice-Pres., 1947–51); Aust. Wool Testing Authority, 1958–63; Council, NFU of Aust., 1951–54; CSIRO State Cttee, 1951–68; Chairman: The Wool Bureau Inc., New York, 1962–69; Trustee: Qld Cancer Fund; Australian Pastoral Research Trust, 1959–71. Coronation Medal, 1953; Golden Fleece Achievement Award (Bd of Dirs of Nat. Assoc. of Wool Manufrs of America), 1962; Award of Golden Ram (Natal Woolgrowers Assoc. of SA), 1973. *Address:* (home) 98 Windermere Road, Ascot, Qld 4007, Australia. *T:* Brisbane 268 2688; (office) Wool Exchange, 69 Eagle Street, Brisbane, Qld 4000. *T:* Brisbane 21 4044. *Clubs:* Queensland, Tattersalls, Queensland Turf (Brisbane); Union (Sydney); Australian (Melbourne).

GUNNELL, (William) John; Leader, West Yorkshire Metropolitan County Council, since 1981; *b* 1 Oct. 1933; *s* of late William Henry and Norah Gunnell; *m* 1955, Jean Louise, *d* of late Frank and of Harriet Louise Lacey; three *s* one *d. Educ:* King Edward's Sch., Birmingham; Univ. of Leeds (BSc Hons). Hospital porter, St Bartholomew's, London, 1955–57; Teacher, Leeds Modern Sch., 1959–62; Head of Science, United Nations International Sch., New York, 1962–70; Lectr, Centre for Studies in Science Education, Univ. of Leeds, 1970–. County Councillor for Hunslet, 1977–; Leader of Opposition, W Yorks MCC, 1979–81. *Publications:* Selected Experiments in Advanced Level Chemistry, 1975, and other texts (all with E. W. Jenkins). *Recreations:* music, opera, watching cricket and soccer. *Address:* 148 Ashbourne Croft, Leeds LS10 2TZ. *T:* Leeds 770592. *Clubs:* East Hunslet Labour (Leeds); Warwickshire CC; Yorkshire CC.

GUNNING, Prof. Brian Edgar Scourse, FRS 1980; FAA 1979; Professor of Developmental Biology, Australian National University, since 1974; *b* 29 Nov. 1934; *s* of William Gunning and Margaret Gunning (*née* Scourse); *m* 1964, Marion Sylvia Forsyth; two *s. Educ:* Methodist Coll., Belfast; Queen's Univ., Belfast (BSc (Hons), MSc, PhD); DSc ANU. Lecturer in Botany, 1957, Reader in Botany, 1965, Queen's Univ., Belfast. *Publications:* Ultrastructure and the Biology of Plant Cells (with Dr M. Steer), 1975; Intercellular Communication in Plants: studies on plasmodesmata (with Dr A. Robards), 1976; contribs to research jls. *Recreations:* hill walking, photography. *Address:* 29 Millen Street, Hughes, ACT 2605, Australia. *T:* (062) 812879.

GUNNING, John Edward Maitland, CBE 1960 (OBE 1945); Barrister-at-law; *b* 22 Sept. 1904; *s* of late John Elgee Gunning, Manor House, Moneymore, Co. Derry, and late Edythe, *er d* of T. J. Reeves, London; *m* 1936, Enid Katherine, *o d* of George Menhinick; two *s. Educ:* Harrow; Magdalene Coll., Cambridge. Called to Bar, Gray's Inn, 1933. Practised South Eastern Circuit, Central Criminal Court, North London Sessions, Herts and Essex Sessions. Joined Judge Advocate General's office, Oct. 1939. War of 1939–45: served BEF, France, 1939–40; N Africa, 1942–43; Italy, 1943–45 (despatches, OBE). Middle East, 1945–50; Deputy Judge Advocate Gen. with rank of Col, CMF, 1945, Middle East, 1946; Deputy Judge Advocate Gen. (Army and RAF): Germany, 1951–53, 1960–63, 1968–70; Far East, 1957–59, 1965–67; Senior Asst Judge Advocate Gen., 1965–70. *Recreations:* bridge, watching cricket, reading. *Address:* 31 Brunswick Court, Regency Street, SW1. *Clubs:* Travellers', MCC.

GUNNING, Sir Robert Charles, 8th Bt, *cr* 1778; gold-mine owner and farmer; *b* 2 Dec. 1901; *o s* of late Charles Archibald John Gunning and Beatrice Constance Purvis; *S* cousin 1950; *m* 1934, Helen Nancy, *d* of late Vice-Adm. Sir T. J. Hallet, KBE, CB; eight *s* two *d. Educ:* St Paul's Sch.; Leeds Univ. Business in the Sudan and Nigeria, 1924–33; prospecting and gold-mining in Nigeria, 1933–38; pegged first Nigerian lode gold-mine of the least importance, this in 1935 at Bin Yauri; served AA Command, 1939–46, temp. Capt. Emigrated to Alberta, 1948. Chairman: Peace River Hosp. Bd; Peace Region Mental Health Council. *Recreations:* gardening, cricket, and almost any ball game. *Heir: s* Lt-Comdr Charles Theodore Gunning, RCN [*b* 19 June 1935; *m* 1969, Sarah, *d* of Col Patrick Arthur Easton; one *d*]. *Address:* c/o Postmaster, Peace River, Alberta, Canada.

GUNSTON, Major Sir Derrick Wellesley, 1st Bt, *cr* 1938; MC; *b* 1891; *s* of late Major Bernard Hamilton Gunston, late 5th Dragoon Guards; *m* 1917, Evelyn (Gardenia), OBE 1944, *d* of Howard St George, Cam House,

Campden Hill, W8; one *s* (and *er s* killed in action 1944). *Educ:* Harrow; Trinity Coll., Cambridge. Pres. of the New Carlton Club at Cambridge; joined Irish Guards, Aug. 1914; second in command 1st Battalion Irish Guards at Armistice; War of 1939–45, Major 7th Bn Glos Regt; MP (C) Thornbury Division Glos, 1924–45; Parliamentary Private Sec. to Rt Hon. Sir Kingsley Wood, Parliamentary Sec. to the Ministry of Health in Conservative Government, 1926–29; Parliamentary Private Sec. to Rt Hon. Neville Chamberlain, Chancellor of the Exchequer, 1931–36, to Sir Edward Grigg, Joint Under-Sec. for War 1940–42. *Heir: s* Richard Wellesley Gunston [*b* 15 March 1924; *m* 1st, 1947, Elizabeth Mary (from whom he obtained a divorce, 1956), *e d* of Arthur Colegate, Hillgrove, Bembridge, IoW; one *d* ; 2nd, 1959, Mrs Joan Elizabeth Marie Coldicott (marr. diss.), *o d* of Reginald Forde, Johannesburg; one *s* ; 3rd, 1976, Veronica Elizabeth ((*née* Haines), *widow* of Captain V. G. Loyd]. *Address:* Fram Cottage, Bembridge, IoW; 14 Pelham Crescent, SW7. *Clubs:* Carlton, Pratt's; MCC; Royal Yacht Squadron (Cowes); Bembridge Sailing (Bembridge, IoW).

GUNTHER, Sir John Thomson, Kt 1975; CMG 1965; OBE 1954; MB, DTM&H Sydney; Vice-Chancellor, University of Papua and New Guinea, 1966–72; Assistant Administrator, Papua and New Guinea, 1957–66; formerly MEC and MLC, Papua and New Guinea; *b* 2 Oct. 1910; *s* of C. M. Gunther; *m* 1938; one *s* three *d. Educ:* Sydney Univ. Dir of Public Health, Papua and New Guinea, 1949–56; Levers Pacific Plantations Pty Ltd, Brit. Solomon Is, 1935–37; Chm., Med. Bd (Mt Isa, Qld), investigating Plumbism, 1938–41; MO, RAAF, 1941–46; Malariologist, RAAF, 1943; CO 1 Trop. Research Fld Unit, 1944–45; Mem. S Pacific Commn Research Coun. (Chm. 1st meeting); Chm. Select Cttee on Polit. Develt for Papua and NG; Mem. Commn on Higher Educn, Papua and NG. *Publications:* reports to govt of Qld on Plumbism, 1939–40; reports to RAAF on Malaria and Scrub Typhus. *Recreation:* gardening. *Club:* University (Sydney).

GURD, Surg. Rear-Adm. Dudley Plunket, CB 1968; Medical Officer-in-Charge, Royal Naval Hospital, Malta, 1966–69; now in private practice; *b* 18 June 1910; *s* of Frederick Plunket Gurd and Annie Jane Glenn; *m* 1939, Thérèse Marie, *d* of John and Frances Delenda, Saloninka,Greece; one *s* one *d. Educ:* Belfast Royal Academy; Queen's Univ., Belfast, MB, BCh, BAO (Hons) 1932; MD (High Commend) 1942; FRACS 1945; MCh 1959; FRCS (Eng.) 1964. Gilbert Blane Medal, 1943. Sen. Consultant and Adviser in Ophthalmology to the Navy, 1952; Warden, Ophthalmic Hosp. of St John, Jerusalem, Jordan, 1952–55. Joined RN as Surg. Lieut, 1934; Lieut-Comdr 1939; Comdr 1945; Capt. 1958; Rear-Adm. 1966; retired 1969; Served in Royal Naval Hosps at Malta, Barrow Gurney, Hong Kong, Plymouth and Haslar. QHS 1964. KStJ 1967. Hon. DSc QUB, 1969. Chevalier de l'Ordre Nationale du Viet-Nam, 1949; Gold Cross, Order of Holy Sepulchre, 1955. *Publications:* various contribs to ophthalmic literature. *Recreations:* interested in all kinds of sport and athletics, also in languages, religion and medical education. *Address:* Shanklin Lodge, Eastern Villas Road, Southsea, Hants. *T:* Portsmouth 731496. *Clubs:* Athenæum; Union (Malta); Royal Naval and Royal Albert Yacht.

GURDEN, Harold Edward; *s* of late Arthur William and late Ada Gurden; *m* 1st, Lucy Isabella Izon (*d* 1976); three *d* ; 2nd, Elizabeth Joan, *widow* of Arthur Taylor. Birmingham City Council, Selly Oak Ward, 1946–56; Pres. Birmingham and Dist Dairymen's Assoc., 1947–50; Chm. Soc. of Dairy Technology, Midland Div.; Pres.-Elect, Nat. Dairyman's Assoc., 1951; Chm., Northfield Div. Conservative Assoc., 1950–52. MP (C) Selly Oak Div. of Birmingham, 1955–Oct. 1974; Mem. of Speaker's Panel, House of Commons, 1966; Chm., Selection Cttee, House of Commons, 1970. Rector's Warden, St Margaret's Westminster, 1973–75, Dep. Rector's Warden, 1975–. *Recreations:* bridge, golf, numismatics. *Address:* 20 Portland Road, Oxford.

GURDON, family name of **Baron Cranworth.**

GURDON, John Bertrand, DPhil; FRS 1971; Member of Staff, Medical Research Council Laboratory for Molecular Biology, Cambridge, since 1972; Fellow of Churchill College, Cambridge, since 1973; Fellow of Eton College, since 1978; *b* 2 Oct. 1933; *s* of late W. N. Gurdon, DCM, formerly of Assington, Suffolk, and of late Elsie Marjorie (*née* Byass); *m* 1964, Jean Elizabeth Margaret Curtis; one *s* one *d. Educ:* Edgeborough; Eton; Christ Church, Oxford; BA 1956; DPhil 1960. Beit Memorial Fellow, 1958–61; Gosney Research Fellow, Calif. Inst. Technol., 1962; Departmental Demonstrator, Dept of Zool., Oxford, 1963–64; Lectr, Dept of Zoology, 1965–72; Research Student, Christ Church, 1962–72. Visiting Research Fellow, Carnegie Instn, Baltimore, 1965; Lectures: Dunham, Harvard, 1974; Croonian, Royal Soc., 1976; Carter-Wallace, Princeton, 1978. Foreign Associate, Nat. Acad. of Sciences, USA, 1980. Hon. Foreign Mem., Amer. Acad. of Arts and Sciences, 1978. Hon. DSc: Chicago, 1978; René Descartes, Paris, 1982. Albert Brachet Prize (Belgian Royal Academy), 1968; Scientific Medal of Zoological Soc., 1968; Feldberg Foundn Award, 1975; Paul Ehrlich Award, 1977; Nessim Habif Prize, Univ. of Geneva, 1979; CIBA Medal, Biochem. Soc., 1980. *Publications:* Control of Gene Expression in Animal Development, 1974; articles in scientific jls, especially on nuclear transplantation. *Recreations:* skiing, horticulture. *Address:* Whittlesford Grove, Whittlesford, Cambridge. *Club:* British Ski.

GURNEY, Oliver Robert, MA, DPhil Oxon; FBA 1959; Shillito Reader in Assyriology, Oxford University, 1945–78; Professor, 1965; Fellow of Magdalen College, 1963–78, now Emeritus; *b* 28 Jan. 1911; *s* of Robert

Gurney, DSc, and Sarah Gamzu, MBE, *d* of Walter Garstang, MD, MRCP; *m* 1957, Mrs Diane Hope Grazebrook (*née* Esencourt); no *c. Educ:* Eton Coll.; New Coll., Oxford. Served War of 1939-45, in Royal Artillery and Sudan Defence Force. Freeman of City of Norwich. For. Mem., Royal Danish Acad. of Sciences and Letters, 1976. *Publications:* The Hittites (Penguin), 1952; (with J. J. Finkelstein and P. Hulin) The Sultantepe Tablets, 1957, 1964; (with John Garstang) The Geography of the Hittite Empire, 1959; Ur Excavations, Texts, VII, 1974; (with S. N. Kramer) Sumerian Literary Texts in the Ashmolean Museum, 1976; Some Aspects of Hittite Religion (Schweich Lectures, 1976), 1977; articles in Annals of Archæology and Anthropology (Liverpool), Anatolian Studies, etc. *Recreations:* lawn tennis, golf. *Address:* Bayworth Corner, Boars Hill, Oxford. *T:* Oxford 735322.

GUTCH, Sir John, KCMG 1957 (CMG 1952); OBE 1947; *b* 12 July 1905; *s* of late Clement Gutch, MA, King's Coll., Cambridge, and late Isabella Margaret Newton; *m* 1938, Diana Mary Worsley; three *s. Educ:* Aldenham Sch.; Gonville and Caius Coll., Cambridge. Classical scholar, 1924; 1st class Classical Tripos, Part I, 1926; 2nd class Classical Tripos, Part II, 1927; BA 1927; MA 1931. Cadet, Colonial Administrative Service, 1928; Asst District Commissioner, Gold Coast, 1928; Asst Colonial Secretary, Gold Coast, 1935; Asst Secretary, Palestine, 1936, Principal Asst Secretary, 1944, Under Sec., 1945; Asst Sec., Middle East Department, Colonial Office, 1947; Chief Secretary, British Administration, Cyrenaica, 1948; Adviser to the Prime Minister, Government of Cyrenaica, 1949; Chief Secretary, British Guiana, 1950-54; High Commissioner for Western Pacific, 1955-60. British Electric Traction Co. Ltd, 1961-69. Governor, Aldenham School, 1964-81; Mem., Cttee of Management, Institute of Opthalmology, 1965-80 (Fellow, 1968). *Publications:* Martyr of the Islands: the life and death of John Coleridge Patteson, 1971; Beyond the Reefs: the life of John Williams, missionary, 1974. *Address:* Littleworth Cross, Seale, near Farnham, Surrey. *T:* Runfold 2081.

GUTFREUND, Prof. Herbert, FRS 1981; Professor of Physical Biochemistry, University of Bristol, since 1972; *b* 21 Oct. 1921; *s* of late Paul Peter Gutfreund and Clara Angela (*née* Pisko); *m* 1958, Mary Kathelen, *er d* of late Mr and Mrs L. J. Davies, Rugby; two *s* one *d. Educ:* Vienna; Univ. of Cambridge (PhD). Research appts at Cambridge Univ., 1947-57; Rockefeller Fellow, Yale Univ., 1951-52; part-time Research Associate, Yale Univ., 1953-58; Principal Scientific Officer, National Inst. for Research in Dairying, Univ. of Reading, 1957-65; Visiting Professor: Univ. of California, 1965; Max Planck Inst., Göttingen, 1966-67; Reader in Biochemistry and Director of Molecular Enzymology Laboratory, Univ. of Bristol, 1967-72. Visiting appointments: Univ. of Leuven, 1972; Univ. of Adelaide, 1979. *Publications:* An Introduction to the Study of Enzymes, 1966; Enzymes: Physical Principles, 1972; ed, Chemistry of Macromolecules, 1974; ed, Biochemical Evolution, 1981; papers and reviews on many aspects of physical biochemistry. *Recreations:* mountain walking in Austria, gardening, reading general literature and philosophy of science, listening to music and all other good things in life. *Address:* University of Bristol Medical School, Bristol. *T:* Bristol 24161; 12a The Avenue, Bristol BS9 1PA. *T:* Bristol 684453. *Club:* United Oxford & Cambridge University.

GUTHRIE, Rev. Donald Angus; Rector, Holy Spirit Episcopal Church, Missoula, Montana, since 1979; *b* 18 Jan. 1931; *s* of Frederick Charles and Alison Guthrie; *m* 1959, Joyce Adeline Blunsden (*d* 1976); two *s* one *d* ; *m* 1977, Lesley Josephine Boardman. *Educ:* Marlborough Coll.; Trinity Coll., Oxford (MA). Rector, St John's Church, Selkirk, 1963-69; Vice-Principal, Episcopal Theological Coll., Edinburgh, 1969-74; Priest-in-Charge, Whitburn Parish Church, Tyne and Wear, 1974-76; Provost, St Paul's Cathedral, Dundee, 1976-77; Episcopal Chaplain to Univ. of Montana, 1977-79. *Recreations:* walking, reading. *Address:* 409 Edith, Missoula, Montana 59801, USA.

GUTHRIE, Air Vice-Marshal Kenneth MacGregor, CB 1946; CBE 1944; CD 1948; retired; *b* 9 Aug. 1900; *s* of Rev. Donald and Jean Stirton Guthrie; *m* 1926, Catherine Mary Fidler; one *d. Educ:* Baltimore, USA; Montreal and Ottawa, Canada. RFC and RAF, 1917-19; RCAMC 1919-20; Canadian Air Board and RCAF since 1920. Asst Director of Military and Air Force Intelligence, General Staff, Ottawa, 1935-38; CO, RCAF Station, Rockcliffe, 1938-39; Senior Air Staff Officer, Eastern Air Command, 1939-41; CO, RCAF Station, Gander, Nfld, 1941; Air Officer i/c Administration, Western Air Command, 1942; Deputy Air Member Air Staff (Plans) AFHQ, Dec. 1942-44; AOC Northwest Air Command, RCAF, 1944-49. Retired, 1949. Legion of Merit (USA), 1946. *Recreations:* hunting, fishing, gardening. *Address:* 506, 9915-115 Street, Edmonton, Alberta T5K 1S5, Canada. *Club:* United Services Institute (Edmonton and Victoria).

GUTHRIE, Sir Malcolm (Connop), 3rd Bt *cr* 1936; *b* 16 Dec. 1942; *s* of Sir Giles Connop McEacharn Guthrie, 2nd Bt, OBE, DSC, and of Rhona, *d* of late Frederic Stileman; *S* father, 1979; *m* 1967, Victoria, *o d* of late Brian Willcock; one *s* one *d. Educ:* Millfield. *Heir: s* Giles Malcolm Welcome Guthrie, *b* 16 Oct. 1972. *Address:* Brent Eleigh, Belbroughton, Stourbridge, Worcs.

GUTHRIE, Robert Isles Loftus; Director, Joseph Rowntree Memorial Trust, since 1979; *b* 27 June 1937; *s* of late Prof. W. K. C. Guthrie, FBA and of Adele Marion Ogilvy, MA; *m* 1963, Sarah Julia Weltman; two *s* one *d. Educ:* Clifton Coll.; Trinity Coll., Cambridge (MA); Liverpool Univ. (CertEd); LSE (MScEcon). Head of Cambridge House (Univ. settlement in S London);

1962-69; teacher, ILEA, 1964-66; Social Develt Officer, Peterborough Develt Corp., 1969-75; Asst Dir, Social Work Service, DHSS, 1975-79. Mem., expedns in Anatolia, British Inst. of Archaeol. at Ankara, 1958-62. Member: Arts Council of GB, 1979-81 (Regional Cttee, 1976-81); Council, Policy Studies Institute, 1979-. FRSA. *Publications:* (ed) Outlook, 1963; (ed) Outlook Two, 1965; articles, esp. in New Society. *Recreations:* music, mountains, travel, sheep. *Address:* Braeside, Acomb, York YO2 4EZ. *Club:* United Oxford & Cambridge University.

GUTHRIE, Roy David, (Gus), PhD, DSc; CChem, FRSC, FRACI; Secretary General, Royal Society of Chemistry, since 1982; *b* 29 March 1934; *s* of David Ephraim Guthrie and Ethel (*née* Kimmins); *m* 1st, 1956, Ann Hoad (marr. diss. 1981); three *s* ; 2nd, 1982, Lyn Fielding. *Educ:* Dorking Grammar Sch.; King's Coll., Univ. of London (BSc, PhD, DSc). Shirley Inst., Manchester, 1958-60; Asst Lectr, then Lectr, Univ. of Leicester, 1960-63; Lectr, then Reader, Univ. of Sussex, 1963-73; Griffith Univ., Brisbane: Foundation Prof. of Chemistry, 1973-81; Inaugural Chm., School of Science, 1973-78; Pro-Vice-Chancellor, 1980-81; Professor Emeritus, 1982. Hon. DUniv. Griffith, 1981. Professor Emeritus Griffith University 1982. *Publications:* An Introduction to the Chemistry of Carbohydrates (with J. Honeyman), 3rd edn 1974; over 120 scientific papers. *Recreations:* Badminton, theatre. *Address:* Royal Society of Chemistry, Burlington House, Piccadilly, W1V 0BN. *T:* 01-734 9971.

GUTHRIE, Hon. Sir Rutherford (Campbell), Kt 1968; CMG 1960; *b* 28 Nov. 1899; *s* of late Thomas O. Guthrie, Rich Avon, Donald; *m* 1927, Rhona Mary McKellar, *d* of late T. McKellar; one *s* (and one *s* decd). *Educ:* Melbourne Church of England Grammar Sch.; Jesus Coll., Cambridge (BA). Farmer and grazier, Skipton, Victoria. Served European War of 1914-18 and War of 1939-45 (wounded, despatches): 9 Australian Div., El Alamein. MP Ripon, Victoria, 1947-50; Minister for Lands and for Soldier Settlement, 1948-50. *Recreations:* fishing and golf. *Address:* Jedburgh Cottage, Howey Street, Gisborne, Vic. 3437, Australia. *Clubs:* Melbourne, Naval and Military; Royal Melbourne Golf; Hawks, Pitt (Cambridge); Leander (Henley on Thames).

GUTTERIDGE, Joyce Ada Cooke, CBE 1962; retired; *b* 10 July 1906; *d* of late Harold Cooke Gutteridge, QC, and late Mary Louisa Gutteridge (*née* Jackson). *Educ:* Roedean Sch.; Somerville Coll., Oxford. Called to the Bar, Middle Temple, Nov. 1938. Served in HM Forces (ATS), War of 1939-45. Foreign Office: Legal Assistant, 1947-50; Asst Legal Adviser, 1950-60; Legal Counsellor, 1960-61; Counsellor (Legal Adviser), UK Mission to the United Nations, 1961-64; Legal Counsellor, FO, 1964-66; re-employed on legal duties, FO, 1966-67. Hon. LLD, Western College for Women, Oxford, Ohio, 1963. *Publications:* The United Nations in a Changing World, 1970; articles in British Year Book of International Law and International and Comparative Law Quarterly. *Recreations:* reading, travel. *Address:* 8 Westberry Court, Grange Road, Cambridge CB3 9BG. *Club:* University Women's.

GUY, Geoffrey Colin, CMG 1964; CVO 1966; OBE 1962 (MBE 1957); farmer; Governor and Commander in Chief, St Helena and its Dependancies, 1976-80, retired; *b* 4 Nov. 1921; *s* of late E. Guy, 14 Woodland Park Road, Headingley, Leeds, and of Constance Reed Guy (*née* Taylor); *m* 1946, Joan Elfreda Smith; one *s. Educ:* Chatham House Sch., Ramsgate; Brasenose Coll., Oxford. Served as Pilot, RAF, 1941-46, Middle East and Burma (Flight Lieut). Colonial Administrative Service, Sierra Leone: Cadet, 1951; District Commissioner, 1955; seconded Administrator, Turks and Caicos Islands, 1958-65; Administrator, Dominica, 1965-67, Governor, March-Nov. 1967; Sec., Forces Help Soc. and Lord Roberts' Workshops, 1970-73; Administrator, Ascension Island, 1973-76. *Recreations:* swimming, riding. *Address:* Tamarisk Cottage, Kirk Hammerton, York; Farm Lodge, St Helena, South Atlantic. *Clubs:* Royal Commonwealth Society, Royal Air Force.

GUY, Leslie George; General Secretary, National Union of Sheet Metal Workers, since 1977; *b* 1 Sept. 1918; *s* of Albert and Annie Guy; *m* 1940, Audrey Doreen (*née* Symonds); two *d. Educ:* secondary modern school. National Union of Sheet Metal Workers: shop steward; Member: Branch and District Cttees; Nat. Executive Cttee; National President, June 1972-74; Asst General Secretary, 1974-77. Member: General Council, TUC, 1977-; Exec., CSEU, 1977-; Engrg Industry Trng Bd, 1979-. *Recreations:* work and politics. *Address:* 75-77 West Heath Road, NW3 7TL. *T:* 01-455 0053.

GUY, Lt-Comdr Robert Lincoln, MVO 1980; RN; *b* 4 Sept. 1947; *s* of late John Guy and Susan Guy; *m* 1981, Rosemary Ann Walker. *Educ:* Radley Coll. Entered BRNC Dartmouth, 1966; ADC to Governor and Commander-in-Chief, Gibraltar, 1973; commanded: HMS Ashton, 1974; HMS Kedleston, 1975; Equerry to the Queen, 1977-80; First Lieut, HMS Antelope, 1981-82. Lieut 1971; Lt-Comdr 1979. *Recreations:* polo, skiing, shooting. *Address:* Stable House, South Warnborough, Basingstoke, Hants. *T:* Long Sutton 254. *Club:* Army and Navy.

GUY, Lt-Gen. Sir Roland (Kelvin), KCB 1981; CBE 1978 (MBE 1955); DSO 1972; Military Secretary, since 1980; *b* 25 June 1928; *s* of Lt-Col Norman Greenwood Guy and Mrs Edna Guy; *m* 1957, Dierdre, *d* of Brig. P. H. Graves Morris, DSO, MC, and Mrs Auriol Graves-Morris; two *d. Educ:* Wellington Coll.; RMA Sandhurst. Commnd KRRC, 1948; 1950-71: Signals Officer, Germany; Adjt Kenya Regt, and 2 KRRC; Weapon Trng Officer 1 KRRC; Staff Coll., Camberley; MoD; Co. Comdr 2 RGJ; DS Staff Coll.; Bn 2 i/c;

Mil. Asst to Adjt Gen.; CO 1 RGJ; Col GS HQ Near East Land Forces, 1971; Comd 24 Airportable Bde, 1972; RCDS, 1975; Principal SO to CDS, 1976-78; Chief of Staff, HQ BAOR, 1978-80; served in Kenya, Libya, British Guiana, Cyprus, Malaysia, W Germany and Berlin. Col Comdt: 1st Bn Royal Green Jackets, 1981-; Small Arms School Corps, 1981-. *Recreations:* music, skiing, golf, gardening. *Address:* c/o Grindlays Bank, 13 St James's Square, SW1. *Club:* Army and Navy.

GUYATT, Richard Gerald Talbot, CBE 1969; Rector, Royal College of Art, 1978-81 (Pro-Rector, 1974-78; Professor of Graphic Arts, 1948-78); *b* 8 May 1914; *s* of Thomas Guyatt, sometime HM Consul, Vigo, Spain and Cecil Guyatt; *m* 1941, Elizabeth Mary Corsellis; one step *d. Educ:* Charterhouse. Freelance designer: posters for Shell-Mex and BP, 1935. War Service: Regional Camouflage Officer for Scotland, Min. of Home Security. Dir and Chief Designer, Cockade Ltd, 1946-48; Co-designer of Lion and Unicorn Pavilion, Festival of Britain, 1951; Consultant Designer to: Josiah Wedgwood & Sons, 1952-55, 1967-70; Central Electricity Generating Bd, 1964-68; British Sugar Bureau, 1965-68; W. H. Smith, 1970-. Vis. Prof., Yale Univ., 1955 and 1962. Ceramic Designs for Min. of Works (for British Embassies), King's Coll. Cambridge, Goldsmiths' Co. and Wedgwood commem. mugs for Coronation, 1953, Investiture, 1969 and Royal Silver Wedding, 1973. Designed: silver medal for Royal Mint, Mint Dirs Conf., 1972; 700th Anniv. of Parlt stamp, 1965; Postal Order forms, 1964 for Post Office; Silver Jubilee stamps, 1977; commem. crown piece for 80th birthday of HM Queen Elizabeth The Queen Mother, 1980. Member: Stamp Adv. Cttee, 1963-74; Internat. Jury, Warsaw Poster Biennale, 1968; Bank of England Design Adv. Cttee, 1968-; Adv. Council, Victoria and Albert Mus., 1978-81. Chm., Guyatt/Jenkins Design Group. Governor, Imperial Coll. of Sci. and Technol., 1979-81. FSIA; Hon. ARCA. *Address:* Flat 1, 5 Onslow Square, SW7. *T:* 01-584 5398; Forge Cottage, Ham, Marlborough, Wilts. *T:* Inkpen 270.

GUYMER, Maurice Juniper, OBE 1982; DL; JP; Metropolitan Stipendiary Magistrate, since 1967; *b* 29 Aug. 1914; *s* of Frank and Florence Mary Guymer. *Educ:* Northcliffe House, Bognor Regis; Westminster School. Admitted Solicitor, 1936. Served with RAF, 1940-45. Chm., Inner London Juvenile Courts, 1967-76. Royal Borough of Kingston upon Thames: Council, 1953; Mayor, 1959-60 and 1960-61; Alderman, 1960-65; JP 1956. DL, Co. Surrey, 1960. Chm., Bd of Visitors, Latchmere House Remand Centre, 1969- (Mem., 1958-). Chm., Kingston and Malden District Scout Council, 1962-76, Pres., 1976-. *Address:* Desborough Cottage, 132 Lower Ham Road, Kingston upon Thames, Surrey. *T:* 01-546 5529.

GWANDU, Emir of; Alhaji Haruna, (Muhammadu Basharu), CFR 1965; CMG 1961; CBE 1955; 18th Emir of Gwandu, 1954; Member, North Western State House of Chiefs, and Council of Chiefs; Member, and Chairman, Executive Council, State Self-Development Funds Council; President, former Northern Nigeria House of Chiefs, since 1957 (Deputy President 1956); *b* Batoranke, 1913; *m* 1933; fifteen *c. Educ:* Birnin Kebbi Primary Sch.; Katsina Training Coll. Teacher: Katsina Teachers Coll., 1933-35; Sokoto Middle Sch., 1935-37; Gusau Local Authority Sub-Treasurer, 1937-43; Gwandu Local Authority Treasurer, 1943-45; District Head, Kalgo, 1945-54. Member former N Reg. Marketing Board. *Recreations:* hunting, shooting. *Address:* Emir's Palace, PO Box 1, Birnin Kebbi, North Western State, Nigeria.

GWILLIAM, John Albert, MA Cantab; Headmaster of Birkenhead School, since Sept. 1963; *b* 28 Feb. 1923; *s* of Thomas Albert and Adela Audrey Gwilliam; *m* 1949, Pegi Lloyd George; three *s* two *d. Educ:* Monmouth Sch.; Trinity Coll., Cambridge. Assistant Master: Trinity Coll., Glenalmond, 1949-52; Bromsgrove Sch., 1952-56; Head of Lower Sch., Dulwich Coll., 1956-63. *Address:* The Lodge, Beresford Road, Birkenhead, Merseyside.

GWILLIAM, Prof. Kenneth Mason, FCIT; Professor of Transport Economics, University of Leeds, since 1967; Director, National Bus Company, since 1978; *b* 27 June 1937; *s* of John and Marjorie Gwilliam; *m* 1961, Jennifer Mary Bell; two *s. Educ:* Magdalen Coll., Oxford (BA 1st Cl. Hons PPE). Res. Asst, Fisons Ltd, 1960-61; Lecturer: Univ. of Nottingham, 1961-65; Univ. of E Anglia, 1965-67. Editor, Jl of Transport Economics and Policy. *Publications:* Transport and Public Policy, 1964; (jtly) Criteria for Investment in Transport Infrastructure, 1973; Economics and Transport Policy, 1975. *Recreations:* badminton, tennis. *Address:* 53 Primley Park Avenue, Alwoodley, Leeds LS17 7HX. *T:* Leeds 681183.

GWILT, George David, FFA; General Manager and Actuary, Standard Life Assurance Company, since 1979; *b* 11 Nov. 1927; *s* of Richard Lloyd Gwilt and Marjory Gwilt (*née* Mair); *m* 1956, Ann Dalton Sylvester; three *s. Educ:* Sedbergh Sch.; St John's Coll., Cambridge (MA). FFA 1952; FBCS. Joined Standard Life Assurance Co., 1949; Asst Official, 1956; Asst Actuary, 1957; Statistician, 1962; Mechanisation Manager, 1964; Systems Manager, 1969; Dep. Pensions Manager, 1972; Pensions Actuary, 1973; Asst General Manager and Pensions Manager, 1977; Asst Gen. Man. (Finance), 1978. Trustee, TSB of South of Scotland, 1966-. Pres., Faculty of Actuaries, 1981-. *Recreation:* flute playing. *Address:* 39 Oxgangs Road, Edinburgh EH10 7BE. *T:* 031-445 1266. *Clubs:* Royal Air Force; New (Edinburgh).

GWYNEDD, Viscount; David Richard Owen Lloyd George; *b* 22 Jan. 1951; *s* and *heir* of 3rd Earl Lloyd George of Dwyfor, qv. *Educ:* Eton. *Address:* 43 Cadogan Square, SW1; Brimpton Mill, near Reading, Berks.

GWYNN, Edward Harold, CB 1961; Deputy Under-Secretary of State, Ministry of Defence, 1966-72; retired 1972; *b* 23 Aug. 1912; *y s* of late Dr E. J. Gwynn, Provost of Trinity Coll., Dublin, and late Olive Ponsonby; *m* 1937, Dorothy, *d* of late Geoffrey S. Phillpotts, Foxrock, Co. Dublin; one *s* four *d. Educ:* Sedbergh School; TCD. Entered Home Office, 1936; Assistant Secretary, 1947; Assistant Under Secretary of State, 1956; Principal Finance Officer (Under-Secretary), Ministry of Agriculture, 1961-62; Deputy Under-Secretary of State, Home Office, 1963-66. *Recreations:* gardening, the countryside. *Address:* The Chestnuts, Minchinhampton, Glos. *T:* Nailsworth 2863.

GWYNN-JONES, Peter Llewellyn; Lancaster Herald of Arms, since 1982; *b* 12 March 1940; *s* of late Major Jack Llewellyn Gwynn-Jones, Cape Town, and late Mary Muriel Daphne, *d* of Col Arthur Patrick Bird Harrison, and step *s* of late Lt-Col Gavin David Young, Long Burton, Dorset. *Educ:* Wellington Coll.; Trinity Coll., Cambridge (MA). Assistant to Garter King of Arms, 1970; Bluemantle Pursuivant of Arms, 1973; Secretary, Harleian Society, 1981; House Comptroller of College of Arms, 1982. *Recreations:* antiques, tropical forests, wild life conservation, fishing. *Address:* Spring House, Long Burton, Sherborne, Dorset. *T:* Holnest 240; 79 Harcourt Terrace, SW10. *T:* 01-373 5859.

GWYNNE-EVANS, Sir Ian William, 3rd Bt, *cr* 1913; Deputy Chairman, Real Estate Corporation of South Africa Ltd, 1973-79 (Managing Director and Chairman, 1950-73); Director, Grootvlei (Proprietary) Mines Ltd, retired 1982; *b* 21 Feb. 1909; *er s* of Sir Evan Gwynne-Evans, 2nd Bt; *S* father, 1959; *m* 1st, 1935, Elspeth Collins (marr. diss.); two *d*; 2nd, 1946, Monica Dalrymple. *Educ:* Royal Naval College, Dartmouth. Entered Royal Navy as Cadet, 1922; retired as Lieut, 1934. Served War, 1940-45, Lieut, Royal Navy. *Recreation:* bowls. *Heir: b* Francis Loring Gwynne-Evans [*b* 22 Feb. 1914; *m* 1st, 1937, Elisabeth Fforde (marr. diss., 1958), *d* of J. Fforde Tipping; two *s* one *d*; 2nd, 1958, Gloria Marie Reynolds; two *s* three *d*]. *Address:* Ivy Farm, St John, Jersey, CI. *Clubs:* Garrick; Victoria (Jersey); Rand (Johannesburg).

GWYNNE JONES, family name of **Baron Chalfont.**

GWYTHER, (Arthur) David; Inspector General, Insolvency Service, Department of Trade, since 1981; *b* 8 Dec. 1924; *s* of late Arthur James Gwyther and of Lily Elizabeth Gwyther; *m* 1949, Agnes, (Nan), Boyd; one *s* two *d. Educ:* Sutton High Sch. for Boys, Plymouth. Dept of Trade Insolvency Service: Asst Examiner, 1948; Examiner, 1951; Assistant Official Receiver: Brighton, 1955; Southampton, 1957; Official Receiver, Plymouth, 1959; Inspector of Official Receivers, 1961; Official Receiver, Birmingham, 1965; Dep. Inspector Gen., 1976. *Recreation:* gardening. *Address:* Tarnhow, 65 Abbots Lane, Kenley, Surrey CR2 5JG. *T:* 01-668 6145.

GYÖRGYI, Albert S.; *see* Szent-Györgyi.

H

HABAKKUK, Sir John (Hrothgar), Kt 1976; FBA 1965; Principal of Jesus College, Oxford, since 1967; a Pro Vice-Chancellor, University of Oxford, since 1977; President, University College, Swansea, since 1975; *b* 13 May 1915; *s* of Evan Guest and Anne Habakkuk; *m* 1948, Mary Richards; one *s* three *d. Educ:* Barry County Sch.; St John's Coll., Cambridge (scholar and Strathcona student), Hon. Fellow 1971. Historical Tripos: Part I, First Class, 1935; Part II, First Class (with distinction), 1936; Fellow, Pembroke Coll., Cambridge, 1938-50, Hon. Fellow 1973; Director of Studies in History and Librarian, 1946-50. Temporary Civil Servant: Foreign Office, 1940-42, Board of Trade, 1942-46. University Lecturer in Faculty of Economics, Cambridge, 1946-50; Chichele Prof. of Economic History, Oxford, and Fellow of All Souls Coll., 1950-67; Vice-Chancellor, Oxford Univ., 1973-77. Visiting Lecturer, Harvard University, 1954-55; Ford Research Professor, University of California, Berkeley, 1962-63. Member: Grigg Cttee on Departmental Records, 1952-54; Advisory Council on Public Records, 1958-70; SSRC, 1967-71; Nat. Libraries Cttee, 1968-69; Royal Comnn on Historic Manuscripts, 1978-; Admin. Bd, Internat. Assoc. of Univs, 1975-. Chairman: Cttee of Vice Chancellors and Principals of Univs of UK, 1976-77; Adv. Gp on London Health Servs, 1980-81; Oxfordshire DHA, 1981-. Pres., RHistS, 1976-80. Foreign Member: Amer. Phil. Soc.; Amer. Acad. of Arts and Sciences. Hon. DLitt: Wales, 1971; Cambridge, 1973; Pennsylvania, 1975; Kent, 1978. *Publications:* American and British Technology in the Nineteenth Century, 1962; Population Growth and Economic Development since 1750, 1971; articles and reviews. *Address:* The Lodgings, Jesus College, Oxford. *T:* Oxford 48140.

HABGOOD, Rt. Rev. John Stapylton; *see* Durham, Bishop of.

HACAULT, Most Rev. Antoine; *see* St Boniface, Archbishop of, (R.C.).

HACKER, Alan Ray; clarinettist and conductor; Lecturer in Music, York University, since 1976; *b* 30 Sept. 1938; *s* of Kenneth and Sybil Hacker; *m* 1st, 1959, Anna Maria Sroka; two *d*; 2nd, 1977, Karen Evans; one *s. Educ:* Dulwich Coll.; Royal Academy of Music. FRAM. Joined LPO, 1958; Prof., RAM, 1960-76. Founded: Pierrot Players (with S. Pruslin and H. Birtwistle), 1965; Matrix, 1971; Music Party for authentic performance of classical music, 1972; Classical Orch., 1977. First modern "authentic" perfs, 1977-81, incl: Mozart's Symphonies 39, 40; Beethoven's Symphonies 3, 7, 9; Haydn's Harmonie and Creation Masses. Revived basset clarinet and restored orig. text, Mozart's concerto and quintet, 1967; revived baroque clarinet (hitherto unplayed), 1975. Premieres of music by Birtwistle, Boulez, Feldman, Goehr, Maxwell Davies, Stockhausen, Blake and Mellers. Sir Robert Mayer Lectr, Leeds Univ., 1972-73. Mem. Fires of London, 1970-76; Dir, York Early Music Festival. Many recordings. *Publications:* Scores of Mozart Concerto and Quintet, 1972; 1st edn of reconstructed Mozart Concerto, 1973; book on rediscovering the Classical Style through the instruments, in preparation. *Recreation:* cookery. *Address:* University of York, Heslington, York YO1 5DD.

HACKER, Rt. Rev. George Lanyon; *see* Penrith, Bishop Suffragan of.

HACKER, Prof. Louis M., MA (Columbia); Emeritus Professor of Economics, Columbia University, USA, 1967 (Economics Department, 1935); Dean of School of General Studies, 1952-58, Director, 1949-52; Professor of Economics, 1948-67); *b* 17 March 1899; *s* of Morris Hacker; *m* 1st, 1921, Lillian Lewis (*d* 1952); one *s* one *d.*; 2nd, 1953, Beatrice Larson Brennan (*d* 1977). *Educ:* Columbia Coll.; Columbia University. Assistant and contributing Editor of New International Encyclopædia, Social Science Encyclopædia, Columbia Encyclopædia; taught economics and history at University of Wisconsin, Ohio State University, Utah State Agricultural College, University of Hawaii, Yeshiva University, Penn State University, Univ. of Puget Sound, Army War College, National War College. Executive sec. American Academic Freedom Study; Editor, American Century Series; Chairman, Academic Freedom Cttee, American Civil Liberties Union, resigned 1968; Guggenheim Fellow, 1948, 1959; Relm Foundation Fellow, 1967. Harmsworth Professor of American History, Oxford Univ., 1948-49; Lecturer, Fulbright Conference on American Studies, Cambridge, 1952. Visiting Distinguished Professor of Economics, Fairleigh Dickinson, 1967-68. Fellow, Queen's Coll., Oxford, and MA (Oxon); Benjamin Franklin Fellow of RSA; Hon. LLD Hawaii; Hon. LHD Columbia. Students Army Training Corps, 1918. *Publications:* (with B. B. Kendrick) United States since 1865, 1932, 4th edn 1949; The Farmer is Doomed, 1933; Short History of the New Deal, 1934; The US: a Graphic History, 1937; American Problems of Today, 1939; Triumph of American Capitalism, 1940; (with Allan Nevins) The US and Its Place in World Affairs, 1943; The Shaping of the American Tradition, 1947; New Industrial Relations (jointly), 1948; Government Assistance and the British Universities (jointly), 1952; (with H. S. Zahler) The United States in the 20th Century, 1952; Capitalism and the Historians (jointly), 1954; Alexander Hamilton in the American Tradition, 1957; American Capitalism, 1957; Larger View of the University, 1961; Major Documents in American Economic History, 2 vols, 1961; The World of Andrew Carnegie, Part 1, 1861-1901, 1968; The Course of American Economic Growth and Development, 1970; (with M. D. Hirsch) Proskauer: his life and times, 1978; contributions to learned journals and reviews. *Recreations:* walking, bridge, travel. *Address:* 430 W 116th Street, New York, NY 10027, USA. *Clubs:* Athenæum (London); Faculty, Columbia University (New York); Pilgrims (USA).

HACKETT, Prof. Brian; Professor of Landscape Architecture, University of Newcastle upon Tyne, 1967-77, now Emeritus Professor; *b* 3 Nov. 1911; *s* of Henry and Ida Adeline Mary Hackett; *m* 1st, 1942, Frederica Claire Grundy (*d* 1979); one *s* two *d*; 2nd, 1980, Dr Elizabeth Ratcliff. *Educ:* Grammar Sch., Burton-on-Trent; Birmingham Sch. of Architecture; Sch. of Planning for Regional Development, London. MA Dunelm, PPILA, RIBA, MRTPI. Professional experience, 1930-40; Flt-Lt, RAFVR, 1941-45; Lectr, Sch. of Planning for Regional Develt, London, 1945-47; Univ. of Durham: Lectr in Town and Country Planning, 1947; Lectr in Landscape Architecture, 1948, Sen. Lectr, 1949-59; Vis. Prof. of Landscape Architecture, Univ. of Illinois, 1960-61; Reader in Landscape Arch., Univ. of Newcastle upon Tyne, 1962-66. Mem., Water Space Amenity Commn, 1973-80. Pres., Inst. of Landscape Architects, 1967-68; Hon. Corresp. Mem., Amer. Soc. of Landscape Architects, 1962. European Prize for Nature Conservation and Landscape Develt, 1975. *Publications:* Man, Society and Environment, 1950; (jtly) Landscape Techniques, 1967; Landscape Planning, 1971; Steep Slopes Landscape, 1971; (jtly) Landscape Reclamation, 1971-72; (jtly) Landscape Reclamation Practice, 1977; Planting Design, 1979; Landscape Conservation, 1980; numerous papers in internat. jls. *Recreation:* musical performance. *Address:* 27 Larkspur Terrace, Jesmond, Newcastle upon Tyne NE2 2DT. *T:* Newcastle upon Tyne 810747. *Club:* Royal Commonwealth Society.

HACKETT, Prof. Cecil Arthur, MA Cantab, Docteur de l'Université de Paris; Professor of French, University of Southampton, 1952-70, now Professor Emeritus; *b* 19 Jan. 1908; *s* of Henry Hackett and Alice Setchell; *m* 1942, Mary Hazel Armstrong. *Educ:* King's Norton Grammar Sch., Birmingham; University of Birmingham; Emmanuel Coll., Cambridge (Scholar and Prizeman). Assistant d'Anglais, Lycée Louis-le-Grand, Paris, 1934-36; Lecturer in French and English, Borough Road Coll., Isleworth, 1936-39. Served War of 1939-45: enlisted 1/8th Bn Middlesex Regt, 1939.

Education Representative, British Council, Paris, 1945-46; Lecturer in French, University of Glasgow, 1947-52. Chevalier de la Légion d'Honneur. *Publications:* Le Lyrisme de Rimbaud, 1938; Rimbaud l'Enfant, 1948; An Anthology of Modern French Poetry, 1952, 4th edn 1976; Rimbaud, 1957; Autour de Rimbaud, 1967; (ed and introd) New French Poetry: an anthology, 1973; Rimbaud, a critical introduction, 1981; contributions to English and French Reviews. *Address:* Shawford Close, Shawford, Winchester, Hants. *T:* Twyford 713506.

HACKETT, Dennis William; publishing and communications consultant; TV critic, The Times; *b* 5 Feb. 1929; *s* of James Joseph Hackett and Sarah Ellen Hackett (*née* Bedford); *m* 1st, 1953, Agnes Mary Collins; two *s* one *d*; 2nd, 1974, Jacqueline Margaret Totterdell; one *d. Educ:* De La Salle College, Sheffield. Served with RN, 1947-49. Sheffield Telegraph, 1945-47 and 1949-54; Daily Herald, 1954; Odhams Press, 1954; Deputy Editor, Illustrated, 1955-58; Daily Express, 1958-60; Daily Mail, 1960; Art Editor, Observer, 1961-62; Deputy Editor, 1962, Editor, 1964-65, Queen; Editor, Nova, 1965-69; Publisher, Twentieth Century Magazine, 1965-72; Editorial Dir, George Newnes Ltd, 1966-69; Dir, IPC Newspapers, 1969-71; Associate Editor, Daily Express, 1973-74. Chm., Design and Art Directors' Assoc., 1967-68. *Publications:* The History of the Future: Bemrose Corporation 1826-1976, 1976; The Big Idea: the story of Ford in Europe, 1978. *Recreations:* reading, walking. *Address:* 4 East Heath Road, NW3 1BN. *Club:* Royal Automobile.

HACKETT, John Wilkings; Director, Financial, Fiscal and Enterprise Affairs, Organisation for Economic Co-operation and Development, Paris, since 1979; *b* 21 Jan. 1924; *s* of Albert and Bertha Hackett; *m* 1952, Anne-Marie Le Brun. *Educ:* LSE (BSc(Econ) 1950); Institut d'Etudes Politiques, Paris (Diplôme 1952); Univ. of Paris (Dr d'état ès sciences economiques 1957). Served RN, 1942-46. Economic research, 1952-57; OECD, 1958-. *Publications:* Economic Planning in France (with A.-M. Hackett), 1963; L'Economie Britannique—problèmes et perspectives, 1966; (with A.-M. Hackett) The British Economy, 1967; articles on economic subjects in British and French economic jls. *Recreations:* music, painting, reading. *Address:* 48 rue de la Bienfaisance, 75008 Paris, France. *T:* 562 2170.

HACKETT, Gen. Sir John Winthrop, GCB 1967 (KCB 1962; CB 1958); CBE 1953 (MBE 1938); DSO 1942 and Bar 1945; MC 1941; BLitt, MA Oxon; FRSL 1982; Principal of King's College, London, 1968-July 1975; *b* 5 Nov. 1910; *s* of late Sir John Winthrop Hackett, KCMG, LLD, Perth, WA; *m* 1942, Margaret, *d* of Joseph Frena, Graz, Austria; one *d* (and two adopted step *d*). *Educ:* Geelong Grammar Sch., Australia; New Coll., Oxford, Hon. Fellow 1972. Regular Army, commissioned 8th KRI Hussars, 1931; Palestine, 1936 (despatches); seconded to Transjordan Frontier Force, 1937-41 (despatches twice); Syria, 1941 (wounded); Sec. Commn of Control Syria and Lebanon; GSO2 9th Army; Western Desert, 1942 (wounded); GSO1 Raiding Forces GHQ, MELF; Comdr 4th Parachute Brigade, 1943; Italy, 1943 (despatches); Arnhem, 1944 (wounded); Comdr Transjordan Frontier Force, 1947; idc 1951; DQMG, BAOR, 1952; Comdr 20th Armoured Bde, 1954; GOC 7th Armoured Div., 1956-58; Comdt, Royal Mil. Coll. of Science, 1958-61; GOC-in-C, Northern Ireland Command, 1961-63; Dep. Chief of Imperial Gen. Staff, 1963-64; Dep. Chief of the Gen. Staff, Ministry of Defence, 1964-66. Comdr-in-Chief, British Army of the Rhine, and Comdr Northern Army Gp, 1966-68. ADC (Gen.), 1967-68. Col. Commandant, REME, 1961-66; Hon. Col: 10th Bn The Parachute Regt, TA, 1965-67; 10th Volunteer Bn, The Parachute Regt, 1967-73; Oxford Univ. Officers Training Corps, 1967-78; Col, Queen's Royal Irish Hussars, 1969-75. Mem., Lord Chancellor's Cttee on Reform of Law of Contempt, 1971-74; Mem., Disciplinary Tribunal, Inns of Court and Bar. Vis. Prof. in Classics, KCL, 1977-80. Lectures: Lees Knowles, Cambridge, 1961; Basil Henriques Meml, 1970; Harmon Meml, USAF Acad., 1970; Jubilee, Imperial Coll., 1979. President: UK Classical Assoc., 1971; English Assoc., 1973-74. Hon. Liveryman, Worshipful Company of Dyers, 1975; Freeman of City of London, 1976. Hon. LLD: Queen's Univ. Belfast; Perth, WA, 1963; Exeter, 1977. FKC, 1968; Hon. Fellow St George's Coll., University of Western Australia, 1965. *Publications:* I Was a Stranger, 1977; (jtly) The Third World War, 1978; (jtly) The Untold Story, 1982; articles and reviews. *Address:* Coberley Mill, Cheltenham, Glos GL53 9NH. *T:* Coberley 207. *Clubs:* Cavalry and Guards, Carlton, United Oxford & Cambridge University, White's.

HACKING, family name of **Baron Hacking.**

HACKING, 3rd Baron *cr* 1945, of Chorley; **Douglas David Hacking;** Bt 1938; Solicitor of Supreme Court of England and Wales; Attorney and Counselor-at-Law of State of New York; *b* 17 April 1938; *er s* of 2nd Baron Hacking, and of Daphne Violet, *e d* of late R. L. Finnis; *S* father, 1971; *m* 1982, Dr Tessa M. Hunt, MB, MRCP, FFARCS, *er d* of Roland C. C. Hunt, *qv*; (two *s* one *d* by former marriage). *Educ:* Aldro School, Shackleford; Charterhouse School; Clare College, Cambridge (BA 1961, MA 1968). Called to the Bar, Middle Temple, Nov. 1963 (Astbury and Harmsworth Scholarships). Served in RN, 1956-58; Ordinary Seaman, 1956; Midshipman, 1957; served in HMS Ark Royal (N Atlantic), 1957; HMS Hardy (Portland) and HMS Brocklesby (Portland and Gibraltar), 1958; transferred RNR as Sub-Lt, 1958, on completion of National Service; transf. List 3 RNR, HMS President, 1961; Lieut 1962; retired RNR, 1964. Barrister-at-Law, 1963-76; in practice, Midland and Oxford Circuits, 1964-75. Admitted to State and

Federal Bar, New York State, 1975; admitted Solicitor of Supreme Court, 1977; with Simpson, Thacher and Bartlett, NYC, 1975-76; with Lovell, White and King, 1976-79. Member: Amer. Bar Assoc.; NY State Bar Assoc.; Bar Assoc. of City of New York. Pres., Assoc. of Lancastrians in London, 1971-72. Apprenticed to Merchant Taylors' Co., 1955, admitted to Freedom, 1962; Freedom, City of London, 1962. FCIArb 1979. *Recreations:* squash, walking. *Heir: s* Hon. Douglas Francis Hacking, *b* 8 Aug. 1968. *Address:* 20 Hanover Gardens, The Oval, SE11; Richards Butler & Co., 5 Clifton Street, EC2A 4DQ. *T:* 01-247 6555. *Clubs:* MCC; Century (NY).

HACKNEY, Archdeacon of; *see* Sharpley, Ven. R. E. D.

HACKNEY, Arthur, RWS 1957 (VPRWS 1974-77); RE 1960; ARCA 1949; Deputy Head of Fine Art Department, West Surrey College of Art and Design (Farnham Centre) (formerly Farnham School of Art), since 1979; *b* 13 March 1925; *s* of late J. T. Hackney; *m* 1955, Mary Baker, ARCA; two *d. Educ:* Burslem Sch. of Art; Royal Coll. of Art, London. Served in Royal Navy, 1942-46. Travelling scholarship, Royal College of Art, 1949; part-time Painting Instructor, Farnham Sch. of Art, 1949, Lecturer, 1962; Head of Dept: Graphic, 1963-68; Printmaking, 1968-79. Work represented in Public Collections, including Bradford City Art Gallery, Victoria and Albert Museum, Ashmolean Museum, Wellington Art Gallery (NZ), Nottingham Art Gallery, Keighley Art Gallery (Yorks), Wakefield City Art Gallery, Graves Art Gallery, Sheffield, GLC, Preston Art Gallery, City of Stoke-on-Trent Art Gall., Kent Educn Cttee, Staffordshire Educn Cttee. Mem., Fine Art Bd, CNAA, 1975-78. *Address:* Woodhatches, Spoil Lane, Tongham, Farnham, Surrey. *T:* Aldershot 23919. *Club:* Chelsea Arts.

HADDEN-PATON, Major Adrian Gerard Nigel, DL, JP; *b* 3 Dec. 1918; *s* of late Nigel Fairholt Paton, Covehithe, Suffolk; *m* 1951, Mary-Rose, *d* of Col A. H. MacIlwaine, DSO, MC, Troutbeck, S Rhodesia; two *s* (and two step *s*). *Educ:* Rugby; Worcester Coll., Oxford. BA. 2nd Lt, 1st The Royal Dragoons, 1940; Adjutant, 1943-44; served 1940-45: Western Desert, Tunisia, Italy, France, Belgium, Holland, Germany and Denmark; (despatches); Maj. 1945. Instructor, RMA, Sandhurst, 1947-50; retired 1950. Mem. Estates Cttee of Nat. Trust, 1956, Properties Cttee, 1970, Finance Cttee, 1973; Mem. Exec. Cttee, 1959-73, and Finance Cttee, 1961-73 (Chm. 1962-68) of Country Landowners Association. Is an Underwriting Mem. of Lloyd's; Chm. Holland & Holland Ltd; Chm. Hertfordshire Agricultural Soc., 1961-69; Past Pres. Hertfordshire & Middlesex Trust for Nature Conservation; Vice-Pres., Royal Forestry Soc., 1980-. Chm. of Governors, Berkhamsted Sch. and Berkhamsted Sch. for Girls, 1973-78 (Governor 1950-78). JP 1951, DL 1962, Herts; High Sheriff, 1961. *Recreations:* shooting, forestry. *Address:* Rossway, Berkhamsted, Herts. *T:* Berkhamsted 3264. *Club:* Cavalry and Guards.

HADDINGTON, 12th Earl of, *cr* 1619; **George Baillie-Hamilton,** KT 1951; MC; TD; FRSE; FSAScot; LLD (Glasgow); Baron Binning, 1613; Scottish Representative Peer, 1922-63; HM Lieutenant County of Berwick, 1952-69; *b* 18 Sept. 1894; *s* of late Lord Binning; *e s* of 11th Earl, and Katharine Augusta Millicent (*d* 1952), *o c* of W. Severin Salting; *S* grandfather, 1917; *m* 1923, Sarah, *y d* of G. W. Cook, of Montreal; one *s* one *d. Educ:* Eton; Sandhurst. Served European War (Royal Scots Greys), 1915-18 (MC, wounded); late Major 19th (L and BH) Armoured Car Coy. Served European War of 1939-45; Wing Comdr RAFVR, 1941-45; Capt. Queen's Body Guard for Scotland, Royal Company of Archers, 1953-74. Pres. Soc. of Antiquaries of Scotland; Pres. Scottish Georgian Soc.; Chm. of Trustees, National Museum of Antiquities, Scotland; Trustee, National Library of Scotland. *Publications:* verse: The Gathering of the Clans, 1968; I Love Mountains, 1970. *Heir: s* Lord Binning, *qv. Address:* Tyninghame, Dunbar, East Lothian.

HADDON, Eric Edwin, CB 1965; CChem, FRSC; retired; Director, Chemical Defence Establishment, Ministry of Defence, 1961-68; *b* 16 March 1908; *s* of late William Edwin Haddon, York; *m* 1934, Barbara Fabian, York; no *c. Educ:* Archbishop Holgate's Grammar Sch., York; Queen Mary Coll., London Univ. BSc (Special) Chemistry, ARIC 1929; FRIC 1943. Joined Scientific Staff of Admiralty, 1929; Scientific Staff of War Dept, 1929; Sec., Scientific Advisory Council, Min. of Supply, 1945-52; Dir, Chemical Defence Research and Development, Min. of Supply, 1957-61. *Recreations:* electronics, gardening, bridge. *Address:* Knavesmire, St Leonards Road, Thames Ditton, Surrey KT7 0RX. *T:* 01-398 5944.

HADDON-CAVE, Sir (Charles) Philip, KBE 1980; CMG 1973; Chief Secretary, Hong Kong, since 1981; *b* 6 July 1925; *m* 1948, Elizabeth Alice May Simpson; two *s* one *d. Educ:* Univ. Tasmania; King's Coll., Cambridge. Entered Colonial Administrative Service, 1952: East Africa High Commn, 1952; Kenya, 1953-62; Seychelles, 1961-62; Hong Kong, 1962-; Financial Secretary, Hong Kong, 1971-81. *Publication:* (with D. M. Hocking) Air Transport in Australia, 1951. *Address:* Victoria House, Hong Kong. *T:* 96696; Government Secretariat, Hong Kong. *T:* 95406. *Clubs:* Oriental; Hong Kong, Royal Hong Kong Jockey, Royal Hong Kong Golf.

HADDOW, Sir (Thomas) Douglas, KCB 1966 (CB 1955); FRSE; Chairman of Court, Heriot-Watt University, since 1978; *b* 9 Feb. 1913; *s* of George Haddow, Crawford, Lanarkshire; *m* 1942, Margaret R. S. Rowat (*d* 1969); two *s. Educ:* George Watson's Coll., Edinburgh; Edinburgh Univ.; Trinity Coll., Cambridge. MA (Edinburgh) 1932; BA (Cambridge) 1934. Department of Health for Scotland, 1935; Private Sec. to Sec. of State for Scotland, 1941-44. Commonwealth Fund Fellow, 1948. Secretary: Dept of

Health for Scot., 1959-62; Scottish Develt Dept, 1962-64; Permanent Under-Sec. of State, Scottish Office, 1965-73. Chm., N of Scotland Hydro-Electric Bd, 1973-78; Mem. (pt-time), S of Scotland Electricity Bd, 1973-78; Dir, British Investment Trust, 1978-. Hon. LLD Strathclyde Univ., 1967; Hon. DLitt Heriot-Watt Univ., 1971. *Recreation:* golf. *Address:* The Coach House, Northumberland Street Lane SW, Edinburgh EH3 6JD. *T:* 031-556 3650; Castle View, Dirleton, East Lothian EH39 5EH. *T:* Dirleton 266. *Club:* Royal Commonwealth Society.

HADDRILL, Harry Victor; County Councillor, West Yorkshire County Council; *b* 15 Nov. 1914; *s* of Harry Charles Haddrill and Sophie Nancy (*née* Davis); *m* 1937, Kathleen Hilda Miller; three *s. Educ:* Ninfield; Bexhill. Served War: Royal Sussex Regt, 1939-43; Royal Hampshire Regt, 1943-45; France, N Africa, Italy, Egypt. Elected: W Riding CC, 1956 (West Riding CA, 1968-74); W Yorks Metropolitan CC, 1973; first Conservative Chm., 1977-78; Chairman: Law and Parly Cttee, 1967-71; Fire Service Cttee, 1971-74; Planning Cttee, 1979-81; Dep. Leader, Cons. Party, W Yorks CC, 1981-. Pres., Ilkley Cons. Assoc., 1981. *Recreations:* playing tennis, watching cricket, reading, listening to music, play-going. *Address:* 41 Grange Estate, Ilkley, W Yorks. *T:* Ilkley 608620. *Clubs:* St Stephen's Constitutional; British Legion (Ilkley).

HADEN, William Demmery, TD, MA; Headmaster, Royal Grammar School, Newcastle upon Tyne, 1960-72, retired; *b* 14 March 1909; *s* of Reverend William Henry and Gertrude Haden, Little Aston; *m* 1939, Elizabeth Marjorie, *d* of R. S. Tewson, Chorley Wood; one *s* two *d. Educ:* Nottingham High Sch.; Wadham Coll., Oxford (2nd Class Lit. Hum.; MA 1934). English Master, Merchant Taylors' Sch., 1938-46; Headmaster, Mercers' Sch., 1946-59. War Service, 1940-45: served as Battery Comdr RA with Fourteenth Army throughout Burma Campaign (despatches twice); Administrative Commandant, Hmawbi Area, S Burma District, 1945. *Recreations:* games, gardening, listening to music. *Address:* 1 High Espley Cottages, Morpeth, Northumberland.

HADEN-GUEST, family name of **Baron Haden-Guest.**

HADEN-GUEST, 3rd Baron *cr* 1950, of Saling, Essex; **Richard Haden Haden-Guest;** *b* 1904; *s* of 1st Baron Haden-Guest, MC, and Edith (*d* 1944), *d* of Max Low; *S* brother, 1974; *m* 1st, 1926, Hilda (marr. diss. 1934), *d* of late Thomas Russell-Cruise; one *d*; 2nd, 1934, Olive Maria, *d* of late Anders Gotfrid Nilsson; one *s* decd; 3rd, 1949, Marjorie, *d* of late Dr Douglas F. Kennard. *Educ:* Bembridge. *Heir: half-b* Hon. Peter Haden Haden-Guest [*b* 1913; *m* 1945, Jean, *d* of late Dr Albert George Hindes; two *s* one *d*]. *Address:* 3 Chemin des Cret de Champel, 1206 Geneva, Switzerland. *T:* Geneva 476940.

HADFIELD, (Ellis) Charles (Raymond), CMG 1954; *b* 5 Aug. 1909; *s* of Alexander Charles Hadfield, South Africa Civil Service; *m* 1945, Alice Mary Miller, *d* of Lt-Col Henry Smyth, DSO; one *s* one *d* (and one *s* decd). *Educ:* Blundell's Sch.; St Edmund Hall, Oxford. Joined Oxford University Press, 1936; Dir of Publications, Central Office of Information, 1946-48; Controller (Overseas), 1948-62. Dir, David and Charles (Publishers) Ltd, 1960-64. Mem., British Waterways Bd, 1962-66. *Publications:* The Young Collector's Handbook (with C. Hamilton Ellis), 1940; Civilian Fire Fighter, 1941; (with Alexander d'Agapayeff) Maps, 1942; (with Frank Eyre) The Fire Service Today, 1944; (with Frank Eyre) English Rivers and Canals, 1945; (with J. E. MacColl) Pilot Guide to Political London, 1945; (with J. E. MacColl) British Local Government, 1948; (as Charles Alexander) The Church's Year, 1950; British Canals, 1950, 6th edn 1979; The Canals of Southern England, 1955; Introducing Canals, 1955; The Canals of South Wales and the Border, 1960; (with John Norris) Waterways to Stratford, 1962; Canals of the World, 1964; Canals and Waterways, 1966; (with Alice Mary Hadfield) The Cotswolds, 1966; The Canals of the East Midlands, 1966; The Canals of the West Midlands, 1966; The Canals of South West England, 1967; Atmospheric Railways, 1967; (with Michael Streat) Holiday Cruising on Inland Waterways, 1968; The Canal Age, 1968; The Canals of South and South East England, 1969; (with Gordon Biddle) The Canals of North West England, 1970; The Canals of Yorkshire and North East England, 1972; Introducing Inland Waterways, 1973; (with Alice Mary Hadfield) Introducing the Cotswolds, 1976; Waterways Sights to See, 1976; Inland Waterways, 1978; (with A. W. Skempton) William Jessop, Engineer, 1979; (with Alice Mary Hadfield) Afloat in America, 1979. *Recreations:* writing; exploring canals. *Address:* 13 Meadow Way, South Cerney, Cirencester, Glos GL7 6HY. *T:* Cirencester 860422. *Club:* United Oxford & Cambridge University.

HADFIELD, Esmé Havelock, FRCS; Consultant Ear, Nose and Throat Surgeon, High Wycombe, Amersham and Chalfont Hospitals; Associate Surgeon (Hon.), Ear, Nose and Throat Department, Radcliffe Infirmary, Oxford; *b* 1921; *o d* of late Geoffrey Hadfield, MD. *Educ:* Clifton High Sch.; St Hugh's Coll., Oxford; Radcliffe Infirmary Oxford. BA (Oxon.) 1942; BM, BCh Oxon 1945; FRCS 1951; MA Oxon. 1952. House Officer appts, Radcliffe Infirmary, Oxford, 1945; Registrar to ENT Dept, Radcliffe Infirmary, Oxford, 1948; Asst Ohren, Nase, Hals Klinik, Kantonspital, University of Zurich, 1949. First Asst ENT Dept, Radcliffe Infirmary, Oxford, 1950. Mem. Court of Examrs, RCS, 1978-. Pres.-elect., Sect. of Laryngology, RSocMed, 1982-83. British Empire Cancer Campaign Travelling Fellow in Canada, 1953; Hunterian Prof., RCS, 1969-70. *Publications:* articles on ENT surgery in medical journals. *Recreation:* travel.

Address: Linaver, Lane End, High Wycombe, Bucks. *T:* High Wycombe 881473.
See also G. J. Hadfield.

HADFIELD, Geoffrey John, CBE 1980; TD 1963; MS, FRCS; Surgeon, Stoke Mandeville Hospital, since 1960; *b* 19 April 1923; *s* of late Prof. Geoffrey Hadfield, MD, and Eileen Irvine; *m* 1960, Beryl, *d* of late Hubert Sleigh, Manchester; three *d. Educ:* Merchant Taylors' Sch.; St Bartholomew's Hosp., London Univ. MB BS 1947, MS 1954, London; MRCS LRCP 1946, FRCS 1948. Ho. Officer Appts, Demonstr. of Anatomy, Registrar and Sen. Lectr in Surgery, St Bart's Hosp.; Fellow in Surgery, Memorial Hosp., New York; served RAMC, Far East, 1948-50; TAVR, 1950-73; Bt-Col, RAMC RARO, Hon. Col 219 Gen. Hosp., TAVR. Royal College of Surgeons of England: Arris and Gale Lectr, 1954; Hunterian Prof., 1959; Erasmus Wilson Demonstr., 1969; Arnott Demonstr., 1972; Mem. Council and Court of Examiners, 1971-. Examiner in Surgery for Univs of Liverpool, Bristol and Leeds, and Vis. Examiner to univs in Middle and Far East. Fellow, Assoc. of Surgs of Gt Britain and Ireland, 1955-; Associate Fellow and Council Mem., Brit. Assoc. of Urol Surgs, 1960-; Mem., Brit. Assoc. of Surg. Oncology, 1973-; Mem. Council, Brit. Assoc. of Clin. Anatamists, 1976-. *Publications:* Current Surgical Practice (with M. Hobsley), vol. 1, 1976, vol. 2, 1978, vol. 3, 1981; articles in jls and chapters in books on diseases of the breast, cancer, urology, trauma, varicose veins and med. educn. *Recreations:* dinghy sailing, travel, walking, golf. *Address:* Milverton House, 3 Spenser Road, Aylesbury, Bucks HP21 7LR. *T:* Aylesbury 5343.
See also E. H. Hadfield.

HADFIELD, John Charles Heywood; author; Proprietor, The Cupid Press, since 1949; Director, Rainbird Publishing Group, 1965-82; *b* 16 June 1907; 2nd *s* of H. G. Hadfield, Birmingham; *m* 1st, 1931, Phyllis Anna McMullen (*d* 1973); one *s*; 2nd, 1975, Joy Westendarp. *Educ:* Bradfield. Editor, J. M. Dent & Sons, Ltd, 1935-42; Books Officer for British Council in the Middle East, 1942-44; Dir of the National Book League, 1944-50; Organiser, Festival of Britain Exhibition of Books, 1951; Editor, The Saturday Book, 1952-73. *Publications:* The Christmas Companion, 1939; Georgian Love Songs, 1949; Restoration Love Songs, 1950; A Book of Beauty, 1952, rev. edn 1976; A Book of Delights, 1954, rev. edn 1977; Elizabethan Love Songs, 1955; A Book of Britain, 1956; A Book of Love, 1958, revd edn 1978; Love on a Branch Line, 1959; A Book of Pleasures, 1960; A Book of Joy, 1962; A Chamber of Horrors, 1965; (ed) The Shell Guide to England, 1970, rev. edn 1981; (ed) Cowardy Custard, 1973; (ed) The Shell Book of English Villages, 1980; (ed) Everyman's Book of English Love Poems, 1980; The Best of The Saturday Book, 1981; (With Miles Hadfield): The Twelve Days of Christmas, 1961; Gardens of Delight, 1964. *Recreations:* books, pictures, gardens. *Address:* 2 Quay Street, Woodbridge, Suffolk. *T:* Woodbridge 7414. *Club:* Savile.

HADFIELD, Ven. John Collingwood; Archdeacon of Caithness, Rector of St John the Evangelist, Wick, and Priest-in-Charge of St Peter and the Holy Rood, Thurso, Caithness, since 1977; *b* 2 June 1912; *s* of Reginald Hadfield and Annie Best Hadfield (*née* Gribbin); *m* 1939, Margretta Mainwaring Lewis Matthews; three *s* three *d. Educ:* Manchester Grammar School; Jesus Coll., Cambridge (Exhibnr, BA 1st cl. Hons, Classical Tripos Pt 2 1934, MA 1938); Wells Theological College. Deacon 1935, priest 1936, Manchester; Curate of S Chad, Ladybarn, Manchester, 1935-44 (in charge from 1940); Vicar of S Mark, Bolton-le-Moors, Lancs, 1944-50; Vicar of S Ann, Belfield, Rochdale, Lancs, 1950-62; Surrogate, 1944-62; Proctor in Convocation for Dio. Manchester, 1950-62. Diocese of Argyll and The Isles: Rector of S Paul, Rothesay, Bute, 1962-64; Itinerant Priest, 1964-77; Canon of S John's Cathedral, Oban, 1965-77; Inspector of Schools, 1966-77; Synod Clerk, 1973-77. *Recreation:* music. *Address:* 4 Sir Archibald Road, Thurso, Caithness KW14 8HN. *T:* Thurso 2047.

HADLEY, David Allen; Under Secretary, Ministry of Agriculture, Fisheries and Food, since 1981; *b* 18 Feb. 1936; *s* of Sydney and Gwendoline Hadley; *m* 1965, Veronica Ann Hopkins; one *s. Educ:* Wyggeston Grammar Sch., Leicester; Merton Coll., Oxford. MA. Joined MAFF, 1959; Asst Sec., 1971; HM Treas., 1975-78. *Recreations:* gardening, music. *Address:* Old Mousers, Dormansland, Lingfield, Surrey. *T:* Lingfield 832259.

HADLEY, Dr George Dickinson; Emeritus Physician, Middlesex Hospital; *b* 30 June 1908; *s* of Laurence Percival Hadley and Norah Katherine Hadley (*née* Alabaster); *m* 1947, Jean Elinor Stewart; three *d. Educ:* King Edward VI Sch., Birmingham; Clare Coll., Cambridge. 1st Class Natural Sciences Tripos, Part I 1930, Part II 1931, Cambridge; MB, ChB Cantab 1934; MRCP 1937; MD Cantab 1939; Elmore Clinical Research Student, University of Cambridge, 1936-38; FRCP 1947. Major RAMC and Medical Specialist, 1939-45 (POW, Germany, 1940-45). Physician, Middlesex Hospital, 1946. Examiner in Medicine: Cambridge Univ., 1955-57; University of London, 1956-60; RCP, 1965-70. *Publications:* articles in various medical journals. *Recreations:* angling, 'cello playing, book-binding. *Address:* 59 Gloucester Crescent, NW1 7EG.

HADLEY, Sir Leonard Albert, Kt 1975; JP; Secretary, Unions of Workers, Wellington, NZ; *b* Wellington, 8 Sept. 1911; *s* of Albert A. Hadley, JP; *m* 1st, 1939, Jean Lyell (*d* 1965), *d* of E. S. Innes; one *s* one *d*; 2nd, 1978, Amelia Townsend. Mem., Nat. Exec., NZ Fedn of Labour, 1946-76; Dir, Reserve Bank of NZ, 1959-; Pres., Wellington Trustee Savings Bank, 1976-79 (Dep. Pres., 1973-76); Bd of Trustees since Bank's formation, 1964; Mem. Industrial

Relns Council since formation, 1974 (and its predecessor, Industrial Adv. Council, 1953); Relieving Mem., Industrial Commn and Industrial Court, 1974 (and its predecessor, Arbitration Court, 1960); Member: NZ Immigration Adv. Council, 1964-; Periodic Detention Work Centre Adv. Cttee (Juvenile), 1964-, and Adult Centre, 1967- (both since formation); Absolute Liability Enquiry Cttee, 1963-, and Govt Cttees to review Exempted Goods, 1959 and 1962; Terawhiti Licensing Trust, 1975-80; Waterfront Industry Tribunal, 1981. Rep., NZ Fedn of Labour Delegns to ILO, Geneva, 1949 and 1966; Internat. Confedn of Free Trade Unions Inaugural Conf., 1949; Social Security Conf., Moscow, 1971; SE Asian Trade Union Conf., Tokyo, 1973; OECD Conf., Paris, 1974. Awarded Smith-Mundt Leader Study Grant in USA, 1953. Life Mem., Wellington Working Men's Club and Literary Inst., 1979. JP 1967. *Recreations:* reading, music, outdoor bowls, Rugby, tennis, and sport generally. *Address:* (private) 3 Cheeseman Street, Wellington 2, New Zealand.

HADOW, Sir Gordon, Kt 1956; CMG 1953; OBE 1945; Deputy Governor of the Gold Coast (now Ghana), 1954-57; *b* 23 Sept. 1908; *e s* of late Rev. F. B. Hadow and Una Ethelwyn Durrant; *m* 1946, Marie, *er d* of late Dr L. H. Moiser; two *s. Educ:* Marlborough; Trinity Coll., Oxford. Administrative Service, Gold Coast, 1932; Dep. Financial Sec., Tanganyika, 1946; Under-Sec. Gold Coast, 1948; Sec. for the Civil Service, 1949; Sec. to Governor and to Exec. Council, 1950-54. *Address:* Little Manor, Coat, Martock, Somerset. *Club:* Athenæum.

HADOW, Sir (Reginald) Michael, KCMG 1971 (CMG 1962); HM Diplomatic Service, retired; *b* 17 Aug. 1915; *s* of Malcolm McGregor Hadow and Constance Mary Lund; *m* 1976, Hon. Mrs Daphne Sieff. *Educ:* Berkhamsted Sch.; King's Coll., Cambridge. Selected for ICS, 1937; Private Sec. to HM Ambassador, Moscow, 1942; Under-Sec., External Affairs Dept, Delhi, 1946-47; transferred to Foreign Office, 1948; FO, 1948-52; Private Sec. to Minister of State, 1949-52; Head of Chancery, Mexico City, 1952-54; FO, 1955; Head of Levant Dept and promoted Counsellor, 1958; Counsellor, Brit. Embassy, Paris, 1959-62; Head of News Dept, FO, 1962-65; Ambassador to Israel, 1965-69; Ambassador to Argentina, 1969-72. *Recreations:* all field sports. *Address:* The Miller's House, Kintbury, Berks RG15 0UR. *Club:* Norfolk (Norwich).

HADRILL, John Michael W.; *see* Wallace-Hadrill.

HAENDEL, Ida; violinist; *b* Poland, 15 Dec. 1928; Polish parentage. Began to play at age of 3½; amazing gift discovered when she picked up her sister's violin and started to play. Her father a great connoisseur of music, saw in her an unusual talent and decided to abandon his own career as an artist (painter) to devote himself to his daughter; studied at Warsaw Conservatorium and finished with a gold medal at age of ten; also studied with such great masters as Carl Flesch and Georges Enesco. Gave concerts for British and US troops, and in factories, War of 1939-45; plays in Europe, US, and Middle East with great conductors like Sir Henry Wood, Sir Thomas Beecham, Sir Malcolm Sargent, Klemperer, Szell, Molinari; played with London Philharmonic in China, 1973; BBC Symphony tour of Australia, 1982. *Publication:* Woman with Violin (autobiog.), 1970. *Address:* c/o Harold Holt, 31 Sinclair Road, W14.

HAFERKAMP, Wilhelm; a Vice-President, Commission of the European Communities, since 1970; *b* Duisburg, 1 July 1923. *Educ:* Universität zu Köln. German Trade Union Federation: Head of Division for Social Questions, 1950-63, Dep. Chm. 1953, Chm. 1957, N Rhine—Westphalia Area; Mem. Fed. Exec., 1962-67. Socialist Mem., Landtag of North Rhine—Westphalia, 1958-67; Mem., Commn of European Communities, 1967-, responsible for Energy policy, Euratom Supply Agency and Euratom Safeguards; Vice-Pres., 1970, resp. for internal market and legal harmonisation; 1973, resp. for economic and financial affairs; 1977, resp. for external relations. *Address:* 200 rue de la Loi, 1049 Brussels, Belgium. *T:* Brussels 235.11.11.

HAFFENDEN, Maj.-Gen. D. J. W.; *see* Wilson-Haffenden.

HAFFNER, Albert Edward, PhD; Chairman, North Eastern Gas Board, 1971-72 (Deputy Chairman, 1966-71); *b* 17 Feb. 1907; 4th *s* of late George Christian and late Caroline Haffner, Holme, near Burnley, Lancs; *m* 1934, Elizabeth Ellen Crossley, Cheadle Heath, Stockport; one *s* one *d. Educ:* Burnley Grammar Sch.; Royal College of Science; Imperial Coll., London; Technische Hochschule, Karlsruhe. BSc (1st Cl. Hons), ARCS, PhD, DIC, London. Burnley Gas Works, 1924-26; Gas Light & Coke Co, 1932-56; Research Chemist and North Thames Gas Bd; Gp Engr, Chief Engineer and later Bd Member, Southern Gas Bd, 1956-66. Past Pres., Instn Gas Engineers (Centenary Pres., 1962-63); Past Vice-Pres., Internat. Gas Union. CEng, MIChemE. *Publications:* Contributor to: Proc. Roy. Soc., Jl Instn Gas Engrs, Instn Chem. Engrs, Inst. of Fuel, New Scientist; papers presented to Canadian Gas Assoc., French Chem. Soc., Japanese Gas Industry and at IGU Confs in USA, USSR and Germany, etc. *Recreations:* photography, travel, gardening, cabinetmaking. *Address:* Burnthwaite, Iwerne Courtney, near Blandford Forum, Dorset DT11 8QL. *T:* Child Okeford 860749.

HAGART-ALEXANDER, Sir C.; *see* Alexander.

HAGEN, Dr John P(eter), Presidential Certificate of Merit (US), 1947; DSM (US), 1959; Professor of Astronomy and Head of Department of Astronomy,

Pennsylvania State University, 1967-75, now Emeritus; Director, Office of United Nations Conference, National Aeronautics and Space Administration, 1960-62 (Director, Vanguard Division, 1958-60); *b* 31 July 1908; *s* of John T. and Ella Bertha Hagen (*née* Fisher); *m* 1935, Edith W. Soderling; two *s*. *Educ:* Boston, Wesleyan, Yale and Georgetown Univs. Res. Associate, Wesleyan Univ., 1931-35; Supt Atmosphere and Astrophysics Div., US Naval Res. Lab., 1935-58; Dir, Project Vanguard, 1955-58. Lecturer, Georgetown Univ., 1949-. FRAS 1969; FIEEE; Fellow: Amer. Acad. of Arts and Sciences; Amer. Assoc. for Advancement of Science; Amer. Astronomical Soc. Chairman: Study Gp 2 (Radioastronomy and Space Res.), Comité Consultative Internat. Radio; IUCAF Cttee of ISCU. Hon. ScD: Boston, 1958; Adelphi, Loyola, Fairfield, 1959; Mt Allison, 1960. Phi Beta Kappa. *Publications:* contrib. to Astrophysical Journal and to Proc. Inst. Radio Engrg; contributor to Encyclopædia Britannica. *Address:* 613 W Park Avenue, State College, Pa 16801, USA. *T:* 237-3031. *Club:* Cosmos (Washington, DC).

HAGEN, Victor W. Von; *see* Von Hagen.

HAGGARD, William; *see* Clayton, Richard Henry Michael.

HAGGART, Most Rev. Alastair Iain Macdonald; *see* Edinburgh, Bishop of.

HAGGERSTON GADSDEN, Sir Peter Drury; *see* Gadsden.

HAGGETT, Prof. Peter; Professor of Urban and Regional Geography, University of Bristol, since 1966; Pro-Vice-Chancellor, since 1979; *b* 24 Jan. 1933; *s* of Charles and Elizabeth Haggett, Pawlett, Somerset; *m* 1956, Brenda Woodley; two *s* two *d*. *Educ:* Dr Morgan's Sch., Bridgwater; St Catharine's Coll., Cambridge (Exhib. and Scholar; MA, PhD). Asst Lectr, University Coll. London, 1955; Demonstrator and University Lectr, Cambridge, 1957; Fellow, Fitzwilliam Coll., 1964; Leverhulme Research Fellow (Brazil), 1959; Canada Council Fellow, 1977; Erskine Fellow (NZ), 1979. Visiting Professor: Berkeley; Pennsylvania State; Western Ontario; Toronto; Monash, Australia. Member, SW Economic Planning Council, 1967-72. Governor, Centre for Environmental Studies, 1975-78; Mem. Council, RGS, 1972-73, 1977-80. Cullum Medal of American Geographical Soc., 1969; Meritorious Contribution Award, Assoc. of American Geographers, 1973. *Publications:* Locational Analysis in Human Geography, 1965; (ed jtly) Frontiers in Geographical Teaching, 1965; Models in Geography, 1967; (with R. J. Chorley) Network Analysis in Geography, 1969; Progress in Geography, vols 1-9, 1969-77; Regional Forecasting, 1971; (with A. D. Cliff and others) Elements of Spatial Structure, 1975; Geography: a modern synthesis, 1975; Processes in Physical and Human Geography: Bristol Essays, 1975; Spatial Diffusion, 1981; research papers. *Recreations:* natural history, cricket. *Address:* 5 Tun Bridge Close, Chew Magna, Somerset.

HÄGGLÖF, Gunnar, GCVO (Hon.), 1954; Swedish Diplomat; *b* 15 Dec. 1904; *s* of Richard Hägglöf and Sigrid Ryding, Stockholm, Sweden; *m* Anna, *d* of Count Folchi-Vici, Rome. *Educ:* Upsala Univ., Sweden. Entered Swedish Diplomatic Service, 1926; Minister without Portfolio, 1939. During War of 1939-45, led various Swedish delegns to Berlin, London, and Washington; Envoy to Belgian and Dutch Govts, 1944; Envoy in Moscow, 1946; permanent delegate to UN, 1947; Ambassador to Court of St James's, 1948-67; Ambassador to France, 1967-71. Delegate to Conf. for Constitution, European Council, 1949; delegate to Suez Confs, 1956; Mem. of Menzies Cttee to Cairo, 1956. Hon. DCL Birmingham, 1960. *Publications:* Diplomat, 1972; several books and essays in economics, politics and history. *Recreations:* ski-ing, swimming, reading and writing. *Address:* Les Hauts de Vaugrenier, 06270 Villeneuve-Loubet, France.

HAGUE, Prof. Sir Douglas (Chalmers), Kt 1982; CBE 1978; Professorial Fellow, Oxford Centre for Management Studies, and Chairman, Oxford Strategy Unit, since 1981; *b* Leeds, 20 Oct. 1926; *s* of Laurence and Marion Hague; *m* 1947, Brenda Elizabeth Fereday; two *d*. *Educ:* Moseley Grammar Sch.; King Edward VI High Sch., Birmingham; University of Birmingham. Assistant Tutor, Faculty of Commerce, Birmingham Univ., 1946; Assistant Lecturer, University College, London, 1947, Lecturer, 1950; Reader in Political Economy in University of London, 1957; Newton Chambers Professor of Economics, University of Sheffield, 1957-63. Visiting Professor of Economics, Duke Univ., USA, 1960-61; Head of Department of Business Studies, University of Sheffield, 1962-63; Professor of Applied Economics, University of Manchester, 1963-65; Prof. of Managerial Economics, Manchester Business Sch., 1965-81, Dep. Dir, 1978-81, Vis. Prof., 1981-. Director: Economic Models Ltd, 1970-78; The Laird Gp, 1976-79. Rapporteur to International Economic Association, 1953-78, Editor General, 1981-; Member Working Party of National Advisory Council on Education for Industry and Commerce, 1962-63; Consultant to Secretariat of NEDC, 1962-63; Member: Treasury Working Party on Management Training in the Civil Service, 1965-67; EDC for Paper and Board, 1967-70; (part-time) N Western Gas Board, 1966-72; Working Party, Local Govt Training Bd, 1969-70; Price Commn, 1973-78 (Dep. Chm., 1977); Director: Manchester School of Management and Administration, 1964-65; Centre for Business Research, Manchester, 1964-66. Member Council, Manchester Business School, 1964-; Chairman, Manchester Industrial Relations Society, 1964-66; President, NW Operational Research Group, 1967-69; British Chm., Carnegie Project on Accountability, 1968-72; Jt Chm., Conf. of Univ. Management Schools, 1971-73; Chm., DoI Working Party, Kirkby

Manufacturing and Engineering Co., 1978. Economic adviser to Mrs Thatcher, Gen. Election campaign, 1979; Adviser to PM's Policy Unit, 10 Downing St, 1979-. Industrial Consultant. *Publications:* (with P. K. Newman) Costs in Alternative Locations: The Clothing Industry, 1952; (with A. W. Stonier) A Textbook of Economic Theory, 1953, 4th edn 1973; (with A. W. Stonier) The Essentials of Economics, 1955; The Economics of Man-Made Fibres, 1957; Stability and Progress in the World Economy (ed), 1958; The Theory of Capital (ed), 1961; Inflation (ed), 1962; International Trade Theory in a Developing World (ed) (with Sir Roy Harrod), 1965; Price Formation in Various Economies (ed), 1967; Managerial Economics, 1969; The Dilemma of Accountability in Modern Government (ed) (with Bruce L. R. Smith), 1970; Pricing in Business, 1971; (with M. E. Beesley) Britain in the Common Market: a new business opportunity, 1973; (with W. E. F. Oakeshott and A. A. Strain) Devaluation and Pricing Decisions: a case study approach, 1974; (with W. J. M. Mackenzie and A. Barker) Public Policy and Private Interests: the institutions of compromise, 1975; articles in economic and financial journals. *Recreations:* church organs, watching Manchester United. *Address:* Oxford Centre for Management Studies, Kennington, Oxford OX1 5NY.

HAGUE, Harry; a Recorder of the Crown Court, 1972-79; *b* 9 April 1922; *o c* of Harry Hague and Lilian (*née* Hindle), Stalybridge and Blackpool; *m* 1967, Vera, *d* of Arthur Frederick and Sarah Ann Smith, Manchester; two step *d*. *Educ:* Arnold Sch., Blackpool; Manchester and London Univs. LLB London. Army, 1941-44. Called to Bar, Middle Temple, 1946; Northern Circuit. Asst Recorder, Burnley, 1969-71. Contested (L): Blackburn East, 1950; Blackpool North, 1959, 1962 (bye-election) and 1964; Mem. Nat. Exec., Liberal Party, 1956-59 and 1962-64. *Recreations:* activities concerning animals, motoring, historical buildings. *Address:* 60 King Street, Manchester M2 4NA. *T:* 061-834 6876; Glenmore, 197 Victoria Road West, Cleveleys, Thornton-Cleveleys, Lancs. *T:* Cleveleys 2104.

HAHN, Prof. Frank Horace, FBA 1975; Professor of Economics, University of Cambridge, since 1972; Fellow of Churchill College, Cambridge, since 1960; *b* 26 April 1925; *s* of Dr Arnold Hahn and Maria Hahn; *m* 1946, Dorothy Salter; no *c*. *Educ:* Bournemouth Grammar School; London School of Economics. PhD London, MA Cantab. Univ. of Birmingham, 1948-60, Reader in Mathematical Economics, 1958-60; Univ. Lectr in Econs, Cambridge, 1960-67; Prof. of Economics, LSE, 1967-72; Frank W. Taussig Res. Prof., Harvard, 1975-76. Visiting Professor: MIT, 1956-57; Univ. of California, Berkeley, 1959-60. Fellow, Inst. of Advanced Studies in Behavioural Sciences, Stanford, 1966-67. Mem. Council for Scientific Policy, later Adv. Bd of Res. Councils, 1972-75. Fellow, Econometric Soc., 1962; Vice-Pres., 1967-68; Pres., 1968-69. Managing Editor, Review of Economic Studies, 1965-68. Foreign Hon. Mem., Amer. Acad. of Arts and Sciences, 1974. Hon. DSocSci Birmingham, 1981. *Publications:* (with K. J. Arrow) General Competitive Analysis, 1971; The Share of Wages in the National Income, 1972; Money and Inflation, 1982; articles in learned journals. *Address:* 16 Adams Road, Cambridge. *T:* Cambridge 352560; 30 Tavistock Court, Tavistock Square, WC1. *T:* 01-387 4293.

HAIDER, Michael Lawrence; Chairman of the Board, Chief Executive Officer, and Chairman of Executive Committee, Standard Oil Co. (NJ), 1965-69, retired; *b* 1 Oct. 1904; *s* of Michael Haider and Elizabeth (*née* Milner). *Educ:* Stanford Univ. BS 1927. Chemical Engineer, Richfield Oil Co., 1927-29; Carter Oil Co., Tulsa, Okla., 1929-38 (Chief Engineer, 1935-38); Manager, Research and Engineering Dept, Standard Oil Development Co., 1938-45; Standard Oil Co. (NJ): Executive, Producing Dept, 1945-46; Deputy Co-ordinator of Producing Activities, 1952-54; Vice-President, 1960-61; Executive Vice-President, 1961-63; President and Vice-Chairman, Executive Cttee, 1963-65. Was with: Imperial Oil Ltd, Toronto, 1946-52 (Vice-President and Director, 1948-52); International Petroleum Co. Ltd (President and Director), 1954-59. President, American Institute of Mining and Metallurgical Engineers, 1952. *Publications:* (ed) Petroleum Reservoir Efficiency and Well Spacing, 1943; articles in technical journals. *Address:* (office) Room 1250, 1 Rockefeller Plaza, New York, NY 10020, USA; (home) 35 Adam Way, Atherton, Calif 94025, USA.

HAIG, family name of **Earl Haig.**

HAIG, 2nd Earl, *cr* 1919; **George Alexander Eugene Douglas Haig,** OBE 1966; Viscount Dawick, *cr* 1919; Baron Haig and 30th Laird of Bemersyde; is a painter; Member, Queen's Body Guard for Scotland; *b* March 1918; *o s* of 1st Earl and Hon. Dorothy Vivian (*d* 1939) (Author of A Scottish Tour, 1935), *d* of 3rd Lord Vivian; *S* father, 1928; *m* 1st, 1956, Adrienne Thérèse, *d* of Derchor Morley; one *s* two *d*; 2nd, 1981, Donna Gerolama Lopez y Royo di Taurisano. *Educ:* Stowe; Christ Church, Oxford. MA Oxon. 2nd Lieut Royal Scots Greys, 1938; retired on account of disability, 1951, rank of Captain; Hon. Major on disbandment of HG 1958; studied painting Camberwell School of Art; paintings in collections of Arts Council and Scottish Nat. Gallery of Modern Art. War of 1939-45 (prisoner). Member: Royal Fine Art Commission for Scotland, 1958-61; Council and Executive Cttee, Earl Haig Fund, Scotland, 1950-65 and 1966- (Pres., 1980-); Scottish Arts Council, 1959-75; President, Scottish Craft Centre, 1950-75. Member Council, Commonwealth Ex-Services League; Chairman, Officers' Association (Scottish Branch), 1977; Vice-President, Scottish National Institution for War Blinded; President Border Area British Legion, 1955-61; Chairman SE Scotland Disablement Advisory Cttee, 1960-73; Vice-Chairman, British Legion, Scotland, 1960, Chairman, 1962-65, Pres., 1980-;

Trustee, Scottish National War Memorial, 1961; Trustee, National Gallery of Scotland, 1962-72; Chairman: Berwickshire Civic Soc., 1971-73; Friends of DeMarco Gall., 1968-71. Berwickshire: DL 1953; Vice-Lieutenant, 1967-70. KStJ 1977. FRSA 1951. *Heir: s* Viscount Dawick, *qv. Address:* Bemersyde, Melrose, Scotland. *T:* St Boswells 22762. *Clubs:* Beefsteak, Cavalry and Guards; New (Edinburgh).

See also Baron Astor of Hever, Baron Dacre of Glanton.

HAIG, General Alexander Meigs, Jr; Secretary of State, United States of America, 1981-82; with Hudson Institute for Policy Research, since 1982; *b* 2 Dec. 1924; *m* 1950, Patricia Fox; two *s* one *d. Educ:* schs in Pennsylvania; Univ. of Notre Dame; US Mil. Acad., West Point (BS); Univs of Columbia and Georgetown (MA); Ground Gen. Sch., Fort Riley; Armor Sch., Fort Knox; Naval and Army War Colls. 2nd Lieut 1947; Far East and Korea, 1948-51; Europe, 1956-59; Vietnam, 1966-67; CO 3rd Regt, subseq. Dep. Comdt, West Point, 1967-69; Sen. Mil. Adviser to Asst to Pres. for Nat. Security Affairs, 1969-70; Dep. Asst to Pres. for Nat. Security Affairs, 1970-73; Vice-Chief of Staff, US Army, Jan.-July 1973, retd; Chief of White House Staff, 1973-74 when recalled to active duty; Supreme Allied Commander Europe, 1974-79, and Commander-in-Chief, US European Command, 1974-79; President and Chief Operating Officer, United Technologies, 1979-81. Hon. LLD: Niagara; Utah; hon. degrees: Syracuse, Fairfield, Hillsdale Coll., 1981. Awarded numerous US medals, badges and decorations; also Vietnamese orders and Cross of Gallantry; Medal of King Abd el-Aziz (Saudi Arabia). *Recreations:* tennis, golf, squash, equitation. *Address:* c/o Hudson Institute, Quaker Ridge Road, Croton-on-Hudson, NY 10520, USA.

HAIG, Mrs Mary Alison G.; *see* Glen Haig.

HAIGH, (Austin) Anthony (Francis), CMG 1954; retired as Director of Education and of Cultural and Scientific Affairs, Council of Europe, 1962-68; *b* 29 Aug. 1907; *s* of late P. B. Haigh, ICS, and Eliza (*d* 1963), *d* of George Moxon; *m* 1st, 1935, Gertrude (marr. diss. 1971), 2nd *d* of late Frank Dodd; two *s* two *d*; 2nd, 1971, Eleanore Margaret, *d* of late T. H. Bullimore and widow of J. S. Herbert. *Educ:* Eton; King's Coll., Cambridge. Entered Diplomatic Service, 1932; served in Foreign Office and at HM Embassies at Rio de Janeiro, Tokyo, Lisbon, Ankara, Cairo and Brussels; Head of Cultural Relations Department, Foreign Office, 1952-62. Chairman Cttee of Cultural Experts, Council of Europe, 1960-61; Chairman, Admin. Board, Cultural Fund of Council of Europe, 1961-62. *Publications:* A Ministry of Education for Europe, 1970; Congress of Vienna to Common Market, 1973; Cultural Diplomacy in Europe, 1974. *Address:* The Furnace, Crowhurst, near Battle, East Sussex. *Club:* Leander.

HAIGH, Brian Roger; Director General, Defence Contracts, since 1980; *b* 19 Feb. 1931; *s* of Herbert Haigh and Ruth Haigh (*née* Lockwood); *m* 1953, Sheila Carter; one *s* one *d. Educ:* Hillhouse Central School, Huddersfield. Min. of Supply, 1949; National Service, RAF, 1949-51; Min. of Supply/Min. of Aviation, 1951-62; NATO Bullpup Production Orgn, 1962-67 (Head of Contracts, Finance and Admin, 1965-67); Min. of Technology, Aviation Supply, Defence (Defence Sales Orgn), 1968-73 (Asst Dir, Sales, 1971-73); Nat. Defence Coll., 1973-74; Ministry of Defence: Asst Dir, Contracts, 1974; Dir of Contracts (Weapons), Dec. 1974; Principal Dir of Navy Contracts, 1978; Under Secretary, 1980. *Recreations:* family, music, opera, bridge. *Address:* 12 Nursery Close, Haywards Heath, Sussex. *T:* Haywards Heath 57172. *Club:* Cormorant (Latimer).

HAIGH, Clement Percy, PhD; FInstP; consultant; *b* 11 Jan. 1920; *m* 1945, Ruby Patricia Hobdey; three *s. Educ:* Univ. of Leeds (BSc); King's Coll., London (PhD). Radiochemical Centre, Thorium Ltd, 1943-49; Medical Physicist, Barrow Hosp., Bristol, 1949-56; joined CEGB, 1956: Director, Berkeley Nuclear Laboratories, 1959-73; Dep. Director-General, Design and Construction Div., Gloucester, 1973-78; Dir of Research, BNOC, 1978-81. Dir, South Western Industrial Res., 1981-. Distinguished Lectr, American Nuclear Soc., San Francisco, 1965; Assessor, Nuclear Safety Adv. Cttee, 1972-76; Member: BBC West Adv. Council, 1972-76; Mechanical Engrg and Machine Tools Requirements Bd, 1973-76; Off-Shore Energy Technology Bd, 1978-81; Board, National Maritime Inst., 1981-; UK Chm., Joint UK/USSR Working Gp on Problems of Electricity Supply, 1974-78. *Publications:* various papers on applied nuclear physics and on nuclear energy. *Recreations:* music; study of magnificent failures in technology. *Address:* Painswick, Old Sneed Park, Bristol, Avon BS9 1RG. *T:* Bristol 68 2065. *Clubs:* Savile, Royal Automobile.

HAIGH, Clifford; Editor, The Friend, 1966-73; *b* 5 Feb. 1906; *yr s* of Leonard and Isabel Haigh, Bradford, Yorks; *m* 1st, 1934, Dora Winifred Fowler (*d* 1959); one *s* one *d*; 2nd, 1970, Grace Elizabeth Cross. Editorial Staff: Yorkshire Observer, 1924-27; Birmingham Post, 1928-46; The Times, 1947-61; Assistant Editor, The Friend, 1961-65. *Recreation:* walking. *Address:* 4 Chichester Road, Sandgate, Kent. *T:* Folkestone 38212.

HAIGH, Maurice Francis; Barrister; a Recorder of the Crown Court, since 1981; *b* 6 Sept. 1929; *s* of William and Ceridwen Francis Haigh. *Educ:* Repton. Asst cameraman in film production; worked for Leslie Laurence Productions Ltd, London, Manchester Film Studios, and finally for Anglo-Scottish Pictures Ltd at London Film Studios, Shepperton, 1946-49; in commerce, 1950-52. Called to the Bar, Gray's Inn, 1955. *Recreations:* reading,

cycling, fell and mountain walking. *Address:* 27 Byrom Street, Manchester M3 4PF. *T:* 061-832 4036. *Club:* English-Speaking Union.

HAIGHT, Gordon Sherman, PhD; Professor of English, Yale University, 1950, Emily Sanford Professor, 1966, Emeritus 1969; General Editor, Clarendon George Eliot, since 1975; *b* 6 Feb. 1901; *s* of Louis Pease Haight and Grace Carpenter; *m* 1937, Mary Treat Nettleton. *Educ:* Yale Univ. BA 1923, PhD 1933. Master in English: Kent Sch., 1924-25; Hotchkiss Sch., 1925-30; taught English at Yale, 1931-69; Master of Pierson Coll., Yale Univ., 1949-53. Visiting Prof. of English: Columbia Univ., 1946-47; Univ. of Oregon, 1949. Guggenheim Fellow, 1946, 1953, 1960. Fellow Royal Society of Literature, Corres. Fellow British Academy. Member: Berzelius; Zeta Psi. Wilbur Cross Medal, Yale, 1977. *Publications:* Mrs Sigourney, 1930; George Eliot and John Chapman, 1940, 1969; George Eliot, A Biography, 1968 (James Tait Black Award, Heinemann Award of Royal Society of Literature, Van Wyck Brooks Award, 1969; Amer. Acad. of Arts and Letters Award, 1970); Editor: Miss Ravenel's Conversion (J. W. De Forest), 1939, 1955; Adam Bede, 1948; The George Eliot Letters, 9 vols, 1954-78; Middlemarch, 1955; The Mill on the Floss, 1961, Clarendon edn, 1980; A Century of George Eliot Criticism, 1965; Portable Victorian Reader, 1971; contribs to various literary jls. *Recreations:* garden, water colours. *Address:* 145 Peck Hill Road, Woodbridge, Conn 06525, USA. *T:* 203-393-0689. *Clubs:* Yale, Century (New York); Elizabethan (New Haven).

HAILEY, Arthur; author; *b* 5 April 1920; *s* of George Wellington Hailey and Elsie Mary Wright; *m* 1st, 1944, Joan Fishwick (marr. diss. 1950); three *s*; 2nd, 1951, Sheila Dunlop; one *s* two *d. Educ:* English elem. schs. Pilot, RAF, 1939-47 (Flt-Lt). Emigrated to Canada, 1947; various positions in industry and sales until becoming free-lance writer, 1956. *Films:* Zero Hour, 1956; Time Lock, 1957; The Young Doctors, 1961; Hotel, 1966; Airport, 1970; The Moneychangers, 1976; Wheels, 1978. *Publications:* (in 32 languages): (with John Castle) Flight Into Danger, 1958; Close-Up (Collected Plays), 1960; The Final Diagnosis, 1959; In High Places, 1962; Hotel, 1965; Airport, 1968; Wheels, 1971; The Moneychangers, 1975; Overload, 1979. *Address:* (home) Lyford Cay, PO Box N7776, Nassau, Bahamas; (office) Seaway Authors Ltd, First Canadian Place-6400, PO 130, Toronto, Ont M5X 1A4, Canada. *Clubs:* River (New York); Lyford Cay (Bahamas).

HAILSHAM, 2nd Viscount, *cr* 1929, of Hailsham; Baron, *cr* 1928 [disclaimed his peerages for life, 20 Nov. 1963]; *see under* Baron Hailsham of St Marylebone.

HAILSHAM OF SAINT MARYLEBONE, Baron *cr* 1970 (Life Peer), of Herstmonceux; **Quintin McGarel Hogg,** PC 1956; CH 1974; FRS 1973; Lord High Chancellor of Great Britain, 1970-74 and since 1979; Editor, Halsbury's Laws of England, 4th edition, since 1972; *b* 9 Oct. 1907; *er s* of 1st Viscount Hailsham, PC, KC, and Elizabeth (*d* 1925), *d* of Judge Trimble Brown, Nashville, Tennessee, USA, and widow of Hon. A. J. Marjoribanks; *S* father, 1950, as 2nd Viscount Hailsham, but disclaimed his peerages for life, 20 Nov. 1963 (Baron *cr* 1928, Viscount *cr* 1929); *m* 1944, Mary Evelyn (*d* 1978), *d* of late Richard Martin of Ross; two *s* three *d. Educ:* Eton (Schol., Newcastle Schol.); Christ Church, Oxford (Scholar). First Class Hon. Mods, 1928; First Class Lit Hum, 1930; Pres., Oxford Union Soc., 1929. Served War of 1939-45: commissioned Rifle Bde Sept. 1939; served Middle East Forces, Western Desert, 1941 (wounded); Egypt, Palestine, Syria, 1942; Temp. Major, 1942. Fellow of All Souls Coll., Oxford, 1931-38, 1961-; Barrister, Lincoln's Inn, 1932; a Bencher of Lincoln's Inn, 1956, Treasurer, 1975; QC 1953. MP (C) Oxford City, 1938-50, St Marylebone, (Dec.) 1963-70; Jt Parly Under-Sec. of State for Air, 1945; First Lord of the Admiralty, 1956-57; Minister of Education, 1957; Dep. Leader of the House of Lords, 1957-60; Leader of the House of Lords, 1960-63; Lord Privy Seal, 1959-60; Lord Pres. of the Council, 1957-59 and 1960-64; Minister for Science and Technology, 1959-64; Minister with special responsibility for: Sport, 1962-64; dealing with unemployment in the North-East, 1963-64; higher education, Dec. 1963-Feb. 1964; Sec. of State for Education and Science, April-Oct. 1964. Chm. of the Conservative Party Organization; Sept. 1957-Oct. 1959. Rector of Glasgow Univ., 1959-62. Pres. Classical Assoc., 1960-61. John Findley Green Foundation Lecture, 1960; Richard Dimbleby Lecture, 1976. Hon. Student of Christ Church, Oxford, 1962; Hon. Bencher, Inn of Court of NI, 1981; Hon. FICE 1963; Hon. FIEE 1972; Hon. FIStructE 1960. Hon. Freeman, Merchant Taylors' Co., 1971. Hon. DCL: Westminster Coll., Fulton, Missouri, USA, 1960; Newcastle, 1964; Oxon, 1974; Hon. LLD: Cambridge, 1963; Delhi, 1972; St Andrews, 1979; Leeds, 1982. *Publications:* The Law of Arbitration, 1935; One Year's Work, 1944; The Law and Employers' Liability, 1944; The Times We Live In, 1944; Making Peace, 1945; The Left was never Right, 1945; The Purpose of Parliament, 1946; Case for Conservatism, 1947; The Law of Monopolies, Restrictive Practices and Resale Price Maintenance, 1956; The Conservative Case, 1959; Interdependence, 1961; Science and Politics, 1963; The Devil's Own Song, 1968; The Door Wherein I Went, 1975; Elective Dictatorship, 1976; The Dilemma of Democracy, 1978. *Heir: (to disclaimed viscountcy): s* Hon. Douglas Martin Hogg, *qv. Recreations:* walking, climbing, shooting, etc. *Address:* House of Lords, SW1. *Clubs:* Carlton, Alpine, MCC.

HAILSTONE, Bernard, RP; painter; *b* 6 Oct. 1910; *s* of William Edward Hailstone; *m* 1934, Joan Mercia Kenet Hastings; one *s. Educ:* Sir Andrew Judd's Sch., Tonbridge. Trained at Goldsmiths' Coll. and Royal Academy Schs; Practising Artist, 1934-39; NFS, London (Fireman Artist), 1939-42;

Official War Artist to Ministry of Transport, 1942-44; Official War Artist to SEAC, 1944-45. Recent portraits include: HM Queen; Prince Charles and Princess Anne; Mrs Anne Armstrong, US Ambassador to UK; Pres. of USA, Jimmy Carter, 1977; HM Queen Elizabeth The Queen Mother, 1980; Prince Andrew, 1981. *Recreation:* tennis. *Address:* 43a Glebe Place, Chelsea, SW3. *T:* 01-352 1309; 49 Roland Gardens, SW7. *T:* 01-373 2970. *Club:* Chelsea Arts.

HAIMENDORF, Christoph von F.; *see* Fürer-Haimendorf.

HAINES, Sir Cyril (Henry), KBE 1962 (CBE 1953; MBE 1930); Chairman, South West London Rent Tribunal, 1962-66; *b* 2 March 1895; *s* of late Walter John Haines, OBE, formerly Deputy Chief Inspector of Customs and Excise; *m* 1934, Mary Theodora, *d* of late Rev. J. W. P. Silvester, BD, Hon. CF, Vicar of Wembley; two *d. Educ:* Hele's Sch., Exeter. Apptd to Scottish Education Dept, 1914. On active service with Army, 1915-19. Appt to Foreign Office, Dec. 1919. Called to Bar, Middle Temple, 1926. Asst Brit. Agent to Anglo-Mexican Revolutionary Claims Commn, 1928; Registrar, HM Supreme Court, for China, 1930 (acted as Asst Judge during absences from China of one of Judges); Asst Judge, HM Consular Court in Egypt, and, for Naval Courts, HM Consul at Alexandria, Egypt, 1943; Judge of HM Consular Court in Egypt, 1946. Indep. Referee for War Pension Appeals in Egypt, 1946; Asst Judge of HM Chief Court for the Persian Gulf, 1949-59, and Head of Claims Dept, Foreign Office, 1949-54; Judge of HM Chief Court for the Persian Gulf, 1959-61. Pres., Abbeyfield Orpington Soc., 1975- (Chm., 1962-75). *Address:* Wood Lea, 6 The Glen, Farnborough Park, Orpington, Kent. *T:* Farnborough, Kent, 54507.

HAINES, Joseph Thomas William; Chief Leader Writer, The Daily Mirror, since 1978 (Feature Writer, 1977-78); *b* 29 Jan. 1928; *s* of Joseph and Elizabeth Haines; *m* 1955, Irene Betty Lambert; no *c. Educ:* Elementary Schools, Rotherhithe, SE16. Parly Correspondent, The Bulletin (Glasgow) 1954-58, Political Correspondent, 1958-60; Political Correspondent: Scottish Daily Mail, 1960-64; The Sun, 1964-68; Dep. Press Sec. to Prime Minister, Jan.-June 1969; Chief Press Sec. to Prime Minister, 1969-70 and 1974-76, and to Leader of the Opposition, 1970-74. Mem. Tonbridge UDC, 1963-69, 1971-74. Mem., Royal Commn on Legal Services, 1976-79. *Publication:* The Politics of Power, 1977. *Recreations:* heresy and watching football. *Address:* 7 Hazel Shaw, Tonbridge, Kent. *T:* Tonbridge 365919.

HAINING, Thomas Nivison; HM Diplomatic Service, retired; independent consultant and writer on international affairs; *b* 15 March 1927; *m* 1955, Dorothy Patricia Robson; one *s.* Foreign Office, 1952; served Vienna, Moscow, Rome and New York; Counsellor, FCO, 1972-79; Ambassador and Consul-Gen. to Mongolia, 1979-82. FRGS 1980. *Address:* 14 Stompond Lane, Walton-on-Thames, Surrey. *Club:* Royal Automobile.

HAINSWORTH, Col John Raymond, CMG 1953; CBE 1945; retired; *b* 14 March 1900; *s* of William Henry Hainsworth, Keighley, Yorks; *m* 1925, Dora Marguerite Skiller, Rochester, Kent; one *s* one *d. Educ:* Taunton Sch.; RMA, Woolwich. Commissioned in Royal Engineers, 1919; posted to India, 1922. Served War of 1939-45 (despatches twice, CBE): Burma Campaign, 1942-45; apptd Dir of Works, GHQ, India, March 1945; seconded to Civil Employment in PWD, NWFP, India, 1946; Chief Engineer and Secretary to Government, PWD, NWFP, Pakistan, 1948-52; retired with rank of Col, 1952. *Recreations:* shooting, fishing. *Address:* 11 Butfield, Lavenham, Sudbury, Suffolk. *T:* Lavenham 247604.

HAINWORTH, Henry Charles, CMG 1961; HM Diplomatic Service, retired; *b* 12 Sept. 1914; *o s* of late Charles S. and Emily G. I. Hainworth; *m* 1944, Mary, *yr d* of late Felix B. and Lilian Ady; two *d. Educ:* Blundell's Sch.; Sidney Sussex Coll., Cambridge. Entered HM Consular Service, 1939; HM Embassy, Tokyo, 1940-42; seconded to Ministry of Information (Far Eastern Bureau, New Delhi), 1942-46; HM Embassy, Tokyo, 1946-51; Foreign Office, 1951-53; HM Legation, Bucharest, 1953-55; NATO Defence Coll., Paris, 1956; Political Office, Middle East Forces (Nicosia), 1956; Foreign Office, 1957-61 (Head of Atomic Energy and Disarmament Dept, 1958-61); Counsellor, United Kingdom Delegation to the Brussels Conference, 1961-63; HM Minister and Consul-Gen. at British Embassy, Vienna, 1963-68; Ambassador to Indonesia, 1968-70; Ambassador and Perm. UK Rep. to Disarm. Conf., Geneva, 1971-74. *Publication:* A Collector's Dictionary, 1980. *Recreations:* reading, fishing. *Address:* c/o Barclays Bank Ltd, 50 Jewry Street, Winchester, Hants.

HAITINK, Bernard, Hon. KBE 1977; Artistic Director and Permanent Conductor, Concertgebouw Orchestra, Amsterdam, since 1964; Musical Director, Glyndebourne Opera, since 1978; *b* Amsterdam, 4 March 1929. *Educ:* Amsterdam Conservatory. Studied conducting under Felix Hupke, but started his career as a violinist with the Netherlands Radio Philharmonic; in 1954 and 1955 attended annual conductors' course (org. by Netherlands Radio Union) under Ferdinand Leitner; became 2nd Conductor with Radio Union at Hilversum with co-responsibility for 4 radio orchs and conducted the Radio Philharmonic in public during the Holland Fest., in The Hague, 1956; conducted the Concertgebouw Orch. (as a subst. for Giulini), Oct. 1956; then followed guest engagements with this and other orchs in the Netherlands and elsewhere. Debut in USA, with Los Angeles Symph. Orch., 1958; 5 week season with Concertgebouw Orch., 1958-59, and toured Britain with it, 1959; apptd (with Eugen Jochum) as the Orchestra's permanent conductor, Sept.

1961; became sole artistic dir and permanent conductor of the orch., 1964; toured Japan and USSR, 1974; Japan, 1977; début at Royal Opera House, Covent Garden, 1977. London Philharmonic Orchestra: Principal Conductor, Artistic Dir, 1967-79; toured: Japan, 1969; USA, 1970, 1971, 1976; Berlin, 1972; Holland, Germany, Austria, 1973; USSR, 1975; has been a guest conductor all over the world, including Glyndebourne Festival Opera 1972, 1973, 1975, 1976, 1977. Hon. RAM 1973. Bruckner Medal of Honour, 1970; Gold Medal, Internat. Gustav Mahler Soc., 1971. Chevalier de L'Ordre des Arts et des Lettres, 1972; Order of Orange Nassau, 1969; Officer, Order of the Crown (Belgium), 1977. *Address:* c/o Harold Holt Ltd, 31 Sinclair Road, W14.

HAJNAL, John, FBA 1966; Professor of Statistics, London School of Economics, since 1975 (Reader, 1966-75); *b* 26 Nov. 1924; *s* of late Kálmán and Eva Hajnal-Kónyi; *m* 1950, Nina Lande; one *s* three *d. Educ:* University Coll. Sch., London; Balliol Coll., Oxford. Employed by: Royal Commission on Population, 1944-48; UN, New York, 1948-51; Office of Population Research, Princeton Univ., 1951-53; Manchester Univ., 1953-57; London Sch. of Economics, 1957-. Vis. Fellow Commoner, Trinity Coll., Cambridge, 1974-75; Vis. Prof., Rockefeller Univ., NY, 1981. Mem. Internat. Statistical Institute. *Publications:* The Student Trap, 1972; papers on demography, statistics, mathematics, etc. *Address:* London School of Economics and Political Science, Houghton Street, WC2A 2AE. *T:* 01-405 7686.

HAKEWILL SMITH, Maj.-Gen. Sir Edmund, KCVO 1967; CB 1945; CBE 1944; MC; psc; JP; Governor, Military Knights of Windsor, 1951-78; Deputy Constable and Lieutenant-Governor of Windsor Castle, 1964-72; *b* Kimberley, S Africa, 17 March 1896; *s* of George Cecil Smith and Mildred, 2nd *d* of J. B. Currey; *m* 1928, Edith, *e d* of Brigadier-Gen. H. Nelson, DSO, Shovel, Somerset; one *d. Educ:* Diocesan Coll., South Africa; RMC Sandhurst. Commissioned into Royal Scots Fusiliers as 2nd Lieut, 1915; ADC to Governor of Bengal, 1921-22; Adjutant, 2nd RSF, 1927-30; Staff Coll., Quetta, 1930-32; Staff Capt., War Office, 1934-36. Employed Air Staff Duties, RAF, 1936-37; DAAG War Office, 1938-40. Comdr 5 Devons, March-June 1940; Comdr 4/5 RSF, 1940-41; Comd 157 Inf. Bde, 1941-42; Dir of Organisation, War Office (Maj.-Gen.), 1942-43; Comdr 155 Inf. Bde (Brig.), Feb.-Nov. 1943; Comdr 52nd Lowland Div. (Maj.-Gen.), 1943 till disbandment, 1946; Commander, Lowland District, 1946; retired pay, 1949. Served European War, 1915-18 (wounded twice, MC); War of 1939-45 (despatches, CBE, CB. Order of St Olaf, Order of Orange-Nassau). Col, The Royal Scots Fusiliers, 1946-57; Berks County Commandant, Army Cadet Force, 1952-57. Grand Officer of Order of Orange Nassau, 1947; Order of St Olaf, Second Class, 1947. *Address:* Apt 28, Tennis Court Lane, Hampton Court Palace, East Molesey, Surrey.

HALABY, Najeeb Elias; President, Halaby International Corporation; Director: Chrysler Corporation; BankAmerica Corporation; BDM International Co.; Menlo Financial Co.; *b* 19 Nov. 1915; *s* of late Najeeb Elias Halaby and of Laura Wilkins Halaby; *m* 1946, Doris Carlquist (marr. diss. 1976); one *s* two *d. Educ:* Stanford Univ. (AB); Yale Univ. (LLB); Bonar Law Coll., Ashridge, (Summer) 1939. Called to the Bar: California, 1940; District of Columbia, 1948; NY, 1973. Practised law in Los Angeles, Calif, 1940-42, 1958-61; Air Corps Flight Instructor, 1940; Test pilot for Lockheed Aircraft Corp., 1942-43; Naval aviator, established Navy Test Pilot Sch., 1943; formerly Chief of Intelligence Coordination Div., State Dept; Foreign Affairs Advisor to Sec. of Defense; Chm., NATO Military Production and Supply Board, 1950; Asst Administrator, Mutual Security Economic Cooperation Administration, 1950-51; Asst Sec. of Defense for Internat. Security, 1952-54; Vice-Chm., White House Advisory Group whose report led to formation of Federal Aviation Agency, 1955-56, Administrator of the Agency, 1961-65; Pan American World Airways: Director, 1965-73; Member, Executive Committee of Board, 1965-68; Senior Vice-President, 1965-68, President, 1968-71; Chief Executive, 1969-72; Chairman, 1970-72; Associate of Laurance and Nelson Rockefeller, 1954-57; Past Exec. Vice-Pres. and Dir, Servomechanisms Inc.; Sec.-Treas., Aerospace Corp., 1959-61; Pres., American Technology Corp. Member of Board: Planned Parenthood- World Population; Mem. Exec. Cttee, (Founder-Chm., 1971-73), US-Japan Econ. Council; Trustee: Aspen Inst., Aspen, Colo.; Internat. Executive Service Corps; Eisenhower Exchange Fellowships, Inc.; Amer. Univ. of Beirut (Chm.). Monsanto Safety Award; FAA Exceptional Service Medal. Fellow, Amer. Inst. of Aeronautics and Astronautics. Hon. LLB: Allegheny Coll., Pa, 1967; Loyola Coll., LA, 1968. *Publication:* Crosswinds (memoir), 1976. *Recreation:* golf. *Address:* (office) 239 Glenville Road, Greenwich, Connecticut 06830, USA; (residence) 1822 Kalorama Square NW, Washington, DC 20008, USA. *Clubs:* F Street, Metropolitan, Chevy Chase (Washington); Bohemian Grove (California); Explorers', University, River (NYC).

HALAS, John, OBE 1972; FSIAD; Chairman, Educational Film Centre, since 1960; President: British Federation of Film Societies, since 1980; International Animated Film Association, since 1975; *b* 16 April 1912; *s* of Victor and Bertha Halas; *m* 1940, Joy Batchelor; one *s* one *d. Educ:* Académie des Beaux-Arts, Paris; Mühely, Budapest. Founded: (with Joy Batchelor) Halas and Batchelor Animation Ltd, 1940; (with Lord Snow, Morris Goldsmith, Joy Batchelor and Roger Manvell) Educational Film Centre, 1960; ASIFA (International Animated Film Assoc.), 1960. Produced 2,000 animated films, 1940-80, incl. first feature-length animated film in GB, Animal Farm. Past President, Internat. Council of Graphic Design Assocs; Hon. Fellow, BKSTS, 1972.

Publications: How to Cartoon, 1959; The Technique of Film Animation, 1961; Film and TV Graphics, 1967; Computer Animation, 1974; Visual Scripting, 1977; Film Animation, a Simplified Approach, 1978; Timing for Animation, 1981; Graphics in Motion, 1981. *Recreations:* painting, music. *Address:* 6 Holford Road, Hampstead, NW3 1AD. *T:* 01-435 8674.

HALDANE, Archibald Richard Burdon, CBE 1968; *b* 18 Nov. 1900; *s* of late Sir William Haldane; *m* 1941, Janet Macrae Simpson-Smith; one *s* one *d*. *Educ:* Edinburgh Academy; Winchester Coll.; Balliol Coll., Oxford; Edinburgh University. LLB Edinburgh, 1926; WS 1926; DLitt Edinburgh, 1950. Dep. Chm., Trustee Savings Banks Assoc., 1959-61; Chm., Trustee Savings Banks Inspection Cttee, 1960-67; Vice-Pres., Trustee Savings Bank Assoc., 1971. *Publications:* By Many Waters, 1940; The Path by the Water, 1944; The Drove Roads of Scotland, 1950, repr. 1973; New Ways through the Glens, 1962, repr 1973; Three Centuries of Scottish Posts, 1971; By River, Stream and Loch, 1973. *Recreations:* fishing, walking. *Address:* Foswell, Auchterarder, Perthshire. *T:* Auchterarder 2610; 4 North Charlotte Street, Edinburgh. *T:* 031-225 4181. *Club:* New (Edinburgh).

HALE, family name of **Baron Hale.**

HALE, Baron *cr* 1972 (Life Peer), of Oldham; **(Charles) Leslie Hale;** *b* 13 July 1902; *s* of Benjamin George Hale, Managing Director of Stableford & Co. Ltd, Coalville, Leics; *m* 1926, Dorothy Ann Latham (*d* 1971); one *s* one *d*. *Educ:* Ashby-de-la-Zouch Boys' Grammar Sch. Articled to Evan Barlow, Solicitor, Leicester; practised in Coalville, Nuneaton and London. Mem. Leics County Council, 1925-50. Contested (L) S Nottingham, 1929. MP (Lab) for Oldham, Lancs. 1945-50, West Division of Oldham, 1950-Jan. 1968, resigned. Freedom of Oldham, 1969. *Publications:* Thirty Who Were Tried, 1955; John Philpot Curran, 1958; Blood on the Scales, 1960; Hanged in Error, 1961; Hanging in the Balance, 1962; None So Blind, 1963. *Recreation:* house painting. *Address:* 92 College Road, SE21.

HALE, Prof. John Rigby, FBA 1977; Professor of Italian, University College London, since 1970; Public Orator, University of London, since 1981; *b* 17 Sept. 1923; *s* of E. R. S. Hale, FRCP, MD, and Hilda Birks; *m* 1st, 1952, Rosalind Williams; one *s* two *d* ; 2nd, 1965, Sheila Haynes MacIvor; one *s*. *Educ:* Neville Holt Preparatory Sch.; Eastbourne Coll., Jesus Coll., Oxford. BA first cl. hons Mod. Hist., 1948; MA (Oxon) 1950. Served War, Radio Operator in Merchant Service, 1942-45. Commonwealth Fellow, Johns Hopkins and Harvard Univs, 1948-49; Fellow and Tutor in Modern History, Jesus Coll., Oxford, 1949-64. Editor, Oxford Magazine, 1958-59; Visiting Prof., Cornell Univ., 1959-60; Vis. Fellow, Harvard Centre for Renaissance Studies, I Tatti, 1963; Prof. of History, Univ. of Warwick, 1964-69; Vis. Prof., Univ. of California, Berkeley, 1969-70; Folger Library, Washington Fellowship, 1970. Chm. of Trustees, Nat. Gallery, 1974-80 (Trustee, 1973-80); Mem., Royal Mint Adv. Cttee, 1979-. Chm., British Soc. for Renaissance Studies, 1973-76. FSA 1962; FRHistS 1968; FRSA 1974. Socio Straniero, Accademia Arcadia, 1972. Academicus ex Classe (Bronze Plaque Award), Academia Medicea, 1980; Commendatore, Ordine al Merito della Repubblica Italiana, 1981; Premio Bolla (services to Venice), 1982. *Publications:* England and the Italian Renaissance, 1954;The Italian Journal of Samuel Rogers, 1956; Machiavelli and Renaissance Italy, 1961; (trans. and ed) The Literary Works of Machiavelli, 1961; (ed) Certain Discourses Military by Sir John Smythe, 1964; The Evolution of British Historiography, 1964; (co-ed) Europe in the Late Middle Ages, 1965; Renaissance Exploration, 1968; Renaissance Europe 1480-1520, 1971; (ed) Renaissance Venice, 1973; Italian Renaissance Painting, 1977; Renaissance Fortification: art or engineering?, 1978; Florence and the Medici: the pattern of control, 1977; The Travel Journal of Antonio de Beatis, 1979; (ed) A Concise Encyclopaedia of the Italian Renaissance, 1981; contributor: New Cambridge Modern History, vols 1, 2, 3; Past and Present; Studi Veneziani, Italian Studies, etc. *Recreation:* Venice. *Address:* Department of Italian, University College, Gower Street, WC1E 6BT. *T:* 01-387 7050; 26 Montpelier Row, Twickenham, Mddx TW1 2NQ. *T:* 01-892 9636. *Club:* Beefsteak.

HALE, Comdr John William, DSO 1940; RN retired; *b* 30 March 1907; 4th *s* of late Warren Stormes Hale and late Cora Hale; *m* 1938, Ada Elizabeth Bowden; one *s* two *d*. *Educ:* Highgate Sch.; RN Coll., Dartmouth. Went to sea as midshipman in HMS Resolution, 1924; Lieut and joined Fleet Air Arm, 1929; Lieut Cdr 1937; at beginning of war of 1939-45, served in HMS Glorious and then HMS Illustrious; took part in attack on Italian Fleet, Taranto, 11 Nov. 1940 (DSO); Commander, 1940; retired, 1957; Freeman of City of London; Past Master of Tallow Chandlers Company. Mem., Historic Houses Assoc. (opens Letheringham Water Mill and Gardens to public during the summer). *Recreation:* gardening. *Address:* Letheringham Mill, Woodbridge, Suffolk.

HALE, Joseph; engineer; formerly Merchant Navy; *b* 28 Oct. 1913; *s* of J. Gordon Tyson Hale and M. Hale (*née* Johnston); *m* 1939, Annie Irene Clowes; one *s* one *d*. *Educ:* elementary and secondary technical schs. Mem. Bolton Town Council until 1950; Junior Whip to Labour Group; Chm. Bolton West Divisional Party, 1949; Mem. Amalgamated Engineering Union District Cttee, 1943-50. MP (Lab) Rochdale, 1950-51. *Recreations:* literature, music. *Address:* 30 Thorpe Street, Bolton, Lancs.

HALE, Kathleen, (Mrs Douglas McClean), OBE 1976; artist; illustrator and author of books for children; *b* 24 May 1898; *d* of Charles Edward Hale and Ethel Alice Aylmer Hughes; *m* 1926, Dr Douglas McClean (*d* 1967); two *s*. *Educ:* Manchester High Sch. for Girls; Manchester Sch. of Art; Art Dept (scholar) of University Coll., Reading; Central Sch. of Art; East Anglian Sch. of Painting and Drawing. Has exhibited paintings at: New English Art Club, London Group, Grosvenor Galleries, Vermont Gallery, Warwick Public Library Gallery; Gallery Edward Harvane, New Grafton Gallery, Parkin Gallery; metal groups and pictures at: Lefèvre Galleries; Leicester Galleries; Oxford Arts Council, Arts Centre. Mural for South Bank (Festival) Schs Section, 1951; Orlando Ballet for Festival Gardens, 1951. *Publications:* The Orlando The Marmalade Cat Series, since 1938: Camping Holiday; Trip Abroad; Buys a Farm; Becomes a Doctor; Silver Wedding; Keeps a Dog; A Seaside Holiday; The Frisky Housewife; Evening Out; Home Life; Invisible Pyjamas; The Judge; Zoo; Magic Carpet; Country Peep-Show; Buys a Cottage; and The Three Graces; Goes to the Moon; and the Water Cats; Henrietta, the Faithful Hen, 1946; Puss-in-Boots Peep-Show, 1950; Manda, 1952; Henrietta's Magic Egg, 1973. TV and radio programmes. *Recreation:* painting. *Address:* Tod House, Forest Hill, near Oxford. *T:* Stanton St John 390.

HALE, Norman Morgan; Under Secretary, Department of Health and Social Security, since 1975; *b* 28 June 1933; *s* of late T. N. Hale and Mrs A. E. Hale, Evesham, Worcs; *m* 1965, Sybil Jean (*née* Maton); one *s* one *d*. *Educ:* Prince Henry's Grammar Sch., Evesham; St John's Coll., Oxford (MA). Min. of Pensions and National Insurance, 1955; Asst Sec., Nat. Assistance Bd, 1966; Min. of Social Security, 1966; CSD, 1970-72. *Address:* 64 Castle Avenue, Ewell, Epsom, Surrey. *T:* 01-393 3507.

HALES, Prof. Charles Nicholas, PhD, MD; FRCPath; FRCP; Professor of Clinical Biochemistry, University of Cambridge, since 1977; *b* 25 April 1935; *s* of Walter Bryan Hales and Phyllis Marjory Hales; *m* 1st, 1959, Janet May Moss; two *s* ; 2nd, 1978, Margaret Griffiths; one *d*. *Educ:* King Edward VI Grammar Sch., Stafford; Univ. of Cambridge (BA 1956, MB, BChir, MA 1959, PhD 1964, MD 1971). MRCPath 1971, FRCPath 1980; MRCP 1971, FRCP 1976. House Surgeon, UCH, 1959, House Physician, 1960; Stothert Res. Fellow, Royal Soc., 1963-64; Lectr, Dept of Biochem., Univ. of Cambridge, 1964-70; Clinical Asst, Addenbrooke's Hosp., Cambridge, 1961-68, Hon. Consultant in Clin. Biochem, 1968-70; Prof. of Med. Biochem., Welsh National Sch. of Medicine, Cardiff, and Hon. Consultant in Med. Biochem., University Hosp. of Wales, Cardiff, 1970-77. Consultant in Med. Biochem., South Glam Health Authority (T). *Recreations:* music, fishing. *Address:* Department of Clinical Biochemistry, Addenbrooke's Hospital, Hills Road, Cambridge CB2 2QR. *T:* Cambridge 245151.

HALEY, Prof. Keith Brian, PhD; FIMA, FOR; Professor of Operational Research since 1968, and Head of Department of Engineering Production since 1981, Birmingham University; *b* 17 Nov. 1933; *s* of Arthur Leslie Haley and Gladys Mary Haley; *m* 1960, Diana Elizabeth Mason; one *s*. *Educ:* King Edward VI, Five Ways, Birmingham; Birmingham Univ. (BSc, PhD). FIMA 1970; FOR 1976. OR Scientist, NCB, 1957-59; Lectr, 1959-63, Sen. Lectr, 1963-68, Birmingham Univ. Pres., ORS, 1982-; Editor, Jl of ORS, 1972-80. Governor, Bromsgrove Sch., 1968-. *Publications:* Mathematical Programming for Business and Industry, 1966; Operational Research '75, 1976; Operational Research '78, 1979; Search Theory and Applications, 1980; Applied Operations Research in Fishing, 1981; many articles. *Recreations:* squash, bridge. *Address:* 22 Eymore Close, Selly Oak, Birmingham B29 4LB. *T:* 021-475 3331. *Club:* Royal Over-Seas League.

HALEY, Philip William Raymond Chatterton, MBE 1956; HM Diplomatic Service, retired 1976; *b* 18 June 1917; 2nd *s* of late Joseph Bertram Haley and late Lilian Anne Chatterton Haley; *m* 1941, Catherine Skene Stewart, LRAM, LRCM; two *d*. *Educ:* Perse Sch.; London University. HM Services, 1940-47 in KOSB and on Gen. Staff; 2nd Lieut 1941, Lieut 1942, Captain 1943, Major 1945, Lt-Col 1946; Control Commn for Germany, 1947-56, serving also with Internat. Commn for the Saar. HM Diplomatic Service, 1956; Consul, Düsseldorf; Hamburg, 1959; 1st Sec. and Embassy spokesman, Bonn, 1960; Dep. Consul-General, Chicago, 1964; Johannesburg, 1968; Consul-Gen., Hanover, 1973. Croix de la Libération, 1946. *Recreations:* gardening, painting, senile delinquency (*eg* bird watching). *Address:* Casa Iris, 6 Calle el Tulipan, San Patricio, Santa Ursula, Tenerife, Canary Isles. *T:* 300814.

HALEY, Sir William (John), KCMG, 1946; Hon. LLD Cambridge 1951, Dartmouth, New Hampshire, 1957, London, 1963, St Andrews, 1965); Hon. Fellow Jesus College, Cambridge 1956; FRSL; Commissioner of Appeal for Income Tax, Jersey, since 1971; *b* Jersey, CI, 24 May 1901; *s* of Frank Haley, Bramley, Leeds, and Marie Sangan; *m* 1921, Edith Susie Gibbons; two *s* two *d*. *Educ:* Victoria Coll., Jersey. Joined Manchester Evening News, 1922; Chief Sub-Editor, 1925; Managing Editor, 1930; Dir Manchester Guardian and Evening News, Ltd, 1930; Jt Managing Dir, 1939-43; Dir Press Association, 1939-43; Dir Reuters, 1939-43; Editor-in-Chief, BBC, 1943-44; Dir-Gen., BBC, 1944-52; Editor of the Times, 1952-66; Dir and Chief Executive, The Times Publishing Co. Ltd, 1965-66; Chm., Times Newspapers Ltd, 1967; Editor-in-Chief, Encylopædia Britannica, 1968-69. Pres., Nat. Book League, 1955-62; Chm., Jersey Arts Council, 1976-77. Chevalier Legion of Honour, 1948; Grand Officer, Order of Orange Nassau, 1950. *Address:* Beau Site, Gorey, Jersey, Channel Islands. *T:* Jersey 51068.

See also Prof. J. N. Hunt.

HALFORD, Maj.-Gen. Michael Charles Kirkpatrick, DSO 1946; OBE 1957; DL; *b* 28 Oct. 1914; *s* of Lieut-Col M. F. Halford, OBE, and Violet Halford (*née* Kirkpatrick); *m* 1945, Pamela Joy (*née* Wright); three *s. Educ:* Wellington Coll.; Trinity Coll., Cambridge. Commissioned Royal Guernsey Militia, 1932; 2nd Lieut York and Lancaster Regt, 1935; served Egypt and Palestine, 1936; France 1940; N Africa, Italy, France and Germany; comd Hallamshire Bn, York and Lancaster Regt, 1945, 1st Bn, 1954; Asst Army Instr, Imperial Defence Coll., 1957; comd 147 Inf. Bde (TA), 1960; GOC 43 (Wessex) Div./District, 1964-67; retd, 1967. Representative Col The York and Lancaster Regt, 1966-79. DL Hants 1975. *Recreations:* fishing, golf. *Address:* Fairfields, Poulner Hill, Ringwood, Hants. *Club:* Army and Navy.

HALFORD-MacLEOD, Aubrey Seymour, CMG 1958; CVO 1965; HM Diplomatic Service, retired; *b* 15 Dec. 1914; *o s* of late Joseph and Clara Halford; changed name by deed poll from Halford to Halford-MacLeod, 1964; *m* 1939, Giovanna Mary, *o d* of late W. H. Durst; three *s* one *d. Educ:* King Edward's Sch., Birmingham; Magdalen Coll., Oxford. Entered HM Diplomatic (subseq. Foreign, now again Diplomatic) Service as Third Sec., 1937; Bagdad, 1939; Second Sec., 1942; transferred to Office of Minister Resident in N Africa, 1943; First Sec., 1943; British mem. of Secretariat of Advisory Council for Italy, 1944; British High Commission in Italy, 1944; Asst Political Adviser to Allied Commission in Italy, Sept, 1944, Political Adviser, 1945; transferred to HM Foreign Office, 1946, Principal Private Sec. to Permanent Under-Sec.; Dep. Exec. Sec. to Preparatory Commission for Council of Europe, May 1949, and promoted Counsellor; Dep. Sec. Gen. of the Council of Europe, 1949-52; Counsellor, HM Embassy, Tokyo, 1953-55; in charge of HM Legation, Seoul, 1954; Counsellor at HM Embassy in Libya, 1955-57; HM Political Agent at Kuwait, 1957-59; HM Consul-Gen., Munich, 1959-65; HM Ambassador to Iceland, 1966-70. Foreign Affairs Adviser, Scottish Council (Develt and Ind.), 1971-78. Dir, Scottish Opera, 1971-78. Pres., Scottish Soc. for Northern Studies, 1973-76. Vice-Pres., Clan MacLeod Soc. of Scotland, 1976-79. *Publication:* (with G. M. Halford) The Kabuki Handbook, 1956. *Recreations:* fishing, shooting, ornithology. *Address:* Mulag House, Ardvourlie, N Harris PA85 3AB. *T:* Harris 2054.

HALIFAX, 3rd Earl of, cr 1944; **Charles Edward Peter Neil Wood;** Bt 1784; Viscount Halifax, 1866; Baron Irwin, 1925; *b* 14 March 1944; *s* of 2nd Earl of Halifax, and of Ruth, *d* of late Captain Rt Hon. Neil James Archibald Primrose, MC, sometime MP; *S* father, 1980; *m* 1976, Camilla, *d* of Col. C. F. J. Younger, *qv*; one *s* one *d. Educ:* Eton; Christ Church, Oxford. Contested (C) Dearne Valley, Feb. and Oct. 1974. Dir, Hambros Bank, 1978-. *Heir: s* Lord Irwin, *qv. Address:* Garrowby, York. *Clubs:* Turf, White's.

HALIFAX (NS), Archbishop of, (RC), since 1967; **Most Rev. James Martin Hayes;** *b* 27 May 1924; *s* of late L. J. Hayes. *Educ:* St Mary's Univ., Halifax; Holy Heart Seminary, Halifax; Angelicum Univ., Rome. Asst, St Mary's Basilica, 1947-54; Chancellor and Sec. of Archdiocese of Halifax, 1957-65; Rector, St Mary's Basilica, 1963-65; Auxil. Bp of Halifax, 1965-66; Apostolic Administrator of Archdiocese of Halifax, 1966-67. Hon. Dr of Letters, St Anne's Coll., Church Point, NS; Hon. Dr of Sacred Theology, King's Coll., Halifax, NS. *Address:* 6541 Coburg Road, PO Box 1527, Halifax, Nova Scotia B3J 2Y3, Canada. *T:* 902-429-9388.

HALIFAX, Archdeacon of; *see* Alford, Ven. J. R.

HALL, family name of **Viscount Hall.**

HALL, 2nd Viscount, cr 1946, of Cynon Valley; **(William George) Leonard Hall;** *b* 9 March 1913; *s* of 1st Viscount Hall, PC, and Margaret, *d* of William Jones, Ynysybwl; *S* father, 1965; *m* 1st, 1935, Joan Margaret (*d* 1962), *d* of William Griffiths, Glamorganshire; two *d*; 2nd, 1963, Constance Ann Gathorne (*d* 1972), *d* of Rupert Gathorne Hardy, London; 3rd, 1975, Marie-Colette Bach, St Viatre. *Educ:* Christ Coll., Brecon; University Coll. Hospital. MRCS; LRCP. Asst MOH, Merthyr Tydfil, 1938-40. Surgeon Lt-Comdr, RNVR, 1940-46. Powell Duffryn Group, 1946-60; Dir of Investments, Africa, Asia and ME, Internat. Finance Corp. (affiliate of IBRD), 1962-64; Advisor for Special Projects, Internat. Finance Corp., 1963-64; Chm., Post Office, 1969-70. Liveryman, Hon. Co. of Carmen. *Recreations:* country activities. *Address:* Solvain, 41210 St Viatre, Loir et Cher, France. *T:* (54) 83 63 67.

HALL, Adam; *see* Trevor, Elleston.

HALL, Alfred Charles, CBE 1977 (OBE 1966); HM Diplomatic Service, retired; Grants Officer, Save the Children Fund, since 1979; Director: Expotec (UK) Ltd, since 1981; Eotap, since 1982; *b* 2 Aug. 1917; *s* of Alfred Hall and Florence Mary Hall; *m* 1945, Clara Georgievna Strunina, Moscow; five *s* one *d. Educ:* Oratory Sch.; Polytechnic of Central London (Rothschild Prize; Local Govt Dip.). Served War, RA and Intell. Corps, 1939-43. LCC, 1934-39 and 1946-49; FO, with service in Saudi Arabia, Algeria, Egypt, Iran and USSR, 1943-46; FCO (formerly CRO and CO), with service in Pakistan, India, Nigeria, Canada and Australia, 1949-75; Dep. High Comr in Southern India, 1975-77. *Publications:* freelance journalism and technical papers. *Recreations:* music, reading, gardening, linguistics. *Address:* White Cliff, St Margaret's Bay, Kent CT15 6HR. *T:* Dover 852230. *Club:* Royal Commonwealth Society.

HALL, Prof. Alfred Rupert, LittD; FBA 1978; Professor of the History of Science and Technology, Imperial College of Science and Technology, University of London, 1963-80; *b* 26 July 1920; *s* of Alfred Dawson Hall and Margaret Ritchie; *m* 1st, 1942, Annie Shore Hughes; two *d*; 2nd, 1959, Marie Boas. *Educ:* Alderman Newton's Boy's Sch., Leicester; Christ's Coll., Cambridge (scholar). LittD Cantab 1975. Served in Royal Corps of Signals, 1940-45. 1st cl. Historical Tripos Part II, 1946; Allen Scholar, 1948; Fellow, Christ's Coll., 1949-59, Steward, 1955-59; Curator, Whipple Science Mus., Cambridge and University Lectr, 1950-59. Medical Research Historian, University of Calif, Los Angeles, 1959-60, Prof. of Philosophy, 1960-61; Prof. of History and Logic of Science, Indiana Univ., 1961-63. FRHistS. Pres., British Soc. for History of Science, 1966-68; Pres., Internat. Acad. of the History of Science, 1977-81. Co-editor, A History of Technology, 1951-58. Corresp. Mem., Soc. for the History of Technology, 1970. Silver Medal, RSA, 1974; (jtly) Sarton Medal, 1981. *Publications:* Ballistics in the Seventeenth Century, 1952; The Scientific Revolution, 1954; From Galileo to Newton, 1963; The Cambridge Philosophical Society: a history, 1819-1969, 1969; Philosophers at War, 1980. With Marie Boas Hall: Unpublished Scientific Papers of Isaac Newton, 1962; Correspondence of Henry Oldenburg, 1965-.; (with Laura Tilling) Correspondence of Isaac Newton, vols 5-7, 1974-77; (ed with Norman Smith) History of Technology, 1976-. Contributor to Isis, Annals of Science, etc. *Address:* 14 Ball Lane, Tackley, Oxford. *T:* Tackley 257.

HALL, Sir Arnold (Alexander), Kt 1954; FRS 1953; MA; Chairman, Hawker Siddeley Group plc, since 1967 (Director, 1955, Vice-Chairman, 1963-67, Managing Director, 1967-81); Chairman: Hawker Siddeley Diesels Ltd; Hawker Siddeley Electric Ltd; Hawker Siddeley Canada Inc.; Hawker Siddeley Rail Ltd; Director: Lloyds Bank, 1966-; Lloyd's Bank UK Management Ltd, 1979-; Phoenix Assurance; ICI; Onan Corporation, 1976-80; Chancellor, Loughborough University of Technology, since 1980; *b* 23 April 1915; married. *Educ:* Clare Coll., Cambridge (Rex Moir Prize in Engineering, John Bernard Seely Prize in Aeronautics, Ricardo Prize in Thermodynamics). Res. Fellow in Aeronautics of the Company of Armourers and Brasiers (held at University of Cambridge), 1936-38; Principal Scientific Officer, Royal Aircraft Establishment, Farnborough, Hants, 1938-45; Zaharoff Prof. of Aviation, University of London, and Head of Dept of Aeronautics, Imperial Coll. of Science and Technology, 1945-51; Dir of the Royal Aircraft Establishment, Farnborough, 1951-55. Chm., Fasco Industries Inc., 1980-81. Pres., Royal Aeronautical Society, 1958-59, Hon. Fellow, 1965; Dep. Pres., BEAMA, 1966-67, Pres., 1967-68; Vice-Pres., Engineering Employers' Fedn, 1968; President: Locomotive and Allied Manufacturers Assoc. of GB, 1968-69, 1969-70; SBAC, 1972-73. Member: Advisory Council on Scientific Policy, 1962-64; Air Registration Board, 1963-73; Electricity Supply Research Council, 1963-72; Advisory Council on Technology (Min. of Technology), 1964-67; Defence Industries Council, 1969-77; Industrial Develt Adv. Bd, 1973-75; Dep. Chm., Engineering Industries Council, 1975-. Pro-Chancellor, Warwick Univ., 1965-70. Fellow, Imperial Coll. of Science and Technology, 1963-; Founder Fellow, Fellowship of Engineering, 1976 (Vice-Pres., 1977); For. Associate, US Nat. Acad. of Engrg, 1976-; Hon. Fellow, Clare Coll., Cambridge, 1966; Hon. ACGI; Hon. FRAeS; Hon. FAIAA; Hon. MIMechE, 1968; Hon. FIEE, 1975; Hon. DTech Loughborough 1976. Gold Medal, RAeS, 1962; Hambro Award (Business Man of the Year), 1975; Gold Medal, BIM, 1981. *Address:* Hawker Siddeley Group plc, 18 St James's Square, SW1. *Club:* Athenæum.

HALL, Arthur Henderson, RWS 1970; RE 1961; MSIA; ARCA; painter, etcher, freelance illustrator; Head of School of Graphic Design, Kingston Polytechnic, 1965-71 (Senior Lecturer in charge, 1952-65); *b* 25 June 1906; *s* of Charles and Mary Hall; *m* 1942, Frances Bruce; one *s* one *d. Educ:* Sedgefield; Royal College of Art; British Sch., Rome. Prix de Rome, Engraving, 1931; Glass Designer for Webb & Corbett, 1933-36; Part-time Teacher, Kingston Sch. of Art, 1933-41; Part-time Teacher, London Central Sch. of Art, 1936-39. RAF, 1942-46. Teacher, London Central Sch. of Art, 1946-52; exhibits paintings and etchings at: RA, RWS, RE. *Publications:* numerous illustrations for children's books and books on gardening. *Recreations:* gardening, travel. *Address:* 15 Church Road, East Molesey, Surrey. *T:* 01-979 5681. *Club:* Nash House.

HALL, Arthur Herbert; Librarian and Curator, Guildhall Library and Museum, 1956-66, retired; Director of Guildhall Art Gallery, 1956-66; *b* 30 Aug. 1901; *y s* of Henry and Eliza Jane Hall, Islington, London; *m* 1927, Dorothy Maud (*née* Barton); two *s* one *d. Educ:* Mercers' Sch., Holborn, London. Entered Guildhall Library as junior asst, 1918; Dep. Librarian, 1943-56. Hon. Librarian, Clockmakers' and Gardeners' Companies, 1956-66. Served with RAOC, 1942-46. Chm. Council, London and Middlesex Archæological Soc., 1957-64, Vice-Pres., 1962-; Member: Council of London Topographical Soc., 1960-67; Exec. Cttee, Friends of Nat. Libraries, 1965-69. Hon. Sec., Middlesex Victoria County History Council, 1966-78; Enfield Archaeological Soc. (Hon. Sec., 1966-71); Master, 1974-75, Hon. Clerk, 1965-74, Asst Hon. Clerk, 1975-, Civic Guild of Old Mercers. Liveryman of the Clockmakers Co.; FLA 1930; FSA 1963. *Address:* 23 Uvedale Road, Enfield, Mddx. *T:* 01-363 2526.

HALL, Sir Basil (Brodribb), KCB 1977 (CB 1974); MC 1945; TD 1952; Chairman, Civil Service Appeal Board, since 1981 (Deputy Chairman, 1980-81); Legal Adviser, Broadcasting Complaints Commission, since 1981; *b* 2 Jan. 1918; *s* of late Alfred Brodribb Hall and of Elsie Hilda Hall, Woking,

Surrey; *m* 1955, Jean Stafford Gowland; two *s* one *d. Educ:* Merchant Taylors' Sch. Articled Clerk with Gibson & Weldon, Solicitors, 1935–39; admitted Solicitor, 1942. Served War of 1939–45: Trooper, Inns of Court Regt, 1939; 2nd Lieut, 12th Royal Lancers, 1940; Captain, 27th Lancers, 1941; Major, 27th Lancers, 1942. Legal Asst, Treasury Solicitor's Dept, 1946; Sen. Legal Asst, 1951; Asst Treasury Solicitor, 1958; Principal Asst Solicitor, 1968; Dep. Treasury Solicitor, 1972; HM Procurator Gen. and Treasury Solicitor, 1975. Mem. Council, Nat. Army Museum, 1981–. *Recreations:* military history, travel. *Address:* Woodlands, Danes Way, Oxshott, Surrey. *T:* Oxshott 2032. *Clubs:* Athenæum, Cavalry and Guards.

HALL, Very Rev. Bernard, SJ; English Assistant to Father General, Society of Jesus, Rome, since 1982; *b* 17 Oct. 1921. *Educ:* St Michael's Coll., Leeds; Heythrop Coll., Oxford. LicPhil, STL. Captain RA, 1941–46. Entered Society of Jesus, 1946; ordained priest, 1955; Provincial of the English Province, Society of Jesus, 1970–76; Rector, Collegio San Roberto Bellarmino, Rome, 1976–82. *Address:* Borgo Santo Spirito 5, 00193 Rome, Italy.

HALL, Betty, CBE 1977; Regional Nursing Officer, West Midlands Regional Health Authority, 1974–81; *b* 6 June 1921; *d* of John Hall and Jane (*née* Massey), Eagley, Lancs. *Educ:* Bolton Sch.; Royal Infirm., Edinburgh (RGN); Radcliffe Infirm., Oxford and St Mary's Hosp., Manchester (SCM); Royal Coll. of Nursing (RNT). Nursed tuberculous patients from concentration camps, Rollier Clinic, Leysin, 1948–49; Ward Sister, Salford Royal Hosp., 1949–51; Sister Tutor, Royal Masonic Hosp., London, 1952–54; Principal Tutor, St Luke's Hosp., Bradford, 1954–61 (Mem. Leeds Area Nurse Trng Cttee); King Edward's Hosp. Fund Admin. Staff Coll., 1961–62; Work Study Officer to United Bristol Hosps, 1961–64; Asst Nursing Officer to Birmingham Regional Hosp. Bd, 1964–65, Regional Nursing Officer, 1966–74. Member: W Mids Regional Nurse Trng Cttee; Cttee, Abbeyfield Homes, Grange-over-Sands. *Recreations:* reading, tapestry making, cricket. *Address:* Chailey, Ash Mount Road, Grange-over-Sands, Cumbria LA11 6BX. *Club:* Naval and Military.

HALL, Dame Catherine (Mary), DBE 1982 (CBE 1967); FRCN; General Secretary, Royal College of Nursing of the United Kingdom, 1957–82; *b* 19 Dec. 1922; *d* of late Robert Hall, OBE and late Florence Irene Hall (*née* Turner). *Educ:* Hunmanby Hall Sch. for Girls, Filey, Yorks. Gen. Infirmary, Leeds: nursing trng, 1941–44 (SRN); Ward Sister, 1945–47; sen. nursing appts, 1949–53; midwifery trng, Leeds and Rotherham, 1948 (SCM); travelling fellowship, US and Canada, 1950–51; student in nursing administration, Royal College of Nursing, 1953–54; Asst Matron, Middlesex Hosp., London, 1954–56. Part-time Member: CIR, 1971–74; British Railways Regional Bd for London and the South East, 1975–77; Mem. GMC, 1979–; Chm., UK Central Council for Nursing, Midwifery and Health Visiting, 1980–. Hon. Mem., Florida Nurses Assoc., 1973. FRCN 1976. OStJ 1977. Hon. DLitt City, 1975.

HALL, Dr Cecil Charles, CB 1968; retired; Director, Warren Spring Laboratory, Ministry of Technology, 1964–68; *b* 10 May 1907; *s* of Frederick Harrington and Alice Hall; *m* 1950, Margaret Rose Nicoll; no *c. Educ:* Beckenham Gram. Sch.; London Univ. Jun. Chemist, S Metropolitan Gas Co., 1925–30; BSc 1st Hons Chem. (London), 1929; MSc (London), 1931. Jun. Asst, Fuel Research Stn, DSIR, 1930: PhD (London), 1934. Research in high pressure hydrogenation of coal tar and synthesis of oils and chemicals from coal by catalytic processes. Special Merit Promotion to Sen. Princ. Scientific Off., 1952; Dep. Chief Chemist, Fuel Res. Stn, DSIR, 1953; Dep. Dir, Warren Spring Lab., 1959. Chm. Governors, N Herts Coll. FRSC (FRIC 1944); FInstE (FinstF 1954). *Publications:* (with T. P. Hilditch) Catalytic Processes in Industrial Chemistry, 1937; numerous research and review papers in scientific and techn. jls dealing with chemistry of high pressure hydrogenation processes and with Fischer Tropsch synthesis. *Recreation:* gardening, specialising in iris growing and hybridising (Pres., British Iris Soc., 1967–70). *Address:* Tanglewood, Sollershott West, Letchworth, Herts. *T:* Letchworth 4339. *Clubs:* Civil Service; Rotary (Stevenage).

HALL, Christopher Myles; Editor of The Countryman, since 1981; *b* 21 July 1932; *s* of Gilbert and Muriel Hall; *m* 1957, Jennifer Bevan Keech (marr. diss. 1980); one *s* one *d* ; since 1981, lives with Linda J. Herbst. *Educ:* New Coll., Oxford. 2nd cl. Hons PPE. Reporter and Feature-writer, Daily Express, 1955–58; Sub-editor and Leader-writer, Daily Mirror, 1958–61; Feature-writer and Leader-writer, Daily Herald/Sun, 1961–65; Special Asst (Information): to Minister of Overseas Develt, 1965–66; to Minister of Transport, 1966–68; Chief Information Officer, MoT, 1968; Sec., Ramblers' Assoc., 1969–74, Mem. Exec. Cttee, 1982–; Dir, Council for Protection of Rural England, 1974–80. Pres., The Holiday Fellowship, 1974–77; Vice-Chm., S Reg. Council of Sport and Recreation, 1976–; Mem., DoT Cttee of Inquiry into Operators' Licensing, 1977–79; Hon. Sec., Chiltern Soc., 1965–68. *Publications:* Motorways in London (contrib.), 1969; How to Run a Pressure Group, 1974; (contrib.) No Through Road, 1975; (contrib.) The Countryman's Britain, 1976; (contrib.) Book of British Villages, 1980; (contrib.) Sunday Times Book of the Countryside, 1981; (contrib.) Walker's Britain, 1982; pamphlets; contrib. to Vole, The Countryman, New Statesman, New Scientist, The Geographical Magazine, The Guardian and various jls. *Recreation:* walking in the countryside. *Address:* c/o The Countryman, Sheep Street, Burford, Oxon OX8 4LH. *Club:* United Oxford & Cambridge University.

HALL, David, QPM 1977; Chief Constable of Humberside Police, since 1976; *b* 29 Dec. 1930; *s* of Arthur Thomas Hall and Dorothy May Charman; *m* 1952, Molly Patricia Knight; two *s. Educ:* Richmond and East Sheen Grammar School for Boys. Joined Metropolitan Police and rose through ranks from PC to Chief Supt, 1950–68; Staff Officer to Chief Inspector of Constabulary, Col Sir Eric St Johnson, 1968; Asst Chief Constable, 1970, Dep. Chief Constable, 1976, Staffordshire Police. Vice-Pres., Assoc. of Chief Police Officers of England, Wales and NI, 1982–83. OStJ 1980. *Recreations:* gardening, walking, playing the piano. *Address:* Humberside Police, Police Headquarters, Queens Gardens, Hull HU1 3DJ. *T:* Hull 220113.

HALL, Rt. Rev. Denis Bartlett; *b* 9 April 1899; *s* of Frank Marshall Hall and Caroline Beatrice Hall (*née* Bartlett), both of Bristol. *Educ:* Tudor House Sch., Henleaze, Bristol; Bristol Grammar Sch.; Bristol Univ. (BA). RNVR, 1917–19. University of Bristol, 1919–23; Ridley Hall, Cambridge, 1923–24. Curate, St Gabriel's Sunderland, 1924–28; Chaplain, HMS Conway Sch. Ship, 1928–30; Vicar of Bishopston, Bristol, 1930–47; Asst Bishop on The Niger, 1947–57; Vicar of St Paul's, Thornton Heath, Surrey, 1957–61; Asst Bishop of Canterbury, 1960–61; Rector of Tormarton with W Littleton, Glos, 1961–66. *Address:* Cowlin House, 26 Pembroke Road, Clifton, Bristol BS8 3BB.

HALL, Denis C.; *see* Clarke Hall.

HALL, Denis Whitfield, CMG 1962; late Provincial Commissioner, Kenya; *b* 26 Aug. 1913; *s* of late H. R. Hall, Haslemere, Surrey; *m* 1940, Barbara Carman; two *s. Educ:* Dover College; Wadham Coll., Oxford. Dist Officer, Kenya, 1936; Personal Asst to Chief Native Comr, 1948; Senior Dist Comr, 1955; Provincial Comr, Coast Province, 1959. *Recreations:* sailing, tennis, walking, motoring. *Address:* Martins, Priory Close, Boxgrove, West Sussex. *Club:* Oxford University Yacht.

HALL, Air Vice-Marshal Donald Percy, CB 1981; CBE 1975; AFC 1963; Air Officer Commanding No 38 Group, RAF, since 1980; *b* 11 Nov. 1930; *s* of William Reckerby Hall and Elsie Hall; *m* 1953, Joyce (*née* Warburton); two *d. Educ:* Hull Grammar Sch.; Royal Air Force Coll., Cranwell. Entered Cranwell, 1949; flying appts until 1963; Staff, Germany, 1964–66; OC, No 111 Sqdn, 1966–68; Staff, IDC, 1968–70; OC, Empire Test Pilots Sch., 1970–73; OC, RAF Akrotiri, 1974–75; SASO, No 11 Gp, 1975–77; AOC No 11 Gp, 1977; ACAS (Operational Requirements), 1977–80. *Recreations:* shooting, walking, swimming. *Address:* Littlecott House, Enford, near Pewsey, Wilts. *Club:* Royal Air Force.

HALL, Sir Douglas (Basil), 14th Bt *cr* 1687; KCMG 1959 (CMG 1958); *b* 1 Feb. 1909; *s* of late Capt. Lionel Erskine Hall and late Jane Augusta Hall (*née* Reynolds); *S* brother, Sir Neville Hall, 13th Bt, 1978; *m* 1933, Rachel Marion Gartside-Tippinge; one *s* two *d* (and one *s* decd). *Educ:* Radley Coll.; Keble Coll., Oxford (MA). Joined Colonial Admin. Service, 1930; posted to N Rhodesia as Cadet; District Officer, 1932; Senior District Officer, 1950; Provincial Commr, 1953; Administrative Sec., 1954; Sec. for Native Affairs to Government of Northern Rhodesia, 1956–59, Acting Chief Sec. for a period during 1958; Governor and C-in-C, Somaliland Protectorate, 1959–60. JP Co. Devon, 1964, Chm., Kingsbridge Petty Sessional Div., 1971–79. *Publications:* various technical articles. *Recreation:* vintage cars. *Heir: s* John Douglas Hoste Hall [*b* 7 Jan. 1945; *m* 1972, Angela Margaret, *d* of George Keys; two *s*]. *Address:* Barnford, Ringmore, near Kingsbridge, Devon. *T:* Bigbury-on-Sea 401.

HALL, Ven. Edgar Francis, MA; Archdeacon of Totnes, 1948–62, Archdeacon Emeritus, 1962; Canon Residentiary of Exeter, 1934–62; Treasurer, Exeter Cathedral, 1951–62; *b* 14 Aug. 1888; *s* of Francis R. Hall, Oxford; *m* 1915, Anstice (*d* 1982) *d* of Dr Louis Tosswill, Exeter; three *d. Educ:* Oxford High Sch.; Jesus Coll., Oxford (Scholar). Asst Master, Exeter Sch., 1911; Deacon 1914; Priest 1915; Curate of St James', Exeter, 1914; Chaplain of Exeter Sch., 1917; Vicar of Leusden, Devon, 1921; Diocesan Dir of Relig. Education, Exeter, 1934; Proctor in Convocation, 1944; Gen. Sec. Nat. Soc., 1943–47; Chm. Church of England Council for Education, 1949–58 (Sec. 1948–49). Retired, 1962. *Address:* The Old Parsonage, Leusdon, Poundsgate, Newton Abbot, Devon. *T:* Poundsgate 329.

HALL, Edward, RP 1958; *b* 5 Feb. 1922; *s* of James and Elizabeth Hall; *m* 1946, Daphne Cynthia, (*née* Grogan); two *s* one *d. Educ:* Wyggeston Sch., Leicester. Leicester Coll. of Art, 1939–41; Royal Air Force, 1941–46; Wimbledon Sch. of Art, 1946–48; Slade Sch. of Fine Art, 1949–52. Since 1952, portrait painting; exhibits annually at Royal Academy; part-time teaching and lecturing in various London and provincial art schools, including Sir John Cass School of Art, Chelsea School of Art, Medway Coll. of Design. Hon. Treasurer, Royal Soc. of Portrait Painters, 1977–. *Recreations:* music, playing the piano. *Address:* 51 St George's Drive, SW1. *T:* 01-834 5366.

HALL, Maj.-Gen. Edward Michael, CB 1970; MBE 1943; DL; *b* 16 July 1915; *s* of late Brig. E. G. Hall, CB, CIE; *m* 1948, Nina Diana (*née* McArthur); three *s. Educ:* Sherborne; RMA; Peterhouse, Cambridge. Commissioned RE, 1935; BA (Cantab) 1937. Served 1939–46, with Royal Bombay Sappers and Miners; Western Desert, India, Burma. CRE, 10th Armd and 3rd Inf. Div., 1957–59; Comd Training Bde, RE, 1962–63; Chief of Staff, Western Command, 1965–66; Military Deputy to Head of Defence Sales, 1966–70. Col Comdt, RE, 1973–76. Comdr and Comr, St John Ambulance,

Cornwall, 1971-80. DL Cornwall, 1971. KStJ 1981. *Recreation:* country pursuits. *Address:* Treworgey Manor, Liskeard, Cornwall.

HALL, Dr Edward Thomas; Professor, Research Laboratory for Archaeology and the History of Art, Oxford University, since 1975 (Director since 1954); Fellow of Worcester College, Oxford, since 1969; *b* 10 May 1924; *s* of late Lt-Col Walter D'Arcy Hall, MC, and of Ann Madelaine Hall; *m* 1957, Jennifer Louise de la Harpe; two *s. Educ:* Eton; Oxford Univ. BA 1948, MA 1953, DPhil 1953, Oxon; FPhysS. Chm., Hon. Scientific Cttee, National Gallery, 1971-; Trustee: British Museum, 1973-; National Gallery, 1977-. Member: Science Mus. Adv. Council, 1979-; Court of Goldsmiths' Co., 1976. FSA. *Publications:* contrib. Archaeometry, various jls concerning science applied to archaeology. *Recreations:* the sea, hot-air ballooning, making things. *Address:* Beenhams, Littlemore, Oxford OX4 4PZ. *T:* Oxford 777800; 11A Elm Park Lane, SW3 6DD. *T:* 01-352 5847.

HALL, Francis Woodall; HM Diplomatic Service, retired; *b* 10 May 1918; *s* of Francis Hall and Florence Adelaide Woodall; *m* 1951, Phyllis Anne Amelia Andrews; one *s* one *d. Educ:* Taunton School. Inland Revenue, 1936-40; Admty (Alexandria, Port Said, Haifa, Freetown), 1940-46; FO, 1946; Bahrain and Baghdad, 1949; Vice-Consul, Malaga, 1950; FO, 1952; 2nd Sec., Cairo, 1955; Consul: Madrid, 1957; Zagreb, 1960; FO 1962; Consul, Stockholm, 1964; Head of Mombasa Office of British High Commn to Kenya, 1969; Consul-Gen., Alexandria, 1971-78; Hon. Consul, Seville, 1979. *Recreations:* music, walking. *Address:* Burton Cottage, Burton Lane, East Coker, Somerset.

HALL, Sir (Frederick) John (Frank), 3rd Bt, *cr* 1923; *b* 14 Aug. 1931; *er s* of Sir Frederick Henry Hall, 2nd Bt, and Olwen Irene, *yr d* of late Alderman Frank Collis, Stokeville, Stoke-on-Trent, and Deganwy, Llandudno; *S* father, 1949; *m* 1st, 1956, Felicity Anne (marr. diss. 1960), *d* of late Edward Rivers-Fletcher, Norwich, and of Mrs L. R. Galloway; 2nd, 1961, Patricia Ann Atkinson (marr. diss., 1967); two *d* ; re-married, 1967, 1st wife, Felicity Anne Hall; two *d. Heir: b* David Christopher Hall [*b* 30 Dec. 1937; *m* 1962, Irene, *d* of William Duncan, Aberdeen; one *s* one *d*]. *Address:* Carradale, 29 Embercourt Road, Thames Ditton, Surrey. *T:* 01-398 2801.

HALL, Frederick Thomas Duncan; Chairman, West Midlands County Council, 1977-78 (Member, since 1974); Lord Mayor of Birmingham, May 1972-May 1973; *b* 12 Jan. 1902; *s* of Frederick James and Catherine Harriett Hall; *m* 1925, Irene Margaret Lawley; one *s. Educ:* Bourne Coll., Quinton, Birmingham. Chairman, Hall & Rice Ltd and associated cos. Member: West Bromwich Educn Cttee, 1933-46 (co-opted); Birmingham City Council, 1949-73 (Alderman, 1961); served Cttees: Educn, 1949-73 (Chm., 1966-69); Finance, 1966-73; Gen. Purposes, 1956-74; Jt Consultative, 1969-72 (Chm.); Allotments, 1949-66. Governor: Birmingham Univ., 1967-73; Aston Univ., 1957-; Handsworth Grammar Sch., 1960-. Member: AMC (Educn) Cttee, 1967-72 (Vice-Chm., 1971-72); Assoc. of Educn Cttees Exec., 1968-72; Chm., Sandwell Ward Conservative Assoc., 1947-65; Pres., Handsworth Div. Conservative Assoc., 1973; Dir, Birmingham Repertory Theatre, 1970-73; formed Handsworth Historical Soc., 1951 (Chm., 1951-65). Vice-Pres., West Bromwich Albion FC, 1979-. *Recreations:* hockey, golf, historical research. *Address:* 32 Englestede Close, Birmingham B20 1BJ. *T:* 021-554 6060. *Clubs:* Aberdovey Golf (Pres., 1967-); Sandwell Park Golf (Captain, 1948-49).

HALL, Maj.-Gen. Frederick William G.; *see* Gordon-Hall.

HALL, Rear-Adm. Geoffrey Penrose Dickinson, CB 1973; DSC 1943; DL; Hydrographer of the Navy 1971-75; retired; *b* 19 July 1916; *er s* of late Major A. K. D. Hall and late Mrs P. M. Hall; *m* 1945, Mary Ogilvie Carlisle; two *s* one *d. Educ:* Haileybury. Served in American waters, 1935-37 and on Nyon Patrol during Spanish Civil War; joined surveying service, 1938, served in Indian Ocean until 1939 when transf. to minesweeping in Far East; hydrographic duties, home waters, Iceland, W Africa; navigational and minesweeping duties, Icelandic waters; transf. to Combined Ops, SE Asia; subseq. comd frigate, British Pacific Fleet; from 1947, hydrographic work: with RNZN, 1949-51; subseq. five comds i/c surveys at home and abroad; served ashore and in Atlantic, Indian Ocean, Antarctic waters (Cuthbert Peek Grant, RGS, for work in furtherance of oceanographical exploration); twice Asst Hydrographer; surveyed between S Africa and Iceland, 1965-67; Asst Dir (Naval), Hydrographic Dept, Taunton. Cadet 1934; Midshipman 1935; Sub-Lt 1938; Lieut 1939; Lt-Comdr 1945; Comdr 1953; Captain 1961; Rear-Adm. 1971. Pres., Hydrographic Soc., 1975. FRGS; FRICS. DL Lincs, 1982. *Publications:* contribs to Nature, Deep Sea Research, Internat. Hydrographic Review, Navy International. *Recreation:* country pursuits. *Address:* Manby House, Manby, Louth, Lincs LN11 8UF. *T:* South Cockerington 777. *Club:* Naval and Military.

HALL, Geoffrey Ronald, FEng, CChem, FRSC, SFInstE; Director, Brighton Polytechnic, since 1970; *b* 18 May 1928; *er s* of late Thomas Harold Hall, JP, and late Muriel Frances Hall, Douglas, IoM; *m* 1950, Elizabeth Day Sheldon; two *s* one *d. Educ:* Douglas High Sch., IoM; Univ. of Manchester (BSc). Research in Nuclear Science and Engineering at AERE, Harwell, 1949-56; sabbatical at Oxford Univ., 1955; Colombo Plan Expert to Indian Atomic Energy Commn, 1956-58; Reader in Nuclear Technology, Imperial Coll., London, 1958-63; Prof. of Nuclear Technology, Imperial Coll., 1963-70. Member: CNAA, 1977-; Engineering Council, 1981-; SERC, 1982- (Mem., Engrg Bd, SRC, later SERC, 1978-); Chm., Engrg Working Gp, Nat. Adv.

Body for Local Authority Higher Educn, 1982-. President: British Nuclear Energy Soc., 1970-71; Inst. of Fuel, 1976-77; Founder Fellow, Fellowship of Engineering, 1976. *Publications:* papers related to nuclear science, fuels and engineering. *Recreations:* travel, caravanning. *Address:* 1 Great Wilkins, Brighton BN1 9QW.

HALL, Harold George; His Honour Judge Hall; a Circuit Judge, since 1975; *b* 20 Sept. 1920; *s* of late Albert Hall and Violet Maud Hall (*née* Etherington); *m* 1950, Patricia Delaney; four *s* one *d. Educ:* Archbishop Holgate's Grammar Sch., York. RAF, 1940-46 (Flt-Lt). Called to Bar, Middle Temple, 1958; practised NE Circuit; Dep. Chm., WR Yorks QS, 1970; a Recorder, 1972-75.

HALL, Harold Percival, CMG 1963; MBE 1947; Director of Studies, Royal Institute of Public Administration, since 1974; *b* 9 Sept. 1913; *s* of late Major George Charles Hall; *m* 1939, Margery Hall, *d* of late Joseph Dickson; three *s* (including twin *s*). *Educ:* Portsmouth Grammar Sch.; Royal Military College, Sandhurst. Commissioned Indian Army, 1933. Indian Political Service, 1937-47. Private Sec. to Resident, Central India States, 1937; Magistrate and Collector, Meerut, 1938-39. Military Service, 1938-43 (Major). Staff Coll., Quetta, 1941. Asst Political Agent, Loralai, 1943, Nasirabad, 1944; Dir, Food and Civil Supplies, and Dep. Sec., Revenue, Baluchistan, 1945-46; Principal, Colonial Office, 1947; Asst Sec. (Head of Pacific and Indian Ocean Dept), Colonial Office, 1955-62; Seconded to Office of UK Comr-Gen. for SE Asia, 1962-63; British Dep. High Comr for Eastern Malaysia, Kuching, Sarawak, 1963-64; Asst Sec., Colonial Office, 1965-66; Assistant Under-Secretary of State: Commonwealth Office, 1966-68; MoD, 1968-73. Mem. Governing Body, Sch. of Oriental and African Studies, 1971-74. *Recreation:* gardening. *Address:* 77 Moss Lane, Pinner, Middlesex HA5 3AZ. *T:* 01-866 1162.

HALL, (Harold) Peter; Legal Adviser and Solicitor, Crown Estate Commissioners, 1976-80; Solicitor of Supreme Court; *b* 10 Dec. 1916; *s* of Arthur William Henry and Ethel Amelia Hall; *m* 1946, Tessibel Mary Mitchell (*née* Phillips); one *s* one *d. Educ:* Bristol Grammar Sch.; Bristol Univ. (LLB Hons). Articled to, and Asst Solicitor with, Burges Salmon & Co., Solicitors, Bristol, 1934-39. Served War of 1939-45: enlisted Somerset Light Inf., Dec. 1939; commnd in E Yorkshire Regt, 1940; service Home and Far East, 1940-45. Asst Provost Marshal (Major), Southern Army, India Command, 1945. Legal Branch, Min. of Agric., Fisheries and Food, 1946-66; Asst Legal Adviser, Land Commn, 1967-71; Asst Solicitor, Dept of the Environment, 1971-76. *Recreations:* reading, photography, walking. *Address:* The Ridings, 9 Steep Hill Court Road, Ventnor, Isle of Wight PO38 1UH.

HALL, Prof. Henry Edgar, FRS 1982; Professor of Physics, University of Manchester, since 1961; *b* 1928; *s* of John Ainger Hall; *m* 1962, Patricia Anne Broadbent; two *s* one *d. Educ:* Latymer Upper Sch., Hammersmith; Emmanuel Coll., Cambridge. BA 1952; PhD 1956. At Royal Society Mond Laboratory, Cambridge, 1952-58; Senior Student, Royal Commission for the Exhibition of 1851, 1955-57; Research Fellow of Emmanuel Coll., 1955-58; Lecturer in Physics, Univ. of Manchester, 1958-61. Simon Memorial Prize (with W. F. Vinen), 1963. Visiting Professor: Univ. of Western Australia, 1964; Univ. of Oregon, 1967-68; Cornell Univ., 1974, 1982-83. *Publications:* Solid State Physics, 1974; papers in scientific journals. *Recreation:* mountain walking. *Address:* The Schuster Laboratory, The University, Manchester M13 9PL.

HALL, Air Vice-Marshal Hubert Desmond, CB 1979; CBE 1972; AFC 1963; Defence Adviser, Canberra, 1980-82; *b* 3 June 1925; *s* of Charles William and Violet Victoria Kate Hall; *m* 1951, Mavis Dorothea (*née* Hopkins). *Educ:* Portsmouth Municipal Coll. FBIM. Commissioned RAF, 1945; RAF Coll., Cranwell QFI, 1951-55; Flt Comdr, 9 Sqdn, 1955-56; 232 OCU Gaydon, Sqdn Ldr, Medium Bomber Force; Instructor, Wing Comdr 1962; 3 Group Headquarters (Training), 1963-65; Air Warfare Coll., 1965; commanded No 57 Sqdn (Victors), 1966-68; Gp Captain Nuclear Operations SHAPE HQ, 1968-71; comd RAF Waddington, 1971-73; Overseas Coll. of Defence Studies India, 1974; MoD: Director (Air Cdre) of Establishments, RAF, 1975-77; Air Comdr Malta, 1977-79. Air Vice-Marshal 1979. Queen's Commendation, 1957. OStJ 1979. *Recreations:* shooting, gardening, reading. *Address:* c/o Lloyds Bank Ltd, 115 Commercial Road, Portsmouth, Hants PO1 1BY. *Clubs:* Royal Air Force, Royal Commonwealth Society.

HALL, Prof. James Snowdon, CBE 1976; Professor of Agriculture, Glasgow University, and Principal, West of Scotland Agricultural College, 1966-80; *b* 28 Jan. 1919; *s* of Thomas Blackburn Hall and Mary Milburn Hall; *m* 1942, Mary Smith; one *s* one *d. Educ:* Univ. of Durham (BSc Hons). FRAgS, FIBiol. Asst Technical Adviser, Northumberland War Agric. Exec. Commn, 1941-44; Lectr in Agriculture, Univ. of Newcastle upon Tyne, 1944-54; Principal, Cumbria Coll. of Agriculture and Forestry, 1954-66. *Address:* 26 Earls Way, Doonfoot, Ayr. *T:* Alloway 41162. *Club:* Farmers'.

HALL, Jean Graham, LLM (London); Her Honour Judge Graham Hall; a Circuit Judge (formerly Deputy Chairman, South-East London Quarter Sessions), since 1971; *b* 26 March 1917; *d* of Robert Hall and Alison (*née* Graham). *Educ:* Inverkeithing Sch., Fife; St Anne's Coll., Sanderstead; London Sch. of Economics. Gold Medal (Elocution and Dramatic Art), Incorporated London Acad. of Music, 1935; Teacher's Dipl., Guildhall Sch. of Music, 1937;

Social Science Cert., London Sch. of Economics, 1937; LLB (Hons), London, 1950. Club Leader and subseq. Sub-Warden, Birmingham Univ. Settlement, 1937-41; Sec., Eighteen Plus (an experiment in youth work), 1941-44; Probation Officer, Hants, subseq. Croydon, 1945-51. Called to Bar, Gray's Inn, 1951. Metropolitan Stipendiary Magistrate, 1965-71. Pres., Gray's Inn Debating Soc., 1953; Hon. Sec., Soc. of Labour Lawyers, 1954-64; Pres., British Soc. of Criminology, 1971-74. Chm. Departmental Cttee on Statutory Maintenance Limits, 1966-68. Contested (Lab) East Surrey, 1955. Hon. LLD Lincoln, USA, 1979. *Publication:* (jtly) Child Abuse: procedure and evidence in juvenile courts, 1978. *Recreations:* travel, congenial debate. *Address:* 2 Dr Johnson's Buildings, Temple, EC4. *Clubs:* University Women's.

HALL, Joan Valerie; Member, Central Transport Consultative Committee, since 1981; *b* 31 Aug. 1935; *d* of late Robert Percy Hall and of Winifred Emily Umbers. *Educ:* Queen Margaret's Sch., York; Ashridge House of Citizenship. Contested (C) Barnsley, 1964 and 1966. MP (C) Keighley, 1970-Feb. 1974; PPS to Minister of State for Agriculture, Fisheries and Food, 1972-74. Vice-Chm., Greater London Young Conservatives, 1964. Mem. Council, University Coll. Buckingham, 1977-. *Address:* Mayfields, Darton Road, Cawthorne, Barnsley, South Yorks S75 4HY. *T:* Barnsley 790230.

HALL, Sir John; *see* Hall, Sir F. J. F.

HALL, John; *see* Hall, W. J.

HALL, John Anthony Sanderson, DFC 1943; QC 1967; *b* 25 Dec. 1921; *s* of late Rt Hon. W. Glenvil Hall, PC, MP, and late Rachel Ida Hall (*née* Sanderson); *m* 1st, Nora Ella Hall (*née* Crowe) (marr. diss. 1974); one *s* two *d* ; 2nd, Elizabeth Mary, widow of Alan Riley Maynard. *Educ:* Leighton Park Sch.; Trinity Hall, Cambridge (MA). Served RAF, 1940-46, 85 Squadron and 488 (NZ) Squadron (Squadron Leader; DFC and Bar). Called to Bar, Inner Temple, 1948, Master of the Bench, 1975; Western Circuit; Dep. Chm., Hants Quarter Sessions, 1967; Recorder of Swindon, 1971. Member: Gen. Council of the Bar, 1964-68, 1970-74; Senate of the Four Inns of Court, 1966-68, 1970-74; Council of Legal Educn, 1970-74. Mem., 1972-79, Chm., 1978-79, UK Deleg. to Consultative Cttee, Bars and Law Socs of EEC. Dir Gen., Internat. Fedn of Producers of Ph■ ▬ams and Videograms, 1979-81. Governor: St Catherine's Sch., Bramley (Chm.); Cranleigh Sch., 1972-. *Recreations:* walking, sailing, fishing. *Address:* 2 Dr Johnson's Buildings, Temple, EC4. *Club:* Garrick.

HALL, Sir John (Bernard), 3rd Bt *cr* 1919; a Vice President, Bank of America NT and SA, since 1982; Director, European Brazilian Bank Ltd; *b* 20 March 1932; *s* of Lieut-Col Sir Douglas Hall, DSO, 2nd Bt, and Ina Nancie Walton, *d* of late Col John Edward Mellor, CB (she *m* 2nd, 1962, Col Peter J. Bradford, DSO, OBE, TD); *S* father, 1962; *m* 1957, Delia Mary, *d* of late Lieut-Col J. A. Innes, DSO; one *s* two *d*. *Educ:* Eton; Trinity Coll., Oxford (MA). FIB 1976. Lieut. Royal Fusiliers (RARO). J. Henry Schroder Wagg & Co. Ltd, formerly J. Henry Schroder & Co, 1955-73 (Dir, 1967-73); Director: The Antofagasta (Chili) and Bolivia Rly Co. Ltd, 1967-73; Bank of America International, 1974-82. Chm., Anglo-Colombian Soc., 1978-81. FIB. *Recreations:* travel, fishing. *Heir: s* David Bernard Hall, *b* 12 May 1961. *Address:* Penrose House, Patmore Heath, Albury, Ware, Herts SG11 2LT. *T:* Albury 255. *Clubs:* Boodle's, Lansdowne, Overseas Bankers'.

HALL, John Edward Beauchamp, CMG 1959; *b* 9 Dec. 1905; *s* of Henry William Hall, MA, and Emily (*née* Odam); *m* 1936, Jane Gordon (*née* Forbes); two *d. Educ:* Bradfield Coll., Berks; Worcester Coll., Oxford. Foundation Scholar, Bradfield Coll., 1919-24; Exhibitioner, Worcester Coll., Oxford, 1924-28. Appointed to Colonial Administrative Service, Nigeria, 1930; Permanent Sec., Federal Government of Nigeria, 1958-60; retired, 1961. *Recreation:* gardening. *Address:* The Croft, Church Road, Sandhurst, Hawkhurst, Kent TN18 5NS. *T:* Sandhurst 302.

HALL, Maj.-Gen. Kenneth, CB 1976; OBE 1962 (MBE 1958); Director of Army Education, 1972-76; *b* 29 July 1916; *s* of Frank Hall and Hannah Hall (*née* Clayton); *m* 1945, Celia Adelaide Elizabeth Francis; two *s. Educ:* Worksop Coll.; St John's Coll., Cambridge (MA). Served War of 1939-45: commissioned in Royal Tank Regt, 1940-49; transf. to Royal Army Educational Corps, 1949; War Office, 1945-52; HQ Malta Garrison, 1953-57; War Office, 1958-62; HQ Aldershot District, 1962-64; Chief Educn Officer, GHQ, MELF, 1965; Comdt Army Sch. of Educn, 1965-66; MoD, 1966-69; Chief Educn Officer, HQ Southern Comd, 1969-71; Comdt RAEC Centre, 1971-72. Col Comdt, RAEC, 1978-82. *Recreations:* boxing (Cambridge Univ. Blue, 1937-38-39), reading, golf. *Address:* 42 Exeter House, Putney Heath, SW15. *T:* 01-788 4794. *Clubs:* Army and Navy; Hawks (Cambridge).

HALL, (Laura) Margaret; *see* MacDougall, Laura Margaret.

HALL, Margaret Dorothy, OBE 1973; RDI 1974; FSIAD; Design Officer, British Museum, since 1964; *b* 22 Jan. 1936; *d* of Thomas Robson Hall and Millicent (*née* Britton). *Educ:* Bromley County Grammar Sch.; Bromley College of Art; Royal College of Art (DesRCA). Design Assistant: Cason, Condor & Partners, 1960-61; Westwood Piet & Partners, 1961-63; Dennis Lennon & Partners, 1963-64; British Museum, 1964-: exhibitions designed include: Masterpieces of Glass, 1968; Museum of Mankind, 1970; Treasures of Tutankhamun, 1972; Nomad and City, 1976; Captain Cook in the South Seas,

1979. Designer, Manuscripts and Men, National Portrait Gallery, 1969. Chm., Gp of Designers/Interpreters in Museums, 1978-81. FSIAD 1975 (MSIAD 1968) (Chm., SIAD Salaried Designers Cttee, 1979-81). Chm., Wynkyn de Worde Soc., 1982. Governor, Ravensbourne College of Art, 1973-78. FRSA 1974. *Address:* The British Museum, WC1B 3DG. *T:* 01-636 1555. *Club:* Double Crown.

HALL, Michael Kilgour H.; *see* Harrison-Hall.

HALL, Sir Noel (Frederick), Kt 1957; Principal, Brasenose College, Oxford, 1960-73, Hon. Fellow 1973; *s* of late Cecil Gallopine Hall and late Constance Gertrude Upcher; *m* 1st, 1927, Edith Evelyn Pearl Haward (marr. diss. 1944); no *c* ; 2nd, 1946, Elinor Hirschhorn Marks; one *s* one *d. Educ:* Royal Grammar Sch., Newcastle on Tyne; Bromsgrove Sch.; Brasenose Coll., Oxford. 1st Class hons Modern History, 1924; Senior Hulme Scholar, 1924-25; Certificate Social Anthropology, 1925; BA 1924; MA 1933. Commonwealth Fund Fellow in Economics, Princeton Univ., 1925-27, AM (Economics) Princeton, 1926; Lecturer in Political Economy, head of Dept of Political Economy, and Civil Service Tutor, University of London, University Coll., 1927-29; Senior Lecturer, 1929-35; Prof. of Political Economy in the University of London (University Coll.,) 1935-38; Sec. of Fellowship Advisory Cttee of Rockefeller Foundation for Social Sciences in Great Britain and Ireland, 1930-36; Dir, National Institute for Economic and Social Research, 1938-43; Mem. of International Commission for Relief of Child Refugees in Spain, 1939; Joint Dir, Ministry of Economic Warfare, 1940; Minister in charge of War Trade Department, British Embassy, Washington, 1941-43; Development Adviser West Africa, 1943-45; Principal of the Administrative Staff Coll., Greenlands, Henley-on-Thames, 1946-61. Ford Foundation Distinguished Visiting Prof., New York Univ., 1958 (University Medal, 1958). Hon. Associate, College of Advanced Technology, Birmingham, 1963. Hon. LLD Univ. of Lancaster, 1964. *Publications:* Measures of a National and International character for Raising Standards of Living (Report to Economic Committee of League of Nations, 1938); The Exchange Equalisation Account, 1935; Report on Grading Structure of Administrative and Clerical Staff in the Hospital Service, 1957; The Making of Higher Executives, 1958. *Recreations:* golf, bridge. *Address:* 1 Northfield End, Henley-on-Thames, Oxon. *T:* Henley-on-Thames 3265. *Club:* English-Speaking Union.

HALL, Peter; *see* Hall, H. P.

HALL, Peter Edward; HM Diplomatic Service; Counsellor, British Embassy, Washington, since 1981 and Head of British Information Services, New York, since 1978; *b* 26 July 1938; *s* of Bernard Hall and late Monica Hall (*née* Blackbourn); *m* 1972, Marnie Kay; one *s* one *d. Educ:* Portsmouth Grammar Sch.; HM Services (Jt Services Sch. for Linguists); Pembroke Coll., Cambridge (Scholar; 1st Cl. parts I and II, Mediaeval and Modern Langs Tripos). Foreign Office, 1961-63; 3rd Sec., Warsaw, 1963-66; 2nd Sec., New Delhi, 1966-69; FCO (European Integration Dept), 1969-72; 1st Sec., UK Permanent Representation to EEC, 1972-76; Asst Head, Financial Relations Dept, FCO, 1976-77; Counsellor, Caracas, 1977-78. *Recreations:* reading (A. Powell, Byron), music (Rolling Stones, Mozart). *Address:* c/o Foreign and Commonwealth Office, King Charles Street, SW1.

HALL, Prof. Peter Geoffrey; Professor, since 1968 and Head of Department of Geography, 1968-80, Chairman, School of Planning Studies, 1971-77, Dean of Urban and Regional Studies, 1975-78, University of Reading; *b* 19 March 1932; *s* of Arthur Vickers Hall and Bertha Hall (*née* Keefe); *m* 1st, 1962, Carla Maria Wartenberg (marr. diss. 1966); 2nd, 1967, Magdalena Mróz; no *c. Educ:* Blackpool Grammar Sch.; St Catharine's Coll., Cambridge Univ. (MA, PhD). Asst Lectr, 1957, Lectr, 1960, Birkbeck Coll., Univ. of London; Reader in Geography with ref. to Regional Planning, London Sch. of Economics and Political Science, 1966. Vis. Prof., City and Regional Planning, 1974, Acting Dir, Inst. of Urban and Regional Develt, 1980-81, Univ. of Calif, Berkeley. Member: SE Regional Planning Council, 1966-79; Nature Conservancy, 1968-72; Transport and Road Research Laboratory Adv. Cttee on Transport, 1973-; Environmental Bd, 1975-79; SSRC, 1975-80 (Chm., Planning Cttee); EEC Expert Gp on New Tendencies of Social and Economic Develt, 1975-77; Standing Adv. Cttee on Trunk Road Assessment, 1978-80; Editorial Bd, (and regular contributor to) New Society, 1965-; Exec. Cttee, Regional Studies Assoc., 1967- (Hon. Jl Editor, 1967-78); Exec. Cttee, Fabian Soc., 1964-80 (Chm. 1971-72); Governor, Centre for Environmental Studies, 1975-80. Vice-Chm., Tawney Soc., 1982-. FRGS; Hon. RTPI, 1975. Editor, Built Environment, 1977-. *Publications:* The Industries of London, 1962; London 2000, 1963 (reprint, 1969); Labour's New Frontiers, 1964; (ed) Land Values, 1965; The World Cities, 1966, 2nd edn, 1977; Containment of Urban England, 1973; Urban and Regional Planning, 1974; Europe 2000, 1977; Great Planning Disasters, 1980; Growth Centres in the European Urban System, 1980. *Recreations:* writing, reading, talking. *Address:* Department of Geography, University of Reading, Whiteknights, Reading RG6 2AB.

HALL, Peter George; Managing Director, Esso Petroleum Co. Ltd, since 1982; *b* 10 Dec. 1924; *s* of Charles and Rosina Hall; *m* 1949, Margaret Gladys (*née* Adams); two *s* two *d. Educ:* Sandown, IoW, Grammar Sch.; Southampton Univ. (BScEng). FInstPet. Anglo-Iranian Oil Co., 1946-51; Esso Petroleum Co. Ltd: various positions at Fawley Refinery, 1951-63; Manager, Milford Haven Refinery, 1963-66; Employee Relations Manager, 1966-70; Vice-Pres., General Sekiyu Seisei, Tokyo, 1971-74; Asst Gen. Man., Refining, Imperial

Oil Ltd, Toronto, 1974-76; Refining Man., Exxon Corp., New York, 1976-77; Director, Esso Petroleum Co. Ltd, London, 1977-78; Vice-Pres., Esso Europe Inc. London, 1979-81. *Recreations:* opera, classical music, walking, gardening. *Address:* Flat A, 65 Warwick Square, SW1V 2AL. *T:* 01-834 8061.

HALL, Sir Peter (Reginald Frederick), Kt 1977; CBE 1963; director of plays, films and operas; Director, National Theatre, since 1973; *b* Bury St Edmunds, Suffolk, 22 Nov. 1930; *s* of Reginald Edward Arthur Hall and Grace Pamment; *m* 1956, Leslie Caron (marr. diss., 1965); one *s* one *d*; *m* 1965, Jacqueline Taylor (marr. diss. 1981); one *s* one *d*; *m* 1982, Maria Ewing; one *d*. *Educ:* Perse Sch., Cambridge; St Catharine's Coll., Cambridge (MA Hons; Hon. Fellow, 1964). Dir, Arts Theatre, London, 1955-56 (directed several plays incl. first productions of Waiting for Godot, South, Waltz of the Toreadors); formed own producing company, International Playwrights' Theatre, 1957, and directed their first production, Camino Real; at Sadler's Wells, directed his first opera, The Moon and Sixpence, 1957. First productions at Stratford: Love's Labour's Lost, 1956; Cymbeline, 1957; first prod. on Broadway, The Rope Dancers, Nov. 1957. Plays in London, 1956-58: Summertime, Gigi, Cat on a Hot Tin Roof, Brouhaha, Shadow of Heroes; Madame de . . ., Traveller Without Luggage, A Midsummer Night's Dream and Coriolanus (Stratford). The Wrong Side of the Park, 1959; apptd Dir of Royal Shakespeare Theatre, Jan. 1960, responsible for creation of RSC as a permanent ensemble, and its move to Aldwych Theatre, 1960; Man. Dir at Stratford-on-Avon and Aldwych Theatre, London, 1960-68; Co-Dir, RSC, 1968-73; plays produced/directed for *Royal Shakespeare Company:* Two Gentlemen of Verona, Twelfth Night, Troilus and Cressida, 1960; Ondine, Becket, Romeo and Juliet, 1961; The Collection, Troilus and Cressida, A Midsummer Night's Dream, 1962; The Wars of the Roses (adaptation of Henry VI Parts 1, 2 and 3, and Richard III), 1963 (televised for BBC, 1965); Sequence of Shakespeare's histories for Shakespeare's 400th anniversary at Stratford: Richard II, Henry IV Parts 1 & 2, Henry V, Henry VI, Edward IV, Richard III, 1964; The Homecoming, Hamlet, 1965; The Government Inspector, Staircase, 1966; The Homecoming (NY), Macbeth, 1967; A Delicate Balance, Silence and Landscape, 1969; The Battle of the Shrivings, 1970; Old Times, 1971 (NY, 1971, Vienna, 1972); All Over, Via Galactica (NY), 1972; Macbeth, Metropolitan Opera, NY, 1982; plays produced/directed for *National Theatre:* The Tempest, 1974; John Gabriel Borkman, 1975; No Man's Land, Happy Days, Hamlet, 1975; Tamburlaine the Great, 1976; No Man's Land (NY), Volpone, Bedroom Farce, The Country Wife, 1977; The Cherry Orchard, Macbeth, Betrayal, 1978; Amadeus, 1979, NY 1981 (Tony Award for Best Director); Othello, 1980; Family Voices, The Oresteia, 1981; Importance of Being Earnest, 1982; Other Places, 1982. *Films:* Work is a Four Letter Word, 1968; A Midsummer Night's Dream, Three into Two Won't Go, 1969; Perfect Friday, 1971; The Homecoming, 1973; Akenfield, 1974. *Opera:* at Covent Garden: Moses and Aaron, 1965; The Magic Flute, 1966; The Knot Garden, 1970; Eugene Onegin, Tristan and Isolde, 1971; at Glyndebourne: La Calisto, 1970; Il Ritorno d'Ulisse in Patria, 1972; The Marriage of Figaro, 1973; Don Giovanni, Così Fan Tutte, 1978; Fidelio, 1979; A Midsummer Night's Dream, 1981; Orfeo ed Euridice, 1982. *Television:* Presenter, Aquarius (LWT), 1975-77. Associate Prof. of Drama, Warwick Univ., 1966-. Mem., Arts Council, 1969-73. DUniv York, 1966; Hon. DLitt Reading, 1973; Hon. LittD: Liverpool; 1974; Leicester, 1977. Tony Award (NY) for best director, 1966; Hamburg Univ. Shakespeare Prize, 1967; Standard Special Award, 1979; Standard Award Best Director, 1981; Standard Award for outstanding achievement in Opera, 1981. Chevalier de l'Ordre des Arts et des Lettres, 1965. *Recreation:* music. *Address:* The National Theatre, Upper Ground, SE1.

HALL, Prof. Philip, FRS 1942; MA; Sadleirian Professor of Pure Mathematics, Cambridge University, 1953-67, now Emeritus (University Lecturer in Mathematics, 1933-51; Reader in Algebra, 1951-53); Fellow of King's College, Cambridge, 1927; *b* 11 April 1904. *Educ:* Christ's Hosp. Hon. Sec. London Mathematical Soc., 1938-41, 1945-48, Pres., 1955-57. Sylvester Medal, Royal Society, 1961; de Morgan Medal and Larmor Prize of the London Mathematical Soc., 1965. Hon. DSc: Tübingen, 1963; Warwick, 1977. Hon. Fellow, Jesus Coll. Cambridge, 1976. *Address:* 50 Impington Lane, Histon, Cambs.

HALL, Prof. Reginald, FRCP; Professor of Medicine, Welsh National School of Medicine, since 1980; *b* 1 Oct. 1931; *s* of Reginald P. Hall and Maggie W. Hall; *m* 1960, Dr Molly Hill; two *s* three *d*. *Educ:* Univ. of Durham (BSc, MB BS, MD). Harkness Fellow of Commonwealth Fund, Clinical and Research Fellow in Medicine, 1960-61; Wellcome Sen. Research Fellow in Clinical Science, 1964-67; Cons. Physician, Royal Victoria Infirmary, Newcastle upon Tyne, 1967-79; Prof. of Medicine, Univ. of Newcastle upon Tyne, 1970-79. *Publications:* Fundamentals of Clinical Endocrinology, 1969, 3rd edn 1980; Atlas of Endocrinology, 1980. *Recreations:* bryology, literature. *Address:* 37 Palace Road, Llandaff, Cardiff CF5 2AG. *T:* Cardiff 567689; (office) Cardiff 755944, ext. 2307.

HALL, Sir Robert de Zouche, KCMG 1953 (CMG 1952); MA; *b* 27 April 1904; *s* of late Arthur William Hall, Liverpool; *m* 1932, Lorna Dorothy (*née* Markham); one *s* one *d*. *Educ:* Willaston Sch.; Gonville and Caius Coll., Cambridge. MA, 1932; Colonial Administrative Service, Tanganyika, 1926; Provincial Comr, 1947; Senior Provincial Comr, 1950; Mem. for Local Government, Tanganyika, 1950-53. Governor, Comdr-in-Chief, and Vice-Adm., Sierra Leone, 1953-56. Hon. Sec. Vernacular Architecture Group,

1959-72, Pres., 1972-73; Chm. Governing Body, Somerset County Museum, 1961-73; Mem. Gisborne Museum Staff, NZ, 1974-80. *Publication:* (ed) A Bibliography on Vernacular Architecture, 1973. *Address:* 1 Lewis Street, Gisborne, New Zealand.

HALL, Robert King, PhD; international consultant, educator and executive; *b* Kewanee, Ill, 13 March 1912; *s* of Dr Nelson Hall and Nellie Jean Hyer; *m* 1938, Margaret Wheeler, Belmont, Mass; one *s* two *d*. *Educ:* Lake Forest Univ. (AB); Harvard Univ. (AM); Univ. of Chicago (AMEduc); Columbia Univ. (AM); Sch. of Asiatic Studies, NY (AM); Univ. of Michigan (PhD). Master: Cranbrook Sch. (Mich), 1936-40; Dir Research Milwaukee Country Day Schs, 1940-41; Asst Dir, Commn on Eng. Lang. Studies, Harvard Univ., 1941-43; Lt-Comdr, USNR, 1943-46; Assoc. Prof. Teachers Coll., Columbia Univ., 1947-50, Prof. of Comparative Education, 1950-55; Dir of Trng, Arabian Amer. Oil Co., Saudi Arabia, 1955-60. Hon. Lectr, Teachers Coll., Columbia Univ., 1955-57; Internat. Consultant, 1960-64; Sen. Advisor, Univ. of Petroleum and Minerals, Dhahran, 1964-. Vis. Prof. and Lectr, English, American and foreign Univs; special assignments in connection with education, in Japan, South America, Iran, Arabia; Jt Editor, Year Book of Education (London), 1952-57. Vice-Pres. and Treasurer, Coll. of Petroleum and Minerals Foundn, 1977-. Deleg. to numerous internat. educnl congresses. Holder of hon. degrees. *Publications:* Federal Control of Education in ABC Republics, 1942; The Teaching of English, 1942; Report of Latin-American Workshop, 1941; A Basic English for South America, 1943; Ingles Basico Para Brasil, 1943; Education for a New Japan, 1949; Kokutai no Hongi (with J. O. Gauntlett), 1949; Shūshin: The Ethics of a Defeated Nation, 1949; Educación en Crisis, 1950; Problemas de Educação Rural, 1950; Report of a Study of YMCA World Services Policy and Practices, 1962; A Strategy for the Inner City, 1963. Articles in English and foreign educnl jls; numerous monographs and consulting reports. *Recreation:* travel. *Address:* University of Petroleum and Minerals, Dhahran, Saudi Arabia. *Club:* Explorers' (New York).

HALL, Prof. the Rev. Stuart George; Professor of Ecclesiastical History, King's College, University of London, since 1978; *b* 7 June 1928; *s* of George Edward Hall and May Catherine Hall; *m* 1953, Brenda Mary Henderson; two *s* two *d*. *Educ:* University Coll. Sch., Hampstead; New Coll., and Ripon Hall, Oxford (BA 1952, MA 1955, BD 1973). National Service, Army, 1947-48. Deacon 1954, priest 1955; Asst Curate, Newark-on-Trent Parish Church, 1954-58; Tutor, Queen's Coll., Birmingham, 1958-62; Lectr in Theology, Univ. of Nottingham, 1962-73, Sen. Lectr, 1973-78. *Publications:* Melito of Sardis On Pascha and fragments: (ed) texts and translations, 1979; contrib. to Jl of Eccles. History, Jl of Theol Studies, Studia Evangelica, Studia Patristica, and Theology. *Recreations:* gardening, choral music, swimming. *Address:* 16 Abbey Avenue, St Albans, Herts AL3 4AZ. *T:* St Albans 56358.

HALL, Prof. Stuart McPhail; Professor of Sociology, The Open University, since 1979; *b* 3 Feb. 1932; *s* of Herman and Jessie Hall; *m* 1964, Catherine Mary Barrett; one *s* one *d*. *Educ:* Jamaica Coll.; Merton Coll., Oxford (MA; Rhodes Scholar, 1951). Editor, New Left Review, 1957-61; Lectr, Film and Mass Media Studies, Chelsea Coll., London Univ., 1961-64; Centre for Cultural Studies, Univ. of Birmingham: Res. Fellow, 1964-68; Actg Dir, 1968-72; Dir, 1972-79. *Publications:* The Popular Arts, 1964; Resistance Through Rituals, 1974; Policing The Crisis, 1978; Culture, Media, Language, 1980. *Address:* 5 Mowbray Road, Kilburn, NW6.

HALL, Thomas William; Under-Secretary, Department of Transport, 1976-79 and since 1981; *b* 8 April 1931; *s* of Thomas William and Euphemia Jane Hall; *m* 1961, Anne Rosemary Hellier Davis; two *d*. *Educ:* Hitchin Grammar Sch.; St John's Coll., Oxford (MA). Asst Principal, Min. of Supply, 1954; Principal: War Office, Min. of Public Building and Works, Cabinet Office, 1958-68; Asst Sec., Min. of Public Building and Works, later DoE, 1968-76; Under Sec., Depts of Environment and Transport, 1979-81. *Recreations:* music, literature, gardening, walking. *Address:* Department of Transport, 2 Marsham Street, SW1. *T:* 01-212 3164.

HALL, Dr Trevor Henry, JP; PhD; FSA; FRICS; writer, historian, lecturer; President, Leeds Library (founded 1768), since 1969; *b* 28 May 1910; *o s* of H. Roxby Hall, Wakefield; *m* 1st, 1937, Dorothy (*d* 1973), *d* of late A. H. Keningley, Nostell; one *s* one *d*; 2nd, 1977, Marguerite, widow of Dr R. L. McMorris, Selby; one step *s* one step *d*. *Educ:* Wakefield Sch.; Trinity Coll., Cambridge (Perrott Student; MA); London Coll. of Estate Management (first place in final prof. exams, 1932). FSA 1978. Served War of 1939-45, Army. Sen. Partner, with Richard Gamble Walker, V. Stanley Walker & Son, chartered surveyors, Leeds, Wakefield, Rothwell and Woodlesford, 1945-82; Pres., Huddersfield or Bradford (now Yorkshire) Building Soc., 1972-74; Chm., Legal & General Assce Soc. (North Regional and Scottish Bds), 1978-80. Cecil Oldman Meml Lectr in bibliography and textual criticism, Univ. of Leeds, 1972-73. One of 300 invited Founder Life Mems, Cambridge Soc., 1977; Mem., Oxford Univ. Soc. of Bibliophiles, 1981 (Lectr, 1980). Chm., Leeds Cttee, Nat. Trust, 1968-70. JP City of Leeds, 1959. *Publications:* The Testament of R. W. Hull, 1945; (with E. J. Dingwall and K. M. Goldney) The Haunting of Borley Rectory: A Critical Survey of the Evidence, 1956; A Bibliography of Books on Conjuring in English from 1580 to 1850, 1957; (with E. J. Dingwall) Four Modern Ghosts, 1958; The Spiritualists: The Story of William Crookes and Florence Cook, 1962; The Strange Case of Edmund Gurney, 1964; The Mystery of the Leeds Library, 1965; New Light on Old Ghosts, 1965; (with J. L. Campbell) Strange Things, 1968; Sherlock Holmes:

Ten Literary Studies, 1969; Mathematical Recreations, 1633: An Exercise in 17th Century Bibliography, 1970; The Late Mr Sherlock Holmes, 1971; Old Conjuring Books: a bibliographical and historical study, 1972; The Card Magic of Edward G. Brown, 1973; The Early Years of the Huddersfield Building Society, 1974; A New Era, 1974; The Winder Sale of Old Conjuring Books, 1975; (with Percy H. Muir) Some Printers and Publishers of Conjuring Books and Other Ephemera, 1800-1850, 1976; Sherlock Holmes and his Creator, 1978; Search for Harry Price, 1978; The Strange Story of Ada Goodrich Freer, 1979; Dorothy L. Sayers: Nine Literary Studies, 1980. *Recreations:* walking, gardening, book collecting, writing. *Address:* The Lodge, Selby, N Yorks YO8 0PW. *T:* Selby 703372. *Club:* Leeds (Leeds).

HALL, Vernon F., CVO 1960; Anæsthetist, King's College Hospital, 1931-69, retired; *b* 25 Aug. 1904; *s* of Cecil S. and M. M. Hall; *m* 1935, C. Marcia Cavell; one *s* two *d. Educ:* Haberdashers' Sch.; King's Coll. Hosp., London. MRCS, LRCP, 1927; DA, 1938; FFARCS, 1948. Served War of 1939-45 in Army (Emergency Commission), 1942-46; Consultant Anæsthetist, India Command (Local Brig.), 1945; Dean, King's Coll. Hosp. Medical Sch., 1951-65. FKC 1958; Hon. FFARCS 1975. *Publications:* History of King's College Hospital Dental School, 1973; chapters on Anaesthesia—Rose & Carless, Surgery, etc. *Recreations:* riding, walking, reading and music. *Address:* Deercombe, Brendon, N Devon. *T:* Brendon 281.

HALL, (Wallace) John; HM Diplomatic Service (on secondment from Department of Trade, since 1979); Consul-General, São Paulo, since 1981; *b* 5 Oct. 1934; *s* of Claude Corbett Hall and Dulcie Hall (*née* Brinkworth); *m* 1962, Janet Bowen; three *d. Educ:* Crypt Sch., Gloucester; Hertford Grammar Sch.; Downing Coll., Cambridge (MA Classics). National Service, RAF, 1953-55. Pirelli-General Cable Works Ltd, 1958-62; Sales Manager, D. Meredew Ltd, 1962-67; Principal, Min. of Technology, 1967-70; Dept of Trade and Industry, Civil Aviation Policy, 1970-72; Consul (Commercial), São Paulo, Brazil, 1972-76; Asst Secretary, Dept of Trade, Shipping Policy, 1976-79; Counsellor (Economic), Brasilia, 1979-81. *Recreations:* bridge, tennis and other sports, daughters. *Address:* c/o Foreign and Commonwealth Office, SW1.

HALL, Prof. William Bateman; Professor of Nuclear Engineering, University of Manchester, since 1959; *b* 28 May 1923; *s* of Sidney Bateman Hall and Doris Hall; *m* 1950, Helen Mary Dennis; four *d. Educ:* Urmston Grammar Sch.; College of Technology, Manchester. Engineering apprenticeship, 1939-44; Royal Aircraft Establishment, 1944-46; United Kingdom Atomic Energy Authority (formerly Dept of Atomic Energy, Min. of Supply), 1946-59: Technical Engineer, 1946-52; Principal Scientific Officer, 1952-56; Senior Principal Scientific Officer, 1956-58; Dep. Chief Scientific Officer, 1958. Mem., Adv. Cttee on Safety of Nuclear Installations, 1972-. Pro-Vice-Chancellor, Univ. of Manchester, 1979-82. *Publications:* Reactor Heat Transfer, 1958; papers to scientific and professional institutions. *Recreations:* music, fell walking. *Address:* Maple Bank, Macclesfield Road, Alderley Edge, Cheshire. *T:* Alderley Edge 583034.

HALL, Brig. Sir William (Henry), KBE 1979 (CBE 1962); Kt 1968; DSO 1942; ED; Comptroller of Stores, State Electricity Commission of Victoria, 1956-70; Colonel Commandant, RAA Southern Command, since 1967; *b* 5 Jan. 1906; *s* of William Henry Hall, Edinburgh, Scotland; *m* 1930, Irene Mary, *d* of William Hayes; one *s* four *d. Educ:* Morgan Acad., Dundee; Melbourne Univ. Joined Staff of State Electricity Commn of Vic, 1924. Enlisted AIF, 1939: Capt. Royal Aust. Artillery, Palestine, Egypt, Syria, Papua, New Guinea, 1941 (Major); Aust. Dir of Armaments at AHQ, 1942 (Lt-Col); Dir of Armament at AHQ, 1945 (Col); CRA 3 Div. Artillery CMF, 1955-59 (Brig.). Director: Royal Humane Society of Vic.; Multiple Sclerosis Soc.; Chairman: Patriotic Funds Coun.; War Widows and Widowed Mothers' Trust; RSL War Veterans' Trust; State Pres. Victorian Br., RSL, 1964-74 (now Chm. Trustees); Nat. Pres., Aust. RSL, 1974-78; Aust. Councillor, World Veterans' Foundn; Patron, Aust.-Free China Economic Assoc.; Patron: Royal Artillery Assoc. (Vic.); Carry On, Vic. Dir, Queen Elizabeth II Silver Jubilee Trust for Young Australians; Trustee, Victorian Overseas Foundn. Associate Fellow, Aust. Inst. Management; Mem., Inst. of Purchasing and Supply (London). *Recreation:* golf. *Address:* Rosémont, 112 Kooyong Road, Caulfield, Vic. 3162, Australia; Montrose, Flinders, Victoria 3929. *Clubs:* Naval and Military (Melbourne); Melbourne Cricket, Peninsula Country Golf, Flinders Golf.

HALL, William Telford, CSI 1947; CIE 1942; *b* 4 June 1895; *s* of John Hall, Edinburgh; *m* 1922, E. Winifred, *d* of late Col Sir George McCrae, DSO, DL; two *s* one *d. Educ:* George Heriot's Sch. Served European War, 1914-18, Capt. Royal Irish Fusiliers and Machine Gun Corps, Salonica and France. Joined Indian Forest Service, 1921; Chief Conservator of Forests, United Provinces, India. *Address:* Rose Cottage, The Street, Effingham, Leatherhead, Surrey.

HALL, Willis; writer; *b* 6 April 1929; *s* of Walter and Gladys Hall; *m* 1973, Valerie Shute; one *s* (and three *s* by previous marriages). *Educ:* Cockburn High Sch., Leeds. TV plays include: The Villa Maroc; They Don't all Open Men's Boutiques; Song at Twilight; TV series: The Fuzz, 1977; The Danedyke Mystery, 1979; (with Keith Waterhouse): The Upper Crusts, 1973; Billy Liar, 1974; Worzel Gummidge, 1979 (adapted as stage musical, 1981). *Publications:* (with Michael Parkinson) The A-Z of Soccer, 1970; Football Report, 1973; Football Classified, 1974; My Sporting Life, Football Final, 1975; *children's*

books: The Royal Astrologer, 1960; The Gentle Knight, 1967; The Incredible Kidnapping, 1975; The Summer of the Dinosaur, 1977; The Last Vampire, 1982; *plays:* The Long and the Short and the Tall, 1959; A Glimpse of the Sea, 1969; Kidnapped at Christmas, 1975; Walk on, Walk on, 1975; Stag Night, 1976; Christmas Crackers, 1976; A Right Christmas Caper, 1977; (with Keith Waterhouse): Billy Liar, 1960; Celebration, 1961; All Things Bright and Beautiful, 1962; England Our England, 1962; Squat Betty and The Sponge Room, 1963; Say Who You Are, 1965; Whoops-a-Daisy, 1968; Children's Day, 1969; Who's Who, 1972; (musical) The Card, 1973; Saturday, Sunday, Monday (adaptation from de Filippo), 1973; Filumena (adaptation from de Filippo), 1977. *Address:* Laverock Hall, Oakworth, near Keighley, W Yorkshire. *Clubs:* Garrick, Lansdowne.

HALL-THOMPSON, Major (Robert) Lloyd, ERD; TD; JP; *b* 9 April 1920; *s* of Lt-Col Rt Hon. S. H. Hall-Thompson, PC (NI), DL, JP, MP; *m* 1948, Alison F. Leitch, MSR; one *s* one *d. Educ:* Campbell Coll. Prep. Sch.; Campbell Coll. Royal School. Major, Royal Artillery, 1939-46; TA, 1946-56. Joined Unionist Party, 1938; Vice-Pres., Clifton Unionist Assoc. (Chm. 1954-57); MP (U) Clifton, 1969-73; Mem (U), N Belfast, NI Assembly, 1973-75 (Leader of the House, 1973-74); Chief Whip, NI Executive, 1973-74; Mem. (UPNI) for N Belfast, NI Constitutional Convention, 1975-76. Director of several companies. Formerly Mem. NI Hosps Authority (Past Vice-Chm. Finance and Gen. Purposes Cttee); Past Vice-Chm., Samaritan Hosp. Management Cttee; Life Governor, Samaritan Hosp.; Pres. and Trustee, North Belfast Working Men's Club; Trustee and Hon. Sec., Belfast Newsboys' Club and W. S. Armour Girls' Club; Vice-Pres., Cliftonville Football and Athletic Club; Founder, Trustee & Pres., Duncairn Friendship Assoc.; Life Mem., (Past Hon. Sec. and Hon. Treas.), Not Forgotten Assoc.; Life Mem., Royal Ulster Agric. Soc.; Freeman and Stewart, Down Royal Corp. of Horse Breeders; Chm., Irish Draught Horse Soc.; Hon. Sec., Half-Bred Horse Breeders' Soc.; Mem. Cttee, NI Nurses Housing Assoc. *Recreations:* horse riding, hunting, racing, eventing, show jumping, breeding; golf, reading. *Address:* Maymount, Ballylesson, Belfast 8, Northern Ireland. *T:* Drumbo 327. *Club:* Ulster (Belfast).

HALLADAY, Eric, MA; Master, Grey College, University of Durham, since 1980; *b* 9 July 1930; *s* of Rev. A. R. Halladay and Helena Renton; *m* 1956, Margaret Baister; one *s* two *d. Educ:* Durham Sch.; St John's Coll., Cambridge (MA History Tripos Pts I and II, Cl. II Div. I); Ripon Hall, Oxford. National Service, commnd 5th Regt, RHA, 1948-50. Exeter Sch., 1954-60, Sen. History Master, 1956-60; Sen. Lectr in History, RMA, Sandhurst, 1960-64; Sen. Tutor, Grey Coll., Univ. of Durham, and part-time Lectr in History, 1964-80; Vice-Master, Grey Coll., 1967-80. Chm., Northumbrian Univs Military Educn Cttee, 1981-; Mem., TA&VRA, N of England, 1980-; Sec., Durham Br., SSAFA, 1977-. Chm., Durham Regatta, 1982-. *Publications:* The Building of Modern Africa (with D. D. Rooney), 1966, 2nd edn 1968; The Emergent Continent: Africa in the Nineteenth Century, 1972. *Recreations:* gardening, rowing. *Address:* The Master's House, Hollingside Lane, Durham. *T:* Durham 65065; Haven Cottage, Over Norton, Chipping Norton, Oxon. *T:* Chipping Norton 2995. *Club:* Leander (Henley-on-Thames).

HALLAM, Bishop of, (RC), since 1980; **Rt. Rev. Gerald Moverley,** JCD; *b* 9 April 1922; *s* of William Joseph Moverley and Irene Mary Moverley (*née* Dewhirst). *Educ:* St Bede's Grammar Sch., Bradford; Ushaw Coll., Durham; Angelicum Univ., Rome. Priest, 1946; Sec. to Bishop Poskitt, Leeds, 1946-51; Angelicum Univ., 1951-54; Chancellor, Dio. Leeds, 1958-68; Domestic Prelate to HH Pope Paul VI, 1965; apptd Bishop, Dec. 1967; Titular Bishop of Tinisa in Proconsulari and Bishop Auxiliary of Leeds, 1968-80; translated to new diocese of Hallam, established May 1980. *Address:* Quarters, Carsick Hill Way, Sheffield S10 3LT. *T:* Sheffield 301596.

HALLAM-HIPWELL, H.; *see* Vivenot, Baroness Raoul de.

HALLCHURCH, David Thomas, TD 1965; barrister-at-law; a Recorder of the Crown Court, since 1980; *b* 4 April 1929; *s* of Walter William Hallchurch and Marjorie Pretoria Mary Hallchurch (*née* Cooper); *m* 1st, 1954, Gillian Mary Jagger (marr. diss. 1972); three *s*; 2nd, 1972, Susan Kathryn Mavor Brennan; one step *s* one step *d. Educ:* Bromsgrove Sch.; Trinity Coll., Oxford (MA Hons). Called to the Bar, Gray's Inn, 1953; Whitehead Travelling Scholarship, Canada and USA, 1953-54; practised as barrister-at-law on Midland and Oxford Circuit, 1954-60 and 1964-. Major, Staffs Yeomanry (Queen's Own Royal Regiment), TA, 1953-66. Legal Mem., Mental Health Review Tribunal for the West Midlands, 1979-. *Recreations:* cricket, drawing (cartoons). *Address:* Neachley House, Tong, near Shifnal, Shropshire TF11 8PH. *T:* Albrighton 3542. *Clubs:* Vincent's (Oxford); Greenflies Cricket (Brewood, Staffs).

HALLETT, Vice-Adm. Sir Cecil Charles; *see* Hughes Hallett.

HALLETT, Cecil Walter; retired as General Secretary, Amalgamated Engineering Union, 1957-64; *b* 10 Dec. 1899; *m*; two *s* two *d. Educ:* New City Road Elementary Sch., London. Messenger, Commercial Cable Co., 1913-15; apprentice fitter and turner, Gas Light and Coke Co., Becton, N Woolwich, 1916-18. HM Forces, 10th London Regt, 1918-19; journeyman fitter and turner, various firms, 1923-48; Asst Gen. Sec. AEU, 1948-57. Former Editor, AEU Monthly Jl and The Way. *Address:* 317 High Street South, Carterton, North Island, New Zealand. *T:* Carterton 8565.

HALLETT, Prof. George Edward Maurice, MDS; Child Dental Health Professor, University of Newcastle upon Tyne (formerly King's College, University of Durham), 1951-77, now Emeritus; Dean, Sutherland Dental School, 1960-77, and Hospital, 1970-77; retired; *b* 30 July 1912; *s* of Edward Henry and Berthe Hallett; *m* 1936, Annetta Eva Grant Napier; three *d. Educ:* Birkenhead Institute; Liverpool Univ. (LDS, Gilmour Medal and other prizes). HDD RCSE 1939; FDS RCS 1948; MDS Durham, 1952; DOrth RCS, 1954; FDS RCSE 1960; FFD RCSI 1964. House Surgeon, Liverpool Dental Hosp., 1934-35; School Dental Officer, Doncaster CB, 1935-36, Notts, 1936-40; served War, 1940-46: Army Dental Corps, Major, despatches. University of Durham: Lecturer in Children's Dentistry, 1946, Reader, 1948; Lectr in Orthodontics, 1946. Examiner in Dental subjects, Universities of Dundee, Durham, Edinburgh and Glasgow; RCS of Eng., 1954-77; Consultant, United Teaching Hosps, Newcastle upon Tyne; Head of Dept of Child Dental Health, Dental Hosp., Newcastle upon Tyne, 1948. Mem. Dental Council, RCSE; Past President: Société Française d'Orthopedie Dento-Faciale; European Orthodontic Soc. (also former Editor; Hon. Life Mem.); North of England Odontological Soc.; Brit. Soc. for the study of Orthodontics (Hon. Life Mem.); Newcastle Medico-Legal Soc.; former Mem., Newcastle RHB; former Mem., Newcastle AHA (T). Hon. Life Mem., British Dental Assoc. Pres., British Med. Pilots' Assoc. Hon. FDSRCPS Glas 1979. Silver Medal, Ville de Paris, 1980. *Publications:* contribs to scientific and dental jls. *Recreations:* dilettantism in the glyptic arts, flying. *Address:* 63 Runnymede Road, Darras Hall, Ponteland, Newcastle upon Tyne NE20 9HJ. *T:* Ponteland 22646. *Club:* Newcastle Aero.

HALLETT, Victor George Henry; Social Security (formerly National Insurance) Commissioner, since 1976; *b* 11 Feb. 1921; *s* of Dr Denys Bouhier Imbert Hallett; *m* 1947, Margaret Hamlyn. *Educ:* Westminster; Queen's Coll., Oxford (MA). Served War, 1939-45 (despatches 1946). Called to Bar, Inner Temple, 1949. Mem., Land Registration Rules Cttee, 1971-76; Conveyancing Counsel of the Court, 1971-76. *Publications:* Key and Elphinstone's Conveyancing Precedents (ed jtly), 15th edn, 1952; Prideaux's Precedents in Conveyancing (ed jtly), 25th edn, 1953; Hallett's Conveyancing Precedents, 1965; (with Nicholas Warren) Settlements, Wills and Capital Transfer Tax, 1979. *Address:* Office of the Social Security Commissioners, 6 Grosvenor Gardens, SW1W 0DH.

HALLGARTEN, Anthony Bernard Richard, QC 1978; *b* 16 June 1937; *s* of Fritz and Friedel Hallgarten; *m* 1962, Katherine Borchard; one *s* three *d. Educ:* Merchant Taylors' Sch., Northwood; Downing Coll., Cambridge (BA). Called to the Bar, Middle Temple, 1961; Barstow Scholar, Inns of Court, 1961. *Recreations:* cricket, canals, cycling. *Address:* 3 Essex Court, Temple, EC4Y 9AL. *T:* 01-583 9294. *Clubs:* Garrick, MCC.

HALLIBURTON, Rev. Canon Robert John; Priest in Charge, All Souls, St Margaret's-on-Thames, since 1982; *b* 23 March 1935; *s* of Robert Halliburton and Katherine Margery Halliburton (née Robinson); *m* 1968, Jennifer Ormsby Turner; one *s* three *d* (and one *s* decd). *Educ:* Tonbridge Sch.; Selwyn Coll., Cambridge (MA); Keble Coll., Oxford (DPhil); St Stephen's House, Oxford. Curate, St Dunstan and All Saints, Stepney, 1961; Tutor, St Stephen's House, Oxford, 1967; Vice-Principal, St Stephen's House, 1971; Lectr, Lincoln Coll., Oxford, 1973; Principal of Chichester Theol Coll., 1975-82, Canon and Prebend of Chichester Cathedral, 1976-82, Canon Emeritus, 1982-. Select Preacher, Oxford Univ., 1976-77. Consultant, Anglican-Roman Catholic Internat. Commn, 1971-75. Mem., Doctrinal Commn of C of E, 1978-. *Publications:* contrib. The Eucharist Today, ed. R. C. D. Jasper, 1974; articles in Studia Patristica, La Revue des Etudes Augustiniennes, Faith and Unity. *Recreations:* music, gardening, dog breeding. *Address:* 30 Ailsa Road, St Margaret's-on-Thames, Twickenham, Middlesex TW1 1QW. *Club:* Athenæum.

HALLIDAY, Edward Irvine, CBE 1973; RP 1952; RBA 1942; ARCA (London) 1925; Immediate Past-President, Royal Society of Portrait Painters; Past-President, Royal Society of British Artists; Vice-President and Chairman, Artists General Benevolent Institution, since 1965; President, Artists League of Great Britain, since 1975; *b* 7 Oct. 1902; *s* of James Halliday and Violet Irvine; *m* 1928, Dorothy Lucy Hatswell; one *s* one *d. Educ:* Liverpool; Paris; Royal College of Art, London; British Sch. at Rome (Rome Scholar 1925). War of 1939-45: service with RAF Bomber Command until seconded for special duties with Foreign Office. Mural paintings in London and Liverpool. Posters of Western Highlands for British Railways. Principal Portraits include: The Queen, for various cities, regiments, etc.; The Queen and The Duke of Edinburgh, for SS Caronia; The Duke of Edinburgh, for Gordonstoun Sch., Baltic Exchange, the Press Club, and Nat. Defence Coll.; The Prince of Wales, for Air Support Comd, RAF, and Naval Club; Queen Elizabeth the Queen Mother; HRH Princess Alice, Countess of Athlone; Admiral of the Fleet the Earl Mountbatten of Burma; Countess Mountbatten of Burma; Pandit Nehru (painted in New Delhi); Sir Edmund Hillary; President Azikiwe (painted in Nigeria); Dr Kaunda (painted in Zambia); King Olaf of Norway; Lord Hunt of Fawley and other doctors. Conversation Pieces include: The Royal Family; The 5th Marquess of Salisbury with his brother and sisters; Undergraduates at Worcester Coll., Oxford, 1937 and 1952. Broadcasts on many subjects. Governor, Fedn of British Artists, 1970-. Gold Medal, Paris Salon, 1953, 1965. FRSA 1970. *Address:* 62 Hamilton Terrace, NW8. *T:* 01-286 7030. *Clubs:* Athenæum, Arts, Chelsea Arts.

HALLIDAY, Sir George Clifton, Kt 1967; Consultant Otolaryngologist, Royal Prince Alfred Hospital and Prince Henry Hospital (Consultant Surgeon, since 1960); *b* 22 April 1901; *s* of late Edward James Halliday, NSW; *m* 1927, Hester Judith Macansh; two *s* one *d. Educ:* The King's Sch., Parramatta; St Paul's Coll., Univ. of Sydney. MB, ChM Sydney Univ., 1925; FRCSE 1934; FRACS 1954. Surg., St George Hosp., 1935; Surg., Royal Prince Alfred Hosp., 1936; Lectr in Otolaryngology, Sydney Univ., 1948-61. Served in AAMC, Middle East, 1940-43 (Lt-Col). Hon. Mem., RSM, 1970; Corresp. Fellow, Amer. Laryngological Assoc., 1970. Patron, Australian Assoc. for Better Hearing. *Recreations:* tennis, cricket, golf. *Address:* 67 Cranbrook Road, Rose Bay, NSW 2029, Australia. *T:* FM 2280. *Clubs:* Union, Royal Sydney Golf, Elanora Country (all Sydney).

HALLIDAY, Ian Francis, FCA; Finance Director, Lowndes Lambert Group Ltd, since 1981; *b* 16 Nov. 1927; *s* of Michael and Jean Halliday; *m* 1952, Mary Busfield; one *s* two *d. Educ:* Wintringham Grammar Sch., Grimsby; Lincoln Coll., Oxford (MA Mathematics). Armitage & Norton, Chartered Accountants, 1951-69; qual. as Chartered Accountant, 1954; Partner, 1957; Finance Director on Main Board, Allied Textile Co. Ltd, 1970-74; on secondment as Dep. Director of Industrial Development Unit, Dept of Industry, 1974-77; Finance Dir on Main Board, Leslie & Godwin (Holdings) Ltd, internat. insce and re-insce Lloyd's Brokers, 1977-80; Chief Exec., NEB, 1980. *Recreations:* gardening, sailing. *Address:* 40 Finthorpe Lane, Huddersfield HD5 8TU.

HALLIDAY, James; see Symington, D.

HALLIDAY, Prof. Michael Alexander Kirkwood; Professor of Linguistics in the University of Sydney, since 1976; *b* 13 April 1925; *s* of late Wilfrid J. Halliday and of Winifred Halliday (née Kirkwood). *Educ:* Rugby School; University of London. BA London; MA, PhD, Cambridge. Served Army, 1944-47. Asst Lectr in Chinese, Cambridge Univ., 1954-58; Lectr in General Linguistics, Edinburgh Univ., 1958-60; Reader in General Linguistics, Edinburgh Univ., 1960-63; Dir, Communication Res. Centre, UCL, 1963-65; Linguistic Soc. of America Prof., Indiana Univ., 1964; Prof. of General Linguistics, UCL, 1965-71; Fellow, Center for Advanced Study in the Behavioral Sciences, Stanford, Calif., 1972-73; Prof. of Linguistics, Univ. of Illinois, 1973-74; Prof. of Language and Linguistics, Essex Univ., 1974-75. Visiting Professor of Linguistics: Yale, 1967; Brown, 1971; Nairobi, 1972. FAHA 1979. Dr *hc* Nancy. *Publications:* The Language of the Chinese 'Secret History of the Mongols', 1959; (with A. McIntosh and P. Strevens) The Linguistic Sciences and Language Teaching, 1964; (with A. McIntosh) Patterns of Language, 1966; Intonation and Grammar in British English, 1967; A Course in Spoken English: Intonation, 1970; Explorations in the Functions of Language, 1973; Learning How To Mean, 1975; (with R. Hasan) Cohesion in English, 1976; System and Function in Language, ed G. Kress, 1976; Language as Social Semiotic, 1978; articles in Jl of Linguistics, Word, Trans of Philological Soc., etc. *Address:* Department of Linguistics, University of Sydney, NSW 2006, Australia.

HALLIDAY, Norman Pryde; Senior Principal Medical Officer (Under Secretary), Department of Health and Social Security, since 1977; *b* 28 March 1932; *s* of late James and Jessie Thomson Hunter Halliday; *m* 1953, Eleanor Smith; three *s* one *d. Educ:* Woodside, Glasgow; King's Coll., London; King's Coll. Hosp. Med. Sch. SRN 1955; MB, BS, MRCS, LRCP 1964; DCH RCPGlas 1969. Various posts in clinical medicine, incl. Registrar (Paediatrics), KCH, London; SMO, DHSS, 1972. *Publications:* articles on medical subjects in professional journals. *Recreations:* photography, sub aqua diving, fashion, DIY, cross-bow shooting. *Address:* 12 Regalfield Close, Guildford, Surrey GU2 6YG. *T:* Worplesdon 233577.

HALLIDAY, Vice-Adm. Sir Roy (William), KBE 1980; DSC 1944; Director General of Intelligence, Ministry of Defence, since 1981; *b* 27 June 1923; *m* 1945, Dorothy Joan Meech. *Educ:* William Ellis Sch.; University College Sch. Joined Royal Navy, 1941; served in Fleet Air Arm (fighter pilot) in World War II, in HMS Chaser, HMSs Victorious and Illustrious; test pilot, Boscombe Down, 1947-48; Comdg Officer 813 Sqdn (Wyverns, HMS Eagle), 1954; Army Staff Coll., Camberley; Comdr, 1958; Exec. Officer Coastal Forces Base (HMS Diligence), 1959; Sen. Officer 104th Minesweeping Sqdn, Far East Flt, in comd (HMS Houghton), 1961-62; Naval Asst to Chief of Naval Information, 1962-64; comdr (Air) HMS Albion, 1964-66; Captain, 1966; Dep. Dir Naval Air Warfare, 1966-70; HMS Euryalus in comd and as Captain D3 Far East Fleet and D6 Western Fleet, 1970-71; Commodore, 1971; Cdre Amphibious Warfare, 1971-73; Cdre Intelligence, Defence Intelligence Staff, 1973-75; Comdr British Navy Staff, Washington, Naval Attaché, and UK Nat. Liaison Rep. to SACLANT, 1975-78; Dep. Chief of Defence Staff (Intelligence), 1978-81. ADC to the Queen, 1975. *Recreations:* gardening, walking. *Address:* c/o Barclays Bank, Lyndhurst, Hants. *Club:* Army and Navy.

HALLIFAX, Vice-Adm. Sir David John, KBE 1982; Deputy Supreme Allied Commander, Atlantic, since 1982; *b* 3 Sept. 1927; *s* of Ronald H. C. Hallifax and Joanne M. Hallifax; *m* 1962, Anne Blakiston Houston; two *s* one *d. Educ:* Winchester. Joined RN 1945; minesweeping, Gulf of Salonika, 1949-51; CO MTB 5008, 1953; Long TAS Course, 1954; HMS Salerno, Suez, 1956; Staff Coll., Camberley, 1959; CO HMS Agincourt, 1964-65; RCDS 1972; CO HMS Fife, 1973-75; Flag Officer, First Flotilla, 1978-80; Chief of Staff to C-in-C Fleet, 1980-82. *Recreations:* sailing, conchology. *Address:* Box C-01,

Naval Party 1964 (Saclant), BFPO Ships. *Clubs:* Pratt's, Farmers', Royal Yacht Squadron.

HALLINAN, Sir (Adrian) Lincoln, Kt 1971; DL; Barrister-at-law; Stipendiary Magistrate, South Glamorgan (Cardiff), since 1976; a Recorder of the Crown Court, since 1972; *b* 13 Nov. 1922; *e s* of late Sir Charles Hallinan, CBE and late Theresa Doris Hallinan, JP (*née* Holman); *m* 1955, Mary Parry Evans, *qv*; two *s* two *d. Educ:* Downside. Lieut, Rifle Bde, 1942–47; TA, 1950–52 (Captain). Called to Bar, Lincoln's Inn, 1950; Wales and Chester Circuit. A Legal Mem., Mental Health Review Tribunal for Wales, 1966–76; Chm., Med. Appeals Tribunal, 1970–76. Cardiff CC, 1949–74 (serving on several educational and cultural cttees); Alderman, 1961–74; Lord Mayor of Cardiff, 1969–70. Contested (C), Aberdare, 1946, Cardiff West, 1951, 1959. Chm., Cardiff Educn Cttee, 1961–63 and 1965–70; Chm., Governing Body, Cardiff Coll. of Art, and Cardiff Coll. of Music and Drama, 1961–73; First Chm., Nat. Court of Governors, Welsh Coll. of Music and Drama, 1970; Chairman: Commemorative Collectors Soc.; S Wales Gp, Victorian Soc.; Founder and Chm., Cardiff 2000–Cardiff Civic Trust, 1964–73, 1st Pres. 1973; Trustee, Cardiff Million Pound Fund, 1972; Chm., Cardiff-Nantes Fellowship, 1961–68. Chevalier, Ordre des Palmes Academiques, 1965; Chevalier de la Légion d'Honneur, 1973; Knight of Mark Twain, 1979. OStJ 1969. DL Glamorgan, 1969. *Recreations:* music, the arts, collecting. *Address:* 42 Heol Isaf, Radyr, Cardiff CF1 9HE. *T:* Cardiff 842454; Sunny Hill, Newquay, Dyfed. *Club:* Cardiff and County (Cardiff).

HALLINAN, Sir Eric, Kt 1955; *b* 27 Oct. 1900; *s* of Edward Hallinan, Midleton, Co. Cork, and Elizabeth, *d* of Maj.-Gen. Sir Thomas Dennehy; *m* 1936, Monica, *d* of George Waters, Midleton, Co. Cork; one *s* one *d. Educ:* Downside; Trinity Coll., Dublin. BA, LLB Dublin, 1924; Barrister-at-Law (King's Inns, 1923; Gray's Inn, 1927). Practised at Irish Bar, 1924–29. Colonial Administrative Service, Nigeria, 1930–36; Colonial Legal Service, Nigeria, 1936–40; Attorney-Gen., Bahamas, 1940–44; Puisne Judge: Trinidad, 1944–48; Nigeria, 1948–52; Chief Justice, Cyprus, 1952–57; Chief Justice of The West Indies, 1958–61; Justice of Appeal, Bahamas and Bermuda, 1966–68. LLD (*jure dig.*) Dublin, 1958. *Address:* Calle Margarita Blanca 5, Pueblo Lopez, Fuengirola, (Málaga), Spain. *T:* 471927. *Club:* Royal Commonwealth Society.

HALLINAN, Sir Lincoln; see Hallinan, Sir A. L.

HALLINAN, Mary Alethea, (Lady Hallinan); see Parry Evans, M.A.

HALLIWELL, Brian; Accountant and Comptroller General, HM Customs and Excise, since 1980; *b* 17 Dec. 1930; *s* of late Norman and Emma Halliwell; *m* 1957, Agnes Lee. *Educ:* Preston Grammar Sch. DMS 1968. Joined HM Customs and Excise as Clerical Officer, 1947; Principal, 1969; Asst Sec., 1973; Dep. Accountant General, 1976. *Recreations:* chess, reading, sport. *Address:* 33 Elm Drive, Rayleigh, Essex SS6 8AB. *T:* Rayleigh 742259.

HALLIWELL, Leslie; Programme Buyer: ITV since 1968; Granada Television, since 1960; Channel Four, since 1981; *b* 23 Feb. 1929; *s* of James and Lily Halliwell; *m* 1958, Ruth (*née* Turner); one *s* (and one step *s* one step *d*). *Educ:* Bolton Sch.; St Catharine's Coll., Cambridge (MA). Journalist, Picturegoer, 1952; Prog. Manager, specialised cinemas in Cambridge, 1953–55; Exec. Trainee, 1956, Administrator of Publicity Div., 1957, Rank Org.; Prog. Buyer, Southern Television, 1958; Film Researcher, Granada Television, 1959. Introduced Home Front, TV series, 1982. Author of plays professionally performed (Harrogate, Bristol, Blackpool, Bolton, Hastings, Leeds etc): Make your own Bed, 1957; A Night on the Island, 1960. *Publications:* The Filmgoer's Companion, 1965 (7th edn 1980); The Filmgoer's Book of Quotes, 1973 (2nd edn 1978); (with Graham Murray) The Clapperboard Book of the Cinema, 1975; Halliwell's Movie Quiz, 1977; Halliwell's Film Guide, 1977, 3rd edn 1981; Mountain of Dreams, 1977; Halliwell's Teleguide, 1979, revd edn as Halliwell's Television Companion, 1982; Halliwell's Hundred, 1982; contrib. Spectator, New Statesman, TLS, Sight and Sound, Photoplay, Variety, Television Radio Age, Television Today. *Recreations:* country driving, travel, chess, collecting, walking. *Address:* Clovelly, 26 Atwood Avenue, Richmond, Surrey.

HALLOWES, Odette Marie Celine, GC 1946; MBE 1945; Légion d'Honneur, 1950; Vice-President, Women's Transport Services (FANY); Member Royal Society of St George; housewife; *b* 28 April 1912; *d* of Gaston Brailly, Croix-de-Guerre, Médaille Militaire; *m* 1931, Roy Sansom (decd); three *d*; *m* 1947, late Captain Peter Churchill, DSO; *m* 1956, Geoffrey Macleod Hallowes. *Educ:* The Convent of Ste Thérèse, Amiens (France) and privately. Entered Special Forces and landed in France, 1942; worked as British agent until capture by Gestapo, 1943; sentenced to death June 1943; endured imprisonment and torture until 28 April 1945, when left Ravensbrück Concentration Camp (MBE, GC). Member: Military Medallists League (Vice-Pres.); Cttee, Victoria Cross and George Cross Assoc. Pres., 282 (East Ham) Air Cadet Sqdn. Vice-Pres., Woman of the Year Luncheon. *Recreations:* reading, travelling, cooking, trying to learn patience. *Address:* Rosedale, Eriswell Road, Burwood Park, Walton-on-Thames, Surrey. *Clubs:* Naval and Military, FANY, Special Forces.

HALLOWS, Ralph Ingham, CMG 1973; MBE 1947; retired from Bank of England, 1973; *b* 4 May 1913; *s* of Ralph Watson Hallows, MA Cantab, TD, and Muriel Milnes-Smith; *m* 1939, Anne Lorna Bond; one *s* one *d. Educ:*

Berkhamsted Sch. Indian Police Service, 1932; Indian Political Service, 1937; India Office/Commonwealth Relations Office, 1947; Kuwait Oil Co., 1948; Bank of England, 1954. Specialist Adv. to Select Cttee on Overseas Develt, 1974. *Recreations:* golf, fishing, sailing. *Address:* Apple Tree Cottage, Thursley Road, Elstead, Surrey. *T:* Elstead 702284.

HALLSWORTH, Prof. Ernest Gordon, DSc, FRSC, FTS; Project Director, IFIAS, Science Policy Research Unit, University of Sussex, since 1979; *b* 1913; *s* of Ernest and Beatrice Hallsworth, Ashton-under-Lyne, Lancs; *m* 1st, 1943, Elaine Gertrude Seddon (*d* 1970), *d* of R. C. Weatherill, Waverley, NSW; two *s* one *d* and one step *s*; 2nd, 1976, Merrily Ramly; one step *d. Educ:* Ashton Grammar Sch., Ashton-under-Lyne, Lancs; Univ. of Leeds. University of Leeds: First Cl. Hons in Agric. Chem., Sir Swire Smith Fellow, 1936; Asst Lectr in Agric. Chem., 1936; PhD 1939; DSc 1964. Lectr in Agric. Chem., Univ. of Sydney, 1939; Prof. of Soil Science, Univ. of West Australia, 1960–61; Prof. of Agric. Chem. and Head Dept Agric. Sci., Univ. Nottingham, 1951–64 (Dean, Faculty of Agric. and Hort., 1951–60); Chief of Div. of Soils, CSIRO, 1964–73; Chm., Land Resources Labs, CSIRO, 1973–78. Pres. Lecturers' Assoc., Sydney Univ., 1946–49. Treas., Aust. Assoc. of Scientific Workers, 1943; Member: Science Advisory Panel, Australian Broadcasting Commn, 1949–51; Pasture Improvement Cttee, Australian Dairy Produce Bd (NSW), 1948–51; Chm. Insecticides and Fungicides Cttee, Australian Standards Inst., 1949–51. President: Internat. Soc. of Soil Science, 1964–68; Sect. 13, Aust. and NZ Assoc. for the Advancement of Science, 1976. Mem. Council, Flinders Univ., 1967–; Chief Scientific Liaison Officer (Aust.), London, 1971. Fellow, Aust. Acad. of Technol Scis, 1976. *Publications:* (Ed) Nutrition of the Legumes, 1958; (ed with D. V. Crawford) Experimental Pedology, 1964; (with others) Handbook of Australian Soils, 1968; (with others) Principles of a Balanced Land Use Policy for Australia, 1976; Where Shall We Build Our New Cities?, 1978; Land and Water Resources of Australia, 1979; Socio-economic Restraints in Tropical Forest Management, 1982; contributions to: Aust. Jl Science, Jl Soc. Chem. Industr., Empire Jl Experimental Agric., Jl Agric. Science, Aust. Medical Jl, Jl Soil Science. *Recreations:* talking, pedology. *Address:* 1 Bellevue Cottages, Blackboys, near Uckfield, Sussex. *T:* Framfield 606; 30 Fowlers Road, Glen Osmond, SA 5064, Australia. *T:* 796318. *Club:* Farmers'.

HALLWARD, Bertrand Leslie, MA; *b* 24 May 1901; *er s* of late N. L. Hallward, Indian Educational Service, and Evelyn A. Gurdon; *m* 1926, Catherine Margaret, 2nd *d* of late Canon A. J. Tait; four *d. Educ:* Haileybury Coll. (Scholar); King's Coll., Cambridge (Scholar). Fellow of Peterhouse, 1923–39. Hon. Fellow 1956. Headmaster of Clifton Coll., 1939–48; Vice-Chancellor, Nottingham Univ., 1948–65. Hon. LLD: Sheffield, 1964; Nottingham, 1965. *Publications:* Chapters II, III, IV, and part of VII (the Second and Third Punic Wars) in Cambridge Ancient History, Vol. VIII, 1930; Editor of the Classical Quarterly, 1935–39. *Address:* Flat 48, Gretton Court, Girton, Cambridge. *T:* Cambridge 277327.

See also Prof. W. O. Chadwick, G. C. H. Spafford.

HALNAN, Patrick John; Metropolitan Stipendiary Magistrate, since 1978; *b* 7 March 1925; *s* of E. T. and A. B. Halnan; *m* 1955, Judith Mary (*née* Humberstone); four *c. Educ:* Perse Sch., Cambridge; Trinity Coll., Cambridge (MA). Army, 1943–47. Solicitor. Asst Solicitor, Hants CC, 1954–58; Clerk to the Justices, Cambs, 1958–78. Sec., Justices' Clerks' Soc., 1972–76, Pres., 1978. Chm., Road Traffic Cttee, Magistrates' Assoc., 1981–. *Publications:* (ed with Prof. R. M. Jackson) Leo Page, Justice of the Peace, 3rd edn 1967; (ed) Wilkinson's Road Traffic Offences, 11th edn, 1982 (also ed 7th, 8th, 9th, 10th edns); (with David Latham) Drink/Driving Offences, 1979; Road Traffic, 1981. *Recreations:* sailing, stamp collecting. *Address:* Thames Magistrates' Court, Aylward Street, E1.

HALPERN, Prof. Jack, FRS 1974; Louis Block Professor of Chemistry, University of Chicago, since 1962; *b* Poland, 19 Jan. 1925 (moved to Canada, 1929; USA 1962); *s* of Philip Halpern and Anna Sass; *m* 1949, Helen Peritz; two *d. Educ:* McGill Univ., Montreal. BSc 1946, PhD 1949. NRC Postdoc. Fellow, Univ. of Manchester, 1949–50; Prof. of Chem., Univ. of Brit. Columbia, 1950–62 (Nuffield Foundn Travelling Fellow, Cambridge Univ., 1959–60); Prof. of Chem., Univ. of Chicago, 1962–71, Louis Block Prof., 1971–. Visiting Prof.: Univ. of Minnesota, 1962; Harvard Univ., 1966–67; California Inst. of Techn., 1969; Princeton Univ., 1970–71; Copenhagen Univ., 1978; Firth Vis. Prof., Sheffield, 1982; Sherman Fairchild Dist. Scholar, California Inst. of Technology, 1979; Guest Scholar, Kyoto Univ., 1981; Lectureships: 3M, Univ. of Minnesota, 1968; FMC, Princeton Univ., 1969; Du Pont, Univ. of Calif., Berkeley, 1970; Frontier of Chemistry, Case Western Reserve Univ., 1971; Venable, Univ. of N Carolina, 1973; Ritter Meml, Miami Univ., 1980; University, Univ. of Western Ontario, 1981; F. J. Toole, Univ. of New Brunswick, 1981. Associate Editor: Jl of Amer. Chem. Soc.; Inorganica Chimica Acta; Mem. Editorial Bds: Accounts of Chemical Research; Jl of American Chemical Soc.; Jl of Catalysis; Catalysis Reviews; Jl of Coordination Chem.; Inorganica Chimica Acta; Inorganic Syntheses; Jl of Molecular Catalysis; Jl of Organometallic Chemistry; Amer. Chem. Soc. Advances in Chemistry series; Co-editor, OUP International Series of Monographs in Chemistry. Mem. Bd of Trustees, Gordon Research Confs, 1968–70; Chm., Gordon Conf. on Inorganic Chem., 1969; Chm., Amer. Chemical Soc. Div. of Inorganic Chem., 1971. Fellow, Amer. Acad. of Arts and Sciences, 1967. Holds several honours and awards, including: Amer. Chem. Soc. Award in Inorganic Chem., 1968; Chem. Soc. Award, 1976; Humboldt Award, 1977; Kokes Award, Johns Hopkins Univ., 1978.

Publications: Editor (with F. Basolo and J. Bunnett) Collected Accounts of Transition Metal Chemistry, vol. I, 1973, vol. II, 1977; contrib. articles on Catalysis and on Coordination Compounds to Encyclopaedia Britannica; numerous articles to Jl of Amer. Chemical Soc. and other scientific jls. *Recreations:* art, music. *Address:* Department of Chemistry, University of Chicago, 5735 South Ellis Avenue, Chicago, Illinois 60637, USA. *T:* (312) 753-8271. *Club:* Quadrangle (Chicago).

HALPIN, Most Rev. Charles A.; *see* Regina, Archbishop of, (R.C.).

HALPIN, Miss Kathleen Mary, CBE 1953 (OBE 1941); Chief Administrator, Regions, WRVS (formerly WVS), 1945-73; *b* 19 Nov. 1903; unmarried. *Educ:* Sydenham High Sch. (GPDST). Organising Sec., Women's Gas Council, 1935, and represented Gas Industry at International Management Congress, Washington, USA, 1936, Sweden, 1947. Appointed Chief of Metropolitan Dept, WVS, 1939; lent to Min. of Health and went to Washington as UK representative on Standing Technical Cttee on Welfare, UNRRA; Comr, Trainer, and Camp Adviser, Girl Guides Assoc., 1924-48; Comdt, BRCS, 1937-39; Mem. Council London Hostels Assoc., 1941-; Chm. Women's Gas Fedn, 1945-49, Pres., 1949-60. A Governor of St Bartholomew's Hospital, 1948-74; President Fedn of Soroptomist Clubs of Gt Britain and Ireland, 1959-60. Trustee, Women's Service Trust. OStJ. *Recreations:* motoring, reading, theatre. *Address:* 7 Chagford House, Chagford Street, NW1 6EG. *T:* 01-262 6226.

HALSBURY, 3rd Earl of, *cr* 1898; **John Anthony Hardinge Giffard,** FRS 1969; Baron Halsbury, 1885; Viscount Tiverton, 1898; Chancellor of Brunel University, since 1966; *b* 4 June 1908; *o s* of 2nd Earl and Esmé (*d* 1973), *d* of late James Stewart Wallace; *S* father, 1943; *m* 1st, 1930, Ismay Catherine, *er d* of late Lord Ninian Crichton-Stuart and Hon. Mrs Archibald Maule Ramsay; one *s*; 2nd, 1936, Elizabeth Adeline Faith, *o d* of late Major Harry Crewe Godley, DSO, Northamptonshire Regt and of late Mrs Godley, of Claremont Lodge, Cheltenham; two *d*. *Educ:* Eton. Man. Dir, Nat. Research Development Corporation, 1949-59; External Examiner, OECD, on mission to Japan, 1965. Chairman: Science Museum Advisory Council, 1951-65; Cttee on Decimal Currency, 1961-63; Cttee of Management, Inst. of Cancer Research, Royal Marsden Hosp., 1962-77; Review Body on Doctors' and Dentists' Pay, 1971-74; Deptl Cttee of Enquiry into pay of Nurses, Midwives and Professions Supplementary to Medicine, 1974-75; Meteorological Cttee, 1970-82; President: Institution of Production Engineers, 1957-59; Inst. of Nuclear Engineers, 1963-65; Nat. Inst. of Industrial Psychol., 1963-75; Machine Tool Industry Res. Assoc., 1964-77; Member: Adv. Council to Cttee of Privy Council for Scientific Research, 1949-54; SRC, 1965-69; Computer Bd for Univs and Research Councils, 1966-69; Decimal Currency Bd, 1966-71; Nationalised Transport Advisory Council, 1963-67; Standing Commn on Museums and Galleries, 1960-76; MRC, 1973-77; Cttee of Managers, Royal Institution, 1976-79. A Governor: BBC, 1960-62; LSE, 1959-; UMIST, 1966- (formerly Mem. Council, Manchester Coll. of Sci. and Technol., 1956-65). Hon. FICE, 1975. Hon. DTech Brunel Univ., 1966; Hon. DUniv Essex, 1968. *Heir: s* Adam Edward Giffard, *qv. Address:* 4 Campden House, 29 Sheffield Terrace, W8. *T:* 01-727 3035.

HALSEY, Prof. Albert Henry; Professor of Social and Administrative Studies, University of Oxford, since 1978; Professorial Fellow of Nuffield College, Oxford, since 1962; *b* 13 April 1923; *m* 1949, Gertrude Margaret Littler; three *s* two *d*. *Educ:* Kettering Grammar Sch.; London Sch. of Econs. BSc (Econ), PhD London, MA Oxon. RAF, 1942-47; student LSE, 1947-52; Research Worker, Liverpool Univ., 1952-54; Lectr in Sociology, Birmingham Univ., 1954-62; Dir, Dept of Social and Admin. Studies, Oxford Univ., 1962-78. Fellow, Center for Advanced Study of Behavioral Sciences, Palo Alto, Calif, 1956-57; Vis. Prof. of Sociology, Univ. of Chicago, 1959-60. Adviser to Sec. of State for Educn, 1965-68; Chm. of CERI at OECD, Paris, 1968-70. Reith Lectr, 1977. Foreign Associate, Amer. Acad. of Educn. *Publications:* (jtly) Social Class and Educational Opportunity, 1956; (jtly) Technical Change and Industrial Relations, 1956; (with J. E. Floud) The Sociology of Education, Current Sociology VII, 1958; (jtly) Education, Economy and Society, 1961; Ability and Educational Opportunity, 1962; (with G. N. Ostergaard) Power in Co-operatives, 1965; (with Ivor Crewe) Social Survey of the Civil Service, 1969; (with Martin Trow) The British Academics, 1971; (ed) Trends in British Society since 1900, 1972; (ed) Educational Priority, 1972; Traditions of Social Policy, 1976; Heredity and Environment, 1977; Change in British Society, 1978, 2nd edn 1981; (jtly) Origins and Destinations, 1980; numerous articles and reviews. *Address:* 28 Upland Park Road, Oxford. *T:* Oxford 58625.

HALSEY, Rt. Rev. Henry David; *see* Carlisle, Bishop of.

HALSEY, Rev. John Walter Brooke, 4th Bt *cr* 1920 (but uses designation Brother John Halsey); *b* 26 Dec. 1933; *s* of Sir Thomas Edgar Halsey, 3rd Bt, DSO, and of Jean Margaret Palmer, *d* of late Bertram Willes Dayrell Brooke; *S* father, 1970. *Educ:* Eton; Magdalene College, Cambridge (BA 1957). Deacon, 1961, priest, 1962, Diocese of York; Curate of Stocksbridge, 1961-65; Brother in Community of the Transfiguration, 1965-. *Heir: uncle* William Edmund Halsey [*b* 8 Jan. 1903; *m* 1931, Barbara Dorothea, *d* of late Charles Lindsay Orr Ewing; one *d* (one *s* decd)]. *Address:* Community of the Transfiguration, Manse Road, Roslin, Midlothian.

HALSEY, Philip Hugh, MVO 1972; Under Secretary, Department of Education and Science, since 1977; *b* 9 May 1928; *s* of Sidney Robert Halsey and Edith Mary Halsey; *m* 1956, Hilda Mary Biggerstaff; two *s*. *Educ:* University Coll. London (BSc). Headmaster, Hampstead Sch., 1961; Principal, DES, 1966.

HALSTEAD, Ronald, CBE 1976; Chairman, Beecham Products, since 1967; Managing Director (Consumer Products), Beecham Group Ltd, since 1973; *b* 17 May 1927; *s* of Richard and Bessie Harrison Halstead; *m* 1968, Yvonne Cecile de Monchaux (*d* 1978); two *s*. *Educ:* Lancaster Royal Grammar Sch.; Queens' Coll., Cambridge. MA, BSc, FRSC. Research Chemist, H. P. Bulmer & Co, 1948-53; Manufg Manager, Macleans Ltd, 1954-55; Factory Manager, Beecham Products Inc. (USA), 1955-60; Asst Managing Dir, Beecham Research Labs, 1960-62; Vice-Pres. (Marketing), Beecham Products Inc. (USA), 1962-64; Pres., Beecham Research Labs Inc. (USA), 1962-64; Chm., Food and Drink Div., Beecham Group Ltd, 1964-67. Dir, Otis Elevator Co. Ltd (UK), 1978-; Non-Exec. Dir, BSC, 1979-. Mem. Egg Re-organisation Commn, 1967-68; Pres., Incorp. Soc. of Brit. Advertisers, 1971-73; Chairman: British Nutrition Foundn, 1970-73; Knitting Sector Working Party, NEDO, 1978-; Vice-Chairman: Proprietary Assoc. of GB, 1968-77; Advertising Assoc., 1973-81; Food and Drink Industries Council, 1973-76; Member: Council and Exec. Cttee, Food Manufrs' Fedn Inc., 1966- (Pres., 1974-76); Council, British Nutrition Foundn, 1967-79; Cambridge Univ. Appts Bd, 1969-73; Council, CBI, 1970-; Council, BIM, 1972-77; Council, University Coll. at Buckingham, 1973-; Nat. Coll. of Food Technol., 1977- (Chm., 1978-) ARC, 1978-; Council, Univ. of Reading, 1978-; Newspaper Panel, Monopolies and Mergers Commn, 1980-. Trustee, Inst. of Economic Affairs, 1980-. Governor, Ashridge Management Coll., 1970- (Vice-Chm., 1977-); President: Nat. Advertising Benevolent Soc., 1978-80; Inst. of Packaging, 1981- (a Vice-Pres., 1979-81). Fellow, Marketing Soc., 1981; FBIM, FInstM; FIGD; FRSA. Hon. DSc Reading, 1982. *Recreations:* sailing, squash racquets, ski-ing. *Address:* 37 Edwardes Square, W8 6HH. *T:* 01-603 9010. *Clubs:* Hurlingham, Carlton, Lansdowne, Royal Thames Yacht.

HAM, Prof. James Milton, OC 1980; ScD; FIEEE; President, University of Toronto, since 1978; *b* 21 Sept. 1920; *s* of James Arthur Ham and Harriet Boomer Gandier; *m* Mary Caroline, *d* of Albert William Augustine; one *s* two *d*. *Educ:* Runnymede Coll. Inst., Toronto, 1936-39; Univ. of Toronto (BASc 1943); MIT (SM, ScD). Served with RCNVR as Elect. Lt, 1944-45. Lectr and Housemaster, Univ. of Toronto, 1945-46; Mass Inst. of Technology: Res. Associate, 1949-51; Res. Fellow in Electronics, 1950; Asst Prof. of Elect. Engrg, 1951-52; Univ. of Toronto: Associate Prof., 1952-59; Prof., 1959-; Fellow, New Coll., 1963; Head, Dept of Elect. Engrg, 1964-66; Dean, Fac. of Applied Science and Engrg, 1966-73; Chm., Research Bd, 1974-76; Dean, Sch. of Graduate Studies, 1976-78. Vis. Scientist, Cambridge Univ. and USSR, 1960-61. Dir, Shell Canada. Mem., Nat. Res. Council (Chm., Associate Cttee on Automatic Control, 1959-65); Governor, Ont. Res. Foundn; Chm., Cttee on Engrg Educn of World Fed. of Engrg Orgs, 1970. Member: Assoc. Prof. Engrs, Ont.; Internat. Fed. Automatic Control (Exec. Council); Fellow, Engrg Inst. Canada. British Assoc. for Advancement of Science Medal, 1943; McNaughton Medal, IEEE; Centennial Medal, Engrg Medal Assoc. Professional Engrs, Ontario; Queens' Jubilee Medal; Engrg Alumni Medal. Hon. DèsScA Montreal; Hon. DSc: New Brunswick, McGill, Queen's, McMaster; Hon. LLD: Manitoba; Hanyang (Korea); Hon. DEng: Tech. Univ. of Nova Scotia; Memorial Univ. *Publications:* Scientific Basis of Electrical Engineering (with G. R. Slemon), 1961; Report of Royal Commission on Health and Safety of Workers in Mines; papers for scientific jls on automatic control. *Recreations:* sailing, skiing, photography. *Address:* 93 Highland Avenue, Toronto, Ontario M4W 2A4, Canada.

HAM, Rear-Adm. John Dudley Nelson, CB 1955; RN retired; *b* 7 Sept. 1902; *s* of Eng. Rear-Adm. John William Ham and Lily Florence Nelson; *m* 1927, Margery Lyne Sandercock; no *c*. *Educ:* Edinburgh House, Lee-on-Solent; RN Colleges, Osborne and Dartmouth. Junior Service, 1920-37; HMS Ramillies, HMS Ceres; staff of RN Engineering College; Destroyers; Commander, 1937; Engineer Officer, Yangtse, China, 1938-40; served War of 1939-45: Chief Engineer, HMS Danae, 1940-41; Asst Dir Combined Operations Material, 1942; Chief Engineer, HMS Indomitable, 1945; Capt., 1946; Fleet Engineer Officer, Home Fleet, 1949; Staff Air Engineer Officer, 1951; Rear-Admiral, 1953; Dir of Aircraft Maintenance and Repair, 1953-55; Flag Officer Reserve Aircraft, 1955-57, retired. *Recreations:* golf, cabinet-making. *Address:* Green Lane Cottage, Lee-on-Solent, Hants. *T:* Lee-on-Solent 550660.

HAMBIDGE, Most Rev. Douglas Walter; *see* New Westminster, Archbishop of.

HAMBLEDEN, 4th Viscount, *cr* 1891; **William Herbert Smith;** *b* 2 April 1930; *e s* of 3rd Viscount and Lady Patricia Herbert, DCVO 1953, *o d* of 15th Earl of Pembroke, MVO; *S* father 1948; *m* 1955, Donna Maria Carmela Attolico di Adelfia, *d* of late Count Bernardo Attolico and of Contessa Eleonora Attolico di Adelfia, Via Porta Latina, Rome; five *s*. *Educ:* Eton. *Heir: s* Hon. William Henry Bernard Smith, *b* 18 Nov. 1955. *Address:* The Manor House, Hambleden, Henley-on-Thames, Oxon. *TA:* Hambleden. *T:* Hambleden 335.

See also Baron Margadale.

HAMBLEN, Derek Ivens Archibald, CB 1978; OBE 1956; *b* 28 Oct. 1917; *s* of Leonard Tom Hamblen and Ruth Mary Hamblen, *d* of Sir William Frederick Alphonse Archibald; *m* 1950, Pauline Alison, *d* of late Gen. Sir William Morgan, GCB, DSO, MC; one *s* one *d*. *Educ:* St Lawrence Coll., Ramsgate; St John's Coll., Oxford (Casberd Exhibn); Portuguese Essay Prize, 1938; BA Hons (Mod. Langs) 1940, MA 1949. Served War, 1940-46: 1st Army, N Africa, 1942-43; Major, GS, AFHQ, N Africa and Italy, and Adv. Mission to British Mil. HQ, Greece, 1944-45; GSO1, Allied Commn for Austria, 1945-46; Lt-Col, 1946. War Office, later Ministry of Defence, 1946-77: seconded HQ British Troops, Egypt, 1946-47; Asst Sec., Office of UK High Commn in Australia, 1951-55; seconded Foreign Office, 1957-60; Asst Sec., 1964-68; a Special Advr to NATO and SHAPE, 1968-74; Under Sec., 1974-77, retired. Mem. Bd of Governors, St Lawrence Coll., 1977-. Medal of Merit, 1st cl. (Czechoslovakia), 1946. *Recreations:* cricket, hockey (represented Oxford v Cambridge, 1940), golf, music, reading. *Address:* c/o Lloyds Bank, East Grinstead, West Sussex. *Clubs:* MCC; Vincent's (Oxford).

HAMBLING, Sir (Herbert) Hugh, 3rd Bt, *cr* 1924; *b* 3 Aug. 1919; *s* of Sir (Herbert) Guy (Musgrave) Hambling, 2nd Bt; *S* father 1966; *m* 1950, Anne Page Oswald, Spokane, Washington, USA; one *s*. *Educ:* Wixenford Preparatory Sch.; Eton Coll. British Airways Ltd, 1937-39. RAF Training and Atlantic Ferry Command, 1939-46. British Overseas Airways: Montreal, 1948; Seattle, 1950; Manager, Sir Guy Hambling & Son, 1956; BOAC Representative, Douglas, Los Angeles, and Boeing Co., Seattle, 1957-75; Royal Brunei Airlines Rep., Boeing Co., Seattle, 1975. *Heir: s* Herbert Peter Hugh Hambling, *b* 6 Sept. 1953. *Address:* 1219 Evergreen Point Road, Bellevue, Washington 98004, USA. *T:* 206-454-0905 (USA); Rookery Park, Yoxford, Suffolk, England. *T:* Yoxford 310.

HAMBRO, Charles Eric Alexander; Chairman, Hambros Bank Ltd, since 1972; *b* 24 July 1930; *s* of late Sir Charles Hambro, KBE, MC, and Pamela Cobbold; *m* 1st, 1954, Rose Evelyn (marr. diss., 1976), *d* of Sir Richard Cotterell, 5th Bt, CBE; two *s* one *d* ; 2nd, 1976, Cherry Twiss, *d* of Sir John Huggins, GCMG, MC. *Educ:* Eton. Lieut Coldstream Guards, 1949-51; joined Hambros Bank Ltd, 1952: Man. Dir 1957; Dep. Chm. 1965; Vice-Chm., Guardian Royal Exchange Assurance. Chm., Royal National Pension Fund for Nurses, 1968. *Recreations:* shooting, cricket, flying. *Address:* Dixton Manor, Gotherington, Cheltenham, Glos GL52 4RB. *T:* Bishops Cleeve 2011. *Clubs:* White's, MCC.

HAMBRO, Jocelyn Olaf, MC 1944; Chairman, Hambros Ltd, since 1970; Managing Director, Hambros Bank Ltd, 1947-72, and Chairman, 1965-72; Chairman: Phoenix Assurance Co. Ltd, since 1978; Charter Consolidated, since 1982 (Director, since 1965); The Hambro Trust Ltd; Hambros Investment Trust Ltd; HIT Securities Ltd; Newmarket Estates & Property Co. Ltd; Rosedimond Investment Trust Ltd; Waverton Property Co. Ltd; Wiltons (St James's) Ltd; *b* 7 March 1919; *s* of late Ronald Olaf Hambro and late Winifred Martin-Smith; *m* 1st, 1942, Ann Silvia (*d* 1972) *d* of R. H. Muir; three *s* ; 2nd, 1976, Margaret Elisabeth, *d* of late Frederick Bradshaw McConnel and *widow* of 9th Duke of Roxburghe. *Educ:* Eton; Trinity Coll., Cambridge. Coldstream Guards, 1939-45. Hambros Bank Ltd, 1945. Member, Jockey Club. *Recreations:* racing, shooting. *Address:* Waverton House, Moreton-in-Marsh, Glos; 16 Victoria Road, W8. *Clubs:* Pratt's, White's.

HAMBURGER, Michael Peter Leopold, MA (Oxon); *b* Berlin, 22 March 1924; *e s* of late Prof. Richard Hamburger and Mrs L. Hamburger (*née* Hamburg); *m* 1951, Anne Ellen File; one *s* two *d*. *Educ:* Westminster Sch.; Christ Church, Oxford. Army Service, 1943-47; Freelance Writer, 1948-52; Asst Lectr in German, UCL, 1952-55; Lectr, then Reader in German, Univ. of Reading, 1955-64. Florence Purington Lectr, Mount Holyoke Coll., Mass, 1966-67; Visiting Professor, State Univ. of NY: at Buffalo, 1969; at Stony Brook, 1971; Vis. Fellow, Center for Humanities, Wesleyan Univ., Conn, 1970; Vis. Prof. Univ. of S Carolina, 1973; Regent's Lectr, Univ. of California, San Diego, 1973; Vis. Prof., Boston Univ., 1975-77; part-time Prof., Univ. of Essex, 1978. Bollingen Foundn Fellow, 1959-61, 1965-66. FRSL 1972. Corresp. Mem., Deutsche Akademie für Sprache und Dichtung, Darmstadt, 1973; Akademie der Künste, Berlin; Akad. der Schönen Künste, Munich. Translation Prizes: Deutsche Akademie für Sprache und Dichtung, Darmstadt, 1964; Arts Council, 1969; Arts Prize, Inter Nationes, Bonn, 1976; Medal, Inst. of Linguists, 1977; Schlegel-Tieck Prize, London 1978, 1981; Wilhelm-Heinse Prize (medallion), Mainz, 1978. *Publications: poetry:* Flowering Cactus, 1950; Poems 1950-1951, 1952; The Dual Site, 1958; Weather and Season, 1963; Feeding the Chickadees, 1968; Penguin Modern Poets (with A. Brownjohn and C. Tomlinson), 1969; Travelling, 1969; Travelling, I-V, 1973; Ownerless Earth, 1973; Travelling VI, 1975; Real Estate, 1977; Moralities, 1977; Variations, 1981; *translations:* Poems of Hölderlin, 1943, rev. edn as Hölderlin: Poems, 1952; C. Baudelaire, Twenty Prose Poems, 1946, repr. 1968; L. van Beethoven, Letters, Journals and Conversations, 1951, repr. 1967, 1978; J. C. F. Hölderlin, Selected Verse, 1961; G. Trakl, Decline, 1952; A. Goes, The Burnt Offering, 1956; (with others) H. von Hofmannsthal, Poems and Verse Plays, 1961; B. Brecht, Tales from the Calendar, 1961; (with C. Middleton) Modern German Poetry 1910-1960, 1962; (with others) H. von Hofmannsthal, Selected Plays and Libretti, 1964; G. Büchner, Lenz, 1966; H. M. Enzensberger, Poems, 1966; (with C. Middleton) G. Grass, Selected Poems, 1966; J. C. F. Hölderlin, Poems and Fragments, 1967, new enlarged edn 1980; (with J. Rothenberg and the author) H. M. Enzensberger, The Poems of Hans Magnus Enzensberger, 1968; H. M.

Enzensberger, Poems For People Who Don't Read Poems, 1968; (with C. Middleton), G. Grass, The Poems of Günter Grass, 1969; P. Bichsel, And Really Frau Blum Would Very Much Like To Meet The Milkman, 1968; G. Eich, Journeys, 1968; N. Sachs, Selected Poems, 1968; Peter Bichsel, Stories for Children, 1971; Paul Celan, Selected Poems, 1972, new enlarged edn 1980; (ed) East German Poetry, 1972; Peter Huchel: Selected Poems, 1974; German Poetry 1910-1975, 1977; Helmut Heissenbüttel: Texts, 1977; Franco Fortini: Poems, 1978; An Unofficial Rilke, 1981; *criticism:* Reason and Energy, 1957; From Prophecy to Exorcism, 1965; The Truth of Poetry, 1970, new edn 1982; Hugo von Hofmannsthal, 1973; Art as Second Nature, 1975; *autobiography:* A Mug's Game, 1973. *Recreations:* gardening, walking. *Address:* c/o Williams & Glyn's Bank Ltd, Kirkland House, Whitehall, SW1.
See also P. B. Hamlyn.

HAMBURGER, Sir Sidney (Cyril), Kt 1981; CBE 1966; JP; DL; Chairman, North Western Regional Health Authority, 1973-82; *b* 14 July 1914; *s* of Isidore and Hedwig Hamburger; *m* 1940; three *s*. *Educ:* Salford Grammar Sch. Served in Army, 1940-46, Capt. Salford City Council: Mem., 1946-70; Alderman, 1961-70; Mayor of Salford, 1968-69. Chairman: NE Manchester Hosp. Management Cttee, 1970-74; Member: Manchester Regional Hosp. Bd, 1966-74 (Chm. Finance Cttee); Supplementary Benefits Commn, 1967-77; BBC NW Adv. Cttee, 1970-73. Pres. Council, Manchester-Salford Jews, 1962-65; Life-President: Manchester Jewish Homes for the Aged, 1965-; Zionist Central Council of Greater Manchester. Hon. Fellow, Bar-Ilan Univ., Israel, 1979; Hon. MA Salford, 1979. JP Salford, 1957; DL Greater Manchester, 1981. *Recreation:* football. *Address:* 26 New Hall Road, Salford M7 0JU.

HAMEED, A. C. Shahul; Minister of Foreign Affairs, Sri Lanka, since 1977; *b* 10 April 1929. Mem., United National Party; Mem. for Harispattuwa, Nat. Parliament, 1960-; former Dep. Chm., Public Accounts Cttee; has been concerned with foreign affairs, public finance and higher education. Leader of delegns to internat. confs. incl. UN; Chm., Ministerial Conf. of Non-Aligned Countries; Mem., Conf. of UN Cttee on Disarmament. Governor, Univ. of Sri Lanka. *Publications:* short stories and poems. *Address:* Ministry of Foreign Affairs, Republic Building, Colombo 1, Sri Lanka.

HAMER, John, MBE 1944; VMH 1975; Secretary, Royal Horticultural Society, 1962-75; *b* 14 June 1910; 2nd *s* of late John and Katherine Hamer; *m* 1st, 1940, Marjorie Agnes Martin (*d* 1970); one *s* one *d* ; 2nd, 1980, Joan Edith MacKinlay (*née* Prior). *Educ:* University of Leeds (BA). Asst Master, 1932-39. War Service, 1939-46 (despatches, MBE): The Loyal Regt, Hertfordshire Regt, Royal Tank Regt, 20 British Mil. Mission (Free French), Combined Operations, 1943-45; Lieut-Col, Comd 18 DLI; Controller of Supplies, Singapore, 1945. Joined Malayan Civil Service, 1946: District Officer, Jasin 1948, Klang 1952; British Adviser, Perlis, 1955; Deputy Chm., Rural Industrial Development Authority, Federation of Malaya, 1957; Ministry of Agriculture, 1958; State Sec., Penang, 1958-61. Joined Royal Horticultural Soc., 1961. *Recreation:* gardening. *Address:* Wildacres, Itchingfield, West Sussex RH13 7NZ. *T:* Slinfold 790467.

HAMER, Hon. Sir Rupert (James), KCMG 1982; ED; Premier of Victoria, Australia, and Treasurer, 1972-81; *b* 29 July 1916; *s* of H. R. Hamer, Wolverhampton, England; *m* 1944, April F., *d* of N. R. Mackintosh; two *s* two *d*. *Educ:* Melbourne Grammar and Geelong Grammar Schs; Trinity Coll., Univ. of Melbourne (LLM). Solicitor, admitted 1940. Served War of 1939-45: 5½ years, AIF, Tobruk, Alamein, NG, Normandy. MLA (Lib.) E Yarra, 1958-71, Kew, Vic., 1971-81; Minister for: Immigration, 1962-64; Local Govt, 1964-71; Chief Sec. and Dep. Premier, Victoria, 1971-72; Minister for: the Arts, 1972-79; State Develt, Decentralization and Tourism, 1979-81. Vice-Chairman: Vic. State Opera; Cttee of Management, Werribee Park; Pres., Vic. Coll. of the Arts; Member: Fountains Trust; Melbourne Scots Council; Trustee, Yarra Bend Park. CO, Vic. Scottish Regt, CMF, 1954-58. *Recreations:* tennis, golf, Australian Rules football. *Address:* 39 Monomeath Avenue, Canterbury, Victoria 3126, Australia. *Club:* Naval and Military.

HAMES, Jack Hamawi, QC 1972; a Recorder of the Crown Court, since 1977; *b* 15 June 1920; *s* of Elie and Edmee Hamawi; *m* 1949, Beryl Julia Cooper; two *s*. *Educ:* English School, Cairo; Queens' Coll., Cambridge (MA, LLB). Called to Bar, Inner Temple, 1948, Bencher, 1979. Vice-Chm, Bd of Governors, John Ruskin Sch., Croydon. *Publications:* Family Law, 1950; The Married Women's Property Act, 1872 (3rd edn 1971); contrib. to Solicitors' Jl. *Recreations:* squash, tennis, painting, music, poetry, history, literature. *Address:* 18 Castlemaine Avenue, South Croydon CR2 7HQ. *T:* 01-688 6326; 10 Old Square, Lincoln's Inn, WC2A 3SO. *T:* 01-405 0758. *Club:* Warlingham Squash (Vice-Chm. 1980-81).

HAMILL, Patrick, QPM 1979; Chief Constable, Strathclyde Police, since 1977; *b* 29 April 1930; *s* of Hugh Hamill and Elizabeth McGowan; *m* 1954, Nellie Gillespie; four *s* one *d*. *Educ:* St Patrick's High Sch., Dumbarton. Joined Dunbartonshire Constabulary, 1950; transf. to City of Glasgow Police, 1972; apptd Assistant Chief Constable: Glasgow, 1974; Strathclyde Police, 1975; attended Royal Coll. of Defence Studies Course, 1976. OStJ 1978. *Recreations:* walking, gardening, golf. *Address:* 173 Pitt Street, Glasgow G2 4JS. *T:* 041-204 2626.

HAMILTON, family name of **Duke of Abercorn,** of **Lord Belhaven,** and of **Barons Hamilton** of **Dalzell** and **HolmPatrick.**

HAMILTON; see Baillie-Hamilton.

HAMILTON; see Douglas-Hamilton.

HAMILTON, 15th Duke of, cr 1643, Scotland, AND BRANDON, 12th Duke of, cr 1711, Great Britain; **Angus Alan Douglas Douglas-Hamilton;** Premier Peer of Scotland; Hereditary Keeper of Palace of Holyroodhouse; b 13 Sept. 1938; e s of 14th Duke of Hamilton and Brandon, PC, KT, GCVO, AFC, and of Lady Elizabeth Percy, er d of 8th Duke of Northumberland, KG; S father, 1973; m 1972, Sarah, d of Sir Walter Scott, Bt, qv ; two s two d. Educ: Eton; Balliol Coll., Oxford (BAEngrg). Flt Lieut RAF; retired, 1967. Flying Instructor, 1965; Sen. Commercial Pilot's Licence, 1967; Test Pilot, Scottish Aviation, 1971–72. Mem. Council, CRC, 1978–. Mem., Queen's Body Guard for Scotland, 1975–. Hon. Mem., Royal Scottish Pipers Soc., 1977; Patron, British Airways Pipe Band, 1977. Hon. Air Cdre, No 2 (City of Edinburgh) Maritime HQ Unit, RAuxAF, 1982–. KStJ 1975 (Prior, Order of St John in Scotland, 1975–82). Heir: s Marquess of Douglas and Clydesdale, qv. Address: 8 Eccleston Mews, SW1. T: 01-235 7213; Lennoxlove, Haddington, E Lothian. Clubs: Naval and Military; New (Edinburgh).
See also Lord James Douglas-Hamilton.

HAMILTON, Marquess of; James Harold Charles Hamilton; b 19 Aug. 1969; s and heir of Duke of Abercorn, qv.

HAMILTON OF DALZELL, 3rd Baron, cr 1886; **John d'Henin Hamilton**, KCVO 1981; MC 1945; JP; Lord Lieutenant of Surrey, since 1973 (Vice-Lieutenant, 1957–73); President, National Association of Probation Officers, 1964–74; a Lord-in-Waiting to the Queen, 1968–81; b 1 May 1911; s of late Major Hon. Leslie d'Henin Hamilton, MVO, and Amy Cecile, e d of late Col Horace Ricardo, CVO; S uncle, 1952; m 1935, Rosemary Olive, d of late Major Hon. Sir John Coke, KCVO; two s one d. Educ: Eton; RMC, Sandhurst. Coldstream Guards, 1931–37 and 1939–45 (Major). Min. of Agriculture's Liaison Officer in South-East, 1960–64. Mem., Council on Tribunals, 1964–72; Chm., Lord Chancellor's Adv. Cttee on Legal Aid, 1972–79. Chairman: Surrey Agricultural Exec. Cttee, 1958–68; Surrey Council of Social Service, 1960–73; Guildford Bench, 1968–78; Guildford Cathedral Council, 1958–69. DL Surrey, 1957; JP Guildford, 1957. KStJ 1973. Heir: s Hon. James Leslie Hamilton [b 11 Feb. 1938; m 1967, Corinna, yr d of late Sir Pierson Dixon, GCMG, CB and of Lady Dixon; four s]. Address: Snowdenham House, Bramley, Guildford, Surrey GU5 0DB. T: Guildford 892002.
See also Hon. A. G. Hamilton.

HAMILTON, Adrian Walter, QC 1973; a Recorder of the Crown Court, since 1974; b 11 March 1923; er s of late W. G. M. Hamilton, banker, Fletching, Sussex and of late Mrs S. E. Hamilton; m 1966, Jill, d of S. R. Brimblecombe, Eastbourne; two d. Educ: Highgate Sch.; Balliol Coll., Oxford. BA 1st cl. Jurisprudence 1948, MA 1954. Served with RN, 1942-46: Ord. Seaman, 1942; Sub-Lt RNVR, 1943, Lieut 1946. Balliol Coll., 1946–48: Jenkyns Law Prize; Paton Mem. Student, 1948–49; Cassel Scholar, Lincoln's Inn, 1949; called to Bar, Lincoln's Inn, 1949 (Bencher 1979) and Middle Temple; Mem., Senate of Inns of Court and the Bar, 1976–, Treas., 1979–. Mem., Council of Legal Educn, 1977–. Inspector, Peek Foods Ltd, 1977. Recreations: family, golf, sailing, gardening. Address: 7 King's Bench Walk, Temple, EC4. T: 01-353 3684. Clubs: Garrick; Piltdown Golf.

HAMILTON, Rt. Rev. Alexander Kenneth, MA; b 11 May 1915; s of Cuthbert Arthur Hamilton and Agnes Maud Hamilton; unmarried. Educ: Malvern Coll.; Trinity Hall, Cambridge; Westcott House, Cambridge. MA 1941. Asst Curate of Birstall, Leicester, 1939–41; Asst Curate of Whitworth with Spennymoor, 1941–45. Chaplain, RNVR, 1945–47. Vicar of S Francis, Ashton Gate, Bristol, 1947-58; Vicar of S John the Baptist, Newcastle upon Tyne, 1958-65; Rural Dean of Central Newcastle, 1962–65; Bishop Suffragan of Jarrow, 1965–80. Publication: Personal Prayers, 1963. Recreations: golf, trout fishing. Address: 3 Ash Tree Road, Burnham-on-Sea, Somerset TA8 2LB. Clubs: Naval; Burnham and Berrow Golf.

HAMILTON, Alexander Macdonald, CBE 1979; Senior Partner, McGrigor, Donald & Co., Solicitors, Glasgow, since 1977; b 11 May 1925; s of John Archibald Hamilton and Thomasina Macdonald or Hamilton; m 1953, Catherine Gray; two s one d. Educ: Hamilton Acad. (Dux, 1943); Glasgow Univ. (MA 1948, LLB 1951). Solicitor. Served War, RNVR, 1943–46. Dir, Royal Bank of Scotland Ltd, 1978–. Law Soc. of Scotland: Mem. Council, 1970–82; Vice-Pres., 1975–76; Pres., 1977–78. Pres., Glasgow Juridical Soc., 1955–56; Vice-Pres. and Chm., Greater Glasgow Social Council, 1978–; Session Clerk, Cambuslang Old Parish Church, 1969–; Vice-Chm., Cambuslang Community Council, 1978–. Recreations: golf, sailing, swimming. Address: 30 Wellshot Drive, Cambuslang, Glasgow G72 8BT. T: 041-641 1445. Club: Royal Scottish Automobile (Glasgow).

HAMILTON, Anthony Norris; b 19 July 1913; 3rd s of Capt. Claude Hamilton, RD, RNR, and Kathleen Sophia Hamilton (née Mack); m 1942, Jean Philippa, 3rd d of Rev. David Railton, MC; one s three d. Educ: Kelly Coll.; Exeter Coll., Oxford. Asst Master Clifton Coll., 1935-40. Served War of 1939–45: commnd 6 Bn Argyll and Sutherland Highlanders, 1940; Gen. Staff, V Corps HQ, 1942, X Corps HQ 1943, VIII Army HQ, 1944. Ops Editor of VIII Army History of Italian Campaign, 1945. House Master, Clifton Coll., 1946–48; Headmaster, Strathallan Sch., 1948–51; Headmaster,

Queen Mary's Grammar Sch., Walsall, 1951–55; Headmaster, Hardye's Sch., Dorchester, 1955-74. Recreations: fishing, painting. Address: Odney Orchard, Chilmark, near Salisbury, Wilts.

HAMILTON, Hon. Archibald Gavin; MP (C) Epsom and Ewell, since April 1978; an Assistant Government Whip, since 1982; b 30 Dec. 1941; yr s of Baron Hamilton of Dalzell, qv ; m 1968, Anne Catharine Napier; three d. Educ: Eton Coll. Borough Councillor, Kensington and Chelsea, 1968-71. Contested (C) Dagenham, Feb. and Oct., 1974. PPS to Sec. of State for Energy, 1979-81, to Sec. of State for Transport, 1981-82. Address: Daneshole, Bramley, Surrey.

HAMILTON, Sir Bruce S.; see Stirling-Hamilton.

HAMILTON, Sir (Charles) Denis, Kt 1976; DSO 1944; TD 1975; Chairman: Times Newspapers Holdings Ltd, 1980–81; Reuters Ltd, since 1979; President, Commonwealth Press Union, since 1981; b 6 Dec. 1918; er s of Charles and Helena Hamilton; m 1939, Olive, author, yr d of Thomas Hedley Wanless and Mary Anne Wanless; four s. Educ: Middlesbrough High Sch. Editorial Staff: Evening Gazette, Middlesbrough, 1937-38; Evening Chronicle, Newcastle, 1938-39; Editorial Asst to Viscount Kemsley, 1946-50; Editorial Dir, Kemsley (now Thomson) Newspapers, 1950-67; Editor of the Sunday Times, 1961-67; Chief Exec., Times Newspapers Ltd, 1967-70, Editor-in-Chief, 1967-81, Chm., 1971-80. Director: Evening Gazette Ltd, 1950-82; Newcastle Chronicle and Journal Ltd, 1950-82; Internat. Thomson Orgn Plc (formerly Kemsley Newspapers, Thomson Newspapers, Thomson British Holdings), 1950-. Chm., British Cttee, 1972-78, first Pres., 1978-, internat. Press Inst. Member: Council, Newspaper Publishers' Association, 1950-80; Press Council, 1959-81; National Council for the Training of Journalists (Chm., 1957); BOTB, 1976-79; British Library Bd, 1975-; IBA, 1981-; Chm., British Museum Publications Ltd; Trustee: British Museum, 1969-; Henry Moore Foundn, 1980-; Visnews, 1981-; Vice-Chm., Exec. Cttee, GB-China Centre, 1981-; Governor, British Inst. Florence, 1974-. Joint Sponsor of exhibitions: Tutankhamun, BM, 1972; China, RA, 1973; 1776-US Bicentennial, Nat. Maritime Mus., 1976; Gold of Eldorado, RA, 1978; Vikings, BM, 1980. Served War of 1939-45, TA, Durham Light Infantry; Lt-Col comdg 11th Bn Durham LI and 7th Bn Duke of Wellington's Regt. Hon. DLitt: Southampton, 1975; City, 1977; Hon. DCL Newcastle upon Tyne 1979. Grande Officiale, Order of Merit (Italy), 1976. Publications: Jt Editor, Kemsley Manual of Journalism, 1952; Who is who on the British Press (Haldane Meml Lecture), 1976. Recreation: fruit farming. Address: 25 Roebuck House, Palace Street, SW1. T: 01-828 0410; Weston House, Nutbourne, Chichester, West Sussex. T: Emsworth 3351. Clubs: Garrick, Royal Automobile, Grillions.

HAMILTON, Cyril Robert Parke, CMG 1972; Director: Rank Organisation and subsidiary companies, 1963-77; A. Kershaw & Sons Ltd, 1966-77; Rank Xerox Ltd, 1967-77; b 4 Aug. 1903; s of Alfred Parke and Annie Hamilton; m 1st, 1929, Cecily May Stearn (d 1966); one s one d ; 2nd, 1971, Betty Emily Brand. Educ: High Sch., Ilford; King's Coll., London Univ. Entered Bank of England, 1923, and retired as Deputy Chief Cashier, 1963, after career mainly concerned with internat. financial negotiations and Exchange Control. Vice-Chm., Standard and Chartered Banking Gp Ltd, 1969-74; Dep. Chm., Standard Bank, 1963-74; Director: Standard Bank of SA, 1963-74; Midland and International Banks, 1964-74; Banque Belge d'Afrique, 1969-74; Chairman: Malta International Banking Corp, 1969-74; Tozer Standard and Chartered Ltd, 1973-74. Recreations: golf, gardening. Address: Peat Moor, Harborough Hill, Pulborough, West Sussex. T: West Chiltington 2171. Clubs: Brooks's, MCC.

HAMILTON, Sir Denis; see Hamilton, Sir C. D.

HAMILTON, Dundas; see Hamilton, J. D.

HAMILTON, Eben William, QC 1981; b 12 June 1937; s of Rev. John Edmund Hamilton, MC and Hon. Lilias Maclay; m 1973, Catherine Harvey (marr. diss. 1977). Educ: Winchester; Trinity Coll., Cambridge. Nat. Service: 4/7 Royal Dragoon Guards, 1955-57; Fife and Forfar Yeomanry/Scottish Horse, TA, 1958-66. Called to the Bar, Inner Temple, 1962. Address: 1 New Square, Lincolns Inn, WC2. T: 01-405 0884. Club: Garrick.
See also Martha Hamilton.

HAMILTON, Sir Edward (Sydney), 7th and 5th Bt, cr 1776 and 1819; b 14 April 1925; s of Sir (Thomas) Sydney (Percival) Hamilton, 6th and 4th Bt, and Bertha Muriel, d of James Russell King, Singleton Park, Kendal; S father, 1966. Educ: Canford Sch. Served Royal Engineers, 1943-47; 1st Royal Sussex Home Guard, 1953-56. Recreations: Spiritual matters, music. Address: The Cottage, East Lavant, near Chichester, West Sussex PO18 0AL. T: Chichester 527414.

HAMILTON, Prof. George Heard; Director, Sterling and Francine Clark Art Institute, 1966-77, now Emeritus; Professor of Art, Williams College, Williamstown, Massachusetts, 1966-75, now Emeritus; Director of Graduate Studies in Art History, Williams College, 1971-75; b 23 June 1910; s of Frank A. Hamilton and Georgia Neale Heard; m 1945, Polly Wiggin; one s one d. Educ: Yale Univ. BA 1932; MA 1934; PhD 1942. Research Asst, Walters Art Gallery, Baltimore, 1934-36; Mem. Art History Faculty, Yale Univ., 1936-66 (Prof., 1956-66); Robert Sterling Clark Prof. of Art, Williams Coll., 1963-64.

Slade Prof. of Fine Art, Cambridge Univ., 1971-72; Kress Prof. in Residence, Nat. Gall of Art, Washington, DC, 1978-79. FRSA 1973; Fellow, Amer. Acad. of Arts and Science, 1979. Hon. LittD Williams Coll., 1977; Wilbur Lucius Cross Medal, Yale Grad. Sch., 1977; Amer. Art Dealers' Assoc. award for excellence in art hist., 1978. *Publications:* (with D. V. Thompson, Jr) De Arte Illuminandi, 1933; Manet and His Critics, 1954; The Art and Architecture of Russia, 1954; Monet's Paintings of Rouen Cathedral, 1960; European Painting and Sculpture, 1880-1940, 1967; (with W. C. Agee) Raymond Duchamp-Villon, 1967; 19th and 20th Century Art: Painting, Sculpture, Architecture, 1970; Articles in Burlington Magazine, Gazette des Beaux-Arts, Art Bulletin, etc. *Recreations:* music, gardening. *Address:* Williamstown, Mass 01267, USA. *T:* (413) 458-8626. *Clubs:* Century Association (New York); Elizabethan (New Haven); Edgartown Yacht (Mass).

HAMILTON, Maj.-Gen. Godfrey John, CB 1966; CBE 1959 (OBE 1956); DSO 1935; *b* 31 March 1912; *s* of late Lieut-Col F. A. Hamilton, OBE, DL, JP, and of Mrs Hamilton, Osbaston, Monmouth; *m* 1st, 1937, Mary Penelope Colthurst; one *d*; 2nd, 1942, Mary Margaret Kaye, *qv*; two *d*. *Educ:* Radley Coll.; RMC, Sandhurst. Commnd, 1932; served in Guides Infantry, IA, 1932-48 (despatches): India, Burma and Malaya; Royal Irish Fusiliers (despatches twice): Palestine, Egypt, Germany, Korea, Kenya, N Ireland, Berlin. Chief, Joint Services Liaison Organization, BAOR, 1963-66. Retired, 1967. *Recreations:* fishing, painting. *Address:* The Old House, Boreham Street, near Hailsham, East Sussex. *Club:* Army and Navy.

HAMILTON, Graeme Montagu, TD; QC 1978; a Recorder of the Crown Court, since 1974; *b* 1 June 1934; *s* of late Leslie Montagu Hamilton and of Joan Lady Burbidge (Joan Elizabeth Burbidge, *née* Moxey); *m* 1978, Mrs Deirdre Lynn. *Educ:* Eton; Magdalene Coll., Cambridge (MA). National Service, 4/7 Royal Dragoon Guards, 1953-55. Called to Bar, Gray's Inn, 1959; Mem., Senate of Inns of Court and Bar, 1975-78. TA City of London Yeomanry, Inns of Court and City Yeomanry, 1955-70. *Recreations:* sailing, shooting. *Address:* 2 Crown Office Row, Temple, EC4Y 7HJ. *Clubs:* Cavalry and Guards, Royal Thames Yacht, Royal Automobile.

HAMILTON, Hamish; President, Hamish Hamilton Ltd, Publishers (Chairman, 1931-81, and Managing Director, 1931-72); *b* Glasgow, 15 Nov. 1900; *o s* of James Neilson Hamilton, and Suzanne van Valkenburg; *m* 1st, 1929, Jean Forbes-Robertson (marr. diss. 1933), *d* of Sir Johnston and Lady Forbes-Robertson; 2nd, 1940, Countess Yvonne Pallavicino, of Rome; one *s*. *Educ:* Rugby; Caius Coll., Cambridge (Medical Student, 1919). MA (Hons Mod. Langs), LLB. Travelled in USA, 1922-23; called to Bar (Inner Temple), 1925; London Manager Harper and Brothers, Publishers, 1926; founded Hamish Hamilton Ltd, 1931; served in Army, 1939-41 (Holland and France, 1940); seconded to American Division, Ministry of Information, 1941-45; Hon. Sec. Kinsmen Trust, 1942-56; founded Kathleen Ferrier Meml Scholarships, 1954; a Governor, the Old Vic, 1945-75; Member Council, English-Speaking Union; a Governor, British Institute, Florence. Chevalier de la Légion d'Honneur, 1953; Grande Ufficiale, Order of Merit (Italy), 1976. *Publications:* articles on publishing, Anglo-American relations and sport. Commemorative Anthologies: Decade, 1941, Majority, 1952. *Recreations:* music, the theatre, travel; formerly rowing (spare stroke Cambridge Eight, 1921; stroked Winning Crews Grand Challenge Cup, Henley, 1927 and 1928, and Olympic Eight, Amsterdam, 1928 (silver medal)), ski-ing, flying, squash. *Address:* Palazzo Guicciardini, 15 Via Guicciardini, Florence, Italy. *T:* 294 830. *Clubs:* Garrick; Leander, MCC.

HAMILTON, Brig. Hugh Gray Wybrants, CBE 1964 (MBE 1945); DL; Chairman, Forces Help Society and Lord Roberts Workshops (in an honorary capacity), since 1974; *b* 16 May 1918; *s* of Lt-Col H. W. Hamilton, late 5th Dragoon Guards; *m* 1944, Claire Buxton; two *d*. *Educ:* Wellington Coll., Berks; Peterhouse, Cambridge; Royal Mil. Academy. Commissioned with Royal Engineers, 1938. War Service in BEF, BNAF, BLA, 1939-45. Post War Service in Australia, BAOR, France and UK. Instructor, Army Staff Coll., Camberley, 1954-56; Student, IDC, 1965; retired, 1968. Gen. Manager, Corby Develt Corp., 1968-80. DL Northants, 1977. *Recreations:* riding, sailing, farming. *Address:* Covert House, East Haddon, Northants. *T:* East Haddon 488. *Club:* Army and Navy.

HAMILTON, Iain (Bertram); author and journalist; *b* 3 Feb. 1920; *s* of John Hamilton and Margaret Laird MacEachran; *m* 1944, Jean Campbell Fisher; one *s* one *d*. *Educ:* Paisley Grammar Sch. Editorial staff: Daily Record, 1944-45; The Guardian, 1945-52; The Spectator, 1952; Asst Editor, 1953, Associate Editor, 1954-56, The Spectator; Editor-in-Chief, 1957, Editorial Director, The Hutchinson group of publishing cos, 1958-62; Editor of The Spectator, 1962-63. Man. Dir, Kern House Enterprises Ltd, 1970-75; Dir of Studies, Inst. for Study of Conflict, 1975-77; Man. Dir, Campbell & Hamilton Ltd, 1978-; Founder Mem., British Irish Assoc. Has contrib. prose and verse to Radio, Daily Telegraph, Encounter, Illustrated London News, Interplay, Country Life, The Times Educational and Literary Supplements, Spectator, World Review, Twentieth Century, Scots Review and other periodicals. *Publications:* Scotland the Brave, 1957; The Foster Gang (with H. J. May), 1966; Embarkation for Cythera, 1974; The Kerry Kyle, 1980; Koestler, 1982; *play:* The Snarling Beggar, 1951. *Address:* c/o Martin Secker & Warburg Ltd, 54 Poland Street, W1V 3NF.

HAMILTON, Iain Ellis, BMus, FRAM; composer; pianist; Mary Duke Biddle Professor of Music, Duke University, North Carolina, USA, 1962-78

(Chairman of the Department, 1966); *b* Glasgow, 6 June 1922; *s* of James and Catherine Hamilton. *Educ:* Mill Hill; Royal Academy of Music. Engineer (Handley Page Ltd), 1939-46; RAM (Scholar) 1947-51; BMus (London University), 1951. Lecturer at Morley Coll., 1952-58; Lecturer, London Univ., 1956-60. Prizes and awards include: Prize of Royal Philharmonic Society, 1951; Prize of Koussevitsky Foundation (America), 1951; Butterworth Award, 1954; Arnold Bax Gold Medal, 1956; Ralph Vaughan Williams Award, Composers' Guild of GB, 1975. FRAM, 1960. Chm. Composers' Guild, 1958; Chm. ICA Music Cttee, 1958-60. *Works:* 4 Symphonies; Sinfonia for two orchestras (Edinburgh Festival Commission); Concertos, for piano, clarinet, organ and violin; The Bermudas, for baritone, chorus and orchestra (BBC Commission); Symphonic Variations for string orchestra; Overture, Bartholomew Fair; Overture, 1912; Ecossaise for orchestra; Concerto for jazz trumpet and orchestra (BBC Commn); Scottish Dances; Sonata for chamber orchestra; 5 Love Songs for tenor and orchestra; (BBC Commission) Cantos for orchestra; Jubilee for orchestra; Arias for small orchestra; Circus for orchestra (BBC Commn); Epitaph for this World and Time: 3 choruses and 2 organs; Vespers, for chorus, 2 pianos, harp and percussion; Voyage for horn and orchestra; Alastor for orchestra; Amphion for violin and orchestra; Commedia for orchestra; Threnos for solo organ; Aubade and Paraphrase for solo organ; Clerk Saunders, a ballet; chamber works include: two String Quartets; String Octet; Sonatas for piano, viola, clarinet and flute; Flute Quartet; Clarinet Quintet; 3 Nocturnes for clarinet and piano; 5 Scenes for trumpet and piano; Sextet; Sonatas and Variants for 10 winds; Dialogues for soprano and 5 instruments; Nocturnes with Cadenzas for solo piano; 4 Border Songs, The Fray of Suport, a Requiem and a Mass for unaccompanied voices; 1 choral work, St Mark Passion; Cleopatra for soprano and orchestra; Opera: Agamemnon; Royal Hunt of the Sun; Pharsalia; The Catiline Conspiracy; Tamburlaine; Anna Karenina; Dick Whittington; Lancelot. Music for theatre and films. Hon. DMus Glasgow, 1970. *Publications:* articles for many journals. *Address:* 1 King Street, WC2.

HAMILTON, Ian; poet; *b* 24 March 1938; *s* of Robert Tough Hamilton and Daisy McKay; *m* 1963, Gisela Dietzel; one *s*. *Educ:* Darlington Grammar Sch.; Keble Coll., Oxford (BA Hons). Editor, Review, 1962-72; Poetry and Fiction Editor, Times Literary Supplement, 1965-73; Lectr in Poetry, Univ. of Hull, 1972-; Editor, The New Review, 1974-79. E. C. Gregory Award, 1963; Malta Cultural Award, 1974. *Publications:* (ed) The Poetry of War 1939-45, 1965; (ed) Alun Lewis: poetry and prose, 1966; (ed) The Modern Poet, 1968; The Visit (poems), 1970; A Poetry Chronicle, 1973; (ed) Robert Frost: selected poems, 1973; The Little Magazines, 1976. *Address:* 18 Dorset Square, NW1. *T:* 01-262 0517.

HAMILTON, Ian Robertson, QC (Scot.) 1980; barrister and advocate; *b* Paisley, Scotland, 13 Sept. 1925; *s* of John Harris Hamilton and Martha Robertson; *m* 1974, Jeannette Patricia Mari Stewart, yr of Lochnabeithe in Parish of Ardchattan and Co. of Argyll; one *s* (one *s* two *d* by former *m*). *Educ:* John Neilson Sch., Paisley; Allan Glens Sch., Glasgow; Glasgow and Edinburgh Univs (BL). Served RAFVR, 1944-48. Called to the Scottish Bar, 1954 and to the Albertan Bar, 1982. Advocate Depute, 1962; Dir of Civil Litigation, Republic of Zambia, 1964-66; Hon. Sheriff of Lanarks, 1967; retd from practice to work for National Trust for Scotland and later to farm in Argyll, 1969; returned to practice, 1974. Chief Pilot, Scottish Parachute Club, 1978-80. *Publications:* No Stone Unturned, 1952 (also New York); The Tinkers of the World, 1957 (Foyle award-winning play); contrib. various jls. *Recreations:* flying, walking, canoeing, dry-fly fishing. *Address:* c/o Advocates' Library, Parliament House, Edinburgh EH1 1RF.

HAMILTON, James, CBE 1979; MP (Lab) Bothwell since 1964; *b* 11 March 1918; *s* of George Hamilton and Margaret Carey; *m* 1945, Agnes McGhee; one *s* three *d* (and one *s* decd). *Educ:* St Bridget's, Baillieston; St Mary's, High Whifflet. District Councillor, 6th Lanarks, 1955-58; Lanarks County Council, 1958-64. National Executive Mem., Constructional Engrg Union, 1958-Pres., 1968-; Constr. Trade Union Group, Parly Labour Party, 1969-. Asst Govt Whip, 1969-70; an Opposition Whip, 1970-74; a Lord Comr of the Treasury and Vice-Chamberlain of the Household, 1974-78; Comptroller of HM Household, 1978-79. *Recreations:* tennis, badminton, golf. *Address:* 12 Rosegreen Crescent, North Road, Bellshill, Lanarks.

HAMILTON, Prof. James; Professor of Physics, Nordic Institute for Theoretical Atomic Physics, since 1964; *b* 29 Jan. 1918; *s* of Joseph Hamilton, Killybegs, Co. Donegal and Jessie Mackay, Keiss, Caithness; *m* 1945, Glen, *d* of Charles Dobbs, Verwood, Dorset; two *s* one *d*. *Educ:* Royal Academical Institution, Belfast; Queen's Univ., Belfast; Institute for Advanced Study, Dublin; Manchester Univ. Scientific Officer (Ops Research), Admiralty, London, and South East Asia Command, 1943-45; ICI Fellow, Manchester Univ., 1945-48; Lectr in Theoretical Physics, Manchester Univ., 1948-49; University Lectr in Mathematics, Cambridge Univ., 1950-60. Fellow of Christ's Coll., Cambridge, 1953-60; Research Associate in Nuclear Physics, Cornell Univ., NY, 1957-58; Prof. of Physics, University Coll., London, 1960-64. Donegall Lectr, TCD, 1969. Foreign Mem., Royal Danish Acad. Hon. Dr Trondheim, 1982. *Publications:* The Theory of Elementary Particles, 1959; (with B. Tromborg) Partial Wave Amplitudes and Resonance Poles, 1972; papers and articles on interaction of radiation with atoms, elementary particle physics, causality, and related topics. *Address:* Nordita, Blegdamsvej 17, 2100 Copenhagen Ø, Denmark. *T:* (01) 421616; Rosenørn's Allé 16v, 1970 Copenhagen V; 25 Lantree Crescent, Trumpington, Cambridge CB2 2NJ.

HAMILTON, Sir James (Arnot), KCB 1978 (CB 1972); MBE 1952; Permanent Under-Secretary of State, Department of Education and Science, since 1976; *b* 2 May 1923; *m* 1947, Christine Mary McKean (marr. diss.); three *s. Educ:* University of Edinburgh (BSc). Marine Aircraft Experimental Estab., 1943: Head of Flight Research, 1948; Royal Aircraft Estab., 1952; Head of Projects Div., 1964; Dir, Anglo-French Combat Aircraft, Min. of Aviation, 1965; Dir-Gen. Concorde, Min. of Technology, 1966-70; Deputy Secretary: (Aerospace), DTI, 1971-73; Cabinet Office, 1973-76. *Publications:* papers in Reports and Memoranda series of Aeronautical Research Council, Jl RAeS, and technical press. *Address:* Pentlands, 9 Cedar Road, Farnborough, Hants. *T:* Farnborough 543254. *Club:* Athenæum.

HAMILTON, (James) Dundas; Senior Partner, Fielding, Newson-Smith & Co., since 1977 (Partner, since 1951); Deputy Chairman, Committee on Invisible Exports, since 1976; *b* 11 June 1919; *o s* of late Arthur Douglas Hamilton and Jean Scott Hamilton; *m* 1954, Linda Jean, *d* of late Sinclair Frank Ditcham and Helen Fraser Ditcham; two *d. Educ:* Rugby; Clare Coll., Cambridge. Served War, Army (Lt-Col RA), 1939-46. Member, Stock Exchange, 1948, Mem. Council, 1972-78 (Dep. Chm., 1973-76). Director: Bluemel Bros plc; Richard Clay & Co. plc (Vice-Chm., 1981-); LWT (Holdings) plc; Pasold Res. Fund Ltd (Chm.). Member: Council of Industrial Soc., 1959-79 (Exec. Cttee, 1963-68); Adv. Bd, RCDS, 1980-; Soc. of Investment Analysts; Exec. Cttee, City Communications Centre. Contested (C) East Ham North, 1951. *Publications:* The Erl King (radio play), 1949; Lorenzo Smiles on Fortune (novel), 1953; Three on a Honeymoon (TV series), 1956; Six Months Grace (play, jointly with Robert Morley), 1957; Stockbroking Today, 1968, 2nd edn, 1979. *Recreations:* writing, swimming, skiing. *Address:* 45 Melbury Court, W8 6NH. *T:* 01-602 3157. *Clubs:* City of London; All England Lawn Tennis and Croquet.

HAMILTON, John Cole; *see* Cole-Hamilton.

HAMILTON, Adm. Sir John (Graham), GBE 1966 (KBE 1963; CBE 1958); CB 1960; National President, Institute of Marketing, 1972-75 (Director-General, 1968-72); *b* 12 July 1910; *s* of late Col E. G. Hamilton, CMG, DSO, MC, and Ethel Marie (*née* Frith); *m* 1938, Dorothy Nina Turner, 2nd *d* of late Col J. E. Turner, CMG, DSO; no *c. Educ:* RN Coll., Dartmouth. Joined RN 1924; specialised in Gunnery, 1936. Served War of 1939-45: destroyers; on staff of Adm. Cunningham, Mediterranean; Gunnery Officer, HMS Warspite; Admiralty; SE Asia; Comdr, 1943 (despatches). In command, HMS Alacrity, Far East, 1946-48; Capt., 1949; Dep. Dir, Radio Equipment, 1950-51; in command, 5th Destroyer Squadron, 1952-53; Dir of Naval Ordnance, Admiralty, 1954-56; in command HMS Newfoundland, Far East, 1956-58; despatches, 1957; Rear-Adm., 1958; Naval Sec. to First Lord of the Admiralty, 1958-60; Vice-Adm., 1961; Flag Officer: Flotillas, Home Fleet, 1960-62; Naval Air Command, 1962-64; C-in-C Mediterranean, and C-in-C Allied Forces, Mediterranean, 1964-67; Adm. 1965. *Recreations:* walking, climbing, photography. *Address:* Chapel Barn, Abbotsbury, Dorset DT3 4LF. *T:* Abbotsbury 507.

HAMILTON, Maj.-Gen. John Robert Crosse, CB 1957; CBE 1950; DSO 1944; late RE; Fellow, Churchill College, Cambridge (Bursar, 1959-72); *b* 1 April 1906; *s* of late Major J. A. C. Hamilton, Fyne Court, Bridgwater, Somerset; *m* 1938, Rosamond Budd, *d* of late Richard Hancock, Hong Kong; one *s* one *d. Educ:* Radley; Royal Military Academy; Caius Coll., Cambridge. idc. 2nd Lieut RE, 1925. Served War of 1939-45 (DSO), France, Belgium, Germany; acting Brig., 1947; Lt-Col 1948; Col, 1950; Maj.-Gen., 1956. Chief of Staff, HQ Malaya Command, 1955-56; Dir of Military Operations, War Office, 1956-59; retired, 1959. Col Comdt, RE, 1962-71. *Address:* Peas Hill End, Shipton Gorge, Bridport, Dorset. *Club:* Naval and Military.

HAMILTON, Loudon Pearson; Principal Establishment Officer, Scottish Office, since 1979; *b* 12 Jan. 1932; *s* of Vernon Hamilton and Jean Mair Hood; *m* 1956, Anna Mackinnon Young; two *s. Educ:* Hutchesons' Grammar Sch., Glasgow; Glasgow Univ. (MA Hons Hist.). National Service, 2nd Lieut RA, 1953-55. Inspector of Taxes, Inland Revenue, 1956-60; Asst Principal, Dept of Agriculture and Fisheries for Scotland, 1960; Private Sec. to Parly Under-Secretary of State for Scotland, 1964; First Secretary, Agriculture, British Embassy, Copenhagen and The Hague, 1966-70; Asst Secretary, Dept of Agriculture and Fisheries for Scotland, 1973-79. *Recreation:* sailing. *Address:* 5 Belgrave Road, Edinburgh EH12 6NG. *T:* 031-334 5398. *Club:* Royal Commonwealth Society.

HAMILTON, Martha, (Mrs R. R. Steedman); Headmistress, St Leonards School, St Andrews, since 1970; *d* of Rev. John Edmund Hamilton and Hon. Lilias Maclay; *m* 1977, Robert Russell Steedman, *qv. Educ:* Roedean Sch.; St Andrews Univ. (MA Hons Hist.); Cambridge Univ. (DipEd); Edinburgh Univ. (Dip. Adult Educn). Principal, Paljor Namgyal Girls' High School, Gangtok, Sikkim, 1959-66. Awarded Pema Dorji (for services to education), Sikkim, 1966. *Recreations:* ski-ing, photography. *Address:* St Leonards School, St Andrews, Fife. *T:* St Andrews 72126.
See also E. W. Hamilton.

HAMILTON, Mary Margaret; *see* Kaye, M. M.

HAMILTON, Michael Aubrey; MP (C) Salisbury since Feb. 1965; *b* 5 July 1918; *s* of late Rt Rev. E. K. C. Hamilton, KCVO; *m* 1947, Lavinia, 3rd *d* of late Col Sir Charles Ponsonby, 1st Bt, TD; one *s* three *d. Educ:* Radley;

Oxford. Served War of 1939-45, with 1st Bn, Coldstream Guards. MP (C) Wellingborough Div. Northants, 1959-64; Asst Govt Whip, 1961-62; a Lord Comr of the Treasury, 1962-64; PPS to Sec. of State for Foreign and Commonwealth Affairs, 1982-. UK Representative: UN Gen. Assembly, 1970; US Bicentennial Celebrations, 1976. *Address:* 27 Kylestrome House, Cundy Street, SW1. *T:* 01-730 1819; Lordington House, Chichester, Sussex.

HAMILTON, Myer A. B. K.; *see* King-Hamilton.

HAMILTON, Nigel John Mawdesley, QC 1981; *b* 13 Jan. 1938; *s* of Archibald Dearman Hamilton and Joan Worsley Mawdesley; *m* 1963; Leone Morag Elizabeth Gordon; two *s. Educ:* St Edward's Sch., Oxford; Queens' Coll., Cambridge. Nat. Service, 2nd Lieut, RE, Survey Dept, 1956-58. Assistant Master: St Edward's Sch., Oxford, 1962-63; King's Sch., Canterbury, 1963-65. Called to the Bar, Inner Temple, 1965. *Recreation:* fishing. *Address:* Moonrakers, Compton Martin, Somerset BS18 6JP. *T:* West Harptree 421.

HAMILTON, North Edward Frederick D.; *see* Dalrymple Hamilton.

HAMILTON, Sir Patrick George, 2nd Bt, *cr* 1937; Director, Possum Controls Ltd; Trustee: Eleanor Hamilton Trust; Sidbury Trust; Disabled Living Foundn Trust; *b* 17 Nov. 1908; *o s* of Sir George Clements Hamilton, 1st Bt, and Eleanor (*d* 1958), *d* of late Henry Simon and *sister* of 1st Baron Simon of Wythenshawe; *S* father, 1947; *m* 1941, Winifred Mary Stone (CBE, MA), *o c* of Hammond Jenkins, Maddings, Hadstock, Cambs. *Educ:* Eton; Trinity Coll., Oxford (MA). First Managing Director and later Chairman of Tyresoles Ltd, 1934-53 (Dir, Propeller Production, MAP, 1943-44); Director: Simon Engineering Ltd and other Simon cos, 1937-78; Renold Ltd, 1952-78; Lloyds Bank Ltd, 1953-79; Chm., Expanded Metal Co. Ltd, 1955-78. Chm., Advisory Cttee on Commercial Information Overseas, 1957-59. Dep. Chm., Export Publicity Council, 1960-63. Chm., Transport Users Consultative Cttee, NW Area, 1957-64; Mem., Central Transport Consultative Cttee, 1963-64. Treas., Fedn of Commonwealth Chambers of Commerce, 1962-64. Mem., ITA, 1964-69. Chm., Central Mddx Gp Hosp. Management Cttee, 1964-70. *Recreations:* gardening, travel. *Heir:* none. *Address:* Maddings, Hadstock, near Linton, Cambs; 39 Hyde Park Gate, SW7. *T:* 01-581 3990.

HAMILTON, Richard; painter; *b* 24 Feb. 1922; *s* of Peter and Constance Hamilton; *m* 1947, Terry O'Reilly (*d* 1962). *Educ:* elementary; Royal Academy Schs; Slade Sch. of Art. Jig and Tool draughtsman, 1940-45. Lectr, Fine Art Dept, King's Coll., Univ. of Durham (later Univ. of Newcastle upon Tyne), 1953-66. Devised exhibitions: Growth and Form, 1951; Man, Machine and Motion, 1955. Collaborated on: This is Tomorrow, 1956; 'an Exhibit', 1957; exhibn with D. Roth, ICA New Gall., 1977. One man art exhibitions: Gimpel Fils, 1951; Hanover Gall., 1955, 1964, Robert Fraser Gall., 1966, 1967, 1969; Whitworth Gall, 1972; Nigel Greenwood Inc., 1972; Serpentine Gall. 1975; Stedelijk Mus., Amsterdam, 1976; Waddington Gall., 1980; Anthony d'Offay Gall., 1980. Retrospective exhibitions: Tate Gallery, 1970 (also shown in Eindhoven and Bern); Guggenheim Museum, New York, 1973 (also shown in Cincinnati, Munich, Tübingen, Berlin); Musée Grenoble, 1977; Kunsthalle Bielefeld, 1978; other exhibitions abroad include: Kassel, 1967, New York, 1967; Milan, 1968, 1969, 1971, 1972; Hamburg, 1969; Berlin, 1970, 1971, 1973. William and Noma Copley award, 1960; John Moores prize, 1969; Talens Prize International, 1970. *Address:* c/o Tate Gallery, Millbank, SW1P 4RG.

HAMILTON, Sir Richard Caradoc; *see* Hamilton, Sir Robert C. R. C.

HAMILTON, Richard Graham; a Recorder of the Crown Court, since 1974; Chancellor, Diocese of Liverpool, since 1976; *b* 26 Aug. 1932; *s* of Henry Augustus Rupert Hamilton and Frances Mary Graham Hamilton; *m* 1960, Patricia Craghill Hamilton (*née* Ashburner); one *s* one *d. Educ:* Charterhouse; University Coll., Oxford (MA). Called to Bar, Middle Temple, 1956. *Publication:* Foul Bills and Dagger Money, 1979. *Recreations:* reading, walking, films. *Address:* 15 Gwydrin Road, Liverpool L18 3HA. *T:* 051-722 5806. *Club:* Athenæum (Liverpool).

HAMILTON, Sir (Robert Charles) Richard (Caradoc), 9th Bt, *cr* 1647; *b* 8 Sept. 1911; *s* of Sir Robert Caradoc Hamilton, 8th Bt, and Irene Lady Hamilton (*née* Mordaunt) (*d* 1969); *S* father, 1959; *m* 1952, Elizabeth Vidal Barton; one *s* three *d. Educ:* Charterhouse; St Peter's Coll., Oxford (MA). Served in the Intelligence Corps, 1940-45. Schoolmaster at Ardingly Coll., Sussex, 1946-60. Owner, Walton Estate, Warwick; Chm., Warwickshire Br., CLA. *Publication:* (trans.) A History of the Royal Game of Tennis, 1979. *Recreations:* dramatist; Real tennis. *Heir:* *s* Andrew Caradoc Hamilton, *b* 23 Sept. 1953. *Address:* Walton, Warwick. *T:* Stratford-on-Avon 840460.

HAMILTON, Robert William, FBA 1960; *b* 26 Nov. 1905; *s* of William Stirling Hamilton and Kathleen Hamilton (*née* Elsmie); *m* 1935, Eileen Hetty Lowick; three *s* two *d. Educ:* Winchester Coll.; Magdalen Coll., Oxford. Chief Insp. of Antiquities, Palestine, 1931-38; Dir of Antiquities, Palestine, 1938-48; Sec.-Librarian, British Sch. of Archæology, Iraq, 1948-49; Senior Lecturer in Near Eastern Archæology, Oxford, 1949-56; Keeper of Dept of Antiquities, 1956-72, Keeper, 1962-72, Ashmolean Museum, Oxford. Fellow Magdalen Coll., Oxford, 1959-72. *Publications:* The Church of the Nativity, Bethlehem, 1947; Structural History of the Aqsa Mosque, 1949; Khirbat al

Mafjar, 1959; (with others) Oxford Bible Atlas, 1974. *Address:* The Haskers, Westleton, Suffolk.

HAMILTON, Walter, MA; Hon. DLitt Durham; FRSL; Master of Magdalene College, Cambridge, 1967-78, Hon. Fellow, since 1978; *b* 10 Feb. 1908; *s* of late Walter George Hamilton and Caroline Mary Stiff; *m* 1951, Jane Elizabeth, *o d* of Sir John Burrows, *qv*, Ridlands Cottage, Limpsfield Chart, Surrey; three *s* one *d*. *Educ:* St Dunstan's Coll.; Trinity Coll., Cambridge (Scholar). 1st Class Classical Tripos, Part I, 1927; Part II, 1929; Craven Scholar, 1927; Chancellor's Classical Medallist, 1928; Porson Prizeman and Craven Student, 1929. Fellow of Trinity Coll., 1931-35; Asst Lecturer, University of Manchester, 1931-32; Asst Master, Eton Coll., 1933-46, Master in Coll., 1937-46, Fellow, 1972-81; Fellow and Classical Lecturer, Trinity Coll., 1946-50; Tutor, 1947-50; University Lectr in Classics, 1947-50; Head Master: of Westminster Sch., 1950-57; of Rugby Sch., 1957-66. Editor, Classical Quarterly, 1946-47. Chairman: Scholarship Cttee, Lord Kitchener Nat. Meml Fund, 1953-59, Exec. Cttee, 1967-77; Headmasters' Conference, 1955, 1956, 1965, 1966; Governing Body, Shrewsbury Sch., 1968-81; Governing Bodies Assoc., 1969-74. Member: Exec. Cttee, British Council, 1958-70; Council of Senate of Cambridge Univ., 1969-74. *Publications:* A new translation of Plato's Symposium, 1951; Plato's Gorgias, 1960; Plato's Phaedrus and Letters VII and VIII, 1973; contributions to Classical Quarterly, Classical Review, etc. *Address:* 6 Hedgerley Close, Cambridge. *T:* Cambridge 63202. *Club:* Athenæum.

HAMILTON, Prof. William Donald, FRS 1980; Professor of Evolutionary Biology, Museum of Zoology and Division of Biological Sciences, University of Michigan, since 1978; *b* 1 Aug. 1936; *s* of Archibald Milne Hamilton and Bettina Matraves Hamilton (*née* Collier); *m* 1967, Christine Ann Friess; three *d*. *Educ:* Tonbridge Sch.; Cambridge Univ. (BA); London Univ. (PhD). Lecturer in Genetics, Imperial Coll., London Univ., 1964-77. For. Member, American Acad. of Arts and Sciences, 1978. *Publications:* contribs to Jl of Theoretical Biology, Science, Nature, Amer. Naturalist. *Address:* 2900 Fuller Road, Ann Arbor, Michigan 48105, USA. *T:* 313 995 4034.

HAMILTON, William Winter; MP (Lab) Fife Central, since 1974 (Fife West, 1950-74); *b* 26 June 1917; *m* (wife died 1968); one *s* one *d*; *m* 1982, Mrs Margaret Cogle. *Educ:* Washington Grammar Sch., Co. Durham; Sheffield Univ. (BA, DipEd). Joined Lab. Party, 1936; contested W Fife, 1945; Chairman, H. of C. Estimates Cttee, 1964-70; Vice-Chm., Parly Labour Party, 1966-70; Mem., European Parlt, 1975-79, Vice-Chm., Rules and Procedure Cttee, 1976-79 (Chm., 1975-76). School teacher; Mem. National Union of Teachers. Served War of 1939-45, Middle East, Capt. *Publication:* My Queen and I, 1975. *Address:* House of Commons, SW1.

HAMILTON-DALRYMPLE, Sir Hew; *see* Dalrymple.

HAMILTON FRASER, Donald; *see* Fraser.

HAMILTON-JONES, Maj.-Gen. (retd) John, CBE 1977; Director of Marketing, General Defense Corporation of Pennsylvania; President, Ordnance Board, 1980-81; *b* 6 May 1926; *s* of George and Lillian Hamilton-Jones; *m* 1952, Penelope Ann Marion Derry; three *d*. *Educ:* Cranbrook Sch.; Edinburgh Univ.; Technical Staff Coll. US Army Guided Missile Grad., 1957. Commnd RA, 1945; Indian Artillery, 1945-47; Regtl Service, Far East/ME, 1947-60; Jt Services Staff Coll., 1966; comd a regt, 1966-69; DS RMCS, 1970-72; MoD Dir, 1975-78 (Brig.). CEng; FRAeS; MIERE; FBIM (MBIM 1979). *Recreations:* rowing, Rugby, squash, music, hi-fi. *Address:* c/o Lloyds Bank Ltd, Cox's & King's Branch, 6 Pall Mall, SW1Y 5NH.

HAMILTON-RUSSELL, family name of **Viscount Boyne.**

HAMILTON-SMITH, family name of **Baron Colwyn.**

HAMILTON-SPENCER-SMITH, Sir John; *see* Spencer-Smith.

HAMILTON STUBBER, Lt-Col John Henry, Lord Lieutenant of Co. Tyrone, since 1979; *b* 1921; *o s* of late Major Robert Hamilton Stubber, DSO, and Lady Mabel Hamilton Stubber, MBE, *d* of 4th Earl of Erne and widow of Captain Lord Hugh William Grosvenor; *m* 1953, Fiona Patricia, *d* of late Captain G. W. Breitmeyer, Dibmardan, Glos; four *s*. *Educ:* Eton; Trinity Coll., Cambridge. Joined Coldstream Guards, 1941; served France and Germany, 1941-45 (despatches 1945); Captain 1944, retired 1948; Major, Ulster Defence Regt, 1970, retired 1978 with rank of Hon. Brevet Lt-Col. Chairman, Dungannon DC, 1973-79. Formerly JP Gloucestershire. DL 1971, High Sheriff 1972, Co. Tyrone. CStJ 1981. *Address:* Aughentaine, Fivemiletown, Co. Tyrone BT75 0LH, Northern Ireland. *T:* Fivemiletown 271. *Clubs:* Turf, MCC; Ulster (Belfast); Kildare Street and University (Dublin).

HAMLEY, Donald Alfred; HM Diplomatic Service; Consul-General, Jerusalem, since 1980; *b* 19 Aug. 1931; *s* of Alfred Hamley and Amy (*née* Brimacombe); *m* 1958, Daphne Griffith; two *d*. *Educ:* Devonport High Sch., Plymouth. Joined HM Foreign (subseq. Diplomatic) Service, 1949; Nat. Service, 1950-52; returned to FO; served in: Kuwait, 1955-57; Libya, 1958-61; FO, 1961-63; Jedda, 1963-65 and 1969-72; Rome, 1965-69; seconded to DTI, 1972-73; Commercial Counsellor, Caracas, 1973-77; seconded to Dept of Trade, 1977-80. *Recreations:* tennis, golf, swimming, squash, choral singing.

Address: c/o Foreign and Commonwealth Office, SW1A 2AL; 1 Forge Close, Bromley, Kent. *T:* 01-462 6696.

HAMLYN, Prof. David Walter; Professor of Philosophy and Head of Philosophy Department, Birkbeck College, University of London, since 1964, and Head of Classics Department, since 1981; *b* 1 Oct. 1924; *s* of late Hugh Parker Hamlyn and late Gertrude Isabel Hamlyn; *m* 1949, Eileen Carlyle Litt; one *s* one *d*. *Educ:* Plymouth Coll.; Exeter Coll., Oxford. BA (Oxon) 1948, MA 1949 (1st cl. Lit. Hum., 1st cl. Philosophy and Psychology, 1950). Research Fellow, Corpus Christi Coll., Oxford, 1950-53; Lecturer: Jesus Coll., Oxford, 1953-54; Birkbeck Coll., London, 1954-63, Reader, 1963-64. Pres., Aristotelian Soc., 1977-78. Mem. Council, Royal Inst. of Philosophy, 1968- (Exec., 1971-). Mem., London Univ. Senate, 1981-; Governor, Birkbeck Coll., 1965-69; Chm. Governors, Heythrop Coll., 1971-78, Fellow, 1978. Editor of Mind, 1972-. *Publications:* The Psychology of Perception, 1957 (repr. with additional material, 1969); Sensation and Perception, 1961; Aristotle's De Anima, Books II and III, 1968; The Theory of Knowledge, 1970 (USA), 1971 (GB); Experience and the Growth of Understanding, 1978 (Spanish trans. 1981); Schopenhauer, 1980; Perception, Learning and the Self, 1982; contrib. to several other books and to many philosophical, psychological and classical jls. *Recreations:* playing and listening to music. *Address:* 7 Burland Road, Brentwood, Essex CM15 9BH. *T:* Brentwood 214842; Department of Philosophy, Birkbeck College, Malet Street, WC1E 7HX. *T:* 01-580 6622.

HAMLYN, Paul (Bertrand); Founder and Chairman: Octopus Publishing Group (London, New York and Sydney), since 1971; Mandarin Publishers (Hong Kong), since 1971; Chairman, Octopus Books; Co-founder (with David Frost) and Director, Sundial Publications, since 1973; Co-founder (with Doubleday & Co., New York) and Director, Octopus Books International BV (Holland), since 1973; Director: News International, since 1971; News America, since 1980; Tigerprint, since 1980; TV-AM, since 1981; *b* 12 Feb. 1926; 2nd *s* of late Prof. Richard Hamburger and Mrs L. Hamburger (*née* Hamburg); *m* 1st, 1952, Eileen Margaret (Bobbie) (marr. diss. 1969), *d* of Col Richard Watson; one *s* one *d*; 2nd, 1970, Mrs Helen Guest. *Educ:* St Christopher's Sch., Letchworth, Herts. Founder of Hamlyn Publishing Gp; Formed: Books for Pleasure, 1949; Prints for Pleasure, 1960; Records for Pleasure, Marketing long-playing classical records, and Golden Pleasure Books (jt co. with Golden Press Inc., NY), 1961; Music for Pleasure (with EMI), 1965. Paul Hamlyn Gp acquired by Internat. Publishing Corp, 1964; joined IPC Bd with special responsibility for all Corporation's book publishing activities; Butterworth & Co. acquired 1968; Director, IPC, 1965-70; Chm., IPC Books, controlling Hamlyn Publishing Gp, 1965-70 (formerly Chm., Paul Hamlyn Holdings Ltd, and associated Cos); Jt Man. Dir, News International Ltd, 1970-71. Mem. Council, ICA, 1977-. *Address:* 64 Old Church Street, SW3. *T:* 01-352 8369.
See also M. P. L. Hamburger.

HAMMARSKJÖLD, Knut (Olof Hjalmar Åkesson); Director-General and Chairman of Executive Committee, International Air Transport Association, since 1966; *b* Geneva, 16 Jan. 1922; Swedish; *m*; four *s*. *Educ:* Sigtunaskolan; Stockholm Univ. Swedish Foreign Service, 1946; Attaché, Swedish Embassy, Paris, 1947-49; Foreign Office, Stockholm, 1949-51; Attaché, Swedish Embassy, Vienna, 1951-52; 2nd Sec., Moscow, 1952-54, 1st Sec, 1954-55; 1st Sec., Foreign Office, 1955-57; Head of Foreign Relations Dept, Swedish Civil Aero. Bd, 1957-59; Counsellor, Paris, also Dep. Head of Swedish Delegn to OEEC, 1959-60; Dep. Sec.-Gen., EFTA, Geneva, 1960-66; Minister Plenipotentiary. Hon. Fellow, Canadian Aeronautics and Space Inst.; Hon. Academician, Mexican Acad. of Internat. Law; Hon. FCIT (London). Pres. and Mem., Alexander S. Onassis Public Benefit Foundn Internat. Jury for award of Athens and Olympia prizes. Comdr (1st cl.), Order of North Star (Sweden); NOR (Sweden); Grand Cross Order of Civil Merit (Spain); Grand Officer, Order of Al-Istiqlal (Jordan); Commander: Order of Lion (Finland); Oranje Nassau (Netherlands); Order of Falcon (1st cl.) (Iceland); Order of Black Star (France). *Publications:* articles on political, economic and aviation topics. *Recreations:* music, painting, ski-ing. *Address:* c/o IATA, 2000 Peel Street, Montreal, PQ H3A 2R4, Canada; IATA, 26 Chemin de Joinville, PO Box 160, 1216 Cointrin-Geneva, Switzerland. *T:* 983366.

HAMMER, James Dominic George; HM Chief Inspector of Factories since 1975; *b* 21 April 1929; *s* of E. A. G. and E. L. G. Hammer; *m* 1955, Margaret Eileen Halse; two *s* one *d*. *Educ:* Dulwich Coll.; Corpus Christi Coll., Cambridge. BA Hons Mod. Langs. Joined HM Factory Inspectorate, 1953. *Address:* Health and Safety Executive, 25 Chapel Street, NW1 4DT. *T:* 01-262 3277.

HAMMER, Rev. Canon Raymond Jack, PhD; Director, Bible Reading Fellowship, since 1977; *b* 4 July 1920; *s* of Paul and Lily Hammer; *m* 1949, Vera Winifred (*née* Reed); two *d*. *Educ:* St Peter's Coll., Oxford (MA, Dip.Theol.); Univ. of London (BD, MTh, PhD). Asst Curate, St Mark's, St Helens, 1943-46; Sen. Tutor, St John's Coll., Durham, 1946-49; Lectr in Theol., Univ. of Durham, 1946-49; Prof., Central Theol Coll., Tokyo, 1950-64; Prof. in Doctrine, St Paul's Univ., Tokyo, 1958-64; Chaplain at British Embassy, Tokyo, 1954-64; Hon. Canon, St Michael's Cathedral, Kobe, Japan, 1964-; Lectr, Queen's Coll., Birmingham, and Lectr in Theol., Univ. of Birmingham, 1965-77. Examining Chaplain to: Bishop of Liverpool, 1965-78; Bishop of Birmingham, 1973-78. Archbishops' Consultant on Relations with Other Faiths, 1978-. Treasurer, Studiorum Novi Testamenti

Societas, 1970-82. *Publications*: Japan's Religious Ferment, 1961 (US 1962); The Book of Daniel (commentary), 1976; contrib: Theological Word Book of the Bible, 1950; Oxford Dictionary of the Christian Church, 1957, 2nd edn 1975; Concise Dictionary of the Bible, 1966; Concise Dictionary of the Christian World Mission, 1970; Man and his Gods, 1971; Shorter Books of the Apocrypha, 1972; Perspectives on World Religions, 1978; The World's Religions, 1982; World Religions, 1982. *Recreations*: travel, literature. *Address*: St Michael's House, 2 Elizabeth Street, SW1W 9RQ. *T*: (office) 01-730 9181; (home) Farnborough (Kent) 57326. *Clubs*: Athenæum; Sion College.

HAMMERSLEY, Dr John Michael, FRS 1976; Reader in Mathematical Statistics, University of Oxford, and Professorial Fellow, Trinity College, Oxford, since 1969; *b* 21 March 1920; *s* of late Guy Hugh Hammersley and Marguerite (*née* Whitehead); *m* 1951, Shirley Gwendolene (*née* Bakewell); two *s*. *Educ*: Sedbergh Sch.; Emmanuel Coll., Cambridge. MA, ScD (Cantab); MA, DSc (Oxon). War service in Royal Artillery, Major, 1940-45. Graduate Asst, Design and Analysis of Scientific Experiment, Univ. of Oxford, 1948-55; Principal Scientific Officer, AERE, Harwell, 1955-59; Sen. Research Officer, Inst. of Economics and Statistics, Univ. of Oxford, 1959-69; Sen. Research Fellow, Trinity Coll., Oxford, 1961-69. FIMS 1959; FIMA 1964; Fulbright Fellow, 1955; Erskine Fellow, 1978. Mem., ISI, 1961. Von Neumann Medal for Applied Maths, Brussels, 1966. *Publications*: (with D. C. Handscomb) Monte Carlo Methods, 1964, rev. edn 1966, repr. 1979, trans. as Les Méthodes de Monte Carlo, 1967; papers in scientific jls. *Address*: Trinity College, Oxford. *T*: Oxford 49631.

HAMMERSLEY, Rear-Adm. Peter Gerald, CB 1982; OBE 1965; Royal Navy, retired; Chief Executive, British Internal Combustion Engine Manufacturers' Association, since 1982; *b* 18 May 1928; *s* of Robert Stevens Hammersley and Norah Hammersley (*née* Kirkham); *m* 1959, Audrey Cynthia Henderson Bolton; one *s* one *d*. *Educ*: Newcastle High Sch., Newcastle under Lyme; Denstone Coll.; RNEC Manadon; Imperial Coll., London (DIC). Served RN, 1946-82; Long Engrg Course, RNEC Manadon, 1946-50; HMS Liverpool, 1950-51; Advanced Marine Engrg Course, RNC Greenwich, 1951-53; HMS Ocean, 1953-54; joined Submarine Service, 1954; HMS Alaric, HMS Tiptoe, 1954-58; Nuclear Engrg Course, Imperial Coll., 1958-59; First Marine Engineer Officer, first RN Nuclear Submarine, HMS Dreadnought, 1960-64; DG Ships Staff, 1965-68; Base Engineer Officer, Clyde Submarine Base, 1968-70; Naval Staff, 1970-72; Asst Director, S/M Project Team, DG Ships, 1973-76; CO, HMS Defiance, 1976-78; Captain, RNEC Manadon, 1978-80; CSO (engrg) to C-in-C Fleet, 1980-82. Comdr 1965; Captain 1971; Rear-Adm. 1980. *Recreations*: squash, tennis, walking, gardening. *Address*: Rusland, 27 Horsecombe Brow, Combe Down, Bath BA2 5QY.

HAMMERTON, Rolf Eric; His Honour Judge Hammerton; a Circuit Judge, since 1972; *b* 18 June 1926; *s* of Eric Maurice Hammerton and Dora Alice Hammerton (*née* Zander); *m* 1953, Thelma Celestine Hammerton (*née* Appleyard), JP; one *s* three *d*. *Educ*: Brighton, Hove and Sussex Grammar Sch.; Peterhouse, Cambridge (MA, LLB). Philip Teichman Prize, 1952; called to Bar, Inner Temple, 1952. Governor, Brighton, Hove and Sussex Sixth Form Coll. *Recreation*: cooking. *Address*: The Shambles, 6 Onslow Road, Hove, East Sussex BN3 6TA. *T*: Hove 551874.

HAMMETT, Sir Clifford (James), Kt 1969; Chief Justice, Fiji, 1967-72; Acting Governor General of Fiji, 1971; Law Revision Commissioner, St Kitts, 1974; *b* 8 June 1917; *s* of late Frederick John and Louisa Maria Hammett; *m* 1946, Olive Beryl Applebee; four *s* one *d*. *Educ*: Woodbridge. Admitted Solicitor, 1939. Indian Army, 1st Punjab Regt, 1939, North Africa, 1940; captured at Singapore, 1942 (despatches); POW on Siam Railway, 1942-45. Magistrate, Nigeria, 1946-52. Called to the Bar, Middle Temple, 1948. Transferred to Fiji, 1952; Senior Magistrate, Fiji, 1954, Puisne Judge, 1955; conjointly Chief Justice, Tonga, 1956-68. *Recreation*: gardening. *Address*: c/o Lloyds Bank, 6 Pall Mall, SW1. *Club*: Naval and Military.

HAMMETT, Harold George; British Deputy High Commissioner, Peshawar, 1964-66; *b* 2 Aug. 1906; 2nd *s* of Arthur Henry Hammett; *m* 1st, 1936, Daphne Margaret Vowler; one *s* ; 2nd, 1947, Natalie Moira Sherratt; one *s* one *d*. *Educ*: St Olave's; Clare Coll., Cambridge. Malayan Civil Service, 1928-57; retired from post of Resident Commissioner, Malacca, on Malayan Independence, 1957; Commonwealth Office (formerly CRO), 1958-66. *Recreations*: woodwork, gardening. *Address*: Hole Head, Holcombe, Dawlish, Devon. *T*: Dawlish 2114. *Clubs*: East India, Devonshire, Sports and Public Schools, Royal Commonwealth Society.

HAMMICK, Sir Stephen (George), 5th Bt, *cr* 1834; *b* 27 Dec. 1926; *s* of Sir George Hammick, 4th Bt; *S* father, 1964; *m* 1953, Gillian Elizabeth Inchbald; two *s* one *d*. *Educ*: Stowe. Royal Navy as Rating (hostilities only), 1944-48; RAC Coll., Cirencester, 1949-50; MFH Cattistock Hunt, 1961 and 1962. County Councillor (Dorset), 1958. High Sheriff, Dorset, 1981-82. Farmer, with 450 acres. *Recreations*: hunting, fishing, sailing. *Heir*: *s* Paul St Vincent Hammick, *b* 1 Jan. 1955. *Address*: Badgers, Wraxall, Dorchester. *T*: Evershot 343.

HAMMOND, Anthony Hilgrove; Principal Assistant Legal Adviser to Home Office and Northern Ireland Office, since 1980; *b* 27 July 1940; *s* of Colonel Charles William Hilgrove Hammond and late Jessie Eugenia Hammond (*née*

Francis). *Educ*: Malvern Coll.; Emmanuel Coll., Cambridge (BA, LLB). Admitted Solicitor of Supreme Court, 1965. Articled with LCC, 1962; Solicitor, GLC, 1965-68; Home Office: Legal Assistant, 1968; Sen. Legal Assistant, 1970; Asst Legal Advr, 1974. *Recreations*: bridge, music, opera, walking, birdwatching. *Address*: 48 Rosebank, Holyport Road, Fulham, SW6. *T*: 01-385 7966. *Club*: Athenæum.

HAMMOND, Catherine Elizabeth, CBE 1950; Colonel, WRAC (retired); *b* 22 Dec. 1909; *d* of late Frank Ernest Rauleigh Eddolls and late Elsie Eddolls (*née* Cooper); *m* ; one *s* one *d*. *Educ*: Lassington House, Highworth, Wilts; Chesterville Sch., Cirencester, Glos. Joined ATS (TA) (FANY), 1938; Private, 7th Wilts MT Co. 1939; 2nd Subaltern 1940; Capt., 1942; Major, Commanding Devon Bn, 1942; Lieut-Col, Asst Dir ATS Oxford, 1943; Col, Dep. Dir ATS (later WRAC), Eastern Command 1947-50; Hon. Col 54 (East Anglia) Div./Dist WRAC/TA, 1964-67. Chm., WRAC Assoc., 1966-70, Life Vice-Pres., 1971. Chm., Highworth and District Br., RNLI, 1970-. Deputy Mayor, Highworth Town Council, 1978, Mayor, 1979-81. *Recreations*: hockey—Army (women), 1947-48; all games; racing. *Address*: Red Down, Highworth, Wilts SN6 7SH. *T*: Swindon 762331.

HAMMOND, Eric Albert Barratt, OBE 1977; Executive Councillor, Electrical, Electronic, Telecommunication and Plumbing Union, since 1963; *b* 17 July 1929; *s* of Arthur Edgar Hammond and Gertrude May Hammond; *m* 1953, Brenda Mary Edgeler; two *s*. *Educ*: Corner Brook Public Sch. Shop Steward, 1953-63; Branch Sec., EETPU, 1958-63. Borough and Urban District Councillor, 1958-63. Member: Electronics EDC, 1967; Engineering Construction EDC, 1976-; Industrial Development Adv. Bd, 1977-; Adv. Council on Energy Conservation, 1974-77; (part-time) Monopolies and Mergers Commn, 1978-; Chm., Electronic Components Sector Working Party, 1975-. *Recreations*: scouting (Chm., 5th Northfleet Scout Gp), gardening, photography. *Address*: 9 Dene Holm Road, Northfleet, Kent DA11 8LF. *T*: Gravesend 63856. *Club*: Northfleet Traders'.

HAMMOND, James Anthony; a Recorder of the Crown Court, since 1980; *b* 25 July 1936; *s* of James Hammond and Phyllis Eileen Hammond; *m* 1963, Sheila Mary Hammond, JP (*née* Stafford); three *d*. *Educ*: Wigan Grammar Sch.; St Catherine's Coll., Oxford (BA). Called to Bar, Lincoln's Inn, 1959; National Service, 1959-61. Councillor: Up Holland UDC, 1962-66; Skelmersdale and Holland UDC, 1970-72. Chairman, NW Branch, Society of Labour Lawyers, 1975-. *Recreations*: hockey, walking, sailing, pub quizzes. *Address*: The Lawns, Sandford Road, Tontine, Orrell, Wigan, Lancs. *T*: Up Holland 622467.

HAMMOND, Dame Joan (Hood), DBE 1974 (CBE 1963; OBE 1953); CMG 1972; Australian operatic, concert, oratorio, and recital singer; *b* 24 May 1912; *d* of late Samuel Hood Hammond and Hilda May Blandford. *Educ*: Presbyterian Ladies Coll., Pymble, Sydney, Australia. Student of violin and singing at Sydney Conservatorium of Music; played with Sydney Philharmonic Orchestra for three years. Sports writer, Daily Telegraph, Sydney. Commenced public appearances (singing) in Sydney, 1929; studied in Europe from 1936; made operatic debut, Vienna, 1939; London debut in Messiah, 1938. World Tours: British Isles, USA, Canada, Australasia, Malaya, India, E and S Africa, Europe, Scandinavia, Russia, etc. Guest Artist: Royal Opera House, Covent Garden; Carl Rosa; Sadler's Wells; Vienna Staatsoper; Bolshoi, Moscow; Marinsky, Leningrad; Riga, Latvia; New York City Centre; Australian Elizabethan Theatre Trust; Netherlands Opera; Barcelona Liceo. Operatic roles: Aida, Madame Butterfly, Tosca, Salome, Otello, Thais, Faust, Don Carlos, Eugene Onegin, Invisible City of Kitej, La Traviata, Il Trovatore, La Bohème, Pique Dame, Manon, Manon Lescaut, La Forza del Destino, Fidelio, Simone Boccanegra, Turandot, Tannhauser, Lohengrin, Damnation of Faust, Martha, Pagliacci, Der Freischutz, Oberon, Magic Flute, Dido and Aeneas; World Premieres: Trojan Women, Wat Tyler, Yerma; British Premiere, Rusalka. HMV Recording artist. Head of Vocal Studies, Victorian College of the Arts; Mem., Victorian Council for the Arts; Trustee, Geelong Performing Arts Centre. Volunteer Ambulance Driver, London, War of 1939-45. Sir Charles Santley Award, Worshipful Co. of Musicians, 1970. Hon. MusD Western Australia, 1979. Coronation Medal 1953. *Publication*: A Voice, A Life, 1970. *Recreations*: golf (won first junior Golf Championship of NSW, 1930 and 1931; NSW. LGU State Title, 1932, 1934, 1935; runner-up Australian Open Championship, 1933; Mem. first LGU team of Australia to compete against Gt Brit., 1935) (runner-up NSW State Squash Championship, 1934), yachting, swimming, tennis, writing, reading. *Address*: Private Bag 101, Geelong Mail Centre, Victoria 3221, Australia. *Clubs*: New Century (London); Barwon Heads Golf (Victoria); Royal Sydney Golf; Royal Motor Yacht (Dorset, England).

HAMMOND, Prof. Nicholas Geoffrey Lemprière, CBE 1974; DSO 1944; FBA 1968; DL; Henry Overton Wills Professor of Greek, University of Bristol, 1962-73; a Pro-Vice-Chancellor, 1964-66; *b* 15 Nov. 1907; *s* of late Rev. James Vavasour Hammond, Rector of St Just-in-Roseland, Cornwall, and Dorothy May; *m* 1938, Margaret Campbell, *d* of James W. J. Townley, CBE, MIEE; two *s* three *d*. *Educ*: Fettes Coll. (schol.); Caius Coll., Cambridge (schol.). 1st Cl. Classical Tripos Pts I and II, dist. in Hist., Pt II; Montagu Butler Prize; Sandys Student; Pres. CU Hockey Club; Treas. Union Soc. Fellow Clare Coll., Cambridge, 1930; University Lectr in Classics, 1936; Junior Proctor, 1939; Sen. Tutor, Clare Coll., 1947-54 (Hon. Fellow, 1974); Headmaster, Clifton Coll., 1954-62. Johnson Prof., Wisconsin Univ., 1973-74; Mellon Prof., Reed Coll., Oregon, 1975-76; Brittingham Prof., Wisconsin

Univ., 1977; Leverhulme Prof., Univ. of Ioannina, 1978; Visiting Professor: Haverford Coll., 1978; Univ. of Auckland, 1980; St Olaf Coll., Minnesota, 1981; Pennsylvania Univ., 1982. Chm., Managing Cttee, British Sch. at Athens, 1972-75. Served War of 1939-45, as Lt-Col, campaigns in Greece, Crete, Syria, and Mem. Allied Mil. Mission, Greece, 1943-44 (despatches twice, DSO). Pres., Hellenic Soc., 1965-68. DL: Bristol, 1965; Cambridge, 1974. Hon. DLett: Wisconsin, 1981; St Olaf Coll., 1982. Officer, Order of the Phoenix, Greece, 1946. *Publications:* Memoir of Sir John Edwin Sandys, 1933; History of Greece, 1959, 2nd edn, 1967; Epirus, 1967; A History of Macedonia, Vol. 1, 1972, Vol. 2, 1979; Studies in Greek History, 1973; The Classical Age of Greece, 1976; Migrations and Invasions in Greece, 1976; Alexander the Great: King Commander and Statesman, 1981; Editor: Clifton Coll. Centenary Essays, 1962; Cambridge Ancient History, 3rd edn, vols I and II; Oxford Classical Dictionary, 2nd edn, 1970; Atlas of the Greek and Roman World in Antiquity, 1981; articles and reviews in learned jls. *Address:* 3 Belvoir Terrace, Trumpington Road, Cambridge. *T:* Cambridge 357151.

HAMMOND, Roy John William; Director, City of Birmingham Polytechnic, since 1979; *b* 3 Oct. 1928; *s* of John James Hammond and Edith May Hammond; *m* 1949, Audrey Cecilia Dagmar Avello; three *d*. *Educ:* East Ham Grammar Sch.; University College of the South West, Exeter; Sorbonne, Paris. BA Hons, 1st Cl. French and Latin, London. Royal Air Force Education Branch, 1952-56; Asst Lectr, Blackburn Municipal Technical Coll. and School of Art, 1956-59; Head of Department: Herefordshire Technical Coll., 1960-66; Leeds Polytechnic, 1966-71; Asst Dir, City of Birmingham Polytechnic, 1971-79. *Recreations:* cricket, theatre, music, walking. *Address:* City of Birmingham Polytechnic, Perry Barr, Birmingham B42 2SU. *T:* 021-356 9193.

HAMMOND INNES, Ralph, CBE 1978; author and traveller; *b* 15 July 1913; *s* of late William Hammond and Dora Beatrice Innes; *m* 1937, Dorothy Mary Lang. Staff of Financial News, 1934-40. Served Artillery, 1940-46. Member: various cttees, Soc. of Authors, sailing foundns, Timber Growers' Orgn; Vice-Pres., Assoc. of Sea Training Orgns. Works regularly translated into numerous languages; many book club and paperback edns throughout the world. *Publications include:* Wreckers Must Breathe, 1940; The Trojan Horse, 1940; Attack Alarm, 1941; Dead and Alive, 1946; The Lonely Skier, 1947; The Killer Mine, 1947; Maddon's Rock, 1948; The Blue Ice, 1948; The White South (Book Society Choice), 1949; The Angry Mountain, 1950; Air Bridge, 1951; Campbell's Kingdom (Book Society Choice), 1952; The Strange Land, 1954; The Mary Deare (chosen by Literary Guild of America, Book Soc. Choice), 1956; The Land God Gave to Cain, 1958; Harvest of Journeys (Book Soc. Choice), 1959; The Doomed Oasis (chosen by Literary Guild of America, Book Soc. Choice), 1960; Atlantic Fury (Book Society Choice), 1962; Scandinavia, 1963; The Strode Venturer, 1965; Sea and Islands (Book Society Choice), 1967; The Conquistadors (Book of the Month and Literary Guild), 1969; Levkas Man, 1971; Golden Soak, 1973; North Star, 1974; The Big Footprints, 1977; The Last Voyage (Cook), 1978; Solomons Seal, 1980; The Black Tide, 1982; *films:* Snowbound, Hell Below Zero, Campbell's Kingdom, The Wreck of the Mary Deare; *TV:* Explorers (Cook), 1975; Golden Soak, 1979; Levkas Man, 1981. *Recreations:* cruising and ocean racing, forestry. *Address:* Ayres End, Kersey, Ipswich IP7 6EB. *T:* Hadleigh (Suffolk) 823294. *Clubs:* Royal Ocean Racing, Royal Cruising.

HAMMOND-STROUD, Derek; concert and opera baritone; *b* 10 Jan. 1929; *s* of Herbert William Stroud and Ethel Louise Elliott. *Educ:* Salvatorian Coll., Harrow, Mddx; Trinity Coll. of Music, London; in Vienna and Munich with Elena Gerhardt and Gerhard Hüsch. Glyndebourne Festival Opera, 1959; Sadler's Wells Opera (later ENO), 1961; Houston Grand Opera, USA, 1975; Royal Opera, Covent Garden, 1975; Netherlands Opera, 1976; Metropolitan Opera, NY, 1977; Teatro Colón, Buenos Aires, 1981. Concerts and Lieder recitals at Edinburgh, Aldburgh, Munich and Vienna Festivals, and in Spain, Iceland and Denmark. Pres., Univ. of London Opera Gp, 1971. Freeman, City of London, 1952; Hon. RAM 1976. Recordings include: The Ring (Goodall); Der Rosenkavalier (de Waart). *Recreations:* chess, badminton, study of philosophy. *Address:* 18 Sutton Road, Muswell Hill, N10 1HE.

HAMNETT, Thomas Orlando; Chairman, Greater Manchester Council, 1975-1976, Vice-Chairman, 1976; *b* 28 Sept. 1930; *s* of John and Elizabeth Hamnett; *m* 1954, Kathleen Ridgway; one *s* five *d*. *Educ:* Stockport Jun. Techn. Sch. Sheetmetal craftsman, 1946-. Member, Manchester City Council, 1963 until re-organisation (Vice-Chm., Health Cttee, Chm. sub cttee on Staff on Cleansing Cttee, Mem. Policy and Finance Cttees), and 1978- (Member Direct works, Markets, and Personnel Cttees); Mem. Transportation, Education, and Recreation and Arts Cttees, Greater Manchester Council. *Recreations:* football, cricket, table tennis. *Address:* 199 Chapman Street, Gorton, Manchester M18 8WP. *T:* 061-223 3098. *Club:* Gorton Trades and Labour (Chm.).

HAMPDEN; see Hobart-Hampden.

HAMPDEN, 6th Viscount *cr* 1884; **Anthony David Brand;** *b* 7 May 1937; *s* of 5th Viscount Hampden and of Imogen Alice Rhys, *d* of 7th Baron Dynevor; *S* father, 1975; *m* 1969, Cara Fiona, *e d* of Claud Proby; two *s* one *d*. *Educ:* Eton. *Publication:* Henry and Eliza, 1980. *Heir:* *s* Hon. Francis Anthony Brand, *b* 17 Sept. 1970. *Address:* Glynde Place, Glynde, Lewes, Sussex. *Club:* White's.

HAMPER, Rev. Richard John, JP; General Secretary, Free Church Federal Council, since 1979; *b* 18 Nov. 1928; *s* of Albert Thomas Hamper and Margaret Catherine Hamper; *m* 1954, Madeline Lewis; two *s* two *d*. *Educ:* Price's Sch., Fareham, Hants; Oxford Univ. (MA). Baptist Minister: Botley and Eynsham, Oxon, 1952-56; Bilborough, Nottingham, 1956-61; Queen's Road, Coventry, 1961-79. Free Church Adviser, Central Indep. Television (formerly ATV), 1970-. JP Inner London Juvenile Bench, 1969-. *Recreations:* fell walking, gardening. *Address:* Free Church Federal Council, 27 Tavistock Square, WC1H 9HH. *T:* 01-387 8413.

HAMPSHIRE, Margaret Grace, MA; JP; Principal of Cheltenham Ladies' College, 1964-79; *b* 7 Sept. 1918; *o d* of Dr C. H. Hampshire, CMG, MB, BS, BSc, sometime Sec. of British Pharmacopœia Commission, and Grace Mary Hampshire. *Educ:* Malvern Girls' Coll.; Girton Coll., Cambridge. BA 1941; MA 1945. Entered Civil Service, Board of Trade, 1941. Joined Staff of Courtaulds, 1951. Head of Government Relations Department, 1959-64. Member: Board of Governors, University Coll. Hosp., 1961-64; Marylebone Borough Council, 1962-64; SW Regional Hosp. Board, 1967-70; Midlands Electricity Consultative Council, 1973-80. JP Cheltenham, 1970. *Recreations:* music, reading, foreign travel. *Address:* Ringwood, 9 The Croft, Painswick, Glos GL6 6QP.

HAMPSHIRE, Sir Stuart (Newton), Kt 1979; FBA 1960; Warden of Wadham College, Oxford University, since 1970; *b* 1 Oct. 1914; *s* of G. N. Hampshire and Marie West; *m* 1961, Renee Ayer. *Educ:* Repton; Balliol Coll., Oxford. 1st Cl. Lit Hum, Oxford, 1936. Fellow of All Souls Coll., and Lectr in Philosophy, Oxford, 1936-40. Service in Army, 1940-45. Personal Asst to Minister of State, Foreign Office, 1945; Lectr in Philosophy, University Coll., London, 1947-50; Fellow of New Coll., Oxford, 1950-55; Domestic Bursar and Research Fellow, All Souls Coll., 1955-60; Grote Prof. of Philosophy of Mind and Logic, Univ. of London, 1960-63; Prof. of Philosophy, Princeton Univ., 1963-70. Fellow, Amer. Acad. of Arts and Sciences, 1968. Hon. DLitt Glasgow, 1973. *Publications:* Spinoza, 1951; Thought and Action, 1959; Freedom of the Individual, 1965; Modern Writers and other essays, 1969; Freedom of Mind and other essays, 1971; (ed jtly) The Socialist Idea, 1975; Two Theories of Morality, 1977; (ed) Public and Private Morality, 1978; articles in philosophical journals. *Address:* Wadham College, Oxford.

HAMPSHIRE, Susan; actress; *b* 12 May 1942; *d* of George Kenneth Hampshire and June Hampshire; *m* 1st, 1967, Pierre Granier-Deferre (marr. diss. 1974); one *s* (one *d* decd); 2nd, 1981, Eddie Kulukundis, *qv*. *Educ:* Hampshire Sch., Knightsbridge. *Stage:* Expresso Bongo, 1958; 'that girl' in Follow That Girl, 1960; Fairy Tales of New York, 1961; Marion Dangerfield in Ginger Man, 1963; Kate Hardcastle in She Stoops to Conquer, 1966; On Approval, 1966; Mary in The Sleeping Prince, 1968; Nora in A Doll's House, 1972; Katharina in The Taming of the Shrew, 1974; Peter in Peter Pan, 1974; Jeannette in Romeo and Jeannette, 1975; Rosalind in As You Like It, 1975; title rôle in Miss Julie, 1975; Elizabeth in The Circle, 1976; Ann Whitefield in Man and Superman, 1977; Siri Von Essen in Tribades, 1978; Victorine in An Audience Called Edouard, 1978; Irene in The Crucifer of Blood, 1979; Ruth Carson in Night and Day, 1979; Elizabeth in The Revolt, 1980; Stella Drury in House Guest, 1981; *TV Serials:* Andromeda (title rôle), Fleur Forsyte in The Forsyte Saga (Emmy Award for Best Actress, 1970), Becky Sharp in Vanity Fair (Emmy Award for Best Actress, 1973), Sarah Churchill, Duchess of Marlborough, in The First Churchills (Emmy Award for Best Actress, 1971), Glencora Palliser in The Pallisers; Lady Melfont in Dick Turpin. *Films include:* During One Night, The Three Lives of Thomasina, Night Must Fall, Wonderful Life, Paris in August, The Fighting Prince of Donegal, Monte Carlo or Bust, Rogan, David Copperfield, Living Free, A Time for Loving, Malpertius (E. Pae Prizes du Film Fantastique, Best Actress, 1972), Neither the Sea Nor the Sand, Roses and Green Peppers, Bang. *Publication:* Susan's Story, 1981. *Recreations:* gardening, music, the study of antique furniture. *Address:* c/o Midland Bank Ltd, 92 Kensington High Street, W8 4SH. *T:* 01-937 0962.

HAMPSON, Prof. Elwyn Lloyd, MDS, FDSRCS; HDD RCSE; Professor of Restorative Dentistry, University of Sheffield, 1960-81, now Emeritus; Hon. Consultant Dental Surgeon to Sheffield Area Health Authority; *b* 31 Jan. 1916; *s* of John and Mary Hampson; *m* 1940, Anne Cottrell; one *s* one *d*. *Educ:* Calday Grange Grammar Sch., W Kirby, Cheshire; Univ. of Liverpool. BDS with 1st Class Hons 1939; HDD RCSE 1944; FDSRCS 1949; MDS 1954; FDSE 1964. House surg., Liverpool Dental Hosp., 1939; Royal Army Dental Corps, 1941-45; Lecturer in Operative Dental Surgery, Edinburgh Dental Sch., 1945-47; Lecturer and later Senior Lecturer in Operative Dental Surgery, Univ. of Sheffield, 1947-60, Dean of Sch. of Clinical Dentistry, 1968-72. Mem., GDC, 1968-73. *Publications:* Hampson's Textbook of Operative Dental Surgery, 1961, 4th edn 1980; many papers in scientific jls. *Recreation:* water colour painting. *Address:* 8 Milborne Close, Chester CH2 1HH.

HAMPSON, Dr Keith; MP (C) Ripon, since Feb. 1974; *b* 14 Aug. 1943; *s* of Bertie Hampson and Mary Elizabeth Noble; *m* 1st, 1975, Frances Pauline (*d* 1975), *d* of Mr and Mrs Mathieu Donald Einhorn; 2nd, 1979, Susan, *d* of Mr and Mrs John Wilkie Cameron. *Educ:* King James I Grammar Sch., Bishop Auckland, Co. Durham; Univ. of Bristol; Harvard Univ. BA, CertEd, PhD. Personal Asst to Edward Heath, 1966 and 1970 Gen. Elections and in his House of Commons office, 1968; Lectr in American History, Edinburgh Univ., 1968-74. PPS to Minister for Local Govt, 1979-. Vice Chm., Cons.

Parly Educn Cttee, 1975–79. Vice Pres., WEA, 1978–; Vice-Chm., Youthaid, 1979–. *Recreations:* tennis, dancing, music. *Address:* House of Commons, SW1A 0AA. *T:* 01-219 4463. *Club:* Carlton.

HAMPSON, Prof. Norman, FBA 1980; Professor of History, University of York, since 1974; *b* 8 April 1922; *s* of Frank Hampson and Elizabeth Jane Fazackerley; *m* 1948, Jacqueline Gardin; two *d. Educ:* Manchester Grammar Sch.; University Coll., Oxford (MA); Dr de l'Univ. Paris. Service in Royal Navy, 1941–45. Manchester Univ., 1948–67: Lectr and Sen. Lectr; Prof. of Modern History, Univ. of Newcastle, 1967–74. *Publications:* La Marine de l'an II, 1959; A Social History of the French Revolution, 1963; The Enlightenment, 1968; The First European Revolution, 1969; The Life and Opinions of Maximilien Robespierre, 1974; A Concise History of the French Revolution, 1975; Danton, 1978. *Address:* 305 Hull Road, York YO1 3LB. *T:* York 412661.

HAMPSTEAD, Archdeacon of; *see* Pickering, Ven. F.

HAMPTON, 6th Baron *cr* 1874; **Richard Humphrey Russell Pakington;** Bt 1846; *b* 25 May 1925; *s* of 5th Baron Hampton, OBE, and Grace Dykes (*d* 1959), 3rd *d* of Rt Hon. Sir Albert Spicer, 1st Bt; *S* father, 1974; *m* 1958, Jane Elizabeth Farquharson, *d* of late T. F. Arnott, OBE, TD, MB, ChB; one *s* two *d. Educ:* Eton; Balliol Coll., Oxford. Observer in Fleet Air Arm, RNVR, 1944–47. Varied employment, mainly with advertising agencies, 1949–58; Worcestershire Branch Council for the Protection of Rural England, 1958–71; Tansley Witt & Co., Chartered Accts, Birmingham, 1971–73. *Publication:* (written with his father, Humphrey Pakington) The Pakingtons of Westwood, 1975. *Heir: s* Hon. John Humphrey Arnott Pakington, *b* 24 Dec. 1964. *Address:* Palace Farmhouse, Upton-on-Severn, Worcester WR8 0SN. *T:* Upton-on-Severn 2512.

HAMPTON, Antony Barmore, TD 1954; DL; President, Record Ridgway Ltd, since 1981 (Chairman, 1958–81); President, Engineering Employers Federation, 1980–82; *b* 6 March 1919; *s* of Charles William Hampton and Winifred Elizabeth Hampton; *m* 1948, Helen Patricia Lockwood; five *s. Educ:* Rydal Sch.; Christ's Coll., Cambridge, 1938–40 (MA). Indian Army 1941–46 (despatches). C. and J. Hampton Ltd, 1947, until merger with Ridgway, 1972 (Chm. of both, 1958–81); Lloyds Bank Ltd: Chm., Yorkshire Board, 1972– (Mem., 1961–); Director, UK Board, 1972–. Mem., Engrg Industry Trng Bd, 1979–; Master Cutler of Hallamshire, 1966–67. Chm., Crucible Theatre Trust, Sheffield, 1970. DL S Yorkshire (previously W Riding) 1972. *Recreations:* sailing, fishing. *Address:* Tideway, 20 Wittering Road, Hayling Island, Hants PO11 9SP. *T:* Hayling Island 4361. *Clubs:* Little Ship; The Club (Sheffield).

HAMPTON, Bryan; Counsellor (Energy), Washington, since 1981; *b* 4 Dec. 1938; *s* of William Douglas Hampton and Elizabeth Cardwell; *m* 1964, Marilyn Joseph; five *d. Educ:* Harrow County Grammar Sch. for Boys. Board of Trade: Exec. Officer, 1957; Asst Private Sec. to Parly Sec., 1961; Private Sec. to Minister of State (Lords), 1963; Asst Principal, 1965; Second Sec., UK Delegn to EFTA/GATT, Geneva, 1966; Principal, DTI, 1969; Asst Sec., Dept of Energy, 1974. *Recreations:* music, cricket, Liverpool FC. *Address:* 5226 Loughboro Road NW, Washington, DC 20016, USA. *T:* (202) 966-1122. *Club:* International (Washington).

HAMPTON, Christopher James, FRSL 1976; playwright; *b* 26 Jan. 1946; *s* of Bernard Patrick Hampton and Dorothy Patience Hampton (*née* Herrington); *m* 1971, Laura Margaret de Holesch; two *d. Educ:* Lancing Coll.; New Coll., Oxford (MA). First play: When Did You Last See My Mother?, 1964 (perf. Royal Court Theatre, 1966; transf. Comedy Theatre; prod. at Sheridan Square Playhouse, New York, 1967). Resident Dramatist, Royal Court Theatre, Aug. 1968–70. *Plays:* Total Eclipse, Prod. Royal Court, 1968; The Philanthropist, Royal Court, 1970 (Evening Standard Best Comedy Award, 1970; Plays & Players London Theatre Critics Best Play, 1970), Ethel Barrymore Theatre, New York, 1971; Savages, Royal Court, 1973, Comedy, 1973, Mark Taper Forum Theatre, Los Angeles, 1974 (Plays & Players London Theatre Critics Best Play, Jt Winner, 1973; Los Angeles Drama Critics Circle Award for Distinguished Playwriting, 1974); Treats, Royal Court, 1976, Mayfair, 1976; Able's Will, BBC TV, 1977; After Mercer, Nat. Theatre, 1980; The History Man (from Malcolm Bradbury) BBC TV, 1981; Total Eclipse (rev. version) Lyric, Hammersmith, 1981; The Portage to San Cristobal of A. H. (from George Steiner), Mermaid, 1982; Tales from Hollywood, Mark Taper Forum Theatre, Los Angeles, 1982; *translations:* Marya, by Isaac Babel, Royal Court, 1967; Uncle Vanya, by Chekhov, Royal Court, 1970; Hedda Gabler, by Ibsen, Fest. Theatre, Stratford, Ont, 1970; A Doll's House, by Ibsen, Playhouse Theatre, New York, 1971, Criterion, London, 1973, Vivian Beaumont Theatre, New York, 1975; Don Juan, by Molière, Bristol Old Vic, 1972; Tales from the Vienna Woods, by Horváth, National Theatre, 1977; Don Juan Comes Back from the War, by Horváth, Nat. Theatre, 1978; Ghosts, by Ibsen, Actors' Co., 1978; The Wild Duck, by Ibsen, Nat. Theatre, 1979; The Prague Trial, Paris Studio, 1980; *films:* A Doll's House, 1973; Tales From the Vienna Woods, 1979. *Publications:* When Did You Last See My Mother?, 1967; Total Eclipse, 1969, rev. version, 1981; The Philanthropist, 1970; Savages, 1974; Treats, 1976; Able's Will, 1979; *translations:* Isaac Babel, Marya, 1969; Chekhov, Uncle Vanya, 1971; Ibsen, Hedda Gabler, 1972; Ibsen, A Doll's House, 1972; Molière, Don Juan, 1972; Horváth, Tales from the Vienna Woods, 1977; Horváth, Don Juan Comes Back from the War, 1978;

Ibsen: The Wild Duck, 1980; Ghosts, 1981. *Recreations:* travel, cinema. *Address:* 2 Kensington Park Gardens, W11. *Club:* Dramatists'.

HAMSON, Prof. Charles John, QC 1975; Professor of Comparative Law, University of Cambridge, 1953–73; Fellow of Trinity College, since 1934; Barrister-at-Law, Gray's Inn, Bencher, 1956, Treasurer, 1975; Correspondent, Institut de France (Acad. Sci. Mor. et Pol.), since 1961; Doctor *hc* Universities of Grenoble, Nancy, Poitiers, Bordeaux, Brussels, Montpellier, Strasbourg; Hon. Fellow, St Edmund's House, Cambridge, 1976; Chevalier de la Légion d'Honneur; *b* 23 Nov. 1905; *er s* of Charles Edward Hamson (formerly of Constantinople), and of Thérèse Boudon; *m* 1933, Isabella (*d* 1978), *y d* of Duncan Drummond and Grace Gardiner of Auchterarder; one *d. Educ:* Downside; Trinity Coll., Cambridge. Entrance and Sen. Scholar in Classics; Classical Tripos Part I 1925, Part II 1927 (distinction); Capt. CU Epée Team, 1928; Davison Scholar, Harvard Law Sch., 1928–29; Linthicum Foundation Prize (North-western Univ.) 1929; Yorke Prize, 1932; LLB 1934; LLM 1935. Asst Lecturer, 1932, Lecturer, 1934, Reader in Comparative Law, 1949; Chm. Faculty Board of Law, 1954–57. Editor, Cambridge Law Jl, 1955–74; Univ. Press Syndic, 1955–69; Library Syndic, 1966–73; Gen. Bd, 1966–69. President: Internat. Acad. of Comparative Law, 1966–79; CU Catholic Assoc., 1964–76; St Edmund's Assoc., 1977–81. Served War of 1939–45; commissioned in Army, 1940; detached for service with SOE; Battle of Crete, 1941; POW Germany, 1941–45. Hamlyn Lectures on Conseil d'Etat, 1954; Visiting Professor: University of Michigan Law Sch. (Ann Arbor), 1957; Paris Faculty of Law, 1959; Univ. of Pennsylvania, 1964; Auckland Univ., 1967; professeur associé, Paris II, 1973–74; Sherill Lectr, Yale Law Sch., 1960; Wiener-Anspach Inaugural Lectr, Univ. of Brussels, 1978. *Address:* Trinity College, Cambridge. *T:* Cambridge 358201.
See also J. R. Cann.

HAMYLTON JONES, Keith, CMG 1979; HM Diplomatic Service, retired; HM Ambassador, to Costa Rica, 1974–79, to Honduras, 1975–78, and to Nicaragua, 1976–79; *b* 12 Oct. 1924; *m* 1953, Eira Morgan; one *d. Educ:* St Paul's Sch.; Balliol Coll., Oxford (Domus Scholar in Classics, 1943); BA 1948; MA 1950. Welsh Guards, 1943; Italy, 1944 (Lieut); S France, 1946 (Staff Captain). HM Foreign Service, 1949; 3rd Sec., Warsaw, 1950; 2nd Sec., Lisbon, 1953; 1st Sec., Manila, 1957; Head of Chancery and HM Consul, Montevideo, 1962; Head of Chancery, Rangoon, 1967; Asst Head of SE Asia Dept, FCO, 1968; Consul-General, Lubumbashi, 1970–72; Counsellor, FCO, 1973–74. *Publication:* (as Peter Myllent) The Ideal World, 1972. *Recreations:* reading, writing, walking, music, tennis. *Address:* Morval House, Morval, near Looe, Cornwall.

HAN SUYIN, (Mrs Elizabeth Comber); doctor and author; (*née* Elizabeth K. Chow); *b* 12 Sept. 1917; *d* of Y. T. Chow (Chinese) and M. Denis (Belgian); *m* 1st, 1938, General P. H. Tang, (*d* 1947); one *d*; 2nd, 1952, L. F. Comber. *Educ:* Yenching Univ., Peking, China; Brussels Univ., Brussels, Belgium; London Univ., London, England. Graduated MB, BS, London (Hons) in 1948, since when has been a practising doctor. *Publications: as Han Suyin:* Destination Chungking, 1942; A Many Splendoured Thing, 1952; And the Rain My Drink, 1956; The Mountain Is Young, 1958; Cast but One Shadow and Winter Love, 1962; The Four Faces, 1963; China in the Year 2001, 1967; The Morning Deluge, 1972; Wind in the Tower, 1976; Lhasa, the Open City, 1977; Les Cent Fleurs: La Peinture Chinoise Aujourd'hui, 1978; La Chine aux Mille Visages, 1980; Chine: Terre Eau et Hommes, 1981; Till Morning Comes, 1982; *autobiography:* The Crippled Tree, 1965; A Mortal Flower, 1966; Birdless Summer, 1968; My House Has Two Doors, 1980. *Recreations:* botany, riding, swimming, lecturing. *Address:* c/o Jonathan Cape Ltd, 30 Bedford Square, WC1.

HANBURY, Lt-Col Hanmer Cecil, MVO 1953; MC 1943; JP; HM Lord-Lieutenant of Bedfordshire, since 1978; *b* 5 Jan. 1916; *yr s* of late Sir Cecil Hanbury, MP, FLS, and late Mrs Hanbury-Forbes, OBE, of Kingston Maurward, Dorchester, Dorset, and La Mortola, Ventimiglia, Italy; *m* 1939, Prunella Kathleen Charlotte, *d* of late Air Cdre T. C. R. Higgins, CB, CMG, DL, JP, Turvey House, Beds; one *s* one *d. Educ:* Eton; RMC, Sandhurst. 2nd Lieut Grenadier Guards, 1936; served 1939–45 with Grenadier Guards, France, Belgium, N Africa, Italy; Capt. 1943; Temp. Major, 1944; Major 1948; Temp. Lt-Col, 1955–57; retired 1958. BRCS, Bedfordshire: Dir, 1959–71; Dep. Pres., 1972–78; Patron, 1978–; Pres., St John's Council for Bedfordshire, 1979–; Chm., Beds T&AVR Cttee, 1970–78, Pres., 1978; Vice-Chm., E Anglia T&AVRA, 1970–78, Vice-Pres., 1978–80, Pres., 1980–. DL 1958, Vice-Lieut, later Vice Lord-Lieut, 1970–78, JP 1959, Beds; High Sheriff, Beds, 1965. KStJ 1980. *Recreations:* shooting and country pursuits. *Address:* Turvey House, Turvey, Beds MK43 8EL. *T:* Turvey 227. *Clubs:* White's, Army and Navy, Pratt's.

HANBURY, Harold Greville, QC 1960; DCL; Vinerian Professor Emeritus of English Law, Oxford; Hon. Fellow, Lincoln College, Oxford; Hon. Master of the Bench, Inner Temple; *b* 19 June 1898; *s* of late Lt-Col Basil Hanbury and late Hon. Patience Verney; *m* 1927, Anna Margaret (*d* 1980), *d* of late Hannibal Dreyer, Copenhagen, Denmark. *Educ:* Charterhouse; Brasenose Coll., Oxford (Scholar). Vinerian Law Scholar, 1921; Fellow of Lincoln Coll., Oxford 1921–49; Fellow of All Souls Coll., 1949–64, Emeritus Fellow, 1980; Vinerian Prof. of English Law, Oxford, 1949–64. Visiting Prof., Univ. of Ife, 1962–63; Dean of Law Faculty, Univ. of Nigeria, 1964–66. Barrister-at-Law, Inner Temple, 1922; Rhodes Travelling Fellow, 1931–32; Senior Proctor, Oxford Univ., 1933–34 and 1944–45. President: Bentham Club, UCL, 1954;

Soc. of Public Teachers of Law, 1958-59. Chairman: Court of Inquiry into Provincial Omnibus Industry, 1954; Board of Inquiry into West Indian Airways, Trinidad, 1958; Tribunal for Industrials, Gibraltar, 1960; Independent Mem. Commns of Inquiry on Retail Distributive Trades, 1946; Minimum Wage Arbitrator in Nigeria, 1955. Hon. Mem., Mark Twain Soc., 1977. *Publications*: Le Système Actuel de l'Équité dans le Système Juridique de l'Angleterre (trans. Robert Kiéfé), 1929; Essays in Equity, 1934, German edn 1977; Modern Equity, 1935 (11th edn *sub nom*. Hanbury and Maudsley, 1981); Traité Pratique des Divorces et des Successions en Droit Anglais (with R. Moureaux), 1939 (2nd edn 1952); English Courts of Law, 1944 (5th edn *sub nom*. Hanbury and Yardley, 1979); Principles of Agency, 1952 (2nd edn, 1960); The Vinerian Chair and Legal Education, 1958; Biafra: a challenge to the conscience of Britain, 1968; articles in legal periodicals. *Recreations*: reading, aelurophily (Vice-Pres. Oxford and District Cat Club), formerly cricket, travelling. *Address*: 14 Dan Pienaar Road, Kloof, Natal, South Africa.

HANBURY, Sir John (Capel), Kt 1974; CBE 1969; Formerly Chairman, Allen and Hanburys Ltd, 1954-73 (Director, 1944); *b* 26 May 1908; *e s* of late Frederick Capel Hanbury; *m* 1935, Joan Terry Fussell; *two s one d* (and one *s* decd). *Educ*: Downside; Trinity Coll., Cambridge. Mem., Pharmacopoeia Commn, 1948-73; Chm., Central Health Services Council, 1970-76; Pres. Assoc. of Brit. Pharmaceutical Industry, 1950-52; Chm., Assoc. of Brit. Chemical Manufacturers, 1961-63; Pres. Franco-British Pharmaceutical Commn, 1955. Mem., Thames Water Authority, 1974-79. FRSC (FRIC 1947); FPS 1955. Fellow, UCL, 1977. *Recreations*: horticulture, archæology. *Address*: Amwellbury House, Ware, Herts. *T*: Ware 2108. *Club*: United Oxford & Cambridge University.

HANBURY-TENISON, Airling Robin, OBE 1981; MA, FLS, FRGS; farmer; Chairman, Survival International, since 1969; *b* 7 May 1936; *s* of late Major Gerald Evan Farquhar Tenison, Lough Bawn, Co. Monaghan, Ireland, and Ruth, *o surv. c* of late John Capel Hanbury, JP, DL, Pontypool Park, Monmouthshire; *m* 1959, Marika Hopkinson (*see* Marika Hanbury Tenison); *one s one d*. *Educ*: Eton; Magdalen Coll., Oxford (MA). Made first land crossing of South America at its widest point, 1958 (Mrs Patrick Ness Award, RGS, 1961); explored Tassili N'Ajjer, Tibesti and Aïr mountains in Southern Sahara, 1962-66; crossed S America in a small boat from the Orinoco to Buenos Aires, 1964-65; Geographical Magazine Amazonas Expedn, by Hovercraft, 1968; Trans-African Hovercraft Expedn (Dep. Leader), 1969; visited 33 Indian tribes as guest of Brazilian Govt, 1971; Winston Churchill Memorial Fellow, 1971; British Trans Americas Expedn, 1972; explored Outer Islands of Indonesia, 1973; Eastern Sulawesi, 1974; Sabah, Brunei, Sarawak, 1976; RGS Mulu (Sarawak) Expedn (Leader), 1977-78; expedns to Ecuador, Brazil and Venezuela, 1980-81. Comr of Income Tax, 1965-; Mem. of Lloyd's, 1976. Mem. Council, RGS, 1968-70, 1971-76, 1979-; Patron's Medal, RGS, 1979; Krug Award of Excellence, 1980. *Publications*: The Rough and the Smooth, 1969; Report of a Visit to the Indians of Brazil, 1971; A Question of Survival, 1973; A Pattern of Peoples, 1975; Mulu: the rain forest, 1980; Aborigines of the Amazon Rain Forest: the Yanomami, 1982; articles in: The Times, Spectator, Blackwood's Magazine, etc; articles and reviews in Geographical Magazine (numerous), Geographical Jl, Ecologist, Expedition, etc. *Recreations*: travelling, riding on Bodmin Moor, enjoying his wife's cooking. *Address*: Maidenwell, Cardinham, Bodmin, Cornwall PL30 4DW. *T*: Cardinham 224 and 282. *Club*: Kildare Street and University (Dublin).
See also R. Hanbury-Tenison.

HANBURY TENISON, Marika; Cookery Editor, Sunday Telegraph, since 1967; Deputy Chairman, Sea Fish Industry Authority, since 1981; *b* 9 Sept. 1938; *d* of Lt-Col John Montgomerie Hopkinson and Alexandra Martha Ingeborg Pauline Stiernstedt; *m* 1959, Airling Robin Hanbury-Tenison, *qv*; *one s one d*. *Educ*: Francis Holland Sch. for Girls. Freelance journalist, 1966-; Cookery Editor: The Cornish Guardian, 1966-67; Nova, 1967-68; The Spectator, 1977-79. Corning Food Writer of the Year, 1981. *Publications*: Soups and Hors d'Oeuvres, 1969; Deep Freeze Cookery, 1970; Left Over for Tomorrow, 1971; Marika Hanbury Tenison's Menus for Each Month of the Year, 1972; For Better, For Worse, 1972; Eat Well and Be Slim, 1974; A Slice of Spice, 1974; Best of British Cooking, 1977; Recipes from a Country Kitchen, 1978; The Magimix and Food Processor Cookery Book, 1978; New Fish Cookery, 1979; Teach Yourself Deep Freezing, 1979; Cooking with Vegetables, 1980 (André Simon Meml Fund Book Award); The Cook's Handbook, 1980; Book of Afternoon Tea, 1980; Sunday Telegraph Cook Book, 1980; The Princess and the Unicorn, 1981; Magimix Cookery, 1982; contribs to nat. newspapers, many journals and magazines. *Recreations*: gardening, cooking, travelling, the pursuit of unicorns. *Address*: Maidenwell, Cardinham, near Bodmin, Cornwall PL30 4DW. *T*: Cardinham 224. *Clubs*: Annabel's, Harry's Bar.

HANBURY-TENISON, Richard, JP; Lord-Lieutenant of Gwent, since 1979; *b* 3 Jan. 1925; *e s* of late Major G. E. F. Tenison, Lough Bawn, Co. Monaghan, Ireland, and Ruth, *o surv. c* of late J. C. Hanbury, JP, DL, Pontypool Park, Monmouthshire; *m* 1955, Euphan Mary, *er d* of late Major A. B. Wardlaw-Ramsay, 21st of Whitehill, Midlothian; *three s two d*. *Educ*: Eton; Magdalen Coll., Oxford. Served Irish Guards, 1943-47 (Captain, wounded). Entered HM Foreign Service, 1949: 1st Sec., Vienna, 1956-58; 1st Sec. (and sometime Chargé d'Affaires), Phnom Penh, 1961-63, and Bucharest, 1966-68; Counsellor, Bonn, 1968-70; Head of Aviation and Telecommunications Dept,

FCO, 1970-71; Counsellor, Brussels, 1971-75; retired from Diplomatic Service, 1975. South Wales Regional Dir, Lloyds Bank, 1980-. Mem. Council and Ct, Nat. Museum of Wales, 1980-. President: Monmouthshire Rural Community Council, 1959-75; Gwent Local Hist. Council; SE Wales Arts Assoc.; Gwent County Scout Council; Chm., Gwent Community Services Council. Hon. Col, 3rd (V) Bn, The Royal Regt of Wales, TAVR, 1982-. DL 1973, High Sheriff 1977, JP 1979, Gwent. CStJ 1980. *Recreations*: shooting, fishing, conservation. *Address*: Clytha Park, Abergavenny, Gwent. *T*: Gobion 300; Lough Bawn, Co. Monaghan. *Clubs*: Boodle's; Kildare Street and University (Dublin).
See also A. R. Hanbury-Tenison.

HANBURY-TRACY, family name of **Baron Sudeley**.

HANCOCK, Lt-Col Sir Cyril (Percy), KCIE 1946 (CIE 1941); OBE 1930; MC; *b* 18 Sept. 1896; *m* Joyce (*d* 1982), *d* of F. R. Hemingway, ICS; *three s one d*. *Educ*: Wellington Coll.; RMC, Sandhurst. Commd Indian Army, 114th Mahrattas, 1914; ADC to GOC 1st Corps MEF (Gen. Sir Alexander Cobbe, VC), 1918; GSO 3 at GHQ Baghdad, 1919; transf. to Bombay Political Dept, 1920; Asst Pvte Sec. to Governor of Bombay (Lord Lloyd), 1921; Asst Pvte Sec. to Viceroy (Lord Reading), 1923; Sec., Rajkot Pol. Agency, 1925; Sec. to Resident for Rajputana, 1929; Prime Minister, Bharatpur State, Rajputana, 1932; Dep. Sec., Govt of India (Pol. Dept, i/c War Br.), 1939; Resident: Eastern States, Calcutta, 1941; Western India States and Baroda Rajkot, 1943. *Address*: Woodhayes, Firgrove Road, Yateley, Hants GU17 7NH. *T*: Yateley 873240. *Club*: MCC.
See also G. F. Hancock.

HANCOCK, David John Stowell; Deputy Secretary, Cabinet Office, since 1982; *b* 27 March 1934; *s* of late Alfred George Hancock and Florence Hancock (*née* Barrow); *m* 1966, Sheila Gillian Finlay; *one s one d*. *Educ*: Whitgift Sch.; Balliol Coll., Oxford. Asst Principal, Bd of Trade, 1957; transf. to HM Treasury, 1959; Principal, 1962; Harkness Fellow, 1965-66; Private Sec. to Chancellor of the Exchequer, 1968-70; Asst Sec., 1970; Financial and Economic Counsellor, Office of UK Permanent Rep. to European Communities, 1972-74; Under Sec., 1975-80; Dep. Sec., 1980-82. Dir, European Investment Bank, 1980-82. *Recreations*: gardening, theatre. *Address*: 157 Rosendale Road, SE21 8HE. *T*: 01-670 3155. *Club*: Civil Service.

HANCOCK, Geoffrey Francis, CMG 1977; HM Diplomatic Service, retired; Foreign and Commonwealth Office, 1979-82; *b* 20 June 1926; *s* of Lt-Col Sir Cyril Hancock, *qv*; *m* 1960, Amelia Juana Aragon; *one s one d*. *Educ*: Wellington; Trinity Coll., Oxford. MA 1951. Third Sec., Mexico City, 1953; Second Sec., Montevideo, 1956; Foreign Office, 1958; Madrid, 1958; FO, 1960; MECAS, 1962; First Sec., Baghdad, 1964-67 and 1968-69; FCO, 1969-73; Counsellor, Beirut, 1973-78. *Recreations*: music, sailing. *Address*: c/o Lloyds Bank Ltd, 6 Pall Mall, SW1Y 5NH.

HANCOCK, Prof. Sir Keith; *see* Hancock, Prof. Sir W. K.

HANCOCK, Prof. Keith Jackson; Vice-Chancellor, since 1980, Professor of Economics, since 1964, The Flinders University of South Australia; *b* 4 Jan. 1935; *s* of late A. S. Hancock and Mrs R. D. Hancock; *m* 1958, Joan, *d* of W. Taggert; *two s one d*. *Educ*: Univ. of Melbourne (BA); Univ. of London (PhD). Tutor in Economic History, Univ. of Melbourne, 1956-57; Lectr in Economics, Univ. of Adelaide, 1959-63; Pro-Vice-Chancellor, Flinders Univ. of South Australia, 1975-79. Pres., Acad. of Social Sciences in Australia, 1981-. FASSA 1968. Hon. Fellow, LSE, 1982. *Publications*: (with P. A. Samuelson and R. H. Wallace) Economics (Australian edn), 1969, 2nd edn 1975; articles in Economic Jl, Economica, Amer. Econ. Rev. and other jls. *Recreations*: bridge, sailing, music. *Address*: 6 Maturin Road, Glenelg, SA 5045, Australia. *T*: 08-294-1875. *Clubs*: South Australian Bridge Association, Royal South Australian Yacht Squadron.

HANCOCK, Maj.-Gen. Michael Stephen, CB 1972; MBE 1953; retired 1972; Planning Inspector, Department of the Environment, since 1972; *b* 19 July 1917; *s* of late Rev. W. H. M. Hancock and late Mrs C. C. Hancock (*née* Sherbrooke); *m* 1941, Constance Geraldine Margaret Ovens, *y d* of late Brig.-Gen. R. M. Ovens, CMG; *one s one d*. *Educ*: Marlborough Coll.; RMA, Woolwich. Commnd into Royal Signals, 1937; Comdr, Corps Royal Signals, 1st British Corps, 1963-66; Sec., Mil. Cttee, NATO, 1967-68; Chief of Staff, FARELF, 1968-70; VQMG, MoD, 1970-72. Col Comdt, Royal Signals, 1970-77. Chm., CCF Assoc., 1972-82, Vice Pres., 1982-. CEng; FIEE. *Recreation*: sailing. *Address*: Brakey Hill, Godstone, Surrey. *T*: Godstone 842273. *Club*: Army and Navy.

HANCOCK, Norman, CB 1976; CEng, FRINA; RCNC; Director of Warship Design, Ministry of Defence, 1969-76; *b* 6 March 1916; *o s* of late Everard Hancock, Plymouth; *m* 1940, Marie E., *d* of William E. Bow; *two s*. *Educ*: Plymouth Grammar Sch.; RNC Greenwich. Asst Constructor, AEW, Haslar, 1940; Constructor, Naval Construction Dept, 1944; British Services Observer (Constructor Comdr), Bikini, 1946. HM Dockyard, Singapore, 1949; Frigate design, Naval Construction Dept, 1952; Chief Constructor in charge of R&D, 1954; Prof. of Naval Architecture, RNC, Greenwich, 1957-62; Asst Dir of Naval Construction, in charge of Submarine Design and Construction, 1963-69. Liveryman, Worshipful Co. of Shipwrights; past Mem. Council, RINA. *Recreations*: organ music, cabinet making, travel.

Address: 41 Cranwells Park, Bath, Avon. *T:* Bath 26045. *Club:* Royal Commonwealth Society.

HANCOCK, P(ercy) E(llis) Thompson, FRCP; Hon. Consultant Physician: The Royal Free Hospital; The Royal Marsden Hospital; Potters Bar and District Hospital; *b* 4 Feb. 1904; *s* of Frank Hancock; *m* 1932, Dorothy Barnes (*d* 1953); two *d*; *m* 1955, Laurie Newton Sharp. *Educ:* Wellington Coll., Berks; Caius Coll., Cambridge; St Bartholomew's Hospital. MB 1937, BCh 1930, Cantab; FRCP 1944. Formerly: Senior Examiner in Medicine, Univ. of London; Dir of Dept of Clinical Res., Royal Marsden Hosp. and Inst. of Cancer Res. Member: Council, Imperial Cancer Res. Fund; Grand Council, British Empire Cancer Campaign for Research; Mem. Exec. Cttee, Action on Smoking and Health. Hosp. Visitor, King Edward's Hosp. Fund for London. FRSocMed (Pres., Section of Oncology, 1974-75); Fellow, Assoc. Européene de Médecine Interne d'Ensemble. Corresp. Mem., Società Italiana de Cancerologia. Hon. Member: American Gastroscopic Soc., 1958; Sociedad Chilena de Cancerología; Sociedad Chilena de Hematología; Sociedad Médica de Valparaíso. *Publications:* (joint) Cancer in General Practice; The Use of Bone Marrow Transfusion with massive Chemotherapy, 1960; (joint) Treatment of Early Hodgkin's Disease, 1967. *Recreations:* dining and wining. *Address:* 23 Wigmore Place, W1H 9DD. *T:* 01-631 4679; Is Morus, Santa Margherita di Pula, Cagliari, Sardinia.

HANCOCK, Ronald John; Chairman, Leyland Vehicles Ltd, since 1981; Managing Director, Leyland Group, since 1981; *b* 11 Feb. 1934; *s* of George and Elsie Hancock; *m* 1970, Valerie Hancock; two *d*. *Educ:* Dudley Grammar Sch., Dudley. FCMA. Served HM Forces, 1952-61. Schweppes Ltd, 1962-63; Mullard Ltd, 1963-66; Valor Group, 1966-68; BL Ltd, 1968-. Chairman: Bus Manufacturers Holdings; Self Changing Gears; Director: British Leyland Internat. Holdings; Ashok Leyland, India; Ennore Foundries, India. *Recreations:* travel, reading. *Address:* 35-38 Portman Square, W1.

HANCOCK, Sheila, OBE 1974; actress and director; *d* of late Enrico Hancock and late Ivy Woodward; *m* 1st, 1955, Alexander Ross (*d* 1971); one *d*; 2nd, 1973, John Thaw; one *d*. *Educ:* Dartford County Grammar Sch.; Royal Academy of Dramatic Art. Acted in Repertory, Theatre Workshop, Stratford East, for 8 years. West End starring roles in: Rattle of a Simple Man, The Anniversary, A Delicate Balance (RSC), So What About Love?, Absurd Person Singular, Déjà Revue, The Bed Before Yesterday, Annie, Sweeney Todd; The Winter's Tale, RSC, Stratford 1981, Barbican 1982. Has starred in several successful revues; repeated stage role in film of The Anniversary. Appeared on Broadway in Entertaining Mr Sloane. Many Television successes, including her own colour spectacular for BBC2, and several comedy series. Dir, The Soldier's Fortune, Lyric, Hammersmith, 1981. Awards: Variety Club, London Critics, Whitbread Trophy (for best Actress on Broadway). *Recreations:* reading, music. *Address:* c/o John Redway and Associates, 16 Berners Street, W1P 3DD.

HANCOCK, Air Marshal Sir Valston Eldridge, KBE 1962 (CBE 1953); CB 1958; DFC 1945; retired; grazier; *b* 31 May 1907; *s* of R. J. Hancock, Perth, W Australia; *m* 1932, Joan E. G., *d* of Col A. G. Butler, DSO, VD; two *s* one *d*. *Educ:* Hale Sch., Perth; RMC, Duntroon; psa; idc. Joined Royal Military College, Duntroon, 1925; transferred RAAF, 1929; Dir of Plans, 1940-41; commanded 71 (Beaufort) Wing, New Guinea, 1945; Commandant RAAF Academy, 1947-49; Deputy Chief of Air Staff, 1951-53; Air Mem. for Personnel, Air Board, 1953-54; Head of Australian Joint Services Staff, UK, 1955-57; Extra Gentleman Usher to the Royal Household, 1955-57; AOC 224 Group, RAF, Malaya, 1957-59; Air Officer Commanding Operational Command, 1959-61; Chief of Air Staff, Royal Australian Air Force, 1961-65. Commissioner-Gen., Australian Exhibit Organization, Expo 1967. *Recreations:* literature and sport. *Address:* 108a Victoria Avenue, Dalkeith, WA 6009, Australia. *Club:* Weld (Perth).

HANCOCK, Prof. Sir (William) Keith, KBE 1965; Kt 1953; MA; FBA 1950; Emeritus Professor and Hon. Fellow; Professor of History, Australian National University, Canberra, 1957-65; *b* Melbourne, 26 June 1898; *s* of Archdeacon William Hancock, MA; *m* 1st, 1925, Theaden Brocklebank (*d* 1960); 2nd, 1961, Marjorie Eyre. Fellow of All Souls Coll., Oxford, 1924-30; Prof. of Modern History in the University of Adelaide, 1924-33; Prof. of History, Birmingham Univ., 1934-44; Chichele Prof. of Economic History, University of Oxford 1944-49; Dir, Institute of Commonwealth Studies, and Prof. of British Commonwealth Affairs in the University of London, 1949-56; Dir of the Research Sch. of Social Sciences, Australian National Univ., 1957-61; appointed to War Cabinet Offices as Supervisor of Civil Histories, 1941, thereafter editor of series. Fellow: Churchill Coll., Cambridge, 1964; St John's Coll., Cambridge, 1971-72. Hon. Fellow, Balliol Coll., Oxford; Corresp. Mem., Sch. of Oriental and African Studies. FAHA (1st Pres.) 1969. Hon. DLitt (Rhodes, Cambridge, Birmingham, Oxford, Cape Town, Melbourne, ANU, Adelaide, WA). Foreign Hon. Member: American Historical Association; American Academy of Arts and Sciences. Order of Merit of Republic of Italy. *Publications:* Ricasoli, 1926; Australia, 1930; Survey of British Commonwealth Affairs, 1937, 1940, and 1942; Politics in Pitcairn, 1947; (with M. M. Gowing) British War Economy, 1949; Country and Calling, 1954; War and Peace in this Century, 1961; Smuts: The Sanguine Years, 1870-1919, Vol. I, 1962; The Fields of Force, 1919-1950, Vol. II, 1968; Discovering Monaro, 1972; Professing History, 1976. *Address:* 49 Gellibrand Street, Campbell, Canberra, ACT 2601, Australia. *Club:* Athenæum.

HAND, Most Rev. Geoffrey David; *see* Papua New Guinea, Archbishop of.

HAND, Prof. Geoffrey Joseph Philip, DPhil; Barber Professor of Jurisprudence in the University of Birmingham, since 1980; *b* 25 June 1931; *s* of Joseph and Mary Macaulay Hand. *Educ:* Blackrock Coll.; University Coll., Dublin (MA); New Coll., Oxford (DPhil); King's Inns, Dublin. Called to Irish Bar, 1961. Lecturer: Univ. of Edinburgh, 1960; Univ. of Southampton, 1961; University Coll., Dublin, 1965; Professor: University Coll., Dublin, 1972-76; European University Inst., Fiesole, 1976-80; Dean of Faculty of Law, University Coll., Dublin, 1970-75. Chairman, Arts Council of Ireland, 1974-75. *Publications:* English Law in Ireland 1290-1324, 1967; Report of the Irish Boundary Commission 1925, 1969; (with Lord Cross of Chelsea) Radcliffe and Cross's English Legal System, 5th edn 1971, 6th edn 1977; (with J. Georgel, C. Sasse) European Election Systems Handbook, 1979; Towards a Uniform System of Direct Elections, 1981; numerous periodicals. *Recreations:* listening to classical music, chess playing. *Address:* c/o Faculty of Law, University of Birmingham, PO Box 363, Birmingham B15 2TT. *T:* 021-472 1301. *Clubs:* United Oxford & Cambridge University; Royal Irish Yacht (Dun Laoghaire); Kildare Street and University (Dublin).

HANDCOCK, family name of **Baron Castlemaine.**

HANDLEY, Ven. Anthony Michael; Archdeacon of Norwich, since 1981; *b* 3 June 1936; *s* of Eric Harvey Handley and Janet Handley; *m* 1962, Christine May Adlington; two *s* one *d*. *Educ:* Spalding Grammar School; Selwyn Coll., Cambridge (MA Hons); Chichester Theological Coll. Asst Curate, Thorpe St Andrew, 1962-66; Anglican Priest on Fairstead Estate, 1966-72; Vicar of Hellesdon, 1972-81; RD of Norwich North, 1979-81. Research Project, The Use of Colour, Shape, and Line Drawings as Experiential Training Resources, 1976. *Publication:* A Parish Prayer Card, 1980. *Recreations:* climbing mountains, painting, bird watching. *Address:* 40 Heigham Road, Norwich NR2 3AU. *T:* Norwich 611808.

HANDLEY, Mrs Carol Margaret; Headmistress, Camden School for Girls, since 1971; *b* 17 Oct. 1929; *d* of Claude Hilary Taylor and Margaret Eleanor Taylor (*née* Peebles); *m* 1952, Eric Walter Handley, *qv*. *Educ:* St Paul's Girls' Sch.; University Coll., London (BA), Fellow 1977. Asst Classics Mistress: North Foreland Lodge Sch., 1952; Queen's Gate Sch., 1952; Head of Classics Dept, Camden Sch. for Girls, 1956; Deputy Headmistress, Camden Sch. for Girls, 1964. Member Council: Royal Holloway Coll., 1977-; Mddx Hosp. Med. Sch., 1980-; Mem. Governors and Council, Bedford Coll., 1981-. *Publications:* articles and book reviews for classical jls. *Recreations:* walking, driving, travel. *Address:* Camden School for Girls, Sandall Road, NW5 2DB. *T:* 01-485 3414.

HANDLEY, Sir David John D.; *see* Davenport-Handley.

HANDLEY, Prof. Eric Walter; FBA 1969; Professor of Greek, University College, London, since 1968, and Director of the Institute of Classical Studies, University of London, since 1967; *b* 12 Nov. 1926; *s* of late Alfred W. Handley and A. Doris Cox; *m* 1952, Carol Margaret Taylor (*see* C. M. Handley). *Educ:* King Edward's Sch., Birmingham; Trinity Coll., Cambridge. Steward of Rannoch Schol. and Browne Medal, 1945. Asst Lectr in Latin and Greek, University Coll. London, 1946, Lectr, 1949, Reader, 1961, Prof. of Latin and Greek, 1967-68. Cromer Greek Prize (jtly), 1958; Vis. Lectr on the Classics, Harvard, 1966; Vis. Mem., Inst. for Advanced Study, Princeton, 1971; Visiting Professor: Stanford Univ., 1977; Melbourne Univ., 1978; Vis. Senior Fellow, Council of the Humanities, Princeton, 1981. Sec. Council Univ. Classical Depts, 1969-70, Chm., 1975-78. Mem. Comité Scientifique, Fondation Hardt, Geneva, 1978-; Foreign Sec., British Academy, 1979-. *Publications:* (with John Rea) The Telephus of Euripides, 1957; The Dyskolos of Menander 1965; Greek literary papyri, papers in class. jls, etc. *Recreations:* boating, hill-walking, travel. *Address:* University College London, Gower Street, WC1E 6BT. *T:* 01-387 7050. *Club:* United Oxford & Cambridge University.

HANDLEY, Richard Sampson, OBE 1946; Surgeon, The Middlesex Hospital, W1, 1946, Surgeon Emeritus, 1974, retired; *b* 2 May 1909; *e s* of late W. Sampson Handley; *m* 1st, 1942, Joan (*d* 1975), *d* of Dr Cyril Gray, Newcastle upon Tyne; one *s* one *d*; 2nd, 1976, Rosemary, *d* of Captain E. Dickinson, Reigate. *Educ:* Uppingham Sch.; Gonville and Caius Coll., Cambridge; The Middlesex Hospital. Entrance Schol., Middx Hosp., 1930; BA Cantab 1930 (Pts 1 and 2, Nat. Sci. Tripos); MRCS, LRCP and MA, MB, BCh Cantab, 1933; University Demonstrator of Anatomy, Cambridge, 1936; Asst Pathologist, 1937, and Surgical Registrar, 1939, Middx Hosp. FRCS 1938; Mem. Council, 1966, Vice-Pres., 1974, RCS; Hon. Sec. RSM, 1967-73, Pres., Surgery Section, 1971; Pres., Assoc. of Surgeons of GB and Ireland, 1973-74. Served, 1939-46 (despatches, OBE); Temp. Major RAMC and Surgical Specialist, serving with BEF, 1939, and MEF, 1940; Temp. Lieut-Col, RAMC, 1944, serving BLA. Late Examiner in Surgery, Cambridge Univ.; late Mem. Court of Examiners, RCS; late Hon. Sec., Assoc. of Surgeons of GB and Ireland. Hon. Member: Hellenic Surgical Soc.; Salonika Med. Soc. Hon. MD Salonika, 1976. *Publications:* papers and lectures on surgical subjects, especially with reference to malignant disease. *Recreations:* sailing, model-making. *Address:* Elmdon Cottage, Chalkpit Lane, Marlow, Bucks SL7 2JE. *T:* Marlow 6155.

HANDLEY, Vernon George, FRCM 1972; Musical Director and Conductor, Guildford Corporation, and Conductor, Guildford Philharmonic Orchestra and Choir, 1962-summer 1983; Associate Conductor, London Philharmonic Orchestra, from Sept. 1983 (Guest Conductor, 1961-Aug. 1983); *b* 11 Nov. 1930; 2nd *s* of Vernon Douglas Handley and Claudia Lilian Handley, Enfield; *m* 1954, Barbara (marr. diss.), *e d* of Kilner Newman Black and Joan Elfriede Black, Stoke Gabriel, Devon; one *s* one *d* (and one *s* decd); *m* Victoria, *d* of Vaughan and Nora Parry-Jones, Guildford, Surrey; one *s* one *d*. *Educ:* Enfield Sch.; Balliol Coll., Oxford (BA); Guildhall Sch. of Music. Conductor: Oxford Univ. Musical Club and Union, 1953-54; OUDS, 1953-54; Tonbridge Philharmonic Soc., 1958-61; Hatfield Sch. of Music and Drama, 1959-61; Proteus Choir, 1962-81; Prof. at RCM: for Orchestra and Conducting, 1966-72; for Choral Class, 1969-72. Guest Conductor from 1961: Bournemouth Symph. Orch.; Birmingham Symph. Orch.; Royal Philharmonic Orch.; BBC Welsh Orch.; BBC Northern Symph. Orch.; Royal Liverpool Philharmonic Orch.; Ulster Orch.; BBC Scottish Symphony Orch.; New Philharmonia Orch.; conducted London Symphony Orch. in internat. series, London, 1971; toured: Germany, 1966, 1980; S Africa, 1974; Holland, 1980; Sweden, 1980, 1981; Germany, Sweden, Holland and France, 1982-83. Regular broadcaster and has made many records. Hon. RCM, 1970; FRCM 1972. Arnold Bax Meml Medal for Conducting, 1962; Conductor of the Year, British Composer's Guild, 1974; Hi-Fi News Audio Award, 1982. DUniv Surrey, 1980. *Recreations:* bird photography, old-fashioned roses. *Address:* Hen Gerrig, Pen-y-Fan, near Monmouth, Gwent. *T:* Trelleck 860318.

HANDLEY-TAYLOR, Geoffrey, FRSL; author; *b* 25 April 1920; 2nd *s* of Walter Edward Taylor and Nellie Hadwin (*née* Taylor), Horsforth. *Educ:* widely. Served War of 1939-45: Duke of Wellington's Regt and War Office. Chairman, British Poetry-Drama Guild, 1948-52; Vice-Pres., Leeds Univ. Tudor Players, 1948-50; Publisher, Leeds University Poetry, 1949; featured in NBC-TV (USA) People series, 1954; Founder, Winifred Holtby Meml Collection, Fisk Univ., Nashville, 1955; Hon. Gen. Sec., Dumas Assoc., 1955-57; Founder, Sir Ralph Perring City of London Collection, Fisk Univ., 1962; Pres., St Paul's Literary Soc., Covent Garden, 1966-68; Chm., General Council, Poetry Society, 1967-68; Mem. Gen. Council, National Book League, 1968; Dep. Pres., Lancashire Authors' Assoc., 1967-69 (Pres., 1969-72); Trustee, Gladstone Meml Library, London, 1974-78; Jt Literary Executor, Estate of Vera Brittain, 1979-. FRSL 1950. Various foreign awards. *Publications:* Mona Inglesby, Ballerina and Choreographer, 1947; Italian Ballet Today, 1949; New Hyperion, 1950; Literary, Debating and Dialect Societies of GB, Ireland and France, 5 pts, 1950-52; A Selected Bibliography of Literature Relating to Nursery Rhyme Reform, 1952; Winifred Holtby Bibliography and Letters, 1955; (with Frank Granville Barker) John Gay and the Ballad Opera, 1956; (with Thomas Rae) The Book of the Private Press, 1958; John Masefield, OM, The Queen's Poet Laureate, 1960; (with Vera Brittain) Selected Letters of Winifred Holtby and Vera Brittain 1920-1935, 1961, 2nd edn 1970; Bibliography of Monaco, 1961, 2nd edn 1968; Bibliography of Iran, 1964, 5th edn 1969; (with Timothy d'Arch Smith) C. Day Lewis, Poet Laureate, 1968; ed, County Authors Today Series, 9 vols, 1971-1973; Pogg (a satire), 1980; (with John Malcolm Dockeray) Vera Brittain, a concise bibliography, 1982; also contribs to Encycl. Britannica, Hinrichsen Music Book, 1949-1958; Airs from The Beggar's Opera, arr. Edith Bathurst, 1953; The Beggar's Opera, ed Edward J. Dent, 1954. *Address:* c/o Lloyds Bank Ltd, 185 Baker Street, NW1 6XB. *Club:* National Liberal.

HANDLIN, Prof. Oscar; Carl H. Pforzheimer University Professor, Harvard University, since 1972; Director, Harvard University Library, since 1979; *b* 29 Sept. 1915; *m* 1st, 1937, Mary Flug; one *s* two *d*; 2nd, 1977, Lilian Bombach. *Educ:* Brooklyn Coll. (AB); Harvard (MA, PhD). Instructor, Brooklyn Coll., 1938-39; Harvard Univ.: Instructor, 1939-44; Asst Prof., 1944-48; Associate Prof., 1948-54; Prof. of History, 1954-65; Charles Warren Prof. of Amer. Hist., and Dir, Charles Warren Center for Studies in Amer. Hist., 1965-72; Harmsworth Prof. of Amer. History, Oxford Univ., 1972-73. Dir, Center for Study of History of Liberty in America, 1958-67; Chm., US Bd of Foreign Scholarships, 1965-66 (Vice-Chm. 1962-65). Hon. Fellow, Brandeis Univ., 1965. Hon. LLD Colby Coll., 1962; Hon. LHD: Hebrew Union Coll., 1967; Northern Michigan, 1969; Seton Hall Univ., 1972; Hon. HumD Oakland, 1968; Hon. LittD Brooklyn Coll., 1972; Hon. DHL: Boston Coll., 1975; Univ. of Lowell, 1980; Univ. of Cincinnati, 1981. *Publications:* Boston's Immigrants, 1790-1865, 1941; (with M. F. Handlin) Commonwealth, 1947; Danger in Discord, 1948; (ed) This Was America, 1949; Uprooted, 1951, 2nd edn 1972; Adventure in Freedom, 1954; American People in the Twentieth Century, 1954 (rev. edn 1963); (ed jtly) Harvard Guide to American History, 1954; Chance or Destiny, 1955; (ed) Readings in American History, 1957; Race and Nationality in American Life, 1957; Al Smith and his America, 1958; (ed) Immigration as a Factor in American History, 1959; John Dewey's Challenge to Education, 1959; (ed) G. M. Capers, Stephen A. Douglas, Defender of the Union, 1959; Newcomers, 1960; (ed jtly) G. Mittleberger, Journey to Pennsylvania, 1960; (ed) American Principles and Issues, 1961; (with M. F. Handlin) The Dimensions of Liberty, 1961; The Americans, 1963; (with J. E. Burchard) The Historian and the City, 1963; Firebell in the Night, 1964; A Continuing Task, 1964; (ed) Children of the Uprooted, 1966; The History of the United States, vol. 1, 1967, vol. 2, 1968; America: a History, 1968; (with M. F. Handlin) The Popular Sources of Political Authority, 1967; The American College and American Culture, 1970; Facing Life: Youth and the Family in American History, 1971; A Pictorial History of Immigration, 1972; (with M. F. Handlin) The Wealth of the American People, 1975; Truth in History, 1979; (with L. Handlin) Abraham Lincoln and the Union, 1980; The Distortion of America, 1981; (with L. Handlin) A Restless People, 1982. *Address:* 18 Agassiz Street, Cambridge, Mass 02140, USA. *Clubs:* St Botolph (Boston); Harvard (NY); Faculty (Cambridge, Mass).

HANDS, Terence David, (Terry Hands); Joint Artistic Director, Royal Shakespeare Company, since 1978 (Associate Director, 1967-77); *b* 9 Jan. 1941; *s* of Joseph Ronald Hands and Luise Berthe Kohler; *m* 1st, 1964, Josephine Barstow (marr. diss. 1967); 2nd, 1974, Ludmila Mikael (marr. diss. 1980); one *d*. *Educ:* Woking Grammar Sch.; Birmingham Univ. (BA Hons Eng. Lang. and Lit.); RADA (Hons Dip.). Founder-Artistic Dir, Liverpool Everyman Theatre, 1964-66; Artistic Dir, RSC Theatregoround, 1966-67; Consultant Dir, Comédie Française, 1975-77. Associate Mem., RADA; Trust Mem., Acacia Theatre Trust. Chevalier des Arts et des Lettres, 1973. *Director* (for Liverpool Everyman Theatre, 1964-66): The Importance of Being Earnest; Look Back in Anger; Richard III; The Four Seasons; Fando and Lis; *Artistic Director* (for RSC Theatregoround): The Proposal, 1966; The Second Shepherds' Play, 1966; The Dumb Waiter, 1967; Under Milk Wood, 1967; *directed for RSC:* The Criminals, 1967; Pleasure and Repentance, 1967; The Latent Heterosexual, 1968; The Merry Wives of Windsor, 1968, Japan tour, 1970; Bartholomew Fair, 1969; Pericles, 1969; Women Beware Women, 1969; Richard III, 1970, 1980; Balcony, 1971; Man of Mode, 1971; The Merchant of Venice, 1971; Murder in the Cathedral, 1972; Cries from Casement, 1973; Romeo and Juliet, 1973; The Bewitched, 1974; The Actor, 1974; Henry IV, Parts 1 and 2, 1975; Henry V, 1975, USA and European Tour, 1976; Old World, 1976; Henry VI parts 1, 2 and 3 (Soc. of West End Theatre Award, Dir of the Year, Plays and Players, Best Production, 1978), Coriolanus, 1977, European tour, 1979; The Changeling, 1978; Twelfth Night, The Children of the Sun, 1979; As You Like It, Richard II, 1980; Troilus and Cressida, 1981; Arden of Faversham, Much Ado About Nothing, 1982; *directed for Comédie Française:* Richard III, 1972 (Meilleur Spectacle de l'Année award); Pericles, 1974; Twelfth Night, 1976 (Meilleur Spectacle de l'Année award); Le Cid, 1977; Murder in the Cathedral, 1978; *directed for Paris Opéra:* Verdi's Otello, 1976 (televised 1978); *directed for Burg Theatre, Vienna:* Troilus and Cressida, 1977; As You Like It, 1979; *directed for Teatro Stabile di Genova, Italy:* Women Beware Women, 1981; *directed for Royal Opera:* Parsifal, 1979; *recording:* Murder in the Cathedral, 1976. *Publications:* trans. (with Barbara Wright) Genet, The Balcony, 1971; Pleasure and Repentance, 1976; (ed Sally Beauman) Henry V, 1976; contribs to Theatre 72, Playback. *Address:* c/o Royal Shakespeare Theatre, Stratford-upon-Avon, Warwicks CV37 6BB. *T:* Stratford-upon-Avon 296655.

HANDY, Gen. Thomas Troy, Hon. KBE 1945; DSC (US) 1918; DSM (US) 1945 (Oak Leaf Clusters, 1947 and 1954); Legion of Merit, 1945; formerly Deputy to General Ridgway (Supreme Allied Commander in Europe and Commander-in-Chief US European Command, 1952-53); *b* Tennessee, 11 March 1892; *s* of Rev. T. R. Handy and Caroline (*née* Hall); *m* 1920, Alma Hudson, Va; one *d*. *Educ:* Va Mil. Inst. (BS). Served European War, 1917-18 (DSC, French Croix de Guerre); War of 1939-45; when US a belligerent, 1942, became Asst Chief of Staff, Ops Div.; Dep. Chief of Staff, US Army, 1944; Gen. 1945. Comdg-Gen. 4th Army, Texas, 1947; C-in-C all Amer. Troops in Europe (except in Austria and Trieste), 1949-52; retired 1954. Grand Officer, Legion of Honour, 1951. *Address:* 122 Brandon Drive East, San Antonio, Texas 78209, USA.

HANES, Prof. Charles Samuel, FRS 1942; FRSC 1956; Professor of Biochemistry, University of Toronto, 1951-68, now Emeritus; Hon. Fellow of Downing College, Cambridge; *b* 1903; *m* 1931, Theodora Burleigh Auret, Johannesburg; one *d*. *Educ:* University of Toronto (BA 1925); University of Cambridge, PhD Cantab 1929; ScD Cantab 1952. Lately Reader in Plant Biochemistry, University of Cambridge, and Director, Agricultural Research Council Unit of Plant Biochemistry; previously Dir of Food Investigation, Dept of Scientific and Industrial Research. Flavelle Medal, Royal Society of Canada, 1958. *Address:* Department of Biochemistry, University of Toronto, Toronto M5S 1A1, Canada; 60 Beech Avenue, Apt 4, Toronto, Ont. M4E 3H4, Canada.

HANHAM, Leonard Edward; HM Diplomatic Service, retired; Consul-General, Amsterdam, 1978-80; *b* 23 April 1921; *m* 1945, Joyce Wrenn; two *s* two *d*. Served War, RN, 1939-48. Foreign Office, 1948; Vice-Consul: Rouen, 1949; Basra, 1950; Ponta Delgada, 1952; Foreign Office, 1955; 1st Sec. and Consul: Rangoon, 1957; Tegucigalpa, 1961; Foreign Office, 1963; Consul: Durban, 1965; Medan, 1969; FCO, 1972; Counsellor and Consul-Gen., Lisbon, 1975-78. *Address:* 26 First Avenue, Gillingham, Kent.

HANHAM, Sir Michael (William), 12th Bt *cr* 1667; DFC 1945; RAFVR; *b* 31 Oct. 1922; *s* of Patrick John Hanham (*d* 1965) and Dulcie (*d* 1979), *yr d* of William George Daffarn and *widow* of Lynn Hartley; *S* kinsman, Sir Henry Phelips Hanham, 11th Bt, 1973; *m* 1954, Margaret Jane, *d* of W/Cdr Harold Thomas, RAF retd, and Joy (*née* MacGeorge); one *s* one *d*. *Educ:* Winchester. Joined RAF 1942, as Aircrew Cadet; served No 8 (Pathfinder) Gp, Bomber Command, 1944-45; FO 1945. At end of war, retrained as Flying Control Officer; served UK and India, 1945-46; demobilised, 1946. Joined BOAC, 1947, Traffic Branch; qualified as Flight Operations Officer, 1954; served in Africa until 1961; resigned, 1961. Settled at Trillinghurst Farmhouse, Kent and started garden and cottage furniture making business, 1963; moved to Wimborne, 1974; now engaged with upkeep of family house and estate.

Governor of Minster and of Dumpton School. *Recreations:* conservation (Vice-Chm. Weald of Kent Preservation Soc., 1972-74 and Wimborne Civic Soc., 1977-); preservation of steam railways; sailing, gardening. *Heir: s* William John Edward Hanham [*b* 4 Sept. 1957; *m* 1982, Elizabeth Anne Keyworth, *yr d* of Paul Keyworth, Farnham and Mrs Keith Thomas, Petersfield]. *Address:* Deans Court, Wimborne, Dorset. *Clubs:* Pathfinder.

HANKEY, family name of **Baron Hankey.**

HANKEY, 2nd Baron *cr* 1939, of The Chart; **Robert Maurice Alers Hankey;** KCMG 1955 (CMG 1947); KCVO 1956; *b* 4 July 1905; *s* of 1st Baron Hankey, PC, GCB, GCMG, GCVO, FRS, and Adeline (*d* 1979), *d* of A. de Smidt; *S* father, 1963; *m* 1st, 1930, Frances Bevyl Stuart-Menteth (*d* 1957); two *s* two *d*; 2nd, 1962, Joanna Riddall Wright, *d* of late Rev. James Johnstone Wright. *Educ:* Rugby Sch.; New Coll., Oxford. Diplomatic Service, 1927; served Berlin, Paris, London, Warsaw, Bucharest, Cairo, Teheran, Madrid, Budapest. HM Ambassador at Stockholm, 1954-60. Permanent UK Delegate to OEEC and OECD, and Chm., Economic Policy Cttee, 1960-65; Vice-Pres., European Inst. of Business Administration, Fontainebleau, 1966-82. Dir, Alliance Bldg Soc., 1970-. Member: Internat. Council of United World Colleges, 1966-78; Council, Internat. Baccalaureati Foundn, Geneva, 1967-76. Pres., Anglo-Swedish Soc., 1969-75. Grand Cross of Order of the North Star (Sweden), 1954. *Recreations:* reading, tennis, ski-ing, music. *Heir: er s* Hon. Donald Robin Alers Hankey [*b* 12 June 1938; *m* 1st, 1963, Margaretha, *yr d* of H. Thorndahl, Copenhagen; 2nd, 1974, Eileen Désirée, *yr d* of Maj.-Gen. Stuart Battye, *qv*; two *d*]. *Address:* Hethe House, Cowden, Edenbridge, Kent. *T:* Cowden 538.
See also Sir John Benn, Hon. H. A. A. Hankey.

HANKEY, Col George Trevor, OBE 1945; TD; late RAMC (TA); Consulting Oral Surgeon; *b* London, 15 March 1900; *er s* of J. Trevor Hankey, Lingfield, Surrey; *m* 1933, Norah (*d* 1939), *y d* of late R. H. G. Coulson, Tynemouth; (one *s* decd); *m* 1945, Mary Isobel, *d* of late R. H. G. Coulson, Tynemouth. *Educ:* Oakham Sch; Guy's Hosp. LDSEng, 1922; LRCP, MRCS 1925; elected FDS, RCS, 1948, FRCS 1977; Consultant Dental Surgeon, St Bartholomew's Hospital, 1928-65, retd; Consultant, The London Hosp. Dental Sch., 1928-66; Lectr in Oral Surg., University of London. Fellow, Royal Society of Medicine; Examr in Dental Surgery, RCS England, 1948-54; Examiner in Dental and Oral Surgery, University of London, 1948-56; Pres. Odontological Section, RSM 1957-58 (now Hon. Mem.); Charles Tomes Lecturer, RCS, 1953; Mem. Bd Dent. Faculty RCS, 1958-73; Vice-Dean, 1966-67. John Tomes Prize, RCS, 1960, Mem. Bd Govs, London Hosp., 1954-63, and NE Metrop. Reg. Hosp. Bd, 1959-62; Founder Fellow, Brit. Assoc. Oral Surgeons, Pres., 1963-64; Sprawson Lectr, 1967. Served War, 1917-19; 2nd Lt, RHA; Commissioned RAMC(TA), 1927; OC 141 Field Ambulance, 1939; OC 12 Gen. Hosp., 1952; Hon. Col 1957-62. Served War of 1939-45 (despatches, prisoner, OBE). Officer, Legion of Merit, USA, 1951. *Publications:* chapter on Mandibular Joint Disorders, in Surgical Progress, 1960; contrib. Brit. Dental Jl and British Jl of Oral Surgery; various communications on Oral Surgery and Pathology to Proc. Royal Society of Medicine. *Recreations:* golf, fishing. *Address:* 22 East Hill Road, Oxted, Surrey RH8 9HZ. *T:* Oxted 3553.

HANKEY, Hon. Henry Arthur Alers, CMG 1960; CVO 1959; HM Diplomatic Service, retired; *b* 1 Sept. 1914; *y s* of 1st Baron Hankey, PC, GCB, GCMG, GCVO, FRS; *m* 1941, Vronwy Mary Fisher; three *s* one *d*. *Educ:* Rugby Sch.; New Coll., Oxford. Entered HM Diplomatic Service, 1937; Third Sec., HM Embassy, Paris, 1939; Second Sec., Madrid, 1942; First Sec., Rome, 1946; Consul, San Francisco, 1950; First Sec., Santiago, 1953; promoted Counsellor and apptd Head of American Dept, Foreign Office, Sept. 1956; Counsellor, HM Embassy, Beirut, 1962-66; Ambassador, Panama, 1966-69; Asst Under-Sec. of State, FCO, 1969-74. Director: Lloyds Bank International, 1975-80; Antofagasta (Chile) & Bolivia Railway Co. Ltd. *Recreations:* ski-ing, tennis, music. *Address:* Hosey Croft, Hosey Hill, Westerham, Kent. *T:* Westerham 62309. *Club:* United Oxford & Cambridge University.

HANKINSON, Cyril Francis James, Editor of Debrett's Peerage, 1935-62; *b* 4 Nov. 1895; *e s* of late Charles James Hankinson, MBE, JP (pseudonym Clive Holland), of Ealing, W5, and formerly of Bournemouth, and late Violet, *d* of William Downs, CE; *m* 1942, Lillian Louise (*d* 1976), *d* of late Walter Herbert Read, FSI, 29 Castlebar Road, Ealing, W5; one *s*. *Educ:* Queen Elizabeth's Grammar Sch., Wimborne, Dorset. European War, 1915-19 with Kite Balloon Section RFC, France, Belgium and subsequently at Air Ministry; Asst Editor of National Roll of the Great War, 1919-21; Asst Editor of Debrett, 1921-35. *Publications:* My Forty Years with Debrett, 1963; A Political History of Ealing, 1972. Contributor to London, Commonwealth, and American Press, and to Encyclopaedia Britannica and Chambers's Encyclopaedia, of articles regarding Royal Family, Peerage, Heraldry, etc; also lectured and broadcast on these subjects. *Recreations:* reading biographies, watching cricket. *Address:* 13 Welsby Court, Eaton Rise, Ealing, W5. *T:* 01-997 5018. *Club:* MCC.

HANKINSON, Sir Walter Crossfield, KCMG 1948 (CMG 1941); OBE 1936; MC; *b* 1894; *y s* of late A. W. Hankinson; *m* 1936, Sheila (*d* 1981), *d* of Dr Frederick Watson, Sydney. *Educ:* Manchester Grammar Sch.; Jesus Coll., Oxford. MA. Served European War, 1914-18 (MC); Colonial Office, 1920; transferred to Dominions Office, 1925; Acting Representative in

Australia of HM Govt in the United Kingdom, 1931-32 and 1935-36; Principal Private Sec. to successive Secretaries of State for Dominion Affairs, 1937-39; Principal Sec., Office of High Commissioner for the United Kingdom in Canada, 1939-41; Principal Sec. to United Kingdom Representative to Eire, 1942-43; Dep. High Comr in Australia, 1943-47; Acting High Comr June 1945-June 1946; UK High Commissioner in Ceylon, 1948-51; British Ambassador to Republic of Ireland, 1951-55, retired. *Recreation:* reading. *Address:* 25 Beauchamp Street, Deakin, Canberra, ACT 2600, Australia. *Club:* United Oxford & Cambridge University.

HANLEY, Gerald Anthony; author; *b* 17 Feb. 1916; *s* of Edward Michael Hanly and Bridget Maria Roche. *Publications:* Monsoon Victory, 1946; The Consul at Sunset, 1951; The Year of the Lion, 1953; Drinkers of Darkness, 1955; Without Love (Book Society Choice), 1957; The Journey Homeward (Book Society Choice), 1961; Gilligan's Last Elephant, 1962; See You in Yasukuni, 1969; Warriors and Strangers, 1971; Noble Descents, 1982. *Recreations:* music, languages. *Address:* c/o Gillon Aitken, 17 South Eaton Place, SW1.

HANLEY, Howard Granville, CBE 1975; MD, FRCS; Urologist, Royal Masonic Hospital London; Consulting Urologist, King Edward VII's Hospital for Officers, W1; Urological Consultant to the Army; Hon. Consulting Urologist, Royal Hospital, Chelsea; Dean of Institute of Basic Medical Sciences, Royal College of Surgeons, 1972-76; *b* 27 July 1909; *s* of F. T. Hanley; *m* 1939, Margaret Jeffrey; two *s*. *Educ:* St Bees Sch., Cumberland. MB 1932; MD 1934; FRCS 1937. Hunterian Prof., Royal College of Surgeons, 1955; Visiting Prof. of Urology: University of Calif, Los Angeles, 1958; Ohio State Univ., Columbus, 1961; University of Texas Southwestern Medical Sch., 1963; Tulane University, New Orleans, 1967; late Dean, Inst. of Urology, London Univ. Pres., Urological Section Royal Society of Medicine, 1964-65; Vice-Pres., RCS, 1979-81 (Mem. Council, 1969-). Fellow, Association of Surgeons of Great Britain and Ireland; Past Pres. (formerly Treasurer, Sec. and Vice-Pres.), British Assoc. Urological Surgeons; Sec., Hunterian Soc.; Hon. Librarian, Royal Society of Medicine. Member: Internat. Soc. Urology; German Urol. Soc.; Soc. Française d'Urologie; Med. Soc. London; Chelsea Clinical Soc. Corresp. Mem., Amer. Assoc. Genito-urinary Surgeons; Hon. Member: Mexican Urological Soc.; Western Sect. Amer. Urological Assoc. Liveryman, Worshipful Soc. of Apothecaries of London. Hon. FACS. *Publications:* Recent Advances in Urology, 1957; chapters in: British Surgical Practice, 1960; Modern Trends in Urology, 1960; A Text Book of Urology, 1960; contribs to jls on urology. *Recreation:* gardening. *Address:* 147 Harley Street, W1. *T:* 01-935 4444; Brandon House, North End Avenue, NW3 7HP. *T:* 01-458 2035. *Club:* Athenæum.

HANLEY, James; novelist; short story writer and playwright; *b* 1901. *Publications: novels:* Drift, 1930; Boy, 1931; Ebb and Flood, 1932; Captain Bottell, 1933; Resurrexit Dominus, 1934; The Furys, 1935; Stoker Bush, 1935; The Secret Journey, 1936; Hollow Sea, 1938; Our Time is Gone, 1940; The Ocean, 1941; No Directions, 1943; Sailor's Song, 1943; What Farrar Saw, 1946; Emily, 1948; Winter Song, 1950; House in the Valley (as Patric Shone), 1951, reissued as Against the Stream, 1982; The Closed Harbour, 1952; The Welsh Sonata, 1954; Levine, 1956; An End and a Beginning, 1958; Another World, 1972; A Woman in the Sky, 1973; A Dream Journey, 1976; A Kingdom, 1978; *short stories:* German Prisoner, 1930; A Passion Before Death, 1930; The Last Voyage, 1931; Men in Darkness, 1931, NY 1932; Stoker Haslett, 1932; Aria & Finale, 1932; Quartermaster Clausen, 1934; At Bay, 1935; Half-an-Eye, 1937; People Are Curious, 1938; At Bay and other stories, 1944; Crilley and other stories, 1945; Selected Stories, 1947; A Walk in the Wilderness, 1950; Collected Stories, 1953; The Darkness, 1973; Lost, 1979; *essays:* Grey Children (a sociological study), 1937; Between the Tides, 1939; Don Quixote Drowned, 1953; The Face of Winter, 1969; John Cowper Powys: A Man in the Corner, 1969; Herman Melville: A Man in the Customs House, 1971; *plays:* Say Nothing, 1962; The Inner Journey, 1965; Plays One, 1968; *Recreations:* fishing, music. *Address:* c/o David Higham Associates, 5/8 Lower John Street, Golden Square, W1R 4HA.

HANLEY, Sir Michael (Bowen), KCB 1974; *b* 24 Feb. 1918; *s* of late Prof. J. A. Hanley, PhD, ARCS; *m* 1957, Hon. Lorna Margaret Dorothy, *d* of late Hon. Claude Hope-Morley. *Educ:* Sedbergh School; Queen's Coll., Oxford (MA). Served War of 1939-45. *Address:* c/o Ministry of Defence, SW1.

HANLON, John Austin Thomas, JP; a Recorder of the Crown Court, 1972-77; *b* 18 Dec. 1905; *s* of late Thomas Peter Hanlon; *m* 1933, Marjorie Edith (Nesta), *d* of late John W. Waltham Taylor, Portsmouth. *Educ:* Portsmouth Grammar Sch. Joined Portsmouth Police, 1924; served through ranks CID, Det. Sgt, Det. Inspector; Dep. Chief Constable, Scarborough, 1934; Chief Constable, Leamington, 1938; Home Office Regional Comr's Staff, 1940; admitted student Gray's Inn, 1934; called to the Bar, 1944; practised NE Circuit. Deputy Chm. of Quarter Sessions: Co. Northumberland, 1955-65; Co. Durham, 1958-65; Chm., Co. Northumberland QS, 1965-71. Chm. of Traffic Comrs, Northern Traffic Area, 1953-75. JP Northumberland, 1954-. *Recreations:* athletics (British Team, Olympic Games, 1928; AAA 220 yds and 440 yds Champion, 1929; many internat. teams and events); fishing, shooting, motoring, music. *Address:* Hartburn, Morpeth, Northumberland NE61 4JB. *T:* Hartburn 269. *Club:* Northern Counties (Newcastle upon Tyne).

HANMER, Sir John (Wyndham Edward), 8th Bt *cr* 1774; JP; DL; *b* 27 Sept. 1928; *s* of Sir (Griffin Wyndham) Edward Hanmer, 7th Bt, and Aileen Mary (*d* 1967), *er d* of Captain J. E. Rogerson; *S* father, 1977; *m* 1954, Audrey Melissa, *d* of Major A. C. J. Congreve; two *s*. *Educ:* Eton. Captain (retired), The Royal Dragoons. JP Flintshire, 1971; High Sheriff of Clwyd, 1977; DL Clwyd, 1978. *Recreation:* shooting. *Heir: s* Wyndham Richard Guy Hanmer, *b* 27 Nov. 1955. *Address:* The Mere House, Hanmer, Whitchurch, Salop. *T:* Hanmer 383. *Club:* Army and Navy.

HANNAM, John Gordon; MP (C) Exeter, since 1970; *b* 2 Aug. 1929; *s* of Thomas William and Selina Hannam; *m* 1956, Wendy Macartney; two *d*. *Educ:* Yeovil Grammar Sch. Studied Agriculture, 1945–46. Served in: Royal Tank Regt (commissioned), 1947–48; Somerset LI (TA), 1949–51. Studied Hotel industry, 1950–52; Managing Dir, Hotels and Restaurant Co., 1952–61; Developed Motels, 1961–70; Chm., British Motels Fedn, 1967–74, Pres. 1974–80; Mem. Council, BTA, 1968–69; Mem. Economic Research Council, 1967–. PPS to: Minister for Industry, 1972–74; Chief Sec., Treasury, 1974. Secretary: Cons. Parly Trade Cttee, 1971–72; All-Party Disablement Gp, 1974–; Chairman: West Country Cons. Cttee, 1973–74; West Country Group of MPs, 1979–81; Cons. Party Energy Commn, 1979–; Vice-Chairman: Arts and Heritage Cttee, 1974–79; British Cttee of Internat. Rehabilitation, 1979–. Captain: Lords and Commons Tennis Club, 1975–; Lords and Commons Ski Club, 1977–81; Cdre, House of Commons Yacht Club, 1975. Mem., Snowdon Working Party on the Disabled, 1975–76. Vice-President: Disablement Income Gp; Royal Assoc. for Disability and Rehabilitation; Council, Action Research for the Crippled Child; Disabled Motorists Gp; Bd, Nat. Theatre. Mem., Glyndebourne Festival Soc. Pres., Exeter Chambers of Trade and Commerce. *Recreations:* music (opera), art (modern), sailing (anything), skiing (fast), Cresta toboganning (foolish); county tennis and hockey (Somerset tennis champion, 1953). *Address:* House of Commons, SW1A 0AA. *Clubs:* Royal Yacht Squadron, All England Lawn Tennis, International Lawn Tennis.

HANNAM, Michael Patrick Vivian, CBE 1980; HM Diplomatic Service, retired; Consul General, Jerusalem, 1976–80; *b* 13 Feb. 1920; *s* of Rev. Wilfrid L. Hannam, BD, and Dorothy (*née* Parker); *m* 1947, Sybil Huggins; one *s* one *d*. *Educ:* Westminster Sch. LMS Railway, 1937–40. Served in Army, 1940–46 (Major, RE). LMS Railway, 1946–50; Malayan Railway, 1950–60. FO, 1960–62; First Sec., British Embassy, Cairo, 1962–65; Principal British Trade Comr, Hong Kong, 1965–69 (and Consul, Macao, 1968–69); Counsellor, Tripoli, 1969–72; Counsellor (Economic and Commercial), Nairobi, 1972–73, Dep. High Commissioner, Nairobi, 1973–76. Chm. Governors, Rose Hill Sch., Tunbridge Wells, 1980. *Recreation:* music. *Address:* Little Oaklands, Langton Green, Kent TN3 0HP. *T:* Langton 2163. *Club:* Army and Navy.

HANNAN, William; insurance agent; *b* 30 Aug. 1906; *m* ; one *d*. *Educ:* North Kelvinside Secondary Sch. MP (Lab) Maryhill, Glasgow, 1945–Feb. 1974; Lord Commissioner of HM Treasury, 1946–51; an Opposition Whip, Nov. 1951–53; PPS to Rt Hon. George Brown as First Sec. and Sec. of State for Economic Affairs, 1964–66, as Sec. of State for Foreign Affairs, 1966–68; retired from Parliament, General Election, Feb. 1974. Mem., British Delegation to Council of Europe. Town Councillor, Glasgow, 1941–45. Mem. SDP, 1981–. *Recreation:* music. *Address:* 24 Galbraith Drive, Milngavie, Dunbartonshire.

HANNAY, David Hugh Alexander, CMG 1981; HM Diplomatic Service; Assistant Under-Secretary of State, Foreign and Commonwealth Office, since 1979; *b* 28 Sept. 1935; *s* of Julian Hannay; *m* 1961, Gillian Rex; four *s*. *Educ:* Winchester; New Coll., Oxford. Foreign Office, 1959–60; Tehran, 1960–61; 3rd Sec., Kabul, 1961–63; 2nd Sec., FO, 1963–65; 2nd, later 1st Sec., UK Delegn to European Communities, Brussels, 1965–70; 1st Sec., UK Negotiating Team with European Communities, 1970–72; Chef de Cabinet to Sir Christopher Soames, Vice President of EEC, 1973–77; Head of Energy, Science and Space Dept, FCO, 1977–79; Head of Middle East Dept, FCO, 1979. *Recreations:* travel, photography. *Address: c/o* Foreign and Commonwealth Office, SW1A 2AH. *Club:* Travellers'.

HANNAY, Elizabeth Anne Scott, MA; Head Mistress, Godolphin School, Salisbury, since 1980; *b* 28 Dec. 1942; *d* of Thomas Scott Hannay and Doreen Hewitt Hannay. *Educ:* Heathfield Sch., Ascot; St Hugh's Coll., Oxford (MA). Assistant Mistress: St Mary's Sch., Calne, 1966–70; Moreton Hall Sch., Shropshire, 1970–72; S Michael's, Burton Park, Petworth, 1973–75; Dep. Headmistress, St George's Sch., Ascot, 1975–80. *Address:* Downend Cottage, Tichborne, near Alresford, Hants SO24 0NA.

HANNEN, Rt. Rev. John Edward; *see* Caledonia, Bishop of.

HANNEN, Mrs Nicholas; *see* Seyler, Athene.

HANNIGAN, James Edgar, CB 1981; Deputy Secretary, Roads and Local Transport, Department of Transport, since 1980; *b* 12 March 1928; *s* of James Henry and Kathleen Hannigan; *m* 1955, Shirley Jean Bell; two *d*. *Educ:* Eastbourne Grammar Sch.; Sidney Sussex Coll., Cambridge (BA). Civil Service, 1951; Asst Sec., Housing Div., Min. of Housing and Local Govt, 1966–70; Asst Sec., Local Govt Div., DoE, 1970–72. Under Sec. 1972; Regional Dir for West Midlands, DoE, 1972–75; Chm., West Midlands Economic Planning Bd, 1972–75; Dir of Housing 'B', DoE, 1975–78; Dep.

Sec., NI Office, 1978–80. *Address:* 4 Pashley Road, Eastbourne, East Sussex.

HANON, Bernard; Officier, Ordre National du Mérite, 1980; Chairman and President, Régie Nationale des Usines Renault, since 1981; *b* 7 Jan. 1932; *s* of Max Hanon and Anne Smulevicz; *m* 1965, Ghislaine de Bragelongne; two *s*. *Educ:* HEC 1955; Columbia Univ. (MBA 1956; PhD 1962). Dir of Marketing, Renault Inc., USA, 1959–63; Asst Prof. of Management Sci., Grad. Sch. of Business, NY Univ., 1963–66; Head, Dept of Economic Studies and Programming, 1966–69, Dir of Corporate Planning and Inf. Systems, 1970–75, Régie Nat. des Usines Renault; Dir, Renault Automotive Ops, 1976; Executive Vice President: i/c Automobile Div., 1976–81; Renault Gp, 1981. *Address:* 34 quai du Point du Jour, 92109 Boulogne, France. *T:* 609 57 25. *Clubs:* Racing Club de France (Paris); Golf de St Germain.

HANROTT, Francis George Vivian, CBE 1981; Chief Officer, Technician Education Council, 1973–82; *b* 1 July 1921; *s* of late Howard Granville Hanrott and Phyllis Sarah Hanrott; *m* 1953, Eileen Winifred Appleton; three *d*. *Educ:* Westminster Sch.; King's Coll., Univ. of London (BA Hons). Served War, RN (Air Br.), 1940–45; Lieut (A) RNVR. Asst Master, St Marylebone Grammar Sch., 1948–50; Lectr, E Berks Coll. of Further Educn, 1950–53; Asst Educn Officer, Wilts, 1953–56; Staff Manager, GEC Applied Electronics Labs, 1956–59; Asst Educn Officer, Herts, 1959–66; Registrar and Sec., CNAA, 1966–73. Governor, Millfield Sch. Hon. MA Open Univ., 1977. *Recreations:* music, angling. *Address:* Coombe Down House, Salcombe Road, Malborough, Kingsbridge, Devon. *T:* Salcombe 2721.

HANSFORD, John Edgar, CB 1982; Under-Secretary, Defence Policy and Matériel Group, HM Treasury, 1976–82, retired; *b* 1 May 1922; *s* of Samuel George Hansford, ISO, MBE, and Winifred Louise Hansford; *m* 1947, Evelyn Agnes Whitehorn; one *s*. *Educ:* Whitgift Middle Sch., Croydon. Clerical Officer, Treasury, 1939. Served War of 1939–45: Private, Royal Sussex Regt, 1940; Lieutenant, Royal Fusiliers, 1943; served in: Africa, Mauritius, Ceylon, India, Burma, on secondment to King's African Rifles; demobilised, 1946. Exec. Officer, Treasury, 1946–50; Higher Exec. Officer, Regional Bd for Industry, Leeds, 1950–52; Exchange Control, Treasury, 1952–54; Agricultural Policy, Treasury, 1954–57; Sen. Exec. Officer, and Principal, Defence Div., Treasury, 1957–61; Principal, Social Security Div., Treasury, 1961–66; Public Enterprises Div., 1966–67; Overseas Develt Div., 1967–70; Asst Sec., Defence Policy and Matériel Div., Treasury, 1970–76; Under-Sec. in charge of Gp, 1976. *Recreations:* gardening, motoring.

HANSON, Sir Anthony (Leslie Oswald), 4th Bt, *cr* 1887; *b* 27 Nov. 1934; *s* of Sir Gerald Stanhope Hanson, 2nd Bt, and Flora Liebe (*d* 1956), *e d* of late Lieut-Col W. A. R. Blennerhassett; *S* half-brother, 1951; *m* 1964, Denise Jane (Tuppence), *e d* of R. S. Rolph. *Educ:* Hawtrey's, Savernake, Wilts; Gordonstoun, Elgin, Morayshire. Career in Royal Navy until 1955; farming, 1956–. *Recreation:* hunting.

HANSON, Dr Bertram Speakman, CMG 1963; DSO 1942; OBE 1941; ED; *b* 6 Jan. 1905; *s* of William Speakman Hanson and Maggie Aitken Hanson; *m* 1932, Mayne, *d* of T. J. Gilpin; three *s* one *d*. *Educ:* St Peter's Coll., Adelaide; University of Adelaide (MB, BS). War Service: Comd 2/8 Aust. Field Amb., 1940–43; ADMS, 9 Aust. Div., 1943–44. Pres., SA Branch of BMA, 1952–53; Pres. College of Radiologists of Australasia, 1961–62; Mem., Radiation Health Cttee of Nat. Health and Med. Research Coun., 1963–67; Hon. Radiotherapist, Royal Adelaide Hospital, 1952–64; Pres., The Australian Cancer Soc., 1964–67 (Gold Medal, 1979); Chairman: Exec. Board, Anti-Cancer Foundation, University of Adelaide, 1955–74; Anti-Cancer Foundation, Universities of South Aust., 1980–; Mem. Council, International Union Against Cancer, 1962–74. Pres., Nat. Trust of South Aust., 1979–82. FFR (Hon.) 1964; FAMA 1967; FRCR (Hon.) 1975. *Publications:* sundry addresses and papers in Med. Jl of Australia. *Recreation:* gardening. *Address:* Private Box, Longwood PO, Longwood, SA 5153, Australia. *Club:* Adelaide.

HANSON, Brian John Taylor; Registrar and Legal Adviser to General Synod of Church of England, since 1980; Joint Principal Registrar, Provinces of Canterbury and York, since 1980; *b* 23 Jan. 1939; *o s* of Benjamin John Hanson and Gwendoline Ada Hanson (*née* Taylor); *m* 1972, Deborah Mary Hazel, *yr d* of Lt-Col R. S. P. Dawson, OBE; two *s* two *d*. *Educ:* Hounslow Coll.; Law Society's Coll. of Law. Admitted solicitor, 1963; in private practice, Wilson Houlder & Co., 1963–65; Solicitor with Church Comrs, 1965–; Asst Legal Advr to General Synod, 1970–75. Sec., Legal Adv. Commn of General Synod, 1970–. *Publications:* (ed) The Canons of the Church of England, 2nd edn 1975; (ed) The Opinions of the Legal Board, 5th edn 1974. *Recreations:* the family, gardening, genealogy. *Address:* 17 Earlsfield Road, Wandsworth Common, SW18 3DB. *T:* 01-874 2895. *Club:* Royal Commonwealth Society.

HANSON, Sir (Charles) John, 3rd Bt *cr* 1918; Member of the London Stock Exchange; *b* 28 Feb. 1919; *o s* of Major Sir Charles Edwin Bourne Hanson, 2nd Bt, and Violet Sybil (*d* 1966), 3rd *d* of late John B. Johnstone, Coombe Cottage, Kingston Hill, Surrey; *S* father 1958; *m* 1st, 1944, Patricia Helen (marr. diss. 1968), *o c* of late Adm. Sir (Eric James) Patrick Brind, GBE, KCB; one *s* one *d*; 2nd, 1968, Mrs Helen Yorke, *d* of late Charles Ormonde Trew. *Educ:* Eton; Clare Coll., Cambridge. Late Captain, The Duke of Cornwall's Light Infantry; served War of 1939–45. *Heir: s* Charles Rupert Patrick Hanson [*b* 25 June 1945; *m* 1977, Wanda, *d* of Don Arturo Larrain, Santiago, Chile; one *s*]. *Address:* Gunn House, Shelfanger, near Diss, Norfolk. *T:* Diss 3207; 4 Holland Park Road, W14. *T:* 01-602 2652. *Club:* MCC.

HANSON, Derrick George; financial consultant; writer, director of companies; Chairman: Moneyguide Ltd, since 1978; Tring Hall Securities plc, since 1978; City of London & European Property Company Ltd, since 1980; Director: Midshires Building Society, since 1982; Phillips Group, Fine Art Auctioneers, since 1977; Albany Investment Trust plc, since 1980; Toye & Co. plc, since 1981; Barrister-at-Law; *b* 9 Feb. 1927; *s* of late John Henry Hanson and of Frances Elsie Hanson; *m* 1st, 1951, Daphne Elizabeth (*née* Marks) (decd); one *s* two *d* ; 2nd, 1974, Hazel Mary (*née* Buckley). *Educ:* Waterloo Grammar Sch.; London Univ. (LLB (Hons)); Liverpool Univ. (LLM). Called to Bar, Lincoln's Inn, 1952. Joined Martins Bank Ltd, 1943; Chief Trustee Manager, Martins Bank Ltd, 1963; Dir and Gen. Manager, Martins Bank Trust Co. Ltd, 1968; Dir and Gen. Manager, Barclays Bank Trust Co. Ltd, 1969-76; Chairman: Barclays Unicorn Ltd, 1972-76; Barclays Unicorn Internat. Ltd, 1974-76; Barclays Life Assce Co. Ltd, 1972-76; Director: Barclaytrust Property Management Ltd, 1971-76; Barclaytrust Internat. Ltd, 1972-76; Barclays Bank plc, Manchester Bd, 1976-77; Sen. Adviser (UK), Manufacturers Hanover Trust Co., 1977-79. Assessor, Cameron Tribunal regarding Bank Staff Relations, 1962; Dir, Oxford Univ. Business Summer Sch., 1971. Member: Commercial Property Cttee, British Property Fedn; NW Industrialists' Council, 1977-; South Sefton Health Authority, 1982-. Pres., Assoc. of Banking Teachers, 1979-. Mem. Council, Liverpool Univ., 1980-; Chm., Christian Arts Trust, 1980-. George Rae Prize of Inst. of Bankers; FIB. Hon. Fellow, City Univ. *Publications:* Within These Walls: a century of Methodism in Formby, 1974; Service Banking, 1979; Moneyguide: The Handbook of Personal Finance, 1981; contribs to financial jls. *Recreations:* golf, gardening, hill-walking. *Address:* Tower Grange, Grange Lane, Formby, Liverpool L37 7BR. *T:* Formby 74040. *Club:* Formby Golf (Formby, Lancs).

HANSON, Sir James (Edward), Kt 1976; Chairman: Hanson Trust, since 1964; Hanson Transport Group, since 1973; *b* 20 Jan. 1922; *s* of late Robert Hanson, CBE and late Louisa Ann (Cis) (*née* Rodgers); *m* 1959, Geraldine (*née* Kaelin); two *s* one *d*. War Service 1939-46, 7th Bn Duke of Wellington's Regt, etc. Underwriting Mem. of Lloyds, 1951-. Trustee: D'Oyly Carte Opera Trust; Hanson Fellowship of Surgery, Oxford Univ. Fellow, Cancer Res. Campaign. Life Member: BHS; BSJA; Hunter Improvement Soc.; Yorks CCC. Liveryman, Saddlers' Co.; Freeman, City of London; FRSA. *Recreations:* riding (former MFH Grove and Rufford), photography. *Address:* 180 Brompton Road, SW3 1HF. *T:* 01-589 7070. *Clubs:* Brooks's; Royal Thames Yacht; The Brook (NY).

HANSON, Sir John; see Hanson, Sir Charles John.

HANSON, John Gilbert, CBE 1979; Controller, Finance Division, British Council, since 1979; *b* 16 Nov. 1938; *s* of Gilbert Fretwell Hanson and Gladys Margaret (*née* Kay); *m* 1962, Margaret Clark; three *s*. *Educ:* Manchester Grammar Sch.; Wadham Coll., Oxford (BA Lit. Hum. 1961, MA 1964). Asst Principal, WO, 1961-63; British Council: Madras, India, 1963-66; ME Centre for Arab Studies, Lebanon, 1966-68; Rep., Bahrain, 1968-72; Dep. Controller, Educn and Science Div., 1972-75; Representative, Iran, and Counsellor (Cultural) British Embassy, Tehran, 1975-79. *Recreations:* books, music, sport, travel. *Address:* c/o The British Council, 10 Spring Gardens, SW1A 2BN. *T:* 01-930 8466. *Club:* Gymkhana (Madras).

HANSON, Neil; Under Secretary, and Controller, Newcastle upon Tyne Central Office, Department of Health and Social Security, since 1981; *b* 21 March 1923; *s* of late Reginald William Hanson and Lillian Hanson (*née* Benson); *m* 1st, 1950, Eileen Ashworth (*d* 1976); two *s* ; 2nd, 1977, Margaret Brown-Smelt. *Educ:* City of Leeds Sch. Served War, 1942-46, N Africa, Sicily, Italy. Jun. Clerk, Leeds Social Welfare Cttee, 1939; Clerical Officer, 1948-50, Exec. Officer, 1950-56, Nat. Assistance Bd; Manager, Suez and Hungarian Refugee Hostels, 1956-59; Higher Exec. Officer, 1959-62, Sen. Exec. Officer, 1963-66, Nat. Assistance Bd; Principal, Min. of Social Security, 1967-73; Sen. Principal, 1973-76, Asst Sec., 1976-80, DHSS. *Recreations:* cricket, music, walking. *Address:* 27 Croham Road, South Croydon CR2 7HB. *T:* 01-680 3494; Seacrest, North Parade, Whitley Bay NE26 1PA. *T:* Whitley Bay 850563.

HANSON, Rt. Rev. Richard Patrick Crosland, MA, DD; MRIA; Assistant Bishop, Diocese of Manchester, since 1973; Professor of Historical and Contemporary Theology, University of Manchester, 1973-82, now Emeritus; *b* 24 Nov. 1916; *s* of late Sir Philip Hanson, CB, and late Lady Hanson; *m* 1950, Mary Dorothy, *d* of late Canon John Powell; two *s* two *d*. *Educ:* Cheltenham Coll.; Trinity Coll., Dublin. 1st Hons BA in Classics also in Ancient Hist., 1938; BD with Theol. Exhibn, 1941; DD 1950; MA 1961. Asst Curate, St Mary's, Donnybrook, Dublin, and later in Banbridge, Co. Down, 1941-45; Vice-Principal, Queen's Coll., Birmingham, 1946-50; Vicar of St John's, Shuttleworth, dio. Manchester, 1950-52; Dept of Theol., Univ. of Nottingham, Lectr, Sen. Lectr and Reader, 1952-62; Lightfoot Prof. of Divinity, Univ. of Durham, and Canon of Durham, 1962-64; Prof. of Christian Theology, Univ. of Nottingham, 1964-70; Hon. Canon of Southwell, 1964-70; Canon Theologian of Coventry Cathedral, 1967-70; Examining Chaplain to the Bishop of Southwell, 1968; Bishop of Clogher, 1970-73. *Publications:* Origen's Doctrine of Tradition, 1954; II Corinthians

(commentary, Torch series), 1954; Allegory and Event, 1959; God: Creator, Saviour, Spirit, 1960; Tradition in the Early Church, 1962; New Clarendon Commentary on Acts, 1967; Saint Patrick: his origins and career, 1968; Groundwork for Unity, 1971; The Attractiveness of God, 1973; Mystery and Imagination: reflections upon Christianity, 1976; (ed, abridged and trans.), Justin Martyr's Dialogue with Trypho, 1963; Saint Patrick, Confession et Lettre à Coroticus, avec la collaboration de Cécile Blanc, 1978; Christian Priesthood Examined, 1979; Eucharistic Offering in the Early Church, 1979; (with A. T. Hanson) Reasonable Belief: a Survey of the Christian Faith, 1980; The Continuity of Christian Doctrine, 1981; contribs to: Institutionalism and Church Unity, 1963; The Anglican Synthesis, 1964; Vindications, 1966; (ed) Difficulties for Christian Belief, 1966; (co-ed) Christianity in Britain 300-700, 1968; (ed) Pelican Guide to Modern Theology, 1969-70; contribs to: A Dictionary of Christian Theology, 1969; Lambeth Essays on Ministry, 1969; Le Traité sur le Saint-Esprit de Saint Basile, 1969; Cambridge History of The Bible, vol. 1, 1970; Dogma and Formula in the Fathers (Studia Patristica XIII 2 etc, 1975); The Christian Attitude to Pagan Religions (Aufstieg und Niedergang der römischen Welt II.23.2, 1980); articles in: Jl of Theol Studies, Vigiliae Christianae, Expository Times, Theology, Modern Churchman, The Times. *Recreations:* tennis, drama. *Address:* 24 Styal Road, Wilmslow, Cheshire SK9 4AG.

HANTON, Alastair Kydd; Deputy Managing Director, National Girobank, Post Office, since 1982; *b* 10 Oct. 1926; *er s* of late Peter Hanton and Maude Hanton; *m* 1956, Margaret Mary (*née* Lumsden); two *s* one *d*. *Educ:* Mill Hill Sch.; Pembroke Coll., Cambridge. Commonwealth Develt Corp., 1948-54; ICFC, 1954-57; Unilever, 1957-66; Rio Tinto-Zinc, 1966-68; Post Office, 1968-. *Recreation:* forestry. *Address:* 8 Gilkes Crescent, Dulwich Village, SE21 7BS. *T:* 01-693 2618.

HANWORTH, 2nd Viscount, *cr* 1936, of Hanworth; **David Bertram Pollock,** CEng, MIMechE, FIEE, FRPS, FIQA; Baron, *cr* 1926; Bt, *cr* 1922; Lt-Col Royal Engineers, retired; Barrister-at-Law (Inner Temple), 1958; *b* 1 Aug. 1916; *s* of Charles Thomas Anderson Pollock and Alice Joyce Becher; *S* grandfather, 1936; *m* 1940, Isolda Rosamond, *yr d* of Geoffrey Parker, of Cairo; two *s* one *d*. *Educ:* Wellington Coll.; Trinity Coll., Cambridge. (Mechanical Science Tripos, 1939). Joined Social Democratic Alliance, 1981. *Publications:* Amateur Carbro Colour Prints, 1950; Amateur Dye Transfer Colour Prints, 1956. *Recreations:* ski-ing, photography, gardening, canal cruising. *Heir: s* Hon. David Stephen Geoffrey Pollock [*b* 16 Feb. 1946; *m* 1968, Elizabeth Liberty, *e d* of Lawrence Vambe; two *d*]. *Address:* Quoin Cottage, Shamley Green, Guildford, Surrey GU5 0UJ.
See also Sir W. L. Farrer.

HAPPOLD, Prof. Frank Charles, PhD, DSc (Manchester); Professor of Biochemistry, University of Leeds, 1946-67, Emeritus Professor, 1967; *b* Barrow-in-Furness, 23 Sept. 1902; *s* of Henry Happold and Emma Happold (*née* Ley); *m* 1926, A. Margaret M. Smith, MA, Brighton; one *s* one *d*. *Educ:* privately; Barrow Gram. Sch.; University of Manchester. PhD (Manchester) 1927; DSc (Manchester) 1934. University of Leeds: Department of Bacteriology, 1926-36; Dept of Physiology, 1936-46; Dept of Biochemistry, 1946-67; Research Prof., University of Florida, 1958-59. First Chm., Fedn of European Biochem. Socs, 1964. Leverhulme Fellowship to Harvard Univ. Post Graduate Medical Sch., 1939; Visiting Prof., University of Ghana, 1967-70; Royal Soc. Vis. Prof., Univ. of Science and Technology, Kumasi, 1972. Co-founder with wife of International Tramping Tours, 1929. Diplôme d'Honneur, Fedn European Biochem. Socs, 1974. Bronze Medal, Ville de Paris, 1964. *Publications:* numerous scientific publications, mainly in Microbiological Chemistry and Enzymology. *Recreations:* gardening and travel. *Address:* Three Roods, Arnside, Carnforth LA5 0BB.

HARARE (formerly **SALISBURY**), **Archbishop of,** (RC), since 1976; **Most Rev. Patrick Chakaipa;** *b* 20 June 1932; *s* of Chakaipa and Chokutaura. *Educ:* Chishawasha Minor and Regional Major Seminary, nr Salisbury; Kutama Teachers' Coll. Ecclesiastic qualifications in Philosophy and Theology; Teacher Training Cert. Asst priest, Makumbi Mission, 1967-69; Priest-in-Charge, All Souls Mission, Mtoko, 1969-73; Episcopal Vicar, Mtoko-Mrewa Area, 1970-73; Auxiliary Bishop of Salisbury, 1973-76. *Publications:* Karikoga, 1958; Pfumo reRopa, 1961; Rudo Ibofu, 1961; Garandichauya, 1963; Dzasukwa, 1967. *Recreation:* chess. *Address:* PO Box 8060, Causeway, Harare, Zimbabwe. *T:* 792125.

HARBERTON, 10th Viscount *cr* 1791; **Thomas de Vautort Pomeroy;** Baron Harberton 1783; *b* 19 Oct. 1910; *s* of 8th Viscount Harberton, OBE, and Mary Katherine (*d* 1971), *d* of A. W. Leatham; *S* brother, 1980; *m* 1978, Vilma, *widow* of Sir Alfred Butt, 1st Bt. *Educ:* Eton. Joined Welsh Guards, 1932; transferred to RAOC, 1939; served BEF, then in India; retired, 1952. *Heir: b* Hon. Robert William Pomeroy [*b* 29 Feb. 1916; *m* 1953, Winifred Anne, *d* of late Sir Arthur Colegate, MP; two *s*]. *Address:* 2 Brook Terrace, The Grange, St Peter Port, Guernsey, CI. *T:* Guernsey 22431. *Club:* Cavalry and Guards.

HARBISON, Air Vice-Marshal William, CB 1977; CBE 1965; AFC 1956; RAF, retired; Vice-President, British Aerospace Inc., Washington, DC, since 1979; *b* 11 April 1922; *s* of W. Harbison; *m* 1950, Helen, *d* of late William B. Geneva, Bloomington, Illinois; two *s*. *Educ:* Ballymena Academy, N Ireland. Joined RAF, 1941; 118 Sqdn Fighter Comd, 1943-46; 263, 257 and 64 Sqdns, 1946-48; Exchange Officer with 1st Fighter Group USAF, 1948-50;

Central Fighter Estabt, 1950-51; 4th Fighter Group USAF, Korea, 1952; 2nd ATAF Germany: comd No 67 Sqdn, 1952-55; HQ No 2 Group, 1955; psc 1956; Air Min. and All Weather OCU, 1957; comd No 29 All Weather Sqdn Fighter Comd, Acklington and Leuchars, 1958-59; British Defence Staffs, Washington, 1959-62; jssc 1962; comd RAF Leuchars Fighter Comd, 1963-65; ndc 1965-66; Gp Capt. Ops: HQ Fighter Comd, 1967-68; No 11 Group Strike Comd, 1968; Dir of Control (Ops), NATCS, 1968-72; Comdr RAF Staff, and Air Attaché, Washington, 1972-75; AOC 11 Group, RAF, 1975-77. *Recreations:* flying, motoring. *Address:* c/o Lloyds Bank, Cox's & King's Branch, 6 Pall Mall, SW1. *Club:* Royal Air Force.

HARBORD, Rev. Derek; a Judge of the High Court of Tanganyika, and Member, Court of Appeal for East Africa, 1953-59, retired; granted arms, 1967; *b* 25 July 1902; *yr s* of F. W. Harbord, Birkenhead, and Isabella (*née* Gardner), Sale; *m* Grace Rosalind (*d* 1969), *o d* of A. S. Fowles, Birmingham; two *s* one *d. Educ:* Mount Radford Sch., Exeter; Gray's Inn; St Michael's Theol Coll., Llandaff. Barrister-at-Law, 1925; Deacon, 1925; Priest, 1926; Curate, W Norwood, 1925-27; Streatham, 1927-29; Vicar, Stoke Lyne, 1929; Royal Army Chaplains Dept, 1929; Chaplain i/c Depot RAMC, Crookham, and V Lt Bde RA, Ewshott, 1929-30; Vicar, Hindolveston, 1930-33; Vicar, Good Shepherd, W Bromwich, 1933-35; resigned to become a Roman Catholic, 1935; reconciled with Anglican Communion and licensed to offic. Accra dioc., 1959-61; Rector of St Botolph-without-Aldgate with Holy Trinity, Minories, 1962-74; Fellow of Sion College, 1964-74; permission to officiate, dio. Rochester, 1974-. Practised at English Bar, 1935-40: Central Criminal Court, SE Circuit, Mddx and N London Sess; Sec., Bentham Cttee for Poor Litigants, 1937-40; Army Officers Emergency Reserve, 1938; HM Colonial Legal Service, 1940; Dist Magistrate and Coroner, Gold Coast, 1940-44; Registrar of High Court of N Rhodesia and High Sheriff of the Territory, 1944-46; Resident Magistrate and Coroner, N Rhodesia, 1946-53; Chm., Reinstatement in Civil Employment (Mining Industry) Cttee; Chm., Liquor Licensing Appeal Tribunal for N Rhodesia; admitted to Ghana Bar, 1959; Senior Lecturer, Ghana Sch. of Law, and Editor of Ghana Law Reports, 1959-61. *Publications:* Manual for Magistrates (N Rhodesia), 1951; Law Reports (N Rhodesia), 1952; Law Reports (Ghana), 1960. *Recreations:* keeping track of 22 grand and great grandchildren, reading modern theology and other whodunnits, pottering about. *Address:* Winterslow, Bayley's Hill, Sevenoaks, Kent TN14 6HS. *T:* Sevenoaks 452544. *Club:* Athenæum.

HARBORD-HAMOND, family name of **Baron Suffield.**

HARBOTTLE, Rev. Anthony Hall Harrison, MVO 1979; Rector of East Dean with Friston and Jevington, since 1981; Chaplain to the Queen, since 1968; *b* 3 Sept. 1925; *y s* of Alfred Charles Harbottle, ARIBA, and Ellen Muriel, *o d* of William Popham Harrison; *m* 1955, Gillian Mary, *o d* of Hugh Goodenough; three *s* one *d. Educ:* Sherborne Sch.; Christ's Coll., Cambridge (MA); Wycliffe Hall, Oxford. Served War in Royal Marines, 1944-46. Deacon 1952, priest 1953; Asst Curacies: Boxley, 1952-54; St Peter-in-Thanet, 1954-60; Rector of Sandhurst with Newenden, 1960-68; Chaplain of the Royal Chapel, Windsor Great Park, 1968-81. Founder Mem., Kent Trust for Nature Conservation, 1954. FRES 1971. *Publications:* contribs to entomological jls, on lepidoptera. *Recreations:* butterflies and moths, nature conservancy, entomology, ornithology, philately, coins, Treasury and bank notes, painting, cooking, lobstering. *Address:* East Dean Rectory, Eastbourne, East Sussex. *T:* East Dean 3266.

HARBOTTLE, (George) Laurence; Senior Partner, Harbottle & Lewis, Solicitors, since 1956; *b* 11 April 1924; *s* of George Harbottle and Winifred Ellen Benson Harbottle. *Educ:* The Leys Sch., Cambridge; Emmanuel Coll., Cambridge (MA). Solicitor 1952. Served War: commnd RA, 1942; Burma and India; Temp. Captain; Adjt 9th Fd Regt, 1945-47. Theatre Companies: Chairman: Theatre Centre, 1959-; Prospect, 1966-77; Royal Exchange (69), 1968-; Cambridge, 1969-; Director: The Watermill, 1970-75; The Bush (Alternative), 1975-77. Arts Council: Mem., 1976-77-78; Mem., Drama Panel, 1974-78; Chairman: Housing the Arts, 1977-78; Trng Cttee, 1977-78; Chm., Central Sch. of Speech and Drama, 1982- (Vice Chm., 1977); Dep. Chm., ICA, 1977-. Pres., Theatrical Management Assoc., 1979-. Member: Justice Cttee on Privacy, 1970; Theatres Trust, 1980-. *Recreations:* works of art, gardening, tennis. *Address:* 34 South Molton Street, W1Y 2BP. *T:* 01-629 7633. *Club:* Savile.

HARBOTTLE, Brig. Michael Neale, OBE 1959; General Secretary, World Disarmament Campaign, since 1980; *b* 7 Feb. 1917; *s* of Thomas Benfield Cecil and Kathleen Milicent Harbottle; *m* 1st, 1940, Alison Jean Humfress; one *s* one *d* ; 2nd, 1972, Eirwen Helen Simonds. *Educ:* Marlborough Coll.; Royal Military Coll., Sandhurst. Commissioned Oxfordshire and Buckinghamshire Light Infantry, 1937 (despatches 1944); commanded 1st Royal Green Jackets, 1959-62; Chief of Staff, UN Peacekeeping Force Cyprus, 1966-68; retired, 1968. Vice-Pres./Consultant, Internat. Peace Academy, 1970-81; Vis. Sen. Lectr (Peace Studies), Bradford Univ., 1974-79; Vice-Pres., UN Assoc. (UK), 1974-81; Cons., United World College of Atlantic, 1974-81; Mem., Management Cttee, Council for Educn in World Citizenship, 1978-81; Educn Planning Dir, British Council for Aid to Refugees (Vietnamese Sec.), 1979-80. *Publications:* The Impartial Soldier, 1970; The Blue Berets, 1971, 2nd edn 1975; (jtly) The Thin Blue Line: International Peacekeeping and its Future, 1974; The Knaves of Diamonds, 1976; (collator) Peacekeeper's Handbook, 1978; contributor to: Unofficial Diplomats, 1977 (USA); The Arab-Israel Conflict, Readings and Documents, 1977 (USA). *Recreations:*

cricket, golf, crossword puzzles. *Address:* 86d Hamilton Terrace, NW8 9UL. *T:* 01-289 0314.

HARCOURT, Geoffrey David, JP; RDI, DesRCA, FSIAD; freelance designer, since 1962; Consultant to Artifort, Dutch furniture manufacturer, since 1963; *b* 9 Aug. 1935; *s* of William and Barbara Harcourt; *m* 1965, Jean Mary Vaughan Pryce-Jones; one *s* one *d. Educ:* High Wycombe Sch. of Art; Royal Coll. of Art; DesRCA, Silver Medal 1960. FSIAD 1968; RDI 1978. Designer: Latham, Tyler, Jensen, Chicago, 1960-61; Jacob Jensen, Copenhagen, 1961; Andrew Pegram Ltd, London, 1961-62. Vis. Lectr, High Wycombe Coll. of Art and Design, 1963-74; Ext. Assessor for BA Hons degrees, Kingston Polytechnic, 1974-77, Loughborough Coll. of Art and Design, 1978-81, and at present for Belfast Polytechnic and Buckinghamshire Coll. of Higher Educn. Chair design for Artifort awarded first prize for creativity, Brussels, 1978; Mem., Design Awards Cttee, Design Council, 1979-80. Work exhibited: Designed in Britain, made abroad, Design Council, London and Glasgow, 1981. FRSA 1979. Freeman, City of London; Liveryman, Worshipful Co. of Furniture Makers. JP 1981. *Recreations:* making things, sailing, cooking. *Address:* The Old Vicarage, Benson, Oxfordshire.

HARCOURT-SMITH, Air Vice-Marshal David, DFC 1957; Assistant Chief of Air Staff (Operational Requirements), since 1980; *b* 14 Oct. 1931; *s* of late Air Vice-Marshal G. Harcourt-Smith, CB, CBE, MVO, and of M. Harcourt-Smith; *m* 1957, Mary (*née* Entwistle); two *s* one *d. Educ:* Felsted Sch.; RAF College. Commnd 1952; flying appts with Nos 11, 8 and 54 Squadrons; Staff Coll., 1962; OC No 54 Squadron, 1963-65; PSO to AOC-in-C, Tech. Training Comd, 1965-67; Defence Planning Staff, 1967-68; OC No 6 Squadron, 1969-70; Central Tactics and Trials Organisation, 1970-72; OC RAF Brüggen, 1972-74; Dir of Op. Requirements, 1974-76; RCDS, 1977; Comdt, RAF Coll., Cranwell, 1978-80. *Recreations:* tennis, walking, golf. *Address:* c/o Barclays Bank, Walters Ash, High Wycombe, Bucks. *Club:* Royal Air Force.

HARCUS, Rear-Adm. Ronald Albert, CB 1976; RN retired; *b* 25 Oct. 1921; *s* of Henry Alexander Harcus and Edith Maud (*née* Brough); *m* 1946, Jean Heckman; two *s* two *d. Educ:* St Olave's Grammar Sch.; RNC Greenwich. FIMarE, MBIM. Entered Royal Navy, 1937; Comdr 1956; Captain 1964; Rear-Adm. 1974; served in HM Ships Nigeria, Jamaica, Ocean, Dainty (despatches, Korea, 1953); Fleet Marine Engr Officer Home Fleet, 1965-67; Dep. Dir Fleet Maintenance, 1968-69; Captain, HMS Sultan, 1971-72; attended Royal Coll. of Defence Studies, 1973; Asst Chief of Fleet Support, MoD (Navy), 1974-76. Managing Director: RWO (Marine Equipment) Ltd, 1976-79; R. W. Owen Ltd, 1976-79. Chairman: Management Cttee, Brixham Seamen's Boys Home, 1981; NSPCC South Devon, 1981. *Recreations:* fishing, sailing. *Address:* Higher Leigh, Kingsbridge, Devon. *T:* Kingsbridge 2436.

HARDCASTLE, Alan John, FCA; Partner, Peat, Marwick, Mitchell & Co., since 1967; Vice-President, Institute of Chartered Accountants in England and Wales, 1982-83; *b* 1934; *m* ; two *s. Educ:* Haileybury Coll. Articled to B. W. Brixley, 1951-56; Nat. Service as Sub-Lieut RNVR, 1956-58. Inst. of Chartered Accountants in England and Wales: Mem. Council, 1974-; Chairman: Parly and Law Cttee, 1976-79; Technical Directorate Planning Cttee, 1977-; Professional Standards Cttee, 1981-; Vice-Chm., Gen. Purposes and Finance Cttee, 1981-; representative for ICA on Consultative Cttee of Accountancy Bodies, 1976-80. Chm., London and District Soc. of Chartered Accountants, 1973-74; Pres., Chartered Accountants Students' Soc. of London, 1976-80. Master, Co. of Chartered Accountants in England and Wales, 1978-79. Hon. Treas., Berkeley Square Ball. Mem. Court, Mary Rose Trust. *Address:* Institute of Chartered Accountants in England and Wales, Chartered Accountants' Hall, Moorgate Place, EC2.

HARDCASTLE, Prof. Jack Donald, FRCS; Professor of Surgery, University of Nottingham, since 1970; *b* 3 April 1933; *s* of Albert Hardcastle and Bertha (*née* Ellison); *m* 1965, Rosemary Hay-Shunker; one *s* one *d. Educ:* St Bartholomew's Grammar Sch., Newbury; Emmanuel Coll., Cambridge (Senior Scholar 1954; BA, MA; Windsor Postgrad. Schol.); London Hospital (Open Scholarship 1955; MB, BChir, MChir (Distinction)). MRCP 1961; FRCS 1962. House Phys./Surg., Resident Accoucheur, London Hosp., 1959-60; Ho. Surg. to Prof. Aird, Hammersmith Postgraduate Hosp., 1961-62; London Hospital: Research Asst, 1962; Lectr in Surgery, 1963; Registrar in Surgery, 1964; Registrar in Surgery, Thoracic Unit, 1965; Sen. Registrar in Surgery, 1965; Sen. Registrar, St Mark's Hosp., London, 1968; Sen. Lectr in Surgery, London Hosp., 1968. *Publications:* Isolated Organ Perfusion (with H. D. Ritchie), 1973; various scientific papers. *Recreation:* field sports. *Address:* Wild Briars, Goverton, Bleasby, Nottingham. *T:* Newark 830316.

HARDEN, Donald Benjamin, CBE 1969 (OBE 1956); MA Cantab, MA Oxon, PhD Mich; FSA; Director of the London Museum, 1956-70; Acting Director of the Museum of London, 1965-70; *b* Dublin, 8 July 1901; *er s* of late John Mason Harden and Constance Caroline Sparrow; *m* 1st, 1934, Cecil Ursula (*d* 1963), *e d* of late James Adolphus Harriss; one *d* ; 2nd, 1965, Dorothy May, *er d* of late Daniel Herbert McDonald. *Educ:* Kilkenny Coll.; Westminster Sch.; Trinity Coll., Cambridge; University of Michigan. Travelled in Italy and Tunisia, 1923-24; Senior Asst, Dept of Humanity, University of Aberdeen, 1924-26; Commonwealth Fund Fellow, University of Michigan, 1926-28; Asst University of Michigan Archæol. Exped. to Egypt, 1928-29; Asst Keeper, Dept of Antiquities, Ashmolean Museum, Oxford, 1929-45; Keeper, Dept of Antiquities, and Sec., Griffith Institute, 1945-56. Temp. Civil Servant Ministries of Supply and Production, 1940-45. Vice-Pres. Soc. of Antiquaries of London, 1949-53, 1964-67; President: Council for British Archæology, 1950-54; Oxford Architectural and Historical Soc., 1952-55; Section H, British Assoc., 1955; London and Middlesex Archæol. Soc., 1959-65; Royal Archæol. Inst., 1966-69; Internat. Assoc. for History of Glass, 1968-74; Chm., Directors' Conf. (Nat. Museums), 1968-70; Hon. Sec. Museums Assoc., 1949-54, Chm. Educ. Cttee 1954-59, Pres. 1960; Hon. Editor, Soc. for Medieval Archæology, 1957-73, Pres., 1975-77; Mem. of Council, British School of Archæology in Iraq; Member: Ancient Monuments Board for England, 1959-74; Royal Commission on Historical Monuments (England), 1963-71; Trustee, RAEC Museum. Mem., German Archaeol. Inst. Leverhulme Fellowship for research on ancient glass, 1953. Gold Medal, Soc. of Antiquaries, 1977. *Publications:* Roman Glass from Karanis, 1936; (with E. T. Leeds) The Anglo-Saxon Cemetery at Abingdon, Berks, 1936; The Phoenicians, 1962, rev. edns 1971, 1980; (jointly) Masterpieces of Glass, British Museum, 1968; Catalogue of Greek and Roman Glass in the British Museum, I, 1981; (ed) Dark-Age Britain, 1956; numerous articles on archæology and museums. *Address:* 12 St Andrew's Mansions, Dorset Street, W1H 3FD. *T:* 01-935 5121. *Club:* Athenæum.

HARDEN, Major James Richard Edwards, DSO; MC; DL; farmer; *b* 12 Dec. 1916; *s* of late Major J. E. Harden, DL, JP, Royal Irish Fusiliers, and L. G. C. Harden; *m* 1948, Ursula Joyce, *y d* of G. M. Strutt, Newhouse, Terling, Chelmsford, Essex; one *s* two *d*. *Educ:* Oriel House, St Asaph; Bedford Sch.; Sandhurst. Commissioned into Royal Tank Regt 1937; retired on agricultural release, 1947; MP (UU) for County Armagh, 1948-54. JP County Armagh, 1956, Cærnarvonshire, later Gwynedd, 1971; DL: Co. Armagh, 1946; Cærnarvonshire, later Gwynedd, 1968; High Sheriff, Cærnarvonshire, 1971-72. *Recreations:* shooting, fishing. *Address:* Nanhoran, Pwllheli, Gwynedd LL53 8DL. *T:* Botwnnog 610.

HARDERS, Sir Clarence Waldemar, Kt 1977; OBE 1969; Lawyer with Freehill, Hollingdale and Page, Canberra, ACT, since 1980; *b* Murtoa, 1 March 1915; *s* of E. W. Harders, Dimboola, Vic; *m* 1947, Gladys, *d* of E. Treasure; one *s* two *d*. *Educ:* Concordia Coll., Unley, S Australia; Adelaide Univ. (LLB). Joined Dept of the Attorney-General, 1947; Dep. Sec., 1965-70; Sec., 1970-79; Legal Adviser, Dept of Foreign Affairs, 1979-80. *Address:* c/o Freehill, Hollingdale and Page, 10th Floor, National Mutual Centre, Darwin Place, Canberra, ACT, Australia; 43 Stonehaven Crescent, Deakin, ACT 2600, Australia. *Clubs:* Commonwealth, National Press, Canberra Bowling (Canberra), Royal Automobile of Victoria.

HARDIE, Ven. Archibald George; Archdeacon of West Cumberland and Hon. Canon of Carlisle Cathedral, 1971-79; also Vicar of Haile, 1970-79; *b* 19 Dec. 1908; *s* of late Archbishop Hardie and late Mrs Hardie; *m* 1936, Rosalie Sheelagh Hamilton (*née* Jacob); three *s* one *d*. *Educ:* St Lawrence Coll., Ramsgate; Trinity Coll., Cambridge (MA); Westcott House, Cambridge. Curate of All Hallows, Lombard St, EC, and London Sec. of Student Christian Movement, 1934-36; Chaplain, Repton Sch., 1936-38; Vicar of St Alban, Golders Green, London, NW11, 1938-44; OCF. Rector of Hexham Abbey, 1944-63; Vicar and Rural Dean of Halifax, 1963-71, and Hon. Canon of Wakefield Cathedral. *Recreations:* tilling the soil and chewing the cud. *Address:* Grasslees Cottage, Swindon, Sharperton, Morpeth, Northumberland.

HARDIE, Sir Charles (Edgar Mathewes), Kt 1970; CBE 1963 (OBE 1943); chartered accountant; Partner in Dixon, Wilson and Co., 1934-81, Senior Partner, 1975-81; *b* 10 March 1910; *s* of Dr C. F. and Mrs R. F. Hardie (*née* Moore), Barnet, Herts; *m* 1st, 1937, Dorothy Jean (*née* Hobson) (*d* 1965); one *s* three *d* ; 2nd, 1966, Mrs Angela Richli, widow of Raymond Paul Richli; 3rd, 1975, Rosemary Margaret Harwood. *Educ:* Aldenham Sch. Qualified as Chartered Accountant, 1932; practised in London, 1934-81. War Service, 1939-44 (Col). Chairman: BOAC, 1969-70; Metropolitan Estate & Property Corp., 1964-71; White Fish Authority, 1967-73; Fitch Lovell Ltd, 1970-77; Director: British American and General Trust Ltd; British Printing Corp. Ltd (Chm., 1969-76); Royal Bank of Canada, 1969-81; Mann Egerton & Co. Ltd, 1959-80; Trust Houses Forte Ltd; Westminster Property Group Ltd; Hill Samuel Group Ltd, 1970-77. Dep. Chm., NAAFI, 1953-72; Member: BEA Board, 1968-70; Council, Inst. of Directors, 1966-80. Legion of Merit, USA, 1944. *Recreation:* yachting. *Address:* The Old School House, Sturminster Newton, Dorset; 207 Cranmer Court, Whiteheads Grove, SW3 3HG. See also C. J. M. Hardie.

HARDIE, (Charles) Jeremy (Mawdesley); Partner, Dixon Wilson & Co., since 1975; *b* 9 June 1938; *s* of Sir Charles Hardie, *qv* ; *m* 1st, 1962, Susan Chamberlain (marr. diss. 1976); two *s* two *d* ; 2nd, 1978, Xandra, Countess of Gowrie, *d* of late Col R. A. G. Bingley, CVO, DSO, OBE. *Educ:* Winchester Coll.; New Coll., Oxford (2nd Cl. Class. Hon. Mods, 1st Cl. Lit. Hum.); Nuffield Coll., Oxford (BPhil Econs). ACA 1965, Peat, Marwick, Mitchell & Co.; Nuffield Coll., Oxford, 1966-67; Jun. Res. Fellow, Trinity Coll., Oxford, 1967-68; Fellow and Tutor in Econs, Keble Coll., Oxford, 1968-75. Director: National Provident Instn, 1972-77, Dep. Chm., 1977-80, Chm., 1980-; Alexanders Discount Co. Ltd, 1978-, Dep. Chm., 1981-; Stockholders Investment Trust Ltd, 1979-; Unilever Pensions Investment Management Ltd, 1980-; IBM UK Pensions Trust Ltd, 1981-; NAAFI, 1981-;

John Swire and Sons, 1982-. Member: Monopolies and Mergers Commn, 1976- (Dep. Chm., 1980-); Council, Oxford Centre for Management Studies, 1978-; Hammersmith Health Authority, 1982-. Trustee, Esmée Fairbairn Charitable Trust, 1972-. *Recreations:* sailing, skiing. *Address:* The Old Rectory, Metton, Norfolk NR11 8QX. *T:* Cromer 761765.

HARDIE, Colin Graham; Official Fellow and Tutor in Classics, Magdalen College, Oxford, 1936-73; Public Orator of Oxford University, 1967-73; Hon. Professor of Ancient Literature, Royal Academy of Arts, since 1971; *b* 16 Feb. 1906; 3rd *s* of William Ross Hardie, Fellow of Balliol Coll. and Prof. of Humanity in Edinburgh Univ., and Isabella Watt Stevenson; *m* 1940, Christian Viola Mary Lucas; two *s*. *Educ:* Edinburgh Acad.; Balliol Coll., Oxford (Warner Exhibitioner and Hon. Scholar); 1st class Classical Moderations, 1926, and Lit Hum BA, 1928; MA, 1931; Craven Scholar, 1925; Ireland Scholar, 1925; Hertford Scholar, 1926; Gaisford Prize for Greek Prose, 1927; Junior Research Fellow of Balliol, 1928-29; Fellow and Classical Tutor, 1930-33; Dir of the British Sch. at Rome, 1933-36. *Publications:* Vitae Vergilianae antiquae, 1954; papers on Virgil and Dante. *Recreation:* gardening. *Address:* Rackham Cottage, Greatham, Pulborough, Sussex. *T:* Pulborough 3170.

HARDIE, Jeremy; see Hardie, C. J. M.

HARDIE, John William Somerville, MA Cantab; Hon. DLitt; Principal, Loughborough College of Education, 1963-73; *b* 21 Aug. 1912; 2nd *s* of late Most Rev. W. G. Hardie, CBE, DD; *m* 1938, Evelyn Chrystal, 5th *d* of J. C. Adkins, Uppingham, Rutland; one *s* two *d*. *Educ:* St Lawrence Coll., Ramsgate; Trinity Coll., Cambridge. Second Cl. Hon. (Div. I) Modern and Medieval Lang. Tripos. Asst Master St Lawrence Coll., 1933-35; Asst Master Uppingham Sch., 1935-40; Headmaster Cornwall Coll., Montego Bay, Jamaica 1940-42; Headmaster Jamaica Coll., Kingston, Jamaica, 1943-46; Asst Master Blundell's Sch., 1946-47; Headmaster, Canford Sch., 1947-60; Headmaster-Elect, Hesarack Sch., Iran, 1960-61; consultant Voluntary Service Overseas, 1961; Managing Dir, The Broadcasting Company of Northern Nigeria Ltd (seconded by Granada TV Ltd), 1961-62; Head of Information and Research, The Centre for Educational Television Overseas, Nuffield Lodge, 1962-63. Chm., HMC Overseas Cttee, 1958-60. Mem. Council Loughborough Univ. of Technology, 1968-76; a Governor, St Luke's Coll., Exeter, 1974-78. Hon. DLitt Loughborough, 1973. *Recreations:* hockey (Cambridge Univ. Hockey XI, 1931, 1932, Captain 1933; Welsh Hockey XI, 1931, 1932, Captain 1933-39); music, painting. *Address:* 15 Parc-an-Dillon, Portscatho, Truro, Cornwall TR2 5DU.

HARDIE, Miles Clayton; Director General, International Hospital Federation, since 1975; *b* 27 Feb. 1924; *s* of late Frederick Hardie and Estelle (*née* Clarke); *m* 1st, 1949, Pauline (marr. diss. 1974), *d* of late Sir Wilfrid Le Gros Clark, FRS; two *s* ; 2nd, 1974, Melissa, *d* of late James Witcher, Houston, Texas; two step *d*. *Educ:* Charterhouse; Oriel Coll., Oxford (MA). Served War, RAF, 1943-46. Admin. Asst, Hosp. for Sick Children, London, 1949-51; Sec., Victoria Hosp. for Children, 1951-55; Sec., Bahrain Govt Med. Dept, 1956-58; joined staff of King Edward's Hosp. Fund for London, 1958, Dep. Dir, King's Fund Centre, 1963-66, Dir, 1966-75. Hon. Sec., British Hosps Export Council, 1964-67, Mem. Council, 1967-75; Mem. Council, Nat. Assoc. of Leagues of Hosp. Friends, 1970-75; Member: Adv. Council, Nat. Corp. Care of Old People, 1973-76; Council of Management, MIND/Nat. Assoc. for Mental Health, 1967-; Man. Cttee of Spinal Injuries Assoc., 1975-79; Bd of Governors, Volunteer Centre, 1977-80; Court of Assistants, Salters' Co., 1969-79. Adviser to WHO, 1978-. *Recreations:* gardening, tennis, fell-walking. *Address:* 4 The Vineyard, Richmond, Surrey TW10 6EW. *T:* 01-940 5530.

HARDIE, William Francis Ross; President, Corpus Christi College, Oxford, 1950-69; Hon. Fellow, 1969; *b* 25 April 1902; *s* of late W. R. Hardie, Professor of Humanity, University of Edinburgh; *m* 1938, Isobel St Maur Macaulay; two *s*. *Educ:* Edinburgh Academy; Balliol Coll., Oxford. Fellow by Examination, Magdalen Coll., 1925; Fellow and Tutor in Philosophy, Corpus Christi Coll., Oxford, 1926-50. *Publications:* A Study in Plato, 1936; Aristotle's Ethical Theory, 1968, 2nd edn 1980; articles in philosophical journals. *Address:* Hogan, Frilford Heath, Abingdon, Oxon. *T:* Frilford Heath 390401.

HARDING, family name of **Baron Harding of Petherton.**

HARDING OF PETHERTON, 1st Baron *cr* 1958, of Nether Compton; **Field-Marshal Allan Francis, (John), Harding,** GCB 1951 (KCB 1944); CBE 1940; DSO 1941; MC; *b* 1896; *s* of late Francis E. Harding, Compton Way, S Petherton, Somerset; *m* 1927, Mary G. M., *d* of late Wilson Rooke, JP, Knutsford, Cheshire; one *s*. *Educ:* Ilminster Grammar Sch. Served European War, 1914-19, with TA and Machine Gun Corps (MC); Lieut Somerset Light Infantry 1920; Capt. 1923; psc 1928; Brigade Major British Force, Saar Plebiscite; Bt Major, 1935; Bt Lieut-Col 1938; Lieut-Col 1939; Brig. 1942; Maj.-Gen. 1942; Lieut-Gen. 1943; General, 1949; Field-Marshal, 1953. Served War of 1939-45 (despatches, CBE, DSO and two Bars, KCB). GOC CMF, 1946-47; GOC-in-C Southern Command, 1947-49; C-in-C, Far East Land Forces, 1949-51; Comdr-in-Chief, British Army of the Rhine, 1951-52; Chief of the Imperial Gen. Staff, 1952-55. Governor and Comdr-in-Chief, Cyprus, 1955-Nov. 1957. Director: Nat. Provincial Bank, 1957-69; Standard Bank, 1965-71; Williams (Hounslow) Ltd, 1962-74 (Chm. 1962-71);

Plessey Co. Ltd, 1967-70 (Dir, 1962-75; Dep. Chm., 1964-67; Chm., 1967-70). ADC Gen. to King George VI, 1950-52, to the Queen, 1952-53. Col 6th Gurkha Rifles, 1951-61; Col Somerset and Cornwall LI (Somerset LI, 1953-60); Col, The Life Guards, and Gold Stick to the Queen, 1957-64. KStJ. Hon. DCL (Durham). *Recreation:* gardening. *Heir:* s Major Hon. John Charles Harding [b 12 Feb. 1928; m 1966, Harriet, yr d of late Maj.-Gen. J. F. Hare, and Mrs D. E. Hare; two s one d]. *Address:* The Barton, Nether Compton, Sherborne, Dorset. *Clubs:* Army and Navy, Cavalry and Guards, Naval and Military.

HARDING, Prof. Dennis William, MA, DPhil; Abercromby Professor of Archaeology, University of Edinburgh, since 1977; b 11 April 1940; s of Charles Royston Harding and Marjorie Doris Harding. *Educ:* Keble Coll., Oxford (BA, MA, DPhil). Assistant Keeper, Dept of Antiquities, Ashmolean Museum, Oxford, 1965-66; Lecturer in Celtic Archaeology, 1966, Sen. Lectr, 1975-77, Univ. of Durham. Member: Board of Trustees, National Museum of Antiquities of Scotland, 1977-; Ancient Monuments Board for Scotland, 1979-. *Publications:* The Iron Age in the Upper Thames Basin, 1972; The Iron Age in Lowland Britain, 1974; (with A. J. Challis) Later Prehistory from the Trent to the Tyne, 1975; ed and contrib., Archaeology in the North: Report of the Northern Archaeological Survey, 1976; ed and contrib., Hillforts: later prehistoric earthworks in Britain and Ireland, 1976; Prehistoric Europe, 1978. *Recreation:* private flying. *Address:* Department of Archaeology, 16-20 George Square, Edinburgh EH8 9JZ. *T:* 031-667 1011. *Club:* Athenæum.

HARDING, Denys Wyatt, MA; Emeritus Professor of Psychology, University of London, since 1968; b 13 July 1906; s of Clement and Harriet Harding; m 1930, Jessie Muriel Ward; no c. *Educ:* Lowestoft Secondary Sch.; Emmanuel Coll., Cambridge. Investigator and Mem. of research staff, National Institute of Industrial Psychology, 1928-33; Asst (later Lecturer) in Social Psychology, London Sch. of Economics, 1933-38; Senior Lecturer in Psychology, University of Liverpool, 1938-45 (leave of absence for national service, 1941-44); part-time Lecturer in Psychology, University of Manchester, 1940-41 and 1944-45; Prof. of Psychology, Univ. of London, at Bedford Coll., 1945-68. Clark Lectr, Trinity Coll., Cambridge, 1971-72. Hon. Gen. Sec., British Psychological Soc., 1944-48. Mem. of editorial board of Scrutiny, a Quarterly Review, 1933-47. Editor, British Journal of Psychology (Gen. Section) 1948-54. *Publications:* The Impulse to Dominate, 1941; Social Psychology and Individual Values, 1953; Experience into Words: Essays on Poetry, 1963; Words into Rhythm, 1976; ed (with Gordon Bottomley) The Complete Works of Isaac Rosenberg, 1937; translated (with Erik Mesterton) Guest of Reality, by Pär Lagerkvist, 1936; various papers on psychology and literary criticism. *Address:* Ashbocking Old Vicarage, near Ipswich, IP6 9LG. *T:* Helmingham 347.

HARDING, Derek William; Secretary-General, British Computer Society, since 1976; b 16 Dec. 1930; o s of William Arthur Harding; m 1954, Daphne Sheila, yr d of Reginald Ernest Cooke; one d. *Educ:* Glendale Grammar Sch., London; Univ. of Bristol (BSc). FInstP, FIM, CEng. Develt Engr, Pye Ltd, 1954-56; Sen. Physics Master, Thornbury Grammar Sch., Bristol, 1956-60; Sen. Lectr in Physical Science, St Paul's Coll., Cheltenham, 1960-64; Asst Organiser, Nuffield Foundn Science Teaching Project, 1964-67; joined staff of Instn Metallurgists, 1967, Registrar-Sec., 1969-76. *Recreations:* sailing, music. *Address:* 16 Exeter Road, N14 5JY. *T:* 01-368 1463. *Clubs:* Athenæum, Little Ship.

HARDING, George William, CMG 1977; CVO 1972; HM Diplomatic Service; Ambassador to Brazil, since 1981; b 18 Jan. 1927; s of late Lt Col G. R. Harding, DSO, MBE, and of Grace Henley (née Darby); m 1955, Sheila Margaret Ormond Riddel; four s. *Educ:* Aldenham; St John's College, Cambridge. Royal Marines, 1945-48. Entered HM Foreign Service, 1950; served in Singapore, 1951-52; Burma, 1952-55; Paris, 1956-59; Santo Domingo, 1960-63; Mexico City, 1967-70; Paris, 1970-74; FCO, 1974-76; Ambassador to Peru, 1977-79; Asst Under-Sec. of State, FCO, 1979-81. *Address:* c/o Foreign and Commonwealth Office, SW1. *Clubs:* Garrick, Leander.

HARDING, Sir Harold (John Boyer), Kt 1968; FEng, FCGI, FICE; Consulting Civil Engineer; individual practice since 1956; b 6 Jan. 1900; s of late Arthur Boyer Harding, Elvetham, Hants, and Helen Clinton (née Lowe); m 1927, Sophie Helen Blair, d of E. Blair Leighton, RI; two s one d. *Educ:* Christ's Hosp.; City and Guilds (Engrg) Coll.; Imperial Coll. of Science and Technology; BSc, DIC. Joined John Mowlem & Co. Ltd, Civil Engrg Contractors, 1922; Dir, John Mowlem & Co., 1950-56; Dir, Soil Mechanics Ltd, 1949-56; Consultant to Channel Tunnel Study Group, 1958-70. Governor: Westminster Techn Coll., 1948-53; Northampton Engrg Coll., 1950-53; Imperial Coll., 1955-75. Mem., Building Res. Bd, 1952-55; Pres., ICE, 1963-64; Mem., Aberfan Disaster Tribunal, 1966-67; Vice-Pres., Parly and Scientific Cttee, 1968-72. James Forrest Lectr, ICE, 1952. Chm., British Tunnelling Soc., 1971-73. AMICE 1927; MICE 1939; FCGI 1952; FEng 1976; Fellow, Imperial Coll. of Science and Technology, 1968. Hon. DSc City Univ., 1970. Prix Coiseau, Soc. des Ingénieurs Civils de France, 1964. *Publications:* Tunnelling History and My Own Involvement, 1981; numerous papers to ICE. *Recreations:* varied. *Address:* 37 Monmouth Street, Topsham, Exeter, Devon. *T:* Topsham 3281.

HARDING, Hugh Alastair, CMG 1958; Under-Secretary, Department of Education and Science, 1967-77; b 4 May 1917; 2nd s of late Roland Charles

Harding, Norton-le-Moors, Staffordshire; m 1943, Florence Esnouf; one s one d. *Educ:* Rugby; Trinity Coll., Cambridge. Colonial Office, 1939; Asst Sec., 1950; Asst Sec., Treasury, 1961; Under-Sec., Treasury, 1962-64; Minister, UK Delegation to OECD, 1964-67. Served War of 1939-45, Army (Captain RA). *Address:* c/o National Westminster Bank, Town Hall Buildings, Tunstall, Stoke-on-Trent, Staffs.

HARDING, John Philip, PhD; Keeper of Zoology, British Museum (Natural History), 1954-71, retired; b 12 Nov. 1911; s of Philip William and Eleanor Harding, Rondebosch, Cape Town; m 1937, Sidnie Manton, PhD, ScD, FRS (d 1979); one s one d. *Educ:* Torquay; University Coll., Exeter; University of Cincinnati; King's Coll., Cambridge. Ministry of Agriculture and Fisheries, 1936-37; British Museum (Natural History), 1937-71. Vis. Prof., Westfield Coll., Univ. of London, 1971-77. *Publications:* scientific papers on Crustacea. *Recreations:* screen-printing, mechanical devices, photography. *Address:* 7 Ashcroft Close, Ringmer, Lewes, East Sussex. *T:* Ringmer 812385.

HARDING, Air Marshal Peter Robin, CB 1980; FBIM; Vice-Chief of the Air Staff, since 1982; b 2 Dec. 1933; s of Peter Harding and Elizabeth Kezia Clear; m 1955, Sheila Rosemary May; three s one d. *Educ:* Chingford High Sch. Joined RAF, 1952; Pilot, 12 Sqdn, 1954-57; QF1 and Flt Comdr, RAF Coll., Cranwell, 1957-60; Pilot, 1 Sqdn, RAAF, 1960-62; sc 1963; Air Secretary's Dept, MoD, 1964-66; OC, 18 Sqdn, Gutersloh and Acklington, 1966-69; jssc, Latimer, 1969-70; Sec. and 'C' Team Mem., Defence Policy Staff, MoD, 1970-71; Director, Air Staff, Briefing, MoD, 1971-74; Comdr, RAF Brüggen, 1974-76; Dir of Defence Policy, MoD, 1976-78; Asst Chief of Staff (Plans and Policy), SHAPE, 1978-80; AOC No 11 Group, 1981-82. ADC to the Queen, 1975. *Recreations:* music, pianoforte, bridge, ornithology. *Address:* Ministry of Defence, Whitehall, SW1A 2HB. *Club:* Royal Air Force.

HARDING, Air Vice-Marshal Ross Philip, CBE 1968; Specialist Adviser to House of Commons Defence Committee, since 1979; b 22 Jan. 1921; s of P. J. Harding, Salisbury; m 1948, Laurie Joy Gardner; three s. *Educ:* Bishop Wordsworth Sch., Salisbury; St Edmund Hall, Oxford (MA). No 41 Sqdn Fighter Comd and 2 TAF, 1943-45; RAF Staff Coll., Andover, 1951; Air Min. (ACAS Ops), 1952-54; CO No 96 Sqdn, Germany, 1955-58; Directing Staff, RAF Staff Coll., Andover, 1958-60; CO Oxford Univ. Air Sqdn, 1960-62; Dep. Chief, British Mil. Mission, Berlin, 1963-65; CO RAF Valley, 1965-68; Senior Directing Staff (Air), Jt Services Staff Coll., 1968-69; Defence and Air Attaché, Moscow, 1970-72; Dir of Personal Services 1, MoD (Air), 1973; Senior RAF Member, RCDS, 1974-76. *Recreations:* ski-ing, shooting. *Address:* Tally-Ho, 8 Hadrian's Close, Lower Bemerton, Salisbury, Wilts. *Club:* Royal Air Force.

HARDING, His Honour Rowe, LLD; DL; a Circuit Judge (formerly County Court Judge), 1953-76; Chairman, Swansea Porcelain Ltd, since 1976; b 10 Sept. 1901; s of late Albert Harding, Swansea, and Elizabeth Harding; m 1933, Elizabeth Adeline, d of John Owen George, Hirwaun, S Wales; one s one d (and one s decd). *Educ:* Gowerton County Sch.; Pembroke Coll., Cambridge. Qualified as solicitor, 1924; called to Bar, Inner Temple, 1928. Captain, Wales, Cambridge and Swansea Rugby football, 1924-28. Home Guard, 1940-44. Contested (Nat. L and C): Swansea East, 1945; Gower, 1950 and 1951. Mem., Swansea Town Council, 1945-48. Deputy Chairman, Quarter Sessions: Haverfordwest, 1945 (Chm., 1948-49): Breconshire, 1953 (Chm., 1955-71); Pembrokeshire, 1953 (Chm., 1971); Carmarthenshire, 1956-65; Glamorganshire, 1959-71; Chm., Radnorshire, QS, 1953-59. Dep. Chm., Local Tribunal for Conscientious Objectors in Wales, 1956-; Pres., Royal Institution of S Wales, 1960-61; Mem., Nat. Adv. Council on the Training of Magistrates, 1964; Chancellor: Diocese of St David's, 1949-; Diocese of Swansea and Brecon, 1974-82; former Mem., Governing and Rep. Bodies of Church in Wales; Judge of the Provincial Court of Church in Wales, 1966-; Member: Council, Lampeter Coll., 1945-80; Court of Governors, UC Swansea, 1956-81 (Council, 1957), Univ. of Wales, 1971-74; Chm., Welsh Regional Cttee, Cheshire Homes, 1961-63; Trustee, Cheshire Foundation, 1962-70. Vice-Pres., Welsh Rugby Union, 1953-56; Chm., Glamorgan County Cricket Club, 1959-76, Pres., 1977-. DL Glamorgan, later West Glamorgan, 1970. Hon. LLD Wales, 1971. *Publications:* Rugby Reminiscences and Opinions, 1929; Rugby in Wales, 1970. *Recreations:* walking, gardening, watching Rugby football and cricket. *Address:* The Old Rectory, Ilston, Gower, near Swansea, West Glamorgan. *T:* Penmaen 243.

HARDING, Wilfrid Gerald, CBE 1978; FRCP, FFCM, DPH; Area Medical Officer, Camden and Islington Area Health Authority (Teaching), since 1974; Consultant Physician in Community Medicine, University College Hospital, London, since 1971; Civil Consultant in Community Medicine to the RAF, since 1974; Hon. Lecturer, Department of Sociology, Bedford College, University of London, since 1969; President, Faculty of Community Medicine, Royal Colleges of Physicians of the UK, since 1975; b 17 March 1915; s of late Dr hc Ludwig Ernst Emil Hoffman and Marie Minna Eugenie (née Weisbach); m 1st, 1938, Britta Charlotta Haraldsdotter, Malmberg (marr. diss. 1970); three s; 2nd, 1973, Hilary Maxwell. *Educ:* Französisches Gymnasium, Berlin; Süddeutsches Landerziehungsheim, Schondorf, Bavaria; Woodbrooke Coll., Selly Oak, Birmingham; University Coll. London; University Coll. Home Med. Sch. (interned twice in 1939 and 1940). MRCS, LRCP 1941; DPH London 1949; MRCP 1968; FFCM 1972; FRCP 1972. Ho. Phys. and Ho. Surg., UCH, 1941-42; Asst MOH, City of Oxford, 1942-43; RAMC, 1943-47, Field Units in NW Europe (wounded in Normandy), 1

Corps Staff and Mil. Govt, Lt-Col (Hygiene Specialist). Public Health Officer, Ruhr Dist of Germany, CCG, 1947-48; London Sch. of Hygiene and Tropical Med., 1948-49; career posts in London public health service, 1949-64. Lectr in Public Health, Midwife Teachers Trng Coll., 1951-62; MOH, London Bor. of Camden, and Principal Sch. MO, ILEA, 1965-74. Chm. of Council, Soc. of MOH, 1966-71 (Pres. 1971-72); Chm., Prov. Bd of FCM, Royal Colls of Physicians of UK, 1971-72 (Vice-Pres., 1972-75, Pres., 1975-78). Member: Central Health Services Council and Standing Med. Adv. Cttee, 1966-71 and 1975-; Standing Mental Health Adv. Cttee, 1966-71; Sub-cttees on Org. of Gp Practices, 1968-71, and on Med. Rehabilitation, 1968-72; Bd of Studies in Preventive Med. and Public Health, Univ. of London, 1965-; Council, UCH Med. Sch., 1965-; Ct of Govs and Bd of Management, London Sch. of Hyg. and Trop. Med., 1968-; Council for Educn and Trng of Health Visitors, 1965-77; Council, ASH, 1970-73 and 1978-; Public Health Laboratory Service Bd, 1972-; Adv. Cttee on Distinction Awards, 1975-; Armed Services Med. Adv. Bd, 1975-; DHSS Working Party on Neural Tube Defects, 1978-; Children's Jt Cttee (Central Health Services Council and Personal Social Services Council), 1978-; GMC, 1979-. Hon. Advr, Office of Health Econs, 1977-. *Publications:* papers on public health and community med. in medical books and jls; Parkes Centenary Meml Lecture (Community, Health and Service), 1976. *Recreations:* watching river birds, music, wine. *Address:* 1 Mill Cottages, High Street, Farningham, Dartford DA4 0DW. *T:* Farningham 862733. *Club:* Athenæum.

HARDING, William; *see* Harding, G. W.

HARDINGE, family name of **Viscount Hardinge** and **Baron Hardinge of Penshurst.**

HARDINGE, 5th Viscount *cr* 1846, of Lahore and of King's Newton, Derbyshire; **Henry Nicholas Paul Hardinge;** Chief Executive, Orion Royal Bank Ltd, since 1981; *b* 15 Aug. 1929; *s* of 4th Viscount Hardinge, MBE, and of Margaret Elizabeth Arnott, *d* of Hugh Fleming, Ottawa; *S* father, 1979; *m* 1st, 1955, Zoë Anne (marr. diss. 1982), *d* of the Hon. H. de M. Molson, OBE, Montreal; three *s*; 2nd, 1982, Baroness Florence von Oppenheim. *Educ:* Harrow School. Commissioned into 7th Queen's Own Hussars, 1949-54. Joined The Royal Bank of Canada, 1954. *Recreations:* hunting, shooting, fishing. *Heir:* *s* Hon. Charles Henry Nicholas Hardinge, *b* 25 Aug. 1956. *Address:* 5 Somerset Square, W14 8EE. *T:* 01-602 5169. *Clubs:* Cavalry and Guards; Mount Royal (Montreal).

HARDINGE OF PENSHURST, 3rd Baron *cr* 1910; **George Edward Charles Hardinge;** *b* 31 Oct. 1921; *o* *s* of 2nd Baron Hardinge of Penshurst, PC, GCB, GCVO, MC, and Helen Mary Cecil (*d* 1979); *S* father, 1960; *m* 1st, 1944, Janet Christine Goschen (marr. diss. 1962, she *d* 1970), *d* of late Lt-Col F. C. C. Balfour, CIE, CVO, CBE, MC; three *s*; 2nd, 1966, Margaret Trezise; one *s*, and one step-*s*, now adopted. *Educ:* Eton; Royal Naval College, Dartmouth. RN 1940-47; subsequently in publishing. *Publication:* An Incompleat Angler, 1976. *Recreations:* reading, fishing, gardening. *Heir:* *s* Hon. Julian Alexander Hardinge, *b* 23 Aug. 1945. *Address:* Chalkfield, Friston, East Sussex. *T:* East Dean 3155. *Club:* Brooks's.
See also Lt-Col Sir J. F. D. Johnston.

HARDINGE, Sir Robert Arnold, 7th Bt *cr* 1801; *b* 19 Dec. 1914; *s* of Sir Robert Hardinge, 6th Bt and Emma Vera, *d* of Charles Arnold; *S* father, 1973. *Heir:* kinsman 5th Viscount Hardinge, *qv.*

HARDINGHAM, Sir Robert (Ernest), Kt 1969; CMG 1953; OBE 1947; Chief Executive, Air Registration Board, 1947-68; *b* 16 Dec. 1903; *s* of late Robert Henry Hardingham and Florence Elizabeth Hardingham; *m* 1929, I. Everett; one *s* one *d. Educ:* Farnborough; de Havilland Technical Coll. RAE Farnborough, 1918-21; de Havilland Aircraft Co., 1921-34; Air Min., 1934-37; Air Registration Board, 1937-68. Pres., Soc. of Licenced Aircraft Engineers and Technologists, 1968-72. Liveryman, Guild of Air Pilots and Navigators, 1966. CEng; FRAeS 1949 (Empire and Commonwealth Lecturer, 1952). Wakefield Gold Medal, RAeS, 1965; Silver Medal, Royal Aero Club, 1965. Cavaliere Ordino Merito della Repubblica Italiana. *Publications:* many technical papers. *Recreation:* golf. *Address:* Wortheal House, Southam Lane, Cheltenham, GL52 3NY. *T:* Cheltenham 36765. *Club:* Naval and Military.

HARDMAN, Amy Elizabeth; Matron, The Royal Free Hospital, London, 1953-70; *b* 23 Dec. 1909; *d* of late Charlton James Hardman and Elizabeth Clark. *Educ:* Godolphin and Latymer Sch., Hammersmith; Rosebery Sch. for Girls, Epsom. General Training, St Bartholomew's Hosp., London, 1930-34 (SRN); Midwifery Training, Kingston County Hosp., 1937 (SCM); Asst Matron, Sister Tutor, Metropolitan Hosp., E8, 1937-42; Matron, The Guest Hospital, Dudley, Worcs, 1942-49; Matron, St Margaret's Hospital, Epping, 1949-53. *Publication:* An Introduction to Ward Management, 1970. *Address:* Apple Tree Cottage, Main Street, Northiam, Rye, East Sussex. *T:* Northiam 2319.

HARDMAN, David Rennie, MA, LLB; JP; Secretary, Cassel Educational Trust; Secretary, Stafford Cripps Memorial Appeal and Trustees; *b* 1901; *s* of David Hardman, MSc, and Isobel Rennie, Mansfield House University Settlement; *m* 1928, Freda Mary Riley; one *d*; *m* 1946, Barbara, *er d* of late Herbert Lambert, Bath; one *s* one *d. Educ:* Coleraine Academical Instn; Christ's Coll., Cambridge. Mem. Railway Clerks' Assoc., 1919-21; Pres.

Cambridge Union Soc., 1925; Contested (Lab) Cambridge Borough, 1929. Cambridge Borough Councillor and Cambridge County Councillor, 1937-46; late Chm. Cambs Education Cttee; JP Cambridge, 1941-47; MP (Lab) Darlington, 1945-51; Parl. Sec., Min. of Education, 1945-51; contested (Lab) Rushcliffe Div. of Notts, 1955; leader UK delegns UNESCO, Paris 1946, Mexico 1947, Beirut 1948, Paris 1949, Florence 1950, Paris 1951; Vice-Pres. Shaw Soc.; Pres., Holiday Fellowship, 1962-69. Visiting Prof. of English Literature, Elmira, New York, 1964-66. Barclay Acheson Prof. Internat. Studies, Macalester Coll., Minn, 1967. *Publications:* What about Shakespeare?, 1939; Poems of Love and Affairs, 1949; Telscombe: A Sussex Village, 1964; History Holiday Fellowship 1913-1940, 1981. *Recreation:* gardening. *Address:* Bankyfield, Hurstpierpoint, West Sussex. *T:* Brighton 833194. *Club:* Savile.

HARDMAN, Sir Fred, Kt 1982; MBE 1972; Board Member, Telford Development Corporation, since 1980; Chairman, Taws (Printers) PLC, Telford, since 1983; *b* 26 Sept. 1914; *s* of Fred Hardman (killed in action, 1915, Hooge; KSLI) and Annie (*née* Walsh); *m* 1941, Ennis Lawson; one *s. Educ:* Basle, Switzerland. Served Royal Air Force, 1936-46. Conservative Political Agent, 1946-52; Senior Executive, Lectr and Public Relations, Rentokil, 1952-74; Industrial Relations Consultant, 1974-. President, Coalbrookdale, Royal British Legion, 1970-. Chairman: Conservative Trade Unionists, 1977-80; Nat. Union of Conservative Assocs, 1980-81; Conservative Party Conference, Blackpool, 1981. *Address:* Coppice House, Coalbrookdale, Telford, Shropshire. *T:* Ironbridge 3423. *Clubs:* St Stephen's Constitutional, Carlton.

HARDMAN, Sir Henry, KCB 1962 (CB 1956); *b* 15 Dec. 1905; *s* of late Harry and late Bertha Hardman; *m* 1937, Helen Diana, *d* of late Robert Carr Bosanquet; one *s* two *d. Educ:* Manchester Central High Sch.; University of Manchester. Lecturer for Workers' Educational Association, 1929-34; Economics Tutor, University of Leeds, 1934-45; joined Ministry of Food, 1940; Deputy Head, British Food Mission to N America, 1946-48; Under-Sec., Ministry of Food, 1948-53; Minister, UK Permanent Delegation, Paris, 1953-54; Dep. Sec., Ministry of Agriculture, Fisheries and Food, 1955-60; Dep. Sec., Ministry of Aviation, 1960; Permanent Sec., 1961-63: Permanent Sec., Ministry of Defence, 1963-64; Permanent Under Sec. of State, Min. of Defence, 1964-66. Mem., Monopolies Commn, 1967-70 (Dep. Chm., 1967-68); Chm., Cttee of enquiry into the Post Office pay dispute, 1971; Consultant to CSD on dispersal of govt work from London, 1971-73 (report published, 1973). Chairman: Covent Garden Mkt Authority, 1967-75; Home-Grown Cereals Authority, 1968-77. Governor and Trustee, Reserve Bank of Rhodesia, 1967-79. Hon. LLD Manchester, 1965. *Address:* 33 Durand Gardens, SW9 0PS. *T:* 01-582 1757. *Club:* Reform. .

HARDMAN, James Arthur, MBE 1968; HM Diplomatic Service; Consul (Commercial) Düsseldorf, since 1979; *b* 12 Sept. 1929; *er s* of late James Sidney Hardman and Rachel Hardman; *m* 1953, Enid Mary Hunter; two *s. Educ:* Manchester Grammar Sch.; Manchester Univ. (BA Hons 1950). FCIS (FCCS 1964). Served in Intelligence Corps, 1951-53; Admiralty, 1953-54. HM Foreign Service, 1954; served: Tehran, 1955; FO, 2nd Sec., 1960; Bonn, 2nd, later 1st, Sec. (Comm.), 1962; Atlanta, Consul, 1967; New York, Consul (Comm.), 1970; FCO, Dep. Dir Diplomatic Service Language Centre, 1972; Consul-Gen., Strasbourg, 1975-79. *Address:* c/o Foreign and Commonwealth Office, SW1. *Club:* Civil Service.

HARDWICK, Charles Aubrey, CMG 1971; QC (Australia); Vice-Patron, Benevolent Society of New South Wales, since 1973 (Director, 1947-73; Vice-President, 1958-61; President, 1961-73); *b* 29 July 1885; 2nd *s* of G. W. Hardwick, Rylstone, NSW; *m* 1922, Maisie Jean (*d* 1971), *er d* of David Fell, MLA, Sydney and Rout's Green, Bledlow Ridge, Bucks; two *s* (and one *s* decd). *Educ:* Rylstone Public Sch.; Univ. of Sydney (evening student). BA 1913, LLB 1915. NSW Dept of Attorney-General and of Justice, 1902-14; called to NSW Bar, 1915, in practice, 1915-76; KC 1934; Actg Judge, Supreme Court of NSW, 1939. Foundn Mem., NSW Inst. of Hospital Almoners, Treas. 1937-63; Dir, Prince Henry's Hosp., 1936-44; Vice-Chm., Metropolitan Hosps Contribution Fund, 1938-44. Mem., Sydney Cricket Ground, 1909-. *Recreation:* reading. *Address:* Wentworth Chambers, 180 Phillip Street, Sydney, NSW 2000, Australia; Unit 2, 4 Milner Crescent, Wollstonecraft, NSW 2065, Australia. *T:* Sydney 43-4825. *Clubs:* Australian, Australian Jockey (Life Mem.), Sydney Cricket Ground (Hon. Mem.) (Sydney).

HARDWICK, Christopher, MD, FRCP; Physician Emeritus, Guy's Hospital, since 1976; *b* 13 Jan. 1911; *s* of Thomas Mold Hardwick and Harriet Taylor; *m* 1938, Joan Dorothy Plummer; two *s. Educ:* Berkhamsted Sch.; Trinity Hall, Cambridge; Middlesex Hospital. MRCS, LRCP 1935; MA (Cambridge) 1937; MD (Cambridge) 1940; FRCP 1947. House Physician, House Surgeon and Med. Registrar, Middlesex Hosp., 1935 and 1938-41; House physician and Registrar, Hosp. for Sick Children, Gt Ormond Street, 1936-38. Wing Comdr, Medical Specialist, RAF Med. Service, 1941-46. Physician, Guy's Hosp., 1946-76. Hon. Vis. Phys., Johns Hopkins Hosp., Baltimore, 1954. Mem. Council, RCP, 1965-68; Mem. Board of Governors, Guy's Hospital, 1967-74. Chm., British Diabetic Assoc., 1974-80. *Publications:* contribs to medical literature. *Recreations:* gardening, reading. *Address:* Blue Firs, Broomfield Park, Westcott, Dorking, Surrey RH4 3QQ.

HARDWICK, Donald, CBE 1980; PhD; Chairman: Steel Division, Johnson & Firth Brown Ltd, since 1975; Sheffield Forgemasters, since 1983 (Firth

Brown Ltd, 1974-83); *b* 1926; *m* 1950, Dorothy Mary Hardwick; two *s. Educ:* Tadcaster Grammar Sch.; Sheffield Univ. (BMet 1st Cl. Hons 1947, Mappin Medal; PhD 1954). FIM. After appointments with English Electric Co., BISRA, and BSA Gp Research Centre, became first C. H. Desch Res. Fellow, Sheffield Univ. Joined Brown Firth Res. Laboratories, 1959; Man. Dir, Firth Brown Ltd, 1974-78; Mem. Bd, Johnson & Firth Brown, on amalgamation with Richard Johnson & Nephew, 1973. Director, Mitchell Somers Gp, 1974-; Pres., BISPA, 1977. *Recreations:* fell walking, gardening. *Address:* Steel Division, Johnson & Firth Brown Ltd, Atlas Works, Sheffield S4 7TE. *T:* Sheffield 20081; 43 Dore Road, Dore, Sheffield.

HARDWICK, Prof. James Leslie, MDS, MSc, PhD; FDSRCS; Professor of Preventive Dentistry, University of Manchester, 1960-78, now Emeritus; *b* 27 March 1913; *o s* of George Hardwicke and Mary Ann Hardwick; *m* 1954, Eileen Margaret Isobel Gibson; two *s* two *d. Educ:* Rugby Sch.; Birmingham Univ. MDS 1948, PhD 1950, Birmingham; FDSRCS 1954; MSc 1964. Private and hospital dental practice, 1935-39. Served War of 1939-45, Army Dental Corps. University of Birmingham: Lecturer, 1945-48, Sen. Lecturer in Operative Dental Surgery, 1948-52; Reader in Dental Surgery, 1952-60. *Publications:* editor of and contributor to dental and other scientific journals and textbooks. *Address:* 167 Stanley Road, Cheadle Hulme, Cheshire SK8 6RF. *T:* 061-437 3555.

HARDWICK, Michael John Drinkrow; author and dramatist; *b* 10 Sept. 1924; *s* of George Drinkrow Hardwick and Katharine Augusta Townend; *m* 1961, Mollie (*née* Greenhalgh), *qv* ; one *s. Educ:* Leeds Grammar Sch. Morley Observer, 1942-43; Indian Army, 1943-47, served in India and Japan, Captain 1944. Dir, NZ Nat. Film Unit, 1948-53; Freedom Newspaper, NZ, 1953-54; Drama Dept, BBC (Radio), 1958-63; freelance, 1963-. FRSA 1966. *Publications:* The Royal Visit to New Zealand, 1954; Emigrant in Motley: letters of Charles Kean and Ellen Tree, 1954; Seeing New Zealand, 1955; Opportunity in New Zealand, 1955; (ed with Baron Birkett) The Verdict of the Court, 1960; Doctors on Trial, 1961; The Plague and Fire of London, 1966; The World's Greatest Air Mysteries, 1970; The Discovery of Japan, 1970; The Osprey Guide to Gilbert and Sullivan, 1972; The Osprey Guide to Jane Austen, 1973; A Literary Atlas and Gazetteer of the British Isles, 1973; The Osprey Guide to Oscar Wilde, 1973; Upstairs Downstairs: Mr Hudson's Diaries, 1973, Mr Bellamy's Story, 1974, On with the Dance, 1975, Endings and Beginnings, 1975; The Osprey Guide to Anthony Trollope, 1974; The Inheritors, 1974; (abridger) The Pallisers, 1974; The Four Musketeers, 1975; A Christmas Carol (play), 1975; The Man Who Would be King, 1976; The Cedar Tree, 1976; The Cedar Tree: Autumn of an Age, 1977, A Bough Breaks, 1978; Regency Royal, 1978; Prisoner of the Devil, 1979; Regency Rake, 1979; Regency Revenge, 1980; Bergerac, 1981; The Chinese Detective, 1981; Regency Revels, 1982; (abridger) The Barchester Chronicles, 1982; as *John Drinkrow:* The Vintage Operetta Book, 1972; The Vintage Musical Comedy Book, 1973; *with Mollie Hardwick:* The Jolly Toper, 1961; The Sherlock Holmes Companion, 1962; Sherlock Holmes Investigates, 1963; The Man Who Was Sherlock Holmes, 1964; Four Sherlock Holmes Plays, 1964; The Charles Dickens Companion, 1965; The World's Greatest Sea Mysteries, 1967; Writers' Houses: a literary journey in England, 1968; Alfred Deller: A Singularity of Voice, 1968, rev. edn 1980; Charles Dickens As They Saw Him, 1969; The Game's Afoot (Sherlock Holmes Plays), 1969; Plays from Dickens, 1970; Dickens's England, 1970; The Private Life of Sherlock Holmes (novel), 1970; Four More Sherlock Holmes Plays, 1973; The Bernard Shaw Companion, 1973; The Charles Dickens Encyclopedia, 1973; The Charles Dickens Quiz Book, 1974; The Upstairs Downstairs Omnibus, 1975; The Gaslight Boy, 1976; The Hound of the Baskervilles and Other Sherlock Holmes Plays, 1982; author of numerous plays and scripts for radio and TV; contribs to many publications. *Recreations:* scripophily, serendipity, watching cricket. *Address:* Barton House, The Street, Kennington, Ashford, Kent TN24 9HB. *T:* Ashford 23838.

HARDWICK, Mollie; author; *b* Manchester; *d* of Joseph Greenhalgh and Anne Frances Atkinson; *m* 1961, Michael Hardwick, *qv* ; one *s. Educ:* Manchester High Sch. for Girls. Announcer, BBC (Radio) N Region, 1940-45; BBC (Radio) Drama Dept, 1946-62; freelance, 1963-. FRSA 1966. *Publications:* Stories from Dickens, 1968; Emma, Lady Hamilton, 1969; Mrs Dizzy, 1972; Upstairs Downstairs: Sarah's Story, 1973, The Years of Change, 1974, The War to end Wars, 1975, Mrs Bridges' Story, 1975, The World of Upstairs Downstairs, 1976; Alice in Wonderland (play), 1975; Beauty's Daughter, 1976 (Elizabeth Goudge Award for best historical romantic novel of year); The Duchess of Duke Street: The Way Up, 1976, The Golden Years, 1976, The World Keeps Turning, 1977; Charlie is my Darling, 1977; The Atkinson Heritage, 1978; Thomas and Sarah, 1978; Thomas and Sarah: Two for a Spin, 1979; Lovers Meeting, 1979; Sisters in Love, 1979; Dove's Nest, 1980; Willowwood, 1980; Juliet Bravo 1, 1980; Juliet Bravo 2, 1980; Monday's Child, 1981; Calling Juliet Bravo: New Arrivals, 1981; I Remember Love, 1982; *with Michael Hardwick:* The Jolly Toper, 1961; The Sherlock Holmes Companion, 1962; Sherlock Holmes Investigates, 1963; The Man Who Was Sherlock Holmes, 1964; Four Sherlock Holmes plays, 1964; The Charles Dickens Companion, 1965; The World's Greatest Sea Mysteries, 1967; Writers' Houses: a literary journey in England, 1968; Alfred Deller: A Singularity of Voice, 1968, rev. edn 1980; Charles Dickens As They Saw Him, 1969; The Game's Afoot (Sherlock Holmes Plays), 1969; Plays from Dickens, 1970; Dickens's England, 1970; The Private Life of Sherlock Holmes, 1970; Four More Sherlock Holmes Plays, 1973; The Charles Dickens Encyclopedia, 1973; The Bernard Shaw Companion, 1973; The Charles Dickens Quiz Book,

1974; The Upstairs Downstairs Omnibus, 1975; The Gaslight Boy, 1976; The Hound of the Baskervilles and Other Sherlock Holmes Plays, 1982; numerous plays and scripts for radio and TV; contribs to women's magazines. *Recreations:* reading, theatre, watching cricket. *Address:* Barton House, The Street, Kennington, Ashford, Kent TN24 9HB. *T:* Ashford 23838.

HARDWICKE, 10th Earl of, *cr* 1754; **Joseph Philip Sebastian Yorke;** Baron Hardwicke 1733; Viscount Royston 1754; *b* 3 Feb. 1971; *s* of Philip Simon Prospero Rupert Lindley, Viscount Royston (*d* 1973) and of Virginia Anne, *d* of Geoffrey Lyon; *S* grandfather, 1974. *Heir: cousin* Richard Charles John Yorke, *b* 25 July 1916. *Address:* The Mustique Company, St Vincent, West Indies.

HARDY; *see* Gathorne-Hardy.

HARDY, Alan; Member for Brent North, Greater London Council, since 1967; Opposition Leader on Industry and Employment, since 1982; *b* 24 March 1932; *s* of John Robert Hardy and Emily Hardy; *m* 1972, Betty Howe. *Educ:* Hookergate Grammar Sch.; Univ. of Manchester; Inst. of Historical Res., Univ. of London (MA). Res. Asst to Sir Lewis Namier, History of Parliament Trust, 1955-56; Res. Officer and Dep. Dir, London Municipal Soc., 1956-63; Mem. British Secretariat, Council of European Municipalities, 1963-64. Chm., Finance and Establishment Cttee, GLC, 1977-81. Member: Local Authorities' Conditions of Service Adv. Bd, 1977-81; Nat. Jt Council for Local Authorities' Services (Manual Workers), 1977-81. Mem. Bd, Harlow Develt Corp., 1968-80. Contested Islington SW (C), 1966. *Publications:* Queen Victoria Was Amused, 1976; The Kings' Mistresses, 1980. *Recreation:* exercising wife's dog. *Address:* 20 Meadowside, Cambridge Park, Twickenham, Mddx. *T:* 01-892 7968. *Club:* Guards' Polo.

HARDY, Sir Alister (Clavering), Kt 1957; FRS 1940; MA, DSc Oxon; FLS, FZS; Hon. Fellow of Exeter College, Oxford; Hon. Fellow of Merton College, Oxford (Fellow, 1946-63); Professor Emeritus, University of Oxford; *b* Nottingham, 10 Feb. 1896; *y s* of late Richard Hardy; *m* 1927, Sylvia Lucy, 2nd *d* of late Prof. Walter Garstang; one *s* one *d. Educ:* Oundle Sch.; Exeter Coll., Oxford. Lieut and Capt. 2/1 Northern Cyclist Bn, 1915-19; attached RE, Asst Camouflage Officer, Staff of XIII Army Corps, 1918; Christopher Welch Biological Research Scholar, 1920; Oxford Biological Scholar at the Stazione Zoologica, Naples, 1920; Asst Naturalist in Fisheries Dept, Min. of Agriculture and Fisheries, 1921-24; Chief Zoologist to the Discovery Expedition, 1924-28; Prof. of Zoology and Oceanography, University Coll., Hull, 1928-42; Regius Prof. of Natural History, University of Aberdeen, 1942-45; Linacre Prof. of Zoology, University of Oxford, 1946-61; Prof. of Zoological Field Studies, Oxford, 1961-63; Gifford Lectr, Univ. of Aberdeen, for 1963-65. Founder, and Dir 1969-76, Religious Experience Res. Unit, Manchester Coll., Oxford. Scientific Medal of Zoological Soc., 1939. Hon. LLD Aberdeen; Hon. DSc: Southampton; Hull. Pierre Lecomte du Noüy Prize, 1968. *Publications:* The Open Sea, Part I, The World of Plankton, 1956; The Open Sea, Part II, Fish and Fisheries, 1958; The Living Stream, 1965; The Divine Flame, 1966; Great Waters, 1967; (with R. Harvie and A. Koestler) The Challenge of Chance, 1973; The Biology of God, 1975; The Spiritual Nature of Man, 1979. *Recreation:* water-colour sketching. *Address:* 7 Emden House, Barton Lane, Old Headington, Oxford OX3 9JU. *T:* Oxford 62775.

HARDY, Prof. Barbara Gladys; Professor of English Literature, Birkbeck College, University of London, since 1970; teacher and author; *d* of Maurice and Gladys Nathan; *m* Ernest Dawson Hardy (decd); two *d. Educ:* Swansea High Sch. for Girls; University Coll. London. BA, MA. Subsequently on staff of English Dept of Birkbeck Coll., London; Prof. of English, Royal Holloway Coll., Univ. of London, 1965-70. DUniv. Open, 1981. *Publications:* The Novels of George Eliot, 1959; The Appropriate Form, 1964; (ed) George Eliot: Daniel Deronda, 1967; (ed) Middlemarch: Critical Approaches to the Novel, 1967; The Moral Art of Dickens, 1970; (ed) Critical Essays on George Eliot, 1970; The Exposure of Luxury: radical themes in Thackeray, 1972; (ed) Thomas Hardy: The Trumpet-Major, 1974; Tellers and Listeners: the narrative imagination, 1975; (ed) Thomas Hardy: A Laodicean, 1975; A Reading of Jane Austen, 1975; The Advantage of Lyric, 1977; Particularities: readings in George Eliot, 1982. *Address:* Birkbeck College, Malet Street, WC1E 7HX.

HARDY, Gen. Sir Campbell Richard, KCB 1957 (CB 1954); CBE 1951; DSO 1944 (and 2 Bars); RM retired; Director of the Coal Utilisation Council, 1960-70; *b* 24 May 1906; *s* of Major Frank Buckland Hardy, OBE; *m* 1931, Phyllis Cole Sutton; one *s* one *d. Educ:* Felsted Sch. 2nd Lieut RM, 1924; HMS Renown, 1927-29; courses, 1929-30; HMS Rodney, 1930-31; Physical Training Officer, Portsmouth Div., RM, 1932-37; RNC Dartmouth, 1937-38; HMS Vindictive, 1938-39; served War of 1939-45; Adjt Ports Div., RM, 1939-40; RM Div., 1940-43; 46 Commando, RM, 1943-44; Comd 3 Commando Bde, 1944-45; Staff, RM Office, 1946-47; Chief Instructor, Sch. of Combined Ops, 1947-48; Comd 3 Commando Bde, 1948-51; CO Depot, RM, Deal, 1951; Chief of Staff Royal Marines, 1952-55; Commandant General of the Royal Marines, 1955-59; retired, 1959; Col Comdt, Royal Marines, 1961-66. *Address:* Bunch Lane Lodge, Haslemere, Surrey. *T:* Haslemere 3177. *Club:* Army and Navy.
See also J. C. Hardy.

HARDY, David William; a Managing Director, Ocean Transport and Trading Ltd, since 1977; Chairman, Ocean Inchcape Ltd, since 1980; Director: Agricultural Mortgage Corporation; Globe Investment Trust Ltd; *b* 14 July 1930; 3rd *s* of late Brig. John H. Hardy, CBE, MC; *m* 1957, Rosemary, *d* of late Sir Godfrey F. S. Collins, KCIE, CSI, OBE; one *s* one *d. Educ:* Wellington Coll.; Harvard Business School (AMP). Chartered Accountant. Served 2nd RHA, 2/Lt, 1953-54. With Funch Edye Inc., and Imperial Tobacco, USA, 1954-70; HM Govt Co-ordinator of Industrial Advrs, 1970-72; Gp Finance Dir, Tate & Lyle Ltd, 1972-77. Member: NEDC Cttee for Agriculture, 1970-72; Export Credit Guarantees Adv. Council, 1973-78; Co-opted Council of Inst. of Chartered Accountants, 1974-78. Mem. Council, BIM, 1974-78 (Chm. Economic and Social Affairs Cttee, 1974-78). Hon. British Consul, Norfolk, Va, 1960-62. *Address:* 47 Russell Square, WC1B 4JP. *T:* 01-636 6844. *Clubs:* Brooks's, MCC.

HARDY, Sir Harry, Kt 1956; JP; ATI; chartered textile technologist; *b* 10 Sept. 1896; *e s* of Friend and Elizabeth Ann Hardy, Rods Mills, Morley; *m* 1922, Remie (*d* 1955), *d* of Benjamin Siddle, Morley; *m* 1957, Mollie, *d* of Henry Dixon, Morley. *Educ:* Univ. of Leeds. Retired as chemical and fibre manufacturer. Lectr in Textiles, Dewsbury Technical Coll., 1920-35, Head of Textile Industries Dept, 1925-35; Lecturer in Textiles, Huddersfield Technical Coll., 1922-25; Examiner to City and Guilds of London Institute, 1941-44. Pres. Morley and District Textile Soc., 1936-; Founder Pres. Morley Musical Soc., 1943-58; Chm. Youth Employment Cttee, 1943-70; Chm. Local Employment Cttee, 1950-68; Founder Pres., Rotary Club of Morley, 1949-; Vice-Pres. Textile Inst., 1956-59; Liveryman, Cordwainers' Co., 1946-. Hon. Life Pres., Batley and Morley Conservative Assoc. (65 years active service). County Councillor, West Riding of Yorks, 1945-49, County Alderman, 1949-70; JP Borough of Morley, 1948-. Hon. Freeman, Borough of Morley, 1972. *Recreations:* education for textiles, science and technology of textiles; youth employment, music and the arts. *Address:* 45 The Roundway, Dartmouth Park, Morley, near Leeds. *T:* Morley 535150.

HARDY, Herbert Charles; Chief Executive and Managing Director, Evening Standard Co. Ltd, since 1980; *b* 13 Dec. 1928; *s* of Charles John Hardy and Margaret Elizabeth (*née* Burniston); *m* 1959, Irene Burrows; one *d. Educ:* RMA, Sandhurst. *Recreations:* golf, horse racing. *Address:* Evening Standard Co. Ltd, Fleet Street, EC4. *T:* 01-353 8000. *Club:* Thirty.

HARDY, Sir James (Douglas), Kt 1962; CBE 1955 (OBE 1953); *b* 8 June 1915; *s* of James Percy Hardy; *m* 1937, Robina, *d* of Robert Bookless; two *s. Educ:* Gonville and Caius Coll., Cambridge. ICS, 1937-47; Pakistan Civil Service, 1947-61. Dist and Sessions Judge and Dep. Comr, Punjab, up to 1952; Jt Sec. to Govt of Pakistan, 1953; served in: Min. of Communications, as Jt Sec. in charge, 1953-56; Cabinet Secretariat; Min. of Law. Apptd Jt Sec. in charge Establt Div., President's Secretariat, 1959; promoted Sec., Govt of Pakistan President's Secretariat, 1960; retired, 1961. Ford Foundation representative, in N Africa, 1961-67; Project Manager and Chief UN Adviser, UN Special Fund Public Service Reform and Trng Project, Tehran, 1968-75; Chief Project Manager and UN Adviser, Admin. Reform, Govt of Morocco, Rabat, 1975-76. Star of Pakistan (SPk), 1961; Comdr Order of Tunisia, 1967. *Recreations:* riding, golf, motoring. *Address:* c/o Midland Bank Ltd, Poultry and Princes Street, EC2.

HARDY, Sir James (Gilbert), Kt 1981; OBE 1975; Chairman of Directors, Thomas Hardy & Sons Pty Ltd, since 1981; *b* 20 Nov. 1932; *s* of Thomas Mayfield Hardy and Eileen C. Hardy; *m* 1956, Anne Christine Jackson; two *s. Educ:* St Peter's Coll., Adelaide, SA; S Australian Sch. of Mines; S Australian Inst. of Technol. (Dip. in Accountancy). AASA. National Service, 13th Field Artillery Regt, Adelaide, 1951. Elder Smith & Co. Ltd, 1951; J. C. Correll & Co., 1952; Thomas Hardy & Sons Pty Ltd, Winemakers, Adelaide, 1953-: Shipping Clerk, Sales Rep., Sales Supervisor and Lab. Asst, 1953-62; Dir and Manager, Sydney Br., 1962-77; Regional Dir, Eastern Australia, 1977-81. Director: S Australian Film Corp., 1981-; America's Cup Challenge 1983 Ltd, 1981-; Dep. Chm., Racing Rules Cttee, Yachting Fedn, 1969-81. Treasurer, Liquor Trade Supervisory Council of NSW, 1965-70; Fellow, Catering Inst. of Australia, 1972; Wine and Brandy Assoc. of NSW: Mem. Exec., 1963; Treas., 1965; Vice Pres., 1968; Pres., 1980-. NSW Chm., Aust. National Travel Assoc., 1976; Vice Pres., Royal Blind Soc. of NSW, 1980- (Mem. Council, 1967-); Pres., NSW Aust. Football League and Sydney Football League, 1982-. Dep. Grand Master, United Grand Lodge of NSW, 1977-80. *Recreation:* yachting (skipper or helmsman in America's Cup and Admiral's Cup races). *Address:* Thomas Hardy & Sons Pty Ltd, 104 Bay Street, East Botany, NSW 2019, Australia. *T:* (02) 666-5855. *Clubs:* Australian, Tattersalls, Royal Sydney Yacht Squadron (Sydney); Cruising Yacht of Australia (NSW); (Cdre) Brighton and Seacliff Yacht (SA); Canberra Yacht (ACT); Southport Yacht (Qld); Fort Worth Boat (Texas, USA).

HARDY, Maj.-Gen. John Campbell, MVO 1978; Chief of Staff to Commandant General Royal Marines, since 1982; *b* 13 Oct. 1933; *s* of General Sir Campbell Hardy, *qv; m* 1961, Jennifer Mary Kempton; one *s* one *d. Educ:* Sherborne School. Joined Royal Marines, 1952; 45 Commando, 1954; HMS Superb, 1956; Instructor, NCOs' School, Plymouth, 1957; 42 Commando, 1959; 43 Commando, 1962; Adjt, Jt Service Amphibious Warfare Centre, 1964; Company Comdr, 45 Commando, 1965; sc Bracknell, 1966; Instr, RNC Greenwich, 1967; Extra Equerry to Prince Philip, 1968-69; SO, Dept of CGRM, 1969; Rifle Company Comdr, 41 Commando, 1971; ndc Latimer, 1972; Staff of Chief of Defence Staff, 1973; Staff Officer HQ Commando

Forces, 1975; CO RM Poole, 1977; CofS and Asst Defence Attaché, British Defence Staff Washington, 1979; ADC to the Queen, 1981-82. *Recreations:* dinghy sailing, shooting. *Address:* c/o National Westminster Bank plc, 51 The Strand, Walmer, Deal, Kent. *Club:* Army and Navy.

HARDY, Peter; MP (Lab) Rother Valley since 1970; *b* 17 July 1931; *s* of Lawrence Hardy and of Mrs I. Hardy, Wath upon Dearne; *m* 1954, Margaret Anne Brookes; two *s* (and one *s* decd). *Educ:* Wath upon Dearne Grammar Sch.; Westminster Coll., London; Sheffield Univ. Schoolmaster in S Yorkshire, 1953-70. Member: Wath upon Dearne UDC, 1960-70 (Chm. Council, 1968-69); Governing Body of Wath Grammar Sch. (Chm. of Governors, 1969-70). Pres., Wath upon Dearne Labour Party, 1960-68; contested (Lab): Scarborough and Whitby, 1964; Sheffield, Hallam, 1966. PPS to Sec. of State for the Environment, 1974-76; PPS to Foreign Sec., 1976-79. Mem., UK delegn to Council of Europe, 1976-. Mem., NUPE. *Publications:* A Lifetime of Badgers, 1975; various articles on educational and other subjects. *Recreation:* watching wild life. *Address:* 53 Sandygate, Wath upon Dearne, Rotherham, South Yorkshire. *T:* Rotherham 874590. *Clubs:* Kennel; Rawmarsh Trades and Labour.

HARDY, Robert; see Hardy, T. S. R.

HARDY, Robert James; His Honour Judge Hardy; a Circuit Judge, since 1979; *b* 12 July 1924; *s* of James Frederick and Ann Hardy; *m* 1951, Maureen Scott; one *s* one *d. Educ:* Mostyn House Sch.; Wrekin Coll.; University Coll., London (LLB). Served, 1942-46, Royal Navy, and Pilot, Fleet Air Arm. Called to Bar, 1950; a Recorder of the Crown Court, 1972-79. *Recreation:* sailing. *Address:* Fallow Green, Overhill Lane, Wilmslow Park, Wilmslow, Cheshire. *T:* Wilmslow 528031; Betlem, Mallorca.

HARDY, Rt. Rev. Robert Maynard; see Maidstone, Bishop Suffragan of.

HARDY, Sir Rupert (John), 4th Bt, *cr* 1876; Lieutenant-Colonel Life Guards, retired; *b* 24 Oct. 1902; *s* of 3rd Bt and Violet Agnes Evelyn (*d* 1972), *d* of Hon. Sir Edward Chandos Leigh, KCB, KC; *S* father 1953; *m* 1930, Hon. Diana Joan Allsopp, *er d* of 3rd Baron Hindlip; one *s* one *d. Educ:* Eton; Trinity Hall, Cambridge. BA 1925. Joined The Life Guards, 1925; Major, 1940; retired, 1948, and rejoined as RARO, 1952; Lieut-Col comdg Household Cavalry Regt, 1952-56; ceased to belong to R of O, Dec. 1956; granted hon. rank of Lieut-Col. *Recreations:* hunting and shooting. *Heir: s* Richard Charles Chandos Hardy [*b* 6 Feb. 1945; *m* 1972, Venetia, *d* of Simon Wingfield Digby, *qv.;* three *d*]. *Address:* Gullivers Lodge, Guilsborough, Northampton. *Club:* Turf.

HARDY, (Timothy Sydney) Robert, CBE 1981; actor and writer; *b* 29 Oct. 1925; *s* of late Major Henry Harrison Hardy, CBE, and Edith Jocelyn Dugdale; *m* 1st, 1952, Elizabeth (marr. diss.), *d* of late Sir Lionel Fox and Lady Fox; one *s* ; 2nd, 1961, Sally, *d* of Sir Neville Pearson, Bt, *qv,* and late Dame Gladys Cooper, DBE; two *d. Educ:* Rugby Sch.; Magdalen Coll., Oxon (Hons degree, Eng. Lit.). Shakespeare Meml Theatre, 1949-51; London, West End, 1951-53; Old Vic Theatre, 1953-54; USA, 1954 and 1956-58 (plays incl. Hamlet and Henry V); Shakespeare Meml 1959 Centenary Season; West End plays. Films and television, 1951-, incl.: David Copperfield; Age of Kings; Trouble-shooters; Elizabeth R; Manhunt; Edward VII; All Creatures Great and Small; Speed King; Fothergill; Winston Churchill—The Wilderness Years. Author of TV documentaries: Picardy Affair, 1962; The Longbow, 1972; Horses in our Blood, 1977; Gordon of Khartoum, 1982. Livery Mem., Worshipful Co. of Bowyers. *Publication:* Longbow, 1976. *Recreations:* archery, horsemanship, bowyery. *Address:* Upper Bolney House, Upper Bolney, near Henley-on-Thames, Oxon RG9 4AQ. *Clubs:* Buck's, Royal Toxophilite, British Longbow.

HARDY-ROBERTS, Brig. Sir Geoffrey (Paul), KCVO 1972; CB 1945; CBE 1944 (OBE 1941); JP; DL; Master of HM's Household, 1967-73; Extra Equerry to the Queen, since 1967; Secretary-Superintendent of Middlesex Hospital, 1946-67; *b* 1907; *s* of A. W. Roberts; *m* 1945, Eldred, widow of Col J. R. Macdonell, DSO. *Educ:* Eton; RMC Sandhurst. Regular Commission, 9th Lancers, 1926-37. Served War of 1939-45 (OBE, CBE, CB). Mem., West Sussex AHA, 1974-82; Dep. Chm., King Edward VII Hospital, Midhurst, 1972-82. JP 1960, DL 1964, West Sussex (formerly Sussex), High Sheriff, 1965, Sussex. Officer, Legion of Merit, 1945. *Address:* The Garden House, Coates, Pulborough, West Sussex RH20 1ES. *T:* Fittleworth 446.

HARDYMAN, Norman Trenchard; Secretary, University Grants Committee, since 1982; *b* 5 Jan. 1930; *s* of late Rev. Arnold Victor Hardyman and late Laura Hardyman; *m* 1961, Carol Rebecca Turner; one *s* one *d. Educ:* Clifton Coll.; Christ Church, Oxford. Asst Principal, Min. of Educn, 1955; Principal 1960; Private Sec. to Sec. of State for Educn and Science, 1966-68; Asst Sec. 1968-75, Under-Sec., 1975-79, DES; Under-Sec., DHSS, 1979-81. *Recreations:* walking, gardening, reading, photography. *Address:* 16 Rushington Avenue, Maidenhead, Berks. *T:* Maidenhead 24179.

HARE, family name of **Viscount Blakenham** and **Earl of Listowel.**

HARE, Hon. Alan Victor, MC 1942; Chairman, since 1978 and Chief Executive, since 1975, Financial Times Ltd (Managing Director, 1971-78); *b* 14 March 1919; 4th *s* of 4th Earl of Listowel and Hon. Freda, *d* of 2nd Baron Derwent; *m* 1945, Jill Pegotty (*née* North); one *s* one *d. Educ:* Eton Coll.;

New Coll., Oxford (MA). Army, 1939–45. Foreign Office, 1947–61; Industrial and Trade Fairs, 1961–63; Financial Times, 1963–; Director: Pearson Longman Ltd, 1975–; Economist Newspaper Ltd, 1975–; Chm., Industrial and Trade Fairs Holdings, 1979– (Dir, 1977–). Mem., Press Council, 1975–78. *Recreations:* walking, opera, swimming. *Address:* Flat 12, 53 Rutland Gate, SW7. *T:* 01-581 2184. *Club:* White's.
See also Viscount Blakenham.

HARE, David; playwright; *b* 5 June 1947; *s* of Clifford Theodore Rippon Hare and Agnes Cockburn Hare; *m* 1970, Margaret Matheson (marr. diss. 1980); two *s* one *d. Educ:* Lancing Coll.; Jesus Coll., Cambridge (MA Hons). Founded Portable Theatre, 1968; Literary Manager and Resident Dramatist, Royal Court, 1969–71; Resident Dramatist, Nottingham Playhouse, 1973; founded Joint Stock Theatre Group, 1975. Author of following plays: Slag, Hampstead, 1970, Royal Court, 1971 (Evening Standard Drama Award, 1970); The Great Exhibition, Hampstead, 1972; Knuckle, Comedy, 1974 (John Llewellyn Rhys Award, 1974); Fanshen, Joint Stock, 1975; Teeth 'n' Smiles, Royal Court, 1975, Wyndhams, 1976; Plenty, Nat. Theatre, 1978; A Map of the World, Adelaide Fest. 1982, NT 1983. *TV plays:* Man Above Men (Play for Today), 1973; Licking Hitler (Play for Today), 1978 (BAFTA award, 1978); Dreams of Leaving (Play for Today), 1980; Saigon, 1983. *Directed:* Brassneck, Nottingham Playhouse, 1973; The Party, Nat. Theatre, 1974; Weapons of Happiness, Nat. Theatre, 1976. US/UK Bicentennial Fellowship, 1977; Total Eclipse, Lyric, Hammersmith, 1981. *Publications:* Slag, 1970; The Great Exhibition, 1972; Knuckle, 1974; Brassneck, 1974; Fanshen, 1976; Teeth 'n' Smiles, 1976; Plenty, 1978; Licking Hitler, 1978; Dreams of Leaving, 1980; Am Mischief!, 1982; A Map of the World, 1982; Saigon, 1983. *Recreation:* collecting regal erotica. *Address:* 95 Linden Gardens, W2.

HARE, Prof. Frederick Kenneth, OC 1978; PhD; FRSC 1968; University Professor, since 1976, Provost, since 1979, University of Trinity College, Toronto; *b* Wylye, Wilts, 5 Feb. 1919; *s* of Frederick Eli Hare and Irene Smith; *m* 1st, 1941, Suzanne Alice Bates (marr. diss. 1952); one *s* ; 2nd, 1953, Helen Neilson Morrill; one *s* one *d. Educ:* Windsor Grammar Sch.; King's Coll., University of London (BSc); Univ. of Montreal (PhD). Lectr in Geography, Univ. of Manchester, 1940–41; War service in Air Min., Meteorological Office, 1941–45; Asst and Assoc. Prof. of Geography, McGill Univ., Montreal, 1945–52; Prof. of Geography and Meteorology, McGill Univ., 1952–64, Chm. of Dept, 1950–61; Dean of Faculty of Arts and Science, 1962–64; Prof. of Geography, Univ. of London (King's Coll.), 1964–66; Master of Birkbeck Coll., Univ. of London, 1966–68; Pres., Univ. of British Columbia, 1968–69; Prof. of Geography and Physics and University Prof., 1969–, Dir, Inst. for Environmental Studies, 1974–79, Univ. of Toronto. Vis. Centenary Prof., Univ. of Adelaide, 1974. FKC 1967. Sci. Advr, Dept of the Environment, Canada, 1972–73. Mem. Nat. Research Council of Canada, 1962–64; Chm. of Bd, Arctic Inst. of N America, 1963; Mem., NERC, 1965–68; Dir, Resources for the Future, 1968–80; Member: SSRC, Canada, 1974–76; Adv. Council, Electric Power Res. Inst., 1977–80. Chairman: Adv. Cttee on Canadian Demonstration Projects, 1974–75, for 1976 UN Conf. on Human Settlements; Special Prog. Panel on Ecoscis, NATO, 1975; Federal Study Gp on Nuclear Waste Disposal, 1977; Climate Planning Bd, Govt of Canada, 1979–. President: Canadian Assoc. of Geographers, 1964; RMetS, 1967–68 (Vice-Pres., 1968–70); Fellow, Amer. Meteorological Soc., 1969; Hon. Fellow, Amer. Geographical Soc., 1963; Hon. Pres., Assoc. of Amer. Geographers, 1964. Hon. Life Mem., Birkbeck Coll., 1969. Hon. LLD: Queen's (Canada) Univ., 1964; Univ. of W Ontario, 1968; Trent Univ., 1979; Hon. DSc: McGill, 1969; York (Canada), 1978; DSc *ad eund.* Adelaide, 1974. Meritorious Achievement Citation, Assoc. Amer. Geographers, 1961; President's Prize, RMetS (Can.), 1961, 1962; Patterson Medal, Can. Met. Service, 1973; Massey Medal, Royal Can. Geographical Soc., 1974; Patron's Medal, RGS, 1977; Award for Scholarly Distinction, Canadian Assoc. of Geographers, 1979; Univ. of Toronto Alumni Assoc. Faculty Award, 1982. *Publications:* The Restless Atmosphere, 1953; On University Freedom, 1968; (with M. K. Thomas) Climate Canada, 1974, 2nd edn 1979; numerous articles in Quarterly Jl Royal Meteorological Soc., Geography, and other learned jls. *Recreation:* music. *Address:* Trinity College, 6 Hoskin Avenue, Toronto, Ont M5S 1H8, Canada. *Clubs:* Athenæum; McGill Faculty (Montreal) (Hon. Life Mem.); Toronto Faculty, York (Toronto).

HARE, Kenneth; *see* Hare, F. K.

HARE, Hon. Mrs Richard; *see* Gordine, Dora.

HARE, Rt. Rev. Richard; *see* Hare, Rt Rev. Thomas Richard.

HARE, Prof. Richard Mervyn, FBA 1964; White's Professor of Moral Philosophy and Fellow of Corpus Christi College, Oxford, since 1966; *b* 21 March 1919; *s* of late Charles Francis Aubone Hare and late Louise Kathleen (*née* Simonds); *m* 1947, Catherine, *d* of Sir Harry Verney, 4th Bt, DSO; one *s* three *d. Educ:* Rugby (Schol.); Balliol Coll., Oxford (Schol.). Commissioned Royal Artillery, 1940; Lieut, Indian Mountain Artillery, 1941; Prisoner of War, Singapore and Siam, 1942–45. 1st Lt. Hum. 1947. Fellow and Tutor in Philosophy, Balliol Coll., Oxford, 1947–66, Hon. Fellow, 1974. Visiting Fellow: Princeton, 1957; ANU, 1966; Center for Advanced Study in Behavioral Sciences, Stanford, 1980; Wilde Lectr in Natural Religion, Oxford, 1963–66; Visiting Professor: Univ. of Michigan, 1968; Univ. of Delaware, 1974. Pres., Aristotelian Soc., 1972–73. Member: Nat. Road Safety Advisory Council, 1966–68; C of E Working Parties on Medical Questions,

1964–75. Hon. Fellow, Inst. of Life Scis, Hastings Center, 1974; For. Hon. Mem., American Acad. of Arts and Sciences, 1975. Tanner Award, 1979. *Publications:* The Language of Morals, 1952; Freedom and Reason, 1963; Essays on Philosophical Method, 1971; Practical Inferences, 1971; Essays on the Moral Concepts, 1972; Applications of Moral Philosophy, 1972; Moral Thinking, 1981. *Recreations:* music, gardening. *Address:* Saffron House, Ewelme, Oxford.

HARE, Ronald, MD (London); Emeritus Professor of Bacteriology in University of London since 1964 and Hon. Consulting Bacteriologist to St Thomas' Hospital since 1951; *b* 30 Aug. 1899; *s* of late Frederick Hare, MD, and Elizabeth Roxby Hare, Esh Winning, Co. Durham; *m* 1932, Barbara Thurgarland Wintle (*d* 1966); one *s. Educ:* Royal Masonic Sch.; Birkbeck Coll.; St Mary's Hosp., London. Scholar, Institute of Pathology and Research, 1925, and asst in Inoculation Dept, St Mary's Hospital, London, 1926–30; first asst in Research Laboratories, Queen Charlotte's Hospital, London, 1931–36; Research Associate in Connaught Laboratories, Univ. of Toronto, and Lectr in Dept of Hygiene and Preventive Medicine, 1936; has carried out extensive researches on the streptococci (Catherine Bishop Harman Prize of BMA and Nicholls Prize of Royal Society of Medicine); largely responsible for the planning and building of the penicillin plant set up in the University of Toronto by the Govt of Canada. Professor of Bacteriology, University of London, 1946–64. Mem. Council: Wright-Fleming Inst., 1952–60; Nuffield Inst. of Comparative Med., 1960–68; Fountains and Carshalton Gp Hospital Management Cttee, 1966–71. Pres., Pathology Sect., 1963–64, and Mem. Council, Royal Society of Medicine, 1965–68; Examr in Universities of: London, Malaya, Birmingham, West Indies, East Africa, Ibadan. *Publications:* Pomp and Pestilence, 1954; An Outline of Bacteriology and Immunity, 1956; Bacteriology and Immunity for Nurses, 1961; The Birth of Penicillin, 1970; many papers in scientific and medical jls. *Recreations:* water-colour painting, the history of pestilence. *Address:* Flat 3, 15 Warwick Square, SW1. *T:* 01-834 6038.

HARE, Sir Thomas, 5th Bt *cr* 1818; *b* 27 July 1930; *s* of Sir Ralph Leigh Hare, 4th Bt, and Doreen Pleasance Anna, *d* of late Sir Richard Bagge, DSO; *S* father, 1976; *m* 1961, Lady Rose Amanda Bligh, *d* of 9th Earl of Darnley; two *d. Educ:* Eton; Magdalene College, Cambridge (MA). ARICS. *Heir: cousin* Philip Leigh Hare [*b* 13 Oct. 1922; *m* 1950, Anne Lisle, *d* of Major Geoffrey Nicholson, CBE, MC; one *s* one *d*]. *Address:* Stow Bardolph, King's Lynn, Norfolk PE34 3HU.

HARE, Rt. Rev. Thomas Richard; *see* Pontefract, Bishop Suffragan of.

HARE DUKE, Rt. Rev. Michael Geoffrey; *see* St Andrews, Dunkeld and Dunblane, Bishop of.

HARES, Phillip Douglas George; Board Member for Finance, since 1981, and a Corporate Managing Director responsible for Finance, Shiprepair (Divisional Vice-Chairman) and Business Development, since 1982, British Shipbuilders; *b* 31 Dec. 1926; *s* of Edgar Sidney George and Edith Winifred Frances Hares; *m* 1955, Violet May Myers; one *s* one *d. Educ:* Richmond and East Sheen Grammar Sch. FIAM; FBCS; FBIM. Involved with management sciences and computing in various commercial, industrial, and consulting organisations, 1952–69, dating from early application of computers in 1952 with J. Lyons & Co. Ltd; Asst Man. Dir (Ops), British Mail Order Corp. Ltd (Great Universal Stores), 1969–77; Man. Dir (Finance), British Shipbuilders, 1978–81. *Publications:* various papers in computing sciences and business administration. *Recreations:* reading, genealogy. *Address:* Linden Barns, Causey Hill, Hexham, Northumberland NE46 2JF. *T:* Hexham 605481.

HAREWOOD, 7th Earl of, *cr* 1812; **George Henry Hubert Lascelles**; Baron Harewood, 1796; Viscount Lascelles, 1812; Managing Director, English National Opera (formerly Sadler's Wells Opera), since 1972; *b* 7 Feb. 1923; *er s* of 6th Earl of Harewood, KG, GCVO, DSO, and HRH Princess Mary (Princess Royal; who *d* 28 March 1965); *S* father, 1947; *m* 1st, 1949, Maria Donata (marr. diss. 1967; she *m* 1973, Rt Hon. (John) Jeremy Thorpe), *d* of late Erwin Stein; three *s* ; 2nd, 1967, Patricia Elizabeth, *d* of Charles Tuckwell, Australia; one *s* and one step *s. Educ:* Eton; King's Coll., Cambridge (MA). Served War of 1939–45, Capt. Grenadier Guards (wounded and prisoner, 1944, released May 1945); ADC to Earl of Athlone, 1945–46, Canada. Editor of magazine "Opera" 1950–53; Royal Opera House, Covent Garden: a Dir, 1951–53; on staff, 1953–60; a Dir, 1969–72; Artistic Director: Edinburgh Internat. Festival, 1961–65; Leeds Festival, 1958–74; Artistic Advr, New Philharmonia Orch., London, 1966–76; Man. Dir, English Nat. Opera North, 1978–81. Chm., Music Advisory Cttee of British Council, 1956–66; Chancellor of the Univ. of York, 1963–67; Member: Arts Council, 1966–72; Gen. Adv. Council of BBC, 1969–77. President: English Football Assoc., 1963–72; Leeds United Football Club. Hon. LLD: Leeds, 1959; Aberdeen, 1966; Hon. DMus Hull, 1962. Janáček Medal, 1978. *Publications:* (ed) Kobbé's Complete Opera Book, 1953, rev. edn 1976; The Tongs and the Bones (autobiog.), 1981. *Heir: s* Viscount Lascelles, *qv. Address:* Harewood House, Leeds LS17 9LG.

HARFORD, Sir James (Dundas), KBE 1956; CMG 1943; *b* Great Yarmouth, 7 Jan. 1899; *s* of late Rev. Dundas Harford, MA; *m* 1st, 1932, Countess Thelma, *d* of Count Albert Metaxa; one *s* ; 2nd, 1937, Lilias Madeline, *d* of Major Archibald Campbell; two *d. Educ:* Repton; Balliol Coll., Oxford (Hon. Scholar, MA). Served European War, France and

Belgium, 1917-19; Asst Master, Eton Coll., 1922-25; Administrative Service, Nigeria, 1926; District administration, Bornu Province, 1926-29; Asst Sec., Nigerian Secretariat, 1930-34 and Clerk to Exec. and Legislative Councils; seconded to Colonial Office, 1934-36; Administrator of Antigua and Federal Sec. of the Leeward Islands, 1936-40; Administrator, St Kitts-Nevis, 1940-47; administered Government of Leeward Islands, on various occasions; seconded to Colonial Office, 1947-48; administered Government of Mauritius, on various occasions; Colonial Sec., Mauritius, 1948-53; Governor and Commander-in-Chief of St Helena, 1954-58. Conference Organiser, Commonwealth Institute, 1959-64. *Address:* Links Cottage, Rother Road, Seaford, East Sussex.

HARFORD, Sir (John) Timothy, 3rd Bt *cr* 1934; Director, Singer & Friedlander Ltd, since 1970 (Local Director, 1967-69); *b* 6 July 1932; *s* of Sir George Arthur Harford, 2nd Bt and Anstice Marion, *d* of Sir Alfred Tritton, 2nd Bt; *S* father, 1967; *m* 1962, Carolyn Jane Mullens; two *s* one *d. Educ:* Harrow Sch.; Oxford Univ.; Harvard Business Sch. Philip Hill Higginson Erlangers Ltd, 1960-63; Dir, Birmingham Industrial Trust Ltd, 1963-67. *Recreations:* wine and food, travel. *Heir: s* Mark John Harford, *b* 6 Aug. 1964. *Address:* South House, South Littleton, Evesham, Worcs. *T:* Evesham 830478.

HARGRAVE, John Gordon, FRSA; artist and writer; *b* 1894; *s* of Gordon Hargrave, landscape painter; *m* 1919, Ruth Clark (marr. diss. 1952); one *s; m* 1968, Gwendolyn Gray. *Educ:* Wordsworth's Sch., Hawkshead. Illustrated Gulliver's Travels, and the Rose and the Ring at the age of fifteen; chief cartoonist, London Evening Times, at the age of seventeen; joined the staff of C. Arthur Pearson Ltd, 1914; enlisted in RAMC, and served with 10th (Irish) Division in Gallipoli campaign (Suvla Bay Landing), and later in Salonika; invalided out, end of 1916; Art Manager, C. Arthur Pearson Ltd, 1917-20; founded the Kibbo Kift, 1920 (later Social Credit Party, The Green Shirts); Hon. Adviser to the Alberta Govt Planning Cttee, 1936-37; issued the Alberta Report, July 1937; invented the Hargrave Automatic Navigator for Aircraft, 1937; created animal character, "Bushy", for The Sketch, 1952. *Publications:* Lonecraft, 1913, and five other handbooks on camping and the outdoor life; At Suvla Bay, 1916; Harbottle, 1924; Young Winkle, 1925; And Then Came Spring, 1926; The Pfenniger Failing, 1927; The Confession of the Kibbo Kift, 1927; The Imitation Man, 1931; Summer Time Ends, 1935; Professor Skinner alias Montagu Norman, 1939; Words Win Wars, 1940; Social Credit Clearly Explained, 1945; The Life and Soul of Paracelsus, 1951; The Paragon Dictionary, 1953; The Suvla Bay Landing, 1964; The Facts of the Case concerning the Hargrave Automatic Navigator for Aircraft (privately pr.), 1969; special articles on Paracelsus, 1971, and L. Hargrave, inventor of the box-kite, in Encyclopaedia Britannica, 1974; The Confession of the Kibbo Kift (special request edn), 1979. *Recreation:* work. *Address:* 3 Rosemary Court, Fortune Green Road, Hampstead, NW6.

HARGREAVES, Eric Lyde; Emeritus Fellow since 1963 (Fellow, 1925, Tutor, 1930, Senior Tutor, 1937-56), Oriel College, Oxford; *b* 13 Oct. 1898; *s* of George Harrison and Emily Frances Hargreaves. *Educ:* St Paul's Sch.; Corpus Christi Coll., Oxford (Scholar). Wounded and taken prisoner, April 1918; 1st Class Lit. Hum., 1921; PhD London, 1924; University Lecturer in Economics, 1929-35, and 1954-59; Historian, Official History of Second World War (Civil Series), 1942-52; Fellow of Royal Economic and Royal Statistical Societies. *Publications:* Restoring Currency Standards, 1926; National Debt, 1930; (with M. M. Gowing) Civil Industry and Trade, 1952; essays and articles on economic subjects. *Recreation:* walking. *Address:* Oriel College, Oxford.

HARGREAVES, Prof. John Desmond; Professor of History, University of Aberdeen, since 1962, part-time since 1982; *b* 25 Jan. 1924; *s* of Arthur Swire Hargreaves and Margaret Hilda (*née* Duckworth); *m* 1950, Sheila Elizabeth (*née* Wilks); one *s* two *d. Educ:* Skipton Grammar Sch.; Bootham; Manchester Univ. War service, 1943-46. Asst Princ., War Office, 1948; Lectr in History: Manchester Univ., 1948-52; Fourah Bay Coll., Sierra Leone, 1952-54; Aberdeen Univ., 1954-62. Vis. Prof., Union Coll. Schenectady, New York, 1960-61; Univ. of Ibadan, 1970-71. Mem., Kidd Cttee on Sheriff Court Records, 1966. Pres., African Studies Assoc. (UK), 1972-73. *Publications:* Life of Sir Samuel Lewis, 1958; Prelude to the Partition of West Africa, 1963; West Africa: the Former French States, 1967; France and West Africa, 1969; West Africa Partitioned: Vol. I, The Loaded Pause, 1974; The End of Colonial Rule in West Africa, 1979; Aberdeenshire to Africa, 1981; many articles and chapters in jls and collaborative volumes. *Recreations:* inhabiting dilapidated shooting-lodge; hill-walking; occasional lawn tennis. *Address:* Balcluain, Raemoir Road, Banchory, Kincardine AB3 3UJ. *T:* Banchory 2655. *Club:* Royal Commonwealth Society.

HARGREAVES, Brig. Kenneth, CBE 1956 (MBE (mil.) 1939); TD 1942; DL; Lord-Lieutenant, West Yorkshire, 1974-78 (West Riding of Yorkshire and City of York, 1970-74); Hon. President, Hargreaves Group Ltd, since 1974 (Managing Director, 1938-64, Chairman, 1964-74); *b* 23 Feb. 1903; *s* of late Henry Hargreaves, Leeds, and late Hope Hargreaves; *m* 1st, 1958, Else Margareta Allen (*d* 1968); one step *s* one step *d* (both adopted); 2nd, 1969, Hon. Mrs Margaret Packe; two step *d. Educ:* Haileybury Coll. Lieut-Col comdg 96th HAA Regt RA, 1939-41; Brig. comdg 3rd Ind. AA Bde, 1942-45; Hon. Col, several TA regiments, 1947-66; Vice-Pres., Yorks TAVR, 1970-78. Director: Lloyds Bank Ltd, 1965-73 (Chm., Yorkshire Regional Bd, 1967-73); Yorkshire Bank, 1969-79; Sadler's Wells Trust Ltd, 1969-75; ENO, 1975-80;

Opera North, 1981-; Pres., Friends of Opera North, 1978-. Mem., Royal Commn on Historical Monuments, 1971-74. Pres., Queen's Silver Jubilee Appeal, W Yorks, 1977-78. Chairman: Coal Industry Soc., 1933-34, Pres. 1973-75; Coal Trade Benevolent Assoc., 1958; British Railways (Eastern) Bd, 1970-73 (Dir, 1964-73). President: Chartered Inst. of Secretaries, 1956 (FCIS 1930); W Yorks Branch, BRCS, 1965-74, now Patron; St John Council (W Yorks), 1970-74, W and S Yorks, 1974-78; Yorks Agricultural Soc., 1972-73; Haileybury Soc., 1974-75; Vice-Pres., Leeds Chamber of Commerce, 1946-47; Dep. Chm., Leeds Musical Festival, 1961-70; Mem. Court, University of Leeds, 1950- (Hon. LLD 1970); Trustee, York Minster, 1970-; High Steward, Selby Abbey, 1974-; Patron, Central Yorkshire Scouts, 1978 (former Chm. and Pres.). Contested: Pontefract, 1947; Keighley, 1950 and 1951; Hon. Treasurer, Yorks Provincial Area Conservative and Unionist Assoc., 1946-54; Governor, Swinton Conservative Coll., 1952-70; Lay Reader, Ripon Diocese, 1954-. Liveryman, Clothworkers' Co., 1938, Master, 1969-70. High Sheriff of Yorks, 1962-63; DL WR Yorks 1956-70, West Yorks, 1978-. KStJ 1970. *Recreations:* gardening, music. *Address:* Easby House, Great Ouseburn, York YO5 9RQ. *T:* Green Hammerton 30548. *Clubs:* Army and Navy, Carlton.

HARGREAVES, Maj.-Gen. William Herbert, CB 1965; OBE 1945; FRCP; *b* 5 Aug. 1908; *s* of Arthur William Hargreaves; *m* 1946, Pamela Mary Westray; one *s* one *d. Educ:* Merchant Taylors' Sch.; St Bartholomew's Hospital. FRCP 1950; FRCPE 1965. Served War of 1939-45. Medical Liaison Officer to Surgeon-Gen., US Army, Washington, DC, 1946-48; Prof. of Medicine, Univ. of Baghdad, 1951-59; Physician to late King Faisal II of Iraq, 1951-58; Hon. Consulting Physician, Iraqi Army, 1953-59; Consulting Physician to the Army, 1960-65; retd 1965. Lectr in Tropical Medicine, Middlesex Hosp. Med. Sch., 1960-65, and London Hosp. Med. Sch., 1963-65; Hon. Consulting Physician, Royal Hosp., Chelsea, 1961-65; Chief Med. Advr, Shell Internat. Petroleum Co. Ltd, 1965-72. Examiner: RCP, 1964-66; Soc. Apothecaries, 1966-73. Mem. of Council, Royal Society of Medicine, 1966-69, Vice-Pres., Library (Scientific Research) Section, 1967-69. Counsellor, Royal Soc. of Tropical Med. and Hygiene, 1961-65; Member: Hosp. Cttee, St John's Ophthalmic Hosp., Jerusalem, 1968-71; Finance Cttee, RCP. OStJ 1965. Iraq Coronation Medal, 1953. *Publications:* The Practice of Tropical Medicine (with R. J. G. Morrison), 1965; chapters in: Textbook of Medicine (Conybeare), 16th edn 1975; Modern Trends in Gastro-Enterology (Avery Jones), 1951; Medicine in the Tropics (Woodruff), 1974; numerous articles in med. jls. *Recreations:* art and music. *Address:* 6/3 Gladswood Gardens, Double Bay, NSW 2028, Australia.

HARINGTON, Gen. Sir Charles (Henry Pepys), GCB 1969 (KCB 1964; CB 1961); CBE 1957 (OBE 1953); DSO 1944; MC 1940; ADC (General) to the Queen, 1969-71; *b* 5 May 1910; *s* of Lt-Col H. H. Harington and Dorothy Pepys; *m* 1942, Victoire Marion Williams-Freeman; one *s* two *d. Educ:* Malvern; Sandhurst. Commissioned into 22nd (Cheshire) Regt, 1930. Served War of 1939-45: France and Belgium, 2nd Bn Cheshire Regt, 1939-40; CO, 1st Bn Manchester Regt and GSO1, 53 (Welch) Div., NW Europe, 1944-45. DS Staff Coll., 1946; GSO1 Mil. Mission Greece, 1948; CO 1st Bn The Parachute Regt, 1949; Mil. Asst to CIGS, 1951; SHAPE, 1953; Comdr 49 Inf. Bde in Kenya, 1955; idc 1957; Comdt Sch. of Infantry, 1958; GOC 3rd Div., 1959; Comdt, Staff Coll., Camberley, 1961; C-in-C Middle East, 1963; DCGS, 1966; Chief of Personnel and Logistics, to the three Services, 1968-71, retired; Col The Cheshire Regt, 1962-68. Col Comdt, Small Arms Sch. Corps, 1964-70; Col Comdt, The Prince of Wales Div., 1968-71. President: Combined Cadet Force Assoc., 1971-80; Milocarian (Tri-Service) Athletic Club. Chm. Governors, Royal Star and Garter Home, 1972-80. Comr, Duke of York's Royal Military Sch. Mem. Council, Officers' Pensions Soc. Mem., London Bd, Northern Rock Building Soc. Knight Officer with swords, Order of Orange Nassau (Netherlands), 1945. *Recreations:* sailing, English watercolours. *Address:* 19 Rivermead Court, SW6 3RT. *Clubs:* Army and Navy, Hurlingham (Pres.).

HARINGTON, (Edward Henry) Vernon; *b* 13 Sept. 1907; *er s* of late His Honour Edward Harington; *m* 1st, 1937, Mary Elizabeth (marr. diss. 1949), *d* of late Louis Egerton; one *d* (and one *d* decd); 2nd, 1950, Mary Johanna Jean, JP, *d* of late Lt-Col R. G. S. Cox, MC; two *d. Educ:* Eton. Called to Bar, Inner Temple, 1930. Private Sec. to Lord Chancellor and Dep. Serjeant-at-Arms, House of Lords, 1934-40; served with HM Forces, 1940-45 (Major, Coldstream Guards); WO, 1944-45; Austrian Control Commn, Legal Div., 1945; Asst Sec. to Lord Chancellor for Commns of the Peace, 1945; Dep. Judge Advocate, 1946; Asst Judge Advocate Gen., 1954-73. Dep. Chm., Herefordshire QS, 1969-71; a Recorder of the Crown Court, 1972-74. Chm., Hereford, Worcester, Warwicks and W Midlands Regional Agricl Wages Cttee, 1976-82. Councillor, Malvern Hill DC, 1979-. JP Herefordshire, 1969-71. *Recreations:* shooting, fishing. *Address:* Woodlands House, Whitbourne, Worcester. *T:* Knightwick 437.

HARINGTON, Maj.-Gen. John, CB 1967; OBE 1958; *b* 7 Nov. 1912; *s* of late Col Henry Harington, Kelston, Folkestone, Kent; *m* 1943, Nancy, *d* of late Stanley Allen, Denne Hill, Canterbury; one *s. Educ:* Lambrook, Bracknell; Aldenham Sch.; RMA Woolwich. Commnd RA, 1933. Served War of 1939-45: BEF, 1939-40; Capt., RHA, France and Germany; Major 1943; 1st Airborne Corps; Lt-Col 1945. GSO1, British and Indian Div., Japan, 1946-47; CO 18th Regt RA, 1954-55; College Comdr, RMA, Sandhurst, 1956-57; Head of Defence Secretariat, Middle East, 1958-59; commanded 1st Artillery Brigade, 1960-61; BRA, Far East Land Forces, 1962; DMS (2), War Office,

1962-64 (Min. of Defence, 1964); Chief of Staff to C-in-C, Far East Comd, 1964-67, retired. *Recreations:* ski-ing, shooting, golf, tennis. *Address:* Harkaway, Goodworth Clatford, Andover, Hants. *Clubs:* Army and Navy, Ski Club of Great Britain.

HARINGTON, Kenneth Douglas Evelyn Herbert; Metropolitan Magistrate since 1967; *b* 30 Sept. 1911; *yr s* of late His Honour Edward Harington; *m* 1st, 1939, Lady Cecilia Bowes-Lyon (*d* 1947), *er d* of 15th Earl of Strathmore; 2nd, 1950, Maureen Helen McCalmont, *d* of Brig.-Gen. Sir Robert McCalmont, KCVO, CBE, DSO; two *s. Educ:* Stowe. War of 1939-45: Served NW Europe (Major, Coldstream Guards). Hon. Attaché, British Legation, Stockholm, 1930-32; Barrister, Inner Temple, 1952; Acting Deputy Chm., Inner London and NE London Quarter Sessions, 1966-67. *Recreations:* shooting, fishing. *Address:* 36 Lennox Gardens, SW1. *T:* 01-589 8951; Sotchers, Bury Gate, Pulborough, West Sussex. *T:* Fittleworth 227. *Club:* Cavalry and Guards.

HARINGTON, Sir Nicholas (John), 14th Bt *cr* 1611; Senior Legal Assistant, Treasury Solicitor's Department, since 1977; *b* 14 May 1942; *s* of His Honour John Charles Dundas Harington, QC (*d* 1980) (*yr s* of 12th Bt) and of Lavender Cecilia Harington, *d* of late Major E. W. Denny, Garboldisham Manor, Diss; *S* uncle, 1981. *Educ:* Eton; Christ Church, Oxford (MA Jurisprudence). Called to the Bar, 1969. Employed in Persian Gulf, 1971-72. Joined Civil Service, 1972. *Recreations:* numerous. *Heir: b* David Richard Harington, *b* 27 June 1944. *Address:* The Ring o'Bells, Whitbourne, Worcester WR6 5RT. *T:* Knightwick 21819.

HARINGTON, Vernon; *see* Harington, E. H. V.

HARINGTON HAWES, Derrick Gordon; *b* 22 May 1907; *s* of late Col Charles Howard Hawes, DSO, MVO, Indian Army; *m* 1932, Drusilla Way; one *s* two *d. Educ:* Wellington Coll.; RMC Sandhurst. 14th Punjab Regt, IA, 1927-34; Indian Political Service, 1934-47; King Edward's Hospital Fund for London, 1949-62; Dir Gen., Internat. Hospital Fedn, 1962-75. *Address:* 8 Northbrook Road, Aldershot, Hants GU11 3HE. *Club:* Oriental.

HARKIN, Brendan; Chairman and Chief Executive, Labour Relations Agency, since 1976; *b* 21 April 1920; *s* of Francis and Catherine Harkin; *m* 1949, Maureen Gee; one *s* two *d. Educ:* St Mary's Christian Brothers' Primary and Grammar Schs, Belfast. Apprentice Electrician, 1936. Asst Sec. 1953, Gen. Sec. 1955-76, NI Civil Service Assoc. (which after amalgamations became Public Service Alliance, 1971). Chm., Strathearn Audio Ltd, 1974-76; Deputy Chairman: NI Finance Corp., 1972-76; NI Development Agency, 1976. Mem., EEC Economic and Social Cttee, 1973-76. Pres., Irish Congress of Trade Unions, 1976. Mem. Council, NUU. Regular television and radio broadcaster, and contributor to several publications, particularly on industrial relations. *Recreations:* theatre, music, reading. *Address:* 524 Antrim Road, Belfast, Northern Ireland. *T:* 21442.

HARKNESS, Lt-Col Hon. Douglas Scott, OC 1978; GM 1943; ED 1944; PC (Canada) 1957; Minister of National Defence, Canada, 1960-63; *b* 29 March 1903; *s* of William Keefer and Janet Douglas Harkness (*née* Scott); *m* 1932, Frances Elisabeth, *d* of James Blair McMillan, Charlottetown and Calgary; one *s. Educ:* Central Collegiate, Calgary; University of Alberta (BA). Served overseas in War (Italy and NW Europe), 1940-45; Major and Lt-Col, Royal Canadian Artillery; with Reserve Army, CO 41st Anti-Tank Regt (SP), Royal Canadian Artillery. MP (Calgary E) gen. elecs, 1945, 1949; Re-elected: (Calgary N) gen. elecs, 1953, 1957, 1958, 1962, 1963, 1965, (Calgary Centre) 1968, retired 1972. Min. for Northern Affairs and Nat. Resources and Actg Minister of Agric., June 1957; Minister of Agric., Aug. 1957; relinquished portfolios of Northern Affairs and Nat. Resources, Aug. 1957, of Agriculture, Oct. 1960. Mem. Alta Military Institute. Hon. LLD Calgary, 1975. *Address:* 716 Imperial Way SW, Calgary, Alta T2S 1N7, Canada. *T:* Calgary (403) 243-0825. *Clubs:* Ranchmen's, Calgary Petroleum (Calgary).

HARKNESS, Rear-Adm. James Percy Knowles, CB 1971; *b* 28 Nov. 1916; *s* of Captain P. Y. Harkness, West Yorkshire Regt, and Gladys Dundas Harkness (*née* Knowles); *m* 1949, Joan, *d* of late Vice-Adm. N. A. Sulivan, CVO; two *d.* Dir-Gen., Naval Manpower, 1970; retired 1972. *Recreation:* sailing.

HARKNESS, Captain Kenneth Lanyon, CBE 1963; DSC 1940; Royal Navy; *b* 24 Aug. 1900; *s* of late Major T. R. Harkness, RA, and late Mrs G. A. de Burgh; *m* 1st, 1932, Joan Phyllis Lovell (*d* 1979); one *d*; 2nd, 1979, Mary Isabel Powell (*née* Stroud), Brettenham, Suffolk. *Educ:* RN Colls, Osborne and Dartmouth; Cambridge Univ. Midshipman, HMS Bellerophon, 1917; Cambridge Univ., 1922; Qual. Gunnery, 1926; Comdr Admty, 1935; Sqdn Gunnery Off., 2nd Battle Sqdn, 1937; Comd HMS Winchelsea, 1938; Comd HMS Fearless, 1939-40; Capt. 1940; Chief of Intell. Service, Far East, 1940-42; Dep. Dir of Naval Ordnance, Admty, 1943-44; Comd HMS Ceylon, 1945; Comd HMS Sheffield, 1946; Chief of Staff to C-in-C Portsmouth, 1947; retired from RN, 1949. Civil Defence Officer, Portsmouth, 1949; Home Office, Asst Chief Trg Off. (CD), 1952; Prin. Off., later Reg. Dir of CD, London Reg., 1954; Temp. seconded as CD Adviser, Cyprus, 1956; later Regional Dir of Civil Defence, London Region, 1954-65. *Recreation:* gardening. *Address:* Far Rockaway, Durford Wood, Petersfield, Hants GU31 5AW. *T:* Liss 3173.

HARLAND, Ven. Ian; Archdeacon of Doncaster, since 1979; *b* 19 Dec. 1932; *s* of Canon Samuel James Harland and Brenda Gwendolyn Harland; *m* 1967, Susan Hinman; one *s* three *d. Educ:* Dragon School, Oxford; Haileybury; Peterhouse, Cambridge (MA); Wycliffe Hall, Oxford. Teaching at Sunningdale School, 1956-58; Curate, Melton Mowbray, 1960-63; Vicar, Oughtibridge, Sheffield, 1963-72; Member, Wortley RDC, 1969-73; Vicar, St Cuthbert, Fir Vale, Sheffield, 1972-75; Priest-in-charge, All Saints, Brightside, 1973-75; RD of Ecclesfield, 1973-75; Vicar of Rotherham, 1975-79; RD of Rotherham, 1976-79. Proctor in Convocation, 1975. *Recreations:* politics; sport. *Address:* 2 Durham Road, Dunscroft, Doncaster, S Yorks DN7 4NQ. *T:* Doncaster 841769.

HARLAND, Rt. Rev. Maurice Henry, MA, DD; *b* 17 April 1896; *s* of late Rev. William George Harland and late Clara Elizabeth Harland; *m* 1923, Agnes Hildyard Winckley, MBE 1967; two *d. Educ:* St Peter's Sch., York; Exeter Coll., Oxford (MA); Leeds Clergy Sch. DD (Lambeth) 1948. 2nd Lieut West Yorks Regt, 1914-15; 2nd Lieut R Field Artillery, 1915-16; Lieut Royal Flying Corps and afterwards RAF, 1916-19; Curate St Peter's, Leicester, 1922-27; Priest in Charge St Anne's Conventional District, 1927-33; Perpetual Curate of St Matthew's Holbeck, Leeds, 1933-38; Vicar of St Mary's, Windermere, 1938-42; Rural Dean of Ambleside; Vicar of Croydon, 1942-47; Archdeacon of Croydon, 1946-47; Hon. Canon of Canterbury, 1942-47; Bishop Suffragan of Croydon, 1942-47; Bishop of Lincoln, 1947-56; Bishop of Durham, 1956-66, retired. Select Preacher, Oxford Univ., 1949-50. Pres., Edinburgh Sir Walter Scott Soc., 1940-50; Hon. Fellow, Exeter Coll., Oxford, 1950; Hon. DD Durham Univ., 1956. Introduced to House of Lords, 1954 and again in 1956 on becoming Bishop of Durham. *Recreations:* fishing, riding. *Address:* White Chimneys, Rookwood Road, West Wittering, near Chichester, West Sussex PO20 8LT. *T:* West Wittering 2351.

See also M. H. W. Wells.

HARLAND, Air Marshal Sir Reginald (Edward Wynyard), KBE 1974; CB 1972; with W. S. Atkins and Partners, Epsom, since 1977; *b* 30 May 1920; *s* of Charles Cecil Harland and Ida Maud (*née* Bellhouse); *m* 1942, Doreen Rosalind, *d* of late W. H. C. Romanis; two *s* two *d* (and one *s* decd). *Educ:* Summer Fields, Oxford; Stowe; Trinity Coll., Cambridge (MA). Served War of 1939-45: RAE Farnborough, 1941-42; N Africa, Italy and S France, 1942-45. Techn. trng, techn. plans and manning depts, Air Min., 1946-49; pilot trng, 1949-50; Chief Engrg Instructor, RAF Coll., Cranwell, 1950-52; Guided Weapon trng, RMCS Shrivenham, 1952-53; Thunderbird Project Officer: RAE Farnborough, 1953-55; Min. of Supply, 1955-56; psa 1957; Ballistic Missile Liaison Officer, (BJSM) Los Angeles, 1958-60; CO, Central Servicing Develt Estab., Swanton Morley, 1960-62; STSO, HQ No 3 (Bomber) Gp, Mildenhall, 1962-64; AO i/c Engrg, HQ Far East Air Force, Singapore, 1964-66; Harrier Project Dir, HQ Min. of Technology, 1967-68; idc 1969; AOC No 24 Group, RAF, 1970-72; AO Engineering, Air Support Command, 1972; AOC-in-C, RAF Support Command, 1973-77. Mem. Council, BIM, 1973-78; Pres., Soc. Environmental Engrs, 1974-78. CEng 1966; FIMechE 1967; FIEE 1964; FRAeS 1967; CBIM (FBIM 1974); FIE (Singapore) 1967; MIE (Malaysia) 1966. *Publications:* occasional articles in Jl RAeS and other engrg jls. *Recreations:* sailing, bridge, reading. *Address:* Battlecrease Hall, Russell Road, Shepperton, Mddx TW17 8JW. *T:* Walton-on-Thames 26060. *Club:* Royal Air Force.

HARLAND, Sydney Cross, DSc (London); FRS 1943; FRSE 1951; FTI (Hon.) 1954; George Harrison Professor of Botany, Manchester University, 1950-58, retired, Emeritus Professor, 1958; Member, Agricultural Research Council, 1950-55; *b* 19 June 1891; *s* of Erasmus and Eliza Harland, Cliff Grange, Snainton, Yorks; *m* 1st, 1915, Emily Wilson Cameron; two *d*; 2nd, 1934, Olive Sylvia Atteck; one *s. Educ:* Municipal Secondary School, Scarborough; King's Coll., London. Asst Supt Agric., St Vincent, BWI, 1915; Asst for Cotton Research, Imp. Dept Agric. for West Indies, 1918; Head Botanical Dept, British Cotton Industry Res. Assoc., Manchester, 1920; Prof. Botany and Genetics, Imperial Coll. Trop. Agric., Trinidad, 1923; Chief Geneticist, Empire Cotton Growing Corp., Cotton Research Station, Trinidad, and Cotton Adviser to Comr of Agric., 1926; Gen. Adviser to State Cotton Industry of Sao Paulo, Brazil, 1935; Dir, Institute of Cotton Genetics, National Agricultural Soc., Peru, 1939-50. Mem., UNESCO Mission to Ecuador, 1962. President: Genetical Soc. of GB, 1953-56; Indian Cotton Congress, 1956; Fellow: Botanical Soc., Edinburgh, 1953; New England Inst. of Medical Res., 1963. Hon. Mem., Internat. Union for R&D, 1964. Hon. MSc Manchester, 1958; Hon. DSc West Indies, 1973. *Publications:* The Genetics of Cotton, 1939; also papers on cotton, cocoa, other tropical crops, and applied genetics. *Recreations:* travel, gardening, human genetics. *Address:* Cliff Grange, Snainton, Scarborough, Yorks. *T:* Snainton 549. *Club:* Athenæum.

HARLAND, Prof. William Arthur; Regius Professor of Forensic Medicine, University of Glasgow, since Oct. 1974; *b* 7 March 1926; *s* of Robert Wallace Harland and Elizabeth Montgomery Robb; *m* 1953, Brenda Foxcroft; three *s* one *d. Educ:* Methodist Coll., Belfast; Queen's Univ., Belfast. MB, BCh Belfast 1948, MD Belfast 1974; FRCP(C) 1959, PhD London 1964, FRCPath 1967, MRCPGlas 1971, FRCPGlas 1974, FRSE 1980. Demonstrator in Pathology, Emory Univ., 1951-53; Resident Pathologist, Presbyterian Hosp., NY, 1954; Dir of Labs, St Joseph's Hosp., Chatham, Ont, 1955-58; Assoc. Path., Jewish Gen. Hosp., Montreal, 1958-60; Sen. Lectr in Pathology, Univ. of West Indies, 1960-64; Path., MRC Atheroma Res. Unit, Western Infirmary, Glasgow, 1964-66; Sen. Lectr in Pathology, Univ. of Glasgow,

1966-74. *Publications:* various articles in sci. jls on thyroid diseases and on atherosclerosis. *Recreation:* sheep farming. *Address:* Department of Forensic Medicine, University of Glasgow, Glasgow G12 8QQ. *T:* 041-339 8855.

HARLE, James Coffin, DPhil; Keeper, Department of Eastern Art, Ashmolean Museum, Oxford, since 1967; Student of Christ Church, Oxford, since 1970; *b* 5 April 1920; *s* of James Wyly Harle and Elfrieda Frances (*née* Baumann); *m* 1st, 1949, Jacqueline Thérèse Ruch (marr. diss. 1966, she *d* 1968); 2nd, 1967, Mrs Carola Sybil Mary Fleming (*d* 1971); 3rd, 1973, Lady (Betty) Hulbert. *Educ:* St George's Sch., Newport, RI; Princeton Univ. (BA 1942, Phi Beta Kappa); Oxford Univ. (BA 1st cl. Sanskrit and Pali, 1956, DPhil 1959). Served War, 1942-46, USNR (Aviation Br.), retd as Lieut; DFC (US). Asst to Dean of the College, Princeton, 1947; Part-time instructor in English, Princeton, 1948-49; Fulbright Lectr, Philippines, 1953-54; Ashmolean Museum: Asst Keeper, 1960; Sen. Asst Keeper, 1962. *Publications:* Tower Gateways in South India, 1963; Gupta Sculpture, 1974; articles in periodicals on Indian Art. *Address:* Hawkswell, Portland Road, Oxford. *T:* Oxford 55236. *Club:* Princeton (New York).

HARLECH, 5th Baron *cr* 1876; **William David Ormsby Gore,** PC 1957; KCMG 1961; *b* 20 May 1918; *e* surv. *s* of 4th Baron Harlech, KG, PC, GCMG, and Lady Beatrice Cecil (Dowager Lady Harlech, DCVO) (*d* 1980); *S* father, 1964; *m* 1st, 1940, Sylvia (*d* 1967), 2nd *d* of late Hugh Lloyd Thomas, CMG, CVO; one *s* three *d* (and one *s* decd); 2nd, 1969, Pamela, *o d* of Ralph F. Colin, New York; one *d*. *Educ:* Eton; New Coll., Oxford. Joined Berks Yeomanry, 1939, Adjutant, 1942; Major (GS), 1945. MP (C) Oswestry Div. of Salop, 1950-61; Parliamentary Private Sec. to Minister of State for Foreign Affairs, 1951; Parliamentary Under-Sec. of State for Foreign Affairs, Nov. 1956-Jan. 1957; Minister of State for Foreign Affairs, 1957-61; British Ambassador in Washington, 1961-65. Dep.-Leader of the Opposition, House of Lords, 1966-67. Dep. Chm., Commn on Rhodesian Opinion, 1972. President: British Bd of Film Censors, 1965-; The Pilgrims (Soc. of UK, 1965-77); Trustee, The Pilgrim Trust, 1965- (Chm., 1974-79); Chairman: Harlech Television; Kennedy Meml Trust; Papworth and Enham Village Settlements; European Movement, 1969-75; RIIA, 1978-. Director: Morgan Crucible, 1965-; Commercial Bank of Wales, 1972-. Chm., Adv. Cttee, Kennedy Inst., Harvard; Mem., Adv. Cttee, V&A Mus., 1979-; Trustee, Tate Gallery, 1971-78; Governor, Yehudi Menuhin Sch. Hon. Chm., Shelter, 1969-73, Pres. 1973-78; Chm., Nat. Cttee for Electoral Reform, 1976-. Hon. Fellow, New Coll., Oxford, 1964. Hon. DCL, Univ. of Pittsburgh, 1962; Hon. LLD: Brown Univ., 1963; New York Univ., 1964; William and Mary Coll., 1965; Manchester, 1966. DL Salop, 1961. KStJ. *Publications:* Must the West Decline?, 1966; (jtly) Europe: the case for going in, 1971. *Heir: s* Hon. Francis David Ormsby Gore, *b* 13 March 1954. *Address:* 14 Ladbroke Road, W11. *T:* 01-229 6701; House of Lords, Westminster, SW1; Glyn, Talsarnau, Gwynedd. *T:* Harlech 780338. *Club:* Pratt's.

See also Rt Hon. M. V. Macmillan, Sir A. L. Mayall, Baron Wardington.

HARLEY, Prof. John Laker, CBE 1979; FRS 1964; FLS; MA, DPhil Oxon; Professor of Forest Science, Oxford University, 1969-79, now Emeritus Professor; Fellow of St John's College, Oxford, 1969-79, now Emeritus Fellow; *b* 17 Nov. 1911; *s* of late Charles Laker Harley and Edith Sarah (*née* Smith); *m* 1938, Elizabeth Lindsay Fitt; one *s* one *d*. *Educ:* Leeds Grammar Sch.; Wadham Coll., Oxford. Open Exhibition, Wadham Coll., 1930, Hon. Scholar 1933, Hon. Fellow, 1972; Christopher Welch Scholar, Oxford, 1933-37; Senior Student 1851 Exhibition, 1937-38. Departmental Demonstrator, Oxford, 1938-44. Served in Royal Signals, 1940-45: attached Operation Research Group No. 1, India, Lieut-Col GSO1. University Demonstrator, Oxford, 1945-62; Browne Research Fellow, Queen's Coll., Oxford, 1946-52; Official Fellow, Queen's Coll., Oxford, 1952-65; Reader in Plant Nutrition, Oxford Univ., 1962-65; Prof. of Botany, Sheffield Univ., 1965-69. Mem., ARC, 1970-80. President: British Mycological Soc., 1967 (Hon. Mem. 1980); British Ecological Soc., 1970-72. Hon. Fellow, Nat. Acad. of Scis, India, 1981. Hon. FilDr Uppsala, 1981. Editor, New Phytologist, 1961-. *Publications:* Biology of Mycorrhiza, 1969; scientific papers in New Phytologist, Annals of Applied Mycology, Annals of Botany, Biochemical Jl, Plant Physiology, Proc. Royal Soc., Jl of Ecology. *Recreation:* gardening. *Address:* The Orchard, Old Marston, Oxford OX3 0PQ.

HARLEY, Sir Thomas (Winlack), Kt 1960; MBE 1944; MC 1918; DL; Consultant with Simpson North Harley & Co., solicitors, Liverpool and with Stanleys & Simpson North, London, admitted 1922; *b* 27 June 1895; *o s* of George Harley and Annie Thomson (*née* Macwatty); *m* 1924, Margaret Hilda (*d* 1981), 2nd *d* of late Canon J. U. N. Bardsley; three *s*. *Educ:* Birkenhead Sch.; Eton. Served European War, 1914-19, France and Balkans, Major The King's Own Regt (despatches, MC); War of 1939-45, Major RA (TA); comd (HG) AA Battery (MBE). Mem., Liverpool Regional Hosp. Bd, 1947- (Chm., 1959-68). Mem. Board of Governors, United Liverpool Hosps, 1955-69; Pres., Bebington and Ellesmere Port Conservative Assoc., etc. DL Cheshire (formerly County of Chester), 1962. *Recreation:* gardening. *Address:* Hesketh Hey, Thornton Hough, Wirral, Merseyside L63 1JA. *T:* 051-336 3439. *Clubs:* Royal Over-Seas League; Royal Liverpool Golf.

HARMAN, Sir Cecil W. F. S. K.; *see* Stafford-King-Harman.

HARMAN, Ernest Henry, CBE 1973 (OBE 1961); Chairman, South Western Gas Region (formerly South Western Gas Board), 1964-73; *b* 1908;

m 2nd, 1958, Dorothy Anne Parsons; (two *d* by 1st *m*). *Educ:* London Univ. BSc (Hons). Sec., 1936, Gen. Manager, 1944, Commercial Gas Co.; Gen. Manager, Sheffield and Rotherham Div., East Midlands Gas Board, 1949; Dep. Chm., East Midlands Gas Board, 1952. *Recreations:* tennis, motoring, music. *Address:* Court Hill, Low Road, Church Lench, Evesham, Worcs WR11 4UH.

HARMAN, Gen. Sir Jack (Wentworth), GCB 1978 (KCB 1974); OBE 1962; MC 1943; Deputy Supreme Allied Commander, Europe, 1978-81; *b* 20 July 1920; *s* of late Lt-Gen. Sir Wentworth Harman, KCB, DSO, and late Dorothy Harman; *m* 1947, Gwladys May Murphy (*widow* of Lt-Col R. J. Murphy), *d* of Sir Idwal Lloyd; one *d* and two step *d*. *Educ:* Wellington Coll.; RMC Sandhurst. Commissioned into The Queen's Bays, 1940, Bt Lt-Col, 1958; Commanding Officer, 1st The Queen's Dragoon Guards, 1960-62; commanded 11 Infantry Bde, 1965-66; attended IDC, 1967; BGS, HQ Army Strategic Command, 1968-69; GOC, 1st Div., 1970-72; Commandant, RMA, Sandhurst, 1972-73; GOC 1 (British) Corps, 1974-76; Adjutant-General, 1976-78. ADC Gen. to the Queen, 1977-80. Col, 1st The Queen's Dragoon Guards, 1975-80; Col Comdt, RAC, 1977-80. *Address:* Sandhills House, Dinton, near Salisbury, Wilts. *T:* Teffont 288. *Club:* Cavalry and Guards.

HARMAN, Jeremiah LeRoy, QC 1968; *b* 13 April 1930; *er s* of late Rt Hon. Sir Charles Eustace Harman; *m* 1960, Erica Jane, *e d* of late Hon. Sir Maurice Richard Bridgeman, KBE; two *s* one *d*. *Educ:* Horris Hill Sch.; Eton Coll. Served Coldstream Guards and Parachute Regt, 1948-51; Parachute Regt (TA), 1951-55. Called to the Bar, Lincoln's Inn, 1954, Bencher, 1977; called to Hong Kong Bar, 1978, Singapore Bar, 1980; Mem., Bar Council, 1963-67. Dir, Dunford & Elliott Ltd, 1972-79. *Recreations:* fishing, shooting, stalking, watching birds. *Address:* Great Shefford House, Newbury, Berks. *T:* Gt Shefford 212; Sra-na-Cloya, near Louisburgh, Co. Mayo; 9 Old Square, Lincoln's Inn, WC2. *T:* 01-405 0846.

HARMAN, John Bishop, FRCS, FRCP; Honorary Consulting Physician, since 1972; *b* 10 Aug. 1907; *s* of late Nathaniel Bishop Harman and of Katharine (*née* Chamberlain); *m* 1946, Anna Charlotte Malcolm Spicer; four *d*. *Educ:* Oundle; St John's Coll., Cambridge (Scholar); St Thomas's Hospital (Scholar). Fearnsides Scholar, Cantab, 1932; 1st Cl. Nat. Sci. Tripos Pt I, 2nd Cl. Pt II, Cantab; MA 1933; MD 1937; FRCS 1932; FRCP 1942. Physician: St Thomas' Hospital, 1938-72; Royal Marsden Hospital, 1947-72. Pres., Medical Defence Union, 1976-; 2nd Vice Pres., RCP, 1981-82. Late Lt-Col RAMC (despatches). *Publications:* contribs to medical literature. *Recreation:* horticulture. *Address:* 108 Harley Street, W1. *T:* 01-935 7822.

HARMAN, Robert Donald, QC 1974; a Recorder of the Crown Court, since 1972; *b* 26 Sept. 1928; *o s* of late Herbert Donald Harman, MC; *m* 1st, 1960, Sarah Elizabeth (*d* 1965), *o d* of late G. C. Cleverly; two *s* ; 2nd, 1968, Rosamond Geraldine, JP, 2nd *d* of late Cmdr G. T. A. Scott, RN; two *d*. *Educ:* privately; St Paul's Sch.; Magdalen Coll., Oxford. Called to Bar, Gray's Inn, 1954; South-Eastern Circuit; a Junior Prosecuting Counsel to the Crown at Central Criminal Court, 1967-72; a Senior Treasury Counsel, 1972-74. Appeal Steward, BBB of C. Liveryman, Goldsmiths' Co. *Address:* 2 Harcourt Buildings, Temple, EC4. *T:* 01-353 2112; 17 Pelham Crescent, SW7 2NR. *T:* 01-584 4304. *Clubs:* Garrick, Beefsteak, Pratt's; Swinley Forest Golf.

HARMAR-NICHOLLS, family name of **Baron Harmar-Nicholls.**

HARMAR-NICHOLLS, Baron *cr* 1974 (Life Peer), of Peterborough, Cambs; **Harmar Harmar-Nicholls,** JP; Bt 1960; Member (C) Greater Manchester South, European Parliament, since 1979; *b* 1 Nov. 1912; 3rd *s* of Charles E. C. Nicholls and Sarah Anne Nicholls, Walsall; *m* 1940, Dorothy Elsie, *e d* of James Edwards, Tipton; two *d*. *Educ:* Dorsett Road Sch., Darlaston; Queen Mary's Gram. Sch., Walsall. Mem. Middle Temple Inn of Court. Chairman: Nicholls and Hennessy (Hotels) Ltd; Malvern Festival Theatre Trust Ltd; Pleasurama, 1970-; Director: J. & H. Nicholls & Co., Paints, etc, 1945-; Radio Luxemburg (London) Ltd; Cannon Assurance Ltd, 1971-72; Mem. of Syndicate at Lloyd's. Mem. Darlaston UDC at age of 26 (Chm., 1949-50); County Magistrate, 1946. Vice-Chm. W Midland Fedn, Junior Imperial League, 1937; contested (C): Nelson and Colne, 1945; Preston by-election, 1946; MP (C) Peterborough Div. of Northants, 1950-Sept. 1974; PPS to Asst Postmaster-Gen., 1951-April 1955; Parly Sec., Min. of Agriculture, Fisheries and Food, April 1955-Jan. 1957; Parliamentary Sec., Min. of Works, 1957-60; Mem. Conservative Housing Cttee; Sec. of Parly Road Safety Cttee (Conservative); Jt Sec. All party Parly Group Empire Migration; Mem. Govt Overseas Settlement Board on migration to Commonwealth. War of 1939-45: volunteered as sapper, commnd Royal Engineers; served India and Burma. *Recreations:* gardening, reading, walking, theatre. *Address:* Abbeylands, Weston, Stafford. *T:* Weston 252. *Clubs:* St Stephen's Constitutional; (Pres.) Unionist, City and Counties (Peterborough); Conservative (Darlaston); Unionist (Walsall).

HARMER, Cyril Henry Carrington; *b* 17 Aug. 1903; *s* of Henry Revell Harmer and Edith Annie Harmer; *m* 1935, Elizabeth Boyd Baird; two *d*. *Educ:* Brighton Grammar Sch. Joined H. R. Harmer, 1921; Partner, 1927; Dir, 1946; Chm. and Man. Dir, 1967-76; Pres., 1976-79. Lieut RA, 1939-45; POW, 1941-45. FInstD; Roll of Distinguished Philatelists, 1969. *Publications:* (with R. E. R. Dalwick) Newfoundland Air Mails, 1953; contribs to philatelic jls. *Recreation:* bowls. *Address:* 20 Wildcroft Manor, SW15 3TS. *T:* 01-788 0710.

Clubs: Hurlingham; Collectors (New York); Western Province Sports (Cape).

HARMER, Sir Dudley; *see* Harmer, Sir J. D.

HARMER, Sir Frederic (Evelyn), Kt 1968; CMG 1945; *b* 3 Nov. 1905; *yr s* of late Sir Sidney Frederic Harmer, KBE, FRS; *m* 1st, 1931, Barbara Susan (*d* 1972), *er d* of late Major J. A. C. Hamilton, JP, Fyne Court, Bridgwater, Som.; one *s* two *d*; 2nd, 1973, Daphne Shelton Agar. *Educ:* Eton; King's Coll., Cambridge. Wrangler, Maths Tripos Part II, 1926; Class 1, Div. 1, Econs Tripos Part II 1927; BA 1927; MA 1934. Entered Treasury, Sept. 1939; Temp. Asst Sec., 1943-45; served in Washington, March-June 1944 and again in Sept.-Dec. 1945 for Anglo-American economic and financial negotiations; resigned Dec. 1945. Dep. Chm., P&OSN Co., 1957-70. Chairman: Cttee of European Shipowners, 1965-68; Internat. Chamber of Shipping, 1968-71; HM Govt Dir, British Petroleum Co. Ltd, 1953-70. Hon. Fellow, LSE, 1970. *Recreations:* sailing, golf. *Address:* Tiggins Field, Kelsale, Saxmundham, Suffolk. *T:* Saxmundham 3156.

HARMER, Sir (John) Dudley, Kt 1972; OBE 1963; JP; farmer; *b* 27 July 1913; *s* of Ernest George William Harmer and Germaine Stuart Harmer (*née* Wells); *m* 1947, Erika Minder-Lanz, Switzerland; two *s. Educ:* Merchant Taylors' Sch.; Wye College. Certif. Agriculture. Mem. 1956, Dep. Chm. 1964-72, Kent Agric. Exec. Cttee; Mem., Kent CC Agric. and Smallholdings Cttee, 1958 (Chm. of Selection of Tenants and Loans Sub-Cttee); Vice-Chm. 1964-66, Chm. 1966-71, SE Area Conservative Provincial Council. Service connected with Home Guard, 1952-56: Hon. Major 1956. Trustee, Develt and Endowment Fund of Kent Inc. Soc. for Promoting Experiments in Horticulture, 1979-. JP Kent, 1962. *Recreations:* gardening, travel. *Address:* Stone Hill, Egerton, Ashford, Kent. *T:* Egerton 241. *Club:* Royal Commonwealth Society.

HARMER, Michael Hedley, MA, MB Cantab, FRCS; Consulting Surgeon, Royal Marsden Hospital and Paddington Green Children's Hospital (St Mary's Hospital); *b* 6 July 1912; *y s* of late Douglas Harmer, MC, FRCS, and May (*née* Hedley); *m* 1939, Bridget Jean, *d* of late James Higgs-Walker, MA, and of Muriel Jessie, *e d* of Rev. Harold Earnshaw Smith; one *s* one *d. Educ:* Marlborough; King's Coll., Cambridge; St Bartholomew's Hosp., London. Surgical Specialist, RAFVR, 1943-46. Bellman Snark Club, Cambridge, 1934-. Freeman of Norwich by Patrimony, 1935. *Publications:* A Handbook of Surgery, 1951; Aids to Surgery, 1962; (Jt Editor) Rose and Carless's Manual of Surgery, 19th edn, 1959; The Forgotten Hospital, 1982; papers on the surgery and classification of malignant disease. *Recreations:* music, the country. *Address:* Perrot Wood, Graffham, Petworth, Sussex GU28 0NZ. *T:* Graffham 307.

HARMOOD-BANNER, Sir George Knowles, 3rd Bt, *cr* 1924; *b* 9 Nov. 1918; *s* of Sir Harmood Harmood-Banner, 2nd Bt, and Frances Cordelia (*d* 1975), *d* of late George Duberly, JP, Plansworth, Co. Durham; *S* father 1950; *m* 1947, Rosemary Jane, *d* of Col M. L. Treston, CBE, FRCS, FRCOG, late IMS, and late Mrs Sheila Treston; two *d. Educ:* Eton; University of Cambridge. Served War of 1939-45; 2nd Lieut Royal Welch Fusiliers, 1942, attached to East African Engineers (SEAC); transferred RASC, 1945. *Recreations:* tennis, ski-ing and swimming. *Heir:* none. *Address:* c/o The Bank of Nova Scotia, 62-63 Threadneedle Street, EC2P 2LS.

HARMSWORTH, family name of **Viscount Rothermere** and **Baron Harmsworth.**

HARMSWORTH, 2nd Baron, *cr* 1939, of Egham; **Cecil Desmond Bernard Harmsworth;** painter; *b* 1903; *e s* of 1st Baron Harmsworth and Emilie Alberta (*d* 1942), *d* of William Hamilton Maffett, Finglas, Co. Dublin; *S* father, 1948; *m* 1926, Dorothy Alexander, *d* of late Hon. J. C. Heinlein, Bridgeport, Ohio, USA; one *d. Educ:* Eton Coll.; Christ Church, Oxford (MA); (in drawing) Académie Julian, Paris; (in painting) public galleries. Was successively newspaperman and book publisher before becoming a painter. Exhibitions: Galerie des Quatre-Chemins, Paris, 1933; Wildenstein Gall., London, 1938; Bonestell Gall., New York, 1944; Swedish Modern, Dallas, Texas, 1950; Messrs Roland, Browse & Delbanco, London, 1954. Has been regular contributor to Salon d'Automne and group exhibitions in Paris; has exhibited in many London and New York galleries, and at the Phillips Memorial Gallery, Washington, DC. Portraits of Norman Douglas, Havelock Ellis, Lord Inverchapel, James Joyce, Consuelo de Saint-Exupéry, Sir Osbert Sitwell, Swami Nikhilananda, etc. Chairman, Dr Johnson's House Trust. Served in British Information Services, New York, 1940-46. *Publications:* occasional prose and verse contributions to English, Irish, and US periodicals, inc. verse translation of Paul Valéry, Le Cimetière Marin (Adam Internat. Review nos 334-336, 1969); drawings and paintings reproduced in US magazines. *Heir:* b Hon. Eric Beauchamp Northcliffe Harmsworth [*b* 28 Aug. 1905; *m* 1935, Hélène (*d* 1962), *d* of Col Jules-Raymond Dehove, Paris; one *s* one *d*; *m* 1964, Mrs Helen Hudson, London. *Educ:* Eton Coll.; Christ Church, Oxford (MA)]. *Address:* Lime Lodge, Egham, Surrey. *T:* Egham 2379.

HARMSWORTH, Sir Hildebrand Harold, 3rd Bt *cr* 1922; *b* 5 June 1931; *s* of Sir Hildebrand Alfred Beresford Harmsworth, 2nd Bt, and Elen, *d* of Nicolaj Billenstein, Randers, Denmark; *S* father, 1977; *m* 1960, Gillian Andrea, *o d* of William John Lewis; one *s* two *d. Educ:* Harrow; Trinity College, Dublin. *Heir:* s Hildebrand Esmund Miles Harmsworth, *b* 1 Sept. 1964. *Address:* Ewlyn Villa, 42 Leckhampton Road, Cheltenham.

HARMSWORTH, St John Bernard Vyvyan; a Metropolitan Magistrate, since 1961; *b* 28 Nov. 1912; *e s* of Vyvyan George Harmsworth and Constance Gwendolen Mary Catt; *m* 1937, Jane Penelope, *er d* of Basil Tanfield Berridge Boothby; three *d. Educ:* Harrow; New Coll., Oxford. Called to the Bar, Middle Temple, 1937. Served in RNVR, Lieut-Comdr, Oct. 1939-Feb. 1946. *Recreations:* fly fishing, tennis. *Address:* 25 Whitelands House, SW3. *Clubs:* Boodle's, Pratt's, Beefsteak.

HARNDEN, Lt-Col Arthur Baker, CB 1969; BSc, CEng, FIEE, MBIM; Chairman, Appeals Tribunals, Supplementary Benefits Commission, since 1970; *b* 6 Jan. 1909; *s* of Cecil Henry Harnden and Susan (*née* Baker); *m* 1st, 1935, Maisie Elizabeth Annie (*d* 1970), *d* of A. H. Winterburn, LRIBA; one *s*; 2nd, 1971, Jean Kathleen, *d* of H. F. Wheeler and *widow* of Eric J. Dedman; one step *s. Educ:* various state schools. Exec. Engr, GPO, 1933; Royal Corps of Signals, 1939-45; GSO1, WO, 1942; DCSO Antwerp, 1944, Hamburg 1945. Dir, London Telecommunications Region, GPO, 1962; Senior Dir, Operations, PO (Telecommunications), 1967-69. Principal, Comrie House Sch., Finchley, 1971-72. *Recreations:* painting and potting. *Address:* Comrie, Dipley, Hartley Wintney, Hants. *T:* Hartley Wintney 3265.

HARPER, Alfred Alexander, MA, MD; Professor of Physiology, University of Newcastle upon Tyne, 1963-72; *b* 19 June 1907; *er s* of James and Elizabeth Harper. *Educ:* Aberdeen Grammar Sch.; Aberdeen Univ. Lecturer in Physiology, University of Leeds, 1935-36; Demonstrator in Physiology, St Thomas's Hosp., London, 1936-39; Lectr, later Reader, in Human Physiology, Univ. of Manchester, 1939-49; Prof. of Physiology, Univ. of Durham, 1949-63. *Publications:* papers in Jl of Physiology mostly on physiology of digestion. *Address:* Wellburn House, Benwell Lane, Newcastle upon Tyne NE15 6LX. *T:* Newcastle 748178.

HARPER, Sir Arthur (Grant), KCVO 1959 (CVO 1954); CBE 1954; JP; now retired; Chairman: Wareham Associates Ltd; Woolshed Restaurant Ltd; Deputy Chairman, Williams Development Holdings Ltd; *b* 16 July 1898; *s* of William John and Robina Harper; *m* 1925, Hilda Mary Evans (decd); two *s* one *d. Educ:* Hastings High Sch. Entered NZ Civil Service, 1914; held various positions; Sec. for Internal Affairs, also Clerk of the Writs, NZ, 1948-58. Chief Electoral Officer, 1945-50; Dir of Royal Tours of NZ, 1953-54, 1956, 1958. Patron, Vice-Pres., Trustee or Mem. of several national and local voluntary organizations. JP 1949. *Recreations:* cricket and hockey, bowls (past); interested in most sports. *Address:* Flat 1, 50 Devonshire Road, Miramar, Wellington, NZ. *T:* 886-425. *Club:* United Services Officers' (Wellington).

HARPER, Bill; *see* Harper, F. A.

HARPER, Prof. Denis Rawnsley, CBE 1975; BArch, PhD, MSc Tech, FRIBA, MRTPI, PPIOB, FCIArb; building consultant; Professor of Building at the University of Manchester Institute of Science and Technology, 1957-74, now Emeritus; *b* 27 May 1907; *s* of James William Harper, Harrogate; *m* 1st, 1934, Joan Mary Coggin (*d* 1968); one *s* one *d*; 2nd, 1971, Dora Phylis Oxenham (widow). *Educ:* Harrogate Grammar Sch.; Univ. of Liverpool Sch. of Architecture. Asst Architect in Hosp. practice in London, 1930-38; RIBA Saxon Snell Prizeman, 1939; Lectr in Sch. of Architecture, University of Cape Town, 1939-49. In private practice (with Prof. Thornton White), in Cape Town, as architect and town planner, 1940-50; Associate Architect in BBC TV Centre, 1950-52; Chief Architect to Corby New Town, Northants, 1952-57. Hanson Fellow, The Master Builder Fedn of South Africa, 1972. Cttee Mem., CNAA. Mem., Summerland Fire Commn, 1973-74. *Publications:* Building: process and product, 1978; various contribs to technical jls. *Recreations:* gardening, boating. *Address:* 89 Earls Barton Road, Great Doddington, Wellingborough, Northants. *T:* Wellingborough 223841.

HARPER, Donald John; Director-General, Research C, Procurement Executive, Ministry of Defence, and Deputy Chief Scientist, RAF (retitled Chief Scientist (RAF), 1980), since 1978; *b* 6 Aug. 1923; *s* of Harry Tonkin and Caroline Irene Harper; *m* 1947, Joyce Beryl Kite-Powell; two *d. Educ:* Purley County Grammar Sch. for Boys; Queen Mary Coll., London. 1st cl. BSc (Eng) 1943; CEng, FRAeS. Joined Aero Dept, RAE Farnborough, 1943; Scientific Officer, Spinning Tunnel, 1947-49; High Speed and Transonic Tunnel, 1950-59; Sen. Scientific Officer; Principal Scientific Officer, 1955; Dep. Head of Tunnel, 1958-59; Space Dept RAE, Satellite Launching Vehicles, 1960-62; Senior Principal Scientific Officer, MoD, Central Staff, 1963-65; Head of Assessment Div., Weapons Dept RAE, 1966-68; Dir of Project Time and Cost Analysis, MoD (PE), 1968-71; Dir-Gen., Performance and Cost Analysis, MoD (PE), 1972-77. *Publications:* contrib. Aeronautical Res. Council reports and memoranda and techn. press. *Recreations:* music, especially choral singing; gardening; home improvement. *Address:* Minstrels, Hockering Road, Woking, Surrey. *T:* Woking 60541.

HARPER, Frank Appleby, (Bill), CB 1979; MBE 1954; Director of Establishments and Organisation, Department of Education and Science, 1974-80; *b* 11 April 1920; *s* of F. S. and M. E. B. Harper; *m* 1st, 1943, Daphne Margaret (*née* Short) (*d* 1965); one *d*; 2nd, 1968, Mrs Jillian Kate Langstaff (*née* Brooks). *Educ:* grammar sch., Birmingham. Regular Army (Royal Engrs) until joined Home Civil Service as Direct Entry Principal, 1964;

Under-Sec. 1974. *Recreation:* home workshop. *Address:* Lochnell, Searle Road, Farnham, Surrey. *T:* Farnham (Surrey) 714127.

HARPER, George Clifford; *b* 8 Aug. 1900; *s* of Charles George and Emily Harper, Newcastle upon Tyne; *m* 1st, 1925, Georgette Marie Aimée Guéry (*d* 1977); two *d* (and one *s* decd); 2nd, 1980, Margaret Rose Miriam Benezra. *Educ:* Shrewsbury Sch.; Christ Church, Oxford. Traffic Apprentice LNER; Asst Master at Stowe and Bedford; Headmaster of King Edward VI Sch., Southampton, until 1946; HM Inspector of Schools, 1947-60 (Metropolitan Divisional Inspector, 1952-60); Mem., Anglo-French Mixed Cultural Commn, 1954-60; Chm. and Dir, British Cttee for Interchange of Teachers with USA, 1960-65. Officier d'Académie. *Address:* 2 Trym Bank, Grove Road, Bristol BS9 2RQ. *T:* Bristol 685243.

HARPER, Heather (Mary), (Mrs E. J. Benarroch), CBE 1965; soprano; *b* 8 May 1930; *d* of late Hugh Harper, Belfast; *m* 1973, Eduardo J. Benarroch. *Educ:* Trinity Coll. of Music, London. Has sung many principal roles incl. Arabella, Ariadne, Marschallin, Chrysothemis, Elsa and Kaiserin, at Covent Garden, Glyndebourne, Sadler's Wells, Bayreuth, Teatro Colon (Buenos Aires), Edinburgh Fest., La Scala, NY Met, San Francisco, Deutsche Oper (Berlin), Frankfurt, Netherlands Opera, Canadian Opera Co., Toronto, and has sung at every Promenade Concert season since 1957; created the soprano role in Benjamin Britten's War Requiem in Coventry Cathedral in 1962; soloist at opening concerts: Maltings, Snape, 1967; Queen Elizabeth Hall, 1967. Toured USA, 1965, and USSR, 1967, with BBC SO; has toured USA annually, 1967-, and appears regularly at European music fests; toured: Japan and S Korea with Royal Opera Co., 1979; Australia and Hong Kong with BBC Symph. Orch., 1982; has also sung in Asia, Middle East, Australia and S America. Has made many recordings, incl. works of Britten, Beethoven, Berg, Mahler, Mozart and Verdi; broadcasts frequently throughout the world; also TV appearances. FTCL; Hon. RAM, 1972. Hon. DMus, Queen's Univ., Belfast, 1966. Edison Award, 1971; Grammy Nomination, 1973; Grammy Award, 1979. *Recreations:* gardening, painting, cooking. *Address:* c/o Harrison-Parrott Ltd, 12 Penzance Place, W11.

HARPER, James Norman; a Recorder of the Crown Court, since 1980; *b* 30 Dec. 1932; *s* of late His Honour Judge Norman Harper and of Iris Irene Harper; *m* 1956, Blanka Miroslava Eva Sigmund; one *s* one *d. Educ:* Marlborough Coll.; Magdalen Coll., Oxford (BA Hons). Called to the Bar, Gray's Inn, 1957. Pres., Northumberland County Hockey Assoc. *Recreations:* cricket, hockey, painting. *Address:* 51 Westgate Road, Newcastle upon Tyne NE1 1SS. *T:* Newcastle 320541. *Club:* MCC.

HARPER, Prof. John Lander, DPhil; FRS 1978; Professor of Botany, 1977-82 and Head of School of Plant Biology, 1967-82, University College of North Wales, Bangor (Professor of Agricultural Botany, Department of Agricultural Botany, 1960); *b* 27 May 1925; *s* of John Hindley Harper and Harriett Mary (*née* Archer); *m* 1954, Borgny Lerø; one *s* two *d. Educ:* Lawrence Sheriff Sch., Rugby; Magdalen Coll., Oxford (BA, MA, DPhil). Demonstr, Dept of Agriculture, Univ. of Oxford, 1951, Lectr 1953; Rockefeller Foundn Fellow, Univ. of Calif, 1960-61. *Publications:* Biology of Weeds, 1960; Population Biology of Plants, 1977; papers in Jl of Ecol., New Phytologist, Annals of Applied Biol., and Evolution. *Recreation:* gardening. *Address:* Cae Groes, Glan y Coed Park, Dwygyfylchi, near Penmaenmawr, N Wales. *T:* Penmaenmawr 622362. *Club:* Farmers'.

HARPER, John Mansfield; Managing Director (Inland), British Telecommunications, since 1981; *b* 17 July 1930; *s* of late T. J. Harper and May (*née* Charlton); *m* 1956, Berenice Honorine, *d* of Harold Haydon; one *s* one *d. Educ:* Merchant Taylors' Sch.; St John's Coll., Oxford. 2nd Lieut Royal Corps of Signals, 1948-49. Asst Principal, Post Office, 1953; Private Sec. to Dir-Gen., 1956-58; Principal, 1958-66; Asst Sec., Reorganization Dept, 1966-69; Dir, North-Eastern Telecommunications Region, 1969-71; Dir, Purchasing and Supply, 1972-75; Sen. Dir, Planning and Provisioning, 1975-77; Asst Man. Dir, Telecommunications, 1978-79; Dep. Man. Dir, British Telecommunications (Post Office), 1979-81. Comp IEE; CBIM; FRSA. *Recreations:* music, gardening, electronics. *Address:* 34 Longfield Drive, Amersham, Bucks. *T:* Amersham 5443.

HARPER, Norman Adamson; Vice President, Gemmological Association of Great Britain, since 1978 (Chairman, 1965-78); Founder-Director, Perry Greaves Ltd, 1964; Director: W. A. Perry & Co. Ltd, since 1963; Gemmological Instruments Ltd, since 1965; Managing Director, H. H. Bray Ltd, since 1977; *b* 15 Oct. 1913; *s* of Andrew Adamson Harper, Newcastle-upon-Tyne; *m* 1st, 1935, Priscilla (*d* 1956), *d* of William George Hoverd; three *s* one *d*; 2nd, 1957, Brenda, *d* of Robert Watts; one *s. Educ:* Rutherford Coll.; Durham Univ. Dip. Nat. Assoc. Goldsmiths, 1946. FGA 1934; FRGS 1946; FInstD 1953; FBIM 1978. Chm., Nat. Assoc. of Goldsmiths, 1961-63; Guardian of Standard of Wrought Plate in Birmingham, 1963-; Sen. Lectr on Gemstones and Jewellery, City of Birmingham Sch. of Jewellery and Silversmithing, 1946-66; Founder, Course on Gem Diamonds for Jewellers, 1962. Freedom of Goldsmiths' Co. (Special Award), 1947; Freedom of City of London, 1947. Winner of Greenough Trophy, 1946. *Publications:* Introduction to Gemstones, 1955; Handbook on Gem Diamonds, 1965; articles in Jl of Gemmology, British Jeweller, Watchmaker and Jeweller, etc. *Recreations:* keyboard music, historical studies. *Address:* 9 Jury Street, Warwick CV34 4EH. *T:* Warwick 42791. *Clubs:* Athenæum, Naval and Military, Number Ten; Portcullis (Warwick).

HARPER GOW, Leonard Maxwell, MBE 1944; CBIM; Vice-Chairman, since 1981, and Director, since 1952, Christian Salvesen Ltd (Chairman, 1964-81); *b* 13 June 1918; *s* of late Leonard Harper Gow and Eleanor Amalie (*née* Salvesen); *m* 1944, Lillan Margaret Kiaer; two *s* one *d. Educ:* Cargilfield; Rugby; Corpus Christi Coll., Cambridge Univ. (BA). CBIM (FBIM 1976). Served War, 1939-46: Major RA 1st Commando Bde. 3 seasons with Antarctic Whaling Fleet, 1946-47, 1948-49 and 1952-53. Director: Scottish Widows' Fund & Life Assurance Society, 1964- (Chm., 1972-75); Royal Bank of Scotland Ltd, 1969- (Vice-Chm., 1980-); Royal Bank of Scotland Group Ltd, 1978-; Edinburgh Investment Trust Ltd, 1965-; Radio Forth Ltd, 1973- (Chm.). Chm., Scottish Hosp. Trust; Member: the Queen's Body Guard for Scotland, Royal Co. of Archers; Exec. Cttee, Scottish Council of Develt and Industry; Lloyd's Underwriters; Convener, Univ. of Edinburgh Adv. Cttee on Business Studies. Liveryman, Worshipful Co. of Shipwrights. Pres., Norwegian-Scottish Assoc., Edinburgh; Hon. Consul for Norway in Edinburgh/Leith. Comdr, Order of St Olav, Norway. *Recreations:* hill farming, shooting, golf. *Address:* Eventyr, Lyars Road, Longniddry, East Lothian. *T:* Longniddry 52142. *Clubs:* Caledonian; New (Edinburgh).

HARPHAM, Sir William, KBE 1966 (OBE 1948); CMG 1953; HM Diplomatic Service, retired; Director, Great Britain-East Europe Centre, 1967-80; *b* 3 Dec. 1906; *o s* of W. Harpham and N. Harpham (*née* Stout); *m* 1943, Isabelle Marie Sophie Droz; one *s* one *d. Educ:* Wintringham Secondary Sch., Grimsby; Christ's Coll., Cambridge. Entered Dept of Overseas Trade, 1929; transferred to Embassy, Brussels, 1931, Rome, 1934; Private Sec. to Parliamentary Sec. for Overseas Trade, 1936; seconded to League of Nations, 1937; reverted to Dept of Overseas Trade, 1939; served: Cairo, 1940-44; Beirut, 1944-47; appointed Counsellor (Commercial) at Berne, 1947; Head of Gen. Dept, Foreign Office, 1950-53; Dep. to UK Delegate to OEEC, 1953-56; Minister, British Embassy, Tokyo, 1956-59; Minister (Economic), Paris, 1959-63; Ambassador to Bulgaria, 1964-66; retd 1967. Order of Madara Horseman, Bulgaria, 1969; Order of Stara Planina, Bulgaria, 1976. *Address:* 9 Kings Keep, Putney Hill, SW15 6RA. *T:* 01-788 1383. *Clubs:* Travellers', Royal Automobile.

HARPLEY, Sydney Charles, RA 1981 (ARA 1974); sculptor since 1956; *b* 19 April 1927; *s* of Sydney Frederick Harpley, electrical engr and cabinet maker, and Rose Isabel Harpley, milliner; *m* 1956, Sally Holliday (marr. diss. 1968), illustrator; two *s* one *d. Educ:* Royal Coll. of Art. ARCA 1956. Realist sculptor, portraits and figure; commnd Smuts Memorial, Cape Town, 1963; sculpture in collections of Nat. Gallery, NZ; Nat. Gallery, Cape Town; Paul Mellon, USA; Anton Rupert, SA; Princess Grace of Monaco; Fleur Cowles Meyer, London; S. & D. Josefowitz, Geneva; Lady Verulam; Lord Jersey; portrait of Edward Heath for Constitutional Club, 1973. Visitors' Choice Prize, RA Summer Exhibition, 1978, 1979. *Recreations:* chess, music. *Address:* 15 Royal Crescent, W11. *T:* 01-602 0470. *Club:* Chelsea Arts.

HARRAP, George Paull Munro, CBE 1974; Chairman, Harrap General Books, since 1981; *b* 10 June 1917; *s* of George Steward and Kathleen Mary Harrap; *m* 1959, Alice Foyle. *Educ:* privately. Entered family firm, 1936; Chm., George G. Harrap & Co. Ltd, 1971-81. *Address:* Tile House, Stebbing Green, Essex. *T:* Stebbing 261; 60 Darwin Court, Gloucester Avenue, NW1 7BQ. *T:* 01-267 8571.

HARRER, Prof. Heinrich; author and explorer; (awarded title of Professor by President of Austrian Republic, 1964); *b* 6 July 1912; *m* ; *s* m 1953, Margaretha Truxa (marr. diss. 1958); *m* 1962, Katharina Haarhaus. *Educ:* University of Graz, Austria (graduated in Geography, 1938). First ascent, Eiger North Wall, 1938; Himalayan Expedition, 1939; interned in India, 1939-44; Tibet, 1944-51; Himalayan Expedition, 1951; expeditions: to the Andes, 1953; to Alaska, 1954; to Ruwenzori (Mountains of the Moon), Africa, 1957; to West New Guinea, 1961-62; to Nepal, 1965; to Xingu Red Indians in Mato Grosso, Brazil; to Bush Negroes of Surinam (Surinam Expedn with King Leopold of Belgium), 1966; to the Sudan, 1970; to North Borneo (Sabah) (with King Leopold of Belgium), 1971; N-S crossing of Borneo, 1972; Valley of Flowers (Alaknanda), 1974; Andaman Islands, 1975; Zangkar-Ladakh, 1976. Austrian National Amateur Golf Champion, 1958; Austrian National Seniors Golf Champion, 1970. Pres., Austrian Golf Association, 1964. *Publications:* Seven Years in Tibet, 1953 (Great Britain, and numerous other countries); Meine Tibet-Bilder, 1953 (Germany); The White Spider, History of the North Face of the Eiger, 1958; Tibet is My Country: Biography of Thubten Jigme Norbu, *e b* of Dalai Lama, 1960 (Eng.); I Come from the Stone Age, 1964 (London); The Last 500, 1975; The Last Caravan, 1976; Lhasa Revisited, 1982. *Address:* Neudorf 577, 9493-Mauren, Liechtenstein.

HARRIES, Rev. Richard Douglas; Dean, King's College, London, since 1981; *b* 2 June 1936; *s* of Brig. W. D. J. Harries, CBE and Mrs G. M. B. Harries; *m* 1963, Josephine Bottomley, MA, MB, BChir, DCH; one *s* one *d. Educ:* Wellington Coll.; RMA, Sandhurst; Selwyn Coll., Cambridge (MA 1965); Cuddesdon Coll., Oxford. Lieut, Royal Corps of Signals, 1955-58. Curate, Hampstead Parish Church, 1963-69; Chaplain, Westfield Coll., 1966-69; Lectr, Wells Theol Coll., 1969-72; Warden, Wells, Salisbury and Wells Theol Coll., 1971-72; Vicar, All Saints, Fulham, 1972-81. GOE examnr in Christian Ethics, 1972-76; Dir, Post Ordination Trng for Kensington Jurisdiction, 1973-79. Vice-Chairman: Council of Christian Action, 1979-; Council for Arms Control, 1982-; Mem., Home Office Adv. Cttee for reform of law on sexual offences, 1981-. Radio and TV work, incl. Prayer for the Day every Friday morning, 1973-. *Publications:* Prayers of Hope, 1975;

Turning to Prayer, 1978; Prayers of Grief and Glory, 1979; Being a Christian, 1981; Should Christians Support Guerrillas?, 1982; The Authority of Divine Love, 1983; contributed to: Teaching Christian Ethics, 1974; Stewards of the Mysteries of God, 1979; What Hope in an Armed World?, 1982; articles in Theology, The Times, The Observer and various other periodicals. *Recreations:* theatre, literature, sport. *Address:* King's College, The Strand, WC2 2LS. *T:* 01-836 5454.

HARRIMAN, Averell; *see* Harriman, William A.

HARRIMAN, (William) Averell; US Ambassador-at-Large, 1965-69; *b* 15 Nov. 1891; *s* of late Edward Henry Harriman and Mary Williamson Averell; *m* 1st, 1915, Kitty Lanier Lawrence (decd); two *d*; 2nd, 1930, Mrs Marie Norton Whitney; 3rd, 1971, Hon. Mrs Leland Hayward, *e d* of 11th Baron Digby, KG, DSO, MC, TD. *Educ:* Groton Sch., Yale Univ., BA 1913. Partner Brown Brothers Harriman & Co. since 1931, Limited partner since 1946; Chairman of the Board, Union Pacific Railroad Co. 1932-46; Mem. Business Advisory Council for the Dept of Commerce since 1933 (Chm., 1937-40). Vice-Pres. in Charge of Purchases and Supplies of Union Pacific Railroad Co., 1914-18; Chm. Board of Merchant Ship-building Corp., 1917-25; Chm. Board of W. A. Harriman & Co., Inc. (merged with Brown Brothers, 1931), 1920-30; Chm. Exec. Cttee Ill. Central Railroad Co., 1931-42; National Recovery Administration: Division Administrator of Div. II, Jan.-March 1934, Special Asst Administrator, March-May, 1934, Administrative Officer, Nov. 1934-June 1935; Associated with Industrial Materials Div., National Defense Advisory Commission, 1940; Chief, Materials Branch, Production Div., Office of Production Management, Jan.-March 1941; Pres. Roosevelt's Special Representative in Great Britain with rank of Minister, March 1941; Special Rep. of the Pres. and Chm. of the President's Special Mission to USSR with rank of Ambassador, 1941; US Representative in London of Combined Shipping Adjustment Board, 1942; Mem. London Combined Production and Resources Board, 1942; US Ambassador to USSR, 1943-46; to Britain, 1946; US Sec. of Commerce, 1946-48; US Special Representative in Europe under Economic Co-operation Act of 1948 (with rank of Ambassador) until 1950; US Rep. on N Atlantic Defence, Financial and Economic Cttee, 1949; Special Asst to Pres. Truman, 1950-51; Dir of Foreign Aid under Mutual Security Act, 1951-53; Governor, State of New York, Jan. 1955-Dec. 1958; US Ambassador-at-Large, Feb.-Dec. 1961 and 1965-69; Asst Sec. of State for Far Eastern Affairs, 1961-63; Under-Sec. for Political Affairs, 1963-65. Negotiated Limited Test Ban Treaty, 1963; US Representative, Vietnam Peace Talks, Paris, 1968-69. Medal for Merit, presented by President Harry S. Truman; Presidential Medal of Freedom, with distinction, presented by President Lyndon B. Johnson, 1969; Foreign Service Cup, American Foreign Service, 1980; Winston Churchill Award, Winston Churchill Foundn, 1981. Hon. LLD: New York, 1947; Columbia, 1954; Yale, 1964; Harvard, 1966; Georgetown, 1970; Yeshiva, 1972; and many other hon. degrees. Democrat. *Publications:* Peace with Russia?, 1960; America and Russia in a Changing World, 1971; (with E. Abel) Special Envoy to Churchill and Stalin 1941-1946, 1975. *Address:* (residence) 3038 N Street, NW, Washington, DC 20007, USA.
See also W. S. Churchill.

HARRINGTON, 11th Earl of, *cr* 1742; **William Henry Leicester Stanhope;** Viscount Stanhope of Mahon and Baron Stanhope of Elvaston, Co. Derby, 1717; Baron Harrington, 1729; Viscount Petersham, 1742; late Captain RAC; *b* 24 Aug. 1922; *o s* of 10th Earl and Margaret Trelawney (Susan) (*d* 1952), *d* of Major H. H. D. Seaton; *S* father, 1929; *m* 1st, 1942, Eileen (from whom he obtained a divorce, 1946), *o d* of late Sir John Grey, Enville Hall, Stourbridge; one *s* one *d* (and one *d* decd); 2nd, 1947, Anne Theodora (from whom he obtained a divorce, 1962), *o d* of late Major Richard Arenbourg Blennerhassett Chute; one *s* two *d*; 3rd, 1964, Priscilla Margaret, *d* of Hon. A. E. Cubitt and Mrs Ronald Dawnay; one *s* one *d*. *Educ:* Eton; RMC, Sandhurst. Served War of 1939-45, demobilised 1946. Owns about 700 acres. Became Irish Citizen, 1964. *Heir:* *s* Viscount Petersham, *qv. Address:* Greenmount Stud, Patrickswell, Co. Limerick, Eire.
See also Baron Ashcombe.

HARRINGTON, Dr Albert Blair, CB 1979; Head of Civil Service Department Medical Advisory Service, 1976-79; Chairman, Civil Service Commission Medical Boards, since 1979; *b* 26 April 1914; *s* of late Albert Timothy Harrington and Lily Harrington; *m* 1939, Valerie White; one *d. Educ:* Brisbane Grammar Sch., Qld; Aberdeen Univ. MB, ChB 1938, MD 1944. House Phys., Woodend Hosp., Aberdeen, 1938-39; service in RAMC (Field Amb., Blood Transfusion Phys., Neurologist), 1940-45; MO (Head Injuries) and Dep. Supt, Stoke Mandeville Hosp., 1946-48; Med. Supt, Dunston Hill Hosp., Gateshead, 1948-50; SMO (Pensions), Cleveleys, 1950-53; Med. Supt, Queen Mary's Hosp., Roehampton, 1954-56; SMO, Dept of Health (Hosp. Bldg and later Regional Liaison Duties), 1956-68; PMO (Hosp. Bldg), 1968-73; SPMO (Under-Sec.), DHSS, 1973-76. FFCM (Foundn Fellow) 1972. *Publications:* articles on Sjögren's Disease, paralytic poliomyelitis, and hospital planning, medical care and the work of the Medical Advisory Service. *Recreations:* gardening, country life; formerly tennis. *Address:* 59 Lauderdale Drive, Petersham, Richmond, Surrey TW1O 7BS. *T:* 01-940 1345. *Club:* Athenæum.

HARRINGTON, Illtyd, JP; Member for Brent South, Greater London Council, since 1973; Deputy Leader of the Council, 1973-77, and since 1981; *b* 14 July 1931; *s* of Timothy Harrington and Sarah (*née* Burchell); unmarried.

Educ: St Illtyd's RC Sch., Dowlais; Merthyr County Sch.; Trinity Coll., Caermarthen. Member: Paddington Borough Council, 1959-64; Westminster City Council, 1964-68 and 1971-78, Leader, Lab. Gp, 1972-74; GLC, 1964-67; Alderman, GLC, 1970-73; Chm., Policy and Resources Cttee, GLC, 1973-77; Dep. Leader of the Opposition, GLC, 1977-81. JP Willesden 1968. First Chairman, Inland Waterways Amenity Adv. Council, 1968-71; Member: British Waterways Bd, 1974-82; BTA, 1976-80. Chm., Kilburn Skills, 1977-. Member: Bd, Theatre Royal, Stratford E, 1978-; Bd, Wiltons Music Hall, 1979-; Nat. Theatre Bd, 1975-77; Bd, National Youth Theatre, 1982-; Chm., Half Moon Theatre, 1978-; Director: Soho Poly Theatre, 1981-; The Young Vic, 1981-. Pres., Grand Union Canal Soc., 1974-; Vice Pres., Coventry Canal Soc., 1970-. Patron, Westminster Cathedral Appeal, 1977-. Trustee: Kew Bridge Pumping Mus., 1976-; Chiswick Family Rescue, 1978-. Governor, Brunel Univ., 1981-. *Recreations:* a slave to local government; laughing, singing and incredulity. *Address:* 16 Lea House, Salisbury Street, NW8 8BJ. *T:* 01-402 6356. *Club:* Paddington Labour.

HARRIS, family name of **Barons Harris, Harris of Greenwich, Harris of High Cross** and of **Earl of Malmesbury.**

HARRIS, 5th Baron (of Seringapatam and Mysore, and of Belmont, Kent, *cr* 1815); **George St Vincent Harris,** CBE 1972; MC; JP; DL; Vice-Lieutenant of Kent, 1948-72; *b* 3 Sept. 1889; *e s* of 4th Baron and Hon. Lucy Ada Jervis, CI (*d* 1930), *d* of 3rd Viscount St Vincent; *S* father, 1932; *m* 1918, Dorothy Mary (*d* 1981) (Order of League of Mercy), *d* of Rev. W. J. Crookes, late Vicar of Borden; one *s. Educ:* Eton; Christ Church, Oxford (MA). Capt. late Royal East Kent Imperial Yeomanry; served European War, 1914-18 (MC, wounded, despatches). Grand Master, Mark Master Masons of England, 1954-73; Grand Master, Masonic Knights Templar of England, 1947-73. Commissioner St John Amb. Brigade for Kent, 1940-45; Chm. Kent Police Authority, 1945-64; KStJ 1949. JP 1919, DL 1936, Kent. *Heir:* *s* Hon. George Robert John Harris, *b* 17 April 1920. *Address:* Belmont Park, Faversham, Kent. *Clubs:* MCC, Carlton, Beefsteak.

HARRIS OF GREENWICH, Baron *cr* 1974 (Life Peer), of Greenwich; **John Henry Harris;** Chairman, Worldtech Ventures, since 1982; director of companies; *b* Harrow, Middlesex, 5 April 1930; *s* of Alfred George and late May Harris; *m* 1952, Patricia Margaret Alstrom; one *s* one *d. Educ:* Pinner County Grammar Sch., Middlesex. Journalist on newspapers in Bournemouth, Leicester, Glasgow and London. National Service with Directorate of Army Legal Services, WO. Personal assistant to Rt Hon. Hugh Gaitskell when Leader of the Opposition, 1959-62; Director of Publicity, Labour Party, 1962-64; Special Assistant: to Foreign Secretary, 1964-65; to Rt Hon. Roy Jenkins as Home Secretary, 1965-Nov. 1967, and as Chancellor, Nov. 1967-1970. Staff of Economist newspaper, 1970-74. Minister of State, Home Office, 1974-79. Chm., Parole Bd for England and Wales, 1979-82; Trustee, Police Foundn (Chm., Exec. Cttee). Chm., Westward TV Ltd, 1980-81. Eisenhower Exchange Fellow from UK, 1972. Mem. Council, Harlow, Essex, 1957-63, Chm. Council 1960-61, Leader of Labour Gp, 1961-63. Mem. Exec. Cttee, Britain in Europe, referendum campaign, 1975. Joined Social Democratic Party, 1981. *Address:* House of Lords, SW1. *Clubs:* Reform, MCC.

HARRIS OF HIGH CROSS, Baron *cr* 1979 (Life Peer), of Tottenham in Greater London; **Ralph Harris;** General Director, Institute of Economic Affairs, since 1957; *b* 10 Dec. 1924; *m* 1949, Jose Pauline Jeffery; one *s* one *d* (and one *s* decd). *Educ:* Tottenham Grammar Sch.; Queens' Coll., Cambridge (Exhibr, Foundn Schol.). 1st Cl. Hons Econs, MA Cantab. Lectr in Polit. Economy, St Andrews Univ., 1949-56. Contested (C): Kirkcaldy, 1951; Edinburgh Central, 1955. Leader-writer, Glasgow Herald, 1956. Trustee and Hon. Secretary, Wincott Foundn; Trustee and Hon. Treasurer, Ross McWhirter Foundn. Mem. Council, Univ. Coll. at Buckingham; Dir, Churchill Press. Free Enterprise Award, 1976. *Publications:* Politics without Prejudice, a biography of R. A. Butler, 1956; Hire Purchase in a Free Society, 1958, 3rd edn 1961; (with Arthur Seldon) Advertising in a Free Society, 1959; Advertising in Action, 1962; Advertising and the Public, 1962; (with A. P. Herbert) Libraries: Free for All?, 1962; Choice in Welfare, 1963; Essays in Rebirth of Britain, 1964; Choice in Welfare, 1965; Right Turn, 1970; Choice in Welfare, 1970; Down with the Poor, 1971; (with Brendan Sewill) British Economic Policy 1970-74, 1975; Crisis '75, 1975; Catch '76, 1976; Freedom of Choice: consumers or conscripts, 1976; (with Arthur Seldon) Pricing or Taxing, 1976; Not from Benevolence, 1977; (ed, with Arthur Seldon) The Coming Confrontation, 1978; (with Arthur Seldon) Over-ruled on Welfare, 1979; End of Government, 1980; Challenge of a Radical Reactionary, 1981; columnist in Truth, Statist, etc. *Recreations:* conjuring and devising spells against over-government. *Address:* 4 Walmar Close, Beech Hill, Hadley Wood, Barnet, Herts. *Clubs:* (Hon. Sec.) Political Economy, Mont Pelerin Society.

HARRIS, Prof. Sir Alan (James), Kt 1980; CBE 1968; BScEng, FEng, FICE, FIStructE, MConsE; Consultant, Harris & Sutherland, Consulting Engineers, since 1981; Professor of Concrete Structures, Imperial College, London, 1973-81, now Emeritus; *b* 8 July 1916; *s* of Walter Herbert Harris and Ethel Roach, Plymouth; *m* 1948, Marie Thérèse, *d* of Prof. Paul Delcourt, Paris; two *s. Educ:* Owen's Sch., Islington; Northampton Polytechnic (London Univ.). Local Government engineer, 1933-40; served Royal Engineers (Mulberry, Rhine Bridges) (despatches), 1940-46; with Eugène Freyssinet in Paris studying prestressing, 1946-49; Director, Prestressed Concrete Co. Ltd,

1949-55; set up in private practice, 1955-. Member: Council, Agrément Board, 1968-81; Engrg Council, 1981-; part-time Board Mem., Property Services Agency, 1974-78. President, Instn of Structural Engineers, 1978-79. Croix de Guerre (France) 1945; Ordre de Mérite (France) 1975. *Publications:* numerous papers in learned jls. *Recreation:* sailing. *Address:* 128 Ashley Gardens, Thirleby Road, SW1P 1HL. *T:* 01-834 6924. *Club:* Athenæum.

HARRIS, Anne Macintosh, (Mrs H. J. L. Harris); National Chairman, National Federation of Women's Institutes, since 1981; *b* 17 April 1925; *d* of Montague Macintosh Williams and Marguerite Anne Williams (*née* Barrington); *m* 1950, Henry John Leshley Harris; one *s* three *d. Educ:* Battle Abbey Sch.; Swanley Horticultural Coll. and Wye Coll. (Swanley Dip. in Horticulture, 1946). Owned and ran nursery/market garden and shop, 1946-50. Mem., WI, 1947-; Mem., NFWI Exec. Cttee, 1973- (Vice-Chm., 1979-81); Chm., NFWI Markets Sub-Cttee, 1972-79. Mem. Council, Nat. Trust, 1981-. Chm., Tunbridge Wells East District Local Assoc. Girl Guides, 1963-79; Vice-Chm., Brenchley PCC, 1978-82. *Recreations:* gardening, walking, reading, music. *Address:* The Old Vicarage, Brenchley, Tonbridge, Kent TN12 7NQ. *T:* Brenchley 2040. *Club:* Agricola Club and Swanley Guild (Wye).

HARRIS, Marshal of the Royal Air Force Sir Arthur Travers, 1st Bt, *cr* 1953; GCB 1945 (KCB 1942; CB 1940); OBE 1927; AFC 1918; *b* 13 April 1892; *m* 1st, 1916; one *s* two *d*; 2nd, 1938, Thérèse Hearne; one *d.* Served European War, 1914-19, 1st Rhodesian Regt, RFC, and RAF; India, 1921-22; Iraq, 1922-24; Egypt, 1930-32; Group Capt. 1933; Air Ministry, Dep. Dir of Plans, 1934-37; Air Commodore, 1937; AOC 4 Bomber Gp, 1937; Head of RAF Mission, USA and Canada, 1938; Air Vice-Marshal, 1939; Air Marshal, 1941; Air Chief Marshal, 1943; AOC, RAF Palestine and Transjordan, 1938-39; AOC, 5 Bomber Group, 1939-40; Deputy Chief of Air Staff, 1940-41; Head of Royal Air Force Delegation to USA, 1941; Commander-in-Chief Bomber Command 1942-45. Marshal of the RAF 1945. Managing Director South African Marine Corporation, 1946-53. Order of Suvorov (1st class) (Russia), 1944, Grand Cross Polonia Restituta (Poland), 1945, Chief Commander Legion of Merit (US), 1944; Grand Cross Order of the Southern Cross (Brazil), 1945; Grand Officier Légion d'Honneur, Croix de guerre avec palme (France), 1945; DSM (US), 1945. Freeman of Honiton and of Chepping Wycombe; Freeman, City of London and Liveryman, Guild of Air Pilots and Air Navigators, 1978. Hon. LLD Liverpool, 1946. *Heir: s* Anthony Kyrle Travers Harris, *b* 18 March 1918. *Address:* The Ferry House, Goring-on-Thames, Oxfordshire RG8 9DX. *Clubs:* Royal Air Force, Army and Navy; Pathfinders; Royal and Ancient (St Andrews).

See also R. J. Harris.

HARRIS, Rt. Rev. Augustine; see Middlesbrough, Bishop of, (RC).

HARRIS, Basil Vivian, CEng, MIEE; Chief Engineer, Communications Division, Foreign and Commonwealth Office, 1979-81, retired; *b* 11 July 1921; *s* of Henry William and Sarah May Harris; *m* 1943, Myra Winifred Mildred Newport. *Educ:* Watford Grammar School. GPO Engineering Dept (Research), 1939; served RAF, 1943-46; GPO Engineering Dept (Radio Branch), 1946; Diplomatic Wireless Service, FCO, 1963; Dep. Chief Engineer, Communications Division, FCO, 1971. *Publications:* contribs to technical jls on communications. *Recreations:* golf, photography, travel. *Address:* 13 Decoy Drive, Eastbourne, Sussex BN22 0AB. *T:* Eastbourne 55819. *Club:* Royal Eastbourne Golf.

HARRIS, Ven. Brian; see Harris, Ven. R. B.

HARRIS, Brian Thomas, QC 1982; Clerk to the Justices, Poole, since 1967; *b* 14 Aug. 1932; *s* of Thomas and Eleanor Harris; *m* 1957, Janet Rosina Harris (*née* Hodgson); one *s* one *d. Educ:* Henry Thornton Grammar Sch.; King's Coll., Univ. of London. LLB (Hons). Called to the Bar, Gray's Inn, 1960; joined London Magistrates' Courts, 1963. Member: Juvenile Courts Committee, Magistrates' Assoc., 1973-; NACRO Juvenile Crime Adv. Cttee, 1982-; former member: CCETSW working party on legal trng of social workers, 1974; NACRO cttee on diversion (Zander report), 1975; HO/DHSS working party on operation of Children and Young Persons' Act, 1969, 1978; ABAFA working party on care proceedings, 1979. Pres., Justices' Clerks Soc., 1981-82. Editor, *Justice of the Peace Review. Publications:* Criminal Jurisdiction of Magistrates, 1969, 8th edn 1982; Warrants of Search and Entry, 1973; The Courts, the Press and the Public, 1976; The Rehabilitation of Offenders Act 1974, 1976; New Law of Family Proceedings in Magistrates' Courts, 1979; (ed jtly) Clarke Hall and Morrison on Children; (ed) entry on Magistrates in Halsbury's Laws of England, 4th edn 1979; contribs to Criminal Law Review, New Law Jl, Law Society Gazette, Family Law. *Recreation:* the contemplation of verse. *Address:* Law Courts, Park Road, Poole, Dorset. *T:* Parkstone 745309.

HARRIS, Cecil Rhodes, FCIS, FSCA; Chief Executive, Commercial Union Assurance Company Ltd, since 1982; *b* 4 May 1923; *s* of Frederick William Harris and Dorothy Violet Plum; *m* 1946, Gwenyth Evans; one *s* two *d. Educ:* private schools. FCIS 1950; FSCA 1951. Joined Employers Liability Assurance, 1949, Asst Sec., 1961-64, Overseas Manager, Northern & Employers, 1965-68; Commercial Union Assurance Co. Ltd: Asst Gen. Man., 1969-73; Dep. Gen. Man., 1974; Dir and Sec., 1975-78; Exec. Dir, 1979; Dep. Chief Gen. Man., 1980-82. *Recreations:* tennis, study of the Scriptures.

Address: Ashley, 35a Plough Lane, Purley, Surrey CR2 3QJ. *T:* 01-668 2820.

HARRIS, Sir Charles Herbert S.; see Stuart-Harris.

HARRIS, Sir Charles Joseph William, KBE 1961 (CBE 1927); Kt 1952; Private Secretary to successive Parliamentary Secretaries to Treasury, 1919-24, 1924-29 and 1931-61; retired as Assistant Secretary, HM Treasury, 1961; *b* 1901; *m* 1924, Emily Kyle Thompson; one *s* two *d. Educ:* Christ Church Sch., Ramsgate; privately. Private Sec. to Conservative Chief Whip, 1924 and 1929-31. Freeman, City of London; Mem., Court of Assistants, Guild of Freemen of City of London; Liveryman, Scriveners' Company. *Address:* 7 Fir Tree Court, Allum Lane, Elstree, Herts WD6 3NF. *T:* 01-953 6618. *Club:* City Livery.

HARRIS, Colin Grendon, CMG 1964; HM Diplomatic Service, retired; *b* 25 Oct. 1912; *m* 1941, Adelaide Zamoiska (decd); *m* 1947, Monique Jacqueline Marcuse-Baudoux; four *s* two *d. Educ:* Rossall Sch.; Pembroke Coll., Cambridge. Entered Foreign (subseq. Diplomatic) Service, 1935; served San Francisco, Antwerp, Elisabethville, Leopoldville, Lisbon, Montevideo, Rio de Janeiro, Vienna, Tokyo, Oslo, retired 1969. *Address:* 263 Avenue Defré, Brussels, Belgium.

HARRIS, David; Director, Commission of the European Communities, Directorate for Social and Demographic Statistics, since 1973; *b* 28 Dec. 1922; *s* of David and Margaret Jane Harris; *m* 1946, Mildred Alice Watson; two *d. Educ:* Bootle Grammar Sch.; LSE (BScEcon). FSS. Statistician, BoT, 1960; Statistician 1966 and Chief Statistician 1968, HM Treasury; Chief Statistician, Central Statistical Office, Cabinet Office, 1969. *Recreations:* tennis, swimming, economics. *Address:* 41 Boulevard Napoleon Ier, Luxembourg. *T:* Luxembourg 445223; 3 Amberwood Drive, Camberley, Surrey. *T:* Camberley 20213.

HARRIS, David Anthony; Member (C) Cornwall and Plymouth, European Parliament, since 1979; *b* 1 Nov. 1937; *s* of late E. C. Harris and Betty Harris; *m* 1962, Diana Joan Hansford; one *s* one *d. Educ:* Mount Radford Sch., Exeter. Jun. Reporter, Express and Echo, Exeter, 1954-58. Nat. Service, commnd Devonshire and Dorset Regt, 1958; Staff Captain (Public Relns) GHQ, MELF, 1959. Reporter, Western Morning News, 1960-61; joined Daily Telegraph, Westminster Staff, 1961; Political Correspondent, Daily Telegraph, 1976-79. Chm., Parly Lobby Journalists, 1977-78. Mem. (C) Bromley, and Bromley, Ravensbourne, GLC, 1968-77; Chm. Thamesmead Cttee, 1971-73. Contested (C), Mitcham and Morden, Feb. 1974. *Recreations:* gardening, walking the dog. *Address:* Little Trehan Farm, Trehan, Saltash, Cornwall. *T:* Saltash 3720. *Club:* Farmers'.

HARRIS, Dame Diana R.; see Reader Harris.

HARRIS, Rev. Donald Bertram; Vicar of St Paul's, Knightsbridge, 1955-78; *b* 4 Aug. 1904; unmarried. *Educ:* King's Coll. Choir Sch., Cambridge; Haileybury Coll.; King's Coll., Cambridge; Cuddesdon Coll., Oxford. Chorister, King's Coll. Choir, 1915-19; Choral Scholar, King's Coll., Cambridge, 1923-26; BA 1925; MA 1929; Ordained Deacon, 1927; Priest, 1928; Curate of Chesterfield Parish Church, 1927-31; St Mary the Less, Cambridge, 1931-36. Chaplain of King's Coll., Cambridge, 1932-33; Examg Chaplain to Bishop of Wakefield, 1932-36; Rector of Great Greenford, Middx, 1936-45; Archdeacon of Bedford 1946-55, and Rector of St Mary's Bedford, 1945-55, Life Governor, Haileybury and Imperial Service Coll., 1946-. Pres., Assoc. for Promoting Retreats, 1968-71. *Address:* 105 Marsham Court, Marsham Street, SW1. *T:* 01-828 1132. *Club:* Royal Thames Yacht.

HARRIS, Dr Edmund Leslie, CB 1981; FRCP, FRCPE, FFCM; Deputy Chief Medical Officer (Deputy Secretary), Department of Health and Social Security, since 1977; *b* 11 April 1928; *s* of late M. H. and S. Harris; *m* 1959, Robina Semple (*née* Potter). *Educ:* Univ. of Witwatersrand. MB, BCh 1952; MRCPE 1959, FRCPE 1971, MRCP 1959, FRCP 1975; MRCP 1978, FFCM 1980. Gen. practice, Benoni, S Africa, 1954; various NHS posts, 1955-61; Medical Dir, pharmaceutical industry, 1962-68; SMO, DHSS, 1969-72; PMO, Cttee on Safety of Medicines and Medicines Commn, 1973; SPMO, Under-Sec., and Head of Medicines Div., DHSS, 1974-77. Chm., Assoc. of Med. Advisers in Pharmaceutical Industry, 1966; Member: Nat. Biol. Bd, 1975-77; Bd, Public Health Lab. Service, 1977-. Rep. Governor, Imperial Cancer Res. Fund, 1977-. *Publications:* various, mainly on aspects of clinical pharmacology and control of medicines. *Recreations:* walking, photography. *Address:* Department of Health and Social Security, Alexander Fleming House, Elephant and Castle, SE1. *T:* 01-407 5522.

HARRIS, Euan Cadogan; Deputy Legal Adviser, Ministry of Agriculture, Fisheries and Food, 1964-71; *b* 6 June 1906; *s* of late Charles Poulett Harris, MD and Violet Harris; *m* 1931, Brenda, *er d* of late William Turnball Bowman, OBE and Jessie Bowman; two *d. Educ:* Epsom Coll.; Clare Coll., Cambridge. BA 1927; LLB 1928. Admitted Solicitor (Edmund Thomas Child Prize), 1930. Entered Legal Dept of Min. of Agric. and Fisheries, 1935; Asst Solicitor, 1949-64. *Recreations:* walking, swimming, gardening; reading, especially history. *Address:* 6 Newlands Road, Rottingdean, East Sussex BN2 7GD. *T:* Brighton 32019.

See also Sir A. K. Rothnie.

HARRIS, Frank; *see* Harris, W. F.

HARRIS, Geoffrey (Herbert); Member, Transport Users' Consultative Committee for London, 1961-77 (Chairman, 1972-77, Deputy Chairman, 1971-72); Chairman, London Transport Passengers' Committee, 1972-74; *b* 31 Jan. 1914; *s* of late W. Leonard Harris and late Sybil M. Harris; *m* 1945, Eve J. Orton; two *d. Educ:* Colchester Royal Grammar School. FCIS. Commercial Union Gp of Cos, 1932-37; Shell Gp of Cos, 1937-73; Manager Office Administration, London, 1963-73. Royal Artillery, 1937-45. *Recreations:* music, architecture, travel. *Address:* Garden End, Spinfield Lane, Marlow, Bucks. *T:* Marlow 72550. *Club:* Phyllis Court (Henley-on-Thames).

HARRIS, Prof. Harry, FRCP; FRS 1966; Harnwell Professor of Human Genetics, University of Pennsylvania, since 1976; *b* 30 Sept. 1919; *m* 1948, Muriel Hargest; one *s. Educ:* Manchester Gram. Sch.; Trinity Coll., Cambridge. (MA, MD); FRCP 1973. Research Asst, Galton Laboratory, Dept of Eugenics, Biometry, and Genetics UC, London, 1947-50; Leverhulme Scholar, RCP, 1947-48; Lund Research Fellow, Diabetic Assoc., 1949; Lectr, Dept of Biochem., UC, London, 1950-53; Sen. Lectr, 1953-58, Reader in Biochem. Genetics, 1958-60, Dept of Biochem., The London Hosp. Med. Coll.; Prof. of Biochem., University of London, at King's Coll., 1960-65; Galton Prof. of Human Genetics, London Univ. at UCL, 1965-76. Hon. Lectr, 1950-55, Hon. Research Associate, 1955-60, Dept of Eugenics, Biometry and Genetics, UCL; Hon. Dir, MRC Human Biochem. Genetics Res. Unit, 1962-76; Hon. Consulting Geneticist, UCH, 1966-76. Joint Editor: Annals of Human Genetics, 1965-79; Advances in Human Genetics, 1970-. Nat. Research Coun. of Canada and Nuffield Foundation Vis. Lectr, British Columbia and McGill, 1967; Fogarty Scholar, Nat. Insts of Health, USA, 1972; Rock Carling Fellowship, Nuffield Provincial Hosps Trust, 1974. Lectures: Thomas Young, St George's Hosp. Med. Sch., 1966; De Frees, University Penna, 1966; Walter R. Bloor, Univ. Rochester, 1967; Langdon Brown, RCP, 1968; Sir William Jackson Pope, RSA, 1968; Darwin, Inst. Biol., 1969; Leonard Parsons, Birmingham Univ., 1969; Sidney Ringer, UCH Med. Sch., 1970; T. H. Huxley, Birmingham Univ., 1971; George Frederic Still, British Paediatric Assoc., 1971; L. S. Penrose Meml, Genetical Soc., 1973; Bicentennial, Coll. of Physicians of Pa, 1976; Noble Wiley Jones, Univ. of Oregon, 1978; Rhodes, Emory Univ., 1978; Thomas S. Hall, Washington Univ., St Louis, 1979; Harvey, Harvey Soc., NY, 1981. For. Associate, Nat. Acad. of Scis, USA, 1976. Hon. Dr Univ. René Descartes, Paris, 1976. William Allan Meml Award, Amer. Soc. of Human Genetics, 1968. *Publications:* An Introduction to Human Biochemical Genetics (Eugenics Laboratory Memoir series), 1953; Human Biochemical Genetics, 1959; The Principles of Human Biochemical Genetics, 1970, 3rd edn 1980; Prenatal Diagnosis and Selective Abortion, 1975; (with D. A. Hopkinson) Handbook of Enzyme Electrophoresis in Human Genetics, 1976. *Address:* 4050 Irving Street, Philadelphia, Pa 19104, USA. *T:* (215) 387-0245.

HARRIS, Prof. Henry, FRCP; FRCPath; FRS 1968; Regius Professor of Medicine, University of Oxford, since 1979; Head of the Sir William Dunn School of Pathology, since 1963; Hon. Director, Cancer Research Campaign, Cell Biology Unit, since 1963; Fellow of Lincoln College, 1963-79, Hon. Fellow 1980; Student of Christ Church; *b* 28 Jan. 1925; *s* of late Sam and late Ann Harris; *m* 1950, Alexandra Fanny Brodsky; one *s* two *d. Educ:* Sydney Boys' High Sch. and University of Sydney, Australia; Lincoln Coll., Oxford. Public Exhibnr, University of Sydney, 1942; BA Mod. Langs, 1944; MB BS 1950; Travelling Schol. of Austr. Nat. Univ. at Univ. of Oxford, 1952; MA; DPhil (Oxon.), 1954, DM 1979. Dir of Research, Brit. Empire Cancer Campaign, at Sir William Dunn Sch. of Pathology, Oxford, 1954-59; Visiting Scientist, Nat. Institutes of Health, USA, 1959-60; Head of Dept of Cell Biology, John Innes Inst., 1960-63; Prof. of Pathology, Univ. of Oxford, 1963-79. Vis. Prof., Vanderbilt Univ., 1968; Walker-Ames Prof., University of Washington, 1968; Foreign Prof., Collège de France, 1974. Member: ARC, 1968-78 (Chm., Animals Res. Bd, 1976-78); Council, European Molecular Biology Organization, 1974-76; Council, Royal Society, 1971-72; Scientific Adv. Cttee, CRC; Governor, European Cell Biology Organization, 1973-75. Lectures: Almroth Wright, 1968; Harvey, Harvey Soc., NY, 1969; Dunham, Harvard, 1969; Jenner Meml, 1970; Croonian, Royal Soc., 1971; Gwladys and Owen Williams, Liverpool Univ., 1971; Nat. Insts of Health, USA, 1971; Foundation, RCPath, 1973; Woodhull, Royal Instn, 1975; Wade Foundn, Southampton Univ., 1976; Rotherham, Lincoln Coll., Oxford, 1979; Herbert Spencer, Oxford Univ., 1979; Opening Plenary, Internat. Congress of Cell Biology, 1980; First Distinguished, in Experimental Pathology, Pittsburgh Univ., 1982. Foreign Hon. Mem., Amer. Acad. Arts and Sciences; Foreign Mem., Max-Planck Soc.; Hon. Mem., Amer. Assoc. of Pathologists; Corresp. Mem., Amer. Assoc. for Cancer Res. Hon. Fellow, Cambridge Philosophical Soc. Hon. FRCPath Aust. Hon. DSc Edinburgh, 1976; Hon. MD Geneva, 1982. Feldberg Foundn Award, Ivison Macadam Meml Prize, RCSE; Prix de la Fondation Isabelle Decazes de Noüe for cancer research; Madonnina Prize for medical scis (City of Milan), 1979; Royal Medal, Royal Soc., 1980. *Publications:* Nucleus and Cytoplasm, 1968, 3rd edn, 1974; Cell Fusion, 1970; La Fusion cellulaire, 1974; papers on cellular physiology and biochemistry, in scientific books and jls. *Recreation:* history. *Address:* Sir William Dunn School of Pathology, South Parks Road, Oxford OX1 3RE. *T:* Oxford 57321; 73 Cumnor Hill, Oxford OX2 9HX.

HARRIS, Lt.-Gen. Sir Ian (Cecil), KBE 1967 (CBE 1958); CB 1962; DSO 1945; Member of Family Partnership and Manager, Ballykisteen Stud, Tipperary, and Owner, Victor Stud, Golden, Cashel, Tipperary; Chairman:

Irish Bloodstock Breeders Association, since 1977; Irish Bloodstock Breeders Federation, since 1978; *b* 7 July 1910; *y s* of late J. W. A. Harris, Victor Stud, Golden, Tipperary; *m* 1945, Anne-Marie Desmotreux; two *s. Educ:* Portora Royal Sch., Enniskillen, Northern Ireland; RMC, Sandhurst. 2nd Lt Royal Ulster Rifles, 1930; served War of 1939-45, NW Frontier of India, 1939 (despatches); comd 2nd Bn Royal Ulster Rifles, 1943-45; GSO1, 25 Ind. Div. and 7 Div. in Burma and Malaya, 1945-46 (despatches), India and Pakistan, 1946-47; AQMG Scottish Comd, 1949-51; comd 6th Bn Royal Ulster Rifles (TA), 1951-52; Chief of Staff, Northern Ireland, 1952-54; Comdr 1 Federal Infantry Bde, Malaya, 1954-57 (despatches); Dep. Dir of Staff Duties (A), WO, 1957-60; GOC Singapore Base District, 1960-62; Chief of Staff, Contingencies Planning, Supreme HQ, Allied Powers, Europe, 1963-66; GOC-in-C, then GOC, N Ireland, 1966-69. Colonel: Royal Ulster Rifles, 1962-68; Royal Irish Rangers, 1968-72. *Recreations:* riding and tennis. *Address:* Acraboy House, Monard, Co. Tipperary. *T:* Tipperary 51564. *Club:* Army and Navy.

HARRIS, Air Cdre Irene Joyce, RRC 1976; QHNS 1981; SRN, SCM; Director, Nursing Services (RAF), and Matron-in-Chief, Princess Mary's Royal Air Force Nursing Service, since 1981; *b* 26 Sept. 1926; *d* of late Robert John Harris and Annie Martha Harris (*née* Breed). *Educ:* Southgate County Sch.; Charing Cross Hosp.; The London Hosp.; Queen Mary's Maternity Home, Hampstead. SRN 1947, SCM 1950. Joined Princess Mary's RAF Nursing Service, 1950; gen. nursing and midwifery duties in UK, Singapore, Germany and Cyprus; Dep. Matron, 1970; Sen. Matron, 1975; Principal Matron, 1978; Dep. Dir, Nursing Services (RAF), 1981. *Recreations:* travel, cine-photography, ornithology, Thames sailing barges, music. *Address:* Ministry of Defence, First Avenue House, High Holborn, WC1V 6HE. *T:* 01-430 5635. *Clubs:* Royal Air Force, Victory Services.

HARRIS, Sir Jack A. S.; *see* Sutherland-Harris.

HARRIS, Sir Jack Wolfred Ashford, 2nd Bt, *cr* 1932; Chairman, Bing Harris & Co. Ltd, Wellington, NZ, since 1935; *b* 23 July 1906; *er s* of Rt Hon. Sir Percy Harris, 1st Bt, PC, and Frieda Bloxam (*d* 1962); *S* father 1952; *m* 1933, Patricia, *o d* of A. P. Penman, Wahroonga, Sydney, NSW; two *s* one *d. Educ:* Shrewsbury Sch.; Trinity Hall, Cambridge. BA (Cantab) History; then one year's study in Europe. Joined family business in New Zealand, 1929, and became director shortly afterwards. Past Pres. Wellington Chamber of Commerce. Served during War of 1939-45, for three years in NZ Home Forces. *Recreations:* gardening, fishing, swimming. *Heir:* s Christopher John Ashford Harris [*b* 26 Aug. 1934; *m* 1957, Anna, *d* of F. de Malmanche, Auckland, NZ; one *s* two *d*.] *Address:* Te Rama, Waikanae, near Wellington, NZ. *Clubs:* Royal Automobile; Wellington (Wellington); Northern (Auckland).

HARRIS, John Frederick, FSA; Curator, British Architectural Library's Drawing Collection and Heinz Gallery, since 1960; Slade Professor of Fine Art, University of Oxford, 1982-83; *b* 13 Aug. 1931; *s* of Frederick Harris and Maud (*née* Sellwood); *m* 1960, Eileen Spiegel, New York; one *s* one *d. Educ:* Cowley C of E School. Itinerant before 1956; Library of Royal Inst. of Architects, 1956. Mem., Mr Paul Mellon's Adv. Bd, 1966-78; Trustee, Amer. Mus. in Britain, 1974-; Chm., Colnaghi & Co., 1982-. President: Internat. Confedn on Architectural Museums, 1981- (Chm., 1979-81); Marylebone Soc., 1978-80; Member: Council, Drawing Soc. of America, 1962-68; Council, Victorian Soc., 1974-; Nat. Council, Internat. Council of Monuments and Sites, 1976-; Soc. of Dilettanti, 1977-; Mem. Committee: Soc. of Architectural Historians of GB, 1958-66; Georgian Gp, 1970-74; Save Britain's Heritage, 1970-; Thirties Soc., 1979-; Stowe Landscape, 1980-; Bldg Museum Proj., 1980-; Garden History, 1980-; Jl of Garden History, 1980-; Mem., Ambrose Congreve Award, 1980-. Andrew W. Mellon Lectr in Fine Arts, Nat. Gall., Washington, 1981. Exhibitions Organizer: The King's Arcadia, 1973; The Destruction of the Country House (with Marcus Binney), 1974; The Garden, 1979; Dir, British Country House Exhibn, Nat. Gall., Washington, 1982-; many exhibns in Heinz Gall.; travelling exhibns and catalogues: Italian Architectural Drawings, 1966; Sir Christopher Wren, 1970. FSA 1968; FRSA 1975; Hon. FRIBA 1972; Hon. Brother Art Workers' Guild, 1972. Editor, Studies in Architecture, 1976-. *Publications:* English Decorative Ironwork, 1960; Regency Furniture Designs, 1961; ed, The Prideaux Collection of Topographical Drawings, 1963; (jtly) Lincolnshire, 1964; contrib. The Making of Stamford, 1965; (jtly) Illustrated Glossary of Architecture, 1966, 2nd edn 1969; (jtly) Buckingham Palace, 1968; Georgian Country Houses, 1968; contrib., Concerning Architecture, 1968; Sir William Chambers, Knight of the Polar Star, 1970 (Hitchcock Medallion 1971); ed, The Rise and Progress of the Present State of Planting, 1970; ed (jtly) The Country Seat, 1970; Catalogue of British Drawings for Architecture, Decoration, Sculpture and Landscape Gardening in American Collections, 1971; A Country House Index, 1971, 2nd edn 1979; Catalogue of the Drawings Collection RIBA: Inigo Jones and John Webb, 1972; contrib., Guide to Vitruvius Britannicus, 1972; (jtly) The King's Arcadia: Inigo Jones and The Stuart Court, 1973; Catalogue of the Drawings Collection RIBA: Colin Campbell, 1973; Headfort House and Robert Adam, 1973; (jtly) The Destruction of the Country House, 1974; Gardens of Delight, The Art of Thomas Robins, 1976; Gardens of Delight, The Rococo English Landscape of Thomas Robins, 1978; (jtly) Catalogue of Drawings by Inigo Jones, John Webb and Isaac de Caus in Worcester College, Oxford, 1979; A Garden Alphabet, 1979; ed, The Garden Show, 1979; The Artist and the Country House, 1979 (Sir Banister Fletcher prize, 1979); contrib., Village England,

1980; The Palladians, 1981; The English Garden 1530-1840: a contemporary view, 1981; contrib., John Claudius Loudon and the Early Nineteenth Century in Great Britain, Washington, 1980; (jtly) Interiors, 1981; The Palladians, 1981; Die Hauser der Lords und Gentlemen, 1982; William Talman Maverick, architect, 1982; contrib., Gibraltar: an architectural appreciation, 1982; Architectural Drawings in the Cooper Hewitt Museum, New York, 1982; articles in Country Life, Arch. Rev., Arch. Hist., and other jls. *Recreations:* grand hotels, history of World War I and flinting. *Address:* 16 Limerston Street, SW10 0HH.

HARRIS, John Percival, DSC 1945; QC 1974; **His Honour Judge Harris;** a Circuit Judge, since 1980; *b* 16 Feb. 1925; *o s* of late Thomas Percival Harris and of Nora May Harris; *m* 1959, Janet Valerie Douglas; one *s* two *d. Educ:* Wells Cathedral Sch.; Pembroke Coll., Cambridge. BA 1947. Served in RN, 1943-46: Midshipman, RNVR, 1944, Sub-Lt 1945. Called to Bar, Middle Temple, 1949, Bencher 1970. A Recorder of the Crown Court, 1972-80. *Recreations:* golf, reading, Victorian pictures. *Address:* Tudor Court, Fairmile Park Road, Cobham, Surrey. *T:* Cobham 4756; 12 King's Bench Walk, Temple, EC4Y 7EL. *T:* 01-353 5892. *Clubs:* United Oxford & Cambridge University; Woking Golf, Burnham and Berrow Golf, Rye Golf.

HARRIS, Leonard John; Assistant Secretary, Cabinet Office, since 1980; *b* 4 July 1941; *s* of Leonard and May Harris; *m* 1965, Jill Christine Tompkins; one *s* two *d. Educ:* Westminster City Sch.; St John's Coll., Cambridge. BA 1964 (Eng. Lit.), MA 1967. HM Customs and Excise: Asst Principal, 1964; Private Sec. to Chairman, 1966-68; Principal, 1968; CS Selection Bd, 1970; HM Customs and Excise, 1971; Cabinet Office, 1971-74; First Sec., UK Rep. to EEC, 1974-76, Counsellor, 1976-77; Asst Sec., HM Customs and Excise, 1977-80. *Recreations:* music, cooking, eating. *Address:* Elm Cottage, Reading Road, Harwell, Oxon. *T:* Harwell 615.

HARRIS, Sir Lewis Edward, Kt 1979; OBE 1960; *b* 25 March 1900; *s* of Joseph Henry Harris and Mable Harris, New Zealand; *m* Myra Nicholson Anderson, *d* of Christopher Nicholson; two *s* one *d. Educ:* Hastings School, New Zealand. Knighthood conferred for services to the handicapped in New Zealand. *Address:* Brooklands, Puketapu, Hawkes Bay, RD2, Napier, New Zealand.

HARRIS, Brigadier Lewis John, CBE 1961 (OBE 1949; MBE 1943); Consultant to Federal Surveys and Mapping, Canada, since 1967; *b* 19 Dec. 1910; *e s* of late David Rees and of Cecilia Harris; *m* 1975, Thelma Opal, *d* of James Marshall Carr and Zettie Lou Witt, and *widow* of Lt-Col A. L. Nowicki, US Corps of Engineers. *Educ:* Christ Coll., Brecon; RMA, Woolwich; Pembroke Coll., Cambridge (Exhibitioner); Mech. Sci. Tripos, MA. Commissioned RE 1930; Triangulation of Jamaica, 1937-39; served War of 1939-45: British Expeditionary Force, 1939-40 (despatches); First Army in North Africa, 1942-43, AFHQ and American Seventh Army, Italy, 1944; Land Forces SE Asia, India, Burma and Malaya, 1944-46; Chief Instructor, Sch. of Mil. Survey, 1946-49; War Office, Geog. Section GS, 1949-52; Ordnance Survey, 1952-53; Dir, Survey GHQ, Middle East, and GHQ, E Africa, 1953-55; Land Survey Adviser, Allied Forces, Mediterranean, 1954-55; Ordnance Survey of Great Britain, 1955-61; Dir, Map Production and Publication, 1956-59; Dir, Field Surveys, 1959-61; Dir of Mil. Survey, MoD and Chief of Geographical Section Gen. Staff, 1961-65. Brig. 1956. Hon. Col 135 Survey Engineer Regt, TA, 1965-67. Chm., Nat. Cttee for Cartography, Royal Society, 1961-67. Hon. Foreign Sec., Royal Geographical Soc., 1964-67; Vice-Pres., Internat. Cartographic Assoc., 1958-61. Hon. Vice-Pres., Army Rugby Union. FRGS, FRICS. *Publications:* various papers on cartography in learned jls. *Recreations:* outdoor sports, travelling. *Address:* 12410 Hound Ears Point, Fox Den, PO Box 22129, Knoxville, Tenn 37922, USA. *Clubs:* Naval and Military, MCC; Hawks (Cambridge); Royal Ottawa Golf; IZ, FF, BB.

HARRIS, Lyndon Goodwin, RI 1958; RSW 1952; RWA 1947; artist in oil, water-colour, stained glass, and etching; *b* 25 July 1928; *s* of late S. E. Harris, ACIS and late Mary Elsie Harris. *Educ:* Halesowen Grammar Sch. Studied Art at: Birmingham Coll. of Art; Slade Sch. of Fine Art, 1946-50; University of London Inst. of Education, 1950-51; Courtauld Inst.; Central Sch. of Art and Crafts, London. Leverhulme Schol., Pilkington Schol., Slade Schol., and Slade Anatomy Prizeman; Dip. Fine Art (London) 1949; Courtauld Certificate, 1950; ATD 1951. *Works exhibited:* Paris Salon (Gold Medal, Oil Painting; Honourable Mention, Etching); RA (first exhibited at age of 13), RSA, RI, RSW, NEAC, RBA, RGI, RWA, and principal provincial galleries. *Works in permanent collections:* Ministry of Works; University Coll., London; Birmingham and Midland Inst.; City of Worcester; (stained glass) Gorsty Hill Methodist Church, Halesowen. *Recreation:* music (organ and pianoforte). *Address:* The Uplands, Waxland Road, Halesowen, West Midlands.

HARRIS, Margaret Frances, OBE 1975; Director of Theatre Design Course at Riverside (formerly, Director of the English National Opera and Sadler's Wells Design Course); *b* 28 May 1904; *d* of William Birkbeck Harris and Kathleen Marion Carey. *Educ:* Downe House. In partnership with Elizabeth Montgomery and late Sophie Devine as firm of Motley, 1931-. Has designed many productions in London and New York of drama, opera and ballet: first notable production, Richard of Bordeaux, for John Gielgud, 1932; recently, sets and costumes for: Prokofiev's War and Peace, Coliseum, 1972; (with Elizabeth Montgomery) Unknown Soldier and His Wife, New London, 1973;

A Family and a Fortune, 1975; Tosca, English Nat. Opera, 1976; Paul Bunyan, English Music Theatre, 1976; The Consul, Coliseum, 1978. *Publications:* Designing and Making Costume, by Motley, 1965; Theatre Props, by Motley, 1976. *Address:* 40 Smith Square, SW1. *T:* 01-222 5431.

HARRIS, Martin Richard; Deputy Chairman, Reckitt and Colman plc, since 1979 (Director, since 1977); Director: National Westminster Bank PLC, since 1977; County Bank Ltd, since 1977; Inmos International plc, since 1980; De La Rue Co. plc, since 1981; Equity & Law Life Assurance Soc. Plc, since 1981; Westland plc, since 1981; *b* 30 Aug. 1922; *m* 1952, Diana Moira (*née* Gandar Dower); four *s. Educ:* Wellington Coll. FCA. Captain, RE, ME and Italy, 1941-46. Joined Price Waterhouse & Co., 1946, Partner, 1956-74; Dir Gen., Panel on Take-Overs and Mergers, 1974-77. Inst. of Chartered Accountants in England and Wales: Mem. Council, 1971-79; Chm., Parly and Law Cttee, 1973-74; Chm., Prof. Standards Cttee, 1977-79; Mem., Accountants Internat. Study Gp, 1972-74. Mem., DTI's Company Law Consultative Gp, 1972-74. Mem. Court, Drapers' Co., 1978-; Co. of Chartered Accountants, 1977-. Governor, QMC, London Univ., 1979-. US Silver Star 1945. *Recreations:* philately, antique furniture and china. *Address:* 29 Belvedere Grove, Wimbledon, SW19 7RQ. *T:* 01-946 0951. *Clubs:* Carlton, MCC.

HARRIS, Maurice Kingston, CB 1976; formerly Secretary, Northern Ireland Ministry of Home Affairs, Jan. 1973, seconded to Northern Ireland Office, 1974-76; *b* 5 Oct. 1916; *s* of late Albert Kingston Harris and late Annie Rebecca Harris; *m* 1948, Margaret McGregor, *d* of Roderick Fraser McGregor; one *s* three *d. Educ:* The Perse Sch.; London Univ. 1st cl. Hons Mod. Langs, 1939. Served in Indian Army, 8th Punjab Regt, 1942-46. Colonial Office, 1946-47. Entered Northern Ireland Civil Service, 1947, and served in various Ministries; retired 1976. *Recreations:* music, walking. *Address:* 27 Strangford Avenue, Belfast BT9 6PG. *T:* Belfast 681409.

HARRIS, Noël H. V.; *see* Vicars-Harris.

HARRIS, Rt. Rev. Patrick Burnet; Rector of Kirkheaton and Assistant Bishop, Diocese of Wakefield, since 1981; *b* 30 Sept. 1934; *s* of Edward James Burnet Harris and Astrid Kendall; *m* 1968, Valerie Margaret Pilbrow; two *s* one *d. Educ:* St Albans School; Keble Coll., Oxford (MA). Asst Curate, St Ebbe's, Oxford, 1960-63; Missionary with S American Missionary Soc., 1963-73; Archdeacon of Salta, Argentina, 1969-73; Diocesan Bishop of Northern Argentina, 1973-80. *Recreations:* ornithology, S American Indian culture, music. *Address:* The Rectory, Kirkheaton, Huddersfield, West Yorks HD5 0JR. *T:* Huddersfield 31449.

HARRIS, Prof. Peter Charles, MD, PhD, FRCP; Simon Marks Professor of Cardiology, University of London, since 1966; Physician, National Heart Hospital; *b* 26 May 1923; *s* of David Jonathan Valentine and Nellie Dean Harris; *m* 1952, Felicity Margaret Hartridge; two *d. Educ:* St Olave's Grammar Sch.; Univ. of London. MB, BS (London) 1946; MRCP 1950; MD (Univ. medal) 1951; PhD 1955; FRCP 1965. House appts at King's Coll. Hospital, and elsewhere, 1946-55. Nuffield Fellow, Columbia Univ., New York, 1955-57; Lectr, Sen. Lectr and Reader in Medicine, Univ. of Birmingham, 1957-66; Dir, Inst. of Cardiology, Univ. of London, 1966-73. Hon. FACC, 1976. *Publications:* The Human Pulmonary Circulation (with D. Heath), 1962, 2nd edn 1977; articles to jls, etc, on cardio-pulmonary physiology and biochemistry. *Recreation:* chamber music. *Address:* 2 Beaumont Street, W1. *T:* 01-486 3043.

HARRIS, Philip; Principal, Monopolies and Mergers Commission, since 1977; *b* Manchester, 15 Dec. 1915; *er s* of S. D. Harris and Sarah Chazan; *m* 1939, Sarah Henriques Valentine; three *d. Educ:* Manchester Grammar Sch.; Trinity Hall, Cambridge (Open Scholarship, BA 1st Cl (with dist.), Historical Tripos, MA 1970). Asst Principal, Board of Trade, 1938-40. Served War, 1940-45; Anti-Aircraft Command and Western Europe; 2nd Lieut RA, 1941; Lieut, 2/8th Lancs Fusiliers, 1944; Capt., 6th Royal Welch Fusiliers, 1945. Principal, Board of Trade, 1946; Asst Sec., Board of Trade, 1948-64; Asst Registrar, Office of the Registrar of Restrictive Trading Agreements, 1964-66, Principal Asst Registrar, 1966-73; Principal Asst Registrar, Fair Trading Div. I, DTI, 1973; Dir, Restrictive Trade Practices Div., Office of Fair Trading, 1973-76. Nuffield Travelling Fellowship, 1956-57 (study of Indian Industrial Development). UK Mem., EEC Adv. Cttee on Cartels and Monopolies, 1973-76. Leader, UK Delgn to Internat. Cotton Advisory Cttee, 1960, 1963. *Recreation:* history. *Address:* 23 Court House Gardens, Finchley, N3 1PU. *T:* 01-346 3138. *Club:* Arts Theatre.

HARRIS, Phillip, FRCSE, FRCPE, FRCS(Glas); FRS(Ed); Consultant Neurosurgeon, Department of Surgical Neurology, Royal Infirmary and Western General Hospital, Edinburgh, and Spinal Unit, Edenhall Hospital, Musselburgh, since 1955; Senior Lecturer, Department of Neurological Surgery, Edinburgh University, since 1975; Member, MRC Brain Metabolism Unit, University of Edinburgh, since 1952; Chairman: Professional and Linguistic Assessments Board, General Medical Council; Committee of Management, School of Occupational Therapy, Edinburgh; Member, Advisory Council, Society of British Neurological Surgeons; *b* Edinburgh, 28 March 1922; *s* of late Simon Harris, Edinburgh; *m* 1949, Sheelagh Shèna (*née* Coutts); one *s* one *d. Educ:* Royal High Sch., Edinburgh; Edinburgh Univ.; Sch. of Med. of Royal Colls, Edinburgh. Medallist in Anatomy, Physiol., Physics, Materia Medica and Therapeutics, Med., Midwifery and Gynaec., and Surgery. LRCP and LRCSEd, LRFP and SG

1944; FRCSE 1948; MRCPE 1954; FRCPE 1959; FRCS(Glas) 1964 (*ad eundem*). Sydney Watson-Smith Lectr, RCPE, 1967; Honeyman-Gillespie Lectr, Edinburgh Univ., 1968; Visiting Prof.: Columbus, Ohio; Cincinnati, Ohio; Phoenix, Arizona; UCLA; Montreal Neurological Inst., Montreal; Chicago; Rangoon; Bangkok; Buenos Aires; La Paz. Guest Chief and Vis. Lectr in Univs in Canada, USA, Japan, Israel, Denmark, Peru, Hong Kong, Uruguay. Member: Amer. Assoc. of Neurolog. Surgeons; Burmese Med. Assoc.; Hong Kong Surg. Soc.; Middle East Neurosurg. Soc.; Brazilian Coll. Surgeons. Chm., Epilepsy Soc. of Edinburgh and SE Reg.; Trustee and Mem. Exec., Scottish Trust for the Physically Disabled Ltd. Pres., Royal High Sch. FP Club, Edinburgh. Captain RAMC, 1945-48. *Publications:* Spinal Injuries, RCSE, 1965; (ed jtly) Epilepsy, 1971; (ed jtly) Head Injuries, 1971; chapters in books on neurological surgery; over 60 papers in scientific jls on various neurosurgical topics. *Recreations:* sport, music, travel. *Address:* 4/5 Fettes Rise, Edinburgh EH4 1QH. *T:* 031-552 8900. *Clubs:* New (Edinburgh); Royal Scottish Automobile (Glasgow); University Staff (Edinburgh).

HARRIS, Ven. (Reginald) Brian; Archdeacon of Manchester, since 1980; a Residentiary Canon of Manchester Cathedral, since 1980; *b* 14 Aug. 1934; *s* of Reginald and Ruby Harris; *m* 1959, Anne Patricia Hughes; one *s* one *d*. *Educ:* Eltham College; Christ's College Cambridge (MA); Ridley Hall, Cambridge. Curate of Wednesbury, 1959-61; Curate of Uttoxeter, 1961-64; Vicar of St Peter, Bury, 1964-70; Vicar of Walmsley, Bolton, 1970-80; RD of Walmsley, 1970-80. *Recreations:* walking, painting, music. *Address:* 4 Victoria Avenue, Eccles, Manchester M30 9HA. *T:* 061-707 6444.

HARRIS, Richard Reader; *b* 4 June 1913; *s* of Richard Reader Harris; *m* 1940, Pamela Rosemary Merrick Stephens; three *d*. *Educ:* St Lawrence Coll., Ramsgate. Called to the Bar, 1941. Fire Service, 1939-45. MP (C) Heston and Isleworth, 1950-70. *Recreations:* squash, Tennis.

HARRIS, Richard Travis; Deputy Chairman, Gallaher Ltd, since 1978 (Director, since 1970); *b* 15 April 1919; 2nd *s* of Douglas Harris and Emmeline Harris (*née* Travis); *m* 1st, 1941, June Constance Rundle (marr. diss. 1953); two *d* ; 2nd, 1953, Margaret Sophia Nye (*née* Aron); one *s* one *d*. *Educ:* Charterhouse; RMA Woolwich. Served War of 1939-45, France, Western Desert, Tunisia, Italy; BAOR, 1945-46; Sudan Defence Force Signal Regt, 1947-50 (CO, 1948-50); retired from Royal Signals, 1950, Lt-Col. Man. Dir, Rediffusion (Nigeria) Ltd and Gen. Manager, Rediffusion in Africa, 1951-54; Dep. Gen. Manager, Associated-Rediffusion Ltd, 1954-57; Man. Dir, Coates & Co. (Plymouth) Ltd, 1957-64; Man. Dir, 1964-78, Chm., 1970-78, Dollond & Aitchison Group Ltd. Director: Dollond & Aitchison Gp (formerly TWW Enterprises), 1964-; Dollard Internat., 1973-; Filotechnica Salmoiraghi SpA, 1974-; Istituto Ottico Vigano SpA, 1974-; Saunders Valve Co. Ltd, 1978-; Mono Pumps Ltd, 1978-; Formatura Iniezione Polimeri SpA, 1978-; Tobacco Kiosks Ltd, 1978-; Gallaher Pensions Ltd, 1975-. Chm., Fedn of Optical Corporate Bodies, 1970-; Chm. Council, Inst. of Dirs, 1982; Mem. Council, Univ. of Birmingham. Governor, Royal Shakespeare Theatre. *Recreations:* fishing, theatre. *Address:* 21 Lucy's Mill, Stratford-upon-Avon, Warks CV37 6BJ. *T:* Stratford-upon-Avon 66016. *Club:* Royal Western Yacht (Plymouth).

HARRIS, Robert; actor since 1922; *b* 28 March 1900; *s* of Alfred H. Harris and Suzanne Amelie (*née* Anstie). *Educ:* Sherborne; New Coll., Oxford. Has appeared in Shakespearean rôles with the Old Vic-Sadler's Wells Company and at Stratford-on-Avon, and in the West End (Hamlet, Oberon, Prospero, Angelo, Henry IV, King John, Shylock, Dr Faustus, J. Robert Oppenheimer). Other parts include: St Bernard, in The Marvellous History of St Bernard; Charles Tritton, in The Wind and The Rain; Eugene Marchbanks, in Candida; Orin Mannon, in Mourning Becomes Electra; Thomas More, in A Man for all Seasons (USA); Pope Pius XII in The Deputy (NY); 40 Years On (Canada); Prendergast, in Decline and Fall (film); Morta in Roma (film); Ransom (film); Love Among the Ruins (film). Television, verse reading, and radio plays incl.: Old Jolyon in The Forsyte Saga; Prof. Gay in C. P. Snow's Strangers and Brothers (serials); Archdeacon Grantly in The Barchester Chronicles; The Mysterious Death of Charles Bravo; Edward and Mrs Simpson (TV serial). *Recreation:* travel. *Address:* 18 Pitt Street, W8 4NY. *Clubs:* Garrick, Chelsea Arts.

HARRIS, Sir Ronald (Montague Joseph), KCVO 1960 (MVO 1943); CB 1956; First Church Estates Commissioner, 1969-82; Chairman, Central Board of Finance of Church of England, 1978-82; *b* 6 May 1913; *o s* of late Rev. J. Montague Harris and Edith A. Harris (*née* Malcolmson); *m* 1st, 1939, Margaret Julia Wharton (*d* 1955); one *s* three *d* ; 2nd, 1957, Marjorie, widow of Julian Tryon, and *e d* of Sir Harry Verney, 4th Bt, DSO, and late Lady Rachel Verney; one step *d* (one step *s* decd). *Educ:* Harrow; Trinity Coll., Oxford. India Office and Burma Office, 1936-38; Private Sec. to Sec. of Cabinet, 1939-43; India Office and Burma Office, 1944-47; Imperial Defence Coll., 1948; HM Treasury, 1949-52; Cabinet Office, 1952-55; Second Crown Estate Commissioner, 1955-60; Third Sec., HM Treasury, 1960-64; Sec. to Church Commissioners, 1964-68. Director: Yorks Insurance Co., 1966-69; Yorkshire General Life Assurance Co., 1969-; General Accident Fire and Life Assurance Corp. Ltd; Triplevest Ltd. Chairman: Benenden Sch. Council, 1971-77; Friends of Yehudi Menuhin Sch., 1972-, Governor, 1976-. *Address:* Slyfield Farm House, Stoke D'Abernon, Cobham, Surrey. *Club:* Boodle's.

HARRIS, Rosemary Jeanne; author; *b* 1923; *yr d* of Marshal of the RAF Sir Arthur Harris, Bt, *qv*, and Barbara Kyrle Money. *Educ:* privately; Thorneloe

Sch., Weymouth; St Martin's, Central and Chelsea Schs of Art. Red Cross Nursing Auxiliary, London, Westminster Div., from 1941. Student, 1945-48; picture restorer, 1949; student at Courtauld Inst. (Dept of Technology), 1950; Reader, MGM, 1951-52; subseq. full-time writer. Reviewer of children's books for The Times, 1970-73. Television plays: Peronik, 1976; The Unknown Enchantment, 1981. *Publications:* The Summer-House, 1956; Voyage to Cythera, 1958; Venus with Sparrows, 1961; All My Enemies, 1967; The Nice Girl's Story, 1968; A Wicked Pack of Cards, 1969; The Double Snare, 1975; Three Candles for the Dark, 1976; *for children:* The Moon in the Cloud, 1968 (Carnegie Medal); The Shadow on the Sun, 1970; The Seal-Singing, 1971; The Child in the Bamboo Grove, 1971; The Bright and Morning Star, 1972; The King's White Elephant, 1973; The Lotus and the Grail, 1974; The Flying Ship, 1974; The Little Dog of Fo, 1976; I Want to be a Fish, 1977; A Quest for Orion, 1978; Beauty and the Beast, 1979; Greenfinger House, 1979; Tower of the Stars, 1980; The Enchanted Horse, 1981; Janni's Stork, 1982; Zed, 1982. *Recreations:* music, theatre, photography. *Address:* 33 Cheyne Court, Flood Street, SW3 5TR.

HARRIS, Rosina Mary; Senior Partner, Joynson-Hicks & Co., Solicitors, since 1977 (Partner, 1954-77); Deputy Chairman, Blundell-Permoglaze Holdings Ltd, since 1981 (non-executive Director, 1979); *b* 30 May 1921; *d* of Alfred Harris, CBE, DSO, and Rosa Alfreda Harris. *Educ:* St Swithun's Sch., Winchester; Oxford Univ. (BA Law, 1946; BCL post grad. law degree). Joined American Ambulance of Gt Britain, 1940. Member, Whitford Committee (a Cttee set up under the Chairmanship of Hon. Mr Justice Whitford to enquire into and report as to copyright law), 1973. The Queen's Silver Jubilee Medal, 1977. *Recreations:* theatre, riding. *Address:* 23 Devonshire Place, W1N 1PD. *T:* (office) 01-387 0909. *Club:* Naval and Military.

HARRIS, Prof. Roy; Professor of General Linguistics, University of Oxford, since Jan. 1978; Fellow of Worcester College, Oxford; *b* 24 Feb. 1931; *s* of Harry and Emmie J. Harris; *m* 1955, Rita Doreen Shulman; one *d*. *Educ:* Queen Elizabeth's Hospital, Bristol; St Edmund Hall, Oxford. MA, DPhil (Oxon), PhD London). Lecteur, Ecole Normale Supérieure, Paris, 1956-57; Asst Lectr, 1957-58, Lectr, 1958-60, Univ. of Leicester; Exeter Coll., Oxford, 1960-76; Keble Coll., Oxford, 1960-67; Magdalen Coll., Oxford, 1960-76; New Coll., Oxford, 1960-67; Faculty of Medieval and Modern Languages, Oxford, 1961-76; Fellow and Tutor in Romance Philology, Keble Coll., Oxford, 1967-76; Prof. of the Romance Langs, Oxford Univ., 1976-77. Council Member, Philological Soc., 1978-82. Editor, Language & Communication, 1980-. *Publications:* Synonymy and Linguistic Analysis, 1973; Communication and Language, 1978; The Language-Makers, 1980; The Language Myth, 1981; F. de Saussure: Course in General Linguistics, 1982; contribs to Analysis, French Studies, Jl of Linguistics, Linguistics, Medium Ævum, Revue de linguistique romane, Theoria, Zeitschrift für romanische Philologie. *Recreations:* cricket, modern art and design. *Address:* 2 Paddox Close, Oxford OX2 7LR. *T:* Oxford 54256.

HARRIS, (Theodore) Wilson; *b* 24 March 1921; *m* 1st, 1945, Cecily Carew; 2nd, 1959, Margaret Whitaker (*née* Burns). *Educ:* Queen's Coll., Georgetown, British Guiana. Studied land surveying, British Guiana, 1939, and subseq. qualified to practise; led many survey parties (mapping and geomorphological research) in the interior; Senior Surveyor, Projects, for Govt of British Guiana, 1955-58. Came to live in London, 1959. Writer in Residence, Univ. of West Indies and Univ. of Toronto, 1970; Commonwealth Fellow, Leeds Univ., 1971; Vis. Prof., Univ. of Texas at Austin, 1972; Guggenheim Fellow, 1973; Henfield Fellow, UEA, 1974; Southern Arts Writer's Fellowship, 1976; Guest Lectr, Univ. of Mysore, 1978; Vis. Lectr, Yale Univ., 1979; Writer in Residence, Univ. of Newcastle, Australia, 1979. *Publications:* Eternity to Season (poems, privately printed), 1954; Palace of the Peacock, 1960; The Far Journey of Oudin, 1961; The Whole Armour, 1962; The Secret Ladder, 1963; Heartland, 1964; The Eye of the Scarecrow, 1965; The Waiting Room, 1967; Tradition, the Writer and Society: Critical Essays, 1967; Tumatumari, 1968; Ascent to Omai, 1970; The Sleepers of Roraima (a Carib Trilogy), 1970; The Age of the Rainmakers, 1971; Black Marsden, 1972; Companions of the Day and Night, 1975; Da Silva da Silva's Cultivated Wilderness, and Genesis of the Clowns, 1977; The Tree of the Sun, 1978; The Angel at the Gate, 1982. *Address:* c/o Faber and Faber, 3 Queen Square, WC1N 3AU.

HARRIS, Thomas Maxwell, FRS 1948; Professor of Botany, University of Reading, 1935-68, Professor Emeritus 1968; *b* 8 Jan. 1903; *s* of Alexander Charles Harris and Lucy Frances Evans; *m* 1928, Katharine Massey; one *s* three *d*. *Educ:* Bootham, York; Wyggeston Sch., Leicester; University Coll., Nottingham; Christ's Coll., Cambridge (scholar). Natural Science Tripos, Parts I and II, 1st Class Hons; London BSc, 1st Class Hons; ScD Cambridge; Mem. of Danish Expedition to E Greenland, 1926-27; Demonstrator in Botany, 1928; Fellow of Christ's Coll., 1928. Vice-Pres., Royal Society, 1960-61; President, Linnæan Soc., 1961-64; Vice-Pres., 1964. Trustee, Natural History Museum, 1963-73. *Publications:* communications to scientific journals on Palæobotany. *Recreation:* gardening. *Address:* 74 Birdhill Avenue, Reading RG2 7JU. *T:* Reading 84930; Department of Geology, The University, Reading, Berks.

HARRIS, Hon. Walter Edward, PC (Canada), QC (Canada); DCL; Director, Homewood Sanitarium Ltd; *b* 14 Jan. 1904; *s* of Melvin Harris and Helen (*née* Carruthers); *m* 1933, Grace Elma Morrison; one *s* two *d*. *Educ:*

Osgoode Hall, Toronto. Served War of 1939-45. First elected to House of Commons, Canada, 1940 (re-elected 1945, 1949, 1953), MP (Canada) until 1957. Parliamentary Asst to Sec of State for External Affairs, 1947; Parly Asst to Prime Minister, 1948; Minister of Citizenship and Immigration, 1950; of Finance, 1954-57. Mem. of the firm of Harris & Dunlop, Barristers, Markdale. *Address:* Markdale, Ontario, Canada.

HARRIS, (Walter) Frank; retired 1982; *b* 19 May 1920; *m* Esther Blanche Hill; two *s* two *d. Educ:* King Edward's Sch., Birmingham; University of Nottingham. Served Royal Air Force, 1939-46. University, 1946-49. Ford Motor Company, 1950-65; Principal City Officer and Town Clerk, Newcastle upon Tyne, 1965-69. Comptroller and Dir, Admin, Massey-Ferguson (UK), 1969-71; Financial Dir, Dunlop SA Ltd, 1972-79; Business Planning Exec., Dunlop Ltd (UK Tyre Gp), 1979-81. *Recreations:* astrophysics (undergraduate at Univ. of S Africa), fell walking, gardening. *Address:* Acomb High House, Northumberland NE46 4PH. *T:* Hexham 602844. *Club:* Reform.

HARRIS, William Barclay, QC 1961; *b* 25 Nov. 1911; *s* of W. Cecil Harris, Moatlands, E Grinstead, Sussex; *m* 1937, Elizabeth, 2nd *d* of Capt. Sir Clive Milnes-Coates, 2nd Bt, and of Lady Celia Milnes-Coates; one *s* two *d. Educ:* Harrow; Trinity Coll., Cambridge (MA). Served 1940-45: with Coldstream Guards, N Africa, Italy, Germany (despatches), Major. Barrister, Inner Temple, 1937. Chm., Rowton Hotels, 1965-. A Church Commissioner, 1966-82 (Chm., Redundant Churches Cttee, 1972-82; Mem., Bd of Governors, 1972-82). Liveryman, Worshipful Co. of Merchant Taylors. *Address:* Moatlands, East Grinstead, West Sussex. *T:* Sharpthorne 810228; 29 Barkston Gardens, SW5. *T:* 01-373 8793. *Clubs:* Athenæum, MCC, Brooks's.

HARRIS, Sir William (Gordon), KBE 1969; CB 1963; MA (Cantab); FEng; FICE; Chairman, B & CE Holiday Management Co., since 1978; *b* 10 June 1912; *s* of late Capt. James Whyte Harris, Royal Naval Reserve, and Margaret Roberta Buchanan Forsyth; *m* 1938, Margaret Emily Harvie; three *s* one *d. Educ:* Liverpool Coll.; Sidney Sussex Coll., Cambridge. Mechanical Sciences Tripos and BA 1932, MA 1937. London Midland & Scottish Railway, 1932-35; Sudan Irrigation Dept, 1935-37; Joined Civil Engineer in Chief's Dept, Admiralty, 1937; Asst Civil Engineer in Chief, 1950; Deputy Civil Engineer in Chief, 1955; Civil Engineer in Chief, 1959; Dir-Gen., Navy Works, 1960-63; Dir-Gen. of Works, MPBW, 1963-65; Dir-Gen., Highways, MoT, later DoE, 1965-73. Partner, Peter Fraenkel & Partners, 1973-78. Chief British Delegate to: Perm. Internat. Assoc. of Navigation Congresses, 1969- (Vice-Pres., 1976-79); Perm. Internat. Assoc. of Road Congresses, 1970-73; Mem., Dover Harbour Bd, 1959-82 (Dep. Chm., 1975-79; Chm., 1980-82); Chm., Construction Industry Manpower Bd, 1976-79. Commonwealth Fund (of New York) Fellowship, 1950-51. A Vice-Pres., Instn Civil Engineers, 1971-74, Pres. 1974-75. FEng. 1977. Mem., Smeatonian Soc. of Civil Engineers. Hon. DSc City, 1977. *Address:* 3 Rofant Road, Northwood, Mddx. *T:* Northwood 25899.

HARRIS, Sir William (Woolf), Kt 1974; OBE 1961; surveyor and company director; *b* London, 19 Aug. 1910; *e s* of Simon Harris and Fanny Harris, London; *m* 1952, Beverly Joyce, *y d* of Howard Bowden, Minneapolis, USA; one *s* two *d. Educ:* King's Coll.; Princeton Univ. Chm. of number of companies concerned with residential and industrial building construction. Chm., Bow Street Magistrates Court, 1955-80; Chm., Inner London Juvenile Courts, 1955-75; Member: Inner London Sessions Appeals Court; London Probation Cttee and Home Office Juvenile Courts Consultative Cttee, 1955-72; a General Commissioner of Taxes; Vice-Pres. (former Chm.), Royal Soc. of St George (City of London); former jt Nat. Treas., Trades Adv. Council; Founder 1951, and Chm. until 1963, Addison Boys Club, Hammersmith; Conservative Party: Chairman: Nat. Union of Conservative Assocs, 1971-73; Party Conf., 1972; Standing Adv. Cttee on Candidates, 1971-73; Greater London Area, 1966-69; former London Area, 1963; Mem., Cons Party Adv. Cttee on Policy, 1965-75 and of other nat. adv. cttees; Mem., Nat. Exec. Cttee and Gen. Purpose Cttee, 1963-75; Chm., S Battersea Conservative Assoc., 1956-63; former Pres. and Chm., Battersea Chamber of Commerce; Branch Chm., NSPCC, 1956-65; Founder and Nat. Chm., Leasehold Reform Assoc., 1956-67. Mem. Council and Ct, City Univ., 1979-. Mem. Council, Imperial Soc. of Knights Bachelor, 1978-. Mem. Court of Assistants, Worshipful Co. of Basketmakers. Freeman, City of London; High Sheriff of Greater London, 1971-72; JP Bow Street, 1952-80. *Publications:* papers on problems of juvenile delinquency, child welfare, mental health and penal reform in various jls. *Recreations:* reading history, theatre, travel, listening to the wiseacres talk. *Address:* 165 Bickenhall Mansions, Gloucester Place, W1H 3DF. *T:* 01-935 3752. *Clubs:* Carlton, St Stephen's Constitutional, City Livery.

HARRIS, Wilson; see Harris, T. W.

HARRISON, (Alastair) Brian (Clarke); DL; Director, Agricultural Investments Australia Ltd; *b* 3 Oct. 1921; *s* of late Brig. E. F. Harrison, Melbourne; *m* 1952, Elizabeth Hood Hardie, Oaklands, NSW, Aust.; one *s* one *d. Educ:* Geelong Grammar Sch.; Trinity Coll., Cambridge. Capt. AIF. MP (C) Maldon, Essex, 1955-Feb. 1974; Parliamentary Private Secretary to: Min. of State, Colonial Office, 1955-56; Sec. of State for War, 1956-58; Min. of Agriculture, Fisheries and Food, 1958-60. Mem. Victoria Promotion Cttee (London); Mem. One Nation Gp which published The Responsible Society,

and One Europe; toured USA on E-SU Ford Foundation Fellowship, 1959; Commonwealth Parliamentary Assoc. Delegations: Kenya and Horn of Africa, 1960; Gilbert and Ellice Islands, New Hebrides and British Solomon Islands Protectorate. Chm., Standing Conf. of Eastern Sport and Physical Recreation, 1974-80. High Sheriff, 1979, DL 1980, Essex. *Recreations:* photography, gardening. *Address:* Green Farm House, Copford, Colchester, Essex; Munethana, Orchid Valley, WA 6395, Australia. *Clubs:* Pratt's; Melbourne (Melbourne); Weld (Perth).

HARRISON, Albert Norman, CB 1966; CVO 1955; OBE 1946; RCNC; Hon. Vice-President RINA; *b* 12 July 1901; *s* of William Arthur and Sarah Jane Harrison, Portsmouth, Hants; *m* 1941, Queenie Perpetua Parker, Luton, Beds; one *d. Educ:* Portsmouth; Royal Naval Coll., Greenwich. Asst Constructor, Royal Corps of Naval Constructors, 1926; Constructor, 1937; Principal Ship Overseer. Vickers-Armstrong, Barrow-in-Furness, 1936-39; Staff of RA (D), Home Fleet, 1940-41; Naval Constructor-in-Chief, Royal Canadian Navy, 1942-48; Chief Constructor, Admiralty, 1948-51; Asst Dir of Naval Construction, Admiralty, 1951-61; Dir of Naval Construction, Min. of Defence (N) (formerly Admiralty), 1961-66. *Address:* Whiteoaks, 126 Bloomfield Road, Bath, Avon. *T:* Bath 29145. *Club:* Bath and County (Bath).

HARRISON, Alexander, CBE 1955; CA; Vice-President, Trustee Savings Bank Association (Deputy-Chairman, 1947-59); *b* 26 Feb. 1890; *s* of John Harrison, CBE, LLD, FRSE, DL, and Helen Georgina Roberts; *m* 1931, Jean Muriel Small; one *s* three *d. Educ:* Merchiston Castle Sch. Chartered Accountant, 1914 (Distinction). Chm. Edinburgh Savings Bank, 1945-54. Mem. Edinburgh Town Council, 1946-48. Served European War, 1914-18; temp. Major, Royal Scots, attached Machine Gun Corps in France and Italy, FRSGS. Hon. Pres., Scottish Mountaineering Club. *Address:* 3a Tipperlinn Road, Edinburgh EH10 5ET. *T:* 031-447 7434. *Clubs:* Alpine; New (Edinburgh).

HARRISON, Brian; see Harrison, A. B. C.

HARRISON, Rev. Cecil Marriott; Vicar of Aislaby, Diocese of York, 1969-79, retired; *b* 16 March 1911; *s* of late Tom Marriott Harrison, Davidson's Mains, Midlothian; *m* 1944, Phyllis Edith McKenzie. *Educ:* Westminster Sch.; Trinity Coll., Cambridge. 1st Class Classical Tripos Pt I, 1930; Pt II, 1932; BA 1932, MA 1936; Classical Sixth Form Master, Nottingham High Sch., 1932; Dulwich Coll., 1934; Charterhouse, 1936-47. Served War of 1939-45; Royal Signals, 1940-46; Headmaster of Felsted Sch., 1947-51; Headmaster, King's School, Peterborough, 1951-69. Deacon, 1966, Priest, 1967. *Address:* 4 Rosedale Abbey, Pickering, N Yorks YO18 8RA. *T:* Lastingham 569. *Club:* Leander.

HARRISON, Prof. Charles Victor; retired; Professor of Pathology, University of Ife, Nigeria, 1972-75; *b* Newport, Mon, 1907; *s* of Charles Henry Harrison, LDS, and Violet Harrison (*née* Witchell); *m* 1937, Olga Beatrice Cochrane; one *s* one *d. Educ:* Dean Close Sch., Cheltenham; University Coll., Cardiff; University Coll. Hosp., London. MB, BCh, BSc (Wales), 1929; MB, BS (London), 1929; MD (London), 1937; FRCPath 1965; FRCP 1967. Demonstrator in Pathology, Welsh National School of Medicine, 1930; Asst Morbid Anatomist, British Postgraduate Medical Sch., 1935; Senior Lecturer, Liverpool Univ., 1939; Reader in Morbid Anatomy, Postgraduate Medical Sch. of London, 1946; Prof., Royal Postgrad. Med. Sch., Univ. of London, 1955-72. Hon. DSc Wales, 1972. Willie Seager Gold Medal in Pathology, 1927. *Publications:* (ed) Recent Advances in Pathology, 1973; various scientific papers in Jl of Pathology and Bacteriology, British Heart Journal, Jl Clin. Pathology, etc. *Recreations:* carpentry and gardening. *Address:* 8 Wattleton Road, Beaconsfield, Bucks HP9 1TS. *T:* Beaconsfield 2046.

HARRISON, Claude William, RP 1961; Artist; portrait painter and painter of conversation pieces, imaginative landscapes and murals, etc; *b* Leyland, Lancs, 31 March 1922; *s* of Charles Harrison and Florence Mildred Ireton; *m* 1947, Audrey Johnson; one *s. Educ:* Hutton Grammar Sch., Lancs. Served in RAF, 1942-46. Royal Coll. of Art, 1947-49; Studio in Ambleside, 1949-52. Exhibited since 1950 at: RA; RSA; Royal Society Portrait Painters; New English Art Club, etc. *Publication:* The Portrait Painter's handbook, 1968. *Recreation:* painting. *Address:* Barrow Wife, Cartmel Fell, near Grange over Sands, Cumbria. *T:* Newby Bridge 31323.

HARRISON, Sir Colin; see Harrison, Sir R. C.

HARRISON, David, ScD; Vice-Chancellor, University of Keele, since 1979; Fellow of Selwyn College, Cambridge, since 1957; *b* 3 May 1930; *s* of Harold David Harrison and Lavinia Wilson; *m* 1962, Sheila Rachel Debes; two *s* one *d. Educ:* Bede Sch., Sunderland; Clacton County High Sch.; Selwyn Coll., Cambridge (1st Cl. Pts I and II Natural Sciences Tripos, BA 1953, PhD 1956, MA 1957, ScD 1979). CEng; FRSC (FRIC 1961), FIChemE 1968. 2nd Lieut, REME, 1949. Research student, Dept of Physical Chemistry, Cambridge, 1953-56; Univ. Asst Lectr in Chem. Engrg, 1956-61; Univ. Lectr, 1961-79; Sen. Tutor, Selwyn Coll., Cambridge, 1967-79; Visiting Professor of Chemical Engineering: Univ. of Delaware, USA, 1967; Univ. of Sydney, 1976. Member, Council of the Senate, Univ. of Cambridge, 1967-75; Chm. of Faculty Bd of Educn, 1976-78; Member Council: Lancing Coll., 1970-; Haileybury, 1974-; St Edward's, Oxford, 1977-; Bolton Girls' Sch., 1981-;

Fellow, Woodard Corporation of Schools, 1972–; Chm., Bd of Trustees, Homerton Coll., Cambridge, 1979–. Hon. Editor, Trans Instn of Chemical Engrs, 1972–78. *Publications:* (with J. F. Davidson, *qv*) Fluidised Particles, 1963; (also with J. F. Davidson) Fluidization, 1971; numerous articles in scientific and technological jls. *Recreations:* music, tennis, hill walking, good food. *Address:* The Clock House, University of Keele, Staffs ST5 5BE. *T:* Newcastle (Staffs) 621111. *Club:* Athenæum.

HARRISON, Denis Byrne; JP; a Local Commissioner for Administration in England, 1974–81, and Vice-Chairman of the Commission for Local Administration, 1975–81; *b* 11 July 1917; *y s* of late Arthur and Priscilla Harrison; *m* 1956, Alice Marion Vickers, *e d* of late Hedley Vickers. *Educ:* Birkenhead Sch.; Liverpool Univ. (LLM). Articled to late E. W. Tame, OBE (Town Clerk of Birkenhead). Admitted Solicitor, 1939; Asst Solicitor to Birkenhead Corp., 1939. Served War, 1939–46: 75th Shropshire Yeo. (Medium Regt) RA, Combined Ops Bombardment Unit; Staff Captain at HQ of OC, Cyprus. First Asst Solicitor, Wolverhampton Co. Borough, 1946–49; Dep. Town Clerk of Co. Boroughs: Warrington, 1949–57; Bolton, 1957–63; Sheffield, 1963–66; Town Clerk and Chief Exec. Officer, Sheffield, 1966–74. Mem., Advisory Council on Noise, 1970–79. Mem. Council, 1975–, Pro-Chancellor, 1980–, Univ. of Sheffield. JP City of London, 1976. *Recreations:* foreign travel, music, ski-ing, golf. *Address:* Doucegrove Farm, Northiam, near Rye, East Sussex TN31 6JG. *T:* Brede 882599; 108A Whitehall Court, SW1. *T:* 01-930 6394.

HARRISON, Maj.-Gen. Desmond, CB 1946; DSO 1940; FICE; Civil Engineer; *b* 11 Nov. 1896; *s* of R. J. Harrison, JP; *m* 1920; one *s* two *d*. *Educ:* Kilkenny Coll.; Mountjoy Sch., Dublin; RMA, Woolwich; Cambridge Univ. Temp. Maj.-Gen. 1944; Maj.-Gen. 1947; Comdt SME 1942; Engineer-in-Chief, SEAC, 1943; Director of Fortifications and Works, War Office, 1946; retired 1947. Mem. Overseas Food Corp., 1947; resigned 1949. Comdr Legion of Merit, USA. *Recreations:* golf, shooting, fishing. *Address:* 55 Hans Road, SW3. *T:* 01-584 4867. *Club:* Army and Navy.

HARRISON, Prof. Donald Frederick Norris, MD, MS, FRCS; Professor of Laryngology and Otology (University of London), at the Institute of Laryngology, Gray's Inn Road, WC1, since 1963; Surgeon, Royal National Throat, Nose and Ear Hospital; Civilian Consultant on ENT to RN; *b* 9 March 1925; *s* of Frederick William Rees Harrison, OBE, JP, and Florence, *d* of Robert Norris, Portsmouth, Hants; *m* 1949, Audrey, *o d* of Percival Clubb, Penarth, Glam.; two *d*. *Educ:* Newport High Sch., Mon.; Guy's Hosp. MD (London) 1960; MS (London) 1959; FRCS 1955. Ho. Surg., Guy's Hosp. and Royal Gwent Hospital, Newport; Surg. Registrar, Shrewsbury Eye and Ear Hosp.; Senior Registrar, Throat and Ear Dept, Guy's Hosp.; University Reader in Laryngology, Inst. of Laryngol. and Otol. Hunterian Prof., RCS, 1962; Chevalier Jackson Lectr, 1964; Erasmus Wilson Demonstrator, RCS, 1971; Yearsley Lectr, 1972; Wilde Lectr, 1972; Litchfield Lectr, 1973; Semon Lectr, 1974; Colles Lectr, RCSI, 1977; Jobson Horne Lectr, BMA, 1979; Conacher Lectr, Toronto, 1978. W. J. Harrison Prize, RSM, 1978. Mem. of Court of Examiners, RCS; Examr, NUI; External Examr, Univs of Melbourne, Sydney, Manchester, Liverpool, Glasgow, Hong Kong and Cambridge; Fellow Medical Soc. London; Scientific Fellow, Royal Zoological Soc. of London; FRSM (former Vice-Pres., Sect. of Laryngology; Mem. Council, Sect. of Oncology); Mem. BMA; Mem. Council: Brit. Assoc. of Otolaryngologists; Brit. Assoc. of Head and Neck Oncologists (Pres.); Former Chairman: Special Adv. Cttee on Human Communication; Bd Postgrad. Med. Studies, London Univ.; Chm., Centennial Conf., Laryngeal Cancer, 1974; Asst Sec., Collegium Oto-Rhino-Laryngologium; Member: Anatomical Soc. of Great Britain; Res. Cttee, Nat. Deaf Children's Soc. (Dep. Chm.); Cttee of Management, Institute of Cancer Research; Internat. Cttee for Cancer of Larynx; Chm., NE Thames Region Postgrad. Cttee. Editorial Board: Acta Otolaryngologica; Practica Oto-Rhino-Laryngologica; Annals of Oto-Rhino-Laryngology; Excerpta Medica (Sect. II); Otolaryngological Digest. Hon. FRCSE 1981; Hon. Fellow: Acad. ENT, America, 1976; Triol. Soc., USA, 1977; Amer. Laryngol Assoc., 1979; Hon. FRACS, 1977. Hon. Member: NZ ENT Soc.; Jamaican ENT Soc.; Polish ENT Soc.; Egyptian ENT Soc.; Otolaryngological Soc., Australia; For. Mem., Internat. Broncho-œsophagological Soc.; Corresp. Member: Amer. Head and Neck Soc.; Soc. Française d'Otorhinolaryngologie; Otolaryngological Soc., Denmark; Amer. Acad. of Facial Plastic Reconstr. Surgery; Pacific Coast Oto-Ophthalmological Soc.; Amer. Laryngological Soc.; Yeoman, Soc. of Apothecaries. *Publications:* (ed jtly) Scientific Basis of Otolaryngology, 1976; articles on familial hæmorrhagic telangiectases, meatal oseomata, cancer chemotherapy, head and neck surgery in learned jls; chapters in Text Books on Ent. and Gen. Surgery. *Recreations:* radio-controlled models, heraldry. *Address:* Institute of Laryngology and Otology, Gray's Inn Road, WC1. *T:* 01-837 8855; Springfield, Fisher's Farm, Horley, Surrey. *T:* Horley 4307.

HARRISON, Douglas Creese, DSc London, PhD Cantab, ARIC; Professor of Biochemistry, Queen's University, Belfast, 1935–67; *b* 29 April, 1901; *s* of Lovell and Lillian E. Harrison, MBE, JP; *m* 1926, Sylva Thurlow, MA, PhD, Philadelphia, USA; one *s*. *Educ:* Highgate Sch.; King's Coll., London; Emmanuel Coll., Cambridge. Keddey Fletcher-Warr Research Studentship, 1925–28; Lecturer at Sheffield Univ., 1926–35. *Publications:* various papers in the Biochemical Journal, Proc. Royal Society, Lancet, etc. *Address:* 4 Broomhill Park Central, Belfast. *T:* Belfast 665685.

HARRISON, Maj.-Gen. Eric George William Warde, CB 1945; CBE 1943; MC 1915; MA (hon.) Oxford; *b* 23 March 1893; *s* of Major W. C. Warde Harrison, Indian Army; *m* 1961, Mrs Roza M. Stevenson, widow of J. B. Stevenson (she *d* 1967). *Educ:* Royal Military Academy, Woolwich. Commissioned Royal Artillery, 1913; European War, France and Belgium, 1914–19, GSOII 58 Div. and III Corps (despatches four times, MC, Crown of Italy, Bt Major); Staff Coll. Camberley, 1925–26; GSOII Lahore District, India, 1928–32; Major, 1932; Bt Lieut-Col 1931; Commanding Oxford Univ. OTC 1934–38; Lieut-Col 1939; Col 1939. War of 1939–45, CRA 12 Div., BRA Northern Ireland, CCRA 9 Corps, MGRA AFHQ, Comdr Surrey and Sussex District. War Service North Africa and Italy, 1943–45 (despatches, CBE, CB); Temp. Maj.-Gen. 1944; ADC to the King, 1945–46; retired pay, 1946. JP 1951, DL 1955, High Sheriff 1958, Cornwall. Chm. St Lawrence's Hospital Management Cttee, 1952–66. *Publications:* Riding, 1949; To Own a Dog, 1951; Gunners, Game and Gardens, 1979. *Recreations:* fishing, gardening, painting; Rugby football Mother Country XV 1919, Army 1920; Athletics, represented England in 120 yds Hurdles, 1914 and 1920, Olympic Games, 1924; Master RA Harriers, 1920–24, Staff Coll. Drag 1925–26, Lahore Hounds 1928–31, South Oxon Foxhounds, 1935–38, North Cornwall Foxhounds, 1940–48. *Address:* Swallowfield Park, near Reading, Berks. *Clubs:* Army and Navy; Houghton Fishing.

HARRISON, Sir Ernest (Thomas), Kt 1981; OBE 1972; FCA; Chairman and Managing Director, Racal Electronics Plc, since 1966; Chairman and Chief Executive, Decca Ltd, since 1980; *b* 11 May 1926; *s* of Ernest Horace Harrison and Gertrude Rebecca Gibbons Harrison; *m* 1960, Phyllis Brenda Knight (Janie); three *s* two *d*. *Educ:* Trinity Grammar Sch., Wood Green, London. FCA 1950. Qualified as Chartered Accountant, 1950; served Articles with Harker Holloway & Co; joined Racal Electronics as Secretary and Chief Accountant, when company commenced manufacturing, 1951; Director, 1958, Dep. Man. Dir, 1961. Mem., RSA; Liveryman, Scriveners' Co. CompIERE 1975; CBIM; CompIEE 1978. Hon. DSc, DUniv Surrey. *Recreations:* gardening, sport, espec. soccer. *Address:* Racal Electronics Plc, Western Road, Bracknell, Berkshire RG12 1RG.

HARRISON, Sir Francis Alexander Lyle, (Sir Frank Harrison), Kt 1974; MBE 1943; QC (NI); DL; President, Lands Tribunal for Northern Ireland, since 1964; *b* 19 March 1910; *s* of Rev. Alexander Lyle Harrison and Mary Luise (née Henderson), Rostrevor, Co. Down; *m* 1940, Norah Patricia (née Rea); two *d*. *Educ:* Campbell Coll., Belfast; Trinity Coll., Dublin. BA (Moderator in Legal Sci.), LLB (Hons). Called to Bar of NI, 1937. Served War: commissioned Gen. List, Oct. 1939; ADC to GOC, NI, 1939–40; Major, Dep. Asst Adjt-Gen., HQ, NI, 1941–45 (MBE). Apptd to determine Industrial Assurance disputes in NI, 1946–62; Counsel to Attorney-Gen., NI, 1946–48; KC 1948. Legal Adviser to Min. of Home Affairs, 1949–64; Sen. Crown Prosecutor, Co. Fermanagh, 1948–54; subseq. for Counties Tyrone, Londonderry and Antrim, 1954–64; Chm., Mental Health Review Tribunal, 1948–64; Counsel to the Speakers of House of Commons and Senate of NI, 1953–64; Mem. Statute Law Cttee, NI, 1953–64; Chm., Advisory Cttee under Civil Authorities Special Powers Acts (NI), 1957–62; Bencher, Inn of Court of NI, 1961; Chm., Shaftesbury Sq. Hosp. Management Cttee, 1964–73; Chm., Glendhu Children's Hostel, 1968–81; Founder Mem., NI Assoc. of Mental Health, 1959–. Boundary Comr under Local Govt (Boundaries) Act (NI), 1971. DL Co. Down, 1973. *Publications:* Report of Working Party on Drug Dependence, 1968; Recommendations as to Local Government Boundaries and Wards in Northern Ireland, 1972. *Recreations:* hybridisation of narcissi, country pursuits, social service. *Address:* Ballydorn Hill, Killinchy, Newtownards, Co. Down, Northern Ireland. *T:* Killinchy 541 250. *Club:* Ulster (Belfast).

HARRISON, Francis Anthony Kitchener; *b* 28 Aug. 1914; *s* of late Fred Harrison, JP, and Mrs M. M. Harrison (née Mitchell); *m* 1955, Sheila Noëlle, *d* of late Lt-Col N. D. Stevenson and Lady Nye; three *s* one *d*. *Educ:* Winchester; New Coll., Oxford. Asst Principal, India Office, Nov. 1937; 1st Sec., UK High Commn, New Delhi, 1949–51; Commonwealth Relations Office, 1951–56; Asst Sec., 1954; Dep. High Comr for the UK at Peshawar, 1956–59; Asst Sec., CRO, 1959–61; British Dep. High Comr, New Zealand, 1961–64; Asst Sec., Cabinet Office, 1965–67; Asst Dir, Civil Service Selection Bd, 1967–79. *Recreations:* golf, gardening. *Address:* Lea Farm, Bramley, near Guildford, Surrey. *T:* Guildford 893138.

HARRISON, Francis Laurence Theodore G.; *see* Graham-Harrison.

HARRISON, Prof. Francis Llewelyn, FBA 1965; Professor of Ethnomusicology, University of Amsterdam, 1970–76, now Emeritus; *b* Dublin, 29 Sept. 1905; *s* of Alfred Francis and Florence May Harrison; *m* 1966, Joan Rimmer; (two *d* of a former marriage). *Educ:* St Patrick's Cathedral Gram. Sch., Dublin; Mountjoy Sch., Dublin; Trinity Coll., Dublin; Oxford Univ. MusB Dublin, 1926; MusD Dublin, 1929; MA, DMus Oxon, 1952; Hon. LLD Queen's (Canada), 1974. Organist: St Canice's Cath., Kilkenny, 1927; Prof. of Music: Queen's Univ., Kingston, Ontario, 1935; Colgate Univ., 1946; Washington Univ., St Louis, 1947; Lectr in Music, 1952, Sen. Lectr, 1956, Reader in History of Music, 1962–70, University of Oxford; Senior Research Fellow, Jesus Coll., 1965–70. Visiting Professor of Musicology: Yale Univ., 1958–59; Utrecht Univ., 1976–79; Mellon, Univ. of Pittsburg, 1981; Vis. Prof. of Music, Princeton Univ., 1961, 1968–69; Vis. Mem., Inst. for Advanced Study, Princeton, 1957; Vis. Scholar, Queen's Univ, Kingston, 1980; Fellow of Center for Advanced Study in the Behavioral Sciences,

Stanford, Calif, 1965-66. General Editor: Early English Church Music, 1961-73; Polyphonic Music of the Fourteenth Century, 1963-73. *Publications:* The Eton Choirbook (3 vols), 1956-61; Music in Medieval Britain, 1958; Collins Music Encyclopaedia (with J. A. Westrup), 1956; Musicology (with M. Hood and C. V. Palisca), 1963; European Musical Instruments (with J. Rimmer), 1964; Polyphonic Music of the Fourteenth Century, vol. V (Motets of French Provenance), 1969, vol. XV (Motets of English Provenance), 1980; Time, Place and Music, 1974; (with E. J. Dobson) Medieval English Songs, 1979; edns of music by William Mundy, John Sheppard and others; contribs to New Oxford History of Music, and to musical jls, etc. *Recreations:* travel, eating, model railways. *Address:* 3 Gore Mews, Canterbury, Kent CT1 1JB. *T:* Canterbury 59752.

HARRISON, Sir Frank; see Harrison, Sir Francis A. L.

HARRISON, Fred Brian, CBE 1982; FCA; Member, National Coal Board, since 1976; *b* 6 March 1927; *s* of Fred Harrison and Annie Harrison; *m* 1950, Margaret Owen; two *s. Educ:* Burnley Grammar Sch. FCA 1960. East Midlands Div., National Coal Board: Divnl Internal Auditor, 1953-55; Financial Accountant, No 3 Area, 1955-57, Cost Accountant, 1957-62; Chief Accountant, No 1 Area, 1962-67; Chief Accountant, N Derbyshire Area, NCB, 1967-68; Finance Dir, Coal Products Div., NCB, 1968-71, Dep. Man. Dir, 1971-73; Dep. Chief Exec., NCB (Coal Products) Ltd, 1973-76, Chm., 1978-. Chm., British Investment Trust, 1978-. *Recreations:* music, theatre. *Address:* 11 Birch Tree Walk, Watford, Herts. *T:* Watford 31967.

HARRISON, Sir Geoffrey (Wedgwood), GCMG 1968 (KCMG 1955; CMG 1949); KCVO 1961; HM Diplomatic Service, retired; *b* Southsea, 18 July 1908; *s* of late Lieut-Comdr Thomas Edmund Harrison, Royal Navy, and Maud, *d* of Percy Godman; *m* 1936, Amy Katharine, *d* of late Rt Hon. Sir R. H. Clive, PC, GCMG; three *s* one *d. Educ:* Winchester; King's Coll., Cambridge. Entered FO, 1932; served HM Embassy, Tokyo, 1935-37; HM Embassy, Berlin, 1937-39; Private Sec. to Parly Under-Sec., FO, 1939-41; First Sec., FO, 1941-45; Counsellor, HM Embassy, Brussels, 1945-47; Brit. Minister in Moscow, 1947-49; Head of Northern Dept, FO, 1949-51; Asst Under-Sec., FO, 1951-56; Ambassador: to Brazil, 1956-58; to Persia, 1958-63; Dep. Under-Sec. of State, FO, 1963-65; Ambassador to the USSR, 1965-68. Mem., West Sussex CC, 1970-77. Order of Homayoun (1st Class), 1959. *Recreations:* music, gardening. *Address:* Timbers, Plummers Plain, near Horsham, Sussex. *T:* Handcross 400266; 6 Ormonde Gate, SW3.
    See also J. C. Harrison.

HARRISON, George Anthony; DL; solicitor; Chief Executive, Greater Manchester Council, since 1976; *b* 20 Aug. 1930; *s* of John and Agnes Catherine Harrison; *m* 1957, Jane Parry; two *s* one *d. Educ:* Roundhay Sch., Leeds; Trinity Coll., Cambridge (MA, LLB). Asst Solicitor, Wolverhampton, 1955-58; ICI, 1958-59; Dep. Town Clerk, Wallasey and Bolton, 1962-65; Town Clerk and Clerk of the Peace, Bolton, 1965-69; Dir-Gen., Greater Manchester Transport Exec., 1969-76. DL Manchester, 1978. *Recreations:* music, squash, sailing. *Address:* 2 Clarebank, Chorley New Road, Bolton. *T:* Bolton 43545.

HARRISON, George Bagshawe, MA Cantab; PhD London; Emeritus Professor of English, University of Michigan, 1964 (Professor, 1949-64); *b* 14 July 1894; *s* of late Walter Harrison, Brighton; *m* 1919, Dorothy Agnes, *o d* of late Rev. Thomas Barker; one *d* (three *s* decd). *Educ:* Brighton Coll.; Queens' Coll., Cambridge (Classical Exhibitioner); 1st Class English Tripos, 1920. Commnd to 5th Bn The Queen's Royal Regt, and served in India and Mesopotamia, 1914-19; Staff Capt. 42nd Indian Infantry Brigade (despatches); War of 1939-45, RASC and Intelligence Corps, 1940-43. Asst Master, Felsted Sch., 1920-22; Senior Lecturer in English, St Paul's Training Coll., Cheltenham, 1922-24; Asst Lecturer in English Literature, King's Coll., University of London, 1924-27; Lecturer, 1927-29; Frederic Ives Carpenter Visiting Prof. of English, University of Chicago, 1929; Reader in English Literature, University of London, 1929-43; Head of English Dept and Prof. of English, Queen's Univ., Kingston, Ont., Canada, 1943-49; lectured at Sorbonne, 1933, in Holland, 1940; Alexander Lecturer, University of Toronto, Canada, 1947. Mem., Internat. Commn on English in the Liturgy. Hon. LittD Villanova, 1960, Holy Cross, 1961; Marquette, 1963; Hon. LLD Assumption, 1962. KSG 1981. Campion Award for long and eminent service in cause of Christian literature, 1970. *Publications:* Shakespeare: the Man and his Stage (with E. A. G. Lamborn), 1923; Shakespeare's Fellows, 1923; John Bunyan: a Study in Personality, 1928; England in Shakespeare's Day; An Elizabethan Journal, 1591-94, 1928; A Second Elizabethan Journal 1595-98, 1931; A Last Elizabethan Journal, 1599-1603, 1933; Shakespeare at Work, 1933; The Life and Death of Robert Devereux, Earl of Essex, 1937; The Day before Yesterday (a Journal of 1936), 1938; Elizabethan Plays and Players, 1940; A Jacobean Journal, 1603-1606, 1941; A Second Jacobean Journal, 1607-1610, 1950; Shakespeare's Tragedies, 1951; Profession of English, 1962; The Fires of Arcadia, 1965; (with John McCabe) Proclaiming the Word: a handbook for church speaking, 1976, etc.; Editor: The Bodley Head Quartos, 1922-26; The New Readers' Shakespeare (with F. H. Pritchard); The Pilgrim's Progress and Mr Badman; The Church Book of Bunyan Meeting, 1928; Breton's Melancholike Humours, 1929; The Trial of the Lancaster Witches, 1612, 1929; The Earl of Northumberland's Advice to his son; translated and edited The Journal of De Maisse (with R. A. Jones), 1931; A Companion to Shakespeare Studies (with Harley Granville-Barker), 1934; The Letters of Queen Elizabeth, 1935; The Penguin Shakespeares, 1937-59; Contributor to The

Road to Damascus, 1949; etc. *Address:* 36A Manson Street, Palmerston North, New Zealand. *T:* 75-895.

HARRISON, George Michael Antony, CBE 1980; Chief Education Officer, City of Sheffield, since 1967; *b* 7 April 1925; *s* of George and Kathleen Harrison; *m* 1951, Pauline (*née* Roberts); two *s* one *d. Educ:* Manchester Grammar Sch.; Brasenose Coll., Oxford. MA (LitHum); DipEd. Military service, Lieut, Parachute Regt, 1947. Asst Master, Bedford Modern Sch., 1951-53; Admin. Asst, W Riding CC, Education Dept, 1953-55; Asst Educn Officer, Cumberland CC Educn Dept, 1955-64; Dep. Educn Officer, Sheffield, 1965-67. Member various cttees, incl.: Taylor Cttee of Enquiry on Govt in Schools, 1975-77; UK Nat. Commn for Unesco Educn Adv. Cttee, 1977-; Yorkshire and Humberside Econ. Planning Council, 1978-79; Technician Educn Council, 1979-; Pres., Soc. of Educn Officers, 1976; Chm., Standing Conf. on Schools' Science and Technology, 1975-79. *Recreations:* sailing, gardening, music. *Address:* Audrey Cottage, 83 Union Road, Sheffield S11 9EH. *T:* Sheffield 53783. *Club:* Royal Over-Seas League.

HARRISON, Rear-Adm. Hubert Southwood, CBE 1951; DSC 1941; *b* Glasgow, 7 Aug. 1898; *s* of T. S. Harrison; *m* 1935, Beth Rowson Saynor (*d* 1962). *Educ:* Trinity Coll., Glenalmond. Cadet, RN, 1916; Midshipman, 1917; Sub-Lieut, 1918; Lieut (E), 1920; Lieut-Comdr (E), 1927; Comdr (E), 1930; Capt. (E), 1941; Rear-Adm. (E), 1948; Asst Dir of Dockyards, Admiralty, 1946-52; retired, 1952. *Recreations:* golf, sailing, fishing. *Address:* House in the Wood, Budock Vean, Falmouth. *T:* Mawnan Smith 250337.

HARRISON, Maj.-Gen. Ian Stewart, CB 1970; Captain of Deal Castle, since 1980; Director, British Consultants Bureau, since 1977; *b* 25 May 1919; *s* of Leslie George Harrison and Evelyn Simpson Christie; *m* 1942, Winifred Raikes Stavert; one *s* one *d. Educ:* St Albans Sch. Commissioned, Royal Marines, 1937; service at sea, in Norway, Middle East, Sicily, BAOR, 1939-45; Staff Coll., Camberley (student), 1948; HQ 3rd Commando Bde, 1949-51 (despatches); Staff of Comdt-Gen., RM, 1951-52; Staff Coll., Camberley (Directing Staff), 1953-55; Commandant, RM Signal Sch., 1956-58; Joint Services Staff Coll. (Student), 1958; CO 40 Commando, RM, 1959-61; Dir, Royal Marines Reserves, 1962; Staff of Comdt-Gen., RM, 1963-64; Joint Warfare Estabt, 1965-67; British Defence Staff, Washington, DC, 1967-68; Chief of Staff to Comdt-Gen., RM, 1968-70, retired. ADC to HM the Queen, 1967-68. Representative Col Comdt, Royal Marines, 1981-82. Dir-Gen. British Food Export Council, 1970-77. MBIM. *Recreations:* sailing, real tennis, lawn tennis, golf. *Address:* Manor Cottage, Runcton, Chichester, W Sussex PO20 6PU. *T:* Chichester 785480. *Clubs:* Army and Navy, St Stephen's Constitutional; Royal Yacht Squadron, Royal Naval Sailing Association, Royal Marines Sailing (Commodore, 1968-70), Itchenor Sailing; Royal St George's Golf.

HARRISON, Jessel Anidjah; Chairman, Slimma Group Holdings Ltd (formerly Emu Wool Industries Ltd), since 1973; *b* 28 May 1923; *s* of Samuel Harrison and Esta (*née* Romain); *m* 1st, 1943, Irene (*née* Olsberg) (marr. diss. 1956); one *s* one *d*; 2nd, 1961, Doreen Leigh. *Educ:* Vernon House Preparatory Sch.; Brondesbury Coll.; Macauley Coll., Cuckfield, Sussex. Chairman: Slimma Ltd, 1964; Slimma (Wales) Ltd, 1971; Dir, Tootals Clothing Div., 1977-. Member: European Trade Cttee, 1975-; Clothing Industry Productivity Resources Agency, 1978-; British Overseas Trade Adv. Council, 1978-. Vice Pres., Clothing Export Council of Great Britain, 1977 (Chm., 1973); Chm., British Overseas Trade Group for Israel, 1978. Pres., Clothing Institute, 1978. *Recreations:* golf, walking. *Address:* Springfield, 6 Madehurst Close, East Preston, Angmering, Sussex BN16 2TH. *T:* Rustington 5084. *Club:* Royal Automobile.

HARRISON, Surgeon Vice-Adm. Sir John (Albert Bews), KBE 1982; QHP; FRCP, FRCR; Medical Director General (Naval), since 1980; *b* 20 May 1921; *s* of late Albert William Harrison and Lilian Eda Bews, Dover, Kent; *m* 1943, Jane (*née* Harris); two *s. Educ:* Queens' Coll., Cambridge; St Bartholomew's Hosp. MRCS, LRCP; DMRD. After house appt, joined RNVR, 1947; served: RM Infirmary, Deal, 1948; HMS Sparrow, Amer. WI stn, 1949; RN Hosp., Plymouth, 1951; HMS Ganges, 1952; Admiralty Med. Bd and St Bartholomew's Hosp., 1953; RN Hosps, Hong Kong, 1955, Chatham, 1958, Haslar, 1959; St Bart's and Middlesex Hosps, 1961; RN Hosps Malta, 1962, Haslar, 1964-75; Adviser in Radiol., 1967-79; Dep. Med. Dir Gen. and Dir Med. Personnel and Logistics, 1975-77; Dean of Naval Medicine and MO i/c, Inst. of Naval Medicine, 1977-80. Mem., Council for Med. Postgrad. Educn of Eng. and Wales, 1977-79. Fellow: RSM; MedSocLond. OStJ 1975. QHP 1976. *Publications:* Hyperbaric Osteonecrosis et al, 1975; articles in med. press on sarcoidosis, tomography, middle ear disease, and dysbaric osteonecrosis. *Recreations:* fishing, cricket, countryman. *Address:* Alexandra Cottage, Swanmore, Hampshire SO3 2PB. *Clubs:* Naval and Military, MCC.

HARRISON, John Audley, CB 1976; a Director, Ministry of Defence, 1969-76; *b* 13 May 1917; *s* of John Samuel Harrison and Florence Rose (*née* Samways); *m* 1940, Dorothea Pearl (*née* West); two *s* one *d. Educ:* Caterham Sch., Surrey. Prudential Assce Co. Ltd, 1935-39. London Rifle Bde (TA), 1939-40; York and Lancaster Regt (emergency commn), 1940-46. Attached War Office (later MoD), 1946-76, retd, May 1976. *Recreations:* golf, bridge. *Address:* 23 Benfield Way, Portslade, Sussex. *T:* Brighton 418302. *Club:* Dyke Golf (Brighton).

HARRISON, John Clive, MVO 1971; HM Diplomatic Service; Counsellor and Head of Chancery, Lagos, since 1981; *b* 12 July 1937; *s* of Sir Geoffrey Harrison, *qv*; *m* 1967, Jennifer Heather Burston; one *s* two *d*. *Educ:* Winchester Coll.; Jesus Coll., Oxford. BA. Entered Foreign Office, 1960; Rangoon, 1961; Vientiane, 1964; FO, 1964; Second, later First, Sec. (Information), Addis Ababa, 1967; Ankara, 1971; seconded to Cabinet Office, 1973; First Sec., FCO, 1976; First Sec., Head of Chancery and Consul, Luxembourg, 1978. *Recreations:* tennis, golf, family holidays. *Address:* c/o Foreign and Commonwealth Office, King Charles Street, SW1A 2AH; Timbers, Plummers Plain, Horsham, Sussex RH13 6PE. *T:* Handcross 400266. *Club:* Ikoyi (Lagos).

HARRISON, Prof. John Fletcher Clews, PhD; Professor of History, University of Sussex, since 1970; *b* 28 Feb. 1921; *s* of William Harrison and Mary (*née* Fletcher); *m* 1945, Margaret Ruth Marsh; one *s* one *d*. *Educ:* City Boys' Sch., Leicester; Selwyn Coll., Cambridge (Schol. and Prizeman; Goldsmiths' Open Exhibnr in History, BA 1st Cl. Hons 1942, MA 1946); PhD Leeds. Served Army, 1941-45 (overseas 1942-45): commnd, Royal Leics Regt and seconded to KAR, 1942; Captain and Adjt, 17th Bn, KAR, 1943-44; Staff Captain, GSOIII, E Africa Comd, 1944-45. Lectr, Dept of Adult Educn and Extra-Mural Studies, Univ. of Leeds, 1947-58; Dep. Dir, Extra-Mural Studies and Dep. Head of Dept, Univ. of Leeds, 1958-61; Prof. of History, Univ. of Wisconsin, USA, 1961-70. Research and teaching (Fulbright Award), Univ. of Wisconsin, 1957-58; Faculty Res. Fellow, SSRC, USA, 1963-64; Vis. Professorial Res. Fellow, ANU, 1968-69 and 1977; Res. Fellow, Harvard Univ., 1972-73; Social Sci. Res. Fellow, Nuffield Foundn, 1975; Vice-Chancellor's Cttee Visitor, NZ, 1977; Herbert F. Johnson Res. Prof., Univ. of Wisconsin, 1977-78. Chm., Soc. for Study of Labour History, 1974-81 (Sec., 1960-61); Mem., Adv. and Editorial Bds, Victorian Studies, 1963-. Hon. Mem., Phi Beta Kappa, Wisconsin, 1978. *Publications:* A History of the Working Men's College 1854-1954, 1954; Social Reform in Victorian Leeds: The Work of James Hole 1820-1895, 1954; Learning and Living 1790-1960: A Study in the History of the English Adult Education Movement, 1961, Toronto 1961; ed, Society and Politics in England 1780-1960, NY 1965; ed, Utopianism and Education: Robert Owen and the Owenites, NY 1968; Quest for the New Moral World: Robert Owen and the Owenites in Britain and America, 1969, NY 1969 (Walter D. Love Meml Prize, USA, 1969); The Early Victorians 1832-1851, 1971, NY 1971, paperbacks 1973, 1979; The Birth and Growth of Industrial England 1714-1867, 1973; ed, Eminently Victorian, BBC 1974; (with Dorothy Thompson) Bibliography of the Chartist Movement 1837-1976, 1978; The Second Coming: Popular Millenarianism 1780-1850, 1979, NJ 1979; articles and reviews in Victorian Studies, TLS and usual academic history jls. *Recreations:* walking, gardening, book collecting. *Address:* 13 Woodlands, Barrowfield Drive, Hove, Sussex BN3 6TJ. *T:* Brighton 554145.

HARRISON, John H.; see Heslop-Harrison.

HARRISON, Maj.-Gen. John Martin Donald W.; see Ward-Harrison.

HARRISON, Hon. Sir (John) Richard, Kt 1980; ED; MP Hawke's Bay, New Zealand, since 1963; Speaker, House of Representatives, since 1978; *b* 23 May 1921; *s* of William Harrison and Jean (*née* Bell); *m* 1948, Margaret Kelly; three *s* one *d*. *Educ:* Wanganui Collegiate Sch.; Canterbury University Coll. (BA). Sheep farmer, 1946-. CO, Hawke's Bay Regt, 1956-59. MP (Nat) for Hawke's Bay, 1963; Govt Whip, 1970-71; Opposition Whip, 1974-75; Chm. of Cttees, 1972, 1976-77. Pres., Commonwealth Parly Assoc., 1978-79. *Recreations:* tennis, swimming, gardening. *Address:* Springfield, Takapau, New Zealand; Parliament House, Wellington, NZ. *Clubs:* Wellington, Hastings.

HARRISON, Kathleen, (Mrs J. H. Back); leading character actress, stage and films; *d* of Arthur Harrison, MICE, Civil Engineer, and Alice Harrison; *m* 1916, John Henry Back; two *s* one *d*. *Educ:* Clapham High Sch. Trained at RADA. *Notable plays include:* Badger's Green, Prince of Wales Theatre, 1930; Night Must Fall, Duchess, 1935; The Corn is Green, Duchess, 1938; Flare Path, Apollo, 1942; The Winslow Boy, Lyric, 1946; All for Mary, Duke of York's, 1955; Nude with Violin, Globe, 1956; How Say You?, Aldwych, 1959; Watch it, Sailor!, Aldwych, 1960; The Chances, Chichester Festival, 1962; Norman, Duchess, 1963; title role in Goodnight Mrs Puffin, New Theatre, Bromley; Harvey, Richmond Theatre, 1971; She Stoops to Conquer, Young Vic, 1972; toured in All for Mary and Goodnight Mrs Puffin, 1970. *Films include:* In Which We Serve; The Huggett films; Alive and Kicking; The Winslow Boy; Bank Holiday; Holiday Camp; Barabbas; West 11; Scrooge; The London Affair. *TV includes:* Martin Chuzzlewit serial (Betsy Prig); title role in Mrs Thursday series; Waters of the Moon; The Coffee Lace; Spring and Autumn, 1973; The Defence, in Shades of Greene, 1975; Mrs Boffin, in Our Mutual Friend, 1976; Danger UXB. *Address:* c/o T. Plunket Greene, 91 Regent Street, W1. *T:* 01-734 7311.

HARRISON, Kenneth Cecil, OBE 1980 (MBE mil. 1945); FLA; City Librarian, Westminster, 1961-80, retired; Executive Secretary, Commonwealth Library Association, since 1980; *b* 29 April 1915; *s* of Thomas and Annie Harrison; *m* 1941, Doris Taylor; two *s*. *Educ:* Grammar Sch., Hyde. Asst, Hyde Public Library, 1931-36; Branch Librarian, Coulsdon and Purley Public Libraries, 1936-39; Borough Librarian: Hyde, 1939-47; Hove (also Curator), 1947-50; Eastbourne, 1950-58; Hendon, 1958-61. HM Forces, 1940-46; Commnd RMC Sandhurst, 1942; served with E Yorks Regt in

Middle East, Sicily and NW Europe (wounded, 1944; Major 1944-46). President: Library Assoc., 1973; Commonwealth Library Assoc., 1972-75; Vice-Pres., Internat. Assoc. Metropolitan Libraries; Member: IFLA Public Libraries Cttee, 1969-81; Central Music Library Council, 1961-80; Library Assoc. Council, 1953-79; MCC Arts and Library Cttee, 1973-; British Council Libraries Advisory Panel, 1974-80; Chm. Jt Organising Cttee for Nat. Library Week, 1964-69. Vice-Pres., Westminster Arts Council (Hon. Sec., 1965-80). British Council Consultant to Sri Lanka, 1974, to India, 1981; UNESCO Consultant to the Seychelles and Mauritius, 1977-78; Commonwealth Relations Trust Consultant to Ghana, Sierra Leone and The Gambia, 1979. Commonwealth Foundn Scholar, E and Central Africa, 1975. C. C. Williamson Meml Lectr, Nashville, Tenn, 1969. Governor, Westminster College, 1962-80. Editor, The Library World, 1961-71. Knight, First Class, Order of the Lion (Finland), 1976. *Publications:* First Steps in Librarianship, 1950, 5th edn 1980; Libraries in Scandinavia, 1961, 2nd edn 1969; The Library and the Community, 1963, 3rd edn 1977; Public Libraries Today, 1963; Facts at your Fingertips, 1964, 3rd edn 1983; British Public Library Buildings (with S. G. Berriman), 1966; Libraries in Britain, 1968; Public Relations for Librarians, 1973, 2nd edn 1982; (ed) Prospects for British Librarianship, 1976; Public Library Policy, 1981; contribs to many British and foreign jls and encyclopædias. *Recreations:* reading, writing, travel, wine, cricket, crosswords, zoo visiting. *Address:* 50 West Hill Way, N20 8QS. *T:* 01-445 1298. *Clubs:* Royal Commonwealth Society, MCC.

HARRISON, Laurence, CMG 1952, retired; *b* 3 Oct. 1897; *s* of late George Henry Harrison; *m* 1st, 1923, Nellie Florence (Serving Sister of Order of St John; *d* 1963); one *d*; 2nd, 1969, Jenny Margaret Wallace Pritchard (*née* Duncan), Sandown, Johannesburg. *Educ:* St Dunstan's Coll.; Strand Sch. Served BEF France (RE), 1916-19. Entered Min. of Pensions, 1919; transf. to Dept of Overseas Trade, 1930; Asst Trade Commissioner, Johannesburg, 1937, Trade Commissioner (Grade II), 1945, Trade Commissioner (Grade I), New Delhi, 1947, Johannesburg, 1953-57. *Recreation:* field natural history. *Address:* 3 Victoria Court, Barberton, 1300 East Transvaal, South Africa.

HARRISON, Lloyd Adnitt, CBE 1977; Chief Executive Officer, Greater Nottingham Co-operative Society Ltd, 1969-77; *b* 15 March 1911; *s* of late Joseph Adnitt Harrison and Frances Louisa Harrison; *m* 1954, Mabel Pauline Hooley. *Educ:* Beeston Higher Sch., Notts; Co-operative Coll. Managing Sec., Nottingham Co-op. Soc. Ltd, 1965-69, and Admin. Officer, 1956-65. Director: Co-operative Insurance Soc. Ltd, 1973-75; Co-operative Bank, 1974-75; Co-operative Wholesale Soc. Ltd, 1968-76 (Chm., CWS, 1973-76). Chm., Building and Social Housing Foundn. Vice-Pres., Nottingham Univ. Council. CBIM. *Recreations:* music, reading, walking, gardening, local radio (formerly Chm. Local Radio Council, Nottingham). *Address:* 63 Parkside, Wollaton, Nottingham NG8 2NQ. *T:* Nottingham 256452.

HARRISON, Sir Michael James Harwood, 2nd Bt *cr* 1961, of Bugbrooke; Director of private companies; *b* 28 March 1936; *s* of Sir (James) Harwood Harrison, 1st Bt, TD, and of Peggy Alberta Mary, *d* of late Lt-Col V. D. Stenhouse, TD; *S* father, 1980; *m* 1967, Rosamund Louise, *d* of Edward Clive; one *s* two *d*. *Educ:* Rugby. Served with 17th/21st Lancers, 1955-56. Member of Lloyds; Mem. Council, Sail Training Assoc. Liveryman, Mercers' Co; Freeman of the City of London. *Recreations:* sailing, ski-ing, riding (horse and bicycle), Daily Telegraph crossword. *Heir: s* Edwin Michael Harwood Harrison, *b* 29 May 1981. *Address:* 35 Paulton's Square, SW3. *T:* 01-352 1760. *Clubs:* MCC, Ski Club of GB.

HARRISON, Mrs Molly, MBE 1967; Curator, Geffrye Museum, 1941-69; *b* Stevenage, 1909; *d* of late Ethel and late Ernest Charles Hodgett; *m* 1940, Gordon Frederick Harrison; three *d*. *Educ:* Friends Sch., Saffron Walden; Convent in Belgium; Sorbonne. Teaching in various Schs, 1934-39; Asst to Curator, Geffrye Museum, 1939-41. FMA 1952; Member: Council Museums Assoc., 1953-56; Council of Industrial Design, 1958-61; Cttee of Management, Society of Authors, 1967. Lectr on varied educational topics. FRSA 1968. Editor, Local Search Series, 1969-77. *Publications:* Museum Adventure, 1950; Picture Source Books for Social History, 1951, 1953, 1955, 1957, 1958, 1960 and 1966; Furniture 1953; Learning out of School, 1954; Food, 1954; Homes, 1960; Children in History, 1958, 1959, 1960, 1961; Your Book of Furniture, 1960; Shops and Shopping, 1963; How They Lived, 1963; Changing Museums, 1967; Hairstyles and Hairdressing, 1968; The English Home, 1969; People and Furniture, 1971; The Kitchen in History, 1972; Homes, 1973; Museums and Galleries, 1973; On Location: Museums, 1974; People and Shopping, 1975; Home Inventions, 1975; Homes in Britain, 1975; Markets and Shops, 1979; Growing Up in Victorian Times, 1980; numerous articles and reviews. *Recreations:* writing, gardening. *Address:* The Coach House, Horse Leas, Bradfield, Berks. *T:* Reading 744437.

HARRISON, Patrick Kennard, CBE 1982; Secretary, Royal Institute of British Architects, since 1969; *b* 8 July 1928; *s* of late Richard Harrison and Sheila Griffin; *m* 1955, Mary Wilson, *y d* of late Captain G. C. C. Damant, CBE, RN; one *d*. *Educ:* Lord Williams's Sch., Thame; Downing Coll., Cambridge (Exhbnr). Asst Principal, Dept of Health for Scotland, 1953; Private Sec. to Deptl Sec. and to Parly Secs, Scottish Office, 1958-60; Principal, Scottish Devel Dept and Regional Devel Div., Scottish Office, 1960-68. Hon. Mem., Amer. Inst. of Architects, 1978. *Address:* 63 Princess Road, NW1. *T:* 01-722 8508. *Clubs:* Reform; New (Edinburgh).

HARRISON, Rex Carey; Commendatore, Order of Merit of the Republic of Italy, 1967; actor; *b* 5 March 1908; *s* of William Reginald and Edith Carey Harrison; *m* 1st, 1934, Marjorie Noel Collette Thomas; one *s* ; 2nd, 1943, Lilli Palmer (marr. diss. 1957); one *s* ; 3rd, 1957, Kay Kendall (*d* 1959); 4th, 1962, Rachel Roberts (marr. diss. 1971); 5th, Hon. Elizabeth Rees Harris (marr. diss. 1976), *d* of 1st Baron Ogmore, PC, TD; 6th, 1978, Mercia Tinker. *Educ:* Birkdale Preparatory Sch.; Liverpool Coll. Made first appearance on the stage at Liverpool Repertory Theatre, 1924; remained until 1927. Toured with Charley's Aunt playing Jack, 1927; also toured at intervals during subsequent years until 1935, and appeared with Cardiff Repertory, and in the West End. First appearance on London stage as Rankin in The Ninth Man, Prince of Wales Theatre, 1931; First appearance on New York stage at Booth Theatre, 1936, as Tubbs Barrow in Sweet Aloes. Played in French Without Tears at Criterion, 1936-37-38, and at Haymarket Theatre, 1939-41, in Design for Living (Leo) and No Time for Comedy (Gaylord Esterbrook). Volunteered RAFVR, 1941, and served till 1944. Released from Forces to make Blithe Spirit (film), and, 1945, Rake's Progress (film). Filmed in Hollywood, 1945-46-47. (Maxwell Anderson's) Anne of the Thousand Days, Schubert Theatre, NY, 1948-49 (Antoinette Perry Award, best actor); in The Cocktail Party, New Theatre, London, 1950; acted in and produced Bell, Book and Candle, Ethel Barrymore Theatre, NY, 1951, and Phœnix Theatre, London, 1954; in Venus Observed, Century Theatre, NY, 1952; directed and played in Love of Four Colonels, Schubert Theatre, NY, 1953; produced Nina, Haymarket Theatre, London, 1955; acted in: My Fair Lady (Henry Higgins), Mark Hellinger Theatre, NY, 1956-57 (Antoinette Perry Award, best actor), and Drury Lane, London, 1958-59; The Fighting Cock, Anta Theatre, NY, 1959; Platonov, Royal Court, 1960 (Evening Standard Award, best actor); August for the People, Edinburgh Festival, 1961, and Royal Court Theatre; The Lionel Touch, Lyric, 1969; Henry IV, Her Majesty's, 1974; Perrichon's Travels, Chichester, 1976; Caesar and Cleopatra, NY, 1977; The Kingfisher, NY, 1978-79, etc. Began acting in films in 1929. Best known films: Storm in a Teacup, 1936; St Martin's Lane, 1937; Over the Moon, 1938; Night Train to Munich, Major Barbara, 1940-41; Blithe Spirit, 1944; I Live in Grosvenor Square, 1944; The Rake's Progress, 1945; (Hollywood, 1945) Anna and the King of Siam, 1946; The Ghost and Mrs Muir, 1947; The Foxes of Harrow, 1947; (Galsworthy's) Escape (in England), 1948; Unfaithfully Yours (in America), 1948; The Long Dark Hall, 1951; King Richard and the Crusaders, 1954; The Constant Husband, 1955; The Reluctant Debutante, 1958; Midnight Lace, 1960; The Happy Thieves, 1961; Cleopatra (Julius Caesar), 1962; My Fair Lady, 1964 (Academy Award, best actor); The Yellow Rolls Royce, 1965; The Agony and the Ecstacy, 1965; The Honey Pot, 1967; Doctor Dolittle, 1967; A Flea in her Ear, 1967; Staircase, 1968; The Prince and the Pauper, 1976; Man in the Iron Mask, 1977; Ashanti, 1979. *Publication:* Rex (autobiog.), 1974. *Recreations:* golf, yachting, fishing. *Address:* 5 Impasse de la Fontaine, Monte Carlo, Monaco 98000. *Clubs:* Beefsteak, Green Room, Garrick; Players' (New York); Travellers' (Paris).

HARRISON, Hon. Sir Richard; *see* Harrison, Hon. Sir J. R.

HARRISON, Prof. Richard John, MD, DSc; FRS 1973; Professor of Anatomy, Cambridge University, 1968-82, now Emeritus; Fellow of Downing College, Cambridge, 1968-82; *b* 8 Oct. 1920; *er s* of late Geoffrey Arthur Harrison, MD, and Theodora Beatrice Mary West; *m* Barbara, *o d* of James and Florence Fuller, Neston, Cheshire. *Educ:* Oundle; Gonville and Caius Coll., Cambridge (Scholar); St Bartholomew's Hosp. Medical Coll. LRCP, MRCS, 1944. House Surgeon, St Bartholomew's Hosp., 1944. MB, BChir, 1944; MA 1946; MD Cantab 1954. Demonstrator in Anatomy, St Bartholomew's Hosp. Medical Coll., 1944; Lectr in Anatomy, Glasgow Univ., 1946, DSc Glasgow 1948; Sen. Lectr, 1947, and Reader in Anatomy, 1950, Charing Cross Hosp. Medical Sch. (Symington Prize for research in Anatomy); Reader in charge of Anatomy Dept, London Hosp. Medical Coll., 1951-54; Prof. of Anatomy, University of London, at London Hosp. Medical Coll., 1954-68; Fullerian Prof. of Physiology, Royal Institution, 1961-67. Chairman: Farm Animal Welfare Adv. Cttee, MAFF, 1974-79; Farm Animal Welfare Council, 1979-. Pres., European Assoc. for Aquatic Mammals, 1974-76. A Trustee, British Museum (Natural History), 1978-. Pres., Anat. Soc. of GB and Ireland, 1978-79; Mem. Council, Royal Soc., 1981-. FZS (Mem. Council, 1974-78, 1980-); Hon. Mem., Societa Italiana Anatomia. *Publications:* Man the Peculiar Animal, 1958; (with J. E. King) Marine Mammals, 1965, 2nd edn 1979; Reproduction and Man, 1967; (with W. Montagna) Man, 2nd edn 1972; Functional Anatomy of Marine Mammals, vol. I, 1972, vol. II, 1974, vol. III, 1977; (with S. H. Ridgway) Handbook of Marine Mammals, vols I and II, 1981; numerous papers on embryology, comparative and human anatomy. *Recreations:* marine biology, painting, golf. *Address:* The Beeches, 8 Woodlands Road, Great Shelford, Cambs. *T:* Cambridge 843287. *Clubs:* Garrick; Sheringham Golf.

HARRISON, Prof. Richard Martin, FSA; Professor of Archaeology, University of Newcastle upon Tyne, since 1972; *b* 16 May 1935; *s* of George Lawrance Harrison and Doris Waring (*née* Ward); *m* 1959, Elizabeth Anne Harkness Browne; one *s* three *d*. *Educ:* Sherborne Sch.; Lincoln Coll., Oxford (BA Greats 1958, MA 1961). FSA 1965. Scholar 1959, and Fellow 1960, Brit. Inst. of Archaeol., Ankara; Rivoira Scholar, Brit. Sch. at Rome, 1960; Controller of Antiquities, Provincial Govt of Cyrenaica, 1960-61; Lectr in Class. Archaeol., Bryn Mawr Coll., 1961-62; Glanville Res. Student, Lincoln Coll., Oxford, 1962-64; Newcastle upon Tyne University: Lectr in Roman and Romano-British History and Archaeol., 1964-68; Prof. of Roman Hist. and Archaeol., 1968-72; Vis. Fellow, Dumbarton Oaks, 1969. Dir,

Excavations at Saraçhane (Istanbul), 1964-69. Chm., Northern Soc. for Anatolian Archaeol., 1976. Corresp. Mem., German Archaeol. Inst., 1973. *Publications:* articles on Roman and Byzantine archaeol. in Anatolian Studies, Dumbarton Oaks Papers, Jl of Roman Studies. *Address:* 23 Linden Road, Gosforth, Newcastle upon Tyne NE3 4EY. *T:* Newcastle upon Tyne 850465.

HARRISON, Sir (Robert) Colin, 4th Bt, *cr* 1922; *b* 25 May 1938; *s* of Sir John Fowler Harrison, 2nd Bt, and Kathleen, *yr d* of late Robert Livingston, The Gables, Eaglescliffe, Co. Durham; *S* brother, 1955; *m* 1963, Maureen, *er d* of E. Leonard Chiverton, Garth Corner, Kirkbymoorside, York; one *s* two *d. Educ:* St Peter's Coll., Radley; St John's Coll., Cambridge. Commissioned with Fifth Royal Northumberland Fusiliers (National Service), 1957-59. Chm., Young Master Printers Nat. Cttee, 1972-73. *Heir:* s John Wyndham Fowler Harrison, *b* 14 Dec. 1972. *Address:* Keld Close, Hutton-le-Hole, York. *T:* Lastingham 329.

HARRISON, Prof. Ronald George; Derby Professor of Anatomy, University of Liverpool, since 1950; *b* 5 April 1921; *s* of James Harrison and Alice Hannah Harrison (*née* Edmondson); *m* 1945; two *s* one *d* ; *m* 1966, Dr M. J. Hoey, Southport, Lancs; one *d. Educ:* Ulverston Grammar Sch.; Oxford Univ. BA Oxon, 1942; BM, BCh, Oxon 1944; MA Oxon, 1946; DM Oxon, 1949. Demy, Magdalen Coll., Oxford, 1939-42; Pres., OU Scientific Club, 1942. Junior Gynæcological House Surg., Nuffield Dept of Obstetrics and Gynæcology, Oxford, 1943; Gynæc. and Obst. House Surgeonships, Radcliffe Infirmary, Oxford, 1944-45; Demonstrator and Lecturer, Dept of Human Anatomy, Univ. of Oxford, 1945-49. Lectr in Anatomy, Ruskin Sch. of Drawing and Fine Art, 1946-50; Univ. Demonstrator, Dept of Human Anatomy, Univ. of Oxford, 1949-50; Lectr in Anatomy, Pembroke Coll., Oxford, 1950; Vis. Prof. of Egyptology, Univ. of Cairo, 1972. Sometime External Examr: RCS; RCSI; Univs of: Belfast, Birmingham, Glasgow, Leeds, London, Manchester, Oxford, TCD, Khartoum, Haile Sellassie I, Addis Ababa. Lectures: First Celebrity, British Acad. Forensic Scis, 1970; Sir John Struthers Meml, 1979. BBC TV film, Tutankhamen Post-mortem, 1969; ITV film, Tutankhamen Kinship, 1973. Fellow: Eugenics Soc.; Zoological Soc. of London. Chm., Bd of Governors, Liverpool Coll. of Occupational Therapy, 1968; President: Inst. of Science Technology, 1972-76; Liverpool Univ. Med. Sciences Club, 1954-55; Wallasey Med. Soc., 1981-82. For. Corr. Mem., Royal Belgian Soc. of Obstetrics and Gynæcology, 1964-68. Pres., Rotary Club of Liverpool, 1971 (Vice-Pres., 1970). Kt of the Dannebrog (Denmark), 1977. *Publications:* A Textbook of Human Embryology, 1959, 1963; The Adrenal Circulation, 1960; Sex and Infertility, 1977; Clinical Embryology, 1978; Chapters in Cunningham's Textbook of Anatomy, 1964, 1972, 1981; Orthopaedics and Traumatology, 1980; contrib. to various medical and scientific journals. Editor, Studies on Fertility, 1954-58. *Recreations:* riding, egyptology. *Address:* The Stables, Fernhill, Upper Brighton, Wallasey, Merseyside. *T:* 051-639 6327.

HARRISON, Theophilus George, OBE 1971; JP; Member, Greater Manchester Council, 1973-77 (Chairman, 1973-1974 and 1974-1975, Deputy Chairman, 1975-76); General Secretary, National Association of Powerloom Overlookers, 1947-76; Member Executive, General Union of Associations of Loom Overlookers, 1947-76 (1946-66); *b* 30 Jan. 1907; *s* of Alfred and Emma Harrison; *m* 1935, Clarissa Plevin; one *s* one *d.* Swinton and Pendlebury Borough Council: Mem., 1941-56; Alderman, 1956-74; Mayor, 1954-55; Chairman: Housing Cttee; Highways and Lighting Cttee; Mem., Div. Planning Cttee; Lancs CC: Mem. Educn Cttee, 1946-74 (Vice-Chm. 1951-53, Chm. 1953-74); Vice-Chairman: Road Safety Cttee; Public Health and Housing Cttee; Greater Manchester Transport Cons. Cttee; Pres., Lancs Non-County Boroughs Assoc., 1960-62; Chairman: Swinton and Pendlebury Youth Employment Cttee; Youth Adv. Cttee and Youth Centres; Mem., Div. Exec., Educn Cttee; Member: Gen. Council, Lancs and Merseyside Ind. Develt Corp.; N Counties Textile Trades Fedn Central Board; Swinton and Pendlebury Trades Council and Labour Party; Manchester Reg. Hosp. Bd, 1961-74; W Manchester HMC, 1957-74 (Chm. 1963-74); Wrightington HMC, 1957-74; Salford Community Health Council (Vice-Chm.; Chm., Develt Cttee); Assoc. of Community Health Councils (Vice-Chm., NW Region). Hon. Vice-Pres., Greater Manchester Council for Voluntary Service. Past Chm. or Mem. many other Co. or local organizations and cttees. Former Pres., SE Lancs and Cheshire Accident Prevention Fedn; Dir, RoSPA; Freeman of Swinton and Pendlebury, 1973 (now Salford DC). JP 1949. *Recreations:* reading, Rugby League football (spectator); much of his political and public activities. *Address:* 271 Rivington Crescent, Bolton Road, Pendlebury, Swinton, Manchester M27 2TQ. *T:* 061-794 1112.

HARRISON, Rt. Hon. Walter, PC 1977; JP; MP (Lab) Wakefield, since 1964; Deputy Chief Opposition Whip, since 1979; *b* 2 Jan. 1921; *s* of Henry and Ada Harrison; *m* 1948, Enid Mary (*née* Coleman); one *s* one *d. Educ:* Dewsbury Technical and Art Coll. Electrical Inspector and Electrical Foreman, Electricity Supply Industry, 1937-64. Asst Govt Whip, 1966-68; a Lord Comr of the Treasury, 1968-70; Dep. Chief Opposition Whip, 1970-74; Treasurer of HM Household and Dep. Chief Govt Whip, 1974-79. West Riding CC, 1958-64; Alderman, Castleford Borough Council, 1959-66 (Councillor, 1952-59); JP West Riding Yorks, 1962. *Address:* House of Commons, SW1. *T:* 01-219 3000.

HARRISON-CHURCH, Prof. Ronald James; Professor of Geography, University of London, at London School of Economics, 1964-77; *b* 26 July

1915; *s* of late James Walter Church and late Jessie May Church; *m* 1944, Dorothy Violet, *d* of late Robert Colchester Harrison and late Rose Harrison; one *s* one *d. Educ:* Westminster City Sch.; Universities of London and Paris. BSc (Econ) 1936, PhD 1943, London. LSE: Asst Lectr, 1944–47; Lectr, 1947–58; Reader, 1958–64. Consultant to UN Economic Commn for Africa on large scale irrigation schemes, 1962. Visiting Professor: University of Wisconsin, 1956; Indiana Univ., 1965; Tel Aviv and Haifa Univs, 1972–73. Has lectured in many other univs in Brazil, US, Canada, West Africa, Belgium, France, Germany, Poland and Sweden. Vice-Pres., Royal Afr. Soc.; Back Award, RGS, 1957; IGU Award, 1978. *Publications:* Modern Colonization, 1951; West Africa, 1957, 8th edn, 1980; Environment and Policies in West Africa, 1963, 2nd edn 1976; Looking at France, 1970, rev. repr. 1976; (jtly) Africa and the Islands, 1964, 4th edn, 1977; (jtly) An Advanced Geography of Northern and Western Europe, 1967, 3rd edn 1980; contribs to Geograph. Jl, W Africa, etc. *Recreations:* travel, television. *Address:* 40 Handside Lane, Welwyn Garden City, Herts. *T:* Welwyn Garden 23293.

HARRISON-HALL, Michael Kilgour; His Honour Judge Harrison-Hall; a Circuit Judge, since 1972; *b* 20 Dec. 1925; *s* of late Arthur Harrison-Hall, Oxford; *m* 1951, Jessie Margaret, *d* of late Rev. Arthur William Brown, Collingbourne Ducis, Wilts; two *s* two *d. Educ:* Rugby; Trinity College, Oxford. Called to Bar, Inner Temple, 1949. Dep. Chm., Warwickshire QS, 1968–71; a Recorder of the Crown Court, 1972. *Address:* Ivy House, Church Street, Barford, Warwick. *T:* Barford 624272. *Clubs:* United Oxford & Cambridge University; Leander.

HARROD, Maj.-Gen. Lionel Alexander Digby, OBE 1969; Inspector of Recruiting (Army), since 1979; *b* 7 Sept. 1924; *s* of Frank Henry Harrod, CBE, and Charlotte Beatrice Emmeline (*née* David); *m* 1952, Anne Priscilla Stormont Gibbs; one *s* two *d. Educ:* Bromsgrove Sch. Grenadier Guards, 1944–63; Bde Major, 19 Bde, 1956–58; WO staff, 1959–60; CO 1 Welch, 1966–69; Brit. Def. Staff, Washington, 1969–70; Military Attaché, Baghdad, 1971; Staff HQ UKLF, 1972–73; Chief, Brit. Mission to Gp of Soviet Forces, Germany, 1974–76; ACOS (Intelligence), SHAPE, 1976–79, retired. Col, Royal Regt of Wales, 1977–. *Recreations:* sport, country life. *Address:* The Grange, Marnhull, Dorset. *T:* Marnhull 820256. *Clubs:* Army and Navy, Special Forces, MCC, Pratt's.

HARROLD, Roy Mealham; Member, Press Council, since 1976; farmer, since 1947; *b* 13 Aug. 1928; *s* of John Frederick Harrold and Ellen Selena Harrold (*née* Mealham); *m* 1968, Barbara Mary, *yr d* of William and Florence Andrews; one *s* one *d. Educ:* Stoke Holy Cross Primary Sch.; Bracondale Sch., Norwich. County Chm., Norfolk Fedn of Young Farmers' Clubs, 1956–57; Mem., Nat. Council of Young Farmers, 1957–60; Mem. Council, Royal Norfolk Agric. Assoc., 1972–75, 1980–. Lay Chm., Norwich East Deanery Synod, 1970–79; Mem., Norwich Dio. Synod, 1970–; Mem., Norwich Dio. Bd of Patronage, 1970–; Church Warden, St Peter Mancroft, Norwich, 1978–82. *Recreations:* music, opera, ballet. *Address:* Salamanca Farm, Stoke Holy Cross, Norwich NR15 8QJ. *T:* Framingham Earl 2322.

HARROP, Peter John, CB 1980; Second Permanent Secretary, Department of the Environment, since 1981; *b* 18 March 1926; *s* of late Gilbert Harrop; *m* 1975, Margaret Joan, *d* of E. U. E. Elliott-Binns, *qv* ; two *s. Educ:* King Edward VII Sch., Lytham, Lancs; Peterhouse, Cambridge. MA (Hist. Tripos). Served RNVR, 1945–47 (Sub-Lt). Min. of Town and Country Planning, 1949; Min. of Housing and Local Govt, 1951; Dept of the Environment, 1970 (Chm., Yorks and Humberside Economic Planning Bd, and Regional Dir, 1971–73); Under Sec., HM Treasury, 1973–76; Deputy Secretary: DoE, 1977–79, 1980–81; Cabinet Office, 1979–80. *Recreations:* sailing, skiing. *Address:* 19 Berwyn Road, Richmond, Surrey. *Clubs:* United Oxford & Cambridge University; Ski Club of Great Britain; Island Cruising (Salcombe).

HARROWBY, 6th Earl of, *cr* 1809; **Dudley Ryder;** Baron Harrowby, 1776; Viscount Sandon, 1809; Major, late RFA (TAR); *b* 11 Oct. 1892; *e s* of 5th Earl of Harrowby and Hon. Mabel Danvers Smith, DBE (*d* 1956), *y d* of late Rt Hon. W. H. Smith, MP, and 1st Viscountess Hambleden; *S* father 1956; *m* 1922, Lady Helena Blanche Coventry (*d* 1974), *e d* of late Viscount Deerhurst; two *s* one *d. Educ:* Eton; Christ Church, Oxford (BA). Asst Private Sec. to Viscount Milner, Sec. of State for the Colonies, Jan. 1919–Aug. 1920; MP (U) Shrewsbury Division of Salop, Nov. 1922–Nov. 1923, and Oct. 1924–May 1929; Parliamentary Private Sec. to Sir S. Hoare, Sec. of State for Air, Dec. 1922–Nov. 1923; Alderman LCC, 1932–37, Mem. for Dulwich, 1937–40; served European War, Major RA, 1914–19 (wounded); served War of 1939–45. Col Commandant Staffs Army Cadet Force, 1946–50. DL Staffs, 1925; JP Staffs, 1929; Mem. of Royal Commission on Historical Manuscripts, 1935–66. Hon. DLitt Oxon, 1964. *Publications:* England at Worship; (joint) Geography of Everyday Things. *Heir: s* Viscount Sandon, *qv. Address:* Sandon Hall, Stafford; Burnt Norton, Chipping Campden, Gloucestershire. *Club:* Travellers'.

HARRY, Ralph Gordon, MChemA, CChem, FRSC; Scientific Adviser to A/S Persano: Medicinal-og Kosmetikfabrik, Farum, Copenhagen, Denmark, since 1973; *b* 25 June 1908; *s* of Jenkin Campbell Harry and Sarah Harrison; *m* 1938, Dorothy Mary Crafter; two *d. Educ:* Monkton House Sch., Cardiff; University Coll. of S Wales and Monmouthshire. Asst to Public Analyst, Cardiff (Inst. of Prev. Med.), 1934–37; Chief Chemist, J. Campbell Harry &

Co., 1937–41; Manager, Toilet Research Dept, Unilever Ltd, 1941–47; Head, Cosmetic and Toilet Preparations Research Dept, Beecham Research, 1947–49; Chief Experimental Chemist, Maclean Gp of Companies, 1949–53; Chief Research and Develt Chemist and Dep. Chief Chemist (Pharmaceuticals and Cosmetics), Internat. Chemical Co. Ltd (American Home Products Corp.), 1954–73. Devised and published ultra-violet, infra-red, chemical and staining techniques to determine skin penetration; internationally recognised as pioneering recognition of cosmetics by medical profession and govt authorities thoughout world by his publications on post-mortem and living skin and acclaimed by leading dermatologists and cancer specialists. Rep., Gt Britain, Cttee of Honour, 2nd Symposium Internat. des Parfums, Synthetiques et Natural, et de Cosmetologie, Versailles, 1956. Premio Internazionale di Estetica e Cosmetologia 'Guiliana Brambilla', for outstanding contribs to the art and science of cosmetics, 1967. Fellow, RSocMed. Founder Vice-Chm., 1948–50, Hon. Mem., 1973, Soc. of Cosmetic Scientists (formerly Soc. of Cosmetic Chemists of GB). Co-patentee, several British, German, Greek, S American and Swiss patents. *Publications:* The Principles and Practice of Modern Cosmetics: Vol. 1, Modern Cosmeticology, NY 1940, Spanish edns 1954, 7th edn London 1982 (reprinted under title Harry's Cosmeticology); Vol. 2, Cosmetic Materials, their origin, uses and dermatological action, 1948, 2nd edn 1963; contrib. Chambers's Encycl., Br. Jl of Dermatology and Syphilis, The Analyst, Chem. & Ind., Paint Manufacture, Mnfg Chemist, Pharm. Jl, Jl of State Medicine (USA). *Recreations:* cine sound films (Double Star awards 16mm); 35mm technical photography (ARPS 1941); Hi-Fi sound. *Address:* 61 Kimberley Road, Penylan, Cardiff CF2 5DL. *T:* Cardiff 495075. *Club:* Royal Society of Medicine.

HARSCH, Joseph Close, CBE (Hon.) 1965; writer and broadcaster; columnist Christian Science Monitor, Boston; *b* Toledo, Ohio, 25 May 1905; *s* of Paul Arthur Harsch and Leila Katherine Close; *m* 1932, Anne Elizabeth Wood; three *s. Educ:* Williams Coll., Williamstown, Mass, (MA); Corpus Christi Coll., Cambridge (MA). Joined staff Christian Science Monitor, 1929; Washington corresp., then foreign corresp.; Asst Dir, Intergovt Cttee, London, 1939; Monitor Corresp. in Berlin, 1940, SW Pacific area, 1941 and 1942. Began radio broadcasting, 1943; Senior European Correspondent, NBC, 1957–65; Diplomatic Correspondent, NBC, 1965–67; Commentator, American Broadcasting Co., 1967–71; Chief Editorial Writer, Christian Science Monitor, 1971–74. Edward Weintal award for writing on foreign affairs, 1979. *Publications:* Pattern of Conquest, 1941; The Curtain Isn't Iron, 1950. *Address:* c/o Christian Science Monitor, 1 Norway Street, Boston, Mass 02115, USA; Highland Drive, Jamestown, Rhode Island 02835, USA. *Clubs:* Garrick; Metropolitan, Cosmos (Washington, DC); Century (New York); St Botolph (Boston).

HART, Alan; Controller, BBC1 Television, since 1981; *b* 17 April 1935; *s* of Reginald Thomas Hart and Lillian Hart; *m* 1961, Celia Mary Vine; two *s* one *d. Educ:* Pinnerwood Primary Sch.; University College Sch., Hampstead. Reporter: Willesden Chronicle and Kilburn Times, 1952–58; Newcastle Evening Chronicle, 1958; London Evening News, 1958–59; Editorial Asst, BBC Sportsview, 1959–61; Television Sports Producer, BBC Manchester, 1962–64; Asst Editor, Sportsview, 1964–65; Editor, Sportsview, 1965–68; Editor, Grandstand, 1968–77; Head of Sport, BBC Television, 1977–81. *Recreations:* sport, music, walking. *Address:* Old Stocks, Halfacre Hill, Chalfont St Peter, Bucks SL9 7PB. *T:* 01-743 8000.

HART, Alexander Hendry, QC (Canada) 1969; Agent General for British Columbia in the United Kingdom and Europe, since 1981; *b* Regina, Sask., 17 July 1918; *s* of Alexander Hart and Mary (*née* Davidson); *m* 1948, Janet MacMillan Mackay; three *s* one *d. Educ:* Dalhousie Law School (LLB). Served War, Royal Canadian Artillery, 1939–45; retired with rank of Major. Read law with McInnis, Mcquarrie and Cooper; called to Bar of Nova Scotia, 1947. Vice-Pres., Marketing, 1967–71; Sen. Vice-Pres., Canadian Nat. Rlwys, 1971–81. Dep. Internat. Pres., Pacific Basin Economic Council, 1980–81; Past Pres., Vancouver Board of Trade; Past Chm., Western Transportation Adv. Council; Past Mem., University Council of British Columbia; Past Pres., Canada Japan Soc. of Vancouver. *Recreation:* golf. *Address:* British Columbia House, 1 Regent Street, SW1Y 4NS. *T:* 01-930 6857. *Clubs:* East India, Devonshire, Sports and Public Schools, Royal Automobile; Vancouver, Men's Canadian, Shaughnessy Golf and Country (Vancouver); Pine Valley.

HART, Anthony Bernard, PhD; Head of Chemistry Division, Research Division of Central Electricity Generating Board, 1976–82; Member for Hornsey, Greater London Council, since 1981; *b* 7 July 1917; *s* of late Oliver and Jessie Hart; *m* 1946, Judith Ridehalgh (see Rt Hon. Dame Judith Hart); two *s. Educ:* Enfield Grammar Sch.; Queen Mary Coll., London. BSc, PhD; CEng, CChem, FRSC, MInstE. RN Cordite Factories, 1940–46; RN Scientific Service, 1946–50; Lectr in Physical Chem., Royal Coll. of Sci. and Technol., Glasgow (now Strathclyde Univ.), 1950–60; Res. Div., CEGB, 1960–. Exec. Mem., later Chm., Glasgow Trades Council, 1952–60; Nat. Exec. Mem., AUT, 1954–59. Mem. Steering Cttee, World Disarmament Campaigns, 1980–81; Exec. Mem. and Co-Founder, Scientists Against Nuclear Arms, 1981–. Mem., Barnes BC, 1962–64; Mem. and Leader of Opposition, Richmond upon Thames Council, 1964–68 and 1971–74; Chm., Richmond upon Thames Local Govt Cttee, 1968–77; Chm., Finance and Gen. Purposes Cttee, GLC, 1981–82. *Publications:* (with G. J. Womack) Fuel Cells, 1967; (with A. J. B. Cutler) Deposition and Corrosion in Gas Turbines, 1973; contribs to scientific jls. *Recreation:* campaigning for peace and socialism.

Address: 3 Ennerdale Road, Kew, Richmond, Surrey TW9 3PG. *T:* 01-948 1989.

HART, Sir Byrne, Kt 1974; CBE 1968; MC; chartered accountant; *b* Brisbane, 6 Oct. 1895; *s* of F. McD. Hart; *m* 1922, Margaret H., *d* of D. Cramond; two *s. Educ:* Southport Sch.; Brisbane Grammar Sch. FCA. Served Wars of 1914-18 and 1939-45. *Address:* 14 Gerald Street, Ascot, Brisbane, Queensland 4007. *Clubs:* Queensland, Queensland Turf (Brisbane); Union (Sydney).

HART, David Michael; General Secretary, National Association of Head Teachers, since 1978; *b* 27 Aug. 1940; *s* of Edwin Henry Hart and Freda Muriel Hart; *m* 1963, Mary Chalmers; two *s. Educ:* Hurstpierpoint Coll., Sussex. Solicitor 1963. *Recreation:* bridge. *Address:* Barn Cottage, Fairmile Lane, Cobham, Surrey. *T:* Cobham 2884. *Clubs:* MCC, Wig and Pen.

HART, Donald, QC 1978; a Recorder of the Crown Court, since 1978; *b* 6 Jan. 1933; *s* of Frank and Frances Hart; *m* 1958, Glenys Thomas; two *s* two *d. Educ:* Altrincham Grammar Sch.; Magdalen Coll., Oxford. MA. Macaskie Scholar, Arden and Atkin Prize, Lee Essay Prize (Gray's Inn), 1956. Called to the Bar, Gray's Inn, 1956; Northern Circuit, 1956-. *Recreations:* opera; Manchester City FC. *Address:* 7 Bunkers Hill, Romiley, Cheshire. *T:* 061-430 3998; (chambers) 18 St John Street, Manchester. *T:* 061-834 9843.

HART, Dr Everard Peter, CChem, FRSC; Rector, Sunderland Polytechnic, since 1981; *b* 16 Sept. 1925; *s* of Robert Daniel Hart and Margaret Stokes; *m* Enid Mary; three *s* one *d. Educ:* Wyggeston Grammar Sch., Leicester; Loughborough Coll. BSc, PhD London. Asst Lectr, Lectr and Sen. Lectr, Nottingham and Dist Technical Coll., 1951-57; Head of Dept of Chemistry and Biology, 1958-69, Vice-Principal, 1963-69, Sunderland Technical Coll.; Dep. Rector, Sunderland Polytechnic, 1969-80. Mem., Cttee for Sci. and Technol., CNAA, 1974-77. Royal Institute of Chemistry: Mem. Council, 1963-65, 1970-73; Vice-Pres., 1973-75. *Recreations:* music, opera, theatre, travel. *Address:* Redesdale, The Oval, North End, Durham City. *T:* Durham 48305.

HART, F(rancis) Dudley, FRCP; Physician, 1946-74, and Physician-in-charge Rheumatism Unit, Westminster Hospital, SW1, retired 1974; Consulting Physician: Hospital of St John and St Elizabeth, London; Westminster Hospital; Chelsea Hospital for Women; lately Consulting Rheumatologist, The Star and Garter Home for Disabled Sailors, Soldiers and Airmen, Richmond; lately Hon. Consulting Physician (Civilian) to the Army; *b* 4 Oct. 1909; *s* of Canon C. Dudley Hart and Kate Evelyn Bowden; *m* 1944, Mary Josephine, *d* of late Luke Tully, Carrigaline, Co. Cork; one *s* two *d. Educ:* Grosvenor Sch., Nottingham; Edinburgh Univ. MB, ChB Edinburgh 1933, MD 1939; MRCP 1937, FRCP 1949. House physician and clinical asst, Brompton Hosp., 1937; Med. Registrar, Royal Northern Hosp., 1935-37; Med. Registrar, Westminster Hosp., 1939-42; Med. Specialist and Officer i/c Med. Div., RAMC, 1942-46. Mem., Cttee on Review of Medicines, 1975-. Ex-Pres. Heberden Soc.; Member: BMA; RSM; Med. Soc. of London. Arris and Gale Lectr, RCS, 1955; Ellman Lectr, RCP, 1969; Stanley Davidson Lectr, Univ. of Aberdeen, 1970; Bradshaw Lectr, RCP, 1975; Alexander Brown Meml Lectr, Univ. of Ibadan, Nigeria, 1979. Exec. Mem., Arthritis and Rheumatism Council; Hon. Member: Ligue Française contre le Rheumatisme; La Societa di Rheumatologia Italia; American Rheumatism Association; Australian Rheumatism Association. *Publications:* (co-author) Drugs: actions, uses and dosage, 1963; (ed) French's Differential Diagnosis, 10th edn, 1973, 11th edn, 1979; (ed) The Treatment of Chronic Pain, 1974; Joint Disease: all the arthropathies, 1975, 3rd edn 1978; (ed) Drug Treatment of the Rheumatic Diseases, 1978; contributions to: Pye's Surgical Handicraft, 1939-72; Cortisone and ACTH, 1953; Miller's Modern Medical Treatment, 1962; Copeman's Textbook of the Rheumatic Diseases (ed J. T. Scott), 3rd edn 1964, 5th edn 1978; Encyclopedia of General Practice, 1964; Chambers's Encyclopædia, 1964; Drug Treatment, 1976; Butterworth's Medical Dictionary (all rheumatological sections), 1978; articles and broadcasts on general medicine and rheumatism. *Recreations:* multi-track recording, travelling. *Address:* 24 Harmont House, 20 Harley Street, W1N 1AN. *T:* 01-935 4252; (private) 19 Ranulf Road, Hampstead, NW2. *T:* 01-794 2525.

HART, Sir Francis Edmund T.; *see* Turton-Hart.

HART, (Frank) Donald; *see* Hart, Donald.

HART, Frank Thomas, BA; JP; *b* London, 9 Nov. 1911; *s* of late Samuel Black and Ada Frances Laura Hart; *m* 1938, Eveline Brenda Deakin, Leek, Staffs; three *s. Educ:* Gravesend and Sheerness Junior Technical Schs. Asst Sec., Buchanan Hospital, St Leonards-on-Sea, 1931-34; Sec., 1934-42; Sec., Central London Eye Hospital, 1942-44; Sec.-Superintendent, Princess Louise Hospital, 1944-48; Superintendent, Royal Infirmary, Sheffield, 1948-52; House Governor and Sec. to the Bd, Charing Cross Hospital, 1952-73; Hospital Manager, Zambia Medical Aid Soc., 1973-75. Mem. Tribunal set up by President of Zambia to hear applications for release from political detainees, 1973-75. Vice-Pres., League of Friends, Charing Cross Hosp.; Past Pres., Assoc. of Hosp. Secretaries; Past Pres. of the Hospital Officers' Club. DPA (London); Diploma of Economics (London); BA Open, 1982. JP: Co. Mddx, 1955-65; Co. Surrey, 1965-77, East Sussex, 1978-81. Mem., Worshipful Soc. of Apothecaries. *Publication:* (jointly) A Study of Hospital Administration,

1948. *Recreations:* all games, walking, reading. *Address:* 11 The Mount, St Leonards on Sea, East Sussex.

HART, George Vaughan; Consultant, Law Reform Division, Department of Justice, Dublin, since 1972; *b* 9 Sept. 1911; *e s* of George Vaughan Hart and Maude (*née* Curran); *m* 1949, Norah Marie, *d* of Major D. L. J. Babington; one *s* one *d. Educ:* Rossall; Corpus Christi Coll., Oxford. Called to Bar, Middle Temple, 1937. Served Royal Irish Fusiliers, 1940-45. Entered Home Office as Legal Asst, 1946; Principal Asst Legal Advr, 1967-72. Sec., Criminal Law Revision Cttee, 1959-72. *Recreations:* walking, bird-watching. *Address:* Annaghloy House, Castlebaldwin, Boyle, Co. Roscommon. *T:* Boyle 245. *Clubs:* Athenæum; Kildare Street and University (Dublin).

HART, Graham Allan; Under Secretary, Central Policy Review Staff, since 1982; *b* 13 March 1940; *s* of Frederick and Winifred Hart; *m* 1964, Margaret Aline Powell; two *s. Educ:* Brentwood Sch.; Pembroke Coll., Oxford. Assistant Principal, 1962, Principal, 1967, Ministry of Health; Asst Registrar, General Medical Council, 1969-71; Principal Private Sec. to Secretary of State for Social Services, 1972-74; Asst Sec., 1974, Under Sec., 1979, DHSS. *Address:* 68 Kings Avenue, Bromley, Kent BR1 4HL. *T:* 01-464 9456.

HART, Prof. Herbert Lionel Adolphus; FBA 1962; Principal, Brasenose College, Oxford, 1973-78, Hon. Fellow 1978; Delegate of the Oxford University Press, 1960-74; *b* 18 July 1907; 3rd *s* of Simeon Hart and Rose (*née* Samson); *m* 1941, Jenifer, 3rd *d* of Sir John Fischer Williams, CBE, KC; three *s* one *d. Educ:* Cheltenham Coll.; Bradford Grammar Sch.; New Coll., Oxford (Hon. Fellow 1968). Open Classical Scholar, New Coll., Oxford, 1926; First Class Lit. Hum., 1929. Practised at the Chancery Bar, 1932-40. Served War of 1939-45, in War Office, 1940-45. Fellow and Tutor in Philosophy, New Coll., Oxford, 1945; University Lecturer in Philosophy, Oxford, 1948; Prof. of Jurisprudence, Oxford, 1952-68; Fellow, University Coll., Oxford, 1952-68, Res. Fellow 1969-73, Hon. Fellow, 1973; Sen. Res. Fellow, Nuffield Foundn, 1969-73. Visiting Professor: Harvard Univ., 1956-57; Univ. of California, LA, 1961-62. Mem., Monopolies Commn, 1967-73. Pres., Aristotelian Soc., 1959-60; Vice-Pres., British Acad., 1976-77. Hon. Master of the Bench, Middle Temple, 1963. For. Mem., Amer. Acad. of Arts and Sciences, 1966. Hon. Dr of Law, Stockholm, 1960; Hon. LLD: Glasgow, 1966; Chicago, 1966; Cambridge, 1978; Harvard, 1980; Edinburgh, 1980; Georgetown, 1982; Hon. DLitt: Kent, 1969; Hull, 1979; Bradford, 1980; Hon. Dr, Nat. Autonomous Univ. of Mexico, 1979. Fellow, Accademia delle Scienze, Turin, 1964; Commonwealth Prestige Fellow (Govt of NZ), 1971. *Publications:* (with A. M. Honoré) Causation in the Law, 1959; The Concept of Law, 1961; Law Liberty and Morality, 1963; The Morality of the Criminal Law, 1965; Punishment and Responsibility, 1968; (ed, with J. H. Burns) Jeremy Bentham: An Introduction to the Principles of Morals and Legislation, 1970; (ed) Jeremy Bentham: Of Laws in General, 1970; A Comment on the Commentaries and A Fragment on Government, 1977; Essays on Bentham: jurisprudence and political theory, 1982; articles in philosophical and legal journals. *Address:* University College, Oxford; 11 Manor Place, Oxford. *T:* 42402.

HART, Rt. Hon. Dame Judith (Constance Mary), DBE 1979; PC 1967; MP (Lab) Lanark Division of Lanarkshire since 1959; *d* of Harry Ridehalgh and late Lily Ridehalgh; *m* 1946, Anthony Bernard Hart, *qv* ; two *s. Educ:* Clitheroe Royal Grammar Sch.; London School of Economics, London University (BA Hons 1945). Contested (Lab) Bournemouth West, 1951, and South Aberdeen, 1955. Jt Parly Under-Sec. of State for Scotland, 1964-66; Minister of State, Commonwealth Office, 1966-67; Minister of Social Security, 1967-68; Paymaster-General (in the Cabinet), 1968-69; Minister of Overseas Develt, 1969-70, 1974-75; Minister for Overseas Develt, 1977-79; front bench opposition spokesman on overseas aid, 1979-80. Govt Co.-Chm., Women's Nat. Commn, 1969-70. Labour Party: Mem., Nat. Executive, 1969-; Vice-Chm., 1980-81, Chm., 1981-82; Chm., Industrial Policy Sub-Cttee. Pres., Internat. Inst. for Resource Develt. *Publication:* Aid and Liberation, 1973. *Recreations:* theatre, gardening, spending time with her family. *Address:* 3 Ennerdale Road, Kew Gardens, Richmond-upon-Thames. *T:* 01-948 1989.

HART, Michael, MA; FRSA; Headmaster of European School, Luxembourg, since 1980; *b* 1 May 1928; *yr s* of late Dr F. C. Hardt; *m* 1956, Lida Dabney Adams, PhD (Wisconsin Univ.). *Educ:* Collège Français, Berlin; Landerziehungsheim Schondorf; Keble Coll., Oxford (Exhib.). 1st Cl. Hons History, 1951. Administrative Asst, UNRRA, 1945-47; Asst Master and Head of History, Sherborne Sch., 1951-56; Head of History, 1956-61, and Housemaster of School House, 1961-67, Shrewsbury Sch.; Headmaster of Mill Hill Sch., 1967-74; HM Inspector of Schs, DES, 1974-76; Headmaster, European Sch., Mol, Belgium, 1976-80. *Publications:* The EEC and Secondary Education in the UK, 1974; contrib. to Reader's Digest World Atlas and Atlas of British Isles. *Recreations:* travel, climbing. *Address:* 10 rue Jean Engling, Dommeldange, Luxembourg.

HART, Prof. Michael, FRS 1982; FInstP; Wheatstone Professor of Physics and Head of Department of Physics, King's College, London University, since 1976; *b* 4 Nov. 1938; *s* of Reuben Harold Victor Hart and Phyllis Mary (*née* White); *m* 1963, Susan Margaret (*née* Powell); three *d. Educ:* Cotham Grammar Sch., Bristol; Bristol Univ. (BSc, PhD, DSc). FInstP 1971. Research Associate: Dept of Materials Science and Engrg, Cornell Univ., 1963-65; Dept of Physics, Bristol Univ., 1965-67; Lectr in Physics, 1967-72, Reader in

Physics, 1972-76, Bristol Univ.; Sen. Resident Res. Associate of Nat. Research Council, Nat. Aeronautics and Space Admin Electronics Research Center, Boston, Mass, 1969-70; Special Advisor, Central Policy Review Staff, Cabinet Office, 1975-77. Amer. Crystallographic Assoc.'s Bertram Eugene Warren Award for Diffraction Physics (jtly with Dr U. Bonse), 1970; Charles Vernon Boys Prize of Inst. of Physics, 1971. *Publications:* numerous contribs to learned jls on x-ray optics, defects in crystals and synchrotron radiation. *Recreations:* squash, weaving, flying kites. *Address:* 31 Chessfield Park, Little Chalfont, Bucks HP6 6RU. *T:* Little Chalfont 2402.

HART, P(hilip) M(ontagu) D'Arcy, CBE 1956; MA, MD (Cambridge), FRCP; Medical Research Council grant holder, National Institute for Medical Research, since 1965 (Director, Tuberculosis Research Unit, Medical Research Council, 1948-65); *b* 25 June 1900; *s* of late Henry D'Arcy Hart and late Hon. Ethel Montagu; *m* 1941, Ruth, *d* of late Herbert Meyer and late Grete Meyer-Larsen; one *s. Educ:* Clifton Coll.; Gonville and Caius Coll., Cambridge; University Coll. Hospital. Dorothy Temple Cross Fellowship to USA, 1934-35; Consultant Physician, UCH, 1934-37; Mem. Scientific Staff, MRC, 1937-48; Mem. Expert Cttee on Tuberculosis, WHO, 1947-64. Goldsmith Entrance Exhibnr, Filliter Exhibnr, Magrath Scholarship, Tuke Medals, UCH Medical Sch., 1922-25; Horton Smith MD Prize, Cambridge, 1930; Royal College of Physicians: Milroy Lecture, 1937; Mitchell Lecture, 1946; Weber-Parkes Prize, 1951; Marc Daniels Lecture, 1967; Stewart Prize, BMA, 1964. *Publications:* scientific papers on respiratory disease, epidemiology and cell biology. *Address:* National Institute for Medical Research, Mill Hill, NW7. *T:* 01-959 3666; 37 Belsize Court, NW3 5QN. *Club:* Athenæum.

HART, Captain Raymond, CBE 1963; DSO 1945; DSC 1941, Bar 1943; Royal Navy; Director, Maritime World Ltd; *b* 24 June 1913; *o s* of late H. H. Hart, Bassett, Southampton; *m* 1945, Margaret Evanson, *o d* of Capt. S. B. Duffin, Danesfort, Belfast; two *s* one *d. Educ:* Oakmount Preparatory Sch.; King Edward VII Sch. Joined Merchant Navy, 1927; Joined Royal Navy, 1937; HMS Hasty, 2nd Destroyer Flotilla, 1939-42; in command: HMS Vidette, 1942-44 (despatches); HMS Havelock, 1944; Sen. Officer, 21st Escort Gp, 1944-45; served in HMS Vanguard during Royal Tour of S Africa, 1947. RN Staff Course, 1949-52; in command, HMS Relentless, 1952-53; Joint Services Staff Course, 1953-54. Staff C-in-C Allied Forces Mediterranean, as Liaison Officer to C-in-C. Allied Forces Southern Europe, HQ Naples, Italy, 1954-56; in command, HMS Undine, and Capt. 6th Frigate Sqdn, 1957-58; Cdre Naval Drafting, 1960-62; retd from RN, 1963. Nautical Advr, British & Commonwealth Shipping Co., 1963-72; Fleet Manager, Cayzer, Irvine & Co. Ltd, 1972-76; Director: Union-Castle Mail Steamship Co. Ltd; Clan Line Steamers Ltd, 1964-76; Cayzer, Irvine & Co. Ltd, 1966-76; British & Commonwealth Shipping Co. Ltd, 1966-76. Vice-Chm. Council, Missions to Seamen; Chm., Cttee of Management, Seamen's Hosp. Soc.; Mem. Council, Sea Cadet Assoc.; Mem., Cttee of Management, Marine Soc. FRIN; FNI. Officer Order of Merit of Republic of Italy, 1958. *Recreations:* swimming, tennis, gardening, fishing. *Address:* Three Firs Cottage, Bramshott Chase, Hindhead, Surrey. *T:* Hindhead 4890.

HART, Thomas Mure, CMG 1957; *b* 1 March 1909; *s* of late Maxwell M. Hart and of Elizabeth Watson, Aiknut, West Kilbride; *m* 1936, Eileen Stewart Lawson; one *s* one *d. Educ:* Strathallan; Glasgow Univ.; Brasenose Coll., Oxford. Colonial Administrative Service, 1933; seconded Colonial Office, 1933-36; Malayan Civil Service, 1936; Dir of Commerce and Industry, Singapore, 1953; Financial Sec., Singapore, 1954; retired, 1959. Bursar, Loretto Sch., Musselburgh, 1959-69. *Recreation:* golf. *Address:* 44 Frogston Road West, Edinburgh EH10 7AJ. *T:* 031-445 2152. *Clubs:* Royal and Ancient (St Andrews); Honourable Company of Edinburgh Golfers.

HART, Maj.-Gen. Trevor Stuart, CB 1982; MRCS, LRCP; FFCM; Director of Medical Services, BAOR, since 1981; *b* 19 Feb. 1926; *s* of R. J. Hart and C. G. Hart (*née* Blyfield); *m* 1954, P. G. Lloyd; two *s* one *d. Educ:* Dulwich Coll.; Guy's Hosp. MB, BS; FFCM; DPH, DTM&H. DDMS HQ 1 (BR) Corps, 1975-78; DMS, UKLF, 1978-81. OStJ 1973. *Recreations:* gardening, growing orchids (more leaves than blooms). *Address:* c/o Barclays Bank Ltd, 72 Cheapside, EC2.

HART, Rt. Rev. Mgr William Andrew; *b* Dumbarton, 9 Sept. 1904; *s* of Daniel Hart and Margaret Gallagher. *Educ:* St Mungo's Academy, Glasgow; St Mary's Coll., Blairs, Aberdeen; Royal Scots Coll. and Pontifical Univ., Valladolid, Spain. Asst Priest, St Mary's, Hamilton, 1929-33; St John's, Glasgow, 1933-39; Army Chaplain, 1939-45; Asst Priest, St Michael's, Glasgow, 1945-48; Vice-Rector, Royal Scots Coll., Valladolid, 1948-49; Parish Priest, St Nicholas', Glasgow, 1949-51, St Saviour's, Glasgow, 1951-55; Bishop of Dunkeld, 1955-81. *Address:* Birchwood House, Birnam, Dunkeld, Perthshire. *T:* Dunkeld 267.

HART-DAVIS, Sir Rupert (Charles), Kt 1967; author, editor and former publisher; Director of Rupert Hart-Davis, Ltd, Publishers, 1946-68; Vice-President, Committee of the London Library, since 1971 (Chairman 1957-69); *b* 28 Aug. 1907; *o s* of Richard Vaughan Hart-Davis and Sybil Mary Cooper, *er sister* of 1st Viscount Norwich; *m* 1st, 1929, Peggy Ashcroft (now Dame Peggy Ashcroft) (marr. diss.); 2nd, 1933, Catherine Comfort Borden-Turner (marr. diss.), *d* of Mary Borden and George Douglas Turner; two *s* one *d*; 3rd, 1964, Winifred Ruth (*d* 1967), *d* of C. H. Ware, Bromyard, and *widow* of Oliver Simon; 4th, 1968, June (*née* Clifford), *widow* of David Williams.

Educ: Eton; Balliol Coll., Oxford. Student at Old Vic, 1927-28; Actor at Lyric Theatre, Hammersmith, 1928-29; office boy at William Heinemann Ltd, 1929-31; Manager of Book Soc., 1932; Dir of Jonathan Cape Ltd, 1933-40. Served in Coldstream Guards, 1940-45. Founded Rupert Hart-Davis Ltd, 1946. Hon. DLitt: Reading, 1964; Durham, 1981. *Publications:* Hugh Walpole: a biography, 1952; The Arms of Time: a memoir, 1979; *edited:* George Moore: Letters to Lady Cunard, 1957; The Letters of Oscar Wilde, 1962; Max Beerbohm: Letters to Reggie Turner, 1964; A Catalogue of the Caricatures of Max Beerbohm, 1972; The Autobiography of Arthur Ransome, 1976; The Lyttelton Hart-Davis Letters, vol. I, 1978, vol. II 1979, vol III, 1981, vol. IV, 1982; Selected Letters of Oscar Wilde, 1979; Two Men of Letters, 1979; Siegfried Sassoon Diaries 1920-1922, 1981. *Recreations:* reading, book-collecting, watching cricket. *Address:* The Old Rectory, Marske-in-Swaledale, Richmond, N Yorks.
See also Baron Silsoe.

HART DYKE, Sir Derek William, 9th Bt *cr* 1677; *b* 4 Dec. 1924; *s* of Sir Oliver Hamilton Augustus Hart Dyke, 8th Bt, and Millicent Zoë (*d* 1975), *d* of Dr Mayston Bond; *S* father, 1969; *m* 1st, 1953, Dorothy Moses, Hamilton, Ont (marr. diss. 1963); one *s* one *d*; 2nd, 1964, Margaret Dickson Elder, Ottawa (marr. diss. 1972). Mem., Royal Canadian Military Inst. *Educ:* Harrow; Millfield. *Heir: s* David William Hart Dyke, *b* 5 Jan. 1955. *Address:* 80 Erie Avenue, Hamilton, Ontario L8N 2W6, Canada. *Club:* Hamilton Press.

HART-LEVERTON, Colin Allen; QC 1979; a Recorder of the Crown Court, since 1979; *b* 10 May 1936; *s* of Monty Hart-Leverton and Betty (*née* Simmonds); *m* 1963, in USA, A. P. Bennett. *Educ:* Stowe; self-taught thereafter. Mem., Inst. of Taxation, 1957 (youngest to have ever qualified); called to the Bar, Middle Temple, 1957 (youngest to have ever qual.). Contested (L): Bristol West, 1959 (youngest cand.); Walthamstow West, 1964. Prosecuting Counsel, Central Criminal Court, 1974-79; Dep. Circuit Judge, 1975; Attorney-at-Law, Turks and Caicos Islands, Caribbean, 1976. Occasional television and radio broadcasts. *Recreations:* ping-pong, jazz. *Address:* 10 King's Bench Walk, EC4Y 7EB. *T:* 01-353 2501; 9533 Brighton Way, Beverly Hills, Calif, USA.

HARTE, Dr Michael John; Chairman, NATO Civil and Military Budget Committees, since 1981; *b* 15 Aug. 1936; *s* of Harold Edward Harte and Marjorie Irene Harte; *m* 1st, 1962, Diana Hayes (marr. diss. 1971); 2nd, 1975, Mary Claire Preston; four step *d. Educ:* Charterhouse; Trinity Coll., Cambridge (BA); University Coll., London (PhD; Dip. in Biochem. Engrg). Sen. Scientific Officer, Micro-biol Res. Estab., MoD, 1963; Principal, MoD, 1967; Private Sec. to Minister of State for Def., 1972; Asst Secretary: Central Policy Rev. Staff, 1973; MoD, 1975; Counsellor, Budget and Infrastructure, UK Delegn to NATO, 1977-81. *Recreation:* wine: tasting, buying, drinking, keeping. *Address:* avenue Lt Gen. Pire 18, 1150 Bruxelles, Belgium. *T:* 02 731 9385.

HARTFALL, Prof. Stanley Jack, TD 1942; BSc, MD; FRCP; Professor of Clinical Medicine, University of Leeds, 1948-64, now Emeritus; *b* 27 Feb. 1899; *m* 1931, Muriel Ann Hunter; two *s* (one *d* decd). *Educ:* University of Leeds; Guy's Hosp. House Surg. and House Physician. Resident Medical Officer, Leeds Gen. Infirmary, 1926-30; Medical Asst to Sir A. Hurst, Guy's Hosp., 1930-32; Leverhulme Research Scholar, Royal College of Physicians, London, 1932-33; Hon. Physician and Consulting Physician, Leeds Gen. Infirmary and Leeds Regional Hosp. Board, Harrogate Royal Bath Hosp., Dewsbury and District Gen. Hosp., Prof. of Therapeutics, University of Leeds, 1937. Lieut-Col RAMC (TA). *Publications:* numerous papers on pathological and clinical subjects, gastro-intestinal diseases, anaemias and blood diseases, arthritis and rheumatism. *Recreations:* cricket and tennis. *Address:* White Gables, Hill Farm Road, Playford, near Ipswich, Suffolk. *T:* Ipswich 623784.

HARTHAN, John Plant, MA, FLA; Keeper of the Library, Victoria and Albert Museum, 1962-76; *b* 15 April 1916; *y s* of late Dr George Ezra Harthan, Evesham, Worcs, and Winifred May Slater. *Educ:* Bryanston; Jesus Coll., Cambridge; University Coll., London. Asst-Librarian, Southampton Univ., 1940-43; Royal Society of Medicine Library, 1943-44; Asst Under-Librarian, Cambridge Univ. Library, 1944-48; Asst-Keeper of the Library, Victoria and Albert Museum, 1948. FLA 1939. *Publications:* Bookbindings in the Victoria and Albert Museum, 1950, 3rd edn 1982; co-editor, F.D. Klingender, Animals in Art and Thought, 1971; Books of Hours, 1977; The History of the Illustrated Book, 1981; Introduction to Illuminated Manuscripts, 1982. *Recreations:* history of religion, royalty, music, botany, writing. *Address:* 15 Palliser Court, Palliser Road, W14 9ED.

HARTINGTON, Marquess of; Peregrine Andrew Morny Cavendish; Director, Devonshire Arms (Bolton Abbey) Ltd, since 1980; Commercial Manager, Chatsworth, since 1980; *b* 27 April 1944; *s* of 11th Duke of Devonshire, *qv*; *m* 1967, Amanda Carmen, *d* of late Comdr E. G. Heywood-Lonsdale, RN, and of Mrs Heywood-Lonsdale; one *s* two *d. Educ:* Eton; Exeter Coll., Oxford. President: Wakefield and N of England Tulip Soc.; British Resorts Assoc., 1980-. Vice-Chm., British Field Sports Soc., 1981-. Mem., Jockey Club, 1980-. *Heir: s* Ear of Burlington, *qv. Address:* 15 Christ Church Road, SW14. *T:* 01-878 2272.

HARTLAND-SWANN, Julian Dana Nimmo; HM Diplomatic Service; Counsellor and Head of Chancery, Brussels, since 1979; *b* 18 Feb. 1936; *s* of late Prof. J. J. Hartland-Swann and of Mrs Kenlis Hartland-Swann (*née* Taylour); *m* 1960, Ann Deirdre Green; one *s* one *d. Educ:* Stowe; Lincoln Coll., Oxford (History). Entered HM Diplomatic Service, 1960; 3rd Sec., Brit. Embassy, Bangkok, 1961-65; 2nd, later 1st Sec., FO, 1965-68; 1st Sec., Berlin, 1968-71; 1st Sec. and Head of Chancery, Vienna, 1971-74; FCO, 1975-77; Ambassador to Mongolian People's Republic, 1977-79. *Recreations:* French food, sailing, music. *Address:* c/o Foreign and Commonwealth Office, SW1A 2AL.

HARTLEY, Arthur Coulton, CIE 1946; OBE 1943; ICS (retired); *b* 24 March 1906; *s* of late John Aspinall Hartley and Jennie Hartley; *m* 1943, Mrs Cecilie Leslie; one *s. Educ:* Cowley Grammar Sch.; Manchester Univ.; Balliol Coll., Oxford. Entered Indian Civil Service, 1929; Asst Magistrate, Comilla, Bengal, 1929-30; Subdivisional Magistrate, Sirajganj, Bengal, 1930-32; Asst Settlement Officer, Rangpur, Bengal, 1932-34; Settlement Officer, Rangpur, Bengal, 1934-37; Asst Sec. to Governor of Bengal, 1938-40; District Magistrate, Howrah, Bengal, 1940-43; Controller of Rationing, Calcutta, Bengal, 1943-45; Dir-Gen. of Food, Bengal, India, 1945-47. *Publication:* Report on Survey and Settlement Operations of Rangpur, 1938. *Recreations:* hill walking, painting. *Address:* c/o Midland Bank Ltd, Terminus Road, Eastbourne, East Sussex.

HARTLEY, Brian Joseph, CMG 1950; OBE 1945 (MBE 1934); *b* 1907; *s* of late John Joseph Hartley, Tring, Herts; *m* 1951, Doreen Mary, *d* of Col R. G. Sanders; three *s* one *d. Educ:* Loughborough; Midland Agricultural Coll.; Wadham Coll., Oxford; Imperial Coll. of Tropical Agriculture, Trinidad. Entered Colonial Service; Agricultural Officer, Tanganyika, 1929; Aden Protectorate: Agricultural Officer, 1938; Agricultural Adviser, 1944; Dir of Agriculture, 1946-54; retd 1954; Chief, FAO(UN), mission in Iraq, 1955; Mem., Tanganyika Agricultural Corporation, 1956-62; Trustee, Tanganyika Nat. Parks, 1957-64; Mem., Ngorongoro Conservation Authority Advisory Board, 1963-64. UN (Special Fund) Consultant Team Leader: Kafue Basin Survey, N Rhodesia, 1960; Livestock Develt Survey, Somalia, 1966; Chief Livestock Adviser, FAO, Somalia, 1967-70; Project Manager, UNSF Survey of Northern Rangelands Project, Somalia, 1970-72; Consultant, FAO-IBRD Project, Anatolia, Turkey, 1972-73; Consultant, Wadi Rima and Montane Plains, Yemen Arab Republic, 1975; Consultant, 1972-76, Technical Manager, 1976-78, World Bank Nomadic Rangelands Project, Ethiopia; Consultant: Oxfam Karamoja Relief Prog. in Uganda, 1980; Oxfam E Africa Office, 1981-82. *Address:* Box 337, Malindi, Kenya.

HARTLEY, Prof. Brian Selby, PhD; FRS 1971; Professor of Biochemistry, Imperial College, University of London, since 1974 and Director, Centre for Biotechnology, since 1982; *b* 16 April 1926; *s* of Norman and Hilda Hartley; *m* 1949, Kathleen Maude Vaughan; three *s* one *d. Educ:* Queens' Coll., Cambridge; Univ. of Leeds. BA 1947, MA 1952, Cantab; PhD 1952, Leeds. ICI Fellow, Univ. of Cambridge, 1952; Helen Hay Whitney Fellow, Univ. of Washington, Seattle, USA, 1958; Fellow and Lectr in Biochemistry, Trinity Coll., Cambridge, 1964; Scientific Staff, MRC Laboratory of Molecular Biology, 1961-74. Mem. Council: EMBO (European Centre for Molecular Biology), 1978; Royal Soc., 1982-. Hon. Mem., Amer. Soc. of Biological Chemists, 1977. British Drug Houses Medal for Analytical Biochemistry, 1969. *Publications:* papers and articles in scientific jls and books. *Recreations:* fishing, gardening. *Address:* Imperial College of Science and Technology, SW7 2AZ.

HARTLEY, Air Marshal Sir Christopher (Harold), KCB 1963 (CB 1961); CBE 1957 (OBE 1949); DFC 1945; AFC 1944; BA Oxon; Director, Westland Aircraft Ltd, since 1971; *b* 31 Jan. 1913; *s* of late Brig.-Gen. Sir Harold Hartley, GCVO, CH, CBE, MC, FRS; *m* 1st, 1937, Anne Sitwell (marr. diss., 1943); 2nd, 1944, Margaret Watson; two *s. Educ:* Eton; Balliol Coll., Oxford (Williams Exhibnr); King's Coll., Cambridge. Zoologist on Oxford Univ. expeditions: to Sarawak, 1932; Spitsbergen, 1933; Greenland, 1937. Asst Master at Eton Coll., 1937-39. Joined RAFVR, 1938. Served War of 1939-45: 604 Sqdn, 256 Sqdn, Fighter Interception Unit, Central Fighter Establishment. Permanent Commission, 1945; AOC 12 Group, Fighter Command, 1959; ACAS (Operational Requirements), Air Min., 1961; DCAS, 1963-66; Controller of Aircraft, Min. of Aviation and Min. of Technology, 1966-70, retired. Dep. Chm., British Hovercraft Corporation, 1979- (Chm., 1974-78). *Recreations:* shooting, fishing. *Address:* c/o Westland Aircraft Ltd, 4 Carlton Gardens, SW1. *Club:* Travellers'.

HARTLEY, Sir Frank, Kt 1977; CBE 1970; PhD London, CChem, FPS, FRSC; Vice-Chancellor, University of London, 1976-78; Dean of the School of Pharmacy, University of London, 1962-76; *b* 5 Jan. 1911; *s* of late Robinson King Hartley and Mary Hartley (*née* Holt); *m* 1937, Lydia May England; two *s. Educ:* Municipal Secondary (later Grammar) Sch., Nelson, Lancs; Sch. of Pharmacy (Fellow, 1977), University Coll. (Fellow, 1972), and Birkbeck Coll. (Fellow, 1970), University of London. Jacob Bell Schol., 1930, Silver Medallist in Pharmaceutics, Pharmaceut. Chem. and Pharmacognosy, 1932. Pharmaceutical Chemist, 1932, Demonstrator and Lectr, 1932-40, at Sch. of Pharmacy; 1st cl. hons BSc (Chem.), University of London, 1936, and PhD, 1941; Chief Chemist, Organon Laboratories Ltd, 1940-43; Sec., Therapeutic Research Corp., 1943-46; Sec., Gen. Penicillin Cttee (Min. of Supply), 1943-46; Dir of Research and Sci. Services, The British Drug Houses, Ltd, 1946-62; Chm. Brit. Pharmaceut. Conf, 1957, and of Sci. Adv. Cttee of

Pharmaceut. Soc. of Great Britain, 1964-66; Mem. Council, 1955-58, 1961-64, Vice-Pres., 1958-60, 1964-65, 1967-69, Pres., 1965-67, of Royal Institute of Chemistry; Hon. Treasurer, 1956-61, Chm. 1964-68 of Chem. Council; Mem. 1953-80, Vice-Chm. 1963-68, Chm. 1970-80, of British Pharmacopoeia Commn, and a UK Deleg., 1964-80, to European Pharmacopoeia Commn; Mem., 1970-, Vice-Chm., 1977-, Medicines Commn; Member: Poisons Bd (Home Office), 1958-66; Cttee on Safety of Drugs (Min. of Health), 1963-70; Cttee on Prevention of Microbiol Contamination of Medicinal Products, 1972-73; Nat. Biological Standards Bd, 1975-; Cttee of Enquiry on Contaminated Infusion Fluids, 1972; Chairman: Bd of Studies in Pharmacy, Univ. of London, 1964-68; Pharmacy Bd, CNAA, 1965-77; Collegiate Council, 1969-73; Panel on Grading of Chief Pharmacists in Teaching Hosps, 1972-74, Qualified Person Adv. Cttee, DHSS, 1979; Comrs for Lambeth, Southwark and Lewisham Health Area, 1979-80; Pharmacy Working Gp, Nat. Adv. Bd for Higher Educn, Local Authorities, 1982-; Mem., Academic Council, 1969-73. Co-opted Mem. Senate, 1968-76, 1978-81, 1981-, ex officio Mem., 1976-78, Senate Mem. of Court, 1970-76, 1978-81, 1981-83, ex officio Mem., 1976-78, Dep. Vice-Chancellor, 1973-76, University of London; Member Council: St Thomas's Hosp. Medical Sch., University of London, 1968-80; Royal Free Hosp. Med. Sch., 1970-; Member Bd of Governors: Royal Free Hosp. Gp, 1970-74; Kingston Polytechnic, 1970-75; British Postgrad. Med. Fedn, London Univ., 1972-; Royal Postgrad. Med. Sch., 1972-; Inst. of Basic Med. Sci, 1973-. Chm., Charing Cross and Westminster Med. Schs, London Univ., 1981-. Lectures: Sir William Pope Meml, RSA, 1962; Wilkinson, Inst. of Dental Surg., 1978; Astor, Middlesex Hosp. Med. Sch., 1980; Bernal, Birkbeck Coll., 1982. Hon. FRCP 1979, Hon. FRCS 1980, Hon. FRSC 1981. Liveryman, Worshipful Soc. of Apothecaries of London. Hon. DSc Warwick, 1978; Hon. LlD Strathclyde, 1980. Charter Gold Medal, Pharm. Soc. of GB, 1974. *Publications:* papers on chem. and pharmaceut. research in Quarterly Jl of Pharmacy, Jl of Pharmacy and Pharmacology and Jl of Chem. Soc. Reviews and articles in sci. and tech. jls. *Recreations:* reading, gardening. *Address:* 146 Dorset Road, Merton Park, SW19 3EF. *T:* 01-542 7198. *Clubs:* Athenæum, Savage.
See also F. R. Hartley.

HARTLEY, Prof. Frank Robinson, CChem, FRSC; Acting Dean, Royal Military College of Science, Shrivenham, since 1982; *b* 29 Jan. 1942; *s* of Sir Frank Hartley, *qv* ; *m* 1964, Valerie Peel; three *d. Educ:* King's College Sch., Wimbledon (Sambrooke Schol.); Magdalen Coll., Oxford (Demy; BA, MA, DPhil). Post-doctoral Fellow, Commonwealth Scientific and Industrial Research Organisation, Div. of Protein Chemistry, Melbourne, Aust., 1966-69; Imperial Chemical Industries Research Fellow and Tutor in Physical Chemistry, University Coll. London, 1969-70; Lectr in Inorganic Chemistry, Univ. of Southampton, 1970-75; Professor of Chemistry and Head of Dept of Chemistry and Metallurgy, Royal Military Coll. of Science, Shrivenham, 1975-82. *Publications:* The Chemistry of Platinum and Palladium (Applied Science), 1973; Elements of Organometallic Chemistry (Chemical Soc.), 1974, Japanese edn 1981; (with C. Burgess and R. M. Alcock) Solution Equilibria, 1980; papers in inorganic, coordination and organometallic chemistry in major English, Amer. and Aust. chemical jls. *Recreations:* Rugby refereeing, golf, swimming, squash, gardening, cliff walking, reading. *Address:* 9 Curtis Road, Shrivenham, Wiltshire SN6 8AY. *Club:* Shrivenham.

HARTLEY, His Honour Gilbert Hillard; a Circuit Judge (formerly Judge of County Courts), 1967-82; *b* 11 Aug. 1917; *s* of late Percy Neave Hartley and late Nellie Bond (*née* Hillard); *m* 1948, Jeanne, *d* of late C. W. Gall, Leeds; one *s* two *d. Educ:* Ashville, Harrogate; Exeter Coll. Oxford. Called to Bar, Middle Temple, 1939. Served with Army, 1940-46. Recorder of Rotherham, 1965-67; Dep. Chm., WR of Yorkshire QS, 1965-71. *Address:* South Lawn, East Keswick, Leeds LS17 9DB.

HARTLEY, Ven. Peter Harold Trahair; Archdeacon of Suffolk, 1970-75, now Archdeacon Emeritus; Priest in Charge of Badingham with Bruisyard and Dennington; *b* 11 July 1909; *m* 1938, Ursula Mary Trahair; two *d. Educ:* Leys School; University of London (BSc 1935); Queen's College, Oxford (MA 1948); Cuddesdon Theological College. Deacon 1953, Priest 1954; Diocese of St Edmundsbury; Curate of Dennington and Badingham, 1953-55; Rector of Badingham, 1955, with Bruisyard, 1960, and Cransford, 1974; Rural Dean of Loes, 1967-70. *Publications:* papers in zoological journals. *Recreations:* natural history, naval and military history. *Address:* Pollards, Badingham, Woodbridge, Suffolk. *T:* Badingham 217.

HARTLEY, Richard Leslie Clifford, QC 1976; *b* 31 May 1932; *s* of late Arthur Clifford Hartley, CBE and late Nina Hartley. *Educ:* Marlborough Coll.; Sidney Sussex Coll., Cambridge (MA). Called to the Bar, Gray's Inn, 1956. *Recreations:* golf, tennis. *Address:* 15 Chesham Street, SW1. *T:* 01-235 2420. *Clubs:* Garrick, MCC; Woking Golf, Rye Golf, St Enodoc Golf.

HARTLINE, Prof. Haldan Keffer; Professor of Biophysics, Rockefeller University, New York, 1953-74, now Emeritus; *b* Bloomsburg, Pa, 22 Dec. 1903; *s* of Daniel S. Hartline and Harriet F. Keffer; *m* 1936, Elizabeth Kraus; three *s. Educ:* Lafayette Coll. (BS); Johns Hopkins Univ. (MD), Nat. Res. Fellow, Medicine, Johns Hopkins Univ., 1927-29; Reeves Johnson Trav. Res. Schol., Universities of Leipzig and Munich, 1929-31; University of Pa; Fellow, Med. Physics, 1931-36; Asst Prof. Biophysics, Eldridge Reeves Johnson Foundn for Med. Physics, 1936-40; Assoc. Prof. Physiology, Cornell Univ. Med. Coll., NY, 1940-41; Asst Prof. Biophysics, Johnson Foundn, Univ. of Pennsylvania, 1941-42, Assoc. Prof. Biophysics, 1943-48, Prof. of

Biophysics, 1948-49; Prof. Biophysics and Chm. of Dept, Johns Hopkins Univ., 1949-53. Mem., Nat. Acad. of Sciences; For. Mem., Royal Soc. (London); Hon. Member: Optical Soc., Amer., 1980; Physiol. Soc., 1980. Hon. ScD: Lafayette Coll., 1959; Pennsylvania, 1971; Rockefeller, 1976; Maryland, Baltimore County, 1978; Syracuse, 1979; Hon. Dr of Laws, Johns Hopkins Univ., 1969; Hon. Dr med Freiburg, 1971. William H. Howell Award (Physiol.), 1927; Howard Crosby Warren Medal, 1948; A. A. Michelson Award, 1964; Nobel Prize in Physiology or Medicine (jointly), 1967; Lighthouse Award, NY Assoc. for the Blind, 1969. *Publications:* contrib. Ratliff: Studies on Excitation and Inhibition in the Retina, 1974; articles in: Amer. Jl Physiol; Jl Gen. Physiol; Jl Cell. Comp. Physiol.; Cold Spring Harbor Symposia on Quant. Biol.; Jl Opt. Soc. Amer.; Harvey Lectures; Science; Rev. Mod. Physics, etc. *Recreation:* mountain hiking. *Address:* Patterson Road, Hydes, Maryland 21082, USA. *T:* 301 592 8162.

HARTLING, Poul; Grand Cross of Dannebrog; United Nations High Commissioner for Refugees, since 1978; Member of Folketing, Denmark, 1957-60 and 1964-78; *b* 14 Aug. 1914; *s* of Mads Hartling and Mathilde (*née* Nielsen); *m* 1940, Elsebeth Kirkemann; three *s* one *d. Educ:* Univ. of Copenhagen (Master of Divinity 1939). Curate, Frederiksberg Church, 1941-45; Chaplain, St Luke Foundn, 1945-50; Principal, Zahle's Teachers' Trng Coll., 1950-68. Chm., Liberal Party Parly Group, 1965-68; Mem., Nordic Council, 1964-68 (Pres., 1966-68); Minister of Foreign Affairs, 1968-71; Prime Minister, 1973-75; Chm., Liberal Party, 1964-78. Secretary: Christian Academic Soc., 1934-35; Christian Movement of Sen. Secondary Students, 1939-43. Dr *hc*, 1981. Grand-Croix: l'Ordre de la Couronne, Belgique; l'Ordre de Mennlik II, Ethiopie; Grosskreuz des Verdienstordens der Bundesrep, Deutschland; Royal Order of St Olav, Norway; Falcon of Iceland; Merit of Luxembourg; Yugoslovenske Zvezde. *Publications:* Sursum Corda; growth of church ideas in the missionary field, 1945; (ed) Church, School, Culture, 1963; The Danish Church, 1964 (2nd edn 1967); From 17 Years in Danish Politics, 1974; Autobiography vol. I, 1980, vol. II, 1981. *Recreation:* music. *Address:* Office of the United Nations High Commissioner for Refugees, Palais des Nations, 1211 Geneva 10, Switzerland. *T:* 31 02 61.

HARTMAN, (Gladys) Marea, CBE 1978 (MBE 1967); team manager, British Athletics team at Olympic and European Games, and English Athletics team at Commonwealth Games, since 1956; *b* 1920. Competed as a runner for Spartan Athletic Club and Surrey County. Chm., Women's Commn of Internat. Amateur Athletic Fedn, 1968-; Hon. Treasurer, British Amateur Athletic Bd, 1972-; Hon. Sec., Women's AAA, 1960- (Hon. Treasurer, 1950; Life Vice-Pres., 1980); Dep. Chm., CCPR, 1981-. *Recreations:* music, reading, theatre. *Address:* c/o Women's Amateur Athletic Association, Francis House, Francis Street, SW1P 1DE. *T:* 01-828 4731.

HARTNETT, Sir Laurence (John), Kt 1967; CBE 1945; BBM (Singapore) 1974; FRSA; MIE (Australia); Industrial Adviser to Singapore Government; industrial consultant, chairman and director of a number of companies; *b* Woking, Surrey, 26 May 1898; *s* of John Joseph Hartnett, MD and Katherine Jane Hartnett; *m* 1925, Gladys Winifred, *d* of Charles Walter Tyler, Bexleyheath, Kent; three *d. Educ:* Kingston Grammar Sch.; Epsom Coll., England. Cadet, Vickers Ltd, England. Served European War, 1914-18, as Flt Sub-Lieut, RNAS and Pilot, RAF; War of 1939-45: Dir of Ordnance Production, Min. of Munitions, and Chm. Army Inventions Bd, Australia. Started own engrg and motor business; Man. Motor Dept, Guthrie & Co. Ltd, Singapore; Zone Man., General Motors, USA; Vice-Pres., General Motors Export Co., NY; Sales Man., General Motors, Nordeska, Sweden; Dir, Vauxhall Motors Ltd, England; Man. Dir, General Motors Holdens, Australia, 1934-46; Regional Dir of the overseas operations; Chm., Ambulance Design Cttee, 1967. Mem. Exec. and Past Pres., Aust. Industries Develt Assoc.; Trustee, Inst. of Applied Sciences, Vic.; Mem. Govt Bd, Corps of Commissionaires. Hon. FAIM. *Publication:* Big Wheels and Little Wheels, 1964. *Recreations:* yachting, tennis. *Address:* Rubra, Mt Eliza, Vic. 3930, Australia. *T:* Melbourne 78-71271; Flat 4, 24 Hill Street, Toorak, Vic. 3142, Australia. *T:* Melbourne 245381. *Club:* Canadian Bay (Mt Eliza).

HARTOG, Harold Samuel Arnold; Knight, Order of the Netherlands Lion; KBE (Hon.) 1970; Advisory Director, Unilever NV, 1971-75; *b* Nijmegen, Holland, 21 Dec. 1910; *m* 1963, Ingeborg Luise Krahn. *Educ:* Wiedemann Coll., Geneva. Joined Unilever, 1931. After service with Dutch forces during War of 1939-45 he joined management of Unilever interests in France, and subseq. took charge of Unilever cos in the Netherlands; elected to Bds of Unilever, 1948; Mem. Rotterdam Group Management and responsible for Unilever activities in Germany, Austria and Belgium, 1952-60; subseq. Mem. Cttee for Unilever's overseas interests, in London; became, there, one of the two world co-ordinators of Unilever's foods interests, 1962; Chm., Unilever NV, 1966-71. *Recreations:* hisotry of art; collecting Chinese pottery and porcelain. *Address:* Kösterbergstrasse 40B, 2000 Hamburg (Blankensee), Germany. *Clubs:* Dutch; Ubersee (Hamburg); Golf (Falkenstein).

HARTOPP, Sir John Edmund Cradock-, 9th Bt, *cr* 1796; TD; *b* 8 April 1912; *s* of late Francis Gerald Cradock-Hartopp, Barbrook, Chatsworth, Bakewell, Derbyshire (kinsman of 8th Bt) and Elizabeth Ada Mary (*née* Stuart); *S* kinsman, Sir George Francis Fleetwood Cradock-Hartopp, 1949; *m* 1953, Prudence, 2nd *d* of Sir Frederick Leith-Ross, GCMG, KCB; three *d. Educ:* Summer Fields, Oxford; Uppingham Sch. Travelled in United States of America before joining at age of 18, Staff of Research Laboratories, Messrs Guss Firth & John Brown Ltd, Steel Makers, Sheffield, 1930; travelled in India

and the Far East, 1948-49; Dir, Firth Brown Tools Ltd, 1961-76. War of 1939-45 (despatches twice); joined TA and served with Royal Engineers in UK; Norway, 1940; North Africa (1st Army), 1943; Italy, 1943-45; released, 1945, with rank of Major. Mem. Council: Machine Tool Research Assoc., 1965-70; Machine Tool Trades Assoc., 1970-73. *Recreations:* golf (semi-finalist English Golf Champ., 1935; first reserve, Eng. *v* France, 1935); cricket, tennis, motoring. *Heir:* cousin Lt-Comdr Kenneth Alston Cradock-Hartopp, MBE, DSC, RN [*b* 26 Feb. 1918; *m* 1942, Gwendolyn Amy Lilian Upton; one *d*]. *Address:* The Cottage, 27 Wool Road, Wimbledon Common, SW20. *Clubs:* East India, MCC; Royal and Ancient (St Andrews).

HARTWELL, Baron, *cr* 1968 (Life Peer), of Peterborough Court in the City of London; **(William) Michael Berry,** MBE 1944; TD; Chairman and Editor-in-Chief of The Daily Telegraph and Sunday Telegraph; *b* 18 May 1911; 2nd *s* of 1st Viscount Camrose and Mary Agnes, *e d* of late Thomas Corns, London; *m* 1936, Lady Pamela Margaret Elizabeth Smith (*d* 1982), *yr d* of 1st Earl of Birkenhead, PC, GCSI, KC; two *s* two *d. Educ:* Eton; Christ Church, Oxford (MA). 2nd Lieut 11th (City of London Yeo.) Light AA Bde, RA (TA), 1938; served War of 1939-45; Capt. and Major, 1940; Lieut-Col 1944 (despatches twice, MBE). Editor, Sunday Mail, Glasgow, 1934-35; Managing Editor, Financial Times, 1937-39; Chm. Amalgamated Press Ltd, 1954-59. *Publication:* Party Choice, 1948. *Address:* 18 Cowley Street, Westminster, SW1. *T:* 01-222 4673; Oving House, Whitchurch, near Aylesbury, Bucks. *T:* Whitchurch 307. *Clubs:* White's, Beefsteak; Royal Yacht Squadron.
See also Viscount Camrose.

HARTWELL, Benjamin James, OBE 1959; Clerk to Southport Borough Justices, 1943-73; *b* Southport, 24 June 1908; *s* of late Joseph Hartwell, Bucks, and late Margaret Ann Hartwell; *m* 1937, Mary (*née* Binns), Southport; one *s* one *d. Educ:* Kirkcudbright Acad.; King George V Sch., Southport; London Univ. (LLM). Admitted a Solicitor of the Supreme Court, 1936; Hon. Sec. Justices' Clerks' Soc., 1947-59; Pres. Lancs and Cheshire Dist of Boys' Brigade, 1950-63; Chm. Council, Congregational Union of England and Wales, 1952-58; Chm. Congregational Union of England and Wales 1959-60. Member: Central Cttee, World Council of Churches, 1954-61; Home Secretary's Advisory Council on the Treatment of Offenders, 1955-63. *Address:* Mayfield, Longden Common Lane, Longden, near Shrewsbury SY5 8AQ. *T:* Dorrington 541.

HARTWELL, Sir Brodrick William Charles Elwin, 5th Bt, *cr* 1805; *b* 7 Aug. 1909; *s* of Sir Brodrick Cecil Denham Arkwright Hartwell, 4th Bt, and Joan Amy (*d* 1962), *o d* of Robert Milne Jeffrey, Esquimault, Vancouver; *S* father, 1948; *m* 1st, 1937, Marie Josephine, *d* of late S. P. Mullins (marriage dissolved 1950); one *s* ; 2nd, 1951, Mary Maude, MBE, *d* of J. W. Church, Bedford; one *d* decd. *Educ:* Bedford Sch. Sometime Pilot Officer RAF. Served War of 1939-45; Capt. Leics Regt, 1943. *Heir:* *s* Francis Antony Charles Peter Hartwell [*b* 1 June 1940; *m* 1968, Barbara Phyllis Rae, *d* of H. Rae Green; one *s*]. *Address:* Little Dale, 50 High Street, Lavendon, Olney, Bucks.

HARTWELL, Eric; Vice-Chairman since 1972 and Joint Chief Executive since 1982, Trusthouse Forte plc (Chief Executive, 1979-82); *b* 10 Aug. 1915; *m* 1st, 1937, Gladys Rose Bennett (marr. diss.); one *s* one *d* ; 2nd, 1952, Dorothy Maud Mowbray; one *s* one *d. Educ:* Mall Sch., Twickenham; Worthing High School. Fellow, Hotel Catering and Institutional Management Assoc. Electrical industry, 1932-37; Dir, Fortes & Co. Ltd, 1938; HM Forces, 1940-45; Jt Man. Dir, Forte Holdings Ltd, 1962; Dep. Man. Dir, Trust Houses Forte Ltd, 1970; Dep. Chief Exec., Trust Houses Forte Ltd, 1972-75, Jt Chief Exec., 1975-78. Chm., BHRCA, 1981-. Mem. Council, Thames Heritage Trust Ltd; Dir, LV Catering Educn Trust Ltd. *Recreations:* yachting, painting, photography. *Address:* Tall Trees, 129 Totteridge Lane, N20 8NS. *T:* 01-445 2321. *Clubs:* National Sporting, River Emergency Service Association, Inner Magic Circle; Thames Motor Yacht.

HARTY, Most Rev. Michael; *see* Killaloe, Bishop of, (RC).

HARUNA, Alhaji; *see* Gwandu, Emir of.

HARVATT, Thomas, CMG 1960; Secretary and Deputy Director, Council of Legal Education, 1934-68; *b* 5 Nov. 1901; *s* of Thomas Joseph Harvatt, Sheffield; *m* 1931, Nellie Adelaide, *d* of James Stephen Blythe, Sydenham; two *d. Educ:* King Edward VII Sch., Sheffield; University Coll., London; Inner Temple. Personal Asst to Dir of Educn, Sheffield, 1923-27; first Sec. for Educn, NALGO, 1927-34; Sec. to Council of Legal Education, 1934-68, and Dep. Dir of Inns of Court Sch. of Law, 1958-68; Mem. Cttee on Legal Education for Students from Africa, 1960. *Address:* 72 Old Lodge Lane, Purley, Surrey.

HARVEY, family name of **Barons Harvey of Prestbury** and **Harvey of Tasburgh.**

HARVEY OF PRESTBURY, Baron *cr* 1971 (Life Peer), of Prestbury in the County Palatine of Chester; **Arthur Vere Harvey,** Kt 1957; CBE 1942; FRAeS; *b* 31 Jan. 1906; *s* of A. W. Harvey, Kessingland, Suffolk; *m* 1st, 1940, Jacqueline Anne (marr. diss., 1954), *o d* of W. H. Dunnett; two *s* ; 2nd, 1955, Mrs Hilary Charmian Williams (marr. diss. 1977); 3rd, 1978, Mrs Carol Cassar Torreggiani. *Educ:* Framlingham Coll. Royal Air Force 1925-30, qualified as flying instructor; Dir of Far East Aviation Co. Ltd and Far East Flying Training Sch. Ltd, Hong-Kong, 1930-35; Adviser to Southern Chinese Air Forces with hon. rank of Maj.-Gen., 1932-35; Sqdn Leader AAF, 1937, and founded 615 County of Surrey Squadron and commanded the Squadron in France, 1939-40 (despatches twice); Group Captain 1942; Air Commodore 1944. MP (C) Macclesfield Div. of Cheshire, 1945-71; Chairman Cons. Members' 1922 Cttee, 1966-70. Dir, Tradewinds Airways Ltd. Vice-Pres. British Air Line Pilots' Assoc., 1965. FRAeS. Hon. Freeman: Macclesfield, 1969; Congleton, 1970. Hon. DSc Salford, 1972. Comdr, Order of Oranje Nassau, 1969. *Recreations:* private flying (4th King's Cup Race, 1937), sailing. *Address:* Cedars, Kappara Road, Malta. *Clubs:* Buck's, Royal Air Force; Royal Yacht Squadron (Cowes).

HARVEY OF TASBURGH, 2nd Baron, *cr* 1954, of Tasburgh, Norfolk; **Peter Charles Oliver Harvey;** Bt 1868; Chartered Accountant; Investment Consultant, Brown, Shipley & Co. Ltd, since 1978; *b* 28 Jan. 1921; *er s* of 1st Baron Harvey of Tasburgh, GCMG, GCVO, CB, and Maud Annora (*d* 1970), *d* of late Arthur Watkin Williams-Wynn; *S* father, 1968; *m* 1957, Penelope Anne, *d* of Lt-Col Sir William Makins, 3rd Bt; two *d. Educ:* Eton; Trinity College, Cambridge. Served 1941-46 with Royal Artillery, Tunisia, Italy. Bank of England, 1948-56; Binder Hamlyn & Co., 1956-61; Lloyds Bank International Ltd (formerly Bank of London and South America), 1961-75; English Transcontinental Ltd, 1975-78. *Recreations:* sailing, music. *Heir: b* Hon. John Wynn Harvey [*b* 4 Nov. 1923; *m* 1950, Elena Maria-Teresa, *d* of late Marchese Giambattista Curtopassi, Rome; two *s* one *d*]. *Address:* 36 Lennox Gardens, SW1; Crownick Woods, Restronguet, Mylor, Cornwall. *Clubs:* Brooks's; Royal Cornwall Yacht, Royal Fowey Yacht.

HARVEY, Alan Frederick Ronald, OBE 1970; HM Diplomatic Service, retired; *b* 15 Dec. 1919; *s* of Edward Frederick and Alice Sophia Harvey; *m* 1946, Joan Barbara (*née* Tuckey); one *s. Educ:* Tottenham Grammar Sch. Air Ministry, 1936-40 (Civil Service appt). Served War, RAF, 1940-46. Air Min., 1946-49; Foreign Office, 1949-52 (on transfer to Diplomatic Service); HM Vice-Consul, Turin, 1953-55; Second Sec.: Rome, 1956; Tokyo, 1957-59; HM Consul (Information): Chicago, 1959-62; FO, 1963-65; First Sec. (Commercial): Belgrade, 1965-67; Tokyo, 1967-72; Commercial Counsellor: Milan, 1973-74; Rome, 1975-76; Consul-General in Perth, 1976-78. *Recreations:* tennis, golf. *Address:* Pengelly Manor, Linkinhorne, Callington, Cornwall. *Club:* Royal Commonwealth Society, Civil Service.

HARVEY, Alexander, PhD, BSc, FInstP; Principal, University of Wales Institute of Science and Technology, 1946-68 (formerly Cardiff Technical College, later Welsh College of Advanced Technology); Pro-Vice-Chancellor, University of Wales, 1967-68; *b* 21 Sept. 1904; *s* of Andrew Harvey, Bangor, Co. Down; *m* 1933, Mona Anderson, Newcastle upon Tyne; one *s* two *d. Educ:* Gateshead Grammar Sch.; Armstrong (King's) Coll., Univ. of Durham. Commonwealth Fund Fellowship, Univ. of California, 1929-31; Scientific Asst, Adam Hilger Ltd, London, 1931-33; Asst Lecturer, Physics Dept, University of Manchester, 1933-34; Head of Physics Dept, Wigan and District Mining and Tech. Coll., 1934-42; Principal, Scunthorpe Tech. Sch., 1942-46. President: Assoc. of Principals of Technical Instns, 1957-58; South Wales Instn of Engineers, 1970-71; Chm. Council of Assoc. of Technical Instns, 1961-62. Hon. LLD Wales, 1970. *Publications:* Science for Miners, 1938; One Hundred Years of Technical Education, 1966; various papers on optical, spectroscopic and educational subjects. *Address:* 110 Pencisely Road, Llandaff, Cardiff. *T:* Cardiff 563795.

HARVEY, Rev. Canon Anthony Ernest; Canon Residentiary of Westminster Abbey, since 1982; *b* 1 May 1930; *s* of Cyril Harvey, QC, and Nina (*née* Darley); *m* 1957, Julian Elizabeth McMaster; four *d. Educ:* Dragon Sch., Oxford; Eton Coll.; Worcester Coll., Oxford (BA, MA); Westcott House, Cambridge. Curate, Christ Church, Chelsea, 1958; research student, Christ Church, Oxford, 1962; Warden, St Augustine's Coll., Canterbury, 1969; Univ. Lectr in Theology and Fellow of Wolfson Coll., Oxford, 1976; Chaplain, The Queen's Coll., 1977; Six Preacher, Canterbury Cathedral, 1977; Bampton Lectr, 1980. *Publications:* Companion to the New Testament (New English Bible), 1970, 2nd edn 1980; Priest or President?, 1975; Jesus on Trial, 1976; Something Overheard, 1977; Jesus and the Constraints of History, 1982; articles in classical and theological jls. *Recreations:* music, walking. *Address:* 3 Little Cloister, Westminster Abbey, SW1. *T:* 01-222 4174.

HARVEY, Arthur Douglas; Assistant Under-Secretary of State, Ministry of Defence, 1969-76; *b* 16 July 1916; *o s* of late William Arthur Harvey and Edith Alice; *m* 1940, Doris Irene Lodge; two *s. Educ:* Westcliff High Sch.; St Catharine's Coll., Cambridge. Wrangler, Maths Tripos, 1938. Entered War Office, 1938; served in Army, 1940-45; Princ. 1945; Registrar, Royal Military College of Science, 1951-54; Asst Sec. 1954; Under-Sec. 1969. *Address:* 36b Lovelace Road, Long Ditton, Surrey. *T:* 01-399 0587.

HARVEY, Barbara Fitzgerald, FSA 1964; FBA 1982; Fellow of Somerville College, Oxford, since 1956; Vice-Principal, 1981-83; *b* 21 Jan. 1928; *d* of Richard Henry Harvey and Anne Fitzgerald (*née* Julian). *Educ:* Teignmouth Grammar Sch.; Bishop Blackall Sch., Exeter; Somerville Coll., Oxford (Schol.). First Cl. Final Honour Sch. of Modern History, Oxford, 1949; Bryce Student, Oxford Univ., 1950-51; BLitt Oxon 1953. Assistant, Dept of Scottish History, Edinburgh Univ., 1951-52; Asst Lectr, subseq. Lectr, Queen Mary Coll., London Univ., 1952-55; Tutor, Somerville Coll., Oxford, 1955-; Vice-Principal, 1976-79. Assessor, Oxford Univ., 1968-69. *Publications:*

Documents Illustrating the Rule of Walter de Wenlok, Abbot of Westminster 1283-1307, 1965; Westminster Abbey and its Estates in the Middle Ages, 1977; (ed, with L. C. Hector) The Westminster Chronicle 1381-94, 1982; contribs to Economic History Rev., Trans Royal Historical Soc., Bulletin of Inst. of Historical Research, etc. *Address:* Somerville College, Oxford OX2 6HD. *T:* Oxford 57595.

HARVEY, Benjamin Hyde, OBE 1968; FCA; IPFA; DPA; General Manager, Harlow Development Corporation, 1955-73; *b* 29 Sept. 1908; *s* of Benjamin Harvey and Elizabeth (*née* Hyde); *m* 1938, Heather Frances Broome; one *d. Educ:* Stationers' Company's Sch. Local Govt, 1924-40; Treas., Borough of Leyton, 1940-47; Comptroller, Harlow Develt Corp., 1947-55. *Publication:* (jtly) Harlow: the story of a new town, 1980. *Recreations:* books, sport. *Address:* 188 Hugh's Tower, Harlow, Essex. *T:* Harlow 24031; Brick House, Broxted, Essex. *T:* Henham 233. *Club:* Royal Automobile.

HARVEY, Prof. Brian Wilberforce; Professor of Property Law, University of Birmingham, since 1973; Dean, Faculty of Law, since 1982; *b* 17 March 1936; *s* of Gerald and Noelle Harvey; *m* 1962, Rosemary Jane Brown; two *s* two *d. Educ:* Clifton Coll., Bristol; St John's Coll., Cambridge (Choral Schol., MA, LLM). Solicitor, 1961. Lectr, Birmingham Univ., 1962-63; Sen. Lectr, Nigerian Law Sch., 1965-67; Lectr, Sen. Lectr and Prof. of Law, QUB, 1967-73; Dir, Legal Studies, Univ. of Birmingham, 1973-76. Member: Statute Law Cttee (NI), 1972-73; Cttee on Legal Educn (NI), 1972-73; Jt Dir, Birmingham Vocational Trng (Law) Courses, 1973-; Adviser, Council of Legal Educn, NI, 1976-79. Fellow, St Michael's Coll., Tenbury, 1975-. *Publications:* Law of Probate Wills and Succession in Nigeria, 1968; (jtly) Survey of Northern Ireland Land Law, 1970; Settlements of Land, 1973; (ed) Vocational Legal Training in UK and Commonwealth, 1975; (ed) The Lawyer and Justice, 1978; The Law of Consumer Protection and Fair Trading, 1978, 2nd edn 1982; various articles. *Recreations:* performing and listening to music. *Address:* Mount Vernon, 5 Rainbow Hill Terrace, Worcester WR3 8NG. *T:* Worcester 22836.

HARVEY, Bryan Hugh, CBE 1978; Chairman, Advisory Committee on Major Hazards, since 1975; Adviser to Employment Committee, House of Commons, since 1980; *b* 17 Oct. 1914; *y s* of late Oliver Harvey and Ellen Harvey (*née* Munn); *m* 1941, Margaret, 2nd *d* of late E. G. Palmer; one *d. Educ:* KES Birmingham; Bristol Grammar Sch.; Corpus Christi Coll., Oxford; Harvard Univ. BA 1936; MA 1945; MSc 1953 (Industrial Hygiene). RAF, 1943-45. Printing industry until 1938, when joined Inspectorate of Factories; Dep. Chief Inspector, 1965; Chief Inspector, 1971-74. Dep. Dir Gen. (Dep. Sec.), Health and Safety Exec., 1975-76. Rockefeller Foundn Fellow, 1952-53; Hon. Lectr, Dept of Occupational Health, Univ. of Manchester, 1954-59; Vis. Prof., Univ. of Aston in Birmingham, 1972-79. Pres. British Occupational Hygiene Soc., 1976-77; FSA 1964; Hon. Fellow, Instn of Occupational Safety and Health. *Publications:* (with R. Murray) Industrial Health Technology, 1958; (ed) Handbook of Occupational Hygiene, 1980; many articles in jls on industrial safety and hygiene, and industrial archaeology. *Recreations:* industrial archaeology, Georgian architecture, steam engines. *Address:* 2 Surley Row, Caversham, Reading, Berks RG4 8LY. *T:* Reading 479453. *Club:* Army and Navy.

HARVEY, Charles Richard Musgrave; (3rd Bt *cr* 1933, but does not use the title); *b* 7 April 1937; *s* of Sir Richard Musgrave Harvey, 2nd Bt, and of Frances Estelle, *er d* of late Lindsay Crompton Lawford, Montreal; *S* father, 1978; *m* 1967, Celia Vivien, *d* of George Henry Hodson; one *s* one *d. Educ:* Marlborough; Pembroke Coll., Cambridge (BA 1960, MA 1964). Fellow, Institute of Development Studies, Sussex. *Heir: s* Paul Richard Harvey, *b* 1971.

HARVEY, Colin Stanley, MBE 1964; TD 1962; DL; a Recorder of the Crown Court, Western Circuit, since 1975; a Solicitor of the Supreme Court; *b* 22 Oct 1924; *s* of Harold Stanley and Lilian May Harvey; *m* 1949, Marion Elizabeth (*née* Walker); one *s* one *d. Educ:* Bristol Grammar Sch.; University Coll., Oxford (BA). Served 1939-45 war in Queen's Regt and RA, India, Burma, Malaya, Java. In private practice as a solicitor. Bt Lt-Col TAVR, 1973. DL Avon, 1977. *Recreations:* TAVR, riding, beagling. *Address:* 12 Southfield Road, Westbury-on-Trym, Bristol BS9 3BH. *T:* Bristol 620404. *Clubs:* Royal Commonwealth Society, Royal Western Yacht (Plymouth).

HARVEY, Ven. Francis William; Archdeacon of London and Canon Residentiary of St Paul's Cathedral, since 1978; *b* 28 Sept. 1930; *s* of Frank and Clara Harvey; *m* 1955, Mavis Wheeler; one *s* three *d. Educ:* Chester College; Lichfield Theological Coll. Mil. service, RAOC, 1948-50. Teaching service, 1952-60; Curate, St Ann, Rainhill, Liverpool, 1962-65; Vicar, St Mark, Edge Lane, Liverpool, 1965-68; Liverpool Diocesan Planning Adviser, 1967-71; Area Sec., London Diocesan Fund, 1971-75; Pastoral Sec., Diocese of London, 1975-78; Prebendary of St Paul's Cathedral, 1975-78. Examining Chaplain to Bishop of London, 1981-. Mem., Gen. Synod Commn on Faculty Jurisdiction, 1980. MA Lambeth, 1982. *Recreations:* music, reading. *Address:* 2 Amen Court, EC4M 7BU. *T:* 01-248 3312.

HARVEY, Ian Douglas, TD 1950; psc 1944; author; public relations consultant; free-lance journalist; Associate, Douglas Stephens Associates Ltd, Management Consultants, 1970-80; *b* 25 Jan. 1914; *s* of late Major Douglas Harvey, DSO, and of late Mrs Bertram Bisgood (*née* Dorothy Cundall); *m* 1949, Clare (legally separated), *y d* of late Sir Basil E. Mayhew, KBE; two *d. Educ:* Fettes Coll.; Christ Church, Oxford. BA, 1937; MA, 1941. President: Oxford Univ. Cons. Assoc., 1935; Oxford Carlton Club, 1936; Oxford Union Soc., 1936. Served War of 1939-45, Adjutant, 123 LAA Regt, RA, 1940; Bde Major, 38 AA Bde, RA, 1943; GSO2 (ops), HQ AA command, 1944; Staff Coll. Camberley, 1944; Bde Major 100 AA Bde, NW Europe, 1945; Lieut-Col Comdg 566 LAA Regt, RA (City of London Rifles) TA, 1947-50. Contested Spelthorne Div. of Mddx, 1945; MP (C) Harrow East, 1950-58; Sec., 1922 Cttee, 1955-57; Parly Sec., Min. of Supply, 1956-57; Jt Parly Under-Sec. of State, FO, 1957-58. Mem. of Council, Royal Borough of Kensington, 1947-52; Mem. of LCC for S Kensington, 1949-52; Rep. of LCC on County of London TA Assoc. 1949-52; Deleg. Advertising Assoc. to Advertising Fedn of America Convention (Detroit), 1950; Chm. Press Relations Cttee of Internat. Advertising Conference (Great Britain), 1951; Member: Advertising Assoc.; Inst. of Public Relations; Parly Select Cttee for reform of the Army and Air Force Acts, 1952-54; Adv. Cttee on Publicity and Recruitment for Civil Defence, 1952-56; London Soc. of Rugby Union Football Referees; Rep. of Church Assembly on Standing Cttee of Nat. Soc., 1951-55; Vice-Pres., Campaign for Homosexual Equality, 1972-; Pres., Cons. Gp for Homosexual Equality, 1980-. Director: W. S. Crawford Ltd, 1949-56; Colman, Prentis and Varley Ltd, 1962-63; Advertising Controller, Yardley of London Ltd, 1963-64 (Advertising Dir., 1964-66). Chairman: Coningsby Club, 1946-47; London Old Fettesian Assoc., 1953-54; Paddington Cons. Assoc., 1980-; Dep. Chm., Westminster Play Assoc., 1980-; Secretary: Iain Macleod Meml Trust, 1974-; Selwyn-Lloyd Meml Library Appeal, 1980-81; Subscriptions Manager, Middle East International, 1978-80. Governor, St George's Sch. (RC), Maida Vale, 1977-; Birkbeck Coll., 1949-52; Paddington Coll., 1979-. *Publications:* Talk of Propaganda, 1947; The Technique of Persuasion, 1951; Arms and To-morrow, 1954; To Fall Like Lucifer, 1971. *Recreations:* squash, cycling, swimming, tennis. *Address:* 62D St Michael's Street, W2 1QR.

HARVEY, John Edgar; consultant in energy policy and public affairs; Director, Burmah Oil Trading Ltd and subsidiary companies in Burmah Oil Group, 1974-80; *b* Londonderry, 24 April 1920; *s* of John Watt Harvey and Charlotte Elizabeth Harvey; *m* 1945, Mary Joyce Lane, BA, JP; one *s. Educ:* Xaverian Coll., Bruges, Belgium; Lyme Regis Grammar Sch. Radio Officer, in the Merchant Navy, 1939-45. Contested (C): St Pancras North, 1950; Walthamstow East, 1951; Mem. Nat. Exec. Cttee., Conservative Party, 1950-55; Chm., Woodford Conservative Assoc., 1954-56. MP (C) Walthamstow East, 1955-66. Mem., NSPCC Central Executive Cttee, 1963-68. Governor, Forest Sch., 1966-78. Verderer of Epping Forest, 1970-. Mem., Guild of Freemen of City of London, 1977- (Master, 1981-82). *Recreations:* various in moderation. *Address:* 43 Traps Hill, Loughton, Essex. *T:* 01-508 8753. *Clubs:* Carlton, City of London, City Livery.

HARVEY, Prof. Jonathan Dean; composer; Professor of Music, University of Sussex, since 1980; *b* 3 May 1939; *s* of Gerald and Noelle Harvey; *m* 1960, Rosaleen Marie Barry; one *s* one *d. Educ:* St Michael's Coll., Tenbury; Repton; St John's Coll., Cambridge (MA, DMus); Glasgow Univ. (PhD). Lectr, Southampton Univ., 1964-77; Reader, Sussex Univ., 1977-80. Harkness Fellow, Princeton Univ., 1969-70. Works performed at many festivals and international centres. *Publications:* The Music of Stockhausen, 1975; compositions: Persephone Dream, for orch., 1972; Inner Light (trilogy), for performers and tape, 1973-77; Quartet, 1977; Hymn, for choir and orch., 1979; Passion and Resurrection, church opera, 1980; Mortuos Plango, Vivos Voco, for tape, 1980; 'Whom ye adore ...', for orch., 1981. *Recreations:* tennis, squash, walking. *Address:* 35 Houndean Rise, Lewes, Sussex BN7 1EQ. *T:* Lewes 71241.
    See also B. W. Harvey.

HARVEY, Prof. Leonard Patrick; Cervantes Professor of Spanish, King's College, University of London, since 1973; *b* 25 Feb. 1929; *s* of Francis Thomas Harvey and Eva Harvey; *m* 1954, June Rawcliffe; two *s. Educ:* Alleyn's Sch., Dulwich; Magdalen Coll., Oxford. 1st cl. hons BA Mod. Langs 1952; 2nd cl. Oriental Studies 1954; MA 1956; DPhil 1958. Lectr in Spanish, Univ. of Oxford, 1957-58; Univ. of Southampton, 1958-60; Queen Mary Coll., Univ. of London: Lectr, 1960-63; Reader and Head of Dept, 1963; Prof. of Spanish, 1967-73; Dean of Faculty of Arts, 1970-73; Dean of Faculty of Arts, KCL, 1979-81. Vis. Prof., Univ. of Victoria, BC, 1966. Mem. UGC, 1979-. *Publications:* articles in Al-Andalus, Bulletin of Hispanic Studies, Jl of Semitic Studies, Modern Philology, Revista de Filología Española, etc. *Address:* Tree Tops, Yester Park, Chislehurst, BR7 5DQ. *T:* 01-467 3565.

HARVEY, Prof. Leslie Arthur; Professor, 1946-69, and Head of Department of Zoology, University of Exeter, 1930-69; *b* 23 Dec. 1903; *s* of Arthur Harvey; *m* 1925, Christina Clare Brockway; one *s* one *d. Educ:* Bancroft's Sch.; Imperial Coll., London. ARCS 1923; BSc 1923; Beit Mem. Research Student, Imperial Coll., 1923-25; MSc 1925. Asst Lecturer, subsequently Lecturer in Zoology, University of Edinburgh, 1925-30. *Publications:* (with D. St Leger Gordon) Dartmoor, 1952; contributions to various learned journals, 1925-. *Recreations:* gardening, bridge. *Address:* Benhams, The Garrison, St Mary's, Isles of Scilly. *T:* Scillonia 22686.

HARVEY, Mary Frances Clare, MA; Headmistress, St Mary's Hall, Brighton, since 1981; *b* 24 Aug. 1927; *d* of Rev. Oliver Douglas Harvey, Highfield, Southampton. *Educ:* St Mary's Sch., Colchester; St Hugh's Coll., Oxford. BA Oxon, Final Honour Sch. of Mod. Hist., 1950; Diploma in Educn, 1951; MA 1954. History Mistress, St Albans High Sch., 1951; Head of History Dept,

Portsmouth High Sch., GPDST, 1956; Headmistress: Sch. of St Clare, Penzance, 1962-69; Badminton Sch., Westbury on Trym, Bristol, 1969-81. Governor, Bristol Cathedral Sch., 1978-81. *Recreations:* music, travel, reading, needlework. *Address:* 233 Eastern Road, Brighton BN2 5JF. *T:* Brighton 683028.

HARVEY, Michael Llewellyn Tucker, QC 1982; *b* 22 May 1943; *s* of Rev. Victor Llewellyn Tucker Harvey and Pauline Harvey (*née* Wybrow); *m* 1972, Denise Madeleine Neary; one *s* one *d. Educ:* St John's Sch., Leatherhead; Christ's Coll., Cambridge (BA Hons Law, LLB, MA). Called to the Bar, Gray's Inn, 1966 (Uthwatt Schol. 1965, James Mould Schol. 1966). *Publication:* joint contributor of title 'Damages' in Halsbury's Laws of England. *Recreations:* shooting, golf. *Address:* 2 Crown Office Row, Temple, EC4Y 7HJ. *T:* 01-353 9337. *Clubs:* United Oxford & Cambridge University; Hawks (Cambridge).

HARVEY, Peter, CB 1980; Legal Adviser, Department of Education and Science, since 1977; *b* 23 April 1922; *o s* of Rev. George Leonard Hunton Harvey and Helen Mary (*née* Williams); *m* 1950, Mary Vivienne, *d* of John Osborne Goss and Elsie Lilian (*née* Bishop); one *s* one *d. Educ:* King Edward VI High Sch., Birmingham; St John's Coll., Oxford (MA, BCL). RAF, 1942-45. Called to the Bar, Lincoln's Inn, 1948. Entered the Home Office as a Legal Assistant, 1948; Principal Asst Legal Advr, 1971-77. *Publications:* contributor to Halsbury's Laws of England (3rd and 4th edns). *Recreations:* history, and walking. *Address:* Mannamead, Old Avenue, Weybridge, Surrey KT13 0PS. *T:* Weybridge 45133.

HARVEY, Rt. Rev. Philip James Benedict, OBE 1973; Auxiliary Bishop of Westminster (Bishop in North London) (RC), since 1977; Titular Bishop of Bahanna; *b* 6 March 1915; *s* of William Nathaniel and Elizabeth Harvey. *Educ:* Cardinal Vaughan Sch., Kensington; St Edmund's Coll., Ware, Herts. Ordained Priest, Westminster, 1939; Assistant Priest: Cricklewood, 1929-45; Kentish Town, 1945-46; Fulham, 1946-53; Asst Administrator, Crusade of Rescue, 1953-63, Administrator 1963-77. *Address:* 73 St Charles Square, W10 6EJ. *T:* 01-960 4029.

HARVEY, Rachel; see Bloom, Ursula.

HARVEY, Richard Jon Stanley, QC 1970; a Recorder of the Crown Court, since 1972; *b* 30 Aug. 1917; *s* of Nehemiah Stanley Harvey, Home Civil Servant, and Alicia Margaret Harvey; *m* 1942, Yvonne Esther, *e d* of A. J. d'Abreu, FRCS, Waterford, Eire; no *c. Educ:* Newtown Sch., Waterford; Mountjoy Sch., Dublin; Trinity Coll., Dublin. 1st cl. sizarship in Irish, 1936; First Scholar of the House, History and Political Science, 1938; 1st cl. Moderatorship History and Political Science, 1940; Pres., Univ. Philosophical Soc., 1940-41; Founder Mem., Students Representative Council, 1941; LLB 1941. Royal Artillery, 1942-45; SUO Tonfanau RA OCTU, 1943; 2nd Lieut RA 1943, subseq. W/Subst. Lieut. Called to the Bar, Gray's Inn, 1947, Holker Scholar, 1947-48, Master of the Bench, 1980. Contested (C): Woolwich East, 1951 and 1952; Romford, 1955 and 1959. Gresham Prof. of Law, 1961-64. Received into Catholic Church, 1952. *Publications:* Harvey on Industrial Relations, 1971; contribs to learned jls; novels and other works written pseudonymously. *Recreations:* music, reading, gardening, swimming, walking, writing novels pseudonymously; formerly cricket and athletics (occasional mem. TCD 1st Cricket XI and Athletics 1st team, 1936-39). *Address:* 3 Raymond Buildings, Gray's Inn, WC1. *T:* 01-405 9420; Francis Taylor Building, Temple, EC4. *T:* 01-353 2182; The Barge, Great Walsingham, Norfolk. *T:* Walsingham 330. *Clubs:* Carlton, Sportsman, Les Ambassadeurs, Newman Association, Catenian Association; Royal West Norfolk Golf.

HARVEY, Major Thomas Cockayne, CVO 1951; DSO 1945; Extra Gentleman Usher to the Queen, since 1952 (to King George VI, 1951-52); *b* 22 Aug. 1918; *s* of late Col John Harvey, DSO; *m* 1940, Lady Katharine Mary Coke, (Woman of the Bedchamber to Queen Elizabeth the Queen Mother, 1961-63), *yr d* of 3rd Earl of Leicester; one *s* two *d. Educ:* Radley; Balliol Coll., Oxford. Joined Scots Guards SRO, 1938. Served Norway, 1940, Italy, 1944; Private Sec. to the Queen, 1946-51. *Recreations:* golf, shooting. *Address:* 2 Catherine Wheel Yard, Little St James's Street, SW1. *T:* 01-499 6692; Warham House, Warham, Wells, Norfolk. *T:* Fakenham 710457. *Clubs:* White's, Beefsteak.

HARVEY-JAMIESON, Lt-Col Harvey Morro, OBE 1969; TD; DL; WS; Member, Queen's Body Guard for Scotland (Royal Company of Archers), since 1934; *b* 9 Dec. 1908; *s* of late Major A. H. Morro Jamieson, OBE, RGA, Advocate, Edinburgh, and Isobel, *d* of late Maj.-Gen. Sir Robert Murdoch Smith, KCMG; *m* 1936, Frances, *o c* of late Col. J. Y. H. Ridout, DSO; three *s* ; assumed additional surname of Harvey, with authority of Lord Lyon King of Arms, 1958. *Educ:* Edinburgh Acad.; RMC Sandhurst (Prize Cadetship); Edinburgh Univ. (BL). Commissioned 1st Bn KOSB, 1928; Capt. RARO 1938; Major, 1939, to raise 291 HAA Battery RA (TA). Served War of 1939-45, Belgium, Holland and Germany, RA and Staff, Lieut-Col, 1942; Comd 3rd Edinburgh HG Bn, 1954-57. France and Germany Star, General Service and Home Defence Medals; Jubilee Medals 1935 and 1977; Coronation Medals, 1937 and 1953. Secretary and Legal Adviser, Co. of Merchants of City of Edinburgh, 1946-71; former Mem., Cttee on Conveyancing Legislation and Practice (apptd by Sec. of State for Scotland, 1964). Mem. Council. Cockburn Assoc. (Edinburgh Civic Trust), 1958-78; Hon. Manager, Edinburgh and

Borders Trustee Savings Bank, 1957-78. Chairman, Scottish Committee: HMC, Assocs of Governing Bodies of Boys' and Girls' Public Schs, 1966-71. DL, County of the City of Edinburgh, 1968. *Publications:* The Historic Month of June, 1953; contrib. to Juridical Review, Scots Law Times and Yachting Monthly. *Address:* Walhampton Cottage, Walhampton, Lymington, Hants SO4 8SA. *T:* Lymington 74589. *Clubs:* Royal Forth Yacht (Granton); Royal Lymington Yacht; Army Sailing Association.

HARVEY-JONES, John Henry, MBE 1952; Chairman, Imperial Chemical Industries Ltd, since 1982; *b* 16 April 1924; *s* of Mervyn Harvey-Jones, OBE, and Eileen Harvey-Jones; *m* 1947, Mary Evelyn, *er d* of F. F. Bignell; one *d. Educ:* Tormore Sch., Deal, Kent; RNC, Dartmouth, Devon. RN, 1937-56: specialised in submarines; qual. as Russian interpreter, 1946, and subseq. as German interpreter; appts in Naval Intell. (MBE); resigned, 1956, Lt-Comdr. Joined ICI as Work Study Officer, Wilton, 1956; commercial appts at Wilton and Heavy Organic Chemicals Div. until apptd Techno-Commercial Dir, 1967; Dep. Chm., HOC Div., 1968; Chm., ICI Petrochemicals Div., 1970-73; Main Bd, ICI, 1973, Dep. Chm., 1978-82. Chm., Phillips-Imperial Petroleum, 1973-75; Non-Exec. Director: Carrington Viyella Ltd, 1974-79 and 1981-82; Reed International Ltd, 1975-; Mem. Bd, Fiber Industries Inc., 1975-78. Member: Tees & Hartlepool Port Authority, 1968-73; NE Develt Bd, 1971-73. *Recreations:* ocean sailing, swimming, countryside, cooking, contemporary literature. *Address:* Imperial Chemical House, Millbank, SW1P 3JF. *T:* 01-834 4444.

HARVIE-CLARK, Ven. Sidney, MA; Archdeacon of Stow, 1967-75 and Vicar of Hackthorn and Rector of Cold Hanworth, 1967-75; *b* 26 July 1905; *s* of John Harvie Clark and Minnie Young Hunter, Glasgow and Chiswick, London; *m* 1936, Sheilah Marjorie, *d* of late Dr G. C. L. Lunt, Bishop of Salisbury; one *s* one *d* (one *d* decd). *Educ:* St Paul's Sch., London; Jesus Coll. and Westcott House, Cambridge. Deacon, 1930; Priest, 1931; Curate, St Mary's, Gateshead, Co. Durham, 1930-34; St Mary's, Portsea, 1934-36; Rector, Jarrow-on-Tyne, 1936-40; St John's, Edinburgh, 1940-47; Rector of Wishaw, 1947-48; Archdeacon of Birmingham, 1947-67; Vicar of Harborne, 1948-67. *Recreations:* walking, camping. *Address:* Stow House, Skillington, Grantham, Lincs NG33 5HQ. *T:* Grantham 860447.

HARVIE-WATT, Sir George Steven, 1st Bt, *cr* 1945, of Bathgate; QC 1945; TD 1942 (with three Bars); *b* 23 Aug. 1903; *s* of late James McDougal Watt of Armadale; *m* 1932, Bettie, *o d* of late Paymaster-Capt. Archibald Taylor, OBE, RN; two *s* one *d. Educ:* George Watson's Coll., Edinburgh; Glasgow Univ.; Edinburgh Univ. Called to Bar, Inner Temple, 1930; practised in London and on North Eastern Circuit. Commissioned RE TA 1924, 52nd (Lowland) Scottish Div., 1924-29; 56th (1st London) Div., 1929-38; Bt Major, 1935; Lt-Col Commanding 31st Bn RE TA, 1938-41; promoted Brig. to command 6th AA Bde, 1941; Brig. Commanding 63rd AA Bde TA, 1948-50; Hon. Col 566 LAA Regt, 1949-62. ADC to King George VI, 1948-52; ADC to the Queen, 1952-58; MP (U) Keighley Div. of Yorks, 1931-35; (U) Richmond, Surrey, Feb. 1937-Sept. 1959; PPS to late Rt Hon. Euan Wallace when Parly Sec. to Board of Trade, 1937-38; Asst Government Whip, 1938-40; PPS to Rt Hon. Winston S. Churchill when Prime Minister, July 1941-July 1945; Hon. Treas. UK Branch of Commonwealth Parly Assoc., 1945-51; Mem. UK Deleg. to CPA Confs, Ottawa and Washington, 1949, Australia and New Zealand, 1950; Mem. of Borough Council, Royal Borough of Kensington, 1934-45. Formerly Mem. of City of London TA Association; TA Rep. Council of RUSI, 1948-57; DL: Surrey, 1942; Greater London, 1966-78; JP County of London, 1944-56. President: Consolidated Gold Fields Ltd, 1973-81 (Chief Executive, 1954-69, Dep. Chm., 1954-60, Chm., 1960-69); Printers' Pension Corp., 1956-57; formerly: Chm., Monotype Corp. Ltd; Director: Eagle Star Insce Co.; Standard Bank Ltd; Midland Bank Ltd; Clydesdale Bank Ltd; Great Western Rly Co.; North British Steel Gp. Member of Queen's Body Guard for Scotland, Royal Company of Archers; Hon. Freeman, City of London, 1976. FRSA 1973. Gold Medal, Inst. Mining and Metallurgy (for distinguished service to world-wide mining), 1969. *Publication:* Most of My Life, 1980. *Heir: s* James Harvie-Watt [*b* 25 Aug. 1940; *m* 1966, Roseline, *d* of late Baron Louis de Chollet; one *s* one *d*]. *Recreation:* Territorial Army. *Address:* Sea Tangle, Earlsferry, Leven, Fife KY9 1AD. *T:* Elie 330506. *Club:* Caledonian (Chm. 1953-61, Vice-Pres. 1961-).

HARVINGTON, Baron *cr* 1974 (Life Peer), of Nantwich; **Robert Grant Grant-Ferris,** PC 1971; Kt 1969; AE; *b* 30 Dec. 1907; *s* of late Robert Francis Ferris, MB, ChB; *m* 1930, Florence, *d* of Major W. Brennan De Vine, MC; one *s* one *d. Educ:* Douai Sch. Called to Bar, Inner Temple, 1937; joined RAuxAF, 1933, 605 (County of Warwick) Fighter Sqdn; Flight Comdr 1939-40; Wing Comdr, 1941; Air Efficiency Award, 1942. MP (C) North St Pancras, 1937-45; MP (C) Nantwich, Cheshire, 1955-Feb. 1974; PPS to Minister of Town and Country Planning (Rt Hon. W. S. Morrison, KC, MP), 1944-45; Temp. Chm. House of Commons and Chairman of Cttees, 1962-70; Chm. of Ways and Means and the Dep. Speaker, House of Commons, 1970-74. Contested Wigan, 1935, North St Pancras, 1945, Central Wandsworth, 1950, 1951. Chm., Bd of Management, Hosp. of St John and St Elizabeth, 1963-70. Pres. Southdown Sheep Soc. of England, 1950-52, 1959-60, 1973; Pres. Nat. Sheep Breeders' Assoc., 1956-58; a Vice-Pres. Smithfield Club, 1964, Pres. 1970. Mem. Council, Imperial Soc. of Knights Bachelor, 1973-. Knight Grand Cross of Magistral Grace, the Sovereign and Military Order of Malta; holds Grand Cross of Merit with Star of same Order; Comdr, Order of Leopold II (Belgium), 1964. *Recreations:* hunting, golf,

yachting (sometime Hon. Admiral, House of Commons Yacht Club). *Address:* La Vielle Maison, The Bulwarks, St Aubin, Jersey, Channel Islands. *Clubs:* Carlton, MCC; Royal and Ancient Golf; Royal Thames Yacht, Royal Yacht Squadron.

HARWOOD, Basil Antony, MA; QC 1971; Barrister-at-Law; a Master of the Supreme Court (Queen's Bench Division), 1950-70; Senior Master and Queen's Remembrancer, 1966-70; 2nd *s* of late Basil Harwood, DMus, Woodhouse, Olveston, Glos; *m* 1929, Enid Arundel, *d* of late Philip Grove, Quorn House, Leamington; two *s. Educ:* Charterhouse; Christ Church, Oxford (MA). Called to the Bar, Inner Temple, 1927. Served War of 1939-45 in Italy. Prosecuting Counsel to Post Office, Western Circuit, 1948-50. Pres. Medico-Legal Soc., 1967-69. *Publication:* Circuit Ghosts, 1980. *Address:* 1 The Mount, Whitchurch, Hants RG28 7AT.

HARWOOD, Elizabeth Jean, (Mrs J. A. C. Royle); international opera singer; *b* 27 May 1938; *d* of Sydney and Constance Harwood; *m* 1966, Julian Adam Christopher Royle; one *s. Educ:* Skipton Girls' High Sch.; Royal Manchester Coll. of Music. FRMCM, GRSM, LRAM. Kathleen Ferrier Memorial Schol., 1960; jt winner, Verdi Competition (Busetto), 1965. Principal operatic roles at Glyndebourne, Sadler's Wells, Covent Garden, Scottish Opera, principal opera houses in Europe incl. Salzburg, Paris and La Scala; toured Australia, 1965, with Sutherland-Williamson Internat. Opera Co. singing principal roles in Lucia de Lammermoor, La Sonnambula and L'Elisir d'Amore; début at NY Metropolitan Opera in Cosi Fan Tutte, 1975; Don Giovanni, 1978; Rosenkavalier, Glyndebourne, 1980; took part in exchange visit to La Scala with Covent Garden Opera, 1976. Has made numerous recordings of oratorio and opera. *Recreations:* swimming, horse riding. *Address:* Masonetts, Fryerning, Ingatestone, Essex. *T:* Ingatestone 3024. *Club:* Oriental.

HARWOOD, Ronald, FRSL; writer since 1960; *b* 9 Nov. 1934; *s* of Isaac Horwitz and Isobel Pepper; *m* 1959, Natasha Riehle; one *s* two *d. Educ:* Sea Point Boys' High Sch., Cape Town; RADA. FRSL 1974. Actor, 1953-60. Artistic Dir, Cheltenham Festival of Literature, 1975; Presenter: Kaleidoscope, BBC, 1973; Read All About It, BBC TV, 1978-79. Chm., Writers Guild of GB, 1969; Mem., Lit. Panel, Arts Council of GB, 1973-78. TV plays incl.: The Barber of Stamford Hill, 1960; (with Casper Wrede) Private Potter, 1961; The Guests, 1972; adapted several of Roald Dahl's Tales of the Unexpected for TV, 1979-80; screenplays incl.: A High Wind in Jamaica, 1965; One Day in the Life of Ivan Denisovich, 1971; Evita Perón, 1981. *Publications: novels:* All the Same Shadows, 1961; The Guilt Merchants, 1963; The Girl in Melanie Klein, 1969; Articles of Faith, 1973; The Genoa Ferry, 1976; Cesar and Augusta, 1978; *short stories:* One. Interior. Day.—adventures in the film trade, 1978; (co-ed) New Stories 3, 1978; *biography:* Sir Donald Wolfit, CBE—his life and work in the unfashionable theatre, 1971; *plays:* Country Matters, 1969; The Ordeal of Gilbert Pinfold (from Evelyn Waugh), 1977; A Family, 1978; The Dresser, 1980 (New Standard Drama Award; Drama Critics Award); *musical libretto:* The Good Companions, 1974. *Recreations:* tennis, cricket. *Address:* c/o Judy Daish Associates, 122 Wigmore Street, W1. *T:* 01-486 5404. *Clubs:* Garrick, MCC.

HASELDEN, Edward Christopher, CMG 1952; *b* 14 Aug. 1903; *s* of E. N. Haselden, Minieh, Upper Egypt; *m* 1929, Lily Jewett Foote; two *d. Educ:* Cheltenham Coll.; Pembroke Coll., Cambridge. Joined Sudan Political Service, 1925; Sudan Agent in Cairo, 1945-53; retired, 1953. Chm. of Anglo-Egyptian Aid Soc. Cttee, 1960. Order of the Nile (4th Class), 1936. *Address:* 14 Gilston Road, SW10. *Club:* Athenæum.

HASELDEN, Prof. Geoffrey Gordon; Brotherton Professor of Chemical Engineering, University of Leeds, since 1960; *b* 4 Aug. 1924; *s* of George A. Haselden and Rose E. (*née* Pleasants); *m* 1945, Eileen Doris Francis; three *d. Educ:* Sir Walter St John's Sch.; Imperial Coll. of Science and Technology. BScChemEng London 1944; ACGI; PhD (Eng) Chem Eng London, 1947; DScEng London, 1962; DIC; CEng; FIMechE; FIChemE; MInstR. Mem. Gas Research Bd, 1946-48; Lectr in Low Temperature Technology, Chemical Engrg Dept, 1948-57, Senior Lectr in Chemical Engrg, 1957-60, Imperial Coll. Chm., British Cryogenics Council, 1967-71. President: Commn A3, Internat. Inst. of Refrigeration, 1971-79; Inst. of Refrigeration, 1981-. Gen. Editor, Internat. Jl of Refrigeration, 1978-. *Publications:* Cyrogenic Fundamentals, 1971; research papers in Trans. Inst. Chem. Eng., etc. *Recreation:* Methodist lay preacher. *Address:* 12 High Ash Drive, Wigton Lane, Leeds LS17 8RA. *T:* Leeds 687047; The University, Leeds. *T:* Leeds 31751.

HASELDINE, (Charles) Norman; public relations consultant; *b* 25 March 1922; *s* of Charles Edward Haseldine and Lily White; *m* 1946, Georgette Elise Michelle Bernard; four *s. Educ:* Nether Edge Grammar Sch., Sheffield. Education Officer, Doncaster Co-operative Soc., 1947-57; PRO, Sheffield & Ecclesall Co-op. Soc., 1957-70. MP (Lab and Co-op) Bradford West, 1966-70; PPS to Minister of Power, 1968-69; PPS to Pres. Bd of Trade, 1969-70; Mem. Select Cttee on Nationalised Inds. *Recreation:* classical music. *Address:* Flat 16, 30 Bramham Gardens, SW5. *T:* 01-373 2940; 115 Psalter Lane, Sheffield S11 8YR. *T:* Sheffield 585974.

HASELER, Dr Stephen Michael Alan; author and lecturer; Member of the Greater London Council, 1973-77; *b* 9 Jan. 1942; *m* 1967, Roberta Alexander. *Educ:* London School of Economics. BSc(Econ), PhD. Contested (Lab)-

Saffron Walden, 1966; Maldon, 1970. Chairman: Labour Political Studies Centre, 1973-78; General Purposes Cttee, GLC, 1973-75. Founder Mem., SDP, 1981. Vis. Prof., Georgetown Univ., Washington DC, 1978. *Publications:* The Gaitskellites, 1969; Social-Democracy—Beyond Revisionism, 1971; The Death of British Democracy, 1976; Eurocommunism: implications for East and West, 1978; The Tragedy of Labour, 1980. *Address:* 4 Carlton Mansions, Holland Park Gardens, W14. *T:* 01-602 3640. *Club:* Reform.

HASELGROVE, Dennis Cliff, CB 1963; MA; Under Secretary, Department of the Environment, 1970-75; *b* 18 Aug. 1914; *s* of late H. Cliff Haselgrove, LLB, Chingford; *m* 1941, Evelyn Hope Johnston, MA, *d* of late R. Johnston, Edinburgh; one *s. Educ:* Uppingham Sch.; King's Coll., Cambridge. 1st Class, Classical Tripos, Parts I and II. Entered Ministry of Transport, Oct. 1937. Private Sec. to Permanent Sec., and Asst Priv. Sec. to Minister, 1941. Served in Intelligence Corps and 10th Baluch Regt, IA, 1941-45. Min. of Transport: Asst Sec., 1948; Under-Sec., 1957-70. Govt Delegate to: ILO Asian Maritime Conf., 1953; Internat. Conf. on Oil Pollution of the Sea, 1954, 1962; Internat. Lab. Conf. (Maritime Session), 1958; Internat. Conf. on Safety of Life at Sea, 1960. Imperial Defence Coll., 1955. *Recreations:* archæology, travel, philately. *Address:* 10 Church Gate, SW6 3LD. *T:* 01-736 5213.

HASELHURST, Alan Gordon Barraclough; MP (C) Saffron Walden, since July 1977; *b* 23 June 1937; *s* of John Haselhurst and Alyse (*née* Barraclough); *m* 1977, Angela (*née* Bailey); two *s. Educ:* King Edward VI Sch., Birmingham; Cheltenham Coll.; Oriel Coll., Oxford. Pres., Oxford Univ. Conservative Assoc., 1958; Sec., Treas. and Librarian, Oxford Union Soc., 1959-60; Nat. Chm., Young Conservatives, 1966-68. MP (C) Middleton and Prestwich, 1970-Feb. 1974. PPS to Sec. of State for Educn, 1979-82. Chairman: Manchester Youth and Community Service, 1974-77; Commonwealth Youth Exchange Council, 1978-81; Trustee, Community Projects Foundn, 1982-. *Recreations:* squash, theatre, music. *Address:* House of Commons, SW1A 0AA. *Club:* MCC.

HASHMI, Dr Farrukh Siyar, OBE 1974; FRCPsych; Consultant Psychiatrist, All Saints' Hospital, Birmingham, since 1969; Psychotherapist, HM Prison, Stafford, since 1973; *b* Gujrat, Pakistan, 12 Sept. 1927; *s* of Dr Ziaullah Qureshi and Majida Qureshi; *m* 1972, Shahnaz; one *s* two *d. Educ:* King Edward Med. Coll., Lahore (Punjab Univ.). MB, BS; MRCPsych; DPM; FRCPsych 1979. Mayo Hosp. and King Edward Med. Coll., Lahore, March-Sept. 1953; New End Hosp., Hampstead, 1954; Children's Hosp., Birkenhead, 1954-55; Sen. House Officer, Brook Gen. Hosp., Woolwich, 1955-56; Snowdon Road Hosp., Bristol, 1956; Asst MOH, Co. Berwicks, 1957; psychiatric medicine: Registrar, Uffculme Clinic and All Saints Hosp., Birmingham, 1960-63, Sen. Registrar, 1966-69; Research Fellow, Dept of Psychiatry, Birmingham Univ., 1963-66. Chm., Psychiatric Div., West Birmingham Health Dist., 1977-; Member: Home Secretary's Adv. Cttee on Race, 1976-81 (formerly Mem., HO Adv. Cttee on Race Relations Research); Commn for Racial Equality, 1980-; Mental Health Services Cttee, RHA, 1976-; SSRC Project, Univ. of East Anglia, 1974-81; Council, Mind (NAMH), 1976-81; UK Cttee, World Fedn for Mental Health, 1978-; Editorial Bd, Medicos, 1977-81; GMC, 1979-; Parole Board, 1981-; Central District Authority, Birmingham, 1982-; Home Office Police Training Council, Working Party on Community and Race Relations Training, 1982-; Cttee of Inquiry into the Education of Children from Ethnic Minority Groups (Swann Cttee), 1982-. Pres., Pakistan Med. Soc., UK, 1974-76; Founder and Chm., Iqbal Acad., Coventry Cathedral, 1972-. Member: Health and Welfare Adv. Panel, Nat. Cttee for Commonwealth Immigrants, 1966-81; Community Relations Working Party, NAYC, 1968-81; Warley Area Social Services Sub-Cttee, 1973-81; Race Relations Bd West Midlands Conciliation Cttee, 1968-81; BBC Regional Adv. Council, 1970-77. *Publications:* Pakistan Family in Britain, 1965; Mores, Migration and Mental Illness, 1966; Psychology of Racial Prejudice, 1966; Community Psychiatric Problems among Birmingham Immigrants, 1968; In a Strange Land, 1970; Measuring Psychological Disturbance in Asian Immigrants to Britain, 1977. *Recreations:* writing, reading, music. *Address:* 71 Wellington Road, Edgbaston, Birmingham B15 2ET. *T:* 021-440 3063. *Clubs:* Oriental; Rotary, Edgbaston Priory (Birmingham).

HASKARD, Sir Cosmo (Dugal Patrick Thomas), KCMG 1965 (CMG 1960); MBE 1945; *b* 25 Nov. 1916; *o c* of late Brig.-Gen. J. McD. Haskard, CMG, DSO; *m* 1957, Phillada, *o c* of Sir Robert Stanley, KBE, CMG; one *s. Educ:* Cheltenham; RMC Sandhurst; Pembroke Coll., Cambridge (MA). Served War of 1939-45 (MBE); 2nd Lieut, TA (Gen. List), 1938; emergency Commn, Royal Irish Fusiliers, 1939; seconded KAR, 1941; served 2nd Bn, E Africa, Ceylon, Burma; Major 1944. Cadet, Tanganyika, 1940; transf. Nyasaland, 1946; Dist Comr, 1948; Provincial Commissioner, 1955; acting Secretary for African Affairs, 1957-58; Sec. for Labour and Social Development, 1961; Sec. for Local Government, 1962; Sec. for Natural Resources, 1963; Governor and C-in-C, Falkland Islands, and High Comr for the British Antarctic Territory, 1964-70. Served on Nyasaland-Mozambique Boundary Commission, 1951-52. Trustee, Beit Trust, 1976-. *Address:* Tragariff, Bantry, Co. Cork, Ireland.

HASKELL, Donald Keith, CVO 1979; HM Diplomatic Service; Head of Nuclear Energy Department, Foreign and Commonwealth Office, since 1981; *b* 9 May 1939; *s* of Donald Eric Haskell and Beatrice Mary Haskell (*née* Blair); *m* 1966, Maria Luisa Soeiro Tito de Morais; two *s* two *d* (and one *s* one *d*

decd). *Educ:* Portsmouth Grammar Sch.; St Catharine's Coll., Cambridge (BA 1961, MA 1964). Joined HM Foreign Service, 1961; served in: London, Lebanon, Iraq, Libya; HM Consul, Benghazi, 1969-70; First Sec., Tripoli, 1970-72; Foreign and Commonwealth Office, 1972-75; Chargé d'Affaires and Consul-Gen., Santiago, 1975-78; Counsellor and Consul-Gen., Dubai, 1978-81. Foundation Medal, Soka Univ. of Japan, 1975. *Recreations:* rifle shooting, squash, tennis, wine and food. *Address:* c/o Foreign and Commonwealth Office, SW1A 2AL; Barn Cottage, Brightstone Lane, Lower Farringdon, near Alton, Hants. *T:* Tisted 485. *Club:* Hawks (Cambridge).

HASKELL, Francis James Herbert, FBA 1971; Professor of Art History, Oxford University and Fellow of Trinity College, Oxford, since October 1967; *b* 7 April 1928; *s* of late Arnold Haskell, CBE, and Vera Saitzoff; *m* 1965, Larissa Salmina. *Educ:* Eton Coll.; King's Coll., Cambridge. Junior Library Clerk, House of Commons, 1953-54; Fellow of King's Coll., Cambridge, 1954-67; Librarian of Fine Arts Faculty, Cambridge Univ., 1962-67. Mem., British Sch. at Rome, 1971-74. A Trustee, Wallace Collection, 1976-. Mem. Exec. Cttee, Nat. Art Collections Fund, 1976-. Foreign Hon. Mem., Amer. Acad. of Arts and Scis, 1979; Corresp. Mem., Accad. Pontaniana, Naples, 1982. *Publications:* Patrons and Painters: a study of the relations between Art and Society in the Age of the Baroque, 1963, 2nd edn 1980; Géricault (The Masters), 1966; An Italian Patron of French Neo-Classic Art, 1972; (ed jtly) The Artist and Writer in France, 1975; Rediscoveries in Art, 1976, 2nd edn 1980 (Mitchell Prize for Art History, 1977); L'arte e il linguaggio delta politica (Florence), 1977; (with Nicholas Penny) Taste and the Antique, 1981; articles in Burlington Mag., Jl Warburg Inst., etc; reviews in New Statesman, NY Review of Books, etc. *Recreation:* foreign travel. *Address:* 7 Walton Street, Oxford; Trinity College, Oxford OX1 2HG; 35 Beaumont Street, Oxford.

HASKELL, Peter Thomas, CMG 1975; PhD, FRES, FIBiol; Director, Centre for Overseas Pest Research, and Chief Adviser on Pest Control, Overseas Development Administration, since 1971; *b* 21 Feb. 1923; *s* of late Herbert James and Mary Anne Haskell; *m* ; one *s. Educ:* Portsmouth Grammar Sch.; Imperial Coll., London. BSc, ARCS, PhD. Asst Lectr, Zoology Dept, Imperial Coll., London, 1951-53; Lectr, 1953-55; Sen. Sci. Officer, Anti-Locust Research Centre, Colonial Office, 1955-57; Principal Sci. Officer, 1957-59; Dep. Dir, 1959-62; Dir, Anti-Locust Research Centre, Min. of Overseas Develt, 1962-71; Consultant, FAO, UN, 1962-; Consultant: UNDP, 1970-; WHO, 1973-; OECD, 1975-; UNEP, 1976-; Agric. Adv. Panel, British Council, 1976-. Vice-Pres., Inst. of Biology, 1982. Professorial Res. Fellow, University Coll., Cardiff, 1971. Mem., Bd of Governors, Internat. Centre for Insect Physiology and Ecology, Kenya, 1972 (Vice-Chm., 1978; Chm., 1979 and 1981-). Vis. Prof., Univ. of Newcastle, 1977. Thamisk Lectr, Royal Swedish Acad. of Scis, 1979. Van Den Brande Internat. Prize, 1982. *Publications:* Insect Sounds, 1962; The Language of Insects, 1962; many papers and articles in scientific and literary jls. *Recreations:* sailing, gardening, reading. *Address:* 19 Drumaline Ridge, Worcester Park, Surrey. *T:* 01-337 4852.

HASKINS, Sam, (Samuel Joseph), FRPS, FSIAD; photographer; *b* 11 Nov. 1926; *s* of Benjamin G. Haskins and Anna E. Oelofse; *m* 1952, Alida Elzabé van Heerden; two *s. Educ:* Helpmekaar Sch.; Witwatersrand Technical Coll.; Bolt Court Sch. of Photography. Freelance work: Johannesburg, 1953-68; London, 1968-. One-man Exhibitions: Johannesburg, 1953, 1960; Tokyo, 1970, 1973, 1976, 1981; London, 1972, 1976, 1978, 1980; Paris, 1973; Amsterdam, 1974; NY, 1981; San Francisco, 1982; Toronto, 1982; Bologna, 1982. *Publications:* Five Girls, 1962; Cowboy Kate and other stories, 1964 (Prix Nadar, France, 1964); November Girl, 1966; African Image, 1967 (Silver Award, Internat. Art Book Contest, 1969); Haskins Posters, 1972 (Gold Medal, New York Art Directors Club, 1974); Photo-Graphics, 1980 (Kodak Book Award); portfolios in most major internat. photographic magazines. *Recreations:* sculpting, books, music. *Address:* 9A Calonne Road, SW19 5HH. *T:* 01-946 9660.

HASLAM, Hon. Sir Alec (Leslie), Kt 1974; Judge of the Supreme Court of New Zealand, 1957-76, Senior Puisne Judge, 1973-76; *b* 10 Feb. 1904; *s* of Charles Nelson Haslam and Adeline Elsie Haslam; *m* 1933, Kathleen Valerie Tennent; two *s* two *d. Educ:* Waitaki Boys' High Sch.; Canterbury UC; Oriel Coll., Oxford. Rhodes Scholar 1927; 1st cl. hons LLM NZ; DPhil, BCL Oxon. Served with 10th Reinf. 2 NZEF, ME and Italy, 1943-46. Barrister and Solicitor, 1925; in private practice, 1936-57. Lectr in Law, Canterbury Univ., 1936-50 (except while overseas). Chm. Council of Legal Educn, 1962-75 (Mem. 1952); Mem., Rhodes Scholarship Selection Cttee, 1936-74; NZ Sec. to Rhodes Scholarships, 1961-74; Mem., Scholarships (Univ. Grants) Cttee, 1962-80; Pres., Canterbury District Law Soc., 1952-53; Vice-Pres., NZ Law Soc., 1954-57; Mem., Waimairi County Council, 1950-56; Mem., NZ Univ. Senate, 1956-61. Sen. Teaching Fellow, Univ. of Canterbury, 1977-81. Hon. LLD Canterbury, 1973. *Publication:* Law Relating to Trade Combinations, 1931. *Recreations:* reading, walking, bowls; formerly athletics (rep. Canterbury Univ. and Oriel Coll.) and rowing (rep. Oriel Coll.). *Address:* 22 Brackendale Place, Burnside, Christchurch 4, NZ. *T:* 588-589.

HASLAM, Rear Adm. David William, CB 1979; OBE 1964; Hydrographer of the Navy, since 1975; *b* 26 June 1923; *s* of Gerald Haigh Haslam and Gladys Haslam (*née* Finley). *Educ:* Ashe Prep. Sch., Etwall; Bromsgrove Sch., Worcs. FRGS, FRIN, FRICS, FNI. Special Entry Cadet, RN, 1941; HMS Birmingham, HMAS Quickmatch, HMS Resolution (in Indian Ocean),

1942-43; specialised in hydrographic surveying, 1944; HMS White Bear (surveying in Burma and Malaya), 1944-46; comd Survey Motor Launch 325, 1947; RAN, 1947-49; HMS Scott, 1949-51; HMS Dalrymple, 1951-53; i/c RN Survey Trng Unit, Chatham, 1953-56; HMS Vidal, 1956-57; comd, HMS Dalrymple, 1958; comd, HMS Dampier, 1958-60; Admty, 1960-62; comd, HMS Owen, 1962-64; Exec. Officer, RN Barracks, Chatham, 1964-65; Hydrographer, RAN, 1965-67; comd, HMS Hecla, 1968-70; Asst Hydrographer, MoD, 1970-72; comd, HMS Hydra, 1972-73; Asst Dir (Naval) to Hydrographer, 1974-75; sowc 1975. Lt-Comdr 1952; Comdr 1957; Captain 1965; Rear Adm. 1975. Pres., Hydrographic Soc., 1977-79. Governor, Bromsgrove Sch., 1977-. *Recreations:* most team games (Pres., English Schs Basketball Assoc.), supporting any youth organisations.

HASLAM, Geoffrey; see Haslam, W. G.

HASLAM, Robert, CEng, MInstME; Chairman, Tate & Lyle plc, since 1982; *b* 4 Feb. 1923; *s* of Percy and Mary Haslam; *m* 1947, Joyce Quin; two *s*. *Educ:* Bolton Sch.; Birmingham Univ. (BSc Coal Mining, 1st Cl.). Joined Manchester Collieries Ltd, 1944; National Coal Board, Jan. 1947; Mining Engr, Oct. 1947, Personnel Director, 1960, ICI Nobel Division; Director, 1963, Dep. Chm., 1966, ICI Plastics Div.; Dep. Chm., 1969, Chm., 1971, ICI Fibres Div.; Director, ICI Ltd, 1974; Chairman: ICI Americas Inc., 1978-81; ICI Canada Ltd, 1979-80; Dep. Chm., ICI Ltd, 1980-82; Non-Exec. Dep. Chm., Tate & Lyle plc, 1982 (Dir, 1978-); Director: Carrington Viyella, 1982-; Cable and Wireless, 1982-. Chairman: Man-Made Fibres Producers Cttee, 1972-74; Common Market Group of CIRFS, 1973-75. Mem., BOTB, 1981- (Chm., N America Adv. Gp, 1982-); Vice-Pres., British Textile Confedn, 1972-74. *Recreations:* golf, travel. *Address:* c/o Tate & Lyle plc, Sugar Quay, Lower Thames Street, EC3R 6DQ. *T:* 01-626 6525. *Clubs:* Wentworth; Sky (New York).

HASLAM, (William) Geoffrey, DFC 1944; Deputy Chairman: Prudential Corporation Ltd, since 1980; Prudential Assurance Co. Ltd, since 1980; *b* 11 Oct. 1914; *yr s* of late William John Haslam and late Hilda Irene Haslam; *m* 1941, Valda Patricia Adamson; two *s* one *d*. *Educ:* New Coll. and Ashville Coll., Harrogate. War Service with RAF, No 25 Sqdn (night fighters), 1940-46. Joined Prudential Assurance Co. Ltd, 1933: Dep. Gen. Manager, 1963; Gen. Manager, 1969; Chief Gen. Manager, 1974-78; Chief Exec., 1979. Chm., Industrial Life Offices Assoc., 1972-74; Chm., British Insurance Assoc., 1977-78. *Recreation:* golf. *Address:* 6 Ashbourne Road, W5 3ED. *T:* 01-997 8164. *Clubs:* City of London, MCC.

HASLEGRAVE, Herbert Leslie, WhSch (Sen.), MA Cantab, PhD London, MSc (Eng), CEng, FIMechE, FIEE, FIProdE; planning consultant; formerly Vice-Chancellor, Loughborough University of Technology; *b* 16 May 1902; *s* of late George Herbert Haslegrave and Annie (*née* Totty), Wakefield; *m* 1938, Agnes Mary, *er d* of Leo Sweeney, Bradford; one *d*. *Educ:* Wakefield Gram. Sch.; Bradford Technical Coll.; Trinity Hall Cambridge (Scholar). Rex Moir Prizeman, John Bernard Seeley Prizeman, Ricardo Prizeman, 1928; 1st Cl. Mechanical Sciences Tripos, 1928. English Electric Co. Ltd: Engineering Apprentice, 1918-23, Asst Designer, Stafford, 1928-30; Lecturer: Wolverhampton and Staffs, Technical Coll., 1931; Bradford Technical Coll., 1931-35; Head of Continuative Education Dept, Loughborough Coll., 1935-38; Principal: St Helens Municipal Technical Coll., 1938-43; Barnsley Mining and Technical Coll., 1943-46; Leicester Coll. of Technology, 1947-53; Loughborough Coll. of Technology, 1953-66. Bernard Price Lectr, SA Inst. of Electrical Engrs, 1971. Member of: Productivity Team on Training of Supervisors, visiting USA, 1951; Delegation on Education and Training of Engineers visiting USSR, 1956; Council, IMechE, 1965-66; Council, IEE, 1956-58. Chairman: Council, Assoc. of Technical Institutions, 1963-64; Cttee on Technician Courses and Examinations, 1967-69; Pres., Whitworth Soc., 1972-73. Hon. DTech Loughborough Univ. of Technology. *Publications:* various on engineering, education and management in proceedings of professional engineering bodies and educational press; chapter in Management, Labour and Community. *Recreations:* motoring, swimming, music. *Address:* 19 Lands Road, Brixham, Devon; 4 Capstan Square, E14 9EU.

HASLEGRAVE, Neville Crompton; Town Clerk, 1965-74, and Chief Executive Officer, 1969-74, Leeds; Solicitor; *b* 2 Aug. 1914; *o s* of late Joe Haslegrave, Clerk of Council, and late Olive May Haslegrave; *m* 1943, Vera May, *o d* of late Waldemar Julius Pedersen, MBE, and Eva Pedersen; two *d*. *Educ:* Exeter Cathedral Choristers School; Leeds Univ. Asst Examr, Estate Duty Office, Bd of Inland Revenue, 1940-44; Asst Solicitor, Co. Borough of Leeds, 1944-46. Chief Prosecuting Solicitor, Leeds, 1951-54; Principal Asst Solicitor, Leeds, 1951-60; Dep. Town Clerk, Leeds, 1960-65. Pres., Leeds Law Soc., 1972-73. Mem., IBA Adv. Council, 1969-73. *Recreations:* music, walking. *Address:* 37 West Court, West Avenue, Roundhay, Leeds LS8 2SP. *Club:* Headingley Taverners'.

HASLEWOOD, Prof. Geoffrey Arthur Dering; Professor of Biochemistry at Guy's Hospital Medical School, University of London, 1949-77, now Emeritus; *b* 9 July 1910; *s* of N. A. F. Haslewood, Architect, and Florence (*née* Hughes); *m* 1943, B. W. Leeburn (*d* 1949); two *d*; *m* 1953, E. S. Blakiston, Geelong, Vic, Australia. *Educ:* St Marylebone Grammar Sch.; University Coll., London. Research on polycyclic aromatic hydrocarbons, etc, at Royal Cancer Hosp. (Free), 1933-35; Asst in Pathological Chemistry at British Postgraduate Med. Sch., 1935-39; Reader in Biochemistry at Guy's Hosp. Med. Sch., 1939-49. Mem., Zaire River Expedition, 1974-75. MSc

1932, PhD 1935, DSc 1946, London. FRSC (FRIC 1946). *Publications:* Bile Salts, 1967; The Biological Importance of Bile Salts, 1978; various articles and original memoirs in scientific literature, mainly on steroids in relation to evolution. *Recreations:* fishing, keeping lizards. *Address:* 28 Old Fort Road, Shoreham-by-Sea, Sussex. *T:* Shoreham-by-Sea 3622.

HASLIP, Joan; author; *b* 27 Feb. 1912; *yr d* of late George Ernest Haslip, MD, original planner of the Health Service. *Educ:* privately in London and on the continent. Grew up in Florence. Sub-editor, London Mercury, 1929-39, contributed verse, reviews, etc; travelled extensively Europe, USA, Middle East; Editor, European Service, BBC, 1941-45 (Italian Section); lectured for British Council, Italy and Middle East; broadcast and contributed articles to BBC and various publications and newspapers. FRSL 1958. *Publications:* (several translated); Out of Focus (novel), 1931; Grandfather Steps (novel), 1932 (USA 1933); Lady Hester Stanhope, 1934; Parnell, 1936 (USA 1937); Portrait of Pamela, 1940; Lucrezia Borgia, 1953 (USA 1954); The Sultan, Life of Abdul Hamid, 1958, repr. 1973; The Lonely Empress, a life of Elizabeth of Austria, 1965 (trans. into ten languages); Imperial Adventurer, 1971 (Book of Month choice, USA, 1972); Catherine the Great, 1976; The Emperor and the Actress, 1982. *Recreations:* travelling and conversation. *Address:* 8 Via Piana, Bellosguardo, Florence, Italy.

HASLUCK, Rt. Hon. Sir Paul (Meernaa Caedwalla), KG 1979; GCMG 1969; GCVO 1970; PC 1966; Governor-General of Australia, 1969-74; *b* 1 April 1905; *s* of E. M. C. Hasluck and Patience (*née* Wooler); *m* 1932, Alexandra Margaret Martin Darker, AD 1978, DStJ 1971; one *s* (and one *s* decd). *Educ:* University of Western Australia (MA). Journalist until 1938. Lectr in History, University of Western Australia, 1939-40; Australian Diplomatic Service, 1941-47; Head of Australian Mission to United Nations, 1946-47; Representative on Security Council, Atomic Energy Commn, General Assembly, etc. Research Reader in History, University of Western Australia, 1948. Official War Historian. Mem. (L) House of Representatives, 1949-69; Minister for Territories in successive Menzies Governments, 1951-63; Minister for Defence, 1963-64; Minister for External Affairs, 1964-69. Fellow, Aust. Acad. of Social Scis. Hon. Fellow, Aust. Acad. of Humanities; Hon. FRAIA; Hon. FRAHS. KStJ 1969. *Publications:* Black Australians, 1942; Workshop of Security, 1946; The Government and the People (Australian Official War History), vol. 1, 1951, vol. 2, 1970; Collected Verse, 1970; An Open Go, 1971; The Office of the Governor-General (Queale Meml Lecture), 1973, rev. edn, 1979; The Poet in Australia, 1975; A Time for Building: Australian administration in Papua New Guinea, 1976; Mucking About (autobiog.), 1977; Sir Robert Menzies (Mannix Lecture), 1980; Diplomatic Witness, 1980. *Recreation:* book collecting (Australiana). *Address:* 2 Adams Road, Dalkeith, WA 6009, Australia. *Clubs:* Weld (Perth); Claremont Football.

HASSALL, Anthony Frank Albert; Group Managing Director and Chief Executive, Torvale Group, since 1979; *b* 6 Aug. 1930; *s* of late Frank Armitage Hassall and Ena Dorothy (*née* Andrews); *m* 1954, Brenda, *d* of late Thomas Harry Freeman; two *s* one *d*. *Educ:* Derby Grammar Sch.; Loughborough Coll. (BSc MechEng, DLC). CEng. Instr Lieut RN, 1954. British Celanese Ltd, 1952; H. C. Slingsby Ltd, 1957; NRDC, 1960; British Technical Service Corp., Washington, DC, 1963; Marketing Dir, Bridon Fibres & Plastics Ltd, 1966-77; Regional Industrial Dir (Under Sec.), Yorks and Humberside, DoI, 1977-78. *Recreations:* squash, golf. *Address:* c/o Torvale Group, Pembridge, Herefordshire. *T:* Pembridge 383. *Club:* Farmers'.

HASSALL, Joan, RE 1948; FSIA 1958; painter and wood engraver; *b* 3 March 1906; *d* of late John Hassall, RI, RWA, and late Constance Brooke-Webb. *Educ:* Parsons Mead, Ashtead; Froebel Educational Institute, Roehampton. Sec. to London Sch. of Art, 1925-27; studied Royal Academy Schs, 1928-33; studied Wood Engraving, LCC Sch. of Photo-engraving and Lithography. Teacher of Book Production (deputy), Edinburgh Coll. of Art, 1940; resumed her own work in London, chiefly wood engraving, 1945. Work represented in: British Museum, Victoria and Albert Museum and collections abroad. Designed the Queen's Invitation Card to her guests for Coronation, 1953. Master, Art Workers Guild, 1972 (Mem., 1964-); Bronze Medal, Paris Salon, 1973. *Publications:* first published engraving in Devil's Dyke, by Christopher Hassall, 1935; The Wood Engravings of Joan Hassall, 1960. Her engraved and drawn work appears in many classic and contemporary books of prose and poetry, and in advertising. *Recreations:* music, literature and printing. *Address:* Priory Cottage, Malham, Skipton, N Yorks BD23 4DD. *T:* Airton 356.

HASSALL, William Owen; Librarian to Earl of Leicester, Holkham, since 1937; Bodleian Library, Oxford, 1938-80 (Senior Assistant Librarian); *b* 4 Aug. 1912; *s* of Lt-Col Owen Hassall and Bessie Florence Hassall (*née* Cory); *m* 1936, Averil Grafton Beaves; three *s* one *d*. *Educ:* Twyford Sch., Hants; Wellington Coll., Berks; (Classical scholar) Corpus Christi Coll., Oxford. Hon. Mods, 1st cl. Modern History, 1936, DPhil 1941. Lent by RA to Min. Economic Warfare, 1942-46. Formerly: External Examnr in History, Univs of Bristol, Durham, Leicester and Oxford Insts of Educn (Trng Colls); Hon. Editorial Sec., British Records Assoc.; Mem. Council, Special Libraries and Information Bureaux. Hon. Sec., Oxfordshire Record Soc., 1947-76. FSA 1942; FRHistS. *Publications:* A Cartulary of St Mary Clerkenwell, 1949; A Catalogue of the Library of Sir Edward Coke, 1950; The Holkham Bible Picture Book, 1954; Wheatley Records, 956-1956, 1956; They saw it happen: an anthology of eye-witnesses' accounts for events in British history, 55BC-AD1485, 1957; Who's Who in History, vol. I, British Isles, 55BC-1485, 1960;

(with A. G. Hassall) The Douce Apocalypse, 1961; How they Lived: an anthology of original accounts written before 1485, 1962; Index of Names in Oxfordshire Charters, 1966; History Through Surnames, 1967; The Holkham Library Illuminations and Illustrations in the Manuscript Library of the Earl of Leicester (printed for presentation to the Members of the Roxburghe Club), 1970; (with A. G. Hassall) Treasures from the Bodleian, 1975; contrib. to various learned publications. *Recreations:* lecturing; research on Holkham records. *Address:* Manor House, Wheatley, Oxford. *T:* Wheatley 2333.

HASSAN, Sir Joshua (Abraham), Kt 1963; CBE 1957; MVO 1954; QC (Gibraltar) 1961; JP; Chief Minister of Gibraltar, 1964–69, and since 1972; *b* 1915; *s* of late Abraham M. Hassan, Gibraltar; *m* 1945, Daniela (marr. diss. 1969), *d* of late José Salazar; two *d* ; *m* 1969, Marcelle Bensimon; two *d. Educ:* Line Wall Coll., Gibraltar. Called to Bar, Middle Temple, 1939. HM Deputy Coroner, Gibraltar, 1941–64; Mayor of Gibraltar, 1945–50 and 1953–69; Mem. Executive Council, Chief Mem. Legislative Council, Gibraltar, 1950–64; Leader of the Opposition, Gibraltar House of Assembly, 1969–72. Chairman: Cttee of Management, Gibraltar Museum, 1952–65; Gibraltar Govt Lottery Cttee, 1955–70; Central Planning Commn, 1947–70. *Address:* 11/18 Europa Road, Gibraltar. *T:* A2295. *Clubs:* United Oxford & Cambridge University; Royal Gibraltar Yacht.

HASSAN, Mamoun Hamid; Managing Director, National Film Finance Corporation, since 1979 (Board Member since 1978); *b* Jedda, 12 Dec. 1937; *s* of Dr Hamid Hassan and Fatma Hassan (*née* Sadat); *m* 1966, Moya Jacqueline Gillespie, MA Oxon; two *s.* Formerly script writer, editor and director; Head of Production Board, British Film Inst., 1971–74; Head of Films Branch, UNRWA, Lebanon, 1974–76. Mem., Cinematograph Films Council, 1977–78. *Address:* National Film Finance Corporation, 22 Southampton Place, WC1A 2BP.

HASSETT, Gen. Sir Francis (George), AC 1975; KBE 1976 (CBE 1966; OBE 1945); CB 1970; DSO 1951; MVO 1954; Chief of the Defence Force Staff, 1975–77, retired; *b* 11 April 1918; *s* of John Francis Hassett, Sydney, Australia; *m* 1946, Margaret Hallie Roberts, *d* of Dr Edwin Spencer Roberts, Toowoomba, Qld; one *s* two *d* (and one *s* deed). *Educ:* RMC, Duntroon, Australia. Graduated RMC, 1938. Served War of 1939–45, Middle East and South West Pacific Area (Lt-Col; despatches twice); CO 3 Bn Royal Australian Regt, Korea, 1951–52; Marshal for ACT Royal Tour, 1954; Comd 28 Commonwealth Bde, 1961–62; idc, 1963; DCGS, 1964–65; Head of Aust. Jt Services Staff, Australia House, 1966–67; GOC Northern Comd, Australia, 1968–70; Chm., Army Rev. Cttee, 1969–70; Vice Chief of Gen. Staff, Australia, 1971–73; CGS, Australia, 1973–75. Extra Gentleman Usher to the Queen, 1966–68. *Recreations:* fishing, boating. *Address:* 42 Mugga Way, Red Hill, Canberra, ACT 2603, Australia. *Clubs:* Commonwealth, Queensland.

HASSETT, Maj.-Gen. Ronald Douglas Patrick, CB 1978; CBE 1975; Director, Orient: New Zealand Trading Co. Ltd, since 1979; *b* 27 May 1923; *s* of Edmond Hassett and Elinor Douglas; *m* 1953, Lilian Ivy Gilmore; two *s* one *d. Educ:* St Patrick's Coll., Wellington; RMC Duntroon. psc, G, rcds. 2nd NZ Expeditionary Force, Italy, 1944–46; NZ Army Liaison Staff, London, 1948–50; served Korea, NZ and Malaya, 1952–62; NZ Instructor, Australian Staff Coll., 1963–65; Dir of Equipment, NZ Army, 1966–67; DQMG, 1967–69; Comdr NZ Inf. Brigade Group, 1969; DCGS, 1970; RCDS, 1971; ACDS (Policy), 1972–74; Dep. Chief of Defence Staff, 1974–76; Chief of General Staff, NZ Army, 1976–78. *Recreations:* gardening, golf. *Address:* (office) 2nd Floor, Straits Trading Building, 4 Leboh Pasar Besar, PO Box 2197, Kuala Lumpur, Malaysia; (home) 70 Lorong Chong Khoon Lin 3, Ukay Heights, Kuala Lumpur, Malaysia.

HASTERT, Roger Joseph Leon; Officer, Order of Adolphe de Nassau, Luxembourg; Hon. CMG 1972; Dr-en-Droit; Ambassador of Luxembourg to the Court of St James's, and Permanent Representative to the Council of the Western European Union, since 1978; concurrently Ambassador to Ireland and Iceland; *b* Luxembourg City, 10 July 1929; *m* Éléonore Heijmerink; one *s* one *d.* Barrister-at-law, Luxembourg, 1956–59; joined Diplomatic Service, 1959 (Political Affairs); First Sec. and Consul Gen., Brussels, 1963–69; Dir of Protocol and Juridical Affairs, Min. of Foreign Affairs; Pres., Commn Internationale de la Moselle; and Mem., Commn de Contrôle des Comptes des Communautés Européennes, 1969–73; Ambassador to The Netherlands, 1973–1978. *Address:* Luxembourg Embassy, 27 Wilton Crescent, SW1X 8SD. *T:* 01-235 6961.

HASTIE-SMITH, Richard Maybury; Deputy Under-Secretary of State, Ministry of Defence, since 1981; *b* 13 Oct. 1931; *s* of Engr-Comdr D. Hastie-Smith and H. I. Hastie-Smith; *m* 1956, Bridget Noel Cox; one *s* two *d. Educ:* Cranleigh Sch. (Schol.); Magdalene Coll., Cambridge (Schol.; MA). HM Forces, commnd Queen's Royal Regt, 1950–51. Entered Administrative Class, Home CS, War Office, 1955; Private Sec. to Permanent Under-Sec., 1957; Asst Private Sec. to Sec. of State, 1958; Principal, 1960; Asst Private Sec. to Sec. of State for Defence, 1965; Private Sec. to Minister of Defence (Equipment), 1968; Asst Sec., 1969; RCDS, 1974; Under-Sec., MoD, 1975, Cabinet Office, 1979–81. Governor: Cranleigh Sch.; St Catherine's Sch., Bramley. *Address:* 18 York Avenue, East Sheen, SW14. *T:* 01-876 4597. *Club:* Army and Navy.

HASTILOW, Michael Alexander; Director, Glynwed Ltd, 1969–81; *b* 21 Sept. 1923; *s* of late Cyril Alexander Frederick Hastilow, CBE, MSc, BCom,

FRIC, and Doreen Madge, MA; *m* 1953, Sheila Mary Tipper (*née* Barker); one *s* two *d. Educ:* Mill Hill Sch.; Birmingham Univ. (Pres., Guild of Undergrads; BSc Civil Engrg, BCom). Served in Fleet Air Arm, RNVR, 1944–46. Commercial Manager, J. H. Lavender & Co. Ltd, 1948–54; Birmid Industries Ltd, 1954–57: Asst Gen. Man., Birmidal Developments Ltd, 1956–57; Commercial Man., Birmetals Ltd, 1957; Commercial and Gen. Sales Man., Bilston Foundries Ltd, 1957–63; Dir, Cotswold Buildings Ltd, 1963–64; Glynwed Ltd, 1964–81: Dir, The Wednesbury Tube Co. Ltd, 1966–81 (Man. Dir, 1968–74; Chm., 1973–76); dir or chm. of various Glynwed divs and subsids. British Non-Ferrous Metals Federation: Mem. Council, 1973–81; Vice Pres., 1975–79; Pres., 1979–80; Chm., Tube Gp, 1975–77. National Home Improvement Council: Mem. Council, 1975–; Mem. Bd, 1975–; Vice Chm., 1979–80; Chm., 1980–81. Member: Commn for New Towns, 1978–; Construction Exports Adv. Bd, 1975–78; Exec. Cttee, 1973–, and Council, 1974–, Nat. Council for Bldg Material Producers; EDC for Building, 1980–. Hon. Treasurer, Midlands Club Cricket Conf., 1969–81, Pres., 1981–82. *Recreations:* cricket, railways. *Address:* The Mount, 3 Kendal End Road, Rednal, Birmingham B45 8PX. *T:* 021-445 2007. *Clubs:* Royal Automobile, Old Millhillians.

HASTINGS, family name of Earl of Huntingdon.

HASTINGS; *see* Abney-Hastings, family name of Countess of Loudoun.

HASTINGS, 22nd Baron, *cr* 1290; **Edward Delaval Henry Astley,** Bt 1660; *b* 14 April 1912; *s* of 21st Baron and Lady Marguerite Nevill (*d* 1975), *d* of 3rd Marquess of Abergavenny; *S* father 1956; *m* 1954, Catherine Rosaline Ratcliffe Coats, 2nd *d* of late Capt. H. V. Hinton; two *s* one *d. Educ:* Eton and abroad. Supplementary Reserve, Coldstream Guards, 1934; served War of 1939–45, Major 1945; farming in Southern Rhodesia, 1951–57. Mem. of Parliamentary delegation to the West Indies, 1958; a Lord in Waiting, 1961–62; Jt Parly Sec., Min. of Housing and Local Govt, 1962–64. Chairman: British-Italian Soc., 1957–62 (Pres., 1972–); Italian People's Flood Appeal, 1966–67; Governor: Brit. Inst. of Florence, 1959–; Royal Ballet, 1971–; Chm., Royal Ballet Benevolent Fund, 1966–; Pres., British Epilepsy Assoc., 1965–. Grand Officer, Order of Merit (Italy), 1968. *Heir: s* Hon. Delaval Thomas Harold Astley, *b* 25 April 1960. *Recreations:* riding, ballet, foreign travel. *Address:* Fulmodeston Hall, Fakenham, Norfolk. *T:* Thursford 231; Seaton Delaval Hall, Northumberland. *Clubs:* Brooks's, Army and Navy; Northern Counties (Newcastle); Norfolk (Norwich).

HASTINGS, Bernard Ratcliffe; Chairman, Merseyside and North Wales Electricity Board, since 1978; *b* 16 March 1930; *s* of Robert Patrick and Mary Frances Hastings; *m* 1956, Mary Roddick Murdoch; one *s* one *d. Educ:* Glasgow Univ. BSc Hons. Various posts, latterly Head of Industrial Engrg Dept, Mullard Radio Valve Co., 1955–67; Management Services Controller, South of Scotland Electricity Bd, 1967–74; Dep. Chm., Merseyside and N Wales Electricity Bd, 1974–77. *Recreations:* golf, piano, gardening. *Address:* Ranfurly, 2 Walnut Croft, Churton, Chester CH3 6NB. *T:* Farndon 270788.

HASTINGS, Hubert De Cronin; Chairman, Architectural Press, 1927–74; Editor, Architectural Review, 1927–73; Editor, Architects' Journal, 1932–73; *b* 18 July 1902; *s* of Percy Hastings and Lilian Bass; *m* 1927, Hazel Rickman Garrard; one *s* one *d.* Royal Gold Medal for Architecture, 1971. *Publications:* The Italian Townscape, 1963; Civilia-The End of Sub-Urban Man, 1971; The Alternative Society, 1980. *Address:* 9/13 Queen Anne's Gate, Westminster, SW1. *Clubs:* Arts, National, ICA.

HASTINGS, Michael; playwright; *b* 2 Sept. 1938; *s* of Max Emmanuel Gerald and Marie Katherine Hastings; *m* 1975, Victoria Hardie; one *s* and one *d* by previous *m. Educ:* Imperial Service Coll., Windsor; Dulwich Coll.; Alleyn's Sch., Dulwich. Bespoke tailoring apprenticeship, Kilgour, French & Stanbury, London, 1953–56. FRGS. *Publications: plays:* Don't Destroy Me, 1956; Yes and After, 1957 (Arts Council Play Award, 1956); The World's Baby, 1962 (Enc. Britannica Award Medal, 1962); Lee Harvey Oswald: 'a far mean streak of independence brought on by neglect', 1966; The Silence of Saint-Just, 1971; For the West (Uganda), 1977; Gloo Joo, 1978 (Evening Standard Comedy of the Year Award, 1978); Full Frontal, 1979; Carnival War a Go Hot, 1979; Midnite at the Starlite, 1980; *novels:* The Game, 1957; The Frauds, 1960; Tussy is Me, 1968 (Somerset Maugham Award, 1969); The Nightcomers, 1971; And in the Forest the Indians, 1975 (Arts Council Fiction Award, 1975); *poems:* Love me Lambeth, 1959; *stories:* Bart's Mornings and other Tales of Modern Brazil, 1975; *criticism:* Rupert Brooke, The Handsomest Young Man in England, 1967; Sir Richard Burton: a biography, 1978; *for film and television:* For the West (Congo), 1963; Blue as his Eyes the Tin Helmet He Wore, 1966; The Search for the Nile, 1972 (Amer. Acad. of Arts and Scis 'emmy', 1972; St Christopher Medallion, 1975; British Screenwriters' Guild Award, 1975); The Nightcomers, 1972; Auntie Kathleen's Old Clothes, 1977; Murder Rap, 1980; Midnight at the Starlight, 1980; Michael Hastings in Brixton, 1980. *Address:* 2 Helix Gardens, Brixton Hill, SW2. *T:* 01-674 2802.

HASTINGS, Lt-Col Robin Hood William Stewart, DSO 1944 (and Bar 1945); OBE (mil.) 1946; MC 1943; despatches twice; Chairman, British Bloodstock Agency Ltd, since 1968; *b* 16 Jan. 1917; *s* of Hon. Osmond Hastings and Mary Caroline Campbell Hastings; *c* and *heir-pres.* to 15th Earl of Huntingdon, qv ; *m* 1950, Jean Suzanne Palethorpe; one *d. Educ:* Stowe Sch.; Christ Church Oxford (Hons History, MA). Commissioned Rifle

Brigade, 1939; Commanded: 6th Bn The Green Howards, 1943–44; 2nd Bn KRRC, 1944; GSOI 11th Armoured Div., 1945; commanded 1 Rifle Bde, 1945-46. Employed by BBA Ltd, 1952-; Director, 1954. Rode steeplechasing, 1945-52. *Publications:* The Rifle Brigade 1939-45, 1950; (jtly) The London Rifle Brigade 1919-50, 1952. *Recreations:* hunting, shooting. *Address:* The Malt House, Bramdean, Alresford, Hampshire SO24 0LN. *T:* Bramdean 243. *Club:* White's.

HASTINGS, Stephen Lewis Edmonstone, MC 1944; MP (C) Mid-Bedfordshire since Nov. 1960; *b* 4 May 1921; *s* of late Lewis Aloysius MacDonald Hastings, MC, and of Edith Meriel Edmonstone; *m* 1st, 1948, Harriet Mary Elisabeth (marr. diss. 1971), *d* of Col Julian Latham Tomlin, CBE, DSO; one *s* one *d* ; 2nd, 1975, Hon. Elisabeth Anne Lady Naylor-Leyland, *yr d* of late Viscount FitzAlan of Derwent and of Countess Fitzwilliam. *Educ:* Eton; RMC, Sandhurst. Gazetted Ensign, Scots Guards, 1939; served 2nd Bn, Western Desert, 1941-43 (despatches); SAS Regt, 1943. Joined Foreign Office, 1948. British Legation, Helsinki, 1950-52; British Embassy, Paris, 1953-58; First Sec., Political Office, Middle East Forces, 1959-60. Director: Dust Suppression Ltd; BMSS (Shrewsbury) Ltd; Fitzwilliam Estates Co. Chairman: Cons. Countryside Conservation Cttee; British Field Sports Soc., 1982-. Jt Master, Fitzwilliam Hounds. *Publication:* The Murder of TSR2, 1966. *Recreations:* fieldsports. *Address:* c/o House of Commons, SW1; 12A Ennismore Gardens, SW7. *Clubs:* White's, Pratt's, Buck's.

HASZELDINE, Prof. Robert Neville, FRS 1968; CChem, FRSC; MA Cantab, PhD Birmingham, PhD Cantab, DSc Birmingham, ScD Cantab; Professor of Chemistry, 1957-82, Head of Department of Chemistry, 1957-76, and Principal, 1976-82, University of Manchester Institute of Science and Technology (Faculty of Technology, The University of Manchester); *b* Manchester, 3 May 1925; *s* of late Walter Haszeldine and late Hilda Haszeldine (*née* Webster); *m* 1954, Pauline Elvina Goodwin; two *s* two *d. Educ:* Stockport Grammar Sch.; University of Birmingham (John Watt Meml Schol., 1942); Sidney Sussex Coll., Cambridge; Queens' Coll., Cambridge. University of Cambridge: Asst in Research in Organic Chemistry, 1949; University Demonstrator in Organic and Inorganic Chemistry, 1951; Asst Dir of Research, 1956; Fellow and Dir of Studies, Queens' Coll., 1954-57, Hon. Fellow, 1976. Mem. various Govt Cttees, 1957-. Former Vice-Pres., Perkin Div., Chemical Soc. Tilden Lectr, 1968; Vis. Lectr at universities and laboratories in the USA, Russia, Switzerland, Austria, Germany, Japan, China and France. Meldola Medal, 1953; Corday-Morgan Medal and Prize, 1960. *Publications:* numerous scientific publications in chemical jls. *Recreations:* mountaineering, gardening, natural history, good food, wine. *Address:* Windyridge, Lyme Road, Disley, Cheshire. *T:* Disley 2223.

HATCH, family name of **Baron Hatch of Lusby.**

HATCH OF LUSBY, Baron *cr* 1978 (Life Peer), of Oldfield in the County of W Yorks; **John Charles Hatch;** author, lecturer, broadcaster; *b* 1 Nov. 1917; *s* of John James Hatch and Mary White. *Educ:* Keighley Boys' Grammar School; Sidney Sussex Coll., Cambridge (BA). Tutor, Nat. Council of Labour Colls, 1942-44; Nat. Organiser, Independent Labour Party, 1944-48; Lectr, Glasgow Univ., 1948-53; Sec., Commonwealth Dept, Labour Party, 1954-61; Dir, Extra-Mural Dept, Univ. of Sierra Leone, 1961-62; Dir, African Studies Programme, Houston, Texas, 1964-70. Commonwealth Correspondent, New Statesman, 1950-70. Hon. Fellow, School of Peace Studies, Univ. of Bradford, 1976. *Publications:* The Dilemma of South Africa, 1953; New from Africa, 1956; Everyman's Africa, 1959; Africa Today and Tomorrow, 1960; A History of Post-War Africa, 1964; The History of Britain in Africa, 1966; Africa: The Re-Birth of Self-Rule, 1968; Tanzania, 1969; Nigeria, 1971; Africa Emergent, 1974; Two African Statesmen, 1976. *Recreations:* cricket, music. *Address:* End Cottage, Lusby, near Spilsby, Lincs. *T:* Winceby 630. *Clubs:* Royal Commonwealth Society, MCC.

HATCH, David Edwin; Controller, Radio Two, since 1980; *b* 7 May 1939; *s* of Rev. Raymond Harold Hatch and Winifred Edith May (*née* Brookes); *m* 1964, Ann Elizabeth Martin; two *s* one *d. Educ:* St John's Sch., Leatherhead; Queens' Coll., Cambridge (MA, DipEd). Actor, Cambridge Circus, 1963; I'm Sorry I'll Read That Again, 1964; Producer, Light Entertainment Radio, 1964, Executive Producer, 1972; Network Editor Radio, Manchester, 1974; Head of Light Entertainment Radio, 1978. *Recreations:* winemaking, laughing, family. *Address:* The Windmill, Ray's Hill, Cholesbury, near Chesham, Bucks HP5 2UJ. *T:* Cholesbury 542. *Club:* Lords' Taverners'.

HATCH, Dr Marshall Davidson, AM 1981; FRS 1980; FAA; Chief Research Scientist, Division of Plant Industry, CSIRO, Canberra, since 1970; *b* 24 Dec. 1932; *s* of Lloyd Davidson Hatch and Alice Endesby Hatch (*née* Dalziel); divorced; two *s. Educ:* Newington Coll., Sydney; Univ. of Sydney (BSc, PhD). FAA. Res. Scientist, Div. of Food Res., CSIRO, 1955-59; Post Doctoral Res. Fellow, Univ. of Calif., Davis, 1959-61; Res. Scientist, Colonial Sugar Refining Co. Ltd, Brisbane, 1961-66 and 1968-69 (Reader in Plant Biochemistry, Univ. of Queensland, Brisbane, 1967). Rank Prize, 1981. *Publications:* 102 papers, reviews and chaps in scientific jls and text books in field of photosynthesis and other areas of plant biochemistry. *Recreations:* skiing, squash, running. *Address: business:* Division of Plant Industry, CSIRO, PO Box 1600, Canberra City, ACT 2601, Australia.

HATCHARD, Frederick Henry; Stipendiary Magistrate for Metropolitan County of West Midlands (Birmingham), since 1981; *b* 22 April 1923; *s* of Francis and May Hatchard; *m* 1955, Patricia Egerton; two *s. Educ:* Yardley Grammar Sch., Birmingham. Justices Clerk: Sutton Coldfield and Coleshill, 1963-67; Walsall, 1967-81. *Recreations:* walking, gardening. *Address:* 3(B) Manor Road, Streetly, Sutton Coldfield B74 3NQ.

HATENDI, Rt. Rev. Ralph Peter; *see* Mashonaland, Bishop of.

HATFIELD, Rt. Rev. Leonard Fraser; *see* Nova Scotia, Bishop of.

HATFIELD, Hon. Richard Bennett; PC (Can.) 1982; Premier of New Brunswick since 1970; MLA (Progressive C) Carleton County since 1961, New Brunswick; *b* 9 April 1931; single. *Educ:* Rothesay Collegiate Sch.; Hartland High Sch.; Acadia Univ.; Dalhousie Univ. BA Acadia 1952; LLB Dalhousie 1956. Admitted to Bar of NS, 1956. Joined law firm of Patterson, Smith, Matthews & Grant in Truro, NS, 1956; Exec. Asst to Minister of Trade and Commerce, Ottawa, 1957-58; Sales Man., Hatfield Industries Ltd, 1958-65. Leader, PC Party of New Brunswick, 1969. Hon. LLD: Moncton, 1971; New Brunswick, 1972; St Thomas, 1973; Mount Allison, 1975. Hon. Chief, Micmac and Maliseet Tribes, 1970. Canada-Israel Friendship Award, 1973. *Address:* Office of the Premier, PO Box 6000, Fredericton, New Brunswick E3B 5H1, Canada. *T:* (506) 453-2144.

HATFULL, Alan Frederick; Counsellor (Labour), Bonn, since 1981; *b* 12 June 1927; *s* of Frederick George Hatfull and Florence May Hatfull (*née* Dickinson); *m* 1951, Terttu Kaarina Wahlroos; one *s* one *d. Educ:* St Olave's and St Saviour's Grammar School; London School of Economics. BSc (Econ) 1951. Assistant Principal, Min. of Labour, 1951, Principal 1957, Assistant Sec., 1965; Director, Commn on Industrial Relations, 1970-73; Counsellor (Labour), Paris, 1977-81. *Address:* c/o Foreign and Commonwealth Office, SW1.

HATHERTON, 7th Baron *cr* 1835; **Thomas Charles Tasman Littleton,** TD 1953; *b* 6 Oct. 1907; *s* of 4th Baron Hatherton and Hester Edithe (*d* 1947), *d* of Thomas Tarrant Hoskins, MD, Tasmania; *S* brother, 1973; *m* 1933, Ann Scott, *o d* of late Lt-Comdr Thomas McLeod, RN; one *d. Educ:* St Edward's School. Commnd TA, 1934; served War of 1939-45; Captain TARO 1945, retd 1956. *Heir: cousin* Edward Charles Littleton [*b* 1950; *m* 1974, Hilda Maria Robert; one *s* one *d*]. *Address:* Walhouse, Hutton Henry, Castle Eden, Co. Durham. *Club:* Naval and Military.

HATTERSLEY, Edith Mary, (Molly Hattersley); Assistant Education Officer, Inner London Education Authority, since 1983; *b* 5 Feb. 1931; *d* of Michael and Sally Loughran; *m* 1956, Rt Hon. Roy Sydney George Hattersley, qv. *Educ:* Consett Grammar Sch.; University College of Hull. BA Hons English (London), CertEd (Hull). Assistant Mistress at schools in Surrey and Yorkshire, 1953-61; Sen. Mistress, Myers Grove Sch., Sheffield, 1961-64; Dep. Headmistress, Kidbrooke Sch., SE3, 1965-69; Head Mistress, Hurlingham Sch., SW6, 1969-74; Headmistress, Creighton Sch., N10, 1974-82. Chairman of Cttee, Assoc. of Head Mistresses, 1975-77; Pres., Secondary Heads Assoc., 1980-81. *Recreation:* reading. *Address:* 14 Gayfere Street, SW1P 3HP. *T:* 01-222 1309.

HATTERSLEY, Rt. Hon. Roy Sydney George, PC 1975; BSc (Econ.); MP (Lab) Sparkbrook Division of Birmingham since 1964; *b* 28 Dec. 1932; *s* of Frederick Roy Hattersley, Sheffield; *m* 1956, Molly Hattersley, qv. *Educ:* Sheffield City Grammar Sch.; Univ. of Hull. Journalist and Health Service Executive, 1956-64; Mem. Sheffield City Council, 1957-65 (Chm. Housing Cttee and Public Works Cttee). PPS to Minister of Pensions and National Insurance, 1964-67; Jt Parly Sec., DEP (formerly Min. of Labour), 1967-69; Minister of Defence for Administration, 1969-70; Labour Party spokesman: on Defence, 1972; on Educn and Sci., 1972-74; Minister of State, FCO, 1974-76; Sec. of State for Prices and Consumer Protection, 1976-79; principal opposition spokesman on environment, 1979-80, on home affairs, 1980-. Vis. Fellow, Inst. of Politics, Univ. of Harvard, 1971, 1972. Dir, Campaign for a European Political Community, 1966-67. Columnist: Punch; The Guardian; The Listener, 1979-82; Columnist of the Year, Granada, 1982. *Publications:* Nelson, 1974; Goodbye to Yorkshire (essays), 1976; Politics Apart, 1982. *Address:* House of Commons, SW1. *Club:* Reform.

HATTO, Prof. Arthur Thomas, MA; Head of the Department of German, Queen Mary College, University of London, 1938-77; *b* 11 Feb. 1910; *s* of Thomas Hatto, LLB and Alice Walters; *m* 1935, Margot Feibelmann; one *d. Educ:* Dulwich Coll.; King's Coll., London (Fellow, 1971); University Coll., London. BA (London) 1931; MA (with Distinction), 1934. Lektor für Englisch, University of Berne, 1932-34; Asst Lectr in German, KCL, 1934-38; Queen Mary Coll., University of London, 1938 (Head of Dept of German). Temp. Sen. Asst, Foreign Office, 1939-45; Part-time Lectr in German, University Coll., London, 1944-45; returned to Queen Mary Coll., 1945; Reader in German Language and Literature, 1946, Prof. of German Language and Literature, 1953, University of London. Governor: SOAS, Univ. of London, 1960 (Foundn Day Lecture, 1970; Hon. Fellow, 1981); QMC, Univ. of London, 1968-70. Chairman: London Seminar on Epic; Cttee 'A' (Theol. and Arts), Central Research Fund, Univ. of London, 1969. Fellow: Royal Anthropological Institute; Royal Asiatic Society (lecture: Plot and character in Kirghiz epic poetry of the mid 19th cent., 1976); Leverhulme Emeritus Fellow (heroic poetry in Central Asia and Siberia), 1977-. Corresp. Mem.,

Finno-Ugrian Soc., 1978; Invited Mem., Rundgespräch, Seminar für Sprach- und Kulturwissenschaft Zentralasiens, Univ. of Bonn, 1978, 1979, 1980. *Publications:* (with R. J. Taylor) The Songs of Neidhart von Reuental, 1958; Gottfried von Strasbourg, Tristan (trans. entire for first time) with Tristran of Thomas (newly trans.) with an Introduction, 1960; The Niblungenlied: a new translation, with Introduction and Notes, 1964; editor of Eos, an enquiry by fifty scholars into the theme of the alba in world literature, 1965; (ed for first time with translation and commentary) The Memorial Feast for Kökötöy-khan: a Kirghiz epic poem, 1977; Essays on Medieval German and Other Poetry, 1980; Parzival, Wolfram von Eschenbach, a new translation, 1980; gen. editor, Traditions of Heroic and Epic Poetry, 2 vols, 1980; articles in learned periodicals. *Recreations:* reading, gardening, walking. *Club:* The Confrères.

HATTON; *see* Finch Hatton, family name of Earl of Winchilsea.

HATTY, Hon. Sir Cyril (James), Kt 1963; Minister of Finance, Bophuthatswana, 1979-82; *b* 22 Dec. 1908; *o s* of James Hatty and Edith (*née* Russen); *m* 1937, Doris Evelyn, *o d* of James Lane Stewart and Mable Grace Stewart; two *s. Educ:* Westminster City Sch. Deputy Dir, O and M Division, UK Treasury, until Jan. 1947; emigrated to S Africa, in industry, Feb. 1947; moved to Bulawayo, in industry, Jan. 1948. MP for Bulawayo North, Sept. 1950-Dec. 1962; Minister of Treasury, Jan. 1954-Sept. 1962, also Minister of Mines, Feb. 1956-Dec. 1962. FCIS; Fellow, Inst. of Cost and Management Accountants; FBIM. *Publication:* Digest of SR Company Law, 1952. *Recreations:* painting, music. *Address:* Merton Park, Norton, Zimbabwe. *Clubs:* Polytechnic, Salisbury, New (Harare, Zimbabwe).

HAUGHEY, Charles James, Teachta Dala (TD) (Fianna Fail) for Dublin (Artane); Taoiseach (Prime Minister of Ireland), 1979-81 and since 1982; *b* 16 Sept. 1925; *s* of John Haughey and Sarah Ann (*née* McWilliams); *m* 1951, Maureen Lemass; three *s* one *d. Educ:* Scoil Mhuire, Marino, Dublin; St Joseph's Christian Brothers' Sch., Fairview, Dublin; University College Dublin (BCom); King's Inns, Dublin. Called to Irish Bar, 1949. Member, Dublin Corporation, 1953-55; Member (Fianna Fail) Dail Eireann for a Dublin constituency, 1957-, now representing Dublin (Artane); Parliamentary Secretary to Minister for Justice, 1960-61; Minister: for Justice, 1961-64; for Agriculture, 1964-66; for Finance, 1966-70; Chairman, Jt Cttee on the Secondary Legislation of the European Communities, 1973-77; Minister for Health and Social Welfare, 1977-79. President, Fianna Fail Party, 1979-. *Recreations:* music, racing, riding, swimming. *Address:* Abbeville, Kinsaley, Co. Dublin, Ireland. *T:* (01) 450111. *Clubs:* St Stephen's Green, Ward Union Hunt (Dublin).

HAUGHTON, Daniel Jeremiah; *b* Dora, Walker County, Ala, 7 Sept. 1911; *s* of Gayle Haughton and Mattie Haughton (*née* Davis); *m* 1935, Martha Jean, *d* of Henry Oliver, Kewanee, Ill, a farmer; no *c. Educ:* Univ. of Alabama. BS degree in commerce and business administration, 1933. Lockheed Aircraft Corp., 1939-76: first as systems analyst; Works Manager, Vega Aircraft Corp. (a subsidiary), 1943; General Manager, Lockheed-Georgia Co. (a div.), 1952-56; elected: a Lockheed Vice-Pres., 1952, Exec. Vice-Pres., 1956; a Dir, 1958; Pres. of Corp., 1961; Chm. of Bd, 1967-76. Member of many professional societies; active in community and national affairs, including, 1967, Chm. of US Treasury Dept's industrial payroll savings bonds campaign. Chm., Nat. Multiple Sclerosis Soc.; Bd of Trustees, Nat. Security Industrial Assoc. Employer of the Year, Nat. Ind. Recreation Assoc., 1973; Management Man of the Year, Nat. Managing Assoc., 1966; Award of Achievement, Nat. Aviation Club, 1969; 16th Annual Nat. Transportation Award, Nat. Defense Transportation Assoc.; Tony Jannus Award, 1970; Salesman of the Year, Sales and Marketing Assoc., Los Angeles, 1970. Hon. LLD: Univ. of Alabama, 1962; George Washington Univ., 1965; Hon. DSc (Business Admin) Clarkson Coll. of Tech., 1973; Hon. LLD Pepperdine Univ., 1975. *Recreation:* fishing. *Address:* 1890 Battlefield Road SW, Marietta, Ga 30064, USA. *T:* (404) 422 9957. *Club:* Capital City (Atlanta).

HAUGHTON, Surgeon Rear-Adm. John Marsden, MVO 1964; FFARCS; *b* 27 Oct. 1924; *s* of Col Samuel George Steele Haughton, CIE, OBE, IMS, and Marjory Winifred Haughton (*née* Porter); *m* 1956, Lucy Elizabeth Lee, Tackley, Oxon; three *s* one *d. Educ:* Winchester Coll.; St Thomas' Hosp., 1942-48 (MRCS, LRCP, DA). Joined Royal Navy, 1949; 45 Commando RM, Malaya, 1950; Anaesthetic Specialist, RN Hosp., Plymouth, 1952; HMS Superb, 1954; RN Hosps, Haslar, 1956, Chatham, 1958; Sen. Anaesthetist, RN Hosp., Malta, 1959; PMO, Royal Yacht Britannia, 1962; Consultant Anaesthetist, RN Hospital: Haslar, 1964; Malta, 1968; Haslar, 1970; Comd MO and MO in charge RN Hosp., Malta, 1975; MO in charge RN Hosp., Plymouth, 1978; Surg. Rear-Adm. (Naval Hosps), Haslar, 1980-82. QHP 1978-82. *Recreations:* fishing, gardening, walking. *Address:* Footaway, Chagford, Devon TQ13 8JF.

HAUSER, Frank Ivor, CBE 1968; free-lance director; *b* 1 Aug. 1922; *s* of late Abraham and of Sarah Hauser; unmarried. *Educ:* Cardiff High Sch.; Christ Church, Oxford. Oxford, 1941-42; RA, 1942-45; Oxford, 1946-48. BBC Drama Producer, 1948-51; Director: Salisbury Arts Theatre, 1952-53; Midland Theatre Co., 1945-55. Formed Meadow Players Ltd, which re-opened the Oxford Playhouse, 1956, Dir of Productions, 1956-73; took Oxford Playhouse Co. on tour of India, Pakistan and Ceylon, 1959-60. Produced at Sadler's Wells Opera: La Traviata, 1961; Iolanthe, 1962; Orfeo, 1965;

produced: at Oxford Playhouse: Antony and Cleopatra, 1965; Phèdre, 1966; The Promise, 1966; The Silent Woman, 1968; Pippa Passes, 1968; Uncle Vanya, 1969; Curtain Up, 1969; The Merchant of Venice, 1973; also: Il Matrimonio Segreto, Glyndebourne, 1965; A Heritage and its History, Phoenix, 1965; The Promise, Fortune, 1967; Volpone, Garrick, 1967; The Magic Flute, Sadler's Wells, 1967; Kean, Globe, 1971; The Wolf, Apollo, 1973; Cinderella, Casino, 1974; On Approval, Haymarket, 1975; All for Love, Old Vic, 1977; The Importance of Being Earnest, Old Vic, 1980; Captain Brassbound's Conversion, Haymarket, 1982. *Recreation:* piano. *Address:* 5 Stirling Mansions, Canfield Gardens, NW6. *T:* 01-624 4690.

HAVARD, John David Jayne, MD; Secretary, British Medical Association, since 1980; *b* 5 May 1924; *s* of Dr Arthur William Havard and Ursula Jayne Vernon Humphrey; *m* 1st, 1950, Margaret Lucy Lumsden Collis (marr. diss. 1982); two *s* one *d* ; 2nd, 1982, Audrey Anne Boutwood, FRCOG, *d* of Rear Adm. L. A. Boutwood, CB, OBE. *Educ:* Malvern Coll.; Jesus Coll., Cambridge (MA, MD, LLB); Middlesex Hosp. Med. Sch. Called to the Bar, Middle Temple, 1953. Professorial Med. Unit, Middlesex Hosp., 1950; National Service, RAF, 1950-52; general practice, Lowestoft, 1952-58 (Sec., E Suffolk LMC, 1956-58). British Medical Assoc.: Asst Sec., 1958-64; Under-Sec., 1964-76; Dep. Sec., 1976-79. Short-term Cons., Council of Europe, 1964-67, OECD 1964-69, WHO 1967-, on Road Accident Prevention. Dep. Chm., Staff Side, Gen. Whitley Council for the Health Services, 1975-; Sec., Managerial, Professional and Staffs Liaison Gp, 1978-; Member: various Govt Working Parties on Coroners' Rules, Visual Standards for Driving, Licensing of Professional Drivers, etc. Gold Medal, Inter-Scandinavian Union for Non-Alcoholic Traffic, 1962. Pres., CUAC, 1945-46; Captain United Hosps AC, 1946-47; London Univ. Record for 100 yards, 1947. *Publications:* Detection of Secret Homicide (Cambridge Studies in Criminology), 1960; Research on Effects of Alcohol and Drugs on Driving Behaviour (OECD), 1968; chapters in textbooks on legal medicine, research advances on alcohol and drugs, etc; many articles in med., legal and sci. periodical lit.; several WHO reports. *Recreations:* Bach Choir, history, English countryside. *Address:* 1 Wilton Square, N1. *T:* 01-359 2802. *Clubs:* United Oxford & Cambridge University; Achilles.

HAVARD-WILLIAMS, Peter; (first) Professor and Head of the Department of Library and Information Studies since 1972, and Warden of Royce Hall since 1978, Loughborough University; *b* 1922; *s* of Graham Havard-Williams and Elizabeth (*née* James); *m* 1st, 1964, Rosine (*d* 1973), *d* of late Paul Cousin, Croix de Guerre; two *d* ; 2nd, 1976, Eileen Elizabeth, *d* of Oliver Cumming; one *d. Educ:* Bishop Gore Grammar Sch., Swansea; University Coll. of Swansea (Smith's Charity Scholar; MA Wales); Oxford Univ. FBIM, FRSA, FLAI, ALA, ANZLA, FIInfSc. Sub-Librarian, Univ. of Liverpool, 1951-56; Libr. and Keeper of Hocken Collection, Univ. of Otago, 1956-60; Fellow, Knox Coll., Dunedin, 1958-60; Dep. Libr., Univ. of Leeds, 1960-61; Libr., QUB, 1961-71 (Dir, Sch. of Lib. and Inf. Studies, 1964-70); Dean and Prof., Lib. Sch., Ottawa Univ., 1971-72; Loughborough University: Dean of Educn and Humanities, 1976-79; Project Head, Centre for Library and Information Management, 1979-. Library Association: Vice-Pres., 1970-; Chm. Council, 1970-71 and 1974-75; Chm. Exec. Cttee, 1976-78; Chm., Cons. Cttee on Nat. Library Co-ordination 1978-80; Chm., Bd of Assessors, 1981; Chm., NI Br., 1963 (when first all-Ireland lib. conf. held at Portrush). President: Internat. Colloquium on Univ. Lib. Bldgs, Lausanne, 1971; Internat. Seminar on Children's Lit., Loughborough, 1976; Vice-Pres., Internat. Fedn of Lib. Assocs, 1970-77. Member: Adv. Cttee on Public Lib. Service, NI, 1965; Lib. Adv. Council, 1976-78; Hon. Soc. of Cymmrodorion, 1970-; Ct of Governors, UWIST, 1979-. Lib. bldg consultant, UK and abroad, 1961-; Cons. and Mem. Brit. Delegn, Unesco Inter-govtl Conf. on Nat. Inf. Systems, Paris, 1974; Consultant: Min. of Educn and Culture, Brazil, 1975; Min. of Educn, Korea, 1976, 1979; Univ. of Ghana, 1977; Kenya Nat. Acad., 1978; Mara Inst. of Technol., 1978; Universidad Nacional Autonoma de Mexico, 1979; Nigeria, 1980; Singapore, 1981, 1982; Thailand, Hong Kong, Korea, Philippines, 1982. Former Ext. Examr, London, Sheffield, Strathclyde, NUI, CNAA, and Univs of Ibadan, WI, Zambia; has lectured in Finland, France, Kenya, Mexico, Poland, Sweden, Morocco, Algiers, Tunisia. Editor, IFLA Communications and Publications, 1971-78; Editorial Consultant, Internat. Library Review, 1969-; Consultant Editor, Library Progress Internat., 1981. *Publications:* (ed) Marsden and the New Zealand Mission, 1961; Planning Information Manpower, 1974; Departmental People, 1981; articles in Jl of Documentation, Libri, Internat. Lib. Rev., Unesco Bull. for Libs, Eng. Studies, Essays in Crit., and Monthly Mus. Record. *Recreations:* collecting Bloomsbury first editions, bears (esp. Winnie the Pooh), music, idling. *Address:* Department of Library and Information Studies, Loughborough University, Loughborough, Leics LE11 3TU. *T:* Loughborough 63171. *Clubs:* Athenæum, Royal Commonwealth Society.

HAVELOCK, Sir Wilfrid (Bowen), Kt 1963; *b* 14 April 1912; *s* of late Rev. E. W. Havelock and Helen (*née* Bowen); *m* 1st, 1938, Mrs M. E. Pershouse (*née* Vincent) (marr. diss. 1967); one *s* ; 2nd, 1972, Mrs Patricia Mumford, widow of Major Philip S. Mumford. *Educ:* Imperial Service Coll., Windsor, Berks. Elected to Kenya Legislative Council, 1948; Chairman, European Elected Members, 1952; Mem., Kenya Executive Council, 1952; Minister for Local Government, Kenya, 1954; Minister for Agriculture, Kenya, 1962-63. Dep. Chm., Agricl Finance Corp., Kenya, 1964-; Member: Nat. Irrigation Bd, 1974-79; Hotels and Restaurant Authority, 1975-81. Dir, Bamburi Portland Cement Co., 1974-. Chm., Kenya Assoc. of Hotelkeepers and Caterers, 1974,

1975, 1976. *Address:* PO Box 154, Malindi, Kenya. *Clubs:* Royal Commonwealth Society; Mombasa, Muthaiga Country, Nairobi (Kenya).

HAVELOCK-ALLAN, Sir Anthony James Allan, 4th Bt *cr* 1858; film producer; *b* 28 Feb. 1905; *s* of Allan (2nd *s* of Sir Henry Havelock-Allan, 1st Bt, VC, GCB, MP), and Annie Julia, *d* of Sir William Chaytor, 3rd Bt; *S* brother, 1975; *m* 1st, 1939, Valerie Louise Hobson, *qv* (marr. diss. 1952), *d* of late Comdr Robert Gordon Hobson, RN; two *s* ; 2nd, 1979, Maria Theresa Consuela (Sara) Ruiz de Villafranca, *d* of late Don Carlos Ruiz de Villafranca (formerly Ambassador to Chile and to Brazil), and Doña Julia Ruiz de Villafranca y Osuño, Villafranca, prov. Madrid. *Educ:* Charterhouse; Switzerland. Artists and Recording Manager, Brunswick Gramophone Co., London and Vox AG, Berlin, 1924-29; entered films as Casting Dir and Producer's Asst, 1933; produced quota films for Paramount; produced for Pinebrook Ltd and Two Cities Films, 1938-40; Assoc. Producer to Noel Coward, 1941; with David Lean and Ronald Neame, formed Cineguild, 1942; Producer, Assoc. Producer or in charge of production for Cineguild, 1942-47; formed Constellation Films, independent co. producing for Rank Org. and British Lion, 1949; Mem. Cinematographic Films Council and Nat. Film Production Council, 1948-51; Mem. Home Office Cttee on Employment of Children in Entertainment; Chm. British Film Academy, 1952; formed with Lord Brabourne and Major Daniel Angel British Home Entertainment to introduce Pay TV, 1958; Chm. Council of Soc. of Film and Television Arts (now BAFTA), 1962, 1963; Mem. Nat. Film Archive Cttee; a Gov. British Film Inst. and Mem. Institute's Production Cttee, 1958-65; Mem. US Academy of Motion Pictures Arts and Sciences, 1970. Films include: This Man is News, This Man in Paris, Lambeth Walk, Unpublished Story, From the Four Corners (documentary prod and dir), Brief Encounter (shared Academy script nomination), Great Expectations (shared Academy script nomination), Take my Life, Blanche Fury, Shadow of the Eagle, Never Take No for an Answer, Interrupted Journey, Young Lovers (dir Anthony Asquith), Orders to Kill (dir Anthony Asquith), Meet Me Tonight, The Quare Fellow, An Evening with the Royal Ballet (directed two ballets); (for television): National Theatre's Uncle Vanya, Olivier's Othello, Zeffirelli's Romeo and Juliet, David Lean's Ryan's Daughter. *Heir:* s Simon Anthony Henry Havelock-Allan, *b* 6 May 1944. *Address:* c/o Messrs Gorrie Whitson & Sons, 9 Cavendish Square, W1.

HAVERGAL, Henry MacLeod, OBE 1965; MA Oxon, BMus Edinburgh; FRCM; FRSAMD; Hon. RAM; *b* 21 Feb. 1902; *er s* of Rev. Ernest Havergal; *m* 1st, 1926, Hyacinth (*d* 1962), *er d* of Arthur Chitty; two *s* ; 2nd, 1964, Nina Davidson, Aberdeen. *Educ:* Choristers Sch., Salisbury; St Edward's Sch. and St John's Coll., Oxford. Dir of Music, Fettes Coll., Edinburgh, 1924-33; Haileybury Coll., 1934-36; Harrow Sch., 1937-45; Master of the Music, Winchester Coll., 1946-53; Principal, Royal Scottish Academy of Music (later Royal Scottish Academy of Music and Drama), 1953-69; Dir, Jamaica Sch. of Music, 1973-75. Hon. DMus Edinburgh, 1958; Hon. LLD Glasgow, 1969. *Recreation:* fishing. *Address:* 2 Bellevue Terrace, Edinburgh EH7 4DU. *T:* 031-556 6525. *Club:* New (Edinburgh).

HAVERS, Rt. Hon. Sir (Robert) Michael (Oldfield), PC 1977; Kt 1972; QC 1964; MP (C) Merton, Wimbledon, since 1974 (Wimbledon, 1970-74); Attorney General, since 1979; *b* 10 March 1923; 2nd *s* of Sir Cecil Havers, QC, and late Enid Snelling; *m* 1949, Carol Elizabeth, *d* of Stuart Lay, London; two *s. Educ:* Westminster Sch.; Corpus Christi Coll., Cambridge. Lieut RNVR, 1941-46. Called to Bar, Inner Temple, 1948; Master of the Bench, 1971. Recorder: of Dover, 1962-68; of Norwich, 1968-71; a Recorder, 1972; Chm., West Suffolk QS, 1965-71 (Dep. Chairman 1961-65). Chancellor of Diocese of St Edmundsbury and Ipswich, 1965-73, of Ely, 1969-73. Solicitor-General, 1972-74; Shadow Attorney-General and Legal Adviser to Shadow Cabinet, 1974-. Chm., Lakenheath Anglo-American Community Relations Cttee, 1966-71. *Publications:* (jtly) The Poisoned Life of Mrs Maybrick, 1977; The Royal Baccarat Scandal, 1977; (jtly) Tragedy in Three Voices: the Rattenbury murder, 1980. *Recreations:* writing, photography, reading. *Address:* 5 King's Bench Walk, Temple, EC4. *T:* 01-353 4713. *Clubs:* Garrick, Carlton.
See also Hon. Dame A. E. O. Butler-Sloss.

HAVERY, Richard Orbell, QC 1980; *b* 7 Feb. 1934; *s* of Joseph Horton Havery and Constance Eleanor (*née* Orbell). *Educ:* St Paul's; Magdalen Coll., Oxford (MA 1961). Called to the Bar, Middle Temple, 1962. *Publication:* (with D. A. McI. Kemp and W. S. Kemp) The Quantum of Damages: personal injury claims, 3rd edn, 1967. *Recreations:* music, croquet. *Address:* Gray's Inn Chambers, Gray's Inn, WC1R 5JA. *T:* 01-405 7211. *Clubs:* Garrick, Hurlingham.

HAVILAND, Denis William Garstin Latimer, CB 1957; MA; FBIM; FIWM; FRSA; idc; Chairman, Technology and Innovation Exchange, since 1981; *b* 15 Aug. 1910; *s* of late William Alexander Haviland and of Edyth Louise Latimer. *Educ:* Rugby Sch., St John's Coll., Cambridge (MA, exam. of AMInstT). LMS Rly, 1934-39. Army, RE (Col), 1940-46. Prin., Control Office for Germany and Austria, 1946; Asst Sec., 1947; transf. FO (GS), 1947; seconded to IDC, 1950; transf. Min. of Supply, 1951; Under Sec., 1953; Dep. Sec., 1959; trans. Min. of Aviation, 1959, Deputy Sec., 1959-64. Chm., Preparatory Commn European Launcher Develt Organisation, 1962-64. Jt Man. Dir and Dep. Chm., 1964, Chm. and Man. Dir, 1965-69, Staveley Industries Ltd; Director: Short Bros & Harland Ltd, 1964-81; Organised Office Designs, 1972-; Consultant. Mem. Council, BIM, 1967- (Vice-Chm.,

1973-74; Chm., Professional Standards Cttee, 1975-82). Member: Management Studies Bd, CNAA, 1974-79; Business and Management Cttee and Academic Cttee, CNAA, 1979-; Ct, Cranfield Inst. of Technology, 1970-. Liveryman, Co. of Coachmakers. Chm., Confedn of Healing Organisations, 1981-. *Address:* 113 Hampstead Way, NW11. *T:* 01-455 2638. *Club:* Naval and Military.

HAVILLAND; *see* de Havilland.

HAWAII, Bishop of, (Episcopal Church in the USA); *see* Browning, Rt Rev. E. L.

HAWARDEN, 8th Viscount, *cr* 1791; **Robert Leslie Eustace Maude;** farming his own estate since 1952; *b* 26 March 1926; *s* of 7th Viscount Hawarden and Viscountess Hawarden (*née* Marion Wright) (*d* 1974); *S* father 1958; *m* 1957, Susannah Caroline Hyde Gardner; two *s* one *d. Educ:* Winchester; Christ Church, Oxford. Cirencester Agricultural Coll., 1948-50. Served for a short time in the Coldstream Guards and was invalided out, 1945-46. *Recreation:* shooting. *Heir: s* Hon. Robert Connan Wyndham Leslie Maude, *b* 23 May 1961. *Address:* Wingham Court, near Canterbury, Kent. *T:* Wingham 222. *Club:* Farmers'.

HAWES, Derrick Gordon H.; *see* Harington Hawes.

HAWES, Maj.-Gen. Leonard Arthur, CBE 1940; DSO 1918; MC; MA (Hon.) Oxon; DL; Royal Artillery; *b* Throcking, Herts, 22 July 1892; *s* of C. A. Hawes, Uckfield, Sussex; *m* 1st, 1919, Gwendolen Mary (*d* 1970), *d* of D. H. Grimsdale, JP, Uxbridge, Middlesex; one *d* (one *s* decd); 2nd, 1972, Yolande, *widow* of Wyndham Robinson. *Educ:* Bedford; RM Academy, Woolwich. Lieut Royal Garrison Artillery, 1911; Capt., 1916; Temp. Major, 1917; Major, 1929; Bt Lieut-Col 1932; Lieut-Col and Col 1938; served European War, 1914-18 (wounded, CBE, DSO, MC, despatches, Order of Crown of Italy); served War of 1939-45; retired pay, 1945. DL West Sussex, 1977. *Address:* Old Manor House, West Harting, Petersfield, Hants. *Club:* Army and Navy.

HAWKE, family name of Baron Hawke.

HAWKE, 9th Baron, *cr* 1776, of Towton; **Bladen Wilmer Hawke;** *b* 31 Dec. 1901; *s* of 8th Baron and late Frances Alice, *d* of Col J. R. Wilmer, Survey of India; *S* father 1939; *m* 1934, Ina Mary, *e d* of late Henry Faure Walker, Highley Manor, Balcombe, Sussex; seven *d. Educ:* Winchester; King's Coll., Cambridge (MA). Bombay Company, India, 1923-38; Temp. Civil Servant, Ministry of Economic Warfare, 1940-43, War Office, 1943-45. Lord-in-Waiting to the Queen and Government Whip, House of Lords, 1953-57. Chm. Conservative Back Bench Peers Assoc., 1949-53; Executive Cttee, National Union Conservatives, 1950-53; Mem., House of Laity, Church Assembly, later Gen. Synod of C of E, 1955-75; Church Commissioner, 1958-73; Chm., Chichester Diocesan Board of Finance, 1962-72. Director: Initial Services Ltd, 1960-78; Ecclesiastical Insurance Office, Ltd, 1961-77. *Recreations:* golf, gardening. *Heir: b* Squadron Leader Hon. (Julian Stanhope) Theodore Hawke, Auxiliary Air Force [*b* 19 Oct. 1904; *m* 1st, 1933, Angela Margaret Griselda (marr. diss., 1946), *d* of late Capt. Edmund W. Bury; two *d* ; 2nd, 1947, Georgette Margaret, *d* of George S. Davidson; one *s* three *d*]. *Address:* Faygate Place, Faygate, Sussex. *T:* Faygate 252. *Club:* Carlton.
See also J. F. Easton, N. P. Scott.

HAWKE, Robert James Lee, AC 1979; MP (Lab) Wills, Melbourne, Parliament of Australia, since 1980; Member, National Executive, Australian Labor Party, since 1971 (President, 1973-78); *b* 9 Dec. 1929; *m* 1956, Hazel Masterson; one *s* two *d. Educ:* Univ. of Western Australia (LLB, BA(Econ)); Oxford Univ. (BLitt). Research Officer and Advocate for Aust. Council of Trade Unions, 1958-69. Pres., ACTU, 1970-80. Member: Governing Body of Internat. Labour Office, 1972-80; Board, Reserve Bank of Australia, 1973-80; Aust. Population and Immigration Council, 1976-80; Aust. Manufacturing Council, 1977-80. *Recreations:* tennis, cricket, reading. *Address:* 57 Waterfield Street, Coburg, Vic 3058, Australia; Parliament House, Canberra, ACT 2600, Australia.

HAWKEN, Lewis Dudley; a Deputy Chairman of the Board of Customs and Excise, since 1980; *b* 23 Aug. 1931; *s* of Richard and Doris May Evelyn Hawken; *m* 1954, Bridget Mary Gamble; two *s* one *d. Educ:* Harrow County Sch. for Boys; Lincoln Coll., Oxford (MA). Comr of Customs and Excise, 1975. *Recreations:* collecting Victorian books, tennis. *Address:* 19 Eastcote Road, Ruislip, Mddx. *T:* Ruislip 32405. *Clubs:* United Oxford & Cambridge University, MCC.

HAWKER, Albert Henry, CMG 1964; OBE 1960; *b* 31 Oct. 1911; *s* of late H. J. Hawker, Cheltenham and late Mrs G. A. Hawker, Exeter; *m* 1944, Margaret Janet Olivia (*d* 1980), *d* of late T. J. C. Acton (ICS) and Mrs M de C. Acton, BEM, Golden Furlong, Brackley, Northants; two *s. Educ:* Pate's Sch., Cheltenham. Served War of 1939-45: Bde Major 12th Bde, 1941-43; Staff Coll., Camberley, 1943-44; Lieut-Col Mil. Asst to CGS in India, 1944-46. RARO; Lieut-Col The Gordon Highlanders, 1946-61. Barclays Bank Ltd, Birmingham and Oxford Local Districts, 1929-39. Joined HM Overseas Civil Service, 1946; served in: Palestine, 1946-48; N Rhodesia, 1948-52; Zanzibar, 1952-64 (Development Sec., Admin. Sec., Perm. Sec. in Min. of Finance, Prime Minister's Office, Vice-President's Office and

President's Office); retd, 1964. Director: Thomson Regional Newspapers Ltd, 1965-69; The Times Ltd and The Sunday Times Ltd, 1968-69; The Thomson Organization, 1969-76. Gold Cross, Royal Order of George I of Greece, 1948; Brilliant Star of Zanzibar, 1957. *Recreations:* sailing, gardening, photography (Cdre, Zanzibar Sailing Club, 1955 and 1961). *Address:* Bowling Green Farm, Cottered, near Buntingford, Herts. *T:* Cottered 234. *Clubs:* Royal Commonwealth Society, Royal Yachting Association.

HAWKER, Rt. Rev. Dennis Gascoyne; *see* Grantham, Bishop Suffragan of.

HAWKER, Sir (Frank) Cyril, Kt 1958; Chairman: The Chartered Bank, 1973-74; The Standard Bank Ltd, 1962-74; Standard and Chartered Banking Group, 1969-74; The Bank of West Africa, 1965-73; Union Zairoise de Banques, 1969-74; Director: Head Wrightson & Co. Ltd, 1962-79; Davy Corporation Ltd, 1977-79; Deputy-Chairman, Midland and International Banks, 1964-72; Vice President, National Playing Fields Association, since 1976 (Hon. Treasurer and Chairman, Finance Committee, 1958-76); *b* 21 July 1900; *s* of late Frank Charley and Bertha Mary Hawker; *m* 1931, Marjorie Ann, *d* of late Thomas Henry and Amelia Harriett Pearce; three *d. Educ:* City of London Sch. Entered service Bank of England, 1920; Dep. Chief Cashier, 1944-48; Chief Accountant, 1948-53; Adviser to Governors, 1953-54; Executive Director, Bank of England, 1954-62. Dep. Chm., Agricultural Mortgage Corporation, 1962-73. High Sheriff of County of London, 1963. President: MCC, 1970-71; Minor Counties Cricket Assoc., 1968-; Amateur Football Alliance; Hon. Vice-Pres., Football Assoc. *Recreation:* cricket. *Address:* Pounsley Lodge, Blackboys, near Uckfield, Sussex. *T:* Hadlow Down 250. *Clubs:* Athenæum, MCC.

HAWKER, Sir Richard (George), Kt 1965; MA Cantab; *b* 11 April 1907; *s* of late R. M. Hawker; *m* 1940, Frances C., *d* of late S. Rymill; two *s* two *d* (and one *s* decd). *Educ:* Geelong Grammar Sch.; Trinity Hall, Cambridge. Returned SA, 1929; took over management Bungaree Merino Stud, 1932. Mem. Blyth Dist Coun., 1936-42, 1946-70. War service: 9/23 Light Horse Regt, 1939-41; 1st Armoured Div., AIF, 1941-44. Member: Cttee SA Stud Merino Breeders Assoc., 1939-40, 1959- (Pres. 1962-63, 1963-64); Council, Aust. Assoc. of Stud Merino Breeders, 1962-71 (Pres., 1968-71); Australian Wool Industry Conf., 1963-65 (as nominee of Federal Graziers' Council). Chm., Roseworthy Agricultural Coll. Council, 1964-73. Director: Adelaide Steamship Co. Ltd, 1949-79 (Chm. 1952-73); Coal & Allied Industries, NSW, 1961-78; (local bd in SA) Queensland Insurance Co. Ltd, 1955-74; Amalgamated Wireless (Australasia) Ltd, 1971-78. *Recreations:* shooting, fishing. *Address:* Bungaree, Clare, SA 5453, Australia. *T:* Clare (088) 422676. *Clubs:* Oriental; Australian (Sydney); Adelaide (SA).

HAWKES, (Charles Francis) Christopher, FBA, FSA; Professor of European Archaeology in the University of Oxford, and Fellow of Keble College, 1946-72, Professor Emeritus, since 1972; Hon. Fellow of Keble College, since 1972; Secretary, Committee of Research Laboratory for Archæology and History of Art, 1955-72; *b* 5 June 1905; *o s* of late Charles Pascoe Hawkes; *m* 1st, 1933, Jacquetta (from whom he obtained a divorce 1953) (*see* Jacquetta Hawkes), *yr d* of late Sir Frederick Gowland Hopkins, OM; one *s* ; 2nd, 1959, Sonia Elizabeth, *o d* of late Albert Andrew Chadwick. *Educ:* Winchester Coll. (Scholar); New Coll. Oxford (Scholar). 1st in Classical Hon. Mods 1926, in Final Lit. Hum. 1928; BA 1928; MA 1931; entered British Museum, Dept. of British and Medieval Antiquities, 1928; Asst Keeper 1st Class, 1938; in charge of Prehistoric and Romano-British Antiquities, 1946. Principal in Ministry of Aircraft Production, 1940-45. Retired from British Museum, 1946. I/c Inst. of Archæology, Oxford, 1961-67, 1968-72. FBA, 1948; FSA 1932; Fellow of Royal Archæological Institute, Hon. Sec. 1930-35, and Editor of Archæological Journal, 1944-50; Pres., Prehistoric Soc., 1950-54; a National Sec. for Great Britain, 1931-48, Mem. of Permanent Council, 1948-71, and Mem. Cttee of Honour, 1971-, International Union of Prehistoric and Protohistoric Sciences; Hon. Sec. of Colchester Excavation Cttee and in joint charge of its excavations, 1930-62; in charge of, or associated with various excavations, 1925-64, on Roman and prehistoric sites, especially for the Hants Field Club, and near Oxford; conducted archæological expedns in N Portugal, 1958-59. Vis. Lectr, Univ. of Manchester, 1947-49; Lectures: Dalrymple, Univ. of Glasgow, 1948; George Grant McCurdy, Harvard Univ., 1953; Davies, Belfast, 1974; Myres Meml, Oxford, 1975; British Acad., and Accad. Naz. Lincei, Rome, 1975; Mortimer Wheeler, 1975; travelled in Europe as Leverhulme Research Fellow, 1955-58, and as Leverhulme Emeritus Fellow, 1972-73; Guest Academician, Budapest, 1971; Guest Prof., Univ. of Munich, 1974; a Visitor, Ashmolean Museum, 1961-67. President: Section H., Brit. Assoc., 1957; Hants Field Club, 1960-63; Member: Council for British Archæology 1944-72 (Pres., 1961-64; Group 9 Convener, 1964-67); Ancient Monuments Board for England, 1954-69. Mem., German Archaeological Inst.; Corresp. Mem., RIA; Swiss Soc. for Prehistory; Patronal Mem., Univ. of Barcelona Inst. of Archaeology and Prehistory. Editor of Inventaria Archæologica for Great Britain, 1954-76. Hon. Dr Rennes, 1971; Hon. DLitt NUI, 1972. Various British Acad. awards, 1963-; Gold Medal, Soc. of Antiquaries, 1981. *Publications:* St Catharine's Hill, Winchester (with J. N. L. Myres and C. G. Stevens), 1931; Archæology in England and Wales, 1914-31 (with T. D. Kendrick), 1932; Winchester College: An Essay in Description and Appreciation, 1933; The Prehistoric Foundations of Europe, 1940, 1974; Prehistoric Britain (with Jacquetta Hawkes), 1943, 1947, 1957; Camulodunum: The Excavations at Colchester, 1930-39 (with M. R. Hull),

1947; (contrib. and ed with Sonia Hawkes) Archaeology into History, vol I, 1973; (contrib. and ed with P. M. Duval) Celtic Art in Ancient Europe, 1976; articles in encyclopædias, collaborative books, and many archæological journals; received complimentary vol. by British and foreign colleagues, 1971. *Recreations:* archæology, travelling, music. *Address:* Keble College, Oxford; 19 Walton Street, Oxford.

HAWKES, David, MA, DPhil; Research Fellow, All Souls College, Oxford, since 1973; *b* 6 July 1923; *s* of Ewart Hawkes and Dorothy May Hawkes (*née* Davis); *m* 1950, Sylvia Jean Perkins; one *s* three *d. Educ:* Bancroft's Sch. Open Scholarship in Classics, Christ Church, Oxford, 1941; Chinese Hons Sch., Oxford, 1945-47; Research Student, National Peking Univ., 1948-51. Formerly University Lecturer in Chinese, Oxford; Prof. of Chinese, Oxford Univ., 1959-71. Visiting Lecturer in Chinese Literature, Harvard Univ., 1958-59. *Publications:* Ch'u Tz'ü, Songs of the South, 1959; A Little Primer of Tu Fu, 1967; The Story of the Stone, vol. 1, 1973, vol. 2, 1977, vol. 3, 1980.

HAWKES, Jacquetta, OBE 1952; author and archaeologist; *b* 1910; *yr d* of Sir Frederick Gowland Hopkins, OM and Jessie Anne Stephens; *m* 1st, 1933, Christopher Hawkes (*see* Prof. C. F. C. Hawkes) (marr. diss. 1953); one *s* ; 2nd, 1953, J. B. Priestley, *qv. Educ:* Perse Sch.; Newnham Coll., Cambridge. MA. Associate, Newnham Coll., 1951. Research and excavation in Great Britain, Eire, France and Palestine, 1931-40; FSA, 1940. Asst Principal, Post-War Reconstruction Secretariat, 1941-43; Ministry of Education, becoming established Principal and Sec. of UK National Commn for UNESCO, 1943-49; retired from Civil Service to write, 1949. John Danz Vis. Prof., Univ. of Washington, 1971. Vice-Pres. Council for Brit. Archæology, 1949-52; Governor, Brit. Film Inst., 1950-55. Archæological adviser, Festival of Britain, 1949-51. Mem., UNESCO Culture Advisory Cttee, 1966-79. *Publications:* Archæology of Jersey, 1939; Prehistoric Britain (with Christopher Hawkes), 1944; Early Britain, 1945; Symbols and Speculations (poems), 1948; A Land, 1951 (£100 Kemsley Award); Guide to Prehistoric and Roman Monuments in England and Wales, 1951; Dragon's Mouth, (play) (with J. B. Priestley); Fables, 1953; Man on Earth, 1954; Journey Down a Rainbow (with J. B. Priestley), 1955; Providence Island, 1959; Man and the Sun, 1962; Unesco History of Mankind, Vol. I, Part 1, 1963; The World of the Past, 1963; King of the Two Lands, 1966; The Dawn of the Gods, 1968; The First Great Civilizations, 1973; (ed) Atlas of Ancient Archaeology, 1975; The Atlas of Early Man, 1976; A Quest of Love, 1980; Mortimer Wheeler: Adventurer in Archaeology, 1982; contrib. learned jls and national periodicals. *Recreation:* natural history. *Address:* Kissing Tree House, Alveston, Stratford-on-Avon, Warwicks.

HAWKES, Prof. John Gregory; Mason Professor of Botany, University of Birmingham, 1967-82; *b* 27 June 1915; *s* of C. W. and G. M. Hawkes; *m* 1941, Ellen Barbara Leather; two *s* two *d. Educ:* Univ. of Cambridge. BA, MA, PhD, ScD. Botanist, Potato Res. Station of Commonwealth Agricultural Bureaux, 1939-48, 1951-52; Dir of Potato Research Project, Min. of Ag., Colombia, S America, 1948-51; Lectr and Sen. Lectr in Taxonomic Botany, 1952-61; Prof. of Taxonomic Botany (Personal Chair), 1961-67. *Publications:* The Potatoes of Argentina, Brazil, Paraguay, and Uruguay (with J. P. Hjerting), 1969; A Computer-Mapped Flora (with D. A. Cadbury and R. C. Readett), 1971; (with O. H. Frankel) Crop Genetic Resources for Today and Tomorrow, 1975; Conservation and Agriculture, 1978; (with R. N. Lester and A. D. Skelding) The Biology and Taxonomy of the Solanaceae, 1979; contribs to various botanical and plant breeding jls. *Recreations:* walking, gardening, travel, art, archaeology. *Address:* 66 Lordswood Road, Birmingham B17 9BY. *T:* 021-427 2944.

HAWKES, Michael John; Deputy Chairman, Kleinwort, Benson Ltd, since 1982; *b* 7 May 1929; *s* of Wilfred Arthur Hawkes and Anne Maria Hawkes; *m* 1st, 1957, Gillian Mary Watts; two *s* two *d* ; 2nd, 1973, Elizabeth Anne Gurton. *Educ:* Bedford School; New College, Oxford (Exhibnr; BA); Gray's Inn. Kleinwort Sons & Co. Ltd, 1954; Kleinwort, Benson Ltd: Director, 1967; Vice Chairman, 1974; Director, Kleinwort, Benson, Lonsdale Ltd, 1974-; Chairman, Sharps Pixley Ltd, 1971-. *Address:* Brookfield House, Burghfield Common, Berks. *T:* Burghfield Common 2912. *Club:* Leander (Henley on Thames).

HAWKES, Raymond; Deputy Director, Naval Ship Production, 1977-78, retired; *b* 28 April 1920; *s* of Ernest Hawkes; *m* 1951, Joyce Barbara King; one *s* one *d. Educ:* RNC Greenwich. 1st cl. Naval Architecture, R.CNC; CEng; FRINA. Ship design, Bath, 1942-45 and 1954-56; aircraft carrier research at RAE Farnborough, 1945-49; hydrodynamic research at A.E.W. (Admiralty Experiment Works) Haslar, 1949-54; Principal Admty Overseer, Birkenhead, 1956-58; ship prodn, Bath, 1958-62; Chief Cons. Design, assault ships, survey fleet, small ships and auxiliaries, 1962-69; Senior Officers War Course 1966; Asst Dir Warship Design and Project Man. for Through Deck Cruiser, 1969-72; Dep. Dir, Warship Design, 1972-77. *Recreation:* golf. *Address:* Wood Meadow, Beechwood Road, Combe Down, Bath. *T:* Combe Down 832885.

HAWKESBURY, Viscount; Luke Marmaduke Peter Savile Foljambe; *b* 25 March 1972; *s* and *heir* of 5th Earl of Liverpool, *qv.*

HAWKESWORTH, Thomas Simon Ashwell; QC 1982; a Recorder of the Crown Court, since 1982; *b* 15 Nov. 1943; *s* of Charles Peter Elmhirst

Hawkesworth and Felicity Hawkesworth; *m* 1970, Jennifer Lewis; two *s*. *Educ*: Rugby Sch.; The Queen's Coll., Oxford. MA. Called to the Bar, Gray's Inn, 1967. Asst Recorder, 1980-82. *Recreations*: squash, gardening, amateur dramatics. *Address*: The Lodge, Kirkby Overblow, Harrogate, N Yorks HG3 1HH. *T*: Harrogate 879355.

HAWKEY, Rt. Rev. Ernest Eric; *b* 1 June 1909; *s* of Richard and Beatrice Hawkey; *m* 1943, Patricia Spark. *Educ*: Trinity Grammar Sch., Sydney, NSW. Deacon, 1933; Priest, 1936. Curate: St Alban's, Ultimo, 1933-34; St Paul, Burwood, 1934-40; Priest-in-charge, Kandos, 1940-46, Rector, 1946-47; Aust. Bd of Missions: Actg Organising Sec., 1947-50; Organising Sec., 1950-68; Canon Residentiary, Brisbane, 1962-68; Bishop of Carpentaria, 1968-74. *Recreations*: music, gardening. *Address*: 2/12 Wellington Street, Clayfield, Queensland 4011, Australia. *T*: 262-2108.

HAWKING, Prof. Stephen William, CBE 1982; FRS 1974; Fellow of Gonville and Caius College, Cambridge; Lucasian Professor of Mathematics, Cambridge University, since 1979; *b* 8 Jan. 1942; *s* of Dr F. and Mrs E. I. Hawking; *m* 1965, Jane Wilde; two *s* one *d*. *Educ*: St Albans Sch.; University Coll., Oxford (BA), Hon. Fellow 1977; Trinity Hall, Cambridge (PhD). Research Fellow, Gonville and Caius Coll., 1965-69; Fellow for distinction in science, 1969-; Mem. Inst. of Theoretical Astronomy, Cambridge, 1968-72; Research Asst, Inst. of Astronomy, Cambridge, 1972-73; Cambridge University: Research Asst, Dept of Applied Maths and Theoretical Physics, 1973-75; Reader in Gravitational Physics, 1975-77, Professor, 1977-79. Fairchild Distinguished Schol., Calif Inst. of Technol., 1974-75. Hon. DSc Oxon, 1978. (Jtly) Eddington Medal, RAS, 1975; Pius XI Gold Medal, Pontifical Acad. of Scis, 1975; Dannie Heinemann Prize for Math. Phys., Amer. Phys. Soc. and Amer. Inst. of Physics, 1976; William Hopkins Prize, Cambridge Philosoph. Soc., 1976; Maxwell Medal, Inst. of Physics, 1976; Hughes Medal, Royal Soc., 1976; Albert Einstein Award, 1978; Albert Einstein Medal, Albert Einstein Soc., Berne, 1979; Franklin Medal, Franklin Inst., USA, 1981. Hon. Degrees: Chicago, 1981; Leicester, New York, Notre Dame, Princeton, 1982. *Publications*: (with G. F. R. Ellis) The Large Scale Structure of Space-Time, 1973; (ed W. W. Israel) General Relativity: an Einstein centenary survey, 1979; (ed with M. Roček) Superspace and Supergravity, 1981. *Address*: 5 West Road, Cambridge. *T*: Cambridge 51905.

HAWKINGS, Sir (Francis) Geoffrey, Kt 1978; Chairman: Stone-Platt Industries Ltd, 1974-80 (Director, 1962; Managing Director, 1967); Chloride Group Ltd, 1977-79 (Director, 1975; Deputy Chairman, 1976); Director, Alliance Investment Co., 1976-81; *b* 13 Aug. 1913; *s* of Harry Wilfred Hawkings and Louise Hawkings, Lymington, Hants; *m* 1940, Margaret Mary, *d* of Alexander Wilson, OBE, MD, DL; one *s* one *d*. *Educ*: Wellington; New Coll., Oxford (MA). Commissioned into Lancashire Fusiliers (TA), 1939; Camberley sc, 1943; Bde Major, Inf. and Air-borne Bdes. Administrative appt, Stewarts & Lloyds Ltd, 1946-49; joined Textile Machinery Makers Ltd, 1950, Dir, 1959, Man. Dir, 1961. Mem., Court of Governors, Manchester Univ., 1964-79; Pres., Engrg Employers' Fedn, 1978-80. *Recreations*: fishing, racing. *Address*: Lovington House, Alresford, Hants SO24 0RD. *T*: Itchen Abbas 371.

HAWKINS, Sir Arthur (Ernest), Kt 1976; BSc (Eng); CEng, FIMechE, FIEE, FInstE; Chairman 1972-77, Member, 1970-77, Central Electricity Generating Board; *b* 10 June 1913; *s* of Rev. H. R. and Louisa Hawkins; *m* 1939, Laura Judith Tallent Draper; one *s* two *d*. *Educ*: The Grammar Sch., Gt Yarmouth; City of Norwich Technical Coll. Served (prior to nationalisation) with Gt Yarmouth Electricity Dept, Central Electricity Bd and Islington Electricity Dept (Dep. Engr and Gen. Manager); Croydon Dist Manager of SE Elec. Bd, 1948; joined Brit. Electricity Authority as Chief Asst Engr in System Operation Br., 1951; Personal Engrg Asst to Chief Engr, 1954. With the CEGB since its formation in 1957, at first as System Planning Engr and then as Chief Ops Engr, 1959-64; Midlands Regional Dir, 1964-70. Mem., Nuclear Power Adv. Bd, 1973-. Chm., F International Ltd, 1978-79. CBIM. *Publications*: contrib. Jl of Management Studies; various papers to technical instns. *Recreations*: fell walking, swimming, motoring. *Address*: 61 Rowan Road, W6. *Club*: Royal Automobile.

HAWKINS, Clive David B.; *see* Black-Hawkins.

HAWKINS, Desmond, OBE 1963; BBC Controller, South and West, 1967-69; *b* 1908; *m* Barbara Hawkins (*née* Skidmore); two *s* two *d*. Novelist, critic and broadcaster, 1935-45; Literary Editor of New English Weekly and Purpose Quarterly; Fiction Chronicler of The Criterion; Features Producer, BBC West Region, 1946; Head of Programmes, 1955; founded BBC Natural History Unit, 1957. FRSL 1977. Hon. LLD Bristol, 1974. Silver Medal, RSPB, 1959; Imperial Tobacco Radio Award for best dramatisation, 1976 and 1978. *Publications*: Poetry and Prose of John Donne, 1938; Hawk among the Sparrows, 1939; Stories, Essays and Poems of D. H. Lawrence, 1939; Lighter than Day, 1940; War Report, 1946; Sedgemoor and Avalon, 1954; The BBC Naturalist, 1957; Hardy the Novelist, 1965; Wild Life in the New Forest, 1972; Avalon and Sedgemoor, 1973; Hardy, Novelist and Poet, 1976; preface to Richard Jefferies' Wild Life in a Southern County, 1978; Cranborne Chase, 1980; Concerning Agnes, 1982. *Address*: 2 Stanton Close, Blandford Forum, Dorset DT11 7RT. *T*: Blandford 54954. *Club*: BBC.

HAWKINS, Air Vice-Marshal Desmond Ernest, CB 1971; CBE 1967; DFC and Bar, 1942; *b* 27 Dec. 1919; *s* of Ernest and Lilian Hawkins; *m* 1947, Joan Audrey (*née* Munro); one *s*, and one step *s*. *Educ*: Bancroft Sch. Commissioned in RAF, 1938. Served War of 1939-45: Coastal Command and Far East, commanding 36, 230 and 240 Sqdns, 1940-46 (despatches). Commanded RAF Pembroke Dock, 1946-47 (despatches). Staff appts, 1947-50; RAF Staff Coll., 1950; Staff appts, 1951-55; commanded 38 Sqdn, OC Flg, RAF Luqa, 1955-57; jssc, 1957; Staff appts, 1958-61; SASO 19 Gp, 1961-63; commanded RAF Tengah, 1963-66; idc 1967; commanded RAF Lyneham, 1968; SASO, HQ, RAF Strike Command, 1969-71; Dir-Gen., Personal Services (RAF), MoD, 1971-74; Dep. Man. Dir, Services Kinema Corp., 1974-80. *Recreations*: sailing, fishing. *Address*: c/o Barclays Bank, Bridgwater, Somerset. *Clubs*: Royal Air Force; Cruising Association; Royal Lymington Yacht.

HAWKINS, Prof. Eric William, CBE 1973; Director, Language Teaching Centre, University of York, 1965-79, now Professor Emeritus; *b* 8 Jan. 1915; *s* of James Edward Hawkins and Agnes Thompson (*née* Clarie); *m* 1938, Ellen Marie Thygesen, Copenhagen; one *s* one *d*. *Educ*: Liverpool Inst. High Sch.; Trinity Hall, Cambridge (Open Exhibn). MA, CertEd, (Hon.) FIL. War Service, 1st Bn The Loyal Regt, 1940-46 (despatches 1945); wounded N Africa, 1943; Major 1945. Asst Master, Liverpool Coll., 1946-49; Headmaster: Oldershaw Grammar Sch., Wallasey, 1949-53; Calday Grange Grammar Sch., Ches, 1953-65. Member: Central Adv. Council for Educn (England) (Plowden Cttee), 1963-66; Rampton Cttee (educn of ethnic minorities), 1979-81. Hon. Professorial Fellow, University Coll. of Wales, Aberystwyth, 1979. Gold Medal, Inst. Linguists, 1971. *Publications*: (ed) Modern Languages in the Grammar School, 1961; (ed) New Patterns in Sixth Form Modern Language Studies, 1970; A Time for Growing, 1971; Le français pour tout le monde, vols 1-5, 1974-79; Modern Languages in the Curriculum, 1981. *Recreations*: walking, cello. *Address*: 9 Tower View, Tranby Lane, Anlaby, Hull HU10 7EG. *Club*: Royal Commonwealth Society.

HAWKINS, Frank Ernest; Chairman, 1959-73, and Managing Director, 1956-73, International Stores Ltd, Mitre Square, EC3; *b* 12 Aug. 1904; 2nd *s* of late George William and Sophie Hawkins; *m* 1933, Muriel, *d* of late Joseph and Isabella Sinclair; two *s* one *d*. *Educ*: Leyton County High Sch. Joined staff of International Stores Ltd as boy clerk, 1919; apptd: Asst Sec., 1934; Sec., 1935; Director, 1949; Managing Dir, 1956; Vice-Chm., 1958; Chairman, 1959. *Recreation*: golf. *Address*: Merton Court, Page's Croft, Wokingham, Berkshire. *Club*: East Berkshire Golf.

HAWKINS, Sir Humphry (Villiers) Cæsar, 7th Bt, *cr* 1778; MB, ChB; Medical Practitioner; *b* 10 Aug. 1923; *s* of Sir Villiers Geoffry Caesar Hawkins, 6th Bt and Blanche Hawkins, *d* of A. E. Hampden-Smithers; *S* father 1955; *m* 1952, Anita, *d* of C. H. Funkey, Johannesburg; two *s* three *d*. *Educ*: Hilton Coll.; University of Witwatersrand. Served War of 1939-45 with 6th SA Armoured Div. *Heir*: *s* Howard Cæsar Hawkins, *b* 17 Nov. 1956. *Address*: 41 Hume Road, Dunkeld, Johannesburg, S Africa. *Club*: Johannesburg Country.

HAWKINS, Sir Paul (Lancelot), Kt 1982; TD 1945; MP (C) South West Norfolk since 1964; *b* 7 Aug. 1912; *s* of L. G. Hawkins and of Mrs Hawkins (*née* Peile); *m* 1937, E. Joan Snow; two *s* one *d*. *Educ*: Cheltenham Coll. Joined Family Firm, 1930; Chartered Surveyor, 1933. Served in TA, Royal Norfolk Regt, 1933-45; POW Germany, 1940-45. An Asst Govt Whip, 1970-71; a Lord Comr of the Treasury, 1971-73; Vice-Chamberlain of HM Household, 1973-74. Mem., Delegn to Council of Europe and WEU, 1976-. CC Norfolk, 1949-70, Alderman, 1968-70. *Recreations*: walking, gardening, travel. *Address*: Stables, Downham Market, Norfolk. *Club*: Carlton.

HAWKINS, Rt. Rev. Ralph Gordon, CMG 1977; ThD; *b* St John's, Newfoundland, 1911; *s* of late Samuel J. and Alfreda Hawkins; *m* 1938, Mary Edna, *d* of late William James and Grace Leslie, Newport, Mon.; one *s* one *d*. *Educ*: Univ. Memorial Coll., St John's; St Boniface Coll., Warminster; Durham Univ. (Hatfield Coll.). BA, LTh 1934; deacon, 1935, priest, 1936, Bristol. Curate of St Anne's, Brislington, 1935-38; Rector of Morawa, 1938-43; Rector of Wembley-Floreat Park, 1943-49; Chaplain, RAAF, 1943-45; Rector of St Hilda's, N Perth, 1949-56; Canon of Perth, 1954; Archdeacon of Perth, 1957; Bishop of Bunbury, 1957-77. *Address*: 9 Cross Street, Bunbury, Western Australia 6230.

HAWKINS, Vice-Adm. Sir Raymond (Shayle), KCB 1965 (CB 1963); *b* 21 Dec. 1909; *s* of late Thomas Hawkins and Dorothy Hawkins, Bedford; *m* 1936, Rosalind (marr. diss. 1980), *d* of late Roger and Ada Ingpen; three *s* one *d*. *Educ*: Bedford Sch. Entered Royal Navy, 1927; HMS Iron Duke 1932; HMS Resolution, 1933; served with Submarines, 1935-43; HMS Orion, 1943. Asst Naval Attaché, Paris, 1954; Commanding Officer, HMS St Vincent, 1957; Rear-Adm., Nuclear Propulsion, 1959; Dir of Marine Engineering, 1961-63; Chief Naval Engineering Officer, 1962-63; Vice-Adm., 1964; a Lord Comr of the Admiralty, Fourth Sea Lord and Vice-Controller, 1963-64; Chief of Naval Supplies and Transport and Vice-Controller of the Navy, MoD, 1964-67; retd, 1967. *Address*: The Old Garden, All Saints Road, Lansdown, Bath, Avon.

HAWKINS, Ven. Richard Stephen; Archdeacon of Totnes, since 1981; Priest-in-charge of Whitestone with Oldridge, since 1981; *b* 2 April 1939; *s* of late Ven. Canon John Stanley Hawkins and of Elsie Hawkins (*née* Briggs); *m* 1966, Valerie Ann Herneman; one *s* one *d* (and one *s* one *d* decd). *Educ*:

Exeter School; Exeter Coll., Oxford; St Stephen's House, Oxford. MA (Oxon); BPhil (Exeter Univ.); CQSW. Asst Curate, St Thomas, Exeter, 1963-66; Team Vicar of Clyst St Mary, Clyst Valley Team Ministry, 1966-78; Bishop's Officer for Ministry and Joint Director, Exeter-Truro Ministry Training Scheme, 1978-81; Team Vicar, Central Exeter Team Ministry, 1978-81; Diocesan Director of Ordinands, 1979-81. *Address:* The Rectory, Whitestone, Exeter EX4 2JT. *T:* Longdown 406.

HAWKINS, Rev. Robert Henry; *b* 3 March 1892; *s* of Rev. Francis Henry Albert Hawkins and Mary Anna Ridley Hawkins (*née* Morris); *m* 1917, Margaret (*d* 1977), *e d* of Rev. T. A. Lacey, DD, Canon of Worcester; two *s* three *d. Educ:* Forest Sch., Essex; St Edmund Hall, Oxford. BA 1913, MA 1919. Served European War: commissioned 3rd S Staffs Regt, 1914; France and Salonika, 1915-17; RFC (Flight Comdr), 1917-19. Ordained Deacon, 1919, Priest, 1920; Vicar of: Maryport, Dio. Carlisle, 1923-27; St George, Barrow in Furness, 1927-34; Dalston, 1934-43; Vicar of St Mary, Nottingham, Rural Dean of Nottingham and Hon. Canon of Southwell, 1943-58; Canon of St George's, Windsor, 1958-70. *Address:* Manormead, Tilford Road, Hindhead, Surrey. *T:* Hindhead 6493.

HAWKSLEY, John Callis, CBE 1946; PhD, MD, FRCP; formerly Physician, University College Hospital and St Peter's, St Paul's and St Philip's Hospitals, London; *b* 30 Nov. 1903; *s* of late Joseph Hawksley, Great Yarmouth; *m* 1933, Margaret, *er d* of late Engineer Vice-Adm. Sir Reginald Skelton, KCB, CBE, DSO; two *s* two *d. Educ:* Dulwich Coll.; University Coll., London; University Coll. Hospital. Appts on resident staff, University Coll. Hosp., 1926-28; ship's surg., BISN Co., 1929; research appts, Birmingham Children's Hosp., 1930-32; Sebag-Montefiore Research Fellow, Hospital for Sick Children, Gt Ormond Street, 1933-34; Bilton Pollard Travelling Fellowship, University Coll. Hosp., 1935, devoted to work at Rigshospitalet, Copenhagen; Asst Physician, University Coll. Hosp., 1936-39; Physician to University Coll. Hosp., 1940; retd, 1969. Temp. commission RAMC 1939; served with rank of Lieut-Col in MEF, 1941-44 (despatches); Consulting Physician, local Brig., with South East Asia Command, 1945. Fellow of University Coll., London, 1966; Dean of University Coll. Hosp. Med. Sch., 1949-54; Senior Vice-Pres., RCP, 1966. *Publications:* contributions to various medical journals. *Recreations:* mountaineering, music. *Address:* The Old Vicarage, East Kennett, Wilts. *T:* Lockeridge 237. *Club:* Alpine.

HAWKSLEY, (Philip) Warren; MP (C) The Wrekin, since 1979; *b* 10 March 1943; *s* of late Bradshaw Warren Hawksley and of Monica Augusta Hawksley; *m* 1967, Cynthia Marie Higgins; two *d. Educ:* Denstone Coll., Uttoxeter. Employed by Lloyd's Bank since leaving school. Member: Salop County Council, 1970-81; West Mercia Police Authority, 1977-81. *Recreations:* badminton, reading, travel, beagling. *Address:* The Old Place, The Racecourse, Oswestry, Salop SY10 7NL; 34 St Andrew's Way, Church Aston, Newport, Shropshire. *T:* Newport 811717.

HAWLEY, Major Sir David Henry, 7th Bt, *cr* 1795; MA; FRICS; DL; late KRRC; formerly with firm of Jas Martin & Co., Chartered Surveyors, Land Agents and Valuers, 8 Bank Street, Lincoln; *b* 13 May 1913; *e s* of Capt. Cyril Francis Hawley and Ursula Mary, *d* of Henry Percy St John; *S* uncle, 1923; *m* 1938, Hermione, 2nd *d* of late Col L. Gregson; one *s* two *d. Educ:* Eton; Magdalene Coll., Cambridge. Served Palestine, 1936-39 (medal and clasp), War of 1939-45 (prisoner, 1939-45 Star, despatches). Hon. Life Mem., Nat. Trust. Chm., Lincoln Dio. Adv. Cttee, 1978-81. Vice-Pres., Lincs Branch, CLA. DL 1952, High Sheriff, 1962-63, Lincs. *Recreation:* shooting. *Heir: s* Henry Nicholas Hawley, *b* 26 Nov. 1939. *Address:* Tumby Lawn, Boston, Lincs PE22 7TA. *T:* Coningsby 42337.

HAWLEY, Sir Donald (Frederick), KCMG 1978 (CMG 1970); MBE 1955; HM Diplomatic Service, retired; British High Commissioner in Malaysia, 1977-81; Barrister-at-law; *b* 22 May 1921; *s* of late Mr and Mrs F. G. Hawley, Little Gaddesden, Herts; *m* 1964, Ruth Morwenna Graham Howes, *d* of late Rev. P. G. Howes and of Mrs Howes, Charmouth, Dorset; one *s* three *d. Educ:* Radley; New Coll., Oxford (MA). Served in HM Forces, 1941. Sudan Political Service, 1944; joined Sudan Judiciary, 1947. Called to Bar, Inner Temple, 1951. Chief Registrar, Sudan Judiciary, and Registrar-Gen. of Marriages, 1951; resigned from Sudan Service, 1955; joined HM Foreign Service, 1955; FO, 1956: Political Agent, Trucial States, in Dubai, 1958; Head of Chancery, British Embassy, Cairo, 1962; Counsellor and Head of Chancery, British High Commission, Lagos, 1965; Vis. Fellow, Dept of Geography, Durham Univ., 1967; Counsellor (Commercial), Baghdad, 1968; HM Consul-General, Muscat, 1971; HM Ambassador to Oman, 1971-75; Asst Under Sec. of State, FCO, 1975-77. Special Adviser to Hongkong and Shanghai Banking Corp.; Dir, Ewbank & Partners; consultant. Vice-Pres., Anglo-Omani Soc.; Mem. Council, Reading Univ. *Publications:* Handbook for Registrars of Marriage and Ministers of Religion, 1963 (Sudan Govt pubn); Courtesies in the Trucial States, 1965; The Trucial States, 1971; Oman and its Renaissance, 1977; Courtesies in the Gulf Area, 1978. *Recreations:* tennis, squash, sailing, book collecting; Hon. Sec., Sudan Football Assoc., 1952-55. *Address:* Little Cheverell House, near Devizes, Wilts. *T:* Lavington 3322. *Club:* Athenæum.

HAWORTH, Sir (Arthur) Geoffrey, 2nd Bt, *cr* 1911; MA; farmer; *b* 5 April 1896; *s* of Sir Arthur Haworth, 1st Bt, and Lily (*d* 1952), *y d* of late John Rigby, Altrincham; *S* father, 1944; *m* 1926, Emily Dorothea (*d* 1980), *er d* of H. E. Gaddum, The Priory, Bowdon; two *s* two *d. Educ:* Rugby Sch.; New

Coll., Oxford. Served European War, 1914-19, Lieut Queen's Own Royal West Kent Regiment and Machine Gun Corps (despatches). Chm., Hallé Concert Soc., 1965-77; Pres., Manchester Palace Theatre Trust Ltd, 1980- (Chm., 1978-80). FRSA 1969. JP Chester, 1937-70. Hon. MA Manchester, 1972. *Recreation:* music. *Heir: s* Philip Haworth [*b* 17 Jan. 1927; *m* 1951, Joan Helen, *d* of late S. P. Clark, Ipswich; four *s* one *d*]. *Address:* The Red Brook, Lower Peover, Cheshire. *Club:* Farmers'.

HAWORTH, Mrs Betsy Ellen; Deaconess; Third Church Estates Commissioner, since 1981; *b* 23 July 1924; *d* of Ambrose and Annie Kenyon; *m* 1953, Rev. Fred Haworth (*d* 1981); one *s* two *d. Educ:* William Temple Coll. IDC (CofE). Licensed as lay worker, dio. Manchester, 1952, dio. Blackburn, 1965; elected Mem., Church Assembly, 1965-70, Gen. Synod, 1970-75, 1975-80, 1980-. Advr for Women's Ministry, dio. Manchester, 1971-81. Deaconess 1980. Hon. Licensed Lay Worker, St Stephen, Astley, dio. Manchester, 1981-; Examining Chaplain to Bishop of Manchester, 1981-. *Address:* 20 Guild Avenue, Walkden, Worsley, Manchester. *T:* 061-799 5364.

HAWORTH, Sir Geoffrey; *see* Haworth, Sir A. G.

HAWORTH, Very Rev. Kenneth William; Dean of Salisbury, 1960-71, Dean Emeritus, since 1971; *b* 21 Jan. 1903; *s* of William Bell and Helen Haworth; *m* 1937, Sybil Mavrojani (*d* 1982); two *s* two *d. Educ:* Cheltenham Coll.; Clare Coll., Cambridge; Wells Theological Coll. Curate of St Giles, Willenhall, 1926; Domestic Chaplain 1931, Examining Chaplain, 1937, to Bp of Lichfield; Chaplain of Wells Theological Coll., 1938; CF (4th cl.), 1939; Rector of Stratton w. Baunton, Dio., Gloucester, 1943; Vice-Principal of Wells Theol. Coll., 1946, Principal, 1947-60; Prebendary of Combe II in Wells Cathedral, 1947-60; Exam. Chap. to Bishop of Bath and Wells, 1947; Proctor in Convocation, 1956-59; Exam. Chap. to Bishop of Salisbury, 1962. *Address:* The Common, Woodgreen, Fordingbridge, Hants. *T:* Downton 22239.

HAWORTH, Lionel, OBE 1958; FRS 1971; RDI; FEng; Senior Partner, Lionel Haworth and Associates; *b* 4 Aug. 1912; *s* of John Bertram Haworth and Anna Sophia Ackerman; *m* 1956, Joan Irene Bradbury; one *s* one *d. Educ:* Rondebosch Boys' High Sch.; Univ. of Cape Town. Cape Town Corp's Gold Medal and schol. tenable abroad. BSc (Eng); FIMechE; FRAeS. Graduate Apprentice, Associated Equipment Co., 1934; Rolls-Royce Ltd, Derby: Designer, 1936; Asst Chief Designer, 1944; Dep. Chief Designer, 1951; Chief Designer (Civil Engines), 1954; Chief Engr (Prop. Turbines), 1962; Bristol Siddeley Engines Ltd: Chief Design Consultant, 1963; Chief Designer, 1964; Dir of Design, Aero Div., 1965, Dir of Design, Aero Div., Rolls-Royce Ltd, 1968-77. Brit. Gold Medal for Aeronautics, 1971; RDI 1976; Founder Fellow, Fellowship of Engineering, 1976. *Recreation:* sailing. *Address:* 10 Hazelwood Road, Sneyd Park, Bristol BS9 1PX. *T:* Bristol 683032.

HAWORTH, Robert Downs, DSc, PhD Victoria, BSc Oxon; FRS 1944; FRSC; Firth Professor of Chemistry, University of Sheffield, 1939-63, now Emeritus; *b* 15 March 1898; *s* of J. T. and Emily Haworth, Cheadle, Cheshire; *m* 1930, Dorothy, *d* of A. L. Stocks, Manchester; one *d. Educ:* Secondary Sch., Stockport; University of Manchester, Mercer Scholar, 1919; Beyer Fellow, 1920; 1851 Exhibition Scholar, 1921-23; 1851 Exhibition Sen. Student, 1923-25; Demonstrator in Organic Chemistry, Oxford, 1925-26; Lecturer in Chemistry, King's Coll., Newcastle upon Tyne, 1927-39. Visiting Prof. of Organic Chemistry, University of Madras, 1963-64. Davy Medal, Royal Society, 1956. Hon. DSc Sheffield, 1974. *Publications:* papers on organic chemistry in Journal of Chemical Society. *Address:* The University, Sheffield S3 7HF; 67 Tom Lane, Sheffield S10 3PA. *T:* Sheffield 302595.

HAWORTH, Hon. Sir William (Crawford), Kt 1969; Director of companies; *b* 15 April 1905; *s* of Edward Haworth; *m* 1927, Winifred Senior. *Educ:* Essendon; Melbourne Univ.; Victorian Pharmacy Coll. PhC 1925; MPS. War of 1939-45: Captain, 2nd AIF, 9th Div.; served in Egypt, Tobruk, Palestine and Syria; R of O 1944. Municipal Councillor, S Melbourne, 1923-38; Mem. Bd of Management, Victoria Infectious Diseases Hosp., 1936-38; Mem. Council, S Melbourne Technical Sch., 1939-62 (Pres., 1947-48) MLA for Albert Park, Vic Parliament, 1937-45; Minister for Health and Housing, Vic Govt, Oct.-Nov. 1945. MHR for Isaacs, Aust. Commonwealth Parliament, 1949-69. Mem., Jt Parly Cttee for Foreign Affairs, 1959-66; Leader of Aust. Deleg. to Inter-Parly Union Conf., Warsaw, 1959 (Mem. IPU Council, 1959-60); Dep. Chm. of Cttees, 1960-69. *Recreation:* golf. *Address:* 25 Grange Road, Toorak, Vic 3142, Australia. *T:* 241-7055. *Clubs:* Australian (Melbourne); Naval and Military, West Brighton, Victoria Racing, Royal Automobile Club of Victoria, Kingston Heath Golf (Vic).

HAWSER, Cyril Lewis, QC 1959; **His Honour Judge Hawser;** a Circuit Judge (Official Referee), since 1978; *b* 5 Oct. 1916; *s* of Abraham and Sarah Hawser; *m* 1940, Phyllis Greatrex; one *s* one *d. Educ:* Cardiff High Sch.; Balliol Coll., Oxford (Williams Law Scholar; MA). Called to the Bar, 1938, Bencher, 1966, Inner Temple. Recorder of Salisbury, 1967-69; Recorder of Portsmouth, 1969-71; a Recorder of the Crown Court, 1972-78. Mem. Council and Vice-Chm. of Exec. Cttee of Justice. *Publication:* (report) Case of James Hanratty, 1975. *Recreations:* tennis, chess, conversation. *Address:* 39D Eaton Square, SW1. *T:* 01-235 6566.

HAWTHORNE, James Burns, CBE 1982; Controller, BBC Northern Ireland, since 1978; *b* 27 March 1930; *s* of Thomas Hawthorne and Florence Hawthorne (*née* Burns); *m* 1958, Patricia King; one *s* two *d. Educ:* Queen's Univ., Belfast (BA); Stranmillis Coll. of Educn. Master at Sullivan Upper Sch., Holywood, 1951–60; joined Educn Dept, BBC, 1960; Schools Producer in charge, N Ireland, 1968; Chief Asst, N Ireland, 1969–70; seconded to Hong Kong Govt, as Controller Television, 1970; Dir of Broadcasting, Hong Kong, 1972–77 (resigned from BBC staff, 1976, *ie* seconded status ended; rejoined BBC, Jan. 1978, on appt as Controller, NI). Mem., NI Council for Educn Develt, 1980–. Queen's Univ. New Ireland Soc. award for community relations work, 1967; Winston Churchill Fellowship, 1968. *Publications:* (ed) Two Centuries of Irish History, 1966, repr. 1967, 1969, rev. edn 1974; Reporting Violence: lessons from Northern Ireland, 1981. *Recreations:* angling, music. *Address:* c/o BBC, Belfast, Northern Ireland BT2 8HQ.

HAWTHORNE, Nigel Barnard; self-employed actor and writer; *b* Coventry, 5 April 1929; *s* of Charles Barnard Hawthorne and Agnes Rosemary (*née* Rice). *Educ:* Christian Brothers' Coll., Cape Town, S Africa. Entered theatre professionally, 1950; returned to England, 1951, where he has worked ever since, with the exception of a small number of engagements abroad. *Stage:* Otherwise Engaged, 1976; Privates on Parade, 1978; *television:* Marie Curie, 1977; Destiny, 1978; Edward and Mrs Simpson, 1978; The Knowledge, 1979; Rod of Iron, 1980; Yes Minister (series), annually 1980–; The Critic, 1982; *films:* Firefox, 1981; Gandhi, 1981; Golda, 1981. SWET (Best Supporting Actor) and Clarence Derwent Award for Privates on Parade; Broadcasting Press Guild Award and BAFTA (Best Actor in Light Entertainment) for Yes Minister. *Recreations:* swimming, gardening, painting. *Address:* 5 Stud Cottages, Burnt Farm Ride, Crewes Hill, Enfield, Mddx. *T:* 01-366 5319.

HAWTHORNE, Prof. Sir William (Rede), Kt 1970; CBE 1959; MA; ScD; FRS 1955; FEng; FIMechE; Master of Churchill College, Cambridge, 1968–July 1983; Hopkinson and ICI Professor of Applied Thermodynamics, University of Cambridge, 1951–80; Head of Department of Engineering, 1968–73; *b* 22 May 1913; *s* of William Hawthorne, MInstCE, and Elizabeth C. Hawthorne; *m* 1939, Barbara Runkle, Cambridge, Massachusetts, USA; one *s* two *d. Educ:* Westminster Sch.; Trinity Coll., Cambridge; Massachusetts Institute of Technology, USA. Development Engineer, Babcock & Wilcox Ltd, 1937–39; Scientific Officer, Royal Aircraft Establishment, 1940–44; British Air Commission, Washington, 1944; Dep. Dir Engine Research, Min. of Supply, 1945; Massachusetts Institute of Technology: Associate Prof. of Mechanical Engineering, 1946; George Westinghouse Prof. of Mechanical Engineering, 1948–51; Jerome C. Hunsaker Prof. of Aeronautical Engineering, 1955–56; Vis. Inst. Prof., 1962–63; Mem. Corporation, 1969–74. Chairman: Home Office Scientific Adv. Council, 1967–76; Adv. Council for Energy Conservation, 1974–79; Member: Energy Commn, 1977–79; Standing Commn on Energy and the Environment, 1978–81. Director: Dracone Developments Ltd, 1958–; Cummins Engine Co. Inc., 1974–. Governor, Westminster Sch., 1956–76. A Vice-Pres., Royal Soc., 1969–70 and 1979–81; Mem. Council, 1968–70, 1979–81. Foreign Associate: US Nat. Acad. of Sciences, 1965; US Nat. Acad. of Engrg, 1976. Hon. DEng: Sheffield, 1976; Liverpool 1982; Hon. DSc: Salford, 1980; Strathclyde, 1981; Bath, 1981; Oxon, 1982. Hon. FAIAA; Hon. FRAeS. Medal of Freedom (US), 1947. *Publications:* papers in mechanical and aeronautical journals. *Address:* The Master's Lodge, Churchill College, Cambridge. *Club:* Athenæum.

HAWTREY, John Havilland Procter, CBE 1958; FICE; *b* 16 Feb. 1905; *e s* of late Edmond Charles Hawtrey and late Helen Mary Hawtrey (*née* Durand); *m* 1947, Kathleen Mary, *d* of late Captain M. T. Daniel, RN, Henley-on-Thames; one *s* one *d. Educ:* Eton; City and Guilds Engineering Coll., London (BSc 1927). Asst Engineer, later Dist Engineer, Burma Railways, 1927–47. Served War of 1939–45: with RE, 1940–46; Major 1942, in India and Burma, 1942–46 (despatches). Entered office of Crown Agents for Oversea Govts and Administrations, 1948: Chief Civil Engineer, 1956; Crown Agent and Engineer-in-Chief, 1965; retired, 1969. *Address:* 11 Curzon Avenue, Beaconsfield, Bucks HP9 2NN. *T:* Beaconsfield 4220.

See also S. C. Hawtrey.

HAWTREY, Stephen Charles, CB 1966; Clerk of the Journals, House of Commons, 1958–72; *b* 8 July 1907; *s* of Edmond C. Hawtrey; *m* 1934, Leila Winifred (*d* 1982), *e d* of late Lieut-Col Wilmot Blomefield, OBE; two *s* one *d. Educ:* Trinity Coll., Cambridge (MA). Asst Clerk, House of Commons, 1930; Senior Clerk, 1944. Temporarily attached: to Min. of Home Security, 1939; to Secretariat of Council of Europe, Strasbourg, France, at various sessions between 1950 and 1964. *Publication:* (With L. A. Abraham) A Parliamentary Dictionary, 1956 and 1964; 3rd edn (with H. M. Barclay), 1970. *Address:* 52 New Street, Henley-on-Thames, Oxon. *T:* Henley 4521. *Clubs:* United Oxford & Cambridge University; Railway.

See also J. H. P. Hawtrey.

HAY, family name of **Earls of Erroll** and **Kinnoull**, and of **Marquis of Tweeddale**.

HAY, Sir (Alan) Philip, KCVO 1960 (CVO 1953); TD; Treasurer to the Duke of Kent, since 1962; *b* 27 Feb. 1918; *y s* of late E. Alan Hay; *m* 1948, Lady Margaret Katharine Seymour, DCVO (*d* 1975); three *s. Educ:* Harrow; Trinity Coll., Cambridge (BA). Herts Yeomanry, TA (135 Field Regt RA), 1939; prisoner, Singapore, 1942–45. Private Sec. to Princess Marina, Duchess

of Kent, 1948–68. Director: National Mutual Life Assoc. of Australasia, 1967; Sotheby & Co., 1969. *Address:* Nottingham Cottage, Kensington Palace, W8. *T:* 01-937 5514. *Clubs:* Boodle's, Buck's; All England Lawn Tennis.

HAY, Allan Stuart, PhD; FRS 1981; Research and Development Manager, Chemical Science and Engineering, General Electric Research & Development Center, Schenectady, New York, since 1980; *b* 23 July 1929; *s* of Stuart Lumsden and Verna Emila Hay; *m* 1956, Janet Mary Keck; two *s* two *d. Educ:* Univ. of Alberta (BSc Hon, MSc); Univ. of Illinois (PhD). Research Associate, General Electric Res. & Develt Center, 1955; Manager, Chemical Laboratory, General Electric, 1968. Adjunct Professor, Polymer Science and Engineering Dept, Univ. of Massachusetts, 1975. Soc. of Plastics Engrs Internat. award in Plastics Science and Engineering, 1975. *Publications:* numerous papers and contribs to learned jls. *Recreations:* philately, reading, swimming. *Address:* 2306 Pine Ridge Road, Schenactady, New York 12309, USA. *T:* 518 393 4087.

HAY, Sir Arthur Thomas Erroll, 10th Bt of Park, *cr* 1663; ISO 1974; DiplArch; ARIBA 1935; retired Civil Servant; *b* 13 April 1909; *o s* of 9th Bt and Lizabel Annie (*d* 1957), *o d* of late Lachlan Mackinnon Macdonald, Skeabost, Isle of Skye; *S* father, 1923; *m* 1st, 1935, Hertha Louise (who was granted a divorce, 1942), *d* of late Herr Ludwig Stölzle, Nagelberg, Austria, and of H. E. Frau Vaugoin, Vienna; one *s*; 2nd, 1942, Rosemarie Evelyn Anne, *d* of late Vice-Adm. Aubrey Lambert and of Mrs Lambert. *Educ:* Fettes Coll., Edinburgh. Student of architecture, University of Liverpool, 1927–31; Diploma in Architecture, Architectural Assoc., July 1934. Served War of 1939–45; 2nd Lieut RE 1943; Lieut 1944; service in Normandy, Belgium, Holland and Germany in 21 Army Group. *Heir:* *s* John Erroll Audley Hay, *b* 3 Dec. 1935. *Address:* c/o Lloyds Bank, Castle Street, Farnham, Surrey.

HAY, Sir David (Osborne), KBE 1979; CBE 1962; DSO 1945; Secretary, Department of Aboriginal Affairs, 1977–80; *b* 29 Nov. 1916; 2nd *s* of late H. A. Hay, Barwon Heads, Victoria; *m* 1944, Alison Marion Parker Adams; two *s. Educ:* Geelong Grammar Sch.; Brasenose Coll., Oxford; Melbourne Univ. Joined Commonwealth Public Service, 1939. Australian Imperial Force, 1940–46: Major, 2nd Sixth Infantry Bn; served in Western Desert, Greece, New Guinea. Rejoined External Affairs Dept, 1947; Imp. Def. Coll., 1954; Minister (later Ambassador) to Thailand, 1955–57; High Comr in Canada, 1961–64; Ambassador to UN, New York, 1964–65; First Asst Secretary, External Affairs, 1966; Administrator of Papua and New Guinea, 1967–70; Sec., Dept of External Territories, Canberra, 1970–73; Defence Force Ombudsman, 1974–76. *Publication:* The Delivery of Services financed by the Department of Aboriginal Affairs, 1976. *Address:* 10 Hotham Crescent, Deakin, ACT 2600, Australia. *Clubs:* Australian, Melbourne (Melbourne); Commonwealth (Canberra).

HAY, Prof. Denys, MA; FBA 1970; FRSE 1977; Emeritus Professor of Medieval History, University of Edinburgh; *b* 29 Aug. 1915; *s* of Rev. W. K. Hay and Janet Waugh; *m* 1937, Sarah Gwyneth, *d* of S. E. Morley; one *s* two *d. Educ:* Royal Grammar Sch., Newcastle upon Tyne; Balliol Coll., Oxford. 1st Cl. hons, Modern History, 1937; senior demy, Magdalen Coll., 1937. Temporary Lecturer, Glasgow Univ., 1938; Bryce Studentship, Oxford Univ., 1939; Asst Lecturer, University Coll., Southampton, 1939; RASC 1940–42; War Historian (Civil Depts), 1942–45; Lecturer, 1945, Professor of Medieval History, 1954–80, Emeritus Professor 1980, Edinburgh Univ., Vice-Principal, 1971–75. Literary Dir, RHistS, 1955–58; Lectures: Italian, British Acad., 1959; Wiles, QUB, 1960; Birkbeck, Trinity Coll., Cambridge, 1971–72; Visiting Professor: Cornell Univ., 1963; Univ. of Virginia, 1980; Prof. of History, European Univ. Inst., Badia Fiesolana, 1980–82; Senior Fellow, Newberry Library, Chicago, 1966; Trustee, Nat. Library of Scotland, 1966–; President: Historical Association, 1967–70; Ecclesiastical Hist. Soc., 1980–81; Mem., Reviewing Cttee on Export of Works of Art, 1976–80. Editor, English Historical Review, 1958–65. Hon. For. Mem., Amer. Acad. of Arts and Scis, 1974. Hon. DLitt, Newcastle, 1970. Comdr, Order of Merit, Italy, 1980. *Publications:* Anglica Historia of P. Vergil, 1950; Polydore Vergil, 1952; From Roman Empire to Renaissance Europe, 1953 (The Medieval Centuries, 1964); ed. R. K. Hannay's Letters of James V, 1954; Europe: the emergence of an idea, 1957, new edn 1968; (ed) New Cambridge Modern History, Vol. I: The Renaissance, 1493–1520, 1957, new edn 1976; Italian Renaissance in its Historical Background, 1961, new edn 1976; Design and Development of Weapons (History of Second World War) (with M. M. Postan and J. D. Scott), 1964; Europe in the 14th and 15th Centuries, 1966; (ed with W. K. Smith) Aeneas Sylvius Piccolomini, De Gestis Concilii Basiliensis, 1967; (ed) The Age of the Renaissance, 1967; Annalists and Historians, 1977; Italian Church in the 15th Century, 1977; articles in historical journals. *Address:* 31 Fountainhall Road, Edinburgh EH9 2LN. *T:* 031-667 2886.

See also Richard Hay.

HAY, Frances Mary, (Mrs Roy Hay); see Perry, F. M.

HAY, Sir Frederick Baden-Powell, 10th Bt of Alderston, *cr* 1703; *b* 24 June 1900; *s* of late Frederick Howard Hay; *S* uncle 1936; *m* 1935, Henrietta Margaret, *d* of Herbert William Reid; no *c. Recreations:* golf, turf, motoring. *Heir:* *b* Ronald Nelson Hay [*b* 9 July 1910; *m* 1940, Rita, *d* of John Munyard; one *s* one *d*]. *Address:* Haddington, 14/32 Mentone Parade, Mentone, Vic 3194, Australia. *T:* 550 3726. *Club:* Royal Caledonian (Melbourne).

HAY, Rt. Rev. Mgr George Adam; Rector of the Venerable English College, Rome, since 1978; *b* 14 Nov. 1930; *s* of late Sir William Rupert Hay, KCMG, KCIE, CSI, and late Sybil Ethel, *d* of Sir Stewart Abram. *Educ:* Ampleforth College, York; New Coll., Oxford (BA History, MA); Venerable English Coll., Rome (STL). National Service as Midshipman RNVR, 1949-50; student, Oxford, 1950-53; Venerable English Coll., Rome, 1953-60. Ordained priest at Rome, 1959; Curate, Sacred Heart Church, Exeter, and part-time RC Chaplain to students at Exeter Univ., 1960; Chaplain to students at Exeter Univ. and Priest-in-charge, Crediton, 1966-78. *Recreations:* fly fishing, squash, mountain walking. *Address:* The Venerable English College, Via di Monserrato 45, 00186 Rome, Italy. *T:* Rome 6541829.

HAY, Sir Hamish (Grenfell), Kt 1982; Mayor of Christchurch, New Zealand, since 1974; Chairman, Alternative Television Network Ltd, since 1980; *b* 8 Dec. 1927; twin *s* of Sir James Lawrence Hay, OBE, and Lady (Davidina) Hay; *m* 1955, Judith Leicester Gill; one *s* four *d*. *Educ:* St Andrew's Coll., Christchurch; Univ. of Canterbury, NZ (BCom). FCA(NZ). Councillor, Christchurch City Council, 1959-74. Chairman: Christchurch Town Hall Board of Management, 1968-; Canterbury Museum Trust Bd, 1981-; President: Christchurch Aged People's Welfare Council, 1974-; Christchurch Civic Music Council, 1974-; Christchurch Symphony Orchestra, 1982-; Chm., Christchurch Arts Festival, 1965-74; past Mem., Queen Elizabeth II Arts Council. Chm., New Zealand Soc. of Accountants (Canterbury Br.), 1958; Dep. Man. Dir, Haywrights Ltd, 1962-74. Mem. Council, Univ. of Canterbury, 1974-; Vice-Pres., Municipal Assoc. of NZ, 1974-; Trustee, Canterbury Savings Bank, 1962- (Pres., 1974-75). *Recreations:* golf, gardening, listening to good music. *Address:* 70 Heaton Street, Merivale, Christchurch 5, New Zealand. *T:* 557-244. *Club:* Christchurch (New Zealand).

HAY, Sir James B. D.; *see* Dalrymple-Hay.

HAY, John Albert; Managing Director, Walport Group, since 1968; *b* 24 Nov. 1919; *er s* of Alderman J. E. Hay; *m* 1st, 1947, Beryl Joan (marr. diss. 1973), *o d* of Comdr H. C. Found, RN (retired); one *s* one *d* ; 2nd, 1974, Janet May, *y d* of A. C. Spruce. *Educ:* Brighton, Hove and Sussex Grammar Sch. Solicitor admitted May 1945. Chairman: Brighton and Hove Young Conservatives, 1945-47; Sussex Federation of Young Conservatives, 1945-47; Young Conservative and Unionist Central Cttee, 1947-49; Conservative Party Housing and Local Govt Cttee, 1956-59; formerly Dir London Municipal Soc.; formerly Vice-Pres. Urban District Councils Assoc.; Hon. Sec. UK Council of the European Movement, 1965-66; Mem. of Exec. Cttee, Nat. Union of Conservative and Unionist Assoc., 1947-49 and 1950-51. Served War of 1939-45, in RNVR; temp. Sub-Lieut, RNVR, 1940-44; temp. Lieut, RNVR, 1944; invalided 1944. Member: British Delegn, Congress of Europe, 1948, and 1973; UK Delegns, Council of Europe and Western European Union, 1956-59. MP (C) Henley, Oxon, 1950-Feb. 1974; PPS to Pres. of BoT, 1951-56; Parly Sec., MoT, 1959-63; Civil Lord of the Admiralty, 1963-64; Parly Under-Sec. of State for Defence for the Royal Navy, April-Oct. 1964. Chm., British Section, Council of European Municipalities, 1971-76, Vice-Chm., 1976-77, Pres., 1977-81, Vice-Pres., 1981-. Mem. Court, Reading Univ., 1968-. Fellow, Royal Philharmonic Soc., 1976. *Recreations:* gardening, music, travel, historical study. *Address:* 62/66 Whitfield Street, W1. *T:* 01-631 4373.

HAY, Prof. John Duncan, MA, MD, FRCP; Professor of Child Health, University of Liverpool, 1957-74, now Professor Emeritus; *b* 6 Feb. 1909; *s* of late Prof. John Hay; *m* 1936, Jannett Ceridwen Evans; one *s* two *d*. *Educ:* Liverpool Coll.; Sidney Sussex Coll., Cambridge; Liverpool Univ. MB, ChB, 1st Cl. Hons, Liverpool, 1933; MA 1934, MB 1935, Cambridge; MD Liverpool, 1936; DCH London, MRCP 1939; FRCP 1951. Holt Fellowship in Pathology, Liverpool, 1935; Cons. Pædiatrician to: Royal Liverpool Children's Hospital, 1939-74; Royal Liverpool Babies' Hospital, 1939-61; Birkenhead Children's Hosp., 1937-54; Liverpool Maternity Hosp. 1946-74; Lancashire County Hosp., Whiston, 1942-51; Liverpool Open-Air Hospital, Leasowe, and Mill Road Maternity Hosp., 1947-74; Alder Hey Children's Hosp., 1957-74; Liverpool Education Cttee, 1951-72. Demonstrator in Pathology, University of Liverpool, 1935 and 1938; Asst Lectr in Clinical Pædiatrics, University of Liverpool, 1948-57. Brit. Paediatric Association: Treasurer, 1964-71; Pres., 1972-73; Hon. Mem., 1973-; President: Liverpool Med. Instn, 1972-73; Liverpool Paediatric Club, 1975-; Hon. Mem. Assoc. European Paediatric Cardiologists, 1975-. RAMC (Major and Lieut-Col), 1942-46. *Publications:* contribs to Archives of Disease in Childhood, British Heart Journal, BMJ, Lancet, Practitioner, Brit. Encyclopædia of Medical Practice, Medical Progress, 1957, Cardiovascular Diseases in Childhood. *Recreations:* music, fell walking. *Address:* Fairfield, Cedarway, Gayton, Merseyside L60 3RH. *T:* 051-342 2607.

HAY, Sir Philip; *see* Hay, Sir Alan Philip.

HAY, Richard; Deputy Director-General, Directorate-General for Personnel and Administration, since 1981; *b* 4 May 1942; *s* of Prof. Denys Hay, *qv*; *m* 1969, Miriam Marguerite Alvin England; two *s*. *Educ:* George Watson's Coll., Edinburgh; Edinburgh Univ.; Balliol Coll., Oxford (BA Hons, Mod. Hist.). Assistant Principal, HM Treasury, 1963-68; Secretary, West Midlands Economic Planning Council, 1966-67; Private Sec. to Financial Sec., Treasury, 1967-68; Principal, Treasury, 1968-73; Member, Cabinet of Sir Christopher (now Lord) Soames, Vice-Pres., European Commn, 1973-75; Dep. Chef de Cabinet, 1975-77; Chef de Cabinet to Mr Christopher Tugendhat, Member, European Commn, 1977-79; Dir, Economic Structures and Community Interventions, Directorate-Gen. for Economic and Financial Affairs, European Commn, 1979-81. *Address:* c/o European Commission, 200 rue de la Loi, 1049 Brussels, Belgium. *T:* (02) 735 80 40. *Club:* United Oxford & Cambridge University.

HAY, Maj.-Gen. Robert Arthur, CB 1970; MBE 1946; Secretary, Australian Council of Professions, since 1978; Australian Army Officer, retired 1977; *b* 9 April 1920; *s* of Eric Alexander Hay and Vera Eileen Hay (*née* Whitehead); *m* 1944, Endree Patricia Hay (*née* McGovern); two *s* one *d*. *Educ:* Brighton Grammar Sch., Melbourne, Victoria; RMC Duntroon, ACT (graduated Dec. 1939). Lt-Col, 1945; Col, 1955; Col GS HQ Eastern Comd; Military Attaché, Washington, DC, 1956; Dir Administrative Planning, AHQ, 1959; Defence Representative, Singapore and Malaya, 1962; Brig., 1964; IDC London, 1965; Dir Military Ops and Plans, AHQ, 1966; Maj.-Gen., 1967; Dep. Chief of the General Staff, AHQ; Comdr, Australian Forces, Vietnam, 1969; Comdr, First Australian Div., 1970; Chief, Mil. Planning Office, SEATO, 1971-73; Comdt, Royal Military Coll., Duntroon, 1973-77. Pres., Veterans Tennis Assoc. of Australia, 1981-. *Recreations:* tennis, golf. *Address:* 5 Borrowdale Street, Red Hill, ACT 2603, Australia. *Clubs:* Melbourne Cricket; Commonwealth, Royal Canberra Golf (Canberra); Tanglin (Singapore).

HAY, Robert Edwin, (Roy Hay), MBE 1970; VMH 1971; formerly Editor, Gardeners' Chronicle (1954-64); *b* 20 Aug. 1910; *o s* of late Thomas Hay, CVO, sometime Superintendent Central Royal Parks; *m* 1st, 1946, Elizabeth Jessie (*d* 1976), *d* of late Rev. H. C. Charter; two *d*; 2nd, 1977, Mrs Frances Perry, *qv*. *Educ:* Marylebone Grammar Sch. Horticultural seed trade, 1928; Asst Editor, Gardeners' Chronicle, 1936; Editor, Royal Horticultural Soc.'s publications, 1939; Min. of Agriculture, 1940; Horticultural Officer, Malta, 1942; Controller of Horticulture and Seed Divs, British zone of Germany, 1945. Officier du Mérite Agricole: Belgium, 1956; France, 1959. *Publications:* Annuals, 1937; In My Garden, 1955; Gardening the Modern Way, 1962; (with P. M. Synge) The Dictionary of Garden Plants, 1969; (jtly) The Dictionary of Indoor Plants in Colour, 1975; (ed) The Complete Guide to Fruit and Vegetable Growing, 1978; (with Frances Perry) Tropical and Subtropical Plants, 1982. *Recreation:* foreign travel. *Club:* Farmers'.

HAY DAVISON, Ian Frederic; *see* Davison, I. F. H.

HAYBALL, Frederick Ronald, CMG 1969; *b* 23 April 1914; *s* of late Frederick Reuben Hayball and late Rebecca Hayball; *m* 1938, Lavinia Violet Palmer; one *s* one *d*. *Educ:* Alleyn's Sch., Dulwich. Accountant, Myers, Gondouin & Co. Ltd, 1932-39. Flying Officer, RAF, 1939-45. Foreign and Commonwealth Office, 1945-69 (Counsellor, retired); Asst Sec., Longman Gp Ltd, 1969-81. *Recreations:* cricket, angling, motoring. *Address:* 42 Theydon Park Road, Theydon Bois, Essex. *T:* Theydon Bois 2195.

HAYCRAFT, Colin Berry; Chairman, Managing Director and controlling shareholder, Gerald Duckworth & Co. Ltd, publishers, since 1971; *b* 12 Jan. 1929; *yr s* of Major W. C. S. Haycraft, MC and Bar, 5/8 Punjab Regt (killed 1929), and late Olive Lillian Esmée (*née* King); *m* 1957, Anna Margaret Lindholm; four *s* one *d* (and one *s* one *d* decd). *Educ:* Wellington Coll. (schol.); The Queen's Coll., Oxford (Open Schol. in Classics; 1st Cl. Classical Mods, 1st Cl. Lit.Hum., MA). Nat. service (army), 1947-49. Personal Asst to Chm., Cecil H. King, Daily Mirror Newspapers Ltd; Dir, Weidenfeld & Nicolson Ltd and Weidenfeld (Publishers) Ltd (original editor and subseq. Man. Dir, World University Library Ltd); joined Duckworth, 1968. Public Schs Rackets Champion (singles and pairs), 1946; Oxford blue for Squash Rackets (4 years, Captain OUSRC, Eng. internat.), Lawn Tennis (Devon Co. player) and Rackets. *Address:* 22 Gloucester Crescent, NW1 7DY.
See also J. S. Haycraft.

HAYCRAFT, John Stacpoole, CBE 1982; Director General, English International (International House), since 1975; *b* 11 Dec. 1926; *s* of late Major W. C. S. Haycraft and Olive Haycraft; *m* 1953, Brita Elisabeth Langenfelt; two *s* one *d*. *Educ:* Wellington Coll.; Jesus Coll., Oxford (Open Exhibnr; MA). E-SU Fellowship. Yale Univ., 1951-52. Founder and Dir, Academia Britanica, Córdoba, 1953; Founder and Principal: International Language Centre, London, 1960; International Teacher Trng Inst., 1963; Founder and Director: International House, London, 1964; International House, Rome, 1967-68; Dir, International House, Paris, 1971-72; Founder: English Teaching Theatre, 1970; English International (International House), 1975. *Publications:* Babel in Spain, 1958, 2nd edn 1958; Getting on in English, 1964, 7th edn 1982 (trans. 9 langs); Babel in London, 1965; George and Elvira, 1970; Choosing Your English, 1972, 8th edn 1982; Action, 1977; Introduction to English Language Teaching, 1978; contrib. Modern English Teacher, etc. *Recreations:* squash, tennis, swimming, chess, cinema, theatre, history, travel. *Address:* 81 Lee Road, SE3. *T:* 01-852 5495. *Club:* Canning.
See also C. B. Haycraft.

HAYDAY, Anthony Victor; HM Diplomatic Service; Deputy High Commissioner, Calcutta, since 1981; *b* 1 June 1930; *s* of Charles Leslie Victor Hayday and Catherine (*née* McCarthy); *m* 1966, Anne Heather Moffat; one *s* one *d*. *Educ:* Beckenham and Penge Grammar School. Royal Air Force, 1949-50; HM Foreign (later Diplomatic) Service, 1950; Brazzaville, 1953; British Information Services, New York, 1955; FO, 1958; Vice Consul, Houston, 1961; 2nd Secretary, Algiers, 1962; FO (later FCO), 1966; 1st

Secretary, New Delhi, 1969; Head of Chancery, Freetown, 1973; on secondment to Commonwealth Secretariat, 1976-80. *Recreations:* birdwatching, athletics. *Address:* c/o Foreign and Commonwealth Office, SW1. *Clubs:* Brooks's, Blackheath Harriers, Mensa; Bengal, Tollygunge (Calcutta).

HAYDAY, Sir Frederick, Kt 1969; CBE 1963; National Industrial Officer, National Union of General and Municipal Workers, 1946-71; Chairman, International Committee, Trades Union Congress; *b* 26 June 1912; *s* of late Arthur Hayday, MP for W Notts; *m.* Member: General Council of the Trades Union Congress, 1950-72 (Chairman, 1962-63, Vice-Chairman, 1964-69); IBA (formerly ITA), 1969-73; British Railways Board, 1962-76. Mem., Police Complaints Bd, 1977-. *Address:* 42 West Drive, Cheam, Surrey. *T:* 01-642 8928.

HAYDEN, Hon. William George; Leader of Australian Labor Party and of the Opposition, since 1977; MHR (Lab) for Oxley, Qld, since 1961; *b* Brisbane, 23 Jan. 1933; *s* of G. Hayden, Oakland, Calif, USA; *m* 1960, Dallas, *d* of W. Broadfoot; one *s* two *d. Educ:* Brisbane State High Sch. BEcon (Q). Police Constable in Queensland, 1953-61. Parly Spokesman on Health and Welfare, 1969-72; Minister for Social Security, Australian Commonwealth Govt, 1972-75; Federal Treasurer, June-Nov. 1975; spokesman on defence, 1976-, and on economic management, 1977-. *Address:* Parliament House, Canberra, ACT, Australia; (home) 16 East Street, Ipswich, Queensland 4305, Australia.

HAYDON, Prof. Denis Arthur, FRS 1975; Professor of Membrane Biophysics, University of Cambridge, since 1980; Fellow, since 1965, Vice-Master, since 1978, Trinity Hall, Cambridge; *b* 21 Feb. 1930; *s* of late Ernest George Haydon and Grace Violet (*née* Wildman); *m* 1958, Ann Primrose Wayman; two *s* one *d. Educ:* Dartford Grammar Sch.; King's Coll., Univ. of London (BSc, PhD). MA Cantab. ICI Res. Fellow, Imperial Coll., London, 1956-58; Asst Dir of Res., Univ. of Cambridge, Dept of Colloid Science, 1959-70, and Dept of Physiology, 1970-74; Dir of Studies in Natural Scis, Trinity Hall, 1965-78; Asst Tutor, Trinity Hall, 1968-73; Tutor for Natural Scientists, Trinity Hall, 1973-74; Reader in Surface and Membrane Biophysics, Univ. of Cambridge, 1974-80. Chem. Soc. Medal for Surface and Colloid Chem., 1976. *Publications:* (with R. Aveyard) An Introduction to the Principles of Surface Chemistry, 1973; papers on surface chemistry and membrane biophysics in Proc. Royal Soc., Trans Faraday Soc., Jl Chem. Soc. and other sci. jls. *Recreations:* climbing, sailing, music. *Address:* Westgate Cottage, 7 Orwell Road, Barrington, Cambridge CB2 5SE. *T:* Cambridge 871305.

HAYDON, Sir Walter Robert, (Sir Robin Haydon), KCMG 1980 (CMG 1970); HM Diplomatic Service, retired; Director of Group Public Affairs, Imperial Group, since 1981; *b* 29 May 1920; *s* of Walter Haydon and Evelyn Louise Thom; *m* 1943, Joan Elizabeth Tewson; one *s* one *d* (and one *d* decd). *Educ:* Dover Grammar Sch. Served in Army in France, India and Burma, 1939-46. Entered Foreign Service, 1946; served at London, Berne, Turin, Sofia, Bangkok, London, Khartoum, UK Mission to UN (New York), Washington; Head of News Dept, FCO, 1967-71; High Comr, Malawi, 1971-73; Chief Press Sec., 10 Downing Street, 1973-74; High Comr, Malta, 1974-76; Ambassador to Republic of Ireland, 1976-80. Governor, E-SU, 1980-. *Recreations:* walking, swimming, tennis. *Address:* c/o Lloyds Bank Ltd, Cox's & King's Branch, 6 Pall Mall, SW1Y 5NH. *Club:* Travellers'.

HAYEK, Friedrich August (von), FBA 1944; Dr Jur, DrScPol, Vienna; DSc (Econ.) London; *b* Vienna, 8 May 1899; *s* of late August von Hayek, Prof. of Botany at University of Vienna; certificate of naturalisation, 1938; *m* 1st, Hella von Fritsch (*d* 1960); one *s* one *d* ; 2nd, Helene Bitterlich. *Educ:* University of Vienna. Austrian Civil Service, 1921-26; Dir, Austrian Institute for Economic Research, 1927-31; Lecturer in Economics, University of Vienna, 1929-31; Tooke Prof. of Economic Science and Statistics in University of London, 1931-50; Prof. of Social and Moral Science, University of Chicago, 1950-62; Prof. of Economics, Univ. of Freiburg i B, 1962-69. Hon. Fellow: LSE; Austrian Acad. of Scis; American Economic Assoc.; Hoover Inst. on War, Revolution and Peace; Argentine Acad. of Economic Sci.; Academia Sinica. Dr jur *hc* Rikkyo Univ., Tokyo, 1964; Dr jur *hc* Univ. of Salzburg, 1974; Dr Lit. Hum. *hc* Univ. of Dallas, 1975; Hon. Dr Soc. Sci., Marroquin Univ., Guatemala, 1977; Hon. Dr: Santa Maria Univ., Valparaiso, 1977; Univ. of Buenos Aires, 1977; Univ. of Giessen, 1982. Nobel Prize in Economic Science (jtly), 1974. Austrian Distinction for Science and Art, 1975; Mem., Orden pour le Mérite für Wissenschaften und Künste, Fed. Rep. of Germany, 1977. *Publications:* Prices and Production, 1931; Monetary Theory and the Trade Cycle, 1933 (German edition, 1929); Monetary Nationalism and International Stability, 1937; Profits, Interest, and Investment, 1939; The Pure Theory of Capital, 1941; The Road to Serfdom, 1944; Individualism and Economic Order, 1948; John Stuart Mill and Harriet Taylor, 1950; The Counter-revolution of Science, 1952; The Sensory Order, 1952; The Political Ideal of the Rule of Law, 1955; The Constitution of Liberty, 1960; Studies in Philosophy, Politics and Economics, 1967; Freiburger Studien, 1969; Law, Legislation & Liberty, vol. I: Rules and Order, 1973, Vol II: The Mirage of Social Justice, 1976, Vol. III: The Political Order of a Free People, 1979; De-Nationalisation of Money, 1976; New Studies in Philosophy, Politics, Economics and the History of Ideas, 1978; edited: Beiträge zur Geldtheorie, 1933; Collectivist Economic Planning, 1935; Capitalism and the Historians, 1954; and the works of H. H. Gossen, 1927; F. Wieser, 1929; C. Menger,

1933-36; and H. Thornton, 1939; articles in Economic Journal, Economica, and other English and foreign journals. *Address:* Urachstrasse 27, D-7800 Freiburg i. Brg, West Germany. *Club:* Reform (London).

HAYES, Sir Brian (David), KCB 1980 (CB 1976); Permanent Secretary, Ministry of Agriculture, Fisheries and Food, since 1979; *b* 5 May 1929; *s* of late Charles and Flora Hayes, Bramerton, Norfolk; *m* 1958, Audrey Jenkins; one *s* one *d. Educ:* Norwich Sch.; Corpus Christi Coll., Cambridge. BA (Hist.) 1952, PhD (Cambridge) 1956. RASC, 1947-49. Joined Min. of Agriculture, Fisheries and Food, 1956; Asst Private Sec. to the Minister, 1958; Asst Sec., 1967; Under-Sec., Milk and Poultry Gp, 1970-73; Dep. Sec., 1973-78. *Recreations:* reading, caravanning, watching cricket. *Address:* c/o Ministry of Agriculture, Fisheries and Food, Whitehall Place, SW1. *Club:* Reform.

HAYES, Sir Claude (James), KCMG 1974 (CMG 1969); MA, MLitt; Chairman, Crown Agents for Oversea Governments and Administrations, 1968-74; *b* 23 March 1912; *er s* of late J. B. F. Hayes, West Hoathly, Sussex; *m* 1940, Joan McCarthy, *yr d* of Edward McCarthy Fitt, Civil Engineer; two *s* one *d. Educ:* Ardingly Coll.; St Edmund Hall, Oxford (Scholar); Sorbonne; New Coll., Oxford (Sen. Scholar). Heath Harrison Travelling Scholarship; Zaharoff Travelling Fellowship; Paget Toynbee Prize; MA, MLitt. Asst Dir of Examinations, Civil Service Commn, 1938. Captain RASC 1st Inf. Div. BEF, 1939; Major 1940, Combined Ops; Lieut-Col, 1942-45 (N Africa, Sicily, Italy, NW Europe). Dep. Dir of Examinations, Civil Service Commn, 1945; Dir and Comr, 1949, also Sec., 1955; Nuffield Foundn Fellowship, 1953-54, toured Commonwealth studying public service recruitment and management. Asst Sec., HM Treasury, 1957; British Govt Mem., Cttee on Dissolution of Central African Fedn, 1963; Under-Sec., HM Treasury, 1964-65; Prin. Finance Officer, Min. of Overseas Development, 1965-68. *Recreations:* music; unaided gardening; antique furniture; 18th century bourgeois chattels; getting value for money from shops. *Address:* Prinkham, Chiddingstone Hoath, Kent. *T:* Cowden 335. *Club:* United Oxford & Cambridge University.

HAYES, Colin Graham Frederick, MA; RA 1970 (ARA 1963); painter; *b* 17 Nov. 1919; *s* of Gerald Hayes and Winifred (*née* Yule); *m* 1949, Jean Westbrook Law; three *d. Educ:* Westminster Sch.; Christ Church, Oxford. Served Royal Engineers, 1940-45 (Middle East) (Capt.). Ruskin Sch. of Drawing, 1946-47. Tutor, Sen. Tutor and Reader, Royal College of Art, 1949-; Hon. ARCA and Fellow, RCA, 1960. Work in Collections: Arts Council; British Council; Carlisle Museum, etc. *Publications include:* Renoir, 1961; Stanley Spencer, 1963; Rembrandt, 1969; many articles on painting in jls. *Address:* 26 Cleveland Avenue, W4. *T:* 01-994 8762.

HAYES, Helen, (Mrs Charles MacArthur); actress; *b* Washington, DC 10 Oct. 1900; *d* of Francis Van Arnum Brown and Catherine Estelle Hayes; *m* 1928, Charles MacArthur (*d* 1956); one *s* one *d. Educ:* Sacred Heart Academy, Washington, DC. As actress has appeared in USA in stage plays, among others: Pollyanna, Dear Brutus, Clarence, Bab, Coquette, The Good Fairy, To the Ladies, Young Blood, Mary of Scotland, Victoria Regina, Ladies and Gentlemen, Twelfth Night, Harriet, Happy Birthday; The Wisteria Trees, 1950; Mrs McThing, 1952. First appearance in England in The Glass Menagerie, 1948. Is also radio actress. Has appeared in films: Farewell to Arms, The Sin of Madelon Claudet, Arrowsmith, The Son-Daughter, My Son John, Anastasia, Airport (Best Supporting Actress Award, 1971), Candleshoe, etc. Awarded gold statuette by Motion Picture Academy of Arts and Sciences, 1932, as outstanding actress, based on performance in the Sin of Madelon Claudet; Hon. degrees: Smith Coll., Hamilton Coll., Columbia Univ., Princeton Univ., St Mary's Coll. *Publications:* A Gift of Joy, 1965; On Reflection, 1968; (with Anita Loos) Twice Over Lightly, 1971; *relevant publication:* Front Page Marriage: Helen Hayes and Charles MacArthur, by Jhan Robbins, 1982. *Address:* Nyack, New York, NY 10960, USA. *Clubs:* Cosmopolitan, River, etc.

HAYES, Most Rev. James Martin; *see* Halifax (NS), Archbishop of, (RC).

HAYES, Vice-Admiral Sir John (Osler Chattock), KCB 1967 (CB 1964); OBE 1945; Lord-Lieutenant of Ross and Cromarty, Skye and Lochalsh, since 1977; *b* 9 May 1913; *er s* of late Major L. C. Hayes, RAMC and Mrs Hayes; *m* 1939, Hon. Rosalind Mary Finlay, *o d* of 2nd and last Viscount Finlay of Nairn; two *s* one *d. Educ:* RN Coll., Dartmouth. Entered RN, 1927. Served War of 1939-45; Atlantic, HMS Repulse, Singapore, Russian Convoys, Malta. The Naval Sec., 1962-64; Flag Officer: Flotillas, Home Fleet, 1964-66; Scotland and NI, 1966-68; retd. Comdr 1948; Capt. 1953; Rear-Adm. 1962; Vice-Adm. 1965. Chm., Cromarty Firth Port Authority, 1974-77. Mem., Queen's Body Guard for Scotland (Royal Company of Archers), 1969. Pres., Scottish Council, King George's Fund for Sailors, 1968-78. Dep. Chm. Bd of Governors, Gordonstoun Sch. King Gustav V of Sweden Jubilee Medal, 1948. *Recreations:* walking, music, writing. *Address:* Arabella House, by Tain, Ross and Cromarty. *T:* Nigg Station 293.

HAYES, John Philip; Assistant Under-Secretary of State (Economics), Foreign and Commonwealth Office, since 1975; *b* 1924; *s* of late Harry Hayes and late Mrs G. E. Hayes (*née* Hallsworth); *m* 1956, Susan Elizabeth, *d* of Sir Percivale Liesching, GCMG, KCB, KCVO; one *s* one *d. Educ:* Cranleigh Sch.; Corpus Christi Coll., Oxford. RAFVR, 1943-46. Barnett Memorial Fellowship, 1948-49; Political and Economic Planning, 1950-53; OEEC,

1953-58; Internat. Bank for Reconstruction and Develt, 1958-64; Head, Economic Develt Div., OECD, 1964-67; Dir, World Economy Div., Economic Planning Staff, ODM, 1967-69; Dep. Dir Gen. of Economic Planning, ODM, later ODA, 1969-71; Dir, Econ. Program Dept, later Econ. Analysis and Projections Dept, IBRD, 1971-73; Dir, Trade and Finance Div., Commonwealth Secretariat, 1973-75. *Recreations:* music, lawn tennis. *Address:* 1 Elgar Avenue, Ealing, W5 3JU. *T:* 01-567 2426.

HAYES, John Trevor, MA Oxon, PhD London; FSA; Director of the National Portrait Gallery, London, since 1974; *b* 21 Jan. 1929; *er s* of late Leslie Thomas Hayes and late Gwendoline (*née* Griffiths), London. *Educ:* Ardingly; Keble Coll. Oxford (Open Exhibr); Courtauld Inst. of Art, London; Inst. of Fine Arts, New York. Asst Keeper, London Museum, 1954-70, Dir, 1970-74; Commonwealth Fund Fellow, 1958-59 (NY Univ.); Vis. Prof. in History of Art, Yale Univ., 1969. Chm., Walpole Soc., 1981-. *Publications:* London: a pictorial history, 1969; The Drawings of Thomas Gainsborough, 1970; Catalogue of Oil Paintings in the London Museum, 1970; Gainsborough as Printmaker, 1971; Rowlandson: Watercolours and Drawings, 1972; Gainsborough: Paintings and Drawings, 1975; The Art of Graham Sutherland, 1980; The Landscape Paintings of Thomas Gainsborough, 1982; various London Museum and Nat. Portrait Gall. pubns; numerous articles in The Burlington Magazine, Apollo and other jls. *Recreations:* music, walking, gardening, travel. *Address:* c/o The National Portrait Gallery, St Martin's Place, WC2H 0HE. *T:* 01-930 1552. *Clubs:* Athenæum, Beefsteak, Arts.

HAYES, Thomas William Henry; *b* 1 Aug. 1912; *s* of Henry Daniel and Joanna Hayes; *m* 1933, Alice Frances; one *s*. *Educ:* Central Foundation Sch., London; London Univ. After 3 years in teaching and 2 in industry joined Prison Service, 1937, as Borstal Housemaster. Served in RA, 1940-45. Dep. Gov. Rochester Borstal, 1945-48; Staff Officer, with British Police and Prisons Mission to Greece, 1948-51; Governor, subseq. of Lewes Prison, Hatfield and Lowdham Grange Borstals, Ashford Remand Centre and Wormwood Scrubs Prison; Asst Dir of Borstals, Home Office, 1964-69; Regional Dir of Prisons, SW Region, 1969-72; Advr to Dir of Prisons, Botswana, 1975-77; Regional Prisons Adviser, British Develt Div., Caribbean, 1978-79, retired. *Recreations:* bowls, gardening, contract bridge. *Address:* 5 Squitchey Lane, North Oxford OX2 7LD.

HAYES, Walter (Leopold Arthur), CBE 1980; Vice President, Ford Motor Company, since 1977; *b* 12 April 1924; *s* of Walter and Hilda Hayes; *m* 1949, Elizabeth (*née* Holland); two *s* one *d*. *Educ:* Hampton Grammar Sch.; Royal Air Force. Editor, Sunday Dispatch, 1956; Associate Editor, Daily Mail, 1959; Director, Ford of Britain, 1965; Vice-Pres., Ford of Europe Incorporated, 1968; Director: Ford Advanced Vehicles Ltd, 1963-; Ford Switzerland, Ford Belgium and Ford Werke A.G., 1970-80. Vice-Pres., Public Affairs, Ford Motor Co. in the United States, 1980-. *Publications:* Angelica: a story for children, 1968; The Afternoon Cat and Other Poems, 1976. *Recreations:* old books, cricket. *Address:* 1341 Glendaloch Circle, Ann Arbor, Michigan 48104, USA. *Clubs:* MCC, Royal Automobile; Detroit (Detroit, Michigan).

HAYES, Prof. William, FRS 1964; FRSE 1968; FAA 1976; Professor and Head of the Department of Genetics, Research School of Biological Sciences, Australian National University, 1974-78, now Emeritus; *b* 18 Jan. 1913; *s* of William Hayes and Miriam (*née* Harris), Co. Dublin, Ireland; *m* 1941, Honora Lee; one *s*. *Educ:* College of St Columba, Rathfarnham, Co. Dublin; Dublin Univ. BA (1st Cl. Mods. Nat. Sci.) Dublin, 1936; MB, BCh, Dublin, 1937; FRCPI 1945; ScD, Dublin, 1949. Served in India as Major, RAMC, Specialist in Pathology, 1942-46. Lectr in Bacteriology, Trinity Coll., Dublin, 1947-50; Sen. Lectr in Bacteriology, Postgraduate Medical Sch. of London, 1950-57, later Hon. Senior Lectr; Dir, MRC Molecular Genetics Unit, 1957-68, Hon. Dir 1968-73; Prof. of Molecular Genetics, Univ. of Edinburgh, 1968-73; Sherman Fairchild Dist. Scholar, Div. of Biology, California Inst. of Technology, 1979-80; Vis. Fellow, Botany Dept, ANU, 1980-. Hon. DSc Leicester, 1966; NUI, 1973; Kent, 1973; Hon. LLD Dublin, 1970. *Publication:* The Genetics of Bacteria and their Viruses, 1964. *Recreations:* painting, reading or doing nothing. *Address:* 17 MacPherson Street, O'Connor, ACT 2601, Australia.

HAYHOE, Bernard John, (Barney), CEng, MIMechE; MP (C) Hounslow, Brentford and Isleworth, since 1974 (Heston and Isleworth, 1970-74); Minister of State, HM Treasury, since 1981; *b* 8 Aug. 1925; *s* of Frank Stanley and Catherine Hayhoe; *m* 1962, Anne Gascoigne Thornton, *o d* of Bernard William and Hilda Thornton; two *s* one *d*. *Educ:* State schools; Borough Polytechnic. Tool Room Apprentice, 1941-44; Armaments Design Dept, Ministry of Supply, 1944-54; Inspectorate of Armaments, 1954-63; Conservative Research Dept, 1965-70. PPS to Lord President and Leader of House of Commons, 1972-74; an additional Opposition Spokesman on Employment, 1974-79; Parly Under Sec. of State for Defence for the Army, 1979-81; Minister of State, CSD, 1981. Hon. Sec., 1970-71, Vice-Chm., 1974, Cons. Parly Employment Cttee; Jt Hon. Sec., 1970-73, Vice-Chm., 1973-76, Cons. Gp for Europe; Vice-Chm., Cons. Party Internat. Office, 1973-79; Mem., Select Cttee on Race Relations and Immigration, 1971-73. Mem., Trilateral Commn, 1977-79. Governor, Birkbeck Coll., 1976-79. *Address:* 20 Wool Road, SW20. *T:* 01-947 0037.

HAYHOE, Prof. Frank George James, MD, FRCP, FRCPath; Leukaemia Research Fund Professor of Haematological Medicine, University of Cambridge, since 1968; Fellow, Darwin College, Cambridge, since 1964;

Vice-Master, 1964-74; *b* 25 Oct. 1920; *s* of Frank Stanley and Catharine Hayhoe; *m* 1945, Jacqueline Marie Marguerite (*née* Dierkx); two *s*. *Educ:* Selhurst Grammar Sch.; Trinity Hall, Cambridge; St Thomas's Hospital Medical Sch. BA Cantab 1942; MRCS, LRCP 1944; MB, BChir Cantab 1945; MRCP 1949; MA Cantab 1949; MD Cantab 1951; FRCP 1965; FRCPath 1971. Captain RAMC, 1945-47. Registrar, St Thomas' Hosp., 1947-49. Elmore Research Student, Cambridge Univ., 1949-51; Royal Soc. Exchange Res. Schol., USSR, 1962-63; Lectr in Medicine, Cambridge Univ., 1951-68; Mem. Council of Senate, 1967-71. Mem., Bd of Governors, United Cambridge Hospitals, 1971-74; Mem., Cambs AHA, 1974-75. Lectures: Langdon Brown, RCP, 1971; Cudlip Meml, Ann Arbor, 1967; vis. lectr at med. schs in N and S America, Europe, Middle East, Africa, India. G. F. Götz Foundn Prize, Zürich Univ., 1974; Suniti Rana Panja Gold Medal, Calcutta Sch. of Trop. Med., 1979. *Publications:* (ed) Lectures in Haematology, 1960; Leukaemia: Research and Clinical Practice, 1960; (jtly) Cytology and Cytochemistry of Acute Leukaemia, 1964; (ed) Current Research in Leukaemia, 1965; (with R. J. Flemans) An Atlas of Haematological Cytology, 1969, 2nd edn 1982; (with J. C. Cawley) Ultrastructure of Haemic Cells, 1973; (jtly) Leukaemia, Lymphomas and Allied Disorders, 1976; (jtly) Hairy Cell Leukaemia, 1980; (with D. Quaglino) Haematological Cytochemistry, 1980; contribs to med. and scientific jls, on haematological topics, especially leukaemia. *Address:* Department of Haematological Medicine, University of Cambridge, Cambridge. *T:* Cambridge 245171.
See also B. J. Hayhoe.

HAYMAN, Mrs Helene (Valerie); *b* 26 March 1949; *d* of Maurice Middleweek and Maude Middleweek; *m* 1974, Martin Hayman; two *s*. *Educ:* Wolverhampton Girls' High Sch.; Newnham Coll., Cambridge (MA). Pres., Cambridge Union, 1969. Worked with Shelter, Nat. Campaign for the Homeless, 1969; Camden Council Social Services Dept, 1971; Dep. Dir, Nat. Council for One Parent Families, 1974. Contested (Lab) Wolverhampton SW, Feb. 1974; MP (Lab) Welwyn and Hatfield, Oct. 1974-1979.

HAYMAN, John David Woodburn; His Honour Judge Hayman; a Circuit Judge, since 1976; *b* 24 Aug. 1918; *m*; two *s* four *d*. *Educ:* King Edward VII Sch., Johannesburg; St John's Coll., Cambridge (MA, LLB). Served with S African Forces, 1940-42. Called to the Bar, Middle Temple, 1945; sometime Lecturer in Law: University Coll. of Wales, Aberystwyth; Leeds Univ.; Cambridge Univ.

HAYMAN, Sir Peter (Telford), KCMG 1971 (CMG 1963); CVO 1965; MBE 1945; HM Diplomatic Service, retired; *b* 14 June 1914; *s* of C. H. T. Hayman, The Manor House, Brackley, Northants; *m* 1942, Rosemary Eardley Blomefield; one *s* one *d*. *Educ:* Stowe; Worcester Coll., Oxford. Asst Principal: Home Office, 1937-39; Min. of Home Security, 1939-41; Asst Priv. Sec. to Home Sec. (Rt Hon. Herbert Morrison, MP), 1941-42; Principal, Home Office, 1942. Served War, 1942-45, Rifle Bde, Major. Principal, Home Office, 1945-49; transf. to Min. of Defence as Personal Asst to Chief Staff Officer to the Minister, 1949-52; Asst Sec, Min. of Defence, 1950; UK Delegation to NATO, 1952-54; transf. to FO, 1954; Counsellor, Belgrade, 1955-58; seconded for temp. duty with Governor of Malta, 1958; Couns., Baghdad, 1959-61; Dir-Gen. of British Information Services, New York, 1961-64; Minister and Dep. Comdt, Brit. Milit. Govt in Berlin, 1964-66; Asst Under-Sec., FO, 1966-69; Dep. Under-Secretary of State, FCO, 1969-70; High Comr in Canada, 1970-74. *Recreations:* shooting, fishing, travel. *Address:* Uxmore House, Checkendon, Oxon. *T:* Checkendon 680 658. *Clubs:* Army and Navy, MCC.

HAYMAN, Prof. Walter Kurt, FRS 1956; MA; ScD (Cambridge); Hon. ARCS (Imperial College); Professor of Pure Mathematics, since 1956, and Dean of the Royal College of Science, 1978-81, at the Imperial College of Science and Technology, London; *b* 6 Jan. 1926; *s* of late Franz Samuel Haymann and Ruth Therese (*née* Hensel); *m* 1947, Margaret Riley Crann, MA Cantab, *d* of Thomas Crann, New Earswick, York; three *d*. *Educ:* Gordonstoun Sch.; St John's Coll., Cambridge. Lecturer at King's Coll., Newcastle upon Tyne, 1947, and Fellow of St John's Coll., Cambridge, 1947-50; Lecturer, 1947, and Reader, 1953-56, Exeter. 1st Smiths prize, 1948, shared Adams Prize, 1949, Junior Berwick Prize, 1955; Senior Berwick Prize, 1964. Visiting Lecturer at Brown Univ., USA, 1949-50, at Stanford Univ., USA (summer) 1950 and 1955, and to the American Mathematical Soc., 1961. Co-founder with Mrs Hayman of British Mathematical Olympiad; Hon. Sec., Soc. for Protection of Science and Learning. For. Mem., Finnish Acad. of Science and Letters; Corresp. Mem., Bavarian Acad. of Science. Hon. DSc Exeter, 1981. *Publications:* Multivalent Functions (Cambridge, 1958) Meromorphic Functions (Oxford, 1964); Research Problems in Function Theory (London, 1967); Subharmonic Functions, vol I, 1976; papers in various mathematical journals. *Recreations:* music, travel. *Address:* Imperial College, Queen's Gate, SW7 2BZ. *T:* 01-589 5111.

HAYMAN, Rev. Canon William Samuel; Chaplain to The Queen's Household, 1961-73; *b* 3 June 1903; *s* of late Rev. William Henry Hayman, Rector of Leckford, and late Louise Charlotte Hayman; *m* 1930, Rosemary Prideaux Metcalfe; one *s* one *d*. *Educ:* Merchant Taylors' Sch.; St John's Coll., Oxford (MA). Deacon, 1926; Priest, 1927; Curate: St Matthew, Brixton, 1926-32; Wimbledon (in charge of St Mark), 1932-34; Vicar of Finstall, Worcs, 1934-38; Rector of Cheam, 1938-72. Hon. Canon of Southwark, 1952-60, Canon Emeritus, 1972. Rural Dean of Beddington, 1955-60; Archdeacon of Lewisham, 1960-72. Scouts Silver Acorn, 1971. *Recreations:*

fly-fishing, photography, music. *Address:* Wayside, Houghton, Stockbridge, Hants SO20 6LH. *T:* King's Somborne 204.

HAYNES, David Francis, (Frank); JP; MP (Lab) Ashfield, since 1979; *b* London, March 1926; *m* ; one *s* two *d*. *Educ:* secondary schs in London. Fireman, Southern Railway; then coalminer. Member: Notts CC, 1965–; Mansfield DC; Chm., Central Notts Community Health Council. Mem., NUM. *Address:* House of Commons, SW1; 27 Lawns Road, Annesley Woodhouse, Kirkby in Ashfield, Notts.

HAYNES, Denys Eyre Lankester; Keeper of Greek and Roman Antiquities, British Museum, 1956–76; *b* 15 Feb. 1913; 2nd *s* of late Rev. Hugh Lankester Haynes and late Emmeline Marianne Chaldecott; *m* 1951, Sybille Edith Overhoff. *Educ:* Marlborough; Trinity Coll., Cambridge. Scholar, British School at Rome, 1936; Asst Keeper: Victoria and Albert Museum, 1937; British Museum, 1939–54 (released for war service, 1939–45); Dep. Keeper, British Museum, 1954. Geddes-Harrower Prof. of Greek Art and Archaeology, Univ. of Aberdeen, 1972–73. Chm., Soc. for Libyan Studies, 1974. Corr. Mem., German Archæological Inst., 1953; Ordinary Mem., 1957. Visitor, Ashmolean Museum, 1979. Lectures: Burlington, 1976; Brown and Hayley, Univ. of Puget Sound, 1977. *Publications:* Porta Argentariorum, 1939; Ancient Tripolitania, 1946; Antiquities of Tripolitania, 1956; The Parthenon Frieze, 1958; The Portland Vase, 1964; Fifty Masterpieces of Classical Art, 1970; The Arundel Marbles, 1975; Greek Art and the Idea of Freedom, 1981. *Address:* Merle Cottage, Dean, near Charlbury, Oxford OX7 3LD.

HAYNES, Edwin William George, CB 1971; *b* 10 Dec. 1911; *s* of Frederick William George Haynes and Lilian May Haynes (*née* Armstrong); *m* 1942, Dorothy Kathleen Coombs; one *s* one *d*. *Educ:* Regent Street Polytechnic Secondary Sch.; University of London (BA, LLM). Barrister-at-law, Lincoln's Inn, 1946. Estate Duty Office, Inland Revenue, 1930–39; Air Min., 1939; Min. of Aircraft Production, 1940; Min. of Supply, 1946; Min. of Aviation, 1959; Under-Sec., 1964; Under-Sec., DTI (formerly Min. of Technology), 1968–71. Sec., Covent Garden Market Authority, 1971–81. *Recreations:* tennis, cats. *Address:* 92 Malmains Way, Beckenham, Kent. *T:* 01-650 0224.

HAYNES, Frank; *see* Haynes, D. F.

HAYNES, Sir George (Ernest), Kt 1962; CBE 1945; *b* 24 Jan. 1902; *e s* of Albert Ernest and Sarah Anne Haynes, Middlewich, Cheshire; *m* 1930, Kathleen Norris Greenhaigh; two *d*. *Educ:* Sandbach Sch.; Liverpool Univ. BSc 1922; school master and educational and social research, 1923–28; Warden of University Settlement, Liverpool, 1928–33; Dir, Nat. Council of Social Service, 1940–67; Mem., Lord Chancellor's Cttee: on Procedure of County Courts, 1948; on Legal Aid, 1944–45 (and Mem., Adv. Cttee, 1950–75); Chm., Standing Conf. on Legal Aid, 1973–75. Chm., Temp. Internat. Council for Educational Reconstruction of UNESCO, 1947–48; Mem. Colonial Office Advisory Cttee, on Social Development, 1947–63. President: Internat. Conf. of Social Work, 1948–56; Standing Conf. for the Advancement of Counselling; Chairman: Preparatory Cttee, World Assembly of Youth, 1947–48; Internat. Congresses at Paris, 1950, Madras, 1952, Toronto, 1954, Munich, 1956; Nat. Children's Bureau, 1963–68; Invalid Children's Aid Association, 1964–69; Rural Industries Loan Fund Ltd, 1949–68; Social Services Cttee, National Association for Mental Health, 1955–58; Standing Conference of British Organisations for Aid to Refugees, 1953–60; Council of British Assoc. of Residential Settlements, 1963–68; Adv. Council, Rural Industries Bureau, 1962–68; Exec. Cttee, British National Conference on Social Welfare, 1950–67; Social Science Cttee, Nat. Fund for Research into Crippling Diseases, 1968–72. Vice-Chm., Family Welfare Assoc., 1961–66. Mem. Council of Brit. Red Cross Soc., 1960–76; Vice-President: Holiday Fellowship; British Assoc. for Disability and Rehabilitation; Assoc. for Spina Bifida; TOC H; Crown Trustee, City Parochial Foundation, 1965–75; Pres., Nat. Assoc. of Citizens Advice Bureaux, 1978–81; Trustee, National Birthday Trust, 1981–82 (Pres., 1966–81). UK Delegate to UN Social Commission, 1962–66, and to UN Commn for Social Develt 1967. René Sand Memorial Award, 1958. *Address:* 103 Richmond Hill Court, Richmond, Surrey. *T:* 01-940 6304.

HAYNES, Very Rev. Peter; Dean of Hereford since 1982; *b* 24 April 1925; *s* of Francis Harold Stanley Haynes and Winifred Annie Haynes; *m* 1952, Ruth, *d* of late Dr Charles Edward Stainthorpe, MRCS, LRCP, Brunton Park, Newcastle upon Tyne; two *s*. *Educ:* St Brendan's Coll., Clifton; Selwyn Coll., Cambridge (MA); Cuddesdon Theol Coll., Oxford. Staff of Barclays Bank, 1941–43; RAF, 1943–47. Deacon 1952, Priest 1953. Asst Curate, Stokesley, 1952–54; Hessle, 1954–58; Vicar, St John's Drypool, Hull, 1958–63; Bishop's Chaplain for Youth and Asst Dir of Religious Educn, Dio. Bath and Wells, 1963–70; Vicar of Glastonbury, 1970–74 (with Godney from 1972); Archdeacon of Wells, Canon Residentiary and Prebendary of Huish and Brent in Wells Cathedral, 1974–82. Proctor in Convocation, 1976–. Mem., Dioceses Commn, 1978–. *Recreations:* sailing, model engineering. *Address:* The Deanery, Hereford HR1 2NG. *T:* Hereford 272525. *Club:* Sloane.

HAYNES, Rear-Adm. William Allen, CB 1968; OBE 1941; retired 1970; *b* 29 Sept. 1913; *s* of late Paymaster Capt. W. F. Haynes, Royal Navy and late Mrs M. W. Haynes (*née* Wilkinson); *m* 1964, Mary Theodosia Peploe; two *d*. *Educ:* Royal Naval Colleges, Dartmouth, Keyham and Greenwich. HMS Leander, 1935–36; HMS Glasgow, 1938–41; HM Dockyard, Chatham,

1941–44; HMS Gabbard, 1944–47; Admty i/c development of steam catapult, 1947–51; HMS Ceylon (Korean War), 1951–53; Apprentice Trng in HMS Fisgard, 1953–55; HM Dockyard, Chatham, 1955–60; Imp. Def. Coll., 1961; Dir of Naval Ship Production, 1962–67; Dir-Gen., Dockyards and Maintenance, 1967–69. Comdr 1947; Capt. 1958; Rear-Adm. 1966. *Recreations:* sailing, gardening. *Address:* Bowden House, Dartmouth, Devon. *T:* Stoke Fleming 234. *Club:* Royal Ocean Racing.

HAYNES-DIXON, Margaret Rumer, (Rumer Godden); writer, playwright, poet; *b* 10 Dec. 1907; *d* of late Arthur Leigh Godden, Lydd House, Aldington, Kent, and Katherine Norah Hingley; *m* 1934, Laurence Sinclair Foster, Calcutta; two *d* ; *m* 1949, James Haynes Dixon, OBE (*d* 1973). *Educ:* abroad and Moira House, Eastbourne. *Publications:* Chinese Puzzle, 1935; Lady and Unicorn, 1937; Black Narcissus (novel and play), 1938; Gypsy Gypsy, 1940; Breakfast with the Nikolides, 1941; Fugue in Time (novel and play), 1945; The River, 1946 (filmed, 1950); Rungli-Rungliot (biography), 1943; Candle for St Jude, 1948; In Noah's Ark (poetry), 1949; A Breath of Air, 1950; Kingfishers Catch Fire, 1953; Hans Christian Andersen (biography), 1955; An Episode of Sparrows, 1955 (filmed 1957); Mooltiki, 1957; The Greengage Summer, 1958 (filmed, 1961); China Court, 1961; The Battle of the Villa Florita, 1963 (filmed 1964); (with Jon Godden) Two Under the Indian Sun, 1966; The Kitchen Madonna, 1967; Swans and Turtles, 1968; In This House of Brede, 1969; (comp.) The Raphael Bible, 1970; The Tale of the Tales, 1971; The Old Woman Who Lived in a Vinegar Bottle, 1972; (with Jon Godden) Shiva's Pigeons, 1972; The Peacock Spring, 1975; Five for Sorrow, Ten for Joy, 1979; Gulbadan Begum: portrait of a Rose Princess at the Mughal Court (biography), 1980; The Dark Horse, 1981; children's books, incl. The Diddakoi, 1972 (Whitbread Award); published internationally (11 languages). *Address:* The Small House, Tundergarth, Lockerbie, Dumfriesshire.

HAYR, Air Vice-Marshal Kenneth William, CB 1982; CBE 1976; AFC 1963 and Bar 1972; Air Officer Commanding No 11 Group, RAF, since 1982; *b* 13 April 1935; *s* of Kenneth James and Jean Templeton Hayr; *m* 1961, Joyce Gardner; three *s*. *Educ:* Auckland Grammar Sch.; RAF Coll. Cranwell. Served Hunter and Lightning Sqns, 1958–64; Central Fighter Estabt/Fighter Comd Trials Unit, 1964–67; Phantom OCU Sqn Comdr, 1968–69; OC 1(F) Sqn (Harriers), 1970–71; RAF Staff Coll., 1972; OC RAF Binbrook (Lightnings), 1973–76; Inspector of Flight Safety (RAF), 1976–79; RCDS 1980; Asst Chief of Air Staff (Ops), 1980–82. *Recreations:* flying, wind surfing, tennis, golf. *Address:* c/o Lloyds Bank, Cox's & King's Branch, 6 Pall Mall, SW1Y 5NH. *T:* (office) 01-950 4000 ext. 400. *Club:* Royal Air Force.

HAYTER, 3rd Baron *cr* 1927 of Chislehurst, Kent; **George Charles Hayter Chubb,** KCVO 1977; CBE 1976; Bt 1900; Managing Director, 1941–71, Chairman, 1957–81, Chubb & Son's Lock & Safe Co. Ltd; a Deputy Chairman, House of Lords, since 1981; *b* 25 April 1911; *e s* of 2nd Baron Hayter and Mary (*d* 1948), *d* of J. F. Haworth; *S* father, 1967; *m* 1940, Elizabeth Anne Rumbold, MBE 1975, JP; three *s* one *d*. *Educ:* Leys Sch., Cambridge; Trinity Coll., Cambridge (MA). Chairman: Royal Society of Arts, 1965–66; Management Cttee, King Edward's Hospital Fund for London, 1965–; Executives Assoc. of GB, 1960; Duke of Edinburgh's Countryside in 1970 Cttee. President: Canada-United Kingdom Chamber of Commerce, 1966–67; Royal Warrant Holders Association, 1967; Business Equipment Trades Association, 1954–55. Mem., CoID, 1964–71; Chairman: EDC International Freight Movement, 1972–79; British Security Industry Assoc., 1973–77. Worshipful Company of Weavers': Liveryman, 1934–; Upper Bailiff, 1961–62. *Publication:* Security offered by Locks and Safes (Lecture, RSA), 1962. *Heir:* s Hon. George William Michael Chubb, *b* 9 Oct. 1943. *Address:* Ashtead House, Ashtead, Surrey. *T:* Ashtead 73476.

HAYTER, Dianne, JP; Researcher, A Week in Politics, Channel Four, since 1982; Director, Galleon World Travel, since 1982; *b* 7 Sept. 1949; *d* of late Alec Hayter and late Nancy Hayter. *Educ:* Trevelyan Coll., Durham Univ. (BA Hons Sociology and Social Admin). Research Assistant: General and Municipal Workers Union, 1970–72; European Trade Union Confedn (ETUC), Brussels, 1973; Research Officer, Trade Union Adv. Cttee to OECD (TUAC-OECD), Paris, 1973–74; Asst Gen. Sec., Fabian Soc., 1974–76, Gen. Sec., 1976–82. Mem. Exec. Cttee, London Labour Party. Mem., Royal Commn on Criminal Procedure, 1978–80. Member: Socialist Medical Assoc.; British Organisation of Non-parents; Labour Parliamentary Assoc.; NCCL; Soc. of Labour Lawyers; Socialist Health Assoc.; NUJ; GMWU; Justice. JP Inner London, 1976–. *Publications:* The Labour Party: crisis and prospects (Fabian Soc.), 1977; (contrib.) Labour in the Eighties, 1980. *Recreations:* reading, politics. *Address:* 213 Battersea Bridge Road, SW11. *T:* 01-228 4591.

HAYTER, Stanley William, CBE 1967 (OBE 1959); Hon. RA 1982; artist; *b* 27 Dec. 1901; *s* of William Harry Hayter and Ellen Mercy Palmer; *m* 1st, 1926, Edith Fletcher (marriage dissolved at Reno, Nevada, 1929); one *s* decd; 2nd, 1940, Helen Phillips (marr. diss., Paris, 1971); two *s*. *Educ:* Whitgift Middle Sch.; King's Coll., London. Chemist, Anglo-Iranian Oil Co., Abadan, Iran, 1922–25. Founded Atelier 17, Paris, 1927. Has exhibited since 1927 in various cities of Europe, America and Japan (incl. London: 1928, 1938, 1957, 1962, 1967). Paintings and prints in principal museums in Gt Britain, France, Belgium, Switzerland, Sweden, Italy, Canada, USA, Japan. Foreign Mem., Amer. Acad. of Arts and Scis, 1978. Hon. Dr Hamline Univ., Minn. Legion of Honour, 1951; Chevalier des Arts et Lettres, 1967. *Publications:* New Ways of Gravure, 1949 (New York also) (revised edn, 1966); Nature and Art of Motion, New York, 1964; About Prints, 1962. *Address:* 12 rue Cassini, 75 Paris 14e, France. *T:* 326 26.60.

HAYTER, Sir William Goodenough, KCMG 1953 (CMG 1948); Warden of New College, Oxford, 1958-76, Hon. Fellow, 1976; *b* 1 Aug. 1906; *s* of late Sir William Goodenough Hayter, KBE; *m* 1938, Iris Marie, *d* of late Lieut-Col C. H. Grey (formerly Hoare), DSO; one *d. Educ:* Winchester; New Coll., Oxford. Entered HM Diplomatic Service, 1930; served Foreign Office, 1930; Vienna, 1931; Moscow, 1934; Foreign Office, 1937; China, 1938; Washington, 1941; Foreign Office, 1944 (Asst Under-Sec. of State, 1948); HM Minister, Paris, 1949; Ambassador to USSR, 1953-57; Deputy Under-Sec. of State, Foreign Office, 1957-58. Fellow of Winchester Coll., 1958-76. Trustee, British Museum, 1960-70. Hon. DL Bristol, 1976; Grosses Goldenes Ehrenzeichen mit dem Stern für Verdienste (Austria), 1967. *Publications:* The Diplomacy of the Great Powers, 1961; The Kremlin and the Embassy, 1966; Russia and the World, 1970; William of Wykeham, Patron of the Arts, 1970; A Double Life (autobiog.), 1974; Spooner, 1977. *Address:* Bassetts House, Stanton St John, Oxford. *T:* Stanton St John 598.

HAYWARD, Sir Alfred, KBE 1961 (CBE 1960); retired; *b* England, 14 Jan. 1896; *s* of Thomas and Minnie Hayward, Sudbourne, Suffolk; *m* 1923, Margaret Fromm; one *s* two *d.* Came to New Zealand, 1911. Served European War, 1914-18, in France, 1916-18. Took up farming in Waikato district. Dir, NZ Co-op. Dairy Co., 1933-61. Chm., 1947-61; Deputy Chm., NZ Dairy Board, 1958. JP 1957. *Address:* 42A Whittaker Street, Otumoetai, Tauranga, New Zealand.

HAYWARD, Sir Anthony (William Byrd), Kt 1978; President and Chief Executive Officer, Private Investment Company for Asia (PICA) SA, since 1982; *b* 29 June 1927; *s* of Eric and Barbara Hayward; *m* 1955, Jenifer Susan McCay; two *s* two *d. Educ:* Stowe Sch., Buckingham; Christ Church, Oxford. Served RNVR, 1945-48. With family business in Calcutta, 1948-57; Shaw Wallace & Co. Ltd, India, 1957-78; Man. Dir, Guthrie Berhad, Singapore, 1978-81. President: Bengal Chamber of Commerce, 1973-74; Associated Chambers of Commerce, 1977-78; UK Citizens Assoc., 1976-78. *Recreations:* shooting, golf, photography. *Address:* Dane Street House, Chilham, near Canterbury, Kent. *T:* Chilham 221; 156 Mount Pleasant Road, Singapore. *T:* 2500670. *Clubs:* Oriental; Rye Golf; Singapore Island, Cricket, Tanglin (Singapore).
See also Ven. J. D. R. Hayward.

HAYWARD, Brian Robin, FCIT; Group Managing Director, National Carriers Ltd, since 1976; Chairman, Fashion Flow Ltd, since 1976; *b* 11 Jan. 1937; *s* of Henry Albert and Jesse Agness Hayward; *m* 1954, Kathleen Mary Scott; three *s. Educ:* Woodlands, Gillingham, Kent. CBIB; MInstM. Depot Manager, Pickfords, 1963-66; Transport Manager, Hotpoint, 1966-69; Director and General Manager, Carryfast Ltd, 1969-72; Supplies Director, British Domestic Appliances, 1972-75; Managing Director, Southern BRSL, 1975-76. *Recreation:* golf. *Address:* 34 Audley Gate, Peterborough. *T:* Peterborough 263711. *Club:* Royal Automobile.

HAYWARD, Sir Charles (William), Kt 1974; CBE 1970; Founder and Trustee, Hayward Foundation and Charles Hayward Trust; *b* 3 Sept. 1892; *s* of John and Mary Hayward, Wolverhampton; *m* 1st, 1915, Hilda (*d* 1971), *d* of late John and Alexandra Arnold; one *s;* 2nd, 1972, Elsie Darnell, *d* of late Charles and Kate George. *Educ:* St John's School, Wolverhampton. Mem. of Post Office Advisory Council, 1952. Held Directorships since 1920 in various companies, public and private, including engineering, farming and horticulture. Vice-Pres., Wildfowl Trust. Pres., Royal Wolverhampton Sch. Liveryman of Barbers' Company; Freeman of the City of London, 1938; Worshipful Company of Masons. Hon. Fellow, Keble Coll., Oxford, 1973, Oriel Coll., Oxford, 1980. Hon. FRCS, 1970; Hon. Fellow, Inst. of Ophthalmology, 1967; Hon. LLD Birmingham, 1975. KStJ 1973. *Address:* Isle of Jethou, PO Box 5, Guernsey, CI. *T:* Guernsey 23844.
See also J. A. Hayward.

HAYWARD, Sir Edward (Waterfield), Kt 1961; grazier and company director, Australia; Chairman, Coca Cola Bottlers Ltd, since 1948; Director, Bennett & Fisher Ltd, since 1960; *b* 10 Nov. 1903; *s* of Arthur Dudley Hayward and Mary Anne Hayward; *m* 1972, Jean Katherine Bridges, widow of Ernest Bushby Bridges. *Educ:* St Peter's Coll., Adelaide, S Australia. Lt-Col, 2nd AIF, Middle East, New Guinea and Borneo (despatches: 1944 in New Guinea, 1945 in Borneo). Pres., Council of St John in South Australia, 1976– (Chm. 1946-76). Purchased Silverton Park, Delamere, SA 1942, and established Border Leicester Stud and later Hereford Stud. KStJ 1960; Bronze Star Medal, USA, 1945. *Recreations:* polo (represented S Australia, Interstate, 1936-57); golf, swimming. *Address:* 100 Rundle Street, Adelaide, SA 5001, Australia. *T:* 23-0200; Carrick Hill, Springfield, SA 5062, Australia. *T:* 79-3886. *Clubs:* Adelaide, Naval, Military & Air Force, Royal Adelaide Golf, Adelaide Polo (Adelaide SA); Melbourne (Melbourne); Australian, Royal Sydney Golf (Sydney, NSW).

HAYWARD, Maj.-Gen. George Victor, BSc; CEng, FICE, FIMechE; Senior Planning Inspector, Department of the Environment; *b* 21 June 1918; *e s* of late G. H. Hayward; *m* 1953, Gay Benson, *d* of late H. B. Goulding, MB, BCh, FRCSI; one *s* one *d. Educ:* Blundells; Birmingham Univ. (BSc). War of 1939-45: commissioned, 1940; transf. to REME, 1942; GSO1 REME

Training Centre, 1958; Comdr, REME 2nd Div., 1960; Asst Mil. Sec., War Office, 1962; Col, RARDE, Fort Halstead, 1963; CO, 38 Central Workshop, 1965; Dep. Comdt, Technical Group, REME, 1966; Comdt, REME Training Centre, 1969; Comdt, Technical Gp, REME, 1971-73, retired. Col Comdt, REME, 1973-78. *Recreations:* sailing, ski-ing, shooting. *Address:* Chart Cottage, Chartwell, Westerham, Kent. *T:* Crockham Hill 253. *Club:* Army and Navy.

HAYWARD, Gerald William; HM Diplomatic Service; Counsellor, Foreign and Commonwealth Office, since 1980; *b* 18 Nov. 1927; *s* of late Frederick William Hayward and Annie Louise (*née* Glasscock); *m* 1956, Patricia Rhonwen (*née* Foster Hall); one *s* three *d. Educ:* Tottenham Grammar School. 1st cl. Interpreter Chinese (Cantonese), 2nd cl. Chinese (Mandarin), 1954. HM Forces, 1946-57. Joined HM Foreign (now HM Diplomatic) Service, 1957; British High Commn, Kuala Lumpur, 1958-60; HM Embassy, Bangkok, 1960-62; Hong Kong, 1962-64; FO, 1964-67; Copenhagen, 1967-71; FCO, 1971-76; Counsellor, Kuala Lumpur, 1976-79. *Recreations:* golf, ski-ing. *Address:* c/o Foreign and Commonwealth Office, SW1; White Mill End, 5 Granville Road, Sevenoaks, Kent TN13 1ES. *T:* Sevenoaks 451227. *Club:* Naval and Military.

HAYWARD, Jack Arnold, OBE 1968; Chairman, Grand Bahama Development Co. Ltd and Freeport Commercial and Industrial Ltd, since 1976; *b* 14 June 1923; *s* of Sir Charles Hayward, *qv*; *m* 1948, Jean Mary Forder; two *s* one *d. Educ:* Northaw Prep Sch.; Stowe Sch., Buckingham. Joined RAF, 1941; flying training in Florida, USA; active service as officer pilot in SE Asia Comd, demobilised as Flt-Lt, 1946. Joined Rotary Hoes Ltd, 1947; served S Africa branch until 1950. Founded USA operations Firth Cleveland Gp of Companies, 1951; joined Grand Bahama Port Authority Ltd, Freeport, Grand Bahama Island, 1956. Hon. LLD Exeter, 1971. *Recreations:* promoting British endeavours, mainly in sport; watching cricket; amateur dramatics; preserving the British landscape, keeping all things bright, beautiful and British. *Address:* Seashell Lane (PO Box F-99), Freeport, Grand Bahama Island, Bahamas. *T:* Freeport 373-1528. *Clubs:* MCC, Pratt's, Royal Air Force, Durban Country (S Africa).

HAYWARD, Ven. John Derek Risdon; Vicar of Isleworth, since 1964; General Secretary, Diocese of London, since 1975; Archdeacon of Middlesex, 1974-75, now Archdeacon Emeritus; *b* 13 Dec. 1923; *s* of late Eric Hayward and of Barbara Olive Hayward; *m* 1965, Teresa Jane Kaye; one *s* one *d. Educ:* Stowe; Trinity Coll., Cambridge (BA 1956, MA 1964). Served War of 1939-45, Lieut 27th Lancers, Middle East and Italy, 1943-45 (twice wounded). Man. Dir, Hayward Waldie & Co., Calcutta (and associated cos), 1946-53. Trinity Coll., Cambridge, 1953-56, Westcott House, Cambridge, 1956-57. Asst Curate, St Mary's Bramall Lane, Sheffield, 1957-58; Vicar, St Silas, Sheffield, 1959-63. Mem., General Synod, 1975. Bronze Star (US) 1945. *Recreations:* riding, skiing, sailing (when opportunity offers). *Address:* 61 Church Street, Isleworth, Mddx TW7 6BE. *T:* 01-560 6662.
See also Sir Anthony Hayward.

HAYWARD, Sir Richard (Arthur), Kt 1969; CBE 1966; *b* 14 March 1910; *m* 1936, Ethel Wheatcroft; one *s* one *d. Educ:* Catford Central Sch. Post Office: Boy Messenger; Counter Clerk; Union of Post Office Workers: Assistant Secretary, 1947; Deputy General Secretary, 1951. Secretary General, Civil Service National Whitley Council (Staff Side), 1955-66; Chm., Supplementary Benefits Commn, 1966-69; Member, Post Office Board, 1969-71; Chairman: NHS Staff Commn, 1972-75; New Towns Staff Commn, 1976-77; Member: Parole Board, England and Wales, 1975-79; Solicitors' Disciplinary Tribunal, 1975-82. UK Rep., Meeting of Experts on Conditions of Work and Service of Public Servants, ILO, 1963; overseas visits, inc. Israel, Mauritius, Canada, to advise on Trade Unionism in Public Services. Life Vice-President: Civil Service Sports Council, 1973 (Chm., 1968-73); Nat. Assoc. of Young Cricketers, 1975; President: Civil Service Cricket Assoc., 1966–; Assoc. of Kent Cricket Clubs, 1970–; Civil Service Assoc. Football, 1974–. Governor, Guy's Hosp., 1949-72. Freedom, City of London, 1980. *Recreations:* topography of Southwark, watching sport. *Address:* 10 Birchwood Avenue, Southborough, Tunbridge Wells, Kent TN4 0UD. *T:* Tunbridge Wells 29134. *Clubs:* MCC, Civil Service.

HAYWARD, Ronald George, CBE 1970; General Secretary of the Labour Party, 1972-82; *b* 27 June 1917; *s* of F. Hayward, small-holder, Oxon; *m* 1943, Phyllis Olive (*née* Allen); three *d. Educ:* Bloxham C of E Sch.; RAF Technical Schools, Halton, Cosford, Locking. Apprenticed Cabinet-maker, 1933-36. NCO, RAF: Technical Training Instructor, 1940-45. Labour Party: Secretary-Agent: Banbury Constituency, 1945-47; Rochester and Chatham Constituency, 1947-50; Asst Regional Organiser, 1950-59; Regional Organiser, 1959-69; National Agent, 1969-72. Vice-Pres., Nat. Union of Labour and Socialist Clubs. *Address:* Haylens, 1 Sea View Avenue, Birchington, Kent. *Club:* The Wellesley (Cliftonville, Kent).

HAYWARD ELLEN, Patricia Mae; *see* Lavers, P. M.

HAYWOOD, Thomas Charles Stanley, OBE 1962; JP; Lieutenant of Leicestershire, since 1974 (Lord Lieutenant of Rutland, 1963-74); *b* 10 March 1911; *s* of late Charles B. Haywood, Woodhatch, Reigate, Surrey; *m* 1937, Anne, *d* of J. B. A. Kessler, London; two *s* one *d. Educ:* Winchester; Magdalene Coll., Cambridge. Served 1939-42 with Leics Yeomanry, Capt. 1940, Hon. Col, 1970-77. Chm. Trustees, Oakham Sch., 1964-81. DL 1962,

JP 1957, High Sheriff 1952, County of Rutland. *Address:* Gunthorpe, Oakham, Rutland. *T:* Manton 203. *Club:* MCC.

HAZAN, John Boris Roderick, QC 1969; Barrister-at-Law; a Recorder of the Crown Court, since 1972; *b* 3 Oct. 1926; *s* of Selik and Eugenie Hazan. *Educ:* King's Coll., Taunton; King's Coll., Univ. of London (LLB 1946). Called to Bar, Lincoln's Inn, 1948, Bencher 1977. Prosecuting Counsel to Inland Revenue, South Eastern Circuit, 1967-69. Dep. Chm., Surrey QS, 1969-71. Member: Criminal Law Revision Cttee, 1971-; Home Secretary's Policy Adv. Cttee on Sexual Offences, 1976-; Dept of Trade Inspector, Hartley Baird Ltd, 1973-76. JP Surrey, 1969. *Recreations:* music, opera, walking. *Address:* 4 Brick Court, Temple, EC4. *T:* 01-353 2725. *Club:* Savile.

HAZELL, Bertie, CBE 1962 (MBE 1946); Chairman, Special Programme Board, North Yorkshire, Manpower Services Commission, since 1978; *b* 18 April 1907; *s* of John and Elizabeth Hazell; *m* 1936, Dora A. Barham; one *d. Educ:* various elementary schs in Norfolk. Agricultural worker, 1921; apptd Sec. and Agent to E Norfolk Divisional Labour Party, Sept. 1933; District Organiser, Nat. Union of Agricl Workers, 1937-64, Pres., 1966-78; Mem. W Riding of Yorks, War Agricultural Executive Cttee, 1939 (Chm. several of its Cttees, throughout war period). Contested (Lab) Barkston Ash Parliamentary Division, 1945 and 1950 Gen. Elections; MP (Lab) North Norfolk, 1964-70. Chairman: E and W Ridings Regional Bd for Industry, 1954-64; N Yorks AHA, 1974-82; York DHA, 1981-; Vice-Chm., Agricultural, Horticultural and Forestry Trng Bd, 1972-74; Member: E Riding Co. Agricultural Exec. Cttee, 1946-64; Agricultural Wages Board, 1946-78; Leeds Regional Hosp. Board, 1948-74 (Chm. Works and Buildings Cttee); Potato Marketing Bd, 1970-. Magistrate, City of York, 1950-; Chairman: York and District Employment Cttee, 1963-74; N Yorks District Manpower Cttee, 1975-80; Vice-Chm., Leeds Regional Hosp. Bd, 1967-74. Mem. Council, Univ. of E Anglia. *Recreation:* gardening. *Address:* 42 Fellbrook Avenue, Beckfield Lane, Acomb, York. *T:* York 78443.

HAZELL, Ven. Frederick Roy; Archdeacon of Croydon, since 1978; Vicar of Holy Saviour, Croydon, since 1968; *b* 12 Aug. 1930; *s* of John Murdoch and Ruth Hazell; *m* 1956, Gwendoline Edna Armstrong (née Vare), widow of Major J. W. D. Armstrong; one step-s. *Educ:* Hutton Grammar School, near Preston; Fitzwilliam Coll., Cambridge (MA); Cuddesdon Coll., Oxford. HM Forces, 1948-50. Asst Master, Kingham Hill School, 1953-54; Asst Curate, Ilkeston Parish Church, 1956-59; Priest-in-Charge, All Saints', Marlpool, 1959-62; First Vicar of Marlpool, 1962-63; Chaplain, Univ. of the West Indies, 1963-66; Asst Priest, St Martin-in-the-Fields, 1966-68; Rural Dean of Croydon, 1972-78. Hon. Canon of Canterbury, 1973-. *Recreations:* music, numismatics. *Address:* Holy Saviour Vicarage, 96 Lodge Road, Croydon CR0 2PF. *T:* 01-684 2526.

HAZELL, Quinton, CBE 1978 (MBE 1961); Chairman, Supra Group plc, since 1973; Director: Phoenix Assurance Co. plc, since 1968; Foreign and Colonial Investment Trust, since 1978; Hawker-Siddeley Group, since 1979; *b* 14 Dec. 1920; *s* of late Thomas Arthur Hazell and Ada Kathleen Hazell; *m* 1942, Morwenna Parry-Jones; one *s. Educ:* Manchester Grammar School. Management Trainee, Braid Bros Ltd, Colwyn Bay, 1936-39; Royal Artillery, 1939-46; formed Quinton Hazell Ltd, 1946; Chm., 1946-73; Chm., Edward Jones (Contractors) Ltd, 1973-74. Chm., W Midlands Econ. Planning Council, 1971-77. Mem., Welsh Adv. Cttee for Civil Aviation, 1961-67; Director: Wales Gas Bd, 1961-65; Winterbottom Energy Trust, 1978-82; Non-Exec. Chm., F&C Enterprise Trust plc; Dep. Chm., Warwickshire Private Hosp. Member Council: UC Bangor, 1966-68; Univ. of Birmingham. *Recreations:* antiques, horology, water ski-ing. *Address:* Birdingbury Manor, Birdingbury, near Rugby, Warwicks. *T:* Leamington Spa 632779.

HAZI, Dr Vencel; Deputy Foreign Minister, Hungary, since 1976; *b* 3 Sept. 1925; *m* 1952, Judit Zell; one *d. Educ:* Technical Univ. and Univ. of Economics, Budapest. Entered Diplomatic Service, 1950; served in Min. of Foreign Affairs, Budapest, 1950; Press Attaché, Hungarian Legation, London, 1951-53; Counsellor, Legation, Stockholm, 1957-58; Ambassador: to Iraq, and to Afghanistan, 1958-61; to Greece, and to Cyprus, 1962-64; Head of Western Dept, Min. of For. Affairs, Budapest, 1964-68; Dep. For. Minister, Budapest, 1968-70; Ambassador to Court of St James's, 1970-76. Golden Grade of Order of Merit for Labour, 1962, and of Medal of Merit of Hungarian People's Republic, 1953; Grand Cordon of Order of Omayoum, 1st Class, Iran. *Recreations:* reading, music, swimming, chess. *Address:* Ministry for Foreign Affairs, Budapest, II Bem rkp 47, Hungary. *Club:* Opera Fans (Budapest).

HAZLERIGG, family name of Baron Hazlerigg.

HAZLERIGG, 2nd Baron, *cr* 1945, of Noseley; **Arthur Grey Hazlerigg,** Bt, *cr* 1622; MC 1945; DL, JP; *b* 24 Feb. 1910; *e s* of 1st Baron and Dorothy Rachel (*d* 1972), *e d* of John Henry Buxton, Easneye, Ware, Herts; *S* father 1949; *m* 1945, Patricia (*d* 1972), *e d* of late John Pullar, High Seat, Fields Hill, Kloof, Natal, SA; one *s* two *d. Educ:* Eton; Trinity Coll., Cambridge. BA 1932. FRICS 1946. Served War of 1939-45, Leics Yeomanry (MC); Major, 1941; served in Italy. DL Leics 1946; JP 1946. *Recreations:* golf, shooting. *Heir: s* Hon. Arthur Grey Hazlerigg, *b* 5 May 1951. *Address:* Noseley Hall, Leicester LE7 9EH. *Clubs:* Army and Navy, MCC.

HAZLEWOOD, Air Vice-Marshal Frederick Samuel, CB 1970; CBE 1967 (OBE 1960); AFC 1951 (Bar to AFC, 1954); retired; *b* 13 May 1921; *s* of Samuel Henry and Lilian Hazlewood; *m* 1943, Isabelle Mary (née Hunt); one *s. Educ:* Kimbolton Sch. Served War of 1939-45: joined RAF, 1939; ops with Bomber Command, 1941; MEAF and UK Coastal Command, 1940-45. CFS, 1948; Lancaster Units, 1948-53 (Sqdn Ldr); Staff Coll. course, 1955; Comdg Officer, No 90 Valiant Sqdn, 1958-61 (Wing Comdr); HQ, Bomber Comd, 1961-63; HQ, RAF, Germany, 1963-64 (Gp Capt.); OC, RAF, Lyneham, 1965-67; HQ, RAF, Germany, 1968-69 (Air Cdre); AOC and Commandant, Central Flying School, 1970-72; Dir of Personnel (Air), 1972; AOC 38 Gp, RAF, 1972-74; Comdt, Jt Warfare Estab., 1974-76. *Recreations:* golf, tennis, rough shooting. *Address:* Holly Ditch Farm, Calne, Wilts. *Club:* Royal Air Force.

HAZLEWOOD, Rt. Rev. John; see Ballarat, Bishop of.

HEAD, family name of Viscount Head.

HEAD, 1st Viscount *cr* 1960, of Throope; **Antony Henry Head;** PC 1951; GCMG 1963 (KCMG 1961); CBE 1946; MC 1940; *b* 1906; *s* of late Geoffrey Head; *m* 1935, Lady Dorothea Ashley-Cooper, *d* of 9th Earl of Shaftesbury, KP, PC, GCVO, CBE; two *s* one *d* (and one *d* decd). *Educ:* Eton; Royal Military Coll., Sandhurst, Adjt Life Guards, 1934-37; Staff Coll., 1939; Brigade Major 20th Gds Bde, 1940; Asst Sec. Cttee Imperial Defence, 1940-41; Guards Armbd Div., 1941-42 (GSO2); representative with Directors of Plans for Amphibious Operations (Brigadier), 1943-45. MP (C) Carshalton Division of Surrey, 1945-60; Sec. of State for War, 1951-56; Minister of Defence, Oct. 1956-Jan. 1957. High Commissioner (first) of the United Kingdom in the Federation of Nigeria, 1960-63; High Commissioner to the new Federation of Malaysia, 1963-66. Trustee of the Thomson Foundation, 1967-75. Pres., RNIB, 1975- (Chm., 1968-75). Col Comdt, SAS Regt, 1968-76. Chm., Wessex Region, National Trust, 1970-76. *Recreations:* sailing, shooting. *Heir: s* Hon. Richard Antony Head [*b* 27 Feb. 1937; *m* 1974, Alicia, *er d* of Julian Salmond, Malmesbury; two *s. Educ:* Eton; Royal Military Coll., Sandhurst]. *Address:* Throope Manor, Bishopstone, near Salisbury, Wilts.

HEAD, Adrian Herbert; His Honour Judge Head; a Circuit Judge since 1972; *b* 4 Dec. 1923; *s* of late Judge Head and Mrs Geraldine Head (née Pipon); *m* 1947, Ann Pamela, *d* of late John Stanning and late Mrs A. C. Lewin, of Leyland and Njoro, Kenya; three *s. Educ:* RNC Dartmouth (invalided, polio); privately; Magdalen Coll., Oxford (MA). Arden Scholar, Gray's Inn, 1947. Called to Bar, Gray's Inn, 1947 (subseq. ad eundem Inner Temple). Chm., Agricultural Land Tribunals (SE Region), 1971; Dep. Chm., Middlesex QS, 1971. Dir, later Chm., Norfolk Lavender Ltd, 1953-71. Tredegar Memorial Lectr, RSL, 1948. *Publications:* (contrib.) Oxford Poetry 1942-1943; The Seven Words and The Civilian, 1946; contrib. Essays by Divers Hands, 1953; Safety Afloat (trans. from Dutch of W. Zantvoort), 1965; Consumer Credit Act Supplement to McCleary's County Court Precedents, 1979. *Recreations:* sailing, writing, trees. *Address:* Overy Staithe, Kings Lynn, Norfolk PE31 8JG. *T:* Burnham Market 312; 5 Raymond Buildings, Gray's Inn, WC1R 5BP. *T:* 01-405 7146. *Clubs:* Norfolk (Norwich); Royal Naval Sailing Association, Cruising Association.

HEAD, Dennis Alec, CBE 1979; Director of Operations, Short Brothers, since 1982; *b* 8 Nov. 1925; *s* of late Alec Head and Florence Head; *m* 1966, Julia Rosser-Owen; one *s. Educ:* Whitgift Sch.; Peterhouse, Cambridge (Mech. Sciences Tripos, MA); Royal Naval Engrg Coll., Manadon. Served FAA, RN, 1943-47: Sub-Lt (A) RNVR, 1945; Air Engr Officer. Rolls-Royce Ltd: grad. apprentice, 1949; Manager, Design Services, Aero Engine Div., 1962, Dir of Personnel and Admin, 1967; Dir and Gen. Man., subseq. Man. Dir, Derby Engine Div., 1973; Managing Director: Aero Div., 1976; Operations, 1980-82; Member Board: Rolls-Royce Ltd, 1973-82; Rolls-Royce Turbomeca, 1973-82 (Chm., 1981-82); Turbo-Union, 1979-82; Chm., Rolls-Royce & Associates, 1981-82. Member: Reg. Adv. Council for Further Educn, 1968-73; Engrg Employers' Fedn Policy Cttee, 1978-82. *Recreations:* photography, history, music. *Address:* Short Brothers Ltd, Airport Road, Belfast BT3 9DZ. *T:* Belfast 58444.

HEAD, Major Sir Francis (David Somerville), 5th Bt, *cr* 1838; late Queen's Own Cameron Highlanders; *b* 17 Oct. 1916; *s* of 4th Bt and Grace Margaret (*d* 1967), *d* of late David Robertson; *S* father, 1924; *m* 1st, 1950, Susan Patricia (marr. diss. 1965), *o d* of A. D. Ramsay, OBE; one *s* one *d*; 2nd, 1967, Penelope, *d* of late Wilfred Alexander. *Educ:* Eton; Peterhouse, Cambridge, BA 1937. Served War of 1939-45 (wounded and prisoner); retired 1951. *Heir: s* Richard Douglas Somerville Head [*b* 16 Jan. 1951. *Educ:* Eton; Magdalene Coll., Cambridge]. *Address:* 10 Fairway, Merrow, Guildford, Surrey. *Club:* Naval and Military.

HEAD, Mildred Eileen, OBE 1971; Senior Partner, Head & Woodward (furnishers); *b* 13 June 1911; *d* of Philip Strudwick Head and Katie Head. *Educ:* Sudbury Girls' Secondary Sch.; Chelsea Coll. of Physical Educn (Dipl.). MCSP. Teacher, Lectr and Organiser of Physical Educn, 1933-50; owner, director and partner in several furniture and drapery shops from 1950. Pres., Nat. Fedn of Business and Professional Women's Clubs of Gt Britain and N Ireland, 1966-69; Pres., Nat. Chamber of Trade, 1977-79 (Chm. Bd of Management, 1971-77). Mayor of Borough of Sudbury, 1970-71; Member: Price Commn, 1973-77; Nat. Economic Cttee for Distributive Trades,

1974-79; Retail Consortium, 1971-; Davignon Cttee for Commerce and Distribution (EEC), 1979-; Franks Panel on pharm. payments, 1979; Discip. Cttee of Assoc. of Certified Accountants, 1980-. Comr of Inland Revenue, 1959-. Pres., Internat. Fedn of Business and Professional Women, 1977-80 (First Vice-Pres., 1974-77). *Recreation:* theatre. *Address:* Rosebank, Ingrams Well Road, Sudbury, Suffolk CO1O 6RT. *T:* Sudbury 72185.

HEADFORT, 6th Marquis of, *cr* 1800; **Thomas Geoffrey Charles Michael Taylour,** FRICS; Bt 1704; Baron Headfort, 1760; Viscount Headfort, 1762; Earl of Bective, 1766; Baron Kenlis (UK), 1831; *b* 20 Jan. 1932; *o s* of 5th Marquis and Elsie Florence (*d* 1972), *d* of J. Partridge Tucker, Sydney, NSW, and *widow* of Sir Rupert Clarke, 2nd Bt of Rupertswood; *S* father, 1960; *m* 1st, 1958, Hon. Elizabeth Nall-Cain (from whom he obtained a divorce, 1969), *d* of 2nd Baron Brocket; one *s* two *d*; 2nd, 1972, Virginia, *d* of late Mr Justice Nable, Manila. *Educ:* Stowe; Christ's Coll., Cambridge (MA; Cert. of Proficiency in Rural Estate Management). 2nd Lieut Life Guards, 1950; acting Pilot Officer, RAFVR, 1952. Dir, Bective Electrical Co. Ltd, 1953; Sales Manager and Chief Pilot, Lancashire Aircraft Co. Ltd, 1959. Freeman, Guild of Air Pilots and Air Navigators, 1958. Piloted Prospector aircraft around Africa, 1960, etc. Fellow, Royal Instn of Chartered Surveyors; Fellow, Chartered Inst. of Arbitrators. Council, Royal Agricultural Society of England, 1961. Inspector, Royal Hongkong Auxiliary Police. Holds commercial pilot's licence. Underwriting Mem. of Lloyds. *Heir: s* Earl of Bective, *qv. Address:* Ellerslie, Crosby, Isle of Man. *T:* Marown 851521; 1425 Figueroa Street, Paco, Manila, Philippines. *T:* Manila 59-38-29; telex 40199 OPRNS PM; Affix Ltd, 302 Hang Chong Building, 5 Queen's Road Central, Hong Kong. *T:* Hong Kong 235166; telex 75204. *Clubs:* Cavalry and Guards; Kildare Street and University (Dublin); Ellan Vannin (Isle of Man); Manila, Makati Sports (Philippines); Hong Kong, Foreign Correspondents (Hong Kong).

HEADLAM-MORLEY, Prof. Agnes, MA, BLit; Montague Burton Professor of International Relations, Oxford University, 1948-71; *b* 10 Dec. 1902; *o d* of late Sir James Wycliffe Headlam-Morley, CBE, Historical Adviser to the Foreign Office. *Educ:* Wimbledon High Sch., GPDST; Somerville Coll., Oxford. Fellow and Tutor, St Hugh's Coll., Oxford, 1932. Adopted Prospective Conservative Candidate, Barnard Castle Div. of Durham, 1936. Hon. Fellow: Somerville Coll., Oxford, 1948; St Hugh's Coll., Oxford, 1970; Mem., St Antony's Coll. Received into the Roman Catholic Church, 1948. Mem., Academic Council, Wilton Park. Founder Mem., Anglo-German Assoc. *Publications:* The New Democratic Constitutions of Europe, 1929; Editor (with K. Headlam-Morley) of Studies in Diplomatic History by J. W. Headlam-Morley, 1930; Arthur Cayley Headlam (a memoir published in The Fourth Gospel as History by A. C. Headlam, 1948); Last Days, 1960; (ed) A Memoir of the Peace Conference of Paris 1919 by J. W. Headlam-Morley, 1972; essay on Gustav Stresemann in The History Makers, ed Sir John Wheeler-Bennett and Lord Longford, 1973; contrib. Longford Report on Pornography, 1976; articles and reviews in Trivium and History Today. *Address:* 29 St Mary's Road, Wimbledon, SW19; St Hugh's College, Oxford. *T:* 01-946 6134.

HEADLAM-MORLEY, Kenneth Arthur Sonntag, OBE 1962; Secretary, The Iron and Steel Institute, 1933-67; *b* 24 June 1901; *o s* of late Sir James Headlam-Morley, CBE (who assumed additional surname of Morley by Royal Licence, 1917), Historical Adviser to the Foreign Office, and of Else, *y d* of late Dr August Sonntag, Lüneburg; *m* 1951, Lorna Dione, *d* of late Francis Kinchin Smith; three *s* two *d. Educ:* Eton; New Coll., Oxford (Schol.). Staff of Dorman, Long & Co Ltd, 1924; Secretary: Inst. of Metals, 1944-47; Instn of Metallurgists, 1945-48; Dep. Controller Chrome Ore, Magnesite and Wolfram Control, Foundry Bonding Materials Control and assoc. Controls of Min. of Supply, 1940-43. Hon. Life Member: Amer. Inst. of Mining and Metallurgical Engrs, 1955; Amer. Soc. for Metals, 1955. Hon. Member: l'Assoc. des Ingénieurs sortis de l'Ecole de Liège, 1955; Verein deutscher Eisenhüttenleute, 1955; Soc. Française de Métallurgie, 1956; The Indian Institute of Metals, 1963. Chevalier Order of Vasa (Sweden), 1954; Chevalier Order of the Crown (Belgium), 1955. *Recreation:* gardening. *Address:* Field House, Whorlton, Barnard Castle, Co. Durham DL12 8XA. *T:* Teesdale 27354.

HEADLEY, 7th Baron *cr* 1797; **Charles Rowland Allanson-Winn;** Bt 1660 and 1776; retired; *b* 19 May 1902; *s* of 5th Baron Headley and Teresa (*d* 1919), *y d* of late W. H. Johnson; *S* brother, 1969; *m* 1927, Hilda May Wells-Thorpe; one *s* three *d. Educ:* Bedford School. *Recreations:* golf, fishing. *Heir: s* Hon. John Rowland Allanson-Winn, *b* 14 Oct. 1934. *Address:* Torton Top, Torton Hill Road, Arundel, West Sussex. *T:* Arundel 882569. *Club:* East India, Devonshire, Sports and Public Schools.

HEADLY, Derek, CMG 1957; lately Malayan Civil Service; Midlands Secretary, Independent Schools Careers Organisation (formerly Public Schools Appointments Bureau), 1966-77; *b* 1908; *s* of L. C. Headly, The House-on-the-Hill, Woodhouse Eaves, Leics; *m* 1946, Joyce Catherine (marr. diss. 1975), *d* of C. F. Freeman; one *s* one *d. Educ:* Repton Sch.; Corpus Christi Coll., Cambridge (BA). Military Service, 1944-46, Lieut-Col, Special Ops Exec., Force 136 (despatches). Cadet, Malaya, 1931; served Muar, Trengganu, etc; Palestine, 1938-44; Resident N Borneo, 1946; ret. as Brit. Adv., Kelantan, 1957. Dir, Vipan & Headly Ltd, 1957-66. Mem. Melton and Belvoir RDC, 1958-67. Officer (Brother) Order of St John. *Publication:* From Learning to Earning (Independent Schools Careers Organisation Careers Guide), 1977.

Recreations: hunting, fishing, tennis, golf. *Address:* Rooftree Cottage, Hoby, Melton Mowbray, Leics. *T:* Rotherby 214. *Club:* Special Forces.

HEAF, Peter Julius Denison, MD, FRCP; Consultant Physician, University College Hospital, since 1958; *b* 1922; *s* of late Prof. F. R. G. Heaf, CMG; *m* 1947, Rosemary Cartledge; two *s* two *d. Educ:* Stamford Sch., Lincs; University Coll., London, Fellow 1973. MB, BS 1946; MD London 1952; MRCP 1954; FRCP 1965. House Physician and Surg., also RMO, University Coll. Hosp., and Capt. RAMC, 1946-51; Research Asst, Brompton Hosp., 1953-54; Sen. Registrar, St Thomas' Hosp., 1955-58. *Publications:* papers on chest disease and pulmonary physiology, in Lancet, etc. *Recreations:* painting, sailing. *Address:* 16 Gordon Mansions, Torrington Place, WC1E 7HE. *T:* 01-580 6981.

HEAKES, Air Vice-Marshal Francis Vernon, CB 1944; Commander, Legion of Merit (US); RCAF retired; *b* 27 Jan. 1894; *s* of Frank R. Heakes, Architect, and Susie Pemberton Heakes; *m* 1920, Edna Eulalie Watson, BA; one *s* three *d. Educ:* University of Toronto. Canadian Expeditionary Force, Lieut 1916-17; RFC (seconded), 1917-18; RAF 1918-19; CAF 1919; CAF and RCAF since 1923; Air Mem. Permanent Joint Board, Canada and US; Dir Air Personnel, RCAF; Dir Plans & Operations; AOC, RCAF, Newfoundland; AOC Western Air Command, Canada. *Recreations:* sports, all kinds, writing prose and verse, oil painting, musical composition. *Address:* 1876 West 63rd Avenue, Vancouver, BC V6P 2J1, Canada.

HEAL, Anthony Standerwick; Head of the Business, Heal & Son Holdings Ltd; *b* 23 Feb. 1907; *s* of Sir Ambrose Heal and Lady Edith Florence Digby Heal; *m* 1941, Theodora Caldwell (*née* Griffin); two *s. Educ:* Leighton Park Sch., Reading. Joined Heal & Son Ltd 1929; Dir 1936; Chm., Heal & Son, later Heal & Son Hldgs, Ltd, 1952-81. Chm. Council, London and S Eastern Furniture Manufrs Assoc., 1947-48; Master, Furniture Makers Guild (now Worshipful Co. of Furniture Makers), 1959-60; Mem. Council of Industrial Design, 1959-67; Mem. Council, City and Guilds of London Inst., 1969-81, Chm., Licentiateship Cttee, 1976-79; Pres., Design and Industries Assoc., 1965; Chm. Indep. Stores Assoc., 1970-72. Hon. FSIAD (Hon. FSIA 1974); Hon. FCGI 1981. RSA Bi-Centenary Medal, 1964. Order of White Rose of Finland, 1970; Chevalier (First Class) Order of Dannebrog, 1974. *Recreations:* vintage cars and steam engines. *Address:* Baylins Farm, Knotty Green, Beaconsfield, Bucks. *Clubs:* Vintage Sports Car, National Traction Engine.
See also O. S. Heal.

HEAL, Oliver Standerwick; Chairman, Heal & Son Holdings Ltd, since 1981 (Director, since 1975); *b* 18 April 1949; *s* of Anthony Standerwick Heal, *qv. Educ:* Leighton Park Sch., Reading. Joined Heal's, 1970; Dir, Heal & Son Ltd, 1974-, Chm., 1977-. *Recreation:* vintage cars. *Address:* 12 Compton Road, N1. *T:* 01-359 5735. *Clubs:* Twenty, Winnowing; Vintage Sports Car (Newbury).

HEALD, Mervyn, QC 1970; *b* 12 April 1930; *s* of Rt Hon. Sir Lionel Heald, QC, and of Daphne Constance, CBE 1976, *d* of late Montague Price; *m* 1954, Clarissa Bowen; one *s* three *d. Educ:* Eton College; Magdalene College, Cambridge. Called to the Bar, Middle Temple, 1954; Bencher, 1978. *Recreations:* country pursuits. *Address:* Headfoldswood, Loxwood, Sussex. *T:* Loxwood 752 248.

HEALD, Thomas Routledge; His Honour Judge Heald; a Circuit Judge (formerly County Court Judge), since 1970; *b* 19 Aug. 1923; *s* of late John Arthur Heald and Nora Marion Heald; *m* 1950, Jean, *d* of James Campbell Henderson; two *s* two *d. Educ:* Merchant Taylors' Sch.; St John's Coll., Oxford. Fish Schol., St John's Coll., Oxford, 1941; Lieut, RAC, 1943-45; BA (Jurisprudence) 1947; MA 1949. Called to Bar, Middle Temple, 1948; Midland Circuit; Prosecuting Counsel to Inland Revenue (Midland Circuit), 1965-70; Deputy Chairman, QS: Lindsey, 1965-71; Notts 1969-71. Mem. Council, Nottingham Univ., 1974- (Chm., Physical Recreation Adv. Cttee; Chm., Law Adv. Cttee); Chm., Law Adv. Cttee, Trent Polytechnic. *Recreations:* golf, local history, family history. *Address:* Rebbur House, Nicker Hill, Keyworth, Nottingham NG12 5ED. *T:* Plumtree 2676. *Clubs:* United Services (Nottingham); Notts Golf, Woking Golf.

HEALEY, Sir Charles Arthur C.; *see* Chadwyck-Healey.

HEALEY, Rt. Hon. Denis Winston, CH 1979; MBE 1945; PC 1964; MP (Lab) Leeds East, since 1955; Leeds East since 1955; Deputy Leader of the Labour Party, since 1980; *b* 30 Aug. 1917; *s* of late William Healey, Keighley, Yorks; *m* 1945, Edna May, *d* of Edward Edmunds, Coleford, Gloucestershire; one *s* two *d. Educ:* Bradford Grammar Sch.; Balliol Coll., Oxford (Hon. Fellow, 1979). First Cl. Hons Mods 1938; Jenkyns Exhib. 1939; Harmsworth Sen. Schol., First Cl. Lit. Hum., BA 1940; MA 1945. War of 1939-45; entered Army, 1940; served N Africa, Italy. Major RE 1944 (despatches). Contested (Lab) Pudsey and Otley Div., 1945; Sec., International Dept, Labour Party, 1945-52. Shadow Cabinet, 1959-64, 1970-74, 1979-; Secretary of State for Defence, 1964-70; Chancellor of the Exchequer, 1974-79; opposition spokesman on Foreign and Commonwealth Affairs, 1980-. Mem. Brit. Delegn to Commonwealth Relations Conf., Canada, 1949; British Delegate to: Consultative Assembly, Council of Europe, 1952-54; Inter Parly Union Conf., Washington, 1953; Western European Union and Council of Europe, 1953-55. Chm., IMF Interim Cttee, 1977-79. Mem. Exec.

Fabian Soc., 1954-61. Mem., Labour Party Nat. Exec. Cttee, 1970-75. Councillor: RIIA, 1948-60; Inst. of Strategic Studies, 1958-61. Grand Cross of Order of Merit, Germany, 1979. *Publications:* The Curtain Falls, 1951; New Fabian Essays, 1952; Neutralism, 1955; Fabian International Essays, 1956; A Neutral Belt in Europe, 1958; NATO and American Security, 1959; The Race Against the H Bomb, 1960; Labour Britain and the World, 1963; Healey's Eye, 1980. *Recreations:* travel, photography, music, painting. *Address:* House of Commons, SW1. *T:* 01-219 4503.

HEALEY, Deryck John; Chairman: Deryck Healey International Ltd, since 1969; Deryck Healey Associates, London, since 1966; *b* 30 Jan. 1937; *s* of Leonard Melvon Healey and Irene Isabella Healey (*née* Ferguson); *m* 1962, Mary Elizabeth Pitt Booth (decd); two *s. Educ:* Northlands High Sch., Natal, SA (Victoria League Empire Scholar); Manchester Polytechnic (DipAd, ADF 1961). Design Man., Good Hope Textiles, SA, 1959-66; Design Man., WPM London (Wallpaper mfrs), 1966-68; Design Co-ordinator consultant, ICI Fibres, 1968-80. Chm., CNAA Textile and Fashion Bd, 1971-81; Member: Design working party, Clothing and Allied Products Trng Bd, 1980; CNAA Art and Design Cttee; Design Council Textile Design Selection Cttee, 1978-81; Craft Council Textile Panel, 1980; SIAD British Design Export Gp, 1980. Governor, London Coll. of Fashion, 1978. External Examiner, Textile and Fashion courses: CNAA BA and MA; Liverpool, BA, 1978-80; Manchester, MA, 1977-79; Kingston, 1978-80; St Martin's, 1978-80; RCA, Textiles, 1980. FSIAD 1964. CoID Design Award, 1964; Queen's Award to Industry for Export, 1974; RSA Bicentenary Medal, 1981. *Publications:* Colour, 1980 (Mem. Editorial Bd and contrib.); Living with Colour, 1982. *Recreations:* drawing, painting, photography, squash, Deryck Healey Trust for the encouragement of Art, Design and Craft graduates. *Address:* 15 Thurloe Square, SW7. *Clubs:* various.

HEALEY, Rt. Rev. Kenneth; an Assistant Bishop, Diocese of Lincoln since 1966; *b* 7 Aug. 1899; *s* of late Harry Healey; *m* 1925, Marjorie, *d* of late Harry Wright Palmer, Friday Bridge, Cambs; two *d. Educ:* Moulton Grammar Sch. Deacon, 1931; Priest, 1932; Asst Curate, Grantham, 1931; Rector of Bloxholm with Digby, 1935; and Vicar of Ashby de la Launde (in plurality), 1939: Rural Dean of Lafford North, 1938; Vicar of Nocton, 1943; Rector of Algarkirk, 1950-58; Archdeacon of Lincoln, 1951-58; Bishop Suffragan of Grimsby, 1958-65. Proctor in Convocation, 1945-70; Church Commissioner, 1952-72. Chm. (formerly Vice-Chm.) Lindsey and Kesteven Agricultural Wages Cttee, 1945-69. MA Lambeth, 1958. *Address:* Gedney Dyke, Spalding, Lincs. *T:* Holbeach 362030.

HEALY, Prof. John Francis, MA, PhD; Professor of Classics, London University, and Head of Department at Royal Holloway College, since 1966; *b* 27 Aug. 1926; *s* of late John Healy and Iris Maud (*née* Cutland); *m* 1957, Carol Ann McEvoy; one *s. Educ:* Trinity Coll., Cambridge (Open Exhbn in Classics 1943; Classical Prelim. Cl. 1 1944; Classical Tripos: 1st Cl. Pt I 1949, 1st Cl. Pt II 1950 (dist. Cl. Archaeol.); Sen. Schol. 1950; BA 1950, MA 1952, PhD 1955). War service, 1944-48; Captain, Intelligence Corps, 1946-48. Walston student, Brit. Sch. of Archaeol., Athens, 1950; G. C. Winter Warr Schol., Cambridge, 1951; Manchester University: Asst Lectr in Classics, 1953-56; Lectr in Classics and Class. Archaeol., 1956-61; London University: Reader in Greek, Bedford Coll., 1961-66; Chm., Bd of Studies in Classics, 1979-81; Dean of Faculty of Arts, Royal Holloway Coll., 1978-81. Chm. Finance Cttee, Inst. of Classical Studies, London, 1967-. FRNS 1950; FRSA 1971; MRI 1979. *Publications:* contrib. (A. Rowe) Cyrenaican Expeditions of the University of Manchester, 1955-57; Mining and Metallurgy in the Greek and Roman World, 1978; articles and reviews in Jl of Hellenic St., Numismatic Chron., Nature, Amer. Num. Soc.'s Mus. Notes, Jl of Metals, Class. Rev., Gnomon. *Recreations:* travel, music, gardening. *Address:* Department of Classics, Royal Holloway College, Egham Hill, Egham, Surrey TW20 0EX. *T:* Egham 34455. *Club:* Cambridge Union Society.

HEALY, Tim T.; see Traverse-Healy.

HEANEY, Brig. George Frederick, CBE 1943; late Royal Engineers (retd); *b* 1 June 1897; 2nd *s* of late George Robert Heaney, Dublin; *m* 1929, Doreen Marguerite, *e d* of late Lieut-Col R. H. Hammersley-Smith, CBE; one *s* two *d* (and one *s* decd). *Educ:* St Lawrence; RMA Woolwich; Christ's Coll., Cambridge. 2nd Lieut RE 1916; European War in France, 1917-18 (wounded, despatches twice); apptd to Survey of India, 1921; in India and Burma, 1920-41; served in Persia-Iraq Forces, 1941-43 (CBE); D Survey, Allied Land Forces, SEAC, 1944-45; retired from Army, 1948; Surveyor-Gen. of India, 1946-51; Pres. Inst. of Surveyors (India), 1950-51; Managing Dir, North Essex Growers Ltd, 1963-64. *Address:* 16 Park Road, Lymington, Hants SO4 9GN.

HEANEY, Henry Joseph, MA, FLA; University Librarian and Keeper of the Hunterian Books and Manuscripts, Glasgow, since 1978; *b* 2 Jan. 1935; *s* of late Michael Heaney and Sarah (*née* Fox); *m* 1976, Mary Elizabeth Moloney. *Educ:* Abbey Grammar Sch., Newry; Queen's Univ. of Belfast (MA). FLA 1967. Asst Librarian, QUB, 1959-62; Libr., Magee University Coll., Londonderry, 1962-67; Dep. Libr., New Univ. of Ulster, 1967-69; Asst Sec., Standing Conf. of National and Univ. Libraries, 1969-72; Librarian: QUB, 1972-74; University Coll., Dublin, 1975-78. Trustee, Nat. Lib. of Scotland, 1980-. *Publication:* (ed) IFLA Annual, 1971. *Address:* Glasgow University Library, Glasgow G12 8QE. *T:* 041-334 2122.

HEANEY, Leonard Martin, CMG 1959; Overseas Civil Service, retired; *b* 28 Nov. 1906; *s* of Alexander John and Lilian Heaney; *m* 1947, Kathleen Edith Mary Chapman; no *c. Educ:* Bristol Grammar Sch.; Oriel Coll., Oxford. Joined Colonial Service on leaving Oxford, 1929; served in Tanganyika, retiring as a Senior Provincial Commissioner, 1959. Military service with East African Forces in Abyssinia, Madagascar, Ceylon, Burma, 1940-45. *Recreations:* reading and golf. *Address:* Northwood, Burgundy Road, Minehead, Somerset. *T:* Minehead 3859.

HEANEY, Seamus Justin; Member of Irish Academy of Letters; Visiting Professor at Harvard University; *b* 13 April 1939; *s* of Patrick and Margaret Heaney; *m* 1965, Marie Devlin; two *s* one *d. Educ:* St Columb's College, Derry; Queen's University, Belfast. BA first cl. 1961. Teacher, St Thomas's Secondary Sch., Belfast, 1962-63; Lectr, St Joseph's Coll. of Educn, Belfast, 1963-66; Lectr, Queen's Univ., Belfast, 1966-72; free-lance writer, 1972-75; Lectr, Carysfort Coll., 1975-81. *Publications:* Eleven Poems, 1965; Death of a Naturalist, 1966 (Somerset Maugham Award, 1967; Cholmondeley Award, 1968); Door into the Dark, 1969; Wintering Out, 1972; North, 1975 (W. H. Smith Award; Duff Cooper Prize); Field Work, 1979; *Preoccupations:* Selected Prose, 1968-1978, 1980; Selected Poems, 1965-1975, 1980. *Address:* c/o Faber & Faber, 3 Queen Square, WC1N 3RU.

HEANEY, Brig. Sheila Anne Elizabeth, CB 1973; MBE 1955; TD; Chairman, Women's Royal Voluntary Service, Scotland, 1977-81; *b* 11 June 1917; 2nd *d* of late Francis James Strong Heaney, MA, MD, FRCSI, Liverpool and Anne Summers McBurney. *Educ:* Huyton Coll.; Liverpool University. BA 1938. Joined ATS, 1939, WRAC, 1949; Director, WRAC, and Hon. ADC to the Queen, 1970-73. *Address:* 41 Wardie Road, Edinburgh EH5 3LJ.

HEANLEY, Charles Laurence, TD 1950; FRCS; Consulting Surgeon; Member of Lloyd's; *b* 28 Feb. 1907; *e s* of Dr C. M. Heanley; *m* 1935; three *s. Educ:* Epsom Coll.; Downing Coll., Cambridge (Exhib., Schol.); London Hosp. BA Cambridge (Nat. Sci. Tripos) 1929, MA 1934; MRCS, LRCP 1932; MB, BCh Cambridge 1934; FRCS 1933; MRCP 1935. London Hosp., 1929; Surg. First Asst, 1936. Served War of 1939-45; France, Surgical Specialist, 17th Gen. Hosp., 1939-40; Surgeon Specialist, RAMC Park Prewitt Plastic Unit, 1941-42; India, OC No 3 British Maxillo-Facial Surgical Unit and Lieut-Col OC Surgical Div., 1942-45; Surg. in charge of Dept of Plastic Surg., London Hosp., 1946-64. Cons. Surg. Worthing Hosp., Bethnal Green Hosp., and Plastic Unit Queen Victoria Hosp., East Grinstead, 1945; Plastic Surg. London Hosp.; Hon. Cons. Plastic Surg. Royal National and Golden Square Hosps, 1969. *Publications:* varied medical articles. *Recreations:* swimming, archæology. *Address:* Vainona, St George, Woodmancote, Henfield, West Sussex BN5 9ST. *T:* Henfield 2947.

HEAP, Sir Desmond, Kt 1970; LLM, Hon. LLD, PPRTPI; solicitor; *b* 17 Sept. 1907; *o s* of late William Heap, Architect, Burnley, Lancs, and Minnie Heap; *m* 1945, Adelene Mai, *o d* of late Frederick Lacey, Harrogate, and of Mrs F. N. Hornby; one *s* two *d. Educ:* The Grammar Sch., Burnley; Victoria University of Manchester. LLB Hons 1929; LLM 1936; Hon. LLD 1973; admitted Solicitor, 1933; Hons Final Law Examination; Pres., Law Soc., 1972-73 (Mem. Council, 1954-78, Chm. Law Reform Cttee, 1955-60, and Chm., Town Planning Cttee, 1964-70). Past Master, Worshipful Company of Solicitors; Liveryman of Worshipful Company of Carpenters. Mem., Court of Worshipful Co. of Chartered Surveyors; Legal Mem., RTPI (formerly TPI), 1935-, Mem. of Council, 1947-77, Pres., 1955-56; Assoc. Mem. Royal Institute of Chartered Surveyors, 1953-, Mem. of Council, 1957-; Mem. of Colonial Office Housing and Town Planning Adv. Panel, 1953-65; Prosecuting Solicitor, 1935-38 and Chief Asst Solicitor for City of Leeds, 1938-40; Dep. Town Clerk of Leeds, 1940-47; Lecturer in the Law of Town and Country Planning and Housing, Leeds Sch. of Architecture, 1935-47; Comptroller and City Solicitor to the Corporation of London, 1947-73. Mem. of Editorial Board of Journal of Planning and Environment Law, 1948-; Mem., Council on Tribunals, 1971-77; Vice-Pres., Statute Law Soc., 1982-. Dep. Pres., City of London Branch, British Red Cross Soc., 1956-76. Chm. of Governors, Hurstpierpoint Coll., 1975-82. FRSA (Mem. Council, 1974-78). Hon. Member: Amer. Bar Foundn, 1971-; Hawaii Chapter, Phi Beta Kappa; Hon. Fellow, Inc. Soc. of Valuers and Auctioneers, 1979-. *Publications:* Planning Law for Town and Country, 1938; Planning and the Law of Interim Development, 1944; The Town and Country Planning Act, 1944, 1945; An Outline of Planning Law, 1943 to 1945, 1945; The New Towns Act, 1946, 1947; Introducing the Town and Country Planning Act, 1947, 1947; Encyclopædia of Planning, Compulsory Purchase and Compensation, Vol. 1, 1949; Heap on the Town and Country Planning Act, 1954, 1955; Encyclopædia of Planning Law and Administration, 4 vols, 1960; Introducing the Land Commission Act 1967, 1967; Encyclopædia of Betterment Levy, 1967; The New Town Planning Procedures, 1969; The Land and the Development; or, the Turmoil and the Torment (Hamlyn Lectures), 1975; An Outline of Planning Law, 7th edn 1978, 8th edn 1982; How to Control Land Development, 1974, 2nd edn 1981; Lectures on tape: The Community Land Act, 1975; articles in legal jls. *Recreations:* swimming, fell walking, the amateur theatre. *Address:* Quarry Cottage, Blackhall Lane, Sevenoaks, Kent. *T:* Sevenoaks 458529; (office) Coward Chance, Royex House, Aldermanbury Square, EC2V 7LD. *T:* 01-600 0808; Last, Suddards & Co., 128 Sunbridge Road, Bradford. *T:* Bradford 33571. *Clubs:* Athenæum, City Livery, Guildhall.

HEAP, Peter William; HM Diplomatic Service; Head of Energy, Science and Space Department, Foreign and Commonwealth Office, since 1980; *b* 13 April 1935; *s* of Roger and Dora Heap; *m* 1st, 1960, Helen Cutting Wilmerding (marr. diss.); two *s* two *d*; 2nd, 1977, Dorrit Breitenstein. *Educ:* Bristol Cathedral Sch.; Merton Coll., Oxford. Army, 1954-56. CRO, 1959; Third Sec., Dublin, 1960; Third and Second Sec., Ottawa, 1960; First Sec., Colombo, 1963-66; seconded to MoD, 1966-68; FO, 1968-71; Dep. Dir-Gen., British Information Services, New York, 1971-76; Counsellor (Political and Economic), 1976-78, Counsellor (Commercial), 1978-80, Caracas. *Address:* c/o Foreign and Commonwealth Office, King Charles Street, SW1A 2AL.

HEARN, David Anthony; General Secretary, Association of Broadcasting and Allied Staffs, since 1972; *b* 4 March 1929; *s* of James Wilfrid Laurier Hearn and Clara (*née* Barlow); *m* 1952, Anne Beveridge; two *s*. *Educ:* Trinity Coll., Oxford (MA). Asst to Gen. Sec., Assoc. of Broadcasting Staff, 1955; subseq. Asst Gen. Sec., then Dep. Gen. Sec.; Sec., Fedn of Broadcasting Unions. *Address:* 4 Stocks Tree Close, Yarnton, Oxford OX5 1LU. *T:* Kidlington 4613.

HEARN, Rear-Adm. Frank Wright, CB 1977; Assistant Chief of Personnel and Logistics, Ministry of Defence, 1974-77; *b* 1 Oct. 1919; *s* of John Henry Hearn, Civil Servant, and Elsie Gertrude Hearn; *m* 1st, 1947, Ann Cynthia Keeble (*d* 1964); two *d*; 2nd, 1965, Ann Christina June St Clair Miller. *Educ:* Abbotsholme Sch., Derbyshire. Joined RN, 1937; HMS Hood, 1937-39. Served War of 1939-45 in various HM Ships in Atlantic, Mediterranean and East Indies. Staff of CinC, Home Fleet, 1951-53; Sec. to Flag Officer, Submarines, 1954-56; after service in USA became Sec. to Dir of Naval Intell., 1958-60, when joined HMS Tiger as Supply Officer; Fleet Supply Officer, Western Fleet, 1962-64; subseq. service in Plans Div, MoD (Navy) and CSO (Admin.) to Flag Officer, Submarines; IDC 1969; commanded HMS Centurion in rank of Cdre, 1970-73; Chm., Review of Officer Structure Cttee, 1973-74. *Recreations:* golf, tennis, gardening, wine-making. *Address:* Hurstbrook Cottage, Hollybank Lane, Emsworth, Hants PO10 7UE. *T:* Emsworth 2149.

HEARN, Rt. Rev. George Arthur; *see* Rockhampton, Bishop of.

HEARN, Prof. John Patrick; Director of Science and Director of Institute of Zoology, The Zoological Society of London, since 1980; Visiting Professor in Zoology, University College London, since 1979; *b* Limbdi, India, 24 Feb. 1943; *s* of Lt-Col Hugh Patrick Hearn and Cynthia Ellen (*née* Nicholson); *m* 1967, Margaret Ruth Patricia McNair; three *s* one *d*. *Educ:* Crusaders' Sch., Headley, Hants; St Mary's Sch., Nairobi, Kenya; University Coll., Dublin (BSc, MSc); ANU, Canberra (PhD). Sen. Demonstrator in Zool., University Coll., Dublin, 1966-67; Lectr in Zool., 1967-69, and Dean of Science, 1968-69, Strathmore Coll., Nairobi; Res. Scholar, ANU, 1969-72; Staff Mem., MRC Reproductive Biology Unit, Edinburgh, 1972-79; Hon. Fellow, Univ. of Edinburgh, 1974-79. Consultant Scientist, WHO Special Prog. of Res. in Human Reproduction, Geneva, 1978-79; Dir, Wellcome Labs of Comparative Physiology, Zoological Soc. London, 1979-80. *Publications:* (ed with H. Rothe and H. Wolters) The Biology and Behaviour of Marmosets, 1978; (ed) Immunological Aspects of Reproduction and Fertility Control, 1980; (ed) Reproduction in New World Primates, 1982; papers on develtl and reproductive physiol. in scientific jls. *Recreations:* music, travel, wildlife, squash, running, swimming. *Address:* The Institute of Zoology, The Zoological Society of London, Regent's Park, NW1 4RY. *T:* 01-722 3333.

HEARNE, Graham James; Chief Executive, Tricentrol, since 1981; *b* 23 Nov. 1937; *s* of Frank Hearne and Emily (*née* Shakespeare); *m* 1961, Carol Jean (*née* Brown); one *s* three *d*. *Educ:* George Dixon Grammar Sch., Birmingham. Admitted solicitor, 1959: Pinsent & Co., Solicitors, 1959-63; Fried, Frank, Harris, Shriver & Jacobson, Attorneys, NYC, 1963-66; Herbert Smith & Co., Solicitors, 1966-67; IRC, 1967-70; N.M. Rothschild & Sons Ltd, 1970-77; Finance Dir, Courtaulds Ltd, 1977-81. Non-exec. Director: N.M. Rothschild & Sons Ltd, 1973-; Northern Foods, Ltd, 1976-82; BPB Industries, 1982-; part-time Member: British National Oil Corp., 1975-78; Dover Harbour Bd, 1976-78. *Address:* 1 East Heath Road, NW3 1BN. *T:* 01-794 4987. *Club:* Reform.

HEARNE, Peter Ambrose; Director and General Manager, Marconi Avionics, since 1970; *b* 14 Nov. 1927; *s* of late Arthur Ambrose Hearne, MD, and Helen Mackay Hearne; *m* 1952, Georgina Gordon Guthrie; three *s*. *Educ:* Sherborne Sch., Dorset; Loughborough Coll. of Technol. (DLC); Cranfield Inst. of Technol. (MSc); MIT. Design Engr, Saunders Roe, 1946-47; Ops Develt Engr, BOAC, 1949-54; Helicopter Proj. Engr, BEA, 1954-58; Marketing Manager, British Oxygen, 1958-59; Divl Man., Guided Weapons, Elliott Flt Automation, 1959; Asst Gen. Man., 1960; Dir and Gen. Man., 1965-70. Vis. Prof., Cranfield Inst. of Technol., 1981. Chm., Cranfield Soc., 1965-67, Pres., 1981; Pres., Royal Aeronautical Society, 1980-81 (Vice-Pres., 1976-79). *Publications:* papers in Jl of RAeS and NATO Agard series. *Recreations:* flying with and without engines, sailing, models. *Address:* The Limes, Wateringbury, Kent. *T:* Maidstone 812385. *Clubs:* Surrey and Hants Gliding, Tiger (Redhill); Whitstable Yacht, Southwold Sailing.

HEARNSHAW, Prof. Leslie Spencer; Professor of Psychology, University of Liverpool, 1947-75, now Emeritus; *b* Southampton, 9 Dec. 1907; *o s* of

late Prof. F. J. C. Hearnshaw, Prof. of History, King's Coll., London; *m* 1937, Gwenneth R. Dickins, Perth, Western Australia; one *s* three *d*. *Educ:* King's Coll. Sch., Wimbledon; Christ Church, Oxford; King's Coll., London. 1st Class Lit Hum, 1930; 1st Class Psychology Hons (London), 1932. Investigator, Nat. Institute of Industrial Psychology, London, 1933-38; Lecturer in Psychology, Victoria Univ., Coll., Wellington, NZ, 1939-47; Dir, Industrial Psychology Div., DSIR, Wellington, NZ, 1942-47; Mem. of Council, British Psychological Soc., 1949-57; Chm., Industrial Section, 1953-54; Pres., British Psychological Soc., 1955-56. Pres. Section J (Psychology), Brit. Assoc., 1954; Hon. Dir, Medical Research Council, Research Group into occupational aspects of ageing, 1955-59, 1963-70. Hobhouse Memorial Lecturer, 1966. Vice-Pres., International Assoc. of Applied Psychology, and Editor of its Journal, 1964-74. *Publications:* (with R. Winterbourn) Human Welfare and Industrial Efficiency, 1945; A Short History of British Psychology, 1840-1940, 1964; Cyril Burt, psychologist, 1979; articles on industrial psychology and the psychology of thinking. *Address:* 1 Devonshire Road, West Kirby, Wirral L48 7HR. *T:* 051-625 5823.
See also C. T. C. Wall.

HEARST, Stephen, CBE 1980; Controller, Future Policy Group, BBC, since 1978; *b* Vienna, Austria, 6 Oct. 1919; *m* 1948, Lisbeth Edith Neumann; one *s* one *d*. *Educ:* Vienna Univ.; Reading Univ. (Dip. Hort.); Brasenose Coll., Oxford (MA). Free lance writer, 1949-52; joined BBC as producer trainee, 1952; Documentary television: script writer, 1953-55; writer producer, 1955-65; Exec. Producer, Arts Programmes Television, 1965-67; Head of Arts Features, Television, 1967-71; Controller, Radio 3, 1972-78. FRSA 1980. *Publications:* Two Thousand Million Poor, 1965; Artistic Heritage and its Treatment by Television, 1982. *Recreations:* gardening, swimming, reading, listening to music. *Address:* c/o British Broadcasting Corporation, Broadcasting House, W1A 1AA.

HEARST, William Randolph, Jun.; journalist; Editor-in-Chief, The Hearst Newspapers, and Chairman of the Executive Committee, The Hearst Corporation; *b* NYC, 27 Jan. 1908; *s* of William Randolph Hearst and Millicent Veronica (*née* Willson); *m* 1st, 1928, Alma Walker (marr. diss., 1932); 2nd, 1933, Lorelle McCarver (marr. diss., 1948); 3rd, 1948, Austine McDonnell; two *s*. *Educ:* Collegiate Sch.; St John's Manlius Mil. Acad., Syracuse; Berkeley High Sch., Berkeley, Calif.; Hitchcock Mil. Acad., San Rafael, Calif; University of Calif. Began career with New York American, NYC, as a reporter, 1928; publisher, 1936-37; publisher, NY Journal-American, 1937-56; The American Weekly, 1945-56; War Correspondent, 1943-45. Member Boards: USO, NY; United Press International; Permanent Charter Mem., For. Correspondents Club of Japan, 1945-. *Address:* (home) 810 Fifth Avenue, New York, NY 10021, USA; (office) 959 Eighth Avenue, New York, NY 10019, USA. *Clubs:* Overseas Press, Marco Polo, Brook, Madison Square Garden (New York City); F Street, Sulgrave, National Press, Metropolitan, Burning Tree, International (Washington); Bohemian, Pacific Union (San Francisco); London Press; Alaska Press; Tokyo Press.

HEARTH, John Dennis Miles; Chief Executive, Royal Agricultural Society of England, since 1972; *b* 8 April 1929; *s* of late Cyril Howard Hearth, MC, and of Dr Pauline Kathleen Hearth, MB, BSc; *m* 1959, Pamela Anne (*née* Bryant); two *s*. *Educ:* The King's Sch., Canterbury; Brasenose Coll., Oxford (MA). Called to the Bar, Gray's Inn, 1962. Administrative Officer, HM Overseas Civil Service, 1953-61; Editor, Fairplay Shipping Journal, Fairplay Publications Ltd, 1961-66; Cunard Steam-Ship Co. Ltd, 1966-71 (various appts and Main Board Joint Ventures Director, 1969-71). CBIM 1980. *Recreations:* travel, history, theatre, golf. *Address:* Bayard's, Fenny Compton, near Leamington Spa, Warwicks CV33 0XY. *T:* Fenny Compton 370. *Clubs:* Farmers', Anglo-Belgian.

HEATH, Sir Barrie, Kt 1978; DFC 1941; Director: Barclays Bank, since 1976; Barclays Bank UK Ltd, since 1975; Pilkington Brothers Ltd, since 1967; Smiths Industries Ltd, since 1970; Tunnel Holdings Ltd, since 1980; Chairman, Hesketh Motorcycles, 1980-82; *b* 11 Sept. 1916; *s* of George Heath and Florence Amina Heath (*née* Jones); *m* 1st, 1939, Joy Anderson (*d* 1980); two *s*; 2nd, 1981, Joan Elizabeth McKee. *Educ:* Wrekin; Pembroke Coll., Cambridge. Trained with Rootes Securities Ltd, 1938-39; fighter pilot, RAF, 1939-45 (Wing Comdr, despatches); Dir, Hobourn Aero Components, Rochester, 1946-50; Managing Dir, Powell Duffryn Carbon Products Ltd, 1950-60; Man. Dir, Triplex Safety Glass Co. Ltd, 1960-68, Chm., 1965-74; non-exec. Dir, GKN Ltd, 1972-74; Group Chm., GKN Ltd, 1975-79. Dep. Pres., Soc. of Motor Manufacturers and Traders, 1980-81 (Vice-Pres., 1973-78, Pres., 1978-80); Vice-President: Engineering Employers' Fedn, 1975-; Inst. of Motor Industry, 1975-; Pres., German Chamber of Industry and Commerce in UK, 1977-80; Founder Mem., Engineering Industries Council, 1975-; Chm., Commonwealth Games UK Jt Appeal Cttee, 1977-78; Member: Industrial Democracy Cttee, 1975-77; British Overseas Trade Adv. Council, 1977-80; BOTB, 1977-80; Tenneco European Adv. Council, 1980-. Governor, and Chm. Vehicle Cttee, Motability, 1977-. Trustee: Nat. Motor Mus., 1975-; RAF Mus., 1976-. Freeman of City of London; Liveryman, Coachmaker and Coach Harness Makers' Co. *Recreations:* yachting, field sports. *Address:* GKN House, 22 Kingsway, WC2B 6LG. *T:* 01-242 1616.

HEATH, Edward Peter, OBE 1946; Consultant, Matheson & Co. Ltd, since 1980; Director: Matheson Motor Holdings, since 1981; Lancaster Group Holdings, since 1981; *b* 6 June 1914; *m* 1953, Eleanor Christian Peck; one *s* three *d*. *Educ:* St Lawrence Coll., Ramsgate. Joined Borneo Co. Ltd, 1934;

interned in Thailand, 1941-45. Gen. Manager, Borneo Co. Ltd, 1953-63; a Man. Dir, 1963-67; a Man. Dir, Inchcape & Co. Ltd, 1967-75, a Dep. Chm., 1976-79. Director: Mann Egerton & Co. Ltd, 1973-79; Dodwell & Co. Ltd, 1974-79; Inchcape Far East Ltd, 1972-79; Chairman: Toyota GB and Pride & Clark, 1978-79; Anglo-Thai Corp. Ltd, 1978-79; Dep. Chm., Bewac Motor Corp., 1970-79. Dep. Chairman: Hong Kong Assoc., 1975-79; Anglo Thai Soc., 1975-. Order of White Elephant (5th Cl.) (Thailand); Officer, Order of Orange Nassau (Netherlands). *Recreations:* hunting, gardening, motoring. *Address:* Cooks Place, Albury, Guildford, Surrey GU5 9BJ. *T:* Shere 2698. *Clubs:* Boodle's, City of London.

HEATH, Rt. Hon. Edward Richard George, PC 1955; MBE 1946; MP (C) Bexley, Sidcup, since 1974 (Bexley, 1950-74); Chairman, International Advisory Council, International Reporting Information Systems, since 1981; Member, Public Review Board, Arthur Andersen & Co.; *b* Broadstairs, Kent, 9 July 1916; *s* of late William George and Edith Anne Heath. *Educ:* Chatham House Sch., Ramsgate; Balliol Coll., Oxford (Scholar; Hon. Fellow, 1969). Pres. Oxford Univ. Conservative Assoc., 1937; Chm. Federation of Univ. Conservative Assocs, 1938; Pres. Oxford Union, 1939; Oxford Union debating tour of American Univs, 1939-40; Pres. Federation of University Conservative and Unionist Associations, 1959-77, Hon. Life Patron, 1977. Served War of 1939-45 (despatches, MBE); in Army, 1940-46, in France, Belgium, Holland and Germany; gunner in RA, 1940; Major 1945. Lieut-Col comdg 2nd Regt HAC, TA, April 1947-Aug. 1951; Master Gunner within the Tower of London, 1951-54. Administrative Civil Service, 1946-47 resigning to become prospective candidate for Bexley. Asst Conservative Whip, Feb. 1951; Lord Commissioner of the Treasury, Nov. 1951, and Joint Deputy Govt Chief Whip, 1952, and Dep. Govt Chief Whip, 1953-55; Parliamentary Sec. to the Treasury, and Government Chief Whip, Dec. 1955-Oct. 1959; Minister of Labour, Oct. 1959-July 1960; Lord Privy Seal, with Foreign Office responsibilities, 1960-63; Sec. of State for Industry, Trade, Regional Development and Pres. of the Board of Trade, Oct. 1963-Oct. 1964; Leader of the Opposition, 1965-70; Prime Minister and First Lord of the Treasury, 1970-74; Leader of the Opposition, 1974-75. Chm., Commonwealth Parly Assoc., 1970-74. Mem., Indep. Commn on Internat. Development Issues, 1977-79. Mem. Council, Royal College of Music, 1961-70; Chm., London Symphony Orchestra Trust, 1963-70; Vice-Pres., Bach Choir, 1970-; Pres., European Community Youth Orchestra, 1977-80; Hon. Mem., LSO, 1974-. Smith-Mundt Fellowship, USA, 1953; Vis. Fellow, Nuffield Coll., Oxford, 1962-70, Hon. Fellow, 1970; Chubb Fellow, Yale, 1975; Montgomery Fellow, Dartmouth Coll., 1980. Lectures: Cyril Foster Meml, Oxford, 1965; Godkin, Harvard, 1966; Montagu Burton, Leeds, 1976; Edge, Princeton, 1976; Romanes, Oxford, 1976. Hon. Bencher, Gray's Inn, 1972; Hon. Freeman, Musicians' Co., 1973. Hon. FRCM; Hon. FRCO; Hon. Fellow, Royal Canadian Coll. of Organists. Hon. DCL Oxon, 1971; Hon. DTech Bradford, 1971; Hon. LLD Westminster Coll., Salt Lake City, 1975; Dr *hc* Univ. of Paris, Sorbonne, 1976; Hon. Dr of Public Admin, Wesleyan Coll., Macon, Ga, 1981; Hon. DL, Westminster Coll., Fulton, Missouri, 1982. Freiherr Von Stein Foundn Prize; Charlemagne Prize, 1963; Estes J. Kefauver Prize 1971; Stresseman Gold Medal, 1971; Gold Medal of City of Paris, 1978; World Humanity Award, 1980; Gold Medal, European Parlt, 1981. Winner, Sydney to Hobart Ocean Race, 1969; Captain: Britain's Admiral's Cup Team, 1971, 1979; Britain's Sardinia Cup Team, 1980. *Publications:* (joint) One Nation-a Tory approach to social problems, 1950; Old World, New Horizons (Godkin Lectures), 1970; Sailing: a course of my life, 1975; Music: a joy for life, 1976; Travels: people and places in my life, 1977; Carols: the joy of Christmas, 1977. *Recreations:* sailing, music. *Address:* House of Commons, SW1. *Clubs:* Buck's, Carlton, St Stephen's Constitutional (Jt Pres., 1979); Royal Yacht Squadron.

HEATH, Henry Wylde Edwards, CMG 1963; QPM; Commissioner of Police, Hong Kong, 1959-67, retired; *b* 18 March 1912; *s* of late Dr W. G. Heath and late Mrs L. B. Heath; *m* Joan Mildred Crichett; two *s* one *d. Educ:* Dean Close Sch.; HMS Conway. Probationer Sub-Inspector of Police, Leeward Islands, 1931; Asst Supt, Hong Kong, 1934; Superintendent, 1944; Asst Commissioner, 1950. Colonial Police Medal, 1953; QPM, 1957. *Recreations:* golf, ski-ing. *Address:* Quintyens Cottage, 4 Firle Drive, Seaford, Sussex. *Clubs:* Seaford Golf; Kandahar Ski.

HEATH, Prof. John Baldwin; Professor of Economics, London Graduate School of Business Studies, since 1970; Director of the Master's Programme; *b* 25 Sept. 1924; *s* of late Thomas Arthur Heath and late Dorothy Meallin; *m* 1953, Wendy Julia Betts; two *s* one *d. Educ:* Merchant Taylors' Sch.; St Andrews Univ.; Cambridge Univ. RNVR, 1942-46. Spicers Ltd, 1946-50; Lecturer in Economics, Univ. of Manchester, 1956-64; Rockefeller Foundation Fellowship, 1961-62; Dir, Economic Research Unit, Bd of Trade, 1964-67; Dir, Economic Services Div., BoT, 1967-70. Member: Mechanical Engrg EDC, 1971-76; British Airports Auth., 1980-; Economic Adviser, CAA, 1972-78. *Publications:* articles in many learned jls on competition and monopoly, productivity, cost-benefit analysis. *Recreations:* music, walking. *Address:* 25 Chalcot Square, NW1. *T:* 01-722 4301.

HEATH, John Moore, CMG 1976; HM Diplomatic Service, retired; Director General, Canning House, since 1982; *b* 9 May 1922; *s* of late Philip George and of Olga Heath; *m* 1952, Patricia Mary Bibby; one *s* one *d. Educ:* Shrewsbury Sch.; Merton Coll., Oxford (MA). Served War of 1939-45, France, Belgium and Germany: commnd Inns of Court Regt, 1942; Capt. GSO3 11th Armoured Div., 1944-45 (despatches). Merton Coll., 1940-42,

1946-47. Entered Foreign Service, 1950; 2nd Sec., Comr-Gen.'s Office, Singapore, 1950-52; 1st Sec. (Commercial), Jedda, 1952-56; 1st Sec., FO, 1956-58; Nat. Def. Coll., Kingston, Ont., 1958-59; Head of Chancery and HM Consul, Brit. Embassy, Mexico City, 1959-62; Head of Chancery, Brit. Embassy, Kabul, Afghanistan, 1963-65; Counsellor and Head of Establishment and Organisation Dept, FCO (formerly DSAO), 1966-69; Counsellor (Commercial), Brit. Embassy, Bonn, 1969-74; Overseas Trade Advr, Assoc. of British Chambers of Commerce, on secondment, 1974; Consul-Gen., Chicago, 1975-79; Ambassador to Chile, 1980-82. *Recreations:* walking, travel. *Address:* 6 Cavendish Crescent, Bath, Avon. *Club:* Naval and Military.

HEATH, Sir Mark (Evelyn), KCVO 1980; CMG 1980; HM Diplomatic Service; Ambassador to the Holy See, since 1982 (Minister, 1980-82); *b* 22 May 1927; *s* of late Captain John Moore Heath, RN; *m* 1954, Margaret, *d* of late Sir (William) Lawrence Bragg, CH, OBE, MC, FRS; two *s* one *d. Educ:* Marlborough; Queens' Coll., Cambridge. Served in RNVR, 1945-48. Joined HM Foreign (subseq. Diplomatic) Service, 1950; served in: Djakarta, 1952-56; Copenhagen, 1956-58; FO, 1958-62; Sofia, 1962-64 (Chargé d'Affaires, 1963 and 1964); Ottawa, 1964-68; FO, later FCO, 1968, Hd of Commodities Dept, 1970-71; Dep. Head, UK Delegn to OECD, 1971-74; seconded to Cabinet Office, 1974-75; Head of W African Dept, FCO, and Ambassador to Chad, 1975-78; Inspector, 1978-80. Officer, Order of Dannebrog, 1957. *Recreations:* books, gardening. *Address:* c/o Foreign and Commonwealth Office, SW1; 47 Arbrook Lane, Esher, Surrey KT10 9EG. *Club:* Athenæum.

HEATH, Air Marshal Sir Maurice (Lionel), KBE 1962 (OBE 1946); CB 1957; CVO 1978; DL; Gentleman Usher to the Queen, 1966-79, Extra Gentleman Usher to the Queen since 1979; *b* 12 Aug. 1909; *s* of Lionel Heath, Artist and Principal of the Mayo Sch. of Arts, Lahore, India; *m* 1938, Kathleen Mary *d* of Boaler Gibson, Bourne, Lincs; one *s* one *d. Educ:* Sutton Valence Sch.; Cranwell. Commissioned RAF, 1929; service with Nos 16 and 28 Squadrons; Specialist Armament duties, 1933-42; Chief Instructor, No 1 Air Armament Sch., 1942; Station Commander, Metheringham, No 5 Group, Bomber Comd, 1944 (despatches). Dep. to Dir-Gen. of Armament, Air Min., 1946-48; CO Central Gunnery Sch., 1948-49; Sen. Air Liaison Officer, Wellington, NZ, 1950-52; CO Bomber Comd Bombing Sch., 1952-53; idc, 1954; Dir of Plans, Air Min., 1955; Deputy Air Secretary, Air Ministry, 1955-57; Commander, British Forces, Arabian Peninsula, 1957-59; Commandant, RAF Staff Coll., 1959-61; Chief of Staff, HQ Allied Air Forces Central Europe, 1962-65, retd. Dir, Boyd and Boyd, Estate Agents, 1971-76; Private Agent, Henderson Financial Management, 1980-. Chief Hon. Steward, Westminster Abbey, 1965-74. Appeal Dir, 1977-79, Appeal Consultant, 1979-, Voluntary Research Trust Nat. Appeal, King's Coll. Hosp. and Med. Sch. Pres., Storrington Br., RAFA, 1966-. DL West Sussex, 1977. *Recreations:* sailing, golf and travel. *Address:* Broom Cottage, Sunset Lane, West Chiltington, Pulborough, Sussex RH20 2NY. *Clubs:* Royal Air Force; West Sussex Golf.

HEATH, Oscar Victor Sayer, FRS 1960; DSc (London); Professor of Horticulture, University of Reading, 1958-69, now Emeritus; *b* 26 July 1903; *s* of late Sir (Henry) Frank Heath, GBE, KCB, and Frances Elaine (*née* Sayer); *m* 1930, Sarah Margery, *d* of Stephen Bumstead, Guestling, Hastings; two *s* one *d. Educ:* Imperial Coll., London (Forbes Medallist), Fellow, 1973. Asst Demonstrator in Botany, Imperial Coll., 1925-26; Empire Cotton Growing Corp. Sen. Studentship, Imperial Coll. of Tropical Agriculture, Trinidad, 1926-27; Plant Physiologist, Empire Cotton Growing Corp., Cotton Experiment Station, Barberton, S Africa, 1927-36; Research Student, Imperial Coll., London, 1936-39; Leverhulme Research Fellow, 1937-39; Research Asst, 1939-40, and Mem. of Staff, Research Inst. of Plant Physiology of Imperial Coll., Rothamsted, 1940-46, London, 1946-58; Sen. Principal Scientific Officer, 1948-58; Special Lectr in Plant Physiology, Imperial Coll., 1945-58; Dir, ARC Unit of Flower Crop Physiology, 1962-70; Mem. ARC, 1965-70; Leverhulme Emeritus Res. Fellow, 1970-72. *Publications:* chapters on physiology of leaf stomata in Encyclopædia of Plant Physiology (ed Ruhland) 1959, in Plant Physiology-a Treatise (ed Steward), 1959, and (with T. A. Mansfield) in Physiology of Plant Growth (ed Wilkins), 1969; The Physiological Aspects of Photosynthesis, 1969 (trans. German, 1972, Russian, 1972); Investigation by Experiment, 1970 (trans. Spanish, 1977, Portuguese, 1981); Stomata, 1975, 2nd edn 1981; papers in scientific jls. *Address:* 10 St Peter's Grove, W6 9AZ. *T:* 01-748 0471.

HEATH-GRACIE, George Handel, BMus (Dunelm), 1932; FRCO 1915; Organist and Master of the Choristers, Derby Cathedral, 1933-57; Diocesan Choirmaster, 1936-57; Founder and Conductor, Derby Bach Choir, 1935; Special Commissioner, Royal School of Church Music, since 1951; *m* 1922, Marjory Josephine Knight. *Educ:* Bristol Grammar Sch.; Bristol Cathedral. Organist of various Bristol Churches, 1909-14; of St John's, Frome, 1914-15; Service with HM forces, 1915-19; Organist of St Peter, Brockley, SE, 1918-33; Conductor South London Philharmonic Soc., 1919-21; Broadcast Church Music Series, 1936-38; Music Dir, Derby Sch., 1938-44; Mem. panel of examnrs, Associated Bd of Royal Schs of Music, 1946-; Sch. Music Adviser, Derbyshire Educn Cttee, 1944-57; Mem. Council, Incorporated Soc. of Musicians for SW England, 1964-67; Mem. Diocesan Adv. Cttee, to 1957; Mem., Artist selection panel, BBC, 1946-74. Extra-mural Lectr, University Coll., Nottingham; Festival Adjudicator and Lectr. Toured Canada and USA as adjudicator, lecturer and performer, 1949, return visit, 1953; travelled in

Asia, and African Tour, 1959; Eastern Tour, Ceylon, Singapore, Malaya, 1960; Tour of W Indies, N and S America and New Zealand, 1966, and New Zealand, 1968. *Publications:* various Church Music and press articles. *Recreations:* gossip, grass-cutting, brewing, domestic repairs, and electrical engineering. *Address:* Shorms, Stockland, Honiton, Devon EX14 9DQ. *T:* Stockland 403. *Clubs:* Savage; Exeter and County; (Hon.) Kiwanis (Peterborough, Ont).

HEATH-STUBBS, John (Francis Alexander); poet; Lecturer in English Literature, College of St Mark and St John, Chelsea, 1963-73; *b* 1918; *s* of Francis Heath Stubbs and Edith Louise Sara (*née* Marr). *Educ:* Bembridge School; Worcester Coll. for the Blind, and privately; Queen's Coll., Oxford. English Master, Hall Sch., Hampstead, 1944-45; Editorial Asst, Hutchinson's, 1945-46; Gregory Fellow in Poetry, Leeds Univ., 1952-55; Vis. Prof. of English: University of Alexandria, 1955-58; University of Michigan, 1960-61. FRSL 1953. Queen's Gold Medal for Poetry, 1973; Oscar Williams/Jean Durwood Award, 1977. *Publications:* verse: Wounded Thammuz; Beauty and the Beast; The Divided Ways; The Swarming of the Bees; A Charm against the Toothache; The Triumph of the Muse; The Blue Fly in his Head; Selected Poems; Satires and Epigrams; Artorius; A Parliament of Birds; The Watchman's Flute; Birds Reconvened; Buzz Buzz, Naming of the Beast; *drama:* Helen in Egypt; *criticism:* The Darkling Plain; Charles Williams; The Pastoral; The Ode; The Verse Satire; *translations:* (with Peter Avery) Hafiz of Shiraz; (with Iris Origo) Leopardi, Selected Prose and Poetry; (with Carol A. Whiteside) The Poems of Anyte; (with Peter Avery) The Rubaiyat of Omar Khayyam; *edited:* Selected Poems of Jonathan Swift; Selected Poems of P. B. Shelley; Selected Poems of Tennyson; Selected Poems of Alexander Pope; (with David Wright) The Forsaken Garden; Images of Tomorrow; (with David Wright) Faber Book of Twentieth Century Verse; (with Martin Green) Homage to George Barker on his Sixtieth Birthday; Selected Poems of Thomas Gray. *Recreation:* taxonomy. *Address:* 35 Sutherland Place, W2. *T:* 01-229 6367.

HEATHCOAT AMORY, Sir Ian, 6th Bt *cr* 1874; JP; DL; *b* 3 Feb. 1942; *s* of Sir William Heathcoat Amory, 5th Bt, DSO, and of Margaret Isabel Dorothy Evelyn, *yr d* of Sir Arthur Havelock James Doyle, 4th Bt; *S* father, 1982; *m* 1972, Frances Louise, *d* of J. F. B. Pomeroy; three *s. Educ:* Eton. JP, DL Devon. *Heir: s* William Francis Heathcoat Amory, *b* 19 July 1975. *Address:* Hayne House, Tiverton, Devon.

HEATHCOTE, Brig. (Gilbert) Simon, CBE 1964 (MBE 1941); *b* 21 Sept. 1913; *s* of late Col R. E. M. Heathcote, DSO, Manton Hall, Rutland and Millicent Heathcote; *heir* to baronetcy of Earl of Ancaster, *qv*; *m* 1939, Patricia Margaret (*née* Leslie); one *s* one *d. Educ:* Eton; RMA Woolwich. Commnd RA, 1933; War Service in Europe, 1939-44; Commdr RA, 1960-62; Chief of Staff, Middle East Comd, 1962-64; retd. *Publications:* articles in service jls. *Recreations:* sailing, ski-ing. *Address:* Stable Cottage, Manton, Oakham, Leics. *Clubs:* Army and Navy, Royal Cruising.

HEATHCOTE, Sir Michael Perryman, 11th Bt, *cr* 1733; *b* 7 Aug. 1927; *s* of Leonard Vyvyan Heathcote, 10th Bt, and Joyce Kathleen Heathcote (*d* 1967); *S* father, 1963; *m* 1956, Victoria Wilford, *e d* of Comdr J. E. R. Wilford, RN, Retd; two *s* one *d. Educ:* Winchester Coll.; Clare Coll., Cambridge. Started farming in England, 1951, in Scotland, 1961. Is in remainder to Earldom of Macclesfield. *Recreations:* fishing, shooting and farming. *Heir: s* Timothy Gilbert Heathcote, *b* 25 May 1957. *Address:* Warborne Farm, Boldre, Lymington, Hants. *T:* Lymington 73478; Carie and Carwhin, Lawers, by Aberfeldy, Perthshire.

HEATHCOTE, Simon; *see* Heathcote, Gilbert S.

HEATHCOTE-DRUMMOND-WILLOUGHBY; family name of **Earl of Ancaster.**

HEATHCOTE-SMITH, Clifford Bertram Bruce, CBE 1963; HM Diplomatic Service, 1936-72; acting Senior Clerk, Department of Clerk of House of Commons, 1973-77; *b* 2 Sept. 1912; *s* of late Sir Clifford E. Heathcote-Smith, KBE, CMG; *m* 1940, Thelma Joyce Engström; two *s. Educ:* Malvern; Pembroke Coll., Cambridge. Entered Consular Service, 1936; served in China, 1937-44; Foreign Office, 1944-47; Political Adviser, Hong-Kong, 1947-50, Montevideo, 1951-56; Commercial Counsellor: Ankara, 1956-60; Copenhagen, 1960-64; Washington, 1964-65; Dep. High Comr, Madras, 1965-68; a Diplomatic Service Inspector, 1969-72. *Address:* Lampool Lodge, Maresfield, East Sussex. *T:* Nutley 2849.

HEATHER, Stanley Frank, CBE 1980; Comptroller and City Solicitor, City of London Corporation, 1974-80; Attorney and General Counsel, City of London (Arizona) Corporation, since 1974; *b* 8 Jan. 1917; *s* of Charles and Jessie Heather; *m* 1946, Janet Roxburgh Adams, Perth; one *s* one *d. Educ:* Downhills Sch.; London Univ. Commnd Reconnaissance Corps, RAC, 1941; India/Burma Campaign, 1942-45. Admitted Solicitor, 1959. Asst Solicitor, City of London, 1963; Dep. Comptroller and City Solicitor, 1968. FRSA 1981. *Recreations:* golf, squash, fishing. *Address:* Kinnoull, 14 Morrell Avenue, Horsham, West Sussex. *T:* Horsham 60109. *Clubs:* City Livery, Guildhall; Ifield Golf and Country.

HEATLY, Peter, CBE 1971; Director, Peter Heatly & Co. Ltd, since 1958; Chairman, Scottish Sports Council, since 1975; *b* 9 June 1924; *s* of Robert

Heatly and Margaret Ann Heatly; *m* 1948, Jean Robertha Hermiston (*d* 1979); two *s* two *d. Educ:* Leith Academy; Edinburgh Univ. (BSc). CEng, FICE. *Recreations:* swimming, golf, gardening. *Address:* Lanrig, Balerno, Edinburgh EH14 7AJ. *T:* 031-449 3998.

HEATON, David; Assistant Under Secretary of State, Home Office, since 1976; *b* 22 Sept. 1923; *s* of late Dr T. B. Heaton, OBE, MD; *m* 1961, Joan, *d* of Group Captain E. J. Lainé, CBE, DFC; two *s* one *d. Educ:* Rugby Sch. Served RNVR, 1942-46. Ghana, 1948-58; Cabinet Office, 1961-69; Home Office, 1969-. *Address:* 53 Murray Road, SW19 4PF. *T:* 01-947 0375.

HEATON, Very Rev. Eric William; Dean of Christ Church, Oxford, since 1979; *b* 15 Oct. 1920; *s* of late Robert William Heaton and late Ella Mabel Heaton (*née* Brear); *m* 1951, Rachel Mary, *d* of late Rev. Charles Harold Dodd, CH, FBA; two *s* two *d. Educ:* Ermysted's, Skipton; (Exhibnr) Christ's Coll., Cambridge (MA). English Tripos, Part I; Theological Tripos, Part I (First Class). Deacon, 1944; Priest, 1945; Curate of St Oswald's, Durham, 1944-45; Staff Sec., Student Christian Movement in University of Durham, 1944-45; Chaplain, Gonville and Caius Coll., Cambridge, 1945-46; Dean and Fellow, 1946-53; Tutor, 1951-53; Bishop of Derby's Chaplain in University of Cambridge, 1946-53; Canon Residentiary, 1953-60, and Chancellor, 1956-60, Salisbury Cathedral; Tutor in Theology, Official Fellow and Chaplain, 1960-74, Senior Tutor, 1967-73, St John's College, Oxford; Dean of Durham, 1974-79. Chm. Council, Headington Sch., Oxford, 1968-74; Chm. Governors, High Sch., Durham, 1975-79. Moderator, Gen. Ordination Exam., 1971-81. Examining Chaplain to: Archbishop of York, 1951-56; Bishop of Portsmouth, 1947-74; Bishop of Salisbury, 1949-64; Bishop of Norwich, 1960-71; Bishop of Wakefield, 1961-74; Bishop of Rochester, 1962-74. Select Preacher: Cambridge University, 1948, 1958; Oxford Univ., 1958-59, 1967, 1971. Hon. Lectr, Univ. of Durham, 1975-79. Hon. Fellow, Champlain Coll., Univ. of Trent, Ont, Canada, 1973-; Hon. Fellow, St John's Coll., Oxford, 1979. *Publications:* His Servants the Prophets, 1949 (revised and enlarged Pelican edn, The Old Testament Prophets, 1958, 2nd rev. edn, 1977); The Book of Daniel, 1956; Everyday Life in Old Testament Times, 1956; Commentary on the Sunday Lessons, 1959; The Hebrew Kingdoms, 1968; Solomon's New Men, 1974; articles in Jl of Theological Studies, Expository Times, etc. *Address:* Christ Church, Oxford. *T:* (office) Oxford 47122, (private) Oxford 43815.

HEATON, Ralph Neville, CB 1951; *b* 4 June 1912; *s* of late Ernest Heaton; *m* 1939, Cecily Margaret Alabaster; three *s* one *d. Educ:* Westminster; Christ Church, Oxford. Formerly Deputy Secretary various Govt Depts, including Education, Transport, and Economic Affairs. Commonwealth Fund Fellow, 1951-52. *Address:* 38 Manor Park Avenue, Princes Risborough, Bucks.

HEATON, Sir Yvo (Robert) Henniker-, 4th Bt *cr* 1912; *b* 24 April 1954; *s* of Sir (John Victor) Peregrine Henniker-Heaton, 3rd Bt, and of Margaret Patricia, *d* of late Lieut Percy Wright, Canadian Mounted Rifles; *S* father, 1971; *m* 1978, Freda, *d* of B. Jones. *Heir: uncle* Clement Algernon Charles Henniker-Heaton, CBE [*b* 11 Dec. 1909; *m* 1940, Marjorie, *d* of W. E. Speight; two *s* one *d*]. *Address:* 7 Borough Street, Keyworth, Leics.

HEATON-WARD, Dr William Alan, FRCPsych; Lord Chancellor's Medical Visitor, since 1978; *b* 19 Dec. 1919; *s* of Ralph Heaton-Ward, MA, and Mabel Orton; *m* 1945, Christine Edith Fraser; two *d. Educ:* Queen Elizabeth's Hosp., Bristol; Univ. of Bristol Med. Sch. MB, ChB, 1944; DPM 1948; FRCPsych 1971. Jun. Clerk, Messrs W. D. & H. O. Wills, 1936-38; House Phys., Bristol Royal Inf., 1944-45; MO, Littlemore Mental Hosp., 1945-46; served RNVR, 1946-48: Surg. Lt-Comdr; Neuropsychiatrist, Nore Comd; Sen. Registrar, St James Hosp., Portsmouth, 1948-50; Dep. Med. Supt, Hortham Brentry Gp, 1950-54; Stoke Park Hosp. Group: Consultant Psych., 1954-78, Hon. Consultant, 1978-; Med. Supt, 1954-61; Cons. Psych. i/c, 1963-74; Clinical Teacher in Mental Health, Univ. of Bristol, 1954-78; Cons. Psych., Glos Royal Hosp., 1962-67. Hon. Cons. Adviser: NAMH, 1966-73; CARE, 1970-78; British Council Vis. Lectr, Portugal, 1971. Royal Coll. of Psychiatrists: Vice Pres., 1976-78; Blake Marsh Lectr, 1976; Burden Res. Gold Medal and Prize Winner, 1978. Pres., Brit. Soc. for Study of Mental Subnormality, 1978-79; Vice-Pres., Fortune Centre, Riding for the Disabled, 1980-; Mem. Council, Inst. of Mental Subnormality, 1972-76; Hon. Mem., Amer. Assoc. of Physician Analysts, 1976-. *Publications:* Notes on Mental Deficiency (jtly), 1952, 3rd edn 1955; Mental Subnormality, 1960, 4th edn 1975; Left Behind, 1977; papers on all aspects of care and treatment of mentally handicapped and on gen. psychiatric topics; book revs. *Recreations:* following all forms of outdoor sport, gardening, seeking the sun, philately. *Address:* 75 Pembroke Road, Clifton, Bristol BS8 3DP. *T:* Bristol 738124. *Club:* Savages (Bristol).

HEAUME, Sir Francis H. du; *see* du Heaume.

HEAVENER, Rt. Rev. Robert William; *b* 28 Feb. 1906; *s* of Joseph and Maria Heavener; *m* 1936, Ada Marjorie, *d* of Rev. Chancellor Thomas Dagg; one *s* one *d. Educ:* Trinity Coll., Dublin (MA). Ordained, 1929; Curate, Clones; Diocesan Curate; 1930; Curate-in-charge, Lack, 1933-38; Rector, Derryvullen N, 1938-46; Rector, Monaghan, 1946-73; Rural Dean, 1946. Examining Chaplain and Canon of Clogher, 1951-62; Canon of St Patrick's Cathedral, Dublin, 1962-68; Archdeacon of Clogher, 1968-73; Bishop of Clogher, 1973-80. OCF, 1938-43; Member of Staff of Command Welfare Officer, NI District, 1938-43. *Publications:* Co. Fermanagh, 1940 (a short topographical and historical account of NI); Diskos, 1970 (a collection of material for Adult Education). *Recreations:* tennis, rare book collecting. *Address:* c/o The See House, Thornfield, Fivemiletown, Co. Tyrone. *T:* Fivemiletown 265. *Club:* Friendly Brother House (Dublin).

HEBB, Prof. Donald Olding, FRSC 1959; FRS 1966; Professor of Psychology, 1947-72 (part-time appointment, 1972-74), and Chancellor, 1970-74, Professor Emeritus, 1975, McGill University (Chairman of Department, 1948-58; Vice-Dean of Biological Sciences, 1964-66); *b* 22 July 1904; *s* of Arthur Morrison Hebb and Mary Clara Olding; *m* 1st, 1931, Marion Isobel Clark (*d* 1933); 2nd, 1937, Elizabeth Nichols Donovan (*d* 1962); two *d*; 3rd, 1966, Margaret Doreen Wright (*née* Williamson). *Educ:* Dalhousie Univ.; McGill Univ.; University of Chicago; Harvard Univ. PhD (Harvard), 1936. Taught in schools, Nova Scotia and Quebec, 1925-34; Instructor, Harvard Univ., 1936-37; Research Fellow, Montreal Neurological Inst., 1937-39; Lectr, Queen's Univ., 1939-42; Research Associate, Yerkes Labs of Primate Biology, 1942-47. Royal Soc. Vis. Prof., UCL, 1974. Hon. Prof., Dalhousie Univ., 1978-. Pres., Canadian Psychol Assoc., 1952; Pres., American Psychol. Assoc., 1960. Hon. DSc: Chicago, 1961; Waterloo, 1963; York, 1966; McMaster, 1967; St Lawrence, 1972; McGill, 1975; Memorial, 1977; Hon. DHL, Northeastern, 1963; Hon. LLD: Dalhousie, 1965; Queen's, 1967; Western Ontario, 1968; Concordia, 1975; Trent, 1976; Victoria, BC, 1976; Hon. DCL Bishop's, 1977. *Publications:* Organization of Behaviour, 1949; Textbook of Psychology, 1958, 3rd edn 1972; Essay on Mind, 1980; papers in technical psychological jls. *Address:* RR1, Chester Basin, Nova Scotia B0J 1K0, Canada. *T:* (902) 275-4367.

HEBBLETHWAITE, Peter; Vatican Affairs Writer for The National Catholic Reporter (USA), since 1979; *b* 30 Sept. 1930; *s* of Charles and Elsie Ann Hebblethwaite; *m* 1974, Margaret I. M. Speaight; two *s* one *d*. *Educ:* Xaverian Coll., Manchester; Campion Hall, Oxford; Heythrop Coll., Oxon. MA (1st Cl.) Oxford; LTh. Editor, The Month, a Jesuit review of Church and world affairs, 1965-73; Asst Editor, Frontier, 1974-76; Lectr in French, Wadham Coll., Oxford, 1976-79; thence to Rome as free-lance and Vatican Affairs Writer, for National Catholic Reporter, 1979-. *Publications:* Georges Bernanos, 1965; The Council Fathers and Atheism, 1966; Theology of the Church, 1968; The Runaway Church, 1975; Christian-Marxist Dialogue and Beyond, 1977; The Year of Three Popes, 1978; The New Inquisition?, 1981; The Papal Year, 1981; Introducing John Paul II, 1982; contribs to TLS. *Recreations:* singing songs: Lieder and chansons. *Address:* 45 Marston Street, Oxford OX4 1JU. *T:* Oxford 723 771.

HEBBLETHWAITE, Sidney Horace, CMG 1964; HM Diplomatic Service, retired; Hon. Vice-Consul at Florence, since 1978; *b* 15 Nov. 1914; *s* of Sidney Horace Hebblethwaite and Margaret Bowler Cooke; *m* 1942, May Gladys Cook; two *d*. *Educ:* Reale Ginnasio-Liceo, Francesco Petrarca, Trieste, Italy; Pembroke Coll., Cambridge. Third Sec., FO, 1939; transferred to: Rome, 1939; FO, 1940; Lisbon, 1942; Second Sec. 1944; transferred to FO, 1945; Foreign Service Officer, 1948; 1st Sec. (Information), Athens, 1949; transferred to: Rome, 1951; FO, 1955; seconded to Treasury, 1957; transferred to Brussels, 1958; Counsellor: HM Embassy, Stockholm, 1958-62, Rangoon, 1962-65; Counsellor (Information), Washington, 1965-68; retired, in order to take up appt as HM Consul, Florence, 1970-74. *Recreations:* music, reading. *Address:* 10 Via San Egidio, Florence, Italy.

HEBDITCH, Maxwell Graham; Director, Museum of London, since 1977 (Deputy Director, 1974-77); *b* 22 Aug. 1937; *s* of late Harold Hebditch, motor engr, Yeovil, and Lily (*née* Bartle); *m* 1963, Felicity Davies; two *s* one *d*. *Educ:* Yeovil Sch.; Magdalene Coll., Cambridge. MA, FSA, FMA. Field Archaeologist, Leicester Museums, 1961-64; Asst Curator in Archaeology, later Curator in Agricultural and Social History, City Museum, Bristol, 1965-71; Dir, Guildhall Mus., London, 1971-74. Chm., UK Nat. Cttee, ICOM, 1981-. *Publications:* contribs to Britannia, Museums Jl, County Archaeological Jls. *Recreation:* archaeology. *Address:* Museum of London, London Wall, EC2Y 5HN. *T:* 01-600 3699.

HECKER, William Rundle, CBE 1963; MA, BSc, FKC; Headmaster of St Dunstan's College, Catford, 1938-67; *b* 1899; *s* of late W. J. Hecker, Margate, and Elizabeth, *d* of Richard Rundle, Hazelbeech, Northants; *m* 1925, Ione Murray, *d* of late J. P. Topping, MD; one *s*. *Educ:* Chatham House, Ramsgate; King's Coll., London. Served European War, 1914-18, in France; London Regt, 1917-19; Senior Science Master, Boston Gram. Sch., 1924-25; Asst Master, Epsom Coll., 1925-28; Headmaster of Tavistock Gram. Sch., 1928-31, Wilson's Gram. Sch., Camberwell, 1931-38. Pres. Incorporated Assoc. of Headmasters, 1951. Chm. Jt Cttee of the Four Secondary Assoc., 1958-59. *Recreations:* walking, gardening, travel. *Address:* 5 Meadowcourt Road, Oadby, Leicester.

HECTOR, Gordon Matthews, CMG 1966; CBE 1961 (OBE 1955); Secretary to the Assembly Council, General Assembly of the Church of Scotland, since 1980; *b* 9 June 1918; *m* 1944, Mary Forrest, MB, ChB; *o d* of late Robert Gray, Fraserburgh, Aberdeenshire; one *s* two *d*. *Educ:* Edinburgh Academy; Lincoln Coll., Oxford. Military Service with East Africa Forces, 1940-45. Apptd Dist Officer, Kenya, 1946; Asst Sec., 1950; Sec. to Road Authority, 1951; Sec. to Govt of Seychelles, 1952; Acting Governor, 1953; Dep. Resident Comr and Govt Sec., Basutoland, 1956; Chief Sec., Basutoland, 1964; Deputy British Government Representative, Lesotho (lately Basutoland), 1965. Sec., Basutoland Constitutional Commn, 1957-58. Clerk to the Univ. Court,

Aberdeen, 1967-76; Dep. Sec. and Establishment Officer, Aberdeen Univ., 1976-80. Fellow of the Commonwealth Fund, 1939. Mem. Bd of Governors, Oakbank D List Sch. Burgess of Guild, Aberdeen City. *Recreation:* railways ancient and modern. *Address:* 18 Magdala Crescent, Edinburgh EH12 5BD. *T:* 031-346 2317. *Clubs:* Royal Over-Seas League; New (Edinburgh); Vincent's (Oxford).

HEDDLE, (Bentley) John; MP (C) Lichfield and Tamworth, since 1979; Consultant Surveyor; Consultant Partner, Elliott Son and Boyton, Chartered Surveyors, since 1980; *b* 15 Sept. 1943; *s* of Oliver Heddle and late Lilian Heddle; *m* 1964, Judith, *d* of Dr R. H. M. Robinson, Hyde Hall, Rettendon, Essex, and Joy Robinson, Hothfield, Kent; two *s* two *d*. *Educ:* Bishop's Stortford Coll.; College of Estate Management, London Univ., 1962-64. FCIArb; FInstD, etc. Partner, Heddle Butler & Co., Cons. Surveyors, 1966-70; John Heddle & Co., 1970-80. Member: Internat. Real Estate Fedn, 1972-; Bd of Management, UK Housing Assoc., 1980-. Underwriting Mem., Lloyds, 1974. Councillor, Kent CC, 1973-80. Contested (C): Gateshead West, Feb. 1974; Bolton East, Oct. 1974; adopted as parly cand., Lichfield and Tamworth, Nov. 1975. Jt Sec., Cons. Parly Environment Cttee, 1979-; Chm., Bow Gp Environment Cttee, 1980-; Sec., Cons. Parly Media Cttee; Mem. H of C Select Cttee on the Environment. Industry and Parlt Trust Fellowship, 1979. Deleg. to Commonwealth Parly Assoc. Conf., Gibraltar, 1981. FRSA 1979. Freeman, City of London, 1979. *Publications:* The Way Through the Woods, 1973; St Cuthbert's Village—an urban disaster, 1976; A New Lease of Life—a solution to Rent Control (CPC), 1975; The Great Rate Debate (CPC), 1980; No Waiting?—a solution to the hospital waiting list problem (CPC), 1982; various contribs on housing, rating, planning and environmental subjects to nat. and profess. press and political jls. *Recreation:* relaxing with family. *Address:* House of Commons, SW1A 0AA. *T:* 01-219 5057; 14A The Close, Lichfield, Staffs. *Club:* Carlton.

HEDDY, Brian Huleatt; HM Diplomatic Service, retired; Regional Co-ordinator, British Council for Aid to Refugees, since 1979; *b* 8 June 1916; *o s* of late Dr William Reginald Huleatt Heddy, Barrister-at-Law, and Ruby Norton-Taylor; *m* 1st, 1940, Barbara Ellen Williams (*d* 1965); two *s* one *d*; 2nd, 1966, Ruth Mackarness (*née* Hogan) (*d* 1967); (one step *s* two step *d*); 3rd, 1969, Horatia Clare Kennedy. *Educ:* St Paul's Sch.; Pembroke Coll., Oxford. Commissioned in 75th (Highland) Field Regt, Royal Artillery, Nov. 1939; served in France 1940; WA, 1943; War Office and France, 1944-45; Mem. of Gray's Inn. Entered Foreign Service, 1945. Appointed to Brussels, 1946; Denver, 1948; Foreign Office, 1952; Tel Aviv, 1953; UK Delegation to ECSC, Luxembourg, 1955; Foreign Office, 1959; promoted Counsellor, 1963; Consul-Gen. at Lourenço Marques, 1963-65; Head of Nationality and Consular Dept, Commonwealth Office, 1966-67; Head of Migration and Visa Dept, FCO, 1968-71; Consul-Gen. in Durban, 1971-76. *Recreations:* tennis, golf. *Address:* Wynyards, Winsham, near Chard, Somerset. *T:* Winsham 260. *Clubs:* East India, Devonshire, Sports and Public Schools, MCC.

HEDGECOE, Prof. John, Dr RCA; FSIAD; Professor of Photography, Royal College of Art, London; Pro Rector, since 1981; *b* 24 March 1937; *s* of William Hedgecoe and Kathleen Don; *m* 1960, Julia Mardon; two *s* one *d*. *Educ:* Gulval Village Sch., Cornwall; Guildford Sch. of Art. Staff Photographer, Queen Magazine, 1957-72; Freelance: Sunday Times and Observer, 1960-70; most internat. magazines, 1958-; Portrait, HM the Queen, for British and Australian postage stamps, 1966; photographed The Arts Multi-Projection, British Exhibn, Expo Japan Show, 1970. Started Photography Sch. at RCA, 1965: Head of Dept and Reader in Photography, 1965-74; Fellow, 1973; awarded Chair of Photography, 1975; started Audio/Visual Dept, RCA, 1980. Mem. Photographic Bd, CNAA, 1976-78; Governor W Surrey Coll. of Art (and Mem. Acad. Adv. Bd), 1975-. Has illustrated numerous books, 1958-. Television: Tonight, Aust. TV, 1967; Folio, Anglia, 1980; 8 progs on Photography, Channel Four, 1983. Exhibitions: London, Sydney, Toronto, Edinburgh, Venice; collections: V&A Museum; Art Gall. of Ontario; Nat. Portrait Gall., London. *Publications:* Henry Moore, 1968 (prize best art book, world-wide, 1969); (jtly) Kevin Crossley-Holland book of Norfolk Poems, 1970; (jtly) Photography, Material and Methods, 1971-74 edns; Henry Moore, Energy in Space, 1973; The Book of Photography, 1976; Manual of Photographic Techniques, 1977; The Art of Colour Photography, 1978 (Kodak Photobuchpreis Stuttgart 1979; Grand Prix Technique de la Photographie, Musée Français de la Photographie, Paris 1980); Possessions, 1978; The Pocket Book of Photography, 1979; Introductory Photography Course, 1979; Master Classes in Photography: Children and Child Portraiture, 1980; (illus.) Poems of Thomas Hardy, 1981; (illus.) Poems of Robert Burns, 1981; The Book of Advanced Photography, 1982. *Recreations:* sculpture, building, gardening. *Address:* Burgates, Little Dunmow, Essex CM6 3HT. *T:* Great Dunmow 820328.

HEDGELAND, Air Vice-Marshal Philip Michael Sweatman, CB 1978; OBE 1957 (MBE 1948); CEng, FIEE; Consultant in Communications and Electronics; *b* 24 Nov. 1922; *s* of Philip and Margaret Hedgeland, Maidstone, Kent; *m* 1946, Jean Riddle Brinkworth, *d* of Leonard and Anne Brinkworth, Darlington, Co. Durham; two *s*. *Educ:* Maidstone Grammar Sch.; City and Guilds Coll., Imperial Coll. of Science and Technology, London. BSc(Eng), ACGI (Siemens Medallist). Served War: commnd into Technical Br., RAF, 1942; Radar Officer, Pathfinder Force and at TRE, Malvern. Radar Develt Officer, Central Bomber Estabt, 1945-48; Radio Introd. Unit Project Officer for V-Bomber Navigation and Bombing System, 1952-57; Wing Comdr Radio (Air) at HQ Bomber Comd, 1957-60; jssc 1960; Air Ministry Technical

Planning, 1961-62; aws 1963; Dir of Signals (Far East), Singapore, 1963-65; commanded RAF Stanbridge (Central Communications Centre), 1966-67; SASO, HQ Signals Comd/90 Gp, 1968-69; IDC, 1970; MoD Procurement Exec., Project Dir for Airborne Radar, 1971-74; Vice-Pres., Ordnance Bd, 1975-77, Pres., 1977-78. FCGI 1977; FBIM. *Recreations:* audio engineering, horticulture, amateur radio. *Address:* 16 Amersham Hill Gardens, High Wycombe, Bucks HP13 6QP. *T:* High Wycombe 25266. *Club:* Royal Air Force.

HEDGER, Eric Frank, CB 1979; OBE 1960; Director General of Defence Contracts, Under Secretary, Ministry of Defence, 1969-80; *b* 15 Sept. 1919; *s* of Albert Frank Hedger and late Ellen Agnes Hedger (*née* Laffey); *m* 1945, Joan Kathleen Bernas; two *s* one *d. Educ:* St Luke's, Southsea. War Service, 1939-46 (despatches 1945): Adjutant, 10 Air Formation Signals; Adjutant, then 2nd i/c, 7 Indian Air Formation Signals. Secretary, Admiralty Awards Council, 1946-49; Admin. Staff Coll., 1958; Dir of Navy Contracts, 1968. Mem. of Council and Bd of Management, Inst. of Purchasing and Supply, 1974-75. FInstPS. *Recreations:* music, reading, doing something. *Address:* 5 Maywood Close, Beckenham Place Park, Beckenham, Kent. *T:* 01-650 3250.

HEDGES, Anthony (John); Reader in Composition, University of Hull, since 1978; *b* 5 March 1931; *s* of late S. G. Hedges; *m* 1957, Delia Joy Marsden; two *s* two *d. Educ:* Bicester Grammar Sch.; Keble Coll., Oxford. MA, BMus, LRAM. National Service as solo pianist and arranger Royal Signals Band, 1955-57. Teacher and Lecturer, Royal Scottish Academy of Music, 1957-63. During this period became a regular contributor to Scotsman, Glasgow Herald, Guardian, Musical Times, etc. Lecturer in Music, Univ. of Hull, 1963, Sen. Lectr, 1968. The Composers' Guild of Great Britain: Chm., Northern Br., 1966-67; Mem. Exec. Cttee of Guild, 1969-73, 1977-81; Chm. of Guild, 1972, Jt Chm., 1973. Member: Council, Central Music Library, Westminster, 1970; Council, Soc. for Promotion of New Music, 1974-81; Music Bd, CNAA, 1974-77; Music Panel, Yorks Arts Assoc., 1974-75, Lincs and Humberside Arts Assoc., 1975-78; Founder-conductor, The Humberside Sinfonia, 1978-. Wrote regularly for Yorkshire Post, 1963-78, and contributed to many jls, incl. Composer, Current Musicology, etc, and also broadcast on musical subjects. *Publications include: (works): orchestral:* Comedy Overture, 1962 (rev. 1967); Overture, October '62, 1962 (rev. 1968); Sinfonia Semplice, 1963; Expressions for Orchestra, 1964; Prelude, Romance and Rondo, strings, 1965; Concertante Music, 1965; Four Miniature Dances, 1967; A Holiday Overture, 1968; Variations on a theme of Rameau, 1969; Kingston Sketches, 1969; An Ayrshire Serenade, 1969; Four Diversions, strings, 1971; Celebrations, 1973; Symphony, 1972-73; Festival Dances, 1976; Overture, Heigham Sound, 1978; Four Breton Sketches, 1980; Sinfonia Concertante, 1980; Scenes from the Humber, 1981; *choral:* Cantiones Festivalis, chorus and orch. (various texts), 1960; Gloria, unaccompanied, 1965; Epithalamium, chorus and orch. (Spencer), 1969; To Music, chorus and orch. (various texts), 1972; Psalm 104, 1973; A Manchester Mass, chorus, orch. and brass band, 1974; A Humberside Cantata, 1976; Song Cycle, 1977; Songs of David, 1978; The Temple of Solomon, 1979; *chamber music:* Five Preludes, piano, 1959; Four Pieces, piano, 1966; Rondo Concertante, v, cl. hn, vc, 1967; Sonata for violin and harpsichord, 1967; Three Songs of Love, s, pf (from Song of Songs), 1968; String Quartet, 1970; Rhapsody, v, pf, 1971; piano sonata, 1974; Fantasy for Violin and Piano, 1981; *opera:* Shadows in the Sun (lib. Jim Hawkins), 1976; *musical:* Minotaur (lib. Jim Hawkins), 1978; *miscellaneous:* many anthems, partsongs, albums of music for children; music for television, film and stage. *Recreations:* family life, reading, walking. *Address:* 13 Norfolk Street, Beverley HU17 7DN. *T:* Beverley 865129.

HEDGES, Sir John (Francis), Kt 1962; CBE 1958; retired solicitor in private practice; *b* 1917; *o s* of late Francis Reade Hedges and Nesta Violet (*née* Cavell); *m* 1957, Barbara Mary (*née* Ward), *widow* of Comdr Richard Scobell Palairet, RN; no *c. Educ:* St Amersham's, Eastbourne; Harrow. Commissioned Royal Signals, 1940; served India and SE Asia, TARO, 1950. Chm. Abingdon Conservative Assoc., 1948-60; Chm. Wessex Area, 1954-57 (Hon. Treas. 1960-67); Pres. Berks, Bucks and Oxon Justices' Clerks' Soc., 1955; Pres. Berks, Bucks and Oxon Inc. Law Soc., 1963; Chm. Turner's Court Sch. for Boys, 1955-75; Pres. League of Friends, Wallingford Hosps, 1953-73; Mem. Berks Exec. Council, NHS, 1960-74 (Chm., 1971-74); Chm., Berkshire AHA, 1973-79; Chm., Oxon Diocese Redundant Churches Uses Cttee, 1974-. Hon. Freeman, Borough of Wallingford, 1971. *Recreations:* shooting, gardening, music. *Address:* The Coach House, Castle Street, Wallingford, Oxon OX10 8DL. *T:* Wallingford 36217.

HEDLEY, Hilda Mabel, CB 1975; Under-Secretary, Department of Health and Social Security (formerly Ministry of Health), 1967-75; *b* 4 May 1918; *d* of late George Ward Hedley, Cheltenham, and late Winifred Mary Hedley (*née* Cockshott). *Educ:* Cheltenham Ladies' Coll.; Newnham Coll., Cambridge. Uncommon Languages Dept., Postal Censorship, 1940-42; Foreign Office, 1942-46; Min. of Health, later DHSS, 1946-75. Sec. to Royal Commn on Mental Health, 1954-57. Nuffield Foundation Travelling Fellowship, 1960-61. Gen. Sec., Cheltenham Ladies' Coll. Guild, 1976-82. *Recreations:* gardening, bird-watching, cooking. *Address:* The Anchorage, Castle Street, Winchcombe, Cheltenham GL54 5JA. *T:* Winchcombe 602314.

HEDLEY, Prof. Ronald; Director, Trent Polytechnic, Nottingham, 1970-80, Emeritus Professor, 1980; *b* 12 Sept. 1917; *s* of Francis Hedley, Hebburn, Co.

Durham; *m* 1942; one *s* one *d. Educ:* Jarrow Grammar Sch.; Durham Univ. (MA, DipEd); Ecole Normale d'Instituteurs, Evreux. Various appts in teaching and educational administration, 1947-64; Dep. Dir of Education, Nottingham, 1964-70. Chm., Regional Acad. Bd, Regional Adv. Council for Further Educn in E Midlands, 1972-76; Member: Central Council for Educn and Trng in Social Work, 1971-77; Nat. Adv. Council for Educn for Ind. and Commerce, 1973-77; Central Council for Educn and Trng of Health Visitors, 1972-77; Cttee for Arts and Social Studies, CNAA, 1974-76; Personal Social Services Council, 1974-78; Cttee on Recreation Management Training, 1977-80; Local Govt Trng Bd, 1978-81; Adv. Cttee for Supply and Educn of Teachers, 1980-81. Hon. Fellow, Trent Polytechnic, 1980. Hon. Senator, Fachhochschule, Karlsruhe, Germany, 1980. Hon. LlD Nottingham, 1981. *Address:* 5 Branksome Close, Pitt Manor, Winchester, Hants. *T:* Winchester 65546.

HEDLEY, Ronald Henderson, DSc, PhD; FIBiol; Director, British Museum (Natural History), since 1976; *b* 2 Nov. 1928; *s* of Henry Armstrong Hedley and Margaret Hopper; *m* 1957, Valmai Mary Griffith, New Zealand; one *s. Educ:* Durham Johnston Sch.; King's Coll., Univ. of Durham. Commissioned in Royal Regt of Artillery, 1953-55. Sen. Scientific Officer, British Museum (Natural History), 1955-61; New Zealand Nat. Research Fellow, 1960-61; Principal Scientific Officer, 1961-64; Dep. Keeper of Zoology, 1964-71; Dep. Dir, 1971-76. Vis. Lectr in Microbiology, Univ. of Surrey, 1968-75. Mem. Council, Fresh Water Biological Assoc., 1972-76; Trustee, Percy Sladen Meml Fund, 1972-77; Pres., British Section, Soc. of Protozoology, 1975-78; Member Council: Marine Biolog. Assoc., 1976-79, 1981-; Zoological Soc., London, 1981- (Hon. Sec., 1977-80; Vice-Pres., 1980-); Mem., Internat. Trust for Zoological Nomenclature, 1977-. Mem. Council, Royal Albert Hall, 1982-. *Publications:* (ed with C. G. Adams) Foraminifera, vols 1-3, 1974, 1976, 1978; (with C. G. Ogden) Atlas of Testate Amoebae, 1980; technical papers, mainly on biology, cytology and systematics of protozoa, 1956-. *Address:* British Museum (Natural History), Cromwell Road, SW7 5BD. *T:* 01-589 6323. *Club:* Athenæum.

HEDLEY-MILLER, Mrs Mary Elizabeth; Under-Secretary, HM Treasury, since 1973; *b* 5 Sept. 1923; *d* of late J. W. Ashe; *m* 1950, Roger Latham Hedley-Miller; one *s* two *d. Educ:* Queen's Sch., Chester; St Hugh's Coll., Oxford (MA). Joined HM Treasury, 1945; served in UK Treasury Delegn, Washington DC, 1947-49. Alternate Mem., Monetary Cttee, EEC, and Alternate Dir, European Investment Bank, 1977-. *Recreations:* family, including family music; reading. *Address:* 108 Higher Drive, Purley, Surrey. *T:* 01-660 1837. *Club:* United Oxford & Cambridge University.

HEDSTROM, Sir (John) Maynard, KBE 1980; retired; company director; *b* 16 May 1908; *s* of Sir John Maynard Hedstrom and Grace Lambert Hedstrom (*née* Eastgate); *m* 1940, Moira Harwood (*née* Dietrich); two *s. Educ:* Geelong Grammar School; Melbourne University. LLB. Joined Morris Hedstrom Ltd, Suva, Fiji, as junior clerk, 1934; retired as General Manager, 1958. Dir, W. R. Carpenter Holdings Ltd; Chm., W. R. Carpenter (South Pacific) Ltd. Knight First Class, Order of Vasa, Sweden, 1964. *Recreation:* learning to grow old. *Address:* 37 Prince's Road, Tamavua, Suva, Fiji. *T:* Suva 381416. *Clubs:* Australian (Sydney); Fiji, Defence, Union (Suva); Royal Suva Yacht.

HEENAN, Maurice, CMG 1966; QC (Hong Kong) 1962; The General Counsel, United Nations Relief and Works Agency for Palestine Refugees in the Near East, 1973-77; *b* NZ, 8 Oct. 1912; 2nd *s* of late David Heenan and of Anne Frame; *m* 1951, Claire, 2nd *d* of late Emil Ciho and Iren Rotbauer, Trenčín, Bratislava, Czechoslovakia; two *d. Educ:* Canterbury Coll., University of New Zealand. Law Professional, LLB, Barrister and Solicitor of Supreme Court of New Zealand, Practised law in NZ, 1937-40. War of 1939-45; Major, 2nd NZEF; active service Western Desert, Libya, Cyrenaica and Italy, 1940-45 (despatches). Crown Counsel, Palestine, 1946-48. Solicitor-Gen., Hong Kong, 1961; HM's Attorney-Gen., Hong Kong, and *ex officio* MEC and MLC, Hong Kong, 1961-66; Dep.-Dir, Gen. Legal Div., Office of Legal Affairs, Offices of the Sec.-Gen., UN, NY, 1966-73. *Recreations:* Rugby football, tennis, squash, ski-ing, golf. *Address:* Plane Trees, West Road, New Canaan, Conn 06840, USA. *Clubs:* Hong Kong; Country (New Canaan).

HEES, Hon. George H., PC (Canada) 1957; MP (Canada) (Progressive C) Northumberland, Ontario, since Nov. 1965 (Prince Edward-Hastings Riding); *b* Toronto, 17 June 1910; *s* of Harris Lincoln Hees, Toronto, and Mabel Good, New York; *m* 1934, Mabel, *d* of late Hon. E. A. Dunlop; three *d. Educ:* Trinity Coll. Sch., Port Hope, Ont; RMC, Kingston, Ont; University of Toronto; Cambridge Univ. Formerly Dir, George H. Hees & Son & Co. Served War of 1939-45: Royal Canadian Artillery, 1941-44; 3rd Anti-Tank Regt, Royal Canadian Artillery; Bde Major, 5th Infantry Bde, Holland (wounded); retd as Major. Contested (Prog. C) Spadina Riding, 1945. Minister of Transport, Canada, 1957-60; Minister of Trade and Commerce, 1960-63. Pres., Montreal and Canadian Stock Exchanges, 1964-65. Executive with George H. Hees Son & Co., Toronto; Director: Expo 67; Wood Green Community Centre. Hon. Dr of Laws, 1961. *Recreations:* reading, ski-ing, swimming, golf, tennis, riding, bridge; formerly boxing. *Address:* 7 Coltrin Place, Ottawa, Ontario K1M 0A5, Canada; Rathbunwood, Cobourg, Canada. *Clubs:* Toronto Golf, Toronto Badminton and Racquet, Osler Bluff Ski (Toronto); Royal Ottawa Golf.

HEFFER, Eric Samuel; MP (Lab) Walton Division of Liverpool since 1964; *b* 12 Jan. 1922; *s* of William George Heffer and Annie Heffer (*née* Nicholls); *m* 1945, Doris Murray. *Educ:* Bengeo Junior Sch. and Longmore Senior Sch., Hertford. Served RAF, 1942-45. Pres. Liverpool Trades Council and Labour Party, 1959-60, 1964-65, and Vice-Pres., 1960 and 1964. Liverpool City Councillor, 1960-66. Member: Council of Europe, 1965-68; WEU, 1965-68 (served on political, social and financial cttees). Labour front bench spokesman on Industrial Relations, 1970-72; Minister of State, Dept of Industry, 1974-75; Mem., Shadow Cabinet and Labour spokesman on European affairs, 1981-. Mem., Lab Party Nat. Exec. Cttee, 1975-. *Publications:* (part author) The Agreeable Autocracies, 1961, (USA); (part author) Election 70, 1970; The Class Struggle in Parliament, 1973; articles in Tribune, Liverpool Daily Post, The Times, Guardian, Daily Telegraph, New Statesmen, Spectator, New Outlook, Labour Voice, New Left Review, and in foreign jls. *Recreations:* hill-walking, mountaineering. *Address:* House of Commons, SW1.

HEGARTY, Most Rev. Séamus; *see* Raphoe, Bishop of, (RC).

HEGGS, Renata Fanny Madeleine; a Social Security Commissioner, since 1981; *b* 29 Nov. 1929; *d* of E. and G. Calderan; *m* 1953, Geoffrey Ellis Heggs; two *s* one *d*. *Educ:* Notting Hill and Ealing High Sch., GPDST; London Univ. (LLB). Admitted Solicitor, 1955; practising Solicitor, 1955-81. Chm., Nat. Insce Local Tribunal, 1976-81; pt-time Chm. of Industrial Tribunals, 1978-81; Pres., Appeal Tribunal under London Building Acts, 1979-81. *Recreations:* music, travelling. *Address:* (office) 6 Grosvenor Gardens, SW1W 0DH. *T:* 01-730 9236.

HEGINBOTHAM, Christopher John; National Director, MIND (National Association for Mental Health), since 1982; *b* 25 March 1948; *s* of Joseph William and Marjorie Higinbotham. *Educ:* Univ. of Birmingham (BSc Hons); Univ. of Essex (MSc). Area Manager, Circle Thirty Three Housing Trust, 1977-80; Assistant Borough Housing Officer, London Borough of Haringey, 1980-82. *Publication:* Housing Projects for Mentally Handicapped People, 1981. *Recreations:* writing, painting, sailing. *Address:* 22 Harley Street, W1. *T:* 01-637 0741.

HEGINBOTHAM, Prof. Wilfred Brooks, OBE 1978; Director General, Production Engineering Research Association of Great Britain (PERA), Melton Mowbray, since 1979; *b* 9 April 1924; *s* of Fred and Alice Heginbotham; *m* 1957, Marjorie Pixton; three *d*. *Educ:* Manchester Univ. (UMIST). BScTech 1949; MScTech 1950; PhD (Manchester) 1956; DSc (Manchester) 1979. FIProdE; MIMechE; FRSA. Started in industry as wood pattern maker; part-time courses to HNC, 1938-46; Walter Preston Schol., Manchester Coll. of Tech., 1946; joined staff, 1951; Lectr in Production Engineering subjects, UMIST, 1951-58; industrial experience for 10 years; Nottingham University: Sen. Lectr, 1958; started first BSc course in Prod. Engrg in UK, 1961; Head of Dept of Prod. Engrg and Prod. Management, 1961-63; Cripps Prof., 1963-79; Dean, Faculty of Applied Science, 1967-71. Developed group to study Automatic Assembly Systems and Industrial Robot devices, including computer vision and tactile sense, and co-operated with industry in development of advanced automation equipment. Chm. Org. Cttee for establishment of Brit. Robot Assoc., 1977, Chm. of Council, 1977-80, Pres., 1980-. Editor-in-Chief: The Industrial Robot; Assembly Automation. Hon. DTech Scis Eindhoven, 1981. *Publications:* contribs to Encyc. Brit. on Robot Devices and to prof. pubns on metal cutting, automated assembly, industrial robots, artificial intelligence and production processes. *Recreations:* gliding, model aircraft construction and operation (radio controlled). *Address:* Bardsley Brow, 14 Middleton Crescent, Beeston, Notts NG9 2TH. *T:* Nottingham 257796.

HEGLAND, David Leroy, DFC 1944; Director: Kemtron Ltd; Galena; Massey-Ferguson Holdings (Australia) Ltd; Carlton and United Breweries Holdings Ltd; Plessey Pacific Pty Ltd; cattle grazier; *b* 12 June 1919; *s* of Lee and Jennie Hegland; *m* 1944, Dagmar Cooke; two *s* one *d*. *Educ:* Whitman Coll., Washington, USA (BA). Served War, 1942-45; USN aircraft pilot in Pacific Ocean areas; Lt Comdr USNR, 1945. Managing Director: GM International, Copenhagen, 1956-58; GM South African, Port Elizabeth, 1958-61; GM Holden's Pty Ltd, Melbourne, 1962-65; Chm. and Man. Dir, Vauxhall Motors Ltd, Luton, 1966-70; Dir, General Motors Ltd, London, 1966-70; Chm., GKN Australia Ltd, and Dir, Ajax GKN Holdings Pty Ltd, and Guest, Keen & Nettlefolds (Overseas) Ltd, 1972-80. Member: Albury-Wodonga Develt Corp., 1980-81; Industry Forum, Aust. Acad. of Science, 1972-; Aust. Inst. of Dirs; Delta Sigma Rho. FIMI. Richard Kirby medal for production engrg, 1964. *Recreations:* flying, tennis, riding. *Address:* c/o Galena Hills, Holbrook, NSW 2644, Australia. *Clubs:* Royal & Ancient Golf (St Andrews); Melbourne; Victoria Racing (Melbourne); Albury (Albury, NSW).

HEIFETZ, Jascha; Commander, Legion of Honour, 1957; violinist, soloist; 1st Vice-President of American Guild of Musical Artists, Inc., New York City; Hon. Member: Society of Concerts of Paris Conservatoire; Association des Anciens Elèves du Conservatoire; Cercle International de la Jeunesse Artistique; Hon. Vice-President of Mark Twain Society, USA; Hon. President, Musicians' Fund of America; on music department staff, University of Southern California, Los Angeles; *b* Vilna, Russia, 2 Feb. 1901; father professional violinist and music teacher. *Recreations:* sailing, ping-pong (table tennis), motoring, reading and dancing. *Address:* Beverly Hills, Calif, USA.

Clubs: Royal Automobile, Savage; Bohemian (New York); Beaux Arts, Inter-Allied (Paris).

HEILBRON, Hon. Dame Rose, DBE 1974; **Hon. Mrs Justice Heilbron;** a Judge of the High Court of Justice, Family Division, since 1974; *b* 19 Aug. 1914; *d* of late Max and Nellie Heilbron; *m* 1945, Dr Nathaniel Burstein; one *d*. *Educ:* Belvedere Sch., GPDST; Liverpool University, LLB 1st Class Hons, 1935; Lord Justice Holker Scholar, Gray's Inn, 1936; LLM 1937. Called to Bar, Gray's Inn, 1939, Bencher, 1968; joined Northern Circuit, Leader, 1973-74, Presiding Judge, 1979-82; QC 1949; Recorder of Burnley, 1956-71, a Recorder, and Hon. Recorder of Burnley, 1972-74. Mem., Bar Council, 1973-74. Chm., Home Sec's Adv. Gp on Law of Rape, 1975-. Hon. Fellow, Lady Margaret Hall, Oxford, 1976; Hon. LLD: Liverpool, 1975; Warwick, 1978; Manchester, 1980. Hon. Col, WRAC(TA). *Address:* Royal Courts of Justice, Strand, WC2.

HEIM, Most Rev. Bruno Bernard, PhD, JCD; Apostolic Pro-Nuncio to the Court of St James's, since 1982 (Apostolic Delegate, 1973-82); *b* Olten, Switzerland, 5 March 1911; *s* of Bernard and Elisabeth Heim-Studer. *Educ:* Olten, Engelberg and Schwyz; St Thomas of Aquino Univ.; Gregorian Univ.; Univ. of Fribourg; Papal Acad. of Diplomacy. Priest 1938; Vicar in Basle and Arbon, 1938-42; Chief Chaplain for Italian and Polish Internees in Switzerland, 1943-45; Sec., Papal Nunciature in Paris; Auditor at Nunciature in Vienna; Counsellor and Chargé d'affaires at Nunciature in Germany; titular Archbp of Xanthos, 1961; Apostolic Delegate to Scandinavia, 1961-69; Apost. Pro-Nuncio (Ambassador): to Finland, 1966-69; to Egypt, 1969-73; President of Caritas Egypt, 1969-73. Lauréat, French Acad.; Corresp. Mem., Real Academia de la Historia, Madrid, 1950; Mem. Council, Internat. Heraldic Acad.; Grand Cross: Order of Malta, 1950; Teutonic Order, 1961; Order of Finnish Lion, 1969; Order of St Maurice and Lazarus, 1973; (1st Class) Order of the Republic, Egypt, 1975; Gr. Officer Order of Holy Sepulchre; Orders of Merit: Germany, Italy, Austria; Officier Légion d'honneur, etc. *Publications:* Die Freundschaft nach Thomas von Aquin, 1934; Wappenbrauch und Wappenrecht in der Kirche, 1947; Coutumes et droit héraldiques de l'Eglise, 1949; L'oeuvre héraldique de Paul Boesch, 1973; Heraldry in the Catholic Church, 1978; Armorial Liber Amicorum, 1981; contrib. Adler, Zeitschrift f. Heraldik und Genealogie, Heraldisk Tidskrift. *Recreations:* heraldry, heraldic painting, cooking, gardening. *Address:* 54 Parkside, SW19 5NF. *T:* 01-946 1410.

HEIN, Sir (Charles Henri) Raymond, Kt 1977; Chevalier de la Légion d'Honneur, 1950; QC 1956; Barrister-at-Law, in practice since 1925; Director of Companies; *b* 26 Sept. 1901; *s* of Jules Hein and Clémence de Charmoy; *m* 1928, Marcelle Piat; four *s* four *d*. *Educ:* Royal Coll., Mauritius (Scholar, 1920); Wadham Coll., Oxford. MA Oxon. Mem., Council of Govt, 1936-48; Mayor of Port Louis, 1948. Dir, 1937-76, Pres., 1975-76, Mauritius Commercial Bank; Chairman: Swan Insurance Ltd, 1967-; Mauritius Life Assurance, 1972-; Anglo-Mauritius Assce Soc. Ltd, 1973-; New Mauritius Dock Co. Ltd, 1960-70 (Dir, 1937-70); Dir, Reinsurance Co. of Mauritius. Former President: Mauritius Chamber of Agric.; Mauritius Sugar Industry Res. Inst.; Mauritius Turf Club. Pres., Alliance Française, 1948-54. Former Pres., Bar Council. *Publications:* trans. Bernardin de St Pierre's Paul et Virginie, 1977; Le Naufrage du Saint Géran (Légende de Paul et Virginie), 1981. *Recreations:* music, gardening, ancient Greek literature. *Address:* Route de Saint Jean, Quatre Bornes, Mauritius; (chambers) Cathedral Square, Port Louis. *T:* 2-0327. *Club:* Mauritius Turf (Port Louis).

HEINE, Prof. Volker, FRS 1974; Professor of Theoretical Physics, University of Cambridge, since 1976; Fellow of Clare College, Cambridge, since 1960; *b* 19 Sept. 1930; *m* 1955, M. Daphne Hines; one *s* two *d*. *Educ:* Otago Univ. (MSc, DipHons); Cambridge Univ. (PhD). FInstP. Demonstrator, Cambridge Univ., 1958-63, Lectr 1963-70; Reader in Theoretical Physics, 1970-76. Vis. Prof., Univ. of Chicago, 1965-66; Vis. Scientist, Bell Labs, USA, 1970-71. *Publications:* Group Theory in Quantum Mechanics, 1960; (jtly) Solid State Physics Vol. 24, 1970, Vol. 35, 1980; articles in Proc. Royal Soc., Jl Physics, Physical Review, etc. *Address:* Cavendish Laboratory, Madingley Road, Cambridge CB3 0HE.

HEINZ, Henry John, II, Hon. KBE 1977; Chairman, H. J. Heinz Company, since 1959 (President, 1941-59); *b* Sewickley, Pa, USA, 10 July 1908; *s* of Howard and Elizabeth Rust Heinz; *m* 1st, 1935, Joan Diehl (marr. diss. 1942); one *s*; *m* 1953, Drue English Maher. *Educ:* Yale (BA 1931); Trinity Coll., Cambridge. Salesman, H. J. Heinz Co., Ltd, London, 1932; with H. J. Heinz Co., Pittsburgh, Pa, Pres., 1941-59; Chm., 1959-. Chm., Governing Bd, Yale Univ. Art Gallery; Member: Adv. Cttee, Yale Univ. Economic Growth Centre; Council of Management, British-Ditchley Foundn; Business Cttee for the Arts; Director: Pittsburgh Symphony Soc.; World Affairs Council, Pittsburgh; Trustee: Carnegie Inst.; Carnegie-Mellon Univ.; Nutrition Foundn; Cttee for Econ. Develt; US Council, ICC. Commander, Royal Order of the Phoenix, Greece, 1950; Chevalier de la Légion d'Honneur, France, 1950; Comdr of Order of Merit, Italian Republic. OStJ. *Recreation:* ski-ing. *Address:* (residence) Goodwood, Sewickley, Pa 15143, USA. *Clubs:* Buck's, White's; The Brook, River (New York); Duquesne, Rolling Rock, Allegheny Country (Pittsburgh).

HEISBOURG, Georges; Ambassador of Luxembourg to Federal Republic of Germany, since 1979; *b* 19 April 1918; *s* of Nicolas Heisbourg and Berthe (*née* Ernsterhoff); *m* 1945, Hélène Pinet; two *s* one *d*. *Educ:* Athénée, Luxembourg;

Univs of Grenoble, Innsbruck and Paris. Head of Govt Press and Information Office, Luxembourg, 1944-45; Attaché 1945-48, Sec. 1948-51, of Legation, London; Head of Internat. Organisations Section, Dir of Political Affairs, Min. of For. Affairs, Luxembourg, 1951-58; Luxembourg Ambassador to USA, Canada and Mexico, 1958-64; Perm. Rep. to UN, 1958-61; Luxembourg Ambassador: to Netherlands, 1964-67; to France, 1967-70; Perm. Rep. to OECD, 1967-70; Sec. Gen., WEU, 1971-74; Ambassador to USSR, 1974-77; Perm. Rep. to Council of Europe, 1978-79. Grand Officer, Nat. Order of Crown of Oak, 1980 (Chevalier, 1958), Comdr, Order of Adolphe de Nassau, 1963, and Grand Officer, Order of Merit, 1976, Luxembourg; also holds decorations from Austria, Belgium, France, Germany, Italy, Mexico, and the Netherlands. *Recreations:* tennis, swimming. *Address:* Adenauerallee 110, 5300 Bonn 1, Germany.

HEISER, Terence Michael; Deputy Secretary, Finance and Local Government, Department of the Environment, since 1981; *b* 24 May 1932; *s* of David and Daisy Heiser; *m* 1957, Kathleen Mary Waddle; one *s* two *d*. *Educ:* Grafton Road Primary Sch., Dagenham; London Evacuee Sch., Sunninghill, Berks; Windsor County Boy's Sch., Berks; Birkbeck Coll., Univ. of London; BA (Hons English). Served in RAF, 1950-52; joined Civil Service 1949, served with Colonial Office, Min. of Works, Min. of Housing and Local Govt; Principal Private Sec. to Sec. of State for the Environment, 1975-76; Under Secretary: Housing Directorate, 1976-79; Local Govt Finance Directorate, 1979-81. *Recreations:* reading, walking, talking. *Address:* 19 Sylvan Hill, Upper Norwood, SE19.

HEISKELL, Andrew; Chairman of the Board, Time Inc., 1960-80; *b* Naples, 13 Sept. 1915; *s* of Morgan Heiskell and Ann Heiskell (*née* Hubbard); *m* 1937, Cornelia Scott (marr. diss.); one *s* one *d*; *m* 1950, Madeleine Carroll (marr. diss.); one *d*; *m* 1965, Marian, *d* of Arthur Hays Sulzberger, and *widow* of Orvil E. Dryfoos. *Educ:* Switzerland; France; University of Paris. Science teacher, Ecole du Montcel, Paris, 1935. Life Magazine: Science and Medicine Editor, 1937-39; Asst Gen. Manager, 1939-42; Gen. Manager, 1942-46; Publisher, 1946-60; Vice-Pres., Time, Inc., 1949-60. Director: Amer. TV & Communications Corp.; Book-of-the-Month Club Inc.; Inland Container Corp.; Internat. Executive Service Corps; Temple-Eastex Inc. Mem. Bd of Advisors, Dumbarton Oaks Research Library and Collection. Trustee: New York Public Library (Chm.); Trust for Cultural Resources of the City of New York; Chm., Bryant Park Restoration Corp. Vice Chm., and Chm. Exec. Cttee, The Brookings Institn. Fellow, Harvard Coll. Wharton Sch. Alumni Soc., Univ. of Pennsylvania, Gold Medal Award of Merit, 1968. Hon. LLD: Shaw Univ., 1968; Lake Erie Coll., 1969; Hofstra Univ., 1972; Hobart and William Smith Colls, 1973; Hon. DLitt Lafayette Coll., 1969. *Address:* Time and Life Building, Rockefeller Center, New York, NY 10020; 870 United Nations Plaza, New York, NY 10017; Darien, Conn., USA.

HELAISSI, Sheikh Abdulrahman Al-; Hon. GCVO; Saudi Arabian Ambassador to the Court of St James's, 1966-76; *b* 24 July 1922. *Educ:* Universities of Cairo and London. Secretary to Embassy, London, 1947-54; Under-Sec., Min. of Agriculture, 1954-57; Head of Delegn to FAO, 1955-61; Ambassador to Sudan, 1957-60; Representative to UN, and to various confs concerned with health and agriculture; Delegate to Conf. of Non-aligned Nations, Belgrade, 1961; Ambassador: Italy and Austria, 1961-66; UK and Denmark (concurrently), 1966-70. Versed in Islamic Religious Law. *Publication:* The Rehabilitation of the Bedouins, 1959. *Address:* c/o Olaya, Division 3, Riyadh, POB 8062, Saudi Arabia.

HELE, Desmond George K.; *see* King-Hele.

HELE, James Warwick; High Master of St Paul's School since 1973; *b* 24 July 1926; *s* of John Warwick Hele, Carlisle; *m* 1948, Audrey Whalley; four *d*. *Educ:* Sedbergh Sch.; Hertford Coll., Oxford; Trinity Hall, Cambridge (Schol., MA). 1st cl. hons History Tripos 1951. Asst Master, Kings College Sch., Wimbledon, 1951-55; Rugby School: Asst Master, 1955-73; Housemaster, Kilbracken, 1965-73; 2nd Master, 1970-73. Chm., Headmasters' Conference, 1982. *Recreations:* Rugby football (Oxford Univ. XV 1944), hill walking, Brathay Exploration Group. *Address:* The High Master's House, St Paul's School, Lonsdale Road, Barnes, SW13 9JT. *T:* 01-748 6420.

HELLABY, Sir (Frederick Reed) Alan, Kt 1981; Managing Director, R. & W. Hellaby Ltd, since 1963; *b* 21 Dec. 1926; *s* of Frederick Allan Hellaby and Mavis Reed; *m* 1954, Mary Dawn Trotter; three *s* one *d*. *Educ:* King's Coll., Auckland; Auckland Univ. Joined R. & W. Hellaby Ltd, 1948, Dir, 1960-, Dep. Chm., 1969-. Chairman: NZ Steel Ltd, 1974- (Dir, 1964-); NZ Insurance Co., 1979- (Dir, 1966-); NZ S British Insurance Gp, 1981-; NZ Steel Develt Co. Ltd, 1981-; Director: NZ Steel Mining; Pacific Steel Ltd; Rheem NZ Ltd; IBM (NZ) Ltd. Mem., Commn of Inquiry into Meat Industry, 1973. Chm., NZ Export Year Cttee, 1978-79. Chm. Bd of Governors, King's Coll.; Trustee: Massey Univ. Agricl Res. Foundn; NZ Red Cross Foundn. Hon. DSc Massey, 1982. *Recreation:* weekend farming. *Address:* 519 Remuera Road, Auckland, New Zealand. *T:* 547423. *Clubs:* Northern, Royal NZ Yacht Squadron, Auckland Golf (all Auckland).

HELLIER, Maj. Gen. Eric Jim, CBE 1977 (OBE 1970, MBE 1967); General Manager, International Military Services, since 1982; *b* 23 July 1927; *s* of Harry and Elizabeth Hellier; *m* 1952, Margaret Elizabeth Leadeham; one *s* one *d* (and one *s* decd). *Educ:* Hugh Saxons Sch.; Cardiff Univ. Served, 1945-66: Navigating Officer, RNVR; regtl duty, Royal Signals; Staff Coll. and Jt

Services Staff Coll; GSO2 WO; DAA&QMG 39 Inf. Bde; CO, 24 Signals Regt, 1967-69; GSO1 Plans (Operational Requirements) MoD, 1970; Col A/Q HQ 4 Div, 1971-72; Comd Bde Royal Signals and Catterick Garrison, 1973-74; RCDS,, 1975; Brig A/Q HQ 1(BR), Corps, 1976-79; Maj. Gen. Admin, UKLF, 1979-81. Col Comdt, Royal Corps of Signals, 1981-. *Recreations:* squash, tennis, sailing. *Address:* Wayside, West Hatch, Taunton TA3 5RJ. *T:* Taunton 480099. *Club:* Army and Navy.

HELLINGS, Gen. Sir Peter (William Cradock), KCB 1970 (CB 1966); DSC 1940; MC 1943; DL; *b* 6 Sept. 1916; *s* of Stanley and Norah Hellings; *m* 1941, Zoya, *d* of Col Bassett; one *d* (one *s* decd). *Educ:* Naut. Coll., Pangbourne. Joined Royal Marines, 1935; Company Cmdr, 40 Commando, 1942; GSO 2, Commando Group, 1944; Comdr 41 and 42 Commandos, 1945-46; Brigade Major, 3 Commando Bde in Malaya, 1949-51; joined Directing Staff of Marine Corps Schs, Quantico, USA, 1954; Comdr 40 Commando, 1958; Brigade Comdr, 3 Commando Bde, 1959; Comdr Infantry Training Centre, Royal Marines, 1960; idc 1962; Dep. Dir, Joint Warfare Staff, 1963; Maj.-Gen., 1964; Chief of Staff to Commandant-Gen., RM, 1964; Group Comdr, HQ Portsmouth Group RM, 1967-68; Lt-Gen., 1968; Comdt-Gen., RM, 1968-71; General, 1970. Col Comdt, Royal Marines, 1977-79, Representative Col Comdt, 1979-80. DL Devon 1973. *Recreations:* shooting, fishing. *Address:* The Leys, Milton Combe, Devon. *T:* Yelverton 3355.

HELLMAN, Lillian; playwright; *b* New Orleans, Louisiana, USA, 20 June 1907; *d* of Max Bernard Hellman and Julia Newhouse; *m* 1925, Arthur Kober (divorced). *Educ:* New York Univ.; Columbia Univ. Worked for Horace Liveright, Publishers, 1925-26. Hon. LLD Wheaton Coll., MA Tufts Univ.; Hon. LLD: Rutgers Univ., 1963, Brandeis Univ., 1965; Yale, 1974; Smith Coll., 1974; New York Univ., 1974; Franklin and Marshall Coll., 1975; Columbia Univ., 1976; Creative Arts Award, Brandeis Univ., 1976; Mem., National Inst. of Arts and Letters (Gold Medal for Drama, 1964); Mem., American Academy of Arts and Sciences. Book reviews, Herald Tribune, wrote short stories. First produced play The Children's Hour, 1934. Wrote movie scenarios The Dark Angel, These Three (screen version of The Children's Hour), Dead End, The Little Foxes, North Star. *Publications:* plays produced: The Children's Hour, 1934; Days to Come, 1936; The Little Foxes, 1939; Watch on the Rhine, 1941; The Searching Wind, 1944; Another Part of the Forest, 1946; adapted from the French, Roblès' play, Montserrat, 1949; The Autumn Garden, 1951; adapted Anouilh's The Lark, 1955; adapted Voltaire's Candide as comic operetta, 1956; Toys in the Attic, 1960; adapted Blechman's novel How Much as play, My Mother, My Father and Me, 1963; edited: The Selected Letters of Anton Chekhov, 1955; (with introduction) Dashiell Hammett, The Big Knockover, 1966; (memoir) An Unfinished Woman, 1969 (National Book Award 1970); Pentimento, 1974; Scoundrel Time, 1976; Maybe, 1980. *Address:* 630 Park Avenue, New York, NY 10021, USA.

HELLYER, Arthur George Lee, MBE 1967; FLS; Gardening Correspondent to the Financial Times; Editor of Amateur Gardening, 1946-67; Editor of Gardening Illustrated, 1947-56; *b* 16 Dec. 1902; *s* of Arthur Lee Hellyer and Maggie Parlett; *m* 1933, Grace Charlotte Bolt (*d* 1977); two *s* one *d*. *Educ:* Dulwich Coll. Farming in Jersey, 1918-21; Nursery work in England, 1921-29; Asst Editor of Commercial Horticulture, 1929; Asst Editor of Amateur Gardening, 1929-46. Associate of Hon. of Royal Horticultural Society; Victoria Medal of Honour in Horticulture. *Publications:* The Amateur Gardener, 1948; Amateur Gardening Pocket Guide, 1941; Amateur Gardening Popular Encyclopædia of Flowering Plants, 1957; Encyclopædia of Garden Work and Terms, 1954; Encyclopædia of Plant Portraits, 1953; English Gardens Open to the Public, 1956; Flowers in Colour, 1955; Garden Pests and Diseases, 1966; Garden Plants in Colour, 1958; Practical Gardening for Amateurs, 1935; Shrubs in Colour, 1966; Your Garden Week by Week, 1938; Your New Garden, 1937; Starting with Roses, 1966; Find out about Gardening, 1967; Gardens to Visit in Britain, 1970; Your Lawn, 1970; Carter's Book for Gardeners, 1970; All Colour Gardening Book, 1972; All Colour Book of Indoor and Greenhouse Plants, 1973; Picture Dictionary of Popular Flowering Plants, 1973; The Collingridge Encyclopaedia of Gardening, 1976; Shell Guide to Gardens, 1977; Gardens of Genius, 1980; The Collingridge Book of Ornamental Garden Shrubs, 1981; The Dobies Book of Greenhouses, 1981; Gardening Through the Year, 1981; Garden Shrubs, 1982. *Recreations:* gardening, photography, travelling. *Address:* Orchard Cottage, Rowfant, near Crawley, West Sussex. *T:* Copthorne 714838.

HELLYER, Hon. Paul Theodore, PC (Canada) 1957; FRSA 1973; Syndicated Columnist, Toronto Sun; *b* Waterford, Ont, Canada, 6 Aug. 1923; *s* of A. S. Hellyer and Lulla M. Anderson; *m* 1945, Ellen Jean, *d* of Henry Ralph, Toronto, Ont; two *s* one *d*. *Educ:* Waterford High Sch., Ont; Curtiss-Wright Techn. Inst. of Aeronautics, Glendale, Calif; University of Toronto (BA). Fleet Aircraft Mfg Co., Fort Erie, Ont. Wartime service, RCAF and Cdn Army. Propr Mari-Jane Fashions, Toronto, 1945-56; Treas., Curran Hall Ltd, Toronto, 1950 (Pres., 1951-62). Elected to House of Commons, 1949; re-elected, 1953; Parly Asst to Hon. Ralph Campney, Minister of Nat. Defence, 1956; Associate Minister of Nat. Defence, 1957; defeated in gen. elections of June 1957 and March 1958; re-elected to House of Commons in by-election Dec. 1958 and again re-elected June 1962, April 1963, Nov. 1965, June 1968, and Oct. 1972; defeated gen. election July 1974; Minister of National Defence, 1963-67; Minister of Transport, 1967-69, and Minister i/c Housing, 1968-69; resigned 1969 on question of principle relating to housing. Chm., Federal Task Force on Housing and Urban Develt, 1968. Served as a Parly Rep. to NATO under both L and C administrations. Joined

Parly Press Gallery, Oct. 1974. Distinguished visitor, York Univ., 1969-70. Founder and Leader, Action Canada, 1971; joined Progressive Cons. Party, 1972; Candidate for leadership of Progressive Cons. Party Feb. 1976. *Publications:* Agenda: a Plan for Action, 1971; Exit Inflation, 1981. *Recreations:* philately, music. *Address:* Suite 506, 65 Harbour Square, Toronto, Ont M5J 2L4, Canada. *Club:* Ontario.

HELMORE, Roy Lionel, CBE 1980; Principal, Cambridgeshire College of Arts and Technology, since 1977; *b* 8 June 1926; *s* of Lionel Helmore and Ellen Helmore (*née* Gibbins); *m* 1969, Margaret Lilian Martin. *Educ:* Montrose Academy; Edinburgh Univ. (BScEng). FIEE, FBIM. Crompton Parkinson Ltd, 1947-49; Asst Lectr, Peterborough Techn. Coll., 1949-53; Lectr, subseq. Sen. Lectr, Shrewsbury Techn. Coll., 1953-57; Head of Electrical Engrg and Science, Exeter Techn. Coll., 1957-61; Principal, St Albans Coll. of Further Education, 1961-77. Pres., Assoc. of Principals of Techn. Instns, 1972-73 (Hon. Sec. 1968-71); Member: BBC Further Educn Adv. Council, 1967-73; Air Transport and Travel ITB, 1967-73; Technician Educn Council, 1973-79 (Vice-Chm.); Manpower Services Commn, 1974-; RAF Trng and Educn Adv. Cttee, 1976-79; Chm., Trng and Further Educn Cons. Gp, 1977-. Fellow, Hughes Hall, Cambridge, 1982. JP St Albans, 1964-78. *Recreations:* gardening, travel, opera. *Address:* Chardingleye, 4 Plaistow Way, Great Chishill, Royston, Herts SG8 8SQ. *T:* Royston 838570. *Club:* Royal Commonwealth Society.

HELMSING, Most Rev. Charles H.; Former Bishop (RC) of Kansas City-St Joseph (Bishop, 1962-77, retired); *b* 23 March 1908; *s* of George Helmsing and Louise Helmsing (*née* Boschert). *Educ:* St Michael's Parochial Sch.; St Louis Preparatory Seminary; Kenrick Seminary. Sec. to Archbishop of St Louis, 1946-49; Auxiliary Bishop to Archbishop of St Louis, and Titular Bishop of Axum, 1949; first Bishop, Diocese of Springfield-Cape Girardeau, Mo, 1956-62. Member: Secretariat of Christian Unity, 1963-76; US Bishops Cttee for Ecumenical Affairs, 1964-76; Preparatory Cttee for Dialogue between Anglican Communion and Roman Catholic Church, 1966-67 (Chm., Roman Catholic Members); Chm., Special Cttee for Dialogue with Episcopal Church, US, 1964-76. Hon. Doctorates: Letters: Avila Coll. 1962; Humanities, Rockhurst Coll., 1963. Law: St Benedict's Coll. 1966. Order of Condor, Bolivia, 1966. *Address:* Cathedral House, 416 West 12th, Kansas City, Missouri 64105, USA.

HELPMANN, Sir Robert Murray, Kt 1968; CBE 1964; dancer, actor (stage and films); choreographer; producer; director; *b* 9 April 1909; *s* of James Murray Helpman, Mount Gambia, South Australia, and Mary Gardiner, Mount Shank, SA. *Educ:* Prince Alfred's Coll., Adelaide. First appeared under J. C. Williamson's Management, Australia, 1926-30; Premier Danseur, Sadler's Wells Ballet, 1933-50; Director, Australian Ballet, 1965-76; Artistic Dir, Adelaide Festival, 1970-. Guest dancer, Royal Opera House, 1958; guest artist, Sadler's Wells Royal Ballet, 1977. *Theatre:* Stop Press, Adelphi, 1936; Oberon, A Midsummer Night's Dream, Old Vic, 1937-38; Gremio, The Taming of the Shrew, 1939; title role, Old Vic prodn Hamlet, New, 1944; Flamineo, The White Devil, 1947; Prince, He Who Gets Slapped, Duchess, 1947; Stratford-on-Avon, 1948 season: Shylock, King John and Hamlet; Sir Laurence Olivier's Shaw-Shakespeare Festival Season, 1951: Apollodorus, Caesar and Cleopatra; Octavius Caesar, Antony and Cleopatra; The Millionairess, New, 1952; Oberon, A Midsummer Night's Dream, Edinburgh Festival, USA and Canada, 1954; Old Vic Australian Tour, 1955: Petruchio, Taming of the Shrew; Shylock, Merchant of Venice; Angelo, Measure for Measure; Old Vic: Shylock, Merchant of Venice, 1956; Launce, The Two Gentlemen of Verona, 1957; Emperor, Titus Andronicus, 1957; Pinch, Comedy of Errors, 1957; King Richard, Richard III, 1957; Georges de Valera, Nekrassov, Edinburgh Festival and Royal Court, 1957; Sebastian, Nude with Violin, London and Australian Tour, 1958; Sarah in America, USA, 1980; Colette, USA, 1981; Valmouth, Chichester, 1982; *produced:* Madame Butterfly, Royal Opera Hse, Covent Gdn, 1950; Murder in the Cathedral, Old Vic, 1953; Coq d'Or, Royal Opera Hse, 1954, 1956, 1962; After the Ball, Globe, 1954; Antony and Cleopatra, Old Vic, 1957; The Marriage-Go-Round, Piccadilly, 1959; Duel of Angels: New York, 1960; Melbourne, 1961; Old Vic S American Tour, 1962; Peter Pan, Coliseum, 1972, 1973, 1974; Palladium, 1975; *choreographer:* Red Shoes (and Premier Danseur), 1948; Australia, 1964: Comus; Hamlet; The Birds; Miracle in the Gorbals; Adam Zero; The Soldier's Tale; Elektra; The Display; Yugen; Cinderella, Covent Gdn, 1965; Elektra, Australia, 1966; Sun Music, Australia; dir., Camelot, Drury Lane, 1964; *films include:* One of our Aircraft is Missing, Wyecroft in Caravan, Henry V (Bishop of Ely), Tales of Hoffmann, The Iron Petticoat, Big Money, Red Shoes, 55 Days in Pekin, The Soldier's Tale, The Quiller Memorandum, Chitty Chitty Bang Bang, Alice in Wonderland (Mad Hatter), Don Quixote, The Mango Tree, Patrick. Has appeared on TV. Knight of the Northern Star (Sweden); Knight of the Cedar (Lebanon). *Address:* c/o Midland Bank Ltd, 70 St Martin's Lane, WC2.

HELY, Brig. Alfred Francis, CB 1951; CBE 1945; DSO 1943; TD 1944; DL; Chief Dental Officer, Cheshire County Council, 1957-68; *b* 3 Aug. 1902; *s* of Alfred Francis Hely; unmarried. *Educ:* St Edward's Coll., Liverpool; Liverpool Univ. Qualified as a Dental Surg., 1923; in private practice, 1923-26. Liverpool Univ. OTC, 1921-25; Cadet Corporal, Duke of Lancaster's Own Imperial Yeomanry, 1925-26; 106 (Lancs Hussars), RHA, 1926-41 (comd, 1937-41); served War of 1939-45 (despatches twice); 60th Field Regt, RA, 1941-42; CRA 7 Ind. Div., 1942-45; Comd 7 Ind. Div. 1945 until end of hostilities in Burma (3 months); war service in Palestine, Western Desert, Greece, Crete, Syria, 1940-42, North-West Frontier, India, 1942, Burma, 1943-45. CRA 42 (Lancs) Inf. Div. (TA), 1947-50. DL Merseyside (formerly County Palatine of Lancaster), 1951. *Recreations:* outdoor country pursuits. *Address:* Flat 2, Inchbroom, 21 Bidston Road, Birkenhead, Merseyside L43 2JY. *T:* 051-652 2132. *Club:* Army and Navy.

HELY, Air Commodore Arthur Hubert McMath, CB 1962; OBE 1945; Air Commodore Operations, HQ Maintenance Command, 1961-64, retired; *b* 16 Feb. 1909; *s* of Hamilton McMath Hely and Lubie Thrine Hely (*née* Jörgensen); *m* 1935, Laura Mary Sullivan, 6th *d* of Serjeant A. M. Sullivan, QC; two *s* two *d*. *Educ:* Mt Albert, Auckland, NZ; Auckland University Coll. Joined Royal Air Force, 1934; Staff Coll., 1942; HQ SACSEA, 1944, 1945; Joint Chiefs of Staff, Australia, 1946-48; Joint Services Staff Coll., 1948; Group Capt. 1950; HQ Fighter Command, 1953-56; HQ Far East Air Force, 1956, 1958; Air Ministry (acting Air Commodore), 1958; Air Commodore, 1959. *Recreations:* golf, painting. *Address:* Windrush, Harborough Hill, West Chiltington, West Sussex. *Clubs:* West Sussex Golf; RAF Changi Golf.

HELY-HUTCHINSON, family name of **Earl of Donoughmore.**

HEMANS, Simon Nicholas Peter; HM Diplomatic Service; Deputy High Commissioner, Nairobi, Kenya, since 1981; *b* 19 Sept. 1940; *s* of Brig. P. R. Hemans, CBE, and Mrs M. E. Hemans (*née* Melsome); *m* 1970, Ursula Martha Naef; three *s* one *d*. *Educ:* Sherborne; London School of Economics (BScEcon). Joined Foreign Office, 1964; British Embassy, Moscow, 1966-68; FO, 1968-69; Dep. Commissioner, Anguilla, March-Oct. 1969; FO, 1969-71; UK Mission to UN, New York, 1971-75; British Embassy, Budapest, 1975-79; FO, 1979-81. *Recreation:* travel. *Address:* c/o Foreign and Commonwealth Office, SW1; British High Commission, Bruce House, Standard Street, Nairobi, Kenya. *T:* Nairobi 335944.

HEMINGFORD, 3rd Baron; *see* Herbert, D. N.

HEMINGWAY, Albert, MSc, MB, ChB; Emeritus Professor, University of Leeds (Professor of Physiology, 1936-67); *b* 1902; *s* of Herbert Hemingway, Leeds; *m* 1930, Margaret Alice Cooper; one *d*. *Educ:* University of Leeds. Demonstrator in Physiology, King's Coll., London, 1925; Senior Asst in Physiology, University Coll., London, 1926; Lecturer in Experimental Physiology, Welsh National Sch. of Medicine, 1927. Vis. Prof., Makerere University Coll., Uganda, 1968. Examiner in Physiology, Universities of St Andrews, Birmingham, Bristol, Cambridge, Durham, Glasgow, Liverpool, London, Manchester, Wales and RCS. Mem. various cttees of MRC on work and exercise physiology; Mem. Cttee, Physiological Soc. (Editor, Jl Physiology); Pres., Section I, British Assoc., 1959. *Publications:* original papers on the physiology of the circulation, exercise and the kidney in scientific and medical journals. *Recreation:* travel. *Address:* 4 Helmsley Drive, Leeds LS16 5HY. *T:* Leeds 785720.

HEMINGWAY, Peter, FCA; Director and Chief General Manager, Leeds Permanent Building Society, since 1982; *b* 19 Jan. 1926; *s* of William Edward and Florence Hemingway; *m* 1952, June Maureen, *d* of Maurice and Lilian A. Senior. *Educ:* Leeds College of Commerce. With John Gordon, Walton & Co., Chartered Accountants, Leeds, 1941-62, Partner 1959-62; Director, Provincial Registrars Ltd, 1955-62; joined Leeds Permanent Bldg Soc. as Secretary, 1962. Hon. Sec. 1970-82, Vice-Chm. 1982-, Yorkshire County Assoc. of Building Societies; Mem. Council: Building Societies Assoc., 1981-; Chartered Building Societies Inst., 1982-. *Recreations:* travel, motor racing, music, gardening. *Address:* Old Barn Cottage, Kearby, near Wetherby, Yorks LS22 4BU. *T:* Harewood 886380.

HEMLOW, Prof. Joyce; Professor Emerita, McGill University, Montreal, Canada; author; *b* 30 July 1906; *d* of William Hemlow and Rosalinda (*née* Redmond), Liscomb, NS. *Educ:* Queen's Univ., Kingston, Ont (MA; Hon. LLD 1967); Harvard Univ., Cambridge, Mass (AM, PhD). Preceding a univ. career, period of teaching in Nova Scotia, Canada; lecturer in English Language and Literature at McGill Univ.; Prof. of English Language and Literature, McGill Univ., 1955-, now part-time. FRSC 1960. Guggenheim Fellow, 1951-52, 1960-62 and 1966. Member: Phi Beta Kappa, The Johnsonians, and of other literary and professional organizations. Hon. LLD Dalhousie, 1972. James Tait Black Memorial Book Prize, 1958; Brit. Academy Award (Crawshay Prize), 1960. *Publications:* The History of Fanny Burney, 1958 (GB); (ed with others) The Journals and Letters of Fanny Burney (Madame d'Arblay), vols i-x, 1972-82; articles in learned jls on Fanny Burney's novels and unpublished plays. *Address:* (home) Liscomb, Nova Scotia, Canada; The Crestwood, 3555 Atwater Avenue, Montreal, Canada. *Club:* English-Speaking Union (Canadian Branch).

HEMMING, Air Commodore Idris George Selvin, CB 1968; CBE 1959 (OBE 1954); retired; *b* 11 Dec. 1911; *s* of late George Hemming, Liverpool; *m* 1939, Phyllis, *d* of Francis Payne, Drogheda, Eire; two *s*. *Educ:* Chalford, Glos.; Wallasey, Cheshire. Joined RAF, 1928; served War of 1939-45, UK, India and Burma; Gp Capt. 1957; Air Cdre 1962; Dir of Equipment (Pol.) (RAF), MoD, 1962-66; Dir of Equipment (1) (RAF), MoD, Harrogate, 1966-68. *Recreations:* cricket, golf. *Address:* Ash House, St Chloe Green, Amberley, near Stroud, Glos GL5 5AP. *T:* Amberley 3581. *Club:* Royal Air Force.

HEMMING, John Henry, DLitt; Joint Chairman, Municipal Journal Ltd, since 1976 (Director, since 1962; Deputy Chairman, 1967-76); Director and Secretary, Royal Geographical Society, since 1975; *b* 5 Jan. 1935; *s* of late Henry Harold Hemming, OBE, MC, and of Alice Louisa Weaver, OBE; *m* 1979, Sukie, *d* of M. J. Babington Smith, *qv*; one *s* one *d. Educ:* Eton College; McGill University; Oxford University (DLitt 1981). Chairman: Brintex Ltd, 1979– (Man. Dir, 1963-70, Dep. Chm. 1976-78); Newman Books, 1979-. Member, Iriri River Expedition, Brazil, 1961. Member Council: Lepra; Anglo-Brazilian Soc.; Mt Everest Foundn. Corres. Mem., Academia Nacional de la Historia, Venezuela. Trustee and Hon. Treas., Survival International; Trustee, L.S.B. Leakey Trust. *Publications:* The Conquest of the Incas, 1970 (Robert Pitman Literary Prize, 1970, Christopher Award, NY, 1971); (jt) Tribes of the Amazon Basin in Brazil, 1972; Red Gold: The Conquest of the Brazilian Indians, 1978; The Search for El Dorado, 1978; Machu Picchu, 1981; Monuments of the Incas, 1982. *Recreations:* writing, travel. *Address:* 178-202 Great Portland Street, W1N 6NH. *T:* 01-637 2400. *Clubs:* Travellers', Beefsteak, Geographical (Mem. Council).
See also L. A. *Service.*

HEMMINGS, David Leslie Edward; actor, director and producer; engaged in entertainment industry since 1949; *b* 18 Nov. 1941; *m* 1st, 1960, Genista Ouvry; one *d*; 2nd, 1969, Gayle Hunnicutt (marr. diss. 1975); one *s*; 3rd, 1976, Prudence J. de Casembroot; two *s. Educ:* Glyn Coll., Epsom, Surrey. The Turn of the Screw, English Opera Group, 1954; Five Clues to Fortune, 1957; Saint Joan, 1957; The Heart Within, 1957; Men of Tomorrow, 1958; In the Wake of a Stranger, 1958; No Trees in the Street, 1959; Some People, 1962; Play it Cool, 1963; Two Left Feet, 1963; The System, 1964; Be my Guest, 1965; Eye of the Devil, 1966; Blow Up, 1966; Camelot, 1967; Barbarella, 1967; Only When I Larf, 1968; The Charge of the Light Brigade, 1968; The Long Day's Dying, 1968; The Best House in London, 1968; Alfred the Great, 1969; Fragment of Fear, 1970; The Walking Stick, 1970; Unman, Wittering & Zigo, 1971; The Love Machine, 1971; Voices, 1973; Don't Worry Momma, 1973; Juggernaut, 1974; Quilp, 1974; Profundo Rosso, 1975; Islands in the Stream, 1975; The Squeeze, 1976; Jeeves (musical), Her Majesty's, 1975; Power Play, 1978; Thirst, 1979; Beyond Reasonable Doubt, 1980; Jekyll and Hyde, 1980; Harlequin, 1980. BBC TV, Scott Fitzgerald, 1975; ITV, The Rime of the Ancient Mariner, 1978; ITV, Charlie Muffin, 1979. Directed: Running Scared, 1972; The 14, 1973 (Silver Bear Award, Berlin Film Festival, 1973); Disappearance, 1977; Power Play, 1977; Just a Gigolo, 1978; David Bowie Stage, 1979; Murder By Decree, 1979; Survivor, 1979; Race to the Yankee Zephyr, 1980; also in Australia, NZ etc. Produced: Strange Behaviour, 1981; Turkey Shoot, 1981. Director: International Home Video FGH Pty Ltd (Melbourne); Film and General Holdings Inc. (California). *Recreation:* painting. *Address:* 94 Onslow Gardens, SW7. *Clubs:* Turf, Chelsea Arts, Magic Circle.

HEMP, Prof. William Spooner, MA, FRAeS; Stewarts and Lloyds Professor of Structural Engineering, Oxford University, since 1965; Professorial Fellow of Keble College, Oxford, since 1965; *b* 21 March 1916; *s* of late Rev. William James Hemp and Daisy Lilian Hemp; *m* 1938, Dilys Ruth Davies; one *s. Educ:* Paston Grammar Sch., North Walsham; Jesus Coll., Cambridge (Scholar, MA). Aeronautical Engineer, Bristol Aeroplane Co., 1938-46. Coll. of Aeronautics: Senior Lecturer, 1946-50; Prof. of Aircraft Structures and Aeroelasticity, 1950-65; Head of Dept of Aircraft Design, 1951-65; Dep. Principal, 1957-65. Mem. of various cttees of Aeronautical Research Council since 1948. Visiting Prof., Stanford Univ., Calif, 1960-61. *Publications:* Optimum Structures, 1973; research papers in the Theory of Structures, Solid Mechanics and Applied Mathematics. *Recreations:* mountain walking, music. *Address:* Department of Engineering Science, Park Road, Oxford. *T:* Oxford 59988.

HEMPHILL, 5th Baron *cr* 1906, of Rathkenny and Cashel; **Peter Patrick Fitzroy Martyn Martyn-Hemphill;** *b* 5 Sept. 1928; *o s* of 4th Baron Hemphill and Emily, *d* of F. Irving Sears, Webster, Mass; *S* father 1957; *m* 1952, Olivia Anne, *er d* of Major Robert Francis Ruttledge, MC, Cloonee, Ballinrobe, County Mayo; one *s* two *d*; assumed surname of Martyn in addition to Hemphill, 1959. *Educ:* Downside; Brasenose Coll., Oxford (MA). *Heir: s* Hon. Charles Andrew Martyn Martyn-Hemphill, *b* 8 Oct. 1954. *Address:* Tulira, Ardrahan, Co. Galway, Eire. *T:* Ardrahan 4. *Clubs:* Royal Automobile, White's; Kildare Street and University (Dublin); County (Galway).

HEMSLEY, Thomas Jeffrey; free-lance opera and concert singer; *b* 12 April 1927; *s* of Sydney William Hemsley and Kathleen Anne Hemsley (née Deacon); *m* 1960, Hon. Gwenllian Ellen James, *d* of 4th Baron Northbourne; three *s. Educ:* Ashby de la Zouch Grammar Sch.; Brasenose Coll., Oxford (MA). Vicar Choral, St Paul's Cathedral, 1950-51; Prin. Baritone, Stadttheater, Aachen, 1953-56; Deutsche Oper am Rhein, 1957-63; Opernhaus, Zurich, 1963-67; Glyndebourne, Bayreuth, Edinburgh Festivals, etc. Hon. RAM 1974. *Address:* 10 Denewood Road, N6. *T:* 01-348 3397.

HENAO, Rev. Sir Ravu, Kt 1982; OBE 1975; Executive Secretary, Bible Society of Papua New Guinea, since 1980; *b* 27 March 1927; *s* of Boga Henao and Gaba Asi; *m* 1944, Lahui Peri; four *s* five *d. Educ:* Port Moresby (completed standard 5); Lawes Theol Coll., Fife Bay, Milne Bay Province. Primary sch. teacher, various schs in Central Dist, 1944-66 (pastor as well as teacher, 1946); Chm. (full-time), Papua Ekalesia (national church related to London Missionary Soc.), 1967; Bishop of United Church for Papua Mainland

Region, 1968-80. *Publications:* (with Raymond Perry) Let's Discuss These Things, 1966; (with Alan Dunstan) Paul's Letter to the Galatians, 1974. *Recreations:* fishing, hunting, gardening. *Address:* PO Box 18, Port Moresby, Papua New Guinea. *T:* (office) 21-7893, (home) 21-4367.

HENARE, Sir James Clendon Tau, KBE 1978 (CBE 1966); DSO 1945; retired farmer, New Zealand; *b* Motatau, NZ, 18 Nov. 1911; *s* of Tau Henare, MP; *m* 1933, Rosie, *d* of Johnson Cherrington; three *s* three *d. Educ:* Motatau Sch., Awanui, Takapuna; Thorndon Normal Sch.; Sacred Heart Coll., Auckland; Massey Coll. (later Univ.). Served War, 2nd NZEF; Private, 1939; commissioned, 1940; finally CO (Lt-Col) Maori Bn (despatches). Member: Waitangi Nat. Trust Bd; Bay of Islands CC; Bay of Islands Maritime and Historic Park Bd; Chm., Taitokerau Trust Bd. Former Member: Rehabilitation Bd; Geographic Bd; Bd of Maori Affairs; Auckland Diocese Synod; Maori Language Runanga, and many other organisations. Awarded KBE for service to the community, especially Maori affairs, New Zealand. *Address:* Moerewa Road 3, Bay of Islands, New Zealand.

HENBEST, Prof. Harold Bernard; Professor of Organic Chemistry at the Queen's University, Belfast, 1958-73; *b* 10 March 1924; *s* of A. Bernard Henbest and Edith Winifred Herbert; *m* 1948, Rosalind Eve Skone James; two *s* one *d. Educ:* Barking Abbey Sch.; Imperial Coll. of Science, London. Beit Research Fellow, 1947-48; Lectr, University of Manchester, 1948-56; Research Fellow, Harvard Univ., 1953-54; Vis. Prof., UCLA, 1954; Reader, KCL, 1956-57. *Publications:* Organic Chemistry (with M. F. Grundon), 1968; contribs to Jl of Chemical Soc. *Address:* 1 St Albans Gardens, Belfast, Northern Ireland.

HENDEL, Prof. Charles William; Professor Emeritus of Moral Philosophy and Metaphysics, Yale University; *b* 16 Dec. 1890; *s* of Charles William Hendel and Emma Stolz, American; *m* 1916, Elizabeth Phoebe Jones (*d* 1977); two *s. Educ:* Princeton Univ. LittB 1913; PhD 1917. United States Army, 1917-18, 2nd Lieut Infantry. Instructor, Williams Coll., 1919-20; Asst and Associate Prof., Princeton Univ., 1920-29; MacDonald Prof. of Moral Philosophy, McGill Univ., 1929-40; Chm. of Philosophy, 1929-40; Dean of Faculty of Arts and Science, 1937-40; Clarke Prof. of Moral Philosophy and Metaphysics, Yale Univ., 1940-59; Chm. of Dept, 1940-45 and 1950-59; Prof. Emeritus, 1959-. Gifford Lecturer, University of Glasgow, 1962-63. Hon. MA Yale, 1940. President: American Philosophical Assoc. (Eastern Div.), 1940; American Soc. for Political and Legal Philosophy, 1959-61. *Publications:* Studies in the Philosophy of David Hume, 1925 (2nd edn enlarged with Supplement, 1963); (jointly) Contemporary Idealism in America, 1932; Jean Jacques Rousseau, Moralist, 2 vols 1934 (2nd edn with Preface, 1963); Citizen of Geneva, 1937; Civilization and Religion, 1948; The Philosophy of Kant and our Modern World; John Dewey: Philosophy and the Experimental Spirit, 1959; many translations, joint authorships, and edns of philosophical works. *Recreations:* music; out-of-doors, in woods, fields and mountains.

HENDER, John Derrik; DL; Chief Executive, West Midlands Metropolitan County Council, since 1973; *b* 15 Nov. 1926; *s* of late Jessie Peter and late Jennie Hender; *m* 1949, Kathleen Nora Brown; one *d. Educ:* Great Yarmouth Grammar School. IPFA, FCA, FBIM. Deputy Borough Treasurer: Newcastle-under-Lyme, 1957-61; Wolverhampton County Borough, 1961-64; City Treas. 1965-69, Chief Exec. and Town Clerk 1969-73, Coventry County Borough. FBIM 1975. DL West Midlands, 1975. *Publications:* numerous articles relating to various aspects of local govt and related matters. *Recreation:* gardening. *Address:* West Midlands County Council, County Hall, 1 Lancaster Circus, Queensway, Birmingham B4 7DJ. *T:* 021-300 6000.

HENDERSON, family name of **Barons Faringdon** and **Henderson.**

HENDERSON, 1st Baron, *cr* 1945, of Westgate in the City and County of Newcastle upon Tyne; **William Watson Henderson,** PC 1950; Director, Alliance Building Society, 1955-75 (Chairman, 1966-72); journalist and political writer; *b* Newcastle upon Tyne, 8 Aug. 1891; *s* of late Rt Hon. Arthur Henderson, MP. *Educ:* Queen Elizabeth Grammar Sch., Darlington. Editorial Sec., Daily Citizen, 1912-14; Parliamentary Correspondent, Labour Press Dept, 1919-21; Lobby Correspondent, Daily Herald, 1919-21; Sec., Press and Publicity Dept, Labour Party, 1921-45; Private Sec. to Rt Hon. John Hodge, MP, Minister of Labour, 1917; Prospective Labour Candidate, Bridgwater Div. of Somerset, 1919-21; MP (Lab) Enfield, 1923-24 and 1929-31; Parliamentary Private Sec. to the Sec. of State for India, 1929-31; Personal Asst to Rt Hon. Arthur Greenwood, MP (Minister without Portfolio and Mem. of the War Cabinet), 1940-42; an additional mem. of the Air Council, 1945-47; a Lord in Waiting to the King, 1945-48; a Parly Under-Sec. of State, FO, 1948-51. A British Representative at Assembly of Council of Europe, 1954 and 1955; Labour Peers representative on Parliamentary Cttee of Parliamentary Labour Party, 1952-55.

HENDERSON, Barry; *see* Henderson, J. S. B.

HENDERSON, Rt. Rev. Charles Joseph; Auxiliary Bishop in Southwark, (RC), since 1972; Titular Bishop of Tricala, since 1972; Area Bishop with responsibility for South East Metropolitan London, since 1980; Parish Priest, St Mary's, Blackheath, since 1969; *b* 14 April 1924; *s* of Charles Stuart Henderson and Hanora Henderson (née Walsh). *Educ:* Mount Sion Sch., Waterford; St John's Seminary, Waterford. Priest, 1948; Curate, St Stephen's,

Welling, Kent, 1948-55; English Martyrs, Streatham, SW16, 1955-58; Chancellor, RC Diocese of Southwark, 1958-70; Vicar General, RC Diocese of Arundel and Brighton, 1965-66; Episcopal Vicar for Religious, Southwark, 1968-73; Vicar General, RC Archdiocese of Southwark, 1969; Canon of Cathedral Chapter, 1972; Provost of Cathedral Chapter, 1973. Member: Ecumenical Commn for England and Wales, 1976-; Nat. Catholic Commn for Racial Justice, 1978-81; English Anglican/RC Relations, 1982-; RC Consultant-Observer, BCC, 1982-. Papal Chamberlain, 1960; Prelate of Papal Household, 1965. Freeman, City of Waterford, 1973. Kt Comdr with Star of Equestrian Order of Holy Sepulchre, Jerusalem, 1973. *Recreation:* special interest in sport. *Address:* Park House, 6A Cresswell Park, Blackheath, SE3 9RD. *T:* 01-318 1094.

HENDERSON, David; *see* Henderson, P. D.

HENDERSON, Derek, FDSRCS; Senior Consultant Oral and Maxillo-facial Surgeon, St Thomas' Hospital, since 1975; Consultant: Royal Dental Hospital, since 1975; St George's Hospital, since 1975; Hon. Consultant, Charing Cross Hospital, since 1977; Hon. Senior Lecturer in Oral Surgery, Royal Dental School, London, since 1977; Recognised Teacher, University of London, since 1977; Hon. Civilian Consultant in Dental Surgery: Royal Navy, since 1971; Army, since 1981; *b* 9 April 1935; *s* of Robert Henderson and Dorothy Edith Henderson; *m* 1961, Jennifer Jill Anderson; one *s* one *d. Educ:* Dulwich Coll.; London Univ. (BDS Hons 1956, MB, BS Hons 1963). FDSRCS (Eng) 1960 (LDS 1956); MRCS, LRCP 1963. Dental and med. trng, KCH, London, 1952-56 and 1959-63 (Prizeman); house surg. appts, KCH and Royal Dental Hosp., 1956-59; King's Coll. Hospital: Cons Registrar in Dental Materials, 1958-65; ENT House Officer, and Casualty Off., 1964; Registrar in Oral Surg., Queen Mary's Hosp., Roehampton, and Westminster Hosp., 1965; Sen. Registrar in Oral Surg., United Cardiff Hosps, 1965-67; Consultant Oral Surgeon to Eastern Reg. Hosp. Bd, Scotland, and Dundee Dental Hosp., 1967-69 (Hon. Sen. Lectr, Univ. of Dundee); Consultant i/c Reg. Maxillo-facial Service to Glasgow and West of Scotland, based on Canniesburn Plastic and Oral Surg. Unit, Glasgow, 1969-75 (Hon. Clinical Teacher, Glasgow Univ.). Hon. Civilian Consultant, Queen Elizabeth Mil. Hosp., Woolwich (formerly Queen Alexandra Mil. Hosp., Millbank), 1976-81. Vis. Prof. and Lectr, Brazil, Argentina, Chile, USA, Spain, Venezuela, Australia, Holland, Saudi Arabia, Uruguay, SA. Hunterian Prof., RCS, 1975-76; Kelsey Fry Adviser in Postgraduate Educnl Trng, RCS Faculty of Dental Surg., 1975-80; Member: Bd of Faculty of Dental Surgery, RCS, 1978- (and Examr, FDSRCS); Central Cttee for Hospital Dental Services, 1978- (Mem. Exec. Cttee, 1980-); Central Cttee for Univ. Dental Teachers and Research Workers, 1978-81; Negotiating Subcttee, CCHMS, 1980-; European Assoc. for Maxillo-Facial Surg.; BMA; BDA; Craniofacial Soc. (Mem. Council, 1973-77); Oral Surgery Club GB. FRSM; Fellow: BAOS (Mem. Council, 1974-76, 1977-80); Internat. Assoc. of Oral Surgeons. Hon. Mem., Amer. Assoc. of Oral Surgeons in Europe; Hon. Associate Life Mem., Soc. of Maxillo-facial and Oral Surgeons of SA; Hon. Pres., Inst. of Maxillo-Facial Technol., 1977-78. *Publications:* contribs on general oral surgery to British Jl of Oral Surgery and British Dental Jl, and especially on surgery of facial and jaw deformity to Brit. Jl of Oral Surg. and Brit. Jl of Plastic Surg. *Recreation:* fly fishing. *Address:* 3 Woodsyre, Sydenham Hill, SE26 6SS. *T:* 01-670 5094; 107 Harley Street, W1N 1DG. *T:* 01-935 6906. *Clubs:* Savage, Flyfishers'; Royal Navy Medical; Piscatorial Soc.

HENDERSON, Dr Derek Scott; Principal and Vice-Chancellor, Rhodes University, Grahamstown, South Africa, since 1975; *b* 28 Oct. 1929; *s* of Ian Scott and Kathleen Elizabeth Henderson; *m* 1958, Thelma Muriel Mullins; two *d. Educ:* Rhodes University Coll. (BSc); Oxford Univ. (MA); Cambridge Univ. (MA); Harvard Univ. (PhD). Exec. Trainee, Anglo American Corp. of S Africa, 1953-56; Lectr in Maths, Univ. of the Witwatersrand, Johannesburg, 1957; Associate Engr, IBM Corp., Poughkeepsie, NY, 1960-62; Univ. of the Witwatersrand, 1962-75: Sen. Lectr, then Dir of Computer Centre; Prof. of Computer Science; Head of Dept of Applied Maths; Dean of Science Faculty. *Publications:* seventeen articles in learned jls. *Recreations:* golf, cricket. *Address:* Rhodes University, PO Box 94, Grahamstown, 6140, S Africa. *T:* 0461-3639. *Club:* Port Elizabeth (Port Elizabeth, S Africa).

HENDERSON, Douglas Mackay, FRSE 1966; FLS; Regius Keeper, Royal Botanic Garden, Edinburgh, since 1970; *b* 30 Aug. 1927; *s* of Captain Frank Henderson and Adine C. Mackay; *m* 1952, Julia Margaret Brown; one *s* two *d. Educ:* Blairgowrie High Sch.; Edinburgh Univ. (BSc). Scientific Officer, Dept of Agriculture and Fisheries for Scotland, 1948-51. Royal Botanic Garden, Edinburgh, 1951-: Sec., Internat. Assoc. of Botanical Gardens, 1969-. Curator of Library and Museum, Royal Soc. of Edinburgh, 1978-. *Publications:* British Rust Fungi (with M. Wilson), 1966; many papers on taxonomy of cryptogams. *Recreations:* music, art, hill walking, field natural history, sailing. *Address:* 12 Afton Terrace, Edinburgh EH5 3NG. *T:* 031-552 3457.

HENDERSON, Rt. Rev. Edward Barry, DSC 1944; DD (Lambeth) 1960; *b* 22 March 1910; 2nd *s* of late Dean of Salisbury, the Very Rev. E. L. Henderson; *m* 1935, Hester Borradaile Taylor; one *s* two *d. Educ:* Radley; Trinity Coll., Cambridge. Curate of St Gabriel's, Pimlico, 1934-36; Priest-in-charge, All Saints, Pimlico, 1936-39; Rector of Holy Trinity, Ayr, 1939-47; Chaplain, RNVR, 1943-44; Vicar of St Paul's, Knightsbridge, 1947-55; Rural Dean of Westminster, 1952-55; Bishop Suffragan of Tewkesbury, 1955-60;

Bishop of Bath and Wells, 1960-75. Chm., Church of England Youth Council, 1961-69. Chaplain and Sub-Prelate, Order of St John of Jerusalem, 1961. Hon. Freeman, City of Wells, 1974. Hon. DLitt Bath, 1975. *Recreations:* fishing, golf, and sailing. *Address:* Hill Cottage, Ryme Intrinseca, near Sherborne, Dorset. *T:* Yetminster 872894.

HENDERSON, Ven. Edward Chance, BD, ALCD; Archdeacon of Pontefract, 1968-81, now Archdeacon Emeritus; *b* 15 Oct. 1916; *s* of William Edward and Mary Anne Henderson; *m* 1942, Vera Massie Pattison; two *s* three *d. Educ:* Heaton Grammar Sch.; London University. Asst Curate, St Stephen, Newcastle upon Tyne, 1939-42; Organising Sec., CPAS, 1942-45; Vicar of St Mary of Bethany, Leeds, 1945-51; Priest i/c: Armley Hall, Leeds, 1948-51; St John, New Wortley, Leeds, 1949-51; Vicar of: All Souls, Halifax, 1951-59; Dewsbury, 1959-68; Darrington with Wentbridge, 1968-75. Examining Chaplain to Bishop of Wakefield, 1972-. *Address:* 12 Park Lane, Balne, Goole, North Humberside DN14 0EP. *T:* Goole 85284.

HENDERSON, Edward Firth, CMG 1972; HM Diplomatic Service, retired; Chairman, American Educational Trust, Washington, DC, since 1982; *b* 12 Dec. 1917; *m* 1960, Jocelyn (*née* Nenk); two *d. Educ:* Clifton Coll.; BNC, Oxford. Served War of 1939-45 in Army (despatches); served in Arab Legion, 1945-47. With Petroleum Concessions Ltd, in Arabian Gulf, 1948-56; Foreign Service, 1956; served in Middle East posts and in Foreign Office; Political Agent, Qatar, 1969-71, and Ambassador there 1971-74. Lectr and Res. Schol., Sch. of Advanced Internat. Studies, Johns Hopkins Univ., 1976, 1977 and 1979; Lectr, Univs of Texas, NY and Princeton, 1979; Hon. Fellow, LSE, 1980-81. Research specialist, Centre for Documentation and Res., Presidential Court, Abu Dhabi, 1976-81; Dir, Council for the Advancement of Arab-British Understanding, 1981-82. *Address:* 4 Purcell Close, Tewin Woods, near Welwyn, Herts AL6 0NN. *Club:* Travellers'.

HENDERSON, Rear-Adm. Geoffrey Archer, CB 1969; retired; *b* 14 Aug. 1913; *s* of late Sir Charles James Henderson, KBE; *m* 1959 Pamela (Rachel), *d* of late Sir Philip Petrides; one *s* one *d. Educ:* Christ's Hosp. Entered RN, 1931. Served War of 1939-45; HMS Onslow, 1941-42 (despatches); Sec. to Asst Chief of Naval Staff (F), 1943-44. HMS Newfoundland, 1952-55; HMS Victorious, 1957-58; Cabinet Office, 1959-61; idc 1962; Director of Naval Officer Appointments (S), 1963-65; Commodore, RN Barracks, Portsmouth, 1965-66; ADC 1966; Naval Mem. of Senior Directing Staff, Imperial Defence Coll., 1966-68; Chief Naval Supply and Secretariat Officer, 1968-70, and Dir, Management and Support Intelligence, MoD, 1969-70. Admin Manager, National Mutual Life Assce Soc., 1970-78. *Address:* Pigeon's Green, St Mary's Platt, Sevenoaks, Kent TN15 8NL. *T:* Borough Green 882462.

HENDERSON, Rt. Rev. George Kennedy Buchanan; *see* Argyll and the Isles, Bishop of.

HENDERSON, Prof. George Patrick, FRSE 1980; Professor of Philosophy in the University of Dundee (formerly Queen's College, Dundee), 1959-80, Dean, Faculty of Arts and Social Sciences, 1973-76; *b* 22 April 1915; *e s* of Rev. George Aitchison Henderson, MA, and Violet Margaret Mackenzie; *m* 1939, Hester Lowry Douglas McWilliam, BSc (*d* 1978), *d* of Rev. John Morell McWilliam, BA. *Educ:* Elgin Academy; St Andrews Univ. (Harkness Scholar); Balliol Coll., Oxford. 1st Class Hons in Philosophy, University of St Andrews, 1936; Miller Prize and Ramsay Scholarship; MA 1936; Ferguson Scholarship in Philosophy, 1936; 2nd Class Lit Hum, University of Oxford, 1938; BA 1938. Asst in Logic and Metaphysics, University of St Andrews, 1938; Shaw Fellow in Mental Philosophy, University of Edinburgh, 1938. MA Oxon, 1943. Army Service, 1940-46; Royal Artillery (commissioned 1940, Adjutant 1942-43) and Gen. Staff (GSO 3 1945); served in UK, Italy and Greece. Lecturer in Logic and Metaphysics, University of St Andrews, 1945; Senior Lecturer, 1953. Corresp. Member: Acad. of Athens, 1973; Ionian Acad., 1975. Editor of the Philosophical Quarterly, 1962-72. *Publications:* The Revival of Greek Thought, 1620-1830, 1970; The Ionian Academy (in Greek trans.), 1980; numerous articles and reviews in principal philosophical periodicals. *Recreations:* modern Greek studies, gardening. *Address:* The Pendicle, Invergowrie, Dundee DD2 5DQ.

HENDERSON, Sir Guy (Wilmot McLintock), Kt 1956; BA, LLB Cantab; QC (Uganda) 1949; Chief Justice of the Bahamas, 1951-60, retired; *b* 13 July 1897; *e s* of late Arthur James and Charlotte West Henderson; *m* 1930, Ann (*d* 1980), *d* of late George and Elizabeth Dring-Campion; two *s* one *d. Educ:* Blundell's, Tiverton; Collegiate Sch., Wanganui, NZ; Trinity Coll., Cambridge. Served European War, 1914-18, Lieut RFA (R). Barrister-at-Law, Inner Temple, 1923; private practice, Rangoon, Burma, 1924-29; professional clerk, prosecuting staff GPO, London, 1930-32; stipendiary and circuit magistrate, Bahamas, 1932-37; Crown Counsel, Tanganyika Territory, 1937-40; legal draftsman, Nigeria, 1940-45; dep. Chief Legal Adviser, British Military Administration, Malaya, 1945-46; Solicitor-Gen., Colony of Singapore, 1946-48; Attorney-Gen., Uganda Protectorate, 1948-51. *Address:* PO Box N 7776, Nassau, Bahamas.

HENDERSON, Ian Dalton, ERD 1960 (1st clasp 1966, 2nd clasp 1972); FRCS; Consultant Surgeon, Tunbridge Wells District, 1956-82; *b* 4 Nov. 1918; *s* of Stewart Dalton Henderson and Grace Aird (*née* Masterson); *m* 1951, Rosa Hertz, MB, BS, MRCOG; two *d. Educ:* Fettes Coll., Edinburgh; Guy's Hosp., Univ. of London (MB, BS 1943). LMSSA 1943; FRCS 1949. Served War, RAMC, 1943-46: served India; Major, 1945-46. Lectr in Anatomy and

Surg. Registrar, Guy's Hosp., 1947-50; Sen. Surg. Registrar, Royal Postgrad. Med. Sch. of London, 1952-56. Hon. Surgeon to the Queen, 1971-73. Member: Kent AHA, 1973-; Société Internat. de Chirurgie, 1972-. FRSM 1947-. Served TA and AER, subseq. T&AVR, 1948-79; former Hon. Col and OC 308 Gen. Hosp., T&AVR. Silver Jubilee Medal, 1978. *Recreations:* archaeology, skiing, golf, photography. *Address:* 23 Calverley Park, Tunbridge Wells, Kent TN1 2SL. *T:* Tunbridge Wells 25471. *Clubs:* Ski of GB, Army Ski.

HENDERSON, James Ewart, MA, DSc; Scientific Adviser to British Aerospace, since 1978; Director, since 1977, Managing Director, since 1982, Mastiff Security Systems Ltd; *b* 29 May 1923; *s* of late Rev. James Ewart Henderson, MA, BD and Agnes Mary (*née* Crawford); *m* 1st, 1949, Alice Joan Hewlitt; one *d*; 2nd, 1966, Nancy Maude Dominy; two *s. Educ:* private sch.; Glasgow Univ.; Edinburgh Univ. Research on air rockets and guns, MAP, 1943-44; hon. commn in RAFVR, 1944-46; operational assessment of air attacks in Belgium, Holland and Germany, 2TAF, 1944-45; exper. research on fighter and bomber capability, and on the use of radar and radio aids: RAF APC Germany, 1945-46, Fighter Comd, 1946-49 and CFE, 1949-52; research on weapons effects and capability: Air Min., 1952-54, AWRE 1955, Air Min., 1955-58; Asst Scientific Adviser (Ops), Air Min., 1958-63; Dep. Chief Scientist (RAF), MoD, 1963-69; Chief Scientist (RAF) and Mem., Air Force Bd, 1969-73. Aviation Conslnt, Hawker Siddeley Aviation Ltd, 1973-77; Financial Conslnt, Charles Stapleton & Co. Ltd, 1973-78; freelance Operational Res. and Management Conslnt, 1975-78; Dir, Lewis Security Systems Ltd, 1976-77. Chm., Air League, 1981- (Mem. Council, 1979-80). MInstD 1978. *Publications:* technical papers on operational capability of aircraft and weapons; UK manual on Blast Effects of Nuclear Weapons. *Recreations:* flying (private pilot's licence), sailing, golf, opera, photography. *Address:* British Aerospace, Weybridge, Surrey KT13 0ST. *Clubs:* Naval and Military, Arts; Royal Scottish Automobile (Glasgow); Moor Park Golf; New Zealand Golf.

HENDERSON, (James Stewart) Barry; MP (C) East Fife, since 1979; management consultant, since 1975; *b* 29 April 1936; *s* of James Henderson, CBE and Jane Stewart McLaren; *m* 1961, Janet Helen Sprot Todd; two *s. Educ:* Lathallan Sch.; Stowe Sch. Mem. British Computer Soc. Nat. Service, 1954-56; electronics and computer industries, 1957-65; Scottish Conservative Central Office, 1966-70; computer industry, 1971-74; MP (C) East Dunbartonshire, Feb.-Sept. 1974. Vice-Chm., Scottish Cons. Back Bench Cttee, 1979-; Member: Select Cttee on Scottish Affairs, 1979-; H of C Chairmen's Panel, 1981-. *Address:* Old Gillingshill, by Anstruther, Fife.

HENDERSON, Sir James Thyne, KBE 1959; CMG 1952; *b* 18 Jan. 1901; *s* of late Sir Thomas Henderson; *m* 1930, Karen Margrethe Hansen; one *s* four *d. Educ:* Warriston, Moffat; Sedbergh Sch.; Queen's Coll., Oxford. Entered Diplomatic Service, 1925, apptd to FO; transf. to Tehran, 1927; Athens, 1929; Helsinki, 1932, where acted as Chargé d'Affaires in 1932, 1933, 1934 and 1935; Foreign Office, 1935. First Sec., 1936; attached to Representative of Finland at the Coronation of King George VI, 1937; Tokyo, 1938; Santiago, 1941; Foreign Office, 1944; Stockholm, 1946, Chargé d'Affaires there in 1946 and 1947; Counsellor, 1947; Consul-Gen., Houston, 1949; HM Minister to Iceland, 1953-56; HM Ambassador to Bolivia, 1956-60, retired. *Recreation:* gardening. *Address:* 4 Merchiston Crescent, Edinburgh EH10 5AN. *T:* 031-229 1185.

HENDERSON, Dame Joan; *see* Kelleher, Dame Joan.

HENDERSON, Prof. John Louis, MD, FRCPE; Professor of Child Health, University of Dundee, 1967-72, retired; *b* 25 March 1907; British; *m* 1st, 1938, Agnes Deneson McHarg, MB, ChB (*d* 1963); one *s* three *d*; 2nd, 1964, Helen Nea Carlisle Richards (*née* Attenborough). *Educ:* Leighton Park Sch., Reading; University of Edinburgh. Sen. Pres., Royal Medical Society, Edinburgh 1934-35; Lecturer, Dept of Child Health, University of Edinburgh, 1939-45; Rockefeller Travelling Fellow at Yale and Harvard, USA, 1946; Senior Lecturer, Dept of Child Health, University of Edinburgh, 1947-51; Physician, Royal Edinburgh Hosp. for Sick Children, 1948-51; Prof. of Child Health, University of St Andrews, 1951-67. Member: Scottish Health Services Council, 1953-62; GMC, 1966-; Chm. Standing Med. Adv. Cttee, Dept of Health for Scotland, 1956-62. *Publications:* Cerebral Palsy in Childhood and Adolescence, 1961; articles in medical journals. *Recreations:* golf, ornithology. *Address:* Wayside West, Castle Road, Longforgan, Dundee DD2 5HA.

HENDERSON, Sir (John) Nicholas, GCMG 1977 (KCMG 1972; CMG 1965); HM Diplomatic Service, retired; re-appointed, Ambassador to Washington, 1979-82; *b* 1 April 1919; *s* of Prof. Sir Hubert Henderson; *m* 1951, Mary Barber (*née* Cawadias); one *d. Educ:* Stowe Sch.; Hertford Coll., Oxford (Hon. Fellow 1975). Mem. HM Diplomatic Service. Served Minister of State's Office, Cairo, 1942-43; Asst Private Sec. to the Foreign Sec., 1944-47; HM Embassy, Washington, 1947-49; Athens, 1949-50; Permanent Under Secretary's Dept, FO, 1950-53; HM Embassy, Vienna, 1953-56; Santiago, 1956-59; Northern Dept, FO, 1959-62; Permanent Under Secretary's Dept, 1962-63; Head of Northern Dept, Foreign Office, 1963; Private Sec. to the Sec. of State for Foreign Affairs, 1963-65; Minister in Madrid, 1965-69; Ambassador to Poland, 1969-72, to Federal Republic of Germany, 1972-75, to France, 1975-79. *Publications:* Prince Eugen of Savoy (biography); various stories and articles in Penguin New Writing, Horizon, Apollo, Country Life and History Today. *Recreations:* tennis, gardening, dogs. *Address:* 31 Dorset

Square, NW1. *T:* 01-724 2598; School House, Combe, near Newbury, Berks. *T:* Inkpen 330. *Clubs:* Brooks's, Garrick, Beefsteak.
See also Viscount Moore.

HENDERSON, John Ronald, MBE 1945; Vice-Lord-Lieutenant of Berkshire, since 1979; *b* 6 May 1920; *s* of Major R. H. W. Henderson and Mrs Marjorie Henderson (*née* Garrard); *m* 1st, 1949, Sarah Katherine Beckwith-Smith (*d* 1972); two *s* one *d*; 2nd, 1976, Catherine Christien; one step *s* two step *d. Educ:* Eton; Cambridge Univ. Served War: ADC to Field Marshal Montgomery, 1942-46; retd Major, 12th Royal Lancers, 1946. Chm., Henderson Admin (Gp); Director: Barclays Bank, 1978-; Barclays International, 1972-. *Recreations:* racing, shooting, golf, tennis. *Address:* West Woodhay House, Newbury, Berks. *T:* Inkpen 271. *Club:* White's.

HENDERSON, John Stuart Wilmot; Director General of Ordnance Factories, Finance, Procurement and Administration, retired 1976; *b* 31 March 1919; *s* of Bruce Wilmot Henderson and Sarah (*née* Marchant); *m* 1941, Elsie Kathleen (*née* Rose) (*d* 1981); one *s* three *d. Educ:* Wade Deacon Grammar Sch., Widnes. Exec. Officer, Royal Ordnance Factories, 1938-39; served War of 1939-45: Royal Fusiliers, 1939-43; Intell. Corps, 1944-47; various appts in Ministries of Supply, Aviation, Technology and Defence, 1947-76. *Recreations:* gardening, enjoying music, bird watching, grandfathering six girls and six boys (so far). *Address:* Rowan, Dixter Lane, Northiam, Rye, East Sussex. *T:* Northiam 3210.

HENDERSON, Julia Juanita; Secretary-General, International Planned Parenthood Federation, 1971-78; *b* 15 Aug. 1915; *d* of Frank and Agnes Henderson. *Educ:* Univs of Illinois (BA, MA) and Minnesota (PhD); Harvard Grad. Sch. of Public Admin. Research Asst, SSRC, 1938-39; Techn. Adviser, Unemployment Compensation Div., Social Security Bd, 1939-42; Lectr in Polit. Science, Wellesley Coll., 1942-44; United Nations: Mem. Secretariat on Organization and Budget Preparatory Commn of UN, London, 1945-46; Chief of Policy Div., Bureau of Finance, 1946-50; Dir, Div. of Social Welfare, Dept of Social Affairs, 1951-54; Dir, Bureau of Social Affairs, Dept of Econ. and Social Affairs, 1955-67; Assoc. Comr and Dir for Techn. Co-operation, 1967-71; Consultant to UN Fund for Population Activities, 1978-82; Mem. Nat. Acad. of Public Admin. Hon. LLD, Smith Coll., 1967; Hon. LittD, Rider Coll., 1969; Hon. DHum, Silliman Univ., 1975; Rene Sand Award, Internat. Council of Social Welfare, 1972; Margaret Sanger Award, Planned Parenthood Fedn of America, 1978. *Recreations:* music, theatre, golf, tennis. *Address:* 1735 Forest Road, Venice, Fla 33595, USA. *T:* 813-488-3935. *Clubs:* United Oxford & Cambridge University; Cosmopolitan (NY).

HENDERSON, Kenneth David Druitt, CMG 1951; Secretary, Spalding Educational Trust and Union for the Study of Great Religions, since 1953; Vice-President, World Congress of Faiths, since 1966; *b* 4 Sept. 1903; *s* of late George Gilfillan Henderson, MA, MB, CM (Edinburgh); *m* 1935, Margery Grant, *d* of John Atkinson, Sydney, NSW; one *s* two *d. Educ:* Glenalmond; University Coll., Oxford. Entered Sudan Political Service, 1926; Dept Asst Civil Sec., 1938-44; Sec. to Governor-General's Council, 1939-44, to N Sudan Advisory Council, 1944; Principal Sch. of Administration and Police, Omdurman, 1944; Deputy-Governor, Kassala Province, Sudan, 1945; Asst Civil Sec., 1946-49; Governor, Darfur Province, Sudan, 1949-53. Officer, Order of the Nile, 1937. *Publications:* History of the Hamar Tribe, 1935; Survey of the Anglo-Egyptian Sudan, 1898-1944, 1945; The Making of The Modern Sudan, 1952; Sudan Republic, 1965; Account of the Parish of Langford, 1973; Younghusband Memorial Lecture (inaugural), 1976; Is Religion Necessary? (Farmington Paper), 1977; contribs to Chambers's Encyclopædia, Encyclopædia Britannica, and Encyclopædia Americana. *Address:* Orchard House, Steeple Langford, Salisbury, Wilts. *T:* Stapleford 388.

HENDERSON, Leslie Edwin, CBE 1982; Director of Contracts, Property Services Agency, since 1978; *b* 16 Dec. 1922; *s* of Thomas Edwin and Mabel Mary Henderson; *m* 1946, Marjorie (*née* Austin); two *s. Educ:* Ealing County Sch., London. Entered Civil Service (BoT) as Clerical Officer, 1939; Min. of Shipping, 1939; served in RAF, 1941-46; Min. of War Transport, 1946; subsequently in: Min. of Transport and Civil Aviation, MoT, DoE; Head of Contracts, Highways, Dept of Transport, 1968-78. *Recreations:* gardening, do-it-yourself. *Address:* 61 Greenacres Avenue, Ickenham, Mddx UB10 8HH. *T:* Ruislip 72536.

HENDERSON, Sir Neville (Vicars), Kt 1975; CBE 1967; Founder of firm of Henderson & Lahey, Solicitors, Brisbane, 1924; retired to become consultant, 1971; grazier and company director, Australia; *b* 21 March 1899; *s* of John Cunningham Henderson, grazier, late of Brougham, Toowong, Brisbane, formerly of Goulburn, NSW, etc, and Ann Janet Henderson, *d* of Capt. Lachlan Macalister, 48th Regt; *m* 1934, Jean Hamilton Brownhill, *d* of David James Brownhill, Sydney, NSW; one *s* two *d. Educ:* Southport Sch., Southport, Qld (Pres., Old Southportians Assoc., 1926); Univ. of Qld, Brisbane; Trinity Coll., Univ. of Melbourne, Vic. Final Hons Schol. in Law and Supreme Ct Prizeman (Melb.) 1922; BA, LLM (Melb.) 1922. Barrister and solicitor of Supreme Ct of Vic., 1923, and of High Ct of Aust., 1923; Solicitor of Supreme Ct of Qld, 1923; Notary Public, 1945. Mem. Council, Qld Law Assoc., 1926-27, Sec., 1926-28; collaborated in drafting the first Conveyancing Scale for use in Qld, 1925-26; assisted in drafting Act, 1927, and has taken part in Law Reform since that time; also Sec. Qld Law Soc. Incorp., 1928-54, and Clerk to Statutory Cttee of the Soc., 1928-31, also its delegate at Aust. Law Conf., Sydney (at which Law Council of Aust. was formed), 1932; Council, St John's Coll., Univ. of Qld, 1932-38; Sec., Law Council of Aust., 1939-40. Captain, AMF, 1932. Served War, 1940-44: Judge Advocate on various Courts Martial, 1940-43; Major, 1942, and apptd Dep. Asst Adj.-Gen., Northern Comd; assisted in organising course for rehabilitation of legal ex-Servicemen, and Hon. Lectr in Law of Life Ins., 1945. Sen. Partner, Henderson & Sons, Graziers, Mahrigong Station, Winton, Qld, 1950-79; Pres., Soc. of Notaries of Queensland, 1954-56; Founder and Governor, Henderson Foundn (educnl and charitable instn), 1957. Man. Editor for Annotated Reprint of Qld Statutes (20 vols), 1962. Hon. Consul for Austria, Qld, 1957; Dean of Consular Corps of Queensland, 1977. Dist. Service Order in gold of Republic of Austria, Kt Cross First Cl., 1964; Grand Decoration of Honour for services to the Republic of Austria, 1982. *Publications:* Estate Planning (Proc. of Second Commonwealth and Empire Law Conf., Ottawa, 1960), etc. *Address:* Glencraig, 63 Eldernell Avenue, Hamilton, Brisbane, Qld 4007, Australia. *T:* 268-3953. *Clubs:* Queensland, United Service, Journalists', Queensland Turf, Tattersalls (all in Brisbane); Australasian Pioneers' (Sydney).

HENDERSON, Sir Nicholas; *see* Henderson, Sir J. N.

HENDERSON, Admiral Sir Nigel Stuart, GBE 1968 (OBE 1944); KCB 1962 (CB 1959); DL; *b* 1 Aug. 1909; *s* of late Lt-Col Selby Herriott Henderson, IMS; *m* 1939, Catherine Mary Maitland; one *s* two *d*. *Educ:* Cheltenham Coll. Entered RN, 1927; served War of 1939-45 in HM Ships and as Fleet Gunnery Officer, Mediterranean; Comdr 1942; Capt. 1948; Naval Attaché, Rome, 1949-51; in comd HMS Protector, 1951; in comd RN Air Station, Bramcote, 1952; Imperial Defence Coll., 1954; in command HMS Kenya, 1955; Rear-Admiral, 1957; Vice-Naval Dep. to Supreme Allied Comdr, Europe, 1957-Dec. 1959; Vice-Adm. 1960; Dir-Gen. of Training, Admiralty, 1960-62; C-in-C Plymouth, 1962-65; Adm. 1963; Head of British Defence Staffs, Washington, and UK Rep., Mil. Cttee, NATO, 1965-68; Chm., Mil. Cttee, NATO, 1968-71; retired 1971. Rear-Admiral of the United Kingdom, 1973-76; Vice-Admiral of the United Kingdom, and Lieutenant of the Admiralty, 1976-79. Pres., Royal British Legion, Scotland, 1974-80. DL Stewartry of Kirkcudbright, 1973. *Address:* Hensol, Mossdale, Castle Douglas, Kirkcudbrightshire. *T:* Laurieston 207.

HENDERSON, (Patrick) David; Professor of Political Economy, University College, London, since 1975; *b* 10 April 1927; *s* of late David Thomson Henderson and late Eleanor Henderson; *m* 1960, Marcella Kodicek; one *s* one *d*. *Educ:* Ellesmere Coll., Shropshire; Corpus Christi Coll., Oxford. Fellow and Tutor in Economics, Lincoln Coll., Oxford, 1948-65; Univ. Lectr in Economics, Oxford, 1950-65; Commonwealth Fund Fellow (Harvard), 1952-53; Junior Proctor, Oxford Univ., 1955-56; Economic Adviser, HM Treasury, 1957-58; Chief Economist, Min. of Aviation, 1965-67; Adviser Harvard Development Advisory Service (Athens and Kuala Lumpur), 1967-68; Vis. Lectr, World Bank, 1968-69; Economist, World Bank, 1969-75, Dir of Economics Dept 1971-72. Mem., Commn on Environmental Pollution, 1977-80; Special Adviser, Sec. of State for Wales, 1978-79; Member: Nat. Ports Council, 1979-81; Bd, Commonwealth Develt Corp., 1980-. *Publications:* India: the energy sector, 1975; (jointly) Nyasaland: The Economics of Federation, 1960; ed and contrib.: Economic Growth in Britain, 1965; contrib: The British Economy in the 1950's, 1962; Public Enterprise, 1968; Public Economics, 1969; Unfashionable Economics, 1970; The World Bank, Multilateral Aid and the 1970's, 1973; The Economic Development of Yugoslavia, 1975; articles in economic and other jls. *Address:* 3 Christchurch Hill, NW3. *T:* 01-435 5866.

HENDERSON, Peter, CB 1965; MD; Senior Principal Medical Officer, Ministry of Education, 1964-69; *b* 16 March 1904; *e s* of Peter and Margaret Henderson, Inverness; *m* 1933, Beatrice Chrissie Pashley, Bridlington, Yorks; no *c*. *Educ:* High Sch. and Royal Academy, Inverness; Aberdeen Univ. MB 1929; MD 1931; DPH London, 1932. Resident MO, Bradford City Sanatorium, 1929-30; House Physician, St Luke's Hospital, Bradford, 1930-31; Resident MO, Inst. of Ray Therapy, London, 1931-32; Asst MO, Somerset CC, 1933-35; Asst MO, St Helens, 1935-36; Dep. MOH, Leyton, 1936-39; MOH, Todmorden, 1939-40; MO, Min. of Educn, 1940-51, PMO, 1951-64. Consultant, WHO. Milroy Lectr, 1968. QHP 1962. *Publications:* various papers on the health and disabilities of children in BMJ, Lancet and Practitioner; contribs to The Theory and Practice of Public Health (ed W. Hobson), 1961, 5th edn 1979; chapter in The Humanist Outlook (ed A. J. Ayer), 1968; Disability in Childhood and Youth, 1974. *Recreation:* gardening. *Address:* Lythe Ghyll, Merrowcroft, Guildford, Surrey. *T:* Guildford 75353.

HENDERSON, Sir Peter (Gordon), KCB 1975; Clerk of the Parliaments since 1974; *b* 16 Sept. 1922; *m* 1950, Susan Mary Dartford; two *s* two *d*. *Educ:* Stowe Sch.; Magdalen Coll., Oxford (Demy). Served War, Scots Guards, 1942-44. Clerk, House of Lords, 1954-60; seconded to HM Treasury as Sec. to Leader and Chief Whip, House of Lords, 1960-63; Reading Clerk and Clerk of Public Bills, 1964-74; Clerk Asst, 1974. Mem., Cttee on Preparation of Legislation, 1973-74. *Address:* 16 Pelham Street, SW7 2NG; Helbeck Cottage, Brough, Kirkby Stephen, Cumbria CA17 4DD. *Clubs:* Boodle's, Pratt's.

HENDERSON, Robert Alistair; Chairman: Kleinwort, Benson, Lonsdale plc, since 1978; Kleinwort, Benson Ltd, 1975-May 1983; President, Klescan

Investments Ltd, since 1971; Chairman: Kleinwort, Benson Inc., since 1971; Kleinwort, Benson (Trustees) Ltd, since 1975; Cross Investment Trust Ltd, since 1969; Director: Cadbury Schweppes PLC; Fuji International Finance Ltd; Hamilton Brothers Oil and Gas Ltd; Hamilton Oil (Great Britain) PLC (formerly Hamilton Brothers Oil Co. (Great Britain) Ltd); Inchcape PLC; Kleinwort Benson Investment Management Ltd; Kleinwort, Benson Investment Trust Ltd; Sharps, Pixley Ltd; *b* 4 Nov. 1917; *s* of Robert Evelyn Henderson and Beatrice Janet Elsie Henderson; *m* 1947, Bridget Elizabeth, *d* of late Col J. G. Lowther, CBE, DSO, MC, TD, and Hon. Lilah White, *er d* of 3rd Baron Annaly; two *s* one *d*. *Educ:* Eton; Magdalene Coll., Cambridge. Hons degree in History. Served War: 60th Rifles, 1940-45, Captain. Jessel Toynbee & Co. Ltd, 1945-48; Borneo Co. Ltd, 1948-51; Robert Benson, Lonsdale & Co. Ltd, 1951 (Dir, 1957); Dir, Kleinwort, Benson Ltd, 1961 (on merger of Robert Benson, Lonsdale & Co. Ltd with Kleinwort Sons & Co.; Vice-Chm., 1970-71, Dep. Chm., 1971-75). Dir, Equitable Life Assurance Soc., 1958-81. Mem., BAB, 1981-. *Recreations:* gardening, shooting. *Address:* North Ecchinswell Farm, Ecchinswell, near Newbury, Berks RG15 8UJ. *T:* Headley 244. *Club:* Brooks's.

HENDERSON, Robert Brumwell, CBE 1979; Deputy Chairman, since 1977, and Managing Director, since 1959, Ulster Television; *b* 28 July 1929; *s* of late Comdr Oscar Henderson, CVO, CBE, DSO, RN, and of Mrs Henderson; *m*; two *d*; *m* 1970, Patricia Ann Davison. *Educ:* Brackenber House Sch., Belfast; Bradfield Coll., Berks; Trinity Coll., Dublin. BA (Hons) 1951, MA 1959. Journalism: London, Liverpool, Glasgow and Belfast, 1951-59. Director: ITN, 1964-68; Independent Television Publications, 1968-; North-South Trading Ltd; Dep. Chm., North West Oil and Gas. Chm., Publicity Assoc. of NI, 1959-60; President: Radio Industries Club of NI, 1963-70, 1972-; NI Chamber of Commerce and Industry, 1980-81; Member: Exec. Council, Cinema and Television Benevolent Fund, 1980- (Chm. of NI Cttee, 1961-); Council for Continuing Educn, 1975-; NI Council for Educnl Develt, 1980-; Cttee to Review Higher Educn in NI, 1964; various cttees of Trinity Coll. Dublin, New Univ. of Ulster, and Queen's Univ. of Belfast; Council, Inst. of Dirs, 1981- (Chm., NI Br., 1973-79); Governor, N Ire. Polytechnic, 1979-. Fellow, Royal Television Soc., 1977 (Mem. Council, 1981-, Chm., 1982-). Hon. DLitt Ulster, 1982. *Publications:* Midnight Oil, 1961; A Television First, 1977. *Recreations:* reading, theatre and cinema, golf. *Address:* Ulster Television, Havelock House, Ormeau Road, Belfast BT7 1EB; 5 Dorchester Park, Belfast BT9 6RH. *Clubs:* Naval and Military; Royal County Down Golf; Moyola Country; Malone Golf.

HENDERSON, Roger Anthony, QC 1980; barrister; *b* 21 April 1943; *s* of Dr Peter Wallace Henderson and Dr Stella Dolores Henderson; *m* 1968; three *d* (and one *d* decd). *Educ:* Radley Coll.; St Catharine's Coll., Cambridge (Scholar; 1st Cl. Hons degree in Law, MA; Adderley Prize for Law, 1964). Inner Temple: Duke of Edinburgh Award, 1962; Major Scholarship, 1964; called to the Bar, 1964; Pupil Studentship, 1965. Mem. Exec. Council, British Acad. of Forensic Sciences, 1977-. *Recreations:* gardening, fishing, shooting. *Address:* 2 Harcourt Buildings, Temple, EC4Y 9DB. *T:* 01-583 9020; 9 Brunswick Gardens, W8.

HENDERSON, Roy (Galbraith), CBE 1970; FRAM; retired baritone; Teacher of Singing (private); Professor of Singing, RAM, London, 1940-74; *b* Edinburgh, 4 July 1899; *er s* of late Rev. Dr Alex. Roy Henderson, formerly Principal of Paton Coll., Nottingham; *m* 1926, Bertha Collin Smyth; one *s* two *d*. *Educ:* Nottingham High Sch.; Royal Academy of Music, London (Worshipful Company of Musicians Medal). Debut as baritone singer, Queen's Hall, London, 1925; has sung at all leading Festivals in England. Internat. Festival for contemporary music, Amsterdam, 1933; recitals at first two Edinburgh Festivals, 1947 and 1948; principal parts in all Glyndebourne Opera festivals, 1934-40, associated chiefly with works of Delius, Elgar and Vaughan Williams, and sang many first performances of contemp. music. Retired from concert platform, 1951, to devote his whole time to teaching (among his pupils was late Kathleen Ferrier). Conductor, Huddersfield Glee and Madrigal Soc., 1932-39; Founder and Conductor, Nottingham Oriana Choir, 1937-52. Conductor of Bournemouth Municipal Choir, 1942-53. Adjudicator at International Concours, Geneva, 1952, and Triennially, 1956-65. Mem. of the Jury of the International Muziekstad s'Hertogenbosch, Holland, 1955-62, 1965, and Barcelona, 1965. Master classes in singing: Royal Conservatory of Music, Toronto, 1956; Toonkunst Conservatorium, Rotterdam, 1957, 1958; s'Hertogenbosch, 1967. Awarded the Sir Charles Santley memorial by Worshipful Company of Musicians for distinguished services to the art of singing, 1958. *Publications:* contributed to: Kathleen Ferrier, ed Neville Cardus, 1954; Opera Annual, 1958. *Recreations:* fishing, gardening and cricket. *Address:* The Cottage, 3 Eton Avenue, Hampstead, NW3 3EL. *T:* 01-794 2374.

HENDERSON, Rupert Albert Geary; Chairman: Australian Newsprint Mills Ltd, 1960-78; Trustees of Reuters Ltd, 1961-78 (Trustee, 1952-78, Director, 1946-51); Amalgamated Television Services Pty Ltd, 1958-74; *b* 26 Feb. 1896; *s* of late Robert Geary Henderson and Isabel Henderson; *m* 1st, 1914, Helene, *d* of Thomas Mason; one *s*; 2nd, 1939, Hazel, *d* of Herbert Harris; one *d*. *Educ:* Glebe Public Sch., Sydney. Literary staff, The Sydney Morning Herald, 1915; London rep., 1923-26; Advertising Manager, Sydney Mail, 1927; Circulation Manager, Sydney Morning Herald, 1928; Sec. to Gen. Manager, 1934; Gen. Manager, 1938; Chm., Australian Associated Press Pty Ltd, 1940-49; Managing Director: John Fairfax & Sons Pty Ltd, 1949-56; John Fairfax Ltd, 1956-64 (Dir 1964-78); Associated Newspapers Ltd, 1954-64;

Pres. Australian Newspaper Proprietors' Association, 1942-47 and 1951-58; Director, Australian Assoc. Press Pty Ltd. *Recreation:* grazier. *Address:* John Fairfax Ltd, 23 Hamilton Street, Sydney, NSW 2000, Australia. *TA:* Herald, Sydney. *T:* 20944. *Clubs:* Union, Royal Prince Alfred Yacht (Sydney).

HENDERSON, William Crichton; Advocate; Sheriff of Tayside, Central and Fife (formerly Stirling, Dunbarton and Clackmannan) at Stirling, since 1972 (also at Alloa, 1972-81); *b* 10 June 1931; *s* of late William Henderson, headmaster, and late Helen Philp Henderson (*née* Crichton); *m* 1962, Norma Sheila Hope Henderson (*née* Grant); two *d. Educ:* George Watson's Boys' Coll., Edinburgh; Edinburgh Univ. MA Edinburgh 1952, LLB Edinburgh 1954. Admitted Solicitor, 1954; Diploma in Administrative Law and Practice, Edinburgh, 1955; called to Scottish Bar, 1957; practised as Advocate, 1957-68; Sheriff of Renfrew and Argyll at Paisley, 1968-72. Chm., Supreme Court Legal Aid Cttee, 1967-68. *Recreations:* gardening, travel. *Address:* Woodcot, Dollar, Clackmannanshire. *T:* Dollar 2528. *Club:* New (Edinburgh).

HENDERSON, Sir William (MacGregor), Kt 1976; FRS 1976; FRSE 1977; Secretary, Agricultural Research Council, 1972-78; Member Science Council, Celltech Ltd, since 1980; *b* 17 July 1913; *s* of late William Simpson Henderson and late Catherine Alice Marcus Berry; *m* 1941, Alys Beryl Goodridge; four *s. Educ:* George Watson's Coll., Edinburgh; Royal (Dick) Veterinary Coll., Edinburgh (MRCVS); Univ. of Edinburgh (BSc, DSc). Assistant, Dept of Medicine, Royal (Dick) Veterinary Coll., Edinburgh, 1936-38; Member Scientific Staff, Animal Virus Research Inst., Pirbright, 1939-56, Dep. Dir, 1955-56; Director, Pan American Foot-and-Mouth Disease Center, Rio de Janeiro, 1957-65; Head, Dept of Microbiology, ARC Inst. for Research on Animal Diseases, Compton, 1966-67, Director, 1967-72; Visiting Prof., Univ. of Reading, 1970-72. Chm., Genetic Manipulation Adv. Gp, 1979-81. Corresp. Member: Argentine Assoc. of Microbiology, 1959; Argentine Soc. of Veterinary Medicine, 1965; Foreign Mem., Argentine National Acad. of Agronomy and Veterinary Science, 1980; Hon. Mem. Brasilian Soc. of Veterinary Medicine, 1965; FRCVS, by election, 1973; Hon. Fellow, RASE, 1979. Hon. DVMS Edinburgh, 1974; Hon. DVSc Liverpool, 1977; FIBiol. Orden de Mayo, Argentina, 1962. Dalrymple-Champneys Award, 1974; Massey-Ferguson National Award, 1980; Underwood-Prescott Award, 1981. *Publications:* Quantitative Study of Foot-and-Mouth Disease Virus, 1949; Man's Use of Animals, 1981; British Agricultural Research and the Agricultural Research Council, 1981; contribs to scientific jls principally on foot-and-mouth disease. *Recreation:* gardening. *Address:* Yarnton Cottage, Streatley, Berks. *Clubs:* Athenæum; New (Edinburgh).

HENDERSON-STEWART, Sir David (James), 2nd Bt *cr* 1957; *b* 3 July 1941; *s* of Sir James Henderson-Stewart, 1st Bt, MP, and of Anna Margaret (*née* Greenwell); *S* father, 1961; *m* 1972, Anne, *d* of Count Serge de Pahlen; three *s. Educ:* Eton Coll.; Trinity Coll., Oxford. *Heir: s* David Henderson-Stewart, *b* 2 Feb. 1973. *Address:* 3 Chepstow Crescent, W11 3EA. *T:* 01-221 6255. *Club:* Travellers'.

HENDRIE, Prof. Gerald Mills; Professor of Music, The Open University, since 1969; Director of Studies in Music, St John's College, Cambridge, since 1981 (Supervisor, 1977-81); *b* 28 Oct. 1935; *s* of James Harold Hendrie and Florence Mary MacPherson; *m* 1962, Marion Florence Barsham; two *s. Educ:* Framlingham Coll., Suffolk; Royal Coll. of Music; Selwyn Coll., Cambridge (MA, MusB, PhD). FRCO, ARCM. Director of Music, Homerton Coll., Cambridge, 1962-63; Lectr in the History of Music, Univ. of Manchester, 1963-67; Prof. and Chm., Dept of Music, Univ. of Victoria, BC, Canada, 1967-69; Reader in Music, subseq. Prof., The Open Univ., 1969-. FRSA. *Publications:* Musica Britannica XX, Orlando Gibbons: Keyboard Music, 1962 (2nd rev. edn, 1967); The Chandos and Related Anthems of George Frideric Handel (4 vols and critical commentary for the Halle Handel Society's complete edn of Handel's works, in press since 1972); (with Dinah Barsham) Iolanthe (critical edn in full score, in press 1982); articles for Die Musik in Geschichte und Gegenwart; various others including musical compositions, recordings for TV, radio and disc. *Address:* The Open University, Walton Hall, Milton Keynes, Bucks MK7 6AA. *T:* Milton Keynes 653280.

HENDRY, Prof. Arnold William; Professor of Civil Engineering, University of Edinburgh, since 1964; *b* 10 Sept. 1921; *s* of late Dr George Hendry, MB, ChB, Buckie, Scotland; *m* 1st, 1946, Sheila Mary Cameron Roberts (*d* 1966), Glasgow; one *s* one *d* (and one *s* decd); 2nd, 1968, Elizabeth Lois Alice Inglis, Edinburgh. *Educ:* Buckie High Sch.; Aberdeen Univ. Civil engineer with Sir William Arrol & Co. Ltd, Bridge builders and Engineers, Glasgow, 1941-43; Asst in Engineering, University of Aberdeen, 1943-46; Lecturer in Civil Engineering, 1946-49; Reader in Civil Engineering, Univ. of London, King's Coll., 1949-51; Prof. of Civil Engrg and Dean of Fac. of Engrg, Univ. of Khartoum, 1951-57; Prof. of Building Science, University of Liverpool, 1957-63. *Publications:* An Introduction to Photo-Elastic Analysis, 1948; (with L. G. Jaeger) The Analysis of Grid Frameworks, 1958; The Elements of Experimental Stress Analysis, 1964, 2nd edn 1977; Structural Brickwork, 1981; An Introduction to the Design of Load Bearing Brickwork, 1981; about 100 papers and articles in professional and technical jls. *Address:* Department of Civil Engineering, University of Edinburgh EH9 3JL.

HENDRY, Prof. David Forbes, PhD; Professor of Economics, University of Oxford, since 1982; Fellow, Nuffield College, Oxford, since 1982; *b* 6 March 1944; *s* of Robert Ernest Hendry and Catherine Helen (*née* Mackenzie); *m* 1966, Evelyn Rosemary (*née* Vass); one *d. Educ:* Aberdeen Univ. (MA 1st

Cl. Hons); LSE (MSc Distinction, PhD). Fellow, Econometric Soc., 1976. Lectr, LSE, 1969, Reader, 1973, Prof. of Econometrics, 1977. Vis. Professor: Yale Univ., 1970; Univ. of Calif, Berkeley, 1976; Catholic Univ. of Louvain, 1980; Univ. of Calif, San Diego, 1981. Editor: Rev. of Econ. Studies, 1971-75; Econ. Jl, 1976-80. *Publications:* papers in econometrics and economics jls. *Recreations:* squash, cricket. *Address:* Nuffield College, Oxford OX1 1NF; 26 Northmoor Road, Oxford.

HENHAM, John Alfred; Stipendiary Magistrate for South Yorkshire, since 1975; a Recorder of the Crown Court, since 1979; *b* 8 Sept. 1924; *s* of Alfred and Daisy Henham; *m* 1946, Suzanne Jeanne Octavie Ghislaine Pinchart (*d* 1972); two *s. Address:* Court House, Sheffield S3 8LW. *T:* Sheffield 78535, ext. 250.

HENIG, Stanley; Head of School of Social Studies, Preston Polytechnic, since 1976; *b* 7 July 1939; *s* of Sir Mark Henig and Grace (*née* Cohen); *m* 1966, Ruth Beatrice Munzer; two *s. Educ:* Wyggeston Grammar Sch.; Corpus Christi Coll., Oxford. BA 1st Cl. Hons, 1961; MA 1965 Oxon. Teaching Asst, Dept of Politics, Univ. of Minnesota, 1961; Research Student, Nuffield Coll., 1962; Lecturer in Politics, Lancaster Univ., 1964-66. MP (Lab) Lancaster, 1966-70; Lectr in Politics, Warwick Univ., 1970-71; Lectr, Civil Service Coll., 1972-75. Governor, British Inst. of Recorded Sound, 1975-. Asst Editor, Jl of Common Market Studies, 1964-72, Editor, 1973-76. *Publications:* (ed) European Political Parties, 1969; External Relations of the European Community, 1971; (ed) Political Parties in the European Community, 1979; Power and Decision in Europe, 1980. *Recreation:* collector of old gramophone records. *Address:* 10 Yealand Drive, Lancaster LA1 4EW. *T:* 69624.

HENLEY, 8th Baron (Ire.), *cr* 1799; **Oliver Michael Robert Eden;** Baron Northington (UK) 1885; *b* 22 Nov. 1953; *er s* of 7th Baron Henley and of Nancy Mary, *d* of Stanley Walton, Gilsland, Cumbria; *S* father, 1977. *Educ:* Clifton; Durham Univ. (BA 1975). Called to the Bar, Middle Temple, 1977. Pres., Cumbria Assoc. of Local Councils, 1981-. *Heir: b* Hon. Andrew Francis Eden, *b* 4 Sept. 1955. *Address:* Scaleby Castle, Carlisle, Cumbria CA6 4LN. *Club:* Brooks's.

HENLEY, Sir Douglas (Owen), KCB 1973 (CB 1970); Comptroller and Auditor General, 1976-81; Advisor to Deloitte, Haskins and Sells, since 1982; *b* 5 April 1919; *m* 1942, June Muriel Ibbetson; four *d. Educ:* Beckenham County Sch.; London Sch. of Economics (Hon. Fellow, 1974). BSc (Econ.), 1939; Gerstenberg Studentship and Leverhulme Res. Studentship (not taken up). Served Army, 1939-46; Queen's Own Royal West Kent Regt and HQ 12th Inf. Bde (despatches twice, 1945). Treasury, 1946; Treas. rep. (Financial Counsellor) in Tokyo and Singapore, 1956-59; Asst Under-Sec. of State, DEA, 1964-69, Dep. Under-Sec. of State, 1969; Second Permanent Sec., HM Treasury, 1972-76. Mem. Council, GPDST, 1982-. Hon. LLD Bath, 1981. *Address:* Walwood House, Park Road, Banstead, Surrey. *T:* Burgh Heath 52626.

HENLEY, Rear-Adm. Sir Joseph (Charles Cameron), KCVO 1963; CB 1962; *b* 24 April 1909; *e s* of Vice-Adm. J. C. W. Henley, CB; *m* 1934, Daphne Ruth (marr. diss. 1965), *d* of late A. A. H. Wykeham, of Pitt Place, Brighstone, IW; one *s* three *d; m* 1966, Patricia Sharp, MBE 1952, *d* of late Roy Eastman, Alberta, Canada. *Educ:* Sherborne. Joined Royal Navy, 1927. Served War of 1939-45, in HMS Birmingham and King George V. Capt., 1951, in command HMS Defender, 1954-55; Naval Attaché; Washington (as Commodore), 1956-57; Dir, Royal Naval Staff Coll., 1958; Chief of Staff, Mediterranean Station, 1959-61, as Commodore; Rear-Adm. 1960; Flag Officer, Royal Yachts and Extra Naval Equerry to the Queen, 1962-65; retd 1965. *Address:* 11a Hopewood Gardens, Darling Point, Sydney, NSW 2027, Australia. *T:* 321068. *Clubs:* Royal Yacht Squadron; Royal Sydney Golf.

HENMAN, Philip Sydney, DL; Founder of Transport Development Group Ltd; FCIT. DUniv Surrey, 1974. Farmer. High Sheriff, Surrey, 1971-72; DL Surrey, 1979. *Address:* 6 Lowburys, Ridgeway Road, Dorking, Surrey. *T:* Dorking 882310.

HENN, Charles Herbert; Assistant Under Secretary of State, Ministry of Defence, since 1979; *b* 11 July 1931; *s* of Herbert George Henn and Ellen Anne Henn; *m* 1955, Ann Turner; one *s* one *d. Educ:* King's Coll. Sch., Wimbledon; Queen's Coll., Oxford (BA). National Service, REME, 1952-54 (2/Lieut). Scientific Officer, WO, 1954; Sen. Scientific Officer, 1957; Principal, 1964; Private Sec. to Minister of State for Defence, 1969; Asst Sec., 1972. *Recreations:* walking, running, listening to music. *Address:* 23 Breamwater Gardens, Ham, Richmond, Surrey TW10 7SF. *T:* 01-940 9449.

HENNELL, Rev. Canon Michael Murray; Residentiary Canon, Manchester Cathedral, since 1970; *b* 11 Sept. 1918; *s* of Charles Murray and Jessie Hennell; *m* 1950, Peggy Glendinning; four *s. Educ:* Bishops Stortford Coll. (Prep.); Royal Masonic Sch.; St Edmund Hall and Wycliffe Hall, Oxford. MA Oxon and, by incorporation, MA Cantab. Asst Curate: St Stephen's With St Bartholomew's, Islington, N1, 1942-44; All Saints, Queensbury, Middx, 1944-48; Tutor, Ridley Hall, Cambridge, 1948-51. St Aidan's Coll., Birkenhead: Sen. Tutor, 1951; Vice-Principal, 1952-59; Principal, 1959-63; Principal, Ridley Hall, Cambridge, 1964-70. Examining Chaplain to the Bishops of Derby and Manchester (Chelmsford, 1964-70; Liverpool, 1964-75). Commissary to the Bishop on the Niger, 1975-. *Publications:* John Venn and the Clapham Sect, 1958; ed and contrib., Charles Simeon, 1759-1836, 1959; contrib., The Anglican Synthesis, 1964; Popular Belief and Practice, 1972; Sons of the Prophets, 1979. *Address:* 21 Morville Road, Chorlton-cum-Hardy, Manchester M21 1UG.

HENNESSEY, Robert Samuel Fleming, CMG 1954; Assistant Research Director, Wellcome Foundation, 1967-70, retired; *b* 8 May 1905; *s* of late W. R. H. Hennessey and late Elizabeth Fleming; *m* 1930, Grace Alberta Coote (*d* 1980); one *s* one d. *Educ:* St Andrew's Coll., Dublin; Dublin and London Universities. MD, FRCPI, DipBact, DTM&H. Pathologist, Uganda, 1929; Dep. Director (Laboratories), Palestine, 1944; Dep. Director, Medical Services, Palestine, 1946; Asst Medical Adviser, Colonial Office, 1947; Director of Medical Services, Uganda, 1949-55; Head of the Wellcome Laboratories of Tropical Medicine, London, 1956-58; Head of Therapeutic Research Division, Wellcome Foundation, 1958-66. *Publications:* papers on pathology in scientific jls. *Recreations:* golf, music, literature. *Address:* 51 Stone Park Avenue, Beckenham, Kent. *T:* 01-650 5336.

HENNESSY, family name of Baron Windlesham.

HENNESSY, Christopher; journalist; Chairman, Associated Catholic Newspapers (1912) Ltd, 1970-79; Trustee, The Universe, since 1979 (Editor, 1954-72); *b* 29 Dec. 1909; *e s* of Daniel and Anne Hennessy; *m* 1942, Kathleen Margaret Cadley, Liverpool. *Educ:* St Edward's Coll., Liverpool. Served War of 1939-45 as Commissioned Officer in British and Indian Armies; commanded a Territorial Army Unit in the North-West, 1950-55. KCSG 1975. *Recreation:* travel. *Address:* Beech House, Montreal Road, Riverhead, Sevenoaks, Kent TN13 2EP. *T:* Sevenoaks 454117.

HENNESSY, Denis William, OBE 1967; HM Diplomatic Service, retired; *b* 5 Dec. 1912; *s* of Daniel Hennessy and Rosina Gertrude Hennessy (*née* Griffiths); *m* 1937, Lorna McDonald Lappin; three *s* one d. *Educ:* private sch. Joined Foreign Office, 1930; served in the Foreign Office and in Prague, Washington, New York, Zürich, Bremen, Miami, Düsseldorf, Accra, and as Consul-Gen., Hanover; Counsellor, Bonn, 1969-72. *Address:* 6 Springside Avenue, Mount Pleasant, Western Australia 6153. *Club:* Travellers'.

HENNESSY, Sir James (Patrick Ivan), KBE 1982 (OBE 1968; MBE 1959); CMG 1975; HM Diplomatic Service; Chief Inspector of Prisons for England and Wales, since 1982; *b* 26 Sept. 1923; *s* of late Richard George Hennessy, DSO, MC; *m* 1947, Patricia, *o d* of late Wing Comdr F. H. Unwin, OBE; five *d* (one *s* decd). *Educ:* Bedford Sch.; Sidney Sussex Coll., Cambridge; LSE. Served RA, 1942-46. Apptd to HM Overseas Service, Basutoland, District Officer, 1948; Judicial Comr, 1953; Dist Comr, 1954-56; Jt Sec., Constitutional Commn, 1957-59; Supervisor of Elections, 1959; Sec. to Exec. Council, 1960; seconded to Office of High Comr, Cape Town/Pretoria, 1961-63; Perm. Sec., 1964; MLC, 1965; Sec. for External Affairs, Defence and Internal Security, 1967; Prime Minister's Office, and Head of Civil Service, 1968. Retired, later apptd to HM Diplomatic Service; FO, 1968-70; Montevideo, 1970; (Chargé d'Affaires 1971-72); Acting, later High Comr to Uganda and Ambassador (non-resident), Rwanda, 1973-76; Consul-Gen., Cape Town, 1977-80; Governor and C-in-C, Belize, 1980-81. *Address:* c/o Prisons Inspectorate, Home Office, 50 Queen Anne's Gate, SW1H 9AT. *Clubs:* Naval and Military, Royal Commonwealth Society.

HENNESSY, Sir John Wyndham P.; see Pope-Hennessy.

HENNIKER, 8th Baron *cr* 1800; **John Patrick Edward Chandos Henniker-Major,** KCMG 1965 (CMG 1956); CVO 1960; MC 1945; Bt 1765; Baron Hartismere (UK) 1866; Director, Wates Foundation, 1972-78; *b* 19 Feb. 1916; *s* of 7th Baron Henniker, and Molly (*d* 1953), *d* of Sir Robert Burnet, KCVO; *S* father, 1980; *m* 1946, Margaret Osla Benning (*d* 1974); two *s* one *d* ; *m* 1976, Julia Marshall Poland (*née* Mason). *Educ:* Stowe; Trinity Coll., Cambridge. HM Foreign Service, 1938; served 1940-45, Army (Major, The Rifle Brigade). HM Embassy Belgrade, 1945-46; Asst Private Secretary to Secretary of State for Foreign Affairs, 1946-48; Foreign Office, 1948-50; HM Embassy, Buenos Aires, 1950-52; Foreign Office, 1952-60 (Counsellor and Head of Personnel Dept, 1953); HM Ambassador to Jordan, 1960-62; to Denmark, 1962-66; Civil Service Commission, 1966-67; Asst Under-Secretary of State, FO, 1967-68. Dir-Gen., British Council, 1968-72. Lay Mem., Mental Health Review Tribunal (Broadmoor), 1975-81; Member: Parole Bd, 1979-; Council and Finance Bd, Univ. of E Anglia, Norwich, 1979-; Council, Toynbee Hall, 1978-, Dep. Chm., 1982. Trustee: City Parochial Foundn, 1973; London Festival Ballet, 1975. *Recreations:* gardening, bridge, ornithology. *Heir: s* Hon. Mark Ian Philip Chandos Henniker-Major [*b* 29 Sept. 1947; *m* 1973, Mrs Lesley Antoinette Masterton-Smith, *d* of Wing Comdr G. W. Foskett; three *d*]. *Address:* Red House, Thornham Magna, Eye, Suffolk. *Clubs:* Boodle's, Special Forces.

HENNIKER, Brig. Sir Mark Chandos Auberon, 8th Bt, *cr* 1813; CBE 1953 (OBE 1944); DSO 1944; MC 1933; DL; retired, 1958; *b* 23 Jan. 1906; *s* of late F. C. Henniker, ICS, and of Ada Russell (*née* Howell); *S* cousin (Lieut-Col Sir Robert Henniker, 7th Bt, MC) 1958; *m* 1945, Kathleen Denys (*née* Anderson); one *s* one d. *Educ:* Marlborough Coll.; Royal Military Academy, Woolwich; King's Coll., Cambridge. Royal Engineers, 1926; served India, 1928-34 (MC); Aldershot, 1937-39; BEF, 1939-40; North Africa, 1943; Sicily, 1943 (wounded); Italy, 1943 (OBE); NW Europe, 1944-45 (immediate award of DSO, Oct. 1944); India, 1946-47; Malaya, 1952-55

(CBE); Port Said, 1956 (despatches). Hon. Col, Parachute Engineer Regt (TA), 1959-68; Hon. Col, REME (TA), 1964-68. DL Gwent (formerly County of Mon), 1963. *Publications:* Memoirs of a Junior Officer, 1951; Red Shadow over Malaya, 1955; Life in the Army Today, 1957. *Recreations:* appropriate to age and rank. *Heir: s* Adrian Chandos Henniker [*b* 18 Oct. 1946; *m* 1971, Ann, *d* of Stuart Britton; twin *d*]. *Address:* c/o Lloyds Bank Ltd, Cox's & King's Branch, 6 Pall Mall, SW1. *Club:* Athenæum.

HENNIKER-GOTLEY, Roger Alwyn, MA Oxon; Headmaster of Sebright School, 1938-63, retired; *b* 8 Feb. 1898; 3rd *s* of late Rev. George Henniker-Gotley and late Louisa Sarah Lefroy; *m* 1931, Helen Hope Campbell, *d* of late Rev. Gerald Campbell Dicker; two s. *Educ:* Cheltenham Coll.; Brasenose Coll., Oxford. Served European War, 1914-18, Lancashire Fusiliers. Asst Master and Housemaster, Stamford School, 1924-25; Asst Master and Housemaster, Worksop Coll., 1925-27; Asst Master and Senior English Master, Cranleigh Sch., 1927-38. *Recreations:* cricket, ornithology, gardening. *Address:* Little Orchard, Codford St Mary, Warminster, Wiltshire. *T:* Codford St Mary 239.

HENNIKER HEATON, Sir Yvo Robert; see Heaton.

HENNIKER-MAJOR, family name of Baron Henniker.

HENNING, Prof. Basil Duke, PhD; Editor, History of Parliament (1660-90 section), since 1962; *b* 16 April 1910; *s* of late Samuel C. Henning and Julia, *d* of Gen. Basil Duke, CSA; *m* 1939, Alison Peake; two *s* one d. *Educ:* Yale Univ. (BA 1932, PhD 1937). Served War: Pacific War, 1943-45; Lieut (JG) USNR, 1942-44; Lieut, 1944-47; Lt-Comdr, 1947-55. Commendation Medal, USA, 1944 and 1945. Yale University: Instr, 1935-39; Sterling Fellow, 1939-40; Instr, 1940-42; Asst Prof., 1945-46; Associate Prof., 1946-70; Master, Saybrook Coll., 1946-75; Colgate Prof. of History, 1970-78. FRHistS 1963. Yale Medal, 1979; William C. de Vane Medal, Phi Beta Psi Soc. (Yale chapter), 1981. *Publications:* (ed) The Parliamentary Diary of Sir Edward Dering, 1670-1673, 1940; (jtly) Ideas and Institutions in European History, 800-1715, 1948; The Quest for a Principle of Authority, 1715 to Present, 1948; Crises in English History, 1066-1945: select problems in historical interpretation, 1952; The Dynamic Force of Liberty in Modern Europe, 1952; Foundations of the Modern State, 1952; Select Problems in Western Civilization, 1956; (ed) Conflict in Stuart England: essays in honour of Wallace Notestein, 1960. *Recreations:* reading, music. *Address:* 34 Tavistock Square, WC1H 9EZ. *T:* 01-636 0272. *Clubs:* Garrick; Yale (NY); Lawn (New Haven, Conn).

HENNINGS, John Dunn, CMG 1968; HM Diplomatic Service, retired; High Commissioner in Singapore, 1978-82; *b* 9 June 1922; *s* of Stanley John and Grace Beatrice Hennings, Ipswich, Suffolk; *m* 1953, Joanna Anita, *er d* of J. Thompson Reed, Northampton; two s. *Educ:* Ipswich Sch.; University College, Oxford. Foreign Office and Berlin, 1947-49; Colonial Office, 1949-53 (Sec., British Guiana Constitutional Commn, 1951); W African Inter-Territorial Secretariat, Accra, 1953-55; Colonial Office, 1955-60; Attaché for Colonial Affairs, British Embassy, Washington, DC, 1960-63; Commonwealth Relations Office, 1963; Counsellor, HM Diplomatic Service, 1965; Head, British High Commission, Residual Staff, Salisbury, Rhodesia, 1966-68; Counsellor and Head of Chancery, High Commn, Delhi, 1968-72; Actg High Commissioner, Uganda, 1972; High Comr, Jamaica, and Ambassador (non-resident) to Haiti, 1973-76; Asst Under Sec. of State, FCO, 1976-78. *Recreations:* reading, photography. *Address:* Rest-Harrow, 3 Heathfield, Chislehurst, Kent. *Club:* Travellers'.

HENNINGS, Richard Owen, CMG 1957; retired as Deputy Chief Secretary, Kenya (1960-63); *b* 8 Sept. 1911; *s* of W. G. Hennings; *m* 1939, Constance Patricia Milton Sexton; one d. *Educ:* Cheltenham; New Coll., Oxford. Newdigate Prize Poem, 1932. District Officer, Kenya, 1935; Political Officer, Ethiopia, 1941; Secretary for Agriculture, Kenya, 1953; Permanent Secretary, Ministry of Agriculture, Animal Husbandry and Water Resources, Kenya, 1956. Nominated Member of Kenya Legislative Council, 1960, and of East African Central Legislative Assembly, 1960. Hon. Editor, Ski Notes and Queries, 1964-71; Editor, Ski Survey, 1972-73. *Publications:* Arnold in Africa, 1941; African Morning, 1951; articles in The Geographical Magazine, Journal of African Administration, Corona, British Ski Year Book, Ski Notes and Queries. *Recreations:* ski-ing, tennis, gardening, reefing. *Address:* July Farm House, Great Chesterford, Saffron Walden, Essex. *Clubs:* Ski Club of Great Britain; Nairobi (Nairobi).

HENREY, Mrs Robert; authoress; *b* Paris, 13 Aug. 1906; maiden name Madeleine Gal; *m* 1928, Robert Selby Henrey (*d* 1982), *o s* of Rev. Thomas Selby Henrey, Vicar of Old Brentford, Mddx, and Euphemia, *d* of Sir Coutts and Lady Lindsay of Balcarres; one s. *Educ:* Protestant Girls' Sch., Clichy; Convent of The Holy Family, Tooting, SW. *Publications:* autobiographical sequence in the following chronological order: The Little Madeleine, 1951, New York, 1953; An Exile in Soho, 1952; Julia, 1971; A Girl at Twenty, 1974; Madeleine Grown Up, 1952, New York 1953; Green Leaves, 1976; Madeleine Young Wife, New York 1954, London 1960; London under Fire 1940-45, 1969; A Month in Paris, 1954; Milou's Daughter, 1955, New York 1956; Her April Days, 1963; Wednesday at Four, 1964; Winter Wild, 1966; She Who Pays, 1969; The Golden Visit, 1979 (read in the above order these volumes make one consecutive narrative); *other books:* A Farm in Normandy, 1941; A Village in Piccadilly, 1943; The Incredible City, 1944; The Foolish Decade,

1945; The King of Brentford, 1946; The Siege of London, 1946; The Return to the Farm, 1947; London (with illustrations by Phyllis Ginger RWS) 1948, New York, 1949; A Film Star in Belgrave Square, 1948; A Journey to Vienna, 1950; Matilda and the Chickens, 1950; Paloma, 1951, New York, 1955; A Farm in Normandy and the Return, 1952; Madeleine's Journal, 1953; This Feminine World, 1956; A Daughter for a Fortnight, 1957; The Virgin of Aldermanbury (illustrations by Phyllis Ginger), 1958; Mistress of Myself, 1959; The Dream Makers, 1961; Spring in a Soho Street, 1962. *Recreations:* most feminine occupations: sewing, knitting, ironing, gardening. *Address:* c/o J. M. Dent & Sons, Aldine House, 33 Welbeck Street, W1M 8LX; Ferme Robert Henrey, 14640 Villers-sur-Mer, Calvados, France. *T:* Calvados (31) 87 03 88.

HENRI, Adrian Maurice; President, Liverpool Academy of Arts, 1972-81; *b* Birkenhead, 10 April 1932; *s* of Arthur Maurice Henri and Emma Johnson; *m* 1957, Joyce Wilson. *Educ:* St Asaph Grammar Sch., N Wales; Dept of Fine Art, King's Coll., Newcastle upon Tyne, 1951-55. Hons BA Fine Art (Dunelm) 1955. Worked for ten seasons in Rhyl fairground, later as a scenic-artist and secondary school teacher; taught at Manchester then Liverpool Colls of Art, 1961-67. Led the poetry/rock group, Liverpool Scene, 1967-70; since then, freelance poet/painter/singer/songwriter/lecturer. Tour of USA, 1973; Bicentennial Poetry Tour of USA, 1976; exchange tour of Canada, 1980. Pres., Merseyside Arts Assoc., 1978-80; Writer-in-Residence, Tattenhall Centre, Cheshire, 1980-82. *Exhibitions:* include: Biennale della Giovane Pintura, Milan, 1968; Pen as Pencil, Brussels, 1973; John Moores Liverpool Exhibns, 1962, 1965, 1974, 1980; Peter Moores Project, Real Life, Liverpool, 1977; Art and the Sea, 1980-81; Hedgerow mural, Royal Liverpool Hosp.; John Moores Liverpool £2000 prize, 1972. *Major One-Man Shows:* ICA, London, 1968; ArtNet, London, 1975; Williamson Art Gall., Birkenhead, 1975; Retrospective 1960-76, Wolverhampton City Art Gall., 1976; Demarco Gall., Edinburgh, 1978. Various recordings. *Publications:* Tonight at Noon, 1968; City, 1969 (out of print); Autobiography, 1971; (with Nell Dunn) I Want (novel), 1972; World of Art Series: Environments and Happenings, 1974; The Best of Henri, 1975; City Hedges 1970-76, 1977; From The Loveless Motel, poems 1976-79, 1980; (for children) Eric, the Punk Cat, 1982; *anthologies:* The Oxford Book of Twentieth Century Verse, 1973; The Liverpool Scene (ed Edward Lucie-Smith), 1967; Penguin Modern Poets No 10: The Mersey Sound, 1967, rev. and enlarged edn, 1974; British Poetry since 1945 (ed Edward Lucie-Smith: Penguin), 1970; *plays:* I Wonder, a Guillaume Apollinaire Show (with Mike Kustow), 1968; Yesterday's Girl (a play with music for Granada TV), 1973; The Big Feller, 1979. *Recreations:* watching Liverpool FC; visiting Shropshire and Normandy; old movies; SF, Gothic and crime novels. *Address:* 21 Mount Street, Liverpool L1 9HD. *T:* 051-709 6682; (literary agent) Deborah Rogers Ltd, 5-11 Mortimer Street, W1. *Club:* Private Chauffeurs' (Liverpool).

HENRION, Frederick Henri Kay, MBE 1951; RDI; PPSIAD; general consulting designer and lecturer; *b* 18 April 1914; *m* ; two *s* one *d*. Textile design in Paris, 1932-33; worked in Paris and London, 1936-39; designed Smoke Abatement Exhibition, Charing Cross Station, and worked on Glasgow Empire Exhibition, 1939, and New York World Fair, 1940-45. Design of all exhibitions for Ministry of Agriculture through Ministry of Information and exhibitions for Army Bureau of Current Affairs (WO), etc., 1943-45. Consultant Designer to US Embassy and US Office of War Information, 1945; Chief Cons. Designer to Sir William Crawford and Partners, 1946-47; Art Editor of Contact Publication, 1947-48; Art Director BOAC Publications, 1949-51, and of Future Magazine, 1951; Designer, Festival of Britain pavilions (Agriculture and Natural History), 1950-51-54; Art Editor and Designer of the Bowater Papers, 1951-53; subseq. Cons. Designer for many firms. Posters for: GPO; BOAC; LPTB; Council of Industrial Design; exhibitions and permanent collections in Europe, USA and S America. One-man show, Designing Things and Symbols, at Institute of Contemporary Arts, 1960. Vis. Lectr, RCA, 1950-60; Member Council and Vice-President, SIAD (President, 1961-63); Member: Council of Industrial Design, 1963-66; Advisory Council to Governors of London School of Printing; Council, CNAA (Chm. Bd of Graphic Design; Mem. Cttee of Art and Design, 1973-78); Court, RCA, 1975; President: Alliance Graphique Internationale, 1962-67; ICOGRADA, 1968-70; Past Governor, Central School of Art; Outside Assessor, Scottish Schools of Art; Consultant Designer to: BTC; KLM Royal Dutch Airlines; British Olivetti Ltd; Tate & Lyle Ltd; The Postmaster General; BEA; Blue Circle Group; Courage, Barclay & Simonds Ltd; Financial Times; Volkswagen, Audi, NSU, Porsche, LEB, Penta Hotels, Braun AG. Co-ordinating graphics designer for British Pavilion, Expo 67. Master of Faculty, RDI, 1971-73; Head of Faculty of Visual Communication, London Coll. of Printing, 1976-79. Consultant to Henrion, Ludlow and Schmidt, 1982. Hon. Dip. Manchester, 1962. SIAD Design Medal, 1976. *Publications:* Design Co-ordination and Corporate Image, 1967 (also USA). Contributor to: Graphis, Gebrauchgraphik, Design Magazine, Architectural Review, Art and Industry, Penrose Annual, Format, Novum Gebrauchsgraphik, Design Magazine, The Designer, Print Magazine (USA), Graphic Design Idea (Tokyo). *Address:* 35 Pond Street, NW3 2PN. *T:* 01-435 7402.

HENRY, David; Senior Director, Postal Services, since 1978; *b* 19 April 1925; *s* of Thomas Glanffrwd Henry and Hylda Frances Henry. *Educ:* Midhurst Grammar Sch.; St John's Coll., Cambridge (MA Hons). Assistant Postal Controller, 1950; Head Postmaster, Norwich, 1961; Postal Controller, 1966; Controller Operations, 1968; Director, Midlands Postal Region, 1969;

Chairman, Midlands Postal Board, 1974; Dir, London Postal Region, 1977. *Recreations:* Rugby football, cricket. *Address:* 46 Boileau Road, Barnes, SW13 9BL. *Clubs:* City Livery, Civil Service.

HENRY, Sir Denis (Aynsley), Kt 1975; OBE 1962; QC Grenada 1968; barrister-at-law; Senior Partner, Henry, Henry & Bristol, St George's, Grenada, WI; *b* 3 Feb. 1917; *s* of Ferdinand H. Henry and Agatha May Henry; *m* 1966, Kathleen Carol (née Sheppard); two *s* three *d*. *Educ:* Grenada Boys' Secondary Sch.; King's Coll., London (LLB Hons). Called to Bar, Inner Temple (Certif. of Honour), 1939. In practice at Bar, Grenada, 1939-. Served three terms as nominated MLC, Grenada, 1952-65; Sen. nominated Mem. Exec. Council, 1956-65; Senator in First Parlt of Associated State of Grenada, 1966-67. Mem. Council, Univ. of West Indies, 1956-68. Pres. and Dir, Windward Islands Banana Growers Assoc., 1957-75; Pres., Commonwealth Banana Exporters Assoc., 1973-75; Chairman: Grenada Banana Co-operative Soc., 1953-75; Grenada Cocoa Assoc., 1973-75. Vice-Pres., Commonwealth Caribbean Society for the Blind, 1972-75; Mem. Exec., West India Cttee, London, 1972-75. *Recreations:* golf, swimming, tennis. *Address:* Mount Parnassus, St George's, Grenada, WI. *T:* 2370. *Clubs:* Royal Commonwealth Society; Grenada Golf, Richmond Hill Tennis (Grenada).

HENRY, Denis Robert Maurice; QC 1977; a Recorder of the Crown Court, since 1979; *b* 19 April 1931; *o s* of late Brig. Maurice Henry and of Mary Catherine (née Irving); *m* 1963, Linda Gabriel Arthur; one *s* one *d* (and one *d* decd). *Educ:* Shrewsbury; Balliol Coll., Oxford (MA). 2nd Lieut, KORR, 1950-51. Called to the Bar, Inner Temple, 1955. *Recreations:* history, golf. *Address:* Fountain Court, Temple, EC4 9DH. *T:* 01-353 7356.

HENRY, (Ernest James) Gordon, FCIB; Chairman, Associated International Insurance Company, USA, since 1976; *b* 16 June 1919; *s* of Ernest Elston Henry and Dolina Campbell (née Smith); *m* 1950, Marion Frew Allan; three *d*. *Educ:* Bellahouston Acad., Glasgow. FCIB 1957. Served War, Army (No 5 Commando), 1939-46. Began career in insurance broking, Glasgow, 1937; founded Gordon Henry & Co., Insurance Brokers, 1952; merged with Matthews Wrightson, 1957; Chm., Stewart Wrightson Holdings Ltd (formerly Matthews Wrightson Holdings Ltd), 1978-81, retd; non-exec. Dir, Stewart Smith Holdings Inc., USA (subsid. of Stewart Wrightson Holdings Ltd), 1981-. Dir, Royal Caledonian Schs, Herts. Member: Worshipful Co. of Insurers; Incorporation of Bakers, Glasgow; Merchants House, Glasgow. *Recreations:* golf, fishing, boating, writing. *Address:* Rannoch, Gryffe Road, Kilmacolm, Renfrewshire. *T:* Kilmacolm 3382. *Clubs:* Caledonian; The Western (Glasgow); Royal & Ancient Golf (St Andrews, Fife); Western Gailes Golf (Ayrshire); Kilmacolm Golf (Renfrewshire).

HENRY, Sir James Holmes, 2nd Bt, *cr* 1922; CMG 1960; MC 1944; TD 1950; QC (Tanganyika) 1953, (Cyprus) 1957; Chairman, Foreign Compensation Commission, since 1977 (Commissioner, 1960-77); *b* 22 Sept. 1911; *er s* of Rt Hon. Sir Denis Stanislaus Henry, 1st Baronet, Cahore, Draperstown, Co. Londonderry, 1st Lord Chief Justice of Northern Ireland, and Violet (*d* 1966), 3rd *d* of late Rt Hon. Hugh Holmes, Court of Appeal, Ireland; *S* father, 1925; *m* 1st, 1941 (marriage terminated by divorce and rescript of Holy Office in Rome); 2nd, 1949, Christina Hilary, *widow* of Lieut-Commander Christopher H. Wells, RN, and *e d* of late Sir Hugh Holmes, KBE, CMG, MC, QC (formerly Mixed Courts, Egypt); three *d*. *Educ:* Mount St Mary's Coll., Chesterfield; Downside Sch.; University College, London. BA (Hons) Classics (1st Class), University Scholarships. Called to Bar, Inner Temple, 1934; practised, London, 1934-39. Served War of 1939-45, London Irish Rifles (wounded). Crown Counsel, Tanganyika, 1946; Legal Draftsman, 1949; jt comr, Revised Edn of Laws of Tanganyika (1947-49), 1950; Solicitor-General, 1952; Attorney-General, Cyprus, 1956-60. *Heir:* *b* Denis Valentine Henry [*b* 29 June 1917; *m* 1956, Elizabeth, *d* of Rowland Walker; one *s* two *d*]. *Address:* Kandy Lodge, 18 Ormond Avenue, Hampton-on-Thames, Mddx. *Clubs:* Travellers', Royal Commonwealth Society.

HENRY, Thomas Cradock, FDS, RCS; MRCS; LRCP; Hon. Consultant Oral Surgeon, Hospital for Sick Children, Great Ormond Street; Consultant Maxillo-Facial Surgeon, Royal Surrey County Hospital; Consultant Oral Surgeon, Italian Hospital, London; *b* 30 Dec. 1910; *s* of late Thomas Henry and Rose Emily Bowdler, Moorgate, Park Retford; *m* 1939, Claire Mary, 7th *c* of late R. A. Caraman, The Grange, Elstree; two *s*. *Educ:* King Edward VI Grammar Sch., Retford; King's Coll., University of London; Middlesex and Royal Dental Hospital; Saunders Scholar; qualified as Doctor, 1935. Formerly: House Physician, House Surgeon and Resident Anæsthetist St James's Hosp., London; Dental House Surgeon, St Bartholomew's Hosp.; Squadron Leader and Surgical Specialist, RAFVR, 1939-46; Surgical Registrar, Plastic and Jaw Injuries Centre, East Grinstead, 1941-42; Surgeon in charge of Maxillo-Facial and Burns Unit, RAF Hosp., Cosford, 1942-46; Hunterian Prof., RCS, 1944-45. FRSocMed; Founder Fellow and Pres., British Assoc. of Oral Surgeons; Member: European Orthodontic Soc.; British Assoc. of Plastic Surgeons (Mem. Council); BMA. *Publications:* Fracture of the Facial Bones (chapter in Fractures and Dislocations in General Practice, 1949); Labial Segment Surgery (chapter in Archer's Oral Surgery, 1971); Melanotic Ameloblastoma (in Trans 3rd ICOS); numerous contrib. to leading medical and dental journals, including BMJ and Jl of Bone and Joint Surgery. *Recreations:* shooting and fishing. *Address:* Private Consulting Rooms, Mount Alvernia Nursing Home, Harvey Road, Guildford, Surrey. *T:* Guildford 67517; Fieldfares, Thursley, Surrey. *T:* Elstead 702279.

HENRY, Hon. Sir Trevor (Ernest), Kt 1970; Judge, Fiji Court of Appeal, since 1974; *b* 9 May 1902; *s* of John Henry and Edith Anna (*née* Eaton); *m* 1930, Audrey Kate Sheriff; one *s* one *d. Educ:* Rotorua District High Sch.; Univ. of New Zealand (Auckland). LLB 1925, LLM Hons 1926, NZ. Solicitor of Supreme Court of NZ, 1923, Barrister, 1925. Judge of the Supreme Court of NZ, 1955-77. *Recreation:* fishing. *Address:* 16 Birdwood Crescent, Parnell, Auckland 1, New Zealand. *Club:* Northern (Auckland).

HENRY, William Robert, CBE 1979; Chairman: Coats Patons Ltd, 1975-81; Scottish Amicable Life Assurance Society, since 1981; *b* 30 April 1915; *s* of William Henry and Sarah (*née* Lindsay); *m* 1947, Esther Macfayden; two *s* one *d. Educ:* Govan High Sch.; London Univ. Entered Company's service, 1934; Head of Financial Dept, 1953; Asst Accountant, 1957; Dir, J. & P. Coats Ltd (Parent Co.), 1966; Dep. Chm., Coats Patons Ltd, 1970. *Recreations:* sailing, gardening. *Address:* Flat 1, 1 Langside Gate, 270 Camphill Avenue, Langside, Glasgow G43.

HENSHALL, Rt. Rev. Michael; *see* Warrington, Bishop Suffragan of.

HENSLEY, John; *b* 28 Feb. 1910; *s* of late Edward Hutton and Marion Hensley; *m* 1st, 1940, Dorothy Betty (*d* 1969), *d* of Percy George and Dorothy Coppard; one *s*; 2nd, 1971, Elizabeth, *widow* of Charles Cross and *d* of Harold and Jessie Coppard. *Educ:* Malvern; Trinity Coll., Cambridge (Chancellor's Classical Medal, MA). Entered Min. of Agriculture and Fisheries, 1933; Priv. Sec. to Chancellor of Duchy of Lancaster and Minister of Food, 1939; Priv. Sec. to Minister of Agriculture and Fisheries, 1945; Asst Sec., 1946; Under Sec., 1957. Member: Agricultural Research Council, 1957-59; Council, Nat. Inst. of Agricultural Botany, 1970-73; Sec., Cttee of Inquiry into Veterinary Profession, 1971-75; retired 1975. *Recreations:* theatre, opera, genealogy, gardening. *Address:* 109 Markfield, Courtwood Lane, Croydon CR0 9HP. *T:* 01-657 6319.

HENSON, Ronald Alfred, MD, FRCP; Physician and Neurologist, The London Hospital, 1949-81; Physician, National Hospitals for Nervous Diseases, Maida Vale Hospital, 1952-81; Member: Medical Appeals Tribunal, since 1980; Attendance Allowance Board, since 1981; *b* 4 Oct. 1915; *s* of Alfred and Nellie Henson, Chippenham, Wilts; *m* 1941, Frances, *d* of A. Francis and Jessie Sims, Bath; three *d. Educ:* King Edward VI Sch., Bath; London Hospital Medical Coll. Major, RAMC, 1940-46. Mem., Archbishops' Commission on Divine Healing, 1953-57. Dir of Studies, Institute of Neurology, University of London, 1955-64; Dir, Cancer Res. Campaign Neuropathological Res. Unit, London Hosp. Med. Coll., 1967-71. Hon. Consulting Neurologist, Royal Soc. Musicians, GB, to 1981; formerly Mem. Board of Governors: The London Hosp.; Nat. Hosps for Nervous Diseases. Chairman: Advance in Medicine, 1976; Scientific Adv. Panel, Action Research, 1983- (Mem., 1977; Vice-Chm., 1981); President: Neurological Section, RSM, 1976-77 (Sec., 1956-58; Vice-Pres., 1974); Assoc. of British Neurologists, 1976-77 (Sec., 1964-68). Commonwealth Fellow 1964. Special Trustee, The London Hosp., 1974-82. Member: Assoc. of Physicians of Great Britain and Ireland; British Neuropathological Soc.; Hon. Corresponding Mem. Amer. Neurological Assoc., 1966; Hon. Member: Canadian Neurological Soc., 1971; Belgian Neurological Soc., 1976. Chm., London Bach Soc., 1977-; Mem., Arts Council of GB, 1981-, Vice-Chm., Regional Adv. Cttee, 1982-. Dep. Editor, Brain, 1974-81. *Publications:* Music and the Brain (ed jtly), 1977; Cancer and the Nervous System (jtly), 1982; various contributions to the neurological literature. *Address:* The Nab, Church Road, Newnham-on-Severn, Glos. *Clubs:* Athenæum, MCC.

HENTSCHEL, Christopher Carl, MSc; FLS, FZS, FIBiol; Principal, Chelsea College of Science and Technology, 1962-65, retired; *b* 4 July 1899; *s* of Carl and Bertha Hentschel; unmarried. *Educ:* St Paul's Sch. (Classical Scholar); King's Coll., London. Demonstrator, in Biology, St Bartholomew's Med. Coll., 1923-31; Chelsea Polytechnic, later Chelsea Coll. of Science and Technology; Lectr in Zoology, 1931-53; Head, Dept of Botany and Zoology, 1953-61; Vice-Principal, 1961-62. Mem. of Senate, University of London, 1956-64, 1966-70. Vice-Pres., Linnean Soc. of London, 1943-44, 1950-51, 1952-53; Formerly Governor: Sloane & Rutherford Schs, London; Paddington Technical Coll.; Pent Valley Sch., Folkestone. Hon. FChS. *Publications:* (with W. R. Ivimey Cook) Biology for Medical Students, 1932; papers on parasitic Protozoa. *Recreations:* motoring; continental travel. *Address:* 6 Winchester Drive, Dere Park, Brandon, Durham DH7 8UG.

HENZE, Hans Werner; composer; *b* 1 July 1926; *s* of Franz Gebhard Henze and Margarete Geldmacher. *Educ:* Bünde i/W; Bielefeld i/W; Braunschweig. Studying music in Heidelberg, 1945; First Work performed (Chamber Concerto), at Darmstadt-Kranichstein, 1946; Musical Dir, Municipal Theatre, Constance, 1948; Artistic Dir of Ballet, Hessian States Theatre, Wiesbaden, 1950; Prof. of Composition, Acad. Mozarteum, Salzburg, 1961. Definite departure for Italy, living first in Forio d'Ischia, then Naples, then Castelgandolfo as a composer; Artistic Director: Internat. Art Workshop, Montepulciano, Tuscany, 1976-80; Philharmonic Acad., Rome, 1981-; Prof. of Composition, Hochschule für Musik, Cologne, 1980-. Frequent international conducting tours. Member: German Acad. of Arts, E Berlin; Philharmonic Acad., Rome. Hon. DMus Edinburgh, 1970. Robert Schumann Prize, 1952; Prix d'Italia, 1953; Nordrhein-Westphalien Award, 1955; Berlin Prize of Artists, 1958; Great Prize for Artists, Hanover, 1962; Louis Spohr Prize, Brunswick, 1977. *Publications:* a book of Essays; 6 symphonies; 9 full length operas, 3 one-act operas, 1 children's opera; 6 normal ballets and 5

chamber ballets; chamber music; choral works; concerti for violin, viola, violoncello, double bass, oboe, clarinet and harp; various symphonic works; song cycle; music theatre works incl. El Cimarrón, La Cubana, Natascha Ungeheuer, and El Rey de Harlem. *Address:* B. Schott's Soehne, 6500 Mainz, Weihergarten 1-5, West Germany.

HEPBURN, Audrey; actress; *b* Brussels, 4 May 1929; *d* of J. A. Hepburn; *m* 1st, 1954, Mel Ferrer (marr. diss. 1968); one *s*; 2nd, 1969, Dr Andrea Dotti; one *s.* Studied ballet in Amsterdam and in Marie Rambert's ballet sch. First stage part in musical production, High Button Shoes; first film appearance in Laughter in Paradise. Played leading rôles in Gigi (play), New York, 1951 (tour of America, Oct. 1952-May 1953); Ondine (play by Jean Giraudoux), 1954. *Films:* One Wild Oat, The Lavender Hill Mob; The Young Wives' Tale; The Secret People; Nous Irons à Monte Carlo; Roman Holiday, 1952; Sabrina Fair, 1954; War and Peace, 1956; Funny Face, 1957; Love in the Afternoon, 1957; The Nun's Story, 1958, also Green Mansions; The Unforgiven, 1960; Breakfast at Tiffany's, 1961; Paris When it Sizzles, 1962; Charade, 1962; My Fair Lady, 1964; How to Make a Million, 1966; Two for the Road, 1967; Wait Until Dark, 1968; Robin Hood and Maid Marion, 1975; Sidney Sheldon's Bloodline, 1979. *Address:* c/o Kurt Frings, 9440 Santa Monica Boulevard, Beverly Hills, Calif 90210, USA.

HEPBURN, Bryan Audley St John, CMG 1962; Financial Secretary, Sarawak, 1958-63; Member, Sarawak Legislative and Executive Councils, 1955-63; Member, Inter-Governmental Committee which led to establishment of Federation of Malaysia; *b* 24 Feb. 1911; *m* 1940, Sybil Isabel Myers; two *d. Educ:* Cornwall Coll., Jamaica. Jamaica Civil Service, 1930; Asst Sec., Colonial Service, 1944; Principal Asst Sec., Sarawak, 1947; Development Sec., 1951. Chm., Sarawak Devel Finance Corp., 1958-63; Chm., Sarawak Electricity Supply Co. Ltd, 1955-63; Dir, Malayan Airways Ltd, 1959-63; Dir, Borneo Airways Ltd, 1958-63; Dep. Chm., Malaysian Tariff Adv. Bd, 1963-65. Ministry of Overseas Development, 1966-73. *Recreations:* golf, fishing. *Address:* 7 Weald Rise, Haywards Heath, West Sussex. *Clubs:* Royal Over-Seas League; Sarawak (Sarawak).

HEPBURN, John William; Under Secretary, Ministry of Agriculture, Fisheries and Food, since 1982; *b* 8 Sept. 1938; *s* of late Dugald S. Hepburn and of Margarita R. Hepburn; *m* 1972, Isla Marchbank; one *s. Educ:* Hutchesons' Grammar Sch.; Glasgow Univ. (MA); Brasenose Coll., Oxford. Assistant Principal, 1961, Principal, 1966, MAFF; First Secretary, UK Delegn to European Communities, Brussels, 1969-71; Private Sec. to Minister of Agriculture, Fisheries and Food, 1971-73; Asst Sec., MAFF, 1973-81. *Recreation:* golf. *Address:* c/o Ministry of Agriculture, Fisheries and Food, SW1.

HEPBURN, Katharine; actress; *b* 9 Nov. 1909; *d* of late Dr Thomas N. Hepburn and Katharine Houghton; *m* Ludlow Ogden Smith (marr. diss.). *Educ:* Hartford; Bryn Mawr College. First professional appearance on stage, Baltimore, 1928, in Czarina; first New York appearance, 1928, in Night Hostess (under name Katherine Burns), The Millionairess, New Theatre, London, 1952. Entered films, 1932; notable films: A Bill of Divorcement; Morning Glory; Little Women; The Little Minister; Mary of Scotland; Quality Street; Stage Door; The Philadelphia Story; Keeper of the Flame; Dragon Seed; Woman of the Year; Under-current; Without Love; Sea of Grass; Song of Love; State of the Union; Adam's Rib; The African Queen; Pat and Mike; Summer Madness; The Iron Petticoat; The Rainmaker; His Other Woman; Suddenly, Last Summer; Long Day's Journey into Night; Guess Who's Coming to Dinner; The Madwoman of Chaillot; The Lion in Winter; The Trojan Women; A Delicate Balance; Rooster Cogburn; On Golden Pond. *Stage:* Warrior's Husband; The Philadelphia Story; Without Love; As You Like It; Taming of the Shrew; Merchant of Venice; Measure for Measure, Australia, 1955; Coco, 1970; A Matter of Gravity, NY, 1976, tour, 1977; The West Side Waltz, NY, 1981. Academy Awards for performances in Morning Glory, Guess Who's Coming to Dinner, The Lion in Winter, On Golden Pond.

HEPBURN, Surg. Rear-Adm. Nicol Sinclair, CB 1971; CBE 1968; *b* 2 Feb. 1913; *s* of late John Primrose and Susan Hepburn, Edinburgh; *m* 1939, Dorothy Blackwood; two *s. Educ:* Broughton; Edinburgh Univ. MB, ChB 1935; DPH London, 1948; DIH London, 1952. Barrister-at-law, Gray's Inn, 1956. Joined RN, 1935; served during war in Atlantic and Pacific Stations; SMO, HM Dockyard: Plymouth, 1952; Portsmouth, 1955; Naval Medical Officer of Health: Portsmouth, 1959; Malta, 1962; Surg. Cdre and Dep. Med. Dir-Gen., 1966; Surg. Rear-Adm. 1969; MO i/c, RN Hosp., Haslar, 1969-72; retd. MO, DHSS, 1972-80. FRSM; FFCM 1973. *Address:* Mallows, 10 Chilbolton Avenue, Winchester, Hants SO22 5HD.

HEPBURN, Sir Ninian B. A. J. B.; *see* Buchan-Hepburn.

HEPBURN, Prof. Ronald William; Professor of Moral Philosophy, University of Edinburgh, since 1975 (Professor of Philosophy, 1964-75); *b* 16 March 1927; *s* of late W. G. Hepburn, Aberdeen; *m* 1953, Agnes Forbes Anderson; two *s* one *d. Educ:* Aberdeen Grammar Sch.; University of Aberdeen. MA 1951, PhD 1955 (Aberdeen). National service in Army, 1944-48. Asst, 1952-55, Lecturer, 1955-60, Dept of Moral Philosophy, University of Aberdeen; Visiting Associate Prof., New York University, 1959-60; Prof. of Philosophy, University of Nottingham, 1960-64. Stanton Lecturer in the Philosophy of Religion, Cambridge, 1965-68. *Publications:*

(jointly) Metaphysical beliefs, 1957; Christianity and Paradox, 1958; chapters in: Collected Papers on Aesthetics, 1965; Christian Ethics and Contemporary Philosophy, 1966; British Analytical Philosophy, 1966; Hobbes and Rousseau, 1972; Education and the Development of Reason, 1972; Philosophy and the Arts, 1973; Contemporary British Philosophy, vol. IV, 1976; Inaugural Address, Proc. Aristotelian Soc. (Supp. Vol. LIV), 1980; The Philosophical Frontiers of Christian Theology, 1982; contrib. to learned journals; broadcasts. *Recreations:* music, hill-walking. *Address:* Department of Philosophy, University of Edinburgh, David Hume Tower, George Square, Edinburgh EH8 9JX.

HEPBURNE-SCOTT, family name of **Lord Polwarth.**

HEPPEL, Richard Purdon, CMG 1959; HM Diplomatic Service, retired; *b* 27 Oct. 1913; 2nd *s* of late Engineer Rear-Admiral Walter George Heppel and Margaret, *d* of late Robert Stevens Fraser; *m* 1949, Ruth Theodora, *d* of late Horatio Matthews, MD; two *s* one *d. Educ:* Rugby Sch.; Balliol Coll., Oxford. Laming Travelling Fellow, Queen's Coll., 1935. Entered Diplomatic Service, 1936; Third Sec., Rome, 1939; Second Sec., Tehran, 1942; First Sec., Athens, 1944; Private Sec. to Min. of State, 1946; First Sec., Karachi, 1948, Madrid, 1951; Counsellor, HM Legation, Saigon, 1953-54; Ambassador to Cambodia, 1954-56; Minister at Vienna, 1956-59; Head of South East Asia Dept, Foreign Office, 1959; Head of Consular Dept, Foreign Office, 1961-63; Imperial Defence Coll., 1960; Consul-Gen. at Stuttgart, 1963-69. Administrative Officer, The City Univ. Grad. Business Centre, 1969-70; Appeals Sec. for Beds, Bucks and Herts, Cancer Res. Campaign, 1970-79. Freeman, Skinners' Company, 1961, Liveryman 1969. *Address:* Barns Piece, Nether Winchendon, Aylesbury, Bucks.

HEPPELL, Thomas Strachan; Under Secretary, Department of Health and Social Security, since 1979; *b* 15 Aug. 1935; *s* of Leslie Thomas Davidson Heppell and Doris Abbey Heppell (*née* Potts); *m* 1963, Felicity Ann Rice; two *s. Educ:* Acklam Hall Grammar Sch., Middlesbrough; The Queen's Coll., Oxford. National Assistance Board, Ministry of Social Security/DHSS: Asst Principal, 1958; Principal, 1963-73 (seconded to Cabinet Office, 1967-69); Asst Director of Social Welfare, Hong Kong, 1971-73; Asst Sec., DHSS, 1973-78 (Social Security Adviser, Hong Kong Govt, 1977). *Publications:* contribs to social administration jls. *Recreations:* gardening, travelling. *Address:* 61 Tor Bryan, Ingatestone, Essex CM4 9HN. *T:* Ingatestone 3418.

HEPPER, Anthony Evelyn, CEng, FIMechE; CBIM; Chairman, Richardsons, Westgarth PLC, since 1982 (Director, since 1980); *b* 16 Jan. 1923; *s* of Lieut-Col J. E. Hepper; *m* 1970, Jonquil Francisca Kinloch-Jones. *Educ:* Wellington Coll.; Berks. Royal Engrs, 1942-47 (retd as Hon. Major); Courtaulds Ltd, 1947-53; Cape Asbestos Co. Ltd 1953-57; Thomas Tilling Ltd, 1957-68 (Dir from 1963 until secondment), seconded as Industrial Adviser, DEA, 1966-67, and Mem., SIB, 1967; Chairman: Upper Clyde Shipbuilders Ltd, 1968-71; Henry Sykes Ltd, 1972-81; Director: Cape Industries Ltd, 1968-; Cardinal Investment Trust PLC, 1982-; General Investors Trustees PLC, 1982-. *Recreation:* golf. *Address:* 70 Eaton Place, SW1X 8AT. *T:* 01-235 7518.

HEPPLE, Prof. Bob Alexander; Professor of English Law, University College, London, since 1982; a part-time Chairman of Industrial Tribunals (England and Wales), 1975-77 and since 1982 (full-time, 1977-82); *b* 11 Aug. 1934; *s* of Alexander Hepple and Josephine Zwarenstein; *m* 1960, Shirley Goldsmith; one *s* one *d. Educ:* Univ. of Witwatersrand (BA 1954, LLB *cum laude* 1957); Univ. of Cambridge (LLB 1966, MA 1968). Attorney, S Africa, 1958; Lectr in Law, Univ. of Witwatersrand, 1959-62; Advocate, S Africa, 1962-63. Left S Africa after detention without trial for anti-apartheid activities, 1963. Called to Bar, Gray's Inn, 1966; Lectr in Law, Nottingham Univ., 1966-68; Fellow of Clare Coll., Cambridge and Univ. Lectr in Law, 1968-76; Prof. of Comparative Social and Labour Law, Univ. of Kent, 1976-77 (Hon. Prof., 1978-83). *Publications:* various books and articles on labour law, race relations, law of tort, etc; Founding Editor, Industrial Law Jl, 1972-77; Gen. Ed (jtly) Encyclopedia of Labour Relations Law, 1972-; Chief Editor, International Encyclopedia of Comparative Law, Vol. XV, Labour Law, 1979-. *Address:* Faculty of Laws, University College, 4-8 Endsleigh Gardens, WC1H 0EG.

HEPPLE, (Robert) Norman, RA 1961 (ARA 1954); PRP 1979 (RP 1948); NEAC, 1950; *b* 18 May 1908; *s* of Robert Watkin Hepple and Ethel Louise Wardale; *m* 1948, Jillian Constance Marigold Pratt; one *s* one *d. Educ:* Goldsmiths' Coll.; Royal Acad. Schools. Figure subject and portrait painter. *Address:* (studio) 16 Cresswell Place, South Kensington, SW10; (home) 10 Sheen Common Drive, Richmond, Surrey. *T:* 01-878 4452. *Club:* Chelsea Arts.

HEPPLESTON, Prof. Alfred Gordon; Professor of Pathology, University of Newcastle upon Tyne (formerly Durham), 1960-77, now Emeritus Professor; *b* 29 Aug. 1915; *s* of Alfred Heppleston, Headmaster, and Edith (*née* Clough); *m* 1942, Eleanor Rix Tebbutt; two *s. Educ:* Manchester Grammar Sch. Chief Asst, Professorial Medical Unit, University of Manchester; Asst Lecturer in Pathology, Welsh Nat. Sch. of Medicine, Univ. of Wales, 1944-47; Dorothy Temple Cross Research Fellow, Univ. of Pennsylvania, 1947-48; Sen. Lectr in Pathology, Univ. of Wales, 1948-60. *Publications:* on pathological topics, largely in reference to pulmonary disorders. *Recreations:*

ornithology, cricket and music. *Address:* Bridgeford Gate, Bellingham, Hexham, Northumberland NE48 2HT.

HEPTINSTALL, Leslie George; HM Diplomatic Service, retired; *b* 20 Aug. 1919; *s* of late Victor George Heptinstall and of Maud Maunder; *m* 1949, Marion Nicholls; one *d. Educ:* Thames Valley County Sch.; London Univ. (BSc Econ.). Served War of 1939-45: Capt., Royal Artillery; Middle East, Mediterranean, North-West Europe. Asst Principal, Colonial Office, 1948; Principal, 1951; seconded to West African Inter-Territorial Secretariat, Accra, 1955; Acting Chief Sec., 1958; Acting Administrator, W African Research Office, 1959; Principal, CRO, 1961; First Sec. on Staff of Brit. High Comr, Wellington, NZ, 1962-64; Brit. Dep. High Comr, Lahore, 1964-65; Head of South Asia Dept, ODM, 1966-68; Dep. Senior Trade Comr, Montreal, 1968-70; Internat. Coffee Orgn, 1971-73. *Recreations:* sailing, golf and tennis. *Address:* 63 Richmond Way, Great Bookham, Surrey.

HEPWORTH, Rear-Adm. David, CB 1976; retired from RN, 1976; Naval Adviser to International Military Services Ltd, since 1977; *b* 6 June 1923; *s* of Alfred Ernest Hepworth and Minnie Louisa Catherine Bennet Tanner (*née* Bowden); *m* 1st, 1946, Brenda June Case (marr. diss. 1974); one *s* one *d* ; 2nd, 1975, Eileen Mary Macgillivray (*née* Robson). *Educ:* Banbury Grammar School. Boy Telegraphist, RN, 1939; HMS Ganges, 1939-40; served in Atlantic, Mediterranean and E Indies Fleets; commnd 1944; submarines and midget submarines, 1945-50; Home, Australian and Far East Stns, 1951-58; Sen. Officer Submarines Londonderry, 1959-61; CO HMS Ashanti, 1961-64; jssc 1964; Dep. Dir Undersea Warfare, MoD, 1964-66; idc 1967; CO HMS Ajax and Captain (D) 2nd Far East Destroyer Sqdn, 1968-69; Dir RN Tactical Sch. and Maritime Tactical Sch., 1969-71; Dir Naval Warfare, MoD, 1971-73; Staff of Vice-Chief of Naval Staff, 1973-76. Lt-Comdr 1952; Comdr 1958; Captain 1964; Rear-Adm. 1974. *Recreations:* gardening, music. *Address:* Darville House, Lower Heyford, Oxon. *T:* Steeple Aston 47460.

HERBECQ, Sir John (Edward), KCB 1977; a Church Commissioner, since 1982; *b* 29 May 1922; *s* of late Joseph Edward and Rosina Elizabeth Herbecq; *m* 1947, Pamela Filby; one *d. Educ:* High Sch. for Boys, Chichester. Clerical Officer, Colonial Office, 1939; Asst Principal, Treasury, 1950; Private Sec. to Chm., UK Atomic Energy Authority, 1960-62; Asst Sec., Treasury, 1964; Asst Sec., 1968, Under Sec., 1970, Dep. Sec., 1973, Second Permanent Sec., 1975-81, CSD. *Recreations:* Scottish country dancing (ISTD Supreme Award with Hons), walking. *Address:* Maryland, Ledgers Meadow, Cuckfield, Haywards Heath, West Sussex RH1 5EW. *T:* Haywards Heath 413387.

HERBERT, family name of **Earls of Carnarvon, Pembroke,** and **Powis,** and **Baron Hemingford.**

HERBERT, Lord; William Alexander Sidney Herbert; *b* 18 May 1978; *s* and *heir* of Earl of Pembroke and Montgomery, *qv.*

HERBERT, Alfred James; British Council Representative, Portugal, since 1980; *b* 16 Oct. 1924; *s* of late Corbyn Herbert and Betty Herbert; *m* 1958, Helga Elberling (*d* 1981); two *s* ; *m* 1982, Dr Wanda Wolska. *Educ:* Royal Masonic Schs; University Coll. London (BA 1950, MA 1952). Guest Prof. of English Lit., Univs of Yokohama and Tokyo, 1958-60; Lectr, English Dept, Birmingham Univ., 1960-62; joined British Council, 1962: Sierra Leone, 1962-65; Brazil, 1965-68; Representative: Somalia, 1968-70; Pakistan, 1974-77; Poland, 1977-80. *Publications:* Modern English Novelists, (Japan), 1960; Structure of Technical English, 1965. *Recreations:* travelling, reading. *Address:* Quinta São Mateus, Dafundo, Lisbon, Portugal.

HERBERT, Christopher Alfred, CB 1973; retired; *b* 15 June 1913; *s* of Alfred Abbot Herbert and Maria Hamilton (*née* Fetherston); *m* 1941, Evelyn Benson Scott (*née* Ross) (*d* 1972); one *s* one *d. Educ:* Mountjoy Sch., Dublin; Trinity Coll., Dublin (BA (Hons)). Indian Civil Service, 1937-47; Eastern Manager, May & Baker (India) Ltd, 1947-50. MoD, 1950-77, Under Sec., 1971-77. *Recreations:* walking, gardening, reading. *Address:* 41 Woodcote Avenue, Wallington, Surrey. *T:* 01-647 5223. *Club:* East India, Devonshire, Sports and Public Schools.

HERBERT, (Dennis) Nicholas; (3rd Baron Hemingford, *cr* 1943, of Watford); Editorial Director, Westminster Press, since 1974; *b* 25 July 1934; *s* of 2nd Baron Hemingford and Elizabeth McClare (*d* 1979), *d* of Col J. M. Clark, Haltwhistle, Northumberland; *S* father, 1982; remains known professionally as Nicholas Hubert; *m* 1958, Jennifer Mary Toresen Bailey, *d* of F. W. Bailey, Harrogate; one *s* three *d. Educ:* Oundle Sch.; Clare Coll., Cambridge (MA). Reuters Ltd, 1956-61; The Times: Asst Washington Corresp., 1961-65; Middle East Corresp., 1965-68; Dep. Features Editor, 1968-70; Editor, Cambridge Evening News, 1970-74. Vice-Pres., Guild of British Newspaper Editors, 1979, Pres., 1980-81. *Heir: s* Hon. Christopher Dennis Charles Herbert, *b* 4 July 1973. *Address:* Old Rectory, Hemingford Abbots, Huntingdon PE18 9AH. *T:* St Ives (Hunts) 66234. *Clubs:* Royal Commonwealth Society, City Livery.

HERBERT, Lieut-Gen. Sir (Edwin) Otway, KBE 1955 (CBE 1944); CB 1946; DSO 1940; retired as General Officer Commanding-in-Chief, Western Command (1957-60); Colonel Commandant, Royal Artillery 1956-66; *b* 18 Nov. 1901; *s* of late Gustavus Otway Herbert; *m* 1925, Muriel Irlam Barlow; one *d. Educ:* Felsted Sch.; Royal Military Academy, Woolwich. Commissioned Royal Artillery, 1921: served war of 1939-45; BEF France and

Belgium, 1939-40 (despatches, DSO); 1st Army, 78 Div., North Africa, 1942-43 (bar to DSO); 21 Army Group, 1943-45 (despatches, CBE, CB); GOC British Troops, Berlin, and British Commandant, Berlin, 1947-49; Dir Territorial Army and Cadets, War Office, 1949-52; GOC 44 (Home Counties) Div. and District, 1952-53; GOC-in-C, West Africa Command, 1953-56. High Sheriff of Anglesey, 1964-65. Officer of Legion of Merit (USA); Knight Commander Orange Nassau (Netherlands); Commander of Leopold II (Belgium). *Recreations:* most outdoor sports available. *Address:* Llanidan House, Brynsiencyn, Anglesey. *T:* Brynsiencyn 393. *Club:* Army and Navy.

HERBERT, Frederick William; Controller of Personnel, Greater London Council, since 1982; *b* London, 18 Dec. 1922; *s* of William Herbert and late Alice Herbert; *m* 1948, Nina Oesterman; two *d. Educ:* Ealing Boys' Grammar Sch. Served RAFVR, 1942-46. Local Govt Finance, Mddx CC, 1939-65; Greater London Council: Local Govt Finance, 1965-72; Personnel Management, Estabt Officer, 1972-77; Asst Dir of Personnel, 1977-80; Head of Industrial Relations, 1980-82. *Recreations:* cricket, music (classical and jazz), theatre, Antient Society of Cogers (debating). *Address:* 20 Priory Hill, Wembley, Mddx HA0 2QF. *T:* 01-904 8634.

HERBERT, Jocelyn, Hon. ARCA 1964; RDI 1971; *b* 22 Feb. 1917; *d* of Sir Alan Patrick Herbert, CH, and Gwendolen (*née* Quilter); *m* 1937, Anthony Lousada (marr. diss. 1960); one *s* three *d. Educ:* St Paul's Girls' Sch.; Paris and Vienna; London Theatre Studio; Slade School of Art. Started painting at André L'Hote's Sch., Paris, 1932-33; studied drawing and painting with Leon Underwood, 1934; trained as theatre designer with Michel St Denis and George Devine, London Th. Studio, 1936-37; joined staff of English Stage Co., Royal Court Th., 1956; became freelance designer, 1958, centred largely on Royal Court. Prefers working on new plays to reading classics. *Plays designed*, 1957-: Royal Court Theatre: Ionesco: The Chairs, The Lesson, Exit the King; W. B. Yeats: Purgatory; Ann Jellico: Sport of My Mad Mother; Samuel Beckett: Krapp's Last Tape, Happy Days, Not I, Footfalls, That Time; Arnold Wesker: Roots, The Kitchen, I'm Talking about Jerusalem, Chips with Everything, The Merchant; Arden: Serjeant Musgrave's Dance; Christopher Logue: Trials by Logue, Antigone, The Trial of Cob and Leach; Middleton: The Changeling; Shakespeare: Richard III, Midsummer Night's Dream, Julius Caesar; John Osborne: Luther, A Patriot for Me, Inadmissible Evidence; Barry Reckford: Skyvers; W. Solvonka: The Lion and the Jewel; O'Neil and Seabrook: Life Price; Donald Howarth: Three Months Gone; David Storey: Home, The Changing Room, Cromwell, Life Class, Early Days; Christopher Hampton: Savages, The Portage to San Cristobal of A. H.; Joe Orton: What the Butler Saw; David Hare: Teeth 'n' Smiles; Mustapha Matura: Rum and Coca Cola; RSC: Richard III; Ibsen's Ghosts; Phoenix: Brecht's Baal; National Theatre: Othello; Brecht's Mother Courage and Life of Galileo; A Woman Killed with Kindness; Adrian Mitchell's Tyger; David Storey's Early Days; Aeschylus' The Oresteia; Queen's Theatre: The Seagull; Brecht's Joan of the Stockyard; Round House: Hamlet; Albery Theatre: Pygmalion; Aldwych: Saratoga; (New York) Wesker's The Merchant. *Opera*, 1967, and 1975-: Sadler's Wells: Gluck's Orpheus and Euridice; Paris Opera: Verdi's The Force of Destiny, 1975; Metropolitan, NY: Alban Berg's Lulu, 1977; Mozart's The Abduction, 1979; Brecht and Weil's Rise and Fall of the City of Mahagonny, 1979. *Films:* Tony Richardson: (colour cons. and costumes) Tom Jones, (prodn designer) Hamlet, Ned Kelly; Karel Reisz: (prodn designer) Isadora; Lindsay Anderson: (prodn designer) If . . . , O Lucky Man!. *Recreations:* the country, painting. *Address:* 45 Pottery Lane, W11. *T:* 01-727 1104.

HERBERT, Nicholas; *see* Herbert, D. N.

HERBERT, Lieut.-Gen. Sir Otway; *see* Herbert, Lieut.-Gen. Sir E. O.

HERBERT, Vice-Adm. Peter Geoffrey Marshall, OBE 1969; Flag Officer Submarines and Commander Submarines Eastern Atlantic, since 1981; *b* 28 Feb. 1929; *s* of A. G. S. Herbert and P. K. M. Herbert; *m* 1953, Ann Maureen (*née* McKeown); one *s* one *d. Educ:* Dunchurch Hall; RN Coll., Dartmouth. Midshipman, Mediterranean Fleet, 1945-47; specialised in submarines, 1949, and served in submarines, 1949-56; Comd HM Submarine Scythian, 1957-58; nuclear course, RN Coll., Greenwich, 1959; Comd HM Submarine Porpoise, 1960-62; Comd nuclear submarine, HMS Valiant, 1963-68; Comd HMS Venus, 1964; Dep. Dir, Naval Equipment, 1969; Comd 10th (Polaris) Submarine Squadron, 1970-72; COS to Flag Officer Submarines, 1972-74; Comd HMS Blake, 1974-75; Dep. Chief, Polaris Exec., 1976-78; Flag Officer Carriers and Amphibious Ships, 1978-79; Dir Gen., Naval Manpower and Training, 1980-81. FBIM, MINucE. *Recreations:* woodwork, gardening, golf, swimming. *Address:* Dolphin Square, SW1. *T:* 01-834 1512. *Club:* Royal Commonwealth Society.

HERBERT, Prof. Robert Louis, PhD; Robert Lehman Professor of the History of Art, Yale University, since 1974; *b* 21 April 1929; *s* of John Newman Herbert and Rosalia Harr Herbert; *m* 1953, Eugenia Randall Warren; one *s* two *d. Educ:* Wesleyan Univ., Middletown, Conn (BA 1951); Yale Univ. (MA 1954, PhD 1957). Fulbright Scholar, Paris, 1951-52; Faculty, Yale Univ., 1956-: Fellow, 1960-61 and 1968-69; Associate Prof., 1963; Prof., 1966; Departmental Chm., 1965-68. Guggenheim Fellow, 1971-72; Slade Prof. of Fine Art, Oxford, 1978. Organizer of exhibitions: Barbizon Revisited, Boston Museum of Fine Arts and others, 1962-63; Neo-Impressionism, Solomon R. Guggenheim Mus., 1968; J. F. Millet, Musées Nationaux, Paris, and Arts Council, London, 1975-76; Léger's Le Grand

Déjeuner, Minneapolis Inst. of Arts and Detroit Inst. of Arts, 1980. Fellow, Amer. Acad. of Arts and Sciences, 1978. Chevalier, Ordre des Arts et des Lettres, 1976. *Publications:* Barbizon Revisited, 1962-63; Seurat's Drawings, 1963; The Art Criticism of John Ruskin, 1964; Modern Artists on Art, 1964; Neo-Impressionism, 1968; David, Voltaire, 'Brutus' and the French Revolution, 1972; J. F. Millet, 1975; articles in learned jls. *Address:* Department of the History of Art, Yale University, Box 2009, 56 High Street, New Haven, Conn 06520, USA. *T:* 436-8347.

HERBERT, Robin Arthur Elidyr, DL; JP; Chairman, Leopold Joseph Holdings Ltd, since 1978; a Director: National Westminster Bank Ltd (Chairman, SW Regional Board); Equity and Law Life Assurance; *b* 5 March 1934; *s* of late Sir John Arthur Herbert, GCIE and Lady Mary Herbert; *m* 1960, Margaret Griswold Lewis; two *s* two *d. Educ:* Eton; Christ Church, Oxford (MA); Harvard Business School (MBA). ARICS. 2nd Lieut Royal Horse Guards, 1953-54; Captain Royal Monmouthshire RE, 1962-68. Dep. Chm., Countryside Commn, 1971-80; Member: Council and Exec. Cttee, National Trust, 1969- (Chm. Cttee for Wales, 1969-); Council, RHS, 1971-74, 1979-; Nat. Water Council, 1980-; Welsh Develt Agency, 1980-. DL 1968, JP 1964, High Sheriff 1972, Monmouthshire. *Recreations:* dendrology, walking. *Address:* Llanover, Abergavenny, Gwent. *T:* Nantyderry 880232. *Club:* Brooks's.

HERBERT, Walter William, (Wally Herbert); *b* 24 Oct. 1934; *s* of Captain W. W. J. Herbert and Helen (*née* Manton); *m* 1969, Marie, *d* of Prof. C. A. McGaughey; two *d.* Trained as surveyor in RE; Egypt, 1953-54, demob. 1955; travelled in Middle East, 1955; Surveyor with Falkland Is Dependencies Survey; Hope Bay, Antarctica, 1955-58; travelled in S America, 1958-59; Mem. expedn to Lapland and Spitzbergen, 1960; travelled in Greenland, 1960; Surveyor, NZ Antarctic Expedn, 1960-62; leader Southern Party; mapped 26,000 sq. miles of Queen Maud Range and descended Amundsen's route to Pole on 50th anniv.; led expedn to NW Greenland, 1966-67; dog-sledged 1,400 miles Greenland to Canada in trng for trans-Arctic crossing; led British Trans-Arctic Expedn, 1968-69, which made 3,800-mile first surface crossing of Arctic Ocean from Alaska via North Pole to Spitzbergen (longest sustained sledging journey in history of Polar exploration); led Ultima Thule expedn (filming Eskimos, Thule District), 1971-73; led expedn to Lapland, 1975; leading expedn to Greenland, 1978- (7,000 miles; first circumnavigation by dog sledge and skin boat). Hon. Mem., British Schools Exploring Soc.; Jt Hon. Pres., World Expeditionary Assoc. FRGS. Polar Medal 1962, and clasp 1969; Livingstone Gold Medal, RSGS, 1969; Founder's Gold Medal, RGS, 1970. *Publications:* A World of Men, 1968; Across the Top of the World, 1969; (contrib.) World Atlas of Mountaineering, 1969; The Last Great Journey on Earth, 1971; Polar Deserts, 1971; Eskimos, 1976 (Jugendbuchpreis, 1977); North Pole, 1978; (contrib.) Expeditions the Expert's Way, 1977; (contrib.) Bell House Book, 1978; Hunters of the Polar North, 1982. *Recreation:* painting. *Address:* c/o Royal Geographical Society, SW7. *Clubs:* Lansdowne; Explorers (NY).

HERBERT-JONES, Hugh (Hugo) Jarrett, CMG 1973; OBE 1963; HM Diplomatic Service, retired; International Affairs Director, Confederation of British Industry, since 1979; *b* 11 March 1922; *s* of late Dora Herbert-Jones (*née* Rowlands), and Captain Herbert-Jones; *m* 1954, Margaret, *d* of Rev. J. P. Veall; one *s* two *d. Educ:* Bryanston; Worcester Coll., Oxford. History Scholar. Commnd Welsh Guards, 1941; served NW Europe and Middle East; wounded 1944; demobilised 1946 (Major). Entered Foreign (later Diplomatic) Service, 1947; served: Hamburg, 1947; Berlin, 1949; Hong Kong, 1951; Phnom Penh, 1955; Saigon, 1956; Nairobi, 1959; Pretoria/Cape Town, 1963; FCO, 1966; Paris, 1973; FCO, 1975-79. *Recreations:* sailing, golf, music, spectator sports. *Address:* Prior's Hill, Park Road, Aldeburgh, Suffolk IP15 5ET. *T:* Aldeburgh 3335; 37 Addison Gardens, W14. *T:* 01-602 7596. *Clubs:* United Oxford & Cambridge University; MCC; London Welsh Rugby Football; Aldeburgh Golf; Aldeburgh Yacht.

HERBISON, Rt. Hon. Margaret McCrorie, PC 1964; Lord High Commissioner to the General Assembly of the Church of Scotland, 1970-71; *b* 11 March 1907. *Educ:* Dykehead Public Sch., Shotts; Bellshill Acad.; Glasgow Univ. Teacher of English and History in Glasgow Schs; MP (Lab) North Lanark, 1945-70; Jt Parly Under-Sec. of State, Scottish Office, 1950-51; Minister of Pensions and National Insurance, Oct. 1964-Aug. 1966, of Social Security, 1966-67. Chm., Select Cttee on Overseas Aid, 1969-. Member National Executive Cttee, Labour Party; Chm. Labour Party, 1957. Mem., Royal Commn on Standards of Conduct in Public Life, 1974-. Scotswoman of the Year, 1970. Hon. LLD Glasgow, 1970. *Recreations:* reading, gardening. *Address:* 8 Mornay Way, Shotts, Lanarkshire ML7 4EG. *T:* Shotts 21944.

HERD, Frederick Charles; Assistant Under-Secretary of State (Civilian Management, General), Ministry of Defence, 1970-75; *b* 27 April 1915. *Educ:* Strode's Sch., Egham; Sidney Sussex Coll., Cambridge. Asst Principal, Admiralty, 1937; Principal, 1941; Asst. Sec., 1950; Asst Under-Sec. of State, 1964. *Recreations:* music, lawn tennis, bridge. *Address:* 21 Cleveland Square, W2. *T:* 01-262 0920. *Clubs:* United Oxford & Cambridge University; Cumberland Lawn Tennis.

HERDON, Christopher de Lancy, OBE 1971; HM Diplomatic Service; Counsellor, Foreign and Commonwealth Office, since 1977; *b* 24 May 1928; *s* of Wilfrid Herdon and Clotilde (*née* Parsons); *m* 1953, Virginia Grace; three *s* two *d. Educ:* Ampleforth; Magdalen Coll., Oxford. Foreign Office, 1951;

Vienna, 1953; 2nd Sec., Baghdad, 1957; Beirut, 1961; 1st Sec., Amman, 1962; FO, 1965; Aden, 1967; FCO, 1970; Counsellor, Rome, 1973. *Recreations:* painting, music, tennis. *Address:* c/o Foreign and Commonwealth Office, SW1; Moses Farm, Lurgashall, Petworth, W Sussex GU28 9EP. *T:* North Chapel 323. *Clubs:* Reform, Special Forces.

HEREFORD, 18th Viscount *cr* 1550; **Robert Milo Leicester Devereux;** Bt 1611; Premier Viscount of England; *b* 4 Nov. 1932; *o s* of Hon. Robert Godfrey de Bohun Devereux (*d* 1934) and Audrey Maureen Leslie, DStJ 1963 (*d* 1978) (she *m* 2nd 1961, 7th Earl of Lisburne, who *d* 1965), *y d* of late James Meakin, Westwood Manor, Staffs and of late Countess Sondes; *S* grandfather, 1952; *m* 1969, Susan Mary, *o c* of Major Maurice Godley, Ide Hill, Sevenoaks, Kent, and of Mrs Glen Godley, Spencer's Cottage, Little Haseley, Oxon; two *s*. *Educ:* Eton. Member: Royal Philharmonic Soc.; Royal Philharmonic Orchestra Assoc. OStJ. *Heir: s* Hon. Charles Robin de Bohun Devereux, *b* 11 Aug. 1975. *Address:* The Lyford Cay Club, Lyford Cay, New Providence, Bahamas. *Clubs:* House of Lords Yacht, Lloyd's Yacht.

HEREFORD, Bishop of, since 1973; **Rt. Rev. John (Richard Gordon) Eastaugh;** *b* 11 March 1920; *s* of Gordon and Jessie Eastaugh; *m* 1963, Bridget Nicola, *y d* of Sir Hugh Chance, CBE; two *s* one *d*. *Educ:* Leeds Univ.; Mirfield. Curate of All Saints, Poplar, 1944; Rector: of W. Hackney, 1951; of Poplar, 1956; Commissary of Bp of Polynesia, 1962; Vicar of Heston, 1963; Archdeacon of Middlesex, 1966–73; Vicar of St Peter, Eaton Square, 1967–74. Sub Prelate, Order of St John, 1978–. *Recreations:* theatre, music. *Address:* Bishop's House, The Palace, Hereford HR4 9BN.

HEREFORD, Dean of; *see* Haynes, Very Rev. Peter.

HEREFORD, Archdeacon of; *see* Woodhouse, Ven. A. H.

HEREN, Louis Philip, FRSL; Director, Times Newspapers Holdings Ltd, 1981; Associate Editor of The Times, 1981; *b* 6 Feb. 1919; *s* of William Heren and Beatrice (*née* Keller); *m* 1948, Patricia Cecilia O'Regan (*d* 1975); one *s* three *d*. *Educ:* St George's Sch., London. FRSL 1974. Army, 1939–46. Foreign Corresp. of The Times, 1947–70; India, 1947–48; Israel and Middle East, 1948–50; Southeast Asian Corresp., 1951–53; Germany, 1955–60; Chief Washington Corresp. and American Editor, 1960–70; Co-Dep. Editor (Foreign), 1970–73; Dep. Editor and Foreign Editor, 1973–78; Dep. Editor, 1978–81. War Correspondent: Kashmir, 1947; Israel-Arab war, 1948; Korean war, 1950. Hannan Swaffer Award for Internat. Reporting, 1967; John F. Kennedy Memorial Award, 1968. *Publications:* New American Commonwealth, 1968; No Hail, No Farewell, 1970; Growing Up Poor in London, 1973; The Story of America, 1976; Growing Up on The Times, 1978; Alas, Alas for England, 1981. *Address:* Fleet House, Vale of Health, NW3. *T:* 01-435 0902. *Club:* Garrick.

HERFORD, Geoffrey Vernon Brooke, CBE 1956 (OBE 1946); MSc; FIBiol; Director of Pest Infestation Research, Agricultural Research Council, 1940–68, retired; *b* 1905; *s* of late Henry J. R. Herford, Hampstead; *m* 1933, Evelyn Cicely (*d* 1969), *d* of W. G. Lambert. *Educ:* Gresham's School, Holt; Magdalen College, Oxford (BA); Minnesota University (MSc). *Address:* Rose Cottage, Wells Road, Eastcombe, Stroud, Glos.

HERIOT, Alexander John, MS, FRCS, FDS; late Senior Surgeon, King's College Hospital; Postgraduate Regional Dean, South East Thames Regional Health Authority; *b* 28 May 1914; *s* of Robert Heriot; *m* 1940, Dr Christine Stacey (*d* 1958); two *s*; *m* 1959, Dr Cynthia Heymeson; one *s* one *d*. Major RAMC. *Address:* 261 Trinity Road, SW18.

HERITAGE, Prof. Robert, CBE 1980; RDI, DesRCA, FSIA; Professor, School of Furniture Design, Royal College of Art, since 1974; *b* 2 Nov. 1927; *m* Dorothy; two *s* one *d*. *Educ:* Royal College of Art, RCA, 1950; freelance designer, 1961. RDI 1963. *Recreations:* tennis, fishing. *Address:* 12 Jay Mews, Kensington Gore, SW7 2EP. *Club:* Chelsea Arts.

HERITAGE, Rev. Canon Thomas Charles; Canon Residentiary of Portsmouth Cathedral, 1964–76, now Canon Emeritus; *b* 3 March 1908; *s* of Thomas and Sarah Ellen Heritage; *m* 1934, Frances Warrington (*d* 1979); twin *d*. *Educ:* The King's Sch., Chester; St Edmund Hall, Oxford. BA 1929; MA 1944; Diploma in Education (Oxford), 1930; ATCL 1931. Deacon, 1934; Priest, 1938. Curate of Christ Church, Chesterfield and Asst Master, Chesterfield Grammar Sch., 1934–38; Asst Master, Portsmouth Grammar Sch., 1938–64; Curate of St Mark, Portsmouth, 1938–40, St Christopher, Bournemouth, 1940–44; Chaplain of Portsmouth Cathedral, 1945–64. Hon. Canon, 1958–64. Examining Chaplain to the Bishop of Portsmouth, 1965–74. Warden, Portsmouth Diocesan Readers' Assoc., 1966–76. *Publications:* A New Testament Lectionary for Schools, 1943; The Early Christians in Britain (with B. E. Dodd), 1966. *Recreations:* music, the theatre, reading, travel. *Address:* 117 The Close, Salisbury, Wilts SP1 2EY. *T:* Salisbury 29104.

HERKLOTS, Geoffrey Alton Craig, CBE 1961; MSc, PhD; FLS; FIBiol; VMH; *b* Naini Tal, India, 10 Aug. 1902; *er s* of late Rev. Bernard Herklots, MA; *m* 1932, Iris, *yr d* of late Capt. Philip Walter, RN; two *s* one *d*. *Educ:* Trent Coll., Derbyshire; University of Leeds; Trinity Hall, Cambridge. Reader in Biology, University of Hong Kong, 1928–45; interned at Stanley Camp, Hong Kong, Jan. 1942-Aug. 1945; Secretary for Development, Hong Kong, 1946–48; Secretary for Colonial Agricultural Research, Colonial

Office, London, 1948–53. Principal and Director of Research, Imperial College of Tropical Agriculture, Trinidad, 1953–60, retired 1961. Colombo Plan Botanical Adviser to HM Government of Nepal, 1961–63. Corresp. Member Zoological Society. *Publications:* Common Marine Food Fishes of Hong Kong, 1936, 3rd edn 1961; The Birds of Hong Kong, Field Identification and Field Note Book, 1946; Vegetable Cultivation in Hong Kong, 1941; The Hong Kong Countryside, 1951; Hong Kong Birds, 1953, 2nd edn 1967; Birds of Trinidad and Tobago, 1961; Vegetable Cultivation in South-East Asia, 1973; Flowering Tropical Climbers, 1976. Editor: Hong Kong Naturalist, 1930–41; Journal of Hong Kong Fisheries Research Station, 1940. *Recreations:* drawing, gardening, walking. *Address:* Vanners, Chobham, Woking, Surrey GU24 8SJ. *T:* Chobham (Woking) 8109.

HERLIE, Eileen; actress; *b* 8 March 1920; *d* of Patrick Herlihy (Irish) and Isobel Cowden (Scottish); *m* 1st, 1942, Philip Barrett; 2nd, 1951, Witold Kuncewicz. *Educ:* Shawlands Academy, Glasgow. Varied repertoire with own company, 1942–44; Old Vic, Liverpool, 1944–45; Lyric Theatre, Hammersmith, 1945–46; Andromache in Trojan Women, Alcestis in Thracian Horses, Queen in Eagle has Two Heads, 1946–47; Gertrude in Hamlet (film), 1948; Medea, 1949; Angel with the Trumpet (film), 1949; Paula in The Second Mrs Tanqueray, Haymarket, 1950–51; Helen D'Oyly Carte in Gilbert and Sullivan (film), 1952; Mother in Isn't Life Wonderful? (film), 1952; John Gielgud Season, 1953: Mrs Marwood in The Way of the World; Belvidera in Venice Preserv'd; Irene in Sense of Guilt, 1953; Mrs Molloy in The Matchmaker, 1954; She Didn't Say No! (film), 1958; acted in George Dillon (New York), 1958; Take Me Along (New York), 1959; All America (New York), 1963; The Queen in Hamlet (New York), 1964; Halfway up the Tree, 1967; Emperor Henry IV, NY, 1973; Crown Matrimonial, 1973; The Seagull (film). *Recreations:* riding, reading, music. *Address:* c/o International Famous Agency, 1301 Avenue of the Americas, New York, NY 10019, USA.

HERMAN, Josef, OBE 1980; painter; *b* 3 Jan. 1911; *m* 1955, Eleanor Ettlinger; one *s* (one *d* decd). *Educ:* Warsaw. First exhibition, Warsaw, 1932; left for Belgium, 1938; arrived in Britain, June 1940; lived in: Glasgow, 1940–43; Ystradgynlais (mining village, Wales), 1944-53. Exhibitions include: Glasgow, 1942; Edinburgh, 1942; London, 1943; Roland, Browse and Delbanco Gallery, 1946–; British Council; Arts Council; (retrospective) Whitechapel Art Gallery, 1956; (retrospective) Camden Arts Centre, 1980. Work in permanent collections: Arts Council; British Council; British Museum; National Museum, Cardiff; Contemporary Art Society; National Museum Bezalel, Jerusalem; National Gallery, Johannesburg; Tate Gallery, London; Victoria and Albert Museum, London; National Gallery, Melbourne; National Gallery, Ottawa; National Gallery, Wellington, etc. Gold Medal, Royal National Eisteddfod, Llanelly, 1962; Contemporary Art Society prize, 1952 and 1953; prize, John Moore Exhibition, 1956; Trust House Award, 1962. *Publication:* Related Twilights (autobiog.), 1975. *Address:* 120 Edith Road, W14.

HERMANN, Alexander Henry Baxter; HM Diplomatic Service, retired; *b* 28 Dec. 1917; *m* 1944, Eudoksia Eugenia Domnina; one *d*. Joined Foreign Service, 1939; served 1942-55; Peking, Ahwaz, Chengtu, Chungking, Shanghai, Quito, Panama, Tamsui; Foreign Office, 1956; Commercial Counsellor and Consul-General, Rangoon, 1957-61; HM Consul-General at Marseilles, also to Monaco, 1961–65; Diplomatic Service Inspector, 1965–66; Counsellor, Hong Kong Affairs, Washington, 1967–70, 1974–77; Consul-General, Osaka, 1971–73. *Address:* 6 Church Farm Lane, Sidlesham, Sussex. *Club:* Oriental.

HERMES, Gertrude, OBE 1982; RA 1971 (ARA 1963); RE; sculptor; wood engraver; Teacher of wood engraving, Royal Academy Schools, W1, until 1976; *b* Bickley, Kent, 1901; *m* ; one *s* one *d*. *Educ:* Belmont, Bickley, Kent; Leon Underwood's Sch., London. Portrait Sculpture and decorative carving for buildings; wood engraving decorations for books; fountain and door furniture, Shakespeare Memorial Theatre, Stratford-on-Avon; Britannia Window, British Pavilion, Paris, 1937; 3 glass panels, British Pavilion, World's Fair, NY, 1939; Engravings for books, for: Cressett Press, Swan Press, Golden Cockerel Press, Penguin Books Ltd, etc.; member of: London Group; Society of Wood-engravers. *Recreations:* swimming and fishing. *Address:* 31 Danvers Street, Chelsea, SW3. *T:* 01-352 4006.

HERMON, Sir John (Charles), Kt 1982; OBE 1975; Chief Constable, Royal Ulster Constabulary, since 1980; *b* 23 Nov. 1928; *s* of late William Rowan Hermon and Agnes Hermon; *m* 1954, Jean Webb; one *s* one *d*. *Educ:* Larne Grammar Sch. Accountancy training and business, 1946-50; joined RUC, 1950. *Recreations:* sailing, canoeing, gardening, walking. *Address:* Brooklyn, Knock Road, Belfast, N Ireland BT5 6LE. *T:* Belfast 652062. *Clubs:* Garrick, Royal Commonwealth Society; Royal Ulster Yacht (Bangor, Co. Down).

HERMON, Peter Michael Robert; Board Member, since 1978, Managing Director, European Services Division, since 1982, British Airways Board; Member Board of Directors, International Aeradio Ltd, since 1966; Chairman, International Aeradio (Caribbean) Ltd, since 1967; *b* 13 Nov. 1928; British; *m* 1954, Norma Stuart Brealey; two *s* two *d*. *Educ:* Nottingham High Sch.; St John's and Merton Colls, Oxford. 1st cl. hons Maths Oxon. Leo Computers Ltd, 1955-59; Manager, Management and Computer Divs, Dunlop Co., 1959-65; Information Handling Dir, BOAC, 1965-68; Management Services Dir, BOAC, and Mem. Bd of Management, 1968-72; Mem. of Board, BOAC, 1972; British Airways: Gp Management Services Dir, 1972-78; Management

Services Dir, 1978-82. *Recreations:* hill walking, music. *Address:* Speedbird House, London (Heathrow) Airport, PO Box 10, Hounslow, Middx.

HERMON-HODGE, family name of **Baron Wyfold.**

HERN, Major William Richard, (Dick), CVO 1980; racehorse trainer; *b* Holford, Somerset, 20 Jan. 1921. Served War of 1939-45, North Irish Horse. Asst Trainer to Major M. B. Pope, MC, 1952-57; licence to train under Jockey Club rules, 1957-; leading trainer, 1962, 1972. Races won include: Derby, 1979, 1980 (Troy, Henbit); 2,000 Guineas, 1971 (Brigadier Gerard); 1,000 Guineas, 1974 (Highclere); St Leger, 1962, 1965, 1974, 1977, 1981 (Hethersett, Provoke, Bustino, Dunfermline, Cut Above); Epsom Oaks, 1977, 1980 (Dunfermline, Bireme); King George VI and Queen Elizabeth Diamond Stakes, 1972, 1979, 1980 (Brigadier Gerard, Troy, Ela-Mana-Mou); Champion Stakes, 1971, 1972 (Brigadier Gerard); Eclipse Stakes, 1972, 1980 (Brigadier Gerard, Ela-Mana-Mou); Coronation Cup, 1974, 1975 (Buoy, Bustino). Leading Trainer, Flat Season, 1980; Flat Trainer of the Year (Derby Award), 1980. *Address:* West Ilsley Stables, West Ilsley, Newbury, Berks RG16 0AE. *T:* East Isley 219; (home) East Isley 251.

HERNIMAN, Ven. Ronald George; Archdeacon of Barnstaple since 1970, and Rector of Shirwell with Loxhore, since 1972; *b* 18 April 1923; *s* of George Egerton and Rose Herniman; *m* 1949, Grace Jordan-Jones; one *s* two *d*. *Educ:* Geneva; Bideford, Devon. Served RAF, 1941-46. Birkbeck Coll., London Univ., 1948-51 (BA); Oak Hill Theological Coll., 1951-53; Tutor, Oak Hill Coll., 1953-54; Asst Curate, Christ Church, Cockfosters, 1954-56; Dir of Philosophical Studies, Oak Hill, 1956-61; Rector of Exe Valley Group of Churches (Washfield, Stoodleigh, Withleigh, Calverleigh Oakford, Morebath, Rackenford, Loxbeare and Templeton), 1961-72. *Recreations:* sailing; making and mending things. *Address:* The Rectory, Shirwell, near Barnstaple, Devon. *T:* Shirwell 371.

HERON, Sir Conrad (Frederick), KCB 1974 (CB 1969); OBE 1953; Permanent Secretary, Department of Employment, 1973-76; *b* 21 Feb. 1916; *s* of Richard Foster Heron and Ida Fredrika Heron; *m* 1948, Envye Linnéa Gustafsson; two *d*. *Educ:* South Shields High Sch.; Trinity Hall, Cambridge. Entered Ministry of Labour, 1938; Principal Private Secretary to Minister of Labour, 1953-56; Under-Secretary, Industrial Relations Dept, 1963-64 and 1965-68, Overseas Dept, 1964-65; Dep. Under-Sec. of State, Dept of Employment, 1968-71; Dep. Chm., Commn on Industrial Relations, 1971-72; Second Permanent Sec., Dept of Employment, 1973. *Address:* Old Orchards, West Lydford, Somerton, Somerset. *T:* Wheathill 387.

HERON, Patrick, CBE 1977; painter; *b* 30 Jan. 1920; *e s* of T. M. and Eulalie Heron; *m* 1945, Delia Reiss (*d* 1979); two *d*. *Educ:* St Ives, Cornwall; Welwyn Garden City; St Georges, Harpenden; Slade School. Art criticism in: New English Weekly, 1945-47; New Statesman and Nation, 1947-50 (Art Critic); London correspondent, Arts (NY), 1955-58. John Power Lectr, Sydney Univ., 1973; Doty Prof., Univ. of Texas at Austin, 1978. Trustee, Tate Gall., 1980-. One-man exhibitions: Redfern Gallery, London, 1947, 1948, 1950, 1951, 1954, 1956 and 1958; Waddington Galleries, London, 1959, 1960, 1963, 1964, 1965, 1967, 1968, 1970 (canvases), 1970 (prints), 1973, 1975, 1977, 1979; Rutland Gallery, London, 1975; Waddington Fine Arts, Montreal, 1970; Bertha Schaefer Gallery, NY, 1960, 1962 and 1965; Galerie Charles Lienhard, Zürich, 1963; Traverse Theatre Gallery, Edinburgh, 1965; São Paulo Bienal VIII, 1965 (Silver Medal) (exhibn toured S Amer., 1966); Harrogate Festival, 1970; Rudy Komon Gall., Sydney, 1970; Whitechapel Gallery, 1972; Bonython Art Gall., Sydney, 1973; Galerie le Balcon des Arts, Paris, 1977; Retrospective exhibitions: Wakefield City Art Gallery, Leeds, Hull, Nottingham, 1952; Richard Demarco Gallery, Edinburgh, 1967; Museum of Modern Art, Oxford, 1968; Kunstnernes Hus, Oslo, 1967; Univ. of Texas at Austin Art Mus., 1978 (69 works); Oriel Gallery, Cardiff, 1979. Twelve paintings shown at São Paulo Bienal II, Brazil, 1953-54. Carnegie International, Pittsburgh, 1961; British Art Today, San Francisco, Dallas, Santa Barbara, 1962-63; Painting and Sculpture of a Decade, 1954-64, Tate Gallery, 1964; British Painting and Sculpture, 1960-70, National Gallery of Art, Washington DC; British Painting 1952-1977, RA, 1977; Color en la Pintura Británica (tour of S Amer.), 1977-78. Exhibited in group and British Council exhibitions in many countries; works owned by: Tate Gallery; Arts Council; British Council; V&A Museum; British Museum; Gulbenkian Foundation; Leeds City Art Gallery; Stuyvesant Foundation; National Portrait Gallery; Broadcasting House; Warwick Univ.; Wakefield City Art Gallery; Manchester City Art Gallery; Contemporary Art Society; Oldham Art Gallery; CEMA, N Ireland; Abbot Hall Art Gallery, Kendal; The Art Gallery, Aberdeen; National Gallery of Wales, Cardiff; Toronto Art Gallery; Montreal Museum of Fine Art; Vancouver Art Gallery; Toledo Museum of Art, Ohio; Smith College Museum of Art, Mass; Brooklyn Museum, NY; Albright-Knox Art Gallery, Buffalo, NY; Univ. of Michigan Museum of Art; Univ. of Texas at Austin Art Museum; Museum of Art, Carnegie Inst., Pittsburgh; Stuyvesant Foundn, Holland; Boymans Museum, Rotterdam; Musée d'Art Contemporain, Montreal; Western Australian Art Gallery, Perth; Pembroke and Nuffield Colleges, Oxford; Stirling Univ.; Bristol City Art Gall.; Exeter Art Gallery; Exeter Univ. (Cornwall House); Plymouth City Art Gallery; Power Collection, Sydney; London Art Gall., London, Ont.; Hatton Art Gall., Newcastle Univ.; Southampton Art Gall.; Norwich Art Gall.; also represented in Fitzwilliam Museum, Cambridge, and in municipal collections at Glasgow, Reading and Sheffield. Hon. DLitt Exeter, 1982. Awarded Grand Prize by international jury, John Moores' 2nd Liverpool Exhibition, 1959.

Publications: Vlaminck: Paintings, 1900-1945, 1947; The Changing Forms of Art, 1955; Ivon Hitchens, 1955; Braque, 1958; The Shape of Colour, 1973; Paintings by Patrick Heron 1965-1977, 1978; The Colour of Colour, 1978; contrib. The Guardian, Studio International, etc. *Address:* Eagles Nest, Zennor, near St Ives, Cornwall. *T:* Penzance 796921; 12 Editha Mansions, Edith Grove, SW10. *T:* 01-352 1787.

HERON, Raymond; Deputy Director, Propellants, Explosives and Rocket Motor Establishment, Ministry of Defence (Procurement Executive), since 1977; *b* 10 April 1924; *s* of Lewis and Doris Heron; *m* 1948, Elizabeth MacGathan; one *s* one *d*. *Educ:* Heath Grammar Sch., Halifax; Queen's Coll., Oxford (BA Physics). Shell Refining and Marketing Co., 1944-47; RN, Instructor Branch, 1947-52; Rocket Propulsion Estabt, Min. of Supply (later Min. of Technology), 1952-67; Cabinet Office, 1967; Asst Dir, Min. of Technology, 1967-73; Dep. Dir, Explosives Research and Development Estabt, MoD, 1973; Special Asst to Sec. (Procurement Exec.), MoD, 1973-74; Head of Rocket Motor Exec. and Dep. Dir/2, Rocket Propulsion Estabt, MoD (PE), 1974-76. *Publications:* articles in scientific and technical jls. *Recreations:* music, hill walking, golf. *Address:* 9 Grange Gardens, Wendover, Aylesbury, Bucks HP22 6HB. *T:* Wendover 622921. *Club:* Ashridge Golf.

HERON, Robert, MA; Director, Duke of Edinburgh's Award Scheme, since 1978; *b* 12 Oct. 1927; *s* of James Riddick Heron and Sophie Leathem; *m* 1953, Patricia Mary Pennell; two *s* one *d*. *Educ:* King Edward's Sch., Birmingham; St Catharine's Coll., Cambridge. Housemaster: Strathallan, Perthshire, 1952-59; Christ Coll., Brecon, 1959-62; Headmaster, King James I Sch., IOW, 1962-66. Head of Educational Broadcasting, ATV Network Ltd, 1966-69, responsible for production of TV programme series in the scis, langs, soc. documentary, leisure interests, music, drama; Deleg., EBU study gps on educnl broadcasting; Programme Dir, The Electronic Video Recording Partnership (CBS Inc. USA/ICI/Ciba-Geigy UK), 1970-77; Managing Dir, EVR Ltd, 1974-77, and of EVR Enterprises Ltd, 1975-77. Freeman, City of London, 1981. Formerly 6/7th Bn, The Black Watch (RHR) TA. *Recreations:* shooting, hill walking, sport. *Address:* Avon Wharf, Bridge Street, Christchurch, Dorset. *Clubs:* Rugby; ISC (Cowes); Hawks (Cambridge).

HERON-MAXWELL, Sir Nigel (Mellor), 10th Bt *cr* 1683; *b* 30 Jan. 1944; *s* of Sir Patrick Ivor Heron-Maxwell, 9th Bt and of D. Geraldine É., *yr d* of late Claud Paget Mellor; *S* father, 1982; *m* 1972, Mary Elizabeth Angela, *o d* of W. Ewing, Co. Donegal; one *s* one *d*. *Educ:* Milton Abbey. *Heir:* *s* David Mellor Heron-Maxwell, *b* 22 May 1975. *Address:* 105 Codicote Road, Welwyn, Herts.

HERRIDGE, Geoffrey Howard, CMG 1962; Chairman, Iraq Petroleum Co. Ltd and Associated Companies, 1965-70, retired (Managing Director, 1957-63; Deputy Chairman, 1963-65); *b* 22 Feb. 1904; 3rd *s* of late Edward Herridge, Eckington, Worcestershire; *m* 1935, Dorothy Elvira Tod; two *s* two *d*. *Educ:* Crypt Sch., Gloucester; St John's Coll., Cambridge. Joined Turkish Petroleum Co. Ltd (later Iraq Petroleum Co. Ltd), Iraq, 1926; served in Iraq, Jordan, Palestine, 1926-47; General Manager in the Middle East, Iraq Petroleum Co. and Associated Companies, 1947-51; Executive Director, 1953-57; Member of London Cttee, Ottoman Bank, 1964-79. Chairman, Petroleum Industry Training Board, 1967-70. *Recreation:* sailing. *Address:* Flint, Sidlesham Common, Chichester, West Sussex. *T:* Sidlesham 357. *Club:* Oriental.

HERRIES, Lady (14th in line, of the Lordship *cr* 1490), of Terregles; **Anne Elizabeth Fitzalan-Howard;** *b* 12 June 1938; *e d* of 16th Duke of Norfolk, EM, KG, PC, GCVO, GBE, TD, and of Lavinia Duchess of Norfolk, *qv* ; *S* to lordship upon death of father, 1975. Racehorse trainer. *Recreations:* riding, golf, breeding spaniels. *Heir:* sister Lady Mary Katharine Fitzalan-Howard, CVO 1982, *b* 14 Aug. 1940. *Address:* Angmering Park, Littlehampton, West Sussex.

HERRIES, Sir Michael Alexander Robert Young-, Kt 1975; OBE 1968; MC 1945; Chairman: The Royal Bank of Scotland plc, since 1976 (Director since 1972); Vice-Chairman, 1974-75; Deputy Chairman, 1975-76); The Royal Bank of Scotland Group plc (formerly National and Commercial Banking Group Ltd), since 1978 (Director since 1976); Scottish Widows' Fund and Life Assurance Society, since 1981 (Deputy Chairman, 1979-81); Deputy Chairman, Williams and Glyn's Bank plc, since 1978; Director: Matheson & Co. Ltd (Chairman, 1971-75); Jardine, Matheson & Co. Ltd; Scottish Mortgage & Trust plc; Lloyds and Scottish PLC; *b* 28 Feb. 1923; *s* of Lt-Col William Dobree Young-Herries and Ruth Mary (*née* Thrupp); *m* 1949, Elizabeth Hilary Russell (*née* Smith); two *s* one *d*. *Educ:* Eton; Trinity Coll., Cambridge (MA). Served KOSB, 1942-47; Temp. Captain, Actg Maj., Europe and ME; Adjt 5th (Dumfries and Galloway) Battalion and 1st Battalion TARO, 1949. Joined Jardine Matheson & Co. Ltd, 1948; served in Hong Kong, Japan and Singapore; Director, 1959; Managing Director, 1962; Chm. and Man. Dir, 1963-70; Chairman: Jardine Japan Investment Trust Ltd, 1972-76; Crossfriars Trust Ltd, 1972-76. Formerly Mem., Exec. Legislative Council, Hong Kong; Chm., Hong Kong Univ. and Polytechnics Grant Cttee, 1965-73. Former Mem. Council, London Chamber of Commerce and Industry, Hon. Mem., 1980-; Chm., Scottish Trust for the Physically Disabled, 1981-; Mem. Council, Missions to Seamen. Mem., Royal Company of Archers (Queen's Body Guard for Scotland), 1973-. Hon. LLD Chinese Univ. of Hong Kong, 1973; Univ. of Hong Kong, 1974. *Recreations:* shooting, walking, swimming, tennis. *Address:* (office) The Royal Bank of Scotland plc, 42 St Andrew Square, Edinburgh EH2 2YE. *T:* 031-556 8555; Spottes, Castle

Douglas, Stewartry of Kirkcudbright. *T:* Haugh of Urr 202; 30 Heriot Row, Edinburgh. *T:* 031-226 2711; Flat 14, Lochmore House, Cundy Street, SW1W 9JX. *T:* 01-730 1119. *Clubs:* Caledonian, Farmers', City of London; New (Edinburgh).

HERRING, Cyril Alfred; Chairman and Managing Director, Southern Airways Ltd, and Chairman of subsidiary companies, since 1978; *b* Dulwich, 17 Jan. 1915; *s* of Alfred James Herring and Minnie Herring (*née* Padfield); *m* 1939, Helen (*née* Warnes); three *s. Educ:* Alleyn's Sch.; London School of Economics. BSc(Econ); FCMA; JDipMA; IPFA; FCIT. Chief Accountant, Straight Corporation Ltd, 1936-46; joined BEA, 1946; Chief Accountant, 1951-57; Personnel Director, 1957-65; Financial Director, 1965-71; Executive Board Member, 1971-74; Mem., BAB, 1972-78; Chief Executive, British Airways Regional Div., 1972-74; Finance Dir, 1975-78; Chm. and Man. Dir, British Air Services Ltd, 1969-76; Chairman: Northeast Airlines Ltd, 1969-76; Cambrian Airways Ltd, 1973-76; London Rail Adv. Cttee, 1976-80; CIPFA Public Corporations Finance Group, 1976-78. Member Council: Chartered Inst. of Transport, 1971-74; Inst. of Cost and Management Accountants, 1967-77 (Vice-Pres., 1971-73, Pres., 1973-74); CBI, 1975-78 (Mem. Financial Policy Cttee, 1975-78, Finance and General Purposes Cttee, 1977-78). Freeman, City of London; Liveryman, Guild of Air Pilots and Air Navigators. *Recreations:* flying, motoring, boating. *Address:* Cuddenbeake, St Germans, Cornwall. *Clubs:* Reform, Royal Aero.

HERRINGTON, Air Vice-Marshal Walter John, CB 1982; RAF retd; Director of Service Intelligence, 1980-82; *b* 18 May 1928; *s* of Henry Herrington and Daisy Restal Gardiner; *m* 1958, Joyce Maureen Cherryman; two *s. Educ:* Peter Symonds, Winchester; Woking Grammar Sch.; RAF Coll., Cranwell. FBIM. Commnd RAF, 1949, Pilot; 1950-69: Long Range Transp. Sqdns; ADC to C-in-C Bomber Comd; Reconnaissance Sqdns; RAF Staff Coll.; Exchange Officer, USAF Acad., Colo; Comd 100 Sqdn; Jt Services Staff Coll.; Air Sec.'s Dept; Comd RAF Honnington, 1969-71; Ops Dept, MoD, 1971-73; RCDS (student), 1974; Defence Attaché, Paris, 1975-77. Hon. ADC to the Queen, 1971-74; Senior RAF Mem., Directing Staff, RCDS, 1978-80. *Publications:* text books for courses on air power for USAF Academy. *Recreations:* reading, international affairs, sport. *Address:* c/o Lloyds Bank, Green Lane, Northwood, Mddx HA6 1AB. *Club:* Royal Air Force.

HERRIOT, James; *see* Wight, J. A.

HERROD, Donald, QC 1972; **His Honour Judge Herrod;** a Circuit Judge, since 1978; *b* 7 Aug. 1930; *o s* of Wilfred and Phyllis Herrod, Doncaster; *m* 1959, Kathleen Elaine Merrington, MB, ChB; two *d. Educ:* grammar schs, Doncaster and Leeds. Entered Army, 1948; commnd 1949. Called to Bar, 1956. A Recorder of the Crown Court, 1972-78. Member: Parole Bd, 1978-81; Judicial Studies Bd, 1982-. Governor Leeds Grammar School, 1978-. *Recreations:* lawn tennis, golf. *Address:* The Crown Court, Leeds 1.

HERRON, Very Rev. Andrew; Clerk to the Presbytery of Glasgow, 1959-81; *b* 29 Sept. 1909; *s* of John Todd Herron and Mary Skinner Hunter; *m* 1935, Joanna Fraser Neill; four *d. Educ:* Glasgow Univ. (MA, BD, LLB). Minister: at Linwood, 1936-40, at Houston and Killellan, 1940-59; Clerk to the Presbytery of Paisley, 1953-59; Moderator of General Assembly of Church of Scotland, 1971-72. Convener: Dept of Publicity and Publications, 1959-68; Gen. Admin Cttee; Business Cttee, Gen. Assembly, 1972-76, 1978; Gen. Trustee, Church of Scotland. Hon. DD St Andrews, 1975. *Publications:* Record Apart, 1974; Guide to the General Assembly of the Church of Scotland, 1976; Guide to Congregational Affairs, 1978. *Address:* 36 Darnley Road, Glasgow G41 4NE. *T:* 041-423 6422. *Clubs:* Glasgow Art; Caledonian (Edinburgh).

HERRON, Henry, CBE 1975; Procurator-Fiscal, Glasgow, 1965-76, retired; Deputy Chairman of Traffic Commissioners and Licensing Authority for Scottish Traffic Area, 1978-81; *b* 6 May 1911; *s* of William and Jessie Herron; *m* 1942, Dr Christina Aitkenhead Crawford; one *s* two *d. Educ:* Hamilton Academy; Glasgow Univ. (MA, LLB). Solicitor. Depute Procurator-Fiscal, Glasgow, 1946; Procurator-Fiscal, Banff, 1946-51; Asst Procurator-Fiscal, Glasgow, 1951-55; Procurator-Fiscal, Paisley, 1955-65. *Recreations:* gardening, jurisprudence, criminology. *Address:* 51 Craw Road, Paisley. *T:* 041-889 3091.

HERRON, Shaun; novelist; *m* ; two *s* two *d.* Northern Irish. Ordained to Ministry of Scottish Congregational Churches, 1940; Minister, United Church of Canada, 1958. Editor, British Weekly, 1950-58; Correspondent in USA, 1960-64, Sen. Leader Writer, 1964-76, Winnipeg Free Press. Has held various lectureships in US and Canada. Finds entries in reference books too dreary to read. *Publications:* novels: Miro, 1968; The Hound and The Fox and The Harper, 1970; Through the Dark and Hairy Wood, 1972; The Whore-Mother, 1973; The Bird in Last Year's Nest, 1974; The Mac Donnell, 1976; Aladale, 1978; The Search for Arthur Barber, 1981. *Recreations:* travelling, writing. *Address:* c/o A. P. Watt Ltd, 26/28 Bedford Row, WC1R 4HL.

HERSCHELL, family name of **Baron Herschell.**

HERSCHELL, 3rd Baron, *cr* 1886; **Rognvald Richard Farrer Herschell;** late Captain Coldstream Guards; *b* 13 Sept. 1923; *o s* of 2nd Baron and Vera (*d* 1961), *d* of Sir Arthur Nicolson, 10th Bt, of that Ilk and Lasswade; *S* father,

1929; *m* 1948, Heather, *d* of 8th Earl of Dartmouth, CVO, DSO; one *d. Educ:* Eton. Page of Honour to the King, 1935-40. *Heir:* none. *Address:* Westfield House, Ardington, Wantage, Berks. *T:* East Hendred 224.

HERSEY, John; writer; *b* 17 June 1914; *s* of Roscoe M. and Grace B. Hersey; *m* 1st, 1940, Frances Ann Cannon (marr. diss. 1958); three *s* one *d* ; 2nd, 1958, Barbara Day Kaufman; one *d. Educ:* Yale Univ.; Clare Coll., Cambridge. Secretary to Sinclair Lewis, 1937; Editor Time, 1937-42; War and Foreign Correspondent, Time, Life, New Yorker, 1942-46. Mem. Council, Authors' League of America, 1946-70 (Vice-Pres., 1948-55, Pres., 1975-80). Fellow, Berkeley Coll., Yale Univ., 1950-65; Master, Pierson Coll., Yale Univ., 1965-70, Fellow, 1965-. Writer in Residence, Amer. Acad. in Rome, 1970-71. Lectr, Yale Univ., 1971-75, Vis. Prof., 1975-76, Adjunct Prof., 1976-; Lectr, Salzburg Seminars in Amer. Studies, 1975; Vis. Prof., MIT, 1975. Chm., Connecticut Cttee for the Gifted, 1954-57; Member: Amer. Acad. Arts and Letters, 1953 (Sec., 1962-76; Chancellor, 1981-); Nat. Inst. Arts and Letters, 1950; Amer. Acad. of Arts and Scis, 1978; Council, Authors' Guild, 1946- (Chm., Contract Cttee, 1963-); Yale Univ. Council cttees on: the Humanities, 1951-56, and Yale Coll., 1959-69 (Chm., 1964-69); Vis. Cttee, Harvard Grad. Sch. of Educn, 1960-65; Nat. Citizens' Commn for the Public Schs, 1954-56; Bd of Trustees, Putney Sch., 1953-56; Trustee: Nat. Citizens' Council for the Public Schs, 1956-58; Nat. Cttee for the Support of the Public Schs, 1962-68. Delegate: to White House Conf. on Educn, 1955; to PEN Congress, Tokyo, 1958. Comr, Nat. Commn on New Technological Uses of Copyrighted Works, 1975-78. Hon. Fellow, Clare Coll., Cambridge, 1967. Hon. MA Yale Univ., 1947; Hon. LLD Washington and Jefferson Coll., 1946; New Haven Univ., 1975; Hon. LHD New Sch. for Social Research, 1950; Hon. DHL Dropsie Coll., 1950; Hon. LittD: Wesleyan Univ., 1957; Bridgeport Univ., 1959; Clarkson Coll. of Technology, 1972. Pulitzer Prize for Fiction, 1945; Sidney Hillman Foundn Award, 1951; Howland Medal, Yale Univ., 1952. *Publications:* Men on Bataan, 1942; Into the Valley, 1943; A Bell for Adano, 1944; Hiroshima, 1946; The Wall, 1950; The Marmot Drive, 1953; A Single Pebble, 1956; The War Lover, 1959; The Child Buyer, 1960; Here to Stay, 1962; White Lotus, 1965; Too Far to Walk, 1966; Under the Eye of the Storm, 1967; The Algiers Motel Incident, 1968; The Conspiracy, 1972; The Writer's Craft, 1974; My Petition for More Space, 1974; The President, 1975; The Walnut Door, 1977; Aspects of the Presidency, 1980. *Address:* 420 Humphrey Street, New Haven, Conn 06511, USA.

HERSHEY, Dr Alfred Day; Director, Genetics Research Unit, Carnegie Institution of Washington, 1962-74, retired; *b* 4 Dec. 1908; *s* of Robert D. Hershey and Alma (*née* Wilbur); *m* 1944, Harriet Davidson; one *s. Educ:* Michigan State Coll. (now Univ.). BS 1930; PhD 1934. Asst Bacteriologist, Washington Univ. Sch. of Medicine, St Louis Missouri, 1934-36; Instructor, 1936-38; Asst Prof., 1938-42; Assoc. Prof., 1942-50; Staff Mem., Dept of Genetics (now Genetics Research Unit), Carnegie Instn of Washington, 1950-. Albert Lasker Award, Amer. Public Health Assoc., 1958; Kimber Genetics Award, Nat. Acad. Sci., US, 1965. Hon. DSc, Chicago, 1967; Hon. Dr Med. Science, Michigan State, 1970. Nobel Prize for Physiology or Medicine (jtly), 1969. *Publications:* numerous articles in scientific jls or books. *Address:* RD Box 1640, Moores Hill Road, Syosset, NY 11791, USA. *T:* 516 692 6855.

HERTFORD, 8th Marquess of, *cr* 1793; **Hugh Edward Conway Seymour;** Baron Conway of Ragley, 1703; Baron Conway of Killultagh, 1712; Earl of Hertford, Viscount Beauchamp, 1750; Earl of Yarmouth, 1793. DL Warwick, 1959; formerly Lieutenant Grenadier Guards; *b* 29 March 1930; *s* of late Brig.-General Lord Henry Charles Seymour, DSO (2nd *s* of 6th Marquess) and Lady Helen Frances Grosvenor (*d* 1970), *d* of 1st Duke of Westminster; *S* uncle, 1940; *m* 1956, Comtesse Louise de Caraman Chimay, *o d* of late Lt-Col Prince Alphonse de Chimay, TD; one *s* three *d. Educ:* Eton. Chm., Hertford Public Relations Ltd, 1962-73. Chief interests are estate management (Diploma, Royal Agricultural Coll., Cirencester, 1956) and opening Ragley to the public. *Heir:* *s* Earl of Yarmouth, *qv. Address:* Ragley Hall, Alcester, Warwickshire. *T:* Alcester 762455/762090/762845. *Clubs:* White's, Pratt's, Turf.

HERTFORD, Bishop Suffragan of, since 1982; **Rt. Rev. Kenneth Harold Pillar;** *b* 10 Oct. 1924; *s* of Harold and Mary Pillar; *m* 1955, Margaret Elizabeth Davies; one *s* three *d. Educ:* Devonport High School; Queens' Coll., Cambridge (MA); Ridley Hall, Cambridge. Asst Curate, Childwall, Liverpool, 1950-53; Chaplain, Lee Abbey, Lynton, N Devon, 1953-57; Vicar: St Paul's, Beckenham, 1957-62; St Mary Bredin, Canterbury, 1962-65; Warden of Lee Abbey, Lynton, N Devon, 1965-70; Vicar of Waltham Abbey, Essex, 1970-82; RD of Epping Forest, 1976-82. *Recreation:* walking. *Address:* Hertford House, Abbey Mill Lane, St Albans, Herts AL3 4HE. *T:* St Albans 66420.

HERTFORDSHIRE, Bishop in, (RC); *see* O'Brien, Rt Rev. J. J.

HERVEY, family name of **Marquess of Bristol.**

HERVEY, Rear Adm. John Bethell, CB 1982; OBE 1970; Marketing Vice President, Western Hemisphere, MEL, since 1982; *b* 14 May 1928; *s* of late Captain Maurice William Bethell Hervey, RN, and Mrs Joan Hervey (*née* Hanbury); *m* 1950, (Audrey) Elizabeth Mote; two *s* one *d. Educ:* Marlborough Coll., Wilts. Joined RN, 1946; specialised in submarines, 1950, nuclear submarines, 1968; command appointments: HMS Miner VI, 1956; HMS Aeneas, 1956-57; HMS Ambush, 1959-62; HMS Oracle, 1962-64; Sixth

Submarine Div., 1964-66; HMS Cavalier, 1966-67; HMS Warspite, 1968-69; Second Submarine Sqdn, 1973-75; HMS Kent, 1975-76; staff appointments: Course Officer, Royal Naval Petty Officers Leadership Sch., 1957-59; Submarine Staff Officer to Canadian Maritime Comdr, Halifax, NS, 1964-66; Ops Officer to Flag Officer Submarines, 1970-71; Def. Op. Requirements Staff, 1971-73; Dep. Chief of Allied Staff to C-in-C Channel and C-in-C Eastern Atlantic (as Cdre), 1976-80; Comdr British Navy Staff, and British Naval Attaché, Washington, and UK Nat. Liaison Rep. to SACLANT, 1980-82, retired. Comdr 1964, Captain 1970, Rear Adm. 1980. *Recreations:* walking, talking, reading. *Address:* c/o National Westminster Bank, 26 Haymarket, SW1Y 4ER. *Club:* Royal Navy of 1765 and 1785.

HERVEY-BATHURST, Sir F.; *see* Bathurst.

HERWARTH von BITTENFELD, Hans Heinrich; Grand Cross (2nd Class), Order of Merit, Federal Republic of Germany, 1963; Hon. GCVO 1958; State Secretary, retired; *b* Berlin, 14 July 1904; *s* of Hans Richard Herwarth von Bittenfeld and Ilse Herwarth von Bittenfeld (*née* von Tiedemann); *m* 1935, Elisabeth Freiin von Redwitz; one *d. Educ:* Universities of Berlin, Breslau and Munich (Law and Nat. Econ.). Entered Auswärtiges Amt, Berlin, 1927; Attaché, Paris, 1930; Second Secretary and Personal Secretary to Ambassador, Moscow, 1931-39. Military Service, 1939-45. Oberregierungsrat, Regierungsdirektor, Bavarian State Chancellery, 1945-49; Ministerialdirigent and Chief of Protocol, Federal Government, 1950, Minister Plenipotentiary, 1952; German Ambassador to Court of St James's, 1955-61; State Secretary and Chief of German Federal Presidential Office, 1961-65; German Ambassador to Republic of Italy, 1965-69; Pres., Commn for Reform of German Diplomatic Service, 1969-71. Chm., Supervisory Council, Unilever, Germany, 1969-77. Chm., Venice Cttee, German Unesco Commn; Pres., Internat. Adv. Cttee for Venice. Pres., Goethe Institut, Munich, 1971-77. *Publication:* Against Two Evils: memoirs of a diplomat-soldier during the Third Reich, 1981. *Recreations:* ski-ing, antiques. *Address:* Menzelstrasse 7, 8000 München 80, Germany.

HERZBERG, Charles Francis; Group Industrial Planning Adviser, Northern Engineering Industries plc, since 1977; *b* 26 Jan. 1924; *s* of Dr Franz Moritz Herzberg and Mrs Marie Louise Palache; *m* 1956, Ann Linette Hoare; one *s* two *d. Educ:* Fettes Coll., Edinburgh; Sidney Sussex Coll., Cambridge (MA). CEng, FIMechE, MIGasE. Alfred Herbert Ltd, 1947-51; Chief Engr and Dir, Hornflowa Ltd, Maryport, 1951-55; Chief Engr, Commercial Plastics Gp of Cos, and Dir, Commercial Plastics Engrg Co. at Wallsend on Tyne, North Shields, and Cramlington, Northumberland, 1955-66; Corporate Planning Dir, Appliance Div., United Gas Industries, and Works Dir, Robinson Willey Ltd, Liverpool, 1966-70; Man. Dir and Chief Exec., Churchill Gear Machines Ltd, Blaydon on Tyne, 1970-72; Regional Industrial Director, Dept of Industry, N Region, 1972-75; Dir of Corporate Develt, Clarke Chapman Ltd, 1975-77. *Recreation:* shooting. *Address:* 3 Furzefield Road, Gosforth, Newcastle upon Tyne NE3 4EA. *T:* Newcastle upon Tyne 855202. *Club:* East India, Devonshire, Sports and Public Schools.

HERZBERG, Gerhard, CC (Canada), 1968; FRS 1951; FRSC 1939; Director, Division of Pure Physics, National Research Council of Canada, 1949-69, now Distinguished Research Scientist, National Research Council of Canada; *b* Hamburg, Germany, 25 Dec. 1904; *s* of late Albin Herzberg and Ella Herzberg; *m* 1929, Luise Herzberg, *née* Oettinger (*d* 1971); one *s* one *d* ; *m* 1972, Monika Herzberg, *née* Tenthoff. *Educ:* Inst. of Technology, Darmstadt, Germany; Univ. of Göttingen, Germany; Univ. of Bristol, England. Lecturer, Darmstadt Inst. of Technology, 1930; Research Professor, Univ. of Saskatchewan, 1935; Prof. of Spectroscopy, Yerkes Observatory, Univ. of Chicago, 1945; Principal Research Officer, National Research Council of Canada, 1948. University Medal, Univ. of Liège, Belgium, 1950; President, RSC, 1966 (Henry Marshall Tory Medal, 1953). Joy Kissen Mookerjee Gold Medal of Indian Association for Cultivation of Science, 1954 (awarded 1957). Gold Medal of Canadian Association Phys., 1957; Bakerian Lecture, Royal Society, 1960; Faraday Lecture and Medal, Chem. Soc., 1970; Nobel Prize for Chemistry, 1971; Royal Medal, Royal Soc., 1971. Hon. Fellow: Indian Academy of Science, 1954; Indian Physical Society, 1957; Chemical Society of London, 1968. Hon. Member: Hungarian Academy of Sciences, 1964; Optical Society of America, 1968; Royal Irish Acad., 1970; Japan Acad., 1976; Chem. Soc. of Japan, 1978; Hon. Foreign Member American Academy Arts and Sciences, 1965; Foreign Associate, National Academy of Sciences, US, 1968; Foreign Mem. (Physics), Royal Swedish Acad. of Sciences, 1981. President, Canadian Association of Physicists, 1956; Vice-Pres., International Union of Pure and Applied Physics, 1957-63. Holds numerous hon. degrees, including Hon. ScD Cantab, 1972. *Publications:* Atomic Spectra and Atomic Structure, 1st edition (USA) 1937, 2nd edition (USA) 1944; Molecular Spectra and Molecular Structure: I, Spectra of Diatomic Molecules, 1st edition (USA), 1939, 2nd edition (USA), 1950; II, Infra-red and Raman Spectra of Polyatomic Molecules (USA), 1945; III, Electronic Spectra and Electronic Structure of Polyatomic Molecules (USA), 1966; IV, (with K. P. Huber) Constants of Diatomic Molecules (USA), 1979; The Spectra and Structures of Simple Free Radicals: an introduction to Molecular Spectroscopy (USA), 1971; original research on atomic and molecular spectra published in various scientific journals. *Address:* National Research Council, Ottawa, Ontario K1A 0R6, Canada. *T:* 99-22350; 190 Lakeway Drive, Rockcliffe Park, Ottawa, Ontario K1L 5B3, Canada. *T:* 746-4126.

HERZIG, Christopher; Director, External Relations, International Atomic Energy Agency, Vienna, since 1981; *b* 24 Oct. 1926; *s* of late L. A. Herzig and late Mrs Elizabeth Herzig (*née* Hallas); *m* 1952, Rachel Katharine Buxton; four *s* one *d. Educ:* Christ's Hosp.; Selwyn Coll., Cambridge (MA). Asst Principal, Min. of Fuel and Power, 1951-56; Principal, Min. of Supply, 1956-58; Min. of Aviation, 1959-61; Private Sec. to Lord President of the Council, 1961-64; Private Sec. to Minister of Technology, 1964-66; Asst Sec., Min. of Technology, 1966-70; Dept of Trade and Industry, 1970-71, Under-Sec., DTI, 1972-73; Under Sec., Dept of Energy, 1974-81. UK Governor, IAEA, 1972-78. *Address:* 13a The Causeway, Horsham, West Sussex RH12 1HE. *T:* Horsham 65239; Wasagasse 4/8, 1090 Vienna.

HERZOG, Frederick Joseph, MC; farmer, retired; *b* 8 Dec. 1890; *s* of late F. C. Herzog, formerly of Mossley Hill, Liverpool; *m* 1918, Constance Cicely Broad; two *s* one *d. Educ:* Charterhouse; Trinity Coll., Cambridge. BA, Economics tripos, 1911. Served European War in Royal Artillery, 1914-19 (MC); retired with rank of Major. High Sheriff of Denbighshire, 1942; JP Denbighshire since 1946. *Recreations:* sketching, gardening. *Address:* The Grange, Ruthin, North Wales. *T:* Ruthin 2124.

HESELTINE, Rt. Hon. Michael (Ray Dibdin); PC 1979; MP (C) Henley, since 1974 (Tavistock, 1966-74); Secretary of State for the Environment, since 1979; *b* 21 March 1933; *s* of late Col R. D. Heseltine, Swansea, Glamorgan; *m* 1962, Anne Harding Williams; one *s* two *d. Educ:* Shrewsbury Sch.; Pembroke Coll., Oxford. BA PPE; Pres. Oxford Union, 1954. National Service (commissioned), Welsh Guards, 1959. Contested (C): Gower, 1959; Coventry North, 1964. Director of Bow Publications, 1961-65; Chm., Haymarket Press, 1966-70. Vice-Chm., Cons. Parly Transport Cttee, 1968; Opposition Spokesman on Transport, 1969; Parly Sec., Min. of Transport, June-Oct. 1970; Parly Under-Sec. of State, DoE, 1970-72; Minister for Aerospace and Shipping, DTI, 1972-74; Opposition Spokesman on: Industry, 1974-76; Environment, 1976-79. Pres., Assoc. of Conservative Clubs, 1978; Vice-Pres., 1978, Pres., 1982-. Nat. Young Conservatives. *Address:* Thenford House, near Banbury, Oxon. *Club:* Carlton.

HESELTINE, Sir William (Frederick Payne), KCVO 1982 (CVO 1969; MVO 1961); CB 1978; Deputy Private Secretary to the Queen since 1977 (Assistant Private Secretary, 1972-77); *b* E Fremantle, W Australia, 17 July 1930; *s* of H. W. Heseltine; *m* 1st, Ann Elizabeth (*d* 1957), *d* of late L. F. Turner, Melbourne; 2nd, Audrey Margaret, *d* of late S. Nolan, Sydney; one *s* one *d. Educ:* Christ Church Grammar Sch., Claremont, WA; University of Western Australia (1st class hons, History). Prime Minister's dept, Canberra, 1951-62; Private Secretary to Prime Minister, 1955-59; Asst Information Officer to The Queen, 1960-61; Acting Official Secretary to Governor-General of Australia, 1962; Asst Federal Director of Liberal Party of Australia, 1962-64; attached to Household of Princess Marina for visit to Australia, 1964; attached to Melbourne Age, 1964; Asst Press Secretary to the Queen, 1965-67, Press Secretary, 1968-72. *Address:* St James's Palace, SW1A 1BG. *Clubs:* Boodle's, Press.

HESKETH, 3rd Baron, *cr* 1935, of Hesketh, **Thomas Alexander Fermor-Hesketh,** Bt 1761; *b* 28 Oct. 1950; *s* of 2nd Baron and Christian Mary, *o d* of Sir John McEwen, 1st Bt of Marchmont, DL, JP; *S* father 1955; *m* 1977, Hon. Claire, *e d* of 3rd Baron Manton, *qv* ; one *d. Educ:* Ampleforth. *Heir:* *b* Hon. Robert Fermor-Hesketh [*b* 1 Nov. 1951; *m* 1979, Jeanne, *d* of Patrick McDowell]. *Address:* Easton Neston, Towcester, Northamptonshire. *T:* Towcester 50445. *Club:* Turf.

HESKETH, (Charles) Peter Fleetwood Fleetwood-, TD 1943; DL; *b* 5 Feb. 1905; 2nd *s* of late Charles Hesketh Fleetwood-Hesketh, and late Anne Dorothea, *e d* of Sir Thomas Brocklebank, 2nd Bt; *m* 1940, Mary Monica (*d* 1982), JP Lancs, 2nd *d* of Sir Ralph Cockayne Assheton, 1st Bt; one *d. Educ:* Eton. Studied architecture at London Univ. under Sir Albert Richardson, and at Architectural Association; Student RIBA and Registered Architect. Worked in office of late H. S. Goodhart-Rendel and later with Seely & Paget and other architects. Member of Lloyd's until 1975. Hon. district rep., for National Trust, 1947-68 (Mem., W Midlands Regional Cttee, 1972-); Member: Covent Gdn Conservation Area Adv. Cttee, 1972-; Archbp's Adv. Bd on Redundant Churches, 1973-78; Cttee, Westminster Soc.; Gen. Synod of Church of England, 1975-80; Prayer Book Soc. (Founder Mem. and Trustee); Cttee of Incorporated Church Building Soc.; Council, Anglo-Rhodesian Soc., 1965-80 (Chm. Lancs and Cheshire Br., 1969-80); Salisbury Gp. Hon. Dist Rep., Georgian Group and other societies; Founder Mem., Victorian Society (Secretary, 1961-63, Hon. Architectural Adviser 1963-, Chm., Liverpool Gp, 1968-); Patron, Thirties Soc., 1980-. Architectural Correspt, Daily Telegraph, 1964-67. Pres., Widnes, Cheshire, Div., Conservative Assoc., 1971-. Special Constable in London during Gen. Strike, 1926. 2nd Lieut DLO Yeomanry (Cavalry) 1926, Captain 1938. Served, 1939-45, with DLO Yeomanry; WO, MI (Liaison); in occupied France with 2nd SAS and Maquis; Monuments, Fine Arts and Archives (Austria). High Sheriff, Lancs., 1960-61; DL Lancs, 1961-74, Cheshire, 1974-. A Burgess of Preston; Freeman of Hale. Assisted with The Master Builder magazine in early 1930's. *Publications:* Guide to the Palace of Schönbrunn, 1945; Murray's Lancashire Architectural Guide, 1955; Lancs section of Collins's Guide to English Parish Churches, 1958 (ed. John Betjeman); Life of Sir Charles Barry, in Peter Ferriday's Victorian Architecture, 1963; 1790-1840 section of Ian Grant's Great Interiors, 1967; chapters in: Shell Guide to England (ed John Hadfield), 1970, rev. edn 1981; The Country Seat (ed Howard Colvin and

John Harris), 1970; contrib. Good Churches Guide, 1982. Illustrated John Betjeman's Ghastly Good Taste, 1933, extended 1970. Contrib. articles and drawings to Country Life, etc. *Address:* The Manor House, Hale, near Liverpool. *T:* 051-425 3116; 57 Great Ormond Street, WC1. *T:* 01-242 3672. *Clubs:* Travellers', MCC, Royal Automobile (Life Mem.).

HESKETH, Roger Fleetwood, OBE 1970; TD 1942; *b* 28 July 1902; *e s of* Charles Hesketh Fleetwood-Hesketh, DL; *m* 1952, Lady Mary Lumley, OBE, DStJ, *e d* of 11th Earl of Scarbrough, KG, PC, GCSI, GCIE, GCVO; one *s* two *d. Educ:* Eton; Christ Church, Oxford (MA). Called to the Bar, Inner Temple, 1928. MP (C) for Southport, 1952-59. High Sheriff, Lancs, 1947; DL 1950, Vice-Lieutenant, 1972-77; JP 1950, Lancs; Mayor of Southport, 1950; Freeman of the Borough, 1966. Chairman, Lancashire Agricultural Executive Cttee, 1965-72. Trustee, Historic Churches Preservation Trust. Served War of 1939-45 (despatches, Bronze Star Medal, USA). Hon. Colonel, Duke of Lancaster's Own Yeomanry, 1956-67. *Address:* Meols Hall, Southport, Merseyside. *T:* Southport 28171; H4 Albany, Piccadilly, W1. *T:* 01-734 5320. *Club:* Travellers'.

HESLOP-HARRISON, Prof. John, FRS 1970; MSc, PhD, DSc, FRSE, MRIA, FRSA, FLS; Royal Society Research Professor, University College of Wales, Aberystwyth, since 1977; *b* 10 Feb. 1920; *s* of late Prof. J. W. Heslop-Harrison, FRS; *m* 1950, Yolande Massey; one *s. Educ:* Grammar School, Chester-le-Street, King's Coll. (University of Durham), Newcastle upon Tyne. MSc (Dunelm), PhD (Belfast), DSc (Dunelm). Radio Officer, Ministry of Supply, 1941-42; 2nd Lieut RAOC, 1942; Captain REME, 1942-45. Lecturer in Agricultural Botany, King's Coll., Univ. of Durham, 1945-46; Lecturer in Botany: Queen's Univ., Belfast, 1946-50; UCL, 1950-53; Reader in Taxonomy, UCL, 1953-54; Prof. of Botany, Queen's Univ., Belfast, 1954-60; Mason Prof. of Botany, Univ. of Birmingham, 1960-67; Prof. of Botany, Inst. of Plant Develt, Univ. of Wisconsin, 1967-71; Dir, Royal Botanic Gardens, Kew, 1971-76. Visiting Professor: (Brittingham) Univ. of Wisconsin, 1965; US Dept of Agriculture Institute of Forest Genetics, Rhinelander, Wis, 1968; Univ. of Massachusetts, Amherst, Mass, 1976-77, 1978-79; Lectures: Sigma Xi, Geneva, NY, 1969; William Wright Smith, Edinburgh, 1972; George Bidder, Soc. Exptl Biol., Leeds, 1973; Ghosh, Univ. of Calcutta, 1973; Kennedy Orton Meml, UCW, Bangor, 1974; Croonian, Royal Society, 1974; Amos Meml, E Malling, 1975; Holden, Univ. of Nottingham, 1976; Bewley, Glasshouse Crops Res. Inst., 1978; Hooker, Linnean Soc., 1979; Bateson, John Innes Inst., 1979; Waller Meml, Univ. of Ohio, 1980; Blackman, Univ. of Oxford, 1980. Mem., ARC, 1977-82; Vice-President: Botanical Soc. of British Isles, 1972; Linnean Soc., 1973; President: Inst. of Biology, 1974-75; Sect. K, British Assoc. for Advancement of Science, 1974. Editor, Annals of Botany, 1961-67. Corresp. Mem., Royal Netherlands Botanical Soc., 1968; For. Fellow, Indian Nat. Sci. Acad., 1974; Mem., German Acad. of Science, 1975; For. Mem., American Botanical Soc., 1976-; For. Hon. Mem., Amer. Acad. Arts and Scis., 1982. Hon. DSc: Belfast, 1971; Bath, 1982. Trail-Crisp Award, Linnean Soc., 1967; Univ. of Liège Medal, 1967; Erdtman Internat. Medal for Palynology, 1971; Cooke Award, Amer. Acad. of Allergy, 1974. *Publications:* New Concepts in Flowering-plant Taxonomy, 1953; (ed) Pollen: development and physiology, 1971; papers on botanical subjects in various British and foreign journals. *Recreations:* hill walking, photography and painting. *Address:* Old Post, Hatfield, near Leominster, Herefordshire; Welsh Plant Breeding Station, Plas Gogerddan, near Aberystwyth SY23 3EB.

HESS, Ellen Elizabeth, NDH; Administrator, Studley College Trust, 1970-80; Principal, Studley College, Warwickshire, 1956-69; *b* 28 Dec. 1908; *d* of Charles Michael Joseph Hess and Fanny Thompson Hess (*née* Alder). *Educ:* Grammar School for Girls, Dalston; Royal Botanic Society, Regents Park. Lecturer in Horticulture, Swanley Horticultural College for Women, 1934-39; Agricultural Secretary, National Federation of Women's Institutes, 1939-46; Ellen Eddy Shaw Fellowship, Brooklyn Botanic Gardens, New York, USA, 1946-47; School of Horticulture, Ambler, Pa., USA, 1947-48; HM Inspector of Schools (Agriculture and Further Education), 1948-56. Veitch Meml Medal, RHS, 1967. *Recreations:* travel, photography, walking. *Address:* The Croft, 54 Torton Hill Road, Arundel, West Sussex BN18 9HH.

HESSAYON, Dr David Gerald; horticultural and agricultural author; Chairman: Pan Britannica Industries Ltd, since 1972; Turbair Ltd, since 1972; Director, Tennants Consolidated Ltd, since 1982; *b* 13 Feb. 1928; *s* of Jack and Lena Hessayon; *m* 1951, Joan Parker Gray; two *d. Educ:* Salford Grammar Sch.; Leeds Univ. (BSc 1950); Manchester Univ. (PhD 1954). FRMS 1960; FRES 1960; FRSA 1970; FIBiol 1971; FBIM 1972. Res. Fellow, UC of Gold Coast, 1953; entered Pan Britannica Industries Ltd, 1955; Technical Manager, 1955; Technical Dir, 1960; Man. Dir, 1964. Chm., British Agrochemicals Assoc., 1980-81. Mem., Guild of Freemen of the City of London, 1977-. *Publications:* Be Your Own Gardening Expert, 1959, revd edn 1977; Be Your Own House Plant Expert, 1960, revd edn 1980; Potato Growers Handbook, 1961; Silage Makers Handbook, 1961; Be Your Own Lawn Expert, 1962, revd edn 1979; Be Your Own Rose Expert, 1964, revd edn 1977; (with J. P. Hessayon) The Garden Book of Europe, 1973; Vegetable Plotter, 1976; Be Your Own House Plant Spotter, 1977; Be Your Own Vegetable Doctor, 1978; Be Your Own Garden Doctor, 1978; The House Plant Expert, 1980; The Rose Expert, 1981; The Lawn Expert, 1982; The Cereal Disease Expert, 1982; The Tree and Shrub Expert, 1983. *Recreations:* American folk music, thinking

about the book I should be writing. *Address:* Hilgay, Mill Lane, Broxbourne, Herts. *Club:* Press.

HESSE, Mary Brenda, MA, MSc, PhD; FBA 1971; Professor of Philosophy of Science, University of Cambridge, since 1975; Fellow of Wolfson College (formerly University College), Cambridge, since 1965; *b* 15 Oct. 1924; *d* of Ethelbert Thomas Hesse and Brenda Nellie Hesse (*née* Pelling). *Educ:* Imperial Coll., London; University Coll., London. MSc, PhD (London); DIC; MA (Cantab). Lecturer: in Mathematics, Univ. of Leeds, 1951-55; in Hist. and Philosophy of Science, UCL, 1955-59; in Philosophy of Science, Univ. of Cambridge, 1960-68; Reader in Philosophy of Sci., Cambridge Univ., 1968-75; Vice-Pres., Wolfson Coll., 1976-80. Member: Council, British Acad., 1979-; UGC, 1980-. Visiting Prof.: Yale Univ., 1961; Univ. of Minnesota, 1966; Univ. of Chicago, 1968. Stanton Lectr, Cambridge, 1977-80; Joint Gifford Lectr, Edinburgh, 1983. Editor, Brit. Jl for the Philosophy of Science, 1965-69. *Publications:* Science and the Human Imagination, 1954; Forces and Fields, 1961; Models and Analogies in Science, 1963; The Structure of Scientific Inference, 1974; Revolutions and Reconstructions in the Philosophy of Science, 1980; articles in jls of philosophy and of the history and the philosophy of science. *Recreations:* walking, Roman roads. *Address:* Department of History and Philosophy of Science, Free School Lane, Cambridge CB2 3RH.

HESTON, Charlton; actor (films, stage and television), USA; *b* Evanston, Ill, 4 Oct. 1924; *s* of Russell Whitford Carter and Lilla Carter (*née* Charlton); *m* 1944, Lydia Marie Clarke (actress), Two Rivers, Wisconsin; one *s* one *d. Educ:* New Trier High Sch., Ill; Sch. of Speech, Northwestern Univ., 1941-43. Served War of 1939-45, with 11th Army Air Forces in the Aleutians. Co-Dir (with wife), also both acting, Thomas Wolfe Memorial Theatre, Asheville, NC (plays: the State of the Union, The Glass Menagerie, etc.). In Antony and Cleopatra, Martin Beck Theatre, New York, 1947; also acting on Broadway, 1949 and 1950, etc. *Films:* (1950-) include: Dark City, Ruby Gentry, The Greatest Show on Earth, Arrowhead, Bad For Each Other, The Savage, Pony Express, The President's Lady, Secret of the Incas, The Naked Jungle, The Far Horizons, The Private War of Major Benson, The Ten Commandments (Moses), The Big Country, Ben Hur (Acad. Award for best actor, 1959), The Wreck of the Mary Deare, El Cid, 55 Days at Peking, The Greatest Story Ever Told, Major Dundee, The Agony and the Ecstacy, Khartoum, Will Penny, Planet of the Apes, Soylent Green, The Three Musketeers, Earthquake, Airport 1975, The Four Musketeers, The Last Hard Men, Battle of Midway, Two-Minute Warning, Gray Lady Down, Crossed Swords, The Mountain Men, The Awakening. TV appearances, esp. in Shakespeare. Mem., Screen Actors' Guild (Pres., 1966-69); Mem., Nat. Council on the Arts, 1967-; Chm., Amer. Film Inst., 1961-; Chm., Center Theatre Group, LA, 1963; Chm. on the Arts for Presidential Task Force on the Arts and Humanities, 1981-. Is Interested in Shakespearian roles. Academy Award, 1978; Jean Hersholt Humanitarian Award, 1978. *Publication:* (ed Hollis Alpert) The Actor's Life: Journals 1956-1976, 1979. *Address:* c/o Mrs Carol M. Lanning, 1369 Avenida de Cortez, Pacific Palisades, Calif 90272, USA.

HETHERINGTON, Alastair; *see* Hetherington, H. A.

HETHERINGTON, (Arthur) Carleton, CBE 1971 (MBE 1945); Secretary of Association of County Councils, 1974-80; *b* 13 Feb. 1916; *s* of late Arthur Stanley and Mary Venters Hetherington, Silloth, Cumberland; *m* 1941, Xenia, *d* of late Nicholas Gubsky, Barnes; three *s. Educ:* St Bees Sch. Admitted Solicitor 1938. Asst Solicitor: Peterborough, 1938-39; Stafford, 1939. Served Royal Artillery, 1939-46 (Hon. Lt-Col); Temp. Lt-Col 1944-46. Dep. Clerk of the Peace and Dep. Clerk of County Council: of Cumberland, 1946-52; of Cheshire, 1952-59; Clerk of the Peace and Clerk of County Council of Cheshire, 1959-64. Sec., County Councils Assoc., 1964-74. Mem., Departmental Cttee on Jury Service, 1963-64; Sec., Local Authorities Management Services and Computer Cttee, 1965-80. *Recreations:* music, golf, family. *Address:* 33 Campden Hill Court, W8 7HS. *Club:* Royal Automobile.

HETHERINGTON, Sir Arthur (Ford), Kt 1974; DSC 1944; Chairman, British Gas Corporation, 1973-76 (Member 1967, Deputy Chairman 1967-72, Chairman 1972, Gas Council); *b* 12 July 1911; *s* of late Sir Roger Hetherington and Lady Hetherington; *m* 1937, Margaret Lacey; one *s* one *d. Educ:* Highgate Sch.; Trinity Coll., Cambridge (BA). Joined staff of Gas Light & Coke Company, 1935. Served War, RNVR, 1941-45. North Thames Gas Board, 1949-55; joined staff of Southern Gas Board, 1955; Deputy Chairman, 1956; Chairman 1961-64; Chairman, E Midlands Gas Board, 1964-66. FEng; Hon. FIGasE. Hon. DSc London, 1974. *Address:* 32 Connaught Square, W2. *T:* 01-723 3128. *Clubs:* Athenæum; Royal Southampton Yacht.
See also R. le G. Hetherington.

HETHERINGTON, Carleton; *see* Hetherington, A. C.

HETHERINGTON, Rear-Adm. Derick Henry Fellowes, CB 1961; DSC 1941 (2 Bars 1944, 1945); MA (Oxon), 1963; Domestic Bursar and Fellow of Merton College, Oxford, 1963-76; Emeritus Fellow, 1976; *b* 27 June 1911; *s* of Commander H. R. Hetherington, RD, Royal Naval Reserve, and Hilda Fellowes; *m* 1942, Josephine Mary, *d* of Captain Sir Leonard Vavasour, 4th Bt, RN; one *s* three *d* (and one *s* decd). *Educ:* St Neot's, Eversley, Hants; RNC Dartmouth. Cadet, HMS Barham, 1928-29; Midshipman-Comdr (HMS Effingham, Leander, Anthony, Wildfire, Kimberley, Windsor, Lookout,

Royal Arthur, Cheviot), 1929-50; Captain 1950; Chief of Staff, Canal Zone, Egypt, 1950-52; Senior British Naval Officer, Ceylon, 1953-55; Captain (D) 4th Destroyer Squadron, 1956-57; Director of Naval Training, Admiralty, 1958-59; Flag Officer, Malta, 1959-61; retired 1961. Croix de Guerre (France) 1945. *Address:* 14 Couching Street, Watlington, Oxon OX9 5QQ.

HETHERINGTON, (Hector) Alastair; journalist; Research Professor, Stirling University, since 1982; former Editor of The Guardian; *b* Llanishen, Glamorganshire, 31 Oct. 1919; *yr s* of late Sir Hector Hetherington and Lady Hetherington; *m* 1st, 1957, Miranda (marr. diss. 1978), *d* of Professor R. A. C. Oliver, *qv* ; two *s* two *d* ; 2nd, 1979, Sheila Janet Cameron, *widow* of Hamish Cameron; one step *s* two step *d*. *Educ:* Gresham's Sch., Holt; Corpus Christi Coll., Oxford (Hon. Fellow, 1971). Royal Armoured Corps, 1940-46. Editorial staff, The Glasgow Herald, 1946-50; joined Manchester Guardian, 1950, Asst Editor and Foreign Editor, 1953-56, Editor, 1956-75; Director: Guardian and Manchester Evening News Ltd, 1956-75; Guardian Newspapers Ltd, 1967-75; Controller, BBC Scotland, 1975-78; Manager, BBC Highland, 1979-80. Member, Royal Commission on the Police, 1960-62. Vis. Fellow, Nuffield Coll., Oxford, 1973-79. Trustee, Scott Trust, 1970-. Journalist of the Year, Nat. Press awards, 1970. *Publication:* Guardian Years, 1981. *Recreations:* hill walking, golf. *Address:* c/o Media Studies Department, University of Stirling, Stirling FK9 4LA; Tigh na-Fraoich, High Corrie, Isle of Arran KA27 8JB. *T:* Brodick 81652. *Club:* Athenæum.

HETHERINGTON, Roger le Geyt, CBE 1974 (OBE 1945); retired; *b* 20 Dec. 1908; *s* of late Sir Roger and Lady Hetherington; *m* 1945, Katharine Elise Dawson; one *d*. *Educ:* Highgate Sch.; Trinity Coll., Cambridge (MA). FEng, FICE, FIWES. Joined Binnie Deacon & Gourley (now Binnie & Partners), as pupil, 1930. Served War, RE, 1940-45. Taken into partnership, Binnie & Partners, 1947, Sen. Partner, 1973. President: Institution of Civil Engineers, 1972-73; Pipeline Industries Guild, 1975-77; Mem., Smeatonian Soc. of Civil Engineers. *Address:* 38 North Road, Highgate N6 4AX. *T:* 01-340 4203. *Club:* United Oxford & Cambridge University.

See also Sir A. F. Hetherington.

HETHERINGTON, Sir Thomas Chalmers, (Tony), KCB 1979; CBE 1970; TD; QC 1978; Director of Public Prosecutions, since 1977; *b* 18 Sept. 1926; *er s* of William and Alice Hetherington; *m* 1953, June Margaret Ann Catliff; four *d*. *Educ:* Rugby Sch.; Christ Church, Oxford. Served in Royal Artillery, Middle East, 1945-48; Territorial Army, 1948-67. Called to Bar, Inner Temple, 1952; Bencher, 1978. Legal Dept, Min. of Pensions and Nat. Insce, 1953; Law Officers' Dept, 1962, Legal Sec., 1966-75; Dep. Treasury Solicitor, 1975-77. *Address:* 4/12 Queen Anne's Gate, SW1.

HEUSTON, Prof. Robert Francis Vere, DCL Oxon 1970; MRIA 1978; Regius Professor of Laws, Trinity College, Dublin, 1970-83; *b* Dublin, 17 Nov. 1923; *e s* of late Vere Douglas Heuston and of Dorothy Helen Coulter; *m* 1962, Bridget Nancy (*née* Bolland), *widow* of Neville Ward-Perkins; four step *c*. *Educ:* St Columba's Coll.; Trinity Coll., Dublin: St John's Coll., Cambridge. Barrister, King's Inns, 1947, Gray's Inn, 1951; Hon. Member, Western Circuit, 1966. Fellow, Pembroke Coll., Oxford, 1947-65 (Hon. Fellow, 1982), Dean, 1951-57, Pro-Proctor, 1953; Professor of Law, Univ. of Southampton, 1965-70. Member, Law Reform Cttee (England), 1968-70, (Ireland), 1975-. Visiting Professor: Univ. of Melbourne, 1956; Univ. of British Columbia, 1960; ANU, 1977; Gresham Professor in Law, 1964-70. *Publications:* (ed) Salmond and Heuston on Torts, 18th edn 1981; Essays in Constitutional Law, 2nd edn 1964; Lives of the Lord Chancellors, 1964; various in learned periodicals. *Address:* Kentstown House, Brownstown, Navan, Ireland. *T:* Drogheda 25195. *Clubs:* United Oxford & Cambridge University; Royal Irish Yacht.

HEWAN, Gethyn Elliot; Hon. Secretary, Surrey Golf Union, since 1977; *b* 23 Dec. 1916; *s* of late E. D. Hewan and Mrs L. Hewan; *m* 1943, Peggy (*née* Allen); one *s* two *d*. *Educ:* Marlborough Coll., Wilts; Clare Coll., Cambridge (Exhibitioner); Yale Univ., USA (Mellon Schol). BA Hons 1938; MA 1943, Cambridge. Served War of 1939-45 (despatches): Middle East; Capt. 3rd Regt RHA 1943; Staff Coll., Camberley, psc 1944; BMRA 51st Highland Div., 1944-45. Asst Master, Wellington Coll., 1946-50; Headmaster, Cranbrook Sch., Bellevue Hill, NSW, 1951-63; Acting Bursar, Marlborough Coll., Wilts, 1963; Asst Master, Winchester Coll., 1963-64, Charterhouse Sch., 1964-65; Headmaster, Allhallows Sch., Rousdon, 1965-74. Sec., NSW branch of HMC of Aust., 1956-63; Standing Cttee of HMC of Aust., 1958-63; Foundation Member, Aust. Coll. of Education, 1958; Exec. Cttee, Australian Outward Bound Foundation, 1958-63. *Recreations:* cricket (Cambridge blue, 1938), golf, fishing; formerly hockey (blue, 1936-37-38, Captain) and billiards (½-blue, 1938). *Address:* Little Hadlow, Worplesdon Hill, Woking, Surrey. *T:* Brookwood 2652. *Clubs:* MCC; I Zingari; Free Foresters; Oxford and Cambridge Golfing Society; Worplesdon Golf; Senior Golfers'.

HEWARD, Air Chief Marshal Sir Anthony Wilkinson, KCB 1972 (CB 1968); OBE 1952; DFC and bar; AFC; Air Member for Supply and Organisation, Ministry of Defence, 1973-76; *b* 1 July 1918; *s* of late C E. J. Heward; *m* 1944, Clare Myfanwy Wainwright, *d* of late Maj.-Gen. C. B. Wainwright, CB; one *s* one *d*. Gp Captain RAF, 1957; IDC 1962; Air Cdre 1963; Dir of Operations (Bomber and Reconnaissance) MoD (RAF), 1963; Air Vice-Marshal 1966; Dep. Comdr, RAF Germany, 1966-69; AOA, HQ RAF Air Support Command, 1969-70; Air Marshal 1970; Chief of Staff, RAF Strike Command, 1970-72; AOC, No 18 (Maritime) Group, 1972-73; Air

Chief Marshal, 1974. County Councillor, Wilts, 1981-. *Address:* Home Close, Donhead St Mary, near Shaftesbury, Dorset.

HEWARD, Edmund Rawlings; Chief Master of the Supreme Court (Chancery Division), since 1980 (Master, 1959-79); *b* 19 Aug. 1912; *s* of late Rev. Thomas Brown Heward and Kathleen Amy Rachel Rawlings; *m* 1945, Constance Mary Sandiford, *d* of late George Bertram Crossley, OBE. *Educ:* Repton; Trinity Coll., Cambridge. Admitted a solicitor, 1937. Enlisted Royal Artillery as a Gunner, 1940; released as Major, DAAG, 1946. Partner in Rose, Johnson and Hicks, 9 Suffolk St, SW1, 1946. LLM 1960. *Publications:* Guide to Chancery Practice, 1962 (5th edn 1979); Matthew Hale, 1972; (ed) Part 2, Tristram and Coote's Probate Practice, 24th edn, 1973, 26th edn, 1983; (ed) Judgments and Orders in Halsbury's Laws of England, 4th edn; Lord Mansfield, 1979; Chancery Practice, 1983. *Address:* 36a Dartmouth Row, Greenwich, SE10 8AW. *T:* 01-692 3525. *Clubs:* United Oxford & Cambridge University, Travellers'.

HEWER, Christopher Langton, MB, BS (London); MRCP; Hon. FFARCS; Consulting Anæsthetist to St Bartholomew's Hospital and to Hospital for Tropical Diseases, London; late Senior Anæsthetist, The Queen's Hospital for Children, Hackney Road; Seamen's Hospital, Royal Albert Dock; St Andrew's Hospital, Dollis Hill; late Anæsthetist to Queen Mary's Hospital, Roehampton, Ministry of Pensions, Brompton Chest Hospital and Anæsthetic Specialist RAMC; Examiner in Anæsthesia to Royal College of Surgeons of England and Royal College of Physicians; late Consultant Anæsthetist to West Herts Hospital, Hemel Hempstead, to Luton and Dunstable Hospital, and to Harpenden Hospital; *s* of Joseph Langton Hewer, MD, FRCS; *m* 1925, Doris Phœbe, *d* of H. D'Arcy Champney, MA, Bristol; two *s* one *d*. *Educ:* University Coll. Sch; St Bartholomew's Hospital. Junior Scholarship in Anatomy and Physiology at St Bartholomew's Hospital Medical Coll.; MB, BS London degree (distinction in Physiology), 1920; served as House Surgeon and Resident Anæsthetist at St Bartholomew's Hospital; FRSM; Sec. of the Anæsthetic Section of same, 1930 and 1931, Pres., 1936-37; late Vice-Pres. Assoc. of Anæsthetists of Great Britain and Ireland, and Editor Emeritus of the Association's Journal, Anæsthesia; Member Anæsthetics Cttee of MRC and RSM; Pres., Section of Anæsthetics, BMA, 1953; Hon. Member: Liverpool Soc. of Anæsthetists; Canadian Soc. of Anæsthetists; late Member Board of Faculty of Anæsthetists, RCS. Frederic Hewitt Lecturer, 1959. Henry Hill Hickman Medallist, 1966, John Snow Medallist, 1966. *Publications:* Anæsthesia in Children, 1922; (with H. E. G. Boyle) Practical Anæsthetics, 1923; (ed) Recent Advances in Anæsthesia and Analgesia, 1932, 14th edn 1982; Thoughts on Modern Anæsthesia, 1970; articles in medical journals and reports; Section on Anæsthesia in Post Graduate Surgery, edited by R. Maingot; formerly editor Section on Anæsthesia in Medical Annual. *Address:* 33 Stormont Road, Highgate, N6. *T:* 01-340 1388.

HEWER, Thomas Frederick, MD (Bristol); FRCP, FLS; Professor of Pathology, 1938-68, and Pro-Vice-Chancellor, 1966-68, University of Bristol; Professor Emeritus, 1968; *b* 12 April 1903; *s* of William Frederick Hewer and Kathleen Braddon Standerwick; *m* 1941, Anne Hiatt Baker, OBE 1977; two *s* two *d*. *Educ:* Bristol Gram. Sch.; University of Bristol. Commonwealth Fund Fellow and Asst Pathologist, Johns Hopkins Univ., USA, 1927-29; Bacteriologist Sudan Government, 1930-35; Sen. Lectr in Pathology, University of Liverpool, 1935-38. Chm., Bristol Br., English-Speaking Union, 1942-67, Vice-Pres., 1967-. Botanical explorer, FAO/UN, 1975-; consultant, WHO, investigating causation of cancer among Turkoman, NE Iran, making botanical exploration of desert E of Caspian Sea, 1976-77. *Publications:* articles in medical and horticultural journals. *Recreations:* gardening and travel. *Address:* Vine House, Henbury, Bristol BS10 7AD. *T:* Bristol 503573. *Club:* English-Speaking Union.

HEWETSON, Christopher Raynor, TD 1967; Partner, Laces & Co., Solicitors, Liverpool, since 1961; Vice President, Law Society, since 1982; *b* 26 Dec. 1929; *s* of Harry Raynor Hewetson and Emma Hewetson; *m* 1962, Alison May Downie; two *s* one *d*. *Educ:* Sedbergh Sch.; Peterhouse, Cambridge (MA). National Service, 2nd Lieut 4th RHA, 1951-53; Territorial Service, 1953-68: Lt-Col commanding 359 Medium Regt, RA, TA, 1965-68. Qualified as solicitor, 1956. Mem. Council, Law Society, 1966-; President, Liverpool Law Society, 1976. *Recreations:* golf, walking. *Address:* 24c Westcliffe Road, Birkdale, Southport, Merseyside PR8 2BU. *T:* Southport 67179. *Clubs:* Army and Navy; Athenæum (Liverpool); Royal Birkdale Golf (Southport).

HEWETSON, Gen. Sir Reginald (Hackett), GCB 1966 (KCB 1962; CB 1958); CBE 1945 (OBE 1943); DSO 1944; Adjutant-General, Ministry of Defence (Army), 1964-67; retired; *b* Shortlands, Kent, 4 Aug. 1908; *s* of late J. Hewetson, ICS, and E. M. M. Hackett-Wilkins; *m* 1935, Patricia Mable, *y d* of late F. H. Burkitt, CIE; one *s* one *d*. *Educ:* Repton; RMA, Woolwich. Regular Commission in RA, 1928; Service in India (including Active Service, 1930-32), 1929-35; RA depot and home stations, 1935-39; psc 1939; Staff Capt. RA 4 Div., 1938; Adjt 30 Fd Regt and Capt. 1939; France, Oct. 1939-Jan. 1940; 2nd war course at Staff Coll., Camberley, Jan.-April 1940; Brigade Major RA 43 (Wessex) Div. May-Sept. 1940. Temp. Major; various GSO2 jobs incl. instructor Senior Officers Sch., 1940-42; GSO1 (Lieut-Col) HQ L of C North Africa, Sept.-Nov. 1942; 78 Div. (in North Africa), 1942-43 (OBE); Lieut-Col Comdg Fd Regt in 56 (London) Div. in Italy, 1943-44 (DSO); BGS HQ 10 Corps, 1944-45; BGS, British Troops, Austria, 1945-47; Student, IDC, 1949; Dep. Dir Staff Duties, WO, 1950-52; CRA 2nd

Infantry Div., BAOR, 1953–55; GOC 11th Armoured Div., March 1956; GOC, 4th Infantry Div. 1956–58; Commandant, Staff Coll., Camberley, 1958–61; Commander, British Forces, Hong Kong, Dec. 1961–March 1963; GOC-in-C, Far East Land Forces, 1963–64. Col Comdt, RA, 1962–73; Col Comdt, APTC, 1966–70; ADC (Gen.), 1966–67. Chm., Exec. Cttee, Army Benevolent Fund, 1968–76. Governor and Mem. Administrative Bd, Corps of Commissioners, 1964– (Pres., 1980-). *Recreations:* cricket (Army and Kent 2nd XI MCC, IZ), hockey (Norfolk and RA), golf. *Address:* Cherry Orchard, Fairwarp, near Uckfield, East Sussex. *Club:* MCC.

HEWETT, Sir John George, 5th Bt, *cr* 1813; MC 1919; Captain KAR; *b* 23 Oct. 1895; *e* surv. *s* of Sir Harold George Hewett, 4th Bt, and Eleanor (*d* 1946), *d* of Capt. Studdy, RN, and Mrs W. T. Summers; *S* father, 1949; *m* 1926, Yuilleen Maude (*d* 1980), *o c* of Samuel F. Smithson, Lauriston, Camberley; two *s*. *Educ:* Cheltenham. Served European War, 1914–18, British East Africa, 1914–19. *Heir: er s* Peter John Smithson Hewett, MM [*b* 27 June 1931; *m* 1958, Jennifer Ann Cooper, *o c* of Emrys Thomas Jones, Bexhill-on-Sea; two *s* one *d*. *Educ:* Bradfield Coll.; Jesus Coll., Cambridge. Called to the Bar, Gray's Inn, 1954; now a practising Advocate in Kenya. Kenya Regt attached Special Branch, Kenya Police, 1957]. *Address:* Lamwia Road, Langata, PO Box 40763, Nairobi, Kenya.

HEWISH, Prof. Antony, MA, PhD; FRS 1968; Professor of Radioastronomy, University of Cambridge, since 1971 (Reader, 1969–71); Fellow of Churchill College since 1962; *b* 11 May 1924; *s* of Ernest William Hewish and late Frances Grace Lanyon Pinch; *m* 1950, Marjorie Elizabeth Catherine Richards; one *s* one *d*. *Educ:* King's Coll., Taunton; Gonville and Caius Coll., Cambridge (Hon. Fellow, 1976). BA (Cantab.) 1948, MA 1950, PhD 1952; Hamilton Prize, Isaac Newton Student, 1952. RAE Farnborough, 1943–46; Research Fellow, Gonville and Caius Coll., 1952–54; Asst Dir of Research, 1954–62; Fellow, Gonville and Caius Coll., 1955–62; Lectr in Physics, Univ. of Cambridge, 1962–69. Visiting Prof. in Astronomy, Yale, 1963; Prof. of the Royal Instn, 1977; Halley Lectr, Oxford, 1979. Hon. DSc: Leicester, 1976; Exeter, 1977. Foreign Hon. Mem., Amer. Acad. of Arts and Sciences; Foreign Fellow, Indian Nat. Sci. Acad., 1982. Eddington Medal, Royal Astronomical Soc., 1969; Charles Vernon Boys Prize, Inst. of Physics and Physical Soc., 1970; Dellinger Gold Medal, Internat. Union of Radio Science, 1972; Michelson Medal, Franklin Inst., 1973; Hopkins Prize, Cambridge Phil Soc., 1973; Holweck Medal and Prize, Soc. Française de Physique, 1974; Nobel Prize for Physics (jtly), 1974; Hughes Medal, Royal Soc., 1977. *Publications:* Papers in Proc. Royal Society, Phys. Soc., Mon. Not. Royal Astr. Soc., etc. *Recreations:* music, gardening, sailing. *Address:* Pryor's Cottage, Kingston, Cambridge. *T:* Comberton 2657.

HEWITT, family name of Viscount Lifford.

HEWITT, Cecil Rolph, (C. H. Rolph); *b* London, 23 Aug. 1901; *s* of Frederick Thompson Hewitt and Edith Mary Speed; *m* 1st, 1926, Audrey Mary Buttery (marr. diss., 1946); one *d*; 2nd, 1947, Jenifer Wayne, author and scriptwriter; one *s* two *d*. *Educ:* State schools. City of London Police, 1921–46 (Chief Inspector); editorial staff, New Statesman, 1947; editor The Author, 1956–60; Dir, New Statesman, 1965–80. Vice-President: The New Bridge; Howard League for Penal Reform; Mem. Council, Soc. of Authors. *Publications:* A Licensing Handbook, 1947; Crime and Punishment, 1950; Towards My Neighbour, 1950; On Gambling, 1951; Personal Identity, 1956; (Ed.) The Human Sum, 1957; Mental Disorder, 1958; Commonsense About Crime and Punishment, 1961; The Trial of Lady Chatterley, 1961; (with Arthur Koestler) Hanged by the Neck, 1961; All Those in Favour? (The ETU Trial), 1962; The Police and The Public, 1962; Law and the Common Man, 1967; Books in the Dock, 1969; Kingsley, 1973; Believe What You Like, 1973; Living Twice (autobiog.), 1974; Mr Prone, 1977; The Queen's Pardon, 1978; London Particulars, 1980; The Police (child's history), 1980; contributor to The Encyclopædia Britannica, Chambers's Encyclopædia, Punch, The Week-End Book, The New Law Journal, the Times Literary Supplement, The Author, The Nation (NY), daily and weekly press. *Recreations:* music, reading, and the contemplation of work. *Address:* Rushett Edge, Bramley, Surrey GU5 0LH. *T:* Guildford 893227.

HEWITT, Sir (Cyrus) Lenox (Simson), Kt 1971; OBE 1963; Chairman: Qantas Airways Ltd, 1975–80 (Director, 1973–80); Qantas Wentworth Holdings Ltd, 1975–80. Q. H. Tours Ltd, 1975–80 (Director, 1974–80); *b* 7 May 1917; *s* of Cyrus Lenox Hewitt and Ella Louise Hewitt; *m* 1943, Alison Hope (*née* Tillyard); one *s* three *d*. *Educ:* Scotch Coll., Melbourne; Melbourne Univ. (BCom). FASA, FCIS, LCA. Broken Hill Proprietary Co. Ltd, 1933–39; Asst Sec., Commonwealth Prices Br., Canberra, 1939–46; Economist, Dept of Post War Reconstruction, 1946–49; Official Sec. and Actg Dep. High Comr, London, 1950–53; Commonwealth Treasury: Asst Sec., 1953–55; 1st Asst Sec., 1955–62; Dep. Sec., 1962–66; Chm., Australian Univs. Commn, 1967; Secretary to: Prime Minister's Dept, 1968–71; Dept of the Environment, Aborigines and the Arts, 1971–72; Dept of Minerals and Energy, 1972–75. Lectr, Econs and Cost Accountancy, Canberra UC, 1940–49, 1954. Acting Chairman: Pipeline Authority, 1973–75; Petroleum and Minerals Authority, 1974–75; Chm., Petroleum and Minerals Co. of Aust. Pty Ltd, 1975–; Director: East/Aust. Pipeline Corp. Ltd, 1974–75; Mary Kathleen Uranium Ltd, 1975–80; Aust. Industry Develt Corp., 1975; Ansett Transport Industries Ltd, 1982–; Santos Ltd, 1981–82; Pontello Constructions Ltd, 1980–82; Aberfoyle Ltd, 1981–; Endeavour Resources Ltd, 1982–; Dep. Chm., Aust. Atomic Energy Commn, 1977–82. Chairman: Exec. Cttee, IATA, 1976–77 (Mem.,

1975–); Orient Airlines Assoc., 1977. *Recreations:* tennis, farming. *Address:* 9 Torres Street, Red Hill, Canberra, ACT 2603, Australia. *T:* 958679; (office) PO Box 33, Redfern, NSW 2016, Australia. *T:* 699 2222. *Clubs:* Brooks's; Melbourne (Melbourne); Union (Sydney).
See also P. H. Hewitt.

HEWITT, Eric John, PhD, DSc; FRS 1982; Head of Plant Physiology and Biochemistry Section, Long Ashton Research Station, and Reader in Plant Physiology, University of Bristol, since 1967; *b* London, 27 Feb. 1919; *s* of Harry Edward Hewitt, OBE, MD, DPH, and Blanche (*née* Du Roveray); *m* 1943, Hannah Eluned (*née* Williams); one *s*. *Educ:* Whitgift Sch., S Croydon; King's Coll., Univ. of London, 1936–40 (BSc 1st Cl., AKC; DipEd); PhD, DSc Bristol; FIBiol. Asst Chemist/Chemist, MoS, 1940–42; Long Ashton Research Station: ARC Res. Grant Research Asst, 1942–45; Sen. Plant Physiologist, 1945–; seconded to ARC Unit of Plant Nutrition (Micronutrients), 1952–59; SPSO (merit promotion), 1967. *Publications:* Sand and Water Culture Methods Used in the Study of Plant Nutrition, 1952, 2nd edn 1966; (with T. A. Smith) Plant Mineral Nutrition, 1975; (ed, with C. V. Cutting): (sympos.) Nitrogen Metabolism in Plants, 1968; (sympos.) Nitrogen Assimilation of Plants, 1979; approx. 150 research contribs to jls. *Recreations:* squash, gardening, fell walking, TV and records. *Address:* Department of Agriculture and Horticulture, University of Bristol, Long Ashton Research Station, Bristol BS18 9AF. *T:* Long Ashton 2181; Langdales, 63 Ridgeway Road, Long Ashton, Bristol BS18 9EZ. *T:* Long Ashton 2274. *Club:* Chesham (King's College Assoc.).

HEWITT, Rev. Canon George Henry Gordon; Residentiary Canon, Chelmsford Cathedral, 1964–78, Canon Emeritus since 1978; *b* 30 May 1912; *s* of Rev. G. H. Hewitt; *m* 1942, Joan Ellen Howden; two *s* one *d*. *Educ:* Trent Coll.; Brasenose, Oxford; Wycliffe Hall, Oxford. Asst Curate, St Clement, Leeds, 1936–39; Chaplain, Ridley Hall, Cambridge, 1939–41; Asst Curate, Leeds Parish Church, 1941–43; Religious Book Editor, Lutterworth Press, 1943–52; Diocesan Education Sec., Sheffield, 1952–58; Residentiary Canon, Sheffield Cathedral, 1953–58; Vicar of St Andrew, Oxford, 1958–64. Chaplain to the Queen, 1969–82. *Publications:* Let the People Read, 1949; The Problems of Success: a history of the Church Missionary Society, 1910–1942, vol. I, 1971, vol. II, 1977. *Address:* 8 Rainsford Avenue, Chelmsford, Essex.

HEWITT, Harold; His Honour Judge Hewitt; a Circuit Judge, since 1980; *b* 14 March 1917; *s* of George Trueman Hewitt and Bertha Lilian Hewitt; *m* 1946, Doris Mary Smith; two *s*. *Educ:* King James I Grammar Sch., Bishop Auckland. Admitted solicitor (Hons), 1938; HM Coroner, S Durham, 1948–80; a Recorder of the Crown Court, 1974–80. Chm. (part-time), Industrial Tribunal, 1975–80. Member Council, Law Society, 1976–80. *Recreations:* gardening, French literature, bird-watching. *Address:* Longmeadows, Etherley, Bishop Auckland, Co. Durham. *T:* Bishop Auckland 832386; Saltings Cottage, Bowness-on-Solway, Cumbria. *Clubs:* Carlton, Lansdowne.

HEWITT, Harold; solicitor, consultant since 1973; *b* 1 Jan. 1908; *m* 1949, Jeannette Myers; one *d*. *Educ:* Bede Collegiate Sch., Sunderland; Armstrong Coll., Univ. of Durham. Solicitor, admitted 1930. Legal Adviser, High Commissioner for Austria, Allied Commission, 1946–49. Member, Law Society; Past Pres., Bexley and Dartford Law Soc. *Recreation:* social welfare work. *Address:* 121 Dorset House, Gloucester Place, NW1 5AQ.

HEWITT, Capt. John Graham, DSO, 1940; RN (retired); *b* 15 Oct. 1902; *s* of J. G. L. Hewitt, SM, Marton, NZ; two *s*; *m* 1947, Mrs Rooney, widow of Col J. J. Rooney, IMS. *Educ:* RN Colls, Osborne and Dartmouth. Midshipman, 1919; Comdr, 1936; commanded HMS Winchelsea, 1937, HMS Auckland, 1940–41; HMS Dauntless, 1941–42; Capt. 1942; HMS Royalist, 1944; HMS Frobisher, 1945–46; Second Naval Member of NZ Navy Board, 1947; Director Tactical Sch., Woolwich, 1949–52; retired list, 1952. Norwegian War Cross, 1942. *Recreation:* fishing. *Address:* 16 Royston Court, Kew Gardens, Richmond, Surrey.

HEWITT, Air Vice-Marshal Joseph Eric, CBE 1951 (OBE 1940); psa 1934; Royal Australian Air Force (retired); Member Panel of Military Experts, United Nations, since 1952; *b* 13 April 1901; *s* of late Rev. J. H. Hewitt, MA, BD and late Rose Alice Hewitt (*née* Harkness), Melbourne, Vic; *m* 1925, Lorna Pretoria (*d* 1976), *d* of late Alfred Eugene Bishop and late Joanne Bishop (*née* Prismall), Melbourne, Vic; three *d*. *Educ:* Scotch Coll., Melbourne; Royal Australian Naval Coll., Jervis Bay, NSW. Served in RAN, RN, RAAF and RAF, 1915–28; Cadet Midshipman, 1915; Midshipman, 1918; Sub-Lieut 1921; Lieut, 1922. Transferred to RAAF, 1928; Comdg Officer RAAF, HMAS Albatross, 1929–32; RAF Staff Coll., Andover, 1934; Asst Liaison Officer, Australia House, London, 1935; Comdg Officer, No 104 Sqdn, RAF, 1936–38; SASO, RAAF, Richmond, NSW, 1938–39; Sen. Admin. Staff Officer, Southern Area, HQ, 1939–40; DPS, HQ, RAAF, 1940–41; DCAS, RAAF, 1941; Director of Air Operations, Staff of C-in-C. Allied Command, NEI, Java, 1942; ACAS, 1942; Director of Allied Air Intelligence, SW Pacific Area, 1942 and 1944; AOC No 9 Op. Group, 1943 (Battle of Bismarck Sea, 1943); Air member for Personnel, RAAF, HQrs, 1945–48; Australian Defence Representative, London, 1949–51; Air Member for Supply and Equipment, Dept of Air, Melbourne, 1951–56, retired April 1956. Member, Council for Adult Education of Victoria, 1956–66. Manager, Education and Training, Internat. Harvester Co. (Aust.) Pty Ltd, 1956–66; Trustee, Services Canteens Trust Fund, 1957–77. FAIM 1956. *Publication:*

Adversity in Success, 1981. *Recreations:* swimming, gardening, reading. *Address:* Unit 1, 24 Oxford Street, South Yarra, Vic 3141, Australia. *Club:* Naval and Military (Melbourne).

HEWITT, Sir Lenox; *see* Hewitt, Sir C. L. S.

HEWITT, Margaret, PhD; Reader in Social Institutions, University of Exeter, since 1970; *b* 25 Oct. 1928; *d* of Robert Henry Hewitt and Jessie Hewitt. *Educ:* Bedford Coll., London; London Sch. of Economics. BA Hons Sociology (1st Cl.) 1950, PhD Sociology 1953. Univ. of London Postgrad. Studentship in Sociology, 1950-52; Asst Lectr in Sociology, University Coll. of the South West, 1952-54; Lectr in Sociology, Univ. of Exeter, 1954-65, Sen. Lectr, 1965-70. Mem. Council, Univ. of Exeter, 1964-70; Governor: Bedford Coll., 1968-; St Luke's Coll., Exeter, 1969-78. Member: Church Assembly, 1961-70; Gen. Synod of Church of England, 1970-; Standing Cttee of Gen. Synod, 1976-; Church Commn on Crown Appts, 1977-. Rep. of Univ. of London on Council of Roedean Sch., 1974-. *Publications:* Wives and Mothers in Victorian Industry, 1958; (with Ivy Pinchbeck) Children in English Society, Vol. I 1969, Vol. II 1973. *Recreation:* doing nothing. *Address:* 14 Velwell Road, Exeter, Devon EX4 4LE. *T:* Exeter 54150. *Club:* University Women's.

HEWITT, Sir Nicholas Charles Joseph, 3rd Bt *cr* 1921; *b* 12 Nov. 1947; *s* of Sir Joseph Hewitt, 2nd Bt and of Marguerite, *yr d* of Charles Burgess; *S* father, 1973; *m* 1969, Pamela Margaret, *o d* of Geoffrey J. M. Hunt, TD; two *s* one *d*. *Heir:* s Charles Edward James Hewitt, *b* 15 Nov. 1970. *Address:* The Forge, Hutton Buscel, Scarborough, North Yorks. *T:* Scarborough 862307.

HEWITT, Patricia Hope; General Secretary, National Council for Civil Liberties, since 1974; *b* 2 Dec. 1948; *d* of Sir (Cyrus) Lenox (Simson) Hewitt, *qv*, and Alison Hope Hewitt. *Educ:* C of E Girls' Grammar Sch., Canberra; Australian Nat. Univ.; Newnham Coll., Cambridge. BA, AMusA (piano). Public Relations Officer, Age Concern (Nat. Old People's Welfare Council), 1971-73; Women's Rights Officer, Nat. Council for Civil Liberties, 1973-74; Trustee: Cobden Trust, 1974-; Areopagitica Trust, 1981-; Member: Sec. of State's Adv. Cttee on Employment of Women, 1977-; Unofficial Cttee of Enquiry into Southall, 23 April 1979; National Labour Women's Cttee, 1979-; Labour Party Enquiry into Security Services, 1980-81; Co-Chm., Human Rights Network, 1979-81. Prospective Parly cand. (Lab) Leicester East, 1981-. *Publications:* Your Rights (Age Concern), 1973, 10th edn 1982; Rights for Women (NCCL), 1975; Civil Liberties, the NCCL Guide (co-ed 3rd edn), 1977; The Privacy Report (NCCL), 1977; Your Rights at Work (NCCL), 1978, 2nd edn 1981; The Abuse of Power, 1981. *Recreations:* reading, theatre, music, politics. *Address:* 53 Willes Road, NW5 3DN. *T:* 01-267 2567. *Club:* Camden Labour.

HEWITT, Richard Thornton, OBE 1945; Consultant, Royal Society of Medicine (Executive Director, 1952-82); Vice-President, The Royal Society of Medicine Foundation, Inc., New York, since 1969; *b* 1917; *yr s* of late Harold and Elsie Muriel Hewitt, Bramhall, Cheshire. *Educ:* King's Sch., Macclesfield; Magdalen Coll., Oxford (Exhibitioner). Served War, Lt-Col, infantry and special forces, 1939-46. Asst Registrary, Cambridge Univ., 1946. Incorporated MA, Magdalene Coll., Cambridge, 1946. Sec., Oxford Univ. Medical Sch., 1947-52. Hon. Fellow, Swedish Med. Soc., 1968. Liveryman, Worshipful Society of Apothecaries of London, 1954. Freeman of the City of London, 1954. *Recreations:* gentle golf and gardening, music. *Address:* 84 Dorset House, NW1. *T:* 01-935 4014; The White House, Iffley, Oxford. *T:* Oxford 779263. *Clubs:* Athenæum, MCC, Royal Automobile; Frewen (Oxford); Royal and Ancient (St Andrews).

HEWLETT-DAVIES, Mrs Janet Mary; Director of Information, Department of Health and Social Security, since 1982; *b* 13 May 1938; *d* of Frederick Charles and Margaret Ellen Hewlett; *m* 1964, John Barry Davies. *Educ:* King Edward VI High School for Girls, Birmingham. Journalist, West Midlands 1956-59; BBC, 1959-65; Films Division, Central Office of Information, 1966-67; Press Officer: Prime Minister's Office, 1967-72; HM Customs and Excise, 1972-73; Principal Information Officer, Dept of Trade and Industry, 1973-74; Dep. Press Secretary to Prime Minister, 1974-76; Head of Information, Dept of Transport, 1976-79; Dir of Inf., DoE, 1979-82. *Recreations:* cooking, theatre, needlework, Radio 4. *Address:* 131a Ashley Gardens, SW1. *T:* 01-834 3738.

HEXHAM AND NEWCASTLE, Bishop of, (RC), since 1974; **Rt. Rev. Hugh Lindsay;** *b* 20 June 1927; *s* of William Stanley Lindsay and Mary Ann Lindsay (*née* Warren). *Educ:* St Cuthbert's Grammar Sch., Newcastle upon Tyne; Ushaw Coll., Durham. Priest 1953. Asst Priest; St Lawrence's, Newcastle upon Tyne, 1953; St Matthew's, Ponteland, 1954; Asst Diocesan Sec., 1953-59; Diocesan Sec., 1959-69; Chaplain, St Vincent's Home, West Denton, 1959-69; Auxiliary Bishop of Hexham and Newcastle and Titular Bishop of Chester-le-Street, 1969-74. *Recreation:* walking. *Address:* Bishop's House, East Denton Hall, 800 West Road, Newcastle upon Tyne NE5 2BJ.

HEXHAM AND NEWCASTLE, Auxiliary Bishop of, (RC); *see* Swindlehurst, Rt Rev. O. F.

HEXT, Maj.-Gen. Frederick Maurice, CB 1954; OBE 1945; CEng; FIMechE; FIEE; *b* 5 May 1901; *s* of Frederick Robert Hext; *m* 1924, Kathleen

Goulden; one *s*. *Educ:* Portsmouth Gram. Sch.; RMA, Woolwich. Commissioned RE 1921; served in India, 1925-28, and 1931-34; Instructor, Sch. of Military Engineering, 1939-42; served NW Europe Campaign (despatches) Comdr, REME, 53rd (Welsh) Div., and Dep. Dir of Mechanical Engineering, 12 Corps; DDME, 1 Corps, 1945-46; DDME, Burma Command, 1946-48; AAG, AG 21, War Office, 1949-51; DME, BAOR, 1951-53; Inspector of REME, 1953-56, retired 1956. Hon. Col 53 (Welsh) Inf. Div. REME, 1956-61. Maj.-Gen., 1953. Formerly Member Wessex RHB; Chm. Isle of Wight Group Hospital Management Cttee, 1961-72. FRSA. *Address:* Orchard Dene, Undercliff, St Lawrence, Isle of Wight. *T:* Niton 730387.

HEY, Donald Holroyde, DSc, PhD; FRS 1955; FRIC; Daniell Professor of Chemistry, University of London, 1950-71, now Emeritus Professor; President, Section B, British Association for the Advancement of Science, 1965; *b* Swansea, 1904; 2nd *s* of Arthur Hey, MusB, FRCO, LRAM, and Frances Jane Hey; *m* 1931, Jessie, MSc (Wales), *d* of Thomas and Katharine Jones; one *s* one *d*. *Educ:* Magdalen Coll. Sch., Oxford; University Coll., Swansea, BSc, MSc Wales; PhD London; DSc Manchester. Asst Lecturer in Chemistry, University of Manchester, 1928-30; Lecturer in Chemistry, University of Manchester, 1930-38; Lecturer in Chemistry, Imperial Coll. of Science and Technology, London, 1939-41; Dir of British Schering Research Institute, 1941-45; University Prof. of Chemistry at King's Coll., London, 1945-50; Asst Principal, King's Coll., 1962-68. Scientific Advr for Civil Defence, SE Region, 1952-58. Vice-Pres. of Chemical Soc. 1951-54 (Tilden Lectr, 1951, Pedler Lectr, 1970, Hon. Secretary, 1946-51, Vice-Pres., Perkin Div., 1971). Reilly Lectr, University of Notre Dame, Indiana, 1952; Visiting Prof. University of Florida, 1967. FKC; Fellow Imp. Coll. of Science and Technology, 1968; Hon. Fellow, Chelsea Coll., 1973. Member: Council, KCL, 1955-78; Adv. Council RMCS, 1961-73. Hon. DSc Wales, 1970. Defence Medal 1945. Intra-Science Res. Conf. Award and Medal, Santa Monica, Calif., 1968; Hon. Fellow, Intra-Science Res. Foundn, 1971. *Publications:* articles in scientific journals, mainly in Jl of Chem. Soc. *Recreations:* music, gardening. *Address:* 5 Wrayfield Avenue, Reigate, Surrey RH2 0NF. *T:* Reigate 47053.

HEY, Air Vice-Marshal Ernest, CB 1967; CBE 1963 (OBE 1954); CEng; Air Member for Technical Services, Department of Air, Canberra, 1960-72, retired; *b* Plymouth, Devon, 29 Nov. 1912; *s* of Ernest Hey, Terrigal, NSW; *m* 1936, Lorna, *d* of Sqdn Ldr A. Bennett, Melbourne; one *s* one *d*. *Educ:* Sydney Technical High Sch.; Sydney University. RAAF cadet, 1934; served War of 1939-45; Dir Technical Services, 1947-54; AOC Maintenance Comd, 1956-57; Imp. Defence Coll., 1957; Liaison Air Materiel Comd, USAF, 1958-59. *Recreations:* painting, lawn bowls. *Address:* 36 Holmes Crescent, Campbell, Canberra, ACT 2601, Australia.

HEY, James Stanley, MBE 1945; DSc; FRS 1978; retired; Research Scientist at Royal Radar Establishment, 1952-69; Chief Scientific Officer, 1966-69; *b* 3 May 1909; *s* of William Rennie Hey and Barbara Elizabeth Hey (*née* Matthews); *m* 1934, Edna Heywood. *Educ:* Rydal Sch.; Manchester Univ. BSc (Physics), 1930; MSc (X-ray Crystallography), 1931; DSc (Radio Astronomy and Radar Research), 1950. Army Operational Research Group, 1940-52 (Head of Estab., 1949-52). Hon. DSc: Birmingham, 1975; Kent, 1977. Eddington Medal, RAS, 1959. *Publications:* The Radio Universe, 1971; The Evolution of Radio Astronomy, 1973; research papers in scientific jls (RAS, Royal Society, Phys Soc., Philosophical Magazine, Nature, etc) including pioneering papers in radio astronomy. *Address:* 4 Shortlands Close, Willingdon, Eastbourne, Sussex BN22 0JE.

HEYCOCK, Baron *cr* 1967 (Life Peer), of Taibach; **Llewellyn Heycock,** CBE 1959; DL, JP; *b* 12 Aug. 1905; *s* of William Heycock and late Mary Heycock; *m* 1930, Olive Elizabeth (*née* Rees); one *s* (and one *s* decd). *Educ:* Eastern Sch., Port Talbot. Engine Driver, Dyffryn Yard Loco Sheds, Port Talbot. Glam CC, 1937-74 (Chm. 1962-63); Chm., West Glamorgan CC, 1973-75. Formerly: Member: Council and Court, University of Wales; Council and Court, University Coll. of S Wales and Mon.; Chairman: Schools Museum Service for Wales; Celtic Sea Adv. Cttee; Exec. Cttee, Royal National Eisteddfod of Wales, Port Talbot, 1966; Chm., Welsh Jt Educn Cttee; President: Coleg Harlech; Assoc. of Educn Cttees, 1964-65; Nat. Assoc. of Div. Execs for England and Wales, 1954-55, 1965-66; Exec. Mem., County Councils Assoc.; Hon. Druid, Nat. Eisteddfod of Wales, 1963; Vice-Pres., Nat. Theatre Co. for Wales. Hon. LLD, University of Wales, 1963. Hon. Freedom of Port Talbot, 1961. CStJ. JP Glam; JP Port Talbot; DL Glam 1963. *Recreation:* Rugby football. *Address:* 1 Llewellyn Close, Taibach, Port Talbot, West Glam. *T:* Port Talbot 2565.

HEYCOCK, Air Cdre George Francis Wheaton, CB 1963; DFC 1941; JP; *b* 17 Sept. 1909; *s* of Rev. F. W. Heycock, MA, and Edith Rowlandson; *m* 1938, Betty Boyd; one *s*. *Educ:* Haileybury and Imperial Service Coll.; Cranwell Cadet Coll. Commnd in RAF, 1929; Flying Instructor at RAF Coll., Cranwell and Central Flying Sch., 111 Sqdn, Fleet Air Arm, 1935-37. Test Pilot, Farnborough, 1937-39. Command of 23 and 141 Sqdns, 1940-42. Dir of Ops, Indian Air Force, 1949; Command of RAF Syerston, 1950-52; Air Ministry, 1952-55; Chief of Staff, British Joint Services Mission (RAF Staff), Washington, and Air Attaché, Washington, 1955; Air Attaché, Paris, 1959-64. JP Northants, 1965. Comdr Légion d'Honneur. *Recreation:* golf. *Address:* The Manor House, Pytchley, Northants. *T:* Kettering 790269. *Club:* Royal Air Force.

HEYERDAHL, Thor; author and anthropologist, since 1938; *b* 6 Oct. 1914; *s* of Thor Heyerdahl and Alison Heyerdahl (*née* Lyng); *m* 1st, 1936, Liv Coucheron Torp (*d* 1969); two *s*; 2nd, 1949, Yvonne Dedekam-Simonsen; three *d*. *Educ*: University of Oslo, 1933-36. Researches in the Marquesas Islands (Pacific), 1937-38; Researches among Coast Indians of Brit. Columbia, 1939-40. Active service Free Norwegian Army-Air Force parachute unit, 1942-45. Organised and led Kon-Tiki expedition, 1947. Continued research in USA and Europe, with authorship, 1948-. Chm. Bd, Kon-Tiki Museum, Oslo; organised and led Norwegian Archæological Expedition to the Galapagos Islands, 1953; experiments revealing tacking principles of balsa raft in Ecuador, 1953; field research, Bolivia, Peru, Colombia, 1954. Organised and led Norwegian Archæological Expedition to Easter Island and the East Pacific, 1955-56. Continued research, 1957-59. Made crossing from Safi, Morocco, to W Indies in papyrus boat, Ra II, 1970; sailed from Qurna, Iraq, to Djibouti in reed boat, Tigris, 1977-78. Participation in: Internat. Congress of Americanists, 1952-; Pacific Science Congresses, 1961-, all with lectures subseq. publ. in Proc. Congress. Vice-Pres., World Assoc. of World Federalists, 1966-; Trustee, Internat. Bd, World Wildlife Fund, 1977-; Internat. Patron, United World Colls, 1980. Mem., Royal Norwegian Acad. of Science, 1958; Fellow: New York Acad. of Sciences, 1960; Amer. Anthropological Assoc., 1966. Hon. Prof., Inst. Politecnico Nacional, Mexico, 1972. Hon. Dir, Explorers' Club, NY, 1982. Hon. Mem. Geog. Soc.: Peru, 1953; Norway, 1953; Brazil, 1954; USSR, 1964. Hon. Doctor: Oslo, 1961; USSR Acad. of Scis, 1980. Retzius Medal, Swedish Soc. for Anthropology and Geography, 1950; Mungo Park Medal, Royal Scottish Geographical Society, 1951; Prix Bonaparte-Wyse from Société de Géographie, Paris, 1951; Elish Kent Kane Gold Medal, Geog. Soc. of Philadelphia, 1952; Vega Medal, Swedish Soc. of Anthropology and Geography, 1962; Lomonosov Medal, Moscow Univ., 1962; Royal Gold Medal, Royal Geog. Society, London, 1964; Oscar Prize for best documentary feature of 1951, Acad. of Motion Picture Arts and Sciences, 1952; Officer of El Order por Meritos Distinguidos, Peru, 1953; Gold Medal City of Lima; Gr.-Officer, Order Al Merito della Repubblica Italiana, Italy, 1965; Comdr, Knights of Malta, 1970; Comdr with Star, Order of St Olav, Norway, 1970; Order of Merit, Egypt, 1971; Grand Officer, Royal Alaouites Order, Morocco, 1971; Hon. Citizen, Larvik, Norway, 1971; Kiril i Metodi Order, Bulgaria, 1972; Internat. Pahlavi Environment Prize, UN, 1978; Order of Golden Ark, Netherlands, 1980. Works trans. into numerous languages. *Publications*: Paa Jakt efter Paradiset, 1938; The Kon-Tiki Expedition, 1948; American Indians in the Pacific: the theory behind the Kon-Tiki expedition, 1952; (with A. Skjolsvold) Archæological Evidence of Pre-Spanish Visits to the Galapagos Islands, 1956; Aku-Aku: The Secrets of Easter Island, 1957; Co-editor (with E. N. Ferdon, Jr) Reports of the Norwegian Archæological Expedition to Easter Island and the East Pacific, Vol. I: The Archæology of Easter Island, 1961, vol. II: Miscellaneous Papers, 1965; Navel of the World (Chapter XIV) in Vanished Civilizations, 1963; Indianer und Alt-Asiaten im Pazifik: Das Abenteuer einer Theorie, 1966 (Vienna); Sea Routes to Polynesia, 1968; The Ra Expeditions, 1970; Chapters in Quest for America, 1971; Fatu-Hiva Back to Nature, 1974; Art of Easter Island, 1974; Zwischen den Kontinenten, 1975; Early Man and the Ocean, 1978; The Tigris Expedition, 1979; contrib. National Geographical Magazine, Royal Geographical Journal, The Geographical Magazine, Archiv für Völkerkunde, Ymer, Swedish Geogr. Year-book, South-western Journal of Anthropology, Russian Academy of Sciences Yearbook, American Antiquity, Antiquity (Cambridge); *relevant publication*: Senor Kon-Tiki, by Arnold Jacoby, 1965. *Recreations*: outdoor life, travelling. *Address*: Colla Micheri, Laigueglia, Italy.

HEYES, Sir Tasman (Hudson Eastwood), Kt 1960; CBE 1953; *b* 6 Nov. 1896; *s* of late Hudson Heyes and of Mary Heyes, Melbourne; *m* 1921, Ethel Brettell (decd), *d* of late Archibald and Phoebe Causer, Melbourne; one *s* one *d*. *Educ*: Melbourne. Served European War, 1914-18, with 3rd Divisional Signal Co., AIF, France and Flanders, 1916-19. Attached to Historical Section, Cttee of Imperial Defence, London, and War Depts, Ottawa, Washington, and Wellington, 1924-28. Dir, Australian War Memorial, Canberra, 1939-42; Dept of Defence, Melbourne, 1942-46; Sec., Dept of Immigration, Australia, 1946-61. Mem., Australian Broadcasting Control Bd, 1963-68, retd. Mem., Immigration Planning Council, 1961-74. Nansen Medal, 1962. *Address*: Creswick, 536 Toorak Road, Toorak, Victoria 3142, Australia. *Club*: Melbourne.

HEYGATE, Sir George Lloyd, 5th Bt *cr* 1831; *S* father, 1976. *Heir*: *b* Richard John Gage Heygate.

HEYHOE FLINT, Rachael, MBE 1972; journalist, broadcaster, public speaker, sportswoman; *b* 11 June 1939; *d* of Geoffrey Heyhoe and Roma (*née* Crocker); *m* 1971, Derrick Flint, BSc; one *s* and one step *s* two step *d*. *Educ*: Wolverhampton High Sch. for Girls; Dartford Coll. of Physical Educn (Dip. in Phys. Educn). Head of Phys. Education: Wolverhampton Municipal Grammar Sch., 1960-62; Northicote Sch., 1962-64; US Field Hockey Assoc. Coach, 1964 and 1965; Journalist, Wolverhampton Express & Star, 1965-72; Sports Editor, Wolverhampton Chronicle, 1969-71; first woman Sports Reporter, ITV, 1972; Daily Telegraph Sports Writer, 1967-; Vice-Chm., 1981-, and Public Relations Officer, 1982-, Women's Cricket Assoc.; Mem., Sportswriters Assoc., 1967. England Hockey rep., 1964 (goalkeeper); Mem., England Women's Cricket team, 1960-77, 1979-, Captain, 1966-77. Best After Dinner Speakers Award, Guild of Professional Toastmasters, 1972. *Publications*: Just for Kicks, (Guide to hockey goalkeeping), 1966; Women's Hockey, 1975; (with Netta Rheinberg) Fair Play, The Story of Women's Cricket, 1976; (autobiog.) "Heyhoe!" 1978. *Recreations*: hockey, cricket; former county squash player (Staffs). *Address*: Danescroft, Wergs Road, Tettenhall, Wolverhampton, West Midlands. *T*: Wolverhampton 752103. *Clubs*: Lord's Taverners; Wolverhampton Lawn Tennis & Squash.

HEYMAN, Allan, QC 1969; *b* 27 Feb. 1921; *e s* of late Erik Heyman and of Rita Heyman (*née* Meyer); *m* 1958, Anne Marie (*née* Castenschiold); one *d*. *Educ*: Stenhus Kostskole, Denmark; Univ. of Copenhagen. Master of Law (Univ. of Copenhagen), 1947. Called to Bar, Middle Temple, 1951, Bencher 1975. Pres., Internat. Lawn Tennis Fedn, 1971-74, Hon. Life Vice-Pres., 1979. Kt of Dannebrog (Denmark). *Recreations*: shooting, stalking, reading, music. *Address*: 1 New Square, Lincoln's Inn, WC2; Marshland House, Iken, Woodbridge, Suffolk. *Clubs*: Naval and Military, Shikar; All England Lawn Tennis and Croquet.

HEYMAN, Sir Horace (William), Kt 1976; BSc; CEng, FIEE; Chairman, English Industrial Estates Corporation, 1970-77; Member, Supervisory Board, Hotelplan AG, Zürich, since 1955; Director, Hotelplan (UK Group) Ltd, since 1980; *b* 13 March 1912; *m* 1st, 1939; one *s* one *d*; 2nd, 1966, Dorothy Forster Atkinson. *Educ*: Ackworth Sch.; Technische Hochschule, Darmstadt; Birmingham Univ. BSc hons, electrical engrg, 1936. Electricars Ltd, 1936-40; Metropolitan Vickers Ltd, Sheffield, 1940-45; Smith's Electric Vehicles Ltd and Subsids, 1945-64 (Man. Dir, 1949-64); Co-Founder, Sevcon Engineering Ltd, 1960; Vice-Pres., Battronic Corp., Philadelphia, 1960-64; Dir, Inghams Travel Gp, 1965-77; Export Marketing Adviser for Northern Region, BoT, 1969-70; Consultant: DOI Invest in Britain Bureau, 1977-79; Elm Wood Sensors Ltd, 1977-. Mem. Council, Soc. of Motor Manufrs and Traders, 1949-64 (Man. Cttee, 1952-64); Chm., Electric Vehicle Assoc. of Gt Britain, 1953-55. Witness at US Senate hearings on air and water pollution, 1967. Chairman: N Region Energy Conservation Group, 1973-77; NEDO Working Party on House Bldg Performance, 1976-79; English Industrial Estates Pension Fund Trustees, 1972-. Governor: Newcastle Polytechnic, 1974-; Northern Regional Management Centre, 1979-. FIEE 1952; FRSA 1969. *Publications*: numerous in professional jls, on urban transport and food distribution. *Address*: Appletree House, Whickham, Newcastle upon Tyne NE16 5AS. *T*: Newcastle upon Tyne 885757.

HEYMAN, Prof. Jacques, MA, PhD; FICE; FSA; Professor of Engineering, University of Cambridge, since 1971; Fellow of Peterhouse, 1949-51, and since 1955; Consultant Engineer: Ely Cathedral, since 1972; St Albans Cathedral, since 1978; *b* 8 March 1925; *m* 1958, Eva Orlans; three *d*. *Educ*: Whitgift Sch.; Peterhouse, Cambridge. Senior Bursar, Peterhouse, 1962-64; University Demonstrator, Engineering Dept, Cambridge Univ., 1951, University Lectr, 1954, Reader, 1968. Vis. Professor: Brown Univ., USA, 1957-58; Harvard Univ., 1966. Member: Architectural Adv. Panel, Westminster Abbey, 1973-; Cathedrals Advisory Commn for England, 1981-. Mem., Council, ICE, 1960-63 and 1975-78. Hon. DSc Sussex, 1975. James Watt Medal, 1973. *Publications*: The Steel Skeleton, vol. 2 (with Lord Baker, M. R. Horne), 1956; Plastic Design of Portal Frames, 1957; Beams and Framed Structures, 1964, 2nd edn 1974; Plastic Design of Frames, vol. 1, 1969 (paperback 1980), vol. 2, 1971; Coulomb's Memoir on Statics, 1972; Equilibrium of Shell Structures, 1977; Elements of Stress Analysis, 1982; The Masonry Arch, 1982; articles on plastic design, masonry construction and general structural theory. *Address*: Engineering Laboratory, Trumpington Street, Cambridge. *T*: Cambridge 66466.

HEYMANN, Prof. Franz Ferdinand, PhD; FInstP; Quain Professor of Physics, and Head of Department of Physics and Astronomy, University College, University of London, since 1975; *b* 17 Aug. 1924; *s* of Paul Gerhard Heymann and Magdalena Petronella Heymann; *m* 1950, Marie Powell. *Educ*: Univ. of Cape Town (BScEng with Distinction, 1944); Univ. of London (PhD 1953). FInstP 1966. Engr, Cape Town, 1944-45; Jun. Lectr in Engrg, Univ. of Cape Town, 1945-47; Special Trainee, Metropolitan Vickers, Manchester, 1947-50; University Coll. London: Asst Lectr in Physics, 1950-52; Lectr, 1952-60; Reader, 1960-66; Prof. of Physics, 1966-75. *Publications*: scientific papers on res. done mainly in fields of particle accelerators and elementary particle physics. *Recreations*: music, gemmology, gardening. *Address*: Department of Physics and Astronomy, University College, Gower Street, WC1E 6BT; 59 The Gateway, Woking, Surrey. *T*: Woking 72304.

HEYMANSON, Sir (Sydney Henry) Randal, Kt 1972; CBE 1965 (OBE 1955); Chairman of the Board, American Australian Association, since 1967; *b* 18 April 1903; *s* of Frederick Heymanson and Elizabeth (*née* McDonnell). *Educ*: Melbourne C of E Grammar Sch.; Melbourne Univ. (MA Hons); London Univ. Australian Newspapers Service: European Corresp., 1928-40; Editor, NY, 1940-69; War Corresp., ETO; Editor and Publisher, Vital News, 1939-42; N American Rep., West Australian Newspapers, 1969-. Pres., Foreign Press Assoc., NY, 1942-43; Pres., Australian Soc. of NY, 1945-46. Exec. Vice-Pres. 1950-65, Pres. 1965-66, American Australian Assoc. *Recreations*: bibliomania, art collecting, travel. *Address*: 7 Mitchell Place, New York, NY 10017, USA. *Clubs*: Overseas Press, Dutch Treat, Ends of the Earth (New York); National Press (Washington).

HEYS, Derek Isaac, CBE 1971; TD 1945; Senior Partner in Heys, Wall & Co, Freight Forwarders, 1949-73; Executive with Wingate & Johnston Ltd, Liverpool, 1973-79; *b* 6 Aug. 1911; twin *s* of Isaac and Laura Heys; *m* 1936, Margaret Helena Ashcroft; one *s* one *d* (and one *s* decd). *Educ*: Birkenhead

Sch. Late Lt-Col RA (TA). Pres., Internat. Fedn of Forwarding Agents' Assocs (FIATA), 1967-71; Nat. Chm., Inst. of Shipping and Forwarding Agents, 1962-63; Chm., Merseyside Chamber of Commerce and Industry, 1970-71; Chm., first Adv. Cttee of three, apptd by Dirs of Mersey Docks & Harbour Co. to represent interest of holders of Co.'s redeemable subordinated unsecured Loan Stock, 1974; Vice-President: Inst. of Freight Forwarders, 1965-; Assoc. of British Chambers of Commerce, 1975. Consul for Belgium in Liverpool, 1966-77. Chm. of Governors, Birkenhead Sch., 1977-. High Sheriff, Merseyside, 1982. Order of the Crown (Belgium), 1977. *Recreation:* golf. *Address:* Fairway Cottage, Pinfold Lane, West Kirby, Wirral, Merseyside. *T:* 051-632 4242. *Clubs:* Athenæum (Liverpool); Royal Liverpool Golf (Hoylake).

HEYTESBURY, 6th Baron *cr* 1828; **Francis William Holmes à Court; Bt** 1795; *b* 8 Nov. 1931; *s* of 5th Baron Heytesbury and Beryl (*d* 1968), *y d* of late A. E. B. Crawford, LLD, DCL, Aston Clinton House, Bucks; *S* father, 1971; *m* 1962, Alison, *e d* of Michael Graham Balfour, CBE; one *s* one *d*. *Educ:* Bryanston; Pembroke College, Cambridge (BA 1954). *Heir: s* Hon. James William Holmes à Court, *b* 30 July 1967.

HEYWARD, Rt. Rev. Oliver Spencer; *see* Bendigo, Bishop of.

HEYWOOD, Francis Melville, MA; Warden of Lord Mayor Treloar College, 1952-69, retired 1969; *b* 1 Oct. 1908; 4th *s* of late Rt Rev. B. O. F. Heywood, DD; *m* 1937, Dorothea Kathleen, *e d* of late Sir Basil Mayhew, KBE; two *s* two *d*. *Educ:* Haileybury Coll. (Scholar); Gonville and Caius Coll. Cambridge (Scholar), 1st Class Hons, Classical Tripos, Part I, 1929; Part II, 1931; Rugby Football blue, 1928. Asst Master, Haileybury Coll., 1931-35; Fellow, Asst Tutor and Praelector, Trinity Hall, Cambridge, 1935-39; Master of Marlborough Coll., 1939-52. *Recreations:* gardening, walking. *Address:* 5 Manor Road, Bexhill-on-Sea, E Sussex TN40 1SP. *T:* Bexhill 214626.

HEYWOOD, Geoffrey, MBE (mil.) 1945; JP; Consulting Actuary; Senior Partner, Duncan C. Fraser & Co., since 1952; *b* 7 April 1916; *s* of Edgar Heywood and Annie (*née* Dawson), Blackpool; *m* 1941, Joan Corinna Lumley; one *s* one *d*. *Educ:* Arnold Sch., Blackpool. Served War, 1940-46: Royal Artillery, N Africa, Italy, Greece; commissioned, 1941, Major, 1944; despatches, 1945. Refuge Assce Co Ltd, 1933-40; Duncan C. Fraser & Co. (Consulting Actuaries), 1946-. Pres., Manchester Actuarial Soc., 1951-53; Chm., Assoc. of Consulting Actuaries, 1959-62; Chm.; Internat. Assoc. of Consulting Actuaries, 1968-72; Pres., Inst. of Actuaries, 1972-74 (Vice-Pres., 1964-67). Mem. Page Cttee to Review National Savings. Dep. Chm., Mersey Docks & Harbour Co.; Mem., Nat. Bus Co., 1978-. Director: Liverpool Bd Barclays Bank; Barclays Bank Trust Co.; Barclays Unicorn Gp; Universities Superannuation Scheme. Governor, Birkenhead Sch. FFA 1939; FIA 1946. Founder Master, Actuaries Co., 1979; Liveryman, Clockmakers' Co. JP Liverpool 1962. *Publications:* contribs to Jl Inst. Actuaries. *Recreations:* golf, tennis, antiquarian horology. *Address:* Drayton, Croft Drive East, Caldy, Wirral, Merseyside. *T:* 051-625 6707. *Clubs:* Army and Navy, Royal Automobile.

HEYWOOD, Geoffrey Henry, CBE 1972; Consultant, Dunlop Heywood & Co., Chartered Surveyors, Manchester, since 1969 (Partner, 1930-69); Chairman, Skelmersdale Development Corporation, 1969-75; President, Manchester Rent Assessment Panel, 1965-74; *b* 22 Aug. 1903; *s* of late Henry Arthur Heywood, Christleton Lodge, Chester; *m* 1931, Magdeleine Jeanne Georgette Marie, *d* of late J. H. Herpin, Paris; one *s* one *d*. *Educ:* Repton School. FRICS. Mem. Council, RICS, 1950-70 (Pres. 1962-63). Mem., Skelmersdale Develt Corp., 1962-75 (Dep. Chm. 1962-69). *Address:* 1 Derrydown, Hook Heath Road, Woking, Surrey GU22 0LD. *T:* Woking 23251.

HEYWOOD, Very Rev. Hugh Christopher Lempriere, MA; Provost Emeritus of Southwell; *b* 5 Nov. 1896; *s* of late Charles Christopher Heywood; *m* 1920, Margaret Marion (*d* 1982), *d* of Herbert Vizard; one *s* one *d*. *Educ:* Haileybury; Trinity Coll., Cambridge (Scholar and Stanton Student). Manchester Regt 1914-17 (wounded, despatches); 74th Punjabis IA 1917-23 (Staff Capt., 1919-22); Ordained, 1926; Curate of St Andrew's the Great, Cambridge, 1926-27; of Holy Cross, Greenford, 1927-28; Fellow and Dean, Gonville and Caius Coll., Cambridge, 1928-45; University Lecturer in Divinity, Cambridge, 1937-45; Provost of Southwell and Rector of S Mary, Southwell, 1945-69; Priest-in-charge of Upton, Diocese of Southwell, 1969-76. Examining Chaplain to Bishop of Southwark, 1932-41, and to Bishop of Southwell, 1941-69. Junior Proctor, Cambridge, 1934-35 and 1942-43. *Publications:* The Worshipping Community, 1938; On a Golden Thread, 1960; Finding Happiness in Remembering, 1978; Still on a Golden Thread, 1980. *Address:* 26 Lyndewode Road, Cambridge.

HEYWOOD, Sir Oliver Kerr, 5th Bt, *cr* 1838; *b* 30 June 1920; *s* of late Maj.-Gen. C. P. Heywood, CB, CMG, DSO (2nd *s* of 3rd Bt) and late Margaret Vere, *d* of late Arthur Herbert Kerr; *S* uncle 1946; *m* 1947, Denise Wymondham, 2nd *d* of late Jocelyn William Godefroi, MVO; three *s*. *Educ:* Eton; Trinity Coll. Cambridge (BA). Served in Coldstream Guards, 1940-46 (despatches). Profession: artist. *Heir: s* Peter Heywood [*b* 10 Dec. 1947; *m* 1970, Jacqueline Anne, *d* of Sir Robert Hunt, *qv* ; two *d*]. *Address:* Viner's Wood, Wickstreet, Stroud, Glos.

HEYWORTH, Peter Lawrence Frederick; Music Critic of The Observer since 1955; *b* 3 June 1921; *er s* of Lawrence Ormerod Heyworth and Ellie Stern. *Educ:* Charterhouse; Balliol Coll., Oxford. HM Forces, 1940-46; Balliol, 1947-50; University of Göttingen, 1950. Music critic of Times Educational Supplement, 1952-56; Record reviewer for New Statesman, 1956-58; Guest of the Ford Foundation in Berlin, 1964-65. Critic of the Year, British Press Awards, 1980, commendation 1979. *Publications:* (ed) Berlioz, Romantic and Classic: selected writings by Ernest Newman, 1972; (ed) Conversations with Klemperer, 1973. *Address:* 32 Bryanston Square, W1H 7LS. *T:* 01-262 8906; Yew Tree Cottage, Hinton St Mary, Sturminster Newton, Dorset. *T:* Sturminster Newton 72203.

HEZLET, Vice-Admiral Sir Arthur Richard, KBE 1964; CB 1961; DSO 1944 (Bar 1945); DSC 1941; *b* 7 April 1914; *s* of late Maj.-Gen. R. K. Hezlet, CB, CBE, DSO; *m* 1948, Anne Joan Patricia, *e d* of late G. W. N. Clark, Carnabane, Upperlands, Co. Derry; two adopted *d*. *Educ:* RN College, Dartmouth. Comd HM Submarines: H44, Ursula, Trident, Thrasher and Trenchant, 1941-45; comd HMS Scorpion, 1949-50; Chief Staff Officer to Flag Officer (Submarines), 1953-54; Capt. (D), 6th Destroyer Squadron 1955-56; Dir, RN Staff Coll., Greenwich, 1956-57; comd HMS Newfoundland, 1958-59; Rear-Adm. 1959; Flag Officer (Submarines), 1959-61; Flag Officer, Scotland, 1961-62; Vice-Adm. 1962; Flag Officer, Scotland and Northern Ireland, 1963-64; retired 1964. Legion of Merit (Degree of Commander) (US), 1945. *Publications:* The Submarine and Sea Power, 1967; Aircraft and Sea Power, 1970; The 'B' Specials, 1972; Electron and Sea Power, 1975. *Address:* Bovagh House, Aghadowey, Co. Derry, N Ireland. *Clubs:* Army and Navy, Royal Ocean Racing.

HIBBARD, Prof. Bryan Montague, MD, PhD; FRCOG; Professor of Obstetrics and Gynaecology, Welsh National School of Medicine, since 1973; Consultant Obstetrician and Gynaecologist, University Hospital of Wales; *b* 24 April 1926; *s* of Montague Reginald and Muriel Irene Hibbard; *m* 1955, Elizabeth Donald Grassie. *Educ:* Queen Elizabeth's Sch., Barnet; St Bartholomew's Hosp. Med. Coll., London (MD); PhD (Liverpool). MRCS. Formerly: Sen. Lectr, Liverpool Univ.; Consultant Obstetrician and Gynaecologist, Liverpool RHB. *Publications:* numerous contribs to world medical literature. *Recreations:* collecting 18th century drinking glasses, fell walking, coarse gardening. *Address:* The Clock House, Cathedral Close, Llandaff, Cardiff CF5 2ED. *T:* Cardiff 564565.

HIBBARD, Prof. Howard, PhD; Professor of Art History, since 1966, Chairman, Department of Art History and Archaeology, 1978-81, Columbia University; *b* 23 May 1928; *s* of Benjamin Horace Hibbard and Margaret Baker Hibbard; *m* 1951, Shirley Irene Griffith; three *d*. *Educ:* Univ. of Wisconsin (BA 1949, MA 1952); Columbia Univ.; Harvard Univ. (PhD 1958). Fulbright Fellow, Paris, 1949-50; Univ. Fellow, Columbia Univ., 1952-53; Harvard Prize Fellow, 1953-54; Fellow, Amer. Acad. in Rome, 1956-58; Vis. Instr, Univ. of Calif, 1958-59; Asst Prof., 1959-62, Associate Prof., 1962-66, Columbia Univ. Amer. Council of Learned Socs Fellow, Rome, 1962-63; Guggenheim Fellow, Rome, 1965-66 and 1972-73; Sen. Fellow, Nat. Endowment for Humanities, Rome, 1967, 1979-80; Vis. Dist. Scholar, City Coll., City Univ. of NY, 1973-74; Vis. Prof., Yale Univ., 1976; Slade Prof. of Fine Art, Oxford Univ., 1976-77. Phi Betta Kappa Vis. Scholar, 1980-81. Fellow, Amer. Acad. of Arts and Sciences, 1969. Hon. MA Oxon 1977. Editor-in-Chief, Art Bulletin, 1974-78. *Publications:* The Architecture of the Palazzo Borghese, 1962; Bernini, 1965; Bernini e il barocco, 1968; (with J. Nissman) Florentine Baroque Art from American Collections, 1969; Carlo Maderno and Roman Architecture 1580-1630, 1972; Poussin: The Holy Family on the Steps, 1974; Michelangelo, 1975, rev. edn 1978; Masterpieces of European Sculpture, 1977; The Metropolitan Museum of Art, 1980; Caravaggio, 1982; contrib. Art Bull., Burlington Mag., Jl Soc. Architect. Historians. *Recreations:* gardening, cooking. *Address:* 176 Brewster Road, Scarsdale, NY 10583, USA. *T:* 914-725-3743.

HIBBERD, (Andrew) Stuart, MBE; *b* 5 Sept. 1893; *y s* of late W. H. Hibberd, Canford Magna, Dorset; *m* 1923, Alice Mary, *e d* of late Lieut-Col Gerard Chichester, North Staffs Regt; no *c*. *Educ:* Weymouth Coll.; St John's Coll., Cambridge (MA). Served European War in 7th and 5th Batt. Dorset Regt; and 46th Punjabis IA; later 2/25th Punjabis IA; served in Gallipoli, Mesopotamia and Waziristan. Joined BBC, at Savoy Hill, 1924; on Headquarter Staff until retirement, 1951; for some years Chief Announcer. Fellow: Royal Society of Arts; Royal Society of St George. *Publication:* "This-is London", 1951. *Recreations:* gardening, music. *Address:* 2 West Field, Budleigh Salterton, Devon.

HIBBERD, Sir Donald (James), Kt 1977; OBE 1956; Chairman, Comalco Ltd, 1969-80 (Chief Executive, 1969-78); *b* 26 June 1916; *s* of William James Hibberd and Laura Isabel Hibberd; *m* 1942, Florence Alice Macandie; one *s* one *d*. *Educ:* Sydney Univ. (BEc). Commonwealth Dept of Trade and Customs, 1939-46; Exec. Asst, Commonwealth Treasury, 1946-53; Mem., Aust. Aluminium Production Commn, 1953-57; First Asst Sec., Banking Trade and Industry Br., Commonwealth Treasury, 1953-57; Exec. Dir, Commonwealth Aluminium Corp., 1957-61; Man. Dir, Comalco Industries Pty Ltd, 1961-69. Director: COR Ltd, 1949-51; G. E. Crane Hldgs Ltd, 1961-78; Conzinc Rio Tinto of Aust. Ltd, 1962-71; Mem., Reserve Bank Bd, 1966-81; Vice Chm., Queensland Alumina Ltd, 1964-80; Chm., Munich Reinsurance Co. of Aust. Ltd, 1970-; Chm., NZ Aluminium Smelters Ltd, 1969-80. Pres., Aust. Mining Industry Council, 1972-73. Mem., Melbourne

Univ. Council, 1967-. *Recreations:* golf, reading. *Address:* 193 Domain Road, South Yarra, Vic 3141, Australia. *T:* 264037. *Clubs:* Athenæum (Melbourne); Commonwealth (Canberra); Royal Melbourne Golf, Frankston Golf.

HIBBERD, Prof. George, PhD; ARTC, CEng, Hon. FIMinE; FRSE; Dixon Professor of Mining, University of Glasgow, and Professor of Mining, University of Strathclyde, Glasgow, 1947-67, now Emeritus; *b* Muirkirk, NB, 17 May 1901; *e s* of Charles Hibberd and Helen Brown; *m* 1931, Marion Dalziel Robb Adamson; two *s* two *d*. *Educ:* Muirkirk Public Sch.; Royal Tech. Coll., Glasgow. Walter Duncan Res. Scholar. Mining official, 1926-28; Coll. Lectr, 1928-46. Past Pres. Mining Inst. of Scotland. Mem. Council, Inst. Mining Engineers. *Publications:* A Survey of the Welsh Slate Industry; A Survey of The Caithness Flagstone Industry; numerous papers on mining and scientific subjects in technical press. (Jointly) A Survey of the Scottish Slate Industry and A Survey of the Scottish Free-Stone Quarrying Industry. *Recreations:* golf, gardening. *Address:* 120 Kings Park Avenue, Glasgow G44 4HS. *T:* 041-632 4608.

HIBBERD, Stuart; *see* Hibberd, A. S.

HIBBERD; *see* Holland-Hibberd, family name of Viscount Knutsford.

HIBBERT, Christopher, MC 1945; author; *b* 5 March 1924; *s* of late Canon H. V. Hibbert; *m* 1948, Susan Piggford; two *s* one *d*. *Educ:* Radley; Oriel Coll., Oxford (MA). Served in Italy, 1944-45; Capt., London Irish Rifles. Partner in firm of land agents, auctioneers and surveyors, 1948-59. Fellow, Chartered Auctioneers' and Estate Agents' Inst., 1948-59. Pres., Johnson Soc., 1980. Won Heinemann Award for Literature, 1962. FRSL, FRGS. *Publications:* The Road to Tyburn, 1957; King Mob, 1958; Wolfe at Quebec, 1959; The Destruction of Lord Raglan, 1961; Corunna, 1961; Benito Mussolini, 1962; The Battle of Arnhem, 1962; The Roots of Evil, 1963; The Court at Windsor, 1964; Agincourt, 1964; (ed) The Wheatley Diary, 1964; Garibaldi and His Enemies, 1965; The Making of Charles Dickens, 1967; (ed) Waterloo: Napoleon's Last Campaign, 1967; (ed) An American in Regency England: The Journal of Louis Simond, 1968; Charles I, 1968; The Grand Tour, 1969; London: Biography of a City, 1969; The Search for King Arthur, 1970; (ed) The Recollections of Rifleman Harris, 1970; Anzio: the bid for Rome, 1970; The Dragon Wakes: China and the West, 1793-1911, 1970; The Personal History of Samuel Johnson, 1971; (ed) Twilight of Princes, 1971; George IV, Prince of Wales, 1762-1811, 1972; George IV, Regent and King, 1812-1830, 1973; The Rise and Fall of the House of Medici, 1974; (ed) A Soldier of the Seventy-First, 1975; Edward VII: a portrait, 1976; The Great Mutiny: India 1857, 1978; Disraeli and His World, 1978; The Court of St James's, 1979; (ed) Boswell's Life of Johnson, 1979; The French Revolution, 1981; (ed) Greville's England, 1981. *Recreations:* gardening, travel, cooking. *Address:* 64 St Andrew's Road, Henley-on-Thames, Oxon.

HIBBERT, Eleanor; author; *b* London. *Educ:* privately. *Publications: as Jean Plaidy:* Together They Ride, 1945; Beyond The Blue Mountains, 1947; Murder Most Royal (and as The King's Pleasure, USA), 1949; The Goldsmith's Wife, 1950; Madame Serpent, 1951; Daughter of Satan, 1952; The Italian Woman, 1952; Sixth Wife, 1953, new edn 1969; Queen Jezebel, 1953; St Thomas's Eve, 1954; The Spanish Bridegroom, 1954; Gay Lord Robert, 1955; The Royal Road to Fotheringay, 1955, new edn 1968; The Wandering Prince, 1956; A Health unto His Majesty, 1956; Here Lies Our Sovereign Lord, 1956; Flaunting Extravagant Queen, 1956, new edn 1960; Triptych of Poisoners, 1958, new edn 1970; Madonna of the Seven Hills, 1958; Light on Lucrezia, 1958; Louis the Wellbeloved, 1959; The Road to Compiegne, 1959; The Rise of the Spanish Inquisition, 1959; The Growth of the Spanish Inquisition, 1960; Castile For Isabella, 1960; Spain for the Sovereigns, 1960; The End of the Spanish Inquisition, 1961; Daughters of Spain, 1961; Katherine, The Virgin Widow, 1961; Meg Roper, Daughter of Sir Thomas More (for children), 1961; The Young Elizabeth (for children), 1961; The Shadow of the Pomegranate, 1962; The King's Secret Matter, 1962; The Young Mary, Queen of Scots, 1962; The Captive Queen of Scots, 1963; Mary, Queen of France, 1964; The Murder in the Tower, 1964; The Thistle and the Rose, 1965; The Three Crowns, 1965; Evergreen Gallant, 1965; The Haunted Sisters, 1966; The Queen's Favourites, 1966; The Princess of Celle, 1967; Queen in Waiting, 1967; The Spanish Inquisition, its Rise, Growth and End (3 vols in one), 1967; Caroline The Queen, 1968; Katharine of Aragon (3 vols in one), 1968; The Prince and the Quakeress, 1968; The Third George, 1969; Catherine de Medici (3 vols in one), 1969; Perdita's Prince, 1969; Sweet Lass of Richmond Hill, 1970; The Regent's Daughter, 1971; Goddess of the Green Room, 1971; Victoria in the Wings, 1972; Charles II (3 vols in one), 1972; The Captive of Kensington Palace, 1972; The Queen and Lord M, 1973; The Queen's Husband, 1973; The Widow of Windsor, 1974; The Bastard King, 1974; The Lion of Justice, 1975; The Passionate Enemies, 1976; The Plantagenet Prelude, 1976; The Revolt of the Eaglets, 1977; The Heart of the Lion, 1977; The Prince of Darkness, 1978; The Battle of the Queens, 1978; The Queen from Provence, 1979; Edward Longshanks, 1979; The Follies of the King, 1980; The Vow on the Heron, 1980; Pasage to Pontefract, 1981; Star of Lancaster, 1981; Epitaph for Three Women, 1981; Red Rose of Anjou, 1982; *as Eleanor Burford:* Daughter of Anna, 1941; Passionate Witness, 1941; Married Love, 1942; When All The World Was Young, 1943; So The Dreams Depart, 1944; Not In Our Stars, 1945; Dear Chance, 1947; Alexa, 1948; The House At Cupid's Cross, 1949; Believe The Heart, 1950; Love Child, 1950; Saint Or Sinner?, 1951; Dear Delusion, 1952; Bright Tomorrow, 1952; When We Are Married, 1953; Leave Me My Love, 1953; Castles in Spain, 1954;

Hearts Afire, 1954; When Other Hearts, 1955; Two Loves In Her Life, 1955; Married in Haste, 1956; Begin To Live, 1956; To Meet A Stranger, 1957; Pride of the Morning, 1958; Blaze of Noon, 1958; Dawn Chorus, 1959; Red Sky At Night, 1959; Night of Stars, 1960; Now That April's Gone, 1961; Who's Calling?, 1962; *as Ellalice Tate:* Defenders of The Faith, 1956 (under name of Jean Plaidy, 1970); Scarlet Cloak, 1957 (2nd edn, under name of Jean Plaidy, 1969); Queen of Diamonds, 1958; Madame Du Barry, 1959; This Was A Man, 1961; *as Elbur Ford:* The Flesh and The Devil, 1950; Poison in Pimlico, 1950; Bed Disturbed, 1952; Such Bitter Business, 1953 (as Evil in the House, USA 1954); *as Kathleen Kellow:* Danse Macabre, 1952; Rooms At Mrs Oliver's, 1953; Lilith, 1954 (2nd edn, under name of Jean Plaidy, 1967); It Began in Vauxhall Gardens, 1955 (2nd edn under name of Jean Plaidy, 1968); Call of the Blood, 1956; Rochester-The Mad Earl, 1957; Milady Charlotte, 1959; The World's A Stage, 1960; *as Victoria Holt:* Mistress of Mellyn, 1961; Kirkland Revels, 1962; The Bride of Pendorric, 1963; The Legend of the Seventh Virgin, 1965; Menfreya, 1966; The King of the Castle, 1967; The Queen's Confession, 1968; The Shivering Sands, 1969; The Secret Woman, 1971; The Shadow of the Lynx, 1972; On the Night of the Seventh Moon, 1973; The Curse of the Kings, 1973; The House of a Thousand Lanterns, 1974; Lord of the Far Island, 1975; The Pride of the Peacock, 1976; My Enemy the Queen, 1978; The Spring of the Tiger, 1979; The Mask of the Enchantress, 1980; The Judas Kiss, 1981; *as Philippa Carr:* The Miracle at St Bruno's, 1972; Lion Triumphant, 1974; The Witch from the Sea, 1975; Saraband for Two Sisters, 1976; Lament for a Lost Lover, 1977; The Love Child, 1978; The Song of the Siren, 1979; The Drop of the Dice, 1980; The Adulteress, 1981. *Address:* c/o Robert Hale Ltd, 45/47 Clerkenwell Green, EC1.

HIBBERT, Maj.-Gen. Hugh Brownlow, DSO 1940; *b* 10 Dec. 1893; *s* of late Adm. H. T. Hibbert, CBE, DSO; *m* 1926, Susan Louisa Mary Feilding (*d* 1975); one *s* one *d*. *Educ:* Uppingham; RMC, Sandhurst. Retired pay, 1946. *Address:* The Lodge, Albrighton Hall, near Wolverhampton.

HIBBERT, Jack; Under Secretary, Statistics 2, Departments of Industry and Trade, since 1982; *b* 14 Feb. 1932; *s* of William Collier Hibbert and Ivy Annie (*née* Wigglesworth); *m* 1957, Joan Clarkson; two *s* one *d*. *Educ:* Leeds Grammar Sch.; London Sch. of Economics (BScEcon). Served Royal Air Force, 1950-52. Exchequer and Audit Dept, 1952-60; Central Statistical Office, 1960-65; London Sch. of Economics, 1965-66; CSO, 1966; Chief Statistician, 1970; Asst Dir, 1977; OECD and EUROSTAT Consultant 1981. *Publications:* contributor to: The Organisation and Retrieval of Economic Knowledge, 1977; articles in Economic Trends, Rev. of Income and Wealth. *Recreations:* bridge, squash. *Address:* Department of Trade, 1 Victoria Street, SW1H 0ET. *Club:* Reform.

HIBBERT, Sir Reginald (Alfred), GCMG 1982 (KCMG 1979; CMG 1966); HM Diplomatic Service, retired; Director, Ditchley Foundation, since 1982; *b* 21 Feb. 1922; *s* of Alfred Hibbert, Sawbridgeworth, Herts; *m* 1949, Ann Alun Pugh, *d* of late Sir Alun Pugh; two *s* one *d*. *Educ:* Queen Elizabeth's Sch., Barnet; Worcester Coll., Oxford. Served with SOE and 4th Hussars in Albania and Italy, 1943-45. Entered Foreign Service, 1946; served in Bucharest, Vienna, Guatemala, Ankara, Brussels; Chargé d'Affaires, Ulan Bator, 1964-66; Research Fellow, Leeds Univ., 1966-67; Political Adviser's Office, Singapore, 1967-69; Political Adviser to C-in-C Far East, 1970-71; Minister, Bonn, 1972-75; Asst Under-Sec. of State, FCO, 1975-76; Dep. Under-Sec. of State, FCO, 1976-79; Ambassador to France, 1979-82. *Address:* Ditchley Park, Enstone, Oxon OX7 4ER. *T:* Enstone 346; Frondeg, Pennal, Machynlleth, Powys SY20 9JX. *T:* Pennal 220. *Club:* Reform.

HICHENS, Mrs Mary Hermione, CBE 1950; ARRC; JP; County Councillor, Oxon, 1937-51, Chairman of Education Committee, 1946-57, Alderman, 1951-74; *b* 15 Oct. 1894; 3rd *d* of Gen. Rt Hon. Sir N. G. Lyttelton, GCB, GCVO; *m* 1919, William Lionel Hichens (Chm. of Cammell Laird; killed by enemy action, 1940); two *s* three *d* (and one *s* killed in action). *Educ:* Alexander Coll., Dublin. Served as Military Probationer QAIMNS in England, 1915; in France, 1916-19 (despatches, ARRC); Mem. of Royal Commission on the Geographical Distribution of the Industrial Population, 1937-39, signed Minority Report; Mem. of Consultative Panel on Post-War Reconstruction to Minister of Works and Buildings; Mem. of Departmental Cttee on Land Utilisation, 1941; Mem. of Departmental Cttee on Training of Teachers, 1942; Commissioner under the Catering Act, 1943-58. Member: County Councils Assoc., 1946-66; Oxon Agric. Exec. Cttee, 1956-61. JP Oxon 1934. *Address:* North Aston Hall, Oxford OX5 4JA. *T:* Steeple Aston 40200.

HICK, Prof. John Harwood; Danforth Professor, Claremont Graduate School, California, since 1979; *b* 20 Jan. 1922; *s* of Mark Day Hick and Mary Aileen (Hirst); *m* 1953, (Joan) Hazel, *d* of F. G. Bowers, CB, CBE, and Frances Bowers; three *s* one *d*. *Educ:* Bootham Sch., York; Edinburgh Univ. (MA 1948 (1st cl. hons Philos); DLitt 1974); Oriel Coll., Oxford (Campbell-Fraser schol.; DPhil 1950); Westminster Coll., Cambridge. Friends' Ambulance Unit, 1942-45. Ordained, Presb. C of E, 1953; Minister, Belford Presb. Church, Northumberland, 1953-56; Asst Prof. of Philosophy, Cornell Univ., 1956-59; Stuart Prof. of Christian Philosophy, Princeton Theolog. Seminary, 1959-64; S. A. Cook Bye-Fellow, Gonville and Caius Coll., Cambridge, 1963-64; PhD by incorporation; Lectr in Divinity, Cambridge Univ., 1964-67; H. G. Wood Prof. of Theology, Univ. of Birmingham, 1967-82. Guggenheim Fellow, 1963-64; Leverhulme Res. Fellow, 1976. Lectures: Mead-Swing, Oberlin Coll., USA, 1962-63; Mary Farnum Brown,

Haverford Coll., USA 1964-65; James W. Richard, Univ. of Virginia, 1969; Distinguished Vis., Univ. of Oregon, 1969; Arthur Stanley Eddington Meml, 1972; Stanton, Cambridge Univ., 1974-77; Teape, Delhi and Madras, 1975; Ingersoll, Harvard, 1977; Hope, Stirling, 1977; Younghusband, London, 1977; Mackintosh, East Anglia, 1978; Riddell, Newcastle, 1978-79; Berkeley, TCD, 1979; Greenhoe, Louisville Pres. Sem., 1979; Potter, Washington State Univ., 1980; Montefiore, London, 1980; Brooks, Univ. of S California, 1982. Visiting Professor: Banares Hindu Univ., 1971; Visva Bharati Univ., 1971; Punjabi Univ., Patiala, 1971; Visiting Fellow: British Acad. Overseas, 1974; Univ. of Ceylon, 1974. Hulsean Preacher, Cambridge Univ., 1969; Select Preacher, Oxford Univ., 1970. Chairman: Religious and Cultural Panel, Birmingham Community Relations Cttee, 1969-74; Coordinating Working Party, Statutory Conf. for Revision of Agreed Syllabus of Religious Educn, Birmingham, 1971-74; All Faiths for One Race, 1972-73, 1978-80; Birmingham Inter-Faiths Council, 1975; Pres., Soc. for the Study of Theology, 1975-76. Mem. Council, Selly Oak Colls, 1967-80; Governor, Queen's Coll., Birmingham, 1972-. Member Editorial Board: The Encyclopedia of Philosophy; Religious Studies; Jl of Religion. Hon. Teol. Dr Uppsala, 1977. *Publications:* Faith and Knowledge, 1957, 2nd edn 1966; Philosophy of Religion, 1963, 2nd edn 1973 (Spanish, Portuguese, Chinese, Japanese, Korean, Finnish and Swedish edns); (ed) Faith and the Philosophers, 1963; (ed) The Existence of God, 1963; (ed) Classical and Contemporary Readings in the Philosophy of Religion, 1963, 2nd edn 1970; Evil and the God of Love, 1966, 2nd edn 1977; (ed) The Many-Faced Argument, 1967; Christianity at the Centre, 1968, 2nd edn as The Centre of Christianity, 1977 (trans. Dutch); Arguments for the Existence of God, 1971; Biology and the Soul, 1972; God and the Universe of Faiths, 1973; (ed) Truth and Dialogue, 1974; Death and Eternal Life, 1976 (trans. Dutch); (ed) The Myth of God Incarnate, 1977 (trans. German); God has Many Names, 1980; (ed with Brian Hebblethwaite) Christianity and Other Religions, 1980. *Address:* Department of Religion, Claremont Graduate School, Claremont, Calif 91711, USA; 21 Greening Drive, Edgbaston, Birmingham B15 2XA.

HICKEY, Sir Justin, Kt 1979; Chairman and Managing Director, Accident Insurance Mutual Ltd, since 1968; *b* 5 April 1925; *s* of Hon. Simon Hickey, Speaker, New South Wales Parliament, and Hilda Ellen Hickey (*née* Dacey); *m* 1964, Barbara Standish Thayer; one *s* four *d. Educ:* De La Salle College, Sydney. Chairman: Australian Family Trust, 1965; Accident Insurance Mutual Ltd, 1968; Thayer Foundation (US), 1972; Mem., Lloyd's of London, 1979. FRSA 1978. JP 1950. *Recreations:* yachting, art collection. *Address:* 44 Emerstan Drive, Castlecove, NSW 2069, Australia. *T:* (02) 406 5023. *Club:* Royal Motor Yacht (Sydney).

HICKEY, Nancy Maureen, OBE 1979; SRN, SCM, MTD, DN; Chairman, Central Midwives Board for England and Wales, since 1979; *b* 31 Aug. 1924; *d* of late Timothy Hickey and Elsie Winifred Hickey. *Educ:* Woking Secondary School for Girls. SRN Guy's Hospital, 1948; SCM Sussex Maternity Hosp., 1949; Sister, Guy's Hosp., 1953-55; MTD Royal College of Midwives, 1954; Midwifery Teacher, Guy's Hosp., 1955-57; Midwifery Supt, Pembury Hosp., 1957-65; Diploma in Nursing, London (Obst.), 1957; Matron, Coventry Maternity Hosp., 1965-70; Chief Nursing Officer, Coventry, 1970-74; Area Nursing Officer, Coventry, 1974-79. *Recreations:* light music, walking. *Address:* 12 Woodfield Road, Earlsdon, Coventry, West Midlands CV5 6AL. *T:* Coventry 72559. *Club:* Coventry Soroptimist (Coventry).

HICKINBOTHAM, Rev. James Peter, DD Lambeth, 1979; *b* 16 May 1914; *s* of late F. J. L. Hickinbotham, JP and late Mrs Hickinbotham; *m* 1948, Ingeborg Alice Lydia Manger; two *s* one *d. Educ:* Rugby Sch.; Magdalen Coll., Oxford; Wycliffe Hall, Oxford. Deacon, 1937; priest, 1938; curate: St John, Knighton, Leicester, 1937-39; St Paul, S Harrow, 1940-42; Chaplain, Wycliffe Hall, Oxford, 1942-45; Vice-Principal, 1945-50. Prof. of Theology, University Coll. of the Gold Coast, 1950-54. Principal, St John's Coll. and Cranmer Hall, Durham, 1954-70; Principal of Wycliffe Hall, Oxford, 1970-79. Examining Chaplain: to Bishop of Manchester, 1947-50; to Bishop of Leicester, 1948-53; to Bishop of Durham, 1955-70. Proctor in Convocation, 1957-70. Hon. Canon, Durham Cathedral, 1959-70. Hon. Curate, Christ Church, Dowend, 1979-. *Address:* 46 Chesterfield Road, Downend, Bristol BS16 5RQ. *T:* Bristol 562054.

HICKINBOTHAM, Sir Tom, KCMG 1953 (CMG 1951); KCVO 1954; CIE 1944; OBE 1939; *b* 27 April 1903; 2nd *s* of James Ryland Hickinbotham, MB, and Beatrice Elliot, *d* of Rev. Theophilus Sharp, MA. *Educ:* Royal Military Coll., Sandhurst. Entered Indian Army, 1923; served North West Frontier, 1924 (medal); posted to 5th Battalion Baluch Regiment, 1924; transferred to Indian Political Service, 1930; served in various appointments in Aden, 1931-32, 1933-35, and 1938-39; Political Agent, Bahrain, 1937, Muscat, 1939-41, Kuwait, 1941-43, Bahrain, 1943-45; Kalat, 1945-47; Chm. of the Aden Port Trust, 1948-51; Governor and Comdr-in-Chief of Colony and Protectorate of Aden, 1951-56, retired from Government Service. Director of various companies, 1956-73. Now lives in Scotland. *Publication:* Aden, 1958. *Recreation:* fishing. *Address:* Newburgh, Ettrick, Selkirk TD7 5HS.

HICKLIN, Denis Raymond, OBE 1969; Member (part-time), Forestry Commission, 1978-81; *b* 15 April 1918; *s* of Joseph Herbert and Florence May Hicklin; *m* 1949, Joyce Grisdale Smith; two *s. Educ:* Merchant Taylors' Sch. Served War, 1939-46, RA (Major). John Dickinson, 1936-48; St Anne's Board Mill Co. Ltd, 1948-78 (Chm. and Man. Dir, 1966-78). *Recreations:* tennis,

golf. *Address:* 1 Bumpers Batch, Midford Road, Bath BA2 5SQ. *T:* Bath 833123.

HICKLING, Rev. Canon Colin John Anderson; Lecturer in New Testament Studies, King's College, University of London, since 1968; Priest in Ordinary to the Queen since 1974; Canon Theologian, Leicester Cathedral, since 1983; *b* 10 July 1931; *s* of late Charles Frederick Hickling, CMG, ScD, and late Marjorie Ellerington, *d* of late Henry Blamey. *Educ:* Taunton Sch.; Epsom Coll.; King's Coll., Cambridge; Chichester Theol Coll. BA 1953, MA 1957. Deacon 1957, Priest 1958. Asst Curate, St Luke's, Pallion, Sunderland, 1957-61; Asst Tutor, Chichester Theol Coll., 1961-65; Asst Priest Vicar, Chichester Cath., 1964-65; Asst Lectr in New Testament Studies, King's Coll., Univ. of London, 1965-68; Dep. Minor Canon, St Paul's Cath., 1969-78; Dep. Priest in Ordinary to the Queen, 1971-74; Subwarden of King's Coll. Hall, 1969-78; Warden of King's Coll. Hostel, 1978-81. Boyle Lectr, 1973-76. *Publications:* contributed to: Church without Walls, 1968; Catholic Anglicans Today, 1968; Bible Bibliography 1967-73, 1974; (also ed) What About the New Testament?, 1975; St Paul: Teacher and Traveller, 1975; L'Evangile de Jean, 1977; Les Actes des Apôtres, 1979; The Ministry of the Word, 1979; This is the Word of the Lord, 1980; Studia Biblica 1978, Vol. III, 1980; Logia: the sayings of Jesus, 1982; reviews and articles. *Recreation:* music. *Address:* 44 Westminster Palace Gardens, Artillery Row, SW1P 1RR.

HICKLING, Reginald Hugh, CMG 1968; PhD (London); QC (Gibraltar) 1970; *b* 2 Aug. 1920; *er s* of late Frederick Hugh Hickling and Elsie May Hickling, Malvern, Worcs; *m* 1945, Beryl Iris (*née* Dennett); two *s* one *d* (and one *s* decd). *Educ:* Buxton Coll.; Nottingham Univ. RNVR, 1941-46. Dep. Solicitor, Evening Standard, London, 1946-50; Asst Attorney-Gen., Sarawak, 1950-55; Legal Adviser, Johore, 1956; Legal Draftsman, Malaya, 1957; Parly Draftsman, Malaya, 1959; Comr of Law Revision, Malaya, 1961; Commonwealth Office, 1964; Legal Adviser to High Comr, Aden and Protectorate of S Arabia, 1964-67; Maritime Law Adviser: Thailand, 1968-69; Malaysia, 1969; Ceylon, 1970; Attorney-General, Gibraltar, 1970-72. Lectr in SE Asian Law, SOAS, 1976-78, 1981-; Vis. Prof., Dept of Law, Univ. of Singapore, 1974-76 and 1978-80. Hon. JMN (Malaya), 1960. *Publications:* The Furious Evangelist, 1950; The English Flotilla, 1954 (US as Falconer's Voyage, 1956); Sarawak and Its Government, 1955; Festival of Hungry Ghosts, 1957; An Introduction to the Federal Constitution, 1960; Lieutenant Okino, 1968. *Recreation:* not watching TV. *Address:* 1 Highfield Road, Malvern, Worcs. *T:* Malvern 3477.

HICKMAN, Sir Glenn; *see* Hickman, Sir R. G.

HICKMAN, John Kyrle, CMG 1977; HM Diplomatic Service; Ambassador to Chile, since 1982; *b* 3 July 1927; *s* of late J. B. Hickman and Joan Hickman; *m* 1956, Jennifer Love; two *s* one *d. Educ:* Tonbridge; Trinity Hall, Cambridge. Served in RA, 1948-50. Asst Principal, WO, 1950; Principal, 1955; transf. to CRO, 1958; UK High Comm, Wellington, 1959-62; HM Diplomatic Service, 1965; British Embassy, Madrid, 1966; Counsellor and HM Consul-General, Bilbao, 1967; Dep. High Comr, Singapore, 1969-71; Head of SW Pacific Dept, FCO, 1971-74; Counsellor, Dublin, 1974-77; Ambassador to Ecuador, 1977-81. *Recreations:* ski-ing, golf. *Address:* c/o Foreign and Commonwealth Office, SW1; 3 Weltje Road, W6. *Club:* United Oxford & Cambridge University.

HICKMAN, Michael Ranulf; His Honour Judge Hickman; a Circuit Judge, since 1974; *b* 2 Oct. 1922; *s* of John Owen Hickman and Nancy Viola Hickman (*née* Barlow); *m* 1943, Diana Richardson; one *s* one *d. Educ:* Wellington; Trinity Hall, Cambridge. 2nd cl. Hons in Law. Served War, RAFVR, 1940-46. Cambridge Univ., 1946-48; called to Bar, Middle Temple, 1949. Actg Dep. Chm., Hertfordshire QS, 1965-72; a Recorder of Crown Court, 1972-74. *Recreations:* shooting, fishing, gun dog training. *Address:* The Acorn, Bovingdon, Herts. *T:* Hemel Hempstead 832226.

HICKMAN, Sir (Richard) Glenn, 4th Bt *cr* 1903; *b* 12 April 1949; *s* of Sir Alfred Howard Whitby Hickman, 3rd Bt, and of Margaret D., *o d* of Leonard Kempson; *S* father, 1979; *m* 1981, Heather Mary Elizabeth, *er d* of late Dr James Moffett, Swindon, and late Dr Gwendoline Moffett. *Educ:* Eton. *Heir:* uncle Patrick Nelson Hickman [*b* 14 March 1921; *m* 1st, 1944, Mary Lena (marr. diss. 1950), *d* of Captain J. A. D. Perrins, MC; one *s* one *d* ; 2nd, 1953, Gail, *d* of Col C. R. St Aubyn; one *s* one *d*]. *Address:* Twin Cottage, Batlers Green, Radlett, Herts. *Club:* Turf.

HICKOX, Richard Sidney, FRCO(CHM); organist, conductor; Music Director: City of London Sinfonia, since 1971; Richard Hickox Singers, since 1971; London Symphony Chorus, since 1976; Bradford Festival Choral Society, since 1978; Artistic Director, Northern Sinfonia, since 1982; Associate Conductor, San Diego Symphony Orchestra, since 1983; *b* Stokenchurch, Bucks, 5 March 1948; *m* 1976, Frances Ina Sheldon-Williams; one *s. Educ:* in organ, piano and composition, Royal Acad. of Music (LRAM); Organ Scholar, Queens' Coll., Cambridge (MA). Début as professional conductor, St John's Smith Square, 1971; Organist and Master of the Music, St Margaret's, Westminster, 1972-82; Prom début, 1973. Artistic Director: Woburn Fest., 1967-; St Endellion Fest., 1974-; Christ Church Spitalfields Fest., 1978-; Principal Guest Conductor, Dutch Radio Orch., 1980-; also regularly conducts LSO, RPO, Bournemouth Symphony Orch. and Sinfonietta, Royal Liverpool Phil. Orch., BBC Concert, Scottish and Welsh Orchs, BBC Singers, Aarhus and Odens Orchs. Conducted ENO, 1979, Royal Opera,

1983, and has appeared at many music festivals incl. Proms, Flanders, Bath and Cheltenham. Many recordings of choral and orchestral music. *Address:* 1c Morpeth Terrace, SW1. *T:* 01-834 1192.

HICKS; *see* Joynson-Hicks.

HICKS, David (Nightingale); interior decorator, designer and author; Director of David Hicks Ltd; *b* 25 March 1929; 3rd surv. *s* of late Herbert Hicks (stockbroker and twice past Master Salter's Company) and late Mrs Hicks; *m* 1960, Lady Pamela Carmen Louise Mountbatten, *yr d* of Admiral of the Fleet 1st Earl Mountbatten of Burma, KG, GCB, OM, GCSI, GCIE, GCVO, DSO, PC, FRS; one *s* two *d. Educ:* Charterhouse; Central School of Arts and Crafts, London. Interiors for: Helena Rubinstein; QE2; HRH the Prince of Wales; Govt of NSW; British Steel Corp.; Aeroflot Offices; Marquess of Londonderry; Library in British Embassy, Washington, etc. Associate offices in: Brussels, Geneva, Munich, Paris, Tokyo. Designer of: fabrics, men's ties, carpets, tiles, furniture, sheets, etc. Master, Salters' Co., 1977-78. FRSA. ColD (now Design Council) design award, 1970. *Publications:* David Hicks on Decoration, 1966; David Hicks on Living— with taste, 1968; David Hicks on Bathrooms, 1970; David Hicks on Decoration—with fabrics, 1971; David Hicks on Decoration—5, 1972; David Hicks Book of Flower Arranging, 1976; David Hicks Living with Design, 1979; David Hicks Garden Design, 1982. *Recreations:* shooting, riding, preservation. *Address:* Albany, Piccadilly, W1. *T:* (office) 01-930 1991.

HICKS, Col Sir Denys (Theodore), Kt 1961; OBE 1950; TD 1943; DL; Member Council of The Law Society, 1948-69; *b* 2 May 1908; *s* of late Cuthbert Hicks, Bristol; *m* 1941, Irene Elizabeth Mansell Leach; four *d. Educ:* Clifton. Admitted a Solicitor of Supreme Court of Judicature, 1931. Served War of 1939-45; with RA in UK and on staff; Col 1953; Hon. Col, 266 (Gloucester Vol. Artillery) Bty RA (Vols), 1972-75. Vice-President of The Law Society, 1959, Pres., 1960; Chm., Internat. Bar Assoc., 1966-70, Pres., 1970-74, Hon. Life Pres., 1974. Dep. Chm., Horserace Betting Levy Board, 1961-76; Mem., Royal Commission on Assizes and QS, 1967. Hon. Member: Amer. Bar Assoc., 1960; Il Ilustre y Nacional Collegio de Abogados de Mexico, 1964; Virginia State Bar Assoc., 1966. DL Avon (formerly Glos), 1957. *Address:* Damson Cottage, Hunstrete, Pensford, Bristol BS18 4NY. *T:* Compton Dando 464; 12 Berkeley Square, Bristol BS8 1HD. *T:* 290221.

HICKS, Donald, OBE 1968; MSc (London), FIChemE, FRSC; Director-General, British Coal Utilisation Research Association, 1962-67; *b* 26 June 1902; *e s* of late Benjamin and Matilda Hicks; *m* May, *y d* of late William and Margaret Sainsbury, Shirenewton, Chepstow; no *c. Educ:* Pontypridd Grammar Sch.; Glamorgan Coll. of Technology. Chief Coal Survey Officer, DSIR, S Wales, 1930-45; Supt of Coal Survey Organisation, DSIR, 1946; Dir of Scientific Control, Nat. Coal Bd, 1947-58; Carbonisation and Scientific Dir and Mem. East Midland Divisional Bd of NCB, 1959-62; Dir of Operational Research and Dir of Pneumoconiosis Field Research, Nat. Coal Bd, 1949-62. *Publications:* Primary Health Care: a review, 1976; papers in various scientific and technical jls. *Recreations:* walking and reading. *Address:* 26 St Kingsmark Avenue, Chepstow, Gwent NP6 5LY. *T:* Chepstow 3147.

HICKS, Sir Edwin (William), Kt 1965; CBE 1956; Company Director and consultant; *b* 9 June 1910; *s* of late William Banks Hicks, Melbourne, Victoria; *m* 1st, 1937, Jean (*d* 1959), *yr d* of late Thomas MacPherson, Brighton, Victoria; four *s* one *d* ; 2nd, 1961, Lois, *o d* of Norman S. Swindon, Canberra; one *s* one *d. Educ:* Haileybury; Melbourne Grammar Sch.; Canberra Univ. Coll. (BCom 1947). Commonwealth Public Service Bd, 1929-31; Commonwealth Statistician's Branch, 1931-38; Trade and Customs Dept, 1938-48; Senior Inspector, then Actg Asst Comr Commonwealth Public Service Bd, investigating organisation and methods of Commonwealth Govt Depts, 1948-51; Secretary: Dept of Air, Commonwealth of Australia, 1951-56; Dept of Defence, 1956-68; Australia High Comr in NZ, 1968-71, retired from Public Service, 1971. Served 1942-45 with Royal Australian Air Force in South West Pacific Area. *Recreations:* formerly: cricket, football, tennis; now golf. *Address:* 73 Endeavour Street, Red Hill, ACT 2603, Australia.

HICKS, Howard Arthur, CBE 1981; Founder and Chairman, IDC Group plc, since 1957; *b* 3 May 1914; *s* of Ivor Lewis Hicks and Gertrude Freda (*née* Shaw); *m* 1940, Anne Maureen (*née* Lang); one *s* one *d. Educ:* Pontypridd; Polytechnic of Wales. DSc, CEng, FICE, FIProdE, FCIOB, FAmSCE, MSocCE(France), FIMH, FRSA, CBIM. Civil Engineer, Bridge Dept, Glamorgan CC, 1934-39; served War, Royal Engineers, 1939-46 (Major); Man. Dir, Beecham Reinforced Concrete Engineers, 1947-56; Chairman, Cold Rolled Sections Ltd, 1968-; Director: Prudential Pensions Ltd, 1980-; Candover Ltd, 1980-. Chm., Aston Technical Management & Planning Services (Aston Univ.) Ltd, 1970-82; President: Inst. of Materials Handling, 1977-80; Instn of Production Engrs, 1980-81. Hon. DSc Aston in Birmingham, 1976; Internat. Engrg Achievements Award, Inst. for the Advancement of Engrg, 1981; Distinguished Internat. Archimedes Engrg Achievements Award, Nat. Soc. of Professional Engrs of America, 1980; SME Engrg Citation, Soc. of Manufacturing Engrs of United States, 1982. *Recreations:* (patron) Pontypridd Rugby Football Club; theatre. *Address:* Avonfield, Stratford upon Avon, Warwickshire CV37 6BJ. *T:* Stratford upon Avon 293594. *Clubs:* Athenæum; Cardiff and County; Phoenix (Lima, Peru).

HICKS, Lt-Col James Hamilton, OBE 1966; TD 1945; *b* 21 April 1909; *yr s* of late Major George Hicks, MC, TD, JP, and Elizabeth Young; *m* 1938, Roberta Kirk (*d* 1971), *y d* of late Thomas Boag, Greenock; no *c. Educ:* Pannal Ash Coll., Harrogate. 2nd Lieut RA, Territorial Army, 1929; Capt., 1934; Major, 1939; served in War of 1939-45, OC Bute Battery RA; POW (Germany), 1940-45; despatches, 1945; Lieut-Col, 1950. Chm. Buteshire T&AFA, 1950-62; County Cadet Commandant, Bute, 1950-53; DL, JP, Bute, 1949, Vice-Lieut, 1957-75. *Address:* 39 Crichton Road, Rothesay PA20 9JT. *T:* Rothesay 2612.

HICKS, John Charles; QC 1980; a Recorder of the Crown Court, Western Circuit, since 1978; *b* 4 March 1928; *s* of late Charles Hicks and late Marjorie Jane Hicks; *m* 1957, Elizabeth Mary, *o d* of late Rev. J. B. Jennings; one *s* one *d. Educ:* King Edward VI Grammar Schs, Chelmsford and Totnes; London Univ. LLM 1954. Served RA (National Service), 1946-48. Admitted solicitor, 1952; called to the Bar, Middle Temple, 1966. Legal Dept, Thomas Tilling Ltd, 1953-54; Partner in Messrs Burchells, solicitors, 1955-65; Methodist Missionary Soc., Caribbean, 1965-66. *Publications:* (ed jtly) The Constitution and Discipline of the Methodist Church in the Caribbean and the Americas, 1967, with annual supplements to date; articles in Mod. Law Rev., Cambridge Law Jl, and Epworth Rev. *Recreations:* squash rackets, music, theatre, opera, the Methodist Constitution. *Address:* 14 St Alban's Avenue, W4 5JP. *T:* 01-994 0315.

HICKS, Sir John (Richard), Kt 1964; FBA 1942; Fellow of All Souls College, since 1952; *b* 1904; *s* of late Edward Hicks, Leamington Spa; *m* 1935, Ursula K. Webb (*see* U. K. Hicks). *Educ:* Clifton Coll.; Balliol Coll., Oxford. Lectr, London Sch. of Economics, 1926-35; Fellow of Gonville and Caius Coll., Cambridge, 1935-38, Hon. Fellow, 1971; Prof. of Political Economy, University of Manchester, 1938-46; Official Fellow of Nuffield Coll., Oxford, 1946-52; Drummond Prof. of Political Economy, University of Oxford, 1952-65; Member: Revenue Allocation Commn, Nigeria, 1950; Royal Commn on the Taxation of Profits and Income, 1951. Hon. Fellow, LSE, 1969. (Jtly) Nobel Memorial Prize for Economics, 1972. *Publications:* The Theory of Wages, 1932 (revised edn, 1963); Value and Capital, 1939; The Taxation of War Wealth (with U. K. Hicks and L. Rostas), 1941; The Social Framework, 1942 (4th edn, 1971); Standards of Local Expenditure (with U. K. Hicks), 1943; The Problem of Valuation for Rating (with U. K. Hicks and C. E. V. Leser), 1944; The Incidence of Local Rates in Great Britain (with U. K. Hicks), 1945; The Problem of Budgeting Reform, 1948; A Contribution to the Theory of the Trade Cycle, 1950; (with U. K. Hicks) Report on Finance and Taxation in Jamaica, 1955; A Revision of Demand Theory, 1956; Essays in World Economics, 1960; Capital and Growth, 1965; Critical Essays in Monetary Theory, 1967; A Theory of Economic History, 1969; Capital and Time, 1973; The Crisis in Keynesian Economics, 1974; Economic Perspectives, 1977; Causality in Economics, 1979; Collected Papers, 2 vols, 1981, 1982. *Address:* All Souls College, Oxford. *Club:* Athenæum.

HICKS, Robert; MP (C) Bodmin, 1970-Feb. 1974 and since Oct. 1974; *b* 18 Jan. 1938; *s* of W. H. Hicks; *m* 1962, Maria Elizabeth Ann Gwyther; two *d. Educ:* Queen Elizabeth Grammar Sch., Crediton; University Coll., London; Univ. of Exeter. Taught at St Austell Grammar Sch., 1961-64; Lecturer in Regional Geography, Weston-super-Mare Technical Coll., 1964-70. An Asst Govt Whip, 1973-74; Mem., Select Cttee of House of Commons, European Legislation, 1973, 1976-; Vice-Chairman, Cons. Parly Cttees for: Agriculture, 1972-73 (Chm., Horticultural Sub-Cttee), and 1974-; European Affairs, 1979-80; Chm., Westcountry Gp of Cons. MPs, 1976-77. *Recreations:* cricket, gardening. *Address:* Little Court, St Ive, Liskeard, Cornwall. *Club:* MCC.

HICKS, Thomas; *see* Steele, Tommy.

HICKS, Ursula Kathleen, (Lady Hicks); University Lecturer in Public Finance, Oxford, 1947-65; Fellow of Linacre College, since 1965; *b* 17 Feb. 1896; *d* of W. F. and I. M. Webb, Dublin; *m* 1935 Sir John Hicks, qv. *Educ:* Roedean; Somerville College, Oxford; London Sch. of Economics (Hon. Fellow, 1980). Asst Lecturer, London Sch. of Economics, Oct. 1935 (resigned on marriage); Lecturer in charge of Dept of Economics, Liverpool University, 1941-46; Fiscal Comr, Uganda, 1962, Eastern Caribbean, 1962-63. Hon. Fellow, Inst. of Social Studies, The Hague, 1967; Hon. DSc (Econ.), Belfast, 1966. *Publications:* Finance of British Government, 1920-36, 1938; Taxation of War Wealth, 1941, Standards of Local Expenditure, 1943, The Problem of Valuation for Rating, 1944, and The Incidence of Local Rates, 1945 (with J. R. Hicks); Indian Public Finance, 1952 (UN); Finance and Taxation in Jamaica (with J. R. Hicks), 1955; Public Finance, 1955; British Public Finances, their Structure and Development, 1880-1952, 1954; Development from Below (Local Government and Finance in Developing Countries of the Commonwealth), 1961; Federalism and Economic Growth (with others), 1961; Report of Fiscal Commission Eastern Caribbean (Command Paper No 1991), 1963; Development Finance: Planning and Control, 1965; The Large City: A World Problem, 1974; Federalism, Failure and Success: a comparative study, 1978; articles in Economic Journal, Economica, Public Administration, etc. *Recreations:* painting, gardening. *Address:* Porch House, Blockley, Glos GL56 9BW. *T:* Blockley 700210.

HICKS, Maj.-Gen. William Michael Ellis, CB 1982; OBE 1967; General Officer Commanding, North West District, since 1980; *b* 2 June 1928; *s* of late Group Captain William Charles Hicks, AFC, and Nellie Kilbourne (*née* Kay); *m* 1950, Jean Hilary Duncan; three *s. Educ:* Eton Coll.; RMA

Sandhurst. Commnd 2 Lieut Coldstream Guards, 1948; served, 1948-67: regtl service, UK, Tripoli and Canal Zone; Instr, Sch. of Inf. (Captain); Staff Coll. (Major); GSO2 (Ops) HQ 4 Div.; regtl service, BAOR, UK and Kenya; JSSC; GSO (DS) Staff Coll.; GSO1 MO1, MoD, 1967-70 (Lt-Col); CO 1st Bn Coldstream Guards, 1970-72; RCDS, 1973 (Col); comd 4th Guards Armoured Bde, 1974-76 (Brig.); BGS Trng HQ UKLF, 1977-79; BGS (Author) attached to DMO, MoD, 1979. *Recreation:* golf. *Address:* c/o Lloyds Bank Ltd, Cox's & King's Branch, 6 Pall Mall, SW1Y 5NH.

HICKS BEACH, family name of **Earl St Aldwyn.**

HIDAYATULLAH, Mohammed; OBE 1946; Chief Justice, Supreme Court of India, 1968-70; Vice-President of India, since 1979 (Acting President, 1969); *b* 17 Dec. 1905; *y s* of Khan Bahadur Hafiz M. Wilayatullah, ISO; *m* 1948, Pushpa Shah, *d* of A. N. Shah, ICS; one *s* (one *d* decd). *Educ:* Govt High Sch., Raipur; Morris Coll., Nagpur (Phillips Schol.; BA; Malak Gold Medal); Trinity Coll., Cambridge (MA); Lincoln's Inn; Bencher 1968. Nagpur High Court: Advocate, 1930-46; Govt Pleader, 1942-43; Advocate General, CP & Berar, 1943-46; Puisne Judge, 1946-54; Chief Justice, 1954-56; Chief Justice, Madhya Pradesh High Court, 1956-58; Puisne Judge, Supreme Court of India, 1958-68. Dean, Faculty of Law, Nagpur Univ., 1950-54; Mem., Faculty of Law, Sagar, Vikram and Aligarh Univs; Pres., Indian Law Inst., 1968-70; Pres., Internat. Law Assoc. (Indian Br.), 1968-70; Pres., Indian Soc. of Internat. Law, 1968-70; Mem., Internat. Inst. of Space Law, Paris; Internat. Coun. of Former Scouts and Guides (awarded Silver Elephant, bronze medal for gallantry); Exec. Coun., World Assembly of Judges; Advr, Council for World Peace through Law; rep. India at Internat. Confs at Bangkok, Helsinki, Durham, Geneva, Port of Spain, Belgrade, Venice, Canberra, Melbourne and Washington. Chancellor, Muslim Nat. Univ., New Delhi; Pro-Chancellor, Delhi Univ., 1968-70. Kt of Mark Twain. Hon. LLD: Univ. of Philippines, 1970; Ravishankar Univ., 1970; Rajasthan Univ., 1976; Benares Hindu Univ. Medallion and plaque of Merit, Philconsa, Manila; Order of Jugoslav Flag with Sash, 1972. *Publications:* Democracy in India and the Judicial Process, 1966; The South-West Africa Case, 1967; Judicial Methods, 1969; (ed) Mulla's Mahomedan Law, 1968, 2nd edn 1977; A Judge's Miscellany, vol. 1, 1972, Second series, 1979; USA and India, 1977; 5th and 6th Schedules to Constitution of India 1970; My Own Boswell; numerous monographs and articles. *Recreations:* golf, bridge. *Address:* A-10 Rockside, 112 Walkeshwar Road, Bombay 6, India. *T:* 819798; 10 Janpath, New Delhi, India. *Clubs:* Delhi Gymkhana (New Delhi); Willingdon (Bombay).

HIDDEN, Anthony Brian, QC 1976; a Recorder of the Crown Court, since 1977; *b* 7 March 1936; *s* of late James Evelyn Harold Hidden, GM and of Gladys Bessie (*née* Brooks); *m* 1982, Mary Elise Torriano Pritchard, *d* of R. C. Pritchard of Barton Abbotts, Tetbury, Glos. *Educ:* Reigate Grammar Sch.; Emmanuel Coll., Cambridge (BA Hons 1957, MA 1960). 2nd Lieut, 1st Royal Tank Regt, Far East Land Forces, Hong Kong, 1958-59. Called to the Bar, Inner Temple, 1961; Mem., Hon. Soc. of Inner Temple, 1956-, and of Lincoln's Inn (*ad eundem*), 1973-. *Recreations:* reading, playing golf, watching football. *Address:* 8 New Square, Lincoln's Inn, WC2A 3QP. *T:* 01-242 4986.

HIDE, Prof. Raymond, FRS 1971; Director of Geophysical Fluid Dynamics Laboratory (Chief Scientific Officer), Meteorological Office, Bracknell, since 1967; Visiting Professor: Department of Mathematics, University College, London University, since 1967; Department of Meteorology, University of Reading, since 1976; Adrian Fellow, Univ. of Leicester, since 1980; *b* 17 May 1929; *s* of late Stephen Hide and Rose Edna Hide (*née* Cartlidge); *m* 1958, (Phyllis) Ann Licence; one *s* two *d. Educ:* Percy Jackson Grammar Sch., near Doncaster; Manchester Univ.; Caius Coll., Cambridge. BSc 1st cl. hons Physics Manchester, 1950; PhD 1953, ScD 1969, Cantab. Res. Assoc. in Astrophysics, Univ. of Chicago, 1953-54; Sen. Res. Fellow, AERE Harwell, 1954-57; Lectr in Physics, Univ. of Durham (King's Coll., Newcastle), 1957-61; Prof. of Geophysics and Physics, MIT, 1961-67. Mem. NERC, 1972-75. Mem. Council: RAS, 1969-72 (Vice-Pres., 1970-72); Royal Meteorological Soc., 1969-72 and 1974-77 (Pres., 1974-76); Eur. Geophysical Soc., 1981-. Lectures: Symons Meml, RMetS, 1970; R. A. Fisher Meml, 1977; Halley, Oxford, 1980; Jeffreys, RAS, 1981. Fellow, Amer. Acad. of Arts and Sciences, 1964. Charles Chree Medal, Inst. Physics, 1975; Holweck Medal, Soc. Franç. de Physique, 1982. *Publications:* papers in scientific jls. *Address:* 11 Clare Avenue, Wokingham, Berks. *T:* Bracknell 20242, ext. 2592.

HIEGER, Izrael, DSc (London); Biochemist, Royal Marsden Hospital, 1924-66; *b* Siedletz, Russian-Poland, June 1901; *s* of F. E. Hieger. *Educ:* Birkbeck Coll. and University Coll., London. With colleagues, Anna Fuller Memorial Prize for Cancer Research, 1939. *Publications:* One in Six: An Outline of the Cancer Problem, 1955; Carcinogenesis, 1961; papers on the discovery of cancer producing chemical compounds. *Address:* Chester Beatty Research Institute, Royal Marsden Hospital, Fulham Road, SW3.

HIGGINBOTTOM, Donald Noble; HM Diplomatic Service, retired; Counsellor, Foreign and Commonwealth Office, 1976-79; *b* 19 Dec. 1925; *s* of late Harold Higginbottom and Dorothy (*née* Needham); *m* 1950, Sarah Godwin. *Educ:* Calday Grange Grammar Sch., Cheshire; King's Coll., Cambridge (1st Cl. Hons Hist.); Yale Univ., USA (MA Hist.). Lectr in Humanities, Univ. of Chicago, 1951. Entered Foreign Office, 1953; Buenos Aires, 1955; Peking, 1958; Saigon, 1960; Phnom Penh, 1962; Singapore, 1964; Bangkok, 1971; Buenos Aires, 1974. *Recreations:* electronic clocks, power

boating. *Address:* 91 Dora Road, Wimbledon, SW19 7JT. *T:* 01-946 8890. *Clubs:* Athenæum; Yacht Club Olivos (Buenos Aires).

HIGGINS, see Longuet-Higgins.

HIGGINS, Alec Wilfred, MBE 1944; MC 1940; TD 1945; JP, DL; Deputy Chairman of Lloyd's, 1975, 1976, 1980 and 1981; Chairman: Higgins & Doble Ltd, since 1962; Crowe Underwriting Agency Ltd, since 1978; *b* 1 Nov. 1914; *s* of late Frederick Gladstone Higgins and Beatrice Louisa Scriven; *m* 1939, Denise May Philcox; two *s* one *d. Educ:* Merton Court Sch., Sidcup; Sutton Valence Sch. Joined Woods & Maslen Ltd, 1937, Chm., 1963-80. Underwriting Mem. of Lloyd's, 1948 (Mem. Cttee, 1967-73, 1975-77, 1980-); Mem. Cttee, Lloyd's Insce Brokers Assoc., 1960-63 and 1965-68 (Dep. Chm. 1965, Chm. 1966); Mem., Gen. Cttee, Lloyd's Register of Shipping, 1978-81; Chm., Insce Section, London Chamber of Commerce, 1963-64; Vice-Pres., Insce Inst. of London, 1967; Member: Council, Chartered Insce Inst., 1972-80; Insce Industry Trng Council, 1969; Export Guarantee Adv. Council, 1977- (Dep. Chm., 1982-). Mem., Court of Assistants, Insurers' Co., 1980, Junior Warden, 1982. Councillor, Chislehurst and Sidcup UDC, 1962-65 (Vice-Chm. of Council, 1964); Alderman, London Borough of Bexley, 1968-78; JP Bexley, 1967; DL Greater London, 1973, Representative DL, Havering, 1978. *Recreation:* swimming. *Address:* Somersby, 12 Priestlands Park Road, Sidcup, Kent DA15 7HR. *T:* 01-300 3792. *Clubs:* City of London, Royal Automobile.

HIGGINS, Sir Christopher (Thomas), Kt 1977; Chairman, Peterborough Development Corporation, 1968-81; *b* 14 Jan. 1914; *s* of late Thomas Higgins and Florence Maud Higgins; *m* 1936, Constance Joan Beck; one *s* one *d. Educ:* West Kensington Central Sch.; London Univ. Executive with Granada Group Ltd, 1939-68. Served War of 1939-45: with RA, 1940-46. Member: Acton Borough Council, 1945-65; GLC, 1964-67; Hemel Hempstead Develt Corp., 1947-52; Bracknell Develt Corp., 1965-68. Chm., North Thames Gas Consumers' Council, 1969-79. *Recreations:* reading, gardening, walking; watching most sports. *Address:* Coronation Cottage, Wood End, Little Horwood, Milton Keynes, Bucks MK17 0PE. *T:* Winslow 2636.

HIGGINS, Frank, FCIT 1979; *b* 30 Aug. 1927; *s* of Wilfred and Hilda Higgins; *m* 1948, Betty Pulford; one *s* one *d. Educ:* Hanley High Sch., Stoke-on-Trent; St Paul's Coll., Cheltenham. Teacher: Stoke-on-Trent, 1946; Notts, 1948-58; Organising Sec., Youth Gp, 1958-60; Teacher, Nottingham, Derby, 1960-73; Mem. Nat. Bus Co., 1974-79. Contested (Lab) Harborough 1966, Grantham 1970. Mem., Nottingham City Council, 1971-74, 1979- (Chm. Transportation Cttee, 1972-74, 1979-81); Mem., Notts CC, 1973-77 and 1981- (Chm. Environment Cttee, 1973-77; Chm. Resources Cttee, 1981-). Chm., Central Transport Consultative Cttee, 1977-80. *Recreations:* travelling, talking. *Address:* 7 Hamilton Road, Nottingham. *T:* Nottingham 608571.

HIGGINS, Jack; see Patterson, Harry.

HIGGINS, Prof. John Christopher, CEng, FIEE; CBIM; Director of Management Centre, University of Bradford, and Professor of Management Sciences, since 1972; *b* 9 July 1932; *s* of James Higgins and Margaret Eileen Higgins (*née* Dealtrey); *m* 1960, Margaret Edna Howells; three *s. Educ:* Gonville and Caius Coll., Cambridge (MA); Univ. of London (BSc, MSc); PhD Bradford. Short service commission, RAF, 1953-56; 1956-70: Electronics Industry; Dept of Chief Scientist (RAF) in MoD; management consultancy; Director of Economic Planning and Research for IPC Newspapers Ltd. Member: Final Selection Bd for Civil Service Commn, 1976-; Defence Scientific Adv. Council's Assessments Bd, 1976- (Chm. of its Cttee on Operational Analysis, 1980-); UGC Sub-Cttee on Management and Business Studies, 1979-; Chm., Social Sciences Res. Council's Accountancy Steering Cttee and Member of its Management and Industrial Relns Cttee, 1976-80. *Publications:* Information Systems for Planning and Control: Concepts and Cases, 1976; Strategic and Operational Planning Systems: Principles and Practice, 1980; numerous papers and articles on corporate planning, information systems and management educn. *Recreations:* violin/viola (ex National Youth Orchestra of Great Britain), Rugby (formerly Member Middlesex RFU Committee), cricket, fell-walking. *Address:* Woodfield, 36 Station Road, Baildon, West Yorkshire BD17 5NW. *T:* Bradford 592836.

HIGGINS, Rev. Canon John Denis P.; see Pearce-Higgins.

HIGGINS, John Patrick Basil, QC; His Honour Judge Higgins; County Court Judge, Northern Ireland, since 1971; Recorder of Belfast, since 1982; *b* 14 June 1927; *e s* of late John A. and Mary Philomena Higgins, Magherafelt; *m* 1960, Bridget, *e d* of late Dr Matthew F. O'Neill, Hollingwood, Chesterfield; two *s* three *d. Educ:* St. Columb's Coll., Derry; Queen's Univ., Belfast (LLB). Called to Bar of N Ireland, 1948, Bencher, 1969-71; QC (N Ire.) 1967; County Court Judge: Armagh and Fermanagh, 1971-79; S Antrim, 1979-82. Chairman: Mental Health Review Tribunal for NI, 1963-71; Legal Aid Adv. Cttee (NI), 1975-; Council of HM County Court Judges, 1978-; Member: County Court Rules Cttee (NI), 1973-; Statute Law Cttee of NI, 1975-; Lowry Cttee on Registration of Title in NI, 1958-67; Jones Cttee on County Courts and Magistrates' Courts in NI, 1972-73; Gardiner Cttee on measures to deal with terrorism in NI, 1974. Chm., Voluntary Service, Belfast, 1975-. Member: Community Peace Conf., 1969; Bd of Management, St Joseph's Coll. of Educn, Belfast, 1969-; Bd of Governors, Dominican Coll.,

Portstewart, 1974-. *Address:* 2 Waterloo Park, Belfast, Northern Ireland. *T:* 777813.

HIGGINS, Prof. Peter Matthew; Professor of General Practice, Guy's Hospital Medical School, University of London, since 1974; *b* 18 June 1923; *s* of Peter Joseph Higgins and Margaret Higgins; *m* 1952, Jean Margaret Lindsay Currie; three *s* one *d. Educ:* St Ignatius' Coll., London; UCH, London. MB, BS; FRCP, FRCGP. House Phys., Medical Unit, UCH, 1947; RAMC, 1948-49; House Phys., UCH, St Pancras, 1950; Resident MO, UCH, 1951-52; Asst Med. Registrar, UCH, 1953; Gen. Practice, Rugeley, Staffs, 1954-66, and Castle Vale, Birmingham, 1966-68; Sen. Lectr, Guy's Hosp. Med. Sch., 1968-74. Vice-Chm., SE Thames RHA, 1976-. Governor, Linacre Centre. *Publications:* articles in Lancet, BMJ, Jl RCGP. *Recreations:* squash, swimming, sailing. *Address:* Wallings, Heathfield Lane, Chislehurst, Kent. *T:* 01-467 2756.

HIGGINS, Reynold Alleyne, LittD; FBA 1972; FSA; *b* Weybridge, 26 Nov. 1916; *er s* of late Charles Alleyne Higgins and late Marjorie Edith (*née* Taylor); *m* 1947, Patricia Mary, *d* of J. C. Williams; three *s* two *d. Educ:* Sherborne Sch.; Pembroke Coll., Cambridge (Scholar). First Cl., Classical Tripos pts I and II, 1937, 1938; MA, 1960; LittD, 1963. Served War: Queen Victoria's Rifles, KRRC, 1939-46 (Captain, PoW). Asst Keeper, Dept of Greek and Roman Antiquities, British Museum, 1947, Dep. Keeper, 1965-77, Acting Keeper, 1976. Visiting Fellow, British School of Archaeology at Athens, 1969, Chm., Managing Cttee, 1975-79. Corr. Mem., German Archaeological Inst. *Publications:* Catalogue of Terracottas in British Museum, vols I and II, 1954, 1959; Greek and Roman Jewellery, 1961, 2nd edn 1980; Greek Terracotta Figures, 1963; Jewellery from Classical Lands, 1965; Greek Terracottas, 1967; Minoan and Mycenaean Art, 1967, 2nd edn 1981; The Greek Bronze Age, 1970; The Archaeology of Minoan Crete, 1973; The Aegina Treasure, 1979; also articles and reviews in British and foreign periodicals. *Recreation:* travel. *Address:* Hartfield, 21 Burstead Close, Cobham, Surrey KT11 2NL. *T:* Cobham 3234.

HIGGINS, Prof. Rosalyn, JSD; Professor of International Law at the London School of Economics, University of London, since 1981; *b* 2 June 1937; *d* of Lewis Cohen and Fay Inberg; *m* 1961, Rt Hon. Terence Langley Higgins, *qv*; one *s* one *d. Educ:* Burlington Grammar Sch., London; Girton Coll., Cambridge (Scholar; BA 1958, 1st Cl. Law Qualifying 1, 1st Cl. Tripos Pt II; 1st Cl. LLB 1959); Yale Law Sch., (JSD 1962). UK Intern, Office of Legal Affairs, UN, 1958; Commonwealth Fund Fellow, 1959; Vis. Fellow, Brookings Instn, Washington, DC, 1960; Jun. Fellow in Internat. Studies, LSE, 1961-63; Staff Specialist in Internat. Law, RIIA, 1963-74; Vis. Fellow, LSE, 1974-78; Prof. of Internat. Law, Univ. of Kent at Canterbury, 1978-81. Vis. Prof. of Internat. Law: Stanford Univ., 1975; Yale Univ., 1977. Sidgwick Meml Lecture, Cambridge, 1977; Montague Burton Lecture, Leeds Univ., 1979; Hague Lectures on Internat. Law, 1982. Vice Pres., Amer. Soc. of Internat. Law, 1972-74 (Certif. of Merit, 1971). Dr *hc* Univ. of Paris XI, 1980. Mem. Board of Editors: International Organization, 1972-78; American Journal of International Law; British Yearbook of International Law. *Publications:* The Development of International Law through the Political Organs of the United Nations, 1963; Conflict of Interests: international law in a divided world, 1965; The Administration of the United Kingdom Foreign Policy through the United Nations, 1966; (ed with James Fawcett) Law in Movement—essays in memory of John McMahon, 1974; UN Peacekeeping: documents and commentary: Vol. I, Middle East, 1969; Vol. II, Asia, 1971; Vol. III, Africa, 1980; Vol. IV, Europe, 1981; articles for law jls and jls of internat. relations. *Recreations:* sport, cooking, eating. *Address:* London School of Economics, Houghton Street, WC2A 2AE; 4 Essex Court, Temple, EC4Y 9AJ. *T:* 01-583 9191.

HIGGINS, Rt. Hon. Terence (Langley); PC 1979; MP (C) Worthing since 1964; *b* 18 Jan. 1928; *s* of Reginald Higgins, Dulwich; *m* 1961, Prof. Rosalyn Higgins, *qv*; one *s* one *d. Educ:* Alleyn's Sch., Dulwich; Gonville and Caius Coll., Cambridge. Brit. Olympic Team (athletics) 1948, 1952; BA (Hons) 1958. MA 1963; Pres. Cambridge Union Soc., 1958. NZ Shipping Co., 1948-55; Lectr in Economic Principles, Dept of Economics, Yale Univ., 1958-59; Economist with Unilever, 1959-64. Director: Warne Wright Gp, 1976-; Lex Service Group, 1980-. Sec., Cons. Parly Finance Cttee, 1965-66; Opposition Spokesman on Treasury and Economic Affairs, 1966-70; Minister of State, Treasury, 1970-72; Financial Sec. to Treasury, 1972-74; Opposition Spokesman: on Treasury and Econ. Affairs, 1974; for Trade, 1974-76; Chairman: Cons. Parly Cttees, on Sport, 1979-81, Transport, 1979-; Select Cttee on Procedure, 1980-; Member: Select Cttee on Treasury and Civil Service, 1980; Exec. Cttee, 1922 Cttee, 1980-. Member: Council, RIIA, 1979-; Council, IAM, 1979. Associate, Inst. of Chartered Shipbrokers. *Address:* 18 Hallgate, Blackheath Park, SE3. *Clubs:* Yale; Hawks (Cambridge).

HIGGINS, Wilfred Frank; *see* Higgins, Frank.

HIGGINS, Rear-Adm. William Alleyne, CBE 1980; Flag Officer Medway, and Port Admiral Chatham, since 1982; *b* 18 May 1928; *s* of Comdr H. G. Higgins, DSO, RN, and Mrs L. A. Higgins; *m* 1963, Wiltraud Hiebaum; two *s* one *d. Educ:* Wellington College. Joined Royal Navy, 1945; Commander 1965; Captain 1973; Commodore, HMS Drake, 1980-82. *Recreations:* skiing, rock climbing and mountaineering. *Address:* East Horsley, Surrey. *Club:* Royal Naval and Royal Marines Mountaineering (President).

HIGGINSON, Prof. Gordon Robert; Professor of Engineering, Durham University, since 1965; *b* 8 Nov. 1929; *s* of Frederick John and Letitia Higginson; *m* 1954, Marjorie Forbes Rannie; three *s* two *d. Educ:* Leeds Univ. BSc, PhD. MICE; MIMechE. Scientific Officer, then Sen. Scientific Officer, Min. of Supply, 1953-56; Lectr, Leeds Univ., 1956-62; Associate Prof., RMCS, Shrivenham, 1962-65; Dean of Faculty of Science, Durham Univ., 1972-75. Mem., UGC, 1979- (Chm., Tech. Sub. Cttee, 1979-). IMechE James Clayton Fund Prize, 1963 and 1979. Gold Medal, Brit. Soc. of Rheology, 1969. *Publications:* Elastohydrodynamic Lubrication (with D. Dowson), 1966, 2nd edn 1977; Foundations of Engineering Mechanics, 1974; papers on mechanics in various jls. *Recreation:* two acres of land. *Address:* White Lea House, Crook, Co. Durham. *T:* Crook 2868. *Club:* Billy Row Working Mens' (Crook).

HIGGON, Col Laurence Hugh, CBE 1958; MC 1916 and Bar 1917; *b* 3 Sept. 1884; 4th (and *o* surv.) *s* of late Capt. J. D. G. Higgon, RA, DL, JP, Scolton, Pembrokeshire; *m* 1922, Neda Kathleen C., *er d* of Lieut-Col F. Rennick (killed 1915); two *d. Educ:* Cheltenham; RMA, Woolwich. Entered RA 1903; retired, 1927; comd 102nd (Pembroke Yeo.) Bde RA, 1930-35 (Bt Col); Hon. Col 1948; Hon. Comr Toc H in Wales, 1931. Rejoined RA (Lieut-Col), 1939. Home Guard, Pembs (Lieut-Col), 1942-45. DL, JP, Pembrokeshire; JP Haverfordwest. Served European War, 1914-19, France and Flanders (despatches twice, MC and Bar). Chm. Pembroke County War Memorial Hospital 1934-53; Mem. West Wales Hosps Management Cttee, 1948-53; Chm. Standing Joint Cttee, 1949-54; Chm., Pembroke TA Assoc., 1944-47; Lord Lieutenant, Pembrokeshire, 1944-54. OStJ. *Address:* Castle Corner, Manorbier, Dyfed. *T:* Manorbier 343. *Clubs:* Army and Navy; Pembroke County (Haverfordwest).

HIGGS, Brian James, QC 1974; a Recorder of the Crown Court, since 1974; Barrister-at-Law; *b* 24 Feb. 1930; *s* of James Percival Higgs and Kathleen Anne Higgs; *m* 1st, 1953, Jean Cameron DuMerton; two *s* three *d*; 2nd, 1980, Vivienne Mary Johnson; one *s. Educ:* Wrekin Coll.; London Univ. Served RA, 1948-50. Called to Bar, Gray's Inn, 1955. Contested (C) Romford, 1966. *Recreations:* gardening, golf, wine, chess, bridge. *Address:* Navestock Woodhouse, Navestock Side, Brentwood, Essex. *T:* Coxtie Green 72032; 2 Harcourt Buildings, Temple, EC4Y 9DB. *T:* 01-353 2622. *Clubs:* Thorndon Park Golf.

HIGGS, Godfrey Walter, CBE 1960; Vice-President, Bahamas Senate, 1964-68; *b* 28 Sept. 1907; *yr s* of late Charles Roger Higgs; *m* 1937, Marion Suzanne (marr. diss.), *y d* of Roscoe Hagen, Rochester, NY; three *s*; *m* Eleanor Claire, *y d* of Charles Frederick Beckmann, New York City, USA. *Educ:* Queen's Coll., Taunton. Called to Bahamas Bar, 1929; English Bar, Inner Temple, 1933 (Profumo Prize); Deputy Speaker, House of Assembly, Bahamas, 1937-42; Mem. Executive Council and Leader for the Govt, Bahamas House of Assembly, 1942-45 and 1946-49; Member: Legislative Council, Bahamas, 1950-64; Senate, 1964-68. *Recreations:* yachting, swimming, golf, shooting, fishing, etc. *Address:* Stanley, PO Box N3247, East Bay Street, Nassau, Bahamas. *Clubs:* Royal Nassau Sailing, Nassau Lawn Tennis.

HIGGS, Rt. Rev. Hubert Laurence, MA Cantab; *b* 23 Nov. 1911; *s* of Frank William and Mary Ann Higgs; *m* 1936, Elizabeth Clare (*née* Rogers); one *s* one *d. Educ:* University Coll. Sch.; Christ's Coll., Cambridge; Ridley Hall, Cambridge. Curate: Holy Trinity, Richmond, 1935; St Luke's, Redcliffe Square, London, 1936-38; St John's, Boscombe (and Jt Sec. Winchester Youth Council), 1938-39. Vicar, Holy Trinity, Aldershot, 1939-45; Editorial Sec., Church Missionary Soc., 1945-52; Vicar, St John's, Woking, 1952-57 (Rural Dean, 1957); Archdeacon of Bradford and Canon Residentiary of Bradford Cathedral, 1957-65; Bishop Suffragan of Hull, 1965-76; RD of Hull, 1972-76. *Recreations:* history, music-listening, gardening. *Address:* The Farmstead, Chediston, Halesworth, Suffolk. *T:* Halesworth 2621.

HIGGS, Sir (John) Michael (Clifford), Kt 1969; DL; solicitor, retired; *b* 30 May 1912; *s* of late Alderman A. W. Higgs, Cranford House, Stourton, Staffs; *m* 1st, 1936, Diana Louise Jerrams (*d* 1950); two *d*; 2nd, 1952, Rachel Mary Jones; one *s* one *d. Educ:* St Cuthberts, Malvern; Shrewsbury. LLB (Birmingham), 1932. Admitted solicitor, 1934. Served War of 1939-45 with 73 HAA Regt RA (TA), 1939-42; JAG Staff, 1942-46; demobilised, 1946, with rank of Lieut-Col. Mem. of Staffs County Council, 1946-49; MP (C) Bromsgrove Div. of Worcs, 1950-55; Mem. of Worcs CC, 1953-73 (Chm. 1959-73); Alderman, 1963; Chm., Hereford and Worcester CC, 1973-77. Mem. West Midlands Economic Planning Council, 1965-79; Chm., W Midlands Planning Authorities' Conf., 1969-73. DL Worcs 1968, Hereford and Worcester, 1974. *Address:* Pixham Cottage, Callow End, Worcester WR2 4TH. *T:* Worcester 830645.

HIGGS, John Walter Yeoman; Secretary and Keeper of the Records, Duchy of Cornwall, since 1981; *b* 1 Sept. 1923; *s* of Walter Frank Higgs and Cecilia Elizabeth (*née* Yeoman); *m* 1948, Elizabeth Patricia, *d* of Lt-Col H. B. Norcott, Rifle Bde; two *d. Educ:* Oundle Sch.; Emmanuel Coll., Cambridge (MA). National Inst. of Agricl Engrg, 1944-46; Agricultural Economics Inst., Univ. of Oxford, 1946-48; Lectr, Faculty of Agric., Univ. of Reading, 1948-57; Keeper, Museum of English Rural Life, 1951-57; Lectr in Agricl Development, Univ. of Oxford, 1957-66; Fellow of Exeter Coll., 1963-73; Finance and Estates Bursar, 1963-68; Sen. Research Fellow, 1969-73; Curator: University Chest, 1963-70; University Theatre, 1963-70. Consultant to UN and FAO and other UN Agencies on rural develt in several countries, 1964-80;

Secretary: UN/FAO/ILO World Conf. on Agrarian Reform, 1966; FAO/Unesco/ILO World Conf. on Agricl Educn and Trng, 1970; Chief, Educn and Extension Service, FAO, Rome, 1971-74; Member: Adv. Cttee, Agrarian History of England & Wales, 1956-; Prince of Wales' Council, 1979-; President: British Agricl History Soc., 1974-76; Internat. Assoc. of Agricl Museums, 1974-76; Trustee, Ernest Cook Trust, 1977-. Partner in family farms in Dumfriesshire and Oxfordshire. *Publications:* The Land: a visual history of modern Britain, 1964; ed, People in the Countryside, 1964; ed, Education for Rural Families in Developing Countries, 1977; numerous papers on agricl and rural development in nat. and internat. jls. *Recreations:* fishing, shooting. *Address:* Arkleton, Langholm, Dumfriesshire DG13 0HL. *T:* Ewes 247; 10 Buckingham Gate, SW1. *T:* 01-828 3550. *Clubs:* Brooks's, Farmers'; Leander.

HIGGS, Sir Michael; see Higgs, Sir J. M. C.

HIGHAM, John Drew, CMG 1956; *b* 28 Nov. 1914; *s* of Richard and Margaret Higham, Pendleton, Lancs; *m* 1st, 1936, Mary Constance Bromage (*d* 1974); three *d*; 2nd, 1976, Katherine Byard Pailing. *Educ:* Manchester Grammar Sch.; Gonville and Caius Coll., Cambridge (Scholar). Asst Principal, Admiralty, 1936; Asst Private Sec. to First Lord, 1939; Private Sec. to Parliamentary Sec. and Parliamentary Clerk, 1940; Principal, Admiralty, 1941; transferred to Colonial Office, 1946; Asst Sec. Colonial Office, 1948; seconded to Singapore as Under Sec., 1953, and as Dir of Personnel, 1955-57 (acted on various occasions as Chief Sec.); Asst Sec., Min. of Housing and Local Govt, 1965; Head of Development Control Div., DoE, 1970-74. Chevalier 1st Cl. Order of St Olaf (Norway), 1948. *Recreations:* history of art, gardening. *Address:* Avonside, Bredon, Tewkesbury, Glos. *T:* Bredon 72468; 6 Chalcot Gardens, NW3 4YB. *T:* 01-722 3157.

HIGHAM, Rear-Adm. Philip Roger Canning, CB 1972; Keeper, HMS Belfast, Imperial War Museum, 1978-83 (Director, HMS Belfast Trust, 1973); *b* 9 June 1920; *s* of Edward Higham, Stoke Bishop, Bristol; *m* 1942, Pamela Bracton Edwards, *er d* of Gerald Edwards, Southport, Lancs; two *s*. *Educ:* RNC Dartmouth. Cadet, 1937; Midshipman, 1938; Sub-Lt 1940; Lieut 1942; qual. Gunnery Officer, 1944; Second Gunnery Off., HMS Vanguard, Royal Tour of S Africa, 1947; psc 1948; Exper. Dept, HMS Excellent, 1951-52; Comdr, Devonport Gunnery Sch., 1953; Trials Comdr, RAE Aberporth, 1954-55; jssc 1956; Exper. Comdr, HMS Excellent, 1957-59; Admty (DTWP), 1960-61; Naval Attaché, Middle East, 1962-64; idc 1965; Dep. Chief Polaris Exec., 1966-68; Cdre i/c Hong Kong, 1968-70; Asst Chief of Naval Staff (Op. Requirements), 1970-72. *Recreations:* gardening, fishing. *Address:* Apple Tree Farm, Prinsted, Emsworth, Hants. *T:* Emsworth 2195. *Club:* Naval and Military.

HIGHET, Helen Clark; see MacInnes, H. C.

HIGHSMITH, Patricia; writer since 1942; *b* 19 Jan. 1921; *o c* of Jay Bernard Plangman and Mary Coates (of German and English-Scots descent respectively); name changed to Highsmith on mother's 2nd marriage; unmarried. *Educ:* Barnard Coll., Columbia Univ., New York. For a year after univ. had a mediocre writing job; after that free-lance until publication of first novel. Lived in Europe and America alternately from 1951, and now has been some years in France. *Publications:* Strangers on a Train, 1950; The Blunderer, 1955; The Talented Mr Ripley, 1956; Deep Water, 1957; A Game for the Living, 1958; This Sweet Sickness, 1960 (filmed 1979); The Cry of the Owl, 1962; The Two Faces of January, 1964; The Glass Cell, 1965; A Suspension of Mercy, 1965; Plotting and Writing Suspense Fiction, 1966; Those Who Walk Away, 1967; The Tremor of Forgery, 1969; Eleven (short stories), 1970; Ripley Under Ground, 1971; A Dog's Ransom, 1972; Ripley's Game, 1974 (filmed as The American Friend, 1978); The Animal-Lover's Book of Beastly Murder (short stories), 1975; Edith's Diary, 1977; Little Tales of Misogyny (short stories), 1977; Slowly, Slowly in the Wind (short stories), 1979; The Boy Who Followed Ripley, 1980; The Black House (short stories), 1981. *Recreations:* drawing, some painting, carpentering, snail-watching, travelling by train. *Club:* Detection.

HIGHTON, Rear-Adm. Jack Kenneth, CB 1959; CBE 1952; *b* 2 Sept. 1904; *s* of John Henry Highton and Kate (*née* Powers); *m* 1933, Eileen Metcalfe Flack; one *s* two *d*. *Educ:* Bedford Modern Sch. Joined Royal Navy, 1922; Captain 1951; Dir of Welfare and Service Conditions, 1955-57; Rear-Adm. 1957; Chief Staff Officer (Administration) to Commander-in-Chief, Plymouth, 1957-60; retired, 1960. *Recreations:* walking, sailing, gardening. *Address:* c/o National Westminster Bank Ltd, Woodbridge, Suffolk.

HIGMAN, Prof. Graham, MA, DPhil; FRS 1958; Waynflete Professor of Pure Mathematics, Oxford University, and Fellow of Magdalen College, Oxford, since 1960; *b* 1917; 2nd *s* of Rev. Joseph Higman; *m* 1941, Ivah May Treleaven; five *s* one *d*. *Educ:* Sutton Secondary Sch., Plymouth; Balliol Coll., Oxford. Meteorological Office, 1940-46; Lecturer, University of Manchester, 1946-55; Reader in Mathematics at Oxford Univ., 1955-60; Senior Research Fellow, Balliol Coll., Oxford, 1958-60. Hon. DSc Exeter, 1979. De Morgan Medal, London Mathematical Soc., 1974; Sylvester Medal, Royal Soc., 1979. *Publications:* papers in Proc. London Math. Soc., and other technical jls. *Address:* 64 Sandfield Road, Headington, Oxford. *T:* 62974.

HIGNETT, John Mulock, FCA; Director-General, Panel on Take-overs and Mergers, since 1981; *b* 9 March 1934; *s* of Reginald and Marjorie Hignett;

m 1961, Marijke Inge de Boer; one *s* one *d*. *Educ:* Harrow Sch.; Magdalene Coll., Cambridge (MA). Kemp Chatteris & Co., 1958-61; Deloitte & Co., 1961-63; joined Lazard Brothers & Co. Ltd, 1963; Manager, Issues Dept; 1971; Dir, 1972; Head of Corporate Finance Div., 1980. *Address:* 61 Roehampton Lane, SW15 5NE. *T:* 01-876 2902. *Clubs:* MCC; Hawks (Cambridge).

HIGNETT, Peter George; General Manager, Hampshire Cattle Breeders' Society, since 1976; *b* 3 June 1925; *s* of Harry Sutton Hignett and Annie Hignett; *m* 1948, Patricia Bishop; two *s* one *d*. *Educ:* Pontesbury CofE Sch.; King Edward VI Sch., Birmingham; Univ. of Liverpool (MRCVS). General practice, 1947-49; Wellcome Veterinary Res. Station, 1949-54; Reader in Veterinary Reproduction, Univ. of Glasgow, 1954-76. Mem. Council, RCVS, 1972-, Pres., 1981-82. Pres., Soc. for Study of Animal Breeding, 1966-68; Secretary: Associated AI Centres, 1977-; Edgar Meml Trust, 1977-; Mem., Trehane Cttee, 1979-. *Publications:* scientific papers on fertility in domestic animals. *Recreations:* gardening, sailing, music. *Address:* Qaisik, Sway Road, Brockenhurst, Hants S04 7SG. *T:* Lymington 22066. *Club:* Farmers'.

HIGTON, Dennis John, CEng, FIMechE, FRAeS; company director; *b* 15 July 1921; *s* of John William and Lillian Harriett Higton; *m* 1945, Joy Merrifield Pickett; one *s* one *d*. *Educ:* Guildford Technical Sch.; RAE Farnborough Technical Sch. Mid-Wessex Water Co., 1937. RAE Engineering Apprentice, 1938-42; RAE Aerodynamics Dept (Aero Flight), 1942-52; learned to fly at No 1 EFTS RAF Panshangar, 1946; A&AEE Boscombe Down, Head of Naval Test and Supt of Performance, 1953-66; British Defence Staff, Washington DC, USA, 1966-70; MoD(PE) Anglo-French Helicopter Production, 1970-72; Director Aircraft Production, 1972-75; Dir-Gen. of Mil. Aircraft Projects, MoD, 1976-79, of Aircraft 4, 1979-80, Under-Sec. and Dir Gen. Aircraft 3, 1980-81. Mem., Fleet Air Arm Officers Assoc. *Publications:* research and memoranda papers mainly on aerodynamic flight testing. *Recreations:* beekeeping, skiing, sailing, gardening, walking on Salisbury Plain, shooting. *Address:* Jasmine Cottage, Rollestone Road, Shrewton, Salisbury, Wiltshire SP3 4HG. *T:* Shrewton 276.

HILALY, Agha, HQA, SPk; Chairman, Board of Governors, Pakistan Institute of Strategic Studies, since 1973; *b* 20 May 1911; *s* of late Agha Abdulla; *m* 1938, Malek Taj Begum, *d* of Mirza Kazim, Bangalore; three *s*. *Educ:* Presidency Coll., Madras (MA); King's Coll., Cambridge (MA). Entered former ICS (Bengal cadre), 1936; Under-Sec., Govt of Bengal, 1939-41; Govt of India, 1941-47; entered Pakistan Foreign Service at time of Partition; Jt Sec., Min. of Foreign Affairs, 1951; Imp. Def. Coll., 1955; Ambassador to Sweden, Norway, Denmark and Finland, 1956; Delegate to UN Gen. Assembly, 1958; Ambassador to USSR and Czechoslovakia, 1959; High Commissioner in India and Ambassador to Nepal, 1961; High Commissioner for Pakistan in the UK and Ambassador to Ireland, 1963-66; Ambassador for Pakistan to the United States, 1966-71, also accredited to Mexico, Venezuela and Jamaica. Dir, State Bank of Pakistan, 1972-. Hilal-i-Quaid-i-Azam, Pakistan; Star of Pakistan; Grand Cross, Order of the North Star, Sweden; Grand Cross, Prabol Gurkha Dakshana Bahu (Nepal). *Recreations:* colour photography, shooting. *Address:* No 48 Fifteenth Street, Phase 5, Defence Housing Society, Karachi 6, Pakistan. *Clubs:* Travellers'; International (Washington); Sind (Karachi).

HILARY, David Henry Jephson; Assistant Under Secretary of State, Home Office, since 1975; *b* 3 May 1932; *s* of late Robert and Nita Hilary; *m* 1957, Phoebe Leonora, *d* of John J. Buchanan; two *s* two *d*. *Educ:* Tonbridge Sch.; King's Coll., Cambridge (Sandys Student 1954, Craven Student 1955; MA). Royal Artillery, 1953-54. Entered Home Office, 1956. *Recreations:* cricket, squash, bridge. *Address:* 17 Victoria Square, SW1. *Clubs:* RAC, MCC.

HILD, Maj.-Gen. John Henry, MBE 1969; CEng, FIEE; FBIM; Chief Signal Officer, British Army of the Rhine, since 1980; *b* 28 March 1931; *m* 1954, Janet Macdonald Brown; one *s* one *d*. *Educ:* Blackfriars; Laxton; Sandhurst. Joined Army, 1949; commissioned, 1952; Korea, 1952-53; sc 1961; MoD, DAQMG, 1962-64; Borneo, 1965; Hong Kong, 1966-67; 1 (BR) Corps, DAQMG, 1968-69; CO 18 Sig. Regt, 1969-71; DS, Staff Coll., 1972-73; Comd 1 Sig. Gp, 1974-76; Comdt, Sch. of Sigs, 1976-78; RCDS 1979; HQ BAOR, DQMG, 1980-. *Recreations:* entertaining friends, travel, sport. *Address:* c/o Lloyds Bank Ltd, Cox's and King's Branch, 6 Pall Mall, SW1. *Club:* Army and Navy.

HILDER, Rev. Geoffrey Frank; Archdeacon of Taunton, 1951-71; Prebendary of Wells Cathedral, 1951-73; Provost of Western Division of Woodard Corporation, 1960-70; *b* 17 July 1906; *s* of Albert Thomas and Lilian Ethel Hilder; *m* 1939, Enid, *d* of Rev. F. E. Coggin. *Educ:* Uppingham Sch.; Lincoln Coll., Oxford; Inner Temple; Ely Theological Coll. Called to the Bar, 1930. Deacon, 1931; Priest, 1932; Rector of Ruardean, Glos., 1937-41; Vicar of St Stephen's, Cheltenham, 1941-48; Vicar of Hambridge, 1948-59. Prolocutor of Lower House of Convocation of Canterbury, 1955-70; Dir of Ecclesiastical Insurance Office Ltd, 1957-61. *Recreations:* music, gardening. *Address:* 4 Falcon Terrace, Bude, Cornwall EX23 8LJ. *T:* Bude 4532.

HILDER, Rowland, RI 1938; painter; *b* Greatneck, Long Island, USA, 28 June 1905, British parents; *m* 1929, Edith Blenkiron; one *s* one *d*. *Educ:* Goldsmiths' Coll. Sch. of Art, London. Exhbn, Furneaux Gall., Wimbledon, 1974, 1976, 1980. PRI 1964-74. *Publications:* Illustrated editions of: Moby Dick, 1926; Treasure Island, 1929; Precious Bane, 1930; The Bible for To-day, 1940; The Shell Guide to Flowers of the Countryside (with Edith Hilder), 1955;

(jointly) Sketching and Painting Indoors, 1957; Starting with Watercolour, 1966; Expressing Land, Sea and Sky in Watercolour, 1982; *relevant publication:* Rowland Hilder: painter and illustrator, by John Lewis, 1978. *Address:* 5 Kidbrooke Grove, Blackheath, SE3. *T:* 01-858 3072.

HILDITCH, Clifford Arthur; Director of Social Services, Manchester District Council, since April 1974 (Manchester City Council, 1970-74); *b* 3 Feb. 1927; *s* of late Arthur Clifford Hilditch and of Lilian Maud Hilditch (*née* Brockman); *m* 1953, Joyce Hilditch (*née* Burgess); one *s. Educ:* Huntingdon Grammar Sch.; London Univ. Dip. in Applied Social Studies. Army Service, 1944-48 (commissioned into Indian Army, 1945). Service as an Administrative Officer, LCC (Welfare Services) until 1961; Manchester City Council: Dep. Chief Welfare Officer, 1962-64; Chief Welfare Officer, 1965-70. Hon. Fellow, Manchester Polytechnic, 1976. *Publications:* contributor to various hosp. and social services jls. *Recreations:* various. *Address:* 14 Priory Road, Wilmslow, Cheshire. *T:* Wilmslow 522109.

HILDRED, Sir William (Percival), Kt 1945; CB 1942; OBE 1936; Grand Officer, Order of Orange-Nassau, 1946; Commander Order of Crown of Belgium; MA; Director-General Emeritus International Air Transport Association (Director-General, 1946-66); *b* 13 July 1893; *s* of late William Kirk Hildred; *m* 1920, Constance Mary Chappell, MB, ChB; two *s* one *d. Educ:* Boulevard Sch., Hull; University of Sheffield. Served European War, 1st York and Lancaster Regt, 1914-17; entered Treasury, 1919; Finance Officer, Empire Marketing Board, 1926-34; Head of Special Measures Branch, Ministry of Agriculture and Fisheries, 1934-35; Deputy General Manager, Export Credits Guarantee Dept, 1935-38; Deputy Dir-Gen. of Civil Aviation, Air Ministry, 1938; Principal Asst Sec., Ministry of Aircraft Production, 1940; assisted in formation of RAF Ferry Command, Montreal, 1941; Director-Gen. of Civil Aviation, Ministry of Civil Aviation, 1941-46. Edward Warner Award of ICAO, 1965. Hon. LLD: Sheffield; McGill Univ.; FRSA. Hon. FRAeS. *Recreations:* cycling, music, carpentry. *Address:* Spreakley House, Frensham, Surrey.

HILDRETH, Maj.-Gen. Sir (Harold) John (Crossley), KBE 1964 (CBE 1952; OBE 1945); *b* 12 June 1908; *s* of late Lt-Col H. C. Hildreth, DSO, OBE, FRCS, and late Mrs Hildreth; *m* 1950, Mary, *d* of late G. Wroe; two *s* three *d. Educ:* Wellington Coll., Berks; RMA, Woolwich. 2nd Lieut, RA, 1928; transferred to RAOC, 1935, as Captain; Major 1944; Lieut-Col 1948; Col 1952; Brig. 1958; Maj.-Gen. 1961. War Office: Col 1942-44; Brig. 1944-47; Inspector of Establishments, 1947-50; Controller of Army Statistics, 1950-51; Comdr RAOC, Ammunition Org., 1951-53; Comdr, Bicester, 1953-57; DOS, BAOR, 1957-60; Inspector, RAOC, War Office, 1960-61; Dir of Ordnance Service, War Office, 1961-64; retired, Dec. 1964. Man. Dir, Army Kinema Corp., 1965-70, Services Kinema Corp., 1970-75. Chm. Greater London Br., SS&AFA, 1977-81. Col Commandant, RAOC, 1963-70. Legion of Merit (degree of Officer), USA. *Recreations:* shooting, sailing. *Address:* 56 The Cottages, North Street, Emsworth, Hants PO10 7PJ. *T:* Emsworth 3466.

HILDRETH, (Henry) Jan (Hamilton Crossley); independent consultant; Director: Minster Trust Ltd, since 1980; Bowmax International Ltd, since 1979; Mixalloy Ltd, since 1982; *b* 1 Dec. 1932; *s* of Maj.-Gen. Sir (Harold) John (Crossley) Hildreth, KBE, and late Mrs Joan Elise Hallett (*née* Hamilton); *m* 1958, Wendy Moira Marjorie, *d* of late Arthur Harold Clough, CMG; two *s* one *d. Educ:* Wellington Coll.; The Queen's Coll., Oxford. National Service in RA, BAOR, 1952-53; 44 Parachute Bde (TA), 1953-58. Oxford, Hon. Mods (Nat. Sci.), BA (PPE) 1956, MA. Baltic Exchange, 1956; Royal Dutch Shell Group, 1957: served Philippines (marketing) and London (finance); Kleinwort, Benson Ltd, 1963; NEDO, 1965; Member of Economic Development Cttees for the Clothing, the Hosiery and Knitwear, and the Wool Textile industries; Mem., London Transport Bd, subseq. LTE, 1968-72: main responsibilities Finance, Marketing, Corp. Plan, Data Processing, and Estates; Asst Chief Exec., John Laing & Son Ltd, 1972-74; Dir-Gen., Inst. of Directors, 1975-78. Member: Cttee, GBA, 1978-82; Council, ISIS; Exec. Cttee, Industrial Soc.; Council, British Exec. Service Overseas; Council and Finance Cttee, Spastic Soc.; Board, Contact A Family. A Governor, Wellington Coll. FCIT. FRSA. *Recreations:* cross-country running, photography, water mills; and others. *Address:* 50 Ridgway Place, Wimbledon, SW19. *Clubs:* Athenæum; Vincent's (Oxford); Thames Hare and Hounds.

HILDREW, Bryan, CBE 1977; Managing Director, Lloyds Register of Shipping, since 1977; *b* 19 March 1920; *s* of Alexander William Hildrew and Sarah Jane (*née* Clark); *m* 1950, Megan Kathleen Lewis; two *s* one *d. Educ:* Bede Collegiate Sch., Sunderland; Technical Coll., Sunderland; City and Guilds, Imperial Coll., London (MSc, DIC). FEng, FIMechE, FIMarE. Engineer Officer, RN, 1941-46. Lloyds Register of Shipping: Research Surveyor, 1948-67 (Admiralty Nuclear Submarine Project, 1956-61); Chief Engineer Surveyor, 1967-70; Technical Dir, 1970-77. Pres., IMechE, 1980-81; Chm., CEI, 1981-82. *Recreations:* orienteering, walking. *Address:* 8 Westholme, Orpington, Kent. *T:* Orpington 25451.

HILDYARD, Rev. Christopher, MVO 1969; MA; *b* 28 April 1901; *s* of Lyonel D'Arcy and Dora Hildyard. *Educ:* St George's, Windsor Castle; Repton; Magdalene Coll., Cambridge; Cuddesdon Theological Coll. Curate at Glass Houghton, West Yorks, 1925-27; Curate at Gisborough, North Yorks, 1927-28; Asst Minor Canon, Westminster Abbey, 1928-32; Minor Canon, Westminster Abbey, 1932-73; Chaplain of Westminster Hospital, 1937-58; Custodian, Westminster Abbey, 1945-55; Sacrist, Westminster Abbey, 1958-73, Sacrist Emeritus, 1977. Chairman, Royal Asylum of St Ann's Soc., 1952-76. Patron of the Living of Rowley, E Yorks. *Recreation:* painting. *Address:* 2 The Cloisters, Westminster, SW1. *T:* 01-222 4982.

HILDYARD, Sir David (Henry Thoroton), KCMG 1975 (CMG 1966); DFC 1943; HM Diplomatic Service, retired; *b* 4 May 1916; *s* of late His Honour G. M. T. Hildyard, QC, and Sybil, *d* of H. W. Hamilton Hoare; *m* 1947, Millicent (*née* Baron), *widow* of Wing Commander R. M. Longmore, OBE; one *s* one *d. Educ:* Eton; Christ Church, Oxford. Served with RAF, 1940-46. Entered HM Foreign (subseq. Diplomatic) Service, 1948; Montevideo, 1950; Madrid, 1953; FO, 1957; Counsellor, Mexico City, 1960-65; Head of Economic Relations Dept, FO, 1965-68; Minister and Alternate UK Rep. to UN, 1968-70; Ambassador to Chile, 1970-73; Ambassador and Permanent UK Rep. to UN and other International Organisations, Geneva, 1973-76. *Recreations:* tennis, golf. *Address:* 97 Onslow Square, SW7. *Clubs:* Reform, Hurlingham.

HILEY, Joseph; DL; *b* 18 Aug. 1902; *s* of Frank Hiley of Leeds; *m* 1932, Mary Morrison, *d* of Dr William Boyd; three *d. Educ:* West Leeds High Sch.; Leeds Univ., 1920-23. Formerly family business, Hiley Brothers, took over firm of J. B. Battye & Co. Ltd, 1924, Managing Dir 1927-59; Dir, Irish Spinners Ltd, 1952-74. Mem. of Lloyd's, 1966-. MP (C) Pudsey, Oct. 1959-Feb. 1974. Leeds City Councillor, 1930, Alderman, 1949, resigned, 1960; Lord Mayor of Leeds, 1957-58; President: West Leeds Conservative Assoc.; Leeds & District Spastics Soc.; Leeds YMCA; Central Yorks Scout Council; Past President: Hand-Knitting Assoc.; Leeds Chamber of Commerce; Chm., Northorpe Hall Trust. DL West Yorks, 1971. *Recreations:* cricket, theatre. *Address:* Elmaran, Layton Road, Horsforth, Leeds. *T:* Horsforth 4787. *Clubs:* Leeds (Leeds); Pudsey Conservative (Pudsey).

HILEY, Sir Thomas (Alfred), KBE 1966; Chartered Accountant, Australia, since 1932; *b* 25 Nov. 1905; *s* of William Hiley and Maria (*née* Savage); *m* 1929, Marjory Joyce (*née* Jarrott) (*d* 1972); two *s. Educ:* Brisbane Grammar Sch.; University of Qld. State Public Service, 1921; Public Accountancy, 1923; in practice (Public Accountant), 1925. Qld Parliament, 1944; Dep. Leader of Opposition, 1950; Treasurer of Qld and Minister for Housing, 1957; Treasurer, 1963; Deputy Premier, 1965; retired from Parliament, 1966. Pres., Inst. of Chartered Accts in Aust., 1946-47. Hon. MCom, University of Qld, 1960. *Recreations:* shooting, fishing, cricket. *Address:* Illawong, 39 The Esplanade, Tewantin, Qld 4565, Australia. *T:* 471-175. *Clubs:* Number 10 (London); Queensland (Brisbane).

HILGENDORF, Sir Charles, Kt 1981; CMG 1971; JP; farmer; *b* 1908; *s* of Prof. Frederick William Hilgendorf and Frances Elizabeth (*née* Murray); *m* 1936, Rosemary Helen Mackenzie; one *s* one *d. Educ:* Christ's College, Christchurch; Univ. of Canterbury, NZ (MA; Hon. LLD 1978). Held various positions in Federated Farmers of NZ, 1946-61. Member: NZ Meat Producers Board, 1961-80 (Chm., 1972-80); University Grants Cttee (of NZ), 1961-74. *Address:* Sherwood, Ashburton, NZ. *T:* Winchmore 643. *Clubs:* Farmers'; Christchurch, Wellington (both in New Zealand).

HILL, family name of **Marquess of Downshire, Baron Hill of Luton** and **Baron Sandys.**

HILL; see Clegg-Hill, family name of Viscount Hill.

HILL, 8th Viscount *cr* 1842; **Antony Rowland Clegg-Hill;** Bt 1726-27; Baron Hill 1814; *b* 19 March 1931; *s* of 7th Viscount Hill and Elisabeth Flora (*d* 1967), *d* of Brig.-Gen. George Nowell Thomas Smyth-Osbourne, CB, CMG, DSO; *S* father, 1974; *m* 1963, Juanita Phyllis, *d* of John W. Pertwee, Salfords, Surrey. *Educ:* Kelly Coll.; RMA, Sandhurst. Formerly Captain, RA. Freeman of Shrewsbury, 1957. *Heir: cousin* Peter David Raymond Charles Clegg-Hill [*b* 17 Oct. 1945; *m* 1973, Sharon Ruth Deane, Kaikohe, NZ; two *d*]. *Address:* House of Lords, SW1.

HILL OF LUTON, Baron, *cr* 1963 (Life Peer); **Charles Hill,** PC 1955; MA, MD, DPH, LLD; *b* 15 Jan. 1904; *s* of late Charles Hill and Florence M. Cook; *m* 1931, Marion Spencer Wallace; two *s* three *d. Educ:* St Olave's Sch.; Trinity Coll., Cambridge; London Hosp. Formerly: House Physician and Receiving Room Officer, London Hospital; London University Extension Lecturer in Biology; Deputy Medical Supt, Coppice Mental Hospital, Nottingham; Deputy MOH, City of Oxford; Sec., BMA, 1944-50; President: World Medical Assoc.; Central Council for Health Educn; Hon. Sec., Commonwealth Medical Conf. Chm., Chest, Heart and Stroke Assoc., 1974-. MP (L and C) Luton, 1950-63; Parly Sec., Min. of Food, 1951-April 1955; Postmaster-Gen., April 1955-Jan. 1957; Chancellor of the Duchy of Lancaster Jan. 1957-Oct. 1961; Minister of Housing and Local Government and Minister for Welsh Affairs, Oct. 1961-July 1962. Chm., Nat. Jt Council for Local Authorities' Administrative, Professional, Technical and Clerical Services, 1963-78. Chm., Independent Television Authority, 1963-67; Chm. of Governors of the BBC, 1967-72. Chairman: Laporte Industries Ltd, 1965-70; Abbey National Building Soc., 1976-78 (Dir, 1964-78). Hon. Fellow Amer. Medical Assoc. *Publications:* What is Osteopathy? (jointly), 1937; Re-printed Broadcasts, 1941-50; Both Sides of the Hill, 1964; Behind the Screen, 1974. *Recreations:* fishing, walking. *Address:* 5 Bamville Wood, East Common,

Harpenden, Herts. *Club:* Reform.
See also D. R. Fairbairn.

HILL, Prof. Alan Geoffrey, MA; Professor of English Language and Literature in the University of London at Royal Holloway College, since 1981; *b* 12 Dec. 1931; *yr s* of Thomas Murton Hill and Alice Marion Hill (*née* Nunn); *m* 1960, Margaret Vincent Rutherford; three *d. Educ:* Dulwich Coll.; St Andrews Univ. (MA 1st Cl. Hons English Lang. and Lit.); Merton Coll., Oxford (BLitt). Asst Lectr/Lectr in English, Exeter Univ., 1958-62; Lectr in English, St Andrews Univ., 1962-68; Sen. Lectr in English, Dundee Univ., 1968-80. Vis. Professor of English, Univ. of Saskatchewan, 1973-74; Crowsley Lectr, Charles Lamb Soc., 1981. Trustee, Dove Cottage Trust, 1969-; General Editor, The Letters of William and Dorothy Wordsworth, 1979-. *Publications:* The Letters of William and Dorothy Wordsworth, vol. III, The Middle Years, Part 2, 1812-1820, 2nd edn (rev. and ed with Mary Moorman), 1970; vol. IV, The Later Years, Part 1, 1821-1828, 2nd edn (rev. and ed), 1978; vol. V, The Later Years, Part 2, 1829-1834, 2nd edn (rev. and ed), 1979; vol. VI, The Later Years, Part 3, 1835-1839, 2nd edn (rev. and ed), 1982; Selected Letters of Dorothy Wordsworth (ed), 1981; articles and reviews in lit. and theological jls. *Recreations:* music, fine arts, ecclesiology. *Address:* 1a Northcroft Road, Englefield Green, Surrey TW2O 0DP. *T:* Egham 31659. *Club:* Savile.

HILL, Alan John Wills, CBE 1972; Managing Director, Heinemann Computers in Education Ltd, since 1981; Consultant to the Heinemann Group of Publishers, since 1979; Chairman, Heinemann Educational Books Ltd (Nigeria), since 1979; *b* of William Wills Hill; *m* 1939, Enid Adela Malin; two *s* one *d. Educ:* Wyggeston Sch., Leicester; Jesus Coll., Cambridge (Schol., MA). RAF, 1940-45: Specialist Armament Officer (Sqdn Ldr). Publishing Asst, Wm Heinemann Ltd, 1936-40; Dir, 1955; Jt Man. Dir, 1959-61; Chm. and Man. Dir, Heinemann Educational Books Ltd, 1961-79; Man. Dir, Heinemann Group of Publishers Ltd, 1973-79; Chm., World's Work Ltd, 1973-79; Pres., Heinemann Educational Books Inc. (USA), 1977-79. Chm., Soc. of Bookmen, 1965-68; Chm., Educational Publishers' Council, 1969-71; Member: Council, Publishers' Assoc., 1972-79; Exec. Cttee, National Book League, 1973-79; British Council Books Adv. Panel, 1973-; CNAA (Business Studies Panel), 1975-; Council, Chelsea Coll., London Univ., 1978- (Vice-Chm., 1981-); UNESCO Cttee on Copyright in third world countries; Cttee, Friends of the Lake District. Governor, Nuffield-Chelsea Trust, 1979-. Pres., Keswick Amateur Athletic Club, 1977-. Closely involved with Commonwealth literature and educn. *Publications:* (with R. W. Finn) And So Was England Born, 1939; History in Action, 1962; articles in jls. *Recreations:* tennis, swimming, mountain-walking. *Address:* 56 Northway, NW11 6PA. *T:* 01-455 8388; New House, Rosthwaite, Borrowdale, Cumbria. *Clubs:* Athenæum, Garrick, Royal Air Force, PEN.

HILL, Alastair Malcolm; QC 1982; a Recorder of the Crown Court, since 1982; *b* 12 May 1936; *s* of Prof. Sir Ian George Wilson Hill, CBE, LLD, FRCP, FRSE and Lady (Audrey) Hill; *m* 1969, Elizabeth Maria Hall (*née* Innes) (marr. diss. 1978); one *d. Educ:* Trinity Coll., Glenalmond; Keble Coll., Oxford (Stevenson-Chatterton Schol.; BA Hons Jurisp. 1959). Nat. Service, RHA, 1954-56. Called to the Bar, Gray's Inn, 1961; South Eastern Circuit. *Recreations:* collecting prints and watercolours, fly-fishing. *Address:* New Court, Temple, EC4Y 9BE. *T:* 01-583 6166.

HILL, Rev. Alexander Currie, CB 1957; Minister Emeritus of Portknockie, Banffshire; Principal Finance Officer, Board of Trade, 1958-64; *b* 23 Jan. 1906; *o s* of late Alexander Hill and Jeanie Currie; unmarried. *Educ:* George Heriot's Sch., Edinburgh; Univ. of Edinburgh; Univ. of Aberdeen (Faculty of Divinity); Christ's Coll., Aberdeen. Entered Administrative Class, Home Civil Service, 1928. Under-Sec., Board of Trade, 1950-58. *Address:* 62a Rubislaw Den North, Aberdeen AB2 4AN. *Club:* Royal Northern (Aberdeen).

HILL, (Arthur) Derek; artist, writer, and organiser of exhibitions; *b* Bassett, Hampshire 6 Dec., 1916; *s* of A. J. L. Hill and Grace Lilian Mercer. *Educ:* Marlborough Coll. Has designed sets and dresses for Covent Garden and Sadler's Wells. *One-man exhibitions:* Nicholson Gall., London, 1943; Leicester Galls, London, 1947, 1950, 1953 and 1956. *Organised exhibitions:* 1934 onwards: Dégas Exhibn for Edinburgh Fest. and Tate Gall., London, 1952; Landseer exhibn (with John Woodward) at Royal Academy, 1961, etc. Represented in exhibns, Europe and USA, 1957-; exhibns in New York, 1966 and 1969; retrospective exhibitions: Whitechapel Gall., London, 1961; Arts Council of NI, Belfast, 1970; Municipal Gall., Dublin, 1971; portraits, Marlborough Fine Arts, London, 1978. *Pictures owned by:* Tate Gall.; Nat. Gall. of Canada; Arts Council; Fogg Museum, Harvard; City Art Galleries of: Southampton, Birmingham, Bradford, Coventry, Carlisle, etc. FRGS. *Publications:* Islamic Architecture and Its Decoration (with Prof. Oleg Grabar), 1965; Islamic Architecture in North Africa (with L. Golvin), 1976; articles in Illustrated London News, Apollo, Burlington Magazine, etc. *Recreations:* gardening, travelling.

HILL, Sir Austin Bradford, Kt 1961; CBE 1951; FRS 1954; PhD (Econ.), 1926, DSc, 1929 (London); Emeritus Professor of Medical Statistics, London School of Hygiene and Tropical Medicine, University of London, and Hon. Director, Statistical Research Unit of Medical Research Council, 1945-61; Dean of the London School of Hygiene and Tropical Medicine, 1955-57,

Honorary Fellow, 1976; *b* 8 July 1897; 3rd *s* of late Sir Leonard Erskine Hill, FRS; *m* 1923, Florence Maud (*d* 1980), *d* of late Edward Salmon, OBE; two *s* one *d. Educ:* Chigwell Sch.; privately; University Coll., London. Flight Sub-Lieut in Royal Naval Air Service, 1916-18; on staff of Medical Research Council and its Industrial Health Research Board, 1923-33; Reader in Epidemiology and Vital Statistics, London Sch. of Hygiene and Tropical Medicine, 1933-45; seconded during the war to Research and Experiments Dept, Ministry of Home Security, 1940-42, and to Medical Directorate, RAF, 1943-45. Hon. Civil Consultant in Medical Statistics to RAF and mem. of Flying Personnel Research Cttee, 1943-78; Civil Consultant in Medical Statistics to RN, 1958-77; Mem., Cttee on Safety of Medicines, 1964-75; Pres. Royal Statistical Soc., 1950-52 (Hon. Sec. 1940-50); Gold Medallist, 1953; Pres. Section of Epidemiology, RSM, 1953-55, Section of Occupational Medicine, 1964-65; Member: Council, MRC, 1954-58; Cttee on Review of Medicines, 1975-78; Fellow of University Coll., London; Hon. FRCP; Hon. FFCM; Hon. FFOM; Hon. FIA; Hon FRSM; Hon. FAPHA; Hon. Fellow: Soc. of Community Medicine; Soc. of Occupational Medicine; Faculty of Medicine, University of Chile; Society for Social Medicine; Internat. Epidemiological Assoc.; Med. Research Club. Cutter Lecturer, Harvard, 1953; Harben Lecturer RIPH&H, 1957; Alfred Watson Memorial Lectr Inst. of Actuaries, 1962; Marc Daniels Lectr RCP, 1963. Hon. DSc Oxford, 1963; Hon. MD Edinburgh, 1968. Galen Medallist, Soc. of Apothecaries, 1969; Harben Gold Medallist, 1961; Jenner Medallist, RSM, 1965; Heberden Medallist, Heberden Soc., 1965. *Publications:* Internal Migration and its Effects upon the Death Rates, 1925; The Inheritance of Resistance to Bacterial Infection in Animal Species, 1934; Principles of Medical Statistics, 1937, 11th edn, as A Short Textbook of Medical Statistics, 1983; Statistical Methods in Clinical and Preventive Medicine, 1962; reports to Industrial Health Research Board on industrial sickness and numerous papers in scientific journals, especially studies of cigarette smoking and cancer of the lung and of the clinical trial of new drugs. *Recreations:* walking in the countryside, gardening. *Address:* April Cottage, Lower Hopton, Nesscliffe, Shropshire SY4 1DL. *T:* Nesscliffe 231.

HILL, Brian, DL; Chief Executive and Clerk, Lancashire County Council, since 1977; *b* 16 Oct. 1930; *s* of late Joseph Hill and of Bessie Hill; *m* 1954, Barbara (*née* Hickson); one *d. Educ:* Wigan Grammar Sch.; Univ. of Manchester (LLB). Solicitor. Asst Solicitor, Manchester Corp., 1953-56; Lancashire County Council: Sen. Solicitor appts, finally Second Dep. Clerk of CC, 1956-74; Dep. Clerk, 1974-76. Clerk of Lancs Lieutenancy; County Electoral Returning Officer. Secretary: Lancs Adv. Cttee; Lord Chancellor's Adv. Cttee on Gen. Comrs of Income Tax; Lancs Probation and After Care Cttee; Adviser to Planning and Transport Cttee, ACC. Past Chairman: Local Govt Legal Soc.; Soc. of County Secs. Vice-Pres., Lancs Youth Clubs Assoc.; Member: Northern Circuit Adv. Cttee; Area Bd, Manpower Services Commn. Clerk to Court, RNCM, Manchester (Hon. RNCM 1979); Mem. Court, Univ. of Lancaster. DL Lancs, 1977. *Recreation:* music. *Address:* 1 Regent Drive, Fulwood, Preston, Lancs. *Club:* Royal Over-Seas League.

HILL, Christopher; *see* Hill, J. E. C.

HILL, Christopher Pascoe, CB 1964; CBE 1956; Charity consultant; *b* 6 July 1903; *s* of late Charles Pascoe Grenfell Hill; *m* 1st, 1926, Elizabeth Redding Oldfield (*d* 1931), *d* of late Lieut-Col H. Oldfield, RMA; one *d*; 2nd, 1934, Joan Elizabeth Smith, *d* of late R. W. Smith; two *s* one *d. Educ:* Merchant Taylors'; St John's Coll., Oxford, Gaisford Prizeman, 1925. Entered Home Office, Asst Principal, 1925; Asst Sec., Ministry of Home Security, 1942; Home Office: Aliens Dept, 1943-47; Children's Dept, 1947-56; Asst Under-Sec. of State, 1957. Attached to Charity Commission, 1956, to prepare Charities Act, 1960; Chief Charity Commissioner, 1960-65; Sec. to Archbishop's Commission on Church and State, 1966-70. Vice Pres., Herts Council of Voluntary Service; Member: Exec. Cttee, Hertfordshire Soc., 1966-79; Standing Conf. on Herts Countryside (Chm., 1967-76); Gen. Adv. Council of BBC; BBC and IBA Central Appeals Adv. Cttees (Chm.), 1969-74; Council, National Trust, 1969-73; Family Welfare Assoc. Inf. Cttee, 1968-78; Legal Bd, Church Assembly, 1966-70; Adv. Council, Christian Orgns Res. and Adv. Trust. Director: WRVS Trustees Ltd, 1966-79; Internat. Standing Conf. on Philanthropy, Geneva. UK correspondent, Foundation News, 1975-. King Haakon VII Liberty Cross, Norway. *Publications:* A Guide for Charity Trustees, 1966, rev. edn 1974; UK section, Trusts and Foundations in Europe, 1972; UK section, Philanthropy in the Seventies, 1973; papers on delinquency and charity subjects in periodicals. *Recreations:* garden, painting, archæology, preserving Herts countryside. *Address:* The Grange, Therfield, Royston, Herts. *T:* Kelshall 358. *Club:* Athenæum.

HILL, Colin de Neufville, CMG 1961; OBE 1959; Business Manager, University of Sussex, 1964-82; *b* 12 Jan. 1917; *s* of Philip Rowland and Alice May Hill; *m* 1950, Mary Patricia Carson Wilson; two *s. Educ:* Cheltenham Coll.; St Edmund Hall, Oxford. BA. hons in Mod. Langs, Oxford, 1938. Selected for appt to Colonial Service, 1938; Administrative Officer, Colonial Admin. Service, Eastern Nigeria, 1939; served with Provincial and Regional Administration, Eastern Nigeria, 1939-53; transferred to Tanganyika and apptd Sec. for Finance, 1954; Permanent Sec. to the Treasury, Tanganyika Government, 1959-64. *Recreations:* photography, gardening, music. *Address:* Mount Pleasant Farm, Barcombe, near Lewes, East Sussex.

HILL, Prof. David Keynes, ScD; FRS 1972; Professor of Biophysics, Royal Postgraduate Medical School, University of London, 1975-82; *b* 23 July 1915;

s of Prof. Archibald Vivian Hill, CH, OBE, ScD, FRS, and late Margaret Neville, *d* of late Dr J. N. Keynes; *m* 1949, Stella Mary Humphrey; four *d.* *Educ:* Highgate Sch.; Trinity Coll., Cambridge. ScD Cantab 1965. Fellow, Trinity Coll., Cambridge, 1940-48; Physiologist on staff of Marine Biological Assoc., Plymouth, 1948-49; Sen. Lectr, 1949-62, Reader in Biophysics, 1962-75, Vice-Dean, 1969-74, Royal Postgrad. Med. Sch., London Univ. Physiological Society: Editor of Journal, 1969-76; Chm., Bd of Monographs, 1979-81. *Publications:* Scientific papers in Jl Physiology. *Recreations:* gardening, photography. *Address:* Harkaway House, Corse Lawn, Gloucester GL19 4LT. *T:* Tirley 371.
See also Polly Hill.

HILL, Derek; see Hill, A. D.

HILL, Prof. Dorothy, CBE 1971; FRS 1965; FAA 1956; Research Professor of Geology, University of Queensland, 1959-72, now Emeritus Professor; President, Professorial Board, 1971-72; Member of Senate, 1976-77; *b* 10 Sept. 1907; *d* of R. S. Hill, Brisbane; unmarried. *Educ:* Brisbane Girls' Grammar Sch.; Univs of Queensland and Cambridge. BSc (Qld) 1928, 1st Cl. Hons in Geol. and Univ. Gold Medal. Foundn Trav. Fellowship of Univ. of Queensland held at Newnham Coll., Cambridge, 1930-32; PhD Cantab 1932; Old Students' Res. Fellowship, Newnham Coll., Cambridge, 1932-35; Sen. Studentship (Exhibn of 1851) held at Cambridge, 1935-37; Coun. for Sci. and Indust. Res. Fellowship, held at Univ. of Queensland, 1937-42; DSc (Qld) 1942. WRANS, Second Off., 1942-45 (RAN Ops Staff). Univ. of Queensland: Lectr in Geol., 1946-56, Reader, 1956-59. Hon. Editor, Geol. Soc. of Aust., 1958-64; Mem. Council, Australian Acad. of Science, 1968-70, Pres. 1970; Pres., Geol Soc. of Aust., 1973-75. Lyell Medal, Geol. Soc. of London, 1964; Clarke Medal, Royal Society of NSW, 1966; Mueller Medal, ANZAAS, 1967; Foreign and Commonwealth Mem. Geol. Soc. London, 1967; Hon. Fellow, Geol Soc. of America, 1971. Hon. LLD Queensland, 1974. W. R. Browne Medal, Geol. Soc. of Australia, 1980. *Publications:* numerous, in geology and palæontology jls on fossil corals, archæocyatha, brachiopods, reef sediments and Australian geology and stratigraphy. *Recreations:* travel, reading. *Address:* University of Queensland, St Lucia, Brisbane, Qld 4067, Australia.

HILL, Douglas William, CBE 1965; DSc; *b* 3 March 1904; *o s* of Henry and Florence Mary Hill; *m* 1st, 1936, Margaret Eluned (*d* 1956), *y d* of Rev. O.M. Owen; one *s* ; 2nd, 1958, Mabel Constance Prothero (*d* 1975), *er d* of James Belford. *Educ:* St George's Sch., Bristol; Univs of Bristol, Liverpool and Illinois, PhD Liverpool, 1926; DSc Bristol, 1936. Research Chemist, Boots Pure Drug Co. Ltd, 1927-30; Commonwealth Fund Fellow, Univ. of Illinois and Rockefeller Inst. for Med. Research, New York, 1930-33; Lectr in Organic Chemistry, UC Exeter and Special Lectr in Biochemistry, Bristol Univ., 1933-37; Asst to Dir, Shirley Inst., 1937-40; Min. of Supply, 1940-43; Combined Production and Resources Board, Washington DC, 1943-44; Dep. Dir, Shirley Inst., 1944-56; Director, 1956-69. Mem. Council RIC, 1948-60 (Chm., Manchester and Dist Sect., 1953-54); Mem. Council, Chemical Soc., 1947-50; Vice-Pres., Parly and Sci. Cttee, 1962-65; Chairman: Cttee of Dirs of Research Assocs, 1960-63; Cttee of Dirs of Textile Research, Assocs, 1964-66; Cttee on Mule Spinners' Cancer; Chm. of Governors, Royal Coll. of Advanced Technology, Salford, 1962-67; Chm. of Council and Pro-Chancellor, Univ. of Salford, 1967-75; Sen. Pro-Chancellor, 1976-82; Member: UGC Cttee on Libraries, 1962-68, Cttee of Management, Science Policy Foundn; Chm., Perkin Centenary Trust; Dir, Shirley Developments Ltd, 1953-74. Chm., Macclesfield Div. Liberal Assoc., 1948-56. Bernard Dyer Memorial Medallist and Lectr, 1962; Mather Lectr, 1970. Hon. DSc Salford, 1969. *Publications:* Insulin: Its Production, Purification and Properties, 1936; Impact and Value of Science, 1944, 2nd edn, 1946; Co-operative Research for Industry, 1946; papers and articles in scientific jls, press and reviews. *Recreations:* sketching, travel, writing and lecturing. *Address:* River Cottage, Cage Lane, Smarden, near Ashford, Kent. *T:* Smarden 588. *Clubs:* Athenæum; Union (Malta).

HILL, Col (Edward) Roderick, DSO 1944; JP; Lord-Lieutenant of Gwent, 1974-79 (HM Lieutenant for Monmouthshire, 1965-74); Director, Chepstow Race Course Co. Ltd, since 1958 (Chairman, 1964-81); *b* 1904; *s* of late Capt. Roderick Tickell Hill; *m* 1934, Rachel, *e d* of Ellis Hicks Beach, Witcombe Park, Glos; one *s* one *d. Educ:* Winchester; Magdalen Coll., Oxford. Gazetted to Coldstream Guards, 1926; served War of 1939-45, with regt (despatches, DSO); commanded 5th Bn and 1st Bn Coldstream Guards and Guards Training Bn; comd Regt, 1949-52. JP Co. Monmouth; High Sheriff of Monmouthshire, 1956; DL Monmouthshire, 1957; Vice-Lieut, 1963-65. Chm. of the Curre Hunt, 1959-65. Chm. of Governors, Monmouth Sch. and Monmouth Sch. for Girls, 1961-66; Chm. Chepstow RDC, 1962-63. Hon. Col, 104 Light AD Regt RA(V), 1967-69. Freeman and Liveryman, Haberdashers Co., 1969. Pres., Royal Welsh Agric. Soc., 1970-71. Pres., TA&VRA for Wales and Monmouthshire, 1971-74. Officer, Order of Orange-Nassau (with swords), 1946. KStJ 1972. *Publication:* (with the Earl of Rosse) The Story of the Guards Armoured Division, 1941-1945, 1956. *Address:* Little Court, St Arvan's, Chepstow, Gwent. *T:* Chepstow 2091. *Club:* Cavalry and Guards.
See also Baron Raglan.

HILL, (Eliot) Michael, QC 1979; a Recorder of the Crown Court, since 1977; *b* 22 May 1935; *s* of Cecil Charles Hill and Rebecca Betty Hill; *m* 1965, Kathleen Irene (*née* Hordern); one *s* two *d. Educ:* Bancroft's Sch., Essex;

Brasenose Coll., Oxford. Called to the Bar, Gray's Inn, 1958; Mem., Senate of the Inns of Court and the Bar, 1976-79. South-Eastern Circuit. Second Prosecuting Counsel to Crown, Inner London Sessions, 1969, First Pros. Counsel to Crown, 1971; Fourth Jun. Pros. Counsel to Crown, Central Criminal Court, 1974, Third Jun. Pros. Counsel to Crown, 1974, First Jun. Pros. Counsel to Crown, 1975; a Sen. Pros. Counsel to Crown, 1977-79. Chm., Criminal Bar Assoc., 1982- (Sec., 1973-75; Vice-Chm., 1979-82). *Recreations:* family, friends, riding, fishing and just living. *Address:* (chambers) 3 Temple Gardens, Temple, EC4Y 9AU. *T:* 01-353 1662.

HILL, Dame Elizabeth (Mary), DBE 1976; Emeritus Professor of Slavonic Studies, Cambridge; *b* 24 Oct. 1900. *Educ:* University and King's Colls, London Univ. BA London 1924, PhD London 1928; MA Cantab 1937. War of 1939-45: Slavonic specialist, Min. of Information. University Lecturer in Slavonic, 1936-48; Prof. of Slavonic Studies, Univ. of Cambridge, 1948-68; Andrew Mellon Prof. of Slavic Languages and Literatures, Pittsburgh Univ., 1968-70. Fellow of University Coll., London; Fellow, Girton Coll., Cambridge. Hon. LittD East Anglia, 1978. *Address:* 10 Croft Gardens, Cambridge.

HILL, Air Cdre Dame Felicity (Barbara), DBE 1966 (OBE 1954); Director of the Women's Royal Air Force, 1966-69; *b* 12 Dec. 1915; *d* of late Edwin Frederick Hill and late Mrs Frances Ada Barbara Hill (*née* Cocke). *Educ:* St Margaret's Sch., Folkestone. Joined WAAF, 1939; commnd, 1940; served in: UK, 1939-46; Germany, 1946-47; Far East Air Force, 1949-51; other appts included Inspector of WRAF, 1956-59; OC, RAF Hawkinge, 1959-60; OC, RAF Spitalgate, 1960-62; Dep. Dir, 1962-65. Hon. ADC to the Queen, 1966-69. *Address:* Worcester Cottage, Mews Lane, Winchester, Hants. *Club:* Royal Air Force.

HILL, (Francis) John, CBE 1976; Hon. DCL UEA 1982; Hon. FCP 1980; FRSA; County Education Officer for Suffolk, 1973-79 (CEO West Suffolk, 1961-73); Member, Suffolk Area Health Authority, 1979-82; *b* July 1915; *m* Roma Lunn, Stourbridge; one *s. Educ:* King Edward VI Sch., Stourbridge; Univ. of Birmingham (English and Educn); Univ. of Poitiers. Royal Signals, 1940-46, Major (despatches). In Educn Depts of, successively, Wiltshire, Hertfordshire and Cornwall (Deputy Education Officer), prior to appt to West Suffolk. Chairman: Council for Educnl Technology (UK) from inception, 1973-80; Eastern Regional Council for Special Educn, 1976-82; Mem. Council, Univ. of E Anglia, 1961- (Chm. Jt Cttee for Academic Staff); Vice-Chm. Governors, Cambridge Inst. of Educn, 1974-80; Trustee, Homerton Coll., Cambridge, 1969- (Vice-Chm., 1980-); Mem. Council and Chm. Educn Cttee, RNIB, 1966-; UK deleg. to World Conf. on Educn of Blind Youth, Boston, USA, 1967; Vice-Chm. Trustees, Central Bureau for Educnl Visits and Exchanges, 1965-77; (first) Chm., UK/USA Schs Exchange Scheme; Member, E-SU Schols Cttee; UK Rep., Commonwealth Educn Conf., Wellington, NZ, 1977; Member Govt Cttees on: Sch. Transport, Educnl Technology, Speech Therapy Sces in Medicine and Educn, Recreation Management Trng; adv. visits to USA (3), Dublin, Gibraltar, France, Austria, Scandinavia. Mem., Sports Council for UK, 1975-82 (Chm. Nat. Centres Cttee, Vice-Chm. Finance Cttee); Chairman: Eastern Council for Sport and Recreation, 1979- (Mem., 1965-); Chm., Finance and Grants Cttee, 1976-79); Sports Aid Foundn (East), 1980-. Hon. Mem., CCPR. Cert. Exceptional Sce to Anglo-Amer. relations, 1975. *Recreations:* most sports, gardening, countryside, imposing democratic solutions. *Address:* Willowfield, Old Newton, Stowmarket, Suffolk. *T:* Haughley 525.

HILL, Geoffrey (William), FRSL; University Lecturer in English and Fellow of Emmanuel College, University of Cambridge, since 1981; *b* 18 June 1932; *s* of late William George Hill and late Hilda Beatrice Hill (*née* Hands); *m* 1956, Nancy Whittaker; three *s* one *d. Educ:* County High Sch., Bromsgrove; Keble Coll., Oxford (BA 1953, MA 1959; Hon. Fellow, 1982). Mem., academic staff, Univ. of Leeds, 1954-80 (Prof. of Eng. Lit., 1976-80). Vis. Lectr, Univ. of Michigan, 1959-60; Vis. Lectr, Dept of English, Univ. of Ibadan, Nigeria, 1967; Churchill Fellow, Dept of English, Univ. of Bristol, 1980. FRSL 1972. English version of Ibsen's Brand produced at National Theatre, London, 1978. Whitbread Award, 1971; RSL Award (W. H. Heinemann Bequest), 1971. *Publications: poetry:* For the Unfallen, 1959 (Gregory Award, 1961); King Log, 1968 (Hawthornden Prize, 1969; Geoffrey Faber Meml Prize, 1970); Mercian Hymns, 1971 (Alice Hunt Bartlett Award, 1971); Somewhere is Such a Kingdom: Poems 1952-1971, 1975; Tenebrae, 1978 (Duff Cooper Meml Prize, 1979); The Poetry and Voice of Geoffrey Hill (gramophone record), 1979; *poetic drama:* Henrik Ibsen, Brand: a version for the English Stage, 1978. *Address:* Emmanuel College, Cambridge CB2 3AP.

HILL, Sir George (Alfred) Rowley, 9th Bt *cr* 1779; retired; *b* 11 Oct. 1899; *s* of Alfred Rowley Hill (*d* 1946) (brother of 7th Bt) and Jean (*d* 1943), *d* of J. Cunninghame; *S* cousin, 1980; *m* 1st, 1924, Rose Ethel Kathleen Spratt, MBE (marr. diss. 1938); one *s* ; 2nd, 1938; one *s* one *d. Educ:* Melville Coll., Edinburgh. Indian Railways, 1919-37; retired, ill health. Served RNVR, 1915-Jan. 1919, and 1940-45. War Ribbons, 1914-18 and 1939-45, inc. Atlantic Star. *Recreations:* Rugby, golf, shooting, tennis. *Heir:* *s* Richard George Rowley Hill, MBE, Major KOSB, retired [*b* 18 Dec. 1925; *m* 1954, Angela Mary (*d* 1974), *o d* of Lt-Col Stanley Herbert Gallon, TD]. *Address:* c/o Barclays Bank, Berwick-upon-Tweed TD15 1AF.

HILL, George Geoffrey David, CMG 1971; late Assistant Secretary, Department of the Environment (Head of International Transport Division, Ministry of Transport, 1964); *b* 15 Aug. 1911; *o s* of late William George Hill, JP; *m* 1935, Elisabeth Wilhelmina (*née* Leuwer); one *d. Educ:* Manchester Grammar Sch.; Gonville and Caius Coll., Cambridge (BA (Hons)). Entered Ministry of Transport as Asst Principal, 1934; Principal, 1941; Asst Sec., 1954; retired 1972. *Recreations:* bridge, languages. *Address:* 125 Ember Lane, Esher, Surrey. *T:* 01-398 1851.

HILL, George Raymond, FCA, FCIT; FHCIMA; Director, Bass Ltd, since 1976 (Member, Executive Committee; formerly Chairman, Southern Beer Division); Chairman: Crest Hotels Ltd; Centre Hotels Ltd; *b* 25 Sept. 1925; *s* of George Mark and Jill Hill; *m* 1948, Sophie (*née* Gilbert); two *d. Educ:* St Dunstan's Coll., London. Royal Marines, 1943–46 (Lieut). Distillers Co. Ltd (Industrial Group), 1952–66; BP Chemicals Ltd, 1967–69; British Transport Hotels Ltd: Chief Exec., 1970–76; Chm., 1974–76; Chm., Bass UK Ltd, 1978–80. Member Boards: British Railways (Scottish), and British Rail Hovercraft Ltd, 1972–76; British Tourist Auth., 1981–. Member: Hotel and Catering Industry Trng Bd, 1973–78; Civil Service Final Selection Bd, 1973–80; Cttee of Inquiry on Motorway Service Areas, 1978; Chm. Bd, 1979–80, Vice-Chm. Nat. Council, 1982–, BHRCA. FRSA 1980. *Recreations:* music, theatre, works of art, country life. *Address:* 23 Sheffield Terrace, W8. *T:* 01-727 3986; The Paddocks, Chedworth, Glos. *Club:* Honourable Artillery Company.

HILL, Gladys, MA, MD; FRCS, FRCOG; retired as Obstetrician and Gynæcologist, Royal Free Hospital (1940–59); *b* 28 Sept. 1894; *d* of late Arthur Griffiths Hill and Caroline Sutton Hill. *Educ:* Cheltenham Ladies' Coll.; Somerville Coll., Oxford; Royal Free Hosp. Med. Sch. MA Oxon, MD, BS London, FRCS 1936; FRCOG 1943. *Publications:* contribs to medical journals. *Recreations:* architecture, amateur dramatics, reading. *Address:* The Captain's Cottage, Bishops Lydeard, near Taunton, Som. *T:* Bishops Lydeard 432533.

HILL, Graham Starforth; Chairman, Guinness Mahon & Co. Ltd, since 1979 (Director, 1977–79); *b* 22 June 1927; *s* of late Harold Victor John Hill and of Helen Dora (*née* Starforth); *m* 1952, Margaret Elise Ambler (marr. diss.); one *s* one *d. Educ:* Dragon Sch., Oxford; Winchester Coll.; St John's Coll., Oxford (MA Hons). Called to the Bar, Gray's Inn, 1951; admitted solicitor, 1961; also admitted solicitor, Malaysia, Singapore and Hong Kong; Notary Public and Comr for Oaths, Singapore. Flying Officer, RAF, 1948–50. Crown Counsel, Colonial Legal Service, Singapore, 1953–56; Partner, subseq. Sen. Partner, Rodyk and Davidson, Advocates and Solicitors, Singapore, 1957–76. Mem., Malayan Bd of Income Tax, 1957–60. Formerly (all Singapore): Hon. Legal Adviser to High Commn; Law Reform Comr; dir of numerous cos; Member: Univ. Faculty of Law; Constl Commn; Council, Law Soc. (Pres., 1970–74, Hon. Mem. 1978); Courts Martial Mil. Ct of Appeal; Council, Internat. Bar Assoc.; Discip. Cttee and Appeal Cttee, ICA, 1980–. Chm., London City Ballet Trust, 1981–; Trustee: Southwark Cathedral Develt Trust Fund, 1980–; Royal Opera House Trust, 1982–. Cavaliere dell'Ordine della Stella della Solidarietà, and Commendatore dell'Ordine al Merito, Italy. *Publications:* co-editor, The Laws of Singapore, revised edition 1970; report of Consitutional Commission of Singapore. *Recreations:* music, Italy. *Address:* 28 St Petersburgh Place, W2 4LA. *T:* 01-221 6585; Casa Claudia, 07020 Porto Cervo, Italy. *T:* Porto Cervo 92317. *Clubs:* Garrick; Singapore Turf (Singapore).
See also I. S. Hill.

HILL, Harry, FCCA, FCIS, FTII; Chairman, Beecham Products International, since 1977; Director, Beecham Group Ltd, since 1979; *b* 22 May 1924; *s* of James and Charlotte Hill; *m* 1944, Vera Brydon; two *d.* War service, 1942–45: flying duties, Fleet Air Arm; Lieut RNVR. John Marshall & Co., Newcastle upon Tyne, 1945–50: professional accountancy and auditing; articled clerk, subseq. managing clerk, and partner; General Motors Ltd, London, 1950–69: sen. financial appts; Group Gen. Comptroller, 1966–69; Parkinson-Cowan Ltd, London, 1969–71: Dir of Finance and Admin; Beecham Products, Brentford, Mddx: Financial Dir, 1972–76; Admin Dir, 1976–77. FCCA 1964; FCIS 1970; FTII 1976. Pres., Assoc. of Certified Accountants, 1975–76. Mem., Price Commn, 1977–79. *Recreations:* golf, gardening, motoring. *Address:* 77 Howards Thicket, Gerrards Cross, Bucks SL9 7NU. *T:* Gerrards Cross 83550.

HILL, Rt. Rev. Henry Gordon; Co-Chairman, Anglican-Orthodox Joint Doctrinal Commission, since 1980; *b* 14 Dec. 1921; *s* of Henry Knox Hill and Kathleen Elizabeth (*née* Cunningham); unmarried. *Educ:* Queen's Univ., Kingston, Ont. (BA 1945); Trinity Coll., Toronto (LTh 1948); St John's Coll., Cambridge (MA 1952). Deacon, Dio. Ont., 1948; Priest (Bp of Ely for Ontario), 1949; Curate, Belleville, Ont., 1950; Rector of Adolphustown, Ont., 1951; Chaplain, St John's Coll., Cambridge, Eng., 1952; Curate, Wisbech, Cambs, 1955; Rector, St Thomas, Reddendale, Ont., 1957; Asst Prof., Canterbury Coll., Univ. of Windsor, 1962–68; (Vice-Principal, 1965–68); Associate Prof. of History, Univ. of Windsor, Ont., 1968–74; Bishop of Ontario, 1975–81. Vice-Pres., Fellowship of St Alban and St Sergius, 1980. Hon. DD: Trinity Coll., Toronto, 1976; Montreal Dio. Theol Coll., 1976; Hon. LLD Univ. of Windsor, 1976; Hon. Dr, Theological Inst., Bucharest, 1977. KLJ 1980. Patriarchal Cross of Romanian Orthodox Church, 1969. *Publications:* articles in Cdn Jl of Theology, Sobornost, Jl Fellowship of St Alban and St Sergius. *Recreations:* walking, reading. *Address:* c/o Synod Office, 1444 Union Avenue, Montreal, PQ H3A 2B8, Canada.

HILL, Ian Macdonald, MS, FRCS; Consultant Thoracic Surgeon: St Bartholomew's Hospital, Lambeth, Southwark and Lewisham Area Health Authority (Teaching), (formerly SE Regional Hospital Board), since 1950; Greenwich District Health Authority, since 1976; *b* 8 June 1919; British; *m* 1944, Agnes Mary Paice; three *s* one *d. Educ:* Stationers' Company's Sch.; St Bartholomew's Hosp. Medical Coll. Undergrad. schols and medals, 1937–41; MB, BS (Hons) London, 1942; MRCS, LRCP 1942; FRCS 1944; MS London 1945. Demonstrator of Anatomy, St Bartholomew's, 1943; Surgical Chief Asst St Bart.'s Hosp., 1944; RAF Medical Branch, 1946; Wing Comdr i/c Surg. Div. No 1 RAF Gen. Hosp., 1947; Senior Registrar, Thoracic Surg. Unit, Guy's Hosp., 1948; Surgical Chief Asst, Brompton Hosp. and Inst. of Diseases of the Chest, 1950. Sub-Dean, St Bart's Hosp. Med. Coll., 1964–73. FR.SocMed. Member: Soc. of Apothecaries; Soc. of Thoracic Surgeons; Thoracic and Cardiac Socs. Freeman of City of London. *Publications:* articles in professional jls, mainly relating to lung and cardiac surgery, 1942–61. *Recreations:* old cars, furniture, keyboard instruments; gardening and house care. *Address:* 98 Fox Lane, Palmers Green, N13 4AX. *T:* 01-886 7324; 152 Harley Street, W1N 1HH. *T:* 01-935 8868.

HILL, (Ian) Starforth, QC 1969; His Honour Judge Starforth Hill; a Circuit Judge, since 1974; *b* 30 Sept. 1921; *s* of late Harold Victor John Hill; *m* 1950, Bridget Mary Footner; one *s* two *d. Educ:* Shrewsbury Sch.; Brasenose Coll., Oxford (MA). 11th Sikh Regt, Indian Army, 1940–45, India, Africa, Italy (despatches). Called to Bar, Gray's Inn, 1949; Dep. Chm., Isle of Wight QS, 1968–71; Western Circuit; a Recorder of the Crown Court, 1972–74. *Address:* 1 Crown Office Row, Temple, EC4. *T:* 01-353 9272; Tulls Hill, Preston Candover, Hants RG25 2EW. *T:* Preston Candover 309. *Club:* Hampshire (Winchester).
See also G. S. Hill.

HILL, Ivan Conrad, CBE 1960; Chairman, Illingworth Morris & Co. Ltd, 1976–80; Chairman, Industrial Coal Consumers Council, since 1965; *b* 22 Jan. 1906; *s* of Wilfred Lawson Hill and Annie Jane (*née* England); *m* 1st, 1931, Alexandrina Ewart (marr. diss. 1962); four *d* ; 2nd, 1963, Sheila Houghton. *Educ:* Oakham Sch.; St John's Coll., Cambridge. Exhibitioner and Open Scholar of St John's Coll. 1st cl. Hons Law Tripos Cantab 1928. Apptd Jt Man. Dir, Kelsall & Kemp Ltd, 1933. Chm. Wool Industries Research Assoc., 1950–53; Mem. Monopolies and Restrictive Practices Commn, and Monopolies Commn, 1951–63; Chm. British Rayon Research Assoc., 1956–61; Chairman, Samuel Courtauld & Co. Ltd, 1962–66. Liveryman, Weavers' Company, 1938–. *Recreations:* travel, architecture, sport. *Address:* Crystal Spring, Duchy Road, Harrogate, N Yorks.

HILL, Brig. James; *see* Hill, Brig. S. J. L.

HILL, James; *see* Hill, S. J. A.

HILL, Sir James Frederick, 4th Bt *cr* 1917; Chairman, Sir James Hill & Sons Ltd; Director: Yorkshire Building Society; Intasun Leisure Group; Air Europe Ltd; *b* 5 Dec. 1943; *s* of Sir James Hill, 3rd Bt and of Marjory, *d* of late Frank Croft; *S* father, 1976; *m* 1966, Sandra Elizabeth, *o d* of J. C. Ingram; one *s* three *d.* **Heir:** *s* James Laurence Ingram Hill, *b* 22 Sept. 1973. *Address:* Moorlands, Moor Lane, Menston, Ilkley, West Yorks LS29 6AS. *T:* Menston 74360. *Clubs:* Royal Automobile; Bradford (Yorks); Ilkley Golf.

HILL, James William Thomas, (Jimmy) Managing Director, Jimmy Hill Ltd, since 1972; Soccer analyst to the BBC, since 1973; *m* 1st, 1950, Gloria Mary (marr. diss. 1961); two *s* one *d* ; 2nd, 1962, Heather Christine; one *s* one *d. Educ:* Henry Thornton School, Clapham. Player, Brentford FC, 1949–52, Fulham FC, 1952–61; Gen. Manager, Coventry City FC, 1961–67, Managing Director, 1975–, Chm., 1980–. London Weekend Television: Head of Sport, 1967–72; Controller of Press, Promotion and Publicity, 1971–72; Deputy Controller, Programmes, 1972–73. Mem., Sports Council, 1971–76. Hon. Chm., The Professional Footballers Assoc., 1957–61. *Publications:* Striking for Soccer, 1961; Improve your Soccer, 1964. *Recreations:* golf, riding, tennis, soccer, bridge. *Address:* c/o BBC Television, Kensington House, Richmond Way, W14 0AX. *Clubs:* The Sportsman, Queen's.

HILL, Jimmy; *see* Hill, James William Thomas.

HILL, John; *see* Hill, F. J.

HILL, John; City Treasurer of Liverpool, 1974–82; *b* 28 April 1922; *s* of William Hallett Hill and Emily Hill (*née* Massey); *m* 1952, Hilda Mary Barratt; one *s. Educ:* Merchant Taylors' Sch., Crosby; Liverpool Univ. (BCom); Inst. of Public Finance and Accountancy, 1954. City Treasury, Liverpool, 1949; apptd Asst City Treasurer, 1962. *Recreation:* music. *Address:* 325 Northway, Lydiate, Merseyside L31 0BW. *T:* 051-526 3699.

HILL, John Edward Bernard; farming in Suffolk since 1946; *b* 13 Nov. 1912; *o s* of late Capt. Robert William Hill, Cambs Regt, and Marjorie Jane Lloyd-Jones, *d* of Edward Scott Miller; *m* 1944, Edith Luard, widow of Comdr R. A. E. Luard, RNVR, and 5th *d* of late John Maxwell, Cove, Dunbartonshire; one adopted *d. Educ:* Charterhouse; Merton Coll., Oxford (MA). Various journeys; Middle East, Far East, India, USA, 1935–37; Far East,

1956-57; USA, 1958. Called to Bar, Inner Temple (Certificate of Honour), 1938. RA (TA), 1939; Air Observation Post Pilot, 1942; War Office, 1942; 651 (Air OP) RAF, Tunisia, 1942; wounded, 1943; invalided out, 1945. MP (C) South Norfolk, Jan. 1955-Feb. 1974; Mem. Parliamentary delegns: W Germany and Berlin, 1959; Ghana, 1965; IPU Conf., Teheran, 1966; CPA Conf., Uganda, 1967; Bulgaria, 1970; Council of Europe and WEU, 1970-72; Mem., European Parlt, 1973-74; Chm., Cons. Educn Cttee, 1971-73; Member: Select Cttee on Agriculture, 1967-69; Select Cttee on Procedure, 1970-71; Asst Govt Whip, 1959-60; a Lord Comr of the Treasury, 1960-64. Mem. East Suffolk and Norfolk River Board, 1952-62. Mem. Exec. Cttee, CLA, 1957-59, 1977-82. Member: Governing Body, Charterhouse Sch., 1958; Langley Sch., Norfolk, 1962-77; GBA Cttee, 1966-79, 1980-; Council, Univ. of East Anglia, 1975-82. *Recreations:* association football (Blue; Sec., OUAFC 1934); shooting, concerts, picture galleries. *Address:* Watermill Farm, Wenhaston, Halesworth, Suffolk. *T:* Blythburgh 207. *Club:* Garrick.

HILL, Prof. (John Edward) Christopher, FBA 1966; DLitt; Master of Balliol College, Oxford, 1965-78; *b* 6 Feb. 1912; *m* 1st, 1944, Inez Waugh; one *d*; 2nd, 1956, Bridget Irene Sutton; one *s* one *d* (and one *d* decd). *Educ:* St Peter's Sch., York; Balliol Coll., Oxford. BA 1931, DLitt 1965. Fellow of All Souls Coll., Oxford, 1934; Asst Lectr, University Coll., Cardiff, 1936; Fellow and Tutor in Modern History, Balliol Coll., Oxford, 1938. Private in Field Security Police, commissioned Oxford and Bucks Light Inf., 1940, Major; seconded to Foreign Office, 1943. Returned to Balliol, 1945; University Lectr in 16th- and 17th-century history, 1959; Ford's Lectr, 1962. Vis. Prof., Open Univ., 1978-80. Hon. DLitt: Hull, 1966; E Anglia, 1968; Exeter, 1979; Wales, 1979; Hon. LittD Sheffield, 1967; Hon. DLitt: Glasgow, 1976; Exeter, 1979; Wales, 1979; Hon. LLD Bristol, 1976; DUniv York, 1978; Hon. Dr Sorbonne Nouvelle, 1979; DUniv Open, 1982. Foreign Hon. Member: Amer. Acad. of Sciences, 1973; Hungarian Acad. of Sciences, 1982. *Publications:* The English Revolution 1640, 1940; (under name K. E. Holme) Two Commonwealths, 1945; Lenin and the Russian Revolution, 1947; The Good Old Cause (ed jointly with E. Dell), 1949; Economic Problems of the Church, 1956; Puritanism and Revolution, 1958; Oliver Cromwell, 1958; The Century of Revolution, 1961; Society and Puritanism in Pre-Revolutionary England, 1964; Intellectual Origins of the English Revolution, 1965; Reformation to Industrial Revolution, 1967; God's Englishman, 1970; Antichrist in 17th Century England, 1971; The World Turned Upside Down, 1972; ed, G. Winstanley, The Law of Freedom and other writings, 1973; Change and Continuity in Seventeenth Century England, 1975; Milton and the English Revolution, 1978 (Heinemann award; Milton Soc. of America award); Some Intellectual Consequences of the English Revolution, 1980; articles in learned journals, etc. *Address:* Woodway House, Sibford Ferris, Banbury, Oxon OX15 5RA. *T:* Oxford 58544.

HILL, John Frederick Rowland, CMG 1955; *b* 20 April 1905; *s* of Judge William Henry Hill; *m* 1930, Phyllys Esmé (*née* Fryer); one *s* two *d. Educ:* Pinewood Sch., Farnborough; Marlborough Coll.; Lincoln Coll., Oxford. BA Oxon, Hon. Sch. Jurisprudence, 1927; Cadet Colonial Civil Service, Tanganyika, 1928; Asst District Officer, 1930; District Officer, 1940; Dep. Provincial Comr, 1947; Provincial Comr, 1948; Sen. Provincial Comr, 1950; Mem. for Communications, Works and Development Planning, Tanganyika Govt, 1951-56; Chm., Tanganyika Broadcasting Corp. and Dir of Broadcasting, 1956-57; Govt Liaison Officer, Freeport, Bahamas, 1957-58; Supervisor of Elections, Zanzibar, 1959-60. *Recreation:* golf. *Address:* Flat 3, 29 Powhiri Avenue, Whangarei, New Zealand.

HILL, Sir John McGregor, Kt 1969; BSc, PhD; FRS 1981; FEng 1982; FInstP, FInstE; Chairman: British Nuclear Fuels Ltd, since 1971; Amersham International Ltd, since 1975; *b* 21 Feb. 1921; *s* of late John Campbell Hill and of Margaret Elizabeth Park; *m* 1947, Nora Eileen Hellett; two *s* one *d. Educ:* King's Coll., London; St John's Coll., Cambridge. Flt Lieut, RAF, 1941. Cavendish Laboratory, Cambridge, 1946; Lecturer, London Univ., 1948. Joined UKAEA, 1950, Mem. for Production, 1964-67, Chm., 1967-81. Member: Advisory Council on Technology, 1968-70; Nuclear Power Adv. Bd, 1973-; Energy Commn, 1977-79. Hon. FIEE 1981; Foreign Associate, US Nat. Acad. of Engineering, 1976. Melchett Medal, 1974; Sylvanus Thompson Medal, 1978. Hon. FIChemE 1977. *Recreation:* golf. *Address:* Dominic House, Sudbrook Lane, Petersham, Surrey. *T:* 01-940 7221. *Club:* East India, Devonshire, Sports and Public Schools.

HILL, Sir John (Maxwell), Kt 1974; CBE 1969; DFC 1945; QPM; Chief Inspector of Constabulary, Home Office, 1972-75; *b* 25 March 1914; *s* of late L. S. M. Hill, Civil Servant, Plymouth; *m* 1939, Marjorie Louisa, *d* of late John Oliver Reynolds, Aylesbury, Bucks; one *s* one *d. Educ:* Plymouth Coll. Metropolitan Police Coll., Hendon, 1938-39; joined Metropolitan Police, 1933. Served with RAF, 1942-45. Dep. Comdr, New Scotland Yard, 1959; Metropolitan Police: Comdr, No 3 District, 1963, Comdr, No 1 District, 1964; HM Inspector of Constabulary, 1965; Asst Comr (Administration and Operations), 1966-68; Asst Comr (Personnel and Training), 1968-71; Dep. Comr, 1971-72. *Recreations:* walking, golf. *Address:* 23 Beacon Way, Banstead, Surrey. *T:* Burgh Heath 52771.

HILL, Rear-Adm. John Richard; Flag Officer, Admiralty Interview Board, since 1981; *b* 25 March 1929; *s* of Stanley Hill and May Hill (*née* Henshaw); *m* 1956, Patricia Anne Sales; one *s* two *d. Educ:* Royal Naval College, Dartmouth. China Station as midshipman, 1946-47; Sub-Lieut's Courses,

1948-49; Lieut, HM Ships: Gambia, 1950; Chevron, 1950-52; Tintagel Castle, 1952-54; Dryad (Navigation Specialist), 1954; Cardigan Bay, 1954-56; Albion, 1956-58; Roebuck, 1958-59; Lt-Comdr, Pembroke Dock, 1959-60; HMS Duchess, 1960-62; Comdr, MoD, 1963-65 and 1967-69; IDC 1965-67; HMS Dryad, 1969-71; Captain, MoD, 1973-75; Defence and Naval Attaché, The Hague, 1975-77; Cdre, MoD, 1977-80; Rear-Adm. 1981. Defence Fellow, University of London King's College, 1972. *Publications:* The Royal Navy Today and Tomorrow, 1981; articles in Survival, Navy International, Brassey's Annual, NATO's 15 Nations, Naval Review. *Recreations:* amateur theatre, cricket groundsman. *Address:* Waltham Chase, Southampton. *Club:* Royal Commonwealth Society.

HILL, Michael; *see* Hill, E. M.

HILL, Michael William, CChem; Director, The British Library, Science Reference Library, since 1973; *b* 1928; *o s* of late Geoffrey William Hill, Ross on Wye and Torquay; *m* 1st, 1957, Elma Jack Forrest (*d* 1967); one *s* one *d*; 2nd, 1969, Barbara Joy Youngman. *Educ:* Nottingham High Sch.; Lincoln Coll., Oxford (BSc, MA). MRIC 1953; CChem; FIInfSc 1982. Research Chemist, Laporte Chemicals Ltd, 1953-56; Morgan Crucible Group: Laboratory Head, 1956; Asst Process Control Manager, 1958; Group Technical Editor, 1963. Asst Keeper, British Museum, 1964. Dep. Librarian, Patent Office Library, 1965; Keeper, Nat. Ref. Library of Science and Invention, 1968-73. Member: Exec. Cttee, Nat. Central Library, 1971-74; EEC/CIDST Working Parties on Patent documentation, 1973-, and on Information for Industry, 1976-; Board, UK Chemical Inf. Service, 1974-77; Chairman: Circle of State Librarians, 1977-79; Council, Aslib, 1979-81; Vice President: IATUL, 1976; Fédn Internat. de Documentation, 1981-. *Publication:* Patent Documentation (with Wittmann and Schiffels), 1979. *Address:* 137 Burdon Lane, Cheam, Surrey SM2 7DB. *T:* 01-642 2418. *Club:* United Oxford & Cambridge University.

HILL, Norman A.; *s ee* Ashton Hill.

HILL, Norman Hammond, MD (London), MRCP; Consulting Physician: Belgrave Hospital for Children; Metropolitan and Wembley Hospitals; *b* 10 March 1893; *s* of Lewis Gordon Hill and Amy Caroline Hammond; *m* 1938, Suzanne Mary, *y d* of Rev. H. S. Rees, Christchurch, Mon. *Educ:* Bradford Grammar Sch.; St Bartholomew's Hosp. MRCS, LRCP 1915. Served in Army, 1915-19, Capt. RAMC (TF); held appointment of House Surgeon, Chief Asst to a Medical Unit, and Casualty Physician St Bartholomew's Hosp. and House Physician and Senior Resident Medical Officer Metropolitan Hosp. *Publications:* articles on medical subjects to Lancet, British Medical Journal, Clinical Journal, and Medical Press and Circular. *Recreations:* golf, photography. *Address:* 22 Acacia Road, NW8. *T:* 01-722 7466.

HILL, Dr Polly; Fellow, Clare Hall, Cambridge, since 1965; *b* 10 June 1914; *d* of Prof. A. V. Hill, CH, OBE, FRS, and Margaret, *d* of Dr J. N. Keynes and F. A. Keynes; *m* 1953, Kenneth Humphreys (marr. diss. 1961); one *d. Educ:* Newnham Coll., Cambridge (PhD). Editorial Asst, REconS, 1936-38; research, Fabian Soc., 1938-39; temp. civil servant, 1940-51; editorial staff, West Africa (weekly), 1951-53; Res. Fellow, then Sen. Res. Fellow, Econs Dept, followed by Inst. of African Studies, Univ. of Ghana, 1954-65; financed by Center for Research on Econ. Develt, Univ. of Mich, Ann Arbor, mainly working in Cambridge and northern Nigeria, 1965-70, and by SSRC, mainly working in northern Nigeria, 1970-72; Smuts Reader in Commonwealth Studies, Cambridge Univ., 1973-79; fieldwork in villages in Karnataka, S India, 1977-78, and (as Leverhulme Emeritus Fellow) in Kerala, S India, 1981-82. *Publications:* The Unemployment Services, 1940; The Gold Coast Cocoa Farmer, 1956; The Migrant Cocoa-Farmers of Southern Ghana, 1963, 3rd edn 1977; Rural Capitalism in West Africa, 1970, 2nd edn 1976; Rural Hausa, 1972; Population, Prosperity and Poverty: rural Kano, 1900 and 1970, 1977 (Amaury Talbot prize for African anthropology, 1977); Dry Grain Farming Families, 1982; articles on rural W Africa in learned jls; chapters in books. *Recreations:* art, travel. *Address:* The Stilts, Hemingford Abbots, Huntingdon, Cambs PE18 9AR. *T:* St Ives (Huntingdon) 63296.
See also D. K. Hill, J. H. Humphrey.

HILL, Robert, ScD Cantab 1942; FRS 1946; biochemist; Member of Scientific Staff of Agricultural Research Council, 1943-66; *b* 2 April 1899; *s* of Joseph Alfred Hill and Clara Maud Jackson; *m* 1935, Anny Priscilla, *d* of Edgar Worthington; two *s* two *d. Educ:* Bedales Sch.; Emmanuel Coll., Cambridge (Scholar). Served European War, 1914-18: RE pioneer Anti-gas Dept, 1917-18. Emmanuel Coll., Cambridge, 1919-22; Senior Studentship (Exhibn of 1851), 1927; Beit Memorial Research Fellow, 1929; Senior Beit Memorial Research Fellow, 1935; Hon. Fellow of Emmanuel Coll., 1963. Royal Medal, Royal Society, 1963; 1st Award for photosynthesis, Soc. of American Plant Physiologists, 1963; Charles E. Kettering Research Award, 1963; Hon. Member: Amer. Soc. of Biological Chemists, 1964; Comité Internat. de Photobiologie, 1968; American Acad. Arts and Sciences, 1971; For. Associate, Nat. Acad. of Sciences, 1975; For. Mem., Accad. Nazionale dei Lincei, 1975. *Publication:* (with C. P. Whittingham) Photosynthesis, 1955. *Recreations:* growing plants and dyeing with traditional plant dyes, water-colour painting. *Address:* 1 Comberton Road, Barton, Cambridge CB3 7BA.

HILL, Sir Robert E.; *see* Erskine-Hill.

HILL, Roderick; *see* Hill, Colonel E. R.

HILL, Rodney, FRS 1961; PhD; ScD; Professor of Mechanics of Solids, University of Cambridge, 1972–79 (Reader, 1969–72); Fellow, Gonville and Caius College, since 1972; *b* 11 June 1921; *o s* of Harold Harrison Hill, Leeds; *m* 1946, Jeanne Kathlyn, *yr d* of C. P. Wickens, Gidea Park; one *d. Educ:* Leeds Grammar Sch.; Pembroke Coll., Cambridge. MA, PhD, ScD Cambridge. Armament Research Dept, 1943–46; Cavendish Laboratory, Cambridge, 1946–48; British Iron and Steel Research Assoc., 1948–50; University of Bristol: Research Fellow, 1950–53, Reader, 1953; Univ. of Nottingham: Prof. of Applied Mathematics, 1953–62; Professorial Research Fellow, 1962–63; Berkeley Bye-Fellow, Gonville and Caius Coll., Cambridge, 1963–69. Hon. DSc: Manchester, 1976; Bath, 1978. Von Karman Medal, ASCE, 1978. Editor, Jl of Mechanics and Physics of Solids, 1952–68. *Publications:* Mathematical Theory of Plasticity, 1950; Principles of Dynamics, 1964. *Address:* Department of Applied Mathematics and Theoretical Physics, Silver Street, Cambridge.

HILL, (Stanley) James (Allen); MP (C) Southampton Test, 1970–Oct. 1974, and since 1979; company director; *b* 21 Dec. 1926; *s* of James and Florence Cynthia Hill; *m* 1958, Ruby Evelyn Ralph; two *s* three *d. Educ:* Regents Park Sch., Southampton; Southampton Univ.; North Wales Naval Training Coll. Former Pilot. Mem., Southampton City Council, 1966–70, 1976–79, Chm. of Housing, 1967–70, 1976–79; Mem. Cttee, Southampton Conservative and Ratepayers Fedn. Secretary: Cons. Parly Cttee on Housing and Construction, 1971–73; Cons. Industry Cttee, 1979–81; Mem., Select Cttee on European Legislation, 1979–. Mem., British Delegn to European Parlt, Strasbourg, and Chm., Regional Policy and Transport Cttee, 1973–75; Mem. Hon. Cttee for Europe Day, Council of Europe; Govt Whip to Council of Europe and WEU. Pres., Motor Schools Assoc.; Mem. Council, IAM. *Recreations:* private aviation, farming. *Address:* 51 Oakley Street, SW3; Gunsfield Lodge, Melchet Park, Plaitford, Hants. *Clubs:* Carlton, St Stephen's Constitutional.

HILL, Brig. (Stanley) James (Ledger), DSO 1942, and Bars, 1944, 1945; MC 1940; Vice-Chairman, Powell Duffryn Ltd, 1970–76 (Director, 1961–76); Chairman, Pauls & Whites Ltd, 1973–76 (Director, since 1970); Director: Lloyds Bank, 1972–81; Lloyds Bank UK Management Committee Ltd, 1979–81; *b* 14 March 1911; *s* of late Maj.-Gen. Walter Pitts Hendy Hill, CB, CMG, DSO, West Amesbury House, Wilts; *m* 1937, Denys, *d* of late E. Hubert Gunter-Jones, MC, JP, Gloucester House, Ledbury; one *d. Educ:* Marlborough; RMC Sandhurst. 2nd Bn, Royal Fusiliers, 1931–35; 2nd Bn, RF, BEF, 1939; DAAG, GHQ, BEF, 1940; comd 1st Bn, Parachute Regt, N Africa landing, 1942; comd 3rd Parachute Bde, 1943–45; took part in Normandy and Rhine crossing (wounded thrice); comdr 4th Parachute Bde (TA), 1947–48. Apptd to Bd of Associated Coal & Wharf Cos Ltd, 1948; Pres., Powell Duffryn Group of Cos in Canada, 1952–58. Legion of Honour (France), 1942; Silver Star (USA), 1945; King Haakon VII Liberty Cross (Norway), 1945. *Recreation:* birdwatching. *Address:* Bristol Court Cottage, Seymour Street, Brighton BN2 1DP. *T:* Brighton 684945; 2 Egerton Place, SW3 2EF. *T:* 01-589 0875. *Clubs:* Boodle's, Army and Navy; Island Sailing (IoW).

HILL, Starforth; *see* Hill, Ian S.

HILL, Susan Elizabeth, (Mrs Stanley Wells); novelist and playwright; *b* 5 Feb. 1942; *d* of R. H. and late Doris Hill; *m* 1975, Dr Stanley W. Wells, *qv* ; one *d. Educ:* grammar schs in Scarborough and Coventry; King's Coll., Univ. of London. BA Hons English 1963; Fellow, 1978. FRSL 1972. Literary critic, various jls, 1963–; numerous plays for BBC, 1970–. *Publications:* The Enclosure, 1961; Do me a Favour, 1963; Gentleman and Ladies, 1969; A Change for the Better, 1969; I'm the King of the Castle, 1970; The Albatross, 1971; Strange Meeting, 1971; The Bird of Night, 1972; A Bit of Singing and Dancing, 1973; In the Springtime of the Year, 1974; The Cold Country and Other Plays for Radio, 1975; (ed) The Distracted Preacher and other stories by Thomas Hardy, 1979; The Magic Apple Tree, 1982; *play:* The Ramshackle Company, 1981. *Recreations:* music, walking in the English countryside, friends, reading, broadcasting. *Address:* Midsummer Cottage, Church Lane, Beckley, Oxon.

HILL, Victor Archibald Lord, MA; *b* 3 July 1905; *o s* of W. E. Hill; *m* 1938, Jean Melicent, *e d* of Dr D. N. Seth-Smith, Bournemouth; two *s. Educ:* Chigwell Sch.; Queen Mary Coll., London (Open Exhibr; University Schol. in Classics; 1st cl. Hons BA); Hertford Coll., Oxford (Open Schol., 1st Cl. Hon. Mods, 3rd Cl. Lit. Hum.). MA (Oxon) 1934. Asst Master, Shrewsbury Sch., 1930-40, 1946-48; Headmaster, Allhallows Sch., 1948-65; Asst Master: Blundell's, 1965-66; Uppingham, 1966-67, 1968-69; Chigwell, 1969-70; Lectr in Classics, Exeter Univ., 1967-68. Served 1940-45, with KSLI and RA (Major). *Recreations:* music, golf. *Address:* Beggars' Roost, Morchard Bishop, near Crediton, Devon. *T:* Morchard Bishop 315. *Club:* National Liberal.

HILL, William Sephton; Principal Assistant Solicitor, HM Customs and Excise, since 1980; *b* 24 July 1926; *s* of late William Thomas and Annie May Hill; *m* 1954, Jean, *d* of Philip Wedgwood; one *d. Educ:* Cowley Sch., St. Helens, Merseyside. BA, LLB Cantab. Served RAF, 1944–48, Japanese interpreter. Called to the Bar, Gray's Inn, 1951; practised Northern Circuit, 1951-54. Joined Solicitor's Office, HM Customs and Excise, 1954. *Recreations:* golf (ex-captain and ex-champion, Civil Service Golfing Society), bridge, listening to and playing piano. *Address:* 31 Hill Rise, Rickmansworth, Herts WD1 2PQ. *T:* Rickmansworth 74756. *Club:* Moor Park Golf (Herts).

HILL-NORTON, family name of **Baron Hill-Norton.**

HILL-NORTON, Baron *cr* 1979 (Life Peer), of South Nutfield, Surrey; **Admiral of the Fleet Peter John Hill-Norton,** GCB 1970 (KCB 1967; CB 1964); Chairman, Military Committee of NATO, 1974–77; *b* 8 Feb. 1915; *s* of Capt. M. J. Norton and Mrs M. B. Norton; *m* 1936, Margaret Eileen Linstow; one *s* one *d. Educ:* RNC Dartmouth. Went to sea, 1932; commnd, 1936; specialised in Gunnery, 1939; War of 1939-45: Arctic Convoys; NW Approaches; Admiralty Naval Staff. Comdr 1948; Capt. 1952; Naval Attaché, Argentine, Uruguay, Paraguay, 1953-55; comd HMS Decoy, 1956-57; comd HMS Ark Royal, 1959-61; Asst Chief of Naval Staff, 1962-64; Flag Officer, Second-in-Command, Far East Fleet, 1964-66; Dep. Chief of the Defence Staff (Personnel and Logistics), 1966; Second Sea Lord and Chief of Naval Personnel, Jan.-Aug. 1967; Vice-Chief of Naval Staff, 1967-68; C-in-C Far East, 1969-70; Chief of the Naval Staff and First Sea Lord, 1970-71; Chief of the Defence Staff, 1971-73. President: Sea Cadets Assoc., 1977–; Defence Manufacturers' Assoc., 1980–; Vice-Pres., RUSI. Liveryman, Shipwrights' Co., 1973, Mem. Court, 1979; Freeman, City of London 1973. *Publications:* No Soft Options, 1978; Sea Power, 1982. *Recreations:* gardening, shooting. *Address:* King's Mill House, South Nutfield, Surrey. *T:* Nutfield Ridge 3309. *Clubs:* Army and Navy; Royal Thames Yacht, Royal Navy of 1765.

HILL-SMITH, Derek Edward, VRD 1958; **His Honour Judge Hill-Smith;** a Circuit Judge, since 1972; *b* 21 Oct. 1922; *s* of Charles Hill-Smith and Ivy (*née* Downs); *m* 1950, Marjorie Joanna, *d* of His Honour Montague Berryman, QC; one *s* one *d. Educ:* Sherborne; Trinity Coll., Oxford (MA). RNVR, 1942-46; Lt-Comdr RNR. Trinity Coll., Oxford, 1941-42 and 1946-47 (MA, Classics and Modern Greats); BEA, 1947-48; business, 1948-50; teaching, 1950-54; called to Bar, Inner Temple, 1954; Dep. Chm., Kent QS, 1970; Recorder, 1972. *Publications:* contrib. Law Guardian. *Recreations:* yacht-racing, the theatre, food and wine. *Address:* c/o National Westminster Bank, Grosvenor House, Park Lane, W1. *Clubs:* Garrick; Bar Yacht.

HILL-TREVOR, family name of **Baron Trevor.**

HILL-WOOD, Sir David (Basil), 3rd Bt *cr* 1921; Director, Guinness Mahon & Co., since 1977; *b* 12 Nov. 1926; *s* of Sir Basil Samuel Hill Hill-Wood, 2nd Bt, and Hon. Joan Louisa Brand, *e d* of 3rd Viscount Hampden; *S* father, 1954; *m* 1970, Jennifer, 2nd *d* of late Peter McKenzie Strang, Adelaide; two *s* one *d. Educ:* Eton. Served in Army (Grenadier Guards), 1945-48. Morgan Grenfell & Co Ltd, 1948-55; Partner, Myers & Co. and Capel-Cure Myers Ltd, 1958-77. Aust. Rep., FA Council. High Sheriff Berks, 1982. *Recreations:* soccer, shooting. *Heir: s* Samuel Thomas Hill-Wood, *b* 24 Aug. 1971. *Address:* Dacre Farm, Farley Hill, Reading, Berks. *T:* Eversley 733185; 58 Cathcart Road, SW10. *T:* 01-352 0389. *Clubs:* White's; Melbourne (Australia).

HILLABY, John; writer, naturalist and traveller; *b* 24 July 1917; *er s* of late Albert Ewart Hillaby, Pontefract, and Mabel Colyer; *m* 1940, Eleanor Riley, Leeds (marr. diss.); two *d* ; *m* 1966, Thelma Gordon (*d* 1972), child analyst, London and Montreal; *m* 1981, Kathleen Burton, Easingwold, Yorks. *Educ:* Leeds; Woodhouse Grove, Yorkshire. Served RA, War of 1939-45. Local journalism up to 1939; magazine contributor and broadcaster, 1944–; Zoological Corresp., Manchester Guardian, 1949; European science writer, New York Times, 1951–; biological consultant, New Scientist, 1953. Formerly a dir, Universities Fedn for Animal Welfare; Founder Pres., Backpackers Club. Has travelled on foot through parts of boreal Canada, Appalachian Trail, USA, Congo, traversed Ituri Forest and Mountains of the Moon (Ruwenzori), Sudan, Tanzania; three months foot safari with camels to Lake Rudolf, Kenya, and walked from Lands End to John o'Groats, from The Hague to Nice via the Alps, from Provence to Tuscany, from Lake District to London. Woodward Lectr, Yale, 1973. Radio and TV series include: Men of the North, Expedition South, Alpine Venture, Hillaby Walks, Globetrotter, etc. FZS (scientific). *Publications:* Within The Streams, 1949; Nature and Man, 1960; Journey to the Jade Sea, 1964; Journey Through Britain, 1968; Journey Through Europe, 1972; Journey through Love, 1976. *Recreations:* talking, reading, music, walking alone; observing peculiarities of man, beast, fowl and flora. *Address:* 85 Cholmley Gardens, NW6. *T:* 01-435 4626; Rosedale-by-Pickering, North Yorkshire. *Club:* Savage.

HILLARD, His Honour Richard Arthur Loraine, MBE 1946; a Circuit Judge (formerly a County Court Judge), 1956-72; *b* 1906; *er s* of Frederick Arthur Hillard, Puriton Manor, Bridgwater, Som; *m* 1st, 1936, Nancy Alford (*d* 1964), *d* of Dr Alford Andrews, Cambridge; one *s* one *d* ; 2nd, 1969, Monica Constance, *er d* of John Healey Carus, Darwen, and *widow* of Paul Hillard; one step *s* one step *d. Educ:* Worcester Royal Grammar Sch.; Christ Church, Oxford. Barrister, Gray's Inn, 1931; South-Eastern circuit. Served, 1940-45: Military Dept, Judge Advocate General's Office, 1941-45, Lt-Col 1945. Asst Reader and Lecturer, Council of Legal Education, 1945-55. Chm. Agricultural Land Tribunal, South Eastern Province, 1955. *Recreation:* gardening. *Address:* Oakchurch House, Staunton-on-Wye, Hereford. *T:* Moccas 345. *Club:* United Oxford & Cambridge University.

HILLARY, Sir Edmund, KBE 1953; Director, Field Educational Enterprises of Australasia Pty Ltd; Consultant to Sears Roebuck & Co., Chicago, on camping and outdoor equipment; author; lecturer; mountaineer; *b* 20 July 1919; *s* of Percival Augustus Hillary and Gertrude Hillary (*née* Clark); *m* 1953, Louise Rose (*d* 1975); one *s* one *d* (and one *d* decd). *Educ:* Auckland Grammar Sch., Auckland, New Zealand. Apiarist, 1936-43. RNZAF, navigator on Catalina flying boats in Pacific Area, 1944–45. Apiarist (in partnership with brother W. F. Hillary), 1951–70. Himalayan Expeditions: NZ Gawhal Expedition, 1951; British Everest Reconnaissance, 1951; British Cho Oyu Expedition, 1952; Everest Expedition, 1953; with Sherpa Tenzing reached summit of Mount Everest, May 1953 (KBE). Leader of NZ Alpine Club Expedition to Barun Valley, East of Everest, 1954. Appointed, 1955, leader of New Zealand Transantarctic Expedition; completed overland journey to South Pole, Jan. 1958. Expeditions in Everest region, 1960–61, 1963, 1964, 1965; built first hosp. for Sherpas in Everest Area, with public subscription and NZ doctor, 1966; led expedition to Antarctic for geological and mountaineering purposes incl. first ascent of Mt Herschel, 1967; expedition to E Nepal (explored Himalayan rivers with two jet boats; first ascent of 180 miles of Sun Kosi river from Indian border to Katmandu), 1968; jet boat expedition up the Ganges, 1977. Hon. LLD: Univ. of Victoria, BC, Canada, 1969; Victoria Univ., Wellington, NZ, 1970. Hubbard Medal (US), 1954; Star of Nepal 1st Class; US Gold Cullum Geographical Medal, 1954; Founder's Gold Medal, Royal Geographical Society, 1958; Polar Medal, 1958. *Publications:* High Adventure; East of Everest, 1956 (with George Lowe); The Crossing of Antarctica, 1958 (with Sir Vivian Fuchs); No Latitude for Error, 1961; High in the Thin Cold Air, 1963 (with Desmond Doig); School House in the Clouds, 1965; Nothing Venture, Nothing Win (autobiog.), 1975; From the Ocean to the Sky: jet boating up the Ganges, 1979. *Recreations:* mountaineering, ski-ing, camping. *Address:* 278a Remuera Road, Auckland, SE2, New Zealand. *Clubs:* New Zealand Alpine (Hon. Mem.; Pres. 1965–67); Hon. Mem. of many other NZ and US clubs.

HILLER, Dame Wendy, DBE 1975 (OBE 1971); actress; *b* 1912; *d* of Frank Watkin and Marie Hiller, Bramhall, Cheshire; *m* 1937, Ronald Gow; one *s* one *d*. *Educ:* Winceby House, Bexhill. Manchester Repertory Theatre; Sir Barry Jackson's tour of Evensong; Sally Hardcastle in Love on the Dole, London and New York; leading parts in Saint Joan and Pygmalion at Malvern Festival, 1936. *Plays include:* Twelfth Night (war factory tour); Cradle Song (Apollo); The First Gentleman (Savoy); Tess of the d'Urbervilles (Piccadilly); The Heiress (Biltmore, NY, and Haymarket, London); Ann Veronica (Piccadilly); Waters of the Moon (Haymarket), 1951–53; The Night of the Ball (New), 1955; Old Vic Season, 1955–56; Moon for the Misbegotten (NY), 1957; Flowering Cherry (Haymarket), 1958; Toys in the Attic (Piccadilly), 1960; Aspern Papers (NY), 1962; The Wings of the Dove (Lyric), 1963; The Sacred Flame (Duke of York's), 1967; When We Dead Awaken (Edinburgh Festival), 1968; The Battle of Shrivings (Lyric), 1970; Crown Matrimonial (Haymarket), 1972; John Gabriel Borkman, (National), 1975; Lies! (Albery), 1975; Waters of the Moon (Chichester), 1977, (Haymarket) 1978; The Old Jest, 1980. *Films:* Pygmalion; Major Barbara; I Know Where I'm Going; Outcast of the Islands; Separate Tables (Academy Award); Sons and Lovers; Toys in the Attic; A Man for All Seasons; David Copperfield; Murder on the Orient Express; The Elephant Man, etc. *TV:* When We Dead Awaken, 1968; Peer Gynt, 1972; Clochemerle, 1973; Last Wishes, 1978; Richard II, 1979; Miss Morison's Ghosts, 1981. *Address:* Spindles, Beaconsfield, Bucks.

HILLERY, Dr Patrick John; Uachtarán na hÉireann (President of Ireland), since Dec. 1976; *b* Miltown Malbay, Co. Clare, 2 May 1923; *s* of Dr Michael Joseph Hillery and Ellen (*née* McMahon); *m* 1955, Dr Mary Beatrice Finnegan; one *s* one *d*. *Educ:* Miltown Malbay National Sch.; Rockwell Coll.; University Coll. Dublin. BSc; MB BCh, BAO, DPH. Mem. Health Council, 1955–57; MO, Miltown Malbay, 1957–59; Coroner for West Clare, 1958–59; TD (Mem. Dáil Eireann), Clare, 1951–73; Minister: for Educn, 1959–65; for Industry and Commerce, 1965–66; for Labour, 1966–69; of Foreign Affairs, 1969–72 (negotiated Ireland's accession to European Communities); Comr for Social Affairs and a Vice-Pres., Commn of the European Communities, 1973–76. MRIA 1963. Hon. FRCSI 1977; Hon. FFDRCSI 1977; Hon. FRCPI 1978; Hon. Fellow, All-India Inst. of Medical Sciences, 1978; Hon. FRCGP 1982. Hon. LLD: NUI, 1962; Univ. of Dublin, 1977. *Address:* Aras an Uachtaráin, Phoenix Park, Dublin 8, Ireland; Spanish Point, Co. Clare, Ireland.

HILLHOUSE, Robert Russell; Under Secretary (Principal Finance Officer), Scottish Office, since 1980; *b* 23 April 1938; *s* of Robert Hillhouse and Jean Russell; *m* 1966, Alison Janet Fraser; two *d*. *Educ:* Hutchesons' Grammar Sch., Glasgow; Glasgow Univ. (MA). Scottish Education Dept, 1962; HM Treasury, 1971; Asst Secretary, Scottish Office, 1974; Scottish Home and Health Dept, 1977. *Recreation:* making music. *Address:* 48 Dreghorn Loan, Colinton, Edinburgh. *T:* 031-441 1587.

HILLIARD, Christopher Richard; His Honour Judge Hilliard; a Circuit Judge, since 1980; *b* 12 June 1930; *s* of late Dr Francis Maybury Hilliard and Mrs Gwen Hilliard; *m* 1955, Anne Margaret, *o d* of late Mr and Mrs Mark Maber; one *s* one *d*. *Educ:* RN Colls, Dartmouth and Greenwich. Served RN, 1947–61: Lieut 1952, Lt-Comdr 1960; retd 1961. Called to the Bar, Middle Temple, 1959; admitted to Cyprus Bar, 1960; practised at the Bar, South Eastern Circuit, 1962–80. *Recreations:* reading, heraldry, keeping Jacob's sheep. *Address:* 6 King's Bench Walk, Temple, EC4Y 7DR. *T:* 01-353 3327. *Clubs:* National, Naval and Military.

HILLIER, Arthur, OBE 1947; retired as Chairman and Managing Director, Sperry Gyroscope Co. Ltd (1938–59); Chairman: Industrial Products (Speco) Ltd, 1949–59; New Holland Machine Co. Ltd, 1954–59; *b* 2 Dec. 1895; *s* of Thomas Hillier and Ann Hillier (*née* Holland); *m* 1st, 1919, Rita Mary (*d* 1955), *d* of John Wakeley; two *d*; 2nd, 1956, Margaret Howard. *Educ:* Judd Sch., Tonbridge, Kent. Joined Sperry Gyroscope Co. Ltd as Asst Sec., 1916; Sec., 1920; Dir, 1922; Dir and Gen. Manager, 1933; Man. Dir, 1934. Freeman of City of London, 1930; Freeman and Liveryman of: Needlemakers' Company, 1930; Shipwrights' Company, 1951. FCIS 1937; FIN 1953 (was Founder Mem.); JP Middlesex, 1951; High Sheriff County of Middlesex, 1956–57. Comdr, Order of Orange Nassau (Netherlands), 1950; Officer, Legion of Honour (France), 1952; Commendatore, Order of Merit (Italy), 1955. *Recreation:* ancient history. *Address:* Cranmore, Little Forest Road, Bournemouth, Dorset. *T:* Bournemouth 765532. *Clubs:* Royal Automobile, City Livery.

HILLIER, Bevis; Deputy Literary Editor, The Times, since 1981; *b* 28 March 1940; *s* of J. R. Hillier and Mary Louise Hillier (*née* Palmer). *Educ:* Reigate Grammar Sch.; Magdalen Coll., Oxford (demy). Gladstone Memorial Prize, 1961. Editorial staff, The Times, 1963–68 (trainee, Home News Reporter, Sale Room Correspondent); Editor, British Museum Society Bulletin, 1968–70; Antiques Correspondent, the Times, 1970–; Guest Curator, Minneapolis Inst. of Arts, USA, 1971; Editor, The Connoisseur, 1973–76. FRSA 1967. *Publications:* Master Potters of the Industrial Revolution: The Turners of Lane End, 1965; Pottery and Porcelain 1700–1914, 1968; Art Deco of the 1920s and 1930s, 1968; Posters, 1969; Cartoons and Caricatures, 1970; The World of Art Deco, 1971; 100 Years of Posters, 1972; introduction to A Boy at the Hogarth Press by Richard Kennedy, 1972; Austerity/Binge, 1975; (ed with Mary Banham) A Tonic to the Nation: The Festival of Britain 1951, 1976; The New Antiques, 1977; Greetings from Christmas Past, 1982; contributor to The Connoisseur, Apollo, Trans English Ceramic Circle, Proc. Wedgwood Soc., etc. *Recreations:* piano; collecting; awarding marks out of ten for suburban front gardens. *Address:* Goldbeaters House, Manette Street, W1. *T:* 01-437 1972. *Clubs:* Beefsteak, Garrick.

HILLIER, Harold George, CBE 1971; President, Hillier Nurseries (Winchester) Ltd, Nurserymen and Seedsmen to Queen Elizabeth the Queen Mother; horticulturalist; *b* 2 Jan. 1905; *s* of Edwin Lawrence and Ethel Marian Hillier; *m* 1934, Barbara Mary Trant; two *s* two *d*. *Educ:* Peter Symonds Sch., Winchester; King Edward's Grammar Sch., Southampton. Joined Hillier Nurseries, 1922. FLS; Hon. FRHS 1972 (a Vice-Pres., 1974–); Hon. Fellow, Japanese Horticultural Soc., 1976. VMH 1957; Veitch Memorial Medal in Gold, 1962; Massachusetts Horticultural Society's Thomas Roland Medal, 1965. *Recreation:* making an arboretum. *Address:* Jermyns House, Ampfield, Romsey, Hants. *T:* Braishfield 68212.

HILLIER, Tristram Paul, RA 1967 (ARA 1957); painter and writer; *b* 11 April 1905; *s* of Edward Guy Hillier, CMG, and Ada Everett; *m* 1st, 1931, Irene Rose Hodgkins (marr. diss. 1935); two *s*; 2nd, 1937, Leda Millicent Hardcastle; two *d*. *Educ:* Downside; Christ's Coll., Cambridge. Studied at Slade Sch. and under André Lhôte, Paris. Has held nine one-man exhibitions in London at Lefevre Gall. (3) and Tooth's Gall. (7); other exhibitions: retrospective, Worthing Art Gall., 1960; Galerie Barreiro, Paris; Langton Gall., London, 1974; Pieter Wenning Gall., Johannesburg, 1975. Rep. by official purchases of pictures in following public collections: Tate Gall.; National Galleries of Canada, NSW, and Victoria; Ferens Art Gall., Hull; Contemporary Art Soc.; City Art Galleries: Manchester, Aberdeen, Leeds, Southampton, Nottingham, Belfast, Exeter; Art Galleries of Toronto, Brisbane, Rochdale, Oldham, Kettering; Min. of Works (for Brit. Embassies Fund); Harris Museum, Preston; Chantrey Bequest; Norton Simon Museum, USA. Served as Lieut RNVR, 1940–45. *Publication:* Leda and the Goose (autobiography), 1954. *Recreations:* riding, walking, swimming. *Address:* c/o Alex Reid & Lefevre, Lefevre Gallery, 30 Bruton Street, W1X 8JD. *T:* 01-629 2250; Yew Tree Cottage, East Pennard, Shepton Mallet, Somerset. *T:* Ditcheat 284.

HILLIER-FRY, (William) Norman, CMG 1982; HM Diplomatic Service; High Commissioner in Uganda, since 1980; *b* 12 Aug. 1923; *o s* of William Henry and Emily Hillier Fry; *m* 1948, Elizabeth Adèle Misbah; two *s* two *d*. *Educ:* Colfe's Grammar School, Lewisham; St Edmund Hall, Oxford (BA 1946). Served Army, 1942–45; commissioned, Loyal Regt, 1942. HM Foreign Service, 1946; served: Iran, 1947–52; Strasbourg (Delegation to Council of Europe), 1955–56; Turkey, 1956–59; Czechoslovakia, 1961–63; Counsellor, UK Disarmament Delegn, Geneva, 1968–71; Hd of ME Dept, ODA, 1971–74; Consul-Gen., Hamburg, 1974–79; Ambassador to Afghanistan, 1979–80. *Recreations:* music, theatre. *Address:* c/o Foreign and Commonwealth Office, SW1.

HILLIS, Arthur Henry Macnamara, CMG 1961; Comptroller General, National Debt Office, 1961–68; *b* 29 Dec. 1905; *s* of late John David Hillis, FRCS, Dublin; *m* 1936, Mary Francis; no *c*. *Educ:* Trinity Coll., Dublin. Called to Bar, Inner Temple, 1931. HM Treasury, 1941; Harkness Fund Fellow, USA, 1950–51; Minister (Treasury Adviser), UK Permanent Mission to United Nations, 1958–61; Under-Sec., Treasury, 1961. Mem., Internat. CS Commn (UN), 1974–81. *Address:* 2 Hare Court, Temple, EC4. *T:* 01-353 3443. *Club:* Athenæum.

HILLMAN, Ellis Simon; GLC Councillor, Hackney Central, since 1964; Principal Lecturer in Environmental Studies, North East London Polytechnic, since 1972, and Head of International Office, since 1981; *b* 17 Nov. 1928; *s* of David and Annie Hillman; *m* 1967, Louise; one *s*. *Educ:* University Coll. Sch.; Chelsea Coll. of Science and Technol. (BSc). Scientific Technical Officer: Soil Mechanics Ltd; NCB Field Investigation Group; Architectural

Assoc.; Organiser of Cttee, NELP/UNESCO Conf. on Solar Energy, 1977. Chm., London Subterranean Survey Assoc., 1968-. Elected to LCC, 1958. Chairman: GLC Arts and Recreation Cttee, 1973-77; AMA Arts and Recreation Cttee, 1974-78; Further and Higher Educn Sub-Cttee, ILEA, 1977-81 (Bldgs Section, 1970-73); Vice-Chm., ILEA, 1980-81. Member: Lee Valley Reg. Park Authority, 1973-; Sports Council, 1975-; Water Space Amenity Commn, 1977-80; Inland Waterways Amenity Adv. Council, 1977-. Founder and Hon. Pres., Lewis Carroll Soc., 1969-. Governor: Imperial Coll. of Science and Technol., and Queen Mary Coll., Univ. of London; Museum of London; Coombe Lodge; Staff Further Educn Coll. Pres., Paddy O'Connor Trust. FRSA 1979. Publications: Essays in Local Government Enterprise, 1964-67; (ed) Towards a Wider Use, 1976; Novellae on the Scroll of Esther, 1982; (ed) Space for the Living or Space for the Dead, 1977; contrib. Underground Services; Architects Jl, Arch. Design, Municipal Rev., and Municipal Jl. Recreations: walking, gardening, allotment holding, classical music, reading, writing poetry. Address: 13 View Road, Highgate, N6 4DJ. T: 01-340 7216.

HILLS, Edwin Sherbon, CBE 1971; FRS 1954; FAA; Professor of Geology, 1944-64, Research Professor, 1964-71, now Professor Emeritus, University of Melbourne; b Melbourne, 31 Aug. 1906; s of Edwin S. Hills, Melbourne; m 1932, Claire D. Fox; two s one d. Educ: Univs of Melbourne and London. DSc Melbourne; PhD London; FIC; DSc (Hon.) Dunelm; Foreign and Commonwealth FGS (Bigsby Medallist, 1951); David Syme Prize for Scientific Research (Melbourne), 1939. Dep. Vice-Chancellor, Univ. of Melbourne, 1962-71. Fellow, Imperial Coll. of Science and Technology, London, 1968; Hon. Fellow Aust. Inst. of Geographers. Inaugural W. R. Browne Medal, Geol. Soc. Australia, 1979. Publications: Outlines of Structural Geology, 1940, new edn 1953; Physiography of Victoria, 1941, new edn 1975; Elements of Structural Geology, 1963, new edn 1971; (ed) Arid Lands: a Geographical Appraisal, 1966. Address: 25 Barry Street, Kew, Victoria 3101, Australia. T: 862.2079.

HILLS, Air Vice-Marshal Eric Donald, CB 1973; CBE 1968 (MBE 1941); SASO Maintenance Command, 1971-73, retired; b 26 Jan. 1917; s of late Henry James Hills; m 1945, Pamela Mary, d of late Col A. P. Sandeman, Cape Town; one s one d. Educ: Maidstone Grammar Sch. Joined RAF 1939; Group Captain 1962; Dir of Equipment 3 (RAF), 1968-69; Air Cdre 1969; Dir of Equipment (Policy) (RAF), MoD, 1969-71; Air Vice-Marshal 1971. Recreations: gardening, sport as spectator. Address: c/o National Westminster Bank Ltd, Stone, Staffs. Club: Royal Air Force.

HILLS, Graham John, PhD, DSc; FRSE, CChem, FRSC; Principal and Vice-Chancellor of the University of Strathclyde, since 1980; b 9 April 1926; s of Albert Victor Hills and Marjorie Hills (née Harper); m 1st, 1950, Brenda Stubbington (d 1974); one s three d; 2nd, 1980, Mary Jane McNaughton. Educ: Birkbeck Coll., London Univ. (BSc 1946, PhD 1950, DSc 1962). Lecturer in Physical Chemistry, Imperial College, 1949-62; Professor of Physical Chemistry, Univ. of Southampton, 1962-80; Visiting Professor: Univ. of Western Ontario, 1968; Case Western Reserve Univ., 1969; Univ. of Buenos Aires, 1977. Publications: Reference Electrodes, 1961; Polarography, 1964; contrib. Faraday Transactions, on physical chemistry, espec. electrochemistry. Recreations: mountain walking, sailing, European political history. Address: University of Strathclyde, Royal College, 204 George Street, Glasgow G1 1XW. T: 041-552 4400. Clubs: Athenæum, Caledonian.

HILLS, Lawrence Donegan; Director, Henry Doubleday Research Association, since 1954; b 2 July 1911; s of William Donegan and Mabel Annie Hills; m 1964, Mrs Hilda Cherry Brooke (née Fea). Educ: at home, owing to ill health. Took up horticulture on medical advice in 1927 and worked for many leading nurseries until 1940. Served War of 1939-45, RAF. Wrote first book, Miniature Alpine Gardening, in hospitals before invalided out on D-Day. Founded Henry Doubleday Research Assoc., 1954, and still Director of this leading internat. body of gardeners and farmers without chemicals. Gardening Correspondent: Observer, 1958-66; Punch, 1966-70; Countryman, 1970; Garden News, 1981; Associated Editor: Compost Science (USA); Ecologist, 1973. Publications: Miniature Alpine Gardening, 1944; Rapid Tomato Ripening, 1946; Propagation of Alpines, 1950; Alpines Without A Garden, 1953; Russian Comfrey, 1953; Alpine Gardening, 1955; Down To Earth Fruit and Vegetable Growing, 1960; Down to Earth Gardening, 1967; Lands of the Morning (Archaeology), 1970; Grow Your Own Fruit and Vegetables, 1971; Comfrey—Its Past, Present and Future, 1976; Organic Gardening, 1977; Fertility Gardening, 1981. Recreations: reading, thinking, non-gardening writing. Address: 32 Convent Lane, Bocking, Braintree, Essex. T: Braintree 24083.

HILLYARD, Patrick Cyril Henry, OBE 1956; Head of Sound Light Entertainment BBC, 1952-64, retd Nov. 1964; s of Rev. Dr H. J. Hillyard and Louie Charlotte Robinson; m 1932, Ena Violet, d of late Rev. C. Porter-Brickwell; one s. Educ: The High Sch., Dublin. Studied stage production under Donald Calthrop. Stage directed and produced plays and musical comedies in England and America, including: A Midsummer Night's Dream, Twelfth Night, The Fake, Jolly Roger, No More Ladies, The Desert Song, Gay Divorce, On Your Toes, Lilac Time. Joined BBC Television Service as Dep. Productions Manager, 1937; Asst Dir of Variety, BBC, 1941; Actg Dir of Variety, BBC, 1946; Dir of Television Presentation, BBC, 1947; Head of Television Light Entertainment, BBC, 1948. Kt of Mark Twain,

1980. Recreations: going to the theatre, golf, tennis and swimming. Address: c/o Barclays Bank, 15 Langham Place, W1. Club: Malta Union.

HILSUM, Prof. Cyril, PhD; FRS 1979; FInstP, FIEE; Chief Scientific Officer, Royal Signals and Radar Establishment, Malvern, since 1974; Visiting Professor in Applied Physics and Electronics, University of Durham, since 1978; b 17 May 1925; s of Benjamin and Ada Hilsum; m 1947, Betty Cooper; two d. Educ: Raines Sch., London; University Coll., London (BSc, PhD). SMIEEE; FEng 1978; FIEE 1967; FInstP 1960. Joined Royal Naval Scientific Service, 1945; Admiralty Res. Lab., 1947-50, and Services Electronics Res. Lab., 1950-64, working first on infra-red res., then on semiconductors; Royal Signals and Radar Estab., 1964-, working first on compound semiconductors, now on flat panel electronic displays. Publications: Semiconducting III-V Compounds, 1961; over 100 scientific and technical papers. Recreations: ballroom dancing, tennis. Address: Royal Signals and Radar Establishment, St Andrews Road, Malvern, Worcs.

HILTON, Sir Derek (Percy), Kt 1966; MBE 1945; b 11 April 1908; o c of Percy Hilton and Mary Beatrice Hilton (née Stott); m 1945, Joanna Stott, er d of late Sir Arnold Stott, KBE; three d. Educ: Rugby Sch.; Trinity Hall, Cambridge. Solicitor, 1932; subsequently private practice in Manchester. War of 1939-45, Manchester Regt; seconded to special operations executive, 1941. Mem. Council, Law Soc., 1951; Hon. Sec., Manchester Law Soc., 1950-59; Pres., Manchester Law Soc., 1957; Pres. of the Law Soc., 1965-66. Dir, Abbey National Building Soc., 1966-81; Chm., Lancashire & Yorkshire Revisionary Interest Co. Ltd, 1956-77; Pres., Immigration Appeal Tribunal, 1970-78. Norwegian Liberty Cross, 1945. Recreations: gardening, walking, fishing. Address: Eaves, Chapel-en-le-Frith, Stockport, Cheshire SK12 6UA. T: Chapel-en-le-Frith 812241. Club: Special Forces.

HILTON, John Robert, CMG 1965; HM Diplomatic Service (appointed to Foreign Service, 1943), retired 1969; b 5 Jan. 1908; s of Oscar Hilton, MD, and Louisa Holdsworth Hilton; m 1933, Margaret Frances Stephens; one s three d. Educ: Marlborough Coll.; Corpus Christi Coll., Oxford (MA); Bartlett Sch. of Architecture; University Coll., London (Diploma). ARIBA. Dir of Antiquities, Cyprus, 1934-36; Architect to E. S. & A. Robinson Ltd and private practice, 1936-41. Capt. RE, 1941-43. Foreign Service, 1943; transferred to Istanbul, 1944; 2nd Sec., Athens, 1945; Foreign Office, 1947; 1st Sec., Istanbul, 1956; Foreign Office, 1960. FRSA. Publications: articles in Architectural Review and other jls, Mind and Analysis; Memoir on Louis MacNeice (as appendix to his autobiography, The Strings are False), 1965. Recreations: philosophy, walking. Address: Hope Cottage, Nash Hill, Lacock, Wilts. T: Lacock 369.

HILTON, Col Peter, MC 1942 and Bars 1943 and 1944; JP; Managing Director, James Smith (Scotland Nurseries) Ltd; Lord-Lieutenant and Custos Rotulorum of Derbyshire, since 1978; b 30 June 1919; er s of late Maj.-Gen. R. Hilton, DSO, MC, DFC, and Phyllis Martha (née Woodin); m 1942, Winifred, d of late Ernest Smith. Man. Dir Scotland Nurseries, Tansley; one s (and one s deed). Educ: Malvern Coll.; RMA Woolwich; psc. Commnd RA, 1939; BEF, 1939-40, 1st Div. Dunkirk; Western Desert, 1942-43, 7th Armd Div. Alamein (RHA Jacket 1942); Italy, 1943-44, 5th American Army, Adjt 3rd Regt RHA; Normandy, 1944, OC J Bty RHA (wounded Falaise Gap); Greece, 1946-49 (despatches 1948); Instructor Royal Hellenic Staff Coll.; Col RA 1949, retd; RARO; recalled Korean Emergency, 1950; TA Commn, 1951; CO 528 W Notts Regt, RA (TA), 1951-54; ACF Commn, 1962; Comdt Derbyshire ACF, 1962-66, Hon. Col 1972-77. Vice-Pres., TA & VRA, E Midlands, 1978; Chm., Derbys War Pensions Cttee; Comdr, Derbys SJAB; Vice-Pres., Derbys Rural Community Council. Trustee: Derby New Theatre; Sherwood Foresters Museum; Crich Meml Trust; Vice-Pres., British Heart Foundn, Derbs; Chm. of Governors, Anthony Gell Sch., Wirksworth. JP 1967, High Sheriff 1970-71, DL 1972, Derbs; Mem. Wirksworth Div. Derbs CC, 1967-77. FRHS. KStJ 1979. Greek Order of Minerva, 1949. Recreations: ex-Service interests, local activities. Address: Alton Manor, Idridgehay, Derbs. T: Wirksworth 2435; James Smith (Scotland Nurseries) Ltd, Tansley, Matlock, Derbs DE4 5GF. T: Matlock 3036.

HILTON, Prof. Peter John, MA, DPhil Oxon, PhD Cantab; Beaumont University Professor, Case-Western Reserve University, since 1972; b 7 April 1923; s of late Dr Mortimer Hilton and of Mrs Elizabeth Hilton; m 1949, Margaret (née Mostyn); two s. Educ: St Paul's Sch.; Queen's Coll., Oxford. Asst Lectr, Manchester Univ., 1948-51, Lectr, 1951-52; Lectr, Cambridge Univ., 1952-55; Senior Lecturer, Manchester Univ., 1956-58; Mason Prof. of Pure Mathematics, University of Birmingham, 1958-62; Prof. of Mathematics, Cornell Univ., 1962-71, Washington Univ., 1971-73. Visiting Professor: Cornell Univ., USA, 1958-59; Eidgenössische Techn. Hochschule, Zürich, 1966-67; Courant Inst., NY Univ., 1967-68. Mathematician-in-residence, Battelle Research Center, Seattle, 1970-; Mathematics Prof., State Univ. of NY at Binghampton, 1982-. Chariman: US Commn on Mathematical Instruction, 1971-74; NRC Cttee on Applied Maths Trng, 1977-; First Vice-Pres., Math. Assoc. of Amer., 1978-80. Corresp. Mem., Brazilian Acad. of Scis, 1979; Hon. Mem. Belgian Mathematical Soc., 1955. Hon. DHum N Michigan, 1977. Silver Medal, Univ. of Helsinki, 1975. Publications: Introduction to Homotopy Theory, 1953; Differential Calculus, 1958; Homology Theory (with S. Wylie), 1960; Partial Derivatives, 1960; Homotopy Theory and Duality, 1965; (with H. B. Griffiths) Classical Mathematics, 1970; General Cohomology Theory and K- Theory, 1971; (with U. Stammbach) Course in Homological Algebra, 1971; (with Y.-C. Wu)

Course in Modern Algebra, 1974; (with G. Mislin and J. Roitberg) Localization of Nilpotent Groups and Spaces, 1975; numerous research articles on algebraic topology, homological algebra and category theory in British and foreign mathematical journals. *Recreations:* travel, sport, reading, theatre, chess, bridge, broadcasting. *Address:* Battelle Research Center, 4000 NE 41st Street, Seattle, Washington 98105, USA.

HILTON, Prof. Rodney Howard, FBA 1977; Professor of Medieval Social History, University of Birmingham, 1963-82; *b* 1916; *s* of John James Hilton and Anne Hilton. *Educ:* Manchester Grammar Sch.; Balliol Coll. and Merton Coll., Oxford (BA, DPhil). Army, 1940-46; Lectr and Reader in Medieval History, Univ. of Birmingham, 1946-63. *Publications:* The Economic Development of Some Leicestershire Estates in the 14th and 15th Centuries, 1947; (with H. Fagan) The English Rising of 1381, 1950; (ed) Ministers' Accounts of the Warwickshire Estates of the Duke of Clarence, 1952; (ed) The Stoneleigh Leger Book, 1960; A Medieval Society, 1966; The Decline of Serfdom in Medieval England, 1969; Bondmen Made Free, 1973; The English Peasantry in the Later Middle Ages, 1975; (ed) Peasants, Knights and Heretics, 1976; (ed) The Transition from Feudalism to Capitalism, 1976; articles and reviews in Past and Present, English Historical Review, Economic History Review, etc. *Address:* School of History, University of Birmingham, Birmingham B15 2TT. *T:* 021-472 1301.

HILTON, William (Samuel); Director, Master Builders' Federation, since 1969; National Director, Federation of Master Builders, since 1970; Managing Director: Trade Press (FMB) Ltd, since 1972; National Register of Warranted Builders Ltd, since 1980; *b* 21 March 1926; *m* 1948, Agnes Aitken Orr; three *s. Educ:* Kyleshill, Saltcoats; Ardrossan Academy. Railway Fireman until 1949; Labour Party Agent to late Lord Kirkwood, 1949-52; Research and Education Officer for Building Trade Operatives, 1952-66. MP (Lab and Co-op) Bethnal Green, 1966- Feb. 1974. Mem. Agrément Bd for Building Industry, 1965-66; Mem. Economic Development Council for Building Industry, 1964-66; Employers' Sec., Building and Allied Trades Jt Industrial Council, 1979-. Editor, Builders Standard, 1954-66. *Publications:* Building by Direct Labour, 1954; Foes to Tyranny, 1964; Industrial Relations in Construction, 1968. *Address:* The Roost, 1 Mavelstone Close, Bromley, Kent.

HIME, Martin; HM Diplomatic Service; Consul General, Cleveland, Ohio, since 1982; *b* 18 Feb. 1928; *s* of Percy Joseph Hime and Esther Greta (*née* Howe); *m* 1st, 1960, Henrietta Fehling (marr. diss.); one *s* three *d* ; 2nd, 1971, Janina Christine Majcher; one *d. Educ:* King's Coll. Sch., Wimbledon; Trinity Hall, Cambridge (MA). Served RA, 1946-48. Called to the Bar, Inner Temple, 1951; Marks and Spencer Ltd, 1952-58; joined HM Diplomatic Service, 1960; served in Tokyo, Kobe, Frankfurt and Buenos Aires, 1960-69; 2nd Sec., FCO, 1970-72; Consul, Johannesburg, 1972-74; 1st Sec. (Econ.), Pretoria, 1974-76; Asst Head, S Pacific Dept, FCO, 1976-79; Dep. High Comr in Bangladesh, 1979-82. *Recreations:* golf, lawn tennis, books, table games. *Address:* c/o Foreign and Commonwealth Office, SW1; Field House, Dover House Road, Roehampton, SW15. *T:* 01-788 5070. *Clubs:* All England Lawn Tennis; Hawks (Cambridge); Kurmitola Golf (Dacca).

HIMMELWEIT, Prof. Hilde T.; Professor of Social Psychology, London School of Economics, University of London, since 1964; *b* Berlin; *d* of S. Litthauer and Feodore Littauer (*née* Remak); *m* 1940, Prof. F. Himmelweit (*d* 1977), MD, FRCPEd; one *d. Educ:* Berlin; Hayes Court, Kent; Newnham Coll., Cambridge. Degrees in Mod. Langs and Psych.; qual. Educational and Clinical Psychologist, 1943; PhD London 1945; Clin. Psychologist, Maudsley Hosp., 1945-48; joined LSE, 1949; Reader in Social Psychology, 1954. Dir Nuffield Television Enquiry, 1954-58; Visiting Professor: Univ. of Calif, Berkeley, 1959; Hebrew Univ., Jerusalem, 1974; Stanford Univ., Calif, 1975; Fellowship to Centre for Advanced Study of Behavioral Sciences, Stanford, Calif, 1967; Fellow, Van Leer Foundn, Jerusalem, 1978-79; Chm., Academic Adv. Cttee of Open Univ., 1969-74; FBPsS 1952; Member: Council, Brit. Psycholog. Soc., 1961-64; Editorial Bds, Brit. Jl of Soc. and Clin. Psychology, 1962-, Jl Communications Research, 1972-, Interdisciplinary Science Reviews; Research Bd, Inst. of Jewish Affairs, 1970-; US SSRC Cttee on TV and Social Behaviour, 1973-79; Annan Cttee on Future of Broadcasting, 1974-77; Trustee, Internat. Broadcasting Inst., 1974-79; Adviser, House of Commons Select Cttee on ITA or IBA, 1972. Vice-Pres., Internat. Soc. of Political Psychology. DUniv Open, 1976. *Publications:* Television and the Child, 1958; How Voters Decide, 1981; articles and chapters on: rôle, structure and effects of broadcasting; attitude development and change; socialization, rôle of school and other instns; societal influences on outlook and behaviour; political attitudes and their change. *Address:* London School of Economics, Houghton Street, WC2. *T:* 01-405 7686.

HIMSWORTH, Eric, CMG 1951; *b* 23 Nov. 1905; *s* of H. Himsworth and M. J. Macdonald; *m* 1941, Ethel Emily, *d* of Major Brook Pratt, DSO, Coldstream Guards; two *s. Educ:* Silcoates Sch., near Wakefield; Merton Coll., Oxford. MA, BCL Oxon; LLB, BSc (Econ.), DPA London. Colonial Administrative Service, 1928-55; Financial Sec., Malaya, 1952-55; UN Technical Assistance Administration, Nepal, 1956-64; IMF Financial Consultant, 1965-71; Consultant, Ta Hing Co., Hong Kong, 1972-81. *Recreation:* travelling. *Address:* 33 Ballachurry Avenue, Onchan, Isle of Man. *Club:* United Oxford & Cambridge University.

HIMSWORTH, Sir Harold (Percival), KCB 1952; MD; FRS 1955; FRCP; Secretary, Medical Research Council, 1949-68, retired (Member and Deputy Chairman, 1967-68); *b* 19 May 1905; *s* of late Arnold Himsworth, Huddersfield, Yorks; *m* 1932, Charlotte, *yr d* of William Gray, Walmer, Kent; two *s. Educ:* King James' Grammar Sch., Almondbury, Yorks; University Coll. and University Coll. Hosp., London. Asst, Medical Unit, University Coll. Hosp., 1930; Beit Memorial Research Fellow, 1932-35; William Julius Mickle Fellow, University of London, 1935; Fellow of University Coll., London, 1936; Deputy Dir, Medical Unit, University Coll. Hospital, 1936; Goulstonian Lecturer, 1939; Oliver-Sharpey Lectr, 1949, RCP; Prof. of Medicine, Univ. of London and Dir of the Medical Unit, University Coll. Hospital, London, 1939-49; Mem. of Medical Research Council, 1948-49; Sydney Ringer Lecturer, 1949; Lowell Lecturer, Boston, Mass, 1947; Harveian Orator, Royal College of Physicians, 1962. Pres., Sect. of Experimental Medicine, Royal Society of Medicine, 1946-47. Chm., Bd of Management, London Sch. of Hygiene and Tropical Med., 1969-76. Prime Warden, Goldsmiths Co., 1975. Docteur *hc* Toulouse, 1950; Hon. LLD: Glasgow, 1953; London, 1956; Wales, 1959; Hon. DSc: Manchester, 1956; Leeds, 1968; Univ. of WI, 1968; Hon. ScD, Cambridge, 1964. New York Univ. Medallist, 1958; Conway Evans Prize, RCP, 1968. Member: Norwegian Med. Soc., 1954; Royal Soc. of Arts and Sciences, Göteborg, Sweden, 1957; Hon. Member: Med. Soc. of Sweden, 1949; Amer. Assoc. of Physicians, 1950; For. Mem., Amer. Philosoph. Soc., 1972; For. Hon. Member: Amer. Acad. of Arts and Sciences, 1957; Belgian Royal Acad. of Medicine, 1958. Hon. FRCR 1958; Hon. FRCPE 1960; Hon. FRSM 1961; Hon. FRCS 1965; Hon. FRCPath 1969; Hon. Fellow LSHTM, 1979; Hon. FRSTM, 1981. *Publications:* The Development and Organisation of Scientific Knowledge, 1970; medical and scientific papers. *Recreation:* fishing. *Address:* 13 Hamilton Terrace, NW8. *T:* 01-286 6996. *Club:* Athenæum.

HINCHCLIFFE, Peter Robert Mossom, CVO 1979; HM Diplomatic Service; Consul-General, Dubai, since 1981; *b* 9 April 1937; *s* of Herbert Peter and Jeannie Hinchcliffe; *m* 1965, Archbold Harriet Siddall; three *d. Educ:* Elm Park, Killylea, Co. Armagh, Prep. Sch.; Radley Coll.; Trinity Coll., Dublin (BA (Hons), MA). Military service, short service commission, W Yorks Regt, 1955-57; TCD, Dublin Univ., 1957-61; HMOCS: West Aden Protectorate, South Arabian Fedn, 1961-67; Admin. Asst, Birmingham Univ., 1968-69; FCO: 1st Sec., Near Eastern Dept, 1969-70; 1st Sec., UK Mission to UN, 1971-74; 1st Sec. and Head of Chancery, Kuwait, 1974-76; Asst Head of Science and Technology and Central and Southern African Depts, FCO, 1976-78; Dep. High Comr, Dar es Salaam, 1978-81. *Recreations:* golf, tennis, philately. *Address:* c/o Foreign and Commonwealth Office, SW1A 2AH. *Clubs:* East India, Devonshire, Sports and Public Schools; North Middlesex Golf; Royal Co. Down Golf (Newcastle, Co. Down).

HINCHEY, Herbert John, CMG 1966; CBE 1955; Financial Adviser to Prime Minister of Mauritius, 1967-72; *b* 13 Feb. 1908; *s* of late Edward and late Mary A. Hinchey, Sydney, NSW; *m* 1944, Amy E., *d* of late William and late Caroline Beddows, Vuni Vasa Estate, Taveuni, Fiji; no *c. Educ:* Sydney Grammar Sch.; University of Sydney; London Sch. of Economics. Bank of New South Wales, Sydney and Brisbane, 1932-40; Colonial Administrative Service, later HMOCS, 1940-65; Financial Secretary: Western Pacific High Commn, 1948-52; Govt of Mauritius, 1952-57; E Africa High Commn/Common Services Organization, 1957-65. Sometime Member: Mauritius Legislative Coun.; E African Central Legislative Assembly; Chairman: E African Industrial Coun.; E African Industrial Research Bd; E African Currency Bd, E African Airways Bd, etc. *Recreations:* reading, writing, walking. *Address:* 45 Launceston Avenue, Banksia Park, Adelaide, SA 5091, Australia. *Clubs:* East India, Devonshire, Sports and Public Schools; Corona; Nairobi (Nairobi).

HINCHINGBROOKE, Viscount; *see* Montagu, J. E. H.

HINCHLIFF, Rev. Canon Peter Bingham, MA, DD Oxon, PhD Rhodes; Chaplain and Fellow, Balliol College, Oxford, since 1972; *b* 25 Feb. 1929; *e s* of Rev. Canon Samuel Bingham Hinchliff and Brenda Hinchliff; *m* 1955, Constance, *d* of E. L. Whitehead, Uitenhage, S Africa; three *s* one *d. Educ:* St Andrew's Coll., Grahamstown, S Africa; Rhodes Univ., Grahamstown; Trinity Coll., Oxford. Deacon, 1952; Priest, 1953, in Anglican Church in S Africa; Asst in Parish of Uitenhage, 1952-55. Subwarden, St Paul's Theological Coll., Grahamstown, 1955-59; Lectr in Comparative Religion, Rhodes Univ., 1957-59; Prof. of Ecclesiastical History, Rhodes Univ., 1960-69; Canon and Chancellor, Grahamstown Cathedral, 1964-69; Sec., Missionary and Ecumenical Council of the General Synod (formerly the Church Assembly), 1969-72; Examng Chaplain to Bishop of Newcastle, 1973, to Bishop of Oxford, 1974-. Public Orator, Rhodes Univ., 1965; Hulsean Lectr, Cambridge Univ., 1975-76; Bampton Lectr, Oxford Univ., 1982. Provincial Hon. Canon, Cape Town Cathedral, 1959-; Hon. Canon, Grahamstown Cathedral, 1969-; Canon Theologian, Coventry Cathedral, 1972-. Pres., Society of Historical Theol., 1978-79. *Publications:* The South African Liturgy, 1959; The Anglican Church in South Africa, 1963; John William Colenso, 1964; The One-Sided Reciprocity, 1966; A Calendar of Cape Missionary Correspondence, 1967; The Church in South Africa, 1968; The Journal of John Ayliff, 1970; Cyprian of Carthage, 1974; (with D. Young) The Human Potential, 1981; Holiness and Politics, 1982; contributor to: Jl of Ecclesiastical History; Studia Liturgica, etc. *Recreations:* crossword puzzles, odd jobbery. *Address:* Balliol College, Oxford.

HINCHLIFF, Stephen, CBE 1976; Chairman, Dexion Group of Companies, since 1976; *b* 11 July 1926; *s* of Gordon Henry and Winifred Hinchliff; *m* 1951, Margaret Arrundale Crossland; one *s* one *d. Educ:* Almondbury Grammar Sch., Huddersfield; Boulevard Nautical Coll., Hull; Huddersfield Coll. of Technology; Cranfield Inst. of Technology (MSc). FIMechE, FIProdE. Production Engr, Dowty Auto Units Ltd, 1953-54; Dowty Seals Ltd: Chief Prodn Engr, 1953-54; Works Manager, 1954-56; Dir, 1956-76; Dep. Man. Dir, 1966-67; Man. Dir, 1967-76; Dep. Chm., Dowty Gp Ltd, 1973-76; Man. Dir, Dowty Gp Industrial Div., 1973-76; Man. Dir, Dexion-Comino Internat. Ltd, 1976-. CBIM; FRSA. *Recreations:* squash, badminton, tennis. *Address:* 18 Newcourt Park, Charlton Kings, Cheltenham, Glos. *T:* Cheltenham 517541.

HIND, Kenneth, ERD 1955; Senior Director, Employment and Industrial Relations, Post Office, 1973-80; *b* 14 March 1920; *er s* of late Harry and Edith Hind; *m* 1942, Dorothy Walton; one *s. Educ:* Central Sec. Sch., Sheffield; Queens' Coll., Cambridge (Munro Schol.). Army, 1940-48: Major, REME. General Post Office: Asst Principal, 1948; Principal, 1950; Asst Sec., 1960; Dir, Radio and Broadcasting, 1967; Central Services, 1969; Senior Dir, 1971. *Recreations:* cricket, gardening. *Address:* 40 Wilbury Crescent, Hove, East Sussex BN3 6FJ. *T:* Brighton 779780.

HINDE, Prof. Robert Aubrey, FRS 1974; Royal Society Research Professor, University of Cambridge, since 1963; Fellow of St John's College, Cambridge, since 1958; *b* 26 Oct. 1923; *s* of late Dr and Mrs E. B. Hinde, Norwich; *m* 1st, 1948, Hester Cecily (marr. diss. 1971), *d* of late C. R. V. Coutts; two *s* two *d* ; 2nd, 1971, Joan Gladys, *d* of F. J. Stevenson; two *d. Educ:* Oundle Sch.; St John's Coll., Cambridge; Balliol Coll., Oxford. Served Coastal Comd, RAF, Flt-Lt, 1941-45. Research Asst, Edward Grey Inst., Univ. of Oxford, 1948-50; Curator, Ornithological Field Station (now sub-Dept of Animal Behaviour), Madingley, Cambridge, 1950-65; St John's Coll., Cambridge: Research Fellow, 1951-54; Steward, 1956-58; Tutor, 1958-63. Hon. Dir, MRC Unit on Develt and Integration of Behaviour, 1970-. Hitchcock Prof., Univ. of California, 1979. For. Hon. Mem., Amer. Acad. of Arts and Sciences, 1974; For. Associate, Nat. Acad. of Scis, USA, 1978; Hon. Fellow, Amer. Ornithologists' Union, 1977; Hon FBPsS 1981. Hon. ScD: Univ. Libre, Brussels, 1974; Univ. of Paris (Nanterre), 1979. Scientific Medal, Zoological Soc., 1961; Leonard Cammer Medal in Psychiatry, Columbia Coll., NY, 1980. *Publications:* Animal Behaviour: a synthesis of Ethology and Comparative Psychology, 1966; (ed) Bird Vocalizations: their relations to current problems in biology and pscyhology, 1969; (ed jtly) Short Term Changes in Neural Activity and Behaviour, 1970; (ed) Non-Verbal Communication, 1972; (ed jtly) Constraints on Learning, 1973; Biological Bases of Human Social Behaviour, 1974; (ed jtly) Growing Points in Ethology, 1976; Towards Understanding Relationships, 1979; Ethology: its nature and relations with other sciences, 1982; sundry papers in biological and psychological journals. *Address:* Park Lane, Madingley, Cambridge. *T:* Madingley 210430.

HINDE, Thomas; see Chitty, Sir Thomas Willes.

HINDERKS, Prof. Hermann Ernst, MA, DrPhil; Professor of German in the Queen's University, Belfast, 1954-70; *b* 19 Dec. 1907; *s* of Elrikus Hinderks and Alma Charlotte Jane (*née* Hildebrand); *m* 1935, Ingeborg (*née* Victor); three *d. Educ:* Lichtwark Schule, Hamburg; Univs of Hamburg, Freiburg i.Br and Basle (MA, DrPhil 1938). Teacher St George's Cathedral Grammar Sch., Capetown, 1935-37; Head of German Dept, Rhodes University Coll., Grahamstown, S Africa, 1938-39; Lecturer in German, University of Cape Town, 1939-53. *Publications:* Friedrich Nietzsche, ein Menschenleben and seine Philosophie (with H. A. Reyburn and J. G. Taylor), 1st edn 1946, 2nd edn 1947 (Eng. version, Nietzsche, The Story of a Human Philosopher, 1948); Uber die Gegenstandsbegriffe in der Kritik der reinen Vernunft, 1948. *Recreations:* music and walking. *Address:* 8821 Gnotzheim, Spielberg 28, Mittelfranken, W Germany.

HINDLEY, Prof. Colin Boothman; Professor of Child Development since 1972, and Director of Centre for Study of Human Development since 1967, Institute of Education, London; *b* Bolton, 1923; *m* 1945; two *s. Educ:* Bolton Sch.; Manchester Univ.; University Coll., London. MB, ChB Manchester 1946; BSc London 1949 (1st cl. Psychol.). Asst Med. Officer, Hope Hosp., Salford; Res. Psychologist and subseq. Sen. Lectr, London Univ. Inst. of Educn, 1949-72; Head of Adolescent Development Dip. Course, 1968-72. Psychol. Adviser, Internat. Children's Centre Growth Studies, Paris, 1954-; Editor, Jl of Child Psychol. and Psychiat., 1959-69; Mem. Council, Brit. Psychol. Soc., 1970-73; Mem. Cttee, Internat. Soc. for Study Behavioural Develt, 1969-75; Mem. Assoc. Child Psychol. and Psychiat. (Chm. 1967-68). FBPsS. *Publications:* chapters in Child Development: International Method of Study, ed Falkner, 1960; Learning Theory and Personality Development, in Psychosomatic Aspects of Paediatrics, ed Mackeith and Sandler, 1961; The Place of Longitudinal Methods in the Study of Development, in Determinants of Behavioural Development, ed Mönks, Hartup and de Wit, 1972; contribs to jls. *Address:* Department of Child Development, Institute of Education, Bedford Way, WC1H 0AL.

HINDLEY, Henry Oliver Rait; *b* 19 June 1906; 3rd *s* of late Sir Clement Hindley; unmarried. *Educ:* Oundle; Trinity Coll., Cambridge; Dundee School of Economics. Industrial Consultant, 1936-40; Treasury, 1940; Air Min., 1940-45; Dir-Gen., Brit. Air Commission, later British Supply Office, USA, 1945-46; Chairman: Northern Divisional Board of National Coal Board, Sept.

1946-47; Raw Cotton Commission, 1947-51. Canadian Civil Servant, 1961; Sec., Adv. Cttee on Broadcasting, 1965; Asst Under-Sec. of State, 1965-69; Dept of Communications, 1969-75. Sec., Cttee on Telecommunications and Canadian Sovereignty, 1979. *Address:* 200 Rideau Terrace 1114, Ottawa, Ontario, K1M 0Z3, Canada.

HINDLEY-SMITH, David Dury, CBE 1972; Registrar, General Dental Council (formerly Dental Board of the UK), 1947-81; Chairman, Council of Royal Dental Hospital, London School of Dental Surgery, since 1981 (Member, since 1976); Member, West Suffolk Health Authority; *b* 20 Feb. 1916; *e s* of late James Dury Hindley-Smith; *m* 1947, Dorothy Westwood Legge, *e d* of Arthur Collins and Mary Fielding; two *d. Educ:* Uppingham; King's Coll., Cambridge (MA); Paris and Vienna. Passed examination for Diplomatic Service, 1939. War Service: Artists' Rifles, 1939; commissioned Royal Fus., 1940; liaison officer to Gén. Leclerc, 1942, to Gén. de Gaulle's first administration, 1944; Acting Col. Vice-Chm., Surrey Assoc. of Youth Clubs, 1950-70 (Vice-Pres., 1970-); Executive Chm., Nat. Assoc. of Youth Clubs, 1970-74 (Vice-Pres., 1974-); Chairman: Sembal Trust, 1972-81; Suffolk Assoc. of Youth, 1982-. Hon. Mem., BDA, 1975; Hon. FDS RCSEd, 1977; Hon. FDS RCS, 1980. Cecil Peace Prize, 1938. *Recreations:* gardening, writing English. *Address:* The Ark House, Whepstead, Bury St Edmunds, Suffolk. *T:* Horringer 351. *Club:* Boodle's.

HINDLIP, 5th Baron *cr* 1886; **Henry Richard Allsopp;** Bt 1880; *b* 1 July 1912; 2nd *s* of 3rd Baron Hindlip and Agatha (*d* 1962), 2nd *d* of late John C. Thynne; *S* brother, 4th Baron, 1966; *m* 1939, Cecily Valentine Jane, *o d* of late Lt-Col Malcolm Borwick, DSO, Hazelbech Hill, Northampton; two *s* one *d. Educ:* Eton; RMC Sandhurst. 2nd Lieut, Coldstream Guards, 1932; Major, 1941; retired, 1948. Served War of 1939-45; NW Europe, 1944. JP 1957, DL 1956, Wilts. Bronze Star Medal, USA, 1945. *Recreations:* travel, shooting. *Heir: s* Hon. Charles Henry Allsopp [*b* 5 Aug. 1940; *m* 1968, Fiona Victoria, *d* of Hon. William McGowan; one *s* two *d*]. *Address:* The Dower House, Charlton, Malmesbury, Wilts. *T:* Malmesbury 3503. *Clubs:* White's, Pratt's, Turf.

See also Sir R. J. Hardy, Bt.

HINDMARSH, Frederick Bell; Under-Secretary, Department of Health and Social Security, 1973-79, retired; *b* 31 Jan. 1919; *yr s* of Frederick Hindmarsh and Margaret May Hindmarsh; *m* 1947, Mary Torrance Coubrough; one *d. Educ:* County Grammar Sch., Acton. Clerical Officer, Min. of Health, 1936; Exec. Officer, 1937. Served war, Army, 1939-46. Min. of Pensions and Nat. Insurance and Min. of Social Security: Higher Exec. Officer, 1946; Sen. Exec. Officer, 1947; Chief Exec. Officer, 1951; Sen. Chief Exec. Officer, 1959; Prin. Exec. Officer, 1964; Asst Sec., DHSS, 1969. *Recreation:* music. *Address:* 3 Hawthorn Close, Nascot Wood Road, Watford, Herts WD1 3SB. *T:* Watford 36769.

HINDMARSH, Irene, JP, MA; Principal, St Aidan's College, University of Durham, since 1970; Second Pro-Vice-Chancellor, University of Durham, since 1982; *b* 22 Oct. 1923; *d* of Albert Hindmarsh and Elizabeth (*née* White). *Educ:* Heaton High Sch.; Lady Margaret Hall, Oxford (MA Hons French); King's Coll., Univ. of Durham (PGCE). Taught at St Paul's Girls' Sch., London, 1947-49, Rutherford High Sch., Newcastle upon Tyne, 1949-55; Interchange Teacher, Lycée de Jeunes Filles, Dax, Landes, France, 1954-55; Lectr in Educn and French, King's Coll., Durham, 1959-64; Headmistress, Birkenhead High Sch., GPDST, 1964-70. Vis. Prof., New York State Univ., Syracuse, Cornell, Harvard, 1962; Delegate of Internat. Fedn of Univ. Women to UNO, NY, to Commns on Human Rights and Status of Women, 1962; Vis. Prof., Fu-Dan Univ., Shanghai, 1979, and again, 1980. Delegate/Translator to internat. confs of FIPESO, 1963-70; Chairman: Internat. Cttee of Headmistresses' Assoc., 1966-70; Internat. Panel of Joint Four, 1967-70. Editor, Internat. Bull. of AHM, 1966-70. JP Birkenhead 1966, Durham 1974. *Publications:* various articles on educnl topics in AGM papers of Assoc. of Head Mistresses; contribs to prelim. papers of FIPESO meetings; seminar papers to symposia on lit. topics, Sèvres, under auspices of Council of Europe; contrib. re St Aidan's to Durham History from the Air. *Recreations:* travel, music, theatre, films. *Address:* St Aidan's College, Durham DH1 3LJ. *T:* Durham 65011.

HINDSON, William Stanley, CMG 1962; BScEng, MIM, FIMechE; engineering and metallurgical consultant since 1974; *b* 11 Jan. 1920; *s* of late W. A. L. Hindson, Darlington; *m* 1944, Mary Sturdy (*d* 1961); one *s* one *d* ; *m* 1965, Catherine Leikine, Paris, France; one *s. Educ:* Darlington Grammar Sch.; Coatham Sch., Redcar. With Dorman Long (Steel) Ltd, Middlesbrough, 1937-55; Metallurgical Equipment Export Co. Ltd and Indian Steelworks Construction Co. Ltd, 1956-62; Wellman Engineering Corp. Ltd, 1963-69; Cementation Co. Ltd, 1970-71; Humphreys & Glasgow, 1971-74. Mem., Inst. of Directors. *Recreations:* chess, philately. *Address:* 36 Eresby House, Rutland Gate, SW7. *T:* 01-589 3194.

HINE, Air Vice-Marshal Patrick Bardon; Assistant Chief of Air Staff (Policy), Ministry of Defence, since 1979; *b* 14 July 1932; parents decd; *m* 1956, Jill Adèle (*née* Gardner); three *s. Educ:* Peter Symonds Sch., Winchester. Served with Nos 1, 93 and 111 Sqdns, 1952-60; Mem., Black Arrows aerobatic team, 1957-59; commanded: No 92 Sqdn, 1962-64; No 17 Sqdn, 1970-71; RAF Wildenrath, 1974-75; Dir, Public Relations (RAF), 1975-77; RCDS 1978; SASO, HQ RAF, Germany, 1979. Queen's Commendation for Valuable Service in the Air, 1960. FBIM. Winner, Carris Trophy, Hants, IoW and Channel Islands Golf Championship, and Brabazon Trophy, 1949; English Schoolboy Golf Internat., 1948-49; Inter-Services Golf, 1952-57. *Recreations:* golf, squash, caravanning, photography. *Address:* Belmont, Clappins Lane, Naphill, near High Wycombe, Bucks. *T:* Naphill 2488. *Clubs:* Royal Air Force; Ashridge Golf.

HINES, Prof. Albert Gregorio; Professor of Economics, University of London, and Head of Department of Economics, Birkbeck College, since 1972; *b* 8 Oct. 1935; Jamaican; *m* 1962, June Rosemary Chesney Carcas (marr. diss. 1976); two *s* one *d. Educ:* Victoria Town Sch., Manchester; London Sch. of Economics, Univ. of London (BSc Econ). Asst Lectr, Univ. of Bristol, 1962-64; Lectr, University Coll. London, 1964-68; Prof. of Economics, Univ. of Durham, 1968-72. Vis. Prof., Massachusetts Inst. of Technology, 1971-72. Vice-Pres., Section F, British Assoc. for the Advancement of Science, 1970-71. Economist, Overseas Development Ministry, 1965-66. Mem., Gen. Adv. Council, BBC, 1974-; Chairman: Enquiry into Minority Arts in UK, 1975; Commn for Economic Stabilisation, Jamaica, 1975-. *Publications:* On the Reappraisal of Keynesian Economics, 1971; articles in: Economic Jl, Review of Economic Studies, Review of Economics and Statistics, Amer. Economic Review, The Times. *Recreations:* theatre, cinema, music, novels, cricket, walking. *Address:* Department of Economics, Birkbeck College, 7/15 Gresse Street, W1P 1PA. *Club:* National Liberal.

HINES, Sir Colin (Joseph), Kt 1976; OBE 1973; President: NSW Returned Services League Clubs Association, since 1971; NSW Branch, Returned Services League of Australia, since 1971; Deputy National President, Returned Services League of Australia, since 1974; *b* 16 Feb. 1919; *s* of J. Hines and Mrs Hines, Lyndhurst, NSW; *m* 1942, Jean Elsie, *d* of A. Wilson, Mandurama, NSW; two *s. Educ:* All Saints' Coll., Bathurst, NSW. Army, 1937-45. Farmer and grazier, 1946-71. Hon. Officer, Returned Services League of Aust., 1971-76. State Comr, Aust. Forces Overseas Fund, 1971-; Trustee, Anzac Meml Trust, 1971-. Chairman: War Veterans Homes, Narrabeen, 1971-; Clubs Mutual Services Ltd, 1972-. *Recreations:* rifle shooting, golf. *Address:* The Meadows, Lyndhurst, NSW 2741, Australia. *T:* Lyndhurst 17. *Club:* Imperial Services (Sydney, NSW).

HINES, Gerald; *see* Hines, V. G.

HINES, His Honour (Vivian) Gerald, QC 1964; a Circuit Judge, 1972-79, retired (Chairman, North East London Quarter Sessions, 1965-68, Greater London Quarter Sessions (Middlesex Area), 1969, Greater London Quarter Sessions (Inner London), 1969-71); *b* 24 Dec. 1912; 2nd *s* of late John Hines and Lizzie Emily (*née* Daniells), Essex; *m* 1st, 1950, Janet Graham, MA (*d* 1957), *e d* of late John Graham, Wigtownshire; 2nd, 1960, Barbara, *y d* of late Herbert Gunton, Colchester. *Educ:* Earls Colne Grammar Sch. Admitted Solicitor, 1935; private practice, 1935-42; Clerk to Colchester Borough Justices, 1942; called to Bar, Inner Temple, 1943; South-Eastern Circuit. Dep. Chairman: Essex QS, 1955-67; County of London QS, 1965; Judge of the Central Criminal Court, 1968-69. Mem., Home Office Adv. Council on the Penal System, 1970-. Member: Council, Magistrates' Assoc., 1967-70; Standing Joint Cttee, Essex, 1962-65. Governor, New Coll., London, 1963-65; Member: Court of Essex Univ., 1966-; Council of Boy Scouts' Assoc., 1961-66; Essex CC, 1946-49. JP Essex, 1955, Greater London, 1965-79. Freeman, City of London, 1975. Liveryman, Fan Makers' Co., 1976. *Publications:* Judicial Discretion in Sentencing, 1982; contrib. to Halsbury's Laws of England, 4th edn (Criminal Law Vol.); articles in British Jl of Criminology, The Magistrate, Reform and other jls. *Address:* Littlefield, Great Bentley, Colchester, Essex CO7 8QE. *T:* Great Bentley 250555.

HINGLEY, Anthony Capper Moore, CVO 1954; *b* 28 Nov. 1908; *e s* of late Lieut-Col S. H. Hingley and Dorothy, *d* of Thomas Capper; *m* 1947, Ruth, *d* of late C. P. Andrews; two *s* one *d. Educ:* Rugby Sch.; Trinity Coll., Oxford (MA). Ceylon Civil Service, 1931-47; Asst Establishment Officer, Kenya, 1947-49; Chief Establishment Officer, Nyasaland, 1949-50; Sec. to Governor-Gen., Ceylon, 1950-54; Chief Establishment Officer, Nyasaland, 1954-60; seconded as Mem., Interim Federal Public Service Commn, Fedn of Rhodesia and Nyasaland, 1955-59; Establishments Adviser, Seychelles, 1965. *Recreations:* golf, bridge. *Address:* Jester's, Queen Square, North Curry, Taunton, Som. *Clubs:* East India, Devonshire, Sports and Public Schools; Somerset County.

HINGSTON, Lt-Col Walter George, OBE 1964; psc; FRGS; *b* Radcliffe on Trent, Notts, 15 Feb. 1905; *s* of late Charles Hingston and late Mildred (*née* Pleydell Bouverie), Cotgrave, Nottingham; *m* 1939, Elizabeth Margaret, *d* of late Brig. Sir Clinton Lewis, OBE, and late Lilian Eyre (*née* Wace); two *d. Educ:* Harrow; RMC Sandhurst; and Staff Coll. 2nd Lieut, KOYLI, 1925; Nigeria Regt, RWAFF, 1931-36; 1st Punjab Regt, Indian Army, 1936. Served War of 1939-45: 4th Indian Div., North Africa, Eritrea (despatches); Dep. Dir Public Relations, GHQ India, 1942; Chief Information Officer to C-in-C, Ceylon, 1943; retired (invalided), 1945. Chief Information Officer, Dept of Scientific and Industrial Research, 1945-63; Editor, the Geographical Magazine, 1963-68. Mem., Marlborough and Ramsbury RDC, 1970-74. *Publications:* The Tiger Strikes, 1942; The Tiger Kills (with G. R. Stevens), 1944; Never Give Up, 1948. *Recreation:* fishing. *Address:* The Old Vicarage, Ramsbury, Marlborough, Wilts. *Club:* Army and Navy.

HINSLEY, Prof. Francis Harry, OBE 1946; FBA 1981; Vice-Chancellor, University of Cambridge, 1981-Oct. 1983; Master of St John's College, since 1979 (Fellow, 1944-79; President, 1975-79), and Professor of the History of International Relations, since 1969; *b* 26 Nov. 1918; *s* of Thomas Henry and Emma Hinsley; *m* 1946, Hilary Brett, *d* of H. F. B. and Helena Brett-Smith, Oxford; two *s* one *d. Educ:* Queen Mary's Grammar Sch., Walsall; St John's Coll., Cambridge. HM Foreign Office, war service, 1939-46; Research Fellow, St John's Coll., Cambridge, 1944-50; Lectr in History, Univ. of Cambridge, 1949-65; Tutor, St John's Coll., Cambridge, 1956-63; Editor, The Historical Journal, 1960-71; Reader in the History of International Relations, Univ. of Cambridge, 1965-69. Chm., Faculty Bd of History, Cambridge, 1970-72; Lees-Knowles Lectr on Military Science, Trinity Coll., 1970-71. UK Rep., Provisional Academic Cttee for European Univ. Inst., 1973-75. Hon. Fellow, TCD, 1981. *Publications:* Command of the Sea, 1950; Hitler's Strategy, 1951; (ed) New Cambridge Modern History, Vol. XI, 1962; Power and the Pursuit of Peace, 1963; Sovereignty, 1966; Nationalism and the International System, 1973; (ed) British Foreign Policy under Sir Edward Grey, 1977; (jtly) British Intelligence in the Second World War, vol. 1, 1979, vol. 2, 1981. *Address:* The Master's Lodge, St John's College, Cambridge. *T:* Cambridge 61621.

HINSLEY, Prof. Frederick Baden, DSc; FEng; Professor of Mining and Head of Department of Mining Engineering, University of Nottingham, 1947-67, now Emeritus; *b* 20 May 1900; *m* 1932, Doris Lucy Spencer; three *s* two *d. Educ:* Coalville Technical Coll.; University of Birmingham. Lecturer and Vice-Principal, County Technical Coll., Worksop, 1932-39; Lecturer in Dept of Mining, University Coll., Cardiff, 1939-47. Pres. IMinE, 1968. Silver medal, Warwicks and S Staffs Inst. of Mining Engineers, 1940; Gold medal, South Wales Inst. of Engineers, 1946; Silver medal, Midland Counties Instn of Engineers, 1951; Douglas Hay medal, 1955, Institution Medal, 1971, Instn of Mining Engineers; Van Waterschoot Van der Gracht medal, Royal Geol. and Mining Soc. of the Netherlands, 1962. *Publications:* contribs to: Proc. S Wales Inst. of Engineers; Proc. Nat. Assoc. of Colliery Managers; Trans Instn of Mining Engineers. *Recreations:* writing history of mining, gardening, reading. *Address:* 7 Puller Road, Boxmoor, Hemel Hempstead, Herts HP1 1QL. *T:* Hemel Hempstead 62011.

HINTON, family name of **Baron Hinton of Bankside.**

HINTON OF BANKSIDE, Baron *cr* 1965 (Life Peer); **Christopher Hinton,** OM 1976; KBE 1957; Kt 1951; FRS 1954; MA; Hon. FICE; Hon. FIMechE; Hon. FIEE; FIChemE; FRSA; *b* 12 May 1901; *s* of late Frederick Henry Hinton, Lacock, Wilts; *m* 1931, Lillian (*d* 1973), *d* of late Thomas Boyer; one *d. Educ:* Chippenham Grammar Sch.; Trinity Coll., Cambridge. Engineering apprenticeship, GWR Co., Swindon, 1917-23; Trinity Coll., Cambridge, 1923-26 (senior scholarship, 1st Class Hons Mech. Sciences Tripos, John Winbolt Prize, Second Yeats Prize). ICI (Alkali), Northwich, 1926-40 (Chief Engineer, 1931-40); on loan from ICI to Ministry of Supply, 1940-46 (Dep. Dir-Gen. of Filling Factories, 1942-46); Dep. Controller Atomic Energy (Production), Min. of Supply, 1946-54; Mem. of Board for Engineering and Production, and Man. Dir (Industrial Gp), UKAEA, 1954-57; Chairman: Central Electricity Generating Board, 1957-64; Internat. Exec. Cttee of World Energy Conf., 1962-68; Dep. Chm., Electricity Supply Research Coun., 1965-; Special Adviser to the Internat. Bank for Reconstruction and Develt, 1965-70; Chancellor of Bath Univ., 1966-80. President: CE1, 1976-; Fellowship of Engineering, 1976-81. Hon. Fellow of Trinity Coll., Cambridge, 1957; Hon. Associate, Manchester Coll. of Science and Technology. Hon. DEng, Liverpool, 1955; Hon. DSc (Eng), London, 1956; Hon. ScD, Cambridge, 1960; Hon. LLD, Edinburgh, 1958; Hon. DSc: Oxford, 1957; Southampton, 1962; Durham, 1966; Bath, 1966. Albert Medal (RSA), 1957; Melchett Medal, Inst. of Fuel, 1957; Glazebrook Medal and Prize, 1966; Rumford Medal (Royal Soc.); Axel Johnson Prize, Roy. Swedish Acad. of Engrg; Wilhelm-Exner Medal, Osterreichischer Gewerbeverein; Castner Medal, Soc. of Chem. Industries; James Watt Internat. Medal, IMechE. Pres., IMechE, 1966-67. Hon. Fellow: Metals Soc.; Instn of Gas Engineers; Inst. of Welding; Welding Soc.; IMunE; Hon. MASME. For. Associate, Amer. Acad. of Engineering; Corresp. Mem., Mexican Acad. of Engineering; Mem., Eur. Acad. of Arts, Sciences and Humanities. Imperial Order of The Rising Sun (Japan), 1966. *Publications:* Engineers and Engineering, 1970; Heavy Current Electricity in the United Kingdom: history and development, 1979. *Address:* Tiverton Lodge, Dulwich Common, SE21 7EW. *T:* 01-693 6447.

HINTON, Prof. Denys James, FRIBA; Chairman, Redditch New Town Development Corporation, since 1978; *b* 12 April 1921; *s* of James and Nell Hinton; *m* 1971, Lynette Payne (*née* Pattinson); one *d. Educ:* Reading Sch.; Architectural Assoc. (MSc; AADip.). FRIBA. Asst, Wells Coates, 1950-52; Birmingham Sch. of Architecture: Lectr, 1952-57; Sen. Lectr, 1957-64; Dir, 1964-72; Prof. of Architecture, Univ. of Aston, 1966-81, now Emeritus. Sen. Partner, Hinton Brown Langstone, Architects, Warwick. Vice-Chm., Exec. Cttee, Internat. New Towns Assoc., 1980-. *Publications:* Performance Characteristics of the Athenian Bouleterion, RIBA Athens Bursary, 1962; Great Interiors: High Victorian Period, 1967; contrib. RIBA and Architects Jl, papers on architectural education, Inst. Bulletin (worship and religious architecture), Univ. of Birmingham. *Recreations:* travel, moving house, water colours. *Address:* 26 Frederick Road, Edgbaston, Birmingham B15 1JN. *T:* 021-454 0350.

HINTON, Michael Herbert; partner in City chartered accountants; *b* 10 Nov. 1934; *s* of late Walter Leonard Hinton and of Freda Millicent Lillian Hinton;

m 1955, Sarah (*née* Sunderland); one *s* two *d*. *Educ:* Ardingly Coll. FCA. Liveryman: Farmers' Co., 1964 (Master, 1981-82); Wheelwrights' Co., 1971; Mem. Court of Common Council, 1970-71, Alderman, 1971-79, Ward of Billingsgate; Clerk to Wheelwrights' Co., 1965-71; Sheriff, City of London, 1977-78. *Recreations:* cricket, collector, City of London interests. *Address:* 178 Burges Road, Thorpe Bay, Essex. *T:* Shoeburyness 2685. *Clubs:* Farmers, MCC, City Livery (Pres., 1976-77).

HINTON, Nicholas John; Director, National Council for Voluntary Organisations (formerly National Council of Social Service), since 1977; *b* 15 March 1942; *s* of Rev. Canon Hinton and late Mrs J. P. Hinton; *m* 1971, Deborah Mary Vivian. *Educ:* Marlborough Coll., Wiltshire; Selwyn Coll., Cambridge (MA). Asst Dir, Northorpe Hall Trust, 1965-68; Nat. Assoc. for Care and Resettlement of Offenders, 1968-77, Dir, 1973-77. Member: Central Council for Educn and Trng in Social Work, 1974-79; Stonham Housing Assoc., 1976-79; Exec. Cttee, London Voluntary Service Council; Cttee of Inquiry into UK Prison Services, 1978-79; Exec Cttees, Councils of Social Service, NI, Scotland and Wales; Exec. Cttee, Business in the Community; Trustee: Charities Aid Foundn; Burnbake Trust. Dir, Edington Music Festival, 1965-70. FRSA 1981. *Recreation:* music. *Address:* 26 Bedford Square, WC1B 3HU. *T:* 01-636 4066.

HINTZ, Orton Sutherland, CMG 1968; former Editor, The New Zealand Herald, Auckland, New Zealand, 1958-70; Trustee, Woolf Fisher Trust (educational); Member, Central North Island Wildlife Conservancy Council; *b* 15 Nov. 1907; *s* of late Alfred and late Cora Hintz; *m* 1st, 1931, Flora Margaret McIver (*d* 1943); 2nd, 1965, Caroline Jean Crawford (*née* Hutchinson). *Educ:* Mt Albert Grammar Sch., Auckland; Auckland Univ. Joined NZ Herald Staff, 1925; Parly Corresp., 1935-38; War service, Naval Intelligence, 1941-46; Night Ed., NZ Herald, 1946; Assoc. Ed., NZ Herald, 1952; Dir, Wilson & Horton Ltd, 1961; Dir, NZ Press Assoc., 1962 (Chm., 1965-66); Reuters Trustee, 1964-68. Mem. Coun., Outward Bound Trust of NZ, 1961; Delegate, Commonwealth Press Conf., India and Pakistan, 1961. *Publications:* The New Zealanders in England, 1931; HMNZS Philomel, 1944; Trout at Taupo, 1955; (ed) Lord Cobham's Speeches, 1962; Fisherman's Paradise, 1975. *Recreations:* trout fishing (Pres. Lake Taupo Angling Fedn, 1970-81), cricket, Rugby football. *Address:* 36 Oregon Drive, Rainbow Point, Taupo, NZ. *T:* 85-568. *Clubs:* Anglers' (New York); Northern (Auckland).

HIPKIN, John; Head of English, Meridian School, Royston, Herts, since 1977; *b* 9 April 1935; *s* of Jack Hipkin and Elsie Hipkin; *m* 1963, Bronwyn Vaughan Dewey; four *s* one *d*. *Educ:* Surbiton Grammar Sch. for Boys; LSE (BScEcon). Asst Teacher, 1957-65; Research Officer: King's Coll., Cambridge, 1965-68; Univ. of East Anglia, 1968-71; Sec., Schools Council Working Party on Whole Curriculum, 1973-74; Dir, Adv. Centre for Educn, 1974-77. *Publications:* (jtly) New Wine in Old Bottles, 1967; (ed jtly) Education for the Seventies, 1970; The Massacre of Peterloo (a play), 1968, 2nd edn 1974. *Recreations:* theatre, photography, history, modern music. *Address:* 82 Chesterton Road, Cambridge CB4 1ER. *T:* Cambridge 67038.

HIPPISLEY-COX, Peter Denzil John; solicitor and parliamentary agent; Senior Partner, Dyson, Bell & Co., London, since 1976; Chairman, Equity & Law Life Assurance Society, since 1977; *b* 22 May 1921; *s* of late Col Sir Geoffrey Hippisley Cox, CBE, and Lady Hippisley Cox; *m* 1st, 1948, Olga Kay (marr. diss. 1956); one *d*; 2nd, 1956, Frieda Marion Wood; two *d*. *Educ:* Stowe; Trinity Coll., Cambridge (MA). Served War, RAF (Signals), 1941-46 (Flt Lieut). Admitted a solicitor, 1949. Dir, Equity & Law Life Assurance Soc., 1965- (Dep. Chm. 1973). Member: Council, Law Soc., 1956-81; Court, Drapers' Co., 1972- (Warden, 1981-). Governor, Bancroft's Sch., 1975-. *Recreation:* music. *Address:* 95 Dovehouse Street, Chelsea, SW3 6JZ. *T:* 01-352 4608. *Club:* Carlton.

HIPWELL, Hermine H.; see Vivenot, Baroness R. de.

HIRAHARA, Tsuyoshi; Ambassador of Japan to the Court of St James's, since 1982; *b* 25 Oct. 1920; *m* Kiyo Nishi; two *d*. *Educ:* Faculty of Law, Tokyo Univ. Dep. Dir-Gen. for Gen. Affairs, Economic Affairs Bureau, Min. of For. Affairs, 1962; Consul-Gen., Milan, 1964; Minister, Brussels, 1966; Dep. Dir-Gen., 1969, Dir-Gen., 1970, Economic Affairs Bureau, Min. of For. Affairs; Ambassador to: Morocco, 1972; OECD, Paris, 1975-80. Commander: Legion of Honour (France); Ordre de la Couronne (Belgium); Grand Officer: Ordre de Leopold II (Belgium); Order of Ouissam Alaouit Cherifiam (Morocco). *Recreation:* golf. *Address:* Japanese Embassy, 46 Grosvenor Street, W1X 0BA. *T:* 01-493 6030.

HIRSCH, Prof. Kurt August; Emeritus Professor of Pure Mathematics, University of London, Queen Mary College; *b* Berlin, 12 Jan. 1906; *s* of Dr Robert Hirsch and Anna (*née* Lehmann); *m* 1928, Elsa Brühl; one *s* two *d*. *Educ:* University of Berlin; University of Cambridge. Dr phil (Berlin), 1930; PhD (Cambridge), 1937. Asst Lecturer, later Lecturer, University Coll., Leicester, 1938-47; Lecturer, later Sen. Lecturer, King's Coll., Newcastle upon Tyne, 1948-51; Reader, University of London, Queen Mary Coll., 1951-57, Prof., 1957-73. Editor, Russian Mathematical Surveys. *Publications:* (with A. G. Kurosh) Theory of Groups, 2 vols, 2nd English edn 1954; (with F. R. Gantmacher) Theory of Matrices, 2 vols, English edn 1960; (with A. G. Kurosh) Lectures on General Algebra, English edn 1964; (with I. R. Shafarevich) Basic Algebraic Geometry, 1974; contribs to learned jls.

Recreations: chess, gardening. *Address:* 101 Shirehall Park, NW4 2QU. *T:* 01-202 7902.

HIRSCH, Prof. Sir Peter (Bernhard), Kt 1975; MA, PhD; FRS 1963; Isaac Wolfson Professor of Metallurgy in the University of Oxford since 1966; Fellow, St Edmund Hall, Oxford, since 1966; Chairman, United Kingdom Atomic Energy Authority, since 1982; *b* 16 Jan. 1925; *s* of Ismar Hirsch and Regina Meyerson; *m* 1959, Mabel Anne Kellar (*née* Stephens), *widow* of James Noel Kellar; one step *s* one step *d*. *Educ:* Sloane Sch., Chelsea; St Catharine's Coll., Cambridge (Hon. Fellow, 1982). BA 1946; MA 1950; PhD 1951. Reader in Physics in Univ. of Cambridge, 1964-66; Fellow, Christ's Coll., Cambridge, 1960-66, Hon. Fellow, 1978. Has been engaged on researches with electron microscope on imperfections in crystalline structure of metals and on relation between structural defects and mechanical properties. Chm., Metallurgy and Materials Cttee and Mem., Eng. Bd, SRC, 1970-73; Member: Elec. Supply Res. Council, 1969-; UKAEA, 1982-. Rosenhain Medal, Inst. of Metals, 1961; C. V. Boys Prize, Inst. of Physics and Physical Soc., 1962; Clamer Medal, Franklin Inst., 1970; Wihuri Internat. Prize, Helsinki, 1971; Royal Soc. Hughes Medal, 1973; Metals Soc. Platinum Medal, 1976; Royal Medal, Royal Soc., 1977. Hon. Fellow: RMS, 1977; Japan Soc. of Electron Microscopy, 1979. Hon. DSc: Newcastle, 1979; City, 1979; Northwestern, 1982. *Publications:* Electron Microscopy of Thin Crystals (with others), 1965; (ed) The Physics of Metals, vol. 2, Defects, 1975; numerous contribs learned jls. *Recreation:* walking. *Address:* United Kingdom Atomic Energy Authority, 11 Charles II Street, SW1Y 4QP. *T:* 01-930 5454; Department of Metallurgy and Science of Materials, Parks Road, Oxford OX1 3PH. *T:* Oxford 59981; 104A Lonsdale Road, Oxford OX2 7ET.

HIRSHFIELD, family name of **Baron Hirshfield.**

HIRSHFIELD, Baron *cr* 1967, of Holborn in Greater London (Life Peer); **Desmond Barel Hirshfield;** Joint Senior Partner, Stoy Horwath & Co., Chartered Accountants; Consultant, Stoy Hayward & Co.; Chairman, Horwath & Horwath (UK) Ltd; President, Horwath & Horwath International; Founder and Chairman, Trades Union Unit Trust Managers Ltd, since 1961; Chairman, MLH Consultants, since 1981; Founder and Director, Foundation on Automation and Human Development, since 1962; *b* 17 May 1913; *s* of late Leopold Hirshfield and Lily Hirshfield (*née* Blackford); *m* 1951, Bronia Eisen. *Educ:* City of London Sch. Chartered Accountant, 1939; Mem., Cttee on Consumer Credit, 1968-71; Dep. Chm., Northampton New Town Develt Corp., 1968-76; Member: Central Adv. Water Cttee, 1969-70; Top Salaries Review Body, 1975-; Admin. Trustee, Chevening Estate, 1970-81; Pres., Brit. Assoc. of Hotel Accountants, 1969-; Treasurer: UK Cttee of UNICEF, 1969-; Nat. Council for the Unmarried Mother and her Child, 1970-71. President: Norwood Charitable Trust, 1960-; Norwood Foundn, 1977-. Capt., British Team, World Maccabi Games, Prague, 1934. *Publications:* pamphlets and reports on The Accounts of Charitable Institutions; Avoidance and Evasion of Income Tax; Scheme for Pay as You Earn; Investment of Trade Union Funds; Organisations and Methods Reviews; articles in periodicals and newspapers. *Recreations:* travel, painting, caricaturing. *Address:* 54 Baker Street, W1M 1DJ. *T:* 01-486 5888.

HIRST, Hon. Sir David (Cozens-Hardy), Kt 1982; Hon. Mr Justice Hirst; a Judge of the High Court, Queen's Bench Division, since 1982; *b* 31 July 1925; *er s* of late Thomas William Hirst and of Margaret Joy Hirst, Aylsham, Norfolk; *m* 1951, Pamela Elizabeth Molesworth Bevan, *d* of Col T. P. M. Bevan, MC; three *s* two *d*. *Educ:* Eton (Fellow, 1976); Trinity Coll., Cambridge. MA. Served 1943-47; RA and Intelligence Corps, Capt. 1946. Barrister, Inner Temple, 1951, Bencher, 1974; QC 1965; Vice-Chm. of the Bar, 1977-78, Chm., 1978-79. Member: Lord Chancellor's Law Reform Cttee; Council on Tribunals, 1966-80; Cttee to review Defamation Act, 1952, 1971-74. *Recreations:* shooting, lawn tennis, theatre and opera, growing vegetables. *Address:* Royal Courts of Justice, Strand, WC2A 2LL. *Clubs:* Boodle's, MCC.

HIRST, Geoffrey Audus Nicholson, TD 1945; *b* 14 Dec. 1904; *s* of late Col E. A. Hirst, CMG, TD, Ingmanthorpe Hall, Wetherby, Yorks. *Educ:* Charterhouse; St John's Coll., Cambridge. Former Director: Samuel Webster & Sons Ltd; J. Hey & Co. Ltd; Hey & Humphries Ltd; Spinks (Caterers) Ltd; FBI: Mem. Grand Council and Executive Cttee, 1932-40, 1958-65; Mem. Economic Policy Cttee; Mem. Leeds Exec., 1930-46; East and West Riding Council and Exec., 1946-65, Vice-Chm., 1956, Chm., 1958-60. Mem. of Council, CBI: Mem., Economic Cttee, East and West Ridings and Humberside (Yorks) Regional Council, 1965-69. Leeds Chamber of Commerce: Mem. Council, 1932-; Junior Vice-Pres., 1948-49; Senior Vice-Pres., 1949-51; Pres., 1952-54; Mem. Council, Bradford Chamber of Commerce, 1950-70; Vice-Pres., Urban Dist Councils' Assoc., 1951-70; Mem., Nat. Advisory Council for Educn in Industry and Commerce, 1948-51; Chm., Yorks Regional Academic Bd, 1947-49; Mem., Leeds and Hull Academic Board, 1947-53 (Chm. 1949-50); Mem., Yorks Council for Further Educn, 1934-40 and 1949-51; Leeds Coll. of Technology: Mem. Bd of Governors, 1932-40; Vice-Chm., 1932-36 and 1938-40. Member: Leeds Nat. Service Cttee, 1938-40; UK Council of European Movement; Economic League, Central Council, 1934-67. Chm., W Yorks Regional Council and Exec., 1945-50; Mem., Nat. Council, Inst. of Marketing and Sales Management, 1932-35, 1960-62; Leeds Executive: Mem., 1930-; Chm., 1932-33; Pres., 1949-50; Vice-Pres. W Yorks Branch, English-Speaking Union. MP (C)

Shipley Div., WR Yorks, 1950-70; Hon. Sec., Conservative Party's Parliamentary Trade and Industry Cttee, 1959-61, Vice-Chm., 1962, Chm., 1963-64. Mem., Parly Delegns to Malta, 1965, Holland, 1966. Member: Leeds Musical Festival Exec., 1934-54; Leeds Philharmonic Soc. Exec., 1930-39. FCS, FSS, FREconS, FInstMSM. TA, 1924-32, rejoined, 1939; served War of 1939-45; Battery Comdr, second in Comd 69th Fd Regt, RA, 1939-44; attached to Staff, 21 Army Gp, 1945. *Publications:* various contribs to the Press. *Recreations:* travel, music. *Address:* 3 King Gardens, Hove BN3 2PE. *T:* Brighton 727978. *Club:* Boodle's.

HIRST, Prof. John Malcolm, DSC 1945; PhD; FRS 1970; FIBiol; Director, Long Ashton Research Station, and Professor of Agricultural and Horticultural Science, Bristol University, since 1975; *b* 20 April 1921; *s* of Maurice Herbert Hirst and Olive Mary (*née* Pank); *m* 1957, Barbara Mary Stokes; two *d. Educ:* Solihull Sch.; Reading University. PhD London 1955. Royal Navy (Coastal Forces), 1941-46; Reading Univ. (BSc Hons Agric. Bot.), 1946-50; Rothamsted Exper. Stn., Harpenden, 1950-75, Hd of Plant Pathology Dept, 1967-75. Vice-Chm. Tech. Adv. Cttee, Consultative Gp, Internat. Agricl Research. Jakob Eriksson Gold Medal (Internat. Botanical Congress), 1959; Research Medal, RASE, 1970. *Publications:* papers in scientific jls mainly in Trans British Mycological Soc., Annals of Applied Biology, Jl of General Microbiology. *Address:* Long Ashton Research Station, Long Ashton, Bristol BS18 9AF. *T:* Long Ashton 2181.

HIRST, Prof. Paul Heywood; Professor of Education, University of Cambridge, and Fellow of Wolfson College (formerly University College), Cambridge, since 1971; *b* 10 Nov. 1927; *s* of late Herbert and Winifred Hirst, Birkby, Huddersfield. *Educ:* Huddersfield Coll.; Trinity Coll., Cambridge. BA 1948, MA 1952, Certif. Educn 1952, Cantab; DipEd 1955, London; MA Oxon (by incorporation), Christ Church, Oxford, 1955. Asst Master, William Hulme's Grammar Sch., Manchester, 1948-50; Maths Master, Eastbourne Coll., 1950-55; Lectr and Tutor, Univ. of Oxford Dept of Educn, 1955-59; Lectr in Philosophy of Educn, Univ. of London Inst. of Educn, 1959-65; Prof. of Educn, King's Coll., Univ. of London, 1965-71. Visiting Professor: Univ. of British Columbia, 1964, 1967; Univ. of Malawi, 1969. De Carle Lectr, Univ. of Otago, 1976; Fink Lectr, Univ. of Melbourne, 1976. Vice-Pres., Philosophy of Educn Soc. of GB. *Publications:* (with R. S. Peters) The Logic of Education, 1970; (ed with R. F. Dearden and R. S. Peters) Education and the Development of Reason, 1971; Knowledge and the Curriculum, 1974; Moral Education in a Secular Society, 1974; papers in: Philosophical Analysis and Education (ed R. D. Archambault), 1965; The Study of Education (ed J. W. Tibble), 1965; The Concept of Education (ed R. S. Peters), 1966; Let's Teach Them Right (ed C. Macy), 1969; also in Brit. Jl Educnl Studies, Jl Curriculum Studies, Proc. Philosophy of Educn Soc. *Recreation:* music, especially opera. *Address:* Dept of Education, 17 Trumpington Street, Cambridge CB2 1PT. *T:* Cambridge 64111. *Club:* Athenæum.

HIRST, Prof. Rodney Julian, MA; Professor of Logic and Rhetoric, University of Glasgow, 1961-81; *b* 28 July 1920; *s* of Rev. William Hirst and Elsie Hirst; *m* 1942, Jessica, *y d* of Charles Alfred Podmore; two *d. Educ:* Leeds Grammar Sch.; Magdalen Coll., Oxford. Demy, 1938-47; 1st Cl. Hons Classical Mods, 1940. War Service, 1940-45, mainly as REME Officer (Radar) at home and in Italy. First Class Hons Lit. Hum., Dec. 1947. Lectr in Logic and Metaphysics, St Andrews Univ., 1948; Glasgow University: Lectr, 1949, and Sen. Lectr, 1959, in Logic; Dean of Arts, 1971-73; Senate Assessor on Univ. Court, 1973-78; Vice-Principal, 1976-79. *Publications:* Problems of Perception, 1959; (co-author) Human Senses and Perception, 1964; Perception and the External World, 1965; Philosophy: an outline for the intending student, 1968; contribs to Encyclopedia of Philosophy and philosophical journals. *Address:* 18 Farmfield Terrace, West Kilbride, Ayrshire KA23 9HD. *T:* West Kilbride 822774.

HISCOCKS, Prof. Charles Richard, MA, DPhil; Professor of International Relations, University of Sussex, 1964-72, now Emeritus; *b* 1 June 1907; *y s* of F. W. Hiscocks; unmarried. *Educ:* Highgate Sch.; St Edmund Hall, Oxford; Berlin University. Asst Master, Trinity Coll. Sch., Port Hope, Ont, 1929-32; Bradfield Coll., 1936-39; Marlborough Coll., 1939-40. Served with Royal Marines, 1940-45, Lieut-Col; seconded to army for mil. govt duties in Germany, 1945; Brit. Council Rep. in Austria, 1946-49, S India, 1949-50; Prof. of Polit. Sci. and Internat. Relations, Univ. of Manitoba, 1950-64. UK Mem., UN Sub-Commn for Prevention of Discrimination and Protection of Minorities, 1953-62. Pres., Winnipeg Art Gall., 1959-60. Vis. Fellow, Princeton Univ., 1970-71; Fellow, Adlai Stevenson Inst. of Internat. Affairs, Chicago, 1971-72. Vice-Pres., UNA 1977-. *Publications:* The Rebirth of Austria, 1953; Democracy in Western Germany, 1957; Poland: Bridge for the Abyss?, 1963; Germany Revived, 1966; The Security Council: a study in adolescence, 1973. *Recreations:* music, art, gardening. *Address:* Dickers, Hunworth, Melton Constable, Norfolk. *T:* Holt 2503. *Club:* Garrick.

HISLOP, George Steedman, CBE 1976; PhD; FEng, FIMechE, FRAeS; FRSE; Director: Caledonian Airmotive, since 1978; Inveresk Research International, since 1978; Chairman, Airworthiness Requirements Board, Civil Aviation Authority, since 1982; *b* 11 Feb. 1914; *s* of George Alexander Hislop and Marthesa Maria Hay; *m* 1942, Joan Daphne, *d* of William Beer and Gwendoline Fincken; two *s* one *d. Educ:* Clydebank High Sch.; Royal Technical Coll., Glasgow (ARTC); Cambridge Univ. (PhD). BScEng London. CEng, FIMechE 1949; FRAeS 1955; Fellowship of Engrg, 1976; FRSE 1976; FRSA 1959. A&AEE, RAF Boscombe Down, 1939-45; RAE,

Farnborough, 1945-46; BEA, 1947-53; Chief Engr/Dir, Fairey Aviation Ltd, 1953-60; Westland Aircraft Ltd, 1960-: Technical Dir (Develt), 1962-66; Dep. Man. Dir, 1966-68; Man. Dir, 1968-72; Vice-Chm., 1972-76. Chm. CEI, 1979-80 (Vice-Chm., 1978-79). Mem. Council, RAeS, 1960- (Pres., 1973-74); Vis. Prof., Univ. of Strathclyde, 1978-. Hon. DSc Strathclyde, 1976. *Publications:* contrib. R & M series and RAeS Jl. *Recreations:* hill walking, photography, bird watching. *Address:* Hadley, St John's Hill, Old Coulsdon, Surrey CR3 1HD. *T:* 01-660 1008. *Clubs:* Royal Air Force, MCC.

HISS, Alger; Commercial printing since 1959 (manufacturing, 1957-59); *b* 11 Nov. 1904; *s* of Charles Alger Hiss and Mary L. Hughes; *m* 1929, Priscilla Fansler Hobson; one *s. Educ:* Johns Hopkins Univ. (AB 1926, Hon. LLD 1947); Harvard Univ. (LLB 1929). Sec. and law clerk to Supreme Court Justice Holmes, 1929-30; law practice, 1930-33; asst to gen. counsel and asst gen. counsel, Agricultural Adjustment Admin., 1933-35; legal asst, special Senate cttee investigating munitions industry, 1934-35; special attorney, US Dept of Justice, 1935-36; asst to Asst Sec. of State, 1936; asst to Adviser on Political Relations, 1939; special asst to Dir, Office of Far Eastern Affairs, 1944; special asst to Dir, Office of Special Political Affairs, May 1944; Dep. Dir, Nov. 1944, Dir, 1945; accompanied Pres. Roosevelt and Sec. of State Stettinius to Malta and Yalta Conferences, Feb. 1945; exec. sec., Dumbarton Oaks Conversations, Aug.-Oct. 1944; sec.-gen., United Nations Conference on International Organization, San Francisco, 1945; Principal Adviser to US Delegation, Gen. Assembly of United Nations, London, 1946; elected Pres. and Trustee of Carnegie Endowment for Internat. Peace, Dec. 1946 (Pres. until 1949). Mem., Massachusetts Bar. Mem., Alpha Delta Phi, Phi Beta Kappa. *Publications:* The Myth of Yalta, 1955; In the Court of Public Opinion, 1957, new edn 1972; Holmes-Laski Letters (abridged edn), 1963. *Recreations:* tennis, swimming, ornithology. *Address:* c/o Davison-Bluth, 295 Lafayette Street, New York, NY 10012, USA. *T:* Worth 6-2492.

HITCH, Brian, CVO 1980; HM Diplomatic Service; Consul-General, Munich, since 1980; *b* 2 June 1932; *m* 1954, Margaret Kathleen Wooller; two *d. Educ:* Wisbech Grammar Sch. (FRCO, LRAM); Magdalene Coll., Cambridge. Joined FO, 1955; asst Dir, Tokyo, 1955-61; FO, 1961-62; 2nd/1st Sec., Havana, 1962-64; 1st Sec., Athens, 1965-68; 1st Sec. and Head of Chancery, Tokyo, 1968-72; Asst Head, Southern European Dept, FCO, 1972-73; Dep. Head, later Head, Marine and Transport Dept, FCO, 1973-75; Counsellor, Bonn, 1975-77 and Algiers, 1977-80. *Recreation:* music. *Address:* c/o Foreign and Commonwealth Office, SW1; (home) 1 Mount Ararat Road, Richmond, Surrey TW10 6PQ. *T:* 01-940 4737. *Club:* United Oxford & Cambridge University.

HITCHCOCK, Dr Anthony John Michael; Head of Transportation and Road Safety Department, Transport and Road Research Laboratory, Department of Transport, since 1978; *b* 26 June 1929; *s* of Dr Ronald W. Hitchcock and Hilda (*née* Gould); *m* 1953, Audrey Ellen (*née* Ashworth); one *s* two *d. Educ:* Bedales; Manchester Grammar Sch.; Trinity Coll., Cambridge; Univ. of Chicago. PhD, BA; MInstP; MCIT. Asst, Univ. of Chicago, 1951-52; AEA, 1953-67; Head of Traffic Dept, TRRL, 1967-71, 1971-75; Head, Res. Policy (Transport) Div., DoE/DoT, 1975-78. Vis. Prof., Transport Studies, Cranfield Inst. of Technology, 1978-81. *Publications:* Nuclear Reactor Control, 1960; (with P. Corcoran and K. MacMahon) Developments in Freight Transport, 1980; articles in learned jls. *Recreation:* bridge. *Address:* Seal Point, Comeragh Close, Golf Club Road, Woking, Surrey GU22 0LZ. *T:* Woking 5219.

HITCHCOCK, Prof. Edward Robert, ChM, FRCS; FRCSE; Professor of Neurosurgery, University of Birmingham, since 1978; *b* 10 Feb. 1929; *s* of Edwin Robert and Martha Hitchcock; *m* 1953, Jillian Trenowath; three *s* one *d. Educ:* Lichfield Grammar Sch.; Univ. of Birmingham (MB ChB; ChM 1952). FRCS 1959; FRCSE, ad eundem, 1971. Leader, Univ. of Birmingham Spitzbergen Expedn, 1951. Lecturer in Anatomy, Univ. of Birmingham, 1953; Captain, RAMC, 1954-56; Registrar: Dept of Traumatic Surgery, General Hosp., Birmingham, 1956; Professorial Surgical Unit, University College Hosp., London, 1957-59; Fellow in Clinical Research, MRC, 1960; 1961-65: Ho. Surg./Registrar/Sen. Registrar, Dept of Neurological Surgery, Radcliffe Inf., Oxford, and Dept of Neurosurgery, Manchester Royal Inf.; Research Fellow, Univ. of Oxford; Sen. Lectr and Reader, Dept of Surgical Neurology, Univ. of Edinburgh, 1966-78. Hon. Specialist in Neurosurgery, Brazilian Neurosurg. Soc.; Corresp. Member: Amer. Assoc. of Neurol Surgeons; Scandinavian Neurosurg. Soc. *Publications:* Initial Management of Head Injuries (Folia Traumatologica), 1971; Management of the Unconscious Patient, 1971; papers on pain, stereotaxic surgery and tumours, in various jls. *Recreations:* reading, hedging, fishing. *Address:* Cubbold House, Ombersley, near Droitwich, Worcs WR9 0HJ. *T:* Worcester 620606.

HITCHCOCK, Geoffrey Lionel Henry, CBE 1975 (OBE 1957); External Relations Consultant, Bell Educational Trust, Cambridge, 1977-81; *b* 10 Sept. 1915; *s* of late Major Frank B. Hitchcock, MC, and Mrs Mildred Hitchcock (*née* Sloane Stanley), Danbury, Essex; *m* 1950, Rosemary, *d* of Albert de Las Casas, Tiverton; two *s* one *d. Educ:* Oratory Sch., Caversham; Hertford Coll., Oxford (Exhibr, MA). British Council, April-Sept. 1939. Commnd London Rifle Bde, 1939; served with KAR in E Africa and SE Asia; Major 1943. Returned to British Council, 1946; served in London; Germany, 1950-54; Representative in Austria, 1954-59; Representative in Yugoslavia, 1962-67; Controller Home Div., British Council, 1970-73; Rep. of British Council in France and Cultural Counsellor, British Embassy, Paris, 1973-76. *Recreations:*

race-going, gardening. *Address:* 1 Storey's Way, Cambridge CB3 0DP. *T:* Cambridge 350112. *Club:* Travellers'.

HITCHCOCK, Prof. Henry-Russell; Adjunct Professor, Institute of Fine Arts, University of New York, since 1969; *b* 3 June 1903; *s* of Henry R. Hitchcock and Alice Whitworth Davis. *Educ:* Middlesex Sch., Concord, Mass, USA; Harvard Univ. MA 1927. Asst Prof. of Art, Vassar Coll., 1927-28; Asst, Assoc., Prof., Wesleyan Univ., 1929-48; Lectr in Architecture, Massachusetts Institute of Technology, 1946-48; Prof. of Art, Smith Coll., Mass, 1948-68; Prof. of Art, Univ. of Massachusetts, 1968. Dir, Smith Coll. Museum of Art, 1949-55; Lectr, Inst. of Fine Arts, New York Univ., 1951-57; Lectr in Architecture, Yale Univ., 1951-52, 1959-60, 1970, Cambridge Univ., 1962, 1964. Fellow Amer. Acad. of Arts and Sciences. Hon. Corr. Mem. RIBA; Franklin Fellow, RSA; Pres., Soc. of Architectural Historians, 1952-54; Fellow, Pilgrim Soc.; Founder-Mem., Victorian Soc.; Pres., Victorian Soc. in America, 1969-74. Hon. DFA New York Univ., 1969; Hon. DLitt Glasgow, 1973; Hon. DHL: Pennsylvania, 1976; Wesleyan, 1979. Award of Merit, AIA, 1978; Benjamin Franklin Award, RSA, 1979. *Publications:* Modern Architecture, 1929, 2nd edn, 1970; J. J. P. Oud, 1931; The International Style (with Philip Johnson), 1932 (2nd edn 1966); The Architecture of H. H. Richardson, 1936 (3rd edn 1966); Modern Architecture in England (with others), 1937; Rhode Island Architecture, 1939 (2nd edn 1968); In the Nature of Materials, the Buildings of Frank Lloyd Wright, 1942 (2nd edn 1973); American Architectural Books, 1946; Painting towards Architecture, 1948; Early Victorian Architecture in Britain, 1954, 2nd edn 1972; Latin American Architecture since 1945, 1955; Architecture: Nineteenth and Twentieth Centuries, 1958 (4th edn 1977); German Rococo: The Brothers Zimmermann, 1968; Rococo Architecture in Southern Germany, 1968; (with William Seale) Temples of Democracy, 1977; Netherlandish Scrolled Gables of the 16th and early 17th Centuries, 1978; German Renaissance Architecture, 1981. *Address:* 152 E 62nd Street, New York, NY 10021, USA. *T:* 758-6554.

HITCHEN, Rt. Rev. Anthony; Titular Bishop of Othona and an Auxiliary Bishop of Liverpool, (RC), since 1979; *b* 23 May 1930. *Educ:* St Cuthbert's College, Ushaw. Priest, 1955; Administrator of St Mary's, Liverpool, 1969. *Address:* The Rectory, Formby, Liverpool L37 3LW.

HITCHEN, John David; a Recorder of the Crown Court, since 1978; *b* 18 July 1935; *s* of late Harold Samuel and of Frances Mary Hitchen; *m* 1966, Pamela Ann Cellan-Jones. *Educ:* Woodhouse Grove Sch., nr Bradford; Pembroke Coll., Oxford (BA(Hons)). Called to Bar, Lincoln's Inn, 1961. *Recreations:* music, reading. *Address:* 39 Rutland Drive, Harrogate, Yorks. *T:* Harrogate 66236.

HITCHIN, Prof. Aylwin Drakeford, CBE 1970; Boyd Professor of Dental Surgery, Director of Dental Studies, University of Dundee (formerly University of St Andrews), 1947-77 and Dean of Dundee Dental Hospital, 1947-73; Dental Consultant, Dundee Royal Infirmary, 1947-77; Civil Consultant Dental Surgeon to Royal Navy, 1957-77; *b* 31 Dec. 1907; *s* of Alfred Leonard Hitchin, FRPS, and Ruth Drakeford; *m* 1942, Alice Stella Michie; one *s* one *d. Educ:* Rutherford College, Newcastle upon Tyne; Durham University Coll. of Medicine. LDS (Dunelm) 1931, BDS 1932, MDS 1935; DDSc 1957; FDSRCS Edinburgh 1951; FFDRCS Ire 1964; FDSRCPS Glasgow 1967. Asst Hon. Dental Surgeon and Demonstrator of Dental Surgery, Newcastle upon Tyne Dental Hosp., 1932-36; Private Dental Practice, Newcastle upon Tyne, 1932-46 (except for 6 yrs with AD Corps during War of 1939-45); Dental Surgical Specialist, Scottish Command, 1943-45, with rank of Major. Chairman: Dental Educn Advisory Council, 1951-52; Dental Hosp. Assoc., 1959-60; Chm., Dental Cttee, Scot. Post-Grad. Med. Council, 1969-79; Member: Dental Cttee of MRC, 1966-72; Advisory Cttee on Medical Research (Scotland), 1967-71; Dental Adv. Cttee, Scottish Health Services Council, 1952-57, 1968-74; Convener, Dental Council, RCSE, 1971-74; Jt Cttee on Higher Training in Dentistry, 1969-74; East Scotland Regional Hosp. Bd, 1948-52; Dental Sub Cttee, UGC, 1969-73; Nominated Mem., Gen. Dent. Council, 1956-74; External Examiner Dental Subjects, Universities, Durham, Edinburgh, Queen's, Belfast, Dublin, Manchester, Liverpool, Birmingham, Leeds, Newcastle, Bristol, Wales, RCS in Ireland; Examiner, LDS, FDSRCS Edinburgh, FFDRCS Ire, and FDSRCPS Glasgow. William Guy Meml Lectr, RCSE, 1972; Founders and Benefactors Lectr, Univ. of Newcastle upon Tyne Dental Sch., 1973. President: Oral Surgery Club, 1956-57; Christian Dental Fellowship, 1966-69; Brit. Soc. Dental Radiology, 1961-63; Royal Odonto-Chir. Soc. of Scotland, 1969-70; Vice-Pres., Inter-Varsity Fellowship (Pres., 1966-67); Foundation Fellow of the British Assoc. of Oral Surgeons; Hon. Mem., Swedish Dental Soc. Dr Odont (*hc*) Lund, 1977; Hon. FDSRCPS Glasgow, 1979. *Publications:* contribs to dental periodical literature. *Address:* Kyleakin, 8 Cedar Road, Broughty Ferry, Dundee DD5 3BB. *TA* and *T:* Dundee 77320.

HITCHINS, Francis Eric, CBE 1954; Member, Australian Wool Realization Commission, 1945-57; President Emeritus, Australian Wool and Meat Producers' Federation; sheep farming, Cranbrook, W Australia; *b* 15 Oct. 1891; *m* 1921, Bessie R. Paltridge; two *s* one *d.* Served European War, 1914-18, AIF, France. Inspector, Agric. Bank of W Australia, 1918-23; Land Valuer, Federal Taxation Dept, 1923-32; resumed sheep farming. Pres., Wool Sect., Primary Producers' Assoc. of WA; Pres., Australian Wool and Meat Producers' Fedn, 1941-52; Wool Grower Rep., Central Wool Cttee, War of

1939-45. Grower Rep., London Wool Confs, 1945 and 1950. *Publications:* Tangled Skeins: A Historic Survey of Australian Wool Marketing, 1956; Skeins Still Tangled: wool events 1952-72, 1972. *Address:* RSL War Veterans Home, Alexander Drive, Mount Lawley, WA, Australia.

HIVES, family name of **Baron Hives.**

HIVES, 2nd Baron, *cr* 1950, of Duffield; **John Warwick Hives;** *b* 26 Nov. 1913; *s* of 1st Baron Hives and of Gertrude Ethel (*d* 1961), *d* of John Warwick; *S* father, 1965; *m* 1st, 1937, Olwen Protheroe Llewellin (*d* 1972); no *c* ; 2nd, 1972, Gladys Mary Seals. *Educ:* Manor School, Mickleover, Derby. *Recreation:* shooting. *Heir: nephew* Matthew Peter Hives, *b* 25 May 1971. *Address:* Bendalls, Milton, Derby. *T:* Burton on Trent 703319. *Club:* Farmers'.

HO, Eric Peter, CBE 1981; Secretary for Social Services, Hong Kong, since 1977; *b* 30 Dec. 1927; *s* of Sai-Ki Ho and Doris (*née* Lo); *m* 1956, Grace Irene, *d* of Mr and Mrs A. V. Young; two *s* one *d. Educ:* Univ. of Hong Kong (BA 1950). Inspector of Taxes (under training), London, 1950-53; Hong Kong Civil Service, 1954-: Inland Revenue, 1954-57; Admin. Service, 1957-. Overseas Service Course B, Cambridge Univ., 1961-62; RCDS, London, 1976. *Recreations:* swimming, lawn tennis. *Address:* 7 Wiltshire Road, Kowloon Tong, Hong Kong. *T:* 3-363567.

HOAD, Air Vice-Marshal Norman Edward, CVO 1972; CBE 1969; AFC 1951 and Bar, 1956; artist; *b* 28 July 1923; *s* of Hubert Ronald Hoad and Florence Marie (*née* Johnson); two *s. Educ:* Brighton. Joined RAF, 1941, pilot trng, S Rhodesia; Lancaster pilot until shot down and taken prisoner in Germany, 1944; various flying and instructional duties, 1945-51; Sqdn Ldr 1951; OC No 192 Sqdn, 1953-55; psc 1956; Wing Comdr, HQ 2 ATAF, 1957-59; pfc 1960; OC No 216 Sqdn, 1960-62; jssc 1963; Gp Capt., MoD, 1963-65; idc 1966; Stn Comdr: RAF Lyneham, 1967, RAF Abingdon, 1968; Defence and Air Attaché, British Embassy, Paris, 1969-72; Dir, Defence Policy (A), 1972-74; Chief of Staff, 46 Gp, RAF Strike Comd, April-Oct. 1974; AOC No 46 Group, and Comdr, UK Jt Airborne Task Force, 1974-75; Senior RAF Mem., RCDS, 1976-78. Director, Air League, 1978-82. Founder Mem., Guild of Aviation Artists; Chm., Soc. of Equestrian Artists. MBIM 1970. *Address:* Little Meadow, Stowupland, Stowmarket, Suffolk. *Clubs:* Royal Air Force, Arts.

HOARE, Cecil Arthur, DSc; FRS 1950; FIBiol; *b* 6 March 1892; *m* Marie Leserson. *Educ:* XII St Petersburg Gymnasium; University of Petrograd (BSc 1917); University of London (DSc 1927). Fellow of Petrograd Univ., 1917-20; Lectr at Military Medical Academy, Petrograd, 1918-20; Researcher to Medical Research Council, 1920-23; Head of Protozoological Dept, Wellcome Laboratories of Tropical Medicine, London, 1923-57; Wellcome Research Fellow, 1957-70; Trypanosomiasis Research Institute, Uganda Medical Service, 1927-29; acting Prof. of Medical Protozoology at London Sch. of Hygiene and Tropical Medicine, 1941-45; Recorder of "Protozoa" in Zoological Record, 1926-57; Mem., Expert Panel, WHO, 1957-73. Hon. Member: Soc. Protozool., USA; Amer. Soc. Parasitol.; Brit. Soc. Parasitol.; Royal Soc. Trop. Med. and Hygiene; Société de Pathologie Exotique, Paris; For. Member: Société Belge de Médecine Tropicale; Soc. Protistol. Franç. G. Vianna Medal, Brazil. Acad. Sci., 1962; Patrick Manson Prize, 1963, Manson Medal, Royal Soc. Trop. Med., 1974. *Publications:* Handbook of Medical Protozoology, 1949; The Trypanosomes of Mammals, 1972; numerous papers dealing with the Protozoa.

HOARE, Prof. Charles Antony Richard, FRS 1982; Professor of Computation, Oxford University, since 1977; Fellow of Wolfson College, since 1977; *b* 11 Jan. 1934; *s* of Henry S. M. Hoare and Marjorie F. Hoare; *m* 1962, Jill Pym; one *s* one *d* (and one *s* decd). *Educ:* King's Sch., Canterbury; Merton Coll., Oxford (MA, Cert. Stats). Computer Div., Elliott Brothers, London, Ltd, 1959-68: successively Programmer, Chief Engr, Tech. Man., Chief Scientist; National Computer Centre, 1968; Prof. of Computer Science, QUB, 1968-77. Dist. FBCS 1978; Hon. DSc Southern California, 1979. A. M. Turing Award, Assoc. Comp. Mach., 1980; Harry Goode Meml Award, Amer. Fedn of Inf. Processing Socs, 1981. *Publications:* Structured Programming (with O.-J. Dahl and E. W. Dijkstra), 1972; articles in Computer Jl, Commun. ACM, and Acta Informatica. *Recreations:* walking, swimming, reading, listening to music. *Address:* Programming Research Group, 45 Banbury Road, Oxford OX2 6PE. *T:* Oxford 58086.

HOARE, Rear-Adm. Desmond John, CB 1962; Vice President, United World Colleges, since 1969; *b* 25 June 1910; *s* of Capt. R. R. Hoare, OBE, Royal Navy; *m* 1941, Naomi Mary Gilbert Scott; one *s* two *d. Educ:* Wimbledon Coll.; King's Sch., Rochester. Joined RN, 1929; Engineering training, RNEC Keyham, 1930-33; Advanced engineering course, RNC Greenwich, 1934-36; HMS Exeter, 1936-39; Admiralty, 1939-41; HMS King George V, 1942-44; Admiralty, 1945-48; HMS Vanguard, 1949-51; HMS Condor (apprentice training), 1951-53; idc, 1955; Admiralty, 1956-59; Chief Staff Officer Technical to C-in-C Plymouth, 1960-62; retired, 1962. Headmaster, Atlantic Coll., 1962-69. *Recreations:* sailing, power boats. *Address:* Bally Island House, Skibbereen, Cork, Ireland.

HOARE, Sir Frederick (Alfred), 1st Bt, *cr* 1962; Kt 1958; Managing Partner of C. Hoare & Co., Bankers, of 37 Fleet Street, since 1947; Director: Messrs Hoare Trustees, since 1947; Mitre Court Securities Ltd, since 1963; Mitre

Court Cranes Ltd, since 1957; Mitre Court Property Holding Co., since 1980; Grimersta Estate Ltd, since 1969; Tuscan Development Co., since 1972; Hoare's Bank Nominees Ltd, since 1936; TR Property Investment Trust plc; *b* 11 Feb. 1913; *s* of late Frederick Henry Hoare, 37 Fleet Street, EC4; *m* 1st, 1939, Norah Mary, OBE (*d* 1973), *d* of A. J. Wheeler; two *d*; 2nd, 1974, Oonah Alice Dew (*d* 1980), *d* of late Brig.-Gen. David Ramsay Sladen, CMG, DSO, and Isabel Sladen (*née* Blakiston-Houston). *Educ:* Wellington Coll. Clerk to C. Hoare & Co., 1931; Bankers' Agent, 1936, Managing Partner, 1947. Chm., General Practice Finance Corp., 1966-73; Deputy Chairman: Nat. Mutual Life Assurance Soc., 1969-72; St George Assurance Co. Ltd, 1969-73. Common Councilman City of London, 1948; Alderman for Ward of Farringdon Without, 1950-71; Sheriff, City of London, 1956; Lord Mayor of London, 1961-62. Formerly one of HM Lieutenants for City of London; former Governor: Christ's Hosp.; Royal Bridewell Hosp.; Past Chm., St Bride's Institute; Mem., Court of Assistants and Prime Warden of Goldsmiths' Company, 1966-67. Pres., British Chess Federation, 1964-67; Past President: London Primary Schs Chess Assoc.; Cosmopolitan Banks Chess Assoc.; Upward Bound Young People's Gliding and Adventure Trust; Vice-Pres., Toc H. Trustee: Lady Hoare Thalidomide Appeal; Historic Churches Preservation Trust; Vice-Pres., Anglers' Co-operative Assoc. (Chm., 1977-82); Chm., John Eastwood Water Protection Trust Ltd, 1977-82; Member: Nat. Coun. for Voluntary Organisations; Nat. Council, Noise Abatement Soc.; Chm., Family Welfare Assoc., 1961-68; Vice-Pres., British Rheumatism and Arthritis Assoc., 1979-. Past Grand Deacon, United Grand Lodge of England. KStJ. Knight of Liberian Humane Order of African Redemption, 1962; Grand Officier de L'Ordre National de la République de Côte d'Ivoire, 1962. *Recreations:* chess, fishing, ornithology, photography, philately. *Heir:* none. *Address:* 34 Cadogan Square, SW1X 0JL. *Clubs:* Garrick, City Livery, Flyfishers'.

HOARE, John Michael; Administrator, Wessex Regional Health Authority, since 1973; *b* 23 Oct. 1932; *s* of Leslie Frank Hoare and Gladys Hoare; *m* 1963, Brita Hjalte; one *s* one *d*. *Educ:* Raynes Park; Christ's Coll., Cambridge (BA). Asst Sec., United Bristol Hosps, 1961; House Governor, St Stephen's Hosp., 1963; Asst Clerk, St Thomas' Hosp., 1965; Administrator, Northwick Park Hosp., 1967. Mem., Defence Medical Services Inquiry, 1971-73. *Recreations:* reading, walking, music, squash. *Address:* 24 Clausentum Road, Winchester, Hants SO23 9QE. *T:* Winchester 4192.

HOARE, Hon. Marcus Bertram, CMG 1965; Justice of Supreme Court of Queensland, 1966-80; *b* 3 March 1910; *s* of John George and Emma Hoare; *m* 1936, Eileen Parker; four *s*. *Educ:* Brisbane Grammar Sch. Solicitor, 1933; Barrister-at-Law, 1944; QC (Australia) 1960. *Address:* 191 Laurel Avenue, Chelmer, Brisbane, Qld 4068, Australia. *T:* 379-4181. *Clubs:* Queensland, Johnsonian (Brisbane).

HOARE, Sir Peter Richard David, 8th Bt *cr* 1786; *b* 22 March 1932; *s* of Sir Peter William Hoare, 7th Bt, and of Laura Ray, *o d* of Sir John Esplen, 1st Bt, KBE; *S* father, 1973; *m* 1st, 1961, Jane (marr. diss. 1967), *o d* of Daniel Orme; 2nd, 1978, Katrin Alexa, Lady Hodson, *o d* of late Erwin Bernstiel. *Educ:* Eton. *Recreations:* travelling, shooting, skiing. *Heir:* b David John Hoare [*b* 8 Oct. 1935; *m* 1965, Mary Vanessa (marr. diss. 1978), *y d* of Peter Gordon Cardew; one *s*]. *Address:* c/o C. Hoare & Co., 37 Fleet Street, EC4. *Club:* Royal Automobile.

HOARE, Rev. Dr Rupert William Noel; Principal of Westcott House, Cambridge, since 1981; *b* 3 March 1940; *s* of Julian Hoare and Edith Hoare (*née* Temple); *m* 1965, Gesine (*née* Pflüger); three *s* one *d*. *Educ:* Rugby School; Trinity Coll., Oxford (BA 1958, MA 1967); Westcott House and Fitzwilliam House, Cambridge (BA 1964); Birmingham Univ. (PhD 1973). Deacon 1964, priest 1965, Dio. Manchester; Curate of St Mary, Oldham, 1964-67; Lecturer, Queen's Theological Coll., Birmingham, 1968-72; Rector, Parish of the Resurrection, Manchester, 1972-78; Residentiary Canon, Birmingham Cathedral, 1978-81. Canon Theologian of Coventry Cathedral, 1970-75. *Publications:* (trans. jtly) Bultmann's St John, 1971; (contrib.) Queen's Sermons, 1973, Queen's Essays, 1980; articles in Theology. *Recreations:* hill walking, sailing, gardening, listening to music. *Address:* Westcott House, Jesus Lane, Cambridge.

HOARE, Sir Timothy Edward Charles, 8th Bt *cr* 1784; Director: Career Plan Ltd; New Metals and Chemicals Ltd; *b* 11 Nov. 1934; *s* of Sir Edward O'Bryen Hoare, 7th Bt and of Nina Mary, *d* of late Charles Nugent Hope-Wallace, MBE; *S* father, 1969; *m* 1969, Felicity Anne, *o d* of Peter Boddington; one *s* twin *d*. *Educ:* Radley College; Worcester College, Oxford (BA Modern Hist.; MA); Birkbeck Coll., London (MA Manpower Studies). Mem., Gen. Synod of Church of England, 1970-. *Heir:* s Charles James Hoare, *b* 15 March 1971. *Address:* 10 Belitha Villas, N1.

HOBAN, Brian Michael Stanislaus; Head Master of Harrow, 1971-81; *b* 7 Oct. 1921; 2nd *s* of late Capt. R. A. Hoban; *m* 1947, Jasmine, 2nd *d* of J. C. Holmes, MC, Charterhouse, Godalming; one *s* one *d* (and one *d* decd). *Educ:* Charterhouse (Scholar); University Coll., Oxford (Schol.). 2nd Cl. Hon. Mods, 1947; 2nd Cl. Lit. Hum.; 1949; BA 1949, MA 1957. Served War of 1939-45: Capt., Westminster Dragoons; NW Europe, 1944-45 (despatches); demobilised, Nov. 1945. Capt. Northants Yeomanry, TA, 1950-56. Asst Master: Uppingham Sch., 1949-52; Shrewsbury Sch., 1952-59; Headmaster, St Edmund's Sch., Canterbury, 1960-64; Head Master, Bradfield Coll., 1964-71. Hon. Associate Mem., HMC, 1981- (Hon. Treasurer, 1975-80). Governor,

Wellington Coll., 1981-. JP Berks, 1967-71. *Recreations:* music, cricket, golf, walking. *Address:* Upcot, Wantage Road, Streatley, Berks. *Clubs:* Athenæum; Vincent's (Oxford).

HOBAN, Russell Conwell; full-time writer, since 1967 (with some interruptions); *b* 4 Feb. 1925; *s* of Abram Hoban and Jenny Dimmerman; *m* 1st, 1944, Lillian Aberman (marr. diss. 1975); one *s* three *d*; 2nd, 1975, Gundula Ahl; three *s*. *Educ:* Lansdale High Sch.; Philadelphia Museum Sch. of Industrial Art. Served US Army, 1943-45: 339th Inf., 85th Div., Italy (Bronze Star Medal, 1945). Various jobs, 1945-56; free-lance illustration, 1956-65; copywriter with Doyle, Dane, Bernbach, New York, 1965-67; resident in London, 1969-. *Publications: children's books:* What Does It Do and How Does It Work?, 1959; The Atomic Submarine, 1960; Bedtime for Frances, 1960; Herman the Loser, 1961; The Song in My Drum, 1962; London Men and English Men, 1963; Some Snow Said Hello, 1963; A Baby Sister for Frances, 1964; Nothing To Do, 1964; Bread and Jam for Frances, 1964; The Sorely Trying Day, 1964; Tom and the Two Handles, 1965; The Story of Hester Mouse, 1965; What Happened When Jack and Daisy Tried To Fool the Tooth Fairies, 1965; Goodnight, 1966; Henry and the Monstrous Din, 1966; Charlie the Tramp, 1966; The Little Brute Family, 1966; Save My Place, 1967; The Mouse and His Child, 1967; The Pedalling Man and Other Poems, 1968; The Stone Doll of Sister Brute, 1968; A Birthday for Frances, 1968; Ugly Bird, 1969; Best Friends for Frances, 1969; Harvey's Hideout, 1969; The Mole Family's Christmas, 1969; A Bargain for Frances, 1970; Emmet Otter's Jug-Band Christmas, 1971; Egg Thoughts and Other Frances Songs, 1972; The Sea-Thing Child, 1972; Letitia Rabbit's String Song, 1973; How Tom Beat Captain Najork and His Hired Sportsmen, 1974 (Whitbread Literary Award); Ten What?, 1974; Dinner at Alberta's, 1975; Crocodile and Pierrot, 1975; A Near Thing for Captain Najork, 1975; The Twenty-Elephant Restaurant, 1977; Arthur's New Power, 1978; The Dancing Tigers, 1979; La Corona and Other Tin Tales, 1979; Ace Dragon Ltd, 1980; Flat Cat, 1980; The Serpent Tower, 1981; The Great Fruit Gum Robbery, 1981; They Came from Aargh!, 1981; The Flight of Bembel Rudzuk, 1982; The Battle of Zormla, 1982; *novels:* The Lion of Boaz-Jachin and Jachin-Boaz, 1973; Kleinzeit, 1974; Turtle Diary, 1975; Riddley Walker, 1980; Pilgermann, 1983. *Recreations:* stones, short wave listening. *Address:* David Higham Associates Ltd, 5-8 Lower John Street, Golden Square, W1R 4HA. *T:* 01-437 7888.

HOBART, Archbishop of, (RC), since 1955; **Most Rev. Sir Guilford Young,** KBE 1978; DD (Rome); *b* Sandgate, Queensland, 10 Nov. 1916. Ordained, Rome, 1939; Auxiliary Bishop of Canberra and Goulburn, 1948; Co-Adjutor Archbishop of Hobart, 1954; succeeded to See of Hobart, Sept. 1955. *Address:* Archbishop's House, 31 Fisher Avenue, Sandy Bay, Hobart, Tasmania 7005, Australia.

HOBART, Maj.-Gen. Patrick Robert Chamier, CB 1970; DSO 1945; OBE 1944; MC 1943; *b* 14 Nov. 1917; *s* of Robert Charles Arthur Stanley Hobart and Elsie Hinds. *Educ:* Charterhouse; Royal Military Academy Woolwich; 2nd Lieut, Royal Tank Corps, 1937; served in war of 1939-45 (despatches 4 times); France, Western Desert, Tunisia, Italy, with 2nd Royal Tank Regt, BM 9th Armd Bde, GSO2 30 Corps, GSO1 7th Armd Div; NW Europe, GSO1 Guards Armd Div. and CO 1st RTR; CO 2nd RTR, BAOR and N Africa, 1958-60; Comdr, 20th Armoured Brigade, BAOR, 1961-63; Chief of Staff, 1 (British) Corps, BAOR, 1964-66; Dir Military Operations, MoD, 1966-68; Chief of Staff Army Strategic Command, 1968-70; Dir, RAC, 1970-72; retired; Lieut-Governor, Royal Hosp., Chelsea, 1973-78. Col Comdt, Royal Tank Regt, 1968-78, Representative Col Comdt, 1971-74. ADC to the Queen, 1961-66. *Address:* c/o Williams & Glyn's Bank Ltd, Kirkland House, Whitehall, SW1.

HOBART, Lt-Comdr Sir Robert (Hampden), 3rd Bt *cr* 1914; RN; *b* 7 May 1915; *o s* of Sir (Claud) Vere Cavendish Hobart, 2nd Bt, DSO, OBE and Violet Verve, MBE (*d* 1935), 2nd *d* of late John Wylie; *S* father 1949; *m* 1st, 1942, Sylvia (*d* 1965), *d* of H. Argo, Durban, Natal; three *s* one *d*; 2nd, 1975, Caroline Fleur, *d* of Colonel H. M. Vatcher, MC, and widow of 11th Duke of Leeds. *Educ:* Wixenford; RN Coll., Dartmouth. Sub-Lieut, RN, 1935; Lieut-Comdr, 1945; served War of 1939-45 (wounded, two medals, four stars); retired, 1950. Contested (Nat Lib) Hillsborough Div. of Sheffield, 1945, (C and L) Itchen Div. of Southampton, 1950. *Heir:* s John Vere Hobart [*b* 9 April 1945; *m* 1982, Kate Iddles; one *s*]. *Address:* Gatcombe Park, Newport, Isle of Wight. *Clubs:* Travellers', Royal London Yacht; Royal Yacht Squadron; Royal Southern Yacht, Bembridge Sailing.

HOBART-HAMPDEN, family name of **Earl of Buckinghamshire.**

HOBBS, Herbert Harry, CB 1956; CVO 1972; Director, Ancient Monuments and Historic Buildings, 1970-72, retired; *b* 7 Nov. 1912; *s* of late Bertie Hobbs and Agnes Dora (*née* Clarke); *m* 1937, Joan Hazel Timmins (*d* 1979); two *s* one *d*. *Educ:* Bedford Sch.; Corpus Christi Coll., Oxford. Entered War Office, 1935; Comptroller of Lands and Claims, 1956-60; Asst Under-Sec. of State (Works), War Office, 1960-63; Under-Sec., MPBW, later DoE, 1963-72. Medal of Freedom with bronze palm (USA), 1946. *Recreation:* golf. *Address:* 9 Hemp Garden, Minehead, Som.

HOBBS, John Charles; Chief Insurance Officer, Department of Health and Social Security, 1971-76; *b* 28 May 1917; British; *m* 1961, Doris Gronow. *Educ:* Portsmouth Southern Grammar Sch.; Portsmouth Coll. of Technology. 1st cl. hons BSc, 1936; 1st cl. hons BSc (Spec.) Maths, 1944. FIS 1950. Asst

Principal, 1946; Principal, 1947; Asst Sec., 1957. *Recreations:* pianoforte, guitar, marquetry.

HOBBS, Ven. Keith; Archdeacon of Chichester, since 1981; *b* 3 March 1925; *s* of late Percival Frank and Gwennyth Mary Hobbs; *m* 1950, Mary, *d* of late Louis Lingg and Mary Elizabeth Ruderman; one *s* one *d. Educ:* St Olave's Grammar School; Exeter Coll., Oxford (MA); Wells Theological Coll. Instr Branch, RN, 1946; retired (Lt Comdr), 1956. Curate, Clewer St Stephen, 1958-60; Soho, 1960-62; St Stephen, S Kensington, 1962-78; Lectr and Co-ordinator of Counselling, Borough Road Coll., 1964-77; Actg Gen. Secretary, Church Union, 1977-78; Chaplain to Bishop of Chichester, 1978-81. *Address:* 4 Canon Lane, Chichester, W Sussex PO19 1PX. *T:* Chichester 784260.

HOBBS, William Alfred, CB 1973; CBE 1965; Chief Valuer, Board of Inland Revenue, 1972-74; *b* 3 March 1912; *s* of A. V. Getland Hobbs; *m* 1937, Rose Winslade; one *s* one *d. Educ:* Brighton, Hove and Sussex Grammar Sch. Chartered Surveyor (FRICS). Private practice, 1928-38; joined Valuation Office, 1938; Dist Valuer (Maidstone), 1945; Superintending Valuer, 1950 (London, Manchester and Birmingham); Asst Chief Valuer, 1958; Dep. Chief Valuer, 1966-71. *Recreations:* fly-fishing, golf. *Address:* 216 Cooden Sea Road, Bexhill-on-Sea, E Sussex. *T:* Cooden 3995.

HOBDAY, Sir Gordon (Ivan), Kt 1979; DL; Chairman, Central Independent Television; Director, Lloyds Bank; Chancellor, Nottingham University (President of the Council, since 1973); *b* 1 Feb. 1916; *e s* of late Alexander Thomas Hobday and Frances Cassandra (*née* Meads); *m* 1940, Margaret Jean Joule; one *d. Educ:* Long Eaton Grammar Sch.; UC Nottingham. BSc, PhD London; FRSC. Joined Boots Co., 1939; Dir of Research, 1952-68; Man. Dir, 1970-72; Chm., 1973-81. A Dep. Chm., Price Commn, 1977-78. DL Notts, 1981. Hon. LLD Nottingham, 1977. *Recreations:* handicrafts, gardening. *Address:* University of Nottingham, University Park, Nottingham NG7 2RD. *T:* Nottingham 56101. *Club:* Athenæum.

HOBDEN, Dennis Harry; *b* 21 Jan. 1920; *s* of Charles Hobden and Agnes Hobden (*née* Smith); *m* 1st, 1950, Kathleen Mary Hobden (*née* Holman) (marr. diss. 1970); two *s* two *d* ; 2nd, 1977, Sheila Hobden, JP (*née* Tugwell). *Educ:* elementary sch. Entered GPO, 1934. Served as Air Crew, RAF, 1941-46 (Flt Lieut). MP (Lab) Kemptown Div. of Brighton, 1964-70. Leader, Labour Gp, E Sussex CC; Mayor of Brighton, 1979-80. *Recreations:* politics, gardening, music, reading; Spiritualist lay preacher. *Address:* 3 Queens Park Terrace, Brighton, East Sussex BN2 2YA.

HOBDEN, Reginald Herbert, DFC 1944; HM Diplomatic Service, retired; *b* 9 Nov. 1919; *s* of William Richard and Ada Emily Hobden; *m* 1945, Gwendoline Ilma Vowles; two *s* one *d. Educ:* Sir William Borlase's Sch., Marlow. Apptd Colonial Office, Dec. 1936. Served War of 1939-45 (despatches, DFC): RAFVR, Sept. 1940-Jan. 1946 (Sqdn Ldr). Returned to Colonial Office, 1946; seconded to Dept of Technical Co-operation, 1961; First Sec., UK Commn, Malta, 1962-64; HM Diplomatic Service, Nov. 1964: CRO until April 1968; Head of British Interests Section, Canadian High Commn, Dar es Salaam, April 1968; British Acting High Comr, Dar es Salaam, July-Oct. 1968, and Counsellor, Dar es Salaam, Oct. 1968-69; Counsellor (Economic and Commercial), Islamabad, 1970-75; Inst. of Develt Studies, Sussex Univ., 1975; High Comr, Lesotho, 1976-78. Clerk in Clerk's Dept, House of Commons, 1978-. *Recreations:* chess, bridge. *Address:* 14 Belmont Close, Uxbridge, Mddx. *T:* Uxbridge 34754. *Club:* Royal Commonwealth Society.

HOBHOUSE, Sir Charles Chisholm, 6th Bt, *cr* 1812; TD; *b* 7 Dec. 1906; *s* of Sir Reginald A. Hobhouse, 5th Bt and Marjorie Chisholm Spencer (*d* 1967); *S* father, 1947; *m* 1st, 1946, Mary (*d* 1955), *widow* of Walter Horrocks, Salkeld Hall, Penrith; no *c* ; 2nd, 1959, Elspeth Jean, *d* of T. G. Spinney, Mazagan, Morocco; one *s. Educ:* Eton. Commissioned North Somerset Yeomanry, 1926; Major 1940; Hon. Col 1966. *Recreations:* hunting, shooting. *Heir: s* Charles John Spinney Hobhouse, *b* 27 Oct. 1962. *Address:* The Manor, Monkton Farleigh, Bradford-on-Avon, Wilts. *T:* Bath 858558. *Clubs:* Brooks's, City of London.

HOBHOUSE, Hermione; *see* Hobhouse, M. H.

HOBHOUSE, (Mary) Hermione, MBE 1981; FSA; Secretary to the Victorian Society, 1977-82; *d* of late Sir Arthur Lawrence Hobhouse and Konradin Huth Hobhouse; *m* 1958, Henry Trevenen Davidson Graham; one *s* one *d. Educ:* Ladies' Coll., Cheltenham; Lady Margaret Hall, Oxford (Hons Mod. Hist.). Researcher/Writer, Associated-Rediffusion TV and Granada TV, 1957-65; Tutor in Architectural History, Architectural Assoc. Sch., London, 1973-. *Publications:* Thomas Cubitt: Master Builder, 1971; Lost London, 1971 (paperback 1977); History of Regent Street, 1975; Oxford and Cambridge, 1980; contrib. Architectural Design, Architectural Review. *Recreations:* gardening, looking at buildings of all periods. *Address:* Westcombe Stables, Evercreech, Shepton Mallet, Somerset BA4 6ES. *T:* Evercreech 830465.

HOBKIRK, Col Elspeth Isabel Weatherley, CBE 1951; TD 1952; WRAC (retired); Governor of HM Prison and of HM Borstal for Girls, and of HM Young Offenders Institute, Greenock, 1955-69; also appointed Woman Adviser to Scottish Home and Health Department on conditions of detention

of Women and Girls in Scotland, 1956, retired from Scottish Prison Service, Aug. 1969; *d* of late Brig.-Gen. C. J. Hobkirk, CMG, DSO, Cleddon Hall, Trellech, Mon., and Nora Louisa Hobkirk (*née* Bosanquet). *Educ:* Sandecotes, Dorset; London Sch. of Art. JP Monmouthshire, 1938-49. Joined FANY, 1938; enrolled ATS, 1939; served War of 1939-45, Sen. Comdr, 1942; Chief Comdr, 1945; Controller and Dep. Dir ATS, HQ London District, 1946; Dep. Dir ATS, War Office, 1947-49; commissioned into Women's Royal Army Corps, 1949; Dep. Dir WRAC, War Office, 1949; Dep. Dir WRAC, HQ Eastern Command, 1950-52; Vice-Pres. Regular Commissions Bd, 1950-52; retired, 1952. Head Warden, Bristol Royal Hospital, 1952-54; Governor, HM Prison, Duke Street, Glasgow, 1954-55 (prison moved to Greenock, 1955). Member: Govt Adv. Cttee on Drug Dependence, 1967-70; Parole Board for Scotland, 1970-73; (Chm.) Civil Service Commn Panel of Interviewers, 1969-73; Adv. Council on Social Work (Scotland), 1970-72; Emslie Cttee on Penalties for Homicide, 1970-72; Edinburgh Appeals Cttee, Campaign for Cancer Research, 1970-73; Bd of Governors and Exec. Cttee, St Columba's Hospice, 1976-80; an Hon. Sec., RUKBA, Edinburgh, 1974-75; Abbeyfield Edinburgh Exec. Cttee, 1975-76 (Chm. Extra Care House); Catholic Social Work Centre Exec. Cttee, 1974-77; Council, Scottish Soldiers', Sailors' and Airmen's Housing Assoc. and Mem., House Cttee. Hon. LLD Glasgow, 1976. *Recreations:* travel, painting, music, gardening; country pursuits generally. *Address:* 8 Moray Place, Edinburgh EH3 6DS.

HOBKIRK, Michael Dalgliesh; Assistant Under-Secretary of State, Ministry of Defence, since 1980; *b* 9 Dec. 1924; *s* of Roy and Phyllis Hobkirk; *m* 1952, Lucy Preble ; two *d. Educ:* Marlborough Coll.; Wadham Coll., Oxford. MA (Social Studies), MA 1949. Served War of 1939-45: Army (RAC, RAEC, Captain), 1943-47. Civil Service: War Office, 1949-63; MoD, 1963-70. Directing Staff, Nat. Defence Coll., 1970-74; Brookings Instn, Washington, DC, USA, 1974-75; Lord Chancellor's Dept, 1975-80 (Principal Establishment and Finance Officer, 1977-80). *Publication:* contrib. to The Management of Defence (ed L. Martin), 1976. *Address:* 48 Woodside Avenue, Beaconsfield, Bucks HP9 1JH. *Club:* United Oxford & Cambridge University.

HOBLER, Air Vice-Marshal John Forde, CB 1958; CBE 1943; *b* Rockhampton, Qld, Australia, 26 Sept. 1907; *s* of late L. E. Hobler, Rockhampton; *m* 1939, Dorothy Evelyn Diana Haines, Wilsford, Wilts; two *s* one *d. Educ:* Rockhampton, Qld. Served whole of War of 1939-45 in Bomber Command; commanded RAF Lossiemouth; Palestine, 1945; Staff Coll., 1946-48; Air Ministry, 1948-50; Comd Habbaniya, Iraq, 1950-52; HQ Flying Trg Comd, 1952-54; Air Ministry, 1954-56; AO i/c Administration, Middle East Air Force, 1956-58; Air Officer Commanding No 25 Gp, 1958-61; Air Officer i/c Administration, Far East Air Force, 1961-63, retd. *Address:* Paradise Point, Gold Coast, Qld 4216, Australia. *Club:* United Services (Brisbane).

HOBLEY, Brian; Chief Urban Archaeologist, City of London, since 1973; *b* 25 June 1930; *s* of William Hobley and Harriet (*née* Hobson); *m* 1953, Laurie Parkes; one *s* one *d. Educ:* Univ. of Leicester. BA Hons Leicester 1965, FSA 1969, AMA 1970. Field Officer, Coventry Corp., 1965; Keeper, Dept Field Archaeology, Coventry Museum, 1970. Lectr, Birmingham Univ. Extra-mural Dept, 1965-74. Mem. Standing Cttee, Arch. Unit Managers; Treasurer, Assoc. for Promotion of Inst. of Field Archaeologists. MBIM 1978. *Publications:* (ed jtly) Waterfront Archaeology in Britain and Northern Europe, 1981; reports in learned jls incl. Proc. 7th, 8th, 9th and 12th Internat. Congresses of Roman Frontier Studies, Tel Aviv, Univ. Israel and Bucharest Univ., Rumania on excavations and reconstructions at The Lunt Roman fort, Baginton near Coventry and excavations in the City of London. *Recreations:* classical music, chess. *Address:* Department of Urban Archaeology, Museum of London, London Wall, EC2Y 5HN. *T:* 01-600 3699.

HOBLEY, John William Dixon, CMG 1976; QC (Hong Kong); *b* 11 June 1929; *s* of John Wilson Hobley and Ethel Anne Hobley; *m* 1953, Dorothy Cockhill; one *s* one *d. Educ:* University Sch., Southport, Lancs; Univ. of Liverpool (LLB). Called to the Bar, Gray's Inn, 1950; Northern Circuit, 1950-53; Hong Kong: Crown Counsel, 1953-62; Sen. Crown Counsel, 1962-65; Principal Crown Counsel, 1965-72; Attorney-Gen., Bermuda, 1972; Solicitor-Gen., 1973, Attorney-Gen., 1973-79, Hong Kong. *Recreations:* music, bridge. *Address:* 33 Sandringham Road, Ainsdale, Southport, Merseyside.

HOBMAN, David Burton; Director, Age Concern England (National Old People's Welfare Council), since 1970; *b* 8 June 1927; *s* of J. B. and D. L. Hobman; *m* 1954, Erica Irwin; one *s* one *d. Educ:* University College Sch.; Blundell's. Community work, Forest of Dean, 1954-56; British Council for Aid to Refugees, 1957; Nat. Council of Social Service, 1958-67; Visiting Lectr in Social Admin, Nat. Inst. for Social Work, 1967; Dir, Social Work Adv. Service, 1968-70. Vis. Prof., Sch. of Social Work, McGill Univ., Montreal, 1977. Member: BBC/ITA Appeals Adv. Council, 1965-69; Steering Cttee, Enquiry into Homelessness, Nat. Asstce Bd, 1967-68; Adv. Council, Nat. Corp. for Care of Old People, 1970-74; Metrication Bd, 1974-80; Lord Goodman's Cttee Reviewing Law of Charity, 1975-76; Chairman: Social Welfare Commn Conf. of Bishops, 1968-71; Family Housing Assoc., 1969-70; Consultant, UN Div. of Social Affairs, 1968-69; Observer, White House Congress on Ageing, 1971-; Pres., Internat. Fedn on Ageing, 1977-80 (Vice-Pres., 1974-77); Mem., Personal Social Services Council, 1978-80; Mem. Exec. Cttee, Nat. Council of Voluntary Orgns, 1981-; Special Advr, British delegn to World Assembly on Ageing, 1982. Governor: Cardinal Newman Comp.

Sch., Hove, 1971-76 (Chm); Volunteer Centre, 1975-79. KSG. *Publications:* A Guide to Voluntary Service, 1964, 2nd edn 1967; Who Cares, 1971; The Social Challenge of Ageing, 1978; The Impact of Ageing, 1981; numerous papers, broadcasts. *Recreations:* caravanning, travel, pebble polishing. *Address:* Robinswood, George's Lane, Storrington, Pulborough, W Sussex. *T:* Storrington 2987. *Club:* Reform.

HOBSBAWM, Prof. Eric John Ernest, FBA 1976; Professor of Economic and Social History, Birkbeck College, University of London, since 1970; *b* 9 June 1917; *s* of Leopold Percy Hobsbawm and Nelly Grün; *m* 1962, Marlene Schwarz; one *s* one *d*. *Educ:* Vienna; Berlin; St Marylebone Grammar Sch.; Univ. of Cambridge (BA, PhD). Lectr, Birkbeck Coll., 1947; Fellow, King's Coll., Cambridge, 1949-55, Hon. Fellow, 1973; Reader, Birkbeck Coll., 1959. Hon. DPhil Univ. of Stockholm, 1970; Hon. Dr Hum. Let., Univ. of Chicago, 1976; Hon. LittD UEA, 1982. Foreign Hon. Mem., American Academy of Arts and Sciences, 1971; Hon. Mem., Hungarian Acad. of Sciences, 1979. *Publications:* Labour's Turning Point, 1948; Primitive Rebels, 1959; *(pseud.* F. Newton) The Jazz Scene, 1959; The Age of Revolution, 1962; Labouring Men, 1964; (ed) Karl Marx, Precapitalist Formations, 1964; Industry and Empire, 1968; (with G. Rudé) Captain Swing, 1969; Bandits, 1969; Revolutionaries, 1973; The Age of Capital, 1975; contribs to jls. *Recreation:* travel. *Address:* Birkbeck College, Malet Street, WC1. *T:* 01-580 6622.

HOBSON, Alec, CBE 1962 (OBE 1946); MVO 1955; *b* 29 Oct. 1899; *s* of Frederick Hobson, Esher, Surrey; *m* 1924, Elizabeth Josephine, *d* of Arthur Newman, Sudbury, Suffolk; one *s* (one *d* decd). Served Inns of Court and Royal West Surrey Regiments, 1918-19. Engaged in pedigree livestock improvement work, 1920-39; joint founder-partner Harry Hobson & Co. (pedigree livestock auctioneers), 1928. Domestic food production work for Min. of Agriculture, 1939-45. Sec., Royal Agricultural Soc. of England and of Nat. Agricultural Examinations Bds, 1946-61; Hon. Sec., Royal Agricultural Society of The Commonwealth, 1957-67, Hon. Fellow, 1977. Founder Mem., Guild of Agricultural Journalists; Founder Pres., Nat. Soc. of Master Thatchers; Liveryman, Past Master, and Court of Assts, Worshipful Co. of Farriers; Freeman, Worshipful Co. of Farmers. *Recreations:* golf, gardening. *Address:* Clare Cottage, Oulton, Norwich NR11 6NX. *T:* Saxthorpe 362. *Club:* Farmers'.

HOBSON, Anthony Robert Alwyn; bibliographical historian; *b* 5 Sept. 1921; *s* of Geoffrey Dudley Hobson, MVO and Gertrude Adelaide, *d* of Rev. Thomas Vaughan, Rector of Rhuddlan, Flintshire; *m* 1959, Elena Pauline Tanya, *d* of Igor Vinogradoff; one *s* two *d*. *Educ:* Eton Coll. (Oppidan Scholar); New Coll., Oxford (MA). Served Scots Guards, 1941-46, Captain; Italy, 1943-46 (mentioned in despatches). Joined Sotheby & Co., 1947: Dir, 1949-71, Associate, 1971-77. Sandars Reader in Bibliography, Univ. of Cambridge, 1974-75; Franklin Jasper Walls Lectr, Pierpont Morgan Library, NY, 1979. Pres., Bibliographical Soc., 1977-79; Hon. Pres., Edinburgh Bibliographical Soc.; Vice Pres., Association Internationale de Bibliophilie. Cavaliere Ufficiale, Al Merito della Repubblica Italiana, 1979. *Publications:* French and Italian Collectors and their Bindings, 1953; Great Libraries, 1970; Apollo and Pegasus: an enquiry into the formation and dispersal of a Renaissance library, 1975; contrib. The Library, TLS, etc. *Recreations:* travel, opera, visiting libraries founded before 1800. *Address:* The Glebe House, Whitsbury, Fordingbridge, Hants. *T:* Rockbourne 221. *Club:* Brooks's.

HOBSON, Basil; see Hobson, J. B.

HOBSON, David Constable; Senior Partner, Coopers & Lybrand, Chartered Accountants, since 1975; *b* 1 Nov. 1922; *s* of late Charles Kenneth Hobson and of Eileen Isabel Hobson; *m* 1961, Elizabeth Anne Drury; one *s* one *d*. *Educ:* Marlborough Coll.; Christ's Coll., Cambridge (Scholar). MA, ACA 1950; FCA 1958. Served War, REME, 1942-47 (Captain). Joined Cooper Brothers & Co. (now Coopers & Lybrand), 1947; Partner, 1953; Senior Partner, 1975; Mem., Exec. Cttee, Coopers & Lybrand (International), 1973-(Chm., 1975-76, 1978-79, 1981-82). Inspector (for Dept of Trade), London & County Securities Group Ltd, 1974. Member: Accounting Standards Cttee, 1970-; City Capital Markets Cttee, 1980-; Board Mem. (repr. UK and Ireland), Internat. Accounting Standards Cttee, 1980-. Member of Council: Marlborough Coll., 1967-; Francis Holland Schools, 1975-. *Recreations:* travel, gardening, golf. *Address:* Magnolia, Chiswick Mall, W4 2PR. *T:* 01-994 7511. *Clubs:* Reform, Gresham.

HOBSON, Sir Harold, Kt 1977; CBE 1971; Special Writer, The Sunday Times, since 1976 (Drama Critic, 1947-76); contributor to: Times Literary Supplement; Drama; *b* Thorpe Hesley, near Rotherham, 4 Aug. 1904; *o s* of late J. and Minnie Hobson; *m* 1st, 1935, Gladys Bessie (Elizabeth) (*d* 1979), *e d* of late James Johns; one *d*; 2nd, 1981, Nancy Penhale. *Educ:* privately; Oriel Coll., Oxford (Hon. Fellow, 1974). Asst Literary Editor, The Sunday Times, 1942-48; TV Critic, The Listener, 1947-51; for many years took part in BBC Radio programme The Critics. Mem., National Theatre Bd, 1976-79. Hon. DLitt Sheffield, 1977. Chevalier of the Legion of Honour, 1959. Knight of Mark Twain, 1976. *Publications:* The First Three Years of the War, 1942; The Devil in Woodford Wells (novel), 1946; Theatre, 1948; Theatre II, 1950; Verdict at Midnight, 1952; The Theatre Now, 1953; The French Theatre of Today, 1953; (ed) The International Theatre Annual, 1956, 1957, 1958, 1959, 1960; Ralph Richardson, 1958; (with P. Knightly and L. Russell) The Pearl of Days: an intimate memoir of The Sunday Times, 1972; The French Theatre

since 1830, 1978; Indirect Journey (autobiog.), 1978. *Recreation:* remembering. *Address:* 905 Nelson House, Dolphin Square, SW1.

HOBSON, His Honour (John) Basil, QC (Kenya, 1950; Nyasaland, 1953); a Circuit Judge (formerly Deputy Chairman, NE London Quarter Sessions), 1968-78; *b* 1905; *s* of late J. D. Hobson, QC, Trinidad, British West Indies, and late Cecilia (*née* Johnstone); *m* 1932, Ursula, *y d* of late William Collie, Trinidad; no *c*. *Educ:* Sherborne. Solicitor, 1929; Dep. Registrar, Supreme Court, Trinidad, 1936; admitted Middle Temple and called to Bar, 1938; Crown Counsel, Uganda, 1939. Served War of 1939-45, King's African Rifles, 1939-41; Dep. Judge-Advocate, East Africa Command, 1941-44; Solicitor-Gen., Kenya, 1947; MLC, Kenya, 1947-51; Chm., Labour Advisory Board, Kenya, 1948-49; Attorney-Gen., MEC and MLC, Nyasaland, 1951-57; acted Chief Justice, April-Nov. 1954; Dep. Chm., Essex QS, 1964-68. Chm. Commn on Fishing Industry, 1956; Chm. Select Cttee on Non-African Agriculture, 1957. *Recreation:* watching cricket. *Address:* The Chantry, Marston Road, Sherborne, Dorset DT9 4BL. *T:* Sherborne 2582. *Club:* MCC.

HOBSON, Lawrence John, CMG 1965; OBE 1960; with Arab-British Chamber of Commerce, since 1977; *b* 4 May 1921; *er s* of late John Sinton Hobson and Marion Adelaide Crawford; *m* 1946, Patricia Fiona Rosemary Beggs (*née* Green); one step *s* (one *s* decd). *Educ:* Taunton Sch.; St Catharine's Coll., Cambridge. BA 1946, MA 1950. Served War, 1941-42. ADC and Private Sec. to Gov., Aden, 1942; Political Officer, 1944; Asst Chief Sec., 1956; Aden govt Student Liaison Officer, UK, 1960-62; Political Adviser to High Comr, Aden, 1963-66; retired from HMOCS, 1966. With BP Ltd, 1966-77. Mem., Newbury DC, 1973-. *Address:* Saffron House, Stanford Dingley, near Reading, Berks. *T:* Bradfield 536.

HOBSON, Valerie Babette Louise, (Mrs Profumo); film and stage actress; *b* Larne, Ireland; *d* of Comdr R. G. Hobson, RN, and Violette Hamilton-Willoughby; *m* 1st, 1939, Sir Anthony James Allan Havelock-Allan, Bt (marr. diss. 1952), *qv*; two *s*; 2nd, 1954, John Dennis Profumo, *qv*; one *s*. *Educ:* St Augustine's Priory, London; Royal Academy of Dramatic Art. Was trained from early age to become ballet dancer; first stage appearance at Drury Lane in Ball at the Savoy, aged 15. The King and I, Drury Lane, 1953. First film, Badgers Green; went to Hollywood and appeared in Werewolf of London, Bride of Frankenstein, The Mystery of Edwin Drood, etc; at 18 returned to England. Films include: The Drum, This Man is News, This Man in Paris, The Spy in Black, Q Planes, Silent Battle, Contraband, Unpublished Story, Atlantic Ferry, The Adventures of Tartu, The Years Between, Great Expectations, Blanche Fury, The Small Voice, Kind Hearts and Coronets, Train of Events, Interrupted Journey, The Rocking Horse Winner, The Card, Who Goes There?, Meet Me Tonight, The Voice of Merrill, Background, Knave of Hearts. *Recreations:* listening to music, writing, reading, painting.

HOBSON, Prof. William, BSc (1st Cl. Hons), MD (Dist.), DPH (Dist.), Leeds; MRCS; LRCP; Consultant in medical education, World Health Organisation, since 1971; *b* 5 Sept. 1911; *s* of William Hobson, The Langdales, Park Lane, Leeds; *m* 1937, Lucy Muriel Wilson; one *s* one *d* ; *m* 1953, Heather McMahon Greer; one *d*. *Educ:* Fulneck; Bradford Grammar Sch.; Leeds Univ. Lecturer in Physiology and Hygiene, University of Leeds, 1936-38; Asst Sch. Medical Officer, Leeds, 1938-39; Asst County MO, Hants CC, 1939-40; Medical Officer of Health Borough of Lymington, Hants, 1940-42. Major, RAMC, 1942-46 (despatches). Senior Lecturer in Preventive Medicine, University of Bristol, 1946-48; Prof. of Social and Industrial Medicine, University of Sheffield, 1949-58; Chief, Educn and Training, WHO European Office, 1958-68; Chief of Staff Training, WHO HQ Geneva, 1968-71; Consultant, WHO Regional Office for E Mediterranean, Alexandria, 1971-72. WHO Visiting Prof. to India, 1957-58. Hon. Patron, Western Foundn of Vertebrate Zoology, Los Angeles, 1968. Commandeur de la Confrérie des Chevaliers de Tastevin de Bourgogne, 1963. *Publications:* The Health of the Elderly at Home (with J. Pemberton), 1955 (Ciba Foundn Prize, 1956); (ed) Modern Trends in Geriatrics, 1956; (ed) Theory and Practice of Public Health, 1961, 5th edn 1979 (trans. into Greek, Turkish and Italian), 1974; World Health and History, 1963; contribs to Jl of Hygiene, BMJ, Jl of Phys. Med., Jl of Social Med., Bristol Med. Chir. Jl, Jl Med. Chir. Soc., The Naturalist, etc. *Recreation:* ornithology. *Address:* Strand Cottage, Myrtleville, Co. Cork, Ireland.

HOCHHAUSER, Victor; impresario; *b* 27 March 1923; *m* 1949, Lilian Hochhauser (*née* Shields); three *s* one *d*. *Educ:* City of London Coll. Impresario for: David Oistrakh; Sviatoslav Richter; Mstislav Rostropovich; Gilels, Kogan; Margot Fonteyn; Natalia Makarova; Nureyev Festival; Bolshoi Ballet season at Covent Garden, 1963, 1969; Leningrad State Kirov Ballet, Covent Garden, 1961, 1966; Sunday Evening Concerts, Royal Albert Hall; Peking Opera and other Chinese companies, 1972-. *Recreations:* reading, swimming, sleeping. *Address:* 4 Holland Park Avenue, W11. *T:* 01-727 0781.

HOCHOY, Sir Solomon, TC 1969; GCMG 1962 (KCMG 1959; CMG 1957); GCVO 1966; OBE 1952; Governor-General and C-in-C of Trinidad and Tobago, 1962-72 (Governor, 1960-62); *b* Jamaica, 20 April 1905; *m* 1935, Thelma Edna Huggins; one adopted *d*. *Educ:* St Mary's Coll., Port-of-Spain, Trinidad. Trinidad Government: Clerk, 1928-44; Labour Officer, 1944-46; Deputy Industrial Adviser, 1946-49; Commissioner of Labour, 1949-55;

Deputy Colonial Sec., 1955-56; Chief Sec., Trinidad and Tobago, 1956-60. KStJ 1961. *Recreation:* fishing. *Address:* Blanchisseuse, Trinidad. *Clubs:* Royal Commonwealth Society, Corona; Clipper (International).

HOCKADAY, Sir Arthur (Patrick), KCB 1978 (CB 1975); CMG 1969; Secretary and Director-General, Commonwealth War Graves Commission, since 1982; *b* 17 March 1926; *s* of late William Ronald Hockaday and of Marian Camilla Hockaday, *d* of Rev. A. C. Evans; *m* 1955, Peggy, *d* of H. W. Prince. *Educ:* Merchant Taylors' Sch.; St John's Coll., Oxford. BA (1st cl. Lit. Hum.) 1949, MA 1952. Apptd to Home Civil Service, 1949; Admty, 1949-62; Private Sec. to successive Ministers of Defence and Defence Secretaries, 1962-65; NATO Internat. Staff, 1965-69 (Asst Sec. Gen. for Defence Planning and Policy, 1967-69); Asst Under-Sec. of State, MoD, 1969-72; Under-Sec., Cabinet Office, 1972-73; Dep. Under-Sec. of State, MoD, 1973-76; 2nd Permanent Under-Sec. of State, MoD, 1976-82. *Publications:* (contrib.) Ethics and Nuclear Deterrence, 1982; occasional articles. *Recreation:* fell-walking. *Address:* 11 Hitherwood Court, Hitherwood Drive, SE19 1UX. *T:* 01-670 7940. *Clubs:* Naval and Military, Civil Service.

HOCKENHULL, Arthur James Weston, OBE 1966; HM Diplomatic Service, retired; *b* 8 Aug. 1915; *s* of late Frederick Weston Hockenhull and late Jessie Gibson Kaye Hockenhull (*née* Mitchell); *m* 1955, Rachel Ann Kimber; two *d. Educ:* Clifton Coll.; Exeter Coll., Oxford. HM Overseas Civil Service; various appts in Far East, Cyprus and British Guiana, 1936-57. Interned by Japanese, in Singapore, 1942-45; First Sec., UK Commn, Singapore, 1958-63; Counsellor, British High Commn, Malaysia, 1964-68; Consul-Gen., Houston, 1969-74. *Recreations:* golf, gardening, swimming. *Address:* Church Cottage, Southmoor, Oxon OX13 5HT. *Club:* United Oxford & Cambridge University.

HOCKER, Dr Alexander; Grosses Verdienstkreuz mit Stern des Verdienstordens der Bundesrepublik Deutschland, 1974; Director-General, European Space Research Organisation (ESRO), 1971-74; *m* 1940, Liselotte Schulze; five *s* one *d. Educ:* Univs of Innsbruck, Hamburg and Leipzig. Asst, Law Faculty, Leipzig Univ.; County Court Judge; Officer, Advanced Scientific Study Div., Min. of Educn, Hannover, 1947-49; Dep. of Sec.-Gen. of German Res. Assoc. (Deutsche Forschungsgemeinschaft), 1949-56; Ministerialrat and Ministerialdirigent (responsible for res., trng and sci. exchanges), Fed. Min. for Atomic Energy, 1956-61; Mem. Directorate, Nuclear Res. Centre (Kernforschungsanlage) Jülich, 1961-69; Sci. Adviser to Foundn Volkswagenwerk, 1969-71. German Deleg. to CERN, Geneva, 1952-61 (Chm. of Finance Cttee, 1960-61); Chm. of Legal, Admin. and Financial Working Gp of COPERS, 1961-63; Chm. of Council, ESRO, 1965-67 (Vice-Chm. 1964); Member: German Commn for Space Res., 1964-71; Kuratorium Max-Planck-Institut für Physik and Astrophysik, 1968-71; Max-Plank-Institut für Plasmaphysik, 1971-80, Hon. Member 1980-. *Publication:* (jtly) Taschenbuch für Atomfragen, 1968. *Address:* Bad Godesberg, Auguststrasse 63, 5300 Bonn 2, Germany. *T:* (0228) 363961.

HOCKING, Frederick Denison Maurice; Cornwall County Pathologist; Consulting Biologist and Toxicologist, Devon River Board; late Consulting Pathologist, South-Western Regional Hospital Board; Acting Director Public Health Laboratory Service, Cornwall, and other hospitals in Cornwall; late Chemical Pathologist, Biochemist, and Assistant Pathologist, Westminster Hospital; Lecturer in General and Clinical Pathology, Westminster Hospital Medical School, University of London; *b* 28 Feb. 1899; *o s* of late Rev. Almund Trevosso Hocking and Gertrude Vernon Mary, *o d* of J. Parkinson; *m* 1st, 1927, Amy Gladys (*d* 1956), *y d* of A. T. Coucher; two *d*; 2nd, 1957, Kathleen, *e d* of Dr G. P. O'Donnell. *Educ:* High Sch., Leytonstone; City and Guilds of London Coll., Finsbury; Middlesex Hospital Medical Sch. RN Experimental and Anti-gas Station, 1917-18; Asst Laboratory Dir to the Clinical Research Assoc. MB, BS, BSc, MSc London, MRCS, LRCP, CChem, FRSC, FCS, FRMS; FRSA, MIBiol, FRSH. Associate of the City and Guilds of London Tech. Coll., Finsbury; Member: Pathological Soc. of Great Britain and Ireland; Association of Clinical Pathologists (Councillor, 1944-46); Society of Public Analysts; Medico-Legal Society; Brit. Assoc. in Forensic Medicine; former Mem. Court, Univ. of Exeter (representing Royal Institute of Chemistry); Pres. South-Western Branch, British Medical Association, 1946; Chm. South-Western Branch, RIC, 1955-57; Mem. Council, RIC, 1959-62, 1965-68. Consulting Biologist, Devon River Bd. Mem. Brit. Acad. of Forensic Sciences; Mem. Soc. for Forensic Science. *Publications:* The Employment of Uranium in the Treatment of Malignant New Growths, British Empire Cancer Campaign International Conference, London, 1928; Disseminated Sclerosis (with Sir James Purves-Stewart), 1930; Seaside Accidents, 1958; Delayed Death due to Suicidal Hanging, 1961; Hanging and Manual Strangulation, 1966; Christmas Eve Crime in Falmouth (Murder in the West Country), 1975; The Porthole Murder: Gay Gibson (Facets of Crime), 1975; numerous scientific papers in medical journals, etc. *Recreations:* hotels, good food, wine, conversation. *Address:* Strathaven, Carlyon Bay, Cornwall. *Clubs:* National Liberal, English-Speaking Union.

HOCKING, Philip Norman; *b* 27 Oct. 1925; *s* of late Fred Hocking, FIOB; *m* 1950, Joan Mable, *d* of Horace Ernest Jackson, CBE, Birmingham; three *d. Educ:* King Henry VIII Sch., Coventry; Birmingham Sch. of Architecture. Dir, F. Hocking & Sons Ltd. Mem. Coventry City Council, 1955-60. Prominent Mem. Young Con. Movement. MP (C) Coventry South, 1959-64; PPS to Minister of State, FO, 1963-64. Contested Coventry S, 1964 and 1966.

Chm., Conservative Back Benchers' Housing and Local Govt Cttee, 1962-64. *Recreations:* gardening and sailing.

HOCKLEY, Sir Anthony Heritage F.; *see* Farrar-Hockley.

HOCKLEY, Rev. Canon Raymond Alan; Canon Residentiary, Precentor, Succentor Canonicorum and Chamberlain of York Minster, since 1976; *b* 18 Sept. 1929; 2nd *s* of late Henry Hockley and Doris (*née* Stonehouse); unmarried. *Educ:* Firth Park School, Sheffield; Royal Academy of Music, London; Westcott House, Cambridge. MA, LRAM. Macfarren Schol., Royal Acad. of Music, 1951-54; Charles Lucas Medal, William Corder Prize, Cuthbert Nunn Prize, etc; Theodore Holland Award, 1955. Clements Memorial Prize for Chamber Music by a British subject, 1954. Curate of St Augustine's, Sheffield, 1958-61; Priest-in-charge of Holy Trinity, Wicker, with St Michael and All Angels, Neepsend, 1961-63; Chaplain of Westcott House, Cambridge, 1963-68; Fellow, Chaplain and Dir of Studies in Music, Emmanuel Coll., Cambridge, 1968-76. Works performed include: Songs for Tenor, Soprano; String Quartet; Divertimento for piano duet; Cantata for Easter and the Ascension; Symphony; My Enemies pictured within, a Bitter-Suite for Orchestra; various anthems and motets; incidental music for plays. Other works include: two more Symphonies, A Woman's Last Word for three sopranos; Oratorio on the Destruction and Salvation of the World. *Publications:* Six Songs of Faith; New Songs for the Church; Divertimento; Intercessions at Holy Communion; contribs to theological and musical jls. *Recreations:* cooking, talking, unfinished work. *Address:* 2 Minster Court, York. *T:* York 24965. *Club:* Yorkshire (York).

HOCKNEY, David; artist; *b* Bradford, 9 July 1937; *s* of Kenneth and Laura Hockney. *Educ:* Bradford Grammar Sch.; Bradford Sch. of Art; Royal Coll. of Art. Lecturer: Maidstone Coll. of Art, 1962; Univ. of Iowa, 1964; Univ. of Colorado, 1965; Univ. of California, Los Angeles, 1966, Berkeley, 1967. One-man shows: Kasmin Ltd, London, 1963, 1965, 1966, 1968, 1969, 1970, 1972; Alan Gallery, New York, 1964-67; Museum of Modern Art, NY, 1964-68; Stedlijk Museum, Amsterdam, 1966; Whitworth Gallery, Manchester, 1969; Louvre, Paris, 1974; Galerie Claude Bernard, Paris, 1975; Nicholas Wilder, LA, 1976; Galerie Neundorf, Hamburg, 1977; Warehouse Gall., 1979; Knoedler Gall., 1979, 1981, 1982; André Emmerich Gall., 1979, 1980, etc; touring show of drawings and prints: Munich, Madrid, Lisbon, Teheran, 1977; USA and Canada, 1978; Tate, 1980. Retrospective Exhibn, Whitechapel Art Gall., 1970. 1st Prize, John Moores Exhibn, Liverpool, 1967. Designer: The Rake's Progress, Glyndebourne, 1975, La Scala, 1979; The Magic Flute, Glyndebourne, 1978; designing costumes and sets for the Metropolitan Opera House, NY, 1980. Film: A Bigger Splash, 1975. *Publications:* (ed and illustrated) 14 Poems of C. P. Cavafy, 1967; (illustrated) Six Fairy Tales of the Brothers Grimm, 1969; 72 Drawings by David Hockney, 1971; David Hockney by David Hockney, 1976; The Glue Guitar, 1977; David Hockney: Travels with Pen, Pencil and Ink: selected prints and drawings 1962-77, 1978; Paper Pools, 1980. *Address:* c/o Knoedler Kasmin Ltd, Knoedler Gallery, 143 New Bond Street, W1.

HODDER, Prof. Bramwell William, PhD; Professor of Geography, School of Oriental and African Studies, University of London, since 1970; *b* 25 Nov. 1923; *s* of George Albert Hodder and Emily Griggs, Eastbourne; *m* 1971, Elizabeth (*née* Scruton); three *s* two *d. Educ:* Oldershaw, Wallasey; Oriel Coll., Oxford (MA, BLitt); PhD London. Served War, 1942-47, commissioned in Infantry (Cameronians), Lieut. Lecturer, Univ. of Malaya, Singapore, 1952-56; Lectr/Sen. Lectr, Univ. of Ibadan, Nigeria, 1956-63; Lectr, Univ of Glasgow, 1963-64; Lectr/Reader, Queen Mary Coll., Univ. of London, 1964-70. Joint Hon. Pres., World Expeditionary Assoc., 1972-. *Publications:* Man in Malaya, 1959; Economic Development in the Tropics, 1968, 3rd edn 1980; (jtly) Markets in West Africa, 1969; (jtly) Africa in Transition, 1967; (jtly) Economic Geography, 1974; Africa Today, 1979; articles in various learned jls. *Recreations:* music, hill walking. *Address:* 329 Hills Road, Cambridge. *T:* Cambridge 246861.

HODDER-WILLIAMS, Paul, OBE 1945; TD; publisher; Consultant Hodder & Stoughton Ltd, since 1975; *b* 29 Jan. 1910; *s* of late Frank Garfield Hodder Williams, sometime Dean of Manchester, and late Sarah Myfanwy (*née* Nicholson); *m* 1936, Felicity, 2nd *d* of late C. M. Blagden, DD, sometime Bishop of Peterborough; two *s* two *d. Educ:* Rugby; Gonville and Caius Coll., Cambridge (MA). Joined Hodder & Stoughton Ltd, 1931; Dir, 1936, Chm., 1961-75. Served with HAC (Major, 1942), 99th (London Welsh) HAA Regt RA (Lt-Col Comdg, 1942-45). *Recreations:* gardening, walking. *Address:* Court House, Exford, Minehead, Somerset. *T:* Exford 268.

HODDINOTT, Prof. Alun, DMus; Hon. RAM; Professor of Music, University College, Cardiff, since 1967; *b* 11 Aug. 1929; *s* of Thomas Ivor Hoddinott and Gertrude Jones; *m* 1953, Beti Rhiannon Huws; one *s. Educ:* University Coll. of S Wales and Mon. Lecturer: Cardiff Coll. of Music and Drama, 1951-59; University Coll. of S Wales and Mon, 1959-65; Reader, University of Wales, 1965-67. Member: BBC Music Central Adv. Cttee, 1971-78; Welsh Arts Council, 1968-74; Member Council: Welsh Nat. Opera, 1972-75; Composers' Guild of GB, 1972-; Nat. Youth Orchestra, 1972-. Chm., Welsh Music Archive, 1977-78. Artistic Dir, Cardiff Music Festival. Governor, Welsh Nat. Theatre, 1968-74. Walford Davies Prize, 1954; Arnold Bax Medal, 1957; John Edwards Meml Award, 1967; Hopkins Medal, St David's Soc., NY, 1980. Hon. FRNCM 1981. *Publications: opera:* The Beach of Falesá, 1974; The Magician, 1975; What the Old Man does is always right,

1975; The Rajah's Diamond, 1979; The Trumpet Major, 1981; *choral:* Rebecca, 1961; oratorio, Job, 1962; Medieval Songs, 1962; Danegeld, 1964; Four Welsh Songs, 1964; Cantata: Dives and Lazarus, 1965; An Apple Tree and a Pig, 1968; Ballad, Black Bart, 1968; Out of the Deep, 1972; The Tree of Life, 1971; Four Welsh Songs, 1971; The Silver Swimmer, 1973; Sinfonia Fidei, 1977; Dulcia Iuventutis, 1978; Voyagers, 1978; Hymnus ante Somnum, 1979; Te Deum, 1982; *vocal:* Roman Dream, 1968; Ancestor Worship, 1972; Ynys Mon, 1975; A Contemplation upon Flowers, 1976; *orchestral:* Symphonies 1955, 1962, 1968, 1969, 1973; Nocturne, 1952; Welsh Dances I, 1958, II 1969; Folk Song Suite, 1962; Variations, 1963; Night Music, 1966; Sinfonietta I, 1968, II, 1969, III, 1970, IV, 1971; Fioriture, 1968; Investiture Dances, 1969; Divertimento, 1969; the sun, the great luminary of the universe, 1970; the hawk is set free, 1972; Welsh Airs and Dances for Symphonic Band, 1975; Landscapes, 1975; French Suite, 1977; Passaggio, 1977; Nightpiece, 1977; Lanterne des Morts, 1981; *concertos:* Clarinet, 1951; Oboe, 1954; Harp, 1958; Viola, 1958; Piano I, 1950, II, 1960, III, 1966; Violin, 1961; Organ, 1967; Horn, 1969; Nocturnes and Cadenzas (cello), 1969; Ritornelli (trombone), 1974; The Heaventree of Stars, for violin and orchestra, 1980; *chamber:* Septet, 1956; Sextet, 1960; Variations for Septet, 1962; Wind Quartet, 1963; String Quartet, 1965; Nocturnes and Cadenzas for Clarinet, Violin and Cello, 1968; Divertimento for 8 instruments, 1968; Piano Trio, 1970; Piano Quintet, 1972; Scena for String Quartet, 1979; Ritornelli for Brass Quintet, 1979; Ritornelli for four double basses, 1981; Doubles for oboe, strings and harpsichord, 1982; *instrumental:* sonatas for: piano, 1959, 1962, 1965, 1966, 1968, 1972; harp, 1964; clarinet and piano, 1967; violin and piano, 1969, 1970, 1971, 1976; cello and piano, 1970, 1977; horn and piano, 1971; organ, 1979; sonatinas for: clavichord, 1963; 2 pianos, 1978; guitar, 1978; Suite for Harp, 1967; Fantasy for Harp, 1970; Italian Suite for Recorder and guitar, 1977; Nocturnes and Cadenzas for Solo Cello. *Address:* Maesawelon, Mill Road, Lisvane, Cardiff CF4 5UG. *Clubs:* Athenæum; Cardiff and County (Cardiff).

HODGART, Prof. Matthew John Caldwell; Professor of English, La Trobe University, Australia, 1979–80; *b* 1 Sept. 1916; *s* of late Matthew Hodgart (Major RE), MC, and Katherine Barbour Caldwell (*née* Gardner); *m* 1st, 1940, Betty Joyce Henstridge (*d* 1948); one *s* one *d*; 2nd, 1949, Margaret Patricia Elliott; one adopted *d. Educ:* Rugby Sch. (Scholar); Pembroke Coll., Cambridge (Scholar); BA 1938, MA 1945). Jebb Studentship, Cambridge, 1938–39. Served War, 1939–45: Argyll and Sutherland Highlanders and in Intelligence (mentioned in despatches). Cambridge University: Asst Lectr in English, 1945–49; Lectr in English, and Fellow of Pembroke Coll., 1949–64; Prof. of English: Sussex Univ., 1964–70; Concordia Univ., Montreal, 1970–76. Vis. Professor: Cornell Univ., 1961–62 and 1969; Univ. of Calif, Los Angeles, 1977–78; Stanford Univ., 1979; Hinckley Prof., Johns Hopkins Univ., 1982. Chevalier de la Légion d'honneur, and Croix de guerre, 1945. *Publications:* The Ballads, 1950; (with Prof. M. Worthington) Song in the Work of James Joyce, 1959; Samuel Johnson, 1962; (ed) Horace Walpole, Memoirs, 1963; (ed) Faber Book of Ballads, 1965; Satire, 1969 (trans. various languages); A New Voyage (fiction), 1969; James Joyce, Student Guide, 1978; contrib. Rev. of English Studies, and TLS. *Recreations:* travel, music, photography. *Address:* 13 Montpelier Villas, Brighton BN1 3DG. *T:* Brighton 26993.

HODGE, Alexander Mitchell, GC 1940; VRD; DL; Captain RNVR, retired; WS; Member of firm of Cowan & Stewart, WS, Edinburgh: Director, Standard Life Assurance Co. (Chairman, 1977–82); *b* 23 June 1916; *y s* of James Mackenzie Hodge, Blairgowrie, Perthshire; *m* 1944, Pauline Hester Winsome, *o d* of William John Hill, Bristol; one *s* two *d. Educ:* Fettes Coll.; Edinburgh Univ. (MA 1936, LLB 1938). Joined RNVR, 1938; served with Royal Navy, 1939–45 (despatches, GC). Comdr RNVR, 1949, Capt. RNVR, 1953; CO of the Forth Div. RNVR, 1953–57. Chm., Edinburgh Dist Sea Cadet Cttee, 1959–63; Chm., Lady Haig's Poppy Factory, 1961–67; Mem. Council, Earl Haig Fund (Scotland), 1963–67; Chm., Livingston New Town Licensing Planning Cttee, 1963–69; Dir, Edinburgh Western Gen. Hosp. Assoc. of Friends, 1962– (Chm., 1962–68); Trustee and Mem. Cttee of Management: Royal Victoria Hosp. Tuberculosis Trust, 1964– (Pres., 1970–); Royal Edinburgh Inst. for Sailors, Soldiers and Airmen, 1964–71; Chm. General Comrs of Income Tax, Edinburgh South Div., 1967–; Pres., Edinburgh Chamber of Commerce, 1968–70; Dir, The Cruden Foundn, 1969–72, 1973–; Governor, Fettes Coll., 1970–75. DL Edinburgh, 1972. *Address:* Springbank, Barnton, Edinburgh. *T:* 031-339 3054. *Clubs:* Royal Automobile; New (Edinburgh).

HODGE, David, CBE 1980; JP; DL; Lord Provost of Glasgow, and Lord Lieutenant of County of City of Glasgow, 1977–80; *b* 30 Sept. 1909; *s* of David Hodge and Sarah (*née* Crilly); *m* 1950, Mary Forbes Hodge (*née* Taylor); four *d. Educ:* St Mungo's Acad., Glasgow. Served War, RAF, 1940–46: air crew, Coastal Comd. On staff of Scottish Gas Bd, 1934–50; Prudential Assurance Co. Ltd, 1950–74, retd. Chm., Ruchill Ward and Maryhill Constituency for 20 yrs. Elected to Glasgow Corp., 1971; Magistrate, Corp. of Glasgow, 1972–74; Vice-Chm., Transport Cttee. Mem., City of Glasgow Dist Council, 1974: Chm., Licensing Court, Licensing Cttee, and Justices Cttee; Sec. of Admin; Council Rep., Convention of Scottish Local Authorities, 1974–77. JP, 1975, DL 1980, Glasgow. Hon. LLD Strathclyde, 1980. OStJ 1978. *Recreations:* interested in all sports (former professional footballer; winner of tennis championships; former swimming and badminton coach); theatre, ballet, music. *Address:* 59 Hillend Road, Glasgow G22 6NY. *T:* 041-336 8727. *Clubs:* Royal Automobile; Royal Air Forces Association; Art, Pres, Marist Centenary (Glasgow).

HODGE, James William; HM Diplomatic Service; Counsellor (Commercial), Tokyo, since 1982; *b* 24 Dec. 1943; *s* of William Hodge and late Catherine Hodge (*née* Carden); *m* 1970, Frances Margaret, *d* of Michael Coyne and Theresa Coyne (*née* Walsh); three *d. Educ:* Holy Cross Academy, Edinburgh; Univ. of Edinburgh (MA(Hons) English Lang. and Lit.). Commonwealth Office, 1966; Third Secretary, Tokyo, 1967; Second Secretary (Information), Tokyo, 1970; FCO, 1972; First Sec. (Development, later Chancery), Lagos, 1975; FCO, 1978; First Sec. (Economic), Tokyo, 1981. *Recreations:* books, Icelandic studies. *Address:* c/o Foreign and Commonwealth Office, SW1A 2AH. *Clubs:* MCC, Travellers'.

HODGE, John Dennis; Associate Administrator, for Policy, Plans and Program Management, Research and Special Programs Administration, Department of Transportation, Washington, since 1979; *b* 10 Feb. 1929; *s* of John Charles Henry Hodge and Emily M. Corbett Hodge; *m* 1952, Audrey Cox; two *s* two *d. Educ:* Northampton Engineering Coll., University of London (now The City Univ.). Vickers-Armstrong Ltd, Weybridge, England (Aerodynamics Dept), 1950–52; Head, Air Loads Section, Avro Aircraft Ltd, Toronto, Canada, 1952–59; Tech. Asst to Chief, Ops Div., Space Task Group, NASA, Langley Field, Va, USA, 1959; Chief, Flight Control Br., Space Task Group, NASA, 1961; Asst Chief of Flight Control, 1962, Chief, Flight Control Div., Flight Ops Directorate, NASA, MSC, 1963–68; Manager, Advanced Missions Program, NASA, Manned Spacecraft Centre, 1968–70; Dir, Transport Systems Concepts, Transport Systems Center, 1970; Vice-Pres., R&D, The Ontario Transportation Develt Corp., 1974–76; Department of Transportation, Washington, 1976–; Chief, R&D Plans and Programs Analysis Div., 1976–77; Actg Dir, Office of Policy, Plans and Admin, 1977–79. Hon. ScD, The City Univ., London, Eng., 1966; NASA Medal for Exceptional Service, 1967 and 1969; Dept of Transportation Meritorious Achievement Award, 1974; Special Achievement Award, 1979. *Publications:* contribs to NASA publications and various aerospace jls. *Recreation:* reading. *Address:* 1105 Challendon Road, Great Falls, Va 22066, USA.

HODGE, John Ernest, CMG 1962; CVO 1956; QPM 1955; Inspector-General of Police, Republic of Nigeria, 1962–64; *b* 3 Nov. 1911; *s* of late Rev. J. Z. Hodge, DD; *m* 1950, Margaret Henrietta, *d* of late Rev. Hugh Brady Brew, Wicklow; one *s* one *d. Educ:* Taunton Sch., Taunton, Som. Jamaica Constabulary, 1931–35; The Nigeria Police, 1935–64. Mem. East Lothian CC, 1972–75. OStJ 1961. CPM 1953. *Recreation:* golf. *Address:* Netherlea, Dirleton, East Lothian, Scotland. *T:* Dirleton 272. *Clubs:* Royal Over-Seas League; North Berwick.

HODGE, Sir John Rowland, 2nd Bt *cr* 1921; MBE 1940; FRHS; company director; *b* 1 May 1913; *s* of Sir Rowland Hodge, 1st Bt, and Mabel (*d* 1923), *d* of William Edward Thorpe; *S* father, 1950; *m* 1936, Peggy Ann (marr. diss. 1939), *o d* of Sydney Raymond Kent; *m* 1939, Joan (marr. diss. 1961), *o d* of late Sydney Foster Wilson; three *d*; *m* 1967, Vivien Jill, *d* of A. S. Knightley; one *s* one *d. Educ:* Wrekin Coll.: Switzerland. Served War of 1939–45, RNVR; Lt-Comdr, RNVR, 1938; formerly Oxford and Bucks Light Infantry. Mem. Inst. of Directors. Dist Grand Master, Dist Grand Lodge of Freemasons, Malta. Freeman, City of Newcastle upon Tyne. *Heir:* s Andrew Rowland Hodge, *b* 3 Dec. 1968. *Address:* 16 Sutherland Drive, Gunton Park, Lowestoft NR32 4LP. *T:* Lowestoft 68943. *Clubs:* British Racing Drivers, Naval, Royal Malta Yacht, Royal Yachting Association, Cruising Association.

HODGE, Sir Julian Stephen Alfred, Kt 1970; Merchant banker; Chairman: Avana Group Ltd, 1973–81; Carlyle Trust Ltd; Commercial Bank of Wales (Founder, 1971); *b* 15 Oct. 1904; *s* of late Alfred and Jane Hodge; *m* 1951, Moira (*née* Thomas); two *s* one *d. Educ:* Cardiff Technical Coll. Certified Accountant, 1930. Fellow, Inst. of Taxation, 1941–. Founded Hodge & Co., Accountants and Auditors; Man. Dir, 1963–75, Exec. Chm., 1975–78, Hodge Group Ltd; former Chairman: Julian S. Hodge & Co. Ltd; Gwent Enterprises Ltd; Hodge Finance Ltd; Hodge Life Assurance Co. Ltd; Dir, Standard Chartered Bank, 1973–75. Founder and Chairman: The Jane Hodge Foundation, 1962–; Sir Julian Hodge Charitable Trust, 1964; Chairman: Aberfan Disaster Fund Industrial Project Sub-Cttee; Member: Welsh Economic Council, 1965–68; Welsh Council, 1968–79; Council, Univ. of Wales Inst. of Science and Technology (Treasurer, 1968–76; Vice-Pres., 1976; Pres., 1981–); Foundation Fund Cttee, Univ. of Surrey; Pres., S Glamorgan Dist, St John Ambulance Bde; Trustee, Welsh Sports Trust. Governor, All Hallows (Cranmore Hall) Sch. Trust Ltd. FTII 1941. Hon. LLD Univ. of Wales, 1971. KStJ 1977 (CStJ 1972); KSG 1978. *Publication:* Paradox of Financial Preservation, 1959. *Recreations:* golf, walking, reading, gardening. *Address:* (business) 31 Windsor Place, Cardiff CF1 3UR; (home) Ty Gwyn, Lisvane, Cardiff CF4 5SG.

HODGES, C(yril) Walter; free-lance writer, book illustrator, theatrical historian and designer; *b* 18 March 1909; *s* of Cyril James and Margaret Mary Hodges; *m* 1936, Greta (*née* Becker); two *s. Educ:* Dulwich Coll.; Goldsmiths' Coll. Sch. of Art. Commenced as stage designer, 1929, then illustrator for advertising, magazines (esp. Radio Times) and children's books; began writing, 1937; served with Army, 1940–46 (despatches); has designed stage productions (Mermaid Theatre, 1951, 1964), permanent Elizabethan stage, St George's Theatre, 1976; exhibns (Lloyds, UK Provident Instn); mural decorations painted for Chartered Insce Inst., UK Provident Instn; Art Dir, Encyclopædia Britannica Films, 1959–61. Judith E. Wilson Lectr in Poetry and Drama, Cambridge, 1974; Co-ordinator, Symposium for the

Reconstruction of Globe Playhouse, 1979, Adjunct Prof. of Theatre, 1980-, Wayne State University, USA. Hon. DLitt Sussex, 1979. Kate Greenaway Medal for illustration, 1965; Hons List, Hans Christian Andersen Internat. Award, 1966. *Publications:* Columbus Sails, 1939; The Flying House, 1947; Shakespeare and the Players, 1948; The Globe Restored, 1953 (rev. edn 1968); The Namesake, 1964; Shakespeare's Theatre, 1964; The Norman Conquest, 1966; Magna Carta, 1966; The Marsh King, 1967; The Spanish Armada, 1967; The Overland Launch, 1969; The English Civil War, 1972; Shakespeare's Second Globe, 1973; Playhouse Tales, 1974; The Emperor's Elephant, 1975; Plain Lane Christmas, 1978; The Battlement Garden, 1979; (ed) The Third Globe, 1981; contrib. Shakespeare Survey. *Recreations:* music (listening), letters (writing), museums (visiting), whenever time allows. *Address:* 36 Southover High Street, Lewes, East Sussex BN7 1HX. *T:* Lewes 6530.

HODGES, Elaine Mary, OBE 1975; HM Diplomatic Service; Counsellor, Foreign and Commonwealth Office, since 1981; *b* 12 Nov. 1928; *d* of late Lancelot James Hodges and of Edith Mary (*née* Crossland). *Educ:* Nottingham High School for Girls; St Anne's Coll., Oxford (BA Hons, MA). Joined Foreign Office, 1952; served in: Germany, 1952-53; Switzerland, 1955-56; Warsaw, 1959; New Delhi, 1963-64; Paris, 1967-69; Brussels, 1974-79. *Recreations:* gardening, antiques, travel. *Address:* 46 Westbridge Road, SW11 3PW. *T:* 01-228 3771. *Club:* Reform.

HODGES, Gerald; Director of Finance, City of Bradford Metropolitan Council, since 1974; *b* 14 June 1925; *s* of Alfred John Hodges and Gertrude Alice Hodges; *m* 1950, Betty Maire (*née* Brading); one *s* (and one *s* decd). *Educ:* King's Sch., Peterborough. IPFA. Accountancy Asst, Bexley Borough Council, 1941-48, and Eton RDC, 1948-49; Sen. Accountancy Asst, Newcastle upon Tyne, 1949-53; Chief Accountant, Hemel Hempstead, 1953-56; Dep. Treas., Crawley UDC, 1956-70; Treas., Ilkley UDC, 1970-74. *Publications:* occasional articles in Public Finance and Accountancy. *Recreations:* travelling, ornithology, reading. *Address:* 23 Victoria Avenue, Ilkley, West Yorks. *T:* Ilkley 607346.

HODGES, Joseph Thomas Charles, FCA, FCIS; Secretary General, Corporation of Lloyd's, since 1980; *b* 25 July 1932; *s* of Joseph Henry Hodges and Hilda Ellen Susan (*née* Hermitage); *m* 1962, Joan Swan; two *s* one *d.* *Educ:* East Ham Grammar Sch. ACIS 1955, FCIS 1980; ACA 1960, FCA 1971. National Service, RAF, 1950-52. Accounts Dept, Corp. of Lloyd's, 1949-50 and 1953-55; articled to Gerard van de Linde & Son, Chartered Accountants, 1955-60; Corporation of Lloyd's: Audit Dept, 1960-66, Manager of Audit Dept, 1966-74; Head of Advisory and Legislation, 1974-80; Dep. Sec. Gen., 1980. *Recreations:* watching West Ham United, caravanning. *Address:* 246 Halfway Street, Sidcup, Kent DA15 8DW. *T:* 01-850 3927. *Club:* Carlton.

HODGES, Air Chief Marshal Sir Lewis (Macdonald), KCB 1968 (CB 1963); CBE 1958; DSO 1944 and Bar 1945; DFC 1942 and Bar 1943; Governor, British United Provident Association, since 1973; Director, Pilkington Bros Ltd (Optical Division), since 1979; *b* 1 March 1918; *s* of late Arthur Macdonald Hodges and Gladys Mildred Hodges; *m* 1950, Elizabeth Mary, *e d* of late G. H. Blackett, MC; two *s. Educ:* St Paul's Sch.; RAF Coll., Cranwell. Bomber Command, 1938-44; SE Asia (India, Burma, Ceylon), 1944-45; Palestine, 1945-47; Air Ministry and Min. of Defence, 1948-52; Bomber Command, 1952-59; Asst Comdt, RAF Coll., Cranwell, 1959-61; AO i/c Admin., Middle East Comd, Aden, 1961-63; Imperial Def. Coll., 1963; SHAPE, 1964-65; Ministry of Defence, Asst Chief of Air Staff (Ops), 1965-68; AOC-in-C, RAF Air Support Comd, 1968-70; Air Mem. for Personnel, MoD, 1970-73; Dep. C-in-C, Allied Forces Central Europe, 1973-76, retired. Air ADC to the Queen, 1973-76. Chm. of Governors, Duke of Kent School, 1979-; Chm., RAF Benevolent Fund Educn Cttee, 1979-; Pres., RAF Escaping Soc., 1979-; Pres., Royal Air Forces Assoc., 1981-. Légion d'Honneur (French) 1950; Croix de Guerre (French) 1944. *Recreations:* gardening, shooting, bee-keeping. *Address:* Allens House, Plaxtol, near Sevenoaks, Kent. *T:* Plaxtol 255. *Clubs:* Royal Air Force, Special Forces.

HODGETTS, Robert Bartley; Clerk to Worshipful Company of Glaziers, since 1978; *b* 10 Nov. 1918; *s* of late Captain Bartley Hodgetts, MN and Florence Hodgetts (*née* Stagg); *m* 1st, 1945, A. K. Jeffreys; one *d* ; 2nd, 1949, Frances Grace, *d* of late A. J. Pepper, Worcester; two *d. Educ:* Merchant Taylors' Sch., Crosby; St John's Coll., Cambridge (Scholar, BA). Served RNVR (A), 1940-45. Asst Principal, Min. of Nat. Insce, 1947; Principal 1951; Asst Sec. 1964; Under-Sec., DHSS, 1973-78. *Recreations:* watching cricket and Rugby football. *Address:* 9 Purley Bury Close, Purley, Surrey. *T:* 01-668 2827.

HODGINS, Ven. Michael Minden; Archdeacon of Hackney, 1951-71; Secretary of London Diocesan Fund, 1946-74; *b* 26 Aug. 1912; *yr s* of late Major R. Hodgins, Indian Army, and Margaret Hodgins (*née* Wilson); unmarried. *Educ:* Wellington; Cuddesdon Theological Coll. Deacon, 1939; Priest, 1940; Curate, S Barnabas, Northolt Park, 1939; Asst Secretary, London Diocesan Fund, 1943. MA Lambeth 1960. *Address:* 2 Pottery Close, Brede, Sussex. *T:* Brede 882224.

HODGKIN, Sir Alan (Lloyd), OM 1973; KBE 1972; FRS 1948; MA, ScD Cantab; Master of Trinity College, Cambridge, since 1978 (Fellow, 1936-78); Chancellor, University of Leicester, since 1971; *b* 5 Feb. 1914; *s* of G. L.

Hodgkin and M. F. Wilson; *m* 1944, Marion de Kay, *d* of late F. P. Rous; one *s* three *d. Educ:* Gresham's Sch., Holt; Trinity Coll., Cambridge. Scientific Officer working on Radar for Air Ministry and Min. of Aircraft Production, 1939-45. Lecturer and then Asst Dir of Research at Cambridge, 1945-52; Foulerton Research Prof., Royal Soc., 1952-69; John Humphrey Plummer Prof. of Biophysics, Univ. of Cambridge, 1970-81. Baly Medal, RCP, 1955; Royal Medal of Royal Society, 1958; Nobel Prize for Medicine (jointly), 1963; Copley Medal of Royal Society, 1965. Pres., Royal Society, 1970-75; Pres., Marine Biological Assoc., 1966-76. Foreign Member: Royal Danish Acad. of Sciences, 1964; Amer. Acad. of Arts and Sciences, 1962; Amer. Philosophical Soc.; Royal Swedish Acad. of Sciences; Member: Physiological Soc.; Leopoldina Acad., 1964; Pontifical Acad. of Sciences, 1968; Hon. Mem., Royal Irish Acad., 1974; Hon. For. Mem., USSR Acad. of Scis, 1976. Fellow, Imperial Coll. London, 1972; Hon. FRSE, 1974; Hon. Fellow: Indian National Science Acad., 1972; Girton Coll., Cambridge, 1979; Pharmaceutical Soc.; For. Assoc., Nat. Acad. of Scis, USA, 1974. Hon. MD: Berne 1956, Louvain 1958; Hon. DSc: Sheffield 1963, Newcastle upon Tyne 1965, E Anglia 1966, Manchester 1971, Leicester 1971, London 1971, Newfoundland 1973, Wales 1973, Rockefeller Univ., 1974, Bristol 1976; Oxford, 1977; Hon. LLD, Aberdeen 1973. *Publications:* scientific papers dealing with the nature of nervous conduction, muscle and vision, Jl Physiology, etc. *Recreations:* travel, ornithology and fishing. *Address:* Physiological Laboratory, Cambridge; The Master's Lodge, Trinity College, Cambridge. *T:* Cambridge 358201.

HODGKIN, Prof. Dorothy Mary Crowfoot, OM 1965; FRS 1947; Emeritus Professor, University of Oxford; Hon. Fellow: Somerville College, Oxford; Linacre College, Oxford; Girton College, Cambridge; Newnham College, Cambridge; Fellow, Wolfson College, Oxford, since 1977; Chancellor, Bristol University, since 1970; *b* 1910; *d* of late J. W. Crowfoot, CBE; *m* 1937, Thomas Lionel Hodgkin (*d* 1982); two *s* one *d. Educ:* Sir John Leman Sch., Beccles; Somerville Coll., Oxford. Fellow, Somerville Coll., 1936-77, Royal Soc. Wolfson Research Prof., 1960-77, Oxford Univ. Pres., BAAS, 1977-78. Fellow: Australian Academy of Science, 1968; Akad. Leopoldina, 1968. Foreign Member: Royal Netherlands Academy of Science and Letters, 1956; Amer. Acad. of Arts and Sciences, Boston, 1958, and other learned bodies. Hon. Foreign Member: US Nat. Acad. of Scis, 1971; USSR Acad. of Scis, 1976; Bavarian Acad., 1980. Hon. DSc Leeds, Manchester and others; Hon. ScD Cambridge; LLD Bristol; DUniv Zagreb and York; Hon. Dr Medicine and Surgery Modena. Royal Medallist of the Royal Society, 1956; Nobel Prize for Chemistry, 1964; Copley Medal, Royal Soc., 1976. First Freedom of Beccles, 1965. *Publications:* various, on the X-ray crystallographic analysis of structure of molecules. *Recreations:* archæology, walking, children. *Address:* Crab Mill, Ilmington, Shipston-on-Stour, Warwicks. *T:* Ilmington 233.

HODGKIN, Eliot; artist and writer; *b* 19 June 1905; *o s* of Charles Ernest Hodgkin and Alice Jane Brooke; *m* 1940, Maria Clara (Mimi) Henderson (*née* Franceschi); one *s. Educ:* Harrow; Royal Academy Schs. Exhibited at Royal Academy and bought under Chantrey Bequest, for Tate Gallery: October, 1936; Undergrowth, 1943; Pink and White Turnips, 1972; One Man Shows: London Leicester Galleries, 1956; New York, Durlacher, 1958; London, Arthur Jeffress Gallery, 1959; New York, Durlacher, 1962; London, Reid Gallery, 1963; Agnew's, 1966. *Publications:* She Closed the Door, 1931; Fashion Drawing, 1932; 55 London Views, 1948; A Pictorial Gospel, 1949. *Address:* 23 Hillcrest, 51-57 Ladbroke Grove, W11 3AX.

HODGKIN, Howard, CBE 1977; painter; *b* 6 Aug. 1932; *m* 1955, Julia Lane; two *s. Educ:* Camberwell Sch. of Art; Bath Academy of Art. Taught at Charterhouse Sch., 1954-56; taught at Bath Academy of Art, 1956-66; occasional tutor, Slade Sch. of Art and Chelsea Sch. of Art. Vis. Fellow in Creative Art, Brasenose Coll. Oxford, 1976-77. A Trustee: Tate Gall., 1970-76; National Gall., 1978-. One-man exhibitions include: Arthur Tooth & Sons, London, 1961, 1962, 1964, 1967; Kasmin Gallery, 1969, 1971, 1976; Arnolfini Gall., Bristol, 1970, 1975; Dartington Hall, 1970; Galerie Müller, Cologne, 1971; Kornblee Gall., NY, 1973; Museum of Modern Art, Oxford, Serpentine Gall., London and provincial tour, Waddington Gall., 1976; André Emmerich Gall., Zürich, André Emmerich Gall., NY, Museum of Modern Art, Oxford, 1977; Third Sydney Biennale, Art Gall. of NSW, 1979; Waddington Galls, Bernard Jacobson NY, 1980; Knoeller Gall. NY, Bernard Jacobson NY and LA, 1981. Works in public collections: Arts Council of GB; British Council, London; Contemp. Arts Soc.; Kettering Art Gall.; Peter Stuyvesant Foundn; São Paulo Museum; Oldham Art Gall.; Tate; V&A Museum; Swindon Central Lib.; Bristol City Art Gall.; Walker Art Center, Minneapolis; Nat. Gall. of S Aust., Adelaide; Fogg Art Museum, Cambridge, Mass; BM; Louisiana Museum, Denmark; Museum of Modern Art, Edinburgh; Southampton Art Gall.; Museum of Modern Art, NY. Prizewinner, John Moores Exhibn, Liverpool, 1976. *Address:* 32 Coptic Street, WC1. *T:* 01-580 7970.

HODGKINS, David John; Under-Secretary, Manpower General Division, Department of Employment, since 1980; *b* 13 March 1934; *s* of Rev. Harold Hodgkins and Elsie Hodgkins; *m* 1963, Sheila Lacey; two *s. Educ:* Buxton Coll.; Peterhouse, Cambridge. BA 1956 (Hist. Tripos Pts I and II, Cl. 2 (1) and 1); MA 1960. Entered Min. of Labour as Asst Principal, 1956; Principal: Overseas Div., Min. of Lab., 1961-64; Safety, Health and Welfare Div., MoL, 1964-65; Treasury, 1965-68; Manpower and Productivity Services, Dept of Employment, 1968-70; Assistant Secretary: Prices and Incomes Div., Dept of

Employment, 1970–72; Industrial Relns Div., 1973–76; Under Secretary, Overseas Division, Dept of Employment, 1977–80. *Address:* Four Winds, Batchelors Way, Amersham, Bucks HP7 9AJ. *T:* Amersham 5207. *Club:* Royal Commonwealth Society.

HODGKINSON, Rev. Canon Arthur Edward; Retired Priest-in-Charge of St Ebba's, Eyemouth, Diocese of Edinburgh, since 1982; Hon. Canon of Aberdeen, since 1981; *b* 29 Oct. 1913; *s* of Arthur and Rose Hodgkinson. *Educ:* Glasgow High School; Edinburgh Theol College. LTh Durham 1942. Deacon 1939; Priest 1940. Curate, St George's, Maryhill, Glasgow, 1939–43; Choir Chaplain, 1943, and Precentor of St Ninian's Cath., Perth, 1944–47; Curate-in-Charge, St Finnian's, Lochgelly, 1947–52, and Rector, 1952–54; Rector, Holy Trinity, Motherwell, 1954–65; Provost of St Andrew's Cathedral, Aberdeen, 1965–78; Area Sec., Diocese of Monmouth, Llandaff, Swansea and Brecon, and St Davids, USPG, 1978–82. Commissary to Bp of St John's, 1961–78; Mem., Anglican Consultative Council, 1971–77; Canon of St Mary's Cath., Glasgow, 1963–65. Hon. Canon of Christ Church Cathedral, Connecticut, 1965–78. *Recreations:* motoring, travel. *Address:* The Parsonage, Eyemouth, Berwickshire.

HODGKINSON, Sir Derek; *see* Hodgkinson, Sir W. D.

HODGKINSON, Terence William Ivan, CBE 1958; Member, Editorial Board, The Burlington Magazine, since 1978 (Editor, 1978–81); *b* 7 Oct. 1913; *s* of late Ivan Tattersall Hodgkinson, Wells, Som, and of late Kathryn Van Vleck Townsend, New York (who *m* 2nd, 1929, Sir Gilbert Upcott, KCB; he *d* 1967); unmarried. *Educ:* Oundle Sch.; Magdalen Coll., Oxford. Served War of 1939–45 Major, Gen. Staff 1943. Joined staff of Victoria and Albert Museum (Dept of Architecture and Sculpture) 1946; Asst to the Dir, 1948–62; Secretary to the Advisory Council, 1951–67; Keeper, Dept of Architecture and Sculpture, 1967–74; Dir, Wallace Collection, 1974–78. Member: Exec. Cttee, Nat. Art Collections Fund, 1975–; Museums and Galleries Commn, 1981–. *Publications:* (part author) Catalogue of Sculpture in the Frick Collection, New York, 1970; Catalogue of Sculpture at Waddesdon Manor, 1970; articles in Burlington Magazine, Bulletin and Yearbook of the Victoria and Albert Museum and for Walpole Society. *Recreation:* music. *Address:* 9 The Grove, N6.

HODGKINSON, Air Chief Marshal Sir (William) Derek, KCB 1971 (CB 1969); CBE 1960; DFC; AFC; *b* 27 Dec. 1917; *s* of late E. N. Hodgkinson; *m* 1939, Heather Goodwin, *d* of late H. W. Goodwin, Southampton; one *s* one *d*. *Educ:* Repton. Commnd, 1937; No 220 Sqdn, 1938–40; POW Germany, 1942–45; OC No 210 Sqdn, 1947–49; RAF Staff Coll., 1951; Chief Instructor, Jt Austr. Anti Submarine Sch., Nowra, Austr., 1952–54; Directing Staff, Jt Services Staff Coll., 1954–57; OC No 240 Sqdn, 1957–58; OC RAF St Mawgan, 1960–61; Staff of Chief of Defence Staff, and ADC to the Queen, 1961–63; Imp. Def. Coll., 1964; Comdt RAF Staff Coll., Andover, 1965; Asst Chief of the Air Staff, Operational Requirements, 1966–68; SASO, RAF Training Command, 1969–70; AOC-in-C, Near East Air Force, Commander British Forces Near East, and Administrator, Sovereign Base Areas, Cyprus, 1970–73; Air Secretary, 1973–76; retired 1976. Pres., Regular Forces Employment Assoc., 1982–. *Recreations:* cricket, fishing. *Address:* Frenchmoor Lodge, West Tytherley, Salisbury, Wilts SP5 1NU. *Clubs:* Royal Air Force, MCC.

HODGSON, Alfreda Rose, (Mrs Paul Blissett); concert singer; *b* 7 June 1940; *d* of Alfred and Rose Hodgson; *m* 1963, Paul Blissett; two *d*. *Educ:* Northern School of Music (GNSM; Hon. Fellow 1972); LRAM. Won Kathleen Ferrier Memorial Scholarship, 1964; first professional concert with Royal Liverpool Philharmonic Orchestra, 1964; since then has sung with all major orchestras in Britain, also throughout Europe, USA, Canada, Mexico, and elsewhere. *Address:* 16 St Mary's Road, Prestwich, Manchester M25 5AP. *T:* 061-773 1541.

HODGSON, Arthur Brian, CMG 1962; Consultant, League of Red Cross Societies, since 1982; *b* 24 Aug. 1916; *s* of late Major Arthur H. F. Hodgson, Westfields, Iffley, Oxford; *m* 1945, Anne Patricia Halse, *d* of late Lt-Col E. M. Ley, DSO, KRRC; two *s* two *d*. *Educ:* Edinburgh Academy; Eton Coll.; Oriel Coll., Oxford; Trinity Coll., Cambridge. Colonial Civil Service, Tanganyika Administration, 1939–62, retiring as Principal Sec. and Dir of Establishments. British Red Cross Society: Sec., 1964; Dep. Dir-Gen., 1966–70; Dir-Gen., 1970–75; Counsellor, 1975–81. *Recreations:* rowing, rifle shooting, gardening. *Address:* Chandlers, Furners Green, near Uckfield, Sussex TN22 3RH. *T:* Danehill 790310. *Clubs:* Naval; Leander.

HODGSON, Hon. Sir Derek; *see* Hodgson, Hon. Sir W. D. T.

HODGSON, George Charles Day, CMG 1961; MBE 1950; lately an Administrative Officer, Nyasaland; retired from HMOCS, Nov. 1964; Secretary, Old Diocesans' Union, Diocesan College, Rondebosch, Cape, South Africa, since 1964; *b* 21 Sept. 1913; *s* of late P. J. Hodgson and of A. E. Joubert; *m* 1st, 1940, Edna Orde (*d* 1977), *d* of late G. H. Rushmere; one *s*; 2nd, 1978, Cecile Paston Dewar (*née* Foster). *Educ:* Diocesan Coll., Rondebosch, Capetown, S Africa; Rhodes Univ., Grahamstown, S Africa; Cambridge Univ. Joined Colonial Administrative Service as Cadet, 1939. Military Service, 1940–42; Lieut, 1st Bn King's African Rifles. Returned to duty as Distr. Officer, Nyasaland, 1943; seconded for special famine relief duties in Nyasaland, 1949–50; Provincial Commissioner, 1952; Adviser on

Race Affairs to Govt of Federation of Rhodesia and Nyasaland, 1958–59; Nyasaland Govt Liaison Officer to Monckton Commn, 1960; Permanent Sec., Ministry of Natural Resources and Surveys, Nyasaland, 1961–62; Permanent Sec., Ministry of Transport and Communications, Nyasaland, 1963–64. *Recreations:* Rugby football, cricket, golf. *Address:* Diocesan College, Rondebosch, Cape, South Africa; Little Barn, 86 Dean Street, Newlands, Cape, South Africa. *Clubs:* Royal Cape Golf, Western Province Cricket (Cape Town).

HODGSON, James; Managing Director, British Telecom International, since 1981 (Director, 1969–75, Senior Director International, 1975–81, Post Office Telecommunications); *b* 14 Oct. 1925; *s* of late Frederick and Lucy Hodgson; *m* Brenda Dawn (*née* Giles). *Educ:* Exeter Sch.; St John's Coll., Cambridge. Entered GPO, 1950; Private Sec. to Asst PMG, 1952–55 and to Dir Gen. GPO, 1955–56; seconded to Cabinet Office, 1961–63; Head of Telephone Operating Div. of GPO Headquarters, 1965–67; Vice-Director of External Telecommunications Executive, 1967–69; Dir (non-exec.), Cable and Wireless Ltd, 1970–78. *Recreations:* travel, archaeology. *Address:* 21 Prentice Court, Leopold Avenue, Wimbledon, SW19. *T:* 01-947 3086; 1 Red Cottages, Grayswood, Haslemere, Surrey. *T:* Haslemere 52597.

HODGSON, John Bury; Special Commissioner of Income Tax, 1970–78; *b* 17 March 1912; *s* of Charles Hodgson and Dorothy Hope Hodgson; *m* 1948, Helen Sibyl Uvedale Beaumont. *Educ:* Derbyshire Grammar Sch.; Manchester Univ. Solicitor, 1942; Asst Solicitor of Inland Revenue, 1956–70. *Publications:* (contrib.) Halsbury's Laws of England; (Consulting Editor) Sergeant on Stamp Duties. *Recreations:* sailing, beekeeping. *Address:* Five Thorns Cottage, Brockenhurst, Hants. *T:* Lymington 22653. *Clubs:* various yacht.

HODGSON, Sir Maurice (Arthur Eric), Kt 1979; Chairman, British Home Stores plc, since 1982; *b* 21 Oct. 1919; *s* of late Walter Hodgson and of Amy Hodgson (*née* Walker); *m* 1945, Norma Fawcett; one *s* one *d*. *Educ:* Bradford Grammar Sch.; Merton Coll., Oxford (Hon. Fellow, 1979). MA, BSc; FEng, FIChemE; CChem, FRIC. Joined ICI Ltd Fertilizer & Synthetic Products Gp, 1942; seconded to ICI (New York) Ltd, 1955–58; Head of ICI Ltd Technical Dept, 1958; Develt Dir, ICI Ltd Heavy Organic Chemicals Div., 1960, Dep. Chm., 1964; Gen. Man., Company Planning, ICI Ltd, 1966; Commercial Dir and Planning Dir, ICI Ltd, 1970; Dep. Chm., ICI Ltd, 1972–78, Chm., 1978–82; Director: Carrington Viyella Ltd, 1970–74; Imperial Chemicals Insce Ltd, 1970–78 (Chm. 1972); Dunlop Hldgs, 1982–; Mem. Internat. Adv. Bd, AMAX Inc., 1982–. Member: Court, British Shippers' Council, 1978–82; Council, CBI, 1978–82; Internat. Council, Salk Inst., 1978–; Court, Univ. of Bradford, 1979–. Vis. Fellow, Sch. of Business and Organizational Studies, Univ. of Lancaster, 1970–. CBIM 1980 (FBIM 1972). Governor, London Grad. Sch. of Business Studies, 1978–82. DUniv Heriot-Watt, 1979; Hon. DTech Bradford, 1979; Hon. DSc Loughborough, 1981; Hon. FUMIST, 1979. Messel Medal, Soc. of Chemical Industry, 1980; George E. Davis Medal, IChemE, 1982. *Recreations:* horse-racing, swimming, fishing. *Address:* British Home Stores plc, Marylebone House, 129–137 Marylebone Road, NW1 5QD.

HODGSON, Prof. Phyllis; Professor of English Language and Mediæval Literature, Bedford College, University of London, 1955–72, retired; *b* 27 June 1909; *d* of late Herbert Henry Hodgson, MA, BSc, PhD, FRIC. *Educ:* Bolling Grammar Sch. for Girls, Bradford; Bedford Coll., University of London (BA); (Sen. Schol.) Lady Margaret Hall, Oxford (BLitt, DPhil). Tutor of St Mary's Coll., Durham Univ., 1936–38; Jex-Blake Fellow, Girton Coll., Cambridge (MA), 1938–40; Lecturer in English Language (Part-time), Queen Mary Coll., University of London, and Lecturer in English, Homerton Coll., Cambridge, 1940–42; Lecturer in English Language and Mediæval Literature, Bedford Coll., University of London, 1942–49; Reader in English Language in the University of London, 1949–55; External examiner for Reading Univ., 1955–57, 1961–63. Mem. Council of Early English Text Soc., 1959–79; Chm., Bd of Studies in English, 1964–66. Sir Israel Gollancz Prize, British Academy, 1971. *Publications:* The Cloud of Unknowing (EETS), 1944, 1958; Deonise Hid Divinite (EETS), 1955, 1958, 1973; The Franklin's Tale, 1960; The Orcherd of Syon and the English Mystical Tradition (Proc. Brit. Acad. 1964), 1965; The Orcherd of Syon (EETS), 1966; Three 14th Century English Mystics, 1967; The General Prologue to the Canterbury Tales, 1969; articles in Review of English Studies, Modern Language Review, Contemporary Review, etc. *Recreations:* music, walking, travel. *Address:* 25 Barton Croft, Barton-on-Sea, New Milton, Hants BH25 7BT. *T:* New Milton 612 349. *Club:* University Women's.

HODGSON, Robin Granville; Managing Director, M. J. H. Nightingale & Co. Ltd, since 1979 (Director, since 1972); Director: Johnson Bros & Co. Ltd, Walsall, since 1970; Community Hospitals plc, since 1982; *b* 25 April 1942; *s* of Henry Edward and Natalie Beatrice Hodgson; *m* 1982, Fiona Ferelith, *o d* of K. S. Allom, Dorking, Surrey. *Educ:* Shrewsbury Sch.; Oxford Univ. (BA Hons 1964); Wharton Sch. of Finance, Univ. of Pennsylvania (MBA 1969). Investment Banker, New York and Montreal, 1964–67; Industry in Birmingham, England, 1969–72. Contested (C) Walsall North, Feb. and Oct. 1974; MP (C) Walsall North, Nov. 1976–1979. Chm., Birmingham Bow Gp, 1972–73; Mem. Central Council, Nat. Union of Cons. Assocs, 1979–. Mem., Council for the Securities Industry, 1980–; Chm., Nat. Assoc. of Security Dealers and Investment Managers (formerly Assoc. of Licensed Dealers in Securities), 1979–. *Publications:* Britain's Home Defence Gamble, 1978.

Recreations: squash, theatre. *Address:* Astley Abbotts, Bridgnorth, Salop. *T:* Bridgnorth 3122; 44 Charlwood Street, SW1. *T:* 01-834 7562.

HODGSON, Stanley Ernest, CBE 1974 (OBE 1966); retired; Education Adviser, British High Commission, New Delhi, 1971-77; *b* 11 July 1918; *s* of Harold Frederick Hodgson, MPS, and Winifred Caroline (*née* Gale); *m* 1945, Joan Beryl (*née* Ballard); two *d. Educ:* Brentwood Grammar Sch.; London Univ. Teacher's Certif., London, 1941; BA Hons Russian, London, 1949. RA, 1941-46. British Council: India, 1949-54; Uganda, 1956-60; Reg. Rep., South India, 1965-68; Controller Estabts, 1969-71. Dir, Fest. of India in Britain 1982, 1981-82. *Recreations:* reading, gardening, walking. *Address:* Clarendon, Netherfield Road, Battle, East Sussex TN33 OHJ. *T:* Battle 2631. *Club:* Royal Commonwealth Society.

HODGSON, Thomas Charles Birkett, CVO 1970; OBE 1966; QPM 1969; Chief Constable, Thames Valley Constabulary, 1968-70; *b* 8 Dec. 1907; *s* of late Thomas Edward Birkett Hodgson, Preston, Lancs; *m* 1936, Gwyneth Cosslett Bowles, *d* of Ivor Willans Bowles, Llandaff, Cardiff; one *s* one *d. Educ:* St Peter's, York. Served with Lancashire Constabulary, 1927-55; Asst Chief Constable, Birmingham, 1955-59; Chief Constable, Berkshire, 1959-68. *Address:* Little Newnham, Sutton Veny, near Warminster, Wilts. *T:* Sutton Veny 254.

HODGSON, Thomas Edward Highton, CB 1958; Assistant Secretary, Office of Population Censuses and Surveys (formerly General Register Office), 1968-72; *b* 22 Aug. 1907; *e s* of late Sir Edward Hodgson, KBE, CB; *m* 1935, E. Catherine, *d* of T. Robin Hodgson; four *s. Educ:* Felsted Sch.; St John's Coll., Oxford. Asst Master, Felsted Sch., 1931; Board of Trade: Principal, 1941; Asst Sec., 1945; Asst Sec., Ministry of Materials, 1951; Under Secretary: Ministry of Supply, 1954; Ministry of Aviation, 1959; Ministry of Health, 1960-68. *Address:* 15 Church Street, Sudbury, Suffolk.

HODGSON, Ven. Thomas Richard Burnham; Archdeacon of West Cumberland, since 1979; Vicar of Mosser, since 1979; *b* 17 Aug. 1926; *s* of Richard Shillito Hodgson and Marion Thomasina Bertram Marshall; *m* 1952, Margaret Esther, *o d* of Evan and Caroline Margaret Makinson; one *s* one *d. Educ:* Harden House Prep. Sch.; Heversham Grammar School; London Coll. of Divinity, Univ. of London. BD, ALCD. Deacon 1952, priest 1953, dio. Carlisle; Curate of Crosthwaite, Keswick, 1952-55; Curate of Stanwix, Carlisle, 1955-59; Vicar of St Nicholas', Whitehaven, 1959-65; Rector of Aikton, 1965-67; Vicar of Raughtonhead with Gaitsgill, 1967-73; Hon. Canon of Carlisle, 1973-; Vicar of Grange-over-Sands, 1973-79. Domestic Chaplain to Bishop of Carlisle, 1967-73, Hon. Chaplain 1973-79; Director of Ordination Candidates, 1970-74; RD of Windermere, 1976-79; Surrogate, 1962-. *Recreations:* listening to music, watching drama, geology. *Address:* Mosser Vicarage, Cockermouth, Cumbria CA13 0RX. *T:* Cockermouth 822479.

HODGSON, Hon. Sir (Walter) Derek (Thornley), Kt 1977; **Hon. Mr Justice Hodgson;** a Judge of the High Court of Justice, Queen's Bench Division, since 1977; *b* 24 May 1917; *s* of late Walter Hodgson, Whitefield, Manchester; *m* 1951, Raymonde Valda (*née* de Villiers) (*d* 1965); no *c. Educ:* Malvern Coll.; Trinity Hall, Cambridge. Scholar, Trinity Hall; Harmsworth Scholar, Middle Temple; 1st Cl. Law Tripos, Part II, 1938; 1st Cl. LLB, 1939. Served throughout War 1939-46, Royal Artillery; Burma 1942-45; released with rank of Captain, 1946. Called to Bar, Middle Temple, 1946 (Master of the Bench, 1967); QC 1961. Member: Senate of Inns of Court, 1966-69; Gen. Council of the Bar, 1965-69. Judge of the Salford Hundred Court of Record, 1965-71; a Law Comr, 1971-77; a Recorder of the Crown Court, 1972-77. Member: Lord Chancellor's Cttees on: Legal Educn, 1968-71; Contempt of Court, 1971-74; Butler Cttee on Mentally Abnormal Offenders, 1973-75; Parole Board, 1981- (Vice-Chm., 1982). *Recreations:* fell walking, travel. *Address:* Royal Courts of Justice, Strand, WC2. *Clubs:* United Oxford & Cambridge University; Tennis and Racquets (Manchester); Hawks (Cambridge).

HODGSON, William Donald John; Director of Development, Independent Television News Ltd, since 1982 (Director since 1973); *b* 25 March 1923; *s* of James Samuel Hodgson and Caroline Maud Albrecht; *m* 1946, Betty Joyce Brown; two *s* six *d. Educ:* Beckenham Grammar School. Served Beds and Herts Regt, 1940-42; pilot, RAF and Fleet Air Arm, 1942-46. Documentary and feature film editor (with Jean Renoir on The River, Calcutta), 1946-50; Organiser, Festival of Britain Youth Programme, 1950-51; Asst Sec., Central Bureau for Educational Visits and Exchanges, 1951-54; Asst Gen. Man., Press Assoc., 1954-60; Gen. Man., ITN, 1960-82. Dir, UPITN Corp., 1967-73. *Recreations:* child and grandchildcare, private flying, cricket, swimming. *Address:* 38 Park Road, Beckenham, Kent. *T:* 01-650 8959.

HODIN, Prof. Josef Paul, LLD; author, art historian, art critic; *b* 17 Aug. 1905; *s* of Eduard D. Hodin and Rosa (*née* Klug); *m* 1945, Doris Pamela Simms; one *s* one *d. Educ:* Kleinseitner Realschule and Neustädter Realgymnasium, Prague; Charles Univ., Prague; London Univ.; Art Academies of Dresden and Berlin. Press Attaché to Norwegian Govt in London, 1944-45; Dir of Studies and Librarian, Inst. of Contemporary Arts, London, 1949-54; Hon. Mem. Editorial Council of The Journal of Aesthetics and Art Criticism, Cleveland, 1955-; Mem. Exec. Cttee British Soc. of Aesthetics; Pres., British Section, AICA; Editor: Prisme des Arts, Paris, 1956-59; Quadrum, Brussels, 1956-66. 1st internat. prize for art criticism,

Biennale, Venice, 1954. Hon. PhD Uppsala, 1969; Hon. Prof. Vienna, 1975. DSM 1st cl. Czechoslovakia, 1947; St Olav Medal, Norway, 1958; Comdr, Order of Merit, Italy, 1966; Grand Cross, Order of Merit, Austria, 1968; Order of Merit, 1st cl., Germany, 1969; Silver Cross of Merit, Austria, 1972. *Publications:* Monographs on Sven Erixson (Stockholm), 1940; Ernst Josephson (Stockholm), 1942, Edvard Munch (Stockholm), 1948, (Frankfurt a/M), 1951; Isaac Grünewald (Stockholm), 1949; Art and Criticism (Stockholm), 1944; J. A. Comenius and Our Time (Stockholm), 1944; The Dilemma of Being Modern (London), 1956, (New York), 1959; Henry Moore (Amsterdam, Hamburg), 1956, (London, New York), 1958, (Buenos Aires), 1963; Ben Nicholson (London), 1957; Barbara Hepworth (Neuchatel, London, New York), 1961; Lynn Chadwick (Amsterdam, Hamburg, London, New York), 1961; Bekenntnis zu Kokoschka (Mainz), 1963; Edvard Munch (Mainz), 1963; Oskar Kokoschka: A Biography (London, New York), 1966; Walter Kern (Neuchatel, London), 1966; Ruszkowski (London), 1967; Bernard Leach (London), 1967; Oskar Kokoschka: Sein Leben Seine Zeit (Mainz), 1968; Kafka und Goethe (Hamburg), 1968; Die Brühliche Terrasse, Ein Künstlerroman, 1970; Emilio Greco, Life and Work (London, New York), 1971; Edvard Munch (London, New York, Oslo), 1972; Modern Art and the Modern Mind (London, Cleveland), 1972; Alfred Manessier (London, NY, Paris), 1972; Bernard Stern (London), 1972; Ludwig Meidner (Darmstadt), 1973; Hilde Goldschmidt (Hamburg), 1974; Paul Berger-Bergner, Leben und Werk (Hamburg), 1974; Die Leute von Elverdingen (Hamburg), 1974; Kokoschka und Hellas (Vienna), 1977; John Milne (London), 1977; Else Meidner, 1979; Elisabeth Frink, 1980; Douglas Portway, 1980; Franz Luby (Vienna), 1982; contribs on literary and art subjects to internat. periodicals. *Address:* 12 Eton Avenue, NW3 3EH. *T:* 01-794 3609. *Clubs:* Athenæum, Arts.

HODKIN, Rev. Canon Hedley; Residentiary Canon, Manchester Cathedral, 1957-70, Canon Emeritus, since 1970; Sub-Dean, 1966-70; *b* 3 Jan. 1902; *s* of Walter and Elizabeth Hodkin; *m* 1932, Mary M., *d* of Dr J. A. Findlay; one *s* one *d. Educ:* University of Sheffield; Christ's Coll. and Westcott House, Cambridge. Curate of: Morpeth, 1935-38; St George's, Newcastle, 1938-40; Vicar of: St Luke's, Newcastle, 1940-47; Holy Trinity, Millhouses, Sheffield, 1947-57. Examining Chaplain: to Bishop of Newcastle, 1939-47; to Bishop of Sheffield, 1951-57; to Bishop of Manchester, 1957. Hon. Canon of Sheffield, 1955-57. Select Preacher, Cambridge, 1968. *Recreation:* music. *Address:* 79 Folds Crescent, Sheffield S8 0EP. *T:* Sheffield 362155.

HODKINSON, William, CBE 1974 (OBE 1952); Part-time Member, British Gas Corporation, 1973-74; *b* 11 Aug. 1909; *s* of late William Hodkinson and late Ann Greenwood; *m* 1934, Ann, *d* of John Buxton; one *s. Educ:* St Anne's, Stretford; Salford Technical Coll. Stretford Gas Co.: Technical Asst, 1930-32; Asst Works Manager, 1932-35; UK Gas Corp. Ltd: Chief Technical Officer, 1935-39; Gen. Man., 1939-46; Tech. Dir and Gen. Man., 1946-49; North Western Gas Board (later North Western Gas Region): Chief Technical and Planning Officer, 1949-56; Dep. Chm., 1956-64; Chm., 1964-74. Pres., InstGasE, 1963-64. OStJ 1968. *Recreation:* golf. *Address:* 19 Harewood Avenue, Sale, Trafford, Cheshire. *T:* 061-962 4653.

HODSON, Baron (Life Peer), *cr* 1960, of Rotherfield Greys; **Francis Lord Charlton Hodson,** PC 1951; Kt 1937; MC; a Lord of Appeal in Ordinary, 1960-71; Member of Permanent Court of Arbitration at The Hague, 1949-73; *b* 1895; *s* of Rev. Thomas Hodson, MA, late Rector of Oddington, Glos, and Catherine Anne Maskew; *m* 1918, Susan Mary (*d* 1965), *d* of late Major W. G. Blake, DL; one *s* (and *er s* killed in Libya 23 Jan. 1942; one *d* decd). *Educ:* Cheltenham Coll.; Wadham Coll., Oxford (Hon. Fellow). 2nd Lieut 7th Bn Glos Regt, Sept. 1914; served in Gallipoli and Mesopotamia, 1915-17 (MC, Cavaliere of the Order of the Crown of Italy); retired as Captain, 1919; called to Bar, Inner Temple, 1921; Junior Counsel to Treasury (Probate), 1935; KC 1937; Judge of High Court of Justice (Probate Divorce and Admiralty Division), 1937-51; Bencher, Inner Temple, 1938; a Lord Justice of Appeal, 1951-60. Past Pres., Internat. Law Assoc., British Branch. *Address:* Rotherfield Greys, Oxon. *T:* Rotherfield Greys 303. *Club:* Huntercombe Golf (Henley-on-Thames).

HODSON, Prof. Cecil John, MB, BS London; FRCP; FRCR; DMRE; Professor of Uroradiology, School of Medicine, Yale University, since 1975; *b* 20 Dec. 1915; *s* of Dr J. E. Hodson and Kate Bassnett; *m* (marr. diss.); one *s. Educ:* Eastbourne Coll.; St Mary's Hosp., Paddington. Junior medical posts: St Mary's Hosp. and St Giles Hosp., Camberwell; Brompton Hosp.; Harefield Emergency Hosp. RAMC, 1942-46 (despatches); served in N Africa, Sicily, Italy and Greece; Major, Specialist in Radiology. Dep. Dir, X-Ray Dept, University Coll. Hosp., 1949; Dir, X-Ray Diagnostic Dept, UCH, 1960-70; Radiologist, Queen Elizabeth Hosp. for Children, 1948-70; Hon. Cons. Radiologist, Queen Alexandra Mil. Hosp., Millbank, 1963-70; Prof. of Radiology, Memorial Univ. of Newfoundland, 1970-75. Sec., Faculty of Radiologists, 1959-64, Vice-Pres., 1964-65. Baker Travelling Prof. of Royal Australasian College of Radiology, 1962. William Julius Mickle Fellow, University of London, 1966; FRSM. Member: The Renal Assoc.; Thoracic Soc.; British Paediatric Assoc.; Harveian Soc.; Medical Soc. of London. Hon. FACR 1981. *Publications:* chapters in radiological textbooks; numerous contributions to medical journals. *Recreations:* mountains, sailing, gardening. *Address:* School of Medicine, Yale University, New Haven, Conn 06518, USA; 720 Mt Carmel Avenue, Hamden, Conn 06510, USA. *Clubs:* Alpine Ski; United Hospitals Sailing; Royal Sussex Yacht.

HODSON, Donald Manly; *b* 10 Sept. 1913; 2nd *s* of late Prof. T. C. Hodson; *m* 1940, Margaret Beatson Bell, *er d* of late Sir Nicholas Beatson Bell, KCSI, KCIE; three *s* one *d. Educ:* Gresham's Sch.; Balliol Coll., Oxford. Editorial staff, the Economist, 1935; Leader writer, Financial Times, 1936; Asst Leader Page Editor, News Chronicle, 1937-38; Leader Page Editor, News Chronicle, 1939. BBC European Services: Sub-Editor, 1940; Chief Sub-Editor, 1942; Duty Editor, 1943; European Talks Editor, 1945; Asst Head of European News Dept, 1946; Head of European Talks and English Dept, 1948-51; Asst Controller, European Services, 1951-58; Controller, Overseas Services, 1958-68; Controller of Programmes, External Broadcasting, 1968-70; Dir of Programmes, External Broadcasting, 1971-73, retired. *Address:* Scotland House, Scotland Street, Stoke by Nayland, Suffolk. *T:* Nayland 262102.

HODSON, Prof. Frank, BSc London 1949; PhD Reading 1951; Professor of Geology in the University of Southampton, 1958-81, now Emeritus; *b* 23 Nov. 1921; *s* of late Matthew and Gertrude Hodson; *m* 1945, Ada Heyworth; three *d. Educ:* Burnley Grammar Sch.; Reading Univ. Demonstrator, Reading Univ., 1947-49; Lecturer, Reading Univ., 1949-58. Dean, Faculty of Science, 1972-74, and 1976-77, Public Orator, 1970-73, Univ. of Southampton. Murchison Fund, Geol. Soc., 1962; Founder Mem. and first Hon. Sec., Palaeontol. Assoc., 1957. Pres. Sect. C (geology), British Assoc. for Adv. of Science, 1975; Mem., Mineralogical Soc. of GB. Hon. Mem. Geol. Soc. de Belg. *Publications:* geological papers in publications of learned societies. *Recreation:* book collecting. *Address:* Department of Geology, The University, Southampton SO9 5NH.

HODSON, Henry Vincent; Editor, The Annual Register (of world events), since 1973; *b* 12 May 1906; *er s* of late Prof. T. C. Hodson; *m* 1933, Margaret Elizabeth Honey, Sydney; four *s. Educ:* Gresham's Sch.; Balliol Coll., Oxford. Fellow of All Souls Coll., Oxford, 1928-35; Staff of Economic Advisory Council, 1930-31; Asst Editor of the Round Table, 1931, Editor, 1934-39; Director, Empire Div., Ministry of Information, 1939-41; Reforms Commissioner, Govt of India, 1941-42; Principal Asst Sec., and later head of Non-Munitions Div., Min. of Production, 1942-45; Asst Editor, Sunday Times, 1946-50, Editor, 1950-61; Provost of Ditchley, 1961-71. Sole Partner, Hodson Consultants, 1971-. Consultant Editor, The International Foundation Directory, 1974-. Past Master, Mercers' Co. *Publications:* Economics of a Changing World, 1933; (part) The Empire in the World, 1937; Slump and Recovery, 1929-37, 1938; The British Commonwealth and the Future, 1939; Twentieth Century Empire, 1948; Problems in Anglo-American Relations, 1963; The Great Divide: Britain-India-Pakistan, 1969; The Diseconomics of Growth, 1972; many articles in reviews, etc. *Address:* 23 Cadogan Lane, SW1X 9DP. *T:* 01-235 5509.

HODSON, Joseph John, BDS; PhD; FRCPath; FDSRCS; Professor Emeritus, 1972; Professor of Oral Pathology, University of Sheffield, 1960-72; formerly Hon. Consultant in Oral Pathology to the United Sheffield Hospitals, and to Sheffield Regional Hospital Board; *b* 7 March 1912; *e s* of late Rev. J. J. Hodson, MA, and late Mrs A. Hodson, Birmingham; *m* 1937, Mary Alice, *d* of late John and Florence Whitman, Hull; one *s* one *d. Educ:* Birmingham Univ.; Royal College of Surgeons, Edinburgh. Dental Surgeon to Warwicks CC, 1938-41. War Service, Capt., Royal Army Dental Corps, 1941-45. University of Sheffield: Research Asst, 1947-49, Lectr, 1949-53, Sen. Lectr, 1953-60, in Oral Pathology. Howard Mummery Research Prize, BDA, 1952-57. *Publications:* various papers in Medical and Dental Jls covering research in oral tumours, dental and other diseases of the mouth. *Recreations:* music, gardening. *Address:* 34 Glamis Avenue, Melton Park, Gosforth, Newcastle upon Tyne NE3 5SX.

HODSON, Leslie Manfred Noel, CMG 1958; OBE 1953; QC 1943; retired as Advocate of the High Court of Southern Rhodesia (1929-63); *b* 2 Dec. 1902; *s* of late A. Hodson, JP, and Mrs Hodson; *m* 1927, Iona May Mackenzie (*d* 1972); two *s* one *d. Educ:* Boys' High Sch., Salisbury, Rhodesia; University of the Witwatersrand. City Councillor, Salisbury, Rhodesia, 1932-36; contested by-election, Hartley, 1937; MP for Salisbury Central, 1946 and 1948. First Chm. Rhodesia Univ. Assoc., 1945-53, of Inaugural Board, 1953, and of 1st Council, 1954-58, University Coll. of Rhodesia and Nyasaland, 1953-62. MP Federal Assembly of Rhodesia and Nyasaland, 1953-62. Dep. Speaker Legislative Assembly, 1951, 1953. Hon. LLD Rhodesia, 1975. *Recreation:* journalism. *Address:* Ellerton Farm, Harare South, PO Box 3261, Harare, Zimbabwe. *T:* Harare 8943610. *Club:* Salisbury (Harare).

HODSON, Rt. Rev. Mark Allin; an Assistant Bishop of London, since 1974; *b* 1907; *s* of Albert Edgar Hodson, Solicitor; *m* 1959, Susanna Grace, *e d* of late Arthur Hugh Lister, CMG. *Educ:* Enfield Grammar Sch.; University Coll., London (BA), Fellow, 1974; Wells Theological Coll. Ordained 1931; Asst Curate, St Dunstan, Stepney, 1931-35; Missioner St Nicholas, Perivale, 1935-40; Rector of Poplar, 1940-55. Officiating Curate-in-charge of All Hallows, E India Docks, 1942-52; St Stephen, Poplar, 1943-52; St Frideswide, Poplar, 1947-52; Prebendary of Newington in St Paul's Cathedral, London, 1951-55; Suffragan Bishop of Taunton, 1955-61, also Prebendary and Rector of St Michael and All Angels, Dinder, diocese of Bath and Wells, 1956-61; Bishop of Hereford, 1961-73. Exam. Chaplain to Bp of London, 1974-81. Chaplain General, Guild of St Barnabas for Nurses, 1974-76; Pres., Retd Clergy Assoc., 1974-76. Foundn Governor, Enfield Grammar Sch, 1973-81. *Recreation:* travel. *Address:* 150 Marsham Court, Marsham Street, SW1P 4LB. *T:* 01-828 8378. *Club:* Athenæum.

HODSON, Sir Michael (Robin Adderley), 6th Bt *cr* 1789; Captain, Scots Guards, retired; *b* 5 March 1932; *s* of Major Sir Edmond Adair Hodson, 5th Bt, DSO, and of Anne Elizabeth Adderley, *yr d* of Lt-Col Hartopp Francis Charles Adderley Cradock, Hill House, Sherborne St John; *S* father, 1972; *m* 1st, 1963, Katrin Alexa (marr. diss. 1978), *d* of late Erwin Bernstiel, Dinas Powis, Glamorgan; three *d* ; 2nd, 1978, Catherine, *d* of John Henry Seymour, Wimpole St, W1. *Educ:* Eton. *Heir: b* Patrick Richard Hodson [*b* 27 Nov. 1934; *m* 1961, June, *o d* of H. M. Shepherd-Cross; three *s*]. *Address:* Bellehatch, Henley-on-Thames, Oxfordshire.

HOFF, Harry Summerfield; *see* Cooper, William.

HOFFENBERG, Prof. Raymond; William Withering Professor of Medicine, University of Birmingham, since 1972; *b* 6 March 1923; *er s* of Benjamin and Dora Hoffenberg; *m* 1949; two *s. Educ:* Grey High Sch., Port Elizabeth; Univ. of Cape Town. MB, ChB 1948, MD, PhD, FRCP. Served with S African Armed Forces, N Africa and Italy, 1942-45. Sen. Lectr, Dept of Medicine, Univ. of Cape Town and Cons. Phys., Groote Schuur Hosp., 1955-67; CSIR (S Africa) Sen. Res. Fellow, 1954-55; Carnegie Corp. of NY Trav. Fellow, 1957-58; Cecil John Adams Trav. Fellow, 1957; Fellow, Univ. of Cape Town, 1966; banned by S African Govt, 1967; emigrated to UK, 1968. Sen. Scientist, MRC (UK), attached Div. of Biophysics, Nat. Inst. of Med. Res., 1968-70 and Clinical Res. Centre, Harrow, 1970-72; Cons. Phys. (Endocrinology), New End Hosp. and Royal Free Hosp. Med. Sch., London, 1968-70. Member: West Midlands RHA; MRC, 1978-. Member: Endocrine Soc. (SA) (Past Pres. and Chm.); Soc. for Endocrinol. (UK); Endocrine Soc. (USA); Central and Exec. Cttee, Internat. Soc. for Endocrinology, 1976-; Royal Soc. Med. (Council, 1978-; Council, Endocr. Sect., 1970-72, 1974-, Pres., 1978-; Council, Med. Educ. Sect., 1974-77); London Thyroid Club; Med. Res. Soc. (Chm., 1978-); Assoc. of Physicians (Exec. Cttee, 1977-80); Europ. Thyroid Assoc.; Europ. Soc. for Clin. Investigation. Member Editorial Board: Clinical Science, 1968-72 (Chm. 1971-72), Clinical Endocrinology, 1971-77; Jl of Endocrinology, 1974-77; Qly Jl of Medicine, 1975-. Oliver-Sharpey Lectr, 1973, Procensor and Censor, 1977-79, Senior Censor and Vice-Pres., 1981-82, RCP. Past Mem. Nat. Council, S African Inst. of Race Relations; Past Chairman: World Univ. Service (SA); Defence and Aid Fund (SA); Adv. Bd to Nat. Union of S African Students (Hon. Vice-Pres. of Union, 1968-). *Publications:* chapters and scientific papers on various aspects of endocrinology and metabolism in med. and biochem. jls. *Recreations:* (largely nostalgic) reading, walking, gardening, golf, tennis, squash. *Address:* Department of Medicine, Queen Elizabeth Hospital, Birmingham B15 2TH. *T:* 021-472 1311.

HOFFMAN, Anna Rosenberg; Senior Partner, Anna M. Rosenberg Associates, public and industrial relations consultants, New York; *b* Budapest, Hungary, 19 July 1902; *d* of Albert Lederer and Charlotte Bacskal; *m* 1919, Julius Rosenberg; one *s* ; *m* 1962, Paul Gray Hoffman (*d* 1974). Member: President's Commn on Income Maintenance Programs, 1968-; States Urban Action Center, 1967-; NY Urban Coalition, Inc. of Nat. Urban Coalition, 1967-; Mayor Lindsay's Cttee on Rent Control, 1967-; National Citizens' Commn for Internat. Cooperation; Bd of Directors, United Nations Assoc. of the United States of America, Inc.; Population Crisis Cttee; Franklin Delano Roosevelt Memorial Commission; Board of Trustees, Eleanor Roosevelt Memorial Foundation; Board of Directors of World Rehabilitation Fund, Inc.; also Mem. of other Boards and Cttees, etc., in the United States. Formerly: Asst Sec. of Defense, USA, 1950-53; Regional Director of: War Manpower Commn, 1942-45; Social Security Admin., 1936-42; Office of Defense, Health and Welfare Services, 1941-42; Nat. Recovery Admin., 1934-35, Personal Representative of President Roosevelt, 1944, and of President Truman, 1945, to European Theatre of War; Sec. to President Roosevelt's Labor Victory Board, 1942-45; Member: US Nat. Commn for Unesco, 1946-50; Advisory Commn of the President on Universal Mil. Training, 1946-47; President Roosevelt's Industrial Relations Commn to Great Britain and Sweden etc.; Bd of Education, City of NY, 1961-63; Nat. Adv. Commn on Selective Service, 1966-67. Medal of Freedom, 1945 (first award by Gen. Eisenhower to a civilian); Medal for Merit, 1947; Dept of Defense Exceptional Civilian Service Award, 1953; Medallion of City of NY (for work on beautification of City), 1966. Holds Hon. Degrees in USA. *Publications:* chapter, Social Security and the National Purpose, in The Family in a World at War, 1942; article on history and status of American woman in business world, in The Great Ideas Today, 1966. *Recreations:* chiefly indoor gardening; collection of modern French art; antique china. *Address:* (office) 444 Madison Avenue, New York, NY 10022, USA; (home) 2 East 88 Street, New York, NY 10028, USA.

HOFFMAN, Dustin Lee; actor; *b* 8 Aug. 1937; *s* of Harry Hoffman and Lillian Hoffman; *m* 1969, Anne Byrne (marr. diss. 1980); two *d* ; *m* 1980, Lisa Gottsegen; one *s. Educ:* Santa Monica City Coll.; Pasadena Playhouse. Stage debut in Sarah Lawrence Coll. prodn, Yes is For a Very Young Man; Broadway debut, A Cook for Mr General, 1961; appeared in: Harry, and Noon and Night, Amer. Place Theatre, NY, 1964-65; Journey of the Fifth Horse, and Star Wagon, 1965; Fragments, Berkshire Theatre Festival, Stockbridge, Mass, 1966; Eh?, 1966-67; Jimmy Shine, Broadway, 1968-69. Dir, All Over Town, Broadway, 1974. Films: The Graduate, 1967; Midnight Cowboy, 1969; John and Mary, 1969, Little Big Man, 1971; Who Is Harry Kellerman and Why Is He Saying Those Terrible Things About Me?, 1971; Straw Dogs, 1972; Alfredo, Alfredo, 1972; Papillon, 1973; Lenny, 1974; All The President's Men, 1975; Marathon Man, 1976; Straight Time, 1978;

Agatha, 1979; Kramer vs Kramer, 1979 (Academy Award). Record: Death of a Salesman. Obie Award as best off-Broadway actor, 1965-66, for Journey of the Fifth Horse; Drama Desk, Theatre World, and Vernon Rice Awards for Eh?, 1966; Oscar Award nominee for The Graduate, Midnight Cowboy, and Lenny. *Address:* Punch Productions, 110 West 57th Street, New York, NY 10019, USA.

HOFFMAN, Rev. Canon Stanley Harold, MA; Chaplain in Ordinary to the Queen, since 1976; Hon. Canon of Rochester Cathedral, 1965-80, now Emeritus; *b* 17 Aug. 1917; *s* of Charles and Ellen Hoffman, Denham, Bucks; *m* 1943, Mary Mifanwy Patricia, *d* of late Canon Creed Meredith, Chaplain to the Queen, and of Mrs R. Creed Meredith, Windsor; one *s* one *d. Educ:* The Royal Grammar Sch., High Wycombe, Bucks; St Edmund Hall, Oxford (BA 1939, MA 1943); Lincoln Theol Coll., 1940-41. Deacon, 1941; Priest, 1942; Curate: Windsor Parish Ch., 1941-44; All Saints, Weston, Bath, 1944-47; Chertsey (in charge of All SS), 1947-50; Vicar of Shottermill, Haslemere, Sy, 1951-64; Diocesan Director of Education, Rochester, 1965-80; Warden of Readers, 1974-80. Proctor in Convocation, Church Assembly, 1969-70; Exam. Chaplain to Bp of Rochester, 1973-80. Member: Kent Educn Cttee, 1965-80; Bromley Educn Cttee, 1967-80; Kent Council of Religious Educn, 1965-80; Archbps' Commn on Christian Initiation, 1970. Vice-Chm., Christ Church Coll., Canterbury, 1973-80. *Publications:* (pt-author): A Handbook of Thematic Material, 1968; Christians in Kent, 1972; Teaching the Parables, 1974; contrib. various pubns on Preaching and Religious Educn; numerous Dio. study papers. *Recreations:* music, walking (in love with Cornwall). *Address:* Cedarwood, Holly Close, Grayshott Road, Headley Down, Bordon, Hants. *T:* Headley Down 713128.

HOFFMANN, Leonard Hubert, QC 1977; barrister-at-law; *b* 8 May 1934; *s* of B. W. and G. Hoffmann; *m* 1957, Gillian Lorna Sterner; two *d. Educ:* South African College Sch., Cape Town; Univ. of Cape Town (BA); The Queen's Coll., Oxford (Rhodes Scholar; MA, BCL, Vinerian Law Scholar). Advocate of Supreme Court of S Africa, 1958-60. Called to the Bar, Gray's Inn, 1964; a Judge, Courts of Appeal of Jersey and Guernsey, 1980-. Stowell Civil Law Fellow, University Coll., Oxford, 1961-73. Member, Royal Commn on Gambling, 1976-78. *Publication:* The South African Law of Evidence, 1963. *Address:* Surrey Lodge, 23 Keats Grove, NW3 2RS.

HOFFMANN, Prof. Roald; John A. Newman Professor of Physical Science, Cornell University, since 1974; *b* 18 July 1937; *s* of Hillel Safran and Clara (*née* Rosen, who *m* 2nd, Paul Hoffmann); *m* 1960, Eva Börjesson; one *s* one *d. Educ:* Columbia Univ. (BA); Harvard Univ. (MA, PhD). Junior Fellow, Society of Fellows, Harvard Univ., 1962-65; Associate Professor, to Professor, Cornell Univ., 1965-74. Hon. DTech Royal Inst. of Technology, Stockholm, 1977; Hon. DSc: Yale, 1980; Hartford, 1982; Columbia, 1982. Nobel Prize for Chemistry, 1981. *Publications:* many scientific articles. *Address:* Department of Chemistry, Cornell University, Ithaca, NY 14853, USA.

HOFFMEISTER, Maj.-Gen. Bertram Meryl, CB 1945; CBE 1944; DSO 1943; ED; *b* 15 May 1907; *s* of Flora Elizabeth Rodway and Louis George Hoffmeister; *m* 1935, Donalda Strauss; one *s* one *d. Educ:* Public Schs, Vancouver. Previous to war of 1939-45 employed by H. R. MacMillan Export Co. Ltd, Vancouver, BC. 1st Lieut Seaforth Highlanders of Canada, 1927; Capt. 1934; Major 1939 and given command of a rifle Co. Served with Seaforth Highlanders in England as Co. Comdr, 1939-40; returned to Canada, 1942, to attend Canadian Junior War Staff Course; given Command of Seaforth Highlanders of Canada and commanded this Bn in assault on Sicily in July 1943 (DSO); Brig. Oct. 1943 and assumed command 2 Canadian Infantry Brigade (Bar to DSO battle of Ortona); Maj.-Gen. and commanded 5 Cdn Armoured Div. March 1944; operations on Hitler Line, May-June 1944 (2nd Bar to DSO, CBE); in NW Europe until conclusion of hostilities (CB). GOC Canadian Army Pacific Force, 1945. Gen. Manager, Canadian White Pine Co. Ltd, and MacMillan Industries Ltd (Plywood Div.), 1945-47; H. R. MacMillan Export Co. Ltd; Gen. Mgr Prod., 1947-49 and Vice-Pres. Prod., 1949; Pres., 1949-51; MacMillan & Bloedel Ltd; Pres. 1951-56; Chm. Bd, 1956-57. Agent-Gen. for British Columbia, 1958-61. Pres., Council of the Forest Industries of BC, Vancouver, 1961-71. Chm., Nat. Second Century Fund of BC, 1971-. *Recreations:* rugby, rowing, shooting, skiing. *Address:* 3040 Procter Avenue, West Vancouver, BC, Canada. *Clubs:* Vancouver, Capilano Golf and Country, Vancouver Rowing (Vancouver); Canadian.

HOFMEYR, Murray Bernard; Member Operating Committee of Executive Committee, Anglo American Corporation of South Africa Limited, since 1980; *b* 9 Dec. 1925; *s* of William and Margareta Hofmeyr; *m* 1953, Johanna Hendrika Hofmeyr (*née* Verdurmen); three *s* two *d. Educ:* BA (Rhodes), MA (Oxon). Joined Anglo American Corp., 1962; in Zambia, 1965-72; in England, 1972-80; Man. Dir, 1972-76, Chm. and Man. Dir, 1976-80, Charter Consolidated Ltd. *Recreations:* golf, tennis; Captain Oxford Univ. Cricket, 1951; played Rugby for England, 1950. *Address:* 54 Melville Road, Illovo, Johannesburg, South Africa.

HOFSTADTER, Prof. Robert; Max H. Stein Professor of Physics, Stanford University, since 1971; Director, High Energy Physics Laboratory, Stanford University, 1967-74; *b* Manhattan, New York, NY, 5 Feb. 1915; *s* of Louis and Henrietta Hofstadter; *m* 1942, Nancy Givan, Baltimore, Md; one *s* two *d. Educ:* City Coll. of New York (BS *magna cum laude*); Princeton Univ. (MA, PhD). Instructor in Physics: University of Pennsylvania, 1940-41; City Coll., New York, 1941-42; Associate Physicist and Physicist, Nat. Bureau of

Standards, Washington DC, 1942-43; Asst Chief Physicist, Norden Laboratories Corp., New York, 1943-46; Asst Prof., physics, Princeton Univ., 1946-50; Associate Prof., physics, Stanford Univ., 1950-54; Prof., physics, 1954-71. Member, Board of Governors: Weizmann Institute of Science, Rehovoth, Israel, 1967-; Technion, Haifa, Israel, 1977-. Mem., Bd of Directors, John Fluke Manufacturing Co., Washington, 1979-. Associate Editor: Physical Review, 1951-53; Investigations in Physics, 1951-; Review of Scientific Instruments, 1954-56; Reviews of Modern Physics, 1958-61. Has held various fellowships, Nobel Prize in Physics, 1961. Fellow American Physical Soc.; FPS (London); Sigma Xi; Phi Beta Kappa. Hon. LLD, City Univ. of NY, 1962; Hon. DSc: Gustavus Adolphus Coll., Minn, 1963; Carleton Univ., Ottawa, 1967; Seoul Nat. Univ., 1967; *Laurea* (*hc*), Padua, 1965; Dr Univ. (*hc*), Univ. of Clermont, 1967. *Publications:* (with Robert Herman) High Energy Electron Scattering Tables, 1960 (US); (ed) Nuclear and Nucleon Structure, 1963 (US); (co-ed with L. I. Schiff) Nucleon Structure (Proc. Internat. Conf. at Stanford Univ., 1963), 1964; numerous scientific papers on various aspects of molecular structure, solid state physics, nuclear physics, elementary particles, quantum electrodynamics, laser fusion and review articles on crystal counters, electron scattering and nuclear and nucleon structure. *Recreations:* ranching, photography. *Address:* Department of Physics, Stanford University, Stanford, California, USA.

HOGAN, Air Vice-Marshal Henry Algernon Vickers, CB 1955; DFC 1940; retired; *b* 25 Oct. 1909; *s* of late Lt-Col Edward M. A. Hogan, IA; *m* 1939, Margaret Venetia, *d* of late Vice-Adm. W. Tomkinson, CB, MVO; one *s* one *d. Educ:* Malvern Coll.; RAF Coll., Cranwell. Commissioned 1930. Served in Fighter Sqdns and Fleet Air Arm; Instructor CFS, 1936-37; Mem. RAF Long Distance Flight (Vickers Wellesleys) to Australia, 1938; commanded No 501 Sqdn throughout Battle of Britain; USA, 1941-43 (Arnold Scheme and RAF Delegation Washington); Asst Comdt, Empire CFS, 1944; commanded No 19 Flying Training Sch., RAF Coll., Cranwell, 1945; Staff Coll., 1946; Air Ministry, 1947-48; SPSO, MEAF, 1949-50; commanded RAF, Wattisham 1951; Air Cdre 1953; Sector Comdr, Northern Sector, 1952-53; AOC No 81 Group, 1954; Air Vice-Marshal, 1956; AOC No 83 Group, 2nd ATAF, Germany, 1955-58; SASO, Flying Training Command, 1958-62. Led RAF Mission to Ghana, 1960, and Joint Services Mission to Ghana, 1961. Regional Dir, Civil Defence (Midland), 1964-68. USA Legion of Merit (Officer), 1945. *Recreation:* country pursuits. *Address:* Farlea, Stert, near Devizes, Wilts. *T:* Devizes 3113. *Club:* Royal Air Force.

HOGAN, Michael Henry; Secretary to the Gaming Board for Great Britain, since 1980; *b* 31 May 1927; *s* of James Joseph Hogan and Edith Mary Hogan; *m* 1st, 1953, Nina Spillane (*d* 1974); one *s* three *d* ; 2nd, 1980, Mollie Burtwell. *Educ:* Ushaw Coll.; LSE. Certif. Social Sci., Certif. Mental Health. Asst Warden, St Vincent's Probation Hostel, 1949-50; London Probation Service: Probation Officer, Old Street, Stamford House, Tower Bridge Courts, 1953-59; Sen. Probation Officer, SE London Juvenile Ct, 1959-61; Home Office Inspectorate, 1961-80, Chief Probation Inspector, 1972-80. *Recreation:* golf. *Address:* Shrub Hill, Calvert Road, Dorking, Surrey. *T:* Dorking 885229.

HOGAN, Hon. Sir Michael (Joseph Patrick), Kt 1958; CMG 1953; DSNB 1970; President, Court of Appeal of Seychelles, since 1977, and Member of that for Gibraltar, since 1970; *b* 15 March 1908; *m* 1946, Patricia, *d* of late Thomas Galliford; no *c. Educ:* Belvedere Coll., Dublin; Stonyhurst Coll., Lancs; Trinity Coll., Dublin Univ. (BA, Gold Medal, 1st cl. hons; LLB). Admitted Solicitor, Ireland, 1930; admitted to Kenya Bar, 1931; called to Irish Bar (Kings Inns), 1936; Chief Magistrate, Palestine, 1936; Crown Counsel, 1937; Attorney-Gen., Aden, 1945; called to English Bar (Inner Temple), 1946; KC (Aden) 1946; Solicitor-Gen., Palestine, 1947; attached Foreign Office, 1949; Malaya: Solicitor-Gen., 1950, QC (Malaya) 1952; Attorney-Gen., Federation of Malaya, 1950-55; Chief Justice of Hong Kong, 1955-70, and of Brunei, 1964-70; Mem., Courts of Appeal of the Bahamas, Bermuda and Belize, 1970-75; Pres., Courts of Appeal of Brunei, 1970-73, the Bahamas, 1975-78, Bermuda and Belize, 1975-79. British Mem., Anglo-Japanese Property Commission, 1960. Hon. LLD Dublin Univ., 1962. KSG 1970. *Publications:* revised edition of the Laws of Aden, 1948. *Recreation:* golf. *Address:* 2 Carlyle Mansions, Cheyne Walk, SW3. *Clubs:* Athenæum; Kildare Street and University (Dublin); Royal Irish Yacht; Hong Kong and Hong Kong Country.

HOGARTH, (Arthur) Paul, ARA 1974; RDI 1979; painter, illustrator and draughtsman; *b* Kendal, Cumbria, 4 Oct. 1917; *s* of Arthur Hogarth and Janet Bownass; *m* 1963, one *s. Educ:* St Agnes Sch., Manchester; Coll. of Art, Manchester; St Martin's Sch. of Art, London. Travels in: Poland and Czechoslovakia, 1953; USSR and China, 1954; Rhodesia and S Africa, 1956; Ireland, with Brendan Behan, 1959; USA, 1961-79. Tutor of Drawing: Cambridge Sch. of Art, 1959-61; RCA, 1964-71; Associate Prof., Philadelphia Coll. of Art, 1968-69; Vis. Lectr, RCA, 1971-. Hon. Pres., Assoc. of Illustrators, 1982. Exhibitions: one-man, Leicester Gall., London, 1955; Agnews, London, 1957; Amer. Embassy, London, 1964; retrospectives, Time-Life Bldg, London, 1968; World of Paul Hogarth, Arts Council, RCA Gall., 1970; Travels through the Seventies, Kyle Gall., London. Dr RCA, 1971. *Publications:* Defiant People, 1953; Looking at China, 1956; People Like Us, 1958; (illus.) Brendan Behan's Island, 1962; Creative Pencil Drawing, 1964 (6th edn 1979); (illus.) Brendan Behan's New York, 1964; (with Robert Graves) Majorca Observed, 1965; (with M. Muggeridge) London à la Mode, 1966; Artist as Reporter, 1967; (with A. Jacob) Russian Journey, 1969;

Drawing People, 1971; Artists on Horseback, 1972; Drawing Architecture, 1973; Paul Hogarth's American Album, 1974; Creative Ink Drawing, 1974 (5th edn 1979); Walking Tours of Old Philadelphia, 1976; Walking Tours of Old Boston, 1978; (with Stephen Spender) America Observed, 1979; Arthur Boyd Houghton, 1982; contrib. Graphis, Arts Rev., Design, Sports Illus., D. Tel. Mag., Illus. London News. *Recreation:* sailing. *Address:* c/o Leresche & Sayle, 11 Jubilee Place, SW3 3TE. *T:* 01-352 4311. *Clubs:* Reform, Chelsea Arts.

HOGARTH, James, CB 1973; Under-Secretary, Scottish Home and Health Department, 1963-74, retired; *b* 14 Aug. 1914; *s* of George Hogarth; *m* 1940, Katherine Mary Cameron; two *s* one *d. Educ:* George Watson's, Edinburgh; Edinburgh Univ.; Sorbonne, Paris. Joined Dept of Health for Scotland as Asst Principal, 1938; Principal, 1944; Asst Sec., 1948; Under-Sec., 1963. *Publications:* Payment of the General Practitioner, 1963; translations from French, German, Russian, etc. *Recreation:* travel. *Address:* 6A Crawfurd Road, Edinburgh EH16 5PQ. *T:* 031-667 3878.

HOGARTH, Paul; *see* Hogarth, A. P.

HOGBEN, Herbert Edward; retired; *b* 21 Dec. 1905; *s* of Herbert Edward Hogben; *m* 1929, Dorothy, *d* of Samuel Eastoe Pearson; three *d. Educ:* Borden Gram. Sch., Sittingbourne; King's Coll., London (BSc). Scientific Officer, Admiralty, 1927-; Princ. Scientific Officer, 1943; Sen. Princ. Sci. Off., 1952; Dep. Chief Sci. Off., 1961; Chief Sci. Off., Min. of Def. (Navy), 1965; Dep. Chief Scientist, Admiralty Surface Weapons Establishment, 1965-68; Scientific Adviser to Comdr, British Navy Staff, Washington, 1968-70. *Publications:* ASE monographs and technical notes, articles for Jl Inst. of Navigation. *Recreations:* gardening, travel. *Address:* 12 Portsdown Hill Road, Bedhampton, Havant PO9 3JX.

HOGBEN, Ven. Peter Graham; Archdeacon of Dorking, since 1982; *b* 5 July 1925; *s* of Harold Henry and Winifred Minnie Hogben; *m* 1948, Audree Sayers; two *s. Educ:* Harvey Grammar School, Folkestone; Bishops' College, Cheshunt. Served Royal Engineers, 1943-47 (three years in Far East). Office Manager for two firms of Agricultural Auctioneers in Kent and Herts, 1948-59; theological college, 1960-61; ordained, 1961; Asst Curate of Hale, 1961-64; Vicar of Westborough, Guildford, 1964-71; Chaplain to WRAC, 1964-71; Vicar of Ewell, 1971-82; Editor, Guildford Diocesan Leaflet, 1978-; Hon. Canon of Guildford, 1979-; RD of Epsom, 1980-82. *Recreations:* walking, gardening and photography. *Address:* Chesters, Reigate Road, Leatherhead KT22 8RB. *T:* Leatherhead 376266.

HOGG, family name of **Hailsham Viscountcy** and of **Baron Hailsham of Saint Marylebone.**

HOGG, Alexander Hubert Arthur, CBE 1973; Secretary, Royal Commission on Ancient Monuments in Wales and Monmouthshire, 1949-73; *b* 2 May 1908; *s* of A. F. Hogg; *m* 1943, Nellie, *d* of G. P. Henderson, MD; one *s* one *d. Educ:* Highgate Sch.; Sidney Sussex Coll., Cambridge (MA). Asst Engineer, Sir R. McAlpine & Sons, 1930-34; Junior Scientific Officer, Roads Research Laboratory, 1934-36; Lecturer, Engineering Dept, King's Coll., Newcastle upon Tyne, 1936-42; Temp. Experimental Officer, Admiralty Undex Works, Rosyth, 1942-45; ICI Fellowship, 1945-47; Lecturer Engineering Laboratory, University of Cambridge, 1947-49. FSA; FSAScot. Hon. DLitt Wales, 1974. *Publications:* Hill-Forts of Britain, 1975; British Hill-forts, an Index, 1979; Surveying for Field Archaeologists, 1980; papers in Philosophical Magazine and in Archæological periodicals. *Address:* Brynfield, Waun Fawr, Aberystwyth SY23 3PP. *T:* Aberystwyth 3479.

HOGG, Christopher Anthony; Chairman, Courtaulds Ltd, since 1980; *b* 2 Aug. 1936; *s* of Anthony Wentworth Hogg and Monica Mary (*née* Gladwell); *m* 1961, Anne Patricia (*née* Cathie); two *d. Educ:* Marlborough Coll.; Trinity Coll., Oxford (MA; Hon. Fellow 1982). Harvard Univ. (MBA). National Service, Parachute Regt, 1955-57. Harkness Fellow, 1960-62; IMEDE, Lausanne, 1962-63; Hill, Samuel Ltd, 1963-66; IRC, 1966-68; Courtaulds Ltd, 1968-. Member: Indust. Develt Adv. Bd, 1976-; Cttee of Award for Harkness Fellowships, 1980-. *Publication:* Masers and Lasers, 1963. *Recreations:* opera, reading, walking. *Address:* 18 Hanover Square, W1A 2BB. *T:* 01-629 9080.

HOGG, Douglas Martin; MP (C) Grantham, since 1979; barrister; *b* 5 Feb. 1945; *er s* of Baron Hailsham of Saint Marylebone, *qv; m* 1968, Sarah, *d* of Baron Boyd-Carpenter, *qv;* one *s* one *d. Educ:* Eton; Christ Church, Oxford. Called to the Bar, Lincoln's Inn, 1968. PPS to Chief Sec., HM Treasury, 1982-. *Address:* House of Commons, SW1.

HOGG, Vice-Adm. Sir Ian (Leslie Trower), KCB 1968 (CB 1964); DSC 1941, Bar to DSC 1944; *b* 30 May 1911; 3rd *s* of Col John M. T. Hogg, IA, and Elma (*née* Brand); *m* 1945, Mary G. J., *e d* of Col and Mrs Marsden; two *s. Educ:* Cheltenham Coll. Entered Royal Navy, 1929; specialised in Navigation, 1937; HMS Cardiff, 1939; HMS Penelope, 1940; HMAS Napier, 1941-43; HMS Mauritius, 1944-45; Master of the Fleet, 1946-47; British Admiralty Delegation, Washington, DC, 1948-49; HMS Sluys, in comd, 1950-51; Staff of C-in-C Med., 1952-53; Captain RN, Dec. 1953; Brit. Joint Staff, Washington, DC, 1955-57; idc 1958; Staff of Chief of Defence Staff, 1959-60; Cdre, Cyprus, 1961-62; Dir, Chief of Defence Staff's Commonwealth Exercise, 1962-63; Rear-Adm. 1963; Flag Officer, Medway,

and Admiral Superintendent, HM Dockyard, Chatham, 1963-66; Vice-Adm. 1966; Defence Services Sec., 1966-67; Vice-Chief of the Defence Staff, 1967-70, retired. FRSA 1971. *Address:* The Old Mill, Wendover, Bucks. *T:* Wendover 623196.

HOGG, Sir John (Nicholson), Kt 1963; TD 1946; Deputy Chairman: Williams & Glyn's Bank Ltd, since 1970; Gallaher Ltd, 1964-78; Director, Prudential Corporation Ltd; Chairman, Banque Française de Crédit International Ltd; *b* 4 Oct. 1912; *o s* of late Sir Malcolm Hogg and of Lorna Beaman; *m* 1948, Barbara Mary Elisabeth, *yr d* of Capt. Arden Franklyn, Shedfield, Southampton and *widow* of Viscount Garmoyle (*d* of wounds, 1942); one *s* one *d. Educ:* Eton; Balliol Coll., Oxford. Joined Glyn, Mills and Co., 1934. Served War of 1939-45, with KRRC in Greece, Crete, Western Desert, Tunisia, NW Europe. Rejoined Glyn, Mills and Co. 1945, a Man. Dir., 1950-70, Dep. Chm. 1963-68, Chm. 1968-70; Dir, Royal Bank of Scotland Gp Ltd, 1969-82. Fellow of Eton Coll., 1951-70. Mem. of Commonwealth War Graves Commission, 1958-64; A Trustee Imperial War Graves Endowment Fund, 1965. Sheriff County of London, 1960; Chm., Export Credits Guarantee Department's Adv. Council, 1962-67. Chm., Abu Dhabi Investment Bd, 1967-75. Hon. Treasurer, Inst. of Child Health. *Recreations:* cricket, tennis, fishing. *Address:* The Red House, Shedfield, Southampton SO3 2HN. *T:* Wickham 832121. *Club:* Brooks's.

HOGG, Sir Kenneth Weir, 6th Bt, *cr* 1846; OBE 1946; Lieutenant-Colonel (retired); *b* 13 Sept. 1894; *s* of Guy Weir Hogg (*d* 1943); *S* to baronetcy of cousin, 4th Baron Magheramorne, 1957; *m* 1936, Hon. Aline Emily Partington, *o d* of 2nd Baron Doverdale. *Educ:* Haileybury; Christ Church, Oxford. Served in European War, 1914-18 and War of 1939-45; Irish Guards, 1915-33. *Recreations:* fishing, ski-ing. *Heir: cousin* Major Arthur Ramsay Hogg, MBE 1945 [*b* 24 Oct. 1896; *m* 1924, Mary Aileen Hester Lee (*d* 1980), *d* of late P. H. Lee Evans; three *s* one *d*]. *Address:* 2 Curzon Place, Park Lane, W1. *Clubs:* White's, Portland.

HOGG, Norman; MP (Lab) Dunbartonshire East, since 1979; *b* 12 March 1938; *s* of late Norman Hogg, CBE, LLD, DL, JP, and of Mary Wilson; *m* 1964, Elizabeth McCall Christie. *Educ:* Causewayend Sch., Aberdeen; Ruthrieston Secondary Sch., Aberdeen. Local Government Officer, Aberdeen Town Council, 1953-67; District Officer, National and Local Govt Officers Assoc., 1967-79. Secretary, Trade Unions' Cttee for the Electricity Supply Industry in Scotland, 1978-79; Hon. Secretary: South Aberdeen Constituency Labour Party, 1960-65; Aberdeen Fabian Soc., 1965-67; Glasgow Fabian Soc., 1971-74; Chm., East Dunbartonshire Constituency Labour Party, 1971-76. Member: Transport Users Consultative Cttee for Scotland, 1977-79; Select Cttee on Scottish Affairs, 1979-. Chm., Scottish Parly Lab Gp, 1981-82. *Recreation:* music. *Address:* House of Commons, SW1A 0AA. *T:* 01-219 5095.

HOGG, Rear-Adm. Peter Beauchamp, CB 1980; Head of British Defence Liaison Staff and Defence Adviser, Canberra, 1977-80, retired; Secretary, Winchester College Sixth Centenary Appeal, since 1980; *b* 9 Nov. 1924; *s* of Beauchamp and Sybil Hogg; *m* 1951, Gabriel Argentine Alington; two *s* two *d. Educ:* Connaught House, Weymouth; Bradfield Coll., Berks; Royal Naval Engineering Coll., Keyham. Lieut, HMS Sirius, 1947-49; Advanced Engrg Course, RNC Greenwich, 1949-51; HMS Swiftsure and HMS Pincher, 1951-53; Lt Comdr, Loan Service with Royal Canadian Navy, 1953-56; Staff of RN Engrg Coll., Manadon, 1956-58; Comdr (Trng Comdr), HMS Sultan, 1959-62; Marine Engr Officer, HMS Hampshire, 1962-64; JSSC, Latimer, 1964; Ship Dept, Bath, 1965-67; Captain, Ship Dept, Bath, 1968-69; CO, HMS Tyne, 1970-71; RCDS, 1972; CO, HMS Caledonia, 1973-74; Dir of Naval Recruiting, 1974-76. *Address:* c/o National Westminster Bank, City Centre, Plymouth PL1 1DG.

HOGG, Sir William Lindsay L.; *see* Lindsay-Hogg.

HOGGART, Richard, LittD; Warden, Goldsmiths' College, University of London, since 1976; *b* 24 Sept. 1918; 2nd *s* of Tom Longfellow Hoggart and Adeline Emma Hoggart; *m* 1942, Mary Holt France; two *s* one *d. Educ:* elementary and secondary schs, Leeds; Leeds Univ. (MA, LittD 1978). Served 1940-46, RA; demobilised as Staff Capt. Staff Tutor and Sen. Staff Tutor, University Coll. of Hull and University of Hull, 1946-59; Sen. Lectr in English, University of Leicester, 1959-62; Prof. of English, Birmingham Univ., 1962-73, and Dir, Centre for Contemporary Cultural Studies, 1964-73; an Asst Dir-Gen., Unesco, 1970-75. Vis. Fellow, Inst. of Development Studies, Univ. of Sussex, 1975. Visiting Prof., University of Rochester (NY), USA, 1956-57; Reith Lectr, 1971. Member: Albemarle Cttee on Youth Services, 1958-60; Brit. Council Brit. Books Overseas Cttee, 1959-64; BBC Gen. Advisory Council, 1959-60 and 1964-; Youth Service Development Council, 1960-62; (Pilkington) Cttee on Broadcasting, 1960-62; Culture Adv. Cttee of the UK Nat. Commn for UNESCO; Arts Council, 1976-81(Chm., Drama Panel, 1977-80; Vice-Chm., 1980-81); Statesman and Nation Publishing Co. Ltd, 1977-81 (Chm., 1978-81); Chm., Adv. Council for Adult and Continuing Educn, 1977-. Governor, Royal Shakespeare Theatre. Pres., British Assoc. of Former UN Civil Servants, 1979-. FRSL, 1957-63. DUniv: Open, 1973; Surrey, 1981; Hon D-ès-L Univ. of Bordeaux, 1975. Mem. Editorial Board, New Universities Quarterly. *Publications:* Auden, 1951; The Uses of Literacy, 1957; W. H. Auden, 1957; W. H. Auden-A Selection, 1961; chap. in Conviction, 1958; chapter in Pelican Guide to English Literature, 1961; Teaching Literature, 1963; chapter in Of Books and Humankind, 1964; The Critical Moment, 1964; How and Why Do We Learn, 1965; The World in

1984, 1965; Essays by Divers Hands XXXIII; Guide to the Social Sciences, 1966; Technology and Society, 1966; Essays on Reform, 1967; Your Sunday Paper (ed), 1967; Speaking to Each Other: vol. I, About Society; vol. II, About Literature, 1970; Only Connect (Reith Lectures), 1972; An Idea and Its Servants, 1978; (ed with Janet Morgan) The Future of Broadcasting, 1982; An English Temper, 1982; numerous introductions, articles, pamphlets and reviews. *Recreation:* pottering about the house and garden. *Address:* Goldsmiths' College, New Cross, SE14 6NW.

HOGGE, Maj.-Gen. (Arthur) Michael (Lancelot), CB 1979; General Manager, Regular Forces Employment Association, since 1981; *b* 4 Aug. 1925; *s* of late Lt-Col A. H. F. Hogge, Punjab Regt, Indian Army, and Mrs K. M. Hogge; *m* 1952, Gunilla Jeane Earley; two *s*. *Educ:* Wellington Coll.; Brasenose Coll., Oxford (war-time course). Commissioned, Oct. 1945; 6th Airborne Armoured Recce Regt and 3rd Hussars, Palestine, 1945-48; regimental appts, 3rd Hussars, BAOR, 1948-58; Queen's Own Hussars, BAOR, and Staff appts, 1958-65; comd Queen's Own Hussars, UK and Aden, 1965-67; Col GS, Staff Coll., 1969-71; Royal Coll. of Defence Studies, 1972; Dir of Operational Requirements, MoD, 1973-74, rank of Brig.; Dir Gen. Fighting Vehicles and Engineer Equipment, 1974-77; Dep. Master-General of the Ordnance, 1977-80. *Recreations:* sailing, horticulture. *Address:* c/o Lloyds Bank Ltd, Dorking, Surrey.

HOGUE, Oliver Alfred John, CVO 1954; literary staff, Mirror Newspapers, Sydney, 1962-75 and 1976; Associate News Editor, Daily Mirror, 1968-75; *b* 16 Sept. 1910; *s* of Frank Arthur Hogue and Vida C. Hogue (*née* Robinson), Sydney; *m* 1st, 1936, Mary Barbour May (marr. diss., 1966); four *s*; 2nd, 1966, Mary Elizabeth Mofflin (*d* 1976), *d* of Solomon Merkel, Lithuania. *Educ:* Newcastle (NSW) High Sch. Literary staff, Newcastle Herald, 1930; War Correspondent in Australia, 1940-43; Press Sec. to Hon. J. A. Beasley, Australian Minister for Supply, 1943-45; Political Corresp. for Sydney Sunday Sun, Canberra, 1945-53; literary staff, Sydney Sun, 1954-62. Pres., C'wealth Parly Press Gall., 1947-49. Aust. Govt PRO for Australian visit of the Queen and Prince Philip, 1954. *Address:* 5 Hill Street, Roseville, NSW 2069, Australia. *T:* 4196614. *Club:* Journalists' (Sydney).

HOGWOOD, Christopher Jarvis Haley; harpsichordist, composer, musicologist and broadcaster; Director, Academy of Ancient Music, since 1973; *b* 10 Sept. 1941; *s* of Haley Evelyn Hogwood and Marion Constance Higgott. *Educ:* Cambridge Univ. (MA); Charles Univ., Prague. Keyboard and orchestral recordings. Editor of books and music. Artistic Director, King's Lynn Festival, 1976-80. FRSA. *Publications:* Music at Court (Folio Society), 1977; The Trio Sonata, 1979; Haydn's Visits to England (Folio Society), 1980. *Address:* 2 Claremont, Hills Road, Cambridge. *T:* Cambridge 63975.

HOHLER, Henry Arthur Frederick, CMG 1954; HM Diplomatic Service, retired; Ambassador to Switzerland 1967-70; *b* 4 Feb. 1911; *e s* of late Lt-Col Arthur Preston Hohler, DSO; *m* 1st, 1932, Mona Valentine (*d* 1944), *d* of late Lieut-Col Arthur Murray Pirie, DSO; two *s*; 2nd, 1945, Eveline Susan, *d* of late Lieut-Col Hon. Neville Albert Hood, CMG, DSO; two *d*. *Educ:* Eton; Sandhurst. 2nd Lieut Grenadier Guards, 1931. 3rd Sec. in Foreign Office, 1934; Budapest, 1936; 2nd Sec., 1939; Foreign Office, 1941; 1st Sec., 1945; Berne, 1945; Helsinki, 1948; Moscow, 1949; Counsellor, 1950; Head of Northern Dept, Foreign Office, 1951; Minister in Rome, 1956-60; Ambassador in Saigon, 1960-63; Minister in Paris, 1963-65; Asst Under-Sec., Foreign Office, 1966-67. Liveryman, Grocers' Company. *Address:* RR3, Box 216-A, Gloucester, Va 23061, USA. *Club:* Boodle's.

See also T. S. Astell Hohler.

HOHLER, Thomas Sidney A.; see Astell Hohler.

HOLBOROW, Eric John, MD, FRCP, FRCPath; Professor of Immunopathology, Consultant Immunologist and Head, MRC Group, Bone and Joint Research Unit, London Hospital Medical College, E1; *b* 30 March 1918; *s* of Albert Edward Ratcliffe Holborow and Marian Crutchley; *m* 1943, Cicely Mary Foister; two *s* one *d*. *Educ:* Epsom Coll.; Clare Coll., Cambridge; St Bart's Hosp. MA, MD (Cantab). Served War of 1939-45, Major, RAMC. Consultant Bacteriologist, Canadian Hosp., Taplow, 1953; Mem. Scientific Staff, MRC Rheumatism Unit, Taplow, 1957; Director, 1975. Visiting Prof., Royal Free Hosp. Med. Sch., 1975. Editor, Jl Immunol. Methods, 1971–. *Publications:* Autoimmunity and Disease (with L. E. Glynn), 1965; An ABC of Modern Immunology, 1968, 2nd edn 1973; Immunology in Medicine (with W. G. Reeves), 1977, 2nd edn 1982; books and papers on immunology. *Address:* The Old Rectory, Fingest, Henley-on-Thames, Oxon RG9 6QE. *T:* Turville Heath 391.

HOLBROOK, David Kenneth, MA; author; Fellow and Director of English Studies, Downing College, Cambridge, since 1981; *b* 9 Jan. 1923; *o s* of late Kenneth Redvers and late Elsie Eleanor Holbrook; *m* 1949, Margot Davies-Jones; two *s* two *d*. *Educ:* City of Norwich Sch.; Downing Coll., Cambridge (Exhibr). Intell., mines and explosives officer, ER Yorks Yeo., Armd Corps, 1942-45. Asst Editor, Our Time, 1948; Asst Editor, Bureau of Current Affairs, 1949; Tutor organiser, WEA, 1952-53; Tutor, Bassingbourn Village Coll., Cambs, 1954-61; Fellow, King's Coll., Cambridge, 1961-65; Sen. Leverhulme Res. Fellow, 1965; College Lectr in English, Jesus Coll., Cambridge, 1968-70; Compton Poetry Lectr, Hull Univ., 1969 (resigned); Arts Council Writer's Grant, 1970; Writer in Residence, Dartington Hall, 1970-73 (grant from Elmgrant Trust); Asst Dir English Studies, Downing Coll., Cambridge,

1973-75; Arts Council Writers Grants, 1976, 1979. Mem. Editorial Bd, New Universities Qly, 1976–. *Publications:* Children's Games, 1957; Imaginings, 1961; English for Maturity, 1961; Iron, Honey, Gold, 1961; Llareggub Revisited, 1962; People and Diamonds, 1962; Against the Cruel Frost, 1963; Lights in the Sky Country, 1963; Thieves and Angels, 1963; English for the Rejected, 1964; The Secret Places, 1964; Visions of Life, 1964; The Quest for Love, 1965; Flesh Wounds, 1966; Object Relations, 1967; The Exploring Word, 1967; Children's Writing, 1967; (with Elizabeth Poston) The Cambridge Hymnal, 1967; (with John Joubert) The Quarry (opera), 1967; Plucking the Rushes, 1968; Old World New World, 1969; Human Hope and the Death Instinct, 1971; The Masks of Hate, 1972; Sex and Dehumanization, 1972; Dylan Thomas, The Code of Night, 1972; ed, The Case Against Pornography, 1972; The Pseudo-revolution, 1973; English in Australia Now, 1973; Gustav Mahler and the Courage to Be, 1975; (with Christine Mackenzie) The Honey of Man, 1975; essay on Ted Hughes, in, The Black Rainbow, ed Peter Abbs, 1975; Sylvia Plath: poetry and existence, 1976; Lost Bearings in English Poetry, 1977; Education, Nihilism and Survival, 1977; essay on The Need for Meaning, in, Human Needs and Politics, ed Ross Fitzgerald, 1977; Chance of a Lifetime, 1978; A Play of Passion, 1978; Moments in Italy, 1978; essay on Magazines, in, Discrimination and Popular Culture, ed Denys Thompson; opera with Wilfred Mellers, The Borderline, perf. London 1958; operetta, The Wild Swans (with John Paynter), 1979; English for Meaning, 1980; Selected Poems, 1980. *Recreations:* painting in oils, cooking, gardening. *Address:* Denmore Lodge, Brunswick Gardens, Cambridge CB5 8DQ. *T:* Cambridge 315081.

HOLBURN, James; *b* 1 Dec. 1900; *s* of late Rev. James Holburn, Alyth, Perthshire; *m* 1931, Elizabeth Margaret (*d* 1972), *d* of late Rev. John McConnachie, DD, Dundee; three *s*. *Educ:* Harris Academy, Dundee; University of Glasgow (MA Hons). Editorial staff, the Glasgow Herald, 1921-34; joined The Times, 1934: asst correspondent and actg corresp. Berlin, 1935-39; correspondent Moscow, 1939-40; Ankara, 1940-41; War Correspondent, Middle East, 1941-42; Correspondent New Delhi, 1942-46; United Nations Headquarters, 1946-48; Diplomatic Corresp., 1948-51; Chief Corresp. Middle East, 1952-55; Editor, The Glasgow Herald, 1955-65. *Publications:* contributions to various periodicals. *Recreations:* golf, angling. *Address:* Pitmacree, Johnshill Road, Alyth, Perthshire PH11 8DX. *T:* Alyth 2476. *Club:* Western (Glasgow).

HOLCROFT, Sir Peter (George Culcheth), 3rd Bt *cr* 1921; JP; *b* 29 April 1931; *s* of Sir Reginald Culcheth Holcroft, 2nd Bt, TD, and Mary Frances (*d* 1963), *yr d* of late William Swire, CBE; *S* father, 1978; *m* 1956, Rosemary Rachel, *yr d* of late G. N. Deas; three *s* one *d*. *Educ:* Eton. High Sheriff of Shropshire, 1969; JP 1976. *Recreation:* the countryside. *Heir: s* Charles Antony Culcheth Holcroft, *b* 22 Oct. 1959. *Address:* Eaton Mascott Hall, Cross Houses, Shrewsbury.

HOLDEN, Basil Munroe; Rector, Glasgow Academy, 1959-75, retired; *b* 10 Nov. 1913; *m* 1951, Jean Watters; two *s* two *d*. *Educ:* Queen Elizabeth's Grammar Sch., Blackburn; King's Coll., Cambridge (Foundation Scholar). BA 1935, Maths Tripos (Wrangler), MA 1939. Mathematical Master, Highgate Sch., 1937. Instructor Lieut RN, 1940. Head of Mathematical Dept, Oundle Sch., 1947; Housemaster, Oundle Sch., 1956. *Address:* Brackenburn Lodge, Manesty, Keswick, Cumbria CA12 5UG. *T:* Borrowdale 637.

HOLDEN, Sir David (Charles Beresford), KBE 1972; CB 1963; ERD 1954; *b* 26 July 1915; *s* of Oswald Addenbrooke Holden and Ella Mary Beresford; *m* 1948, Elizabeth Jean Odling; one *s* one *d*. *Educ:* Rossall Sch.; King's Coll., Cambridge. Northern Ireland Civil Service, 1937-76; Permanent Sec., Dept of Finance, NI, and Head of NI Civil Service, 1970-76; Dir, Ulster Office, 1976-77. Royal Artillery, 1939-46. *Address:* Falcons, Wilsford Cum Lake, Amesbury, Salisbury SP4 7BL. *T:* Amesbury 22493.

HOLDEN, Derek; Solicitor; a Recorder of the Crown Court, since 1980; *b* 7 July 1935; *s* of Frederic Holden and Audrey Holden (*née* Hayes); *m* 1961, Dorien Elizabeth Holden (*née* Bell); two *s*. *Educ:* Cromwell House, Staines Grammar Sch. Served Army; Lieut East Surrey Regt, 1953-56. Qualified as Solicitor, 1966; Partner, Derek Holden & Co., Staines and Egham, 1966–; Consultant, Batt Holden & Co., Solicitors, 1970–; Partner: Dorien Property & Investment Co., 1970–; Blacklake Securities, 1979–; Dorien Leasing, 1979–. Mem., Royal Yachting Assoc., 1975– (Yachtmaster, Instr and Ocean certs). Principal, Chandor Sch. of Sailing, Lymington, 1978–. Pres., Staines Amateur Regatta, 1980–. *Recreations:* sailing, ski-ing, photography, tennis. *Address:* Walnut Tree Farm, Windlesham, Surrey. *T:* Bagshot 73422. *Clubs:* Law Society; Ski Club of Great Britain; Remenham (Henley); Staines Boat; Burway Rowing (Laleham); Eton Excelsior Rowing (Windsor); Royal Solent Yacht (Yarmouth, IoW); Queen Mary Sailing (Ashford); Penney Hill Park (Bagshot); Westerly Association.

HOLDEN, Sir Edward, 6th Bt, *cr* 1893; Consultant Anæsthetist, Darlington & Northallerton Group Hospitals, 1957-74; *b* 8 Oct. 1916; *s* of Sir Isaac Holden Holden, 5th Bt, and Alice Edna Byrom (*d* 1971), *S* father, 1962; *m* 1942, Frances Joan, *e d* of John Spark, JP, Ludlow, Stockton-on-Tees; two adopted *s*. *Educ:* Leys Sch. and Christ's Coll., Cambridge (MA); St Thomas's Hosp. MRCS; LRCP 1942; DA Eng., 1946; FFA, RCS, 1958. Formerly Vis. Anæsth., Cumb. Infirm., Carlisle; Cons. Anæsth. W Cumb. Hospital Group. Mem. Council, Harlow Car Gardens. *Recreations:* fishing and gardening. *Heir: b* Paul Holden [*b* 3 March 1923; *m* 1950, Vivien Mary Oldham; one *s* two *d*]. *Address:* Moorstones, Osmotherley, Northallerton, N Yorks DL6 3BG. *Club:* Farmers'.

HOLDEN, Sir John David, 4th Bt *cr* 1919; *b* 16 Dec. 1967; *s* of David George Holden (*d* 1971) (*e s* of 3rd Bt), and of Nancy, *d* of H. W. D. Marwood, Foulrice, Whenby, Brandsby, Yorks; *S* grandfather, 1976. *Heir:* uncle Brian Peter John Holden, *b* 12 April 1944.

HOLDEN, Maj.-Gen. John Reid, CB 1965; CBE 1960 (OBE 1953); DSO 1941; *b* 8 Jan. 1913; 2nd *s* of late John Holden, MA, Edinburgh; *m* 1939, Rosemarie Florence (*d* 1980), *d* of late William Henry de Vere Pennefather, Carlow; one *d.* *Educ:* Hamilton Academy; Glasgow Univ.; RMC, Sandhurst. 2nd Lieut Royal Tank Corps, 1937; Adjutant, 7th Royal Tank Regt, 1940-41 (despatches, DSO); Bde Major, 32nd Army Tank Bde, 1942; POW, 1942-45. GSO1, GHQ, Far ELF, Singapore, 1951-52 (OBE); CO 3rd Royal Tank Regt, BAOR, 1954-57; AAG, War Office, 1958. Comdr, 7th Armoured Bde Group, BAOR, 1958-61 (CBE). Royal Naval War Coll., 1961. Chief of Mission, British Comdrs-in-Chief Mission to the Soviet Forces in Germany, 1961-63; GOC 43 (Wessex) Div. Dist, 1963-65; Dir, RAC, 1965-68, retired 1968. Col Comdt, RTR, 1965-68. Hon. Col, The Queen's Own Lowland Yeomanry, RAC, T&AVR, 1972-75. *Recreations:* books, gardening. *Address:* c/o Williams and Glyn's Bank Ltd, Kirkland House, Whitehall, SW1.

HOLDEN, Kenneth Graham; retired; *b* 6 May 1910; *e s* of Norman Neill Holden; *m* 1937, Winifred Frances, *d* of Lt-Col T. F. S. Burridge; two *d.* *Educ:* Wellington Coll.; Pembroke Coll., Cambridge. Admitted Solicitor, 1935. Director: (and sometime Chm.) Hardman & Holden Ltd, Manchester, 1936-64; Williams & Glyn's Bank Ltd (formerly as Williams Deacon's Bank Ltd), 1949-78 (Chm., 1964-72); Royal Bank of Scotland Ltd, 1950-69; Geigy (Holdings) Ltd (later CIBA-Geigy (UK) Ltd), 1955-75; Borax Consolidated Ltd, 1961-64; Haden-Carrier Ltd, 1967-75; The Trustee's Corp. Ltd, 1967-80; Manchester Ship Canal Co., 1968-74; National Commercial Banking Group Ltd, 1969-76; Yorkshire Bank Ltd, 1970-78; The Industrial and General Trust Ltd, 1971-80. Part-time Mem., NW Gas Bd, 1965-72. Formerly Mem. Bd of Management (and sometime Jt Hon. Treasurer), Manchester Royal Infirmary. Governor, Manchester Grammar School. *Address:* 40 Lee Road, Aldeburgh, Suffolk. *T:* Aldeburgh 3159. *Club:* All England Lawn Tennis.

HOLDEN, Patrick Brian, MA, FCIS; Chairman, Consolidated Scientific Instruments; Director: British Potash Development Co.; Felix Mortgage Guarantee; Group Secretary, Fisons, since 1981; *b* 16 June 1937; *s* of Reginald John and Winifred Isobel Holden; *m* 1912, Jennifer Ruth (*née* Meddings), MB, BS. *Educ:* Allhallows Sch. (Major Schol.); St Catharine's Coll., Cambridge (BA Hons Law 1960, MA 1963). FCIS 1965. Served Royal Hampshire Regt, 1955-57 regular commn), seconded 1 Ghana Regt, RWAFF. Fine Fare Group: Sec., 1960-69; Legal and Property Dir, 1965-69; Pye of Cambridge Gp, 1969-74; Dir, Pye Telecom. Ltd, 1972-74; Dir and Sec., Oriel Foods Gp, 1975-81. Sec., New Town Assoc., 1974-75. FBIM. *Recreations:* squash, sailing. *Address:* The Old School House, Lower Green, Tewin, Herts AL6 0LD. *T:* Tewin 7573. *Club:* Naval and Military.

HOLDEN, Philip Edward; an Underwriting Member of Lloyd's since 1954; *b* 20 June 1905. *Educ:* King Edward VI Schs, Birmingham. Qualified, CA, 1929; Managing Dir Amalgamated Anthracite Collieries, from 1940. Past Chm., Amalgamated Anthracite Holdings Group of Cos. Has served on Exec. of Monmouthshire and S Wales Coal Owners Assoc., and as Chm. of its Commercial Cttee; also served on Exec. Bd of S Wales Coal Mines Scheme. Pres. Swansea Chamber of Commerce, 1952-53; Vice-Chm. Chamber of Coal Traders, 1953-65; Vice-Chm. Nat. Council of Coal Traders (Chm. 1953-65); Pres. Brit. Coal Exporters' Assoc., 1958-63; Mem. Industrial Coal Consumers' Council, 1958. A Dir of public and private cos (coal, shipping, manufactures, electronics, electro-chemical and general engineering, etc). *Recreations:* Pres. Swansea City AFC Ltd; Vice-Pres. Clyne Golf Club, Ltd. *Address:* La Maison Blanche, Jerbourg Road, St Martin, Guernsey, CI. *T:* Guernsey 37985. *Club:* Royal Automobile.

HOLDEN-BROWN, Sir Derrick, Kt 1979; Chairman and Chief Executive, Allied-Lyons (formerly Allied Breweries) plc, since 1982; *b* 14 Feb. 1923; *s* of Harold Walter and Beatrice Florence (*née* Walker); *m* 1950, Patricia Mary Ross Mackenzie; one *s* one *d.* *Educ:* Westcliff. Mem., Inst of Chartered Accountants of Scotland. Served War, Royal Navy, 1941-46, Lt RNVR, Coastal Forces. Chartered Accountant, 1948; Hiram Walker & Sons, Distillers, 1949; Managing Director: Cairnes Ltd, Brewers, Eire, 1954; Grants of St James's Ltd, 1960; Dir, Ind Coope Ltd, 1962; Chm., Victoria Wine Co., 1964; Dir, Allied Breweries Ltd, 1967, Finance Dir, 1972, Vice-Chm., 1975-82, Chm., Beer Div., 1978-82; Dir, Sun Alliance & London Insurance Co. Ltd, 1977-. Dep. Chm., FDIC, 1974-76. Chm., Brewers' Soc., 1978-80. *Recreations:* sailing, offshore cruising. *Address:* Copse House, Milford-on-Sea, Hants. *T:* Milford-on-Sea 2247. *Clubs:* Carlton; Royal Lymington Yacht; Royal Naval Sailing Association.

HOLDER, Sir John (Eric Duncan), 3rd Bt, *cr* 1898; late Flight Lieutenant RAFVR; *b* 2 Aug. 1899; *s* of Sir Henry Holder, 2nd Bt, and Evelyn (*d* 1956), *d* of Sir Robert Ropner, 1st Bt; *S* father, 1945; *m* 1st, 1927, Evelyn Josephine (marr. diss.), *er d* of late William Blain; one *s* two *d*; 2nd, Marjorie Emily, *d* of late F. R. Markham. *Educ:* Uppingham; Brasenose Coll., Oxford (MA). *Heir: s* John Henry Holder, Royal Armoured Corps [*b* 12 March 1928; *m* 1960, Catharine Harrison, *yr d* of late Leonard Baker; two *s* (twins) one *d*].

Address: Mulberry House, 17 Johnsons Drive, Hampton, Middx TW12 2EQ.

HOLDER, Air Marshal Sir Paul (Davie), KBE 1965; CB 1964; DSO 1942; DFC 1941; *b* 2 Sept. 1911; *s* of Hugh John and Frances Rhoda Holder; *m* 1940, Mary Elizabeth Kidd; two *s.* *Educ:* Bristol Univ.; University of Illinois, USA. Graduated Bristol Univ., 1931; MSc 1933; Robert Blair Fellow, 1934; PhD 1935. Vice-Pres., RAF Selection Board, 1947-48; Student, Administrative Staff Coll., Henley on Thames, 1949; CO, RAF, Shallufa, Egypt, 1950-51; CO, RAF, Kabrit, Egypt, 1952; Dep. Dir, Air Staff Policy, Air Min., 1953-55; Student, Imperial Defence Coll., 1956; AOC, Singapore, 1957; AOC, Hong Kong, 1958-59; ACAS (Trng), Air Min., 1960-62; AOC No 25 Gp, RAF Flying Trng Comd, 1962-64; AOC-in-C, RAF Coastal Comd, NATO Comdr Maritime Air, Channel Comd, and Comdr Maritime Air, Eastern Atlantic Area, 1965-68, retired 1968. Mem., Waverley District Council, 1976. FRAeS 1966. *Recreations:* golf, sailing, bridge. *Address:* Spring Cottage, Churt, Surrey. *T:* Frensham 2388. *Club:* Royal Air Force.

HOLDERNESS, Baron *cr* 1979 (Life Peer), of Bishop Wilton in the County of Humberside; **Richard Frederick Wood;** PC 1959; DL; *b* 5 Oct. 1920; 3rd *s* of 1st Earl of Halifax, KG, PC, OM, GCSI, GCMG, GCIE, TD; *m* 1947, Diana, *d* of late Col E. O. Kellett, DSO, MP, and Hon. Mrs W. J. McGowan; one *s* one *d.* *Educ:* Eton; New College, Oxford. Hon. Attaché, British Embassy, Rome, 1940; served War of 1939-45 as Lieutenant, KRRC, 1941-43; retired, wounded, 1943; toured US Army hospitals, 1943-45; New College, Oxford, 1945-47. MP (C) Bridlington, Yorkshire, 1950-79; Parliamentary Private Secretary: to Minister of Pensions, 1951-53; to Minister of State, Board of Trade, 1953-54; to Minister of Agriculture and Fisheries, 1954-55; Joint Parliamentary Secretary: Ministry of Pensions and National Insurance, 1955-58; Ministry of Labour, 1958-59; Minister of Power, October 1959-63, of Pensions and National Insurance, Oct. 1963-64; Minister of Overseas Develt, ODM, June-Oct. 1970, FCO, 1970-74. Dir, Hargreaves Group Ltd, 1974-; Regional Dir, Yorkshire and Humberside regional board, Lloyds Bank, 1981-. Mem., Hansard Soc. Commn on Electoral Reform, 1975-76. DL E Riding Yorks, 1967. Hon. LLD: Sheffield Univ., 1962; Leeds, 1978. Hon. Colonel: Queen's Royal Rifles, 1962; 4th (Volunteer) Bn Royal Green Jackets, 1967-. *Address:* Flat Top House, Bishop Wilton, York YO4 1RY. *T:* Bishop Wilton 266; 49 Cadogan Place, SW1 9RT. *T:* 01-235 1597; 65 Les Collines de Guerrevieille, 83120 Ste Maxime, France.

See also Col Sir E. W. Brooksbank, Bt.

HOLDERNESS, Rt. Rev. George Edward, ERD (with 2 clasps) 1955; Dean Emeritus of Lichfield; an Assistant Bishop, Diocese of York, since 1980; *b* 5 March 1913; 2nd *s* of A. W. Holderness, Roundhay, Leeds; *m* 1940, Irene Mary, *er d* of H. G. Hird, Bedale, Yorkshire; one *s* two *d.* *Educ:* Leeds Grammar Sch.; Keble Coll., Oxford (MA); Westcott House, Cambridge. Assistant Curate of Bedale, 1936-39; Chaplain and Asst Master, Aysgarth School, Bedale, 1939-47. CF (RARO), 1940; SCF, 81st W African Div., 1943; DACG, India Command, 1945. Vicar of Darlington, 1947-55; Hon. Canon of Durham Cathedral, 1954; Suffragan Bishop of Burnley, 1955-70; Rector of Burnley, 1955-70; Canon of Blackburn Cathedral, 1955-70; Dean of Lichfield, 1970-79. DACG, TA, Northern Command, 1951-55. *Recreations:* shooting, fishing. *Address:* Riseborough Cottages, Marton, Sinnington, York YO6 6RD. *Clubs:* MCC, Forty, Lord's Taverners', I Zingari.

HOLDERNESS, Sir Richard William, 3rd Bt, *cr* 1920; Partner, Whiteheads, Estate Agents and Surveyors, since 1967; *b* 30 Nov. 1927; *s* of Sir Ernest William Elsmie Holderness, 2nd Bt, CBE, and Emily Carlton (*d* 1950), *y d* of late Frederick McQuade, Sydney, NSW; *S* father, 1968; *m* 1953, Pamela, *d* of Eric Chapman, CBE; two *s* one *d.* *Educ:* Dauntsey's Sch.; Corpus Christi Coll., Oxford. FRICS 1976. *Heir: s* Martin William Holderness, *b* 24 May 1957. *Address:* Rosetree House, Boxgrove, Chichester; (office) 12 Chapel Road, Worthing, West Sussex.

HOLDGATE, Martin Wyatt, CB 1979; PhD; FIBiol; Deputy Secretary and Chief Scientist (formerly Director General of Research), Departments of the Environment and Transport, since 1976; *b* 14 Jan. 1931; *s* of late Francis Wyatt Holdgate, MA, JP, and of Lois Marjorie Bebbington; *m* 1963, Elizabeth Mary (*née* Dickason), widow of Dr H. H. Weil; two *s.* *Educ:* Arnold Sch., Blackpool; Queens' Coll., Cambridge. BA Cantab 1952; MA 1956; PhD 1955; FIBiol 1967. Senior Scientist, Gough Is Scientific Survey, 1955-56; Lecturer in Zoology, Manchester Univ., 1956-57; Lecturer in Zoology, Durham Colleges, 1957-60; Leader, Royal Society Expedition to Southern Chile, 1958-59; Asst Director of Research, Scott Polar Research Institute, Cambridge, 1960-63; Senior Biologist, British Antarctic Survey, 1963-66; Sec., Working Gp on Biology, Scientific Cttee on Antarctic Res., 1964-68; Dep. Dir (Research), The Nature Conservancy, 1966-70; Director: Central Unit on Environmental Pollution, DoE, 1970-74; Inst. of Terrestrial Ecology, NERC, 1974-76. Hon. Professorial Fellow, UC Cardiff, 1976-. Member: NERC, 1976-; SERC (formerly SRC), 1976-; ABRC, 1976-; Chm., Review of Scientific Civil Service, 1980. Chairman: British Schools Exploring Society, 1967-78; Young Explorer's Trust, 1972, 1979-81. *Publications:* Mountains in the Sea, The Story of the Gough Island Expedition, 1958; (ed jtly) Antarctic Biology, 1964; (ed) Antarctic Ecology, 1970; (with N. M. Wace) Man and Nature in the Tristan da Cunha Islands, 1976; A Perspective of Environmental Pollution, 1979; (ed jtly) The World Environment 1972-82, 1982; numerous papers in biological journals and works on Antarctic.

Address: 35 Wingate Way, Trumpington, Cambridge CB2 2HD. *T:* Cambridge 840086. *Club:* Athenæum.

HOLDING, Malcolm Alexander; HM Diplomatic Service; Consul-General, Edmonton, since 1981; *b* 11 May 1932; *s* of Adam Anderson Holding and Mary Lillian (*née* Golding); *m* 1955, Pamela Eve Hampshire; two *d. Educ:* King Henry VIII Sch., Coventry. Foreign Office, 1949-51; HM Forces, 1951-53; FO, 1953-55; Middle East Centre for Arab Studies, 1956-57; Third Secretary (Commercial), Tunis, 1957-60; Second Sec. (Commercial), Khartoum, 1960-64; Second, later First Sec. (Commercial), Cairo, 1964-68; Consul, Bari, 1969; FCO, 1970-73; First Sec., British Dep. High Commission, Madras, 1973-75; FCO, 1976-78; Canadian National Defence Coll., Kingston, Ontario, 1978-79; Counsellor (Commercial), Rome, 1979-81. *Recreations:* sailing, skiing. *Address:* c/o Foreign and Commonwealth Office, SW1.

HOLDSWORTH, Albert Edward; His Honour Judge Holdsworth, QC; a Circuit Judge, since 1972; *b* 1909; *e s* of Albert Edward and Catherine Sarah Holdsworth; *m* 1st, 1941, Barbara Frances (*d* 1968), *e d* of Ernest Henry and Beatrice Maud Reeves; one *s*; 2nd, 1970, Brianne Evelyn Frances, *d* of Arthur James and Evelyn Lock; two *s. Educ:* Sir George Monoux Sch., Walthamstow; Gonville and Caius Coll., Cambridge (Exhibitioner). Pres., Cambridge Union, 1932; Economics and Politics tripos; MA. Formerly journalist: Financial News, 1932-33; Special Correspondent, World Economic Conf., 1933; Yorkshire Post, 1933-46, Polit. Correspondent, later London Editor. Broadcasts for BBC on current affairs topics, 1935-56. Called to Bar, Middle Temple, 1936. Conservative Candidate Ipswich, 1951; moved resolution in favour of UK entry into European Common Market, Conservative Conf., Llandudno, 1962. Dep.-Chm., SW Metropolitan Mental Health Tribunal, 1962-65. QC 1969. *Address:* 2 Middle Temple Lane, Temple, EC4Y 9AA. *T:* 01-353 7926; Sutton Gate, Sutton, Pulborough, West Sussex RH20 1PN. *T:* Sutton (West Sussex) 230. *Club:* Reform.

HOLDSWORTH, Sir (George) Trevor, Kt 1982; Chairman, Guest, Keen & Nettlefolds plc, since 1980; Director: Midland Bank Ltd, since 1979; Thorn EMI Ltd, since 1977; Equity Capital for Industry Ltd, since 1979; *b* 29 May 1927; *s* of late William Albert Holdsworth and Winifred Holdsworth (*née* Bottomley); *m* 1951, Patricia June Ridler; three *s. Educ:* Hanson Grammar Sch., Bradford; Keighley Grammar Sch. FCA 1950. Rawlinson, Greaves & Mitchell, Bradford, 1944-52; Bowater Paper Corp., 1952-63; joined Guest, Keen & Nettlefolds, 1963; Dep. Chief Accountant, 1963-64; Gp Chief Accountant, 1965-67; General Man. Dir, GKN Screws & Fasteners Ltd, 1968-70; Dir and Gp Controller, 1970-72; Gp Exec. Vice Chm., 1973-74; Dep. Chm., 1974; Man. Dir, 1977. Confederation of British Industry: Mem. Council, 1974-; Mem., Econ. and Financial Policy Cttee, 1978-80; British Institute of Management: Vice-Chm., 1979; Mem., Bd of Fellows, 1979; Chm., 1980-82; a Vice-Pres., 1982-; Mem., Council, 1974-. Vice Pres., Engineering Employers' Fedn, 1980-. Member: Business and Commercial Enterprises Gp, Duke of Edinburgh's Award, 1980-; Exec. Cttee, SMMT, 1980-; Engineering Industries Council, 1980-; Court of British Shippers' Council, 1981-. Trustee: Anglo-German Foundn for the Study of Industrial Society, 1980-; Royal Opera House Trust, 1981-; Philharmonia Trust, 1982-. Governor, Ashridge Management Coll., 1978. Vice-Pres, Ironbridge Gorge Museum Develt Trust, 1981-. Freeman, City of London; Liveryman, Worshipful Co. of Chartered Accountants in England and Wales. Hon. DTech Loughborough, 1981; Hon. DSc Aston, 1982. *Recreations:* music, theatre. *Address:* 7 Cleveland Row, St James's, SW1A 1DB.

HOLDSWORTH, Sir Trevor; *see* Holdsworth, Sir G. T.

HOLE, George Vincer, CBE 1969; ICAO Consultant on Airport Affairs, since 1975; Chief Executive, British Airports Authority, 1965-72; *b* 26 Jan. 1910; *s* of George William Hole and Louisa Hole (*née* Vincer); *m* 1938, Gertraud Johanna Anna Koppe (Baroness von Broesigke); two *s. Educ:* Wilson's Grammar Sch., London; London Sch. of Economics. BSc (Econ.) 1933. Asst Auditor, Exchequer and Audit Dept, 1929; passed First Div. Exam., 1935; Under-Sec., 1958; Min. of Aviation, 1959-65; student Imperial Defence Coll., 1948; Chm. First Div. Assoc., 1949-50; Chm. OEEC Productivity Group, on Traffic Engineering and Control, in the United States, 1954; Chm. W European Airports Assoc., 1970; Member: Council, Internat. Bd of Airport Operators, 1970; Bd, Internat. Civil Airports Assoc. (Chm.); Bd, Airport Assocs Co-ordinating Council (first Chm.). FCIT. Hon. Treas., Caravan Club, 1960-66. Dir, J. E. Greiner Co. Ltd, Consulting Engineers, Edinburgh, 1972-75. ICAO Lectr on Airport Affairs, Beirut, 1972-75. Officer, Order of Orange Nassau, Netherlands, 1946; Officer, Order of the Crown, Belgium, 1946. *Recreation:* pottering. *Address:* 6 St Germans Place, Blackheath, SE3. *T:* 01-858 3917. *Club:* Reform.

HOLE, Tahu Ronald Charles Pearce, CBE 1956; Director of Administration and Member, Board of Management, BBC, 1958-60, retired; *b* Christchurch, NZ, 29 March 1908; *s* of Charles Hole and Susan Eliza Hole; *m* Joyce Margaret Wingate. *Educ:* Sydenham School, Christchurch; Canterbury University Coll. (journalism), NZ. Reporter on New Zealand and Australian newspapers, 1926-35; first news editor, Sydney Morning Herald, 1935-37; London corresp. and war corresp., Sydney Morning Herald, 1937-40; special corresp., The Herald, Melbourne, 1940-41; BBC: commentator, 1940-41; joined Overseas Service, 1941; Empire Services, 1942; producer of War Review, 1942-43; Overseas Talks Manager, 1944; Asst Editor, News Div. and Mem., Edtl Bd, 1946; Editor-Controller, News Div. (Home, Overseas and

TV news), 1948-58. Member: Adv. Council, Empire Press Union, 1937-41; Edtl Bd, RIIA, 1949-54; Press, Broadcasting and Armed Services (Defence Notice) Cttee, 1945-58; BBC adviser to UK Govt's delegation to UN Information Conf., Paris, 1953; BBC rep. at Internat. Convention of Radio and TV News Directors, Washington, 1954, Miami, 1957; Mem., BBC delegation to Commonwealth Broadcasting Conf., London, 1947, Sydney, 1956; organised with Rank Orgn and Reuter for establishment of British Commonwealth International Newsfilm Agency Ltd (Visnews), 1956, Dep. Chm., 1957, Chm., 1958. First journalist to fly to news assignment in NZ; NZ Journalists' Assoc. Award for best journalism, 1929. Frequently attacked by Nazi propaganda dept for war-time broadcasts, cards listing his activities found in Gestapo HQ files after fall of Berlin. Life Mem., Royal Soc. of St George. *Publications:* Anzacs into Battle, 1941; Experiment in Freedom, 1944; The Responsibilities of Editing News and Current Affairs in Radio and Television, 1957; contribs to The Times, Daily Telegraph, Time and Tide, National Review. *Recreations:* travel, music, reading. *Address:* Iwerne Minster, Blandford Forum, Dorset. *Club:* Carlton.

HOLFORD, Rear-Adm. Frank Douglas, CB 1969; DSC 1944; Director General of Naval Manpower, Ministry of Defence, 1967-69, retired 1970; *b* 28 June 1916; *y s* of late Capt. C. F. Holford, DSO, OBE, and Ursula Isobel Holford (*née* Corbett); *m* 1942, Sybil Priscilla, *d* of late Comdr Sir Robert and Lady Micklem; two *s. Educ:* RN Coll., Dartmouth. Cadet, 1929, Midshipman, HMS Hood, 1933; Sub-Lieut, HMS Wolverine, 1937; Lieutenant: HMS Kent, 1938; HMS Anson, 1941; HMS Sheffield, 1943; Lieut-Comdr: HMS Excellent, 1945; HMS Triumph, 1948; Commander: Admlty, Naval Ordnance Dept, 1951; British Joint Services Mission, USA, 1953; HMS Excellent, 1955; Captain: Admlty, Dir Guided Weapons, 1957; Naval and Mil. Attaché, Buenos Aires, 1960; Staff C-in-C Portsmouth, 1962; Cdre-i-C Hong Kong, 1965. Rear-Adm. 1967. jssc 1947. *Address:* Great Down Cottage, Soberton, Hants. *T:* Droxford 448.

HOLFORD, Surgeon Rear-Adm. John Morley, CB 1965; OBE 1954; Senior Principal Medical Officer, Department of Health and Social Security, 1973-74, retired; *b* 10 Jan. 1909; *o s* of late Rev. W. J. Holford and Amy Finnemore Lello; *m* 1935, Monica Peregrine, *d* of late Preb. P. S. G. Propert; two *s. Educ:* Kingswood, Bath; Trinity Hall, Cambridge. MA, MB, Cantab; FRCP; joined RN 1935. War service in HMS Nelson, 1940-42; RN Hosp. Plymouth, 1942-44; consultant in Medicine to RN, 1954-56; Surgeon Capt., 1957; Surgeon Rear-Adm. 1963; Medical Officer in Charge, RN Hosp. Haslar, 1963-66. Retired, 1966. MO, Min. of Health, 1966, SMO, 1967, SPMO, 1973. Gilbert Blanc Medal, 1956; F. E. Williams Prize in Geriatric Medicine, RCP, 1972. CStJ 1964. *Publications:* Articles in medical journals. *Recreations:* chess (jt champion of South Africa, 1946), bridge. *Address:* c/o Lloyds Bank, 84 Park Lane, W1. *Club:* Army and Navy.

HOLGATE, Hon. Harold Norman, MHA; Premier of Tasmania, Treasurer and Minister for Racing and Gaming, 1981-82; *b* 5 Dec. 1933; *s* of late H. W. Holgate; *m* 1963, Rosalind, *d* of E. C. Wesley; two *s* two *d. Educ:* Maitland (NSW) High Sch.; Univ. of Tasmania (BA). Journalist: Sydney Morning Herald, 1952-55; Melbourne Herald, 1955-62; Political Journalist, Dep. Chief of Staff, Launceston Examiner, 1963-66; Public Relns Manager, Tasmanian Directorate of Industrial Development, 1966-70; Exec. Producer, ABC TV Public Affairs Programme, This Day Tonight, Hobart, 1970-73; Press Sec. to Dep. Prime Minister and Minister for Defence, Govt of Australia, Mr Lance Barnard, 1973-74; MHA (Lab) for Bass, Tasmania, 1974-; Speaker of House of Assembly, 1975-76; Minister (Govt of Tasmania): for Housing and Construction and Minister assisting the Dep. Premier, 1976-77; for Education, Recreation and the Arts and for Racing and Gaming, 1977-79; for Education, Recreation and the Arts, and for Police and Emergency Services, 1979-80; for Education, for Police and Emergency Services, for Racing and Gaming, 1980-81; for Police and Emergency Services, for Local Govt, for the Environment, for Water Resources, for Racing and Gaming, 1981. *Recreations:* horse racing, music, reading, dinghy sailing, swimming. *Address:* 145 Canning Street, Launceston, Tasmania 7250. *T:* 003. 317572.

HOLGATE, Dr Sidney, CBE 1981; Master of Grey College, University of Durham, 1959-80; Member, Academic Advisory Committee, Open University, 1969-81 (Vice-Chairman, 1972-75; Chairman, 1975-77); *b* Hucknall, Notts, 9 Sept. 1918; *e s* of late Henry and Annie Elizabeth Holgate; *m* 1942, Isabel Armorey; no *c. Educ:* Henry Mellish Sch., Nottingham; Durham Univ. Open Scholar, Hatfield Coll., Durham, 1937; Univ. Mathematical Scholarship, 1940; BA (1st Cl. Hons Mathematics) 1940; MA 1943; PhD 1945. Asst Master, Nottingham High Sch., 1941-42; Lecturer in Mathematics, University of Durham, 1942-46; Sec. of the Durham Colls, 1946-59; Pro-Vice-Chancellor, Univ. of Durham, 1964-69. Member: Schools Council Gen. Studies Cttee, 1967-70; Chm., BBC Radio Durham Council, 1968-72; Vice-Chm., BBC Radio Newcastle Council, 1972-74. Hon. DUniv. Open, 1980. *Publications:* mathematical papers in Proc. Camb. Phil. Soc. and Proc. Royal Soc. *Recreations:* cricket and other sports, railways, bridge. *Address:* 6 Howlcroft Villas, Neville's Cross, Durham DH1 4DU.

HOLGATE, Surgeon Rear-Adm. (D) William, CB 1962; OBE 1951; Chief Dental Officer, Ministry of Health, 1961-71, and Ministry of Education and Science, 1963-71; *b* 6 July 1906; *s* of Anthony and Jane Holgate; *m* 1933, Inga Ommanney Davis; one *s* one *d. Educ:* Scarborough Coll.; Guy's Hospital. LDS, RCS Eng., 1927; FDS, RCS Eng., 1963. Royal Navy, 1928-61.

Director of Dental Services, 1960. *Address:* Upalong, The Highway, Luccombe, Shanklin, Isle of Wight. *Club:* Savage.

HOLLAMBY, Edward Ernest, OBE 1970; FRIBA, FRTPI, FSIAD; Chief Architect and Planner to London Docklands Development Corporation, since 1981; *b* 8 Jan. 1921; *s* of Edward Thomas Hollamby and late Ethel Mary (*née* Kingdom); *m* 1941, Doris Isabel Parker; one *s* two *d*. *Educ:* School of Arts and Crafts, Hammersmith; University Coll. London. DipTP London. Served RM Engrs, 1941-46. Architect, Miners' Welfare Commn, 1947-49; Sen. Architect, LCC, 1949-62; Borough Architect, Lambeth, 1963-65; Dir. Architect and Town Planning Officer, 1965-69, Dir of Architecture, Planning and Develt, 1969-81. Works, 1957-, incl.: Christopher Wren and N Hammersmith Sec. Schs; Brandon Estate, Southwark; Housing at Elephant and Castle; study for Erith Township, Kent (prototype study for Thamesmead); pioneered rehabil. old houses, LCC Brixton Town Centre Develt Plan; housing schemes, Lambeth, 1965-, incl.: Lambeth Towers; Central Hill, Norwood; Stockwell; Brixton; flats, houses, old people's home, doctors' gp practice, Clapham. Area rehabil. and renewal schemes, Clapham Manor and Kennington; Norwood Libr. and Nettlefold Hall; schs for mentally retarded, Clapham and Kennington; rehabil. centre for disabled, Clapham; home for elderly, Kennington; offices for Tarmac, Brixton; recreation centre; prelim. study, Civic Centre, Brixton; holiday hotel for severely disabled, Netley, near Southampton; Girls' Secure Unit, Croydon, 1978; scheme for village development, Shirley Oaks, 1979; (with David Gosling) Isle of Dogs Urban Design Study. Has lectured on architecture and environmental planning; numerous radio and TV appearances. RIBA: Mem. Council, 1961-70, Hon. Treas., 1967-70; Mem., Historic Buildings Council; Founder Mem., William Morris Soc. Numerous design and Civic Trust awards. *Publications:* contrib. architectural and town planning jls. *Recreations:* travel, classical music, gardening. *Address:* Red House, Red House Lane, Upton, Bexleyheath, Kent DA6 8JF. *T:* 01-303 8808.

HOLLAND, Rt. Rev. Alfred Charles; *see* Newcastle, NSW, Bishop of.

HOLLAND, Arthur David, CB 1973; TD 1947; Chief Highway Engineer, Department of the Environment, 1970-74; *b* 1 Nov. 1913; *o s* of Col. Arthur Leslie Holland, MC, TD, and Dora Helena Hassé; *m* 1938, Jean Moyra Spowart; two *s*. *Educ:* Malvern Coll.; University of Bristol (BSc(Eng)Hons). Asst Engineer, Great Western Railway Co, 1935-36; N Devon CC, 1936-37; Min. of Transport: Manchester, 1937-38; London, 1938-39. Served War with RE, 1939-46; in Air Defence Gt Britain, 1939-42; with Middle East Forces, 1942-46, finally as Lt-Col RE (now Hon. Lt-Col), Sen. Staff Officer to Chief Engineer, Italy. Min. of Transport, Nottingham, 1946-47; Bridge Section, London, 1947-61; Divl Road Engr, E Midland Div., Nottingham, 1961-63; Asst Chief Engr (Bridges), 1963-65; Dep. Chief Engr, HQ London, 1965-70. FICE, FIStructE, FInstHE; Mem., Smeatonian Soc. of Civil Engrs. *Publications:* contribs to Proc. Instn of Civil Engineers and Instn of Highway Engineers. *Address:* Pine Tree Cottage, Pembroke Road, Woking, Surrey. *T:* Woking 62403.

HOLLAND, Brian Arthur; Solicitor to the Post Office, since 1981; *b* 14 June 1935; *s* of George Leigh Holland and Hilda Holland, MBE; *m* 1964, Sally Edwards; one *s* one *d*. *Educ:* Manchester Grammar Sch.; Manchester Univ. (LLB Hons). Admitted Solicitor, 1961. Joined Solicitor's Dept, GPO, 1961; Solicitor's Office, Post Office: Head of Civil Litigation Div., 1977-79; Dir, Litigation and Prosecution Dept, 1979-81. *Publication:* (contrib.) Halsbury's Laws of England, 4th edn, vol. 36. *Recreations:* scouting, photography, studying railways, sketching, gardening. *Address:* 23 Grasmere Road, Purley, Surrey CR2 1DY. *T:* 01-660 0479.

HOLLAND, Christopher John, QC 1978; barrister-at-law; *b* 1 June 1937; *er s* of late Frank and of Winifred Mary Holland; *m* 1967, Jill Iona Holland; one *s* one *d*. *Educ:* Leeds Grammar Sch.; Emmanuel Coll., Cambridge (MA, LLB). National Service (acting L/Cpl), 3rd Royal Tank Regt, 1956-58. Called to the Bar, Inner Temple, 1963; commenced practice on North Eastern Circuit. *Address:* 37 Park Square, Leeds LS1 2PD. *T:* Leeds 452702; 2 Harcourt Buildings, Temple, EC4Y 9DB. *Clubs:* United Oxford & Cambridge University; Leeds (Leeds).

HOLLAND, Sir Clifton Vaughan, (Sir John), Kt 1973; BCE; FTS; FIE(Aust), FAIM, FAIB; Chairman: John Holland (Holdings) Ltd, since 1962; John Holland Construction Group, since 1949; Process Plant Construction Pty Ltd, since 1949; Director: T&G Life Society, since 1972; Australia and New Zealand Banking Group, 1976-81; *b* Melbourne, 21 June 1914; *s* of Thomas and Mabel Ruth Elizabeth Holland; *m* 1942, Emily Joan Atkinson; three *s* one *d*. *Educ:* Flinders State Sch.; Frankston High Sch.; Queen's Coll., Univ. of Melbourne (BCE). Junior Engineer, BP, 1936-39. Served War of 1939-45, RAE and 'Z' Special Force, Middle East, SW Pacific (Lt-Col). Construction Engr, BP Aust. 1946-49; Founder, John Holland Construction Group, 1949, Man. Dir 1949-72. Foundn Pres., Australian Fedn of Civil Contractors (Life Mem., 1971). Member: Rhodes Scholar Selection Cttee, 1970-73; Econ. Consultative Adv. Gp to the Treasurer, 1975-79; Mem. Bd, Royal Melbourne Hosp., 1963-79; Nat. Chm., Outward Bound, 1973-74, Chm. Victorian Div., 1964-77; Councillor, Inst. of Public Affairs, 1970; Mem., Churchill Fellowship Selection Cttee, 1968-; Director: Winston Churchill Meml Trust, 1976- (Chm., Vic. Br., 1977-); Child Accident Prevention Foundn, 1979-81; Chairman: La Trobe Centenary Commemoration Council, 1975-76; Matthew Flinders Bi-Centenary Council, 1973-75; History Adv. Council of Victoria,

1975-; Loch Ard Centenary Commemoration Cttee, 1976-78; Citizens' Council, 150th Anniversary Celebrations, Victoria, 1979-; Victorian Cttee for Anzac Awards, 1982-; Nat. Chm., Queen's Silver Jubilee Trust, 1981- (Vic. Chm., 1977-80); Mem., Centenary Test Co-ordinating Cttee, 1976-77. Director: Corps of Commissionaires (Victoria) Ltd, 1978-; Australian Bicentenary Celebrations, 1980-. Construction projects include: Jindabyne pumping station; Westgate Bridge; Tasman Bridge restoration. Foundation Fellow, Australian Acad. of Technological Scis. Hon. DEng Monash, 1978. Peter Nicoll Russell Meml Medal, 1974; Kernot Medal, Univ. of Melbourne, 1979. *Recreations:* golf, music, gardening, cricket. *Address:* 14 North Road, Brighton, Victoria 3186, Australia. *T:* 596.1558. *Clubs:* Australian, Naval and Military (Melbourne); Royal Melbourne Golf, Frankston Golf.

HOLLAND, David Cuthbert Lyall, CB 1975; Librarian of the House of Commons, 1967-76; *b* 23 March 1915; *yr s* of Michael Holland, MC, and Marion Holland (*née* Broadwood); *m* 1949, Rosemary Griffiths, *y d* of David Ll. Griffiths, OBE; *two s one d*. *Educ:* Eton; Trinity Coll., Cambridge (MA). War service, Army, 1939-46; PoW. Appointed House of Commons Library, 1946. Chm., Study of Parlt Gp, 1973-74. *Publications:* book reviews, etc. *Recreation:* book collecting. *Address:* The Barn, Milton Street, Polegate, East Sussex. *T:* Alfriston 870379. *Club:* Athenæum.

HOLLAND, David George, CMG 1975; a Chief Adviser, Bank of England, since 1980; *b* 31 May 1925; *s* of late Francis George Holland and Mabel Ellen Holland; *m* 1954, Marian Elizabeth Rowles; two *s* one *d*. *Educ:* Taunton Sch.; Wadham Coll., Oxford. Inst. of Economics and Statistics, Oxford, 1949-63; Internat. Bank for Reconstruction and Development, Washington, DC, 1963-65; Min. of Overseas Development, 1965-67; Chief Economic Adviser, FCO, 1967-75; a Dep. Chief, Economic Intelligence and Overseas Depts, Bank of England, 1975-80. *Address:* 20 Woodside Avenue, Highgate, N6.

HOLLAND, Edward Richard Charles, MBE 1969; HM Diplomatic Service, retired; *b* 26 March 1925; *s* of Cecil Francis Richard Holland and Joyce Mary (*née* Pyne); *m* 1952, Dorothy Olive Branthwaite; two *s*. *Educ:* Launceston Coll. Served RAF, 1943-48. Joined FO, 1948; served in Batavia, Bangkok, Oslo, Prague and Helsinki, 1949-57; Consul, Saigon, 1957; FO, 1959; Cape Town, 1962; First Sec., Monrovia, 1964; Consul: Stuttgart, 1969; Düsseldorf, 1971; FCO, 1972; First Sec., Islamabad, 1977; Consul-Gen., Alexandria, 1981-82. *Recreations:* gardening, walking, reading, painting, listening to music. *Address:* 1 Prospect Cottages, Boughton Aluph, Ashford, Kent TN25 4JA. *T:* Ashford 28539. *Club:* Civil Service.

HOLLAND, Frank Robert Dacre; Chairman: C. E. Heath & Co. Ltd, since 1973; C. E. Heath & Co. (Insurance Broking) Ltd, since 1981; *b* 24 March 1924; *s* of Ernest Albert Holland and Kathleen Annie (*née* Page); *m* 1948, Margaret Lindsay Aird; one *d*. *Educ:* Whitgift Sch., Croydon. Joined C.E.Heath & Co. Ltd, 1941; entered Army, 1942; Sandhurst, 1943; commissioned 4th Queen's Own Hussars, 1944; served, Italy, 1944-45, Austria and Germany, 1945-47; returned to C.E.Heath & Co. Ltd, 1947; Joint Managing Director, North American Operation, 1965; Director, C.E.Heath & Co. Ltd, 1965, Dep. Chm., 1969. *Recreations:* travel, gardening. *Address:* Moatside, 68 Ashley Road, Walton-on-Thames, Surrey KT12 1HR. *T:* Walton-on-Thames 27591.

HOLLAND, Geoffrey; Deputy Secretary and Director, Manpower Services Commission, since 1981; *b* 9 May 1938; *s* of late Frank Holland, CBE and of Elsie Freda Holland; *m* 1964, Carol Ann Challen. *Educ:* Merchant Taylors' Sch., Northwood; St John's Coll., Oxford (BA 1st cl. Hons; MA). 2nd Lieut, RTR, 1956-58. Entered Min. of Labour, 1961, Asst Private Sec., 1964-65; Principal Private Sec. to Sec. of State for Employment, 1971-72; Manpower Services Commission: Asst Sec., Hd of Planning, 1973; Dir of Special Progs, 1977. Mem. Industrial Cttee, C of E Bd of Social Responsibility, 1980-. Liveryman, Merchant Taylors' Co., 1967-. *Publications:* Young People and Work, 1977; many articles on manpower, educn, training, management etc in professional jls. *Recreations:* journeying, opera, exercising the dog. *Address:* St Anthony, Stag Lane, Chorleywood, Herts WD3 5HE. *Club:* East India, Devonshire, Sports and Public Schools.

HOLLAND, Sir Guy (Hope), 3rd Bt *cr* 1917; *b* 19 July 1918; *s* of Sir Reginald Sothern Holland, 1st Bt and Stretta Aimée Holland (*née* Price) (*d* 1949); *S* brother, 1981; *m* 1945, Joan Marianne Street, *d* of late Captain Herbert Edmund Street, XXth Hussars, and of Lady Tottenham; two *d*. *Educ:* privately and Christ Church, Oxford. Served War of 1939-45 (wounded); Captain, Royal Scots Greys; ADC to Gen. Sir Andrew Thorne, 1944. *Heir:* none. *Address:* Sheepbridge Barn, Eastleach, Cirencester, Gloucestershire GL7 3PS. *T:* Southrop 296. *Clubs:* Boodle's, Pratt's.

HOLLAND, Sir John; *see* Holland, Sir C. V.

HOLLAND, Rt. Rev. John Tristram, CBE 1975; *b* 31 Jan. 1912; *s* of Rt Rev. H. St B. Holland; *m* 1937, Joan Theodora Arundell, *d* of Dr R. Leslie Ridge, Carlton House, Enfield, Mddx; three *d*. *Educ:* Durham School; University College, Oxford; Westcott House, Cambridge. BA 1933, MA 1937, Oxford. Deacon, 1935; Priest, 1936; Curate of St Peter's, Huddersfield, 1935-37; Commissary to Bishop of Wellington, 1936-37; Vicar of Featherston, 1938-41; CF (2 NZEF), 1941-45; Vicar of: St Peter's, Upper Riccarton, 1945-49; St Mary's, New Plymouth, 1949-51; Bishop of Waikato, 1951-69; Bishop in Polynesia, 1969-75; Officiating Minister: Diocese of Canterbury, 1975-76;

Diocese of Waiapu, 1976. *Address:* 8 Short Street, Tauranga, New Zealand.

HOLLAND, Sir Kenneth (Lawrence), Kt 1981; CBE 1971; QFSM 1974; HM Chief Inspector of Fire Services, 1972–80; Consultant, Fire Safety Engineering; Director, Chloride Gent Ltd; *b* 20 Sept. 1918; *s* of Percy Lawrence and Edith Holland; *m* 1941, Pauline Keith (*née* Mansfield); two *s* one *d. Educ:* Whitcliffe Mount Grammar Sch., Cleckheaton, Yorks. Entered Fire Service, Lancashire, 1937; Divisional Officer: Suffolk and Ipswich, 1948; Worcestershire, 1952; Dep. Chief Fire Officer, Lancashire, 1955. Chief Fire Officer: Bristol, 1960; West Riding of Yorkshire, 1967. Fellow, Instn Fire Engineers. OStJ 1964. Defence Medal; Fire Brigade Long Service and Good Conduct Medal. *Recreations:* motor sport, vintage cars, gardening. *Address:* Erif, Blandford Road, Iwerne Minster, Dorset. *Club:* St John House.

HOLLAND, Philip Welsby; MP (C) Carlton since 1966; *b* 14 March 1917; *s* of late John Holland, Middlewich, Cheshire; *m* 1943, Josephine Alma Hudson; one *s. Educ:* Sir John Deane's Grammar Sch., Northwich. Enlisted RAF 1936; commissioned 1943. Factory Manager, Jantzen Knitting Mills, 1946–47; Management Research, 1948–49; Manufacturers' Agent in Engineering and Refractories Products, 1949–60. Contested (C) Yardley Div. of Birmingham, Gen. Election, 1955; MP (C) Acton, 1959–64; PPS: to Minister of Pensions and Nat. Insurance, 1961–62; to Chief Sec. to Treasury and Paymaster-Gen., 1962–64; to Minister of Aviation Supply, 1970; to Minister for Aerospace, 1971; to Minister for Trade, 1972. Pres., Cons. Trade Union Nat. Adv. Cttee, 1972–74. Personnel Manager, The Ultra Electronics Group of Companies, 1964–66; Personnel Consultant to Standard Telephones and Cables Ltd, 1969–81. Chm., Cttee of Selection, HofC, 1979–. Councillor, Royal Borough of Kensington, 1955–59. *Publications:* The Quango Explosion (jtly), 1978; Quango, Quango, Quango, 1979; Costing the Quango, 1979; The Quango Death List, 1980; The Governance of Quangos, 1981. *Recreations:* travel, hunting the quango. *Address:* 2 Holland Park Mansions, Holland Park Gardens, W14. *T:* 01-603 5640; Orston, Notts.

HOLLAND, Robert Einion, FIA; Chief General Manager, Pearl Assurance Co. Ltd, since 1977; *b* 23 April 1927; *s* of late Robert Ellis Holland and of Bene Holland; *m* 1955, Eryl Haf Roberts; one *s* two *d. Educ:* University Coll. of N Wales, Bangor (BSc). FIA 1957. Joined Pearl Assurance Co. Ltd, 1953; Dir, 1973. Chm., Industrial Life Offices Assoc., 1976–78; Director: Pearl American Corp., 1972–; Aviation & General Insurance Co. Ltd, 1972– (Chm. 1976–78); Community Reinsurance Corp. Ltd, 1973– (Chm., 1973–76); Monarch Insurance Co. of Ohio, 1977–; Chm., London City Underwriting Agencies Ltd. Mem., Welsh Develt Agency, 1976–. Mem., CS Pay Research Unit Bd, 1980–81. *Recreations:* golf and Welsh literature. *Address:* 55 Corkscrew Hill, West Wickham, Kent BR4 9BA. *T:* 01-777 1861.

HOLLAND, Stuart (Kingsley); MP (Lab) Lambeth, Vauxhall, since 1979; *b* 25 March 1940; *y s* of Frederick Holland and May Holland, London; *m* 1976, Jenny Lennard; two *c. Educ:* state primary schs; Christ's Hosp.; Univ. of Missouri (Exchange Scholar); Balliol Coll., Oxford (Domus Scholar; 1st Cl. Hons Mod. History); St Antony's Coll., Oxford (Sen. Scholar; DPhil Econs). Econ. Asst, Cabinet Office, 1966–67; Personal Asst to Prime Minister, 1967–68; Res. Fellow, Centre for Contemp. European Studies, Univ. of Sussex, 1968–71, Assoc. Fellow and Lectr, 1971–79, Vis. Fellow, Sussex European Res. Centre, 1979–. Vis. Scholar, Brookings Instn, Washington, DC, 1970. Special Adviser: Commons Expenditure Cttee, 1971–72; Minister of Overseas Develt, 1974–75. Res. Specialist, RIIA, 1972–74; Associate, Inst. of Develt Studies, 1974–. Consultant: Econ. and Social Affairs Cttee, Council of Europe, 1973; Open Univ., 1973. Rapporteur, Trades Union Adv. Cttee, OECD, 1977. Chm., Public Enterprise Gp, 1973–75. Member: Council, Inst. for Workers' Control, 1974–; Expert Cttee on Inflation, EEC Commn, 1975–76; UN Univ. Working Party on Socio-Cultural Factors in Develt, Tokyo, 1977. Lubbock Lectr, Oxford Univ., 1975; Tom Mann Meml Lectr, Australia, 1977. Mem., Labour Party, 1962–; Mem. sub-cttees (inc. Finance and Econ. Policy, Indust. Policy, EEC, Economic Planning, Defence, Development Cooperation, Public Sector), Nat. Exec. Cttee, Labour Party, 1972–; Executive Member: Labour Coordinating Cttee, 1978–; European Nuclear Disarmament Campaign, 1980–. Hon. MRTPI 1980. *Publications:* (jtly) Sovereignty and Multinational Corporations, 1971; (ed) The State as Entrepreneur, 1972; Strategy for Socialism, 1975; The Socialist Challenge, 1975; The Regional Problem, 1976; Capital versus the Regions, 1976; (ed) Beyond Capitalist Planning, 1978; Uncommon Market, 1980; contrib. symposia; articles in specialist jls and national and internat. press. *Recreation:* singing in the bath. *Address:* House of Commons, SW1. *T:* 01-219 3000.

HOLLAND, Rt. Rev. Thomas; *see* Salford, Bishop of, (RC).

HOLLAND-HIBBERT, family name of Viscount Knutsford.

HOLLAND-MARTIN, Robert George, (Robin); Hon. Deputy Treasurer of Conservative and Unionist Party, since 1979; *b* 6 July 1939; *y s* of Cyril Holland-Martin and Rosa, *d* of Sir Gerald Chadwyck-Healey, 2nd Bt, CBE; *m* 1976, Dominique, 2nd *d* of Maurice Fromaget; two *d. Educ:* Eton. Cazenove & Co., 1960–74 (partner, 1968–74); Finance Director, Paterson Products Ltd, 1976–. Member of Council: Metropolitan Hospital-Sunday Fund, 1963– (Chm. of Council, 1977–); Homoeopathic Trust, 1970– (Dep. Chm., 1975–). Victoria & Albert Museum: Member of Advisory Council, 1972–; Member of Cttee, Associates of V & A, 1976– (Chm., 1981). *Address:*

18 Tite Street, SW3 4HZ. *T:* 01-352 7871. *Clubs:* White's, Royal Automobile.

HOLLENDEN, 3rd Baron *cr* 1912; **Gordon Hope Hope-Morley;** I. & R. Morley Ltd, 1933–67, retired as Chairman; *b* 8 Jan. 1914; *s* of Hon. Claude Hope-Morley (*d* 1968) (*yr s* of 1st Baron) and Lady Dorothy Edith Isabel (*d* 1972), *d* of 7th Earl of Buckinghamshire; *S* uncle, 1977; *m* 1945, Sonja Sundt, Norway; three *s. Educ:* Eton. War medals of 1939–45; King Haakon of Norway Liberation medal. *Heir: s* Hon. Ian Hampden Hope-Morley [*b* 23 Oct. 1946; *m* 1972, Beatrice Saulnier, *d* of Baron Pierre d'Anchald, Paris; one *s* one *d*]. *Address:* Hall Place, Leigh, Tonbridge, Kent. *T:* Hildenborough 832255. *Club:* Brooks's.
See also Sir Michael Hanley.

HOLLENWEGER, Prof. Walter Jacob; Professor of Mission, University of Birmingham, since 1971; *b* 1 June 1927; *s* of Walter Otto and Anna Hollenweger-Spörri; *m* 1951, Erica Busslinger. *Educ:* Univs. of Zürich and Basel. Dr theol Zürich 1966 (and degrees leading up to it). Stock Exchange, Zürich, and several banking appts, until 1948. Pastor, 1949–57; ordained, Swiss Reformed Church, 1961. Study Dir, Ev. Acad., Zürich, 1964–65; Research Asst, Univ. of Zürich, 1961–64; Exec. Sec., World Council of Churches, Geneva, 1965–71. *Publications:* Handbuch der Pfingstbewegung, 10 vols, 1965/66; (ed) The Church for Others, 1967 (also German, Spanish and Portuguese edns); (ed) Die Pfingstkirchen, 1971; Kirche, Benzin und Bohnensuppe, 1971; The Pentecostals, 1972 (also German and Spanish edns); Pentecost between Black and White, 1975 (also German and Dutch edns); Glaube, Geist und Geister, 1975; (ed) Studies in the Intercultural History of Christianity, 20 vols, 1975–; Evangelism Today, 1976 (also German edn); (with Th. Ahrens) Volkschristentum und Volksreligion in Pazifik, 1977; Interkulturelle Theologie, vol. I, 1979, vol. II, 1982; Erfahrungen in Ephesus, 1979; Wie Grenzen zu Brücken werden, 1980; Besuch bei Lukas, 1981; Conflict in Corinth: memoirs of an old man, 1982 (also in German edn). *Address:* Department of Theology, University of Birmingham, PO Box 363, Birmingham B15 2TT. *T:* 021-472 1301.

HOLLEY, Prof. Robert W., PhD; Resident Fellow, The Salk Institute, since 1968; *b* 28 Jan. 1922; *s* of Charles and Viola Holley, Urbana, Ill, USA; *m* 1945, Ann Dworkin; one *s. Educ:* Univ. of Illinois (AB); Cornell Univ. (PhD); Washington State Coll. Research Biochemist, Cornell Univ. Med. Coll., 1944–46; Instructor, State Coll. of Wash., 1947–48; Assistant Prof. and Associate Prof. of Organic Chemistry, NY State Agricultural Experimental Station, Cornell Univ., 1948–57; Research Chemist, US Plant, Soil and Nut. Lab., ARS, USDA, 1957–64; Prof. of Biochem. and Molecular Biol., Biol. Div., Cornell Univ., 1964–69. Various awards for research, 1965–. Hon. DSc Illinois, 1970. Nobel Prize in Physiology or Medicine, 1968. *Publications:* many contribs to: Jl Amer. Chem. Soc., Science, Jl Biol. Chem., Arch. Biochem., Nature, Proc. Nat. Acad. Sci., etc. *Recreations:* sculpture; family enjoys walks along ocean and trips to mountains. *Address:* The Salk Institute, PO Box 85800, San Diego, California 92138, USA. *T:* 453-4100 (ext. 341).

HOLLEY, (William) Stephen, CBE 1979; General Manager, Washington Development Corporation, 1965–80; *b* 26 March 1920; *m* 1947, Dinah Mary Harper; three *s. Educ:* King William's Coll. Student Accountant, 1937–39. War service, RA (TA), 1939–45 (Major). Colonial Service, and Overseas Civil Service, 1945–64; Mem. Legislature and State Sec., Head of Civil Service, Sabah, Malaysia, 1964. Hon. ADK (Malaysia). DL Tyne and Wear, 1975–81. *Publications:* contribs to Sarawak Museum Jl and press articles on New Town Development. *Recreations:* gardening, theatre. *Address:* Forge Cottage, The Green, Abthorpe, Northants. *Club:* Royal Commonwealth Society.

HOLLIDAY, Prof. Frederick George Thomas, CBE 1975; FRSE; Vice-Chancellor and Warden, University of Durham, since 1980; *b* 22 Sept. 1935; *s* of Alfred C. and Margaret Holliday; *m* 1957, Philippa Mary Davidson; one *s* one *d. Educ:* Bromsgrove County High Sch.; Sheffield Univ. BSc 1st cl. hons Zool. 1956; FIBiol 1970, FRSE 1971. Fisheries Research Trng Grant (Develt Commn) at Marine Lab., Aberdeen, 1956–58; Sci. Officer, Marine Lab., Aberdeen, 1958–61; Lectr in Zoology, Univ. of Aberdeen, 1961–66; Prof. of Biology, 1967–75, Dep. Principal, 1972, Acting Principal, 1973–75, Univ. of Stirling; Prof. of Zoology, Univ. of Aberdeen, 1975–79. Member: Scottish Cttee, Nature Conservancy, 1969; Council, Scottish Field Studies Assoc., 1970–78 (Pres., 1981–); Council, Scottish Marine Biol Assoc., 1967– (Pres., 1979–); Scottish Wildlife Trust (Vice-Pres.); Council, Freshwater Biol Assoc., 1969–72; NERC Oceanography and Fisheries Research Grants Cttee, 1971; Council, NERC, 1973–79; Nature Conservancy Council, 1975–80 (Dep. Chm., 1976–77, Chm., 1977–80); Scottish Economic Council, 1975–80; Council, Marine Biol Assoc. UK, 1975–78; Oil Develt Council for Scotland, 1976–78; Standing Commn on Energy and the Environment, 1978–. Dir, Shell UK, 1980–. Trustee: Nat. Heritage Meml Fund, 1980–; Civic Trust for NE, 1980–. Mem., Bd of Governors, Rowett Res. Inst., 1976–. *Publications:* (ed and contrib.) Wildlife of Scotland, 1979; numerous on fish biology and wildlife conservation in Adv. Mar. Biol., Fish Physiology, Oceanography and Marine Biology, etc. *Recreations:* shooting, fishing, local history, gardening. *Address:* Old Shire Hall, Durham. *T:* Durham 64466. *Club:* Royal Commonwealth Society.

HOLLIDAY, Leslie John, FCIOB, CBIM; Chairman and Chief Executive, John Laing plc, since 1982 (Director, 1978); Chairman, John Laing Construction Ltd, since 1980 (Director, 1966); *b* 9 Jan. 1921; *s* of John and Elsie Holliday; *m* 1943, Kathleen Joan Marjorie Stacey; two *s. Educ:* St John's, Whitby. FCIOB 1969; CBIM 1982. Denaby & Cadby Colliery, 1937-40; served Merchant Navy, 1940-45; joined John Laing & Son Ltd, 1947, Dir 1977; Chairman: Laing Homes Ltd, 1978-81; Super Homes Ltd, 1979-81; Laing Management Contracting Ltd, 1980-81; John Laing Internat. Ltd, 1981-82. Mem., EDC for Bldg, 1979-. *Recreations:* yachting, golf. *Address:* 261 Edgwarebury Lane, Edgware, Mddx HA8 8QL. *Clubs:* Royal Ocean Racing; Royal Southern Yacht (Hamble).

HOLLIDAY, Dr Robin, FRS 1976; Head, Division of Genetics, National Institute for Medical Research, since 1970; *b* 6 Nov. 1932; *s* of Clifford and Eunice Holliday; *m* 1957, Diana Collet (*née* Parsons); one *s* three *d. Educ:* Hitchin Grammar Sch.; Univ. of Cambridge (BA, PhD). Member, Scientific Staff: Dept of Genetics, John Innes Inst., Bayfordbury, Herts, 1958-65; Division of Microbiology, Nat. Inst. for Med. Research, 1965-70. *Publications:* The Science of Human Progress, 1981; numerous scientific papers on mechanisms of genetic recombination, repair and cellular ageing. *Recreations:* travel, sculpture. *Address:* National Institute for Medical Research, Mill Hill, NW7 1AA. *T:* 01-959 3666.

HOLLIGER, Heinz; oboist and composer; *b* Langenthal, Switzerland, 1939; *m* Ursula Holliger, harpist. *Educ:* Berne Conservatoire; Paris; Basle; studied with Cassagnaud, Veress, Pierlot and Boulez. Played with Basle Orch., 1959-63; Prof. of oboe, Freiburg Music Acad., 1965-. Appeared at all major European music festivals. Has inspired compositions by Berio, Penderecki, Stockhausen, Henze, Martin and others. Compositions include: Der magische Tänzer, Trio, Dona nobis pacem, Pneuma, Psalm, Cardiophonie, Kreis, Siebengesang, H for wind quintet, string quartet Atembogen, Jahreszeiten, Come and Go. Has won many international prizes, incl. Geneva Competition first prize, 1959, and Munich Competition first prize, 1961. *Address:* c/o Ingpen & Williams Ltd, 14 Kensington Court, W8 5DN.

HOLLINGS, Hon. Sir (Alfred) Kenneth, Kt 1971; MC 1944; **Hon. Mr Justice Hollings;** Judge of the High Court of Justice, Family Division (formerly Probate, Divorce and Admiralty Division), since 1971; *b* 12 June 1918; *s* of Alfred Holdsworth Hollings and Rachel Elizabeth Hollings; *m* 1949, Harriet Evelyn Isabella, *d* of W. J. C. Fishbourne, OBE, Brussels; one *s* one *d. Educ:* Leys Sch., Cambridge; Clare Coll., Cambridge. Law Qualifying and Law Tripos, Cambridge, 1936-39; MA. Served RA (Shropshire Yeomanry), 1939-46. Called to Bar, Middle Temple, 1947 (Harmsworth Schol.); Master of the Bench, 1971. Practised Northern Circuit; Prosecuting Counsel for Inland Revenue, Northern Circuit, 1965; QC 1966; Recorder of Bolton, 1968; Judge of County Courts, Circuit 5 (E Lancs), 1968-71; Presiding Judge, Northern Circuit, 1975-78. *Recreations:* walking, music. *Address:* Royal Courts of Justice, Strand, WC2; The Hermitage, Holmes Chapel, Cheshire. *T:* Holmes Chapel 33130. *Club:* Tennis and Racquets (Manchester).

HOLLINGS, Rev. Michael Richard, MC 1943; Parish Priest, St Mary of the Angels, Bayswater, since 1978; *b* 30 Dec. 1921; *s* of Lieut-Commander Richard Eustace Hollings, RN, and Agnes Mary (*née* Hamilton-Dalrymple). *Educ:* Beaumont Coll.; St Catherine's Society, Oxford (MA). St Catherine's, 1939; Sandhurst, 1941. Served War of 1939-45 (despatches): commnd Coldstream Guards, 1941; served N Africa, Italy, Palestine, 1942-45; Major. Trained at Beda Coll., Rome, 1946-50. Ordained Rome, 1950; Asst Priest, St Patrick's, Soho Square, W1, 1950-54; Chaplain, Westminster Cathedral, 1954-58; Asst Chaplain, London Univ., 1958-59; Chaplain to Roman Catholics at Oxford Univ., 1959-70; Parish Priest, St Anselm's, Southall, Middx, 1970-78. Religious Adviser: ATV, 1958-59; Rediffusion, 1959-68; Thames Television, 1968. Member: Nat. Catholic Radio and TV Commn, 1968; Westminster Diocesan Schools Commn, 1970-; Southall Chamber of Commerce, 1971-78; Oxford and Cambridge Catholic Educn Bd, 1971-78; Executive, Council of Christians and Jews, 1971-79; Lay Mem., Press Council, 1969-75; Nat. Conf. of Priests Standing Cttee, 1974-76; Rampton Cttee, 1979-81; Swann Cttee, 1981-; Exec., Ealing Community Relations Council, 1973-76; Exec., Notting Hill Social Council, 1980-; Chm., N Kensington Action Group, 1980-81. Chaplain: to Sovereign Military Order of Malta, 1957; to Nat. Council of Lay Apostolate, 1970-74; to Catholic Inst. of Internat. Relations, 1971-80. *Publications:* Hey, You!, 1955; Purple Times, 1957; Chaplaincraft, 1963; The One Who Listens, 1971; The Pastoral Care of Homosexuals, 1971; It's Me, O Lord, 1972; Day by Day, 1972; The Shade of His Hand, 1973; Restoring the Streets, 1974; I Will Be There, 1975; You Must Be Joking, Lord, 1975; The Catholic Prayer Book, 1976; Alive to Death, 1976; Living Priesthood, 1977; His People's Way of Talking, 1978; As Was His Custom, 1979; St Thérèse of Lisieux, 1981; Hearts not Garments, 1982; Chaplet of Mary, 1982; contrib. Tablet, Clergy Review, Life of the Spirit. *Recreations:* reading, walking, people. *Address:* St Mary of the Angels, Moorhouse Road, Bayswater, W2 5DJ. *T:* 01-229 0487.

HOLLINGSWORTH, Dorothy Frances, OBE 1958; *b* 10 May 1916; *d* of Arthur Hollingsworth and Dorothy Hollingsworth (*née* Coldwell). *Educ:* Newcastle upon Tyne Church High Sch.; Univ. of Durham (BSc 1937); Royal Infirmary, Edinburgh, Dip. of Dietetics (Dip. in Dietetics). Hosp. Dietitian, Royal Northern Hosp., London, N7, 1939-41; Govt Service, 1941-70: mainly at Min. of Food until its merger with Min. of Agric. and Fisheries, 1955, to form present Min. of Agric., Fisheries and Food. Principal Scientific Officer and Head of a Scientific Br., 1949-70; Dir-Gen., British Nutrition Foundn, 1970-77. Chairman: British Dietetic Assoc., 1947-49; Internat. Cttee of Dietetic Assocs; 3rd Internat. Cong. Dietetics, 1961; Nutrition Panel, Food Gp, Soc. Chem. Ind., 1966-69 (Mem. Food Gp Cttee, 1969-72); Member: Nat. Food Survey Cttee, 1951-; Dietetics Bd, Council for Professions Supp. to Med., 1962-74; Cttee on Med. Aspects of Food Policy, 1970-79; Physiological Systems and Disorders Bd, MRC, 1974-77; Environmental Medicine Res. Policy Cttee, MRC, 1975-76; Council, Inst. Food Sci. and Technol., 1970-; Council, Nutrition Soc., 1974-77; (Dep. Chm.) Adv. Cttee on Protein, ODA, FCO, 1970-73; Jt ARC/MRC Cttee on Food and Nutrition Res., 1970-74; Royal Soc. British Nat. Cttee for Nutritional Scis, 1970-; IBA Med. Adv. Panel, 1970-; Univ. of Reading Delegacy for Nat. Inst. for Res. in Dairying, 1973-. Vice-Pres., Inst. of Biology, 1978-80; Sec. Gen., Internat. Union of Nutritional Scis, 1978-. FRIC 1956; State Registered Dietitian (SRD) 1963; Fellow of Inst. of Food Science and Technology, 1965; FIBiol 1968. *Publications:* The Englishman's Food, by J. C. Drummond and Anne Wilbraham (rev. and prod. 2nd edn), 1958; Hutchison's Food and the Principles of Nutrition (rev. and ed 12th edn with H. M. Sinclair), 1969; Nutritional Problems in a Changing World (ed, with Margaret Russell), 1973; (ed with E. Morse) People and Food Tomorrow, 1976; many papers in scientific jls. *Recreations:* talking with intelligent and humorous friends; appreciation of music, theatre and countryside; gardening. *Address:* 2 The Close, Petts Wood, Orpington, Kent BR5 1JA. *T:* Orpington 23168. *Clubs:* University Women's, Arts Theatre.

HOLLINGWORTH, John Harold; Director and General Manager, Cambridge Symphony Orchestra, since 1980; *b* 11 July 1930; *s* of Harold Hollingworth, Harborne, Birmingham; *m* 1968, Susan Barbara, *d* of J. H. Walters, Ramsey, IoM. *Educ:* Chigwell House Sch.; King Edward's Sch., Edgbaston. MP (C) All Saints Division of Birmingham, 1959-64. Chm., Edgbaston Div. Conservative Assoc., 1967-72; Vice-Chm., Birmingham Conservative Assoc., 1959-61, 1972-78 (Vice-Pres. 1960-66). *Publications:* contributions to political journals. *Recreations:* cricket, tennis. *Address:* Cantlow House, Little London, Berden, Bishop's Stortford, Herts CM22 1BD. *T:* Brent Pelham 567. *Clubs:* Lansdowne; Clavering Cricket (Vice-Pres.).

HOLLIS, Rear-Adm. Hubert Walter Elphinstone, CB 1974; General Manager, Middle East Navigation Aids Service, Bahrain, since 1977; *b* 8 June 1923; *s* of Lt-Col W. T. Hollins; *m* 1963, Jillian Mary McAlpin; one *s* one *d. Educ:* Stubbington House; Britannia RNC Dartmouth. Cadet RN, 1937; Comdr 1957; Captain 1963; Rear-Adm. 1972; comd HM Ships Petard, Dundas, Caesar and Antrim; Flag Officer, Gibraltar, 1972-74; Admiral Commanding Reserves, 1974-77. Younger Brother of Trinity House. MRIN, MNI, FBIM. *Recreations:* fishing, shooting. *Address:* Roselands, Bucklebury, Berks. *T:* Bradfield 744551; Middle East Navigation Aids Service, PO Box 66; Manama, Bahrain. *T:* Bahrain 244298.

HOLLIS, Hon. Sir Anthony Barnard, Kt 1982; **Hon. Mr Justice Barnard;** a Judge of the High Court of Justice, Family Division, since 1982; *b* 11 May 1927; *er s* of late Henry Lewis Hollis and of Gladys Florence Hollis (*née* Barnard); *m* 1956, Pauline Mary (*née* Skuce); no *c. Educ:* Tonbridge Sch.; St Peter's Hall, Oxford. Called to Bar, Gray's Inn, 1951 (Bencher, 1979); QC 1969; a Recorder of the Crown Court, 1976-82. Chm., Family Law Bar Assoc., 1974-76. *Recreation:* golf. *Address:* 1 King's Bench Walk, Temple, EC4. *T:* 01-353 4423. *Clubs:* Woking Golf; Royal St George's Golf (Sandwich).

HOLLIS, Rt. Rev. (Arthur) Michael; *b* 23 June 1899; *s* of late Right Rev. George Arthur Hollis, Bishop of Taunton; *m* 1935, Mary Cordelia, *d* of late Very Rev. Andrew Ewbank Burn, Dean of Salisbury. *Educ:* Leeds Grammar Sch.; Trinity Coll., Oxford (Scholar). Army, 1918-19; BA (2nd class Classical Hon. Mods) 1920; 1st class Litt. Hum., 1922; MA, 1924; BD, 1931; Leeds Clergy Sch., 1922; ordained deacon, 1923; priest, 1924; Curate S Andrew's, Huddersfield, 1923-24; Chaplain and Lecturer in Theology, Hertford Coll., Oxford, Fellow, 1926-31; Lecturer St Peter's Leeds, 1931; SPG Missionary, Bishop's Theological Seminary, Nazareth, diocese of Tinnevelly, India, 1931-37; Perpetual Curate of S Mary's Charlton Kings, diocese of Gloucester, 1937-42; CF 4th class (RARO), 1939-42; Bishop of Madras, 1942-47; Bishop in Madras, 1947-54; Moderator, Church of South India, 1948-54; Professor of Church History, United Theological Coll., Bangalore, 1955-60; Rector of Todwick, 1961-64; Second Assistant Bishop to the Bishop of Sheffield, 1963-66; Asst Bishop, Dio. of St Edmundsbury and Ipswich, 1966-75. Teaching, USA, 1960-61. *Publications:* Paternalism and the Church; The Significance of South India; Mission, Unity and Truth. *Address:* Flat 6, Manormead, Tilford Road, Hindhead, Surrey GU26 6RA. *T:* Hindhead 6951.

HOLLIS, Daniel Ayrton, VRD; QC 1968; a Recorder of the Crown Court, since 1972; *b* 30 April 1925; *s* of Norman Hollis; *m* 1st, 1950, Gillian Mary Turner (marr. diss., 1961), *d* of J. W. Cecil Turner, Cambridge; one *s* one *d*; 2nd, 1963, Stella Hydleman, *d* of Mark M. Gergel; one *s. Educ:* Geelong Grammar Sch., Australia; Brasenose Coll., Oxford. Served N Atlantic and Mediterranean, 1943-46. Lieut-Commander, RNVR. Called to Bar, Middle Temple, 1949; Bencher, 1975. Standing Counsel to Inland Revenue at Central Criminal Court and London Sessions, 1965-68; Dep. Chm., Kent QS, 1970-71. *Recreation:* travel. *Address:* Queen Elizabeth Building, Temple, EC4.

HOLLIS, Ven. Gerald; Archdeacon of Birmingham, since 1974; *b* 16 May 1919; *s* of Canon Walter Hollis and Enid (*née* Inchbold); *m* 1946, Doreen Emmet Stancliffe; one *s* three *d. Educ:* St Edward's Sch., Oxford; Christ Church, Oxford (MA); Wells Theological College. RNVR, 1940-45: on Staff RN Coll., Dartmouth, 1941-45. Curate: All Saints, Stepney, E1, 1947-50; i/c St Luke's, Rossington, 1950-55; Rector, Armthorpe, 1955-60; Vicar of Rotherham and Rural Dean, 1960-74; Proctor in Convocation, dio. Sheffield, 1967-75; Hon. Canon Sheffield Cathedral, 1970. Mem. Gen. Synod, C of E, 1975-. *Publication:* Rugger: do it this way, 1946. *Recreation:* gardening. *Address:* Glengariff, 59 Salisbury Road, Moseley, Birmingham B13 8LB. *T:* 021-449 1642. *Club:* Vincent's (Oxford).

HOLLIS, Hugh; part-time Chairman for Civil Service Commission Appointments Board, 1972-77; *b* 25 July 1910; *s* of Ash and Emily Geraldine Hollis; *m* 1939, Muriel Bewick Hollis (*née* Nattrass); two *s. Educ:* Stockton Sec. Sch.; Constantine Techn. College. BSc Hons London; CChem; FRIC. Imperial Chemical Industries, 1928-36; Chemist, War Office, 1936-40; Principal Scientific Officer, Min. of Supply, 1940-56; Army Dept, MoD, 1956-71: Asst Dir Chemical Inspectorate; Dir 1963, title changed to Dir of Quality Assce (Materials), MoD, 1969-71 (CSO 1970), retired 1971. *Publications:* articles in Jl of Oil and Colour Chemists Assoc. and Inst. of Petroleum. *Recreations:* gardening, trout and salmon fishing. *Address:* Green Point, Fossebridge, Cheltenham, Glos. *T:* Fossebridge 463.

HOLLIS, Rt. Rev. Michael; *see* Hollis, Rt Rev. A. M.

HOLLIS, Posy; *see* Simmonds, P.

HOLLIS, Rt. Rev. Reginald; *see* Montreal, Bishop of.

HOLLMAN, Arthur, MD; FRCP; Consultant Cardiologist to University College Hospital, London, since 1962; Fellow, University College London, since 1978; Hon. Consultant Cardiologist: Kingston Hospital, since 1964; Hospital for Sick Children, London, since 1978; *b* 7 Dec. 1923; *s* of W. J. and I. R. Hollman; *m* 1949, Catharine Elizabeth Large; four *d. Educ:* Tiffin Boys' Sch., Kingston upon Thames; University Coll. London; UCH Med. Sch. (MD). FRCP 1967. Jun. hosp. appts, London, Banbury and Taplow, 1946-57; Bilton Pollard Fellow of UCH Med. Sch. at Children's Meml Hosp., Montreal, 1951-52; Clinical Asst, National Heart Hosp., 1954-56; Sen. Registrar and Asst Lectr, Royal Postgraduate Med. Sch., 1957-62. Advisor in Cardiology: to Mauritius Govt, 1966-; to Republic of Seychelles, 1974-. Councillor, RCP, 1976-79. Member: Cttee of Management, Chelsea Physic Garden, 1971-; Council, British Heart Founds, 1975-80; British Cardiac Soc. (Mem. Council, Asst Sec., and Sec., 1971-76); Assoc. of Physicians of GB and Ireland; Osler Club. Mem. Editorial Bd, Jl of RSM, 1977-81. *Publications:* articles on cardiovascular subjects in British and Amer. jls. *Recreations:* gardening, especially medicinal plants; medical history. *Address:* Cardiac Department, University College Hospital, Gower Street, WC1E 6AU. *T:* 01-387 9300.

HOLLOM, Sir Jasper (Quintus), KBE 1975; Chairman: Panel on Take-overs and Mergers, since 1980; Commonwealth Development Finance Co., since 1980; *b* 16 Dec. 1917; *s* of Arthur and Kate Louisa Hollom; *m* 1954, Patricia Elizabeth Mary Ellis. *Educ:* King's Sch., Bruton. Entered Bank of England, 1936; appointed Deputy Chief Cashier, 1956; Chief Cashier, 1962-66; Director, 1966-70, 1980-; Deputy Governor, 1970-80. *Address:* High Wood, Selborne, Hants. *T:* Selborne 317.

HOLLOWAY, Derrick Robert Le Blond; Registrar of the Family Division, Principal Registry, since 1966; *b* 29 May 1917; *s* of Robert Fabyan Le Blond and Mary Beatrice Holloway; *m* 1942, Muriel Victoria Bower; one *s. Educ:* Brentwood; Univ. of London (LLB (Hons)). Principal Probate Registry, 1937. Served War of 1939-45: DCLI, RASC, Claims Commn. Sec., Cttee on Law of Intestate Succession, 1951; Sec., Cttee on Ancient Probate Records, 1953; Asst Sec., Royal Commn on Marriage and Divorce, 1952-56; Acting Registrar, Probate, Divorce and Admiralty Div., 1965. *Publications:* (ed jtly) Latey on Divorce (14th edn), 1952; Editor: Proving a Will (2nd edn), 1952; Obtaining Letters of Administration, 1954; Divorce Forms and Precedents, 1959; Probate Handbook, 1961, 6th edn 1982; Phillips' Probate Practice (6th edn), 1963; contrib. to Butterworths' Costs (4th edn), 1971; Acting in Person: how to obtain an undefended divorce, 1977. *Recreations:* marriage, gardening, foreign travel, music. *Address:* 1 Chiltern Manor Park, Great Missenden, Bucks.

HOLLOWAY, Frank, FCA; Managing Director, Supplies and Transport, since 1980 (Finance and Supplies, 1976-80) and Board Member, since 1978, British Steel Corporation; *b* 20 Oct. 1924; *s* of Frank and Elizabeth Holloway; *m* 1949, Elizabeth Beattie; three *d. Educ:* Burnage High Sch., Manchester. Served War, Royal Navy, 1943-46. Various senior finance appts in The United Steel Companies Ltd and later in British Steel Corp., 1949-72. Managing Dir, Supplies and Production Control, British Steel Corp., 1973-76. *Recreations:* cricket; collecting books. *Address:* 11 Copperfield Way, Chislehurst, Kent BR7 6RY. *T:* 01-467 9559.

HOLLOWAY, Prof. John, MA, DPhil, DLitt, LittD; Professor of Modern English, Cambridge, 1972-82 (Reader, 1966-72); Fellow of Queens' College, 1955; *b* 1 Aug. 1920; *s* of George Holloway and Evelyn Astbury; *m* 1946, Audrey Gooding; one *s* one *d; m* 1978, Joan Black. *Educ:* County Sch.,

Beckenham, Kent; New Coll., Oxford (Open History Scholar). 1st class Modern Greats, 1941; DPhil Oxon 1947; DLitt Aberdeen 1954; LittD Cambridge, 1969. Served War of 1939-45, commnd RA, 1942; subsequently seconded to Intelligence. Temporary Lecturer in Philosophy, New Coll., 1945; Fellow of All Souls Coll., 1946-60; John Locke Scholar, 1947; University Lecturer in English, Aberdeen, 1949-54; University Lecturer in English, Cambridge, 1954-66; Sec., 1954-56, Librarian, 1964-66, Chm., 1970, 1971, English Faculty. FRSL 1956. Lecture Tour, Ceylon, India, Pakistan, 1958; Middle East, 1965; Byron Professor, University of Athens, 1961-63; Alexander White Professor, Chicago, 1965; Hinkley Prof., Johns Hopkins Univ., 1972; Virginia Lectr, Charlottesville, 1979. *Publications:* Language and Intelligence, 1951; The Victorian Sage, 1953; (ed) Poems of the Mid-Century, 1957; The Charted Mirror (Essays), 1960; (ed) Selections from Shelley, 1960; Shakespeare's Tragedies, 1961; The Colours of Clarity (essays), 1964; The Lion Hunt, 1964; Widening Horizons in English Verse, 1966; Blake, The Lyric Poetry, 1968; The Establishment of English, 1972; (ed with J. Black) Later English Broadside Ballads, vol. I, 1975, vol II, 1979; The Proud Knowledge, 1977; Narrative and Structure, 1979; contributions to journals; *verse:* The Minute, 1956; The Fugue, 1960; The Landfallers, 1962; Wood and Windfall, 1965; New Poems, 1970; Planet of Winds, 1977. *Recreation:* enjoyment. *Address:* Queens' College, Cambridge.

HOLLOWAY, Reginald Eric; HM Diplomatic Service; Consul-General, Toronto, since 1981; *b* 22 June 1932; *s* of late Ernest and Beatrice Holloway; *m* 1958, Anne Penelope, *d* of Walter Robert Pawley and late Doris Lilian Pawley; one *d. Educ:* St Luke's, Brighton. Apprentice reporter, 1947-53; served RAF, 1953-55; journalist in Britain and E Africa, 1955-61; Press Officer, Tanganyika Govt, 1961-63; Dir, British Inf. Service, Guyana, 1964-67; Inf. Dept, FCO, 1967-69 (Anguilla, 1969); 2nd, later 1st Sec., Chancery in Malta, 1970-72; E African Dept, FCO, 1972-74; Consul and Head of Chancery, Kathmandu, 1974-77 (Chargé d'Affaires *ai*, 1975 and 1976); Asst Head, S Asian Dept, FCO, 1977-79; Counsellor, 1979; Inspector, 1979-81. *Recreations:* woodworking, old wirelesses. *Address:* c/o Foreign and Commonwealth Office, SW1. *Club:* Royal Commonwealth Society.

HOLLOWAY, Maj.-Gen. Robin Hugh Ferguson, CB 1976; CBE 1974; Director of Civil Defence, New Zealand; *b* Hawera, 22 May 1922; *s* of late Hugh Ferguson Holloway and Phyllis Myrtle Holloway; *m* 1947, Margaret Jewell, *d* of E. G. Monk, Temple Cloud, Somerset; one *s* two *d. Educ:* Hawera Technical High Sch.; RMC, Duntroon, Australia. Commnd NZ Staff Corps, 1942; served in 2nd NZEF, Solomon Is, Italy and Japan, 1943-47; qual. Air Observation Post Pilot, 1948-49; Staff Coll., Camberley, 1952; Jt Services Staff Coll., Latimer, 1958; Dir of Mil. Intelligence, 1959-61; Dep. Adjt Gen., 1962-63; Head, NZ Defence Liaison Staff, Singapore and Malaysia, 1964-65; ACDS, 1967-68; IDC, 1969; Comdr Northern Mil. Dist, and Comdr 1st Inf. Bde Gp, 1970; DCGS, 1971-73; CGS, 1973-76; R of O, March 1977. Referee, Small Claims Tribunal, Dist Court, Lower Hutt, 1982-. Pres., Scout Assoc. of NZ, 1979-; Dep. Chief Scout, 1979-. *Recreations:* gardening, walking. *Address:* 435 Te Moana Road, Waikanae, New Zealand.

HOLM, Ian; actor, since 1954; *b* 12 Sept. 1931; *s* of Dr James Harvey Cuthbert and Jean Wilson Cuthbert; *m* 1955, Lynn Mary Shaw (marr. diss. 1965); two *d* ; and one *s* one *d* ; *m* 1982, Sophie Baker; one *s. Educ:* Chigwell Grammar Sch., Essex. Trained RADA, 1950-53 (interrupted by Nat. Service); joined Shakespeare Memorial Theatre, 1954, left after 1955; Worthing Rep., 1956; tour, Olivier's Titus Andronicus, 1957; re-joined Stratford, 1958: roles include: Puck; Ariel; Gremio; Lorenzo; Prince Hal; Henry V; Duke of Gloucester; Richard III; The Fool in Lear; Lennie in The Homecoming (also on Broadway, 1966) (Evening Standard Actor of the Year, 1965); left RSC, 1967. Major film appearances include: Young Winston, The Fixer, Oh! What a Lovely War, The Bofors Gun, Alien, All Quiet on the Western Front, Chariots of Fire (Best Supporting Actor: Cannes, 1981; BAFTA, 1982); Return of the Soldier. TV series include: J. M. Barrie in BBC trilogy The Lost Boys (RTS Best Actor Award, 1979); We, the Accused, BBC 2, 1980; The Bell, BBC 2, 1981; other TV appearances include: Lech Walesa in Strike, 1981; Goebbels in Inside the Third Reich, 1982. *Recreations:* tennis, walking, general outdoor activities. *Address:* c/o Leading Artists, 60 St James Street, SW1.

HOLMAN, Norman Frederick; *b* 22 Feb. 1914; *s* of late Walter John and Violet Holman, Taunton; *m* 1940, Louisa Young; one *s* two *d. Educ:* Huish's, Taunton. Entered Post Office as Exec. Officer, 1932; Higher Exec. Officer, 1942. Served in Royal Corps of Signals, 1942-46. Sen. Exec. Officer, 1950; Asst Accountant-Gen., 1953; Dep. Dir, 1956; Dir of Postal Finance, 1967; Dir of Central Finance and Accounts, PO, 1971-74. *Recreations:* bowls, bridge, The Observer crossword. *Address:* Crosswinds, 32 Richmond Road, Exmouth, Devon EX8 2NA. *T:* Exmouth 75298.

HOLMAN, Dr Portia Grenfell; Senior Physician in Psychological Medicine, Elizabeth Garrett Anderson Hospital, 1954-69, retired; *b* 20 Nov. 1903; *d* of Hon. William Arthur Holman, KC, Premier of New South Wales, 1914-18, and Ada Augusta Kidgell. *Educ:* The Women's Coll., Sydney, NSW; Newnham Coll., Cambridge. Economics Tripos, 1923-26, BA Cantab. 1926. Research and lecturing at St Andrews Univ., 1927-33; MA Cantab 1923. Medical student, Cambridge and Royal Free Hospital, 1934-39. Consultant Psychiatrist to Twickenham Child Guidance Clinic, 1944, West Middlesex Hospital, 1945, Elizabeth Garrett Anderson Hospital, 1946. MD 1950; Burlingame Prize, 1952; FRCP 1961; FRCPsych 1971. Founder and first

Chairman Association of Workers for Maladjusted Children, 1951. *Publications:* Bedwetting, 1954; Psychology and Psychological Medicine for Nurses, 1957; (with Amy Sycamore) Sebastians: hospital school experiment in therapeutic education, 1971; contributions to Journal of Mental Science. *Recreations:* mountain climbing, swimming. *Address:* 2 Prince Albert Road, NW1. *Club:* Royal Society of Medicine.

HOLMBERG, Eric Robert Reginald; Deputy Chief Scientist (Army), Ministry of Defence, 1972-77; *b* 24 Aug. 1917; *s* of Robert and May Holmberg; *m* 1940, Wanda Erna Reich; one *s* one *d. Educ:* Sandown (Isle of Wight) Grammar Sch.; St John's Coll., Cambridge (MA); Imperial Coll., London (PhD). Joined Mine Design Department, Admiralty, 1940; Admiralty Gunnery Establishment, 1945; Operational Research Department, Admiralty, 1950; appointed Chief Supt Army Operational Research Group, 1956; Dir, Army Operational Science and Res., subseq. Asst Chief Scientist (Army), MoD, 1961-72. *Publications:* papers in Proc. Royal Astronomical Society. *Address:* 29 Westmoreland Road, Barnes, SW13. *T:* 01-748 2568.

HOLME, Maj.-Gen. Michael Walter, CBE 1966; MC 1945; *b* 9 May 1918; *s* of Thomas Walter Holme and Ruth Sangster Holme (*née* Rivington); *m* 1948, Sarah Christian Van Der Gucht; one *s* two *d. Educ:* Winchester College. Directing Staff, Staff Coll., Camberley, 1952-55; Comdr 1st Bn 3rd East Anglian Regt, 1960-62; Comdr Land Forces Persian Gulf, 1963-66; Chief of Staff, Western Comd, 1966-67; Divisional Brig., The Queen's Div., 1968-69; GOC Near East Land Forces, 1969-72, retired; Dep. Col, The Royal Anglian Regiment, 1970-77. *Recreations:* various. *Address:* c/o C. Hoare & Co., 37 Fleet Street, EC4; Glen Cottage, 145 Park Road, Camberley, Surrey. *Club:* Army and Navy.

HOLME, Richard Gordon; Director, Campaign for Electoral Reform, since 1976; *b* 27 May 1936; *s* of J. R. Holme and E. M. Eggleston; *m* 1959, Kathleen Mary Powell; two *s* two *d. Educ:* Royal Masonic Sch.; St John's Coll., Oxford; Harvard Business Sch. Commnd 10th Gurkha Rifles, Malaya, 1954-56. Vice-Chm., Liberal Party Exec., 1966-67; Pres., Liberal Party, 1980-81; contested (L): East Grinstead, 1964 and a by-election, 1965; Braintree, Oct. 1974. Sec., Parly Democracy Trust, 1977-; Hon. Treasurer, Green Alliance, 1978-. *Publications:* No Dole for the Young, 1975; A Democracy Which Works, 1978. *Address:* 38 Murray Road, Wimbledon, SW19 4PE. *Club:* Reform.

HOLMER, Paul Cecil Henry, CMG 1973; HM Diplomatic Service; Ambassador to Romania, since 1979; *b* 19 Oct. 1923; *s* of late Bernard Cecil and Mimi Claudine Holmer; *m* 1946, Irene Nora, *e d* of late Orlando Lenox Beater, DFC; two *s* two *d. Educ:* King's Sch., Canterbury; Balliol Coll., Oxford. Served in RA, 1942-46. Entered Civil Service, 1947; Colonial Office, 1947-49; transferred to HM Foreign Service, 1949; FO, 1949-51; Singapore, 1951-55; FO, 1955-56; served on Civil Service Selection Bd, 1956; FO, 1956-58; Moscow, 1958-59; Berlin, 1960-64; FO, 1964-66; Counsellor, 1966; Dep. High Comr, Singapore, 1966-69; Head of Security Dept, FCO, 1969-72; Ambassador, Ivory Coast, Upper Volta and Niger, 1972-75; Minister and UK Dep. Perm. Rep. to NATO, 1976-79. Dir, African Develt Fund, 1973-75. *Address:* c/o Foreign and Commonwealth Office, SW1. *Club:* Travellers'.

HOLMES, Anthony, CBE 1982; Chief Passport Officer, since 1980; *b* 4 Sept. 1931; *s* of Herbert and Jessie Holmes; *m* 1954, Sheila Frances Povall. *Educ:* Calday Grange Grammar School. Joined HM Customs and Excise, 1949; served HM Forces, 1950-52; Passport Office, 1955; Dep. Chief Passport Officer, 1977. *Recreations:* golf, sailing. *Address:* c/o Passport Office, Clive House, 70 Petty France, SW1H 9HD. *Clubs:* Cowdray Park Golf (Midhurst); Royal Liverpool Golf; West Kirby Sailing.

HOLMES, Barry Trevor; HM Diplomatic Service; Counsellor (Commercial), Helsinki, since 1980; *b* 23 Sept. 1933; *s* of Edwin Holmes and Marion (*née* Jones); *m* 1956, Dorothy Pitchforth; three *d. Educ:* Bishopshalt Grammar School. Entered HM Foreign Service, 1950; Wages Clerk, 1950-53; Foreign Office, 1955-58; Quito, 1958-62; FO, 1962-65; Vancouver, 1965-68; First Secretary, FCO, 1968-72; Nairobi, 1972-75; FCO, 1975-80. National Service: Captain, Royal Artillery, Egypt, 1953-55. *Recreations:* chess, lay-preaching when anyone will listen. *Address:* c/o Foreign and Commonwealth Office, SW1A 2AH.

HOLMES, David; Under Secretary, Department of Transport, since 1976; *b* 6 March 1935; *s* of late George A. Holmes and Annie Holmes; *m* 1963, Ann Chillingworth; one *s* two *d. Educ:* Doncaster Grammar Sch.; Christ Church, Oxford (MA). Asst Principal, Min. of Transport and Civil Aviation, 1957; Private Sec. to Jt Parly Sec., 1961-63; HM Treasury, 1965-68; Principal Private Sec. to Minister of Transport, 1968-70; Asst Sec., 1970. *Recreation:* music. *Address:* 15 The Orchard, Winchmore Hill, N21 2DN. *T:* 01-360 7134.

HOLMES, David Vivian; Chief Assistant to the Director-General of the BBC, since 1980; *b* 12 Oct. 1926; *s* of Vivian and Kathleen Holmes; *m* 1st, 1957, Rhoda Ann (marr. diss. 1978), *d* of late Col N. J. Gai; two *d* ; 2nd, 1979, Linda Ruth Alexander, *d* of late G. L. Kirk and of Mrs M. M. Kirk. *Educ:* Ipswich Sch.; Allhallows Sch. Served KRRC, 1944-47. Entered journalism, 1948; Evening Standard, Londoner's Diary, 1951-56; Reporter, BBC News, 1956-61; various roles as BBC political reporter, 1961-72; Asst Head, BBC Radio Talks and Documentary Programmes; launched Kaleidoscope arts programme, 1973; Presenter: News Extra, BBC2, 1973-75; Westminster, BBC2,

intermittently, 1969-79; Political Editor, BBC, 1975-80. Mem. Council, Hansard Soc., 1981-. *Recreations:* gardening, music. *Address:* 23 Offley Road, The Oval, SW9 1AS. *T:* 01-582 6096.

HOLMES, E(ric) M(ontagu) Price, CBE 1970; Manager, Legal Department, Beecham Group Ltd, 1946-74; Chairman, Town & Country Building Society; *b* 26 Nov. 1909; *o s* of late Montagu Price Holmes, FSI, FAI and late Rose Holmes (*née* Chevens). *Educ:* University College Sch., London; University Coll., Oxford (MA). Called to Bar, Inner Temple, 1933; Oxford Circuit. Served RA (TA), 1939-45; Major, GSO2, War Office. UNA: Chm. of Gen. Council, 1948-70; Chm., London Regional Council, 1947- (Pres. 1965); Chm. Exec. Cttee, 1970-72 and 1974-76, Vice-Chm., 1972-74; Pres., 1977. Delegate to World Fedn of UNAs, Marianske Lazne, Geneva, Warsaw, New York, Luxembourg, Moscow. Sec. to Governors, Ashridge Management Coll., 1962-74. Chairman: St Marylebone Council of Churches, 1963-64; St Marylebone Almshouses, 1978-. *Recreations:* reading, travel. *Address:* 42 St Stephens Close, Avenue Road, NW8 6DD. *T:* 01-722 0394. *Club:* Royal Over-Seas League.

HOLMES, Sir Frank (Wakefield), Kt 1975; JP; Chairman, New Zealand Planning Council, since 1977; *b* 8 Sept. 1924; *s* of James Francis Wakefield and Marie Esme Babette Holmes; *m* 1947, Nola Ruth Ross; two *s. Educ:* Waitaki Boys' Jun. High Sch. (Dux 1936); King's High Sch. (Dux 1941); Otago Univ.; Auckland University Coll. (Sen. Schol. 1948); Victoria University Coll. MA (1st Cl. Hons) 1949. Flying Officer, Royal NZ Air Force, 1942-45 (despatches). Economic Div., Prime Minister's and External Affairs Depts 1949-52; Lectr to Prof., Victoria Univ. of Wellington, 1952-67: Macarthy Prof. of Economics, 1959-67; Dean, Faculty of Commerce, 1961-63; Economics Manager, Tasman Pulp & Paper Co Ltd, 1967-70; Prof. of Money and Finance, Victoria Univ. of Wellington, 1970-77. Adviser, Royal Commn on Monetary, Banking and Credit Systems, 1955; Consultant, Bank of New Zealand, 1956-58 and 1964-67; Chm., Monetary and Economic Council, 1961-64 and 1970-72; Jt Sec., Cttee on Universities, 1959; Mem., NZ Council Educnl Research, 1965-77 (Chm. 1970-74); Chairman: Adv. Council on Educnl Planning and Steering Cttee, Educnl Develt Conf., 1973-74; NZ Govt Task Force on Economic and Social Planning, 1976. President: NZ Assoc. of Economists, 1961-63; Economic Section, ANZAAS, 1967, Education Section, 1979; Central Council, Economic Soc. of Australia and NZ, 1967-68. Life Mem., VUW Students' Assoc., 1967. JP 1960. FRSA. *Publications:* Money, Finance and the Economy, 1972; Government in the New Zealand Economy, 1977, 2nd edn 1980; pamphlets and articles on econs, finance, educn and internat. affairs. *Recreations:* camping, walking, swimming, tennis. *Address:* 61 Cheviot Road, Lowry Bay, Wellington, New Zealand. *T:* Wellington 684-719. *Club:* Wellington (Wellington).

HOLMES, Dr George Arthur; Fellow and Tutor, St Catherine's College, Oxford, since 1962; *b* 22 April 1927; *s* of late John Holmes and Margaret Holmes, Aberystwyth; *m* 1953, Evelyn Anne, *d* of late Dr John Klein and Audrey Klein; one *s* two *d* (and one *s* decd). *Educ:* Ardwyn County Sch., Aberystwyth; UC, Aberystwyth; St John's Coll., Cambridge (MA, PhD). Fellow, St John's Coll., Cambridge, 1951-54; Tutor, St Catherine's Society, Oxford, 1954-62; Mem., Inst. for Advanced Study, Princeton, 1967-68; Vice-Master, St Catherine's Coll., 1969-71. Chm., Victoria County Hist. Cttee, Inst. of Hist. Res., 1979-. Jt Editor, English Historical Review, 1974-81. *Publications:* The Estates of the Higher Nobility in Fourteenth-Century England, 1957; The Later Middle Ages, 1962; The Florentine Enlightenment 1400-1450, 1969; Europe: hierarchy and revolt 1320-1450, 1975; The Good Parliament, 1975; Dante, 1980; articles in learned jls. *Address:* 431 Banbury Road, Oxford. *T:* Oxford 58135.

HOLMES, George Dennis, CB 1979; FRSE; Director-General and Deputy Chairman, Forestry Commission, since 1977; *b* 9 Nov. 1926; *s* of James Henry Holmes and Florence Holmes (*née* Jones); *m* 1953, Sheila Rosemary Woodger; three *d. Educ:* John Bright's Sch., Llandudno; Univ. of Wales (BSc (Hons)). Post-grad Research, Univ. of Wales, 1947; appointed Forestry Commission, 1948; Asst Silviculturist, Research Div., 1948; Asst Conservator, N Wales, 1962; Dir of Research, 1968; Comr for Harvesting and Marketing, 1973. FICFor; FIWSc. *Publications:* contribs to Forestry Commission pubns and to Brit. and Internat. forestry jls. *Recreations:* sailing, golf, walking. *Address:* Greskine, 7 Cammo Road, Barnton, Edinburgh EH4 8EF. *T:* 031-339 7474.

HOLMES, Prof. Kenneth Charles, PhD; FRS 1981; Director of the Department of Biophysics, Max-Planck-Institute for Medical Research, Heidelberg, since 1968; Professor of Biophysics, Heidelberg University, since 1972; *b* 19 Nov. 1934; *m* 1957, Mary Scruby; one *s* three *d. Educ:* St John's Coll., Cambridge (MA 1959); London Univ. (PhD 1959). Res. Associate, Childrens' Hosp., Boston, USA, 1960-61; Mem., Scientific Staff, MRC Lab. of Molecular Biology, Cambridge, 1962-68. Mem., European Molecular Biol. Organisation. Corresp. Mem., Soc. Royale des Scis, Liège. *Publications:* (with D. Blow) The Use of X-ray Diffraction in the Study of Protein and Nucleic Acid Structure, 1965; papers on virus structure and molecular mechanism of muscular contraction. *Recreations:* rowing, singing. *Address:* Biophysics Department, Max-Planck-Institute for Medical Research, Jahnstrasse 29, 6900 Heidelberg 1, Germany. *T:* Heidelberg 4861.

HOLMES, Brig. Kenneth Soar, CB 1963; CBE 1954; Managing Director, Posts, Postal Headquarters, 1971-72 (Senior Director, 1970-71); *b* 1912; *s* of

W. J. Holmes, Ellesmere, Chaddesden Park Road, Derby; *m* 1936, Anne, *d* of C. A. Chapman, Leicester; one *s*. *Educ*: Bemrose Sch., Derby, and at Derby Technical Coll. Entered Post Office as Asst Traffic Superintendent (Telephones), 1930; Asst Surveyor, 1936; Principal, 1947; Asst Secretary, 1950. Served War of 1939-45 as Officer Commanding 43rd Division Postal Unit, with 21st Army Group and 2nd Army Headquarters, and as Asst Director of Army Postal Services, British Army of the Rhine. Director of: Army Postal Services, War Office, 1950-59; Mechanisation and Buildings, GPO, 1956-60; Postal Services, GPO, 1960-65; London Postal Region, 1965-70. Chairman Executive Cttee of Universal Postal Union, 1960-64. *Address*: 1 Wanderdown Road, Ovingdean, Brighton BN2 7BT. *T*: Brighton 37847.

HOLMES, Brigadier Leonard Geoffrey, CBE 1943; *b* 15 Jan. 1899; *s* of Lt-Col L. Holmes, TD; *m* 1940, Gladys May (*d* 1982), *d* of Sir Robert James Black, 1st Bt; one *s*. *Educ*: Brighton Coll.; RMA, Woolwich. 2nd Lieut RA, Aug. 1916; European War, 1917-18; Staff Coll., Camberley, 1934-35; Middle East and North Africa, 1941-43; Brigadier 1949; retired 1953. *Address*: Headlams Well, Ipsden, Oxford.

HOLMES, Sir Maurice (Andrew), Kt 1969; Barrister-at-Law; *b* 28 July 1911; *o s* of Rev. A. T. Holmes and Ellen Holmes; *m* 1935, Joyce Esther, *d* of late E. C. Hicks, JP, CC; no *c*. *Educ*: Felsted Sch., Essex. Served with RASC, 1941-45 (Major, despatches). Called to Bar, Gray's Inn, 1948; Practised at Bar, 1950-55. Director, 1955-60, Chairman, 1960-65, The Tilling Association Ltd; Chairman, London Transport Board, 1965-69. Circuit Administrator, South Eastern Circuit, 1970-74. Governor of Felsted School. *Recreations*: golf, music. *Address*: The Limes, Felsted, near Dunmow, Essex. *T*: Great Dunmow 820352. *Clubs*: Forty, MCC.

HOLMES, Maj.-Gen. Sir Noel Galway, KBE 1946 (CBE 1940); CB 1943; MC; *b* Galway, Ireland, 25 Dec. 1891; 4th *s* of late Capt. H. W. Holmes, Rockwood, Galway; *m* 1st, 1920, Mary (*d* 1978), *er d* of late Sir Hugh Clifford, GCMG, GBE; one *s* one *d*; 2nd, 1979, Irene, *widow* of Maj. T. L. B. Tennant, RA. *Educ*: Bedford Sch. Joined Royal Irish Regt, 1912; India, 1912-14; served War of 1914-18, France (wounded, despatches four times. MC 1917, 1915 Star, War Medal, Victory Medal); Staff Course, Hesden, 1916, Cambridge, 1918; Bt Major, 1919; Temp. Lt-Col, AAQMG, Upper Silesia, 1921-22; trans. to East Yorkshire Regt, 1922; Staff Coll., 1926-27; Bde Major, Dover, 1929-31; GSO Southern Command, India, 1933-37; Bt Lt-Col, 1935; Commanded 1 Bn East Yorkshire Regt, 1938-39; served War of 1939-45 (Burma Star, Italy Star, France and Germany Medal, War Medal, Victory Medal); Maj.-Gen. 1943; Dir of Movements, War Office, 1939-43; attended Chiefs of Staff confs, Washington, Quebec, Cairo, Teheran, Yalta and Potsdam; DQMG War Office, 1943-46; Commander Aldershot and Hampshire District, 1946; retired at own request, 1946; Chm., NE Divisional Coal Board (Yorkshire), 1946-57. Croix d'Officier of the Legion d'Honneur and Croix de Guerre with Palme, 1945; American Legion of Merit (Commander), 1946. *Recreations*: Davis Cup Lawn Tennis (Ireland), 1930; golf, shooting, etc. *Address*: 59 Braemore Road, Hove, Sussex BN3 4HA.

HOLMES, Prof. Patrick, PhD; Professor of Hydraulics, Imperial College of Science and Technology, University of London, 1974-83; *b* 23 Feb. 1939; *s* of Norman Holmes and Irene (*née* Shelbourne); *m* 1963, Olive (*née* Towning); one *s* one *d*. *Educ*: University Coll. of Swansea, Univ. of Wales (BSc 1960, PhD 1963). CEng, MICE. Res. Engr, Harbour and Deep Ocean Engrg, US Navy Civil Engrg Lab., Port Hueneme, Calif, 1963-65; Lectr, Dept of Civil Engrg, Univ. of Liverpool, 1966-72, Sen. Lectr, 1972-74. Chm., Environment Cttee, SERC, 1981-. *Publications*: articles on ocean and coastal engineering, wave motion, wave loading, coastal erosion and accretion, and harbour and breakwater design, in Proc. ICE and Proc. Amer. Soc. of Civil Engrs. *Recreations*: squash, sailing, walking, music. *Address*: Department of Civil Engineering, Imperial College of Science and Technology, SW7 2AZ; Stepaside, Brancote Road, Oxton, Merseyside L43 6TL. *T*: 051-652 7117. *Club*: Royal Commonwealth Society.

HOLMES, Sir Stanley, Kt 1974; DL; Director, Mersey Docks and Harbour Co., since 1978; Chief Executive, Merseyside Metropolitan County Council, 1974-77; *b* 15 Dec. 1912; *s* of Stanley and Ethel Holmes, Liverpool; *m* 1939, Doris Elizabeth Burton; one *d*. *Educ*: Liverpool Collegiate School. Deputy Town Clerk, Liverpool, 1956, Town Clerk 1967; Chief Exec. and Town Clerk, 1969. DL County of Merseyside, 1974. Hon. LLD Liverpool, 1974. Kt 1st class Royal Norwegian Order of St Olaf, 1974. *Recreations*: people, places, paintings. *Address*: 44 Green Lane, Liverpool L18 6HD. *T*: 051-724 5432.

HOLMES, Prof. William; Professor of Agriculture, Wye College, University of London, since 1955; *b* Kilbarchan, Renfrewshire, 16 Aug. 1922; *s* of William John Holmes, Bank Manager; *m* 1949, Jean Ishbel Campbell, BSc; two *d*. *Educ*: John Neilson Sch., Paisley; Glasgow Univ.; West of Scotland Agricultural Coll. BSc (Agric), NDD, 1942; NDA (Hons), 1943; PhD Glasgow, 1947; DSc London, 1966. FIBiol 1974. Asst Executive Officer, S Ayrshire AEC, 1943-44; Hannah Dairy Research Inst.: Asst in Animal Husbandry, 1944-47; Head of Department of Dairy and Grassland Husbandry, 1947-55. Member, Cttee on Milk Composition in the UK, 1958-60; Governor, Grassland Research Inst., 1960-75; Pres., British Grassland Soc., 1968-69 (1st recipient, British Grassland Soc. Award, 1979); Pres., British Soc. of Animal Production, 1969-70; Member technical cttees of ARC, JCO MAFF and Meat and Livestock Commn, 1960-. *Publications*: (ed) Grass, its production and

utilization, 1980; papers in technical agricultural journals. *Recreations*: gardening, beekeeping, travel, study of organizations. *Address*: Amage, Wye, Kent. *T*: Wye 812372.

HOLMES à COURT, family name of **Baron Heytesbury**.

HOLMES à COURT, (Michael) Robert (Hamilton); Chairman: Associated Communications Corporation plc, since 1982; The Bell Group Ltd, Australia, since 1970; *b* 27 July 1937; *s* of Peter Worsley Holmes à Court and Ethnée Celia Holmes à Court; *m* 1965, Janet Lee Ranford; three *s* one *d*. *Educ*: Michaelhouse, Natal, S Africa; Univ. of Western Australia (LLB). Barrister and Solicitor of the Supreme Court of Western Australia, 1965. *Recreations*: thoroughbred horse breeding and racing. *Address*: 6 Osborne Parade, Claremont, Western Australia 6010. *T*: Perth 384 3894.

HOLMES SELLORS, Patrick John; *see* Sellors.

HOLMPATRICK, 3rd Baron *cr* 1897; **James Hans Hamilton**; *b* 29 Nov. 1928; *s* of 2nd Baron HolmPatrick and Lady Edina Ainsworth (*d* 1964), 4th *d* of 4th Marquess Conyngham; *S* father, 1942; *m* 1954, Anne Loys Roche, *o d* of Commander J. E. P. Brass, RN (retired); three *s*. *Heir*: *s* Hon. Hans James David Hamilton, *b* 15 March 1955. *Address*: Tara Beg, Dunsany, Co. Meath, Ireland.
See also Baron Swansea.

HOLROYD, John Hepworth; Director of Establishments, Ministry of Agriculture, Fisheries and Food, since 1981; *b* 10 April 1935; *s* of Harry Holroyd and Annie Dodgshun Holroyd; *m* 1963, Judith Mary Hudson; one *s* one *d*. *Educ*: Kingswood Sch., Bath; Worcester Coll., Oxford (Open Schol.; BA(Hist.)). Joined MAFF, 1959; Asst Private Sec. to Minister, 1961-63; Principal, Forestry Commn and MAFF, 1963-69; Regional Controller, MAFF, Yorks and Lancs Region, 1969-71; Head of R&D Div., MAFF, 1971-74; Head of Beef Div., MAFF, 1974-78; Under Secretary 1978; Resident Chm., Civil Service Selection Bd, 1978-80. Member: Yorks and Humberside Econ. Planning Bd, 1969-71; NW Econ. Planning Bd, 1969-71. Lay Reader; Methodist Local Preacher. *Recreations*: music, carpentry, bee-keeping, the topography of Great Britain. *Address*: 9 Beech Place, St Albans, Herts.

HOLROYD, Margaret, (Mrs M. de C. F. Holroyd); *see* Drabble, M.

HOLROYD, Michael de Courcy Fraser; author; *b* London, 27 Aug. 1935; *s* of Basil Holroyd and Ulla (*née* Hall); *m* 1982, Margaret Drabble, *qv*. *Educ*: Eton Coll.; Maidenhead Public Library. Saxton Memorial Fellowship, 1964; Bollingen Fellowship, 1966; Winston Churchill Fellowship, 1971; Vis. Fellow, Pennsylvania State Univ., 1979. Chm., Soc. of Authors, 1973-74; Chm., Nat. Book League, 1976-78. Member: BBC Archives Adv. Cttee, 1976-79; Phoenix Trust, 1976-; Vice-Chm., Arts Council Literature Panel, 1982-83. FRSL 1968 (Mem. Council, 1977-); FRHistS. *Publications*: Hugh Kingsmill: a critical biography, 1964 (rev. edn 1971); Lytton Strachey: The Unknown Years, 1967 (rev. edn 1971); Lytton Strachey: The Years of Achievement, 1968 (rev. edn 1971); A Dog's Life: a novel, 1969; (ed) The Best of Hugh Kingsmill, 1970; (ed) Lytton Strachey By Himself, 1971; Unreceived Opinions, 1973; Augustus John (2 vols), 1974, 1975; (with M. Easton) The Art of Augustus John, 1974; (ed) The Genius of Shaw, 1979; (ed with Paul Levy) The Shorter Strachey, 1980; (ed with Robert Skidelsky) William Gerhardie's God's Fifth Column, 1981; (ed) Essays by Divers Hands, vol. XLII, 1982; contribs to Times, TLS, etc; various radio and television scripts. *Recreations*: listening to stories, avoiding tame animals, being polite, music, trying to sleep. *Address*: c/o William Heinemann Ltd, 10 Upper Grosvenor Street, W1X 9PA. *T*: 01-493 4141.

HOLROYDE, Geoffrey Vernon; Director, Coventry (Lanchester) Polytechnic (formerly Lanchester Polytechnic), since 1975; *b* 18 Sept. 1928; *s* of Harold and Kathleen Holroyde; *m* 1960, Elizabeth Mary, *d* of Rev. E. O. Connell; two *s* two *d*. *Educ*: Wrekin Coll.; Birmingham Univ.; BSc. ARCO. Royal Navy, 1949-54 and 1956-61; Welbeck Coll., 1954-56; English Electric, becoming Principal of Staff Coll., Dunchurch, 1961-70; British Leyland, Head Office Training Staff, 1970-71; Head, Sidney Stringer Sch. and Community Coll., Coventry, 1971-75. Governor, 1978-, Trustee, 1979-, Brathay Hall Trust; Governor, Mid-Warwickshire Coll. of Further Educn, 1978-. *Publications*: Managing People, 1968; Delegation, 1969; Organs of St Mary, Warwick, 1969. *Recreations*: music (organ and choir), canals, sailing, outdoor pursuits. *Address*: 38 Coten End, Warwick. *T*: Warwick 492329.

HOLST, Imogen Clare, CBE 1975; musician; *b* 12 April 1907; *d* of Gustav Holst and Isobel (*née* Harrison). *Educ*: St Paul's Girls' Sch.; Royal Coll. of Music (ARCM). CEMA organiser, 1940-42; Dir of Music, Arts Centre, Dartington Hall, 1943-51; Musical Asst to Benjamin Britten, 1952-64; Conductor of Purcell Singers, 1953-67; Artistic Dir of Aldeburgh Festival, 1956-77. FRCM 1966; Hon. Dr, Essex, 1968; Hon. DLitt Exeter, 1969; Hon. RAM, 1970. *Publications*: Gustav Holst: a biography, 1938, 2nd edn 1969; The Music of Gustav Holst, 1951, 2nd edn 1968; Tune, 1962; An ABC of Music, 1963; Bach, 1964; Britten, 1966, 3rd edn 1980; Byrd, 1972; Conducting a Choir, 1973; Holst, 1974; A Thematic Catalogue of Gustav Holst's Music, 1974. *Recreation*: walking. *Address*: 9 Church Walk, Aldeburgh, Suffolk IP15 5DU. *Club*: University Women's.

HOLT, Arthur Frederick; Chairman, Holt Hosiery Co. Ltd, Bolton, 1971-73; *b* 8 Aug. 1914; *m* 1939, Kathleen Mary, MBE, *d* of A. C. Openshaw, Turton, nr Bolton; one *s* one *d. Educ:* Mill Hill Sch.; Manchester Univ. Army Territorial Officer (5th Loyals), 1939-45; taken prisoner, Singapore, 1942-45; despatches twice, 1946. MP (L) Bolton West, 1951-64; Liberal Chief Whip, 1962-63. Pres., Liberal Party, Sept. 1974-Sept. 1975. *Recreation:* golf. *Address:* Trees, High Wray, Ambleside, Cumbria. *T:* Ambleside 2258. *Club:* Reform.

HOLT, Christopher Robert Vesey, CVO 1976; VRD 1952; Member of London Stock Exchange, 1938-82; *b* 17 Oct. 1915; *s* of late Vice-Adm. R. V. Holt, CB, DSO, MVO, and Evelyn Constance Holt; *m* 1945, Margaret Jane Venetia, *d* of late Sir Michael Albert James Malcolm, 10th Bt; one *s* one *d. Educ:* Eton. Partner, James Capel & Co., Stockbrokers, 1938, Sen. Partner, 1968-70, Chm. (on firm becoming a company), 1970-75, Dir, 1975-76. Served RNVR, War of 1939-45, mostly in destroyers; retd with rank of Lieut-Comdr, 1957. *Recreations:* painting, wildlife, shooting. *Address:* Westbury Manor, West Meon, Petersfield, Hants GU32 1ND. *T:* West Meon 381. *Clubs:* Boodle's, Lansdowne.

HOLT, Constance, CBE 1975; Area Nursing Officer, Manchester Area Health Authority (Teaching), 1973-77; *b* 5 Jan. 1924; *d* of Ernest Biddulph and of Ada Biddulph (*née* Robley); *m* 1975, Robert Lord Holt, OBE, FRCS. *Educ:* Whalley Range High Sch. for Girls, Manchester; Manchester Royal Infirmary (SRN); Queen Charlotte's Hosp., London; St Mary's Hosp., Manchester (SCM); Royal Coll. of Nursing, London Univ. (Sister Tutor Dipl.); Univ. of Washington (Florence Nightingale Schol., Fulbright Award). Nursing Officer, Min. of Health, 1959-65; Chief Nursing Officer: United Oxford Hosps, 1965-69; United Manchester Hosps, 1969-73. Pres., Assoc. of Nurse Administrators (formerly Assoc. of Hosp. Matrons), 1972-. Hon. Lectr, Dept of Nursing, Univ. of Manchester, 1972. Hon. MA Manchester, 1980. *Publications:* articles in British and internat. nursing press. *Recreations:* reading, gardening, music. *Address:* Seabank, Marine Terrace, Port St Mary, Isle of Man.

HOLT, Jack; *see* Holt, John Lapworth.

HOLT, Sir James (Arthur), Kt 1960; Co-ordinator General of Public Works, Queensland, 1954-68, retired; director of companies, 1969-79; *b* 30 April 1899; *s* of James and Delia Holt; *m* 1932, Audrey May Benson; three *s* one *d. Educ:* Sydney High Sch.; Sydney Univ. (BE). Engineering draftsman, Sydney Harbour Bridge, 1922-27; Supervising Engineer, Sydney Harbour Bridge, 1927-32; Engineer-in-Charge, District Office, Department of Main Roads, NSW, 1933; Supervising Engineer, for design and construction contract for Story Bridge, Brisbane, 1934-40; Chief Engineer, Bridge Board, Queensland, 1940-49 (Engineer-in-charge, Allied Works Council, Cairns, 1943-44); Chief Engineer, Co-ordinator General's Dept, Queensland, 1949-53. Peter Nicol Russell Memorial Medal, Instn of Engineers, Australia, 1961, Hon. FIEAust, 1971. DEng (*hc*), University of Queensland, 1965. *Publications:* contributions to Journal of Institution of Engineers, Australia; papers on: The Story Bridge, Brisbane; The Fitzroy Bridge, Rockhampton. *Recreations:* bowls and surfing. *Address:* 11 Hawken Drive, St Lucia, Brisbane, Queensland 4067, Australia. *T:* 370 7707. *Clubs:* University of Queensland; St Lucia Bowls.

HOLT, Prof. James Clarke, FBA 1978; Professor of Medieval History, since 1978, and Master of Fitzwilliam College, since 1981, Cambridge University; *b* 26 April 1922; *s* of late Herbert and Eunice Holt; *m* 1950, Alice Catherine Elizabeth Suley; one *s. Educ:* Bradford Grammar Sch.; Queen's Coll., Oxford (Hastings Schol.). MA 1947; 1st cl. Modern Hist.; DPhil 1952. Served with RA, 1942-45 (Captain). Harmsworth Sen. Schol., Merton Coll., Oxford, 1947; Univ. of Nottingham: Asst Lectr, 1949; Lectr, 1951; Sen. Lectr, 1961; Prof. of Medieval History, 1962; Reading University: Prof. of History, 1966-78; Dean, Faculty of Letters and Soc. Scis, 1972-76; Professorial Fellow, Emanuel Coll., Cambridge, 1978-81. Mem., Adv. Council on Public Records, 1974-81. Pres., Royal Historical Soc., 1980-. Raleigh Lectr, British Acad., 1975. *Publications:* The Northerners: a study in the reign of King John, 1961; Praestita Roll 14-18 John, 1964; Magna Carta, 1965; The Making of Magna Carta, 1966; Magna Carta and the Idea of Liberty, 1972; The University of Reading: the first fifty years, 1977; Robin Hood, 1982; papers in English Historical Review, Past and Present, Economic History Review, Trans Royal Hist. Soc. *Recreations:* mountaineering, cricket, fly-fishing. *Address:* 5 Holben Close, Barton, Cambs. *T:* Comberton 3074. *Clubs:* United Oxford & Cambridge University, National Liberal, MCC; Wayfarers' (Liverpool).

HOLT, Sir James (Richard), KBE 1977 (CBE 1972); Managing Director, Sinobrit Ltd (formerly Sino-British Ltd), since 1957; *b* 24 Dec. 1912; *s* of Albert Edward Holt and Margaret Ann Holt; *m* 1974, Jennifer May Squires; one adopted *s* one adopted *d. Educ:* Bishop Vesey's Grammar Sch. Manager, Meklong Railway Co., Ltd, 1938-41; interned, Bangkok, 1942-45; Dir, Sino-British Ltd, 1946-56. Trustee and Mem. Exec. Cttee, Asian Inst. of Technology, 1977-. *Recreations:* racing, swimming. *Address:* c/o Sinobrit Ltd, 287 Surawong Road, PO Box 307, Bangkok, 10500 Thailand; 11 Soi Pranang, Rajvithi Road, Bangkok, Thailand. *T:* 2454071; 71 Belwell Lane, Four Oaks, Sutton Coldfield, West Midlands B74 4TS. *T:* 021-308 0932. *Clubs:* East India, Devonshire, Sports and Public Schools, Royal Automobile; Royal Bangkok Sports (Bangkok, Thailand).

HOLT, Sir John Anthony L.; *see* Langford-Holt.

HOLT, Rear-Adm. John Bayley, CB 1969; DL; Director: Premmit Associates Ltd; Premmit Engineering Services Ltd; Elint Engineering Ltd; *b* 1 June 1912; *s* of Arthur Ogden Holt and Gertrude (*née* Bayley); *m* 1940, Olga Esme Creake; three *d. Educ:* William Hulme Grammar Sch., Manchester; Manchester Univ. BScTech (hons) 1933. FIEE. Electrical Engineer with various cos and electric power undertakings, 1933-41. Joined RN; engaged on degaussing and minesweeping research and development, later on radar and electrical engineering, for Fleet Air Arm, 1941-48; served in HMS Cumberland on Gunnery Trials, Naval Air Stations, HQ and Staff appointments; comd HMS Ariel, 1961-63; subsequently Director of Naval Officer Appointments (Engineering Officers), and Dir-Gen. Aircraft (Naval), 1967-70, Ministry of Defence. Former Naval ADC to HM The Queen. Commander 1948; Captain 1958; Rear-Admiral 1967. Chm., Surrey Br., SS&AFA; Hon. Treas., Diocese of Guildford Endowment Fund. DL Surrey, 1981. *Recreations:* sailing, gardening, sacred music. *Address:* Rowley Cottage, Thursley, Godalming, Surrey. *T:* Elstead 702140. *Club:* Naval and Military.

HOLT, John Lapworth, (Jack Holt), OBE 1979; Founder and Director of Jack Holt Ltd and Holt group of companies, designers and suppliers of small boats and their fittings (Managing Director, 1946-76); *b* 18 April 1912; *s* of Herbert Holt and Annie (*née* Dawson); *m* 1936, Iris Eileen Thornton; one *s* one *d. Educ:* St Peter's Sch., London; Shoreditch Techn. Inst. (Schol.). Joiner, boat builder and designer, 1929-46; formed Jack Holt Ltd, 1946; designed: first British post-war sailing dinghy class, Merlin; first British factory-made do-it-yourself boat building kit to construct Internat. Cadet, for Yachting World magazine; International Enterprise, National Solo and Hornet, Heron, Rambler, Diamond, Lazy E, GP14, Vagabond, Mirror Dinghy, Mirror 16, and Pacer; Pandamaran, for World Wildlife Fund. Techn. Adviser to Royal Yachting Assoc. dinghy cttee, 1950-. Jt winner (with Beecher Moore) of 12ft Nat. Championship, 1946 and Merlin Championships, 1946, 1947 and 1949; Merlin Silver Tiller series winner, 1954-56; won Solo Dutch Nat. Championships, 1962. Yachtsman's Award for service to yachting, RYA, 1977. *Recreation:* small boat sailing. *Address:* Cliveden, The Embankment, Putney, SW15 1LB. *T:* 01-788 0330. *Clubs:* Ranelagh Sailing, Wraysbury Lake Sailing, Chichester Yacht, Aldenham Sailing, Carrum Yacht, Black Rock Sailing.

HOLT, John Michael, MD, FRCP; Consultant Physician, John Radcliffe Hospital, Oxford; Fellow of Linacre College, Oxford, since 1968; *b* 8 March 1935; *s* of Frank and Constance Holt; *m* 1959, Sheila Margaret Morton; one *s* three *d. Educ:* St Peter's Sch., York; Univ. of St Andrews. MA Oxon; MD St Andrews; MSc Queen's Univ. Ont. Registrar and Lectr, Nuffield Dept of Medicine, Radcliffe Infirmary, Oxford, 1964-66, Cons. Physician 1968; Med. Tutor, Univ. of Oxford, 1967-73; Dir of Clinical Studies, Univ. of Oxford, 1971-76. Examiner in Medicine: Univ. of Oxford; Hong Kong Univ. Member: Assoc. of Physicians; Soc. of Apothecaries; Cttee on Safety of Medicines, 1979-. *Publications:* papers on disorders of blood and various med. topics in BMJ, Lancet, etc. *Recreations:* sailing, riding. *Address:* Old Whitehill, Tackley, Oxon OX5 3AB. *T:* Tackley 241. *Club:* United Oxford & Cambridge University.

HOLT, Prof. John Riley, FRS 1964; Professor of Experimental Physics, University of Liverpool, since 1966; *b* 15 Feb. 1918; *er s* of Frederick Holt and Annie (*née* Riley); *m* 1949, Joan Silvester Thomas; two *s. Educ:* Runcorn Secondary Sch.; University of Liverpool. PhD 1941. British Atomic Energy Project, Liverpool and Cambridge, 1940-45. University of Liverpool: Lecturer, 1945-53, Senior Lecturer, 1953-56, Reader, 1956-66. *Publications:* papers in scientific journals on nuclear physics and particle physics. *Recreation:* gardening. *Address:* Rydalmere, Stanley Avenue, Higher Bebington, Wirral L63 5QE. *T:* 051-608 2041.

HOLT, Mary; Her Honour Judge Holt; a Circuit Judge, since 1977; *d* of Henry James Holt, solicitor, and of Sarah Holt (*née* Chapman); unmarried. *Educ:* Park Sch., Preston; Girton Coll., Cambridge (MA, LLB, 1st cl. Hons). Called to the Bar, Gray's Inn, 1949. Practised on Northern circuit. Former Vice-Chm., Preston North Conservative Assoc.; Member: Nat. Exec. Council, 1969-72; Woman's Nat. Advisory Cttee, 1969-70; representative, Central Council, 1969-71. MP (C) Preston N, 1970-Feb. 1974. Contested (C) Preston N, Feb. and Oct. 1974. *Publication:* 2nd edn, Benas and Essenhigh's Precedents of Pleadings, 1956. *Recreation:* walking. *Address:* The Sessions House, Preston, Lancs; Rose Bank, Garstang Road, Fulwood, Preston, Lancs PR2 4RD. *Club:* Royal Commonwealth Society.

HOLT, Prof. Peter Malcolm; FBA 1975; Professor of History of the Near and Middle East, University of London, 1975-82; *b* 28 Nov. 1918; *s* of Rev. Peter and Elizabeth Holt; *m* 1953, Nancy Bury (*née* Mawle); one *s* one *d. Educ:* Lord Williams's Grammar Sch., Thame; University Coll., Oxford (Schol.) (MA, DLitt). Sudan Civil Service: Min. of Education, 1941-53; Govt Archivist, 1954-55. School of Oriental and African Studies, London, 1955-; Prof. of Arab History, 1964-75. FRHistS 1973; FSA 1980. Gold Medal of Science, Letters and Arts, Repub. of Sudan, 1980. *Publications:* The Mahdist state in the Sudan, 1958, 2nd edn 1970; A Modern History of the Sudan, 1961, 2nd edn 1963; (co-ed with Bernard Lewis) Historians of the Middle East, 1962; Egypt and the Fertile Crescent, 1966; (ed) Political and Social Change in Modern Egypt, 1968; (co-ed with Ann K. S. Lambton and Bernard Lewis)

The Cambridge History of Islam, 1970; Studies in the History of the Near East, 1973; (ed) The Eastern Mediterranean Lands in the period of the Crusades, 1977; (with M. W. Daly) The History of the Sudan from the Coming of Islam to the Present Day, 1980; articles in: Encyclopaedia of Islam, Bulletin of SOAS, Sudan Notes and Records, Der Islam, English Historical Rev., etc. *Address:* School of Oriental and African Studies, Malet Street, WC1E 7HP. *T:* 01-637 2388. *Club:* United Oxford & Cambridge University.

HOLT, Richard Anthony Appleby; Managing Director, Hutchinson Ltd, 1978-80 (Chairman, 1959-78); Chairman: Hutchinson Publishing Group, 1965-80; Hutchinson Printing Trust, 1957-80; Director, Constable & Co. Ltd; *b* 11 March 1920; *s* of Frederick Appleby Holt and Rae Vera Franz (*née* Hutchinson); *m* 1945, Daphne Vivien Pegram; three *s* two *d. Educ:* Harrow Sch.; King's Coll., Cambridge. Served War of 1939-45, commissioned 60th Rifles, 1941; demobilised, 1946 (Major). Admitted Solicitor, 1949. Governor, Harrow Sch. *Recreation:* lawn tennis. *Address:* 21 Pelham Crescent, SW7. *T:* 01-589 8469. *Clubs:* All England Lawn Tennis, MCC.

HOLT, Victoria; *see* Hibbert, Eleanor.

HOLT SMITH, Charles; *see* Smith, Charles H.

HOLTBY, Very Rev. Robert Tinsley; Dean of Chichester, since 1977; *b* 25 Feb. 1921; *o s* of William and Elsie Holtby, Thornton-le-Dale, Yorkshire; *m* 1947, Mary, *er d* of late Rt Rev. Eric Graham; one *s* two *d. Educ:* York Minster Choir Sch.; Scarborough Coll. and High School. St Edmund Hall, Oxford, 1939; MA (2nd Class Mod. Hist.), 1946; BD 1957. Choral Scholar, King's Coll., Cambridge, 1944; MA (2nd Class Theol.), 1952. Cuddesdon Theological Coll. and Westcott House, Cambridge, 1943-46. Deacon, 1946; Priest, 1947. Curate of Pocklington, Yorks, 1946-48. Chaplain to the Forces, 1948-52: 14/20th King's Hussars, Catterick; Singapore; Priest-in-charge, Johore Bahru. Acting Chaplain, King's Coll., Cambridge, 1952; Chaplain and Asst Master, Malvern Coll., 1952-54; Chaplain and Assistant Master, St Edward's Sch., Oxford, 1954-58; Canon Residentiary of Carlisle and Diocesan Dir of Educn, 1959-67, Canon Emeritus, 1967-. Gen. Sec., Nat. Soc. for Promoting Religious Education, 1967-77; Sec., Schs Cttee, 1967-74, Gen. Sec., 1974-77, Church of England Bd of Educn. Chm., Cumberland Council of Social Service, 1962-67. Chaplain to High Sheriff of Cumberland, 1964, 1966. *Publications:* Daniel Waterland, A Study in 18th Century Orthodoxy, 1966; Carlisle Cathedral Library and Records, 1966; Eric Graham, 1888-1964, 1967; Carlisle Cathedral, 1969. *Recreations:* music, walking, history. *Address:* The Deanery, Chichester, West Sussex PO19 1PX. *T:* Chichester 783286. *Club:* United Oxford & Cambridge University.

HOLTHAM, Mrs Carmen Gloria, JP; Advice/Information Officer, Earls Court Centre, Royal Borough of Kensington and Chelsea, since 1980; *b* Kingston, Jamaica, 13 July 1922; *née* Bradshaw. *Educ:* Adventist Girls Sch.; Kingston Technical Coll., Kingston, Jamaica; London Univ. (Extra-Mural Course, Dip. Sociol.); NW London Polytech. (Cert. Office Management); SW London Polytech. (Cert. in Counselling); NE London Polytech. (Post Grad. Dip. Inf. and Advice Studies). Govt of Jamaica, 1942-57; United Jewish Appeal, NY, USA, 1958; Resident, England, 1959-; HM Factory Inspectorate, 1959; ILEA, 1959-64; Inst. of Med. Social Workers, 1964-66; Social Services Dept, London Borough of Camden, 1966; Willesden Citizens' Advice Bureau, London Bor. of Brent, 1967-70; Organiser, Thurrock Citizens' Advice Bureau, Grays, Essex, 1971-79. Member: ILEA Sch. Care Cttee, 1963-67; Brent Community Relns Council, 1968-70; Brent Youth Service, 1969-70; British Caribbean Assoc., 1969-; Magistrates Assoc., 1969-; Grays Probation and After-Care Service, 1971; Thurrock Social Services for Elderly, 1971-; Supplementary Benefits Commn, 1976-78. Mem., Bd of Governors, Treetops Sch., Grays, 1975-. JP Mddx (Highgate Magistrates' Court), 1969-71, Essex (Grays Magistrates' Court), 1972-. *Recreations:* reading, the theatre, ceramics. *Address:* 52 Davall House, Grays, Essex. *T:* Grays Thurrock 70838. *Club:* Friends International.

HOLTON, Michael; Assistant Secretary, Ministry of Defence, since 1976; *b* 30 Sept. 1927; 3rd *s* of late George Arnold Holton and Ethel (*née* Fountain), Hampstead Garden Suburb, London; *m* 1951, Daphne Elizabeth Bache; one *s* two *d. Educ:* Finchley County Grammar Sch.; London Sch. of Economics. National Service, RAF, 1946-48; Min. of Food, 1948-54; Air Ministry, 1955-61; MoD, 1961-68; Sec., Countryside Commn for Scotland, 1968-70; Sec., Carnegie UK Trust, 1971-75. Sec., European Conservation Year Cttee for Scotland, 1970; Member: Consultative Cttee, Family Fund, 1973-75; Bd, Cairngorm Sports Develt Co., 1973-; Council, Royal Soc. for Nature Conservation, 1976-. Hon. Sec., RAF Mountaineering Assoc., 1952-54; Hon. Sec., British Mountaineering Council, 1954-59. *Publication:* Training Handbook for RAF Mountain Rescue Teams, 1953. *Address:* 6 Chatham Close, NW11 6HE. *T:* 01-455 5421. *Clubs:* Athenæum, Alpine; Himalayan (Bombay).

HOLTTUM, Richard Eric, MA; ScD; FLS; Honorary Research Associate: Royal Botanic Gardens, Kew, since 1977; Rijksherbarium, Leiden, Netherlands, since 1955; *b* Linton, Cambs, 20 July 1895; *s* of Richard Holttum; *m* 1927, Ursula, *d* of J. W. Massey, Saffron Walden; two *d. Educ:* Friends' Sch., Saffron Walden; Bootham Sch., York; St John's Coll., Cambridge (Foundation Scholar). Natural Sciences Tripos, Part 2 (Botany) Class 1, and Frank Smart Prize, 1920; Junior Demonstrator in Botany, Cambridge Univ.,

1920-22; Assistant Director, Botanic Gardens, Singapore, 1922-25, Director, 1925-49. Professor of Botany, University of Malaya, 1949-54; President: Singapore Gardening Society, 1937-39, 1947-53; Singapore Rotary Club, 1939-41; British Pteridological Society, 1960-63; Section K (Botany), BAAS, 1961; Internat. Assoc. of Pteridologists, 1981. Editor, Series II (Pteridophyta), Flora Malesiana, 1959-. Hon. DSc, University of Malaya, 1949. Linnean gold medal, 1964; VMH 1972; has foreign gold medals, etc., for orchids. *Publications:* Orchids of Malaya, 1953; Gardening in the Lowlands of Malaya, 1953; Plant Life in Malaya, 1954; Ferns of Malaya, 1955; botanical and horticultural papers, especially on ferns and orchids. *Address:* 50 Gloucester Court, Kew Gardens, Richmond, Surrey. *T:* 01-940 6157.

HOLYOAKE, Rt. Hon. Sir Keith Jacka, KG 1980; GCMG 1970; CH 1963; PC 1954; Governor-General of New Zealand, 1977-80; *b* 11 Feb. 1904; *s* of Henry Victor and Esther Holyoake; *m* 1935, Norma Janet Ingram (*see* Dame Norma Holyoake); two *s* three *d. Educ:* Tauranga; Hastings; Motueka. President Golden Bay Rugby Union, 1930-33; Nelson Provincial Pres. Farmers' Union, 1930-41; Member Dominion Executive, Farmers' Union, 1940-50. Dominion Vice-Pres., 1940-50. President, NZ Hop Marketing Cttee, 1938-41; Member Exec.: NZ Tobacco Growers' Federation; NZ Fruit Exporters' Association. MP (Nat) (for Motueka, 1932-38, for Pahiatu, 1943-77); Dep. Leader Opposition, NZ, 1947; Cabinet, 1949; Dep. Prime Minister and Minister of Agriculture, Marketing and Scientific Research, 1949-57; Prime Minister and Minister for Maori Affairs, Sept.-Dec. 1957; Leader of Opposition, 1957-60; Prime Minister and Minister of Foreign Affairs (formerly of External Affairs), 1960-72; Minister of State, 1975-77. Farmer; Represented NZ farmers at World Conf. in London, 1946; Chairman FAO Conference, Rome, 1955; Member: SEATO meetings, 1962-; Conf. on Cambodia, Djakarta, 1970; Commonwealth Heads of Govt Conf., Singapore, 1971; Five-Power Conf. on Defence and Annual Ministerial Meeting of SEATO, London, 1971; S Pacific Forum, Canberra, 1972. Freeman, City of London, 1969. Hon. LLD: Victoria University of Wellington; Seoul Univ., Korea. KStJ 1977. *Recreations:* tennis, gardening. *Address:* 52 Aurora Terrace, Wellington 1, New Zealand. *Clubs:* Ruahine (Dannevirke); Pahiatua (Pahiatua); Wellington, National (Wellington).

HOLYOAKE, Dame Norma Janet, DCMG 1980; *b* 7 March 1909; second *d* of Gordon and Flora Ingram; *m* 1935, Rt Hon. Sir Keith Jacka Holyoake, *qv*; two *s* three *d. Educ:* Motueka Primary and High Schools. Hon. LHD Ewha Women's Univ., Korea, 1968. *Recreations:* golf, gardening. *Address:* 52 Aurora Terrace, Wellington 1, New Zealand. *Club:* Wellington Women's.

HOMAN, Maj.-Gen. John Vincent, CB 1980; CEng, FIMechE; Senior Army Member, Royal College of Defence Studies, 1980-82; *b* 30 June 1927; *s* of Charles Frederic William Burton Homan and Dorothy Maud Homan; *m* 1953, Ann Bartlett; one *s* two *d. Educ:* Haileybury; RMA Sandhurst; RMCS Shrivenham. BSc (Eng). Commnd, REME, 1948; Lt-Col 1967; Comdr REME 2nd Div., 1968-70; Col 1970; MoD 1970-72; CO 27 Comd Workshop REME, 1972-74; Brig. 1974; Dep. Dir, Electrical and Mechanical Engineering, 1st British Corps, 1974-76; Dir of Equipment Management, MoD, 1976-77; Dir Gen., Electrical and Mechanical Engrg, MoD, 1978-79; Maj.-Gen. 1978. Col Comdt, REME, 1982-. *Recreations:* hill walking, woodwork. *Address:* Roedean, 25 The Avenue, Andover, Hants. *T:* Andover 51196. *Club:* Army and Navy.

HOMAN, Philip John Lindsay; Director, Metrication Board, 1974-76; *b* 20 July 1916; *e s* of late Arthur Buckhurst Homan and Gertrude Homan; *m* 1940, Elisabeth Clemency Hobson; two *s* one *d. Educ:* Maidstone Grammar Sch.; LSE. Estate Duty Office, Inland Revenue, 1935-49. Served in RN, 1941-46. Board of Trade, 1949-69: Asst Sec., Controller, Midland Region, 1960; Principal Controller, Scotland, 1966; Min. of Technology, 1969-70; Under-Sec. and Dir, Office for Scotland, DTI, 1970-71; Under-Sec., Vehicles and Mechanical Engrg Products Div., later Mechanical Engrg Div., DTI, 1971-74. *Address:* Redlands, Kiln Lane, Stokenham, Kingsbridge, S Devon. *See also* T. B. Homan.

HOMAN, Rear-Adm. Thomas Buckhurst, CB 1978; Sub-Treasurer of the Inner Temple, since 1978; *b* 9 April 1921; *s* of late Arthur Buckhurst Homan and Gertrude Homan, West Malling, Kent; *m* 1945, Christine Oliver; one *d. Educ:* Maidstone Grammar Sch. RN Cadet, 1939; served War of 1939-45 at sea; Comdr 1958; Captain 1965; Defence Intell. Staff, 1965; Sec. to Comdr Far East Fleet, 1967; idc 1970; Dir Naval Officer Appts (S), 1971; Captain HMS Pembroke, 1973; Rear-Adm. 1974; Dir Gen., Naval Personal Services, 1974-78. *Recreations:* reading, theatre, golf, cooking. *Address:* 4 Paper Buildings, Temple, EC4Y 7EX. *T:* 01-353 6184. *Club:* Army and Navy. *See also* P. J. L. Homan.

HOMANS, Prof. George Caspar; Professor of Sociology, Harvard University, 1953-81, now Emeritus; *b* 11 Aug. 1910; *s* of Robert Homans and Abigail (*née* Adams); *m* 1941, Nancy Parshall Cooper; one *s* two *d. Educ:* St Paul's Sch., Concord, New Hampshire; Harvard Univ. (AB). Harvard Univ.: Junior Fellow, 1934-39; Instructor in Sociology, 1939-41; Associate Professor of Sociology, 1946-53; Simon Vis. Prof., Univ. of Manchester, 1953; Prof. of Social Theory, Univ. of Cambridge, 1955-56; Vis. Prof., Univ. of Kent, 1967. Overseas Fellow, Churchill Coll., Cambridge, 1972. Pres., American Sociological Assoc., 1963-64; Mem., Nat. Acad. of Sciences, USA, 1972. Officer, US Naval Reserve (Lieut-Commander), 1941-45. *Publications:*

Massachusetts on the Sea, 1930; An Introduction to Pareto, 1934; Fatigue of Workers, 1941; English Villagers of the 13th Century, 1941; The Human Group, 1950; Marriage, Authority and Final Causes, 1955; Social Behaviour, 1961, rev. edn 1974; Sentiments and Activities, 1962; The Nature of Social Science, 1967. *Recreations:* forestry, sailing. *Address:* 11 Francis Avenue, Cambridge, Mass 02138, USA. *T:* 617-547-4737. *Club:* Tavern (Boston, USA).

HOME; see Douglas-Home.

HOME, 14th Earl of [Disclaimed his peerages for life, 23 Oct. 1963]; see under Home of the Hirsel, Baron and Douglas-Home, Hon. D.A.C.

HOME OF THE HIRSEL, Baron *cr* 1974 (Life Peer), of Coldstream; **Alexander Frederick Douglas-Home,** KT 1962; PC 1951; DL; Chancellor, Order of the Thistle, since 1973; First Chancellor of Heriot-Watt University, 1966–77; *b* 2 July 1903; *e s* of 13th Earl of Home (*d* 1951), KT, and Lilian (*d* 1966), *d* of 4th Earl of Durham; *S* father, 1951, but disclaimed his peerages for life, 23 Oct. 1963; *m* 1936, Elizabeth Hester, 2nd *d* of late Very Rev. C. A. Alington, DD; one *s* three *d*. *Educ:* Eton; Christ Church, Oxford. MP (U) South Lanark, 1931–45; MP (C) Lanark Div. of Lanarkshire, 1950–51; Parliamentary Private Sec. to the Prime Minister, 1937–40; Joint Parliamentary Under-Sec., Foreign Office, May–July 1945; Minister of State, Scottish Office, 1951–April 1955; Sec. of State for Commonwealth Relations, 1955–60; Dep. Leader of the House of Lords, 1956–57; Leader of the House of Lords, and Lord Pres. of the Council, 1957–60; Sec. of State for Foreign Affairs, 1960–63; MP (U) Kinross and W Perthshire, Nov. 1963–Sept. 1974; Prime Minister and First Lord of the Treasury, Oct. 1963–64; Leader of the Opposition, Oct. 1964–July 1965; Sec. of State for Foreign and Commonwealth Affairs, 1970–74. Hon. Pres., NATO Council, 1973. Captain, Royal Co. of Archers, Queen's Body Guard for Scotland, 1973. Mem., National Farmers' Union, 1964. DL Lanarkshire, 1960. Hon. DCL Oxon., 1960; Hon. Student of Christ Church, Oxford, 1962; Hon. LLD: Harvard, 1961; Edinburgh, 1962; Aberdeen, 1966; Liverpool, 1967; St Andrews, 1968; Hon. DSc Heriot-Watt, 1966. Hon. Master of the Bench, Inner Temple, 1963; Grand Master, Primrose League, 1966; Pres. of MCC, 1966–67. Freedom of Selkirk, 1963; Freedom of Edinburgh, 1969; Freedom of Coldstream, 1972. Hon. Freeman: Skinners' Co., 1968; Grocers' Co., 1977. *Publications:* The Way the Wind Blows (autobiog.), 1976; Border Reflections, 1979. *Address:* House of Lords, SW1; The Hirsel, Coldstream, Berwickshire. *T:* Coldstream 2345; Castlemains, Douglas, Lanarkshire. *T:* Douglas, Lanark 241.
   See also Hon. D. A. C. Douglas-Home, Hon. William Douglas-Home, Duke of Sutherland, J. C. V. Wilkes.

HOME, Captain Archibald John Fitzwilliam M.; see Milne Home.

HOME, Sir David George, 13th Bt, *cr* 1671; late Temp. Major Argyll and Sutherland Highlanders; *b* 21 Jan. 1904; *o s* of Sir John Home, 12th Bt and Hon. Gwendolina H. R. Mostyn (*d* 1960), *sister* of 7th Baron Vaux of Harrowden; *S* father, 1938; *m* 1933, Sheila, *d* of late Mervyn Campbell Stephen; two *s* two *d*. *Educ:* Harrow; Jesus Coll., Cambridge (BA 1925). Member Royal Company of Archers (HM Body Guard for Scotland). FSA (Scotland). Heir: *s* John Home [*b* 1 June 1936; *m* 1966, Nancy Helen, *d* of H. G. Elliott, Perth, Western Australia, and *widow* of Commander Ian Macgregor, RAN; one *s* one *d*.] *Address:* Winterfield, North Berwick, East Lothian. *Clubs:* Brooks's; New (Edinburgh); Royal and Ancient (St Andrews).
   See also Sir D. P. M. Malcolm, Bt.

HOME, Prof. George, BL; FIB (Scot); Professor of International Banking, Heriot-Watt University, Edinburgh, since 1978; *b* 13 April 1920; *s* of George Home and Leah Home; *m* 1946, Muriel Margaret Birleson; two *s* one *d*. *Educ:* Fort Augustus Village Sch.; Trinity Academy, Edinburgh; George Heriot's Sch., Edinburgh; Edinburgh Univ. (BL 1952). FIB (Scot); FBIM. Joined Royal Bank of Scotland, 1936; served RAF, 1940–46; Dep. Man. Dir, Royal Bank of Scotland Ltd, 1973–80; Dep. Gp Man. Dir, Royal Bank of Scotland Gp Ltd, 1976–80; Director: Williams & Glyn's Bank Ltd, 1975–80; The Wagon Finance Corp. plc, 1980–. Vice-Pres., Inst. of Bankers in Scotland, 1977–80. *Recreations:* fishing, gardening, reading, travel. *Address:* Bickley, 12 Barnton Park View, Edinburgh EH4 6HJ. *T:* 031-336 7648. *Club:* Caledonian.

HOME, Hon. William Douglas-; dramatic author; *b* Edinburgh, 3 June 1912; *s* of 13th Earl of Home, KT; *m* 1951, Rachel Brand (*see* Baroness Dacre); one *s* three *d*. *Educ:* Eton; New Coll., Oxford (BA). Studied at Royal Academy of Dramatic Art, and has appeared on the West End stage. Formerly Captain RAC. Contested (Progressive Ind) Cathcart Division of Glasgow, April 1942, Windsor Division of Berks, June 1942, and Clay Cross Division of Derbyshire (Atlantic Charter), April 1944, (Liberal) South Edinburgh, 1957. Author of the following plays: Great Possessions, 1937; Passing By, 1940; Now Barabbas, 1947; The Chiltern Hundreds, 1947; Ambassador Extraordinary, 1948; Master of Arts, 1949; The Thistle and the Rose, 1949; Caro William, 1952; The Bad Samaritan, 1953; The Manor of Northstead, 1954; The Reluctant Debutante, 1955; The Iron Duchess, 1957; Aunt Edwina, 1959; Up a Gum Tree, 1960; The Bad Soldier Smith, 1961; The Cigarette Girl, 1962; The Drawing Room Tragedy, 1963; The Reluctant Peer, 1964; Two Accounts Rendered, 1964; Betzi, 1965; A Friend in Need, 1965; A Friend Indeed, 1966; The Secretary Bird, 1968; The Queen's Highland Servant, 1968; The Grouse Moor Image,

1968; The Jockey Club Stakes, 1970; Lloyd George Knew My Father, 1972; At the End of the Day, 1973; The Bank Manager, 1974; The Dame of Sark, 1974; In The Red, The Kingfisher, Rolls Hyphen Royce, The Perch, 1977; The Editor Regrets, 1978. *Publication:* Mr Home Pronounced Hume: an autobiography, 1979. *Address:* Drayton House, East Meon, Hants. *T:* East Meon 250. *Club:* Travellers'.
   See also Baron Home of the Hirsel.

HOME ROBERTSON, John David; MP (Lab) Berwick and East Lothian, since Oct. 1978; *b* 5 Dec. 1948; *s* of late Lt-Col J. W. Home Robertson and of Mrs H. M. Home Robertson; *m* 1977, Catherine Jean Brewster; two *s*. *Educ:* Ampleforth Coll.; West of Scotland Coll. of Agriculture. Farmer. *Address:* Paxton South Mains, Berwick-on-Tweed; House of Commons, SW1. *T:* 01-219 4135. *Clubs:* East Lothian Labour, Prestonpans Labour.

HOMEWOOD, William Dennis; MP (Lab) Kettering, since 1979; *b* Bermondsey, March 1920; *m*. *Educ:* Ruskin Coll., Oxford. Full-time trade union officer, ISTC (formerly branch sec. and dist cttee sec.). Rural Dist Councillor, Market Harborough, 1958–65. Mem., Labour Party, 1946–. *Address:* House of Commons, SW1.

HONE, David; landscape and portrait painter; President, Royal Hibernian Academy of Arts, since 1978; *b* 14 Dec. 1928; *s* of Joseph Hone and Vera Hone (*née* Brewster); *m* 1962, Rosemary D'Arcy; two *s* one *d*. *Educ:* Baymount School; St Columba's College; University College, Dublin. Studied art at National College of Art, Dublin, and later in Italy. Hon. RA, HRSA (ex-officio). *Recreations:* fishing, photography. *Address:* 4 Ailesbury Gardens, Dublin 4, Ireland. *T:* Dublin 692809.

HONE, Maj.-Gen. Sir (Herbert) Ralph, KCMG 1951; KBE 1946 (CBE Mil. 1943); MC; TD; GCStJ 1973; QC Gibraltar 1934, QC Uganda 1938; barrister-at-law; *b* 3 May 1896; *s* of late Herbert Hone and Miriam Grace (*née* Dracott); *m* 1st, 1918, Elizabeth Daisy, *d* of James Matthews (marr. diss. 1944); one *s* one *d* ; 2nd, 1945, Sybil Mary, *widow* of Wing Commander G. Simond; one *s*. *Educ:* Varndean Grammar Sch., Brighton; London Univ. LLB (Hons). Barrister-at-law, Middle Temple. Inns of Court OTC. Gazetted London Irish Rifles, 1915; Lieut, 1916; Captain, 1918; served with BEF, France, 1916 and 1917–18 (wounded, MC), Staff Captain, Ministry of Munitions, 1918–20; Major R of O (TA); Asst Treas., Uganda, 1920; called to Bar; practised and went South Eastern Circuit, 1924–25; Registrar, High Court, Zanzibar, 1925; Resident Magistrate, Zanzibar, 1928; Crown Counsel, Tanganyika Territory, 1930; acted Asst Legal Adviser to the Colonial and Dominions Offices, Jan.–Aug. 1933; Attorney-General, Gibraltar, 1933–36; Commissioner for the Revision of the laws of Gibraltar, 1934; King's Jubilee medal, 1935; Chm., Gibraltar Govt Commn on Slum Clearance and Rent Restriction, 1936; Coronation Medal, 1937; Acting Chief Justice, Gibraltar, on several occasions; Attorney-General, Uganda, 1937–43; Chairman, Uganda Government Cttee on Museum policy, 1938; Commandant, Uganda Defence Force, 1940; Chief Legal Adviser, Political Branch, GHQ, Middle East, 1941; Chief Political Officer, GHQ, Middle East, 1942–43; General Staff, War Office, 1943–45; Chief Civil Affairs Officer, Malaya, 1945–46; Maj.-Gen., 1942–46 (despatches twice, CBE (mil.)); Secretary-General to Governor-General of Malaya, 1946–48; Dep. Commissioner-General in SE Asia, 1948–49; Coronation Medal, 1953. Governor and C-in-C, North Borneo, 1949–54; Head of Legal Division, CRO, 1954–61. Resumed practice at the Bar, 1961. Retd TA with Hon. rank Maj.-Gen., 1956. GCStJ 1973; Mem. Chapter Gen. Order of St John, 1954–. Vice-Pres., Royal Commonwealth Society; Constitutional Adviser, Kenya Govt, Dec. 1961–Jan. 1962; Constitutional Adviser to Mr Butler's Advisers on Central Africa, July–Oct. 1962; Constitutional Adviser to South Arabian Government, Oct. 1965–Jan. 1966, and to Bermuda Government, July–Nov. 1966. Appeal Comr under Civil Aviation Licensing Act, 1961–71; Standing Counsel, Grand Bahama Port Authority, 1962–75. *Publications:* Index to Gibraltar Laws, 1933; revised edn of Laws of Gibraltar, 1935; revised edn of Laws of the Bahamas, 1965; Handbook on Native Courts, etc. *Recreations:* tennis, badminton and philately. *Address:* 1 Paper Buildings, Temple, EC4. *T:* 01-583 7355; 56 Kenilworth Court, Lower Richmond Road, SW15. *T:* 01-788 3367. *Clubs:* Athenæum, Royal Commonwealth Society.

HONE, Robert Monro, MA; Headmaster, Exeter School, 1966–79; *b* 2 March 1923; *s* of late Rt Rev. Campbell R. Hone; *m* 1958, Helen Isobel, *d* of late Col H. M. Cadell of Grange, OBE; three *d*. *Educ:* Winchester Coll. (Scholar); New Coll., Oxford (Scholar). Rifle Brigade, 1942–45. Asst Master, Clifton Coll., 1948–65 (Housemaster, 1958–65). *Address:* Little Hawkridge, Coldridge, Crediton, Devon. *T:* Lapford 289.

HONEYCOMBE, Prof. Robert William Kerr, FRS 1981; Goldsmiths' Professor of Metallurgy, University of Cambridge, since 1966; *b* 2 May 1921; *s* of William and Rachel Honeycombe (*née* Kerr); *m* 1947, June Collins; two *d*. *Educ:* Geelong Coll.; Univ. of Melbourne. Research Student, Department of Metallurgy, University of Melbourne, 1941–42; Research Officer, Commonwealth Scientific and Industrial Research Organization, Australia, 1942–47; ICI Research Fellow, Cavendish Laboratory, Cambridge, 1948–49; Royal Society Armourers and Brasiers' Research Fellow, Cavendish Laboratory, Cambridge, 1949–51; Senior Lecturer in Physical Metallurgy, University of Sheffield, 1951–55; Professor, 1955–66. Fellow of Trinity Hall, Cambridge, 1966–73, Hon. Fellow, 1975; Pres. of Clare Hall, Cambridge, 1973–80. Pres., Instn of Metallurgists, 1977; Pres., Metals Soc., 1980–81;

Vice-Pres., Royal Institution, 1977-78. Visiting Professor: University of Melbourne, 1962; Stanford Univ., 1965; Monash Univ., 1974; Kyoto Univ., 1979. Hatfield Meml Lectr, 1979. Hon. Member: Iron and Steel Inst. of Japan, 1979; Soc. Française de Métallurgie, 1981. Mem. Ct of Assts, Goldsmiths' Co., 1977-. FEng 1980. Hon. DAppSc Melbourne, 1974. Rosenhain Medal of Inst. of Metals, 1959; Sir George Beilby Gold Medal, 1963; Ste-Claire-Deville Medal, 1971; Inst. of Metals Lectr and Mehl Medallist, AIME, 1976. *Publications:* The Plastic Deformation of Metals, 1968; Steels— Microstructure and Properties, 1981; Papers in Proc. Royal Soc., Metal Science, etc. *Recreations:* gardening, photography, walking. *Address:* Barrabool, 46 Main Street, Hardwick, Cambridge CB3 7QS. *T:* Madingley 210501.

HONEYMAN, Prof. Alexander Mackie, MA, BLitt, PhD; Professor of Oriental Languages in University of St Andrews, 1936-67; Fellow of Royal Asiatic Society; *b* 25 Nov. 1907; *s* of late A. M. Honeyman, Cupar, Fife; *m* 1935, Cecilia Mary (*d* 1980), 2nd *d* of late J. Leslie Milne, Edinburgh; one *s* one *d* (and one *d* decd). *Educ:* Universities of St Andrews, Edinburgh, London (School of Oriental Studies), Zürich and Chicago (Oriental Institute). 1st Class Hons Classics, 1929; BLitt in Ancient Languages, 1930; Guthrie Scholar, 1930, University of St Andrews; Commonwealth Fellow, New York and Chicago, 1932-34; PhD Chicago, 1934; Maclean Scholar of University of Glasgow, 1934-35, in Palestine, etc; Interim Lectr in Hebrew and Oriental Languages, Univ. of St Andrews, 1935-36. External Examiner to Univ. of Glasgow, 1941-44, 1946, 1951-54; Univ. of Edinburgh, 1946-48; Queen's Univ., Belfast, 1947-49; Univ. of Leeds, 1954-56, 1959; Univ. of London, 1959; Univ. of Brussels, 1972. Schweich Lecturer of British Academy, 1950; Leverhulme Fellowship, 1954. Travelled and excavated in S Arabia, 1950, 1954 and 1958. Trustee of National Library of Scotland, 1951-56; Mem. Council, Royal Asiatic Soc., 1952-56; Vice-Pres., British Branch, Hebrew Language Academy, 1954-. *Publications:* The Mission of Burzoe in the Arabic Kalilah wa-Dimnah, 1936; articles and reviews in archæological, philological and historical journals. *Address:* Oldtown, Ardgay, Ross-shire. *T:* Ardgay 423.

HONGLADAROM, Sunthorn; Knight Grand Cordon, Order of Crown of Thailand, and Order of White Elephant; Secretary-General, South-East Asia Treaty Organisation, 1972-77; Hon. Assistant Secretary-General, Thai Red Cross Society, since 1977; *b* 23 Aug. 1912; *m* 1937; five *s* one *d*. *Educ:* Trinity Coll., Cambridge. Asst Sec.-Gen. to Cabinet, 1946; Sec.-Gen., Nat. Economic Council, 1950; Ambassador to Fedn of Malaya (now Malaysia), 1957; Minister of Economic Affairs, 1959; Minister of Finance, 1960; Chairman of Boards of Governors; IBRD, IMF, IFC, and Internat. Development Assoc., 1961; Minister of Economic Affairs, 1966; Ambassador to UK, 1968-69, to USA, 1969-72. Hon. LLD, St John's Univ., NY, 1970. *Recreations:* golf, motoring. *Address:* Thai Red Cross Society, Chulalongkorn Memorial Hospital, Bangkok, Thailand. *Club:* Roehampton.

HONIG, Frederick; His Honour Judge Honig; a Circuit Judge (formerly a County Court Judge), since 1968; *b* 22 March 1912; 2nd *s* of late Leopold Honig; *m* 1940, Joan, *o d* of late Arthur Burkart. *Educ:* Berlin and Heidelberg Univs. LLD (Hons) Heidelberg, 1934. Barrister, Middle Temple, 1937. War service, 1940-47: Capt., JAG's Dept; Judge Advocate in civilian capacity, 1947-48; subseq. practised at Bar. *Publications:* (jtly) Cartel Law of the European Economic Community, 1963; contribs to Internat. Law Reports (ed. Lauterpacht) and legal jls, incl. Amer. Jl of Internat. Law, Internat. and Comparative Law Quarterly, Law Jl, Propriété Industrielle, etc. *Recreations:* foreign languages, country walking. *Address:* Lamb Building, Temple, EC4. *T:* 01-353 1612; 23 Shilling Street, Lavenham, Suffolk. *T:* Lavenham 247565.

HONORÉ, Prof. Antony Maurice, DCL Oxon; FBA 1972; Regius Professor of Civil Law, University of Oxford, since 1971; Fellow of All Souls College, Oxford, since 1971; *b* 30 March 1921; *s* of Frédéric Maurice Honoré and Marjorie Erskine (*née* Gilbert); *m* 1st, Martine Marie-Odette Genouville (marr. diss. 1978); one *s* one *d*; 2nd, Deborah Mary Cowen (*née* Duncan). *Educ:* Diocesan Coll., Rondebosch; Univ. of Cape Town; New Coll., Oxford. Rhodes Scholar, 1940. Union Defence Forces, 1940-45; Lieut, Rand Light Infantry, 1942. BCL 1948. Advocate, South Africa, 1951; called to Bar, Lincoln's Inn, 1952, Hon. Bencher, 1971. Lectr, Nottingham Univ., 1948; Rhodes Reader in Roman-Dutch Law, 1957-71, Fellow of Queen's Coll., Oxford, 1949-64, of New Coll., 1964-71. Visiting Professor: McGill, 1961; Berkeley, 1968. *Publications:* (with H. L. A. Hart) Causation in the Law, 1959; Gaius, 1962; The South African Law of Trusts, 2nd edn 1976; Tribonian, 1978; Sex Law, 1978; (with J. Menner) Concordance to the Digest Jurists, 1980; Emperors and Lawyers, 1981; The Quest for Security, 1982; Ulpian, 1982. *Address:* 126 Freehold Street, Lower Heyford, Oxford. *T:* Steeple Aston 40680.

HONOUR, (Patrick) Hugh; writer; *b* 26 Sept. 1927; *s* of late Herbert Percy Honour and Dorothy Margaret Withers. *Educ:* King's Sch., Canterbury; St Catharine's Coll., Cambridge (BA). Asst to Dir, Leeds City Art Gall. and Temple Newsam House, 1953-54. Guest Curator for exhibn, The European Vision of America, National Gall. of Art, Washington, Cleveland Museum of Art, and, as L'Amérique vue par l'Europe, Grand Palais, Paris, 1976. *Publications:* Chinoiserie, 1961 (2nd edn 1973); Companion Guide to Venice, 1965 (4th edn 1977); (with Sir Nikolaus Pevsner and John Fleming) The Penguin Dictionary of Architecture, 1966 (7th edn 1976); Neo-classicism,

1968 (4th edn 1977); The New Golden Land, 1976; (with John Fleming) The Penguin Dictionary of Decorative Arts, 1977; Romanticism, 1979; (with John Fleming) A World History of Art, 1982. *Recreation:* gardening. *Club:* Travellers'.

HONYWOOD, Sir Filmer (Courtenay William), 11th Bt *cr* 1660; FRICS; Regional Surveyor and Valuer, South Eastern Region, Central Electricity Generating Board, since 1978; *b* 20 May 1930; *s* of Col Sir William Wynne Honywood, 10th Bt, MC, and Maud Naylor (*d* 1953), *d* of William Hodgson Wilson, Hexgreave Park, Southwell, Notts; *S* father, 1982; *m* 1956, Elizabeth Margaret Mary Cynthia, *d* of Sir Alastair George Lionel Joseph Miller of Glenlee, 6th Bt; two *s* two *d*. *Educ:* Downside; RMA Sandhurst; Royal Agricultural College, Cirencester (MRAC Diploma). Served 3rd Carabiniers (Prince of Wales' Dragoon Guards). Asst Surveyor, Min. of Agriculture, Fisheries and Food, Maidstone, 1966-73; Surveyor, Cockermouth, Cumbria, 1973-74; Senior Lands Officer, CEGB, SE Region, 1974-78. *Heir:* *s* Rupert Anthony Pagan Honywood, *b* 2 March 1957. *Address:* Greenway Forstal Farmhouse, Hollingbourne, Maidstone, Kent.

HOOD, family name of Viscounts Bridport and Hood.

HOOD, 7th Viscount *cr* 1796; **Alexander Lambert Hood;** Bt 1778; Baron (Ire.) 1782, (GB) 1795; Chairman: Tanks Consolidated Investment plc, since 1976; Petrofina (UK) Ltd, since 1982 (Director, since 1958); Director: J. Henry Schroder Wagg & Co., 1957-75; George Wimpey plc, since 1957; *b* 11 March 1914; *s* of Rear-Adm. Hon. Sir Horace Hood, KCB, DSO, MVO (*d* 1916) (3rd *s* of 4th Viscount) and Ellen Floyd (*d* 1950), *d* of A. E. Touzalin; *S* brother, 1981; *m* 1957, Diana Maud, CVO 1957, *d* of late Hon. G. W. Lyttelton; three *s*. *Educ:* RN Coll., Dartmouth; Trinity Coll., Cambridge; Harvard Business Sch. RNVR, 1939-45. Director: Union Minière; Abbott Laboratories Inc. Part-time Mem., British Waterways Bd, 1963-73. *Heir:* *s* Hon. Henry Lyttelton Alexander Hood, *b* 16 March 1958. *Address:* 67 Chelsea Square, SW3. *T:* 01-352 4952; Loders Court, Bridport, Dorset. *T:* Bridport 22983. *Club:* Brooks's.

HOOD, Sir Harold (Joseph), 2nd Bt *cr* 1922, of Wimbledon, Co. Surrey; TD; Circulation Director, Catholic Herald, since 1961; Circulation Director, Universe, 1953-60; *b* 23 Jan. 1916; *s* of Sir Joseph Hood, 1st Bt, and Marie Josephine (*d* 1956), *e d* of Archibald Robinson, JP, Dublin; *S* father, 1931; *m* 1946, Hon. Ferelith Rosemary Florence Kenworthy, *o d* of 10th Baron Strabolgi and of Doris, Lady Strabolgi, 137 Gloucester Road, SW7; two *s* two *d* (and one *s* decd). *Educ:* Downside Sch. Mem. Editorial Staff, The Universe, 1936-39; Asst Editor, The Catholic Directory, 1950, Managing Ed., 1959-60; Editor, The Catholic Who's Who, 1952 Edition. 2nd Lieutenant 58th Middx Battalion RE (AA) (TA) 1939; Lieut RA, 1941. KSG (Holy See), 1964; KCSG (Holy See), 1978; Kt of Magistral Grace, SMO Malta, 1972. *Heir:* *s* John Joseph Harold Hood, *b* 27 Aug. 1952. *Address:* 31 Avenue Road, NW8 6BS. *T:* 01-722 9088. *Clubs:* Royal Automobile, MCC, Challoner.

HOOD, Rear-Adm. John, CBE 1981; CEng, FIMechE; Director General Aircraft (Naval), 1978-81; *b* 23 March 1924; *s* of Charles Arthur Hood, architect, and Nellie Ormiston Brown Lamont; *m* 1948, Julia Mary Trevaskis; three *s*. *Educ:* Plymouth Coll.; RN Engineering Coll., Keyham. Entered Royal Navy, 1945; RNEC, 1945-48; served in Illustrious, 1948; RN Air Stations, Abbotsinch, Anthorn, RAF West Raynham (NAFDU), 1948-51; HQ Min. of Supply, 1951-53; Air Engineer Officer, 1834 Sqdn, 1953-55, Aeroplane and Armament Experimental Estabt, 1955-57; Staff of Dir Aircraft Maintenance and Repair, 1957-59; AEO, HMS Albion, 1959-61; Sen. Air Engr, RNEC, Manadon, 1961-62; Development Project Officer, Sea Vixen 2, Min. of Aviation, 1962-65; AEO, RNAS, Lossiemouth, 1965-67; Staff of Dir of Officer Appointments (E), 1967-70; Defence and Naval Attaché, Argentina and Uruguay, 1970-73; Sen. Officers War Course, 1973; Asst Dir, Naval Manpower Requirements (Ships), 1974-75; Head of Aircraft Dept (Naval), 1975-78. Comdr 1962, Captain 1969, Rear-Adm. 1979. *Recreations:* sailing, gardening. *Address:* High Pines, Drews Park, Knotty Green, Bucks HP9 2TT. *T:* Beaconsfield 2071. *Clubs:* Army and Navy; RN Sailing Association.

HOOD, (Martin) Sinclair (Frankland); Archaeologist; *b* 31 Jan. 1917; *s* of late Lt-Comdr Martin Hood, RN, and late Mrs Martin Hood, New York; *m* 1957, Rachel Simmons; one *s* two *d*. *Educ:* Harrow; Magdalen Coll., Oxford. British Sch. at Athens: student, 1947-48 and 1951-53; Asst Dir, 1949-51; Dir, 1954-62. Student, British Inst. Archaeology, Ankara, 1948-49. Geddes-Harrower Vis. Prof. of Greek Art and Archaeology, Univ. of Aberdeen, 1968. Took part in excavations at: Dorchester, Oxon, 1937; Compton, Berks, 1946-47; Southwark, 1946; Smyrna, 1948-49; Atchana, 1949-50; Sakca-Gozu, 1950; Mycenae, 1950-52; Knossos, 1950-51, 1953-55, 1957-61; Jericho, 1952; Chios, 1952-55. *Publications:* The Home of the Heroes: The Aegean before the Greeks, 1967; The Minoans, 1971; The Arts in Prehistoric Greece, 1978; various excavation reports and articles. *Address:* The Old Vicarage, Great Milton, Oxford OX9 7PB. *T:* Great Milton 202. *Club:* Athenæum.

HOOD, Prof. Neil; Professor of Business Policy, University of Strathclyde, since 1979; *b* 10 Aug. 1943; *s* of Andrew Hood and Elizabeth Taylor Carruthers; *m* 1966, Anna Watson Clark; one *s* one *d*. *Educ:* Wishaw High Sch.; Univ. of Glasgow. MA, MLitt. Res. Fellow, Scottish Coll. of Textiles, 1966-68; Lectr, later Sen. Lectr, Paisley Coll. of Technol., 1968-78; Economic

Advr, Scottish Economic Planning Dept, 1979. Vis. Prof. of Internat. Business, Univ. of Texas, Dallas, 1981. Trade Adviser, UNCTAD-GATT, 1980-; Economic Consultant to Sec. of State for Scotland, 1980-; Consultant to: Internat. Finance Corp., World Bank, 1982-; UN Centre on Transnational Corporations, 1982-. *Publications:* (with S. Young): Chrysler UK: Corporation in transition, 1977; Economics of Multinational Enterprise, 1979; European Development Strategies of US-owned Manufacturing Companies Located in Scotland, 1980; Multinationals in Retreat: the Scottish experience, 1982; articles on internat. business, marketing and business policy, in various jls. *Recreations:* reading, writing, swimming, golf, gardening. *Address:* Teviot, 12 Carlisle Road, Hamilton ML3 7DB. *T:* Hamilton 424870.

HOOD, Roger Grahame; University Reader in Criminology and Fellow of All Souls College, Oxford, since 1973; *b* 12 June 1936; 2nd *s* of Ronald and Phyllis Hood; *m* 1963, Barbara Blaine Young; one *d. Educ:* King Edward's Sch., Five Ways, Birmingham; LSE (BSc Sociology); Downing Coll., Cambridge (PhD). Research Officer, LSE, 1961-63; Lectr in Social Admin, Univ. of Durham, 1963-67; Asst Dir of Research, Inst. of Criminology, Univ. of Cambridge, 1967-73; Fellow of Clare Hall, Cambridge, 1969-73. Vis. Prof., Univ. of Virginia Sch. of Law, 1980-. Member: Parole Bd, 1972-73; SSRC Cttee on Social Sciences and the Law, 1975-79. Mem., Judicial Studies Bd, 1979-. Mem. Editorial Bd, British Jl of Criminology. *Publications:* Sentencing in Magistrates' Courts, 1962; Borstal Re-assessed, 1965; (with Richard Sparks) Key Issues in Criminology, 1970; Sentencing the Motoring Offender, 1972; (ed) Crime, Criminology and Public Policy: Essays in Honour of Sir Leon Radzinowicz, 1974; (with Sir Leon Radzinowicz) Criminology and the Administration of Criminal Justice: a bibliography, 1976. *Address:* All Souls College, Oxford. *T:* Oxford 722251.

HOOD, Sinclair; *see* Hood, M. S. F.

HOOD, Col Sir Tom (Fielden), KBE 1967 (OBE 1944); CB 1959; TD 1944; DL; Chairman, Portman Building Society, since 1960; Director, National Employers' Mutual General Insurance Association Ltd (Chairman, 1970-76); *s* of late Tom Hood, AMICE, AMIMechE, and Emmeline Clayton Hood (*née* Fielden); *m* 1931, Joan, *d* of Richmond P. Hellyar; two *s. Educ:* Clifton Coll. ACA 1930, FCA 1938. Partner, Lawrence, Gardner & Co., Chartered Accountants, Bristol, 1931-57. 2nd Lieut RE (TA), 1923; CRE 61 Div., 1939-42; DCE Scottish Command, 1942-44; DCE Second Army, 1944-45; Col 1945. Chm., Commn of Enquiry into Port of Aden, 1963. Governor of Clifton Coll., 1954-; Mem. of Court of Univ. of Bristol, 1956-. DL Co. Gloucester, 1950-. *Recreation:* reading. *Address:* Sion Cottage, Sion Hill, Bath BA1 2UL. *T:* Bath 25123. *Clubs:* Army and Navy; Bath and County (Bath).

HOOD, Sir William Acland, 8th Bt *cr* 1806 and 6th Bt *cr* 1809; *b* 5 March 1901; *s* of William Fuller-Acland-Hood (*d* 1933) and Elizabeth (*d* 1966), *d* of M. Kirkpatrick, Salt Lake City, USA; *S* to baronetcies of kinsman, 2nd Baron St Audries, 1971; *m* 1925, Mary, *d* of late Augustus Edward Jessup, Philadelphia; one *d* (one *s* decd). *Educ:* Wellington; RMA Woolwich; Univ. of California (MA). Naturalized American citizen, 1926. Formerly Lieutenant RE. Professor, Los Angeles City College, retired. *Heir:* none. *Address:* SR2, Box 577, 29 Palms, California 92277, USA. *T:* 714 3679345.

HOOD PHILLIPS, Owen; *see* Phillips.

HOOFT, Willem Adolf Visser 't; *see* Visser 't Hooft.

HOOK, Rt. Rev. Ross Sydney, MC 1945; Chief of Staff to the Archbishop of Canterbury, since 1980; an Assistant Bishop, Diocese of Canterbury, since 1981; *b* 19 Feb. 1917; *o s* of late Sydney Frank and Laura Harriet Hook; *m* 1948, Ruth Leslie, *d* of late Rev. Herman Masterman Biddell and Violet Marjorie Biddell; one *s* one *d. Educ:* Christ's Hosp.; Peterhouse, Cambridge (MA); Ridley Hall, Cambridge. Asst Curate, Milton, Hants, 1941-43. Chaplain, RNVR (Royal Marine Commandos), 1942-46. Chaplain, Ridley Hall, Cambridge, 1946-48. Select Preacher, University of Cambridge, 1948; Rector, Chorlton-cum-Hardy, Manchester, 1948-52; Rector and Rural Dean, Chelsea, 1952-61; Chaplain: Chelsea Hosp. for Women, 1954-61; St Luke's Hosp., Chelsea, 1957-61; Residentiary Canon of Rochester and Precentor, 1961-65; Treasurer, 1965; Diocesan Dir of Post Ordination Training, 1961-65; Bishop Suffragan of Grantham, 1965-72; Bishop of Bradford, 1972-80. Examining Chaplain to Bishop of Rochester, 1961-65, to Bishop of Lincoln, 1966-72; Prebendary of Brampton (Lincoln Cathedral), 1966-72; Dean of Stamford, 1971-72. Chm., Inspections Cttee, Central Advisory Council for the Ministry, 1966-71 (Sec., 1960-66). Hon. DLitt Bradford, 1981. *Recreation:* cricket. *Address:* Lambeth Palace, SE1 7JU.

HOOK, Prof. Sidney; Professor, Department of Philosophy, Graduate School of Arts and Science, New York University, 1939-72, now Emeritus Professor; Senior Research Fellow on War, Revolution and Peace, at Hoover Institution, Stanford University, since 1973; Founder of The New York University Institute of Philosophy; *b* 20 Dec. 1902; *s* of Isaac Hook and Jennie Halpern; *m* 1924; one *s*; *m* 1935, Ann Zinken; one *s* one *d. Educ:* College of the City of New York; BS 1923; Columbia Univ. (MA 1926, PhD 1927); Columbia Univ. Fellowship in Philosophy, 1926-27; Guggenheim Research Fellowship in Philosophy for Study Abroad, 1928-29, 1953-; Ford Fellowship for the Study of Asian philosophy and culture, 1958. Teacher, New York City Public Schs, 1923-27; Instr in Philosophy, Washington Square Coll., New York Univ., 1927-32; Asst Prof., 1932-34; Assoc. Prof. and Chm. of Dept of Philosophy, 1933-39; Lectr, New Sch. for Social Research, NYC, 1931-. Vis. Prof., Univ. of California, 1950, Harvard Univ., 1961; Thomas Jefferson Memorial Lectr, Univ. of California at Berkeley, 1961; Regents Prof., Univ. of California at Santa Barbara, 1966; Vis. Prof., Univ. of California at San Diego, 1975. Fellow at Center for Advanced Study in the Behavioral Sciences, Stanford Univ., 1961-62. Butler Silver Medal for distinction in Philosophy, Columbia Univ., 1945. Organiser: conf. on Methods in Philosophy and Sci., conf. on Sci. Spirit and Dem. Faith, and Cttee for Cultural Freedom; Organiser and Co-Chm., Americans for Intellectual Freedom; President: Univ. Centers for Rational Alternatives; John Dewey Foundn (and Treasurer); Mem., American Philosophical Assoc. Vice-Pres., Eastern Div., 1958, Pres., 1959-60. Am. Assoc. Univ. Profs (past Council Mem.); Vice-President: Internat. Cttees for Academic Freedom; Council, Nat. Endowment for the Humanities. Hon. DHL: Univ. of Maine, 1960; Univ. of Utah, 1970; Univ. of Vermont, 1979; Hon LLD: Univ. of California, 1966; Rockford Coll., 1970; Univ. of Florida, 1971. Fellow: American Academy of Arts and Sciences, 1965; Nat. Acad. of Educn, 1968. *Publications:* The Metaphysics of Pragmatism, 1927; Towards the Understanding of Karl Marx, 1933; American Philosophy-To-day and To-morrow, 1935; From Hegel to Marx, 1936; Planned Society-Yesterday, To-day, To-morrow, 1937; John Dewey: An Intellectual Portrait, 1939; Reason, Social Myths and Democracy, 1940; The Hero in History, 1943; Education for Modern Man, 1946; Heresy, Yes-Conspiracy No, 1953; The Ambiguous Legacy; Marx and the Marxists, 1955; Common Sense and the Fifth Amendment, 1957; Political Power and Personal Freedom, 1959; The Quest for Being, 1961; The Paradoxes of Freedom, 1962; The Fail-Safe Fallacy, 1963; Religion in a Free Society, 1967; Academic Freedom and Academic Anarchy, 1970; Education and the Taming of Power, 1973; Pragmatism and the Tragic Sense of Life, 1975; Revolution, Reform and Social Justice, 1976; Philosophy and Public Philosophy, 1980; Editor of various works; contrib. numerous articles to philosophical journals. *Recreation:* gardening. *Address:* New York University, New York, NY 10003, USA. *T:* 212-598-3262; Hoover Institution, Stanford, Calif 94305, USA. *T:* 415-497-1501.

HOOK, Sheriff William Thomson; a Sheriff of Lothian and Borders, since 1968 (of Renfrew and Argyll at Greenock, 1956-68); *b* 6 Dec. 1918; *s* of Peter Dewar Hook, JP and Marianne Elizabeth Thomson; *m* 1947, Margaret, *d* of Robert Barr, Shadwell House, Leeds; one *s. Educ:* Edinburgh Acad.; Old Coll., Edinburgh (MA, LLB). Royal Northumberland Fusiliers, 1939-46 (despatches). Faculty of Advocates, 1948; Mem., College of Justice; Standing Jun. Counsel, Min. of Labour; a Chairman, Lothians Nat. Insce Tribunal; Mem. Cttee, Deaconess Hosp.; Mem., Probation and After Care Councils. Elder, West Kirk, Edinburgh. *Publication:* Gaelic Place Names of Bute. *Recreation:* Classical Association. *Address:* 10 Moray Place, Edinburgh. *Clubs:* New (Edinburgh); Royal Gourock Yacht.

HOOKER, Michael Ayerst, PhD; Chief Executive Governor, Truman and Knightley Educational Trust, since 1981 (Governor since 1977); *b* 22 Jan. 1923; *s* of Albert Ayerst Hooker, late of Broomsleigh Park, Seal Chart, Kent, and late Marjorie Mitchell Hooker (*née* Gunson). *Educ:* Marlborough; St Edmund Hall, Oxford (MA 1944); Univ. of the Witwatersrand (PhD 1952). Home Guard, Oxford Univ. Sen. Trng Corps and Army Cadet Force (TARO), 1940-48. British Council, 1945-47; Schoolmaster, England and S Africa, 1947-51; London Diocesan Bd of Educn, 1952-66; Visual Aids and Public Relations, 1953-59. Chm., Fedn of Conservative Students, 1944; Parly Candidate (C) Coventry East, 1955; various offices, Conservative Commonwealth Council, 1955-60. Wells Organisation, fund raising in UK and NZ, 1957-58; Man. Dir, Hooker Craigmyle & Co. Ltd (first institutional fund raising consultants in UK), 1959-72; Man. Dir, Michael Hooker and Associates Ltd, 1972-79; Develt Dir, The Look Wide Trust, 1979-80. From 1957, has helped to raise nearly £70 million for various good causes, incl. 13 historic cathedrals, univs, colleges, schools, medical causes, welfare charities, etc. Mem., Adv. Cttee on Charitable Fund Raising, Nat. Council of Social Service, 1971-73. Trustee: Ross McWhirter Foundn, 1976-; Dicey Trust, 1978-; Jerwood Foundn, 1981-; Hon. Councillor, NSPCC, 1981-; Governor, Oakham Sch., 1971-. *Publications:* various pamphlets and broadcasts on charities, historic churches, educnl issues, law and taxation, Christian stewardship of money. *Address:* 10 Myddelton Gardens, N21 2PA. *T:* 01-360 3206. *Clubs:* Carlton, Royal Commonwealth Society.

HOOKER, Prof. Morna Dorothy; Lady Margaret's Professor of Divinity, University of Cambridge, since 1976; Fellow of Robinson College, Cambridge, since 1976; *b* 19 May 1931; *d* of Percy Francis Hooker, FIA, and Lily (*née* Riley); *m* 1978, Rev. Dr W. David Stacey, MA. *Educ:* Univ. of Bristol (research schol.); Univ. of Manchester (research studentship). MA (Bristol, Oxford and Cambridge); PhD (Manchester). Research Fellow, Univ. of Durham, 1959; Lectr in New Testament Studies, King's Coll., London, 1961; Visiting Prof., McGill Univ., 1968; Lectr in Theology, Oxford, and Fellow, Linacre Coll., 1970-76 (Hon. Fellow, 1980); Lectr in Theology, Keble Coll., 1972-76; Visiting Fellow, Clare Hall, Cambridge, 1974. FKC 1979. *Publications:* Jesus and the Servant, 1959; The Son of Man in Mark, 1967; (ed jtly) What about the New Testament?, 1975; Pauline Pieces, 1979; Studying the New Testament, 1979; (ed jtly) Paul and Paulinism, 1982; contribs to New Testament Studies, Jl of Theological Studies, Theology, etc. *Recreations:* Molinology, music. *Address:* Divinity School, St John's Street, Cambridge.

HOOKER, Ronald George, CEng; CBIM; Chairman: James Austin Steel Holdings plc, since 1981; Dubilier plc, since 1978; Management & Business Services Ltd, since 1972; Henry Sykes plc, since 1981; *b* 6 Aug. 1921; *m* 1954, Eve Pigott; one *s* one *d*. *Educ:* Wimbledon Technical Coll.; London Univ. (external). CEng 1965; CBIM 1972. Apprentice, Philips Electrical Ltd, 1937-41, Develt Engr, 1945-48; FBI, 1948-50; Dir and Gen. Man., Brush Electrical Engineering Co. Ltd, 1950-60; Man. Dir, K & L Steelfounders & Engineers Ltd, 1960-65; Man. Dir, Associated Fire Alarms Ltd, 1965-68; Chm. and Man. Dir, Crane Fruehauf Trailers Ltd, 1968-71; Dir of Manufacture, Rolls Royce (1971) Ltd, 1971-73; Chm. and Man. Dir, John M. Henderson (Holdings) Ltd, 1973-75. Dep. Chairman: Agricultural Hldgs Ltd, 1980-; Grimshawe Hldgs plc, 1974-; UKO Internat. plc, 1966-. Director: Dorada Hldgs plc, 1976-; GEI Internat. plc, 1974; Ruberoid plc, 1977-; Hambros Industrial Management Ltd, 1966-; Gibraltar & Iberian Bank Ltd, 1981-. Chairman: Engrg Careers Inf. Service, 1976-; Manufg Management Fellowship Scheme, 1978-; Member: Engrg Council, 1982-; Engrg Industry Trng Bd, 1976-; Management Bd and Policy Cttee, Engrg Employers' Fedn, 1977-. Past Pres., IProdE, 1974-75 (Hon. Life MIProdE 1980). Freeman, City of London. *Publications:* papers on management and prodn engrg to BIM, ICMA, IProdE and IMechE. *Recreations:* gardening, reading, music. *Address:* Loxborough House, Bledlow Ridge, near High Wycombe, Bucks HP14 4AA. *T:* Bledlow Ridge 486; 6 Tufton Court, Tufton Street, SW1P 3QH. *T:* 01-222 6669. *Clubs:* Athenæum, Lansdowne.

HOOKER, Sir Stanley (George), Kt 1974; CBE 1964 (OBE 1946); FRS 1962; DSc; DPhil; Technical Adviser to the Chairman, 1977-81, Consultant, since 1981, Rolls-Royce Ltd; *b* 30 Sept. 1907; 5th *s* of William Harry and Ellen Mary Hooker; *m* 1st, 1936, Hon. Margaret Bradbury; one *d* ; 2nd, 1950, Kate Maria Garth; one *d*. *Educ:* Borden Grammar Sch.; Imperial Coll., London; Brasenose Coll., Oxford (Hon. Fellow 1980). Scientific and Research Dept, Admiralty, 1935-38; Rolls Royce Ltd, 1938-48; Bristol Aero Engines, 1948-59. Apptd Chief Engr, Engine Div., Bristol Aeroplane Co. Ltd, 1951 and a Dir, 1952; Technical Dir (Aero) Bristol Siddeley Engines Ltd, 1959; Technical Dir, Bristol Engine Div. of Rolls-Royce Ltd, 1966-71; Gp Technical Dir, Rolls-Royce Ltd, 1971-77. FIMechE (Mem. Council, 1958-); FRAeS; Fellow, Imperial Coll.; Hon. Mem. ASME, 1980; Fellow, Amer. Acad of Engineering, 1981; Hon. Prof., Peking Inst. of Aeronautical Scis, 1973. British Silver Medal for Aeronautics, awarded by RAeS, 1955; Diplôme Paul Tissandier, by Féd. Aero Internationale, 1955; Thulin Bronze Medal by Swedish Aero. Soc., 1960; Brit. Gold Medal for Aeronautics, by RAeS, 1961; James Clayton Prize (jointly), 1966; Gold Medal, RAeS, 1967; Churchill Gold Medal, Soc. of Engineers, 1968; Goddard Medal, Amer. Inst. of Aeronautics and Astronautics, 1969. *Address:* Rolls-Royce Ltd, PO Box 3, Filton, Bristol; Orchard Hill, Milbury Heath, Wotton-under-Edge, Glos. *Clubs:* Athenæum; Wings (NY).

See also Sir John Barran, Bt.

HOOKS, Air Vice-Marshal Robert Keith, CBE 1979; CEng, FRAeS; Director General Aircraft 2, Ministry of Defence (Procurement Executive), since 1981; *b* 7 Aug. 1929; *s* of late Robert George Hooks and of Phyllis Hooks; *m* 1954, Kathleen (*née* Cooper); one *s* one *d*. *Educ:* Acklam Hall Sch.; Constantine Coll., Middlesbrough. Bsc(Eng) London. Commissioned RAF, 1951; served at RAF stations West Malling, Fassberg, Sylt, 1952-55; RAF Technical Coll., Henlow, 1956; Fairey Aviation Co., 1957-58; Air Ministry, 1958-60; Skybolt Trials Unit, Eglin, Florida, 1961-63; Bomber Command Armament Sch., Wittering, 1963-65; OC Engrg Wing, RAF Coll., Cranwell, 1967-69; HQ Far East Air Force, 1969-71; Supt of Armament A&AEE, 1971-74; Director Ground Training, 1974-76; Director Air Armament, 1976-80. Vice-Pres. (Air), Ordnance Board, 1980. *Recreations:* gardening, photography, water-skiing. *Address:* c/o Lloyds Bank Ltd, Cox's & King's Branch, 6 Pall Mall, SW1Y 5NH. *Club:* Royal Air Force.

HOOKWAY, Sir Harry (Thurston), Kt 1978; Deputy Chairman and Chief Executive, The British Library Board, since 1973; *b* 23 July 1921; *s* of William and Bertha Hookway; *m* 1956, Barbara Olive, *o d* of late Oliver and Olive Butler; one *s* one *d*. *Educ:* Trinity Sch. of John Whitgift; London Univ. (BSc, PhD). Various posts in industry, 1941-49; DSIR, 1949-65; Asst Dir, National Chemical Laboratory, 1959; Dir, UK Scientific Mission (North America), Scientific Attaché, Washington, DC, and Scientific Adviser to UK High Comr, Ottawa, 1960-64; Head of Information Div., DSIR, 1964-65; CSO, DES, 1966-69, Asst Under-Sec. of State, DES, 1969-73. Chairman: UNESCO Internat. Adv. Cttee for Documentation, Libraries and Archives; British Council Libraries Adv. Cttee, 1982-; Pres., Inst. of Information Scientists, 1973-76; Hon. FIInfSc. Mem., Royal Commn on Historical Monuments (England), 1981-. Governor, British Inst. for Recorded Sound, 1981-. Dir, Arundel Castle Trustees Ltd, 1976-. Hon. LLD Sheffield, 1976; Hon. DLitt Loughborough, 1980. *Publications:* various contribs to jls of learned societies. *Recreations:* music, travel. *Address:* 35 Goldstone Crescent, Hove, East Sussex. *Club:* Athenæum.

HOOKWAY, Reginald John Samuel, FRTPI; consultant planner; Director of the Countryside Commission, 1971-81; *b* 7 June 1920; *er s* of Charles and Florence Hookway, Bideford, Devon; *m* 1942, Ethel Lylie Ashford; one *s* two *d*. *Educ:* Bideford Grammar Sch.; University Coll. of the South West, Exeter (BSc). Served War, 1940-46 (dispatches); commnd RE; served in N Africa, Italy, Jugoslavia, Greece. Devon County Council: Research Officer, 1948-55; Asst County Planning Officer, 1955-58; Dep. County Planning Officer, Norfolk CC, 1958-64; Principal Planning Officer, Countryside Commn,

1965-69; Dep. Chief Planning Officer, Min. of Housing and Local Govt, 1969-71. Mem., Nat. Parks Policies Review Cttee, 1972-74, and many other govt cttees. British Travel Authority: Chm., Caravan and Camping Sub Cttee, 1981-; Mem., Marketing Cttee, 1981-; Adviser to Council for Environmental Consultation, 1982-. Hon. LLD Exeter, 1981. *Publications:* a number of papers on rural and recreational planning, incl. many for Countryside Commn. *Recreations:* walking, swimming. *Address:* 1 Albert Court, Albert Road, Cheltenham, Glos GL52 2TN. *T:* Cheltenham 519483. *Club:* Reform.

HOOLAHAN, Anthony Terence, QC 1973; a Recorder of the Crown Court, since 1976; *b* 26 July 1925; *s* of late Gerald Hoolahan and of Val Hoolahan; *m* 1949, Dorothy Veronica Connochie; one *s* one *d*. *Educ:* Dorset House, Littlehampton, Sussex; Framlingham Coll., Suffolk; Lincoln Coll., Oxford (MA). Served War, RNVR, 1943-46. Oxford Univ., 1946-48. Called to Bar, Inner Temple, 1949, Bencher, 1980; called to the Bar of Northern Ireland, 1980, QC (Northern Ireland) 1980. *Publications:* Guide to Defamation Practice (with Colin Duncan, QC), 2nd edn, 1958; contrib. to Halsbury's Laws of England, Atkin's Court Forms. *Recreations:* squash, swimming. *Address:* 1 Brick Court, Temple, EC4Y 9BY. *T:* 01-353 8845; Fair Lawn, Ormond Avenue, Richmond, Surrey TW10 6TN. *T:* 01-940 1194.

HOOLEY, Frank Oswald; MP (Lab) Sheffield, Heeley, 1966-70 and since Feb. 1974; *b* 30 Nov. 1923; *m* 1945, Doris Irene Snook; two *d*. *Educ:* King Edward's High Sch., Birmingham; Birmingham Univ. Admin. Asst, Birmingham Univ., 1948-52; Sheffield Univ.: Asst Registrar, 1952-65; Sen. Asst Registrar, 1965-66; Registrar, Fourah Bay Coll., Sierra Leone, 1960-62 (secondment from Sheffield); Sen. Admin. Asst, Manchester Poly., 1970-71; Chief Admin. Offr, Sheffield City Coll. of Educn, 1971-74. Chm., Co-ordinating Cttee, Internat. Anti-Apartheid Year, 1978. Chm., Parly Liaison Gp for Alternative Energy Strategies, 1978; Member: Select Cttee on Foreign Affairs; Select Cttee on Procedure. *Address:* House of Commons, SW1A 0AA.

HOOLEY, Maj.-Gen. St John Cutler, CB 1958; CBE 1954; *b* 30 Sept. 1902; *s* of late S. P. Hooley, Tharston, Norfolk; *m* 1931, Molly Isobel, *d* of late Dr A. Scott-Turner, MRCS, LRCP, JP, London; one *d*. *Educ:* RMA, Woolwich. Royal Artillery, 2nd Lieut 1923; Captain RAOC, 1934; Dep. Dir Ordnance Services: AA Comd, 1945-46; British Mil. Mission, Greece, 1947-50; HQ Eastern Comd, 1950-52; Dir, Ordnance Services, HQ BAOR and Northern Army Gp, 1952-57; Brig. 1954, Maj.-Gen. 1957; Inspector RAOC, 1957-58; Comdt, Mechanical Transport Organisation, Chilwell, 1958-60, retired. Served War of 1939-45 in Norway, Middle East and India (despatches). *Recreations:* golf, travel, photography. *Address:* Storrington Cottage, Sea Avenue, Rustington, Sussex.

HOOPER, Sir Anthony (Robin Maurice), 2nd Bt *cr* 1962; *b* 26 Oct. 1918; *o s* of Sir Frederic Collins Hooper, 1st Bt, and Eglantine Irene (Bland); *S* father, 1963; *m* 1970, Cynthia (marr. diss. 1973), *yr d* of Col W. J. H. Howard, DSO. *Educ:* Radley; New Coll., Oxford. Royal Artillery, 1939-41; Asst to Hubert Philips, News Chronicle, 1941-42; Political Research Centre, 1942-44; Actor (Liverpool, Windsor, Birmingham, Oxford, London, BBC), 1944-50; temp. Civil Servant, Cabinet Office, 1950-52. Asst Design Manager, Schweppes Ltd, 1952-64; Director, Couper Gallery, 1964-68. *Recreations:* music, conversation and people. *Club:* Savile.

HOOPER, Ven. Charles German, MA; Archdeacon of Ipswich, 1963-76, now Archdeacon Emeritus; *b* 16 April 1911; 2nd *s* of A. C. Hooper, Solicitor; *m* 1936, Lilian Mary, *d* of late Sir Harold Brakspear, KCVO; one *s* one *d*. *Educ:* Lincoln Coll., Oxford (MA 2nd cl. English). Curacies: Corsham, Wilts, 1934-36; Claremont, CP, South Africa, 1936-39; Rector, Castle Combe, Wilts, 1940; Chaplain, RAFVR, 1942-46 (despatches); Rector, Sandy, Beds, 1946-53; Vicar and Rural Dean, Bishop's Stortford, Herts, 1953-63; Rector of Bildeston, Suffolk, 1963-67; Rector of St Lawrence's and St Stephen's, Ipswich, 1967-74. Chaplain to Cutlers Co., Sheffield, 1964-65, to Drapers Co., 1972-73. *Recreations:* painting in water colours, sailing. *Address:* East Green Cottage, Kelsale, Saxmundham, Suffolk. *T:* Saxmundham 2702.

See also Baron Methuen.

HOOPER, Gloria; Member (C) Liverpool, European Parliament, since 1979; *b* 25 May 1939; *d* of Frances and Frederick Hooper. *Educ:* University of Southampton (BA Hons Law); Universidad Central, Quito, Ecuador (Lic. de Derecho Internacional). Admitted to Law Society, Solicitor, 1973; Partner, Taylor & Humbert, 1974-. Mem., Environment and Consumer Affairs Cttees, European Parlt, 1979-. *Publications:* Cases on Company Law, 1967; Law of International Trade, 1968. *Recreations:* theatre and walking. *Address:* 11 Cleveland Row, St James's, SW1. *T:* 01-839 3929. *Clubs:* Carlton; International (Bruxelles).

HOOPER, Sir Leonard (James), KCMG 1967 (CMG 1962); CBE 1951; idc; a Deputy Secretary, Cabinet Office, 1973-78, retired; *b* 23 July 1914. *Educ:* Alleyn's, Dulwich; Worcester Coll., Oxford. Joined Air Ministry, 1938, transferred Foreign Office, 1942; Imperial Defence Coll., 1953; Dir, Govt Communications HQ, 1965-73. *Recreation:* sport. *Address:* Yew Tree Cottage, Farm Lane, Bredon, Tewkesbury, Glos GL20 7HF. *T:* Bredon 72533. *Club:* New (Cheltenham).

HOOPER, Mrs Mia Lilly Kellmer; *see* Pringle, Dr M. L. K.

HOOPER, Noel Barrie; Hon. Mr Justice Hooper; Judge of the High Court, Hong Kong, since 1981; *b* 9 Nov. 1931; twin *s* of Alfred Edward Hooper and Constance Violet Hooper; *m* 1959, Pauline Mary (*née* Irwin); two *d. Educ:* Prince of Wales Sch., Kenya; St Peter's Hall, Oxford (BA 1954). Called to the Bar, Gray's Inn, 1956. Advocate of High Court, Uganda, 1956-61; Magistrate, Basutoland, 1961-63 and Hong Kong, 1964-68; Sen. Magistrate, Hong Kong, 1968-73; Principal Magistrate, 1973-76; Dist Judge, 1976-81. *Recreations:* tennis, cricket, reading. *Address:* The Courts of Justice, Hong Kong. *Clubs:* MCC; Hong Kong Cricket, Victoria Recreation, Ladies' Recreation (Hong Kong).

HOOPER, Sir Robin (William John), KCMG 1968 (CMG 1954); DSO 1943; DFC 1943; HM Diplomatic Service, retired; Special Representative of Foreign and Commonwealth Secretary, since 1976; Member, NATO Appeals Board, since 1976; *b* 26 July 1914; *s* of late Col John Charles Hooper, DSO, and late Irene Annie Palmer Hooper (*née* Anderson), Harewell, Faversham, Kent; *m* 1941, Constance Mildred Ayshford, *d* of late Lieut-Col Gilbert Ayshford Sanford, DSO, DL, Triley Court, Abergavenny, Mon; three *s. Educ:* Charterhouse; The Queen's Coll., Oxford. 3rd Sec., Foreign Office, 1938-40. Served War of 1939-45; on active service with RAF, 1940-44 (Wing-Comdr). Second Sec., HM Embassy, Paris, 1944-47; First Sec., HM Embassy, Lisbon, 1947-49; transferred to FO, 1949; Counsellor, 1950; Head of Personnel Dept, 1950-53; Counsellor, HM Embassy, Bagdad, 1953-56; Head of Perm. Under-Sec.'s Dept, FO, 1956-60; Asst Sec.-Gen. (Political), NATO, 1960-66; Ambassador to Tunisia, 1966-67; Ambassador to Southern Yemen, 1967-68; Dep. Sec., Cabinet Office, 1968-71; Ambassador to Greece, 1971-74. Chm., Anglo-Hellenic League, 1975-78. Dir, Benguela Railway Co., 1976-. Mem., NATO Appeals Bd, 1977-. Chevalier, Legion of Honour, 1945. Croix de Guerre, 1939-45 (2 Palms), 1945. *Address:* F3, Albany, Piccadilly, W1; Brook House, Egerton, near Ashford, Kent TN27 9AP. *Club:* Travellers'.

HOOSON, family name of **Baron Hooson.**

HOOSON, Baron *cr* 1979 (Life Peer), of Montgomery in the County of Powys and of Colomendy in the County of Clwyd; **Hugh Emlyn Hooson;** QC 1960; a Recorder of the Crown Court, since 1972 (Recorder of Swansea, 1971); *b* 26 March 1925; *s* of late Hugh and Elsie Hooson, Colomendy, Denbigh; *m* 1950, Shirley Margaret Wynne, *d* of late Sir George Hamer, CBE; two *d. Educ:* Denbigh Gram. Sch.; University Coll. of Wales; Gray's Inn (Bencher, 1968). Called to Bar, 1949; Wales and Chester Circuit (Leader, 1971-74); Dep. Chm., Flint QS, 1960-71; Dep. Chm., Merioneth QS, 1960-67, Chm., 1967-71; Recorder of Merthyr Tydfil, 1971. MP (L) Montgomery, 1962-79. Leader, Welsh Liberal Party, 1966-79. Vice-Chm. Political Cttee, North Atlantic Assembly, 1975-79. Hon. Professorial Fellow, University Coll. of Wales, 1971. Farms Pen-y-banc farm, Llanidloes. *Address:* 1 Dr Johnson's Buildings, Temple, EC4. *T:* 01-353 9328; Summerfield, Llanidloes, Powys. *T:* Llanidloes 2298.

HOOSON, Tom (Ellis); MP (C) Brecon and Radnor, since 1979; *b* 16 March 1933; *s* of late David Maelor Hooson and Ursula Ellis Hooson. *Educ:* Rhyl Grammar School; University College, Oxford (MA); Gray's Inn. Career in publishing, advertising and marketing in Britain, USA and France. With Benton & Bowles Inc., 1961-76 (Senior Vice-Pres., Dir of European Operations, 1971-76); Dir of Communications, Cons. Party, 1976-78; Dir-Gen., Periodical Publishers Assoc., 1978-. Contested (C) Caernarvon, 1959. Chm., Bow Group and Bow Publications, 1960-61; founded Welsh Farm News, 1957. *Publications:* (jtly) Work for Wales, 1959; (contrib.) Lessons from America, 1973. *Recreations:* walking, sailing, tennis, reading. *Address:* House of Commons, SW1. *Club:* Carlton.

HOOVER, Herbert William, Jr; President, 1954-66, and Chairman of the Board, 1959-66, The Hoover Company, North Canton, Ohio; *b* 23 April 1918; *s* of late Herbert William Hoover and Grace Hoover (*née* Steele); *m* 1941, Carl Maitland Good; one *s* one *d. Educ:* Choate Sch., Wallingford, Conn.; Rollins Coll. (AB). Served in US Army as 2nd Lieut, 1943-45. Offices held with Hoover Co.: Exec. Sales, 1941; Dir Industrial Relations, 1945; Asst Vice-Pres., 1948; Vice-Pres. Field Sales, 1952; Exec. Vice-Pres., 1953. The Hoover Co. Ltd, Canada: Pres., 1954; Dir, 1952; Hoover Ltd, England: Dir 1954, Chm. 1956. Hoover Inc., Panama: Dir and Pres., 1955; Hoover (America Latina) SA, Panama: Dir and Pres., 1955; Hoover Mexicana, Mexico: Dir and Pres., 1955; Hoover Industrial y Comercial SA, Colombia: Dir and Pres., 1960; Hoover Worldwide Corp., NY City: Pres. and Chm., 1960; Dir, S. A. Hoover, France, 1965. Dir, Harter Bank & Trust Co., Canton, Ohio. Past Regional Vice-Chm., US Cttee for the UN. Dir, Miami Heart Inst.; Mem., Bd of Trustees, Univ. of Miami. Hon. LLD, Mount Union Coll., 1959. Chevalier Légion d'Honneur, France, 1965. *Address:* 70 Park Drive, Bal Harbour, Fla 33154, USA.

HOPCROFT, George William; HM Diplomatic Service, retired; consultant on international relations; *b* 30 Sept. 1927; *s* of late Frederick Hopcroft and Dorothy Gertrude (*née* Bourne); *m* 1951, Audrey Joan Rodd; three *s* one *d. Educ:* Chiswick Grammar Sch.; London Univ. (BCom); Brasenose Coll., Oxford; INSEAD, Fontainebleau. Auditor with Wm R. Warner, 1946; entered Export Credits Guarantee Dept, 1946; Asst Trade Comr, Madras, 1953-57; Sen. Underwriter, ECGD, 1957-65; joined FO, 1965; First Sec. (Commercial), Amman, 1965-69; First Sec. (Econ.), Bonn, 1969-71; First Sec. (Comm.), Kuala Lumpur, 1971-75; FCO, 1975-78; Counsellor (Comm. and Econ.), Bangkok, 1978-81; FCO 1981. Lloyd's Underwriter, 1981-. Founder

Mem., Export and Overseas Trade Adv. Panel (EOTAP), 1982-; operational expert in for. affairs, attached to Govt of Belize, 1982-. *Recreations:* leisure and circumnavigation. *Address:* British High Commission, Belize House, Belmopan, Belize. *T:* 2146; (home) Ffrogs, Pond Road, Hook Heath, Woking, Surrey GU22 0JT. *T:* Woking 5121. *Clubs:* Yvonne Arnaud Theatre; Thames Valley Harriers (Vice-Pres., 1965-); British (Bangkok).

HOPE, family name of **Baron Glendevon, Marquess of Linlithgow** and **Baron Rankeillour.**

HOPE, Maj.-Gen. Adrian Price Webley, CB 1961; CBE 1952; *b* 21 Jan. 1911; *s* of late Adm. H. W. W. Hope, CB, CVO, DSO; *m* 1958, Mary Elizabeth, *e d* of Graham Partridge, Cotham Lodge, Newport, Pembrokeshire; no *c. Educ:* Winchester Coll.; RMC, Sandhurst. 2/Lt KOSB, 1931; Adjt, 1/KOSB, 1937-38; Staff Capt. A, Palestine, Egypt, 1938-40; DAQMG (Plans) Egypt, 1940-41; Instructor, Staff Coll., 1941; AQMG, Egypt, Sicily, Italy, 1941-44; Col Asst Quartermaster, Plans, India, 1945; Brig., Quartermaster, SE Asia, 1946; Comdt Sch. of Military Admin., 1947-48; Instructor, jssc, 1948-50; DQMG, GHQ, MELF, 1951-53; Student, idc, 1954; Brig. Quartermaster (ops), War Office, 1955-57; BGS, HQ, BAOR, 1958-59; MGA, GHQ, FARELF, 1959-61; Dir of Equipment Policy, War Office, 1961-64; Dep. Master-Gen. of the Ordnance, Ministry of Defence, 1964-66; retd 1966. *Address:* Monks Place, Charlton Horethorne, Sherborne, Dorset. *Club:* Army and Navy.

HOPE, Alan, JP; Leader, West Midlands County Council, since 1980; *b* 5 Jan. 1933; *s* of George Edward Thomas Hope and Vera Hope; *m* 1960, Marilyn Dawson; one *s* one *d. Educ:* George Dixon Grammar Sch., Birmingham. Councillor, Birmingham CC, 1964-73; West Midlands County Council: Councillor, 1973; Chairman: Trading Standards, 1977-79; Finance, 1979-80. JP Birmingham 1974. *Address:* Whitehaven, Rosemary Drive, Little Aston Park, Sutton Coldfield, West Midlands B74 3AG. *T:* 021-353 3011. *Club:* Royal Commonwealth Society.

HOPE, Sir Archibald (Philip), 17th Bt of Craighall, *cr* 1628; OBE 1945; DFC 1940; AE 1943; retired 1977; *b* 27 March 1912; *s* of 16th Bt and Hon. Mary Bruce, OBE, JP Midlothian, *e d* of 10th Lord Balfour of Burleigh; *S* father, 1924; *m* 1938, Ruth, *y d* of Carl Davis, Fryern, Storrington, Sussex; two *s. Educ:* Eton; Balliol Coll., Oxford. BA 1934; ACA 1939; FCA 1960; Mem. of Queen's Body Guard for Scotland (Royal Company of Archers). Served, RAFO, 1931-35; 601 (County of London) Sqdn AAF, 1935-39. Served War of 1939-45 (despatches twice, DFC, OBE). Wing Comdr (acting Group Capt.), AAF. Joined Airwork, 1945; Dir, 1951; resigned, June 1956; Dir, D. Napier & Son Ltd, 1956-61; Dir, Napier Aero Engines Ltd, 1961-68; Chief Exec., Napier Aero Engines Ltd, 1962-68; English Electric Co., 1968-70; Gp Treasurer, GEC Ltd, 1970-77. Mem., Air Transport Users Cttee, CAA, 1973-79, Dep. Chm. 1974-77, Chm. 1977-79. Chm., The Air League, 1965-68. FRAeS 1968. *Heir: s* John Carl Alexander Hope [*b* 10 June 1939; *m* 1968, Merle Pringle, *d* of Robert Douglas, Southside, Holbrook, Ipswich; one *s* one *d*]. *Address:* The Manor House, Somerford Keynes, near Cirencester, Glos GL7 6DL. *T:* Cirencester 861250. *Clubs:* Royal Air Force; New (Edinburgh); Nairobi (Nairobi).

HOPE, Bob, (Leslie Townes Hope), CBE (Hon.) 1976; Congressional Gold Medal, US, 1963; film, stage, radio, TV actor; *b* England, 29 May 1903; family migrated to US, 1907; *m* 1934, Dolores Reade; two adopted *s* two adopted *d. Educ:* Fairmont Gram. Sch. and High Sch., Cleveland, O. Started career as dance instructor, clerk, amateur boxer; formed dancing act for Fatty Arbuckle review. After Mid-West tours formed own Company in Chicago; toured New York and joined RKO Vaudeville and Keith Circuit; first important stage parts include: Ballyhoo, 1932; Roberta, 1933; Ziegfield Follies, 1935; first radio part, 1934. Entered films, 1938. *Films include:* Big Broadcast of 1938; Some Like It Hot; The Cat and the Canary; Road to Singapore; The Ghost Breakers; Road to Zanzibar; Star Spangled Rhythm; Nothing but the Truth; Louisiana Purchase; My Favorite Blonde; Road to Morocco; Let's Face It; Road to Utopia; Monsieur Beaucaire; My Favorite Brunette; They Got Me Covered; The Princess and the Pirate; Road to Rio; Where There's Life; The Great Lover; My Favorite Spy; Road to Bali; Son of Paleface; Here Come the Girls; Casanova's Big Night; The Seven Little Foys; The Iron Petticoat; That Certain Feeling; Beau James; The Facts of Life; Bachelor in Paradise; The Road to Hong Kong; Call Me Bwana; A Global Affair; Boy, Did I Get a Wrong Number!; Eight on the Run; How to Commit Marriage; Cancel My Reservation. *TV Series:* The Bob Hope Show, 1950-; numerous guest appearances. First Royal Command Performances. Awarded 44 honorary degrees; more than a thousand awards and citations for humanitarian and professional services. *Publications:* They've Got Me Covered, 1941; I Never Left Home, 1944; So This is Peace, 1946; This One's on Me, 1954; I Owe Russia $1200, 1963; Five Women I Love, 1966; The Last Christmas Show, 1974; Road to Hollywood, 1977. *Address:* Hope Enterprises Inc., 10,000 Riverside Drive, Suite 3, North Hollywood, Calif 91602, USA.

HOPE, Sir (Charles) Peter, KCMG 1972 (CMG 1956); TD 1945; Ambassador to Mexico, 1968-72; *b* 29 May 1912; *s* of G. L. N. Hope and H. M. V. Riddell, Weetwood, Mayfield, Sussex; *m* 1936, H. M. Turner, *d* of late G. L. Turner, company director; three *s. Educ:* Oratory Sch., Reading; London and Cambridge Univs. BSc (Hons), ACGI. Asst War Office, 1938; RA, TA, 1939; served until 1946 (TD). Transferred to Foreign Office and posted HM Embassy, Paris, as Temp. First Sec., 1946; transferred to United Nations Dept, Foreign Office, 1950; to HM Embassy, Bonn, as Counsellor, 1953; Foreign Office Spokesman (Head of News Dept Foreign Office), 1956–59; Minister, HM Embassy, Madrid, 1959–62; Consul-General, Houston, USA, 1963–64; Minister and Alternate UK Rep. to UN, 1965–68. Mem., Acad. of International Law. Grand Cross: Order of the Aztec Eagle; Constantine Order of St George; Grand Officer, Order of Merito Militense. *Recreations:* shooting and fishing. *Address:* North End House, Heyshott, Midhurst, Sussex. *Club:* White's.

HOPE, Rev. Dr David Michael; Vicar of All Saints', Margaret Street, since 1982; Warden, Community of St Mary the Virgin, Wantage, since 1980; *b* 14 April 1940. *Educ:* Nottingham Univ. (BA Hons Theol.); Linacre Coll., Oxford (DPhil). Curate of St John, Tuebrook, Liverpool, 1965–70; Chaplain, Church of Resurrection, Bucharest, 1967–68; Vicar, St Andrew, Warrington, 1970–74; Principal, St Stephen's House, Oxford, 1974–82. Examining Chaplain to: Bp of Bath and Wells, 1976–; Bp of Wakefield, 1979–; Bp of Norwich, 1981–. *Publication:* The Leonine Sacramentary, 1971. *Address:* 7 Margaret Street, W1N 8JQ. *T:* 01-636 1788.

HOPE, James Arthur David, QC (Scotland) 1978; *b* 27 June 1938; *s* of Arthur Henry Cecil Hope, OBE, WS, Edinburgh and Muriel Ann Neilson Hope (*née* Collie); *m* 1966, Katharine Mary Kerr, *d* of W. Mark Kerr, WS, Edinburgh; twin *s* one *d. Educ:* Edinburgh Acad.; Rugby Sch.; St John's Coll., Cambridge (Scholarship 1956, BA 1962, MA 1978); Edinburgh Univ. (LLB 1965). National Service, Seaforth Highlanders, 1957–59 (Lieutenant 1959). Admitted Faculty of Advocates, 1965; Standing Junior Counsel in Scotland to Board of Inland Revenue, 1974–78; Advocate-Depute, 1978–82. *Publications:* (ed jtly) Gloag & Henderson's Introduction to the Law of Scotland, 7th edn, 1968, asst editor, 8th edn, 1980; (ed jtly) Armour on Valuation for Rating, 4th edn, 1971. *Recreations:* walking, ornithology, music. *Address:* 34 India Street, Edinburgh EH3 6HB. *T:* 031-225 8245. *Club:* New (Edinburgh).

HOPE, James Kenneth, CBE 1946; DL; MA (Hon.); Recorder of City of Durham, 1942–74; Clerk of the Peace of County of Durham, Clerk of Durham County Council, and County Registration Officer, 1937–61; County Controller of Civil Defence, 1942–61; Clerk of Durham County Magistrates' Courts Cttee, 1952–61; *b* 12 July 1896; *s* of late J. Basil Hope, OBE, JP, and of Amy L. Hope, Bedford; *m* 1928, Mary Joyce, *yr d* of late Lieut-Col Rouse Orlebar, JP, DL, Hinwick, Beds; three *d. Educ:* Bedford Sch. Served European War, 1915–19: Commissioned Officer, 1st Bn Bedfordshire Regt. Solicitor, 1922; Asst Solicitor, Beds County Council, 1922–27; Dep. Clerk of the Peace and of County Council, Durham, 1927–37; T&AFA, County of Durham, 1937–61. Pres., Durham County Assoc. of Parish Councils, 1963–69. DL, Co. Durham, 1944; High Sheriff of Durham, 1966. *Address:* West Park, Lanchester, Co. Durham. *T:* Lanchester 520339. *Club:* Durham County (Durham).

See also Earl of Mexborough, Baron Vivian.

HOPE, Laurence Frank, OBE 1968; HM Diplomatic Service, retired; HM Consul General, Seattle, 1975–76; *b* 18 May 1918; *y s* of late Samuel Vaughan Trevylian Hope and late Ellen Edith Hope (*née* Cooler); *m* 1940, Doris Phyllis Rosa Hulbert; one *s* one *d. Educ:* County Grammar Sch., Lewes, Sussex. Served War, reaching rank of Major, in British Army (12th (2nd City of London Regt) Royal Fusiliers, TA and York and Lancaster Regt); Indian Army (7th Rajput Regt); Mil. Govt of Germany (Economic Div.), 1939–46. Bd of Trade, London, 1946–47; Asst Brit. Trade Comr, Pretoria, 1947–51; Cape Town, 1951–53; Bd of Trade, London, 1953–56; British Trade Comr, Sydney, 1956–60; Canberra, 1960–61; Lahore, 1961–63; Singapore, 1964; transferred to HM Diplomatic Service; Head of Commercial Section, High Commn, Singapore, 1965–68; Counsellor (Economic and Commercial), Lagos, 1969–72; HM Consul-Gen., Gothenburg, 1972–75. *Recreations:* oil painting, reading. *Address:* 22 Cranford Avenue, Exmouth, Devon EX8 2HU. *Club:* Oriental.

HOPE, Sir Peter; *see* Hope, Sir C. P.

HOPE, Sir Robert Holms-Kerr, 3rd Bt *cr* 1932; *b* 12 April 1900; *s* of Sir Harry Hope, 1st Bt and Margaret Binnie Holms-Kerr; *S* brother, 1979; *m* 1928, Eleanor (*d* 1967), *d* of late Very Rev. Marshall Lang, DD, Whittingehame, East Lothian. *Heir:* none. *Address:* Barneyhill, Dunbar, East Lothian.

HOPE-DUNBAR, Sir David, 8th Bt *cr* 1664; *b* 13 July 1941; *o s* of Sir Basil Douglas Hope-Dunbar, 7th Bt, and of his 2nd wife, Edith Maude Maclaren, *d* of late Malcolm Cross; *S* father, 1961; *m* 1971, Kathleen, *yr d* of late J. T. Kenrick; one *s* two *d. Educ:* Eton; Royal Agricultural College, Cirencester. Qualified: ARICS 1966. *Recreations:* fishing, shooting. *Heir:* *s* Charles Hope-Dunbar, *b* 11 March 1975. *Address:* Banks Farm, Kirkcudbright. *T:* Kirkcudbright 30424.

HOPE GILL, Cecil Gervase, MA; *b* 14 Dec. 1894; *s* of late Rt Rev. Charles Hope Gill and late Mary Hope Gill (*née* Thorp); *m* 1937, Kiti Colin, *e d* of Dr Alexander Campbell-Smith, Nelson, NZ. *Educ:* Windlesham House, Brighton; King William's Coll., IoM; Brighton Coll.; St John's Coll., Cambridge. Served in Royal Monmouthshire RE (Special Reserve), 1914–19 (wounded, despatches); Major 1919 (CRE Tournai); entered Levant Consular Service, 1920; served at Tangier (Vice-Consul), 1921; Casablanca, 1922; Saffi,

1923; Tetuan, 1923–25; Tangier (Asst Oriental Sec.), 1925–30; Jedda (Head of Chancery and Chargé d'Affaires), 1930–33; Alexandria (Consul), 1933–36; Addis Ababa, 1936; Imperial Defence Coll., 1937; Seattle, 1938–40; Baghdad (Asst Oriental Sec.), 1941; Léopoldville (Actg Consul-Gen.), 1941–42; Addis Ababa (First Sec.), 1942–44; Foreign Office, 1944–45; Tetuan (Consul-Gen.), 1945–52; retired from HM Foreign Service with rank of Consul-Gen., 1952. *Recreations:* travel, fruit growing, wine making, bee keeping, cinematography. *Address:* Interpares 51, Cerrado de Calderón, Málaga, Spain. *T:* 952 290 229. *Club:* Royal Automobile.

HOPE-JONES, Sir Arthur, KBE 1964; CMG 1956; Chairman, London Sumatra Plantations Ltd, since 1978; Director and/or Adviser to companies in UK and abroad, since 1960; *b* 26 May 1911; *s* of William and Dinah Elizabeth Hope-Jones; *m* 1938, Lucile Owen, New York; one *s* one *d. Educ:* Kirkby Lonsdale; Christ's Coll., Cambridge (1st cl. hons Hist. Tripos); Columbia Univ., New York (Commonwealth Fund Fellow); Brookings Inst., Washington, DC. Fellow of Christ's Coll., Cambridge, 1937–46. Served War, 1939–45 (TA Gen. List); seconded for duties at home and abroad; Economic Adviser in Persia to Anglo-Iranian Oil Co. (now BP), 1944–46; Economic Adviser Govt of Kenya, 1946–48; Mem., later Minister, for Commerce and Industry, Govt of Kenya, 1948–60; Member: Kenya Legislature, 1947–60; East African Legislative Assembly, 1955–60. Pres., Mesopotamia and Paiforce Officers Dinner Club. *Publications:* Income Tax in the Napoleonic Wars, 1939; contribs to learned society and financial periodicals. *Recreations:* walking, fishing, reading. *Address:* 1 Buckland Court, Buckland, Betchworth, Surrey. *T:* Betchworth 2179; PO Box 43561, Nairobi, Kenya, East Africa. *Clubs:* East India; Muthaiga Country, Nairobi (Nairobi).

HOPE-JONES, Ronald Christopher, CMG 1969; HM Diplomatic Service, retired; *b* 5 July 1920; *s* of William Hope-Jones and Winifred Coggin; *m* 1944, Pamela Hawker; two *s* one *d. Educ:* Eton (scholar); King's Coll., Cambridge (scholar). Served with HM Forces, 1940–45. 3rd Sec., Foreign Office, 1946, Paris, 1947; 2nd Sec., Beirut, 1949; 1st Sec., FO, 1952; Head of Chancery and Consul, Quito, 1955; Commercial Sec., Budapest, 1959; Head of Chancery, 1960; FO, 1961, Counsellor, 1963; UK Rep. to Internat. Atomic Energy Agency, Vienna, 1964–67; FCO 1967; Head of Disarmament Dept, 1967–70; Head of N African Dept, 1970–71; Counsellor, Brasilia, 1972–73; Ambassador in La Paz, 1973–77. *Address:* Wellfield House, Milk Lane, Headley, Bordon, Hants. *T:* Bordon 2793.

HOPE-MORLEY, family name of **Baron Hollenden.**

HOPE-WALLACE, (Dorothy) Jaqueline, CBE 1958; Member Board, National Corporation for the Care of Old People (now Centre for Policy on Ageing), 1973–81 (Chairman, 1978–80); *b* 1909; 2nd *d* of Charles Nugent Hope-Wallace and Mabel Chaplin. *Educ:* Lady Margaret Hall, Oxford. Entered Ministry of Labour, 1932; transferred to National Assistance Board, 1934; Under-Sec., 1958–65; Under-Sec., Min. of Housing and Local Govt, 1965–69, retired. Commonwealth Fellow, 1952–53. Comr, Public Works Loan Bd, 1974–78; Member Board: Corby Develt Corp., 1969–80; Governors, UCH, 1970–74; Inst. for Recorded Sound, 1971–74, 1979– (Chm. 1975–76); Chm., Friends of UCH, 1973–. *Recreations:* arts, travel, gardening. *Address:* 17 Ashley Court, Morpeth Terrace, SW1; Whitegate, Alciston, East Sussex.

HOPETOUN, Earl of; Adrian John Charles Hope; Stockbroker; *b* 1 July 1946; *s* and *heir* of Marquess of Linlithgow, *qv*; *m* 1968, Anne (marr. diss. 1978), *e d* of A. Leveson, Hall Place, Hants; two *s*; *m* 1980, Peta C. Binding; one *d. Educ:* Eton. Joined HM Navy, 1965. *Heir:* *s* Viscount Aithrie, *qv*. *Address:* Hopetoun House, South Queensferry, West Lothian; 36 Edwardes Square, W8. *Clubs:* Turf, White's.

HOPEWELL, John Prince; Consultant Surgeon (Urology), Royal Free Hospital, since 1957; *b* 1 Dec. 1920; *s* of Samuel Prince and Wilhelmina Hopewell; *m* 1959, Dr Natalie Bogdan (*d* 1975); one *s* one *d. Educ:* Bradfield Coll., Berks; King's Coll. Hosp., London. RAMC, 1945–48. Postgrad. education at King's Coll. Hosp. and Brighton, Sussex, and Hosp. for Sick Children, Gt Ormond Street. Formerly Cnslt Surgeon, Putney Hosp. and Frimley Hosp., Surrey. Mem., Hampstead DHA, 1982–; Past Chairman: Med. Cttee Royal Free Hosp.; N Camden Dist Med. Cttee. Founder Mem., British Transplantation Soc., 1972; Member: Internat. Soc. of Urology; British Assoc. Urol. Surgeons; Pres., Section of Urology, RSM, 1982–83. Founder Mem., Assoc. of Univ. Hospitals. Hon. Mem., NY Section, AUA. Hunterian Prof., RCS, 1958. *Publications:* contribs to Surgical Aspects of Medicine, Modern Treatment Year Book, and various medical journals. *Recreations:* photography, travel. *Address:* 11 Harley House, Upper Harley Street, NW1. *T:* 01-935 5291.

HOPKIN, Sir Bryan; *see* Hopkin, Sir W. A. B.

HOPKIN, David Armand; Chief Metropolitan Stipendiary Magistrate, since 1982; *b* 10 Jan. 1922; *s* of Daniel and Edmée Hopkin; *m* 1948, Doris Evelyn (*née* Whitaker); one *s* three *d. Educ:* St Paul's Sch., W Kensington; University Coll., Aberystwyth; Corpus Christi Coll., Cambridge (BA). Called to the Bar, Gray's Inn, 1949. Served in Army, 1942–47, Hon. Major, 1947. Member of Staff of Director of Public Prosecutions, 1950–70; Metropolitan Stipendiary Magistrate, 1970–. *Recreations:* fencing, tennis; administrative steward, British Boxing Board of Control. *Address:* 8 Crane Grove, N7. *T:* 01-607 0349.

HOPKIN, John Raymond; His Honour Judge Hopkin; a Circuit Judge, since 1979; *b* 23 June 1935; *s* of George Raymond Buxton Hopkin and Muriel Hopkin; *m* 1965, Susan Mary Limb; one *s* one *d. Educ:* King's Sch., Worcester. Called to Bar, Middle Temple, 1958; in practice at the Bar, 1959–. A Recorder of the Crown Court, 1978-79. *Recreations:* showing and judging pedigree dogs, fell walking and climbing, gardening. *Address:* Crownie, 19 Heath Avenue, Mansfield, Notts. *T:* Mansfield 643816. *Club:* Kennel.

HOPKIN, Sir (William Aylsham) Bryan, Kt 1971; CBE 1961; Professor of Economics, University College Cardiff, 1972-82 (on leave of absence, 1974-77); *b* 7 Dec. 1914; *s* of late William Hopkin and Lilian Hopkin (*née* Cottelle); *m* 1938, Renée Ricour; two *s. Educ:* Barry (Glam.) County Sch.; St John's Coll., Cambridge; Manchester Univ. Ministry of Health, 1938-41; Prime Minister's Statistical Branch, 1941-45; Royal Commn on Population, 1945-48; Econ. Sect., Cabinet Office, 1948-50; Central Statistical Office, 1950-52; Dir, Nat. Inst. of Econ. and Soc. Research, 1952-57; Sec., Council on Prices, Productivity, and Incomes, 1957-58; Dep. Dir, Econ. Sect., HM Treasury, 1958-65; Econ. Planning Unit, Mauritius, 1965; Min. of Overseas Devlt, 1966-67; Dir-Gen. of Economic Planning, ODM, 1967-69; Dir-Gen., DEA, 1969; Dep. Chief Econ. Adviser, HM Treasury, 1970-72; Head of Govt Economic Service and Chief Economic Advr, HM Treasury, 1974-77. Mem., Commonwealth Develt Corp., 1972-74. Chm., Manpower Services Cttee for Wales, 1978-79. *Address:* Aberthin House, Aberthin, near Cowbridge, South Glamorgan CF7 7HB. *T:* Cowbridge 2303.

HOPKINS, Alan Cripps Nind, MA Cantab, LLB Yale; Chairman, Wellman Engineering Corporation; *b* 27 Oct. 1926; *s* of late Rt Hon. Sir Richard V. N. Hopkins, GCB and Lady Hopkins; *m* 1st, 1954, Margaret Cameron (from whom divorced, 1962), *d* of E. C. Bolton, Waco, Texas, USA; one *s* ; 2nd, 1962, Venetia, *d* of Sir Edward Wills, Bt, *qv* ; twin *s. Educ:* Winchester Coll.; King's Coll., Cambridge; Yale University Law Sch., USA. BA Cantab 1947, MA 1950; LLB Yale 1952. Barrister, Inner Temple, 1948. MP (C and Nat L) Bristol North-East, 1959-66; PPS to Financial Sec. to Treasury, 1960-62. Dir, Dexion-Comino International Ltd. *Recreation:* travelling. *Address:* Hugditch, Ramsbury, near Marlborough, Wilts. *T:* Ramsbury 405; 59 Cadogan Place, SW1. *T:* 01-235 1846. *Club:* Brooks's.

HOPKINS, Anthony; actor since 1961; *b* Port Talbot, S Wales, 31 Dec. 1937; *s* of Richard and Muriel Hopkins; *m* 1st, 1968, Petronella (marr. diss. 1972); one *d* ; 2nd, 1973, Jennifer, *d* of Ronald Lynton. *Educ:* Cowbridge, S Wales; RADA; Cardiff Coll. of Drama. London debut as Metellus Cimber in Julius Caesar, Royal Court, 1964; National Theatre, 1966-73: Juno and the Paycock, A Flea in Her Ear, 1966; The Dance of Death, The Three Sisters, As You Like It (all male cast), 1967; The Architect and the Emperor of Assyria, A Woman Killed with Kindness, Coriolanus, 1971; Macbeth, 1972; The Taming of the Shrew, Chichester, 1972; Equus, USA, 1974-75, 1977; The Tempest, LA, 1979. *Films:* The Lion in Winter, 1967; The Looking Glass War, 1968; Hamlet, 1969; When Eight Bells Toll, 1971; Young Winston, 1972; A Doll's House, 1973; The Girl from Petrovka, 1973; All Creatures Great and Small, 1974; Dark Victory, 1975; Audrey Rose, 1976; A Bridge Too Far, 1976; International Velvet, 1977; Magic, 1978; The Elephant Man, 1980; A Change of Seasons, 1980. *American television films:* QB VII, 1973; Bruno Hauptmann in The Lindbergh Kidnapping Case, 1976; The Voyage of the Mayflower, 1979; The Bunker, The Acts of Peter and Paul, 1980; The Hunchback of Notre Dame, 1981; *BBC television:* Pierre Bezuhov in serial, War and Peace, 1972; Kean, 1978; Othello, 1981; Little Eyolf, 1982. Best TV Actor Award, SFTA, 1973; Best Actor Award, NY Drama Desk, 1975; Outer Critics Circle Award, 1975; American Authors and Celebrities Forum Award, 1975; Emmy award, 1976 and 1981; LA Drama Critics' Award, 1977. *Recreations:* reading, walking, piano. *Address:* c/o Peggy Thompson, 7 High Park Road, Kew, Surrey TW9 4BL.

HOPKINS, Antony, CBE 1976; composer and conductor; *b* 21 March 1921; *s* of late Hugh and of Marjorie Reynolds; adopted *c* of Major and Mrs T. H. C. Hopkins since 1925; *m* 1947, Alison Purves. *Educ:* Berkhamsted Sch.; Royal Coll. of Music. Won Chappell Gold Medal and Cobbett Prize at RCM, 1942; shortly became known as composer of incidental music for radio; numerous scores composed for BBC (2 for programmes winning Italia prize for best European programme of the year, 1952 and 1957). Composed music for many productions at Stratford and in West End. Dir, Intimate Opera Co., 1952-, and has written a number of chamber operas for this group; *ballets:* Etude and Café des Sports, for Sadler's Wells; *films (music) include:* Pickwick Papers, Decameron Nights, Cast a Dark Shadow, Billy Budd; John and the Magic Music Man (narr. and orch.; Grand Prix, Besançon Film Festival, 1976). Regular broadcaster with a series of programmes entitled Talking about Music. Formerly Gresham Prof. of Music, City Univ. Hon. FRCM 1964; Hon. RAM 1979; Hon. Fellow, Robinson Coll., Cambridge, 1980. DUniv. Stirling, 1980. *Publications:* Talking about Symphonies, 1961; Talking about Concertos, 1964; Music All Around Me, 1968; Lucy and Peterkin, 1968; Talking about Sonatas, 1971; Downbeat, 1977; Understanding Music, 1979; The Nine Symphonies of Beethoven, 1980; Songs for Swinging Golfers, 1981; Sounds of Music, 1982; Beating Time (autobiog.), 1982. *Recreations:* motoring, golf. *Address:* Woodyard Cottage, Ashridge, Berkhamsted, Herts. *T:* Little Gaddesden 2257.

HOPKINS, David Rex Eugène; Financial Counsellor, UK Delegation to NATO, since 1981; *b* 29 June 1930; *s* of Frank Hopkins and Vera (*née* Wimhurst); *m* 1955, Brenda Joyce Phillips; two *s* two *d. Educ:* Worthing High Sch.; Christ Church, Oxford (MA 1950; Dip. in Econs and Pol. Science, 1951). National Service Commn, RA, 1952; service in Korea. Asst Principal, WO, 1953; Principal, WO, 1957, MoD 1964; Asst Sec., 1967; Home Office, 1969-70; RCDS, 1971; Defence Equipment Secretariat, 1972; Dir, Headquarters Security, 1975. *Recreations:* church work, archaeological digging, fell-walking, military history. *Address:* 16 Hitherwood Drive, SE19 1XB. *T:* 01-670 7504.

HOPKINS, Douglas Edward, DMus (London); FRAM, FRCO, FGSM; Examiner, Royal Schools of Music, since 1937; Conductor, Stock Exchange Male Voice Choir, since 1956; *b* 23 Dec. 1902; *s* of Edward and Alice Hopkins; unmarried. *Educ:* St Paul's Cathedral Choir Sch.; Dulwich Coll.; Guildhall Sch. of Music (Ernest Palmer and Corporation Scholarships); Royal Academy of Music. Organist, Christ Church, Greyfriars, EC, 1921; Sub-Organist, St Paul's Cathedral, 1927; Prof., Royal Acad. of Music, 1937-78; Master of the Music, Peterborough Cathedral, 1946; Organist, Canterbury Cathedral, 1953-55; Musical Dir, St Felix Sch., Southwold, 1956-65; Organist, St Marylebone Parish Church, 1965-71; Founder, and Dir 1962-74, Holiday Course for Organists; Organist, Royal Meml Chapel, RMA Sandhurst, 1971-76. Since 1957 has done many overseas tours, inc. NZ, Africa, Malaysia, W Indies and Hong Kong. Conductor of Handel Soc., 1928-33, and, since that, of various other musical societies. Liveryman, Worshipful Co. of Musicians. *Address:* 244 Mytchett Road, Mytchett, Camberley, Surrey GU16 6AF.

HOPKINS, Admiral Sir Frank (Henry Edward), KCB 1964 (CB 1961); DSO 1942; DSC 1941; DL; Commander-in-Chief, Portsmouth, 1966-67; retired, 1967; *b* 23 June 1910; *s* of late E. F. L. Hopkins and Sybil Mary Walrond; *m* 1939, Lois Barbara, *d* of J. R. Cook, Cheam, Surrey. *Educ:* Stubbington House; Nautical Coll., Pangbourne. Joined Navy as Cadet, 1927; served in HM Ships: London, Tiger, Whitehall, Vortigern, Winchester, Courageous, Furious, 1928-38; War of 1939-45 (despatches, 1941), in No 826 Fleet Air Arm Squadron (Formidable), 1940-41, and comd No 830 Sqdn, 1941-42, based on Malta; USS Hancock and USS Intrepid, American Pacific Fleet, 1944-45; took part in following operations: Dunkirk, air operations over Europe, Battle of Matapan, evacuation of Crete, bombardment of Tripoli, Malta, Battle of Leyte Gulf; Korean War, Theseus, 1950 (despatches); Capt., 1950; Dir of Air Warfare, Admiralty, comd Myngs, Tyrian, Grenville, and Ark Royal, 1954-58; comd RNC Dartmouth, 1958-60; Rear-Adm. 1960; Flag Officer: Flying Training, 1960-62; Aircraft Carriers, 1962-63; Vice-Adm. 1962; a Lord Comr of the Admiralty, Deputy Chief of Naval Staff and Fifth Sea Lord, 1963-64; Dep. Chief of Naval Staff, MoD, 1964-66; Adm. 1966. DL Devon, 1982. American Legion of Merit, 1948; Comdr, Order of Sword, Sweden, 1954. *Recreations:* sailing, golf. *Address:* Kingswear Court Lodge, Kingswear, S Devon. *Clubs:* Naval and Military, Royal Yacht Squadron; Royal Naval Sailing Assoc.; Britannia Yacht.

HOPKINS, Prof. Harold Horace, FRS 1973; Professor of Applied Optics, University of Reading, since 1967; Head of Department of Physics, 1977-80; *b* 6 Dec. 1918; *s* of William Ernest and Teresa Ellen Hopkins; *m* 1950, Christine Dove Ridsdale; three *s* one *d. Educ:* Gateway Sch., Leicester; Univs of Leicester and London. BSc, PhD, DSc, FInstP. Physicist, Taylor, Taylor & Hobson, 1939-42; Royal Engrs, 1942; Physicist: MAP, 1942-45; W. Watson & Sons, 1945-47; Research Fellow, then Reader in Optics, Imperial Coll., 1947-67. Hon. Papers Sec. and Mem. Council, Physical Soc., 1947-59; President: Internat. Commn for Optics, 1969-72; Maths and Phys Sect., British Assoc., 1977. Thomas Young Orator, Inst. of Physics, 1960. Fellow: Optical Soc. of Amer., 1972; Soc. for Photo-Instrumentation Engrs, 1975; Hon. Member: Amer. Assoc. of Gynæcologic Laparoscopy, 1977; Brit. Assoc. of Urological Surgeons, 1977; Brit. Soc. for Gastroenterology, 1980; Hon. FRCS, 1979. Hon. DrèsSc Besançon, 1960; Hon. DSc Bristol, 1980; Hon. Dr Med. Munich, 1980. Ives Medal, Optical Soc. of Amer., 1978; St Peter's Medal, Brit. Assoc. of Urological Surgeons, 1979; First Distinguished Service Award, Amer. Soc. for Gastrointestinal Endoscopy, 1980. Inventions incl. zoom lenses, fibre optics and medical endoscopes. *Publications:* Wave Theory of Aberrations, 1951; (with J. G. Gow) Handbook of Urological Endoscopy, 1978; papers in Proc. Royal Soc., Proc. Phys. Soc., Optica Acta, Jl Optical Soc. Amer. *Recreations:* keyboard music, sailing, languages, woodwork. *Address:* 26 Cintra Avenue, Reading, Berks. *T:* Reading 871913.

HOPKINS, Sir James S. R. S.; *see* Scott-Hopkins.

HOPKINS, John; writer; *b* 27 Jan. 1931. *Plays:* This Story of Yours, Royal Court, 1968, Long Wharf Theatre, 1981; Find Your Way Home, Open Space, 1970, NY, 1974; Economic Necessity, Haymarket Theatre, Leicester, 1973; Next of Kin, Nat. Theatre, 1974; Losing Time, Manhattan Theatre Club, 1979; Valedictorian, Williston-Northampton Sch., 1982; *TV:* includes: Talking to a Stranger (quartet), 1968; That Quiet Earth; Walk into the Dark; Some Distant Shadow; The Greeks and their Gifts; A Story to Frighten the Children, 1976; Fathers and Families (sextet), 1977; scripts for Z-Cars (series); (with John Le Carré) Smiley's People (series), 1982; adaptations of classic novels; *film scripts:* The Offence, 1973; Murder by Decree, 1979. *Publications:* This Story of Yours, 1969; Find Your Way Home, 1971. *Address:* PO Box 157, Cutchogue, NY 11935, USA.

HOPKINS, Julian; *see* Hopkins, R. J.

HOPKINS, Rev. Canon Leslie Freeman; Canon Residentiary and Treasurer, Liverpool Cathedral, 1964-79, now Canon Emeritus; *b* 1914; *o s* of Joseph

Freeman and Mabel Hopkins, London; *m* 1940, Violet, *d* of Edgar Crick, Crayford; three *s* one *d*. *Educ*: City of London Sch. (Abbott Schol.); Exeter Coll., Oxford (Squire Schol. and Exhib.); Wells Theological Coll. BA 1937, 2nd Cl. Hon. Mods, 2nd Cl. Hons Theology; MA 1940; BD Oxon 1953. Deacon 1938, priest 1939; Curate of Crayford 1938, Nympsfield 1942; Priest-in-Charge, Holy Trinity, Charlton, 1942-45; Vicar of St Chrysostom's, Peckham, 1945-56; Surrogate, 1946-62; Vicar of All Saints, Battersea Park, 1956-62; Chief Inspector of Schools, Dio. of Southwark, 1954-62; Dir of Religious Education, Dio. of Liverpool, 1962-72; Chaplain of Josephine Butler Coll., 1962-72; Governor of Chester Coll., St Elphin's, Darley Dale and of Grammar Schs; Visiting Lectr in Religious Education; Mem. of Council: Guild of St Raphael, 1944 -; USPG. Liveryman, Glass Sellers Co.; Freeman, City of London. FRSA 1982. *Publications*: contribs to press and Syllabuses of Religious Education. *Recreations*: architecture and music. *Address*: Laurel Cottage, Peasmarsh, Rye, Sussex. *T*: Peasmarsh 559.

HOPKINS, (Richard) Julian; General Manager, Charity Christmas Card Council; *b* 12 Oct. 1940; *s* of Richard Robert Hopkins and late Grace Hilda (*née* Hatfield); *m* 1971, Maureen Mary (*née* Hoye); two *s* one *d*. *Educ*: Bedford School. Asst Manager, London Palladium, 1963; Central Services Manager, BBC, 1965; joined RSPCA as Accounts Manager, 1972, appointed Admin. and Finance Officer, 1976; Exec. Dir, 1978-82. Dir, and Mem. Exec. Cttee, World Soc. for Protection of Animals, 1980-. Mem., Farm Animal Welfare Council, 1980-. FBIM. *Recreation*: all theatre, but especially opera. *Address*: Dens Farm, Wadhurst, Sussex. *Club*: Royal Over-Seas League.

HOPKINS, Maj.-Gen. Ronald Nicholas Lamond, CBE 1943; Legion of Merit (US) 1944; psc; Australian Regular Army, retired; *b* 24 May 1897; *s* of Dr Wm F. Hopkins and Rosa M. B. Lamond; *m* 1926, Nora Frances Riceman; one *s*. *Educ*: Melbourne Grammar Sch.; RMC, Duntroon. Lieut Aust. Permt Forces, 1 Jan. 1918 and seconded 1st AIF; served with 6th Australian Light Horse Regt, Palestine, 1918; Staff Capt. 3rd Australian Light Horse Bde, 1919; Staff Coll., Quetta, 1927-28; attached Royal Tank Corps, England, 1937-38; 2nd AIF 1940; service in Middle East and New Guinea; Hon. ADC to Governor-Gen., 1943-45; late Dep. Chief of Gen. Staff (Australia). Chief Exec. Officer, Adelaide Festival of Arts, 1959-60. Hon. Fellow, St Mark's Coll., Univ. of Adelaide, 1977. *Publication*: Australian Armour, 1978. *Address*: 24 Wilsden Street, Walkerville, SA 5081, Australia. *Club*: Adelaide (Adelaide).

HOPKINSON, family name of **Baron Colyton.**

HOPKINSON, Albert Cyril, CBE 1970; FRIBA; consultant architect; *b* 2 Aug. 1911; *s* of Albert Hopkinson and Isaline Pollard (*née* Cox); *m* 1943, Lesley Evelyn Hill; one *s* one *d*. *Educ*: Univs of Sheffield and London. BA 1933; MA 1934. FRIBA 1949 (ARIBA 1934); Dipl. Town Planning and Civic Architecture, London, 1938. Min. of Public Building and Works, 1937-64; Dir of Works and Chief Architect, Home Office, 1964-75. *Recreations*: reading, walking. *Address*: 110b High Street, Berkhamsted, Herts. *T*: Berkhamsted 5256.

HOPKINSON, David Hugh; Chief Night Editor of The Times, since 1982; *b* 9 June 1930; *er s* of late C. G. Hopkinson. *Educ*: Sowerby Bridge Grammar Sch. Entered journalism on Huddersfield Examiner, 1950; Yorkshire Observer, 1954; Yorkshire Evening News, 1954; Evening Chronicle, Manchester, 1956; Chief Sub-Editor, Sunday Graphic, London, 1957; Asst Editor, Evening Chronicle, Newcastle upon Tyne, 1959; Chief Asst Editor, Sunday Graphic, 1960; Dep. Editor, Sheffield Telegraph, 1961, Editor, 1962-64; Editor, The Birmingham Post, 1964-73; Dir, Birmingham Post & Mail Ltd, 1967-80; Editor, Birmingham Evening Mail, 1974-79; Editor-in-Chief, Evening Mail series, 1975-79, Birmingham Post and Evening Mail, 1979-80; Asst to Editor of The Times, 1981. Member: Lord Justice Phillimore's Cttee inquiring into law of contempt; International Press Institute; Associate Mem., Justice (British br. of Internat. Commn of Jurists). National Press Award, Journalist of the Year, 1963. *Address*: 77 Woodlands Road, Moseley, Birmingham B11 4EJ.

HOPKINSON, Maj.-Gen. Gerald Charles, CB 1960; DSO 1945; OBE 1953; MC 1938; retired; *b* Wellington, Som, 27 May 1910; *s* of Capt. Charles Reginald Hopkinson; *m* 1938, Rhona Marion (*d* 1979), *d* of Henry Turner, Farnham, Surrey; one *d*. *Educ*: Imperial Service Coll.; RMC Sandhurst. Second Lieut, Royal Tank Corps, 1930; served War of 1939-45 (India, Middle East, Italy and Europe); comd 1st RTR, Korea, 1952-53; 33rd Armoured Bde, BAOR, 1953-57; GOC 4th Div., BAOR, 1958-59; Dir, RAC, War Office, Oct. 1959-62. Lieut-Col 1952; Col 1953; Maj.-Gen. 1958. Order of the Crown and Croix de Guerre (Belgium). *Address*: Rosemount, Wrantage, Taunton, Somerset. *Club*: Army and Navy.

HOPKINSON, Giles; Under-Secretary, Department of Transport, since 1979; *b* 20 Nov. 1931; *s* of late Arthur John Hopkinson, CIE, ICS, and of Eleanor (*née* Richardson); *m* 1956, Eleanor Jean Riddell; three *d*. *Educ*: Marlborough Coll.; Leeds Univ. (BSc). E. & J. Richardson Ltd, 1956-57; Forestal Land, Timber and Rly Co. Ltd, 1957-58; DSIR: Scientific Officer, 1958-61; Sen. Scientific Officer, 1961-64; Private Sec. to Perm. Sec., 1963-64; Principal, MoT, 1964-71; Asst Sec., DoE, 1971; Under-Sec., DoE, 1976. *Recreations*: music, landscape gardening. *Address*: Digswell Water Mill, Digswell Lane, Welwyn Garden City, Herts AL7 1SW. *Club*: Royal Commonwealth Society.

HOPKINSON, Col (Henry) Somerset (Parnell), OBE 1944; DL; *b* 16 Oct. 1899; *s* of Col H. C. B. Hopkinson, CMG, CBE, and Hon. M. F. L. Parnell, *d* of 3rd Baron Congleton; *m* 1928, Josephine Marie de Gilibert Addison, *d* of Lieut-Col A. J. R. Addison, Royal Irish Rifles; one *d* (and one *d* decd). *Educ*: Winchester and RMC. 2nd Lt Rifle Brigade, 1919; Major, 1938; Staff Coll., 1933-34; Brig. 1945; served War of 1939-45, Palestine, Burma, India; retd 1948. County Councillor Monmouthshire, 1958-64; JP 1950, DL 1951, High Sheriff 1964, Gwent, formerly Monmouthshire. FSA, FSG. *Recreations*: shooting, foreign travel. *Address*: Llanfihangel Court, Abergavenny, Gwent. *T*: Crucorney 217. *Club*: Army and Navy.
See also D. B. Johnson.

HOPKINSON, Sir (Henry) Thomas, Kt 1978; CBE 1967; author, journalist; *b* 19 April 1905; 2nd *s* of late Archdeacon J. H. Hopkinson; *m* 1st, Antonia White; one *d* (and one step *d*); 2nd, Gerti Deutsch; two *d*; 3rd, 1953, Dorothy, widow of Hugh Kingsmill. *Educ*: St Edward's Sch., Oxford; Pembroke Coll., Oxford (Scholar). BA, 1927; MA, 1932; Hon. Fellow, 1978. After working as a freelance journalist and in advertising and publicity, was appointed Asst Editor of the Clarion, 1934; Asst Editor, Weekly Illustrated, 1934-38; helped in preparation and launching of Picture Post; Editor, 1940-50; also edited Lilliput, 1941-46; Features Editor, News Chronicle, 1954-56; Editor, Drum Magazine, 1958-61. Dir for Africa of Internat. Press Inst., 1963-66. Senior Fellow in Press Studies, Univ. of Sussex, 1967-69; Vis. Prof. of Journalism, University of Minnesota, 1968-69; Dir, Course in Journalism Studies, UC Cardiff, 1971-75, Hon. Professorial Fellow, 1978. Hon. FRPS 1976. *Publications*: A Wise Man Foolish, 1930; A Strong Hand at the Helm, 1933; The Man Below, 1939; Mist in the Tagus, 1946; The Transitory Venus (short stories), 1948; Down the Long Slide, 1949; Love's Apprentice, 1953; short life of George Orwell, 1953, in British Council series Writers and Their Work; The Lady and the Cut-Throat (short stories), 1958; In the Fiery Continent, 1962; South Africa, 1964 (New York); (ed) Picture Post, 1938-1950, 1970; (with D. Hopkinson) Much Silence: the life and work of Meher Baba, 1974; Treasures of the Royal Photographic Society, 1980; Of This Our Time (autobiog.), 1982; stories in English and American magazines, and for radio. *Address*: 6 Marine Parade, Penarth, Cardiff. *T*: Cardiff 703354.

HOPKINSON, Maj.-Gen. John Charles Oswald Rooke; Chief-of-Staff, Headquarters Allied Forces Northern Europe, since 1982; *b* 31 July 1931; *s* of Lt-Col John Oliver Hopkinson and Aileen Disney Hopkinson (*née* Rooke); *m* 1956, Sarah Elizabeth, *d* of Maj.-Gen. M. H. P. Sayers, *qv*; three *s* one *d*. *Educ*: Stonyhurst Coll.; RMA, Sandhurst. sc 1963, jssc 1968, rcds 1979. Commanding Officer, 1st Bn Queen's Own Highlanders, 1972-74 (despatches); Dep. Comdr 2nd Armoured Division, and Comdr Osnabrück Garrison, 1977-78; Director Operational Requirements 3 (Army), 1980-82. Colonel Queen's Own Highlanders, 1983. *Recreations*: shooting, fishing, sailing. *Address*: Bigsweir, Gloucestershire. *Club*: Army and Navy.

HOPKINSON, Prof. Ralph Galbraith; Haden-Pilkington Professor of Environmental Design and Engineering, University College London, 1965-76, now Emeritus; *b* 13 Aug. 1913; *s* of late Ralph Galbraith Hopkinson and Beatrice Frances Wright; *m* 1938, Dora Beryl (*née* Churchill); two *s* one *d* (and one *s* decd). *Educ*: Erith Grammar Sch.; Faraday House. BSc (Eng), PhD, CEng, FIEE, FRPS. Research Engr, GEC, 1934-47, lighting and radar; Principal Scientific Officer, DSIR Building Research Stn, 1947-64 (Special Merit appointment, 1960); Dean, Faculty of Environmental Studies, UCL, 1972-74. Work on: human response to buildings, leading to concept of environmental design by engr-physicists and architects in collab.; schools with Min. of Educn Develt Gp and on hosps with Nuffield Foundn, 1949-65; lighting design of new Tate Gallery extension and Stock Exchange Market Hall (Design Award of Distinction, Illum. Engrg Soc. of USA, 1974); visual and noise intrusion (urban motorways) for DoE, 1970; consultant, DoE Road Construction Unit. Pres., Illuminating Engrg Soc., 1965-66 (Gold Medallist, 1972; Hon. Mem., 1976); Mem., Royal Soc. Study Gp on Human Biology in the Urban Environment, 1972-74. Trustee, British Institution Fund, 1972-77. Hon. FRIBA 1969, Hon. FCIBS 1977. *Publications*: Architectural Physics: Lighting, 1963; Hospital Lighting, 1964; Daylighting, 1966; (with J. D. Kay) The Lighting of Buildings, 1969; Lighting and Seeing, 1969; The Ergonomics of Lighting, 1970; Visual Intrusion (RTPI), 1972; papers in Nature, Jl Optical Soc. of America, Jl Psychol., Illum. Eng, etc. *Recreations*: music, human sciences, boating, walking. *Address*: Bartlett School of Architecture and Planning, University College London, Wates House, 22 Gordon Street, WC1H 0QB.

HOPKINSON, Col Somerset; see Hopkinson, Col H. S. P.

HOPKINSON, Sir Thomas; see Hopkinson, Sir H. T.

HOPPE, Iver; Kt of Danish Dannebrog; Kt of Icelandic Falcon; Chairman and Chief Executive, Navalicon Ltd A/S, Denmark; *b* Denmark, 25 July 1920; *s* of Arthur Hans Knudsen Hoppe and Gerda (*née* Raun Byberg); *m* 1943, Ingeborg Lassen; one *d*. *Educ*: Aarhus Katedralskole; Copenhagen Univ. (Law Faculty), 1944. Acting Lecturer, Copenhagen Univ., 1946; Advocate to High Court and Court of Appeal, 1948; Jurisprudential Lecturer, Copenhagen Univ., 1952-58; study sojourn in Switzerland, 1949. A. P. Møller Concern, Copenhagen, 1955-71: Asst Dir, 1960; Man. Dir of Odense Steel Shipyard, Ltd, Odense and Lindø, 1964-71. Chm. A/S Svendborg Skibsvaerft, 1968-71; Mem. Bd of Dansk Boreselskab A/S and other cos until 1971; Man. Dir and Chief Exec., Harland and Wolff Ltd, Belfast, 1971-74; Member: Bd of Den

Danske Landmandsbank A/S, 1970-72; Council of Danish National Bank, 1967-71; Bd of Danish Ship Credit Fund, 1965-71; Assoc. of Danish Shipyards, 1964-71; Assoc. of Employers within the Iron and Metal Industry in Denmark, 1967-71; Assoc. of Danish Industries, 1965-72; West of England Steam Ship Owners Protection and Indemnity Assoc., Ltd, 1960-66; Danish Acad. of Technical Sciences; Shipbuilders and Repairers Nat. Assoc. Exec. Council and Management Bd, 1971-74; British Iron and Steel Consumers' Council, 1971-74; Gen. Cttee, Lloyd's Register of Shipping; British Cttee, Det Norske Veritas; Amer. Bureau of Shipping, and other Danish and foreign instns. *Recreations:* reading, swimming, mountain walking, farming. *Address:* Malmmosegaard, Dyreborgvej 7, DK-5600 Faaborg, Denmark. *Club:* Travellers'.

HOPPER, Prof. Frederick Ernest, MDS, FDSRCS; FFDRCSI; Professor of Dental Surgery and Dean of the School of Dentistry, University of Leeds, since 1959; Consultant Dental Surgeon, Leeds Area Health Authority, since 1959; Chairman, Board of Faculty of Medicine, University of Leeds, 1975-78; *b* 22 Nov. 1919; *s* of Frederick Ernest Hopper, MPS and Margaret Ann Carlyle; *m* 1949, Gudrun Eik-Nes, LDSRCS, *d* of Prost Knut Eik-Nes and Nina Eik-Nes, Trondheim, Norway; three *s*. *Educ:* Dame Allan's Sch., Newcastle upon Tyne; King's Coll., University of Durham. BDS (with dist.) 1943; FDSRCS 1948; MDS 1958. House Surg., Newcastle upon Tyne Dental Hosp. and Royal Dental Hospital, 1943-44; served in EMS in Maxillo-Facial Centres at E Grinstead and Shotley Bridge, 1944-46; successively Lecturer, 1946, and Sen. Lecturer, 1956, in Periodontal Diseases, King's Coll., University of Durham; Lecturer in Dental Pharmacology and Therapeutics, 1947-59; Examiner in Dental subjects, Univs of Durham, Edinburgh, St Andrews, Bristol, Liverpool; Dental Surgeon in charge Parodontal Dept, Newcastle upon Tyne Dental Hosp., and Sen. Dental Surg., Plastic and Jaw Unit, Shotley Bridge, 1946-59; Cons. Dent. Surg., United Newcastle Hosps, 1955-59. Hon. Treas., Brit. Soc. of Periodontology, 1949-53, Pres. 1954. Member: General Dental Council, 1959- (Chm., Educn Cttee, 1980-); Brit. Dental Assoc., 1943-; Internat. Dental Fedn, 1948-. *Publications:* contribs to med. and dental jls. *Recreations:* photography (still and ciné); golf. *Address:* School of Dentistry, Leeds LS2 9LU. *T:* 440111. *Clubs:* Savage; Alwoodley Golf (Leeds).

HOPPER, Prof. Robert John; Professor of Ancient History, University of Sheffield, 1955-75, now Emeritus; *b* 13 Aug. 1910; *s* of Robert and Alice Hopper, Cardiff, Glamorgan; *m* 1939, Henriette, *d* of Edward and Ella Kiernan, Timperley, Cheshire; no *c*. *Educ:* Mount Radford Sch., Exeter; University of Wales; Gonville and Caius Coll., Cambridge. Served Royal Welch Fusiliers and Intelligence Corps, 1941-45. Macmillan Student of British Sch. at Athens, 1935-37; Fellow of Univ. of Wales (in Athens and Rome), 1936-38; Lectr in Classics, UCW Aberystwyth, 1938-41 and 1945-47; Senior Lecturer in Ancient History, Univ. of Sheffield, 1947-55, Dean of Faculty of Arts, 1967-70. FRNS 1949; FSA 1951. *Publications:* The Acropolis, 1971; The Early Greeks, 1976; Greek Trade and Industry, 1978; articles in classical and archæological periodicals. *Recreations:* numismatics; foreign travel. *Address:* 41 Barholm Road, Sheffield S10 5RR. *T:* Sheffield 302587. *Club:* National Liberal.

HOPPER, William Joseph; Member (C) European Parliament, Greater Manchester West, since 1979; *b* 9 Aug. 1929; *s* of I. Vance Hopper and Jennie Josephine Hopper; *m* 1959, Melisa Carmen Humphreys (marr. diss.); one *d*. *Educ:* Langside Elementary Sch., Glasgow; Queen's Park Secondary Sch., Glasgow; Glasgow Univ. (MA Hons (Mod. Langs) 1953). Financial Analyst, W. R. Grace & Co., NY, 1956-59; London Office Manager, H. Hentz & Co., Members, NY Stock Exchange, 1960-66; Gen. Manager, S. G. Warburg & Co. Ltd, 1966-69; Hill Samuel & Co. Ltd, 1969-74; Consultant, Morgan Grenfell & Co. Ltd, 1979- (Dir, 1974-79). Co-founder (1969) and first Chm. (now Mem., Exec. Cttee), Inst. for Fiscal Studies, London. *Publication:* A Turntable for Capital, 1969. *Recreations:* listening to music, gardening. *Address:* 23 Great Winchester Street, EC2P 2AX. *T:* 01-588 4545. *Club:* St James's (Manchester).

HOPTHROW, Brig. Harry Ewart, CBE 1946 (OBE 1940); Council Member, Solent Protection Society; *b* 13 Nov. 1896; *s* of Frederick Hopthrow; *m* 1925, Audrey Kassel (*d* 1975), *d* of J. Lewer; one *s* one *d*. *Educ:* Queen Elizabeth's Grammar Sch., Gainsborough; City Sch., Lincoln; Loughborough Coll. Served European War 1915-1918, RE, France and Flanders. Civil and Mechanical Engineer, ICI Ltd, 1925-39; Commanded 107 Co. RE, 1931-35, Major; Asst Dir of Works, GHQ, BEF, 1939-40, Lt-Col; served France and Flanders, 1939-40 and 1944; Dep. Chief Engineer: Home Forces, 1940-41, and Western Comd, 1941; Dep. Controller Mil. Works Service, War Office, 1941-43; Dir of Fortifications and Works, WO, 1943-45; Asst Sec., ICI Ltd, 1945-58; Hon. Secretary and a Vice-Pres., Royal Institution, 1960-68. AMIMechE 1924, FIMechE 1933. Mem. Central Advisory Water Cttee (Min. of Housing and Local Govt), 1946-70; Mem. Cttee of Inquiry into Inland Waterways (Bowes Cttee), 1956-58; Vice-Chm. IoW River and Water Authority, 1964-73; UK Rep. to Council of European Industrial Fedns, 1965-73. Vice-Pres., Round Tables on Pollution, 1965-73. Officer of American Legion of Merit, 1946. *Recreation:* yachting. *Address:* Surrey House, Cowes, Isle of Wight. *T:* Cowes 292430. *Clubs:* Army and Navy; Royal Engineer Yacht; Royal London Yacht, Island Sailing (Cowes).

HOPWOOD, family name of **Baron Southborough**.

HOPWOOD, Prof. David Alan, FRS 1979; John Innes Professor of Genetics, University of East Anglia and Head of the Genetics Department, John Innes Institute, since 1968; *b* 19 Aug. 1933; *s* of Herbert Hopwood and Dora Hopwood (née Grant); *m* 1962, Joyce Lilian Bloom; two *s* one *d*. *Educ:* Purbrook Park County High Sch., Hants; Lymm Grammar Sch., Cheshire; St John's Coll., Cambridge (MA, PhD). DSc (Glasgow). Whytehead Major Scholar, St John's Coll., Cambridge, 1951-54; John Stothert Bye-Fellow, Magdalene Coll., Cambridge, 1956-58; Res. Fellow, St John's Coll., 1958-61; Univ. Demonstrator, Univ. of Cambridge, 1957-61; Lectr in Genetics, Univ. of Glasgow, 1961-68. *Publications:* numerous articles and chapters in scientific jls and books. *Address:* John Innes Institute, Colney Lane, Norwich NR4 7UH. *T:* Norwich 52571.

HOPWOOD, Brig. John Adam, CBE 1958; DSO 1943 (and Bar 1944); *b* 26 Jan. 1910; *s* of Ernest Hopwood and Constance Marion Adam; *m* Cressida Mona Browning, *d* of R. Campbell Browning, Armsworth, Alresford, Hants; no *c*. *Educ:* St David's, Reigate; Eton; RMC Sandhurst. Commissioned Black Watch, 1930; served with 1st Bn in India, 1931-35; ADC to Governor of Bengal, 1935-37; with 1st Bn Black Watch, and BEF in France, 1939-40; Staff Coll., 1940; Bde Major, 154 Inf. Bde, 1941; Second in Comd, 7th Bn Black Watch, N Africa and Sicily, 1942; comd 1st Bn Black Watch, Sicily and NW Europe, 1943-45; comd 154 and 156 Inf. Bdes, Germany, 1946; Mem. Training Mission to Iraq Army, Baghdad, 1946-48; attended jssc, Latimer, 1948; Liaison Appt, RAF Fighter Comd, 1949; comd 44 Parachute Bde (TA) London, 1950-53; Col i/c Admin., Hong Kong, 1953-55; comd 3 Inf. Bde, Canal Zone, UK, Cyprus, 1955-58; Vice-Pres., Regular Commissions Board, 1958-60, retd. Chm., Honiton Div. Cons. Assoc., 1977-80. Awarded Bronze Lion of Netherlands. *Recreations:* ornithology (MBOU), field sports, travel. *Address:* Gilletts Farm, Yarcombe, Honiton, Devon. *T:* Chard 3121. *Club:* Naval and Military.

HORAM, John Rhodes; MP Gateshead West since 1970 (Lab, 1970-81, SDP, since 1981); *b* 7 March 1939; *s* of Sydney Horam, Preston; *m* 1977, Iris Crawley. *Educ:* Silcoates Sch., Wakefield; Univ. of Cambridge. Market research officer, Rowntree & Co., 1960-62; leader and feature writer: Financial Times, 1962-65; The Economist, 1965-68; Jt Man. Dir, Commodities Res. Unit Ltd, 1968-70. Contested (Lab) Folkestone and Hythe, 1966. Parly Under-Sec. of State, Dept of Transport, 1976-79; Labour spokesman on econ. affairs, 1979-81; Parly spokesman on econ. affairs, SDP, 1981-. Mem., SDP Nat. Steering Cttee, 1981-. *Address:* 19 West Street, King's Cliffe, Peterborough PE8 6XB; 2 Howard House, Dolphin Square, SW1.

HORAN, Rt. Rev. Forbes Trevor; *b* 22 May 1905; *s* of Rev. Frederick Seymour Horan and Mary Katherine Horan; *m* 1939, Veronica, *d* of late Rt Rev. J. N. Bateman-Champain, sometime Bishop of Knaresborough; two *s* two *d*. *Educ:* Sherborne and Trinity Hall, Cambridge. RMC Sandhurst, 1924-25; Oxford and Bucks Lt Infantry, Lieutenant, 1925-29; Trinity Hall, Cambridge, 1929-32; Westcott House, Cambridge, 1932-33; Curate, St Luke's, Newcastle upon Tyne, 1933-35; Curate, St George's, Jesmond, Newcastle upon Tyne, 1935-37; Priest-in-charge, St Peter's, Balkwell, 1937-40; RNVR, 1940-45; Vicar of St Chad's, Shrewsbury, 1945-52; Vicar of Huddersfield Parish Church, 1952-60; Bishop Suffragan of Tewkesbury, 1960-73. *Recreations:* gardening, walking. *Address:* 79 Naunton Lane, Leckhampton, Cheltenham, Gloucestershire. *T:* Cheltenham 27313.

HORD, Brian Howard; Member (C) London West, European Parliament, since 1979; Whip of European Democratic Group, since 1982; Partner, Howard Hord & Palmer, Chartered Surveyors, since 1975; *b* 20 June 1934; *s* of Edwin Charles and Winifred Hannah Hord; *m* 1960, Christine Marian Lucas; two *s*. *Educ:* Reedham Sch.; Purley Grammar Sch. FRICS. County Planning Dept, Mddx CC, 1950-51; Surveyor, private practice, 1951-57; National Service, RAF, 1957-59; Estates Surveyor, United Drapery Stores, 1959-66; Richard Costain Ltd, 1966-70; Director, Capcount UK Ltd, principal subsid. of Capital & Counties Property Co. Ltd, 1970-75. *Publication:* (jtly) Rates-Realism or Rebellion. *Recreations:* squash racquets, top-fruit growing, bee-keeping. *Address:* Whitesides, Pilgrims Way East, Otford, Sevenoaks, Kent TN14 5QN. *T:* Otford 3743. *Club:* Carlton.

HORDER, family name of **Baron Horder**.

HORDER, 2nd Baron *cr* 1933, of Ashford in the County of Southampton; **Thomas Mervyn Horder**; Bt, of Shaston, 1923; *b* 8 Dec. 1910; *s* of 1st Baron Horder, GCVO, MD, FRCP, and Geraldine Rose (*d* 1954), *o d* of Arthur Doggett, Newnham Manor, Herts; *S* father, 1955. *Educ:* Winchester; Trinity Coll., Cambridge. BA 1932; MA 1937. Served War of 1939-45: HQ, RAF Fighter Comd (despatches); Air HQ, India, 1942-44; Headquarters, South-East Asia Command, 1944-45; United Kingdom Liaison Mission, Tokyo, 1945-46; Chairman, Gerald Duckworth & Co. Ltd, 1948-70. *Publications:* The Little Genius, 1966; (ed) Ronald Firbank: memoirs and critiques, 1977; *music:* (ed) The Orange Caro Book, 1962; Norfolk Dances for string orchestra, 1965; Six Betjeman Songs, 1967; A Shropshire Lad (songs), 1980; (ed) The Easter Carol Book, 1982. *Recreations:* music, idling. *Address:* c/o Gerald Duckworth & Co. Ltd, 43 Gloucester Crescent, NW1 7DY.

HORDER, Dr John Plaistowe, CBE 1981 (OBE 1971); FRCP, FRCPE, FRCGP, FRCPsych; general practitioner of medicine, retired; President, Royal College of General Practitioners, 1979-82; *b* 9 Dec. 1919; *s* of Gerald

Morley Horder and Emma Ruth Horder; *m* 1940, Elizabeth June Wilson; two *s* two *d*. *Educ*: Lancing Coll.; University Coll., Oxford (BA 1945); London Hosp. (BM BCh 1948). FRCP 1972 (MRCP 1951); FRCGP 1970 (MRCGP 1957); FRCPsych 1980 (MRCPsych 1975); FRCPE 1982. Consultant, 1959, Travelling Fellow, 1964, WHO; Lectr, London School of Economics and Pol. Sci., 1964-69; Sir Harry Jeffcott Vis. Professor, Univ. of Nottingham, 1975; John Hunt Fellow, 1974-77, Wolfson Travelling Prof., 1978, Royal Coll. of Gen. Practitioners. Consultant Adviser, DHSS, 1978-. Pres., Sect. of Gen. Practice, RSM, 1970. Hon. Mem., Coll. of Family Physicians of Canada. *Publications*: ed and co-author, The Future General Practitioner—learning and teaching, 1972; articles on general practice—training for and psychiatry in. . . ., 1953-81. *Recreations*: painting, music. *Address*: 98 Regent's Park Road, NW1. *T*: 01-267 4411.

HORDERN, Michael Murray, CBE 1972; actor; *b* 3 Oct. 1911; *s* of Capt. Edward Joseph Calverly Hordern, CIE, RIN, and Margaret Emily (*née* Murray); *m* 1943, Grace Eveline Mortimer; one *d*. *Educ*: Brighton Coll. Formerly in business with The Educational Supply Assoc., playing meanwhile as an amateur at St Pancras People's Theatre. First professional appearance as Lodovico in Othello, People's Palace, 1937. Two seasons of repertory at Little Theatre, Bristol, 1937-39; War service in Navy, 1940-46; demobilised as Lieut-Comdr, RNVR. Parts include: Mr Toad in Toad of Toad Hall, at Stratford, 1948 and 1949; Ivanov in Ivanov, Arts Theatre, 1950. Stratford Season, 1952: Jacques, Menenius, Caliban. Old Vic Season, 1953-54: Polonius, King John, Malvolio, Prospero. "BB" in The Doctor's Dilemma, Saville, 1956; Old Vic Season, 1958-59: Cassius, Macbeth. Ulysses (Troilus and Cressida), Edinburgh Fest., 1962; Herbert Georg Beutler in The Physicists, Aldwych, 1963; Southman in Saint's Day, St Martin's, 1965; Relatively Speaking, Duke of York's, 1967; A Delicate Balance, Aldwych, 1969; King Lear, Nottingham Playhouse, 1969; Flint, Criterion, 1970; National Theatre: Jumpers, 1972 and 1976, Gaunt in Richard II, 1972, The Cherry Orchard, 1973; The Ordeal of Gilbert Pinfold, Manchester, 1977, Round House, 1979; RSC Stratford: Prospero in The Tempest, Armado in Love's Labour's Lost, 1978; also many leading parts in films, radio and television. *Recreation*: fishing. *Address*: Flat Y, Rectory Chambers, Old Church Street, SW3 5DA. *Clubs*: Garrick; Flyfishers'.

HORDERN, Peter Maudslay; MP (C) Horsham and Crawley, since 1974 (Horsham, 1964-74); *b* 18 April 1929; British; *s* of C. H. Hordern, MBE; *m* 1964, Susan Chataway; two *s* one *d*. *Educ*: Geelong Grammar Sch., Australia; Christ Church, Oxford, 1949-52 (MA). Mem. of Stock Exchange, London, 1957-74. Director: Petrofina (UK) Ltd, 1973-; Atlas Electric & General Trust, 1975-; Alliance Investment Co., 1978-. Chm., Cons. Parly Finance Cttee, 1970-72; Member: Exec., 1922 Cttee, 1968-; Public Accts Cttee, 1970-. *Recreations*: golf, reading and travel. *Address*: 55 Cadogan Street, SW3.

HORE-RUTHVEN, family name of Earl of Gowrie.

HORLICK, Vice-Adm. Sir Edwin John, (Sir Ted Horlick), KBE 1981; FIMechE, MIMarE; Director General Ships, Ministry of Defence (Navy), since 1979; Chief Naval Engineer Officer, since 1981; *b* 1925; *m* ; four *s*. *Educ*: Bedford Modern Sch. Joined RN, 1943; Sqdn Eng. Officer, 2nd Frigate Sqdn, 1960-63; Ship Dept, MoD, 1963-66; First Asst to Chief Engineer, HM Dockyard, Singapore, 1966-68; Asst Dir Submarines, 1969-72; SOWC 1973; Fleet Marine Engineering Officer, Staff of C-in-C Fleet, 1973-75; RCDS 1976; Dir Project Team Submarine/Polaris, 1977-79. FIMechE, MIMarE. *Recreations*: golf, Rugby administration, DIY. *Address*: Director General Ships, Ministry of Defence (Navy), Foxhill, Bath BA1 5AB. *Clubs*: Army and Navy, Royal Commonwealth Society.

HORLICK, Sir John (James Macdonald), 5th Bt *cr* 1914; Chairman, Highland Fish Farmers, since 1978; Partner, Tournaig Farming Company, since 1973; *b* 9 April 1922; *s* of Lt-Col Sir James Horlick, 4th Bt, OBE, MC, and Flora Macdonald (*d* 1955), *d* of late Col Cunliffe Martin, CB; *S* father, 1972; *m* 1948, June, *d* of Douglas Cory-Wright, CBE; one *s* two *d*. *Educ*: Eton; Babson Institute of Business Admin, Wellesley Hills, Mass, USA. Served War as Captain, Coldstream Guards. Dep. Chairman, Horlicks Ltd, retired 1971. *Recreations*: shooting, model soldier collecting. *Heir*: *s* James Cunliffe William Horlick, *b* 19 Nov. 1956. *Address*: Tournaig, Poolewe, Achnasheen, Ross-shire. *T*: Poolewe 250; Howberry Lane Cottage, Nuffield, near Nettlebed, Oxon. *T*: Nettlebed 641454. *Club*: Beefsteak.

HORLICK, Sir Ted; *see* Horlick, Sir Edwin John.

HORLOCK, Henry Wimburn Sudell; Underwriting Member of Lloyd's, since 1957; Director, Stepping Stone School, since 1962; *b* 19 July 1915; *s* of Rev. Henry Darrell Sudell Horlock, DD, and Mary Haliburton Laurie; *m* 1960, Jeannetta Robin, *d* of F. W. Tanner, JP. *Educ*: Pembroke Coll., Oxford (MA). Served Army, 1939-42. Civil Service, 1942-60. Mem., Court of Common Council, City of London, 1969-; Deputy, Ward of Farringdon Within, 1978-; Sheriff, City of London, 1972-73; Liveryman: Saddlers Co., 1937-, Mem., Court of Assistants, 1968-, Master, 1976-77; Plaisterers' Co. (Hon.), 1975-; Fletchers' Co., 1977-; Gardeners' Co., 1980-; Member: Parish Clerks' Co., 1966-, Court of Assistants, 1976-, Master, 1981-82; Guild of Freemen, 1972-, Court of Assistants, 1977-; Farringdon Ward Club, 1970-, Pres., 1978-79; United Wards Club, 1972-, Pres., 1980-81; Royal Soc. of St George, 1972-. Commander, Order of Merit, Federal Republic of Germany, 1972; Commander, National Order of the Aztec Eagle of Mexico, 1973.

Recreations: gardening, travel, walking. *Address*: 33 Fitzjohn's Avenue, NW3 5JY. *T*: 01-435 9641/2. *Clubs*: Athenæum, Guildhall, City Livery (Pres., 1981-82), National.

HORLOCK, Dr John Harold, FRS 1976; Vice-Chancellor, Open University, since 1981; *b* 19 April 1928; *s* of Harold Edgar and Olive Margaret Horlock; *m* 1953, Sheila Joy Stutely; one *s* two *d*. *Educ*: Edmonton Latymer Sch.; (Scholar) St John's Coll., Cambridge. 1st Class Hons Mech. Sci. Tripos, Pt I, 1948, Rex Moir Prize; Pt II, 1949; MA 1952; PhD 1955; ScD 1975. Design and Development Engineer, Rolls Royce Ltd, Derby, 1949-51; Research Fellow, St John's Coll., Cambridge, 1954-57; Univ. Demonstrator, 1952-56; University Lecturer, 1956-58, at Cambridge Univ. Engineering Lab.; Harrison Prof. of Mechanical Engineering and Head of Dept, Liverpool Univ., 1958-66; Prof. of Engineering, 1967-74, Dep. Head of Engineering Dept, 1969-73, Dir, SRC Turbomachinery Lab., 1971-74, Cambridge Univ.; Professorial Fellow of St John's Coll., Cambridge, 1967-74; Vice-Chancellor, 1974-80, Prof. of Engineering, 1976-80, Univ. of Salford. Visiting Asst Prof. in Mech. Engineering, Massachusetts Inst. of Technology, USA, 1956-57; Vis. Prof. of Aero-Space Engineering, Pennsylvania State Univ., USA, 1966. Dir, BICERA Ltd, 1964-65; Chm., ARC, 1979-80 (Mem., 1960-63, 1969-72); Member: SRC, 1974-77; Cttee of Inquiry into Engineering Profession, 1977-80; Engineering Council, 1981-. Director: Cambridge Water Co., 1971-74; British Engine Insurance Ltd, 1979-; BL (Technol.) Ltd, 1979-. A Vice-Pres., Royal Soc., 1982-. FEng, FIMechE, FRAeS; Fellow ASME. Hon. DSc: Heriot-Watt, 1980; Salford, 1981. Thomas Hawksley Gold Medal, IMechE, 1969. *Publications*: The Fluid Mechanics and Thermodynamics of Axial Flow Compressors, 1958; The Fluid Mechanics and Thermodynamics of Axial Flow Turbines, 1966; Actuator Disc Theory, 1978; contribs to mech. and aero. engineering jls and to Proc. Royal Society. *Recreations*: music, golf. *Address*: The Open University, Walton Hall, Milton Keynes MK7 6AA. *T*: Milton Keynes 653214; Wednesden House, Aspley Guise, Beds. *Clubs*: Athenæum, Royal Automobile, MCC.

HORN, Alan Bowes, CVO 1971; HM Diplomatic Service, retired; *b* 6 June 1917; *m* 1946, Peggy Boocock; one *s* one *d*. *Educ*: London Sch. of Economics. Served in Army, 1940-46. Joined Foreign Service, 1946; Vice-Consul, Marseilles, 1948-49; 2nd Sec., HM Embassy, Tel Aviv, 1949; promoted 1st Sec. and later apptd: London, 1951-53; New York, 1953-56; Helsinki, 1957-60; FO, 1960-63; Ambassador to the Malagasy Republic, 1963-67; Counsellor, Warsaw, 1967-70; Consul-General, Istanbul, 1970-73. *Address*: Oak Trees, Shere Road, Ewhurst, Cranleigh, Surrey.

HORN, Prof. Gabriel, MA, MD, ScD; Professor of Zoology, University of Cambridge, and Fellow of King's College, Cambridge, since 1978; *b* 9 Dec. 1927; *s* of late A. Horn and Mrs Horn; *m* 1st, 1952, Ann Loveday Dean Soper (marr. diss. 1979)); two *s* two *d*; 2nd, 1980, Edith Priscilla Barett. *Educ*: Handsworth Technical Sch. and Coll., Birmingham (Nat. Cert. in Mech. Engrg); Univ. of Birmingham (BSc Anatomy and Physiology; MD, ChB). MA, ScD Cantab. Served in RAF (Educn Br.), 1947-49. House appts, Birmingham Children's and Birmingham and Midland Eye Hosps, 1955-56; Univ. of Cambridge: Univ. Demonstrator in Anat., 1956-62; Lectr in Anat., 1962-72; Reader in Neurobiology, 1972-74; Fellow of King's Coll., 1962-74; Prof. and Head of Dept of Anat., Univ. of Bristol, 1974-77. Sen. Res. Fellow in neurophysiol., Montreal Neurol Inst., McGill Univ., 1957-58; Vis. Prof. of Physiol Optics, Univ. of Calif, Berkeley, 1963; Vis. Res. Prof., Ohio State Univ., 1965; Vis. Prof. of Zool., Makerere University Coll., Uganda, 1966; Leverhulme Res. Fellow, Laboratoire de Neurophysiologie Cellulaire, France, 1970-71. Member: Biol Sciences Cttee, SRC, 1973-75; Jt MRC and SRC Adv. Panel on Neurobiol., 1971-72; Res. Cttee, Mental Health Foundn, 1973-78; Council, Anatomical Soc.; Adv. Gp, ARC Inst. of Animal Physiology, Babraham. Dir, Co. of Biologists, 1980-. FIBiol 1978. Kenneth Craik Award in Physiol Psychol., 1962. *Publications*: (ed with R. A. Hinde) Short-Term Changes in Neural Activity and Behaviour, 1970; contrib. scientific jls, mainly on topics in neurosciences. *Recreations*: walking, cycling, music, riding. *Address*: King's College, Cambridge. *T*: Cambridge 350411.

HORNBY, Sir Antony; *see* Hornby, Sir R. A.

HORNBY, Derrick Richard; *b* 11 Jan. 1926; *s* of late Richard W. Hornby and Dora M. Hornby; *m* 1948, June Steele; two *s* one *d*. *Educ*: University Coll., Southampton (DipEcon). Early career in accountancy; Marketing Dir, Tetley Tea Co. Ltd, 1964-69; Man. Dir, Eden Vale, 1969-74; Chm., Spillers Foods Ltd, 1974-77; Divisional Managing Director: Spillers Internat., 1977-80; Spillers Grocery Products Div., 1979-80. Pres., Food Manufrs Fedn Incorp., 1977-79; Mem., Food and Drinks EDC. Member Council: CBI, to 1979; Food and Drinks Industry Council, to 1979. FBIM, FIGD, ACommA. *Recreation*: golf. *Address*: Hillcrest, Dover Road, Branksome Park, Poole, Dorset. *Clubs*: National Sporting; Wentworth (Surrey).

HORNBY, Frank Robert, CBE 1972 (MBE 1944); Chief Officer and Vice-Chairman, Council for National Academic Awards, 1964-72, retired; *b* 20 Aug. 1911; *yr s* of late Robert Wilson Hornby and Jane Hornby; *m* 1939, Kathleen Margaret, *yr d* of late Dr Sidney Berry and Helen Berry. *Educ*: Heversham Sch., Westmorland; Magdalene Coll., Cambridge. 1st Class Natural Sciences Tripos Pts 1 and 2. Schoolmaster, 1933-41. RAOC, 1941-46 (Lieut-Col). Asst Educn Officer, Nottingham Co. Borough, 1946-56; Sec., Nat. Coun. for Technological Awards, 1956-64. Hon. LLD CNAA, 1972.

Address: 35 High Firs, Gills Hill, Radlett, Herts WD7 8BH. *T:* Radlett 5083.

HORNBY, Prof. James Angus; Professor of Law in the University of Bristol since 1961; *b* 15 Aug. 1922; twin *s* of James Hornby and Evelyn Gladys (*née* Grant). *Educ:* Bolton County Grammar Sch.; Christ's Coll., Cambridge. BA 1944, LLB 1945, MA 1948 Cantab. Called to Bar, Lincoln's Inn, 1947. Lecturer, Manchester Univ., 1947-61. *Publications:* An Introduction to Company Law, 1957, 5th edn 1975; contribs to legal journals. *Recreations:* hill walking, chess. *Address:* The Faculty of Law, The University, Bristol. *Club:* United Oxford & Cambridge University.

HORNBY, James William, MA; Secretary, Incorporated Association of Preparatory Schools, since 1982; *b* 14 March 1924; *s* of late Rt Rev. and Mrs Hugh Leycester Hornby; *m* 1957, Clare Hedley Visick; two *s* two *d. Educ:* Winchester Coll.; Trinity Coll., Oxford (MA). Asst Master, Bramcote Sch., Scarborough, 1947-57, Headmaster, 1957-67; Headmaster, Clifton Coll. Prep. Sch., Bristol, 1967-82. Chairman: Incorporated Assoc. of Prep. Schs, 1966, 1971 and 1978; ISIS, 1981-82. *Recreations:* fishing, sport generally; interest in educational matters. *Address:* 138 Church Street, Kensington, W8 4BN. *T:* 01-727 2316.

HORNBY, Michael Charles St John; retired as Vice-Chairman, W. H. Smith & Son Ltd (1944-65); *b* 2 Jan. 1899; *e s* of C. H. St J. Hornby and Cicely Hornby; *m* 1928, Nicolette Joan, *d* of Hon. Cyril Ward, MVO; two *s* one *d. Educ:* Winchester; RMC Sandhurst; New Coll., Oxford. Joined Grenadier Guards, 1918; served in France and Germany. New Coll., Oxford, 1919-21. Entered W. H. Smith & Son, 1921. Prime Warden, Goldsmiths' Company, 1954-55. Chm., National Book League, 1959. *Recreations:* fox-hunting, shooting, cricket, gardening. *Address:* Pusey House, Faringdon, Oxon. *T:* Buckland 222. *Clubs:* White's, MCC.

See also Sir R. A. Hornby, S. M. Hornby.

HORNBY, Richard Phipps, MA; Director, since 1976, and a Vice-Chairman, since 1981, Halifax Building Society; Director: Cadbury Schweppes plc, since 1982; McCorquodale plc, since 1982; *b* 20 June 1922; *e s* of late Rt Rev. Hugh Leycester Hornby, MC; *m* 1951, Stella Hichens; three *s* one *d. Educ:* Winchester Coll.; Trinity Coll., Oxford (Scholar). Served in King's Royal Rifle Corps, 1941-45. 2nd Cl. Hons in Modern History, Oxford, 1948 (Soccer Blue). History Master, Eton Coll., 1948-50; with Unilever, 1951-52; with J. Walter Thompson Co., 1952-63, 1964-. Contested (C) West Walthamstow: May 1955 (gen. election) and March 1956 (by-election); MP (C) Tonbridge, Kent, June 1956-Feb. 1974. PPS to Rt Hon. Duncan Sandys, MP, 1959-63; Parly Under-Sec. of State, CRO and CO, Oct. 1963-Oct. 1964. Dir, J. Walter Thompson Co. Ltd, 1974-81. Member: BBC Gen. Adv. Council, 1969-74; Cttee of Inquiry into Intrusions into Privacy, 1970-72; British Council Exec. Cttee, 1971-74. *Recreations:* shooting, fishing, walking, riding and tennis. *Address:* 10 Hereford Square, SW7.

HORNBY, Sir (Roger) Antony, Kt 1960; President, Savoy Hotel Ltd, since 1977 (Vice-Chairman to Dec. 1976); *b* 5 Feb. 1904; *s* of late C. H. St J. Hornby, Shelley House, Chelsea; *m* 1st, 1931, Lady Veronica Blackwood (marr. diss. 1940); one *d* ; 2nd, 1949, Lily Ernst. *Educ:* Winchester Coll.; New Coll., Oxford. MA Oxon. Vice-Chm. King's Coll. Hosp., 1959-74. Served War of 1939-45, Grenadier Guards. A Trustee of the Wallace Collection, 1963-77; Chm., Nat. Art Collections Fund, 1970-75. *Recreation:* collecting pictures. *Address:* Claridge's Hotel, W1. *Clubs:* Garrick, MCC.

See also M. C. St J. Hornby.

HORNBY, Simon Michael; Director, since 1974, Chairman, since 1982, W. H. Smith & Son (Holdings) Ltd; Director, S. Pearson & Son Ltd, since 1978; *b* 29 Dec. 1934; *s* of Michael Hornby, *qv* ; *m* 1968, Sheran Cazalet. *Educ:* Eton; New Coll., Oxford; Harvard Business Sch. 2nd Lieut, Grenadier Guards, 1953-55. Entered W. H. Smith & Son, 1958, Dir, 1965; Gp Chief Exec., W. H. Smith & Son (Holdings), 1978-82. Mem. Exec. Cttee, 1966-, Property Cttee, 1979-, Council 1976-, National Trust; Mem. Adv. Council, Victoria and Albert Museum, 1971-75; Trustee, British Museum, 1975-; Chm., Nat. Book League, 1978-80 (Dep. Chm., 1976-78). *Recreations:* gardening, golf. *Address:* 8 Ennismore Gardens, SW7 1LN. *T:* 01-584 1597; Lake House, Pusey, Faringdon, Oxon SN7 8QB. *T:* Buckland 659. *Club:* Garrick.

HORNE, Sir Alan Edgar, 2nd Bt *cr* 1929; MC; *b* 19 Sept. 1889; *s* of Sir Edgar Horne, 1st Bt, and Margery (*d* 1939), *d* of George Anderson May, Elford, Staffs; *S* father, 1941; *m* 1st, 1915, Henriette Kelly (*d* 1918); one *d* ; 2nd, 1923, Roslyn (*d* 1961), *d* of John Brian Robinson; (one *s* decd). *Educ:* Eton; University Coll., Oxford. Served European War, 1914-19, in France and Balkans as Capt. Surrey Yeomanry and on Staff (despatches 4 times, MC, French Croix de Guerre); War of 1939-45, Basutoland and MELF, 1940-48, as Lt-Col Royal Pioneer Corps (African and Native Troops). *Heir: g s* Alan Gray Antony Horne, *b* 11 July 1948. *Address:* 1 The Paragon (Flat 4), Blackheath, SE3 0NX. *Clubs:* Cavalry and Guards, MCC.

HORNE, Alistair Allan; author, journalist, farmer and lecturer; *b* 9 Nov. 1925; *s* of late Sir (James) Allan Horne and Lady (Auriol Camilla) Horne (née Hay); *m* 1953, Renira Margaret, *d* of Adm. Sir Geoffrey Hawkins, KBE, CB, MVO, DSC; three *d. Educ:* Le Rosey, Switzerland; Millbrook, USA; Jesus Coll., Cambridge (MA). Served War of 1939-45: RAF, 1943-44; Coldstream Gds, 1944-47; Captain, attached Intelligence Service (ME). Dir, Ropley Trust Ltd, 1948-77; Foreign Correspondent, Daily Telegraph, 1952-55. Founded Alistair Horne Res. Fellowship in Mod. History, St Antony's Coll., Oxford, 1969, Supernumerary Fellow, 1978-. Fellow, Woodrow Wilson Center, Washington, DC, USA, 1980-81. Member: Management Cttee, Royal Literary Fund, 1969-; Franco-British Council, 1979-; Cttee of Management, Soc. of Authors, 1979-; Trustee, Imperial War Museum, 1975-. FRSL. Knight of Mark Twain. *Publications:* Back into Power, 1955; The Land is Bright, 1958; Canada and the Canadians, 1961; The Price of Glory: Verdun 1916, 1962 (Hawthornden Prize, 1963); The Fall of Paris: The Siege and The Commune 1870-71, 1965; To Lose a Battle: France 1940, 1969; Death of a Generation, 1970; The Terrible Year: The Paris Commune, 1971; Small Earthquake in Chile, 1972; A Savage War of Peace: Algeria 1954-62, 1977 (Yorkshire Post Book of Year Prize, 1978; Wolfson Literary Award, 1978); Napoleon, Master of Europe 1805-1807, 1979; contribs to books: Combat: World War I, ed Don Congdon, 1964; Impressions of America, ed R. A. Brown, 1966; Marshal V. I. Chuikov, The End of the Third Reich, 1967; Sports and Games in Canadian Life, ed N. and M. L. Howell, 1969; Decisive Battles of the Twentieth Century, ed N. Frankland and C. Dowling, 1976; The War Lords: Military Commanders of the Twentieth Century, ed Field Marshal Sir M. Carver, 1976; Regular Armies and Insurgency, ed R. Haycock, 1979; contribs various periodicals. *Recreations:* skiing, painting, gardening, travel. *Address:* c/o Macmillan & Co., 4 Little Essex Street, WC2. *Club:* Garrick.

HORNE, Frederic Thomas; Master of the Supreme Court (Taxing Office) since 1967; *b* 21 March 1917; *y s* of Lionel Edward Horne, JP, Moreton-in-Marsh, Glos; *m* 1944, Madeline Hatton; two *s* two *d. Educ:* Chipping Campden Grammar Sch. Admitted a Solicitor (Hons), 1938. Served with RAFVR in General Duties Branch (Pilot), 1939-56. Partner in Iliffe Sweet & Co., 1956-67. *Recreations:* cricket, music. *Address:* Dunstall, Quickley Lane, Chorleywood, Herts. *Club:* MCC.

HORNE, Prof. Michael Rex, OBE 1981; MA, PhD, ScD Cantab; MSc (Manchester); FRS 1981; FEng, FICE; FIStructE; Beyer Professor of Civil Engineering, University of Manchester, since 1978 (Professor of Civil Engineering, 1960-78); *b* 29 Dec. 1921; *s* of late Rev. Ernest Horne, Leicester; *m* 1947, Molly, *d* of late Mark Hewett, Royston, Herts; two *s* two *d. Educ:* Boston (Lincs) Grammar Sch.; Leeds Grammar Sch.; St John's Coll., Cambridge. MA Cantab 1945; PhD Cantab 1950, ScD Cantab 1956. John Winbolt Prize for Research, Cambridge Univ., 1944. Asst Engineer, River Great Ouse Catchment Bd, 1941-45; Scientific Officer, British Welding Research Assoc., 1945-51; Asst Dir of Research in Engineering, 1951-56, Lectr in Engineering, 1957-60, Fellow of St John's Coll., 1957, Univ. of Cambridge. Instn of Civil Engineers, Telford Premiums, 1956, 1966, 1978. Chm., NW Branch, 1969-70, Pres., 1980-81, IStructE; Pres., Section G, BAAS, 1981-82; Mem., Merrison Cttee on Box Girders, 1970-73. Hon. DSc Salford, 1981. Diploma, 1971, Bronze Medal, IStructE, 1973; Baker Medal, ICE, 1977. *Publications:* (with J. F. Baker and J. Heyman) The Steel Skeleton, 1956; (with W. F. Merchant) The Stability of Frames, 1965; The Plastic Theory of Structures, 1971; (with L. J. Morris) Plastic Design of Low Rise Frames, 1981; contribs on structures, strength of materials and particulate theory of soils to learned journals. *Recreations:* photography, wine-making, music. *Address:* 19 Park Road, Hale, Altrincham, Cheshire WA15 9NW.

HORNER, Arthur William, CMG 1964; TD and clasp 1946; *b* 22 June 1909; *s* of Francis Moore and Edith Horner; *m* 1938, Patricia Denise (née Campbell); two *s* one *d. Educ:* Hardenwick; Felsted. Marine Insurance, 1926-39. Served War, 1939-46, Rifle Brigade; Lieut-Col; psc. Farming in Kenya, 1948-50. Colonial Administrative Service (later HM Overseas Civil Service), Kenya, 1950-64; Commissioner of Lands, 1955-61; Permanent Sec., 1961-64; Dir of Independence Celebrations, 1963; Principal, ODM, 1964-73; seconded Diplomatic Service, 1968-70, retired 1973. *Recreations:* music, gardening. *Address:* St Margaret's Cottage, Northiam, Rye, East Sussex.

HORNER, Douglas George, FIB; Director, Barclays Bank PLC, since 1977; Chairman, Mercantile Credit Company, since 1980; Director, Barclays Bank UK Limited, since 1975 (Vice Chairman, 1979-81); *b* Dec. 1917; *s* of Albert and Louise Horner; *m* 1941, Gwendoline Phyllis Wall; one *s. Educ:* Enfield Grammar Sch. Asst Manager/Manager at various bank branches, 1954-71; Local Dir, Lombard Street, 1971; Regional Gen. Manager, London, 1973; Gen. Man., 1975; Senior Gen. Man., 1977. *Recreations:* golf, gardening. *Address:* Barclays Bank PLC, 54 Lombard Street, EC3P 3AH.

HORNER, Frederick, DSc; CEng, FIEE; Director, Appleton Laboratory, Science Research Council, 1977-79; *b* 28 Aug. 1918; *s* of late Frederick and Mary Horner; *m* 1946, Elizabeth Bonsey; one *s* one *d. Educ:* Bolton Sch.; Univ. of Manchester (Ashbury Scholar, 1937; Fairbairn Engrg Prize, 1939; BSc 1st Cl. Hons 1939; MSc 1941; DSc 1968). CEng, FIEE 1959. On staff of DSIR, NPL, 1941-52; UK Scientific Mission, Washington DC, 1947; Appleton Lab. of SRC (formerly Radio Research Station), 1952-79, Dep. Dir, 1969-77; Admin. Staff Coll., Henley, 1959. Delegate: Internat. Union of Radio Science, 1950- (Chm., Commn VIII, 1966-69); Internat. Radio Consultative Cttee, 1953- (Internat. Chm., Study Group 2, 1980-). Member: Inter-Union Commn on Frequency Allocations for Radio Astronomy and Space Science, 1965- (Sec., 1975-82); Electronics Divl Bd, IEE, 1970-76. Mem. Council, Royal Holloway Coll., 1979- (Hon. Associate, 1975-). *Publications:* more than 50 scientific papers. *Recreations:* tennis, gardening. *Address:* Gralyn, Clarence Drive, Egham, Surrey TW20 0NL. *T:* Egham 33127.

HORNER, Hallam; *see* Horner, L. J. H.

HORNER, John; *b* 5 Nov. 1911; *s* of Ernest Charles and Emily Horner; *m* 1936, Patricia, *d* of Geoffrey and Alice Palmer; two *d. Educ:* elementary sch. and Sir George Monoux Grammar Sch., Walthamstow. Apprenticed Merchant Navy, 1927; Second Mate's Certificate, 1932. Joined London Fire Brigade, 1933; Gen. Sec. Fire Brigades Union, 1939-64; MP (Lab) Oldbury and Halesowen, 1964-70. Mem. Select Cttee on Nationalised Industries. *Publication:* Studies in Industrial Democracy, 1974. *Recreations:* walking, gardening, talking, listening to music, studying history and art. *Address:* Yew Tree, Howle Hill, Ross on Wye, Herefordshire. *T:* Ross on Wye 2932.

HORNER, (Lawrence John) Hallam, CBE 1973 (OBE 1959); Director, Chamber of Shipping of UK, 1966-72; *b* 14 June 1907; *o s* of late David Aitken Horner and Louise Stuart Black; *m* 1935, Kathleen Joan (*d* 1976), *o d* of late Charles D. Taite, Bowdon, Cheshire; two *d. Educ:* Malvern Coll.; Corpus Christi Coll., Oxford (MA). Served War of 1939-45, RSF and 52nd Recce Regt, RAC (despatches). Admitted Solicitor (hons), 1931; Asst Solicitor, Cheshire CC, 1932-34; Rees & Freres, parly agents, 1934-51 (Partner, 1936); Sec., Canal Assoc., 1945-48; Parly Solicitor (later also Sec.), Dock and Harbour Authorities' Assoc., 1946-51; Asst Gen. Man. and Solicitor and Parly Agent, Chamber of Shipping of UK, 1951, Gen. Man., 1959. Sec. Adv. Cttee on New Lighthouse Works, etc, 1951-66; Mem. Adv. Cttee on Oil Pollution of the Sea, 1952-66; Mem., City of London Coll. Shipping Adv. Cttee, 1966-72; Mem., Cttee of Management, British Ship Adoption Soc., 1968-72. Hon. FICS, 1972. Netherlands Bronze Cross, 1945. *Recreation:* watching birds. *Address:* 2 Hamstone Court, Great Gates, Salcombe, South Devon TQ8 8JY. *T:* Salcombe 3420. *Club:* Reform.

HORNSBY, Harry Reginald, MBE 1944; *b* 19 Dec. 1907; *s* of Rev. E. F. Hornsby, Hon. CF; *m* 1946, Mary Elizabeth Whitley; no *c. Educ:* Bromsgrove Sch.; Brasenose Coll., Oxford. MA 1936. Asst Master, Christ's Hosp., Horsham, 1929-39; Headmaster, The King's Sch., Peterborough, 1939-51; Headmaster: Christ's Coll., Christchurch, NZ, 1951-63; St Paul's Sch., Hamilton, NZ, 1963-69; St Andrew's School, Nukuálofa, Tonga, 1970-72. Lay Canon of Christchurch Cathedral, 1962-63; Mem. of Council, Univ. of Canterbury, NZ, 1962-63. War Service, 1940-45 (despatches): Gunner RA, 1940; commissioned Worcs Regt, 1941; served 3rd Queen Alexandra's Own Gurkha Rifles, 1941-45. Chm. Independent Schools Assoc. of New Zealand, 1960-63; Member: Outward Bound Trust of New Zealand, 1961-64; Council, Univ. of Waikato, 1965-68. Lay Canon of Waikato Cathedral, 1967, 1968, 1969. *Recreations:* golf, gardening. *Address:* 13 Bay View Road, Nelson, New Zealand.

HORNSBY-SMITH, family name of **Baroness Hornsby-Smith.**

HORNSBY-SMITH, Baroness *cr* 1974 (Life Peer), of Chislehurst; **Margaret Patricia Hornsby-Smith,** PC 1959; DBE 1961; *b* 17 March 1914; *o d* of F. C. Hornsby-Smith. *Educ:* Richmond. Ministry of Economic Warfare, 1941-45; Barnes Borough Council, 1945-49. MP (C) Kent, Chislehurst, 1950-66 and 1970-Feb. 1974; Parly Sec., Ministry of Health, 1951-57; UK delegate to Assembly of UN, 1958; Jt Parly Under-Sec. of State, Home Office, 1957-59; Jt Parly Sec., Min. of Pensions and Nat. Insurance, 1959-61. Led UK Parliamentary Delegation to Australasia, 1961, Kenya 1972. Pres., EAW, 1975-; Vice-Chm., Arthritis and Rheumatism Council for Research, 1974- (Chm., Appeals Cttee, 1966-). FRSA 1971. *Address:* 31 Stafford Mansions, Stafford Place, SW1E 6NL. *Clubs:* Carlton, Special Forces.

HOROWITZ, Myer, EdD; President, University of Alberta, Canada, since 1979; *b* 27 Dec. 1932; *s* of Philip Horowitz and Fanny Cotler; *m* 1956, Barbara, *d* of Samuel Rosen, Montreal; two *d. Educ:* High Sch., Montreal; Sch. for Teachers, Macdonald Coll.; Sir George Williams Univ. (BA); Univ. of Alberta (MEd); Stanford Univ. (EdD). Teacher, Schs in Montreal, Sch. Bd, Greater Montreal, 1952-60. McGill University: Lectr in Educn, 1960-63; Asst Prof., 1963-65; Associate Prof., 1965-67; Asst to Dir, 1964-65; Prof. of Educn, 1967-69 and Asst Dean, 1965-69. Univ. of Alberta: Prof. and Chm., Dept Elem. Educn, 1969; Dean, Faculty of Educn, 1972-75; Vice-Pres. (Academic), 1975-79. *Address:* University of Alberta, Edmonton, Alberta T6G 2J9, Canada; 14319, 60 Avenue, Edmonton, Alberta T6G 1J9.

HOROWITZ, Vladimir; pianist; *b* Kieff, Russia, 1 Oct. 1904; *s* of Samuel Horowitz and Sophie Bodik; *m* 1933, Wanda Toscanini; one *d. Educ:* Kieff Conservatory; studied under Sergi Tarnowsky and Felix Blumenfeld. European Début, 1925; début with New York Philharmonic Orchestra, 1928. Soloist, New York Symphony Orchestra and other American orchestras. Winner 18 Grammy Awards. Royal Philharmonic Soc. Gold Medal, 1972. *Address:* c/o Columbia Artists Management, Inc., 165 West 57th Street, New York, NY 10019, USA.

HORRELL, John Ray, CBE 1979; TD; DL; farmer; Chairman, Association of County Councils, since 1981 (Vice-Chairman, 1979-81); *b* 1929. Director: Horrell's Farmers Ltd; Horrell's Dairies Ltd. Mem. bd, Peterborough New Town Develt Corp. Mem., Cambs (formerly Huntingdon and Peterborough) CC, 1965- (Chm., 1973-77); Chm., Educn Cttee; Chm., Council of Local Educn Authorities, 1976-79. Major, TA; a Vice-Chm., E Anglia TA&VRA, 1977-. DL Hunts and Peterborough, 1973. *Address:* The Grove, Longthorpe, Peterborough. *T:* Peterborough 262618.

HORRIDGE, Prof. (George) Adrian, FRS 1969; FAA 1971; Professor of Neurobiology, Research School of Biological Sciences, Australian National University, ACT 2601, since 1969; *b* Sheffield, England, 12 Dec. 1927; *s* of George William Horridge and Olive Stray; *m* 1954, Audrey Anne Lightburne; one *s* three *d. Educ:* King Edward VII Sch., Sheffield. Fellow, St John's Coll., Cambridge, 1953-56; on staff, St Andrews Univ., 1956-69; Dir, Gatty Marine Laboratory, St Andrews, 1960-69. *Publications:* Structure and Function of the Nervous Systems of Invertebrates (with T. H. Bullock), 1965; Interneurons, 1968; (ed) The Compound Eye and Vision of Insects, 1975; Monographs of the Maritime Museum at Greenwich nos 38, 39, 40, 1979; The Prahu: traditional sailing boat of Indonesia, 1981 (Oxford in Asia); contribs numerous scientific papers on behaviour and nervous systems of lower animals, to jls, etc. *Recreations:* optics, mathematics, marine biology; sailing, language, arts, boat construction in Indonesia. *Address:* PO Box 475, Canberra City, ACT 2601, Australia. *T:* Canberra 062-494532, Telex 62219.

HORROCKS, Lt-Gen. Sir Brian Gwynne, KCB 1949 (CB 1943); KBE 1945; DSO 1943; MC; Gentleman Usher of the Black Rod, House of Lords, 1949-63; *b* 7 Sept. 1895; *o s* of late Col Sir William Heaton Horrocks, KCMG, CB; *m* 1928, Nancy, *d* of Brook and Hon. Mrs Brook Kitchin; one *d* decd. *Educ:* Uppingham; RMC Sandhurst. 2nd Lieut Middlesex Regt, 1914; served European War, France and Belgium, 1914, Russia, 1919 (wounded, MC); War of 1939-45 (wounded, DSO, CB, KBE); Comd 44 (HC Div.), 9 Armd Div., 13 Corps, 10 Corps in Egypt and Africa, 9 Corps Tunis, 30 Corps in BLA. GOC-in-C Western Comd, 1946; GOC-in-C British Army of the Rhine, 1948; invalided out of Army, 1949. Dir, Bovis Holdings, 1963-77. Hon. LLD (Belfast). *Publications:* A Full Life, 1960, new edn, 1974; Corps Commander, 1977; Editor, Famous Regiments Series. *Address:* The Old School House, Singleton, Chichester, Sussex. *T:* Singleton 783. *Club:* Naval and Military.

HORROCKS, Raymond; Executive Director and Board Member, BL plc, since 1981; Group Chief Executive, Cars, since 1982; *b* 9 Jan. 1930; *s* of Elsie and Cecil Horrocks; *m* 1953, Pamela Florence Russell; three *d. Educ:* Bolton Municipal Secondary School. Textile Industry, 1944-48 and 1950-51; HM Forces, Army Intelligence Corps, 1948-50; Sales Rep., Proctor & Gamble, 1951-52; Merchandiser, Marks & Spencer, 1953-58; Sub Gp Buying Controller, Littlewoods Mail Order Stores, 1958-63; various plant, departmental and divisional management positions, Ford Motor Co., 1963-72; Regional Dir, Europe and Middle East, Materials Handling Gp, Eaton Corp., 1972-77; Chm. and Man. Dir, Austin Morris Ltd, 1978-80; Man. Dir, BL Cars, 1980-81; Chm. and Chief Exec., BL Cars Gp, 1981-82; Chm., Unipart Gp, 1981-82. FIMI; CBIM. *Recreations:* fly fishing, gardening, walking. *Address:* 35-38 Portman Square, W1H 0HQ.

HORSBRUGH-PORTER, Sir Andrew (Marshall), 3rd Bt, *cr* 1902; DSO 1940; Col retired, 1953; *b* 1 June 1907; *s* of Sir John Horsbrugh-Porter, 2nd Bt, and Elaine Maud, *y d* of Thomas Jefferies; *S* father, 1953; *m* 1933, Annette Mary, *d* of late Brig.-Gen. R. C. Browne-Clayton, DSO, Browne's Hill, Carlow; one *s* two *d. Educ:* Winchester; RMC, Sandhurst. Subaltern 12th Royal Lancers, 1927. Served War of 1939-45 (DSO and Bar); commanded 27th Lancers, 1941-45; GSO1, Liaison attached to US Army, 1947; commanded 12th Royal Lancers, 1948-52; Military Adviser to UK High Commissioner, New Delhi, 1952. *Recreations:* watching polo and hunting. *Heir: s* John Simon Horsbrugh-Porter [*b* 18 Dec. 1938; *m* 1964, Lavinia Rose, *d* of Ralph Turton, Kildale Hall, Whitby, Yorks; one *s* two *d*]. *Address:* Manor Farm House, Salford, Chipping Norton, Oxon. *Club:* Cavalry and Guards.

See also Sir J. D. Barlow, Bt.

HORSBURGH, John Millar Stewart, QC (Scot.) 1980; *b* 15 May 1938; *s* of late Alexander Horsburgh and of Helen Margaret Watson Millar or Horsburgh; *m* 1966, Johann Catriona Gardner, MB, ChB, DObst RCOG; one *s* one *d. Educ:* Hutchesons' Boys' Grammar Sch., Glasgow; Univ. of Glasgow (MA Hons, LLB). Admitted to Scots Bar, 1965. *Address:* 8 Laverockbank Road, Edinburgh EH5 3DG. *T:* 031-552 5328.

HORSEFIELD, John Keith, CB 1957; Historian, International Monetary Fund, 1966-69; *b* 14 Oct. 1901; *s* of Rev. Canon F. J. Horsefield, Bristol; *m* 1934, Lucy G. G. Florance. *Educ:* Monkton Combe Sch.; University of Bristol; MA 1948, DSc 1971; London Sch. of Economics. Lecturer, LSE, 1939; Min. of Aircraft Production, 1940; International Monetary Fund, 1947; Under-Sec., Min. of Supply, 1951; Dep. Asst Sec.-Gen. for Economics and Finance, NATO, 1952; Supply and Development Officer, Iron and Steel Bd, 1954; Dir of Finance and Accounts, Gen. Post Office, 1955-60; Chief Editor, International Monetary Fund, 1960-66. *Publications:* The Real Cost of the War, 1940; British Monetary Experiments, 1650-1710, 1960; The International Monetary Fund, 1945-1965, 1970; articles in Economica, etc. *Address:* 37 Clatterford Road, Carisbrooke, Newport, Isle of Wight PO30 1PA. *T:* Newport (IoW) 523675.

HORSEY, Gordon, JP; a Recorder of the Crown Court, since 1978; *b* 20 July 1926; *s* of late E. W. Horsey, MBE, and of H. V. Horsey; *m* 1951, Jean Mary (*née* Favill); one *d. Educ:* Magnus Grammar Sch., Newark, Notts; St Catharine's Coll., Cambridge. BA, LLB. Served RN, 1944-45, RE, 1945-48 (Captain). Admitted solicitor, 1953; private practice in Nottingham, 1953-71; Registrar: Coventry County Court, 1971; Leicester County Court, 1973. JP

Leics, 1975. *Recreations:* fly-fishing, golf, gardening. *Address:* Bronavon, Rothley, Leics. *T:* Leicester 302080.

HORSFALL, Geoffrey Jonas, CBE 1967; Judge of the Grand Court of the Cayman Islands, West Indies, 1965–73, retired; *b* 22 Jan. 1905; *s* of late Major A. H. Horsfall, DSO, TD, Newcastle, NSW, Australia; *m* 1947, Robin, *y d* of late Curwin Maclure, Albury, NSW; one *s* two *d. Educ:* The King's Sch., Parramatta, NSW; Cheltenham Coll.; Keble Coll., Oxford. BA 1927; Barrister-at-Law, 1928, Gray's Inn; South-Eastern Circuit. Entered Colonial Legal Service, 1936, as Crown Counsel, Nigeria; Crown Counsel, Sierra Leone, 1943; Senior Magistrate, Fiji, 1947; Judicial Commissioner, British Solomon Islands Protectorate, 1953; Judge of the High Court, Zanzibar, 1958; Chief Justice of Zanzibar, 1964, but office abolished in Zanzibar revolution. *Recreations:* bowls, walking, gardening. *Address:* 78 Hawthorne Avenue, Chatswood, NSW 2067, Australia. *T:* 02-411-3892.

HORSFALL, Sir John (Musgrave), 3rd Bt *cr* 1909; MC 1946; TD 1949 and clasp 1951; JP; *b* 26 Aug. 1915; *s* of Sir (John) Donald Horsfall, 2nd Bt, and Henrietta (*d* 1936), *d* of William Musgrave; *S* father, 1975; *m* 1940, Cassandra Nora Bernardine, *d* of late G. E. Wright; two *s* one *d. Educ:* Uppingham. Major, Duke of Wellington's Regt. Dir, Skipton Building Society. Mem. Skipton RDC, 1952–74; Pres. Skipton Divl Conservative Assoc., 1966–79. JP North Yorks, 1959. *Recreation:* shooting. *Heir: s* Edward John Wright Horsfall [*b* 17 Dec. 1940; *m* 1965, Rosemary, *d* of Frank N. King; three *s*]. *Address:* Greenfield House, Embsay, Skipton, North Yorkshire. *T:* Skipton 4560.

HORSFIELD, Maj.-Gen. David Ralph, OBE 1962; FIEE; Associate Consultant, PA Management Consultants Ltd, since 1972; *b* 17 Dec. 1916; *s* of late Major Ralph B. and Morah Horsfield (*née* Baynes); *m* 1948, Sheelah Patricia Royal Eagan; two *s* two *d. Educ:* Oundle Sch.; RMA Woolwich; Cambridge Univ. (MA). Commnd in Royal Signals, 1936; comd Burma Corps Signals, 1942; Instr, Staff Coll., 1944–45; comd 2 Indian Airborne Signals, 1946–47; Instr, RMA Sandhurst, 1950–53; comd 2 Signal Regt, 1956–59; Principal Army Staff Officer, MoD, Malaya, 1959–61; Dir of Telecommunications (Army), 1966–68; ADC to the Queen, 1968–69; Deputy Communications and Electronics, Supreme HQ Allied Powers, Europe, 1968–69; Maj.-Gen. 1969; Chief Signal Officer, BAOR, 1969–72; Col Comdt, Royal Signals, 1972–78. Vice Pres., Nat. Ski Fedn, 1978–81. *Recreations:* ski-ing (British Ski Champion, 1949), the visual arts. *Address:* Southill House, Cranmore, Shepton Mallet, Somerset. *T:* Cranmore 395. *Club:* Ski Club of Great Britain.

HORSFIELD, Peter Muir Francis, QC 1978; *b* 15 Feb. 1932; *s* of Henry Taylor Horsfield, AFC, and Florence Lily (*née* Muir); *m* 1962, Anne Charlotte, *d* of late Sir Piers Debenham, 2nd Bt, and Lady (Angela) Debenham; three *s. Educ:* Beaumont; Trinity Coll., Oxford (BA 1st Cl. Hons Mods and Greats). Served RNR, 1955–57; Lieut RNR, 1960. Called to the Bar, Middle Temple, 1958; in practice at Chancery Bar, 1958–. *Recreation:* observational astronomy. *Address:* 24 Liverpool Road, Kingston Hill, Surrey. *T:* 01-546 3388.

HORSFORD, Maj.-Gen. Derek Gordon Thomond, CBE 1962 (MBE 1953); DSO 1944 and Bar 1945; *b* 7 Feb. 1917; *s* of late Captain H. T. Horsford, The Gloucestershire Regt, and Mrs V. E. Horsford, Bexhill-on-Sea; *m* 1948, Sheila Louise Russell Crawford; one *s* (and one step *s* two step *d*). *Educ:* Clifton Coll.; RMC, Sandhurst. Commissioned into 8th Gurkha Rifles, 1937; despatches 1943 and 1945; comd 4/1 Gurkha Rifles, Burma, 1944–45; transf. to RA, 1948; Instructor Staff Coll., 1950–52; transf. to King's Regt, 1950; GSO1, 2nd Infantry Div., 1955–56; comd 1st Bn, The King's Regt, 1957–59; AAG, AG2, War Office, 1959–60; Comdr 24th Infantry Brigade Group, Dec. 1960–Dec. 1962; Imperial Defence Coll., 1963; Brig., Gen. Staff, HQ, BAOR, 1964–66. Maj.-Gen. 1966; GOC 50 (Northumbrian) Div./Dist, 1966–67; GOC Yorks Dist, 1967–68; GOC 17 Div./Malaya District, 1969–70; Maj.-Gen., Brigade of Gurkhas, 1969–71; Dep. Comdr Land Forces, Hong Kong, 1970–71, retired. Col, The King's Regt, 1965–70; Col, The Gurkha Transport Regt, 1973–78. *Recreations:* travel, outdoor life. *Address:* St Mary's Cottage, Semley, Shaftesbury, Dorset. *Club:* Army and Navy.

HORSHAM, Bishop Suffragan of, since 1975; **Rt. Rev. Ivor Colin Docker;** *b* 3 Dec. 1925; *s* of Colonel Philip Docker, OBE, TD, DL, and Doris Gwendoline Docker (*née* Whitehill); *m* 1950, Thelma Mary, *d* of John William and Gladys Upton; one *s* one *d. Educ:* King Edward's High Sch., Birmingham; Univ. of Birmingham (BA); St Catherine's Coll., Oxford (MA). Curate of Normanton, Yorks, 1949–52; Lecturer of Halifax Parish Church, 1952–54; CMS Area Sec., 1954–59; Vicar of Midhurst, Sussex, 1959–64; RD of Midhurst, 1961–64; Vicar and RD of Seaford, 1964–71; Canon and Prebendary of Colworth in Chichester Cathedral, 1966–81; Vicar and RD of Eastbourne, 1971–75; Proctor in Convocation, 1970–75. *Recreations:* photography, travel, reading. *Address:* Bishop's Lodge, Worth, Crawley, Sussex RH10 4RT. *T:* Crawley 883051.

HORSHAM, Archdeacon of; *see* Kerr-Dineen, Ven. F. G.

HORSHAM, Jean, CBE 1979; Deputy Parliamentary Commissioner for Administration, 1981–82, retired; *b* 25 June 1922; *d* of Albert John James Horsham and Janet Horsham (*née* Henderson). *Educ:* Keith Grammar Sch. Forestry Commn, 1939–64, seconded to Min. of Supply, 1940–45; Min. of

Land and Natural Resources, 1964–66; Min. of Housing and Local Govt, 1966; Office of Parly Comr for Administration, 1967–82. *Address:* 14 Cotelands, Chichester Road, Croydon, Surrey CR0 5UD. *T:* 01-686 1557.

HORSLEY, Air Marshal Sir (Beresford) Peter (Torrington), KCB 1974; CBE 1964; MVO 1956; AFC 1945; idc; psc; pfc; Chairman: Horsley Wood & Co. Ltd, since 1975; Horsley Wood Printing Ltd, since 1975; Director: M. L. Holdings Ltd; M. L. Aviation Ltd; Aeromaritime (UK) Ltd; Member, Honeywell Advisory Council, since 1978; *b* 26 March 1921; *s* of late Capt. Arthur Beresford Horsley, CBE; *m* 1st, 1943, Phyllis Conrad Phinney (marr. diss. 1976); one *s* one *d* ; 2nd, 1976, Ann MacKinnon, *d* of Gareth and Frances Crwys-Williams; two step *s* two step *d. Educ:* Wellington Coll. Joined Royal Air Force, 1940; served in 2nd TAF and Fighter Command. Adjt Oxford Univ. Air Sqdn, 1948; Commands: No 9 and No 29 Sqdns, RAF Wattisham, RAF Akrotiri. Equerry to Princess Elizabeth and to the Duke of Edinburgh, 1949–52; Equerry to the Queen, 1952–53; Equerry to the Duke of Edinburgh, 1953–56. Dep. Comdt, Jt Warfare Establishment, RAF Old Sarum, 1966–68; Asst CAS (Operations), 1968–70; AOC No 1 (Bomber) Gp, 1971–73; Dep. C-in-C, Strike Comd, 1973–75. Retired RAF, 1975. Croix de Guerre, 1944. Holds Orders of Christ (Portugal), North Star (Sweden), and Menelik (Ethiopia). *Publication:* (as Peter Beresford) Journal of a Stamp Collector, 1972. *Recreations:* ski-ing, philately. *Address:* c/o Barclays Bank Ltd, High Street, Newmarket.

HORSLEY, Colin, OBE 1963; FRCM 1973; Hon. RAM 1977; Pianist; Professor, Royal College of Music, London; *b* Wanganui, New Zealand, 23 April 1920. *Educ:* Royal College of Music. Debut at invitation of Sir John Barbirolli at Hallé Concerts, Manchester, 1943. Soloist with all leading orchestras of Great Britain, the Royal Philharmonic Soc. (1953, 1959), Promenade Concerts, etc. Toured Belgium, Holland, Spain, France, Scandinavia, Malta, Ceylon, Malaya, Australia and New Zealand. Festival appearances include Aix-en-Provence, International Contemporary Music Festival, Palermo, British Music Festivals in Belgium, Holland and Finland. Broadcasts frequently, and records for His Master's Voice and Meridian Records. *Recreation:* gardening. *Address:* Tawsden Manor, Brenchley, Kent. *T:* Brenchley 2323.

HORSLEY, (George) Nicholas (Seward); Chairman, Northern Foods Ltd, since 1970; *b* 21 April 1934; *s* of Alec Stewart Horsley and Ida Seward Horsley; *m* 1st, 1958, Valerie Anne Edwards (marr. diss. 1975); two *s* one *d* ; 2nd, 1975, Sabita Sarkar. *Educ:* Keswick Grammar Sch.; Bootham Sch., York; Worcester Coll., Oxford (BA). Freelance journalist, 1957–58. Northern Dairies Ltd: Trainee Manager, 1958; Director, 1963; Vice-Chairman, 1968–70 (Northern Dairies Ltd changed its name to Northern Foods Ltd in 1972). Pres., Dairy Trade Fedn, 1975–77 and 1980–. Chm., BBC Consultative Group on Industrial and Business Affairs, 1980–; Mem., BBC Gen. Adv. Council, 1980–. *Recreations:* music, bridge, local pub, watching cricket, reading. *Address:* Northern Foods Ltd, Beverley House, St Stephen's Square, Hull, East Yorkshire HU1 3XG. *T:* Hull 25432; (home) Welton Lodge, Dale Road, Welton, near Brough, East Yorkshire HU15 1PE. *T:* Hull 668341.

HORSLEY, Sir Peter; *see* Horsley, Sir B. P. T.

HORSMAN, Malcolm; Managing Director, Tozer Kemsley & Millbourn (Holdings) Ltd, since 1981 (Director, since 1975); *b* 28 June 1933. Director, Slater Walker Securities Ltd, 1967–70; Chairman, Ralli International Ltd, 1969–73; Director, The Bowater Corporation Ltd, 1972–77. Member: Study Group on Local Authority Management Structures, 1971–72; South East Economic Planning Council, 1972–74; Royal Commission on the Press, 1974–77; Institute of Contemporary Arts Ltd, 1975–78; Exec. Council, British Centre, Internat. Theatre Inst., 1980–. Mem. Council, Oxford Centre for Management Studies, 1973–. Visiting Fellow, Cranfield Institute of Technology/The School of Management, 1977–. Vis. Lectr, Univ. of Transkei, 1977. Chm., Nat. Youth Theatre, 1982– (Dep. Chm. 1971–82); Member: Court, RCA, 1977–80; Editorial Bd, DRAMA, 1978–81; Council, Birthright, 1974–. *Address:* 28 Great Tower Street, EC3R 5DE.

HORSTEAD, Rt. Rev. James Lawrence Cecil, CMG 1962; CBE 1956; DD (Hon.) 1956; Canon Emeritus of Leicester Cathedral; *b* 16 Feb. 1898; *s* of James William and Mary Leah Horstead; *m* 1926, Olive Davidson; no *c. Educ:* Christ's Hosp.; University and St John's Coll., Durham (Mathematical Scholar, Lightfoot Scholar). BA 2nd Cl. Maths Hons 1921; Theol. Hons 1923; MA 1924; Deacon, 1923; Priest, 1924; Curate St Margaret's Church, Durham, 1923–26; Sec. for Durham Student Christian Movement, 1923–26; Principal Fourah Bay Coll., 1926–36; Canon Missioner Diocese of Sierra Leone, 1928–36; Sec. Church Missionary Soc., Sierra Leone, 1936–36; Bishop of Sierra Leone, 1936–61; Archbishop of West Africa, 1955–61; Rector of Appleby Magna, 1962–68; Asst Bp, Diocese of Leicester, 1962–76. *Publication:* Co-operation with Africans, International Review of Missions, April 1935.

HORT, Sir James Fenton, 8th Bt *cr* 1767; *b* 6 Sept. 1926; *s* of Sir Fenton George Hort, 7th Bt, and Gwendolene (*d* 1982), *d* of late Sir Walter Alcock, MVO; *S* father 1960; *m* 1951, Joan, *d* of late Edward Peat, Swallownest, Sheffield; two *s* two *d. Educ:* Marlborough; Trinity Coll., Cambridge. MA, MB, BChir, Cambridge, 1950. *Recreation:* fishing. *Heir: s* Andrew Edwin Fenton Hort, *b* 15 Nov. 1954. *Address:* Poundgate Lodge, Uckfield Road, Crowborough, Sussex.

HORTON, Dr Eric William; Director of Regulatory Affairs, Glaxo Group Research Ltd, since 1980; *b* 20 June 1929; *e s* of late Harold and of Agnes Horton; *m* 1956, Thalia Helen, *er d* of late Sir George Lowe; two *s* one *d*. *Educ:* Sedbergh Sch.; Edinburgh Univ. BSc, MB, ChB, PhD, DSc, MD, FRCPE. Mem. Scientific Staff, MRC, Nat. Inst. for Med. Res., London, 1958-60; Dir of Therapeutic Res. and Head of Pharmacology, Miles Labs Ltd, Stoke Poges, 1960-63; Sen. Lectr in Physiology, St Bartholomew's Hosp., London, 1963-66; Wellcome Prof. of Pharmacology, Sch. of Pharmacy, Univ. of London, 1966-69; Prof. of Pharmacology, Univ. of Edinburgh, 1969-80. Hon. Sen. Res. Fellow, Med. Coll. of St Bartholomew's Hosp., London, 1980-; Hon. Lectr in Pharmacol., Royal Free Hosp. Med. Sch., London, 1960-63. Member, Governing Body, Inveresk Res. Foundn (formerly International), 1971-80; Non-executive Director: Inveresk Res. Internat. Ltd, 1977-80; GLP Systems Ltd, 1978-80. Member: Adv. Cttee on Pesticides, MAFF, 1970-73; Biological Research and Cell Boards, MRC, 1973-75; Pharmacy Panel, SRC, 1980-81; Editorial Bd, British Jl of Pharmacology, 1960-66; Editorial Bd, Pharmacological Reviews, 1968-74. Hon. Treasurer, Brit. Pharmacological Soc., 1976-80. Baly Medal, RCP, 1973. *Publications:* Prostaglandins, 1972; papers in learned jls on peptides and prostaglandins. *Address:* Bury Farm House, Langley Upper Green, Saffron Walden, Essex CB11 4RU. *T:* Clavering 783.

HORTON, Maj.-Gen. Frank Cyril, CB 1957; OBE 1953; RM; *b* 31 May 1907; *s* of late Lieut-Comdr F. Horton, Royal Navy, and late Emma M. Hopper; *m* 1934, Jennie Ellaline Hammond: one *d*. *Educ:* Sir Roger Manwood's Sch. 2nd Lieut RM 1925; Lieut RM 1928; HMS Cumberland, China Station, 1928-29; HMS Royal Oak, Mediterranean Station, 1929-31; Captain RM, 1936; HMS Ajax, America and West Indies Station, 1936-37; Brevet Major, 1940; psc 1941; Actg Lieut-Col 1942; GSO1, Staff of Chief of Combined Operations, 1942-43; Comdg Officer, 44 (RM) Commando, SE Asia, 1943-44; Directing Staff, Army Staff Coll., 1945-46; Plans Div., Admiralty, 1946-48; Directing Staff, Jt Services Staff Coll., 1948-51; Comdt, Amphibious Sch., RM, 1951-52; idc 1953; Col GS, Staff of Comdt Gen., RM, 1954; Chief of Staff to Commandant Gen. Royal Marines, 1955-58; Maj. 1946; Lieut-Col 1949, Col 1953; Maj.-Gen. 1955; retired, 1958. County Civil Defence Officer, Essex, 1959; Regional Dir of Civil Defence, S Eastern Region, 1961-68. *Address:* Southland, Florance Lane, Groombridge, Sussex. *T:* Groombridge 355. *Club:* Royal Naval and Royal Albert Yacht (Portsmouth).

HORWOOD, Hon. Owen Pieter Faure, DMS; MP; Minister of Finance, South Africa, since 1975; Chancellor, University of Durban-Westville, since 1973; *b* 6 Dec. 1916; *e s* of late Stanley Ebden Horwood and of Anna Johanna Horwood (*née* Faure); *m* 1946, Helen Mary Watt; one *s* one *d*. *Educ:* Boys' High Sch., Paarl, CP; University of Cape Town (BCom). South African Air Force, 1940-42. Associate Prof. of Commerce, University of Cape Town, 1954-55; Prof. of Economics, University Coll. of Rhodesia and Nyasaland, 1956-57; Univ. of Natal: William Hudson Prof. of Economics, 1957-65; Dir of University's Natal Regional Survey; Principal and Vice-Chancellor, 1966-70. Mem., 1970-80, Leader, 1978-80, South African Senate; Minister of Indian Affairs and Tourism, 1972-74; Minister of Economic Affairs, 1974-75. Formerly Director: Netherlands Bank of South Africa Ltd; Rembrandt Tobacco Corp. SA Ltd; Nat. Building Soc.; Trans-Natal Coal Corp.; Bonus Investment Corp. of S Africa; Netherlands Insurance Co. of SA Ltd. Financial Adviser to Govt of Lesotho. Hon. DCom Port Elizabeth, 1980; Hon. Scriptural degree, Israel Torah Res. Inst. and Adelphi Univ., 1980; Hon. DEcon Rand Afrikaans, 1981. *Publications:* (jtly) Economic Systems of the Commonwealth, 1962; contribs to SA Jl of Economics, SA Bankers' Jl, Economica (London), Optima, etc. *Recreations:* cricket, gardening, sailing. *Address:* Private Bag X115, Pretoria, South Africa. *Clubs:* Durban (Durban); Kloof Country (Natal); Western Province Cricket; Cape Town Cricket (Captain 1943-48).

HOSE, John Horsley; National Trade Group Chairman, National Union of Agricultural and Allied Workers/Transport and General Workers' Union, since 1982 (President, National Union of Agricultural and Allied Workers, 1978-82); Forest Craftsman, Forestry Commission, since 1975 (Forest Worker, 1949, Skilled Forest Worker, 1950); *b* 21 March 1928; *s* of Harry and Margaret Eleanor Hose; *m* 1967, Margaret Winifred Gaskin. *Educ:* Sneinton Boulevard Council Sch.; Nottingham Bluecoat Sch. Architects' Junior Asst, 1943-46. National Service, with Royal Engineers, 1946-48. *Recreations:* walking, reading, drinking real ale. *Address:* 11 Sandringham Road, Sneinton Dale, Nottingham NG2 4HH. *T:* Nottingham 580494.

HOSEGOOD, Philip James; Under-Secretary, Welsh Office, 1976-80, retired; *b* 9 Sept. 1920; *s* of late George Frank and Madeleine Clarisse Hosegood; *m* 1948, Heather (*née* Roriston); two *d*. *Educ:* Heanor Grammar Sch.; correspondence courses. Joined Civil Service as Tax Officer, 1937; Exec. Officer, India Office, 1939. Served War Army, 1941-46. Asst Principal, Min. of Civil Aviation, 1948; Principal, Min. of Civil Aviation, 1951 (later Min. of Transport); Asst Sec., Welsh Office, 1965. *Recreations:* music, outdoor activities. *Address:* 16 Rheidol Close, Llanishen, Cardiff CF4 5NQ. *T:* Cardiff 756445.

HOSFORD, John Percival, MS, FRCS; retired; Surgeon, Lecturer on Surgery, St Bartholomew's Hospital (1936-60); Surgeon, King Edward VII Hospital for Officers and Florence Nightingale Hospital; Consulting Surgeon to Hospitals at Watford, Leatherhead, Hitchin, St Albans and to the Foundling

Hospital and Reedham Orphanage; *b* 24 July 1900; 2nd *s* of Dr B. Hosford, Highgate; *m* 1932, Millicent Sacheverell Violet Sybil Claud, *d* of late Brig.-Gen. C. Vaughan Edwards, CMG, DSO; one *s* one *d*. *Educ:* Highgate Sch.; St Bartholomew's Hosp. MB, BS (London) 1922; FRCS Eng. 1925; MS (London); University Gold Medal, 1925. Formerly Registrar St Bartholomew's Hosp. and of Royal National Orthopædic Hosp. Hunterian Prof., Royal College of Surgeons, 1932. Retired, Oct. 1960. Formerly: Mem. of Court of Examiners of Royal College of Surgeons; Examiner in Surgery at Universities of Oxford, London, Sheffield, Belfast; Fellow Assoc. of Surgeons (on Council) and Royal Society Med. *Publications:* numerous articles in medical and surgical journals and encyclopædias. *Recreation:* gardening. *Address:* Rua de Castelo Branco L4, Amoreira, 2765 Estoril, Portugal.

HOSIE, James Findlay, CBE 1972 (OBE 1955); a Director, Science Research Council, 1965-74; *b* 22 Aug. 1913; *m* 1951, Barbara Mary Mansell. *Educ:* Glasgow Univ. (MA Hons); St John's Coll., Cambridge (BA). Indian Civil Service, 1938-47; Principal, 1947-56, Asst Sec., 1956-58, Min. of Defence, London; Asst Sec. QMGF, War Office, 1958-61; Office of Minister for Science, later Dept of Educn. and Science, 1961-65. *Recreations:* bird-watching, gardening. *Address:* White Gables, West Street, Alfriston, Sussex. *T:* Alfriston 791.

HOSIER, John; Principal, Guildhall School of Music and Drama, since 1978; *b* 18 Nov. 1928; *s* of Harry J. W. Hosier and Constance (*née* Richmond). *Educ:* Preston Manor Sch.; St John's Coll., Cambridge. MA 1954. Taught in Ankara, Turkey, 1951-53; Music Producer, BBC Radio for schools, 1953-59; seconded to ABC, Sydney, to advise on educational music programmes, 1959-60; Music Producer, subseq. Sen. and Exec. Producer, BBC TV, pioneering first regular music broadcasts to schools, 1960-73; ILEA Staff Inspector for music, and Dir of Centre for Young Musicians, 1973-76. Member: Council, National Youth Orch., 1980; Radio London Adv. Council, 1981; various bds and cttees, incl. ISME, CNAA, and Macnaghten concerts; Vice-Chm., UK Council for Music Educn. Mem., Gulbenkian enquiry into training musicians, 1978. FRSA 1976; FGSM 1978; Hon. RAM 1980; FRCM 1981. *Compositions:* music for: Cambridge revivals of Parnassus, 1949, and Humorous Lovers, 1951; Something's Burning, Mermaid, 1974; many radio and TV productions. *Publications:* The Orchestra, 1961, revd edn 1977; various books, songs and arrangements for children; contribs on music to educnl jls. *Address:* Guildhall School of Music and Drama, Barbican, EC2Y 8DT. *T:* 01-628 2571. *Club:* City Livery.

HOSKING, Eric (John), OBE 1977; photographer, ornithologist, broadcaster; *b* 2 Oct. 1909; 3rd *s* of late Albert Hosking and Margaret Helen, *d* of William Steggall; *m* 1939, Dorothy, *d* of late Harry Sleigh; two *s* one *d*. *Educ:* Stationers' Company's Sch. London, N8. Hon. Fellow, Royal Photographic Society; a Vice-Pres., Royal Society for the Protection of Birds; Hon. Vice-Pres., London Natural History Soc.; a Vice-Pres., British Naturalists' Assoc.; Vice-President: Nature Photographic Society; British Ornithologists' Union; Chm., Photographic Advisory Cttee to Nature Conservancy. Scientific Fellow of Zoological Society; Fellow, Inst. Incorp. Photographers. Exhibited at Royal Photographic Society, 1932- (Council, 1950-56; Fellowship & Associateship Admissions Cttee, 1951-56, 1960-65 and 1967-); Member: BOU, 1935-; Brit. Trust for Ornithology, 1938-; Cornell Laboratory of Ornithology, America, 1961-. Dir of Photography to Coto Doñana Expedn, Spain, 1956 and 1957; Leader of Cazoria Valley Expedition, Spain, 1959; Dir of Photography, British Ornithologists' Expedition to Bulgaria, 1960, to Hungary, 1961; other expeditions: Mountfort-Jordan, 1963; British-Jordan, 1965; Pakistan, 1966; World Wildlife Fund, Pakistan, 1967; Lindblad Galapagos Islands, 1970; Kenya and Rhodesia, 1972; Tanzania and Kenya, 1974 and 1977; Seychelles, 1978; India and Nepal, 1979; Falklands and Antarctic, 1979; circumnavigation of Antarctic, and New Zealand and Australia, 1981. Photographic Editor: of New Naturalist, 1942-; of British Birds, 1960-76. RGS Cherry Kearton Award, 1968; RSPB Gold Medal, 1974; Zoological Soc. Silver Medal, 1975. *Publications:* Intimate Sketches from Bird Life, 1940; The Art of Bird Photography, 1944; Birds of the Day, 1944; Birds of the Night, 1945; More Birds of the Day, 1946; The Swallow, 1946; Masterpieces of Bird Photography, 1947; Birds in Action, 1949; Birds Fighting, 1955; Bird Photography as a Hobby, 1961; Nesting Birds, Eggs and Fledglings, 1967; An Eye for a Bird (autobiog.), 1970; Wildlife Photography, 1973; Birds of Britain, 1978; Eric Hosking's Birds, 1979; Eric Hosking's Owls, 1982; Antarctic Wildlife, 1982. Illustrator of many books on natural history, by photographs. *Address:* 20 Crouch Hall Road, N8 8XH. *T:* 01-340 7703.

HOSKINS, Prof. William George, CBE 1971; FBA 1969; MA, PhD; *b* Exeter, 22 May 1908; *e s* of late William George Hoskins and Alice Beatrice Dymond; *m* 1933, Frances Jackson; one *s* one *d*. *Educ:* Hele's Sch., Exeter; University Coll., Exeter. Lectr in Economics, University Coll., Leicester, 1931-41; 1946-48; Central Price Regulation Cttee, 1941-45; Reader in English Local History, University Coll. (now Univ.) of Leicester, 1948-51; Reader in Econ. Hist., University of Oxford, 1951-65; Hatton Prof. of English History, University of Leicester, 1965-68, retired in despair, 1968; Emeritus Professor, 1968. BBC TV Series, Landscapes of England, 1976, 1977, 1978. Mem. Royal Commission on Common Land, 1955-58; Adv. Cttee on Bldgs of Special Architectural and Historical Interest (Min. of Housing and Local Govt), 1955-64; Vice-Pres. Leicestershire Archæol and Hist. Soc., 1952; President: Dartmoor Preserv. Assoc., 1962-76; Devonshire Assoc., 1978-79;

British Agricultural History Soc., 1972-74; Leverhulme Res. Fellow, 1961-63; Leverhulme Emeritus Fellowship, 1970-71. Murchison Award, RGS, 1976. Hon. FRIBA, 1973. Hon. DLitt: Exon, 1974; CNAA, 1976; DUniv Open, 1981. *Publications:* Industry, Trade and People in Exeter, 1935; Heritage of Leicestershire, 1946; Midland England, 1949; Essays in Leicestershire History, 1950; Chilterns to Black Country, 1951; East Midlands and the Peak, 1951; Devonshire Studies, (with H. P. R. Finberg), 1952; Devon (New Survey of England), 1954; The Making of the English Landscape, 1955; The Midland Peasant, 1957; The Leicestershire Landscape, 1957; Exeter in the Seventeenth Century, 1957; Local History in England, 1959; Devon and its People, 1959; Two Thousand Years in Exeter, 1960; The Westward Expansion of Wessex, 1960; Shell Guide to Rutland, 1963; The Common Lands of England and Wales (with L. Dudley Stamp), 1963; Provincial England, 1963; Old Devon, 1966; Fieldwork in Local History, 1967; Shell Guide to Leicestershire, 1970; History from the Farm, 1970; English Landscapes, 1973; The Age of Plunder, 1976; One Man's England, 1978. *Recreation:* parochial explorations. *Address:* 2 Lyndhurst Road, Exeter. *T:* 56604.

HOSKYNS, Sir Benedict (Leigh), 16th Bt, *cr* 1676; *b* 27 May 1928; *s* of Rev. Sir Edwyn Clement Hoskyns, 13th Bt, MC, DD and Mary Trym, *d* of Edwin Budden, Macclesfield; *S* brother 1956; *m* 1953, Ann Wilkinson; two *s* two *d. Educ:* Haileybury; Corpus Christi Coll., Cambridge; London Hospital. BA Cantab 1949; MB, BChir Cantab 1952. House Officer at the London Hospital, 1953. RAMC, 1953-56. House Officer at Royal Surrey County Hospital and General Lying-In Hospital, York Road, SE1, 1957-58; DObstRCOG 1958; in general practice, 1958–. *Heir: s* Edwyn Wren Hoskyns [*b* 4 Feb. 1956. *Educ:* Nottingham Univ. Medical School (BM, BS 1979)]. *Address:* Harewood, Great Oakley, Essex. *T:* Ramsey 880341.

HOSKYNS, Sir John (Austin Hungerford Leigh), Kt 1982; Director, ICL Plc, since 1982; *b* 23 Aug. 1927; *s* of Lt-Colonel Chandos Benedict Arden Hoskyns and Joyce Austin Hoskyns; *m* 1956, Miranda Jane Marie Mott; two *s* one *d. Educ:* Winchester College. Served in The Rifle Brigade, 1945-57 (Captain); IBM United Kingdom Ltd, 1957-64; founded John Hoskyns & Co. Ltd, later part of Hoskyns Group Ltd (Chm. and Man. Dir), 1964-75. Hd of PM's Policy Unit, 1979-82. *Recreations:* opera, shooting. *Address:* 83 Clapham Common West Side, SW4. *T:* 01-228 9505. *Club:* Travellers'.

HOTHAM, family name of **Baron Hotham.**

HOTHAM, 8th Baron, *cr* 1797; **Henry Durand Hotham;** Bt 1621; DL; *b* 3 May 1940; *s* of 7th Baron Hotham, CBE, and Lady Letitia Sibell Winifred Cecil, *er d* of 5th Marquess of Exeter, KG; *S* father, 1967; *m* 1972, Alexandra Stirling Home, *d* of late Maj. Andrew S. H. Drummond Moray; two *s* one *d. Educ:* Eton; Cirencester Agricultural Coll. Late Lieut, Grenadier Guards; ADC to Governor of Tasmania, 1963-66. DL Humberside, 1981. *Heir: s* Hon. William Beaumont Hotham, *b* 13 Oct. 1972. *Address:* Dalton Hall, Dalton Holme, Beverley, Yorks; Scorborough Hall, Driffield, Yorks.

HOTHFIELD, 4th Baron, *cr* 1881; **Thomas Sackville Tufton;** Bt 1851; *b* 20 July 1916; *s* of Hon. Sackville Philip Tufton (*d* 1936; 2nd *s* of 1st Baron), and Winifred Mary Ripley Dalton (*d* 1970); *S* cousin, 1961. *Educ:* Eton; Cambridge Univ. *Heir: cousin* Lieut-Col George William Anthony Tufton, TD [*b* 28 Oct. 1904; *m* 1936, Evelyn Margarette Mordaunt; two *s* one *d*]. *Address:* House of Lords, SW1.

HOTSON, Leslie, LittD (Cambridge); FRSL; Shakespearean scholar and writer; *b* Delhi, Ont, Canada, 16 Aug. 1897; *s* of John H. and Lillie S. Hotson; *m* 1919, Mary May, *d* of Frederick W. Peabody. *Educ:* Harvard Univ. Sheldon Travelling Fellow, Harvard, 1923-24; Sterling Research Fellow, Yale, 1926-27; Associate Prof. of English, New York Univ., 1927-29; Guggenheim Memorial Fellow, 1929-31; Prof. of English, Haverford Coll., Pa, 1931-41; served War of 1939-45, 1st Lieut and Capt. Signal Corps, US Army, 1943-46; Fulbright Exchange Scholar, Bedford Coll., London, 1949-50; Research Associate, Yale, 1953; Fellow, King's Coll., Cambridge, 1954-60. *Publications:* The Death of Christopher Marlowe, 1925; The Commonwealth and Restoration Stage, 1928; Shelley's Lost Letters to Harriet, 1930; Shakespeare versus Shallow, 1931; I, William Shakespeare, 1937; Shakespeare's Sonnets Dated, 1949; Shakespeare's Motley, 1952; Queen Elizabeth's Entertainment at Mitcham, 1953; The First Night of Twelfth Night, 1954; Shakespeare's Wooden O, 1959; Mr W. H., 1964; Shakespeare by Hilliard, 1977. *Recreation:* boating. *Address:* Northford, Conn 06472, USA.

HOTTER, Hans; opera and concert singer; producer; Professor at Vienna Musik-Hochschule; teaches masterclasses in Austria, Great Britain, Holland, USA, and Australia, and private students in Munich; *b* Offenbach, Germany; *m* 1936, Helga Fischer; one *s* one *d. Educ:* Munich. Concert career began in 1929 and opera career in 1930. Mem. of Munich, Vienna and Hamburg State Operas; guest singer in opera and concerts in all major cities of Europe and USA; concert tours in Australia; for the past 10 years, connected with Columbia Gramophone Co., England; guest singer, Covent Garden Opera, London, 1947-. Festivals: Salzburg, Edinburgh and Bayreuth. *Address:* Emil Dittlerstrasse 26, München 71, West Germany.

HOUGH, George Hubert, CBE 1965; PhD; FRAeS; Chairman: Forthstar Ltd, since 1980; Medwing Ltd, since 1981; *b* 21 Oct. 1921; *m* Hazel Ayrton (*née* Russel); one *s* two *d. Educ:* Winsford Grammar Sch.; King's Coll., London. BSc (Hons Physics), PhD; FIEE. Admiralty Signals Estabt, 1940-46. Standard

Telecommunication Laboratories Ltd (ITT), 1946-51 (as external student at London Univ. prepared thesis on gaseous discharge tubes); de Havilland Propellers Ltd: early mem. Firestreak team in charge of develt of guidance systems, 1951-59; Chief Engr (Guided Weapons), 1959; Chief Executive (Engrg), 1961; Dir, de Havilland Aircraft Co., 1962; Hawker Siddeley Dynamics Ltd: Technical Dir, 1963; Dep. Managing Dir, 1968; Man. Dir, 1977; Dep. Chief Exec., Dynamics Group British Aerospace, 1977. Dep. Chm., 1977, Chief Exec., 1977-80, Chm., 1978-80, British Smelter Constructions Ltd; Director: Sheepbridge Engrg Ltd, 1977-79; Scientific Finance Ltd, 1979–; Programmed Neuro Cybernetics Ltd, 1979–; Landis & Gyr Ltd, 1980–. *Recreations:* sailing, golf. *Address:* Trelyon, Rock, near Wadebridge, Cornwall. *T:* Trebetherick 3454. *Club:* St James's.

HOUGH, Prof. Graham Goulder; Praelector and Fellow of Darwin College, Cambridge, 1964-75, now Emeritus Fellow; Professor of English, 1966-75, now Emeritus, University Reader in English, 1965-66; *b* 14 Feb. 1908; *s* of Joseph and Clara Hough; *m* 1st, 1942, Rosamund Oswell; one *s* one *d* ; 2nd, 1952, Ingeborg Neumann. *Educ:* Prescot Grammar Sch.; University of Liverpool; Queens' Coll., Cambridge. Lecturer in English, Raffles Coll., Singapore, 1930. Served War of 1939-45, with Singapore Royal Artillery (Volunteer), 1942-45. Professor of English, University of Malaya, 1946; Visiting Lecturer, Johns Hopkins Univ., 1950; Fellow of Christ's Coll., Cambridge, 1950 (Tutor, 1955-60); Visiting Prof. Cornell University, 1958. Hon. DLitt, Malaya, 1955; LittD, Cambridge, 1961. *Publications:* The Last Romantics, 1949; The Romantic Poets, 1953; The Dark Sun, 1957; Image and Experience, 1960; Legends and Pastorals, 1961; A Preface to the Faerie Queene, 1962; The Dream and the Task, 1963; An Essay on Criticism, 1966; Style and Stylistics, 1969; Selected Essays, 1978. *Recreation:* travel. *Address:* The White Cottage, Grantchester, Cambridge. *T:* Trumpington 2227.

HOUGH, John Patrick; *b* 6 July 1928; *s* of William Patrick Hough, MBE, Lt-Cmdr RN and Eva Harriet Hough; *m* 1956, Dorothy Nadine Akerman; four *s* one *d. Educ:* Purbrook High School. FCA, MIMC, FBCS. Articled M. R. Cobbett & Co., Portsmouth, 1950-53; Derbyshire & Co., 1953-54; Turquand Youngs & Co., 1954-57; Computer Specialist, IBM United Kingdom Ltd, 1957-61; Consultant 1961-62, Partner 1962-69, Robson Morrow & Co.; Dep. Sec., Inst. of Chartered Accountants in England and Wales, 1969-71, Sec., 1972-82. *Recreations:* music, food and wine. *Address:* 3 Talbot Place, Blackheath, SE3. *Clubs:* Travellers'; London Rowing.

HOUGH, Julia Marie, (Judy); *see* Taylor, Judy.

HOUGH, Richard Alexander; writer; *b* 15 May 1922; *s* of late George and Margaret May Hough; *m* 1st, 1943, Helen Charlotte (marr. diss.) *o d* of Dr Henry Woodyatt; four *d* ; 2nd, 1980, Judy Taylor, *qv. Educ:* Frensham Heights. Served War, RAF Pilot, Fighter Command, home and overseas, 1941-46. Publisher, 1947-70: Bodley Head until 1955; Hamish Hamilton as Dir and Man. Dir, Hamish Hamilton Children's Books Ltd, 1955-70. Contrib. to: Guardian; Observer; Washington Post; NY Times; Encounter; History Today; New Yorker. Mem. Council, 1970-73, 1975–, Vice-Pres., 1977–, Navy Records Society. Chm., Auxiliary Hospitals Cttee King Edward's Hospital Fund, 1975-80. *Publications:* The Fleet that had to Die, 1958; Admirals in Collision, 1959; The Potemkin Mutiny, 1960; The Hunting of Force Z, 1963; Dreadnought, 1964; The Big Battleship, 1966; First Sea Lord: an authorised life of Admiral Lord Fisher, 1969; The Blind Horn's Hate, 1971; Captain Bligh and Mr Christian, 1972 (Daily Express Best Book of the Sea Award); Louis and Victoria: the first Mountbattens, 1974; One Boy's War: per astra ad ardua, 1975; (ed) Advice to a Grand-daughter (Queen Victoria's letters), 1975; The Great Admirals, 1977; The Murder of Captain James Cook, 1979; Man o' War, 1979; Nelson, 1980; Mountbatten: Hero of Our Time, 1980; *novels:* Angels One Five, 1978; The Fight of the Few, 1979; The Fight to the Finish, 1979; Buller's Guns, 1981; Razor Eyes, 1981; Buller's Dreadnought, 1982; numerous books for children under *pseudonym* Bruce Carter. *Address:* Denfurlong, Lower Chedworth, near Cheltenham, Glos GL54 4AP. *T:* Fossebridge 422; Flat 7, 217 Sussex Gardens, W2 2RJ. *T:* 01-723 7327. *Clubs:* Garrick, MCC.

HOUGHTON, family name of **Baron Houghton of Sowerby.**

HOUGHTON OF SOWERBY, Baron *cr* 1974 (Life Peer), of Sowerby, W Yorks; **Arthur Leslie Noel Douglas Houghton,** PC 1964; CH 1967; *b* 11 Aug. 1898; *s* of John and Martha Houghton, Long Eaton, Derbyshire; *m* 1939, Vera Travis; no *c. Educ:* Inland Revenue Staff Fedn, 1922-60. Broadcaster in "Can I Help You?" Programme, BBC, 1941-64. Alderman LCC, 1947-49; Mem. Gen. Council, TUC, 1952-60. Chm., Staff Side, Civil Service National Whitley Council, 1956-58. MP (Lab) Sowerby, WR Yorks, March 1949-Feb. 1974; Chm. Public Accounts Cttee, 1963-64; Chancellor of the Duchy of Lancaster, 1964-66; Minister Without Portfolio, 1966-67. Chm., Parly Lab. Party, 1967-70, Nov. 1970-1974. Chairman: British Parly Gp, Population and Develt, 1978–; House of Lords Industry Study Gp, 1979–. Member: Commn on the Constitution, 1969-73; Royal Commn on Standards of Conduct in Public Life, 1974–. Chairman: Commonwealth Scholarships Commn, 1967-68; Young Volunteer Force Foundation, 1967-70 (Jt Vice-Chm. 1970-71); Teachers' Pay Inquiry, 1974; Cttee on aid to Political Parties, 1975-76; Cttee on Security of Cabinet Papers, 1976; Cttee for Reform of Animal Experimentation, 1977–; Vice-Pres., RSPCA, 1978-82. *Publication:* Paying for the Social Services, 2nd edn, 1968. *Address:* 110 Marsham Court, SW1.

T: 01-834 0602; Becks Cottage, Whitehill Lane, Bletchingley, Surrey. *T:* Godstone 3340. *Club:* Reform.

HOUGHTON, Albert Morley; retired 1972 as Under-Secretary, Department of Trade and Industry; *b* 26 June 1914; *m* 1939, Lallie Whittington Hughes; no *c*. Entered Civil Service, Administrative class, 1946; Civil Service Selection Board, 1946-49; Ministry of Transport, 1949-65; UK Delegn to NATO 1954-56; Shipping Attaché to Comr Gen. for SE Asia, 1956-60; Under-Sec., and Hd of Electronics and Telecommunications Div., Min. of Technology, 1965-70. *Recreations:* reading, music, gardening. *Address:* High Beeches, North Pickenham, Swaffham, Norfolk. *T:* Holme Hale 440489.

HOUGHTON, Rev. Alfred Thomas, MA, LTh; General Secretary Bible Churchmen's Missionary Society, 1945-66, Vice-President 1968; Hon. Canon, Diocese of Morogoro, Central Tanganyika, 1965; *b* Stafford, 11 April 1896; *s* of Rev. Thomas Houghton (Editor of the Gospel Magazine and Vicar of Whitington, Stoke Ferry, Norfolk) and Elizabeth Ann Houghton; *m* 1924, Coralie Mary, *d* of H. W. Green, and *g d* of Maj.-Gen. Green, Indian Army; two *s* four *d. Educ:* Clarence Sch. (now Canford Sch.); Durham Univ. (University Coll.); London Coll. of Divinity. BA Durham, 1923; MA Durham, 1929. Commissioned 2/5th PA Som LI, Burma, 1917; Staff Officer to Inspector of Infantry, South, AHQ India, 1918; Staff Capt., QMG's Br, AHQ India, 1919; demobilised, 1919; Deacon, 1921; Priest, 1922; Missionary Sch. of Medicine, 1923-24; Supt of BCMS Mission in Burma, 1924-40; Asst Bishop-Designate of Rangoon, 1940-44 (cancelled owing to Japanese occupation of Burma); Travelling Sec., Inter-Varsity Fellowship of Evangelical Unions, 1941-44, and Asst Sec., Graduates' Fellowship, 1944-45. Pres. Missionary Sch. of Medicine, 1948-77; Trustee Keswick Convention Council, 1948, and Chm., 1951-69; Chairman: Conference of British Missionary Socs, 1960; Church of England Evangelical Council, 1960-66; Pres. Mt Hermon Missionary Training Coll., 1960-71; Vice-President: Evangelical Alliance; Lord's Day Observance Soc. *Publications:* Tailum Jan, 1930; Dense Jungle Green, 1937; Preparing to be a Missionary, 1956. *Address:* 14 Alston Court, St Albans Road, Barnet, Herts EN5 4LJ. *T:* 01-449 1741.

HOUGHTON, Arthur A., Jr; Chairman, Steuben Glass, since 1973 (President, 1933-73); *b* Corning, New York, USA, 12 Dec. 1906; *s* of Arthur Amory and Mabel Hollister Houghton; *m* 1973, Nina Rodale; one *s* three *d* of a previous marriage. *Educ:* St Paul's Sch.; Harvard Univ. Entered employment of Corning Glass Works, 1929; successively in manufacturing dept, in treasury dept, Asst to Pres., and Vice-Pres. Served War of 1942-45; Chm., Academic Planning Bd, US Army Air Forces Intelligence Sch. (Lieut-Col); Chm., Wye Institute (Maryland). Dir, Corning Glass Works; formerly Director: US Steel Corporation; New York Life Insurance Company; formerly Trustee: United States Trust Company; New York Public Library; Trustee Emeritus: Metropolitan Museum of Art; Pierpont Morgan Library; Mem., Bibliographical Socs of London, Oxford and Cambridge; Past President: Keats-Shelley Assoc. of America; Shakespeare Assoc. of America. A Senior Fellow: Royal College of Art, London; RSA, London. Holds numerous hon. doctorates in Humanities, Law, Letters, Science, Literature and the Arts. Michael Friedsam Medal in Industrial Art. Officer Legion of Honour (France); Commandeur de l'Ordre des Arts et des Lettres. Assoc. CStJ. *Address:* Wye Plantation, Queenstown, Maryland 21658, USA. *Clubs:* Century, Union, Harvard, Knickerbocker, Fifth Avenue (New York); Club of Odd Volumes (Boston); Philobiblon (Philadelphia).

HOUGHTON, Brian Thomas; Under Secretary and Principal Finance Officer, Inland Revenue, since 1977; *b* 22 Aug. 1931; *s* of Bernard Charles Houghton and Sadie Houghton; *m* 1953, Joyce Beryl (*née* Williams); three *s* one *d. Educ:* City Boys' Sch., Leicester; Christ's Coll., Cambridge. BA (Mod. Langs), MA 1957. Inland Revenue, 1957; Private Sec. to Chief Sec., HM Treasury, 1966-68; Assistant Secretary: Inland Revenue, 1968-75; HM Treasury, 1975-77. *Address:* 1 Barns Dene, Harpenden, Herts AL5 2HH. *T:* Harpenden 5905.

HOUGHTON, Herbert; Chairman, Stenhouse Holdings Ltd, 1980-82; Director: Reed Stenhouse Cos Ltd, since 1977; British Vita Co. Ltd, since 1969; *b* 4 Oct. 1920; *s* of Herbert Edward and Emily Houghton; *m* 1939, Dorothy Ballantyne; one *s* one *d. Educ:* William Hulmes' Grammar School. Director, Cockshoots Ltd, 1955; Man. Dir, Stenhouse Northern Ltd, 1968; Chairman: Sir Wm Garthwaite (Holdings) Ltd, 1973; Sten-Re Ltd, 1973; Director and Chief Executive, A. R. Stenhouse & Partners Ltd, 1977. *Recreations:* overseas travel, golf, reading, gardening. *Address:* Hazleford Hall, Leadmill, Hathersage, Sheffield S30 1BA. *T:* Hope Valley 50297.

HOUGHTON, Dr John, JP; Director, Teesside Polytechnic, 1971-79, retired (Principal, Constantine College of Technology, 1961-70); *b* 12 June 1922; *s* of George Stanley Houghton and Hilda (*née* Simpson); *m* 1951, Kathleen Lamb; one *s* one *d. Educ:* King Henry VIII Sch., Coventry; Hanley High Sch.; Coventry Techn. Coll.; King's Coll., Cambridge; Queen Mary Coll., London Univ. BSc (hons) Engrg 1949; PhD 1952. CEng, MIMechE, FRAeS. Aircraft Apprentice, Sir W. G. Armstrong-Whitworth Aircraft Ltd, 1938-43; design and stress engr, 1943-46; student at univ. (Clayton Fellow), 1946-51; Lectr, Queen Mary Coll., London Univ., 1950-52; Sen. Lectr and Head of Aero-Engrg, Coventry Techn. Coll., 1952-57; Head of Dept of Mech. Engrg, Brunel Coll. Advanced Technology, 1957-61. Freeman, City of Coventry, 1943. JP Middlesbrough, 1962. *Publications:* (with D. R. L. Smith) Mechanics

of Fluids by Worked Examples, 1959; various research reports, reviews and articles in professional and learned jls. *Recreations:* keen sportsman (triple Blue), do-it-yourself activities, gardening, photography. *Address:* 14 Marton Moor Road, Nunthorpe, Middlesbrough, Cleveland. *T:* Middlesbrough 35263. *Club:* Middlesbrough Rotary.

HOUGHTON, Prof. John Theodore, FRS 1972; on secondment as Director (Appleton), since 1979 and Deputy Director, since 1981, Rutherford Appleton Laboratory, Science and Engineering Research Council (formerly Science Research Council); Professor of Atmospheric Physics, Oxford University, since 1976; Fellow of Jesus College, Oxford, since 1960; *b* 30 Dec. 1931; *s* of Sidney M. Houghton, schoolmaster and Miriam Houghton; *m* Margaret Edith Houghton (*née* Broughton), MB, BS, DPH; one *s* one *d. Educ:* Rhyl Grammar Sch.; Jesus Coll., Oxford (Scholar). BA hons Physics 1951, MA, DPhil 1955. Research Fellow, RAE Farnborough, 1954-57; Lectr in Atmospheric Physics, Oxford Univ., 1958-62; Reader, 1962-76. Member: Astronomy, Space and Radio Bd, SERC (formerly SRC), 1970-73 and 1976-81; Meteorological Cttee, 1975-80; Jt Organising Cttee, Global Atmospheric Res. Programme, 1976-79; Chm., Jt Scientific Cttee, World Climate Research Programme, 1981-. Pres., RMetS, 1976-78. Buchan Prize, RMetS, 1966; Charles Chree medal and prize, Inst. of Physics, 1979. FInstP. *Publications:* (with S. D. Smith) Infra-Red Physics, 1966; The Physics of Atmospheres, 1977; papers in learned jls on atmospheric radiation, spectroscopy and remote sounding from satellites. *Recreations:* sailing, walking, gardening. *Address:* Lindfield, 1 Begbroke Lane, Begbroke, Oxford; Rutherford Appleton Laboratory, Chilton, Didcot, Oxford.

HOUGHTON, Maj.-Gen. Robert Dyer, CB 1963; OBE 1947; MC 1942; DL; *b* 7 March 1912; *s* of late J. M. Houghton, Dawlish, Devon; *m* 1940, Dorothy Uladh, *y d* of late Maj.-Gen. R. W. S. Lyons, IMS; two *s* one *d. Educ:* Haileybury Coll. Royal Marines Officer, 1930-64; Col Comdt, Royal Marines, 1973-76. Gen. Sec., Royal UK Beneficent Assoc., 1968-78. DL East Sussex, 1977. *Recreations:* gardening, sailing, model engineering. *Address:* Vert House, Whitesmith, near Lewes, East Sussex. *Club:* Army and Navy.

HOUGHTON, Rev. Canon William Reginald; Canon Residentiary of Gloucester Cathedral, 1969-78, now Emeritus; *b* 28 Sept. 1910; *s* of late William Houghton and late Elizabeth Houghton; unmarried. *Educ:* St John's Coll., Durham; Westcott House, Cambridge. BA (Durham) 1940; Dipl. in Th. (Durham) 1941; MA (Durham) 1943. Curate, St Clement, Leeds, 1941-43, Leeds Parish Church, 1943-47 (Senior Curate, 1945-47); Vicar of Beeston, Leeds, 1947-54. Surrogate, 1949-54. Public Preacher, Dio. Southwark, 1954-62; Asst Sec. South London Church Fund and Southwark Diocesan Board of Finance, 1954-56, Dep. Sec., 1956-60, Sec., 1960-61; Sec. Southwark Dio. Bd of Dilapidations, 1956-60; Canon Residentiary (Treas.) of Southwark Cathedral, 1959-62. Rector of St Mary le Crypt with St John the Baptist, Gloucester, 1962-69. *Recreations:* travel and reading. *Address:* Church Cottage, Diddlebury, Craven Arms, Shropshire SY7 9DH. *T:* Munslow 208.

HOULDEN, Rev. Canon James Leslie; Lecturer in New Testament Studies, King's College, London University, since 1977; *b* 1 March 1929; *s* of James and Lily Alice Houlden. *Educ:* Altrincham Grammar Sch.; Queen's Coll., Oxford. Asst Curate, St Mary's, Hunslet, Leeds, 1955-58; Chaplain, Chichester Theological Coll., 1958-60; Chaplain Fellow, Trinity Coll., Oxford, 1960-70; Principal, Cuddesdon Theol Coll., later Ripon Coll., Cuddesdon, 1970-77. Hon. Canon of Christ Church Oxford, 1976-77. Member: Liturgical Commn, 1969-76; Doctrine Commn of C of E, 1969-76; Gen. Synod of C of E, 1980-. *Publications:* Paul's Letters from Prison, 1970; (ed) A Celebration of Faith, 1970; Ethics and the New Testament, 1973; The Johannine Epistles, 1974; The Pastoral Epistles, 1976; Patterns of Faith, 1977; (contrib.) The Myth of God Incarnate, 1977; Explorations in Theology 3, 1978; (contrib.) Incarnation and Myth, 1979; What Did the First Christians Believe?, 1982; reviews and articles in learned jls. *Address:* 33 Raleigh Court, Lymer Avenue, SE19. *T:* 01-670 6648. *Club:* Athenæum.

HOULDER, John Maurice, CBE 1977 (MBE (mil.) 1941); Chairman, Houlder Offshore Ltd, since 1961; *b* 20 Feb. 1916; *m* 1981, Rody, *d* of late Major Luke White. Licensed Aircraft Engineer. Mem. Exec. Board, Lloyds Register of Shipping; Director of Furness Withy & Co. Limited, and Chairman or Director of 26 shipping, engineering and aviation companies. Pres., Soc. for Underwater Technology, 1978-80. *Recreations:* ski-ing, flying, bird-watching, computer programming. *Address:* 53 Leadenhall Street, EC3A 2BR. *T:* 01-481 2963. *Clubs:* Air Squadron; Kandahar Ski, B & B Ski, 1001.

HOULDSWORTH, Sir (Harold) Basil, 2nd Bt, *cr* 1956; Consultant Anæsthetist, Barnsley and District Hospitals, since 1954; *b* 21 July 1922; *s* of Sir Hubert Stanley Houldsworth, 1st Bt, QC and (Hilda Frances) Lady Houldsworth (*née* Clegg) (*d* 1978); *S* father 1956; *m* 1946, Norah Clifford Halmshaw; one *d. Educ:* Heckmondwike Grammar Sch.; Leeds Sch. of Medicine, MRCS, LRCP 1946; FFA RCS 1954; DA Eng. 1951. Junior Registrar Anæsthetist, Leeds Gen. Infirmary, 1946-48; Graded Specialist Anæsthetist, RAMC, 1948-50; Registrar Anæsthetist, Leeds General Infirmary and St James Hospital, Leeds, 1950-53; Senior Registrar, Sheffield City General Hospital, 1953-54. *Recreations:* theatre, ballet and gardening. *Heir:* none. *Address:* Shadwell House, Lundhill Road, Wombwell, near Barnsley, South Yorks. *T:* Barnsley 753191.

HOULDSWORTH, Sir Reginald (Douglas Henry), 4th Bt, *cr* 1887, OBE 1945; TD 1944; DL; landowner; *b* 9 July 1903; *s* of Sir Thomas Houldsworth, 3rd Bt, CBE; *S* father 1961; *m* 1934, Margaret May, *d* of late Cecil Emilius Laurie; one *s* two *d*. *Educ:* Shrewsbury Sch.; Cambridge Univ. Hon. Col Ayrshire ECO Yeomanry, 1960-67; Commanded: Ayrshire Yeomanry, 1940-42; 4 Pack Mule Group, 1943-45. DL Ayrshire, 1970-. *Heir: s* Richard Thomas Reginald Houldsworth [*b* 2 Aug. 1947; *m* 1970, Jane, *o d* of Alistair Orr, Sydehead, Beith; two *s*]. *Address:* Kirkbride, Maybole, Ayrshire. *T:* Crosshill 202. *Clubs:* Cavalry and Guards; Western Meeting (Ayr); Prestwick (Prestwick).

HOULT, Norah; novelist and journalist; *b* Dublin; *d* of Powis Hoult and Margaret O'Shaughnessy. *Educ:* various boarding schools. *Publications:* Poor Women, 1928; Time, Gentlemen! Time!, 1929; Apartments to Let, 1931; Youth Can't be Served, 1933; Holy Ireland, 1935; Coming From the Fair, 1937; Nine Years is a Long Time, 1938; Four Women Grow Up, 1940; Smilin' on The Vine, 1941; Augusta Steps Out, 1942; Scene for Death, 1943; There Were No Windows, 1944; House Under Mars, 1946; Farewell, Happy Fields, 1948; Cocktail Bar, 1950; Frozen Ground, 1952; Sister Mavis, 1953; Journey into Print, 1954; A Death Occurred, 1954; Father Hone and the Television Set, 1956; Father and Daughter, 1957; Husband and Wife, 1959; Last Days of Miss Jenkinson, 1962; Poet's Pilgrimage, 1966; Only Fools and Horses Work, 1969; Not for Our Sins Alone, 1972; Two Girls in the Big Smoke, 1977. *Address:* Jonquil Cottage, Greystones, Co. Wicklow, Ireland.

HOUNSFIELD, Sir Godfrey (Newbold), Kt 1981; CBE 1976; FRS 1975; Senior Staff Scientist, THORN EMI Central Research Laboratories (formerly Central Research Laboratories of EMI), Hayes, Mddx, since 1977 (Head of Medical Systems section, 1972-76; Chief Staff Scientist, 1976-77); *b* 28 Aug. 1919; *s* of Thomas Hounsfield, Newark, Notts. *Educ:* Magnus Grammar Sch., Newark; City and Guilds Coll., London (Radio Communications qualif.); Faraday House Electrical Engineering Coll. (Diploma); grad. for IEE. Volunteered for RAF, 1939; served 1939-46 (incl. period as Lectr at Cranwell Radar Sch.); awarded Certificate of Merit (for work done in RAF), 1945. Attended Faraday House, where he studied elec. and mech. engrg, 1947-51. Joined EMI Ltd, 1951, working initially on radar systems and, later, on computers; led design team for the first large, all transistor computer to be built in Great Britain, the EMIDEC 1100, 1958-59; invented the EMI-scanner computerised transverse axial tomography system for X-ray examination, 1969-72 (now used at Atkinson Morley's Hosp., Wimbledon, and leading hosps in the USA and European continent, which are buying the invention); the technique can be applied to cranial examinations and the whole of the body; the system has overcome obstacles to the diagnosis of disease in the brain which have continued since Röntgen's day (1895); it includes a patient-scanning unit; developer of a new X-ray technique (the EMI-scanner system) which won the 1972 MacRobert Award of £25,000 for the invention, and a Gold Medal for EMI Ltd. Professorial Fellow in imaging sciences, Manchester Univ., 1978-. Dr Medicine (*hc*) Universität Basel, 1975; Hon. DSc: City, 1976; London, 1976; Hon. DTech Loughborough, 1976. Hon. FRCP 1976; Hon. FRCR 1976. Wilhelm-Exner Medal, Austrian Industrial Assoc., 1974; Ziedses des Plantes Medal, Physikalisch Medizinische Gesellschaft, Würzburg, 1974; Prince Philip Medal Award, CGLI, 1975; ANS Radiation Industry Award, Georgia Inst. of Technology, 1975; Lasker Award, Lasker Foundn, 1975; Duddell Bronze Medal, Inst. Physics, 1976; Golden Plate Award, Amer. Acad. of Achievement, 1976; Reginald Mitchell Gold Medal, Stoke-on-Trent Assoc. of Engrs, 1976; Churchill Gold Medal, 1976; Gairdner Foundn Award, 1976; (jtly) Nobel Prize for Physiology or Medicine, 1979; Ambrogino d'Oro Award, City of Milan, 1980; Deutsche Roentgen Plakette, Deutsche Roentgen Museum, 1980. *Publications:* contribs: New Scientist; Brit. Jl of Radiology; Amer. Jl of Röntgenology. *Recreation:* mountain walking. *Address:* THORN EMI Central Research Laboratories, Trevor Road, Hayes, Mddx UB3 1HH. *T:* 01-573 3888, ext. 2872; 15 Crane Park Road, Twickenham TW2 6DF. *T:* 01-984 1746. *Club:* Athenæum.

HOUSDEN, Rt. Rev. James Alan George, BA; *b* Birmingham, England, 16 Sept. 1904; *s* of William James and Jane Housden; *m* 1935, Elfreda Moira Hennessey; two *s* one *d*. *Educ:* Essendon High School; University of Queensland; St Francis College. BA 1st class, Mental and Moral Philosophy, 1928; ThL 1st Class, 1929. Deacon, 1928; Priest, 1929. Curate, St Paul's Ipswich, Qld, 1928-30; Chaplain, Mitchell River Mission, 1930-32; Curate, All Souls' Cathedral, Thursday Island, 1932-33; Rector of Darwin, NT, 1933-37; Vicar of Coolangatta, Qld, 1936-40; Rector and Rural Dean, Warwick, 1940-46; Vicar of Christ Church, S Yarra, Melbourne, 1946-47; Bishop of Rockhampton, 1947-58; Bishop of Newcastle, NSW, 1958-72. *Recreation:* bowls. *Address:* 38 Maltman Street, Caloundra, Qld 4551, Australia. *Club:* Australian (Sydney, NSW).

HOUSE, Lt-Gen. Sir David (George), GCB 1977 (KCB 1975); CBE 1967; MC 1944; Gentleman Usher of the Black Rod, House of Lords, since 1978; Serjeant-at-Arms, House of Lords, and Secretary to the Lord Great Chamberlain, since 1978; *b* 8 Aug. 1922; *s* of A. G. House; *m* 1947, Sheila Betty Darwin; two *d*. *Educ:* Regents Park Sch., London. War service in Italy; and thereafter in variety of regimental (KRRC and 1st Bn The Royal Green Jackets) and staff appts. Comd 51 Gurkha Bde in Borneo, 1965-67; Chief BRIXMIS, 1967-69; Dep. Mil. Sec., 1969-71; Chief of Staff, HQ BAOR, 1971-73; Dir of Infantry, 1973-75; GOC Northern Ireland, 1975-77. Colonel

Commandant: The Light Division, 1974-77; Small Arms School Corps, 1974-77. *Address:* House of Lords, SW1A 0PW. *Club:* Army and Navy.

HOUSE, Donald Victor; Lay Member, Restrictive Practices Court, 1962-70, retired; *b* 31 Jan. 1900; *s* of Dr S. H. House, Liverpool; *m* 1925, Cicely May Cox-Moore (*d* 1980); one *s* two *d*. *Educ:* Liverpool Coll. Lieut, Royal Garrison Artillery, 1918. Mem. (Fellow) Inst. of Chartered Accountants in England and Wales, 1922- (Mem. Council, 1942-62; Pres. 1954-55). Senior Partner, Harmood Banner & Co., 1946-62. Mem. Board of Governors, Guy's Hosp., 1955-74, and Chm. of Finance Cttee, 1957-74; Director: National Film Finance Corporation, 1954-70; Finance Cttee, Friends of the Poor and Gentlefolks Help, 1946-70; Mem., London Rent Assessment Panel, 1967-75. Hon. Sec., Herts Golf Union, 1964-75, Pres., 1976-78; Mem. Council, English Golf Union. Dir of several public and other companies (to 1962); Chm., House Cttee enquiring into Northern Ireland shipping facilities. Special Constabulary Long Service Medal, 1943. *Recreations:* golf, amateur dramatics. *Address:* 8 Greyfell Close, Stanmore Hill, Stanmore, Mddx HA7 3DQ. *T:* 01-954 0525. *Clubs:* Royal Commonwealth Society; Sandy Lodge Golf (Hon. Mem.), Porters Park Golf (Hon. Mem.).

HOUSE, Ven. Francis Harry, OBE 1955; MA; Officer Royal (Hellenic) Order of Phoenix, 1947; Archdeacon of Macclesfield, 1967-78, now Archdeacon Emeritus; Rector of St James, Gawsworth, 1967-78; *b* 9 Aug. 1908; *s* of late Canon William Joseph House, DD; *m* 1938, Margaret Neave; two *d*. *Educ:* St George's Sch., Harpenden; Wadham Coll., Oxford; Cuddesdon Theological Coll. Sec. of Student Christian Movement of Gt Britain and Ireland, 1931-34; Deacon, 1936; Priest, 1937. Asst Missioner, Pembroke Coll. (Cambridge) Mission, Walworth, 1936-37; Travelling sec. of World's Student Christian Federation, Geneva, 1938-40; Curate of Leeds Parish Church, 1940-42; Overseas Asst, Religious Broadcasting Dept, BBC, London, 1942-44; representative of World Student Relief in Greece, 1944-46; Sec. Youth Dept World Council of Churches, Geneva, and World Conference of Christian Youth, Oslo, 1946-47; Head of Religious Broadcasting BBC, London, 1947-55; Associate Gen. Sec. of the World Council of Churches, Geneva, 1955-62; Vicar of St Giles, Pontefract, 1962-67. Select Preacher, Cambridge Univ., 1949. Member: Gen. Synod of Church of England, 1970-78; Gen. Synod's Commn on Broadcasting, 1971-73; Bd for Mission and Unity, 1971-80 (Vice-Chm., 1971-75). *Publications:* articles contributed to: The Student Movement, The Student World, East and West, the Ecumenical Review, Theology, Crucible, One in Christ, etc. *Address:* 11 Drummond Court, Far Headingley, Leeds LS16 5QE. *T:* Leeds 783646.

HOUSE, Harry Wilfred, DSO 1918; MC; MA; Master of Wellington College, 1941-Aug. 1956; *b* Malvern, 26 Sept. 1895; 2nd *s* of late H. H. House, Acre End, Eynsham, Oxon; *m* 1926, Marjorie Stracey, *yr d* of late Arthur Gibbs, of Bramley, Surrey; two *s* one *d*. *Educ:* Lockers Park, Hemel Hempstead; Rugby Sch.; Queen's Coll., Oxford. Served in HM Forces on leaving Rugby in 1914; temp. 2nd Lieut 7th East Lancs Regt, Sept. 1914; served in France from July 1915 (wounded July 1916; MC; DSO); relinquished commission with rank of Temp. Major, March 1919; total service in France 3 years 5 months; temp. appointment Colonial Office, March to Dec. 1919; matriculated Oxford Univ., Jan. 1920; 2nd Class Hon. Mods, March 1921; studied at the University of Paris, 1921-23; Fellow and Lecturer Queen's Coll., Oxford, 1923-41; Laming Resident Fellow, Queen's Coll., Oxford, 1924-41; Junior Proctor, Oxford Univ., 1931-32; Major, Oxford and Bucks Light Infantry, 1939-41; Military Asst to Quarter Master Gen., 1940-41. Supernumerary Fellow, Queen's Coll., Oxford, 1953. *Address:* The Old Rectory, Stutton, near Ipswich, Suffolk. *T:* Holbrook 328205.

HOUSE, Prof. John William, MA; FRGS; Halford Mackinder Professor of Geography, University of Oxford, since 1974; Fellow of St Peter's College, Oxford, since 1974; *b* 15 Sept. 1919; *s* of John Albert House and Eveline (*née* Brunton), Bradford; *m* 1942, Eva (*née* Timm); two *s* two *d*. *Educ:* Bradford Grammar Sch.; Jesus Coll., Oxford (Open Exhibr). BA 1940, MA 1946, DLitt 1980. HM Forces, 1940-46, Major Intell. Corps; Médaille de la Reconnaissance Française 1944. Univ. of Durham: Lectr in Geography, 1946-58; Sen. Lectr, 1958-61; Reader, 1961-63; Leverhulme Research Fellow, 1957-58; Fulbright Prof., Univ. of Nebraska, 1962-63; Univ. of Newcastle upon Tyne: Reader in Applied Geography, 1963-64; Prof., 1964-66; Prof. and Head of Dept, 1966-74. Mem., Northern Econ. Planning Council, 1966-74; Mem., Northern Pennines Rural Develt Bd, 1967-70. Murchison Award, RGS, 1970. *Publications:* Bellingham and Wark, 1952; Northumbrian Tweedside, 1956; Teesside at Mid Century, 1960; (ed) Northern Geographical Essays, 1966; Industrial Britain: the North East, 1969; (ed) The UK Space, 1973; France: an applied geography, 1978; The Rio Grande Frontier, 1982; papers on migration and mobility. *Recreations:* drama, gardening. *Address:* School of Geography, Mansfield Road, Oxford OX1 3TB. *T:* Oxford 41791.

HOUSEHOLD, Geoffrey Edward West, TD; Author; *b* 30 Nov. 1900; *s* of H. W. Household, MA, Barrister-at-Law; *m* 1942, Ilona M. J. Zsoldos-Gutmán; one *s* two *d*. *Educ:* Clifton Coll.; Magdalen Coll., Oxford. Mostly commerce in foreign capitals. *Publications:* novels: The Third Hour, 1937; Rogue Male, 1939; Arabesque, 1948; The High Place, 1950; A Rough Shoot, 1951; A Time to Kill, 1952; Fellow Passenger, 1955; Watcher in the Shadows, 1960; Thing to Love, 1963; Olura, 1965; The Courtesy of Death, 1967; Dance of the Dwarfs, 1968; Doom's Caravan, 1971; The Three Sentinels, 1972; The Lives and Times of Bernardo Brown, 1973; Red Anger, 1975; Hostage: London, 1977; The Last Two Weeks of Georges Rivac, 1978; The Sending,

1980; Summon the Bright Water, 1981; *autobiography:* Against the Wind, 1958; *short stories:* The Salvation of Pisco Gabar, 1938; Tales of Adventurers, 1952; The Brides of Solomon, 1958; Sabres on the Sand, 1966; The Cats To Come, 1975; The Europe That Was, 1979; Capricorn and Cancer, 1981; *for children:* The Spanish Cave, 1940; Xenophon's Adventure, 1955; Prisoner of the Indies, 1967; Escape into Daylight, 1976. *Recreation:* Atlantic Spain. *Address:* Church Headland, Whitchurch, Aylesbury, Bucks.

HOUSEMAN, Alexander Randolph, FEng, FIMechE, FIProdE; Director: British Rail Engineering Ltd, since 1979; P-E Consulting Group Ltd, since 1968; President, Institution of Production Engineers, 1983–84; *b* 9 May 1920; *e s* of Captain Alexander William Houseman and Elizabeth Maud (*née* Randolph); *m* 1942, Betty Edith Norrington; one *d. Educ:* Stockport Grammar School and College. FIMC, CBIM, FRSA. Apprenticed Crossley Motors, 1936–40; Production Engineer: Ford Motor Co. (Aero Engines) Ltd, 1940–43; Saunders-Roe Ltd, 1943–48, General Works Manager, 1948–54; Consultant, Director, Man. Dir and Dep. Chm., P-E International Ltd, 1954–81; Chm., W. Canning Ltd, 1975–80; Dir, Record Ridgway Ltd, 1978–81. Chm., NEDO Sector Wkg Party for Gauge and Tool Industry, 1979–; Chm., Technical Policy Bd, Instn of Production Engrs, 1978–82; Vice-Pres. of the Instn, 1982–83. Member, Industrial Adv. Panels of Fellowship of Engineering, 1980–; Mem. Council, Inst. of Management Consultants, 1968–. *Publications:* articles to learned jls and technical and management press on manufacturing technology and management. *Recreations:* DIY, sailing, photography, walking. *Address:* 11 Kings Avenue, Ealing W5 2SJ. *T:* 01-997 3936. *Clubs:* Caledonian; Royal Anglesey Yacht (Beaumaris).

HOUSSEMAYNE du BOULAY, (Edward Philip) George, FRCR, FRCP; Professor of Neuroradiology, University of London at Institute of Neurology, since 1975; Head, Lysholm Radiological Department, National Hospital for Nervous Diseases, since 1975; Head, X-Ray Department, Nuffield Laboratories, Institute of Zoology, Zoological Society of London, since 1965; *b* 28 Jan. 1922; *yr s* of Philip Houssemayne du Boulay and Mercy Tyrrell (*née* Friend); *m* 1944, Vivien M. Glasson (marr. diss.); four *s* (and two *s* decd); *m* 1968, Pamela Mary Verity; two *d. Educ:* Christ's Hospital; King's Coll., London; Charing Cross Hosp. (Entrance Schol. 1940; MB, BS, DMRD). Served RAF (Medical), 1946–48; Army Emergency Reserve, 1952–57. House appts, Charing Cross Hosp. and Derby City Hosp., 1945–46; Registrar (Radiology), Middlesex Hosp., 1948–49; Sen. Registrar (Radiology): St Bartholomew's Hosp., 1949–54; St George's Hosp., 1951–52; Consultant Radiologist: Nat. Hosp. for Nervous Diseases, Maida Vale, 1954–68; St Bartholomew's Hosp., 1954–71; Nat. Hosp. for Nervous Diseases, Queen Square, 1968–75. Editor, Neuroradiology. Pres., Brit. Inst. of Radiology, 1976–77, Appeal Co-ordinator 1976–; Associate Mem., Société Française de Neuroradiologie; Corresp. Mem., Amer. Soc. of Neuroradiology; Hon. Mem., Swedish Soc. of Neuroradiology. Glyn Evans Meml Lectr, RCR, 1970; Ernestine Henry Lectr, RCP, 1976. Barclay Medal, BIR, 1968. *Publications:* Principles of X-Ray Diagnosis of the Skull, 1965, 2nd edn 1979; (jtly) A Text Book of X-Ray Diagnosis by British Authors: Neuroradiology Vol. 1, 4th edn 1970; (jtly) The Cranial Arteries of Mammals, 1973; (jtly) An Atlas of Normal Vertebral Angiograms, 1976; works in specialist jls. *Recreation:* gardening. *Address:* Old Manor House, Brington, Huntingdon, Cambs PE18 0PX. *T:* Bythorn 353.

HOUSSEMAYNE du BOULAY, Sir Roger (William), KCVO 1982 (CVO 1972); CMG 1975; HM Diplomatic Service, retired; Vice Marshal of the Diplomatic Corps, 1975–82; *b* 30 March 1922; *s* of Charles John Houssemayne du Boulay, Captain, RN, and Mary Alice Veronica, *née* Morgan; *m* 1957, Elizabeth, *d* of late Brig. Home, late RM, and of Molly, Lady Pile; one *d,* and two step *s. Educ:* Winchester; Oxford. Served RAFVR, 1941–46 (Pilot). HM Colonial Service, Nigeria, 1949–58; HM Foreign, later Diplomatic, Service, 1959; FO, 1959; Washington, 1960–64; FCO 1964–67; Manila, 1967–71; Alternate Director, Asian Development Bank, Manila, 1967–69, and Director, 1969–71; Counsellor and Head of Chancery, Paris, 1971–73; Resident Comr, New Hebrides, 1973–75. *Address:* Anstey House, near Buntingford, Herts.

HOUSTON, Aubrey Claud D.; *see* Davidson-Houston.

HOUSTON, Maj.-Gen. David, CBE 1975 (OBE 1972); President, Regular Commissions Board, since 1980; *b* 24 Feb. 1929; *s* of late David Houston and late Christina Charleson Houston (*née* Dunnett); *m* 1959, Jancis Veronica Burn; two *s. Educ:* Latymer Upper Sch. Commissioned, Royal Irish Fusiliers, 1949; served Korea, Kenya, BAOR, N Africa; Staff Coll., Camberley, 1961; commanded 1 Loyals and newly amalgamated 1st QLR, 1969–71; in comd 8th Inf. Bde, Londonderry, N Ireland, 1974–75; Mem. RCDS, 1976; Military Attaché and Commander, British Army Staff, Washington, 1977–79; HQ UKLF, 1979–80. *Recreations:* fishing, shooting, bird watching (feathered). *Address:* c/o National Westminster Bank, 94 Kensington High Street, W8 4SJ.

HOUSTON, James Caldwell, CBE 1982; MD, FRCP; Physician to Guy's Hospital, since 1965; Dean of the Medical and Dental Schools, Guy's Hospital, since 1965; *b* 18 Feb. 1917; *yr s* of late David Houston and Minnie Walker Houston; *m* 1946, Thelma Cromarty Cruickshank, MB, ChB, 2nd *d* of late John Cruickshank, CBE; four *s. Educ:* Mill Hill Sch.; Guy's Hosp. Medical Sch. MRCS, LRCP 1939; MB, BS (London) 1940; MRCP 1944; MD 1946;

FRCP 1956. Late Major RAMC; Medical Registrar, Guy's Hospital, 1946; Asst Ed., 1954, Jt Ed., 1958–67, Guy's Hosp. Reports; Member: Bd of Governors, Guy's Hosp., 1965–74; SE Metropolitan Regional Hosp. Bd, 1966–71; Lambeth, Lewisham and Southwark AHA (Teaching), 1974–78; Court of Governors, London Sch. of Hygiene and Tropical Med., 1969–; Senate, Univ. of London, 1970; Bd of Faculty of Clinical Medicine, Cambridge Univ., 1975–81; Cttee of Vice-Chancellors and Principals, 1977–; Special Trustee, Guy's Hosp., 1974–; Trustee, Hayward Foundn, 1978–81. Dir, Clerical, Medical & Gen. Life Assurance Soc., 1965; Vice-Pres., Medical Defence Union, 1970–. *Publications:* Principles of Medicine and Medical Nursing (jtly), 1956, 5th edn 1978; A Short Text-book of Medicine (jtly), 1962, 7th edn 1981; articles in Quart. Jl Med., Brit. Med. Bull., Lancet, etc. *Recreations:* golf, gardening. *Address:* 108 Harley Street, W1. *T:* 01-935 9338; 16 Hocroft Road, NW2. *T:* 01-435 3434; Cockhill Farm, Detling, Maidstone, Kent. *T:* Medway 31395.

HOUSTON, Prof. William John Ballantyne, PhD, FDSRCS Edin; Professor of Orthodontics, London University, since 1974; Dean, Royal Dental Hospital School of Dental Surgery, since 1978; *b* 6 June 1938; *s* of George and Mary Houston; *m* 1962, Turid Herdis Böe; one *s* one *d. Educ:* Edinburgh Univ. (BDS); London Univ. (PhD). FDSRCS Edin 1964. Lectr, Edinburgh Univ., 1962–64; Lectr, London Univ., at Royal Dental Hosp. Sch. of Dental Surg., 1964–66, Sen. Lectr 1966–74. *Publications:* Orthodontic Diagnosis, 1976; Orthodontic Notes, 1976; papers in Brit. Jl of Orthodontics and Eur. Jl of Orthodontics. *Recreations:* sailing, skiing, music. *Address:* 4 Oaken Coppice, Ashtead, Surrey.

HOUSTOUN-BOSWALL, Sir (Thomas) Alford, 8th Bt *cr* 1836; international economics and business consultant; *b* 23 May 1947; *s* of Sir Thomas Houstoun-Boswall, 7th Bt, and of Margaret Jean, *d* of George Bullen-Smith; *S* father, 1982; *m* 1971, Eliana Michele, *d* of Dr John Pearse, New York; one *s* one *d. Educ:* Lindisfarne College. Chairman, Metropolitan Car Parks and Excelsior Properties Ltd, UK; Partner, Rosedale-Engel, Houstoun-Boswall Partnership, Bermuda; Director, Stair & Co., New York (specialising in fine 18th century English furniture and works of art); Pres., Houstoun-Boswall Inc. (Fine Arts), New York. Lecturer, New York Univ. and Metropolitan Museum of Art, New York. *Heir: s* Alexander Alford Houstoun-Boswall, *b* 16 Sept. 1972. *Address:* 22 Edwardes Square, W8. *T:* 01-602 6763; 15 East 77 Street, New York, NY 10021, USA.

HOVDE, Frederick Lawson; President's Medal for Merit (USA), 1948; President, Purdue University, 1946–71, now President Emeritus; *b* 7 Feb. 1908; *s* of Martin Rudolph Hovde and Julia Essidora Hovde (*née* Lawson); *m* 1933, Priscilla Louise Boyd; one *s* two *d. Educ:* University of Minnesota; Oxford Univ. Asst Dir Gen. Coll., University of Minnesota, 1932–36; Asst to Pres. and Exec. Sec. of Rochester Prize Scholarships, University of Rochester, 1936–41; Head, London Mission, Office of Scientific Research and Development, 1941–42; Exec. Asst to Chm., Nat. Defense Research Cttee, 1942–43; Chief, Rocket Ordnance Research Div., Nat. Defense Research Cttee, 1943–46. Hon. degrees: DSc: Hanover Coll., 1946; Case Inst. of Technology, 1948; Tri-State College, 1967; DEng Rose Polytechnic Inst., 1948; LLD: Wabash Coll., 1946; North Dakota Agricultural Coll., 1949; New York Univ., 1951; Michigan State Univ., 1955; Minnesota, 1956; Northwestern Univ., 1960; Notre Dame, 1964; Ball State Univ., 1965; Indiana State Univ., 1966; Indiana Univ., 1969; Purdue Univ., 1975; DHL Cincinnati, 1956; DCL Oxford, 1957; Dr *hc* University Rural do Estado de Minas Gerais, Brazil, 1965; DEd Valparaiso Univ., 1967; PdD Findlay Coll., 1961; DHum Northwood Inst., 1969. King's Medal for Service in the Cause of Freedom (Britain), 1948; President's Medal for Merit, USA, 1948; Washington Award, Western Soc. of Engineers, 1967; Gold Medal, Nat. Football Foundn and Hall of Fame, 1967; Theodore Roosevelt Award, Nat. Collegiate Athl. Assoc., 1970; Dist. Public Service Medal, Dept of Defense, 1970. Comdr, Order of the Southern Cross, Brazil, 1968. *Recreation:* golf. *Address:* 1701 Redwood Lane, Lafayette, Indiana 47905, USA. *T:* (office) 317-743-4266; (home) 317-447-0808. *Clubs:* Pauma Valley (Calif); Vincent's (Oxford, England).

HOVELL-THURLOW-CUMMING-BRUCE, family name of **Baron Thurlow,** and *see* Cumming-Bruce.

HOVEN, Helmert Frans van den; Knight, Order of Netherlands Lion, 1978; Hon. KBE 1980; Chairman, Unilever NV, since 1975; Vice-Chairman, Unilever Ltd, since 1975; *b* 25 April 1923; *m* 1st, 1950, Dorothy Ida Bevan (marr. diss. 1981); one *s* ; 2nd, 1981, Cornelia Maria van As. *Educ:* Grammar and Trade schs in The Netherlands. Joined Unilever N. V., Rotterdam, 1938; transf. to Unilever Ltd, London, 1948, then to Turkey, 1951, becoming Chm. of Unilever's business there, 1958; Chm., Unilever's Dutch margarine business, Van den Bergh en Jurgens B. V., 1962; sen. marketing post, product gp, Margarine, Edible Fats and Oils, 1966; Mem. Bds of Unilever, and responsible for product gp, Sundry Foods and Drinks, 1970. *Recreations:* summer and winter sports in general. *Address:* c/o Unilever Ltd, Unilever House, EC4P 4BQ.

HOVING, Thomas; President, Hoving Associates, Inc., since 1977; Arts Correspondent, ABC News and ABC Television, since 1978; Arts and Entertainment Correspondent for ABC's 20/20; Editor-in-Chief, The Connoisseur, since 1981; *b* 15 Jan. 1931; *s* of Walter Hoving and Mary Osgood (*née* Field); *m* 1953, Nancy Melissa Bell; one *d. Educ:* Princeton Univ. BA Highest Hons, 1953; Nat. Council of the Humanities Fellowship, 1955;

Kienbusch and Haring Fellowship, 1957; MFA 1958; PhD 1959. Dept of Medieval Art and The Cloisters, Metropolitan Museum of Art: Curatorial Asst, 1959; Asst Curator, 1960; Associate Curator, 1963; Curator, 1965; Commissioner of Parks, New York City, 1966; Administrator of Recreation and Cultural Affairs, New York City, 1967; Dir, Metropolitan Museum of Art, 1967-77. Board Member: IBM World Trade Corporation/Americas-Far East; Manhattan Industries Inc.; H. S. Stuttman Co., Inc. Distinguished Citizen's Award, Citizen's Budget Cttee, 1967. Hon. Mem. AIA, 1967. Hon. LLD, Pratt Inst., 1967; Dr hc : Princeton; New York Univ. Middlebury and Woodrow Wilson Awards, Princeton. *Publications:* The Sources of the Ada Group Ivories (PhD thesis), 1959; Guide to The Cloisters, 1962; Metropolitan Museum of Art Calendar, 1966; The Chase and The Capture, 1976; Wyeth Catalogue, 1977; Tutankhamun, the Untold Story, 1978; King of the Confessors, 1981; articles in Apollo magazine and Metropolitan Museum of Art Bulletin. *Recreations:* sailing, ski-ing, skating, tennis, bicycling. *Address:* 150 East 73rd Street, New York, NY 10021, USA.

HOW, Sir Friston (Charles), Kt 1958; CB 1948; *b* 17 Sept. 1897; *o c* of Charles Friston and Jane Ethel How, Leytonstone; *m* 1932, Ann Stewart, *e d* of late Alexander Chisholm Hunter, Aberdeen; no *c. Educ:* County High Sch. for Boys, Leyton; London Univ. Joined HAC, 1916; commissioned RM, 1917; served in France, 1917-18; demobilised 1919. Exchequer and Audit Dept, 1920; HM Inspector of Taxes, 1920-37; Air Ministry, 1937-40; MAP, 1940-45; Ministry of Supply, 1946-53; Sec., Atomic Energy Office, 1954-59; retired, 1959; Member: Air Transport Advisory Council, 1960-61; Air Transport Licensing Bd, 1960-70. BSc (War) (London), 1917. Called to Bar, Middle Temple, 1927. *Address:* Desswood, Dess, Aboyne, Aberdeenshire. *T:* Kincardine O'Neil 246.

HOWARD; *see* Fitzalan-Howard.

HOWARD, family name of **Earls of Carlisle, Effingham,** and **Suffolk,** and of **Barons Howard of Penrith** and **Strathcona.**

HOWARD DE WALDEN, 9th Baron *cr* 1597; **John Osmael Scott-Ellis,** TD; Baron Seaford, 1826; *b* 27 Nov. 1912; *s* of 8th Baron and Margherita, CBE 1920 (*d* 1974), *d* of late Charles van Raalte of Brownsea Island, Dorset; *S* father, 1946; *m* 1st, 1934, Countess Irene Harrach (*d* 1975), *y d* of Count Hans Albrecht Harrach; four *d* ; 2nd, 1978, Gillian Viscountess Mountgarret. *Educ:* Eton; Magdalene Coll., Cambridge (BA 1934, MA). Dir, Howard de Walden Estates Ltd (Chm.). Member of the Jockey Club (Senior Steward, 1957, 1964, 1976). *Heir:* (to Barony of Howard de Walden) four co-heiresses; (to Barony of Seaford) Colin Humphrey Felton Ellis [*b* 19 April 1946; *m* 1971, Susan Magill; one *s* two *d*]. *Address:* Avington Manor, Hungerford, Berks. *T:* Kintbury 58229; Flat K, 90 Eaton Square, SW1. *T:* 01-235 7127. *Club:* Turf.
See also Capt. D. W. S. Buchan of Auchmacoy.

HOWARD OF PENRITH, 2nd Baron, *cr* 1930; **Francis Philip Howard,** DL; Captain late RA; *b* 5 Oct. 1905; *s* of 1st Baron and Lady Isabella Giustiniani-Bandini (*d* of Prince Giustiniani-Bandini, 8th Earl of Newburgh); *S* father, 1939; *m* 1944, Anne, *widow* of Anthony Bazley; four *s. Educ:* Downside; Trinity Coll., Cambridge (BA). Harvard Univ. Called to Bar, Middle Temple, 1931; served in War, 1939-42 (wounded). DL County of Glos, 1960. *Heir:* *s* Hon. Philip Esme Howard [*b* 1 May 1945; *m* 1969, Sarah, *d* of late Barclay Walker and of Mrs Walker, Perthshire; one *s* two *d*]. *Address:* Dean Farm, Coln St Aldwyns, Glos.
See also Hon. Edmund B. C. Howard.

HOWARD, Alan (Mackenzie); actor; Associate Artist, Royal Shakespeare Company, since 1967; *b* 5 Aug. 1937; *s* of Arthur John Howard and Jean Compton Mackenzie; *m* 1st, Stephanie Hinchcliffe Davies (marr. diss. 1976); 2nd, Sally Beauman; one *s. Educ:* Ardingly Coll. Belgrade Theatre, Coventry, 1958-60, parts incl. Frankie Bryant in Roots (also at Royal Court and Duke of York's); Wesker Trilogy, Royal Court, 1960; A Loss of Roses, Pembroke, Croydon, 1961; The Changeling, Royal Court, 1961; The Chances, and The Broken Heart, inaugural season, Chichester Festival, 1962; Virtue in Danger, Mermaid and Strand, 1963; Bassanio in The Merchant of Venice, Lysander in A Midsummer Night's Dream, in tour of S America and Europe, 1964; Simon in A Heritage and its History, Phoenix, 1965; Angelo in Measure for Measure, Bolingbroke in Richard II, Nottingham, 1965-66; Cyril Jackson in The Black and White Minstrels, Traverse, Edinburgh, 1972, Hampstead, 1973; A Ride Across Lake Constance, Hampstead and Mayfair, 1973. *Royal Shakespeare Company:* joined company, 1966, playing Orsino in Twelfth Night, Lussurioso in The Revenger's Tragedy; 1967: Jaques in As You Like It (also LA, 1968), Young Fashion in The Relapse; 1968: Edgar in King Lear, Achilles in Troilus and Cressida, Benedick in Much Ado about Nothing; 1969: Benedick (also in LA and San Francisco), Achilles, Lussurioso, and Bartholomew Cokes in Bartholomew Fair; 1970: Mephistophilis in Dr Faustus, Hamlet, Theseus/Oberon in A Midsummer Night's Dream, Ceres in The Tempest; 1971: Theseus/Oberon (NY debut); 1971-72: Theseus/Oberon, Nikolai in Enemies, Dorimant in The Man of Mode, The Envoy in The Balcony; 1972-73: Theseus/Oberon, in tour of E and W Europe, USA, Japan, Australia; 1974: Carlos II in The Bewitched; 1975: Henry V, Prince Hal in Henry IV parts I and II; 1976: Prince Hal (SWET Award for Best Actor in revival), Henry V in tour of Europe and USA, Jack Rover in Wild Oats (also Piccadilly); 1977: Henry V, Henry VI parts I, II and III, Coriolanus (Plays and Players London Critics Award, SWET Award for Best Actor in revival,

Evening Standard Best Actor Award, 1978); 1978: Antony in Antony and Cleopatra; 1979: Coriolanus in tour of Europe, The Children of the Sun; 1980: title rôles in Richard II and Richard III (Variety Club Best Actor Award); 1981-82: Neschastlivsev in The Forest; Good (Standard Best Actor Award, 1981). Best Actor (jt), 1981, Drama (British Theatre Assoc.) awards for Richard II, Good and The Forest. *Films include:* The Heroes of Telemark; Works is a Four Letter Word. *Television appearances include:* The Way of the World; Comet Among the Stars; Cover (series). *Recreations:* reading, music. *Address:* c/o Leading Artists, 60 St James's Street, SW1. *T:* 01-491 4400.

HOWARD, Alexander Edward, CBE 1972; Lecturer in Education, London University Centre for Teachers, 1977-81; *b* 2 Aug. 1909; *o s* of Alexander Watson Howard and Gertrude Nellie Howard; *m* 1937, Phyllis Ada Adams; no *c. Educ:* Swindon Coll.; University Coll. and Westminster Coll., London Univ. BSc (London) 1930; Pt I, BSc (Econ.) 1934. Flt-Lieut, RAF, 1940-46. Asst Master, Sanford Boys' Sch., Swindon, 1931-34; Lectr in Maths, Wandsworth Techn. Coll., 1935-40; Maths Master, Wilson's Grammar Sch., 1946-48; Headmaster: Northfleet Sch. for Boys, Kent, 1948-51; Borough-Beaufoy Sch., London, 1951-54; Forest Hill Sch., London, 1955-63; Wandsworth Sch., 1963-74. Co-ordinating Officer Teaching Practice Organisation, London Univ. Inst. of Educn, 1975-77. Member: Naval Educn Adv. Cttee, 1966-80; Army Educational Adv. Bd, 1957-74. Academic Council, RMA, 1970-75. FRSA 1970. Hon. Mem., CGLI, 1979. *Publications:* The Secondary Technical School in England, 1955; Longman Mathematics Stages 1-5, 1962-67, new Metric edns, 1970-71; Teaching Mathematics, 1968; articles in Times Educational Supplement, The Teacher, Technology, Inside the Comprehensive Sch. *Recreations:* amateur theatre, old-time dancing, music, cricket, travel, rotary. *Address:* 19 Downsway, Sanderstead, Surrey CR2 0JB. *T:* 01-657 3399. *Club:* Surrey County Cricket.

HOWARD, Anthony Michell; Deputy Editor, The Observer, since 1981; *b* 12 Feb. 1934; *s* of late Canon Guy Howard and of Janet Rymer Howard; *m* 1965, Carol Anne Gaynor. *Educ:* Westminster Sch.; Christ Church, Oxford. Chm., Oxford Univ. Labour Club, 1954; Pres., Oxford Union, 1955. Called to Bar, Inner Temple, 1956. Nat. Service, 2nd Lieut, Royal Fusiliers, 1956-58; Political Corresp., Reynolds News, 1958-59; Editorial Staff, Manchester Guardian, 1959-61 (Harkness Fellowship in USA, 1960); Political Corresp., New Statesman, 1961-64; Whitehall Corresp., Sunday Times, 1965; Washington Corresp., Observer, 1966-69 and Political Columnist, 1971-72; Asst Editor, 1970-72, Editor, 1972-78, New Statesman; Editor, The Listener, 1979-81. *Publications:* (contrib.) The Baldwin Age, 1960; (contrib.) Age of Austerity, 1963; (with Richard West) The Making of the Prime Minister, 1965; (ed) The Crossman Diaries: selections from the Diaries of a Cabinet Minister, 1979. *Address:* 17 Addison Avenue, W11 4QS. *T:* 01-603 3749.

HOWARD, Very Rev. Donald; Provost, St Andrew's Cathedral, Aberdeen, since 1978; *b* 21 Jan. 1927; *s* of William Howard and Alexandra Eadie (*née* Buchanan); unmarried. *Educ:* Hull Coll. of Technology; London Univ. (BD, AKC). AFRAeS, 1954-58. Design Engineer, Blackburn Aircraft, 1948-52; Hunting Percival Aircraft, 1952-54; English Electric Co., 1954-55. Assistant Minister, Emmanuel Church, Saltburn-by-the-Sea, Yorks, 1959-62; Rector and Mission Director, Dio. Kimberley and Kuruman, S Africa, 1962-65; Rector of St John the Evangelist, East London, S Africa, 1965-72; Rector of Holy Trinity Episcopal Church, Haddington, Scotland, 1972-78. Hon. Canon, Christ Church Cathedral, Hartford, Conn, USA, 1978. *Recreations:* photography, music. *Address:* 145 Gray Street, Aberdeen, Scotland AB1 6JJ. *T:* Aberdeen 56754. *Clubs:* Rotary (Aberdeen), St Nicholas.

HOWARD, Sir Douglas Frederick, KCMG 1953 (CMG 1944); MC; *b* 15 Feb. 1897; *s* of late John Howard Howard and of late Mrs Howard, Biddenham House, Bedford. *Educ:* Harrow. Served European War, 1915-18, France 1916 and 1918. Entered Diplomatic Service as 3rd Sec. Christiania, 1922; Bucharest, 1924; 2nd Sec., 1925; Rome, 1926; FO 1929. BA 1932. 1st Sec., 1934; Sofia, 1935; FO 1936; Madrid, 1939; Counsellor, FO, 1941; Madrid, 1945, where he was Chargé d'Affaires, Dec. 1946-Nov. 1949; Ambassador to Uruguay, 1949-53; HM Minister to the Holy See, 1953-57, retired. *Address:* Clophill House, Clophill, Bedford. *T:* Silsoe 60285.

HOWARD, Hon. Edmund Bernard Carlo, CMG 1969; MVO 1961; HM Diplomatic Service, retired; *b* 8 Sept. 1909; *s* of 1st Baron Howard of Penrith, PC, GCB, GCMG, CVO, and Lady Isabella Giustiniani-Bandini (*d* of Prince Giustiniani-Bandini, 8th Earl of Newburgh); *m* 1936, Cécile Geoffroy-Dechaume; three *s* one *d* (and one *d* decd). *Educ:* Downside Sch.; Newman Sch., Lakewood, NJ; New Coll., Oxford. Called to the Bar, 1932; Sec., Trustees and Managers, Stock Exchange, 1937. Served in HM Forces, KRRC, 1939-45. Joined HM Diplomatic Service, 1947; served in: Rome, 1947-51; Foreign Office, 1951-53; Madrid, 1953-57; Bogotá, 1957-59; Florence, 1960-61; Rome, 1961-65; Consul-Gen., Genoa, 1965-69. Comdr, Order of Merit, Italy, 1973. *Publications:* Genoa: history and art in an old seaport, 1971 (Duchi di Galliera prize, 1973); trans. The Aryan Myth, 1974. *Recreations:* travel, gardening, walking. *Address:* Jerome Cottage, Marlow Common, Bucks. *T:* Marlow 2129.

HOWARD, Sir Edward; *see* Howard, Sir H. E. de C.

HOWARD, Elizabeth Jane; novelist; *b* 26 March 1923; *d* of David Liddon and Katharine M. Howard; *m* 1st, 1942, Peter M. Scott; one *d* ; 2nd, 1959,

James Douglas-Henry; 3rd, 1965, Kingsley Amis, *qv. Educ:* home. Trained at London Mask Theatre Sch. Played at Stratford-on-Avon, and in repertory theatre in Devon; BBC, Television, modelling, 1939–46; Sec. to Inland Waterways Assoc., 1947; subsequently writing, editing, reviewing, journalism and writing plays for television, incl. serials of After Julius in three plays and Something in Disguise in six plays. John Llewellyn Rhys Memorial Prize for The Beautiful Visit, 1950; Book Critic, Queen Magazine, 1959–61. Hon. Artistic Dir, Cheltenham Literary Festival, 1962; Artistic co-Dir, Salisbury Festival of Arts, 1973. *Publications:* The Beautiful Visit, 1950; The Long View, 1956; The Sea Change, 1959; After Julius, 1965; Something in Disguise, 1969 (TV series, 1982); Odd Girl Out, 1972; Mr Wrong, 1975; (ed) A Companion for Lovers, 1978; Getting It Right, 1982. *Recreations:* music, gardening, enjoying all the arts, travelling, natural history. *Address:* c/o Jonathan Clowes, 22 Prince Albert Road, NW1 7ST.

HOWARD, Francis Alex, (Frankie Howerd), OBE 1977; *b* 6 March 1922. *Educ:* Shooters Hill Sch., Woolwich, London. *Revues:* Out of this World, 1950; Pardon my French, 1953; Way Out in Piccadilly, 1966. *Plays:* Charlie's Aunt, 1955; Hotel Paradiso, 1957; A Midsummer Night's Dream (playing Bottom), 1958; Alice in Wonderland, 1960; A Funny Thing Happened on the Way to the Forum, 1963 (Critics' Award for Best Musical Actor, 1964); The Wind in the Sassafras Trees, Broadway, 1968; Simple Simon in Jack and the Beanstalk, Palladium, 1973; *opera:* Frosch in Die Fledermaus, Coliseum, 1982; *films:* The Ladykillers, 1956; Runaway Bus, 1956; Touch of the Sun, 1956; Jumping for Joy, 1956; Further up the Creek, 1958; Carry On, Doctor, 1968; Carry on Up the Jungle, 1970; Up Pompeii, 1971; Up the Chastity Belt, 1972; Up the Front, 1972; The House in Nightmare Park, 1973; Sergeant Pepper's Lonely Hearts Club Band, 1978. *TV Series:* Fine Goings On, 1959; Up Pompeii, 1970–71; Up the Convicts (Australia), 1975; The Frankie Howerd Show (Canada), 1976; Frankie Howerd Strikes Again, 1981; in Gilbert and Sullivan series: HMS Pinafore, 1982; Trial by Jury, 1982. Royal Variety Performances, 1950, 1954, 1961, 1966, 1968, 1969, 1978. Variety Club of GB Award (Show Business Personality of the Year), 1966, 1971; Radio and TV Industries Award (Show Business Personality of the Year), 1971. *Publication:* Trumps, 1982. *Recreations:* tennis, swimming, music, reading. *Address:* c/o RSO Management Ltd, 67 Brook Street, W1.

HOWARD, George Anthony Geoffrey, DL; Chairman of the BBC, since 1980 (a Governor, since 1972); *b* 22 May 1920; *o* surv. *s* of late Hon. Geoffrey Howard; *m* 1949, Lady Cecilia FitzRoy (*d* 1974), *d* of 8th Duke of Grafton; four *s. Educ:* Eton; Balliol Coll., Oxford. Served war of 1939–45: Green Howards, and attached Indian Army (wounded, Burma, 1945), Major 1945. RDC, Malton, 1946–74; CC, North Riding Yorks, 1947–55; Hon. NE Rep. for National Trust, 1948–58; Chm., York Georgian Soc., 1951–71 (Pres. 1971); Mem. Council, Country Landowners' Assoc., 1951 (Chm.: Yorks Br., 1955–65, GP Cttee, 1956–61, Legal and Planning Cttee, 1961–68, Exec. Cttee, 1967–69; Pres. of Assoc., 1969–71). Chm., Meat and Livestock Commn, 1974–77. President: Yorkshire Philosophical Soc., 1969–; Historic Houses Assoc., 1978–82. Member: National Parks Commn/Countryside Commn, 1966–74; Council, Royal Coll. of Art, 1968– (Chm., 1981; Sen. Fellow, RCA, 1974); Central Adv. Water Cttee, 1969–71; Museums and Galleries Commn, 1981–. Mayor of the Company of Merchants of the Staple of England, 1964–65. DL, NR Yorks, 1971; Co-founder Agricultural Forum, 1971. FRAgS 1972. DUniv York, 1980. *Address:* Castle Howard, York; 18 Ennismore Mews, SW7. *Clubs:* White's, Brooks's, Pratt's.

HOWARD, Lt Comdr Hon. Greville (Reginald), VRD; RNR; *b* 7 Sept. 1909; 3rd *s* of 19th Earl of Suffolk and Berkshire; *m* 1945, Mary Ridehalgh; one *d. Educ:* Eton; RMC Sandhurst. Commissioned in King's Shropshire LI, 1930–35. London Manager of G. W. Joynson, Cotton Merchants and Brokers, 1935–39. Councillor Westminster City Council, 1937; Naval Service, War of 1939–45; destroyers commanded: HMS Viscount (temp.), 1943; HMS Sabre, 1943–44; HMS Nith, 1944. Rejoined Westminster City Council, 1945; Mayor of Westminster, 1946–47; Chm. Public Cleansing, Transport, Baths and Contracts Cttee, 1945 and 1947–49; Vice-Chm. Establishments Cttee, 1949; Vice-Chm. Refuse Sub-Cttee, Metropolitan Boroughs Standing Joint Cttee, 1947–49. MP (Nat L and C) St Ives Division of Cornwall 1950–66; retired, 1966. Hon. Overseas Director and European Consultant, Colour Processing Laboratories Ltd. Overseas Mem. Cttee of Management and Hon. Vice-Pres., RNLI; Pres., City of Westminster Dist, Scout Assoc.; Hon. Pres., Fisheries Orgn Soc.; Vice-Chm. Sailing (Overseas), Sail Trng Assoc. Patron, Discovery Dockland Trust. *Recreations:* photography, sailing, bicycling, riding, fishing. *Address:* Redlynch, Brouch, near Mersch, Grand Duché de Luxembourg. *T:* 63560. *Clubs:* (supernumerary or overseas member of all) White's, Pratt's, Naval, Norwegian; Royal Yacht Squadron, Royal Norwegian Yacht, Royal Naval Sailing Assoc., Royal Cornwall Yacht.

HOWARD, Sir (Hamilton) Edward (de Coucey), 2nd Bt *cr* 1955; GBE 1972; Partner of Stockbroking Firm of Charles Stanley and Company; Chairman, LRC International Ltd, to 1982, now President; *b* 29 Oct. 1915; *s* of Sir (Harold Walter) Seymour Howard, 1st Bt, and Edith M. (*d* 1962), *d* of Edward Turner; *S* father 1967; *m* 1943, Elizabeth Howarth Ludlow; two *s. Educ:* Le Rosey, Rolle, Switzerland; Radley Coll., Abingdon; Worcester Coll., Oxford. Mem. of the Stock Exchange, London, 1946. Sheriff of the City of London, 1966 (Common Councillor, 1951; Alderman, 1963); Lord Mayor of London, 1971–72; one of HM Lieutenants, City of London, 1976–. Master of the Gardeners' Company, 1961. DSc City Univ., 1971. KStJ 1972. *Recreation:* gardening. *Heir: s* David Howarth Seymour Howard [*b* 29 Dec.

1945; *m* 1968, Valerie Picton, *o d* of Derek W. Crosse; two *s* two *d*]. *Address:* Courtlands, Bishops Walk, Shirley Hills, Surrey. *T:* 01-656 4444. *Clubs:* Guildhall, City Livery, United Wards.

HOWARD, James Boag, CB 1972; Assistant Under-Secretary of State, Home Office, 1963–75; *b* 10 Jan. 1915; *yr s* of William and Jean Howard, Greenock; *m* 1943, Dorothy Jean Crawshaw; two *d. Educ:* Greenock High Sch.; Glasgow Univ. (MA, BSc; 1st cl. Hons Mathematics and Natural Philosophy). Asst Principal, Home Office, 1937; Private Sec. to Permanent Sec., Ministry of Home Security, 1940–41; Principal, 1941; Asst Sec., 1948. *Address:* 12 Windhill, Bishop's Stortford, Herts. *T:* Bishop's Stortford 51728.

HOWARD, Sir John, Kt 1954; DL; FICE; Founder, 1927, and President, since 1982, John Howard and Co. Plc, Civil Engineering Contractors (Founder Chairman and Managing Director, 1927–82); *b* 17 Nov. 1901; *s* of John Golding Howard, Biddenham, Bedford; *m* 1931, Margaret Mary, *d* of Herbert Edward Kemp; three *s* one *d. Educ:* Bedford Sch. Chm., National Union of Conservative and Unionist Assocs, 1972. Chm., Harpur Trust, Bedford, 1966–78 (now Life Governor). Treasurer, Imperial Soc. of Knights Bachelor, 1968–. Hon. DSc Cranfield, 1971. DL Beds, 1978. *Recreations:* shooting, golf. *Address:* Crossland Fosse, Box End, Bedford. *T:* Bedford 854708. *Clubs:* Carlton, Royal Automobile.

HOWARD, Mrs John E.; *see* Laski, Marghanita.

HOWARD, John James; Chief General Manager and Director, Royal Insurance Company Ltd, since 1980; *b* 9 March 1923; *s* of late Sir Henry Howard, KCIE, CSI, and Lady Howard; *m* 1949, Julia Tupholme Mann; one *s* one *d* (and one *d* decd). *Educ:* Rugby Sch.; Trinity Hall, Cambridge (MA). Pilot, RAFVR, 1942–46 (Flt Lieut). Royal Insurance Company Ltd, 1947–: Financial Secretary, 1964–69; General Manager and Director, 1970–80. Dep. Chm., British Insurance Assoc., 1981–. *Address:* Royal Insurance Company Ltd, 1 Cornhill, EC3V 3QR.

HOWARD, Hon. John Winston; Federal Treasurer, Australia, since 1977; MP(Lib) for Bennelong, NSW, since 1974; *b* 26 July 1939; *m* 1971, Alison Janette Parker; two *s* one *d. Educ:* Canterbury Boys' High Sch.; Sydney Univ. Solicitor of NSW Supreme Court. Minister for Business and Consumer Affairs, Australia, 1975; Minister assisting Prime Minister, May 1977; Minister for Special Trade Negotiations, July 1977. *Recreations:* reading, golf, cricket. *Address:* 19 Milner Crescent, Wollstonecraft, NSW 2065, Australia. *T:* 02-4394360. *Clubs:* Australian (Sydney), Commonwealth (Canberra).

HOWARD, Leonard Henry, RD 1941; retired; *b* 5 Aug. 1904; *m* 1st, 1938, Betty Scourse; one *s* one *d*; 2nd, 1960, Barbara Davies-Colley. *Educ:* Stubbington House Sch.; Nautical Coll., Pangbourne. Sea career in Royal Navy and P&O-Orient Lines (Merchant Navy), 1922–64; commanded several RN units, War of 1939–45; Comdr, troop ship Empire Fowey, and passenger ships Strathmore, Himalaya and Arcadia, P&O Co.; Commodore, P&O-Orient Lines, 1963–64 (now P&O Steam Navigation Co.), retired. *Recreations:* golf, gardening. *Address:* Port, Heyshott, Midhurst, W Sussex. *T:* Midhurst 2560. *Club:* Cowdray Park Golf.

HOWARD, Michael, QC 1982; *b* 7 July 1941; *s* of late Bernard Howard and of Hilda Howard; *m* 1975, Sandra Clare, *d* of Wing-Comdr Saville Paul; one *s* one *d* (and one step *s*). *Educ:* Llanelli Grammar School; Peterhouse, Cambridge. MA, LLB; President of the Union, 1962. Major Scholar, Inner Temple, 1962; called to the Bar, Inner Temple, 1964. Junior Counsel to the Crown (Common Law), 1980–82. Contested (C) Liverpool, Edge Hill, 1966 and 1970; adopted as Cons. Parly Cand., Folkestone and Hythe, 1982; Chm., Bow Group, 1970–71. *Recreations:* watching football (Swansea, Liverpool) and baseball (New York Mets). *Address:* 2 Paper Buildings, Temple, EC4Y 7ET. *T:* 01-353 5835. *Clubs:* Carlton, Coningsby (Chm., 1972–73).

HOWARD, Michael Eliot, CBE 1977; MC 1943; DLitt; FBA 1970; FRHistS; FRSL; Regius Professor of Modern History and Fellow of Oriel College, Oxford, since 1980; *b* 29 Nov. 1922; *y s* of late Geoffrey Eliot Howard, Ashmore, near Salisbury, and of Edith Julia Emma, *o d* of Otto Edinger. *Educ:* Wellington; Christ Church, Oxford. BA 1946, MA 1948. Served War, Coldstream Guards, 1942–45. Asst Lecturer in History, University of London, King's Coll., 1947; Lecturer, 1950; Lecturer in War Studies, 1953–61; Prof. of War Studies, 1963–68; Fellow of All Souls Coll., Oxford, 1968–80; Chichele Prof. of History of War, Univ. of Oxford, 1977–80. Vis. Prof. of European History, Stanford Univ., 1967. Ford's Lectr in English History, Oxford, 1971; Radcliffe Lectr, Univ. of Warwick, 1975; Trevelyan Lectr, Cambridge, 1977; FKC. Vice-Pres. and co-Founder, Internat. Institute for Strategic Studies; Trustee: Imp. War Museum; National Army Museum. Governor, Wellington Coll. Hon. LittD Leeds, 1979. Chesney Meml Gold Medal, RUSI, 1973. *Publications:* The Coldstream Guards, 1920–46 (with John Sparrow), 1951; Disengagement in Europe, 1958; Wellingtonian Studies, 1959; The Franco-Prussian War, 1961 (Duff Cooper Memorial Prize, 1962); The Theory and Practice of War, 1965; The Mediterranean Strategy in the Second World War, 1967; Studies in War and Peace, 1970; Grand Strategy, vol IV (in UK History of 2nd World War, Military series), 1971 (Wolfson Foundn History Award, 1972); The Continental Commitment, 1972; War in European History, 1976; (with P. Paret) Clausewitz On War, 1977; War and the Liberal Conscience, 1978; (ed) Restraints on War, 1979; contributions to

The New Cambridge Modern History. *Recreations:* music, weeding. *Address:* Oriel College, Oxford OX1 4EW. *Club:* Garrick.

HOWARD, Michael Stockwin; Director, Cantores in Ecclesia, since 1964; Co-founder and Artistic Director, Rye Spring Music, 1976; Musical Director, Rye Spring Opera, and Principal Conductor, Dushkin Chamber Ensemble, since 1977; Organist to the Franciscans of Rye, since 1979; *b* London, 14 Sept. 1922; *er s* of late Frank Henry Howard (viola, Internat. String Quartet, Foundn principal, Beecham's Philharmonic) and Florence Mabel Howard. *Educ:* Ellesmere; Royal Acad. of Music; privately. Organist, Tewkesbury Abbey, 1943-44; Dir of Music, Ludgrove Sch.; Founder, Renaissance Society, and conductor, Renaissance Singers, 1944-64; Organist and Master of the Choristers, Ely Cath., 1953-58; Dir of Music, St George's Sch., Harpenden, 1959-61; Asst, Music Presentation, BBC, 1968-78; Dir of Music, St Marylebone Parish Church, 1971-79, Dir Emeritus, 1979. Freelance organist, harpsichordist, conductor, broadcaster and writer. Hon. ARAM 1976. Prix Musicale de Radio Brno, 1967; Gustave Charpentier Grand Prix du Disque, 1975. Recordings with essays include: Tallis/Byrd 1575 Cantiones Sacrae, 1969; Tallis at Waltham Abbey, 1974; Palestrina's The Garden of Love, 1974. *Principal compositions include:* mass, Sonnet VIII, 1961; Scaena Dramatis for Antoinette Michael, 1978; Dances for a Mountain Goat, 1979; opera, The Lion's Mouth, 1980; Sequentia de Insomnia, 1981; Diptych (Arnold and St Ambrose), 1981. *Publications:* The Private Inferno (autobiog.), 1974; contrib. Musical Times, Monthly Musical Record, Dublin Review, Listener, EMG Monthly Letter. *Recreations:* steam railway traction, village fairgrounds. *Address:* c/o The Franciscan Friary, Watchbell Street, Rye, Sussex.

HOWARD, Philip Nicholas Charles; Literary Editor of The Times, since 1978; *b* 2 Nov. 1933; *s* of Peter Dunsmore Howard and Doris Emily Metaxa; *m* 1959, Myrtle, *d* of Sir Reginald Houldsworth, *qv* ; two *s* one *d*. *Educ:* Eton Coll. (King's Scholar); Trinity Coll., Oxford (MA). Glasgow Herald, 1959-64; The Times, 1964-: reporter, writer, columnist. Liveryman, Wheelwrights' Co. London Editor, Verbatim, 1977-. *Publications:* The Black Watch, 1968; The Royal Palaces, 1970; London's River, 1975; New Words for Old, 1977; The British Monarchy, 1977; Weasel Words, 1978; Words Fail Me, 1980. *Recreations:* walking, talking, music, the classics, beagles not beagling. *Address:* Flat 1, 47 Ladbroke Grove, W11 3AR. *T:* 01-727 1077. *Clubs:* Classical Association, Horatian Society; Ad Eundem (Oxford and Cambridge).

HOWARD, Robert, (Bob); Northern Regional Secretary, Trades Union Congress, since 1980; *b* 4 April 1939; *s* of Robert and Lily Howard. *Educ:* Gregson Lane County Primary Sch.; Deepdale Secondary Modern Sch.; Queen Elizabeth's Grammar Sch., Blackburn, Lancs; Cliff Training Coll., Calver via Sheffield, Derbyshire. British Leyland, Lancs, 1961-68: Member, Clerical and Admin. Workers' Union Br. Exec.; Councillor, Walton le Dale UDC, 1962-65; GPO, Preston, Lancs, 1969-80: Telephone Area UPW Telecomms Representative Member: Jt Consultative Council, Jt Productivity Council, Council of PO Unions Area Cttee, Delegate to Preston Trades Council; Secretary, Lancashire Assoc. of Trades Councils, 1977-79; created 14 specialist cttees for LATC; appointment as N Reg. Sec., Trades Union Congress, 1980-, by Gen. Sec., TUC, first full-time secretary to a TUC region. Dir, Industrial Common Ownership Finance, 1981-. Member, Industrial Tribunals, 1979-80. JP Duchy of Lancaster, 1969-74. *Publications:* North-East Lancashire Structure Plan—The Trades Councils' View (with Peter Stock), 1979; Organisation and Functions of TUC Northern Regional Council, 1980. *Recreations:* fell walking, classical music, camping, outdoor sports, reading, chess. *Address:* 4 Rydal Road, Chester le Street, County Durham DH2 3DR. *Clubs:* Newcastle upon Tyne Labour; CIU Affiliate.

HOWARD, Robin Jared Stanley, CBE 1976; Director-General, Contemporary Dance Trust Ltd, since 1966; *b* 17 May 1924; *s* of Hon. Sir Arthur Howard, KBE, CVO, DL, and of Lady Lorna Howard. *Educ:* Eton; Trinity Coll., Cambridge (MA). Served War, 1942-45, Lieut, Scots Guards. Called to Bar, Inner Temple. Hon. Dir, Internat. Service Dept, United Nations Assoc., 1956-64. *Recreation:* sleep. *Address:* 7 Sandwich Street, WC1H 9AB. *Clubs:* Garrick, MCC.

HOWARD, Rev. Canon Ronald Claude; Headmaster, Hurstpierpoint College, 1945-64; *b* 15 Feb. 1902; 2nd *s* of Henry H. and Florence Howard, The Durrant, Sevenoaks. *Educ:* Sidney Sussex Coll., Cambridge; Westcott House, Cambridge. Ordained, 1926; Curate of Eastbourne, 1926-28; Chaplain, Bradfield Coll., 1928-30; Asst Master, Tonbridge Sch., 1930-37; Asst Master, Marlborough Coll., 1937, Chaplain there, 1938-43; Chaplain and Asst Master, Radley Coll., 1943-45. Canon of Chichester, 1957; Communar of Chichester Cathedral, 1964-67. Canon Emeritus, 1967. *Recreations:* painting, collecting water-colours. *Address:* 3 Adelaide Crescent, Hove, East Sussex.

HOWARD, Trevor Wallace; actor; *b* 29 Sept. 1916; father English, mother Canadian; *m* 1944, Helen Mary Cherry. *Educ:* Clifton Coll. Shakespeare Festival, Stratford-on-Avon, 1936 and 1939; French Without Tears, Criterion, 1936-38. Served War in Army, 1940-43, 1st Airborne Division. Played in the Recruiting Officer and Anna Christie, 1944; Old Vic Season, 1947-48, Petruchio in the Taming of the Shrew. *Films include:* Brief Encounter, 1945; The Third Man, 1949; An Outcast of the Islands, 1951; The Heart of the Matter, 1953 (Acad. award); Lovers of Lisbon (French); Cockleshell Heroes, 1955; The Key, Roots of Heaven, 1958; Sons and Lovers, 1960 (Acad. nomination); Mutiny on the Bounty, 1962; Von Ryan's Express, 1965; Father

Goose, 1965; The Liquidator, 1966; The Charge of the Light Brigade, 1968; Ryan's Daughter, 1970; Mary Queen of Scots, 1971; Ludwig, 1972; The Offence, 1973; A Doll's House, 1973; The Visitor, 1974; 11 Harrowhouse, 1974; Hennessy, 1975; Conduct Unbecoming, 1975; Count of Monte Cristo, 1976 (Acad. nomination); The Last Remake of Beau Geste, 1977; Slavers, 1978; Stevie, 1978; Superman, 1978; Hurricane, 1980; The Sea Wolves, 1980; Sir Henry at Rawlinson End, 1980; Windwalker, (Cheyenne), 1980; Light Years Away, 1981. *Plays include:* The Devil's General, 1953; Lopahin in The Cherry Orchard, Lyric, 1954; Two Stars for Comfort, Garrick, 1962; The Father, Piccadilly, 1964; Waltz of the Toreadors, Haymarket, 1974; Scenario, Toronto, 1977. *Television:* Hedda Gabler, 1962; The Invincible Mr Disraeli, 1963 (Acad. Award); Napoleon at St Helena, 1966 (Acad. nom.); Catholics, 1974; Staying On, 1980; Jonathan Swift, 1981. *Recreations:* cricket, travel. *Address:* Rowley Green, Arkley, Herts. *Club:* MCC.

HOWARD, Sir Walter Stewart, Kt 1963; MBE 1944; DL; *b* 1888; *y s* of late Henry Blunt Howard; *m* 1917, Alison Mary Wall, *e d* of late Herbert F. Waring, Farningham Hill, Kent. *Educ:* Wellington; Trinity Coll., Cambridge. Vice-Chm., Warwicks CC, 1955 (Chm., 1956-60); Chm. Whiteley Village Trust, 1952-62; Governor: King Edward VI Sch., Birmingham; Warwick Sch.; Pres., Association of Education Cttees, 1962-63. Trustee of Shakespeare's birthplace. JP 1931, CC 1939, CA 1948, DL 1952, Warwicks. *Recreation:* foreign travel. *Address:* Barford, Warwick. *T:* Barford 624208. *Club:* United Oxford & Cambridge University.

HOWARD, William Brian; Joint Managing Director, Marks & Spencer Ltd, since 1976; *b* 16 July 1926; *s* of William James and Annie Howard; *m* 1952, Audrey Elizabeth (née Jenney); one *s* one *d*. *Educ:* Revoe Junior Sch., Blackpool; Blackpool Grammar Sch.; Manchester Univ. (BA (Hons) Mod. Hist., Economics and Politics); Harvard Graduate Business Sch., 1973. Royal Signals, 1944-47. Marks & Spencer Ltd, 1951-. A Church Comr, 1977-. Member: Council, St George's House, Windsor; Franco-British Council. *Address:* 57 Baker Street, W1A 1DN.

HOWARD, William McLaren, QC 1964; a Recorder, since 1972; Judge Advocate of the Fleet, since 1973; *b* 27 Jan. 1921; 3rd *s* of William George Howard and Frances Jane (née McLaren). *Educ:* Merchant Taylors' Sch. Entered RN as Cadet, 1938. Served at sea throughout War of 1939-45; Lieut 1942; resigned commission, 1946. Called to the Bar, Lincoln's Inn, 1947, Bencher, 1972; joined Inner Temple (ad eundem), 1960; Dep. Chm., Norfolk QS, 1967-71; Recorder of Ipswich, 1968-71. Mem., Bar Council, 1965-69 (also Mem., Bar Council Special Cttee on Sentencing and Penology). Vice-Pres., Norfolk Assoc. for Care and Resettlement of Offenders. Mem., British Acad. Forensic Sci. *Address:* The Red House, Holkham, Wells-next-the-Sea, Norfolk; 3 King's Bench Walk, Temple, EC4. *T:* 01-353 0431. *Clubs:* Garrick; Norfolk (Norwich).

HOWARD-DOBSON, Gen. Sir Patrick John, GCB 1979 (KCB 1974; CB 1973); National President, Royal British Legion, since 1981; *b* 12 Aug. 1921; *s* of Canon Howard Dobson, MA; *m* 1946, Barbara Mary Mills; two *s* one *d*. *Educ:* King's Coll. Choir Sch., Cambridge; Framlingham College. Joined 7th Queen's Own Hussars, Egypt, Dec. 1941; served in: Burma, 1942; Middle East, 1943; Italy, 1944-45; Germany, 1946; psc 1950; jssc 1958; comd The Queen's Own Hussars, 1963-65 and 20 Armoured Bde, 1965-67; idc 1968; Chief of Staff, Far East Comd, 1969-71; Comdt, Staff Coll., Camberley, 1972-74; Military Secretary, 1974-76; Quartermaster General, 1977-79; Vice-Chief of Defence Staff (Personnel and Logistics), 1979-81; ADC Gen. to the Queen, 1978-81. Col Comdt, ACC, 1976-82. Virtuti Militari (Poland), 1945; Silver Star (US), 1945. *Recreations:* sailing, golf. *Address:* The Cottage, Benington, near Stevenage, Herts. *Club:* Cavalry and Guards.

HOWARD-DRAKE, Jack Thomas Arthur; Assistant Under-Secretary of State, Home Office, 1974-78; *b* 7 Jan. 1919; *o s* of Arthur Howard and Ruby (née Cherry); *m* 1947, Joan Mary, *o d* of Hubert and Winifred Crook; one *s* two *d*. *Educ:* Hele's Sch., Exeter. Asst Inspector, Ministry of Health Insurance Dept, 1937-39 and 1946-47. Served War, RA, 1939-46 (Major, despatches). Colonial Office: Asst Principal, 1947; Principal, 1949; Private Sec. to Sec. of State, 1956-62; Asst Sec., 1962; Asst Sec., Cabinet Office, 1963-65; Asst Sec., Home Office, 1965-72; Asst Under-Sec. of State, NI Office, 1972-74. *Recreations:* gardening, local history, golf. *Address:* 26 Sinnels Field, Shipton-under-Wychwood, Oxon OX7 6EJ. *T:* Shipton-under-Wychwood 830792.

HOWARD-JOHNSTON, Rear-Admiral Clarence Dinsmore, CB 1955; DSO 1942; DSC 1940; naval historian; *b* 13 Oct. 1903; *m* 1955, Paulette, *d* of late Paul Helleu. *Educ:* Royal Naval Colls Osborne and Dartmouth. Midshipman, 1921; Commander, 1937; Capt., 1943; Rear-Adm., 1953; Dir of Studies, Greek Naval War Coll., Athens, 1938-40; Anti-submarine Operations, 1940-43; mentioned in despatches 1940; Dir Anti-U-Boat Div., Admiralty, 1943-45; Naval Attaché, Paris, 1947-50; apptd Naval ADC to the Queen, 1952; Chief of Staff to Flag Officer Central Europe, 1953-55; retired RN 1955. Inventor of simple hydraulic mechanisms; commended by Lords Comrs of the Admiralty for invention and develt of anti-submarine training devices including Johnston Mobile A/S target, 1937. Order of Phœnix (Greece), 1940; Legion of Merit (USA), 1945. *Recreations:* fishing, pisiculture, hill-walking, gardening. *Address:* 45 Rue Emile Ménier, 75116 Paris, France; Le Coteau, Chambre d'Amour, 64600 Anglet, France. *Clubs:*

White's, Naval and Military, (Naval Member) Royal Yacht Squadron; Jockey (Paris).

HOWARD-JONES, Maj.-Gen. Leonard Hamilton, CB 1959; CBE 1945 (OBE 1942); *b* 4 April 1905; *s* of late Hubert Stanley Howard-Jones, Maindee Park, Newport, Mon; *m* 1st, 1934, Irene Lucy Gillespie (*d* 1944); 2nd, 1945, Violet, *d* of Sidney Alfred Butler, and *widow* of Lieut-Col Francis John Leland; one *s* one *d*. *Educ:* Imperial Service Coll.; Cardiff Univ. (BSc Eng). Served War of 1939-45 (despatches; OBE; CBE). Commandant REME Training Centre, 1953-57; Inspector, Royal Electrical and Mechanical Engineers, War Office, 1957-60. MIMechE; AMIEE. *Address:* Rifle Range Farm, Fleet Road, Hartley Wintney, Hants RG27 8ED. *T:* Hartley Wintney 2358.

HOWARD-VYSE, Lt.-Gen. Sir Edward (Dacre), KBE 1962 (CBE 1955); CB 1958; MC 1941; DL; *b* 27 Nov. 1905; *s* of late Lieut-Col Cecil Howard-Vyse, JP, Langton Hall, Malton, Yorks; *m* 1940, Mary Bridget, *er d* of late Col Hon. Claude Henry Comaraich Willoughby, CVO; two *s* one *d*. *Educ:* Wellington Coll., Berks; RMA. 2nd Lieut, Royal Artillery, 1925; served War of 1939-45: British Expeditionary Force, France, 1939-40; Lieut-Col, 1941; Mediterranean Expeditionary Force, 1941-44; In command 1st Royal Horse Artillery, Central Mediterranean Force, 1944-45. Brigadier, 1949; CRA 7th Armoured Division, BAOR, 1951-53; Commandant, Sch. of Artillery, 1953; Maj.-Gen., 1957; Maj.-Gen., Artillery, Northern Army Group, 1956-59; Dir, Royal Artillery, War Office, 1959-61; GOC-in-C, Western Command, 1961-64; retired, 1964. Lieut-Gen., 1961. Col Comdt: RA 1962-70; RHA 1968-70. Vice-Pres., Army Cadet Force Assoc., 1974-, Chm., 1964-74; Vice-Pres., Nat. Artillery Assoc., 1965-. DL E Riding of Yorks and Kingston upon Hull, 1964, Vice-Lieut, 1968-74; DL N Yorkshire, 1974-. *Recreations:* country pursuits. *Address:* Langton House, Malton, North Yorks. *Club:* Army and Navy.

HOWARTH, Alan Thomas, CBE 1982; with Baring Brothers & Co. Ltd, since 1982; *b* 11 June 1944; *e s* of T. E. B. Howarth, *qv*; *m* 1967, Gillian Martha, *d* of Mr and Mrs Arthur Chance, Dublin; one *s* two *d*. *Educ:* Rugby Sch. (scholar); King's Coll., Cambridge (major scholar in History; BA 1965). Sen. Res. Asst to Field-Marshal Montgomery on A History of Warfare, 1965-67; Asst Master, Westminster Sch., 1968-74; Personal Asst to Chm. of Conservative Party, 1975-79; Dir, Cons. Res. Dept, 1979-81; Vice-Chm., Conservative Party, 1980-81. *Recreations:* books, travel, the arts, running. *Address:* 8 Bishopsgate, EC2. *T:* 01-283 8833. *Club:* Buck's.

HOWARTH, David Armine; author; *b* 18 July 1912; *s* of Dr O. J. R. Howarth and Mrs E. K. Howarth. *Educ:* Tonbridge Sch.; Trinity Coll., Cambridge. BBC Talks Asst etc, 1934-39. War Correspondent, 1939-40; RNVR, 1940-45. Knight 1st class, Order of St Olav (Norway), 1955; Cross of Freedom (Norway) 1945. *Publications:* The Shetland Bus, 1951; We Die Alone (also under title Escape Alone), 1955; The Sledge Patrol, 1957; Dawn of D-Day, 1959; The Shadow of the Dam, 1961; The Desert King, A Biography of Ibn Saud, 1964; The Golden Isthmus, 1966; A Near Run Thing: the Day of Waterloo, 1968; Trafalgar: The Nelson Touch, 1969; Sovereign of the Seas, 1974; The Greek Adventure, 1976; 1066, The Year of the Conquest, 1977; The Voyage of the Armada: the Spanish story, 1981; *fiction:* Group Flashing Two, 1952; One Night in Styria, 1953; *for children:* Heroes of Nowadays, 1957; Great Escapes, 1969. As Editor: My Land and My People (by HH The Dalai Lama), 1962. *Address:* Wildlings Wood, Blackboys, Sussex. *T:* Hadlow Down 233.

HOWARTH, Elgar; freelance musician; *b* 4 Nov. 1935; *s* of Oliver and Emma Howarth; *m* 1958, Mary Bridget Neary; one *s* two *d*. *Educ:* Manchester Univ. (MusB); Royal Manchester Coll. of Music (ARMCM 1956; FRMCM 1970). Royal Opera House, Covent Garden (Orchestra), 1958-63; Royal Philharmonic Orchestra, 1963-69; Mem., London Sinfonietta, 1968-71; Mem., Philip Jones Brass Ensemble, 1965-76; freelance conductor, 1970-; Musical Advisor, Grimethorpe Colliery Brass Band, 1972-. *Publications:* various compositions mostly for brass instruments. *Address:* 27 Cromwell Avenue, N6.

HOWARTH, Prof. Leslie, OBE 1955; FRS 1950; FRAeS; BSc, MA, PhD; Henry Overton Wills Professor of Mathematics, University of Bristol, 1964-76, now Emeritus; *b* 23 May 1911; *s* of late Fred and Elizabeth Ellen Howarth; *m* 1934, Eva Priestley; two *s*. *Educ:* Accrington Grammar Sch.; Manchester Univ.; Gonville and Caius Coll., Cambridge. Mathematical tripos, 1933; Smith's Prize, 1935; PhD, 1936. Berry-Ramsey Research Fellow, King's Coll., Cambridge, 1936-45; Lecturer in Mathematics in the University of Cambridge, 1936-49; Fellow of St John's Coll., Cambridge, 1945-49; Prof. of Applied Mathematics, University of Bristol, 1949-64; Adams Prize, 1951. Worked at External Ballistics Dept, Ordnance Board, 1939-42, and at Armament Research Dept, 1942-45. *Publications:* (ed) Modern Developments in Fluid Dynamics: High Speed Flow; papers on aerodynamics. *Address:* 10 The Crescent, Henleaze, Bristol BS9 4RW. *T:* Bristol 629621.

HOWARTH, Robert Lever; Senior Lecturer in General Studies, Wigan College of Technology, since 1977; Leader, Labour Group, Bolton Metropolitan Borough, since 1975; Leader, Bolton Metropolitan Borough Council, since 1980; *b* 31 July 1927; *s* of James Howarth and Bessie (*née* Pearson); *m* 1952, Josephine Mary Doyle; one *s* one *d*. *Educ:* Bolton County Grammar Sch.; Bolton Technical Coll. Draughtsman with Hawker Siddeley Dynamics. MP (Lab) Bolton East, 1964-70. Lectr in Liberal Studies, Leigh Technical Coll., 1970-76. *Recreations:* gardening, reading, walking, films. *Address:* 93 Markland Hill, Bolton, Lancs BL1 5EQ. *T:* Bolton 44121.

HOWARTH, Thomas Edward Brodie, MC 1945; TD; Headmaster, Campion School, Athens, 1980-82; *b* 21 Oct. 1914; *e s* of Frank Fielding Howarth; *m* 1943, Margaret Teakle; two *s* one *d* (and one *s* decd). *Educ:* Rugby Sch.; Clare Coll., Cambridge (Scholar, MA, 1st cl. Hons Parts I and II, History Tripos). Asst Master, Winchester Coll., 1938-39, 1946-48; Headmaster King Edward's Sch., Birmingham, 1948-52; Second Master, Winchester Coll., 1952-62; High Master, St Paul's School, 1962-73; Fellow and Sen. Tutor, Magdalene Coll., Cambridge, 1973-80. Served War of 1939-45, King's (Liverpool) Regt; Brigade Major, HQ Mersey Garrison; Brigade Major 207 Infantry Bde; NW Europe, June 1944; Personal Liaison Officer to C-in-C 21st Army Group. Trustee, Imperial War Museum, 1964-79; Governor: St John's Sch., Leatherhead; Rugby Sch.; British Sch. of Paris. Mem., Public Schs Commission, 1966. Chm., Headmasters' Conference, 1969. *Publications:* Citizen-King, 1961; Culture, Anarchy and the Public Schools, 1969; Cambridge Between Two Wars, 1978. *Recreation:* golf. *Address:* 112A Elgin Crescent, W11. *T:* 01-221 7549. *Clubs:* Garrick, Savile, Beefsteak.

See also A. T. Howarth.

HOWAT, Prof. Henry Taylor, CBE 1971; MSc (Manch.); MD, FRCP, FRCPE; Professor of Gastroenterology, University of Manchester, 1972-76, now Emeritus; Physician, Manchester Royal Infirmary, 1948-76; *b* 16 May 1911; *s* of late Adam Howat, MA, and late Henrietta Howat, Pittenweem, Fife; *m* 1940, Rosaline, *o d* of late Miles Green, Auckland, NZ; two *s* one *d*. *Educ:* Cameron Public Sch. and Madras Coll., St Andrews; Univ. of St Andrews. MB, ChB (St And) 1933; MD with Hons and Univ. Gold Medal (St And), 1960; MRCP 1937, FRCP 1948; MRCPE 1961, FRCPE 1965. Resident MO, Manchester Royal Infirmary, 1938-40. Served War, MEF and BLA; RMO, Physician Specialist, Officer in charge of Med. Div., Mil. Hosps, 1940-45; temp. Lt-Col, RAMC. Univ. of Manchester: Asst Lectr in Applied Physiology, 1946-48; Lectr in Med., 1948-69 (Chm., Faculty of Med., 1968-72); Reader, 1969-72; Physician, Ancoats Hosp., Manchester, 1946-62. United Manchester Hospitals, 1948-76: Chm., Med. Exec. Cttee, 1968-73; Mem., Bd of Governors, 1966-74. President: European Pancreatic Club, 1965; British Soc. of Gastroenterology, 1968-69; Assoc. of Physicians of GB and Ireland, 1975-76; Manchester Med. Soc., 1975-76; Pancreatic Soc. of GB and Ireland, 1978-79. Hon. MD, Univ. of Louvain, Belgium, 1945. Manchester Man of the Year, 1973. Medallist, J. E. Purkyně Czechoslovak Med. Soc., 1968. *Publications:* (ed) The Exocrine Pancreas, 1979; articles on gastrointestinal physiology and disease. *Recreation:* golf. *Address:* 19 Manor Road, Cheadle Hulme, Cheadle, Cheshire SK8 7DQ. *T:* 061-485 3146; 40 High Street, Pittenweem, Fife KY10 2PL. *T:* Anstruther 311325. *Clubs:* Athenæum; Royal and Ancient Golf (St Andrews).

HOWD, Mrs Isobel; Regional Nursing Officer, Yorkshire Regional Health Authority, since 1973; *b* 24 Oct. 1928 (*née* Young); *m* 1951, Ralph Howd. SRN, RMN, BTA Cert. Matron, Naburn Hosp., York, 1960-63; Asst Regional Nursing Officer, Leeds Regional Hosp. Bd, 1963-70; Chief Nursing Officer, South Teesside Hosp. Management Cttee, 1970-73. *Address:* Yew Tree Cottage, Upper Dunsforth, York YO5 9RU. *T:* Boroughbridge 2534. *Club:* Naval and Military.

HOWE, 6th Earl, *cr* 1821; **Edward Richard Assheton Penn Curzon**, CBE 1961; DL; JP; Baron Howe, 1788; Baron Curzon, 1794; Viscount Curzon, 1802; Lieutenant-Commander RNVR; President, Chesham and Amersham Conservative Association, since 1972; *b* 7 Aug. 1908; a godson of King Edward VII; *o s* of 5th Earl Howe, PC, CBE, VD; *S* father, 1964; *m* 1st, 1935, Priscilla (whom he divorced, 1942), *o c* of Lieut-Col Sir Archibald Weigall, 1st Bt, KCMG; 2nd, 1946, Gay, *e d* of late Stephen Frederick Wakeling, Durban, South Africa; two *d*. *Educ:* Eton; Corpus Christi Coll., Cambridge. RNVR, 1928-46; war service in Atlantic and Pacific, 1940-46. Mem. (MR) LCC for South Battersea, 1937-46. Commissioner of Bucks St John Ambulance Bde, 1953-55; President: S Bucks Cons. and Unionist Assoc., 1965-72; St John Ambulance, Bucks; Trustee, King William IV Naval Asylum. JP 1946, DL 1960, Bucks. Alderman, Buckinghamshire, 1958, County Councillor, 1973-, Vice Chm., Bucks County Council, 1976-. President: Brit. Automobile Racing Club; Inst. of Road Safety Officers; Fiat Motor Club (GB); RAC Steward; Vice-Chm., RAC; Dir, Automobile Proprietary Ltd; Member: RAC Public Policy Cttee; British Motor Sports Council; Motoring Services Ltd; RNLI Cttee of Management. Hon. FIRTE. CStJ. *Recreations:* motoring, cricket, shooting, golf. *Heir:* cousin Frederick Richard Penn Curzon, *b* 29 Jan. 1951. *Address:* Penn House, Amersham, Bucks. *T:* High Wycombe 713366; 20 Pitts Head Mews, W1. *T:* 01-499 4706. *Club:* Naval.

HOWE, Allen; Chairman, Medical Appeals Tribunal for Wales, since 1982; *b* 6 June 1918; *s* of late Frank Howe and Dora Howe, Monk Bretton, Yorks; *m* 1952, Katherine, *d* of late Mr and Mrs Griff Davies, Pontypridd; two *d*. *Educ:* Holgate Grammar Sch., Barnsley. Served with E Yorks Regt and RWAFF, 1939-46, France, Africa, India and Burma (Major). HM Colonial Admin. Service, Gold Coast, 1946-55 (Sen. Dist Comr). Called to Bar, Middle Temple, 1953; Judicial Adviser, Ashanti, 1954-55; practised Wales and Chester Circuit, 1955-59; Legal Dept, Welsh Bd of Health, 1959-65; Legal Dept, Welsh Office, 1965-74; Circuit Administrator, Wales and Chester Circuit,

Lord Chancellor's Dept, 1974-82. *Recreations:* golf, gardening, walking. *Address:* 2 Orchard Drive, Whitchurch, Cardiff CF4 2AE. *T:* Cardiff 66626. *Clubs:* Cardiff and County; Radyr Golf.

HOWE, Prof. Christopher Barry, PhD; Professor of Economics with reference to Asia, University of London, since 1979; *b* 3 Nov. 1937; *s* of Charles Roderick Howe and Patricia (*née* Creeden); *m* 1967, Patricia Anne Giles; one *s* one *d. Educ:* William Ellis Sch., London; St Catharine's Coll., Cambridge (MA). PhD London. Economic Secretariat, FBI, 1961-63; Sch. of Oriental and African Studies, London Univ., 1963-: Head, Contemp. China Inst., 1972-78. Member: Hong Kong Univ. and Polytechnic Grants Cttee, 1974-; UGC, 1979-. *Publications:* Employment and Economic Growth in Urban China 1949-57, 1971; Wage Patterns and Wage Policy in Modern China 1919-1972, 1973; China's Economy: a basic guide, 1978; (ed) Shanghai: revolution and development, 1980. *Recreations:* music, gardening, Burmese cats. *Address:* 12 Highgate Avenue, N6 5RX. *T:* 01-340 8104.

HOWE, Derek Andrew; Special Adviser to Chancellor of Duchy of Lancaster, since 1981; *b* 31 Aug. 1934; *o s* of late Harold and Elsie Howe; *m* 1st, 1958, Barbara (*née* Estill); two *d* ; 2nd, 1975, Sheila (*née* Digger); one *s. Educ:* City of Leeds Sch.; Cockburn High Sch., Leeds. Journalist, Yorkshire Evening News, 1951-61; Conservative Central Office, 1962-70; Parliamentary Liaison Officer, 1970-73; Special Adviser, 1973-75; Press Officer, Leader of HM Opposition, 1975-79; special advr to Paymaster Gen., 1979-81. *Recreations:* gardening, reading, philately. *Address:* The Vines, Kimpton, near Andover, Hampshire. *Club:* St Stephen's Constitutional.

HOWE, Elspeth Rosamund Morton, (Lady Howe), JP; Deputy Chairman, Equal Opportunities Commission, 1975-79; Chairman, Greenwich Juvenile Court, since 1981; *b* 8 Feb. 1932; *d* of late Philip Morton Shand and Sybil Mary (*née* Sissons); *m* 1953, Rt Hon. Sir Geoffrey Howe, *qv* ; one *s* two *d. Educ:* Bath High Sch.; Wycombe Abbey. Vice-Chm., Conservative London Area Women's Adv. Cttee, 1966-67, also Pres. of the Cttee's Contact Gp, 1973-77; Mem., Conservative Women's Nat. Adv. Cttee, 1966-71. Chm., Southwark North Juvenile Ct, 1970-81; Member: Lord Chancellor's Adv. Cttee on appointment of Magistrates for Inner London Area, 1965-75; Lord Chancellor's Adv. Cttee on Legal Aid, 1971-75; Parole Board, 1972-75. Co-opted Mem., ILEA, 1967-70; Mem., Briggs Cttee on Nursing Profession, 1970-72. Mem., Finance Cttee, BFI, 1979-. Governor: Wycombe Abbey, 1968-; Froebel Educn Inst., 1968-75; Cumberlow Lodge Remand Home, 1967-70. Has served as Chm. or Member: several sch. governing bodies in Tower Hamlets; London Adventure Playgroups Assoc.; Vice-Pres., Pre-School Playgroups Assoc., 1979-; President: Women's Gas Fedn, 1979-; Fedn of Personnel Services, 1980-; Peckham Settlement, 1976-. JP Inner London Juvenile Court Panel, 1964. *Publication:* Under Five (a report on pre-school education), 1966. *Address:* c/o Barclays Bank, 4 Vere Street, W1.
See also B. M. H. Shand.

HOWE, Rt. Hon. Sir Geoffrey; *see* Howe, Rt Hon. Sir R. E. G.

HOWE, Prof. Geoffrey Leslie, TD 1962 (Bars 1969 and 1974); Professor of Oral Surgery and Oral Medicine, and Dean of Dental Studies, University of Hong Kong, since 1978; Director, The Prince Philip Dental Hospital, since 1981; *b* 22 April 1924; *e s* of late Leo Leslie John Howe, Maidenhead, Berks; *m* 1947, Heather Patricia Joan Hambly; one *s. Educ:* Royal Dental and Middlesex Hospitals. LDS RCS 1946; LRCP, MRCS 1954; FDS RCS 1955; MDS Dunelm, 1961; FFD RCSI 1964; FICD 1981. Dental and Medical Sch. Prizeman; Begley Prize, RCS, 1951; Cartwright Prize, RCS, 1961. Dental Officer, Royal Army Dental Corps, 1946-49. House appointments, etc., Royal Dental and Middlesex Hospitals, 1949-55. Registrar in Oral Surgery, Eastman Dental Hosp. (Institute of Dental Surgery), 1955-56; Senior Registrar in Oral Surgery, Plastic and Oral Surgery Centre, Chepstow, Mon, 1956; Senior Registrar in Oral Surgery, Eastman Dental Hospital, 1956-59; Professor of Oral Surgery, University of Newcastle upon Tyne (formerly King's Coll., University of Durham), 1959-67; Prof. of Oral Surgery, Royal Dental Hosp., London Sch. of Dental Surgery, 1967-78 (Dean of School, 1974-78). Cons. Oral Surgeon, United Newcastle upon Tyne Hosps, 1959-67; Chm., Central Cttee for Hosp. Dental Services, 1971-73; Chm., Council, BDA, 1973-78 (Vice-Chm., 1971-73); Pres., Internat. Assoc. of Oral Surgeons, 1980-. Hon. Col Comdt, RADC, 1975-. OStJ. *Publications:* The Extraction of Teeth, 1961, 2nd edn 1970; Minor Oral Surgery, 1966, 2nd edn 1972; (with F. I. H. Whitehead) Local Anaesthesia in Dentistry, 1972, 2nd edn 1981; contribs to: Medical Treatment Yearbook, 1959; Modern Trends in Dental Surgery, 1962, and to numerous medical and dental journals. *Recreations:* sailing; Territorial Army Volunteer Reserve (lately Col, OC 217 (L) Gen. Hosp. RAMC (V), graded Cons. Dental Surgeon RADC, TAVR). *Address:* Flat 11, Block C, 350 Victoria Road, Hong Kong. *T:* Hong Kong 870691; 70 Croham Manor Road, South Croydon, Surrey CR2 7BF. *Clubs:* Savage, Oral Surgery; Royal Hong Kong Yacht; United Services Recreational (Hong Kong).

HOWE, George Edward; HM Diplomatic Service, retired; Counsellor, Foreign and Commonwealth Office, 1977-82; *b* 18 June 1925; *s* of late George Cuthbert Howe and Florence May (*née* Baston); *m* 1949, Florence Elizabeth Corrish; one *s. Educ:* Highbury Grammar Sch.; Westminster Coll. Served British Army, 1943; Indian Army, 2nd Bn The Burma Rifles, 1945-48 (Major). HMOCS, Malaya, 1949; joined Foreign Service, later Diplomatic Service, 1957; served Pnomn Penh, Hong Kong, Singapore, Paris, Milan and

FCO. Mem., RUSI. *Recreations:* fishing, military history. *Address:* Flat 5, 35 Buckingham Gate, SW1. *T:* 01-828 8201. *Club:* Travellers'.

HOWE, Prof. G(eorge) Melvyn; Professor of Geography, University of Strathclyde, since 1967; *b* Abercynon, 7 April 1920; *s* of Reuben and Edith Howe, Abercynon; *m* 1947, Patricia Graham Fennell, *d* of Edgar and Miriam Fennell, Pontypridd; three *d. Educ:* Caerphilly Grammar Sch.; UCW Aberystwyth. BSc 1940; BSc 1st cl. hons Geog. and Anthrop., 1947; MSc 1949; PhD 1957; DSc 1974. FRSE, FRGS, FRSGS, FRMetS. Served with RAF, 1940-46: Meteorological Br., 1940-42; Intell. (Air Photographic Interpretation) Br., 1942-46, in Middle East Commnd 1942. Lectr, later Sen. Lectr, in Geography, UCW Aberystwyth, 1948; Reader in Geog., Univ. of Wales, 1964. Vis. Prof. (Health and Welfare, Canada), 1977. Mem. Council, Inst. of British Geographers; Mem. Medical Geography Cttee, RGS; British Rep. on Medical Geog. Commn of IGU; Mem., Nat. Cttee for Geography. Editor, Ecology of Disease. Gill Memorial Award, RGS, 1964. *Publications:* Wales from the Air, 1957, 2nd edn 1966; (with P. Thomas) Welsh Landforms and Scenery, 1963; National Atlas of Disease Mortality in the United Kingdom, 1963, 2nd edn 1970; The Soviet Union, 1968, 2nd edn 1982; The USSR, 1971; Man, Environment and Disease in Britain, 1972, 2nd edn 1976; (ed and contrib.) Atlas of Glasgow and the West of Scotland, 1972; (contrib.) Wales (ed E. G. Bowen), 1958; (contrib.) Modern Methods in the History of Medicine (ed E. Clarke), 1970; (ed with J. A. Loraine, and contrib.) Environmental Medicine, 1973, 2nd edn 1980; (contrib.) Environment and Man (ed J. Lenihan and W. W. Fletcher), 1976; (ed and contrib.) A World Geography of Human Diseases, 1977; articles in geographical, meteorological, hydrological and medical jls. *Recreation:* travel. *Address:* Hendre, 29 Birnam Crescent, Bearsden, Glasgow. *T:* 041-942 7223.

HOWE, Jack, RDI 1961; FRIBA 1953; FSIAD 1955; Architect and Industrial Designer; *b* 24 Feb. 1911; *s* of Charles Henry and Florence Eleanor Howe; *m* 1960, Margaret Crosbie Corrie (*d* 1979); one *s* one *d* (by former marriage); *m* 1981, Jennifer Mary Dixon (*née* Hughes D'Aeth). *Educ:* Enfield Grammar Sch.; Polytechnic Sch. of Architecture. Asst to E. Maxwell Fry, 1933-37; Chief Asst to Walter Gropius and Maxwell Fry, 1937-39; Drawing Office Manager to Holland, Hannan & Cubitts Ltd for Royal Ordnance Factories at Wrexham and Ranskill, 1939-43; Associate Partner, Arcon, 1944-48; private practice, 1949; Partnership with Andrew Bain, 1959-76. Architectural work includes: Highbury Quadrant Primary School, (LCC); Windmill House, Lambeth (LCC Housing Scheme); Television Research Lab. for AEI Ltd; Kodak Pavilion, Brussels Exhibn, 1958; Official Architects for British Trade Fair, Moscow, 1961; Industrial Designs include: Diesel Electric Locomotives and Express Pullman Trains; also Rly equipment. Industrial Design Consultant to various large firms and to BR Board. Mem. Design Index Cttee and Street Furniture Cttee, Design Council (formerly CoID), 1956-; Member: Cttee on Traffic Signs, Min. of Transport, 1962, 1963; Nat. Council for Diplomas in Art and Design. FSIAD (Pres. 1963-64); Master of Faculty, RDI, 1975-77. Duke of Edinburgh's design prize, 1969. *Publications:* articles for various architectural and design jls. *Recreations:* music, theatre. *Address:* 4 Leopold Avenue, Wimbledon, SW19. *T:* 01-946 7116.

HOWE, John Francis, OBE 1974; Defence Counsellor, UK Delegation to NATO, since 1981; *b* 29 Jan. 1944; *s* of Frank and Marjorie Howe; *m* 1981, Angela Ephrosini Nicolaides; one step *d. Educ:* Shrewsbury Sch.; Balliol Coll., Oxford (Scholar; MA). Pirelli General Cable Works, 1964; joined MoD as Asst Principal, 1967; Principal, 1972; Civil Adviser to GOC NI, 1972-73; Private Sec. to Perm. Under-Sec. of State, 1975-78; Asst Sec., 1979. *Recreation:* travel. *Address:* 12 Clarendon Court, Kew Gardens Road, Kew, Richmond, Surrey TW9 3HE.

HOWE, Air Vice-Marshal John Frederick George, CBE 1980; AFC 1961; Commander, Southern Maritime Air Region, since 1980; *b* 26 March 1930; *m* 1961, Annabelle Gowing; three *d. Educ:* St Andrew's Coll., Grahamstown, SA. SAAF, 1950-54 (served in Korea, 2nd Sqdn SAAF and 19 Inf. Regt, US Army, 1951); 222 Sqdn, Fighter Comd, 1956; 40 Commando RM, Suez Campaign, 1956; Fighter Command: Flt Comdr, 222 Sqdn, 1957; Flt Comdr, 43 Sqdn, 1957-59; Sqdn Comdr, 74 Sqdn, 1960-61; Air Staff, HQ Fighter Command, 1961-63; RAF Staff Coll., 1964; USAF Exchange Tour at Air Defence Comd HQ, Colorado Springs, 1965-67; 229 Operational Conversion Unit, Chivenor, 1967-68; OC 228 OCU, Coningsby, 1968-69; Central Tactics and Trials Org., HQ Air Support Comd, 1969-70; MoD, 1970-72; Station Comdr, RAF Gutersloh, 1973-74; RCDS, 1975; Gp Capt. Ops, HQ No 11 Gp, 1975-77; Comdt, ROC, 1977-80. American DFC 1951; Air Medal 1951. *Recreations:* country pursuits, skiing, sailing. *Address:* c/o Barclays Bank International Ltd, Oceanic House, 1 Cockspur Street, SW1. *Club:* Royal Air Force.

HOWE, Rt. Rev. John William Alexander; Research Fellow of the Research Project, Anglican Consultative Council, since 1983; *b* 1920. *Educ:* Westcliff High Sch.; St Chad's Coll., Durham Univ. BA 1943; MA, BD 1948. Ordained, 1943; Curate, All Saints, Scarborough, 1943-46; Chaplain, Adisadel Coll., Gold Coast, 1946-50; Vice-Principal, Edinburgh Theological Coll., 1950-55; Hon. Chaplain, St Mary's Cathedral, Edinburgh, 1951-55; Bishop of St Andrews, Dunkeld and Dunblane, 1955-69. Hon. Canon, St Mary's Cath., Glasgow, 1969; Exec. Officer of the Anglican Communion, 1969-71; Secretary General, Anglican Consultative Council, 1971-82. Hon. DD: General Theological Seminary, NY, 1974; Lambeth, 1978. *Address:* Lambeth Palace, SE1 7JU. *T:* 01-928 1160.

HOWE, Josephine Mary O'C.; *see* O'Connor Howe.

HOWE, Rt. Hon. Sir (Richard Edward) Geoffrey, PC 1972; Kt 1970; QC 1965; MP (C) Surrey East, since 1974 (Reigate, 1970-74); Chancellor of the Exchequer, since 1979; *b* 20 Dec. 1926; *er s* of late B. E. Howe and Mrs E. F. Howe, JP (*née* Thomson), Port Talbot, Glamorgan; *m* 1953, Elspeth Rosamund Morton Shand (*see* Lady Howe); one *s* two *d. Educ:* Winchester Coll. (Exhibitioner); Trinity Hall, Cambridge (Scholar, MA, LLB); Pres., Trinity Hall Assoc., 1977-78. Lieut Royal Signals 1945-48. Chm. Cambridge Univ. Conservative Assoc., 1951; Chm. Bow Group, 1955; Managing Dir, Crossbow, 1957-60, Editor 1960-62. Called to the Bar, Middle Temple, 1952; Bencher, 1969; Mem. General Council of the Bar, 1957-61; Mem. Council of Justice, 1963-70. Dep. Chm., Glamorgan QS, 1966-70. Contested (C) Aberavon, 1955, 1959; MP (C) Bebington, 1964-66. Sec. Conservative Parliamentary Health and Social Security Cttee, 1964-65; an Opposition Front Bench spokesman on labour and social services, 1965-66; Solicitor-General, 1970-72; Minister for Trade and Consumer Affairs, DTI, 1972-74; opposition front bench spokesman on social services, 1974-75, on Treasury and economic affairs, 1975-79. Director: Sun Alliance & London Insce Co. Ltd, 1974-79; AGB Research Ltd, 1974-79; EMI Ltd, 1976-79. Member: (Latey) Interdeptl Cttee on Age of Majority, 1965-67; (Street) Cttee on Racial Discrimination, 1967; (Cripps) Cons. Cttee on Discrimination against Women, 1968-69; Chm. Ely Hospital, Cardiff, Inquiry, 1969; Pres., Cons. Political Centre Nat. Adv. Cttee, 1977-79. Mem. Council of Management, Private Patients' Plan, 1969-70; an Hon. Vice-Pres., Consumers Assoc., 1974-. *Publications:* various political pamphlets for Bow Group and Conservative Political Centre. *Address:* c/o Barclays Bank, Cavendish Square Branch, 4 Vere Street, W1.

HOWELL, Rt. Hon. David Arthur Russell; PC 1979; MP (C) Guildford since 1966; Secretary of State for Transport, since 1981; *b* 18 Jan. 1936; *s* of late Colonel A. H. E. Howell, DSO, TD, DL and of Beryl Howell, 5 Headfort Place, SW1; *m* 1967, Davina Wallace; one *s* two *d. Educ:* Eton; King's Coll., Cambridge. BA 1st class hons Cantab, 1959. Lieut Coldstream Guards, 1954-56. Joined Economic Section of Treasury, 1959; resigned, 1960. Leader-Writer and Special Correspondent, The Daily Telegraph, 1960; Chm. of Bow Gp, 1961-62; Editor of Crossbow, 1962-64; contested (C) Dudley, 1964; a Lord Comr of Treasury, 1970-71; Parly Sec., CSD, 1970-72; Parly Under-Sec.: Dept of Employment, 1971-72; NI Office, March–Nov. 1972; Minister of State: NI Office, 1972-74; Dept of Energy, 1974; Sec. of State for Energy, 1979-81. Dir of Conservative Political Centre, 1964-66. Trustee, Federal Trust for Educn and Research. Jt Hon. Sec., UK Council of European Movement, 1968-70. *Publications:* (co-author) Principles in Practice, 1960; The Conservative Opportunity, 1965; Freedom and Capital, 1981; various pamphlets and articles. *Recreations:* travel, books. *Address:* House of Commons, SW1. *Club:* Buck's.

HOWELL, Rt. Hon. Denis Herbert, PC 1976; MP (Lab) Small Heath since 1961; *b* 4 Sept. 1923; *s* of Herbert and Bertha A. Howell; *m* 1955, Brenda Marjorie, *d* of Stephen and Ruth Willson, Birmingham; three *s* one *d. Educ:* Gower Street Sch.; Handsworth Grammar Sch., Birmingham. Mem., Birmingham City Council, 1946-56; Hon. Sec. Birmingham City Council Labour Group, 1950-55 (served Catering Establishment, General Purposes, Health and Watch Cttees); Chm. Catering Cttee, 1952-55; Health (Gen. Purposes) Sub-Cttee for setting up of first smokeless zones. MP (Lab) All Saints Div., Birmingham, 1955-Sept. 1959; Jt Parly Under-Sec. of State, Dept of Educn and Science (with responsibility for sport), 1964-69; Minister of State, Min. of Housing and Local Govt (with responsibility for sport), 1969-70; Opposition Spokesman for Local Govt and Sport, 1970-74; Minister of State, DoE (responsible for environment, water resources and sport), 1974-79; Opposition Spokesman on Environment (Environment and Services, Water Resources, Sport, Recreation and Countryside), 1979-. Mem., Labour Party NEC, 1982-. Member: Dudley Road Hosp. Group Management Cttee, 1948-64; the Albemarle Cttee on the Youth Service; Management Cttee, City of Birmingham Symphony Orchestra, 1950-55. Governor, Handsworth Grammar Sch. Chairman: Birmingham Assoc. of Youth Clubs, 1963-64; Birmingham Settlement, 1963-64; Sports Council, 1965-70; Youth Service Develt Council, 1964-69 (report: Youth and Community Work in the 70's); Central Council of Physical Recreation, 1973-74; Cttee of Enquiry into Sponsorship of Sport, 1981. Pres., Assoc. of Professional, Exec. Clerical and Computer Staffs (APEX) (formerly CAWU), 1971-. Football League Referee, 1956-70. Silver Medal, Olympic Order, 1981. *Publication:* Soccer Refereeing, 1968. *Recreations:* sport, theatre, music. *Address:* 33 Moor Green Lane, Moseley, Birmingham B13 8NE. *Clubs:* Reform; Warwickshire County Cricket (Birmingham); Birmingham Press.

HOWELL, Air Vice-Marshal Evelyn Michael Thomas, CBE 1961; CEng, FRAeS; *b* 11 Sept. 1913; *s* of Sir Evelyn Berkeley Howell, KCIE, CSI; *m* 1st, 1937, Helen Joan, *o d* of late Brig. W. M. Hayes, CBE, FRICS (marr. diss. 1972); one *s* three *d* ; 2nd, 1972, Rosemary, *e d* of I. A. Cram, CEng, MICE; one *s* one *d. Educ:* Downside Sch.; RAF Coll., Cranwell. Commissioned, 1934; Dir of Air Armament Research and Devt, Min. of Aviation, 1960-62; Comdt, RAF Techn. Coll., 1963-65; SASO, HQ Technical Training Command RAF, 1966-67; retired, 1967. Gen. Manager, Van Dusen Aircraft Supplies, Oxford, Minneapolis, St Louis, Helsingborg, 1967-79. Mem. Livery of Clothworkers' Co., 1938. *Recreations:* swimming, rifle shooting, tennis, boating. *Address:* Bank Farm, Lorton, Cockermouth, Cumbria CA13 0RQ. *Club:* Royal Air Force.

HOWELL, Gwynne Richard; Principal Bass, Royal Opera House, since 1971; *b* Gorseinon, S Wales, 13 June 1938; *s* of Gilbert and Ellaline Howell; *m* 1968, Mary Edwina Morris; two *s. Educ:* Pontardawe Grammar Sch.; Univ. of Wales, Swansea (BSc); Manchester Univ. (DipTP); MRTPI 1966. Studied singing with Redvers Llewellyn while at UCW; pt-time student, Manchester RCM, with Gwilym Jones, during DipTP trng at Manchester Univ.; studied with Otakar Kraus, 1968-72. Planning Asst, Kent CC, 1961-63; Sen. Planning Officer, Manchester Corp., 1965-68, meanwhile continuing to study music pt-time and giving public operatic performances which incl. the rôle of Pogner, in Die Meistersinger; as a result of this rôle, apptd Principal Bass at Sadler's Wells, 1968; also reached final of BBC Opera Singers competition for N of Eng., 1967. In first season at Sadler's Wells, sang 8 rôles, incl. Monterone and the Commendatore; appearances with Hallé Orch., 1968 and 1969; Arkel in Pelleas and Melisande, Glyndebourne and Covent Garden, 1969; Goffredo, in Il Pirato, 1969. *Royal Opera House, Covent Garden:* début as First Nazarene, Salome, 1969-70 season; the King, in Aida; Timur, in Turandot; Mephisto, in Damnation of Faust; Prince Gremin, in Eugene Onegin; High Priest, in Nabucco; Reinmar, in Tannhauser, 1973-74 (later rôle, Landgraf); Colline, in La Boheme; Pimen, in Boris Godunov; Ribbing, Un ballo in maschera; Padre Guardiano, in La forza del destino; Hobson, in Peter Grimes, 1975; Sparafucile, in Rigoletto, 1975-76 season; Ramfis in Aida, 1977; Tristan und Isolde, 1978, 1982; Luisa Miller, 1978; Samson et Delilah, 1981; Fiesco in Simon Boccanegra, 1981; Pogner in Die Meistersinger, 1982; Arkell in Pelléas et Mélisande, 1982; *English National Opera:* Don Carlos, Die Meistersinger, 1974-75; The Magic Flute, Don Carlos, 1975-76; Duke Bluebeard's Castle, 1978; The Barber of Seville, 1980; Tristan and Isolde, 1981; *sacred music:* Verdi and Mozart Requiems, Missa Solemnis, St Matthew and St John Passions; sings in Europe and USA; records for BBC and for major recording companies. *Recreations:* tennis, squash, Rugby enthusiast, gardening. *Address:* 197 Fox Lane, N13 4BB. *T:* 01-886 1981.

HOWELL, Prof. John Bernard Lloyd; Professor of Medicine, since 1969 and Dean of the Faculty of Medicine, since 1978, University of Southampton; Hon. Consultant Physician, Southampton General Hospital, since 1969; *s* of late David John Howells and Hilda Mary Hill, Ynystawe, Swansea; *m* 1952, Heather Joan Rolfe; two *s* one *d. Educ:* Swansea Grammar Sch.; Middx Hosp. Med. Sch. (Meyerstein Scholar 1946). BSc, MB, BS, PhD; FRCP. House Officer posts, Middx and Brompton Hosps; MO RAMC, 1952-54; Lectr in Physiol Medicine, 1954-56, in Pharmacol Medicine, 1958-60, Middlesex Hosp. Med. Sch.; Manchester Royal Infirmary: Sen. Lectr in Medicine and Hon. Consultant Physician, 1960-66; Consultant Physician, 1966-69. Examiner in Medicine: Welsh Nat. Sch. of Medicine, 1968-70; Univ. of Newcastle, 1969-72; Univ. of Manchester, 1972-75. Eli Lilly Travelling Fellow, Johns Hopkins Hospital, 1957-58; Goulstonian Lectr, RCP, 1966. Member: GMC, 1979-; Physiol Soc., 1956-; Med. Res. Soc., 1956; Thoracic Soc., 1959; Assoc. of Physicians of GB and Ire., 1964-. Hon. Life Mem., Canadian Thoracic Soc., 1978; Hon. FACP 1982. *Publications:* (ed jtly) Breathlessness, 1966; chapters in: Cecil and Loeb's Textbook of Medicine, 13th edn 1970, 14th edn 1974; Recent Advances in Chest Medicine, 1976; Thoracic Medicine, 1981; Oxford Textbook of Medicine, 1982; scientific papers on respiratory physiology and medicine. *Recreations:* DIY, wine. *Address:* The Coach House, Bassett Wood Drive, Southampton SO2 3PT. *T:* Southampton 768878.

HOWELL, Rt. Rev. Kenneth Walter, MA; *b* 4 Feb. 1909; *s* of Frederick John and Florence Sarah Howell; *m* 1st, 1937, Beryl Mary Hope (*d* 1972), *d* of late Capt. Alfred and Mrs Hope, Bedford; two *s* one *d* ; 2nd, 1978, Mrs Siri Colvin. *Educ:* St Olave's; St Peter's Hall, Oxford; Wycliffe Hall, Oxford. Curate of St Mary Magdalene, Peckham, 1933-37; Chaplain of Paraguayan Chaco Mission, 1937-38; Chaplain Quepe Mission, Chile, 1938-40; Superintendent of South American Missionary Society's Mission to Araucanian Indians in S Chile, 1940-47; Vicar of Wandsworth, 1948-63, Rural Dean, 1957-63; Chaplain, Royal Hosp. and Home for Incurables, Putney, 1957-63; Hon. Canon of Southwark, 1962-63; Bishop in Chile, Bolivia and Peru, 1963-71; Minister of St John's, Downshire Hill, Hampstead, 1972-79; an Asst Bishop, Diocese of London, 1976-79. Sec., Spanish and Portuguese Church Aid Soc., 1981-. *Address:* 147 Southgate Street, Bury St Edmunds, Suffolk.

HOWELL, Maj.-Gen. Lloyd, CBE 1972; Consultant, Technical Education Development, University College, Cardiff, since 1980 (Fellow, 1982); Director (non-executive), Building Trades Exhibitions Ltd, since 1980; *b* 28 Dec. 1923; *s* of Thomas Idris Howell and Anne Howell; *m* 1st, 1945, Hazel Barker (*d* 1974); five *s* three *d* ; 2nd, 1975, Elizabeth June Buchanan Husband (*née* Atkinson); two step *s. Educ:* Barry Grammar Sch.; University Coll. of S Wales and Monmouthshire (BSc); Royal Military Coll. of Science. CEng, MRAeS. Commissioned RA, 1944; Field Regt, RA, E Africa, 1945-46; Staff, Divl HQ, Palestine, 1946-47; RAEC 1949; Instr, RMA Sandhurst, 1949-53; TSO II Trials Estabt, 1954-57; SO II (Educn), Divl HQ, BAOR, 1957-59; DS, Royal Mil. Coll. of Science, 1960-64; SEO, Army Apprentices Coll., 1964-67; Headmaster/Comdg, Duke of York's Royal Mil. Sch., 1967-72; Col (Ed), MoD (Army), 1972-74; Chief Educn Officer, HQ UKLF, 1974-76; Dir, Army Educn, 1976-80. Col Comdt, RAEC, 1982-. Mem. Council, CGLI, 1977-; Mem., Ct of Governors, University Coll., Cardiff, 1980-. Hon. MA Open Univ., 1980. *Recreations:* gardening, golf, reading. *Address:* Wanborough House, Lower Wanborough, near Swindon, Wilts. *T:* Wanborough 237. *Club:* Army and Navy.

HOWELL, Paul Frederic; Member (C) Norfolk, European Parliament, since 1979; farmer; *b* 17 Jan. 1951; *s* of Ralph Frederic Howell, *qv. Educ:* Gresham's Sch., Holt, Norfolk; St Edmund Hall, Oxford (BA Agric. and Econ.). Conservative Research Dept, 1973-75. Prospective Party candidate (C) Normanton, 1976-79. *Recreations:* all sports. *Address:* Willy's Croft, Church Road, Wreningham, Norwich, Norfolk NR16 1BA. *T:* Fundenhall 596.

HOWELL, Paul Philip, CMG 1964; OBE 1955; Fellow, and Director of Development Studies, Wolfson College, Cambridge; Director, Cambridge University Courses in Development Studies; *b* 13 Feb. 1917; *s* of Brig.-Gen. Philip Howell, CMG (killed in action, 1916) and Mrs Rosalind Upcher Howell (*née* Buxton); *m* 1949, Bridgit Mary Radclyffe Luard; two *s* two *d. Educ:* Westminster Sch.; Trinity Coll., Cambridge (Sen. Schol., MA, PhD); Christ Church, Oxford (MA, DPhil). Asst District Comr, Sudan Polit. Service, 1938; commnd in Sudan Defence Force, ADC to Gov.-Gen., 1940; Overseas Enemy Territory Administration, Eritrea, 1941; Asst District Comr, Zeraf Valley, 1942; District Comr, Central Nuer, 1944; District Comr, Baggara, Western Kordofan, 1946; Chm., Jonglei Investigation Team, 1948; Chm. (Dep. Gov.), Southern Development Investigation, 1953; Asst Chief Sec., Uganda Protectorate, 1955; Min. of Natural Resources, 1955; Perm. Sec., Min. of Corporations and Regional Communications, 1957; Perm. Sec. Min. of Commerce and Industry, 1959; Chm., E African Nile Waters Co-ordinating Cttee, 1956-61; seconded to FO and Min. of Overseas Development; Head of Middle East Develt Div., Beirut, 1961-69. Chm., Faculty of Archaeology and Anthropology, Univ. of Cambridge, 1977-82. Member: Bd of Governors, Inst. of Development Studies, 1971-; Council, Overseas Development Inst., 1972-. *Publications:* A Manual of Nuer Law, 1954; (ed) The Equatorial Nile Project and its Effects in the Anglo-Egyptian Sudan, 1954; (ed) Natural Resources and Development Potential in the Southern Sudan, 1955. *Recreations:* fishing and country pursuits. *Address:* Wolfson College, Cambridge. *T:* Cambridge 353951; 4 Marlborough Court, Grange Road, Cambridge. *T:* Cambridge 62601; Burfield Hall, Wymondham, Norfolk. *T:* Wymondham 603389. *Club:* Royal Commonwealth Society.

HOWELL, Ralph Frederic; MP (C) North Norfolk since 1970; *b* 25 May 1923; *m* 1950, Margaret (*née* Bone); two *s* one *d. Educ:* Diss Grammar Sch., Norfolk. Navigator/Bomb-aimer, RAF, 1941-46; farming near Dereham, Norfolk, 1946-. Mem., European Parlt, 1974-79. Vice-Chm., Cons. Parly Finance Cttee, 1979-; Mem., Treasury and Civil Service Select Cttee, 1981-. *Publication:* Why Work, 1976, 2nd edn 1981. *Address:* Wendling Grange, Dereham, Norfolk. *T:* Wendling 247. *Clubs:* Carlton, Farmers'.
See also P. F. Howell.

HOWELLS, Anne, (Mrs Stafford Dean), FRMCM (ARMCM); opera, concert and recital singer; *b* 12 Jan. 1941; *d* of Trevor William Howells and Mona Hewart; *m* 1st, 1966, Ryland Davies, *qv* (marr. diss. 1981); 2nd, 1981, Stafford Dean; one *s. Educ:* Sale County Grammar Sch.; Royal Manchester Coll. of Music. Three seasons (Chorus), with Glyndebourne, 1964-66; at short notice, given star rôle there, in Cavalli's L'Ormindo, 1967; rôles, there, also include: Dorabella in Cosi fan Tutte; Cathleen in (world première of) Nicholas Maw's Rising of the Moon, 1970; also the Composer in Ariadne; Diana in Calisto; Unitel Film of Salzburg prodn of Mozart's Clemenza di Tito. Royal Opera House, Covent Garden: under contract for three years, 1969-71, where rôles included: Lena in (world première of) Richard Rodney Bennett's Victory; Rosina in Barber of Seville; Cherubino in Marriage of Figaro. Currently, 1973-, Guest artist with Royal Opera House. Recitals in Brussels and Vienna; operatic guest performances in Chicago, Metropolitan (NY), San Francisco, Geneva, Brussels, Salzburg, Amsterdam, Hamburg (W German début), W Berlin; sings with Scottish Opera, English Nat. Opera, major orchestras in UK. *Recreations:* cinema, reading. *Address:* c/o Harrison Parrott, 12 Penzance Place, W11 4PA.

HOWELLS, Christopher John; HM Diplomatic Service; Head of Nationality and Treaty Department, Foreign and Commonwealth Office, since 1981; *b* 2 March 1933; *s* of late Rev. Brinley Howells; *m* 1959, Jane Hayes; two *s* one *d. Educ:* Oakham Sch.; Merton Coll., Oxford (1st Cl. Hons Mod. Hist.). Royal Leicestershire Regt; Royal West African Frontier Force. Joined HM Diplomatic Service, 1958; Hong Kong, 1959; Third Sec., Peking, 1960; Foreign Office, 1962; First Sec., Vienna, 1965; MoD, 1967; Asst Political Adviser, Hong Kong, 1969; Counsellor and Head of Chancery, Warsaw, 1973; FCO, 1975; Hd of Chancery, UK Deleg. to NATO, 1978. *Address:* c/o Foreign and Commonwealth Office, SW1. *Clubs:* Athenæum; Hong Kong (Hong Kong).

HOWELLS, Derek William; His Honour Judge Howells; a Circuit Judge, since 1980; *b* 8 Oct. 1928; *s* of William Howells and Dinnie Maud (*née* Weeks); *m* 1965, Anne Griffiths. *Educ:* Cardiff High Sch.; Univ. of London. Called to the Bar, Lincoln's Inn, 1955. *Recreations:* golf, gardening. *Address:* 63 Owl's Lodge Lane, Mayals, Swansea SA3 5DP. *T:* Swansea 403845. *Club:* Bristol Channel Yacht.

HOWELLS, Geraint Wyn; MP (L) Cardigan since Feb. 1974; *b* 15 April 1925; *s* of David John Howells and Mary Blodwen Howells; *m* 1957, Mary Olwen Hughes Griffiths; two *d. Educ:* Ponterwyd Primary Sch.; Ardwyn Grammar School. Farmer; Vice-Chm., British Wool Marketing Bd, 1971-; Man. Dir, Wilkinson & Stanier Ltd, Meat Wholesalers, Manchester. Sec., Ponterwyd Eisteddfod, 1944-. *Recreations:* walking, sport. *Address:* Glennydd, Ponterwyd, Ceredigion, Dyfed. *T:* Ponterwyd 258.

HOWELLS, Dr Gwyn, CB 1979; MD; FRCP, FRACP; Director-General and Permanent Head, Federal Department of Health, Canberra, Australia, since 1973; *b* 13 May 1918; *s* of Albert Henry and Ruth Winifred Howells; *m* 1942, Simone Maufe; two *s* two *d. Educ:* University College Sch., London; St Bartholomew's Hosp., Univ. of London (MB BS 1942, MD 1950). MRCS 1941; FRCP 1974 (MRCP 1950, LRCP 1941); FRACP 1971 (MRACP 1967). Cons. Phys., Thoracic Annexe, Toowoomba, Qld, Aust.; Chest Phys., Toowoomba Gen. Hosp., Qld, 1957-66; Federal Dept of Health, Canberra: First Asst Director-General (Tuberculosis), 1966-73; Dep. Dir-Gen., Feb.-Sept. 1973. Chairman, Nat. Health and Med. Res. Council, 1973-; Director of Quarantine for Australia, 1973-. *Publications:* several articles in Lancet, BMJ, Aust. Med. Jl and other specialist jls. *Recreations:* squash, tennis, reading. *Address:* 23 Beauchamp Street, Deakin, ACT 2600, Australia. *T:* Canberra 812575. *Clubs:* Commonwealth, National Press, National Tennis and Squash Centre (Canberra); Imperial Service (Sydney).

HOWELLS, Herbert Norman, CH 1972; CBE 1953; DMus Oxon; MusDoc *hc* Cantab; Hon. DMus RCM; FRCO; FRCM; Hon. RAM; composer; King Edward Professor of Music, University of London, Emeritus 1962; Professor of Composition at Royal College of Music; Director of Music, St Paul's Girls' School, Brook Green, 1936-62; sometime Editor RCM Magazine; Master, Worshipful Company of Musicians, 1959 (first John Collard Fellow; elected to John Collard Life Fellowship, 1959); *b* 17 Oct. 1892; *y s* of late Oliver Howells and Elizabeth Burgham; *m* 1920, Dorothy (*d* 1975), *y d* of late William Goozee; one *d* (one *s* decd). *Educ:* Lydney Grammar Sch.; Gloucester Cathedral; RCM. Became pupil of Sir Herbert Brewer, Gloucester Cathedral, 1905; Open Schol. in Composition at RCM, 1912; studied there under Stanford, Parratt, Parry, Charles Wood, and Walford Davies till 1917; succeeded to the Grove Scholarship, 1915, and became Bruce Scholar, 1916; first work heard in London was the Mass produced by Sir Richard Terry at Westminster Cathedral, 1912; was for short time sub-organist at Salisbury Cathedral. President: RCO, 1958-59; Incorporated Soc. of Musicians, 1952; Plainsong and Mediæval Soc. Hon. MusD Cambridge, 1961; Hon. DMus RCM 1982; Hon. FRSCM, 1963; Hon. Fellow: St John's Coll., Cambridge, 1962; Queen's Coll., Oxford, 1977. *Publications:* Sir Patrick Spens; Sine Nomine (Chorus and Orchestra) Procession; Puck's Minuet; Piano Concerto; Elegy for Strings; Concerto for Strings; Lady Audrey's Suite; Phantasy Quartet; Piano Quartet; Rhapsodic Quintet (Clar. and Str.); First and Third Sonatas for violin and pianoforte; Lambert's Clavichord; In Green Ways, five songs for Soprano and Orchestra; Peacock Pie song-cycle; Sonata for Organ; Hymnus Paradisi for Sopr., Ten., Chor. and Orchestra; Missa Sabrinensis for 4 solo voices, Chorus and Orchestra; Pageantry (Suite for Brass Band); A Kent Yeoman's Wooing Song for 2 Soli, Choir and Orchestra; Four Organ Rhapsodies; Six Psalm Preludes; Music for a Prince (for HRH Prince Charles); Introit (composed for Coronation Service, 1953); Inheritance (commissioned by The Arts Council of Great Britain for A Garland for the Queen, 1953); An English Mass, 1955 (for Chorus and Orch.); Howell's Clavichord (20 pieces); Missa Aedis Christi (for Christ Church, Oxford); Missa, Collegium Regale (for King's Coll., Cambridge); Three Figures (suite for Brass Band); Sequence for St Michael (commnd by St John's Coll., Cambridge); Coventry Antiphon (commnd for Coventry Cath.); Stabat Mater for Tenor, Chorus and Orchestra (commnd by the London Bach Choir); The Coventry Mass. *Recreations:* seeking quiet; English literature. *Address:* 3 Beverley Close, Barnes, SW13. *T:* 01-876 5119. *Club:* Savile.

HOWERD, Frankie; see Howard, F. A.

HOWES, Rear-Adm. Peter Norris, CB 1966; DSC 1941; Private Secretary to Lord Mayor of London, 1968-72; *b* 1 July 1916; *s* of Percy Groom Howes; *m* 1952, Priscilla Hamilton, *d* of Maj.-Gen. G. W. E. Heath, CB, CBE, DSO, MC; three *s* one *d. Educ:* St Peter's Court, Broadstairs; Royal Naval College, Dartmouth. Served in HM Ships Hood, Furious, Fortune, Albury, Aberdeen, Westminster, Adamant, Newcastle, Liverpool; commanded 6th Motor Gunboat Flotilla; HMS Chaplet; HMS Mercury; Dartmouth Training Sqdn; HMS Devonshire; specialised as Communications Officer, 1942; Senior Aide-de-Camp to Viceroy of India, 1947; Naval Asst to First Sea Lord, 1955-58; Flag Officer, Middle East Station, 1964-66. *Publication:* The Viceregal Establishments in India, 1948. *Recreations:* riding, shooting, fishing, photography. *Address:* Sutton Parva House, Heytesbury, Wilts. *T:* Sutton Veny 333.

HOWES, Sally Ann; actress (stage, film and television); *b* 20 July; *d* of late Bobby Howes; *m* 1958, Richard Adler (marr. diss.); *m* 1969, Andrew Maree (marr. diss.). *Educ:* Glendower, London; Queenswood, Herts; privately. *Films include:* Thursday's Child; Halfway House; Dead of Night; Nicholas Nickleby; Anna Karenina; My Sister and I; Fools Rush In; History of Mr Polly; Stop Press Girl; Honeymoon Deferred; The Admirable Crichton; Chitty, Chitty Bang Bang. First appeared West End stage in (revue) Fancy Free, at Prince of Wales's, and at Royal Variety Performance, 1950. *Stage Shows include:* Caprice (musical debut); Paint Your Wagon; Babes in the Wood; Romance by Candlelight; Summer Song; Hatful of Rain; My Fair Lady; Kwamina, NY; What Makes Sammy Run?, NY; Brigadoon (revival), NY City Center, 1962; Sound of Music, Los Angeles and San Francisco, 1972; Lover, St Martin's; The King and I, Adelphi, 1973, Los Angeles and San Francisco, 1974; Hans Andersen, Palladium, 1977. Has appeared on television:

in England from 1949 (Short and Sweet Series, Sally Ann Howes Show, etc); in USA from 1958 (Dean Martin Show, Ed Sullivan Show, Mission Impossible, Marcus Welby MD); Play of the Week; Panel Shows: Hollywood Squares; Password; Bell Telephone Hour; US Steel Hour, etc. *Recreations:* reading, riding, theatre. *Address:* c/o Kramer and Reiss, 9100 Sunset Boulevard, Los Angeles, Calif 90069, USA.

HOWICK OF GLENDALE, 2nd Baron *cr* 1960; **Charles Evelyn Baring;** a Managing Director, Baring Brothers & Co. Ltd, 1969-82; *b* 30 Dec. 1937; *s* of 1st Baron Howick of Glendale, KG, GCMG, KCVO, and of Lady Mary Cecil Grey, *er d* of 5th Earl Grey; *S* father, 1973; *m* 1964, Clare Nicolette, *y d* of Col Cyril Darby; one *s* three *d. Educ:* Eton; New Coll., Oxford. Director: The London Life Association Ltd, 1972-82; Swan Hunter Group Ltd, 1972-79. Member: Exec. Cttee, Nat. Art Collections Fund, 1973-; Council, Friends of Tate Gall., 1973-78. *Heir: s* Hon. David Evelyn Charles Baring, *b* 26 March 1975. *Address:* Howick, Alnwick, Northumberland. *T:* Longhoughton 624; 42 Bedford Gardens, W8. *T:* 01-221 0880. *Club:* Brooks's.
See also Sir E. H. T. Wakefield.

HOWIE, family name of **Baron Howie of Troon.**

HOWIE OF TROON, Baron *cr* 1978 (Life Peer), of Troon in the District of Kyle and Carrick; **William Howie;** civil engineer, journalist; General Manager, New Civil Engineer, since 1976; Professional Conduct Liaison Officer, Institution of Civil Engineers, since 1980; *b* Troon, Ayrshire, 2 March 1924; *er s* of Peter and Annie Howie, Troon; *m* 1951, Mairi Margaret, *o d* of Martha and late John Sanderson, Troon; two *s* two *d. Educ:* Marr Coll., Troon; Royal Technical Coll., Glasgow (BSc, Diploma). MP (Lab) Luton, Nov. 1963-70; Asst Whip, 1964-66; Lord Comr of the Treasury, 1966-67; Comptroller, HM Household, 1967-68. A Vice-Chm., Parly Labour Party, 1968-70. MICE 1951; Member: Council, Instn of Civil Engineers, 1964-67; Cttee of Inquiry into the Engineering Profession, 1977-80; Pres., Assoc. of Supervisory and Exec. Engrs, 1980-. Member: Governing Body, Imperial Coll. of Science and Technology, 1965-67; Council, City Univ., 1968-. *Recreations:* opera, watching football, trying to find time to play golf. *Address:* 34 Temple Fortune Lane, NW11 7UL. *T:* 01-455 0492. *Clubs:* Seretse, Luton Labour.

HOWIE, Archibald, PhD; FRS 1978; Reader in Physics, since 1979, and Head of Metal Physics Research Group, since 1967, Cavendish Laboratory, University of Cambridge; Fellow of Churchill College, Cambridge, since 1960; *b* 8 March 1934; *s* of Robert Howie and Margaret Marshall McDonald; *m* 1964, Melva Jean Scott; one *s* one *d. Educ:* Kirkcaldy High Sch.; Univ. of Edinburgh (BSc); California Inst. of Technology (MS); Univ. of Cambridge (PhD). English Speaking Union, King George VI Memorial Fellow (at Calif. Inst. of Technology), 1956-57; Research Scholar, Trinity Coll., Cambridge, 1957-60; Research Fellow, Churchill Coll., Cambridge, 1960-61; ICI Research Fellow, Cavendish Lab., 1960-61; Demonstrator in Physics, 1961-65, Lecturer, 1965-79, Cavendish Lab.; Visiting Scientist, Nat. Research Council, Canada, 1966-67; Vis. Prof. of Physics, Univ. of Aarhus, Denmark, 1974. C. V. Boys Prize, Inst. of Physics (jtly with M. J. Whelan), 1965. Hon. Fellow Royal Microscopical Soc., 1978. *Publications:* (co-author) Electron Microscopy of Thin Crystals, 1965, 2nd edn 1977; papers on electron microscopy and diffraction in scientific jls. *Recreations:* gardening, wine-making, sailing. *Address:* 194 Huntingdon Road, Cambridge CB3 0LB. *T:* Cambridge 276131.

HOWIE, Sir James (William), Kt 1969; MD (Aberdeen); FRCP, FRCPGlas; FRCPEd; FRCPath; Director of the Public Health Laboratory Service, 1963-73; *b* 31 Dec. 1907; *s* of late James Milne Howie and Jessie Mowat Robertson; *m* 1935, Isabella Winifred Mitchell, BSc; two *s* one *d. Educ:* Robert Gordon's Coll., Aberdeen; University of Aberdeen. University lectureships in Aberdeen and Glasgow, 1932-40; Pathologist, RAMC, 1941-45 (served Nigeria and War Office); Head of Dept of Pathology and Bacteriology, Rowett Research Institute, Aberdeen, 1946-51; Prof. of Bacteriology, University of Glasgow, 1951-63. Mem. Agricultural Research Council, 1957-63. Convener, Medical Research Council Working Party on Sterilisers, 1957-64; Pres., Royal College of Pathologists, 1966-69 (Vice-Pres., 1962-66); President: BMA, 1969-70; Assoc. of Clinical Pathologists, 1972-73. QHP, 1965-68. Hon. ARCVS 1977; Honorary Member: Pathological Soc. of GB and Ireland, 1977; ACP, 1977. Hon. LLD Aberdeen, 1969. *Publications:* various publications in medical and scientific periodicals, particularly on bacteriology and nutrition. *Recreations:* golf, music. *Address:* 34 Redford Avenue, Edinburgh EH13 0BU. *T:* 031-441 3910.

HOWIE, Prof. John Mackintosh; Regius Professor of Mathematics, University of St Andrews, since 1970; Dean, Faculty of Science, 1976-79; *b* 23 May 1936; *s* of Rev. David Y. Howie and Janet McD. Howie (*née* Mackintosh); *m* 1960, Dorothy Joyce Mitchell Miller; two *d. Educ:* Robert Gordon's Coll., Aberdeen; Univ. of Aberdeen; Balliol Coll., Oxford. MA, DPhil, DSc; FRSE 1971. Asst in Mathematics: Aberdeen Univ., 1958-59; Glasgow Univ., 1961-63; Lectr in Mathematics, Glasgow Univ., 1963-67; Visiting Asst Prof., Tulane Univ., 1964-65; Sen. Lectr in Mathematics, Stirling Univ., 1967-70; Vis. Prof., Monash Univ., 1979. Mem., Cttee to Review Examination Arrangements (Dunning Cttee), 1975-77; Chm., Scottish Central Cttee on Mathematics, 1975-82. Keith Prize for 1979-81, RSE, 1982. *Publications:* An Introduction to Semigroup Theory, 1976; articles in British

and foreign mathematical jls. *Recreations:* music, gardening. *Address:* Mathematical Institute, North Haugh, St Andrews, Fife KY16 9SS. *T:* St Andrews 76161.

HOWIE, Prof. Robert Andrew, PhD, ScD; FGS; Professor of Mineralogy, King's College, University of London, since 1972; *b* 4 June 1923; *s* of Robert Howie; *m* 1952, Honor Eugenie, *d* of Robert Taylor; two *s. Educ:* Bedford Sch.; Trinity Coll., Cambridge (MA, PhD, ScD). FGS 1950. Served War, RAF, 1941-46. Research, Dept of Mineralogy and Petrology, Univ. of Cambridge, 1950-53; Lectr in Geology, Manchester Univ., 1953-62; Reader in Geol., King's Coll., London, 1962-72, Fellow 1980; Dean, Faculty of Science, Univ. of London, 1979-. Geological Society: Mem. Council, 1968-71, 1972-76; Vice-Pres., 1973-75. Mineralogical Society: Mem. Council, 1958-61, 1963-; Gen. Sec., 1965; Vice-Pres., 1975-77; Pres., 1978-80; Managing Trustee, 1978-. Fellow, Mineral Soc. of America, 1962. Member: Council, Internat. Mineral Assoc., 1974-82; Senate, Univ. of London, 1974-78, 1980-. Murchison Medal, Geol Soc., 1976. Editor, Mineralogical Abstracts, 1966-. *Publications:* Rock-forming Minerals (with Prof. W. A. Deer and Prof. J. Zussman), 5 vols, 1962-63 (2nd edn 1978, 1982); An Introduction to the Rock-forming Minerals, 1966; scientific papers dealing with charnockites and with silicate mineralogy. *Recreations:* mineral collecting, writing abstracts. *Address:* King's College, Strand, WC2R 2LS. *T:* 01-836 5454; Gayhurst, Woodland Drive, East Horsley, Surrey. *Club:* Geological.

HOWIE, Thomas McIntyre; Principal, Paisley College of Technology, since 1972; *b* 21 April 1926; *m* 1951, Catherine Elizabeth Logan; three *s. Educ:* Paisley Coll. of Technology; Strathclyde Univ. BSc (Eng); CEng, FICE. Civil Engrg Asst, Clyde Navigation Trust, 1947-50; Paisley Coll. of Technology: Lectr in Civil Engrg, 1950-55; Sen. Lectr in Civil Engrg, 1955-58; Head, Dept of Civil Engrg, 1958-72; Vice-Principal, 1970-72. *Recreations:* golf, curling. *Address:* Dunscore, 38 Main Road, Castlehead, Paisley PA2 6AW. *T:* 041-889 5723. *Club:* Caledonian.

HOWITT, Anthony Wentworth; Senior Consultancy Partner, Peat, Marwick, Mitchell & Co., Management Consultants, since 1957; *b* 7 Feb. 1920; *o s* of late Sir Harold Gibson Howitt, GBE, DSO, MC, and late Dorothy Radford; *m* 1951, June Mary Brent. *Educ:* Uppingham; Trinity Coll., Cambridge (MA). FCA, FCMA, JDipMA, CBIM, FIMC, FBCS. Commissioned RA; served in UK, ME and Italy, 1940-46 (Major). With Peat, Marwick, Mitchell & Co., Chartered Accountants, 1946-57. British Consultants Bureau: Sen. Vice-Chm., 1981-; Mem. Council, 1968-75 and 1979-; led mission to Far East, 1969. Member Council: Inst. of Management Consultants, 1964-77 (Pres., 1967-68); Inst. of Cost and Management Accountants, 1966-76 (Pres., 1972-73); Management Consultants Assoc., 1966- (Chm., 1976); Mem., Devlin Commn of Inquiry into Industrial Representation, 1971-72. Member: Bd of Fellows of BIM, 1973-76; Adv. Panel to Overseas Projects Gp, 1973-76; Price Commn, 1973-77. Mem., Court of Assistants, Merchant Taylors' Co., 1971- (Master 1980-81). *Publications:* papers and addresses on professional and management subjects. *Recreations:* fox-hunting, tennis, golf. *Address:* Peat, Marwick, Mitchell & Co., 1 Puddle Dock, EC4V 3PD. *T:* 01-236 8000. *Clubs:* Army and Navy; MCC; Harlequins.

HOWITT, W(illiam) Fowler, DA (Dundee), FRIBA; Partner in Firm of Cusdin Burden and Howitt, Architects, since 1965; *b* Perth, Scotland, May 1924; *s* of late Frederick Howitt, Head Postmaster, Forfar; *m* 1951, Ann Elizabeth, *o d* of late A. J. Hedges, Radipole, Dorset; three *s* one *d. Educ:* Perth Academy. Royal Marines, 1943-46. Sch. of Architecture, Dundee, 1948; RIBA Victory Scholar, 1949. Asst Louis de Soissons, London (housing and flats), 1949-52; Prin. Asst to Vincent Kelly, Dublin (hosps & offices), 1952-55; Architect to St Thomas' Hosp. (Hosp. rebuilding schemes, flats, offices), 1955-64. Present projects include: design and supervision of Faculty of Medicine and King Khalid Hosp., Univ. of Riyad, S Arabia; extensions to: Addenbrooke's Hosp. and Univ. of Cambridge Clinical Sch.; Bedford Coll., Univ. of London; Hospital for Sick Children, Gt Ormond St; hospital planning consultancy: Teaching Hosp., Tlemcen, Algeria; gen. hosps, Sharjah and Fujairah, UAE; Tralee County Hosp.; Mater Misericordiae Hosp., Dublin; teaching hosps in Abuja and Niger State, and children's hosps in Anambra and Plateau States, Nigeria. *Recreations:* reading, golf, childish pursuits. *Address:* Greencoat House, Francis Street, SW1P 1DB. *T:* 01-828 4051; (home) 32 Gloucester Road, Teddington, Mddx TW11 0NU. *T:* 01-977 5772.

HOWKINS, John, MD, FRCS; Gynæcological Surgeon to St Bartholomew's Hospital, 1946-69 (Hon. Consultant Gynæcologist since 1969), to Hampstead General Hospital 1946-67 (Hon. Consultant Gynæcologist, since 1968), and to Royal Masonic Hospital, 1948-73; *b* 17 Dec. 1907; *m* 1940, Lena Brown; one *s* two *d. Educ:* Shrewsbury Sch.; London Univ. Arts Scholar, Middlesex Hospital, 1926; MRCS, LRCP, 1932; MB, BS, London, 1933; FRCS, 1936; MS London, 1936; MD (Gold Medal) London, 1937; MRCOG 1937, FRCOG 1947. House Surgeon and Casualty Surgeon, Middlesex Hosp., 1932-34; RMO Chelsea Hosp. for Women, 1936; Gynæcological Registrar, Middlesex Hosp., 1937-38; Resident Obstetric Surg., St Bartholomew's Hosp., 1938 and 1945; Temp. Wing-Comdr, RAFVR Med. Br., 1939-45. Hunterian Prof., RCS 1947. William Meredith Fletcher Shaw Lectr, RCOG, 1975. Sometime Examiner in Midwifery to Univs of Cambridge and London, RCOG, Conjoint Bd of England. Chm., Council Ski Club of Great Britain, 1964-67 (Hon. Life Member, 1968, Trustee, 1969-); Mem., Gynaecological Travellers' Club. *Publications:* Shaw's Textbook of Gynæcology, 1956 (9th edn 1971); Shaw's Textbook of Gynæcological Surgery, 4th edn, 1977; (jointly) Bonney's Textbook of Gynæcological Surgery, 1963, 8th edn 1974. *Recreations:* ski-ing, salmon fishing and sheep farming. *Address:* Caen Hen, Abercegir, Machynlleth, Powys, Wales. *Clubs:* Ski Club of Great Britain; Wilks XV (Hon. Mem.).

HOWLAND, Lord; Andrew Ian Henry Russell; *b* 30 March 1962; *s* and *heir* of Marquess of Tavistock, *qv. Educ:* Heatherdown; Harrow; Harvard. *Recreations:* shooting, golf. *Address:* Woburn Abbey, Bedfordshire MK43 0TP. *Club:* Annabel's.

HOWLAND, Robert Leslie, MA; Fellow of St John's College, Cambridge, since 1929; *b* 25 March 1905; *s* of Robert and Mary Howland; *m* 1930, Eileen, *d* of Robert Reid Tait; two *s* one *d. Educ:* Shrewsbury Sch.; St John's Coll., Cambridge; 1st Cl. Classical Tripos Part I, 1926, Part II, 1928, Strathcona Student, 1928; Fellow of St John's Coll., 1929, Tutor 1932-65, Senior Tutor, 1956-65, President, 1963-67. University Lectr in Classics, 1934-72; Senior Proctor, 1951-52; Warden of Madingley Hall, 1965-75. Mem., Goldsmiths' Co., 1958. Mem. of Cambridge Univ. Athletic Team, 1925-28; Mem. of British National Athletic Team, 1927-39 (Capt. 1934-35), and British Olympic Team, 1928. Holder of English native record for putting the weight, 1930-48; took part in British Empire Games, 1930, 1934, in British Empire *v* USA Matches, 1930, 1936; Pres., Cambridge Univ. AFC, 1946-76, and Cambs AAA, 1960-75. RAF 1941-46, Fighter Controller (Radar), GB, Mediterranean, SE Asia; France and Italy Star, Burma Star. *Publications:* reviews and articles in classical jls and Oxford Classical Dict. *Address:* Elizabethan Cottage, Littlebury, Saffron Walden, Essex; St John's College, Cambridge. *Clubs:* United Oxford & Cambridge University; Achilles; Hawks (Cambridge).

HOWLAND, Hon. Chief Justice William Goldwin Carrington; Chief Justice of Ontario, since 1977; *b* 7 March 1915; *s* of Goldwin William Howland and Margaret Christian Carrington; *m* 1966, Margaret Patricia Greene. *Educ:* Upper Canada Coll.; Univ. of Toronto (BA 1936, LLB 1939); Osgoode Hall Law Sch. Barrister-at-law. Practised law, McMillan Binch, 1936-75; Justice of Appeal, Court of Appeal, Supreme Court of Ontario, 1975-77. Law Society of Upper Canada: Bencher, 1960, 1965; Life Bencher, 1969; (Head) Treasurer, 1968-70. President: Fedn of Law Socs of Canada, 1973-74; UN Assoc. in Canada, 1959-60. Hon. lectr, Osgoode Hall Law Sch., 1951-67. Hon. LLD: Queen's Univ., Kingston, Ont., 1972; Univ. of Toronto, 1981. *Publications:* special Lectures, Law Soc. of Upper Canada, 1951, 1960. *Recreation:* travel. *Address:* 2 Bayview Wood, Toronto, Canada M4N 1R7. *T:* 483-4696. *Clubs:* Toronto, Toronto Hunt (Toronto).

HOWLETT, Anthony Douglas, RD 1971; Remembrancer of the City of London, since 1981; *b* 30 Dec. 1924; *s* of late Ernest Robert Howlett and Catherine (*née* Broughton), Grantham, Lincs; *m* 1952, Alfreda Dorothy Pearce, *yr d* of Arthur W. Pearce, Hove, Sussex. *Educ:* King's Sch., Rochester; Wellingborough; King's Sch., Grantham; Trinity Coll., Cambridge. BA Hons 1948, LLB 1949, MA 1950. Served War, 1939-46, RNVR; RNVSR, 1951-60; RNR, 1960-75 (Lt Comdr 1968). Called to the Bar, Gray's Inn, 1950; joined Legal Br., BoT, 1951; Sen. Legal Assistant, 1960; Asst Solicitor, 1972, i/c Export Credit Guarantees Br., 1972-75, i/c Merchant Shipping Br., 1975-81. UK delegate: London Diplomatic Conf. on Limitation of Liability for Maritime Claims, 1976; Geneva Diplomatic Conf. on Multi-Modal Transport, 1980, and other internat. maritime confs. Founder Mem., Sherlock Holmes Soc. of London, 1951 (Chm., 1960-63). Freedom of City of London, 1981. Various foreign decorations. *Publications:* articles on Conan Doyle and Holmesiana. *Recreations:* book browsing, Sherlock Holmes, opera, photography, foreign travel. *Address:* Rivendell, 30 Curthwaite Gardens, Oakwood, Enfield, Middlesex EN2 7LN. *T:* 01-363 5802. *Club:* Naval.

HOWLETT, Maj.-Gen. Geoffrey Hugh Whitby, OBE 1972; MC 1952; Commandant, Royal Military Academy, Sandhurst, since 1982; *b* 5 Feb. 1930; *s* of Brig. B. Howlett, DSO, and Mrs Joan Howlett (later Latham); *m* 1955, Elizabeth Anne Aspinal; one *s* two *d. Educ:* Wellington Coll.; RMA, Sandhurst. Commnd Queen's Own Royal W Kent Regt, 1950; served, 1951-69: Malaya, Berlin, Cyprus and Suez; 3 and 2 Para, 16 Parachute Bde and 15 Para (TA); RAF Staff Coll. and Jt Services Staff Coll.; Mil. Asst to CINCNORTH, Oslo, 1969-71; CO 2 Para, 1971-73; RCDS, 1973-75; Comd 16 Parachute Bde, 1975-77; Dir, Army Recruiting, 1977-79; GOC 1st Armoured Div., 1979-82. Col Comdt, ACC, 1981-. *Recreations:* cricket, shooting. *Address:* Government House, Royal Military Academy, Sandhurst, Camberley, Surrey; c/o Lloyds Bank, Tonbridge, Kent. *Clubs:* Naval and Military, MCC.

HOWLETT, Jack, CBE 1969; MA Oxon, PhD Manchester; MIEE, FSS, FBCS, FIMA; Consultant to International Computers Ltd, since 1975 and Editor, ICL Technical Journal, since 1978; *b* 30 Aug. 1912; *s* of William Howlett and Lydia Ellen Howlett; *m* 1939, Joan Marjorie Simmons; four *s* one *d. Educ:* Stand Grammar Sch., Manchester; Manchester Univ. Mathematician, LMS Railway, 1935-40 and 1946-48; mathematical work in various wartime research estabts, 1940-46; Head of Computer Group, Atomic Energy Research Establt, Harwell, 1948-61; Dir, Atlas Computer Lab., Chilton Didcot, Berks, 1961-75 (under SRC, 1965-75). Chm., Nat. Cttee on Computer Networks, 1976-78. Fellow by special election, St Cross Coll., Oxford, 1966. Hon. Sec., British Cttee of Honour for Celebration of 1300th Anniversary of Foundn of Bulgarian State, 1980-82; 1300th Anniversary

Medal of Bulgarian State, 1982. *Publications:* reviews and gen. papers on numerical mathematics and computation. *Recreations:* hill walking, music. *Address:* 20B Bradmore Road, Oxford OX2 6QP. *T:* Oxford 52893. *Clubs:* New Arts, Savile.

HOWLETT, Air Vice-Marshal Neville Stanley, CB 1982; RAF retired, 1982; Member, Panel of Independent Inquiry Inspectors, Department of the Environment, since 1982; *b* 17 April 1927; *s* of Stanley Herbert Howlett and Ethel Shirley Howlett (*née* Pritchard); *m* 1952, Sylvia, *d* of J. F. Foster; one *s* one *d. Educ:* Liverpool Inst. High Sch.; Peterhouse, Cambridge. RAF pilot training, 1945-47; 32 and 64 (Fighter) Squadrons, 1948-56; RAF Staff Coll. Course, 1957; Squadron Comdr, 229 (Fighter) OCU, 1958-59; OC Flying Wing, RAF Coltishall, 1961-63; Directing Staff, RAF Staff Coll., 1967-69; Station Comdr, RAF Leuchars, 1970-72; RCDS, 1972; Dir of Operations (Air Defence and Overseas), 1973-74; Air Attaché, Washington DC, 1975-77; Dir, Management Support of Intelligence, MoD, 1978-80; Dir Gen. of Personal Services (RAF), MoD, 1980-82. *Recreations:* golf, fishing. *Clubs:* Royal Air Force; Huntercombe Golf.

HOWLETT, Ronald William; Managing Director, Cwmbran Development Corporation, since 1978; *b* 18 Aug. 1928; *s* of Percy Edward Howlett and Lucy Caroline Howlett; *m* 1954, Margaret Megan Searl; two *s. Educ:* University Coll. London. BSc Eng.(Hons); MICE, FIMunE. Crawley Develt Corp., 1953-56; Exec. Engr, Roads and Water Supply, Northern Nigeria, 1956-61; Bor. of Colchester, 1961-64; Cwmbran Develt Corp., 1964-65; Bor. of Slough, 1965-69; Dep. Chief Engr and Chief Admin. Officer, Cwmbran Develt Corp., 1969-78. *Recreations:* fishing, music. *Address:* Cwmbran Development Corporation, Gwent House, Town Centre, Cwmbran, Gwent NP44 1XZ. *T:* Cwmbran 67777.

HOWSAM, Air Vice-Marshal George Roberts, CB 1945; MC 1918; RCAF, retired: also retired from Federal Emergency Measures Organization, 1962 (Coordinator, Alberta Civil Defence, 1950-57) and from business; *b* 29 Jan. 1895; *s* of Mary Ida and George Roberts Howsam, Port Perry, Ont; *m* 1st, 1918, Lillian Isobel (*d* 1970), *d* of Mary and William Somerville, Toronto; one *s*; 2nd, 1972, Marion Isobel Garrett, *d* of Clarence Albert Mitchell and Mary Blanche McCurdy, New Brunswick and Nova Scotia. *Educ:* Port Perry and Toronto. Joined Canadian Expeditionary Force, March 1916 and RFC 70 Sqdn and 43 Sqdn, 1917-18; served as fighter pilot France and Belgium, 1917-18 (wounded twice, MC); with Army of Occupation in Germany; returned to Canada, 1921; RCAF photographic survey, NW Canada; RAF Staff Coll., England, 1930 (psa); Senior Mem., RCAF 1st Aerobatic Team (Siskin) Display, Cleveland, USA, 1929; Staff Mem. CGAO Operations at AFHQ, 1931-32; SASO MD2 Toronto, 1933-36; OC 2 Army Co-operation Sqdn, Ottawa, 1937; Dir of Training for RCAF, Ottawa, 1938-40; England and France, 1940; later in 1940, SASO, No 4 Training Command, Regina; commanded No 11 Service Flying Training Sch., Yorkton, 1941; AOC No 4 Training Command, Calgary, 1942-44, also AOC Air Staging Route to Alaska, 1942-43 (thereby holding double command for two years); Chm. Organisation Cttee, Air Force HQ, Ottawa, 1945; retired 1946. Dominion Dir The Air Cadet League of Canada, 1946-47; Alberta Chm. RCAF Assoc., 1958-59. Canadian Deleg. to Emergency Measures NATO Assembly, Paris, Oct. 1960. Legion of Merit in Degree of Comdr (US), 1945; Order of White Lion (Czecho-Slovakia), 1946; Commandeur de l'ordre de la Couronne (Belgium), 1948. *Publications:* Rocky Mountain Foothills Offer Great Chance to Gliders (Calgary Daily Herald), 1923; Industrial and Mechanical Development: War (Canadian Defence Qtly Prize Essay), 1931. *Recreations:* gardening, writing, shooting. *Address:* (home) 2040 Pauls Terrace, Victoria, BC V8N 2Z3, Canada; Bank of Montreal, Government Street, Victoria, BC. *Clubs:* Union, Canadian, Victoria Golf (Victoria, BC); Empire (Toronto); Ranchmen's (Calgary).

HOWSE, Lt-Comdr Humphrey Derek, MBE 1954; DSC 1945; FRIN, FRAS; RN retired; Caird Research Fellow, National Maritime Museum, 1982; *b* Weymouth, 10 Oct. 1919; *s* of late Captain Humphrey F. Howse, RN and late Rose Chicheliana (*née* Thornton); *m* 1946, Elizabeth de Warrenne Waller; three *s* one *d. Educ:* RN Coll., Dartmouth. FRIN 1976; FRAS 1967; Midshipman, RN, 1937-39; Sub-Lt, 1939, Lieut 1941; First Lieut of Destroyers, 1940-43; specialized in navigation, 1944, in aircraft direction, 1947 (despatches 3 times 1943-45); Lt-Comdr 1949; cruiser, Korean War, 1952-54, Inshore Flotilla, 1954-56; retd 1958. Atomic Energy Div., Gen. Electric Co., 1958-61; Associated Industrial Consultants, 1961-62; Continental Oil Co., 1962-63; Asst Keeper, Dept of Navigation and Astronomy, National Maritime Museum, 1963; Head of Astronomy, 1969; Dep. Keeper and Head of Navigation and Astronomy, 1976; Keeper, 1979-82. Pres., British Astronomical Assoc., 1980-82; Member: Council, Antiquarian Horological Soc., 1976-82; Council, Royal Astronomical Soc., 1982; Council, Soc. for Nautical Research, 1982. Liveryman, Clockmakers' Co., 1981. *Publications:* Clocks and Watches of Captain James Cook, 1969; The Tompion Clocks at Greenwich, 1970; (with M. Sanderson) The Sea Chart, 1973; Greenwich Observatory: the buildings and instruments, 1975; Francis Place and the Early History of Greenwich Observatory, 1975; Greenwich Time and the Discovery of the Longitude, 1980; papers to Mariners' Mirror, L'Astronomie, Antiquarian Horology and Jl of British Astronomical Assoc. *Recreations:* reading, writing, sticking in photos, pottering in the vegetable beds. *Address:* 12 Barnfield Road, Riverhead, Sevenoaks, Kent TN13 2AY. *T:* Sevenoaks 454366. *Club:* Royal Over-Seas League.

HOWSON, Rear-Adm. John, CB 1963; DSC 1944; *b* 30 Aug. 1908; *s* of late George Howson and Mary Howson, Glasgow; *m* 1937, Evangeline Collins; one *s* one *d. Educ:* Kelvinside Academy, Glasgow; Royal Naval College, Dartmouth, 1922-25; Lieut, 1930; specialised in gunnery, 1934; Gunnery Officer, HMS Furious, 1936-38; served War of 1939-45 (despatches, DSC); HMS Newcastle, 1939-41; HMS Nelson, 1943-44; Comdr 1945; Fleet Gunnery Officer, British Pacific Fleet, 1947-48; Staff of C-in-C, Far East Stn, 1948-49; Exec. Officer, HMS Superb, 1949-50; Capt. 1951; served on Ordnance Bd, 1950-52; Comdg Officer, HMS Tamar, 1952-54; at SHAPE, 1955-57; Chief of Staff to C-in-C, Plymouth, 1958-61; Rear-Adm. 1961; Comdr, Allied Naval Forces, Northern Europe, 1961-62; Naval Dep. to C-in-C Allied Forces, Northern Europe, 1963-64. Regional Officer, N Midlands, British Productivity Council, 1964-71. FRSA. *Address:* Osborne House, 14 Yorke Road, Dartmouth, Devon TQ6 9HN. *T:* Dartmouth 2854. *Club:* Naval and Military.

HOY, Rev. David, SJ; Rector of Stonyhurst College, since 1980; *b* 1 March 1913; *s* of Augustine Hilary Hoy and Caroline Lovelace. *Educ:* Mount St Mary's Coll. Entered Society of Jesus, 1931. Senior English Master, Wimbledon Coll., 1947, Asst Head Master, 1957-59. Rector of St Robert Bellarmine, Heythrop, Chipping Norton, 1959-64; Rector of Stonyhurst College, 1964-71; Superior of Farm St Church, 1972-75. *Recreation:* walking. *Address:* Stonyhurst College, Lancashire.

HOYER-MILLAR, Dame Elizabeth, DBE 1960 (OBE 1952); DL; Director, Women's Royal Naval Service, 1958-61; Hon. ADC to the Queen, 1958-61; *b* 17 Dec. 1910; *o d* of late Robert Christian Hoyer Millar, Craig, Angus, Scotland, and Muriel (*née* Foster). *Educ:* privately. VAD 1939-41; joined WRNS, 1942. JP 1968-76, DL 1971, Angus. *Recreations:* needlework, gardening, country pursuits. *Address:* The Croft, Hillside, Angus. *T:* Hillside 304.

HOYLE, (Eric) Douglas (Harvey); MP (Lab) Warrington, since July 1981; consultant; *b* 17 Feb. 1930; *s* of late William Hoyle and Leah Ellen Hoyle; *m* 1953, Pauline Spencer; one *s. Educ:* Adlington C of E Sch.; Horwich and Bolton Techn. Colls. Engrg apprentice, British Rail, Horwich, 1946-51; Sales Engr, AEI, Manchester, 1951-53; Sales Engr, Charles Weston Ltd, Salford, 1953-75. Mem., Manchester Regional Hosp. Bd, 1968-74; Mem., NW Regional Health Authority, 1974-75. Contested (Lab): Clitheroe, 1964; Nelson and Colne, 1970 and Feb. 1974; MP (Lab) Nelson and Colne, Oct. 1974-1979. Mem. Nat. Exec., Labour Party, 1978-82. Vice-Pres., ASTMS, 1981- (Pres., 1977-81); Chm., ASTMS Parly Cttee, 1975-76. JP 1958. *Recreations:* sport, cricket, theatre-going, reading. *Address:* 30 Ashfield Road, Anderton, Chorley, Lancs.

HOYLE, Prof. Sir Fred, Kt 1972; FRS 1957; MA Cantab; Hon. Research Professor, Manchester University, since 1972; University College, Cardiff, since 1975; Visiting Associate in Physics, California Institute of Technology, since 1963; *b* 24 June 1915; *s* of Ben Hoyle, Bingley, Yorks; *m* 1939, Barbara Clark; one *s* one *d. Educ:* Bingley Grammar Sch.; Emmanuel Coll., Cambridge. Mayhew Prizeman, Mathematical Tripos, 1936; Smith's Prizeman, Goldsmith Exhibnr, Senior Exhibnr of Royal Commn for Exhibn of 1851, 1938. War Service for British Admiralty, 1939-45. Fellow, St John's Coll., Cambridge, 1939-72; University Lecturer in Mathematics, Cambridge, 1945-58; Plumian Prof. of Astronomy and Exptl Philosophy, Cambridge Univ., 1958-72; Dir, Inst. of Theoretical Astronomy, Cambridge, 1967-73; Prof. of Astronomy, Royal Instn of GB, 1969-72; Staff Mem., Mount Wilson and Palomar Observatories, 1957-62. California Institute of Technology: Vis. Prof. of Astrophysics, 1953, 1954; Vis. Prof. of Astronomy, 1956; Sherman Fairchild Scholar, 1974-75; Addison White Greenaway Vis. Prof. of Astronomy; Andrew D. White Prof.-at-Large, Cornell Univ., 1972-78. Mem. SRC, 1967-72. Vice-Pres., Royal Society, 1970-71; Pres., Royal Astronomical Soc., 1971-73. Hon. MRIA (Section of Science), 1977; Mem., Amer. Philos. Soc., 1980; Hon. Member: Amer. Acad. of Arts and Sciences, 1964; Mark Twain Soc., 1978; Foreign Associate, US Nat. Acad. of Sciences, 1969. Hon. Fellow, St John's Coll., Cambridge, 1973. Hon. ScD E Anglia, 1967; Hon DSc: Leeds 1969; Bradford 1975; Newcastle 1976. Royal Astronomical Soc. Gold Medal, 1968; UN Kalinga Prize, 1968; Bruce Gold Medal, Astronomical Soc. of Pacific, 1970; Royal Medal, Royal Soc., 1974. *Publications: astronomy:* Some Recent Researches in Solar Physics, 1949; The Nature of the Universe, 1951; A Decade of Decision, 1953; Frontiers of Astronomy, 1955; Man and Materialism, 1956; Astronomy, 1962; Star Formation, 1963; Of Men and Galaxies, 1964; Encounter with the Future, 1965; Galaxies, Nuclei and Quasars, 1965; Man in the Universe, 1966; From Stonehenge to Modern Cosmology, 1972; Nicolaus Copernicus, 1973; The Relation of Physics and Cosmology, 1973; (with J. V. Narlikar) Action-at-a-Distance in Physics and Cosmology, 1974; Astronomy and Cosmology, 1975; Highlights in Astronomy, 1975 (in England, Astronomy Today, 1975); Ten Faces of the Universe, 1977; On Stonehenge, 1977; Energy or Extinction, 1977; (with N. C. Wickramasinghe) Lifecloud, 1978; The Cosmogony of the Solar System, 1978; (with N. C. Wickramasinghe) Diseases from Space, 1979; (with G. Hoyle) Commonsense and Nuclear Energy, 1979; (with J. V. Narlikar) The Physics-Astronomy Frontier, 1980; (with N. C. Wickramasinghe) Space Travellers: the Bringers of Life, 1981; Ice, 1981; (with N. C. Wickramasinghe) Evolution from Space, 1981; *novels:* The Black Cloud, 1957; Ossian's Ride, 1959; (with J. Elliot) A for Andromeda, 1962; (with G. Hoyle) Fifth Planet, 1963; (with J. Elliot) Andromeda Breakthrough, 1964; October the First is Too Late, 1967; Element 79, 1967; (with G. Hoyle) Rockets in Ursa Major,

1969; (with G. Hoyle) Seven Steps to the Sun, 1970; (with G. Hoyle) The Molecule Men, 1971; (with G. Hoyle) The Inferno, 1973; (with G. Hoyle) Into Deepest Space, 1974; (with G. Hoyle) The Incandescent Ones, 1977; (with G. Hoyle) The Westminster Disaster, 1978; *children's stories with G. Hoyle:* The Energy Pirate; The Giants of Universal Park; The Frozen Planet of Azuron; The Planet of Death; *play:* Rockets in Ursa Major, 1962; *libretto:* The Alchemy of Love; space serials for television; scientific papers. *Address:* c/o The Royal Society, 6 Carlton House Terrace, SW1Y 5AG.

HOYLE, Ven. Frederick James; Archdeacon of Bolton, since 1982; Team Vicar, East Farnworth and Kearsley, since 1982; *b* 14 Dec. 1918; *s* of Henry and Annie Hoyle; *m* 1939, Lillian Greenlees; two *d. Educ:* S John's College, Univ. of Durham (BA 1947, DiplTh 1949, MA 1957). Served War of 1939-45; Imphal, 1944 (despatches). Asst Curate, S Paul, Withington, 1949; Curate in charge, S Martin, Wythenshawe, 1952; Vicar 1960; Vice-Chm. and Exec. Officer, Diocesan Pastoral Cttee (full-time), 1965; Hon. Canon of Manchester, 1967; Vicar of Rochdale, and Rural Dean, 1971; Rector of Rochdale Team Ministry, 1978. *Recreations:* rowing, sailing, boat building. *Address:* 52 Manchester Road, Swinton, Manchester M27 1ET. *T:* 061-794 8235.

HOYOS, Hon. Sir (Fabriciano) Alexander, Kt 1979; former Lecturer, Cave Hill, University of the West Indies; retired History Teacher, Lodge School, St John; *b* Brazil, 5 July 1912; *s* of Emigdio and Adelina Hoyos, Peru; *m* 1st, 1940, Kathleen Carmen (*d* 1970); three *s* one *d* ; 2nd, 1973, Gladys Louise. *Educ:* Wesley Hall Boys' School; Harrison Coll.; Codrington Coll., Durham Univ. (Sen. Island Schol.). BA 1936; MA 1943; Hon. MEd 1963. Taught at: Combermere Sch., Barbados; St Benedict's Coll., Trinidad; Lodge Sch., 1943-72; Moderator, Caribbean History Survey Course, Cave Hill, UWI, 1963-70. Leader-writer of Daily Advocate, 1937-43; Correspondent, London Times, 1938-65. Member: Barbados Christian Council, 1976-; Privy Council for Barbados, 1977-; Constitution Review Commn, 1977-78. Queen's Jubilee Medal, 1977. *Publications:* Some Eminent Contemporaries, 1944; Two Hundred Years, 1945; Story of Progressive Movement, 1948; Our Common Heritage, 1953; Memories of Princess Margaret and Our Past, 1955; Road to Responsible Government, 1960; Barbados, Our Island Home, 1960; Rise of West Indian Democracy, 1963; Background to Independence, 1967; Builders of Barbados, 1972; Grantley Adams and the Social Revolution, 1974; Barbados: From the Amerindians to Independence, 1978. *Recreations:* gardening, swimming. *Address:* Beachy Crest, Belair Cross Road, St Philip, Barbados, WI. *T:* 36323.

HSIUNG, Shih I; author; President, Tsing Hua College, Hong Kong (Founder, and Director, since 1963); Hon. Secretary of China Society, London, since 1936 (Secretary 1934-36); Member of Universities China Committee, London, since 1935; *b* Nanchang, China, 14 Oct. 1902; *s* of Hsiung, Yuen-Yui and Chou, Ti-Ping; *m* 1923, Tsai, Dymia, (author of Flowering Exile, 1952); three *s* three *d. Educ:* Teachers' Coll., National Univ., Peking. Associate Manager of Chen Kwang Theatre, Peking, 1923; Managing Director of Pantheon Theatre, Shanghai, 1927; Special Editor of Commercial Press, Shanghai; Prof. at Agriculture Coll., Nanchang; Prof. at Min-Kuo Univ., Peking, till 1932. Chinese Delegate to International PEN Congress at Edinburgh, 1934; at Barcelona, 1935; at Prague, 1938; at London, 1941; at Zürich, 1947; Chinese Delegate to First Congress of International Theatre Institute at Prague, 1948; lectured on Modern Chinese and Classical Chinese Drama, University of Cambridge, 1950-53; Visiting Prof., University of Hawaii, Honolulu. Dean, College of Arts, Nanyang Univ., 1954-55; Man.-Dir, Pacific Films Co. Ltd, Hong Kong, 1955-; Dir, Konin Co. Ltd, Hong Kong, 1956-; Dir, Success Co. Ltd, Hong Kong, 1956; Chm., Bd of Dirs Standard Publishers, Ltd, Hong Kong, 1961-. *Publications:* various Chinese books including translations of Bernard Shaw, James Barrie, Thomas Hardy, Benjamin Franklin, etc; English Publications: The Money-God, 1934; Lady Precious Stream, 1934; The Western Chamber, 1935; Mencius Was A Bad Boy, 1936; The Professor From Peking, 1939; The Bridge of Heaven, 1941; The Life of Chiang Kai-Shek, 1943; The Gate of Peace, 1945; Changing China: History of China from 1840 to 1911, 1946; The Story of Lady Precious Stream, 1949; Chinese Proverbs, 1952; Lady on the Roof, 1959. *Recreation:* theatre-going. *Address:* 170 Boundary Street, Kowloon, Hongkong. *T:* K366883. *TA:* DRHSIUNG, Hongkong.

HUANG, Rayson Lisung, Hon. CBE 1976; DSc, DPhil; Vice-Chancellor, University of Hong Kong, since Sept. 1972; *b* 1 Sept. 1920; *s* of Rufus Huang; *m* 1949, Grace Wei Li; two *s. Educ:* Munsang Coll., Hong Kong; Univ. of Hong Kong (BSc); Univ. of Oxford (DPhil, DSc); Univ. of Chicago. DSc (Malaya) 1956. Demonstrator in Chemistry, Nat. Kwangsi Univ., Kweilin, China, 1943; Post-doctoral Fellow and Research Associate, Univ. of Chicago, 1947-50; Univ. of Malaya, Singapore: Lecturer in Chemistry, 1951-54; Reader, 1955-59; Univ. of Malaya, Kuala Lumpur: Prof. of Chemistry, 1959-69, and Dean of Science, 1962-65. Vice-Chancellor, Nanyang Univ., Singapore, 1969-72. Chm. Council, ACU, 1980-81; Pres., Assoc. of SE Asian Instns of Higher Learning, 1981-. MLC Hong Kong, 1977-. JP. Hon. DSc Hong Kong, 1968. *Publications:* Organic Chemistry of Free Radicals, 1974 (London); about 50 research papers on chemistry of free radicals, molecular rearrangements, etc, mainly in Jl of Chem. Soc. (London). *Recreation:* music. *Address:* The Lodge, 1 University Drive, Hong Kong. *T:* H-494790. *Club:* Hong Kong Country.

HUBBACK, David Francis, CB 1970; Clerk of the Financial Committees of the House of Commons, 1979-81 (Special Advisor to the Expenditure Committee, 1976-79); *b* 2 March 1916; *s* of late Francis William and Eva Hubback; *m* 1939, Elais Judith, *d* of late Sir John Fischer Williams; one *s* two *d. Educ:* Westminster Sch.; King's Coll., Cambridge. Mines Dept, Bd of Trade, 1939. War of 1939-45: Army, 1940-44; Capt., Royal Signals; Western Desert, Sicily, Normandy; Cabinet Office, 1944. UK Delegn to OEEC, 1948; Treasury, 1950; Principal Private Sec. to Chancellor of the Exchequer, 1960-62; Under-Sec., Treasury, 1962-68, Board of Trade, 1969, DTI, 1970-71; Dep. Sec., DTI, later Dept of Trade, 1971-76. Mem., London Library Cttee, 1971-78. *Recreations:* mountain walking, reading. *Address:* 4 Provost Road, NW3 4ST. *T:* 01-586 4341. *Club:* Reform.

HUBBARD, family name of **Baron Addington.**

HUBEL, Prof. David Hunter, MD; John Franklin Enders University Professor, Harvard Medical School, since 1982; *b* Canada, 27 Feb. 1926; US citizen; *s* of Hesse H. Hubel and Elsie M. Hunter; *m* 1953, S. Ruth Izzard; three *s. Educ:* McGill Univ. (BSc Hons Maths and Physics, 1947); McGill Univ. Med. Sch. (MD 1951). Rotating Intern, Montreal Gen. Hosp., 1951-52; Asst Resident in Neurology, Montreal Neurol Inst., 1952-53, and Fellow in Electroencephalography, 1953-54; Asst Resident in Neurol., Johns Hopkins Hosp., 1954-55; Res. Fellow, Walter Reed Army Inst. of Res., 1955-58; Res. Fellow, Wilmer Inst., Johns Hopkins Univ. Med. Sch., 1958-59; Harvard Medical School: Associate in Neurophysiology and Neuropharmacology, 1959-60; Asst Prof. of Neurophys. and Neuropharm., 1960-62; Associate Prof. of Neurophys. and Neuropharm., 1962-65; Prof. of Neurophys., 1965-67; George Packer Berry Prof. of Physiol. and Chm., Dept of Physiol., 1967-68; George Packer Berry Prof. of Neurobiol., 1968-82. Sen. Fellow, Harvard Soc. of Fellows, 1971-; Mem., Bd of Syndics, Harvard Univ. Press, 1979-. Associate, Neurosciences Res. Program, 1974. Fellow, Amer. Acad. of Arts and Sciences, 1965; Member: Amer. Physiol Soc., 1959-; National Acad. of Sciences, USA, 1971; Deutsche Akademie der Naturforscher Leopoldina, DDR, 1971; Soc. for Neuroscience, 1970; Assoc. for Res. in Vision and Ophthalmology, 1970; Amer. Philosophical Soc., 1982; Foreign Mem., Royal Soc., 1982. Lectures: George H. Bishop, Washington Univ., St Louis, 1964; Bowditch, Amer. Physiol Soc., 1966; Jessup, Columbia Univ., 1970; Ferrier, Royal Soc., 1972; James Arthur, Amer. Mus. of Nat. Hist., 1972; Harvey, Rockefeller Univ., 1976; Grass Foundn, Soc. for Neuroscience, 1976; Weizmann Meml, Weizmann Inst. of Science, Israel, 1979; Vanuxem, Princeton Univ., 1981; Hughlings Jackson, Montreal Neurol Inst., 1982; first David Marr, Cambridge Univ., 1982. Hon. AM Harvard, 1962; Hon. DSc McGill, 1978. Awards: Res. to Prevent Blindness Trustees, 1971; Lewis S. Rosenstiel for Basic Med. Res., Brandeis Univ., 1972; Friedenwald, Assoc. for Res. in Vision and Ophthalmol., 1975. Prizes: Karl Spencer Lashley, Amer. Phil Soc., 1977; Louisa Gross Horwitz, Columbia Univ., 1978; Dickson in Medicine, Univ. of Pittsburgh, 1979; Ledlie, Harvard Univ., 1980; Nobel Prize in Medicine or Physiol., 1981. *Publications:* articles in scientific jls. *Recreations:* music, photography, astronomy, Japanese. *Address:* Harvard Medical School, 25 Shattuck Street, Boston, Mass 02115, USA. *T:* (617) 732-1655.

HUCKER, Ernest George, CBE 1972; Senior Director, Post Office, 1969-71; *b* Wembdon, Som, 20 March 1908; *s* of Albert Hucker; *m* 1934, Mary Louise Jowett; one *s* one *d. Educ:* Hele's Sch., Exeter. Post Office Telephones, 1929; Asst Surveyor of Posts, 1932-39; 2nd Lieut RE, SRO, 1935; served War of 1939-45, Army: France, 1939-40; India, 1942-45 (Lt-Col); London Postal Region, 1946-52; Controller of Ops, 1952; Comdt PO Management Trng Centre, 1952-55; Chief Inspector of Postal Services, 1956-62; Asst Sec. 1962-63; Dep. Dir 1963-65, Dir 1965-69, Midland Region. Freeman, City of London, 1952. *Recreation:* music. *Address:* 6 Ratton Drive, Eastbourne, East Sussex BN20 9BJ. *T:* Eastbourne 51414.

HUCKFIELD, Leslie (John); MP (Lab) Nuneaton since March 1967; *b* 7 April 1942; *s* of Ernest Leslie and Suvla Huckfield. *Educ:* Prince Henry's Grammar Sch., Evesham; Keble Coll., Oxford; Univ. of Birmingham. Lectr in Economics, City of Birmingham Coll. of Commerce, 1963-67. Contested (Lab) Warwick and Leamington, 1966. PPS to Minister of Public Building and Works, 1969-70; Parly Under-Secretary of State, Dept of Industry, 1976-79. Member: Nat. Exec. Cttee, Labour Party, 1978-82; W Midlands Reg. Exec. Cttee, Labour Party, 1978-; Political Sec., Nat. Union Lab. and Socialist Clubs, 1979-81. Chairman: Lab. Party Transport Gp, 1974-76; Independent Adv. Common on Transport, 1975-76; Pres., Worcs Fedn of Young Socialists, 1962-64; Member: Birmingham Regional Hosp. Bd, 1970-72; Political Cttee, Co-op. Retail Soc. (London Region), 1981-. *Publications:* various newspaper and periodical articles. *Recreation:* keep-fit enthusiast. *Address:* House of Commons, SW1A 0AA.

HUCKLE, Sir (Henry) George, Kt 1977; OBE 1969; Chairman: Agricultural Training Board, 1970-80; Home-Grown Cereals Authority, since 1977; Deputy Chairman, Extrans Technical Services Ltd, since 1980; *b* 9 Jan. 1914; *s* of George Henry and Lucy Huckle; *m* 1st, 1935, L. Steel (*d* 1947); one *s* ; 2nd, 1949, Mrs Millicent Mary Hunter; one *d* and one step *d. Educ:* Latymer Sch.; Oxford Univ. (by courtesy of BRCS via Stalag Luft III, Germany). Accountant trng, 1929-33; sales management, 1933-39; RAF bomber pilot, 1940-41; POW, Germany, 1941-45; Shell Group, 1945-70: Man. Dir, Shellstar Ltd, 1965-70, retd. *Recreations:* competition bridge, gardening, following

daughter's interest in horse eventing. *Address:* Thatchways, Burgate, Fordingbridge, Hants. *T:* Fordingbridge 53152. *Club:* Farmers'.

HUCKSTEP, Prof. Ronald Lawrie, CMG 1971; MD, FRCS, FRCSE, FRACS; Professor of Traumatic and Orthopaedic Surgery, since 1972, and Chairman, School of Surgery, since 1975, University of New South Wales; Chairman of Departments of Orthopaedic Surgery and Director of Accident Services, Prince of Wales and Prince Henry Hospitals, Sydney, Australia, since 1972; Consultant Orthopaedic Surgeon, Royal South Sydney and Sutherland Hospitals, since 1974; *b* 22 July 1926; *er s* of late Herbert George Huckstep and Agnes Huckstep (*née* Lawrie-Smith); *m* 1960, Margaret Ann, *e d* of Ronald Græme Macbeth, DM, FRCS; two *s* one *d. Educ:* Cathedral Sch., Shanghai, China; Queens' Coll., Cambridge; Mddx Hosp. Med. Sch., London. MA, MB, BChir(Cantab) 1952; MD(Cantab) 1957; FRCS (Edinburgh) 1957; FRCS 1958; FRACS (by election) 1973. Registrar and Chief Asst, Orthopaedic Dept, St Bartholomew's Hosp., and various surgical appts Mddx and Royal Nat. Orthopaedic Hosps, London, 1952-60; Hunterian Prof., RCS of Eng., 1959-60. Makerere Univ. Coll., Kampala, Uganda: Lectr, 1960-62, Sen. Lectr, 1962-65 and Reader, 1965-67, in Orthopaedic Surgery, with responsibility for starting orthopaedic dept in Uganda; Prof. of Orthopaedic Surgery, Makerere Univ., Kampala, 1967-72. Became Hon. Cons. Orthopaedic Surgeon, Mulago and Mengo Hosps, and Round Table Polio Clinic, Kampala; Adviser on Orthopaedic Surgery, Ministry of Health, Uganda, 1960-72. Corresp. Editor: Brit. and Amer. Jls of Bone and Joint Surgery, 1965-72; Jl Western Pacific Orthopædic Assoc.; British Jl of Accident Surgery. Fellow, British Orthopaedic Assoc., 1967; Hon. Fellow, Western Pacific Orthopaedic Assoc., 1968. Irving Geist Award, 11th World Congress of Internat. Soc. for Rehabilitation of the Disabled, 1969; Commonwealth Foundn Travelling Lectr, 1970, 1978-79 and 1982. FRSM; Patron Med. Soc., Univ. of NSW; Founder, World Orthopaedic Concern, 1973 (Hon. Mem. 1978); Chairman, Fellow or Mem. various med. socs and of assocs, councils and cttees concerned with orthopaedic and traumatic surgery, accident services and rehabilitation of physically disabled. Inventions incl. Huckstep Femoral Fracture nail, hip and circlip. Hon. Mem., Mark Twain Soc., 1978. *Publications:* Typhoid Fever and Other Salmonella Infections, 1962; A Simple Guide to Trauma, 1970, 3rd edn 1982 (trans. Italian 1978, Japanese 1982); Poliomyelitis—A Guide for Developing Countries, 1975 (ELBS and repr. edns 1979); various booklets, papers and films on injuries, orthopaedic diseases, and appliances. *Recreations:* photography, designing orthopaedic appliances and implants for cripples in developing and developed countries, swimming, travel. *Address:* Department of Traumatic and Orthopaedic Surgery, University of New South Wales, PO Box 1, Kensington, Sydney, NSW 2033, Australia. *T:* Sydney 3990111.

HUDDIE, Sir David (Patrick), Kt 1968; retired; *b* 12 March 1916; *s* of James and Catherine Huddie; *m* 1941, Wilhelmina Betty Booth; three *s. Educ:* Mountjoy Sch., Dublin; Trinity Coll., Dublin. FIQA 1980; FIMechE 1974; FEng 1981. Aero Engine Division, Rolls-Royce Ltd: Asst Chief Designer, 1947; Chief Development Engineer, 1953; Commercial Dir, 1959; General Manager, 1962; Dir, Rolls-Royce Ltd, 1961; Man. Dir, Aero Engine Div., 1965; Chm. Rolls-Royce Aero Engines Inc., 1969-70; Senior Res. Fellow, Imperial Coll., London, 1971-80. Hon. Fellow, 1981. Hon. DSc Dublin, 1968. *Recreations:* gardening, music, archaeology. *Address:* The Dower House, Winster, Derbyshire DE4 2DH. *T:* Winster 213. *Club:* Athenæum.

HUDDLESTON, Most Rev. (Ernest Urban) Trevor; *see* Indian Ocean, Archbishop of the.

HUDLESTON, Air Chief Marshal Sir Edmund C., GCB 1963 (KCB 1958; CB 1952); CBE 1943; Air ADC to the Queen, 1962-67, retired 1967; *b* 30 Dec. 1908; *s* of late Ven. C. Hudleston; *m* 1st, 1936, Nancye Davis (*d* 1980); one *s* one *d* ; 2nd, 1981, Mrs Brenda Withrington. *Educ:* Guildford Sch., W Australia; Royal Air Force Coll., Cranwell. Entered Royal Air Force 1927; served in UK until 1933; India, NWFP, 1933-37 (despatches); RAF Staff Coll., 1938; lent to Turkish Govt 1939-40; served Middle East and N Africa, Sicily, Italy, 1941-43 (despatches thrice); AOC No 84 Group, 2 TAF, Western Front, 1944; Imperial Defence Coll., 1946; Head of UK's military delegation to the Western Union Military Staff Cttee, 1948-50; AOC No 1 Group, Bomber Command, 1950-51; Deputy Chief of Staff, Supreme Headquarters, Allied Command, Europe, 1951-53; AOC No 3 Group, Bomber Command, 1953-56; RAF Instructor, Imperial Defence Coll., 1956-57; Vice-Chief of the Air Staff, 1957-62; Air Officer Commanding-in-Chief, Transport Command, 1962-63; Comdr Allied Air Forces, Central Europe, 1964-67, and C-in-C Allied Forces Central Europe, 1964-65. Dir, Pilkington Bros (Optical Div.), 1971-79. Comdr Legion of Merit (USA), 1944; Knight Commander Order of Orange-Nassau (Netherlands), 1945; Commander Order of Couronne, Croix de Guerre (Belgium), 1945; Officer, Legion of Honour, 1956, Croix de Guerre (France), 1957. *Recreations:* cricket, squash, tennis, shooting, etc. *Address:* 156 Marine Court, St Leonards-on-Sea, East Sussex TN38 0DZ. *Club:* Royal Air Force.

HUDSON, Prof. Anthony Hugh, PhD; Professor of Common Law, Liverpool University, since 1977; *b* 21 Jan. 1928; *s* of late Dr Thomas A. G. Hudson and Bridget Hudson; *m* 1952, Joan O'Malley; one *s* three *d. Educ:* St Joseph's Coll., Blackpool; Pembroke Coll., Cambridge (LLB 1950, MA 1953); PhD Manchester 1966. Called to Bar, Lincoln's Inn, 1954. Lecturer in Law: Hull Univ., 1951-57; Birmingham Univ., 1957-62; Manchester Univ., 1962-64; Liverpool Univ.: Sen. Lectr, 1964-71; Professor of Law, 1971-77;

Dean of Faculty of Law, 1971–78. *Publications:* (with Prof. O. Hood Phillips) Hood Phillips: A First Book of English Law, 7th edn 1977; (with Prof. R. R. Pennington) Commercial Banking Law, 1978; (with Prof. J. K. Macleod) Stevens and Borrie Mercantile Law, 17th edn 1978; contribs to various legal periodicals. *Recreations:* gardening, walking, history. *Address:* 18 Dowhills Road, Blundellsands, Crosby, Liverpool L23 8SW. *T:* 051-924 5830.

HUDSON, Rt. Rev. A(rthur) W(illiam) Goodwin, ThD; Hon. Assistant Bishop, Diocese of Derby, since 1981; *s* of Alfred and Anne Goodwin Hudson; *m* Dr Elena E. de Wirtz; one *s*. *Educ:* London Univ.; London Coll. of Divinity. Ordained Deacon, 1940; Priest, 1941. Curate of St Paul, Chatham, 1940–42; Hon. CF, 1942–45; Vicar of Good Easter, Essex, 1942–45; Diocesan Missioner, Chelmsford Diocese, 1943–45; Head Master, Windsor Sch., Santiago, 1945–48; Chaplain, Santiago, Chile, 1945–48; Vicar of St Mary Magdalene, Holloway, 1948–55 (with St James, 1953–55); Vicar of All Saints, Woodford Wells, 1955–60; Coadjutor Bishop and Dean of Sydney, 1960–65; Vicar of St Paul's, Portman Square, W1, 1965–79. Hon. Gen. Sec., S Amer. Missionary Soc., 1949–60; Hon. Sec., Spanish and Portuguese Church Aid Soc., 1950–55. Chairman: Jerusalem Garden Tomb Assoc.; Council of Christian Churches. *Recreations:* yachting, tennis; and profession! *Address:* 14 Newton Park, Newton Solney, Burton-on-Trent, Staffs DE15 0SX. *T:* Burton-on-Trent 702367. *Clubs:* National; Army and Navy.

HUDSON, Eleanor Erlund, RE 1946 (ARE 1938); RWS 1949 (ARWS 1939); ARCA (London) 1937; Artist; *b* 18 Feb. 1912; *d* of Helen Ingeborg Olsen, Brookline, Boston, USA, and Harold Hudson. *Educ:* Torquay; Dorking; Royal College of Art (Diploma 1937, Travelling Scholarship 1938). Mem. Chicago Print Soc. and Soc. of Artist Print-Makers. Studied and travelled in Italy summer 1939. Interrupted by war. Exhibited in London, Provinces, Scandinavia, Canada, USA, etc.; works purchased by War Artists Advisory Council, 1942–43. *Recreations:* music, country life. *Address:* 6 Hammersmith Terrace, W6. *T:* 01-748 3778.

HUDSON, Eric Hamilton, FRCP; Hon. Consulting Physician: West London Hospital; London Chest Hospital; King Edward VII Hospital, Midhurst; Papworth Village Settlement; retired as: Consultant Physician, Manor House Hospital; Senior Medical Officer, Prudential Assurance Co.; *b* 11 July 1902; *s* of James Arthur and Edith Hudson; *m* 1st, 1940, Jessie Marian MacKenzie (*d* 1968); two *s* one *d*; 2nd, 1972, Nora Joan Pitman. *Educ:* Radley Coll.; Emmanuel Coll., Cambridge; Guy's Hosp., London. MRCS, LRCP, 1927; MA, MB, BCh Cantab, 1931; MRCP 1933, FRCP 1941. Late Wing Commander RAF, Officer in charge Medical Div., 1941–45. Late Examr in Medicine, RCP; Past Pres., W London Medico-Chirurgical Soc., 1959. *Publications:* Section on diagnosis and treatment of respiratory Tuberculosis, Heaf's Symposium of Tuberculosis, 1957; contrib. to Perry and Holmes Sellors Diseases of the Chest, 1964; contrib. to medical jls on diseases of the lungs. *Recreation:* fishing. *Address:* The Shieling, Highclere, near Newbury, Berks. *T:* Highclere 253574.

HUDSON, Frank Michael Stanislaus; barrister; a Recorder of the Crown Court, since 1981; *b* 28 Sept. 1916; *s* of Frederick Francis Hudson and Elizabeth Frances (*née* O'Herlihy); *m* 1947, Jean Colburn (*née* Gordon); one *d*. *Educ:* Wimbledon Coll.; London Univ. (BA). Called to the Bar, Middle Temple, 1961; practised Northern Circuit, 1969–. Served War: 77th Field Regt RA, 1939–41; Glider Pilot Regt, 1941–45. Post-war employment in local govt and in trade assocs; Dep. Circuit Judge, 1977–80. *Recreations:* bee-keeping, history of English monasticism. *Address:* 33 Sherwood Avenue, Radcliffe, Manchester M26 0LE. *T:* 061-764 3807; (chambers) 67 Princess Street, Manchester M2 4EG. *T:* 061-228 1764.

HUDSON, Sir Havelock (Henry Trevor), Kt 1977; Lloyd's Underwriter since 1952; Chairman of Lloyd's, 1975, 1976 and 1977 (Deputy Chairman, 1968, 1971, 1973); *b* 4 Jan. 1919; *er s* of late Savile E. Hudson and Dorothy Hudson (*née* Cheetham); *m* 1st, 1944, Elizabeth (marr. diss., 1956), *d* of Brig. W. Home; two *s*; 2nd, 1957, Cathleen Blanche Lily, *d* of 6th Earl of St Germans; one *s* one *d*. *Educ:* Rugby. Merchant Service, 1937-38. Served War of 1939–45: Royal Hampshire Regt (Major), 1939–42; 9 Parachute Bn, 1942-44. Member: Cttee Lloyd's Underwriters Assoc., 1963; Cttee of Lloyd's, 1965-68, 1970-73, 1975-78; Exec. Bd, Lloyd's Register of Shipping, 1967-78. Dir, Ellerman Lines Ltd, 1979-. Vice-Pres., Chartered Insurance Inst., 1973-76. Dep. Pres., 1976-; Chairman: Arvon Foundn, 1973-; Oxford Artificial Kidney and Transplant Unit, 1976-; Pres., City of London Outward Bound Assoc., 1979-; Member, Board of Governors: Pangbourne Coll., 1976-; Bradfield Coll., 1978-. Lloyd's Gold Medal, 1977. *Recreation:* shooting. *Address:* The Old Rectory, Stanford Dingley, Berkshire. *T:* Bradfield 744346. *Club:* Boodle's.

HUDSON, Ian Francis, CB 1976; Deputy Secretary, Department of Employment, 1976-80; *b* 29 May 1925; *s* of Francis Reginald Hudson and Dorothy Mary Hudson (*née* Crabbe); *m* 1952, Gisela Elisabeth Grettka; one *s* one *d*. *Educ:* City of London Sch.; New Coll., Oxford. Royal Navy, 1943-47. Customs and Excise, 1947-53; Min. of Labour, 1953-56, 1959-61, 1963-64; Treasury, 1957-58; Dept of Labour, Australia, 1961-63; Asst Sec., 1963; DEA, 1964-68; Under-Sec., 1967; Dept of Employment, 1968-73; Dep. Sec. 1973; Sec., Pay Board, 1973-74; Sec., Royal Commn on Distribution of Income and Wealth, 1974-76. *Address:* 9 Birchwood, Banbury, Oxon OX16 9UF.
See also J. A. Hudson.

HUDSON, James Ralph, CBE 1976; FRCS; Surgeon, Moorfields Eye Hospital, 1956-81, now Honorary Consultant Surgeon; Ophthalmic Surgeon, Guy's Hospital, 1963-76; Hon. Ophthalmic Surgeon: Hospital of St John and St Elizabeth, since 1953; King Edward VII Hospital for Officers, since 1970; Teacher of Ophthalmology, Guy's Hospital, 1964-76, Institute of Ophthalmology, University of London, 1961-81; Consultant Adviser in Ophthalmology, Department of Health and Social Security, 1969-82; *b* 15 Feb. 1916; *o s* of late William Shand Hudson and Ethel Summerskill; *m* 1946, Margaret May Oulpé; two *s* two *d*. *Educ:* The King's Sch., Canterbury; Middlesex Hosp. (Edmund Davis Exhibnr), Univ. of London, MRCS, LRCP 1939; MB, BS London 1940; DOMS (England) 1948; FRCS 1949. Res. Med. Appts, Tindal House Emergency Hosp. (Mddx Hosp. Sector), 1939-42. RAFVR Med. Service, 1942-46; Sqdn Ldr, 1944-46. Moorfields Eye Hosp., Clin. Asst, 1947, Ho. Surg., 1947-49; Sen. Resident Officer, 1949, Chief Clin. Asst, 1950-56; Middlesex Hosp., Clin. Asst Ophth. Outpatients, 1950-51; Ophth. Surg., W Middlesex Hosp., 1950-56, Mount Vernon Hosp., 1953-59. Civil Consultant in Ophthalmology to RAF, 1970-82. Examr in Ophthalmology (Dipl. Ophth. of Examg Bd of Eng., RCP and RCS, 1960-65; Mem. Court of Examrs, RCS, 1966-72). FRSocMed 1947 (Vice-Pres. Sect. of Ophthalmology, 1965); Member: Ophthal. Soc. UK, 1948 (Hon. Sec. 1956-58, Vice-Pres., 1969-71); Faculty of Ophthalmologists, 1950 (Mem. Council, 1960-; Hon. Sec. 1960-70; Vice-Pres., 1970-74; Pres., 1974-77; Rep. on Council of RCS, 1968-73); Soc. Française d'Ophtal., 1950- (membre délégue étranger, 1970-); Scientific Cttee Les Entretiens Annuels d'Ophtalmologie, 1970-; Internat. Council of Ophthalmology, 1978-; UK Rep., Union Européenne des Médicins Spécialistes (Ophthalmology Section), 1973-; Hon. Fellow, Royal Aust. Coll. Ophthalmologists; Pilgrims of Gt Britain. Liveryman, Soc. of Apothecaries, and Freeman of City of London. *Publications:* (with T. Keith Lyle) chapters in Matthews's Recent Advances in the Surgery of Trauma; contrib. to chapters in Rob and Rodney Smith's Operative Surgery, 1969; articles in: Brit. Jl of Ophthalmology; Trans Ophth. Soc. UK; Proc. Royal Soc. Med. *Recreations:* motoring, travel. *Address:* 8 Upper Wimpole Street, W1M 7TD. *T:* 01-935 5038; 1A Montagu Mews South, W1H 1TE. *T:* 01-402 6511. *Club:* Garrick.

HUDSON, John Arthur, CB 1970; Deputy Under-Secretary of State, Department of Education and Science, 1969-80; *b* 24 Aug. 1920; *s* of Francis Reginald Hudson and Dorothy Mary (*née* Crabbe); *m* 1960, Dwynwen Davies; one *s* one *d*. *Educ:* City of London Sch.; Jesus Coll., Oxford. Served Royal Corps of Signals, 1941-45 (despatches). Entered Ministry of Education, 1946. Mem., South Bank Theatre Bd, 1967-. *Recreations:* gardening, microscopy. *Address:* The Rosary, Green Lane, Leominster, Herefordshire HR6 8QN. *T:* Leominster 4413.
See also I. F. Hudson.

HUDSON, Prof. John Pilkington, CBE 1975 (MBE 1943); GM 1944 and Bar 1945; BSc, MSc, PhD; NDH; FIBiol; now Emeritus Professor; former Director, Long Ashton Research Station, and Professor of Horticultural Science, University of Bristol, 1967-75; *b* 24 July 1910; *o s* of W. A. Hudson and Bertha (*née* Pilkington); *m* 1936, Mary Gretta, *d* of late W. N. and Mary Heath, Westfields, Market Bosworth, Leics; two *s*. *Educ:* New Mills Grammar Sch.; Midland Agricultural Coll.; University Coll., Nottingham. Hort. Adviser, E Sussex CC, 1935-39. Served War of 1939-45, Royal Engineers Bomb Disposal (Major). Horticulturist, Dept of Agric., Wellington, NZ, 1945-48; Lecturer in Horticulture, University of Nottingham Sch. of Agric., 1948-50; Head of Dept of Horticulture, University of Nottingham, 1950-67 (as Prof. of Horticulture, 1958-67), Dean, Faculty of Agriculture and Horticulture, 1965-67); seconded part-time to Univ. of Khartoum, Sudan, to found Dept of Horticulture, 1961-63. Associate of Honour, Royal New Zealand Institute of Horticulture, 1948. Member: Res. Adv. Cttee, Forestry Commn; Advisory Cttee on Agricultural Education (Chm.); RHS Exam. Bd; Vice-Pres., Inst. of Biology; PP and Hon. Mem., Hort. Educn Assoc. Editor, Experimental Agriculture, 1965-; Mem. Editorial Bds, Jl Hort. Sci, SPAN. Hon. Fellow, RASE, 1977. Victoria Medal of Honour, RHS, 1977. *Publications:* (ed) Control of the Plant Environment, 1957; contributions on effects of environment on plant behaviour to scientific jls. *Recreations:* music, gardening. *Address:* The Spinney, Wrington, Bristol.

HUDSON, Keith William, FRICS; Director of Construction and Cost Intelligence, and Chief Surveyor, Department of Health and Social Security, since 1979; *b* 2 June 1928; *s* of William Walter Hudson and Jessie Sarah Hudson; *m* 1952, Ailsa White; two *s* two *d*. *Educ:* Sir Charles Elliott Sch.; Coll. of Estate Management. FRICS 1945. Served Army, 1948-50 (Lieut). Private practice, 1945-48 and 1950-57; Min. of Works, Basic Grade, 1957-64; Min. of Health (later DHSS), 1964-: Main Grade, 1964-66; Sen. Grade, 1966-74; Superintending, 1974-76; Dir B, 1976-79; Under Sec., 1979. *Publications:* articles in Chartered Surveyor and in Building. *Recreations:* Rugby coaching, athletics coaching. *Address:* Silver Birch, Mill Lane, Felbridge, East Grinstead, West Sussex RH19 2PE. *T:* East Grinstead 25817. *Club:* Felbridge Rugby Football Union (East Grinstead).

HUDSON, Prof. Liam, MA, PhD; Professor of Psychology, Brunel University, since 1977; *b* 20 July 1933; *er s* of Cyril and Kathleen Hudson; *m* 1st, 1955, Elizabeth Ward; 2nd 1965, Bernadine Jacot de Boinod; three *s* one *d*. *Educ:* Whitgift Sch.; Exeter Coll., Oxford. Post-graduate and post-doctoral research, Psychological Laboratory, Cambridge, 1957-65, and King's Coll., Cambridge, 1965-68; Fellow, King's Coll., Cambridge, 1966-68; Prof. of Educnl Scis, Univ. of Edinburgh, 1968-77, and Dir, Res. Unit on

Intellectual Develt., 1964-77. Mem., Inst. for Advanced Study, Princeton, 1974-75. *Publications:* Contrary Imaginations, 1966; Frames of Mind, 1968; (ed) The Ecology of Human Intelligence, 1970; The Cult of the Fact, 1972; Human Beings, 1975; The Nympholepts, 1978; Bodies of Knowledge, 1982. *Recreations:* painting and photography, making things, otherwise largely domestic. *Address:* 34 North Park, Gerrards Cross, Bucks.

HUDSON, Maurice William Petre; Hon. Consulting Anæsthetist: National Dental Hospital (University College Hospital); Westminster Hospital; St Mary's Hospital; Emeritus Consultant Anæsthetist, Princess Beatrice Hospital; Part-time Consultant Anæsthetist, Queen Mary's Hospital, Roehampton; *b* 8 Nov. 1901; *s* of late Henry Hudson, ARCA, and Anna Martha Rosa (*née* Petre); *m* 1922, Fredrica Helen de Pont; one *s* one *d* (and two *s* decd). *Educ:* Sherborne Sch.; St Thomas' Hosp. MB, BS London, 1925; MRCS, LRCP, 1924; DA England, 1936; FFARCS, 1948. Formerly: Resident House Surg., Resident Anæsthetist, and Clin. Asst, Nose and Throat Dept, St Thomas' Hosp. Fellow Assoc. Anæsthetists of Gt Brit. Mem. Royal Soc. Med. *Publications:* contrib. to med. jls. *Recreations:* swimming, photography. *Address:* 15 Harley Street, W1. *T:* 01-580 1850, 01-580 3977.

HUDSON, Norman Barrie; Under Secretary (Principal Establishments Officer), Overseas Development Administration, since 1981; *b* 21 June 1937; *s* of William and Mary Hudson; *m* 1963, Hazel (*née* Cotterill); two *s* one *d*. *Educ:* King Henry VIII Sch., Coventry; Univ. of Sheffield (BA Hons 1958); University Coll., London (MScEcon 1960). Economist, Tube Investments Ltd, 1960; Economist, Economist Intell. Unit, 1962; National Accounts Statistician (UK Technical Assistance to Govt of Jordan), 1963; Statistician, ODM, 1966; Econ. Adviser, ME Develt Div., Beirut, 1967; Econ. Adviser, ODA, 1972, Sen. Econ. Adviser, 1973; Head, SE Asia Develt Div., Bangkok, 1974; Asst Sec., 1977. *Recreations:* theatre, reading, music, watching football and cricket. *Address:* The Galleons, Sallows Shaw, Sole Street, Cobham, Kent DA13 9BP. *T:* Meopham 814419.

HUDSON, Lt-Gen. Sir Peter, KCB 1977; CBE 1970 (MBE 1965); Secretary-General of the Order of St John, since 1981; *b* 14 Sept. 1923; *s* of Captain William Hudson, late The Rifle Bde, and Ivy (*née* Brown); *m* 1949, Susan Anne Knollys; one adopted *s* one *d* and one adopted *d*. *Educ:* Wellingborough; Jesus Coll., Cambridge. Commnd into The Rifle Bde, 1944; psc 1954; comd company in Mau Mau and Malayan campaigns, 1955-57; jssc 1963; comd 3rd Bn The Royal Green Jackets, 1966-67; Regimental Col The Royal Green Jackets, 1968; Comdr 39 Infantry Bde, 1968-70; IDC 1971; GOC Eastern Dist, 1973-74; Chief of Staff, Allied Forces Northern Europe, 1975-77; Dep. C-in-C, UKLF, 1977-80; Inspector-Gen., T&AVR, 1978-80. Col Comdt, The Light Div., 1977-80. Mem., Gen. Adv. Council, BBC, 1981-. Chairman: Council, T&AVRA, 1981-; Governors, Royal Sch. Bath, 1981-; Rifle Brigade Club and Assoc., 1979-. FBIM. KStJ. *Recreations:* travel, fishing, most games. *Address:* Little Orchard, Frilsham, Newbury, Berks. *Clubs:* Naval and Military, MCC; I Zingari; Green Jackets; Free Foresters.

HUDSON, Peter Geoffrey; Under-Secretary, Department of Industry, since 1975; *b* 26 July 1926; *s* of late Thomas Albert Hudson and late Gertrude Hudson; *m* 1954, Valerie Mary, yr *d* of late Lewis Alfred Hart and late Eva Mary Hart; two *s*. *Educ:* King Edward VII Sch., Sheffield; Queen's Coll., Oxford (Hastings Scholar, MA). Gold Medallist, Royal Schs of Music, 1940. Sub-Lt RNVR, 1944-46. Min. of Transport, 1949; Private Sec. to Minister of Transport and Civil Aviation, 1951-53; Principal, Min. of Transport and Civil Aviation, 1953-57; Admin. Staff Coll., Henley, 1957; British Civil Air Attaché, SE Asia and Far East, 1958-61; Asst Sec., Overseas Policy Div. and Estabt Div., Min. of Aviation and BoT, 1963-68; Counsellor (Civil Aviation), British Embassy, Washington, 1968-71; Under-Sec., DTI, subseq. Dept of Trade, 1971-75. Governor, Coll. of Air Trng, Hamble, 1974-75. *Recreations:* music, travel. *Address:* Candle Hill, Raggleswood, Chislehurst, Kent. *T:* 01-467 1761. *Club:* East India.

HUDSON, Peter John, CB 1978; Deputy Under-Secretary of State (Finance and Budget), Ministry of Defence, 1976-79; *b* 29 Sept. 1919; *o s* of late A. J. Hudson; *m* 1954, Joan Howard FitzGerald; one *s* one *d*. *Educ:* Tollington Sch.; Birkbeck Coll., London. Exchequer and Audit Dept, 1938; RNVR, 1940-46 (Lieut); Air Ministry, Air Min., 1947; Private Sec. to Perm. Under Sec. of State for Air, 1948-51; Asst Sec., 1958; Head of Air Staff Secretariat, 1958-61; Imperial Defence Coll., 1962; Head of Programme and Budget Div., MoD, 1966-69; Under-Sec., Cabinet Office, 1969-72; Asst Under-Sec. of State, MoD, 1972-75; Dep. Under-Sec. of State (Air), MoD, 1975-76. *Address:* Folly Hill, Haslemere, Surrey GU27 2EY. *T:* Haslemere 2078. *Club:* Royal Air Force.

HUDSON, Prof. Robert Francis, PhD; FRS 1982; Professor of Organic Chemistry, University of Kent at Canterbury, since 1967 (part-time since 1981); *b* 15 Dec. 1922; *s* of late John Frederick Hudson and Ethel Hudson; *m* 1945, Monica Ashton Stray; one *s* twin *d*. *Educ:* Brigg Grammar Sch.; Imperial Coll. of Science and Technol., London (BSc, ARCS, PhD, DIC). Asst Lectr, Imperial Coll., London, 1945-47; Consultant, Wolsey Ltd, Leicester, 1945-50; Lectr, Queen Mary Coll., London, 1947-59; Res. Fellow, Purdue Univ., 1954; Gp Dir, Cyanamid European Res. Inst., Geneva, 1960-66. Vis. Professor: Rochester, USA, 1970; Bergen, 1971; CNRS, Thiais, Paris, 1973, Calgary, 1975; Mainz, 1979. Lectures: Frontiers, Case-Western Reserve Univ., USA, 1972; Nuffield, Canada, 1975. Pres., Inst. of Science Technol., 1970-76; Member: Council, Chemical Soc., 1967-75 (Foundn Chm., Organic

Reaction Mechanism Gp, 1973); Dalton Council, 1973-76; Perkin Council, 1980-. *Publications:* (with P. Alexander) Wool-its physics and chemistry, 1954, 2nd edn 1960; Structure and Mechanism in Organophosphorus Chemistry, 1965; papers mainly in Jl of Chem. Soc., Helvetica Chemica Acta and Angewendte Chemie. *Address:* The Chemical Laboratory, University of Kent at Canterbury, Canterbury, Kent CT2 7NH. *T:* Canterbury 66822; 37 Puckle Lane, Canterbury CT1 3LA. *T:* Canterbury 61340. *Club:* Athenæum.

HUDSON, Thomas Charles, CBE 1975; Chairman, ICL Ltd, 1972-80; Chartered Accountant (Canadian); *b* Sidcup, Kent, 23 Jan. 1915; British parents; *m* 1944, Lois Alma Hudson (marr. diss. 1973); two *s* one *d*. *Educ:* Middleton High Sch., Nova Scotia. With Nightingale, Hayman & Co, Chartered Accountants, 1935-40. Served War, Royal Canadian Navy, Lieut, 1940-45. IBM Canada, as Sales Rep., 1946-51 (transf. to IBM, UK, as Sales Manager, 1951, and Managing Dir, 1954-65). Plessey Company: Financial Dir, 1967; Dir, 1969-76; Dir, ICL, 1968. Councillor for Enfield, GLC, 1970-73. *Recreations:* tennis, ski-ing, gardening. *Address:* Hele Farm, North Bovey, Devon TQ13 8RW. *T:* Moretonhampstead 249. *Clubs:* Carlton, American, Inst. of Directors; Montreal Amateur Athletic Assoc. (Montreal).

HUDSON, William Meredith Fisher, QC 1967; Barrister-at-law; *b* 17 Nov. 1916; *o s* of late Lt-Comdr William Henry Fisher Hudson, RN (killed in action, Jutland, 1916); *m* 1st, 1938, Elizabeth Sophie (marr. diss., 1948), *d* of late Reginald Pritchard, Bloemfontein, SA; one *s* one *d*; 2nd, 1949, Pamela Helen, *d* of late William Cecil Edwards, Indian Police; two *d*. *Educ:* Imperial Service Coll.; Trinity Hall, Cambridge. BA 1938; Harmsworth Law Scholar, 1939; MA 1940. Called to the Bar, Middle Temple, 1943, Bencher, 1972; South Eastern Circuit, 1945; Mem. of Central Criminal Court Bar Mess. Commissioned Royal Artillery (TA), 1939; served War of 1939-45, Eritrea and Sudan. Chm., Blackfriars Settlement, 1970-. *Recreations:* trains, travel, theatre; formerly athletics (Cambridge Blue, Cross Country half Blue; rep. England and Wales, European Student Games, 1938). *Address:* 5 King's Bench Walk, Temple, EC4. *T:* 01-353 4713; (home) 3 Rivercourt Road, W6. *T:* 01-741 3125; The Park House, Berkeley, Glos. *Clubs:* Hurlingham; Achilles; Hawks (Cambridge).

HUDSON DAVIES, (Gwilym) Ednyfed; see Davies, G. E. H.

HUDSON-WILLIAMS, Prof. Harri Llwyd, MA; Professor of Greek in the University of Newcastle upon Tyne (formerly King's College, Newcastle upon Tyne, University of Durham), 1952-76 and Head of Department of Classics, 1969-76; now Emeritus Professor; *b* 16 Feb. 1911; *yr s* of late Prof. T. Hudson-Williams; *m* 1946, Joan, *er d* of late Lieut-Col H. F. T. Fisher; two *d*. *Educ:* University College of North Wales; King's Coll., Cambridge (Browne Medallist; Charles Oldham Scholar); Munich University. Asst Lectr in Greek, Liverpool Univ., 1937-40; Intelligence Corps, 1940-41; Foreign Office, 1941-45; Lectr in Greek, Liverpool Univ., 1945-50; Reader in Greek, King's Coll., Newcastle upon Tyne, 1950-52; Dean of the Faculty of Arts, 1963-66. *Publications:* contribs to various classical jls, etc. *Recreation:* gardening. *Address:* The Pound, Mill Street, Islip, Oxford OX5 2SZ. *T:* Kidlington 5893.

HUFFINLEY, Beryl; Secretary: Leeds Trades Council, since 1966; Yorkshire and Humberside TUC Regional Council, since 1974; *b* 22 Aug. 1926; *d* of Wilfred and Ivey Sharpe; *m* 1948, Ronald Brown Huffinley. Chairman: Leeds and York Dist Cttee, T&GWU, 1974-; Regional Cttee, T&GWU No 9 Region, 1972-. Member: Regional Econ. Planning Council (Yorkshire and Humberside), 1975-79; Leeds AHA, 1977-; Press Council, 1978-. *Address:* Cornerways, South View, Menston, Ilkley, Yorks. *T:* Menston 75115. *Club:* Trades Council (Leeds).

HUFTON, Prof. Olwen, (Mrs B. T. Murphy), PhD; Professor of Modern History, University of Reading, since 1975; *d* of Joseph Hufton and Caroline Hufton; *m* 1965, Brian Taunton Murphy; two *d*. *Educ:* Hulme Grammar Sch., Oldham; Univ. of London (BA 1959, PhD 1962). Lectr, Univ. of Leicester, 1963-66; Lectr, then Reader, Univ. of Reading, 1966-75. *Publications:* Bayeux in the Late Eighteenth Century, 1967; The Poor of Eighteenth Century France, 1974; Europe, Privilege and Protest, 1730-1789, 1980; articles in Past and Present, Eur. Studies Rev., and French Hist. Studies. *Address:* 40 Shinfield Road, Reading, Berks. *T:* Reading 871514.

HUGGETT, Mrs Helen K.; see Porter, Prof. H. K.

HUGGINS, family name of Viscount Malvern.

HUGGINS, Hon. Sir Alan (Armstrong), Kt 1980; Hon. Mr Justice Huggins; Vice-President, Court of Appeal, Hong Kong, since 1980; *b* 15 May 1921; *yr s* of late William Armstrong Huggins and Dare (*née* Copping); *m* 1950, Catherine Davidson, *d* of late David Dick; two *s* one *d*. *Educ:* Radley Coll.; Sidney Sussex Coll., Cambridge (MA). TARO (Special List), 1940-48 (Actg Major); Admiralty, 1941-46. Called to Bar, Lincoln's Inn, 1947. Legal Associate Mem., TPI, 1949-70. Resident Magistrate, Uganda, 1951-53; Stipendiary Magistrate, Hong Kong, 1953-58; Diocesan Reader, Dio. of Hong Kong and Macao, 1954; District Judge, Hong Kong, 1958-65. Chm., Justice (Hong Kong Br.), 1965-68; Judicial Comr, State of Brunei, 1966-; Judge of Supreme Court, Hong Kong, 1965-76; Justice of Appeal, Hong Kong, 1976-80. Hon. Lectr, Hong Kong Univ., 1979. Hon. Life Governor, Brit. and

For. Bible Soc. Liveryman, Leathersellers' Company. *Recreations:* boating, archery, amateur theatre, tapestry. *Address:* Courts of Justice, Hong Kong. *Club:* Royal Over-Seas League.

HUGGINS, Prof. Charles B.; Professor of Surgery, University of Chicago, since 1936; William B. Ogden Distinguished Service Professor since 1962; *b* Halifax, Canada, 22 Sept. 1901; *s* of Charles Edward Huggins and Bessie Huggins (*née* Spencer); citizen of USA by naturalization, 1933; *m* 1927, Margaret Wellman; one *s* one *d*. *Educ:* Acadia (BA 1920; DSc 1946); Harvard (MD 1924). University of Michigan: Interne in Surgery, 1924–26; Instructor in Surgery, 1926–27; Univ. of Chicago, 1927–: Instructor in Surgery, 1927–29; Asst Prof., 1929–33; Assoc. Prof., 1933–36; Prof., 1936–; Dir, Ben May Laboratory for Cancer Research, 1951–69. Chancellor, Acadia Univ., 1972–79. Alpha Omega Alpha, 1942; Mem. Nat. Acad. of Sciences, 1949; Mem. Amer. Philosophical Soc., 1962. Sigillum Magnum, Bologna Univ., 1964; Hon. Prof., Madrid Univ., 1956; Hon. FRSocMed (London), 1956; Hon. FRCSE 1958; Hon. FRCS 1959; Hon. FACS 1963. Hon. MSc, Yale, 1947; Hon. DSc: Washington Univ., St Louis, 1950; Leeds Univ., 1953; Turin Univ., 1957; Trinity Coll., Hartford, Conn., 1965; Wales, 1967; Univ. of California, Berkeley, 1968; Univ. of Michigan, 1968; Medical Coll. of Ohio, 1973; Gustavus Adolphus Coll., 1975; Wilmington Coll. of Ohio, 1980; Univ. of Louisville, 1980; Hon. LLD: Aberdeen Univ., 1966; York Univ., Toronto, 1968; Hon. DPS, George Washington Univ., 1967. Has given many memorial lectures and has won numerous gold medals, prizes and awards for his work on urology and cancer research, including Nobel Prize for Medicine (jtly), 1966. Holds foreign orders. *Publications:* Experimental Leukemia and Mammary Cancer: Induction, Prevention, Cure, 1979; over 275 articles. *Address:* Ben May Laboratory for Cancer Research, University of Chicago, 950 East 59th Street, Chicago, Ill 60637, USA.

HUGGINS, Kenneth Herbert, CMG 1960; *b* 4 Dec. 1908; *m* 1934, Gladys E. Walker; one *s* one *d*. *Educ:* Hitchin Grammar Sch.; Tollington Sch.; University Coll., London. BSc London 1930; PhD Glasgow, 1940. Asst and Lecturer in Geography, Glasgow Univ., 1930–41; Ministry of Supply, 1941; Staff of Combined Raw Materials Board, Washington, 1942–46; Board of Trade, 1947; Staff of Administrative Staff Coll., Henley, 1954–55; Commercial Counsellor, British Embassy, Washington, 1957–60; UK Trade Commissioner, subsequently Consul-General, Johannesburg, 1960–62. Dir, British Industrial Develt Office, NY, 1962–68. *Publications:* atlases and articles in geographical journals. *Recreation:* keeping paths open. *Address:* 3 Skeyne Mews, Pulborough, W Sussex. *T:* Pulborough 2365.

HUGGINS, Peter Jeremy William; *see* Brett, Jeremy.

HUGH-JONES, Wynn Normington, MVO 1961; Secretary-General of the Liberal Party, since 1977; *b* 1 Nov. 1923; *s* of Huw Hugh-Jones and May Normington; *m* 1958, Ann (*née* Purkiss); one *s* one *d*. *Educ:* Ludlow; Selwyn Coll., Cambridge (Scholar; MA) Served in RAF, 1943–46. Entered Foreign Service (now Diplomatic Service), 1947; Foreign Office, 1947–49; Jedda, 1949–52; Paris, 1952–56; FO, 1956–59; Chargé d'Affaires, Conakry, 1959–60; Head of Chancery, Rome, 1960–64; FO, 1964–66, Counsellor, 1964; Consul, Elizabethville (later Lubumbashi), 1966–68; Counsellor and Head of Chancery, Ottawa, 1968–70; FCO, 1971, attached Lord President's Office; Cabinet Office, 1972–73; Director-Gen., E-SU, 1973–77. FBIM. *Recreations:* golf, gardening. *Address:* 1 Poyle Road, Guildford, Surrey. *Clubs:* National Liberal, Foreign Affairs; Hindhead Golf.

HUGH SMITH, Lt-Col Henry Owen, MVO 1976; General Staff Officer Grade 1, Ministry of Defence, since 1980; *b* 19 June 1937; *s* of Lt-Comdr Colin Hugh Smith and late Hon. Mrs C. Hugh Smith. *Educ:* Ampleforth; Magdalene Coll., Cambridge. BA Hons 1961. Commnd Royal Horse Guards, 1957; Blues and Royals, 1969; psc 1969; served Cyprus and Northern Ireland (wounded); Equerry in Waiting to The Duke of Edinburgh, 1974–76; CO The Blues and Royals, 1978–80. *Recreations:* riding, sailing. *Address:* 26 Stack House, Cundy Street, SW1. *Clubs:* Boodle's, Pratt's, Cavalry and Guards; Royal Yacht Squadron.

HUGHES, family name of **Barons Hughes** and **Cledwyn of Penrhos.**

HUGHES, Baron, *cr* 1961, of Hawkhill (Life Peer); **William Hughes,** PC 1970; CBE 1956 (OBE 1942); DL; Chairman, East Kilbride Development Corporation, since 1975; President: Scottish Federation of Housing Associations, since 1975; Scottish Association for Mental Health, since 1975; Member, Council of Europe and Western European Union, since 1976; company director; *b* 22 Jan. 1911; *e s* of late Joseph and Margaret Hughes; *m* 1951, Christian Clacher, *o c* of late James and Sophia Gordon; two *d*. *Educ:* Balfour Street Public Sch., Dundee; Dundee Technical Coll. ARP Controller Dundee, 1939–43; Armed Forces, 1943–46; Commissioned RAOC, 1944; demobilised as Capt., 1946. Hon. City Treasurer, Dundee, 1946–47; Chairman, Eastern Regional Hospital Board, Scotland, 1948–60; Lord Provost of Dundee and HM Lieut of County of City of Dundee, 1954–60; Member: Dundee Town Council, 1933–36 and 1937–61; Council of St Andrews Univ., 1954–63; Council of Queen's Coll., Dundee, 1954–63; Cttee on Civil Juries, 1958–59; Cttee to Enquire into Registration of Title to Land in Scotland, 1960–62; North of Scotland Hydro-Electric Bd, 1957–64; Scottish Transport Council, 1960–64; Chairman: Glenrothes Develt Corp., 1960–64; Royal Commn on Legal Services in Scotland, 1976–80. Jt Parly Under-Sec. of State for Scotland, 1964–69; Minister of State for Scotland, 1969–70, 1974–75. Contested (Lab)

E Perthshire, 1945 and 1950. Fellow, Inst. of Dirs. Hon. LLD St Andrews, 1960. JP County and City of Dundee, 1943–76; DL Dundee 1960. Chevalier, Légion d'Honneur, 1958. *Recreation:* gardening. *Address:* Muircroft, Auchterarder, Perthshire PH3 1JJ. *T:* Auchterarder 2646.

HUGHES, Albert Henry, OBE 1961; HM Diplomatic Service, retired; HM Ambassador to El Salvador, 1975–77; *b* 20 Sept. 1917; *s* of George Albert Hughes; *m* 1939, Nancy Russell; two *s* one *d*. *Educ:* The Judd Sch., Tonbridge, Kent. Appointed to the Foreign Office, 1935. War of 1939–45: Served in HM Forces, 1940–45, HM Vice-Consul, Rouen, France, 1949; HM Consul, Tehran, Iran, 1949–52; HM Consul, Philadelphia, USA, 1953–55; HM Consul, Bilbao, Spain, 1962–64; Counsellor (Administration) and HM Consul-General, Washington, 1964–68; Head of Finance Dept, FCO, and Finance Officer of the Diplomatic Service, 1968–71; HM Consul-General, Amsterdam, 1971–75. *Recreations:* reading, gardening, photography. *Address:* The Cottage, Matfield Green, near Tonbridge, Kent. *T:* Brenchley 2462.

HUGHES, Andrew Anderson, MA; Director, Grampian Holdings Ltd, since 1973; *b* 27 Dec. 1915; *s* of Alexander and Euphemia Hughes; *m* 1st, 1944, Dorothy Murdoch (marr. diss. 1946); 2nd, 1946, Margaret Dorothy Aikman; no *c*. *Educ:* Waid Academy; St Andrews Univ.; Marburg Univ.; Emmanuel Coll., Cambridge. Colonial Administrative Service, 1939; Private Sec. to Governor, Gold Coast, 1940–42; Colonial Office, 1946; Dept of Health for Scotland, 1947; Asst Sec., 1956; Under-Sec., 1964; Under-Sec., Scottish Development Dept, 1966–69; Man. Dir, Crudens Ltd, 1969–71; Chm., Grampian Construction Ltd, 1971. Member: Scottish Tourist Bd, 1969–81; Central Arbitration Cttee, 1977–; Chm., Scottish Crafts Consultative Cttee, 1979–. Director: Gilmour and Dean Holdings Ltd, 1980–; Cairngorm Chairlift Co., 1981–. Mem. Ct, Heriott-Watt Univ., 1981–. *Recreation:* golf. *Address:* 9 Palmerston Road, Edinburgh EH9 1TL. *T:* 031-667 2353. *Clubs:* Royal Commonwealth Society; New (Edinburgh).

HUGHES, Major Arthur John, MC 1945; TD and Clasp 1950; DL; Chairman, Hertfordshire County Council, 1977–80; *b* 29 June 1914; *s* of Arthur Hubert Hughes and Dorothy Maud Hughes; *m* 1946, Penelope Joan Parker; one *s* one *d*. *Educ:* Highgate Sch. Entered family business, Wm Hughes Ltd, 1931; Chm. and Man. Dir, 1951. Commnd, Mddx Regt, 1936; served War of 1939–45 (Lt-Col 1943) (despatches twice, MC); subst. Major, 1949. Mem., Hatfield RDC, 1955–58 and 1961–64; Herts CC: Councillor, 1958; Alderman, 1966–73; Vice-Chm., 1968–69, 1971–73, 1974–77 (Chm., 1973;) Conservative Gp Leader, 1974. Chairman: Herts Police Authority, 1980–; Herts Society, 1980–. DL Herts, 1974. *Recreations:* golf, gardening, good food, good wine, grand-children. *Address:* The Vineyards, Welwyn, Herts AL6 9NE. *T:* Welwyn 4242.

HUGHES, Maj.-Gen. Basil Perronet, CB 1955; CBE 1944; *b* 13 Jan. 1903; *s* of late Rev. E. B. A. Hughes; *m* 1932, Joan Marion Worthington; two *s*. *Educ:* Eton Coll.; RMA, Woolwich. Commissioned RFA 1923; Staff Coll., 1935–36; Directing Staff, Staff Coll., 1940. Served NW Frontier of India, 1930–31 (medal and clasp); Mohmand, 1933 (clasp); War of 1939–45 (star and despatches). Formerly: Hon. Col 2nd (London) Bn, Mobile Defence Corps; Hon. Colonel 571 LAA Regt (9th Battalion The Middx Regt DCO) RA, TA. ADC to the Queen, 1952–54; GOC 4 Anti-Aircraft Group, 1954; Maj.-Gen. RA (AA), War Office, 1955–58; retired, 1958. Controller, Royal Artillery Instn, 1958–75. Col Comdt RA 1961–63; Hon. Colonel: 5th Bn, The Middx Regt (DCO), TA, 1964–69; 10th Bn, The Queen's Regt (Mddx), T&AVR, 1970–71. *Publications:* British Smooth-Bore Artillery, 1969; The Bengal Horse Artillery 1800–1861, 1971; Firepower, 1974. *Address:* St Nicholas Close, Stour Row, near Shaftesbury, Dorset. *Club:* Leander.

HUGHES, Brodie; *see* Hughes, E. B. C.

HUGHES, Sir David (Collingwood), 14th Bt *cr* 1773; heraldic sculptor; Managing Director, Louis Lejeune Ltd, since 1978; *b* 29 Dec. 1936; *s* of Sir Richard Edgar Hughes, 13th Bt and Angela Lilian Adelaide Pell (*d* 1967); *S* father, 1970; *m* 1964, Rosemary Ann Pain, MA, LLB (Cantab), *d* of Rev. John Pain; four *s*. *Educ:* Oundle and Magdalene College, Cambridge (MA). National Service, RN, 1955–57. United Steel Cos Ltd, 1960–65; Unicam Instruments Ltd (subsequently Pye Unicam Ltd), export executive, 1965–70, E Europe manager, 1970–73. Builder, 1974–76. *Recreations:* carpentry, shooting, fishing. *Heir: s* Thomas Collingwood Hughes, *b* 16 Feb. 1966. *Address:* The Berristead, Wilburton, Ely, Cambs. *T:* Ely 740770.

HUGHES, David Evan Peter, MA; Headmaster, St Peter's School, York, since 1980; *b* 27 April 1932; *s* of late Evan Gwilliam Forrest-Hughes, OBE; *m* 1956, Iris (*née* Jenkins); one *s* two *d*. *Educ:* St Paul's Sch.; St John's Coll., Oxford (Gibbs Schol. in Chemistry; MA). National Service, 5 RHA, 1954. Assistant Master, Shrewsbury School, 1956; Head of Chemistry, 1958, Science, 1965; Nuffield Foundation, 1967–68; Second Master, Shrewsbury Sch., 1972. *Publications:* Advanced Theoretical Chemistry (with M. J. Maloney), 1964; Chemical Energetics, 1967. *Recreations:* music, bridge, hill-walking. *Address:* St Catherine's, 11 Clifton, York YO3 6AB. *T:* York 22590. *Club:* East India and Devonshire.

HUGHES, David Glyn; National Agent of the Labour Party, since 1979; *b* 1 March 1928; *s* of Richard and Miriam Hughes; *m* 1958, Mary Atkinson; one *d*. *Educ:* Darwin St Secondary Modern Sch. Apprentice, later fitter and turner, 1944–52; Labour Party Agent: Northwich, Bolton, Tonbridge,

Portsmouth, 1952-69; Asst Regional Organiser, 1969-75, Regional Organiser, 1975-79, Northern Region. *Recreations:* gardening, walking. *Address:* 42 Langroyd Road, SW17. *T:* 01-672 2959. *Clubs:* Stella Maris Social (Life-Mem.), Usworth and District Workmen's (Washington, Tyne and Wear).

HUGHES, Prof. David Leslie, CBE 1977; PhD, FRCVS, DipBact; Professor of Veterinary Pathology, University of Liverpool, 1955-78, now Emeritus Professor; *b* 26 Oct. 1912; *s* of John and Eva Hughes; *m* 1st, 1938, Ann Marjorie Sparks (*d* 1971) 2nd, 1974, Jean Mavis, *yr d* of C. B. Saul. *Educ:* Wycliffe Coll., Stonehouse; Royal Veterinary Coll., London (MRCVS). PhD Nottingham, 1959. Agricultural Research Council Studentship in Animal Health, 1934-37 (DipBact London, 1936); Research Officer, Veterinary Laboratory, Min. of Agriculture, 1937-38; Lecturer in Bacteriology, Royal Veterinary College, 1938-40; Second Scientific Asst, Agricultural Research Council's Field Station, Compton, 1940-46; Head of Veterinary Science Div., Research Dept, Boots Pure Drug Co. Ltd, 1948-55; Dean of Faculty of Veterinary Science, University of Liverpool, 1965-68; Warden, Roscoe Hall, Univ. of Liverpool, 1965-72; Pro-Vice-Chancellor, Univ. of Liverpool, 1975-78. Mem., ARC, 1973-. FRCVS 1952; Mem. Council, RCVS, 1964-76 (Pres. 1974-75; Sen. Vice Pres., 1975-76); Pres., British Veterinary Assoc., 1963-64; Governor, Howells Sch., Denbigh, 1974-. *Publications:* scientific articles in Veterinary Record, British Veterinary Journal, Journal of Comparative Pathology, Journal of Hygiene, etc. *Recreations:* gardening, painting and travel. *Address:* Ty Maen, Llwyn-y-Rhos, Llanrhaeadr, Denbigh, Clwyd LL16 4NH. *T:* Llanynys 364.

HUGHES, David Morgan; His Honour Judge Morgan Hughes; a Circuit Judge, since Nov. 1972; *b* 20 Jan. 1926; *s* of late Rev. John Edward Hughes and Mrs Margaret Ellen Hughes; *m* 1956, Elizabeth Jane Roberts; *one s two d.* *Educ:* Beaumaris Grammar Sch.; LSE (LLB). Army, 1944-48: Captain, Royal Welch Fusiliers; attached 2nd Bn The Welch Regt; Burma, 1945-47. London Univ., 1948-51; Rockefeller Foundn Fellowship in Internat. Air Law, McGill Univ., 1951-52; called to Bar, Middle Temple, 1953; practised Wales and Chester Circuit; Dep. Chm., Caernarvonshire QS, 1970-71; a Recorder, Jan.-Nov. 1972; Dep. Chm., Agricultural Lands Tribunal, 1972. *Recreations:* tennis, cricket, gardening. *Address:* Bryn, Kelsall, Cheshire. *T:* Kelsall 51349.

HUGHES, Hon. Sir Davis, Kt 1975; Agent-General for New South Wales, in London, 1973-78; *b* 24 Nov. 1910; *m* 1940, Joan Philip Johnson; *one s two d.* *Educ:* Launceston High Sch., Tasmania; Phillip Smith Teachers' Coll., Hobart, Tas. Teacher, Tasmania, incl. Friends' Sch., Hobart, 1930-35; Master, Caulfield Grammar Sch., Melbourne, 1935-40. Served War, Sqdn Ldr, RAAF, Australia and overseas, 1940-45. Dep. Headmaster, Armidale Sch., Armidale, NSW, 1946-49; Mayor of Armidale, 1953-56. MLA, NSW, 1950-53 and 1956-65; Minister for Public Works, NSW, 1965-73. Rep., Derek Crouch Aust. Ltd; Chm., Regni River Corp. Ltd. Dir, Société Générale Australia Ltd. Freeman: City of London; City of Armidale, NSW. *Recreations:* tennis, golf, fishing, racing. *Address:* 25 Bligh Street, Sydney, NSW 2000, Australia. *Clubs:* Union, Australasian Pioneers, Australian Golf (Sydney); Armidale (Armidale).

HUGHES, Desmond; *see* Hughes, F. D.

HUGHES, Rev. Edward Marshall, MTh, PhD (London); Vicar of St Mary's, Dover, since 1971; Chaplain to the Queen, since 1973; *b* London, 11 Nov. 1913; *o s* of late Edward William Hughes, Newhouse, Mersham, Ashford, Kent, and Mabel Frances (*née* Faggetter); descendant of Edward Hughes, *b* 1719, of Little Swanton, Mersham; unmarried. *Educ:* City of London Sch.; King's Coll., London; Cuddesdon Coll., Oxford. Deacon, 1936, Priest, 1937, Canterbury; Curate, St Martin's, Canterbury, 1936-41; Chaplain RAFVR 1941 (invalided Oct. 1941); Curate Bearsted, Kent, 1941-46; Vicar of Woodnesborough, Kent, 1946-52; Chap. St Bartholomew's Hosp., Sandwich, 1947-52; Off. Chap. RAF Station, Sandwich, 1948-52; Warden of St Peter's Theological Coll., Jamaica, 1952-61; Canon Missioner of Jamaica, 1955-61; Examining Chap. to the Bp of Jamaica, 1953-61; Hon. Chap. Jamaica, RAFA, 1954-61; Mem. Board of Governors Nuttall Memorial Hospital, Kingston, 1956-61, and St Jago High Sch., Spanish Town, 1957-61; Visiting Lecturer, McGill Univ., Canada, 1957; Hon. Lecturer, Union Theological Seminary, Jamaica, 1957-58; Visiting Lecturer, Séminaire de Théologie, Haiti, 1959; Acting Rector, St Matthew's Church, Kingston, and Chap. Kingston Public Hospital, 1959-60; JP (St Andrew, Jamaica), 1959-63; Commissary to Bishop of Jamaica, 1968-. Fellow (Librarian, 1962-65), St Augustine's Coll., Canterbury (Central Coll. of the Anglican Communion), 1961-65; Hon. helper, RAF Benevolent Fund, for Kent, 1961-65, for London (Croydon), 1965-71, for Kent, 1971-; Divinity Master, VI Forms, The King's Sch., Canterbury, 1962-63; Officiating Chap., Canterbury Garrison, 1963-64; Vicar of St Augustine's, S Croydon, 1965-71. Proctor in Convocation, Dio. Canterbury, 1966-75. Examining Chaplain to Archbishop of Canterbury, 1967-76; Rural Dean of Dover, 1974-80; Hon. Chaplain: East and South Goodwin Lightships, 1979-; Assoc. of Men of Kent and Kentish Men (of which his father was founder-member, 1897), 1979-. *Publications:* various papers on theological education overseas. *Recreations:* cultivating Japanese bonsai, exercising the dogs. *Address:* The Vicarage, Taswell Street, Dover, Kent CT16 1SE. *T:* Dover 206842. *Club:* Royal Cinque Ports Yacht (Dover).

HUGHES, Prof. Sir Edward (Stuart Reginald), Kt 1977; CBE 1971; Chairman and Professor, Department of Surgery, Monash University, Alfred Hospital, since 1973; *b* 4 July 1919; *s* of Reginald Hawkins Hughes and Annie Grace Langford; *m* 1944, Alison Clare Lelean; *two s two d.* *Educ:* Melbourne C of E Grammar Sch.; Univ. of Melbourne. MB, BS 1943; MD 1945; MS 1946; FRCS 1946, FRACS 1950. Resident Medical Officer, Royal Melbourne Hosp., 1943-45, Asst Surgeon 1950-53, Surgeon 1954-74; Surgeon, Alfred Hosp., 1974. Consultant Surgeon to Australian Army, 1976-. Royal Australasian College of Surgeons: Mem. Council, 1967-78; Chm. Exec. Cttee, 1971; Sr Vice-Pres., 1974; Pres., 1975-78. First Dir, Menzies Foundn for Health, Fitness and Physical Achievement, 1979-. Hon. FACS, Hon. FRCS (C), Hon. FRCSE, Hon. FRCSI, Hon. FPCS, 1977. Sir Hugh Devine Medal, RACS, 1977. *Publications:* Surgery of the Anal Canal and Rectum, 1957; All about an Ileostomy, 1966, 3rd edn 1971; All about a Colostomy, 1970, 2nd edn 1977; Ano-Rectal Surgery, 1972. *Recreations:* tennis, racing. *Address:* 24 Somers Avenue, Malvern, Victoria 3144, Australia. *T:* 20.7688. *Clubs:* Melbourne, Melbourne Cricket, Athenæum, Victoria Racing, Victoria Amateur Turf (Melbourne).

HUGHES, Prof. Emmet John; Professor of Politics, Eagleton Institute, Rutgers University, since 1970; *b* 26 Dec. 1920; *s* of Judge John L. Hughes, Summit, NJ; *m* ; *two d* (one *s two d* by previous marriages). *Educ:* Princeton Univ. (AB *summa cum laude*); Columbia Univ. (Graduate Sch.). Press Attaché, American Embassy, Madrid, 1942-46. Chief of Bureau for Time and Life Magazines: Rome, 1947-48, Berlin, 1948, 1949; Articles Editor, for Life Magazine, New York, 1949-53. Administrative Asst to the President of the United States, 1953, Special European Correspondent, Life Magazine, 1953-57; Chief of Foreign Correspondents, Time and Life, 1957-60; Senior Advisor on Public Affairs to the Rockefeller Brothers, 1960-63; Newsweek columnist and editorial consultant, Washington Post Co., 1963-68; Special Asst to Governor of NY State, 1968-70. *Publications:* The Church and the Liberal Society, 1944; Report from Spain, 1947; America the Vincible, 1959; The Ordeal of Power, 1963; The Living Presidency, 1973. *Address:* c/o Eagleton Institute, Rutgers University, New Brunswick, NJ 08903, USA.

HUGHES, (Ernest) Brodie (Cobbett), FRCS; Professor of Neurosurgery, 1948-78, and Dean of the Faculty of Medicine and Dentistry, 1974-78, University of Birmingham; *b* 21 Sept. 1913; *o s* of E. T. C. Hughes, surgeon, and D. K. Cobbett, Richmond, Surrey; *m* 1971, Frances Wendy Alexander. *Educ:* Eastbourne Coll.; University Coll. and Hospital, London. MB, BS London 1937, FRCS 1939, ChM Birmingham 1949; resident appointments, UC Hospital, and at National Hospital for Nervous Diseases, Queen Square, London. After various appointments in neurosurgery was appointed Neurosurgeon, Birmingham United Hospitals, 1947. *Publications:* The Visual Fields, 1955; various publications in medical journals on neurosurgery and on perimetry and visual fields in particular. *Recreations:* playing the oboe, fly-fishing for trout; unsuccessful attempts to paint and draw in oils, water-colour, pen-and-ink and other media. *Address:* Fairfield House South, Saxmundham, Suffolk IP17 1AX. *T:* Saxmundham 2060. *Club:* Athenæum.

HUGHES, Air Vice-Marshal (Frederick) Desmond, CB 1972; CBE 1961; DSO 1945; DFC and 2 bars, 1941-43; AFC 1954; *b* Belfast, 6 June 1919; *s* of late Fred C. Hughes, company dir, Donaghadee, Co. Down, and late Hilda (*née* Hunter), Ballymore, Co. Donegal; *m* 1941, Pamela, *d* of late Julius Harrison, composer and conductor; *two s.* *Educ:* Campbell Coll., Belfast; Pembroke Coll., Cambridge (MA). Joined RAF from Cambridge Univ. Air Sqdn, 1939; Battle of Britain, No. 264 Sqdn, 1940; night fighting ops in Britain and Mediterranean theatre, 1941-43; comd No. 604 Sqdn in Britain and France, 1944-45; granted perm. commn, 1946; served in Fighter Comd, 1946-53; Directing Staff, RAF Staff Coll., 1954-56; Personal Staff Off. to Chief of Air Staff, 1956-58; comd. RAF Stn Geilenkirchen, 1959-61; Dir of Air Staff Plans, Min. of Def., 1962-64; ADC to the Queen, 1963; Air Officer i/c Administration, HQ Flying Training Command, RAF, 1966-68; AOC, No 18 Group, RAF Coastal Command, and Air Officer, Scotland and N Ireland, 1968-70; Comdt, RAF Coll., Cranwell, 1970-72; SASO Near East Air Force, 1972-74, retired. Hon. Air Cdre, No 2503 RAuxAF Regt Sqdn, 1982-. Dir, Trident Trust, 1976-78. *Recreations:* fishing, shooting, music. *Address:* c/o Midland Bank Ltd, Sleaford, Lincs. *Club:* Royal Air Force.

HUGHES, George; Chairman and Chief Executive: Hughes International Ltd, since 1970; Willowbrook World Wide Ltd, since 1971; Castle Hughes Group Ltd, since 1975; *b* 4 May 1937; *s* of Peter and Ann Hughes; *m* 1963, Janet; *two s.* *Educ:* Liverpool Collegiate (Sen. City Scholar); Gonville and Caius Coll., Cambridge (Open Scholar; MA Hons 1st Cl. German Mod. Lang. Tripos); Harvard Business Sch. (MBA 1968). Ski instructor, 1959; Banking, Paris, 1960; IBM, London, 1960-69 (Strategy Develt Man., 1968-69); Merchant Banking, London, 1969-70; Gp Man. Dir, Duple Gp Ltd, 1970-71. *Publications:* The Effective Use of Computers, 1968; Military and Business Strategy, 1968; papers on mobility: a basic human need; traffic congestion in capital cities; development as strategic choice; getting action and making things happen; integrated cattle development program; choosing the best way; scenario for the president; new towns; control. *Recreations:* cattle farming, historic buildings, shooting, soccer, tennis, squash, racehorses. *Address:* Hampton Court, Herefordshire HR6 0PN; Chateau Beauchamps, Sarthe, France. *Clubs:* MCC, Carlton.

HUGHES, Prof. George Morgan; Professor of Zoology, Bristol University, since 1965; Head of Research Unit for Comparative Animal Respiration, since 1970; *b* 17 March 1925; *s* of James Williams Hughes and Edith May Hughes; *m* 1954, Jean Rosemary, *d* of Rowland Wynne Frazier and Jessie Frazier; two *s* one *d. Educ:* Liverpool Collegiate Sch.; King's Coll., Cambridge (Scholar). Martin Thackeray Studentship, 1946–48, MA, PhD, ScD (Cantab); Frank Smart Prize, 1946. Cambridge Univ. Demonstrator, 1950–55, Lectr, 1955–65; successively Bye-Fellow, Research Fellow and Fellow of Magdalene Coll., Cambridge, 1949–65. Univ. of Bristol: Head of Dept of Zoology, 1965–70. Research Fellow, California Inst. of Technology, 1958–59; Visiting Lectr in Physiology, State Univ. of New York, at Buffalo, 1964; Visiting Professor: Duke Univ., 1969; Japan Society for the Promotion of Science, Kochi, Kyoto, Kyushu and Hokkaido Univs, 1974; Univ. of Regensburg, 1977; Univs of Bhagalpur and Bretagne Occidentale, 1979. Invited Prof., Nat. Inst. of Physiolog. Sciences, Okazaki, 1980. Mem., Internat. Coelacanth Expdn, 1972. *Publications:* Comparative Physiology of Vertebrate Respiration, 1963; Physiology of Mammals and other Vertebrates (jt), 1965; (ed) several symposium vols; papers in Jl of Experimental Biology and other scientific jls, mainly on respiration of fishes. *Recreations:* travel, golf, photography; hockey for Cambridge Univ., 1945, and Wales, 1952-53. *Address:* 11 Lodge Drive, Long Ashton, Bristol BS18 9JF. *T:* Long Ashton 3402.

HUGHES, George Ravensworth, CVO 1943; *b* 16 June 1888; *s* of Thomas McKenny Hughes, formerly Professor of Geology at Cambridge Univ.; *m* 1917, Margaret (*d* 1967), *d* of His Honour Judge Graham; one *s* one *d. Educ:* Eton; Trinity Coll., Cambridge. Clerk of the Worshipful Company of Goldsmiths, 1938–53. *Publications:* The Plate of the Goldsmiths' Co. (with J. B. Carrington), 1926; The Goldsmiths' Company as Patrons of their craft, 1919 to 1953; Articles on Antique and Modern Silverwork. *Recreations:* music, gardening, and golf. *Address:* Plummers, Bishopstone, Seaford, East Sussex. *T:* Seaford 892958. *Club:* Athenæum.

HUGHES, Brig. Gerald Birdwood V.; *see* Vaughan-Hughes.

HUGHES, Glyn Tegai, MA, PhD; Warden of Gregynog, University of Wales, since 1964; *b* 18 Jan. 1923; *s* of Rev. John Hughes and Keturah Hughes; *m* 1957, Margaret Vera Herbert, Brisbane, Qld; two *s. Educ:* Newtown and Towyn County Sch.; Liverpool Institute; Manchester Grammar Sch.; Corpus Christi Coll., Cambridge (Schol., MA, PhD). Served War, Royal Welch Fusiliers, 1942-46 (Major). Lector in English, Univ. of Basel, 1951-53; Lectr in Comparative Literary Studies, Univ. of Manchester, 1953-64, and Tutor to Faculty of Arts, 1961-64. Contested (L) Denbigh Div., elections 1950, 1955 and 1959. Mem., Welsh Arts Council, 1967-76; Nat. Governor for Wales, BBC, and Chm., Broadcasting Council for Wales, 1971-79; Member: Bd, Channel Four Television Co., 1980-; Welsh Fourth TV Channel Auth., 1981-; Vice-Pres., N Wales Arts Assoc.; Chm., Undeb Cymru Fydd, 1968-70. *Publications:* Eichendorffs Taugenichts, 1961; Romantic German Literature, 1979; (ed) Life of Thomas Olivers, 1979; articles in learned journals and Welsh language periodicals. *Recreation:* book-collecting. *Address:* Gregynog, Newtown, Powys. *T:* Tregynon 295.

HUGHES, (Harold) Paul; Director of Finance, British Broadcasting Corporation, since 1971; Director: Kleinwort Benson Farmland Trust (Managers) Ltd, since 1976; *b* 16 Oct. 1926; *o s* of Edmund and Mabel Hughes; *m* 1955, Beryl Winifred Runacres; one *s* one *d. Educ:* Stand Grammar Sch., Whitefield, near Manchester. Certified Accountant. Westminster Bank Ltd, 1942-45; Royal Marines and Royal Navy, 1945-49; Arthur Guinness Son & Co. Ltd, 1950-58; British Broadcasting Corporation: Sen. Accountant, 1958-61; Asst Chief Accountant, Finance, 1961-69; Chief Accountant, Television, 1969-71. *Recreations:* opera, gardening. *Address:* 26 Downside Road, Guildford, Surrey. *T:* Guildford 69166.

HUGHES, Harold Victor; Principal, Royal Agricultural College, Cirencester, since 1978; *b* 2 Feb. 1926; *s* of Thomas Brindley Hughes and Hilda Hughes (*née* Williams). *Educ:* Tenby County Grammar Sch.; UCW, Aberystwyth. Lectr, Glamorgan Training Centre, Pencoed, 1947-49; Crop Husbandry Adv. Officer, W Midland Province, Nat. Agricultural Adv. Service, 1950; Lectr in Agric., RAC, 1950-54; Vice Principal, Brooksby Agricultural Coll., Leics, 1954-60; Royal Agricultural College: Farms Dir and Principal Lectr in Farm Management, 1960-76; Vice Principal and Farms Dir, 1976-78. *Publications:* articles in learned jls and agric. press. *Recreations:* shooting, rugby. *Address:* Royal Agricultural College, Cirencester, Glos. *T:* Cirencester 2531. *Club:* Farmers'.

HUGHES, Rear-Adm. Henry Hugh, CB 1966; retired, 1968; *b* 9 March 1911; British; *m* 1939, Margaret (*née* Lycett); two *d. Educ:* Clydebank High Sch.; Glasgow Univ. (BSc Hons). English Electric Co. Ltd, Stafford, 1932-42; Electrical Officer, RNVR, 1942-45; transf. to RN as Lieut-Comdr, 1945; Comdr 1947; Capt. 1956; Rear-Adm. 1964. HMS Vanguard, 1947-49; subsequently: various appts in Admty and Dockyards; in comd, HMS Collingwood, 1962-63; Dep. Dir of Electrical Engrg, 1963-64; Dir, Naval Electrical Engrg, 1964; Chief Naval Engineer Officer, 1967-68. *Recreation:* tennis. *Address:* Tigh Failté, Argyll Terrace, Tobermory, Isle of Mull, Scotland. *T:* Tobermory 06882432.

HUGHES, Rev. Henry Trevor, MA; *b* 27 Feb. 1910; *s* of late Rev. Dr H. Maldwyn Hughes; *m* 1946, Elizabeth Catherine Williams; one *s* one *d. Educ:* Perse Sch., Cambridge. National Provincial Bank, 1926-31; Wesley House,

Cambridge, 1932-35 (2nd Class Hons Theol Tripos, 1935); Chaplain, Culford Sch., Bury St Edmunds, 1935-41; Chaplain, Royal Air Force, 1941-45 (despatches). Asst Minister, Central Hall, Westminster, 1945-46; Vice-Principal and Chaplain, Westminster College of Education, 1946-53, Principal, 1953-69; Minister, Attleborough Methodist Church, 1969-75. Incorporated MA, Oxford Univ. through Lincoln Coll., 1959. Governor: Culford Sch., Bury St Edmunds; Wymondham Coll. First Methodist Select Preacher, University of Oxford, 1965; Methodist representative, British Council of Churches Preachers' Exchange with the USA, 1964. *Publications:* Prophetic Prayer, 1947; Teaching the Bible to Seniors, 1948; Teaching the Bible to Juniors, 1949; Why We Believe, 1950; The Piety of Jeremy Taylor, 1960; Faith and Life, 1962; Life Worth Living, 1965; A Progress of Pilgrims, 1979; pamphlets: Letters to a Christian, 1947; Teaching the Bible Today, 1957; contributor to London Quarterly Review. *Recreation:* painting. *Address:* 102 New Road, Hethersett, Norfolk NR9 3HQ. *T:* Norwich 811038.

HUGHES, Herbert Delauney, MA; Principal of Ruskin College, Oxford, 1950-79; *b* 7 Sept. 1914; *s* of late Arthur Percy Hughes, BSc, and late Maggie Ellen Hughes; *m* 1937, Beryl Parker. *Educ:* Cheadle Hulme Sch.; Balliol Coll., Oxford (State and County Major Scholar). BA (Hons) in Modern History, 1936. Served War of 1939-45, with 6 Field Regt Royal Artillery. Asst Sec., New Fabian Research Bureau, 1937-39; Organising Sec., Fabian Soc., 1939-46; Mem. Exec. Fabian Soc., 1946- (Vice-Chm. 1950-52, 1958-59, Chm. 1959-60, Vice-Pres., 1971-); MP (Lab) Wolverhampton (West), 1945-50; Parliamentary Private Sec. to Minister of Education, 1945-47; to Financial Sec. to War Office, 1948-50; Mem. Lambeth Borough Council, 1937-42. Governor of Educational Foundation for Visual Aids, 1948-56. Member: Civil Service Arbitration Tribunal, 1955-81; Commonwealth Scholarship Commn, 1968-74; Cttee on Adult Educn, 1969-73. Vice-Pres., Workers' Educational Assoc., 1958-67, Dep. Pres., 1968-71, Pres., 1971-81, Hon. Treasurer, 1981-; Chm. Management Cttee, Adult Literacy Resource Agency, 1975-78; Mem., Adv. Council on Adult and Continuing Educn, 1978-. Hon. Fellow Sheffield Polytechnic, 1979. *Publications:* (part author) Democratic Sweden, 1937, Anderson's Prisoners, 1940, Six Studies in Czechoslovakia, 1947. Advance in Education, 1947; Towards a Classless Society, 1947; A Socialist Education Policy, 1955; The Settlement of Disputes in The Public Service, 1968; (jt author) Planning for Education in 1980, 1970; (part author) Education Beyond School, 1980. *Recreations:* walking and foreign travel. *Address:* Crossways, Mill Street, Islip, Oxford. *T:* Kidlington 6935.

HUGHES, Sir Jack (William), Kt 1980; chartered surveyor; Consultant, Jones, Lang, Wootton, International Real Estate Advisers, since 1976; Chairman, Property Advisory Group, Department of the Environment, since 1978; Director: South Bank Estates, since 1960; URPT, since 1961; Public Property Companies, MEPC, since 1971; Brighton Marina Co. (Representative, Brighton Corporation), since 1974; British Rail Property Board, since 1976; British Rail Investment Co., since 1981; TR Property Investment Trust, since 1982; Property and Reversionary Investment, since 1982; *b* 26 Sept. 1916; 2nd *s* of George William Hughes and Isabel Hughes, Maidstone, Kent; *m* 1939, Marie-Theresa (Slade School trained artist), *d* of Graham Parmley Thompson. *Educ:* Maidstone Grammar Sch.; Univ. of London. BSc (Est. Man.); FRICS. Served with Special Duties Br., RAF, 1940-46; demobilised Squadron Leader. A Sen. Partner, Jones, Lang, Wootton, 1949-76. Chm., Bracknell Develt Corp., 1971-82; Dir, Housing Corporation (1974) Ltd, 1974-78; Mem. Cttee, Mercantile Credit Gp Property Div.; Mem. Cttee of Management, Charities Property Unit Trust, 1967-74; Chm., South Hill Park Arts Centre Trust, 1972-79; Member: Adv. Gp to DoE on Commercial Property, 1974-78; DoE Working Party on Housing Tenure, 1976-77. Trustee, New Towns Pension Fund, 1975-82. Freeman, City of London, 1959-; Liveryman, Painter Stainers Guild, 1960-. FRSA. *Publications:* (jtly) Town and Country Planning Act 1949 (RICS); (Chm. of RICS Cttee) The Land Problem: a fresh approach; techn. articles on property investment, develt and finance. *Recreations:* golf, travel, reading. *Address:* Flat 11, 102 Rochester Row, SW1. *Clubs:* Buck's, Carlton, RAFVR.

HUGHES, John; *see* Hughes, R. J.

HUGHES, Prof. John, PhD; Director, Parke-Davis Research Unit, Addenbrooke's, Cambridge, since 1983; Senior Research Fellow, Wolfson College, University of Cambridge, since 1983; Professor of Pharmacological Biochemistry, Department of Biochemistry, Imperial College of Science and Technology, University of London, 1979-82, Visiting Professor, since 1983; *b* 6 Jan. 1942; *s* of Joseph and Edith Hughes; *m* 1967, Madelaine Carol Jennings (marr. diss. 1981); one *d. Educ:* Mitcham County Grammar Sch. for Boys; Chelsea Coll., London (BSc); Inst. of Basic Med. Sciences, London (PhD). Res. Fellow, Yale Univ. Med. Sch., 1967-69; Univ. of Aberdeen: Lectr in Pharmacology, 1969-77; Dep.-Dir, Drug Res. Unit, 1973-77; Reader in Pharmacol Biochemistry, Imperial Coll. of Science and Technol., 1977-79. Dr *hc* Univ. of Liège, 1978. Lasker Prize, Albert and Mary Lasker Foundn, NY, 1978; W. Feldberg Foundn Award, 1981. *Publications:* Centrally Acting Peptides, 1978; articles in Nature, Science, Brit. Jl Pharmacol., and Brain Res. *Address:* Parke-Davis Research Unit, Addenbrooke's Hospital, Red Cross Lane, Cambridge.

HUGHES, Very Rev. John Chester; Vicar of Bringhurst with Great Easton and Drayton, since 1978; *b* 20 Feb. 1924; *m* 1950, Sybil Lewis McClelland; three *s* two *d* (and one *s* decd). *Educ:* Dulwich Coll.; St John's Coll., Durham. Curate of Westcliffe-on-Sea, Essex, 1950-53; Succentor of Chelmsford

Cathedral, 1953-55; Vicar of St Barnabas, Leicester, 1955-61; Vicar of Croxton Kerrial with Branston-by-Belvoir, 1961-63; Provost of Leicester, 1963-78. ChStJ 1974. *Address:* The Vicarage, Great Easton, Market Harborough, Leics LE16 8SX. *T:* Rockingham 770279.

HUGHES, John Dennis; Principal, Ruskin College, Oxford, since 1979 (Tutor in Economics and Industrial Relations, 1957-70, and Vice Principal, 1970-79); *b* 28 Jan. 1927; *s* of John (Ben) Hughes and Gwendoline Hughes; *m* 1949, Violet (*née* Henderson); four *d*. *Educ:* Westminster City Sch.; Lincoln Coll., Oxford (MA). Lieut, RAEC, 1949-50. Extramural Tutor, Univs of Hull and Sheffield, 1950-57. Dir, Trade Union Res. Unit, 1970-; Dep. Chm., Price Commn, 1977-79. Member: Industrial Develt Adv. Bd, 1975-79; Nat. Consumer Council, 1982-. Governor, London Business School. Mem. Council, St George's House, 1978-; Trustee, Merchant Navy and Airline Officers Assoc., 1981-. *Publications:* Trade Union Structure and Government, 1968; (with R. Moore) A Special Case? Social Justice and the Miners, 1972; (with H. Pollins) Trade Unions in Great Britain, 1973; Industrial Restructuring: some manpower aspects, 1976; Britain in Crisis, 1981; Fabian Soc. pamphlets. *Recreation:* cycling. *Address:* Rookery Cottage, Stoke Place, Old Headington, Oxford. *T:* Oxford 63076.

HUGHES, John Richard Poulton; DL; County Clerk and Chief Executive, Staffordshire County Council, and Clerk to the Lieutenancy, since 1978; *b* 21 Oct. 1920; *s* of Rev. John Evan Hughes and Mary Grace Hughes; *m* 1943, Mary Margaret, *e d* of Thomas Francis Thomas; one *s*. *Educ:* Bromsgrove Sch.; LLB Hons London; DPA; LMRTPI. Solicitor. Served War, RN and RNVR, 1940-46; discharged with rank of Lieut, RNVR. Articled in private practice, 1937-40; Asst Solicitor: West Bromwich County Borough Council, 1947-48; Surrey CC, 1948-50; Staffs County Council: Sen. Asst Solicitor, subseq. Chief Asst Solicitor, and Dep. Clerk, 1950-74; Dir of Admin, 1974-78; Sec., Staffs Probation and After Care Cttee, 1978-. DL Staffs, 1979. *Recreations:* forestry, antiques restoration, sailing, fishing. *Address:* Brookside, Milford, near Stafford. *T:* Stafford 61005; Tyn Siglen, Cynwyd, Clwyd.

See also Sir T. P. Hughes.

HUGHES, Rt. Rev. John Richard Worthington P.; *see* Poole Hughes.

HUGHES, Rt. Rev. John Taylor, CBE 1975; an Assistant Bishop, Diocese of Canterbury, since 1977; *b* 12 April 1908; *s* of Robert Edward and Annie Hughes. *Educ:* Castle Hill Sch., Ealing; Uxbridge County Sch.; Bede Coll., University of Durham (BA 1931, MA 1935). Ordained 1931; Asst Chaplain and Tutor, Bede Coll., Durham, 1931-34; Lecturer, Bede Coll., 1934-35; Curate, St John's, Shildon Co. Durham, 1934-37; Vicar, St James, West Hartlepool, 1937-48; Canon Residentiary and Missioner of Southwark Cathedral. Warden of Diocesan Retreat House, Southwark, 1948-56; Bishop Suffragan of Croydon, 1956-77; Archdeacon of Croydon, 1967-77; Bishop to the Forces, 1966-75. *Recreations:* music, reading. *Address:* 1 Burgate House, Burgate, Canterbury, Kent CT1 2HB. *T:* Canterbury 69351.

HUGHES, Prof. Leslie Ernest, FRCS, FRACS; Professor of Surgery, Welsh National School of Medicine, since 1971; *b* 12 Aug. 1932; *s* of Charles Joseph and Vera Hughes; *m* 1955, Marian Castle; two *s* two *d*. *Educ:* Parramatta High Sch.; Sydney Univ. MB, BS (Sydney); DS (Queensland), 1975; FRCS, 1959; FRACS, 1959. Reader in Surgery, Univ. of Queensland, 1965-71. Eleanor Roosevelt Internat. Cancer Fellow, 1970. *Publications:* numerous papers in medical jls, chiefly on immune aspects of cancer, and diseases of the colon. *Recreation:* music. *Address:* Department of Surgery, University Hospital of Wales, Heath Park, Cardiff CF4 4XW. *T:* Cardiff 755944.

HUGHES, Mark; *see* Hughes, W. M.

HUGHES, Paul; *see* Hughes, H. P.

HUGHES, Paul Grant; His Honour Judge Paul Hughes; a Circuit Judge, since 1978; *b* 22 March 1928; *s* of Charles Alban Hughes and Kathleen Gough Hughes. *Educ:* Giggleswick School; King's Coll., Cambridge (MA, LLB). RAF, 1946-48. Called to Bar, Inner Temple, 1952. Housemaster, Merton House, Penmaenmawr, 1953-58; Barrister, Nottingham, 1958-78. Part-time Chm., Mental Health Review Tribunal, 1971-78. *Recreations:* nature conservation (Treasurer, Notts Trust for Nature Conservation, 1972-), walking, gardening, opera. *Address:* 203 Loughborough Road, Ruddington, Nottingham. *T:* Nottingham 212275.

HUGHES, Philip Arthur Booley, CBE 1982; artist; Chairman, Logica Holdings Ltd, since 1972; Member, Science and Engineering Research Council, since 1981; *s* of Leslie Booley Hughes and Elizabeth Alice Hughes (*née* Whyte); *m* 1964, Psiche Maria Anna Claudia Bertini; two *d* and two step-*d*. *Educ:* Bedford Sch.; Clare Coll., Cambridge (BA). Engineer, Shell Internat. Petroleum Co., 1957-61; Computer Consultant, SCICON Ltd (formerly CEIR), 1961-69; Co-Founder, Logica, 1969; Man. Dir, Logica Ltd, 1969-72. Vis. Prof., UCL, 1981-. Governor, Technical Change Centre, 1980-. Exhibn of paintings with Beryl Bainbridge, Monks Gall., Sussex, 1972; one-man exhibitions: Parkway Focus Gall., London, 1976; Angela Flowers Gall., London, 1977; Gal. Cance Manguin, Vaucluse, 1979; Francis Kyle Gall., London, 1979. *Publications:* articles in nat. press and learned jls on management scis and computing. *Address:* 18 Rochester Terrace, NW1. *T:* 01-485 1635.

HUGHES, Major Richard Charles, MBE 1951; TD 1945; Director, Federation of Commodity Associations, 1973-78; *b* 24 Dec. 1915; *s* of late Frank Pemberton Hughes and Minnie Hughes, Northwich. *Educ:* Wrekin Coll., Wellington, Telford. TA commn, 4/5th (E of C) Cheshire Regt, 1935; regular commn, 22nd (Cheshire) Regt, 1939. Served War of 1939-45: 2 i/c 5th, 2nd and 1st Bns 22nd (Cheshire) Regt. Palestine, 1945-47; S/Captain MS and DAAG Western Comd, 1948-51; Korea, 1954; GSO2 Sch. of Infantry, 1955-56; Sec. of Sch. of Inf. Beagles, 1955-56; retd pay, 1958. Apptd Sec. to Sugar Assoc. of London, British Sugar Refiners Assoc. and Refined Sugar Assoc., 1958; formed British Sugar Bureau and apptd Sec., 1964-66. Hon. Treas., W Kensington Environment Cttee, 1974-75; Mem. Barons Keep Management Cttee, 1975. Member: City Liaison Cttee, Bank of England and City EEC Cttee, 1975; City Adv. Panel to City Univ., and Adviser to City of London Polytechnic, 1975; City Communications Consultative Gp, 1976. *Recreations:* travel, sailing, golf, beagling, antiques. *Address:* 8 Barons Keep, Barons Court, W14 9AT. *T:* 01-603 0429. *Club:* Hurlingham.

HUGHES, Robert; MP (Lab) Aberdeen North since 1970; *b* Pittenweem, Fife, 3 Jan. 1932; *m* 1957, Ina Margaret Miller; two *s* three *d*. *Educ:* Robert Gordon's Coll., Aberdeen; Benoni High Sch., Transvaal; Pietermaritzburg Techn. Coll., Natal. Emigrated S Africa, 1947, returned UK, 1954. Engrg apprentice, S African Rubber Co., Natal; Chief Draughtsman, C. F. Wilson & Co. (1932) Ltd, Aberdeen, until 1970. Mem., Aberdeen Town Council, 1962-70; Convener: Health and Welfare Cttee, 1963-68; Social Work Cttee, 1969-70. Mem., AEU, 1952-. Contested (Lab) North Angus and Mearns, 1959. Mem., Standing Cttee on Immigration Bill, 1971; former Mem., Select Cttee, Scottish Affairs; introd. Divorce (Scotland) Bill 1971 (failed owing to lack of time); Parly Under-Sec. of State, Scottish Office, 1974-75; sponsored (as Private Member's Bill) Rating (Disabled Persons) Act 1978; Junior opposition spokesman on transport, 1981-. Chm., Aberdeen City Labour Party, 1961-69. Founder Mem. and Aberdeen Chm., Campaign for Nuclear Disarmament; Vice-Chm., 1975-76, Chm., 1976-, Anti-Apartheid Movement; Member: Gen. Med. Council, 1976-79; Movement for Colonial Freedom, 1955- (Chm. Southern Africa Cttee); Scottish Poverty Action Group; Aberdeen Trades Council and Exec. Cttee, 1957-69; Labour Party League of Youth, 1954-57. *Recreation:* golf. *Address:* House of Commons, SW1; 23 Lisburne Road, Hampstead, NW3.

HUGHES, (Robert) John; Assistant Secretary of State for Public Affairs, USA, since 1982; *b* Neath, S Wales, 28 April 1930; *s* of Evan John Hughes and Dellis May Hughes (*née* Williams); *m* 1955, Vera Elizabeth Pockman; one *s* one *d*. *Educ:* Stationers' Company's Sch., London. Reporter, sub-editor, corresp. for miscellaneous London and S African newspapers and news agencies (Natal Mercury, Durban; Daily Mirror, Daily Express, Reuter, London News Agency), 1946-54; joined The Christian Science Monitor, Boston, USA, 1954: Africa Corresp., 1955-61; Asst Foreign Editor, 1962-64; Far East Corresp., 1964-70; Man. Editor, 1970; Editor, 1970-76; Editor and Manager, 1976-79; Pres. and Publisher, Hughes Newspapers Inc., USA, 1979-81; Dir, Voice of America, 1982. Nieman Fellow, Harvard Univ., 1961-62. Pres., Amer. Soc. of Newspaper Editors, 1978-79. Pulitzer Prize for Internat. Reporting, 1967; Overseas Press Club of America award for best daily newspaper or wire service reporting from abroad, 1970; Sigma Delta Chi's Yankee Quill Award, 1977. Hon. LLD Colby Coll., 1978. *Publications:* The New Face of Africa, 1961; Indonesian Upheaval (UK as The End of Sukarno), 1967; articles in magazines and encyclopaedias. *Recreations:* reading, walking, raising Labrador retrievers. *Address:* Box 1053, Orleans, Mass 02653, USA. *T:* (617) 255-3133. *Clubs:* Foreign Correspondents', Hong Kong Country (Hong Kong); Overseas Press (New York); Harvard (Boston).

HUGHES, Robert Studley Forrest; Senior Writer (Art Critic), Time Magazine, New York, since 1970; *b* Sydney, Aust., 28 July 1938; *s* of Geoffrey E. F. Hughes and Margaret Sealey Vidal; (marr. diss. 1981); one *s*; *m* 1981, Victoria Whistler. *Educ:* St Ignatius' Coll., Riverview, Sydney; Sydney Univ. (architecture course, unfinished). Contributed articles on art to The Nation and The Observer, Sydney, 1958-62; to Europe, 1964, living in Italy until 1966, when moved to London; freelancing for Sunday Times, BBC and other publications/instns, 1966-70. TV credits include: Landscape with Figures, ten-part series on Australian art for ABC, Australia; Caravaggio, Rubens and Bernini, for BBC, 1976-77; The Shock of the New, eight-part series for BBC, 1980. Hon. Dr Fine Arts, Sch. of Visual Arts, NY, 1982. *Publications:* The Art of Australia, 1966; Heaven and Hell in Western Art, 1969; The Shock of the New (BBC publication), 1980. *Recreations:* gardening, shooting, river and sea fishing, cooking. *Address:* 143 Prince Street, New York, NY 10012, USA.

HUGHES, Air Marshal Sir Rochford; *see* Hughes, Air Marshal Sir S. W. R.

HUGHES, Royston John; MP (Lab) Newport, Gwent, since 1966; *b* 9 June 1925; *s* of John Hughes, Coal Miner; *m* 1957, Florence Marion Appleyard; three *d*. *Educ:* Ruskin Coll., Oxford. Mem. Coventry City Council, 1962-66; various offices in Transport and General Workers' Union, 1959-66. PPS to Minister of Transport, 1974-75; Chairman: Parly Labour Party Sports Gp, 1974-; PLP Steel Group, 1978-; Parly Gp, TGWU, 1979-. *Recreations:* gardening, watching rugby and soccer. *Address:* 34 St Kingsmark Avenue, Chepstow, Gwent. *T:* 3266. *Clubs:* United Service Mess (Cardiff); Pontllanfraith Workingmen's Social.

HUGHES, Prof. Sean Patrick Francis, FRCS, FRCSEd, FRCSI; George Harrison Law Professor of Orthopaedic Surgery, University of Edinburgh, since 1979; *b* 2 Dec. 1941; *s* of Patrick Joseph Hughes and Kathleen Ethel Hughes (*née* Bigg); *m* 1972, Felicity Mary (*née* Anderson); one *s* two *d*. *Educ*: Downside Sch.; St Mary's Hospital, Univ. of London (MB BS, MS). Senior Registrar in Orthopaedics, Middlesex and Royal National Orthopaedic Hosp., 1974-76; Research Fellow in Orthopaedics, Mayo Clinic, USA, 1975; Sen. Lectr, and Director Orthopaedic Unit, Royal Postgraduate Medical Sch., Hammersmith Hosp., 1977-79. Fellow: Brit. Orthopaedic Assoc.; Royal Soc. Med.; Member: Orthopaedic Research Soc.; British Orth. Res. Soc.; Soc. Internat. de Chirurgie Orth. et de Traumatologie; World Orth. Concern. *Publications*: Astons Short Text Book of Orthopaedics, 2nd edn 1976, 3rd edn 1982; Basis and Practice of Orthopaedics, 1981; Basis and Practice of Trauma, 1982; papers on blood flow and mineral exchange, bone scanning, antibiotics in bone, external fixation of fractures. *Recreations*: sailing, golf. *Address*: 9 Corrennie Gardens, Edinburgh EH10 6DG. *T*: 031-337 1443.

HUGHES, Air Marshal Sir (Sidney Weetman) Rochford, KCB 1967 (CB 1964); CBE 1955 (OBE 1942); AFC 1947; Chairman, Mazda Motors (NZ); Director: NZ Steel; NZ Steel Development; Dillingham Industries (NZ) Ltd; General Accident Fire & Life (NZ); *b* 25 Oct. 1914; *s* of late Capt. H. R. Hughes, Master Mariner, and late Mrs Hughes (*née* Brigham), Auckland, NZ; *m* 1942, Elizabeth, *d* of A. Duncum, Colombo, Ceylon; one *d*. *Educ*: Waitaki High School; Oamaru, NZ. Editorial Staff, NZ Herald, 1933-36; RNZ Air Force, 1937-38; RAF, Far East and Middle East, 1939-44 (despatches; Greek DFC); Chief Ops, USAF All Weather Centre, 1948-49; Air Min. and CO Farnborough, 1950-54; Imperial Defence Coll., 1955; CO RAF Jever, Germany, 1956-59; Air Mem. and Chm., Defence Res. Policy Staff, MoD, 1959-61; Air Officer Commanding No 19 Group, 1962-64; Dep. Controller Aircraft (RAF), Ministry of Aviation, 1964-66; Air Comdr, Far East Air Force, 1966-69, retd 1969. Air Adviser, Civil and Military, to Govt of Singapore, 1969-72; Comr, Northland Harbour Bd, 1974. Pres., NZ Nat. Children's Health Res. Foundn. Livery Guild of Air Pilots and Air Navigators; FRAeS. *Recreations*: yachting, motoring, photography. *Address*: Tirimoana, 14 Cliff Road, Torbay, Auckland, New Zealand. *Club*: Royal NZ Yacht Squadron.

HUGHES, Ted, OBE 1977; author; *b* 1930; *s* of William Henry Hughes and Edith Farrar Hughes; *m* 1956, Sylvia Plath (*d* 1963); one *s* one *d*; *m* 1970, Carol Orchard. *Educ*: Pembroke Coll., Cambridge Univ. Author of Orghast (performed at 5th Festival of Arts of Shiraz, Persepolis, 1971). Awards: first prize, Guinness Poetry Awards, 1958; John Simon Guggenheim Fellow, 1959-60; Somerset Maugham Award, 1960; Premio Internazionale Taormina, 1973; The Queen's Medal for Poetry, 1974. *Publications*: The Hawk in the Rain, 1957 (First Publication Award, NY, 1957); Lupercal, 1960 (Hawthornden Prize, 1961); Meet My Folks! (children's verse), 1961; The Earth-Owl and Other Moon People (children's verse), 1963 (US as Moon Whales, 1976); How the Whale Became (children's stories), 1963; (ed, jtly) Five American Poets, 1963; Selected Poems of Keith Douglas (with Introduction), 1964; Nessie, The Mannerless Monster (children's verse story), 1964 (US as Nessie the Monster, 1974); Recklings, 1966; The Burning of the Brothel, 1966; Scapegoats and Rabies, 1967; Animal Poems, 1967; Wodwo, 1967 (City of Florence Internat. Poetry Prize, 1969); Poetry in the Making, 1967 (US as Poetry Is, 1970); The Iron Man (children's story) (US as The Iron Giant, 1968); (ed) A Choice of Emily Dickinson's Verse, 1968; Five Autumn Songs for Children's Voices, 1968; Adaptation of Seneca's Oedipus, 1969 (play, National Theatre, 1968); (libretto) The Demon of Adachigahara, 1969; The Coming of the Kings (4 plays for children), 1970 (US as The Tiger's Bones, 1974); Crow, 1970; A Few Crows, 1970; Crow Wakes, 1970; (ed) A Choice of Shakespeare's Verse, 1971 (US as With Fairest Flowers while Summer Lasts); Shakespeare's Poem, 1971; (with R. Fainlight and Alan Sillitoe) Poems, 1971; Eat Crow, 1971; Prometheus on His Crag, 1973; Spring Summer Autumn Winter, 1974; (libretto) The Story of Vasco, 1974; Cave-Birds (limited edn with illustrations by Leonard Baskin), 1975; Season Songs, 1976; Earth-Moon, 1976; (introd. and trans. jtly) János Pilinsky, Selected Poems, 1976; Gaudete, 1977; (ed and introd.) Sylvia Plath, Johnny Panic and the Bible of Dreams, by Sylvia Plath, 1977; Orts, 1978; Moortown Elegies, 1978; Cave Birds, 1978; Moon-Bells and other poems (verse for children), 1978 (Signal Award); (intr. and trans. jtly) Yehuda Amichai's Amen, 1978; Adam and the Sacred Nine, 1979; Remains of Elmet, 1979; Moortown, 1979 (Heinemann Bequest, RSL, 1980); 12 poems in Michael Morpurgo's All Around the Year, 1979; Henry Williamson—A Tribute, 1979; (ed) Sylvia Plath: Collected Poems, 1981; Under the North Star (poems for children), 1981; Selected Poems 1957-1981, 1982. *Address*: c/o Faber and Faber Ltd, 3 Queen Square, WC1.

HUGHES, Thomas Lowe; President and Trustee, Carnegie Endowment for International Peace, New York, Washington, Geneva, since 1971; *b* 11 Dec. 1925; *s* of Evan Raymond Hughes and Alice (*née* Lowe); *m* 1955, Jean Hurlburt Reiman; two *s*. *Educ*: Carleton Coll., Minn (BA); Balliol Coll., Oxford (Rhodes Schol., BPhil); Yale Law Sch. (LLB, JD). USAF, 1952-54 (Major). Member of Bar: Supreme Court of Minnesota; US District Court of DC; Supreme Court of US. Professional Staff Mem., US Senate Sub-cttee on Labour-Management Relations, 1951; part-time Prof. of Polit. Sci. and Internat. Relations, Univ. of Southern California, Los Angeles, 1953-54, and George Washington Univ., DC, 1957-58; Exec. Sec. to Governor of Connecticut, 1954-55; Legislative Counsel to Senator Hubert H. Humphrey, 1955-58; Admin. Asst to US Rep. Chester Bowles, 1959-60; Staff Dir of Platform Cttee, Democratic Nat. Convention, 1960; Special Asst to Under-Sec. of State, Dept of State, 1961; Dep. Dir of Intelligence and Research, Dept of State, 1961-63; Dir of Intell. and Res. (Asst Sec. of State), 1963-69; Minister and Dep. Chief of Mission, Amer. Embassy, London, 1969-70; Mem., Planning and Coordination Staff, Dept of State, 1970-71. Chm., Nuclear Proliferation and Safeguards Adv. Panel, Office of Technology Assessment, US Congress; Chm., Bd of Editors, Foreign Policy Magazine; Sec., Bd of Dirs, German Marshall Fund of US; Dir, Arms Control Assoc. Chairman: Oxford-Cambridge Assoc. of Washington; US-UK Bicentennial Fellowships Cttee on the Arts. Member Bds of Visitors: Harvard Univ. (Center for Internat. Studies); Princeton Univ. (Woodrow Wilson Sch. of Public and Internat. Affairs); Georgetown Univ. (Sch. of Foreign Service); Bryn Mawr Coll. (Internat. Adv. Bd.); Univ. of Denver (Soc. Sci. Foundn). Member Bds of Trustees: Civilian Military Inst.; Amer. Acad. of Political and Social Sci.; Amer. Cttee, IISS; Hubert H. Humphrey Inst. of Public Affairs. Member: Internat. Inst. of Strategic Studies; Amer. Assoc. of Rhodes Scholars; Amer. Political Sci. Assoc.; Amer. Bar Assoc.; Amer. Assoc. of Internat. Law; Amer. For. Service Assoc.; Internat. Studies Assoc.; Washington Inst. of Foreign Affairs; Trilateral Commn; Assoc. for Restoration of Old San Juan, Puerto Rico. Arthur S. Flemming Award, 1965. Hon. LLD Washington Coll., 1973; Denison Univ., 1979; Hon. HLD: Carleton Coll., 1974; Washington and Jefferson Coll., 1979. *Publications*: occasional contribs to professional jls, etc. *Recreations*: swimming, tennis, music, 18th century engravings. *Address*: 5636 Western Avenue, Chevy Chase, Md 20015, USA; Carnegie Endowment for International Peace, 30 Rockefeller Plaza, New York, NY 10020, USA. *T*: (301)6561420; (212)572-8212; 11 Dupont Circle NW, Washington, DC 20036. *T*: (202)797-6411. *Clubs*: Yale, Century Association, Council on Foreign Relations (New York); Cosmos (Washington).

HUGHES, Sir Trevor Denby L.; *see* Lloyd-Hughes.

HUGHES, Sir Trevor (Poulton), KCB 1982 (CB 1974); CEng, FICE, FIMunE, FIWES; Permanent Secretary, Welsh Office, since 1980; *b* 28 Sept. 1925; *y s* of late Rev. John Evan and Mary Grace Hughes; *m* 1st, 1950, Mary Ruth Walwyn (marr. diss.); two *s*; 2nd, 1978, Barbara June Davison. *Educ*: Ruthin Sch. RE, 1945-48, Captain 13 Fd Svy Co. Municipal engineering, 1948-57; Dep. Borough Engineer, Colwyn Bay, 1957-61; Min. of Transport, 1961-62; Min. of Housing and Local Govt: Engineering Inspectorate, 1962-70; Dep. Chief Engineer, 1970-71; Dir, 1971-72 and Dir-Gen., 1972-74, Water Engineering, DoE; Dep. Sec., DoE, 1974-77; Dep. Sec., Dept of Transport, 1977-80. Hon. FInstWPC; Hon. FIPHE. *Recreations*: music, gardening, golf. *Address*: Welsh Office, Cathays Park, Cardiff. *T*: Cardiff 824215.

See also J. R. P. Hughes.

HUGHES, William, CB 1953; Deputy Secretary, Department of Trade and Industry, 1970-71; *b* 21 Aug. 1910; *o s* of late William Hughes, Bishop's Stortford, Herts, and of Daisy Constance, *y d* of Charles Henry Davis; *m* 1941, Ilse Erna, *o d* of late E. F. Plohs; one *s* one *d*. *Educ*: Bishop's Stortford Coll.; Magdalen Coll., Oxford (demy). Board of Trade, 1933; Asst Sec., 1942; Under-Sec., 1948-63 (Sec., Monopolies and Restrictive Practices Commission, 1952-55); Second Sec., 1963-71. Consultant to British Overseas Trade Bd, 1972-73; Under-Sec., Prices Commn, 1973-75. Mem. Exec. Cttee, Wandsworth Council for Community Relations, 1976-. *Recreation*: music. *Address*: 250 Trinity Road, SW18. *T*: 01-870 3652; Page's, Widdington, Essex. *Clubs*: Reform; Leander.

HUGHES, Maj.-Gen. (Retd) William Dillon, CB 1960; CBE 1953; MD; FRCP(I); DTM&H; Commandant, Royal Army Medical College, 1957-60; *b* 23 Dec. 1900; *s* of R. Hughes, JP; *m* 1929, Kathleen Linda Thomas; one *s*. *Educ*: Campbell Coll., Belfast; Queen's Univ., Belfast. MB, BCh, BAO, 1923; Lieut, RAMC, 1928; Officer i/c Medical Div. 64 and 42 Gen. Hosps, MEF, 1940-42; Officer i/c Medical Div. 105 Gen. Hosp., BAOR, 1944-46; Sen. MO, Belsen, 1945; consulting Physician, Far East Land Forces, 1950-53; ADMS, Aldershot Dist, 1954. Prof. in Tropical Medicine and Consulting Physician, RAM Coll., 1955-56; Vice-Pres., Royal Society of Tropical Medicine and Hygiene, 1959-60; Col Comdt RAMC, 1961-65. QHP 1957; Mitchiner Medal, RCS, 1960. *Address*: Littleport Farm, Sedgeford, Norfolk.

HUGHES, William Henry; His Honour Judge Hughes; a Circuit Judge, since 1972; *b* 6 Jan. 1915; *s* of late William Howard Hamilton Hughes; *m* 1961, Jenny, *d* of Theodore Francis Turner, *qv* ; one *d*. *Educ*: privately; Keble Coll., Oxford. Served War of 1939-45; AA & QMG, BEF, France and Belgium, N Africa, Italy (despatches, Croix de Guerre and palm); Staff Coll.; Lieut-Col 1944. Called to the Bar, Inner Temple, 1949. Deputy Chairman: Isle of Ely QS, 1959-63; Essex QS, 1961-63; London Sessions, 1962-63, 1968-71; a Metropolitan Magistrate, 1963-71. Formerly a Mem., General Council of the Bar. Governor, Camden Sch. for Girls, 1977-. *Recreations*: books, wine, shooting, travel. *Address*: Old Wardour House, Tisbury, Wilts. *T*: Tisbury 431; 112 Bedford Court Mansions, Bedford Avenue, WC1B 3AG. *Clubs*: Beefsteak, Garrick.

See also C. G. Turner, M. J. Turner.

HUGHES, (William) Mark; MP (Lab) Durham since 1970; *b* 18 Dec. 1932; *s* of late Edward Hughes, sometime Prof. of History at Durham, and Sarah (*née* Hughes), Shincliffe, Durham; *m* 1958, Jennifer Mary, *d* of Dr G. H. Boobyer; one *s* two *d*. *Educ*: Durham Sch.; Balliol Coll., Oxford (MA). BA Oxon 1956; PhD Newcastle 1963. Sir James Knott Research Fellow,

Newcastle-upon-Tyne, 1958-60; Staff Tutor, Manchester Univ. Extra-Mural Dept, 1960-64; Lectr, Durham Univ., 1964-70. PPS to Chief Sec. of Treasury, 1974-75; opposition spokesman on agriculture, 1980-; Member: Select Cttee on Expenditure (Trade and Industry Sub-Cttee), 1970-74; Select Cttee on Parly Comr, 1970-75; Delegn to Consultative Assembly of Council of Europe and WEU, 1974-75; European Parlt, 1975-79 (Vice-Chm., Agric. Cttee and Chm., Fisheries Sub-Cttee, 1977-79); Exec. Cttee, British Council, 1974- (Vice-Chm., 1978-); Gen. Adv. Council, BBC, 1976-. An Hon. Vice-Pres., BVA, 1976-. *Recreations:* varied and private. *Address:* Grimsdyke, Vicarage Road, Potten End, Berkhamsted, Herts.

HUGHES, William Reginald Noel, FRINA, RCNC; *b* 14 Dec. 1913; *s* of Frank George Hughes and Annie May Hughes (*née* Lock); *m* 1936, Doris Margaret (*née* Attwool); two *s* two *d. Educ:* Prince Edward Sch., Salisbury, Rhodesia; Esplanade House Sch., Southsea, Hants; Royal Dockyard Sch., Portsmouth; RN Coll., Greenwich. Constr Sub Lieut, Chatham, 1933; Constr Sub Lieut and Lieut, RN Coll., Greenwich, 1934; Admty, London, 1937; HM Dockyard, Chatham, 1938; Admty, Bath, 1940; Constr Comdr, Staff of C-in-C Home Fleet, 1944; HM Dockyard, Hong Kong, 1947; Admty, Bath, 1951; Chief Constr, HM Dockyard, Devonport, 1954; Admty, Bath, 1958; Admty Repair Manager, Malta, 1961; Manager, Constructive Dept, Portsmouth, 1964; Dep. Dir of Dockyards, Bath, 1967-70; Gen. Manager, HM Dockyard, Chatham, 1970-73. *Recreations:* sailing, foreign travel, photography. *Address:* Capstan House, Tower Street, Old Portsmouth, Hants. *T:* Portsmouth 812997. *Clubs:* Little Ship; Royal Naval and Royal Albert Yacht; Royal Naval Sailing Association.

HUGHES HALLETT, Vice-Adm. (retd) Sir (Cecil) Charles, KCB 1954 (CB 1950); CBE 1942; Chairman: Gas Purification and Chemical Co. Ltd, 1958-60; Edwards High Vacuum International Ltd, 1964-68; Mount Row Holdings Ltd, 1962-68; Director, John Tysack & Partners Ltd, 1960-75; *b* 6 April 1898; *s* of Col W. Hughes Hallett and Clementina Mary Loch; *m* 1920, Eileen Louise Boulanger; two *d* (one *s* one *d* decd); *m* 1944, Joyce Plumer Cobbold; one *s* one *d. Educ:* Bedford; RN Colls, Osborne and Dartmouth; Emmanuel Coll., Cambridge. Went to sea as Midshipman in Aug. 1914; present at Dardanelles and Battle of Jutland: specialised in gunnery, 1921, in staff duties, 1933; Comdr 1932; Capt. 1939; Rear-Adm. 1949; Vice-Adm. 1952; retd Feb. 1955. Comdg destroyer 1934-35, anti-aircraft ship, 1940-42, aircraft carrier, 1944-46, during War of 1939-45 (despatches twice, CBE); present at operations against Japanese mainland, 1945. Dir of Administrative Plans and Joint Planning Staff, 1942-44; Dep. Chief of Naval Air Equipment, 1946-48; Admiralty for Special Duty, 1948-50; Chief of Staff to C-in-C Home Fleet, 1950-51; Admiral, British Joint Services Mission, Washington, 1952-54; Personal Asst to Chm., Charterhouse Group, 1955-59. Younger Brother of Trinity House, 1938; Renter Warden, Co. of Glovers, 1967, Master, 1968. Fellow, British Inst. of Management. Legion of Merit, Degree of Officer (USA), 1945. *Address:* Glebe House, Odstock, Salisbury, Wiltshire SP5 4JB. *T:* Salisbury 23854.

HUGHES-MORGAN, Maj.-Gen. Sir David (John), 3rd Bt *cr* 1925; CBE 1973 (MBE 1959); Director, Army Legal Services, Ministry of Defence, since 1980; *b* 11 Oct. 1925; *s* of Sir John Hughes-Morgan, 2nd Bt and of Lucie Margaret, *d* of late Thomas Parry Jones-Parry; *S* father, 1969; *m* 1959, Isabel Jean, *d* of J. M. Lindsay; three *s. Educ:* RNC, Dartmouth. Royal Navy, 1943-46. Admitted solicitor, 1950. Commissioned, Army Legal Services, 1955; Brig., Legal Staff, HQ UKLF, 1976-78; Dir, Army Legal Services, BAOR, 1978-80. *Heir: s* Ian Parry David Hughes-Morgan, *b* 22 Feb. 1960. *Address:* c/o National Westminster Bank Ltd, Brecon.

HUGHES-PARRY, Robert, MD (London), BS, FRCP, MRCS, DPH; retired; formerly Principal Medical Officer to the Bristol City Council; formerly Professor of Preventive Medicine, University of Bristol; Past President Society of Medical Officers of Health; President Preventive Medicine Section, BMA (1949); Hon. FAPHA; *b* 3 Nov. 1895; *s* of J. Hughes-Parry, JP, Penllwyn, Pwllheli, and Anne Hughes, Cwmcoryn, Caernarvonshire; *m* Elsie Joan Williams, LRCP, MRCS, two *s* two *d. Educ:* Pwllheli (Chairman Scholar); University College of Wales, Aberystwyth; University of London, The Middlesex Hospital (Lyell Scholar and Leigh Medallist, Junior Broderip Scholar). Lieut, RAF. MS; Asst to Professor of Experimental Pathology at the Middlesex Cancer Hospital, London, 1922-24; Medical Officer of Health of Bristol, 1930-56; Visiting Prof., Yale Univ., USA, 1956; formerly KHP to King George VI and QHP to the Queen. Medical Consultant, WHO, 1959. Member, Local Government Commission for England, 1959-63. High Sheriff of Caernarvonshire, 1958-59. *Publications:* Under the Cherry Tree (autobiography), 1969; Within Life's Span, 1973; various publications on cancer, health centres and other public health problems. *Recreation:* gardening. *Address:* 7 Gwaen Ganol, Criccieth, Gwynedd LL52 0TB.

HUGHES-YOUNG, family name of **Baron St Helens.**

HUGHESDON, Charles Frederick, AFC 1943; FRAeS; *b* 10 Dec. 1909; *m* 1937, Florence Elizabeth, *widow* of Captain Tom Campbell Black (actress, as Florence Desmond); one *s. Educ:* Raine's Foundation School. Entered insurance industry, 1927; learned to fly, 1932; Flying Instructor's Licence, 1934; commnd RAFO, 1934; Commercial Pilot's Licence, 1936; has Fixed Wing and Helicopter Licences; joined Stewart, Smith & Co. Ltd, 1936; Chief Test Pilot, General Aircraft, 1939-43; rejoined Stewart, Smith & Co. Ltd,

1946, retired as Chm. of Stewart Wrightson 1976; Chm., Aeronautical Trusts Ltd; Director: Tradewinds Airways; The Charles Street Co. Hon. Treas., RAeS, FRAeS 1971. Order of the Cedar, Lebanon, 1972. *Recreations:* flying (fixed wing and helicopter), shooting, horseracing, dressage, riding, yachting, water ski-ing, farming. *Address:* Dunsborough Park, Ripley, Surrey. *T:* Ripley 3366; Flat 12, 5 Grosvenor Square, W1. *T:* 01-493 1494. *Clubs:* Royal Air Force, Royal Thames Yacht, Lloyd's Yacht.

HUGILL, John, QC 1976; a Recorder of the Crown Court, since 1972; *b* 11 Aug. 1930; *s* of John A. and Alice Hugill; *m* 1956, Patricia Elizabeth Hugill (*née* Welton); two *d. Educ:* Fettes; Trinity Hall, Cambridge (MA). 2nd Lieut, RA, 1949. Called to the Bar, Middle Temple, 1954; Assistant Recorder, Bolton, 1971. *Recreation:* yachting. *Address:* The Boundary House, Lower Withington, Cheshire. *T:* Marton Heath 368.

HUGILL, Michael James; Assistant Master, Westminster School, since 1972; *b* 13 July 1918; 2nd *s* of late Rear-Adm. R. C. Hugill, CB, MVO, OBE. *Educ:* Oundle; King's Coll., Cambridge, Exhibitioner, King's Coll., 1936-39; MA 1943. War Service in the RN; Mediterranean, Home and Pacific Fleets, 1939-46; rank on demobilisation, Lieut-Comdr. Mathematics Master, Stratford Grammar Sch., 1947-51; Senior Mathematics Master, Bedford Modern Sch., 1951-57; Headmaster, Preston Grammar Sch., 1957-61; Headmaster, Whitgift School, Croydon, 1961-70; Lectr, Inst. of Education, Keele Univ., 1971-72. *Address:* 42 Kersfield House, Kersfield Road, SW15. *Club:* Army and Navy.

HUGO, Lt-Col Sir John (Mandeville), KCVO 1969 (CVO 1959); OBE 1947; Gentleman Usher to the Queen, 1952-69, an Extra Gentleman Usher since 1969; *b* 1 July 1899; *s* of R. M. Hugo; *m* 1952, Joan Winifred, *d* of late D. W. Hill; two *d. Educ:* Marlborough Coll.; RMA, Woolwich, Commissioned RA, 1917; transf. to Indian Cavalry, 1925; Military Sec. to Governor of Bengal, 1938-40; rejoined 7th Light Cavalry, 1940; Military Sec. to Governor of Bengal 1946-47; Asst Ceremonial Sec., Commonwealth Relations Office, 1948-52; Ceremonial and Protocol Secretary, 1952-69. *Address:* The Cottages, Nizels, Hildenborough, Kent. *T:* Hildenborough 832359. *Club:* Army and Navy.

HUIJSMAN, Nicolaas Basil Jacques, CMG 1973; *b* 6 March 1915; *s* of Nikolaas Kornelis Huijsman, Amsterdam and Hendrika Huijsman (*née* Vorkink). *Educ:* Selborne Coll., E London, S Africa; Univ. of Witwatersrand (BCom); Gonville and Caius Coll., Cambridge (Econ. Tripos). Commnd Royal Scots Fusiliers, 1940; HQ 17 Inf. Bde, 1940; GS03, WO, 1941-42; psc 1942; GSO2, HQ of Chief of Staff to Supreme Cmdr (Des) and SHAEF, 1943-45 (despatches 1944); Controller of Press and Publications, Control Commn for Germany, 1945-48; Colonial Office, 1948-62; Principal Private Sec. to Sec. of State for Commonwealth Relations and Colonies, 1962-64; Asst Sec., Min. of Overseas Develt, 1964-70, and 1974-75, Overseas Develt Admin/FCO, 1970-74. Bronze Star, US, 1945. *Recreations:* Byzantine history, music, opera, painting. *Address:* 13 Regent Square, Penzance TR18 4BG. *Club:* Reform.

HULL, Bishop Suffragan of, since 1981; **Rt. Rev. Donald George Snelgrove,** TD 1972; *b* 21 April 1925; *s* of William Henry Snelgrove and Beatrice Snelgrove (*née* Upshell); *m* 1949, Sylvia May Lowe; one *s* one *d. Educ:* Queens' Coll. and Ridley Hall, Cambridge (MA). Served War, commn (Exec. Br.) RNVR, 1943-46. Cambridge, 1946-50; ordained, 1950; Curate: St Thomas, Oakwood, 1950-53; St Anselm's, Hatch End, 1953-56; Vicar of: Dronfield with Unstone, Dio. Derby, 1956-62; Hessle, Dio. York, 1963-70; Archdeacon of the East Riding, 1970-81. Rural Dean of Hull, 1966-70; Canon of York, 1969. Chaplain T&AVR, 1960-73. *Recreation:* travel. *Address:* Hullen House, Woodfield Lane, Hessle, N Humberside HU13 0ES. *T:* Hull 649019.

HULL, John Folliott Charles; Chairman, J. Henry Schroder Wagg & Co Ltd, since 1977; *b* 21 Oct. 1925; *er s* of Sir Hubert Hull, CBE, and of Judith, *e d* of P. F. S. Stokes; *m* 1951, Rosemarie Waring; one *s* three *d. Educ:* Downside; Jesus Coll., Cambridge (MA). 1st cl. hons Law. Captain, RA, 1944-48, served with Royal Indian Artillery. Called to Bar, Inner Temple, 1952. J. Henry Schroder Wagg & Co. Ltd, 1957-72, 1974- (a Man. Dir, 1961-72, Dep. Chm., 1974-77); Dir, Schroders Ltd, 1969-72, 1974- (Jt Dep. Chm., 1977-); Dep. Chm., Land Securities Investment Trust, 1976-; Director: Lucas Industries Ltd, 1975-; Legal and General Assurance Soc., 1976-79; Legal & General Group Ltd, 1979-. Dir-Gen., City Panel on Take-overs and Mergers, 1972-74; Chm., City Company Law Cttee, 1976-79. Mem., Council, Manchester Business Sch. *Recreations:* reading political history and 19th century novelists, supporting Chelsea Football Club. *Address:* 33 Edwardes Square, W8. *T:* 01-603 0715. *Club:* MCC.

See also Lord Seymour.

HULL, Field Marshal Sir Richard (Amyatt), KG 1980; GCB 1961 (KCB 1956; CB 1945); DSO 1943; Lord-Lieutenant of Devon, 1978-82; *b* 7 May 1907; *s* of Maj.-Gen. Sir Charles Patrick Amyatt Hull, KCB; *m* 1934, Antoinette Mary Labouchère de Rougemont; one *s* two *d. Educ:* Charterhouse; Trinity Coll., Cambridge (MA). Joined 17th/21st Lancers, 1928; Commanded 17/21st Lancers, 1941; Commanded 12th Infantry Bde, 1943; Commanded 26 Armd Bde, 1943; Comd 1st Armd Div., 1944; Cmd 5th Infantry Div., 1945; Commandant Staff Coll. Camberley, 1946-48; Dir of Staff Duties, War Office, 1948-50; Chief Army Instructor, Imperial Defence

Coll., 1950-52; Chief of Staff, GHQ, MELF, 1953-54; General Officer Commanding, British Troops in Egypt, 1954-56; Dep. Chief of the Imperial Gen. Staff, 1956-58; Comdr-in-Chief, Far East Land Forces, 1958-61; Chief of the Imperial Gen. Staff, 1961-64; ADC Gen. to the Queen, 1961-64; Chief of the Gen. Staff, Ministry of Defence, 1964-65; Chief of the Defence Staff, 1965-67. Constable of the Tower of London, 1970-75. Pres., Army Benevolent Fund, 1968-71; Dir, Whitbread & Co. Ltd, 1967-76. Col Comdt, RAC, 1968-71. DL Devon 1973; High Sheriff, Devon, 1975. Hon. LLD Exeter, 1965. *Address:* Beacon Downe, Pinhoe, Exeter. *Club:* Cavalry and Guards.

HULME, Bishop Suffragan of, since 1975; **Rt. Rev. David George Galliford;** *b* 20 June 1925; *s* of Alfred Edward Bruce and Amy Doris Galliford; *m* 1954, Enid May Drax; one *d. Educ:* Bede Coll., Sunderland; Clare Coll., Cambridge (Organ Scholar 1942, BA 1949, MA 1951); Westcott House, Cambridge. Served 5th Royal Inniskilling Dragoon Guards, 1943-47. Curate of St John Newland, Hull, 1951-54; Minor Canon of Windsor, 1954-56; Vicar of St Oswald, Middlesbrough, 1956-61; Rector of Bolton Percy and Diocesan Training Officer, 1961-70; Canon of York Minster, 1969; Canon Residentiary and Treasurer of York Minster, 1970-75. *Publications:* God and Christian Caring, 1973; Pastor's Post, 1975; (ed) Diocese in Mission, 1968. *Recreations:* pottery, music, painting in oils. *Address:* Hulme House, 31 Bland Road, Prestwick, Manchester. *T:* 061-773 1504. *Clubs:* Royal Over-Seas League; Manchester.

HULME, Hon. Sir Alan (Shallcross), KBE 1971; FCA; grazier; *b* 14 Feb. 1907; *s* of Thomas Shallcross Hulme and Emily Clara (*née* Hynes); *m* 1938, Jean Archibald; two *s* one *d. Educ:* North Sydney Boys' High School. Pres., Qld Div. of Liberal Party of Aust., 1946-49, 1962-63. Director: Chandlers (Aust.) Ltd, 1952-58; J. B. Chandler Investment Co. Ltd, 1962-63. Hon. Treas., King's Univ. Coll., 1944-49. Former Vice-Consul for Portugal in Brisbane. Mem., Commonwealth Parlt, Australia, 1949-72; Minister for Supply, 1958-61; acted as Minister: for Army, May-July 1959; for Air, Dec. 1960; Postmaster-General, 1963-72; Minister for Defence, 1965-66 and on subseq. occasions; Vice-Pres., Exec. Council, 1966-72. Member: House Cttee, 1950-58; Jt Cttee of Public Accounts, 1952-58; Chairman: Commonwealth Cttee on Rates of Depreciation, 1954-55; Commonwealth Immigration Planning Council, 1956-58. *Recreations:* gardening, bowls. *Address:* Alcheringa Droughtmaster Stud, Eudlo, Qld 4554, Australia. *T:* Palmwoods 459267. *Club:* Brisbane (Brisbane).

HULME, Geoffrey Gordon; Deputy Secretary and Principal Finance Officer, Department of Health and Social Security, since 1981; *b* 8 March 1931; *s* of Alfred and Jessie Hulme; *m* 1956, Shirley Leigh Cumberlidge; one *s* one *d. Educ:* Daybrook Street Elem. Sch.; King's Sch., Macclesfield; Corpus Christi Coll., Oxford (MA, 1st Cl Hons Mod. Langs). Nat. Service, Intelligence Corps, 1949-50; Oxford, 1950-53; Asst Principal, Min. of Health, 1953-59; Principal, 1959-64; Principal Regional Officer, W Midlands, 1964-67; Asst Sec., 1967-74; Under-Sec., 1974-81. *Recreations:* the usual things and collecting edible fungi. *Address:* 3 Woodhyrst Gardens, Kenley, Surrey CR2 5LX. *T:* 01-660 5713; 163A Kennington Park Road, SE11. *T:* 01-735 4461. *Club:* Royal Automobile.

HULME, Dr Henry Rainsford; Chief of Nuclear Research, Atomic Weapons Research Establishment, 1959-73, retired; *b* 9 Aug. 1908; *s* of James Rainsford Hulme and Alice Jane Smith; *m* 1955, Margery Alice Ducker, *d* of late Sir James A. Cooper, KBE, and of Lady Cooper. *Educ:* Manchester Grammar Sch.; Gonville and Caius Coll., Cambridge; University of Leipzig. BA (Math. Tripos) 1929; Smiths' Prizeman, 1931; PhD (Cambridge) 1932; ScD (Cambridge) 1948. Fellow of Gonville and Caius Coll., Cambridge, 1933-38; Chief Asst Royal Observatory, Greenwich, 1938-45; on loan to Admiralty during war. Scientific Adviser Air Ministry, 1946-48. *Publications:* on Mathematical Physics and Astronomy in learned jls. *Recreations:* various. *Address:* Birch Row, Ramsdell, near Basingstoke, Hants.

HULSE, Sir (Hamilton) Westrow, 9th Bt, *cr* 1739; Barrister-at-Law, Inner Temple; *b* 20 June 1909; *s* of Sir Hamilton Hulse, 8th Bt, and Estelle (*d* 1933) *d* of late William Lorillard Campbell, of New York, USA; *S* father, 1931; *m* 1st, 1932, Philippa Mabel (marr. diss. 1937), *y d* of late A. J. Taylor, Strensham Court, Worcs; two *s* ; 2nd, 1938, Amber (*d* 1940), *o d* of late Captain Herbert Stanley Orr Wilson, RHA, Rockfield Park, Mon; 3rd, 1945 (marr. diss.); 4th, 1954, Elizabeth, *d* of late Col George Redesdale Brooker Spain, CMG, TD, FSA. *Educ:* Eton; Christ Church, Oxford. Wing Comdr RAFVR, served 1940-45 (despatches). *Heir:* s Edward Jeremy Westrow Hulse [*b* 22 Nov. 1932; *m* 1957, Verity Ann, *d* of William Pilkington, Ivy Well, St John, Jersey; one *s* one *d*]. *Address:* Breamore, Hants. *TA:* Breamore. *T:* Downton 22270. *Clubs:* Carlton, Bath; Leander.

HULSE, Sir Westrow; see Hulse, Sir H. W.

HULTON, Sir Edward (George Warris), Kt 1957; Magazine publisher; writer; *b* 29 Nov. 1906; *s* of late Sir Edward Hulton, former proprietor of Evening Standard; *m* 1st, Kira (marr. diss.), *d* of General Goudime-Levkovitsch, Imperial Russian Army; no *c* ; 2nd, 1941, Princess Nika Yourievitch (marr. diss., 1966), 2nd *d* of Prince Serge Yourievitch, Russian sculptor, and Helene de Lipovatz, *d* of Gen. de Lipovatz; two *s* one *d. Educ:* Harrow; Brasenose Coll., Oxford (open scholarship. Contested Leek Div. Staffs, as Unionist, 1929; Harwich Div., 1931. Called to Bar, Inner Temple;

practised on South-Eastern Circuit; Chm., Hulton Publications Ltd. Pres., European Atlantic Group, 1969-70; Mem., British Atlantic Cttee; Vice-Pres., European League for Economic Co-operation; Mem. Nat. Council, British Council of the European Movement. FRSA. Liveryman and Freeman of Company of Stationers; Freeman of City of London. NATO Peace Medal, 1969. *Publications:* The New Age, 1943; When I Was a Child, 1952; Conflicts, 1966; contrib. various newspapers and books. *Recreation:* reading. *Address:* c/o Hulton Publications Ltd, 95 Peel Street, W8. *Clubs:* Athenæum, Beefsteak, Carlton, Garrick, Travellers', Buck's.

HULTON, Sir Geoffrey (Alan), 4th Bt, *cr* 1905; JP; DL; *b* 21 Jan. 1920; *s* of Sir Roger Braddyll Hulton, 3rd Bt and Hon. Marjorie Evelyn Louise (*d* 1970), *o c* of 6th Viscount Mountmorres; *S* father 1956; *m* 1945, Mary Patricia Reynolds. *Educ:* Marlborough. Entered Royal Marines, Sept. 1938; Lieut, 1940; sunk in HMS Repulse, Dec. 1941; prisoner-of-war, Far East, Feb. 1942-Aug. 1945; Captain, 1948; retired (ill-health), 1949. Owner of Hulton Park estate. Chief Scout's Commissioner. Pres., Westhoughton Divisional Conservative Association; Life Patron, Bolton and District Agricultural Discussion Soc.; Vice-President: Royal Lancs Agricultural Soc., 1974-80; Country Landowners' Assoc. (Lancashire); Lancashire County Cricket Club; Bolton Cricket League; Greater Manchester West Scout County; St Ann's Hospice Ltd; President: Greater Manchester North Scout County; Bolton Scout Trust; Hon. Life Vice-Pres., Westhoughton Cricket Club. JP Lancs, 1955; DL Lancs, later Greater Manchester, 1974. KCSG 1966. *Recreations:* country pursuits. *Heir:* none. *Address:* The Cottage, Hulton Park, Over Hulton, Bolton BL5 1BH. *T:* Bolton 651324. *Clubs:* Lansdowne, Royal Over-Seas League, Spanish, Victory.

HULTON, John, MA; *b* 28 Dec. 1915; *e s* of late Rev. Samuel Hulton, Knaresborough; *m* 1940, Helen Christian McFarlan; two *d. Educ:* Kingswood Sch., Bath; Hertford Coll., Oxford. DipLA; graduate of Landscape Inst. Leeds City Art Gallery and Temple Newsam House (Hon. Asst), 1937-38. Served War, RA, 1939-46. Keeper at Brighton Art Gall., Museum and Royal Pavilion, 1946-48; British Council Fine Arts Dept, 1948; Dir, 1970-75; resigned to study landscape design. Organised many art exhibns abroad. *Recreations:* looking at painting and sculpture; landscape and gardens. *Address:* 70 Gloucester Crescent, NW1 7EG. *T:* 01-485 6906. *Club:* Athenæum.

HUMBLE, James Kenneth; Chief Executive, Local Authorities Coordinating Body on Trading Standards; Director, National Metrological Co-ordinating Unit, since 1980; *b* 8 May 1936; *s* of Joseph Humble and Alice (*née* Rhodes); *m* 1961, Freda (*née* Holden); three *d.* Fellow, Inst. of Trading Standards. Served RN, 1954-56. Weights and Measures, Oldham, 1956-62; Fed. Min. of Commerce and Industry, Nigeria, 1962-66; Chief Trading Standards Officer, Croydon, 1966-74; Asst Dir of Consumer Affairs, Office of Fair Trading, 1974-79; Dir of Metrication Bd, 1979-80. Sec., Trade Descriptions Cttee, Inst. of Trading Standards, 1968-73; Examr, Dip. in Trading Standards, 1978-; Vice Chm., Council of Europe Cttee of Experts on Consumer Protection, 1976-79. Member: Council for Vehicle Servicing and Repair, 1972-75; Methven Cttee, 1974-76; OECD Cttee, Air Package Tours, 1978-79; BSI Divl Council, 1976-79. Sport, Devonport Services, 1954-56; Captain, Oldham Rugby Union, 1957-59; Professional Rugby, Leigh RFC, 1959-65. *Publications:* (contrib.) Marketing and the Consumer Movement, 1978; contrib. to various jls. *Recreations:* theatre, golf, bridge. *Address:* PO Box 6, Fell Road, Croydon. *T:* (home) 01-657 6170. *Club:* Royal Commonwealth.

HUME, Sir Alan (Blyth), Kt 1973; CB 1963; *b* 5 Jan. 1913; *s* of late W. Alan Hume; *m* 1943, Marion Morton Garrett; one *s* one *d. Educ:* George Heriot's Sch.; Edinburgh Univ. Entered Scottish Office, 1936. Under-Sec., Scottish Home Department, 1957-59; Asst Under-Sec. of State, Scottish Office, 1959-62; Under-Sec., Min. of Public Bldg and Works, 1963-64; Secretary, Scottish Develt Dept, 1965-73. Chairman: Ancient Monuments Bd, Scotland, 1973-81; Edinburgh New Town Conservation Cttee, 1975-. *Recreations:* golf, fishing. *Address:* 12 Oswald Road, Edinburgh EH9 2HJ. *T:* 031-667 2440. *Clubs:* English-Speaking Union, Royal Commonwealth Society; New (Edinburgh).

HUME, His Eminence Cardinal (George) Basil; see Westminster, Archbishop of, (RC).

HUME, James Bell; Under-Secretary, Scottish Home and Health Department, since 1977; *b* 16 June 1923; *s* of Francis John Hume and Jean McLellan Hume; *m* 1950, Elizabeth Margaret Nicolson. *Educ:* George Heriot's Sch., Edinburgh; Edinburgh Univ. MA Hons History. RAF, 1942-45. Asst Principal, Dept of Health for Scotland, 1947; Principal 1951; Jt Sec., Royal Commn on Doctors' and Dentists' Remuneration, 1958-59; Asst Sec. 1959; Nuffield Trav. Fellowship, 1963-64; Head of Edinburgh Centre, Civil Service Coll., 1969-73; Under-Sec., Scottish Education Dept, 1973-77. *Recreations:* dance music, gardening. *Address:* 24 Cherry Tree Gardens, Balerno, Edinburgh EH14 5SP. *T:* 031-449 3781. *Clubs:* Royal Commonwealth Society; New (Edinburgh).

HUME, John; Member (SDLP) Northern Ireland, European Parliament, since 1979; Leader, Social Democratic and Labour Party, since 1979; *b* 18 Jan. 1937; *s* of Samuel Hume; *m* 1960, Patricia Hone; two *s* three *d. Educ:* St Columb's Coll., Derry; St Patrick's Coll., Maynooth, NUI (MA). Pres., Credit Union League of Ireland, 1964-68; MP for Foyle, NI Parlt, 1969-73; Member

(SDLP), Londonderry: NI Assembly, 1973–75; NI Constitutional Convention, 1975–76; Minister of Commerce, NI, 1974. Contested (SDLP) Londonderry, UK elections, Oct. 1974. *Address:* 6 West End Park, Derry, N Ireland. *T:* Londonderry 65340.

HUME, Thomas Andrew, CBE 1977; FSA, FMA; Director, Museum of London, 1972–77; *b* 21 June 1917; *o s* of late Thomas Hume, Burnfoot, Oxton, and late Lillias Dodds; *m* 1942, Joyce Margaret Macdonald; two *s* one *d. Educ:* Heaton Grammar Sch.; King's Coll., Univ. of Durham (BA Hons Hist.). Gladstone Prizeman, Joseph Cowen Prizeman. Curator: Kirkstall Abbey House Museum, Leeds, 1949–52; Buckinghamshire County Museum, Aylesbury, 1952–60; Dir, City of Liverpool Museums, 1960–72. Mem., Museums and Galleries Commn (formerly Standing Commn on Museums and Galleries), 1977–. Past Pres., NW Fedn of Museums; Past Vice-Pres., Internat. Assoc. of Transport Museums; Past Chm., ICOM British Nat. Cttee; Museum Consultant, Unesco; Dir Mus. Exchange Programme, ICOM, Unesco, 1978–79. Mem. Finance Cttee, Soc. of Antiquaries. *Publications:* contribs Thoresby Soc., Records of Bucks; excavation reports and historical articles. *Recreations:* travel, gardening. *Address:* Homegarth, Church Lane, Whittington, King's Lynn, Norfolk.

HUMMEL, Frederick Cornelius, MA, DPhil, BSc; Head of Forestry Division, Commission of the European Communities, 1973–80, retired; *b* 28 April 1915; *s* of Cornelius Hummel, OBE, and Caroline Hummel (*née* Riefler); *m* 1st, 1941, Agnes Kathleen Rushforth (marr. diss., 1961); one *s* (and one *s* decd); 2nd, 1941, Floriana Rosemary Hollyer; three *d. Educ:* St Stephan, Augsburg, Germany; Wadham Coll., Oxford. District Forest Officer, Uganda Forest Service, 1938–46; Forestry Commn, 1946–73; Mensuration Officer, 1946; Chief, Management Sect., 1956; released for service with FAO as Co-Dir, Mexican Nat. Forest Inventory, 1961–66; Controller, Management Services, Forestry Commn, 1966–68, Comr for Harvesting and Marketing, 1968–73. Dr *hc* Munich, 1978. *Recreations:* walking, ski-ing. *Address:* Ridgemount, 8 The Ridgeway, Guildford, Surrey. *T:* Guildford 72383.

HUMPHREY, Arthur Hugh Peters, CMG 1959; OBE 1952; Hon. PMN (Malaya), 1958; Controller of Special Projects, Overseas Development Administration, Foreign and Commonwealth Office, 1961–71; Malayan Civil Service, 1934–60, retired; *b* 18 June 1911; *s* of late Arthur George Humphrey, Bank Manager; *m* 1948, Mary Valentine, *d* of late Lieut-Col J. E. Macpherson; three *d. Educ:* Eastbourne Coll.; Merton Coll., Oxford (Open Exhbr 1930, 1st class Maths, 1933). Appointed Malayan Civil Service, 1934; Private Sec. to Governor of Straits Settlements and High Comr for Malay States, 1936–38; Resident, Labuan, 1940–42; interned by Japanese in Borneo, 1942–45; idc 1948; Sec. for Defence and Internal Security, Fedn of Malaya, 1953–57; Mem. of Federal Legislative and Executive Councils, 1953–56; Sec. to the Treasury, Federation of Malaya, 1957–59; Director of Technical Assistance, Commonwealth Relations Office, 1960–61; Controller of Special Projects, ODM, 1961. Official Leader, United Kingdom delegations at Colombo Plan conferences: Tokyo, 1960, and Kuala Lumpur, 1961. Coronation Medal, 1953. *Recreations:* music, tennis. *Address:* 14 Ambrose Place, Worthing, Sussex. *T:* Worthing 33339. *Club:* East India, Devonshire, Sports and Public Schools.

HUMPHREY, Frank Basil, CB 1975; Parliamentary Counsel, 1967–80; *b* 21 Sept. 1918; *s* of late John Hartley Humphrey and Alice Maud Humphrey (*née* Broadbent); *m* 1947, Ol'ga Černá, *y d* of late František Cerny, Trenčin, Czechoslovakia; two *s. Educ:* Brentwood Sch.; St Catharine's Coll., Cambridge (Schol.). 2nd cl. hons Pt I. Mod. Langs Tripos, 1st cl. hons Pt II Law Tripos. Served RA, 1939–45: Adjt 23rd Mountain Regt and DAAG 4 Corps, India and Burma. Called to Bar, Middle Temple, 1946 (Harmsworth Schol.). Seconded as First Parly Counsel, Fedn of Nigeria, 1961–64, and as Counsel-in-charge at Law Commn, 1971–72. *Recreations:* gardening, mountain walking, music. *Address:* The Yews, Rookery Close, Fetcham, Surrey KT22 9BG. *T:* Leatherhead 372619.

HUMPHREY, Prof. John Herbert, CBE 1970; BA; MD; FRS 1963; FRCP 1971; Professor of Immunology, Royal Postgraduate Medical School, London University, 1976–81, now Emeritus Professor; *b* 16 Dec. 1915; *s* of Herbert Alfred Humphrey and Mary Elizabeth Humphrey (*née* Horniblow); *m* 1939, Janet Rumney, *d* of Prof. Archibald Vivian Hill, CH, OBE, FRS, ScD, and late Margaret Neville, *d* of late Dr J. N. Keynes; two *s* three *d. Educ:* Winchester Coll.; Trinity Coll., Cambridge; UCH Med. Sch. Jenner Research Student, Lister Inst., 1941–42; Asst Pathologist, Central Middx Hosp., 1942–46; External Staff, Med. Research Council, 1946–49; Member: Scientific Staff, Nat. Inst. for Med. Research, 1949–76, Dep. Dir, 1961–76, Head of Div. of Immunology and Experimental Biology, 1957–76; Expert Cttee on Biological Standardization, WHO, 1955–70; Expert Cttee on Immunology, WHO, 1962–; Nat. Biol. Standards Bd. Editor, Advances in Immunology, 1960–67; Asst Editor, Immunology, 1958–68. Mem. Council, Royal Society, 1967–69. Past Pres., Internat. Union of Immunological Socs. Chm., Medical Campaign against Nuclear Weapons, 1980–. Hon. DSc Brunel, 1979. *Publications:* Immunology for Students of Medicine (with Prof. R. G. White), 1963; contribs to Jls of immunology, biochemistry, physiology, etc. *Address:* 17 Mortimer Crescent, NW6 5NP. *T:* 01-624 9376; Topcliffe's Mill, Meldreth, Royston, Herts. *T:* Royston 60376.

HUMPHREY, William Gerald, MA Oxon and Cantab, DPhil Oxon; Assistant Secretary, University of Cambridge Appointments Board, 1962–72; Headmaster of The Leys School, Cambridge, 1934–58; Group personnel officer, Fisons Ltd, 1958–62; *b* 2 Aug. 1904; *e s* of late Rev. William Humphrey and Helen Lusher; *m* 1936, Margaret, *er d* of late William E. Swift, Cornwall, Conn., USA; one *s. Educ:* King Edward VII Sch., Sheffield; Queen's Coll., Oxford (Hastings Scholar, Taberdar, University Sen. Research Student); 1st Class Final Honour Sch. of Natural Science, 1926; DPhil, 1928; Commonwealth Fund Fellow, Harvard Univ., 1929–31; Senior Science Master, Uppingham Sch., 1932–34. Mem. Ministry of Agriculture Cttee on demand for Agricultural Graduates. *Publications:* The Christian and Education, 1940; Papers in Journal of the Chemical Soc. *Recreation:* painting. *Address:* 14 Wingate Way, Trumpington, Cambridge. *T:* Cambridge 840296.

HUMPHREYS, Arthur Leslie Charles, CBE 1970; Director: ICL Ltd (Managing Director, 1968–72; Deputy Chairman, 1972–77); Data Recording Instrument Co. Ltd, since 1976; *b* 8 Jan. 1917; *s* of late Percy Stewart Humphreys and late Louise (*née* Weston); *m* 1st, 1943, Marjorie Irene Murphy-Jones (decd); two *s* one *d*; 2nd, 1975, Audrey Norah Urquhart (*née* Dunningham). *Educ:* Catford Grammar Sch.; Administrative Staff Coll., Henley. International Computers & Tabulators Ltd: Dir 1963; Dep. Man. Dir 1964; Man. Dir 1967. *Recreations:* table tennis, bridge, music. *Address:* The Sycamores, 24 Middle Street, Thriplow, Royston, Herts SG8 7RD. *T:* Royston 82594.

HUMPHREYS, Prof. Arthur Raleigh; Professor of English, University of Leicester, 1947–76; *b* 28 March 1911; *s* of William Ernest Humphreys and Lois (*née* Rainforth); *m* 1947, Kathryn Jane, *d* of James and Jessie Currie, Drumadoon, Isle of Arran. *Educ:* Grammar Sch., Wallasey, Ches; St Catharine's Coll., Cambridge; Harvard Univ., USA. Charles Oldham Shakespeare Schol., Cambridge, 1932; BA (Cambridge), 1933, MA 1936; Commonwealth Fund Fellow, Harvard, 1933–35; AM (Harvard), 1935. Supervisor in English, Cambridge Univ., 1935–37; Lectr in English, Liverpool Univ., 1937–46. Served War of 1939–45, RAF Intelligence, 1940–42 (Flying Officer); British Council Lecturer in English, Istanbul Univ., 1942–45. Fellow Folger Shakespeare Library, Washington, DC, 1960, 1961, 1964; Visiting Fellow: All Souls Coll., Oxford, 1966; Huntington Library, Calif, 1978–79; Vis. Prof., Bogaziçi Univ., Istanbul, 1979–80, 1981–82. *Publications:* William Shenstone, 1937; The Augustan World, 1954; Steele, Addison, and their Periodical Essays, 1959; (ed) Henry IV, Part I, 1960, Part II, 1966; Melville, 1962; (ed) Joseph Andrews, 1962; (ed) Tom Jones, 1962; (ed) Amelia, 1963; (ed) Jonathan Wild, 1964; (ed) Melville's White-Jacket, 1966; Shakespeare, Richard II, 1967; (ed) Henry V, 1968; (ed) Henry VIII, 1971; Shakespeare, Merchant of Venice, 1973; Defoe, Robinson Crusoe, 1980; (ed) Much Ado About Nothing, 1981; contrib: From Dryden to Johnson (ed B. Ford), 1957; Alexander Pope (ed P. Dixon), 1972; Shakespeare's Art (ed M. Crane), 1973; Shakespeare: Select Bibliographical Guides (ed S. Wells), 1973, and to learned journals. *Recreations:* music, architecture, hill walking. *Address:* 144 Victoria Park Road, Leicester LE2 1XD. *T:* Leicester 705118.

HUMPHREYS, Christmas; *see* Humphreys, T. C.

HUMPHREYS, David Colin, CMG 1977; Deputy Under Secretary of State (Air), Ministry of Defence, since 1979; *b* 23 April 1925; *s* of late Charles Roland Lloyd Humphreys and Bethia Joan (*née* Bowie); *m* 1952, Jill Allison (*née* Cranmer); two *s* one *d. Educ:* Eton Coll. (King's Scholar); King's Coll., Cambridge (MA). Air Min., 1949; Private Sec. to Sec. of State for Air, 1959–60; Counsellor, UK Deleg'n to NATO, 1960–63; Air Force Dept, 1963–69; IDC 1970; Dir, Defence Policy Staff, 1971–72; Asst Sec. Gen. (Defence Planning and Policy), NATO, 1972–76; Asst Under Sec. of State (Naval Staff), MoD, 1977–79. *Address:* Rivendell, North Drive, Virginia Water, Surrey. *T:* Wentworth 2130. *Clubs:* Royal Air Force; Wentworth.

HUMPHREYS, Emyr Owen; Author; *b* 15 April 1919; *s* of William and Sarah Rosina Humphreys, Prestatyn, Flints; *m* 1946, Elinor Myfanwy, *d* of Rev. Griffith Jones, Bontnewydd, Caerns; three *s* one *d. Educ:* University Coll., Aberystwyth; University Coll., Bangor. Gregynog Arts Fellow, 1974–75. *Publications:* The Little Kingdom, 1946; The Voice of a Stranger, 1949; A Change of Heart, 1951; Hear and Forgive, 1952 (Somerset Maugham Award, 1953); A Man's Estate, 1955; The Italian Wife, 1957; Y Tri Llais, 1958; A Toy Epic, 1958 (Hawthornden Prize, 1959); The Gift, 1963; Outside the House of Baal, 1965; Natives, 1968; Ancestor Worship, 1970; National Winner, 1971 (Welsh Arts Council Prize, 1972); Flesh and Blood, 1974; Landscapes, 1976; The Best of Friends, 1978; Penguin Modern Poets No 27, 1978 (Soc. of Authors Travelling Award, 1979); The Kingdom of Brân, 1979; The Anchor Tree, 1980; Pwyll a Riannon, 1980; Miscellany Two, 1981. *Recreations:* rural pursuits. *Address:* 13 Fordd Llangors, Cyncoed, Caerdydd CF2 6PF.

HUMPHREYS, Maj.-Gen. George Charles, CB 1952; CBE 1948 (OBE 1945); *b* 5 Oct. 1899; *s* of late George Humphreys, formerly of Croft House, Croft-on-Tees, Co. Durham, and Caroline Huddart; *m* 1931, Doris Isabelle, *d* of late A. B. Baines, Shanghai; no *c. Educ:* Giggleswick Sch., Yorks; RMC Sandhurst. 2nd Lieut Royal Northumberland Fusiliers, 1918; Lieut 1920; Capt. 1930; Bt-Major, Major 1938; Lieut-Col 1946; Col 1947; Brig. 1951; Maj.-Gen. 1952. Served with 2nd Bn Royal Northumberland Fusiliers, Iraq, India and China, 1919–31, Adjt 1925–28 (Iraq medal and clasp, 1920); Bde Major, E Lancs and Border TA Bde, 1935–37; GSO2 Public Relations, War Office, 1938–39; War of 1939–45, in UK and Italy; GSO1 War Office, 1939–40; successively (Jan. 1941–May 1946), AA and QMG 55th Inf. Div., 1st and 3rd Armd Gps, 79th Armd Div., Col (Q) ops War Office, Col A/Q (BUCO) 21 Army Gp, Col A/Q, 1944-46; Dep. Chief Mil. Div. (Brig.), 1946, Allied Commn for Austria; Brig. i/c Admin Burma Comd, 1946-48; BGS, HQ Scottish Comd, 1948-51; Maj.-Gen. Adminstration, GHQ Middle East Land Forces, 1951-54; Chairman: PAO and PPO Cttees, Middle East, 1951-54; Military Adviser to Contractors for Canal Base (War Office, July 1954-31 May 1955); retired from Army, June 1955, and appointed General Manager, Suez Contractors Management Co. Ltd; appointed Chief Executive to Governing Body of Suez Contractors (Services) Ltd, Jan. 1956 until Liquidation of Suez enterprise, July 1957; Chief Organizer, Dollar Exports Council Conference, 1958. *Recreations:* reading, travel and shooting. *Address:* Lauriston Cottage, Old Green Lane, Camberley, Surrey. *T:* Camberley 21078.

HUMPHREYS, John Henry; Chairman, Industrial Tribunals (Ashford, Kent), since 1976; Legal Officer, Law Commission, since 1973; *b* 28 Feb. 1917; British; *m* 1939, Helen Mary Markbreiter; one *s* one *d. Educ:* Cranleigh School. Solicitor. Served with Co. of London Yeomanry, and Northampton Yeomanry, 1939-47; Treasury Solicitor Dept, 1947-73. *Recreations:* sailing, golf, gardening. *Address:* Gate House Cottage, Sandown Road, Sandwich, Kent. *T:* Sandwich 612961. *Club:* Prince's (Sandwich).

HUMPHREYS, Kenneth William, BLitt, MA, PhD; FLA; Librarian, European University Institute, Florence, 1975-81; Professor of Library Studies, University of Haifa, 1982-83; *b* 4 Dec. 1916; *s* of Joseph Maxmillian Humphreys and Bessie Benfield; *m* 1939, Margaret, *d* of Reginald F. Hill and Dorothy Lucas; two *s. Educ:* Southfield Sch., Oxford; St Catherine's Coll., Oxford. Library Asst, All Souls Coll., Oxford, 1933-36; Asst, Bodleian Library, 1936-50; Dep. Librarian, Brotherton Library, University of Leeds, 1950-52; Librarian, Univ. of Birmingham, 1952-75. Hon. Lectr in Palaeography, University of Leeds, 1950-52; Hon. Lectr in Palaeography, University of Birmingham, 1952-75; Hon. Sec., Standing Conf. of Nat. and University Libraries, 1954-69, Vice-Chm., 1969-71, Chm. 1971-73; Mem. Library Adv. Council for England, 1966-71; Mem. Council, Library Assoc., 1964-75, Chm. Council 1973; Chm. Exec. Cttee, West Midlands Regional Library Bureau, 1963-75; Chairman: Jt Standing Conf. and Cttee on Library Cooperation, 1965-75; Nat. Cttee on Regional Library Cooperation, 1970-75; Mem. Comité International de Paléographie, and Colloque International de Paléographie, 1955-; President: Nat. and University Libraries Section, Internat. Fedn of Library Assocs, 1968-69, Pres., University Libraries Sub-Section, 1967-73; Ligue des Bibliothèques Européennes de Recherche, 1974-80; Round Table on Library History, 1978-. Editor, Studies in the History of Libraries and Librarianship; Associate Editor, Libri; Jt Editor, Series of Reproductions of Medieval and Renaissance Texts. Hon. LittD Dublin (Trinity Coll.), 1967. Hon. FLA 1980; Socio d'onore, Italian Library Assoc., 1982. *Publications:* The Book Provisions of the Medieval Friars, 1964; The Medieval Library of the Carmelites at Florence, 1964; The Library of the Franciscans of the Convent of St Antony, Padua at the Beginning of the fifteenth century, 1966; The Library of the Franciscans of Siena in the Fifteenth Century, 1977; articles in library periodicals. *Recreation:* collection of manuscripts. *Address:* c/o 7 Salisbury Crescent, Oxford. *Clubs:* Athenæum; Kildare Street and University (Dublin).

HUMPHREYS, Sir Myles; see Humphreys, Sir R. E. M.

HUMPHREYS, Sir Olliver (William), Kt 1968; CBE 1957; BSc, FInstP, CEng, FIEE, FRAeS; *b* 4 Sept. 1902; *s* of late Rev. J. Willis Humphreys, Bath; *m* 1933, Muriel Mary Hawkins. *Educ:* Caterham Sch.; University Coll., London. Joined staff GEC Research Labs, 1925, Dir, 1949-61; Director 1953, Vice-Chm., 1963-67, GEC Ltd; Chm. all GEC Electronics and Telecommunications subsidiaries, 1961-66 and GEC (Research) Ltd, 1961-67. Mem. Bd, Inst. Physics, 1951-60 (Pres., 1956-58); Mem. Coun., IEE, 1952-55 (Vice-Pres., 1959-63; Pres., 1964-65); Faraday Lectr, 1953-54. Mem., BoT Cttee on Organisation and Constitution of BSI, 1949-50; Chm., BSI Telecommunications Industry Standards Cttee, 1951-63 (Mem. Gen. Coun., 1953-56; Mem. Exec. Cttee, 1953-60); Chm., Internat. Special Cttee on Radio Interference (CISPR), 1953-61; Chm., Electrical Res. Assoc., 1958-61; Chm., DSIR Radio Res. Bd, 1954-62; Pres., Electronic Engrg Assoc., 1962-64; Founder Chm., Conf. of Electronics Industry, 1963-67; Mem., Nat. ERC, 1963-67. Fellow UCL, 1963. Liveryman, Worshipful Co. of Makers of Playing Cards. *Publications:* various technical and scientific papers in proceedings of learned societies. *Recreations:* travel, walking, reading. *Address:* The Penthouse, Teak Close, Branksome Park, Poole, Dorset BH13 6JH. *T:* Bournemouth 766195. *Club:* Royal Motor Yacht.

HUMPHREYS, Sir (Raymond Evelyn) Myles, Kt 1977; JP; *b* 24 March 1925; *s* of Raymond and May Humphreys; *m* 1963, Joan Tate; two *s. Educ:* Skegoniel Primary Sch.; Londonderry High Sch.; Belfast Royal Acad. Research Engr, NI Transport Bd, 1946-55; Transport Manager, Nestle's Food Products (NI) Ltd, 1955-59; Director: Walter Alexander (Belfast) Ltd, 1959-; Quick Service Stations Ltd, 1971-; Bowring Martin Ltd, 1978-; Abbey National Bldg Soc., 1981-. Member of Board: Ulster Transport Authority, 1966-69; NI Transport Holding Co. Ltd, 1967-74; Chm., NI Railways Co. Ltd, 1966-. Mem., Belfast City Council, 1964-81; Chairman: Belfast Corp. Housing Cttee, 1966-69; City Council Planning Cttee, 1973-75; Town Planning and Environmental Hlth Cttee, 1973-75; Finance and Gen. Purposes Cttee, 1978-80; High Sheriff of Belfast, 1969; Dep. Lord Mayor, 1970; Lord Mayor, 1975-77. Chm., NI Police Authority, Royal Ulster Constabulary,

1976-; Pres., NI Polio Fellowship. Mem., May Cttee of Inquiry into UK Prison Services. Mem., Nat. Exec. Cttee of Nat. Housing and Town Planning Council, 1970-81 (Nat. Chm., 1976-77); Past Chairman: Bd of Visitors, HM Prison, Belfast; Chm., Bd of Management, Dunlambert Secondary Sch. Past-Pres., Belfast Junior Chamber of Commerce; Mem. Council, NI Chamber of Commerce and Industry; NI Rep., Mobility Internat.; Chm., Ulster Tourist Develt Assoc., 1974; Senator, Junior Chamber Internat.; Belfast Harbour Comr, 1979-. Member: NI Housing Exec., 1975-78; NI Tourist Bd, 1973-80; TA&VRA for NI, 1980; Council, Queen's Silver Jubilee Appeal. President: City of Belfast Youth Orch.; Ulster Folk & Transport Mus. District Transport Officer, St John Ambulance Brigade, 1946-66. Freeman of City of London, 1976. FCIT; OStJ. *Address:* Mylestone, Chichester Park, Belfast BT15 5DW. *T:* Belfast 771518. *Clubs:* Lansdowne.

HUMPHREYS, Prof. Robert Arthur, OBE 1946; MA, PhD Cantab; Director, Institute of Latin-American Studies, University of London, 1965-74; Professor of Latin-American History in University of London, 1948-74, now Emeritus; *b* 6 June 1907; *s* of late Robert Humphreys and Helen Marion Bavin, Lincoln; *m* 1946, Elisabeth, *er d* of late Sir Bernard Pares, KBE, DCL. *Educ:* Lincoln Sch.; Peterhouse, Cambridge (Scholar). Commonwealth Fund Fellow, Univ. of Michigan, 1930-32. Asst Lectr in American History, UCL, 1932, Lectr 1935; Reader in American History in Univ. of London, 1942-48; Prof. of Latin-American History, UCL, 1948-70. Research Dept, FO, 1939-45. Mem., UGC Cttee on Latin American Studies, 1962-64; Chairman: Cttee on Library Resources, Univ. of London, 1969-71; Management Cttee, Inst of Archæology, 1975-80; Mem. Adv. Cttee, British Library Reference Div., 1975-79. Governor, SOAS, 1965-80, Hon. Fellow 1981. Pres., RHistS, 1964-68 (Hon. Vice-Pres., 1968). Lectures: Enid Muir Meml, Univ. of Newcastle upon Tyne, 1962; Creighton, Univ. of London, 1964; Raleigh, Brit. Acad., 1965. Corresp. Member: Hispanic Soc. of America; Argentine Acad. of History; Instituto Histórico e Geográfico Brasileiro; Academia Chilena de la Historia; Sociedad Chilena de Historia y Geografia; Instituto Ecuatoriano de Ciencias Naturales; Sociedad Peruana de Historia; Instituto Histórico y Geográfico del Uruguay; Academia Nacional de la Historia, Venezuela. Hon. DLitt: Newcastle, 1966; Nottingham, 1972; Hon. LittD Liverpool, 1972; DUniv Essex, 1973. Comdr, Order of Rio Branco, Brazil, 1972. Machado de Assis Medal, Academia Brasileira de Letras, 1974. *Publications:* British Consular Reports on the Trade and Politics of Latin America, 1940; The Evolution of Modern Latin America, 1946; Liberation in South America, 1806-1827, 1952; Latin American History: A Guide to the Literature in English, 1958; The Diplomatic History of British Honduras, 1638-1901, 1961; (with G. S. Graham), The Navy and South America, 1807-1823 (Navy Records Soc.), 1962; (with J. Lynch) The Origins of the Latin American Revolutions, 1808-1826, 1965; Tradition and Revolt in Latin America and other Essays, 1969; The Detached Recollections of General D. F. O'Leary, 1969; The Royal Historical Society, 1868-1968, 1969; Robert Southey and his History of Brazil, 1978; Latin American Studies in Great Britain (autobiog.), 1978; Latin America and the Second World War, vol. I, 1939-1942, 1981, vol. II, 1942-1945, 1982; Co-edited: (with A. D. Momigliano) Byzantine Studies and Other Essays by N. H. Baynes, 1955; (with Elisabeth Humphreys) The Historian's Business and Other Essays by Richard Pares, 1961; contrib. to The New Cambridge Modern History, vols VIII, IX and X. *Address:* 5 St James's Close, Prince Albert Road, NW8 7LG. *T:* 01-722 3628.

HUMPHREYS, (Travers) Christmas, QC 1959; an Additional Judge, Central Criminal Court, 1968-76; *b* London, 1901; *o surv. s* of late Hon. Sir Travers Humphreys, PC; *m* 1927, Aileen Maude (*d* 1975), *d* of Dr Charles Irvine and Alice Faulkner of Escrick, Yorks and Tunbridge Wells. *Educ:* Malvern Coll.; Trinity Hall, Cambridge (MA, LLB). Called to the Bar, Inner Temple, 1924; Bencher, 1955. Junior Counsel to Treasury for certain Appeals, 1932; Junior Counsel to Treasury at Central Criminal Court, 1934; Recorder of: Deal, 1942-56; Guildford, 1956-68; Deputy Chairman: E Kent QS, 1947-71; Co. of Kent QS, 1962-71. Senior Prosecuting Counsel to the Crown at the Central Criminal Court, 1950-59; a Commissioner, 1962-68. Founding Pres. of Buddhist Lodge, London, 1924 (now Buddhist Society); Past Pres. The Shakespearean Authorship Soc.; Joint Vice-Chm. Royal India, Pakistan and Ceylon Society; a Vice-Pres. Tibet Soc., 1962. *Publications:* The Great Pearl Robbery of 1913, 1928; What is Buddhism?, 1928, and Concentration and Meditation, 1935; The Development of Buddhism in England, 1937; Studies in the Middle Way, 1940; Poems of Peace and War, 1941; Seagulls, and other Poems, 1942; Karma and Rebirth, 1943; Shadows and other Poems, 1945; Walk On, 1947; Via Tokyo, 1948; Zen Buddhism, 1949; Buddhism (Pelican books), 1951; The Way of Action, 1960; Zen Comes West, 1960; The Wisdom of Buddhism, 1960; Poems I Remember, 1960; A Popular Dictionary of Buddhism, 1962; Zen, A Way of Life, 1962; Sixty Years of Buddhism in England, 1968; The Buddhist Way of Life, 1969; Buddhist Poems, 1971; A Western Approach to Zen, 1972; Exploring Buddhism, 1974; The Search Within, 1977; Both Sides of the Circle (autobiog.), 1978; pamphlets, articles, etc. *Recreations:* music, entertaining; Eastern philosophy and Chinese Art. *Address:* 58 Marlborough Place, NW8 0PL. *T:* 01-624 4987.

HUMPHREYS-DAVIES, (George) Peter, CB 1953; Deputy Secretary, Ministry of Agriculture, Fisheries and Food, 1960-67; *b* 23 June 1909; *e s* of late J. W. S. Humphreys-Davies, Southfields, Eastbourne; *m* 1935, Barbara, *d* of late Lieut-Col F. G. Crompton, White Court, Alfriston, Sussex; two *s* one *d. Educ:* Sherborne; New Coll., Oxford. Craven Scholar, 1931. Asst Principal, Admiralty, 1932; HM Treasury, 1934; Private Sec. to Prime

Ministers, 1936-38; Under-Sec., HM Treasury, 1949-56; Deputy Sec., Ministry of Supply, 1956-60; Directing Staff, Imperial Defence Coll., 1954. *Address:* Weyhurst Farm, Rudgwick, Sussex. *T:* Rudgwick 2221.

HUMPHRIES, Barry; *see* Humphries, J. B.

HUMPHRIES, David Ernest; Director General Future Projects, Procurement Executive, Ministry of Defence, since 1981; *b* 3 Feb. 1937; *er s* of late Ernest Augustus Humphries and of Kathleen Humphries; *m* 1959, Wendy Rosemary Cook; one *s* one *d*. *Educ:* Brighton Coll.; Corpus Christi Coll., Oxford (Scholar; MA). RAE Farnborough: Materials Dept., 1961; Avionics Dept, 1966; Head of Inertial Navigation Div., 1974; Head of Bombing and Navigation Div., 1975; Head of Systems Assessment Dept, 1978. *Recreations:* music, pipe organ building and playing. *Address:* Quits, 130 High Street, Sandhurst, Camberley, Surrey GU17 8HA. *T:* Yateley 873335.

HUMPHRIES, Gerard William; His Honour Judge Humphries; a Circuit Judge since 1980; *b* 13 Dec. 1928; *s* of late John Alfred Humphries and Marie Frances Humphries (*née* Whitwell), Barrow-in-Furness; *m* 1957, Margaret Valerie, *o d* of late W. W. Gelderd and of Margaret Gelderd (*née* Bell), Ulverston; four *s* one *d*. *Educ:* St Bede's Coll., Manchester; Manchester Univ. (LLB Hons). Called to Bar, Middle Temple, 1952; admitted to Northern Circuit, 1954; Asst Recorder of Salford, 1969-71; a Recorder of the Crown Court, 1974-80. Chairman: Medical Appeals Tribunal, 1976-80; Vaccine Damage Tribunals, 1979-80. Foundn Governor, St Bede's Coll., Manchester, 1978-. *Recreations:* tennis, squash, golf, music, caravanning. *Address:* 1 Deans Court, Crown Square, Manchester M3 3JL. *Clubs:* Lansdowne; Northern Lawn Tennis; Serra (N Cheshire) (Charter Mem. and Past Pres.).

HUMPHRIES, John Anthony Charles, OBE 1980; Chairman, Water Space Amenity Commission, since 1973; *b* 15 June 1925; *s* of Charles Humphries; *m* 1951, Olga June, *d* of Dr Geoffrey Duckworth, MRCP; four *d*. *Educ:* Fettes; Peterhouse, Cambridge (1st Law). Served War, RNVR, 1943-46. Solicitor (Hons), 1951. Vice-Pres., Inland Waterways Assoc., 1973- (Chm., 1970-73); Mem. Inland Waterways Amenity Adv. Council, 1971-; Adviser to HM Govt on amenity use of water space, 1972-; Mem. Nat. Water Council, 1973-. *Recreations:* inland waters, gardening. *Address:* 21 Parkside, Wimbledon, SW19. *T:* 01-946 3764. *Clubs:* RNVR, City.

HUMPHRIES, (John) Barry, AO 1982; music-hall artiste and author; *b* 17 Feb. 1934; *s* of J. A. E. Humphries and L. A. Brown; *m* 1st, 1959, Rosalind Tong; two *d* ; 2nd, 1979, Diane Millstead; one *s*. *Educ:* Melbourne Grammar Sch.; Univ. of Melbourne. Repertory seasons, Union Theatre, Melbourne, 1953-54; Phillip Street Revue Theatre, Sydney, 1956; Demon Barber, Lyric, Hammersmith, 1959; Oliver, New Theatre, 1960. One-man shows (author and performer): A Nice Night's Entertainment, 1962; Excuse I, 1965; Just a Show, 1968; A Load of Olde Stuffe, 1971; At Least You Can Say That You've Seen It, 1974; Housewife Superstar, 1976; Isn't It Pathetic at His Age, 1979; A Night with Dame Edna, 1979; An Evening's Intercourse with Barry Humphries, 1981-82. Numerous plays, films and broadcasts. *Publications:* Bizarre, 1964; Innocent Austral Verse, 1968; (with Nicholas Garland) The Wonderful World of Barry McKenzie, 1970; (with Nicholas Garland) Bazza Holds His Own, 1972; Dame Edna's Coffee Table Book, 1976; Les Patterson's Australia, 1979; Treasury of Australian Kitsch, 1980; A Nice Night's Entertainment, 1981; Dame Edna's Bedside Companion, 1982. *Recreations:* shopping, painting Portugal, profiting in strange concealments. *Address:* c/o Allen, Allen and Hemsley, PO Box 50, Sydney, NSW 2001, Australia. *Clubs:* Athenæum, Garrick.

HUMPIDGE, Kenneth Palmer, CMG 1957; *b* 18 Nov. 1902; *s* of James Dickerson Humpidge, Stroud; *m* 1938, Jill Mary Russell, *d* of Russell Pountney, Bristol; two *d*. *Educ:* Wycliffe Coll.; Univ. of Bristol. BSc (Engineering). Public Works Dept, Nigeria, 1926; Director of Public Works, Northern Region, Nigeria, 1948-54; Director of Federal Public Works, 1954-57; Min. of Transport, Nottingham and Cheltenham, 1958-69. FICE. *Address:* Corner Walls, Amberley, Stroud, Glos. *T:* Amberley 3212.

HUNN, Sir Jack (Kent), KT 1976; CMG 1964; LLM; Retired as Secretary of Defence, New Zealand (1963-66); *b* 24 Aug. 1906; *m* 1932, Dorothy Murray; two *s*. *Educ:* Wairarapa Coll.; Auckland Univ. Public Trust Office, 1924-46; Actg Sec. of Justice, 1950; Public Service Comr, 1954-61; Actg Sec. of Internal Affairs and Dir of Civil Defence, 1959; Sec. for Maori Affairs and Maori Trustee, 1960-63. Reviewed Cook Islands Public Service, 1949 and 1954; Mem. NZ delegn to Duke of Edinburgh's Conf, 1956; Mem. UN Salary Review Cttee, 1956; reviewed organisation of South Pacific Commn, Noumea and Sydney, 1957, and of SEATO, Bangkok, 1959. Chairman: Wildlife Commission of Inquiry, 1968; Fire Safety Inquiry, 1969; Fire Service Council, 1973; Fire Service Commn, 1974. *Publication:* Hunn Report on Maori Affairs, 1960. *Address:* 17 Kereru Street, Waikanae, Wellington, New Zealand. *T:* 5033.

HUNNINGS, Dr Gordon; Professor and Head of the Department of Philosophy, University of Natal, Pietermaritzburg, since 1977; *b* 8 March 1926; *s* of late William Butters Hunnings and Ellen Hunnings (*née* Robinson); *m* 1947, Jean Mary Hunnings (*née* Marland); one *s*. *Educ:* Christie Hospital & Holt Radium Inst., Manchester (MSRT); Univ. of Bristol (BA); University Coll., London (PhD). Radium Curator, Hogarth Radiotherapy Centre, Nottingham, 1948-61; Lectr in Philosophy, Univ. of Khartoum,

1966-69; Sen. Lectr in Philosophy, Univ. of Malaŵi, 1969-70; Prof. of Philosophy, Univ. of Malaŵi, 1970-73; Vice-Chancellor, Univ. of Malaŵi, 1973-77. *Publications:* various papers in sci. and philos. jls. *Recreations:* theology, music, philately. *Address:* Department of Philosophy, University of Natal, PO Box 375, Pietermaritzburg, Republic of South Africa. *T:* 64800.

HUNNISETT, Dr Roy Frank, FSA, FRHistS; on staff of Public Record Office, since 1953; *b* 26 Feb. 1928; *s* of Frank Hunnisett and Alice (*née* Budden); *m* 1954, Edith Margaret Evans. *Educ:* Bexhill Grammar Sch.; New Coll., Oxford (1st Cl. Hons Mod. Hist., 1952; Amy Mary Preston Read Scholar, 1952-53; MA, DPhil 1956). FRHistS 1961; FSA 1975. Lectr, New Coll., Oxford, 1957-63. Royal Historical Society: Alexander Prize, 1957; Mem. Council, 1974-77; Vice-Pres., 1979-82. Treasurer, Pipe Roll Soc., 1973-; Mem. Council, Selden Soc., 1975-. *Publications:* Calendar of Inquisitions Miscellaneous: (ed jtly) vol. IV, 1957 and vol. V, 1962; (ed) vol. VI, 1963 and vol. VII, 1968; The Medieval Coroners' Rolls, 1960; The Medieval Coroner, 1961; (ed) Bedfordshire Coroners' Rolls, 1961; (ed) Calendar of Nottinghamshire Coroners' Inquests 1485-1558, 1969; (contrib.) The Study of Medieval Records: essays in honour of Kathleen Major, 1971; Indexing for Editors, 1972; Editing Records for Publication, 1977; (ed jtly and contrib.) Medieval Legal Records edited in memory of C.A.F. Meekings, 1978; (ed) Wiltshire Coroners' Bills, 1752-1796, 1981; articles and revs in historical and legal jls. *Recreations:* Sussex, music, cricket. *Address:* 23 Byron Gardens, Sutton, Surrey SM1 3QG. *T:* 01-661 2618.

HUNSDON OF HUNSDON, Baron; *see* Aldenham, Baron.

HUNSWORTH, John Alfred; Director, Banking Information Service, 1954-81; *b* 23 Dec. 1921; *s* of late Fred Sheard Hunsworth and Lillian Margaret (*née* Wetmon); *m* 1972, Phyllis Sparshatt. *Educ:* Selhurst Grammar Sch.; LSE (BCom). Served War, 1941-46: commnd E Surrey Regt; served 2nd Punjab Regt, Indian Army, 1942-45. Dep. Editor, Bankers' Magazine, 1948-54. Freeman, City of London. *Publications:* contrib. prof. jls. *Recreations:* gardening, world travel, philately; formerly lawn tennis and Rugby football. *Address:* 29 West Hill, Sanderstead, Surrey. *T:* 01-657 2585. *Clubs:* Reform; Surrey County Cricket.

HUNT; *see* Crowther-Hunt.

HUNT, family name of **Barons Hunt, Hunt of Fawley** and **Hunt of Tanworth.**

HUNT, Baron, *cr* 1966, of Llanfair Waterdine (Life Peer); **(Henry Cecil) John Hunt;** KG 1979; Kt 1953; CBE 1945; DSO 1944; *b* 22 June 1910; *s* of late Capt. C. E. Hunt, MC, IA, and E. H. Hunt (*née* Crookshank); *m* 1936, Joy Mowbray-Green; four *d*. *Educ:* Marlborough Coll.; RMC, Sandhurst. Commissioned King's Royal Rifle Corps, 1930; seconded to Indian Police, 1934-35 and 1938-40 (Indian Police Medal, 1940). War of 1939-45: Comd 11th Bn KRRC, 1944; Comd 11th Indian Inf. Bde, 1944-46. Staff Coll., 1946; Joint Services Staff Coll., 1949; GSO 1, Jt Planning Staffs, MELF, 1946-48; Western Europe C's-in-C Cttee, 1950-51; Allied Land Forces, Central Europe, 1951-52; Col, Gen. Staff, HQ I (British) Corps, 1952; Asst Comdt, The Staff Coll., 1953-55; Comdr 168 Inf. Bde, TA, 1955-56; retired, 1956; Hon. Brigadier. Dir, Duke of Edinburgh's Award Scheme, 1956-66. Rector, Aberdeen Univ., 1963-66. Personal Adviser to Prime Minister during Nigerian Civil War, 1968-70. Chairman: Parole Bd for England and Wales, 1967-74; Adv. Cttee on Police in N Ireland, 1969; President: Council for Volunteers Overseas, 1968-74; Nat. Assoc. of Probation Officers, 1974-80; Mem., Royal Commn on the Press, 1974-77. Joined Social Democratic Party, 1981. Leader, British Expedition to Mount Everest, 1952-53. President: The Alpine Club, 1956-58; Climbers' Club, 1963-66; British Mountaineering Council, 1965-68; The National Ski Fedn, 1966-72; RGS, 1977-80 (Hon. FRGS). Order 1st Class Gurkha Right Hand, 1953; Indian Everest Medal, 1953; Hubbard Medal (US), 1954; Founder's Medal, RGS, 1954; Lawrence Memorial Medal, RCAS, 1954; Hon. DCL Durham 1954; Hon. LLD: Aberdeen 1954; London 1954; City 1976; Leeds 1979. *Publications:* The Ascent of Everest, 1953; Our Everest Adventure, 1954; (with C. Brasher) The Red Snows, 1959; Life is Meeting, 1978; (ed) My Favourite Mountaineering Stories, 1978. *Recreations:* mountaineering, ski-ing. *Address:* Highway Cottage, Aston, Henley-on-Thames. *Clubs:* Alpine, Ski Club of Great Britain.
See also Hugh Hunt.

HUNT OF FAWLEY, Baron *cr* 1973 (Life Peer), of Fawley in the County of Buckingham; **John Henderson Hunt,** CBE 1970; MA, DM Oxon, FRCP, FRCS, FRCGP; Hon. Fellow, Green College, Oxford, since 1980; President, Royal College of General Practitioners, 1967-70; Consulting Physician, St Dunstan's, 1948-66; PMO, Provident Mutual Life Assurance Association, since 1947; Governor: Charterhouse School; Sutton's Hospital, Old Charterhouse; National Hospital, Queen Square; *b* 3 July 1905; *s* of late Edmund Henderson Hunt, MCh, FRCS, and Laura Mary Buckingham; *m* 1941, Elisabeth Ernestine, *d* of Norman Evill, FRIBA; two *s* two *d*. (and one *s* decd). *Educ:* Charterhouse School; Balliol College, Oxford; St Bartholomew's Hospital. Theodore Williams Scholar in Physiology, Oxford Univ., 1926; Radcliffe Scholar in Pharmacology, 1928. RAF Medical Service, 1940-45 (Wing Comdr). Hon. Cons. in Gen. Practice, RAF; President: Hunterian Soc., 1953; Gen. Practice Section, Royal Soc. Med., 1956; Harveian Soc., 1970; Chelsea Clinical Soc., 1971; Med. Soc. London, 1973-; Soc. of Chiropodists, 1974;

Carthusian Soc., 1980; Vice-Pres. Brit. Med. Students' Assoc., 1956–; Hon. Sec. Council, Coll. of Gen. Practitioners, 1952-67; Med. Soc. of London, 1964-65; Mem. Council: RCS (co-opted), 1957-61; Med. Protection Soc., 1948-69; St Dunstan's, 1966–; Member: General Advisory Council, BBC, 1958-66; Med. Services Review Cttee, 1958-61; Med. Commn on Accident Prevention, 1967. Fellow, 1981, and Gold Medallist, 1980, BMA; Honorary Fellow: RSM, 1975; Aust. Coll. Gen. Practitioners; Amer. Acad. of Family Physicians; Hon. Mem. and Victor Johnston Medallist, Coll. of Family Physicians of Canada. Lloyd Roberts Lecturer (Manchester), 1956; Albert Wander Lectr (RSM), 1968; Paul Hopkins Memorial Orator (Brisbane), 1969; James MacKenzie Lectr, 1972. Late House Surgeon, and Chief Assistant Medical Professorial Unit, St Bart's Hosp. and House Physician National Hosp. Queen Square. *Publications:* (ed) Accident Prevention and Life Saving, 1965; various papers in medical journals; chapter on Raynaud's Phenomenon, in British Encyclopædia of Medical Practice, 1938 and 1948; chapter on Peripheral Vascular Disease, in Early Diagnosis, by Henry Miller, 1959. *Recreation:* gardening. *Address:* Seven Steep, Fawley Green, near Henley-on-Thames, Oxon. *T:* Henley-on-Thames 5853. *Club:* Royal Air Force.

HUNT OF TANWORTH, Baron *cr* 1980 (Life Peer), of Stratford-upon-Avon in the county of Warwickshire; **John Joseph Benedict Hunt**, GCB 1977 (KCB 1973; CB 1968); Secretary of the Cabinet, 1973-79; Chairman, Banque Nationale de Paris plc, since 1980; Deputy Chairman, Prudential Assurance Co. Ltd and Prudential Corporation plc, since 1982; Director: Prudential Pensions Ltd; IBM (UK) Ltd; Advisory Director, Unilever plc; Chairman, Disasters Emergency Committee, since 1981; *b* 23 Oct. 1919; *er* s of Major Arthur L. Hunt and Daphne Hunt; *m* 1st, 1941, Hon. Magdalen Mary Lister Robinson (*d* 1971), *yr d* of 1st Baron Robinson; two *s* one *d*; 2nd, 1973, Madeleine Frances, *d* of Sir William Hume, CMG, FRCP, and widow of Sir John Charles, KCB, FRCP. *Educ:* Downside; Magdalene College, Cambridge (Hon. Fellow, 1977). Served Royal Naval Volunteer Reserve, 1940-46, Lieut; Convoy escort, Western Approaches and in Far East. Home Civil Service, Admin. Class, 1946; Dominions Office, 1946; Priv. Sec. to Parly Under-Sec., 1947; 2nd Sec., Office of UK High Comr in Ceylon, 1948-50; Principal, 1949; Directing Staff, IDC, 1951-52; 1st Sec., Office of UK High Comr in Canada, 1953-56; Private Secretary to: Sec. of Cabinet and Perm. Sec. to Treasury and Head of Civil Service, 1956-58; Asst Secretary: CRO 1958; Cabinet Office, 1960; HM Treasury, 1962-67, Under-Sec., 1965; Dep. Sec., 1968 and First Civil Service Comr, Civil Service Dept, 1968-71; Third Sec., Treasury, 1971-72; Second Permanent Sec., Cabinet Office, 1972-73. *Recreation:* gardening. *Address:* 8 Wool Road, Wimbledon, SW20 0HW. *T:* 01-947 7640.

HUNT, Arthur James, OBE 1971; FRTPI, FRICS; Chief Reporter for Public Inquiries, Scottish Office, 1974-79; *b* 18 Nov. 1915; *s* of Edward Henry and Norah Hunt; *m* 1946, Fanny Betty Bacon; one *s* three *d*. *Educ:* Tauntons Sch., Southampton. Ordnance Survey, 1938-44; Planning Officer with West Sussex, Kent and Bucks County Councils, 1944-48; Asst County Planning Officer, East Sussex CC, 1948-52; Town Planning Officer, City of Durban, SA, 1953-61; Sen. and Principal Planning Inspector, Min. of Housing and Local Govt, 1961-68; Mem., Roskill Commn on the Third London Airport, 1968-70; Superintending Inspector, Dept of the Environment, 1971-74. *Recreations:* sailing, gardening, caravan touring. *Address:* Pentlands, 4 West Avenue, Middleton-on-Sea, West Sussex PO22 6EF.

HUNT, David James Fletcher, MBE 1973; MP (C) Wirral, since March 1976; an Assistant Government Whip, since 1981; *b* 21 May 1942; *s* of Alan Nathaniel Hunt, OBE and Jessie Edna Ellis Northrop Hunt; *m* 1973, Patricia Margery (*née* Orchard); two *s* two *d*. *Educ:* Liverpool Coll.; Montpellier Univ.; Bristol Univ. (LLB); Guildford Coll. of Law. Solicitor of Supreme Court of Judicature, admitted 1968; Partner, Stanley & Simpson North, 1977–; Consultant, Stanley Wasbrough & Co., 1965–. Chm., Cons. Shipping and Shipbuilding Cttee, 1977-79; Pres., British Youth Council, 1978-80; Vice-Chm., Parly Youth Lobby, 1978-80; Chm., Cons. Group for Europe, 1981- (Vice-Chm., 1978-81). PPS to Sec. of State for Trade, 1979-81, to Sec. of State for Defence, 1981. Chm., Bristol Univ. Conservatives, 1964-65; winner of Observer Mace for British Universities Debating Competition, 1965-66; Nat. Vice-Chm., FUCUA, 1965-66; Chm., Bristol City CPC, 1965-68; Nat. Vice-Chm., YCNAC, 1967-69; Chm., Bristol Fedn of YCs, 1970-71; Chm., British Youth Council, 1971-74; Nat. YC Chm., 1972-73; Vice-Chm., Nat. Union of Cons. and Unionist Assocs, 1974-76. Contested (C) Bristol South, 1970, Kingswood, 1974. Member: South Western Economic Planning Council, 1972-76; Adv. Cttee on Pop Festivals. *Publications:* Europe Right Ahead, 1978; A Time for Youth, 1978. *Recreations:* cricket, walking. *Address:* 23 Cable Road, Hoylake, Wirral L47 2AY. *T:* 051-632 4033; 14 Cowley Street, Westminster, SW1P 3LZ. *T:* 01-222 7149. *Club:* Hurlingham.

HUNT, Sir David (Wathen Stather), KCMG 1963 (CMG 1959); OBE 1943; Chairman, Board of Governors, Commonwealth Institute, since 1974; *b* 25 Sept. 1913; *s* of late Canon B. P. W. Stather Hunt, DD, and late Elizabeth Milner; *m* 1st, 1948, Pamela Muriel Medawar; two *s*; 2nd, 1968, Iro Myrianthousi. *Educ:* St Lawrence Coll.; Wadham Coll., Oxford. 1st Class Hon. Mods. 1934; 1st Class Lit. Hum. 1936; Thomas Whitcombe Greene Prize, 1936; Diploma in Classical Archæology, 1937; Fellow of Magdalen Coll., 1937. Served 1st Bn Welch Regt and General Staff in Middle East, Balkans, North Africa, Sicily, Italy, 1940-46 (despatches 3 times, OBE, US Bronze Star); GSO1 18th Army Group, 1943; 15th Army Group, 1943-45;

Col General Staff, Allied Force HQ, 1945-46; attached staff Governor-General Canada, 1946-47; released and granted hon. rank of Colonel, 1947. Principal, Dominions Office, 1947; 1st Secretary, Pretoria, 1948-49; Private Secretary to Prime Minister (Mr Attlee), 1950-51, (Mr Churchill) 1951-52; Asst Secretary, 1952; Deputy High Commissioner for UK, Lahore, 1954-56; Head of Central African Dept, Commonwealth Relations Office, 1956-59; Asst Under Secretary of State, Commonwealth Relations Office, 1959-60; accompanied the Prime Minister as an Adviser, on African tour, Jan.-Feb. 1960; Dep. High Comr for the UK in Lagos, Fedn of Nigeria, Oct. 1960-62; High Comr in Uganda, 1962-65; in Cyprus, 1965-67; in Nigeria, 1967-69; Ambassador to Brazil, 1969-73. Dep. Chm., Exim Credit Management and Consultants, 1974-77, Consultant, 1978-82. Mem. Appts Commn, Press Council, 1977-82; Dir, Observer Newspapers Ltd, 1982–. Montague Burton Vis. Prof. of Internat. Relations, Univ. of Edinburgh, 1980. Pres., Classical Assoc., 1981-82. Corresp. Mem., Brazilian Acad. of Arts, 1972. BBC TV Mastermind, 1977 and winner, Tenth Anniversary Mastermind Championship, 1982. US Bronze Star 1945. *Publications:* A Don at War, 1966; On the Spot, 1975; Footprints in Cyprus, 1982; articles in Annual of British School of Archæology at Athens and Journal of Hellenic Studies; Editor, The Times Yearbook of World Affairs, 1978–. *Recreations:* reading, writing and gardening. *Address:* Old Place, Lindfield, West Sussex RH16 2HU. *T:* Lindfield 2298. *Clubs:* Athenæum; Pen Clube do Brasil.

HUNT, Rt. Rev. Desmond Charles; a Suffragan Bishop of Toronto, since 1981; *b* 14 Sept. 1918; *s* of George P. and Kathleen Hunt; *m* 1944, Naomi F. Naylor; two *s* two *d*. *Educ:* Univ. of Toronto (BA). Rector: Trinity Church, Quebec City, 1943; St John's, Johnstown, USA, 1949; St James, Kingston, Ont., 1953; Church of the Messiah, Toronto, 1969. Hon. DD, Wycliffe Coll., Toronto, 1980. *Address:* Bishopslodge, Box 1150, Lakefield, Ontario, Canada. *T:* 705-652-7372.

HUNT, Gilbert Adams, CBE 1967; Chairman: Thurgar Bardex Ltd, since 1977; Hedin Ltd, since 1978; Director: Technology Transfer Associates Ltd, since 1980; Emray Group, since 1982; *b* Wolverhampton, 29 Dec. 1914; *s* of late Harold William Hunt, MBE, St Helen's, IoW; *m* 1938, Sarah (marr. diss. 1946), *d* of Captain Wadman-Taylor; *m* 1946, Olive Doreen, *d* of late Maurice Martin O'Brien; no *c*; *m* 1975, Diane Rosemary, *d* of Eric O. Cook; one *d*. *Educ:* Old Hall, Wellington; Malvern Coll., Worcester. Director, High Duty Alloys, Slough, 1950-54; Dir and Gen. Man., High Duty Alloys (Dir, HDA, Canada, Northern Steel Scaffold & Engrg Co., all subsids Hawker Siddeley Gp), 1954-60; Man. Dir, Massey-Ferguson (UK) Ltd; Jt Man. Dir, Massey-Ferguson-Perkins; Dir, Massey-Ferguson Holdings Ltd; Chm. and Man. Dir, Massey-Ferguson (Eire) Ltd; Chairman: Massey-Ferguson (Farm Services Ltd), 1960-67; Managing Dir, 1967-73, Chief Exec. Officer, 1967-76, Chm., 1973-79, Rootes Motors Ltd, later Chrysler UK Ltd (Pres., April-June 1979). Chm., Cttee for Industrial Technologies, DTI, 1972-78. President: Agricultural Engrs Association Ltd, 1965; The Society of Motor Manufacturers and Traders Ltd, 1972-74. Freeman, City of London, 1968. CEng, CIMechE, FIProdE, MIBF. Hon. DSc Cranfield, 1973. *Recreations:* golfing, sailing. *Address:* The Dutch House, Sheepstreet Lane, Etchingham, E Sussex.

HUNT, (Henry) Holman; Managing Director, PA Computers and Telecommunications, since 1976; Member, Monopolies and Mergers Commission, since 1980; *b* 13 May 1924; *s* of Henry Hunt and Jessie Brenda Beale; *m* 1954, Sonja Blom; one *s* two *d*. *Educ:* Squires Park Sch., Glasgow; Glasgow Univ. (MA). FCMA, FIMC, FBCS, FInstAM. Caledonian Insce Co., 1940-43; RAF, 1943-46; Glasgow Univ., 1946-50; Cadbury Bros, 1950-51; PA Management Consultants: Consultant, 1952-57; Manager, Office Organisation, 1958-63; Dir, Computer Div., 1964-69; Bd Dir, 1970–. Pres., Inst. of Management Consultants, 1974-75. *Recreations:* music, reading, walking, travel, photography, vegetable gardening. *Address:* 28 The Ridings, Epsom, Surrey KT18 5JJ. *T:* Epsom 20974. *Club:* Caledonian.

HUNT, Hugh (Sydney), CBE 1977; MA; Professor of Drama, University of Manchester, 1961-73, now Emeritus; *b* 25 Sept. 1911; *s* of Captain C. E. Hunt, MC, and late Ethel Helen (*née* Crookshank); *m* 1940, Janet Mary (*née* Gordon); one *s* one *d*. *Educ:* Marlborough Coll.; Magdalen Coll., Oxford. BA Oxon 1934, MA Oxon 1961. Hon. MA Manchester 1965. Pres. of OUDS, 1933-34; Producer: Maddermarket Theatre, Norwich, 1934; Croydon Repertory and Westminster Theatres, 1934-35; Producer, Abbey Theatre, Dublin, 1935-38; produced The White Steed, Cort Theatre, NY. Entered HM Forces, 1939; served War of 1939-45, with Scots Guards, King's Royal Rifle Corps, and Intelligence Service; demobilised, 1945. Director of Bristol Old Vic Company, 1945-49; Director Old Vic Company, London, 1949-53; Adjudicator Canadian Drama Festival Finals, 1954; Executive Officer, Elizabethan Theatre Trust, Australia, 1955-60; Artistic Dir, Abbey Theatre, Dublin, 1969-71. *Produced:* The Cherry Orchard, 1948, Love's Labour's Lost, 1949, Hamlet, 1950, New Theatre; Old Vic Seasons, 1951-53: Twelfth Night, Merry Wives of Windsor, Romeo and Juliet, Merchant of Venice, Julius Caesar; The Living Room, New York, 1954; in Australia, Medea, 1955, Twelfth Night, 1956, Hamlet, 1957, Julius Caesar, 1959; The Shaughraun, World Theatre Season, Dublin, 1968; Abbey Theatre Productions include: The Well of the Saints, 1969; The Hostage, 1970; The Morning after Optimism, 1971; Arrah-na-Pogue, 1972; The Silver Tassie, 1972; The Three Sisters, 1973; The Vicar of Wakefield, 1974; Red Roses for Me, 1980; Sydney Opera House: Peer Gynt, 1975; The Plough and the Stars, 1977. *Publications:* Old Vic Prefaces, 1954; The Director in the Theatre, 1954; The Making of

Australian Theatre, 1960; The Live Theatre, 1962; The Revels History of Drama in the English Language, vol. VII, sections 1 and 2, 1978; The Abbey, Ireland's National Theatre, 1979; Sean O'Casey, 1980; author or co-author of several Irish plays including The Invincibles and In The Train. *Address:* Cae Terfyn, Criccieth, Gwynedd LL52 0SA. *Club:* Garrick.
See also Baron Hunt.

HUNT, Prof. (Jack) Naylor, DSc, MD; FRCP; Professor of Physiology at Baylor College of Medicine, Houston, Texas, since 1977; *b* 29 April 1917; *s* of Charles Frank Hunt and Mary Anne Moss; *m* 1948, Claire, *d* of Sir William Haley, *qv*; no *c. Educ:* Royal Masonic School, Bushey; Guy's Hospital Medical School. Resident MO, Hertford British Hosp., Paris, 1940. Temp. Surgeon Lieutenant, RNVR, 1940-45. Dept of Physiology, Guy's Hospital Medical School, 1945-76, Prof. of Physiology, 1962-76. Mem. Senate, Univ. of London, 1974-76. Rockefeller Fellow, 1951; Arris and Gale Lecturer, 1951; Gillson Scholar, 1952. Med. Licence, Texas. *Publications:* various papers on the alimentary tract. *Address:* Physiology Department, Baylor College of Medicine, Houston, Texas 77030, USA.

HUNT, John Leonard; MP (C) Bromley, Ravensbourne, since 1974 (Bromley, 1964-74); *b* 27 Oct. 1929; *s* of late William John Hunt and of Dora Maud Hunt, Keston, Kent; unmarried. *Educ:* Dulwich Coll. Councillor, Bromley Borough Council, 1953-65; Alderman, Bromley Borough Council, 1961-65; Mayor of Bromley, 1963-64. Contested (C) S Lewisham, Gen. Election, 1959. Member: Select Cttee on Home Affairs (and Mem., Sub-Cttee on Race Relations and Immigration); Speaker's Panel of Chairmen, 1980-. Jt-Chm., British-Caribbean Assoc., 1968-77; Chm., Indo-British Parly Gp; UK Rep. at Council of Europe and WEU, 1973-77. Chm., Conservative Greater London Members' Cttee. Mem., BBC Gen. Adv. Council, 1975-. Mem. of London Stock Exchange, 1958-70. *Recreations:* foreign travel and good food. *Address:* 164 Sutherland Avenue, W9. *T:* 01-286 8324.

HUNT, John Maitland, MA, BLitt; Headmaster of Roedean since Jan. 1971; *b* 4 March 1932; *s* of Richard Herbert Alexander Hunt and Eileen Mary Isabelle Hunt (*née* Witt); *m* 1969, Sarah, *d* of Lt-Gen. Sir Derek Lang, *qv* ; two *s. Educ:* Radley College; Wadham College, Oxford. BA 1956; BLitt 1959; MA 1960. Assistant Master, Stowe School, 1958-70 (Sixth Form tutor in Geography). Chm., Bd of Managers, Common Entrance Exam. for Girls' Schs, 1974-81. *Publications:* various articles on fine arts and architecture. *Recreations:* estate management, fine arts, writing, travel. *Address:* Roedean School, Brighton, East Sussex BN2 5RQ. *T:* Brighton 680791. *Club:* English-Speaking Union.

HUNT, Brig. Kenneth, OBE 1955; MC 1943; Director, British Atlantic Committee, 1978-81; *b* 26 May 1914; *s* of late John Hunt and Elizabeth Hunt; *m* 1939, Mary Mabel Crickett; two *s* (and one *d* decd). *Educ:* Chatham House Sch., Ramsgate; sc Camberley; idc. Commissioned into Royal Artillery, 1940; served, Africa, Italy, Austria, with HAC, 1 RHA and 2 RHA, 1942-46 (despatches thrice); Bt Lt-Col 1955; CO 40 Fd Regt RA, 1958-60; CRA 51 Highland Div., 1961-63; IDC 1963; Dep. Standing Gp Rep. to N Atlantic Council, 1964-66; resigned commission, 1967. Dep. Dir, Internat. Inst. for Strategic Studies, 1967-77; Specialist Adviser to House of Commons Defence Cttee, 1971-. Visiting Professor: Fletcher Sch. of Law, Cambridge, Mass, 1975; Univ. of S California, 1978-79; Univ. of Surrey, 1978-. Mem. Council, RUSI, 1977; Fellow: IISS, 1977; Inst. of Security, Tokyo, 1979. Freeman, City of London, 1977. Hon. Dr (PolSci), Korea Univ., 1977. *Publications:* NATO without France, 1967; The Requirements of Military Technology, 1967; Defence with Fewer Men, 1973; ed, The Military Balance, 1967-77; (jt) The Third World War, 1978; contribs to learned jls, and chapters in many books, in UK, USA, E Asia. *Recreations:* fly-fishing, listening to jazz; formerly skiing. *Address:* 22 The Green, Ewell, Surrey KT17 3JN. *T:* 01-393 7906. *Club:* Army and Navy.

HUNT, Prof. Naylor; see Hunt, J. N.

HUNT, Rear Adm. Nicholas John Streynsham, MVO 1961; Director General, Naval Manpower and Training, since 1981; *b* 7 Nov. 1930; *s* of Brig. and Mrs J. M. Hunt; *m* 1966, Meriel Eve Givan; two *s* one *d. Educ:* BRNC, Dartmouth. CO HMS Burnaston, HMS Palliser, HMS Troubridge, HMS Intrepid, and BRNC, Dartmouth; Asst Private Sec. to late Princess Marina, Duchess of Kent; Executive Officer, HMS Ark Royal, 1969-71; RCDS 1974; Dir of Naval Plans, 1976-78; Flag Officer, Second Flotilla, 1980-81. *Recreation:* family. *Club:* Boodle's.

HUNT, Prof. Norman Charles, CBE 1975; Professor of Business Studies, since 1967, Vice-Principal, since 1980, University of Edinburgh; *b* 6 April 1918; *s* of Charles Hunt and Charlotte (*née* Jackson), Swindon, Wilts; *m* 1942, Lorna Mary, 2nd *d* of Mary and William Arthur Mann, Swindon, Wilts; two *s. Educ:* Commonweal Sch.; Swindon Coll.; University of London (Sir Edward Stern Schol., BCom 1st cl. hons); PhD (Edinburgh). On Staff (Research Dept and Personal Staff of Chief Mechanical Engineer); former GWR Co., 1934-45. Lectr in Organisation of Industry and Commerce, University of Edinburgh, 1946-53; Dir of Studies in Commerce, 1948-53; Prof. of Organisation of Industry and Commerce, 1953-66; Dean of Faculty of Social Sciences, 1962-64. Member: Departmental Cttee on Fire Service, 1967-70; Rubber Industry NEDC, 1968-71; UGC, 1969-78 (Vice-Chm., 1974-76); ODM Working Party on Management Educn and Training in Developing Countries, 1968-69; Bd of Governors (and Chm., Management

Develt Cttee), Council for Technical Educn and Training in Overseas Countries, 1971-75; Police Adv. Bd for Scotland, 1971-75; Council for Tertiary Educn in Scotland, 1979-; CNAA, 1979-. Chairman: R. and R. Clark Ltd, 1967-70; William Thyne Ltd, 1967-70; Director: William Thyne (Holdings) Ltd, 1963-70; William Thyne (Plastics) Ltd, 1967-70. Hon. DLitt Loughborough, 1975. *Publications:* Methods of Wage Payment in British Industry, 1951; (with W. D. Reekie) Management in the Social and Safety Services, 1974; articles in economic and management jls on industrial organisation, industrial relations, and management problems. *Recreations:* photography, motoring, foreign travel. *Address:* 65 Ravelston Dykes Road, Edinburgh EH4 3NU.

HUNT, Gen. Sir Peter (Mervyn), GCB 1973 (KCB 1969; CB 1965); DSO 1945; OBE 1947; DL; Chief of the General Staff, 1973-76; ADC (General) to the Queen, 1973-76; retired; Constable of the Tower of London, since 1980; *b* 11 March 1916; *s* of H. V. Hunt, Barrister-at-law; *m* 1st, 1940, Anne Stopford (*d* 1966), *d* of Vice-Adm. Hon. Arthur Stopford, CMG; one *s* one *d* ; 2nd, 1978, Susan, *d* of Captain D. G. Davidson, late Queen's Own Cameron Highlanders. *Educ:* Wellington Coll.; RMC Sandhurst. Commissioned QO Cameron Highlanders, 1936; commanded 7 Seaforth Highlanders, 1944-45; graduated Command and Gen. Staff Coll., Ft Leavenworth, USA. 1948; Instructor, Staff Coll., Camberley, 1952-55; Instructor, Imperial Defence Coll., 1956-57; commanded 1 Camerons, 1957-60; Comdr 152 (H) Infantry Brigade, TA, 1960-62; Chief of Staff, Scottish Command, 1962-64; GOC, 17 Div., also Comdr, Land Forces, Borneo, and Major-Gen., Bde of Gurkhas, 1964-65; Comdt, Royal Military Academy, Sandhurst, 1966-68; Comdr, FARELF, 1968-70; Comdr Northern Army Gp and C-in-C, BAOR, 1970-73. Col Queen's Own Highlanders (Seaforth and Camerons), 1966-75; Col 10th Princess Mary's Own Gurkha Rifles, 1966-75. Pres., 1940 Dunkirk Veterans' Assoc., 1976; Vice-Pres., NRA, 1976; Pres., NSRA, 1978; HM Special Comr, Duke of York's Royal Mil. Sch., Dover, 1977; Chairman: Council, King Edward VII Hosp., 1978; OStJ 1978, OStJ Council for Cornwall, 1978. DL Cornwall, 1982. CBIM (FBIM 1975). Chevalier of the Order of Leopold II and Croix de Guerre (Belgium), 1940 (awarded 1945). *Recreations:* philately, travel with a camera. *Address:* Rose Cottage, Portloe, Truro, Cornwall TR2 5RA. *Club:* Naval and Military.

HUNT, Philip Bodley; Director, Welsh Office Industry Department, 1975-76; *b* 28 July 1916; *s* of Bernard and Janet Hunt; *m* 1940, Eleanor Margaret Parnell; three *s* one *d. Educ:* Sedbergh Sch.; Christ Church, Oxford (MA). Joined Board of Trade, 1946; Trade Commissioner, Montreal, 1952; Principal Trade Commissioner, Vancouver, 1955; Commercial Counsellor, Canberra, 1957; returned Board of Trade, 1962; Dept of Economic Affairs, 1964-65; Director, London & SE Region, BoT, 1968; Dir, DTI Office for Wales, 1972-75. Chm., S Wales Marriage Guidance Council, 1974-; Mem. Nat. Exec., Nat. Marriage Guidance Council, 1977-; Deptl Mem. of Panel, County Structure Plans of S and W Glamorgan, 1978, of Gwent and Mid Glamorgan, 1979; Vice-Pres., Develt Corporation for Wales, 1980-. Silver Jubilee Medal, 1977. *Recreations:* gardening, music. *Address:* 93 Station Road, Llanishen, Cardiff CF4 5UU. *T:* Cardiff 750480.

HUNT, Ralph Holmes V.; see Vernon-Hunt.

HUNT, Sir Rex (Masterman), Kt 1982; CMG 1980; HM Diplomatic Service; Civil Commissioner, Falkland Islands, since 1982 (Governor and Commander-in-Chief, Falkland Islands, and High Commissioner, British Antarctic Territory, 1980-82); *b* 29 June 1926; *s* of H. W. Hunt and Ivy Masterman; *m* 1951, Mavis Amanda Buckland; one *s* one *d. Educ:* Coatham Sch.; St Peter's Coll., Oxford (BA). Served with RAF, 1944-48; Flt Lt RAFO. Entered HM Overseas Civil Service, 1951; District Comr, Uganda, 1962; CRO, 1963-64; 1st Sec., Kuching, 1964-65; Jesselton, 1965-67; Brunei, 1967; 1st Sec. (Econ.), Ankara, 1968-70; 1st Sec. and Head of Chancery, Jakarta, 1970-72; Asst ME Dept, FCO, 1972-74; Counsellor, Saigon, 1974-75, Kuala Lumpur, 1976-77; Dep. High Comr, Kuala Lumpur, 1977-79. *Recreations:* golf, flying, fishing. *Address:* c/o Foreign and Commonwealth Office, SW1A 2AH. *Club:* Royal Commonwealth Society.

HUNT, Richard Henry; Chief Registrar of the High Court of Justice in Bankruptcy, since 1980; *b* 19 Jan. 1912; *s* of late Francis John and Lucy Edwyna Louise Hunt; *m* 1947, Peggy Ashworth Richardson; two *s. Educ:* Marlborough Coll.; Queen's Coll., Oxford. Called to Bar, 1936. Served with RA, 1939-45: Western Desert, Greece and Crete campaigns (PoW, Crete, 1941). Elected Bencher, Middle Temple, 1964. Registrar of the High Court of Justice in Bankruptcy, 1966-80. *Recreations:* foreign travel, languages. *Club:* Royal Ocean Racing.

HUNT, Sir Robert (Frederick), Kt 1979; CBE 1974; DL; Chairman and Chief Executive, Dowty Group PLC, since 1975; Deputy Chairman, BL PLC, since 1982 (Director, since 1980); Director: Eagle Star Holdings Ltd, since 1980; Eagle Star Insurance Co. Ltd, since 1980; *b* 11 May 1918; *s* of late Arthur Hunt, Cheltenham and Kathleen Alice Cotton; *m* 1947, Joy Patricia Molly, *d* of late Charles Leslie Harding, Cheltenham; four *d. Educ:* Pates Grammar Sch., Cheltenham; N Glos Techn. Coll. Apprenticed Dowty Equipment Ltd, 1935; Chief Instructor to Co.'s Sch. of Hydraulics, 1940; RAF Trng Comd, 1940; Export Man., Dowty Equipment Ltd, 1946; Vice-Pres. and Gen. Man., 1949, Pres., 1954, Dowty Equipment of Canada Ltd; Dir, Dowty Gp Ltd, 1956, Dep. Chm. 1959-75. Chm., Bd of Trustees, Improvement District of Ajax, Ont., 1954; Dir, Ajax and Pickering Gen. Hosp., 1954; Chm.,

Cheltenham Hosp. Gp Man. Cttee, 1959; Chm., Glos AHA, 1974–81; Pres., 1967–68, Treas., 1973, Vice-Pres., 1976, Pres., 1977–78, SBAC. FEng; FCASI 1976; FRAeS 1968, Hon. FRAeS 1981. Hon. DSc Bath, 1979. DL Glos, 1977; Hon. Freeman of Cheltenham, 1980. *Recreations:* family interests, gardening. *Address:* Dowty Group PLC, Arle Court, Cheltenham, Glos. *T:* Cheltenham 21411. *Club:* New (Cheltenham).

HUNT, Roger; a Recorder of the Crown Court, since 1978; *b* 15 Jan. 1935; *s* of Richard Henry Hunt and Monica Hunt; *m* 1963, Barbara Ann Eccles; two *d. Educ:* Giggleswick Sch.; Pembroke Coll., Oxford (MA). Commnd Royal Signals, 1955; served Germany, HQ 4th Guards Bde, 1956; TA 49th Inf. Div., Signal Regt, 1956–63. Called to the Bar, Lincoln's Inn, 1960; joined NE Circuit, 1961. *Recreations:* golf, gardening. *Address:* 6 Park Square, Leeds LS1 2LW. *T:* Leeds 459763. *Club:* Moortown Golf.

HUNT, Roland Charles Colin, CMG 1965; HM Diplomatic Service, retired; Director, British National Committee, International Chamber of Commerce, 1973–76; *b* 19 March 1916; *s* of Colin and Dorothea Hunt, Oxford; *m* 1939, Pauline, 2nd *d* of late Dr J. C. Maxwell Garnett, CBE; three *s* two *d. Educ:* Rugby Sch. (scholar); The Queen's Coll., Oxford (scholar). Entered Indian Civil Service, 1938. Served in various districts in Madras as Sub-Collector, 1941–45; Joint Sec. and Sec., Board of Revenue (Civil Supplies), Madras, 1946–47; joined Commonwealth Relations Office, 1948; served on staff of United Kingdom High Commissioner in Pakistan (Karachi), 1948–50; Mem. UK Delegation to African Defence Facilities Conference, Nairobi, 1951; served in Office of UK High Comr in S Africa, 1952–55; Asst Sec., 1955; attached to Office of High Comr for Fedn of Malaya, Kuala Lumpur, 1956; Dep. High Commisioner for the UK in the Federation of Malaya, Kuala Lumpur, 1957–59; Imperial Defence Coll., 1960; Asst Sec., Commonwealth Relations Office, 1961; British Dep. High Comr in Pakistan, 1962–65; British High Commissioner in Uganda, 1965–67; Asst Under-Sec. of State, CO and FCO, 1967–70; High Comr, Trinidad and Tobago, 1970–73. *Publication:* (ed jtly) The District Officer in India, 1930–1947, 1980. *Recreations:* ball-games, piano-playing. *Address:* Spindlewood, Whitchurch Hill, Reading, Berks.

HUNT, Vernon Arthur Moore, CBE 1958; farmer; *b* 27 Dec. 1912; *s* of late Cecil Arthur Hunt, RWS, MA, LLB and late Phyllis Clara Hunt (*née* Lucas); *m* 1949, Betty Yvonne Macduff; two *s* one *d. Educ:* Sherborne; Trinity Coll., Cambridge (BA); Coll. of Aeronautical Engrg (Pilot's Licence). Airline Pilot, 1938; Capt., BOAC, 1939–46; Min. of Civil Aviation: Dep. Dir of Ops, 1947; Dir of Control and Navigation, 1949; Dir of Control (Plans), Nat. Air Traffic Control Service, 1962–68; Chief Inspector of Accidents, DTI (formerly BoT), 1968–73. Mollison Trophy, 1939; George Taylor Gold Medal, RAeS, 1954. CEng; FRAeS 1956; FRIN (FIN 1956). *Publications:* contribs to RAeS and Inst. Navigation Jls. *Recreation:* photography. *Address:* Neadon, Manaton, near Newton Abbot, Devon TQ13 9UY. *T:* Manaton 310. *Clubs:* Naval and Military; Hayling Island Sailing.

HUNT, Rt. Rev. Warren; *see* Hunt, Rt Rev. W. W.

HUNT, Rt. Rev. (William) Warren, MA; Hon. Assistant Bishop to the Dioceses of Chichester and Portsmouth, since 1978; *b* 22 Jan. 1909; *s* of Harry Hunt, Carlisle; *m* 1939, Mollie, *d* of Edwin Green, Heswall, Cheshire; four *d. Educ:* Carlisle Grammar School; Keble College, Oxford; Cuddesdon Theological College, Oxford. Deacon 1932; Priest 1933; Curate: Kendal Parish Church, 1932–35; St Martin-in-the-Fields, London, 1935–40. Chaplain to the Forces, 1940–44. Vicar, St Nicholas, Radford, Coventry, 1944–48; Vicar, Holy Trinity, Leamington Spa, 1948–57, and Rural Dean of Leamington; Vicar and Rural Dean of Croydon, 1957–65; Bishop Suffragan of Repton, 1965–Jan. 1977. Hon. Canon Canterbury Cathedral, 1957. *Recreations:* golf, vicarage lawn croquet (own rules); travel, reading. *Address:* 15 Lynch Down, Funtington, Chichester, West Sussex PO18 9LR. *T:* West Ashling 536.

HUNTER, family name of **Baron Hunter of Newington.**

HUNTER, Hon. Lord; John Oswald Mair Hunter, VRD; a Senator of the College of Justice in Scotland, since 1961; *b* 21 Feb. 1913; *s* of John Mair Hunter, QC(Scot) and Jessie Donald Drew; *m* 1939, Doris Mary Simpson; one *s* one *d. Educ:* Edinburgh Acad.; Rugby; New Coll., Oxford (BA 1934, MA 1961); Edinburgh Univ. (LLB 1936, LLD 1975). Entered RNVR, 1933; served War 1939–45 (despatches); Lt-Comdr RNVR; retired list 1949. Called to Bar, Inner Temple, 1937; admitted to Faculty of Advocates, 1937; QC(Scot) 1951. Advocate Depute (Home), 1954–57; Sheriff of Ayr and Bute, 1957–61. Chairman: Deptl Cttee on Scottish Salmon and Trout Fisheries, 1961–64; Lands Valuation Appeal Court, 1966–71; Scottish Law Commn, 1971–81; Scottish Council on Crime, 1972–75; Dep. Chm., Boundary Commn for Scotland, 1971–76. Pres., Scottish Univs Law Inst., 1972–77; Member: Scottish Records Adv. Council, 1966–81; Statute Law Cttee, 1971–81; Chm., later Hon. Pres., Cttee, RNLI (Dunbar), 1969–80 and 1981–; Hon. Pres., Scottish Assoc. for Study of Delinquency, 1971–. *Recreation:* angling. *Address:* Court of Session, Parliament Square, Edinburgh.

HUNTER OF NEWINGTON, Baron *cr* 1978 (Life Peer), of Newington in the District of the City of Edinburgh; **Robert Brockie Hunter,** Kt 1977; MBE 1945; FRCP; DL; Vice-Chancellor and Principal, University of Birmingham, 1968–81; *b* 14 July 1915; *s* of Robert Marshall Hunter and Margaret Thorburn Brockie; *m* 1940, Kathleen Margaret Douglas; three *s* one

d. Educ: George Watson's Coll. MB, ChB Edinburgh, 1938; FRCPE 1950; FACP 1963; FRSEd 1964; FInstBiol 1968; FFCM 1975. Personal Physician, Field-Marshal Montgomery, NW Europe, 1944–45. Asst Dir, Edinburgh Post-Graduate Bd for Medicine, 1947; Lectr in Therapeutics, University of Edinburgh, 1947; Commonwealth (Harkness) Fellow in Medicine, 1948; Lectr in Clinical Medicine, University of St Andrews, 1948; Dean of the Faculty of Medicine, 1958–62; Prof. of Materia Medica, Pharmacology and Therapeutics, University of St Andrews, 1948–67, and in University of Dundee, 1967–68; late Consultant Physician to Dundee General Hosps and Dir, Post-graduate Medical Education. Hon. Lectr in Physiology, Boston Univ. Sch. of Medicine, USA, 1950. Member: Clinical Res. Bd, MRC, 1960–64; GMC, 1962–68; Ministry of Health Cttee on Safety of Drugs, 1963–68 (Chm., Clinical Trials Sub-Cttee); UGC, 1964–68 (Chm., Medical Sub-Cttee, 1966–68); West Midlands RHA, 1974–; Nuffield Cttee of Inquiry into Dental Educn, 1977–80; DHSS Working Party on Medical Administrators in Health Service, 1970–72 (Chm.); DHSS Independent Scientific Cttee on Smoking and Health, 1973–80; Med. Adv. Cttee of Cttee of Vice-Chancellors and Principals, 1976–81; Management Cttee, King Edward's Hospital Fund, 1980–; House of Lords Select Cttee on Science and Technology, 1980–. Malthe Foundation Lecturer, Oslo, 1958. Editor, Quarterly Journal of Medicine, 1957–67. Fellow (ex-President) Royal Medical Society. Major, Royal Army Medical Corps. Gained Purdue Frederick Medical Achievement Award, 1958. Senior Commonwealth Travelling Fellowship, 1960; Vis. Professor of Medicine: Post-Graduate school, University of Adelaide, 1965; McGill Univ., 1968. Christie Gordon Lectr, Birmingham, 1978; Raymond Priestley Lectr, Birmingham Univ., Goodman Lectr, Royal Soc., 1981; Wade Lectr, Keele Univ., 1982. DL West Midlands, 1975. Hon. LLD: Dundee, 1969; Birmingham, 1974; Hon. DSc Aston, 1981. *Publications:* Clinical Science; contrib. to Br. Med. Jl, Lancet, Edinburgh Med. Jl, Quarterly Jl of Medicine. *Recreation:* fishing. *Address:* 3 Oakdene Drive, Fiery Hill Road, Barnt Green, Birmingham. *Club:* Oriental.

HUNTER, Adam; miner; *b* 11 Nov. 1908; *m* ; one *s* one *d. Educ:* Kelty Public Elem. Sch. Joined Labour Party, 1933; Member: Exec. Cttee NUM (Scot. Area); Lochgelly Dist Council, 1948–52; Sec., Fife Co-op. Assoc. and Dist Council, 1947–64. MP (Lab) Dunfermline Burghs, 1964–74, Dunfermline, 1974–79. Mem. Fife CC, 1961–64. Voluntary Tutor, Nat. Council of Labour Colls. *Recreation:* reading. *Address:* Whitegates Terrace, Kelty, Fife, Scotland.

HUNTER, Adam Kenneth Fisher; Sheriff of North Strathclyde at Paisley; *b* 1920; *o s* of late Thomas C. Hunter, MBE, AMIEE, and Elizabeth Hunter; *m* 1949, Joan Stella Hiscock, MB, ChB; one *s* two *d. Educ:* Dunfermline High Sch.; St Andrews Univ. (MA Hons); Edinburgh Univ. (LLB). Called to Bar, 1946; Chm. of the Supreme Court Legal Aid Cttee of the Law Society of Scotland, 1949–53; Standing Junior Counsel to HM Commissioners of Customs and Excise, 1950–53; Sheriff-Substitute, later Sheriff, of Renfrew and Argyll (subseq. N Strathclyde) at Paisley, 1953–. *Recreations:* photography, music, motor boating. *Address:* Ravenswood, Bridge of Weir, Renfrewshire. *T:* 612017.

HUNTER, Dr Alan, CBE 1975; Director, Royal Greenwich Observatory, 1973–75; *b* 9 Sept. 1912; *s* of late George Hunter and Mary Edwards; *m* 1937, W. Joan Portnell; four *s. Educ:* Imperial Coll. of Science and Technology. PhD, DIC; FRAS. Research Asst, Applied Mech. Dept, RNC, 1940–46; Royal Observatory, Greenwich: Asst, 1937–61; Chief Asst, 1961–67; Dep. Dir, 1967–73. Editor, The Observatory, 1943–49. Treas., Royal Astronomical Soc., 1967–76 (Sec. 1949–56, Vice-Pres. 1957, 1965, 1976); Pres., British Astronomical Assoc., 1957–59; Chm., Large Telescope Users' Panel, 1974–75 (sec. 1969–73). Liveryman, Worshipful Co. of Clockmakers, 1975. *Recreation:* gardening. *Address:* Thatched Cottage, Frettenham Road, Hainford, Norwich NR10 3BW. *T:* Norwich 890179.
See also Prof. Louis Hunter.

HUNTER, Alastair; *see* Hunter, M. I. A.

HUNTER, Sir Alexander (Albert), KBE 1976; Speaker of the House of Representatives of Belize, since 1974; *b* Belize, British Honduras, 21 May 1920; *s* of Alexander J. Hunter, KSG, and Laura Hunter (*née* Reyes); *m* 1947, Araceli Cayetana Marin S., Alajuela, Costa Rica; one *s* two *d. Educ:* St John's Coll. (Jesuit), Belize City; Regis Coll. (Jesuit), Denver, Colo; Queen's Univ., Kingston, Ont. In Accounting Dept, United Fruit Co., Costa Rica, 1940–41 and 1945–47. Served War, NCO, Radar Br., RCAF, 1942–45: active service in UK, Azores, Gibraltar, with 220 Sqdn Coastal Comd, RAF. Joined staff of James Brodie & Co. Ltd, as Accountant, 1947; Company Sec., 1948; Dir 1952–61; Consultant: James Brodie & Co. Ltd, 1975–; Anschutz Overseas Corp., Denver, Colo, 1975–; Chm., Belize Airways Ltd, 1979–. MLA (PUP), Fort George Div., 1961; Minister of Natural Resources, Commerce and Industry, March 1961; MHR (PUP), Fort George, under new Constitution, 1965; Minister of Natural Resources and Trade, 1965–69; Minister of Trade and Industry, 1969–74; Mem., Constitutional Ministerial External Affairs Cttee, 1965–74. Represented Belize: Bd of Governors, Caribbean Develt Bank, 1969–74; Council of Ministers, CARIFTA, 1971–73; Council of Ministers, Caribbean Economic Community, 1973–74. Acted as Dep. Governor, Aug. 1975. Pres., Belize Br., CPA; Chairman: Standing Orders Cttee; Regulations Cttee; House Cttee. People's United Party: Treasurer and Mem. Central Party Council, 1961–74; Mem. Exec. Cttee, 1961–74; Chm. Fort

George Div., 1961-74. Former Vice-Pres., Belize Chamber of Commerce; Member: Property Valuation Appeal Bd, 1960; Citrus Industry Investigation Cttee, 1960. Member: West India Cttee; Internat. Game Fish Assoc.; Belize Rifle Club; Nat. Geographic Soc. *Recreations:* pistol-shooting, hunting, light and heavy tackle salt-water fishing. *Address:* 6 St Matthew Street, Caribbean Shores, Belize City, Belize. *T:* 4482.

HUNTER, Alistair John; HM Diplomatic Service; Head of Chancery, Bonn, since 1980; *b* 9 Aug. 1936; *s* of Kenneth Clarke Hunter and Joan Tunks; *m* 1st, 1963; one *s* two *d* ; 2nd, 1978, Helge Milton (*née* Kahle). *Educ:* Felsted; Magdalen Coll., Oxford. 1st Cl. Hons English. Royal Air Force, 1955-57; Oxford Univ., 1957-60; CRO, 1961-65; Private Sec. to Permanent Under-Sec., 1961-63; 2nd Sec., British High Commn, Kuala Lumpur, 1963-65; 1st Sec. (Commercial), British Office, Peking, 1965-68; seconded to Cabinet Office, 1969-70; FCO, 1970-73; 1st Sec., Rome, 1973-75; FCO, 1975-80. *Address:* c/o Foreign and Commonwealth Office, SW1.

HUNTER, Rt. Rev. Anthony George Weaver; *b* 3 June 1916; *s* of Herbert George Hunter and Ethel Frances Weaver; *m* 1948, Joan Isobel Marshall (*d* 1981); *m* 1982, Emlyn Marianne Garton (*née* Dent). *Educ:* Wanstead; Leeds Univ. (BA); Coll. of the Resurrection, Mirfield. Deacon, 1941; Priest, 1942; Curate of St George's, Jesmond, 1941-43; Orlando Mission Dist, 1943-47; Johannesburg Coloured Mission, 1947-48; Curate of St George's, Jesmond, 1948-49; Vicar of Ashington, 1949-60; Proctor in Convocation, 1959-60; Vicar of Huddersfield, 1960-68; Rural Dean of Huddersfield, 1960-68; Hon. Canon of Wakefield, 1962-68; Proctor in Convocation, 1962-68; Bishop of Swaziland, 1968-75; Rector of Hexham, Dio. Newcastle, 1975-79; Asst Bishop, Dio. Newcastle, 1976-80; Supernumerary Bishop, 1980-81; Acting Archdeacon of Lindisfarne, 1981; retd Oct. 1981. OStJ. *Recreations:* walking, gardening, travel. *Address:* Knocklaw Cottage, Alnwick Road, Rothbury, Northumberland. *T:* Rothbury 20281. *Club:* St John's.

HUNTER, Prof. Archibald Macbride, MA, BD, PhD Glasgow, Hon. DD Glasgow, DPhil Oxon; Professor of New Testament Exegesis (formerly Biblical Criticism) in Aberdeen University, 1945-71; Master of Christ's College, Aberdeen, 1957-71; *b* 16 Jan. 1906; *s* of late Rev. Archibald Hunter, Kilwinning, and Crissie Swan MacNeish; *m* 1934, Margaret Wylie Swanson; one *s* one *d. Educ:* Hutchesons' Grammar Sch., Glasgow; Universities of Glasgow, Marburg and Oxford. Minister in Comrie, Perthshire, 1934-37; Prof. of New Testament, in Mansfield Coll., Oxford, 1937-42; Minister in Kinnoull, Perth, 1942-45. Hastie Lecturer, Glasgow Univ., 1938; Lee Lecturer, 1950; Sprunt Lecturer (Richmond, Va), 1954. *Publications:* Paul and His Predecessors, 1940; The Unity of the New Testament, 1943; Introducing the New Testament, 1945; The Gospel according to St Mark, 1949; The Work and Words of Jesus, 1950; Interpreting the New Testament, 1951; Design for Life, 1953; Interpreting Paul's Gospel, 1954; The Epistle to the Romans, 1955; Introducing New Testament Theology, 1957; The Layman's Bible Commentary, Vol. 22, 1959; Interpreting The Parables, 1960; Teaching and Preaching the New Testament, 1963; The Gospel according to John, 1965; The Gospel according to St Paul, 1966; According to John, 1968; Bible and Gospel, 1969; Exploring the New Testament, 1971; The Parables Then and Now, 1971; Taking the Christian View, 1974; On P. T. Forsyth, 1974; The New Testament Today, 1974; Gospel and Apostle, 1975; Jesus Lord and Saviour, 1976; The Gospel Then and Now, 1978; Christ and the Kingdom, 1980; The Fifth Evangelist, 1980; Preaching the New Testament, 1981; articles and reviews in theological journals. *Recreation:* fishing. *Address:* 3 Carwinshoch View, Ayr. *T:* Ayr 264403.

HUNTER, Rt. Rev. Barry Russell; *see* Riverina, Bishop of.

HUNTER, Dr Colin Graeme, DSC 1939; physician, National Health Service, retired; *b* 31 Jan. 1913; *s* of Robert Hunter and Evelyn Harrison; *m* 1944, Betty Louise Riley; one *s* one *d. Educ:* Scots Coll., Univ. of Otago, New Zealand. MD 1958, DSc 1970. Christchurch Hosp. NZ, 1937-38; Royal Naval Medical Service, 1938-55; Univ. of Toronto, Canada, 1955-58; Shell Research Ltd, 1958-73. Fellow: RCP (Lond.); Roy. Coll. of Pathologists; etc; also Mem. many societies; Freeman of City of London. *Publications:* scientific papers in many jls devoted to chemical and radiation toxicology. *Recreations:* sailing, squash. *Address:* 77 Ocean Court, Richmond Walk, Plymouth, Devon. *T:* Plymouth 558505. *Clubs:* Army and Navy; Royal Naval Sailing Association.

HUNTER, Hon. David Stronach; Hon. Mr Justice Hunter; a Judge of the Supreme Court of Hong Kong, since 1982; *b* 5 Oct. 1926; *s* of late Robert John Hunter and late Jayne Evelyn Hunter; *m* 1959, Janet Muriel Faulkner; one *s* two *d. Educ:* Harrow Sch., Hertford Coll., Oxford (Baring Scholar); MA Jurisprudence. Called to Bar, Middle Temple, 1951, Bencher, 1979; QC 1971; a Recorder of the Crown Court, 1975-81. *Recreations:* golf, gardening, painting. *Address:* Supreme Court, Hong Kong; 6E Barnton Court, Harbour City, Tsim Sha Tsui, Kowloon. *Club:* MCC.

HUNTER, Sir (Ernest) John, Kt 1964; CBE 1960; DL; Executive Chairman, Swan Hunter Group Ltd, 1972-79 (Chairman and Managing Director, 1957-72); Chairman, North East Broadcasting Company Ltd; *b* 3 Nov. 1912; 2nd *s* of George Ernest Hunter and Elsie Hunter (*née* Edwards); *m* 1st, 1937, Joanne Winifred Wilkinson; one *s* ; 2nd, 1949, Sybil Malfroy (*née* Gordon); one *s* one step *d. Educ:* Oundle Sch.; Cambridge Univ.; Durham Univ. (BSc). Apprentice, Swan, Hunter and Wigham Richardson Ltd, 1930-31; St John's

Coll., Cambridge Univ., 1931-32; Durham Univ. (BSc) 1932-35; Draughtsman, SH and WR Ltd, 1935-37; Asst Manager: Barclay, Curle & Co. 1937-39; SH and WR Dry Docks, 1939-41; Asst Gen. Manager, SH and WR Dry Docks, 1941-43, Gen. Manager, 1943-45; Dir, Swan Hunter and Wigham Richardson Ltd, 1945, Chm., 1957-66. Director: Newcastle & Gateshead Water Co.; Common Bros Ltd, 1966-82; Midland Bank. Chairman: N-E Coast Ship-repairers' Association, 1957-58; Tyne Shipbuilders' Association, 1956-57; Dry Dock Owners' and Repairers' Central Council, 1961-62; President: NEC Institution, 1958-60; Shipbuilding Employers' Fedn, 1956-57; British Employers' Confedn, 1962-64; Shipbuilders' and Repairers' Nat. Assoc., 1968-. Mem. NEDC, 1962-64. First Chm., Central Training Council, 1964-68. Mem. of Cttees connected with shipping and with youth. Liveryman, Company of Shipwrights; Freeman: of City of London (by redemption); of Borough of Wallsend, 1972. DL Northumberland, 1968. Hon. DSc Newcastle, 1968. *Publications:* contrib. to Trans NEC Instn. *Recreations:* golf and gardening. *Address:* Beech Close Farm, Newton, Stocksfield, Northumberland. *T:* Stocksfield 3124. *Clubs:* Garrick; Northern Counties (Newcastle upon Tyne).

HUNTER, Evan; writer; *b* New York, 15 Oct. 1926; *s* of Charles F. Lombino and Marie Lombino; *m* 1st, 1949, Anita Melnick (marr. diss.); three *s* ; 2nd, 1973, Mary Vann Finley; one step *d. Educ:* Cooper Union; Hunter Coll. (BA 1950). Served USNR. Literary Father of the Year, 1961; Phi Beta Kappa. *Publications include: as Evan Hunter:* The Blackboard Jungle, 1954; Second Ending, 1956; Strangers When We Meet, 1958; A Matter of Conviction, 1959; The Remarkable Harry, 1960; The Wonderful Button, 1961; Mothers and Daughters, 1961; Happy New Year, Herbie, 1963; Buddwing, 1964; The Paper Dragon, 1966; A Horse's Head, 1967; Last Summer, 1968; Sons, 1969; Nobody Knew They Were There, 1971; Every Little Crook and Nanny, 1972; The Easter Man, 1972; Seven, 1972; Come Winter, 1973; Streets of Gold, 1974; The Chisholms, 1976; Me and Mr Stenner, 1977; Walk Proud, 1978; Love, Dad, 1981; *as Ed McBain:* Cop Hater, 1956; The Mugger, 1956; The Pusher, 1956; The Con Man, 1957; Killer's Choice, 1958; Killer's Payoff, 1958; Lady Killer, 1958; Killer's Wedge, 1959; 'Til Death, 1959; King's Ransom, 1959; Give the Boys a Great Big Hand, 1960; Lady, Lady, I Did It, 1961; The Empty Hours, 1962; Like Love, 1962; Ten Plus One, 1963; Ax, 1964; The Sentries, 1965; He Who Hesitates, 1965; Doll, 1965; Eighty Million Eyes, 1966; Fuzz, 1968; Shotgun, 1969; Jigsaw, 1970; Hail, Hail, the Gang's All Here!, 1971; Sadie When She Died, 1972; Let's Hear It for the Deaf Man, 1972; Hail to the Chief, 1973; Bread, 1974; Where There's Smoke, 1975; Blood Relatives, 1975; So Long as You Both Shall Live, 1976; Guns, 1977; Long Time No See, 1977; Goldilocks, 1978; Calypso, 1979; Ghosts, 1980; Rumpelstiltskin, 1981; Heat, 1981; Beauty and the Beast, 1982; *screenplays:* Strangers When We Meet, 1959; The Birds, 1962; Fuzz, 1972; Walk Proud, 1979; *plays:* The Easter Man, 1964; The Conjuror, 1969. *Recreation:* travelling. *Address:* John Farquharson Ltd, Bell House, Bell Yard, WC2A 2JU.

HUNTER, Guy, CMG 1973; author and consultant; Overseas Development Institute since 1967; *b* 7 Nov. 1911; *s* of Lt-Col C. F. Hunter, DSO, and Mrs A. W. Hunter (*née* Cobbett); *m* 1941, Agnes Louisa Merrylees. *Educ:* Winchester Coll.; Trinity Coll., Cambridge. 1st cl. hons Classics, MA. Called to Bar, Middle Temple, 1935. Civil Defence, Regional Officer, Edinburgh and Principal Officer, Glasgow and W Scotland, 1939-43; Dir (Admin), Middle East Supply Centre, GHQ, Cairo, 1943-45; Dir, PEP, 1945-46; Warden, Urchfont Manor, Wilts, and Grantley Hall, Yorks, Adult Colleges, 1946-55; Dir of Studies, 1st Duke of Edinburgh's Conf., 1955-56; from 1957, research and consultancy for developing countries overseas, mainly E, W and Central Africa, India, Pakistan, SE Asia, Fiji. Launching and 1st Dir, East African Staff Coll., 1966; Inst. of Race Relations, 1959-66. Visiting Prof., Univ. of Reading, 1969-75. Member: Economic and Social Cttee, EEC, 1975-78; Council for Internat. Develt (ODM), 1977-. Bd of Governors, Inst. of Develt Studies, Sussex Univ. *Publications:* Studies in Management, 1961; The New Societies of Tropical Africa, 1962; Education for a Developing Region, 1963; (ed) Industrialization and Race Relations, 1965; South East Asia: Race, Culture and Nation, 1966; The Best of Both Worlds, 1967; Modernising Peasant Societies, 1969; The Administration of Agricultural Development, 1970; (ed jtly) Serving the Small Farmer, 1974; (ed jtly) Policy and Practice in Rural Development, 1976. *Recreations:* gardening, nature, travel. *Address:* The Miller's Cottage, Hartest, Bury St Edmunds, Suffolk. *T:* Hartest 334. *Club:* Travellers'.

HUNTER, Ian Bruce Hope, MBE 1945; Impresario; Chairman and Managing Director, Harold Holt Ltd; *b* 2 April 1919; *s* of late W. O. Hunter; *m* 1949, Susan (*d* 1977), *d* of late Brig. A. G. Russell; four *d. Educ:* Fettes Coll., Edinburgh; abroad as pupil of Dr Fritz Busch and at Glyndebourne. Served War of 1939-45, Lieut-Col. Asst to Artistic Dir, Edinburgh Festival, 1946-48; Artistic Administrator, Edinburgh Festival, 1949-50; Artistic Dir, Edinburgh Festival, 1951-55. Director, Bath Festivals, 1948, 1955, 1958-68; Adviser, Adelaide Festivals, 1960-64; Artistic Director: Festivals of the City of London, 1962-80; Brighton Festivals, 1967-; (with Yehudi Menuhin) Windsor Festivals, 1969-72; Hong Kong Arts Festivals, 1973-75; Malvern Festival, 1977-; Dir-General, Commonwealth Arts Festival, 1965. Dir, British Nat. Day Entertainment, Expo' 67. Member: Opera/Ballet Enquiry for Arts Council, 1967-69; Arts Administration Course Enquiry for Arts Council, 1970-71; Arts Council Trng Cttee, 1974-76; Exec. Cttee, Musicians' Benevolent Fund; Centenary Appeal Cttee, RCM; Adv. Cttee, Britain Salutes New York, 1983; Chm., Entertainments Cttee, Queen's Silver Jubilee Appeal; Pres., British Arts

Festivals Assoc., 1978-81; Dep. Chm., Stravinsky Festival Trust; Trustee, Chichester Festival Theatre Trust; Governor, Yehudi Menuhin Sch. R. B. Bennett Commonwealth Prize for 1966. Hon. Mem., Guildhall Sch. of Music and Drama. FRSA (Mem. Council, 1968-73, 1976-; Chm. Council and a Vice-Pres., 1981-). Mem. Ct of Assistants, Musicians' Co., 1981-. *Recreation:* gardening. *Address:* Harold Holt Ltd, 31 Sinclair Road, W14 0NS. *T:* 01-603 4600. *Club:* Garrick.

HUNTER, Ian Gerald Adamson, QC 1980; *b* 3 Oct. 1944; *s* of Gerald Oliver Hunter and late Jessie Hunter; *m* 1975, Maggie (*née* Reed); two *s. Educ:* Reading Sch.; Pembroke Coll., Cambridge (Open Scholar, Squire Univ. Law Scholar, Trevelyan Scholar, BA (double first in Law), MA, LLB); Harvard Law Sch. (Kennedy Memorial Scholar, LLM). Called to the Bar, Inner Temple, 1967 (Duke of Edinburgh Entrance Scholar, Major Scholar). Mem. and Rapporteur, Internat. Law Assoc. Anti-Trust Cttee, 1968-72. *Publications:* articles on public international law. *Recreations:* bebop, other good music, French cooking. *Address:* 4 Essex Court, Temple, EC4. *T:* 01-583 9191. *Club:* Piltdown Golf.

HUNTER, Brig. Ian Murray, CVO 1954; MBE 1943; psc 1943; fsc (US) 1955; FAIM 1964; Chairman, Allied Rubber Products (Qld) Pty Ltd; *b* Sydney, Aust., 10 July 1917; *s* of late Dr James Hunter, Stranraer, Scotland; *m* 1947, Rosemary Jane Batchelor; two *s* two *d. Educ:* Cranbrook Sch., Sydney; RMC, Duntroon. Lieut Aust. Staff Corps, and AIF 1939; 2/1 MG Bn, 1939-40; T/Capt. 1940; Staff Capt., 25 Inf. Bde, 1940-41; Middle East Staff Coll., Haifa, 1941; DA QMG (1), HQ 6 Div., 1941-42; T/Major 1942; AQMG, NT Force (MBE), 1942-43; Staff Sch. (Aust.), 1943; Gen. Staff 3 Corps and Advanced HQ Allied Land Forces, 1943-44; Lieut-Col 1945; Instructor, Staff Sch., 1945; AQMG, and Col BCOF, 1946-47; AQMG, AHQ and JCOSA, 1947; AA & QMG, HQ, 3 Div., 1948-50; Royal Visit, 1949; Exec. Commonwealth Jubilee Celebrations, 1950-51; CO 2 Recruit Trg Bn, 1952; CO 4 RAR, 1953; Executive and Commonwealth Marshal, Royal Visit, 1952, and 1954; Command and Gen. Staff Coll., Fort Leavenworth, USA, 1954-55; Military Mission, Washington, 1955-56; Officer i/c Admin., N Comd, 1956-59; Comd 11 Inf. Bde, 1959-60; Command 2nd RQR 1960-62; Chief of Staff 1st Div., 1963; Commandant, Australian Staff Coll., 1963-65; Comdr, Papua New Guinea Comd, 1966-69; DQMG, Army HQ, 1969. Indep. Mem., Presbyterian Church Property Commn, 1974-80. *Recreations:* golf, squash, swimming, riding. *Address:* Garthland, 42 Charlton Street, Ascot, Brisbane, Queensland 4007, Australia; Finchley, Hargreaves Street, Blackheath, NSW 2785, Australia. *Clubs:* Australian (Sydney); Queensland (Brisbane); Royal Sydney Golf.

HUNTER, Sir John; *see* Hunter, Sir E. J.

HUNTER, Surg. Rear-Adm. (D) John, CB 1973; OBE 1963; Director of Naval Dental Services, Ministry of Defence, 1971-74; *b* 21 Aug. 1915; *s* of Hugh Hunter and Evelyn Marian Hunter (*née* Jessop), Hale, Cheshire; *m* 1947, Anne Madelaine Hardwicke, Friarmayne, Dorset; three *s* two *d. Educ:* Bowdon Coll., Cheshire; Manchester Univ. LDS 1939. Surg. Lieut (D) RNVR 1940; HMS Kenya and 10th Cruiser Sqdn, 1941-42; HMS Newcastle and HMS Howe, British Pacific Fleet, 1944-47; transf. to RN; HMS Forth on Staff of Rear-Adm. Destroyers, Mediterranean (Surg. Lt-Comdr), 1948-50; Dartmouth, Royal Marines; Surg. Comdr, Staff of Flag Officer Flotillas Mediterranean, 1956; service ashore in Admty, 1960-63; Surg. Captain (D), Staff of C-in-C Mediterranean, 1965-66; Staff of C-in-C Plymouth Comd, 1967-68; Fleet Dental Surgeon on Staff of C-in-C Western Fleet, 1969-70. QHDS 1971-74. FRSocMed. Mem., South Hams DC, 1979-. *Recreations:* ocean racing, cruising, shooting. *Address:* Horsewells, Newton Ferrers, Plymouth PL8 1AT. *T:* Plymouth 872254. *Clubs:* Royal Ocean Racing, Army and Navy; Royal Western Yacht.

HUNTER, John; His Honour Judge Hunter; a Circuit Judge, since 1980; *b* 12 April 1921; *s* of Charles and Mary Hunter; *m* 1956, Margaret Cynthia Webb; one *s* two *d. Educ:* Fitzwilliam House, Cambridge (MA). Called to the Bar, Lincoln's Inn, 1952. Served War, Army, 1939-46. Industry, 1952-62; practised at the Bar, 1962-80. *Recreations:* sailing, gardening. *Address:* 6 Pump Court, Temple, EC4Y 7AP. *Clubs:* London Rowing; Sussex Yacht.

HUNTER, John Murray, CB 1980; MC 1943; Commissioner for Administration and Finance, Forestry Commission, 1976-81; *b* 10 Nov. 1920; *s* of Rev. Dr John Hunter and Frances Hunter (*née* Martin); *m* 1948, Margaret, *d* of late Stanley Cursiter, CBE, RSW, RSA, and Phyllis Eda (*née* Hourston); two *s* three *d. Educ:* Fettes Coll.; Clare Coll., Cambridge. Served Army, 1941-45: Captain, The Rifle Bde. Served in Diplomatic Service at Canberra, Bogotá, Baghdad, Prague, Buenos Aires and in FCO (Head of Consular Dept, 1966, and of Latin America Dept, 1971-73); idc 1961, sowc 1965, jssc (Senior Directing Staff), 1967-69. Sec., Forestry Commn, 1973-75. *Recreations:* music, golf, curling; formerly Rugby football (Cambridge 1946, Scotland 1947). *Address:* 21 Glencairn Crescent, Edinburgh EH12 5BT. *Club:* Scottish Arts (Edinburgh).

HUNTER, John Oswald Mair; *see* Hunter, Hon. Lord.

HUNTER, Major Joseph Charles, CBE 1959; MC 1918; DL; Chairman Leeds Regional Hospital Board, 1955-63; *b* 1 Sept. 1894; *s* of W. S. Hunter, Gilling Castle, Yorks; *m* 1st, 1920, Cicely Longueville Heywood-Jones (marr. diss. 1930); one *s* two *d*; 2nd, 1934, Prudence Josephine Whetstone; two *s. Educ:*

Harrow. Commissioned Yorkshire Hussars Yeo., 1912. Served European War, 1914-18, Europe; Regular Commission RA 1916; retired, 1920 (Major, R of O); War of 1939-45, in RA. Alderman W Riding of Yorks County Council, 1955-61 (Mem. 1947-55); DL W Riding of Yorks and York, 1959, N Yorkshire, 1974. *Address:* Havikil Lodge, Scotton, Knaresborough, N Yorks. *T:* Harrogate 863400.

HUNTER, Keith Robert, OBE 1981; Secretary of the Board, and Head of Director-General's Department, British Council, since 1982; *b* 29 May 1936; *s* of Robert Ernest Williamson and Winifred Mary Hunter; *m* 1959, Ann Patricia Fuller; one *s* two *d. Educ:* Hymers Coll., Hull; Magdalen Coll., Oxford (MA). Joined British Council, 1962; Lectr, Royal Sch. of Admin, Phnom Penh, 1960-64; Schs Recruitment Dept, 1964-66; SOAS, 1966-67; Asst Rep., Hong Kong, 1967-69; Dir, Penang, 1970-72; Dep. Rep., Kuala Lumpur, 1972-74; London Univ. Inst. of Educn, 1974-75; Rep., Algeria, 1975-78; First Sec. (Cultural), subseq. Cultural Counsellor (British Council Rep.), Peking, 1979-82. *Recreations:* music, DIY. *Address:* British Council, 10 Spring Gardens, SW1A 2BV.

HUNTER, Prof. Laurence Colvin; Professor of Applied Economics, University of Glasgow, since 1970; Chairman, Post Office Arbitration Tribunal, since 1974; *b* 8 Aug. 1934; *s* of Laurence O. and Jessie P. Hunter; *m* 1958, Evelyn Margaret (*née* Green); three *s* one *d. Educ:* Hillhead High Sch., Glasgow; Univ. of Glasgow (MA); University Coll., Oxford (DPhil). Asst, Manchester Univ., 1958-59; National Service, 1959-61; Post-Doctoral Fellow, Univ. of Chicago, 1961-62; Univ. of Glasgow: Lectr, 1962; Sen. Lectr, 1967; Titular Prof., 1969. Member: Ct of Inquiry into miners' strike, 1972; Council, Advisory, Conciliation and Arbitration Service, 1974-; Royal Commn on Legal Services in Scotland, 1976-80; Dep. Chm., Police Negotiating Bd, 1980-. *Publications:* (with G. L. Reid) Urban Worker Mobility, 1968; (with D. J. Robertson) Economics of Wages and Labour, 1969, 2nd edn (with C. Mulvey), 1981; (with G. L. Reid and D. Boddy) Labour Problems of Technological Change, 1970; (with A. W. J. Thomson) The Nationalised Transport Industries, 1973; (with R. B. McKersie) Pay, Productivity and Collective Bargaining, 1973; several articles in economic jls. *Recreations:* golf, painting. *Address:* 23 Boclair Road, Bearsden, Glasgow. *T:* 041-942 0793. *Club:* Royal Commonwealth Society.

HUNTER, Rt. Rev. Leslie Stannard, MA; DD Lambeth; Hon. LLD Sheffield; Hon. DCL Dunelm; Hon. DD Toronto, 1954; *b* 1890; *yr s* of late Rev. John Hunter, DD, Minister of the King's Weigh House Church, London, and Trinity Church, Glasgow, and Marion Martin; *m* 1919, Grace Marion (*d* 1975), *yr d* of late Samuel McAulay, JP, of Aylesby, Lincs. *Educ:* Kelvinside Academy; New Coll., Oxford. Pres. of the Oxford University Lawn Tennis Club, 1911-12; Asst Sec. of the Student Christian Movement of Great Britain and Ireland, 1913-20; Curate of St Peter's, Brockley, SE, 1915-18; served with YMCA, BEF, 1916, and the Army of Occupation, 1919; Mem. of the Army and Religion Inquiry Commission, 1917-19; Asst Curate of St Martin-in-the-Fields and Chaplain of Charing Cross Hospital, London, 1921-22; Residentiary Canon of Newcastle on Tyne, 1922-26 and 1931-39; Vicar of Barking, Essex, 1926-30; Archdeacon of Northumberland, 1931-39; Chm., Tyneside Council of Social Service, 1933-39; Chaplain to the King, 1936-39; Bishop of Sheffield, 1939-62; Chm. of Sheffield Hospitals Council, 1940-49. House of Lords, 1944-62. Foundation Mem., British Council of Churches; Select Preacher, Universities of: Oxford, Cambridge, Glasgow, Aberdeen, St Andrews and Edinburgh, various years; Birks Memorial Lecturer, McGill Univ., Montreal, 1951. Hon. Freeman of City of Sheffield, 1962. Comdr Order of the Dannebrog, 1952. *Publications:* John Hunter, DD: A Life, 1921; A Parson's Job: Aspects of Work in the English Church, 1931; Let Us Go Forward, 1944; Church Strategy in a Changing World, 1950; The Seed and the Fruit, 1953; A Mission of the People of God, 1961; (Editor and part author) A Diocesan Service Book, 1965; Scandinavian Churches, 1965; The English Church: a New Look, 1966. *Address:* c/o Williams & Glyn's Bank, Columbia House, 69 Aldwych, WC2.

HUNTER, Prof. Louis, PhD, DSc (London); FRSC; retired as Professor of Chemistry and Head of Department of Chemistry, University of Leicester (previously University College) (1946-65); Professor Emeritus, 1966; *b* 4 Dec. 1899; *s* of late George Hunter and Mary Edwards; *m* 1926, Laura Thorpe (decd). *Educ:* East London College (subsequently Queen Mary College), University of London. Assistant Lecturer, University Coll. of North Wales, Bangor, 1920-25; Lecturer and Head of Dept of Chemistry, University Coll., Leicester, 1925, Prof. of Chemistry, 1946, and Vice-Principal, 1952-57, Pro-Vice-Chancellor, University of Leicester, 1957-60. Visiting Professor: Univ. of Ibadan, Nigeria, 1963, and Ahmadu Bello Univ., 1966. Mem. of Council: Chemical Soc., 1944-47, 1950-53, 1956-59; Royal Institute of Chemistry, 1947-50, 1961-64 (Vice-Pres., 1964-66; Chm. E Midlands Section, 1938-40); Sec. Section B (Chemistry), British Assoc. for the Advancement of Science, 1939-51, Recorder, 1951-56, mem. of Council, 1956-60. Hon. Fire Observer, Home Office, 1942-54; Scientific Adviser for Civil Defence, N Midlands, 1951-75; Dep. Chm., 1939, Chm., 1952, Leicester Jt Recruiting Bd. *Publications:* mainly in Jl Chem. Soc. *Address:* Thatched Cottage, Frettenham Road, Hainford, Norwich NR10 3BW.
See also A. Hunter.

HUNTER, (Mark Ian) Alastair, MD, FRCP; Physician, St George's Hospital, SW1, 1946-76, now Emeritus; *b* 18 June 1909; *s* of Mark Oliver Hunter and Diana Rachel (*née* Jones); unmarried. *Educ:* Winchester Coll.

(Entrance Exhibition); Trinity Coll., Cambridge. Qualified as Doctor, 1933. MD Cambridge, 1945; FRCP (London), 1947. Dean, St George's Hosp. Med. Sch., 1956-71. Asst Registrar, 1950-57, Censor, 1971-73, Vice-Pres. and Sen. Censor, 1974-75, RCP. Mem., GMC. Dep. Vice-Chancellor, Univ. of London, 1972-73. Medical Awards Administrator, Commonwealth Scholarship Commn, 1974-. Hon. Keeper, 20th Century Painting, Fitzwilliam Museum, Cambridge. *Publications*: medical subjects. *Recreations*: various. *Address*: 42 Festing Road, Putney, SW15. *T*: 01-789 8644. *Clubs*: Royal Automobile, MCC.

HUNTER, Muir Vane Skerrett, QC 1965; Lt-Col (Hon.); MA Oxon; MRI; Barrister-at-Law; *b* 19 Aug. 1913; *s* of late H. S. Hunter, Home Civil Service; *m* 1939, Dorothea Eason (JP), *e d* of late P. E. Verstone; one *d*. *Educ*: Westminster Sch.; Christ Church, Oxford (Scholar). Called, Gray's Inn, 1938 (*ad eundem* Inner Temple, 1965); Holker Senior Scholar; Bencher, Gray's Inn, 1976. Served 1940-46: Royal Armoured Corps; GS Intelligence, GHQ (India), GSO 1 attd War and Legislative Depts, Govt of India; returned to the Bar, 1946; standing counsel (bankruptcy) to Bd of Trade, 1949-65; Dep. Chm., Advisory Cttee on Service Candidates, HO; Member: EEC Bankruptcy Adv. Cttee, Dept of Trade, 1973-76; Insolvency Law Review Cttee, Dept of Trade, 1977-82; Founder-Chairman, N Kensington Neighbourhood Law Centre, 1969-71; Mem. Exec. Cttee and Council of "Justice". Amnesty International Observer: Burundi, 1962; Rhodesia, 1969; Turkey, 1972. Governor, Royal Shakespeare Theatre, 1978-. Member: Council, Royal Shakespeare Theatre Trust; Royal Shakespeare Theatre Centenary Appeal Cttee. *Publications*: Senior Editor, Williams on Bankruptcy, 1958-78, Williams and Muir Hunter on Bankruptcy, 1979-; Emergent Africa and the Rule of Law, 1963; Jt editor: Halsbury's Laws (4th edn), Vol 3; Atkins' Forms, Vol 7; Specialist Editor, Kerr on Receivers, 15th edn. *Recreations*: theatre, travel. *Address*: 49 Hurlingham Court, SW6 3UP. *T*: 01-736 1757; (chambers) 3 Paper Buildings, Temple, EC4Y 7EU. *T*: 01-353 3721. *Clubs*: Army and Navy, Hurlingham.

HUNTER, Dame Pamela, DBE 1981; Vice-Chairman, National Union of Conservative and Unionist Associations, 1981; *b* 3 Oct. 1919; *d* of late Col T. G. Greenwell, TD, JP, DL, and M. W. Greenwell; *m* 1942, Gordon Lovegrove Hunter; one *s* one *d*. *Educ*: Westonbirt Sch., Tetbury; Eastbourne Sch. of Domestic Economy. Served WRNS, 1942-45. Mem., Conservative Nat. Union Exec. Cttee, 1972-; Chairman: Northern Area Cons. Women's Adv. Cttee, 1972-75; Cons. Women's Nat. Adv. Cttee, 1978-81. Mem., Northumbrian Water Authority, 1973-76. Mem., Berwick-upon-Tweed Borough Council, 1973-. School Governor. *Recreations*: charity work for NSPCC, SCF and RNLI, antiques. *Address*: The Coach House, Chatton, Alnwick, Northumberland NE66 5PY. *T*: Chatton 259. *Club*: Lansdowne.

HUNTER, Philip Brown, TD; Chairman, John Holt & Co. (Liverpool) Ltd, 1967-71; *b* 30 May 1909; *s* of Charles Edward Hunter and Marion (*née* Harper); *m* 1937, Joyce Mary (*née* Holt); two *s* two *d*. *Educ*: Birkenhead Sch.; London University. Practised as Solicitor, 1933-80. Chm., Guardian Royal Exchange Assurance (Sierra Leone) Ltd, 1972-79; Director: Cammell Laird & Co. Ltd, 1949-70 (Chm. 1966-70); John Holt & Co. (Liverpool) Ltd, 1951-71 (Exec. Dir, 1960); Guardian Royal Exchange, 1969-79; Guardian Assurance Co. Ltd, 1967-79; Royal Exchange (Nigeria) Ltd, 1972-79; Lion of Africa Insurance Co. Ltd, 1972-79; Enterprise Insurance Co. Ltd, Ghana, 1972-79. *Recreations*: sailing, gardening. *Address*: Bryn Hyfryd, Lixwm, Holywell, Clwyd. *T*: Halkyn 780059. *Club*: Caledonian.

HUNTER, Rita, CBE 1980; prima donna; leading soprano, Sadler's Wells, since 1958; *b* 15 Aug. 1933; *d* of Charles Newton Hunter and Lucy Hunter; *m* 1960, John Darnley-Thomas; one *d*. *Educ*: Wallasey. Joined Carl Rosa, 1950. Debut: Berlin, 1970; Covent Garden, 1972; Metropolitan, NY, 1972; Munich, 1973; Australia, 1978 (returned 1980 and 1981); Seattle Wagner Fest., 1980. Sang Brünnhilde in first complete Ring cycle with Sadler's Wells, 1973; first perf. of Norma, NY Metropolitan, 1975. Has sung leading roles in Aida, Trovatore, Masked Ball, Cavalleria Rusticana, Lohengrin, Flying Dutchman, Idomeneo, Don Carlos, Turandot, Nabucco, Macbeth. Many recordings, including complete Siegfried and complete Euryanthe. Hon. DLitt Warwick, 1978. RAM 1978. *Recreations*: sewing, oil painting, reading, gardening (Mem. Royal Nat. Rose Soc.), caravanning (Mem. Caravan Club). *Address*: The Cornerways, 70 Embercourt Road, Thames Ditton, Surrey KT7 0LW. *T*: 01-398 7502. *Club*: White Elephant.

HUNTER, William Hill, CBE 1971; CA; JP; Partner in McLay, McAlister & McGibbon, Chartered Accountants, since 1946; *b* 5 Nov. 1916; *s* of Robert Dalglish Hunter and Mrs Margaret Walker Hill or Hunter; *m* 1947, Kathleen, *d* of William Alfred Cole; two *s*. *Educ*: Cumnock Academy. Chartered Accountant, 1940. Served War: enlisted as private, RASC, 1940; commissioned RA, 1941; Staff Capt., Italy, 1944-46. Director: Abbey National Building Soc. (Scottish Adv. Bd); City of Glasgow Friendly Soc.; J. & G. Grant Glenfarclas Distillery. President: W Renfrewshire Conservative and Unionist Assoc., 1972-; Scottish Young Unionist Assoc., 1958-60; Scottish Unionist Assoc., 1964-65. Contested (U) South Ayrshire, 1959 and 1964. Chm., Salvation Army Adv. Bd in Strathclyde, 1982- (Vice-Chm., 1972-82); Hon. Treasurer, Quarrier's Homes, 1979-; Pres., City of Glasgow Friendly Soc., 1980-. JP Renfrewshire, 1970. *Recreations*: gardening, golf, swimming. *Address*: Armitage, Kilmacolm, Renfrewshire PA13 4PH. *T*: Kilmacolm 2444. *Club*: Royal Scottish Automobile.

HUNTER BLAIR, Sir James, 7th Bt, *cr* 1786; *b* 7 May 1889; *s* of Capt. Sir E. Hunter Blair, 6th Bt, and Cecilia (*d* 1951), *d* of late Sir W. Farrer; *S* father 1945; *m* 1st, 1917, Jean (*d* 1953), *d* of late T. W. McIntyre, Sorn Castle, Ayrshire; two *s*; 2nd, 1954, Mrs Ethel Norah Collins (*d* 1966). *Educ*: Wellington; Balliol Coll., Oxford (1st Hon. Mod., 2nd Greats); Christ's Coll., Cambridge (Forestry). Articled to solicitor, 1911-14; served with Seaforth Highlanders, 1915-19; District Officer with Forestry Commission, 1920-28. Forestry and Farming at Blairquhan, 1928-. *Publications*: articles on Forestry and cognate subjects in various journals. *Recreation*: collecting pictures. *Heir*: *s* Edward Thomas Hunter Blair [*b* 15 Dec. 1920; *m* 1956, Norma (*d* 1972), *d* of W. S. Harris; one adopted *s* one adopted *d*. *Educ*: Eton; Balliol Coll., Oxford]. *Address*: Milton, Maybole, Ayrshire. *Clubs*: United Oxford & Cambridge University; New (Edinburgh).

HUNTER JOHNSTON, David Alan; Director: British American & General Trust; Trans Oceanic Trust; *b* 16 Jan. 1915; *s* of James Ernest Johnston and Florence Edith Johnston (*née* Hunter); *m* 1949, Philippa Frances Ray; three *s* one *d*. *Educ*: Christ's Hospital; King's Coll., London. Royal Ordnance Factories, Woolwich, 1936-39; S Metropolitan Gas Co., 1939-44; Min. of Economic Warfare (Economic and Industrial Planning Staff), 1944-45; Control Office for Germany and Austria, 1945-47; Sec. to Scientific Cttee for Germany, 1946; FO (German Section), Asst Head, German Gen. Economic Dept, 1947-49; HM Treasury, Supply, Estabt and Home Finance Divs, 1949-53. Central Bd of Finance of Church of England: Sec. (and Fin. Sec. to Church Assembly), 1953-59, and Investment Manager, 1959-65; concurrently, Dir, Local Authorities Mutual Investment Trust, 1961-65, and Investment Man. to Charities Official Investment Fund, 1963-65; a Man. Dir, J. Henry Schroder Wagg & Co. Ltd, 1965-74; Chairman: Reserve Pension Bd, 1974-75; Assoc. of Investment Trust Cos, 1975-77; Director: Clerical, Medical & General Life Assurance Soc., 1970-74; Lindustries Ltd, 1970-79. Mem., Monopolies Commn, 1969-73. Fellow of King's Coll., London. *Address*: Eastfield House, North Perrott, Crewkerne, Somerset TA18 7SW. *T*: Crewkerne 75156. *Clubs*: Farmers', City of London.

HUNTER SMART, William Norman, CA; Partner, Hays Allan, Chartered Accountants, since 1950; *b* 25 May 1921; *s* of William Hunter Smart, CA, and Margaret Thorburn Inglis; *m* 1st, 1948, Bridget Beryl Andreae (*d* 1974); four *s*; 2nd, 1977, Sheila Smith Stewart (*née* Speirs). *Educ*: George Watson's Coll., Edinburgh. Served War, 1939-45; commnd 1st Lothians & Border Horse, 1941; Warwickshire Yeomanry, 1942; served Middle East and Italy; Adjutant-Captain, 1945, mentioned in despatches. Qualified as Chartered Accountant, 1948. Joined Hays, Akers & Hays, 1948. Chm., Assoc. of Scottish Chartered Accountants in London, 1972-73; Institute of Chartered Accountants of Scotland: Council Mem., 1970-75; Vice-Pres., 1976-78; Pres., 1978-79. *Recreations*: sailing, shooting, gardening. *Address*: Flat 4, 19 Royal Crescent, W11 4SL. *T*: 01-602 0386. *Clubs*: Gresham, Caledonian; Royal Motor Yacht (Poole).

HUNTER-TOD, Air Marshal Sir John (Hunter), KBE 1971 (OBE 1957); CB 1969; Head of Engineer Branch and Director-General of Engineering (RAF), 1970-73, retired; *b* 21 April 1917; *s* of late Hunter Finlay Tod, FRCS; *m* 1959, Anne, *d* of late Thomas Chaffer Howard; one *s*. *Educ*: Marlborough; Trinity Coll., Cambridge (MA). DCAe 1948. Commissioned, 1940; Fighter Command and Middle East, 1939-45. Group Capt. 1958; Air Cdre 1963. Dir, Guided Weapons (Air), Min. of Aviation, 1962-65; AOEng, RAF Germany, 1965-67; AOC No 24 Group, RAF, 1967-70; Air Vice-Marshal, 1968; Air Marshal, 1971. CEng. Hon. DSc Cranfield Inst. of Technol., 1974. *Address*: 21 Ridge Hill, Dartmouth, S Devon TQ6 9PE. *T*: Dartmouth 3130. *Club*: Royal Air Force.

HUNTING, (Charles) Patrick (Maule), CBE 1975; TD 1952; FCA; Chairman of Hunting Group, 1962-74; *b* 16 Dec. 1910; *s* of late Sir Percy Hunting; *m* 1941, Diana, *d* of late Brig. A. B. P. Pereira, DSO, of Tavistock, Devon; two *s* two *d*. *Educ*: Rugby Sch.; Trinity Coll., Cambridge. BA (Hons) Mod. and Mediaeval Langs; MA 1975; ACA 1936, FCA 1960. Served Royal Sussex Regt, 1939-45: France and Belgium, 1940; 8th Army, Western Desert, 1942; also in Palestine and Persia; Staff Coll., Camberley (psc), 1945. Entered Hunting Group 1936, Dir, 1946, Vice-Chm., 1961; Director: Hunting Associated Industries Ltd (Chm., 1965-74); Hunting Gibson Ltd (Chm., 1970-74); Hunting Gp Ltd (Chm., 1972-74). Mem. Council, Chamber of Shipping of UK, 1960 (Chm. Tramp Tanker Section, 1962); Master, Ironmongers' Company, 1978 (Mem. Court, 1970-). *Recreations*: golf, fishing. *Address*: The Old House, Birch Grove, Horsted Keynes, Sussex RH17 7BT. *T*: Chelwood Gate 254. *Clubs*: Naval and Military, MCC; Royal Ashdown Forest (Golf).

HUNTING, (Lindsay) Clive; Chairman, Hunting Group of Companies, since 1975; *b* 22 Dec. 1925; *s* of late Gerald Lindsay Hunting and Ruth (*née* Pyman); *m* 1952, Shelagh (*née* Hill-Lowe); one *s* one *d*. *Educ*: Loretto; Trinity Hall, Cambridge (MA). Royal Navy, 1944-47; Cambridge, 1947-50; joined Hunting Group, 1950, Dir 1952, Vice-Chm. 1962. Group comprises Hunting Gibson plc (Hunting Stag Management Ltd, E. A. Gibson Shipbrokers Ltd, Hunting Painting Contractors Ltd, Stag Line Ltd; Inskill Ltd, Systemsolve (computer services) Ltd, New England Estates Ltd); Hunting Associated Industries plc (Hunting Engineering Management Ltd, Hunting Surveys and Consultants Ltd, Field Aviation Ltd, Halmatic Ltd, Field Industries Africa Ltd, Field Aviation Co. Ltd, Canada); Hunting Petroleum Services plc (Hunting Fuel Distribution Ltd, Hunting Oilfield Services Ltd, Fretoil SA, France,

Gibson Petroleum Co. Ltd, Canada, Hunting Oil Exploration Inc. USA, Filtrate Ltd, and Hunting Group Ltd. Chm., Donkin & Co. Ltd, 1952. Pres., British Independent Air Transport Assoc., 1960-62; Pres., Fedn Internationale de Transporte Aerien Privée, 1961-63; Chm., Air League, 1968-71; Pres., Air Educn and Recreation Organisation, 1970-. Mem. Ct, Cranfield Inst. of Technol., 1980-. Renter Warden, Coachmakers' and Coach Harness Makers' Co. CBIM 1980. Nile Gold Medal for Aerospace Educn, 1982. *Recreation:* yachting. *Address:* 14 Conduit Mews, W2 3RE. *T:* 01-402 7914. *Clubs:* City Livery; Royal London Yacht; Royal Yacht Squadron (Cowes).

HUNTING, Patrick; *see* Hunting, C. P. M.

HUNTINGDON, 15th Earl of, *cr* 1529; **Francis John Clarence Westenra Plantagenet Hastings,** MA; artist; *b* 30 Jan. 1901; *s* of 14th Earl and Maud Margaret (*d* 1953), 2nd *d* of Sir Samuel Wilson, sometime MP for Portsmouth; *S* father, 1939; *m* 1st, 1925, Cristina (who obtained a divorce, 1943 and *m* 2nd, 1944, Hon. Wogan Philipps, who *S*, 1962, as 2nd Baron Milford, *qv*; she died 1953), *d* of the Marchese Casati, Rome; one *d*; 2nd, 1944, Margaret Lane, *qv*; two *d*. *Educ:* Eton; Christ Church, Oxford. MA Hons, History; Slade School, London Univ. Played Oxford Univ. Polo team. Prof., Sch. of Arts & Crafts, Camberwell, 1938. ARP Officer and Dep. Controller Andover Rural district, 1941-45. Jt Parly Sec., Min. of Agriculture and Fisheries, 1945-50. Prof., Central Sch. of Arts & Crafts, London, 1950. A pupil of Diego Rivera; *Exhibitions:* Paris, London, Chicago, San Francisco; Mural paintings, Evanston, Ill; Monterey, Calif; Hall of Science, World's Fair, Chicago, 1933; Marx House; Buscot Park, Faringdon; Birmingham Univ.; Women's Press Club, London; Casa dello Strozzato, Tuscany; The Priory, Reading; Vineyards, Beaulieu, etc. Chm. of Cttee Soc. of Mural Painters, 1953-57. Pres., Solent Protection Soc., 1958-68. Mem., Wine Trade Art Soc. *Publications:* Commonsense about India; The Golden Octopus. *Heir:* cousin Lt-Col Robin Hood William Stewart Hastings, *qv*. *Address:* Blackbridge House, Beaulieu, Hants.
See also W. L. Wyatt.

HUNTINGDON, Bishop Suffragan of, since 1980; **Rt. Rev. William Gordon Roe;** *b* 5 Jan. 1932; *s* of William Henry and Dorothy Myrtle Roe; *m* 1953, Mary Andreen; two *s* two *d*. *Educ:* Bournemouth School; Jesus Coll., Oxford (MA, DipTh (with distinction), DPhil); St Stephen's House, Oxford. Curate of Bournemouth, 1958-61; Priest-in-charge of St Michael's, Abingdon, 1961-69; Vice-Principal of St Chad's Coll., Durham, 1969-74; Vicar of St Oswald's, Durham, 1974-80; RD of Durham, 1974-80; Chaplain of Collingwood Coll., Durham, 1974-80; Hon. Canon of Durham Cathedral, 1979-80. *Publications:* Lamennais and England, 1966; (with A. Hutchings) J. B. Dykes, Priest and Musician, 1976. *Recreations:* French literature, and camping. *Address:* Whitgift House, Ely, Cambs CB7 4DP. *T:* Ely 2137.

HUNTINGDON, Archdeacon of; *see* Sledge, Ven. R. K.

HUNTINGFIELD, 6th Baron *cr* 1796; **Gerard Charles Arcedeckne Vanneck;** Bt 1751; international civil servant with United Nations Secretariat, 1946-75; *b* 29 May 1915; *er s* of 5th Baron Huntingfield, KCMG, and Margaret Eleanor (*d* 1943) *o d* of late Judge Ernest Crosby, Grasmere, Rhinebeck, NY; *S* father, 1969; *m* 1941, Janetta Lois, *er d* of Capt. R. H. Errington, RN, Tostock Old Hall, Bury St Edmunds, Suffolk; one *s* two *d* (and one *d* decd). *Educ:* Stowe; Trinity College, Cambridge. *Heir:* *s* Hon. Joshua Charles Vanneck, *b* 10 Aug. 1954. *Address:* 34 Rue Gambetta, 1815 Clarens, Switzerland.
See also Hon. Sir Peter Vanneck.

HUNTINGTON-WHITELEY, Sir Hugo (Baldwin), 3rd Bt *cr* 1918; DL; Partner, Price Waterhouse, Chartered Accountants; *b* 31 March 1924; *e* surv. *s* of Captain Sir Maurice Huntington-Whiteley, 2nd Bt, RN, and Lady (Pamela) Margaret Huntington-Whiteley (*d* 1976), 3rd *d* of 1st Earl Baldwin of Bewdley, KG, PC; *S* father, 1975; *m* 1959, Jean Marie Ramsay, CStJ (JP 1973); two *d*. *Educ:* Eton. Served in Royal Navy, 1942-47. Worcs: High Sheriff 1971; DL 1972. *Recreations:* music, travel. *Heir:* *b* (John) Miles Huntington-Whiteley, VRD, Lieut-Comdr RNR [*b* 18 July 1929; *m* 1960, Countess Victoria Adelheid Clementine Louise, *d* of late Count Friedrich Wolfgang zu Castell-Rudenhausen; one *s* two *d*]. *Address:* Ripple Hall, Tewkesbury, Glos. *T:* Upton-on-Severn 2431. *Club:* Brooks's.

HUNTLY, 12th Marquess of, *cr* 1599, Earl of, *cr* 1450; **Douglas Charles Lindsey Gordon;** Lord of Gordon before 1408; Earl of Enzie, Lord of Badenoch, 1599; Bt 1625; Baron Aboyne, 1627; Earl of Aboyne, Lord Strathavon and Glenlivet, 1660; Baron Meldrum, 1815; sits under creation of 1815; Premier Marquess of Scotland; Chief of House of Gordon; Gordon Highlanders; *b* 3 Feb. 1908; *s* of late Lieut-Col Douglas Gordon, CVO, DSO, and Violet Ida, *d* of Gerard Streatfeild; *S* great-uncle, 1937; *m* 1st, 1941, Hon. Mary Pamela Berry (marr. diss. 1965), *o d* of 1st Viscount Kemsley; one *s* one *d*; 2nd, 1977, Elizabeth Haworth Leigh, *d* of Lt Cdr F. H. Leigh. *Heir:* *s* Earl of Aboyne, *qv*. *Address:* Hollybrook, Ewhurst Road, Cranleigh, Surrey. *T:* Cranleigh 71500. *Club:* Army and Navy.
See also Lord Adam Gordon.

HURD, Derrick Guy Edmund, JP; Head of the European School, since 1978; *b* 22 June 1928; *s* of Clifford Rowland Hurd and Viola Beatrice Hurd; *m* 1962, Janet Barton; one *s* two *d*. *Educ:* Peter Symonds' Sch., Winchester; Culham Coll. (Teacher's Cert., 1948); Birkbeck Coll., Univ. of London (BA

Hons History 1952, MA (thesis) 1961). Assistant, Hugh Myddelton Sec. Sch., London EC1, 1948-52; Lecteur, Lycée Chaptal, Paris, 1952-53; Head of History Dept, Librarian, Hatfield School, 1953-60 (Exchange, Helmholtz Gymnasium, Bielefeld, 1956); Headmaster, John Mason High Sch., Abingdon, 1960-70; Headmaster, Blandford Upper Sch., Dorset, 1970-72; Principal, Easthampstead Park Educational Centre, Wokingham, 1972-78. JP Berkshire, 1967. *Publication:* Sir John Mason (1503-1566), 1975. *Recreations:* walking, philately, music, ecclesiastical architecture, travel. *Address:* The European School, Culham, Abingdon, Oxon OX14 3DZ. *T:* Abingdon 28410.

HURD, Rt. Hon. Douglas (Richard), CBE 1974; PC 1982; MP (C) Mid-Oxon, since Feb. 1974; Minister of State, Foreign and Commonwealth Office, since 1979; *b* 8 March 1930; *e s* of Baron Hurd (*d* 1966) and Stephanie Corner; *m* 1st, 1960, Tatiana Elizabeth Michelle (marr. diss. 1982), *d* of A. C. Benedict Eyre, Westburton House, Bury, Sussex; three *s*; 2nd, 1982, Judy, *d* of Sidney and Pamela Smart. *Educ:* Eton (King's Scholar and Newcastle Scholar); Trinity Coll., Cambridge (Major Scholar). Pres., Cambridge Union, 1952. HM Diplomatic Service, 1952-66; served in: Peking, 1954-56; UK Mission to UN, 1956-60; Private Sec. to Perm. Under-Sec. of State, FO, 1960-63; Rome, 1963-66. Joined Conservative Research Dept, 1966; Head of Foreign Affairs Section, 1968; Private Sec. to Leader of the Opposition, 1968-70; Political Sec. to Prime Minister, 1970-74; Opposition Spokesman on European Affairs, 1976-79. Vis. Fellow, Nuffield Coll., Oxford, 1978. *Publications:* The Arrow War, 1967; (with Andrew Osmond) Send Him Victorious, 1968; The Smile on the Face of the Tiger, 1969; (with Andrew Osmond) Scotch on the Rocks, 1971; Truth Game, 1972; Vote to Kill, 1975; An End to Promises, 1979; (with Andrew Osmond) War Without Frontiers, 1982. *Recreation:* writing thrillers. *Address:* 5 Mitford Cottages, Westwell, Burford, Oxon. *Clubs:* Travellers', Beefsteak.

HURFORD, Peter John; organist; *b* 22 Nov. 1930; *e c* of H. J. Hurford, Minehead; *m* 1955, Patricia Mary Matthews; two *s* one *d*. *Educ:* Blundells Sch.; Royal Coll. of Music; Jesus Coll., Cambridge. MA, MusB Cantab, FRCO, FRSCM, ARCM. Director of Music, Bablake Sch., Coventry and Conductor, Leamington Spa Bach Choir, 1956-57; Master of the Music, Cathedral and Abbey Church of St Alban, 1958-78, Conductor, St Albans Bach Choir, 1958-78; Founder, Internat. Organ Festival Soc., 1963; Mem. Council, RCO, 1963-, Pres., 1980-82; Artist-in-Residence: Univ. of Cincinnati, 1967-68; Sydney Opera Ho., 1980; Vis. Prof. of organ, Univ. of Western Ontario, 1976-77; Acting organist, St John's Coll., Cambridge, 1979-80; recital and lecture tours throughout Europe, USA, Canada, Japan, Philippines, Australia and NZ from 1960. Has made numerous LP records, incl. complete organ works of J. S. Bach. Gramophone Award, 1979. Hon. Dr, Baldwin-Wallace Coll., Ohio, 1981. Hon. Mem., RAM, 1981. *Publications:* Suite: Laudate Dominum; sundry other works for organ; Masses for Series III and Rite II of Amer. Episcopal Church; sundry church anthems. *Recreations:* walking and silence. *Address:* Broom House, St Bernard's Road, St Albans, Herts AL3 5RA.

HURLEY, Ven. Alfred Vincent, CBE 1945 (OBE 1944); TD 1944; Archdeacon of Dudley, 1951-68; Rector of Old Swinford, 1948-64; *b* 12 Jan. 1896; *s* of Alfred Walter and Phoebe Hurley, Reading; *m* 1929, Jenny Drummond, 2nd *d* of Henry John Sansom, Pennsylvania Castle, Portland, Dorset; one *s* three *d*. *Educ:* Queen's Sch., Basingstoke; Keble Coll., Oxford (MA); Cuddesdon Coll. Artists' Rifles, 1915; Royal Flying Corps, 1916-19. Curate, Armley, Leeds, 1922; Chaplain: Leeds Prison, 1923-24; Portland Borstal Instn, 1924; Dep. Gov. Portland Borstal Instn, 1928; Rector of Portland, 1931; Rural Dean of Weymouth, 1937; Canon and Preb. of Salisbury, 1939. Chaplain to Forces, 4th Dorsets, 1939; SCF, 42 East Lancs Div. 1940; Asst Chaplain General, 8th Army, 1944 (despatches); Dep. Chaplain General, South East Asia Allied Land Forces, 1945-46; Hon. Canon of Worcester, 1951-; Exam. Chap. to Bishop of Worcester, 1951-68. *Address:* c/o 55 Belbroughton Road, Halesowen, West Midlands B63 4LS. *T:* 021-550 3575.

HURLEY, Sir Hugh; *see* Hurley, Sir W. H.

HURLEY, Sir John Garling, Kt 1967; CBE 1959; FAIM; FIDCA; JP; Managing Director, Berlei United Ltd, Sydney, 1948-69; *b* Bondi, NSW, 2 Oct. 1906; *s* of late John Hurley, MLA, and late Annie Elizabeth (*née* Garling); *g g g s* of Frederick Garling (1775-1848), free settler, 1815 and senior of first two solicitors admitted to practise in original Supreme Court of Civil Judicature in NSW; *m* 1st 1929, Alice Edith Saunders (*d* 1975); three *d*; 2nd, 1976, Desolie M. Richardson. *Educ:* Sydney Techn. High Sch. FAIM 1949; FIDCA 1980. With Berlei group of cos, 1922-69, incl. Berlei (UK) Ltd, London, 1931-36; Chm., William Adams Ltd, 1963-74 (Dep. Chm. 1974-76); Director: Manufacturers' Mutual Insurance Ltd, Sydney, 1954-82; Develt Finance Corporation Ltd, 1967-79; Australian Fixed Trusts Ltd, 1970-79; Royal North Shore Hosp. of Sydney, 1969-76. President: Associated Chambers of Manufactures of Austr. 1955-56; Chamber of Manufactures of NSW, 1955-57; Member: Inst. of Directors in Australia; Techn. and Further Educn Adv. Council of NSW, 1958-76; Industrial Design Council of Australia, 1958-76 (Dep. Chm., 1970-76); Council, Abbotsleigh Sch., 1960-66; Australian Advertising Standards Adv. Authority, 1974-; Councillor, Nat. Heart Foundn of Australia (NSW Div.), 1969-. Mem., St Andrew's Cathedral Restoration Appeal Cttee; Patron, St Andrew's Cathedral Sch. Building Fund Appeal, 1977-. Chm., Standing Cttee on Productivity, Ministry of Labour Adv. Coun., 1957; Leader of Austr. Trade Mission to India and Ceylon, 1957.

Chm. and Trustee, Museum of Applied Arts and Sciences, NSW, 1958-76. Member: Royal Agricultural Soc.; Sydney Cricket Ground; Australian-American Assoc.; Australia-Britain Soc.; Nat. Trust of Australia. Knighted for distinguished service to Government, industry and the community. *Recreations:* swimming, bowls. *Address:* 12 Locksley Street, Killara, NSW 2071, Australia. *Clubs:* Australian (Sydney); Royal Sydney Yacht Squadron; Australasian Pioneers' (NSW); Warrawee Bowling.

HURLEY, Prof. Rosalinde, (Mrs Peter Gortvai), MD; FRCPath; Professor of Microbiology, University of London, at Institute of Obstetrics and Gynaecology, since 1975; Consultant Microbiologist, Queen Charlotte's Maternity Hospital, since 1963; *b* 30 Dec. 1929; *o d* of late William Hurley and Rose Clancey; *m* 1964, Peter Gortvai, FRCS. *Educ:* Academy of the Assumption, Wellesley Hills, Mass, USA; Queen's Coll., Harley St, London; Univ. of London; Inns of Court. LLB, MD. Called to the Bar, Inner Temple, 1958. House Surg., Wembley Hosp., 1955; Ho. Phys., W London Hosp., 1956; Sen. Ho. Officer, 1956-57, Registrar, 1957-58, Lectr and Asst Clin. Pathologist, 1958-62, Charing Cross Hosp. and Med. Sch. Chm., Medicines Commn, 1982-. Examiner, RCPath, and univs at home and abroad; Founder Mem., Mem. Council, 1977-, and Asst Registrar, 1978-, RCPath; Pres., Section of Pathology, and Vice-Pres., Royal Soc. of Medicine, 1979-; Chm., 1980-, formerly Vice-Chm., Cttee on Dental and Surgical Materials. *Publications:* (jtly) Candida albicans, 1964; (jtly) Symposium on Candida infections, 1966; (jtly) Neonatal and Perinatal Infections, 1979; chapters in med. books; papers in med. and sci. jls. *Recreations:* gardening, reading. *Address:* 2 Temple Gardens, Temple, EC4Y 9AY. *T:* 01-353 0577.

HURLEY, Sir (Wilfred) Hugh, Kt 1963; Chief Justice, High Courts of Northern States of Nigeria, 1967-69; retired, 1969; *b* 16 Oct. 1910; *s* of Henry Hutchings Hurley and Elizabeth Louise (*née* Maguire); *m* 1940, Una Kathleen (*née* Wyllie); one *s* two *d*. *Educ:* St Stephen's Green Sch., Dublin; Trinity Coll., Dublin. Barrister-at-Law (King's Inns, Dublin), 1935; Magistrate, Nigeria, 1940; Chief Registrar, Supreme Court, Nigeria, 1949; Puisne Judge, Supreme Court, Nigeria, 1953-55, Judge, 1955-57, Senior Puisne Judge, 1957-60 and Chief Justice, 1960-67, High Court, Northern Nigeria. Chm., Judicial Service Commn, Northern Nigeria, and Mem., Judicial Service Commission, Federation of Nigeria, 1960-63. Called to the Bar, Gray's Inn, 1976. Hon. LLD Ahmadu Bello Univ., Nigeria, 1968. *Address:* 8 Castle Street, Calne, Wilts.

HURLL, Alfred William, CVO 1970; CBE 1955; Member of Council, The Scout Association, since 1948 (Chief Executive Commissioner, 1948-70); *b* 10 Sept. 1905; *s* of Charles Alfred Hurll; *m* 1933, Elsie Margaret, *d* of Frederick Sullivan; one *s* one *d*. *Educ:* Grammar Sch., Acton. Joined staff, The Scout Assoc. HQ, 1921; Sec., Home Dept, 1935; Asst Gen. Sec., 1938; Gen. Sec., 1941. *Publication:* (co-author) BP's Scouts, 1961. *Recreations:* cricket, theatre. *Address:* 106 Montrose Avenue, Twickenham, TW2 6HD. *T:* 01-894 1957.

HURON, Bishop of, since 1974; **Rt. Rev. Theodore David Butler Ragg,** DD; *b* 23 Nov. 1919; *s* of late Rt Rev. Harry Richard Ragg and Winifred Mary Ragg (*née* Groves); *m* 1945, Dorothy Mary Lee; one *s* two *d*. *Educ:* Univ. of Manitoba; Trinity Coll., Univ. of Toronto (BA, LTh); General Synod (BD). Deacon, 1949; priest, 1950; Asst Curate, St Michael and All Angels, Toronto, 1949; Rector: Nokomis, 1951; Wolseley, 1953; St Clement's, N Vancouver, 1955; St Luke's, Victoria, 1957; Bishop Cronyn Memorial, London, 1962; St George's, Owen Sound, 1967. Examining Chaplain to Bishop of Huron, 1964-67; Archdeacon of Saugeen, 1967; elected Suffragan Bishop of Huron, 1973, elected Bishop of Huron, 1974. Hon. DD: Huron Coll., London, Ont., 1975; Trinity Coll., Toronto, Ont., 1975. *Recreations:* woodworking, golf, camping. *Address:* 4-220 Dundas Street, London, Ontario, Canada N6A 1H3. *T:* (office) (519) 434-6893. *Clubs:* London, London Hunt and Country (London, Ont.).

HURRELL, Anthony Gerald; Under-Secretary, Asia and Oceans Division, Overseas Development Administration (formerly Ministry of Overseas Development), Foreign and Commonwealth Office, since 1978; *b* 18 Feb. 1927; *s* of late William Hurrell and Florence Hurrell; *m* 1951, Jean Wyatt; two *d*. *Educ:* Norwich Sch.; St Catharine's Coll., Cambridge. RAEC, 1948-50; Min. of Labour, 1950-53; Min. of Educn, 1953-64; Min. of Overseas Develt, 1964-; Fellow, Center for International Affairs, Harvard, 1969-70; Head of SE Asia Develt Div., Bangkok, 1972-74; Under Secretary: Internat. Div. ODM, 1974-75; Central Policy Rev. Staff, Cabinet Office, 1976; Duchy of Lancaster, 1977. *Recreations:* bird-ringing, bird-watching, digging ponds, music. *Address:* Benacre, Mill Road, Stock, Essex CM4 9LL. *T:* Stock 840254.

HURRELL, Col Geoffrey Taylor, OBE 1944; Lord-Lieutenant of Cambridgeshire, 1974-75 (of Cambridgeshire and Isle of Ely, 1965-74); *b* 12 March 1900; *s* of Arthur Hurrell and Emily Taylor; *m* 1934, Mary Crossman; one *s* one *d*. *Educ:* Rugby; Sandhurst. Gazetted 17th Lancers, 1918; Lieut-Col comdg 17th/21st Lancers, 1940; Col 1944. High Sheriff, Cambridgeshire and Huntingdonshire, 1963; JP Cambs 1952, DL 1958. KStJ 1972. *Recreations:* hunting, shooting. *Address:* Park House, Harston, near Cambridge. *Club:* Cavalry and Guards.

HURRELL, Ian Murray, MVO 1961; HM Diplomatic Service, retired; *b* 14 June 1914; *s* of Capt. L. H. M. Hurrell and Mrs Eva Hurrell; *m* 1939, Helen Marjorie Darwin; no *c*. *Educ:* Dover Coll. Anglo-Iranian Oil Co., 1932-34; Indian Police (United Provinces), 1934-48; entered HM Foreign (subseq. Diplomatic) Service, 1948; Vice-Consul, Shiraz, 1948-51; Consul, Benghazi, 1952; FO, 1952-53; 1st Sec., Quito, 1954 (Chargé d'Affaires, 1955); Bangkok, 1956-60; Tehran, 1960-64; Ankara (UK Delegn to CENTO), 1964-67; Ambassador, Costa Rica, 1968-72. Life FRSA, 1979; Fellow, British Interplanetary Soc., 1981. Imperial Order of the Crown (Iran). *Recreations:* rambling, photography, skin-diving, gardening, chess, etc. *Address:* Quarr House, Sway, Hants. *Club:* Royal Over-Seas League.

HURST, George; Staff Conductor, Western Orchestral Society (Bournemouth Symphony Orchestra and Bournemouth Sinfonietta), since 1973; *b* 20 May 1926; Rumanian father and Russian mother. *Educ:* various preparatory and public schs. in the UK and Canada; Royal Conservatory, Toronto, Canada. First prize for Composition, Canadian Assoc. of Publishers, Authors and Composers, 1945. Asst Conductor, Opera Dept, Royal Conservatory of Music, of Toronto, 1946; Lectr in Harmony, Counterpoint, Composition etc, Peabody Conservatory of Music, Baltimore, Md, 1947; Conductor of York, Pa, Symph. Orch., 1950-55, and concurrently of Peabody Conservatory Orch., 1952-55; Asst Conductor, LPO, 1955-57, with which toured USSR 1956; Associate conductor, BBC Northern Symphony Orchestra, 1957; Principal Conductor, BBC Northern Symphony Orchestra (previously BBC Northern Orchestra), 1958-68; Artistic Adviser, Western Orchestral Soc., 1968-73. Vice-Pres., Western Orch. Soc., 1979. Since 1956 frequent guest conductor in Europe, Israel, Canada, South Africa. *Publications:* piano and vocal music (Canada). *Recreations:* yachting, horse-riding, chess. *Address:* 21 Oslo Court, NW8. *T:* 01-722 3088.

HURST, Henry Ronald Grimshaw; Overseas Labour Adviser, Foreign and Commonwealth Office, 1976-81, retired; *b* 24 April 1919; *s* of Frederick George Hurst and Elizabeth Ellen (*née* Grimshaw); *m* 1942, Norah Joyce, *d* of John Stanley Rothwell; one *s* one *d*. *Educ:* Darwen and Blackpool Grammar Schs; St Catharine's Coll., Cambridge (MA). Served War, Army, 1940-46. Colonial Service, 1946-70: Permanent Sec., Min. of Labour, Tanzania, 1962-64; Labour Adviser, Tanzania, 1965-68, and Malawi, 1969-70; Dep. Overseas Labour Adviser, FCO, 1970-76. *Recreations:* tennis, cricket, gardening. *Address:* 43 Chatsworth Road, St-Annes-On-Sea, Lancashire FY8 2JL. *T:* St Annes 712263. *Club:* Civil Service.

HURST, Margery, OBE 1976; Joint Chairman, Brook Street Bureau of Mayfair Ltd (Managing Director, 1947-76); *b* 23 May 1913; *d* of late Samuel and Deborah Berney; *m* 1948, Eric Hurst, Barrister-at-law; two *d*. *Educ:* Brondesbury and Kilburn High Sch.; Minerva Coll. RADA. Joined ATS on Direct Commission, 1943 (1939-45 war medal); invalided out of the service, 1944. Commenced business of Brook St Bureau of Mayfair Ltd, 1946; founded Margery Hurst Schs and Colls for administrative and secretarial studies. Co-opted Mem. of LCC Children's Cttee, 1956. Started non-profit making social clubs for secretaries, called Society for International Secretaries, in London, 1960; now in New York, Boston and Sydney; awarded Pimm's Cup for Anglo-American friendship in the business world, 1962. Member: American Cttee, BNEC, 1967-70; Exec. Cttee, Mental Health Research Fund, 1967-72. One of first women elected Underwriting Mem. of Lloyds, 1970. First Lady Mem., Worshipful Co. of Marketors, 1981-; Freeman, City of London, 1981. *Publication:* No Glass Slipper (autobiog.), 1967. *Recreations:* tennis, swimming, drama, opera. *Address:* 125 Edgware Road, W2 2HX. *Clubs:* Royal Corinthian Yacht; Royal Southern Yacht; Lloyds Yacht.

HURST, Peter Thomas; Master of the Supreme Court Taxing Office, since 1981; *b* Troutbeck, Westmorland, 27 Oct. 1942; *s* of Thomas Lyon Hurst and Nora Mary Hurst; *m* 1968, Diane Dulcie Irvine, BA; one *s* two *d*. *Educ:* Stonyhurst College. LLB London. Admitted as Solicitor of the Supreme Court, 1967; Partner: Hurst and Walker, Solicitors, Liverpool, 1967-77; Gair Roberts Hurst and Walker, Solicitors, Liverpool, 1977-81. *Recreations:* gardening, music, stamp collecting. *Address:* Fairfield, Quarry Road East, Heswall, Wirral L61 6XD. *T:* 051-342 6764. *Club:* Athenæum (Liverpool).

HURST, Dr Robert, CBE 1973; GM 1944; FRSC; retired; *b* Nelson, NZ, 3 Jan. 1915; *s* of late Percy Cecil Hurst and late Margery Hurst; *m* 1946, Rachael Jeanette (*née* Marsh); three *s*. *Educ:* Nelson Coll.; Canterbury Coll., NZ (MSc); Cambridge Univ. (PhD). FRIC 1977. Experimental Officer, Min. of Supply, engaged in research in bomb disposal and mine detection, 1940-45. Group Leader Transuranic Elements Group, AERE, Harwell, 1948-55; Project Leader, Homogeneous Aqueous Reactor Project, AERE, Harwell, 1956-57; Chief Chemist, Research and Development Branch, Industrial Group UKAEA, 1957-58; Director, Dounreay Experimental Reactor Establishment, UKAEA, 1958-63; Dir of Res., British Ship Res. Assoc., 1963-76. *Publication:* Editor, Progress in Nuclear Engineering, Series IV (Technology and Engineering), 1957. *Recreations:* gardening, sailing. *Address:* 15 Elms Avenue, Parkstone, Poole, Dorset. *Club:* Athenæum.

HURT, John; actor; stage, films and television; *b* 22 Jan. 1940; *s* of Rev. Arnould Herbert Hurt and Phyllis Massey. *Educ:* The Lincoln Sch., Lincoln; RADA. Started as a painter. *Stage:* début, Arts Theatre, London, 1962; Chips With Everything, Vaudeville, 1962; The Dwarfs, Arts, 1963; Hamp (title role), Edin. Fest., 1964; Inadmissible Evidence, Wyndhams, 1965; Little Malcolm and his Struggle Against the Eunuchs, Garrick, 1966; Belcher's Luck, Aldwych (RSC), 1966; Man and Superman, Gaiety, Dublin, 1969; The

Caretaker, Mermaid, 1972; The Only Street, Dublin Fest. and Islington, 1973; Travesties, Aldwych (RSC), 1974; The Arrest, Bristol Old Vic, 1974; The Shadow of a Gunman, Nottingham Playhouse, 1978. *Films and Television:* began films with The Wild and the Willing, 1962; A Man for All Seasons, 1966; Sinful Davey, 1967, film 1968; The Waste Places (ATV), 1968; later films and TV include: Before Winter Comes, 1969; In Search of Gregory, 1970; Mr Forbush and the Penguins, 1971; (Evans in) 10 Rillington Place, 1971; The Ghoul, 1974; Little Malcolm, 1974; The Naked Civil Servant (ITV), 1975 (Emmy Award, 1976); East of Elephant Rock, 1977; Caligula, in I Claudius (series BBC TV) 1976; Treats (TV), 1977; The Disappearance, The Shout, Spectre, The Alien, and Midnight Express (BAFTA award, 1978), all 1978; Heaven's Gate, 1979; Crime and Punishment (BBC TV series), 1979; The Elephant Man, 1980 (BAFTA award, 1981); History of the World Part 1, 1981; Partners, 1982. *Address:* c/o Leading Artists Ltd, 60 St James's Street, SW1. *T:* 01-491 4400.

HURWITZ, Vivian Ronald; His Honour Judge Hurwitz; a Circuit Judge, since 1974; *b* 7 Sept. 1926; *s* of Alter Max and Dora Rebecca Hurwitz; *m* 1963, Dr Ruth Cohen, Middlesbrough; one *s* two *d*. *Educ:* Roundhay Sch., Leeds; Hertford Coll., Oxford (MA). Served RNVR: Univ. Naval Short Course, Oct. 1944-March 1945, followed by service until March 1947. Called to Bar, Lincoln's Inn, 1952, practised NE Circuit. A Recorder of Crown Court, 1972-74. *Recreations:* tennis, bridge, music (listening), art (looking at), sport—various (watching). *Address:* 2 Bentcliffe Drive, Leeds LS17 6QX. *T:* Leeds 687174.

HUSAIN, Abul Basher M.; *see* Mahmud Husain.

HUSBAND, Sir (Henry) Charles, Kt 1975; CBE 1964; BEng, DSc, FICE, PPIStructE, FIMechE, FAmSCE; Senior Partner, Husband & Co., Consulting Engineers, Sheffield, London and Colombo, since 1937; *b* 30 Oct. 1908; *s* of Prof. Joseph Husband, DEng, MICE and Ellen Walton Husband; *m* 1932, Eileen Margaret, *d* of late Henry Nowill, Sheffield; two *s* two *d*. *Educ:* King Edward VII Sch., Sheffield; Sheffield Univ. Asst to Sir E. Owen Williams, MICE, 1931-33; Engr and Surveyor to First Nat. Housing Trust Ltd, 1933-36; planning and construction of large housing schemes in England and Scotland; from 1936, designed public works at home and overseas incl. major road and railway bridges, drainage and water supply schemes; Princ. Techn. Officer, Central Register, Min. of Labour and Nat. Service, 1939-40; Asst Dir, Directorate of Aircraft Prodn Factories, Min. of Works, 1943-45; designed first high altitude testing plant for continuous running of complete jet engines, 1946, also research estabs for Brit. Iron and Steel Res. Assoc., Prodn Engrg Res. Assoc. and other industrial organisations; designed and supervised construction of 250 ft diameter radio telescope, Jodrell Bank, and other large radio telescopes at home and abroad incl. steerable aerials for GPO satellite stn, Goonhilly Downs, Cornwall. Chm., Yorks Assoc. ICE, 1949; Pres., Instn Struct. Engrs, 1964-65; Chm., Adv. Cttee on Engrg and Metallurgy, University of Sheffield, 1962-65; Mem. Ct, University of Sheffield; Mem. Cons. Panel in Civil Engrg, Bradford Univ. (formerly Inst. of Technology), 1962-68; Mem., Council of Engrg Instns, 1965-66, Board Mem., 1979-; Chm., Assoc. of Consulting Engineers, 1967. Hon. DSc Manchester Univ., 1964; Hon. DEng Sheffield Univ., 1967. Sir Benjamin Baker Gold Medal, ICE, 1959; (first) Queen's Gold Medal for Applied Science, Royal Society, 1965; Wilhelm Exner Medal for Science and Technology, University of Vienna, 1966; Instn Gold Medal, IStructE, 1974; James Watt Medal, ICE, 1976. *Publications:* contributions to British and foreign engrg jls. *Recreations:* sailing, walking. *Address:* Okenhold, School Green Lane, Sheffield S10 4GP. *T:* 303395. *Clubs:* Royal Thames Yacht, St Stephen's, Royal Automobile; Sheffield (Sheffield).

HUSBAND, Prof. Thomas Mutrie, PhD; CEng, FIProdE; Professor of Engineering Manufacture, Imperial College, University of London, since 1981; *b* 7 July 1936; *s* of Thomas Mutrie Husband and Janet Clark; *m* 1962, Pat Caldwell; two *s*. *Educ:* Shawlands Acad., Glasgow; Univ. of Strathclyde. BSc(Eng), MA, PhD; CEng, FIProdE. Weir Ltd, Glasgow: Apprentice Fitter, 1953-58; Engr/Jun. Manager, 1958-62; sandwich degree student (mech. engrg), 1958-61; various engrg and management positions with ASEA Ltd in Denmark, UK and S Africa, 1962-65; postgrad. student, Strathclyde Univ., 1965-66; Teaching Fellow, Univ. of Chicago, 1966-67; Lectr, Univ. of Strathclyde, 1967-70; Sen. Lectr, Univ. of Glasgow, 1970-73; Prof. of Manufacturing Organisation, Loughborough Univ., 1973-81. Member: Manufg Technol. Cttee, SRC, 1976-79; Management and Industrial Relations Cttee, SSRC, 1977-81. *Publications:* Work Analysis and Pay Structure, 1976; Maintenance and Terotechnology, 1977; articles in Terotechnica, Industrial Relations Jl, Microelectronics and Reliability, etc. *Recreations:* watching First Division soccer, jazz, orchestral concerts, theatre, books on humour. *Address:* 47 Chandos Way, Wellgarth Road, NW11 7HF. *T:* 01-458 5267.

HUSKISSON, Alfred, OBE 1951; MC 1917, and Bar 1918; Director of S. Simpson and of Simpson (Piccadilly), 1940-74 (Dep. Chm. 1959-64; Managing Director Simpson (Piccadilly), 1940-59, S. Simpson Ltd, 1942-59); *b* 27 June 1892; *s* of Joseph Cliffe and Martha Huskisson; *m* 1st, 1922, Constance (marr. diss.), *d* of late Arthur Frederick Houfton, Nottingham; one *s* one *d*; 2nd, 1972, Sheila Mary Bullen Huskisson. *Educ:* privately. Served European War, 1914-18 (despatches); granted rank of Major, 1920. Managing Dir William Hollins & Co., Nottingham, 1929-38. Mem. Allies Welcome Cttee, 1943-50. Life Member: Overseas League, 1943; National Playing Fields Assoc. 1952. Hon. Treas. Abbey Div., Westminster Conservative Assoc.,

1945-54; No 1 Assoc. Mem. Variety Club of GB, 1950-; Chm. Wholesale Clothing Manufacturers Assoc., 1952; Pres. Appeal Cottage Homes, Linen and Woollen Drapers, 1953; Master of the Worshipful Co. of Woolmen, 1952-53, 1964-65; Past Pres. The Piccadilly and St James's Assoc. (Chm. 1950-53); Vice-Pres. Westminster Philanthropic Soc. (Chm. 1956); Vice-Chm. Machine Gun Corps Officers' Club, 1960; Member: Grand Council of FBI, 1953-65; British Olympic Assoc. Appeals Cttee, 1955-56; British Empire & Commonwealth Games Appeal Cttee, 1958; British Olympic Assoc. Appeals Cttee, 1959-60; Export Council for Europe, 1960-66; Empire & Commonwealth Games UK Industrial Appeal Cttee, 1961; Chm. various Westminster and other appeals in the past. *Address:* 3 Edenhurst, 21 Grosvenor Road, Bournemouth, Dorset BH4 8BQ. *Club:* Lord's Taverners (Pres. 1954, 1955).

HUSKISSON, Robert Andrews, CBE 1979; Chairman, Lloyd's Register of Shipping, 1973-June 1983 (Deputy Chairman, 1972-73); *b* 2 April 1923; *y s* of Edward Huskisson and Mary Huskisson (*née* Downing); *m* 1969, Alice Marian Swaffin. *Educ:* Merchant Taylors' Sch.; St Edmund Hall, Oxford. Served Royal Corps of Signals, 1941-47 (Major). Joined Shaw Savill & Albion Co. Ltd 1947; Dir 1964-72; Dep. Chief Exec., 1971-72; Director: Overseas Containers Ltd, 1967-72; Container Fleets Ltd, 1967-72; Cairn Line of Steamships Ltd, 1969-72. President: British Shipping Fedn, 1971-72 (Chm. 1968-71); International Shipping Fedn, 1969-73; Chairman: Hotels and Catering EDC, 1975-79; Marine Technology Management Cttee, SRC, 1977-. *Recreations:* golf, gardening, music. *Address:* Lanterns, Luppitt Close, Hutton Mount, Brentwood, Essex. *Clubs:* Vincent's (Oxford); Thorndon Park Golf.

HUSSAIN, Karamat; Councillor (Lab) Mapesbury Ward, London Borough of Brent, since 1971; Chairman, National Standing Conference of Afro-Caribbean and Asian Councillors, since 1980 (Founder Member); *b* Rawalpindi, 1926; *m*; one *d*. *Educ:* Aligarh Muslim Univ., India (BA Hons Humanities, MPhil). Formerly Mem., Housing, Brent and Finance Cttees, Brent Council; Mayor of Brent, 1981-82 (Dep. Mayor, 1980-81); formerly Mem. and Vice-Chm., Brent Community Relations Council. Sitara-i-Quaid-i-Azam 1982. *Address:* Members' Room, Brent Town Hall, Forty Lane, Wembley HA9 9HX.

HUSSEIN bin Onn, Datuk, SPMJ 1972; SPDK 1974; SIMP 1975; PIS 1968; MP for Sri Gading, 1974-81; Prime Minister of Malaysia, 1976-81; *b* Johore Bharu, 12 Feb. 1922; *s* of late Dato' Onn bin Jaafar and of Datin Hajjah Halimah binte Hussein; *m* Datin Suhailah; two *s* four *d*. *Educ:* English Coll., Johore Bharu; Military Acad., Dehra Dun, India. Called to the Bar, Gray's Inn. Cadet, Johore Mil. Forces, 1940; commnd Indian Army; served Egypt, Syria, Palestine, Persia, Iraq, and GHQ, New Delhi; seconded to Malayan Police Recruiting and Trng Centre, Rawalpindi; returned to Malaya with liberation forces, 1945; Comdt, Police Depot, Johore Bharu; demobilised. Joined Malay Admin. Service; served in Selangor State; Officer i/c Kampong (village) guards, Johore, in Communist emergency, 1948. Entered politics; National Youth Leader and Sec.-Gen., United Malays Nat. Org. (UMNO), 1950; Member: Fed. Legislative Council; Johore Council of State; Johore State Exec. Council; left UMNO when his father Dato' Onn bin Jaafar resigned from the organisation in 1951. Studied law in England; in practice, Kuala Lumpur, 1963. Rejoined UMNO, 1968; MP for Johore Bharu Timor, 1969; Minister of Educn, 1970-73; Dep. Prime Minister, 1973-76; Minister of Trade and Industry, 1973-74; Minister of Finance, and Minister of Coordination and Public Corporations, 1974-76. Chairman: Commonwealth Parly Assoc., Malaysia, 1975-76; Inter Parly Union Malaysia Gp. President: Malayan Assoc. for the Blind; Kelab Golf Negara, Subang. *Recreation:* golf. *Address:* 3 Jalan Kenny, Kuala Lumpur, Malaysia.

HUSSEY, Prof. Joan Mervyn, MA, BLitt, PhD; FSA; FRHistS; Professor of History in the University of London, at Royal Holloway College, 1950-74, now Emeritus. *Educ:* privately; Trowbridge High Sch.; Lycée Victor Duruy, Versailles; St Hugh's Coll., Oxford. Research Student, Westfield Coll., London, 1932-34; Internat. Travelling Fellow (FUW), 1934-35; Pfeiffer Research Fellow, Girton, 1934-37; Gamble Prize, 1935. Asst Lectr in Hist., Univ: of Manchester, 1937-43; Lectr in Hist., 1943-47, Reader in Hist., 1947-50, at Bedford Coll., Univ. of London. Visiting Prof. at Amer. Univ. of Beirut, 1966; Pres., Brit. Nat. Cttee for Byzantine Studies, 1961-71; Hon. Vice-Pres., Internat. Cttee for Byzantine Studies, 1976. Governor, Girton Coll., Cambridge, 1935-37; Mem. Council; St Hugh's Coll., Oxford, 1940-46; Mem. Council, Royal Holloway Coll., 1966-; Hon. Fellow, St Hugh's Coll., Oxford, 1968. Hon. Fellow, Instituto Siciliano de Studi Bizantini, 1975. *Publications:* Church and Learning in the Byzantine Empire 867-1185, 1937 (repr. 1961); The Byzantine World, 1957, 3rd edn 1966; Cambridge Medieval History IV, Pts I and II: ed and contributor, 1966-67; The Finlay Papers, 1973; reviews and articles in Byzantinische Zeitschrift, Byzantinoslavica, Trans Roy. Hist. Soc., Jl of Theological Studies, Enc. Britannica, Chambers's Enc., New Catholic Enc., etc. *Address:* 16 Clarence Drive, Englefield Green, Egham, Surrey TW20 0NL.

HUSSEY, Very Rev. John Walter Atherton; Dean of Chichester, 1955-77, Dean Emeritus since 1977; *b* 15 May 1909; *yr s* of Rev. Canon John Rowden and Lilian Mary Hussey. *Educ:* Marlborough Coll.; Keble Coll., Oxford (MA); Cuddesdon Coll., Oxford. Asst Curate, S Mary Abbots, Kensington, 1932-37; Vicar of S Matthew, Northampton, 1937-55; Canon of Peterborough Cathedral, 1949-55; Master of S John's Hosp., Weston Favell, 1948-55; Rural

Dean of Northampton, 1950-55. Chm. Diocesan Art Council, 1966-77; Mem., Redundant Churches Fund, 1969-78. Hon. FRIBA. Hon. DLitt Sussex, 1977. *Recreation:* enjoying the arts. *Address:* 5 Trevor Street, SW7. *T:* 01-581 1819.

HUSSEY, Marmaduke James; special consultant to Times Newspapers Ltd, since 1981; Director, Times Newspapers Ltd, since 1982 (Chief Executive and Managing Director, 1971-80); *b* 1923; *s* of late E. R. J. Hussey, CMG and Mrs Christine Hussey; *m* 1959, Lady Susan Katharine Waldegrave (*see* Lady Susan Hussey); one *s* one *d. Educ:* Rugby Sch.; Trinity Coll., Oxford (Scholar, MA). Served War of 1939-45, Grenadier Guards, Italy. Joined Associated Newspapers, 1949, Dir 1964; Man. Dir, Harmsworth Publications, 1967-70; joined Thomson Organisation Exec. Bd, 1971. A Rhodes Trustee, 1972-. *Address:* 86 Chelsea Park Gardens, SW3. *T:* 01-352 1042. *Club:* Brooks's.

HUSSEY, Lady Susan Katharine, CVO 1971; Woman of the Bedchamber to the Queen, since 1960; *b* 1 May 1939; 5th *d* of 12th Earl Waldegrave, KG, *qv* ; *m* 1959, Marmaduke James Hussey, *qv* ; one *s* one *d. Address:* 86 Chelsea Park Gardens, SW3. *T:* 01-352 1042.

HUSTON, John; film director and writer; *b* Nevada, Missouri, 5 Aug. 1906; *s* of Walter Huston and Rhea Gore; *m* 1st, Dorothy Harvey (marr. diss.); 2nd, Lesley Black (marr. diss.); 3rd, 1946, Evelyn Keyes (marr. diss. 1950); 4th 1950, Enrica Soma (*d* 1969); one *s* one *d* ; 5th, 1972, Celeste Shane (marr. diss. 1975). Became an Irish Citizen, 1964. At beginning of career was reporter, artist, writer and actor at various times. Formerly: Writer for Warner Bros Studios, 1938; Director for Warner Bros 1941; Writer and Dir, Metro-Goldwyn-Mayer, 1949. Dir of several Broadway plays. Films directed or produced include: The Maltese Falcon; Key Largo; The Treasure of Sierra Madre; The Asphalt Jungle; The African Queen; Moulin Rouge; Beat the Devil; Moby Dick; Heaven Knows, Mr Allison; The Barbarian and the Geisha; The Roots of Heaven; The Unforgiven; The Misfits; Freud; The Night of the Iguana; The Bible . . . In the Beginning; Reflections in a Golden Eye; Sinful Davey; A Walk with Love and Death; The Kremlin Letter; Fat City; The Life and Times of Judge Roy Bean; The Mackintosh Man; The Man who would be King; Wise Blood; Phobia; Escape to Victory; Annie. Served US Army 1942-45, Major; filmed documentaries of the War. Hon. LittD Trinity Coll., Dublin, 1970. *Publication:* (autobiog.) An Open Book, 1981. *Recreation:* foxhunting. *Address:* c/o Jess S. Morgan & Co. Inc., 6420 Wilshire Boulevard, 19th Floor, Los Angeles, Calif 90048, USA.

HUTCHINGS, Andrew William Seymour, CBE 1973; General Secretary, Assistant Masters Association, 1939-78, Joint General Secretary, Assistant Masters and Mistresses Association, Sept-Dec. 1978; Chairman, National Foundation for Educational Research in England and Wales, since 1973; *b* 3 Dec. 1907; *o s* of William Percy and Mellony Elizabeth Louisa Hutchings; unmarried. *Educ:* Cotham Sch., Bristol; St Catharine's Coll., Cambridge (MA). Asst Master: Downside Sch., 1929-30; Methodist Coll., Belfast, 1930-34; Holt Sch., Liverpool, 1934-36; Asst Sec., Asst Masters Assoc., 1936-39; Hon. Sec., Jt Cttee of Four Secondary Assocs, 1939-78; Sec.-Gen. 1954-65, Pres. 1965-71 and 1972-73, Internat. Fedn of Secondary Teachers; Member: Exec. Cttee, World Confedn of Organisations of Teaching Profession, 1954-80; Secondary Schs Examination Council, and subseq. of Schools Council, 1939-78; Norwood Cttee on Curriculum and Examinations in Secondary Schs, 1941-43; Chm., Teachers' Panel, Burnham Primary and Secondary Cttee, 1965-78; Vice-Chm., Associated Examining Bd, 1982- (Chm., Exec. Cttee, 1979-). FEIS 1963; FCP 1975. *Publications:* educnl and professional articles and memoranda for Asst Masters Assoc. *Recreation:* breeding and showing Great Danes (Mem. Kennel Club). *Address:* Sticklebridge Farm, Charlton Adam, near Somerton, Som. *T:* Charlton Mackrell 3676.

HUTCHINGS, Arthur James Bramwell; Professor of Music, University of Exeter, 1968-71, now Emeritus; *b* Sunbury on Thames, 14 July 1906; *s* of William Thomas Hutchings, Bideford, N Devon, and Annie Bramwell, Freckleton, Lytham, Lancs; *m* 1940, Marie Constance Haverson; one *d.* Formerly schoolmaster and organist; contributor to musical periodicals, critic and reviewer; served with RAF in SEAC; Prof. of Music, University of Durham, 1947-68, now Emeritus. Mem., Editorial Cttee, The English Hymnal, 1954-. Mem. Bd of Governors of Trinity Coll. of Music, 1947-. BA, BMus, PhD London; Hon. FTCL, FRSCM, Hon. RAM. Compositions include: works for strings, comic operas and church music. *Publications:* Schubert (Master Musicians Series), 1941, 5th edn 1978; Edmund Rubbra (contribution to Penguin Special, Music of Our Time), 1941; Delius (in French, Paris), 1946; A Companion to Mozart's Concertos, 1947; Delius, 1947; The Invention and Composition of Music, 1954; The Baroque Concerto, 1960, 4th edn 1978; Pelican History of Music, Vol 3 (The 19th Century), 1962; Church Music in the Nineteenth Century, 1967; Mozart (2 vols), 1976. Contributions to: Die Musik in Geschichte und Gegenwart, 1956; The Mozart Companion, 1956; New Oxford History of Music, 1962; The Beethoven Companion, 1970; Grove's Dictionary of Music and Musicians, 6th edn, 1975; Purcell (BBC Music Guides), 1982. *Address:* 8 Rosemary Lane, Colyton, Devon EX13 6NJ. *T:* Colyton 52542.

HUTCHINGS, Geoffrey Balfour, CMG 1946; Formerly Senior Partner in Lovell, White & King, Solicitors; *b* 24 Feb. 1904; 2nd *s* of late Charles Graham Hutchings, Seaford, Sussex; *m* 1st, 1928, Dorothy Guest (*d* 1967), *o d* of late

Rev. J. Guest Gilbert; one *s* one *d* ; 2nd, 1969, Mrs Stella Graham. *Educ:* Giggleswick Sch., Yorks. Served with 1/4 Bn South Lancs Regt, Sept. 1939-41; Principal Dir of Salvage and Recovery, Ministry of Supply, 1941-44; Dir-Gen. of British Ministry of Supply Commission, North West Europe, 1944-45; resumed professional practice, 1945. *Recreation:* golf. *Address:* Dunaverty Lodge, Southend by Cambeltown, Argyll. *T:* Southend 634.

HUTCHINS, Frank Ernest, CEng, FIEE, FIMarE; RCNC; retired 1981; consultant engineer, since 1982; *b* 27 Sept. 1922; *s* of Sidney William Hutchins and Eleanor Seager; *m* 1946, Patricia Mary Wakeford-Fullagar; one *d. Educ:* Sir Joseph Williamson's Mathematical Sch., Rochester, Kent; Royal Dockyard Sch., Chatham; Royal Naval Coll., Greenwich. BSc(Eng) 1st cl. Hons London. Asst Electrical Engr, Admiralty, Bath, 1945-49; Asst Staff Electrical Officer, BJSM, Washington DC, USA, 1949-51; Electrical Engr, Admiralty, Bath, 1951-63; Suptg Elec. Engr, Weapon Development and Ship Design, MoD (Navy), Bath, 1963-65; HM Dockyard, Devonport: Dep. Elec. Engrg Manager, 1965-68; Dep. Production Manager, 1968-69; Productivity Manager, 1969-70; attended Senior Officers' War Course, RN War Coll., Greenwich, 1970-71; Asst Director Naval Ship Production (Procurement Executive), MoD (Navy), Bath, 1971-73, Dep. Dir of Electrical Engrng, 1973-78; Chief Electrical Engr, Ship Dept, MoD (Navy), 1978-81. Panel Mem., CS Comr's Interview Selection Bd, 1981-. FBIM. *Recreations:* sketching, carpentry, gardening. *Address:* Bonnie Banks, Ralph Allen Drive, Bath BA2 5AE. *Club:* Civil Service.

HUTCHINS, Captain Ronald Edward, CBE 1961; DSC 1943; RN; *b* 7 Jan. 1912; *s* of Edward Albert Hutchins and Florence Ada (*née* Sharman); *m* 1937, Irene (*née* Wood); two *s. Educ:* St John's (elem. sch.), Hammersmith; TS Mercury, Hamble, Hants (C. B. Fry); RN Coll., Greenwich. Royal Navy, 1928-61; Computer Industry, 1961-75; company director, 1964-75. *Recreations:* walking, gardening.

HUTCHINSON; *see* Hely-Hutchinson.

HUTCHINSON, family name of **Baron Hutchinson of Lullington.**

HUTCHINSON OF LULLINGTON, Baron *cr* 1978 (Life Peer), of Lullington in the County of E Sussex; **Jeremy Nicolas Hutchinson,** QC 1961; *b* 28 March 1915; *o s* of late St John Hutchinson, KC; *m* 1st, 1940, Dame Peggy Ashcroft (marr. diss. 1966); one *s* one *d* ; 2nd, 1966, June Osborn. *Educ:* Stowe Sch.; Magdalen Coll., Oxford. Called to Bar, Middle Temple, 1939, Bencher 1963. RNVR, 1939-46. Practised on Western Circuit, N London Sessions and Central Criminal Court. Recorder of Bath, 1962-72; a Recorder of the Crown Court, 1972-76. Member: Cttee on Immigration Appeals, 1966-68; Cttee on Identification Procedures, 1974-76. Mem., Arts Council of GB, 1974-79 (Vice-Chm., 1977-79); Trustee, Tate Gallery, 1977- (Chm., 1980-). *Address:* Queen Elizabeth Building, Temple, EC4. *T:* 01-583 9744. *Club:* MCC.

HUTCHINSON, Arthur Edward; QC 1979; a Recorder of the Crown Court, since 1974; *b* 31 Aug. 1934; *s* of late George Edward Hutchinson and Kathleen Hutchinson; *m* 1967, Wendy Pauline Cordingley, one *s* two *d. Educ:* Silcoates Sch.; Emmanuel Coll., Cambridge (MA). Commissioned, West Yorkshire Regt, 1953; served in Kenya with 5th Fusiliers, 1953-54. Called to Bar, Middle Temple, 1958; joined NE Circuit, 1959. *Recreations:* cricket, gardening, music. *Address:* 6 Park Square, Leeds LS1 2LW. *T:* Leeds 459763.

HUTCHINSON, Rear-Adm. Christopher Haynes, CB 1961; DSO 1940; OBE 1946; RN retired; *b* 13 March 1906; 2nd *s* of late Rev. Canon Frederick William Hutchinson; *m* 1941, Nancy Marguerite Coppinger. *Educ:* Lydgate House Prep. Sch., Hunstanton; Royal Naval Colleges, Osborne and Dartmouth. Naval Cadet RNC Osborne, Sept. 1919; served largely in submarines; served War of 1939-45, commanding submarine Truant which sank German cruiser Karlsruhe, 9 April 1940 (DSO); submarine base, Malta, 1942 (despatches); Staff Officer, British Pacific Fleet 1945 (OBE); Qualified RN Staff Coll. (1946) and Joint Services Staff Coll. (Directing Staff); Commanding 3rd Submarine Flotilla, 1950-52; Senior Naval Adviser to UK High Commissioner, Australia, 1952-54; Captain, RN Coll., Greenwich, 1954-56; Commodore, 1st Class, Chief of Staff Far East Station, 1956-59; Director-General of Personal Services and Officer Appointments, 1959-61; retired, 1962. *Address:* Pipits Hill, Avington, near Winchester, Hants. *T:* Itchen Abbas 363.

HUTCHINSON, Prof. George William, MA, PhD, Cantab; Professor of Physics, Southampton University, since 1960; *b* Feb. 1921; *s* of George Hutchinson, farmer, and Louisa Ethel (*née* Saul), Farnsfield, Notts; *m* 1943, Christine Anne (marr. diss. 1970), *d* of Matthew Rymer and Mary (*née* Proctor), York; two *s. Educ:* Abergele Grammar Sch.; Cambridge. MA 1946, PhD 1952, Cantab. State Schol. and Schol. of St John's Coll., Cambridge, 1939-42. Research worker and factory manager in cotton textile industry, 1942-47; Cavendish Lab., Cambridge, 1947-52; Clerk-Maxwell Schol. of Cambridge Univ., 1949-52; Nuffield Fellow, 1952-53, and Lecturer, 1953-55, in Natural Philosophy, University of Glasgow; Research Assoc. of Stanford Univ., Calif, 1954. Lecturer, 1955, Sen. Lectr, 1957, in Physics, University of Birmingham. Member: Nat. Exec. Cttee, CND; Nat. Exec. Cttee, AUT. Duddell Medal, Physical Soc., 1959. FPhysS; FRAS; FRSA. *Publications:* papers on nuclear and elementary particle physics, nuclear instrumentation and cosmic rays. *Recreations:* music, volley-ball, sailing. *Address:* Physical Laboratory, University of Southampton, Southampton SO9 5NH. *T:* Southampton 559122.

HUTCHINSON, Sir Joseph (Burtt), Kt 1956; CMG 1944; ScD Cantab; FRS 1951; Drapers' Professor of Agriculture, Cambridge, 1957-69, now Emeritus; Fellow, St John's College; *b* 21 March 1902; *s* of L. M. and Edmund Hutchinson; *m* 1930, Martha Leonora Johnson; one *s* one *d*. *Educ:* Ackworth and Bootham Schs; St John's Coll., Cambridge. Asst Geneticist, Empire Cotton Growing Corporation's Cotton Research Station, Trinidad, 1926-33; Geneticist and Botanist, Institute of Plant Industry, Indore, Central India, 1933-37; Geneticist, Empire Growing Corporation's Cotton Research Station, Trinidad, and Cotton Adviser to the Inspector-General of Agriculture, BWI, 1937-44. Chief Geneticist, Empire Cotton Growing Corp., 1944-49; Dir of its Cotton Research Station, Namulonge, Uganda, 1949-57. Chm. of Council of Makerere Coll., University Coll. of East Africa, 1953-57; Hon. Fellow, Makerere Coll., 1957. Pres., British Assoc., 1965-66; Foreign Fellow, Indian Nat. Science Acad., 1974. Royal Medal, Royal Society, 1967. Hon. DSc: Nottingham, 1966; East Anglia, 1972. *Publications:* The Genetics of Gossypium, 1947; Genetics and the Improvement of Tropical Crops, 1958; Application of Genetics to Cotton Improvement, 1959; Farming and Food Supply, 1972; (ed) Evolutionary Studies in World Crops, 1974; The Challenge of the Third World, 1975; Change and Innovation in Norfolk Farming, 1980; numerous papers on the genetics, taxonomy, and economic botany of cotton. *Address:* Huntingfield, Huntingdon Road, Cambridge. *T:* Cambridge 276272.

HUTCHINSON, Patricia Margaret, CMG 1981; CBE 1982; HM Diplomatic Service; Ambassador to Uruguay, since 1980; *b* 18 June 1926; *d* of late Francis Hutchinson and Margaret Peat. *Educ:* abroad; St Paul's Girls' Sch.; Somerville Coll., Oxford (PPE, MA, Hon Fellow, 1980). ECE, Geneva, 1947; Bd of Trade, 1947-48; HM Diplomatic Service, 1948: 3rd Sec., Bucharest, 1948-50; Foreign Office, 1950-52; 2nd (later 1st) Sec., Berne, 1955-58; 1st Sec. (Commercial), Washington, 1958-61; FO, 1961-64; 1st Sec., Lima, 1964-67 (acted as Chargé d'Affaires); Dep. UK Permanent Rep. to Council of Europe, 1967-69; Counsellor: Stockholm, 1969-72; UK Delegn to OECD, 1973-75; Consul-Gen., Geneva, 1975-80. *Recreations:* music, reading. *Address:* c/o Foreign and Commonwealth Office, SW1. *Club:* United Oxford & Cambridge University.

HUTCHINSON, Richard Hampson; His Honour Judge Hutchinson; a Circuit Judge, since 1974; *b* 31 Aug. 1927; *s* of late John Riley Hutchinson and May Hutchinson; *m* 1954, Nancy Mary (*née* Jones); two *s* three *d*. *Educ:* St Bede's Grammar Sch., Bradford; UC Hull. LLB London. National Service, RAF, 1949-51. Called to Bar, Gray's Inn, 1949; practised on NE Circuit, 1951-74. Recorder: Rotherham, 1971-72; Crown Court, 1972-74. *Recreations:* reading, conversation. *Address:* c/o Crown Court, Holborn House, 10A Newport, Lincoln.

HUTCHINSON, Hon. Sir Ross, Kt 1977; DFC 1944; Speaker, Legislative Assembly, Western Australia, 1974-77, retired; MLA (L) Cottesloe, 1950-77; *b* 10 Sept. 1914; *s* of Albert H. Hutchinson and Agnes L. M. Hutchinson; *m* 1939, Amy Goodall Strang; one *s* one *d*. *Educ:* Wesley Coll. RAAF, 1942-45. School teacher, 1935-49. Chief Sec., Minister for Health and Fisheries, 1959-65; Minister for Works and Water Supplies, 1965-71. Australian Rules Football, former Captain Coach; East Fremantle, West Perth and South Fremantle; Captain Coach, WA, 1939. *Recreations:* tennis, reading. *Address:* 42 Griver Street, Cottesloe, WA 6011, Australia. *T:* 312680. *Club:* Royal King's Park Tennis (Perth, WA).

HUTCHINSON, William James, TD; Chief Executive, County of Avon, 1974-82 (Town Clerk and Chief Executive Officer, Bristol County Borough, 1969-74); *b* 12 Dec. 1919; *s* of William James Hutchinson and Martha Allan Hutchinson (*née* Downie); *m* 1944, Barbara Olive Benaton; one *s* one *d*. *Educ:* Brighton Hove and Sussex Grammar School. Admitted Solicitor, 1947. Bury County Borough Council, 1947-49; Bristol CBC, 1949-. *Recreations:* gardening, walking, theatre. *Address:* 32 Woodland Grove, Coombe Dingle, Bristol BS9 2BB. *T:* 683415.

HUTCHISON, A(lan) Michael Clark; *b* 26 Feb. 1914; *y s* of late Sir George A. Clark Hutchison, KC, MP, of Eriska, Argyll; *m* 1937, Anne, *yr d* of Rev. A. R. Taylor, DD, of Aberdeen; one *s* one *d*. *Educ:* Eton; Trinity Coll., Cambridge. Called to Bar, Gray's Inn, 1937. War of 1939-45 (despatches); served AIF, Middle East and Pacific theatres, psc. Mem. Australian Mil. Mission, Washington, USA, 1945-46. Entered Colonial Admin. Service, 1946, and served as Asst Dist Comr in Palestine till 1948; thereafter as Political Officer and Asst Sec. in Protectorate and Colony of Aden; resigned, 1955. Contested (C) Motherwell Div. of Lanarks, 1955; MP (C) Edinburgh South, May 1957-79; Parliamentary Private Secretary to: Parliamentary and Financial Sec. to the Admiralty, and to the Civil Lord, 1959; the Lord Advocate, 1959-60; Sec. of State for Scotland, 1960-62. Scottish Conservative Members' Committee: Vice-Chm., 1965-66, 1967-68; Chm., 1970-71. Introduced a Private Mem.'s Bills: Solicitors (Scotland) Act; Wills Act; Intestate Succession (Scotland) Act; Confirmation to Small Estates (Scotland) Act. *Recreations:* reading, Disraeliana. *Address:* Wellcroft End, Bucklebury, Reading RG7 6PB. *T:* Woolhampton 3462. *Club:* New (Edinburgh).
See also Lieut-Comdr Sir G. I. C. Hutchison.

HUTCHISON, Bruce; see Hutchison, W. B.

HUTCHISON, Hon. Sir Douglas; see Hutchison, Hon. Sir J. D.

HUTCHISON, Douglas; see Hutchison, J. D.

HUTCHISON, Geordie Oliphant; Managing Director, Calders & Grandidge Ltd, since 1974; *b* 11 June 1934; *s* of late Col Ronald Gordon Oliphant Hutchison and of Ruth Gordon Hutchison-Bradburne; *m* 1964, Virginia Barbezat; two *s* one *d*. *Educ:* Eton Coll. Served RN, 1952-54: commnd as aircraft pilot, 1953. Calders Ltd, 1952-59; Calders & Grandidge Ltd, 1959-: Dir, 1969. Comr, Forestry Commn, 1981-. *Recreations:* golf, shooting. *Address:* Swallowfield House, Welby, Grantham, Lincs NG32 3LR. *T:* Loveden 30510. *Club:* Royal and Ancient Golf (St Andrews).

HUTCHISON, Lt-Comdr Sir (George) Ian Clark, Kt 1954; DL; Royal Navy, retired; Member of the Queen's Body Guard for Scotland, Royal Company of Archers; *b* 4 Jan. 1903; *e s* of late Sir George Clark Hutchison, KC, MP, Eriska, Argyllshire; *m* 1926, Sheena (*d* 1966), *o d* of late A. B. Campbell, WS; one *d*. *Educ:* Edinburgh Academy; RN Colleges, Osborne and Dartmouth. Joined Navy as Cadet, 1916; Lieut, 1926; Lieut-Comdr 1934; specialised in torpedoes, 1929; emergency list, 1931; Mem., Edinburgh Town Council, 1935-41; Chm., Public Assistance Cttee, 1937-39; contested Maryhill Div. of Glasgow, 1935; rejoined Navy Sept. 1939; served in Naval Ordnance Inspection Dept, 1939-43; MP (U) for West Div. of Edinburgh, 1941-59. Mem. National Executive Council of British Legion (Scotland), 1943-51; Governor of Donaldson's Sch. for the Deaf, Edinburgh, 1937-75; Mem. Cttee on Electoral Registration, 1945-46; Mem. Scottish Leases Cttee, 1951-52. DL County of City of Edinburgh, 1958. *Recreations:* golf, fishing, walking, philately. *Address:* 16 Wester Coates Gardens, Edinburgh EH12 5LT. *T:* 031-337 4888. *Club:* New (Edinburgh).
See also A. M. C. Hutchison, J. V. Paterson.

HUTCHISON, Lt-Comdr Sir Ian Clark; see Hutchison, Sir G. I. C.

HUTCHISON, Hon. Sir (James) Douglas, Kt 1959; Judge of Supreme Court of New Zealand, 1948-66, retired; *b* 29 Sept. 1894; *s* of Sir James Hutchison; *m* 1st, 1924, Mary Bethea Johnston (*d* 1943); two *s* two *d*; 2nd, 1954, Mary Elizabeth Averill. *Educ:* Otago Boys' High Sch.; Otago Univ.; Victoria University Coll. (now Victoria Univ. of Wellington). Served European War, 1914-18, with 1st NZEF in Gallipoli and France; War of 1939-45, DAAG, Southern Military District, NZ. Practised Carterton, 1920-24, Christchurch, 1924-48. *Recreations:* radio and television sports. *Address:* Flat 2, 2 Grafton Road, Roseneath, Wellington 3, New Zealand. *Clubs:* Wellington, Canterbury (NZ).

HUTCHISON, Prof. James Holmes, CBE 1971 (OBE 1945); FRCP 1947; FRCPE 1960; FRCPGlas 1962; MD (Hons) 1939 (Glasgow); FRSE 1965; Professor of Paediatrics, University of Hong Kong, 1977-80; *b* 16 April 1912; *s* of Alexander Hutchison and Catherine Holmes; *m* 1940, Agnes T. A. Goodall; one *s* one *d*. *Educ:* High Sch. of Glasgow; University of Glasgow. Qualified MB, ChB (Glasgow) 1934; Resident Hosp. Posts, 1934-36; Royal Hosp. for Sick Children, Glasgow: McCunn Research Schol., 1936-38; Asst Vis. Phys., 1938-39; Physician in charge of Wards, 1947-61; also Consulting Paediatrician, Queen Mother's Hospital, Glasgow; Leonard Gow Lectr on Med. Diseases of Infancy and Childhood, 1947-61, Samson Gemmell Prof. of Child Health, 1961-77, Univ. of Glasgow. Dean, Fac. of Medicine, Univ. of Glasgow, 1970-73. President: Royal College of Physicians and Surgeons of Glasgow, Nov. 1966-Nov. 1968. British Paediatric Assoc., 1969-70; Assoc. of Physicians of GB and Ireland, 1973-74; Hong Kong Paediatric Soc., 1979-80. Hon. FACP 1968. RAMC, Major and Lieut-Col, 1939-45. *Publications:* Practical Paediatric Problems, 1964, 5th edn 1980; Rickets, in British Encyclopædia of Medical Practice, 2nd edn, 1952; Disorders of Storage, Obesity and Endocrine Diseases; chapters 50-57, in Pædiatrics for the Practitioner, 1953 (ed Gaisford and Lightwood); Hypothyroidism, in Recent Advances in Pædiatrics, 1958 (ed Gairdner), 2nd edn 1975; chapter in Emergencies in Medical Practice (ed C. Allan Birch); chapter in Textbook of Medical Treatment (ed Davidson, Dunlop and Alstead); chapter in Endocrine and Genetic Diseases of Childhood (ed L. I. Gardner), 1969, 2nd edn 1976; Thyroid section in Paediatric Endrocrinology (ed D.Hubble), 1969; chapter in Textbook of Pædiatrics (ed J. O. Forfar and G. C. Arneil), 1973, 2nd edn, 1978; many contributions to medical journals. *Recreations:* golf, country dancing (Scottish), motoring. *Address:* 3 Kelvin Court, Glasgow G12 0AB. *T:* 041-334 7545. *Clubs:* Caledonian; Royal Scottish Automobile.

HUTCHISON, James Seller; Chairman, The British Oxygen Co. Ltd and Associated Companies, 1950-72 (Director, 1940-72); *b* 15 Oct. 1904; *s* of late R. F. Hutchison, Glasgow; *m* Kathleen, *d* of late William Maude, Leeds; two *d*. *Educ:* Greenock Academy; Glasgow Univ. Chartered Accountant, 1928. *Recreations:* golf, gardening. *Address:* 3 Elm Gardens, Bearsden, Glasgow.

HUTCHISON, (Joseph) Douglas, CBE 1972; MC 1944; TD 1952; Director, Ranks Hovis McDougall Ltd, since 1956; *b* 3 April 1918; *s* of late John K. Hutchison, Kinloch, Collessie, Fife and late Ethel Rank, OBE; unmarried. *Educ:* Loretto; Clare Coll., Cambridge. BA Agric. 1939. Served Fife and Forfar Yeomanry, 1939-46 (Major); comd Regt, 1951-53. Director: R. Hutchison & Co. Ltd, 1951-73; Ranks Ltd (later RHM), 1956. Mem., ARC, 1973-78. Pres., Nat. Assoc. British and Irish Millers, 1963-64 and 1974-75;

Pres., Research Assoc. Flour Millers and Bakers, 1967-72; Chm., Game Conservancy, 1970-75. *Recreations:* shooting, gardening, music. *Address:* Bolfracks, Aberfeldy, Perthshire. *Club:* New (Edinburgh).

HUTCHISON, Sir Kenneth; *see* Hutchison, Sir W. K.

HUTCHISON, Michael, QC 1976; a Recorder of the Crown Court, since 1975; *b* 13 Oct. 1933; *s* of Ernest and Frances Hutchison; *m* 1957, Mary Spettigue; two *s* three *d. Educ:* Lancing; Clare College, Cambridge (MA). Called to Bar, Gray's Inn, 1958. *Address:* Hare Dene, Albury, Guildford, Surrey GU5 9DB. *T:* Shere 2240.

HUTCHISON, Sir Peter, 2nd Bt, *cr* 1939; *b* 27 Sept. 1907; *er s* of Sir Robert Hutchison, 1st Bt, MD, CM, and Lady Hutchison (then Dr and Mrs Robert Hutchison); *S* father 1960; *m* 1949, Mary-Grace (*née* Seymour); two *s* two *d. Educ:* Marlborough; Lincoln Coll., Oxford. Admitted as a Solicitor, 1933. Dep.-Clerk of the Peace and of the CC, E Suffolk, 1947-71, Clerk of the Peace, 1971. *Recreations:* walking, gardening, reading. *Heir: s* Robert Hutchison, *b* 25 May 1954. *Address:* Melton Mead, near Woodbridge, Suffolk. *T:* Woodbridge 2746. *Club:* Ipswich and Suffolk (Ipswich).

HUTCHISON, Sir Peter Craft, 2nd Bt *cr* 1956; *b* 5 June 1935; *s* of Sir James Riley Holt Hutchison, 1st Bt, DSO, TD, and of Winefryde Eleanor Mary, *d* of late Rev. R. H. Craft; *S* father, 1979; *m* 1966, Virginia, *er d* of John Millar Colville, Gribloch, Kippen, Stirlingshire; one *s. Educ:* Eton; Magdalene Coll., Cambridge. Chm., Hutchison & Craft Ltd, Insurance Brokers, Glasgow, 1979-; Dir, Stakis plc and other cos; Mem., Scottish Tourist Bd, 1981-. *Heir: s* James Colville Hutchison, *b* 7 Oct. 1967. *Address:* Milton House, Milton, by Dumbarton.

HUTCHISON, Robert Edward; Keeper, Scottish National Portrait Gallery, 1953-82; *b* 4 Aug. 1922; *y s* of late Sir William Hutchison; *m* 1946, Heather, *d* of late Major A. G. Bird; one *s* one *d. Educ:* Gresham's Sch., Holt. Served War, 1940-46, Infantry and RA; Asst Keeper, Scottish National Portrait Gallery, 1949. Hon. MA Edinburgh, 1972. *Publication:* (with Stuart Maxwell) Scottish Costume 1550-1850, 1958. *Address:* North House, Firth Home Farm, Roslin, Midlothian. *T:* Penicuik 75118.

HUTCHISON, Sidney Charles, CVO 1977 (MVO 1967); Hon. Archivist, Royal Academy of Arts, since 1982; *b* 26 March 1912; *s* of Henry Hutchison; *m* 1937, Nancy Arnold Brindley; no *c. Educ:* Holloway Sch., London; London Univ. (Dip. in Hist. of Art, with Dist.). Joined staff of Royal Academy, 1929. Served War of 1939-45: Royal Navy, rising to Lieut-Comdr (S), RNVR. Librarian of Royal Academy, 1949-68, also Sec. of Loan Exhibitions, 1955-68; Sec., Royal Academy, 1968-82. Secretary: E. A. Abbey Meml Trust Fund for Mural Painting, 1960-; Incorporated E. A. Abbey Scholarships Fund, 1965-; E. Vincent Harris Fund for Mural Decoration, 1970-; British Institution Fund, 1968-82; Chantrey Trustees, 1968-82; Richard Ford Award Fund, 1977-82. Lectr in the History of Art, for Extra-Mural Dept of Univ. of London, 1957-67. Gen. Comr of Taxes, 1972-. Governor, Holloway Sch., 1969-81. Trustee, Chantrey Bequest. Organist and Choirmaster of St Matthew's, Westminster, 1933-37. Associate Mem., ICOM, 1964. FRSA 1950; FSA 1955; FMA 1962; Fellow, Assoc. of Art Historians, 1974-. Officer, Polonia Restituta, 1971; Chevalier, Belgian Order of the Crown, 1972; Grand Decoration of Honour (silver), Austria, 1972; Cavaliere Ufficiale, Al Merito della Repubblica Italiana, 1980. *Publications:* The Homes of the Royal Academy, 1956; The History of the Royal Academy, 1768-1968, 1968; articles for Walpole Society, Museums Jl, Encyclopædia Britannica, DNB, Apollo, etc. *Recreations:* music, travel, golf. *Address:* 60 Belmont Close, Mount Pleasant, Cockfosters, Herts EN4 9LT. *T:* 01-449 9821. *Clubs:* Athenæum, Arts.

HUTCHISON, Prof. Terence Wilmot; Professor of Economics, University of Birmingham, 1956-78, now Emeritus Professor; Dean of the Faculty of Commerce and Social Science, 1959-61; *b* 13 Aug. 1912; *m* 1935, Loretta Hack (*d* 1981); one *s* two *d. Educ:* Tonbridge Sch.; Peterhouse, Cambridge. Lector, Univ. of Bonn, 1935-38; Prof., Teachers' Training Coll., Bagdad, 1938-41. Served Indian Army, in intelligence, in Middle East and India, 1941-46; attached to Govt of India, 1945-46. Lecturer, University Coll., Hull, 1946-47; Lecturer, 1947-51 and Reader, 1951-56, London Sch. of Economics. Visiting Professor: Columbia Univ., 1954-55; Univ. of Saarbrücken, 1962, 1980; Yale Univ., 1963-64; Dalhousie Univ., 1970; Keio Univ., Tokyo, 1973; Univ. of WA, 1975; Univ. of California, Davis, 1978; Visiting Fellow: Univ. of Virginia, 1960; Aust. Nat. Univ., Canberra, 1967. Mem. Council, Royal Economic Soc., 1967-72. *Publications:* The Significance and Basic Postulates of Economic Theory, 1938 (2nd edn 1960); A Review of Economic Doctrines 1870-1929, 1953; Positive Economics and Policy Objectives, 1964; Economics and Economic Policy 1946-66, 1968; Knowledge and Ignorance in Economics, 1977; Keynes v the Keynesians, 1977; Revolutions and Progress in Economic Knowledge, 1978; The Politics and Philosophy of Economics, 1981; articles, reviews in jls. *Address:* 75 Oakfield Road, Birmingham B29 7HL. *T:* 021-472 2020.

HUTCHISON, (William) Bruce, OC 1967; formerly Editorial Director, Vancouver Sun, now Editor Emeritus; *b* 5 June 1901; *s* of John and Constance Hutchison; *m* 1925, Dorothy Kidd McDiarmid; one *s* one *d. Educ:* Public and high schs, Victoria, BC. Political writer: Victoria Times, 1918; Vancouver Province, 1925; Vancouver Sun, 1938; editor, Victoria Times, 1950-63;

associate editor, Winnipeg Free Press, 1944. Hon. LLD University of British Columbia, 1951. *Publications:* The Unknown Country, 1943; The Hollow Men, 1944; The Fraser, 1950; The Incredible Canadian, 1952; The Struggle for the Border, 1955; Canada: Tomorrow's Giant, 1957; Mr Prime Minister, 1964; Western Windows, 1967; The Far Side of the Street, 1976; Uncle Percy's Wonderful Town, 1981. *Recreations:* fishing, gardening. *Address:* 810 Rogers Avenue, Victoria, BC, Canada. *T:* Granite 9-2269. *Club:* Union (Victoria).

HUTCHISON, Sir (William) Kenneth, Kt 1962; CBE 1954; FRS 1966; FEng; FIChemE; Hon. FIGasE; *b* 30 Oct. 1903; *s* of late William Hutchison; *m* 1929, Dorothea Marion Eva, *d* of late Commander Bertie W. Bluett, Royal Navy; one *d. Educ:* Edinburgh Academy; Corpus Christi Coll., Oxford. FEng 1976. Joined staff of Gas, Light and Coke Co. as Research Chemist, 1926; seconded to Air Ministry as Asst Dir of Hydrogen Production, 1940, Dir, 1942; Dir of Compressed Gases, 1943; Controller of By-Products, Gas, Light and Coke Co., 1945, and a Managing Dir of the Company from 1947; Chm., South Eastern Gas Board, 1948-59; Deputy Chm., Gas Council, 1960-66; Chm., International Management and Engineering Group, 1967-69; Dir, Newton Chambers & Co. Ltd, 1967-73. President: Institution of Gas Engineers, 1955-56; British Road Tar Assoc., 1953-55; Inst. of Chem. Engineers, 1959-61; Soc. of British Gas Industries, 1967-68; Nat. Soc. for Clean Air, 1969-71. *Publications:* papers in Proc. Royal Society and other jls, 1926-. *Recreations:* garden, golf. *Address:* 2 Arlington Road, Twickenham, Mddx TW1 2BG. *T:* 01-892 1685. *Clubs:* Athenæum, Royal Cruising.

HUTCHISON, Prof. William McPhee; Personal Professor in Parasitology, University of Strathclyde, since 1971; *b* 2 July 1924; *s* of William Hutchison and Ann McPhee; *m* 1963, Ella Duncan McLaughland; two *s. Educ:* Eastwood Secondary Sch.; Glasgow Univ. BSc, PhD, DSc; FLS, FIBiol, FRSE. Glasgow Univ. Fencing Blue, 1949; Ford Epée Cup; Glasgow Univ. Fencing Champion, 1950. Strathclyde Univ.: Asst Lectr, 1952; Lectr, 1953; Sen. Lectr, 1969. Engaged in res. on toxoplasma and toxoplasmosis. Robert Koch Medal, 1970. *Publications:* contrib. Trans Royal Soc. Trop. Med. and Hygiene, BMJ, Acta Path. Microbiol. Scand. *Recreations:* general microscopy, woodwork, collection of zoological specimens. *Address:* 597 Kilmarnock Road, Newlands, Glasgow G43 2TH. *T:* 041-637 4882.

HUTSON, Sir Francis (Challenor), Kt 1963; CBE 1960; Senior Partner, D. M. Simpson & Co., Consulting Engineers, Barbados, 1943-70, retired; *b* 13 Sept. 1895; *s* of Francis and Alice Sarah Hutson; *m* 1st, 1925, Muriel Allen Simpkin (*d* 1945); two *s* one *d*; 2nd, 1947, Edith Doris Howell. *Educ:* Harrison Coll., Barbados; Derby Technical Coll., Derby. Resident Engineer, Booker Bros, McConnell & Co. Ltd, British Guiana, 1920-30; Consulting Engineer, Barbados, 1930-35; D. M. Simpson & Co., 1935-70. MLC, 1947-62, MEC, 1958-61, Barbados; PC (Barbados), 1961-70. FIMechE. *Recreation:* bridge. *Address:* Fleetwood, Erdison Hill, St Michael, Barbados. *T:* 93905. *Clubs:* Bridgetown, Royal Barbados Yacht, Savannah, (all in Barbados).

HUTSON, Maj.-Gen. Henry Porter Wolseley, CB 1945; DSO 1917; OBE 1919; MC 1915; *b* 22 March 1893; *s* of late Henry Wolseley Hutson, Wimbledon, SW19; *m* 1922, Rowena, *d* of Surg.-Gen. Percy Hugh Benson, IA; two *s* one *d. Educ:* King's Coll. Sch.; RMA; 2nd Lieut RE, 1913; Capt. 1917; Major, 1929; Lieut-Col 1937; Col 1939; Temp. Brig. 1940; Maj.-Gen. 1944. Employed with Egyptian Army, 1920-24; under Colonial Office (Road Engineer Nigeria), 1926-28; Chief Instructor, Field Works and Bridging, Sch. of Military Engineering, 1934-36; Chief Engineer, Forestry Commn, 1947-58. Served European War, 1914-18, France, Belgium, Egypt and Mesopotamia (wounded, despatches thrice, DSO, OBE, MC); War of 1939-45 (despatches, CB); retired pay, 1947. *Publications:* The Birds about Delhi, 1954; (ed) The Ornithologist's Guide, 1956; Majority Rule—Why?, 1973; Rhodesia: ending an era, 1978. *Address:* 23 Hoskins Road, Oxted, Surrey. *T:* Oxted 2354.

HUTSON, John Whiteford, OBE 1966; HM Diplomatic Service; Consul-General, Frankfurt, since 1980; *b* 21 Oct. 1927; *s* of John Hutson and Jean Greenlees Laird; *m* 1954, Doris Kemp; one *s* two *d. Educ:* Hamilton Academy; Glasgow Univ. (MA (Hons)). HM Forces, 1949-51; Foreign Office, 1951; Third Secretary, Prague, 1953; FO, 1955; Second Sec., Berlin, 1956; Saigon, 1959; First Sec., 1961; Consul (Commercial) San Francisco, 1963-67; First Sec. and Head of Chancery, Sofia, 1967-69; FCO, 1969; Counsellor, 1970; Baghdad, 1971-72; Inspector, FCO, 1972-74; Head, Communications Operations Dept, FCO, 1974-76; Counsellor (Commercial), Moscow, 1976-79. *Address:* c/o Foreign and Commonwealth Office, SW1.

HUTT, Prof. William Harold; Distinguished Professor of Economics, University of Dallas, Texas, 1971-77; Professor of Commerce and Dean of the Faculty of Commerce, University of Cape Town, 1931-64; Professor Emeritus since 1965; *b* 3 Aug. 1899; *s* of William Hutt and Louisa (*née* Fricker); *m* 1946, Margarethe Louise Schonken. *Educ:* LCC Schs; Hackney Downs Sch.; London Sch. of Economics, University of London. Personal Asst to Chm., Benn Bros Ltd, and Manager, Individualist Bookshop Ltd, 1924-28; Senior Lecturer, University of Cape Town, 1928-30. Visiting Professor of Economics at various Univs and Colls in USA, 1966-69; Vis. Research Fellow, Hoover Instn, Stanford Univ., Calif., 1969-71; Distinguished Vis. Prof. of Economics, Calif. State Coll., 1970-71. LLD (*hc*) Cape Town, 1977. *Publications:* The Theory of Collective Bargaining, 1930, 2nd edn, 1975; Economists and the Public, 1936; The Theory of Idle Resources, 1939, 2nd edn 1977; Plan for Reconstruction, 1943; Keynesianism-Retrospect and Prospect, 1963; The

Economics of the Colour Bar, 1964; Politically Impossible?, 1971; The Strike-Threat System, 1973; A Rehabilitation of Say's Law, 1975; Individual Freedom: a symposium of articles 1934-75 selected and ed by Klingaman and Pejovich, 1976; The Keynesian Episode, 1980; numerous articles in economic jls and symposia. *Recreations:* travel, listening to symphonies, watching football, ballet and opera. *Address:* c/o Standard Bank Ltd, ABC Branch, Adderley Street, Cape Town, South Africa. *Club:* Civil Service and City (Cape Town).

HUTTER, Prof. Otto Fred, PhD; Regius Professor of Physiology, University of Glasgow, since 1971; *b* 29 Feb. 1924; *s* of Isak and Elisabeth Hutter; *m* 1948, Yvonne T. Brown; two *s* two *d. Educ:* Chajes Real Gymnasium, Vienna; Bishops Stortford Coll., Herts; University Coll., London (BSc, PhD). Univ. of London Postgrad. Student in Physiology, 1948; Sharpey Scholar, UCL, 1949-52; Rockefeller Travelling Fellow and Fellow in Residence, Johns Hopkins Hosp., Baltimore, 1953-55; Lectr, Dept of Physiology, UCL, 1953-61; Hon. Lectr, 1961-70. Visiting Prof., Tel-Aviv Univ., 1968, 1970; Scientific Staff, Nat. Inst. for Medical Research, Mill Hill, London, 1961-70. *Publications:* papers on neuromuscular and synaptic transmission, cardiac and skeletal muscle, in physiological jls. *Address:* Institute of Physiology, University of Glasgow, Glasgow G12 8QQ. *T:* 041-339 8855.

HUTTON, Alasdair Henry, TD 1977; Member (C) South Scotland, European Parliament, since 1979; *b* 19 May 1940; *s* of Alexander Hutton and Margaret Elizabeth (*née* Henderson); *m* 1975, Deirdre Mary Cassels; two *s. Educ:* Dollar Academy; Brisbane State High Sch., Australia. Radio Station 4BH, Brisbane, 1956; John Clemenger Advertising, Melbourne, 1957-59; Journalist: The Age, Melb., 1959-61; Press and Journal, Aberdeen, Scotland, 1962-64; Broadcaster, BBC: Scotland, N Ireland, London, Shetland, 1964-79. First Vice-Chm., Information sub-cttee, European Parlt, 1981-. *Recreations:* TA: Second in Command, 15th Scottish Parachute Battalion; hill-walking, sailing, reading. *Address:* 7th Floor, 121 St Vincent Street, Glasgow G2 5HW. *T:* 041-221 7850.

HUTTON, (David) Graham, OBE 1945; economist, author; *b* 13 April 1904; *er s* of late David James and Lavinia Hutton; *m* 1st, Magdalene Ruth Rudolph, Zürich (marr. diss. 1934); 2nd, Joyce Muriel Green (marr. diss. 1958); three *d*; 3rd, Marjorie, *d* of late Dr and Mrs David Bremner, Chicago. *Educ:* Christ's Hospital; London Sch. of Economics; French and German Univs. Gladstone Meml Prizeman, London Univ., 1929; Barrister-at-Law, Gray's Inn, 1932; Research Fellowship and teaching staff, LSE, 1929-33, Hon. Fellow 1971; Asst Editor, The Economist, 1933-38; FO and Min. of Information, 1939-45. *Publications:* Nations and the Economic Crisis, 1932; The Burden of Plenty (as ed. and contributor, 1935); Is it Peace?, 1936; Danubian Destiny, 1939; Midwest at Noon, 1946; English Parish Churches, 1952; We Too Can Prosper, 1953; All Capitalists Now, 1960; Inflation and Society, 1960; Mexican Images, 1963; Planning and Enterprise, 1964; Politics and Economic Growth, 1968; (with Olive Cook) English Parish Churches, 1976; Whatever Happened to Productivity? (Wincott Lecture), 1980. *Recreations:* ecclesiology, music, travel. *Address:* 38 Connaught Square, W2 2HL. *T:* 01-723 4067. *Clubs:* Reform, English-Speaking Union.

HUTTON, Gabriel Bruce; His Honour Judge Hutton; a Circuit Judge, since 1978; *b* 27 Aug. 1932; *y s* of late Robert Crompton Hutton, and of Elfreda Bruce; *m* 1st, 1963, Frances Henrietta Cooke (*d* 1963); 2nd, 1965, Deborah Leigh Windus; one *s* two *d. Educ:* Marlborough; Trinity Coll., Cambridge (BA). Called to Bar, Inner Temple, 1956; Dep. Chm., Glos QS, 1971. A Recorder of the Crown Court, 1972-77. *Recreations:* hunting (Chm., Berkeley Hunt), shooting, fishing. *Address:* Chestal House, Dursley, Glos. *T:* Dursley 3285. *Club:* Gloucester (Gloucester).

HUTTON, Graham; *see* Hutton, D. G.

HUTTON, (Hubert) Robin; Director-General, Accepting Houses Committee, since 1982; *b* 22 April 1933; *e s* of Kenneth Douglas and Dorothy Hutton; *m* 1st, 1956, Valerie Riseborough (marr. diss. 1967); one *s* one *d* ; 2nd, 1969, Deborah Berkeley; two step *d. Educ:* Merchant Taylors' Sch.; Peterhouse, Cambridge (Scholar). MA Cantab 1960. Royal Tank Regt, 1952-53 (commnd). Economic Adviser to Finance Corp. for Industry Ltd, 1956-62; economic journalist and consultant; Dir, Hambros Bank Ltd, 1966-70; Special Adviser: to HM Govt, 1970-72; Min. of Posts and Telecommunications, 1972-73. Chm., Cttee of Inquiry into Public Trustee Office, 1971; Dir of Banking, Insurance and Financial Instns in EEC, Brussels, 1973-78; Exec. Dir, S. G. Warburg & Co. Ltd, 1978-82. Mem. London Bd, Northern Rock Building Soc. Chm., Soc. des Banques S. G. Warburg et Leu SA, Luxembourg, 1979-82. *Recreations:* cricket, ski-ing, gardening, travel. *Address:* c/o Accepting Houses Committee, 101 Cannon Street, EC4N 5BA; Church Farm, Athelington, Suffolk. *T:* Worlingworth 361. *Club:* MCC.

HUTTON, Hon. James Brian Edward; Hon. Mr Justice Hutton; a Judge of the High Court of Justice in Northern Ireland, since 1979; *b* 29 June 1931; *s* of late James and Mabel Hutton, Belfast; *m* 1975, Mary Gillian, *o d* of J. R. W. Murland, Saintfield, Co. Down; two *d. Educ:* Shrewsbury Sch.; Balliol Coll., Oxford (1st Cl. final sch. of Jurisprudence); Queen's Univ. of Belfast. Called to Northern Ireland Bar, 1954; QC (NI) 1970; Bencher, Inn of Court of Northern Ireland, 1974; called to English Bar, 1972. Junior Counsel to Attorney-General for NI, 1969; Legal Adviser to Min. of Home Affairs, NI, 1973; Sen. Crown Counsel in NI, 1973-79. Mem., Jt Law Enforcement

Commn, 1974. *Publications:* articles in Modern Law Review. *Address:* Royal Courts of Justice (Ulster), Belfast. *Club:* Ulster (Belfast).

HUTTON, Prof. John Philip, MA; Professor of Economics and Econometrics, University of York, since 1982; *b* 26 May 1940; *s* of Philip Ernest Michelson Hutton and Hester Mary Black Hutton; *m* 1964, Sandra Smith Reid; one *s* one *d. Educ:* Daniel Stewart's Coll., Edinburgh; Edinburgh Univ. (MA 1st Cl.). York University: Junior Research Fellow, 1962; Lecturer, 1963; Sen. Lectr, 1973; Reader, 1976. Economic Adviser, HM Treasury, 1970, 1971; Adviser to Malaysian Treasury, for Internat. Monetary Fund, 1977; Consultant to: NEDO, 1963; Home Office, 1966; Royal Commission on Local Govt in Englandand Wales, 1967; NIESR, 1980. Chairman, HM Treasury Academic Panel, 1980, 1981; Mem. Council, Royal Economic Soc., 1981-. Jt Managing Editor, Economic Journal, 1980-. *Publications:* contribs to learned jls, incl. Economic Jl, Rev. of Economic Studies, Oxford Economic Papers. *Recreations:* family; golf, badminton. *Address:* 1 The Old Orchard, Fulford, York Y01 4LT. *T:* York 38363.

HUTTON, Sir Leonard, Kt 1956; professional cricketer, retired 1956; Director, Fenner International (Power Transmission) Ltd; *b* Fulneck, near Pudsey, Yorks, 23 June 1916; *s* of Henry Hutton; *m* 1939, Dorothy Mary Dennis, *d* of late G. Dennis, Scarborough; two *s.* First played for Yorks, 1934. First played for England *v* New Zealand, 1937; *v* Australia, 1938 (century on first appearance); *v* South Africa, 1938; *v* West Indies, 1939; *v* India, 1946. Captained England *v* India, 1952; *v* Australia, 1953; *v* Pakistan, 1954; *v* Australia, 1954. Captained MCC *v* West Indies, 1953-54. Made record Test score, 364, *v* Australia at the Oval, 1938; record total in a single month, 1294, in June 1949; has made over 100 centuries in first-class cricket. Hon. Mem. of MCC, 1955 (first Professional to be elected). A selector, MCC, 1975-77. Served War of 1939-45: in RA and APTC. Hon. MA Bradford, 1982. *Publications:* Cricket is my Life, 1950; Just my Story, 1956. *Recreation:* golf. *Address:* 1 Coombe Neville, Warren Road, Kingston-on-Thames, Surrey KT2 7HW. *T:* 01-942 0604.

HUTTON, Maurice, PhD, FIMA; Rector, Sunderland Polytechnic, 1969-76; *b* 4 Nov. 1914; *s* of William and Sarah Hutton; *m* 1939, Barbara Stark; one *s* one *d. Educ:* Univ. of Durham (BA, PhD). North Manchester High Sch., 1937-41; Oldham Technical Coll., 1941-44; Sunderland Technical Coll.: Lectr, 1945-53; Head of Dept, 1953-61; Vice-Principal, 1958-61; Principal, 1961-68. Comdr, Royal Norwegian Order of St Olav, 1966. *Publication:* (jt) Engineering Mathematics, 1959. *Recreations:* gardening, walking, music. *Address:* 17 Newlands Avenue, Sunderland SR3 1XW. *T:* Sunderland 285643.

HUTTON, Sir Noël (Kilpatrick), GCB 1966 (KCB 1957; CB 1950); QC, 1962; *b* 27 Dec. 1907; *s* of late William Hutton and of late Mrs D. M. Hutton, Whiteacre, Kippington, Sevenoaks; *m* 1936, Virginia Jacomyn, *d* of Sir George Young, 4th Bt, MVO; two *s* two *d. Educ:* Fettes Coll. (Scholar); University Coll., Oxford (Scholar, Hon. Fellow, 1973). OUBC crew 1930. Called to the Bar, Lincoln's Inn, 1932; entered Parly Counsel Office, 1938; First Parly Counsel, 1956-68. Governor, Alleyn's College; Chm., Trusteeship Bd, Nat. Soc. for Mentally Handicapped Children and Adults, 1966-81. *Recreations:* music, skiing, motoring. *Address:* Greenacre, Steeple Aston, Oxon OX5 3RT. *T:* Steeple Aston 40386. *Clubs:* Athenæum; Leander.

HUTTON, Maj.-Gen. Reginald Antony, CIE 1947; DSO 1944, and Bar 1945; OBE 1942; DL; *b* 18 April 1899; *s* of Charles Antony and Laura Beatrice Hutton, Earls Colne, Essex; *m* 1934, Margaret Isabel, *d* of Mark Feetham; two *d. Educ:* Haileybury and RMC, Sandhurst. Commissioned 1917, 2nd KEO Gurkha Rifles; Staff Coll., Camberley, 1934-35; Bde Major, 1938; GSO1 1940; Deputy Dir Military Intelligence, 1941; Bde Commander, 1944; Chief of Staff, 1 Corps, 1946. Served European War, 1914-18, General Service, 1917-18; 3rd Afghan War, 1919; Mahsud and NWF, 1919-20; Mohmand-Bajaur, 1933; Waziristan and NWF, 1938-40; War of 1939-45: (despatches 1940); Western Desert, Crete, Somaliland, Abyssinia, and Eritrea, 1940-42; Burma and Malaya, 1944-46; Chief of the General Staff, Pakistan Army, 1947-51; retired list, 1951. DL, Devon, 1962. *Address:* The Haven, Newton Ferrers, Devon. *T:* Newton Ferrers 325. *Club:* Naval and Military.

HUTTON, Robin; *see* Hutton, H. R.

HUTTON, Thomas Edward; Managing Director and Chief Executive, Total Oil GB Ltd, since 1967; Chairman, Eastern Region Advisory Board, British Rail, since 1981 (Director, since 1975); *b* 10 Jan. 1921; *s* of Thomas Oswald Powell Hutton and Doris Hutton; *m* 1946, Margaret June Ward; four *s. Educ:* Shrewsbury; St John's Coll., Cambridge. Commnd RNVR (MTBs), 1940-46. Joined Shell as Industrial Rep., 1946; Asphalt Manager, Shell, W of England, 1949; Shell Canada: Asst to Div. Manager, Ont, 1951; Fuel Oil and Asphalt Manager, Ont, 1953; Area Manager, E Ont, 1955; Retail Manager: Ontario, 1957; Shell Canada, 1959; Shell International, 1962; Co-Ordinator, Anglo Saxon subsids, Co. Française des Pétroles (Total), 1965. Director: Renwick Gp Ltd, 1973-81; Wilmot Breeden (Hldgs) Ltd, 1974-81; Berkeley Exploration and Production Ltd, 1981-82. *Recreations:* fishing, walking, golf. *Address:* Birdswood, Ashley Park, Walton-on-Thames, Surrey KT12 1EU. *T:* Walton-on-Thames 21674. *Club:* Oriental.

HUTTON, Maj.-Gen. Walter Morland, CB 1964; CBE 1960; DSO 1943; MC 1936 and bar, 1942; MA (by decree, 1967); FIL (Arabic); Fellow, 1967-72

and Home Bursar, 1966–72, Jesus College, Oxford; *b* 5 May 1912; *s* of Walter Charles Stritch Hutton and Amy Mary Newton; *m* 1945, Peronelle Marie Stella Luxmoore-Ball; two *s* one *d. Educ:* Parkstone Sch.; Allhallows Sch.; RMC Sandhurst. Commissioned into Royal Tank Corps, 1932; served in Palestine, 1936 (MC); 1st Class Army Interpreter in Arabic, 1937; War of 1939–45: Western Desert, Alamein and N Africa (comdg 5 RTR); Italy (comdg 40 RTR); Comdt, Sandhurst, 1944–45; Instructor, Staff Coll., Camberley, 1949–51; BGS, Arab Legion, 1953–56; Imperial Defence Coll., 1957; Deputy Comd (Land), BFAP (Aden), 1957–59; Dir of Administrative Plans, War Office, 1959–60, Dir-Gen. of Fighting Vehicles, 1961–64; Chief Army Instructor, Imperial Defence Coll., 1964–66. Mem., Bd of Governors, United Oxford Hosps, 1969–72. *Address:* c/o Williams & Glyn's Bank, Kirkland House, Whitehall, SW1.

HUTTON, William, CBE 1962; FRSE; Solicitor; retired; Member Council, Law Society of Scotland, 1962–67; *b* 2 Feb. 1902; *e s* of late John Hutton, MPS, Brechin; *m* 1932, Marjorie Elizabeth, MStJ, *d* of late John Philip Gibb, Director of Raimes, Clark & Co. Ltd, Leith; one *s* one *d. Educ:* Brechin High Sch.; Edinburgh Univ., MA 1925, LLB (dist.) 1927, Thow Schol. 1927. Legal experience with Tait & Crichton, WS and Davidson & Syme, WS; admitted Solicitor, 1928; Legal Asst to Dept of Health for Scotland and Asst Draftsman to Scottish Office, 1929–32; Town Clerk of Kirkcaldy, 1932–39; Sen. Deputy Town Clerk of Edinburgh, 1939–48; Dep. Chm. former SW Scotland Electricity Bd, 1948–55; Deputy Chm. South of Scotland Electricity Board, 1955–63. Comp. IEE, 1949–63. Notary Public, 1958; FRSE 1960; JP (Glasgow), 1960–64. *Address:* 21 Craiglockhart Loan, Edinburgh EH14 1JR. *T:* 031-443 3530.

HUTTON-WILLIAMS, Derek Alfred, MBE 1947; BSc, ACGI; CEng, FIMechE, MIEE; Director-General, Royal Ordnance Factories, 1969–75, retired; *b* 26 April 1914; *s* of William Hutton-Williams and Violet Woodfall Hutton-Williams; *m* 1948, Yvonne Irene Anthony; one *s* three *d. Educ:* Oundle Sch.; London Univ.; grad. NATO Defence Coll., Paris. Pupil, Winget Ltd, Rochester, 1935; Techn. Asst, Royal Arsenal, Woolwich, 1938; Asst to Director, Small Arms and Fuzes, Ordance Factories, 1939; Manager, Royal Ordnance Factory, Theale, Berks, 1942; Dep.-Dir, Housing Supplies, Ministry of Supply, 1945; Partner, Hutton-Williams and Partners (Industrial Consultant), 1946; Supt, Royal Ordnance Factory, Maltby, Yorks, 1949; NATO Defence Coll., 1957; Asst Dir, Guided Weapons Production, Min. of Aviation, 1958; Dir, Inspectorate of Armaments, 1959; Dir, Royal Small Arms Factory, Enfield, 1964. *Recreations:* gardening, building, clock repair, music; recognising and accepting the inevitable; admiring craftsmanship. *Address:* The School House, Palgrave, near Diss, Norfolk.

HUWS JONES, Robin; see Jones, R. H.

HUXLEY, Sir Andrew Fielding, Kt 1974; PRS (FRS 1955); MA Cantab; Royal Society Research Professor, in Department of Physiology, University College London, since 1969 (Jodrell Professor 1960–69; Hon. Fellow, 1980); President of the Royal Society; *b* 22 Nov. 1917; *s* of late Leonard Huxley and Rosalind Bruce; *m* 1947, Jocelyn Richenda Gammell Pease; one *s* five *d. Educ:* University College Sch.; Westminster Sch.; Trinity Coll., Cambridge (MA). Operational research for Anti-Aircraft Command, 1940–42, for Admiralty, 1942–45. Fellow, 1941–60, and Dir of Studies, 1952–60, Trinity Coll., Cambridge; Hon. Fellow, Trinity Coll., 1967; Demonstrator, 1946–50, Asst Dir of Research, 1951–59, and Reader in Experimental Biophysics, 1959–60, in Dept of Physiology, Cambridge Univ. Lectures: Herter, Johns Hopkins Univ., 1959; Jesup, Columbia Univ., 1964; Alexander Forbes, Grass Foundation, 1966; Croonian, Royal Society, 1967; Review Lectr on Muscular Contraction, Physiological Soc., 1973; Hans Hecht, Univ. of Chicago, 1975; Sherrington, Liverpool, 1977; Florey, ANU, 1982; John C. Krantz Jr, Maryland Univ. Sch. of Medicine, 1982; Darwin, Darwin Coll., Cambridge, 1982. Fullerian Prof. of Physiology and Comparative Anatomy, Royal Institution, 1967–73; Cecil H. and Ida Green Vis. Prof., Univ. of British Columbia, 1980. Mem., ARC, 1977–81; President: BAAS, 1976–77; Royal Soc., 1980- (Mem. Council, 1977–79); Vice-Pres., Muscular Dystrophy Gp of GB, 1980-; Chm., British Nat. Cttee for Physiological Scis, 1979–80. Trustee, BM (Nat. Hist.), 1981-. Hon. Mem., Physiolog. Soc., 1979; Foreign Associate: Nat. Acad. of Scis, USA, 1979; Amer. Philosophical Soc., 1975; Foreign Hon. Member: Amer. Acad. of Arts and Sciences, 1961; Royal Acad. of Medicine, Belgium; Hon. MRI, 1981; Associate Mem., Royal Acad. of Scis, Letters and Fine Arts, Belgium, 1978; Mem., Leopoldina Academy, 1964; For. Mem. Danish Acad. of Sciences, 1964-. Hon. Fellow: Imperial Coll., London, 1980; Darwin Coll., Cambridge, 1981. Hon. FIBiol 1981; Hon. FRSC (Canada) 1982. Hon. MD University of the Saar, 1964; Hon. DSc: Sheffield, 1964; Leicester, 1967; London, 1973; St Andrews, 1974; Aston, 1977; Western Australia, 1982; Hon. ScD Cambridge, 1978; Hon. LLD Birmingham, 1979; DUniv York, 1981; Hon. DHL New York, 1982; Hon. Dr Marseille Fac. of Medicine, 1979. Nobel Prize for Physiology or Medicine (jtly), 1963; Copley Medal, Royal Soc., 1973. *Publications:* Reflections on Muscle (Sherrington Lectures XIV), 1980; (contrib.) The Pursuit of Nature, 1977; papers in the Journal of Physiology, etc. *Recreations:* walking, shooting, designing scientific instruments. *Address:* Manor Field, Grantchester, Cambridge. *T:* Cambridge 840207.

HUXLEY, Anthony Julian; author, free-lance writer and photographer; *b* 2 Dec. 1920; *s* of Sir Julian Huxley, FRS; *m* 1st, 1943, Priscilla Ann Taylor; three *d*; 2nd, 1974, Alyson Ellen Vivian, *d* of late Beavan Archibald; one *d.*

Educ: Dauntsey's Sch.; Trinity Coll., Cambridge (MA). Operational Research in RAF and Min. of Aircraft Production, 1941–47; Economic Research in BOAC, 1947–48; with Amateur Gardening, 1949–71 (editor, 1967–71). Mem. Council, RHS, 1979-. Veitch Meml Medal, RHS, 1979; VMH 1980. *Publications:* (trans.) Exotic Plants of the World, 1955; (trans. and adapted) Orchids of Europe, 1961; (gen. editor) Standard Encyclopedia of the World's Mountains, 1962; (gen. editor) Standard Encyclopedia of Oceans and Islands, 1962; Garden Terms Simplified, 1962, 1971; Flowers in Greece: an outline of the Flora, 1964; (with O. Polunin) Flowers of the Mediterranean, 1965; (gen. ed.) Standard Encyclopedia of Rivers and Lakes, 1965; Mountain Flowers, 1967; (ed) Garden Perennials and Water Plants, 1971; (ed) Garden Annuals and Bulbs, 1971; House Plants, Cacti and Succulents, 1972; (ed) Deciduous Garden Trees and Shrubs, 1973; (ed) Evergreen Garden Trees and Shrubs, 1973; Plant and Planet, 1978; (ed) The Financial Times Book of Garden Design, 1975; (with W. Taylor) Flowers of Greece and the Aegean, 1977; (ed) The Encyclopedia of the Plant Kingdom, 1977; (with Alyson Huxley) Huxley's House of Plants, 1978; An Illustrated History of Gardening, 1978; (gen. editor) Success with House Plants, 1979; Penguin Encyclopaedia of Gardening, 1981. *Recreations:* photography, wild flowers, travel, gardening. *Address:* 50 Villiers Avenue, Surbiton, Surrey KT5 8BD. *T:* 01-399 1479.

HUXLEY, Elspeth Josceline, (Mrs Gervas Huxley), CBE 1962; JP; *b* 23 July 1907; *d* of Major Josceline Grant, Njoro, Kenya; *m* 1931, Gervas Huxley (*d* 1971); one *s. Educ:* European Sch., Nairobi, Kenya; Reading Univ. (Diploma in Agriculture); Cornell Univ., USA. Asst Press Officer to Empire Marketing Board, London, 1929–32; subsequently travelled in America, Africa and elsewhere; Mem. BBC Gen. Advisory Council, 1952–59; UK Independent Mem., Monckton Advisory Commission on Central Africa, 1959. *Publications:* White Man's Country; Lord Delamere and the Making of Kenya, 2 vols, 1935; Red Strangers (novel), 1939; Three detective stories; Atlantic Ordeal, 1943; Race and Politics in Kenya (with Margery Perham), 1944; The Walled City (novel), 1948; The Sorcerer's Apprentice (travel), 1948; I Don't Mind If I Do (light novel), 1951; Four Guineas (travel), A Thing to Love, 1954; The Red Rock Wilderness, 1957; The Flame Trees of Thika, 1959 (filmed, 1981); A New Earth, 1960; The Mottled Lizard, 1962; The Merry Hippo, 1963; Forks and Hope, 1964; A Man from Nowhere, 1964; Back Street New Worlds, 1965; Brave New Victuals, 1965; Their Shining Eldorado: A Journey through Australia, 1967; Love Among the Daughters, 1968; The Challenge of Africa, 1971; Livingstone and his African Journeys, 1974; Florence Nightingale, 1975; Gallipot Eyes, 1976; Scott of the Antarctic, 1977; Nellie: letters from Africa, 1980; Whipsnade: captive breeding for survival, 1981; The Prince Buys the Manor, 1982. *Recreations:* resting, gossip. *Address:* Green End, Oaksey, near Malmesbury, Wilts. *TA:* Oaksey, Malmesbury. *T:* Crudwell 252.

HUXLEY, Prof. George Leonard; Professor of Greek, Queen's University of Belfast, since 1962; *b* Leicester, 23 Sept. 1932; *s* of Sir Leonard Huxley, *qv*; *m* 1957, Davina Best; three *d. Educ:* Blundell's Sch.; Magdalen Coll., Oxford. 2nd Mods, 1st Greats, Derby Scholar 1955. Commnd in RE, 1951. Fellow of All Souls Coll., Oxford, 1955–61; Asst Dir, British School at Athens, 1956–58. Vis. Lectr, Harvard Univ., 1958 and 1961; Leverhulme Fellow, European Sci. Foundn, 1980–81. Mem. of Exec., NI Civil Rights Assoc., 1971–72. Member: Managing Cttee, British Sch. at Athens, 1967–79; Irish Nat. Cttee Greek and Latin Studies, 1972- (Chm., 1976–79); Irish Mem., Standing Cttee on Humanities, European Science Foundn, Strasbourg, 1978-. Sec., Polite Literature and Antiquities Cttee, RIA, 1979-; Mem. Bureau, Fédn Internat. d'Etudes Classiques, 1981-. FSA; MRIA. Cromer Greek Prize, British Acad., 1963. *Publications:* Achaeans and Hittites, 1960; Early Sparta, 1962; The Early Ionians, 1966; Greek Epic Poetry from Eumelos to Panyassis, 1969; (ed with J. N. Coldstream) Kythera, 1972; Pindar's Vision of the Past, 1975; On Aristotle and Greek Society, 1979; articles on Hellenic and Byzantine subjects. *Recreation:* siderodromophilia. *Address:* 48 Marlborough Park North, Belfast, N Ireland BT9 6HJ. *Club:* Athenæum.

HUXLEY, Mrs Gervas; see Huxley, Elspeth J.

HUXLEY, Hugh Esmor, MBE 1948; FRS 1960; MA, PhD; ScD; Deputy Director, Medical Research Council Laboratory of Molecular Biology, Cambridge, since 1977; Fellow, Churchill College, Cambridge, since 1967; *b* 25 Feb. 1924; *s* of late Thomas Hugh Huxley and Olwen Roberts, Birkenhead, Cheshire; *m* 1966, Frances Fripp, *d* of G. Maxon, Milwaukee; one *d*, and two step-*s* one step-*d. Educ:* Park High Sch., Birkenhead; Christ's Coll., Cambridge (Exhibitioner and Scholar; Hon. Fellow 1981). Natural Science Tripos, Cambridge, 1941–43 and 1947–48 (Pt II Physics); BA 1948, MA 1950, PhD 1952. Served War of 1939–45, Radar Officer, RAF Bomber Command and Telecommunications Research Establishment, Malvern, 1943–47; Mem. Empire Air Armaments Sch. Mission to Australia and NZ, 1946. Research Student, Med. Research Council Unit for Molecular Biology, Cavendish Lab., Cambridge, 1948–52; Commonwealth Fund Fellow, Biology Dept, Massachusetts Inst. of Technology, 1952–54; Research Fellow, Christ's Coll., Cambridge, 1953–56; Mem. of External Staff of MRC, and Hon. Res. Associate, Biophysics Dept, University Coll., London, 1956–61; Scientific Staff, MRC Lab. of Molecular Biol., 1961-. Ziskind Vis. Prof., Brandeis Univ., 1971; Lectures: Harvey Soc., New York, 1964–65; Hooke, Univ. of Texas, 1968; Dunham, Harvard Med. Sch., 1969; Croonian, Royal Soc., 1970; Mayer, MIT, 1971; Penn, Pennsylvania Univ., 1971; Carter-Wallace, Princeton Univ., 1973; Adam Muller, State Univ. of NY, 1973; Pauling, Stanford, 1980; Jesse Beams, Virginia, 1980; Ida Beam, Iowa, 1981. Fellow,

King's Coll., Cambridge, 1961-67. Member: Council, Royal Soc., 1973-75; President's Adv. Bd, Rosentiel Basic Med. Scis Center, Brandeis Univ., 1971-77; Scientific Adv. Council, European Molecular Biol. Lab., 1976-81. Feldberg Foundation Award for Experimental Medical Research, 1963; William Bate Hardy Prize (Camb. Phil. Soc.) 1965; Louisa Gross Horwitz Prize, 1971; Internat. Feltrinelli Prize, 1974; Gairdner Award, 1975; Baly Medal, RCP, 1975; Royal Medal, Royal Soc., 1977. Mem., German Acad. of Science, Leopoldina, 1964; Foreign Hon. Mem., Amer. Acad. of Arts and Sciences, 1965; Hon. For. Mem., Danish Acad. of Sciences, 1971; For. Associate, US Nat. Acad. of Sciences, 1978. Hon. Dr of Science: Harvard Univ., 1969; Chicago Univ., 1974; Univ. of Pennsylvania, 1976. *Publications:* contrib. to learned jls. *Recreations:* ski-ing, sailing. *Address:* Churchill College, Cambridge. *T:* Cambridge 61200; 7 Chaucer Road, Cambridge. *T:* Cambridge 356117.

HUXLEY, Rev. Keith; Home Secretary, Board for Mission and Unity of the Church of England, since 1977; Chaplain to the Queen, since 1981; *b* 17 Sept. 1933; *s* of George and Eluned Huxley. *Educ:* Birkenhead Sch.; Christ's Coll., Cambridge (MA); Cuddesdon Theol Coll. Curate: St Mary's, Bowdon, 1959-61; Christ Church, Crewe, 1961-62; Chester Diocesan Youth Chaplain, 1962-68; Leader, Runcorn Ecumenical Team Ministry, 1968-75; Vicar, St Andrew's, Runcorn, 1968-73; Rector, East Runcorn Team Ministry, 1973-77. *Recreations:* ornithology, the Scout movement. *Address:* Board for Mission and Unity, Church House, Dean's Yard, Westminster, SW1P 3NZ. *T:* 01-222 9011.

HUXLEY, Sir Leonard (George Holden), KBE 1964; MA, DPhil Oxon; PhD Adelaide; FAA; Emeritus Professor, University of Adelaide; Vice-Chancellor, The Australian National University, 1960-Dec. 1967; *b* London, UK, 29 May 1902; *s* of George H. and Lilian S. Huxley; *m* 1929, Ella M. C. (*d* 1981), *d* of F. G. and E. Copeland; one *s* one *d. Educ:* The Hutchins Sch., Hobart; University of Tasmania; New Coll., Oxford. Rhodes Scholar, Tas., 1923; Jessie Theresa Rowden Scholar, New Coll., 1927; Scott Scholar, University of Oxford, 1929. Scientific staff, CSIR, Sydney, 1929-31; Head of Dept of Physics, University Coll. Leicester, 1932-40; Principal Scientific Officer, Telecommunications Research Estabt, MAP, 1940-46; Reader in Electromagnetism, University of Birmingham, 1946-49; Elder Prof. of Physics, University Adelaide, 1949-60; Mem. Executive, CSIRO, 1960; Mem. Council, University of Adelaide, 1953-60; Mem. Council, Aust. Nat. Univ., 1956-59; Foundation FAA, 1954 (Sec., Physical Sciences, 1959-62); Chm. Australian Radio Research Board, 1958-64; Chm. National Standards Commission, 1953-65; Chm. Radio Frequency Allocation Cttee, 1960-64; Mem. Nat. Library Council, 1961-72; Mem. Bd, US Educnl Foundn in Austr., 1960-65; Australian Deleg. on Cttee on Space Research (COSPAR), 1959-60. First President Aust. Inst. of Physics, 1962-65. Mem., Queen Elizabeth II Fellowships Cttee, 1963-66; Chm., Gen. Coun. Encyclopædia Britannica Australia Awards, 1964-74; Chm. Bd, Aust./Amer. Educl Foundn, 1965-69; Trustee, Aust. Humanities Res. Council, 1968-70; Mem. Council, Canberra Coll. of Advanced Educn, 1968-74. Hon DSc: Tasmania, 1962; ANU, 1980. *Publications:* Wave Guides, 1949; (with R. W. Crompton) The Diffusion and Drift of Electrons in Gases, 1974; numerous scientific papers on gaseous Electronics, the ionosphere, upper atmosphere and related subjects. *Address:* 19 Glasgow Place, Hughes, Canberra, ACT 2605, Australia. *Club:* Commonwealth (Canberra).

See also Prof. G. L. Huxley.

HUXLEY, Dr Peter Arthur, PhD; FIBiol; Senior Research Scientist, International Council for Research in Agroforestry, Nairobi, since 1979; *b* 26 Sept. 1926; *s* of Ernest Henry Huxley and Florence Agnes (*née* King); *m* 1st, 1954, Betty Grace Anne Foot (marr. diss. 1980); two *s* one *d* ; 2nd, 1980, Jennifer Margaret Bell (*née* Pollard); one *s* one *d. Educ:* Alleyn's Sch.; Edinburgh Univ.; Reading Univ. (BSc, PhD). FIBiol 1970. RNVR, 1944-46. Asst Lectr to Sen. Lectr, Makerere University Coll., Uganda, 1954-64; Dir of Res., Coffee Res. Foundn, Kenya, 1965-69; Prof. of Horticulture, Univ. of Reading, 1969-74; Prof. of Crop Science, Univ. of Dar es Salaam/FAO, 1974-76; Agric. Res. Adviser/FAO, Agric. Res. Centre, Tripoli, 1977-78. Member: E African Nat. Hist. Soc.; E African Music Soc.; Nairobi Orchestra. FRSA. *Publications:* (jtly) Soils Research in Agroforestry, 1980; approx. 85 pubns in agric., horticult., agroforestry, meteorol and agricl botany jls. *Recreation:* music (double bass) and music-making. *Address:* c/o National Westminster Bank, 49 South Street, Dorchester, Dorset. *Clubs:* Nairobi, Kentmere (Nairobi).

HUXSTEP, Emily Mary, CBE 1964; BA London: Headmistress of Chislehurst and Sidcup Girls' Grammar School, Kent, 1944-66; *b* 15 Sept. 1906; *d* of George T. and Nellie M. Huxstep (*née* Wood). *Educ:* Chatham Girls' Grammar Sch.; Queen Mary Coll. Headmistress, Hanson Girls' Grammar Sch., Bradford, Yorks, 1938-44. Hon. DCL Kent, 1974. *Address:* 23 Homewood Crescent, Chislehurst, Kent. *T:* 01-467 3690.

HUXTABLE, Rev. (William) John (Fairchild), DD; Executive Officer, Churches' Unity Commission, 1975-78; *b* 25 July 1912; *s* of Rev. John Huxtable and Florence Huxtable (*née* Watts); *m* 1939, Joan Lorimer Snow; one *s* two *d. Educ:* Barnstaple Gram. Sch.; Western Coll., Bristol; Mansfield and St Catherine's Colls, Oxford. BA Bristol 1933; BA Oxon 1937, MA 1940. Minister: Newton Abbot Congreg. Church, 1937-42; Palmers Green Congreg. Church, 1942-54; Princ., New Coll., University of London, 1953-64. Chm., 1962-63, Sec., 1964-66, Minister Sec., 1966-72, Congregational Union of

England and Wales; Jt Gen. Sec., United Reformed Church, 1972-74; Moderator, United Reformed Church, 1972-73. Vice-President: British Coun. of Churches, 1967-71; World Alliance of Reformed Churches, 1970-77; Vice-Moderator, Free Church Federal Council, 1975-76, Moderator, 1976-77; Member: Central Cttee, World Council of Churches, 1968-75; Jt Cttee of Translation of New English Bible, 1948-74. Vice-Pres. Council, St Dunstan's, 1973-. Hon. DD: Lambeth, 1973; Aberdeen, 1973. *Publications:* The Ministry, 1943; (ed) John Owen's True Nature of a Gospel Church, 1947; (ed jtly) A Book of Public Worship, 1948; The Faith that is in Us, 1953; The Promise of the Father, 1959; Like a Strange People, 1961; Church and State in Education (C. J. Cadoux Meml Lect.), 1962; The Bible Says (Maynard Chapman Lects), 1962; Preaching the Law, (Joseph Smith Meml Lect.), 1964; The Preacher's Integrity (A. S. Peake Meml Lect), 1966; Christian Unity: some of the issues (Congreg. Lects), 1966; contribs to symposia: The Churches and Christian Unity, 1962; From Uniformity to Unity, 1962; A Companion to the Bible, 1963; Renewal of Worship, 1965; Outlook for Christianity, 1967; contrib. to Christian Confidence, 1970; A New Hope for Christian Unity, 1977; also contribs to Congreg. Quarterly, Theology, Epworth Review, London Quarterly and Holborn Review, and Proc. Internat. Congreg. Council. *Recreation:* reading. *Address:* Manor Cottage, East Ogwell, South Devon.

HUYDECOPER, Jonkheer (Jan Louis) Reinier, Hon. KCVO 1972; Chevalier, Order of Netherlands Lion, 1980; Officer, Order of Orange Nassau, 1966; Ambassador of the Netherlands to the Court of St James's, and concurrently to Iceland, since 1982; *b* 23 Feb. 1922; *s* of Jonkheer Louis Huydecoper and Jonkvrouwe Laurence B. W. Ram; *m* 1944, Baroness Constance C. van Wassenaer; one *s* two *d. Educ:* Univ. of Utrecht (LLM). Banking, 1942-44; Legal Dept, Min. of Finance, The Hague, 1945-46; entered Min. of For. Affairs, 1946; UN, NY, 1946; Ottawa, 1947-48; Mil. Mission, Berlin, 1949-50; Bonn, 1950-52; London, 1952-56; Djakarta, 1956-59; Washington, 1959-62; Rome, 1962-66; Min. of For. Affairs, 1966-70; London, 1970-73; Ambassador, Hd of Delegn to Conf. on Security and Co-operation in Europe, Helsinki and Geneva, 1973-74; Ambassador: Moscow, 1974-77; Lisbon, 1978-80; Inspector of For. Service, Min. of For. Affairs, 1981-82. Holds various foreign orders. *Address:* 8 Palace Green, W8. *T:* 01-584 5040. *Clubs:* Boodle's, Dutch, Special Forces, Royal Automobile, Hurlingham; Haagsche (The Hague).

HUYGHE, René; Grand Officier de la Légion d'Honneur; Member of the Académie Française since 1960; Hon. Professor of Psychology of Plastic Arts, Collège de France (Professor, 1950-76); Hon. Head Keeper, Musée de Louvre; Director, Museum Jacquemart-André, Paris, since 1974; *b* Arras, Pas-de-Calais, France, 3 May 1906; *s* of Louis Huyghe and Marie (*née* Delvoye); *m* 1950, Lydie Bouthet; one *s* one *d. Educ:* Sorbonne; Ecole du Louvre, Paris. Attached to Musée du Louvre, 1927; Asst Keeper, 1930; Head Keeper, Départment des Peintures, Dessins, Chalcographie, 1937. Mem. of Council, Musées Nationaux, 1952 (Vice-Pres. 1964, Pres. 1975); Pres. Assoc. internationale du Film d'Art, 1958. Holds foreign decorations. Praemium Erasmianum, The Hague, 1966. *Publications:* Histoire de l'Art contemporain: La Peinture, 1935; Cézanne 1936 and 1961; Les Contemporains, 1939 (2nd edn, 1949); Vermeer, 1948; Watteau, 1950; various works on Gauguin, 1951, 1952, 1959; Dialogue avec le visible, 1955 (trans. Eng.); L'Art et l'homme, Vol. I, 1957, Vol. II, 1958, Vol. III, 1961 (trans. Eng.); Van Gogh, 1959; Merveilles de la France, 1960; L'Art et l'Ame, 1960 (trans. Eng.); La peinture française aux XVIIe et XVIIIe Siècles, 1962; Delacroix ou le combat solitaire, 1963 (trans. Eng.); Puissances de l'Image, 1965; Sens et Destin de l'Art, 1967; L'Art et le monde moderne, Vol. I, 1970, Vol. II, 1971; Formes et Forces, 1971; La Relève du réel, 1974; La Relève de l'imaginaire, 1976; Ce que je crois, 1976; De l'Art à la Philosophie, 1980; (with D. Ikeda) La Nuit appelle l'Aurore, 1980. *Address:* 3 rue Corneille, Paris 75006, France. *Club:* Union interalliée (Paris).

HYAMS, Daisy Deborah, (Mrs C. Guderley), OBE 1974; Managing Director, Tesco (Wholesale) Ltd, 1965-82; *b* 25 Nov. 1912; *d* of Hyman Hyams and Annie Burnett; *m* 1936, Sidney Hart; no *c* ; *m* 1975, C. Guderley. *Educ:* Coborn Grammar Sch. for Girls, Bow. FGI. Joined Tesco, 1931. Director: Tesco (Wholesale) Ltd, 1955; Tesco Stores Ltd, 1961; Tesco (Holdings) Ltd, 1970. *Recreations:* travel, reading. *Address:* 10 Noblefield Heights, Great North Road, Highgate, N2 0NX. *T:* 01-348 1591.

HYATALI, Hon. Sir Isaac (Emanuel), Kt 1973; TC 1974; Chief Justice and President of the Court of Appeal, Trinidad and Tobago, since 1972; *b* 21 Nov. 1917; *s* of late Joseph Hyatali and Mrs Hyatali; *m* 1943, Audrey Monica Joseph; two *s* one *d. Educ:* Naparima Coll., San Fernando; Gray's Inn and Council of Legal Education, London. Called to Bar, Gray's Inn, 1947. Private practice at the Bar, 1947-59; Judge, Supreme Court, 1959-62; Justice of Appeal, 1962-72; Pres., Industrial Court, 1965-72. Chm., Arima Rent Assessment Bd, 1953-59; Chm., Agricultural Rent Bd (Eastern Counties), 1953-59. Chairman: Agricultural Wages Council, 1958-59; Oil and Water Bd, 1959-62. Arbitrator and Umpire, ICAO, 1981-. Trinidad and Tobago Editor of West Indian Law Reports, 1961-65. Member: World Assoc. of Judges; Council of Management, British Inst. of Internat. and Comparative Law; Hon. Mem., World Peace through Law Center. *Recreations:* gardening, tennis, cricket, reading, social work. *Address:* (office) Chief Justice's Chambers, Supreme Court, PO Box 494, Port-of-Spain, Trinidad and Tobago; (home) 12 Prada Street, St Clair, Port-of-Spain. *T:* 62/32417. *Clubs:* (Hon. Mem.) Union Park Turf (Trinidad); Rotary (Port of Spain).

HYATT KING, Alexander; see King, A. H.

HYDE, Lord; George Edward Laurence Villiers; b 12 Feb. 1976; s and heir of 7th Earl of Clarendon, qv.

HYDE, H(arford) Montgomery, MA Oxon, DLit Belfast, FRHistS; FRSL; MRIA; author and barrister; b Belfast, 14 Aug. 1907; o s of late James J. Hyde, JP, Belfast, and Isobel Greenfield Montgomery; m 1st, 1939, Dorothy Mabel Brayshaw (from whom he obtained a divorce, 1952), e d of Dr J. Murray Crofts, CBE, Disley, Cheshire; 2nd, 1955, Mary Eleanor (marr. diss., 1966), d of Col L. G. Fischer, IMS; 3rd, 1966, Rosalind Roberts, y d of Comdr J. F. W. Dimond, RN. Educ: Sedbergh (Scholar); Queen's Univ. Belfast (Emily Lady Pakenham Scholar); 1st Class Hons Modern History, 1928; Magdalen Coll., Oxford (Open History Exhibitioner); 2nd Class Hons Jurisprudence, 1930; Harmsworth Law Scholar, Middle Temple, 1932. Called to Bar, Middle Temple, 1934; joined NE Circuit; Extension Lecturer in History, Oxford Univ., 1934; Private Sec. to Marquess of Londonderry, 1935–39; Asst Censor, Gibraltar, 1940; commissioned in Intelligence Corps, 1940; Military Liaison and Censorship Security Officer, Bermuda, 1940–41; Asst Passport Control Officer, New York, 1941–42; with British Army Staff, USA, 1942–44; Major, 1942; attached Supreme HQ Allied Expeditionary Force, 1944; Allied Commission for Austria, 1944–45; Lt-Col 1945; Asst Editor, Law Reports, 1946–47; Legal Adviser, British Lion Film Corp. Ltd, 1947–49; MP (U) North Belfast, 1950–59; UK Delegate to Council of Europe Consultative Assembly, Strasbourg, 1952–55; Hon. Col Intelligence Corps (TA), NI, 1958–61; Professor of Hist. and Polit. Sci., University of the Punjab, Lahore, 1959–61; RAF Museum Leverhulme Research Fellowship, 1971–75. Active in campaign for abolition of capital punishment; has travelled extensively in Russia, The Far East, West Indies, Mexico, and South America. Publications: The Rise of Castlereagh, 1933; The Russian Journals of Martha and Catherine Wilmot (with the Marchioness of Londonderry), 1934; More Letters from Martha Wilmot, Impressions of Vienna (with the Marchioness of Londonderry), 1935; The Empress Catherine and Princess Dashkhov, 1935; Air Defence and the Civil Population (with G. R. Falkiner Nuttall), 1937; Londonderry House and Its Pictures, 1937; Princess Lieven, 1938; Judge Jeffreys, 1940, new edn, 1948; Mexican Empire, 1946; A Victorian Historian, 1947; Privacy and the Press, 1947; John Law, 1948, new edn 1969; The Trials of Oscar Wilde, 1948, 3rd edn 1973; Mr and Mrs Beeton, 1951; Cases that changed the Law, 1951; Carson, 1953; The Trial of Craig and Bentley, 1954; United in Crime, 1955; Mr and Mrs Daventry, a play by Frank Harris, 1957; The Strange Death of Lord Castlereagh, 1959; The Trial of Roger Casement, 1960, 2nd edn 1964; The Life and Cases of Sir Patrick Hastings, 1960; Recent Developments in Historical Method and Interpretation, 1960; Simla and the Simla Hill States under British Protection, 1961; An International Crime Case Book, 1962; The Quiet Canadian, 1962; Oscar Wilde: the Aftermath, 1963; Room 3603, 1964; A History of Pornography, 1964; Norman Birkett, 1964; Cynthia, 1965; The Story of Lamb House, 1966, 2nd edn 1975; Lord Reading, 1967; Strong for Service: The Life of Lord Nathan of Churt, 1968; Henry James At Home, 1969; The Other Love, 1970; Their Good Names, 1970; Stalin, 1971; Baldwin: the unexpected Prime Minister, 1973; Oscar Wilde, 1975; The Cleveland Street Scandal, 1976; British Air Policy between the Wars, 1976; Neville Chamberlain, 1976; Crime has its Heroes, 1976; Solitary in the Ranks, 1977; The Londonderrys, 1979; The Atom Bomb Spies, 1980; (ed) Oscar Wilde: Three Plays, 1981; Secret Intelligence Agent, 1982; (ed) The Annotated Oscar Wilde, 1982; chapter 12 (The Congress of Vienna) in the Cambridge History of Poland, etc. Recreations: criminology, music. Address: Westwell House, Tenterden, Kent. T: Tenterden 3189. Clubs: Garrick; Dormy House (Rye); Grolier (New York).

HYDE, John Bean; Chairman and Chief Executive, Charterhouse Japhet plc, since 1981; Deputy Chief Executive, The Charterhouse Group plc, since 1982; b 7 Jan. 1928; s of John Bean Hyde and Ivy Howard Hyde (née Gannon); m 1953, Patricia Gabrielle Mebes Gray; one d (and one s decd). Educ: Shrewsbury Sch.; Magdalen Coll., Oxford (BA PPE 2nd Cl.). AIB 1954; FIB 1972. Vice President, Citibank, 1951–68; Director, Hill Samuel & Co., 1968–70; Chief Executive, London Multinational Bank/Chemical Bank International Ltd, 1970–81. Recreations: bridge, music, theatre. Address: Chagfords, Burdenshot Hill, Worplesdon, Surrey GU3 3RL. T: Worplesdon 232619. Club: City of London.

HYDE, W(illiam) Leonard, FCIBS; President, Leeds Permanent Building Society, since 1981 (Chief General Manager, 1973–78; Vice-President, 1978–81); Regional Director, Lloyds Bank Ltd, since 1976; Local Director, Royal Insurance Co. Ltd, since 1973. Joined Leeds Permanent Building Soc., 1936. Member Council: Building Socs Assoc., 1973–78; Nat. House Builders, 1973–78; Chm., Yorkshire County Assoc. of Building Socs, 1978–80. Recreations: golf, walking. Address: 5 Burn Bridge Road, Harrogate, Yorks. T: Harrogate 871748. Clubs: Lansdowne; Pannal Golf.

HYDE-PARKER, Sir R. W.; see Parker.

HYDE-SMITH, Marisa; see Robles, Marisa.

HYDE WHITE, Wilfrid; b 12 May 1903; s of William Edward White, Canon of Gloucester and Ethel Adelaide (née Drought); m 1927, Blanche Hope Aitken; one s; m 1957, Ethel Korenman (stage name Ethel Drew); one s one d. Educ: Marlborough. First appeared in London in Beggar on Horseback, Queen's Theatre, 1925; successful appearances include: Rise Above

It, Comedy; It Depends What You Mean, Westminster; Britannus in Cæsar and Cleopatra, St James's, London, and Ziegfield, New York; Affairs of State, Cambridge; Hippo Dancing, Lyric; The Reluctant Debutante, Cambridge, and Henry Miller's Theatre, New York (nominated for Tony award, 1956); Not in the Book, Criterion; Miss Pell is Missing, Criterion; The Doctor's Dilemma, Haymarket; Lady Windermere's Fan, Phoenix; Meeting at Night, Duke of York's; The Jockey Club Stakes, Duke of York's, and Cort Theatre, NYC (nominated for Tony award for best actor, 1973); The Pleasure of his Company, Phoenix; Rolls Hyphen Royce, Shaftesbury. Films include: The 3rd Man, The Browning Version, Golden Salamander, The Million Pound Note, Libel, Two Way Stretch, North West Frontier, Let's Make Love, His and Hers, On the Double, Ada, The Castaways, Crooks Anonymous, On the Fiddle, Aliki, My Fair Lady, 10 Little Indians, The Liquidator, In God We Trust. Address: 67157 Santa Barbara Drive, Palm Springs, Calif 92262, USA. T: (714) 327-3276. Clubs: Green Room, Buck's.

HYLTON, 5th Baron, cr 1866; **Raymond Hervey Jolliffe,** MA; ARICS; DL; b 13 June 1932; er s of 4th Baron Hylton and of the Dowager Lady Hylton, d of late Raymond Asquith and sister of 2nd Earl of Oxford and Asquith, qv; S father, 1967; m 1966, Joanna Ida Elizabeth, d of late Andrew de Bertodano; four s one d. Educ: Eton (King's Scholar); Trinity Coll., Oxford (MA). Lieut R of O, Coldstream Guards. Asst Private Sec. to Governor-General of Canada, 1960–62; Trustee, Shelter Housing Aid Centre 1970–76; Chairman: Catholic Housing Aid Soc., 1972–73; Nat. Fedn of Housing Assocs, 1973–76; Housing Assoc. Charitable Trust; Help the Aged Housing Trust, 1976–82; Hugh of Witham Foundn, 1978–; Vice-Pres., Age Concern (Nat. Old People's Welfare Council), 1971–77; Pres., SW Reg. Nat. Soc. for Mentally Handicapped Children, 1976–79; Mem. Council, Foundn for Alternatives; Founder and Mem., Mendip and Wansdyke Local Enterprise Gp, 1979–. Trustee, Christian Internat. Peace Service, 1977–82; Governor, Christian Coll. for Adult Educn, 1972–. Mem., Frome RDC, 1968–72. DL Somerset, 1975. Heir: s Hon. William Henry Martin Jolliffe, b April 1967. Address: Ammerdown, Radstock, Bath.

HYLTON-FOSTER, family name of Baroness Hylton-Foster.

HYLTON-FOSTER, Baroness, cr 1965, of the City of Westminster (Life Peer); **Audrey Pellew Hylton-Foster;** President and Chairman, London Branch, British Red Cross Society, since 1960; Convenor, Cross Bench Peers, since 1974; b 19 May 1908; d of 1st Viscount Ruffside, PC, DL (d 1958), and Viscountess Ruffside (d 1969); m 1931, Rt Hon. Sir Harry Hylton-Foster, QC (d 1965); no c. Educ: St George's, Ascot; Ivy House, Wimbledon. Recreations: gardening, trout fishing. Address: The Coach House, Tanhurst, Leith Hill, Holmbury St Mary, Dorking, Surrey RH5 6LU. T: Dorking 6575.

HYMAN, Joe; Chairman, John Crowther Group Ltd, 1971–81; Underwriting member of Lloyd's; b 14 Oct. 1921; yr s of late Solomon Hyman and Hannah Hyman; m 1st, 1948, Corinne I. Abrahams (marriage dissolved); one s one d; 2nd, 1963, Simone Duke; one s one d. Educ: North Manchester Gram. Sch. Has been in Textiles, 1939–; Chm., Viyella International, 1961–69. Trustee, Pestalozzi Children's Village Trust, 1967–; Governor, LSE. FRSA 1968; FBIM. Comp. TI. Recreations: music, golf, gardening. Address: Lukyns, Ewhurst, Surrey; 24 Kingston House North, Prince's Gate, SW7. Clubs: Royal Automobile, MCC.

HYMAN, Robin Philip; Chairman and Managing Director, Bell & Hyman Ltd, Book Publishers, since 1977; b 9 Sept. 1931; s of late Leonard Hyman and of Helen Hyman (née Mautner); m 1966, Inge Neufeld; two s one d. Educ: Henley Grammar Sch.; Christ's Coll., Finchley; Univ. of Birmingham (BA (Hons) 1955). National Service, RAF, 1949–51. Editor, Mermaid, 1953–54; Bookselling and Publishing: joined Evans Brothers Ltd, Educnl Publishers, 1955: Dir, 1964; Dep. Man. Dir, 1967; Man. Dir, 1972–77; Dir, Rivingtons (Publishers) Ltd, 1967–77; Mem. Editorial Bd, World Year Book of Education, 1969–73. Member: Council, Publishers' Assoc., 1975– (Treasurer, 1982–); Exec. Cttee, Educnl Publishers' Council, 1971–76 (Treas., 1972–75). Mem., First British Publishers' Delegn to China, 1978. Publications: A Dictionary of Famous Quotations, 1962; (with John Trevaskis) Boys' and Girls' First Dictionary, 1967; Universal Primary Dictionary (for Africa), 1976; (with Inge Hyman) 11 children's books, incl. Barnabas Ball at the Circus, 1967; Runaway James and the Night Owl, 1968; The Hippo who Wanted to Fly, 1973; The Magical Fish, 1974; The Greatest Explorers in the World, 1978; The Treasure Box, 1980; Peter's Magic Hide-and-Seek, 1982. Recreations: theatre, reading, cricket. Address: 101 Hampstead Way, NW11 7LR. T: 01-455 7055. Clubs: Garrick, MCC.

HYND, Henry; b Perth, Scotland, 4 July 1900; s of Henry Hynd; m, 1st, 1925, Phyllis Jarman (marr. diss. 1971); one d; 2nd, 1971, Mrs Anne Nadine Scott. Educ: Perth Academy. Railway Clerk, 1915–20; Trade Union Official, 1920–45; Member Hornsey Borough Council, 1939–52; MP (Lab) for Central Hackney, 1945–50, for Accrington, 1950–66; Parliamentary Private Sec. to First Lord of the Admiralty, Dec. 1945–46 and to Min. of Defence, 1946–50. Hon. Pres., London Perthshire Assoc. JP Middlesex. Commander of Belgian Order of the Crown and Officer of Luxembourg Order of the Oak Crown. Recreation: travelling. Address: 31 Alford House, Stanhope Road, N6 5AL. T: 01-340 3308.

HYND, Ronald; choreographer; b 22 April 1931; s of William John and Alice Louisa Hens; m 1957, Annette Page, qv; one d. Educ: erratically throughout

England due to multiple wartime evacuation. Joined Rambert School, 1946; Ballet Rambert, 1949; Royal Ballet (then Sadlers Well's Ballet), 1952, rising from Corps de Ballet to Principal Dancer, 1959; danced Siegfried (Swan Lake), Florimund (Sleeping Beauty), Albrecht (Giselle), Poet (Sylphides), Tsarevitch (Firebird), Prince of Pagodas, Moondog (Lady and Fool), Tybalt (Romeo), etc; produced first choreography for Royal Ballet Choreographic Group followed by works for London Festival Ballet, Royal Ballet, Dutch National Ballet and Munich Ballet; Dir, Munich Ballet, 1970-73. *Ballets include:* Le Baiser de la Fée, 1968, new production 1974; Pasiphaë, 1969; Dvorak Variations, 1970; Wendekreise, 1972; In a Summer Garden, 1972; Das Telefon, 1972; Mozartiana, 1973; Charlotte Brontë, 1974; Mozart Adagio, 1974; Galileo (film), 1974; Orient/Occident, 1975; La Valse, 1975; Valses Nobles et Sentimentales, 1975; The Merry Widow, 1975; L'Eventail, 1976; The Nutcracker (new version for Festival Ballet), 1976; ice ballets for John Curry, 1977; Rosalinda, 1978; La Chatte, 1978; Papillon, 1979; The Seasons, 1980; Alceste, 1981; Scherzo Capriccoso, 1982; *musical:* Sound of Music, 1981. *Recreation:* the gramophone. *Address:* 51 Sutherland Place, W2 5BY. *T:* 01-229 1020.

HYND, Mrs Ronald; *see* Page, Annette.

HYSLOP, Dr James Morton; Principal and Vice-Chancellor, Rhodes University, 1963-75; *b* Dumbarton, 12 Sept. 1908; *s* of William Hyslop; *m* 1935, Helen Margaret, *d* of W. W. Hyslop, Glasgow; one *d*. *Educ:* High Sch. of Glasgow; Univ. of Glasgow (MA, DSc); Christ's Coll., Cambridge (BA, PhD). War Service as Flt-Lt, RAF, mainly in Middle East, 1941-45. Lectr, Univ. of Glasgow, 1933-41 and 1945-47; Prof. of Maths, Univ. of the Witwatersrand, 1947-60; Principal, Royal Coll., Nairobi (now University of Nairobi), 1960-63. Hon. LLD: Glasgow, 1967; Rhodes, 1976. Coronation Medal, 1953. *Publications:* Infinite Series, 1941; Real Variable, 1960; papers in learned jls on mathematical topics. *Recreations:* golf, bowls. *Address:* 36 Grand Street, Port Alfred, South Africa. *Clubs:* Port Elizabeth, Albany (Grahamstown).

HYSLOP, James Telfer, OBE 1968; HM Diplomatic Service, retired; Consul General, Detroit, 1971-76; *b* 21 Sept. 1916; *s* of Mr and Mrs John J. Hyslop; *m* 1942, Jane Elizabeth Owers; one *s* one *d*. *Educ:* Queen Elizabeth's Grammar Sch., Hexham. Royal Navy, 1939-46. Entered Diplomatic Service, 1948; served at: Baltimore, 1948; Valparaiso, 1951; Amman, 1954; Tegucigalpa, 1958; San Francisco, 1961; Johannesburg, 1964; Bogota, 1968. *Recreations:* reading, music. *Address:* 12 Quay Walls, Berwick-on-Tweed.

HYSLOP, Robert John M.; *see* Maxwell-Hyslop.

HYTNER, Benet Alan, QC 1970; a Recorder of the Crown Court, since 1972; Judge of Appeal, Isle of Man, since 1980; *b* 29 Dec. 1927; *s* of late Maurice and of Sarah Hytner, Manchester; *m* 1954, Joyce Myers (marr. diss. 1980); three *s* one *d*. *Educ:* Manchester Grammar Sch.; Trinity Hall, Cambridge (Exhibr). MA. National Service, RASC, 1949-51 (commnd). Called to Bar, Middle Temple, 1952; Bencher, 1977. Member: Gen. Council of Bar, 1969-73; Senate of Inns of Court and Bar, 1977-81. *Recreations:* fell walking, music, theatre, reading. *Address:* 5 Essex Court, Temple, EC4.

I

IBBOTSON, Lancelot William Cripps, CBE 1971 (MBE 1948); General Manager of Southern Region, British Railways, and Chairman, Southern Railway Board, 1968-72; *b* 10 Feb. 1909; *s* of William Ibbotson, FRCS and Mrs Dora Ibbotson (*née* Chapman), London; *m* 1931, Joan Marguerite Jeffcock; one *s* one *d*. *Educ:* Radley Coll. Traffic Apprentice, LNER, 1927; Chief Clerk to Dist. Supt, Newcastle, 1939; Asst Dist Supt, York, 1942; Dist Supt, Darlington, 1945; Asst to Operating Supt, Western Region, 1950; Asst Gen. Man., Western Region, 1959; Chief Operating Officer, British Railways, 1963; Gen. Man., Western Region, BR, and Chm., Western Railway Board, 1966-68. Gen. Man., A. Pearce, Partners & Assoc., 1975-79; Dir, Flameless Furnaces Ltd, 1976-. *Recreations:* foreign travel, photography. *Address:* Monks Well House, Waverley, Farnham, Surrey. *T:* Runfold 2328.

IBBOTT, Alec; HM Diplomatic Service; Counsellor and Head of Chancery, Khartoum, since 1979; *b* 14 Oct. 1930; *s* of Francis Joseph Ibbott and Madge Winifred Ibbott (*née* Graham); *m* 1964, Margaret Elizabeth Brown; one *s* one *d*. Joined Foreign (subseq. Diplomatic) Service, 1949; served in HM Forces, 1949-51; FCO, 1951-54; ME Centre for Arab Studies, 1955-56; Second Secretary and Vice Consul, Rabat, 1956-60; Second Secretary, FO, 1960-61; Second Sec. (Information), Tripoli, 1961; Second Sec., Benghazi, 1961-65; First Sec. (Information), Khartoum, 1965-67; First Sec., FO (later FCO), 1967-71; Asst Political Agent, HM Political Agency, Dubai, 1971; First Secretary, Head of Chancery and Consul, HM Embassy: Dubai, 1971-72; Abu Dhabi, 1972-73; First Secretary and Head of Chancery: HM High Commn, Nicosia, 1973-74; FCO, 1975-77; HM Embassy, Caracas, 1977-79. *Address:*

c/o Foreign and Commonwealth Office, SW1. *Club:* Royal Commonwealth Society.

IBBS, Sir John Robert, (Sir Robin Ibbs), Kt 1982; Director, Imperial Chemical Industries, since 1976; *Educ:* Univ. of Toronto; Trinity Coll., Cambridge (MA). Called to the Bar, Lincoln's Inn. Joined ICI, 1952; Director, 1976; on secondment as Head, Central Policy Review Staff, Cabinet Office, 1980-82. *Address:* Imperial Chemical House, Millbank, SW1P 3JL.

IBIAM, Sir (Francis) Akanu, GCON 1963; LLD, DLit; medical missionary; Eze Ogo Isiala I: Unwana, and the Osuji of Uburu; Chairman, Imo State Council of Traditional Rulers; *b* Unwana, Afikpo Division, Nigeria, 29 Nov. 1906; *s* of late Ibiam Aka Ibiam and late Alu Owora; *m* 1939, Eudora Olayinka Sasegbon (*d* 1974); one *s* two *d*. *Educ:* Hope Waddell Training Instn Calabar; King's Coll., Lagos; University of St Andrews, Scotland. FMCP (GP) Nigeria. Medical Missionary with the Church of Scotland Mission, Calabar, Nigeria, 1936; started and built up new Hosp. in Abiriba, Bende Div., under Calabar Mission, 1936-45; Medical Supt, CSM Hosp., Itu, 1945-48; CSM Hosp., Uburu, 1952-57. MLC, Nigeria, 1947-52; MEC, 1949-52; retd from Politics, 1953; Principal, Hope Waddell Training Instn, Calabar, 1957-60; (on leave) Governor, Eastern Nigeria, 1960-66; Adviser to Military Governor of Eastern Provinces, 1966. Founder (1937) and former Pres., Student Christian Movement of Nigeria, now Hon. President; Trustee: Presbyterian Church of Nigeria, 1945-; Queen Elizabeth Hosp., Umuahia-Ibeku, 1953-; Scout Movement of Eastern Nigeria, 1957-; Mem. Bd of Governors: Hope Waddell Trng Instn, Calabar, 1945-60; Queen Elizabeth Hosp., 1950-60; Mem. Provl Council of University Coll., Ibadan, 1948-54; Mem. Privy Council, Eastern Nigeria, 1954-60; Pres., Christian Council of Nigeria, 1955-58; Mem. Calabar Mission Council, 1940-60 (now integrated with Church); Mem. Admin. Cttee of Internat. Missionary Council, 1957-61; Chm. Provisional Cttee of All Africa Churches Conf., 1958-62; Chairman: Council of University of Ibadan, Nigeria, 1958-60; Governing Council of Univ. of Nigeria, Nsukka, 1966; a Pres. of World Council of Churches, 1961; a Pres. of All Africa Church Conf., 1963; Pres., World Council of Christian Educn and Sunday Sch. Assoc.; Chm. Council, United Bible Socs, 1966-72, Vice-Pres. 1972-; Founder and Pres., Bible Soc. of Nigeria, 1963-74, Patron 1974; Founder and former Pres., All Africa Council of Churches; Founder, Nigerian SPCC; President: Soc. for Promotion of Ibo Lang. and Culture; Cancer Soc. of Nigeria. Patron, Akanu Ibiam Nat. Ambulance; Grand Patron, World Women Christian Temperance Union. Presbyterian Church of Nigeria: Mem. Educ. Authority, 1940-; Mem. Missionaries' Cttee, Med. Bd, and Standing Cttee of Synod; Advanced Training Fund Management Cttee of Synod; Elder, 1940-. Appointed OBE 1949, KBE 1951, KCMG 1962, and renounced these honours 1967 in protest at British Govt policy on Biafra. Upper Room Citation, 1966. Hon. LLD Ibadan; Hon. DSc Ife, 1966. Kt of Mark Twain. Humanitarian of Rosicrucian Order. Golden Cross with crown, Order of Orthodox Knights of Holy Sepulchre, Jerusalem, 1965; Golden Star Medal (1st degree), Order of Russian Orthodox Church, 1965. *Recreation:* reading. *Address:* Ganymede, Unwana, Afikpo Local Government Area, PO Box 240, Imo State, Nigeria.

IBRAHIM, Sir Kashim, GCON 1963; KCMG 1962; CBE 1960 (MBE 1952); Governor of Northern Nigeria, 1962-66; Chancellor, Lagos University, since 1976; *b* 10 June 1910; *s* of Mallam Ibrahim Lakkani; *m* 1st, 1943, Halima; 2nd, 1944, Khadija; 3rd, 1957, Zainaba; four *s* three *d* (and two *d* decd). *Educ:* Bornu Provincial Sch.; Katsina Teachers' Trng Coll. Teacher, 1929-32; Visiting Teacher, 1933-49; Educ. Officer, 1949-52. Federal Minister of Social Services, 1952-55; Northern Regional Minister of Social Develt and Surveys, 1955-56; Waziri of Bornu, 1956-62. Advr to Military Governor, N Nigeria, 1966-. Chm. Nigerian Coll. of Arts, Science and Technology, 1958-62; Chancellor, Ibadan Univ., 1967-75; Chm. Provisional Council of Ahmadu Bello Univ. Hon. LLD: Ahmadu Bello, 1963; Univ. of Ibadan; Univ. of Nigeria (Nsukka); University of Lagos. *Publications:* Kanuri Reader Elementary, I-IV; Kanuri Arithmetic Books, I-IV, for Elementary Schs and Teachers' Guide for above. *Recreations:* walking, riding, polo playing.

IDALIE, Mme Heinric; *see* Oldenbourg-Idalie, Zoë.

IDDESLEIGH, 4th Earl of, *cr* 1885; **Stafford Henry Northcote,** DL; Bt 1641; Viscount St Cyres, 1885; Chairman, South West Trustee Savings Bank, since 1981; Director, Television South West, since 1982; *b* 14 July 1932; *er s* of 3rd Earl of Iddesleigh and of Elizabeth, *er d* of late F. S. A. Lowndes and late Marie Belloc; *S* father, 1970; *m* 1955, Maria Luisa Alvarez-Builla y Urquijo (Condesa del Real Agrado in Spain), *d* of late Don Gonzalo Alvarez-Builla y Alvera and of Viscountess Exmouth, *widow* of 9th Viscount Exmouth; one *s* one *d*. *Educ:* Downside. 2nd Lieut, Irish Guards, 1951-52. DL Devon, 1979. Kt SMO Malta. *Heir:* *s* Viscount St Cyres, *qv*. *Address:* Shillands House, Upton Pyne Hill, Exeter, Devon EX5 5EB. *T:* Exeter 58916. *Club:* Army and Navy.

IEVERS, Frank George Eyre, CMG 1964; Postmaster-General, East Africa, 1962-65, retired; *b* 8 May 1910; *s* of Eyre Francis and Catherine Ievers; *m* 1936, Phyllis Robinson; two *s*. *Educ:* Dover Coll. Asst Traffic Supt, Post Office, 1933; Traffic Supt, East Africa, 1946; Telecommunications Controller, 1951; Regional Dir, 1959. *Recreations:* golf, photography. *Address:* 20 Heron Close, Worcester WR2 4BW. *T:* Worcester 427121. *Clubs:* Nairobi (Kenya); Sudan (Khartoum).

IEVERS, Rear-Adm. John Augustine, CB 1962; OBE 1944; *b* 2 Dec. 1912; *s* of Eyre Francis Ievers, Tonbridge, Kent; *m* 1937, Peggy G. Marshall; one *s* two *d. Educ:* RN Coll., Dartmouth. CO Naval Test Squadron, Boscombe Down, 1945-47; RN Staff Coll., 1948-49; HMS Ocean, 1949; HMS Glory, 1949-50; HMS Burghead Bay, 1951-52; CO, RN Air Station, Lossiemouth, 1952-54; Dep. Dir Naval Air Warfare Div., 1954-57; Captain Air, Mediterranean, 1957-60; Deputy Controller Aircraft, Min. of Aviation, 1960-63; retd, 1964. *Recreation:* golf. *Address:* 3 Hollywood Court, Hollywood Lane, Lymington, Hants. *T:* Lymington 77268.

IGGO, Prof. Ainsley, PhD, DSc; FRS 1978; FRSE; Professor of Veterinary Physiology, University of Edinburgh, since 1962; *b* 2 Aug. 1924; *s* of late Lancelot George Iggo and late Catherine Josefine Fraser; *m* 1952, Betty Joan McCurdy, PhD, *d* of late Donald A. McCurdy, OBE; three *s. Educ:* Gladstone Sch., NZ; Southland Technical High Sch., NZ; Lincoln Coll., NZ (Sen. Scholar; MAgrSc 1947); Univ. of Otago (BSc 1949). PhD Aberdeen, 1954; DSc Edinburgh, 1962. FRSE 1962. Asst Lectr in Physiology, Otago Univ. Med. Sch., 1948-50; NZ McMillan Brown Trav. Fellow, Rowett Inst., 1950-51; Lectr in Physiol., Univ. of Edinburgh Med. Sch., 1952-60; Nuffield Royal Soc. Commonwealth Fellow, ANU, 1959; Royal Soc. Locke Res. Fellow, 1960-62; Dean, Faculty of Veterinary Med., Univ. of Edinburgh, 1974-77. Vis. Professor: Univ. of Ibadan, Nigeria, 1968; (also Leverhulme Res. Fellow) Univ. of Kyoto, 1970; Univ. of Heidelberg, 1972. Chm., IUPS Somatosensory Commn, 1974-. Mem. Council: RCVS, 1975-78; Royal Soc., 1982-; Pres., Internat. Assoc. for Study of Pain, 1980-. Governor, E of Scotland Coll. of Agriculture, 1968-77. *Publications:* (ed) Sensory Physiology: Vol. II, Somatosensory System, 1973; articles on neurophysiol topics in Jl Physiol., etc. *Recreations:* bee-keeping, gardening. *Address:* 5 Relugas Road, Edinburgh EH9 2NE. *T:* 031-667 4879.

IGNATIEFF, George, CC 1973; Chancellor, University of Toronto, since 1980; Hon. Professor, University of Trinity College, Toronto (Vice-Chancellor and Provost, 1972-79); *b* 16 Dec. 1913; *s* of Count Paul N. Ignatieff and Princess Natalie Mestchersky; *m* 1945, Alison Grant, MVO; two *s. Educ:* St Paul's, London; Lower Canada Coll., Montreal; Jarvis Coll., Toronto; Univs of Toronto and Oxford. Rhodes Schol., Ont, 1935; BA Toronto 1935; BA Oxon 1938, MA 1960. Dept of External Affairs, Ottawa, 1940; 3rd Sec., London, 1940-44; Ottawa, 1944-45; Adviser, Canadian Delegn, UN Atomic Energy Commn, 1946; UN Assembly, 1946-47; Alt. Rep., UN Security Council, 1948-49; Councillor, Canadian Embassy, Washington, DC, 1948-53; Imp. Def. Coll., London, 1953-54; Head of Defence Liaison Div., External Affairs, Ottawa, 1954-55; Canadian Ambassador to Yugoslavia, 1956-58; Dep. High Comr, London, 1959-60; Asst Under-Sec. of State for External Affairs, Ottawa, 1960-62; Perm. Rep. and Canadian Ambassador to NATO, 1962-65; Canadian Perm. Rep. and Ambassador to UN: NY, 1965-68; to Cttee on Disarmament, Geneva, 1968-71; to UN and other Internat. Organisations, Geneva, 1970-71. Pres., UNA Canada, 1979-. Chm., Bd of Trustees, Nat. Museums of Canada Corp., 1973-79. Hon. Fellow, St John's Coll., Winnipeg, 1973. Hon. LLD: Toronto, 1969; Brock, 1969; Guelph 1970; Saskatchewan, 1973; York, 1975; Hon. DCL Bishop's, 1973; Hon. DLitt, Victoria Coll., Toronto, 1977. *Address:* 18 Palmerston Gardens, Toronto, Ont M6G 1V9, Canada; University of Trinity College, Toronto, Ontario M5S 1H8, Canada.

IKERRIN, Viscount; David James Theobald Somerset Butler; *b* 9 Jan. 1953; *s* and heir of 9th Earl of Carrick, *qv*; *m* 1975, Philippa V. J., *yr d* of Wing Commander L. V. Craxton; three *s* (including twin *s*). *Educ:* Downside. *Heir: e s* Hon. Arion Thomas Piers Hamilton Butler, *b* 1 Sept. 1975.

IKIN, Rutherford Graham; Headmaster of Trent College, 1936-68; *b* 22 Jan. 1903; *s* of late Dr A. E. Ikin, formerly Dir of Education, Blackpool; *m* 1936, Elizabeth Mary Mason; two *d. Educ:* King Edward VI Sch., Norwich; King's Coll., Cambridge (Choral Scholar). BA 1925; MA 1928; Asst Master at King's Sch., Ely, 1926-29; History Master and House Master, St Bees Sch., 1929-36. *Publications:* A Pageant of World History; The Modern Age; The History of the King's School, Ely. *Address:* Green Eaves, Whatstandwell, Matlock, Derbyshire. *T:* Ambergate 2315. *Club:* East India, Devonshire, Sports and Public Schools.

ILCHESTER, 9th Earl of, *cr* 1756; **Maurice Vivian de Touffreville Fox-Strangways;** Baron Ilchester of Ilchester, Somerset, and Baron Strangways of Woodsford Strangways, Dorset, 1741; Baron Ilchester and Stavordale of Redlynch, Somerset, 1747; Group Captain, Royal Air Force (rtd); *b* 1 April 1920; *s* of 8th Earl of Ilchester and Laure Georgine Emilie (*d* 1970), *d* of late Evanghelos Georgios Mazaraki, sometime Treasurer of Suez Canal Company; *S* father, 1970; *m* 1941, Diana Mary Elizabeth, *e d* of late George Frederick Simpson, Cassington, Oxfordshire. *Educ:* Kingsbridge Sch. CEng; MRAeS; FINucE; Fellow, Soc. of Engineers (Pres., 1974); FBIM; FRSA. Pres., SE Area, RAF Assoc., 1978-. *Recreations:* outdoor activities, enjoyment of the arts. *Heir: b* Hon. Raymond George Fox-Strangways [*b* 11 Nov. 1921; *m* 1941, Margaret Vera, *d* of late James Force, North Surrey, BC; two *s*]. *Address:* Farley Mill, Westerham, Kent TN16 1UB. *T:* Westerham 62314. *Clubs:* Brooks's, Royal Air Force.

ILERSIC, Prof. Alfred Roman; Professor of Social Studies, Bedford College, University of London, since 1965; *b* 14 Jan. 1920; *s* of late Roman Ilersic and Mary (*née* Moss); *m* 1st, 1944, Patricia Florence Bertram Liddle (marr. diss.

1976); one *s* one *d* ; 2nd, 1976, June Elaine Browning. *Educ:* Polytechnic Sec. Sch., London; London Sch. of Economics, Lectr in Econs, University Coll. of S West, Exeter, 1947-53; Lectr in Social Statistics, Beford Coll., 1953; Reader in Economic and Social Statistics, Bedford Coll., London, 1963. Mem., Cost of Living Adv. Cttee, 1970-. Chm., Inst. of Statisticians, 1968-70. Hon. Mem., Rating and Valuation Assoc., 1968. *Publications:* Statistics, 1953; Government Finance and Fiscal Policy in Post-War Britain, 1956; (with P. F. B. Liddle) Parliament of Commerce 1860-1960, 1960; Taxation of Capital Gains, 1962; Rate Equalisation in London, 1968; Local Government Finance in Northern Ireland, 1969. *Recreations:* listening to music, walking. *Address:* 4 Dewhurst House, Winnett Street, W1. *Club:* Reform.

ILIFFE, family name of **Baron Iliffe.**

ILIFFE, 2nd Baron, *cr* 1933, of Yattendon; **Edward Langton Iliffe;** Vice-Chairman of the Birmingham Post and Mail Ltd, 1957-74; Director of the Coventry Evening Telegraph and of the Cambridge News; *b* 25 Jan. 1908; *er s* of 1st Baron Iliffe, GBE, and Charlotte Gilding (*d* 1972); *S* father 1960; *m* 1938, Renée, *er d* of René Merandon du Plessis, Mauritius. *Educ:* Sherborne; France; Clare Coll., Cambridge. Served, 1940-46, with RAFVR (despatches). Trustee, Shakespeare's Birthplace; Mem. Council, Univ. of Warwick, 1965-71; Past Pres., Internat. Lawn Tennis Club of Gt Britain. High Sheriff of Berks, 1957. Hon. Freeman, City of Coventry. *Heir: n* Robert Peter Richard Iliffe, *qv. Address:* 38 St James's Place, SW1. *T:* 01-493 1938; Basildon House, Lower Basildon, near Reading, Berks. *T:* Pangbourne 4409. *Clubs:* Brooks's, Carlton; Royal Yacht Squadron.

ILIFFE, Robert Peter Richard; Chairman, BPM Holdings Ltd, since 1982 (Deputy Chairman, 1980, Director, subsidiary companies); *b* Oxford, 22 Nov. 1944; *s* of late Hon. W. H. R. Iliffe and Mrs Iliffe; *m* 1966, Rosemary Anne Skipwith; three *s* one *d. Educ:* Eton; Christ Church, Oxford. Chairman: West Midlands Press Ltd; Coventry Newspapers Ltd; British Transfer Printing Co. Ltd; Cambridge Newspapers Ltd; The Birmingham Post & Mail Ltd, 1978-81; Director: T. Dillon & Co. Ltd; Birmingham Boat Shows Ltd. Member of Council, Royal Agricultural Soc. of England. *Recreations:* yachting, shooting, fishing and old cars. *Address:* The Old Rectory, Ashow, Kenilworth, Warwickshire CV8 2LE.

ILLINGWORTH, Sir Charles (Frederick William), Kt 1961; CBE 1946; Regius Professor of Surgery, University of Glasgow, 1939, Emeritus, 1964; Hon. Surgeon to the Queen, in Scotland, 1961-65; Extra Surgeon since 1965; *b* 8 May 1899; *s* of John and Edith Illingworth; *m* 1928, Eleanor Mary Bennett (*d* 1971); four *s. Educ:* Heath Grammar Sch., Halifax; Univ. of Edinburgh. Graduated Medicine, 1922. 2nd Lieut, RFC 1917. FRCSE 1925; FRCSGlas, 1963. Hon. FACS, 1954; Hon. FRCS, 1958; Hon. FRCSI, 1964; Hon. FRCS (Canada), 1965; Hon. Fellow, Coll. Surg. S Africa, 1965. DSc (Hon.): University of Sheffield, 1962; University of Belfast, 1963; Hon. LLD (Glasgow, Leeds) 1965. *Publications:* (jtly) Text Book of Surgical Pathology, 1932; Short Text Book of Surgery, 1938; Text Book of Surgical Treatment, 1942; Monograph on Peptic Ulcer, 1953; The Story of William Hunter, 1967; The Sanguine Mystery, 1970; University Statesman: Sir Hector Hetherington, 1971; various contributions to surgical literature, mainly on digestive disorders. *Address:* 57 Winton Drive, Glasgow G12 0QB. *T:* 041-339 3759.

ILLINGWORTH, David Gordon, MVO 1980; MD, FRCPE; Surgeon Apothecary to HM Household at Holyrood Palace, Edinburgh, since 1970; Lecturer in General Practice Teaching Unit, Edinburgh University, since 1965; *b* 22 Dec. 1921; *yr s* of Sir Gordon Illingworth; *m* 1946, Lesley Beagrie, Peterhead; two *s* one *d. Educ:* George Watson's Coll.; Edinburgh University. MB, ChB Edinburgh, 1943; MRCPE 1949; MD (with commendation) 1963; FRCPE 1965; FRCGP 1970. Nuffield Foundn Travelling Fellow, 1966. RN Medical Service, 1944-46; medical appts, Edinburgh Northern Hosps Group, 1946-. Dep. CMO, Scottish Life Assurance Co., 1973-. Hon. Sen. Lectr in Rehabilitation Studies, Dept of Orthopaedic Surgery, Edinburgh Univ., 1977-. Member: Cancer Planning Group, Scottish Health Service Planning Council, 1976-; Tenovus, Edinburgh, 1978-; ASH, Royal Colleges Jt Cttee, 1978-; Specialty Sub-Cttee on Gen. Practice, 1980-; Nat. Med. Cons. Cttee, 1980-. Mem., Harveian Soc. Life Governor, Imperial Cancer Res. Fund, 1978. *Publications:* Practice (jtly), 1978; contribs to BMJ, Jl of Clinical Pathology, Gut, Lancet, Medicine. *Recreations:* golf, gardening. *Address:* 19 Napier Road, Edinburgh EH10 5AZ. *T:* 031-229 8102. *Clubs:* University (Edinburgh); Bruntsfield Links Golfing Soc.

ILLINGWORTH, Rear-Adm. Philip Holden Crothers, CB 1969; *b* 29 Nov. 1916; *s* of late Norman Holden Illingworth, Woking; *m* 1944, Dorothy Jean, *d* of George Wells, Southbourne; three *s* three *d. Educ:* RN Coll., Dartmouth, RNEC. Joined RN 1930, Rear-Adm. 1967. Dep. Controller of Aircraft, Min. of Technology, 1969, MoD, 1971-72; retd 1973; Vice-Chm., EPS (Western) Ltd, 1980-82. *Address:* Manor House, Marston Magna, Somerset. *T:* Marston Magna 850294.

ILLINGWORTH, Raymond, CBE 1973; cricketer; Manager, Yorkshire County Cricket Club, since 1979, and Captain, since 1982; *b* 8 June 1932; *s* of late Frederick Spencer Illingworth and Ida Illingworth; *m* 1958, Shirley Milnes; two *d. Educ :* Wesley Street Sch., Farsley, Pudsey. Yorkshire County cricketer; capped, 1955. Captain MCC, 1969; Captain, Leics CCC, 1969-78. Toured: West Indies, 1959-60; Australia twice (once as Captain), 1962-63 and

1970-71. Played in 66 Test Matches (36 as Captain). *Publications:* Spinners Wicket, 1969; The Young Cricketer, 1972; Spin Bowling, 1979; Captaincy, 1980; Yorkshire and Back, 1980; (with Kenneth Gregory) The Ashes, 1982. *Recreations:* golf, bridge. *Address:* 386 Bradford Road, Stanningley, Pudsey, West Yorkshire LS28 7TQ. *T:* Pudsey 578137.

ILLINGWORTH, Ronald Stanley; Professor of Child Health, University of Sheffield, 1947-75; *b* 7 Oct. 1909; *s* of late H. E. Illingworth, ARIBA, ARPS, Fairleigh, Skipton Road, Ilkley; *m* Dr Cynthia Illingworth, MB, BS, FRCP, Consultant in Paediatric Accident and Emergency, Children's Hosp., Sheffield; one *s* two *d. Educ:* Clifton House Sch., Harrogate; Bradford Grammar Sch. MB, ChB Leeds, 1934; MRCS, LRCP, 1934; MD Leeds, 1937; MRCP, 1937; DPH Leeds (distinction), 1938; DCH (RCP and S), 1938; FRCP 1947; FRPS, Fellow, Royal Society Medicine; Mem. BMA; Hon. Member: British Paediatric Assoc.; Swedish Pædiatric Assoc.; Finnish Pædiatric Assoc.; Amer. Acad. of Pediatrics; Academy of Pædiatricians of the USSR. West Riding County Major Scholar, 1928; Nuffield Research Studentship, Oxford, 1939-41; Rockefeller Research Fellowship, 1939 and 1946. Formerly Resident Asst, Hospital for Sick Children, Great Ormond Street, London, 1938-39; Medical Specialist and officer in charge of Medical Division (Lt-Col), RAMC, 1941-46. Asst to Prof. of Child Health, Univ. of London, 1946. Freedom, City of Sheffield, 1982. Hon. DSc: Univ. of Baghdad, Iraq, 1975; Leeds, 1982; Hon. MD Sheffield, 1976. Medal, Univ. of Turku, Finland, 1974; Aldrich Award, Amer. Acad. of Pediatrics, 1978; Spence Medal, BPA, 1979; Dawson Williams Prize, BMA, 1981. *Publications:* The Normal Child, 1953, 8th edn 1983 (trans. Greek 1966, 1978, Spanish 1969, Japanese 1970, 1975, Farsi 1979, French, 1981); (with C. M. Illingworth) Babies and Young Children: Feeding, Management and Care, 1954, 7th edn 1983; (ed) Recent Advances in Cerebral Palsy, 1958; Development of Infant and Young Child, Normal and Abnormal, 1960, 8th edn 1983 (trans. Japanese 1968, French and Polish 1978); An Introduction to Developmental Assessment in the First Year, 1962; The Normal Schoolchild: His Problems, Physical and Emotional, 1964; (with C. M. Illingworth) Lessons from Childhood: some aspects of the early life of unusual men and women, 1966 (Japanese trans., 1969); Common Symptoms of Disease in Children, 1967, 7th edn 1982 (trans. Greek and Spanish 1968, Italian 1974, 1980, German, 1979); Treatment of the Child at Home: a guide for family doctors, 1971 (Greek trans., 1975); Basic Developmental Screening, 1973, 3rd edn 1982 (trans. Greek and Italian 1978); The Child at School: a Paediatrician's Manual for Teachers, 1974; Your Child's Development in the First Five Years, 1981; various medical and photographic papers. *Recreations:* photography, philately, travel. *Address:* 8 Harley Road, Sheffield S11 9SD. *T:* 362774.

ILLSLEY, Prof. Raymond, CBE 1979; PhD; Professor of Medical Sociology and Director, Institute of Medical Sociology, University of Aberdeen, since 1975; Honorary Director, MRC Medical Sociology Unit, since 1965; *b* 6 July 1919; *s* of James and Harriet Illsley; *m* 1948, Jean Mary Harrison; two *s* one *d. Educ:* St Edmund Hall, Oxford (BA 1948). PhD Aberdeen 1956. Served War, 1939-45: active service in GB and ME, 1939-42; PoW, Italy and Germany, 1942-45. Econ. Asst, Commonwealth Econ. Cttee, London, 1948; Social Res. Officer, New Town Develt Corp., Crawley, Sussex, 1948-50; Sociologist, MRC, working with Dept of Midwifery, Univ. of Aberdeen, as Mem., Social Med. Res. Unit and later Mem., Obstetric Med. Res. Unit, 1951-64; Prof. of Sociology, Univ. of Aberdeen, 1964-75, Head of Dept of Sociology, 1966-71. Vis. Prof., Cornell Univ., NY, 1963-64; Vis. Scientist, Harvard Univ., 1968; Sen. Foreign Scientist, National Sci. Foundn, Boston Univ., 1971-72; Vis. Prof., Dept of Sociology, Boston Univ., 1971-72, Adjunct Prof., 1972-76. Chairman: Scottish TUC Inquiry on Upper Clyde Shipbuilders Ltd, 1971; Social Sciences Adv. Panel, Action for the Crippled Child, 1971-76; Health Services Res. Cttee, Chief Scientist's Org., SHHD, 1976-. Member: Sec. of State's Scottish Council on Crime, 1972-76; Exec. Cttee, Nat. Fund for Res. into Crippling Diseases, 1972-76; Chief Scientist's Cttee, SHHD, 1973-; EEC Cttee on Med. Res., 1974-77; SSRC, 1976-78 (Chairman: Sociol. and Soc. Admin Cttee, 1976-79; Social Affairs Cttee, 1982-); Chief Scientist's Adv. Cttee, DHSS, 1980-; European Adv. Cttee for Med. Res., WHO, 1981-. Rock Carling Fellow, Nuffield Prov. Hosps Trust, 1980. *Publications:* Mental Subnormality in the Community: a clinical and epidemiological study (with H. Birch, S. Richardson, D. Baird et al), 1970; Professional or Public Health, 1980; articles in learned jls on reproduction, migration, social mobility, mental subnormality. *Recreation:* rough husbandry. *Address:* Mains of Kebbaty, Midmar, Inverurie, Aberdeenshire. *T:* (office) Aberdeen 681818. *Club:* National Liberal.

ILLSTON, Dr John Michael, CEng, FICE; Director of the Hatfield Polytechnic, since 1982; *b* 17 June 1928; *s* of Alfred Charles Illston and Ethel Marian Illston; *m* 1951, Olga Elizabeth Poulter; one *s* two *d. Educ:* Wallington County Grammar Sch.; King's Coll., Univ. of London (BScEng, PhD, DScEng). CEng, FICE 1975. Water engr, then schoolmaster, 1949-59; Lectr, Sen. Lectr and Reader in Civil Engrg, King's Coll., London, 1959-77; Dir of Studies in Civil Engrg, Dean of Engrg, and Dep. Dir, Hatfield Polytechnic, 1977-82. *Publications:* (with J. M. Dinwoodie and A. A. Smith) Concrete, Timber and Metals, 1979; contrib. Cement and Concrete Res. and Magazine of Concrete Res. *Address:* Hatfield Polytechnic, PO Box 109, Hatfield, Herts AL10 9AB. *T:* Hatfield 68100.

IMBERT, Peter Michael, QPM 1980; Chief Constable, Thames Valley Police, since 1979; *b* 27 April 1933; *s* of late William Henry Imbert and of Frances May (*née* Hodge); *m* 1956, Iris Rosina (*née* Dove); one *s* two *d. Educ:* Harvey

Grammar Sch., Folkestone, Kent; Holborn College of Law, Languages and Commerce. Joined Metropolitan Police, 1953; Asst Chief Constable, Surrey Constabulary, 1976, Dep. Chief Constable, 1977. Dep. operational head, Metropolitan Police Anti-Terrorist Squad, 1973-75; Police negotiator at Balcombe Street siege, Dec. 1975; visited Holland following Moluccan sieges, and Vienna following siege of OPEC building by terrorists, Dec. 1975. Lectures in UK to police and military on terrorism and siege situations; also in Europe (incl. Berlin, 1978); lecture tours to Australia, 1977 and 1980 to advise on terrorism/sieges, and to Canada, 1981 re practical effects on police forces of recommendations of Royal Commn on Criminal Procedure. Sec., Nat. Crime Cttee-ACPO Council, 1980-. Mem. Gen. Advisory Council, BBC, 1980-. CBIM 1982. *Publications:* book reviews re terrorism/security/sieges police negotiating. *Recreations:* golf, gardening. *Address:* Thames Valley Police Headquarters, Kidlington, Oxford OX5 2NX. *T:* Kidlington 4343.

IMBERT-TERRY, Sir Andrew Henry Bouhier, 4th Bt *cr* 1917; *b* 5 Oct. 1945; *s* of Major Sir Edward Henry Bouhier Imbert-Terry, 3rd Bt, MC, and of Jean, *d* of late Arthur Stanley Garton; *S* father, 1978; *m* 1979, Georgina Anne Massie-Taylor. *Educ:* Eton. Formerly Captain, The Life Guards. *Heir: b* Michael Edward Stanley Imbert-Terry [*b* 18 April 1950; *m* 1975, Frances D., *d* of Peter Scott]. *Address:* Mead Meadow House, near Chobham, Surrey.

IMESON, Kenneth Robert, MA; Headmaster, Nottingham High School, 1954-70; *b* 8 July 1908; *s* of R. W. Imeson; *m* 1st, 1934, Peggy (*d* 1967), *d* of late A. H. Mann, Dulwich; two *d* ; 2nd, Peggy (*d* 1979), widow of Duncan MacArthur, *d* of late Harold Pow; 3rd, Barbara Thorpe (*see* Barbara Reynolds). *Educ:* St Olave's; Sidney Sussex Coll., Cambridge (Schol.). Mathematical Tripos, Part 1 1928; Part II 1930. Asst Master, Llandovery Coll., 1930-33; Sen. Mathematical Master, Watford Grammar Sch., 1933-44; Headmaster, Sir Joseph Williamson's Mathematical Sch., 1944-53; Mem. Council SCM in Schools, 1948-58; Council of Friends of Rochester Cathedral, 1947-53; Board of Visitors, Nottingham Prison, 1956-57; Teaching Cttee, Mathematical Association, 1950-58; Trustee, Nottingham Mechanics Institution, 1955-70; Court of Nottingham Univ., 1955-64, 1968-70; Member: Oxford and Cambridge Examinations Board, 1957-61, 1962-70; Council Christian Education Movement, 1965-69; Council, Arts Educational Schools, 1971-; Cttee, Notts CCC, 1969-72; London Diocesan Bd of Educn, 1971-76; Central Council of Physical Recreation, 1971-. Governor: Lady Margaret Sch., Parson's Green; Purcell Sch. of Music, 1975-78. *Publications:* articles in Journal of Education. *Recreations:* cricket and other games; music. *Address:* 16 Chesterton Towers, Old Chesterton, Cambridge CB4 1DZ. *T:* Cambridge 358008. *Clubs:* MCC, Yellowhammers Cricket, Forty.

IMMS, George, CB 1964; Commissioner and Director of Establishments and Organisation, HM Customs and Excise, 1965-71; *b* 10 April 1911; *o s* of late George Imms; *m* 1938, Joan Sylvia Lance; two *s. Educ:* Grange High Sch., Bradford; Emmanuel Coll., Cambridge (Scholar). Joined HM Customs and Excise, 1933; Asst Sec., 1946; Commissioner, 1957-65. Mem. Civil Service Appeals Bd, 1971-79. *Address:* 26 Lynceley Grange, Epping, Essex.

IMRAY, Colin Henry; HM Diplomatic Service; Deputy High Commissioner, Bombay, since 1980; *b* 21 Sept. 1933; *s* of late Henry Gibbon Imray and of Frances Olive Imray; *m* 1957, Shirley Margaret Matthews; one *s* three *d. Educ:* Highgate Sch.; Hotchkiss Sch., Conn; Balliol Coll., Oxford (2nd cl. Hons PPE). Served in Seaforth Highlanders and RWAFF, Sierra Leone, 1952-54. CRO, 1957; Canberra, 1958-61; CRO, 1961-63; Nairobi, 1963-66; FCO, 1966-70; British Trade Comr, Montreal, 1970-73; Counsellor, Head of Chancery and Consul-Gen., Islamabad, 1973-77; RCDS, 1977; Commercial Counsellor, Tel Aviv, 1977-80; Rayner Project Officer, 1980. *Recreations:* travel, walking. *Address:* c/o Foreign and Commonwealth Office, SW1A 2AH. *Club:* Royal Commonwealth Society.

INCE, Brigadier Cecil Edward Ronald, CB 1950; CBE 1946 (OBE 1941); *b* 5 March 1897; 3rd *s* of late C. H. B. Ince, Barrister-at-Law; *m* 1924, Leslie, *o d* of late Robert Badham, Secretary of Midland & GW Rly, Ireland; two *d. Educ:* Sevenoaks. Regular Army; RA 1915, RASC 1919-79. Deputy Dir (Supplies), Middle East, 1940-42; War Office, 1943-47; Commandant RASC Trng Centre, 1947-49. Dir of Enforcement, subseq. Dir of Warehousing, Min. of Food and Agric., 1949-55. *Publications:* various military pamphlets and articles in Service publications. *Recreation:* progressive gardening. *Address:* 76 West Grove, Walton-on-Thames, Surrey. *T:* Walton-on-Thames 25035.

INCE, Wesley Armstrong, CMG 1968; Solicitor and Company Director; *b* 27 Nov. 1893; *s* of John and Christina Ince, Melbourne; *m* 1919, Elsie Maud Ince, *d* of Wm H. Smith, Melbourne; two *d. Educ:* Wesley Coll., Melbourne; Melbourne Univ. Admitted practice Barrister and Solicitor, 1917; Partner, Arthur Robinson & Co., 1919-67. Chm., Claude Neon Industries Ltd, 1932-70; Chm., Rheem Australia Ltd, 1937-67; Foundn Mem. Coun., Inst. of Public Affairs, 1942-; Foundn Mem., Australian-American Assoc., 1941- (Federal Pres., 1962-63, 1965-67); Chm., Petroleum Refineries (Aust.) Ltd, 1952-61; Director: International Harvester Co. of Australia Pty Ltd, 1945-74; Hoyts Theatres Ltd, 1934-76; Dulux Australia Ltd, 1945-74. *Recreations:* golf, bowls, swimming. *Address:* 372 Glenferrie Road, Malvern, Vic 3144, Australia. *T:* 20 9516. *Clubs:* Athenæum (Melbourne); Royal Melbourne Golf, Melbourne Cricket.

INCH, Sir John Ritchie, Kt 1972; CVO 1969; CBE 1958; QPM 1961; Chief Constable, Edinburgh City Police, 1955-75; *b* 14 May 1911; *s* of James Inch, Lesmahagow, Lanarkshire; *m* 1941, Anne Ferguson Shaw; one *s* two *d*. *Educ*: Hamilton Academy; Glasgow Univ. (MA, LLB). Joined Lanarkshire Constabulary, 1931; apptd Chief Constable, Dunfermline City Police, 1943, and of combined Fife Constabulary, 1949. OStJ 1964. Comdr, Royal Order of St Olav (Norway), 1962; Comdr, Order of Al-Kawkal Al Urdini (Jordan), 1966; Cavaliere Ufficiale, Order of Merit (Italy), 1969; Comdr, Order of Orange-Nassau (Netherlands), 1971; Order of the Oak Crown Class III (Luxembourg), 1972. *Recreations*: shooting, fishing, golf. *Address*: Fairways, 192 Whitehouse Road, Barnton, Edinburgh EH4 6DA. *T*: 031-339 3558. *Club*: Royal Scots (Edinburgh).

INCHBALD, Michael John Chantrey, FSIAD; designer; Director, Michael Inchbald Ltd, since 1953; *b* 8 March 1920; *s* of Geoffrey H. E. Inchbald and late Rosemary Evelyn (*née* Ilbert); *m* 1955, Jacqueline Anne Bromley (marr. diss. 1964; *see* J. A. Thwaites); one *s* one *d*. *Educ*: Sherborne; Architect. Assoc. Sch. of Architecture. FSIAD 1970. Work exhibited: Triennale, Milan; Design Centres London, New York, Helsinki. Design projects for: Dunhill; John Player; Plessey Co; Savoy Group; Trust Houses Forte; ships, QE2 and Windsor Castle; Bank of America; Hanover Trust; Crown Estate Comrs; Cunard; Law Soc.; hotels and restaurants. Inchbald schs founded under his auspices, 1960. *Publications*: contrib. Arch. Rev., Arch. Digest, Connaissance des Arts, Connoisseur, Country Life, Harpers/Queen, House & Garden, Internat. Lighting Rev., and Vogue. *Recreations*: arts, travel, antiques. *Address*: Stanley House, 10 Milner Street, SW3 2PU. *T*: 01-584 8832.

INCHCAPE, 3rd Earl of, *cr* 1929; **Kenneth James William Mackay;** Viscount Glenapp of Strathnaver, *cr* 1929; Viscount Inchcape, *cr* 1924; Baron Inchcape, *cr* 1911; Chairman and Chief Executive, Inchcape PLC, 1958-82, now Life President; Deputy Chairman, P & O Steam Navigation Co., from June 1983 (Chairman, 1973-June 1983; Chief Executive, 1978-81); Director: Standard Chartered Bank Ltd; Guardian Royal Exchange Assurance; British Petroleum Co. Ltd; President, Commonwealth Society for the Deaf; *b* 27 Dec. 1917; *e s* of 2nd Earl and Joan (*d* 1933), *d* of late Lord Justice Moriarty; *S* father 1939; *m* 1st, 1941, Mrs Aline Thorn Hannay (marr. diss. 1954), *widow* of Flying Officer P. C. Hannay, AAF, and *d* of Sir Richard Pease, 2nd Bt; two *s* one *d*; 2nd, 1965, Caroline Cholmeley, *e d* of Cholmeley Dering Harrison, Emo Court, Co. Leix, Eire, and Mrs Corisande Harrison, Stradbally, Co. Waterford; two *s* and one adopted *s*. *Educ*: Eton; Trinity Coll., Cambridge (MA). Served War of 1939-45: 12th Royal Lancers BEF France; Major 27th Lancers MEF and Italy. Chm., Council for Middle East Trade, 1963-65; Pres., Gen. Council of British Shipping, 1976-77. Pres., Royal Soc. for India, Pakistan and Ceylon, 1970-76. Prime Warden: Shipwrights' Co., 1967; Fishmongers' Co., 1977-78. One of HM Comrs of Lieutenancy for the City of London, 1980-. Freeman, City of London. *Recreations*: all field sports. *Heir*: *s* Viscount Glenapp, *qv*. *Address*: Addington Manor, Addington, Bucks; Pearsie House, Kirriemuir, Angus. *Clubs*: White's, Brooks's, Buck's, Turf, City, Oriental.

See also Baron Craigmyle, Baron Tanlaw.

INCHIQUIN, 18th Baron of, *cr* 1543; **Conor Myles John O'Brien;** Bt 1686; *b* 17 July 1943; *s* of Hon. Fionn Maryons O'Brien (*d* 1977) (*y s* of 15th Baron) and of Josephine Reine, *d* of late Joseph Eugene Bembaron; *S* uncle, 1982. *Educ*: Eton. Succeeded a Captain, 14th/20th King's Hussars. *Heir*: *cousin* Murrough Richard O'Brien [*b* 25 May 1910; *m* 1st, 1942, Irene Clarice (marr. diss. 1951), *o d* of H. W. Richards; 2nd, 1952, Joan, *d* of Charles Pierre Jenkinson and *widow* of Captain Woolf Barnato; one *s* one *d*]. *Address*: Thomond House, Dromoland, Co. Clare, Ireland.

INCHYRA, 1st Baron *cr* 1961; **Frederick Robert Hoyer Millar,** GCMG 1956 (KCMG 1949; CMG 1939); CVO 1938; *b* 6 June 1900; *s* of late R. Hoyer Millar; *m* 1931, Elizabeth de Marees van Swinderen; two *s* two *d*. *Educ*: Wellington Coll.; New Coll., Oxford. Hon. Attaché, HM Embassy, Brussels, 1922; entered HM Diplomatic Service, 1923; served as Third Sec. at Berlin and Paris, and as Second Sec. at Cairo; Asst Private Sec. to Sec. of State for Foreign Affairs, 1934-38; First Sec. at Washington, 1939; Counsellor, 1941-42; Sec., British Civil Secretariat, Washington, 1943; Counsellor, FO, 1944; Asst Under-Sec. 1947; Minister, British Embassy, Washington, 1948; UK Deputy, North Atlantic Treaty Organisation, 1950; UK Permanent Representative on NATO Council, 1952; UK High Commissioner in Germany, 1953-55; British Ambassador to Bonn, 1955-57; Permanent Under-Sec. of State, Foreign Office, 1957-61. *Recreation*: shooting. *Heir*: *s* Hon. Robert Charles Reneke Hoyer Millar [*b* 4 April 1935; *m* 1961, Fiona Sheffield; one *s* two *d*]. *Address*: Inchyra House, Glencarse, Perthshire. *Clubs*: Boodle's, Turf; New (Edinburgh); Metropolitan (Washington).

INCLEDON-WEBBER, Lt-Col Godfrey Sturdy, TD 1943; DL; MA; *b* 1 July 1904; *er s* of William Beare Incledon-Webber, DL, JP, Buckland, Braunton, N Devon; *m* 1931, Angela Florence, *d* of Sir Pierce Lacy, 1st Bt; three *d*. *Educ*: Eton (1st classical schol. Radley, 1918); Magdalen Coll., Oxford (BA 1926, MA 1947). Joined Royal Devon Yeomanry Artillery, 1924; served in War of 1939-45 (Lieut-Col Comdg 136 Lt AA Regt RA, 1942-45). Partner, Cutler and Lacy, Stockbrokers, Birmingham, 1933-53; Man. Dir, British Trusts Assoc. Ltd, 1953-73; Director: United Dominions Trust Ltd, 1959-73; English Insurance Co. Ltd, 1955-78; Chm., Incledon Estate Co. Ltd, 1949. Alderman and JP, City of London, 1963-71; one of HM's Lieutenants of City of London; Sheriff, City of London, 1968-69; Master,

Worshipful Co. of Clothworkers, 1975-76 (excused service); Master, Worshipful Co. of Saddlers, 1961-62. Hereditary Freeman of Barnstaple (1925); Lord of the Manor of Croyde and Putsborough, Devon. DL Devon, 1969; High Sheriff, Devon, 1970-71. FRSA 1971. OStJ 1968. *Recreations*: shooting; represented Eton at rackets (Public School Rackets winning pair 1922) and cricket, 1922-23, Oxford Univ. at real tennis and squash rackets, 1925-26; mem. British Squash Rackets Team which toured USA and Canada, 1927, winning Lapham Trophy, USA, Canada and GB competing. *Address*: Buckland Manor, Braunton, N Devon EX33 1HN. *T*: Braunton 812016. *Clubs*: Carlton, City Livery.

IND, Jack Kenneth; Headmaster of Dover College, since 1981; *b* 20 Jan. 1935; *s* of Rev. William Price Ind and Mrs Doris Maud Ind (*née* Cavell); *m* 1964, Elizabeth Olive Toombs; two *s* two *d*. *Educ*: Marlborough Coll.; St John's Coll., Oxford (BA Hons Mods, 2nd Cl. Class. Lit. and Lit. Hum.). Asst Master: Wellingborough Sch., 1960-63; Tonbridge Sch., 1963-81 (Housemaster, 1970-81). *Recreations*: tennis, Rugby football, music, reading. *Address*: Headmaster's House, Dover College, Dover, Kent CT17 9RH. *T*: Dover 205905.

INDIAN OCEAN, Archbishop of the, since 1978; **Most Rev. Trevor Huddleston,** DD; Bishop of Mauritius, since 1978; *b* 15 June 1913; *s* of late Capt. Sir Ernest Huddleston, CIE, CBE; unmarried. *Educ*: Lancing; Christ Church, Oxford; Wells Theological College. 2nd class Hon. Mod. Hist., Oxford, 1934 (BA), MA 1937. Deacon, 1936; Priest, 1937. Joined Community of the Resurrection; Professed, 1941. Apptd Priest-in-charge Sophiatown and Orlando Anglican Missions, diocese Johannesburg, Nov. 1943; Provincial in S Africa, CR, 1949-55; Guardian of Novices, CR, Mirfield, 1956-58; Prior of the London House, Community of the Resurrection, 1958-60; Bishop of Masasi, 1960-68; Bishop Suffragan of Stepney, 1968-78. A Vice-Pres., Anti-Apartheid Movement, 1969-81, Pres., 1981-. Trustee, Runnymede Trust, 1972-. Hon. DD (Aberdeen Univ.), 1956; Hon. DLitt Lancaster, 1972. *Publications*: Naught for Your Comfort, 1956; The True and Living God, 1964; God's World, 1966. *Recreations*: walking and listening to music. *Address*: Phoenix, Mauritius.

INGAMELLS, John Anderson Stuart; Director of the Wallace Collection, since 1978; *b* 12 Nov. 1934; *s* of George Harry Ingamells and late Gladys Lucy (*née* Rollett); *m* 1st, 1960, Iolanthe Hill (marr. diss. 1964); 2nd, 1964, Hazel Wilson; two *d*. *Educ*: Hastings Grammar School; Eastbourne Grammar School; Fitzwilliam House, Cambridge. National Service, Army (Cyprus), 1956-58; Art Asst, York Art Gallery, 1959-63; Asst Keeper, Dept of Art, National Museum of Wales, 1963-67; Curator, York Art Gallery, 1967-77; Asst to the Director, Wallace Collection, 1977-78. *Publications*: The Davies Collection of French Art, 1967; The English Episcopal Portrait, 1981; numerous catalogues, including Philip Mercier (with Robert Raines), 1969; Portraits at Bishopthorpe Palace, 1972; museum catalogues at York, Cardiff and the Wallace Collection; articles in Apollo, Connoisseur, Burlington Magazine, Walpole Soc., etc. *Address*: 39 Benson Road, SE23 3RL.

INGE-INNES-LILLINGSTON, George David, MA, DL; a Crown Estates Commissioner, since 1974; *b* 13 Nov. 1923; *s* of late Comdr H. W. Innes-Lillingston, RN, and of Mrs Innes-Lillingston, formerly of Lochalsh House, Balmacara, Kyle, Ross-shire; *m* 1st, 1946, Alison Mary (*d* 1947), *er d* of late Canon F. W. Green, MA, BD, Norwich; one *d*; 2nd, 1955, Elizabeth Violet Grizel Thomson-Inge, *yr d* of late Lt-Gen. Sir William Thomson, KCMG, CB, MC; two *s* one *d*. *Educ*: Stowe, Buckingham; Merton Coll., Oxford (MA Hons Agric.). Served War as Lieut RNVR, 1942-45, Lt-Comdr RNR, 1966. Member: Agricultural Land Tribunal, 1962-72; Minister's Agricultural Panel for W Midlands, 1972-76; Chairman: N Birmingham and District Hosps, 1968-72; Staffordshire Br., Country Landowners' Assoc., 1968-71, and Headquarters Exec. Cttee, 1977-79; Agr. and Hort. Cttee, BSI, 1980-; Dep. Pres., CLA, 1977-79, Pres., 1979-81; Pres., Staffs Agricultural Soc., 1970-71. JP 1967-74, DL 1969-, Staffs; High Sheriff, Staffs, 1966. *Recreations*: growing trees, yachting. *Address*: Thorpe Hall, Tamworth, Staffs B79 0LH. *T*: Tamworth 830224. *Clubs*: Boodle's, Farmers', Royal Thames Yacht; Royal Highland Yacht (Oban).

INGERSOLL, Ralph McAllister; Editor and Publisher, USA; *b* 8 Dec. 1900; *s* of Colin Macrae and Theresa (McAllister) Ingersoll; *m* 1st, 1925, Mary Elizabeth Carden (marr. diss., 1935; she *d* 1965); 2nd, 1945, Elaine Brown Keiffer (*d* 1948); two *s*; 3rd, 1948, Mary Hill Doolittle (marr. diss., 1962; she *d* 1980); 4th, 1964, Thelma Bradford. *Educ*: Hotchkiss Sch., Lakeville, Connecticut; Yale and Columbia Univs. BS Yale, 1921; student, Columbia, 1922. Mining Engineer; Reporter for The New Yorker (mag.), 1925, Managing Editor, 1926-29; Assoc. Editor, Fortune Magazine, 1930, Managing Editor, 1930-35; Vice-Pres. and General Manager, Time, Inc., publishing Time, Life, Fortune, etc. Publisher of Time Magazine, 1937-39; resigned to organise and finance company subsequently to publish PM (NY daily newspaper); Editor, PM, 1940-46. Enlisted as Private, Engr. Amphibian Command, US Army, 1942; advanced to Lt-Col, Gen. Staff Corps; served overseas, 1943-45; in Africa, England, Italy, France, Belgium, Luxembourg and Germany, on staffs of Gen. Jacob Devers, Field-Marshal Montgomery, and Gen. Omar Bradley. Legion of Merit, Bronze Arrowhead for assault landing in Normandy, and 7 campaign stars; Officer of Order of Crown (Belgium); returned to Editorship of PM; resigned, 1946; Pres., The RJ Company, Inc., 1948-59, investments, principally newspapers; President and Director of numerous newspapers and publishing concerns, in RI, NY, NJ, Pa, Conn, NH,

Mich, Ohio, Vt and Mass; Pres., General Publications, Inc. (newspaper management), 1959-75; Pres., Ingersoll Publications Co., 1975-; Director: Central Home Trust Co., Eliz., NJ, 1963-67; Public Welfare Foundn, Washington DC, 1970-74; Recording for the Blind Foundn, NY, 1973-74. Hon. DHum Boston, 1980. *Publications:* Report on England, 1940; America is Worth Fighting For, 1941; Action on All Fronts, 1941; The Battle is the Pay-Off, 1944; Top Secret, 1946; The Great Ones, 1948; Wine of Violence, 1951; Point of Departure, 1961. *Address:* (home) Cornwall Bridge, Conn 06754, USA. *Club:* The Brook (NYC).

INGESTRE, Viscount; James Richard Charles John Chetwynd-Talbot; *b* 11 Jan. 1978; *s* and *heir* of 22nd Earl of Shrewsbury and Waterford, *qv*.

INGHAM, Bernard; Chief Press Secretary to the Prime Minister, since 1979; *b* 21 June 1932; *s* of Garnet and Alice Ingham; *m* 1956, Nancy Hilda Hoyle; one *s*. *Educ:* Hebden Bridge Grammar Sch., Yorks. Reporter: Hebden Bridge Times, 1948-52; Yorkshire Post and Yorkshire Evening Post, Halifax, 1952-59; Yorkshire Post, Leeds, 1959-61; Northern Industrial Correspondent, Yorkshire Post, 1961; Reporter, The Guardian, 1962-65; Labour Staff, The Guardian, London, 1965-67. Press and Public Relns Adviser, NBPI, 1967-68; Chief Inf. Officer, DEP, 1968-73; Dir of Information: Dept of Employment, 1973; Dept of Energy, 1974-77; Under Sec., Energy Conservation Div., Dept of Energy, 1978-79. *Recreations:* walking, gardening, reading. *Address:* 9 Monahan Avenue, Purley, Surrey CR2 3BB. *T:* 01-660 8970.

INGHAM, John Henry, CMG 1956; MBE 1947; retired; *b* 1910. *Educ:* Plumtree School, S Rhodesia; Rhodes University College, S Africa; Brasenose College, Oxford. Administrative Officer, Nyasaland, 1936; Secretary for Agricultural and Natural Resources, Kenya, 1947; Administrative Secretary, 1952; Senior Secretary, East African Royal Commission, 1953-55; Secretary for African Affairs, Nyasaland, 1956-60; MEC, Nyasaland, 1961. Minister of Urban Development, Malawi, 1961. Representative of Beit Trust and Dulverton Trust in Central Africa, 1962-81. Hon. MA Rhodesia, 1979. *Address:* 25 Canterbury Road, Avondale, Harare, Zimbabwe.

INGHAM, Prof. Kenneth, OBE 1961; MC 1946; Professor of History, University of Bristol, since 1967; *b* 9 Aug. 1921; *s* of Gladson and Frances Lily Ingham; *m* 1949, Elizabeth Mary Southall; one *s* one *d*. *Educ:* Bingley Grammar Sch.; Keble Coll., Oxford (Exhibitioner). Served with West Yorks Regt, 1941-46 (despatches, 1945). Frere Exhibitioner in Indian Studies, University of Oxford, 1947; DPhil 1950. Lecturer in Modern History, Makerere Coll., Uganda, 1950-56, Prof., 1956-62; Dir of Studies, RMA, Sandhurst, 1962-67. MLC, Uganda, 1954-61. *Publications:* Reformers in India, 1956; The Making of Modern Uganda, 1958; A History of East Africa, 1962; The Kingdom of Toro in Uganda, 1975; contrib. to Encyclopædia Britannica, Britannica Book of the Year. *Address:* The Woodlands, 94 West Town Lane, Bristol BS4 5DZ.

INGHAM, Stanley Ainsworth; Deputy Director (Under Secretary), Department for National Savings, 1979-82; *b* 21 Feb. 1920; *s* of David Ingham and Ann (*née* Walshaw); *m* 1944, Ethel Clara (*née* Jordan); one *s*. *Educ:* King's School, Pontefract, Yorkshire. Clerical Officer, Post Office Savings Bank, 1937; served Royal Artillery, 1940-46; Post Office Savings Bank: Executive Officer, 1946; Higher Executive Officer, 1956; Sen. Executive Officer, 1960; Principal, 1964; Asst Sec., Dept for National Savings, 1972. *Recreations:* Church affairs, gardening. *Address:* 2 Manor Crescent, Surbiton, Surrey KT5 8LQ. *T:* 01-399 1078.

INGILBY, Sir Thomas (Colvin William), 6th Bt *cr* 1866; MRAC; part-time Assistant, Strutt & Parker, Land Agents, Harrogate, since 1981; otherwise managing own estate; *b* 17 July 1955; *s* of Sir Joslan William Vivian Ingilby, 5th Bt, DL, JP, and of Diana, *d* of late Sir George Colvin, CB, CMG, DSO; *S* father, 1974. *Educ:* Aysgarth Sch., Bedale; Eton Coll. Student Teacher, Springvale School, Marandellas, Rhodesia, Sept. 1973-April 1974. Joined Army, May 1974, but discharged on death of father; student at Royal Agricultural Coll., Cirencester, until 1978. Asst to Dir, Great Yorkshire Show, 1977-81; Sec., Yorkshire Bachelors Soc., 1982-. Lecture tours, USA, speaking on castles and historic houses, 1978, 1979. Internat. Hon. Citizen, New Orleans, 1979. *Recreations:* cricket, tennis, squash. *Address:* Ripley Castle, Ripley, near Harrogate, North Yorkshire HG3 3AY. *T:* Harrogate 770186.

INGLE, Charles Fiennes; Barrister-at-law; a Recorder (formerly Recorder of Penzance), 1964-78, retired; *b* 30 April 1908; *s* of F. S. Ingle and M. A. Ingle, Bath; *m* 1933, Mary (*née* Linaker); one *s* one *d*. *Educ:* Oundle; Jesus Coll., Cambridge (MA). Called to Bar, Inner Temple, 1931; Western Circuit; Dep. Chm., Devon QS, 1963-71. Sqdn Ldr, RAFVR, 1940-45. *Recreations:* yachting, shooting. *Address:* West Soar, Malborough, Devon. *T:* Galmpton 561334.

INGLEBY, 2nd Viscount, *cr* 1955, of Snilesworth; **Martin Raymond Peake;** Landowner; Director, Hargreaves Group Ltd, 1960-80; *b* 31 May 1926; *s* of 1st Viscount Ingleby, and Joan, Viscountess Ingleby (*d* 1979); *S* father, 1966; *m* 1952, Susan, *d* of late Henderson Russell Landale; four *d* (one *s* decd). *Educ:* Eton; Trinity Coll., Oxford (MA). Called to the Bar, Inner Temple, 1956. Sec., Hargreaves Group Ltd, 1958-61. Administrative Staff Coll., 1961. CC Yorks (North Riding), 1964-67. Mem., N Yorks Moors Nat. Park Planning

Cttee, 1968-78. *Heir:* none. *Address:* Snilesworth, Northallerton, North Yorks DL6 3QD. *T:* Osmotherley 214.

INGLEFIELD, Sir Gilbert (Samuel), GBE 1968; Kt 1965; TD; MA, ARIBA, AADip; *b* 13 March 1909; 2nd *s* of late Adm. Sir F. S. Inglefield, KCB; *m* 1933, Laura Barbara Frances, *e d* of late Captain Gilbert Thompson, Connaught Rangers; two *s* one *d*. *Educ:* Eton; Trinity Coll., Cambridge. Architect; served War of 1939-45 with Sherwood Foresters, France, Far East. British Council Asst Rep. in Egypt, 1946-49 and in London, 1949-56. Alderman, City of London (Aldersgate Ward), 1959-79; Sheriff, 1963-64; Chm., Barbican Cttee, 1963-66; Lord Mayor of London, 1967-68; one of HM Lieutenants for City of London; Church Commissioner for England, 1962-78; Governor: Thomas Coram Foundation; Royal Shakespeare Theatre; Fedn of British Artists, 1972-; Trustee, London Symphony Orchestra; Chm., City Arts Trust, 1968-76; Member: Royal Fine Art Commission, 1968-75; Redundant Churches Fund, 1972-76. Dep. Kt Principal, Imp. Soc. of Knights Bachelor, 1972-. Master, Haberdashers' Co., 1972; Master, Musicians Co., 1974; Assistant, Painter Stainers Co. Chancellor of the Order of St John of Jerusalem, 1969-78; GCStJ. FRSA; Hon. RBA; Hon. GSM; Hon. FLCM. Hon. DSc City Univ., 1967. Comdr Order of the Falcon (Iceland), 1963; Order of the Two Niles, Class III (Sudan), 1964. *Recreations:* music, travel. *Address:* 6 Rutland House, Marloes Road, W8 5LE. *T:* 01-937 3458. *Clubs:* Athenæum, City Livery.

INGLEFIELD, Col Sir John (Frederick) C.; *see* Crompton-Inglefield.

INGLEFIELD-WATSON, Captain Sir Derrick W. I; *see* Watson.

INGLESON, Philip, CMG 1945; MBE 1926; MC 1918; President, Grampian Furniture Ltd (formerly Revel Industrial Products Ltd), 1973-74 (Chairman, 1958-72); retired; *b* 14 June 1892; *s* of William Frederick and Phoebe H. Ingleson; *m* 1921, Gwendoline, *o d* of Col R. Fulton, 1st KGVO Gurkha Rifles, IA; one *d*. *Educ:* Rossall Sch.; Queens' Coll., Cambridge (Senior Classical Scholar; MA 1981). Served European War (France), 1914-19, Royal Fusiliers and Staff Captain 198th Infantry Brigade 66 Div. (MC, despatches); joined Sudan Political Service, 1919; Governor Halfa Province 1931; Governor Berber Province, 1932; Governor Bahr-el-Ghazal Province, 1934; Governor Darfur Province, 1935-44; Ministry of Production, 1944; Board of Trade, 1945; UK Trade Commissioner in Queensland, 1949-53, and in Western Australia, 1954-56; Chm., Chair Centre Ltd, 1958-72. Order of the Nile, 4th Class, 1929; Order of the Nile, 3rd Class 1935. *Recreation:* travel. *Address:* 36 Campden Hill Court, W8. *T:* 01-937 8993.

INGLEWOOD, 1st Baron, *cr* 1964; **William Morgan Fletcher-Vane;** TD; DL; *b* 12 April 1909; *s* of late Col Hon. W. L. Vane and Lady Katharine Vane; assumed name of Fletcher-Vane by deed poll, 1931; *m* 1949, Mary (*d* 1982) (late Sen. Comdr ATS (despatches), JP, Mem. LCC, 1949-52, Cumberland CC, 1961-74), *e d* of Major Sir Richard G. Proby, 1st Bt, MC; two *s*. *Educ:* Charterhouse; Trinity Coll., Cambridge (MA). ARICS. 2nd Lt 6 Bn Durham Light Infantry, 1928; served Overseas: 1940, France, with 50 (N) Div. (despatches); 1941-44, Middle East with Durham LI and on the Staff, Lt-Col, 1943. MP (C) for Westmorland, 1945-64; Parliamentary Private Sec. to Minister of Agriculture, 1951-54, to Joint Under-Sec. of State, Foreign Office, 1954-55, and to Minister of Health, Dec. 1955-July 1956; Joint Parliamentary Secretary: Min. of Pensions and National Insurance, 1958-60; Min. of Agriculture, Oct. 1960-July 1962. DL Westmorland 1946, Cumbria 1974; Landowner; Mem. Chartered Surveyors Institution; formerly Mem. of Historic Buildings Council for England; Leader of UK Delegation to World Food Congress (FAO) Washington, June 1963. Chm., Anglo-German Assoc., 1973- (Vice-Chm., 1966-73). Order of the Phoenix, Greece; Order of the Cedar, Lebanon; Commander, German Order of Merit, 1977. *Heir:* s Hon. William Richard Fletcher-Vane, MA (Cantab) [*b* 31 July 1951. Called to the Bar, Lincoln's Inn, 1975; ARICS]. *Address:* Hutton-in-the-Forest, Penrith, Cumbria CA11 9TH. *T:* Skelton 207; 19 Stack House, Cundy Street, Ebury Street, SW1. *T:* 01-730 1559. *Club:* Travellers'.

INGLIS, Allan, CMG 1962; Director of Public Works, Hong Kong, retired; *b* 25 Feb. 1906; *m* 1936, Constance M. Maclachlan; two *d*. *Educ:* Royal High Sch., Edinburgh; Heriot-Watt Coll., Edinburgh. Chartered Civil Engineer (FICE). Joined Colonial Service, 1930; Engrg Surveyor, Singapore, SS, 1930; Asst Engr, 1935, Exec. Engr, 1939, Malaya. Served War of 1939-45, Major Royal Engineers. Sen. Exec. Engr, 1946, State Engr, 1953, Malaya. *Address:* 26 Cramond Road South, Edinburgh EH4 6AA. *T:* 031-336 1695.

INGLIS, Brian (St John), PhD; FRSL; journalist; *b* 31 July 1916; *s* of late Sir Claude Inglis, CIE, FRS, and late Vera St John Blood; *m* 1958, Ruth Langdon; one *s* one *d*. *Educ:* Shrewsbury Sch.; Magdalen Coll., Oxford. BA 1939. Served in RAF (Coastal Command), 1940-46; Flight Comdr 202 Squadron, 1944-45; Squadron Ldr, 1944-46 (despatches). Irish Times Columnist, 1946-48; Parliamentary Corr., 1950-53. Trinity Coll. Dublin: PhD 1950; Asst to Prof. of Modern History, 1949-53; Lectr in Economics, 1951-53; Spectator: Asst Editor, 1954-59; Editor, 1959-62; Dir, 1962-63. TV Commentator: What the Papers Say, All Our Yesterdays, etc., 1957-. *Publications:* The Freedom of the Press in Ireland, 1954; The Story of Ireland 1956; Revolution in Medicine, 1958; West Briton, 1962; Fringe Medicine, 1964; Private Conscience: Public Morality, 1964; Drugs, Doctors and Disease, 1965; A History of Medicine, 1965; Abdication, 1966; Poverty and the Industrial Revolution, 1971; Roger Casement, 1973; The Forbidden Game:

the social history of drugs, 1975; The Opium War, 1976; Natural and Supernatural, 1977; The Book of the Back, 1978; Natural Medicine, 1979; The Diseases of Civilisation, 1981. *Address:* Garden Flat, 23 Lambolle Road, NW3. *T:* 01-794 0297.

INGLIS, Sir Brian Scott, Kt 1977; Chairman, Ford Motor Co of Australia Ltd, since 1981; Vice-President, Ford Asia-Pacific Inc., since 1981; *b* Adelaide, 3 Jan. 1924; *s* of late E. S. Inglis, Albany, WA; *m* 1953, Leila, *d* of E. V. Butler; three *d. Educ:* Geelong Church of England Grammar School; Trinity Coll., Univ. of Melbourne. Served War of 1939-45; Flying Officer, RAAF, 453 Sqdn, 1942-45. Director and Gen. Manufacturing Manager, 1963-70, first Australian Man. Dir, 1970-81, Ford Motor Co. of Australia Ltd. James N. Kirby Medal, IProdE, 1979; Kernot Meml Medal, Faculty of Engrg, Univ. of Melbourne, 1979. *Address:* 10 Bowley Avenue, Balwyn, Victoria 3103, Australia. *Clubs:* Australian (Melbourne); Geelong (Geelong); Barwon Heads Golf.

INGLIS, Maj.-Gen. Sir Drummond, KBE 1945 (OBE 1939); CB 1944; MC 1916; *b* 4 May 1895; *s* of late Major Thomas Drummond Inglis, RA, Colchester; *m* 1st, 1919, Monica (*d* 1976), *d* of late Philip Percival Whitcombe, MB, London; one *s* (one *d* decd); 2nd, 1977, Joan Proudlove, *d* of Pieter Johannes Jacobus Vrint. *Educ:* Wellington Coll.; RMA, Woolwich. 2nd Lt RE 1914; served European War, 1914-19 (4th Class Order of White Eagle of Serbia with swords, Bt Major); Palestine, 1937-39 (despatches, OBE); War of 1939-45, France, Belgium, Holland, Germany; Chief Engineer, 21st Army Group, 1943-45 (Officer of the Legion of Honour, Croix de Guerre with palms, Knight Grand Officer of the Order of Orange Nassau with swords); retired pay, 1945; Col Comdt RE, 1955-60. *Address:* The Thatched Cottage, Chignal Smealey, near Chelmsford, Essex. *Club:* Army and Navy.

INGLIS, James Craufuird Roger, WS; Partner, Shepherd & Wedderburn, WS, since 1976; Chairman, British Assets Trust plc, since 1978; Director: Edinburgh American Assets Trust plc, since 1957; Atlantic Assets Trust plc, since 1957; Royal Bank of Scotland plc, since 1967; Scottish Provident Institution, since 1962; *b* 21 June 1925; *s* of Lt-Col John Inglis and Helen Jean Inglis; *m* 1952, Phoebe Aeonie Murray-Buchanan; two *s* four *d. Educ:* Winchester Coll.; Cambridge Univ. (BA); Edinburgh Univ. (LLB). *Recreation:* golf. *Address:* Inglisfield, Gifford, East Lothian, Scotland. *T:* Gifford 339. *Clubs:* Army and Navy; New (Edinburgh); Royal and Ancient Golf (St Andrews), Hon. Company of Edinburgh Golfers.

INGLIS, Maj.-Gen. Sir (John) Drummond; *see* Inglis, Maj.-Gen. Sir Drummond.

INGLIS, Prof. Kenneth Stanley, DPhil; Professor of History, Australian National University, since 1977; *b* 7 Oct. 1929; *s* of S. W. Inglis; *m* 1st, 1952, Judy Betheras (*d* 1962); one *s* two *d* ; 2nd, 1965, Amirah Gust. *Educ:* Univ. of Melbourne (MA); Univ. of Oxford (DPhil). Sen. Lectr in History, Univ. of Adelaide, 1956-60; Reader in History, 1960-62; Associate Prof. of History, Australian National Univ., 1962-65; Prof., 1965-66; Prof. of History, Univ. of Papua New Guinea, 1966-72, Vice-Chancellor, 1972-75; Professorial Fellow in Hist., ANU, 1975-77. Prof. of Australian Studies, Harvard, 1982. *Publications:* Hospital and Community, 1958; The Stuart Case, 1961; Churches and the Working Classes in Victorian England, 1963; The Australian Colonists, 1974. *Address:* History Department, Research School of Social Sciences, Australian National University, Canberra, ACT 2600, Australia.

INGLIS, Sheriff Robert Alexander; Sheriff of North Strathclyde (formerly Renfrew and Argyll) at Paisley, since 1972; *b* 29 June 1918; *m* 1950, Shelagh Constance St Clair Boyd (marriage dissolved, 1956); one *s* one *d. Educ:* Malsis Hall, Daniel Stewart's Coll.; Rugby Sch.; Christ Church, Oxford (MA); Glasgow Univ. (LLB). Army, 1940-46; Glasgow Univ., 1946-48; called to Bar, 1948. Interim Sheriff-Sub., Dundee, 1955; perm. appt, 1956; Sheriff of Inverness, Moray, Nairn and Ross and Cromarty, 1968-72. *Recreations:* golf, fishing, bridge. *Address:* 1 Cayzer Court, Ralston, Paisley, Renfrewshire. *T:* 041-883 6498.

INGLIS of Glencorse, Sir Roderick (John), 10th Bt *cr* 1703 (then Mackenzie of Gairloch); MB, ChB; *b* 25 Jan. 1936; *s* of Sir Maxwell Ian Hector Inglis of Glencorse, 9th Bt and Dorothy Evelyn (*d* 1970), MD, JP, *d* of Dr John Stewart, Tasmania; *S* father, 1974; *m* 1960, Rachel, *d* of Lt-Col N. M. Morris, Dowdstown, Ardee, Co. Louth; three *s* (incl twin *s*) one *d. Educ:* Winchester; Edinburgh Univ. (MB, ChB 1960). *Heir: s* Alastair Mackenzie Inglis, younger of Glencorse, *b* 28 July 1961. *Address:* 35 Villiers Drive, Pietermaritzburg, S Africa.

INGLIS-JONES, Nigel John, QC 1982; Barrister-at-Law; a Recorder of the Crown Court, since 1976; *b* 7 May 1935; 2nd *s* of Major John Alfred Inglis-Jones and Hermione Inglis-Jones; *m* 1965, Lenette Bromley-Davenport; two *s* two *d. Educ:* Eton; Trinity Coll., Oxford (BA). Nat. Service with Grenadier Guards (ensign). Called to the Bar, Inner Temple, 1959, Bencher, 1981. *Recreations:* conversation, fishing. *Address:* 4 Sheen Common Drive, Richmond, Surrey. *T:* 01-878 1320. *Club:* MCC.

INGOLD, Cecil Terence, CMG 1970; DSc 1940; FLS; Professor of Botany in University of London, Birkbeck College, 1944-72; Vice-Master, Birkbeck College, 1965-70, Fellow, 1973; *b* 3 July 1905; *s* of late E. G. Ingold; *m* 1933, Leonora Mary Kemp; one *s* three *d. Educ:* Bangor (Co. Down) Grammar Sch.; Queen's Univ., Belfast. Graduated BSc, QUB, 1925; Asst in Botany, QUB, 1929; Lectr in Botany, University of Reading, 1930-37; Lecturer-in-charge of Dept of Botany, University Coll., Leicester, 1937-44; Dean of Faculty of Science, London Univ., 1956-60. Dep. Vice-Chancellor, London Univ., 1966-68, Chm. Academic Council, 1969-72. Chm., University Entrance and School Examinations Council, 1958-64; Vice-Chm., Inter-Univ. Council for Higher Educn Overseas, 1969-74. Chm., Council Freshwater Biolog. Assoc., 1965-74; Pres., Internat. Mycological Congress, 1971. Hooker Lectr, Linnean Soc., 1974. Hon. DLitt Ibadan, 1969; Hon. DSc Exeter, 1972; Hon. DCL Kent, 1978. *Publications:* Spore Discharge in Land Plants, 1939; Dispersal in Fungi, 1953; The Biology of Fungi, 1961; Spore Liberation, 1965; Fungal Spores: their liberation and dispersal, 1971. *Address:* 11 Buckner's Close, Benson, Oxford OX9 6LR.

INGOLD, Dr Keith Usherwood, FRS 1979; FRSC 1969; Associate Director, Division of Chemistry, National Research Council of Canada, since 1977; *b* Leeds, 31 May 1929; *s* of Christopher Kelk Ingold and Edith Hilda (*née* Usherwood); *m* 1956, Carmen Cairine Hodgkin; two *s* one *d. Educ:* University Coll. London (BSc Hons Chem., 1949); Univ. of Oxford (DPhil 1951). Emigrated to Canada, 1951; Post-doctorate Fellow (under Dr F. P. Lossing), Div. of Pure Chem., Nat. Res. Council of Canada, 1951-53; Def. Res. Bd Post-doctorate Fellow (under Prof. W. A. Bryce), Chem. Dept, Univ. of BC, 1953-55; National Research Council of Canada: joined Div. of Appl. Chem., 1955; Head, Hydrocarbon Chem. Section of Div. of Chem., 1965. Amer. Chemical Soc. Award in Petroleum Chem., 1968; Award in Kinetics and Mechanism, Chem. Soc., 1978; Medal of Chem. Inst. of Canada, 1981. Silver Jubilee Medal, 1977. *Publications:* over 200 scientific papers in field of physical organic chemistry, partic. free-radical chemistry. *Recreation:* skiing. *Address:* PO Box 712, RR No 5, Ottawa, Ont, Canada. *T:* (613) 822-1123.

INGOLDBY, Eric, CIE 1943; *b* 7 Jan. 1892; *m* 1925, Zyvee Elizabeth Taylor (*d* 1954); two *s.* Served European War of 1914-18, RGA. Joined Indian State Railways, 1921; Chief Mechanical Engineer, GIP Railway, 1934; Dir Railway Board, India, 1935-40; Chief Controller of Standardisation, Railway Board, Govt of India, 1941-47; retired 1949; mem. firm of Rendel, Palmer and Tritton, consulting engineers, 1947-55. *Address:* 5 Lynne Court, Chesham Road, Guildford, Surrey. *T:* Guildford 70878.

INGRAM, Dr David John Edward, MA, DPhil; DSc Oxon 1960; FInstP; Vice-Chancellor, University of Kent at Canterbury, since 1980; *b* 6 April 1927; *s* of late J. E. Ingram and late Marie Florence (*née* Weller); *m* 1952, Ruth Geraldine Grace McNair; two *s* one *d. Educ:* King's Coll. Sch., Wimbledon; New Coll., Oxford. Postgraduate research at Oxford Univ., 1948-52; Research Fellow and Lectr, University of Southampton, 1952-57; Reader in Electronics, University of Southampton, 1957-59; Prof. and Head of Dept of Physics, Univ. of Keele, 1959-73; Dep. Vice-Chancellor, University of Keele, 1964-65, 1968-71; Principal, Chelsea Coll., London Univ., 1973-80. Mem., UGC, Physical Sciences Cttee, 1971-74. Member, Governing Body: Wye Coll., London Univ.; St Dunstan's Coll.; St Lawrence Coll.; King's Coll. Hosp. Medical Sch.; Roehampton Inst. Chairman: London Univ. Cttee for Non-Teaching Staff, 1979-80; London Univ. Central Coordinating Cttee for Computers, 1978-80. Member: Carnegie UK Trust, 1980-; Council, SPCK, 1980-; Camberwell DHA, 1982-. Hon. DSc (Clermont-Ferrand). *Publications:* Spectroscopy at Radio and Microwave Frequencies, 1955, 2nd edn, 1967; Free Radicals as Studied by Electron Spin Resonance, 1958; Biological and Biochemical Applications of Electron Spin Resonance, 1969; Radiation and Quantum Physics, 1973; Radio and Microwave Spectroscopy, 1976; various papers in Proc. Royal Soc., Proc. Phys. Soc., etc. *Recreations:* sailing, debating. *Address:* The University, Canterbury, Kent; 22 Ethelbert Road, Canterbury. *Club:* Athenæum.

INGRAM, Sir James (Herbert Charles), 4th Bt *cr* 1893; *b* 6 May 1966; *s* of (Herbert) Robin Ingram (*d* 1979) and of Shiela (now Countess Von Der Schulenburg), *d* of late Charles Peczenik; *S* grandfather, 1980. *Educ:* Eton. *Recreations:* golf and shooting. *Heir: half b* Nicholas David Ingram, *b* 1975. *Address:* 8 Pitt Street, W8. *T:* 01-937 0727.

INGRAM, Dame Kathleen Annie; *see* Raven, Dame Kathleen.

INGRAM, Prof. R. P. W.; *see* Winnington-Ingram.

INGRAM, Stanley Edward; Under Secretary (Legal), Department of Health and Social Security, since 1978; *b* 5 Dec. 1922; *o s* of late Ernest Alfred Stanley Ingram and Ethel Ann Ingram; *m* 1948, Vera (*née* Brown); one *s* one *d. Educ:* Charlton Central School. Articled clerk with Wright & Bull, Solicitors; admitted Solicitor, 1950. Served RAF, 1942-46. Legal Asst, Min. of Nat. Insurance, 1953; Sen. Legal Asst, Min. of Pensions and Nat. Insurance, 1958; Asst Solicitor, DHSS, 1971. Member Council: Civil Service Legal Soc. and of Legal Section of First Division Assoc., 1971-; Mem., Salaried Solicitors' Cttee of Law Society, 1978-81. *Recreations:* novel writing, gardening, country walking. *Address:* Department of Health and Social Security, State House, High Holborn, WC1R 4SX. *T:* 01-242 9020. *Club:* Law Society.

INGRAM, Prof. Vernon Martin, FRS 1970; Professor of Biochemistry, Massachusetts Institute of Technology, since 1961; *b* Breslau, 19 May 1924;

s of Kurt and Johanna Immerwahr; *m* 1950, Margaret Young; one *s* one *d*. *Educ:* Birkbeck Coll., Univ. of London. PhD Organic Chemistry, 1949; DSc Biochemistry, 1961. Analytical and Res. Chemist, Thos Morson & Son, Mddx, 1941-45; Lecture Demonstrator in Chem., Birkbeck Coll., 1945-47; Asst Lectr in Chem., Birkbeck Coll., 1947-50; Rockefeller Foundn Fellow, Rockefeller Inst., NY, 1950-51; Coxe Fellow, Yale, 1951-52; Mem. Sci. Staff, MRC Unit for Molecular Biology, Cavendish Lab., Cambridge, 1952-58; Assoc. Prof. 1958-61, MIT; Lectr (part-time) in Medicine, Columbia, 1961-73; Guggenheim Fellow, UCL, 1967-68. Jesup Lectr, Columbia, 1962; Harvey Soc. Lectr, 1965. Member: Amer. Acad. of Arts and Sciences, 1964; Amer. Chem. Soc.; Chemical Soc.; Biochemical Soc.; Genetical Society. William Allen Award, Amer. Soc. for Human Genetics, 1967. *Publications:* Haemoglobin and Its Abnormalities, 1961; The Hemoglobins in Genetics and Evolution, 1963; The Biosynthesis of Macromolecules, 1965, new edn, 1971; articles on human genetics, nucleic acids and differentiation in Nature, Jl Mol. Biol., Jl Cell Biol., Develt Biol., Jl Biol Chem., etc. *Recreation:* music. *Address:* Massachusetts Institute of Technology, Massachusetts Avenue, Cambridge, Mass 02139, USA. *T:* 617-253-3706.

INGRAMS, family name of **Baroness Darcy de Knayth.**

INGRAMS, Richard Reid; Editor, Private Eye, since 1963; *b* 19 Aug. 1937; *s* of Leonard St Clair Ingrams and Victoria (*née* Reid); *m* 1962; one *s* one *d* (and one *s* decd). *Educ:* Shrewsbury; University Coll., Oxford. Joined Private Eye, 1962. *Publications:* (with Christopher Booker and William Rushton) Private Eye on London, 1962; Private Eye's Romantic England, 1963; (with John Wells) Mrs Wilson's Diary, 1965; Mrs Wilson's 2nd Diary, 1966; The Tale of Driver Grope, 1968; (with Barry Fantoni) The Bible for Motorists, 1970; (ed) The Life and Times of Private Eye, 1971; (as Philip Reid, with Andrew Osmond) Harris in Wonderland, 1973; (ed) Cobbett's Country Book, 1974; (ed) Beachcomber: the works of J. B. Morton, 1974; The Best of Private Eye, 1974; God's Apology, 1977; Goldenballs, 1979; (with Fay Godwin) Romney Marsh and the Royal Military Canal, 1980; (with John Wells) Dear Bill: the collected letters of Denis Thatcher, 1980; (with John Wells) The Other Half: further letters of Denis Thatcher, 1981; (with John Wells) One for the Road, 1982. *Recreation:* litigation. *Address:* c/o Private Eye, 34 Greek Street, W1. *T:* 01-437 4017.

INGRESS BELL, P.; *see* Bell, Philip I.

INMAN, Herbert, CBE 1977; Regional Administrator, Yorkshire Regional Health Authority, 1973-77; Hon. Adviser to the Sue Ryder Foundation; *b* 8 Jan. 1917; *s* of Matthew Herbert Inman and Rose Mary Earle; *m* 1939, Beatrice, *d* of Thomas Edward Lee and Florence Lee; twin *s*. *Educ:* Wheelwright Grammar Sch., Dewsbury; Univ. of Leeds. FHA (Nat. Pres. 1968-69); DPA. Various hosp. appts, Dewsbury, Wakefield and Aylesbury, 1933-48; Dep. Gp Sec., Leeds (A) Gp HMC and Dep. Chief Admin. Officer, 1948-62; Gp Sec. and Chief Admin. Officer, Leeds (A) Gp HMC, 1962-70; Gp Sec. and Chief Admin. Officer, Leeds (St James's) Univ. HMC, 1970-73. *Publications:* occasional articles in Hospital and Health Services jls. *Recreations:* travel, gardening, Rugby football, cricket, swimming. *Address:* 7 Potterton Close, Barwick in Elmet, Leeds LS15 4DY. *T:* Leeds 812538.

INMAN, Peter Donald, CBE 1977; TD 1946; DL; Chief Executive/Clerk, Lancashire County Council, 1974-76; *b* 21 Oct. 1916; *s* of Robert and Sarah Inman, Bradford; *m* 1947, Beatrice Dallas; one *s* one *d*. *Educ:* Bradford Grammar Sch.; Leeds Univ. (LLB). Solicitor. Served War, 1939-45: KOYLI; France, India and Germany (Major). Asst Solicitor, Dewsbury, 1946; Lancashire County Council: Asst Solicitor, 1948; Dep. Clerk, 1951; Clerk, 1973-74. DL Lancs 1974; Clerk of Lieutenancy, Lancs, 1974. Hon. Treasurer, Lancs Youth Clubs Assoc., 1948-68, Vice-Pres. 1968. *Recreations:* golf, gardening. *Address:* 1 Beech Drive, Fulwood, Preston PR2 3NB. *T:* Preston 862361.

INMAN, Col Roger, OBE (mil.) 1945 (MBE (mil.) 1944); TD 1945; Vice Lord-Lieutenant of South Yorkshire, since 1981; Joint Managing Director, Harrison Fisher Group, since 1951; *b* 18 April 1915; *y s* of S. M. Inman, Sheffield; *m* 1939, Christine Lucas, *e d* of Lt-Col J. Rodgers, Sheffield; two *s*. *Educ:* King Edward VII Sch., Sheffield. Commissioned into 71st (WR) Field Bde, RA TA, 1935; served War, with RA and General Staff, Western Desert, Middle East, Italy, 1939-45; released, 1946, with rank of Lt-Col; reformed and commanded 271 (WR) Fd Regt, RA TA, 1947-51; Brevet Col 1953; Hon. Col, Sheffield Artillery Volunteers, 1964-70; Member, W Riding T&AFA, 1947-; Vice-Chm., Yorkshire and Humberside TAVRA, 1973-80. JP 1954 (Chm. Sheffield City Bench, 1974-80), DL 1967, West Riding. General Commissioner of Income Tax, 1969-; Chm. of Comrs, Don Div. of Sheffield, 1975-. *Recreation:* golf. *Address:* 228 Graham Road, Sheffield S10 3GS. *T:* Sheffield 301315. *Clubs:* Army and Navy; Sheffield, Hallamshire Golf (Sheffield).

INMAN, Rt. Rev. Thomas George Vernon; Secretary, Commission on Mission, Australian Council of Churches, since 1981; *b* 1904; *s* of late Capt. William James Inman, RE, Durban; *m* 1st, 1935, Alma Coker (*d* 1970), *d* of late Advocate Duncan Stuart Campbell, Bulawayo, Rhodesia; three *s* one *d*; 2nd, 1971, Gladys Marjory Hannah, MB, ChB (she *m* 1st, 1947, Charles William Lysaght, who *d* 1969), *d* of late David Rees Roberts, Cape Town. *Educ:* Selwyn Coll., Cambridge; St Augustine's Coll., Canterbury, MA 1932. Deacon, 1930; priest, 1931; Asst Missioner, Wellington Coll. Mission,

Walworth, 1930-33; Curate of Estcourt, Natal, 1933; Curate of St Paul, Durban, 1933-37, Vicar, 1937-51; Canon of Natal, 1944-51; Archdeacon of Durban, 1950-51; Bishop of Natal, 1951-74; retired, 1974. Dean, Province of S Africa, 1966-74. Chaplain and Sub-prelate, Order of St John of Jerusalem, 1953. Hon. DD Univ. of the South, Tenn., USA, 1958. *Address:* 74 Ray Road, Epping, NSW 2121, Australia. *T:* Sydney 869-2050.

INNES, Sir Berowald; *see* Innes, Sir R. G. B.

INNES of Coxton, Sir Charles (Kenneth Gordon), 11th Bt *cr* 1686; *b* 28 Jan. 1910; *s* of Major Charles Gordon Deverell Innes (*d* 1953), and Ethel Hilda, *d* of George Earle; *S* 1973 to baronetcy of Innes of Coxton, dormant since the death of Sir George Innes, 8th Bt, 1886; *m* 1936, Margaret Colquhoun Lockhart, *d* of F. C. L. Robertson and *g d* of Sir James Colquhoun of Luss, 5th Bt; one *s* one *d*. *Educ:* Haileybury Coll., Herts. War Service, 1939-45, Royal Artillery; Captain, Ayrshire Yeomanry. *Recreations:* photography, music, art, gardening. *Heir:* *s* David Charles Kenneth Gordon Innes [*b* 17 April 1940; *m* 1969, Marjorie Alison, *d* of E. W. Parker; one *s* one *d*. *Educ:* Haileybury; London Univ. BScEng; ACGI]. *Address:* October Cottage, Haslemere, Surrey GU27 2LF.

INNES, Fergus Munro, CIE 1946; CBE 1951; Chairman, India General Navigation and Railway Co. Ltd, 1973-78; *b* 12 May 1903; *s* of late Sir Charles Innes; *m* 1st, Evangeline, *d* of A. H. Chaworth-Musters (marriage dissolved); two *d*; 2nd, Vera, *d* of T. Mahoney; one *s* one *d*. *Educ:* Charterhouse; Brasenose Coll., Oxford. Joined Indian Civil Service, 1926; various posts in Punjab up to 1937; Joint Sec., Commerce Dept, Govt of India, 1944; Mem., Central Board of Revenue, 1947; retired, 1947; Adviser in Pakistan to Central Commercial Cttee, 1947-53; Sec., The West Africa Cttee, 1956-61. Company director. *Address:* The Hippins, Hook Heath Road, Woking, Surrey. *T:* Woking 4626. *Club:* Oriental.

INNES, Hammond; *see* Hammond Innes, Ralph.

INNES of Edingight, Malcolm Rognvald, CVO 1981; Baron of Yeochrie; Lord Lyon King of Arms, since 1981; Secretary to the Order of the Thistle, since 1981; *b* 25 May 1938; 3rd *s* of late Sir Thomas Innes of Learney, GCVO, LLD, and Lady Lucy Buchan, 3rd *d* of 18th Earl of Caithness; *m* 1963, Joan, *o d* of Thomas D. Hay, CA, Edinburgh; three *s*. *Educ:* Edinburgh Acad.; Univ. of Edinburgh (MA, LLB). WS 1964. Falkland Pursuivant Extraordinary, 1957; Carrick Pursuivant, 1958; Lyon Clerk and Keeper of the Records, 1966; Marchmont Herald, 1971. Mem., Queen's Body Guard for Scotland (Royal Company of Archers), 1971. Pres., Heraldry Soc. of Scotland. Trustee, Sir William Fraser's Foundn. FSA (Scot.); KStJ. Grand Officer of Merit, SMO Malta. *Recreations:* archery, fishing, shooting, visiting places of historic interest. *Address:* 35 Inverleith Row, Edinburgh EH3 5QH. *T:* 031-552 4924; Edingight House, Banffshire. *T:* Knock 270. *Clubs:* New, Puffins (Edinburgh).

INNES, Maughan William; Controller Finance, National Research Development Corporation, 1965-77; *b* 18 Nov. 1922; *s* of Leslie W. Innes and Bridget Maud (*née* Humble-Crofts); *m* 1950, Helen Mary, *d* of Roper Spyers; one *s* (and one *s* decd). *Educ:* Marlborough College. FCA; FBIM. RAF, 1941-46. Chartered Accountant, 1949; in Canada, 1953-60; retired 1977. *Recreations:* music, theatre. *Address:* Brook Cottage, Four Elms, Edenbridge, Kent TN8 6PA. *T:* Four Elms 232. *Club:* MCC.

INNES, Michael; *see* Stewart, John I. M.

INNES, Lt-Col Sir (Ronald Gordon) Berowald, 16th Bt *cr* 1628, of Balvenie; OBE 1943; *b* 24 July 1907; *s* of Captain J. W. G. Innes, CBE, RN (*d* 1939) and Sheila (*d* 1949), *d* of Col J. F. Forbes of Rothiemay; *S* kinsman, Sir Walter James Innes, 15th Bt, 1978; *m* 1st, 1933, Elizabeth Haughton (*d* 1958), *e d* of late Alfred Fayle; two *s* one *d*; 2nd, 1961, Elizabeth Christian, *e d* of late Lt-Col C. H. Watson, DSO, IMS. *Educ:* Harrow; RMC Camberley. Commissioned Seaforth Highlanders, 1927; PSC; served War of 1939-45; France, 1939-40; Middle East, 1941-43 (wounded); Sicily, 1943; Holland and Germany, 1944-45; GSO1 50 (Northumbrian) Div., 1942-43; GSO1 Directing Staff, Staff Coll., 1943-44; in comd 7th Bn, Seaforth Highlanders, 1945; GSO1 (Infantry), War Office, 1946-48; in comd 4th (Uganda) Bn, KAR, and OC Troops, Uganda, 1948-49; retired as Lt-Col, 1949. *Recreations:* needlepoint embroidery, foreign touring by caravan. *Heir:* *s* Peter Alexander Berowald Innes, MICE [*b* 6 Jan. 1937; *m* 1959, Julia Mary, *d* of A. S. Levesley; two *s* one *d*]. *Address:* The Loom House, Aultgowrie, by Muir of Ord, Ross and Cromarty. *T:* Urray 216. *Club:* Naval and Military.

See also Lt-Col W. A. D. Innes.

INNES, Lt-Col William Alexander Disney, JP; Vice Lord-Lieutenant of Banffshire, since 1971; *b* 19 April 1910; 2nd *s* of Captain James William Guy Innes, CBE, DL, JP, RN, of Maryculter, Kincardineshire; *m* 1939, Mary Alison, *d* of late Francis Burnett-Stuart, Howe Green, Hertford; two *s*. *Educ:* Marlborough Coll., RMC, Sandhurst. Gordon Highlanders: 2nd Lieut, 1930; Captain 1938; Temp. Major 1941; Major, 1946; Temp. Lt-Col, 1951; retd, 1952. Served War of 1939-45: Far East (PoW Malaya and Siam, 1942-45). Chm. Banffshire T&AFA, 1959. DL 1959, JP 1964, Banffshire. *Recreations:* shooting, gardening. *Address:* The Old Manse of Marnoch, Huntly,

Aberdeenshire AB5 5RS. *T:* Bridge of Marnoch 273.
See also Sir Berowald Innes, Bt.

INNES-KER, family name of **Duke of Roxburghe.**

INNESS, Air Cdre William Innes Cosmo, CB 1962; OBE 1954; DL; *b* 25 March 1916; *y s* of Henry Atkinson Inness; *m* 1942, Margaret Rose Nolan, *er d* of Lt-Col P. E. Nolan, MBE, Royal Signals; two *s. Educ:* Richmond Sch., Yorkshire. Commissioned, RAF Coll., 1936; India, 1936-39; Iraq, 1939-41; Bomber Command, Flt, Sqdn and Station Comdr and Group Captain, Plans, 1941-45. Air Ministry Directorate-Gen. of Personnel, Brit. Bombing Survey Unit, and Directorate of Staff Duties, 1946-48; Air Attaché, Teheran, 1948-51; Sen. Personnel Staff Officer, No. 23 Gp, 1951-54; RAF Flying Coll., 1954-55; Station Comdr, St Eval, 1955-57; Dep. Asst Chief of Staff (Plans), HQ Allied Forces, Mediterranean, 1957-59; Air Officer i/c Administration, Coastal Command, 1959-62; AOC Gibraltar, 1962-65; Dir Personal Services (Provost Marshal), RAF, 1965-68, retired 1968. ADC 1966-68. Regional Comdt, London and SE, Air Cadets, 1968-81; Pres., London Wing, ATC, 1981. Liveryman, Basketmakers' Co., 1975. DL Greater London, 1973. Chevalier of the Military Order of Aviz (Portugal), 1956. *Recreation:* flying. *Address:* c/o National Westminster Bank Ltd, Market Place, Sutton-in-Ashfield, Nottingham NG17 1AS. *Clubs:* Royal Air Force, City Livery.

INNISS, Hon. Sir Clifford (de Lisle), Kt 1961; Judge of the Court of Appeal of Belize, 1974-81; Chairman, Integrity Commission of Belize, since 1981; *b* Barbados, 26 Oct. 1910; *e s* of late Archibald de Lisle Inniss and Lelia Emmaline, *e d* of Elverton Richard Springer. *Educ:* Harrison Coll., Barbados; Queen's Coll., Oxford. BA (hons jurisprudence), BCL. Called to bar, Middle Temple, 1935. QC (Tanganyika) 1950, (Trinidad and Tobago) 1953; Practised at bar, Barbados; subseq. Legal Draughtsman and Clerk to Attorney-Gen., Barbados, 1938; Asst to Attorney General and Legal Draughtsman, 1941; Judge of Bridgetown Petty Debt Court, 1946; Legal Draughtsman, Tanganyika, 1947; Solicitor Gen., Tanganyika, 1949; Attorney-Gen., Trinidad and Tobago, 1953; Chief Justice, British Honduras, later Belize, 1957-72; Judge of the Courts of Appeal of Bermuda, the Bahamas, and the Turks and Caicos Is, 1974-75. *Recreations:* cricket, tennis, swimming. *Address:* 11/13 Oriole Avenue, Belmopan, Belize. *Clubs:* Royal Over-Seas League; Barbados Yacht; Kenya Kongonis (hon. mem.).

INSALL, Donald William, OBE 1981; FSA, FRIBA, FRTPI; architect and planning consultant; Principal, Donald W. Insall & Associates, since 1958; *b* 7 Feb. 1926; *o s* of late William R. Insall and Phyllis Insall, Henleaze, Bristol; *m* 1964, Amy Elizabeth, BA, *er d* of Malcolm H. Moss, Nanpantan, Leics; two *s* one d. *Educ:* private prep; Bristol Grammar Sch.; Bristol Univ.; RA; Sch. of Planning, London (Dip. (Hons)); SPAB Lethaby Schol. 1951. FRIBA 1968, FRTPI 1973. Coldstream Guards, 1944-47. Architectural and Town-Planning Consultancy has included town-centre studies, civic and univ., church, domestic and other buildings, notably in conservation of historic towns and buildings; Medal (Min. of Housing and Local Govt), Good Design in Housing, 1962. Visiting Lecturer: RCA, 1964-69; Internat. Centre for Conservation, Rome, 1969-; Coll. d'Europe, Bruges, 1976-81; Catholic Univ. of Leuven, 1982-; Adjunct Prof., Univ. of Syracuse, 1971-81. Mem., Council of Europe Working Party, 1969-70; Nat. Pilot Study, Chester: A Study in Conservation, 1968; Consultant, Chester Conservation Programme (EAHY Exemplar; European Prize for Preservation of Historic Monuments, 1981). Member: Historic Buildings Council for England, 1971-; Grants Panel, EAHY, 1974; Nat. Cttee, ICOMOS; Council, RSA, 1976- (FRSA, 1948). Member: Council, SPAB; Jt Cttee SPAB, Georgian Gp, Victorian Soc. and Civic Trust; Ancient Monuments Bd for England, 1980-. Hon. Sec., Conf. on Trng Architects in Conservation. RIBA: Banister Fletcher Medallist, 1949; Neale Bursar, 1955; Examnr, 1957; Competition Assessor, 1971. Conferences: White House (on Natural Beauty), 1965; IUA (on Architectural Trng), Pistoia, 1968; UNESCO, 1969. Lecture Tours: USA, 1964, 1972 (US Internat. Reg. Conf. on Conservation); Mexico, 1972; Yugoslavia, 1973; Canada, 1974; Argentina, 1976; India, 1979; Portugal, 1982. European Architectural Heritage Year Medal (for Restoration of Chevening), 1973; Queen's Silver Jubilee Medal, 1977. *Publications:* (jtly) Railway Station Architecture, 1966; (jtly) Conservation Areas 1967; The Care of Old Buildings Today, 1973; Historic Buildings: action to maintain the expertise for their care and repair, 1974; Conservation in Action: Chester's Bridgegate, 1982; contrib. to Encyclopædia Britannica, professional, environmental and internat. jls. *Recreations:* visiting, photographing and enjoying places; appreciating craftsmanship; Post-Vintage Thoroughbred Cars (Mem., Rolls Royce Enthusiasts' Club). *Address:* 73 Kew Green, Richmond, Surrey TW9 3AH; (office) 19 West Eaton Place, Eaton Square, SW1X 8LT. *T:* 01-245 9888. *Club:* Athenæum.

INSCH, James Ferguson, CBE 1974; CA; Director, Guest Keen & Nettlefolds plc, 1964-82, Deputy Chairman, 1980-82; Chairman, Birmid-Qualcast Ltd, since 1977 (Deputy Chairman, 1975-77); *b* 10 Sept. 1911; *s* of John Insch and Edina (*née* Hogg); *m* 1937, Jean Baikie Cunningham; one *s* two *d. Educ:* Leith Academy. Chartered Accountant (Scot.). Director, number of GKN companies, 1945-66; Guest Keen & Nettlefolds Ltd: Group Man. Dir, 1967; Gp Dep. Chm. and Man. Dir, 1968-74; Jt Dep. Chm., 1979. Pres., Nat. Assoc. of Drop Forgers and Stampers, 1962-63 and 1963-64. *Recreations:* golf, fishing. *Address:* Watling House, Twatling Road, Barnt Green, Birmingham. *T:* 021-445 2517.

INSKIP, family name of **Viscount Caldecote.**

INSKIP, John Hampden, QC 1966; a Recorder (formerly Recorder of Bournemouth), since 1970; *b* 1 Feb. 1924; *s* of Sir John Hampden Inskip, KBE, and Hon. Janet, *d* of 1st Baron Maclay, PC; *m* 1947, Ann Howell Davies; one *s* one d. *Educ:* Clifton Coll.; King's Coll., Cambridge. BA 1948. Called to the Bar, Inner Temple, 1949; Master of the Bench, 1975. Mem. of Western Circuit; Dep. Chm., Hants QS, 1967-71. Mem., Criminal Law Revision Cttee, 1973-; Pres., Transport Tribunal, 1982-. *Address:* 3 Pump Court, Temple, EC4. *T:* 01-353 0711; Clerks, Bramshott, Liphook, Hants.

INSOLE, Douglas John, CBE 1979; Marketing Director, Trollope & Colls Holdings Ltd, since 1975; *b* 18 April 1926; *s* of John Herbert Insole and Margaret Rose Insole; *m* 1948, Barbara Hazel Ridgway (*d* 1982); two *d* (and one *d* decd). *Educ:* Sir George Monoux Grammar Sch.; St Catharine's Coll., Cambridge. MA Cantab. Cricket: Cambridge Univ., 1947-49 (Captain, 1949); Essex CCC, 1947-63 (Captain, 1950-60); played 9 times for England; Vice-Captain, MCC tour of S Africa, 1956-57. Chairman: Test Selectors, 1965-68; Test and County Cricket Bd, 1975-78; Mem., MCC Cttee, 1955-; Manager, England cricket team, Australian tours, 1978-79 and 1982-83. Soccer: Cambridge Univ., 1946-48; Pegasus, and Corinthian Casuals; Amateur Cup Final medal, 1956. Member: Sports Council, 1971-74; FA Council, 1979-. JP Chingford, 1962-74. *Publication:* Cricket from the Middle, 1960. *Recreations:* cricket, soccer. *Address:* 34 Warren Road, North Chingford, E4 6QS. *T:* 01-529 6546. *Clubs:* Carlton, MCC.

INVERFORTH, 4th Baron *cr* 1919, of Southgate; **Andrew Peter Weir;** *b* 16 Nov. 1966; *s* of 3rd Baron Inverforth and of Jill Elizabeth, *o d* of John W. Thornycroft, *qv*; *S* father, 1982. *Educ:* Marlborough College. *Heir: uncle* Hon. John Vincent Weir, *b* 8 Feb. 1935. *Address:* 27 Hyde Park Street, W2 2JS. *T:* 01-283 1266; Walber House, Walberswick, Southwold, Suffolk IP18 6TS.

INVERNESS, Provost of (St Andrew's Cathedral); *see* Wheatley, Very Rev. Arthur.

INVERURIE, Lord; Michael Canning William John Keith; Master of Kintore; *b* 22 Feb. 1939; *s* and *heir* of 12th Earl of Kintore, *qv*; assumed surname of Keith in lieu of Baird; *m* 1972, Mary Plum, *d* of late Sqdn Leader E. G. Plum, Rumson, NJ, and of Mrs Roy Hudson; one *s* one d. *Educ:* Eton; RMA Sandhurst. Lately Lieutenant, Coldstream Guards. ACII. *Heir: s* Master of Inverurie, *qv*. *Address:* The Coach House, Keith Hall, Inverurie, Aberdeenshire. *T:* Inverurie 20495.

INVERURIE, Master of; Hon. James William Falconer Keith; *b* 15 April 1976; *s* and *heir* of Lord Inverurie, *qv*.

IONESCO, Eugène; Chevalier de la Légion d'Honneur, 1970; Officier des Arts et lettres, 1961; homme de lettres; Membre de l'Académie française, since 1970; *b* 13 Nov. 1912; *m* 1936, Rodica; one *d. Educ:* Bucharest and Paris. French citizen living in Paris. Ballet: The Triumph of Death, Copenhagen, 1972. *Publications:* (most of which appear in English and American editions) Théâtre I; La Cantatrice chauve, La Leçon, Jacques ou La Soumission, Les Chaises, Victimes du devoir, Amédée ou Comment s'en débarrasser, Paris, 1956; Théâtre II: L'Impromptu de l'Alma, Tueur sans gages, Le Nouveau Locataire, L'Avenir est dans les œufs, Le Maître, La Jeune Fille à marier, Paris, 1958. Rhinocéros (play) in Collection Manteau d'Arlequin, Paris, 1959, Le Piéton de l'air, 1962, Chemises de Nuit, 1962; Le Roi se meurt, 1962; Notes et Contre-Notes, 1962; Journal en Miettes, 1967; Présent passé passé présent, 1968; Découvertes (Essays), 1969; Jeux de Massacre (play), 1970; Macbett (play), 1972; Ce formidable bordel (play), 1974; The Hermit (novel), 1975; The Man with the Suitcase, 1975; (with Claude Bonnefoy) Entre la vie et le rêve, 1977; Antidotes (essays), 1977; L'homme en question (essays), 1979; Variations sur un même thème, 1979; Voyages chez les Morts ou Thème et Variations (play), 1980; Noir et Blanc, 1980; contrib. to: Avant-Garde (The experimental theatre in France) by L. C. Pronko, 1962; Modern French Theatre, from J. Giraudoux to Beckett, by Jean Guicharnaud, 1962; author essays and tales. *Relevant publications:* The Theatre of the Absurd, by Martin Esslin, 1961; Ionesco, by Richard N. Coe, 1961; Eugène Ionesco, by Ronald Hayman, 1972. *Address:* c/o Editions Gallimard, 5 rue Sébastien Bottin, 75007 Paris, France.

IONESCU, Prof. George Ghita; Professor of Government, University of Manchester, 1970-80, now Emeritus; Editor, Government and Opposition, since 1965; Chairman, Research Committee, International Political Science Association, since 1975; *b* 21 March 1913; *s* of Alexandre Ionescu and Hélène Sipsom; *m* 1950, Valence Ramsay de Bois Maclaren. *Educ:* Univ. of Bucharest (Lic. in Law and Polit. Sci.). Gen. Sec., Romanian Commn of Armistice with Allied Forces, 1944-45; Counsellor, Romanian Embassy, Ankara, 1945-47; Gen. Sec., Romanian Nat. Cttee, NY, 1955-58; Dir, Radio Free Europe, 1958-63; Nuffield Fellow, LSE, 1963-68. Hon. MA(Econ) Manchester. *Publications:* Communism in Romania, 1965; The Politics of the Eastern European Communist States, 1966; (jtly) Opposition, 1967; (jtly) Populism, 1970; (ed) Between Sovereignty and Integration, 1973; (ed) Centripetal Politics, 1975; The Political Thought of Saint-Simon, 1976; The European Alternatives, 1979. *Recreations:* music, bridge, racing. *Address:* 36 Sandileigh Avenue, Manchester M20 9LW. *T:* 061-445 7726. *Club:* Athenæum.

IPSWICH, Viscount; Henry Oliver Charles FitzRoy; *b* 6 April 1978; *s* and *heir* of Earl of Euston, *qv.*

IPSWICH, Bishop of; *see* St Edmundsbury.

IPSWICH, Archdeacon of; *see* Walsh, Ven. G. D. J.

IRBY, family name of **Baron Boston.**

IRELAND; *see* de Courcy-Ireland.

IRELAND, Frank, FCA; IPFA; Principal City Officer and Town Clerk, Newcastle upon Tyne, 1969–74; *b* 2 May 1909; *s* of C. A. Ireland, Clitheroe, Lancs; *m* 1935, Elsie Mary (*née* Ashworth); one *s* two *d. Educ:* Clitheroe Royal Grammar Sch.; Victoria Univ., Manchester BA (Com). Chartered Accountant, 1931; Hons, IMTA, 1936. Derby County Borough, 1933–37; Newcastle upon Tyne, 1937–74; City Treasurer, 1962–69. *Recreations:* music, photography. *Address:* 61 Kenton Road, Newcastle upon Tyne NE3 4NJ. *T:* Gosforth 856930.

IRELAND, Frank Edward, BSc, CChem; FRSC; FEng; FIChemE; SFInstE; consultant in air pollution control; HM Chief Alkali and Clean Air Inspector, 1964–78; *b* 7 Oct. 1913; *s* of William Edward Ireland and Bertha Naylor; *m* 1941, Edna Clare Meredith; one *s* three *d. Educ:* Liverpool Univ. (BSc). CChem, FRSC (FRIC 1945); CEng, FIChemE 1950; SFInstF 1956. Plant Superintendent, Orrs Zinc White Works, Widnes, Imperial Smelting Corp. Ltd, 1935–51; Prodn Man., Durham Chemicals Ltd, Birtley, Co. Durham, 1951–53; Alkali Inspector based on Sheffield, 1953–58; Dep. Chief Alkali Inspector, 1958–64. Pres., Inst. of Fuel, 1974–75; Vice Pres., Instn of Chem. Engrs, 1969–72. George E. Davis Gold Medal, Instn of Chem. Engrs, 1969. Founder Fellow, Fellowship of Engineering, 1976. *Publications:* Annual Alkali Reports, 1964–77; papers to nat. and internat. organisations. *Recreations:* golf, gardening. *Address:* 59 Lanchester Road, Highgate, N6. *T:* 01–883 6060.

IRELAND, Ronald David, QC (Scotland) 1964; Sheriff of Lothian and Borders (formerly Lothians and Peebles) at Edinburgh, since 1972; *b* 13 March 1925; *o s* of William Alexander Ireland and Agnes Victoria Brown. *Educ:* George Watson's Coll., Edinburgh; Balliol Coll., Oxford (Scholar); Edinburgh Univ. Served Royal Signals, 1943–46. BA Oxford, 1950, MA 1958; LLB Edinburgh, 1952. Passed Advocate, 1952; Clerk of the Faculty of Advocates, 1957–58; Prof. of Scots Law, 1958–71, Dean of Faculty of Law, 1964–67, Aberdeen Univ. Governor, Aberdeen Coll. of Education, 1959–64 (Vice-Chm., 1962–64). Comr. under NI (Emergency Provisions) Act, 1974–75. Member: Bd of Management, Aberdeen Gen. Hosps, 1961–71 (Chm., 1964–71); Departmental Cttee on Children and Young Persons, 1961–64; Cttee on the Working of the Abortion Act, 1971–74; Hon. Sheriff for Aberdeenshire, 1963–. Member: North Eastern Regional Hosp. Bd, 1964–71 (Vice-Chm. 1966–71); After Care Council, 1962–65; Nat. Staff Advisory Cttee for the Scottish Hosp. Service, 1964–65; Chm., Scottish Hosps Administrative Staffs Cttee, 1965–72. Dir, Scottish Courts Admin, 1975–78. *Recreations:* music, bird-watching. *Address:* 6a Greenhill Gardens, Edinburgh EH10 4BW. *Clubs:* New (Edinburgh); Royal Northern and University (Aberdeen).

IREMONGER, Thomas Lascelles; *o s* of Lt-Col H. E. W. Iremonger, DSO, Royal Marine Artillery, and Julia St Mary Shandon, *d* of Col John Quarry, Royal Berks Regiment; *m* Lucille Iremonger, MA (Oxon), FRSL, author and broadcaster; one *d. Educ:* Oriel Coll., Oxford (MA). HM Overseas Service (Western Pacific), 1938–46. RNVR (Lt), 1942–46. MP (C) Ilford North, Feb. 1954–Feb. 1974, Redbridge, Ilford North, Feb.–Sept. 1974; PPS to Sir Fitzroy Maclean, Bt, CBE, MP, when Under-Sec. of State for War, 1954–57. Contested (C Ind. Democrat) Redbridge, Ilford N, March 1978 and (C, independently), 1979. Member: Royal Commn on the Penal System, 1964–66; Home Sec.'s Adv. Council on the Employment of Prisoners; Gen. Council, Institute for Study and Treatment of Delinquency. Underwriting Mem. of Lloyd's. *Publications:* Disturbers of the Peace, 1962; Money, Politics and You, 1963. *Recreations:* sailing, riding, shooting. *Address:* 34 Cheyne Row, SW3; The Giant's House, Newbourn, near Woodbridge, Suffolk; La Voûte, Montignac-le-Coq, 16390 St Séverin, France.

IRENS, Alfred Norman, CBE 1969; Chairman: British Electrotechnical Approvals Board for Household Appliances since 1974; British Approvals Board for Telecommunications, since 1982; *b* 28 Feb. 1911; *s* of Max Henry and Guinevere Emily Irens; *m* 1934, Joan Elizabeth, *d* of John Knight, FRIBA, Worsley, Manchester; two *s. Educ:* Blundell's Sch., Tiverton; Faraday House, London. College apprentice, Metropolitan Vickers, Ltd, Manchester. Subsequently with General Electric Co., Ltd, until joining Bristol Aeroplane Co., Ltd, 1939, becoming Chief Electrical Engineer, 1943; Consulting Engineer to Govt and other organisations, 1945–56. Part-time mem., SW Electricity Bd, 1948–56, Chm., 1956–73. Past Chm. IEE Utilization Section and IEE Western Sub-Centre; Chairman: British Electrical Development Assoc., 1962–63; SW Economic Planning Council, 1968–71. Chm., Bristol Waterworks Co., 1975–81 (Dir, 1967–81); Dir, Avon Rubber Co. Ltd, 1973–81. JP Long Ashton, Som, 1960–66. Hon. MSc Bristol, 1957. *Recreations:* general outdoor activities. *Address:* Crete Hill House, Cote House Lane, Bristol BS9 3UW. *T:* Bristol 622419.

IRESON, Rev. Canon Gordon Worley; Warden, Community of the Holy Name, since 1974; *b* 16 April 1906; *s* of Francis Robert and Julia Letitia Ireson; *m* 1939, Dorothy Elizabeth Walker; two *s* one *d. Educ:* Edinburgh Theological Coll.; Hatfield Coll., Durham. Asst Curate of Sheringham, 1933–36; Senior Chaplain of St Mary's Cathedral, Edinburgh, with charge of Holy Trinity, Dean Bridge, 1936–37; Priest-Lecturer to National Soc., 1937–39; Diocesan Missioner of Exeter Diocese, 1939–46; Hon. Chaplain to Bishop of Exeter, 1941–46; Canon Residentiary of Newcastle Cathedral, 1946–58; Canon-Missioner of St Albans, 1958–73; Examining Chaplain to Bishop of Newcastle, 1949–59. *Publications:* Church Worship and the Non-Churchgoer, 1945; Think Again, 1949; How Shall They Hear?, 1957; Strange Victory, 1970. *Recreation:* making and mending in the workshop. *Address:* St Mary's, Ranelagh Road, Malvern Link, Worcs WR14 1BQ.

IRISH, Sir Ronald (Arthur), Kt 1970; OBE 1963; Partner, Irish Young & Outhwaite, Chartered Accountants, retired; Chairman, Rothmans of Pall Mall (Australia) Ltd, 1955–81, retired; *b* 26 March 1913; *s* of late Arthur Edward Irish; *m* 1960, Noella Jean Austin Fraser; three *s. Educ:* Fort Street High School. Chm., Manufacturing Industries Adv. Council, 1966–72. Pres., Inst. of Chartered Accountants in Australia, 1956–58; Pres., Tenth Internat. Congress of Accountants, 1972; Life Member: Australian Soc. of Accountants, 1972; Inst. of Chartered Accountants in Australia, 1974. *Publications:* Practical Auditing, 1935; Auditing, 1947, new edn 1972. *Recreations:* golf, swimming. *Address:* 3/110 Elizabeth Bay Road, Elizabeth Bay, NSW 2011, Australia. *Clubs:* Australian, Union (Sydney).

IRON, Air Cdre Douglas, CBE 1944; *b* 1 Aug. 1893; *s* of Captain John Iron, OBE, and Anne Iron; *m* 1917, Dorothy Bentham (from whom he obtained a divorce); one *d* ; *m* 1930, Mrs P. V. Sankey (from whom he obtained a divorce). *Educ:* Tudor Hall Sch., Hawkhurst. Prob. Flight Sub.-Lt RNAS Sept. 1914; Flight Lt May 1915; Acting Lt-Col GSO1 (Air) April 1918; permanent commission, RAF, as Flight Lt 1919. Sqdn Leader, 1924; Wing Comdr 1930; attended Royal Naval Staff Coll., 1935; Group Capt. 1937; Air Officer i/c Administration, 4 Training Command, RCAF, Canada, with rank of Air Commodore, Dec. 1943; Air Officer Commanding 51 Group RAF, 1944–45; retired, 1945. *Recreation:* fishing. *Club:* Army and Navy.

IRONMONGER, Sir (Charles) Ronald, Kt 1970; Personnel Officer, GEC Traction Ltd (formerly AEI) Attercliffe, 1966–79, retired; *b* 20 Jan. 1914; *s* of late Charles and Emily Ironmonger; *m* 1938, Jessie Green (decd); one *s* one *d. Educ:* Huntsmans Gardens Elementary Sch., Firth Park Secondary Sch., Sheffield. Elected Sheffield City Council, Nov. 1945; Chairman, Water Cttee, 1951–66; Leader of City Council and Chairman, Policy Cttee, 1966–74; Chm., S Yorks Local Govt Reorganisation Jt Cttee, 1972; Leader, S Yorkshire CC, 1973–79, Dep. Leader, 1979–; Chm., Policy Cttee, 1973–79, Vice-Chm., 1979–. Vice-Chm., AMA, 1977–78. *Recreations:* reading, sport. *Address:* 70 Chestnut Avenue, Sheffield S9 4AP. *T:* Sheffield 442329.

IRONSIDE, family name of **Baron Ironside.**

IRONSIDE, 2nd Baron, *cr* 1941, of Archangel and of Ironside; **Edmund Oslac Ironside;** International Research and Development Co., since 1968; *b* 21 Sept. 1924; *o s* of 1st Baron Ironside, Field Marshal, GCB, CMG, DSO, and Mariot Ysobel Cheyne; *S* father, 1959; *m* 1950, Audrey Marigold, *y d* of late Lt-Col Hon. Thomas Morgan-Grenville, DSO, OBE, MC; one *s* one *d. Educ:* Tonbridge Sch. Joined Royal Navy, 1943; retd as Lt, 1952. English Electric Gp, 1952–63; Cryosystems Ltd, 1963–68; Dir, Gemini Computer Systems Ltd, 1973; Dep. Chm., Parly and Scientific Cttee, 1974. Mem., Organising Cttee, British Library, 1971–72. President: Electric Vehicle Assoc., 1976; European Electric Road Vehicle Assoc., 1980; Vice-Pres., Inst. of Patentees and Inventors, 1977; Chm., Adv. Cttee, Science Reference Lib., 1976–. Governor, Tonbridge Sch. and others; Mem. Ct, City Univ., 1971–. Master, Skinners' Co., 1981–82. *Publication:* (ed) High Road to Command: the diaries of Major-General Sir Edmund Ironside, 1920–22, 1972. *Heir:* s Hon. Charles Edmund Grenville Ironside, *b* 1 July 1956. *Address:* Broomwood Manor, Chignal St James, Chelmsford, Essex. *T:* Chelmsford 440231. *Club:* Royal Ocean Racing.

IRONSIDE, Christopher, OBE 1971; FRBS; Artist and Designer; *b* 11 July 1913; *s* of Dr R. W. Ironside and Mrs P. L. Williamson (2nd *m* ; *née* Cunliffe); *m* 1st, 1939, Janey (*née* Acheson) (marriage dissolved, 1961); one *d* ; 2nd, 1961, Jean (née Marsden); one *s* two *d. Educ:* Central Sch. of Arts and Crafts. Served War of 1939–45, Dep. Sen. Design Off., Directorate of Camouflage, Min. of Home Security. In charge of Educn Sect., Coun. of Industrial Design, 1946–48; part-time Teacher, Royal College of Art, 1953–63. Paintings in public and private collections. *One-man shows:* Redfern Gall., 1941; Arthur Jeffries Gall., 1960. *Design work includes:* Royal Coat of Arms, Whitehall and decorations in Pall Mall, Coronation, 1953; coinages for Tanzania, Brunei, Qatar and Dubai; reverses for Decimal Coinage, UK and Jamaican; many medals, coins and awards; theatrical work (with brother, late R. C. Ironside); various clocks; coat of arms and tapestry for Leather Sellers' Hall; firegrate for Goldsmiths' Co.; brass and marble meml to 16th Duke of Norfolk, Arundel. FSIA 1970; FRBS 1977. *Recreation:* trying to keep abreast of modern scientific development. *Address:* 22 Abingdon Villas, W8. *T:* 01–937 9418; Church Farm House, Smannell, near Andover, Hants. *T:* Andover 3909.

IRVINE, Alan Montgomery, RDI 1964; DesRCA, ARIBA; architect in private practice; *b* 14 Sept. 1926; *s* of Douglas Irvine and Ellen Marler; *m* 1st, 1955, Betty Middleton (marr. diss. 1963); one *s* ; 2nd, 1966, Katherine Mary Buzas; two *s*. *Educ:* Regent Street Polytechnic, Secondary Sch. and Sch. of Architecture; Royal College of Art. RAF (Aircrew), 1944-47. In private practice since 1956, specialising in design of interiors, museums and exhibitions; formed partnership with Stefan Buzas in 1965. Work has included interior design for Schroder Wagg & Co., Lazards, Bovis, S Australian Govt, Nat. Enterprise Bd; Mem. of design team for QE2, 1968. Various exhibns for V&A Museum, Tate Gall., Royal Acad., British Council including: Treasures of Cambridge, 1959; Book of Kells, 1961; Mellon Collection, 1969; Age of Charles I, 1972; Pompeii AD 79, 1976; Gold of El Dorado, 1978; Horses of San Marco, London, NY, Milan, Berlin, 1979-82; Great Japan Exhibn, 1981; Art and Industry, 1982; museum work includes: New Galleries for Royal Scottish Museum, 1968; Old Master Drawings Gallery, Windsor Castle, 1965; Crown Jewels display, Tower of London, 1968; Treasuries at Winchester Cathedral, 1968, Christ Church, Oxford, 1975, and Winchester Coll., 1982; Heinz Gallery for Architectural Drawings, RIBA, London, 1972; Museum and Art Gallery for Harrow Sch., 1975; Heralds' Museum, London, 1980. Consultant architect to BM, 1981-. Liveryman, Worshipful Co. of Goldsmiths. Hon. Fellow, RCA. *Recreations:* travel, photography. *Address:* 2 Aubrey Place, St John's Wood, NW8 9BH. *T:* 01-328 2229.

IRVINE, Alexander Andrew Mackay, QC 1978; *b* 23 June 1940; *s* of Alexander Irvine and Margaret Christina Irvine; *m* 1974, Alison Mary, *y d* of Dr James Shaw McNair, MD, and Agnes McNair, MA; two *s*. *Educ:* Inverness Acad.; Hutchesons' Boys' Grammar Sch., Glasgow; Glasgow Univ. (MA, LLB); Christ's Coll., Cambridge (Scholar; BA 1st Cl. Hons with distinction; LLB 1st Cl. Hons; George Long Prize in Jurisprudence). Called to the Bar, Inner Temple, 1967; Univ. Lectr, LSE, 1965-69. Contested (Lab) Hendon North, Gen. Election, 1970. *Recreation:* collecting paintings. *Address:* 1 Harcourt Buildings, Temple, EC4Y 9DA. *T:* 01-583 0610. *Club:* Garrick.

IRVINE, Rt. Hon. B(ryant) Godman, PC 1982; MP (C) Rye Division of East Sussex since 1955; Barrister-at-Law; Farmer; *b* Toronto, 25 July 1909; *s* of late W. Henry Irvine and late Ada Mary Bryant Irvine, formerly of St Agnes, Cornwall; *m* 1945, Valborg Cecilie, *d* of late P. F. Carslund; two *d*. *Educ:* Upper Canada Coll.; St Paul's Sch.; Magdalen Coll., Oxford (MA). Sec. Oxford Union Soc., 1931. Called to Bar, Inner Temple, 1932. Chm. Agricultural Land Tribunal, SE Province, 1954-56. Mem. Executive Cttee, East Sussex NFU, 1947-; Branch Chm., 1956-58. Chm. Young Conservative Union, 1946-47; Prospective Candidate, Bewdley Div. of Worcs, 1947-49; contested Wood Green and Lower Tottenham, 1951. PPS to Minister of Education and to Parly Sec., Ministry of Education, 1957-59, to the Financial Sec. to the Treasury, 1959-60. Mem., Speaker's Panel of Chairmen, House of Commons, 1965-76; a Dep. Chm. of Ways and Means, and a Deputy Speaker, 1976-82; Jt Sec., Exec. Cttee, 1922 Cttee, 1965-68, Hon. Treasurer, 1974-76; Vice-Chm., Cons. Agric. Cttee, and spoke on Agriculture from Opposition Front Bench, 1964-70; Mem., House of Commons Select Cttee on Agriculture, 1967-69; Commonwealth Parliamentary Association: Hon. Treasurer, 1970-73; Mem., General Council, 1970-73; Mem., Exec. Cttee, UK Branch, 1964-76; Jt Sec. or Vice-Chm., Cons. Commonwealth Affairs Cttee, 1957-66; Jt Sec., Foreign and Commonwealth Affairs Cttee, 1967-73 (Vice-Chm., 1973-76); Chm., Cons. Horticulture Sub-Cttee, 1960-62; All Party Tourist and Resort Cttee, 1964-66; Pres., British Resorts Assoc., 1962-80. Served War of 1939-45, Lt-Comdr RNVR, afloat and on staff of C-in-C Western Approaches and Commander US Naval Forces in Europe. Comp. InstCE, 1936-74. *Recreations:* ski-ing, travel by sea. *Address:* Great Ote Hall, Burgess Hill, West Sussex. *T:* Burgess Hill 2179; 91 Millbank Court, 24 John Islip Street, SW1. *T:* 01-834 9221; 2 Dr Johnson's Buildings, Temple, EC4. *Clubs:* Carlton, Pratt's, Naval; Dormy House (Rye).

IRVINE, Dr Donald Hamilton, OBE 1979; FRCGP; Principal in General Practice, Ashington, since 1960; Regional Adviser in General Practice, University of Newcastle, since 1973; *b* 2 June 1935; *s* of Dr Andrew Bell Hamilton Irvine and Dorothy Mary Irvine; *m* 1960, Margaret Mary McGuckin; two *s* one *d*. *Educ:* King Edward Sixth Grammar Sch., Morpeth; Medical Sch., King's Coll., Univ. of Durham (MB BS); DObstRCOG 1960; MD Newcastle 1964; FRCGP 1972 (MRCGP 1965). Ho. Phys. to Dr C. N. Armstrong and Dr Henry Miller, 1958-59. Vice-Chm. Council, RCGP, 1981-; Hon. Sec. of the College, 1972-78; Jt Hon. Sec., Jt Cttee on Postgraduate Trng for General Practice, 1976-; Fellow, BMA, 1976; Mem., Gen. Medical Council, 1979-; Governor, MSD Foundn, 1982-. Vice-Pres., Medical Defence Union, 1974-78; Vis. Professor in Family Practice, Univ. of Iowa, USA, 1973; (first) Vis. Prof. to Royal Australian Coll. of General Practitioners, 1977; Vis. Cons. on Postgrad. Educn for Family Medicine to Virginia Commonwealth Univ., 1971, Univ. of Wisconsin-Madison, 1973, Medical Univ. of S Carolina, 1974. *Publications:* The Future General Practitioner: learning and teaching, (jtly), 1972 (RCGP); chapters to several books on gen. practice; papers on clinical and educnl studies in medicine, in BMJ, Lancet, Jl of RCGP. *Recreations:* bird watching, motor cars, politics, watching television. *Address:* Redesdale, Wansbeck Road, Ashington NE63 8JE. *T:* Ashington 813139.

IRVINE, Surg. Captain Gerard Sutherland, CBE 1970; RN retired; Medical Officer, Department of Health and Social Security, 1971-78; *b* 19 June 1913; *s* of Major Gerard Byrom Corrie Irvine and Maud Andrée (*née* Wylde); *m*

1939, Phyllis Lucy Lawrie; one *s*. *Educ:* Imperial Service Coll., Windsor; Epsom Coll.; University Coll. and Hosp., London. MRCS, LRCP, MB, BS 1937; DLO 1940; FRCS 1967. Jenks Meml Schol. 1932; Liston Gold Medal for Surgery 1936. Surg. Sub-Lt RNVR 1935, Surg. Lt RNVR 1937; Surg Lt RN 1939; Surg. Lt-Comdr 1944; Surg. Comdr 1953; Surg. Capt. 1963. Served War of 1939-45 (1939-45 Star, Atlantic Star with Bar for France and Germany, Burma Star, Defence Medal, Victory Medal); subseq. service: Ceylon, 1946; Haslar, 1947-49 and 1957-60; Malta, 1953-56; HMS: Maidstone (Submarine Depot Ship), 1949-51; Osprey (T&A/S Trng Sch.), 1951-53; Collingwood, 1956-57; Lion, 1960-62; Vernon (Torpedo Sch.), 1962-63; Sen. Cons. in ENT, 1953-70; Adviser in ENT to Med. Dir-Gen. (Navy), 1966-70; Sen. MO i/c Surgical Div., RN Hosp. Haslar, 1966-70; QHS 1969-70; retd 1970. Member: BMA 1938; Sections of Otology and Laryngology, RSM, 1948-77 (FRSM 1948-77); British Assoc. of Otolaryngologists, 1945-71 (Council, 1958-70); S Western Laryngological Assoc., 1951-71; Hearing Sub-Cttee of RN Personnel Res. Cttee, 1947-70; Otological Sub-Cttee of RAF Flying Personnel Res. Cttee, 1963-70. OStJ 1969. *Publications:* numerous articles in various medical jls. *Recreations:* gardening, philately, do-it-yourself. *Address:* 9 Alvara Road, Alverstoke, Gosport PO12 2HY. *T:* Gosport 80342.

IRVINE, James Eccles Malise; His Honour Judge Irvine; a Circuit Judge, since 1972; *b* 10 July 1925; *y s* of late Brig.-Gen. A. E. Irvine, CB, CMG, DSO, Wotton-under-Edge; *m* 1954, Anne, *e d* of late Col G. Egerton-Warburton, DSO, TD, JP, DL, Grafton Hall, Malpas; one *s* one *d*. *Educ:* Stowe Sch. (Scholar); Merton Coll., Oxford (Postmaster). MA Oxon. Served Grenadier Guards, 1943-46 (France and Germany Star); Hon. Captain Grenadier Guards, 1946. Called to Bar, Inner Temple, 1949 (Poland Prizeman in Criminal Law, 1949); practised Oxford Circuit, 1949-71; Prosecuting Counsel for Inland Revenue on Oxford Circuit, 1965-71; Dep. Chm., Glos QS, 1967-71. Lay Judge of Court of Arches of Canterbury and Chancery Court of York, 1981-. *Publication:* Parties and Pleasures: the Diaries of Helen Graham 1823-26, 1957. *Address:* 2 Harcourt Buildings, Temple, EC4; c/o Oxford County Court, Harcourt House, Marston Road, Oxford OX3 0EF.

IRVINE, Maj.-Gen. John, OBE 1955; Director of Medical Services, British Army of the Rhine, 1973-75; *b* 31 May 1914; *s* of late John Irvine and late Jessie Irvine (*née* McKinnon); *m* 1941, Mary McNicol, *d* of late Andrew Brown Cossar, Glasgow; one *d*. *Educ:* Glasgow High Sch.; Glasgow Univ. MB, ChB 1940. MFCM 1973. Commnd into RAMC, 1940; served War of 1939-45 (despatches and Act of Gallantry, 1944): Egypt, Greece, Crete, Western Desert, 1941-43; Sicily, Italy and Yugoslavia, 1943-45; served with British Troops, Austria, 1947-49; Korea, 1953-54 (OBE); Malaya, 1954-56 (despatches); Germany, 1958-61; Ghana, 1961; Germany, 1962-64; DDMS, HQ BAOR, 1968-69; DDMS, 1st British Corps, 1969-71; Dep. Dir-Gen., AMS, 1971-73. QHS 1972-75. OStJ 1971. *Recreations:* tennis, ski-ing. *Address:* PO Box 1962, Limassol, Cyprus.

IRVINE, John Ferguson; Permanent Secretary, Department of the Environment for Northern Ireland, since 1981; *b* 13 Nov. 1920; *s* of Joseph Ferguson Irvine and Helen Gardner; *m* 1st, 1945, Doris Partridge (*d* 1973); one *s* one *d* ; 2nd, 1980, Christine Margot Tudor; one *s* and two step *s*. *Educ:* Ardrossan Acad.; Glasgow Univ. (MA). RAF, 1944-46; Scottish Home Dept, 1946-48; NI Civil Service, 1948-66; Chief Exec., Ulster Transport Authority, 1966-68; Chief Exec., NI Transport Holding Co., 1968; NI Civil Service, 1969-; Dep. Sec., DoE, NI, 1971-76; Permanent Secretary: attached NI Office, 1977-80; Dept of Manpower Services, 1980-81. Chm. Management Cttee, 1974-75, and Vice-Chm. General Council, 1975, Action Cancer; Chm., NI Marriage Guidance Council, 1976-78. *Recreations:* distance running, yoga, Majorca, football. *Address:* Department of the Environment, Stormont, Belfast 4.

IRVINE, Very Rev. (John) Murray; Provost and Rector of Southwell Minster, since 1978; *b* 19 Aug. 1924; *s* of Andrew Leicester Irvine and Eleanor Mildred (*née* Lloyd); *m* 1961, Pamela Shirley Brain; one *s* three *d*. *Educ:* Charterhouse; Magdalene Coll., Cambridge; Ely Theological Coll. BA 1946, MA 1949. Deacon, 1948; Priest, 1949; Curate of All Saints, Poplar, 1948-53; Chaplain of Sidney Sussex Coll., Cambridge, 1953-60; Selection Sec. of CACTM, 1960-65; Canon Residentiary, Prebendary of Hunderton, Chancellor and Librarian of Hereford Cathedral, and Dir of Ordination Training, Diocese of Hereford, 1965-78; Warden of Readers, 1976-78. *Address:* The Residence, Vicars Court, Southwell, Notts NG25 0HP. *T:* Southwell 812593.

IRVINE, Norman Forrest, QC 1973; a Recorder of the Crown Court, since 1974; *b* 29 Sept. 1922; *s* of William Allan Irvine and Dorcas Forrest; *m* 1964, Mary Lilian Patricia Edmunds (*née* Constable); one *s*. *Educ:* High Sch. of Glasgow; Glasgow Univ. BL 1941. Solicitor (Scotland), 1943. Served War, 1942-45: Lieut Royal Signals, Staff Captain. HM Claims Commn, 1945-46; London Claims Supt, Provincial Insurance Co. Ltd, 1950-52. Called to Bar, Gray's Inn, 1955. *Recreations:* reading, piano, walking, swimming. *Address:* (chambers) 2 Garden Court, Temple, EC4Y 9BL.

IRVINE, Dr Robin Orlando Hamilton, FRCP, FRACP; Vice-Chancellor, University of Otago, Dunedin, New Zealand, since 1973; *b* 15 Sept. 1929; *s* of late Claude Turner Irvine; *m* 1957, Elizabeth Mary, *d* of late Herbert Gray Corbett; one *s* two *d*. *Educ:* Wanganui Collegiate Sch.; Univ. of Otago. Otago University Med. Sch., 1948-53; MB, ChB, 1953; MD (NZ), 1958;

FRCP, FRACP. House Phys., Auckland Hosp., 1954; Dept of Medicine, Univ. of Otago: Research Asst (Emily Johnston Res. Schol.), 1955; Asst Lectr and Registrar, 1956-57. Leverhulme Research Scholar, Middlesex Hosp., London, 1958; Registrar, Postgraduate Medical Sch., London, 1959-60; Isaacs Medical Research Fellow, Auckland Hosp., 1960-61; Med. Tutor and Med. Specialist, Auckland Hosp., 1962-63; Lectr, Sen. Lectr in Med., Univ. of Otago, 1963-67; Associate Prof., 1968; Clinical Dean and Personal Professor, Univ. of Otago Medical Sch., 1969-72. Consultant, Asian Development Bank, 1974-. Member: Selwyn Coll. Bd, 1966-; Pharmacology and Therapeutic Cttee, Min. of Health, 1967-73; Otago Hosp. Bd, 1969-; Med. Educn Cttee of Med. Council of NZ, 1969-73; Cent. Educn Cttee, NZ Med. Assoc., 1970-73; Social Council of Nat. Develt Council of NZ, 1971-74; Cttee on Nursing Educn, Min. of Educn, 1972; Social Develt Council, 1974-79; Commn for the Future, 1976-80; NZ Planning Council, 1977-; Council, Assoc. of Commonwealth Univs, 1979-80; Otago Polytech. Council, 1973-; Dunedin Teachers Coll. Council, 1973-; NZ Adv. Cttee, Nuffield Foundn, 1973-; NZ Rhodes Scholarships Selection Cttee, 1976-; Chairman: Otago Med. Res. Foundn, 1975-81; Ministerial working party on novel genetic techniques, 1977; NZ Vice-Chancellors' Cttee, 1979-80; Convenor, Med. Educn Mission to Univ. of S Pacific, 1971; Trustee: McMillan Trust, 1973- (Chm., 1977-); Rowheath Trust, 1973-. Hon. ADC 1969, and Hon. Physician 1970, to the Governor-General, Sir Arthur Porritt. Hon. Mem., Australian Soc. of Nephrology. Dr *hc* Edinburgh, 1976. FRSA 1980. Mem. Editorial Bd, Jl of Molecular Medicine. *Publications:* various papers on high blood pressure, renal med. and medical educn. *Recreations:* walking, reading, music. *Address:* University Lodge, St Leonards, Dunedin, New Zealand. *T:* 710.541. *Club:* Fernhill (Dunedin).

IRVINE, Rev. Thomas Thurstan; Rector of St John's, Perth, since 1966; *b* 19 June 1913; 5th *s* of late William Fergusson Irvine; *m* 1943, Elizabeth Marian, *er d* of late Francis More, CA, Edinburgh; five *d. Educ:* Shrewsbury; Magdalen Coll., Oxford. BA 2nd Class History, 1934; Diploma in Theology, 1935; MA 1938. Cuddesdon Coll., 1937; deacon, 1938, priest, 1939, St Albans; Curate, All Saints, Hertford, 1938-40; Precentor, St Ninian's Cathedral, Perth, 1940-43; Priest in charge, Lochgelly, 1943-45; Rector of Bridge of Allan, 1945-47; Rector of Callander, 1947-66; Examining Chaplain to Bishop of St Andrews, 1950; Dean of United Diocese of St Andrews, Dunkeld and Dunblane, 1959-82. *Recreations:* fishing, walking. *Address:* St John's Rectory, Dupplin Terrace, Perth. *T:* Perth 21379.

IRVINE SMITH, Thomas, OBE 1945; DL; *b* 27 Oct. 1908; *er s* of late Sir Thomas Smith and of Lady (Elsie) Smith (*née* Ledgard); *m* 1942, Mary Peters (*d* 1981). *Educ:* Fettes Coll., Edinburgh; Oriel Coll., Oxford. MA 1935. War Service, 1941-45; commnd 8th Gurkha Rifles; GHQ, MEF; ME Supply Centre, 1943; Liaison Officer with Govt of India, 1944-45; Lt-Col 1945. Business in Cawnpore, India, 1931-47; Mem. London Stock Exchange, 1949-69. Surrey County Council: Mem., 1955-77; Alderman, 1965-74; Vice-Chm., 1969-72; Chm., 1972-74; 1st Chm. of re-constituted Council, 1973-75; Chm., Surrey Educn Cttee, 1965-72. Member: Court, London Univ., 1967-78; Council, Surrey Univ., 1966- (Chm., 1975-79, Vice-Chm., 1980-82); Council, Royal Holloway Coll., 1970-79; Murray Cttee, London Univ., 1970-72; Governor: Ottershaw Sch., 1959-77 (Chm. 1961-72); Gordon Boys' Sch., 1965-. DL Surrey, 1973; High Sheriff, Surrey, 1976-77. *Recreation:* gardening. *Address:* Thorney, Onslow Road, Sunningdale, Berks SL5 0HW. *T:* Ascot 22334.

IRVING, family name of **Baron Irving of Dartford.**

IRVING OF DARTFORD, Baron *cr* 1979 (Life Peer), of Dartford in the County of Kent; **Sydney Irving;** PC 1969; DL; *b* 1 July 1918; *s* of Sydney Irving, Newcastle upon Tyne; *m* 1942, Mildred, *d* of Charlton Weedy, Morpeth, Northumberland; one *s* one *d* (and one *s* decd). *Educ:* Pendower Sch., Newcastle upon Tyne; London School of Economics, University of London. BSc (Econ.); DipEd. War Service, 1939-46: West Yorks Regt, Major. Chairman Southern Regional Council of Labour Party, 1965-67. Alderman, Dartford Borough Council; Mem. North-West Kent Divisional Executive, Kent Education Cttee, 1952-74. MP (Lab and Co-op) Dartford, 1955-70 and Feb. 1974-1979; Opposition Whip (S and S Western), 1959-64; Treasurer of the Household and Deputy Chief Government Whip, 1964-66; Dep. Chm. of Ways and Means, 1966-68; Chm. of Ways and Means, and Deputy Speaker, 1968-70; Chairman Select Committees: on Procedure, 1974-79; on Direct Elections to EEC, 1976-77; Chm., Manifesto Gp, 1976-77; Member: Cttee of Privileges, 1974-79; Select Cttee on Members' Interests, 1974-79; Select Cttee on the Member for Walsall, 1975; Liaison Cttee, Parly Lab Party, 1976-79. Mem. CPA delegations: to Hong Kong and Ceylon, 1958; to Council of Europe and WEU, 1963-64; to Canada, 1974; Leader All Party Delegn: to Malta, 1965; to Israel, 1975; to Australia, 1978. Mem. Exec. Cttee, Council European Municipalities 1972-77. Chairman: Dartford Dist Council, 1973-74; Dartford and Darenth Hosp. Management Cttee, 1972-74; Kent County Jt Cttee Chairman, 1957-77. Vice-Chm., Nat. Assoc. of CAB, 1979-. Pres., Thames-side Assoc. of Teachers, NUT, 1955; Mem. Min. of Education's Adv. Cttee on Handicapped Children, 1957-67; a Dep. Pro-Chancellor, Univ. of Kent, 1968-71; Dir, Foundn Fund, Univ. of Kent, 1971-74. Chm., Industry and Parlt Trust, 1982-. DL Kent, 1979. *Address:* 10 Tynedale Close, Dartford, Kent. *T:* 25105.

IRVING, Charles Graham; MP (C) Cheltenham, since Oct. 1974; Director of Public Relations, Dowty Group Ltd (46 companies), since 1947; County

and District Councillor. *Educ:* Glengarth Sch., Cheltenham; Lucton Sch., Hereford. Mem. Cheltenham Borough Council, 1947-74 (Alderman 1959-May 1967, and Sept. 1967-74); Mem., Cheltenham DC, 1974-; Mem. Gloucestershire CC, 1948- (Chm., Social Services Cttee, 1974-); Mayor of Cheltenham, 1958-60 and 1971-72; Dep. Mayor, 1959-63; Alderman of Gloucestershire County, 1965-74; Contested (C): Bilston, Staffs, 1970; Kingswood, Glos, Feb. 1974; Member Cons. Parly Cttees: Aviation; Social Services; Mem., Select Cttee on Administration; Vice-Chm., All Party Cttee CHAR; Chairman: Select Cttee on Catering, 1979-; All Party Mental Health Cttee, 1979-. Pres., Cheltenham Young Conservatives. Dir, Cheltenham Art and Literary Festival Co. (responsible for the only contemp. Festival of Music in England); Founder Mem., Univ. Cttee for Gloucestershire; Pres., Cheltenham and Dist Hotels' Assoc. Member: Bridgehead Housing Assoc. Ltd; Nat. Council for the Care and Resettlement of Offenders (Nat. Dep. Chm., 1974); (Chm.) NACRO Regional Council for South West; Nat. Council of St Leonard's Housing Assoc. Ltd; (Chm.) SW Midlands Housing Assoc. Ltd; SW Regional Hosp. Bd, 1971-72; Glos AHA, 1974-; (Chm.) Cheltenham and Dist Housing Assoc. Ltd, 1972; (Chm.) Cheltenham Dist Local Govt Re-Organisation Cttee, 1972; Founder and Chm., Nat. Victims Assoc., 1973; Chm., Stonham Housing Assoc., 1976-. Chairman: Irving Hotels Ltd; Irving Engineering Co. Mem. NUJ; MIPR 1964. Freedom, Borough of Cheltenham, 1977. *Publications:* pamphlets (as Chm. SW Region of NACRO and SW Midlands Housing Assoc. Ltd, 1970-73) include: Prisoner and Industry; After-care in the Community; Penal Budgeting; What about the Victim; Dosser's Dream—Planner's Nightmare. Pioneered Frontsheet (1st prison newspaper); reported in national papers, Quest, Social Services, Glos. Life, etc. *Recreations:* antiques, social work. *Address:* Drake House, Malvern Road, Cheltenham, Glos. *T:* Cheltenham 23083. *Club:* St Stephen's Constitutional.

IRVING, Clifford; *see* Irving, E. C.

IRVING, David Blair; Chairman, London Electricity Board, 1956-68; *b* 9 Nov. 1903; *s* of late Mitchell B. Irving, Sorn, Ayrshire, and Mary Ross, Broadford, Isle of Skye; *m* 1933, Isabel Gibson; one *s. Educ:* Ayr Academy. BSc Hons (London), 1923. British Thomson-Houston Co. Ltd; trained Rugby; subseq. positions in London, Sheffield, Bombay and Calcutta. Joined Central Electricity Bd, 1932, and London Electricity Bd at Vesting Day, 1 April 1948: Chief Engineer, 1949-53; Dep. Chm., 1953-56. MIEE, 1945; FIEE, 1966; Mem. Société des Ingénieurs Civils de France, 1949-70; Mem. Royal Institution, 1957-69. Chm., British Electrical Development Assoc., 1960-61; Chm., Power Division IEE, 1962-63. Governor, Ashridge Management Coll., 1965-68. *Publications:* papers to British and internat. engineering and scientific bodies. *Recreation:* golf. *Address:* Nettlecombe, Poughill, Bude, North Cornwall. *T:* Bude 3496. *Club:* Caledonian.

IRVING, Rear-Adm. Sir Edmund (George), KBE 1966 (OBE 1944); CB 1962; Hydrographer of the Navy, 1960-66, retired; *b* 5 April 1910; *s* of George Clerk Irving, British North Borneo, and Ethel Mary Frances (*née* Poole), Kimberley, SA; *m* 1st, 1936, Margaret Scudamore Edwards (*d* 1974); one *s* one *d*; 2nd, 1979, Esther Rebecca Ellison. *Educ:* St Anthony's, Eastbourne; RN College, Dartmouth. Joined HMS Royal Oak, as Cadet and Midshipman, 1927; Sub-Lieut's Courses, 1930-31; HMS Kellett Surveying Service, Dec. 1931 (various surveying ships); HMS Franklin, in command, 1944; Hydrographic Dept, 1946; HMS Sharpshooter, in command, 1948; Hydrographic Dept, 1949; HMS Dalrymple, in command, 1950; HMS Vidal, in command, 1953; Hydrographic Dept, Asst Hydrographer, 1954; HMS Vidal, in command, Oct. 1956; Hydrographic Dept, Asst Hydrographer, 1959. Acting Conservator of the River Mersey, 1975-. ADC, 1960. Trustee, Nat. Maritime Museum, 1972-81. FRGS; FRICS; FRSA. Patron's Medal, RGS, 1976. *Recreation:* golf. *Address:* Camer Green, Meopham, Kent DA13 0XR. *T:* Meopham 813253. *Club:* Army and Navy.

IRVING, Edward, ScD; FRS 1979; FRSC 1973; FRAS; Research Scientist, Pacific Geoscience Centre, Sidney, BC, since 1981; *b* 27 May 1927; *s* of George Edward and Nellie Irving; *m* 1957, Sheila Ann Irwin; two *s* two *d. Educ:* Colne Grammar Sch.; Cambridge Univ., 1948-54 (BA, MA, MSc, ScD). Served Army, 1945-48. Research Fellow, Fellow and Sen. Fellow, ANU, 1954-64; Dominion Observatory, Canada, 1964-66; Prof. of Geophysics, Univ. of Leeds, 1966-67; Res. Scientist, Dominion Observatory, later Earth Physics Br., Dept of Energy, Mines and Resources, Ottawa, 1967-81; Adjunct Prof., Carleton Univ., Ottawa, 1975-81. FRAS 1958; Fellow: Amer. Geophysical Union, 1976 (Walter H. Bucher Medal, 1979); Geological Soc. of America, 1979. Gondwanaland Medal, Mining, Geological and Metallurgical Soc. of India, 1962; Logan Medal, Geol Assoc. of Canada, 1975. Hon. DSc Carleton, 1979. *Publications:* Paleomagnetism, 1964; numerous contribs to learned jls. *Recreations:* gardening, carpentry, choral singing. *Address:* Pacific Geoscience Centre, 9860 West Saanich Road, Box 6000, Sidney, BC V8R 6C8, Canada. *T:* (604) 656-8438.

IRVING, (Edward) Clifford, CBE 1981; Chairman, Executive Council, Isle of Man Government 1977-81 (Member, 1968-81); Member, House of Keys, 1955-61 and 1966-81, Acting Speaker, 1971-81; *b* 24 May 1914; *s* of late William Radcliffe Irving and Mabel Henrietta (*née* Cottier); *m* 1941, Nora, *d* of Harold Page, Luton; one *s* one *d. Educ:* Isle of Man; Canada. Member, IOM Government Boards: Airports, 1955-58; Assessment, 1955-56; Social Security, 1956; Local Govt, 1956-62; Tourist, 1956-62; Finance, 1966-71; Member: Industrial Adv. Council, 1961-62, 1971-81; CS Commn, 1976-81.

Chairman: IOM Tourist Bd, 1971-81; IOM Sports Council, 1971-81. President: IOM Assoc. of Veteran Athletes; Wanderers Male Voice Choir; Patron: Manx Variety Club; IOM TT Races. *Recreations:* powerboating, angling. *Address:* Highfield, Belmont Hill, Douglas, Isle of Man. *T:* Douglas 3652.

IRVING, Prof. Harry Munroe Napier Hetherington; Professor of Inorganic and Structural Chemistry, University of Leeds, 1961-71, Professor Emeritus, since 1972; Professor of Analytical Science, University of Cape Town, since 1979 (of Theoretical Chemistry, 1978); *b* 19 Nov. 1905; *s* of John and Clara Irving; *m* 1st, 1934, Monica Mary Wildsmith (*d* 1972); no *c* ; 2nd, 1975, Dr Anne Mawby. *Educ:* St Bees Sch., Cumberland; The Queen's Coll., Oxford. BA 1927; First Class in Final Honour Sch. (Chemistry), 1928; MA, DPhil 1930; DSc 1958 (all Oxon); LRAM 1930. Univ. Demonstrator in Chemistry, Oxford, 1934-61; Lectr in Organic Chemistry, The Queen's Coll., 1930-34; Fellow and Tutor, St Edmund Hall, 1938-51; Vice-Principal, 1951-61; Emeritus-Fellow, 1961-. Member: Chem. Soc. 1935- (Council, 1954, Perkin Elmer Award, 1974); Soc. Chm. Ind., 1935- (Gold Medal, 1980); Soc. for Analytical Chemists, 1950- (Council, 1952-57, 1965-67; Vice-Pres. 1955-57; Gold Medal, 1971); Fellow Royal Inst. of Chemistry, 1948- (Council, 1950-52, 1962-65; Vice-Pres. 1965-67); Mem., S African Chem. Inst., 1979. Has lectured extensively in America, Africa and Europe; broadcasts on scientific subjects. FRSSAf. Hon. DTech Brunel Univ., 1970. *Publications:* (trans.) Schwarzenbach and Flaschka's Complexometric Titrations; Short History of Analytical Chemistry, 1974; Dithizone, 1977; numerous papers in various learned jls. *Recreations:* music, foreign travel, ice-skating. *Address:* 1 North Grange Mount, Leeds LS6 2BY.

IRVING, James Tutin, MA Oxon and Cantab, MD, PhD Cantab; Professor of Physiology in the School of Dental Medicine at Harvard University and the Forsyth Dental Center, 1961-68, Professor Emeritus, 1968, Visiting Lecturer in Oral Biology, 1973-77; Emeritus Professor, National Institute on Aging, Baltimore, 1978-81; *b* Christchurch, New Zealand, 3 May 1902; *m* 1937, Janet, *d* of Hon. Nicholas O'Connor, New York. *Educ:* Christ's Coll., New Zealand; Caius Coll., Cambridge; Trinity Coll., Oxford; Guy's Hospital. Double First Class Hons, Nat. Sci. Tripos, Cambridge, 1923-24; Scholar and Prizeman, Caius Coll., 1923; Benn. W. Levy and Frank Smart Student, 1924-26; Beit Memorial Fellow, 1926-28; Lecturer in Physiology, Bristol Univ., 1931, and Leeds Univ., 1934; Head of Physiology Dept, Rowett Research Inst., and part-time lecturer, Aberdeen Univ., 1936; Prof. of Physiology, Cape Town Univ., 1939-53, Fellow 1948; Professor of Experimental Odontology, and Dir of the Joint CSIR and Univ. of Witwatersrand Dental Research Unit, 1953-59; Prof. of Anatomy, Harvard Sch. of Dental Med., 1959-61. Visiting Professor: Univ. of Illinois Dental Sch. 1947 and 1956; Univ. of Pennsylvania, 1951; Univ. of California, 1956. Chm., Gordon Conference on Bone and Teeth, 1969. Editor, Archives of Oral Biology, 1962-. AM (Hon.) Harvard. Late Hon. Physiologist to Groote Schuur Hosp.; Fellow Odont. Soc. S Africa. Hon. Life Mem. of New York Academy of Sciences. Mem. of Soc. of Sigma Xi. Hon. Mem. of Soc. of Omicron Kappa Upsilon. S African Medal for war services (non-military), 1948. Isaac Schour Meml Award for Res. in Anatomical Scis, 1972. *Publications:* Calcium Metabolism, 1957; Calcium and Phosphorus Metabolism, 1973; many papers in physiological and medical journals, chiefly on nutrition, and bone and tooth formation; also publications on nautical history. *Recreations:* music, gardening, nautical research. *Address:* (home) 5 Peele House Square, Manchester, Mass 01944, USA; (office) 140 The Fenway, Boston, Mass 02115, USA. *Club:* Inanda (Johannesburg).

IRVING, Prof. John; Freeland Professor of Natural Philosophy (Theoretical Physics), University of Strathclyde, Glasgow, since 1961; *b* 22 Dec. 1920; *s* of John Irving and Margaret Kent Aird; *m* 1948, Monica Cecilia Clarke; two *s. Educ:* St John's Grammar Sch.; Hamilton Academy; Glasgow Univ. MA (1st Class Hons in Maths and Nat. Phil.), Glasgow Univ., 1940; PhD (Mathematical Physics), Birmingham Univ., 1951. FInstP 1980. Lectr, Stow Coll., Glasgow, 1944-45; Lectr in Maths, Univ. of St Andrews 1945-46; Lectr in Mathematical Physics, University of Birmingham, 1946-49; Nuffield Research Fellow (Nat. Phil.), University of Glasgow, 1949-51; Sen. Lectr in Applied Maths, University of Southampton, 1951-59; Prof. of Theoretical Physics and Head of Dept of Applied Mathematics and Theor. Physics University of Cape Town, 1959-61. Dean of Sch. of Mathematics and Physics, Strathclyde Univ., 1964-69. *Publications:* Mathematics in Physics and Engineering, 1959 (New York); contrib. to: Proc. Physical Soc.; Philosophical Magazine, Physical Review. *Recreations:* gardening, motoring. *Address:* Department of Natural Philosophy, University of Strathclyde, John Anderson Building, 107 Rotten Row, Glasgow G4 0NG. *T:* 041-552 4400.

IRVING, Laurence Henry Forster, OBE; RDI 1939; *b* 11 April 1897; *s* of late H. B. Irving, actor and author; *m* 1920, Rosalind Woolner (*d* 1978); one *s* one *d. Educ:* by Thomas Pellatt; Royal Academy Schools. Served in RNAS and RAF, 1914-19 (Croix de Guerre, France); rejoined RAF Oct. 1939; served on Staff of British Air Forces in France, 1940 (despatches), and in 2nd Tactical Air Force, France, Belgium, 1943-44. Dir of the Times Publishing Co., 1946-62. Exhibited pictures at Royal Academy; held four exhibitions at the Fine Art Soc., 1925, 1928, 1936, 1950, and at Agnew and Sons, 1957; Art Dir to Douglas Fairbanks, 1928 and 1929, for film productions of The Iron Mask and The Taming of the Shrew; has designed a number of stage and film productions, including Pygmalion, Lean Harvest, The Good Companions, Punchinello, The First Gentleman, Marriage à la Mode, Hamlet (Old Vic),

1950, Man and Superman, 1951; The Happy Marriage, 1952; Pygmalion, 1953; The Wild Duck, 1955; produced and designed film production of Lefanu's Uncle Silas. Master of Faculty, RDI, 1963-65. *Publications:* Windmills and Waterways, 1927; Henry Irving; The Actor and his World, 1951; The Successors, 1967; The Precarious Crust, 1971; edited and illustrated: The Maid of Athens; Bligh's narrative of The Mutiny of the Bounty; A Selection of Hakluyt's Voyages; illustrated: Masefield's Philip the King; Conrad's The Mirror of the Sea; St Exupery's Flight to Arras. *Address:* The Lea, Wittersham, Kent. *Club:* Garrick.

See also Sir Felix Brunner.

IRVING, Robert Augustine, DFC and Bar, 1943; Musical Director, New York City Ballet, New York, 1958; *b* 28 Aug. 1913; *s* of late R. L. G. Irving; unmarried. *Educ:* Winchester; New Coll., Oxford; Royal College of Music. Répétiteur, Royal Opera House, 1936; Music master, Winchester Coll., 1936-40. RA, 1940-41; RAF (Coastal Command), 1941-45. Associate Conductor, BBC Scottish Orchestra, 1945-48; Conductor, Royal Opera House (The Royal Ballet), 1949-58. Many recordings for HMV and Decca, with Philharmonia and Royal Philharmonic Orchestras, also public concerts with these orchestras, London Philharmonic Orchestra and leading Amer. symphony orchestras. Wrote music for film, Floodtide, 1948; for New York production of As You Like It, 1949. *Recreations:* racing, bridge, mountaineering. *Address:* c/o New York City Ballet, New York State Theatre, Columbus Avenue and 62nd Street, New York, NY 10023, USA. *Club:* Brooks's.

IRWIN, Lord; James Charles Wood; *b* 24 Aug. 1977; *s* and *heir* of 3rd Earl of Halifax, *qv*.

IRWIN, Maj.-Gen. Brian St George, CB 1975; Director General, Ordnance Survey, 1969-77, retired; *b* 16 Sept. 1917; *s* of late Lt-Col Alfred Percy Bulteel Irwin, DSO, and late Eileen Irwin (*née* Holberton); *m* 1939, Audrey Lilla, *d* of late Lt-Col H. B. Steen, IMS; two *s. Educ:* Rugby Sch.; RMA Woolwich; Trinity Hall, Cambridge (MA). Commnd in RE, 1937; war service in Western Desert, 1941-43 (despatches); Sicily and Italy, 1943-44 (despatches); Greece, 1944-45; subseq. in Cyprus, 1956-59 (despatches) and 1961-63; Dir of Military Survey, MoD, 1965-69. Col Comdt, RE, 1977-82. FRICS (Council 1969-70, 1972-76); FRGS (Council 1966-70; Vice-Pres., 1974-77). *Recreations:* sailing, gardening, genealogy. *Address:* 16 Northerwood House, Swan Green, Lyndhurst, Hants SO4 7DT. *T:* Lyndhurst 3499. *Club:* Army and Navy.

IRWIN, Francis (Charles), QC 1974; a Recorder (formerly Recorder of Folkestone), since 1971; *b* 5 June 1928; *s* of late R. Stanley Irwin; *m* 1955, Rosalind Derry Wykes, *d* of late Canon W. M. Wykes, Sedgefield, Co. Durham; four *s* one *d. Educ:* Glasgow Academy; Queen's Coll., Oxford (Scholar, BA). Served in Army, 1946-48. Called to Bar, Middle Temple, 1953; SE Circuit. Prosecuting Counsel, GPO (SE Circuit), 1964-69; Dep. Chm., W Suffolk QS, 1967-71. Contested (C): Bridgeton Div. of Glasgow, 1950; Small Heath Div. of Birmingham, 1951. *Address:* 8 New Square, Lincoln's Inn, WC2A 3QP. *T:* 01-242 4986.

IRWIN, Ian Sutherland, CBE 1982; Deputy Chairman and Managing Director, Scottish Transport Group, since 1975; *b* Glasgow, 20 Feb. 1933; *s* of Andrew Campbell Irwin and Elizabeth Ritchie Arnott; *m* 1959, Margaret Miller Maureen Irvine; two *s. Educ:* Whitehill Sen. Secondary Sch., Glasgow; Glasgow Univ. BL; CA, IPFA, FCIT. Commercial Man., Scottish Omnibuses Ltd, 1960-64; Gp Accountant, Scottish Bus Gp, 1964-69; Gp Sec., Scottish Transport Gp, 1969-75; Scottish Bus Gp Ltd (and all subsids) and Caledonian MacBrayne Ltd (and all subsids): Exec. Dir, 1972-; Chm., 1975-; Director: Swan National (Scotland) Ltd, 1974; Nat. Bus Co., Nat. Bus Management Ltd, 1975; Scotcros Ltd, 1978. Pres., Confedn Brit. Road Passenger Transport, 1980-81; Vice-Pres., Internat. Union of Public Transport, 1981-; Mem. Council, CIT, 1978-. Governor, British Transport Staff Coll., 1976. CBIM. *Publications:* various papers. *Recreations:* squash, reading, gardening. *Address:* Baldornie, 4 Glenlockhart Bank, Edinburgh EH14 1BL. *T:* 031-443 2108. *Clubs:* Caledonian, MCC; Colinton Castle Sports.

IRWIN, Sir James (Campbell), Kt 1971; OBE 1945; ED 1947; psc; FRIBA, LFRAIA; Partner in Woods, Bagot, Laybourne-Smith & Irwin, Architects, Adelaide, 1930-74; *b* 23 June 1906; *s* of Francis James and Margaret Irwin; *m* 1933, Kathleen Agnes, *d* of G. W. Orr, Sydney; one *s* one *d. Educ:* Queen's Sch., N Adelaide; St Peter's Coll., Adelaide; St Mark's Coll., Univ. of Adelaide (Hon. Fellow, 1973). Served War, AIF, on active service in Middle East, New Guinea, Philippine Islands, 1940-46; Lt-Col RAA. Col Comdt, RAA, 1966-71. Mem. Adelaide City Council, 1935-72 (except for war years); Lord Mayor of Adelaide, 1963-66; Mem. Nat. Capital Planning Cttee, Canberra, 1964-70. President: RAIA, 1962-63; Adelaide Festival of Arts, 1964-66 (Chm. 1969-73); SA Sch. of Art, 1966-72; Home for Incurables, 1966-82; Pioneers Assoc. of S Australia, 1968-73. Chm., Co-op. Foundn, 1979-. *Publication:* The Irwin Family: Junior South Australian Branch, 1977. *Address:* 124 Brougham Place, North Adelaide, SA 5006, Australia. *T:* 2672839. *Clubs:* Adelaide, Naval Military and Air Force of SA (Adelaide).

IRWIN, John Conran; Keeper, Indian Section, Victoria and Albert Museum, 1959-78, with extended responsibility for new Oriental Department, 1970-78; *b* 5 Aug. 1917; *s* of late John Williamson Irwin; *m* 1947, Helen Hermione Scott (*née* Fletcher), *d* of late Herbert Bristowe Fletcher; three *s. Educ:*

Canford Sch., Wimborne, Dorset. Temp. commission, Gordon Highlanders, 1939. Private Sec. to Gov. of Bengal, 1942-45; Asst Keeper, Victoria and Albert Museum, 1946; Exec. Sec., Royal Academy Winter Exhibition of Indian Art, 1947-48; UNESCO Expert on museum planning: on mission to Indonesia, 1956; to Malaya, 1962. British Acad. Travelling Fellowship, 1974-75; Leverhulme Res. Fellow, 1978-80. Working with research grants from Leverhulme Trust and British Acad., 1978-. Lectures: Birdwood Meml, 1972; Tagore Meml, 1973; Lowell Inst., Boston, Mass, 1974; guest lectr, Collège de France, 1976; Dept of History of Religions, Univ. of Chicago, etc. FRSA 1972; FRAS 1946; FRAI 1977; FSA 1978. *Publications:* Jamini Roy, 1944; Indian art (section on sculpture), 1947; The Art of India and Pakistan (sections on bronzes and textiles), 1951, Shawls, 1955; Origins of Chintz, 1970; (with M. Hall) Indian Painted and Printed Fabrics, 1972; Indian Embroideries, 1974; articles in Encyclopædia Britannica, Chambers's Encyclopædia, Jl of Royal Asiatic Soc., Burlington Magazine, etc. *Recreations:* music, walking. *Address:* Ashford Chace, Steep, Petersfield, Hants GU32 1AB. *T:* Petersfield 4746.

IRWIN, Dr Michael Henry Knox; Senior Adviser (Childhood Disabilities) to the United Nations Children's Fund (UNICEF), since 1980; *b* 5 June 1931; *s* of late William Knox Irwin, FR.CS and of Edith Isabel Mary Irwin; *m* 1958, Elizabeth Miriam, *d* of late John and Nancie Naumann; three *d*. *Educ:* St Bartholomew's Hosp. Med. Coll., London (MB, BS 1955); Columbia Univ., New York (MPH 1960). House Phys. and House Surg., Prince of Wales' Hosp., London, 1955-56; MO, UN, 1957-61; Dep. Resident Rep., UN Technical Assistance Bd, Pakistan, 1961-63; MO, 1963-66, SMO, 1966-69, and Med. Dir, 1969-73, United Nations; Dir, Div. of Personnel, UNDP, 1973-76; UNICEF Rep., Bangladesh, 1977-80; Sen. Consultant, UN Internat. Year of Disabled Persons, 1981. Pres., Assistance for Blind Children Internat., 1978-. FRSM. *Publications:* Check-ups: safeguarding your health, 1961; Overweight: a problem for millions, 1964; Travelling without Tears, 1964; Viruses, Colds and Flu, 1966; Blood: new uses for saving lives, 1967; What Do We Know about Allergies?, 1972. *Recreations:* squash rackets, travelling, bicycling. *Address:* One West 89th Street, New York, NY 10024, USA. *T:* (212) 595-7714.

ISAAC, Alfred James; Chairman, Recruitment Boards, Civil Service Commission (part-time), since 1978; *b* 1 Aug. 1919; *s* of Alfred Jabez Isaac and Alice Marie Isaac (both British); *m* 1943, Beryl Marjorie Rist; one *s* two *d*. *Educ:* Maidenhead Grammar Sch. Post Office Engineering Dept, 1936-49. Served War, RAFVR, Flt Lt (pilot), Coastal Command, 1941-46. Min. of Works, Asst Principal, 1949; Regional Dir, Southern Region, 1960-67; Dir of Professional Staff Management, 1967; Dir of Home Regional Services, DoE, 1971-75. Business Coordinator, Danbury Drilling Ltd, 1977-78. Part-time Clerk, Bigbury Parish Council, 1981-. *Recreations:* amateur radio, cycling, fishing. *Address:* Wave Crest, Marine Drive, Bigbury on Sea, Kingsbridge, Devon TQ7 4AS. *T:* Bigbury on Sea 387. *Clubs:* Civil Service; Victoria.

ISAAC, Anthony John Gower; a Deputy Chairman, Board of Inland Revenue, since 1982 (a Commissioner of Inland Revenue, 1973-77 and since 1979); *b* 21 Dec. 1931; *s* of Ronald and Kathleen Mary Gower Isaac; *m* 1963, Olga Elizabeth Sibley; one *s* two *d* (and two *d* decd). *Educ:* Malvern Coll.; King's Coll., Cambridge (BA). HM Treasury, 1953-70: Private Sec. to Chief Sec. to Treasury, 1964-66; Inland Revenue, 1971; on secondment to HM Treasury, 1976-78. *Recreations:* gardening, fishing. *Address:* Moonsfield, Brenchley, Kent. *T:* Brenchley 2810.

ISAAC, James Keith, FCIT; Director General, West Midlands Passenger Transport Executive, since 1977; *b* 28 Jan. 1932; *s* of late Arthur Burton Isaac and of Doreen (*née* Davies); *m* 1957, Elizabeth Mary Roskell; two *d*. *Educ:* Leeds Grammar Sch. Mem., Inst. of Traffic Admin; FCIT 1978. Asst to Traffic Manager, Aldershot and Dist Traction Co. Ltd, 1958-59; Asst Traffic Man. Jamaica Omnibus Services Ltd, Kingston, Jamaica, 1959-64; Dep. Traffic Man., Midland Red (Birmingham and Midland Motor Omnibus Co. Ltd), Birmingham, 1965-67; Traffic Manager: North Western Road Car Co. Ltd, Stockport, Cheshire, 1967-69; Midland Red, Birmingham, 1969-73; Dir of Ops, W Midlands Passenger Transp. Exec., Birmingham, 1973-77. *Recreations:* golf, gardening, walking. *Address:* 24B Middlefield Lane, Hagley, Stourbridge, West Midlands DY9 0PX. *T:* Hagley 884757. *Clubs:* Army and Navy; Rotary of Hagley (Hereford/Worcester); Churchill and Blakedown Golf (near Kidderminster).

ISAAC, Maurice Laurence Reginald, MA; Headmaster, Latymer Upper School, Hammersmith, W6, since 1971; *b* 26 April 1928; *s* of late Frank and Lilian Isaac; *m* 1954, Anne Fielden; three *d*. *Educ:* Selhurst Grammar Sch., Croydon; Magdalene Coll., Cambridge. BA Hist. Tripos, 1950; MA 1955, Cambridge; Certif. in Educn, 1952. Asst Master: Liverpool Collegiate Sch., 1952-56; Bristol Grammar Sch., 1956-62; Head of History, Colchester Royal Grammar Sch., 1962-65; Headmaster, Yeovil Sch., 1966-71. *Publications:* A History of Europe, 1870-1950, 1960; contributor to The Teaching of History, 1965. *Address:* Latymer Upper School, Hammersmith, W6 9LR. *T:* 01-741 1851.

ISAAC, Prof. Peter Charles Gerald; Professor of Civil and Public Health Engineering, 1964-81, now Emeritus, and Head of Department of Civil Engineering, 1970-81, University of Newcastle upon Tyne; Partner, Watson Hawksley (consulting engineers); *b* 21 Jan. 1921; *s* of late Herbert George Isaac

and Julienne Geneviève (*née* Hattenberger); *m* 1950, Marjorie Eleanor White; one *s* one *d*. *Educ:* Felsted Sch.; London and Harvard Universities. BSc(Eng), SM. Asst Engineer, GWR, 1940-45; Lecturer in Civil Engineering, 1946; Senior Lecturer in Public Health Engineering, 1953, Reader, 1960, Univ. of Durham; Dean of Faculty of Applied Science, Univ. of Newcastle upon Tyne, 1969-73; Sandars Reader in Bibliography, Univ. of Cambridge, 1983-84. Member: Working Party on Sewage Disposal, 1969-70; WHO Expert Adv. Panel on Environmental Health, 1976-; specialist advr, House of Lords Select Cttee on Sci. and Technol. II (Hazardous Waste), 1980-81 and House of Lords Select Cttee on Sci. and Technol. I (Water), 1982. Chm., History of the Book Trade in the North, 1965-. Member of Council: ICE, 1968-71, 1972-75, 1977-80; Bibliographical Soc., 1970-74, 1979- (Hon. Editor of Monographs, 1982-); IPHE, 1973- (Pres., 1977-78); Pres., British Occupational Hygiene Soc., 1962-63; Mem. Bd, CEI, 1978-79. Trustee, Asian Inst. Technology, Bangkok, 1968-82 (Vice-Chm., 1979-82). Director: Thorne's Students' Bookshop Ltd, 1969-74; Environmental Resources Ltd, 1972-74. FICE, FIWES, FIPHE, FIWPC, FHKIE, MISWM. Clemens Herschel Prize in Applied Hydraulics, 1952; Telford Premium, 1957; Thomas Bedford Award, 1978. *Publications:* Electric Resistance Strain Gauges (with W. B. Dobie), 1948; Public Health Engineering, 1953; Trade Wastes, 1957; Waste Treatment, 1960; River Management, 1967; William Davison of Alnwick: pharmacist and printer, 1968; Farm Wastes, 1970; Civil Engineering-The University Contribution, 1970; Management in Civil Engineering, 1971; Davison's Halfpenny Chapbooks, 1971; (ed) The Burman Alnwick Collection, 1973; contribs to various learned and technical jls. *Recreations:* bibliography, printing, Roman engineering. *Address:* Allenholme, Wylam, Northumberland NE41 8HT. *T:* Wylam 3174. *Clubs:* National Liberal, Royal Commonwealth Society; Royal Scottish Automobile (Glasgow).

ISAACS, family name of **Marquess of Reading.**

ISAACS, Dame Albertha Madeline, DBE 1974; former Senator, now worker for the community, in the Bahamas; *b* Nassau, Bahamas, 18 April 1900; *d* of late Robert Hanna and Lilla (*née* Minns); *m* ; three *s* one *d*. *Educ:* Cosmopolitan High Sch. and Victoria High Sch., Nassau. Member: Progressive Liberal Party, Senator, 1968-72; also of PLP's Nat. Gen. Council, and of Council of Women. Has joined a Good Samaritan Group. *Address:* c/o Progressive Liberal Party, Head Office, Nassau Court, Nassau, Bahamas.

ISAACS, Jeremy Israel; Chief Executive, Channel Four Television Company, since 1981; *b* 28 Sept. 1932; *s* of Isidore Isaacs and Sara Jacobs; *m* 1958, Tamara (*née* Weinreich), Cape Town; one *s* one *d*. *Educ:* Glasgow Acad.; Merton Coll., Oxford (MA). Pres. of the Union, Hilary, 1955. Television Producer, Granada TV (What the Papers Say, All Our Yesterdays), 1958; Associated-Rediffusion (This Week), 1963; BBC TV (Panorama), 1965; Controller of Features, Associated Rediffusion, 1967; with Thames Television, 1968-78: Controller of Features, 1968-74; Producer, The World at War, 1974; Director of Programmes, 1974-78; special indep. consultant, TV series: Hollywood, ITV; A Sense of Freedom, ITV; Ireland, a Television History, BBC; Battle for Crete, NZ TV. Governor, BFI, 1979- (Chm., BFI Production Bd, 1979-). James MacTaggart Meml Lectr, Edinburgh TV Fest., 1979. Desmond Davis Award for outstanding creative contrib. to television, 1972; George Polk Meml Award, 1973. Fellow, Royal Television Soc., 1978. *Recreations:* reading, walking, listening to music, sleeping. *Address:* 66 Wavendon Avenue, W4 4NS.

ISAACS, Mrs Nathan; *see* Lawrence, E. M.

ISHAM, Sir Ian (Vere Gyles), 13th Bt *cr* 1627; *b* 17 July 1923; *s* of Lt-Col Vere Arthur Richard Isham, MC (*d* 1968) and Edith Irene (*d* 1973), *d* of Harry Brown; *S* cousin, Sir Gyles Isham, 12th Bt, 1976. Served War of 1939-45, Captain RAC. *Heir: b* Norman Murray Crawford Isham [*b* 28 Jan. 1930; *m* 1956, Joan, *d* of late Leonard James Genet; two *s* one *d*]. *Address:* 40 Turnpike Link, Croydon, Surrey CR0 5NX.

ISHERWOOD, Christopher; author; *b* High Lane, Cheshire, 26 Aug. 1904; *s* of Lt-Col Francis B. Isherwood and Kathleen Machell-Smith. *Educ:* Repton Sch.; Corpus Christi, Cambridge. Private Tutor in London, 1926-27; Medical Student, Kings, London, 1928-29; Teacher of English, Berlin, 1930-33; Journalism, etc. in London, 1934-36; Film-Script work for Gaumont-British; went to China with W. H. Auden, 1938; worked for Metro-Goldwyn-Mayer, 1940, American Friends Service Cttee, 1941-42; editor of Vedanta and the West, 1943. Became a US citizen, 1946; travelled in South America, 1947-48. Elected Mem. US Nat. Inst. of Arts and Letters, 1949. Guest Prof., Los Angeles State Coll., and at University of California, Santa Barbara, 1959-62; Regents' Prof., University of California, 1965-66. Brandeis Medal for Fiction, 1975. *Publications: fiction:* All the Conspirators, 1928; The Memorial, 1932; Mr Norris Changes Trains, 1935; Goodbye to Berlin, 1939 (I Am a Camera, play by John van Druten, perf. US 1951, and Cabaret, musical by Joe Masteroff, John Kander and Fred Ebb, perf. US 1966, both based on stories from Goodbye to Berlin); Prater Violet, 1945; The World in The Evening, 1954; Down There on a Visit, 1962; A Single Man, 1964; A Meeting by the River, 1967 (play, adapted from the novel, by C. I. and Don Bachardy, perf. US, 1972); The Berlin of Sally Bowles, 1975; *biography:* Ramakrishna and his Disciples, 1965; *autobiography:* Lions and Shadows, 1938; Kathleen and Frank, 1971; Christopher and His Kind, 1977; My Guru and His Disciple, 1980; *plays:* The Dog Beneath the Skin (with W. H. Auden), 1935; Ascent of F6 (with W. H. Auden), 1937; On the Frontier (with W. H. Auden), 1938; *travel:*

Journey to a War (with W. H. Auden), 1939; The Condor and the Cows, 1949; *miscellaneous:* Exhumations, 1966; *translation:* (with Swami Prabhavananda) The Bhagavad-Gita, 1944; (with Swami Prabhavananda) Shankara's Crest-Jewel of Discrimination, 1947; Baudelaire's Intimate Journals, 1947; (with Swami Prabhavananda) How to Know God: the Yoga Aphorisms of Patanjali, 1953. *Recreations:* usual. *Address:* 145 Adelaide Drive, Santa Monica, Calif 90402, USA.

ISHERWOOD, Rt. Rev. Harold, MVO 1955; OBE 1959; Auxiliary Bishop, Diocese of Gibraltar in Europe, since 1977; an Assistant Bishop, Diocese of Canterbury, since 1978; *b* 23 June 1907; *s* of James and Margaret Ellen Isherwood; *m* 1940, Hannah Mary Walters. *Educ:* Selwyn Coll., Cambridge; Ely Theol Coll. BA 1938, MA 1946. Deacon 1939; priest 1940; Curate of Beeston, Notts, 1939-43; Chaplain: Nat. Nautical Sch., Portishead, 1943-51; Helsinki and Moscow, 1951-54; Oslo, 1954-59; Brussels, 1959-70; Vicar General, Dio. Gibraltar and Jurisdiction of North and Central Europe, 1970-75; Canon of Gibraltar, 1971-74; Asst Bishop, Dio. Gibraltar, 1974-77. *Recreations:* music, cricket, Rugby and Association football, tennis. *Address:* 16A Burgate, Canterbury, Kent CT1 2HG. *T:* Canterbury 52790. *Club:* Royal Commonwealth Society.

ISLE OF WIGHT, Archdeacon of; *see* Carpenter, Ven. F. C.

ISLES, Maj.-Gen. Donald Edward, CB 1978; OBE 1968; Director (Deputy Managing), British Manufacture & Research Co. Ltd, since 1979; *b* 19 July 1924; *s* of Harold and Kathleen Isles; *m* 1948, Sheila Mary Stephens (formerly Thorpe); three *s* one *d. Educ:* Roundhay; Leeds Univ.; RMCS. MRAeS; FBIM. Italian campaign, with 1st Bn, Duke of Wellington's Regt, 1944-45; Palestine, Egypt, Sudan, Syria, with 1DWR, 1945-47; GSO2, HQ BAOR, 1955-58; Asst Mil. Attaché, Paris, 1963-65; CO, 1DWR, BAOR and UN Forces in Cyprus, 1965-67; AMS, MoD, 1968; Col GS, MoD, 1968-71; Col GS, Royal Armament Res. and Develt Estab., 1971-72; Dir of Munitions, Brit. Defence Staff Washington, 1972-75; Dir-Gen. Weapons (Army), 1975-78, retired. Col, The Duke of Wellington's Regt, 1975-82; Col Comdt, The King's Div., 1975-79; Hon. Col, 3rd Bn, The Yorkshire Volunteers, 1977-. *Recreations:* tennis, squash. *Address:* c/o Lloyds Bank Ltd, 6 Pall Mall, SW1. *Clubs:* Army and Navy, Institute of Directors.

ISMAY, Sir George, KBE 1947; CB 1939; *b* 1891; *s* of late George Ismay, Carlisle; *m* 1919, Jeanette May, *d* of John Lloyd, Tredegar, Mon; two *d. Educ:* private schools, Carlisle. Entered Treasury, 1911; Asst Sec., 1934; Sec. Macmillan Cttee on Finance and Industry, 1929-31; Comptroller and Accountant General, GPO, 1937; Asst Dir-General, 1942; Deputy Dir-Gen., General Post Office, 1947-52; Dir, Woolwich Equitable Building Society, 1952-72; served European War, 1915-19, in Queen's Westminster Rifles. *Address:* Newstead, 105 Golden Avenue, Angmering-on-Sea, West Sussex BN16 1QT. *T:* Rustington 2855.

ISMAY, Walter Nicholas; Managing Director, Worcester Parsons Ltd, 1975-82; *b* 20 June 1921; *s* of late John Ismay, Maryport, Cumberland. *Educ:* Taunton's Sch., Southampton; King's Coll., University of London (BSc). Royal Aircraft Establishment, 1939-40; Ministry of Supply, 1940-43; Served Army (Capt., General List), 1943-46; Imperial Chemical Industries, Metals Division, 1948-58 (Technical Dir, 1957-58); Dir, Yorkshire Imperial Metals, 1958-67; Dep. Chm. Yorkshire Imperial Plastics, 1966-67; Dep. Chm. and Man. Dir, Milton Keynes Develt Corp., 1967-71; McKechnie Britain Ltd, 1972-75. FIMechE. *Recreation:* sailing. *Address:* Springfield, Penn Lane, Tanworth-in-Arden, Warwickshire. *T:* Tanworth 2289.

ISOLANI, Casimiro Peter Hugh Tomasi, CBE 1975 (OBE 1960; MBE 1945); MVO 1961; Representative (Europe), United Nations University, since 1978; *b* 2 Sept. 1917; *s* of late Umberto Tomasi Isolani, Bologna, and late Georgiana Eleanor Lyle-Smyth, Great Barrow, Ches; *m* 1943, Karin Gunni Signe Zetterström, *d* of Henry Zetterström, Gothenburg; one *s. Educ:* Aldenham Sch.; Clare Coll., Cambridge; Major open schol., 1936, 1st cl. Mod. and Med. Lang. Tripos I; Senior Foundn schol., 1937; BA 1939. Commnd RA 1940, Intell. Corps 1941; attached 1st Canadian Div., 1943 (Sicily, Italy landings); Psychol Warfare Br., 1944; GS1 (Civil Liaison, Liaison Italian Resistance), 1945; FO 1946; Vice-Consul, Bologna, 1946; Attaché, later 1st Sec. (Information), British Embassy, Rome, 1947-61; resigned Foreign Service; Dep. Dir, Inst. for Strategic Studies, 1961-63; rejoined Foreign Service; Regional Information Officer, Paris, 1963-72; Counsellor (Information), British Embassy (and UK delegn NATO and UK Representation, EEC), Brussels, 1972-77. *Address:* 44 Pont Street, SW1X 0AD. *T:* 01-584 1543. *Club:* Anglo-Belgian.

ISSERLIS, Alexander Reginald; Senior Research Fellow, Policy Studies Institute, since 1980; *b* 18 May 1922; *y s* of Isaak Isserlis, Ilford, Essex; *m* 1949, Eleanor Mary Ord, *d* of Prof. R. D. Laurie, Aberystwyth; two *d. Educ:* Ilford High Sch.; Keble Coll., Oxford. British and Indian Army, 1942-46. Entered Civil Service, 1947. Principal, Min. of Health, 1950; Principal Private Secretary: to Lord President of the Council and Minister for Science, 1960-61; to Minister of Housing and Local Govt, 1962; Asst Sec., Min. of Housing and Local Govt, 1963; Under-Secretary: Cabinet Office, 1969; Min. of Housing and Local Government, 1969-70; Principal Private Secretary to the Prime Minister, 1970; Asst Under-Sec. of State, Home Office, 1970-72; Dir, Centre for Studies in Social Policy, 1972-77; Dir of Investigations, Office of Parly Comr for Administration, 1977-80. Mem., W Oxon DC, 1982-. *Recreations:*

walking, gardening. *Address:* Rose and Crown Cottage, Upton, Burford, Oxon. *T:* Burford 3434. *Clubs:* Athenæum, Farmers'.

ISSIGONIS, Sir Alec (Arnold Constantine), Kt 1969; CBE 1964; RDI 1964; FRS 1967; Advanced Design Consultant, British Leyland (Austin-Morris) Ltd, since 1972; *b* Smyrna, 1906; British citizen. *Educ:* Battersea Polytechnic, London (Engrg Dip.). Draughtsman, Rootes Motors Ltd, 1933-36; Suspension Engineer, Morris Motors Ltd, 1936, subsequently Chief Engineer; Deputy Engineering Co-ordinator and Chief Engineer, British Motor Corporation, 1957-61; Technical Director, 1961; Dir of R&D, BMC later British Leyland (Austin-Morris) Ltd, 1961-72; designs include: Morris Minor, 1948; Mini-Minor and Austin Seven, 1959; Morris 1100, 1962. Leverhulme Medal, Royal Society, 1966.

IVAMY, Prof. Edward Richard Hardy; Professor of Law, University of London, since 1960; *b* 1 Dec. 1920; *o s* of late Edward Wadham Ivamy and late Florence Ivamy; *m* 1965, Christine Ann Frances, *o d* of William and Frances Culver; one *s. Educ:* Malvern Coll.; University Coll., London. Served War of 1939-45, RA: 67 Field Regt, N Africa, Italy and Middle East; 2nd Lieut 1942; Temp. Capt. 1945; Staff Capt., GHQ, Cairo, 1946. LLB (1st cl. hons) 1947; PhD 1953; LLD 1967. Barrister-at-law, Middle Temple, 1949. University Coll., London: Asst Lectr in Laws, 1947-50; Lectr, 1950-56; Reader in Law, 1956-60; Dean of Faculty of Laws, 1964 and 1965; Fellow, 1969. Hon. Sec., Soc. of Public Teachers of Law, 1960-63; Hon. Sec., Bentham Club, 1953-58; Mem. Editorial Board: Jl of Business Law; Lloyd's Maritime and Commercial Law Quarterly. *Publications:* Show Business and the Law, 1955; (ed) Payne and Ivamy's Carriage of Goods by Sea, 7th edn 1963-11th edn, 1979; Hire-Purchase Legislation in England and Wales, 1965; Casebook on Carriage by Sea, 1965 (5th edn, 1982); Casebook on Sale of Goods, 1966 (4th edn, 1980); (ed) Chalmers's Marine Insurance Act 1906, 6th edn, 1966-8th edn, 1976; General Principles of Insurance Law, 1966 (4th edn, 1979, supp. 1982); (ed) Topham and Ivamy's Company Law, 13th edn, 1967-16th edn, 1978; Casebook on International Law, 1967 (3rd edn, 1979); Fire and Motor Insurance, 1968 (3rd edn, 1978); Casebook on Insurance Law, 1969 (3rd edn, 1977); Marine Insurance, 1969 (3rd edn, 1979, supp. 1982); Casebook on Shipping Law, 1970 (3rd edn, 1982); Casebook on Partnership, 1970 (2nd edn, 1982); Casebook on Agency, 1971 (2nd edn, 1980); Personal Accident, Life and Other Insurances, 1973 (2nd edn, 1980); (ed) Underhill's Partnership, 10th edn, 1975, 11th edn, 1981; (ed) Halsbury's Laws of England, 4th edn, 1978, vol. 25 (Insurance), 1982, vol. 43 (Shipping and Navigation); Dictionary of Insurance Law, 1981; contrib. to Encyclopædia Britannica, Chambers's Encyclopædia, Current Legal Problems, Jl of Business Law; Annual Survey of Commonwealth Law, 1967-77. *Recreations:* railways, cricket, tennis. *Address:* 7 Egliston Mews, SW15 1AP. *T:* 01-785 6718.

IVEAGH, 3rd Earl of, *cr* 1919; Arthur Francis Benjamin Guinness; Bt 1885; Baron Iveagh 1891; Viscount Iveagh 1905; Viscount Elveden 1919; Member, Seanad Eireann, 1973-77; Chairman, Arthur Guinness & Sons PLC; *b* 20 May 1937; *o s* of Viscount Elveden (killed in action, 1945) and Lady Elizabeth Hare, *yr d* of 4th Earl of Listowel; *S* grandfather, 1967; *m* 1963, Miranda Daphne Jane, *d* of Major Michael Smiley, Castle Fraser, Aberdeenshire; two *s* two *d. Educ:* Eton; Trinity Coll., Cambridge. Heir: *s* Viscount Elveden, *qv. Address:* Farmleigh, Castleknock, Co. Dublin. *Clubs:* White's; Royal Yacht Squadron (Cowes); Kildare Street and University (Dublin).

IVENS, Michael William; Director, Aims of Industry, since 1971; Director of the Foundation for Business Responsibilities, since 1967; *b* 15 March 1924; *s* of Harry Guest Ivens and Nina Ailion; *m* 1st, 1950, Rosalie Turnbull (marr. diss. 1971); three *s* one *d* ; 2nd, 1971, Katherine Laurence; two *s.* Dir, Foundn for Business Responsibilities, 1967; Jt Editor, Twentieth Century, 1967; Vice-Pres., Junior Hosp. Doctors Assoc., 1969; Director: Standard Telephone, 1970; Working Together Campaign, 1972-73. Jt Founder and Mem. Council, Freedom Assoc. *Publications:* (poetry) Another Sky, 1963; Practice of Industrial Communication, 1963; (poetry) Last Waltz, 1964; Case Studies in Management, 1964; Case Studies in Human Relations, 1966; Case for Capitalism, 1967; (poetry) Private and Public, 1968; Industry and Values, 1970; Which Way?, 1970; (poetry) Born Early, 1975; Prophets of Freedom and Enterprise, 1975; (ed jtly) Bachman's Book of Freedom Quotes, 1978. *Recreation:* campaigning. *Address:* 40 Doughty Street, WC1N 2LF. *T:* 01-405 5195. *Clubs:* Carlton, Beefsteak, Wig and Pen.

IVERSEN, Leslie Lars, PhD; FRS 1980; Executive Director, Merck, Sharp & Dohme Neuroscience Research Centre, Hoddesdon, Herts; Fellow of Trinity College, Cambridge, since 1964; *b* 31 Oct. 1937; *s* of Svend Iversen and Anna Caia Iversen; *m* 1961, Susan Diana (née Kibble); one *s* one *d* (and one *d* decd). *Educ:* Trinity Coll., Cambridge (BA Biochem, PhD Pharmacol). Harkness Fellow, United States: with Dr J. Axelrod, Nat. Inst. of Mental Health, and Dr E. Kravitz, Dept of Neurobiology, Harvard Med. Sch., 1964-66; Locke Research Fellow of Royal Society, Dept of Pharmacology, Univ. of Cambridge, 1967-71; Dir, MRC Neurochemical Pharmacology Unit, Cambridge, 1971-82. *Publications:* The Uptake and Storage of Noradrenaline in Sympathetic Nerves, 1967; (with S. D. Iversen) Behavioural Pharmacology, 1975, 2nd edn 1981. *Recreations:* reading, gardening. *Address:* Merck, Sharp & Dohme Neuroscience Research Centre, Hertford Road, Hoddesdon, Herts EN11 9BU. *T:* Hoddesdon 67272.

IVES, Arthur Glendinning Loveless, CVO 1954 (MVO 1945); *b* 19 Aug. 1904; *s* of late Rev. E. J. Ives, Wesleyan Minister; *m* 1929, Doris Marion, *d* of Thomas Coke Boden; three *s* one *d. Educ:* Kingswood Sch.; Queen's Coll., Oxford (classical scholar); MA. George Webb Medley Junior Scholarship for Economics, Oxford Univ., 1926. London Chamber of Commerce, 1928-29; joined staff of King Edward's Hosp. Fund for London, 1929; Sec., 1938-60; retired 1960. Seriously injured in railway accident at Lewisham, Dec. 1957. A Governor of Kingswood Sch., 1954-72. *Publications:* British Hospitals (Britain in Pictures), 1948; Kingswood School in Wesley's Day and Since, 1970; contrib. to The Times, Lancet, etc, on hospital administration and allied topics. *Address:* The Cedars, Bordyke, Tonbridge, Kent. *Club:* Athenæum.
See also Rev. A. K. Lloyd.

IVES, Robert; a Recorder, 1963-77 (formerly Recorder of Bury St Edmunds); *b* 25 Aug. 1906; *o s* of Robert Ives; *m* 1931, Evelyn Harriet Hairby Alston (*d* 1965), *er d* of Rev. F. S. Alston; two *d* ; *m* 1966, Vera Bowack, widow of Pilot Officer N. H. Bowack. *Educ:* privately; Gonville and Caius Coll., Cambridge (MA). Called to Bar, Gray's Inn, 1928. War Service, 1940-45: RASC and Judge Advocate General's Dept. Judge of Norwich Guildhall Court of Record, 1952-71; Dep. Chm., Norfolk QS, 1967-71. Chairman: Mental Health Review Tribunal (E Anglia Region), 1960-63; Agricultural Land Tribunal (Eastern Area), 1961-79; Mem. panel of Chairmen of Medical Appeal Tribunals, 1969-78. *Recreations:* garden, photography. *Address:* Pinewood, Heydon Road, Aylsham, Norfolk NR11 6QT. *T:* Aylsham 3369.

IVINS, Prof. John Derek; Professor of Agriculture, University of Nottingham, since 1958; *b* Eccleshall, Staffs, 11 March 1923; *s* of Alfred Ivins and Ann Ivins (*née* Holland); *m* 1952, Janet Alice Whitehead, BSc; one *s* one *d. Educ:* Wolstanton County Grammar Sch., Newcastle, Staffs. BSc Reading 1944, MSc 1951; PhD Nottingham 1954. Technical Officer, Seed Production Cttee of Nat. Inst. of Agricultural Botany, 1944-46; Regional Trials Officer, Nat. Inst. of Agricultural Botany, 1946-48; Nottingham University: Lectr in Agriculture, 1948-58; Dean: Faculty of Agriculture and Horticulture, 1962-65; Faculty of Agricl Sci., 1976-79; Deputy Vice-Chancellor, 1969-74. Mem., UK Seeds Exec., 1973- (Chm., 1978-). Chm. Council, NIAB, 1974-75; Mem. UGC sub-cttee, Agriculture and Veterinary Studies, 1975-81. FRAgS 1973. *Publications:* papers in technical and agricultural journals. *Recreations:* shooting, gardening. *Address:* University of Nottingham School of Agriculture, Sutton Bonington, near Loughborough. *T:* Kegworth 2386.

IVORY, James Francis; film director; Partner in Merchant Ivory Productions, since 1961; *b* 7 June 1928; *s* of Edward Patrick Ivory and Hallie Millicent De Loney. *Educ:* Univ. of Oregon (BA Fine Arts); Univ. of Southern California (MFA Cinema). Guggenheim Fellow, 1974. Collaborator with Ruth Prawer Jhabvala and Ismail Merchant on the following films: The Householder, 1963; Shakespeare Wallah, 1965; The Guru, 1969; Bombay Talkie, 1970; Autobiography of a Princess, 1975; Roseland, 1977; Hullabaloo over Georgie and Bonnie's Pictures, 1978; The Europeans, 1979; Jane Austen in Manhattan, 1980; Quartet, 1981; Heat and Dust, 1982. Other films: (with Nirad Chaudhuri) Adventures of a Brown Man in Search of Civilization, 1971; (with George W. S. Trow and Michael O'Donoghue) Savages, 1972; (with Walter Marks) The Wild Party, 1975; (with Terence McNally) The Five Forty Eight, 1979. Documentaries: Venice, Theme and Variations, 1957; The Sword and the Flute, 1959; The Delhi Way, 1964. *Publication:* Autobiography of a Princess (Also Being the Adventures of an American Film Director in the Land of the Maharajas), 1975. *Recreation:* looking at pictures. *Address:* 400 East 52nd Street, New York, NY 10022, USA. *T:* 212 759 3694; (country) Patroon Street, Claverack, New York 12513, USA. *T:* 518 851 7808.

J

JACK, Hon. Sir Alieu (Sulayman), Grand Commander and Chancellor, National Order of The Gambia, 1972; Kt 1970; Speaker, House of Representatives of the Republic of The Gambia, 1962-72, and since 1977; *b* 14 July 1922; *m* 1944, Yai Marie Cham; four *s* four *d* (and one *d* decd). *Educ:* St Augustine's School. Entered Gambia Civil Service, 1939; resigned and took up local appt with NAAFI, 1940-44; Civil Service, 1945-48; entered commerce, 1948; Man. Dir, Gambia National Trading Co. Ltd, 1948-72. Mem., Bathurst City Council, 1949-62. Minister for Works and Communications, The Gambia, 1972-77. Represented The Gambia Parlt at various internat. gatherings; Pres., CPA Gambia Branch. Comdr, National Order of Senegal, 1967; Comdr, Order of Merit of Mauritania, 1967; Commander, Order of Fed. Republic of Nigeria, 1970; Kt Grand Band, Liberia, 1977. *Recreation:* golf. *Address:* PO Box 376, Banjul, The Gambia; House of Representatives, The Republic of The Gambia. *T:* (home) 93.2204, (office) 241. *Club:* Bathurst (Banjul).

JACK, Sir Daniel (Thomson), Kt 1966; CBE 1951; Hon. LLD Glasgow; MA; Chairman, Air Transport Licensing Board, 1961-70; David Dale Professor of Economics, University of Durham, King's College, Newcastle upon Tyne,

1935-61; Sub-Rector, King's College, 1950-55; *b* 18 Aug. 1901; *m* 1st, 1945, Nan (*d* 1949), widow of Prof. John Dall, Queen's Univ., Canada; 2nd, 1954, Elizabeth Witter Stewart (*d* 1970), Kingston, Ont. *Educ:* Bellahouston Academy, Glasgow; University of Glasgow. Lecturer in Political Economy, University of Glasgow, 1923-28; Lecturer in Political Economy, University of St Andrews, 1928-35. *Publications:* The Economics of the Gold Standard, 1925; The Restoration of European Currencies, 1927; International Trade, 1931; The Crises of 1931, 1931; Currency and Banking, 1932; Studies in Economic Warfare, 1940; Economic Survey of Sierra Leone, 1958; Report on Industrial Relations in the Sisal Industry, 1959; Report on Wage Fixing Machinery in Tanganyika, 1959; (jtly) Economic Survey of Nyasaland, 1959; articles in various journals. *Address:* Austenmead, School Lane, Chalfont St Peter, Bucks. *T:* Gerrards Cross 85577.

JACK, David M.; *see* Morton Jack.

JACK, Prof. Ian Robert James; Professor of English Literature, University of Cambridge, since 1976; Fellow of Pembroke College, Cambridge, since 1961; *b* 5 Dec. 1923; *s* of John McGregor Bruce Jack, WS, and Helena Colburn Buchanan; *m* 1st, 1948, Jane Henderson MacDonald; two *s* one *d* ; 2nd, 1972, Margaret Elizabeth Crone; one *s. Educ:* George Watson's Coll.; Univ. of Edinburgh (John Welsh Classical Schol., 1941; James Boswell Fellow, 1946; MA 1947); Merton Coll., Oxford (DPhil 1950); LittD Cantab 1973. Brasenose College, Oxford: Lectr in Eng. Lit., 1950-55; Sen. Res. Fellow, 1955-61; Cambridge University: Lectr in English, 1961-73; Reader in English Poetry, 1973-76; Librarian, Pembroke Coll., 1965-75. Vis. Professor: Alexandria, 1960; Chicago, 1968-69; California at Berkeley, 1968-69; British Columbia, 1975; Virginia, 1980-81; Tsuda Coll., Tokyo, 1981; de Carle Lectr, Univ. of Otago, 1964; Warton Lectr in English Poetry, British Acad., 1967; Guest Speaker, Nichol Smith Seminar, ANU, 1976; Guest Speaker, 50th anniversary meeting of English Literary Soc. of Japan, 1978; numerous lecture-tours for British Council and other bodies. President: Charles Lamb Soc., 1970-80; Browning Soc., 1980-; Vice-President: Johnson Soc., 1964-; Brontë Soc., 1973-. *Publications:* Augustan Satire, 1952; English Literature 1815-1832 (Vol. X, Oxf. Hist. of Eng. Lit.), 1963; Keats and the Mirror of Art, 1967; Browning's Major Poetry, 1973; (ed) Sterne: A Sentimental Journey, etc, 1968; (ed) Browning: Poetical Works 1833-1864, 1970; (ed with Hilda Marsden) Emily Brontë: Wuthering Heights, 1976; general editor: Brontë novels (Clarendon edn); The Poetical Works of Browning, vols 1-2, 1983; contrib. TLS, etc. *Recreations:* collecting books, travelling hopefully. *Address:* Highfield House, High Street, Fen Ditton, Cambridgeshire CB5 8ST. *T:* Teversham 2697. *Club:* MCC.

JACK, James, CBE 1967; JP; General Secretary, Scottish Trades Union Congress, 1963-75; retired; Member: Scottish Postal Board, 1972-79; Board of the Crown Agents, 1975-77; *b* 6 Dec. 1910; *s* of late Andrew M. Jack and late Margaret Reid; *m* 1936; one *s. Educ:* Auchinraith Primary Sch., Blantyre; St John's Gram. Sch., Hamilton. Chm., Glasgow N and E Cttee, Manpower Services Commn, 1975-79; Member: Scottish Economic Council, 1964-76; Scottish Oil Develt Council, 1974-76; Scottish Develt Agency, 1975-78; Lanarkshire Health Bd, 1975-; Employment Appeal Tribunal, 1976-. JP Lanark. *Address:* 7 Stonefield Place, Blantyre, Glasgow G72 9TH. *T:* Blantyre 823304.

JACK, Prof. Kenneth Henderson, PhD, ScD; FRS 1980; CChem, FRSC; Professor of Applied Crystal Chemistry, University of Newcastle upon Tyne, since 1964, and Director of Wolfson Research Group for High-Strength Materials, since 1970; *b* 12 Oct. 1918; *e s* of late John Henderson Jack, DSC, and Emily (*née* Cozens), North Shields, Northumberland; *m* 1942, Alfreda Hughes (*d* 1974); two *s. Educ:* Tynemouth Municipal High Sch.; King's Coll., Univ. of Durham, Newcastle upon Tyne (BSc 1939, DThPT 1940, MSc 1944); Fitzwilliam Coll., Univ. of Cambridge (PhD 1950, ScD 1978). Experimental Officer, Min. of Supply, 1940-41; Lectr in Chemistry, King's Coll., Univ. of Durham, 1941-45, 1949-52, 1953-57; Sen. Scientific Officer, Brit. Iron and Steel Res. Assoc., 1945-49; research at Crystallographic Lab., Cavendish Laboratory, Cambridge, 1947-49; Research Engr, Westinghouse Elec. Corp., Pittsburgh, Pa, 1952-53; Research Dir, Thermal Syndicate Ltd, Wallsend, 1957-64. Saville-Shaw Medal, Soc. of Chem. Industry, 1944; Sir George Beilby Meml Award, Inst. of Metals, RIC and Soc. of Chem. Industry, 1951; J. W. Mellor Memorial Lecturer, Brit. Ceramic Soc., 1973; Kroll Medal and Prize, Metals Soc., 1979. *Publications:* papers in scientific jls and conf. proc. *Recreation:* playing with grandchildren. *Address:* 147 Broadway, Cullercoats, Tyne and Wear NE30 3TA. *T:* North Shields 573664; Crystallography Laboratory, University of Newcastle upon Tyne, NE1 7RU. *T:* Newcastle upon Tyne 328511, ext. 3201.

JACK, Raymond Evan, QC 1982; *b* 13 Nov. 1942; *s* of Evan and Charlotte Jack; *m* 1976, Elizabeth Alison, *d* of Rev. Canon James Seymour Denis Mansel, *qv* ; two *d. Educ:* Rugby; Trinity Coll., Cambridge (BA). Called to Bar, Inner Temple, 1966. *Recreations:* gardening and wood. *Address:* 1 Hare Court, Temple, EC4.

JACK, Prof. Robert Barr; Partner, McGrigor, Donald & Co., Solicitors, Glasgow, since 1957; Professor of Mercantile Law, Glasgow University, since 1978; *b* 18 March 1928; *s* of Robert Hendry Jack and Christina Alexandra Jack; *m* 1958, Anna Thorburn Thomson; two *s. Educ:* Kilsyth Acad.; High Sch., Glasgow; Glasgow Univ. MA 1948, LLB 1951. Admitted a solicitor in Scotland, 1951. Member: Company Law Cttee of Law Society of Scotland,

1971- (Convener, 1978-); Scottish Law Commn, 1974-77. Scottish observer on Dept of Trade's Insolvency Law Review Cttee, 1977-82; Mem., DoT Adv. Panel on Company Law, 1980-. Director: Brownlee plc, Timber Merchants, Glasgow, 1974-; Scottish Metropolitan Property plc, 1980-; Clyde Football Club Ltd, 1980-. Chm., Scottish Nat. Council of YMCAs, 1966-73; Mem. Council of Management, 1971-, and Mem. Exec. Cttee, 1972-, Quarrier's Homes. Governor, Hutchesons' Educational Trust, Glasgow, 1978- (Chm. 1980-). *Publications:* lectures on various aspects of company law, and articles on the legal implications of current cost accounting and recent company legislation. *Recreations:* golf, hopeful support of one of Glasgow's less fashionable football teams; a dedicated lover of Isle of Arran which serves as a retreat and restorative. *Address:* (home) 39 Mansewood Road, Glasgow G43 1TN. *T:* 041-632 1659; (office) 224 Ingram Street, Glasgow G1 1JP. *T:* 041-248 5981. *Clubs:* Caledonian; Western (Glasgow); Pollok Golf; Western Gailes Golf; Shiskine Golf and Tennis (Isle of Arran) (Captain 1973-75).

JACKLIN, Anthony, OBE 1970; professional golfer; *b* 7 July 1944; *s* of Arthur David Jacklin; *m* 1966, Vivien; two *s* one *d.* Successes include: British Assistant Pro Championship, 1965; Pringle Tournament, 1967; Dunlop Masters, 1967; Greater Jacksonville Open, USA, 1968; British Open Championship, 1969; US Open Championship, 1970; Benson & Hedges, 1971; British Professional Golfers Assoc., 1972, 1982; Gtr Jacksonville Open, 1972; Bogota Open, 1973 and 1974; Italian Open, 1973; Dunlop Masters, 1973; Scandinavian Open, 1975; Kerrygold International, 1976; English National PGA Championship, 1977; German Open, 1979; Jersey Open, 1981; Ryder Cup player, 1967-80. Life Vice-Pres., Professional Golfers' Assoc., 1970. *Publications:* Golf with Tony Jacklin, 1969; The Price of Success, 1979. *Recreations:* shooting, flying. *Address:* Chestnut Lea, St Mary, Jersey, CI. *Clubs:* Potters Bar Golf; Hon. Mem. of others.

JACKLING, Sir Roger William, GCMG 1976 (KCMG 1965; CMG 1955); HM Diplomatic Service, retired; *b* 10 May 1913; *s* of P. Jackling, OBE, and Lucy Jackling; *m* 1938, Joan Tustin; two *s* (and one *s* decd). *Educ:* Felsted. DPA, London Univ., 1932; Solicitor, Supreme Court, 1935; Actg Vice-Consul, New York, 1940; Commercial Sec., Quito, 1942; 2nd Sec., Washington, 1943; 1st Sec., 1945; transf. Foreign Office, 1947; seconded to Cabinet Office, 1950 (Asst Sec.); Counsellor (commercial), The Hague, 1951; Economic and Financial Adviser to UK High Commr, Bonn; and UK commercial rep. in Germany, 1953; Minister (Economic), British Embassy, Bonn, 1955; Counsellor, British Embassy, Washington, 1957-59; Asst Under-Sec. of State, FO, 1959-63; Dep. Permanent UK Rep. to United Nations, 1963-67 (with personal rank of Ambassador from 1965); Dep. Under-Sec. of State, FO, 1967-68; Ambassador to Federal Republic of Germany, 1968-72; Leader, UK Delegn to UN Conf. on Law of the Sea, 1973-75. Chm., Bd of Trustees, Anglo-German Foundn for Study of Industrial Society, 1973-77. *Recreations:* gardening, golf. *Address:* 37 Boundary Road, St John's Wood, NW8. *Club:* Travellers'.

JACKMAN, Air Marshal Sir Douglas, KBE 1959 (CBE 1943); CB 1946; RAF; idc 1948; Air Officer Commanding-in-Chief, Royal Air Force Maintenance Command, 1958-61, retired; *b* 26 Oct. 1902; twin *s* of late A. J. Jackman; *m* 1931, Marjorie Leonore, *d* of late A. Hyland, Kingsdown, Kent. *Educ:* HMS Worcester. Officer Royal Mail Line until 1926; joined RAF, 1926; served in Iraq, 1928-30, in No 55 Squadron; in UK with Wessex Bombing Area and at Cranwell until 1934; to Middle East Command in 1934 and served at Aboukir until 1938, when posted to HQ Middle East until 1943; with Mediterranean Air Command and Mediterranean Allied Air Forces HQ until 1944; HQ Balkan Air Force, 1944-45 (despatches five times, CB, CBE, Comdr Order George 1st of Greece with Swords, AFC [Greek]); Dir of Movements Air Ministry, 1946-47; Dir of Organization (forecasting and planning), Air Ministry, 1949-52; AOC No 40 Group, 1952-55; Dir-Gen. of Equipment, Air Ministry, 1955-58; Co-ordinator, Anglo-American Relations, Air Ministry, 1961-64. *Publication:* technical, on planning, 1942. *Recreations:* golf (Member: RAF Golfing Soc.; Seniors Golfing Soc., Natal); woodworking. *Address:* 107 Musgrave Heights, Musgrave Road, Durban, South Africa. *Clubs:* Royal Over-Seas League; Durban Country.

JACKS, Hector Beaumont, MA; Headmaster of Bedales School, 1946-July 1962; *b* 25 June 1903; *s* of late Dr L. P. Jacks; *m* 1st, Mary (*d* 1959), *d* of Rev. G. N. Nuttall Smith; one *s* one *d* ; 2nd, Nancy, *d* of F. E. Strudwick. *Educ:* Magdalen Coll. Sch. and Wadham Coll., Oxford. Asst master, Wellington Coll., Berks, 1925-32; Headmaster of Willaston Sch., Nantwich, 1932-37; Second Master, Cheltenham Coll. Junior Sch., 1940-46. *Recreation:* gardening. *Address:* Applegarth, Spotted Cow Lane, Buxted, Sussex. *T:* Buxted 2296.

JACKSON, family name of **Baron Allerton.**

JACKSON, Albert Leslie Samuel, JP; Member, Birmingham City Council, since 1952; Lord Mayor of Birmingham, 1975-1976, Deputy Lord Mayor, 1978-79; *b* 20 Jan. 1918; *s* of Bert Jackson and Olive Powell; *m* Gladys Burley; one *s* one *d. Educ:* Handsworth New Road Council Sch. War service, Radio Mechanic, RAF. Subseq. formed building company, 1952, of which he is now Man. Dir. JP 1968. *Recreations:* chess, sailing. *Address:* 10 St Helier House, Manor Close, Melville Road, Birmingham B16 9NG. *T:* 021-558 2266 and 021-454 0849.

JACKSON, Brig. Alexander Cosby Fishburn, CVO 1957; CBE 1954 (OBE 1943); *b* 4 Dec. 1903; *s* of late Col S. C. F. Jackson, CMG, DSO, and Lucy B. Jackson (*née* Drake); *m* 1934, Margaret Hastings Hervey, Montclair, NJ, USA; one *s* (and one *s* decd). *Educ:* Yardley Court, Tonbridge; Haileybury Coll.; RMC Sandhurst. 2nd Lt, R Hants Regt, 1923; Brig. 1952; employed RWAFF, 1927-33; served in Middle East, 1940-45 (despatches twice, OBE); Dep. Dir of Quartering, War Office, 1945-48; Comdr Northern Area, Kenya, 1948-51; Comdr Caribbean Area, 1951-54; HBM Military Attaché, Paris, 1954-58. ADC to the Queen, 1955-58. Order of Kutuzov 2nd Class, USSR, 1944; Comdr Legion of Honour, France, 1957. *Publication:* Rose Croix: a history of the ancient and accepted rite for England and Wales, 1981. *Recreation:* bowls. *Address:* Glenwhern, Grouville, Jersey.

JACKSON, Sir Anthony Henry Mather M.; *see* Mather-Jackson.

JACKSON, Maj.-Gen. Arthur James, BSc; CEng; FIEE; independent consultant; *b* Barrow-upon-Humber, Lincs, 31 March 1923; *e s* of late Comdr A. J. Jackson, RD, RNR, Barrow-upon-Humber; *m* 1948, Joan Marguerite, *d* of late Trevor Lyons Relton, MBE, Whyteleafe, Surrey; two *s* two *d. Educ:* Barton Sch.; RMCS. BSc London, 1951. Joined Royal Signals, 1944; commnd 1946; served Italy and British Embassy, Belgrade, 1946-47; Austria, WO, Staff Coll., Far East, RMCS, BAOR, 1948-64; GSO1, Defence Ops Requirements Staff, MoD, 1965-66; CO 4th Div. Signal Regt, BAOR, 1967-68; psc, ptsc, psc†; Comdr (Brigadier), 12 Signal Gp, 1969-71; Dir of Telecommunications (Army), 1972-73; Dep. Comdt and Sen. Military Dir of Studies, RMCS, 1974-75; Mil. Dep., Head of Defence Sales, MoD, 1975-78, retired. Col Comdt, Royal Signals, 1978-; Chm., Royal Signals Instn. *Recreations:* golf, shooting, gardening, organ music. *Address:* Roughwood House, Fleet, Hampshire; Tower Lodge, Brampford Speke, Devon. *Club:* Army and Navy.

JACKSON, Mrs (Audrey) Muriel W.; *see* Ward-Jackson.

JACKSON, Very Rev. Brandon Donald; Provost of Bradford Cathedral, since 1977; *b* 11 Aug. 1934; *s* of Herbert and Millicent Jackson; *m* 1958, Mary Lindsay, 2nd *d* of John and Helen Philip; two *s* one *d. Educ:* Stockport School; Liverpool Univ.; St Catherine's Coll. and Wycliffe Hall, Oxford (LLB, DipTh). Curate: Christ Church, New Malden, Surrey, 1958-61; St George, Leeds, 1961-65; Vicar, St Peter, Shipley, Yorks, 1965-77. Religious Adviser to Yorkshire Television, 1969-79; Church Commissioner, 1971-73; Examining Chaplain to Bp of Bradford, 1974-; Governor, Harrogate College, 1974-; Member: Council of Wycliffe Hall, Oxford, 1971-; Marriage Commission, 1975-78. *Recreations:* sport (cricket, squash), fell-walking, fishing. *Address:* Provost's House, Cathedral Close, Bradford BD1 4EG. *T:* Bradford 32023.

JACKSON, Christopher Murray; Member (C) Kent East, European Parliament, since 1979; *b* 24 May 1935; *s* of Rev. Howard Murray Jackson and Doris Bessie Jackson (*née* Grainger); *m* 1971, Carlie Elizabeth Keeling; one *s* one *d. Educ:* Kingswood Sch., Bath; Magdalen Coll., Oxford (Open Exhibnr, BA Hons (Physics) 1959, MA 1964); Goethe Univ., Frankfurt; London Sch. of Economics. National Service, commnd RAF, Pilot, 1954-56. Management Trainee, Unilever, 1959; PA to Director of Lever Brothers, 1962; Marketing Manager, Lever Brothers, 1965; Sen. Man., Unilever Ltd, 1967; Gen. Marketing Man., Save and Prosper Gp, 1969; Head of Corporate Planning, D. MacPherson Gp, 1971-74; Dir, Corporate Development Spillers Ltd, 1974-80. Dir, Radio Invicta Ltd, 1981-. Chm., Ludgate Gp, 1963-67. Contested (C): East Ham South, 1970; Northampton North, Feb. 1974. Member, Gen. Council, Cons. Gp for Europe, 1974-76. European Democratic Gp spokesman on develt and co-operation, European Parlt, 1981-. Treas. and Council Mem., St Martin-in-the-Fields, 1975-77; Member: Exec. Cttee, Soc. for Long Range Planning, 1976-79; Economic and Social Affairs Cttee, BIM, 1978-79; Council, Centre for European Agricl Studies, 1981-. *Publications:* Report on UK Apple Industry, European Democratic Group, 1980; numerous articles on development aid and on corporate planning. *Recreations:* music, gardening, ski-ing. *Address:* Rock House, London Road, Maidstone, Kent. *T:* Tonbridge 456688.

JACKSON, Edward; *see* Jackson, J. E.

JACKSON, Edward Francis, MA; Director, Oxford University Institute of Economics and Statistics, and Professorial Fellow of St Antony's College, Oxford, since 1959; *b* 11 July 1915; *o s* of F. E. Jackson, schoolmaster, and Miriam Eveline (*née* Jevon); *m* 1st, 1942, Anne Katherine Cloake (marr. diss.); 2nd, 1954, Mrs Marion Marianne Marris (*d* 1972), *o c* of late Arthur Ellinger; two *s. Educ:* West Bromwich Grammar Sch.; Univ. of Birmingham; Magdalen Coll., Oxford. BCom Birmingham with 1st cl. hons, 1934; Magdalen Coll., Oxford (Demy): 1st in PPE, 1937; Jun. G. W. Medley Schol., 1935-36; Sen. Demy, 1937; Lecturer in Economics: New Coll., 1938; Magdalen Coll., 1939. Temp. Civil Servant in War Cabinet Offices, 1941-45; established Civil Servant (Central Statistical Office), 1945; Dep. Dir, Res. and Planning Div., UN Econ. Commn for Europe, 1951-56. University Lectr in Economic Statistics, Oxford, and Research Fellow of St Antony's Coll., Oxford, 1956-59. Mem. Transport Adv. Council, 1965. *Publications:* The Nigerian National Accounts, 1950-57 (with P. N. C. Obigbo), 1960; articles in economic journals. *Address:* Institute of Economics and Statistics, St Cross Building, Manor Road, Oxford; 62 Park Town, Oxford. *Club:* Reform.

JACKSON, Eric Stead, CB 1954; *b* 22 Aug. 1909; *yr s* of Stead Jackson, Shipley Glen, Yorks; *m* 1938, Yvonne Renée (*d* 1982), *o d* of Devereaux Doria De Brétigny, Victoria, BC; one *s* one *d. Educ:* Bradford Grammar Sch.; Corpus Christi Coll., Oxford (Scholar). 1st Class Hons Math. Mods, Math. Finals and Nat. Sci. Finals, Jun. Math. schol., 1930; MA. Asst Principal, Air Ministry, 1932; Sec., British Air Mission to Australia and NZ, 1939; Private Sec. to Minister of Aircraft Production, 1942, and to Resident Minister in Washington, 1943; Sec., British Supply Council in N America, 1944; Dir-Gen. Aircraft Branch, Control Commission, Berlin, 1945; Dep. Pres. Economic Sub-Commission, 1947; British Head of Bizonal Delegation to OEEC, Paris, 1948; Under Sec., Ministry of Supply, 1950-56; Dir-Gen., Atomic Weapons, Ministry of Supply, 1956-59; Under-Secretary: Min. of Aviation, 1959-67; Min. of Technology, 1967-70; Dept of Trade and Industry, 1970-71. *Address:* 10 Ditchley Road, Charlbury, Oxfordshire. *T:* Charlbury 810682.

JACKSON, Francis Alan, OBE 1978; Organist and Master of the Music, York Minster, 1946-82; *b* 2 Oct. 1917; *s* of W. A. Jackson; *m* 1950, Priscilla, *d* of Tyndale Procter; two *s* one *d. Educ:* York Minster Choir Sch.; Sir Edward Bairstow. Chorister, York Minster, 1929-33; ARCO, 1936; BMus Dunelm 1937; FRCO (Limpus Prize), 1937; FRSCM, 1963; DMus Dunelm 1957. Organist Malton Parish Church, 1933-40. Served War of 1939-45, with 9th Lancers in Egypt, N Africa and Italy, 1940-46. Asst Organist, York Minster, 1946; Conductor York Musical Soc., 1947; Conductor York Symphony Orchestra, 1947-80. Pres. Incorp. Assoc of Organists, 1960-62; Pres., RCO, 1972-74. Hon. Fellow, Westminster Choir Coll., Princeton, NJ, 1970. *Publications:* Organ and Church Music, Songs, Monodramas. *Recreation:* gardening. *Address:* Nethergarth, Acklam, Malton, N Yorks YO17 9RG. *T:* Burythorpe 395.

JACKSON, Frederick Hume, CMG 1978; OBE 1966; HM Diplomatic Service, retired; Consul-General, Düsseldorf, 1975-78; *b* 8 Sept. 1918; *o s* of late Maj.-Gen. G. H. N. Jackson, CB, CMG, DSO, Rathmore, Winchcombe, Glos and Eileen, *d* of J. Hume Dudgeon, Merville, Booterstown, Co. Dublin; *m* 1950, Anne Gibson; two *s* one *d* (and one *s* decd). *Educ:* Winchester; Clare Coll., Cambridge (MA). Military service, 1939-46: GSO3 (Intelligence), HQ 1 Corps District; Colonial Service (Tanganyika), 1946-57; FO, 1957-60; Head of Chancery, Saigon, 1960-62; 1st Sec., Washington, 1962-67; Counsellor and Dep. Head, UK Delegn to European Communities, Brussels, 1967-69; UK Resident Representative, Internat. Atomic Energy Agency, 1969-75; UK Perm. Representative to UNIDO, 1971-75. Chm., Sevenoaks Cons. Assoc., 1982-. *Recreations:* fishing, sailing, shooting, riding. *Address:* The Old Vicarage, Leigh, Tonbridge, Kent TN11 8QJ. *T:* Hildenborough 833495; c/o Barclays Bank Ltd, St Nicholas Street, Scarborough, North Yorks. *Club:* Flyfishers'.

JACKSON, Sir Geoffrey (Holt Seymour), KCMG 1971 (CMG 1963); HM Diplomatic Service, retired; Member, BBC General Advisory Council, 1976-80; *b* 4 March 1915; *s* of Samuel Seymour Jackson and Marie Cecile Dudley Ryder; *m* 1939, Patricia Mary Evelyn Delany; one *s. Educ:* Bolton Sch.; Emmanuel Coll., Cambridge. Entered Foreign Service, 1937; Vice-Consul, Beirut, Cairo, Bagdad; Acting Consul-Gen., Basra, 1946; 1st Sec., Bogotá, 1946-50; Berne, 1954-56; Minister, Honduras, 1956, HM Ambassador to Honduras, 1957-60; Consul-Gen., Seattle, 1960-64; Senior British Trade Commissioner in Ontario, Canada, 1964; Minister (Commercial), Toronto, 1965-69; Ambassador to Uruguay, 1969-72; kidnapped by terrorists and held prisoner for 8 months, Jan.-Sept. 1971; Dep. Under-Sec. of State, FCO, 1973. Mem. London Bd, Burnley Building Soc. Chm., BBC Adv. Gp on Social Effects of TV, 1975-77. Pres., Assoc. of Lancastrians, 1974. Freeman, City of London, 1976. *Publications:* The Oven-Bird, 1972; People's Prison, 1973; Surviving the Long Night, 1974; Concorde Diplomacy, 1981. *Recreations:* remembering ski-ing, golf, Latin-Americana. *Address:* 63B Cadogan Square, SW1. *Club:* Canning.

JACKSON, Most Rev. George Frederic Clarence; *b* 5 July 1907; *s* of James Sandiford Jackson; *m* 1939, Eileen de Montfort Wellburne; two *s* two *d. Educ:* University of Toronto. Deacon, 1934; Priest, 1935, Diocese of Niagara. Diocese of: Toronto, 1937-38; Chester, 1938-46; Niagara, 1946-58; Qu'Appelle, 1958-77. Hon. Canon, Christ Church Cathedral, Hamilton, Ontario, 1952; Dean of Qu'Appelle, 1958; Bishop of Qu'Appelle, 1960; Archbishop of Qu'Appelle and Metropolitan of Rupert's Land, 1970-77; Bishop-Ordinary to the Canadian Armed Forces, 1977-80. Priest-in-charge, Abernethy-Balcarres, 1980. Mayor, Katepwe Beach Village, 1980. DD (*hc*) 1959. *Recreations:* curling, gardening. *Address:* Box 519, Fort Qu'Appelle, Saskatchewan S0G 1S0, Canada.

JACKSON, Gerald Breck; *b* 28 June 1916; *o s* of Gerald Breck Jackson and Mary Jackson, Paterson, NJ; *m* 1940, Brenda Mary, *o d* of William and Mary Titshall; one *s. Educ:* various schs in USA; Canford Sch., Dorset; Faraday House Engrg Coll. Graduate Trainee, Central Electricity Bd, 1938. HM Forces, RE, 1939-43. Various appts in HV transmission with CEB and BEA, 1943-55; Overhead Line Design Engr, BEA, 1955-61; Asst Regional Dir, CEGB, 1961-64; Chief Ops Engr, CEGB, 1964-66; Regional Dir, NW Region, CEGB, 1966-68; Dir Engineering, English Electric Co. Ltd, 1968-69; Sen. Exec., Thomas Tilling Ltd, and Dir subsid. cos, 1969-71; Man. Dir, John Mowlem & Co. Ltd, 1971-72; Man. Dir, NCB (Ancillaries) Ltd, 1972-78. DFH, CEng, FIEE. *Publications:* Network for the Nation, 1960; Power Controlled, 1966. *Recreations:* photography, pen-and-ink drawing. *Address:*

Larchwood, 1A Lansdowne Square, Tunbridge Wells, Kent TN1 2NF. *T:* Tunbridge Wells 44112.

JACKSON, Glenda, CBE 1978; actress; *b* Birkenhead, 9 May 1936; *d* of Harry and Joan Jackson; *m* 1958, Roy Hodges (marr. diss. 1976); one *s. Educ:* West Kirby Co. Grammar Sch. for Girls; RADA. Actress with various repertory cos, 1957-63, stage manager, Crewe Rep.; joined Royal Shakespeare Co., 1963. Pres., Toy Libraries Assoc., 1976-. *Plays:* All Kinds of Men, Arts, 1957; The Idiot, Lyric, 1962; Alfie, Mermaid and Duchess, 1963; Royal Shakespeare Co.: Theatre of Cruelty Season, LAMDA, 1964; The Jew of Malta, 1964; Marat/Sade, 1965, NY and Paris, 1965; Love's Labour's Lost, Squire Puntila and his Servant Matti, The Investigation, Hamlet, 1965; US, Aldwych, 1966; Three Sisters, Royal Ct, 1967; Fanghorn, Fortune, 1967; Collaborators, Duchess, 1973; The Maids, Greenwich, 1974; Hedda Gabler, Australia, USA, London, 1975; The White Devil, Old Vic, 1976; Stevie, Vaudeville, 1977; Antony and Cleopatra, Stratford, 1978; Rose, Duke of York's, 1980; Summit Conference, Lyric, 1982; *films:* This Sporting Life, 1963; Marat/Sade, 1967; Negatives, 1968; Women in Love (Oscar Award, 1971), 1970; The Music Lovers, 1971; Sunday, Bloody Sunday, 1971; The Boyfriend, 1972; Mary, Queen of Scots, 1972; Triple Echo, 1972; Il Sorviso de Grande Tentatore (The Tempter), 1973; Bequest to the Nation, 1973; A Touch of Class (Oscar Award, 1974), 1973; The Maids, 1974; The Romantic Englishwoman, 1974; Hedda Gabler, 1975; The Incredible Sarah, 1976; House Calls, 1978; Stevie, 1978; The Class of Miss MacMichael, 1978; Lost and Found, 1979; Hopscotch, 1980; Return of the Soldier, 1982; Health, 1982; *TV:* Elizabeth in Elizabeth R, 1971; The Patricia Neal Story (Amer.). Best film actress awards: Variety Club of GB, 1971, 1975, 1978; NY Film Critics, 1971; Nat. Soc. of Film Critics, US, 1971. *Recreations:* cooking, gardening, reading Jane Austen. *Address:* c/o Crouch Associates, 59 Frith Street, W1.

JACKSON, Gordon Noel, CMG 1962; MBE; HM Ambassador to Ecuador, 1967-70, retired; *b* 25 Dec. 1913; *m* 1959, Mary April Nettlefold, *er d* of late Frederick John Nettlefold and of Mrs Albert Coates; one *s* two *d.* Indian Political Service until 1947; then HM Foreign Service; Political Officer, Sharjah, 1947; transf. to Kuwait, Persian Gulf, 1949; transf. to Foreign Office, 1950; Consul, St Louis, USA, 1953; Foreign Service Officer, Grade 6, 1955; Consul-General: Basra, 1955-57; Lourenço Marques, 1957-60; Benghazi, 1960-63; HM Ambassador to Kuwait, 1963-67. *Publications:* Effective Horsemanship (for Dressage, Hunting, Three-day Events, Polo), 1967; (with W. Steinkraus) The Encyclopædia of the Horse, 1973. *Address:* Lowbarrow House, Leafield, Oxfordshire. *Club:* Travellers'.

JACKSON, Harvey; Hon. Consulting Surgeon, The National Hospital, Queen Square; Hon. Consulting Neurosurgeon, Westminster Hospital; Hon. Neurological Surgeon, St Thomas' Hospital; Hon. Consulting Surgeon, Acton General Hospital, since 1930; *b* 16 Oct. 1900; *s* of Richard Barlow Jackson and Elizabeth Shepherd; *m* 1930, Freda Mary Frampton; one *s* one *d. Educ:* Royal Grammar School, Newcastle upon Tyne; Middlesex Hospital. Hon. Asst Surg., West London Hosp., 1935-38. Past Pres., West London Medico-Chirurgical Soc.; Past Pres., Soc. of Brit. Neurological Surgeons; Fellow of Assoc. of Surgeons; Hunterian Prof. RCS of England, 1947, 1951; Elsberg Lectr, Neurological Soc. of New York, 1960; Visiting Prof. in Neurosurgery, University of Cairo, Guest Lectr, Univ. of Cincinnati, 1959; Lectr, Neurological Soc. of Chicago, 1959; Guest Lectr, Univ. of Santiago de Compostela, Spain, 1969. Past President: Section of Neurology, RSM; Surrey Branch, BMA. *Address:* 56 Fairacres, Roehampton Lane, SW15 5LY.

JACKSON, Herbert, FRIBA; FRTPI; architect and planning consultant, in private practice since 1931; *b* 25 June 1909; *s* of John Herbert Jackson; *m* 1930, Margaret Elizabeth Pearson. *Educ:* Handsworth Grammar Sch.; Birmingham Sch. of Architecture. RIBA Bronze Medal, 1928; RIBA Saxon Snell Prizeman, 1930. Mem. RIBA Council, 1956-58; Vice-Pres. RIBA 1960-62; Chm., RIBA Allied Socs Conf., 1960-62. Gov., Birmingham Coll. of Art; Chm. Birmingham Civic Soc., 1960-65; Pres. Birmingham and Five Counties Architectural Assoc., 1956-58; Pres. Royal Birmingham Society of Artists, 1960-62 (Prof. of Architecture, 1961). *Publications:* (jt) Plans for Minister of Town and Country Planning): S Wales, 1947; W Midlands and N Staffs, 1948. *Recreations:* travelling, reading. *Address:* 14 Clarendon Square, Leamington Spa, Warwicks. *T:* Leamington 24078.

JACKSON, Ian (Macgilchrist), BA Cantab, MB, BChir, FRCS, FRCOG; Obstetric and Gynæcological Surgeon, Middlesex Hospital, 1948-79, retired; Gynæcological Surgeon: Chelsea Hospital for Women, 1948-79; King Edward VII Hospital for Officers, 1961; Royal Masonic Hospital, 1963-79; Consulting Gynæcologist, King Edward VII Hospital, Midhurst, 1959; Consultant Obstetrician and Gynæcologist, RAF, 1964; *b* Shanghai, 11 Nov. 1914; *s* of Dr Ernest David Jackson; *m* 1943 (marr. diss., 1967); two *s* one *d* ; *m* 1970, Deirdre Ruth Heitz. *Educ:* Marlborough Coll.; Trinity Hall, Cambridge (scholar; double 1st cl. hons, Nat. Sci. tripos pts I, II). London Hospital: open scholarship, 1936; house appointments, 1939; First Asst, Surgical and Obstetric and Gynæcol Depts, 1940-43. Served as Surgical Specialist, RAMC, 1943-47 (Major); Parachute Surgical Team, 224 Para. Field Amb.; Mobile Surgical Unit, 3 Commando Brigade. Royal College of Obstetricians and Gynæcologists: Council, 1951-61, 1962-70; Hon. Sec., 1954-61; Chm., Examination Cttee, 1962-65, Hon. Treas., 1966-70; Hon. Librarian, RSM, 1969-75. Examiner for Univs of Cambridge, Oxford, and London, Conjoint Bd and RCOG. Mem., Court of Assts, Worshipful Soc. of Apothecaries, 1966, Senior Warden 1977, Master 1978; Pres., Chelsea

Clinical Soc., 1979. Order of the Star of Africa (Liberia), 1969; Grand Officer of Order of Istiqlal, Jordan, 1970. *Publications:* British Obstetric and Gynæcological Practice (jtly), 1963; Obstetrics by Ten Teachers (jtly), 1966, 2nd edn 1972; Gynæcology by Ten Teachers (jtly), 1971; numerous contribs to medical literature. *Recreations:* fishing, golf, photography. *Address:* 23 Springfield Road, NW8. *T:* 01-624 3580; 104 Harley Street, W1. *T:* 01-935 1801.

JACKSON, James Barry; *see* Barry, Michael.

JACKSON, (John) Edward, CMG 1977; HM Diplomatic Service; Ambassador to Belgium, since 1982; *b* 24 June 1925; *s* of late Edward Harry Jackson and of Mrs Margaret Jackson, Cambridge; *m* 1952, Evelyn Stainton Harris, *d* of late George James Harris, MC and of Mrs Friede Rowntree Harris, York; two *s* one *d*. *Educ:* Ardingly; Corpus Christi Coll., Cambridge. RNVR (Sub-Lt), 1943-46; joined Foreign (now Diplomatic) Service, 1947; FO, 1947-49; 3rd Sec., Paris, 1949-52; 2nd Sec., FO, 1952-56; Bonn, 1956-57; 1st Sec., Bonn, 1957-59; Guatemala City, 1959-62; FO, 1963-68; Counsellor, 1968; NATO Defence Coll., Rome, 1969; Counsellor (Political Adviser), British Mil. Govt, Berlin, 1969-73; Head of Defence Dept, FCO, 1973-75; Ambassador to Cuba, 1975-79; Head of UK Delegn to Negotiations on Mutual Reduction of Forces and Armaments and Associated Measures in Central Europe, with personal rank of Ambassador, 1980-82. *Recreations:* pictures, antiques, tennis, golf. *Address:* c/o Foreign and Commonwealth Office, SW1A 2AH. *Clubs:* Travellers'; Hurlingham.

JACKSON, John Wharton, JP; *b* 25 May 1902; *s* of John Jackson and Mary Wharton; *m* 1928, Mary Rigg; two *d*. *Educ:* Shrewsbury. Formerly Chm., Jackson's (Hurstead) Ltd, Rochdale. High Sheriff of Radnorshire, 1944-45; JP County of Lancaster, 1952. *Recreation:* golf. *Address:* Brackens, Mottram St Andrew, near Macclesfield, Cheshire. *T:* Prestbury 89277.

JACKSON, Joseph, QC 1967; *b* 21 Aug. 1924; *s* of late Samuel Jackson and of Hetty Jackson; *m* 1952, Marjorie Henrietta (*née* Lyons) (marr. diss. 1982); three *d*. *Educ:* Queens' Coll., Cambridge; University Coll., London. MA, LLB Cantab, LLM London. Barrister, 1947, Gibraltar Bar; Bencher, Middle Temple, 1980. Chairman: Probate and Divorce Bar Assoc., 1968-69; Family Law Bar Assoc., 1980-. Member: General Council of the Bar, 1969-73; Senate of the Inns of Court, 1975-78; Bar Cttee, 1980-81. Mem., Matrimonial Causes Rules Cttee, 1969-73 and 1977-81; Special Divorce Comr, 1969-70. Dept of Trade Inspector, Dowgate and General Investments Ltd, 1975-78. Mem. legal aid cttees including: Law Soc. Legal Aid Cttee, 1975-78; Lord Chancellor's Working Party to review legal aid legislation. Lectures: Weir Meml, Alberta, 1981; Opas Meml, NSW, 1982. *Publications:* English Legal History, 1951 (2nd edn 1955); Formation and Annulment of Marriage, 1951, 2nd edn, 1969; Rayden on Divorce, 5th edn (supp.) 1951 to 14th edn 1982; Matrimonial Finance and Taxation, 1972, 3rd edn, 1980; (consulting editor) Clarke Hall and Morrison on Children, 9th edn, 1977; contrib. to Halsbury's Laws of England, Encyclopædia Britannica, Atkin's Encyclopædia of Court Forms, Law Quarterly Review, Modern Law Review, Canadian Bar Review, etc. *Recreations:* gardening, painting, ceramics. *Address:* 1 Mitre Court Buildings, Temple, EC4. *T:* 01-353 0434/2277.

JACKSON, Prof. Kenneth Hurlstone, FBA 1957; FSAScot 1951; FRSE 1977; Professor of Celtic Languages, Literatures, History and Antiquities, Edinburgh University, 1950-79; *b* 1 Nov. 1909; *s* of Alan Stuart Jackson and Lucy Hurlstone; *m* 1936, Janet Dall Galloway, of Hillside, Kinross-shire; one *s* one *d*. *Educ:* Whitgift Sch., Croydon; St John's Coll., Cambridge (Exhibitioner and Scholar). First Cl. Hons with Distinction, Classical Tripos, 1930 and 1931 (Senior Classic, 1931); BA 1931; First Cl. Hons with Distinction, Archæology and Anthropology Tripos, 1932; Sir William Brown medals for Greek and Latin verse, 1930 (two), 1931; Allen Research Studentship, 1932-34; research in Celtic at University Colls of North Wales and Dublin. Fellowship at St John's Coll., and Faculty Lectr in Celtic, Cambridge Univ., 1934-39; MA 1935; LittD 1954; Hon. Fellow, St John's Coll., 1979; Lectureship, 1939, Assoc. Professorship, 1940-49, Professorship, 1949-50, Celtic Languages and Literatures, Harvard Univ. Hon. AM Harvard, 1940. Editor of the Journal of Celtic Studies, 1949-57. Corr. Fellow of Mediæval Acad. of America, 1951; Pres. of Scottish Anthropological and Folklore Soc., 1952-60; Vice-Pres. of Soc. of Antiquaries of Scotland, 1960-63; Vice-Pres., English Place-Name Soc., 1973-79, Pres., 1979-; Mem., Comité Internat. des Sciences Onomastiques, 1955-; Mem. Council for Name Studies in Great Britain and Ireland, 1961-; one of HM Commissioners for Ancient Monuments (Scotland), 1963-. War service in the British Imperial Censorship, Bermuda (Uncommon Languages), 1942-44; in the US censorship, 1944. Hon. DLitt Celt. Ireland, 1958; Hon. DLitt Wales, 1963; Hon. DUniv Haute-Bretagne, 1971. Hon. Mem. Mod. Language Assoc. of America, 1958; Hon. Mem. Royal Irish Academy, 1965; Assoc. Mem., Royal Belgian Acad. for Scis, Letters and Fine Arts, 1975. Derek Allen Prize, British Acad., 1979. *Publications:* Early Welsh Gnomic Poems, 1935; Studies in Early Celtic Nature Poetry, 1935; Cath Maighe Léna, 1938; Scéalta ón mBlascaod, 1939; A Celtic Miscellany, 1951, repr. 1971; Language and History in Early Britain, 1953; Contribs to the Study of Manx Phonology, 1955; The International Popular Tale and Early Welsh Tradition, 1961; The Oldest Irish Tradition, 1964; A Historical Phonology of Breton, 1967; The Gododdin, 1969; The Gaelic Notes in the Book of Deer, 1972; articles on Celtic Languages, literature, history and folklore in Zeitschrift für Celtische Philologie, Etudes Celtiques, Bulletin of the Bd of Celtic Studies, Antiquity, Journal of Roman Studies, Folklore, Journal of Celtic Studies, Scottish Gaelic Studies, Speculum, Modern Philology, etc. *Recreation:* walking. *Address:* 34 Cluny Drive, Edinburgh EH10 6DX. *Club:* Edinburgh University Staff.

JACKSON, Laura (Riding), (Mrs Schuyler B. Jackson); *see* Riding, Laura.

JACKSON, Very Rev. Lawrence, AKC; Provost of Blackburn, since 1973; *b* Hessel, Yorks, 22 March 1926; *s* of Walter and Edith Jackson; *m* 1955, Faith Anne, *d* of Philip and Marjorie Seymour; four *d*. *Educ:* Alderman Newton's Sch.; Leicester Coll. of Technology; King's Coll., Univ. of London (AKC 1950); St Boniface Coll., Warminster. Asst Curate, St Margaret, Leicester, and Asst Chaplain, Leicester Royal Infirmary, 1951-54; Vicar of: Wymeswold, Leicester, 1954-59; St James the Greater, Leicester, 1959-65; Coventry (Holy Trinity), 1965-73. Canon of Coventry Cath., 1967-73; Rural Dean of Coventry N, 1969-73. Senior Chaplain: Leicester and Rutland ACF, 1955-65; Warwickshire ACF, 1965-73; Chaplain, Coventry Guild of Freemen, 1968-73; Dio. Chaplain, CEMS, 1969-71. Mem., Gen. Synod of C of E, 1975-; a Church Comr, 1981. Dir, The Samaritans of Leicester, 1960-65; Pres., Coventry Round Table, 1968; Chm. Governors, Coventry Blue Coat Sch.; Governor: Barr's Hill Sch.; Bablake Sch.; Queen Elizabeth Grammar Sch., Blackburn. Chm., Blackburn Diocesan Bd for Social Responsibility. *Recreations:* music, archæology, architecture, countryside, after dinner speaking. *Address:* The Provost's House, Preston New Road, Blackburn BB2 6PS. *T:* Blackburn 52502. *Clubs:* Eccentric, Forty; Lighthouse; Lord's Taverners'.

JACKSON, Hon. Sir Lawrence (Walter), KCMG 1970; Kt 1964; BA, LLB; Judge, 1949-77, and Chief Justice, 1969-77, Supreme Court of Western Australia; Chancellor, University of Western Australia, 1968-81; *b* Dulwich, South Australia, 27 Sept. 1913; *s* of L. S. Jackson; *m* 1937, Mary, *d* of T. H. Donaldson; one *s* two *d*. *Educ:* Fort Street High Sch., Sydney; University of Sydney. *Recreations:* swimming, golf. *Address:* 13 Cliff Way, Claremont, WA 6010, Australia. *Club:* Weld (Perth, WA).

JACKSON, Margaret M.; *see* Beckett, M. M.

JACKSON, Sir Michael (Roland), 5th Bt, *cr* 1902; MA; MIEE; FIQA; *b* 20 April 1919; *s* of Sir W. D. Russell Jackson, 4th Bt, and Kathleen (*d* 1975), *d* of Summers Hunter, CBE, Tynemouth; *S* father 1956; *m* 1st, 1942, Hilda Margaret (marr. diss. 1969), *d* of Cecil George Herbert Richardson, CBE, Newark; one *s* one *d*; 2nd, 1969, Hazel Mary, *d* of Ernest Harold Edwards. *Educ:* Stowe; Clare Coll., Cambridge. Served War of 1939-45; Flight-Lt, Royal Air Force Volunteer Reserve. *Heir:* *s* Thomas St Felix Jackson [*b* 27 Sept. 1946; *m* 1980, Victoria, *d* of George Scatliff, Wineham, Sussex; one *d*]. *Address:* Dragon Cottage, Dragon's Green, Horsham, West Sussex.

JACKSON, Mrs Muriel W.; *see* Ward-Jackson.

JACKSON, Sir Nicholas (Fane St George), 3rd Bt *cr* 1913; organist, harpsichordist and composer; Organist and Master of the Choristers, St David's Cathedral, since 1977; *b* 4 Sept. 1934; *s* of Sir Hugh Jackson, 2nd Bt, and of Violet Marguerite Loftus, y *d* of Loftus St George; *S* father, 1979; *m* 1972, Nadia Françoise Genevieve (*née* Michard); one *s*. *Educ:* Radley Coll.; Wadham Coll., Oxford; RAM. LRAM; ARCM. Organist: St Anne's, Soho, 1963-68; St James's, Piccadilly, 1971-74; St Lawrence, Jewry, 1971-77. Musical Dir, St David's Cathedral Bach Fest., 1979. Member of The London Virtuosi. Organ recitals and broadcasts: Berlin, 1967; Paris, 1972, 1975; USA (tour), 1975, 1978; Minorca, 1977; Spain, 1979; Madrid Bach Festival, 1980. Début as harpsichordist, Wigmore Hall, 1963; appeared frequently with Soho Concertante, Queen Elizabeth Hall, 1964-72. Mem. Music Cttee, Welsh Arts Council, 1981-. Recordings: Mass for a Saint's Day, 1971; organ and harpsichord music, incl. works by Arnell, Bach, Couperin, Langlais, Mozart, Vierne and Walther. Liveryman, Drapers' Co., 1965. *Publications:* compositions: Mass for a Saint's Day, 1966; 20th Century Merbecke, 1967; 4 Images (for organ), 1971; Solemn Mass, 1977. *Recreations:* sketching, riding. *Heir:* *s* Thomas Graham St George Jackson, *b* 5 Oct. 1980. *Address:* Organist's Lodgings, St Davids, Pembrokeshire. *T:* St Davids 364.

JACKSON, Oliver James V.; *see* Vaughan-Jackson.

JACKSON, Patrick; *see* Jackson, W. P.

JACKSON, Peter (Michael); Senior Lecturer, Institute of Extra-mural Studies, National University of Lesotho, since 1980; *b* 14 Oct. 1928; *s* of Leonard Patterson Jackson; *m* 1961, Christine Thomas. *Educ:* Durham Univ.; University Coll., Leicester. Lecturer, Dept of Sociology, University of Hull, 1964-66; Fellow, Univ. of Hull, 1970-72; Tutor, Open Univ., 1972-74; Senior Planning Officer, S Yorks CC, 1974-77. MP (Lab) High Peak, 1966-70; contested (Lab) Birmingham North, European Parly elecns, 1979. Mem., Peak Park Jt Planning Bd, 1973-77, 1979-82. *Recreations:* numismatics, book collecting, ski-ing. *Address:* PO Box 1585, Maseru 100, Lesotho, South Africa. *Club:* Maseru (Lesotho).

JACKSON, Air Vice-Marshal Sir Ralph (Coburn), KBE 1973; CB 1963; Adviser in Insurance and Company Medicine; Honorary Civil Consultant in Medicine to RAF; Consultant Medical Referee, Confederation Life Insurance Co.; Deputy Chief Medical Officer: Victory Re-insurance Co.; World Wide

Insurance Co.; *b* 22 June 1914; *s* of Ralph Coburn Jackson and Phillis Jackson (*née* Dodds); *m* 1939, Joan Lucy Crowley; two *s* two *d*. *Educ:* Oakmount Sch., Arnside; Guy's Hosp., London. MRCS 1937; FRCPE 1960 (MRCPE 1950); FRCP 1972 (MRCP 1968, LRCP 1937); FRSM. Qualified in Medicine Guy's Hosp., 1937; House Officer appts, Guy's Hosp., 1937-38; commnd in RAF as MO, Nov. 1938; served in France, 1939-40; Russia, 1941; W Africa, 1942-43 (despatches); Sen. MO, 46 Gp for Brit. Casualty Air Evac., 1944-45 (despatches). Med. Specialist, RAF Hosps Wroughton, Aden and Halton, 1946-52 (Consultant in Med., Princess Mary's RAF Hosp. Halton, 1952-63; RAF Hosp., Wegberg, Germany, 1964-66); Consultant Advr in Medicine, 1966-74; Sen. Consultant to RAF, 1971-75; Advr in Medicine to CAA, 1966-75; Chm., Defence Med. Services, Postgrad. Council, 1973-75. QHP 1969-75. MacArthur Lectr, Univ. Edinburgh, 1959. Member: Assurance Med. Soc.; Main Grants Cttee, RAF Benevolent Fund; Hon. Mem., Chiltern Med. Soc.; Liveryman, Worshipful Soc. of Apothecaries; Freeman, City of London. Fellow RSPB. Lady Cade Medal, RCS, 1960. *Publications:* papers on acute renal failure, the artificial kidney and routine electrocardiography in various medical books and journals, 1959-1974. *Recreations:* birdwatching, ancient buildings, history of City of London. *Address:* Piper's Hill, Marwell, Westerham, Kent TN16 1SB. *T:* Westerham 64436; (office) Room 502/6, New Lloyds Building, 51 Lime Street, EC3. *T:* 01-626 6732. *Club:* Royal Air Force.

JACKSON, Col Richard John Laurence, CBE 1971; DL, JP; FRIBA, DipArch; Architect; Member, North Yorkshire County Council, since 1974 (Chairman, 1977-81); *b* 17 Oct. 1908; *s* of John Robert and Kathleen Emma Jackson; *m* 1936, Sara Alexander Wilson; one *s*. *Educ:* Scarborough Coll.; Liverpool Univ. Served War of 1939-45, Green Howards; Middle East, Western Desert, Libya, Tunisia, Sicily and Normandy invasions. Mem., North Riding of Yorkshire CC, 1949-74 (Alderman, 1961-74). JP 1951; DL North Riding, 1967. *Recreation:* angling. *Address:* Bridgeholme, Egton Bridge, Whitby, North Yorks. *T:* Whitby 85221.

JACKSON, Prof. Richard Meredith, FBA 1966; LLD; JP; Downing Professor of the Laws of England, 1966-70; Fellow, St John's College, Cambridge, since 1946; *b* 19 Aug. 1903; *s* of James Jackson, JP, Northampton and Jenny May Jackson (*née* Parnell); *m* 1st, Lydia Jibourtovitch (marr. diss.); 2nd, 1936, Lenli, *d* of Alexander Tie Ten Quee, Kingston, Jamaica; one *d* (and one *s* decd). *Educ:* Sidcot; Leighton Park; St John's Coll., Cambridge. Admitted solicitor, 1928. Cambridge Law Sch., LLD 1939; Home Office, 1941-45; Sec. Royal Commn on JPs, 1946-48; Reader in Public Law and Admin., Cambridge, 1950; Member: Royal Commn on Mental Health Services, 1954-57; Deptl Cttee on Children and Young Persons, 1956-60; Council of the Magistrates' Assoc., 1948-72 (Vice-Pres., 1972-). JP Cambs. 1942. *Publications:* History of Quasi-Contract in English Law, 1936; Machinery of Justice in England, 1940 (7th edn, 1977); Machinery of Local Government, 1958 (2nd edn, 1965); Enforcing the Law, 1967 (2nd edn, 1972); ed, 3rd edn, Justice of the Peace, by Leo Page, 1967; articles in learned jls. *Recreation:* yacht cruising. *Address:* St John's College, Cambridge. *T:* 61621; 10 Halifax Road, Cambridge. *T:* 358179. *Club:* Royal Cruising.

JACKSON, Richard Michael; HM Diplomatic Service; Counsellor, Stockholm, since 1982; *b* 12 July 1940; *s* of Richard William Jackson and Charlotte (*née* Wrightson); *m* 1961, Mary Elizabeth Kitchin; one *s* one *d*. *Educ:* Queen Elizabeth Grammar Sch., Darlington; Paisley Grammar Sch.; Glasgow Univ. (MA Hons 1961). Joined Home Civil Service, 1961; Scottish Office, 1961-70; seconded to MAFF, 1971-72; seconded to FCO and served in The Hague, 1973-74; trans. to HM Diplomatic Service, 1974; European Integration Dept (External), FCO, 1975-76; Panama City, 1976-79; Arms Control and Disarmament Dept, FCO, 1979-81; Buenos Aires, 1981-82. *Address:* c/o Foreign and Commonwealth Office, King Charles Street, SW1.

JACKSON, Sir Robert, 7th Bt *cr* 1815; *b* 16 March 1910; *s* of Major Francis Gorham Jackson (*d* 1942) (2nd *s* of 4th Bt) and Ana Maria Biscar Brennan; *S* kinsman, Sir John Montrésor Jackson, 6th Bt, 1980; *m* 1943, Maria E. Casamayou; two *d*. *Educ:* St George's College. Career on estancia. *Heir:* kinsman Keith Arnold Jackson [*b* 1921; *m* Pauline Mona, *d* of B. P. Climo, Wellington, NZ; four *s* one *d*]. *Address:* Santiago de Chile 1243, Montevideo, Uruguay. *T:* 905487. *Club:* English (Montevideo).

JACKSON, Comdr Sir Robert (Gillman Allen), KCVO 1962; Kt 1956; CMG 1944; OBE 1941; Under Secretary General, in charge of UN humanitarian operations in Kampuchea and Thailand, since 1979; Consultant to Volta River Authority, Ghana, since 1962 (Member of Board 1965-76); Senior Consultant to McKinsey & Company since 1970; *b* 1911; *m* 1950, Barbara Ward (Baroness Jackson of Lodsworth) (*d* 1981); one *s*. RAN, 1929-37; transf. to Malta and RN, 1937; Chief Staff Officer to Gov. and C-in-C, Malta, 1940; Planning Malta Comd Defence Scheme; re-armament of the Fortress; devalt Co-ordinated Supply Scheme, 1940 (OBE); Dir-Gen., ME Supply Centre and Principal Asst to UK Minister of State, 1942-45; co-ordin civilian supply ops/mil. ops; devalt Aid to Russia Supply route: estab. anti-locust campaign, 1942 (CMG); AFHQ for special duties in Greece, 1944-45; transf. to HM Treasury, 1945; Sen. Dep. Dir-Gen. of UNRRA, 1945-47, and, in 1945, i/c of UNRRA's ops in Europe (inc. 8,500,000 displaced persons); supervised transfer of UNRRA's residual functions to WHO, FAO, and assisted in establishment of IRO (now UNHCR), and International Children's Emergency Fund, 1947 (UNICEF); services

recognised by various governments in Europe and Asia; Asst Sec.-Gen. for Co-ordination in the UN, 1948; HM Treasury, for duties with Lord Pres. of Council, 1949; Perm. Sec., Min. of Nat. Development, Australia, 1950-52 (Snowy Mountains Scheme); Adviser to Govt of India on Development Plans, 1952, 1957 and 1962-63, and to Govt of Pakistan, 1952; Chm. of Preparatory Commission for Volta River multi-purpose project, Gold Coast, 1953-56; Chm., Development Commission, Ghana, 1956-61 (Kt); Organisation of Royal Tours in Ghana, 1959 and 1961(KCVO); Mem. Adv. Bd, Mekong Project, SE Asia, 1962-76; Adviser to President of Liberia, 1962-79; Special Consultant to Administrator, UNDP, 1963-72, Special Adviser, 1978-80; Chm., UN gp reporting on Zambia's security, 1963; Comr i/c, Survey of UN Develt System, 1968-71; Under Sec.-Gen. i/c UN Relief Ops in Bangladesh, 1972-74; Under Sec.-Gen. i/c UN assistance to Zambia, 1973-78, to Indo-China, 1975-78, to Cape Verde Is, 1975-78, to São Tomé and Príncipe, 1977-78; Counsellor to Interim Mekong Cttee, 1978-. Member: Cttee, Fédération Mondiale des Villes Jumelées Cités Unies, 1972-; IUCN Commn on Environmental Policy, 1972-; Dag Hammarskjöld Foundn, Stockholm, 1981-. Mem. Internat. Jury, Prize of Institut de la Vie, 1972-. Hon. DL Syracuse. *Publications:* An International Development Authority, 1955; Report of the Volta River Preparatory Commission, 1956; A Study of the United Nations Development System, 1969; Report on Sen. Volunteers in UN System, 1978; Report on reinforcement of UN Indust. Develt Orgn, 1979. *Address:* United Nations, New York City, NY 10017, USA; Palais des Nations, Geneva, Switzerland. *Clubs:* Brooks's; Victoria (Jersey); Melbourne (Victoria).

JACKSON, Robert Victor; Member (C) Upper Thames, European Parliament, since 1979; *b* 24 Sept. 1946; *m* 1975, Caroline Frances (*née* Harvey). *Educ:* Falcon Coll., S Rhodesia; St Edmund Hall, Oxford (H. W. C. Davis Prize, 1966; 1st Cl. Hons Mod. Hist. 1968); President Oxford Union, 1967. Prize Fellowship, All Souls Coll., 1968 (Fellow, 1968-). Councillor, Oxford CC, 1969-71; Political Adviser to Sec. of State for Employment, 1973-74; Member, Cabinet of Sir Christopher (now Baron) Soames, EEC Commn, Brussels, 1974-76; Chef de Cabinet, President of EEC Economic and Social Cttee, Brussels, 1976-78; Special Adviser to Governor of Rhodesia (Lord Soames), 1979-80; European Parlt's Rapporteur-Gen. on 1983 European Community Budget. Contested (C) Manchester Central Div., general election, Oct. 1974. Editor: The Round Table: Commonwealth Jl of Internat. Relations, 1970-74; International Affairs (Chatham House), 1979-80. *Publications:* South Asian Crisis: India, Pakistan, Bangladesh 1972, 1975; The Powers of the European Parliament, 1977; The European Parliament: Penguin Guide to Direct Elections, 1979; Reforming the European Budget, 1981. *Recreations:* reading, music, walking. *Address:* 4 Churton Place, SW1. *T:* 01-930 9673; 53 avenue des Nerviers, Brussels, Belgium. *Clubs:* Garrick, Athenæum, Travellers'.

JACKSON, Thomas; General Secretary, Union of Communication Workers (formerly Post Office Workers), 1967-82; HM Government Director, British Petroleum Co. Ltd, since 1975; *b* 9 April 1925; *s* of George Frederick Jackson and Ethel Hargreaves; *m* 1947, Norma Burrow; one *d*. *Educ:* Jack Lane Elementary Sch. Boy Messenger, GPO, 1939; Royal Navy, 1943; Postman, 1946; Executive Mem., Union of Post Office Workers, 1955; Asst Sec., Union of Post Office Workers, 1964. Member: Gen. Council of TUC, 1967-82 (Chm., 1978-79; Chm., Internat. Cttee, 1978-82); Press Council, 1973-76; Annan Cttee on the Future of Broadcasting, 1974-77; Broadcasting Complaints Commn, 1982-; CRE, 1977-78; Court and Council, Sussex Univ., 1974-. Vice-Pres., WEA, 1977-. A Governor: BBC, 1968-73; NIESR, 1974-. *Recreations:* cooking, photography. *Address:* 22 Parish Ghyll Road, Ilkley, West Yorks LS29 9NE.

JACKSON, (Walter) Patrick; Under-Secretary, Department of Transport, since 1981; *b* 10 Feb. 1929; *m* 1952, Kathleen (*née* Roper); one *s* one *d*. *Educ:* University Coll., Oxford (BA). John Lewis Partnership, 1952-66; Principal, Min. of Transport and DoE, 1966-72; Asst Sec., DoE, 1972-78; Under Sec. and Regional Dir (E Midlands), DoE and Dept of Transport, 1978-81. *Recreation:* concert- and theatre-going. *Address:* c/o Department of the Environment, 2 Marsham Street, SW1.

JACKSON, Gen. Sir William (Godfrey Fothergill), GBE 1975 (OBE 1958); KCB 1971; MC 1940, and Bar, 1943; Governor and Commander-in-Chief, Gibraltar, 1978-82; *b* 28 Aug. 1917; *s* of late Col A. Jackson, RAMC, Yanwath, Cumberland, and E. M. Jackson (*née* Fothergill), Brownber, Westmorland; *m* 1946, Joan Mary Buesden; one *s* one *d*. *Educ:* Shrewsbury; RMA, Woolwich; King's Coll., Cambridge; King's medal, RMA Woolwich, 1937. Commnd into Royal Engineers, 1937; served War of 1939-45: Norwegian Campaign, 1940; Tunisia, 1942-43; Sicily and Italy, 1943-44; Far East, 1945; GSO1, HQ Allied Land Forces SE Asia, 1945-48; Instructor, Staff Coll., Camberley, 1948-50; Instructor, RMA, Sandhurst, 1951-53; AA & QMG (War Plans), War Office, during Suez ops, 1956; Comdr, Gurkha Engrs, 1958-60; Col GS, Minley Div. of Staff Coll., Camberley, 1961-62; Dep. Dir of Staff Duties, War Office, 1962-64; Imp. Def. Coll., 1965; Dir, Chief of Defence Staff's Unison Planning Staff, 1966-68; Asst Chief of General Staff (Operational Requirements), MoD, 1968-70; GOC-in-C, Northern Command, 1970-72; QMG, 1973-76. Military Historian, Cabinet Office, 1977-78. Colonel Commandant: RE, 1971-81; Gurkha Engrs, 1971-76; RAOC, 1973-78; Hon. Col, Engineer and Rly Staff Corps, RE, TAVR, 1977-; ADC (Gen.) to the Queen, 1974-76. *Publications:* Attack in the West, 1953; Seven Roads to Moscow, 1957; The Battle for Italy, 1967; Battle for

Rome, 1969; Alexander of Tunis as Military Commander, 1971; The North African Campaigns, 1975; Overlord: Normandy 1944, 1978; contribs to Royal United Service Instn Jl (gold medals for prize essays, 1950 and 1966). *Recreations:* fishing, writing, gardening. *Address:* Williams & Glyn's Bank Ltd, Holt's Branch, Whitehall, SW1. *Club:* Army and Navy.

JACKSON, William Theodore, CBE 1967 (MBE 1946); ARIBA; MRTPI; Director of Post Office Services, Ministry of Public Building and Works, 1969-71, retired; *b* 18 July 1906; *y s* of Rev. Oliver Miles Jackson and Emily Jackson; *m* 1932, Marjorie Campbell; one *s* two *d. Educ:* Cheltenham Gram. Sch. Chief Architect, Iraq Govt, 1936-38; Dir, Special Repair Service, Min. of Works, 1939-45; Min. of Public Building and Works, 1946-69; Dir, Mobile Labour Force; Dir of Maintenance; seconded to World Bank as Advr to Iran Technical Bureau of Development Plan organisation, 1956-57; Regional Dir; Dir, Regional Services; Dir, Headquarters Services, 1957-69. *Recreations:* gardening, painting. *Address:* Church Farm, Blyford, Halesworth, Suffolk. *T:* Blythburgh 455.

JACKSON, William Unsworth; Chief Executive, Kent County Council, since 1974; *b* 9 Feb. 1926; *s* of William Jackson and Margaret Esplen Jackson (*née* Sunderland); *m* 1952, Valerie Annette (*née* Llewellyn); one *s* one *d. Educ:* Alsop High Sch., Liverpool. Solicitor. Entered local govt service, Town Clerk's Office, Liverpool, 1942; Dep. County Clerk, Kent, 1970. Hon. Sec., Soc. of Local Authority Chief Execs, 1980-. *Address:* 34 Yardley Park Road, Tonbridge, Kent. *T:* Tonbridge 351078. *Club:* Royal Over-Seas League.

JACKSON, Yvonne Brenda; Chairman, West Yorkshire Metropolitan County Council, 1980-81; *b* 23 July 1920; *d* of Charles and Margaret Wilson; *m* 1946, Edward Grosvenor Jackson; twin *s* one *d. Educ:* Edgbaston C of E Coll., Birmingham; Manchester Teachers' Trng Coll. (Dip. Domestic Science and qualified teacher). School Meals Organizer, West Bromwich, Staffs, 1940-45. Mem., W Riding CC, 1967-73 (local govt reorganisation); Mem. W Yorks CC, 1973-; Chm., Fire and Public Protection Cttee, 1977-80; Dep. Leader and Shadow Chm., Public Transport Cttee, 1981-. Mem. Exec. Cttee, Nat. Union of Cons. Assocs (Mem., Yorks Area Finance and Gen. Purposes Cttee; Divl Chm., Barkston Ash). *Recreations:* badminton, fishing; formerly County hockey and tennis player; former motor rally driver (competed in nat. and internat. events inc. Monte Carlo, Alpine and Tulip rallies). *Address:* The Field House, East Rigton, East Keswick, West Yorkshire LS17 9AR. *T:* Collingham Bridge 73452. *Club:* English-Speaking Union.

JACKSON-LIPKIN, Miles Henry; Hon. Mr Justice Jackson-Lipkin; a Judge of the High Court of Hong Kong, since 1981; *b* Liverpool, 24 May 1919; *s* of late I. J. Jackson-Lipkin, RAMC and Florence Adelaide Garrison-Patley; *m* 1960, Lucille Yun-Shim Fung, barrister; one *s. Educ:* Harrow; Trinity Coll., Oxford. Served RN, 1939-51, Lt-Comdr. Called to the Bar, Middle Temple, 1951; admitted Hong Kong Bar, 1963, NSW Bar, 1980; QC Hong Kong, 1974. Panel Mem., Inland Revenue Bd of Review, Hong Kong, 1975; Chm. Exec. Cttee, and Man. Dir, Hong Kong Children and Youth Services, 1978-. Founder Member: Medico-Legal Soc., 1952; Justice, 1956; Hong Kong Br., Justice, 1963; Hong Kong Medico-Legal Soc., 1974 (Mem. Cttee, 1976-). JP Hong Kong, 1977-81. CLJ 1975, KLJ 1977 (Grand Priory of Lochore); Council of Honour, Monarchist League. *Publications:* The Beaufort Legitimation, 1957; Scales of Justice, 1958; Israel Naval Forces, 1959. *Recreations:* gardening, heraldry, classical music, philately, walking. *Address:* 58 Mount Nicholson Gap, Hong Kong. *T:* (5) 892 1818; 62 Eaton Terrace, SW1. *T:* 01-730 1818. *Clubs:* Naval and Military, MCC; Hong Kong, Hong Kong Cricket, Royal Hong Kong Golf, Royal Hong Kong Jockey, American (Hong Kong).

JACOB, Ven. Bernard Victor; Archdeacon of Kingston-upon-Thames, since 1977; *b* 20 Nov. 1921; *m* 1946, Dorothy Joan Carey; one *s* two *d. Educ:* Liverpool Institute; St Peter's College (MA) and Wycliffe Hall, Oxford. Curate, Middleton, Lancs, 1950-54; Vicar, Ulverston, Lancs, 1954-59; Vicar, Bilston, Staffs, 1959-64; Warden of Scargill House, Yorks, 1964-68; Rector of Mortlake, 1968-77. *Recreations:* travel, reading, enjoying life. *Address:* 7 Cornwall Road, Cheam, Sutton SM2 6DT.

JACOB, Lt-Gen. Sir (Edward) Ian (Claud), GBE 1960 (KBE 1946; CBE 1942); CB 1944; DL; late RE, Colonel, retired and Hon. Lieutenant-General; Chairman, Matthews Holdings Ltd, 1970-76; *b* 27 Sept. 1899; *s* of late Field Marshal Sir Claud Jacob, GCB, GCSI, KCMG; *m* 1924, Cecil Bisset Treherne; two *s. Educ:* Wellington Coll.; RMA, Woolwich; King's Coll., Cambridge (BA). 2nd Lieut, Royal Engineers, 1918; Capt. 1929; Bt Major, 1935; Major, 1938; Bt Lt-Col, 1939; Col, 1943. Waziristan, 1922-23. Staff Coll., 1931-32; GSO3 War Office, 1934-36; Bde-Maj., Canal Bde, Egypt, 1936-38; Military Asst Sec., Cttee of Imperial Defence, 1938; Military Asst Sec. to the War Cabinet, 1939-46; retired pay, 1946. Controller of European Services, BBC, 1946; Dir of Overseas Services, BBC, 1947 (on leave of absence during 1952); Chief Staff Officer to Minister of Defence and Deputy Sec. (Mil.) of the Cabinet during 1952; Dir-Gen. of the BBC, 1952-60; Director: Fisons, 1960-70; EMI, 1960-73; Chm., Covent Garden Market Authority, 1961-66; a Trustee, Imperial War Museum, 1966-73. CC, E Suffolk, 1960-70, Alderman, 1970-74; CC Suffolk, 1974-77. JP Suffolk, 1961-69; DL Suffolk, 1964. US Legion of Merit (Comdr). *Address:* The Red House, Woodbridge, Suffolk. *T:* Woodbridge 2001. *Club:* Army and Navy.

JACOB, Prof. François; Croix de la Libération; Grand-Croix de la Légion d'Honneur; Departmental Head, Pasteur Institute; Professor of Cellular Genetics, at the College of France, since 1964; *b* Nancy (Meurthe & Moselle), 17 June 1920; *m* 1947, Lysiane Bloch; three *s* one *d. Educ:* Lycée Carnot, France. D en M 1947; D ès S 1954. Pasteur Institute: Asst, 1950; Head of Laboratory, 1956. Mem., Acad. of Scis, Paris, 1977. Charles Léopold Mayer Prize, Acad. des Sciences, Paris, 1962; Nobel Prize for Medicine, 1965. Foreign Member: Royal Danish Acad. of Letters and Sciences, 1962; Amer. Acad. of Arts and Sciences, 1964; Nat. Acad. of Scis, USA, 1969; Royal Soc., 1973; Acad. Royale de Médecine, Belgique, 1973. Dr *hc* University of Chicago, 1965. *Publications:* The Logic of Life, 1970; The Possible and the Actual, 1981; various scientific. *Recreation:* painting. *Address:* 28 rue du Dr Roux, 75015 Paris, France.

JACOB, Frederick Henry; retired; Director, Ministry of Agriculture, Fisheries and Food's Pest Infestation Control Laboratory, 1968-77; *b* 12 March 1915; *s* of Henry Theodore and Elizabeth Jacob; *m* 1941, Winifred Edith Sloman; one *s* one *d. Educ:* Friars Sch., Bangor; UC North Wales. BSc, MSc, FIBiol. Asst Entomologist: King's Coll., Newcastle upon Tyne, 1942-44; Sch. of Agriculture, Cambridge, 1944-45; Adviser in Agric. Zoology, UC North Wales, 1945-46; Adv. Entomologist, Min. of Agriculture and Fisheries, Nat. Agric. Adv. Service, N Wales, 1946-50; Head of Entomology Dept, MAFF, Plant Pathology Lab., 1950-68. Pres., Assoc. of Applied Biologists, 1976-77. *Publications:* papers mainly on systematics of Aphididae in learned jls. *Recreations:* hill walking, rock climbing. *Address:* Llys y Gwynt, Llandegai, Bangor, Gwynedd LL57 4BG. *T:* Bangor 53863. *Clubs:* Farmers', Climbers; Wayfarers (Liverpool).

JACOB, Gordon (Percival Septimus), CBE 1968; DMus; FRCM; Hon. RAM; Composer; Professor of Theory, Composition, and Orchestration, Royal College of Music, retired 1966; Editor of Penguin Musical Scores, 1947-57; *b* 5 July 1895; 7th *s* of late Stephen Jacob, CSI; *m* 1st, 1924, Sidney Wilmot (*d* 1958), *er d* of Rev. A. W. Gray, Ipswich; 2nd, 1959, Margaret Sidney Hannah, *d* of C. A. Gray, Helions Bumpstead; one *s* one *d. Educ:* Dulwich Coll.; Royal College of Music. Served European War, 1914-18; UPS and Queen's Royal West Surrey Regt (Prisoner of War in Germany, April 1917-Dec. 1918); Studied composition at the Royal College of Music under the late Sir Charles V. Stanford; Conducting under Adrian Boult, and Theory under Herbert Howells. Compositions include Orchestral, Choral and Chamber music, many concertos for various instruments, works for Wind Orchestra and Brass Band, also orchestrations and arrangements. Holder of John Collard Fellowship (Worshipful Company of Musicians), 1943-46; Cobbett Medal for Services to Chamber Music, 1949. *Publications:* Orchestral Technique, a Manual for Students; How to Read a Score; The Composer and his Art; The Elements of Orchestration; most of the works alluded to above; also many other smaller compositions. Contributed to Chambers's Encyclopædia and Groves Dictionary of Music. *Recreations:* cross-words, motoring, reading; interested in all forms of art, and in natural history. *Address:* 1 Audley Road, Saffron Walden, Essex CB11 3HW. *T:* 22406.

JACOB, Lieut-Gen. Sir Ian; *see* Jacob, Lieut-Gen. Sir E. I. C.

JACOB, Sir Isaac Hai, (Sir Jack Jacob), Kt 1979; QC 1976; Senior Master of the Supreme Court, Queen's Bench Division, and Queen's Remembrancer, 1975-80; Fellow of University College, London, 1966; *b* 5 June 1908; 3rd *s* of late Jacob Isaiah and Aziza Jacob; *m* 1940, Rose Mary Jenkins (*née* Samwell); two *s. Educ:* Shanghai Public Sch. for Boys; London Sch. of Economics; University Coll., London. LLB (1st class Hons), London; Joseph Hume Scholar in Jurisprudence, University Coll., London, 1928 and 1930; Arden Scholar, Gray's Inn, 1930; Cecil Peace Prizeman, 1930. Called to the Bar, Gray's Inn, Nov. 1930; Hon. Bencher, 1978; Mem., Senate of Inns of Court and the Bar, 1975-78. Served in ranks from 1940 until commissioned in RAOC 1942; Staff Capt., War Office (Ord. I), 1943-45. Master, Supreme Court, Queen's Bench Div., 1975-80. Prescribed Officer for Election Petitions, 1975-80. Hon. Lectr in Law, University Coll., London, 1959-74; Hon. Lectr in Legal Ethics, Birmingam Univ., 1969-72; Hon. Visiting Lecturer: Imperial Coll. of Science and Technology, 1963-64; Birmingham Univ., 1964-65; Bedford Coll., 1969-71; European Univ. Institute, Florence, 1978; Vis. Professor: Sydney Univ., 1971; Osgoode Hall Law Sch., York Univ., Toronto, 1971; of English Law, UCL, 1974-; Central London Polytechnic, 1981-. Member: Lord Chancellor's (Pearson) Cttee on Funds in Court, 1958-59; Working Party on the Revision of the Rules of the Supreme Court, 1960-65; (Payne) Cttee on Enforcement of Judgment Debts, 1965-69; (Winn) Cttee on Personal Injuries Litigation, 1966-68; (Kerr) Working Party on Foreign Judgments, 1976-80. Pres., Assoc. of Law Teachers, 1978- (Vice Pres., 1965-78); Vice-President: Industrial Law Soc.; Selden Soc., 1978- (Mem. Cttee of Management, 1976-78); Inst. of Legal Executives, 1978-; Dep. Chm. and Governor, Central London Polytechnic; Member, Cttee of Management: Inst. of Judicial Admin; Brit. Inst. of Internat. and Comparative Law; Law Adv. Cttee of Associated Examining Bd; Friends of Hebrew Univ., Jerusalem; Mem. Council, Justice. Chm., Bentham Club, UCL, 1964-. Hon. Mem., SPTL, 1981. Hon. Freeman, City of London, 1976. Mem., Broderers' Co. Hon. LLD: Birmingham, 1978; London, 1981 Dr Jur. *hc* Würzburg, Bavaria, 1982. Adv. Editor, Court Forms, 1962-; Editor, Annual Practice, 1961-66; Gen. Editor, Supreme Court Practice, 1967-; Civil Justice Quarterly, 1982-. *Publications:* Law relating to Hire Purchase, 1938; Chitty and Jacob's Queen's Bench Forms (19th, 20th and 21st edns); Bullen, Leake and Jacob's Precedents of Pleadings (12th edn); chapter on Civil Procedure including Courts and

Evidence, in Annual Survey of Commonwealth Law, 1965-77; contributed titles: Discovery, Execution (jtly), Practice and Procedure, to Halsbury's Laws of England, 4th edn; Compromise and Settlement, Default Judgments, Interlocutory Proceedings, Interim Orders, Issues, Judgments and Orders (part), Order 14 Proceedings, Service of Proceedings, Stay of Proceedings, Third Party Procedure, to Court Forms. *Recreations:* walking, painting. *Address:* 16 The Park, Golders Green, NW11 7SU. *T:* 01-458 3832. *Clubs:* City Livery, Reform, Royal Automobile; Hendon Golf.

See also R. R. H. Jacob.

JACOB, Robert Raphael Hayim, (Robin Jacob), QC 1981; *b* 26 April 1941; *s* of Sir Jack I. H. Jacob, *qv*; *m* 1967, Wendy Jones; three *s*. *Educ:* King Alfred Sch., Hampstead; Mountgrace Secondary Comprehensive Sch., Potter's Bar; St Paul's Sch.; Trinity Coll., Cambridge (BA, MA); LSE (LLB). Called to the Bar, Gray's Inn, 1965 (Atkin Scholar); teacher of law, 1965-66; pupillage with Nigel (now Lord) Bridge, 1966-67, with A. M. Walton, 1967; entered chambers of Thomas Blanco White, 1967. Junior Counsel to Treasury in Patent Matters, 1976-81. *Publications:* Kerly's Law of Trade Marks (ed jtly), 1972 and 1982 edns; Patents, Trade Marks, Copyright and Designs (ed jtly), 1970 and 1978; Encyclopedia of UK and European Patent Law (ed jtly), 1977; Editor, Court Forms Sections on Copyright (1978-), Designs and Trade Marks (1975-). *Recreations:* photography, country garden. *Address:* Francis Taylor Building, Temple, EC4Y 7BY. *T:* 01-353 5657.

JACOB, Very Rev. William Ungoed; Dean of Brecon Cathedral, 1967-78; Vicar of St Mary's, Brecon with Battle, 1967-78; *b* 6 Oct. 1910; *s* of Wm and L. M. M. Jacob; *m* 1935, Ivy Matilda Hall; one *d*. *Educ:* Llanelly Gram. Sch.; Llandovery Coll.; Jesus Coll., Oxford; Wycliffe Hall, Oxford. BA 2nd cl. History, 1932; 2nd cl. Theology, 1933; MA 1937. Ordained deacon, 1934; priest, 1935; Curate of Holy Trinity, Aberystwyth, 1934-36; Lampeter, 1936-40; Vicar of Blaenau Ffestiniog 1940-51; Rector of Hubberston, 1951-55; Vicar of St Peter's, Carmarthen, 1955-67; Canon of St David's Cathedral, 1957-67. Rural Dean of Carmarthen, 1958-60; Archdeacon of Carmarthen, 1960-67. Pres., Council of Churches for Wales 1971-76 (Sec., 1960-65). Mem., Coun. for Wales and Mon, 1963-66. Gen. Sec. Church in Wales Prov. Council for Mission and Unity, 1967-73; Chm., Provincial Selection Panel, 1974. *Publications:* Meditations on the Seven Words, 1960; Three Hours' Devotions, 1965; A Guide to the Parish Eucharist, 1969. *Address:* 110 Sketty Road, Swansea SA2 0JX.

JACOBI, Derek George; actor; *b* 22 Oct. 1938; *s* of Alfred George Jacobi and Daisy Gertrude Masters. *Educ:* Leyton County High Sch.; St John's Coll., Cambridge (MA Hons). Artistic Associate, Old Vic Co. (formerly Prospect Theatre Co.), 1976-81. *Stage:* Birmingham Repertory Theatre, 1960-63 (first appearance in One Way Pendulum, 1961); National Theatre, 1963-71; Prospect Theatre Co., 1972, 1974, 1976, 1977, 1978; Hamlet (for reformation of Old Vic Co., and at Elsinore), 1979; Royal Shakespeare Co.: Benedick in Much Ado About Nothing, title rôle in Peer Gynt, Prospero in The Tempest, 1982; *TV appearances include:* She Stoops to Conquer, Man of Straw, The Pallisers, I Claudius, Philby, Burgess and Maclean, Richard II, Hamlet, Inside the Third Reich; *films:* 1971-: Odessa File; Day of the Jackal; The Medusa Touch; Othello; Three Sisters; Interlude; The Human Factor; Charlotte; The Man Who Went Up in Smoke; Enigma. *Awards:* BAFTA Best Actor, 1976-77; Variety Club TV Personality, 1976. *Address:* c/o ICM, 388-396 Oxford Street, W1.

JACOBS, Arthur David; Head of Music Department, Huddersfield Polytechnic, since 1979; Editor, British Music Yearbook, formerly Music Yearbook, 1971-79, Advisory Editor since 1979; Critic, Audio and Record Review, now Hi-Fi News & Record Review, since 1964; record reviewer, Sunday Times, since 1968; *b* 14 June 1922; *s* of late Alexander S. and Estelle Jacobs; *m* 1953, Betty Upton Hughes; two *s*. *Educ:* Manchester Grammar Sch.; Merton Coll., Oxford (MA). Music Critic, Daily Express, 1947-52; Mem. Editl Bd, Opera, 1962- (Associate Editor, 1962-71); Music Critic, Jewish Chronicle, 1963-75; Professor, RAM, 1964-79. Leverhulme Res. Fellow in Music, 1977-78. Vis. Fellow, Wolfson Coll., Oxford, 1979. Centennial Lectr, Univ. of Illinois, 1967; Vis. Professor: Univ. of Victoria, BC, 1968; Univ. of California at Santa Barbara, 1969; Temple Univ., Philadelphia, 1970, 1971; UCLA, 1973; Univ. of Western Ontario, 1974; McMaster Univ., 1975. Hon. RAM 1969. *Publications:* Music Lover's Anthology, 1948; Gilbert and Sullivan, 1951; A New Dictionary of Music, 1958 (also Spanish, Portuguese, Danish and Swedish edns), new edn, as The New Penguin Dictionary of Music, 1978; Choral Music, 1963 (also Japanese edn); Libretto of opera One Man Show by Nicholas Maw, 1964; (with Stanley Sadie) Pan Book of Opera, 1966 (US edn, Great Operas in Synopsis); A Short History of Western Music, 1972 (also Italian edn); (ed) Music Education Handbook, 1976; many opera translations incl. Berg's Lulu (first US perf. of complete work, Santa Fe, New Mexico, 1979); contrib. Musical Times, foreign jls, etc. *Recreations:* puns, swimming, walking, theatre. *Address:* 26 Healey House, Huddersfield HD4 7DG. *T:* Huddersfield 662738.

JACOBS, David Lewis; radio and television broadcaster; *b* 19 May 1926; *s* of David Jacobs and Jeanette Victoria Jacobs; *m* 1st, 1949, Patricia Bradlaw (marr. diss. 1972); three *d* (one *s* decd); 2nd, 1975, Caroline Munro (*d* 1975); 3rd, 1979, Mrs Lindsay Stuart-Hutcheson. *Educ:* Belmont Coll.; Strand Sch. RN, 1944-47. First broadcast, Navy Mixture, 1944; Announcer, Forces Broadcasting Service, 1944-45; Chief Announcer, Radio SEAC, Ceylon, 1945-47; Asst Stn Dir, Radio SEAC, 1947; News Reader, BBC Gen. Overseas

Service, 1947, subseq. freelance. Major radio credits include: Book of Verse, Housewives' Choice, Journey into Space, Dateline London, Grande Gingold, Curioser and Curioser, Puffney Post Office, Follow that Man, Man about Town, Jazz Club, Midday Spin, Music Through Midnight, Scarlet Pimpernel, DJ Show, Pick of the Pops, Saturday Show Band Show, Melodies for You, Saturday Star Sounds, Any Questions, Any Answers; Internat. Fest. of Light. TV credits incl.: Focus on Hocus, Vera Lynn Show, Make up your Mind, Tell the Truth, Juke Box Jury, Top of the Pops, Hot Line, Miss World, Top Town, David Jacobs' Words and Music, Sunday Night with David Jacobs, Little Women, There Goes that Song Again, Make a Note, Where are they Now, What's My Line, Who What or Where, Frank Sinatra Show, Mario Lanza Show, Walt Disney Christmas Show, Wednesday Show, Wednesday Magazine, Eurovision Song Contest, TV Ice Time, Twist, A Song for Europe, Ivor Novello Awards, Aladdin, Airs and Graces, There Goes That Song Again, Tell Me Another, Those Wonderful TV Times, Blankety Blank. Numerous film performances incl. Golden Disc, You Must Be Joking, It's Trad Dad, Stardust; former commentator, British Movietone News. 3 Royal Command Performances; 6 yrs Britain's Top Disc Jockey on both BBC and Radio Luxembourg; Variety Club of Gt Brit., BBC TV Personality of Year, 1960, and BBC Radio Personality of the Year, 1975. Vice-Pres., Stars Organisation for Spastics (Past Chm.); Mem. Council, RSPCA, 1969-77, Vice-Chm. 1975-76. *Publications:* (autobiog.) Jacobs' Ladder, 1963; Caroline, 1978; (with Michael Bowen) Any Questions?, 1981. *Recreations:* talking and listening, hotels. *Address:* 19 Launceston Place, W8 5RL.

JACOBS, Prof. John Arthur; Professor of Geophysics, since 1974, and Fellow, Darwin College, since 1976 (Vice Master, 1978-82), University of Cambridge; *b* 3 January 1916; *m* 1st, 1941, Daisy Sarah Ann Montgomerie (*d* 1974); two *d*; 2nd, 1974, Margaret Jones. *Educ:* Univ. of London. BA 1937, MA 1939, PhD 1949, DSc 1961. Instr Lieut RN, 1941-46; Lectr, Royal Holloway Coll., Univ. of London, 1946-51; Assoc. Prof., Univ. of Toronto, 1951-57; Prof., Univ. of British Columbia, 1957-67; Dir, Inst. of Earth Sciences, Univ. of British Columbia, 1961-67; Killam Meml Prof. of Science, Univ. of Alberta, 1967-74; Dir, Inst. of Earth and Planetary Physics, Univ. of Alberta, 1970-74. Sec., Royal Astronomical Soc., 1977-. FRSC 1958; Centennial Medal of Canada, 1967; Medal of Canadian Assoc. of Physicists, 1975. *Publications:* (with R. D. Russell and J. T. Wilson) Physics and Geology, 1959, 2nd edn 1974; The Earth's Core and Geomagnetism, 1963; Geomagnetic Micropulsations, 1970; A Textbook on Geonomy, 1974; The Earth's Core, 1975. *Recreations:* walking, music. *Address:* Department of Earth Sciences, Bullard Laboratories, Madingley Rise, Madingley Road, Cambridge CB3 0EZ. *T:* Cambridge 51686.

JACOBS, Brig. John Conrad S.; *see* Saunders-Jacobs.

JACOBS, John Robert Maurice; Golf Commentator, Independent Television, since 1967; Golf Adviser, Golf World Magazine, since 1962; Golf Instructor: Golf Digest Magazine Schools, 1971-76; Golf Magazine Schools, US, 1977; *b* 14 March 1925; *s* of Robert and Gertrude Vivian Jacobs; *m* 1949, Rita Wragg; one *s* one *d*. *Educ:* Maltby Grammar School. Asst Professional Golfer, Hallamshire Golf Club, 1947-49; Golf Professional: Gezira Sporting Club, Cairo, 1949-52; Sandy Lodge Golf Club, 1952-64; Man. Dir, Athlon Golf, 1967-75, Professional Golfers' Association: Tournament Dir-Gen., 1971-76, Advr to Tournament Div., 1977; European Ryder Cup Captain, 1979-81. Currently associated with John Jacobs' Practical Golf Schools, based in USA. *Publications:* Golf, 1961; Play Better Golf, 1969; Practical Golf, 1973; John Jacobs Analyses the Superstars, 1974; Golf Doctor, 1979; contrib.: Golf World Magazine; Golf Magazine (US). *Recreations:* shooting, fishing. *Address:* Stable Cottage, Chapel Lane, Lyndhurst, Hants SO4 7FG. *T:* Lyndhurst 2743. *Clubs:* Lucayan Country (Grand Bahamas); Sandy Lodge Golf, New Forest Golf, Brockenhurst Golf, Bramshaw Golf.

JACOBS, Hon. Sir Kenneth (Sydney), KBE 1976; Justice of High Court of Australia, 1974-79; *b* 5 Oct. 1917; *s* of Albert Sydney Jacobs and Sarah Grace Jacobs (*née* Aggs); *m* 1952, Eleanor Mary Neal; one *d*. *Educ:* Knox Grammar Sch., NSW; Univ. of Sydney (BA, LLB). Admitted to NSW Bar, 1947; QC 1958; Supreme Court of NSW: Judge, 1960; Judge of Appeal, 1966; Pres., Court of Appeal, 1972. *Publication:* Law of Trusts, 1958. *Recreations:* printing and bookbinding; gardening. *Address:* Crooks Lane Corner, Axford, Marlborough, Wilts SN8 2HA.

JACOBS, Sir Wilfred (Ebenezer), GCMG 1981; KCVO 1977; Kt 1967; OBE 1959; QC 1959; Governor-General of Antigua and Barbuda, since 1981; *b* 19 Oct. 1919; 2nd *s* of late William Henry Jacobs and Henrietta Jacobs (*née* Du Bois); *m* 1947, Carmen Sylva, 2nd *d* of late Walter A. Knight and Flora Knight (*née* Fleming); one *s* two *d*. *Educ:* Grenada Boys' Secondary Sch.; Gray's Inn, London. Called to Bar, Gray's Inn, 1946; Registrar and Additional Magistrate, St Vincent, 1946; Magistrate, Dominica, 1947, and St Kitts, 1949; Crown Attorney, St Kitts, 1952; Attorney-Gen., Leeward Is, 1957-59, and Antigua, 1960. Acted Administrator, Dominica, St Kitts, Antigua, various periods, 1947-60. MEC and MLC, St Vincent, Dominica, St Kitts, Antigua, 1947-60; Legal Draftsman and Acting Solicitor-Gen., Trinidad and Tobago, 1960. Barbados: Solicitor-Gen., and Actg Attorney-Gen., 1961-63; PC and MLC, 1962-63; Dir of Public Prosecutions, 1964; Judge of Supreme Court of Judicature, 1967; Governor of Antigua, 1967-81. KStJ. *Recreations:* swimming, gardening, golf. *Address:* Governor-General's Residence, Antigua, West Indies. *Club:* Royal Commonwealth Society.

JACOBSEN, Frithjof Halfdan; Norwegian Ambassador to the Court of St James's and to Ireland, 1975-82; *b* 14 Jan. 1914; *m* 1941, Elsa Tidemand Anderson; one *s* two *d. Educ:* Univ. of Oslo (Law). Entered Norwegian Foreign Service, 1938; Legation, Paris, 1938-40; Norwegian Foreign Ministry, London, 1940-45; held posts in Moscow, London, Oslo, 1945-55; Director-Gen., Political Affairs, Oslo, 1955-59; Norwegian Ambassador to: Canada, 1959-61; Moscow, 1961-66; Under-Sec. of State, Oslo, 1966-70; Ambassador to Moscow, 1970-75. *Address:* Schwachsgate 4, Oslo 3, Norway.

JACOBSON, family name of **Baron Jacobson.**

JACOBSON, Baron *cr* 1975 (Life Peer), of St Albans; **Sydney Jacobson,** MC 1944; Editorial Director, International Publishing Corporation Newspapers, 1968-74, Deputy Chairman, 1973-74; *b* 26 Oct. 1908; *m* 1938, Phyllis June Buck; two *s* one *d. Educ:* Strand Sch., London; King's Coll., London. Asst Editor: Statesman, India, 1934-36; Lilliput Magazine, 1936-39. Served in Army, 1939-45. Special Correspondent, Picture Post, 1945-48; Editor, Leader Magazine, 1948-50; Political Editor, Daily Mirror, 1952-62; Editor, Daily Herald, 1962-64; Editor, Sun, 1964-65; Chairman, Odhams Newspapers, 1968. Member Press Council, 1969-75. *Recreations:* tennis, walking, reading. *Address:* 6 Avenue Road, St Albans, Herts. *T:* St Albans 53873.

JACOMB, Martin Wakefield; Vice-Chairman, Kleinwort, Benson Ltd, since 1976; *b* 11 Nov. 1929; *s* of Hilary W. Jacomb and Félise Jacomb; *m* 1960, Evelyn Heathcoat Amory; two *s* one *d. Educ:* Eton Coll.; Worcester Coll., Oxford (MA Law 1953). Called to the Bar, Inner Temple, 1955. 2nd Lieut RA, 1948-49. Practised at the Bar, 1955-68; joined Kleinwort, Benson Ltd, 1968; Dir, Kleinwort, Benson, Lonsdale Ltd, 1974-; Chairman: Kleinwort, Benson Investment Management Ltd, 1977-; Harley Mullion & Co. Ltd, 1977-; Merchants Trust Ltd, 1974-; Transatlantic Fund Inc., 1978-. Director: Christian Salvesen Ltd, 1974-; Mercantile Credit Co., 1973-; Hudson's Bay Co., Canada, 1971-; Montagu Boston Investment Trust Ltd, 1975-; Mem., European Adv. Bd, Touche Remnant & Co., 1982-. Part-time mem., British Gas Corp., 1981-. Chm., City Capital Markets Cttee, 1980-; External Mem., Finance Cttee, Delegacy of the OUP, 1971-; Mem., Greenwich Hosp. Cttee, 1976-. Trustee, Nat. Heritage Meml Fund, 1982-. *Recreations:* theatre, family bridge, tennis. *Address:* 20 Fenchurch Street, EC3P 3DB. *T:* 01-623 8000.

JACQUES, family name of **Baron Jacques.**

JACQUES, Baron *cr* 1968 (Life Peer), of Portsea Island; **John Henry Jacques;** Chairman of the Co-operative Union Ltd, 1964-70; *b* 11 Jan. 1905; *s* of Thomas Dobson Jacques and Annie Bircham; *m* 1929, Constance White; two *s* one *d. Educ:* Victoria Univ., Manchester; Co-operative Coll. Sec-Man., Moorsley Co-operative Society Ltd, 1925-29; Tutor, Co-operative Coll., 1929-42; Accountant, Plymouth Co-operative Soc. Ltd, 1942-45; Chief Executive, Portsea Island Co-operative Soc. Ltd, Portsmouth, 1945-65; Pres., Co-operative Congress, 1961. Pres., Retail Trades Education Council, 1971-75. A Lord in Waiting (Govt Whip), 1974-77 and 1979; a Dep. Chm. of Cttees, 1977-. *Publications:* Book-Keeping I, II and III, 1940; Management Accounting, 1966; Manual on Co-operative Management, 1969. *Recreations:* walking, snooker, gardening, West-Highland terriers. *Address:* 23 Hilltop Crescent, Cosham, Portsmouth, Hants PO6 1BB. *T:* Cosham 375511. *Club:* Co-operative (Portsmouth).

JACQUES, Peter Roy Albert; Secretary, TUC Social Insurance and Industrial Welfare Department, since 1971; *b* 12 Aug. 1939; *s* of George Henry Jacques and Ivy Mary Jacques (*née* Farr); *m* 1965, Jacqueline Anne Sears; one *s* one *d. Educ:* Archbishop Temple's Secondary Sch.; Newcastle upon Tyne Polytechnic (BSc Sociology); Univ. of Leicester. Building labourer, 1955-58; market porter, 1958-62; Asst, TUC Social Insce and Industrial Welfare Dept, 1968-71. Member: Industrial Injuries Adv. Council, 1972; Nat. Insce Adv. Cttee, 1972-78; Health and Safety Commn, 1974; Royal Commn on the Nat. Health Service, 1976-79; EEC Cttee on Health-Safety, 1976; NHS London Adv. Cttee, 1979-; Social Security Adv. Cttee, 1980-. Jt Sec., BMA/TUC Cttee, 1972-; Sec., TUC Health Services Cttee, 1979-; Mem. Exec. Cttee, Royal Assoc. for Disability and Rehabilitation, 1975-. *Publications:* responsible for TUC pubns Health-Safety Handbook; Occupational Pension Schemes. *Recreations:* reading, yoga, walking, camping, vegetable growing. *Address:* TUC, Congress House, Great Russell Street, WC1B 3LS. *T:* 01-636 4030.

JACQUOT, Général d'Armée Pierre Elie; Grand Cross of Legion of Honour, 1961; *b* 16 June 1902; *s* of Aimé Jacquot and Marie (*née* Renault); *m* 1929, Lucie Claire Mamet; one *d* (and one *s* killed in action, Algeria, 1962). *Educ:* Saint-Cyr Military Academy, France. Commissioned 30th Chasseur Bn, 1922; Foreign Legion Service, 1925-29; French Ecole de Guerre, 1929-31, Belgian, 1931-33; Capt. 1933; posted to GHQ, Sept. 1939; Comdr 3rd Bn of 109th Inf. Regt, 1940; with André Malraux (alias Col Berger) organised French Resistance in the Corrèze, Dordogne and Lot areas, 1943-44; served in First French Army, 1944-45 (Alsace-Lorraine Bde); Brig.-Gen. 1946; Dep. Chief of Army Staff, 1947; Maj.-Gen. 1950; comd 8th Inf. Div., 1951-54; Lieut-Gen. 1954; High Comr and C-in-C, Indo-China, 1955-56; C-in-C French Forces in Germany, 1956-59; Gen. 1957; Inspector-Gen. of French Land Forces, 1959-61; Commander-in-Chief, Allied Forces Central Europe, 1961-63; Cadre de Réserve, Dec. 1963. *Publications:* Essai de stratégie occidentale, 1953; La Stratégie périphérique devant la bombe atomique, 1954.

Address: (winter) 15 Avenue de Villars, 75007 Paris, France; (summer) Vrécourt, 88140 Contrexéville, France.

JAEGER, Prof. Leslie Gordon; FRSE 1966; Academic Vice-President, Technical University of Nova Scotia, since 1980; *b* 28 Jan. 1926; *s* of Henry Jaeger; *m* 1st, 1948, Annie Sylvia Dyson; two *d* ; 2nd, 1981, Kathleen Grant. *Educ:* King George V Sch., Southport; Gonville and Caius Coll., Cambridge. Royal Corps of Naval Constructors, 1945-48; Industry, 1948-52; University College, Khartoum, 1952-56; Univ. Lectr, Cambridge, 1956-62; Fellow and Dir of Studies, Magdalene Coll., Cambridge, 1959-62; Prof. of Applied Mechanics, McGill Univ., Montreal, 1962-65. Regius Prof. of Engineering, Edinburgh Univ., 1965-66; Prof. of Civil Engineering, McGill Univ., 1966-70; Dean, Faculty of Engineering, Univ. of New Brunswick, 1970-75; Acad. Vice-Pres., Acadia Univ., NS, 1975-80. *Publications:* The Analysis of Grid Frameworks and Related Structures (with A. W. Hendry), 1958; Elementary Theory of Elastic Plates, 1964; Cartesian Tensors in Engineering Science, 1965; various papers on grillage analysis in British, European and American Journals. *Recreations:* golf, curling, contract bridge. *Address:* PO Box 1000, Halifax, NS B3J 2X4, Canada. *T:* 429-8300. *Club:* Halifax (Halifax, Canada).

JAFFÉ, (Andrew) Michael, LittD; Director, Fitzwilliam Museum, Cambridge, since 1973; Professor of the History of Western Art, since 1973; Fellow of King's College, Cambridge, since 1952; *b* 3 June 1923; *s* of Arthur Daniel Jaffé, OBE, and Marie Marguerite Strauss; *m* 1964, Patricia Ann Milne-Henderson; two *s* two *d. Educ:* Eton Coll.; King's Coll., Cambridge (MA, LittD 1980); Courtauld Inst. of Art. Lt-Comdr, RNVR, retd. Commonwealth Fund Fellow, Harvard and New York Univ., 1951-53; Asst Lectr in Fine Arts, Cambridge, 1956; Prof. of Renaissance Art, Washington Univ., St Louis, 1960-61; Vis. Prof., Harvard Univ., Summer 1961; Lectr in Fine Arts, Cambridge, 1961; Reader in History of Western Art, Cambridge, 1968; Head of Dept of History of Art, Cambridge, 1970-73; a Syndic, Fitzwilliam Museum, 1971-73. Mem., Adv. Council, V&A Museum, 1971-76. Organiser (for Nat. Gall. of Canada) of Jordaens Exhibn, Ottawa, 1968-69; Vis. Prof., Harvard Univ., Fall 1968-69. FRSA 1969. Officier, Ordre de Léopold (Belgium), 1980. *Publications:* Van Dyck's Antwerp Sketchbook, 1966; Rubens, 1967; Jordaens, 1968; Rubens and Italy, 1977; articles and reviews (art historical) in European and N American jls, etc. *Recreation:* viticulture. *Address:* Grove Lodge, Trumpington Street, Cambridge. *Clubs:* Athenæum, Turf, Beefsteak.

JAFFRAY, Alistair Robert Morton, CB 1978; Deputy Under-Secretary of State, Ministry of Defence, since 1975; *b* 28 Oct. 1925; *s* of Alexander George and late Janet Jaffray; *m* 1st, 1953, Margaret Betty Newman (decd); two *s* one *d* ; 2nd, 1980, Edna Mary, *e d* of S. J. Tasker, Brasted Chart. *Educ:* Clifton Coll.; Corpus Christi Coll., Cambridge. BA First Cl. Hons., Mod. Langs. Served War, RNVR, 1943-46. Apptd Home Civil Service (Admty), 1948; Private Sec. to First Lord of Admty, 1960-62; Private Sec. to successive Secretaries of State for Defence, 1969-70; Asst Under-Sec. of State, MoD, 1971-75. *Address:* Okeford, 10 Lynch Road, Farnham, Surrey. *T:* Farnham 716572.

JAFFRAY, Sir William Otho, 5th Bt, *cr* 1892; *b* 1 Nov. 1951; *s* of Sir William Edmund Jaffray, 4th Bt, TD, JP, DL, and Anne, *d* of late Captain J. Otho Paget; *S* father, 1953; *m* 1981, Cynthia Ross Corrington, Montreal. *Educ:* Eton. *Address:* The Manor House, Priors Dean, Petersfield, Hants. *T:* Hawkley 204.

JAGAN, Cheddi, DDS; Guyanese Politician; Leader of Opposition in National Assembly; *b* March 1918; *m* 1943; one *s* one *d. Educ:* Howard Univ.; YMCA Coll., Chicago (BSc); Northwestern Univ. (DDS). Member of Legislative Council, British Guiana, 1947-53; Minister of Agriculture, Lands and Mines, May-Oct. 1953; Minister of Trade and Industry, 1957-61; (first) Premier, British Guiana, and Minister of Development and Planning, 1961-64. Hon. Pres., Guyana Agricl and General Workers' Union; Pres., Guyana Peace Council; Mem. Presidential Cttee, World Peace Council. Order of Friendship, USSR, 1978. *Publications:* Forbidden Freedom, 1954; Anatomy of Poverty, 1964; The West on Trial, 1966; Caribbean Revolution, 1979. *Recreations:* swimming, tennis. *Address:* Freedom House, 41 Robb Street, Georgetown, Guyana.

JAGATSINGH, Hon. Sir Kher, Kt 1981; Officier, Ordre National Malgache, 1969; MLA (Lab) Montagne Blanche and Grand River South East, Mauritius, since 1976; Minister of Education and Cultural Affairs, 1977-82; President, Conseil d'Administration, Institut Africain et Mauricien de Bilinguisme, since 1977; *b* Amritsar, 23 July 1931; *m* Radhika; two *s* two *d. Educ:* Beau Bassin Primary Sch.; privately. Civil servant in Dept of Health, 1950-54; co-founded Mauritius Times, weekly newspaper, 1954; journalist on Times of India, later on Slough Observer and Paddington Times; joined Labour Party, 1958, Sec.-Gen., 1961-; Chairman: Govt and non-Govt Gen. Workers' Union, 1961-67; Central Housing Auth., 1963-67. MLC for Beau Bassin-Petite Rivière, 1959, for Montagne Blanche and Grand River SE, 1967; Minister: of Health, 1967-71; of Economic Planning and Develt, 1971-76. Mem. Exec. Bd, UNESCO, 1977-80. Co-founder, The Nation, 1970, now Vice-Chm. Governor for Mauritius, IBRD, Washington; Chairman: Giants Internat. Mauritius Br.; Mauritius Nat. Peace Council. *Publication:* Petals of Dust, 1981. *Address:* c/o Ministry of Education and Cultural Affairs, Port Louis, Mauritius. *T:* (office) 01-1103, 01-1732; (home) 54-1767.

JAGO, David Edgar John; Assistant Under Secretary of State (Naval Staff), Ministry of Defence, since 1982; *b* 2 Dec. 1937; *s* of Edgar George Jago and Violet Jago; *m* 1963, Judith (*née* Lissenden); one *s* one *d. Educ:* King Edward's Sch., Bath; Pembroke Coll., Oxford (MA). National Service, RA, 1956-58. Asst Principal, Admiralty, 1961; Private Sec. to Permanent Under Sec. of State (RN), 1964-65; Principal 1965; Directing Staff, IDC, 1968-70; Private Sec. to Parly Under Sec. of State for Defence (RN), 1971-73; Asst Sec., MoD, 1973; Asst Under Sec. of State (Aircraft), 1979-82. *Recreations:* theatre, opera, military history. *Address:* 7 College Place, Snaresbrook, E17 3PY. *T:* 01-521 8060.

JAHODA, Prof. Marie, (Mrs A. H. Albu), CBE 1974; DPhil; Professor Emeritus, University of Sussex; Senior Research Consultant to Science Policy Research Unit, University of Sussex, since 1971; *b* 26 Jan. 1907; *d* of Carl Jahoda and Betty Jahoda; *m* 1st, 1927, Paul F. Lazarsfeld; one *d*; 2nd, 1958, Austen Albu, *qv. Educ:* Univ. of Vienna (DPhil). Prof. of Social Psychology, NY Univ., 1949-58; Res. Fellow and Prof. of Psychol., Brunel Univ. 1958-65; Prof. of Social Psychol., Sussex Univ., 1965-73. Hon. DLit: Sussex, 1973; Leicester, 1973. *Publications:* Die Arbeitslosen von Marienthal, 1933 (Eng. trans. 1971); Research Methods in Human Relations, 1953; Current Concepts of Positive Mental Health, 1958; Freud and the Dilemmas of Psychology, 1977; (ed) World Futures: the great debate, 1977. *Recreations:* cooking, cello, chess. *Address:* 17 The Crescent, Keymer, Sussex BN6 8RB. *T:* Hassocks 2267.

JAKEWAY, Sir (Francis) Derek, KCMG 1963 (CMG 1956); OBE 1948; *b* 6 June 1915; *s* of Francis Edward and Adeline Jakeway; *m* 1941, Phyllis Lindsay Watson, CStJ; three *s. Educ:* Hele's Sch., Exeter; Exeter Coll., Oxford (BA Hons Mod. Hist.). Colonial Administrative Service, Nigeria, 1937-54, seconded to Seychelles, 1946-49, to Colonial Office, 1949-51; Chief Sec., British Guiana, 1954-59; Chief Sec., Sarawak, 1959-63; Governor and C-in-C, Fiji, 1964-68. Chm., Devon AHA, 1974-82. KStJ 1964. *Address:* 78 Douglas Avenue, Exmouth, Devon. *T:* Exmouth 71342.

JAKOBOVITS, Rabbi Sir Immanuel, Kt 1981; Chief Rabbi of the United Hebrew Congregations of the British Commonwealth of Nations, since 1967; *b* 8 Feb. 1921; *s* of Rabbi Dr Julius Jakobovits and Paula (*née* Wreschner); *m* 1949, Amelie Munk; two *s* four *d. Educ:* London Univ. (BA; PhD 1955); Jews' Coll. and Yeshivah Etz Chaim, London. Diploma, 1944; Associate of Jews' Coll. Minister: Brondesbury Synagogue, 1941-44; SE London Synagogue, 1944-47; Great Synagogue, London, 1947-49; Chief Rabbi of Ireland, 1949-58; Rabbi of Fifth Avenue Synagogue, New York, 1958-67. Hon. DD Yeshiva Univ., NY, 1975. *Publications:* Jewish Medical Ethics, 1959 (NY; 4th edn 1975); Jewish Law Faces Modern Problems, 1965 (NY); Journal of a Rabbi, 1966 (NY), 1967 (GB); The Timely and the Timeless, 1977; contrib. learned and popular jls in America, England and Israel. *Address:* Adler House, Tavistock Square, WC1. *T:* 01-387 1066.

JALLAND, William Herbert Wainwright, JP; His Honour Judge Jalland; a Circuit Judge, Manchester, since 1975 (now sitting in Crown Court, Manchester, and County Courts, Manchester and Salford); *b* 1922; *o s* of Arthur Edgar Jalland, QC, JP and Elizabeth Hewitt Jalland; *m* 1945, Helen Monica, *o d* of John and Edith Wyatt; one *s* one *d. Educ:* Manchester Grammar Sch.; Manchester Univ. LLB 1949. Served War of 1939-45, HM Forces at home and abroad, 1941-46: Captain, King's Own Royal Regt, attached 8th Bn Durham LI. Called to Bar, Gray's Inn, 1950; practised Northern Circuit; part-time Dep. Coroner, City of Salford, 1955-65; part-time Dep. Recorder, Burnley, 1962-70; part-time Dep. Chm., Lancs County Sessions, 1970-71; Recorder, 1972; a Circuit Judge, Liverpool and Merseyside, 1972-75. JP Lancs, 1970; Liaison Judge at Magistrates' Courts, Rochdale, Middleton and Heywood, 1974-. Vice-Pres., Old Mancunians' Assoc., 1979-. *Recreations:* rambling, gardening, photography. *Address:* Broad Oak, Hollin Lane, Styal, Wilmslow, Cheshire SK9 4JH. *Club:* Manchester (Manchester).

JAMES, family name of Barons James of Rusholme, Northbourne and Saint Brides.

JAMES OF RUSHOLME, Baron *cr* 1959, of Fallowfield (Life Peer); **Eric John Francis James,** Kt 1956; Chairman, Royal Fine Art Commission, 1976-79 (Member, 1973-79); *b* 1909; *yr s* of F. W. James; *m* 1939, Cordelia, *d* of late Maj.-Gen. F. Wintour, CB, CBE; one *s. Educ:* Taunton's School, Southampton; Queen's Coll., Oxford (Exhibitioner and Hon. Scholar, 1927. Hon. Fellow, 1959). Goldsmiths' Exhibitioner, 1929; BA, BSc 1931; MA, DPhil 1933; Asst Master at Winchester Coll., 1933-45; High Master of Manchester Grammar Sch., 1945-62; Vice-Chancellor, Univ. of York, 1962-73. Mem. of University Grants Cttee, 1949-59; Chm. of Headmasters' Conference, 1953-54; Mem. Central Advisory Council on Education, 1957-61; Member: Standing Commission on Museums and Galleries, 1958-61; Press Council, 1963-67; SSRC, 1965-68; Chairman: Personal Social Services Council, 1973-76; Cttee to Inquire into the Training of Teachers, 1970-71. Hon. FRIBA 1979. Hon. LLD: McGill, 1957; York, (Toronto) 1970; Hon. DLitt New Brunswick, 1974; DUniv York, 1974. Fellow, Winchester Coll., 1963-69. *Publications:* (in part) Elements of Physical Chemistry; (in part) Science and Education; An Essay on the Content of Education; Education and Leadership; articles in scientific and educational journals. *Address:* Penhill Cottage, West Witton, Leyburn, N Yorks.

JAMES, Anne Eleanor S.; *see* Scott-James.

JAMES, Anthony Trafford, CBE 1979; PhD; Member of Executive Committee of Unilever Research Colworth Laboratory, also Head of Division of Biosciences, since 1972; *b* Cardiff, Wales, 6 March 1922; *s* of J. M. and I. James; *m* 1945, O. I. A. Clayton (*d* 1980); two *s* one *d. Educ:* University College Sch.; Northern Polytechnic; University Coll. London (BSc, PhD), Fellow 1975; Harvard Business Sch. (AMP). MRC Junior Fellowship at Bedford Coll., Univ. of London (with Prof. E. E. Turner, subject: Antimalarials), 1945-47; Jun. Mem. staff, Lister Inst. for Preventive Med., London (with Dr R. L. M. Synge, Nobel Laureate, subject: Structure of Gramicidin S), 1947-50; Mem. scientific staff, Nat. Inst. for Med. Res., London (special appt awarded, 1961), 1950-62 (with Dr A. J. P. Martin, FRS, Nobel Laureate, 1950-56); Unilever Research Lab., Sharnbrook: Div. Manager and Head of Biosynthesis Unit, 1962-67; Head of Div. of Plant Products and Biochemistry, 1967-69; Gp Manager, Biosciences Gp, 1969-72. Industrial Prof. of Chemistry, Loughborough Univ. of Technology, 1966-71. Member: SRC, 1973-77; Food Sci. and Technol. Bd, MAFF, 1975-80; Manpower Cttee, SERC, 1981-; Chairman: Food Composition, Quality and Safety Cttee, MAFF, 1975-80; Biotechnol. Management Cttee, SERC, 1981-. Hon. Dr Dijon, 1981. Has had various awards incl. some from abroad. *Publications:* New Biochemical Separations (ed A. T. James and L. J. Morris), 1964; Lipid Biochemistry—an introduction (M. I. Gurr and A. T. James), 1972. *Recreations:* glass engraving, antique collecting, gardening. *Address:* Unilever Research Colworth Laboratory, Colworth House, Sharnbrook, Beds MK44 1LQ. *T:* Bedford 781781.

JAMES, (Arthur) Walter; Principal, St Catharine's, Windsor, 1974-82; *b* 30 June 1912; *s* of late W. J. James, OBE; *m* 1st, 1939, Elisabeth (marr. diss. 1956), *e d* of Richard Rylands Howroyd; one *d*; 2nd, 1957, Ann Jocelyn, *y d* of late C. A. Leavy Burton; one *d* and one adopted *s* two adopted *d. Educ:* Uckfield Grammar Sch.; Keble Coll., Oxford (Scholar); 1st Cl. Mod. Hist.; Liddon Student; Arnold Essay Prizeman. Senior Demy of Magdalen Coll., 1935; Scholar in Mediæval Studies, British School at Rome, 1935; Editorial staff, Manchester Guardian, 1937-46. NFS 1939-45. Contested (L) Bury, Lancs, 1945. Dep. Editor, The Times Educational Supplement, 1947-51, Editor, 1952-69; Special Advisor on Educn, Times Newspapers, 1969-71; also Editor, Technology, 1957-60. Reader in Journalism, Univ. of Canterbury, NZ, 1971-74. Member: BBC Gen. Advisory Council, 1956-64; Council of Industrial Design, 1961-66; Council, Royal Society of Arts, 1964; Cttee, British-American Associates, 1964; Governor, Central School of Art and Design, 1966. Woodard Lecturer, 1965. *Publications:* (Ed.) Temples and Faiths 1958; The Christian in Politics, 1962; The Teacher and his World, 1962; A Middle-class Parent's Guide to Education, 1964; (contrib.) Looking Forward to the Seventies, 1967. *Recreation:* gardening. *Address:* 1 Cumberland Mews, The Great Park, Windsor, Berks. *Club:* National Liberal.

JAMES, Aubrey Graham Wallen; Deputy Chief Land Registrar, 1975-81; *b* 5 Jan. 1918; *s* of Reginald Aubrey James and Amelia Martha James; *m* 1952, Audrey Elizabeth, *er d* of Dr and Mrs A. W. F. Edmonds; two *s. Educ:* Nantgyle Grammar Sch.; London Univ. (LLB 1939). Solicitor, 1940. Served Second World War, 1940-46, Major, Cheshire Regt. Legal Asst, HM Land Registry, 1948; Asst Land Registrar, 1954; Land Registrar, 1963; Dist Land Registrar, Nottingham, 1963. Chm., E Midlands Region, CS Sports Council, 1970-75. *Recreations:* gardening, motoring, golf; has played Rugby, cricket and tennis with enthusiasm and in latter years, has turned to admin of these and other sports. *Address:* 10 Thameside, Teddington, Mddx TW11 9PW.

JAMES, Basil; Special Commissioner, since 1963; *b* 25 May 1918; *s* of late John Elwyn James, MA (Oxon.), Cardiff, and Mary Janet (*née* Lewis), Gwaelodygarth, Glam; *m* 1943, Moira Houlding Rayner, MA (Cantab.), *d* of late Capt. Benjamin Harold Rayner, North Staffs Regt, and Elizabeth (*née* Houlding), Preston, Lancs; one *s* twin *d. Educ:* Llandovery Coll.; Canton High Sch., Cardiff; Christ's Coll., Cambridge (Exhibnr). Tancred Law Student, Lincoln's Inn, 1936; Squire Law Scholar, Cambridge, 1936. BA 1939; MA 1942. Called to Bar, Lincoln's Inn, 1940. Continuous sea service as RNVR officer in small ships on anti-submarine and convoy duties in Atlantic, Arctic and Mediterranean, 1940-45. King George V Coronation Scholar, Lincoln's Inn, 1946. Practised at Chancery Bar, 1946-63. Admitted to Federal Supreme Court of Nigeria, 1962. *Publications:* contrib. to Atkin's Court Forms and Halsbury's Laws of England. *Recreations:* music, gardening.

JAMES, Cecil; *see* James, T. C. G.

JAMES, Christopher Philip; His Honour Judge C. P. James; a Circuit Judge, since 1980; *b* 27 May 1934; *s* of late Herbert Edgar James, CBE, and late Elizabeth Margaret James. *Educ:* Felsted School; Magdalene Coll., Cambridge (MA). Commnd RASC, 1953. Called to the Bar, Gray's Inn, 1959; a Recorder of the Crown Court, 1979. *Address:* Flat 10, 93 Elm Park Gardens, SW10 9QE. *Club:* United Oxford & Cambridge University.

JAMES, Clive Vivian Leopold; writer and broadcaster; feature writer for The Observer, since 1972 (also television critic, 1972-82); *b* 7 Oct. 1939; *s* of Albert Arthur James and Minora May (*née* Darke). *Educ:* Sydney Technical High Sch.; Sydney Univ.; Pembroke Coll., Cambridge. President of Footlights when at Cambridge. Record albums as lyricist for Pete Atkin: Beware of the Beautiful Stranger; Driving through Mythical America; A King at Nightfall;

The Road of Silk; Secret Drinker; Live Libel; The Master of the Revels. Song-book with Pete Atkin: A First Folio. *Television series:* Cinema, Up Sunday, So It Goes, A Question of Sex, Saturday Night People, Clive James on Television. *television documentaries:* Shakespeare in Perspective: Hamlet, 1980; The Clive James Paris Fashion Show, Clive James and the Calendar Girls, 1981; The Return of the Flash of Lightning, 1982; Clive James Live in Las Vegas, 1982. *Publications:* The Metropolitan Critic, 1974; The Fate of Felicity Fark in the Land of the Media, 1975; Peregrine Prykke's Pilgrimage through the London Literary World, 1976; Britannia Bright's Bewilderment in the Wilderness of Westminster, 1976; Visions Before Midnight, 1977; Fan-Mail, 1977; At the Pillars of Hercules, 1979; Unreliable Memoirs, 1980; First Reactions, 1980; The Crystal Bucket, 1981; Charles Charming's Challenges on the Pathway to the Throne, 1981; From the Land of Shadows, 1982; Glued to the Box, 1982. *Address:* c/o The Observer, 8 St Andrew's Hill, EC4.

JAMES, Rt. Rev. Colin Clement Walter; *see* Wakefield, Bishop of.

JAMES, Cynlais Morgan, CMG 1976; HM Diplomatic Service; Ambassador to Poland, since 1981; *b* 29 April 1926; *s* of Thomas James and Lydia Ann James (*née* Morgan); *m* 1953, Mary Teresa, *d* of R. D. Girouard and Lady Blanche Girouard; two *d. Educ:* Trinity Coll., Cambridge. Service in RAF, 1944-47. Cambridge 1948-51. Entered Senior Branch of Foreign Service, 1951; Foreign Office, 1951-53; Third Sec., Tokyo, 1953-56; Second Sec., Rio de Janeiro, 1956-59; First Sec. and Cultural Attaché, Moscow, 1959-62; FO, 1962-65; Paris, 1965-69; promoted Counsellor, 1968; Counsellor and Consul-General, Saigon, 1969-71; Head of W European Dept, FCO, 1971-75; NATO Defence Coll., Rome, 1975-76; Minister, Paris, 1976-81. *Recreation:* tennis. *Address:* c/o Foreign and Commonwealth Office, SW1. *Clubs:* Brooks's, Beefsteak; Travellers' (Paris).

JAMES, Dr (David) Geraint, FRCP; Consultant Physician since 1959, and Dean since 1968, Royal Northern Hospital, London; Consultant Ophthalmic Physician, St Thomas Hospital, London, since 1973; Teacher, University of London, since 1979; *b* 2 Jan. 1922; *s* of David James and Sarah (*née* Davies); *m* 1951, Sheila Sherlock, *qv* ; two *d. Educ:* Jesus Coll., Cambridge (MA 1945); Mddx Hosp. Med. Sch., London (MD 1953); Columbia Univ., NYC. FRCP 1964. Adjunct Prof. of Medicine, Univ. of Miami, Fla, 1973-, and Prof. of Epidemiology, 1981-; Consulting Phys. to RN, 1972-; Hon. Consultant Phys., US Veterans Admin, 1978-; Hon. Consulting Phys., Sydney Hosp., Australia, 1969-; World Exec. Sec., Internat. Cttee on Sarcoidosis, 1980-. Past President: Med. Soc. of London; Harveian Soc.; Osler Club (Hon. Fellow); London Glamorgan Soc. Mem. Council, Cymmrodorion Soc. Hon. LLD Wales, 1982. Mem. Editorial Board: French Thoracic Jl; Postgraduate Medical Jl; British Jl of Antimicrobial Chemotherapy; On Call; Medical Ophthalmology. *Publications:* Diagnosis and Treatment of Infections, 1957; Sarcoidosis, 1970; Circulation of the Blood, 1978; Atlas of Respiratory Diseases, 1981. *Recreations:* history of medicine, international Welshness, Rugby football. *Address:* 149 Harley Street, W1N 1HG. *T:* 01-935 4444. *Club:* Athenæum.

JAMES, David Guthrie, MBE, 1944; DSC 1944; author; *b* 25 Dec. 1919; *s* of Sir Archibald James, KBE, MC; *m* 1950, Hon. Jaquetta Digby, *y d* of 11th Baron Digby, KG, DSO, MC, TD; four *s* two *d. Educ:* Eton; Balliol. Served before the mast, Finnish 4-m. barque Viking, 1937-38; Balliol Coll., Oxford, 1938-39. Served War of 1939-45, RNVR, 1939-46; PoW 1943; escaped from Germany to Sweden, 1944. Mem. Antarctic Exped., 1945-46; Polar Adviser, Film Scott of the Antarctic, 1946-48. Joined Burns & Oates Ltd, Publishers, 1951. MP (C) Kemp Town Division of Brighton, 1959-64; MP (C) Dorset North, 1970-79. Council Mem., Outward Bound Trust, 1948-72; Trustee National Maritime Museum, 1953-65. Knight of Malta, 1962. *Publications:* A Prisoner's Progress, 1946; That Frozen Land, 1952; Scott of the Antarctic: The Film, 1950; The Life of Lord Roberts, 1954; (ed) Wavy Navy, 1948; (ed) Outward Bound, 1957; (ed) In Praise of Hunting, 1960. *Recreations:* gardening, stalking. *Address:* Torosay Castle, Craignure, Isle of Mull, Scotland. *T:* Craignure 421.

JAMES, Dr David Gwynfor; Head of Meteorological Research Flight, Royal Aircraft Establishment, Farnborough, since 1971; *b* 16 April 1925; *s* of William James and Margaret May Jones; *m* 1953, Margaret Vida Gower; two *d. Educ:* Univ. of Wales, Cardiff (BSc, PhD). Joined Meteorological Office, 1950; Met. Res. Flight, Farnborough, 1951; Forecasting Res., Dunstable, 1953; Christmas Island, Pacific, 1958; Satellite Lab., US Weather Bureau, 1961; Cloud Physics Res., Bracknell, 1966; Met. Res. Flight, RAE, 1971. *Publications:* papers in Qly Jl Royal Met. Soc., Jl Atmospheric Sciences, Met. Res. Papers, and Nature. *Recreations:* golf, choral singing. *Address:* 38 Oak Tree Close, Virginia Water, Surrey. *T:* Wentworth 3433. *Club:* Wentworth (Virginia Water).

JAMES, David Pelham; *see* James, David Guthrie.

JAMES, Dr David William Francis; Chief Executive, British Ceramic Research Association, since 1982 (Director of Research, 1978-82); *b* 29 March 1929; *s* of Thomas M. and Margaret A. James, Merthyr Tydfil; *m* 1953, Elaine Maureen, *d* of Thomas and Gladys Hewett, Swansea; two *d. Educ:* Cyfarthfa Castle Sch., Merthyr Tydfil; Univ. of Wales (BSc); Univ. of London (PhD). Research Asst. Inst. of Cancer Research, Royal Marsden Hosp., 1950-54; Flying Officer, RAF, 1954-56; Research Officer, Imperial Chemical

Industries (now Mond Div.), 1956-60; Lectr and Sen. Lectr, UC North Wales, Bangor, 1960-71; Dep. Principal, Glamorgan Polytechnic, 1971-72; Principal and Director, Polytechnic of Wales, 1972-78. Member: WJEC Techn. Educn Cttee, 1972-78, Techn. Examns Cttee and Management Adv. Cttee, 1972-75; SRC Polytechnics Cttee, 1975-78; Mid-Glamorgan Further Educn Cttee, 1974-78; CNAA, 1976- (Cttee for Research, 1976-; Cttee on Entry Qualifications, 1976-79; Cttee for Academic Policy, 1979-80; General Cttee, 1979-; Chm., Sub-Cttee on College Research Degrees, 1981-); Court, Univ. of Wales; Court, UWIST, 1972-78; Court, Univ. of Surrey, 1978-. FRSA. *Publications:* research papers in various jls; several patents. *Recreations:* photography, reading, church work. *Address:* Fairways, Birchall, Leek, Staffs. *T:* Leek 373311.

JAMES, Derek Claude; Director of Social Services, Leeds, since 1978; *b* 9 March 1929; *s* of Cecil Claude James and Violet (*née* Rudge); *m* 1954, Evelyn (*née* Thomas); one *s* one *d. Educ:* King Edward's Grammar Sch., Camp Hill, Birmingham; Open Univ. (BA). Dip. in Municipal Admin. Local Government: Birmingham, 1946-60; Coventry, 1960-63; Bradford, 1963-69; Leeds, 1969-. Mem., Yorks and Humberside RHA, 1976-. *Recreations:* watching sport, garden pottering. *Address:* Hill House, Woodhall Hills, Calverley, Pudsey, West Yorks LS28 5QY. *T:* Pudsey 578044.

JAMES, Air Vice-Marshal Edgar, CBE 1966; DFC 1945; AFC 1948 (Bar 1959); Aviation Consultant; *b* 19 Oct. 1915; *s* of Richard George James and Gertrude (*née* Barnes); *m* 1941, Josephine M. Steel; two *s. Educ:* Neath Grammar School. Joined RAF, 1939; commnd; flying instr duties, Canada, until 1944; opl service with Nos 305 and 107 Sqdns, 1944-45. Queen's Commendation for Valuable Service in the Air (1943, 1944, 1956). Empire Flying Sch. and Fighter Comd Ops Staff, until Staff Coll., 1950. Ops Requirements, Air Min., 1951-53; 2nd TAF Germany, 1953-56; comd No 68 Night Fighter Squadron, 1954-56; CFE, 1956-58; HQ Fighter Comd Staff, 1958-59; Asst Comdt, CFS, 1959-61; CO, RAF Leeming, 1961-62; Dir Ops Requirements 1, Min. of Def. (Air Force Dept), 1962-66; Comdr British Forces, Zambia, Feb.-Sept. 1966. Dep. Controller of Equipment, Min. of Technology, 1966-69. Wing Comdr 1953; Gp Capt. 1959; Air Cdre 1963; Air Vice-Marshal 1967. FRAeS 1971. *Recreations:* sailing, golf. *Address:* Lowmead, Traine Paddock, Modbury, Devon PL21 0RN. *T:* Modbury 0548; 70 Burton Court, SW3. *T:* 01-730 8482. *Clubs:* Royal Air Force; Royal Western Yacht.

JAMES, Edmund Purcell S.; *see* Skone James.

JAMES, Edward Foster, CMG 1968; OBE 1946; Deputy Director-General, Confederation of British Industry, since 1976; *b* 18 Jan. 1917; *s* of late Arthur Foster James; *m* 1951, Caroline Warwick Bampfylde, *d* of Hon. Francis Warwick Bampfylde; one *s* two *d. Educ:* Chiswick Grammar Sch. Served HM Forces, 1939-46, India, Burma, Malaya, Indonesia; Lieut-Colonel (GSO1) (OBE, despatches twice). Joined HM Diplomatic Service, 1947; Rangoon, 1948; Hong Kong, 1951; Foreign Office, 1953; Rome, 1955; Foreign Office, 1958; Berlin, 1960; FO (later FCO), 1961-74. Exec. Dir, Inst. of Directors, 1975-76. *Address:* Springfield House, West Clandon, Guildford, Surrey. *T:* Guildford 222412. *Club:* Boodle's.

JAMES, Edwin Kenneth George; Managing Director, PAG Power Ltd, since 1977; Chief Scientific Officer, Civil Service Department, 1970-76; *b* 27 Dec. 1916; *s* of late Edwin and Jessie Marion James; *m* 1941, Dorothy Margaret Pratt; one *d. Educ:* Latymer Upper Sch.; Northern Polytechnic. BSc London; FRIC. Joined War Office, 1938; Chem. Defence Exper. Stn, 1942; Aust. Field Exper. Stn, 1944-46; Operational Research Gp, US Army, Md, 1950-54; Dir, Biol and Chem. Defence, WO, 1961; Army (later Defence) Op. Res. Estab., Byfleet, 1965; HM Treasury (later Civil Service Dept), 1968. Silver Medal, Op. Res. Soc., 1979. *Address:* 5 Watersmeet Road, East Harnham, Salisbury, Wilts. *T:* Salisbury 4099. *Club:* Athenæum.

JAMES, (Eliot) Antony B.; *see* Brett-James.

JAMES, (Ernest) Gethin, FRICS; Director, Estate Surveying Services, Property Services Agency, since 1977; *b* 20 March 1925; *s* of Ernest Bertram James and Gwladys James; *m* 1st, 1949 (marr. diss.); 2nd, 1981, Mrs Margaret Hollis. *Educ:* Christ Coll., Brecon; Coll. of Estate Management. FRICS 1954. Defence Land Agent: Colchester, 1968-69; Aldershot, 1969-72; Dep. Chief Land Agent, MoD, 1972-74, Chief Land Agent and Valuer, 1974-75; Asst Dir (Estates), PSA, London Reg., 1975-77. *Recreations:* living each day, golf, shooting. *Address:* 9 Tredenham Close, Farnborough, Hants. *T:* Farnborough 511825. *Club:* Officers' (Aldershot).

JAMES, Evan Maitland; *b* 14 Jan. 1911; *er s* of late A. G. James, CBE, and late Helen James (*née* Maitland); *m* 1939, Joan Goodnow, *d* of late Hon. J. V. A. MacMurray, State Dept, Washington, DC; one *s* two *d. Educ:* Durnford; Eton (Oppidan Scholar); Trinity Coll., Oxford. Served War of 1939-45: War Reserve Police (Metropolitan), 1939; BBC Overseas Dept, 1940-41; Ordinary Seaman, then Lieut, RNVR, 1941-46. Clerk of the Merchant Taylors' Company, 1948-62; Steward of Christ Church, Oxford, 1962-78. *Address:* Upwood Park, Besselsleigh, Abingdon, Oxon OX13 5QE. *T:* Frilford Heath 390535. *Club:* Travellers'.

JAMES, Geraint; *see* James, D. G.

JAMES, Gethin; see James, E. G.

JAMES, Henry Leonard, CB 1980; Director-General, National Association of Pension Funds, since 1981; b 12 Dec. 1919; o s of late Leonard Mark James and late Alice Esther James; m 1949, Sylvia Mary Bickell. Educ: King Edward VI Sch., Birmingham. Entered Civil Service in Min. of Health, 1938; Founder Editor, The Window, Min. of Nat. Insce, 1948-51; Dramatic Critic and London Corresp. of Birmingham News, 1947-51; Press Officer, Min. of Pensions and Nat. Insce, 1951-55; Head of Films, Radio and Television, Admty, 1955-61; Head of Publicity, Min. of Educn, 1961-63; Chief Press Officer, Min. of Educn, 1963-64; Dep. Public Relations Adviser to Prime Minister, 1964; Dep. Press Sec. to Prime Minister, 1964-68; Chief Information Officer, Min. of Housing and Local Govt, 1969-70; Press Sec. to Prime Minister, 1970-71; Dir of Information, DoE, 1971-74; Dir-Gen., COI, 1974-78; Chief Press Sec. to the Prime Minister, 1979; Public Relations Advr to Main Bd, Vickers Ltd, 1978-80. Member: Pub. Cttee, Internat. Year of the Child, 1979; Council, RSPCA, 1980-; BOTB, 1980-. Alumni Guest Lectr, Gustavus Adolphus Coll., Minnesota, 1977. F CAM 1980 (Dep. Chm., 1979-). FRSA. FIPR (Pres., 1979; President's Medal, 1976). Recreation: visual arts. Address: 53 Beaufort Road, W5 3EB. T: 01-997 3021.

JAMES, Prof. Ioan Mackenzie, FRS 1968; MA, DPhil; Savilian Professor of Geometry, Oxford University, since 1970; Fellow of New College, Oxford, since 1970; Editor, Topology, since 1962; b 23 May 1928; o s of Reginald Douglas and Jessie Agnes James; m 1961, Rosemary Gordon Stewart, Fellow of Oxford Centre for Management Studies; no c. Educ: St Paul's Sch. (Foundn Schol.); Queen's Coll., Oxford (Open Schol.). Commonwealth Fund Fellow, Princeton, Berkeley and Inst. for Advanced Study, 1954-55; Tapp Res. Fellow, Gonville and Caius Coll., Cambridge, 1956; Reader in Pure Mathematics, Oxford, 1957-69, and Senior Research Fellow, St John's Coll., 1959-69. London Mathematical Society: Treasurer, 1970-; Whitehead Prize and Lectr, 1978. Mem. Council, Royal Soc., 1982-. Gov. of St Paul's Sch, 1970-. Publications: (ed) The Mathematical Works of J. H. C. Whitehead, 1963; The Topology of Stiefel Manifolds, 1976; sundry papers in mathematical jls. Address: Mathematical Institute, 24-29 St Giles, Oxford. T: Oxford 54295.

JAMES, John, CBE 1981; Founder and Chairman: John James Group of Companies Ltd, Bristol, 1961-79; Broadmead Group of Companies, 1946-60; Dawn Estates Ltd, since 1945; b 25 July 1906; m 1st (marr. diss.); one s two d (and one d decd); 2nd, Margaret Theodosia Parkes. Educ: Merchant Venturers, Bristol. Chm. Bd of Trustees, Dawn James Charitable Foundn. Recreations: chess, swimming. Address: Tower Court, Ascot, Berks. T: Ascot 21094.

JAMES, John A.; see Angell-James.

JAMES, John Anthony, CMG 1973; FRACS; Visiting Neurosurgeon, Wellington Hospital Board, Wellington, NZ, 1965-77; b 2 April 1913; s of Herbert L. James and Gladys E. Paton; m 1941, Millicent Ward, Australia; three s one d. Educ: Melbourne Grammar Sch. (Church of England); Melbourne Univ. (MB, BS). Served War: Surgeon-Lieut, RANR, 1940-43. Neurosurgeon, Neurosurgical Unit, Dunedin Hosp., 1947-52; Dir, Neurosurgical Unit, Otago Univ.; Sen. Lectr in Neurosurgery, Otago Univ., 1951-64. Publications: contribs to surgical jls. Address: 136 Vipond Road, Whangaparaoa, New Zealand. Club: Wellington (Wellington, NZ).

JAMES, John Christopher Urmston; Secretary, Lawn Tennis Association, since 1981 (Assistant Secretary, 1973-81); b 22 June 1937; s of John Urmston James and Ellen Irene James; two s. Educ: Hereford Cathedral Sch. Harrods, 1954; Jaeger, 1961; Pringle, 1972. Recreations: lawn tennis, Rugby football, walking, architecture, the countryside. Address: c/o Lawn Tennis Association, Barons Court, West Kensington, W14 9EG. T: 01-385 2366. Clubs: Queen's, London Welsh, International of GB; West Hants (Bournemouth).

JAMES, Prof. John Ivor Pulsford, MB, MS London; FRCS; FRCSE; George Harrison Law Professor of Orthopædic Surgery, Edinburgh University, 1958-79, now Emeritus Professor; Consultant in Orthopædic Surgery to the Navy since 1956; Head of Orthopaedic Services, Kuwait, since 1980; b 19 Oct. 1913; s of late Stanley B. James and Jessica Heley; m 1968, Margaret Eiriol Samuel, MB, ChB; one s one d. Educ: Eggars Grammar Sch., Alton, Hants; University Coll. and Hosp., London, Hampshire County Schol., 1932-38; Ferrière Schol., University Coll., 1935; Goldsmid Schol., University Coll. Hosp., 1935; Magrath Schol., University Coll. Hosp., 1937; Rockefeller Fellowship, 1947-48; Consultant Orthopædic Surgeon, Royal National Orthopædic Hospital, 1946-58; Asst Dir of Studies, Institute of Orthopædics, University of London, 1948-58. Fellow Univ. Coll., London. Hunterian Prof., RCS, 1957; Past Pres., British Orthopædic Assoc. (Fellow); Past Pres., British Soc. for Surgery of the Hand; Mem. Société Internationale de Chirurgie Orthopédique et de Traumatologie; Corresp. Member: Amer. Orthopædic Assoc.; Austr. Orthopædic Assoc.; Scandinavian Orthopædic Assoc.; Hon. Member: Amer. Acad. of Orthopædic Surgeons; Dutch Orthopædic Assoc.; Assoc. for Orthopædic Surgery and Traumatology of Yugoslavia; Canadian Orthopædic Assoc.; New Zealand Orthopædic Assoc.; Hellenic Assoc. of Orthopædics and Traumatology; Société Française d'Orthopédie et de Traumatologie. Hon. FRACS. Late Temp. Lieut-Col RAMC. Golden Star, Order of Service to the Yugoslav People, 1970. Publications: Scoliosis, 1967, 2nd edn 1976; articles relating to curvature of the spine and surgery of the

hand in medical journals, etc. Recreations: sailing, fishing, gardening. Address: 2 Regent Terrace, Edinburgh EH7 5BN.

JAMES, John Jocelyn S.; see Streatfeild-James.

JAMES, John Nigel Courtenay, FRICS; Trustee of the Grosvenor Estate, since 1971; b 31 March 1935; s of Frank Courtenay James and Beryl May Wilford; m 1961, Elizabeth Jane St Clair-Ford; one s one d. Educ: Sherborne Sch., Dorset. Chief Agent and Estate Surveyor, Grosvenor Estate, 1968-71. Director: Sun Alliance & London Insurance Gp, 1972-; Woolwich Equitable Building Soc., 1982-. Member: Commn for the New Towns, 1978-; Cttee of Management, RNLI, 1980-. Pres., RICS, 1980-81. Recreation: sailing. Address: Heybote, Ellesborough, near Aylesbury, Bucks. T: Aylesbury 622758. Club: Brooks's.

JAMES, John Wynford George, OBE 1950; FRAeS 1963; FCIT (MInstT 1954); Member of Board, BEA, 1964-74; Chairman: BEA Airtours, 1972-74; British Airways Helicopters, 1967-74; Gulf Helicopters Ltd, 1970-76; Deputy Chairman, International Aeradio Ltd, 1971-74 (Director, 1956); British Airways Group Air Safety Adviser, 1973-74; retired 1976; b 13 Feb. 1911; s of William George and Elizabeth James; m 1934, Bertha Mildred Joyce Everard; one s two d. Educ: Royal Grammar School, Worcester. Joined Imperial Airways as a pilot, 1933; Capt., Imperial Airways/BOAC, 1935-46; BEA Chief Pilot, 1946; Operations Dir, BEA, 1954-68. Chm. BALPA, 1943-48. Mem. Bd, International Helicopters Ltd, 1965. Governor, College of Air Training, 1959- (Chm. 1959-61, 1963-66, 1968-70). Liveryman, GAPAN, 1960. Recreations: golf, gardening, fishing, shooting. Address: Wynsfield, Mill Lane, Gerrards Cross, Bucks. T: Gerrards Cross 84038.

JAMES, Lionel Frederic Edward, CBE 1977 (MBE (mil.) 1944); Comptroller, Forces Help Society and Lord Roberts Workshops, 1970-82; b 22 Feb. 1912; s of late Frederic James, Westmount, Exeter; m 1933, Harriet French-Harley; one s one d. Educ: Royal Grammar Sch., Worcester. Investment Co., 1933-39. Served War with Royal Engineers, 1939-46: BEF; Planning Staff, Sicilian Invasion; N Africa, Sicily, Greece and Italy (Major). Dep. Dir, Overseas Service, Forces Help Soc., 1946, Dir, 1948; Asst Sec. of Society, 1953, Company Sec., 1963. Recreation: restoration of antiques. Address: 122 Brompton Road, SW3.

JAMES, Michael Leonard; Director, Plutonium Management Programme, International Atomic Energy Agency, Vienna, since 1978; b 7 Feb. 1941; s of Leonard and Marjorie James, Portreath, Cornwall; m 1975, Jill Elizabeth, d of late George Tarján, OBE and Etelka Tarján, formerly of Budapest; two d. Educ: Latymer Upper Sch.; Christ's Coll., Cambridge (Holland Rose and Wren Prizes). British govt service, latterly Asst Sec., Department of Energy, 1963-78; Private Sec. to Rt Hon. Jennie Lee, MP, Minister for the Arts, 1966-68. UK Governor, IIMT, Milan, 1973-75; Consultant to OECD, 1972-75. FRSA. Publications: (jtly) Internationalization to Prevent the Spread of Nuclear Weapons, 1980; articles on internat. relations and nuclear energy. Recreations: writing, music, shooting. Address: Ziegelofengasse 100, A-3400 Klosterneuburg, Austria. T: (office) Vienna 23600.

JAMES, Dame Naomi (Christine), DBE 1979; author and yachtswoman; b 2 March 1949; d of Charles Robert Power and Joan Power; m 1976, Robert Alan James. Educ: Rotorua Girls' High Sch., NZ. Hair stylist, 1966-71; language teacher, 1972-74; yacht charter crew, 1975-77. Sailed single handed round the world via the three great Capes, incl. first woman solo round Cape Horn, on 53 ft yacht, Express Crusader, Sept. 1977-June 1978; sailed in 1980 Observer Transatlantic Race, winning Ladies Prize and achieving women's record for single-handed Atlantic crossing, on 53 ft yacht Kriter Lady; won 1982 Round Britain Race with Rob James, on multihull Colt Cars GB. Royal Yacht Sqdn Chichester Trophy, 1978; NZ Yachtsman of the Year, 1978. Publications: Woman Alone, 1978; At One with the Sea, 1979; At Sea on Land, 1981. Recreations: boardsailing, riding, skiing, antique furniture. Address: c/o Postgrove Farmhouse, Upper Enham, Andover, Hants. Clubs: Royal Dart Yacht (Dartmouth); Royal Lymington Yacht (Lymington); Royal Western Yacht (Plymouth).

JAMES, Noel David Glaves, OBE 1964; MC 1945; TD 1946; b 16 Sept. 1911; o s of late Rev. D. T. R. James, and Gertrude James; m 1949, Laura Cecilia (d 1970), yr d of late Sir Richard Winn Livingstone; two s (and one s decd). Educ: Haileybury Coll.; Royal Agricultural Coll., Cirencester (Gold Medal and Estate Management Prize). In general practice as a land agent, 1933-39. Served War, 1939-46 (MC, despatches); 68 Field Regt RA (TA), France, Middle East, Italy. Bursar, Corpus Christi Coll., Oxford, 1946-51; MA (Oxon.) 1946. Fellow, Corpus Christi Coll., Oxford, 1950-51; Land Agent for Oxford Univ., 1951-61; Estates Bursar and Agent for Brasenose Coll., 1959-61; Fellow, Brasenose Coll., Oxford, 1951-61; Agent for Clinton Devon Estates, 1961-76. President: Land Agents Soc., 1957-58; Royal Forestry Soc. of England and Wales and N Ireland, 1962-64; Member: Central Forestry Examination Bd of UK, 1951-75; Regional Advisory Cttee, Eastern Conservancy, Forestry Commn, 1951-61; Regional Advisory Cttee, SW Conservancy, Forestry Commission, 1962-75; Departmental Cttee on Hedgerow and Farm Timber, 1953; UK Forestry Cttee, 1954-59; Governor Wye Coll., Kent, 1955-61; Governor Westonbirt Sch., 1959-68. FLAS; FRICS (Diploma in Forestry and Watney Gold Medal). Gold Medal for Distinguished Service to Forestry, 1967; Royal Agricultural Coll. Bledisloe Medal for services to agriculture and forestry, 1970. Publications: Artillery

Observation Posts, 1941; Working Plans for Estate Woodlands, 1948; Notes on Estate Forestry, 1949; An Experiment in Forestry, 1951; The Forester's Companion, 1955 (3rd edn, 1982); The Trees of Bicton, 1969; The Arboriculturalist's Companion, 1972; A Book of Trees (anthology), 1973; Before the Echoes Die Away, 1980; A History of English Forestry, 1981; A Forestry Centenary, 1982. *Recreations:* forestry, shooting. *Address:* Blakemore House, Kersbrook, Budleigh Salterton, Devon. *T:* Budleigh Salterton 3886. *Club:* Army and Navy.

JAMES, Patrick Leonard, FDSRCS, MRCS; Senior Consultant Oral and Maxillo-facial Surgeon, London Hospital, Whitechapel, since 1965; Consultant Oral and Maxillo-facial Surgeon, North East Thames Regional Hospital Board Hospitals, since 1963; Recognized Teacher in Oral Surgery, London University, since 1965; Civilian Consultant in Oral Surgery to RAF, since 1979; *b* 7 Jan. 1926; *s* of late John Vincent James and Priscilla Elsie (*née* Hill), Cuffley, Herts; *m* 1951, Jean Margaret, *er d* of Leslie and Ruth Hatcher, Woking, Surrey; one *s* two *d*. *Educ:* Hertford and Cheshunt Grammar Schs; King's Coll., London; Royal Dental Hosp.; London Hosp. FDSRCS 1958 (LDSRCS 1948); MRCS, LRCP 1956. Served RAF, Flt Lieut, ME Comd, 1949–51. Resident Ho. Surg., Ho. Phys., Cas. Officer, King George Hosp., 1956–57; Sen. Registrar, Queen Victoria Hosp., E Grinstead, 1959–63; Consultant Oral and Maxillo-facial Surgeon: to London Hosp., Honey Lane Hosp., Waltham Abbey, Herts and Essex Hosp., Bishop's Stortford, 1963–; to King George Hosp., 1967–; St Margaret's Hosp., Epping, 1966–; Black Notley Hosp., 1969–. Exchange Fellow, Henry Ford Hosp., Detroit, Mich., 1962; Hunterian Prof., RCS, 1970–71. Member: Academic Bd, London Hosp. Med. Coll., 1968–71; Adv. Cttee in Plastic Surgery, NE Met. Reg. Hosp. Bd, 1969–77; NE Thames Reg. Manpower Cttee, 1975–; Chairman: NE Met. BDA Hosps Gp, 1970–71; NE Thames Reg. Adv. Cttee in hosp. dental surgery, 1982–. Fellow: BAOS, 1963– (Mem. Council, 1971–74); Internat. Assoc. of Oral Surgs (BAOS Rep. on council, 1974–78); Chm., Sci. Session, 6th Internat. Congress of Oral Surgs, Sydney, 1977; Associate Mem., Brit. Assoc. of Plastic Surgs, 1958–77. FRSM; Mem. Council, Chelsea Clin. Soc. Liveryman, Soc. of Apothecaries, 1969; Freeman, City of London, 1978. *Publications:* (chapter in Oral Surgery) Malignancies in Odontogenic Cysts, 1967; (chapter in Oral Surgery) Correction of Apertognathia with Osteotomies and Bone Graft, 1970; (chapter in Oral Surgery, vol. 7) Surgical Treatment of Mandibular Joint Disorders, 1978; numerous articles on surgical treatment of mandibular joint disorders, surgery of salivary glands and maxillo facial surgery in med. and surg. jls. *Recreations:* shooting, fishing, sailing (Cdre, United Hosps Sailing Club, 1968–75), skiing. *Address:* Meesden Hall, Meesden, Buntingford, Herts SG9 0AZ; 19 Harcourt House, 19 Cavendish Square, W1. *T:* 01-580 5123. *Club:* Naval and Military.

JAMES, Prof. Peter Maunde Coram, VRD 1964; John Humphreys Professor of Dental Health since 1966, and Director of the Dental School, 1978–82, University of Birmingham; *b* 2 April 1922; *s* of Vincent Coram James, MRCS, LRCP, and Mildred Ivy (*née* Gooch); *m* 1945, Denise Mary Bond, LDS; four *s*. *Educ:* Westminster Sch.; Royal Dental Hosp., Univ. of London (MDS); Univ. of St Andrews (DPD). LDSRCS. House Surgeon, then Sen. House Surg., Royal Dental Hosp., 1945; Surg. Lieut (D) RNVR, 1945–48; Registrar, Res. Asst and Hon. Lectr, Inst. of Dental Surgery (Eastman Dental Hosp.), 1949–55; Gibbs Travelling Scholar, 1952; Royal Dental Hosp. Sch. of Dental Surgery, Univ. of London: Sen. Lectr, 1955–65; Asst Dean, 1958–66; Dir, Dept of Children's Dentistry, 1962–66; Hon. Cons. Dental Surg., 1961–; Reader in Preventive Dentistry, Univ. of London, 1965; Head, Dept of Dental Health, Univ. of Birmingham, 1966–. Consultant, Internat. Dental Fedn Commn on Dental Res., 1976–; Cons. Advisor in Community Dentistry to DHSS, 1977–; Reg. Advisor (W Midlands), Faculty of Dental Surgery, RCS, 1976–. President: Brit. Paedodontic Soc., 1962; Central Counties Br., BDA, 1981–82; Founding Pres., Brit. Assoc. for Study of Community Dentistry, 1973. Chm., Specialist Adv. Cttee in Community Dental Health, 1981–; Member: Dental Working Party, Cttee on Child Health Services, 1974–77; Birmingham AHA (Teaching), 1979–82, Birmingham Central DHA, 1982–; Jt Cttee for Higher Training in Dentistry, 1981–. Ext. Assessor, Univ. of Malaya, 1977–; ext. examr in dental subjects, univs and colls, 1955–. *Publications:* contrib. to dental and scientific jls. *Recreations:* music, photography, camping. *Address:* The Pump House, Bishopton Spa, Stratford-upon-Avon, Warwicks. *T:* Stratford-upon-Avon 4330. *Club:* Royal Society of Medicine.

JAMES, Prof. Philip Seaforth; Professor of English Law, University College at Buckingham, since 1975; *b* 28 May 1914; *s* of Dr Philip William James, MC, and Muriel Lindley James; *m* 1954. Wybetty, *d* of Claas P. Gerth, Enschede, Holland; two *s*. *Educ:* Charterhouse; Trinity Coll., Oxford (MA), Research Fellow, Yale Univ., USA, 1937-38. Called to the Bar, Inner Temple, 1939. Served War of 1939-45, in Royal Artillery, India, Burma (despatches). Fellow of Exeter Coll., Oxford, 1946–49; Prof. and Hd of Dept of Law, Leeds Univ., 1952-75. Visiting Professor: Univs of Yale and of Louisville, Kentucky, USA, 1960-61; Univ. of South Carolina, 1972-73; NY Law Sch., 1981-83. Chairman: Yorks Rent Assessment Panel, 1966-75; Thames Valley Rent Assessment Panel, 1976–; Assessor to County Court under Race Relations Acts. Pres., Soc. of Public Teachers of Law, 1971-72. Governor, Swinton Conservative College, 1970–. Hon. Mem., Mark Twain Soc., 1979. *Publications:* An Introduction to English Law, 1950; General Principles of the Law of Torts, 1959; Shorter Introduction to English Law, 1969; Six Lectures on the Law of Torts, 1980 (trans. Spanish); various articles, notes and reviews on legal and biographical subjects. *Recreations:* golf and gardening. *Address:*

Chestnut View, Mill Lane, Whitfield, near Brackley, Northants NN13 5TQ. *Club:* National Liberal.

JAMES, Phyllis Dorothy, (Mrs C. B. White); JP; author (as P. D. James); *b* 3 Aug. 1920; *d* of Sidney Victor James and Dorothy Amelia James (*née* Hone); *m* 1941, Connor Bantry White; two *d*. *Educ:* Cambridge Girls' High Sch. Administrator, National Health Service, 1949-68; Civil Service: apptd Principal, Home Office, 1968; Police Dept, 1968-72; Criminal Policy Dept, 1972-79. Member, Crime Writers' Assoc. JP Willesden, 1979. *Publications:* Cover Her Face, 1962; A Mind to Murder, 1963; Unnatural Causes, 1967; Shroud for a Nightingale, 1971; (with T. A. Critchley) The Maul and the Pear Tree, 1971; An Unsuitable Job for a Woman, 1972 (filmed 1982); The Black Tower, 1975; Death of an Expert Witness, 1977; Innocent Blood, 1980; The Skull beneath the Skin, 1982. *Recreations:* exploring churches, walking by the sea. *Address:* c/o Elaine Greene Ltd, 31 Newington Green, N16 9PU. *Club:* Detection.

JAMES, Richard Austin, CB 1980; MC 1945; Receiver for Metropolitan Police District, 1977-80; *b* 26 May 1920; *s* of late Thomas Morris James, Headmaster of Sutton Valence Sch., and Hilda Joan James; *m* 1948, Joan Boorer; two *s* one *d*. *Educ:* Clifton Coll.; Emmanuel Coll., Cambridge. British American Tobacco Co., 1938; Royal Engrs, 1939-41; Queen's Own Royal W Kent Regt, 1941-46; Home Office, 1948; Private Sec. to Chancellor of Duchy of Lancaster, 1960; Asst Sec., 1961; Dep. Receiver for Metropolitan Police District, 1970-73; Asst Under-Sec. of State, Police Dept, Home Office, 1974-76; Dep. Under-Sec. of State, 1980. Gen. Sec., Distressed Gentlefolk's Aid Assoc., 1981-82. Freeman, City of London, 1980. *Recreation:* cricket. *Address:* Cedarwood, Redbrook Lane, Buxted, Sussex. *T:* Buxted 2364. *Clubs:* Athenæum, MCC.

JAMES, Robert Michael; HM Diplomatic Service; Commercial Counsellor and Deputy High Commissioner, Accra, Ghana, since 1980; *b* 2 Oct. 1934; *s* of late Rev. B. V. James and of Mrs D. M. James; *m* 1959, Sarah Helen (*née* Bell); two *s* one *d*. *Educ:* St John's, Leatherhead; Trinity Coll., Cambridge (BA Hons History). Schoolmaster: Harrow Sch., 1958-60; Cranleigh Sch., 1960-62; joined CRO, 1962; 3rd Sec., Wellington, NZ, 1963-65; 1st Sec., Colombo, Sri Lanka, 1966-69; FCO, 1969-71; Dep. High Comr and Head of Chancery, Georgetown, Guyana, 1971-73; Econ. Sec., Ankara, Turkey, 1974-76; FCO, 1976-80. *Recreations:* sport (cricket Blue, 1956-58), drawing, travel. *Address:* c/o Foreign and Commonwealth Office, King Charles Street, SW1. *T:* 01-233 3000; Warwicks Mount, Warwicks Bench Road, Guildford, Surrey GU1 3TQ. *T:* Guildford 504989. *Club:* MCC.

JAMES, Robert Vidal R.; *see* Rhodes James.

JAMES, Prof. Dame Sheila (Patricia Violet); *see* Sherlock, Prof. Dame S. P. V.

JAMES, Stanley Francis; Head of Statistics Division 1, Departments of Industry and Trade, since 1981; *b* 12 Feb. 1927; *s* of H. F. James; unmarried. *Educ:* Sutton County Sch.; Trinity Coll., Cambridge. Maths Tripos Pt II; Dip. Math. Statistics. Research Lectr, Econs Dept, Nottingham Univ., 1951; Statistician, Bd of Inland Revenue, 1956; Chief Statistician: Bd of Inland Revenue, 1966; Central Statistical Office, 1968; Asst Dir, Central Statistical Office, 1970-72; Dir, Stats Div., Bd of Inland Revenue, 1972-77; Head, Econs and Stats Div. 6, Depts of Industry and Trade, 1977-81. Hon. Treasurer, Royal Statistical Soc., 1978–. *Recreations:* travel, theatre, gardening. *Address:* 3 Briary Close, Fellows Road, NW3 3JZ. *T:* 01-722 6232. *Club:* Royal Automobile.

JAMES, Steven Wynne Lloyd; Circuit Administrator, Wales and Chester Circuit, Lord Chancellor's Department, since 1982; *b* 9 June 1934; *s* of late Trevor Lloyd James and of Olwen Ellis; *m* 1962, Carolyn Ann Rowlands, *d* of late James Morgan Rowlands and of Mercia Rowlands; three *s*. *Educ:* Queen Elizabeth Grammar Sch., Carmarthen; LSE. LLB 1956. Admitted solicitor, 1959. Asst Solicitor in private practice, 1959-61; Legal Asst, HM Land Registry, 1961; Asst Solicitor, Glamorgan CC, 1962-70; Asst Clerk of the Peace, 1970-71; Lord Chancellor's Dept, 1971–: Sen. Principal Courts Administrator, Chester/Mold gp of courts, Wales and Chester Circuit, 1971-76; Asst Sec., 1976; Dep. Circuit Administrator, Wales and Chester Circuit, 1976-82; Under Sec., 1982. *Recreations:* walking, gardening, reading. *Address:* Wales and Chester Circuit Office, 3rd Floor, Churchill House, Churchill Way, Cardiff. *T:* Cardiff 396925. *Club:* Civil Service.

JAMES, (Thomas) Cecil (Garside), CMG 1966; Assistant Under-Secretary of State, Ministry of Defence, 1968-77; *b* 8 Jan. 1918; *s* of Joshua James, MBE, Ashton-under-Lyne; *m* 1941, Elsie Williams, Ashton-under-Lyne; one *s* two *d*. *Educ:* Manchester Grammar Sch.; St John's Coll., Cambridge. Prin. Priv. Sec. to Sec. of State for Air, 1951-55; Asst Sec., Air Min., 1955; Civil Sec., FEAF, 1963-66; Chief of Public Relations, MoD, 1966-68. *Recreation:* golf. *Address:* 4 Park View, Pinner, Mddx HA5 4LN.

JAMES, Thomas Garnet Henry, FBA 1976; Keeper of Egyptian Antiquities, British Museum, since 1974; *b* 8 May 1923; *s* of late Thomas Garnet James and Edith (*née* Griffiths); *m* 1956, Diana Margaret, *y d* of H. L. Vavasseur-Durell; one *s*. *Educ:* Neath Grammar Sch.; Exeter Coll., Oxford. 2nd Cl. Lit. Hum. 1947; 1st Cl. Oriental Studies 1950, MA 1948. Served War of 1939-45, RA; NW Europe; 2nd Lieut 1943; Captain 1945. Asst Keeper, Dept of

Egyptian and Assyrian Antiquities, 1951; Dep. Keeper (Egyptian Antiquities), 1974. Laycock Student of Egyptology, Worcester Coll., Oxford, 1954-60; Wilbour Fellow, Brooklyn Museum, 1964; Editor, Jl of Egyptian Archæology, 1960-70; Editor, Egyptological pubns of Egypt Exploration Soc., 1960-. Mem., German Archæological Inst., 1974. *Publications:* The Mastaba of Khentika called Ikhekhi, 1953; Hieroglyphic Texts in the British Museum I, 1961; The Hekanakhte Papers and other Early Middle Kingdom Documents, 1962; (with R. A. Caminos) Gebel es-Silsilah I, 1963; Egyptian Sculptures, 1966; Myths and Legends of Ancient Egypt, 1969; Hieroglyphic Texts in the British Museum, 9, 1970; Archæology of Ancient Egypt, 1972; Corpus of Hieroglyphic Inscriptions in the Brooklyn Museum, I, 1974; (ed) An Introduction to Ancient Egypt, 1979; (ed) Excavating in Egypt, 1982; (contrib.) W. B. Emery: Great Tombs of the First Dynasty II, 1954; (contrib.) T. J. Dunbabin: Perachora II, 1962; (contrib.) Cambridge Ancient History, 3rd edn, 1973; (contrib.) Encyclop. Britannica, 15th edn, 1974; (ed English trans.) H. Kees: Ancient Egypt, 1961; articles in Jl Egyptian Arch., etc; reviews in learned jls. *Recreations:* music, wine and food. *Address:* 14 Turner Close, NW11 6TU. *T:* 01-455 9221.

JAMES, Thomas Geraint Illtyd, FRCS; Hon. Surgeon, Central Middlesex Hospital; Late Teacher of Surgery, Middlesex Hospital, and Hon. Surgical Tutor, Royal College of Surgeons of England; *b* 12 July 1900; *s* of late Evan Thomas and Elizabeth James, Barry; *m* 1932, Dorothy Marguerite, *o d* of late David John, Cardiff; two *s*. *Educ:* Barry, Glam; University Coll., Cardiff; Welsh National Sch. of Medicine; St Mary's Hosp., London; Guy's Hosp., London. BSc Wales, 1921, Alfred Sheen Prize in Anat. and Physiol.; MRCS, LRCP, 1924; MB, ChB, 1925, Maclean Medal and Prize in Obst. and Gynæcol.; FRCSE, 1927; FRCS, 1928; MCh Wales, 1932; FRSocMed; Fellow Association of Surgeons of Great Britain and Ireland; Erasmus Wilson Lectr, RCS, 1972. Mem., Internat. Soc. for Surgery; Corr. Mem. Spanish-Portuguese Soc. of Neurosurgery. Mem. Soc. of Apothecaries; Freeman of City of London. Formerly: Assoc. Examr University of London; Mem. and Chm., Court of Examiners RCS of England; Examr in Surgery, University of Liverpool; Ho. phys., Ho. surg. and Resident Surgical Officer, Cardiff Royal Infirmary; Clinical Asst St Mark's, St Peter's and Guy's Hosps, London; Asst to Neurosurg. Dept, London Hosp.; Mem., Management Cttee, Leavesden Gp of Hosps. *Publications:* in various jls on surg. and neurosurg. subjects. *Recreations:* literature, travelling. *Address:* 1 Freeland Road, W5. *T:* 01-992 2430.

JAMES, Walter; see James, Arthur Walter.

JAMES, Prof. Walter, CBE 1977; Professor of Educational Studies, Open University, since 1969; *b* 8 Dec. 1924; *s* of late George Herbert James and Mary Kathleen (*née* Crutch); *m* 1948, Joyce Dorothy Woollaston; two *s*. *Educ:* Royal Grammar Sch., Worcester; St Luke's Coll., Exeter; Univ. of Nottingham. BA 1955. School teacher, 1948-52; Univ. of Nottingham: Resident Tutor, Dept of Extra-Mural Studies, 1958-65; Lectr in Adult Educn, Dept of Adult Educn, 1965-69; Dean and Dir of Studies, Faculty of Educnl Studies, Open Univ., 1969-77. Consultant on Adult Educn and Community Develt to Govt of Seychelles and ODA of FCO, 1973; Adviser: to Office of Educn, WCC, 1974-76; on Social Planning, to State of Bahrain, 1975; Council of Europe: UK Rep., Working Party on Develt of Adult Education, 1973-81; UK Rep., Chm. of Project Gp and Project Adviser, Adult Educn for Develt, 1982-; Chairman: Nat. Council for Voluntary Youth Services, 1970-76; Review of Training of part-time Youth and Community Workers, 1975-77; Religious Adv. Bd, Scout Assoc., 1977-82; Inservice Training and Educn Panel for Youth and Community Service, 1978-; Member: DES Cttee on Youth and Community Work in 70s, 1967-69; ILO Working Party on Use of Radio and TV for Workers' Educn, 1968; Gen. Synod, C of E, 1970-75; Exec. Cttee, Nat. Council of Social Service, 1970-75; Univs' Council for Educn of Teachers, 1970-; Univs Council for Adult Educn, 1971-76; BBC Further Educn Adv. Council, 1971-75; Exec. Cttee and Council, Nat. Inst. of Adult Educn, 1971-77; Library Adv. Council for England, 1974-76; Adv. Council, HM Queen's Silver Jubilee Appeal, 1976-78; Trustee: Young Volunteer Force Foundn, 1972-77; Community Projects Foundn, 1977-; Trident Educnl Trust, 1972-; President: Inst. of Playleadership, 1972-74; Fair Play for Children, 1979-. *Publications:* (with F. J. Bayliss) The Standard of Living, 1964; (ed) Virginia Woolf, Selections from her essays, 1966; (contrib.) Encyclopaedia of Education, 1968; (contrib.) Teaching Techniques in Adult Education, 1971; (contrib.) Mass Media and Adult Education, 1971; (with H. Janne and P. Dominice) The Development of Adult Education, 1980; numerous TV programmes, articles and reviews on youth, adult and higher educn. *Recreation:* living. *Address:* 40 Brecon Way, Bedford MK41 8DD. *T:* Bedford 54819.

JAMES, William Henry E.; see Ewart James.

JAMESON, Derek; Editor, News of the World, since 1981; *b* 29 Nov. 1929; *e s* of Mrs Elsie Jameson; *m* 1st, 1948, Jacqueline Sinclair (marr. diss. 1966); one *s* one *d*; 2nd, 1971, Pauline Tomlin (marr. diss. 1978); two *s*. *Educ:* elementary schools, Hackney. Office boy rising to Chief Sub-editor, Reuters, 1944-60; Editor, London American, 1960-61; features staff, Daily Express, 1961-63; Picture Editor, Sunday Mirror, 1963-65; Asst Editor, Sunday Mirror, 1965-72; Northern Editor, Sunday and Daily Mirror, 1972-76; Managing Editor, Daily Mirror, 1976-77; Editor, Daily Express, 1977-79; Editor-in-Chief, The Daily Star, 1978-80. TV and radio commentator. *Recreations:*

opera, music, reading. *Address:* 25 Clare Court, Judd Street, WC1H 9QW. *T:* 01-837 8571. *Clubs:* Press, Macreadys.

JAMESON, John Richard; Accountant General, Department of Education and Science, since 1978; *b* 18 Oct. 1930; *s* of late John Harrison and late Gwendoline May Jameson; *m* 1st, 1958, Wendy Rhodes (marr. diss. 1970); one *s* one *d*; 2nd, 1970, Karin Quick; one *d*. *Educ:* Giggleswick Sch.; Balliol Coll., Oxford. Min. of Educn, 1952-59 and 1961-64; Cabinet Office, 1959-61; DES, 1964-; Under Sec., 1973. *Address:* 3A New Ground Road, Aldbury, Tring, Herts. *T:* Aldbury Common 306.

JAMESON, (Margaret) Storm, MA; Hon. LittD (Leeds); Writer; *b* Whitby, Yorks; *d* of William Storm Jameson; *m* Prof. Guy Chapman, OBE, MC (*d* 1972); one *s*. *Educ:* Leeds Univ. Hon. Mem., American Acad. and Inst. of Arts and Letters. *Publications:* Happy Highways, 1920; Modern Drama in Europe, 1920; The Lovely Ship, 1927; The Voyage Home, 1930; A Richer Dust, 1931; That was Yesterday; A Day Off; No Time Like the Present, 1933; Company Parade, 1934; Love in Winter, 1935; In the Second Year, 1936; None Turn Back, 1936; Delicate Monster, 1937; Civil Journey, 1939; Farewell Night, Welcome Day, 1939; Europe to Let, 1940; Cousin Honoré, 1940; The Fort, 1941; The End of this War, 1941; Then We Shall Hear Singing, 1942; Cloudless May, 1943; The Journal of Mary Hervey Russell, 1945; The Other Side, 1945; Before the Crossing, 1947; The Black Laurel, 1948; The Moment of Truth, 1949; Writer's Situation, 1950; The Green Man, 1952; The Hidden River, 1955; The Intruder, 1956; A Cup of Tea for Mr Thorgill, 1957; A Ulysses Too Many, 1958; A Day Off and other stories, 1959; Last Score, 1961; Morley Roberts: The Last Eminent Victorian, 1961; The Road from the Monument, 1962; A Month Soon Goes, 1963; The Aristide Case, 1964; The Early Life of Stephen Hind, 1966; The White Crow, 1968; (autobiography) Journey from the North, Vol. I 1969, Vol. II 1970; Parthian Words, 1970; There will be a Short Interval, 1972; (ed) A Kind of Survivor, autobiog. of Guy Chapman, 1975; Speaking of Stendhal, 1979. *Recreation:* travelling. *Address:* c/o Macmillan & Co., 4 Little Essex Street, WC2.

JAMESON, Air Cdre Patrick Geraint, CB 1959; DSO 1943; DFC 1940 (and Bar 1942), psa; Royal Air Force, retired, 1960; *b* Wellington, NZ, 10 Nov. 1912; *s* of Robert Delvin Jameson, Balbriggan, Ireland, and Katherine Lenora Jameson (*née* Dick), Dunedin, NZ; *m* 1941, Hilda Nellie Haiselden Webster, *d* of B. F. Webster, Lower Hutt, NZ; one *s* one *d*. *Educ:* Hutt Valley High Sch., New Zealand. Commissioned in RAF, 1936. War of 1939-45 (despatches 5 times, DFC and Bar, DSO): 46 Squadron, 1936-40, 266 Squadron, 1940-41; Wing Commander Flying, Wittering, 1941-42; Wing Commander (Flying), North Weald, 1942-43; Group Capt. Plans, HQ No 11 Group, 1943-44; 122 Wing in France, Belgium, Holland, Germany and Denmark, 1944-46; Staff Coll., Haifa, 1946; Air Ministry, 1946-48; CFE, West Raynham, 1949-52; Wunsdorf (2nd TAF), 1952-54; SASO, HQ No II Group, 1954-56; SASO HQ RAF Germany (2nd TAF) 1956-59. Norwegian War Cross, 1943; Netherlands Order of Orange Nassau, 1945; American Silver Star, 1945. *Recreations:* fishing, shooting, sailing, golf. *Address:* 70 Wai-Iti Crescent, Lower Hutt, New Zealand. *Clubs:* Royal Air Force; Hutt Golf; Hutt; Mana Cruising.

JAMESON, Storm; see Jameson, M. S.

JAMESON, Maj-Gen. Thomas Henry, CBE 1946 (OBE 1937); DSO 1919; RM, retired; *b* 10 Dec. 1894; *s* of Robert W. Jameson, JP, and Katherine Anne Jameson; *m* 1918, Barbara Adèle Bayley (*d* 1958); one *d*. *Educ:* Monkton Combe Sch., near Bath, Somerset. Commission in Royal Marines, 1913; served Belgium, France, Gallipoli (despatches) HMS Resolution, HMS Kent, 1914-18; Siberia, 1919 (DSO). War of 1939-45: staff of C-in-C Home Fleet, 15 RM Battalion, Admiralty; Commandant Plymouth, Jan. 1944 and Depot, Deal, June 1944; Commandant Portsmouth Division RM, 1944-46 (CBE); retired, 1946. *Address:* Flete House, Ermington, Devon. *T:* Holbeton 335.

JAMIESON, Major David Auldjo, VC 1944; Member of HM Body Guard, Hon. Corps of Gentlemen at Arms, since 1968, Clerk of the Cheque and Adjutant, since 1981; *b* 1 Oct. 1920; *s* of late Sir Archibald Auldjo Jamieson, KBE, MC; *m* 1st, 1948, Nancy Elwes (*d* 1943), *y d* of Robert H. A. Elwes, Congham, King's Lynn; one *s* two *d*; 2nd, 1969, Joanna, *e d* of Edward Woodall. *Educ:* Eton Coll. Commissioned Royal Norfolk Regt May 1939; served War of 1939-45, incl. Normandy, 1944 (VC); retired, 1948. Dir, Australian Agricultural Co., 1949-78 (Governor, 1952-76); Dir, 1963-, Dep. Chm., 1973-, UK Branch, Australian Mutual Provident Society. High Sheriff of Norfolk, 1980. *Recreations:* shooting, golf. *Address:* The Drove House, Thornham, Hunstanton, Norfolk. *T:* Thornham 206.

JAMIESON, Air Vice-Marshal David Ewan, CB 1981; OBE 1967; Chief of Air Staff, Royal New Zealand Air Force, since 1979; *b* Christchurch, 19 April 1930; *s* of R. D. Jamieson; *m* 1957, Margaret Elaine, *d* of L. J. Bridge; three *s* one *d*. *Educ:* Christchurch and North Plymouth Boys' High Sch. Joined RNZAF, 1949; OC Flying, Ohakea, 1964; CO Malaysia, 1965-66; Jt Services Staff Coll., 1969; CO Auckland, 1971-72; AOC Ops Group, 1974-76; RCDS 1977. *Address:* c/o Ministry of Defence, Wellington, New Zealand.

JAMIESON, Hon. Donald Campbell, PC (Can.); Liberal Leader, Newfoundland Legislature, 1979-80; *b* St John's, Newfoundland, 30 April 1921; *s* of Charles Jamieson and Isabelle Bennett; *m* 1946, Barbara Elizabeth Oakley; one *s* three *d*. *Educ:* Prince of Wales Coll.; St John's, Newfoundland.

Served War with Canadian Naval Special Services and United Service Org. Camp Shows. Regular broadcasts, 1941-46; news broadcasting nightly, 1946; Attaché, Parly Press Gallery, Ottawa, 1948; former Pres., Newfoundland Broadcasting Co. Ltd; also Dir of Broadcast News; Past Chm., Affiliates Sect. Network Advt Cttee, CBC. Pres., Canadian Assoc. of Broadcasters, 1961-65. With Dept of Rural Reconstruction; then Crosbie & Co. Ltd, fishery; Sales Manager, Coca Cola, Newfoundland. MP (Liberal), 1966-, St John's, Newfoundland; Minister: of Supply and Services, 1968-69; of Transport, 1969-72; of Regional Economic Expansion, 1972-75; of Industry, Trade and Commerce, Sept. 1975-76; Sec. of State for External Affairs, Canada, 1976-79. Past Chm., financial campaign of Canadian Cancer Soc.; Past Director: Canadian Centennial Council; Nat. Theatre School. Hon. LLD: Memorial, 1970; Acadia; St Francis Xavier. *Publication:* The Troubled Air, 1966. *Recreations:* fishing, hunting, boating. *Address:* Swift Current, Newfoundland, Canada.

JAMIESON, Rt. Rev. Hamish Thomas Umphelby; *see* Carpentaria, Bishop of.

JAMIESON, Lt-Col Harvey Morro H.; *see* Harvey-Jamieson.

JAMIESON, Rear-Adm. Ian Wyndham, CB 1970; DSC 1945; Home Bursar and Fellow, Jesus College, Oxford, since 1972; *b* 13 March 1920; *s* of late S. W. Jamieson, CBE; *m* 1949, Patricia Wheeler, Knowle, Warwickshire; two *s* one *d. Educ:* RNC, Dartmouth. Served War of 1939-45: Anti Submarine Warfare Specialist, 1943. Comdr, 1953; Staff of RN Tactical Sch., 1953-56; HMS Maidstone, 1956-58; Dir, Jt Tactical Sch., Malta, 1958; Capt. 1959; Asst Dir, Naval Intelligence, 1959-61; Comd HMS Nubian and 6th Frigate Sqdn, 1961-64; Dir, Seaman Officers Appts, 1964-66; Comd Britannia RN Coll., Dartmouth, 1966-68; Rear-Adm. 1968; Flag Officer, Gibraltar, and Admiral Superintendent, HM Dockyard, Gibraltar; also NATO Comdr, Gibraltar (Mediterranean Area), 1968-69; C of S to C-in-C Western Fleet, 1969-71; retired. Hon. MA Oxon, 1973. *Recreations:* hockey (Scotland and Combined Services), cricket, golf, tennis. *Address:* Buckels, East Hagbourne, near Didcot, Oxfordshire. *Clubs:* Army and Navy, MCC.

JAMIESON, John Kenneth; Chairman of Board, Chief Executive Officer and Chairman of Management Committee, Exxon Corporation (formerly Standard Oil Co. (NJ)), 1969-75; *b* Canada, 28 Aug. 1910; *s* of John Locke and Kate Herron Jamieson; *m* 1937, Ethel May Burns; one *s* one *d. Educ:* Univ. of Alberta; Massachusetts Inst. of Technology (BS). Northwest Stellarene Co. of Alberta, 1932; British American Oil Co., 1934; Manager, Moose Jaw Refinery; served War of 1939-45 in Oil Controller's Dept of Canadian Govt; subseq. Manager, Manufrg Dept, British American Oil Co.; joined Imperial Oil Co., 1948: Head of Engrg and Develt Div., Sarnia Refinery, 1949; Asst Gen. Man. of Manufrg Dept, 1950; on loan to Canadian Dept of Defence Production, 1951; Dir, Imperial Oil, 1952, Vice-Pres. 1953; Pres. and Dir International Petroleum Co., 1959; Vice-Pres., Dir and Mem. Exec. Cttee Exxon Co., USA (formerly Humble Oil & Refining Co.), 1961, Exec. Vice-Pres. 1962, Pres. 1963-64; Exec. Vice-Pres. and Dir 1964, Pres. 1965, Jersey Standard. Director: The Equitable Life Assurance Soc. of US; Raychem Corp.; Crutcher Resources Inc. (Chm.). *Address:* 1100 Milam Building, Suite 4601, Houston, Texas 77002, USA. *Clubs:* Augusta National Golf (Augusta); Ramada, Houston Country (Houston).

JAMIESON, Kenneth Douglas, CMG 1968; HM Diplomatic Service, retired; *b* 9 Jan. 1921; *s* of late Rt Hon. Lord Jamieson, PC, KC, Senator of College of Justice in Scotland and Violet Brodie; *m* 1946, Pamela Hall; two *s* one *d. Educ:* Rugby; Balliol Coll., Oxford. War Service: 5th Regt RHA, 1941-45; HQ, RA 7th Armoured Div., 1945-46. Joined Foreign Service, 1946; served in: Washington, 1948; FO, 1952; Lima, 1954; Brussels, 1959; FO, 1961; Caracas, 1963; Dir of Commercial Training, DSAO, 1968; Head of Export Promotion Dept, FCO, 1968-70; Minister and UK Dep. Permanent Representative, UN, NY, 1970-74; Ambassador to Peru, 1974-77; Sen. Directing Staff, RCDS, 1977-80. *Address:* Mill Hill House, Bucks Green, Rudgwick, W Sussex.

JAMIL RAIS, Tan Sri Dato' Abdul; *see* Abdul Jamil Rais.

JAMISON, James Hardie, OBE 1974; chartered accountant; Partner, Coopers & Lybrand, Chartered Accountants, 1939-78, retired; *b* 29 Nov. 1913; *s* of late W. I. Jamison; *m* 1940, Mary Louise, *d* of late W. R. Richardson; two *s* one *d. Educ:* Sydney Church of England Grammar Sch. Chm., Commn of Inquiry into Efficiency and Admin of Hosps, 1979-80. Mem., Nat. Council, Aust. Inst. of Chartered Accountants, 1969-77, Vice Pres., 1973-75, Pres., 1975-76. *Recreation:* sailing. *Address:* 8 McLeod Street, Mosman, NSW 2088, Australia. *Clubs:* Australasian Pioneers' (Pres. 1970-72), Australian, Royal Sydney Yacht Squadron (Sydney).

JAMISON, James Kenneth, OBE 1978; Director, Arts Council of Northern Ireland, since 1969; *b* 9 May 1931; *s* of William Jamison and Alicia Rea Jamison; *m* 1964, Joan Young Boyd; one *s* one *d. Educ:* Belfast College of Art (DA). Secondary school teacher, 1953-61; Art Critic, Belfast Telegraph, 1956-61; Art Organiser, Arts Council of Northern Ireland, 1962-64, Dep. Director, 1964-69. *Publications:* miscellaneous on the arts in the North of Ireland. *Recreations:* the arts, travel. *Address:* 64 Rugby Road, Belfast BT7 1PT. *T:* Belfast 23063. *Club:* Queen's University Common Room (Belfast).

JAMISON, Dr Robin Ralph, FRS 1969, FEng, FRAeS, CChem, MRSC; Chief Technical Executive (Research), Rolls Royce (1971) Ltd (formerly Rolls Royce Ltd), Bristol Engine Division, 1971-75, retired; *b* 12 July 1912; *s* of Reginald Jamison, MD, FRCS, and Eanswyth Heyworth; *m* 1937, Hilda Watney Wilson, Cape Town; two *s* two *d. Educ:* South African Coll.; Univ. of Cape Town. BSc, PhD. S African Govt research grant, 1936-37; research and development of aero engines, Rolls Royce Ltd, 1937-50; Head of Ramjet Dept, Bristol Siddeley Engines Ltd, 1950-62 (Asst Chief Engr, 1956); advanced propulsion res., 1962-65; Chief Engr, Res., 1965-71. Vis. Prof., Bath Univ. of Technology, 1969-73. FEng 1976. Herbert Ackroyd-Stuart Prize, RAeS, 1958; Thulin Bronze Medal, Swedish Aero. Soc., 1960; Silver Medal of RAeS, 1965. *Publications:* papers in aeronautical and scientific jls. *Recreations:* sailing, gardening, music. *Address:* 2 The Crescent, Henleaze, Bristol BS9 4RN. *T:* Bristol 620328.

JANES, Barbara, (Mrs Norman Janes); *see* Greg, B.

JANES, (John) Douglas (Webster), CB 1975; Secretary, The Bach Choir, since 1981; Deputy Secretary, Northern Ireland Office, 1974-79; *b* 17 Aug. 1918; *s* of late John Arnold Janes and Maud Mackinnon (*née* Webster); *m* 1943, Margaret Isabel Smith (*d* 1978); one *s* two *d. Educ:* Southgate County Sch., Mddx; Imperial Coll. of Science and Technology. 1st cl. BSc (Eng) London, ACGI, DIC. Entered Post Office Engineering Dept, Research Branch, 1939. Served Royal Signals, RAOC, REME, 1939-45: War Office, 1941-45; Major. Min. of Town and Country Planning, 1947; Min. of Housing and Local Govt, 1951; seconded to Min. of Power, 1956-58; HM Treasury, 1960-63; Min. of Land and Natural Resources, 1964-66; Prin. Finance Officer and Accountant Gen., Min. of Housing and Local Govt, 1968-70; Prin. Finance Officer (Local Govt and Develt), DoE, 1970-73, Dep. Sec., 1973; Chief Executive, Maplin Develt Authority, 1973-74. Chm., Home Grown Timber Adv. Cttee, 1981- (Mem., 1979-); various management and organisation reviews, 1979-81. *Recreations:* singing, do-it-yourself. *Address:* 136 Waterfall Road, N14 7JN. *T:* 01-886 2133.

JANES, Maj.-Gen. Mervyn, CB 1973; MBE 1944; *b* 1 Oct. 1920; *o s* of W. G. Janes; *m* 1946, Elizabeth Kathleen McIntyre; two *d. Educ:* Sir Walter St John's Sch., London. Commnd 1942; served with Essex Yeo. (104 Regt RHA), 1942-46, Middle East and Italy; psc 1951; served with 3 RHA, 1952-53; 2 Div., BMRA, 1954-55; Chief Instructor, New Coll., RMAS, 1956-57; Batt. Comd, 3 RHA, 1958-60; Asst Army Instructor (GSO1), Imperial Defence Coll., 1961-62; comd 1st Regt RHA, 1963-65; Comdr, RA, in BAOR, 1965-67; DMS2 (MoD(A)), 1967-70; GOC 5th Division, 1970-71; Dir, Royal Artillery, 1971-73. Col Comdt, RA, 1973-81. *Recreations:* music, egyptology, ornithology, tennis. *Address:* 115 Wardo Avenue, SW6. *Club:* Army and Navy.

JANION, Rear-Adm. Sir Hugh (Penderel), KCVO 1981; Flag Officer, Royal Yachts, 1975-81; *b* 28 Sept. 1923; *s* of Engr Captain Ralph Penderel Janion, RN, and Mrs Winifred Derwent Janion; *m* 1956, Elizabeth Monica Ferard; one *s* one *d. Educ:* Malvern Link Sch., Worcs; RNC Dartmouth. Served War of 1939-45, Russian convoys, invasions of Sicily and Italy; Korean War, 1950-52, Inchon landing. Specialised in navigation; Comdr, 1958, i/c HMS Jewel, and Exec. Officer HMS Ark Royal; Captain, 1966, i/c HMS Aurora and HMS Bristol; Rear-Adm. 1975. Extra Equerry to the Queen, 1975-. Younger Brother, Trinity House, 1976-. *Recreations:* sailing, golf. *Address:* King's Hayes, Batcombe, Shepton Mallet, Somerset BA4 6HF. *T:* Upton Noble 300. *Clubs:* Royal Yacht Squadron (Cowes); Royal Naval and Royal Albert Yacht (Portsmouth); Imperial Poona Yacht.

JANNEH, Bocar Ousman S.; *see* Semega-Janneh.

JANNER, Lady; Elsie Sybil Janner, CBE 1968; JP; *b* Newcastle upon Tyne; *d* of Joseph and Henrietta Cohen; *m* 1927, Barnett Janner (later Baron Janner) (*d* 1982); one *s* one *d. Educ:* Central Newcastle High Sch.; South Hampstead High Sch.; Switzerland. Founder and first Hon. Club Leader, Brady Girls' Club, Whitechapel, 1925 (now Pres., Brady Clubs and Settlement); Jt Pres., Brady/Maccabi. War of 1939-45: Captain, Mechanised Transp. Corps (Def. Medal). Chm., Bridgehead Housing Assoc., to acquire property for residential purposes for homeless ex-offenders, 1967-75; Chairman: Adv. Bd, Stonham Housing Assoc. (amalgamation of S Western Housing Assoc., St Leonards Housing Assoc., and Bridgehead), 1975-; Stonham Meml Trust; Mem., Stonham Housing Assoc. Finance and Policy Cttee. Magistrates Assoc.: Vice-Pres.; Hon. Treasurer, 1971-76; formerly Dep. Chm., Road Traffic Cttee, and Mem., Exec. Cttee; Vice Pres., Inner London Br. (former Chm.); former Mem., Jt Standing Cttee, Magistrates Assoc. and Justices' Clerks Soc. JP, Inner London, 1936; contested (Lab), Mile End, LCC, 1947; a Visiting Magistrate to Holloway Women's Prison, 1950-62; Chm., Thames Bench of Magistrates, 1975; Mem., Juvenile Courts Panel, 1944-70 (Chm. 1960-70); Former Member: Inner London and NE London Licensing Planning Cttees; Inner London Licensing Compensation Cttee; Inner London Mem., Cttee of Magistrates. Vice-Pres., Assoc. for Jewish Youth; Hon. Vice-Pres., Fedn of Women Zionists of Gt Brit. and Ire.; Mem., Bd of Deputies, British Jews Educn and Youth Cttee (Chm., 1943-66); Chm., United Jewish Educnl and Cultural Org. (internat. body to re-construct Jewish educn in countries of Europe which had been occupied by Germans), 1947-50; Founder and former Chm., Jewish Youth Organisations Cttee; Mem., Central Council of Jewish Religious Educn. Trustee and Mem. Bursaries and Investment Cttees, Mitchell City of London Charity and Educnl Foundn; Mem., former Nat. Road Safety

Adv. Council, 1965-68; Vice-Chm., Inst. Advanced Motorists, 1980-. Freeman, City of London, 1975. *Recreations:* weeding, grandchildren. *Address:* 45 Morpeth Mansions, Morpeth Terrace, SW1P 1ET; The Jungle, Stone Road, Broadstairs, Kent. *T:* Thanet 61642.

See also Hon. G.E. Janner, Lord Morris of Kenwood.

JANNER, Hon. Greville Ewan, MA Cantab; QC 1971; MP (Lab) Leicester West, since 1974 (Leicester North West, 1970-74); barrister-at-law; author, lecturer, journalist and broadcaster; President, Board of Deputies of British Jews, since 1979; *b* 11 July 1928; *s* of late Baron Janner and of Lady Janner, *qv; m* 1955, Myra Louise Sheink, Melbourne; one *s* two *d. Educ:* Bishop's Coll. Sch., Canada; St Paul's Sch. (Foundn Schol.); Trinity Hall, Cambridge (Exhbnr); Harvard Post Graduate Law School (Fulbright and Smith-Mundt Schol.); Harmsworth Scholar, Middle Temple, 1955. Nat. Service: Sgt, RA, BAOR, War Crimes Investigator. Pres., Cambridge Union, 1952; Chm., Cambridge Univ. Labour Club, 1952; Internat. Sec., Nat. Assoc. of Labour Students, 1952; Pres., Trinity Hall Athletic Club, 1952. Contested (Lab) Wimbledon, 1955. Mem., Select Cttee on Employment, 1982-; Chm., All-Party Parly Industrial Safety Gp; Founder, Trustee and former Chm., All-Party Parly Cttee for Homeless and Rootless People; Vice-Chm., All-Party Parly Cttee for Release of Soviet Jewry; Jt Vice-Chm., British-Israel Parly Gp; Hon. Sec., All-Party Parly Retirement Gp. Vice-President: Assoc. for Jewish Youth; Assoc. of Jewish Ex-Serviceman; European Vice-Pres., World Jewish Congress; Member: Nat. Union of Journalists; Soc. of Labour Lawyers; President: Retired Executives Action Clearing House; Founder Mem., Internat. Cttee for Human Rights in USSR; Chm., Slepak Charitable Trust. Former Dir, Jewish Chronicle Newspaper Ltd. Mem., Magic Circle; FIPM 1976. *Publications:* 33 Books, mainly on employment, industrial relations, company law and product liability (some under pen name Ewan Mitchell). *Address:* (home) 2 Linnell Drive, NW11; (chambers) 1 Garden Court, Temple, EC4. *T:* 01-353 5524/4927; House of Commons, SW1. *T:* 01-219 3000.

JANSEN, Elly, (Mrs Elly Whitehouse-Jansen), OBE 1980; Founder and Director, The Richmond Fellowship for mental welfare and rehabilitation, since 1959; *b* 5 Oct. 1929; *d* of Jacobus Gerrit Jansen and Petronella Suzanna Vellekoop; *m* 1969, Alan Brian Stewart Whitehouse (known as George); three *d. Educ:* Paedologisch Inst. of Free Univ., Amsterdam; Boerhave Kliniek (SRN); London Univ. Founded: Richmond Fellowship of America, 1968; Richmond Fellowship of Australia, 1973; Richmond Fellowship of New Zealand, 1978; Richmond Fellowship of Austria, 1979; Richmond Fellowship of Canada, Richmond Fellowship Internat., 1981. Organised first internat. confs on therapeutic communities, 1973, 1975, 1976, 1979; has acted as consultant to several govts on issues of community care. Fellowship, German Marshall Meml Fund, 1977-78. *Publications:* (ed) The Therapeutic Community Outside the Hospital, 1980; contribs to Amer. Jl of Psychiatry, L'Inf. Psychiatrique, and other jls. *Recreations:* literature, photography, interior design. *Address:* 8 Addison Road, Kensington, W14 8DL. *T:* 01-603 6373.

JANVRIN, Vice-Adm. Sir (Hugh) Richard Benest, KCB 1969 (CB 1965); DSC 1940; *b* 9 May 1915; *s* of late Rev. Canon C. W. Janvrin, Fairford, Glos.; *m* 1938, Nancy Fielding; two *s. Educ:* RNC, Dartmouth. Naval Cadet, 1929; Midshipman, 1933; Sub-Lt, 1936; Lt, 1937; Qualified Fleet Air Arm Observer, 1938. Served War of 1939-45 (took part in Taranto attack, 1940). In Command: HMS Broadsword, 1951-53; HMS Grenville, 1957-58; RNAS Brawdy, 1958; HMS Victorious, 1959-60. Imperial Defence Coll., 1961; Dir, Tactics and Weapons Policy, Admiralty, 1962-63; Flag Officer, Aircraft Carriers, 1964-66; Dep. Chief of Naval Staff, MoD, 1966-68; Flag Officer, Naval Air Comd, 1968-70; retired 1971. Lieut-Comdr, 1945; Comdr, 1948; Capt., 1954; Rear-Adm., 1964; Vice-Adm. 1967. *Recreation:* gardening. *Address:* Allen's Close, Chalford Hill, near Stroud, Glos. *T:* Brimscombe 882336.

JANZON, Mrs Bengt; *see* Dobbs, Mattiwilda.

JAQUES, Prof. Elliott; Director of Institute of Organisation and Social Studies, Brunel University, since 1970 (Professor of Sociology, 1970-82); *b* 18 Jan. 1917; *m* 1953, Kathleen (*née* Walsh); one *d. Educ:* Univ. of Toronto (BA, MA); Johns Hopkins Med. Sch. (MD); Harvard Univ. (PhD). Qual. Psycho-analyst (Brit. Psycho-An. Soc.) 1951. Rantoul Fellow in Psychology, Harvard, 1940-41; Major, Royal Can. Army Med. Corps, 1941-45; Founder Mem., Tavistock Inst. of Human Relations, 1946-51; private practice as psycho-analyst and industrial consultant, 1952-65; Head of Sch. of Social Sciences, Brunel Univ., 1965-70. Adviser to BoT on organisation for overseas marketing, 1965-69; Mem. Management Study Steering Cttee on NHS Reorganisation, 1972. *Publications:* The Changing Culture of a Factory, 1951; Measurement of Responsibility, 1956; Equitable Payment, 1961; (with Wilfred Brown) Product Analysis Pricing, 1964; Time-Span Handbook, 1964; (with Wilfred Brown) Glacier Project Papers, 1965; Progression Handbook, 1968; Work, Creativity and Social Justice, 1970; A General Theory of Bureaucracy, 1976; Health Services, 1978; articles in Human Relations, New Society, Internat. Jl of Psycho-Analysis, etc. *Recreations:* art, music, ski-ing. *Address:* Brunel University, Uxbridge, Mddx. *T:* Uxbridge 56461.

JARDINE, Sir (Andrew) Rupert (John) Buchanan-, 4th Bt *cr* 1885; MC 1944; DL; landowner and farmer; *b* 2 Feb. 1923; *s* of Sir John William Buchanan-Jardine, 3rd Bt and of Jean Barbara, *d* of late Lord Ernest Hamilton; *S* father, 1969; *m* 1950, Jane Fiona (marr. diss. 1975), 2nd *d* of Sir Charles Edmonstone, 6th Bt; one *s* one *d. Educ:* Harrow; Royal Agricultural College. Joined Royal Horse Guards, 1941; served in France, Holland and Germany; Major 1948; retired, 1949. Joint-Master, Dumfriesshire Foxhounds, 1950. JP Dumfriesshire, 1957; DL Dumfriesshire, 1978. Bronze Lion of the Netherlands, 1945. *Recreations:* hunting, shooting, fishing. *Heir: s* John Christopher Rupert Buchanan-Jardine [*b* 20 March 1952; *m* 1975, Pandora Lavinia, *d* of Peter Murray Lee; one *d*]. *Address:* Dixons, Lockerbie, Dumfriesshire. *T:* Lockerbie 2508. *Club:* MCC.

JARDINE, Christopher Willoughby, CB 1967; Assistant Secretary, Monopolies and Mergers Commission, 1975-76; *b* 5 Aug. 1911; *e s* of Judge Willoughby Jardine, KC; *m* 1940, Eva Katharine, *er d* of Sir George Duckworth-King, 6th Bart; three *d. Educ:* Eton (Scholar); King's Coll., Cambridge (Scholar; 1st Cl. Hons. History); and in France and Germany. BoT, later DTI: Asst Principal, 1934; Principal, 1939; Asst Sec., 1945; Under-Sec., 1962; Adviser on Commercial Policy, 1962-64; Insurance and Companies Dept, 1964-72; Principal, Monopolies and Mergers Commn, 1972-75. *Address:* 8 St Loo Court, St Loo Avenue, SW3. *T:* 01-352 1246. *Club:* MCC.

JARDINE, Brig. Sir Ian (Liddell), 4th Bt *cr* 1916; OBE 1966; MC 1945; *b* 13 Oct. 1923; *o s* of Maj.-Gen. Sir Colin Arthur Jardine, 3rd Bt; *S* father 1957; *m* 1948, Priscilla Daphne, *d* of Douglas Middleton Parnham Scott-Phillips, Halkshill, Largs, Ayrshire; two *s* two *d. Educ:* Charterhouse. Served War, 1942-45, Coldstream Guards (MC); 2nd Lieut, 1943; Major, 1950; Lt-Col 1964; Col 1968; Brig., 1969; Brig., GS, 1973-75, Brig., Inf., 1975-78, UKLF, retired. ADC to the Queen, 1976-78. *Heir: s* Andrew Colin Douglas Jardine, *b* 30 Nov. 1955. *Address:* Coombe Place, Meonstoke, Southampton. *T:* Droxford 569. *Club:* Brooks's.

JARDINE, James Christopher Macnaughton; Sheriff of Glasgow and Strathkelvin, since 1979; *b* 18 Jan. 1930; *s* of James Jardine; *m* 1955, Vena Gordon Kight; one *d. Educ:* Glasgow Academy; Gresham House, Ayrshire; Glasgow Univ. (BL). National Service (Lieut RASC), 1950-52. Admitted as Solicitor, in Scotland, 1953. Practice as principal (from 1955) of Nelson & Mackay, and as partner of McClure, Naismith, Brodie & Co., Solicitors, Glasgow, 1956-69; Sheriff of Stirling, Dunbarton and Clackmannan, later N Strathclyde, at Dumbarton, 1969-79. A Vice-Pres., Sheriffs' Assoc., 1976-79. Sec., Glasgow Univ. Graduates Assoc., 1956-66; Mem., Business Cttee of Glasgow Univ. Gen. Council, 1964-67. Mem. Professional Advisory Cttee, Scottish Council on Alcoholism. *Recreations:* boating, enjoyment of music. *Address:* Sheriffs' Library, County Buildings, Ingram Street, Glasgow.

JARDINE, John Frederick James; Under Secretary, Regional Support and Inward Investment Division, Department of Industry, since 1980; *b* 22 Dec. 1926; *s* of late James Jardine; *m* 1957, Pamela Joyce; four *s* two *d. Educ:* Rock Ferry High Sch., Birkenhead. RAF, 1945-48; Inland Revenue, 1948-55; BoT, 1955-58; British Trade Comr, Karachi, 1958-63; BoT, 1963-66; Midland Regional Controller, 1966-71; DTI, 1971-73; seconded to HM Diplomatic Service (Under-Sec.), 1973; HM Consul-General, Johannesburg, 1973-78; Dept of Trade, 1978-80. *Recreations:* tennis, golf, bridge. *Address:* 7 Lynwood Avenue, Epsom, Surrey KT17 4LQ. *T:* Epsom 29156. *Club:* Royal Automobile.

JARDINE, Michael James, CB 1976; Deputy Director of Public Prosecutions, 1974-79; *b* 20 Nov. 1915; *s* of Judge James Willoughby Jardine, KC; *m* 1939; two *s* one *d. Educ:* Eton; King's Coll., Cambridge (BA). Called to Bar, Middle Temple, 1937. Served War with Scots Guards, 1940-46: active service in North Africa and Italy. Legal Asst to Director of Public Prosecutions, 1946; Asst Solicitor, 1965; Asst Director of Public Prosecutions, 1969. *Recreation:* bridge.

JARDINE, Robert Frier, CMG 1928; OBE 1926; Third Class of the Order of Al Rafidain of Iraq, 1937; *b* 9 June 1894; *s* of late Robert Brown Jardine; *m* 1932, Averil (*d* 1975), *o d* of late H. O. Dickin; twin *s* (both Mems of 1960, 1964, 1968 British Olympic Yachting teams). *Educ:* Downing Coll., Cambridge. Commissioned Sept. 1914 from Cambridge Univ. OTC; served European War in Egypt, Gallipoli and Mesopotamia (despatches); in political charge of districts in Northern Iraq and Kurdistan, 1917-21; repatriated Assyrians to their original homes in Hakkiari, 1922; Political Officer to columns in Kurdistan, 1923; Mem. of HMG Delegation to Turkey and League of Nations upon Turkish frontier question, 1924; HM Assessor on League of Nations' Commission in connection with Turco-Iraq frontier, and upon other Commissions, 1925; Administrative Inspector, Mosul Province, 1925-28; Adviser to British Ambassador in Turkey for Tripartite Treaty, 1926; Frontier Commissioner, 1927; Administrative Inspector, Basra Province, 1928-33; Pres. of Commission for settlement of titles to land in Iraq, 1933-36; acted in various capacities in Palestine, 1936-48, including Dir of Settlement and Registration of titles to Land, Civil Aviation, Commissioner for Auqaf, Irrigation, Commissioner of Compensation for Rebellion and War Damages, 1945; Land Settlement and Water Commissioner; Advisory Councillor. During War of 1939-45 assisted with political advice as Lt-Col, Gen. Staff, Jerusalem Bureau. *Publications:* Grammar of Bahdinan Kurmanji (Kurdish), 1922; Gazetteer of Place Names in Palestine and Trans-Jordan, 1941. *Recreation:* yachting.

Address: Walhampton March, Lymington, Hants. *T:* Lymington 72481.
Clubs: Royal Lymington Yacht, etc.

JARDINE, Sir Rupert Buchanan-; *see* Jardine, Sir A. R. J. B.

JARDINE OF APPLEGIRTH, Col Sir William Edward, 11th Bt of Nova Scotia, *cr* 1672; OBE 1966; TD; DL; JP; Chief of the Clan Jardine; late The KOSB; *b* 15 April 1917; *s* of Sir Alexander Jardine of Applegirth, 10th Baronet, and Winifred Mary Hamilton (*d* 1954), *d* of Major Young, Lincluden House, Dumfries; *S* father, 1942; *m* 1944, Ann Graham, *yr d* of late Lt-Col Claud Maitland, DSO, Gordon Highlanders, of Dundrennan and Cumstoun, Kirkcudbright; two *s.* Mem. of The Queen's Body Guard for Scotland, The Royal Company of Archers. Commnd KOSB 1939, retd as Major, 1960. Lt-Col Comd 4/5 KOSB (TA), 1963-67, Bt Col 1967. Chm., Dumfriesshire SSAFA, 1965-78; Mem., Lowland T&AVRA, 1970 (Chm., Border Area Cttee, 1977). Mem., Dumfries CC, 1960-75, Chm. Roads Cttee, 1970-75; Mem., Annandale and Eskdale DC, 1975-, Chm., Gen. Purposes Cttee, 1976-; Chm., Solway River Purification Bd, 1976; Mem., Scottish River Purification Bds Assoc., 1976; Chm., Annan Dist Salmon Fishery Bd, 1980-. JP 1962, DL 1970, co. of Dumfries. *Heir:* *s* Alexander Maule Jardine, yr of Applegirth [*b* 24 Aug. 1947; *m* 1982, Mary Beatrice, *d* of late Hon. John Michael Inigo Cross and of Mrs James Parker-Jervis]. *Address:* Denbie, Lockerbie, Dumfriesshire. *T:* Carrutherstown 631. *Clubs:* Army and Navy; Puffin's (Edinburgh).

JARDINE PATERSON, Lt-Col Arthur James, OBE 1958; TD 1945; Lord Lieutenant of Dumfries, since 1982; *b* 14 July 1918; *s* of late R. Jardine Paterson; *m* 1948, Mary Fearne Balfour-Kinnear; one *d. Educ:* Eton; Jesus Coll., Cambridge. TA, 1939; served War of 1939-45, KOSB, NW Europe; comd 5th Bn KOSB, 1955-58. CC Dumfriesshire, 1960; Reg. Council, Dumfries and Galloway, 1974-82. DL 1964, JP 1965, Dumfriesshire. *Recreation:* shooting. *Address:* Skairfield, Lockerbie, Dumfriesshire DG11 1JL. *T:* Lochmaben 201. *Club:* Army and Navy.
See also Sir J. Jardine Paterson.

JARDINE PATERSON, Sir John (Valentine), Kt 1967; Chairman, McLeod Russel & Co. Ltd, London, since 1979 (Director, since 1967); *b* 14 Feb. 1920; *y s* of late Robert Jardine Paterson, Balgray, Lockerbie, Dumfriesshire; *m* 1953, Priscilla Mignon, *d* of late Sir Kenneth Nicolson, MC; one *s* three *d. Educ:* Eton Coll.; Jesus Coll., Cambridge. Emergency commn, The Black Watch, RHR, 1939. Dir of Jardine Henderson Ltd, Calcutta, 1952-67 (Chm. 1963-67). Chm., Indian Jute Mills Assoc., 1963; Pres., Bengal Chamber of Commerce and Industry and Associated Chambers of Commerce of India, 1966. *Recreations:* golf, shooting. *Address:* Norton Bavant Manor, Warminster, Wilts. *T:* Sutton Veny 378. *Clubs:* Oriental; Bengal, Royal Calcutta Turf (Calcutta).

JARMAN, Air Cdre Lance Elworthy, DFC 1940; RAF (retired); Director, Engineering Industries Association, 1958-73, retired; *b* 17 Aug. 1907; *s* of Hedley Elworthy and Mary Elizabeth Jarman (*née* Chatterway-Clarke); *m* 1940, Elizabeth Evelyn Litton-Puttock (*d* 1978); one *s* one *d. Educ:* Christchurch High Sch., NZ; Canterbury Coll., Univ. of NZ. Commissioned, RAF, 1929; No 12 Bomber Sqdn, Andover, 1930; No 14 Bomber Sqdn, Amman, 1931; Officers' Engineering Course, Henlow, 1932-35; RAF, Abukir, Atbara, Sudan, Cairo, 1935-38; Maintenance Command, 1938. Served War of 1939-45: Nos 214 and 9 Bomber Sqdns, 1939; Chief Flying Instructor, Nos 11-20 and 23 Operational Training Units, 1940; CO, No 27 OTU, Lichfield, 1941; SASO, No 93 Bomber Gp, 1942; CO, RAF Stations, Kidlington and Wyton, 1943; SASO, No 205 Gp, Italy, 1945, qualified as Pathfinder; OC RAF Stations, Oakington and Abingdon, 1947; Senior Officer Administration, RAF, No 42 Gp, 1949; OC, RAF Jet Training Stations, Full Sutton and Merryfield, 1951; Chief of Staff, Royal Pakistan Air Force, 1952; AO Defence Research Policy Staff, Cabinet Office, 1955-56; RAF Rep., Commonwealth Conf. on Defence Sci., Canada; AOA, NATO, Channel and Atlantic Commands, 1957; retired from RAF, 1958. CEng, MIMechE, AFRAeS, MBIM, MAIE. *Publications:* Editor, Engineering Industries Jl. *Recreation:* sailing; lectr, offshore and ocean navigation; examr, RYA/DTI yachtmaster certificate. *Address:* Merryfield, 9 Mewnham Road, Lymington, Hants. *T:* Lymington 74577. *Clubs:* Royal Air Force, Royal Ocean Racing; RAF Yacht (Hamble); Royal New Zealand Yacht Squadron.

JARMAN, Roger Whitney; Under Secretary, Land Use Planning Group, Welsh Office, since 1980; *b* 16 Feb. 1935; *s* of Reginald Cecil Jarman and Marjorie Dix Jarman; *m* 1959, Patricia Dorothy Odwell; one *s. Educ:* Cathays High Sch., Cardiff; Univ. of Birmingham (BSocSc Hons; Cert. in Educn). Recruitment and Selection Officer, Vauxhall Motors Ltd, 1960-64; Asst Sec., Univ. of Bristol Appts Bd, 1964-68; Asst Dir of Recruitment, CSD, 1968-72; Welsh Office: Principal, European Div., 1972-74; Asst Sec., Devolution Div., 1974-78; Asst Sec., Perm. Sec.'s Div., 1978-80. *Recreations:* walking, reading, gardening. *Address:* Coopers Lea, 72 Mill Road, Lisvane, Cardiff CF4 5XJ. *T:* Cardiff 756405. *Club:* Civil Service.

JARRATT, Sir Alexander Anthony, (Sir Alex), Kt 1979; CB 1968; Chairman, Reed International, since 1974 (Director, since 1970); a Deputy Chairman, Midland Bank, since 1980; *b* 19 Jan. 1924; *o s* of Alexander and Mary Jarratt; *m* 1946, Mary Philomena Keogh; one *s* two *d. Educ:* Royal Liberty Gram. Sch., Essex; University of Birmingham. War Service, Fleet Air Arm, 1942-46. University of Birmingham, BCom, 1946-49. Asst Principal, Min. of Power, 1949, Principal, 1953, and seconded to Treas., 1954-55; Min. of Power: Prin. Priv. Sec. to Minister, 1955-59; Asst Sec., Oil Div., 1959-63; Under-Sec., Gas Div., 1963-64; seconded to Cabinet Office, 1964-65; Secretary to the National Board for Prices and Incomes, 1965-68; Dep. Sec., 1967; Dep. Under Sec. of State, Dept of Employment and Productivity, 1968-70; Dep. Sec., Min. of Agriculture, 1970. Man. Dir, IPC, 1970-73; Chm. and Chief Executive, IPC and IPC Newspapers, 1974; Director: ICI; Thyssen-Bornemisza Group. Mem., President's Cttee, CBI; Mem., NEDC, 1976-80. Pres., Advertising Assoc., 1979-. Mem., Industrial Soc. (Chm., 1975-79); Chm., Henley Admin. Staff Coll.; Governor: London Business Sch.; Ashridge Management Coll.; Cranfield Inst. of Technol.; NIESR. Vice-President: Periodical Publishers Assoc.; Inst. of Marketing; Chm., Adv. Bd, Inst. of Occup. Health; Panel Mem., Internat. Centre for Settlement of Investment Disputes. FRSA. Hon. DSc Cranfield, 1973; DUniv Brunel, 1979; Hon. LLD Birmingham, 1982. *Recreations:* the countryside, reading. *Address:* c/o Reed International Ltd, Reed House, 83 Piccadilly, W1. *Club:* Savile.

JARRETT, Sir Clifford (George), KBE 1956 (CBE 1945); CB 1949; Chairman: Tobacco Research Council, 1971-78; Dover Harbour Board, 1971-80; *b* 1909; *s* of George Henry Jarrett; *m* 1st, 1933, Hilda Alice Goodchild (*d* 1975); one *s* two *d* ; 2nd, 1978, Mary, *d* of C. S. Beacock. *Educ:* Dover County Sch.; Sidney Sussex Coll., Cambridge. BA 1931. Entered Civil Service, 1932; Asst Principal, Home Office, 1932-34, Admiralty, 1934-38; Private Sec. to Parl. Sec., 1936-38; Principal Private Sec. to First Lord, 1940-44; Principal Establishments Officer, 1946-50; a Dep. Sec., Admiralty, 1950-61; Permanent Sec., Admiralty, 1961-64; Permanent Under-Sec., Min. of Pensions and Nat. Insurance, later Min. of Social Security, later Dept of Health and Social Security, 1964-70. A Trustee, Nat. Maritime Museum, 1969-81. *Address:* The Coach House, Derry Hill, Menston, Ilkley, W Yorks. *Club:* United Oxford & Cambridge University.

JARRETT, Prof. William Fleming Hoggan, FRS 1980, FRSE 1965; Professor of Veterinary Pathology, University of Glasgow, since 1968; *b* 2 Jan. 1928; *s* of James and Jessie Jarrett; *m* 1952, Anna Fraser Sharp; two *d. Educ:* Lenzie Academy; Glasgow Veterinary Coll.; Univ. of Glasgow; PhD, MRCVS, FRCPath. Gold Medal, 1949; John Henry Steele Meml Medal, 1961; Steele Bodger Meml Schol. 1955. ARC Research Student, 1949-52; Lectr, Dept of Veterinary Pathology, Univ. of Glasgow Vet. Sch., 1952-53; Head of Hospital Path. Dept of Vet. Hosp., Univ. of Glasgow, 1953-61; Reader in Pathology, Univ. of Glasgow, 1962-65; seconded to Univ. of E Africa, 1963-64; Titular Prof. of Experimental Vet. Medicine, Univ. of Glasgow, 1965. *Publications:* various, on tumour viruses, leukaemia and immunology. *Recreations:* sailing, skiing, mountaineering, music. *Address:* 60 Netherblane, High Pines, Blanefield, Glasgow G63 9JP. *T:* Blanefield 70332. *Clubs:* Clyde Cruising, West Highland Yacht, Glencoe Ski, Scottish Ski.

JARRING, Gunnar, PhD; Grand Cross, Order of the North Star, Sweden; Swedish Ambassador and Special Representative of the Secretary-General of the United Nations on the Middle East question since Nov. 1967; *b* S Sweden, 12 Oct. 1907; *s* of Gottfrid Jönsson and Betty Svensson; *m* 1932, Agnes, *d* of Prof. Carl Charlier, Lund; one *d. Educ:* Lund; Univ. of Lund (PhD). Family surname changed to Jarring, 1931. Associate Prof. of Turkish Langs, Lund Univ., 1933-40; Attaché, Ankara, 1940-41; Chief, Section B, Teheran, 1941; Chargé d'Affaires *ad interim:* Teheran and Baghdad, 1945; Addis Ababa, 1946-48; Minister: to India, 1948-51, concurrently to Ceylon, 1950-51; to Persia, Iraq and Pakistan, 1951-52; Dir, Polit. Div., Min. of Foreign Affairs, 1953-56; Permanent Rep. to UN, 1956-58; Rep. on Security Council, 1957-58; Ambassador to USA, 1958-64, to USSR, 1964-73, and to Mongolia, 1965-73. *Publications:* Studien zu einer osttürkischen Lautlehre, 1933; The Contest of the Fruits - An Eastern Turki Allegory, 1936; The Uzbek Dialect of Quilich, Russian Turkestan, 1937; Uzbek Texts from Afghan Turkestan, 1938; The Distribution of Turk Tribes in Afghanistan, 1939; Materials to the Knowledge of Eastern Turki (vols 1-4), 1947-51; An Eastern Turki-English Dialect Dictionary, 1964; Literary Texts from Kashghar, 1980. *Address:* Karlavägen 85, 114 59 Stockholm, Sweden.

JARROW, Bishop Suffragan of, since 1980; **Rt. Rev. Michael Thomas Ball,** CGA; *b* 14 Feb. 1932; *s* of Thomas James Ball and Kathleen Bradley Ball. *Educ:* Lancing Coll., Sussex; Queens' Coll., Cambridge (BA 1955, MA 1959). Schoolmastering, 1955-76; Co-Founder, Community of the Glorious Ascension, 1960; Prior at Stroud Priory, 1963-76; Curate, Whiteshill, Stroud, Glos, 1971-76; Priest-in-charge of Stanmer with Falmer, and Senior Anglican Chaplain to Higher Education in Brighton, including Sussex Univ., 1976-80. *Recreations:* music, sport. *Address:* Melkridge House, Gilesgate, Durham. *T:* Durham 43797.
See also Bishop of Lewes.

JARVIS, Mrs Doris Annie, CBE 1969; Headmistress, Tower Hamlets Comprehensive Girls' School, 1963-74; *b* 18 April 1912; *d* of William George Mabbitt (killed on active service, 1918) and Ada Marie Mabbitt; *m* 1940, George Harry Jarvis; one *s. Educ:* South Hackney Central Sch.; City of London Sch. for Girls; King's Coll., London (BSc); Furzedown Training Coll., London. Commenced teaching in Bethnal Green, E, Sept. 1935; worked in E London schools and evacuation areas during War period; post-war, taught at Daniel Secondary Sch., E2; Emergency Training College Lecturer, Camden Trg Coll., 1949-50; Headmistress, Wilmot Secondary Girls' Sch., Bethnal Green, E2, 1950-63. *Recreations:* home affairs, reading, walking, gardening; furthering knowledge of education and social work in E London, generally. *Address:* 1a Tolmers Avenue, Cuffley, Herts. *T:* Cuffley 3780.

JARVIS, Hon. Eric William George, CMG 1961; Judge of the High Court, Rhodesia, 1963–77; *b* 22 Nov. 1907; *s* of late William Stokes Jarvis and Edith Mary Jarvis (*née* Langley), both of Essex, England; *m* 1937, Eveline Mavis Smith; one *s* one *d. Educ:* Salisbury Boys High Sch. (now Prince Edward Sch.), Salisbury, R; Rhodes Univ., Grahamstown, SA. BA; LLB; admitted as Advocate High Court of Southern Rhodesia, 1929; appointed Law Officer of Crown, 1934; KC 1949; Solicitor-Gen. for Southern Rhodesia, 1949–55; Attorney-Gen. for Southern Rhodesia, 1955–62. *Recreations:* tennis, golf, bowls. *Address:* 680 Glenwood Drive, PO Chisipite, Harare, Zimbabwe. *T:* 471180. *Club:* Salisbury (Harare).

JARVIS, Frederick Frank, (Fred Jarvis); General Secretary, National Union of Teachers, since 1975; Member of General Council, Trades Union Congress, since 1974; *b* 8 Sept. 1924; *s* of Alfred and Emily Ann Jarvis; *m* 1954, Elizabeth Anne Colegrove, Stanton Harcourt, Oxfordshire; one *s* one *d. Educ:* Plaistow Secondary Sch., West Ham; Oldershaw Grammar Sch., Wallasey; Liverpool Univ.; St Catherine's Society, Oxford. Dip. in Social Science with dist. (Liverpool Univ.); BA (Hons) in Politics, Philosophy and Economics (Oxon), MA (Oxon). Contested (Lab) Wallasey, Gen. Elec., 1951; Chm., Nat. Assoc. of Labour Student Organisations, 1951; Pres., Nat. Union of Students, 1952–54 (Dep. Pres., 1951–52); Asst Sec., Nat. Union of Teachers, 1955–59; Head of Publicity and Public Relations, 1959–70; Dep. Gen. Sec., NUT, 1970–74 (apptd Gen. Sec. Designate, March 1974). Mem. Council, Nat. Youth Theatre. Hon. FEIS 1980. *Publications:* The Educational Implications of UK Membership of the EEC, 1972. Ed, various jls incl.: 'Youth Review', NUT Guide to Careers; NUT Univ. and Coll. Entrance Guide. *Recreations:* swimming, golf, tennis, gardening, cinema, theatre. *Address:* 92 Hadley Road, New Barnet, Herts EN5 5QR. *Club:* Ronnie Scott's.

JARVIS, Patrick William, CEng, FIEE; RCNC; Director of Ship Design and Engineering, Ship Department, and Deputy Head, Royal Corps of Naval Constructors (Electrical), Ministry of Defence (PE), Bath, since 1981; *b* 27 Aug. 1926; *s* of Frederick Arthur and Marjorie Winifred Jarvis; *m* 1951, Amy (*née* Ryley); two *s. Educ:* Royal Naval Coll., Greenwich; Royal Naval Engrg Coll., Keyham, Devonport. BScEng. Trade apprentice, HM Dockyard, Chatham, 1942–46; Design Engineer, Admiralty, Bath, 1946–62; Warship Electrical Supt, Belfast, 1962–63; Suptg Engr, MoD(N), Bath, 1963–72; Ship Department, MoD (PE), Bath: Asst Dir and Dep. Dir, 1972–78; Under Sec., 1978; Dir of Naval Ship Production, 1979–81. *Recreations:* indoor sports, chess. *Address:* (home) Ranworth, Bathampton Lane, Bathampton, Bath BA2 6ST. *T:* Bath 65378; (office) DSDE, Ship Department, Ministry of Defence (PE), Foxhill, Bath. *T:* Bath 61211, ext. 2712.

JASPER, Cyril Charles; County Treasurer, Hertfordshire County Council, 1972–81; *b* 16 Oct. 1923; *s* of James Edward Jasper and Daisy (*née* Brown); *m* 1949, Vera Newington; three *s* two *d. Educ:* Brockley County Grammar Sch. DPA London 1950; CIPFA (double Hons) 1959; FBIM. Comptroller's Dept, LCC, 1941–60; Asst County Treas., W Sussex CC, 1961–69; Dep. Co. Treas., Herts CC, 1970–72. Dir, New Court Property Fund; Consultant to: Rowan Investment Managers; Lazard Securities Ltd. Financial Adviser to Educn Cttee, Assoc. of County Councils, 1972–81. Pres., Soc. of County Treasurers, 1978–79. Collins Gold Medal, CIPFA, 1959. *Publications:* contrib. local govt papers. *Recreations:* amateur dramatics, youth work, circuit treasurer in Methodist church. *Address:* Dovedale, 47 Walton Road, Ware, Herts SG12 9PF.

JASPER, Robin Leslie Darlow, CMG 1963; HM Diplomatic Service, retired; *b* 22 Feb. 1914; *s* of T. D. Jasper, Beckenham; *m* 1st, 1940, Jean (marr. diss.), *d* of late Brig.-Gen. J. K. Cochrane, CMG; one *d*; 2nd, 1966, Diana Speed (*née* West), two step *d. Educ:* Dulwich; Clare Coll., Cambridge. Apprentice, LNER Hotels Dept, 1936–39; Bursar, Dominion Students Hall Trust (London House), 1939–40; RAFVR (Wing Comdr), 1940–45; Principal, India Office (later Commonwealth Relations Office), 1945; concerned with resettlement of the Sec. of State's Services in India, 1947–48; British Dep. High Commissioner, Lahore, Pakistan, 1949–52; Adviser to London Conferences on Central African Federation, and visited Central Africa in this connection, 1952–53; Counsellor, HM Embassy, Lisbon, 1953–55; visited Portuguese Africa, 1954; Commonwealth Relations Office, 1955–60 (Head of Information Policy Dept, 1958–60); attached to the United Kingdom delegation to the United Nations, 1956 and 1956; British Dep. High Commissioner, Ibadan, Nigeria, 1960–64; Counsellor, Commonwealth Office, 1965–67; Consul-Gen., Naples, 1967–71, retired 1972. *Recreations:* tennis, Rugby fives, wind music, 17th Century Church Sculpture, claret. *Address:* c/o Royal Bank of Scotland (Drummonds Branch), 49 Charing Cross, SW1. *Clubs:* MCC, Jesters.

JASPER, Very Rev. Ronald Claud Dudley, CBE 1981; DD; Dean of York, since 1975; *b* 17 Aug. 1917; *s* of late Claud Albert and late Florence Lily Jasper; *m* 1943, Ethel, *o d* of David and Edith Wiggins; one *s* one *d. Educ:* Plymouth Coll.; University of Leeds; College of the Resurrection, Mirfield. MA (with distinction), 1940; DD 1961. FRHistS 1954. Curate of Ryhope, 1940–42; St Oswald's, Durham, 1942–43; Esh, 1943–46; Chaplain of University Coll., Durham, 1946–48; Vicar of Stillington, 1948–55; Succentor of Exeter Cathedral, 1955–60; Lecturer in Liturgical Studies: King's Coll., London, 1960–67, Reader, 1967–68; RSCM, 1965–69; Canon of Westminster, 1968–75;

Archdeacon, 1974–75. Chm., Church of England Liturgical Commn, 1964–81. Hon. DLitt Susquehanna, 1976. *Publications:* Prayer Book Revision in England, 1800–1900, 1954; Walter Howard Frere: Correspondence and Memoranda on Liturgical Revision and Construction, 1954; Arthur Cayley Headlam, 1960; George Bell: Bishop of Chichester, 1967; A Christian's Prayer Book, 1972; (ed) The Renewal of Worship, 1965; (ed) The Calendar and Lectionary, 1967; (ed) The Daily Office, 1968; (ed) Holy Week Services, 1971; (ed) Initiation and Eucharist, 1972; (ed) The Eucharist Today, 1974; Prayers of the Eucharist, 1975; Pray Every Day, 1976; The Daily Office Revised, 1978; contribs to Church Quarterly Review, Jl of Ecclesiastical History, Church Quarterly, London Quarterly, Expository Times, Ecumenica, Heythrop Jl. *Recreations:* reading, writing, television. *Address:* The Deanery, York.

JAUNCEY, Hon. Lord; Charles Eliot Jauncey; a Senator of the College of Justice in Scotland, since 1979; *b* 8 May 1925; *s* of late Captain John Henry Jauncey, DSO, RN, Tullichettle, Comrie, and Muriel Charlie, *d* of late Adm. Sir Charles Dundas of Dundas, KCMG; *m* 1st, 1948, Jean (marr. diss. 1969), *d* of Adm. Sir Angus Cunninghame Graham of Gartmore, KBE, CB; two *s* one *d*; 2nd, 1973, Elizabeth (marr. diss. 1977), widow of Major John Ballingal, MC; 3rd, 1977, Camilla, *d* of late Lt-Col Charles Cathcart, DSO, Pitcairlie; one *d. Educ:* Radley; Christ Church, Oxford; Glasgow Univ. BA 1947, Oxford; LLB 1949, Glasgow. Served in War, 1943–46, Sub-Lt RNVR. Advocate, Scottish Bar, 1949; Standing Junior Counsel to Admiralty, 1954; QC (Scotland) 1963; Kintyre Pursuivant of Arms, 1955–71; Sheriff Principal of Fife and Kinross, 1971–74; Judge of the Courts of Appeal of Jersey and Guernsey, 1972–79. Hon. Sheriff-Substitute of Perthshire, 1962. Mem. of Royal Co. of Archers (Queen's Body Guard for Scotland), 1951. Mem., Historic Buildings Council for Scotland, 1971–. *Recreations:* shooting, fishing, genealogy. *Address:* Tullichettle, Comrie, Perthshire. *T:* 349; 12 Moray Place, Edinburgh 3. *T:* 031-225 4612. *Club:* Royal (Perth).

JAUNCEY, Charles Eliot; see Jauncey, Hon. Lord.

JAWARA, Hon. Sir Dawda Kairaba, Kt 1966; President of the Republic of The Gambia, since 1970; Vice-President of the Senegambian Confederation, since 1982; *b* Barajally, MacCarthy Island Div., 16 May 1924. *Educ:* Muslim Primary Sch. and Methodist Boys' Grammar Sch., Bathurst; Achimota Coll. (Vet. School); Glasgow Univ. MRCVS, 1953; Dipl. in Trop. Vet. Med., Edinburgh, 1957. Veterinary Officer for The Gambia govt, 1954–57, Principal Vet. Officer, 1957–60. Leader of People's Progressive Party (formerly Protectorate People's Party), The Gambia, 1960; MP 1960; Minister of Education, 1960–61; Premier, 1962–63; Prime Minister, 1963–70. Grand Cross: Order of Cedar of Lebanon, 1966; Nat. Order of Republic of Senegal, 1967; Order of Propitious Clouds of China (Taiwan), 1968; Nat. Order of Republic of Guinea, 1973; Grand Officer, Order of Islamic Republic of Mauritania, 1967; Grand Cordon of Most Venerable Order of Knighthood, Pioneers of Republic of Liberia, 1968; Grand Comdr, Nat. Order of Federal Republic of Nigeria, 1970; Grand Master, Order of the Republic of The Gambia, 1972; Hon. GCMG, 1974; Comdr of Golden Ark (Netherlands), 1979; Hon LLD Univ. of Ife, 1978; Peutinger Gold Medal, Peutinger-Collegium, Munich, 1979. *Recreations:* golf, gardening, sailing. *Address:* State House, Banjul, The Gambia.

JAY, Barrie Samuel, MD, FRCS; Surgeon, Moorfields Eye Hospital, since 1969; Dean, Institute of Ophthalmology, since 1980; *b* 7 May 1929; *er s* of late Dr M. B. Jay and Julia Sterling; *m* 1954, Marcelle Ruby Byre; two *s. Educ:* Perse Sch., Cambridge; Gonville and Caius Coll., Cambridge (MA, MD); University Coll. Hosp., London. FRCS 1962. House Surgeon and Sen. Resident Officer, Moorfields Eye Hosp., 1959–62; Sen. Registrar, Ophthalmic Dept, London Hosp., 1962–65; Inst. of Ophthalmology, Univ. of London: Shepherd Res. Scholar, 1963–64; Clinical Sub-Dean, 1973–77 Ophthalmic Surgeon, The London Hosp., 1965–79. Examiner: Dip. in Ophthal., 1970–75; British Orthoptic Council, 1970–; Ophthalmic Nursing Bd, 1971–; Mem. Ct of Examrs, RCS, 1975–80. Brit. Rep., Monospecialist Section of Ophthal., Eur. Union of Med. Specialists, 1973–. Mem. Council: Section of Ophthal., RSM, 1965–77 (Editorial Rep., 1966–77); Faculty of Ophthalmologists, 1970– (Asst Hon. Sec., 1976–78; Hon. Sec., 1978–); Nat. Ophthalmic Treatment Bd Assoc., 1971–75; Club Européen de Conseil Génétique, 1974–; Internat. Pediatric Ophthal. Soc., 1975–; Mem. Orthoptists Bd, Council for Professions Supplementary to Medicine, 1977–. Fellow, Eugenics Soc., 1973; Hon. Mem., Canadian Ophthalmol Soc. Liveryman: Soc. of Apothecaries; Co. of Barbers. Mem., Bd of Governors, Moorfields Eye Hosp., 1971–. Editor, Ophthalmic Literature, 1978– (Mem. Ed. Bd, 1962–; Asst Editor, 1977–78); Mem. Editorial Board: British Jl of Ophthalmology, 1965–; Jl of Medical Genetics, 1971–76; Metabolic Ophthalmology, 1975–78; Survey of Ophthalmology, 1976–. *Publications:* contrib. on ophthalmology and genetics to med. jls. *Recreations:* postal history, gardening. *Address:* 10 Beltane Drive, SW19 5JR. *T:* 01-947 1771. *Club:* Athenæum.

JAY, Rt. Hon. Douglas Patrick Thomas, PC 1951; MP (Lab) Wandsworth, Battersea North, since 1974 (Battersea North, July 1946–1974); *b* 23 March 1907; *s* of Edward Aubrey Hastings Jay and Isobel Violet Jay; *m* 1st, 1933, Margaret Christian (marr. diss. 1972), *e d* of late J. C. Maxwell Garnett, CBE, ScD; two *s* two *d*; 2nd, 1972, Mary Lavinia Thomas, *d* of Hugh Lewis Thomas. *Educ:* Winchester Coll.; New Coll., Oxford (Scholar). First Class, Litteræ Humaniores; Fellow of All Souls' Coll., Oxford, 1930–37, and 1968–; on the staff of the Times, 1929–33, and the Economist, 1933–37; City Editor

of the Daily Herald, 1937–41; Asst Sec., Ministry of Supply, 1941–43; Principal Asst Sec., BoT, 1943–45; Personal Asst to Prime Minister, 1945–46; Economic Sec. to Treasury, 1947–50; Financial Sec. to Treasury, 1950–51; President, BoT, 1964–67. Chairman: Common Market Safeguards Campaign, 1970–77; London Motorway Action Group, 1968–. Director: Courtaulds Ltd, 1967–70; Trades Union Unit Trust, 1967–; Flag Investment Co., 1968–71. *Publications:* The Socialist Case, 1937; Who is to Pay for the War and the Peace, 1941; Socialism in the New Society, 1962; After the Common Market, 1968; Change and Fortune, 1980. *Address:* 6 Hampstead Grove, NW3; Monument Cottage, Britwell Salome, Watlington, Oxford. *T:* Watlington 2615.
See also Peter Jay.

JAY, Rev. Canon Eric George; Professor of Historical Theology, Faculty of Divinity, McGill University, 1958–75, Emeritus, 1977; *b* 1 March 1907; *s* of Henry Jay, Colchester, Essex; *m* 1937, Margaret Hilda, *d* of Rev. Alfred W. Webb; one *s* two *d. Educ:* Colchester High Sch.; Leeds Univ. BA 1st Cl. Hons Classics, 1929; MA 1930; BD (London) 1937; MTh 1940; PhD 1951. Deacon, 1931; priest, 1932; Curate, St Augustine, Stockport, 1931–34; Lecturer in Theology, King's Coll., London, 1934–47; Curate, St Andrew Undershaft, City of London, 1935–40. Served War as Chaplain in RAFVR 1940–45. Rector, St Mary-le-Strand, 1945–47; Dean of Nassau, Bahamas, 1948–51; Senior Chaplain to the Archbishop of Canterbury, 1951–58; Principal, Montreal Diocesan Theological Coll., 1958–64; Dean, Faculty of Divinity, McGill Univ., 1963–70. Fellow of King's Coll., London, 1948; Canon of Montreal, 1960. Hon. DD: Montreal Diocesan Theolog. Coll., 1964; Trinity Coll., Toronto, 1975; United Theol Coll., Montreal, 1976. *Publications:* The Existence of God, 1946; Origen's Treatise on Prayer, 1954; New Testament Greek; an Introductory Grammar, 1958; Son of Man, Son of God, 1965; The Church: its changing image through twenty centuries, 1977. *Recreations:* reading "thrillers"; crossword puzzles, watching ice hockey, cricket and Rugby football. *Address:* Apt 15, 570 Milton Street, Montreal H2X 1W4, Canada.

JAY, Peter; Chairman and Chief Executive: TV-am Ltd, since 1980; TV-am News, since 1982; Chairman, National Council for Voluntary Organisations, since 1981; Director, Economist Intelligence Unit, since 1979; *b* 7 Feb. 1937; *s* of Rt Hon. Douglas Patrick Thomas Jay, *qv*; *m* 1961, Margaret Ann, *d* of Rt Hon. James Callaghan, *qv*; one *s* two *d. Educ:* Winchester Coll.; Christ Church, Oxford. MA 1st cl. hons PPE, 1960. President of the Union, 1960. Nuffield Coll., 1960. Midshipman and Sub-Lt RNVR, 1956–57. Asst Principal 1961–64, Private Sec. to Jt Perm. Sec. 1964, Principal 1964–67, HM Treasury; Economics Editor, The Times, 1967–77, and Associate Editor, Times Business News, 1969–77; Presenter, Weekend World (ITV Sunday morning series), 1972–77; The Jay Interview (ITV series), 1975–76; Ambassador to US, 1977–79. Vis. Scholar, Brookings Instn, Washington, 1979–80; Wincott Meml Lectr, 1975; Copland Meml Lectr, Australia, 1980. Consultant, Economist Gp, 1979–81; Chm., TV-am (successful applicant for ITV nat. breakfast time franchise), 1980; Dir, Landen Press Ltd, 1982–. Chm., NACRO Working Party on Children and Young Persons in Custody, 1976–77; Trustee, Charities Aid Foundn, 1981–; Chairman: United Way (UK) Ltd, 1982–; United Way Feasibility Studies Steering Cttee, 1982–; Mem. Council, Cinema and TV Benevolent Fund, 1982–; Governor, Ditchley Foundn, 1982–. Dir, New Nat. Theater, Washington, DC, 1979–81. Political Broadcaster of Year, 1973; Harold Wincott Financial and Economic Journalist of Year, 1973; Royal TV Soc.'s Male Personality of Year (Pye Award), 1974; SFTA Shell Internat. TV Award, 1974. FRSA 1975; FRGS 1977. Hon. DH Ohio State Univ., 1978; Hon. DLitt Wake Forest Univ., 1979; Berkeley Citation, Univ. of Calif, 1979. *Publications:* The Budget, 1972; (contrib.) America and the World 1979, 1980; contrib. Foreign Affairs jl. *Recreation:* sailing. *Address:* 39 Castlebar Road, W5 2DJ. *T:* 01-998 3570; Elm Bank, Glandore, West Co. Cork. *T:* (028) 33198. *Clubs:* Garrick; Royal Naval Sailing Association, Royal Cork Yacht.

JAYAWARDANA, Brig. Christopher Allan Hector Perera, CMG 1956; CVO 1954; OBE 1944 (MBE 1941); ED 1936; JP; FLS; KStJ; *b* 29 March 1898; 4th *s* of Gate Muhandiram Herat Perera Jayawardana; *m* 1924, Sylvia Dorothy Samarasinhe, *e d* of Mudaliyar Soloman Dias Samarasinhe; (one *s* one *d* decd). *Educ:* Trinity Coll., Kandy, Ceylon; Keble Coll., Oxford (MA). Sen. Asst Conservator of Forests, Ceylon (retd); Dep. Warden of Wild Life, Ceylon (retd), 1924–29; served War of 1939–45; OC 1st Bn the Ceylon LI, 1938–43; Chief Comr, Ceylon Boy Scouts' Association, 1949–54; Extra Aide de Camp to HE the Governor Gen. of Ceylon, 1949–; Equerry to HM the Queen, during Royal Visit to Ceylon, 1954; Hon. ADC to the Queen, 1954–. Awarded Silver Wolf, 1944. FLS, 1924. Carnegie School., 1931; Smith-Mundt Schol., 1951; KStJ, 1959 (CStJ, 1954). Diploma of Forestry. *Recreations:* rifle shooting, big game hunting, deep sea fishing, golf, tennis, riding, painting, camping, photography. *Address:* 12 Sukhastan Gardens, Ward Place, Colombo 7, Sri Lanka. *T:* (home) 91354; (office) 33131. *Clubs:* Corona; Sea Anglers' (Sri Lanka).

JAYES, Percy Harris, MB, BS, FRCS; Plastic Surgeon: St Bartholomew's Hospital, London, 1952–73; Queen Victoria Hospital, East Grinstead, 1948–73; Consultant in Plastic Surgery to the Royal Air Force, since 1960; Consultant Plastic Surgeon, King Edward VII Hospital for Officers since 1966; *b* 26 June 1915; *s* of Thomas Harris Jayes; *m* 1945, Kathleen Mary Harrington (*d* 1963); two *s* one *d* ; *m* 1964, Aileen Mary McLaughlin; one *s* one *d. Educ:* Merchant Taylors' Sch.; St Bartholomew's Hosp. Resid. Plastic Surg., EMS Plastic Unit, East Grinstead, 1940–48; Surgeon in Charge, UNRRA Plastic Unit, Belgrade,

1946; Mem. Council, Brit. Assoc. Plastic Surgeons, 1954–64 (Pres., Assoc., 1960). *Publications:* contrib. British Journal of Plastic Surgery, Annals of Royal College of Surgeons and other journals. *Recreation:* tennis. *Address:* Barton St Mary, Lewes Road, East Grinstead. *T:* East Grinstead 23461; 149 Harley Street, W1N 2DE. *T:* 01-935 4444.

JAYEWARDENE, Junius Richard; President of Sri Lanka, since 1978; Minister of Defence, and of Plan Implementation, since 1977; Minister of Power and of Energy, since 1981; *b* Colombo, 17 Sept. 1906; *s* of Mr Justice E. W. Jayewardene, KC and A. H. Jayewardene; *m* 1935, Elina B. Rupesinghe; one *s. Educ:* Royal Coll., Colombo; Ceylon University Coll.; Ceylon Law Coll. Sworn Advocate of Supreme Court of Ceylon, 1932. Joined Ceylon Nat. Congress, later United Nat. Party, 1938; Hon. Sec., 1940–47; Hon. Treasurer, 1946–48, 1957–58; Vice-Pres., 1954–56, 1958–72; Sec., 1972–73; Pres., 1973–. Member: Colombo Municipal Council, 1940–43; State Council, 1943–47; House of Representatives, 1947–56, 1960–77 (Leader, 1953–56); Minister of: Agriculture and Food, 1953–56; Finance, 1947–52, 1952–53, 1960; Chief Opposition Whip, 1960–65; Minister of State and Parly Sec. to Prime Minister, Minister of Defence and External Affairs, and Chief Govt Whip, 1965–70; Leader of the Opposition, House of Representatives, 1970–72, Nat. State Assembly, 1972–77; Prime Minister, and Minister of Planning and Economic Affairs, 1977. Was a co-author of Colombo Plan, 1950; has been leader of delegations to many UN and Commonwealth conferences; Governor, World Bank and IMF, 1947–52. *Publications:* Some Sermons of Buddha, 1940; Buddhist Essays; In Council, 1946; Buddhism and Marxism, 1950, 3rd edn 1957; Selected Speeches. *Address:* President's House, Colombo, Sri Lanka.

JEAFFRESON, David Gregory, CBE 1981; Secretary for Security, Hong Kong Government, since 1982; *b* 21 Nov. 1931; *s* of Bryan Leslie Jeaffreson, MD, FRCS, MRCOG and Margaret Jeaffreson; *m* 1959, Elisabeth Marie Jausions; two *s* two *d* (and one *d* decd). *Educ:* Bootham Sch., York; Clare Coll., Cambridge (MA). 2nd Lieut, RA, 1950. Dist Officer, Tanganyika, 1955–58; Asst Man., Henricot Steel Foundry, 1959–60; Admin. Officer, Hong Kong Govt, 1961; Dep. Financial Sec., 1972–76; Sec. for Economic Services, 1976–82. *Recreations:* French and Chinese history, music, photography, sailing and walking. *Address:* 64 Mount Nicholson, Hong Kong. *T:* 5-730551. *Clubs:* World Traders; Royal Hong Kong Yacht.

JEANES, Leslie Edwin Elloway, CBE 1982; Chief of Public Relations, Ministry of Defence, 1978–81; *b* 17 Dec. 1920; *er s* of late Edwin Eli Jubilee Jeanes and of Mary Eunice Jeanes; *m* 1942, Valerie Ruth, *d* of Ernest and Ethel Vidler; one *d. Educ:* Westcliff High Sch. Entered Civil Service, 1939; Inf. Officer, DSIR, 1948–65; Chief Press Officer, Min. of Technol., 1965–68; Dep. Head of Inf., MoT, 1968–70; Head of News, DoE, 1970–73; Chief Inf. Officer, MAFF, 1973–78. *Recreations:* gardening, motoring, DIY. *Address:* 14 Whistley Close, Bracknell, Berks. *T:* Bracknell 29429.

JEANS, Isabel; Actress; *b* London; *d* of Frederick George Jeans; *m* 1st, Claud Rains (marr. diss.); 2nd, Gilbert Edward, *y s* of late Rt Rev. Henry Russell Wakefield, Bishop of Birmingham; no *c. Educ:* London. Made first appearance under Sir Herbert Tree's management at His Majesty's; first acting role was at the Garrick as Peggy in The Greatest Wish; went to United States with Granville Barker's Company, playing Titania in A Midsummer Night's Dream and Fanny in Fanny's First Play; on returning to England appeared in musical comedy and then joined the Everyman Repertory Company, playing Fanny, Raina in Arms and the Man, Hypatia in Misalliance, and Olivia in Twelfth Night, and also appeared in a number of Elizabethan and Restoration revivals by the Phœnix Society including Volpone, The Maid's Tragedy, The Jew of Malta, The Old Bachelor, and as Margery Pinchwife In The Country Wife; went to Holland to play Laura Pasquale in At Mr Beam's, and later played Yasmin in Hassan at His Majesty's and Lydia Languish in The Rivals at the Lyric, Hammersmith; since 1924 has appeared as Zelie in The Rat, Nell Gwynne in Mr Pepys, Lady Dare Bellingham in Conflict, Amytis in The Road to Rome, Estelle in Beauty, Crystal Wetherby in The Man in Possession, subsequently playing the same part in New York, Leslie in Counsel's Opinion, Mrs Jelliwell in Springtime for Henry, Lady Coperario in Spring 1600, Lucy Lockit in The Beggar's Opera, Lola in Full House, La Gambogi in The Happy Hypocrite, Alice Galvoisier in Mademoiselle, Susanna Venables in Second Helping, Lady Utterwood in Heartbreak House, Mrs Erlynne in Lady Windermere's Fan; went to New York, Jan. 1948, to play Lucia in Make Way for Lucia; since returning to London has appeared as Madame Arkadina in The Seagull; The Countess in Ardele; Florence Lancaster in The Vortex; Mrs Allonby in A Woman of No Importance; Lady Elizabeth Mulhammer in The Confidential Clerk (created rôle at Edinburgh Festival, 1953, and appeared in it finally at Paris Festival of Dramatic Art, 1954; made first appearance on Television, in this rôle, 1955); Sophie Faramond in the Gates of Summer. In 1957 created rôle of Aunt Alicia in the film Gigi; Duchess of Berwick in Lady Windermere's Fan, 1966; Mrs Malaprop in The Rivals, 1967; Lady Bracknell in The Importance of Being Earnest, Haymarket, 1968; Mme Desmortes in Ring Round the Moon, Haymarket, 1969; Dear Antoine, Piccadilly, 1971. Films and TV plays in Hollywood, Paris, Rome and Vienna. *Recreation:* reading historical biographies. *Address:* 66/24 John Islip Street, SW1.

JEBB, family name of **Baron Gladwyn.**

JEBB, Dom Anthony Philip, MA; Head Master, Downside School, since 1980; b 14 Aug. 1932; 2nd s of late Reginald Jebb and Eleanor, d of Hilaire Belloc. *Educ:* Downside; Christ's Coll., Cambridge, 1957–60 (MA Classics). Professed at Downside, 1951; priest, 1956; Curate, Midsomer Norton, 1960–62; teaching at Downside, 1960–; House master, 1962–75; Dep. Head Master, 1975–80. Archivist and Annalist, English Benedictine Congregation, 1972–; Mem., EBC Theological Commn, 1969–82 (Chm., 1979–82); Mem. Council, Somerset Records Soc., 1975–; Vice-Pres., SW Amateur Fencing Assoc., 1970–. Chaplain of Magistral Obedience, British Assoc., Sovereign Mil. Order of Malta, 1978–. *Publications:* Missale de Lesnes, 1964; Religious Education, 1968; Widowed, 1973, 2nd edn 1976; contrib. Consider Your Call, 1978, 2nd edn 1979; A Touch of God, 1982; contribs to Downside Review, The Way, The Sword. *Recreations:* fencing, archaeology, astronomy, canoeing. *Address:* Downside School, Stratton-on-the-Fosse, Bath BA3 4RJ. *T:* Stratton-on-the-Fosse 232206.

JEDDERE-FISHER, Arthur; Solicitor, Customs and Excise, since 1982; b 15 July 1924; s of late Major Harry and Sarah Jeddere-Fisher; m 1947, Marcia Vincent, d of Kenneth Clarence Smith; three s one d. *Educ:* Harrow Sch.; Christ Church, Oxford (MA). Served War of 1939–45, Air Engineer, Royal Navy, 1942–46 (despatches). Called to Bar, Inner Temple, 1949; Magistrate, Senior Magistrate and Chairman Land Tribunal, Fiji, 1953–69; joined Solicitor's Office, HM Customs and Excise, 1970, Principal Asst Solicitor, 1977–82. *Recreations:* the collection and use of historic machinery, cricket, bird photography. *Address:* Apsley Cottage, Kingston Blount, Oxford. *T:* Kingston Blount 51300. *Clubs:* MCC, Vintage Sports Car.

JEELOF, Gerrit, CBE (Hon.) 1981; Director, Philips Lamps, Eindhoven, since 1981; b 13 May 1927; m 1951, Jantje Aleida Plinsinga; two d. *Educ:* Dutch Trng Inst. for Foreign Trade, Nijenrode. Philips Industries: Eindhoven, Holland, 1950–53; Spain and S America, 1953–65; Eindhoven, Holland, 1965–70; Varese, Italy, 1970–76; Chm. and Man. Dir, Philips Industries UK, 1976–80. Commendatore nel Ordine al Merito della Repubblica Italiana, 1974. *Recreations:* sailing and golf. *Address:* NV Philips' Gloeilampenfabrieken, Eindhoven, Netherlands. *T:* Eindhoven 79 11 11. *Clubs:* Buck's, Royal Thames Yacht, Royal Ocean Racing, American; Royal Yacht Squadron.

JEEPS, Richard Eric Gautrey, CBE 1977; fruit farmer; Chairman, Sports Council, since 1978; b 25 Nov. 1931; s of Francis Herbert and Mildred Mary Jeeps; m 1954, Jean Margaret Levitt; three d. *Educ:* Bedford Modern Sch. Rugby career: Cambridge City, 1948–49; Northampton, 1949–62 and 1964; Eastern Counties, 1950–62; England, 1956–62 (24 caps); Barbarians, 1958–62; British Lions: SA, 1955; NZ, 1959; SA 1962; 13 Tests. Rugby Football Union: Mem. Cttee, 1962–; Pres., 1976–77. *Recreations:* Rugby Union football, sport. *Address:* 1 High Street, Willingham, Cambridge CB4 5ES. *T:* Willingham (Cambs) 60450. *Club:* Lord's Taverners.

JEEWOOLALL, Sir Ramesh, Kt 1979; Member, Mauritius Parliament, since 1976; Speaker, House of Assembly, Mauritius, since 1979; b 20 Dec. 1940; s of Shivprasad Jeewoolall; m 1971, Usweenee (née Reetoo); two s. *Educ:* in Mauritius; Inns of Court Sch. of Law. Called to the Bar, Middle Temple, 1968; practising at the Bar, 1969–71; Magistrate, 1971–72; practising at the Bar and Chm., Mauritius Tea Develt Authority, 1972–76; Dep. Speaker, Mauritius Parlt, 1977–79. *Recreations:* reading, conversation, chess. *Address:* Q1, Farquhar Avenue, Quatre Bornes, Mauritius. *T:* 4-5918.

JEFFARES, Prof. Alexander Norman, (Derry Jeffares); MA, PhD, DPhil; Docteur de l'Université (hc) Lille, 1977; FRSA 1963; FRSL 1965; FRSE 1981; Professor of English Studies, Stirling University, since 1974; b 11 Aug. 1920; s of late C. Norman Jeffares, Dublin; m 1947, Jeanne Agnès, d of late E. Calembert, Brussels; one d. *Educ:* The High Sch., Dublin; Trinity Coll., Dublin (Hon. Fellow, 1978); Oriel Coll., Oxford. Lectr in Classics, Univ. of Dublin 1943–44; Lector in English, Univ. of Groningen, 1946–48; Lectr in English, Univ. of Edinburgh, 1949–51; Jury Prof. of English Language and Literature, Univ. of Adelaide, 1951–56; Prof. of English Lit., Leeds Univ., 1957–74. Sec., Australian Humanities Res. Council, 1954–57; Corresp. Mem. for Great Britain and Ireland, 1958–70; Hon. Fellow, Aust. Acad. of the Humanities, 1970–. Vice-Chm., Scottish Arts Council, 1980– (Chm., Literature Cttee, 1977–); Mem., Arts Council of GB, 1980–. Vice-Pres., Film and Television Council of S Aust., 1951–56; Chairman: Assoc. for Commonwealth Literature and Language Studies, 1966–68, Hon. Fellow, 1971; Internat. Assoc. for Study of Anglo-Irish Literature, 1968–70, Co-Chm., 1971–73, Hon. Life Pres., 1973–; Dir, Yeats Internat. Summer Sch., Sligo, 1969–71. Editor, A Review of English Literature, 1960–67; General Editor: Writers and Critics, 1960–73; New Oxford English Series, 1963–; Joint Editor, Biography and Criticism, 1963–73; Literary Editor, Fountainwell Drama Texts, 1968–75; Editor, Ariel, A Review of Internat. English Literature, 1970–72. *Publications:* Trinity College, Dublin: drawings and descriptions, 1944; W. B. Yeats: man and poet, 1949, rev. edn 1962; Seven Centuries of Poetry, 1955, rev. edn 1960; (with M. Bryn Davies) The Scientific Background, 1958; The Poetry of W. B. Yeats, 1961; (ed with G. F. Cross) In Excited Reverie: a centenary tribute to W. B. Yeats, 1965; Fair Liberty was All His Cry: a tercentenary tribute to Jonathan Swift 1667–1743, 1967; A Commentary on the Collected Poems of W. B. Yeats, 1968; (ed) Restoration Comedy, 4 vols, 1974; (with A. S. Knowland) A Commentary on the Collected Plays of W. B. Yeats, 1975; (ed) Yeats: the critical heritage, 1977; A History of Anglo-Irish Literature, 1982; also: edns of works by

Congreve, Farquhar, Goldsmith, Sheridan, Cowper, Maria Edgeworth, Disraeli, Whitman and Yeats; edns of criticisms of Swift, Scott and Yeats; various monographs on Swift, Goldsmith, George Moore, Yeats, Oliver St John Gogarty; contribs to learned jls. *Recreations:* drawing, motoring. *Address:* Department of English Studies, University of Stirling, Stirling. *Clubs:* Athenæum, Royal Commonwealth Society.

JEFFCOATE, Sir (Thomas) Norman (Arthur), Kt 1970; Professor of Obstetrics and Gynæcology, University of Liverpool, 1945–72, now Emeritus; Hon. Consultant Obstetrical and Gynæcological Surgeon, Liverpool Area Health Authority (Teaching); b 25 March 1907; s of Arthur Jeffcoate and Mary Ann Oakey; m 1937, Josephine Lindsay (d 1981); four s. *Educ:* King Edward VI Sch., Nuneaton; University of Liverpool. MB, ChB (Liverpool) 1st class Hons 1929; MD (Liverpool) 1932; FRCS (Edinburgh) 1932; MRCOG 1932; FRCOG 1939 (Vice-Pres., 1967–69; Pres. 1969–72). Hon. Asst Surgeon: Liverpool Maternity Hosp., 1932–45; Women's Hosp., Liverpool, 1935–45. Lectures: Blair-Bell Memorial, Royal College of Obst. and Gynaec. 1938; Sir Arcot Mudalier, Univ. of Madras, 1955; Margaret Orford, S African Coll. of Physicians, Surgeons and Gynaecologists, 1969; J. Y. Simpson, RCSE, 1976. Joseph Price Orator, Amer. Assoc. of Obstetricians and Gynaecologists, 1966. Sims Black Travelling Commonwealth Prof., 1958; Visiting Professor: New York State Univ., 1955; University of Qld, 1964; Univ. of Melbourne, 1964; Univ. of Texas, 1965; Hon. Visiting Obstetrician and Gynæcologist, Royal Prince Alfred Hospital, Sydney, Australia, 1955–. Chairman, Med. Advisory Council of Liverpool Regional Hosp. Bd, 1962–69; President: N of England Obst. and Gynaec. Soc., 1960; Sect. of Obst. and Gynaec., RSM, 1965–66; Liverpool Med. Inst. 1966–67; Vice-Pres. Family Planning Assoc., 1962–79; Member: Gen. Med. Council, 1951–61; Clinical Research Bd, MRC, 1961–65; Clinical Trials Sub-Cttee of Safety of Drugs Cttee, 1963–69; Bd of Science and Educn, BMA, 1968–69; Standing Maternity and Midwifery Adv. Cttee, Dept of Health and Social Security (formerly Min. of Health), 1963–72 (Chm., 1970–72); Standing Med. Adv. Cttee and Central Health Services Council, Dept of Health and Social Security, 1969–72; Jt Sub-Cttee on Prevention of Haemolytic Disease of the Newborn, 1968–72 (Chm., 1969–72). Hon. FCOG(SA), 1972; Hon. FACOG, 1972; Hon. FRCS (C), 1973; Hon. Member: Amer. Gynec. Club; Amer. Gynec. Soc.; Amer. Assoc. Obst. and Gynec.; Central Assoc. Obst. and Gynec.; Assoc. Surg., Ceylon; Obst. and Gynaec. Socs of: Canada, Finland, Honolulu, Malta, Montreal, Panama, S Africa, Uruguay, Venezuela. Hon. LLD, TCD, 1971. Eardley Holland Gold Medal, RCOG, 1975; Simpson Gold Medal, RCSE, 1976. *Publications:* Principles of Gynæcology, 1957 (4th edn, 1975); communications to medical journals. *Address:* 6 Riversdale Road, Liverpool L19 3QW. *T:* 051-427 1448.

JEFFERIES, David George; Chairman, London Electricity Board, since 1981; b 26 Dec. 1933; s of Rose and George Jefferies; m 1959, Jeanette Ann Hanson. *Educ:* SE Coll. of Technology. CEng, FIEE, CBIM. Southern Electricity Board: Area Manager, Portsmouth, 1967–72; Staff Coll., Henley, 1970; Chief Engr, 1972–74; Dir, NW Region, CEGB, 1974–77; Dir Personnel, CEGB, 1977–81. Mem., Bd of Governors, London Business Sch., 1980–. *Recreations:* golf, gardening. *Address:* Wychenwood, Gorse Hill Lane, Virginia Water, Surrey. *T:* Wentworth 3623.

JEFFERIES, Sheelagh; Controller (Home), Central Office of Information, since 1978; b 25 Aug. 1926; d of late Norman and Vera Jefferies. *Educ:* Harrogate Grammar Sch.; Girton Coll., Cambridge (MA); Smith Coll., Northampton, Mass, USA (MA). MIPR. Archivist, RIIA, 1947–50, 1951–52; COI, 1953–60; Office of Chancellor of Duchy of Lancaster, 1960–61; Press Officer, Prime Minister's Office, 1961–67; Principal Inf. Officer, Privy Council Office, 1967–69; Chief Press Officer, Min. of Housing and Local Govt, 1969–71; Head of Parly Liaison Unit and later Head of News, DoE, 1971–74; Chief Inf. Officer, Dept of Prices and Consumer Protection, 1974–77; Dir, Overseas Press and Radio, COI, 1977–78. *Recreations:* reading, conversation. *Address:* 6 Eversfield Road, Richmond, Surrey TW9 2AP. *T:* 01-940 9229.

JEFFERIES, Stephen; Senior Principal Dancer, Royal Ballet, since 1979 (Principal Dancer, 1973–76 and 1977–79); b 24 June 1951; s of George and Barbara Jefferies; m 1972, Rashna Homji. *Educ:* Turves Green Sch., Birmingham; Royal Ballet Sch. ARAD (Advanced Hons). Joined Sadler's Wells Royal Ballet, 1969; created 10 leading roles whilst at Sadler's Wells; joined National Ballet of Canada as Principal Dancer, 1976; created role of Morris, in Washington Square, 1977; returned to Royal Ballet at Covent Garden, 1977; major roles include: Prince in Sleeping Beauty, Swan Lake and Giselle, Prince Rudolf in Mayerling, Petruchio in Taming of the Shrew, Romeo and Mercutio in Romeo and Juliet, Lescaut in Manon; roles created: Yukinojo (mime role), in world première of Minoru Miki's opera An Actor's Revenge, 1979; male lead in Bolero, Japan, 1980 (choreographed by Kenneth Okamoto); Antonio in The Duenna, S Africa (choreographed by Ashley Killar), 1980; lead, in Dances of Albion (choreographed by Glen Tetley), 1980; Esenin in Kenneth Macmillan's ballet, Isadora, Covent Garden, 1981; lead, in L'Invitation au Voyage, Covent Garden, 1982. Choreographed ballets: Bits and Pieces, in Canada, 1977; Mes Souvenirs, in London, 1978. Dances in Europe, USA, S America and Far East. Organiser of charity galas, 1982–. *Recreations:* golf, football, sleeping, gardening, swimming and various other sports. *Address:* c/o Royal Ballet, Royal Opera House, Covent Garden, WC2.

JEFFERS, John Norman Richard, FIS, FIBiol, FIFor; Director, Institute of Terrestrial Ecology, Natural Environment Research Council, since 1976; *b* 10 Sept. 1926; *s* of late Lt-Col John Harold Jeffers, OBE, and Emily Matilda Alice (*née* Robinson); *m* 1951, Edna May (*née* Parratt); one *d. Educ:* Portsmouth Grammar Sch.; Forestry Commission Forester Trng Sch., 1944-46. Forester in Forestry Commn Research Br., 1946-55; joined Min. of Agriculture, 1955, as Asst Statistician, after succeeding in limited competition to Statistician Class; rejoined Forestry Commn as Head of Statistics Section of Forestry Commn Research Br., 1956; Dir, Nature Conservancy's Merlewood Research Station, 1968; Dep. Dir, Inst. of Terrestrial Ecology, 1973. *Publications:* Experimental Design and Analysis in Forest Research, 1959; Mathematical Models in Ecology, 1972; Introduction to Systems Analysis: with ecological applications, 1978; Modelling, 1982; numerous papers in stat., forestry and ecolog. jls. *Recreations:* military history and wargaming, amateur dramatics. *Address:* Ellerhow, Lindale, Grange-over-Sands, Cumbria LA11 6NA. *T:* Grange-over-Sands 3731. *Club:* Athenæum.

JEFFERSON, Bryan; *see* Jefferson, J. B.

JEFFERSON, Sir George Rowland, Kt 1981; CBE 1969; Hon. BSc (London); FEng, FRAeS; FRSA; FBIM; FCGI; Chairman, British Telecommunications, since 1980; *b* 26 March 1921; *s* of Harold Jefferson and Eva Elizabeth Ellen; *m* 1943, Irene Watson-Browne; three *s. Educ:* Grammar Sch., Dartford, Kent. Engrg Apprentice, Royal Ordnance Factory, Woolwich, 1937-42; commnd RAOC, 1942; transf. REME, 1942; served 1942-45, Anti-Aircraft Comd on heavy anti-aircraft power control systems and later Armament Design Dept, Fort Halstead, on anti-aircraft gun mounting development; subseq. Mem. Min. of Supply staff, Fort Halstead, until 1952; joined Guided Weapons Div., English Electric Co. Ltd, 1952; Chief Research Engr, 1953; Dep. Chief Engr, 1958; Dir, English Electric Aviation Ltd, 1961 (on formation of co.); British Aircraft Corporation: Dir and Chief Exec., BAC (Guided Weapons) Ltd, 1963 (on formation of Corp.), Dep. Man. Dir, 1964, Mem. Board, 1965-77, Man. Dir, 1966-68, Chm. and Man. Dir, 1968-77; a Dir, British Aerospace, and Chm. and Chief Exec., Dynamics Gp, British Aerospace, 1977-80 (Mem., Organizing Cttee, 1976-77); Chm., Stevenage/Bristol and Hatfield/Lostock Divs, Dynamics Gp, 1978-80; Chm., BAC (Anti-Tank), 1968-78; Director: British Aerospace (Australia) Ltd, 1968-80; British Scandinavian Aviation AB, 1968-80; Hawker Siddeley Dynamics, 1977-80; Engineering Sciences Data Unit Ltd, 1975-80; a Dep. Chm., PO, 1980-81. Member: NEB, 1979-80; NEDC, 1981-; NICG, 1980-; Member Council: SBAC, 1965-80; Electronic Engineering Assoc., 1968-72; RAeS, 1977-79 (Vice-Pres., 1979). Hon. FIMechE.

JEFFERSON, (John) Bryan; Senior Partner, Jefferson Sheard and Partners, since 1957; President, Royal Institute of British Architects, 1979-June 1981; *b* 26 April 1928; *s* of John Jefferson and Marjorie Jefferson (*née* Oxley); *m* 1954, Alison Gray (marr. diss. 1965); three *s. Educ:* Lady Manners Sch., Bakewell; Sheffield Univ. DipArch 1954. ARIBA 1954; Chm., RIBA Yorkshire Region, 1974-75. Morrison and Partners, Derby, 1955-57; established practice in Sheffield and London with Gerald F. Sheard, 1957. President: Sheffield Soc. of Architects, 1973-74; Concrete Soc., 1977-78. *Publications:* broadcasts; articles in lay and professional jls. *Recreations:* music, sailing offshore, observing social change. *Address:* Fern Hill, Hollow Meadows, near Sheffield S6 6GH. *T:* Sheffield 302737; 70 Wimpole Street, W1. *Clubs:* Savile; Royal Western Yacht.

JEFFERSON, Sir Mervyn Stewart D.; *see* Dunnington-Jefferson.

JEFFERY, George Henry Padget, CMG 1965; FASA; Auditor General for South Australia, 1959-72; Chairman, Board of Trustees, Savings Bank of South Australia, 1972-76 (Trustee, 1965-76); *b* 6 June 1907; *s* of late George Frederick Jeffery and late Adelaide Jeffery (*née* Padget), Victor Harbour, S Aust.; *m* 1934, Jean Loudon Watt, *d* of late Thomas Watt, Adelaide; two *s. Educ:* Adelaide High Sch.; Victor Harbour High Sch.; University of Adelaide. Associate, University of Adelaide, 1933; Auditor, SA Public Service, 1936-40, Chief Inspector, 1940-51; Sec., Public Buildings Dept, 1951-53; Chief Executive, Radium Hill Uranium Project, 1953-59; Mem., SA Public Service Board, 1956-59. Pres., SA Div., Aust. Soc. of Accountants, 1965-67. Chm., Royal Commission of Enquiry into Grape Growing Industry, 1965. Member: Parly. Salaries Tribunal, 1966-79; Royal Commn on State Transport Services, 1966-67; Cttee of Inquiry into S Australian Racing Industry, 1974-75. Dep. Chm., S Australian Egg Bd, 1973-79. Mem., Bd of Management, Queen Victoria Hosp., 1972-76. FASA 1958. *Recreations:* bowls, cricket. *Address:* 49 Anglesey Avenue, St Georges, South Australia 5064, Australia. *T:* 79-2929. *Clubs:* Commonwealth, SA Cricket Association, Glenunga Bowling (Adelaide).

JEFFERY, Lilian Hamilton, FBA 1965; FSA 1956; Fellow and Tutor in Ancient History, Lady Margaret Hall, Oxford, 1952-80, retired, now Honorary Fellow; *b* 5 Jan. 1915; 3rd *d* of late Thomas Theophilus Jeffery, MA Cantab, and Lilian Mary (*née* Hamilton). *Educ:* Cheltenham Ladies' Coll.; Newnham Coll., Cambridge. BA (Class. Tripos) 1936; MA 1941; Dipl. in Class. Archæology, 1937; DPhil (Oxon) 1951. Mem. British Sch. of Archæology, Athens, 1937-; Mem. Soc. for Promotion of Hellenic Studies, 1937-. Nurse in Military Hosp., 1940-41; WAAF (Intelligence), 1941-45. First Katherine McBride Vis. Prof., Bryn Mawr Coll., USA, 1971-72. Ed. Annual of British School at Athens, 1955-61. *Publications:* (collab.) Dedications from the Athenian Akropolis, 1948; The Local Scripts of Archaic Greece, 1961; (contrib.) A Companion to Homer, 1962; (contrib.) Perachora ii, 1964; Archaic Greece, 1976; articles in Jl of Hellenic Studies, Annual of Brit. Sch. at Athens, Hesperia, Amer. Jl of Philology, Historia, Philologus, etc. *Recreation:* drawing. *Address:* c/o Lady Margaret Hall, Oxford.

JEFFERY, Ven. Robert Martin Colquhoun; Archdeacon of Salop, since 1980; *b* 30 April 1935; *s* of Norman Clare Jeffery and Gwenyth Isabel Jeffery; *m* 1968, Ruth Margaret Tinling; three *s* one *d. Educ:* St Paul's School; King's Coll., London (BD, AKC). Assistant Curate: St Aidan, Grangetown, 1959-61; St Mary, Barnes, 1961-63; Asst Sec., Missionary and Ecumenical Council of Church Assembly, 1964-68; Sec., Dept of Mission and Unity, BCC, 1968-71; Vicar, St Andrew, Headington, Oxford, 1971-78; RD of Cowley, 1973-78; Lichfield Diocesan Missioner, 1978-79. *Publications:* (with D. M. Paton) Christian Unity and the Anglican Communion, 1965, 3rd edn 1968; (with T. S. Garret) Unity in Nigeria, 1964; (ed) Lambeth Conference 1968 Preparatory Information; Areas of Ecumenical Experiment, 1968; Ecumenical Experiments: A Handbook, 1971; Case Studies in Unity, 1972. *Recreations:* local history, cooking. *Address:* Tong Vicarage, Tong, Shifnal, Salop TF11 8PW. *T:* Albrighton 2622.

JEFFORD, Barbara Mary, OBE 1965; Actress; *b* Plymstock, Devon, 26 July 1930; *d* of late Percival Francis Jefford and Elizabeth Mary Ellen (*née* Laity); *m* 1953, Terence Longdon (marr. diss., 1961); *m* 1967, John Arnold Turner. *Educ:* Weirfield Sch., Taunton, Som. Studied for stage, Bristol and Royal Academy of Dramatic Art (Bancroft Gold Medal). *Stratford-on-Avon:* (1950-54) Isabella in Measure for Measure; Desdemona in Othello; Rosalind in As You Like It; Katharina in The Taming of the Shrew; toured NZ with NZ Players' Company in The Lady's Not for Burning, 1954-55; Andromache in Tiger at the Gates, London and USA, 1955 and 1956; *Old Vic Company:* (1956-62) Imogen in Cymbeline; Beatrice in Much Ado About Nothing; Portia in The Merchant of Venice; Queen Margaret in Henry VI; Ophelia in Hamlet; Lady Macbeth; Beatrice in The Cenci; Gwendolen Fairfax in The Importance of Being Earnest; Saint Joan; Lavinia in Mourning Becomes Electra; *for Prospect, at Old Vic:* (1977-79) Gertrude in Hamlet; Cleopatra in All for Love; Cleopatra in Antony and Cleopatra; Nurse in Romeo and Juliet; Anna in The Government Inspector; RSC Nat. Tour, 1980, Mistress Quickly in Henry IV pts 1 and 2. *Other London stage appearances include:* Lina in Misalliance, Royal Court and Criterion, 1963; step-daughter in Six Characters in Search of an Author, Mayfair, 1963; Nan in Ride a Cock Horse, Piccadilly, 1965; Patsy Newquist in Little Murders, Aldwych, 1967; Mother Vauzou in Mistress of Novices, Piccadilly, 1973; Gertrude in Hamlet and Zabina in Tamburlaine the Great, Nat. Theatre, 1976; Filumena, Lyric, 1979; Has appeared regularly since 1962 at Oxford Playhouse, Nottingham Playhouse, and Bristol Old Vic, at festivals in Aldeburgh, Bath, Chichester and Edinburgh; has toured extensively in UK, Europe, USA, Near East, Far East, Africa and Australia. *Films:* Ulysses, 1967; A Midsummer Night's Dream, 1967; The Shoes of the Fisherman, 1968; To Love a Vampire, 1970; Hitler: the last ten days, 1973. Has appeared in numerous television and radio plays; Canterbury Tales, TV serial, 1969. Silver Jubilee Medal, 1977. *Recreations:* music, swimming, gardening. *Address:* c/o Fraser and Dunlop Ltd, 91 Regent Street, W1R 8RU.

JEFFREYS, family name of **Baron Jeffreys.**

JEFFREYS, 2nd Baron, *cr* 1952, of Burkham; **Mark George Christopher Jeffreys;** Major, Grenadier Guards, retired; *b* 2 Feb. 1932; *er s* of Capt. Christopher John Darell Jeffreys, MVO, Grenadier Guards (*o s* of 1st Baron; killed in action, 1940) and of Lady Rosemary Beatrice Agar, *y d* of 4th Earl of Normanton; *S* grandfather, 1960; *m* 1st, 1956, Sarah Annabelle Mary (marr. diss., 1967), *o d* of Major Henry Claude Lyon Garnett; two *s* two *d*; 2nd, 1967, Anne Louise, *d* of Sir Shirley Worthington-Evans, 2nd Bt, and of Mrs Joan Parry; one *d*; 3rd, 1981, Suzanne, *d* of James Stead, Goudhurst, Kent. *Educ:* Eton; RMA, Sandhurst. *Heir:* s Hon. Christopher Henry Mark Jeffreys, *b* 22 May 1957. *Address:* Saddlewood Manor, Leighterton, Tetbury, Glos. *Club:* White's.

JEFFREYS, Anthony Henry, CB 1961; *b* 13 Aug. 1896; *yr s* of late Major-Gen. H. B. Jeffreys, CB, CMG; *m* 1922, Dorothy Bertha, *d* of late Lieut-Col Edward Tufnell. *Educ:* Eton. Served War of 1914-18 (despatches; wounded); 2nd Lieut RFA, 1915; Lieut 'D' Battery RHA, 1917-19; Staff Captain, GHQ, France, and War Office, 1939-41. Entered Parliament Office, House of Lords, 1919; called to the Bar Inner Temple, 1924. Examiner of Petitions for Private Bills, 1941; Chief Clerk of Cttees and Private Bills and Taxing Officer, 1945; Reading Clerk, House of Lords, 1953; Clerk Asst of the Parliaments, 1959-61, retd. Chm., City of Westminster Boy Scouts' Assoc., 1953-60. *Address:* Doom Bar House, Trebetherick, Wadebridge, Cornwall PL27 6SA. *T:* Trebetherick 3380. *Club:* Lansdowne.

JEFFREYS, David Alfred, QC 1981; a Recorder of the Crown Court, since 1979; *b* 1 July 1934; *s* of Coleman and Ruby Jeffreys; *m* 1964, Mary Ann Elizabeth Long; one *s* one *d. Educ:* Harrow; Trinity Coll., Cambridge (BA Hons). Served, Royal Signals, 1952-54; City, 1958. Called to the Bar, Gray's Inn, 1958; Junior Prosecuting Counsel to the Crown: Inner London Crown Court, 1974; Central Criminal Court, 1975; Sen. Prosecuting Counsel to the Crown, CCC, 1979-81. Member, Bar Council and Senate of the Inns of Court and Bar, 1977-80. *Address:* (chambers) 3 King's Bench Walk, Temple, EC4.

JEFFREYS, Sir Harold, Kt 1953; MA Cambridge; DSc Durham; FRS 1925; Fellow of St John's College, Cambridge, since 1914; Plumian Professor of Astronomy and Experimental Philosophy, 1946-58; *b* 22 April 1891; *o s* of R. H. and E. M. Jeffreys, Birtley, Durham; *m* 1940, Bertha, *d* of late W. A. Swirles and H. Swirles, Northampton. *Educ:* Armstrong Coll., Newcastle upon Tyne; St John's Coll., Cambridge. University Reader in Geophysics, 1931-46. Mathematical Tripos, 1913; Isaac Newton Student, 1914; Smith's Prize, 1915; Adams Prize, 1927; commended, 1923; Buchan Prize of Royal Meteorological Society, 1929. Gold Medal of Royal Astronomical Society, 1937; Murchison Medal of Geological Soc., 1939; Victoria Medal of RGS, 1942; Royal Medal of Royal Society, 1948; Ch. Lagrange Prize, Acad. Royal Sci., Belg., 1948; Bowie Medal, Amer. Geophys. Union, 1952; Copley Medal, Royal Society, 1960; Vetlesen Prize, 1962; Guy Medal, Royal Statistical Society, 1963; Wollaston Medal, Geological Soc., 1964; Medal of Seismologic. Soc. of Amer., 1979. President: Royal Astronomical Soc., 1955-57; Internat. Seism. Assoc., 1957-60; For. Associate, US Nat. Acad. of Sciences; Accad. dei Lincei, Rome, Acad. Sci. Stockholm, New York Acad. Sci., Amer. Acad. of Arts and Sciences, Acad. Roy. de Belgique; Hon. FRSNZ; Corresp. Member: Amer. Geophys. Union; Geolog. Soc. America; RIA; Hon. Member: Inst. of Mathematics; Amer. Seismological Soc.; RMetS. Hon. LLD Liverpool, 1953; Hon. ScD Dublin, 1956; Hon. DCL Durham, 1960; Hon. DSc, Southern Methodist Univ., Dallas, 1967; Hon. DPhil Uppsala, 1977. *Publications:* The Earth: Its Origin, History, and Physical Constitution, 1924, 1929, 1952, 1959, 1962, 1970, 1976; Operational Methods in Mathematical Physics, 1927, 1931; The Future of the Earth, 1929; Scientific Inference, 1931, 1937, 1957, 1973; Cartesian Tensors, 1931, 1953; Earthquakes and Mountains, 1935, 1950; Theory of Probability, 1939, 1948, 1962, 1967; Methods of Mathematical Physics (with B. Jeffreys), 1946, 1950, 1956, 1962, 1972; Asymptotic Approximations, 1962, 1968; papers on Astronomy, Geophysics, Theory of Scientific Method, and Plant Ecology, republished in Collected Papers of Sir Harold Jeffreys, vols 1-6, 1971-77. *Address:* 160 Huntingdon Road, Cambridge CB3 0LB.

JEFFREYS, Mrs Judith Diana; Assistant Director (Keeper), the Tate Gallery, since 1975; *b* 22 Sept. 1927; *d* of Prof. Philip Cloake, FRCP and Letitia Blanche (*née* MacDonald); *m* 1968, William John Jeffreys. *Educ:* Bedales; Courtauld Inst. of Art, Univ. of London (BA Hons History of Art). Tate Gallery: Asst Keeper, 1951-64; Publications Manager, 1960-65; Dep. Keeper, 1964-75. *Recreations:* renovation of country house, reading, music, gardening. *Address:* The Tate Gallery, Millbank, SW1. *T:* 01-821 1313.

JEFFREYS, Montagu Vaughan Castelman, CBE 1953; MA Oxon; Emeritus Professor, University of Birmingham; *b* 16 Dec. 1900; *s* of late Col F. V. Jeffreys, RE, and late Annie Augusta Jeffreys (*née* Barton); *m* 1941, Joan Sheila, *d* of late Col R. D. Marjoribanks and Sheila Balfour Maclean Marjoribanks (*née* Jack); one *s* one *d. Educ:* Wellington Coll.; Hertford Coll., Oxford. Asst Master, Oundle Sch., 1924-27; Lecturer in Education, Armstrong Coll., Newcastle upon Tyne, 1927-32; Lecturer in Educ., University of London Institute of Education, 1932-39; Prof. of Educn in University of Durham, 1939-46. Prof. of Educn in University of Birmingham and Dir of University of Birmingham Inst. of Educn, 1946-64. Pres. Inst. of Christian Educn, 1958-63. Does occasional broadcasting. *Publications:* Play Production: for Amateurs and Schools (3 edns), 1933 (with R. W. Stopford); History in Schools: The Study of Development, 1939; Education-Christian or Pagan, 1946; Kingdom of This World, 1950; Glaucon: an Inquiry into the Aims of Education (3 edns and 5 reprints), 1950; Beyond Neutrality, 1955; Mystery of Man, 1957; Revolution in Teacher Training, 1961; Personal Values in the Modern World, 1962 (rev. edns 1966, 1968); The Unity of Education, 1966; The Ministry of Teaching, 1967; John Locke, Prophet of Common Sense, 1967; Religion and Morality, 1967; You and Other People, 1969; Education: its nature and purpose, 1972; articles on educational and religious topics in various periodicals. *Address:* Skymers Minor, Minstead, near Lyndhurst, Hants.

JEFFRIES, Graham Montague; *see* Graeme, Bruce.

JEFFRIES, Lionel Charles; actor since 1949, screen writer since 1959, and film director since 1970; *b* 10 June 1926; *s* of Bernard Jeffries and Elsie Jackson; *m* 1951, Eileen Mary Walsh; one *s* two *d. Educ:* Queen Elizabeth's Grammar Sch., Wimborne, Dorset; Royal Academy of Dramatic Art (Dip., Kendal Award, 1947). War of 1939-45: commissioned, Oxf. and Bucks LI, 1945; served in Burma (Burma Star, 1945); Captain, Royal West African Frontier Force. Stage: (West End) *plays:* Carrington VC; The Enchanted; Blood Wedding; Brouhaha; *films:* Colditz Story; Bhowani Junction; Lust for Life; The Baby and The Battleship; Doctor at Large; Law and Disorder; The Nun's Story; Idle on Parade; Two Way Stretch; The Trials of Oscar Wilde; Fanny; The Notorious Landlady (Hollywood); The Wrong Arm of the Law; The First Men in the Moon; The Truth about Spring; Arrivederci Baby; The Spy with a Cold Nose; Camelot (Hollywood); Chitty, Chitty, Bang Bang; Eyewitness; Baxter (also dir.); The Prisoner of Zenda. Wrote and directed: The Railway Children, 1970; The Amazing Mr Blunden, 1972 (Gold Medal for Best Screen Play, Internat. Sci. Fiction and Fantasy Film Fest., Paris, 1974); Wombling Free, 1977; The Water Babies, 1979; *television:* Cream in my Coffee, 1980; Shillingbury Tales, 1981. *Recreations:* swimming, painting. *Address:* c/o ICM, 388/396 Oxford Street, W1N 9HE. *Club:* St James's.

JEFFS, Group Captain (George) James (Horatio), CVO 1960 (MVO 1943); OBE 1950; *b* 27 Jan. 1900; *s* of late James Thomas Jeffs, Chilvers Coton,

Warwicks; *m* 1921, Phyllis Rosina (*née* Bell); two *s* one *d. Educ:* Kedleston Sch., Derby. Served European War: RNAS, 1916-18; RAF, 1918-19. Air Ministry, 1919-23; Croydon Airport, 1923-34; Heston Airport, 1934-37; Air Ministry, 1937-39. Served War of 1939-45, RAF: Fighter, Ferry, and Transport Commands, Group Captain. Ministry of Transport and Civil Aviation, 1945; Airport Commandant, Prestwick, 1950-57; Airport Commandant, London Airport, 1957-60. Legion of Merit, USA, 1944. *Address:* Pixham Firs Cottage, Pixham Lane, Dorking, Surrey. *T:* Dorking 884084. *Club:* Naval and Military.

JEFFS, Julian, QC 1975; Barrister; a Recorder of the Crown Court since 1975; *b* 5 April 1931; *s* of Alfred Wright Jeffs, Wolverhampton, and Janet Honor Irene (*née* Davies); *m* 1966, Deborah, *d* of Peter James Stuart Bevan; three *s. Educ:* Mostyn House Sch.; Wrekin Coll.; Downing Coll., Cambridge (MA). Royal Navy (nat. service), 1949-50. Sherry Shipper's Asst, Spain, 1956. Barrister, Gray's Inn, 1958 (Bencher 1981), Inner Temple, 1971; Midland and Oxford Circuit. Chm., Patent Bar Assoc., 1980-. Editor, Wine and Food, 1965-67; Mem., Cttee of Management, International Wine & Food Soc., 1965-67, 1971-82; Chm., 1970-72, Vice-Pres., 1975-, Circle of Wine Writers. Glenfiddich wine writer awards, 1974 and 1978. General Editor, Faber's Wine Series. *Publications:* Sherry, 1961 (3rd edn 1982); (an editor) Clerk and Lindsell on Torts, 13th edn 1969 (15th edn 1982); The Wines of Europe, 1971; Little Dictionary of Drink, 1973; (jtly) Encyclopedia of United Kingdom and European Patent Law, 1977. *Recreations:* writing, wine, walking, old cars, musical boxes, follies, Iberian things. *Address:* Francis Taylor Building, Temple, EC4. *T:* 01-353 5657, telex 25182; Church Farm House, East Ilsley, Newbury, Berks. *T:* East Ilsley 216. *Clubs:* Beefsteak, Garrick, Reform, Saintsbury.

JEFFS, Kenneth Peter; Assistant Under Secretary of State, Ministry of Defence, since 1979; *b* 30 Jan. 1931; *s* of Albert Jeffs and Theresa Eleanor Jeffs; *m* Iris Woolsey; one *s* two *d. Educ:* Richmond and East Sheen County Sch. jssc. National Service, RAF, 1949-51. Entered CS as Clerical Officer, Bd of Control, 1947; Air Min., 1952; Principal, 1964; JSSC, 1966-67; Private Secretary: to Under-Sec. of State (RN), MoD, 1969-71; to Minister of Defence, 1971-72; Asst Sec., Dir Defence Sales, MoD, 1972-75; Counsellor, Defence Supply, Washington, 1976-79. *Recreation:* rowing. *Address:* Old Studley, Howell Hill Grove, Ewell, Surrey.

JEGER, Baroness *cr* 1979 (Life Peer), of St Pancras in Greater London; **Lena May Jeger;** *b* 19 Nov. 1915; *e d* of Charles and Alice Chivers, Yorkley, Glos; *m* 1948, Dr Santo Wayburn Jeger (*d* 1953); no *c. Educ:* Southgate County Sch., Middx; Birkbeck Coll., London University (BA). Civil Service: Customs and Excise, Ministry of Information, Foreign Office, 1936-49; British Embassy Moscow, 1947; Manchester Guardian London Staff, 1951-54, 1961-; Mem. St Pancras Borough Council, 1945-59; Mem. LCC for Holborn and St Pancras South, 1952-55. Mem., Nat. Exec. Cttee, Labour Party, 1968-80 (Vice-Chm., 1978-79; Chm., 1980). MP (Lab) Holborn and St Pancras South, Nov. 1953-1959 and 1964-74, Camden, Holborn and St Pancras South, 1974-79. Mem., Chairmen's Panel, House of Commons, 1971-79. Chm., Govt Working Party on Sewage Disposal, 1969-70. Member, Consultative Assembly: Council of Europe, 1969-71; WEU, 1969-71; UK delegate, Status of Women Commn, UN, 1967. *Address:* 9 Cumberland Terrace, Regent's Park, NW1.

JEHANGIR, Sir Hirji, 3rd Bt, *cr* 1908; *b* 1 Nov. 1915; 2nd *s* of Sir Cowasjee Jehangir, 2nd Bt, GBE, KCIE, and Hilla, MBE, *d* of late Hormarji Wadia, Lowji Castle, Bombay; *S* father, 1962; *m* 1952, Jinoo, *d* of K. H. Cama; two *s. Educ:* St Xavier Sch., Bombay; Magdalene Coll., Cambridge. Chm., Jehangir Art Gallery, Bombay. *Heir: s* Jehangir, *b* 23 Nov. 1953. *Address:* Readymoney House, 49 L. Jagmohandas Marg, Bombay 36, India; 24 Kensington Court Gardens, W8. *Clubs:* Brooks's; Willingdon (Bombay).

JEJEEBHOY, Sir Jamsetjee, 7th Bt *cr* 1857; *b* 19 April 1913; *s* of Rustamjee J. C. Jamsetjee Jejeebhoy (*d* 1947), and Soonabai Rustomjee Byramjee Jejeebhoy (*d* 1968); *S* cousin, Sir Jamsetjee Jejeebhoy, 6th Bt, 1968, and assumed name of Jamsetjee Jejeebhoy in lieu of Maneckjee Rustomjee Jamsetjee Jejeebhoy; *m* 1943, Shirin Jehangir H. Cama; one *s* one *d. Educ:* St Xavier's Coll., Bombay (BA). Chairman: Sir Jamsetjee Jejeebhoy Charity Funds; Sir J. J. Parsee Benevolent Instn; Wadiaji's Atash-behram; M. F. Cama Athornan Instn; Iran League; Parsi Charity Orgn Soc.; Rustomjee Jamsetjee Jejeebhoy Gujrat Schools Fund; Swabal Stores; Trustee: Sir J. J. Sch. of Arts; Byramjee Jejeebhoy Parsee Charitable Instn; A. H. Wadia Charity Trust; Zoroastrian Bldg Fund; Exec. Cttee, B. D. Petit Parsee Gen. Hosp. *Heir: s* Rustom Jejeebhoy, *b* 16 Nov. 1957. *Address:* (residence) Beaulieu, 95 Worli Sea Face, Bombay 25, India. *T:* 4220955; (office) Maneckjee Wadia Building, Mahatma Gandhi Road, Fort, Bombay 1. *T:* 273843. *Clubs:* Willingdon Sports, Royal Western India, Turf (Bombay).

JELF, Maj.-Gen. Richard William, CBE 1948 (OBE 1944); *b* 16 June 1904; *s* of late Sir Ernest Jelf, King's Remembrancer and Master of the Supreme Court; *m* 1928, Nowell, *d* of Major Sampson-Way, RM, Manor House, Henbury; three *s* one *d. Educ:* Cheltenham Coll.; RMA Woolwich. Commissioned Royal Artillery, 1924; Staff Coll., Quetta, 1936; Dep. Dir Staff Duties, War Office, 1946; Imperial Defence Coll., 1948; CRA 2nd Division, 1949; Dep. Chief, Organization and Training Div., SHAPE, 1951; Comdr 99 AA Bde (TA), 1953; Chief of Staff, Eastern Command, 1956; Maj.-Gen., 1957; Commandant, Police Coll., Bramshill, 1957-63; Dir of Civil

Defence, Southern Region, 1963-68. ADC to the Queen, 1954. Served North-West Frontier, India (Loe Agra), 1934; NW Europe, 1939-45. Hon. Sec., Lyme Regis RNLI. *Recreation:* yachting. *Address:* 1 Library Cottage, Marine Parade, Lyme Regis, Dorset. *T:* 3284.

JELLICOE, family name of **Earl Jellicoe.**

JELLICOE, 2nd Earl, *cr* 1925; **George Patrick John Rushworth Jellicoe,** DSO 1942; MC 1944; PC 1963; Viscount Brocas of Southampton, *cr* 1925; Viscount Jellicoe of Scapa, *cr* 1918; Chairman, Medical Research Council, since 1982; Director: S. G. Warburg & Co., since 1973; Sotheby Holdings, since 1973; Smiths Industries, since 1973; Morgan Crucible, since 1974; Tate & Lyle (Chairman, 1978-82); *b* 4 April 1918; *o s* of Admiral of the Fleet 1st Earl Jellicoe and late Florence Gwendoline, *d* of Sir Charles Cayzer, 1st Bt; godson of King George V; *S* father, 1935; *m* 1st, 1944, Patricia Christine (marr. diss., 1966), *o d* of Jeremiah O'Kane, Vancouver, Canada; two *s* two *d*; 2nd, 1966, Philippa, *o d* of late Philip Dunne; one *s* two *d*. *Educ:* Winchester; Trinity Coll., Cambridge (Exhibnr). Hon. Page to King George VI; served War of 1939-45, Coldstream Guards, 1 SAS Regt (despatches, DSO, MC, Légion d'Honneur, Croix de Guerre, Greek Military Cross). Entered HM Foreign Service, 1947; served as 1st Sec. in Washington, Brussels, Baghdad (Deputy Sec. General Baghdad Pact). Lord-in-Waiting, Jan.-June 1961; Jt Parly. Sec., Min. of Housing and Local Govt, 1961-62; Minister of State, Home Office, 1962-63; First Lord of the Admiralty, 1963-64; Minister of Defence for the Royal Navy, April-Oct. 1964; Deputy Leader of the Opposition, House of Lords, 1967-70; Lord Privy Seal and Minister in Charge, Civil Service Dept, 1970-73; Leader of the House of Lords, 1970-73. Chairman: Brit. Adv. Cttee on Oil Pollution of the Sea, 1968-70; 3rd Int. Conf. on Oil Pollution of the Sea, 1968. Chm., BOTB, 1983- (Mem., 1982-); Pres., London Chamber of Commerce and Industry, 1979-82. Chm., Anglo-Hellenic League, 1978-. A Governor, Centre for Environmental Studies, 1967-70; President: National Federation of Housing Societies, 1965-70; Parly and Scientific Cttee, 1980-; Chm. of Council, KCL, 1977-. FKC 1979. *Recreation:* ski-ing. *Heir: s* Viscount Brocas, *qv. Address:* Tidcombe Manor, Tidcombe, near Marlborough, Wilts. *T:* Oxenwood 225; 97 Onslow Square, SW7. *T:* 01-584 1551. *Club:* Brooks's.
See also Adm. Sir Charles Madden, Bt.

JELLICOE, Ann; *see* Jellicoe, P. A.

JELLICOE, Sir Geoffrey (Alan), Kt 1979; CBE 1961; FRIBA (Dist TP); PPILA; FRTPI; formerly Senior Partner of Jellicoe & Coleridge, Architects; *b* London, 8 Oct. 1900; *s* of George Edward Jellicoe; *m* 1936, Ursula, *d* of late Sir Bernard Pares, KBE, DCL. *Educ:* Cheltenham Coll.; Architectural Association. Bernard Webb Student at British School at Rome; RIBA Neale Bursar. Vis. Fellow, Thames Polytechnic Sch. of Landscape, 1979. Pres., Inst. of Landscape Architects, 1939-49; Hon. Pres. Internat. Fed. of Landscape Architects; Mem. Royal Fine Art Commission, 1954-68; former Trustee of the Tate Gallery; Hon. Corr. Mem. American and Venezuelan Societies of Landscape Architects. Gardens for: Sandringham, Royal Lodge (Windsor); Ditchley Park, RHS central area, Wisley; Chequers; Horsted Place (Sussex); Hartwell House (Aylesbury); Shute House (Wilts); Delta Works (W Bromwich); Hilton Hotel (Stratford-upon-Avon); Dewlish House, Dorchester; The Grange, Winchester; Sutton Place, Surrey; Barnwell Manor, Northants; Town Plans for: Guildford, Wellington (Salop), Hemel Hempstead New Town. Arch. Cons. to N Rhodesian Govt, 1947-52. Housing for Basildon, Scunthorpe, LCC; Plymouth Civic Centre; Chertsey Civic Centre; Cheltenham Sports Centre; GLC Comprehensive Sch., Dalston; Durley Park, Keynsham; Grantham Crematorium and Swimming Pool; comprehensive plans for central area, Gloucester, and for Tollcross, Edinburgh; civic landscape for Modena, Italy; Kennedy Memorial, Runnymede; Plans for Sark, Isles of Scilly, and Bridgefoot, Stratford-upon-Avon. Medal of Amer. Soc. of Landscape Architects, 1981. *Publications:* Italian Gardens of the Renaissance (joint), 1925; (with J. C. Shepherd) Gardens and Design, 1927; Baroque Gardens of Austria, 1931; Studies in Landscape Design, Vol. I 1959, Vol. II 1966, Vol. III 1970; Motopia, 1961; (with Susan Jellicoe) Water, 1971; The Landscape of Man, 1975; The Guelph Lectures on Landscape, 1983. *Address:* 19 Grove Terrace, Highgate, NW5. *T:* 01-485 1823.

JELLICOE, (Patricia) Ann, (Mrs Roger Mayne); playwright and director; Founder, 1979, and Director, Colway Theatre Trust to produce community plays; *b* 15 July 1927; *d* of John Andrea Jellicoe and Frances Jackson Henderson; *m* 1st, 1950, C. E. Knight-Clarke (marr. diss., 1961); 2nd, 1962, Roger Mayne; one *s* one *d*. *Educ:* Polam Hall, Darlington; Queen Margaret's, York; Central Sch. of Speech and Drama (Elsie Fogarty Prize, 1947). Actress, stage manager and dir, London and provinces, 1947-51; privately commnd to study relationship between theatre architecture and theatre practice, 1949; founded and ran Cockpit Theatre Club to experiment with open stage, 1952-54; taught acting and directed plays, Central Sch., 1954-56; Literary Manager, Royal Court Theatre, 1973-75. *Plays:* The Sport of My Mad Mother, Royal Court, 1958; The Knack, Arts (Cambridge), 1961, Royal Court, 1962, New York, 1964, Paris, 1967 (filmed, 1965); Shelley, Royal Court, 1965; The Rising Generation, Royal Court, 1967; The Giveaway, Garrick, 1969; Flora and the Bandits, Dartington Coll. of Arts, 1976; The Bargain, SW Music Theatre, 1979; *community plays:* The Reckoning, Lyme Regis, 1978; The Tide, Seaton, 1980; *plays for children:* You'll Never Guess!, Arts, 1973; Clever Elsie, Smiling John, Silent Peter, Royal Court, 1974; A

Good Thing or a Bad Thing, Royal Court, 1974; *translations include:* Rosmersholm, Royal Court, 1960; The Lady from the Sea, Queen's, 1961; The Seagull (with Ariadne Nicolaeff), Queen's, 1963; Der Freischütz, Sadlers Wells, 1964. *Principal productions include:* The Sport of My Mad Mother (with George Devine), 1958; For Children, 1959; The Knack (with Keith Johnstone), 1962; Skyvers, 1963; Shelley, 1965; A Worthy Guest, 1974; The Poor Man's Friend, 1981. *Publications:* (apart from plays) Some Unconscious Influences in the Theatre, 1967; (with Roger Mayne) Shell Guide to Devon, 1975. *Address:* c/o Margaret Ramsay Ltd, 14a Goodwin's Court, St Martin's Lane, WC2.

JENKIN, Rt. Hon. (Charles) Patrick (Fleeming), PC 1973; MA; MP (C) Redbridge, Wanstead and Woodford, since 1974 (Wanstead and Woodford, 1964-74); Secretary of State for Industry, since 1981; *b* 7 Sept. 1926; *s* of late Mr and Mrs C. O. F. Jenkin; *m* 1952, Alison Monica Graham; two *s* two *d*. *Educ:* Dragon Sch., Oxford; Clifton Coll.; Jesus Coll., Cambridge. MA (Cantab.) 1951. Served with QO Cameron Highlanders, 1945-48; 1st Class Hons in Law, Cambridge, 1951; Harmsworth Scholar, Middle Temple, 1951; called to the Bar, 1952. Distillers Co. Ltd, 1957-70. Member: Hornsey Borough Council, 1960-63; London Coun. of Social Service, 1963-67. An Opposition front bench spokesman on Treasury, Trade and Economics, 1965-70; Jt Vice-Chm., Cons. Parly Trade and Power Cttee, 1966-67; Chm., All Party Parly Group on Chemical Industry, 1968-70; Financial Sec. to the Treasury, 1970-72; Chief Sec. to Treasury, 1972-74; Minister for Energy, 1974; Opposition front bench spokesman: on Energy, 1974-76; on Soc. Services, 1976-79; Sec. of State for Social Services, 1979-81. Director: Tilbury Contracting Gp Ltd, 1974-79; Royal Worcester Ltd, 1975-79; Continental and Industrial Trust Ltd, 1975-79. Governor: Westfield Coll., 1964-70; Clifton Coll., 1969- (Mem. Council, 1972-79). *Recreations:* music, gardening, sailing. *Address:* House of Commons, SW1. *Club:* West Essex Conservative (Wanstead).
See also Rear-Adm. D. C. Jenkin.

JENKIN, Rear Adm. David Conrad; Commandant, National Defence College, since 1981; *b* 25 Oct. 1928; *s* of Mr and Mrs C. O. F. Jenkin; *m* 1958, Jennifer Margaret Nowell; three *s* one *d*. *Educ:* Dragon Sch., Oxford; RNC, Dartmouth. Entered RN at age of 13½, 1942; qual. in Gunnery, 1953; commanded: HMS Palliser, 1961-63; HMS Cambrian, 1964-66; HMS Galatea, 1974-75; HMS Hermes (aircraft carrier), 1978-79; Flag Officer, First Flotilla, 1980-81. *Recreations:* sailing, skiing, do-it-yourself. *Address:* Knapsyard House, West Meon, Hants GU32 1LF. *T:* West Meon 227.
See also Rt Hon. C. P. F. Jenkin.

JENKIN, Rt. Hon. Patrick; *see* Jenkin, Rt Hon. C. P. F.

JENKIN, Sir William Norman Prentice, Kt 1947; CSI 1946; CIE 1931; KPM 1924; *b* 11 Aug. 1899; *m* 1924, Ayliffe Wansborough, *d* of Percy Stevens. *Educ:* Scottish Academy. Commnd RFC, 1917; joined Indian Police Service, 1919; Superintendent, 1927; late Deputy Dir, Intelligence Bureau, Home Department, Government of India; Dir of Intelligence, Malaya, 1950-51. *Address:* Seven, Oaks Road, Tenterden, Kent TN30 6RD. *T:* Tenterden 2760.

JENKINS; *see* Martin-Jenkins.

JENKINS, family name of **Baron Jenkins of Putney.**

JENKINS OF PUTNEY, Baron *cr* 1981 (Life Peer), of Wandsworth in Greater London; **Hugh Gater Jenkins;** *b* 27 July 1908; *s* of Joseph Walter Jenkins and Florence Emily (*née* Gater), Enfield, Middlesex; *m* 1936, Marie (*née* Crosbie), *d* of Sqdn Ldr Ernest Crosbie and Ethel (*née* Hawkins). *Educ:* Enfield Grammar Sch. Personal exploration of employment and unemployment, and political and economic research, 1925-30; Prudential Assce Co., 1930-40. ROC, 1938; RAF: Fighter Comd, 1941; became GCI Controller (Flt Lt); seconded to Govt of Burma, 1945, as Dir Engl. Programmes, Rangoon Radio. Nat. Union of Bank Employees: Greater London Organiser, 1947; Res. and Publicity Officer; Ed., The Bank Officer, 1948; British Actors' Equity Assoc.: Asst Sec., 1950; Asst Gen. Sec., 1957-64. LCC: Mem. for Stoke Newington and Hackney N, 1958-65 (Public Control and Town Planning Cttees). Fabian Soc. lectr and Dir of Summer Schools in early post-war years; Chairman: H Bomb Campaign Cttee, 1954; Campaign for Nuclear Disarmament, 1979-81 (Vice-Pres., 1981-); CND, Aldermaston Marcher, 1957-63; Chm. Victory for Socialism, 1956-60; Mem. Exec. Cttee Greater London Labour Party. Contested (Lab): Enfield W, 1950; Mitcham, 1955; MP (Lab) Wandsworth, Putney, 1964-79; Minister for the Arts, 1974-76. Former Mem., Public Accounts Cttee. Member: Arts Council, 1968-71; Drama Panel, 1972-74; Nat. Theatre Bd, 1976-80; Dep. Chm., Theatres Trust, 1977-79, Dir, 1979-. Chairman: Theatres' Adv. Council; Battersea Arts Centre. *Publications:* Essays in Local Government Enterprise (with others), 1964; The Culture Gap, 1979; Rank and File, 1980; various pamphlets; contrib. to Tribune, New Statesman, The Times, Guardian, etc. Occasional broadcasts and lectures on communications, theatrical and political subjects. *Recreations:* reading, writing, talking, walking, viewing, listening and occasionally thinking. *Address:* 75 Kenilworth Court, Lower Richmond Road, Putney, SW15. *T:* 01-788 0371.

JENKINS, Alan Roberts; Editorial executive, The Times, since 1981; *b* 8 June 1926; *s* of Leslie Roberts Jenkins and Marjorie Kate Cawston; *m* 1st, 1949,

Kathleen Mary Baker (*d* 1969); four *s*; 2nd, 1971, Helen Mary Speed; one *s*. *Educ:* Aylesbury Grammar Sch. Commnd Royal Berks Regt, 1945; Captain, W African Liaison Service, GHQ India; Staff Captain Public Relations, Royal W African Frontier Force, Lagos; DADPR W Africa Comd (Major). Reporter, Reading Mercury and Berkshire Chronicle, 1948; Sub-editor, Daily Herald; Daily Mail: Sub-editor; Night Editor, 1962-69; Northern Editor, 1969-71; Asst Editor, Evening Standard, 1971; Dep. Editor, Sunday People, 1971-72; Asst Editor, Sunday Mirror, 1972-77; Editor, Glasgow Herald, 1978-80. *Recreations:* golf, travel, moving house. *Address:* 44 Belsize Square, Hampstead, NW3.

JENKINS, Arthur Robert, CBE 1972; JP; Chairman: Robert Jenkins & Co. Ltd, Rotherham, since 1958; Robert Jenkins (Holdings) Ltd, since 1968; *b* 20 June 1908; *s* of Edgar Jackson Jenkins and Ethel Mary Bescoby; *m* 1933, Margaret Fitton Jones; one *s* three *d*. *Educ:* Rotherham Grammar Sch.; Sheffield Univ. CEng, FIMechE. Chairman: British Welding Res. Assoc., 1956-68; Tank and Industrial Plant Assoc., 1958-61; of Council, Welding Inst., 1968-71; of Council, Process Plant Assoc., 1971-75 (Vice-Pres., 1975); Pres., Welding Inst., 1951-53 and 1973-75; Vice-Pres., British Mechanical Engrg Confedn, 1972-. Mem. Exec. Bd, BSI, 1974. JP 1948. *Recreation:* gardening. *Address:* Orchard End, Sunderland Street, Tickhill, Doncaster DN11 9QJ.

JENKINS, Prof. Aubrey Dennis; Professor of Polymer Science, University of Sussex, since 1971; *b* 6 Sept. 1927; *s* of Arthur William Jenkins and Mabel Emily (*née* Street); *m* 1950, Audrey Doreen Middleton; two *s* one *d*. *Educ:* Dartford Grammar Sch.; Sir John Cass Technical Inst.; King's Coll., Univ. of London. BSc 1948, PhD 1951; DSc 1961. FRIC 1957. Research Chemist, Courtaulds Ltd, Fundamental Research Laboratory, Maidenhead, 1950-60; Head of Chemistry Research, Gillette Industries Ltd, Reading, 1960-64 (Harris Research Labs, Washington, DC, 1963-64); University of Sussex, 1964-: Sen. Lectr in Chemistry, 1964-68; Reader, 1968-71; Dean, Sch. of Molecular Scis, 1973-78. Visiting Professor: Inst. of Macromolecular Chemistry, Prague, 1978; Univ. of Massachusetts, Amherst, 1979. Member: Internat. Union of Pure and Applied Chemistry, Commn on Macromolecular Nomenclature, 1974- (Chm., 1977-); UNESCO European Expert Cttee on Polymer Chemistry, Industry and Environment, 1977-. Mem., GB/East Europe Centre. Examining chaplain to Bishop of Chichester, 1980-. *Publications:* Kinetics of Vinyl Polymerization by Radical Mechanisms (with C. H. Bamford, W. G. Barb and P. F. Onyon), 1958; Polymer Science, 1972; (with A. Ledwith) Reactivity, Mechanism and Structure in Polymer Chemistry, 1974; Progress in Polymer Science (7 vols), 1967-; papers in learned jls. *Recreations:* music, travel (esp. Czechoslovakia), photography. *Address:* 32 Silverdale Road, Burgess Hill, Sussex RH15 0EF. *T:* Burgess Hill 3332.

JENKINS, Lt-Col Charles Peter de Brisay, MBE 1960; MC 1945; Clerk, Worshipful Company of Goldsmiths, since 1975; *b* 19 Aug. 1925; *s* of late Brig. A. de B. Jenkins and of Mrs Elizabeth Susan Jenkins; *m* 1949, Joan Mary, *e d* of late Col and Mrs C. N. Littleboy, Thirsk; one *s*. *Educ:* Cheltenham Coll.; Selwyn Coll., Cambridge. Commnd RE, 1944; served in Italy, 1944-45; subseq. Hong Kong, Kenya and Germany; jssc 1960; Instructor, Staff Coll., Camberley, 1961-63; Comdr, RE 1st Div., 1965-67; retd 1967. Asst Clerk, Goldsmiths' Co., 1968. Mem., Hallmarking Council, 1977-. Trustee, Nat. Centre for Orchestral Studies, 1980-. *Recreations:* swimming, tennis, gardening. *Address:* Goldsmiths' Hall, Foster Lane, EC2; Oak Hill, South Brent, Devon.

JENKINS, Christopher; *see* Jenkins, J. C.

JENKINS, Clive; *see* Jenkins, D. C.

JENKINS, David, CBE 1977; MA, JP; Librarian, National Library of Wales, 1969-79; *b* 29 May 1912; *s* of late Evan Jenkins and Mary (*née* James), Blaenclydach, Rhondda; *m* 1948, Menna Rhys, *o d* of late Rev. Owen Evans Williams, Penrhyn-coch, Aberystwyth; one *s* one *d*. *Educ:* Ardwyn Grammar Sch., Aberystwyth; UCW, Aberystwyth. BA Hons Welsh Lit. 1936, MA 1948; W. P. Thomas (Rhondda) Schol. 1936; Sir John Williams Research Student, 1937-38. Served War of 1939-45, Army; Major, 1943; NW Europe. National Library of Wales: Asst, Dept MSS, 1939-48; Asst Keeper, Dept of Printed Books, 1949, Keeper, 1957, Sen. Keeper, 1962. Professorial Fellow, UCW Aberystwyth, 1971-79. Gen. Comr of Income Tax, 1968-; Chairman: Mid-Wales HMC, 1969-70; Welsh Books Council, 1974-80 (Vice-Chm. 1971-74); Library Adv. Council (Wales), 1979-; Member: Court of Governors, Univ. of Wales; Ct and Council, UC Aberystwyth; Adv. Council, British Library, 1975-82; BBC Archives Adv. Cttee, 1976-79; Hon. Soc. of Cymmrodorion; Pantyfedwen Trust, 1969-79; Coll. of Librarianship Wales; Governor: Ardwyn Grammar Sch., 1963-72; Penweddig Compreh. Sch., 1973-77. Editor: NLW Jl, 1968-79; Jl Welsh Bibliog. Soc., 1964-79; Ceredigion, Trans Cards Antiq. Soc., 1973-. JP Aberystwyth 1959-82: Chm. Llanbadarn Bench 1965-69; Vice-Chm., Aberystwyth Bench, 1980; Member: Dyfed Magistrates' Courts Cttee, 1975-79; Dyfed-Powys Police Authority, 1977-81. Hon. DLitt Wales, 1979. Sir Ellis Griffith Meml Prize, Univ. of Wales, 1975. *Publications:* Cofiant Thomas Gwynn Jones, 1973 (biog.; Welsh Arts Council Prize, 1974); (ed) Erthyglau ac Ysgrifau Kate Roberts, 1978; articles in NLW Jl, Bull. Bd of Celtic Studies and many other jls; contrib. Dictionary of Welsh Biography. *Recreation:* walking. *Address:* Maesaleg, Penrhyn-coch, Aberystwyth, Dyfed. *T:* Aberystwyth 828 766.

JENKINS, (David) Clive; General Secretary, Association of Scientific, Technical and Managerial Staffs, since 1970 (Joint General Secretary, 1968-70); Member of the General Council of the TUC, since 1974 (Member, Economic Committee, since 1978; Chairman, Education Committee, since 1979); *b* 2 May 1926; *s* of David Samuel Jenkins and Miriam Harris Jenkins (*née* Hughes); *m* 1963, Moira McGregor Hilley; one *s* one *d*. *Educ:* Port Talbot Central Boys' Sch.; Port Talbot County Sch.; Swansea Techn. Coll. (evenings). Started work in metallurgical test house, 1940; furnace shift supervisor, 1942; i/c of laboratory, 1943; tinplate night shift foreman, 1945; Mem., Port Talbot Cooperative Soc. Educn. Cttee, 1945; Branch Sec. and Area Treas., AScW, 1946; Asst Midlands Divisional Officer, ASSET, 1947; Transport Industrial Officer, 1949; Nat. Officer, 1954; Gen. Sec., ASSET, 1961-68. Metrop. Borough Councillor, 1954-60 (Chm. Staff Cttee, St Pancras Borough Coun.); Chm., Nat. Jt Coun. for Civil Air Transport, 1967-68; Member: NRDC, 1974-80; Bullock Cttee on Industrial Democracy, 1975-; Wilson Cttee to Review the Functioning of Financial Institutions, 1977-80; BNOC, 1979-82; BOTB, 1980-; Commn of Inquiry into Labour Party, 1979 (Chm., Finance Panel, 1979); TUC-Labour Party Liaison Cttee, 1980-; Chairman: TUC Educnl Trust, 1979-; Roosevelt Meml Trust, 1979-; Trustee, Nat. Heritage Meml Fund, 1980-. Editor, Trade Union Affairs, 1961-63. Sometime columnist, Tribune, Daily Mirror, Daily Record. *Publications:* Power at the Top, 1959; Power Behind the Screen, 1961; (with J. E. Mortimer) British Trade Unions Today, 1965; (with J. E. Mortimer) The Kind of Laws the Unions Ought to Want, 1968; with B. D. Sherman: Computers and the Unions, 1977; Collective Bargaining: what you always wanted to know about trade unions and never dared ask, 1977; The Collapse of Work, 1979; The Rebellious Salariat: white collar unionism, 1979; The Leisure Shock, 1981; also pamphlets and essays. *Recreations:* bargaining with employers, organising the middle classes; arguing for British withdrawal from the EEC. *Address:* (home) 16 St Marks Crescent, NW1. *T:* 01-485 4509; (office) 79 Camden Road, NW1. *T:* 01-267 4422.
See also T. H. *Jenkins.*

JENKINS, Rev. Prof. David Edward; Professor of Theology, University of Leeds, since 1979; Joint Director, William Temple Foundation, Manchester, since 1979 (Director, 1973-78); *b* 26 Jan. 1925; *er s* of Lionel C. Jenkins and Dora (*née* Page); *m* 1949, Stella Mary Peet; two *s* two *d*. *Educ:* St Dunstan's Coll., Catford; Queen's Coll., Oxford (MA). EC, RA, 1943-45 (Captain). Priest, 1954. Succentor, Birmingham Cath. and Lectr, Queen's Coll., 1953-54; Fellow, Chaplain and Praelector in Theology, Queen's Coll., Oxford, 1954-69; Dir, Humanum Studies, World Council of Churches, Geneva, 1969-73 (Consultant, 1973-75). Exam. Chaplain to Bps of Lichfield, 1956-69, Newcastle, 1957-69, Bristol, 1958-, Wakefield, 1978- and Bradford, 1979-; Canon Theologian, Leicester, 1966-82, Canon Emeritus, 1982-. Bampton Lectr, 1966; Hale Lectr, Seabury-Western, USA, 1970; Moorhouse Lectr, Melbourne, 1972; Cadbury Lectr, Birmingham Univ., 1974; Lindsay Meml Lectr, Keele Univ., 1976; Heslington Lectr, York Univ., 1980; Drummond Lectr, Stirling Univ., 1981. Jt Editor, Theology, 1976-82. *Publications:* Guide to the Debate about God, 1966; The Glory of Man, 1967; Living with Questions, 1969; What is Man?, 1970; The Contradiction of Christianity, 1976; contrib. Man, Fallen and Free, 1969, etc. *Recreations:* music, reading, walking. *Address:* The University, Leeds LS2 9JT. *T:* Leeds 431751; William Temple Foundation, Manchester Business School, Manchester M15 6PB. *T:* 061-273 8228.

JENKINS, David Edward Stewart; Director of the Howard League, since 1982; *b* 9 May 1949; *s* of William Stephen Jenkins and Jean Nicol Downie; *m* 1972, Maggie Lack, *d* of Dr C. H. and Mrs J. D. Lack; two *s* one *d*. *Educ:* Univ. of London Goldsmiths' College (BA(Soc) 1977); LSE. Warden, Ellison Hse Adult Probation Hostel, SE17, 1973-74; Lecturer: (part-time) in Sociology, Brunel Univ., 1980-81; (part-time) in Social Administration, LSE and Goldsmiths' Coll., 1980-81; in Criminology, Univ. of Edinburgh, 1981. *Recreations:* music, swimming, cycling. *Address:* 12 Court Lane, Dulwich, SE21. *T:* 01-693 2494.

JENKINS, Elizabeth, OBE 1981. *Educ:* St Christopher School, Letchworth; Newnham College, Cambridge. *Publications:* The Winters, 1931; Lady Caroline Lamb, a Biography, 1932; Harriet (awarded the Femina Vie Heureuse Prize), 1934; The Phoenix' Nest, 1936; Jane Austen, a Biography, 1938; Robert and Helen, 1944; Young Enthusiasts, 1946; Henry Fielding (The English Novelists Series), 1947; Six Criminal Women, 1949; The Tortoise and the Hare, 1954; Ten Fascinating Women, 1955; Elizabeth the Great (biography), 1958; Elizabeth and Leicester, 1961; Brightness, 1963; Honey, 1968; Dr Gully, 1972; The Mystery of King Arthur, 1975; The Princes in the Tower, 1978. *Address:* 8 Downshire Hill, Hampstead, NW3. *T:* 01-435 4642.

JENKINS, Sir Evan Meredith, GCIE 1947 (KCIE 1944; CIE 1936); KCSI 1945 (CSI 1941); *b* 2 Feb. 1896; *s* of late Sir John Lewis Jenkins, KCSI. *Educ:* Rugby; Balliol Coll., Oxford. Served European War, 1914-19; joined Indian Civil Service, 1920, and served in Punjab; Chief Commissioner, Delhi, 1937; Sec., Dept of Supply, 1940-43; Private Sec to the Viceroy and Sec. to the Governor-General (Personal), 1943-45; Governor of the Punjab, 1946-47. *Address:* 24 Ashley Gardens, SW1. *Club:* Travellers'.
See also Sir Owain *Jenkins.*

JENKINS, Very Rev. Frank Graham; Dean of Monmouth and Vicar of St Woolos, since 1976; *b* 24 Feb. 1923; *s* of Edward and Miriam M. Jenkins; *m* 1950, Ena Doraine Parry; two *s* one *d. Educ:* Cyfarthfa Sec. Sch., Merthyr Tydfil; Port Talbot Sec. Sch.; St David's Coll., Lampeter (BA Hist); Jesus Coll., Oxford (BA Theol., MA); St Michael's Coll., Llandaff. HM Forces, 1942-46. Deacon 1950, priest 1951, Llandaff; Asst Curate, Llangeinor, 1950-53; Minor Canon, Llandaff Cathedral, 1953-60; CF (TA), 1956-61; Vicar of Abertillery, 1960-64; Vicar of Risca, 1964-75; Canon of Monmouth, 1967-76; Vicar of Caerleon, 1975-76. *Address:* The Deanery, Stow Hill, Newport, Gwent NPT 4ED. *T:* Newport 63338.

JENKINS, Garth John; Under Secretary, Ministry of Agriculture, Fisheries and Food, since 1981; *b* 7 Dec. 1933; *s* of John Ernest Jenkins and Amy Elizabeth Jenkins; *m* 1965, Patricia Margaret Lindsay; one *d. Educ:* Birmingham Royal Inst. for the Blind; Royal National College for the Blind; Birmingham Univ. (LLB). Called to Bar, Gray's Inn, 1963. Birmingham Corporation, 1954; South Shields Corporation, 1964; The Land Commission, 1967; MAFF, 1971. *Recreations:* literature, theatre, music, chess; food, drink and conversation. *Address:* 98 Dora Road, Wimbledon, SW19. *T:* 01-947 4598.

JENKINS, Prof. George Charles, MB, BS, PhD; FRCPath; Consultant Haematologist, The London Hospital, since 1965; Hon. Consultant, St Peter's Hospitals, since 1972; Professor of Haematology in the University of London, since 1974; Consultant to the Royal Navy; *b* 2 Aug. 1927; *s* of late John R. Jenkins and Mabel Rebecca (*née* Smith); *m* 1956, Elizabeth, *d* of late Cecil J. Welch, London; one *s* two *d. Educ:* Wyggeston, Leicester; St Bartholomew's Hosp. Med. Coll. MB, BS, PhD; MRCS, LRCP 1951; FRCPath 1975 (MRCPath 1964). House Phys. and Ho. Surg., St Bart's Hosp., 1951-52. Sqdn Ldr, RAF Med. Br., 1952-54. Registrar in Pathology, St Bart's Hosp., 1954-57; MRC Research Fellow, Royal Postgraduate Med. Sch., 1957-60; Sen. Registrar, Haematology, London Hosp., 1960-63; Cons. Haematologist, N Middlesex Hosp., 1963-65. Examiner, Univ. of London, 1971-; Sen. Examiner, RCPath, 1971-. Mem. Council, 1979-, Vice-Pres., 1981-. Mem. subcttee on biologicals, Cttee on Safety of Medicines, 1976-. Member: British Soc. for Haematology (formerly Hon. Sec.), 1962-; Internat. Soc. of Haematology, 1975-; Assoc. of Clinical Pathologists, 1958-; British Acad. of Forensic Scis, 1977-. *Publications:* Advanced Haematology (jtly), 1974; papers and contribs to med. and sci. books and jls. *Recreations:* theatre, music. *Address:* The London Hospital, Whitechapel, E1 1BB. *T:* 01-247 5454. *Club:* Royal Navy Medical.

JENKINS, Gilbert Kenneth; Keeper, Department of Coins and Medals, British Museum, 1965-78; *b* 2 July 1918; *s* of late Kenneth Gordon Jenkins and of Julia Louisa Jenkins (*née* Colbourne); *m* 1939, Cynthia Mary, *d* of late Dr Hugh Scott, FRS; one *s* two *d. Educ:* All Saints Sch., Bloxham; Corpus Christi Coll., Oxford. Open Classical Scholar (Corpus Christi Coll.), 1936; First Class Honour Mods, 1938. War Service in Royal Artillery, 1940-46 (SE Asia, 1944-46). BA, 1946. Asst Keeper, British Museum, 1947; Dep. Keeper, 1956. An Editor of Numismatic Chronicle, 1964-. Mem., German Archaeological Inst., 1967; Corresp. Mem., Amer. Numismatic Soc., 1958; Hon. Mem., Swiss Numismatic Soc., 1979; Hon. FRNS, 1980. Akbar Medal, Numismatic Soc. of India, 1966; Royal Numismatic Soc. Medal, 1975; Archer Huntington Medal, Amer. Numismatic Soc., 1976. *Publications:* Carthaginian Gold and Electrum Coins (with R. B. Lewis), 1963; Coins of Greek Sicily, 1966; Sylloge Nummorum Graecorum (Danish Nat. Museum), part 42, N Africa (ed), 1969, part 43, Spain-Gaul (ed), 1979; The Coinage of Gela, 1970; Ancient Greek Coins, 1972; (with U. Westermark) The Coinage of Kamarina, 1980; articles in numismatic periodicals. *Recreations:* music, cycling. *Address:* 3 Beechwood Avenue, Kew Gardens, Surrey.

JENKINS, Prof. Harold, MA, DLitt; Professor Emeritus, University of Edinburgh; *b* 19 July 1909; *s* of late Henry and Mildred Jenkins, Shenley, Bucks; *m* 1939, Gladys Puddifoot; no *c. Educ:* Wolverton Grammar Sch.; University Coll., London. George Smith Studentship, 1930. Quain Student, University Coll., London, 1930-35; William Noble Fellow, University of Liverpool, 1935-36; Lecturer in English, University of the Witwatersrand, South Africa, 1936-45; Lecturer in English, University Coll., London, 1945-46, then Reader in English, 1946-54; Prof. of English, University of London (Westfield Coll.), 1954-67; Regius Prof. of Rhetoric and English Lit., Edinburgh Univ., 1967-71. Visiting Prof., Duke Univ., USA, 1957-58; Univ. of Oslo, 1974. Jt Gen. Editor, Arden Shakespeare, 1958-82. *Publications:* The Life and Work of Henry Chettle, 1934; Edward Benlowes, 1952; The Structural Problem in Shakespeare's Henry IV, 1956; The Catastrophe in Shakespearean Tragedy, 1968; John Dover Wilson (British Acad. memoir), 1973; (ed) Hamlet (Arden edn), 1982; articles in Modern Language Review, Review of English Studies, The Library, Shakespeare Survey, Studies in Bibliography, etc. *Address:* 22 North Crescent, Finchley, N3 3LL.

JENKINS, Hugh Royston, FRICS; Director General of Investments, National Coal Board, since Dec. 1972; *b* 9 Nov. 1933. *Educ:* Llanelli Grammar Sch.; National Service, Royal Artillery, 1954-56. Valuer, London County Council, 1956-62; Assistant Controller, 1962-68, Managing Director, 1968-72, Coal Industry (Nominees) Ltd. *Recreation:* golf. *Address:* 10 Bouverie Street, EC4. *T:* 01-353 1500.

JENKINS, Dr Ivor, CBE 1970; freelance Consultant, since 1979; Group Director of Research, Delta Metal Co. Ltd, 1973-79; Managing Director, 1973-77, Deputy Chairman, 1977-79, Delta Materials Research Ltd; *b* 25 July 1913; *m* 1941, Carolina Wijnanda James; two *s. Educ:* Gowerton Grammar Sch.; Univ. of Swansea. BSc, MSc, DSc. Bursar, GEC Research Labs, Wembley, 1934; Mem. Scientific Staff, GEC, 1935; Dep. Chief Metallurgist, Whitehead Iron & Steel Co., Newport, Mon, 1944; Head of Metallurgy Dept, 1946, Chief Metallurgist, 1952, GEC, Wembley; Dir of Research, Manganese Bronze Holdings Ltd, and Dir, Manganese Bronze Ltd, 1961-69; Dir of Research, Delta Metal Co., and Dir, Delta Metal (BW) Ltd, 1969-73. Vis. Prof., Univ. of Surrey, 1978-. FEng 1979; FIM 1948 (Pres. 1965-66); Fellow, Amer. Soc. of Metals, 1974; Pres., Inst. of Metals, 1968-69; Mem., Iron and Steel Inst., 1937- (Williams Prize, 1946). Platinum medallist, Metals Soc., 1978. *Publications:* Controlled Atmospheres for the Heat Treatment of Metals, 1946; contribs to learned jls at home and abroad on metallurgical and related subjects. *Recreations:* music, gardening, swimming. *Address:* Drift Cottage, Worthing, Dereham, Norfolk NR20 5HF. *T:* Elmham 601. *Clubs:* Athenæum, Anglo-Belgian.

JENKINS, (James) Christopher; Parliamentary Counsel, since 1978; *b* 20 May 1939; *s* of Percival Si Phillips Jenkins and Dela (*née* Griffiths); *m* 1962, Margaret Elaine Edwards, *yr d* of late Rt Hon. L. John Edwards, PC, OBE, MP and of Mrs D. M. Edwards; two *s* one *d. Educ:* Lewes County Grammar Sch.; Magdalen Coll., Oxford. Solicitor, 1965. Joined Office of Parly Counsel, 1967. *Address:* 36 Whitehall, SW1. *Club:* United Oxford & Cambridge University.

JENKINS, Mrs Jennifer; see Jenkins, Mrs M. J.

JENKINS, John George, CBE 1971; farmer; *b* 26 Aug. 1919; *s* of George John Jenkins, OBE, FRCS and Alice Maud Jenkins, MBE; *m* 1948, Chloe Evelyn (*née* Kenward); one *s* three *d. Educ:* Winchester; Edinburgh University. Farmed in Scotland, 1939-62; farmed in England (Cambs and Lincs), 1957-. Pres., NFU of Scotland, 1960-61; Chm., Agricultural Marketing Development Exec. Cttee, 1967-73. Director: Agricultural Mortgage Corporation Ltd; FMC Ltd; Childerley Estates Ltd; United Oilseeds Ltd, Compère, Anglia Television programme Farming Diary, 1963-80. *Publications:* contrib. Proc. Royal Soc., RSA Jl, etc. *Recreations:* tennis, bridge, wine, music and the arts generally. *Address:* Childerley Hall, Dry Drayton, Cambridge CB3 8BB. *T:* Madingley 210271. *Club:* Farmers'.

JENKINS, Ven. (John) Owen; *b* 13 June 1906; *m* 1939, Gwladys Margaret Clark Jones, *d* of Ven. D. M. Jones, sometime Archdeacon of Carmarthen. *Educ:* St David's Coll., Lampeter; Jesus Coll., Oxford. Deacon 1929, priest 1930; Curate of: Cwmamman, 1929-33; Llanelly, 1933-39; Vicar of Spittal with Trefgarn, 1939-48; TCF, 1943-46; Vicar of Llangadock, 1948-60; Canon of St David's, 1957-62; Rector of Newport, Pembs, 1960-67; Archdeacon of Cardigan, 1962-67; Archdeacon of Carmarthen and Vicar of Llanfihangel Aberbythick, 1967-74. Editor, St David's Dio. Year Book, 1954-63. *Address:* Morfa Gwyn, Aberporth, Cardigan SA43 2EN. *T:* Aberporth 810060.

JENKINS, John Owen, MBE 1978; Senior Teacher, St Mary's Hospital School of Physiotherapy, W2, since 1959; *b* 4 Nov. 1922; *s* of late J. O. Jenkins, JP, and M. E. Jenkins, Great House, Dilwyn, Hereford; *m* 1953, Catherine MacFarlane Baird, MCSP; three *d. Educ:* Worcester College for the Blind; NIB School of Physiotherapy, London. MCSP, TMMG, TET. Chartered Society of Physiotherapy: Mem. Council, 1952- (Chm., Finance and Gen. Purposes Cttee, 1955-); Member: Education Cttee, 1953-71; Executive Cttee, 1955-; Trustee, Members' Benevolent Fund, 1955-. Physiotherapy Representative: Min. of Health Working Party on Statutory Registration, 1954; Council for Professions Supplementary to Medicine, 1961-76; Chm., Physiotherapists' Board, 1962-76. Hon. Director, LAMPS, 1969-; Trustee, Moira Pakenham-Walsh Foundn, 1978. Churchwarden, St James the Great, N20. *Publications:* contribs to Physiotherapy. *Recreations:* chess, rowing. *Address:* Fintray, 8 Ravensdale Avenue, N12 9HS. *T:* 01-445 6072. *Club:* Terenure Country.

JENKINS, John Robin; *b* Cambuslang, Lanarks, 11 Sept. 1912; *s* of late James Jenkins and of Annie Robin; *m* 1937, Mary McIntyre Wyllie; one *s* two *d. Educ:* Hamilton Academy; Glasgow Univ. (MA Hons). *Publications:* (as Robin Jenkins) Happy for the Child, 1953; The Thistle and the Grail, 1954; The Cone-Gatherers, 1955; Guests of War, 1956; The Missionaries, 1957; The Changeling, 1958; Some Kind of Grace, 1960; Dust on the Paw, 1961; The Tiger of Gold, 1962; A Love of Innocence, 1963; The Sardana Dancers, 1964; A Very Scotch Affair, 1968; The Holy Tree, 1969; The Expatriates, 1971; A Toast to the Lord, 1972; A Far Cry from Bowmore, 1973; A Figure of Fun, 1974; A Would-be Saint, 1978; Fergus Lamont, 1979. *Recreations:* travel, golf. *Address:* Fairhaven, Toward, by Dunoon, Argyll, Scotland. *T:* Toward 288.

JENKINS, Mrs (Mary) Jennifer; Chairman, Historic Buildings Council for England, since 1975; *b* 18 Jan. 1921; *d* of late Sir Parker Morris; *m* 1945, Rt Hon. Roy Harris Jenkins, *qv*; two *s* one *d. Educ:* St Mary's Sch., Calne; Girton Coll., Cambridge. Chm., Cambridge Univ. Labour Club. With Hoover Ltd, 1942-43; Min. of Labour, 1943-46; Political and Economic Planning (PEP), 1946-48; part-time extra-mural lectr, 1949-61; part-time teacher, Kingsway Day Coll., 1961-67. Chm., Consumers' Assoc., 1965-76; Member: Exec. Bd, British Standards Instn, 1970-73; Design Council, 1971-

74; Cttee of Management, Courtauld Inst., 1981–; Ancient Monuments Bd, 1982–; Sec., Ancient Monuments Soc., 1972-75. Chm., N Kensington Amenity Trust, 1974-77. Trustee, Wallace Collection, 1977–. Dir, J. Sainsbury Ltd, 1981–. JP London Juvenile Courts, 1964-74. Hon. FRIBA, Hon. RICS. *Address:* 2 Kensington Park Gardens, W11; St Amand's House, East Hendred, Oxon.

JENKINS, Michael Romilly Heald; HM Diplomatic Service; Deputy Secretary General, Commission of the European Communities, since 1981; *b* 9 Jan. 1936; *s* of Prof. Romilly Jenkins and Celine Juliette Haeglar; *m* 1968, Maxine Louise Hodson; one *s* one *d*. *Educ:* privately; King's Coll., Cambridge (Exhibr, BA). Entered Foreign (subseq. Diplomatic) Service, 1959; served in Paris, Moscow and Bonn; Deputy Chef de Cabinet, 1973-75, Chef de Cabinet, 1975-76, to Rt Hon. George Thomson, EEC; Principal Advr to Mr Roy Jenkins, Pres. EEC, Jan.-Aug. 1977; Head of European Integration Dept (External), FCO, 1977-79; Hd of Central Adv. Gp, EEC, 1979-81. *Publications:* Arakcheev, Grand Vizier of the Russian Empire, 1969; contrib. History Today. *Address:* 200 rue de la Loi, 1049 Brussels, Belgium. *Club:* MCC.

JENKINS, Sir Owain (Trevor), Kt 1958; *b* 1907; 5th *s* of late Sir John Lewis Jenkins, KCSI, ICS; *m* 1940, Sybil Léonie, *y d* of late Maj.-Gen. Lionel Herbert, CB, CVO. *Educ:* Charterhouse; Balliol Coll., Oxford. Employed by Balmer Lawrie & Co. Ltd, Calcutta, 1929; Indian Army, 1940-44; Man. Dir, Balmer Lawrie, 1948-58. Pres. of the Bengal Chamber of Commerce and Industry and Pres. of the Associated Chambers of Commerce of India, 1956-57. *Address:* Boles House, East Street, Petworth, West Sussex. *Club:* Oriental.
See also Sir Evan Jenkins.

JENKINS, Ven. Owen; *see* Jenkins, Ven. J. O.

JENKINS, Peter; Political Commentator and Policy Editor, The Guardian, since 1974; *b* 11 May 1934; *s* of Kenneth E. Jenkins and Joan E. Jenkins (*née* Croger); *m* 1st, 1960, Charlotte Strachey (decd); one *d*; 2nd, 1970, Polly Toynbee, *qv*; two *d*. *Educ:* Culford Sch.; Trinity Hall, Cambridge (BA Hist., MA). Journalist, Financial Times, 1958-60; The Guardian: Journalist, 1960–; Labour Correspondent, 1963-67; Washington Correspondent, 1972-74. Theatre Critic, The Spectator, 1978-81. First stage play, Illuminations, performed at Lyric, Hammersmith, 1980. Vis. Fellow, Nuffield Coll., Oxford, 1980–. Awards include: Granada TV Journalist of the Year, 1978. *Publication:* The Battle of Downing Street, 1970. *Address:* 1 Crescent Grove, SW4 7AF. *T:* 01-622 6492. *Club:* Garrick.

JENKINS, Peter White; County Treasurer, Merseyside County Council, since 1973; *b* 12 Oct. 1937; *s* of John White Jenkins, OBE, and Dorothy Jenkins; *m* 1961, Joyce Christine Muter; one *s* one *d*. *Educ:* Queen Mary's Grammar Sch., Walsall; King Edward VI Grammar Sch., Nuneaton. CIPFA. Local govt service in Finance Depts at Coventry, Preston, Chester, Wolverhampton; Dep. Treasurer, Birkenhead, 1969-73. *Recreations:* squash-rackets, gardening, reading. *Address:* Rydal House, Golf Links Road, Prenton, Wirral, Merseyside L42 8LW. *T:* 051-608 1000.

JENKINS, Robin; *see* Jenkins, J. R.

JENKINS, Rt. Hon. Roy Harris, PC 1964; MP (SDP) Glasgow, Hillhead, since March 1982; First Leader, Social Democratic Party, since 1982 (Member of Joint Leadership, 1981-82); President of the European Commission, 1977-81; *b* 11 Nov. 1920; *o s* of late Arthur Jenkins, MP, and of Hattie Jenkins; *m* 1945, Jennifer Morris (*see* M. J. Jenkins); two *s* one *d*. *Educ:* Abersychan Grammar Sch.; Balliol Coll., Oxford, Hon. Fellow, 1969. Sec. and Librarian, Oxford Union Society; Chairman, Oxford Univ. Democratic Socialist Club; First Class in Hon. Sch. of Philosophy, Politics and Economics, 1941. Served War of 1939-45, in RA, 1942-46; Captain, 1944-46. Contested (Lab) Solihull Div. of Warwicks, at Gen. Election, 1945. Mem. of Staff of Industrial and Commercial Finance Corp. Ltd, 1946-48. Mem. Exec. Cttee of Fabian Soc., 1949-61; Chm., Fabian Soc., 1957-58; Mem. Cttee of Management, Soc. of Authors, 1956-60; Governor, British Film Institute, 1955-58; Dir of Financial Operations, John Lewis Partnership, 1962-64. Dir, Morgan Grenfell Hldgs Ltd, 1981–. MP (Lab): Central Southwark, 1948-50; Stechford, Birmingham, 1950-76; PPS to Sec. of State for Commonwealth Relations, 1949-50; Minister of Aviation, 1964-65; Home Sec., 1965-67, 1974-76; Chancellor of the Exchequer, 1967-70; Dep. Leader, Labour Party, 1970-72. UK Deleg. to Council of Europe, 1955-57. Vice-Pres., Inst. of Fiscal Studies, 1970–. Formerly: Dep. Chm. Federal Union; Pres., Britain in Europe, Referendum Campaign, 1975; Chm., Labour European Cttee. A President: of United Kingdom Council of the European Movement; Labour Cttee for Europe. Pres., UWIST, 1975-81. Trustee, Pilgrim Trust, 1973–. Freeman, City of Brussels, 1980. Hon. Foreign Mem., Amer. Acad. Arts and Scis, 1973. Hon. Fellow, Berkeley Coll., Yale, 1972. Hon. LLD: Leeds, 1971; Harvard, 1972; Pennsylvania, 1973; Dundee, 1973; Loughborough, 1975; Bath, 1978; Michigan, 1978; Wales, 1979; Bristol, 1980; Hon. DLitt: Glasgow, 1972; City, 1976; Warwick, 1978; Reading, 1979; Hon. DCL Oxford, 1973; Hon. DSc Aston, 1977; DUniv: Keele, 1977; Essex, 1978; Open, 1979; Hon. DPhil Katholieke Univ., Leuven, 1979; Hon. doctorates: Urbino, 1979; TCD, 1979. Charlemagne Prize, 1972; Robert Schuman Prize, 1972; Prix Bentinck, 1978. Order of European Merit (Luxemburg), 1976; Grand Cross, Order of Charles III (Spain), 1980. *Publications:* (ed) Purpose and Policy (a vol. of the Prime

Minister's Speeches), 1947; Mr Attlee: An Interim Biography, 1948; Pursuit of Progress, 1953; Mr Balfour's Poodle, 1954; Sir Charles Dilke: A Victorian Tragedy, 1958; The Labour Case (Penguin Special), 1959; Asquith, 1964; Essays and Speeches, 1967; Afternoon on the Potomac?, 1972; What Matters Now, 1972; Nine Men of Power, 1975; contrib. to New Fabian Essays, 1952; contrib. to Hugh Gaitskell, A Memoir, 1964. *Address:* 2 Kensington Park Gardens, W11; St Amand's House, East Hendred, Oxon. *Clubs:* Athenæum, Brooks's, Reform.

JENKINS, Simon David; Political Editor, The Economist, since 1979; *b* 10 June 1943; *s* of Dr Daniel Jenkins and Nell Jenkins; *m* 1978, Gayle Hunnicutt; one *s* and one step *s*. *Educ:* Mill Hill Sch.; St John's Coll., Oxford (BA Hons); Research Student, Univ. of Sussex, 1964-65. Country Life magazine, 1965; Research Asst, Univ. of London Inst. of Educn, 1966; News Editor, Times Educational Supplement, 1966-68; joined Evening Standard, 1968; wrote Living in London column, 1969-74; Insight Editor, Sunday Times, 1974-75; Dep. Editor, Evening Standard, 1976, Editor, 1976-78. Mem., British Railways Bd, 1979–; Dir, Municipal Journal Ltd, 1980–. Mem. Council, Bow Group, and Editor of Crossbow, 1968-70; Stockholm Working Party on the Human Habitat, 1973; Member: Cttee Save Britain's Heritage, 1976–; Council, Inst. of Contemporary Arts, 1976–; Council Old Vic Co., 1979-81; Dep. Chm., Thirties Soc., 1979–. *Publications:* A City at Risk, 1971; Landlords to London, 1974; (ed) Insight on Portugal, 1975; Newspapers: the power and the money, 1979; The Companion Guide to Outer London, 1981; various pamphlets and articles in political and architectural jls. *Recreations:* architecture, music, London. *Address:* 174 Regent's Park Road, NW1. *Club:* Garrick.

JENKINS, Stanley Kenneth; HM Diplomatic Service, retired; *b* 25 Nov. 1920; *s* of Benjamin and Ethel Jane Jenkins; *m* 1957, Barbara Mary Marshall Webb; four *d*. *Educ:* Brecon; Cardiff Tech. Coll. President, Nat. Union of Students, 1949-51. LIOB 1950. Served War, Royal Artillery and Royal Engineers, 1942-46, retiring as Major. Joined Foreign (later Diplomatic) Service, 1951; Singapore, 1953; Kuala Lumpur, 1955; FO, 1957; Singapore, 1959; Rangoon, 1959; FO, 1964; Nicosia, 1967; FO, 1970-78, Counsellor. *Recreations:* gardening, tennis. *Address:* Willow Cottage, 1 Beehive Lane, Ferring, Worthing, Sussex BN12 5NL. *T:* Worthing 47356. *Club:* Royal Commonwealth Society.

JENKINS, Very Rev. Thomas Edward; *b* 14 Aug. 1902; *s* of late David Jenkins, Canon of St David's Cathedral and Vicar of Abergwili, and of Florence Helena Jenkins; *m* 1928, Annie Laura, *d* of late David Henry, Penygroes, Carms; one *s*. *Educ:* Llandyssul Grammar Sch.; St David's Coll., Lampeter; Wycliffe Hall, Oxford. St David's Coll., Lampeter, BA 1922, BD 1932, Powys Exhibitioner, 1924; Welsh Church Schol., 1921. Ordained, 1925; Curate of Llanelly, 1925-34; Rector of Begelly, 1934-38; Vicar: Christ Church, Llanelly, 1938-46; Lampeter, 1946-55 (Rural Dean, 1949-54); Canon, St David's Cathedral, 1951-57; Vicar of Cardigan, 1955-57; Dean of St David's, 1957-72. *Address:* 18 North Road, Cardigan, Dyfed SA43 1AA.

JENKINS, Thomas Harris, CBE 1981; General Secretary, Transport Salaried Staffs' Association, 1977-82; *b* 29 Aug. 1920; *s* of David Samuel Jenkins and Miriam Hughes (*née* Harris); *m* 1946, Joyce Smith; two *d*. *Educ:* Port Talbot Central Boys' Sch.; Port Talbot County Sch.; Shrewsbury Technical Coll. (evenings); Pitmans Coll., London (evenings). MCIT 1980. Served War, RAMC, 1941-46 (Certif. for Good Service, Army, Western Comd, 1946). Railway clerk, 1937-41; railway/docks clerk, 1946-49. Full-time service with Railway Clerks' Assoc., subseq. re-named Transport Salaried Staffs' Assoc., 1949–: Southern Reg. Divl Sec., 1959; Western Reg. Divl Sec., 1963; LMR Divl Sec., 1966; Sen. Asst Sec., 1968; Asst Gen. Sec., 1970, also Dep. to Gen. Sec., 1973. Member: Cttee of Transport Workers in European Community, 1976-82; Transport Industry, Nationalised Industries, and Hotel and Catering Industry Cttees of TUC, 1977-82; Management and Indus. Relns Cttee, SSRC, 1979-81; Air Transport and Travel Industry Trng Bd, 1976-82; Hotel and Catering Industry Trng Bd, 1978-82; Employment Appeal Tribunal, 1982–. Mem. Labour Party, 1946–; Mem., Lab. Party Transport Sub-Cttee. *Recreations:* I am paid for my hobby, but enjoy watching cricket, athletics and Rugby football. *Address:* 23 The Chase, Edgware, Mddx. *T:* 01-952 5314. *Clubs:* MCC, Middlesex County Cricket.
See also D. C. Jenkins.

JENKINS, Vivian Evan, MBE 1945; Director of Social Services, Cardiff City Council, 1971-74, retired; *b* 12 Sept. 1918; *s* of late Arthur Evan Jenkins and late Mrs Blodwen Jenkins; *m* 1946, Megan Myfanwy Evans; one *s* one *d*. *Educ:* UC Cardiff (BA). Dipl. Social Science. Army, 1940; commnd Royal Signals, 1943; served with 6th Airborne Div. as parachutist, Europe, Far East and Middle East, 1943-46 (Lieut). Child Care Officer, Glamorgan CC, 1949; Asst Children's Officer, 1951; Mem. Home Office Children's Dept Inspectorate, 1952. *Recreations:* Rugby football (former Captain of Univ. XV and Pontypridd RFC; awarded two Wales Rugby caps as schoolboy, 1933 and 1937); cricket, golf. *Address:* Ty Gwyn, 10 Y Parc, Groesfaen, near Pontyclun, Mid Glamorgan. *T:* Cardiff 890574. *Club:* Radyr Golf.

JENKINS, Sir William, Kt 1966; JP; Agent in London for Government of Northern Ireland, 1966-70; *b* 25 July 1904; *m* 1942, Jessie May Watson, Otago, NZ; no *c*. *Educ:* Whitehouse Sch.; Belfast Coll. of Technology. Joined W. H. Brady & Co. Ltd, Bombay, 1931; became Sen. Dir; retd 1956. JP Bombay, 1946; Hon. Presidency Magistrate Bombay, 1948. Dir various joint cos in Bombay. Chairman: Gilbert-Ash (NI) Ltd; Old Bushmills Distillery Co. Ltd; Director: Belfast Banking Co.; Arthur Guinness Son & Co. (B) Ltd, 1963-79. Entered Belfast Corp., 1957; JP Belfast, 1958; High Sheriff, Belfast, 1961; Dep. Lord Mayor, 1962; Lord Mayor of Belfast, 1964, 1965, 1966. Mem. Senate of N Ireland, 1963-66; Mem. Senate of Queen's Univ., 1963-66; Hon. Treas., Queen's Univ., 1965; first recipient of "Community Award" by New Ireland Soc. of Queen's Univ. for outstanding services to community during term as Lord Mayor. Mem. Council, 1967-70 (Chm. NI Br., 1967-75), Inst. of Directors. *Recreation:* golf. *Address:* 130 Merville Garden Village, Newtown Abbey, Belfast, N Ireland. *Clubs:* Royal Automobile; Willingdon (Bombay); Ulster Reform (Belfast); Royal Belfast Golf, Fortwilliam Golf.

JENKINSON, Sir Anthony Banks, 13th Bt, *cr* 1661; *b* 3 July 1912; *S* grandfather, 1915; *s* of Captain John Banks Jenkinson (killed European War, Sept, 1914) and Joan, *o d* of late Col Joseph Hill, CB (she *m* 2nd, 1920, Maj.-Gen. Algernon Langhorne, CB, DSO, who died 1945); *m* 1943, Frances, *d* of Harry Stremmel; one *s* two *d. Educ:* Eton; Balliol Coll., Oxford (Editor, The Isis, 1933-34). Foreign Correspondent, 1935-40: first British reporter to interview Mao Tse-tung in Yenan, NW China, Daily Sketch, 1938; Mediterranean Snoop Cruise Series, Daily Express, 1939; Caribbean Snoop Cruise, N American Newspaper Alliance & Reader's Digest, 1940; Editor, Allied Labour News Service, London and New York, 1940-46. Managing Director: Cayman Boats Ltd, Cayman Is, 1967-; Morgan's Harbour Ltd, Port Royal, Jamaica, 1953-73; Director: Port Royal Co. of Merchants Ltd, 1965-; Spanish Main Investments Ltd, Grand Cayman, 1962-; Caribbean Bank (Cayman) Ltd, 1973-; Cayman Free Press Ltd, 1974-. *Publications:* America Came My Way, 1935; Where Seldom a Gun is Heard, 1937. *Recreations:* sailing, travel. *Heir: s* John Banks Jenkinson, *b* 16 Feb. 1945. *Address:* 491 South Church Street, Grand Cayman, West Indies. *Clubs:* United Oxford & Cambridge University; MCC; Bembridge Sailing; Cayman Islands Yacht.

JENKS, Sir Richard Atherley, 2nd Bt, *cr* 1932; *b* 26 July 1906; *er s* of Sir Maurice Jenks, 1st Bt, and Martha Louise Christabel, *d* of late George Calley Smith; *S* father 1946; *m* 1932, Marjorie Suzanne Arlette, *d* of late Sir Arthur du Cros, 1st Bt; two *s. Educ:* Charterhouse. Chartered Accountant, retired. *Heir: s* Maurice Arthur Brian Jenks [*b* 28 Oct. 1933; *m* 1962, Susan, *e d* of Leslie Allen, Surrey; one *d*]. *Address:* 42 Sussex Square, W2 2SP. *T:* 01-262 8356.

JENKYNS, Henry Leigh; Under-Secretary, Department of the Environment, 1969-75; *b* 20 Jan. 1917; *y s* of H. H. Jenkyns, Indian Civil Service; *m* 1947, Rosalind Mary Home; two *s* one *d. Educ:* Eton and Balliol Coll., Oxford. War Service in Royal Signals; Lt-Col, East Africa Command, 1944. Treasury, 1945-66; Private Sec. to Chancellor, 1951-53. Treasury Representative in Australia and New Zealand, 1953-56; UK Delegation to OECD, Paris, 1961-63; Asst Under-Sec. of State, DEA, 1966-69; Chm., SE Economic Planning Bd, 1968-71. Mem., Southwark Diocesan Adv. Cttee for Care of Churches, 1977-78. Mem., Exmoor Study Team, 1977. *Recreations:* music, garden, sailing, mending things. *Address:* Westcroft, Priors Hill Road, Aldeburgh, Suffolk. *T:* Aldeburgh 2357. *Club:* United Oxford & Cambridge University.

JENNER, Ann Maureen; Ballerina, Australian Ballet, 1978-80; Guest Ballet Teacher, since 1980: Victorian College of the Arts, and National Ballet School, Melbourne; and many other schools in Sydney and Melbourne; *b* 8 March 1944; *d* of Kenneth George Jenner and Margaret Rosetta (*née* Wilson); *m* 1980, Dale Robert Baker. *Educ:* Royal Ballet Junior and Senior Schools. Royal Ballet Co., 1961-78: Soloist 1964; Principal Dancer 1970. Roles include: Lise, Fille Mal Gardée, 1966; Swanhilda, Coppelia, 1968; Cinderella, 1969; Princess Aurora, Sleeping Beauty, 1972; Giselle, 1973; Gypsy, Deux Pigeons, 1974; White Girl, Deux Pigeons, 1976; Juliet, Romeo and Juliet, 1977; Countess Larisch, Mayerling, 1978; Flavia, Spartacus, 1979; Kitri, Don Quixote, 1979; Anna, Anna Karenina, 1980; Poll, Pineapple Poll, 1980; one-act roles include: Symphonic Variations, 1967; Firebird, 1972; Triad, 1973; Les Sylphides; Serenade; Les Patineurs; Elite Syncopations, Concert, Flower Festival Pas de Deux, etc. *Address:* c/o Australian Ballet, 11 Mount Alexander Road, Flemington, Vic. 3031, Australia.

JENNETT, Prof. (William) Bryan, FRCS, FRCSGlas; Professor of Neurosurgery, since 1968, Dean of the Faculty of Medicine, since 1981, University of Glasgow; Member, Medical Research Council, since 1979; *b* 1 March 1926; *s* of Robert William Jennett and Jessie Pate Loudon; *m* 1950, Sheila Mary Pope; three *s* one *d. Educ:* Univ. of Liverpool (MB ChB 1949, MD 1960). House Physician to Lord Cohen of Birkenhead, 1949; Ho. Surg. to Sir Hugh Cairns, 1950; Surgical Specialist, RAMC, 1951-53; Registrar in Neurosurgery, Oxford and Cardiff, 1954-56; Lectr in Neurosurgery, Univ. of Manchester, 1957-62; Rockefeller Travelling Fellow, Univ. of California, LA, 1958-59; Cons. Neurosurgeon, Glasgow, 1963-68. *Publications:* Epilepsy after Blunt Head Injury, 1962, 2nd edn 1975; Introduction to Neurosurgery, 1964, 3rd edn 1977; (with G. Teasdale) Management of Head Injuries, 1981; many papers in Lancet, BMJ and elsewhere. *Recreations:* cruising under sail (Cdre, Serpent Yacht Club), writing. *Address:* 4 Cleveden Drive, Glasgow G12 0SE. *T:* 041-334 5148. *Club:* Royal Society of Medicine.

JENNINGS, Sir Albert (Victor), Kt 1969; Founder and Chairman, A. V. Jennings Industries (Australia) Ltd, 1932, retired 1972; *b* 12 Oct. 1896; *s* of John Thomas Jennings; *m* 1922, Ethel Sarah, *d* of George Herbert Johnson;

two *s. Educ:* Eastern Road, Sch., Melbourne. Served First World War, AIF. Council Mem., Master Builders Assoc., 1943-; Vice.Pres. Housing, Master Builders Fedn of Aust., 1970-71; Member: Commonwealth Building Research and Advisory Cttee, 1948-72; Manufacturing Industries Adv. Council to Australian Govt, 1962-; Decentralisation and Devel Adv. Cttee to Victorian State Govt, 1965-; Commonwealth of Aust. Metric Conversion Bd, 1970-72; Trustee, Cttee for Economic Devel of Australia. Fellow: Aust. Inst. of Building (Federal Bres., 1964-65 and 1965-66); UK Inst. of Building, 1971. Aust. Inst. of Building Medal 1970; Urban Land Inst. Total Community Devel Award, 1973; Sir Charles McGrath Award for Services to Marketing, 1976. *Recreations:* swimming, golf. *Address:* Ranelagh House, Rosserdale Crescent, Mount Eliza, Victoria 3930, Australia. *T:* 7871350. *Clubs:* Commonwealth (Canberra); Melbourne, Savage (Melbourne).

JENNINGS, Arnold Harry, CBE 1977; MA; Headmaster, Ecclesfield School, Sheffield, 1959-79 (formerly, 1959-67, Ecclesfield Grammar School); *b* 24 May 1915; *s* of Harry Jennings and Alice Mary (*née* Northrop); *m* 1939, Elizabeth Redman; one *s* one *d. Educ:* Bradford Grammar Sch.; Corpus Christi Coll., Oxford (Classical Schol.; MA). Tutor, Knutsford Ordination Test Sch., Hawarden, 1939-40. Served War, Captain RA, England, N Ireland, France, Belgium, Holland and Germany, 1940-46. Sen. Classical Master, Chesterfield Grammar Sch., 1946-53; Headmaster, Tapton House Sch., Chesterfield, 1953-58; part-time extra-mural Lectr, Sheffield Univ., 1946-54. Mem., NUT Executive, 1958-59 and 1960-72 (Chm., Secondary Adv. Cttee, 1968-72); Pres., Head Masters' Assoc., 1977; Hon. Sec., 1978-79; Membership Sec., 1979-81, Secondary Heads Assoc.; Pres., Jt Assoc. of Classical Teachers, 1975-77; Mem., Secondary Schs Examinations Council, 1961-64; Schools Council: Mem., 1964-; Dep. Chm. and Acting Chm. 1982-; Chm., Steering Cttee 'C', 1975-78; Chm., Second Examinations Cttee, 1968-76; Jt Chm., Jt Examinations Sub-Cttee, 1971-76; Chm., Exams Cttee, 1978-; Chm., Classics Cttee. Mem. Court, Sheffield Univ., 1959-78. Sheffield City Councillor, 1949-58; contested (Lab) Heeley, Sheffield, 1950 and 1951. *Publications:* (ed) Management and Headship in the Secondary School, 1977; (ed) Discipline in Primary and Secondary Schools Today, 1979; articles on educn *passim. Recreations:* work, wine, opera, photography, travel. *Address:* 74 Clarkegrove Road, Sheffield S10 2NJ. *T:* Sheffield 662520.

JENNINGS, Audrey Mary; Metropolitan Stipendiary Magistrate, since 1972; *b* 22 June 1928; *d* of Hugh and Olive Jennings, Ashbrook Range, Sunderland; *m* 1961, Roger Harry Kilbourne Frisby, *qv* (marr. diss. 1980); two *s* one *d. Educ:* Durham High Sch.; Durham Univ. (BA); Oxford Univ. (DPA). Children's Officer, City and County of Cambridge, 1952-56. Called to Bar, Middle Temple, 1956 (Harmsworth Schol.); practised at Criminal Bar, London, 1956-61 and 1967-72. Mem., Criminal Law Revision Cttee, 1977-.

JENNINGS, Bernard Antony; Legal Adviser, BBC, since 1977; *b* 29 May 1939; *s* of Bernard Joseph Francis Jennings and Constance Nora Jennings (*née* O'Shea). *Educ:* St Bede's Coll., Manchester; Christ's Coll., Cambridge (MA). Articled Clerk, John Gorna & Co., Manchester; admitted Solicitor, 1964; BBC Solicitor's Dept, 1964-74; BBC Head of Copyright, 1974-77. *Address:* Broadcasting House, W1A 1AA. *T:* 01-580 4468.

JENNINGS, (Edgar) Owen, RWS 1953 (ARWS 1943); RE 1970 (ARE 1944); ARCA London 1925; FRSA; Principal, School of Art, Tunbridge Wells, 1934-65; *b* Cowling, Yorks, 28 Dec. 1899; *s* of Wesley Jennings, JP and Ann Elizabeth Jennings (*née* Hardy); *m* 1929, May (*d* 1977), *d* of Arthur Cullingworth; one *s* one *d. Educ:* Sch. of Art, Skipton; Coll. of Art, Leeds; Royal College of Art, London. Examr in Three Dimensional Design for Ministry of Education. Exhibited: Royal Academy, 1929-79; RWS, RE, NEAC, Paris Salon, New York, Chicago, Antwerp, Vienna. CEMA and Brit. Coun. Exhibns in England, China, Russia, Poland, etc. Works in: British Museum; London Museum; Victoria and Albert Museum; Albertina; Brooklyn Museum, New York; Art Inst.; Chicago; Public Collections Leeds, Birmingham, Wakefield. Logan Prize Winner, Chicago International, 1930; Silver Medallist, City and Guilds of London Inst.; ATD 1926. Pres., Royal Water-Colour Society Art Club, 1966-70. *Publications:* contrib. to various art jls (line engravings, wood engravings, watercolours). *Relevant publication:* review by Adrian Bury, with illustrations, in Old Water-Colour Soc.'s Annual Volume, 1973. *Recreations:* reading, drawing. *Address:* Linton, 26 Wilman Road, Tunbridge Wells, Kent TN4 9AP. *T:* 20581. *Club:* Chelsea Arts.

JENNINGS, Elizabeth (Joan); Author; *b* 18 July 1926; *d* of Dr H. C. Jennings, Oxon. *Educ:* Oxford High Sch.; St Anne's Coll., Oxford. Asst at Oxford City Library, 1950-58; Reader for Chatto & Windus Ltd, 1958-60. *Publications:* Poems (Arts Council Prize), 1953; A Way of Looking, poems, 1955 (Somerset Maugham Award, 1956); A Sense of the World, poems, 1958; (ed) The Batsford Book of Children's Verse, 1958; Let's Have Some Poetry, 1960; Every Changing Shape, 1961; Song for a Birth or a Death, poems, 1961; a translation of Michelangelo's sonnets, 1961; Recoveries, poems, 1964; Robert Frost, 1964; Christianity and Poetry, 1965; The Mind Has Mountains, poems, 1966 (Richard Hillary Prize, 1966); The Secret Brother (poems for children), 1966; Collected Poems, 1967; The Animals' Arrival, poems, 1969 (Arts Council Bursary, 1969); (ed) A Choice of Christina Rossetti's Verse, 1970; Lucidities, poems, 1970; Relationships, 1972; Growing Points, poems, 1975; Seven Men of Vision, 1976; Consequently I Rejoice, poems, 1977; After the Ark (poems for children), 1978; Selected Poems, 1980; Moments of Grace, poems, 1980; (ed) The Batsford Book of Religious Verse, 1981; Celebrations and Elegies, poems, 1982; also poems and articles in: New Statesman, New Yorker, Botteghe Oscure, Observer, Spectator, Listener, Vogue, The Scotsman, etc. *Recreations:* travel, swimming, looking at pictures, the theatre, conversation. *Address:* c/o David Higham Associates Ltd, 5–8 Lower John Street, W1R 4HA. *Club:* Society of Authors.

JENNINGS, Henry Cecil; Chairman, Co-operative Wholesale Society Ltd, 1966–72; Chief Executive Officer, North Eastern Co-operative Society Ltd, 1970–72; *b* 2 Jan. 1908; *s* of late Alfred Ernest Jennings and Gertrude Sybil Jennings; *m* 1934, Winifred Evelyn Radford; one *s* decd. *Educ:* Gerard Street Sch., Derby. Inspector of Shops, Derby Co-operative Soc. Ltd, 1947–49; Blackburn Co-operative Soc. Ltd: Grocery Manager and Buyer, 1949–51; Gen. Man., 1951–54; Gen. Man., Darlington Co-operative Soc. Ltd, 1954–70. Dir of Co-operative Insurance Soc. Ltd, 1968–70; Chm., Associated Co-operative Creameries Ltd, 1968–70; Chm., Birtley Distributive Centre, 1964–70. Pres., Co-operative Congress, 1967. FRSA. *Recreations:* reading, gardening, travel. *Address:* 28 Gladelands Way, Corfe Lodge Park, Broadstone, Dorset BH18 9JB. *T:* Broadstone 696388.

JENNINGS, John Charles; *b* 10 Feb. 1903; *m* 1927, Berta Nicholson (*d* 1979); one *s*. *Educ:* Bede Coll., Durham; King's Coll., Durham Univ. Headmaster. Contested (C), SE Derbyshire, 1950 and 1951. MP (C) Burton-on-Trent, Staffs, 1955–Feb. 1974; Chm., Cttees of House of Commons, 1964–74. *Recreation:* politics. *Address:* Two Trees, Meadowfield Road, Stocksfield, Northumberland. *T:* Stocksfield 3565.

JENNINGS, Very Rev. Kenneth Neal; Dean of Gloucester, since 1983; *b* 8 Nov. 1930; *s* of Reginald Tinsley and Edith Dora Jennings; *m* 1972, Wendy Margaret Stallworthy; one *s* one *d*. *Educ:* Hertford Grammar School; Corpus Christi College, Cambridge (MA); Cuddesdon College, Oxford. Asst Curate, Holy Trinity, Ramsgate, 1956–59; Lecturer 1959–61, Vice-Principal 1961–66, Bishop's College, Calcutta; Vice-Principal, Cuddesdon Theological Coll., 1967–73; Vicar of Hitchin, 1973–76; Team Rector of Hitchin, 1977–82. *Recreations:* music, fell-walking. *Address:* The Deanery, Miller's Green, Gloucester GL1 2BP. *T:* Gloucester 24167.

JENNINGS, Owen; *see* Jennings, E. O.

JENNINGS, Paul (Francis), FRSL; writer; *b* 20 June 1918; *s* of William Benedict and Mary Gertrude Jennings; *m* 1952, Celia Blom; three *s* three *d*. *Educ:* King Henry VIII, Coventry, and Douai. Freelance work in Punch and Spectator began while still in Army (Lt Royal Signals); Script-writer at Central Office of Information, 1946–47; Copy writer at Colman Prentis Varley (advertising), 1947–49; on staff of The Observer, 1949–66. Trustee, New Philharmonia Trust. *Publications:* Oddly Enough, 1951; Even Oddlier, 1952; Oddly Bodlikins, 1953; Next to Oddliness, 1955; Model Oddlies, 1956; Gladly Oddly, 1957; Idly Oddly, 1959; I Said Oddly, Diddle I?, 1961; Oodles of Oddlies, 1963; The Jenguin Pennings, 1963; Oddly Ad Lib, 1965; I Was Joking, of Course, 1968; The Living Village, 1968; Just a Few Lines, 1969; It's An Odd Thing, But..., 1971; (ed) The English Difference, 1974; Britain As She Is Visit, 1976; The Book of Nonsense, 1977; I Must Have Imagined It, 1977; Companion to Britain, 1980; (ed) A Feast of Days, 1982; (ed) My Favourite Railway Stories, 1982; *novel:* And Now for Something Exactly the Same, 1977; *for children:* The Hopping Basket, 1965; The Great Jelly of London, 1967; The Train to Yesterday, 1974. *Recreations:* madrigal singing and thinking about writing another vast serious book. *Address:* Hill House, Rectory Hill, East Bergholt, Suffolk.

JENNINGS, Percival Henry, CBE 1953; *b* 8 Dec. 1903; *s* of late Rev. Canon H. R. Jennings; *m* 1934, Margaret Katharine Musgrave, *d* of late Brig.-Gen. H. S. Rogers, CMG, DSO; three *d*. *Educ:* Christ's Hospital. Asst Auditor, N Rhodesia, 1927; Asst Auditor, Mauritius, 1931; Auditor, British Honduras, 1934; Dep. Dir of Audit, Gold Coast, 1938; Dep. Dir of Audit, Nigeria, 1945; Dir of Audit, Hong Kong, 1948; Dep. Dir-Gen. of the Overseas Audit Service, 1955; Dir-Gen. of the Overseas Audit Service, 1960–63, retd. *Recreation:* golf. *Address:* Littlewood, Lelant, St Ives, Cornwall. *T:* Hayle 753407. *Clubs:* Royal Commonwealth Society; West Cornwall Golf.

JENNINGS, Rev. Peter; Superintendent Minister, Whitechapel Mission, since 1982; *b* 9 Oct. 1937; *s* of Robert William Jennings and Margaret Irene Jennings; *m* 1963, Cynthia Margaret Leicester; two *s*. *Educ:* Manchester Grammar Sch.; Keble Coll., Oxford (MA); Hartley Victoria Methodist Theological Coll.; Manchester Univ. (MA). Ordained 1965. Minister: Swansea Methodist Circuit, 1963–67; London Mission (East) Circuit, 1967–78, and Tutor Warden, Social Studies Centre, 1967–74; Gen. Sec., Council of Christians and Jews, 1974–81; Associate Minister, Wesley's Chapel, 1978–81; Asst Minister, Walthamstow and Chingford Methodist Circuit, 1981–82. Hon. Treasurer, London Rainbow Group; Mem., Exec. Cttee, London Soc. of Jews and Christians. *Publications:* papers and articles on aspects of Christian-Jewish relations. *Recreations:* photography, being educated by Tim and Nick. *Address:* The Whitechapel Mission, 212 Whitechapel Road, E1 1BJ. *T:* 01-247 8280.

JENNINGS, Sir Raymond (Winter), Kt 1968; QC 1945; Master, Court of Protection, 1956–70; *b* 12 Dec. 1897; *o s* of late Sir Arthur Oldham Jennings and Mabel Winter; *m* 1930, Sheila (*d* 1972), *d* of Selwyn S. Grant, OBE; one *s* one *d*. *Educ:* Rugby; RMC, Sandhurst; Oriel Coll., Oxford (MA, BCL).

Served 1916–19 in Royal Fusiliers. Called to Bar, 1922; Bencher of Lincoln's Inn, 1951. *Recreation:* fishing. *Address:* 14C Upper Drive, Hove, East Sussex BN3 6GN. *T:* Brighton 773361. *Club:* Athenæum.

JENNINGS, Sir Robert (Yewdall), Kt 1982; QC 1969; MA, LLB Cantab; a Judge of the International Court of Justice, since 1982; *b* 19 Oct. 1913; *o s* of Arthur Jennings; *m* 1955, Christine, *yr d* of Bernard Bennett; one *s* two *d*. *Educ:* Belle Vue Grammar Sch., Bradford; Downing Coll., Cambridge (scholar; 1st cl. pts I & II Law Tripos; LLB; Hon. Fellow, 1982). Served War, Intelligence Corps, 1940–46; Hon. Major, Officers' AER. Called to the Bar, Lincoln's Inn, 1943 (Hon. Bencher, 1970). Whewell Scholar in Internat. Law, Cambridge, 1936; Joseph Hodges Choate Fellow, Harvard Univ., 1936–37; Asst Lectr in Law, LSE, 1938–39; Jesus College, Cambridge: Fellow, 1939, Hon. Fellow, 1982; Sen. Tutor, 1949–55; Sometime Pres. Whewell Prof. of Internat. Law, Cambridge Univ., 1955–81; Reader in Internat. Law, Council of Legal Educn, 1959–70. Mem., Inst. of Internat. Law (Pres., 1982-83). Joint Editor: International and Comparative Law Quarterly, 1956–61; British Year Book of International Law, 1960–82. *Publications:* The Acquisition of Territory, 1963; General Course on International Law, 1967; articles in legal periodicals. *Address:* Jesus College, Cambridge.

JENOUR, Sir (Arthur) Maynard (Chesterfield), Kt 1959; TD 1950; JP; Chairman and Joint Managing Director: Aberthaw & Bristol Channel Portland Cement Co. Ltd (Director, 1929); T. Beynon & Co., Ltd (Director, 1938); Chairman, Ruthin Quarries (Bridgend) Ltd (Director 1947); Director: Associated Portland Cement Manufacturers Ltd, 1963–75; Blue Jacket Motel (Pty) Ltd, Australia, 1964; *b* 7 Jan. 1905; *s* of Brig.-Gen. A. S. Jenour, CB, CMG, DSO, Crossways, Chepstow and Emily Anna (*née* Beynon); *m* 1948, Margaret Sophie (who *m* 1927, W. O. Ellis Fielding-Jones, *d* 1935; three *d*), *d* of H. Stuart Osborne, Sydney, NSW. *Educ:* Eton. Entered business, 1924. Served War of 1939–45, in England and Middle East, Royal Artillery, Major. High Sheriff of Monmouthshire, 1951–52; Pres., Cardiff Chamber of Commerce, 1953–54; Chm. Wales & Mon. Industrial Estates Ltd, 1954–60; Mem. Board, Development Corporation for Wales, 1958–. JP Mon 1946; DL Mon, 1960; Vice-Lieut of Mon, 1965–74, Vice Lord-Lieut of Gwent, 1974–79. KStJ 1969. *Recreations:* walking, gardening, shooting. *Address:* Stonycroft, 13 Ridgeway, Newport, Gwent. *T:* Newport 63802. *Clubs:* Army and Navy; Cardiff and County (Cardiff); Union (Sydney, NSW).

JEPHCOTT, Sir (John) Anthony, 2nd Bt *cr* 1962; *b* 21 May 1924; *s* of Sir Harry Jephcott, 1st Bt, and of Doris, *d* of Henry Gregory; *S* father, 1978; *m* 1st, 1949, Sylvia Mary, *d* of Thorsten Frederick Relling, Wellington, NZ; two *d*; 2nd, 1978, Josephine Agnes Sheridan. *Educ:* Aldenham; St John's Coll., Oxford; London School of Economics (BCom). Served with REME and RAEC, 1944–47. Director, Longworth Scientific Instrument Co. Ltd, 1946; Managing Director and Chairman, 1952–73; Managing Director and Chairman, Pen Medic Ltd (NZ), 1973–78. *Publications:* correspondence in Anaesthesia (UK) and Anaesthesia and Intensive Care (Australia). *Recreations:* gardening, photography. *Heir:* *b* Neil Welbourn Jephcott [*b* 3 June 1929; *m* 1st, 1951, Mary Denise (*d* 1977), *d* of Arthur Muddiman; two *s* one *d*; 2nd, 1978, Mary Florence Daly]. *Address:* 144 Puriri Park Road, Whangarei, New Zealand.

JEPHSON-JONES, Brig. Robert Llewellyn, GC 1940; Commandant Central Ordnance Depot, Branston, 1957–60, retired; *b* 7 April 1905; *s* of Rev. J. D. Jones, and Margaret Noble Jones (*née* Jephson); *m* 1934, Irene Sykes; one *d*. *Educ:* St Edmund's Sch., Canterbury; RMC, Sandhurst. Commissioned as 2nd Lieut Duke of Wellington's Regt, 1925; served in Singapore and India, 1926–30; served in Royal West African Frontier Force, Adjt, 1930–34; transferred to RAOC, 1936; served War, Malta, Palestine, Egypt, Sudan, Italy, 1939–44 (GC Malta); Col, 1943; Brig., 1954; Deputy Dir of Ordnance Services, Scottish Command, 1954–57. *Address:* 11 Gorselands Court, Glenmoor Road, Ferndown, Dorset BH22 8QF. *T:* Ferndown 873411. *Club:* Naval and Military.

JEPSON, Selwyn; author and occasional soldier; *o s* of late Edgar Jepson. *Educ:* St Paul's Sch. War of 1939–45, Major, The Buffs, Military Intelligence and SOE. Editorial journalism, 1919. *Publications: novels:* The Qualified Adventurer, 1921; That Fellow MacArthur, 1922; The King's Red-Haired Girl, 1923; Golden Eyes, 1924; Rogues and Diamonds, 1925; Snaggletooth, 1926; The Death Gong, 1928; Tiger Dawn, 1929; I Met Murder, 1930; Rabbit's Paw, 1932; Keep Murder Quiet, 1940; Man Running, 1948; The Golden Dart, 1949; The Hungry Spider, 1950; Man Dead, 1951; The Black Italian, 1954; The Assassin, 1956; Noise in the Night, 1957; The Laughing Fish, 1960; Fear in the Wind, 1964; The Third Possibility, 1965; Angry Millionaire, 1968; Dead Letters, 1970; Letter to a Dead Girl, 1971; The Gill Interrogators, 1974; *short stories:* (with Michael Joseph) Heads or Tails, 1933; *stage play:* (with Lesley Storm) Dark Horizon, 1933; *screen plays:* Going Gay, 1932; For the Love of You, 1932; Irresistible Marmaduke, 1933; Monday at Ten, 1933; The Love Test, 1934; The Riverside Murders, 1934; White Lilac, Hyde Park Corner (Hackett), 1935; Well Done, Henry, 1936; The Scarab Murder, 1936; Toilers of the Sea (adapted and directed), 1936; Sailing Along, 1937; Carnet de Bal: Double Crime on the Maginot Line (English Version), 1938; *television plays:* Thought to Kill, 1952; Dialogue for Two Faces, 1952; My Name is Jones, 1952; Little Brother, 1953; Last Moment, 1953; Forever my Heart, 1953; Leave it to Eve (serial), 1954; The Interloper, 1955; Noise in the Night (USA), 1958; The Hungry Spider, 1964; The Peppermint Child, 1976; *radio serial:* The Hungry Spider, 1957; *radio plays:* The Bath that Sang, 1958; Noise in the

Night, 1958; Art for Art's Sake, 1959; Small Brother, 1960; Call it Greymail, 1961; Dark Corners, 1963. *Recreations:* book collecting, painting. *Address:* The Far House, Liss, Hants. *Club:* Savile.

JEREMIAH, Melvyn Gwynne; Principal Finance Officer (Under Secretary), Welsh Office, since 1979; *b* 10 March 1939; *s* of Bryn Jeremiah and Evelyn (*née* Rogers); *m* 1960, Lilian Clare (*née* Bailey) (marr. diss. 1966). *Educ:* Abertillery County Sch. Apptd to Home Office, 1958; HM Customs and Excise, 1963-75; Cabinet Office, 1975-76; Treasury, 1976-79. Sec., Assoc. of First Div. Civil Servants, 1967-70. *Recreations:* work, people. *Address:* Rhandir, 11 Cherry Orchard Road, Lisvane, Cardiff CF4 5UE. *T:* (office) Cardiff 825220. *Club:* Reform.

JERMYN, Earl; Frederick William John Augustus Hervey; Governing Partner, Jermyn Shipping; Director, Estate Associates Ltd; *b* 15 Sept. 1954; *s* and *heir* of 6th Marquess of Bristol, *qv. Educ:* Harrow; Neuchatel Univ. MInstD. *Address:* Sun Tower, Square Beaumarchais, Monte Carlo. *Clubs:* House of Lords Yacht, Royal Thames Yacht; Travellers' (Paris); Monte Carlo Country.

JERNE, Prof. Niels Kaj, MD; FRS 1980; *b* London, 23 Dec. 1911; *s* of Hans Jessen Jerne and Else Marie (*née* Lindberg); *m* 1964, Ursula Alexandra (*née* Kohl); two *s. Educ:* Univ. of Leiden, Holland; Univ. of Copenhagen, Denmark (MD). Res. worker, Danish State Serum Inst., 1943-56; Res. Fellow, Calif Inst. of Technol., Pasadena, 1954-55; CMO for Immunology, WHO, Geneva, 1956-62; Chm., Dept of Microbiology, Univ. of Pittsburgh, 1962-66; Director: Paul-Ehrlich-Institut, Frankfurt, 1966-69; Basel Inst. for Immunology, 1969-80. Prof., Pasteur Inst., Paris, 1981-82. Member: Amer. Acad. of Arts and Sciences, 1967; Royal Danish Acad. of Sciences, 1968; National Acad. of Sciences, USA, 1975; Amer. Philosophical Soc., 1979; Acad. des Scis de l'Institut de France, 1981. DSc *hc* : Chicago, 1972; Columbia, 1978; Copenhagen, 1979; PhD *hc* Basel, 1981. *Publications:* scientific papers on immunology in learned jls. *Address:* Château de Bellevue, Castillon-du-Gard, Gard 30210, France. *T:* 66/370075.

JEROME, James Alexander; PC (Can); QC (Can.) 1976; **Hon. Mr Justice Jerome;** Associate Chief Justice, Federal Court of Canada, since 1980; lawyer, since 1958; *b* Toronto, 4 March 1933; *s* of Joseph Leonard Jerome and Phyllis Devlin; *m* 1958, Barry Karen Hodgins; three *s* two *d. Educ:* Our Lady of Perpetual Help Sch., Toronto; St Michael's Coll. High Sch., Toronto; Univ. of Toronto; Osgoode Hall. Alderman, Sudbury, Ont., 1966-67. MP, Sudbury, 1968-80; Parly Sec. to President of Privy Council, 1970-74; Speaker of the House of Commons, 1974-80. Pres., Commonwealth Parly Assoc., 1976-. *Recreations:* golf, ski-ing, tennis, piano. *Address:* 22 Eisenhower Crescent, Nepean, Ontario, Canada. *T:* 825-3113.

JERRAM, Maj.-Gen. Richard Martyn, MBE 1960; Director, Royal Armoured Corps, since 1981; *b* Bangalore, India, 14 Aug. 1928; *e s* of late Brig. R. M. Jerram, DSO, MC, and late Monica (*née* Gillies), Trevanson, Wadebridge, Cornwall. *Educ:* Stubbington House; Marlborough Coll.; RMA, Sandhurst. Commissioned into Royal Tank Regt, 1948; served in 2, 3 or 4 RTRs, or in Staff appts in Hong Kong, Malaya (twice) (MBE), Libya, N Ireland, USA, Germany (four times), MoD (twice). Instr, Staff Coll., Camberley, 1964-67; CO 3 RTR, 1969-71. Col Comdt, RTR, 1982-. *Recreations:* travel, countryside, literature, chess. *Address:* c/o Williams & Glyn's Bank Ltd, Kirkland House, Whitehall, SW1. *Clubs:* MCC, Army and Navy, Cavalry and Guards.

JERSEY, 9th Earl of, *cr* 1697; **George Francis Child-Villiers;** Viscount Grandison (of Limerick), 1620; Viscount Villiers (of Dartford), and Baron Villiers (of Hoo), 1691; Chairman: Jersey Island Semen Exports Ltd; Associated Hotels Ltd; Hotel L'Horizon Ltd; *b* 15 Feb. 1910; *e s* of 8th Earl and Lady Cynthia Almina Constance Mary Needham (who *m* 2nd, 1925, W. R. Slessor (*d* 1945); she died 1947), *o d* of 3rd Earl of Kilmorey; *S* father, 1923; *m* 1st, 1932, Patricia Kenneth (who obtained a divorce, 1937; she *m* 2nd, 1937, Robin Filmer Wilson, who *d* 1944; 3rd, 1953, Col Peter Laycock, who *d* 1977), *o d* of Kenneth Richards, Cootamundra, NSW, and of late Eileen Mary (who *m* later Sir Stephenson Kent, KCB); one *d* ; 2nd, 1937, Virginia (who obtained a divorce, 1946), *d* of James Cherrill, USA; 3rd, 1947, Bianca Maria Adriana Luciana, *er d* of late Enrico Mottironi, Turin, Italy; two *s* one *d.* Director: Jersey General Investment Trust Ltd; Jersey General Executor and Trustee Co. Ltd. *Heir:* *s* Viscount Villiers, *qv. Address:* Radier Manor, Longueville, Jersey, Channel Islands. *T:* Jersey Central 53102.

JERSEY, Dean of; *see* Goss, Very Rev. T. A.

JERVIS, family name of Viscount St Vincent.

JERVIS, Charles Elliott, OBE 1966; Editor-in-Chief, Press Association, 1954-65; *b* Liverpool, 7 Nov. 1907; *y s* of late J. H. Jervis, Liverpool; *m* 1931, Ethel Braithwaite (*d* 1979), Kendal, Westmorland; one *d.* Editorial Asst, Liverpool Express, 1921-23; Reporter, Westmorland Gazette, 1923-28; Dramatic Critic and Asst Editor, Croydon Times, 1928-37; Sub-Editor, Press Assoc., 1937-47; Asst Editor, 1947-54. Pres., Guild of British Newspaper Editors, 1964-65; Mem. of the Press Council, 1960-65. *Address:* Orchard End, Cart Lane, Grange-over-Sands, Cumbria. *T:* 2335. *Club:* Press.

JERVIS, Charles Walter Lionel; a Recorder of the Crown Court, since 1978; Senior Partner, 1962-80, Consultant, since 1980, Vivian Thomas & Jervis, Solicitors, Penzance; *b* 9 Dec. 1914; *s* of Henry Jervis, MA Oxon, and Elsie Jervis; *m* 1939, Mary Aileen Clarke; two *s* one *d. Educ:* Exeter Sch., Exeter. Solicitor of the Supreme Court. Served War, 1942-46; RNVR, in Asdic Ships (Atlantic Star 1944); demobilized, Lieut RNVR, 1946. Articled in IoW; Asst Solicitor, Penzance, 1939; practised as country solicitor, 1946; Dep. Coroner, Penzance Bor., 1948; Dep. Circuit Judge, 1975-. Pres., Cornwall Law Soc., 1965-66. Mem., Legal Aid Area Cttee, 1967-78. Director: Porthminster Hotel Co. Ltd; Tregarthens Hotel (Scilly) Ltd. Mem., W of England Steam Engine Soc., Redruth. *Publications:* contrib. Justice of Peace, Law Jl, and Criminal Law Rev. *Recreations:* gardening, steam locomotion, wearing old clothes. *Address:* Ros-Vale, St Buryan, Penzance, Cornwall. *T:* St Buryan 272.

JESSEL, family name of Baron Jessel.

JESSEL, 2nd Baron, *cr* 1924, of Westminster; **Edward Herbert Jessel,** Bt, *cr* 1917; CBE 1963; a Deputy Speaker, House of Lords, 1963-77; Chairman, Associated Leisure Ltd; *b* 25 March 1904; *o s* of 1st Baron, CB, CMG, and Maud (*d* 1965), 5th *d* of late Rt Hon. Sir Julian Goldsmid, Bt, MP; *S* father 1950; *m* 1st, 1935, Lady Helen Maglona Vane-Tempest-Stewart (from whom he obtained a divorce, 1960), 3rd *d* of 7th Marquess of Londonderry, KG, PC, MVO; two *d* (one *s* decd); 2nd, 1960, Jessica, *d* of late William De Wet and Mrs H. W. Taylor, Cape Town. *Educ:* Eton; Christ Church, Oxford (MA). Called to Bar, Inner Temple, 1926. Formerly Director: Textile Machinery Makers Ltd; Truscon Ltd; Westminster Trust. Chm., Assoc. of Indep. Unionist Peers, 1959-64. *Address:* 4 Sloane Terrace Mansions, SW1. *T:* 01-730 7843. *Clubs:* Garrick, White's.

See also Sir G. W. G. Agnew.

JESSEL, Sir Charles (John), 3rd Bt *cr* 1883; farmer; *b* 29 Dec. 1924; *s* of Sir George Jessel, 2nd Bt, MC, and Muriel (*d* 1948), *d* of Col J. W. Chaplin, VC; *S* father, 1977; *m* 1st, 1956, Shirley Cornelia (*d* 1977), *d* of John Waters, Northampton; two *s* one *d* ; 2nd, 1979, Gwendolyn Mary, *d* of late Laurance Devereux, OBE, and of Mrs Devereux, and *widow* of Charles Langer, MA. *Educ:* Eton; Balliol College, Oxford. Served War of 1939-45, Lieut 15/19th Hussars (despatches). Hon. Fellow, Psionic Med. Soc., 1977. JP Kent 1960-78. *Recreation:* gardening. *Heir:* *s* George Elphinstone Jessel, *b* 15 Dec. 1957. *Address:* South Hill Farm, Hastingleigh, near Ashford, Kent. *T:* Elmsted 325. *Club:* Cavalry and Guards.

JESSEL, David Charles George, FIB; Chairman, Intervention Board for Agricultural Produce, since 1980; Deputy Chairman, Eagle Star Holdings, and Deputy Chairman and Managing Director, Eagle Star Properties, since 1980; *b* 20 June 1924; *s* of late Sir Richard Hugh Jessel and Margaret Ella Jessel; *m* 1st, 1950, Amelia Grace FitzRoy (marr. diss. 1978), 5th *d* of Viscount Daventry, *qv* ; one *s* one *d* ; 2nd, 1980, Matilda McCormick, Kentucky, USA. *Educ:* Eton. FIB 1964. Served Coldstream Gds, 1942-48 (Captain). Joined Jessel Toynbee & Co. Ltd, 1948; Asst Man. Dir, 1950; Chm. and Man. Dir, 1963-77. Chm. and Dep. Chm., London Discount Market Assoc., 1967-71; Chm., Bernard Sunley Investment Trust, 1977-80. *Recreations:* fishing, shooting, sailing. *Address:* 22 Cambridge Road, SW11 4RR. *Club:* Cavalry and Guards.

JESSEL, Oliver Richard; Chairman: Jessel Trust Ltd, since 1971; Rotaco Domestic Appliances Ltd, since 1977; *b* 24 Aug. 1929; *s* of Comdr R. F. Jessel, DSO, OBE, DSC, RN; *m* 1950, Gloria Rosalie Teresa (*née* Holden); one *s* five *d. Educ:* Rugby. Founded group of companies, 1954; opened office in City of London, 1960; Chm., London, Australian and General Exploration Co. Ltd., 1960-75; formed New Issue Unit Trust and other trusts, 1962-68; responsible for numerous mergers, incl. Johnson & Firth Brown Ltd, and Maple Macowards Ltd; Chm., Charles Clifford Industries Ltd, 1978-81. *Address:* The Grange, Marden, Kent. *T:* Maidstone 831264. *Club:* Garrick.

See also T. F. H. Jessel.

JESSEL, Toby Francis Henry; MP (C) Twickenham since 1970; *b* 11 July 1934; *y s* of Comdr R. F. Jessel, DSO, OBE, DSC, RN, Grange Cottage, Marden, Kent; *m* 1st, 1967 (marr. diss. 1973); one *d* decd; 2nd, 1980, Eira Gwen, *y d* of late Horace and Marigwen Heath. *Educ:* Royal Naval Coll., Dartmouth; Balliol Coll., Oxford (MA). Sub-Lt, RNVR, 1954. Conservative Candidate: Peckham, 1964; Hull (North), 1966. Parly deleg. to India and Pakistan, 1971; Member: Council of Europe, 1976-; WEU, 1976-. Chm., South Area Bd GLC Planning and Transportation Cttee, 1968-70. (Co-opted) LCC Housing Cttee, 1961-65; Councillor, London Borough of Southwark, 1964-66; Mem. for Richmond-upon-Thames, GLC, 1967-73; Hon. Sec. Assoc. of Adopted Conservative Candidates, 1961-66; Jt Sec., Indo-British Parly Gp; Sec., Anglo-Benelux Parly Gp, 1979; Vice-Chm., Cons. Parly Arts Cttee, 1979. Hon. Sec., Katyn Meml Fund, 1972-75. Mem. Metropolitan Water Bd, 1967-70; Mem., London Airport Consultative Cttee, 1967-70. Dir, Clairmace Ltd, 1976-. Mem. Council, Fluoridation Soc., 1976. Liveryman, Worshipful Co. of Musicians. Chevalier, Ordre de la Couronne (Belgium), 1980; Order of Polonia Restituta (Polish Govt in Exile); Order of Merit (Liechtenstein), 1979. *Recreations:* music (has performed Mozart and Schumann piano concertos), gardening, croquet (Longworth Cup, Hurlingham, 1961), ski-ing. *Address:* Old Court House, Hampton Court, East Molesey, Surrey. *Clubs:* Garrick, Hurlingham.

See also O. R. Jessel, A. Panufnik.

JESSUP, Frank William, CBE 1972; Director, Department for External Studies, Oxford University, 1952–76; Librarian of Wolfson College, Oxford, since 1974 (Fellow, 1965–80, Homorary Fellow, 1980); *b* 26 April 1909; *s* of Frederick William Jessup and Alice Sarah (*née* Cheeseman); *m* 1935, Dorothy Hilda Harris; two *s* one *d*. *Educ:* Gravesend Boys' Grammar Sch.; Univ. of London (BA, LLB); Univ. of Oxford (MA). Called to Bar, Gray's Inn, 1935. Dep. County Educn Officer, Kent, until 1952. Chairman: Library Adv. Council (England), 1965–73; British Library Adv. Council, 1976–81; Oxon Rural Community Council, 1976–82; Vice-Chm., Universities Council for Adult Educn, 1973–76. Pres., Kent Archaeol Soc., 1976–82. Chm. of Governors, Rose Bruford Coll. of Speech and Drama, 1960–72. FSA; Hon. FLA. Hon. DCL Kent 1976. *Publications:* Problems of Local Government, 1949; Introduction to Kent Feet of Fines, 1956; A History of Kent, 1958, repr. 1974; Sir Roger Twysden, 1597-1672, 1965, etc; contrib. to Archæologia Cantiana, Studies in Adult Educn, Möbius. *Recreations:* reading, music, gardening. *Address:* Striblehills, Thame, Oxon. *T:* Thame 2027.

JESSUP, Philip C.; United States teacher and lawyer; Judge of International Court of Justice, 1961-70; Teacher of International Law, Columbia University, 1925–61; Hamilton Fish Professor of International Law and Diplomacy, 1946–61; *b* 5 Jan. 1897; *s* of Henry Wynans and Mary Hay Stotesbury Jessup; *m* 1921, Lois Walcott Kellogg; one *s*. *Educ:* Hamilton Coll., Clinton, NY (AB 1919); Columbia Univ. (AM 1924, PhD 1927); Yale Univ. (LLB). US Army Exped. Forces, 1918. Asst to Pres., and Asst Cashier, First Nat. Bank of Utica, NY, 1919–21; Parker & Duryea Law Firm, New York, 1927–43. Asst Solicitor, Dept of State, 1924–25; Asst to Elihu Root, Conf. of Jurists, Permanent Court of International Justice, Geneva, 1929; Legal Adviser to American Ambassador to Cuba, 1930; Chief, Div. of Office of Foreign Relief, Dept of State, 1943; Associate Dir, Naval Sch. of Military Government and Administration, 1942–44; Asst Sec. Gen. UNRRA and Bretton Woods Confs, 1943–44; Asst on Judicial Organisation, San Francisco Conf. on UNO, 1945; US Dep. Rep. to Interim Cttee of Gen. Assembly and Security Council, UN, 1948; Deleg. Sessions: UN Gen. Assembly, 3rd, Paris-New York, 1948–49, 4th New York, 1949, 6th, Paris, Nov. 1951–Jan. 1952, 7th New York 1952. Ambassador at Large of USA, 1949-53. Trustee, Woodrow Wilson Foundn, 1948–57, Pres., 1957–58. Storrs Lectr, Yale Univ. Law Sch., 1956; Cooley Lectr, Michigan Univ. Law Sch., 1958; Blaustein Lectr, Columbia Univ., 1970; Sibley Lectr, Univ. of Georgia Law Sch., 1970; first Fowler Harper Fellow, Yale Law Sch., 1966. Institute of Pacific Relations: Chm., Amer. Council, 1939–40; Chm., Pacific Council, 1939–42; Mem. Curatorium, Hague Acad. of Internat. Law, 1957–68; Trustee: Carnegie Endowment for Internat. Peace, 1937–60; Hamilton Coll., 1949–61; Associate Rockefeller Foundation, 1960–61; Vice-Pres. Institut de droit international, 1959–60, 1974–75. Hon. Mem. Inter-American Institute of International Legal Studies, 1964–. Chairman: Chile-Norway Permanent Conciliation Commn, 1958–; Austro-Swedish Commn for Reconciliation and Arbitration, 1976–; Mem. Governing Council, Inst. for Unification of Private Law, 1964–67, Hon. Mem., 1967–. Hon. President: Amer. Soc. of Internat. Law, 1969–73; Amer. Branch, Internat. Law Assoc., 1970–73. Senior Fellow, Council on Foreign Relations (NYC), 1970–71. Fellow, World Acad. of Art and Sci. Member: Amer. Philosophical Soc.; Amer. Acad. of Arts and Scis. Hon. LLD: Western Reserve Univ., Nat. Univ. of Korea, Rutgers Univ., Middlebury Coll., Yale Univ., St Lawrence Univ., Univ. of Michigan; Johns Hopkins Univ.; Brandeis Univ.; Columbia Univ.; Colby Coll.; Pennsylvania Univ.; Hon. LCD: Colgate Univ., Union Coll.; Hon. JD Oslo; Doc (*hc*) Univ. of Paris; Hon. LittD, Univ. of Hanoi. Hon. Mem., Academia Mexicana de Derecho International. Hungarian Cross of Merit, Class II; Oficial Ordem Nacional do Cruzeiro do Sul, Brazil; Grand Officer, Order of the Cedars, Lebanon; Manley O. Hudson Gold Medal of the American Soc. of International Law, 1964; Distinguished Service Award, Connecticut Bar Assoc., 1970; Wolfgang G. Friedmann Meml Award, 1975; Columbia Univ. Sch. of Law Alumni Assoc. Medal for Excellence, 1977; Graduate Faculties Alumni of Columbia Univ. Award for Excellence, 1977. *Publications:* The Law of Territorial Waters and Maritime Jurisdiction, 1927; United States and the World Court, 1929; Neutrality, Its History, Economics and Law, Vol. I, The Origins (with F. Deak), 1935; Vol. IV, Today and Tomorrow, 1936, repr. 1976; Elihu Root, 1938, repr. 1964; International Problem of Governing Mankind, 1947; A Modern Law of Nations, 1948 (trans. German, Korean, Thai); Transnational Law, 1956 (trans. Arabic, Portuguese, Spanish, Japanese); The Use of International Law, 1959; Controls for Outer Space (with H. J. Taubenfield), 1959; The Price of International Justice, 1971; The Birth of Nations, 1974. *Address:* Windrow Road, Norfolk, Conn 06058, USA. *Clubs:* Century (New York); Cosmos (Washington).

JEVONS, Prof. Frederic Raphael; Vice-Chancellor, Deakin University, Australia, since 1976; *b* 19 Sept. 1929; *s* of Fritz and Hedwig Bettelheim; *m* 1956, Grete Bradel; two *s*. *Educ:* Langley Sch., Norwich; King's Coll., Cambridge (Major Schol.). 1st Cl. Hons Nat. Scis Pt II (Biochem) Cantab 1950; PhD Cantab 1953; DSc Manchester 1966. Postdoctoral Fellow, Univ. of Washington, Seattle, 1953-54; Fellow, King's Coll., Cambridge, 1953–59; Univ. Demonstrator in Biochem., Cambridge, 1956-59; Lectr in Biol Chem., Manchester Univ., 1959–66; Prof. of Liberal Studies in Science, Manchester Univ., 1966–75. Mem. Editorial Adv. Bds, R and D Management and Studies in Science Educn; Mem. Jt Matriculation Bd, 1969–75; Chm. Gen. Studies Cttee, Schools Council, 1974–75; Member: Jt Cttee, SRC and SSRC, 1974–75; Educn Res. and Develt Cttee, 1980–81; Council, Sci. Mus. of Vic., 1980–; Aust. Vice-Chancellors' Exec. Cttee, 1981–; Chm., Grad. Careers Council of Australia, 1976–80. Interviewer for Civil Service Commn on Final Selection Bd, 1970–75; Adviser to Leverhulme project on educnl objectives in applied science, Strathclyde Univ., 1972–75; British Council tours in India, E Africa, Nigeria. *Publications:* The Biochemical Approach to Life, 1964, 2nd edn 1968 (trans. Italian, Spanish, Japanese, German); The Teaching of Science: education, science and society, 1969; (ed jtly) University Perspectives, 1970; (jtly) Wealth from Knowledge: studies of innovation in industry, 1972; (ed jtly) What Kinds of Graduates do we Need?, 1972; Science Observed: science as a social and intellectual activity, 1973; Knowledge and Power, 1976; numerous papers on biochem., history of science, science educn and science policy. *Recreations:* music, theatre, reading. *Address:* Deakin University, Belmont, Geelong, Vic 3217, Australia.

JEWELL, David John, MA, MSc; Headmaster of Repton School, since Jan. 1979; *b* 24 March 1934; *s* of Wing Comdr John Jewell, OBE, FRAeS, and Rachel Jewell, Porthleven, Cornwall; *m* 1958, Katharine Frida Heller; one *s* three *d*. *Educ:* Blundell's Sch., Tiverton; St John's Coll., Oxford. Honours Sch. of Natural Science (Chemistry), BA 1957, MA 1961; BSc Physical Sciences, 1959, MSc 1981. National Service with RAF, 1952-54. Head of Science Dept, Eastbourne Coll., 1958-62; Winchester Coll., 1962-67; Dep. Head, Lawrence Weston Comprehensive Sch., Bristol, 1967-70; Head Master, Bristol Cathedral Sch., 1970–78. Chairman: Choir Schools' Assoc., 1976–77; Direct Grant Sub-Cttee of Headmasters' Conference, 1977-78. FRSA 1981. *Publications:* papers and articles in various scientific and educnl jls. *Recreations:* music, cricket, cooking, Cornwall. *Address:* The Hall, Repton, Derby DE6 6FH. *T:* Burton-on-Trent 702375; Chapel Downs Cottage, Breageside, Porthleven, Cornwall. *Clubs:* East India, Devonshire, Sports and Public Schools; Bristol Savages.

JEWELL, Prof. Peter Arundel, PhD, FIBiol; Mary Marshall and Arthur Walton Professor of Physiology of Reproduction in the University of Cambridge, since Oct. 1977; *b* 16 June 1925; *s* of Percy Arundel Jewell and Ivy Dorothea Enness; *m* 1958, Juliet Clutton-Brock; three *d*. *Educ:* Wandsworth Sch.; Reading Univ. (BSc Agric.); Cambridge Univ. (BA, MA, PhD). Lectr, Royal Veterinary Coll., 1950–60; Research Fellow, Zoological Soc. of London, 1960–66; Dir, Div. of Biological Sciences, Univ. of Biafra, 1966–67; Sen. Lectr and Dir of Conservation Course, University Coll. London, 1967-72; Prof. of Zoology, Royal Holloway Coll., 1972-77. Mem. ICA. *Publications:* Island Survivors: the Ecology of the Soay Sheep of St Kilda, 1974; scientific papers in Jl Animal Ecology, Jl Wildlife Management, Zool. Soc. Symposia, Jl Physiology, etc. *Recreations:* drinking real ale; safaris, watching wild animals; listening, saving rare breeds, theatre, keeping up with three daughters. *Address:* St John's College, Cambridge CB2 1TP.

JEWERS, William George, CBE 1982 (OBE 1976); Managing Director, Finance, and Member, British Gas Corporation, since 1976; *b* 18 Oct. 1921; *s* of late William Jewers and Hilda Jewers (*née* Ellison); *m* 1955, Helena Florence Rimmer; one *s* one *d*. *Educ:* Liverpool Inst. High Sch. for Boys. Liverpool Gas Co., 1938–41. Served War: RAFVR Observer (Flying Officer), 1941–46: Indian Ocean, 265 Sqdn (Catalinas), 1943–44; Burma 194 Sqdn (Dakotas), 1945. Liverpool Gas Co./NW Gas Bd, Sen. Accountancy Asst, 1946–52; W Midlands Gas Bd: Cost Acct, Birmingham and Dist Div., 1953–62; Cost Acct, Area HQ, 1962–65; Asst Chief Acct, 1965–66; Chief Acct, 1967; Dir of Finance, 1968; Gas Council, Dir of Finance, 1969–73; British Gas Corp., Dir of Finance, 1973–76. FCMA, FCCA, JDipMA, CompIGasE. *Publications:* papers and articles to gas industry jls. *Recreations:* music, reading, golf. *Address:* 17 South Park View, Gerrards Cross, Bucks SL9 8HN. *T:* Gerrards Cross 86169.

JEWKES, Gordon Wesley, CMG 1980; HM Diplomatic Service; Consul-General, Chicago, since 1982; *b* 18 Nov. 1931; *er s* of late Jesse Jewkes; *m* 1954, Joyce Lyons; two *s*. *Educ:* Barrow Grammar Sch.; Magnus Grammar Sch., Newark-on-Trent. Colonial Office, 1948; served HM Forces, Army, 1950–52; Gen. Register Office, 1950–63; CS Pay Res. Unit, 1963–65; Gen. Register Office, 1965–68; transf. to HM Diplomatic Service, 1968; CO, later FCO, 1968–69; Consul (Commercial), Chicago, 1969–72; Dep. High Comr, Port of Spain, 1972–75; Head of Finance Dept, FCO, and Finance Officer of Diplomatic Service, 1975–79; Consul-Gen., Cleveland, 1979–82. *Recreations:* music, travel, walking, boating. *Address:* c/o Foreign and Commonwealth Office, SW1A 2AL. *Club:* Travellers'.

JEWKES, John, CBE 1943; MA (Oxon); MCom; *b* June 1902; *m* 1929, Sylvia Butterworth; one *d*. *Educ:* Barrow Grammar Sch.; Manchester Univ. MCom. Asst Sec., Manchester Chamber of Commerce, 1925-26; Lecturer in Economics, University of Manchester, 1926-29; Rockefeller Foundation Fellow, 1929-30; Professor of Social Economics, Manchester 1936-46; Stanley Jevons Prof. of Political Economy, Manchester, 1946–48; Prof. of Economic Organisation, Oxford, and Fellow of Merton College, 1948-69, Emeritus Fellow 1969. Visiting Prof., University of Chicago, 1953-54; Visiting Prof., Princeton Univ., 1961. Dir, Economic Section, War Cabinet Secretariat, 1941; Dir-Gen. of Statistics and Programmes, Ministry of Aircraft Production, 1943; Principal Asst Sec., Office of Minister of Reconstruction, 1944; Mem. of Fuel Advisory Cttee, 1945; Independent Mem. of Cotton Industry Working Party, 1946; Mem. of Royal Commission on Gambling, Betting and Lotteries, 1949. Mem. of Royal Commission on Doctors' and Dentists' Remuneration, 1957–60; Dir, Industrial Policy Gp, 1969–74. Hon. DSc Hull, 1973. *Publications:* An Industrial Survey of Cumberland and Furness (with A. Winterbottom), 1931; Juvenile Unemployment (with A. Winterbottom), 1933; Wages and Labour in the Cotton Spinning Industry (with E. M. Gray),

1935; The Juvenile Labour Market (with Sylvia Jewkes) 1938; Ordeal by Planning, 1948; The Sources of Invention (with David Sawers and Richard Stillerman), 1958; The Genesis of the British National Health Service (with Sylvia Jewkes), 1961; Value for Money in Medicine (with Sylvia Jewkes), 1962; Public and Private Enterprise, 1965; New Ordeal by Planning, 1968; A Return to Free Market Economics?, 1978. *Recreation:* gardening. *Address:* Entwood, Red Copse Lane, Boars Hill, Oxford.
See also B. C. Clarke.

JHABVALA, Mrs Ruth Prawer; author; *b* in Germany, of Polish parents, 7 May 1927; *d* of Marcus Prawer and Eleonora Prawer (*née* Cohn); came to England as refugee, 1939; *m* 1951, C. S. H. Jhabvala; three *d*. *Educ:* Hendon County Sch.; Queen Mary Coll., London Univ. Started writing after graduation and marriage, alternating between novels and short stories; occasional original film-scripts (with James Ivory and Ismail Merchant), including: Shakespeare-wallah, 1965; The Guru, 1969; Bombay Talkie, 1971; Autobiography of a Princess, 1975; Roseland, 1977; Hullabaloo over Georgie and Bonnie's Pictures, 1978; Jane Austen in Manhattan, 1980; Quartet, 1981. *Publications:* novels: To Whom She Will, 1955; The Nature of Passion, 1956; Esmond in India, 1958; The Householder, 1960; Get Ready for Battle, 1962; A Backward Place, 1965; A New Dominion, 1973; Heat and Dust, 1975 (Booker Prize, 1975); *short story collections:* Like Birds, like Fishes, 1964; A Stronger Climate, 1968; An Experience of India, 1971; How I became a Holy Mother and other Stories, 1976. *Recreation:* writing film-scripts. *Address:* c/o John Murray, 50 Albemarle Street, W1.
See also Prof. S. S. Prawer.

JIDDU KRISHNAMURTI; see Krishnamurti, J.

JILANI, Asaf; Editor, Daily Jang, London (first Urdu Daily in UK), since 1973; *b* 24 Sept. 1934; *s* of Abdul Wahid Sindhi and Noor Fatima Jilani; *m* 1961, Mohsina Jilani; two *s* one *d*. *Educ:* Jamia Millia, Delhi; Sindh Marrsa, Karachi; Karachi Univ. (BA, Economics and Persian). Sub-Editor, Daily Imroze, Karachi (Progressive Papers Ltd), 1952; Political Corresp., Daily Imroze, 1954; Special Corresp., Daily Jang, Karachi (posted in India), 1959-65; London Editor: Daily Jang (Karachi, Rawalpindi, Quetta); Daily News, Karachi, and Akhbar-Jehan, Karachi, 1965-73. *Recreations:* cricket, swimming, painting. *Address:* (office) 57 Lant Street, SE1. *T:* 01-403 5833/4122; (home) 23 Horsham Avenue, N12. *T:* 01-368 5697.

JILLETT, Dr Raymond Leslie, TD 1964; AE 1977; Medical Superintendent/Governor, HM Prison, Grendon, Grendon Underwood, since 1975; *b* 24 March 1925; *s* of Leslie George and Ethel Florence Jillett, London; *m* 1955, Mary Patricia (*née* Lewis); two *d*. *Educ:* Bec Sch., London; King's Coll., Univ. of London; King's Coll. Hosp. Med. Sch., London. MB, BS London 1949, DPM 1964, MRCPsych 1971; FBIM 1980 (MBIM 1976). Various hosp. appts, 1949-62; Asst Psychiatrist, Exe Vale Hosp., Exeter, 1962-68. TA, 1954-66: various appts to regts and 128 Field Amb., RAuxAF, Sqdn/Ldr Med., 1967-. HM Prison Service: MO, 1968; Sen. MO, Wakefield Prison, 1975. Oxford Postgrad. Fellowship in Psychiatry, 1964. Divl Surg. and Area Staff Officer, St John Amb. Bde, 1955-60; County Staff Officer, Cadets, 1960-68 (Devon); Area Comr, N Bucks, 1969-; County Surgeon, 1977. OStJ 1970. *Publications:* articles in Lancet and Brit. Jl of Psychiatry. *Recreations:* theatre, dramatic and operatic production. *Address:* c/o The Home Office, 89 Eccleston Square, SW1V 1PU; HM Prison, Grendon, Grendon Underwood, Aylesbury. *Club:* Royal Air Force.

JIMENEZ DE ARECHAGA, Eduardo, DrJur; Professor of International Law, Montevideo Law School, since 1946; *b* Montevideo, 8 June 1918; *s* of E. Jiménez de Aréchaga and Ester Sienra; *m* 1943, Marta Ferreira; three *s* two *d*. *Educ:* Sch. of Law, Univ. of Montevideo. Under-Sec., Foreign Relations, 1950-52; Sec., Council of Govt of Uruguay, 1952-55; Mem., Internat. Law Commn of UN, 1961-69 (Pres., 1963); Cttee *Rapporteur*, Vienna Conf. on Law Treaties, 1968-69; Minister of the Interior, Uruguay, 1968; Pres. of the International Ct of Justice, The Hague, 1976-79 (Judge of the Ct, 1970-79). Inter-Amer. Bar Assoc. Book Award, 1961. *Publications:* Reconocimiento de Gobiernos, 1946; Voting and Handling of Disputes in the Security Council, 1951; Treaty Stipulations in Favour of Third States, 1956; Derecho Constitucional de las Naciónes Unidas, 1958; Curso de Derecho Internacional Público, 2 vols, 1959-61; International Law in the Past Third of a Century, vol. I, 1978. *Address:* Casilla de Correo 539, Montevideo, Uruguay.

JINKS, Prof. John Leonard, FRS 1970; Professor of Genetics and Head of Department of Genetics, since 1965, Pro-Vice-Chancellor, since 1981, Birmingham University; *b* 21 Oct. 1929; *s* of Jack and Beatrice May Jinks; *m* 1955, Diana Mary Williams; one *s* one *d*. *Educ:* Longton High Sch., Stoke-on-Trent; Univ. of Birmingham. BSc Botany 1950, PhD Genetics 1952, DSc Genetics 1964, Birmingham. ARC Research Student: Univ. of Birmingham, 1950-52; Carlsberg Labs, Copenhagen; Istituto Sieroterapico, Milan, 1952-53; Scientific Officer, ARC Unit of Biometrical Genetics, Univ. of Birmingham, 1953-59; Harkness Fellow, California Inst. of Technology, 1959-60; Principal Scientific Officer, ARC Unit of Biometrical Genetics, 1960-65; Birmingham University: Hon. Lectr, 1960-62; Reader, 1962-65; Dean, Faculty of Sci. and Engrg, 1972-75. Member: SRC, 1975-79; ARC, 1979-; Chm., Governing Body, Nat. Veg. Research Station, 1979-. Pres., Genetical Soc. of GB, 1981-. FIBiol 1968. Editor of Heredity, 1960-75, Acting Editor, 1976-77; Editor, Jl of Agricl Scis, 1981-. *Publications:* Extrachromosomal Inheritance, 1964; (jtly) Biometrical Genetics, 1971;

Cytoplasmic Inheritance, 1976; (jtly) Introduction to Biometrical Genetics, 1977; numerous papers and chapters in books on microbial genetics, biometrical genetics and behavioral genetics. *Recreations:* piano, gardening. *Address:* 81 Witherford Way, Selly Oak, Birmingham B29 4AN. *T:* 021-472 2008.

JOB, Rev. Canon (Evan) Roger (Gould); Canon Residentiary, Precentor and Sacrist of Winchester Cathedral, since 1979; *b* 15 May 1936; 2nd *s* of Thomas Brian Job and Elsie Maud Job (*née* Gould), Ipswich; *m* 1964, Rose Constance Mary, *o d* of Stanley E. Gordon and late Audrey H. Gordon, Hooton, Wirral; two *s*. *Educ:* Cathedral Choir School and King's Sch., Canterbury; Magdalen Coll., Oxford; Cuddesdon Theol Coll. BA 1960, MA 1964; ARCM 1955. Deacon 1962, priest 1963. Asst Curate, Liverpool Parish Church, 1962-65; Vicar of St John, New Springs, Wigan, 1965-70; Precentor of Manchester Cath., 1970-74; Precentor and Sacrist of Westminster Abbey, 1974-79; Chaplain of The Dorchester, 1976-79. *Publications:* contrib. Churchman. *Recreations:* gardening, piano. *Address:* 8 The Close, Winchester SO23 9LS. *T:* Winchester 4771.

JOBERT, Michel; Officier de la Légion d'Honneur; Croix de Guerre (1939-45); Minister of State, and Minister for Overseas Trade, France, since 1981; Founder, Mouvement des Démocrates, 1974; Editor, La Lettre de Michel Jobert, since 1974; *b* Meknès, Morocco, 11 Sept. 1921; *s* of Jules Jobert and Yvonne Babule; *m* Muriel Frances Green; one *s*. *Educ:* Lycée de Rabat; Lycée de Meknès; Dip. de l'Ecole libre des sciences politiques; Ecole nationale d'Administration. Cour des comptes: Auditor, 1949; Conseiller Référendaire, 1953. Member of Ministerial Cabinets: Finance, Work and Social Security, President of the Council, 1952-56; Director of the Cabinet of the High Commission of the Republic in French West Africa, 1956-58; Dir of Cabinet of Minister of State, 1959-61; Jt Dir, 1963-66, then Director, 1966-68, of the Prime Minister's Cabinet (Georges Pompidou); Pres., Council of Admin. of Nat. Office of Forests, 1966-73; Admin. of Havas, 1968-73; Secretary-Gen., Presidency of the Republic, 1969-73; Minister for Foreign Affairs, 1973-74. Conseiller-maitre, Cour des comptes, 1971. *Publications:* Mémoires d'avenir, 1974; L'autre regard, 1975; Lettre ouverte aux femmes politiques, 1976; Parler aux Français, 1977; La vie d'Hella Schuster, 1977; Maroc: Extrême Maghreb du Soleil Couchant, 1978; La rivière aux grenades, 1982. *Address:* (home) 21 quai Alphonse-Le Gallo, 92100 Boulogne-sur-Seine, France; (office) 108 quai Louis Blériot, 75016 Paris, France.

JOBLING, Captain James Hobson, RN; Metropolitan Stipendiary Magistrate, since 1973; a Deputy Circuit Judge, since 1976; *b* 29 Sept. 1921; *s* of late Captain and Mrs J. S. Jobling, North Shields, Northumberland; *m* 1946, Cynthia, *o d* of late F. E. V. Lean, Beacon Park, Plymouth; one *s* one *d*. *Educ:* Tynemouth High Sch.; London Univ. (LLB Hons, 1971). Entered Royal Navy, 1940; awarded Gedge Medal and Prize, 1946; called to Bar, Inner Temple, 1955; Comdr, 1960; JSSC course, 1961-62; Dir, Nat. Liaison, SACLANT HQ, USA, 1962-65; Chief Naval Judge Advocate, in rank of Captain, 1969-72; retd, 1973. Planning Inspector, DoE, 1973. *Recreations:* gardening, walking. *Address:* Pinewell Lodge, Wood Road, Hindhead, Surrey. *T:* Hindhead 4426.

JOCELYN, family name of Earl of Roden.

JOCELYN, Dr Henry David, FBA 1982; Hulme Professor of Latin, University of Manchester, since 1973; *b* 22 Aug. 1933; *s* of late John Daniel Jocelyn and Phyllis Irene Burton; *m* 1958, Margaret Jill, *d* of Bert James Morton and Dulcie Marie Adams; two *s*. *Educ:* Canterbury Boys' High Sch.; Univ. of Sydney (BA); St John's Coll., Univ. of Cambridge (BA, PhD). Teaching Fellow in Latin, Univ. of Sydney, 1955; Scholar in Classics, British Sch. at Rome, 1957-59; Univ. of Sydney: Lectr in Latin, 1960-64; Sen. Lectr in Latin, 1964-66; Reader in Latin, 1966-70; Prof. of Latin, 1970-73. Visiting Lectr in Classics, Yale Univ., 1967; Vis. Fellow, ANU, 1979. FAHA 1970. *Publications:* The Tragedies of Ennius, 1967 (corr. reprint 1969); (with B. P. Setchell) Regnier de Graaf on the Human Reproductive Organs, 1972; papers on Greek and Latin subjects in various periodicals. *Address:* 4 Clayton Avenue, Manchester M20 0BN. *T:* 061-434 1526.

JÖDAHL, Ole Erik, GCVO (Hon.) 1975; Swedish Ambassador to the Court of St James's, 1972-76; *b* 18 Nov. 1910; *s* of Oscar Jödahl and Elida Rapp; *m* 1934, Karin, *d* of Hadar Rissler and Signe Ouchterlony; two *s* one *d*. Journalist, editor and Foreign Affairs commentator in Swedish social democratic and co-operative periodicals and newspapers, 1933-45. Entered Swedish Foreign Service as Press Attaché, Helsinki, 1945, Moscow, 1945-48; Head, Foreign Min. Press and Information Dept, 1948-53; Envoy, Belgrade, 1953-56 (Mem. Neutral Nations Supervisory Commn Korea, 1954); Ambassador to Bonn, 1956-67; Sec.-Gen., Min. for Foreign Affairs, 1967-72. Grand Cross, Swedish Order of the North Star; Grand Cross, Order of Merit of Federal Republic of Germany; Grand Cross of Yugoslav Flag; Chevalier, French Legion of Honour, etc. *Publication:* contrib. The War 1939-45 (in Swedish), 1945-47. *Recreations:* mountain walking, reading. *Address:* Bastugatan 27, S-117 25 Stockholm, Sweden. *Club:* Travellers'.

JOEL, Hon. Sir Asher (Alexander), KBE 1974 (OBE 1956); Kt 1971; Member of Legislative Council of New South Wales, 1957-78; Company Director and Public Relations Consultant; *b* 4 May 1912; *s* of Harry and Phoebe Joel, London and Sydney; *m* 1st, 1937 (marr. diss. 1948); two *s*; 2nd, 1949, Sybil, *d* of Frederick Mitchell Jacobs; one *s* one *d*. *Educ:* Enmore Public

ww—38

Sch.; Cleveland Street High Sch., Sydney. Served War of 1939–45: AIF, 1942, transf. RAN; Lieut RANVR, 1943; RAN PRO staff Gen. MacArthur, 1944–45, New Guinea, Halmaheras, Philippines. Chairman: Asher Joel Media Gp; Carpentaria Newspapers Pty Ltd; Mount Isa TV Pty Ltd; Nat. Pres., Anzac Mem. Forest in Israel; Dir, Royal North Shore Hosp. of Sydney, 1959–81. Mem., Sydney Cttee (Hon. Dir, 1956–64); Hon. Dir and Organiser, Pageant of Nationhood (State welcome to the Queen), 1963; Exec. Mem., Citizens Welcoming Cttee visit Pres. Johnson, 1966; Chm., Citizens Cttee Captain Cook Bi-Centenary Celebrations, 1970; Dep. Chm., Citizens Welcoming Cttee visit Pope Paul VI to Australia, 1970; Chm., Sydney Opera Hse Official Opening Citizens Cttee, 1972; Dep. Chm., Aust. Govt Adv. Commn on US Bi-Centenary Celebrations, 1976; Mem., Nat. Australia Day Cttee. Mem., Sydney Opera Hse Trust, 1969–79; Chm., Sydney Entertainment Centre, 1979–. Fellow: Advertising Inst. of Austr. (Federal Patron); Public Relations Inst. of Austr.; Austr. Inst. Management; FInstD; FRSA; Mem., Public Relations Soc. of America; Hon. Mem., Royal Australian Historical Soc., 1970. Hon. Fellow, Internat. Coll. of Dentists, 1975. US Bronze Star, 1943; Ancient Order of Sikatuna (Philippines), 1975; Kt Comdr, Order of Rizal (Philippines), 1978. *Publication:* Without Chains Free (novel), 1977. *Recreations:* fishing, gardening. *Address:* 2 Ormiston Avenue, Gordon, NSW 2072, Australia. *T:* 4985913. *Clubs:* Australian Jockey, Sydney Turf, Tattersall's, American, Imperial Service, Journalists, (Hon. Mem.) Australian Pioneers, Royal Agricultural Society (Sydney); Royal Sydney Yacht Squadron.

JOEL, Harry Joel; *b* 4 Sept. 1894; *o s* of Jack Barnato Joel, JP. *Educ:* Malvern Coll. Served European War 1914–18 with 15th Hussars. *Recreations:* racing and shooting. *Address:* The Stud House, Childwick Bury, St Albans, Herts; Sefton Lodge, Newmarket. *Clubs:* Buck's; Jockey (Newmarket).

JOHANNESBURG, Bishop of, since 1974; **Rt. Rev. Timothy John Bavin;** *b* 17 Sept. 1935; *s* of Edward Sydney Durrance and Marjorie Gwendoline Bavin. *Educ:* Brighton Coll.; Worcester Coll., Oxford (2nd Cl. Theol., MA); Cuddesdon Coll. Curate, St Alban's Cathedral, Pretoria, 1961–64; Chaplain, St Alban's Coll., Pretoria, 1965–68; Curate of Uckfield, Sussex, 1969–71; Vicar of Good Shepherd, Brighton, 1971–73; Dean and Rector of Cathedral of St Mary the Virgin, Johannesburg, 1973–74. ChStJ 1975. *Recreations:* music, theatre, walking, gardening. *Address:* PO Box 1131, Johannesburg, Transvaal, 2000, S Africa. *T:* 834-5181. *Club:* Rand (Johannesburg).

JOHANNESBURG, Assistant Bishops of; *see* Pickard, Rt Rev. S. C.; Tutu, Rt Rev. D. M.

JOHANSEN-BERG, Rev. John; Minister, St Andrew's United Reformed Church, Ealing, since 1977; *b* 4 Nov. 1935; *s* of John Alfred and Caroline Johansen-Berg, Middlesbrough; *m* 1971, Joan, *d* of James and Sally Ann Parnham, Leeds; two *s* one *d. Educ:* Acklam Hall Grammar Sch., Middlesbrough; Leeds Univ. (BA Hons Eng. Lit., BD); Fitzwilliam Coll., Cambridge Univ. (BA Theol Tripos, MA); Westminster Theol Coll. (Dip. Theol.). Tutor, Westminster Coll., Cambridge, 1961; ordained, 1962; pastoral charges: St Ninian's Presbyterian Church, Luton, 1962–70 (Sec., Luton Council of Churches); Founder Minister, St Katherine of Genoa Church, Dunstable (dedicated 1968); The Rock Church Centre, Liverpool (Presbyterian, then United Reformed), 1970–77, work begun in old public house, converted into Queens Road Youth Club, new Church Centre dedicated 1972, a building designed for youth, community and church use. Convener, Church and Community Cttee of Presbyterian C of E, 1970–72; Chm. Church and Society Dept, URC, 1972–79; Moderator of the Gen. Assembly of the URC, 1980–81. British Council of Churches: former Mem., Div. of Community Affairs and Div. of Internat. Affairs. Chm. Gp on Violence, Non-violence and Social Change (for Britain Today and Tomorrow Programme, 1977); Convener, Commission on Non-Violent Action (report published 1973). Chm., Christian Fellowship Trust; Founder Mem. and Sponsor, Christian Concern for Southern Africa. Jt Editor, Jl of Presbyterian Historical Soc. of England, 1964–70. *Publication:* Arian or Arminian? Presbyterian Continuity in the Eighteenth Century, 1969. *Recreations:* mountain walking, badminton, drama. *Address:* St Andrew's Manse, 2 King's Avenue, Ealing, W5 2SH. *T:* 01-998 7405.

JOHANSON, Rev. Dr Brian; Minister of the City Temple, London, since 1976; *b* 8 March 1929; *s* of Bernard Johanson and Petra Johanson; *m* 1955, Marion Shirley Giles; one *s* two *d. Educ:* Univ. of South Africa (BA, DD); Univ. of London (BD). Parish Minister, S Africa, 1956–63; Sen. Lectr in Theology, 1964–69, Prof. of Theol., 1970–76, Univ. of SA; Vis. Res. Fellow: Princeton Theol Seminary, 1970; Univ. of Aberdeen, 1976. *Publications:* univ. pubns in S Africa; booklets; essays in collections; articles in theol jls. *Address:* The City Temple, Holborn Viaduct, EC1. *T:* 01-583 5532.

JOHN, Arthur Walwyn, CBE 1967 (OBE 1945); FCA; Financial Consultant; Chairman: Property Holding and Investment Trust Ltd, since 1977 (Director, since 1976); Stenhouse Holdings Ltd, since 1982 (Director, since 1976); Director: J. H. Sankey & Son Ltd, since 1965; Schroder Property Fund, since 1971; Reed Stenhouse Companies Ltd, Canada, since 1977; Underwriting Member of Lloyds, since 1977; *s* of Oliver Walwyn and Elsie Maud John; *m* 1949, Elizabeth Rosabelle (*d* 1979), *yr d* of Ernest David and Elsie Winifred Williams; one *s* two *d. Educ:* Marlborough Coll. Mem. Institute of Chartered Accountants, 1934 (Mem. Council, 1965–81). Asst to Commercial Manager (Collieries), Powell Duffryn Associated Collieries Ltd,

1936. Joined Army, 1939; served War of 1939–45: commissioned, 1940; War Office, 1941; DAQMG First Army, 1942, and HQ Allied Armies in Italy; AQMG Allied Forces HQ, 1944 (despatches, 1943, 1945). Chief Accountant, John Lewis & Co. Ltd, 1945; Dep. Dir-Gen. of Finance, National Coal Board, 1946; Dir-Gen. of Finance, 1955; Member, NCB, 1961–68; Chm., NCB Coal Products Divn, 1962–68. Dir, Unigate Ltd, 1969–75. Mem., Price Commn, 1976–77. Mem. and Court, Worshipful Co. of Chartered Accts in England and Wales, 1977– (Master, 1981–82). *Recreations:* golf, gardening. *Address:* Limber, Top Park, Gerrards Cross, Bucks SL9 7PW. *T:* Gerrards Cross 84811. *Club:* Army and Navy.

JOHN, Brynmor Thomas; MP (Lab) Pontypridd since 1970; *b* 18 April 1934; *s* of William Henry and Sarah Jane John; *m* 1960, Anne Pryce Hughes; one *s* one *d. Educ:* Pontypridd Boys' Grammar Sch.; University Coll., London. LLB Hons 1954. Articled, 1954; admitted Solicitor, 1957; National Service (Officer, Educn Br., RAF), 1958–60; practising Solicitor, Pontypridd, 1960–70. Parly Under-Sec. of State for Defence (RAF), MoD, 1974–76; Minister of State, Home Office, 1976–79; Opposition spokesman on NI, 1979, on defence, 1980–81, on social security, 1981–. *Recreation:* watching Rugby football. *Address:* House of Commons, SW1A 0AA.

JOHN, Admiral of the Fleet Sir Caspar, GCB 1960 (KCB 1956; CB 1952); Vice-President, Star and Garter Home, since 1973 (Chairman, 1967–72); First Sea Lord and Chief of Naval Staff, 1960–64; *b* 22 March 1903; *s* of late Augustus John, OM, RA; *m* 1944, Mary Vanderpump; one *s* two *d. Educ:* Royal Naval College, Dartmouth. Joined Royal Navy, 1916. Served War of 1939–45, Home and Mediterranean Fleets, Captain, 1941; Rear-Adm., 1951; Flag Officer, Commanding Third Aircraft Carrier Squadron and Heavy Squadron, 1951–52; Deputy Controller Aircraft, 1953–54; Vice-Adm. 1954; Flag Officer, Air, 1955–57; Admiral 1957; Vice-Chief of Naval Staff, 1957–60; Principal Naval ADC to the Queen, 1960–62; Admiral of the Fleet, 1962. Chm., Housing Corp., 1964–68; Mem., Govt Security Commn, 1964–73. *Address:* Trethewey, Mousehole, Penzance, Cornwall TR19 6QQ.

JOHN, David Dilwyn, CBE 1961; TD; DSc; Director, National Museum of Wales, Cardiff, 1948–68; *b* 20 Nov. 1901; *e s* of Thomas John, St Bride's Major, Glam; *m* 1929, Marjorie, *d* of J. W. Page, HMI, Wellington, Salop; one *s* one *d. Educ:* Bridgend County Sch.; University Coll. of Wales, Aberystwyth. Zoologist on scientific staff, Discovery Investigations, engaged in oceanographical research in Antarctic waters, 1925–35; awarded Polar Medal. Appointed Asst Keeper in charge of Echinoderms at British Museum (Natural History), 1935; Deputy Keeper, 1948. Joined Territorial Army, 1936; promoted Major, RA, 1942. Hon. LLD Univ. of Wales, 1969. *Publications:* papers, chiefly on Echinoderms, in scientific journals. *Address:* 7 Cyncoed Avenue, Cardiff CF2 6ST. *T:* Cardiff 752499.

JOHN, DeWitt; Editor, Christian Science periodicals, since 1981; *b* 1 Aug. 1915; *s* of Franklin Howard John and Frances DeWitt; *m* 1942, Morley Marshall; one *s* one *d. Educ:* Principia Coll. (BA); University of Chicago (MA); Columbia (MS). Editorial Page Ed., St Petersburg (Fla) Times, 1938–39; Political Writer, Christian Science Monitor (Boston), 1939–42; US Navy, 1942–45 (Bronze Star); Editorial Staff, Christian Science Monitor, 1945–49; associated with Christian Science Cttee on Publication of First Church of Christ, Scientist, Boston, Mass, 1949–64 (Asst Man., 1954–62 and Man. of Cttees on Publication, 1962–64); Editor, The Christian Science Monitor, 1964–70; Dir, First Church of Christ, Scientist, Boston, 1970–80. Authorized teacher of Christian Science, 1964–. *Publication:* The Christian Science Way of Life, 1962. *Address:* Old Concord Road, Lincoln, Mass 01773, USA.

JOHN, Elton Hercules, (Reginald Kenneth Dwight); musician, composer; *b* 25 March 1947; *s* of Stanley Dwight and Sheila (now Farebrother). *Educ:* Pinner County Grammar Sch.; Royal Acad. of Music, London. Played piano in Northwood Hills Hotel, 1964; joined local group, Bluesology, 1965; signed to Dick James Music as writer and singer, 1967; visited America for concert and was overnight success, 1970; formed Elton John Band, 1970; regularly tours America, Europe, Australia and Japan; first internat. pop singer to perform in Russia, 1979. Vice-Pres. and Mem. Council, National Youth Theatre of GB, 1975–; Chm., Watford Football Club, 1976– (Dir, 1974–). *Hit Records include: albums:* Empty Sky, 1969; Elton John, Tumbleweed Connection, 1970; Friends, 11.17.70, Madman Across the Water, 1971; Honky Chateau, 1972; Don't Shoot Me, Goodbye Yellow Brick Road, 1973; Caribou, Greatest Hits, 1974; Captain Fantastic, Rock of the Westies, 1975; Here and There, Blue Moves, 1976; Greatest Hits vol. II, 1977; A Single Man, 1978; Victim of Love, 1979; 21 at 33, Lady Samantha, 1980; The Fox, 1981; Jump Up, 1982; *singles:* Your Song, 1971; Rocket Man, Crocodile Rock, 1972; Daniel, Goodbye Yellow Brick Road, 1973; Candle in the Wind, Don't Let the Sun Go Down On Me, The Bitch is Back, Lucy in the Sky with Diamonds, 1974; Philadelphia Freedom, Someone Saved My Life Tonight, 1975; Don't Go Breaking My Heart, Sorry Seems to be the Hardest Word, 1976; Ego, Part Time Love, Song for Guy, 1978; Little Jeannie, 1980; Nobody Wins, 1981; Blue Eyes, Empty Garden, Princess, 1982. *Films:* Goodbye to Norma Jean, 1973; To Russia with Elton, 1980; played Pinball Wizard, in Tommy, 1973. Recipient of gold discs for all albums; Ivor Novello Award, Best Pop Song, 1976–77, Best Instrumental, 1978–79. *Recreations:* include playing tennis. *Address:* c/o John Reid Enterprises, 104 Lancaster Gate, W2. *T:* 01-258 3585.

JOHN, Michael M.; *see* Morley-John, M.

JOHN, Sir Rupert (Godfrey), Kt 1971; Governor of St Vincent, 1970–76; Member, Barclays Bank International Ltd Policy Advisory Committe (St Vincent), since 1977; Director, St Vincent Building and Loan Association, since 1977; Consultant to UNITAR, since 1978; *b* 19 May 1916; 2nd *s* of late Donelley John; *m* 1937, Hepsy, *d* of late Samuel Norris; three *s* one *d* (and one *s* decd). *Educ:* St Vincent Grammar Sch.; Univ. of London (BA, DipEd); Gray's Inn; New York University. First Asst Master, St Kitts/Nevis Grammar Sch., 1944; Asst Master, St Vincent Grammar Sch., 1944–52; private practice at Bar of St Vincent, 1952–58; Magistrate, Grenada, 1958–60; Actg Attorney-General, Grenada, 1960–62; Human Rights Officer, UN, 1962–69; Mem. Internat. Team of Observers, Nigeria, 1969–70; Senior Human Rights Officer, 1970. Has attended numerous internat. seminars and confs as officer of UN. Mem. Editorial Adv. Bd, Jl of Third World Legal Studies, 1981–. KStJ 1971. *Publications:* St Vincent and its Constitution, 1971; Pioneers in Nation-Building in a Caribbean Mini-State, 1979; Racism and its Elimination, 1980; papers in various jls. *Recreations:* cricket, walking, swimming. *Address:* PO Box 677, Cane Garden, St Vincent, West Indies. *T:* 61500. *Club:* Royal Commonwealth Society.

JOHN CHARLES, Rt. Rev. Brother; *see* Vockler, Rt. Rev. J. C.

JOHN-MACKIE, Baron *cr* 1981 (Life Peer), of Nazeing in the County of Essex; **John John-Mackie;** Chairman, Forestry Commission, 1976–79; *b* 24 Nov. 1909; *s* of late Maitland Mackie, OBE, Farmer, and Mary Ann Mackie (*née* Yull); *m* 1934, Jeannie Inglis Milne; three *s* two *d. Educ:* Aberdeen Gram. Sch.; North of Scotland Coll. of Agriculture. Managing director of family farming company at Harold's Park Farm, Nazeing, Waltham Abbey, Essex, 1953–; Vicarage and Plumridge Farms, Hadley Wood, Enfield, 1968–79. MP (Lab) Enfield East, 1959-Feb. 1974; Jt Parly Sec., Min. of Agriculture, 1964–70. Mem., Aberdeen and Kincardine Agricl Exec. Cttee, 1939–47; Governor, North of Scotland Coll. of Agriculture, 1942–64, Vice Chm. 1956–64; Chm., Aberdeen and Kincardine Health Exec. Cttee, 1948–51; Governor, Nat. Inst. of Agricl Engn, 1949–61; Member: Secretary of State for Scotland's Adv. Council, 1944–54; Plant Cttee on Poultry Diseases, 1963–64. Chm., Glentworth Scottish Farms Ltd, 1947–68. *Publication:* (for Fabian Soc.) Land Nationalisation. *Recreations:* golf and tennis. *Address:* Harold's Park, Nazeing, Waltham Abbey, Essex. *T:* Nazeing 2202. *Club:* Farmers'.
See also Baron Mackie of Benshie, Sir Maitland Mackie.

JOHN PAUL II, His Holiness Pope, (Karol Jozef Wojtyla); *b* Wadowice, Poland, 18 May 1920; *s* of Karol Wojtyla. *Educ:* Jagiellonian Univ., Cracow; Pontificio Ateneo 'Angelicum' (Dr in Theology). Ordained Priest, 1946; Prof. of Moral Theology, Univs of Lublin and Cracow, 1954–58; titular Bishop of Ombi, and Auxiliary Bishop of Cracow, 1958; Vicar Capitular, 1962; Archbishop and Metropolitan of Cracow, 1964–78. Cardinal, 1967; elected Pope, 16 Oct. 1978. Formerly Member, Congregations Pro Institutione Catholica, Pro Sacramentis et Cultu Divino, and Pro Clero. *Publications:* The Goldsmith Shop (play), 1960; Love and Responsibility, 1962; Person and Act, 1969; The Foundations of Renewal, 1972; Sign of Contradiction, 1976; The Future of the Church, 1979; Easter Vigil and other poems, 1979; Collected Poems (trans. Jerzy Peterkiewicz), 1982. *Address:* Apostolic Palace, 00120 Vatican City.

JOHNES, Herbert J. L.; *see* Lloyd-Johnes.

JOHNS, Alun Morris, MD, FRCOG; Hon. Consulting Gynæcological and Obstetric Surgeon, Queen Charlotte's Hospital, London; *m* 1927, Joyce, *d* of T. Willoughby, Carlton-in-Coverdale, Yorks; one *s* two *d. Educ:* Manchester Univ. MB, ChB 1923, MD Manchester (Commend) 1925; FRCOG 1947. Late Consulting Surgeon, Surbiton Hospital and Erith and Dartford Hospitals. Examiner Central Midwives Board; Fellow Royal Society of Medicine; Fellow Manchester Med. Soc.; Fellow Manchester Path. Soc. *Address:* Loosley Row, near Princes Risborough, Bucks HP17 0PE. *T:* Princes Risborough 5298.

JOHNS, Glynis; actress; *b* Pretoria, South Africa; *d* of Mervyn Johns and Alice Maude (*née* Steel-Payne); *m* 1st, Anthony Forwood (marr. diss.); one *s* ; 2nd, David Foster, DSO, DSC and Bar (marr. diss.); 3rd, Cecil Peter Lamont Henderson; 4th, Elliott Arnold. *Educ:* Clifton and Hampstead High Schs. First stage appearance in Buckie's Bears as a child ballerina, Garrick Theatre, London, 1935. Parts include: Sonia in Judgement Day, Embassy and Strand, 1937; Miranda in Quiet Wedding, Wyndham's, 1938 and in Quiet Weekend, Wyndham's, 1941; Peter in Peter Pan, Cambridge Theatre, 1943; Fools Rush In, Fortune; The Way Things Go, Phœnix, 1950; Gertie (title role), NY, 1952; Major Barbara (title role), NY, 1957; The Patient in Too True to Be Good, NY, 1962; The King's Mare, Garrick, 1966; Come as You Are, New, 1970; A Little Night Music, New York, 1973 (Tony award for best musical actress); Ring Round the Moon, Los Angeles, 1975; 13 Rue de l'Amour, Phœnix, 1976; Cause Célèbre, Her Majesty's, 1977 (Best Actress Award, Variety Club). Entered films as a child. *Films include:* South Riding, 49th Parallel, Frieda, An Ideal Husband, Miranda (the Mermaid), State Secret, No Highway, The Magic Box, Appointment with Venus, Encore, The Card, Sword and the Rose, Personal Affair, Rob Roy, The Weak and the Wicked, The Beachcomber, The Seekers, Poppa's Delicate Condition, Cabinet of Dr Caligari, Mad About Men, Josephine and Men, The Court Jester, Loser Takes All, The Chapman Report, Dear Bridget, Mary Poppins. Also broadcasts; television programmes include: Star Quality; The Parkinson Show (singing Send in the Clowns); Mrs Amworth (USA); All You Need is Love; Across

a Crowded Room; Little Gloria, Happy at Last. *Address:* c/o Harold L. Schiff, 555 Fifth Avenue, New York, NY 10017, USA.

JOHNS, Patricia Holly, MA; Headmistress, St Mary's School, Wantage, Oxon, since 1980; *b* 13 Nov. 1933; *d* of William and Violet Harris; *m* 1958, Michael Charles Bedford Johns (*d* 1965), MA; one *s* one *d. Educ:* Blackheath High Sch.; Girton Coll., Cambridge (BA 1956, MA 1959, CertEd with distinction 1957). Asst Maths Mistress; Cheltenham Ladies' Coll., 1957–58; Macclesfield Girls' High Sch., 1958–60; Asst Maths Mistress, then Head of Maths and Dir of Studies, St Albans High Sch., 1966–75; Sen. Mistress, and Housemistress of Hopeman House, Gordonstoun, 1975–80. *Recreations:* choral singing, walking, camping, dogs (corgis). *Address:* St Mary's School, Newbury Street, Wantage, Oxon OX12 8BZ; 8 Garden Close, Salisbury Avenue, St Albans, Herts AL1 4TX. *T:* St Albans 52185.

JOHNS, Peter Magrath, OBE 1981; Secretary, All England Lawn Tennis Ground Ltd, since 1977; *b* 8 June 1914; *s* of late Robert Johns and Gladys Johns (*née* Booth); *m* 1949, Kathleen Joan Whitefield; two *s. Educ:* Mill Hill School. Served War of 1939–45; commnd 1940; demobilised 1946 (Captain). Lawn Tennis Association: Asst Sec., 1955–73; Sec., 1973–80. Silver Jubilee Medal, 1977. *Recreations:* lawn tennis, real tennis, bowls. *Address:* 54 The Ridgeway, Friern Barnet, N11 3LJ. *T:* 01-368 4655. *Clubs:* Army and Navy, All England Lawn Tennis, Old Millhillians, Queen's; International Lawn Tennis Club of Great Britain.

JOHNSON; *see* Croom-Johnson.

JOHNSON, Alan Campbell; *see* Campbell-Johnson.

JOHNSON, Alan Woodworth, MA, ScD, PhD, ARCS, DIC; FRS 1965, FRSC; Professor of Chemistry and Hon. Director, Agricultural Research Council Unit of Invertebrate Chemistry and Physiology, University of Sussex, since 1968; Member, British Technology Group, since 1981; *b* 29 Sept. 1917; *s* of late James William and Jane Johnson, Forest Hall, Newcastle upon Tyne; *m* 1941, Lucy Ida Celia (*née* Bennett); one *s* one *d. Educ:* Morpeth Grammar Sch., Northumberland; Rutherford Coll., Newcastle-upon-Tyne; Royal College of Science, London. Chemist, Swan, Hunter & Wigham Richardson, Ltd, 1934; Thos Hedley & Co. Ltd, 1935–36; Royal Schol., Imperial Coll. of Science, 1937; BSc, ARCS; PhD, DIC 1940; Research Asst in Organic Chemistry, RCS, 1940–42; Research Chemist, ICI Dyestuffs Div., 1942–46; University of Cambridge: ICI Fellow, 1946–48; Asst Dir of Research in Organic Chemistry, 1948–53; Lecturer in Organic Chemistry, 1953–55; Sir Jesse Boot Prof. of Organic Chemistry and Head of Dept of Chemistry, University of Nottingham, 1955–68; Fellow and Steward, Christ's Coll., Cambridge, 1951–55. Member: ARC Adv. Cttee on Plants and Soils, 1966–71; SRC Chemistry Cttee, 1976–78; Enzyme Panel, 1976; NRDC, 1976–81. Vis. Professor: University of Melbourne, 1960; University of Calif, Berkeley, 1962. Lectures: Tilden, Chemical Soc., 1953; Reilly, Univ. Notre Dame, Ind, USA, 1962; Simonsen, Chemical Soc., 1967; Pedler, Chemical Soc., 1974; Amer. Chem. Soc. W Coast Lectr, 1976; Wheeler, UC Dublin, 1979; Peboc, UC Bangor, 1979. Member Council: Royal Society, 1966–67, 1971–73 (Vice-Pres., 1982–); Chemical Soc., 1955, 1957, 1970–; Hon. Sec. Chemical Society, 1958–65, Vice-Pres., 1965–68, Pres., 1977–78. Corday-Morgan Lecturer, India and Ceylon, 1963; Trustee, Uppingham Sch., 1961–66, 1970–. Fellow, Imperial Coll. of Science and Technology, 1972. Hon. DSc: Memorial Univ., Newfoundland, 1969; Newcastle upon Tyne, 1978; Liverpool, 1978. Meldola Medallist, RIC, 1946; first award for Synthetic Organic Chemistry, Chem. Soc., 1972; Davy Medal, Royal Soc., 1980. *Publications:* Chemistry of Acetylenic Compounds, Vol. I 1946, Vol. II 1950; numerous papers in chemical and biochemical journals. *Recreations:* tennis, philately. *Address:* School of Chemistry and Molecular Sciences, The University of Sussex, Falmer, Brighton, East Sussex. *T:* Brighton 606755.

JOHNSON, Anne Montgomrey; Matron, The Royal Star and Garter Home for Disabled Sailors, Soldiers and Airmen, since 1975; *b* 12 June 1922; *y c* of late Frederick Harold Johnson and late Gertrude Le Quesne (*née* Martin). *Educ:* St John's, Bexhill-on-Sea; Queen Elizabeth Hosp. (SRN); Brompton Hosp. (BTA Hons); Simpson Memorial Maternity Pavilion, Edinburgh (SCM). Asst Matron, Harefield Hosp., 1956–59; Dep. Matron, St Mary's Hosp., Paddington, 1959–62; Matron, Guy's Hosp., 1962–68; Mem. Directing and Tutorial Staff, King Edward's Hosp. Fund for London, 1968–71; Regional Dir, Help the Aged, 1971–73. Member: King's Fund Working Party, 'The Shape of Hospital Management 1980', 1966–67 (report publd 1967); Jt Cttee of Gen. Synod Working Party 'The Hospital Chaplain' (report publd 1974); Hosp. Chaplaincies Council, 1963–81; Nursing Cttee, Assoc. of Indep. Hosps, 1978–83. Central Sec., Mothers' Union, 1973. *Recreations:* ornithology, straight theatre, travel. *Address:* Flat 2, Ancaster House, Richmond Hill, Richmond-on-Thames, Surrey TW10 6RR.

JOHNSON, Rev. Prof. Aubrey Rodway, PhD; Emeritus Professor of Semitic Languages, University College of South Wales and Monmouthshire, Cardiff; *b* Leamington Spa, 23 April 1901; *y s* of Frank Johnson, Baptist Minister, and Beatrice Mary Bebb; *m* 1947, Winifred Mary Rowley; two *d. Educ:* Newport (Mon) Intermediate Sch.; South Wales Baptist Coll., Cardiff; Universities of Wales (University Coll., Cardiff), London (King's Coll.), Oxford (University Coll.) and Halle-Wittenberg. PhD Wales, 1931; Fellow of the University of Wales, 1931–33; Asst Lecturer and subsequently Lecturer in Semitic Languages, University Coll. of South Wales and Mon, Cardiff,

1934-44, Prof., 1944-66. Dean, Faculty of Theology, University Coll., Cardiff, and Chm. of the Cardiff Sch. of Theology, 1944-65; Dean, Faculty of Theology, University of Wales, 1952-55. Haskell Lectr, Graduate Sch. of Theology, Oberlin, 1951. Pres., Soc. for Old Testament Study, 1956. FBA, 1951. Hon. DD Edinburgh, 1952; Hon. DTheol Marburg, 1963; Hon. teol dr Uppsala, 1968. Burkitt Medal of British Academy, 1961. *Publications:* The One and the Many in the Israelite Conception of God, 1942 (2nd edn, 1961); The Cultic Prophet in Ancient Israel, 1944 (2nd edn revised, 1962); The Vitality of the Individual in the Thought of Ancient Israel, 1949 (2nd edn revised, 1964); Sacral Kingship in Ancient Israel, 1955 (2nd edn revised, 1967); The Cultic Prophet and Israel's Psalmody, 1979. *Recreation:* gardening. *Address:* Carisbrooke, Rectory Drive, Slimbridge, Glos GL2 7BL. *T:* Cambridge (Glos) 651.

JOHNSON, Prof. Barry Edward, PhD; FRS 1978; Professor since 1969, and Head of Department of Pure Mathematics since 1976, University of Newcastle upon Tyne; *b* 1 Aug. 1937; *s* of Edward Johnson and Evelyn May (*née* Bailey); *m* (marr. diss. 1979); two *s* one *d. Educ:* Epsom County Grammar Sch.; Hobart State High Sch.; Univ. of Tasmania (BSc 1956); Cambridge Univ. (PhD 1961). Instr, Univ. of Calif, Berkeley, 1961-62; Vis. Lectr, Yale Univ., 1962-63; Lectr, Exeter Univ., 1963-65; Lectr, Univ. of Newcastle upon Tyne, 1965-68, Reader, 1968-69. Vis. Prof., Yale Univ., 1970-71. Member: Council, London Math. Soc., 1975-78 (Pres., 1980-82); Amer. Math. Soc. *Publications:* Cohomology of Banach Algebras, 1972; papers in Jl of London Math. Soc. and Amer. Jl of Maths. *Recreations:* reading, travel. *Address:* 12 Roseworth Crescent, Gosforth, Newcastle upon Tyne NE3 1NR. *T:* Gosforth 845363.

JOHNSON, Bruce Joseph F.; *see* Forsyth-Johnson.

JOHNSON, Carol Alfred, CBE 1951. Admitted a Solicitor, 1933 (Hons). Secretary of the Parliamentary Labour Party, 1943-59. MP (Lab) Lewisham S, Sept. 1959-Feb. 1974; Chairman: Britain and Italy Co-ordinating Cttee; History of Parliament Trust; Vice-Pres., Lab. Cttee for Europe; Member, Council on National Parks; Chm., Commons, Footpaths and Open Spaces Soc.; Mem. Council, National Trust; Trustee, William Morris Soc.; Governor, British Inst., Florence; Pres., Southern Region Ramblers Assoc. Comdr, Italian Order of Merit. *Address:* 19 Melior Court, Shepherds Hill, N6; 204 Lloyd Court, Deal, Kent.

JOHNSON, David Burnham, QC 1978; *b* 6 Aug. 1930; *s* of late Thomas Burnham Johnson and of Elsie May Johnson; *m* 1968, Julia Clare Addison Hopkinson, *o d* of Col H. S. P. Hopkinson, *qv*; one *s* three *d. Educ:* Truro Sch.; Univ. of Wales. Solicitor and Notary Public, Oct. 1952. Commissioned, National Service, with Royal Artillery, 1952-54. Private practice as solicitor, Cardiff and Plymouth, 1954-67; called to Bar, Inner Temple, 1967. *Recreations:* sailing, walking, shooting, reading, music. *Address:* 25 Murray Road, Wimbledon, SW19. *T:* 01-947 9188; (chambers) 3 Essex Court, Temple, EC4Y 9AL. *T:* 01-353 2624. *Clubs:* Army and Navy; Royal Western Yacht (Plymouth).

JOHNSON, Prof. David Hugh Nevil; Professor of International Law, Sydney University, since Jan. 1976; *b* 4 Jan. 1920; 2nd *s* of James Johnson and Gladys Mary (*née* Knight); *m* 1952, Evelyn Joan Fletcher. *Educ:* Winchester Coll.; Trinity Coll., Cambridge; Columbia Univ., New York. MA, LLB Cantab. Served Royal Corps of Signals, 1940-46. Called to Bar, Lincoln's Inn, 1950. Asst Legal Adviser, Foreign Office, 1950-53; Reader in Internat. Law, 1953-59, in Internat. and Air Law, 1959-60, Prof., 1960-Dec. 1975, Dean of Faculty of Laws, 1968-72, Univ. of London. Sen. Legal Officer, Office of Legal Affairs, UN, 1956-57. Registrar, the Court of Arbitration, Argentine-Chile Frontier Case, 1965-68. *Publications:* Rights in Air Space, 1965; articles in legal jls. *Address:* 91 Eastwood Avenue, Epping, NSW 2121, Australia.

JOHNSON, (Denis) Gordon, CBE 1969; Chairman, Geo. Bassett Holdings Ltd, 1955-78 (Managing Director, 1955-71); Chairman: W. R. Wilkinson & Co. Ltd, Pontefract, 1961-78; Drakes Sweets Marketing Ltd, 1961-78; B. V. de Faam, Holland, 1964-78; Barratt & Co. Ltd, London, 1968-78; *b* 8 Oct. 1911; *s* of late Percy Johnson; unmarried. *Educ:* Harrow; Hertford Coll., Oxford (MA). President: Cocoa, Chocolate and Confectionery Alliance, 1964-66 (Hon. Treas., 1972-77); Confectioners' Benevolent Fund, 1967-68; Member: Yorks Electricity Bd, 1965-75; Food Manufacturing Economic Develt Cttee, 1967-70; Council of CBI, 1968-; Council, Sheffield Univ., 1972-; Chm., S Yorks Industrialists' Council, 1976-78. Chm., Hallam Conservative Assoc., 1966-69, and 1973-76; Hon. Treas., City of Sheffield Conservative Fedn, 1969-73; Chm., City of Sheffield Cons. Assocs, 1976-78. Pres., Sheffield and Hallamshire Lawn Tennis Club. Vis. Fellow, Yorks and Humberside Regional Management Centre. FBIM; MInstD. *Publications:* address to British Assoc. (Economics Section), 1964; contributor to: Business Growth (ed Edwards and Townsend), 1966; Pricing Strategy (ed Taylor and Wills), 1969. *Recreations:* walking, travel, philosophy. *Address:* 7 Broadbent Street, W1X 9HJ. *T:* 01-629 1642.

JOHNSON, Donald Edwin, RIBA, FRTPI; Under Secretary, 1978-80, and Deputy Chief Planner, 1975-80, Department of the Environment; *b* 4 July 1920; *s* of Henry William Johnson and Ann Catherine (*née* Lake); *m* 1947, Thérèse Andrée Simone Marquant; two *s* one *d. Educ:* Haberdashers' Aske's, Hatcham; School of Architecture, Regent Polytechnic; APRR School of Planning. Served War, Royal Artillery and Royal Engineers, 1940-45. Planning Officer, Min. of Town and Country Planning, 1947; Sen. Planning

Officer, 1950, Principal Planner, 1965, Asst Chief Planner, 1972. *Publications: fiction:* Project 38, 1963; Crooked Cross, 1964; Flashing Mountain, 1965; Devil of Bruges, 1966. *Address:* Flat D, 1 Morpeth Terrace, SW1P 1EW. *T:* 01-834 7300.

JOHNSON, Hon. Dame Doris (Louise), DBE 1979; President of the Senate of the Bahamas, since 1973, Senator, since 1967; Acting Governor General, 1979; *b* 19 June 1921; *d* of John A. and Sarah E. Sands; *m* 1943, Carl Johnson; one *s. Educ:* Virginia Union Univ. (BA Hons 1956); Univ. of Toronto (MEd 1959); New York Univ. (EdD Hons 1962). Teacher, 1936-51; Principal, All-age Sch., 1951-53; Lectr, Prince William High Sch., 1962-65; Head, Dept of Social Studies, Southern Univ., Baton Rouge, La, 1965-67; Lectr, Florida Memorial Coll., 1967-69. Cabinet Minister without Portfolio, Govt Leader in the Senate, 1968-69; Minister of Transport, 1969-72. Member: Commonwealth Human Ecology Council, 1979-; Internat. Alliance of Women, 1973-; Caribbean Women's Assoc., 1972-; Caribbean Baptist Women's Union, 1978- (Co-ordinator Bahamas Baptist Nat. Women's Convention, 1968); Delta Sigma Theta Sorority, 1955; Nat. Women's Movement, 1968-; Chm., Nat. Commn for Internat. Women's Year, 1975. Hon. LLD Va Union Univ., 1978. Order of the Eastern Star, 1943. *Publication:* The Quiet Revolution, 1972. *Recreations:* reading, boating. *Address:* PO Box N4646, Nassau, Bahamas. *T:* (office) 32 21565, (home) 32 34824 (area code 809).

JOHNSON, Prof. Douglas William John; Professor of French History, since 1968, Chairman of the Department of History, and Dean of the Faculty of Arts, University College London; *b* Edinburgh, 1 Feb. 1925; *o s* of John Thornburn Johnson and Christine Mair; *m* 1950, Madeleine Rébillard; one *d. Educ:* Royal Grammar Sch., Lancaster; Worcester Coll., Oxford (BA, BLitt); Ecole Normale Supérieure, Paris. Birmingham Univ.: Lectr in Modern History, 1949; Prof. of Modern History and Chm. of Sch. of History, 1963-68. Vis. Prof., Univs of Aix-en-Provence, Nancy, Paris, British Columbia, Toronto. Mem. Nat. Council, Historical Assoc.; Chm. Bd of Examrs in History, Univ. of London; Mem. CNAA. FRHistS. *Publications:* Guizot: Aspects of French History 1787-1874, 1963; France and the Dreyfus Affair, 1966; France, 1969; Concise History of France, 1970; The French Revolution, 1970; (ed jtly) Britain and France: Ten Centuries, 1980; (General Editor) The Making of the Modern World. *Recreations:* music, French politics. *Address:* University College, Gower Street, WC1E 6BT; 29 Rudall Crescent, NW3 1RR; 4 rue de la Cité, Saint-Servan-sur-Mer, 35400 Saint-Malo, France.

JOHNSON, Eric Alfred George, CBE 1953; retired chartered engineer; *b* 3 Sept. 1911; *s* of Ernest George Johnson and Amelia Rhoda Johnson; *m* 1936, Barbara Mary Robin; one *d. Educ:* Taunton's Sch., Southampton; UC Southampton. Grad. Engrg, 1931; specialist in flood control, sea defences and land drainage engineering; served for periods with Great Ouse and Trent Catchment Boards, 1933-37; joined Min. of Agriculture, 1937; Chief Engr, 1949-72. Has been associated with most major flood alleviation schemes carried out 1931-81, incl. Thames Barrier; formerly Consultant, Sir Murdoch MacDonald & Partners. Former chm. of several internat. and nat. cttees, and Vice-Pres., Internat. Commn of Irrigation and Drainage. *Publications:* papers in ICE and other professional jls. *Recreation:* visiting the countryside and sea coast to see some of the areas with which he has been associated through floods and protection schemes. *Address:* 94 Park Avenue, Orpington, Kent. *T:* Orpington 23802.

JOHNSON, Prof. Francis Rea; Professor of Anatomy, London Hospital Medical College, since 1968; Pre-clinical Sub-Dean, since 1979; *b* 8 July 1921; *s* of Marcus Jervis Johnson and Elizabeth Johnson; *m* 1951, Ena Patricia Laverty; one *s* one *d. Educ:* Omagh Academy, N Ire.; Queen's Univ., Belfast. MB, BCh, BAO 1945, MD 1949. House appts, Belfast City Hosp., 1946; Demonstrator in Anatomy and Physiology, QUB, 1947-50; Lectr in Anatomy, Sheffield Univ., 1950-57; Reader in Anatomy, London Hosp. Med. Coll., 1957-64; Prof. of Histology, London Hosp. Med. Coll., 1964-68. *Publications:* papers on histochemistry and ultrastructure of tissues and organs in various jls. *Recreations:* motoring, camping, gardening. *Address:* 11 Beacon Rise, Sevenoaks, Kent. *T:* Sevenoaks 53343.

JOHNSON, Air Vice-Marshal Frank Sidney Roland, CB 1973; OBE 1963; CBIM; Base Manager, British Aircraft Corporation RSAF, Dhahran, Saudi Arabia, 1977-82; *b* 4 Aug. 1917; *s* of Major Harry Johnson, IA, and Georgina Marklew; *m* 1943, Evelyn Hunt; two *s. Educ:* Trinity County Secondary Sch., Wood Green. Enlisted, 1935; served in UK and India; commnd, 1943; Germany (Berlin Airlift), 1948; Western Union Defence Organisation, 1955-57; Directing Staff, RAF Staff Coll., 1958-60; comd 113 MU, RAF Nicosia, 1960-63; Chief Instructor Equipment and Secretarial Wing, RAF Coll. Cranwell, 1963-64; Dep. Dir MoD, 1965-66; idc 1967; Chief Supply Officer, Fighter and Strike Comds, 1968-70; Dir-Gen. of Supply, RAF, 1971-73; Supply Manager, BAC, Saudi Arabia, 1974-76; Base Manager, BAC RSAF, Khamis Mushayt, Saudi Arabia, 1976-77. *Recreations:* golf, squash, hockey, cricket. *Address:* 9 Hazely, Tring, Herts. *T:* Tring 6535. *Club:* Royal Air Force.

JOHNSON, Frederick Alistair, PhD; FInstP; Chief Scientist (Royal Navy) and Director General Research A, Ministry of Defence, since 1980; *b* Christchurch, NZ, 9 April 1928; *s* of Archibald Frederick Johnson and Minnie, *d* of William Frederick Pellew; *m* 1952, Isobel Beth, *d* of Horace George Wilson; two *d. Educ:* Christchurch Boys' High Sch.; Univ. of Canterbury,

New Zealand (MSc, PhD). Rutherford Meml Fellow, 1952; Lectr, Univ. of Otago, 1952; post graduate research, Bristol Univ., 1953–55. Royal Radar Establishment, 1956–75: Individual Merit Promotion, 1964; Head of Physics Dept, 1968–73; Dep. Director, 1973–75; Dep. Dir, Royal Armament Research & Development Estabt, 1975–77; Dir of Scientific and Technical Intell., MoD, 1977–79. Visiting Professor, Massachusetts Inst. of Technology, 1967–68; Hon. Prof. of Physics, Birmingham Univ., 1969–75. *Publications:* numerous papers on spectroscopy, optics and lattice dynamics in Proc. Physical Soc. and Proc. Royal Soc. *Recreation:* sailing. *Address:* Otia Tuta, Grassy Lane, Sevenoaks, Kent TN13 1PL.

JOHNSON, Gordon; see Johnson, D. G.

JOHNSON, Graham Rhodes; concert accompanist; *b* 10 July 1950; *s* of John Edward Donald Johnson and Violet May Johnson (*née* Johnson). *Educ:* Hamilton High Sch., Bulawayo, Rhodesia; Royal Acad. of Music, London. ARAM. Concert début, Wigmore Hall, 1972; has since accompanied Elisabeth Schwarzkopf, Jessye Norman, Victoria de los Angeles (USA Tour 1977), Dame Janet Baker, Sir Peter Pears, Felicity Lott, Peter Schreier. Work with contemporaries led to formation of The Songmakers' Almanac (Artistic Director); has devised more than 40 London recitals for this group since Oct. 1976. Tours of US with Sarah Walker, Richard Jackson, and of Australia and NZ with The Songmakers' Almanac, 1981. Writer and presenter of major BBC Radio 3 series on Poulenc songs, and BBC TV series on Schubert songs. Lectr at song courses in Savonlinna (Finland), US and at Pears-Britten Sch., Snape; Artistic advr and accompanist, Alte Oper Festival, Frankfurt, 1981–. Recordings incl. those with Songmakers' Almanac. *Publications:* reviews in TLS, articles for music jls. *Recreations:* book and record collecting. *Address:* 83 Fordwych Road, NW2 3TL. *T:* 01-452 5193.

JOHNSON, Ven. Hayman; Archdeacon of Sheffield, 1963–78, Archdeacon Emeritus 1978; a Canon Residentiary of Sheffield Cathedral, 1975–78; Chaplain to HM The Queen, 1969–82; *b* 29 June 1912; *s* of late W. G. Johnson, Exeter; *m* 1943, Margaret Louise Price; one *d.* *Educ:* Exeter Sch.; New Coll., Oxon. Chaplain, RAFVR, 1941–46; Chaplain and Vicar Temporal, Hornchurch, 1953–61; Examining Chaplain to Bishop of Sheffield, 1962–78. *Address:* Flat 1, Parklands, 56 Kibbles Lane, Southborough, Tunbridge Wells, Kent.

JOHNSON, Sir Henry (Cecil), KBE 1972 (CBE 1962); Kt 1968; FCIT; Chairman: Dennis Waring & Co., since 1971; MEPC Ltd, 1971–76; *b* 11 Sept. 1906; *s* of William Longland and Alice Mary Johnson, Lavendon, Bucks; *m* 1932, Evelyn Mary Morton; two *d.* *Educ:* Bedford Modern Sch. Traffic Apprentice L & NER, 1923–26; series of posts in Operating Dept; Asst Supt, Southern Area, L & NER, 1942; Chief Operating Supt of Eastern Region, BR, 1955; Asst Gen. Man., Eastern Region, Dec. 1955, Gen. Man., 1958; Gen. Man., London Midland Region, BR, 1962, Chm. and Gen. Man., 1963–67; Chm., BR Bd, 1968–71 (Vice-Chm., 1967). Mem., GB Adv. Bd, Imperial Life of Canada. *Recreations:* golf, continuing interest in farming. *Address:* Rowans, Harewood Road, Chalfont St Giles, Bucks. *T:* Little Chalfont 2409. *Clubs:* MCC; Royal and Ancient (St Andrews).

JOHNSON, Henry Leslie, FTI; farmer; *b* 4 March 1904; *s* of Henry and Annie Letitia Johnson, formerly of Macclesfield, Cheshire and Coventry; *m* 1939, Mabel Caroline Hawkins, Woking, Surrey; one *s* two *d.* *Educ:* Rugby. Joined Courtaulds Ltd, 1922; Dir, 1933–68; Managing Dir, 1935–47. Vice-Chm., Warwicks CC, 1974–75. Pres., Textile Institute, 1942 and 1943. Liveryman, Worshipful Co. of Farmers; Freeman, City of London, 1959. *Address:* Offchurch Bury, near Leamington Spa, Warwicks CU33 9AR. *TA* and *T:* Leamington Spa 24293.

JOHNSON, Howard Sydney; solicitor; Director, Alliance Building Society, since 1970; *b* 25 Dec. 1911; *s* of Sydney Thomas Johnson; *m* 1939, Betty Frankiss, actress. *Educ:* Brighton; Highgate. Served War of 1939–45, Africa; invalided out as Major. Joined TA before the war. Mem. of Brighton Town Council, 1945–50. MP (C) Kemptown Div. of Brighton, 1950-Sept. 1959. *Address:* 3 Sylvester Way, Hove, East Sussex. *T:* Brighton 422249; c/o Howard Johnson & McQue, 37 East Street, Brighton BN1 1JD. *T:* Brighton 27173.

JOHNSON, Hugh Eric Allen; author and editor; *b* 10 March 1939; *s* of late Guy Francis Johnson, CBE and Grace Kittel; *m* 1965, Judith Eve Grinling; one *s* two *d.* *Educ:* Rugby Sch.; King's Coll., Cambridge (MA). Staff writer, Condé Nast publications, 1960–63; Editor, Wine & Food, and Sec., Wine and Food Soc., 1963–65; Wine Corresp., 1962–67, and Travel Editor, 1967, Sunday Times; Editor, Queen, 1968–70. Pres., Direct Sunday Times Wine Club, 1973–. Chm., Conservation Cttee, Internat. Dendrology Soc., 1979–. Editorial Director: Jl of RHS, 1975–; The Plantsman, 1979–. *Publications:* Wine, 1966 (rev. edn 1974); The World Atlas of Wine 1971, rev. edn 1977; The International Book of Trees, 1973; (with Bob Thompson) The California Wine Book, 1976; Hugh Johnson's Pocket Wine Book, annually 1977–; The Principles of Gardening, 1979; Understanding Wine, 1980; (with Paul Miles) The Pocket Encyclopedia of Garden Plants, 1981; Hugh Johnson's Wine Handbook, 1982; articles on gastronomy, travel and gardening. *Recreations:* travelling, staying at home. *Address:* Saling Hall, Great Saling, Essex. *Clubs:* Garrick, Saintsbury.

JOHNSON, James, BA, DPA; MP (Lab) Kingston upon Hull West since 1964; *b* 16 Sept. 1908; *s* of James and Mary Elizabeth Johnson; *m* 1937, Gladys Evelyn Green; one *d.* *Educ:* Duke's Sch., Alnwick; Leeds Univ. BA 1st Cl. Hons Geography, 1931; Diploma in Education, 1932; Diploma in Public Administration (London), 1944. FRGS. Schoolmaster: Queen Elizabeth Grammar Sch., Atherstone, 1931; Scarborough High Sch., 1934; Bablake Sch., Coventry, 1944. Lecturer, Coventry Tech. Coll., 1948–50. MP (Lab) Rugby Div. of Warwicks, 1950–59. Trade Union Advr, Kenya Local Govt Workers, 1959–60; Student Adviser, Republic of Liberia, 1960–64. Treasurer, Commonwealth Parly Assoc., 1979–. Played soccer for British Univs and Corinthians. Grand Comdr Order of Star of Africa (Liberia), 1967. *Address:* 70 Home Park Road, SW19. *T:* 01-946 6224. *Clubs:* Royal Over-Seas League; Humber St Andrews Engineering Social and Recreation.

JOHNSON, Air Vice-Marshal James Edgar, (Johnnie Johnson), CB 1965; CBE 1960; DSO 1943 and Bars, 1943, 1944; DFC 1941 and Bar, 1942; DL; Chief Executive, Johnnie Johnson Housing Trust, Ltd; Director of Companies in Canada, South Africa and UK; *m* Pauline Ingate; two *s.* *Educ:* Loughborough Sch.; Nottingham Univ. Civil Engr and Mem. of RAFVR until 1939; served with 616 Sqdn AAF, 1940–42; 610 Sqdn AAF, 1943; Wing Comdr Flying: Kenley, 1943; 127 Wing, 1944; Officer Comdg: 125 Wing (2nd TAF), 1944–45; 124 Wing (2nd TAF), 1945–46; RCAF Staff Coll., 1947–48; USAF (Exchange Officer), 1948–50; served Korea (with USAF), 1950–51; OC, RAF Wildenrath (2nd TAF), 1952–54; Air Ministry, 1954–57; Officer Commanding, RAF Cottesmore, Bomber Command, 1957–60; idc 1960; Senior Air Staff Officer, No 3 Group, Bomber Command, Mildenhall, Suffolk, 1960–63; AOC, Air Forces Middle East, Aden, 1963–65; retired. DL Leicester, 1967. Order of Leopold, 1945, Croix de Guerre, 1945 (Belgium); Legion of Merit, 1950, DFC 1943, Air Medal, 1950 (USA). *Publications:* Wing Leader, 1956; Full Circle, 1964. *Recreations:* shooting, golf. *Address:* The Stables, Hargate Hall, Buxton, Derbyshire SK17 8TA. *Club:* Royal Air Force.

JOHNSON, John Robin; His Honour Judge Johnson; a Circuit Judge, since 1973; *b* 27 Nov. 1927; *s* of Sir Philip Bulmer Johnson, Hexham, Northumberland; *m* 1958, Meriel Jean, *d* of H. B. Speke, Aydon, Corbridge; one *s* one *d.* *Educ:* Winchester; Trinity Coll., Cambridge. Called to Bar, Middle Temple, 1950. Dep. Chm., Northumberland QS, 1966–71; a Recorder of the Crown Court, 1972–73. *Address:* c/o Crown Court, Moot Hall, Newcastle upon Tyne.

JOHNSON, John Rodney, CMG 1981; HM Diplomatic Service; High Commissioner to Zambia, since 1980; *b* 6 Sept. 1930; *s* of Edwin Done Johnson, OBE and Florence Mary (*née* Clough); *m* 1956, Jean Mary Lewis; three *s* one *d.* *Educ:* Manchester Grammar Sch.; Oxford Univ. (MA). HM Colonial Service, Kenya, 1955–64; Dist Comr, Thika, 1962–64; Administrator, Cttee of Vice-Chancellors and Principals of UK Univs, 1965; First Sec., FCO, 1966–69; Head of Chancery, British Embassy, Algiers, 1969–72; Dep. High Comr, British High Commn, Barbados, 1972–74; Counsellor, British High Commn, Lagos, 1975–78; Head of W African Dept, FCO, and Ambassador (non-resident) to Chad, 1978–80. *Recreations:* climbing, reaching remote places, gardening. *Address:* c/o Foreign and Commonwealth Office, SW1; The Gables, High Street, Old Amersham, Bucks. *T:* Amersham 7324. *Clubs:* Travellers'; Climbers; Bridgetown (Barbados).

JOHNSON, Air Vice-Marshal Johnnie; see Johnson, James Edgar.

JOHNSON, Kenneth James, OBE 1966; Director, Dunlop Holdings Ltd, since 1978; Member: Board of Crown Agents for Oversea Governments and Administrations, since 1980; Crown Agents Holding and Realisation Board, since 1980; *b* 8 Feb. 1926; *s* of Albert Percy Johnson and Winifred Florence (*née* Coole); *m* 1951, Margaret Teresa Bontoft Jenkins; three *s* two *d.* *Educ:* Rishworth School, near Halifax; Wadham Coll., Oxford; LSE; SOAS. Indian Army (14 Punjab Regt), 1945–47. Colonial Admin. Service, Nigeria, 1949–61, senior appts in Min. of Finance and Min. of Commerce and Industry; Head of Economic Dept, later Dir of Industrial Affairs, CBI, 1961–70; Courtaulds Ltd, 1970–73: Chm. and Man. Dir, various subsidiary cos. Dep. Chm., Pay Board, 1973–74. FRSA 1972; FIPM 1976. *Recreations:* family pursuits, travel. *Address:* Woodgetters, Shipley, Horsham, West Sussex. *T:* Southwater 730481. *Clubs:* East India, Royal Commonwealth Society.

JOHNSON, Prof. Kenneth Langstreth, PhD; FRS 1982; Professor of Engineering, Cambridge University, since 1977; Fellow of Jesus College, Cambridge, since 1957; *b* 19 March 1925; *s* of Frank Herbert Johnson and Ellen Howorth Langstreth; *m* 1954, Dorothy Rosemary Watkins; one *s* two *d.* *Educ:* Barrow Grammar Sch.; Manchester Univ. (MScTech, MA, PhD). MIMechE. Engr, Messrs Rotol Ltd, Gloucester, 1944–49; Asst Lectr, Coll. of Technology, Manchester, 1949–54; Lectr, then Reader in Engrg, Cambridge Univ., 1954–77. *Publications:* contrib. scientific and engrg jls, and Proc. IMechE. *Recreations:* mountain walking, swimming. *Address:* 13 Park Terrace, Cambridge. *T:* Cambridge 355287.

JOHNSON, Merwyn; see Johnson, W. M.

JOHNSON, Michael Howard; a Recorder of the Crown Court, since 1980; *b* 9 May 1930. Called to the Bar, Gray's Inn, 1964; Asst Parliamentary Boundary Commissioner, 1976–. *Address:* 6 Pump Court, Temple, EC4Y 7AR. *T:* 01-353 7242.

JOHNSON, Dame Monica; see Golding, Dame (Cecilie) Monica.

JOHNSON, Nevil; Nuffield Reader in the Comparative Study of Institutions, University of Oxford, and Professorial Fellow, Nuffield College, since 1969; b 6 Feb. 1929; s of G. E. Johnson and Doris Johnson, MBE, Darlington; m 1957, Ulla van Aubel; two s. Educ: Queen Elizabeth Grammar Sch., Darlington; University Coll., Oxford (BA PPE 1952, MA 1962). Army service, 1947-49. Admin. Cl. of Home Civil Service: Min. of Supply, 1952-57; Min. of Housing and Local Govt, 1957-62; Lectr in Politics, Univ. of Nottingham, 1962-66; Sen. Lectr in Politics, Univ. of Warwick, 1966-69. Chm. Board, Faculty of Social Studies, Oxford, 1976-78. Visiting Professor: Ruhr Univ. of Bochum, 1968-69; Univ. of Munich, 1980. Mem., SSRC, 1981-. Civil Service Comr (pt-time), 1982-. Mem. Exec. Council, Royal Inst. of Public Admin, 1965-. Hon. Editor, Public Administration, 1967-81. Publications: Parliament and Administration: The Estimates Committee 1945-65, 1967; Government in the Federal Republic of Germany, 1973; In Search of the Constitution, 1977 (trans. German, 1977); (with A. Cochrane) Economic Policy-Making by Local Authorities in Britain and Western Germany, 1981; articles in Public Admin, Political Studies, Parly Affairs, Ztschr. für Politik, Die Verwaltung, and Der Staat. Recreations: jogging, swimming, gardening. Address: 50 Norman Avenue, Abingdon, Oxon OX14 2HL. T: Abingdon 20078. Club: United Oxford & Cambridge University.

JOHNSON, Patrick, OBE 1945; MA; b 24 May 1904; 2nd s of A. F. W. Johnson, JP, and F. E. L. Cocking; unmarried. Educ: RN Colls, Osborne and Dartmouth; Tonbridge Sch.; Magdalen Coll., Oxford. Fellow and Lecturer in Natural Science, Magdalen Coll., 1928-47, Dean, 1934-38, Vice-Pres., 1946-47. Flying Officer, RAFO, 1929-34; commissioned in RA (TA), 1938; served War of 1939-45, in Middle East and NW Europe, Lt-Col, Asst Dir of Scientific Research, 21st Army Group and comdg No. 2 operational research section. Dir of Studies, RAF Coll., Cranwell, 1947-52; Dean of Inst. of Armament Studies, India, 1952-55; Scientific Adviser to the Army Council, 1955-58; Asst Scientific Adviser, SHAPE, 1958-62; Head of Experimental Develt Unit, Educnl Foundn for Visual Aids, 1962-70. Recreations: rowing (rowed against Cambridge, 1927), sailing, shooting. Address: 5 Linley Court, Rouse Gardens, SE21 8AQ. Clubs: Reform; Leander.

JOHNSON, Paul (Bede); author; b 2 Nov. 1928; s of William Aloysius and Anne Johnson; m 1957, Marigold Hunt; three s one d. Educ: Stonyhurst; Magdalen Coll., Oxford. Asst Exec. Editor, Réalités, 1952-55; Editorial Staff, New Statesman, 1955, Dir, Statesman and Nation Publishing Co., 1965, Editor of the New Statesman, 1965-70. Mem., Royal Commn on the Press, 1974-77. Publications: The Suez War, 1957; Journey into Chaos, 1958; Left of Centre, 1960; Merrie England, 1964; Statesmen and Nations, 1971; The Offshore Islanders, 1972; (with G. Gale) The Highland Jaunt, 1973; Elizabeth I, 1974; A Place in History, 1974; Pope John XXIII, 1975 (Yorkshire Post Book of the Year Award, 1975); A History of Christianity, 1976; Enemies of Society, 1977; The National Trust Book of British Castles, 1978; The Recovery of Freedom, 1980; British Cathedrals, 1980; Ireland: Land of Troubles, 1980; Pope John Paul II and the Catholic Restoration, 1982. Recreations: mountaineering, painting. Address: Copthall, Iver, Bucks. T: Iver 653350.

JOHNSON, Sir Peter (Colpoys Paley), 7th Bt cr 1755; Publishing Director, Nautical Books, Macmillan London Ltd, since 1981; b 26 March 1930; s of Sir John Paley Johnson, 6th Bt, MBE, and of Carol, d of late Edmund Haas; S father, 1975; m 1st, 1956, Clare (marr. diss. 1973), d of Dr Nigel Bruce; one s two d; 2nd, 1973, Caroline Elisabeth, d of late Sir John Hodsoll, CB; one s. Educ: Wellington Coll.; Royal Military Coll. of Science. Served RA, 1949; retired 1961, Captain. Dir, Sea Sure Ltd, 1965-73; Dir and Editor, Nautical Publishing Co. Ltd, 1970-81. British Delegate, Internat. Offshore (Yachting) Council, 1970-79 (Chm. Internat. Technical Cttee, 1973-76); Ocean Racing Correspondent, Yachting World, London, 1971-81. Publications: Ocean Racing and Offshore Yachts, 1970, 2nd edn 1972; Boating Britain, 1973; Guinness Book of Yachting Facts and Feats, 1975; Guinness Guide to Sailing, 1981. Recreation: sailing. Heir: s Colpoys Guy Johnson, b 13 Nov. 1965. Address: Dene End, Buckland Dene, Lymington, Hants SO4 9DT. T: Lymington 75921. Clubs: Royal Ocean Racing; Royal Southern Yacht (Hamble).

JOHNSON, Philip Cortelyou; architect, with own firm, 1953-67, with Johnson/Burgee Architects, since 1967; b Cleveland, Ohio, 8 July 1906; s of Homer H. Johnson and Louise Pope Johnson. Educ: Harvard (AB 1927, cum laude). Dir, Dept of Architecture, The Museum of Modern Art, New York, 1932-54, Trustee, 1958-; Graduate Sch. of Design, Harvard, 1940-43 (BArch). Has taught and lectured at: Yale Univ.; Cornell Univ.; Pratt Inst. (Dr Fine Arts, 1962). Mem. AIA (New York Chapter); Architectural League, NY. Hon. Dr Fine Arts Yale, 1978. Gold Medal, AIA, 1978; Pritzker Architecture Prize, 1979. Publications: Machine Art, 1934; Mies van der Rohe, 1st edn 1947, 2nd edn 1953; (with Henry-Russell Hitchcock) The International Style, Architecture since 1922, 1932, new edn 1966; (with others) Modern Architects, 1932; Architecture 1949-65, 1966; Philip Johnson Writings, 1979; contributor to Architectural Review. Address: (business) Philip Johnson, 375 Park Avenue, New York, NY 10022, USA. T: 751-7440; (home) Ponus Ridge Road, New Canaan, Conn. T: 966-0565. Clubs: Athenæum, Century.

JOHNSON, Rex; Director of Social Services, Lancashire County Council, since 1978; b 19 Aug. 1921; s of Samuel and Ellen Johnson; m 1946, Mary Elizabeth Whitney; two d. Educ: Accrington Grammar Sch.; St Paul's Trng

Coll., Cheltenham (qual. teacher); Leeds Univ. (MA). Served War, RAF, 1942-46; radar mechanic, educn instr; served Ireland, India, Singapore (Burma Star). Asst Master, Darwen, 1946-49; Dep. Supt, Boys' Remand Home, Lincoln, 1949-52; Head of Springfield Reception Centre, Bradford, 1953-64; Home Office Inspector, Children's Dept, 1964-65; Educnl Psychologist, Bradford, 1965-67; Univ. Lectr, Leeds, 1967-69; Social Work Service Officer, DHSS (formerly Home Office Inspector), 1969-72; Dep. Dir of Social Services, Lancs, 1972-78. Mem., Personal Social Services Council, 1977-80. Publicatiolns: (ed) ABC of Behaviour Problems, 1962 (2nd edn 1969); (ed) ABC of Social Problems and Therapy, 1963; (ed) ABC of Social Services, 1964; articles in Soc. Work Today, Residential Soc. Work, Community Care, Hosp. and Soc. Services Jl, and Jl RSH. Address: Ebor, 5 Links Road, St Annes-on-Sea, Lancs. T: St Annes 724014.

JOHNSON, Robert Lionel; QC 1978; a Recorder of the Crown Court, since 1977; barrister-at-law; b 9 Feb. 1933; er s of Edward Harold Johnson, MSc, FRIC, and Ellen Lydiate Johnson, Cranleigh; m 1957, Linda Mary, er d of late Charles William Bennie and Ena Ethel Bennie, Egglescliffe; one s two d. Educ: Watford Grammar Sch. (1940-51); London Sch. of Econs and Polit. Science. 5th Royal Inniskilling Dragoon Guards, 1955-57, Captain; ADC to GOC-in-C Northern Comd, 1956-57; Inns of Court Regt, 1957-64. Called to the Bar, Gray's Inn, 1957; Jun. Counsel to Treasury in Probate Matters, 1975-78. Legal Assessor, GNC, 1977-. Trustee: (and Founder Mem.) Council, Cystic Fibrosis Res. Trust, 1964-; Robert Luff Charitable Foundn, 1977-. Publications: (with James Comyn) Wills & Intestacies, 1970; Contract, 1975; (with Malcolm Stitcher) Atkin's Trade, Labour and Employment, 1975. Recreations: charitable work, gardening. Address: Queen Elizabeth Building, Temple, EC4Y 9BS. T: 01-583 7837.

JOHNSON, Robert White, CBE 1962; Director, Cammell Laird & Co. Ltd, 1946-70; Chairman: Cammell Laird & Co. (Shipbuilders and Engineers) Ltd, 1957-68; Cammell Laird (Shiprepairers) Ltd, 1963-68; b 16 May 1912; s of late Sir Robert (Stewart) Johnson, OBE; m 1950, Jill Margaret Preston; two s one d. Educ: Rossall Sch. Robt Bradford & Co. Ltd (Insurance Brokers), 1931-35. Served War of 1939-45, Provost Marshal's Dept, RAF, becoming Wing Comdr. Director: Patent Shaft & Axletree Co. Ltd, Wednesbury, Staffs, 1946-51; Metropolitan-Cammell Carriage and Wagon Co. Ltd, Birmingham, 1946-64; English Steel Corp. Ltd, Sheffield, 1949-51 and 1954-; North Western Line (Mersey) Ltd, 1964-70; Bradley Shipping Ltd, 1964-70; formerly Dir, Scottish Aviation Ltd; Coast Lines Ltd; Chm. of North West Tugs Ltd, Liverpool, 1951-66; Mem. Mersey Docks and Harbour Board, 1948-70; Pt-time Mem. Merseyside and North Wales Electricity Board, 1956-66; Chm., Merseyside Chamber of Commerce and Industry, 1972-74. Underwriting Mem., Lloyd's, 1937-. Pres., Shipbuilding Employers' Federation, 1958-59. Recreations: fishing, shooting, golf. Address: The Oaks, Well Lane, Heswall, Wirral, Merseyside L60 8NE. T: 051-342 3304.

JOHNSON, Sir Ronald (Ernest Charles), Kt 1970; CB 1962; JP; b 3 May 1913; o c of Ernest and Amelia Johnson; m 1938, Elizabeth Gladys Nuttall; two s (and one s decd). Educ: Portsmouth Grammar Sch.; St John's Coll., Cambridge. Entered Scottish Office, 1935; Sec., Scottish Home and Health Dept, 1963-72. Chm., Civil Service Savings Cttee for Scotland, 1963-78. Sec. of Commissions for Scotland, 1972-78. Chm., Scottish Hosp. Centre, 1964-72. Mem., Scottish Records Adv. Council, 1975-81; Chm., Fire Service Res. and Training Trust. Served RNVR on intelligence staff of C-in-C, Eastern Fleet, 1944-45. President: Edinburgh Bach Soc.; Edinburgh Soc. of Organists, 1980-82. JP Edinburgh, 1972. Publications: articles in religious and musical jls. Recreation: church organ. Address: 14 Eglinton Crescent, Edinburgh EH12 5DD. T: 031-337 7733. Club: New (Edinburgh).

JOHNSON, Stanley, CBE 1970; FCA; FCIT; Managing Director, British Transport Docks Board, 1967-75; European Agent, Northland Harbour Board, New Zealand, since 1980; b 10 Nov. 1912; s of late Robert and Janet Mary Johnson; m 1940, Sheila McLean Bald; two s two d. Educ: King George V Sch., Southport. Served as Lieut (S) RINVR, 1942-45. Joined Singapore Harbour Board, 1939; Asst Gen. Man. 1952; Chm. and Gen. Man. 1958-59; Chief Docks Man., Hull Docks, 1962; Asst Gen. Man. 1963, Mem. and Dep. Man. Dir 1966, British Transport Docks Board. Chm. Major Ports Cttee, Dock and Harbour Authorities Assoc., 1971-72. Mem., Exec. Council, British Ports Assoc., 1973-75; Vice-Pres., Internat. Assoc. of Ports and Harbours, 1975-77. Vice-Pres., CIT, 1973-75. Recreations: walking, reading, travel. Address: The Red House, Bearswood End, Beaconsfield, Bucks. T: Beaconsfield 3440. Club: Naval and Military.

JOHNSON, Stanley Patrick; Member (C) Wight and Hants East, European Parliament, since 1979; b 18 Aug. 1940; s of Wilfred Johnson and Irène (née Williams); m 1st, 1963, Charlotte Offlow Fawcett (marr. diss.); three s one d; 2nd, 1981, Mrs Jennifer Kidd; one d. Educ: Sherborne Sch.; Exeter Coll., Oxford (Trevelyan Schol., Sen. Classics Schol.); Harkness Fellow, USA, 1963-64. MA Oxon 1963; Dip. Agric. Econs Oxon 1964. World Bank, Washington, 1966-68; Project Dir, UNA-USA Nat. Policy Panel on World Population, 1968-69; Mem. Conservative Research Dept, 1969-70; Staff of Internat. Planned Parenthood Fedn, London, 1971-73; Consultant to UN Fund for Population Activities, 1971-73; Mem. Countryside Commn, 1971-73; Head of Prevention of Pollution and Nuisances Div., EEC, 1973-77; Adviser to Head of Environment and Consumer Protection Service, EEC, 1977-79. Newdigate Prize for Poetry, 1962. Publications: Life Without Birth, 1970; The Green Revolution, 1972; The Politics of the Environment, 1973; (ed) The

Population Problem, 1973; The Pollution Control Policy of the EEC, 1979; *novels:* Gold Drain, 1967; Panther Jones for President, 1968; God Bless America, 1974; The Doomsday Deposit, 1980; The Marburg Virus, 1982. *Recreations:* writing, travel. *Address:* Nethercote, Winsford, Minehead, Somerset. *Club:* Savile.

JOHNSON, Sir Victor Philipse Hill, 6th Bt, *cr* 1818; *b* 7 May 1905; *s* of late Hugh Walters Beaumont Johnson, Kingsmead, Windsor Forest, and Winifred Mena Johnson (*née* Hill, later W. M. Livingstone), Fern Lea, Southampton; *S* cousin, Sir Henry Allen Beaumont Johnson, 5th Bt, 1965; unmarried. *Educ:* Cheltenham Coll. Ranched in BC, Canada, 1926-38. Served with RAF, 1939-45. *Recreations:* gardening, playing at golf. *Heir: kinsman* Robin Eliot Johnson [*b* 1929; *m* 1954, Barbara Alfreda, *d* of late Alfred T. Brown; one *s* two *d*]. *Address:* Beach House, 64 Sea Lane, Goring-by-Sea, Worthing, West Sussex. *T:* Worthing 43630.

JOHNSON, Walter Hamlet; MP (Lab) Derby South since 1970; *b* Hertford, 21 Nov. 1917; *s* of John Johnson; *m* 1945. *Educ:* Devon House Sch., Margate. Councillor, Brentford and Chiswick for 6 years. Nat. Treasurer, Transport Salaried Staffs' Assoc., 1965-. Joined Labour Party, 1945. Contested (Lab) Bristol West, 1955 and South Bedfordshire, 1959, in General Elections; also Acton (Lab), 1968, in by-election. An Assistant Govt Whip, 1974-75. Is particularly interested in welfare services, transport, labour relations and aviation matters; Chm., PLP Aviation Cttee, 1979-. Principal Executive Assistant, London Transport, 1980- (formerly a Sen. Exec., Staff Trng). Pres., Transport Salaried Staffs' Assoc., 1977-81. Governor, Ruskin Coll., Oxford, 1966-. *Recreation:* sport. *Address:* House of Commons, SW1; 10 Melton Street, NW1. *T:* 01-387 2101.

JOHNSON, Prof. William, DSc Manchester, MA Cantab; FRS 1982; CEng, FIMechE; Professor of Mechanics, Cambridge University, since 1975; Professorial Fellow, Fitzwilliam College, Cambridge, since 1975; *b* 20 April 1922; *er s* of James and Elizabeth Johnson; *m* 1946, Heather Marie (*née* Thornber); three *s* two *d*. *Educ:* Central Grammar Sch., Manchester; Manchester Coll. of Science and Technology (BScTech); BSc London. Served War, Lt REME, UK and Italy, 1943-47. Asst Principal, Administrative Grade, Home Civil Service, 1948-50; Lecturer, Northampton Polytechnic, London, 1950-52; Lectr in Engineering, Sheffield Univ., 1952-56; Senior Lectr in Mechanical Engineering, Manchester Univ., 1956-60; Prof. of Mechanical Engrg, 1960-75, Chm. of Dept of Mechanical Engrg, 1960-69, 1971-73, Dir of Medical Engrg, 1973-75, UMIST. Springer Prof. (Visiting), Univ. of Calif, Berkeley, 1980. Hon. Sec., Yorks Br. of IMechE, 1953-56, and Chm., NW Br., 1974-75. Founder, and Editor, Internat. Jl Mech. Sciences, 1960-; Chm., Internat. Jl Mech. Engrg Educn, 1960-. Fellow UCL, 1982. For. Fellow, Nat. Acad. of Greece, 1982. Hon. DTech Bradford, 1976. Premium Award, Jl RAeS, 1956; T. Constantine Medal, Manchester Soc. of Engrs, 1962; Bernard Hall Prize (jt), IMechE, 1965-66 and 1966-67; James Clayton Fund Prize (jt), IMechE, 1972, 1978. *Publications:* Plasticity for Mechanical Engineers (with P. B. Mellor), 1962; Mechanics of Metal Extrusion (with H. Kudo), 1962; Slip Line Fields: Theory and Bibliography (with R. Sowerby and J. B. Haddow), 1970; Impact Strength of Materials, 1972; Engineering Plasticity with P. B. Mellor), 1973; Lectures in Engineering Plasticity (with A. G. Mamalis), 1978; Crashworthiness of Vehicles (with A. G. Mamalis), 1978; (jtly) Plane-Strain Slip-Line Fields for Metal-Deformation Processes, 1982; papers in mechanics of solids, metal forming, impact engineering and mechanics of sports and games; bioengineering. *Recreation:* landscape gardening. *Address:* Engineering Department, University of Cambridge, Cambridge CB2 1QA.

JOHNSON, His Honour William; QC (NI); County Court Judge for County Tyrone, 1947-78; *b* 1 April 1903; *s* of late William Johnson, CBE, and Ellen Johnson. *Educ:* Portora Royal Sch., Enniskillen; Trinity Coll., Dublin (BA; Sen. Moderator Legal and Polit. Sci.; LLB (1st cl.); King's Inns, Dublin (Certif. of Honour at Final Examinations for Call to Bar). Called to Irish Bar and Bar of N Ireland, 1924; Hon. Bencher, Inn of Court of N Ireland. Served War of 1939-45, France, Germany, Holland, Belgium (despatches); ADJAG, Actg Lt-Col. Lectr in Law, QUB, 1933-36; Chm. Court of Referees 1928-30, Dep. Umpire 1930-35, Umpire 1935-47, NI Unemployment Insce and Pensions Acts; KC (Northern Ireland) 1946; Sen. Crown Prosecutor, Co. Antrim, 1947. Chairman: Cttee on Law of Intestate Succession in NI, 1951; Cttee on Law of Family Provision in NI, 1953; Cttee on Examns for Secondary Intermediate Schs in NI, 1958; Vice-Chm., Jt Cttee on Civil and Criminal Jurisdictions in NI, 1971; Council of HM's County Ct Judges in NI, 1975-78. Has held various positions as Leader and Comr in Scout Assoc., 1923-70; Mem., NI Youth Cttee, 1939; Mem. Council, Scout Assoc., 1958-; Chief Comr for NI, Boy Scouts Assocs, 1955-65; Vice-Pres., NI Scout Council; Pres., Belfast County Scout Council. *Address:* Bar Library, Royal Courts of Justice, Belfast BT1.

JOHNSON, William Harold Barrett; Commissioner of Inland Revenue, 1965-76; *b* 18 May 1916; *s* of late William Harold Johnson and Mary Ellen (*née* Barrett); *m* 1940, Susan Gwendolen, *d* of Rev. H. H. Symonds; one *s* one *d*. *Educ:* Charterhouse; Magdalene Coll., Cambridge. Served in Royal Artillery, 1939-45. Entered Inland Revenue Dept, 1945. Vice-Pres., Cruising Assoc., 1974-77. *Recreations:* cruising under sail, gardening. *Address:* 45 Granville Park, SE13 7DY; Barrow Cottage, Ravenglass, Cumbria CA18 1ST.

JOHNSON, (Willis) Merwyn; Agent General for Saskatchewan in the United Kingdom, since 1977; *b* 9 May 1923; *s* of Robert Arthur Johnson and Gudborg Kolbinson; *m* 1946, Laura Elaine Aseltine; two *s* two *d*. *Educ:* McKenzie High Sch., Kindersley; Univ. of Saskatchewan. BSA, BA. MP for Kindersley, Parliament of Canada, 1953-57 and 1957-58. *Recreations:* fishing, golf. *Address:* 21 Pall Mall, SW1Y 5LP. *T:* 01-930 7491. *Clubs:* Wig and Pen, Farmers', Royal Automobile, Canada.

JOHNSON-FERGUSON, Sir Neil (Edward), 3rd Bt, *cr* 1906; TD; Lt-Col Royal Corps of Signals; Vice-Lieutenant, Dumfriesshire, since 1965; *b* 2 May 1905; *s* of Sir Edward Alexander James Johnson-Ferguson, 2nd Bt, and Hon. Elsie Dorothea McLaren (*d* 1973), *d* of 1st Baron Aberconway; *S* father 1953; *m* 1931, Sheila Marion, *er d* of late Col H. S. Jervis, MC; four *s*. *Educ:* Winchester; Trinity Coll., Cambridge (BA). Capt. Lanarks Yeomanry, TA, 1928; Major 1937; Major, Royal Signals, 1939; Lt-Col 1945. JP 1954, DL 1957, Dumfriesshire. American Legion of Merit. *Heir: s* Ian Edward Johnson-Ferguson [*b* 1 Feb. 1932; *m* 1964, Rosemary Teresa, *d* of C. J. Whitehead, The Old House, Crockham Hill, Kent; three *s*]. *Address:* Fairyknowe, Eaglesfield, Dumfriesshire.

JOHNSON-GILBERT, Ronald Stuart, OBE 1976; Secretary, Royal College of Surgeons of England, since 1962; *b* 14 July 1925; *s* of late Sir Ian A. Johnson-Gilbert, CBE and late Rosalind Bell-Hughes; *m* 1951, Ann Weir Drummond; three *d*. *Educ:* Edinburgh Acad.; Rugby; Brasenose Coll., Oxford (Classical Exhbnr and Open Schol., 1943; MA). Intelligence Corps, 1943-46. Trainee, John Lewis Partnership, 1950-51; Admin. Staff, RCS, 1951-; Secretary: Faculties of Dental Surgery and of Anaesthetists, 1958; Jt Conf. of Surgical Colls, 1963-; Internat. Fedn of Surgical Colls, 1967-74. John Tomes Medal, BDA, 1980. *Recreations:* music, painting, literature, golf. *Address:* Potters Wheel, Ruxley Crescent, Claygate, Surrey KT10 0TX. *Club:* Confrères.

JOHNSON-MARSHALL, Percy Edwin Alan, CMG 1975; RIBA; FRTPI; Professor of Urban Design and Regional Planning, University of Edinburgh, since 1964; Head of New Department of Urban Design and Regional Planning, since 1967; in practice as planning consultant since 1960; *b* 20 Jan. 1915; *s* of Felix William Norman Johnson-Marshall and Kate Jane Little; *m* 1944, April Bridger; three *s* four *d*. *Educ:* Liverpool Univ. Sch. of Architecture; Dip. in Arch.(Dist) (RIBA) RTPI; (RIBA) DisTP; MA (Edin). Planning Architect, Coventry, 1938-41; Served War: with Royal Engrs (India and Burma), 1942-46. Asst Regional Planner, Min. of Town and Country Planning, 1946-49; Gp Planning Officer, in charge of reconstr. areas gp, LCC, 1949-59 (Projects incl.: Lansbury and Stepney/Poplar South Bank, (jtly with City Corp.) Barbican Area, Tower Hill area, etc). Apptd Sen. Lectr, Dept of Architecture, Univ. of Edinburgh, 1959. Director: Architectural Research Unit, 1961-64; Planning Research Unit, 1962. Consultant on Human Settlements for UN Stockholm Conf. on Environment, 1972. Principal of Planning Consultancy, Percy Johnson-Marshall and Associates (Projects incl. Edin. Univ. Plan, Kilmarnock and Bathgate Town Centres, Porto Regional Plan, etc). *Publications:* Rebuilding Cities, 1966; contribs to technical jls. *Address:* Bella Vista, Duddingston Village, Edinburgh EH15 3PZ. *T:* 031-661 2019.

JOHNSON SMITH, Sir Geoffrey, Kt 1982; MP (C) East Grinstead since Feb. 1965; *b* 16 April 1924; *s* of late J. Johnson Smith; *m* Jeanne Pomeroy, MD; two *s* one *d*. *Educ:* Charterhouse; Lincoln Coll., Oxford. Served War of 1939-45: Royal Artillery, 1942-47; Temp. Capt. RA, 1946. BA Hons, Politics, Philosophy and Economics, Oxford, 1949. Mem., Oxford Union Soc. Debating Team, USA, 1949. Information Officer, British Information Services, San Francisco, 1950-52; Mem. Production Staff, Current Affairs Unit, BBC TV, 1953-54; London County Councillor, 1955-58; Interviewer, Reporter, BBC TV, 1955-59. MP (C) Holborn and St Pancras South, 1959-64; PPS, Board of Trade and Min. of Pensions, 1960-63; Opposition Whip, 1965; Parly Under-Sec. of State for Defence for the Army, MoD, 1971-72; Parly Sec., CSD, 1972-74. Mem. Exec., 1922 Cttee, 1979-. A Vice-Chm., Conservative Party, 1965-71. Member: IBA Gen. Adv. Council, 1975-80; N Atlantic Assembly Political and Military Cttee, 1980-. Governor, BFI, 1980-. *Address:* House of Commons, SW1. *Club:* Travellers'.

JOHNSTON; *see* Lawson Johnston.

JOHNSTON, Hon. Lord; Douglas Harold Johnston, TD; a Senator of the College of Justice in Scotland, 1961-78; *b* 1907; *s* of late Joseph Johnston, Advocate, Aberdeen; *m* 1936, Doris Isobel, *d* of late James Kidd, MP; two *s* two *d*. *Educ:* Aberdeen Grammar Sch.; St John's Coll., Oxford; Edinburgh Univ. Called to Bar, Inner Temple, 1931; Scottish Bar, 1932; Advocate-Depute, 1945; QC (Scot.) 1947; Solicitor-Gen. for Scotland, 1947-51. MP (Lab) Paisley, 1948-61. Chm., Royal Fine Art Commission for Scotland, 1965-78. Served War of 1939-45. Hon. FRIAS. *Address:* 22 Cammo Crescent, Barnton, Edinburgh. *T:* 031-339 3102.

JOHNSTON, Alan Charles Macpherson, QC (Scot.) 1980; Treasurer, Faculty of Advocates, since 1977; *m* 1966, Anthea Jean Blackburn; three *s*. *Educ:* Edinburgh Academy; Loretto School; Jesus Coll., Cambridge (BA Hons); Edinburgh Univ. (LLB). Called to the Bar, 1967. *Publication:* (asst editor) Gloag and Henderson, Introduction to Scots Law, 7th edn 1968. *Recreations:* shooting, fishing, golf, walking. *Address:* 3 Circus Gardens, Edinburgh. *Clubs:* University Pitt (Cambridge); New (Edinburgh).

JOHNSTON, Alastair McPherson; see Dunpark, Hon. Lord.

JOHNSTON, Sir Alexander, GCB 1962 (CB 1946); KBE 1953; Deputy Chairman: Council for the Securities Industry, since 1978; Panel on Take-overs and Mergers, since 1970; b 27 Aug. 1905; s of Alexander Simpson Johnston and Joan Macdiarmid; m 1947, Betty Joan Harris (see Lady Johnston); one s one d. Educ: George Heriot's Sch.; University of Edinburgh. Entered Home Office, 1928; Principal Asst Sec., Office of the Minister of Reconstruction, 1943–45; Under-Sec., Office of Lord Pres. of the Council, 1946–48; Dep. Sec. of the Cabinet, 1948–51; Third Sec., HM Treasury, 1951–58; Chm., Bd of Inland Revenue, 1958–68. Dep. Chm., Monopolies and Mergers Commn, 1969–76. Hon. DSc(Econ) London, 1977. Address: 18 Mallord Street, SW3. T: 01-352 6840. Club: Reform.

JOHNSTON, Alexander Graham; Sheriff of Grampian, Highland and Islands, since 1982; b 16 July 1944; s of Hon. Lord Kincraig, qv; m 1st, 1972, Susan (marr. diss. 1982); two s; 2nd, 1982, Angela; two step d. Educ: Edinburgh Acad.; Strathallan Sch.; Univ. of Edinburgh (LLB); University Coll., Oxford (BA). Admitted as Solicitor and Writer to the Signet, 1971; Partner, Hagart and Burn-Murdoch, Solicitors, Edinburgh, 1972–82. Hon. Fellow, Inst. of Professional Investigators, 1980. Recreations: golf, piping, curling. Address: 61 Fountainhall Road, Aberdeen. T: Aberdeen 22460. Clubs: Honorable Company of Edinburgh Golfers; Oxford and Cambridge Golfing Society; Vincent's (Oxford).

JOHNSTON, Most Rev. Allen Howard, CMG 1978; LTh; b Auckland, NZ, 1912; s of Joseph Howard Johnston; m 1937, Joyce Rhoda, d of John A. Grantley, Auckland; four d. Educ: Seddon Memorial Technical College; St John's College, Auckland; Auckland Univ. College. Deacon, 1935; Priest, 1936. Assistant Curate of St Mark's, Remuera, 1935–37; Vicar of Dargaville, 1937–42; Vicar of Northern Wairoa, 1942–44; Vicar of Otahuhu, 1944–49; Vicar of Whangarei, 1949–53; Archdeacon of Waimate, 1949–53; Bishop of Dunedin, 1953–69; Bishop of Waikato, 1969–80; Primate and Archbishop of New Zealand, 1972–80. Fellow, St John's Coll., Auckland, 1970. Hon. LLD Otago, 1969. ChStJ 1974. Address: 3 Wymer Terrace, Hamilton, New Zealand.

JOHNSTON, Archibald Gilchrist, PhD; CEng, FIMinE; Director of Research and Laboratory Services Division and Head of Safety in Mines Research Establishment, since 1980; b 3 June 1931; s of late John Johnston and Cecilia Marshall Gilchrist Johnston; m 1958, Elizabeth Smith Orr; one s. Educ: Wishaw High Sch.; Royal College of Science and Technology (ARCST); Glasgow Univ. (PhD). Strata Control/Mechanisation Engineer, National Coal Board, 1955–57; Mine Management, NCB, 1957–62; HM Inspectorate of Mines and Quarries, 1962–77; Research Laboratory Director, 1977–80. Publications: various, in technical jls, incl. Mining Engr, Colliery Guardian, and others. Recreations: gardening, golf. Address: Belhaven, Tickhill, Doncaster DN11 9QF. T: Doncaster 742994.

JOHNSTON, Betty Joan, (Lady Johnston), JP; Chairman: Girls' Public Day School Trust, since 1975; Association of Governing Bodies of Girls Public Schools, since 1979; Deputy Parliamentary Counsel, Law Commission, since 1975; d of Edward and Catherine Anne Harris; m 1947, Sir Alexander Johnston, qv; one s one d. Educ: Cheltenham Ladies' Coll.; St Hugh's Coll., Oxford (1st Cl. Hons Jurisprudence). Called to Bar, Gray's Inn, 1940 (1st cl., Bar Final exams; Arden and Lord Justice Holker Sen. schols). Asst Parly Counsel, 1942-52. Vice-Chm., Direct Grant Schs Jt Cttee, 1975–81; Chm., Francis Holland (Church of England) Schools Trust, 1978–. Member: Indep. Schs Jt Council, 1974– (Chm., Assisted Places Cttee, 1981–); Council, Queen's Coll., London. Governor, Howell's Sch., Llandaff. JP Inner London 1966. Address: 18 Mallord Street, SW3. T: 01-352 6840.

JOHNSTON, Brian (Alexander), MC 1945; freelance broadcaster and commentator; b 24 June 1912; s of Lt-Col C. E. Johnston, DSO, MC; m 1948, Pauline, d of late Col William Tozer, CBE, TD; three s two d. Educ: Eton; New Coll., Oxford (BA). Family coffee business, 1934-39. Served War of 1939-45: in Grenadier Guards; in 2nd Bn throughout, taking part in Normandy Campaign, advance into Brussels, Nijmegen Bridge and Crossing of Rhine into Germany. Joined BBC, 1945, retired 1972; specialises in cricket commentary for TV and radio (BBC Cricket Corresp., 1963-72), interviews, ceremonial commentary (eg Funeral of King George VI, 1952; Coronation of Queen Elizabeth II, 1953; Weddings of Princess Margaret, 1960, Princess Anne, 1973, Prince of Wales, 1981; Queen's Silver Jubilee, 1977); Let's Go Somewhere feature in In Town Tonight, Down Your Way, Twenty Questions, etc. Radio Sports Personality Award, Soc. of Authors/Pye Radio, 1981. Publications: Let's Go Somewhere, 1952; Armchair Cricket, 1957; Stumped for a Tale, 1965; The Wit of Cricket, 1968; All About Cricket, 1972; It's Been a Lot of Fun, 1974; It's a Funny Game ..., 1978; Rain Stops Play, 1979. Recreations: cricket, golf, theatre and reading newspapers. Address: 43 Boundary Road, NW8. T: 01-286 2991. Club: MCC.

JOHNSTON, Sir Charles (Collier), Kt 1973; TD; b 4 March 1915; e s of late Captain Charles Moore Johnston and Muriel Florence Mellon; m ; two s; m 1981, Mrs Yvonne Shearman. Educ: Tonbridge Sch., Kent. Served War: HM Forces, Territorial, commissioned 1938; served throughout war, in RA, retd, 1946, rank Major. Managing Dir, 1948-76, Chm., 1951-77, of Standex International Ltd (formerly Roehlen-Martin Ltd), Engravers and Engineers, of Ashton Road, Bredbury, Cheshire. Chm., Macclesfield Constituency

Conservative Assoc., 1961-65; Hon. Treas., NW Conservatives and Mem. Conservative Bd of Finance, 1965-71; Chm., NW Area Conservatives, 1971-76; a Vice Pres., Nat. Union of Conservative and Unionist Assocs (Mem. Exec. Cttee, 1965-, Chm. 1976-81). Mem., Boyd Commn, as official observers of elecns held in Zimbabwe/Rhodesia, April 1980. Recreations: fly fishing, spectator sports, travelling. Address: 5A Burton Mews, South Eaton Place, SW1. Club: Royal Corinthian Yacht (Cowes).

JOHNSTON, Sir Charles (Hepburn), GCMG 1971 (KCMG 1959; CMG 1953); Member of Council of Toynbee Hall, since 1974; Member of Lloyd's since 1962; Registrar, Order of St Michael and St George, since 1981; b 11 March 1912; s of Ernest Johnston and Emma Hepburn; m 1944, Princess Natasha Bagration; no c. Educ: Winchester; Balliol Coll., Oxford (1st Class Hon. Mods, 1932, Lit. Hum., 1934). Entered Diplomatic Service, 1936; 3rd Sec., Tokyo, 1939; 1st Sec., Cairo, 1945, and Madrid, 1948; Counsellor, FO, 1951, and British Embassy, Bonn, 1955; HM Ambassador in Amman, 1956; Gov. and C-in-C, Aden, 1960-63; High Comr for Aden and Protectorate of South Arabia, 1963; Dep. Under-Sec. of State, Foreign Office, 1963-65; High Commissioner, Australia, 1965-71. KStJ 1961. Publications: The View from Steamer Point, 1964; Mo and Other Originals, 1971; The Brink of Jordan, 1972; Estuary in Scotland (poems), 1974; trans., Pushkin, Eugene Onegin, 1977; Poems and Journeys, 1979; Rivers and Fireworks, 1980; Talk about the Last Poet, 1981; Choisevl and Talleyrand, 1982. Address: 32 Kingston House South, SW7 1NF. Club: White's.

JOHNSTON, Rear-Adm. Clarence Dinsmore H.; see Howard-Johnston.

JOHNSTON, Prof. David, MD, ChM; FRCS, FRCSE, FRCSGlas; Professor of Surgery and Head of Department, University of Leeds at Leeds General Infirmary, since 1977; b Glasgow, 4 Sept. 1936; s of Robert E. and Jean Johnston; m 1963, Jocelyn V. Houghton, BSc, MB, ChB; three s one d. Educ: Hamilton Acad.; Glasgow Univ. (MB, ChB Hons; MD Hons, ChM). FRCSE 1963; FRCSGlas 1964; FRCS 1979. House Surgeon, Western Infirmary, Glasgow, 1961-62; Res. Asst and Registrar, Univ. Dept of Surg., Leeds Gen. Infirm., 1962-64; Lectr in Surg., Univ. of Sheffield, 1965-68; Sen. Lectr and Consultant, Univ. Dept of Surg., Leeds Gen. Infirm., 1968-75; Prof. of Surg. and Head of Dept, Univ. of Bristol (Bristol Royal Infirm.), 1975-77. Publications: papers on physiology and surgery of the stomach and colon. Recreations: reading, running, tennis, fishing. Address: 22 Kepstorn Road, West Park, Leeds LS16 5HL. T: Leeds 757898.

JOHNSTON, David Alan H.; see Hunter Johnston.

JOHNSTON, Prof. David Lloyd; Principal and Vice-Chancellor, and Professor of Law, McGill University, since 1979; b 28 June 1941; s of Lloyd Johnston and Dorothy Stonehouse Johnston; m 1963, Sharon Downey; five d. Educ: Harvard Univ., Cambridge, Mass; Cambridge Univ.; Queen's Univ. at Kingston, Ont. Asst Prof., Faculty of Law, Queen's Univ., Kingston, 1966-68; Faculty of Law, Univ. of Toronto: Asst Prof., 1968-69; Associate Prof., 1969-72; Prof., 1972-74; Dean and Prof., Faculty of Law, Univ. of Western Ont, 1974-79. LLD hc Law Soc. of Upper Canada, 1980. Publications: Computers and the Law, 1968; Canadian Securities Regulation, 1977; (jtly) The Law of Business Associations, 1979; (with R. Forbes) Canadian Companies and the Stock Exchange, 1979; articles and reports. Recreations: jogging, skiing, tennis. Address: McGill University, 845 Sherbrooke Street West, Montreal, Que H3A 2T5, Canada. T: 514-392-5347; 76 Sunnyside Avenue, Montreal, Que H3Y 1C2. T: 514-487-0997. Clubs: University, Faculty (Montreal).

JOHNSTON, (David) Russell; MP (L) Inverness since 1964; b 28 July 1932; s of late David Knox Johnston and Georgina Margaret Gerrie Russell; m 1967, Joan Graham Menzies; three s. Educ: Carbost Public Sch.; Portree High Sch.; Edinburgh Univ. (MA). Commissioned into Intelligence Corps (Nat. Service), 1958; subseq., Moray House Coll. of Educn until 1961; taught in Liberton Secondary Sch., 1961-63. Research Asst, Scottish Liberal Party, 1963-64. Chm., Scottish Liberal Party, 1970- (Vice-Chm., 1965-70), Leader, 1974-; Mem., UK Delegn to European Parlt, 1973-75 and 1976-79, Vice Pres., Political Cttee, 1976-79. Contested (L) Highlands and Islands, European Parly elecn, 1979. Mem., Royal Commission on Local Govt in Scotland, 1966-69. Publications: (pamphlet) Highland Development, 1964; (pamphlet) To Be a Liberal, 1972; Scottish Liberal Party Conf. Speeches, 1979. Recreations: reading, photography. Address: Glendruidh, by Inverness IV1 2AA. T: Inverness 36431. Clubs: Special Forces; Scottish Liberal (Edinburgh).

JOHNSTON, Denis; see Johnston, (William) Denis.

JOHNSTON, Douglas Harold; see Johnston, Hon. Lord.

JOHNSTON, Edward Alexander, CB 1975; Government Actuary, since 1973; b 19 March 1929; 2nd s of Edward Hamilton Johnston, DLitt, and Iris Olivia Helena May; m 1st, Veronica Mary Bernays (marr. diss.); two s two d; 2nd, Christine Elizabeth Nash. Educ: Groton Sch., USA; Marlborough Coll.; New Coll., Oxford. BA 1952; FIA 1957; Founder Fellow, Pensions Management Inst. Equity & Law Life Assce Soc., 1952-58; Govt Actuary's Dept: Asst Actuary, 1958; Actuary, 1961; Principal Actuary, 1970. Address: c/o Government Actuary's Department, 22 Kingsway, WC2. Club: Reform.

JOHNSTON, Very Rev. Frederick Mervyn Kieran; Dean of Cork, 1967-71, retired; *b* 22 Oct. 1911; *s* of Robert Mills Johnston and Florence Harriet O'Hanlon; *m* 1938, Catherine Alice Ruth FitzSimons; two *s. Educ:* Grammar Sch., Galway; Bishop Foy Sch., Waterford; Trinity Coll., Dublin. BA 1933. Deacon, 1934; Priest, 1936; Curate, Castlecomer, 1934-36; Curate, St Luke, Cork, 1936-38; Incumbent of Kilmeen, 1938-40; Drimoleague, 1940-45; Blackrock, Cork, 1945-58; Bandon, 1958-67; Rector of St Fin Barre's Cathedral and Dean of Cork, 1967. *Address:* Ardkilly, Sandycove, Kinsale, Co. Cork.

JOHNSTON, Frederick Patrick Mair; Chairman, Johnston Newspaper Group, since 1973; Member of the Press Council, since 1973 (Member, Complaints Committee, since 1977); *b* Edinburgh, 15 Sept. 1935; *e s* of late Frederick M. Johnston and of Mrs M. K. Johnston, Falkirk; *m* 1961, Elizabeth Ann Jones; two *s. Educ:* Morrison's Acad., Crieff; Lancing Coll., Sussex; New Coll., Oxford (MA, Mod. Hist.). Commissioned in Royal Scots Fusiliers, 1955; served in E Africa with 4th (Uganda) Bn, KAR, 1955-56. Joined Editorial Dept of Liverpool Daily Post & Echo, 1959; joined The Times Publishing Co. Ltd, as Asst Sec., 1960; Company Sec., F. Johnston & Co. Ltd, 1969; Managing Dir, F. Johnston & Co. Ltd, 1973; Chm., Dunn & Wilson Gp Ltd, 1976. President: Young Newspapermen's Assoc., 1968-69; Forth Valley Chamber of Commerce, 1972-73; Scottish Newspaper Proprietors' Assoc., 1976-78; Chm., Central Scotland Manpower Cttee, 1976-; Treasurer, Soc. of Master Printers of Scotland, 1981-. *Recreations:* reading, travelling. *Address:* 1 Grange Terrace, Edinburgh EH9 2LD. *Clubs:* Royal Commonwealth Society; New (Edinburgh).

JOHNSTON, George Alexander, MA, DPhil; *b* Jamaica, 11 Nov. 1888; *e s* of Rev. Robert Johnston, BD; *m* 1919, Pauline Violet, *y d* of late Sir George Roche; one *s* one *d. Educ:* University of Glasgow (MA, 1st cl. Hons Classics and Philosophy, 1912; DPhil, 1918); University of Berlin. Lecturer in Moral Philosophy, St Andrews Univ., 1912-14; Lecturer in Moral Philosophy, Glasgow Univ., 1914-19; served in Macedonia, at the War Office, and GHQ, Palestine and Cairo, 1916-19; Ministry of Labour, 1919-20; International Labour Office, 1920-40; Vis. Prof. of Social Legislation; Columbia Univ., New York, 1931-32; Ministry of Labour, 1940-45; Asst Dir, ILO, 1945-48; Treasurer ILO, 1948-53; Chm. UN Joint Staff Pensions Board, 1951; Sec.-Gen., Govt Training Inst., Istanbul, 1954; Mem. UN Economic Mission to Viet-Nam, 1955-56; Dir ILO London Office, 1956-57. Officer of Order of Orange-Nassau (Netherlands). *Publications:* An Introduction to Ethics, 1915; Selections from the Scottish Philosophy of Common Sense, 1915; The Development of Berkeley's Philosophy, 1923; International Social Progress, 1924; Citizenship in the Industrial World, 1928; Berkeley's Commonplace Book, 1930; The International Labour Organisation: its work for social and economic progress, 1970; articles in periodicals and encyclopædias. *Address:* Talbot Lodge, Blackrock, Co. Dublin, Ireland.

JOHNSTON, Henry Butler M.; *see* McKenzie Johnston.

JOHNSTON, Hugh Philip, CB 1977; Deputy Secretary, Property Services Agency, Department of the Environment, since 1974; *b* 17 May 1927; *s* of late Philip Rose-Johnston and Dora Ellen Johnston; *m* 1949, Barbara Frances Theodoridi; one *s* three *d. Address:* Wimbledon Coll.; Faraday House. DFH (Hons); FIEE, FCIBS. Air Ministry Works Dept: Asst Engr, 1951; Engr, 1956; Ministry of Public Buildings and Works: Prin. Engr, 1964; Asst Dir, 1969; Dir (Under-Sec.), Dept of Environment and Property Services Agency, Engrg Services Directorate, 1970. *Recreations:* motoring, music. *Address:* 9 Devas Road, Wimbledon, SW20 8PD. *T:* 01-946 2021.

JOHNSTON, Ian Henderson, CB 1981; Deputy Controller Aircraft, Procurement Executive, Ministry of Defence, since 1982; *b* 29 April 1925; *s* of late Peter Johnston and Barbara Johnston (*née* Gifford); *m* 1949, Irene Blackburn; two *d. Educ:* George Heriot's Sch., Edinburgh; Edinburgh Univ. (BSc Eng); Imperial Coll., London (DIC Aeronautics). D. Napier & Sons, 1945-46; National Gas Turbine Estabt, 1947-64; Ramjet Project Officer, Min. of Aviation, 1964-66; Exchange Officer to Wright Patterson Air Force Base, Ohio, 1966-68; Asst Dir (Engine Develt), Min. of Technology, 1968-70; Dep. Dir, National Gas Turbine Estabt, 1970-73; Ministry of Defence: Dir-Gen., Multi-Role Combat Aircraft, (PE), 1973-76; Dir, Mil. Vehicles and Engrg Estabt, 1976-78; Dep. Controller, Estabts and Res. B, and Chief Scientist (Army), 1978-80; Dep. Controller, Estabt Resources and Personnel, MoD, 1980-82. *Publications:* papers on turbine research in Aeronautical Research Council Reports and Memoranda Series. *Recreations:* golf, bridge. *Address:* 49 Salisbury Road, Farnborough, Hants. *T:* Farnborough 41971.

JOHNSTON, Maj.-Gen. James Alexander Deans, OBE 1945; MC 1937; Director of Medical Services, BAOR, 1969-70, retired; *b* 28 Feb. 1911; *s* of Walter Johnston and I. C. Gilchrist; *m* 1940, Enid O. Eldridge; one *s* two *d. Educ:* Glasgow Univ. MB, ChB Glasgow, 1933. House Surgeon, Taunton and Somerset Hosp., 1933-34. Commnd into RAMC, 1934; served in India, 1935-40 (Quetta Earthquake, 1935; Mohmand Ops, 1935; Waziristan Ops, 1936-37); served in NW Europe, 1944-45; SMO during and after liberation of Belsen Concentration Camp, April 1945; ADMS HQ Malaya Comd, 19 Ind. Div. and 2 Br. Inf. Div. in Far East, 1945-47; ADMS Southern Comd, UK, 1947-49; DDMS HQ MELF, 1949-52; ADMS 2 Div., and DDMS HQ BAOR, 1952-57; OC British Military Hosp., Dhekelia, Cyprus, 1957-61; ADG WO, 1961-64; Comdt, Depot and Training Establishment and HQ AER, RAMC, 1964-66; DMS, FARELF, 1966-69. Major 1943; Lt-Col 1948;

Col 1957; Brig. 1964; Maj.-Gen. 1966. QHP 1967-70. *Recreations:* swimming, tennis, country pursuits. *Address:* Park Cottage, Ewhurst Lane, Northiam, East Sussex.

JOHNSTON, James Campbell, CBE 1972; Chairman: Capel Court Corporation Ltd, since 1969; Australian Foundation Investment Co., since 1967; Director, T. & G. Mutual Life Society Group, since 1976; Commissioner, State Electricity Commission of Victoria, since 1978; *b* 7 July 1912; *s* of late Edwin and Estelle Johnston; *m* 1938, Agnes Emily, *yr d* of late Richard Thomas; two *s* one *d. Educ:* Prince Alfred Coll., Adelaide; Scotch Coll., Melbourne; University of Melbourne. Admitted to Inst. Chartered Accountants, Australia, 1933; joined J. B. Were & Son, Stock and Share Brokers, 1935, Sen. Partner, 1967-78; Stock Exchange of Melbourne: Mem., 1947; Chm., 1972-77. *Address:* 13 Monaro Road, Kooyong, Victoria 3144, Australia. *T:* 20 2842. *Clubs:* Melbourne, Australian, Athenæum, Victoria Racing, Royal Melbourne Golf (Melbourne).

JOHNSTON, Jennifer, (Mrs David Gilliland), FRSL; author; *b* 12 Jan. 1930; *d* of Denis Johnston, *qv* ; *m* 1st, 1951, Ian Smyth; two *s* two *d* ; 2nd, 1976, David Gilliland, *qv. Educ:* Park House Sch., Dublin; Trinity Coll., Dublin. FRSL 1979. *Publications:* The Captains and the Kings, 1972; The Gates, 1973; How Many Miles to Babylon?, 1974; Shadows on Our Skin, 1978 (dramatised for TV, 1979); The Old Jest, 1979; The Nightingale and not the Lark (play, performed Dublin, 1979); The Christmas Tree, 1981. *Recreations:* theatre, cinema, gardening, travelling. *Address:* Brook Hall, Culmore Road, Derry, N Ireland BT48 8JE. *T:* Londonderry 51297.

JOHNSTON, Sir John (Baines), GCMG 1978 (KCMG 1966; CMG 1962); KCVO 1972; HM Diplomatic Service, retired; *b* 13 May 1918; *e s* of late Rev. A. S. Johnston, Banbury, Oxon; *m* 1969, Elizabeth Mary, *d* of late J. F. Crace; one *s. Educ:* Banbury Grammar Sch.; Queen's Coll., Oxford (Eglesfield Scholar). Served War, 1940-46: Adjt 1st Bn Gordon Highlanders, 1944; DAQMG HQ 30 Corps District, 1945. Asst Principal, Colonial Office, 1947; Principal, 1948; Asst Sec., West African Council, Accra, 1950-51; UK Liaison Officer with Commission for Technical Co-operation in Africa South of the Sahara, 1952; Principal Private Sec. to Sec. of State for the Colonies, 1953; Asst Sec., 1956; Head of Far Eastern Dept, Colonial Office, 1956; transferred to Commonwealth Relations Office, 1957; Dep. High Commissioner in S Africa, 1959-61; British High Commissioner: in Sierra Leone, 1961-63; in the Federation of Rhodesia and Nyasaland, 1963, Rhodesia, 1964-65; Asst, later Dep. Under-Secretary of State, FCO, 1968-71; British High Commissioner: in Malaysia, 1971-74; in Canada, 1974-78. A Governor, BBC, 1978-. Chm., ARELS Exams Trust, 1982-. *Address:* 5 Victoria Road, Oxford OX2 7QF.

JOHNSTON, Lt-Col Sir John (Frederick Dame), KCVO 1981 (CVO 1977; MVO 1971); MC 1945; Comptroller, Lord Chamberlain's Office, since 1981 (Assistant Comptroller, 1964-81); *b* 24 Aug. 1922; *m* 1949, Hon. Elizabeth Hardinge, JP Windsor 1971, *d* of late 2nd Baron Hardinge of Penshurst, PC, GCB, GCVO, MC, and late Lady Hardinge of Penshurst; one *s* one *d. Educ:* Ampleforth. Served in Grenadier Guards, 1941-64. Extra Equerry to the Queen, 1965-. *Address:* Adelaide Cottage, Windsor Home Park, Berks. *T:* Windsor 68286; Stone Hill, Newport, Dyfed. *Clubs:* Pratt's, MCC; Swinley Forest Golf.

JOHNSTON, Kenneth Robert Hope; QC 1953; *b* 18 June 1905; *e s* of Dr J. A. H. Johnston, Headmaster of Highgate Sch., 1908-36, and Kate Winsome Gammon; *m* 1937, Dr Priscilla Bright Clark, *d* of Roger and Sarah Clark, Street, Somerset; one *s* three *d. Educ:* Rugby Sch.; Sidney Sussex Coll., Cambridge Univ.; Harvard Univ., USA. Called to the Bar, Gray's Inn, 1933; Bencher, 1958. RAFVR, 1939-45. *Address:* 28 Leigh Road, Street, Somerset. *T:* Street 43559. *Club:* MCC.

JOHNSTON, Margaret; *see* Parker, Margaret Annette McCrie J.

JOHNSTON, Lt-Gen. Sir Maurice (Robert), KCB 1982; OBE 1971; Deputy Chief of Defence Staff (Operational Requirements), since 1981; *b* 27 Oct. 1929; *s* of late Brig. Allen Leigh Johnston, OBE, and Gertrude Geraldine Johnston (*née* Templer); *m* 1960, Belinda Mary Sladen; one *s* one *d. Educ:* Wellington College; RMA Sandhurst. rcds, psc. Commissioned RA, 1949; transf. The Queen's Bays, 1954; served in Germany, Egypt, Jordan, Libya, N Ireland, Borneo. Instr, Army Staff Coll., 1965-67; MA to CGS, 1968-71; CO 1st The Queen's Dragoon Guards, 1971-73; Comdr 20th Armoured Brigade, 1973-75; BGS, HQ UKLF, 1977-78; Senior Directing Staff, RCDS, 1979; Asst Chief of Gen. Staff, 1980. *Recreations:* fishing, shooting, gardening, music. *Address:* Ivy House, Worton, Devizes, Wilts. *T:* Devizes 3727. *Club:* Army and Navy.

JOHNSTON, Michael Errington; Under-Secretary, Ministry of Agriculture, Fisheries and Food, 1970-76; *b* 22 Jan. 1916; *s* of late Lt-Col C. E. L. Johnston, RA, and late Beatrix Johnston; *m* 1938, Ida Brown; two *d. Educ:* Wellington; Peterhouse, Cambridge (Scholar). BA, 1st cl. Hist. Tripos, 1937; MA 1947. Served War of 1939-45, Rifle Bde (Capt., despatches), Asst Principal, Board of Education, 1938; Principal, 1946; Asst Sec., HM Treasury, 1952, Under-Sec., 1962-68; Under-Sec., Civil Service Dept, 1968-70. *Recreations:* painting and birdwatching. *Address:* 3 The Terrace, Barnes, SW13. *T:* 01-876 5265.

JOHNSTON, Ninian Rutherford Jamieson, RSA 1965; architect and town planner in private practice since 1946; *b* 6 March 1912; *s* of John Neill Johnston and Agnes Johnston; *m* 1937, Helen, *d* of Robert Henry Jackson and Jean Patrick Jackson; one *s* two *d. Educ:* Allan Glen's Sch.; Glasgow Sch. of Architecture. Served with Army, 1939-45. BArch 1934; FRIAS 1935; FRTPI (MTPI 1946); FRIBA 1951. *Principal Works:* Pollokshaws Central Redevelopment Area; Woodside Central Redevelopment Area, Glasgow; Central Hospitals at Dumfries, Greenock and Rutherglen. Mem. Roy. Fine Art Commission for Scotland, 1969-76. *Recreations:* music, painting, gardening. *Address:* Tithe Barn, Compton Abdale, Cheltenham, Glos; 18 Woodlands Terrace, Glasgow, G3 6DF. *T:* 041-332 9184. *Club:* Art (Glasgow).

JOHNSTON, Robert Gordon Scott; Under Secretary, Department of the Environment, and Director of Civil Accommodation, Property Services Agency, since 1979; *b* 27 Aug. 1933; *s* of Robert William Fairfield Johnston, *qv*; *m* 1960, Jill Maureen Campbell; one *s* one *d. Educ:* Clifton; Clare Coll., Cambridge (1st Cl. Hons Classical Tripos, MA). 2/Lieut Scots Guards (National Service), 1955-57. Entered Air Min. as Asst Principal, 1957; Private Sec. to Parly Under Sec. of State for Air, 1959-62; transf. to MPBW, Def. Works Secretariat, 1963; Sec., Bldg Regulation Adv. Cttee, 1964; Principal Private Sec. to successive Ministers of Public Bldg and Works, 1965-68; seconded to Shell Internat. Chemical Co., Finance Div., 1968-70; Asst Dir of Home Estate Management, Property Services Agency, 1970-73; seconded to Cabinet Office, 1973-75; Asst Sec., Railways Directorate, Dept of Transport, 1975-79; Under Sec., seconded to Price Commn, 1979. *Address:* 184 Beckenham Hill Road, Beckenham, Kent BR3 1SZ.

JOHNSTON, Robert Smith; *see* Kincraig, Hon. Lord.

JOHNSTON, Robert William Fairfield, CMG 1960; CBE 1954; MC 1917; TD 1936 (and three Bars, 1947); Assistant Secretary, Ministry of Defence, 1946-62; retired from the Civil Service, 1962; *b* 1 May 1895; *e s* of late Capt. Robert Johnston, Army Pay Dept and Royal Scots; *m* 1922, Agnes Scott (*d* 1980), *o c* of late Peter Justice, Edinburgh; one *s.* Entered Civil Service, Dec. 1910: served in War Office, Bd of Trade, Min. of Labour, Home Office, Office of Minister without Portfolio, Min. of Defence, and seconded to FO, as Counsellor in UK Delegation in Paris to NATO and OEEC, 1953-61. Territorial Army, 1910-47; served European War, 1914-18, The Royal Scots (1st, 9th and 16th Battalions) in France, Flanders, Macedonia and Egypt; commissioned 1917; War of 1939-45, Lieut-Col, Comdg 8th Bn Gordon Highlanders, 1940-42, and 100th (Gordons) Anti-Tank Regt, RA, 1942-44, in 51st (Highland) and 2nd (British) Inf. Divs respectively; retired as Lieut-Col TA, Sept. 1947. *Address:* 8 Broad Avenue, Queen's Park, Bournemouth, Dorset.

See also R. G. S. Johnston.

JOHNSTON, Prof. Ronald Carlyle; Professor of Romance Philology and Medieval French Literature, Westfield College, London, 1961-74; *b* 19 May 1907; *m* ; one *s* three *d. Educ:* Ackworth Sch., Yorks; Bootham Sch., York; Merton Coll., Oxford. Travel in France, Germany and Spain, 1929-30. MA Oxon; 1st Cl. Hons Mediaeval and Modern Languages, French, 1929; Docteur de l'Université de Strasbourg, 1935. Asst Master Uppingham Sch., 1930-35; Lectr in French Philology and Old Fr. Lit., Oxford, 1935-45; Fellow of Jesus Coll., Oxford, 1945-48; Professor of French Language and Literature, University of St Andrews, 1948-61. Sometime external examiner in French, Universities of Oxford, Cambridge, Edinburgh, Aberdeen, and Manchester. Pres., Anglo-Norman Text Soc., 1982- (Hon. Treasurer, 1969-82). Officier d'Académie. Chevalier de la Légion d'Honneur. *Publications:* Les Poésies lyriques du troubadour Arnaut de Mareuil (Paris), 1935; The Crusade and Death of Richard I (Anglo-Norman Text Soc.), 1961; The Versification of Jordan Fantosme, 1974; (with A. Ewert) Selected Fables of Marie de France, 1942; (with D. D. R. Owen) Fabliaux, 1957; Two Old French Gauvain Romances, part 1, 1972; Jordan Fantosme's Chronicle, 1981; *translations:* (with Ana Cartianu): Creanga's Povesti si Povestiri, 1973; Amintiri din copilărie, etc, 1978; reviews in Medium Aevum, Modern Language Review, French Studies, etc. *Recreations:* rough gardening, travel. *Address:* 5 Rawlinson Road, Oxford OX2 6UE. *T:* Oxford 55481.

JOHNSTON, Russell; *see* Johnston, D. R.

JOHNSTON, Sir Thomas Alexander, 13th Bt of Caskieben, *cr* 1626; Attorney-at-Law; partner in legal firm of Howell, Johnston, Langford, Finkbohner and Lawler, Alabama, USA; *b* 7 Sept. 1916; *s* of Sir Thomas Alexander Johnston, 12th Bt and of Pauline Burke, *d* of Leslie Bragg Sheldon, Mobile; *S* father, 1959; *m* 1941, Helen Torrey, *d* of Benjamin Franklin Du Bois; one *s* two *d. Educ:* University of Alabama (LLB). Mem., Alabama House of Representatives, 1941-49; Mem., Alabama State Senate, 1949-54; Pres., Mobile Co. Bar Assoc., 1963. Member: Alabama Constitution Revision Cttee, 1970-76; Alabama Judicial Compensation Commn, 1976-. *Recreations:* hunting, fishing. *Heir: s* Thomas Alexander Johnston, *b* 1 Feb. 1956. *Address:* Howell, Johnston, Langford, Finkbohner and Lawler, Commercial Guaranty Bank Building, Mobile, Alabama, USA. *T:* 205-432-2677. *Clubs:* Athelstan, Country (Mobile).

JOHNSTON, Thomas Lothian; Principal and Vice-Chancellor of Heriot-Watt University, since 1981; *b* 9 March 1927; *s* of late T. B. Johnston and Janet Johnston; *m* 1956, Joan, *d* of E. C. Fahmy, surgeon; two *s* three *d. Educ:*

Hawick High Sch.; Univs of Edinburgh and Stockholm. MA 1951, PhD 1955, Edinburgh. FRSE 1979; FRSA 1981. Served RNVR, 1944-47 (Sub-Lt). Asst Lectr in Polit. Economy, Univ. of Edinburgh, 1953-55, Lectr 1955-65; Res. Fellow, Queen's Univ., Canada, 1965; Prof. and Hd of Dept of Econs, Heriot-Watt Univ., 1966-76. Visiting Professor: Univ. of Illinois, 1962-63; Internat. Inst. for Labour Studies, Geneva, 1973; Western Australia Inst. of Technol., 1979. Sec., Scottish Econ. Soc., 1958-65 (Pres., 1978-81); Member: Scottish Milk Marketing Bd, 1967-72; Nat. Industrial Relations Court, 1971-74; Scottish Cttee on Licensing Laws, 1971-73; Nat. Youth Employment Council, 1968-71; Scottish Telecommunications Bd, 1977-; Scottish Economic Council, 1977-; Council for Tertiary Educn in Scotland, 1979-; Chm., Manpower Services Cttee for Scotland, 1977-80; Economic Consultant to Sec. of State for Scotland, 1977-. Dir, First Charlotte Assets Trust, 1981-. Chm. Council, Fraser of Allander Inst., Univ. of Strathclyde, 1975-78. Chm. of Wages Councils; Chm., Enquiry into staff representation, London Clearing Banks, 1978-79; consultant, UN Human Resources Develt Project, Suez Canal region, 1980; Arbitrator; Overseas Corresp., Nat. Acad. of Arbitrators, USA. *Publications:* Collective Bargaining in Sweden, 1962; (ed and trans.) Economic Expansion and Structural Change, 1963; (jtly) The Structure and Growth of the Scottish Economy, 1971; Introduction to Industrial Relations, 1981; articles in learned jls. *Recreations:* camping, gardening, walking. *Address:* 14 Mansionhouse Road, Edinburgh EH9 1TZ. *T:* 031-667 1439.

JOHNSTON, Rt. Rev. William; *b* 7 July 1914; *s* of late Dr W. Johnston; *m* 1943, Marguerite Pemberton, 2nd *d* of late H. Macpherson, Headingley Hall, Leeds; no *c. Educ:* Bromsgrove Sch.; Selwyn Coll., Cambridge; Westcott House, Cambridge. Asst Curate, S Michael, Headingley, Leeds, 1939-43; Asst Curate, Knaresborough, 1943-45; Vicar of Stourton, Yorks, 1945-49; Vicar of Armley, Leeds, 1949-56; Vicar of St Chad, Shrewsbury, 1956-64; Archdeacon of Bradford, 1965-77; Bishop Suffragan of Dunwich, 1977-80. *Address:* 40 Shrewsbury Road, Church Stretton, Shropshire SY6 6EU. *T:* Church Stretton 722687.

JOHNSTON, Very Rev. William Bryce; Minister of Colinton Parish Church, Edinburgh, since 1964; Chaplain to the Queen in Scotland, since 1981; *b* 16 Sept. 1921; *s* of William Bryce Johnston and Isabel Winifred Highley; *m* 1947, Ruth Margaret, *d* of Rev. James Arthur Cowley; one *s* two *d. Educ:* George Watson's Coll., Edinburgh; Edinburgh Univ. (MA Hons Classics 1942); New Coll., Edinburgh (BD (Dist.) 1945). Ordained as Chaplain to HM Forces, 1945; served in Germany and as Staff Chaplain, PoW Directorate, War Office, 1945-48; Minister: St Andrew's, Bo'ness, 1949; St George's, Greenock, 1955. Moderator of General Assembly of Church of Scotland, 1980-81. Convener: Board of St Colm's Coll., 1966-70; General Assembly Cttee on Adult Educn, 1970; Church and Nation Cttee, 1972; Inter-Church Relations Cttee, 1978; Cttee on Role of Men and Women, 1976. Mem., British Council of Churches, 1970- (Chm., Exec. Cttee, 1981-); Delegate to 5th Assembly of World Council of Churches, 1975; Cunningham Lectr, New Coll., 1968-71; Vis. Lectr in Social Ethics, Heriot-Watt Univ., 1966-. President, Edinburgh Rotary Club, 1975-76. Hon. DD Aberdeen, 1980. *Publications:* translations: K. Barth, Church Dogmatics, vol. 2, 1955; Calvin, Commentaries on Hebrews, 1 Peter, 1960; (jtly) Devolution and the British Churches, 1978; various Bible study pamphlets and theological articles for SCM, Scottish Jl of Theology. *Recreations:* organ-playing, bowls. *Address:* The Manse of Colinton, Edinburgh EH13 0JR. *T:* 031-441 2315. *Clubs:* New, University Staff (Edinburgh).

JOHNSTON, (William) Denis, OBE 1946; Writer, Broadcaster and Professor; *b* Dublin, 18 June 1901; *o s* of late Hon. William John Johnston, Judge of the Supreme Court; *m* 1st, 1928, Shelah Kathleen (marr. diss.), *d* of John William Richards, Dublin; one *s* one *d* ; 2nd, 1945, Betty, *d* of John William Chancellor, Dublin; two *s. Educ:* St Andrew's Coll., Dublin; Merchiston, Edinburgh; Christ's Coll., Cambridge (MA, LLM 1926, Pres. of the Union); Harvard Univ., USA (Pugsley Scholar). Barrister Inner Temple and King's Inns, 1925 and Northern Ireland, 1926; Dir, Dublin Gate Theatre, 1931-36; joined British Broadcasting Corporation, 1936; BBC War Correspondent, Middle East, Italy, France and Germany, 1942-45 (despatches); Programme Dir, BBC Television Service, 1945-47. Professor in English Dept, Mount Holyoke Coll., Mass; 1950-60; Guggenheim Fellowship, 1955; Head of Dept of Theatre and Speech, Smith Coll., 1961-66; Visiting Lecturer: Amherst Coll., 1966-67; Univ. of Iowa, 1967-68; Univ. of California, Davis, 1970-71. Berg Prof., New York Univ., 1971-72; Arnold Prof., Whitman Coll., 1972-73. Allied Irish Banks Award for literature, 1977. Hon. DLitt Ulster, 1979. *Publications:* plays: The Old Lady says 'No!', 1929; The Moon in the Yellow River, 1931; A Bride for the Unicorn, 1933; Storm Song, 1934; The Golden Cuckoo, 1939; The Dreaming Dust, 1940; A Fourth for Bridge, 1948; Strange Occurrence on Ireland's Eye, 1956; The Scythe and the Sunset, 1958; operatic version of Six Characters in Search of an Author (comp. Hugo Weisgall), 1959; *autobiography:* Nine Rivers from Jordan, 1953, operatic version (comp. Hugo Weisgall), 1968; The Brazen Horn, 1976; *biographies:* In Search of Swift, 1959; J. M. Synge, 1965. *Address:* 7 Adelaide Road, Glasthule, Co. Dublin. *Club:* Royal Irish Yacht (Dun Laoghaire).

See also Jennifer Johnston.

JOHNSTON, Ven. William Francis; Chaplain-General to the Forces since 1980; *b* 29 June 1930; *m* ; two *s* one *d. Educ:* Trinity Coll., Dublin (BA 1955). Ordained 1955; Curate of Orangefield, Co. Down, 1955-59. Commissioned into Royal Army Chaplains Dept, 1959; served, UK, Germany, Aden, Cyprus;

ACG South East District, 1977-80. *Address:* Chaplains Department, Ministry of Defence (Army), Bagshot Park, Bagshot, Surrey GU19 5PL.

JOHNSTON, William James; Secretary, Association of Local Authorities of Northern Ireland, 1979-82; *b* 3 April 1919; *s* of late Thomas Hamilton Johnston and of Mary Kathleen Johnston; *m* 1943, Joan Elizabeth Nancye (*née* Young); two *d. Educ:* Portora Royal Sch., Enniskillen. FCA(Ire.). Professional accountancy, 1937-44; Antrim CC, 1944-68, Dep. Sec., 1951-68; Dep. Town Clerk, Belfast, 1968-73, Town Clerk, 1973-79. Member: NI Tourist Bd, 1980-; Local Govt Staff Commn, 1974-; Public Service Trng Council (formerly Public Service Trng Cttee), 1974- (Chm., 1974-); Arts Council of NI, 1974-81. *Recreations:* golf, live theatre. *Address:* 47 Layde Road, Cushendall, Co. Antrim. *T:* Cushendall 211.

JOHNSTON, William Robert Patrick K.; *see* Knox-Johnston, Robin.

JOHNSTONE, VANDEN-BEMPDE-, family name of **Baron Derwent.**

JOHNSTONE, Prof. Alan Stewart; Professor of Radiodiagnosis, University of Leeds, 1948-68, now Emeritus; Director of Radiodiagnosis (General Infirmary, Leeds), United Leeds Hospitals, 1939-68; *b* 12 May 1905; *s* of Dr David A. and Margaret E. Johnstone, The Biggin, Waterbeck, Dumfriesshire; *m* 1934, Elizabeth Rowlett; one *s* one *d. Educ:* St Bees Sch.; Edinburgh Univ. Radiologist, Hammersmith Post-Graduate Hospital, 1935; Radiologist, Leicester Royal Infirmary, 1936-39. Baker Travelling Prof. in Radiology, Coll. of Radiologists of Australasia, 1959. Pres. Radiology Sect., Royal Society of Med., 1959-60; Pres. Thoracic Soc. of Great Britain, 1961-62. *Publications:* contributor to A Text Book of X-ray Diagnosis by British Authors; many in Br. Jl of Radiology, Jl of Faculty of Radiologists, Post Graduate Med. Jl, Edinburgh Med. Jl, Jl of Anatomy. *Recreations:* golf, fly fishing, chess. *Address:* 46 Stanford Road, Rondebosch, Cape Province, South Africa. *T:* Cape Town 667404.

JOHNSTONE, Air Vice-Marshal Alexander Vallance Riddell, CB 1966; DFC 1940; AE; DL; Director, Climax Cleaning Co.; Vice-Chairman, Council, TA&VRA, 1969-79; *b* 2 June 1916; *s* of late Alex. Lang Johnstone and Daisy Riddell; *m* 1940, Margaret Croll; one *s* two *d. Educ:* Kelvinside Academy, Glasgow. 602 (City of Glasgow) Sqdn, AAF, 1934-41; CO RAF Haifa, 1942; Spitfire Wing, Malta, 1942-43 (despatches, 1942); RAF Staff Coll., 1943; OC Fairwood Common, 1943-44; HQ AEAF, 1944; Air Attaché Dublin, 1946-48; OC RAF Ballykelly, 1951-52; OC Air/Sea Warfare Devel. Unit, 1952-54; SASO HQ No 12 Gp, 1954-55; Founder and First CAS Royal Malayan Air Force, 1957; OC Middleton St George, 1958-60; idc, 1961; Dir of Personnel, Air Min., 1962-64; Comdr, Air Forces, Borneo, 1964-65; AO Scotland and N Ireland, AOC No 18 Group, and Maritime Air Comdr N Atlantic (NATO), 1965-68. DL Glasgow, 1971. Johan Mengku Negara (Malaya), 1958. *Publications:* Television Series, One Man's War, 1964; Where No Angels Dwell, 1969; Enemy in the Sky, 1976; Adventure in the Sky, 1978. *Recreations:* golf, sailing. *Address:* 36 Greystoke Lodge, Hanger Lane, W5. *Club:* Royal Air Force.

JOHNSTONE, Sir Frederic (Allan George), 10th Bt of Westerhall, Dumfriesshire, *cr* 1700; *b* 23 Feb. 1906; *o s* of Sir George Johnstone, 9th Bt and Ernestine (*d* 1955), *d* of Col Porcelli-Cust; *S* father, 1952; *m* 1946, Doris, *d* of late W. L. Shortridge; two *s. Educ:* Imperial Service Coll. *Heir:* *s* George Richard Douglas Johnstone, *b* 21 Aug. 1948.

JOHNSTONE, James Arthur; Commissioner of Inland Revenue 1964-73; *b* 29 July 1913; *o s* of Arthur James Johnstone, solicitor, Ayr, and Euphemia Tennant (*née* Fullarton); *m* 1946, Dorothy C. L. Hacket, CBE (*d* 1981), *d* of William Hacket; one *s. Educ:* Ayr Academy; Glasgow Univ.; St John's Coll., Cambridge. Entered Inland Revenue Dept, 1936. Sec., Royal Commission on Taxation of Profits and Income, 1952-55; Chm., Hong Kong Inland Revenue Ordinance Rev. Cttee, 1976. *Address:* 63 Cottesmore Court, Stanford Road, W8 5QW. *T:* 01-937 8726. *Club:* Reform.

JOHNSTONE, Michael Anthony; Metropolitan Stipendiary Magistrate, since 1980; *b* 12 June 1936; *s* of late Thomas Johnstone and Violet Johnstone. *Educ:* St Edmund's College, Ware. Called to the Bar, Inner Temple, 1968; formerly Solicitor of the Supreme Court, admitted 1960; former Dep. Circuit Judge. Member: Soc. for Nautical Res.; Navy Records Soc. Mem., Campaign for Real Ale. *Recreations:* real ale (whilst permitting), the study and collection of books on military and naval history. *Address:* Highbury Corner Magistrates' Court, 51 Holloway Road, N7 8JA.

JOHNSTONE, Maj.-Gen. Ralph E.; *see* Edgeworth-Johnstone.

JOHNSTONE, R(obert) Edgeworth, DSc (London); FIChemE; FIMechE; FRSC; Lady Trent Professor of Chemical Engineering, University of Nottingham, 1960-67; *b* 4 Feb. 1900; *e s* of Lieut-Col Sir Walter Edgeworth-Johnstone, KBE, CB; *m* 1931, Jessie Marjorie (*d* 1981), *d* of late R. M. T. Greig; two *s* one *d. Educ:* Wellington; RMA Woolwich; Manchester Coll. of Technology; University Coll., London. Fellow Salters' Inst. of Industrial Chem., 1926-27. Held various posts at home and abroad with Magadi Soda Co., Trinidad Leaseholds, Petrocarbon, Min. of Supply and UK Atomic Energy Authority. Vice-Pres., IChemE, 1951; Liveryman, Worshipful Co. of Salters, 1956. Council Medal, IChemE, 1969, Hon. Fellow, 1981. *Publications:* Continuing Education in Engineering, 1969; (with Prof. M. W. Thring) Pilot

Plants, Models and Scale-up Methods in Chemical Engineering, 1957; papers in scientific and engineering jls, especially on distillation, process development and engineering education; as *Robert Johnstone:* The Lost World, 1978; (ed) Samuel Butler on the Resurrection, 1980. *Recreations:* music, philosophy. *Address:* c/o Barclays Bank, 139 North Street, Brighton, Sussex. *Club:* Athenæum.

JOHNSTONE, Maj.-Gen. Robert Maxwell, MBE 1954; MC 1942; MA, MD, FRCPE; Assistant Director (Overseas), British Postgraduate Medical Federation, 1970-76; *b* 9 March 1914; *s* of late Prof. Emer. R. W. Johnstone, CBE; *m* 1958, Marjorie Jordan Beattie (*d* 1960). *Educ:* Edinburgh Acad.; Craigflower; Fettes Coll.; Christ's Coll., Cambridge; Univ. of Edinburgh. MRCPE 1940; FRCPE 1944; MD Edinburgh 1954; MRCP 1966. Resident House Phys. and Surg., Royal Infirmary, Edinburgh, 1938-39. Sen. Pres., Royal Med. Soc., 1938-39. RMO, 129 Fd Regt RA, 1938-41; Company Comdr, 167 Fd Amb., RAMC, 1941-43; Staff Coll., Haifa, 1943; CO, 3 Fd Amb., 1945-46. Adviser in Medicine: HQ, E Africa Comd, 1950-51; Commonwealth Forces Korea, 1954-55; Officer i/c Med. Division: Cambridge Mil. Hosp., 1955-57; QAMH, Millbank, 1957-59; Prof. of Med., Univ. of Baghdad and Hon. Cons. Phys., Iraqi Army, 1959-63; CO, BMH, Iserlohn, 1963-65; Cons. Phys., HQ, FARELF, 1965-67; Dep. Director of Med. Services: Southern Comd, 1967-68; Army Strategic Comd, 1968-69; retd; Postgrad. Med. Dean, SW Metropolitan Region, 1969-70. CStJ 1969. *Recreation:* music. *Address:* c/o Royal Bank of Scotland, West End Office, 142/144 Princes Street, Edinburgh; 76 Central Road, Rossmoyne, WA 6155, Australia.

JOHNSTONE, Prof. Thomas Muir; Professor of Arabic, University of London, since 1970; *b* 18 Jan. 1924; *s* of Thomas Cunningham Johnstone and Margaret Connolly Johnstone (*née* Muir); *m* 1949, Bernice Jobling; two *s* three *d. Educ:* Grove Academy, Broughty Ferry; School of Economics, Dundee. BCom 1944, BA 1954, PhD 1962, London. ICI, Manchester, 1944-57; Lectr in Arabic, School of Oriental and African Studies, 1957; Reader in Arabic, Univ. of London, 1965. Travelled extensively in Eastern Arabia and Oman; Mem., Middle East Comd Expedn to Socotra, 1967. Hon. Mem., Bd of Trustees, Univ. of Sanaa, Yemen. Member Editorial Board: Cambridge Hist. of Arabic Literature; Jl of Arabic Linguistics. *Publications:* Eastern Arabian Dialect Studies, 1967; Harsusi Lexicon, 1977; Jibbali Lexicon, 1981; articles, mainly on Arabian dialects and folklore and modern South Arabian languages, in Bulletin of School of Oriental and African Studies, Jl of Semitic Studies, Jl of Arabic Linguistics, Mariner's Mirror, Geographical Jl, Jl of Arabic Literature, Arabian Studies and Encyclopaedia of Islam. *Address:* School of Oriental and African Studies, Malet Street, WC1E 7HP. *T:* 01-637 2388, ext. 495.

JOHNSTONE, William, CBE 1981; Chairman, British Agricultural Export Council, since 1977; *b* 26 Dec. 1915; *s* of late David Grierson Johnstone and Janet Lang Johnstone (*née* Malcolm); *m* 1942, Mary Rosamund Rowden; one *s* two *d. Educ:* Dalry High Sch.; Glasgow Univ. (BSc (Agric)). NDA, NDD. Technical Officer, Overseas Dept of Deutches Kalisyndikat, Berlin, 1938-39; joined ICI Ltd, 1940; seconded to County War Agricl Exec. Cttees in SE England on food prodn campaigns, 1940-45; Reg. Sales Management, ICI, 1950-61; Commercial Dir, Plant Protection Ltd, 1961-63, Man. Dir, 1963-73; Dir, Billingham/Agricl Div., 1961-73; Dep. Chm., Plant Protection Div., 1974-77. Chm. Subsid. Cos: Scotland (Italy), 1967-73; Sopra (France), 1971-75; Zeltia Agraria (Spain), 1976-77; Vis. Dir, ICI (United States) Inc., 1974-77; retd from ICI, 1977. Chairman: Meat and Livestock Commn, 1977-80; Agricl Working Gp, European Trade Cttee, BOTB. FRSA. *Recreations:* gardening, travel. *Address:* Drayton Mill, East Meon, Petersfield, Hants GU32 1PW. *T:* East Meon 216. *Clubs:* Caledonian, Farmers'.

JOHNSTONE, Rev. Prof. William; Professor of Hebrew and Semitic Languages, University of Aberdeen, since 1980; *b* 6 May 1936; *s* of Rev. T. K. Johnstone and Evelyn Hope Johnstone (*née* Murray); *m* 1964, Elizabeth Mary Ward; one *s* one *d. Educ:* Hamilton Academy; Glasgow Univ. (MA 1st Cl. Hons Semitic Langs, BD Distinction in New Testament and Old Testament); Univ. of Marburg. Lectr 1962, Sen. Lectr 1972, in Hebrew and Semitic Languages, Univ. of Aberdeen. Member, Mission archéologique française: Ras Shamra, 1963, 1964, 1966; Enkomi, 1963, 1965, 1971; Member, Marsala Punic Ship Excavation, 1973-79. *Publications:* trans. Fohrer: Hebrew and Aramaic Dictionary of the Old Testament, 1973; contrib. Ugaritica VI, 1969, VII, 1978, Alasia I, 1972; articles in Expository Times, Kadmos, Notizie degli Scavi, Palestine Exploration Qly, Trans. Glasgow Univ. Oriental Soc., Scottish Jl of Theology, Theology. *Recreation:* alternative work. *Address:* 37 Rubislaw Den South, Aberdeen AB2 6BD. *T:* Aberdeen 36022; Makkevet Bor, New Galloway, Castle Douglas DG7 3RN.

JOICEY, family name of **Baron Joicey.**

JOICEY, 4th Baron, *cr* 1906; **Michael Edward Joicey;** Bt 1893; *b* 28 Feb. 1925; *s* of 3rd Baron Joicey and Joan (*d* 1967), *y d* of 4th Earl of Durham; *S* father, 1966; *m* 1952, Elisabeth Marion, *y d* of late Lieut-Col Hon. Ian Leslie Melville; two *s* one *d. Educ:* Eton; Christ Church, Oxford. *Heir:* *s* Hon. James Michael Joicey, *b* 28 June 1953. *Address:* Etal Manor, Berwick-upon-Tweed, Northumberland. *T:* Crookham 205. *Clubs:* Lansdowne, Kennel; Northern Counties (Newcastle upon Tyne).

JOLL, Prof. James Bysse, MA; FBA 1977; Stevenson Professor of International History, University of London, 1967-81, now Professor Emeritus; *b* 21 June 1918; *e s* of Lieut-Col H. H. Joll and Alice Muriel Edwards. *Educ:* Winchester; University of Bordeaux; New Coll., Oxford. War Service, Devonshire Regt and Special Ops Exec., 1939-45. Fellow and Tutor in Politics, New Coll., Oxford, 1946-50; Fellow, 1951-67, now Emeritus, and Sub-Warden, 1951-67, St Antony's Coll., Oxford. Vis. Mem., Inst. for Advanced Study, Princeton, 1954 and 1971; Visiting Professor of History: Stanford Univ., Calif., 1958; Sydney Univ., 1979; Univ. of Iowa, 1980; Vis. Lectr in History, Harvard University, 1962. Hon. Prof. of History, Warwick Univ., 1981. *Publications:* The Second International, 1955, rev. edn 1974; Intellectuals in Politics, 1960; The Anarchists, 1964, rev. edn 1979; Europe since 1870, 1973; Gramsci, 1977. *Recreation:* music. *Address:* 24 Ashchurch Park Villas, W12 9SP. *T:* 01-749 5221.

JOLLIFFE, family name of **Baron Hylton.**

JOLLIFFE, Sir Anthony (Stuart), GBE 1982; FCA; JP; Lord Mayor of London for 1982-83; Partner, Thornton Baker & Co., since 1982 (formerly Senior Partner, Jolliffe Cork & Co.); International Chairman, Jolliffe Cork Ingram; *b* Weymouth, Dorset, 12 Aug. 1938; *s* of Robert and Vi Dorothea Jolliffe; *m* 1962, Anne Phillips; one *s* two *d. Educ:* Porchester Sch., Bournemouth. Qualified chartered accountant, 1964; articled to Morison Rutherford & Co.; commenced practice on own account in name of Kingston Jolliffe & Co. (later, Jolliffe Cork & Co.), 1965. ATII. Director: Parent Bd, E. Fogarty & Co. Ltd; SAS Catering Ltd; Nikko Trading UK Ltd; Capital for Industry Ltd; Erskine House Investments Ltd; Marlborough Property Holdings (Developments) Ltd; Marlborough Property Holdings Ltd and subsids; Albany Commercial & Industrial Developments Ltd; Gantry Railing Ltd; Gantry Railing (Overseas) Ltd; Specialweld Ltd. Alderman, Ward of Candlewick, 1975-; Sheriff, City of London, 1980-81. Vice-Pres., Europ. League for Economic Cooperation; Hon. Treas., Britain in Europe Residual Fund; Hon. Treas., Sheriff's and Recorder's Fund; Trustee, Police Foundn; Vice-Chm., City of London Br., SJA Assoc.; Member: Governing Body, United Wards Club; Bd of Govs, Mermaid Theatre Trust; President: British Home and Hosp. for Incurables; Candlewick Ward Club; Member: Guild of Freemen; Ct, Worshipful Co. of Painter Stainers; Ct, Worshipful Co. of Chartered Accountants in England and Wales; Worshipful Co. of Wheelwrights. Nat. Treas., Nat. Marr. Guidance Council, 1973-78; past Chm., Royal Soc. of St George, City of London Br.; Member: Council, Operation Drake Fellowship; Special Cttee, Heritage of London Trust; Variety Club of GB; FRSA; JP, City Bench. *Recreations:* classic cars, boating, theatre. *Address:* c/o Thornton Baker & Co., Fairfax House, Fulwood Place, WC1; Mansion House, EC4N 8HH. *Clubs:* City Livery (Pres., 1979-80), City Pickwick, Saints and Sinners; Royal London Yacht (Cowes, IoW); Moor Park Golf (Herts).

JOLLIFFE, Christopher, CBE 1971; Chairman, Abbeyfield Richmond Society, since 1980; Director, Science Division, Science Research Council, 1969-72 (Director for University Science and Technology, 1965-69); *b* 14 March 1912; *s* of William Edwin Jolliffe and Annie Etheldreda Thompson; *m* 1936, Miriam Mabel Ash. *Educ:* Gresham's Sch., Holt; University Coll., London. Asst Master, Stowe Sch., 1935-37; Dept of Scientific and Industrial Research, 1937-65. Vice-Chm., Council for Science and Society, 1978-82; Dir, Leverhulme Trust Fund, 1976-77. *Address:* 8 Broomfield Road, Kew, Richmond, Surrey TW9 3HR. *T:* 01-940 4265.

JOLLIFFE, John William, MA; Bodley's Librarian, since 1982; Fellow, Nuffield College, since 1971; *b* 15 July 1929; *s* of William Benjamin Jolliffe and Gwendolen Ada Mary Jolliffe; *m* 1957, Inez Beryl Estelle Bailey; three *d. Educ:* The Grammar Sch., Hastings; University College London (BA). MA Oxon 1970. Assistant Keeper, Dept of Printed Books, British Museum, 1955-70; Keeper of Catalogues, Bodleian Library, Oxford, 1970-82. *Publications:* (ed) J. Du Bellay: Les Regrets, 1966; Computers and Early Books, 1974; contribs to Bibliothèque d'Humanisme et Renaissance, Jl of Documentation, The Library. *Recreations:* chess, computing, music, reading. *Address:* Bodleian Library, Oxford OX1 3BG. *T:* Oxford 44675.

JOLLIFFE, William Orlando, IPFA, FCA; County Treasurer of Lancashire since 1973; *b* 16 Oct. 1925; *s* of late William Dibble Jolliffe and Laura Beatrice Jolliffe; *m* 1st (marr. diss.); one *s* one *d*; 2nd, 1975, Audrey (née Dale); one step *d. Educ:* Bude County Grammar Sch. Institute of Public Finance Accountant. Chartered Accountant (first place in final exam. of (former) Soc. of Incorporated Accountants, 1956). Joined Barclays Bank Ltd, 1941. Served War of 1939-45 (HM Forces, 1944-48). Subseq. held various appts in Treasurers' depts of Devon CC, Winchester City Council, Doncaster CB Council, Bury CB Council (Dep. Borough Treas.), and Blackpool CB Council (Dep. 1959, Borough Treas., 1962). Mem. Council, Chartered Inst. of Public Finance and Accountancy, 1969- (Pres., 1979-80); Financial Adviser, ACC, 1976-; Mem. Council (Pres. 1974-75), Assoc. of Public Service Finance Officers, 1963-76; Chm., Officers' Side, JNC for Chief Officers of Local Authorities in England and Wales, 1971-76; Mem. Exec. Cttee (Pres. 1970-71), NW Soc. of Chartered Accountants, 1966-76; Chm., NW and N Wales Region of CIPFA, 1974-76; Mem., Soc. of County Treasurers (Mem. Exec. Cttee, 1977-); Hon. Treas., Lancashire Playing Fields Assoc. Financial Adviser to Assoc. of Municipal Corporations, 1969-74; Mem. (Govt) Working Party on Collab. between Local Authorities and the National Health Service, 1971-74. *Publications:* articles for Public Finance and Accountancy

and other local govt jls. *Address:* 4 Whitewood Close, Lytham, Lancs FY8 4RN. *T:* Lytham 736201. *Club:* Royal Over-Seas League.

JOLLY, Anthony Charles; His Honour Judge Jolly; a Circuit Judge since 1980; *b* 25 May 1932; *s* of Leonard and Emily Jolly; *m* 1962, Rosemary Christine Kernan; two *s* one *d. Educ:* Royal Naval Coll., Dartmouth; Balliol Coll., Oxford (Exhibnr history; 1st Hon. Sch. Jurisprudence; MA). Called to Bar, Inner Temple, 1954; a Recorder of the Crown Court, 1975-80. *Recreations:* sailing, reading, stern sculling. *Address:* (home) Naze House, Freckleton, Lancs PR4 1UN. *T:* Freckleton 632285.

JOLLY, (Arthur) Richard, PhD; development economist; Deputy Executive Director, UNICEF, New York, since 1982; *b* 30 June 1934; *s* of Arthur Jolly and late Flora Doris Jolly (née Leaver); *m* 1963, Alison Bishop, PhD; two *s* two *d. Educ:* Brighton Coll.; Magdalene Coll., Cambridge (BA 1956, MA 1959); Yale Univ. (MA 1960, PhD 1966). Community Develt Officer, Baringo Dist, Kenya, 1957-59; Associate Chubb Fellow, Yale Univ., 1961-62; Res. Fellow, E Africa Inst. of Social Res., Makerere Coll., Uganda, 1963-64; Res. Officer, Dept of Applied Econs, Cambridge Univ., 1964-68 (seconded as Advr on Manpower to Govt of Zambia, 1964-66); Fellow, 1968-, Dir, 1972-81, Inst. of Develt Studies; Professorial Fellow, Univ. of Sussex, 1971-. Advr on Manpower Aid, ODM, 1968; Sen. Economist, Min. of Develt and Finance, Zambia, 1970; Advr to Parly Select Cttee on Overseas Aid and Develt, 1974-75; ILO Advr on Planning, Madagascar, 1975; Member: Triennial Rev. Gp, Commonwealth Fund for Tech. Co-operation, 1975-76; UK Council on Internat. Develt, 1974-78; UN Cttee for Develt Planning, 1978-81; Special Consultant on N-S Issues to Sec.-Gen., OECD, 1978; sometime member and chief of ILO and UN missions, and consultant to various governments and international organisations. Sec., British Alpine Hannibal Expedn, 1959. Member: Founding Cttee, European Assoc. of Develt Insts, 1972-75; Governing Council and N-S Round Table, SID, 1976- (Vice-Pres., UK Chapter, 1978-). Mem., Editorial Bd, World Development, 1973-. Master, Curriers' Co., 1977-78. *Publications:* (jtly) Cuba: the economic and social revolution, 1964; Planning Education for African Development, 1969; (ed) Education in Africa: research and action, 1969; (ed jtly) Third World Employment, 1973; (jtly) Redistribution with Growth, 1974 (trans. French 1977); (ed) Disarmament and World Development, 1978, 2nd edn 1979; (ed jtly) Recent Issues in World Development, 1981; contributions to: Development in a Divided World, 1971; The Widening Gap: development in the 1970s, 1971; Employment, Income Distribution and Development Strategy, 1976; Dialogue for a New Order, 1980; World Economic Order: past and prospects, 1981; The Poverty of Progress, 1982; articles in professional and develt jls. *Recreations:* billiards, croquet, nearly missing trains and planes. *Address:* Institute of Development Studies, University of Sussex, Brighton, Sussex BN1 9RE. *T:* Brighton 606261; UNICEF, United Nations, New York 10017, USA. *T:* (212) 754-7854.

JOLLY, Hugh R., MA, MD, FRCP, DCH; Physician in charge of Pædiatric Department, Charing Cross Hospital, London, since 1965; *b* 5 May 1918; *s* of late Canon R. B. Jolly; *m* 1944, Geraldine Mary Howard; two *s* one *d. Educ:* Marlborough Coll.; Sidney Sussex Coll., Cambridge; The London Hospital. MB, BChir (Cantab), 1942; MA (Cantab), 1943; MRCP 1948; DCH (England), 1949; MD (Cantab), 1951 (Raymond Horton-Smith Prize); FRCP 1965. House posts, London Hosp. and N Middlesex Hosp., 1943; Capt., RAMC (Dermatologist), 1944-47; Hosp. for Sick Children, Great Ormond Street, London, 1948-51; Prof. of Paediatrics, Univ. Coll., Ibadan, Nigeria, 1961-62; Vis. Prof. of Child Health, Ghana Med. Sch., 1965-67; Consultant Pædiatrician: Plymouth, 1951-60; Charing Cross Hosp., 1960-; Chailey Heritage, 1966-; British Airways, 1980-; Vis. Consultant, Liverpool Sch. of Tropical Medicine, 1969-. Mem., Old Achimotan Assoc., Ghana. Vice-President: Health Visitor's Assoc.; FPA. Trustee, London Br., Assoc. for Spina Bifida and Hydrocephalus. Past President: Pæd. Sect., RSM; Kingston Br., Royal Coll. of Midwives. Mem., Adv. Bd, Parents' Centres, Australia. Consultant Editor, Annals of Tropical Pædiatrics, 1980-. Medical Journalists Award, 1978; (jtly) Bronze Film Award, BMA, 1978; Meering Award, Nat. Assoc. of Nursery Matrons, 1980. *Publications:* Sexual Precocity, 1955; Diseases of Children, 1964, 4th edn 1981 (trans. Spanish); (with Camilla Jessel) Paul in Hospital, 1972; Common Sense about Babies and Children, 1973; Book of Child Care, 1975 (trans. into German, Japanese, Danish, Spanish and Dutch), 3rd edn 1981; More Common Sense about Babies and Children, 1978 (trans. Dutch, Japanese); contribs (on pædiatric subjects) to: Lancet, Archives Dis. Childr., BMJ, Jl Pediatrics, etc. *Recreations:* aviculture, giving gardening instructions to my wife. *Address:* The Garden House, Warren Park, Kingston Hill, Surrey. *T:* 01-942 7855.

JOLLY, Richard; see Jolly, A. R.

JOLLY, Air Cdre Robert Malcolm, CBE 1969; *b* 4 Aug. 1920; *s* of Robert Imrie Jolly and Ethel Thompson Jolly; *m* 1946, Josette Jacqueline (née Baindcky); no *c. Educ:* Skerry's Coll., Newcastle upon Tyne. Commnd in RAF, 1943; Air Cdre 1971; Dir of Personal Services, MoD, 1970-72; Dir of Automatic Data Processing (RAF), 1973-75, retd. Fellow British Computer Soc., 1972; CBIM (formerly FBIM) 1973. *Address:* 1 Felbridge Close, Streatham, SW16 2RH. *T:* 01-769 4088. *Clubs:* Royal Air Force, Arts, Institute of Directors.

JOLOWICZ, Prof. John Anthony; Professor of Comparative Law, University of Cambridge, since 1976; Fellow, Trinity College, Cambridge, since 1952; *b* 11 April 1926; *e s* of late Prof. Herbert Felix Jolowicz and Ruby Victoria Wagner; *m* 1957, Poppy Stanley; one *s* two *d. Educ:* Oundle Sch.; Trinity Coll., Cambridge (Scholar; MA 1st Cl. Hons Law Tripos 1950). Served HM Forces (commnd RASC), 1944-48. Called to the Bar, Inner Temple and Gray's Inn, 1952; Bencher, Gray's Inn, 1978. Univ. of Cambridge: Asst Lectr in Law, 1955, Lectr, 1959; Reader in Common and Comparative Law, 1972. Professeur associé, Université de Paris 2, 1976. Editor, Jl of Soc. of Public Teachers of Law, 1962-80. *Publications:* (ed) H. F. Jolowicz's Lectures on Jurisprudence, 1963; Winfield and Jolowicz on Tort, 1971, 11th edn 1979; (with M. Cappelletti) Public Interest Parties and the Active Role of the Judge, 1975; contrib. to Internat. Encyc. of Comparative Law and to legal jls. *Address:* Trinity College, Cambridge CB1 1TQ. *T:* Cambridge 358201; West Green House, Barrington, Cambridge CB2 5SA. *T:* Cambridge 870495. *Clubs:* Royal Automobile; Leander (Henley-on-Thames).

JOLY de LOTBINIÈRE, Lt-Col Sir Edmond, Kt 1964; Chairman, Eastern Provincial Area Conservative Association, 1961-65, President, 1969-72; Chairman, Bury St Edmunds Division Conservative Association, 1953-72, President, 1972-79; *b* 17 March 1903; *er s* of late Brig.-Gen. H. G. Joly de Lotbinière, DSO; *m* 1st, 1928, Hon. Elizabeth Alice Cecilia Jolliffe (marr. diss. 1937); two *s*; 2nd, 1937, Helen Ruth Mildred Ferrar (*d* 1953); 3rd, 1954, Evelyn Adelaide (*née* Dawnay), widow of Lt-Col J. A. Innes, DSO. *Educ:* Eton Coll.; Royal Military Academy, Woolwich. 2nd Lieut Royal Engineers, 1923; served in India; RARO, 1928; re-employed, 1939. Served War of 1939-45: in Aden, Abyssinian Campaign and East Africa (despatches); Major 1941; Lieut-Col 1943; retired 1945. Chm. and Managing Dir of several private companies connected with the building trade. *Recreations:* shooting, golf, bridge. *Address:* Horringer Manor, Bury St Edmunds, Suffolk. *T:* Horringer 208. *Club:* Naval and Military.
    See also S. J. de Lotbinière.

JOLY de LOTBINIÈRE, S.; *see* de Lotbinière.

JONES; *see* Armstrong-Jones, family name of Earl of Snowdon.

JONES; *see* Elwyn-Jones.

JONES; *see* Gwynne Jones, family name of Baron Chalfont.

JONES; *see* Hope-Jones.

JONES; *see* Lloyd Jones and Lloyd-Jones.

JONES; *see* Morris-Jones.

JONES; *see* Wynne-Jones.

JONES, family name of **Baron Maelor.**

JONES, Alan Payan P.; *see* Pryce-Jones.

JONES, (Albert) Arthur; *b* 23 Oct. 1915; *s* of late Frederick Henry Jones; *m* 1939, Peggy Joyce (*née* Wingate); one *s* one *d. Educ:* Bedford Modern Sch. FSVA. Territorial, Beds Yeomanry, RA, 1938; Middle East with First Armd Div., 1941; captured at Alamein, 1942; escaped as POW from Italy, 600 miles walk to Allied Territory. Mem. Bedford RDC, 1946-49; Mem. Bedford Borough Council, 1949-74, Alderman, 1957-74; Mayor of Bedford, 1957-58, 1958-59; Member: Beds CC, 1956-67; Central Housing Advisory Cttee, 1959-62; Internat. Union of Local Authorities; Chm., Local Govt Nat. Adv. Cttee, Cons. Central Office, 1963-73; UK Rep., Consultative Assembly, Council of Europe and Assembly of WEU, 1971-73. Contested (C) Wellingborough, 1955; MP (C) Northants S, Nov. 1962-1974, Daventry, 1974-79; Mem., Speaker's panel of Chairmen, 1974-79. Member: Select Cttee on Immigration and Race Relations, 1969-70; Select Cttee on Expenditure, 1974-79; Chm., Environment Sub-Cttee, 1974-79; Vice-Chm., Cons. Back-Bench Cttee for the Environment, 1974-79. Hon. Treas., Town and Country Planning Assoc., 1975-81; Mem., Cttee of Management, UK Housing Assoc., 1972-81; Vice-Pres., Inland Waterways Assoc., 1970-; Dep. Chm., New Towns Commn, 1982; Mem., Anglian Water Authority, 1980-82. Governor: Harpur Charity, 1953-; St Andrew's Hosp., Northampton, 1979-. *Publications:* Future of Housing Policy, 1960; War on Waste, 1965; Local Governors at Work, 1968; For the Record; Bedford 1945-74; Land Use and Financial Planning, 1981. *Address:* Moor Farm, Pavenham, Bedford.

JONES, Prof. Albert Stanley, PhD; DSc; Professor of Chemistry, University of Birmingham, since 1969; *b* 30 April 1925; *s* of Albert Ernest Jones and Florence Jones (*née* Rathbone); *m* 1950, Joan Christine Gregg; one *s* one *d. Educ:* Waverley Grammar Sch.; Univ. of Birmingham (BSc (1st Cl. Hons) 1944, PhD 1947, DSc 1957). Beit Memorial Fellow for Medical Research, 1949-52; University of Birmingham: Lectr in Chemistry, 1952-61; Sen. Lectr, 1961-63; Reader in Organic Chemistry, 1963-69. Chemical Society London: Birmingham Representative, 1959-62; Mem. Council, 1966-69; Chm., Nucleotide Group, 1967-72. *Publications:* 150 papers, incl. three review articles, in scientific jls, on various aspects of organic chemistry and biological chemistry, particularly concerning nucleic acid derivatives. *Recreations:* church activities, walking, music, reading. *Address:* Waverley, 76 Manor House Lane, Yardley, Birmingham B26 1PR. *T:* 021-743 2030.

JONES, Rt. Hon. Alec; *see* Jones, Rt Hon. T. A.

JONES, Allen, ARA 1981; artist; *b* 1 Sept. 1937; *s* of William Jones and Madeline Jones (*née* Aveson); *m* 1964, Janet Bowen (marr. diss. 1978); two *d. Educ:* Ealing Grammar Sch. for Boys; Hornsey Sch. of Art (NDD; ATD); Royal Coll. of Art. Teacher of Lithography, Croydon Coll. of Art, 1961-63; Teacher of Painting, Chelsea Sch. of Art, 1966-68; now teaches occasionally in N America and Germany; travels frequently. One-man exhibns include: Arthur Tooth and Sons, London, 1963, 1964, 1967, 1970; Richard Feigen Gall., New York, Chicago and LA, 1964, 1965 and 1970; Marlborough Fine Art, London, 1972; Arts Council sponsored exhibn tour, UK, 1974; Seibu, Tokyo, 1974; Waddington Galls, London, 1976, 1980, 1982; ICA Graphic Retrospective, 1978; first Retrospective of Painting, Walker Art Gall., Liverpool, and tour of England and Germany, 1979; first internat. exhibn, Paris Biennale, 1961; numerous museum and group exhibns in UK and abroad; works included in many public and private collections; has designed sets for television and stage in UK and Germany; designs commercial murals. Television films have been made on his work. *Publications:* Allen Jones Figures, 1969; Allen Jones Projects, 1971; Waitress, 1972, Japanese edn 1973; Sheer Magic, 1979, UK 1980; articles in various jls. *Recreations:* very private, also gardening. *Address:* c/o Waddington Galleries, 2 Cork Street, W1. *T:* 01-439 1866. *Club:* Zanzibar.

JONES, Rt. Rev. Alwyn Rice; *see* St Asaph, Bishop of.

JONES, Maj.-Gen. Anthony George Clifford, CB 1978; MC 1945; President, Regular Commissions Board, 1975-78; *b* 20 May 1923; *s* of late Col R. C. Jones, OBE, and M. D. Jones; *m* Kathleen Mary, *d* of Comdr J. N. Benbow, OBE, RN; two *d. Educ:* St Paul's School; Trinity Hall, Cambridge. Commissioned RE, 1942; service includes: Troop Comdr, Guards Armd Div., Nijmegen, 1945 (MC 1945; despatches, 1947); Indian Sappers and Miners; Staff Coll., 1954; Bde Major, 63 Gurkha Inf. Bde, 1955 (despatches, 1957); jssc; OC 25 Corps Engineer Regt, 1965-67; Comdr, RE Trng Bde, 1968-72; Head of Ops Staff, Northern Army Group, 1972-74; Dep. Comdr SE District, 1974-75. Hon. Col, RE Volunteers (Sponsored Units), 1978-. *Address:* The Gatehouse, Salisbury Road, St Margaret's Bay, Kent CT15 6DP. *Club:* Army and Navy.

JONES, Arthur; *see* Jones, (Albert) Arthur.

JONES, Maj.-Gen. Sir Arthur Guy S.; *see* Salisbury-Jones.

JONES, Rt. Hon. Aubrey, PC 1955; Director: Thomas Tilling Ltd, since 1970; Cornhill Insurance Company Ltd, since 1971 (Chairman, 1971-74); *b* 20 Nov. 1911; *s* of Evan and Margaret Aubrey Jones, Merthyr Tydfil; *m* 1948, Joan, *d* of G. Godfrey-Isaacs, Ridgehanger, Hillcrest Road, Hanger Hill, W5; two *s. Educ:* Cyfarthfa Castle Secondary Sch., Merthyr Tydfil; London School of Economics. BSc (Econ). 1st Cl. Hons, Gladstone Memorial Prizewinner, Gerstenberg Post-grad. Schol., LSE. On foreign and editorial staffs of The Times, 1937-39 and 1947-48. Joined British Iron and Steel Federation, 1949; General Dir, June-Dec. 1955. Served War of 1939-45, Army Intelligence Staff, War Office and Mediterranean Theatre, 1940-46. Contested (C) SE Essex in General Election, 1945 and Heywood and Radcliffe (by-election), 1946; MP (U) Birmingham, Hall Green, 1950-65; Parliamentary Private Sec. to Minister of State for Economic Affairs, 1952, and to Min. of Materials, 1953; Minister of Fuel and Power, Dec. 1955-Jan. 1957; Minister of Supply, 1957-Oct. 1959. Mem., Plowden Cttee of Inquiry into Aircraft Industry, 1965-66. Chairman: Staveley Industries Ltd, 1964-65 (Dir 1962-65); Laporte Industries (Holdings) Ltd, 1970-72; Director: Guest, Keen & Nettlefolds Steel Company Limited, 1960-65; Courtaulds Ltd, 1960-63; Black & Decker, 1977-81. Chm., Nat. Bd for Prices and Incomes, 1965-70; Vice-Pres., Consumers' Assoc., 1967-72; leading consultant to: Nigerian Public Service Commn, 1973-74; Iranian Govt, 1974-78; Plessey Ltd, 1978-80; Mem. Panel of Conciliators, Internat. Centre for Settlement of Investment Disputes, 1974-81. Pres., Oxford Energy Policy Club, 1976-. Regent Lectr, Univ. of California at Berkeley, 1968. Vis. Fellow, New Coll., Oxford, 1978; Sen. Res. Associate, St Antony's Coll., Oxford, 1979-. Industrial Fellow Commoner, Churchill Coll., Cambridge, 1972; Hon. Fellow, LSE, 1959; Mem., Court of Governors, 1964. Hon. DSc Bath, 1968. *Publications:* The Pendulum of Politics, 1946; Industrial Order, 1950; The New Inflation: the politics of prices and incomes, 1973; (contrib.) My LSE, 1977; Oil: the missed opportunity, 1981. *Address:* 89 Northend House, Fitzjames Avenue, W14 0RX; Arnen, Limmer Lane, Felpham, Bognor Regis, West Sussex. *T:* Middleton-on-Sea 2722. *Club:* Brooks's.

JONES, Barry; *see* Jones, Stephen B.

JONES, Maj.-Gen. Basil Douglas, CB 1960; CBE 1950; *b* 14 May 1903; *s* of Rev. B. Jones; *m* 1932, Katherine Holberton, *d* of Col H. W. Man, CBE, DSO; one *s* two *d. Educ:* Plymouth Coll.; RMC, Sandhurst. 2nd Lieut, Welch Regt, 1924; transferred to RAOC, 1935; Major 1939; served with Australian Military Forces in Australia and New Guinea, 1941-44; Temp. Brig. 1947; Brig. 1955; Maj.-Gen. 1958. ADC to the Queen, 1956-58; Inspector, RAOC, 1958-60, retired. Col Commandant, RAOC, 1963-67. *Recreation:* golf. *Address:* Churchfield, Sutton Courtenay, Abingdon, Oxon. *T:* Sutton Courtenay 261.

JONES, Benjamin George, CBE 1979; formerly Partner, Linklaters & Paines, Solicitors; *b* 18 Nov. 1914; *s* of Thomas Jones, Llanarth; *m* 1946, Menna, *d* of Rev. Evelyn Wynn-Jones, Holyhead; one *s* one *d. Educ:* Aberaeron County Sch.; UCW Aberystwyth. Chairman: Council for the Welsh Language, 1973-78; Hon. Soc. of Cymmrodorion, 1973-78 (Dep. Sec., 1960-63, Sec., 1963-73; Pres., 1982-). Contested (L) Merioneth, 1959. Mem. Gen. Adv. Council, BBC, 1970-78. Vice-Pres., UCW Aberystwyth, 1975-; Mem. Court, Univ. of Wales; Mem. Council, Nat. Library of Wales. Dep. Chm., Agricultural Land Tribunal (SE Area). *Recreations:* walking, music, visiting art galleries. *Address:* 12 Thornton Way, NW11 6RY. *Club:* Reform.

JONES, Beti, CBE 1980; *b* 23 Jan. 1919; *d* of Isaac Jones and Elizabeth (*née* Rowlands). *Educ:* Rhondda County Sch. for Girls; Univ. of Wales. BA (Hons) History, Teaching Diploma. Grammar Sch. teaching, 1941-43; S Wales Organiser, Nat. Assoc. of Girls' Clubs, 1943-47; Youth Officer, Education Branch, Control Commission, Germany, 1947-49; Children's Officer, Glamorgan CC, 1949-68; Chief Adviser on Social Work, Scottish Office, 1968-80. Fellow, University Coll., Cardiff, 1982 (Hon. Fellow, Dept of Social Administration). *Recreations:* people and places. *Address:* 14 Royal Circus, Edinburgh EH3 6SR. *T:* 031-225 1548; Craigie Cottage, Craigie, Blairgowrie, Perthshire. *T:* Essendy 373. *Clubs:* Royal Over-Seas League (London and Edinburgh).

JONES, Hon. Brian Leslie; Hon. Mr Justice Jones; Judge of the High Court of Justice, Hong Kong, since 1981; *b* 19 Oct. 1930; *s* of late William Leslie Jones and Gladys Gertrude Jones; *m* 1966, Yukiko Hirokane; one *s* two *d. Educ:* Bromsgrove Sch.; Birmingham Univ. Admitted Solicitor, 1956. Solicitor, private practice, England, 1956-64; Asst Registrar, Supreme Court, Hong Kong, 1964-68; Legal Officer, Attorney General's Dept, Canberra, 1968-69; Asst Registrar, Hong Kong, 1969-74; District Judge, Hong Kong, 1974-81. *Recreations:* squash, chess, walking, reading. *Address:* 16B Severn Road, The Peak, Hong Kong. *T:* 5-96327. *Clubs:* Hong Kong, Hong Kong Cricket.

JONES, Sir Brynmor, Kt 1968; PhD Wales and Cantab, ScD Cantab, FRSC; Chairman, Foundation Committee for Engineering Technology, since 1978; Vice-Chancellor, University of Hull, 1956-72; *b* Sept. 1903; *o c* of late W. E. Jones, Rhos, Wrexham; *m* 1933, Dora Jones. *Educ:* The Grammar School, Ruabon; University Coll. of North Wales, Bangor (Exhibitioner and Research Scholar); St John's Coll., Cambridge (Hon. Fellow, 1970); Sorbonne, Paris; Fellow, Univ. of Wales, 1928-31. Asst Demonstrator, Cambridge, 1930; Lecturer in Organic Chemistry, University of Sheffield, 1931-46; Leverhulme Research Fellowship, 1939; Mem. Extra-Mural Research Team, Min. of Supply, University of Sheffield, 1940-45; G. F. Grant Professor of Chemistry, University Coll. and University of Hull, 1947-56; Dean of Faculty of Science and Dep. Principal, 1949-52, Vice-Principal, 1952-54; Pro-Vice-Chancellor, 1954-56; Chm., Univ's Foundn Cttee for Engineering, 1978-. Sometime Examiner for Univs of St Andrews, London, Leeds, Oxford, Manchester, Edinburgh and the Inst. of Civil Engineers. Dir, Yorkshire TV, 1970-72. Chairman: Nat. Council for Educational Technology, 1967-73; UGC and Min. of Educn's sub-cttee on Audio-Visual Aids (Report, HMSO, 1965); Academic Council, BMA; Univs Council for Adult Educn, 1961-65; Pres., Assoc. for Programmed Learning and Educational Technology, 1969-72; Chairman: Vis. Grants Cttee to Univ. of Basutoland, Bechuanaland Protectorate and Swaziland, 1965; Programme Cttee on Higher Educn, BBC Further Educn Adv. Council, 1967-70, Vice-Chm., 1970-72; Member: Kennedy Memorial Trust, 1964-74; GMC, 1964-74; DSIR Postgraduate Trng Awards Cttee, 1963-65; Univ. Science and Technology Bd (SRC), 1965-68; Brit. Cttee of Selection for Frank Knox Fellowships to Harvard Univ., 1962-72; Inter-Univ. Council (and Exec.) for Higher Educn, Overseas; India Cttee of IUC and British Council, 1972-; Adv. Cttee, Planning Cttee and Council of Open Univ., 1967-72; Royal Commn on Higher Educn in Ceylon, 1969-70; University Council, Nairobi; Provisional Council of Univ. of E Africa and of University Coll., Dar es Salaam, 1961-64; Council of University Coll., Dar es Salaam, 1964-68; Provisional Council, Univ. of Mauritius, 1965-67; General Nursing Council, 1960-66; Acad. Adv. Cttee, Welsh Coll. of Advanced Technology 1964-67; East Riding Educn Cttee, 1956-74; Hull Chamber of Commerce and Shipping; Council of Chemical Soc., 1945-48, and 1953-56; Senior Reporter, Annual Reports of Chemical Soc., 1948; Chm., Humberside Br., British Digestive Foundn, 1978-; President: Hull Civic Soc.; Hull Lit. and Philosoph. Soc., 1955-57; Hull Bach Choir; E Riding Local History Soc. Chm., Beverley Minster Restoration Appeal, 1982- (Vice-Chm., 1977-82). Mem., Court of Universities of Nottingham and Sheffield, 1956-72; Governor: Hymers Coll.; Pocklington Sch.; E Riding Coll. of Agriculture. Roscoe Lectr, Univ. of Manchester, 1967. Hon. FCP (Sir Philip Magnus Meml Lectr, 1973). Hon. LLD Wales, 1968, Leeds, 1974; Hon. DLitt Hull, 1972. *Publications:* numerous papers on Physical Organic and on Organic Chemistry, mainly on kinetics and mechanism of organic reactions and on mesomorphism, in Journal of Chemical Soc. and other scientific periodicals; articles and published addresses on new learning resources and Educational Technology. University of Sheffield Record of War Work, 1939-45. *Recreations:* music, photography and walking. *Address:* 46 Westwood Road, Beverley, North Humberside HU17 8EJ. *T:* Beverley 861125.

JONES, Charles Beynon Lloyd, CMG 1978; Chairman of Directors, David Jones Ltd, 1963-80; Consul General of Finland in Sydney, since 1971; *b* 4 Dec. 1932; *s* of late Sir Charles Lloyd Jones and Lady (Hannah Beynon) Lloyd Jones, OBE. *Educ:* Cranbrook Sch., Sydney; Univ. of Sydney (not completed). Joined David Jones Ltd, 1951; Alternate Director, 1956; Director, 1957; Joint Managing Director, 1961. Pres. Bd of Trustees, Art Gall. of NSW (Trustee, 1972-; Vice-Pres., 1976-81). Officer, Order of Merit, Republic of Italy (Cavaliere Ufficiale). *Address:* Kincoppal House, Elizabeth Bay, NSW 2011, Australia; Summerlees Farm, Yarramalong, NSW 2259. *Club:* Royal Sydney Golf.

JONES, Charles Ian McMillan; Head Master of Bedford School, since 1975; *b* 11 Oct. 1934; *s* of Wilfred Charles Jones and Bessie Jones (*née* McMillan); *m* 1962, Jennifer Marie Potter; two *s. Educ:* Bishop's Stortford Coll.; St John's Coll., Cambridge. Certif. Educn 1959, MA 1962; FBIM, FRSA. 2nd Lieut RA, 1953-55. Head of Geog. Dept, Bishop's Stortford Coll., 1960-70, Asst to Headmaster, 1967-70; Vice-Principal, King William's Coll., IoM, 1971-75. Man., England Schoolboy Hockey XI, 1967-74; Man., England Hockey XI, 1968-69; Pres., English Schoolboys Hockey Assoc., 1980-; Mem. IoM Sports Council, 1972-75. *Publications:* articles in Guardian. *Recreations:* hockey (Captain Cambridge Univ. Hockey XI, 1959; England Hockey XI, 1959-64, 17 caps; Gt Britain Hockey XI, 1959-64, 28 caps), cricket (Captain IoM Cricket XI, 1973-75), squash, gardening. *Address:* School House, 15 Park Avenue, Bedford MK40 2LB. *T:* Bedford 53436. *Clubs:* MCC, East India, Devonshire, Sports and Public Schools; Hawks (Cambridge).

JONES, General Sir Charles (Phibbs), GCB 1965 (KCB 1960; CB 1952); CBE 1945; MC 1940; Governor of Royal Hospital, Chelsea, 1969-75; Chief Royal Engineer, 1967-72; *b* 29 June 1906; *s* of late Hume Riversdale Jones and Elizabeth Anne (*née* Phibbs); *m* 1934, Ouida Margaret Wallace; two *s. Educ:* Portora Royal School, Enniskillen, N Ireland; Royal Military Academy, Woolwich; Pembroke Coll., Cambridge. Commissioned in RE, 1925; service with Royal Bombay Sappers and Miners in India, 1928-34; Adjt of 42nd (EL) Divl Engineers (TA), 1934-39; student at Staff Coll., Camberley, 1939. War of 1939-45: service in BEF, France and Belgium, as Bde Major 127 Inf. Bde, 1940; Instructor at Staff Coll., Camberley, 1940-41; GSO1 at GHQ Home Forces, 1941-42; CRE Guards Armoured Div. in UK and in NW Europe, 1943-44; BGS XXX Corps in NW Europe, 1945. Chief of Staff, Malaya Comd, 1945-46; BGS HQ Western Comd, UK, 1946; idc, 1947; Comdr 2nd Inf. Bde, 1948-50; Dir of Plans, War Office, 1950; GOC 7th Armoured Div., BAOR, 1951-53; Comdt, Staff Coll., Camberley, 1954-56; Vice AG, WO, 1957-58; Dir, Combined Military Planning Staff, CENTO, 1959; GOC, 1st Corps 1960-62; GOC-in-C, Northern Comd, 1962-63; Master General of the Ordnance, 1963-66; ADC (General) to the Queen, 1965-67. A Governor, Corps of Commissionaires, 1969-. Nat. Pres., Royal British Legion, 1970-81. Col Comdt, RE, 1961-72; Hon. Col, Engineer and Rly Staffs Corps, RE, T&AVR, 1970-77. Order of Leopold, Croix de Guerre (Belgium), 1945. *Recreations:* golf and fishing. *Address:* Westwick, Point Hill, Rye, East Sussex. *Clubs:* Army and Navy; Dormy House (Rye).

JONES, Rev. Canon Cheslyn Peter Montague, MA; Rector of Lowick with Sudborough and Shipton, and Priest-in-charge of Islip, Northants, since 1981; *b* 4 July 1918; *e s* of late Montague William and Gladys Muriel Jones; unmarried. *Educ:* Winchester Coll.; New Coll., Oxford. BA 1st cl. Hons Theology, 1939; Senior Demy, Magdalen Coll., 1940-41. Deacon 1941; Priest 1942. Curate of St Peter, Wallsend, 1941-43; St Barnabas, Northolt Park, 1943-46; at Nashdom Abbey, 1946-51; Chaplain, Wells Theological Coll., 1951-52; Librarian, Pusey House, Oxford, 1952-56; Chaplain, Christ Church Cathedral, Oxford, 1953-56; Principal, Chichester Theological Coll., and Chancellor, Chichester Cathedral, 1956-69, Canon Emeritus, 1971; Principal of Pusey House, Oxford, 1971-81. Select Preacher: Oxford Univ., 1960, 1977, 1978 and 1981; Cambridge Univ., 1962; Sir Henry Stephenson Fellow, Univ. of Sheffield, 1969-70; Bampton Lectr, Oxford Univ., 1970. *Publications:* (ed) A Manual for Holy Week, 1967; contributions to: Studies in the Gospels, 1955; Studies in Ephesians, 1956; Thirty 20th century hymns, 1960; Christian Believing, 1976; (editor and contributor): For Better For Worse, 1977; The Study of Liturgy, 1978. *Recreations:* travel, music. *Address:* The Rectory, Lowick, Kettering, Northants NN14 3BQ. *T:* Thrapston 3216.

JONES, Sir Christopher L.; *see* Lawrence-Jones.

JONES, Clement; *see* Jones, John C.

JONES, Clive Lawson; Under Secretary, Gas Division, Department of Energy, since 1981; *b* 16 March 1937; *s* of Celyn John Lawson Jones and Gladys Irene Jones; *m* 1961, Susan Brenda (*née* McLeod); one *s* one *d. Educ:* Cranleigh School; University of Wales. BSc (Chemistry). With British Petroleum, 1957-61; Texaco Trinidad, 1961-68; Principal, Min. of Power, 1968-69; Min. of Technology, 1969-70; DTI, 1970-73; Asst Sec., Oil Emergency Group, 1973-74; Asst Sec., Dept of Energy, 1974-77; Counsellor (Energy), Washington, 1977-81. *Recreations:* art, antiques. *Address:* 5 Burlington Gardens, W4 4LT.

JONES, Daniel, BEM 1945; MP (Lab) Burnley since Oct. 1959; *b* 26 Sept. 1908; *m* 1932, Phyllis, *d* of John Williams Maesteg, Glam.; two *s* one *d. Educ:* Ynyshir County Sch.; NCLC. In coal-mines of Rhondda Valley for 12 years, 1920-32; unemployed for 4 years; in engineering as a SR Engineer, 1939-54; Aircraft Industry, 1939-45 (BEM; commended by Russian Embassy, 1945); Aircraft Official, part-time 1940-54, full-time 1954-59, AEU. Mem. British Legion and Ex-Servicemen's Clubs, London, Burnley and Rhondda Valley.

Recreations: music and walking. *Address:* 124 Marsden Road, Burnley. *T:* Burnley 25638.

JONES, Daniel Gruffydd; Under-Secretary, Department of the Environment, since 1979; *b* 7 Dec. 1933; *o s* of late Ifor Ceredig Jones and Gwendolen Eluned Jones; *m* 1969, Maureen Anne Woodhall; three *d. Educ:* Ardwyn Grammar Sch., Aberystwyth; University Coll. of N Wales, Bangor (BA). Asst Principal, Min. of Housing and Local Govt, 1960; Private Sec. to Parly Sec., 1962-63; Principal, 1963; Private Sec. to Sec. of Cabinet, 1967-69; Asst Sec., 1969; Sec., Water Resources Bd, 1969-73; Asst Sec., DoE, 1973; Sec., Prime Minister's Cttee on Local Govt Rules of Conduct, 1973-74; Asst Sec., DoE, 1974-75; Under Sec. (Principal Finance Officer), Welsh Office, 1975-79. *Address:* c/o Department of the Environment, 2 Marsham Street, SW1P 3EB. *T:* 01-212 3434. *Club:* East India.

JONES, David A.; see Akers-Jones.

JONES, David Evan Alun; Commissioner for Local Administration in Wales, since 1980; *b* 9 Aug. 1925; *s* of David Jacob Jones, Master Mariner, and Margaret Jane Jones; *m* 1952, Joan Margaret Erica (*née* Davies); two *s. Educ:* Aberaeron County Sch.; University Coll. of Wales, Aberystwyth (LLB). Solicitor. Served War, RAF, 1943-47 (Flt Lieut). Articled service, Exeter, 1949-52; asst solicitor posts with Ilford Bor., Southampton County Bor., Berks County and Surrey County Councils, 1952-61; Dep. Clerk, Denbighshire CC, subseq. Clerk of CC and Clerk of the Peace, 1961-74; Chief Exec., Gwynedd CC, 1974-80. Mem., Broadcasting Council for Wales, 1980-. Mem. Council, UCNW, 1982-. *Recreations:* gardening, travel, a little golf. *Address:* Min-y-Don, West End, Beaumaris, Gwynedd LL58 8BG. *T:* Beaumaris 810225; 11 Dunraven House, Westgate Street, Cardiff CF1 1DL. *T:* Cardiff 41574. *Clubs:* National Liberal; Baron Hill Golf (Beaumaris).

JONES, David Hugh; Associate Director, Royal Shakespeare Company, since 1966; *b* 19 Feb. 1934; *s* of John David Jones and Gwendolen Agnes Langworthy (*née* Ricketts); *m* 1964, Sheila Allen; two *s. Educ:* Taunton Sch.; Christ's Coll., Cambridge (MA 1st Cl. Hons English). 2nd Lieut RA, 1954-56. Production team of Monitor, BBC TV's 1st arts magazine, 1958-62, Editor, 1962-64; joined RSC, 1964; Aldwych Co. Dir, 1968-72; Artistic Dir, RSC (Aldwych), 1975-77; Producer, Play of the Month, BBC TV, 1977-78; Artistic Dir, Brooklyn Acad. of Music Theatre Co., 1979-81. Productions for RSC incl. plays by Arden, Brecht, Gorky, Granville Barker, Günter Grass, Graham Greene, Mercer, O'Casey, Shakespeare, and Chekhov. Dir. prodns for Chichester and Stratford, Ontario, Festival Theatres. Dir, films for BBC TV, incl. biography of poet, John Clare, 1969; adaptations of Hardy and Chekhov short stories, 1972 and 1973, and Pinter's screenplay, Langrishe, Go Down, 1978. Obie Awards, NY, for direction of RSC Summerfolk, 1975, for innovative programming at BAM Theatre Co., 1980. *Recreations:* chess, reading modern poetry, exploring mountains and islands. *Address:* 227 Clinton Street, Brooklyn, NY 11201, USA.

JONES, Rev. David Ian Stewart; Rector-designate of Bristol, since 1982; *b* 3 April 1934; *s* of Rev. John Milton Granville Jones and Evelyn Moyes Stewart Jones (formerly Chedburn); *m* 1967, Susan Rosemary Hardy Smith; twin *s* and *d. Educ:* St John's Sch., Leatherhead; Selwyn Coll., Cambridge (MA). Commnd Royal Signals, 1952-54. Curate at Oldham Parish Church, 1959-62; Vicar of All Saints, Elton, Bury, 1963-66; Asst Conduct and Chaplain of Eton Coll., 1966-70; Conduct and Sen. Chaplain of Eton Coll., 1970-74; Headmaster of Bryanston School, 1974-82. *Recreations:* reading (theology, philosophy, politics), music, rowing (coaching). *Address:* The Rectory, 1 Goldney Avenue, Clifton, Bristol 8. *T:* Bristol 736576. *Club:* East India, Devonshire, Sports and Public Schools.

JONES, David le Brun, CB 1975; Director, Long Term Office, International Energy Agency, since 1982; *b* 18 Nov. 1923; *s* of Thomas John Jones and Blanche le Brun. *Educ:* City of London Sch.; Trinity Coll., Oxford. Asst Principal, Min. of Power, 1947; Principal, MOP, 1952; Asst Sec., Office of the Minister for Science, 1962; Asst Sec., MOP, 1963; Under-Sec., MOP, later Min. of Technology and DTI, 1968-73; Dep. Sec., DTI, later DoI, 1973-76; Cabinet Office, 1976-77; Dept of Energy, 1978-82. *Recreations:* walking, reading, chess. *Address:* 47 Grove End Road, NW8 9NB. *Club:* United Oxford & Cambridge University.

JONES, David M.; see Mansel-Jones.

JONES, Prof. David Morgan, MA; Professor of Classics in the University of London (Westfield College), 1953-80; *b* 9 April 1915; *m* 1965, Irene M. Glanville. *Educ:* Whitgift Sch.; Exeter Coll., Oxford (Scholar). 1st Class, Classical Hon. Mods, 1936; 1st Class, Lit Hum, 1938; Derby Scholar, 1938; Junior Research Fellow, Exeter Coll., Oxford, 1938-40; Oxford Diploma in Comparative Philology, 1940; Lecturer in Classics, University Coll. of North Wales, 1940-48; Reader in Classics in the University of London (Birkbeck Coll.), 1949-53. *Publications:* papers and reviews in classical and linguistic journals. *Address:* Kemyell Vean, 3 Laregan Hill, Penzance TR18 4NY. *T:* Penzance 3389.

JONES, Derek John Claremont, CMG 1979; Minister for Hong Kong Relations with the European Communities and Member States, since 1982; *b* 2 July 1927; *er s* of Albert Claremont Jones and Ethel Lilian Jones (*née* Hazell); *m* 1st, 1951, Jean Cynthia Withams; one *s* two *d*; 2nd, 1970, Kay

Cecile Thewlis; one *s. Educ:* Colston Sch., Bristol; Bristol Univ.; London Sch. of Economics and Political Science. Economic Asst, Economic Section, Cabinet Office, 1950-53; Second Sec., UK Delegn to OEEC/NATO, Paris, 1953-55; Asst Principal, Colonial Office, 1955-57; Principal, Colonial Office, 1957-66; First Secretary, Commonwealth Office, 1966-67; Counsellor (Hong Kong Affairs), UK Mission, Geneva, 1967-71; Government of Hong Kong: Dep. Economic Sec., 1971-73; Sec. for Economic Services, 1973-76; Sec. for the Environment, 1976-81; Sec. for Transport, 1981-82. *Recreations:* reading, travel, conversation. *Address:* 56 rue Jules Léjeune, 1060 Brussels, Belgium. *Clubs:* Hong Kong, Royal Hong Kong Jockey.

JONES, Derek R.; see Rudd-Jones.

JONES, Captain Desmond V.; see Vincent-Jones.

JONES, Rev. Prof. Douglas Rawlinson; Lightfoot Professor of Divinity, University of Durham, and Residentiary Canon of Durham Cathedral since 1964; *b* 11 Nov. 1919; *s* of Percival and Charlotte Elizabeth Jones; *m* 1946, Hazel Mary Passmore; three *s* two *d. Educ:* Queen Elizabeth's Hosp., Bristol; St Edmund Hall, Oxford; Wycliffe Hall, Oxford. Squire Scholar, 1938; BA 1941; MA 1945; deacon, 1942; priest, 1943. Curate of St Michael and All Angels, Windmill Hill, Bristol, 1942-45; Lectr, Wycliffe Hall, Oxford, 1945-50; Chaplain, Wadham Coll., Oxford, 1945-50; Lectr in Divinity, 1948-50; University of Durham: Lectr, 1951; Sen. Lectr, 1963. Mem., Gen. Synod of C of E, 1970-80. Chairman of the Liturgical Commn, 1981-. *Publications:* Haggai, Zechariah and Malachi, 1962; Isaiah, 56-66 and Joel, 1964; Instrument of Peace, 1965; contrib. to: Peake's Commentary on the Bible, 1962; Hastings' Dictionary of the Bible, 1963; The Cambridge History of the Bible, 1963; articles in Jl of Theolog. Studies, Zeitschrift für die Alttestamentliche Wissenschaft, Vetus Testamentum, Theology, Scottish Jl of Theology. *Recreation:* carpentry. *Address:* 12 The College, Durham DH1 3EQ. *T:* Durham 64295.

JONES, Prof. Douglas Samuel, MBE 1945; FRS 1968; Ivory Professor of Mathematics, University of Dundee, since 1965; *b* 10 Jan. 1922; *s* of late J. D. Jones and B. Jones (*née* Streather); *m* 1950, Ivy Styles; one *s* one *d. Educ:* Wolverhampton Grammar Sch.; Corpus Christi Coll., Oxford (MA 1947; Hon. Fellow, 1980); DSc Manchester 1957. Flt-Lt, RAFVR, 1941-45. Commonwealth Fund Fellow, MIT, 1947-48; Asst Lectr in Maths, University of Manchester, 1948-51; Lectr 1951-54, Research Prof. 1955, New York Univ.; Sen. Lectr in Maths, Univ. of Manchester, 1955-57; Prof. of Maths, Univ. of Keele, 1957-64. Vis. Prof., Courant Inst., 1962-63. Member: UGC, 1976-; Computer Bd, 1977-. Mem. Council, Royal Soc., 1973-74. FIMA 1964; FRSE 1967. Hon. DSc Strathclyde, 1975. Keith Prize, RSE, 1974; van der Pol Gold Medal, Internat. Union of Radio Sci., 1981. *Publications:* Electrical and Mechanical Oscillations, 1961; Theory of Electromagnetism, 1964; Generalised Functions, 1966; Introductory Analysis, vol. 1, 1969, vol 2, 1970; Methods in Electromagnetic Wave Propagation, 1979; Elementary Information Theory, 1979; The Theory of Generalised Functions, 1982; articles in mathematical and physical jls. *Recreations:* golf, walking, photography. *Address:* Department of Mathematical Sciences, The University, Dundee DD1 4HN. *T:* Dundee 23181.

JONES, Edgar Stafford, CBE 1960 (MBE 1953); *b* 11 June 1909; *s* of late Theophilus Jones; *m* 1938, Margaret Aldis, *d* of late Henry Charles Askew; one *s* one *d. Educ:* Liverpool Institute High Sch. Mem. of Local Government Service, 1925-34; joined Assistance Board, 1934. Seconded to Air Min., as Hon. Flt-Lt RAFVR, 1943; Hon. Sqdn-Ldr, 1945. Transferred to Foreign Office, 1946; transferred to Washington, 1949; Dep. Finance Officer, Foreign Office, 1953; Head of Finance Dept, Foreign Office, 1957 and Diplomatic Service Administration Office, 1965, retired 1968. *Address:* 27 Cole Park Gardens, Twickenham, Mddx. *T:* 01-892 5435. *Clubs:* London Welsh Rugby Football, Rugby; Glamorgan Cricket.

JONES, Edmund Angus, CMG 1963; company director; Managing Director, 1954-65, Chairman, 1962-67, Mobil Oil Australia Ltd; *b* 8 Jan. 1903; *s* of Frederick E. Jones; *m* 1926, Elsie May Townley; two *s* one *d. Educ:* Christchurch Boys' High Sch., NZ; Harvard Business Sch. (Advanced Management Programme). Vacuum Oil Co. Pty Ltd, 1928, Salesman, Christchurch, NZ; Branch Manager, Christchurch, NZ, 1932; Asst Gen. Man., 1935, Gen. Man., 1939, Wellington, NZ; Dir, Melbourne, Australia, 1944; Area Consultant, Standard Vacuum, New York, USA, 1948; Dir, 1951, Man. Dir, 1954, Vacuum Oil Co. Pty Ltd, Melbourne, Australia. Hon. DEd State Coll. of Vic, Melbourne, 1980. *Publications:* various articles on Management. *Recreations:* golf, reading. *Address:* 61/546 Toorak Road, Toorak, Victoria 3142, Australia. *T:* 208181. *Clubs:* Athenæum (Melbourne); Royal Melbourne Golf.

JONES, His Honour Judge Edward; see Jones, J. E.

JONES, Air Marshal Sir Edward G.; see Gordon Jones.

JONES, Sir Edward Martin F.; see Furnival Jones.

JONES, Edward Norton, CMG 1952; OBE 1940; *b* 28 Jan. 1902; *s* of Daniel Norton Jones; *m* 1940, Cecilia Lucy Shaen (*née* Hamersley) (*d* 1976). *Educ:* St Paul's Sch., W Kensington; Corpus Christi Coll., Cambridge (BA). Gold Coast: Asst District Comr, 1925; District Commissioner, 1932; Sec. for Social

Services, 1943; Dir of Social Welfare and Housing, 1946; Chief Commissioner, Northern Territories, 1948; Sec. for Development and Chm. of Marketing and Development Corporations, 1950; Permanent Sec. to the Ministry of Defence and External Affairs, Gold Coast, 1952; Mem., Public Service Commission, Ghana, 1955-61. *Recreation:* golf. *Address:* Walden, Innhams Wood, Crowborough, East Sussex.

JONES, Edward W.; *see* Wilson Jones.

JONES, Rt. Hon. Sir Edward (Warburton), PC 1979; PC (N Ireland) 1965; Kt 1973; **Rt. Hon. Lord Justice Jones;** Lord Justice of Appeal, Supreme Court of Judicature, N Ireland, since 1973 (Judge of the High Court of Justice in Northern Ireland, 1968-73); *b* 3 July 1912; *s* of late Hume Riversdale Jones and Elizabeth Anne (*née* Phibbs); *m* 1st, 1941, Margaret Anne Crosland Smellie (*d* 1953); three *s*; 2nd, 1953, Ruth Buchan Smellie; one *s.* *Educ:* Portora Royal School, Enniskillen, N Ireland; Trinity Coll., Dublin. BA (TCD), with First Class Moderatorship, Legal Science, and LLB (TCD) 1935; called to Bar for Northern Ireland, 1936; QC (N Ireland), 1948; called to Bar (Middle Temple), 1964. Junior Crown Counsel: County Down, 1939; Belfast, 1945-55. Enlisted, 1939; commissioned Royal Irish Fusiliers, 1940; Staff Coll., Camberley, 1943; AAG, Allied Land Forces, SEA, 1945; released with Hon. rank Lt-Col, 1946. MP (U) Londonderry City, Parliament of Northern Ireland, 1951-68; Attorney-Gen. for Northern Ireland, 1964-68. Chancellor: Dio. Derry and Raphoe, 1945-64; Dio. Connor, 1959-64 and 1978-; Dio. Clogher, 1973; Lay Mem. Court of Gen. Synod, Church of Ireland. Bencher, Inn of Court of NI, 1961. *Recreations:* golf, sailing. *Address:* The Lodge, Spa, Ballynahinch, Co. Down, N Ireland. *T:* Ballynahinch 2240; Craig-y-Mor, Trearddur Bay, Anglesey. *T:* Trearddur Bay 860406. *Club:* Army and Navy.

JONES, Eifion, CMG 1964; OBE 1953; Permanent Secretary, Ministry of Works, Northern Nigeria, 1959-66; Member, Northern Nigerian Development Corporation, 1959-66; retired; *b* Llanelly, Carmarthenshire, 10 June 1912; *s* of I. J. Jones and R. A. Jones (*née* Bassett); *m* 1944, Kathleen, *d* of Donald and E. J. MacCalman, Argyllshire. *Educ:* Llanelli Grammar Sch.; University Coll., Swansea. BSc (Wales). Executive Engineer, Nigeria, 1942; Senior Executive Engineer, 1951; Chief Engineer, 1954; Dep. Dir of Public Works, Nigeria, 1958. Member: Lagos Exec. Develt Bd, 1954-57; Governing Cttee, King's Coll., Lagos, 1956-59; Cttee for Develt of Tourism and Game Reserves in N Nigeria, 1965. Mem., West African Council, ICE, 1960-65. JP N Nigeria, 1963-66. FICE 1957; FIWES 1957. *Recreations:* golf, gardening, reading. *Address:* c/o Barclays Bank Ltd, Llanelli, Dyfed.

JONES, Elfryn; Chief Statistician, Royal Commission on the Distribution of Income and Wealth, 1974-79; *b* 9 July 1913; *m* 1940, Vera Anne Owen; two *s.* *Educ:* Enfield Grammar Sch.; Institute of Actuaries. FIA 1942. Prudential Assurance Co. Ltd, 1930-42; statistical staff Admiralty, 1942-54; Head of Naval Statistics, 1954-68; Under-Sec. (Statistics), MoD, 1968-74. *Publications:* papers on manpower planning in actuarial and operational research jls and in proceedings of NATO science confs; Estimation of the magnitude of accumulated and inherited wealth (Inst. of Actuaries prize paper), 1978. *Recreations:* chess, statistics, gardening. *Address:* 7 Downside Close, Charmouth, Dorset DT6 6BH. *T:* Charmouth 60737.

JONES, Sir Elwyn; *see* Jones, Sir W. E. E.

JONES, Emlyn Bartley, MBE 1975; Director General, The Sports Council, since 1978; *b* 9 Dec. 1920; *s* of Ernest Jones and Sarah Bartley; *m* 1944, Constance Inez Jones; one *d.* *Educ:* Alun Grammar School, Mold, Clwyd; Bangor Normal Coll.; Loughborough Coll. of Physical Education. Diploma Loughborough Coll. (Hons). Flight Lieut, RAF, 1941-46; Teacher, Flint Secondary Modern Sch., 1946; Technical Representative, N Wales, 1947-51; Technical Adviser, Central Council of Physical Recreation, 1951-62; Dir, Crystal Palace Nat. Sports Centre, 1962-78. *Publication:* Learning Lawn Tennis, 1958. *Recreations:* golf, ski-ing, travel, conversation. *Address:* Chwarae Teg, 1B Allison Grove, Dulwich Common, SE21 7ER. *T:* 01-693 7528.

JONES, Emrys; *see* Jones, J. E.

JONES, Sir Emrys; *see* Jones, Sir W. E.

JONES, Prof. Emrys, MSc, PhD (Wales); FRGS; Professor of Geography, University of London, at London School of Economics, since 1961; *b* Aberdare, 17 Aug. 1920; *s* of Samuel Garfield and Anne Jones; *m* 1948, Iona Vivien, *d* of R. H. Hughes; one *d* (and one *d* decd). *Educ:* Grammar Sch. for Boys, Aberdare; University Coll. of Wales, Aberystwyth. BSc (1st Class Hons in Geography and Anthropology), 1941; MSc, 1945; PhD, 1947; Fellow of the University of Wales, 1946-47; Asst Lectr at University Coll., London, 1947-50; Fellow, Rockefeller Foundation, 1948-49; Lectr at Queen's Univ., Belfast, 1950-58. Sen. Lectr, 1958. O'Donnel Lectr, Univ. of Wales, 1977. Chm., Regional Studies Assoc., 1967-69; Mem. Council, RGS, 1973-77 (Vice-Pres., 1978-81). Mem. Council, University Coll. of Wales, Aberystwyth, 1978-. Consultant on urbanisation and planning. Victoria Medal, RGS, 1977. Hon. DSc Belfast, 1978. *Publications:* Hon. Editor, Belfast in its Regional Setting, 1952; (jointly) Welsh Rural Communities, 1960; A Social Geography of Belfast, 1961; Human Geography, 1964; Towns and Cities, 1966; Atlas of London, 1968; (ed jtly) Man and his Habitat, 1971;

(contrib.) The Future of Planning, 1973; (with E. van Zandt) The City, 1974; Readings in Social Geography, 1975; (with J. Eyles) Introduction to Social Geography, 1977; (Chief Editor) The World and its Peoples, 1979; articles in geographical, sociological and planning jls. *Recreations:* books, music. *Address:* 2 Pine Close, North Road, Berkhamsted, Herts. *T:* Berkhamsted 75422. *Club:* Athenæum.

JONES, Sir Eric (Malcolm), KCMG 1957; CB 1953; CBE 1946; Director, Government Communications Headquarters, Foreign Office, 1952-60, retired; *b* 27 April 1907; *m* 1929, Edith Mary Taylor; one *s* one *d.* *Educ:* King's Sch., Macclesfield. Textile Merchant and Agent, 1925-40. RAFVR 1940-46, Civil Servant, 1946-60; Dir, Simon Engineering Ltd, 1966-77. Legion of Merit (US), 1946. *Recreations:* ski-ing, golf. *Address:* Guild House, Denmark Road, Gloucester GL1 3HW.

JONES, Eric S.; *see* Somerset Jones.

JONES, Ernest Edward; Chairman, South Yorkshire County Council, 1975-76; Member, Doncaster Metropolitan Borough Council, since 1980; *b* 15 Oct. 1931; *s* of William Edward Jones and Eileen Gasser; *m* 1955, Mary Armstrong; one *s* one *d.* *Educ:* Bentley Catholic Primary Sch., Doncaster; Sheffield De La Salle Coll.; Hopwood Hall Coll. of Educn, Middleton, Lancs; Manch. Univ. Sch. of Educn; Management Studies Unit, Sheffield Polytech. Min. of Educn Teaching Certif. (CertEd); Univ. Dipl. in Science Studies (DipSc); Dipl. in Educn Management (DEM). School Master, 1953-. Doncaster County Borough: Councillor, 1962-74 (Chm. Health Cttee, 1971-74; Chm. Social Services Cttee, 1972-73; served on 15 other cttees at various times). South Yorkshire CC: Mem. 1973-77; Dep. Chm., 1973-75; Chm., Rec., Culture and Health Cttee, 1973-75; Doncaster Metropolitan Borough Council: Chm., Libraries, Museums and Arts Cttee, 1982-; Vice-Chm., Educn Services Cttee, 1982-. Member: Nat. Health Exec. Council, 1964-74; Doncaster and Dist Water Bd, 1972-74; AMC (Social Services), 1972-74; Doncaster Community Health Council, 1981-. Member: Peak Park Planning Bd; MRSH; former Member: Yorks Arts Assoc.; Yorks Regional Land Drainage Cttee; Univ. of Hull Educn Delegacy; AMA; Yorks and Humberside Museums and Art Galleries Fedn; Yorks and Humberside Regional Sports Council; Yorks, Humberside and Cleveland Tourist Bd; Exec. Mem., Youth Assoc. of South Yorks; Mem., Doncaster Community Health Council. FRSA 1980. *Recreations:* music and fine arts, general interest in sport, fell-walking, keen caravanner. *Address:* 11 Norborough Road, Doncaster, South Yorks DN2 4AR. *T:* Doncaster 66122.

JONES, Evan David, CBE 1965; FSA 1959; FLA 1973; Librarian of the National Library of Wales, 1958-69; *b* 6 Dec. 1903; *e s* of Evan Jones and Jane (*née* Evans), Llangeitho; *m* 1933, Eleanor Anne, *o d* of John Humphrey Lewis, master mariner, Aberystwyth; one *s.* *Educ:* Llangeitho Primary Sch.; Tregaron County Sch.; University Coll. of Wales, Aberystwyth. BA 1926, Hons Welsh, Class 1, History 2a; Sir John Williams Research Student, 1928-29. Archivist Asst, National Library of Wales, 1929-36; Dep. Keeper of MSS and Records, 1936-38, Keeper, 1938-58. Lecturer in Archive Administration, UCW, 1957-58. President: Cambrian Archæological Assoc., 1962-63; New Wales Union, 1965-67; Welsh Harp Soc., 1965-; Welsh Bibliographical Soc., 1968-; Cymdeithas Emynau Cymru, 1968-; Cymdeithas Bob Owen, 1976-; Pres., Union of Welsh Independents, 1974-75. Chairman: Governors of Welsh Sch., Aberystwyth, 1946-47; Executive Cttee, Urdd Gobaith Cymru, 1954-57; Cambrian Archæological Assoc., 1954-57; Cardigans. Congregational Quarterly Meeting, 1960; Undeb y Cymdeithasau Llyfrau, 1959-61; Welsh Books Centre, 1966-70; Welsh Books Council, 1968-70; Govs, Coll. of Librarianship, Wales, 1968-74 (Vice-Chm., 1964-68); Three Counties Congregational Assoc., 1972-73; Sec., Welsh Congregational Church, Aberystwyth, 1938-; Treasurer: New Wales Union, 1970-; Interdenominational Cttee on Welsh Lang., 1970-. Mem. Court of Governors: Nat. Museum of Wales, 1958-69; University of Wales, 1958-71; Member: Council of UCW; Congregational Memorial Coll., Swansea; Bala-Bangor Congregational Coll.; Union of Welsh Independents; Bd of Celtic Studies; Hist. and Law Cttee; Ancient Monuments Bd for Wales, 1970-79; Council of Brit. Records Assoc., 1958-69; Pantyfedwen Trust, 1958-69; Council of Hon. Soc. of Cymmrodorion; National Eisteddfod Council; Broadcasting Council for Wales, 1966-71; Library Advisory Council (Wales), 1965-69; Hon. Mem. of the Gorsedd (also Examr). Hon. FLA 1973. Hon LLD Wales, 1972. Editor: NLW Jl, 1958-69; Jl of Merioneth History and Record Soc.; DWB Supplements. *Publications:* Gwaith Lewis Glyn Cothi, 1953; Victorian and Edwardian Wales, 1972; Gwaith Lewis Glyn Cothi 1837-39, 1973; Ystyriaethau ar Undeb Eglwysig, 1974; Trem ar Ganrif, 1978; articles in Archæologia Cambrensis, Bulletin of Board of Celtic Studies, and many other journals; contrib. Dictionary of Welsh Biography. *Recreations:* colour photography, walking, gardening. *Address:* Penllerneuadd, North Road, Aberystwyth SY23 2EE. *T:* Aberystwyth 612112.

JONES, Ewan Perrins W.; *see* Wallis-Jones.

JONES, Sir Ewart (Ray Herbert), Kt 1963; DSc Victoria, PhD Wales, MA Oxon; FRS 1950, FRSC; Waynflete Professor of Chemistry, University of Oxford, 1955-78, now Emeritus; Fellow of Magdalen College, 1955-78, Hon. Fellow, 1978; Chairman, Anchor and Guardian Housing Associations, since 1979; *b* Wrexham, Denbighshire, 16 March 1911; *m* 1937, Frances Mary Copp; one *s* two *d.* *Educ:* Grove Park Sch., Wrexham; University Coll. of North Wales, Bangor; Univ. of Manchester. Fellow of Univ. of Wales,

1935-37; Lecturer, Imperial Coll. of Science and Technology, 1938; Reader in Organic Chemistry, University of London, and Asst Prof., 1945; Sir Samuel Hall Prof. of Chemistry, The University, Manchester, 1947-55; Arthur D. Little Visiting Prof. of Chemistry, Massachusetts Institute of Technology, 1952; Karl Folkers Lecturer at Universities of Illinois and Wisconsin, 1957. Mem. Council for Scientific and Industrial Research, and Chm., Research Grants Cttee, 1961-65; Mem. SRC and Chm., Univ. Science and Technology Bd, 1965-69; Mem., Science Bd, 1969-72. Chemical Society: Tilden Lectr, 1949; Pedler Lectr, 1959; Robert Robinson Lectr, 1978; Award for Service to the Society, 1973; Award in Natural Product Chem., 1974; Meldola Medal, Royal Institute of Chemistry, 1940; Davy Medal, Royal Society, 1966. Fritzsche Award, American Chemical Soc., 1962. President: Chemical Soc., 1964-66; RIC, 1970-72 (Chm., Chem. Soc./RIC Unification Cttee, 1975-80); Royal Soc. of Chemistry, 1980-82. Fellow, Imperial Coll., 1967; Foreign Mem. Amer. Acad. of Arts and Sciences, 1967. Hon. DSc: Birmingham, 1965; Nottingham, 1966; New South Wales, 1967; Sussex, 1969; Salford, 1971; Wales, 1971; East Anglia, 1978; Ulster, 1978; Hon. LLD Manchester, 1972. *Publications:* scientific papers in Jl of the Chem. Soc. *Address:* 6 Sandy Lane, Yarnton, Oxford OX5 1PB. *T:* Kidlington 2581. *Club:* Athenæum.

JONES, Major Francis, CVO 1969; TD (3 clasps); MA, FSA; DL; Wales Herald Extraordinary since 1963; County Archivist, Carmarthenshire, 1958-74; *b* Trevine, Pembrokeshire, 5 July 1908; *s* of James Jones, Grinston, Pembs, and Martha Jones; *m* Ethel M. S. A., *d* of late J. J. Charles, Trewilym, Pembs; two *s* two *d*. *Educ:* Fishguard County Sch., Pembs. Temp. Archivist of Pembs, 1934-36; Archivist, Nat. Library of Wales, 1936-39. Lt 4th Bn Welch Regt (TA), 1931-39; trans. Pembroke Yeomanry (RA, TA), 1939, Battery Captain; served War of 1939-45: RA (Field), N Africa (despatches), Middle East, Italy; Battery Comdr, and 2nd-in-comd of regt; GSO2 War Histories; Mil. Narrator, Hist. Section, Cabinet Office, 1945-58 (Compiled Official narrative of Sicilian and Italian Campaigns); Battery Comdr, The Surrey Yeomanry, QMR (RA, TA), 1949-56; Mil. Liaison Officer, Coronation, 1953; served on the Earl Marshal's staff, State Funeral of Sir Winston Churchill, 1965; Mem., Prince of Wales Investiture Cttee, 1967-69. Local Sec. and Mem., Cambrian Assoc.; Vice-Pres., Council, Hon. Soc. of Cymmrodorion; Member: Gorsedd, Royal National Eisteddfod of Wales; Court and Council, Nat. Library of Wales, 1967-77; Council, Nat. Museum of Wales; Historical Soc. of the Church in Wales; Carmarthenshire Local History Soc.; Pembrokeshire Records Soc. (Vice-Pres.); Croeso '69 Nat. Cttee; Academie Internationale d'Heraldique; Heraldry Soc. Trustee, Elvet Lewis Memorial (Gangell), 1967-. Vice-Pres., Dyfed Local Councils, 1974-81. DL Dyfed, 1965. Broadcaster (TV and sound radio). Hon. MA Univ. of Wales. CStJ. *Publications:* The Holy Wells of Wales, 1954; The History of Llangunnor, 1965; God Bless the Prince of Wales, 1969; The Princes and Principality of Wales, 1969; (jtly) Royal and Princely Heraldry in Wales, 1969; numerous articles on historical, genealogical and heraldic matters to learned jls. *Recreations:* genealogical research and heraldry, fly-fishing, study of ancient ruins. *Address:* Hendre, Springfield Road, Carmarthen. *T:* Carmarthen 7099.

JONES, Sir Francis Avery, Kt 1970; CBE 1966; FRCP; retired; Consulting Physician, Gastroenterological Department, Central Middlesex Hospital (Physician, 1940-74); Consulting Gastroenterologist: St Mark's Hospital (Consultant, 1948-78); Royal Navy (Consultant, 1950-78); Hon. Consulting Physician, St Bartholomew's Hospital, 1978; *b* 31 May 1910; *s* of Francis Samuel and Marion Rosa Jones; *m* 1934, Dorothea Pfirter; one *s*. *Educ:* Sir John Leman Sch., Beccles; St Bartholomew's Hosp. Baly Research Scholarship, St Bart's, 1936; Julius Mickle Fellowship, University of London, 1952. Goulstonian Lecturer, Royal College of Physicians, 1947; Lumleian Lectr, RCP; Nuffield Lectr in Australia, 1952; First Memorial Lectr, Amer. Gastroenterological Assoc., 1954; Croonian Lectr, RCP, 1969; Harveian Orator, RCP, 1980. Formerly Examiner: RCP; Univ. of London; Univ. of Leeds. Chairman: Emergency Bed Service, 1967-72; Med. Records Cttee, Dept of Health and Social Security; Medical Adv. Cttee, British Council, 1973-79; Member: Med. Sub-cttee, UGC, 1966-71; Brent and Harrow AHA, 1975-78; Dep. Chm., Management Cttee, King Edward VII Hosp. Fund, 1976-79; Mem. Council, Surrey Univ., 1975-. Pres., United Services Section, RSM, 1974-75 (formerly Pres., section of Proctology); 2nd Vice-Pres., RCP, 1972-73; President: Medical Soc. of London, 1977-78; British Digestive Foundn, 1981-. Editor of Gut, 1965-70. Hon. FRCS 1981; Hon. Mem., Amer., Canadian, French, Scandinavian and Australian Gastroenterological Assocs. Master, Worshipful Co. of Barbers, 1977-78. Hon. MD Melbourne, 1952; DUniv Surrey, 1980. Ambuj Nath Bose Prize, RCP, 1971; Moxon Medal, RCP, 1978; Fothergillian Gold Medal, Med. Soc., 1980; Henry L. Bockus Medal, World Orgn of Gastroenterology, 1982. *Publications:* Clinical Gastroenterology (jt author), 2nd edn 1967; Editor of Modern Trends in Gastroenterology First and Second Series, 1952 and 1958; many articles on Gastroenterology in the Medical Press. *Recreation:* water-side gardening. *Address:* 44 Cleveland Square, W2 6DA. *T:* 01-262 2027; Mill House, Nutbourne, Pulborough, West Sussex. *Club:* Athenæum.

JONES, Francis Edgar, MBE 1945; PhD, DSc; FRS 1967; FEng, FIEE, FRAeS; FInstP; Director: Philips Industries, 1973-76; Unitech Ltd, since 1974; *s* of Edgar Samuel Jones and Annie Maude Lamb; *m* 1942, Jessie Gladys Hazell; four *s* one *d*. *Educ:* Royal Liberty Sch., Romford; King's Coll., London. Demonstrator in Physics, King's Coll., London, 1938-39; at Min. of Aircraft Production Research Estab., finishing as Dep. Chief Scientific Officer, 1940-52; Chief Scientific Officer and Dep. Dir, RAE, Farnborough, 1952-56; Technical Dir, Mullard Ltd, 1956-62, Man. Dir, 1962-72; Chm., Associated Semiconductor Manufacturers Ltd, 1962-72. Chairman: Adv. Council on Road Research, 1966-68; Electronic Components Bd, 1967-69; Radio & Electronic Component Manufacturers Fedn, 1967-69; Electronic Valve & Semiconductor Manufacturers Assoc., 1968; Member: Inland Transport Research and Develt Council, 1969; Cttee on Manpower Resources for Sciences and Technology (Chm., Working Group on Migration, 1967); Council for Scientific Policy, 1965-70; Central Adv. Council for Science and Technology, 1966-70; Nat. Defence Industries Council, 1969-76; Council, IEE, 1965-69 (Vice-Pres. 1972); Council, Royal Society, 1968, 1979-81; Cttee of Enquiry into Research Assocs; (part-time) Monopolies and Mergers Commn, 1973-81; Chairman: EDC for Mech. Engrg, 1973-76; Rank Prize Fund for Optoelectronics. Pres., Engineering Industries Assoc., 1977-81. Fellow, King's Coll., London, 1968. Mem. Delegacy, KCL, 1976. Vis. Prof. of Electrical Engineering, University Coll., London, 1968-. Trustee: Anglo-German Foundn for the Study of Industrial Soc., 1973-79; Rank Prize Funds, 1977-. Hon. Fellow, Univ. of Manchester Inst. of Science and Technology, 1970. Hon. DSc: Southampton, 1968; Nottingham, 1968; Cranfield, 1976; Heriot-Watt, 1978; DUniv Surrey, 1968; Hon. DTech Brunel, 1969; Duddell Premium, IEE, 1949; Glazebrook Medal and Prize, Inst. of Physics, 1971. *Publications:* (with R. A. Smith and R. P. Chasmar) The Detection and Measurement of Infrared-Radiation, 1956; articles in Proc. Royal Society, RAeS Jl, Jl IEE, Nature. *Address:* Wendacre, Burton's Way, Chalfont St Giles, Bucks HP8 4BP. *T:* Little Chalfont 2228. *Club:* Athenæum.

JONES, Prof. F(rank) Llewellyn-, CBE 1965; MA, DPhil, DSc Oxon; Hon. LLD; Principal, University College of Swansea, 1965-74 (Vice-Principal, 1954-56 and 1960-62; Acting Principal, 1959-60); Professor Emeritus, since 1974; *b* 30 Sept. 1907; *er s* of Alfred Morgan Jones, JP, Penrhiwceiber, Glamorgan; *m* 1938, Eileen (*d* 1982), *d* of E. T. Davies, Swansea; one *s* (one *d* decd). *Educ:* West Monmouth Sch.; Merton Coll., Oxford. Science Exhibnr 1925; 1st Cl. Nat. Sci. physics, BA 1929; Research Scholar, Merton Coll., 1929, DPhil, MA, 1931; Senior Demy, Magdalen Coll., 1931. DSc 1955. Demonstrator in Wykeham Dept of Physics, Oxford, 1929-32; Lecturer in Physics, University Coll. of Swansea, 1932-40; Senior Scientific Officer, Royal Aircraft Establishment, 1940-45; Prof. of Physics, Univ. of Wales, and Head of Dept of Physics, University Coll. of Swansea, 1945-65. Vice-Chancellor, Univ. of Wales, 1969-71. Member: Radio Research Board, DSIR, 1951-54; Standing Conference on Telecommunications Research, DSIR, 1952-55; Board of Institute of Physics, 1947-50; Council of Physical Society, 1951-58 (Vice-Pres., 1954-59). Visiting Prof. to Univs in Australia, 1956; Supernumerary Fellow, Jesus Coll., Oxford, 1965-66, 1969-70; Hon. Professorial Res. Fellow, Univ. of Wales, 1974-; Leverhulme Emeritus Fellow, 1977-79. Regional Scientific Adviser for Home Defence, Wales, 1952-59, Sen. and Chief Reg. Sci. Adv., 1959-77; Pres., Royal Institution of South Wales, 1957-60; Mem. of Council for Wales and Mon, 1959-63, 1963-66; Dir (Part-time), S Wales Gp, BSC, 1968-70; Chm., Central Adv. Council for Education (Wales), 1961-64. Sen. Consultant in Plasma Physics, Radio and Space Research Station of SRC, 1964-65. Vice-Pres., Hon. Soc. of Cymmrodorian, 1982. Hon. LLD Wales, 1975. C. V. Boys' Prizeman, The Physical Soc., 1960; Ragnar Holm Scientific Achievement Award, 6th Internat. Conf. on Electric Contact Phenomena, Chicago, 1972. *Publications:* Fundamental Processes of Electrical Contact Phenomena, 1953; The Physics of Electrical Contacts, 1957; Ionization and Breakdown in Gases, 1957, 2nd edn 1966; The Glow Discharge, 1966; Ionization, Avalanches and Breakdown, 1966; papers in scientific jls on ionization and discharge physics. *Recreations:* railways, walking and gardening. *Address:* Brynheulog, 24 Sketty Park Road, Swansea SA2 9AS. *T:* Swansea 202344. *Club:* Athenæum.

JONES, Fred, CB 1978; CBE 1966; Deputy Secretary, HM Treasury, 1975-80, retired; *b* 5 May 1920; *s* of late Fred Jones and of Harriet (*née* Nuttall); *m* 1954, Joy (*née* Field); two *s*. *Educ:* Preston Grammar Sch.; St Catherine's Coll., Oxford. Economist, Trades Union Congress, 1951-59; Tutor in Economics and Industrial Relations, Ruskin Coll., Oxford, 1960-62; Economist, National Economic Development Office, 1962-64; Dept of Economic Affairs: Senior Economic Adviser, 1964-66; Asst Sec., 1966-68; Asst Under-Sec. of State, 1968-69; HM Treasury, Asst Under-Sec. of State, 1969-75. *Recreations:* walking, reading. *Address:* The Glen, Haighton Green Lane, Haighton, Grimsargh, Preston, Lancs.

JONES, Prof. Gareth (Hywel), FBA 1982; Fellow of Trinity College, Cambridge, since 1961; Downing Professor of the Laws of England, Cambridge University, since 1975; *b* 10 Nov. 1930; *o c* of late B. T. Jones, FRICS, and late Mabel Jones, Tylorstown, Glam; *m* 1959, Vivienne Joy, *o d* of C. E. Puckridge, FIA, Debden Green, Loughton; two *s* one *d*. *Educ:* Porth County Sch.; University Coll. London (PhD); St Catharine's Coll., Cambridge (Scholar); Harvard Univ. (LLM). LLB London 1951; MA, LLB 1953, LLD 1972, Cantab. Choate Fellow, Harvard, 1953; Yorke Prize, 1960. Called to Bar, Lincoln's Inn, 1955 (Scholar); Hon. Bencher 1975. Lecturer: Oriel and Exeter Colls, Oxford, 1956-58; KCL, 1958-61; Trinity Coll., Cambridge: Lectr, 1961-74, Tutor, 1967, Sen. Tutor, 1972; Univ. Lectr, Cambridge, 1961-74; Chm., Faculty of Law, 1978-81. Vis. Professor: Harvard, 1966 and 1975; Chicago, 1976-; California at Berkeley, 1967 and 1971; Indiana, 1971, 1975. *Publications:* (with Hon. Mr Justice Goff) The Law of Restitution, 1966, 2nd edn 1978; The History of the Law of Charity 1532-1827, 1969; The Sovereignty of the Law, 1973; various articles. *Address:* Trinity College, Cambridge CB2 1TQ. *T:* Cambridge 358201; 64 Cavendish Avenue, Cambridge CB1 4UT. *T:* Cambridge 245366. *Club:* Beefsteak.

JONES, Geoffrey; see Jones, John G.

JONES, Ven. Geoffrey G.; see Gower-Jones.

JONES, Prof. Geoffrey M.; see Melvill Jones.

JONES, Geoffrey Rippon R.; see Rees-Jones.

JONES, Air Marshal Sir George, KBE 1953 (CBE 1942); CB 1943; DFC; RAAF; *b* 22 Nov. 1896; *m* 1st, 1919, Muriel Agnes (decd), *d* of F. Stone; one *s* (and one *s* decd); 2nd, 1970, Mrs Gwendoline Claire Bauer. Served Gallipoli and European War, 1914–18 (despatches, DFC); joined RAAF, 1921; Dir Personnel Services, RAAF, 1936–40; Dir of Training, 1940–42; Chief of Air Staff, 1942–52. *Address:* Flat 10, 104 Cromer Road, Beaumaris, Victoria 3193, Australia. *Club:* Naval and Military (Melbourne).

JONES, Prof. George William; Professor of Government, University of London, since 1976; *b* 4 Feb. 1938; *er s* of George William and Grace Annie Jones; *m* 1963, Diana Mary Bedwell; one *s* one *d. Educ:* Wolverhampton Grammar Sch.; Jesus Coll., Oxford; Nuffield Coll., Oxford. Oxf. BA 1960, MA 1965, DPhil 1965. Univ. of Leeds: Asst Lectr in Govt, 1963; Lectr in Govt, 1965; London Sch. of Economics and Political Science: Lectr in Political Science, 1966; Sen. Lectr in Polit. Sci., 1971; Reader in Polit. Sci., 1974. Sec., Polit. Studies Assoc. of the UK, 1965–68; Exec. Cttee of PSA, 1969–75; Exec. Council, Hansard Soc., 1968–70; Mem., Editorial Cttee of The London Journal, 1973–80. Member: Layfield Cttee of Inquiry into Local Govt Finance, 1974–76; Exams Cttee, and Admin. Staff Qualifications Council, Local Govt Trng Bd, 1977–80; Political Science and Internat. Relns Cttee, SSRC, 1977–81; Chm., Central–Local Govt Relations Panel, SSRC, 1978–81. Mem. Governing Council, Wolverhampton Polytechnic, 1978–. FRHistS 1980. Hon. Fellow, Inst. of Local Govt Studies, Birmingham Univ., 1979. *Publications:* Borough Politics, 1969; (with B. Donoughue) Herbert Morrison: portrait of a politician, 1973; (ed with A. Norton) Political Leadership in Local Authorities, 1978; (ed) New Approaches to the Study of Central–Local Government Relationships, 1980; contribs to Political Studies, Public Admin., Political Qly, Parliamentary Affairs, Jl of Admin. Overseas. *Recreations:* cinema, politics. *Address:* Department of Government, London School of Economics, Houghton Street, WC2A 2AE. *T:* 01-405 7686.

JONES, Geraint Iwan; *b* 16 May 1917; *s* of Rev. Evan Jones, Porth, Glam; *m* 1st, 1940, M. A. Kemp; one *d*; 2nd, 1949, Winifred Roberts. *Educ:* Caterham Sch.; Royal Academy of Music (Sterndale Bennett Scholar). National Gallery Concerts, 1940–44; played complete organ works of Bach in 16 recitals in London, 1946. Musical dir of Mermaid Theatre performances of Purcell's Dido and Aeneas with Kirsten Flagstad, 1951–53. Formed Geraint Jones Singers and Orchestra, 1951, with whom many Broadcasts, and series of 12 Bach concerts, Royal Festival Hall, 1955; series of all Mozart's piano concertos, Queen Elizabeth Hall, 1969–70. Frequent European engagements, 1947– and regular US and Canadian tours, 1948–. Musical Director: Lake District Festival, 1960–78; Kirckman Concert Soc., 1963–; Artistic Director: Salisbury Festival, 1973–77; Manchester Internat. Festival, 1977–. Recordings as organist and conductor; Promenade Concerts; also concerts and recordings as harpsichordist, including sonatas with violinist wife, Winifred Roberts. Grand Prix du Disque, 1959 and 1966. *Recreations:* motoring, photography, antiques, reading. *Address:* The Long House, Arkley Lane, Barnet Road, Arkley, Herts.

JONES, Geraint Stanley; Controller, BBC–Wales, since 1981; *b* 26 April 1936; *s* of Olwen and David Stanley Jones; *m* 1961, Rhiannon Williams; two *d. Educ:* Pontypridd Grammar Sch.; University Coll. of N Wales (BA Hons; Dip. Ed.). BBC–Wales: Studio Manager, 1960–62; Production Asst, Current Affairs (TV), 1962–65; TV Producer: Current Affairs, 1965–69; Features and Documentaries, 1969–73; Asst Head of Programmes, Wales, 1973–74; Head of Programmes, Wales, 1974–81. *Recreations:* music, painting. *Address:* Y Goedlan, 8 Nant Fawr Road, Cyncoed, Cardiff, S Glamorgan. *T:* Cardiff 751038. *Club:* Cardiff and County (Cardiff).

JONES, Gerallt; see Jones, R. G.

JONES, Sir Glyn (Smallwood), GCMG 1964 (KCMG 1960, CMG 1957); MBE 1944; *b* 9 Jan. 1908; *s* of late G. I. Jones, Chester; *m* 1942, Nancy Madoc, *d* of J. H. Featherstone, CP, South Africa; one *d* (and one *s* decd). *Educ:* King's Sch., Chester; St Catherine's, Oxford Univ. (MA); Hon. Fellow, 1977. OUAFC 1928, 1929, 1930. HM Colonial Service (now HM Overseas Civil Service) N Rhodesia: Cadet, 1931; District Officer, 1933; Commissioner for Native Development, 1950; Acting Development Sec., 1956; Prov. Comr, 1956; Resident Comr, Barotseland, 1957; Sec. for Native Affairs, 1958; Minister of Native Affairs and Chief Comr, 1959; Chief Sec., Nyasaland, 1960–61, Governor, 1961–64; Governor-Gen. of Malawi, 1964–66. Advr on Govt Admin to Prime Minister of Lesotho, 1969–71; Dep. Chm., Lord Pearce Commn on Rhodesian Opinion, 1971–72; British Govt Observer, Zimbabwe Elections, 1980. KStJ. *Recreations:* shooting, fishing, golf, tennis. *Address:* Little Brandfold, Goudhurst, Kent. *Clubs:* Athenæum, Royal Commonwealth Society, MCC; Chester City.

JONES, Graham Julian; a Recorder of the Crown Court, since 1978; solicitor; *b* 17 July 1936; *s* of late David John Jones, CBE, and of Edna Lillie Jones; *m* 1961, Dorothy, *o d* of late James Smith and Doris Irene Tickle,

Abergavenny; two *s* one *d. Educ:* Porth County Grammar Sch.; St John's Coll., Cambridge. MA, LLB (Cantab). Admitted Solicitor, 1961; Partner, Morgan Bruce and Nicholas, 1961. Pres., Pontypridd Rhondda and Dist Law Soc., 1973–75; Member Council: Cardiff Law Soc., 1975–78; Associated Law Socs of Wales, 1974– (Pres., 1982–); Mem., Lord Chancellor's Legal Aid Adv. Cttee, 1980–. Sat as Dep. Circuit Judge, 1975–78. *Recreations:* golf, boats. *Address:* 17 Windsor Road, Radyr, Cardiff CF4 8BQ. *T:* Radyr 842669. *Clubs:* Cardiff and County, Radyr Golf (Cardiff).

JONES, Griffith Winston Guthrie, QC 1963; a Recorder, 1972–74 (Recorder of Bolton, 1968–71); *b* 24 Sept. 1914; second *s* of Rowland Guthrie Jones, Dolgellau, Merioneth; *m* 1st, 1959, Anna Maria McCarthy (*d* 1969); 2nd, 1978, Janet, *widow* of Commodore Henry Owen L'Estrange, DSC. *Educ:* Bootham Sch., York; University of Wales; St John's Coll., Cambridge. Called to the Bar, Gray's Inn, 1939. Dep. Chm., Cumberland QS, 1963–71. War service in Royal Artillery, 1940–46. *Recreation:* gardening. *Address:* Culleenamore, Sligo, Ireland. *Club:* Kildare Street and University (Dublin).

JONES, (Gwilym) Wyn, CBE 1977; Governor, Montserrat, 1977–80; Administrator, Cwmni Theatr Cymru (Welsh National Theatre), since 1982; *b* 12 July 1926; *s* of late Rev. John Jones, MA, BD, and Elizabeth (*née* Roberts); *m* 1951, Ruth (*née* Thomas); one *s* one *d. Educ:* Llanrwst Grammar Sch.; UCNW, Bangor (BA Hons); London Univ. Served RN, 1944–47. Cadet, Colonial Admin. Service, Gilbert and Ellice Islands, 1950; DO, DC and Secretariat in Tarawa, Line Islands, Phoenix Islands and Ocean Island, 1950–61; Solomon Islands, 1961; Asst Sec., 1961–67; Sen. Asst Sec., 1967–74; Dep. Chief Sec., 1974; Sec. to Chief Minister and Council of Ministers, 1974–77. Mem. Court, UCNW Bangor, 1980–. *Recreation:* walking alone. *Address:* Y Frondeg, Warren Drive, Deganwy, Gwynedd. *T:* Deganwy 83377.

JONES, Prof. Gwyn, CBE 1965; Professor of English Language and Literature, University College of South Wales, Cardiff, 1965–75, Fellow, 1980; *b* 24 May 1907; *s* of George Henry Jones and Lily Florence (*née* Nethercott); *m* 1st, 1928, Alice (*née* Rees) (*d* 1979); 2nd, 1979, Mair (*née* Sivell), *widow* of Thomas Jones. *Educ:* Tredegar Grammar School; University of Wales. Schoolmaster, 1929–35; Lecturer, University Coll., Cardiff, 1935–40; Prof. of Eng. Language and Lit., University Coll. of Wales, Aberystwyth, 1940–64. Ida Beam Vis. Prof., Iowa Univ., 1982. Dir of Penmark Press, 1939–. Mem. of various learned societies; Pres. of Viking Soc. for Northern Research, 1950–52; Mem. of Arts Council and Chm. of Welsh Arts Council, 1957–67. Hon. DLitt: Wales, 1977; Nottingham, 1978. Fellow, Institut Internat. des Arts et des Lettres, 1960. Christian Gauss Award, 1973. Knight, Order of the Falcon (Iceland), 1963. *Publications:* A Prospect of Wales, 1948; Welsh Legends and Folk-Tales, 1955; *novels:* Richard Savage, 1935; Times Like These, 1936, repr. 1979; Garland of Bays, 1938; The Green Island, 1946; The Flowers Beneath the Scythe, 1952; The Walk Home, 1962; *short stories:* The Buttercup Field, 1945; The Still Waters, 1948; Shepherd's Hey, 1953; Selected Short Stories, 1974; *translations:* The Vatnsdalers' Saga, 1942; (with Thomas Jones) The Mabinogion, 1948; Egil's Saga, 1960; Eirik the Red, 1961; The Norse Atlantic Saga, 1964; A History of the Vikings, 1968; Kings, Beasts and Heroes, 1972; (ed) Welsh Review, 1939–48; Welsh Short Stories, 1956; (ed with I. F. Elis) Twenty-Five Welsh Short Stories, 1971; The Oxford Book of Welsh Verse in English, 1977; *non-fiction:* Being and Belonging (BBC Wales Annual Radio Lecture), 1977; contrib. to numerous learned journals. *Address:* Castle Cottage, Sea View Place, Aberystwyth, Dyfed.

JONES, Gwyn Owain, CBE 1978; MA, DSc Oxon; PhD Sheffield; FMA; Director, National Museum of Wales, 1968–77; *b* 29 March 1917; *s* of Dr Abel John Jones, OBE, HMI, and Rhoda May Jones, Cardiff and Porthcawl; *m* 1st, 1944, Sheila Heywood (marr. diss.); two *d*; 2nd, 1973, Elizabeth Blandino. *Educ:* Monmouth Sch.; Port Talbot Secondary Sch.; Jesus Coll., Oxford. Glass Delegacy Research Fellow of University of Sheffield, later mem. of academic staff, 1939–41; Mem. UK Government's Atomic Energy project, 1942–46; Nuffield Foundation Research Fellow at Clarendon Laboratory, Oxford, 1946–49; Reader in Experimental Physics in University of London, at Queen Mary Coll., 1949–53; Prof. of Physics in Univ. of London, and Head of Dept of Physics at Queen Mary Coll., 1953–68; Fellow of Queen Mary Coll. Visiting Prof. Univ. of Sussex, 1964. Member: Court and Council, UWIST, 1968–74; Court, University Coll., Swansea, 1981–; Hon. Professorial Fellow, University Coll., Cardiff, 1969–79. Yr Academi Gymreig (English Language Section) 1971 (Chm., 1978–81); Gorsedd y Beirdd (Aelod er Anrhydedd) 1974; Governor, Commonwealth Institute, 1974–77. *Publications:* Glass, 1956; (in collab.) Atoms and the Universe, 1956; papers on solid-state, glass, low-temperature physics; *novels:* The Catalyst, 1960; Personal File, 1962; Now, 1965; *story sequence:* The Conjuring Show, 1981. *Address:* Ivy Cottage, Hudnall's Loop, St Briavels Common, near Lydney, Glos GL15 6SG. *T:* Dean 530510.

JONES, Gwyneth, CBE 1976; a Principal Dramatic Soprano: Royal Opera House, Covent Garden, since 1963; Vienna State Opera, since 1966; Bavarian State Opera, since 1967; *b* 7 Nov. 1936; *d* of late Edward George Jones and late Violet (*née* Webster). *Educ:* Twmpath Sec. Mod. Sch., Pontypool, Mon; Royal College of Music, London; Accademia Chigiana, Siena; Zürich Internat. Opera Studio; Maria Carpi Prof., Geneva. Oratorio and recitals as well as opera. Guest Artiste: La Scala, Milan; Berlin State Opera; Munich State Opera; Bayreuth Festival; Salzburg Festival; Tokyo; Zürich; Metropolitan

Opera, New York; Paris; Geneva; Dallas; San Francisco; Los Angeles; Teatro Colon, Buenos Aires; Edinburgh Festival; Welsh National Opera; Rome; Hamburg; Cologne; Maggio Musicale, Florence; Chicago. Numerous recordings, radio and TV appearances. FRCM. Kammersängerin, Austria and Bavaria. Hon. DMus Wales. *Address:* Box 380, 8040 Zürich, Switzerland.

JONES, G(wyneth) Ceris; Chief Nursing Officer, British Red Cross Society, 1962-70, retired; *b* 15 Nov. 1906; 2nd *d* of late W. R. Jones, OBE, JP, Tre Venal, Bangor, N Wales. *Educ:* Bangor County Sch. for Girls. State Registered Nurse; trained at Nightingale Training Sch., St Thomas' Hosp., 1927-31; Sister Tutor's Certificate, Univ. of London; Diploma in Nursing, Univ. of London. Sister Tutor, St Thomas' Hosp., 1936-39; served with QAIMNS Reserve, 1939-41; Sister-in-charge, Leys School Annexe to Addenbrooke's Hospital, Cambridge, 1941-43; Asst Matron, London Hospital, 1943-47; Matron, Westminster Hospital, 1947-51; London Hospital, 1951-61. Florence Nightingale Medal, Internat. Cttee, Red Cross, 1971. *Address:* 7 Menai View Terrace, Bangor, Gwynedd LL57 2HF.

JONES, Gwynoro Glyndwr; Assistant Education Officer, Development Forward Planning, West Glamorgan County Council, since 1977; *b* 21 Nov. 1942; *s* of J. E. and late A. L. Jones, Minyrafon, Foelgastell, Cefneithin, Carms; *m* 1967, A. Laura Miles; two *s* one *d. Educ:* Gwendraeth Grammar Sch.; Cardiff Univ. BSc Econ (Hons) Politics and Economics. Market Research Officer with Ina Needle Bearings Ltd, Llanelli, 1966-67; Economist Section, Wales Gas Bd, 1967-69; Public Relations Officer, Labour Party in Wales, March 1969-June 1970; Dir of Res., West Glam. CC, 1974-77. Member: INLOGOV Working Gp on Res. and Intelligence Units in Local Govt, 1975-77; S Wales Standing Conf. Working Gp, 1975-77; Council of European Municipalities, 1975-77, 1980-; Local Govt Exec. Cttee of European movement, 1975-77, 1980-; MP (Lab) Carmarthen, 1970-Sept. 1974; Member: House of Commons Expenditure Cttee, 1972-74; Standing Orders Cttee, 1972-74; Council of Europe and WEU, 1974; PPS to Home Sec., 1974. Vice-Pres., District Council Assoc., 1974. Pres., Nat. Eisteddfod of Wales, 1974. Political Educn Officer: Swansea Labour Assoc., 1976-77; Soc. of Educn Officers, 1978-. Co-ordinator, Wales in Europe campaign, 1975; Sponsor, Wales Lab and TU Cttee for Europe, 1975; joined SDP, May 1981; contested (SDP) Gower, Sept. 1982. *Publications:* The Record Put Straight (booklet), 1973; articles in Soc. Commentary, etc. *Recreations:* sport (played Rugby for both 1st and 2nd class teams). *Address:* Fonthill, 24 Glanmor Park Road, Sketty, Swansea, West Glam. *T:* Swansea 202278.

JONES, Harry, FRS 1952; BSc, PhD Leeds, PhD Cantab; *b* Pudsey, Yorks, 1905; *m* 1931, Frances Molly O'Neill; one *s* two *d. Educ:* University of Leeds; Trinity Coll., Cambridge. Lecturer at Bristol Univ., 1932-37; Imperial College, London: Reader in Mathematics, 1938-46; Prof. of Mathematics, 1946-72, now Professor Emeritus; Head of Dept, 1955-70; Pro-Rector, 1970-72; Sen. Res. Fellow, 1972-81, Fellow, 1975. *Publications:* (with N. F. Mott) The Theory of the Properties of Metals and Alloys, 1936; Theory of Brillouin Zones and Electronic States in Crystals, 1960; various contributions to scientific journals on Theoretical Physics. *Address:* 41 Berwyn Road, Richmond, Surrey. *T:* 01-876 1931.
　　See also A. C. R. Rumbold.

JONES, Sir Harry (Ernest), Kt 1971; CBE 1955; Agent in Great Britain for Northern Ireland, 1970-76; *b* 1 Aug. 1911; *m* 1935, Phyllis Eva Dixon; one *s* one *d. Educ:* Stamford Sch.; St John's Coll., Cambridge. Entered Northern Ireland Civil Service, 1934; Min. of Commerce: Principal Officer 1940; Asst Sec. 1942; Perm. Sec. 1955; Industrial Development Adviser to Ministry of Commerce, 1969. *Recreation:* fishing. *Address:* 51 Station Road, Nassington, Peterborough. *T:* Stamford 782675.

JONES, Rt. Rev. Haydn Harold; *see* Venezuela, Bishop of.

JONES, Henry Arthur, CBE 1974; MA; Professor Emeritus, University of Leicester, since 1981 (Vaughan Professor of Education, 1967-81; Head of the Department of Adult Education, 1967-78; Pro-Vice-Chancellor, 1978-81); *b* 7 March 1917; *er s* of Henry Lloyd Jones; *m* 1st, 1942, Molly (*d* 1971), 4th *d* of Richard Shenton; two *s*; 2nd, 1972, Nancy Winifred (*née* Cox), widow of Lt R. B. B. Jack, RN. *Educ:* Chorlton Grammar Sch.; Manchester Univ. George Gissing Prizeman, Manchester Univ., 1936; Graduate Research Fellow, Manchester Univ., 1937, MA 1938. Served War of 1939-45 with Lancs Fusiliers and DLI, 1940-42. Sen. English Master, Chorlton Grammar Sch., 1942-47; Resident Staff Tutor, Manchester Univ., 1947-49; Asst Dir of Extra-Mural Studies, Liverpool Univ., 1949-52, Dep. Dir 1953-57; Principal, The City Literary Institute, 1957-67. Chairman: Assoc. for Adult Education, 1964-67; Adult Educn Cttee, IBA, 1973-77; Exec. Chm., Nat. Inst. of Adult Education; Hon. Life Mem., Educnl Centres Assoc.; Vice-Pres., Pre-retirement Assoc.; Member: Library Adv. Council, DES, 1965-68; Sec. of State's Cttee on Adult Educn, DES, 1968-72; Adv. Council for Adult and Continuing Educn, DES, 1977-. Chm., Leics Consultative Cttee for Voluntary Orgns, 1974-77. Editor: Vaughan Papers in Educn, 1967-; Studies in Adult Education, 1974-. *Publications:* Adult Literacy: a study of the impact, 1978; The Concept of Success in Adult Literacy, 1978; Adult Literacy: the UK experience, 1978; Education and Disadvantage, 1978. *Address:* Stokes House, Great Bowden, Market Harborough, Leics. *T:* Market Harborough 62846.

JONES, Sir Henry (Frank Harding), GBE 1972 (KBE 1965; MBE 1943); Kt 1956; Chairman of the Gas Council, 1960-71; Vice-Chairman,

International Executive Council, World Energy Conference, 1970-73, Hon. Vice-Chm. since 1973 (Chairman, British National Committee, 1968-71); *b* 13 July 1906; *s* of Frank Harding Jones, Housham Tye, Harlow, Essex; *m* 1934, Elizabeth Angela, *d* of J. Spencer Langton, Little Hadham, Herts; three *s* one *d. Educ:* Harrow; Pembroke Coll., Cambridge (Hon. Fellow 1973). Served War of 1939-45 with Essex Regt and on staff: France and Belgium, 1939-40; India and Burma, 1942-45. Lieut-Col 1943; Col 1945; Brigadier 1945. Before nationalisation of gas industry was: Deputy Chairman, Watford and St Albans Gas Co., Wandsworth and District Gas Co.; Dir of South Metropolitan, South Suburban and other gas companies. Chm. East Midlands Gas Board, 1949-52; Dep. Chm. Gas Council, 1952-60. Chairman: Benzene Marketing Co., 1972-77; Benzole Producers Ltd, 1972-77. Mem., Royal Commn on Standards of Conduct in Public Life, 1974-76. Chm., EDC for Chemical Industry, 1972-75. Liveryman, Clothworkers' Co., 1928, Master 1972-73. Hon. FInstGasE (Pres. 1956-57); FEng; FICE; FIChemE; FRSA 1964. Hon. LLD Leeds, 1967; Hon. DSc: Leicester, 1970; Salford, 1971. *Recreations:* fishing, gardening. *Address:* Pathacres, Weston Turville, Aylesbury, Bucks HP22 5RW. *T:* Stoke Mandeville 2274. *Clubs:* Athenæum, Naval and Military, MCC.

JONES, (Henry) John (Franklin); writer; *b* 6 May 1924; *s* of late Lt-Col James Walker Jones, DSO, IMS, and Doris Marjorie (*née* Franklin); *m* 1949, Jean Verity Robinson; one *s* one *d. Educ:* Blundell's Sch.; Colombo Public Library; Merton Coll., Oxford. Served War, Royal Navy: Ordinary Seaman, 1943; Intell. Staff, Eastern Fleet, 1944. Merton Coll., Oxford: Harmsworth Sen. Scholar, 1948; Fellow and Tutor in Jurisprudence, 1949; Univ. Sen. Lectr, 1956; Fellow and Tutor in Eng. Lit., 1962; Prof. of Poetry, Univ. of Oxford, 1979-. Football Correspondent, The Observer, 1956-59. *Publications:* The Egotistical Sublime, 1954 (5th edn 1978); (contrib.) The British Imagination, 1961; On Aristotle and Greek Tragedy, 1962 (5th edn 1980); (contrib.) Dickens and the Twentieth Century, 1962; (ed) H. W. Garrod, The Study of Good Letters, 1963; John Keats's Dream of Truth, 1969 (2nd edn 1980); (contrib.) The Morality of Art, 1969; The Same God, 1971. *Address:* Holywell Cottage, Oxford. *T:* Oxford 47702; Yellands, Brisworthy, Shaugh Prior, Plympton, Devon. *T:* Shaugh Prior 310.

JONES, Rev. Prof. Hubert C.; *see* Cunliffe-Jones.

JONES, Rev. Hugh; *see* Jones, Rev. R. W. H.

JONES, Hugh (Hugo) Jarrett H.; *see* Herbert-Jones.

JONES, Humphrey Lloyd, CMG 1961; Secretary of the Ashmolean Museum, Oxford, 1962-76; *b* 5 April 1910; *s* of Arthur Davis Jones, London; *m* 1938, Edith, *d* of W. H. Tatham, Natal; one *s* two *d. Educ:* Westminster (King's Scholar); Christ Church, Oxford (MA). Colonial Administrative Service, Northern Rhodesia, Cadet, 1932; Dist Officer, 1934; Private Sec. to Gov., 1937; Asst Sec., 1948. In 1952: acted as Economic Sec.; MEC and MLC; Chm. Maize Control Bd; Chm. Cold Storage Control Bd; attended Commonwealth Economic Conf. in London as rep. of Northern Rhodesia Govt. Seconded to Federal Govt of Rhodesia and Nyasaland as Under-Sec., 1954; Administrative Sec., Govt of Northern Rhodesia, 1956; MLC; Chm. Whitley Council. Acted as Chief Sec. and Deputy for the Governor on a number of occasions. MEC and MLC, 1961; Minister of Labour and Mines and of Local Government and Social Welfare, Northern Rhodesia Govt, 1961; retired 1962. *Recreations:* travel and photography. *Address:* 2B Carlton Road, Oxford.

JONES, Rt. Rev. Hywel James; *see* British Columbia, Bishop of.

JONES, Prof. Ian C.; *see* Chester Jones.

JONES, Ian E.; *see* Edwards-Jones.

JONES, Ilston Percival Ll.; *see* Llewellyn Jones.

JONES, Ivan Ellis, CIE 1944; *b* 26 June 1903; *s* of James L. Jones, 9 Castlewood Park, Rathmines, Dublin; *m* 1948, Anna, *d* of Peter MacNeil, Eoligarry, Barra; one *s* one *d. Educ:* The High Sch., Harcourt Street, Dublin; Trinity Coll., Dublin. Entered Indian Civil Service, 1927; Asst Commissioner in Punjab, 1927; Under-Sec. to Punjab Govt 1929; Deputy Commissioner (Shahpur, Hissar, Multan, Amritsar), 1931-39; Registrar, Co-operative Societies, Punjab, 1940; Dir Food Purchases, Punjab, 1944; Sec. to Govt Punjab Civil Supplies Dept, 1945; Comr Jullundur, 1947; retired from ICS, 1947. Asst Classics Master, Royal High School, Edinburgh, 1949; Principal Classics Master, John Watson's Sch., Edinburgh, 1958, retd 1973. *Address:* 13 Forbes Road, Edinburgh EH10 4EG. *T:* 031-229 7819; 28 Eoligarry, Northbay, Barra, Hebrides. *T:* Northbay 363.

JONES, Ivor R.; *see* Roberts-Jones.

JONES, Jack L.; *see* Jones, James Larkin.

JONES, Sir James (Duncan), KCB 1972 (CB 1964); Policy Adviser, School for Advanced Urban Studies, Bristol University, since 1976; *b* 28 Oct. 1914; *m* 1943, Jenefer Mary Wade; one *s. Educ:* Glasgow High Sch.; Glasgow Univ.; University Coll., Oxford. Admiralty, 1941; Ministry of Town and Country Planning: joined 1946; Prin. Priv. Sec., 1947-50; Under-Sec., Min. of Housing and Local Govt, 1958-63; Sec., Local Govt Commn for England, 1958-61;

Dep. Sec., Min. of Housing and Local Govt, 1963–66; Dep. Sec., Min. of Transport, 1966–70; Sec., Local Govt and Develt, DoE, 1970–72; Permanent Sec., DoE, 1972–75. Hon. FRIBA. *Recreations:* cooking, reading, looking at buildings, walking. *Address:* The Courtyard, Ewelme, Oxford OX9 6HP. *T:* Wallingford 39270. *Clubs:* Athenæum; Oxford Union.

JONES, James Idwal; Welsh Geographer; retired MP; *b* 30 June 1900; *s* of James and Elizabeth Bowyer Jones; *m* 1931, Catherine Humphreys; one *s* (one *d* decd). *Educ:* Ruabon Grammar Sch.; Normal Coll., Bangor. Certificated Teacher, 1922. BSc Econ., London Univ. (Externally), 1936. Headmaster, Grango Secondary Modern Sch., Rhosllanerchrugog, near Wrexham, 1938. MP (Lab) Wrexham Div. of Denbighshire, 1955–70. Mem., Circle of Bards, Nat. Eisteddfod of Wales. Pastor (non-professional) with Scotch Baptists in Wales, 1924–. *Publications:* A Geography of Wales, 1938; An Atlas of Denbighshire, 1950; Atlas Hanesyddol o Gymru, 1952, new edn 1972 (A Welsh Historical Atlas of Wales); A Geographical Atlas of Wales, 1955; A Historical Atlas of Wales, 1955; A New Geography of Wales, 1960; J. R. Jones (Ramoth), 1967. *Recreations:* photography and landscape painting. *Address:* Maelor, Ponciau, Wrexham, Clwyd, Wales.

JONES, James Larkin, (Jack), CH 1978; MBE 1950; FCIT; General Secretary, Transport and General Workers' Union, 1969–78; Chairman, TUC International, Transport and Nationalised Industries Committees, 1972–78; Deputy Chairman, National Ports Council, 1967–79; *b* 29 March 1913; *m* 1938, Evelyn Mary Taylor; two *s*. *Educ:* elementary sch., Liverpool. Worked in engineering and docks industries, 1927–39. Liverpool City Councillor, 1936–39; served in Spanish Civil War; wounded Ebro battle, Aug. 1938; Coventry District Sec., Transport and General Workers' Union, also District Sec., Confedn of Shipbuilding and Engineering Unions, 1939–55; Midlands Regional Sec., Transport and General Workers' Union, 1955–63; Executive Officer, 1963–69. Mem., Midland Regional Bd for Industry, 1942–46, 1954–63; Chm., Midlands TUC Advisory Cttee, 1948–63; Mem., TUC Gen. Council, 1968–78. Coventry City Magistrate, 1950–63; Executive Chm., Birmingham Productivity Cttee, 1957–63; Member: Labour Party Nat. Exec. Cttee, 1964–67; Nat. Cttee for Commonwealth Immigrants, 1965–69; Council, Advisory, Conciliation and Arbitration Service, 1974–78; Bd, Crown Agents, 1978–80; Royal Commn on Criminal Procedure, 1978–80. Vice-Pres., ITF, 1974–79. Vice-Chm., Age Concern, England, 1978–; Pres., Retired Members Assocs, 1979–. Vis. Fellow, Nuffield Coll., Oxford, 1978. Associate Fellow, LSE, 1978–. Dimbleby Lecture, BBC, 1977. Hon. DLitt Warwick, 1978. *Publication:* (with Max Morris) A–Z of Trade Unionism and Industrial Relations, 1982. *Recreation:* walking. *Address:* 74 Ruskin Park House, Champion Hill, SE5. *T:* 01-274 7067.

JONES, Jeffrey Richard, CBE 1978; **Hon. Mr Justice Jones;** Chief Justice, since 1980, and President of the Court of Appeal, since 1982, Kiribati; Puisne Judge of the High Court of the Solomon Islands, since 1982; Acting Puisne Judge of the Supreme Court of Vanuatu, since 1982; *b* 18 Nov. 1921; *s* of Rev. Thomas Jones and Winifred (*née* Williams); *m* 1955, Anna Rosaleen Carberry; one *s* one *d*. *Educ:* Grove Park Sch., Wrexham; Denstone Coll., Staffs; Keble Coll., Oxford, 1946–49 (MA (Hons) PPE); Middle Temple, 1950–52 (Bar Finals, Council of Legal Educn; called, 1954). Served RAFVR, Flt Lieut (Pilot), 1940–46. Schoolmaster, Mountgrace Comprehensive, Potters Bar, 1953–55; private practice, Zaria, Nigeria, 1955–57; Magistrate, 1957, High Court Judge, 1965, Sen. Puisne Judge, 1970, Northern Nigeria; Chief Justice, Kano State, N Nigeria, 1975, Chief Judge (change of title, decree 41 of 1976), 1976–80. President, Rotary Club, Kano, 1977. Editor, Northern Nigeria Law Reports, 1966–74. *Publications:* Some Cases on Criminal Procedure and Evidence in Northern Nigeria 1968, 1968; Some Cases on Criminal Procedure and Evidence in Northern Nigeria 1969, 1969, 2nd edn combining 1968–69, 1970; Criminal Procedure in the Northern States of Nigeria (annotated), 1975, repr. 1978, 2nd edn 1979. *Recreations:* golf, painting, gardening, bridge, duck shooting, sea fishing. *Address:* Chief Justice's Chambers, High Court of Kiribati, PO Box 501, Betio, Tarawa, Kiribati; Bradley Cottage, Bradley Lane, Holt, near Trowbridge, Wilts. *T:* North Trowbridge 782004.

JONES, Jennifer, (Mrs Norton Simon); film actress (US); *b* Tulsa, Okla; *d* of Philip R. Isley and Flora Mae (*née* Suber); *m* 1st, 1939, Robert Walker (marr. diss. 1945); two *s*; 2nd, 1949, David O. Selznick (*d* 1965); one *d* decd; 3rd, 1971, Norton Simon. *Educ:* schools in Okla and Tex; Northwestern Univ., Evanston, Illinois; American Academy of Dramatic Arts, New York City. Films, since 1943, include: The Song of Bernadette; Since You Went Away; Cluny Brown; Love Letters; Duel in the Sun; We Were Strangers; Madame Bovary; Portrait of Jenny; Carrie; Wild Heart; Ruby Gentry; Indiscretion of an American Wife; Beat the Devil; Love is a Many-Splendoured Thing; The Barretts of Wimpole Street; A Farewell to Arms; Tender is the Night; The Idol; The Towering Inferno. Awards include: American Academy of Motion Pictures, Arts and Sciences Award, 1943; 4 other Academy nominations, etc. Medal for Korean War Work.

JONES, John; see Jones, H. J. F.

JONES, (John) Clement, CBE 1972; writer, broadcaster, technical adviser to developing countries; Executive Director (programming), Beacon Broadcasting, Wolverhampton, since 1974; *b* 22 June 1915; *o s* of Clement Daniel Jones; *m* 1939, Marjorie, *d* of George Gibson, Llandrindod Wells; three *s*. *Educ:* Ardwyn, Aberystwyth. Various journalistic positions; News Editor, Express and Star, Wolverhampton, 1955; Editor, 1960–71; Editorial Director,

1971–74. Pres., Guild of British Newspaper Editors, 1966–67, Hon. Life Vice-Pres., 1972. Member: Press Council, 1965–74; Adv. Bd, Thomson Foundn, 1965–; BBC W Midlands Adv. Council, 1971–75; (part-time) Monopolies and Mergers Commn (Newspaper Panel), 1973–; W Midlands Arts Assoc., 1973–78; Exec. Cttee, Soc. Internat. Develt, 1974–78; Vice Chm., Lichfield Dio. Media Council, 1976–82; Mem. Council, and Chm. Press Freedom Cttee, Commonwealth Press Union, 1975–80; Chm., Media Panel, Commn for Racial Equality, 1981–; Vice-Chm., British Human Rights Trust, 1975–78; Governor, British Inst. Human Rights, 1971–82. Founder Mem., Circle of Wine Writers, 1966. Pres., Staffordshire Soc., 1971–74. FRSA, 1970. *Publications:* UNESCO World Survey of Media Councils and Codes of Ethics, 1976; Racism and Fascism, 1981; Race and the Media: thirty years on, 1982. *Recreations:* travel, gardening, bee keeping. *Address:* 17 Swallowdale, Wightwick Bank, Wolverhampton WV6 8DT. *T:* Wolverhampton 763253; 7 South View Drive, Walton on the Naze, Essex CO14 8EP. *T:* Frinton 77087. *Clubs:* Athenæum, Press.

JONES, John Cyril, CBE 1951; BSc; MICE, FIMechE; Technical Education Consultant, World Bank, since 1968; *b* 30 Oct. 1899; *s* of John Jones, Swindon, Wilts; *m* 1928, Doris Anne, *d* of A. Tanner, Swindon, Wilts; one *d*. *Educ:* The College, Swindon; Loughborough Coll., Leics. Design and Research asst, GWR Co., 1922–31; Head of Dept, Loughborough Coll., 1931–34; Principal: St Helen's Municipal Coll., 1934–37, Cardiff Tech. Coll., 1937–41, Royal Tech. Coll., Salford, 1941–44; Dir of Educn, The Polytechnic, Regent Street, W1, 1944–56; Adviser for Tech. Educn to Colonial Office, 1956–61, Dept of Tech. Co-operation, 1961–64, and Min. of Overseas Development, 1964–67. Hon. Sec. Assoc. of Tech. Instns, 1944–56; Hon. Treas. Assoc. of Tech. Instns, 1956–67; Pres., Assoc. of Prins of Tech. Instns, 1951; Mem. Central Advisory Council for Education (Eng.), 1947–56; RAF Educ. Advisory Cttee, 1948–56; Advisory Cttee on Educ. in Colonies, 1953–56; Council for Overseas Colls of Art, Science and Technology, and Council for Tech. Educ. and Training in Overseas Countries, 1949–69. Member: Fulton Commn on Education in Sierra Leone, 1954; Keir Commn on Technical Education in N Rhodesia, 1960. Mem. Council for External Students, University London, 1954–66. Mem. of Council, RSA, 1960–66. Dir Asian Study Tour of Vocational Educ. and Training in the USSR, 1961, 1963; International Bank for Reconstruction and Development Missions to: Pakistan, 1962, 1963; Morocco and Kenya, 1965; Jamaica and Tunisia, 1966; Mem. International Commn on Tech. Educ. in Sudan, 1966. Officier d'Académie (France), 1950; elected Hon. Mem. City and Guilds of London Inst., 1964. *Publications:* papers on higher technological education and reports on development of technical education in various overseas countries. *Recreations:* books, music, and foreign travel. *Address:* 26 Grand Marine Court, Durley Gardens, Bournemouth BH2 5HS.

JONES, (John) Edward; His Honour Judge Edward Jones; a Circuit Judge (formerly County Court Judge since 1969); *b* 23 Dec. 1914; *s* of Thomas Robert Jones, Liverpool; *m* 1945, Katherine Elizabeth Edwards, SRN, *d* of Ezekiel Richard Edwards, Liverpool; one *s* one *d*. *Educ:* Liverpool Institute High School. ACIS 1939–70; BCom London 1942; LLB London 1945. Called to Bar, Gray's Inn, 1945; Member of Northern Circuit, 1946; Dep. Chm., Lancs QS, 1966–69. Dep. Chm., Workmen's Compensation (Supplementation) and Pneumoconiosis and Byssinosis Benefit Boards, 1968–69. Vice President: Merseyside Br., Magistrates' Assoc., 1974–; Liverpool Welsh Choral Union, 1973–; Governor, Aigburth Vale Comprehensive Sch., 1976; Pres., Merseyside Branch, British Red Cross Soc., 1980–. Welsh Presbyterian Church: Deacon, 1947; Liverpool Presbytery Moderator, 1971. JP Lancs, 1966. *Address:* India Buildings, Water Street, Liverpool.

JONES, John Elfed, CEng, MIEE; Chairman, Welsh Water Authority, since 1982; *b* 19 March 1933; *s* of Urien Maelgwyn Jones and Mary Jones; *m* 1957, Mary Sheila (*née* Rosser); two *d*. *Educ:* Blaenau Ffestiniog Grammar Sch.; Denbighshire Technical Coll., Wrexham; Heriot Watts Coll., Edinburgh. Student apprentice, 1949–53, graduate trainee, 1953–55, CEGB; National Service, RAF, 1955–57 (FO); Rock Climbing Instr, Outward Bound Sch., Aberdyfi, 1957; Technical Engr with CEGB, 1957–59; Dep. Project Manager, Rheidol Hydro-Electric Project, 1959–61; Sen. Elec. Engr, Trawsfynydd Nuclear Power Station, 1961–63; Deputy Manager: Mid Wales Gp of Power Stations, 1963–67; Connah's Quay Power Station, 1967–69; Anglesey Aluminium Metal Ltd: Engrg Manager, 1969–73; Production Manager, 1973–76; Admin Director, 1976–77; Dep. Man. Dir, 1977–79; Industrial Dir, Welsh Office (Under Sec. rank), 1979–82. Treasurer, Urdd Gobaith Cymru, 1964–67; Member Court: Univ. of N Wales, Bangor, 1978–82; Royal National Eisteddfod of Wales, 1981–; Member, BBC Broadcasting Council for Wales, 1979–. Hon. Col, Commonwealth of Kentucky, 1976. *Recreations:* fishing for salmon and trout, reading, attending Eisteddfodau. *Address:* Ty Mawr, Coity, Bridgend, Mid Glamorgan.

JONES, (John) Emrys, CBE 1979; Regional Organiser and Secretary, Labour Party, Wales, 1965–79, retired; *b* 12 March 1914; *s* of William Jones and Elizabeth Susan Jones; *m* 1935, Stella Davies; one *d*. *Educ:* Secondary Sch., Mountain Ash, S Wales. Shop assistant, 1928–29; railwayman, 1929–33; Rootes motor factory, 1933–36; railwayman, 1936–49. Regional Organiser, Labour Party: S West, 1949–60; W Midlands, 1960–65. *Recreations:* reading and writing. *Address:* 11 Ael y Bryn, Energlyn, Caerphilly, Mid Glam. CF8 2QX. *T:* Caerphilly 882848.

JONES, Air Vice-Marshal John Ernest A.; see Allen-Jones.

JONES, John Ernest P.; see Powell-Jones.

JONES, John Eryl O.; see Owen-Jones.

JONES, (John) Geoffrey; His Honour Judge Geoffrey Jones; a Circuit Judge since 1975; *b* 14 Sept. 1928; *s* of Wyndham and Lilias Jones; *m* 1954, Sheila (*née* Gregory); three *s*. *Educ*: Brighton and Hove Grammar Sch.; St Michael's Sch., Llanelli; St David's Coll., Lampeter; University Coll., London. LLB London 1955. Army service, 1946-48, commnd into RASC, 1947. Electrical wholesale business, 1948-52. Called to Bar, Gray's Inn, 1956; practised Leicester, 1958-70 and London, 1970-75. *Recreation*: golf. *Address*: c/o The Crown Court, Leicester LE1 6HG. *T*: Leicester 706669.

JONES, John H.; see Hamilton-Jones.

JONES, John Henry H.; see Harvey-Jones.

JONES, John Hubert E.; see Emlyn Jones.

JONES, Air Marshal Sir John Humphrey E.; see Edwardes Jones.

JONES, John Iorwerth, CBE 1977; retired; Lord Mayor of Cardiff, 1976-77; Member, Cardiff City Council, since 1958; *b* 22 Oct. 1901; *s* of David Nicholls Jones and Minnie Jones (*née* Rees); single. *Educ*: Carmarthen (public and private). Apprenticed Electrical Engineering, 1918-23. Chm., Cardiff Trades Council, 1960-67. Elected to Cardiff City Council, 1958; on reorganisation elected to new City Council and also to South Glamorgan County Council, May 1974; Dep. Lord Mayor, 1974-75; re-elected to City Council, 1976; re-elected to County Council, 1977. Chm., Cardiff Searchlight Tattoo Cttee, 1979-80 and 1980-82. Governor: WNO; Nat. Museum of Wales. *Recreations*: Rugby fan; interested in opera, music. *Address*: 11 Anderson Place, Cardiff. *T*: Cardiff 494195. *Club*: Cardiff Athletic (Cardiff).

JONES, Sir (John) Kenneth (Trevor), Kt 1965; CBE 1956; QC 1976; Legal Adviser to the Home Office, 1956-77; *b* 11 July 1910; *s* of John Jones and Agnes Morgan; *m* 1940, Menna, *d* of Cyril O. Jones; two *s*. *Educ*: King Henry VIII Grammar Sch., Abergavenny; University Coll. of Wales, Aberystwyth; St John's Coll., Cambridge. Called to the Bar, Lincoln's Inn, 1937. Served Royal Artillery, 1939-45. Entered the Home Office as a Legal Asst, 1945. Mem. of the Standing Cttee on Criminal Law Revision, 1959-. *Address*: 54 Westminster Gardens, SW1. *T*: 01-834 4950. *Club*: Athenæum.

JONES, John Morgan, CB 1964; CBE 1946; Secretary Welsh Department, Ministry of Agriculture, 1944-68; *b* 20 July 1903; *s* of late Richard and Mary Ellen Jones, Pertheirin, Caersws, Montgomeryshire; *m* 1933, Dorothy Morris, yr *d* of late David Morris, and Margaret Anne Wigley, Llanbrynmair, Montgomeryshire; no *c*. *Educ*: Newtown County Sch.; University Coll. of Wales, Aberystwyth. BA 1922; Hons in Econ. 1923, History 1924; MA 1926. Research Staff Dept of Agric. Economics, University Coll. of Wales, 1924-30; Marketing Officer, Min. of Agric. and Fisheries, 1930-35; Registrar Univ. Coll. of Wales, Aberystwyth, 1936; seconded to Min. of Agric. as Minister's Liaison Officer for mid- and south-west Wales, 1940; Chm. Cardigan War Agric. Exec. Cttee, 1943. Sec./Treas. Aberystwyth and Dist Old People's Housing Soc. Ltd, 1972-76. Life Governor, UCW (Mem. Council, 1950-77). Hon. LLD Wales, 1973. *Publications*: Economeg Amaethyddiaeth, 1930; articles on rural economics, mainly in Welsh Journal of Agriculture. *Address*: Maesnewydd, North Road, Aberystwyth. *T*: Aberystwyth 612507.

JONES, Brig. John Murray R.; see Rymer-Jones.

JONES, Sir John Prichard; see Prichard-Jones.

JONES, Rev. Prebendary John Stephen Langton; Residentiary Canon and Precentor of Wells Cathedral, 1947-67, Prebendary, since 1967; *b* 21 May 1889; *m* 1921, Jeanne Charlotte Dujardin; three *s* one *d*. *Educ*: Dover College; Jesus College, Cambridge. Asst Curate of Halifax Parish Church, 1914; Asst Curate, Hambleden, Berks, 1919; Vicar of Yiewsley, Middx, 1921; Rector of W Lydford, Taunton, 1939-47. Proctor in Convocation for Bath and Wells, 1946-50.

JONES, Prof. Kathleen; Professor of Social Administration, University of York, since 1965; *b* 7 April 1922; *d* of William Robert Savage and Kate Lilian Barnard; *m* 1944, Rev. David Gwyn Jones (*d* 1976); one *s*. *Educ*: North London Collegiate Sch.; Westfield Coll., Univ. of London (BA, PhD). Research Asst in Social Administration, Univ. of Manchester, 1951-53, Asst Lectr 1953-55; Sen. History Teacher, Victoria Instn, Kuala Lumpur, 1956-58; also Asst Lectr in History, Univ. of Malaya (part-time); Lectr in Social Administration, Univ. of Manchester, 1958-62, Sen. Lectr 1962-65. Chm., Social Scis Cttee, UK Commn for UNESCO, 1966-69; Mem., Gen. Synod of C of E, 1975-80; Member: Archbp's Commn on Church and State, 1966-71; Lord Gardiner's Cttee on NI, 1974-75; Archbishop's Commn on Marriage, 1976-78. Pres., Assoc. of Psychiatric Social Workers, 1968-70; Chm., Social Admin Assoc., 1980-. Hon. FRCPsych, 1976. *Publications*: Lunacy, Law and Conscience, 1955; Mental Health and Social Policy, 1960; Mental Hospitals at Work, 1962; The Compassionate Society, 1965; The Teaching of Social Studies in British Universities, 1965; A History of the Mental Health Services, 1972; Opening the Door: a study of new policies for the mentally handicapped, 1975; Issues in Social Policy, 1978; (ed) Year Book of Social Policy in Britain, 1971-76; (ed) Living the Faith: a call to the Church, 1980; (series editor) International Library of Social Policy, 1968-. *Address*: Woodland View, Barton-le-Willows, York YO6 7PD. *T*: Whitwell-on-the-Hill 526. *Club*: University Women's.

JONES, Keith H.; see Hamylton Jones.

JONES, Hon. Mrs Keith Miller; see Askwith, Hon. Betty E.

JONES, Sir Keith (Stephen), Kt 1980; FRCSE; FRACS; *b* 7 July 1911; *s* of Stephen William and Muriel Elsy Jones; *m* 1936, Kathleen Mary Abbott; three *s*. *Educ*: Newington Coll.; Univ. of Sydney (MB,BS). General practitioner, Army MO, Surgeon; President, Aust. Medical Assoc., 1973-76; Chief MO, NSW State Emergency Service, 1966-74; retired. Chairman: Australasian Medical Publishing Co., 1976-82; Nat. Spec. Qualifications Adv. Cttee, 1980-. Hon. FRACGP 1975. Gold Medal, AMA, 1976. *Recreations*: golf, swimming. *Address*: 63/1 Addison Road, Manly, NSW 2095, Australia. *T*: 977 1328. *Club*: Union (Sydney).

JONES, Sir Kenneth; see Jones, Sir J. K. T.

JONES, Hon. Sir Kenneth (George Illtyd), Kt 1974; **Hon. Mr Justice Kenneth Jones;** a Judge of the High Court, Queen's Bench Division, since 1974; *b* 26 May 1921; *s* of Richard Arthur Jones and late Olive Jane Jones, Radyr, Cardiff; *m* 1st, 1947, Dulcie (*d* 1977); one *s* two *d*; 2nd, 1978, June Patricia (prev. marr. diss.), *o d* of Leslie Arthur and late Winifred Doxey, Harrogate. *Educ*: Brigg Gram. Sch.; University Coll., Oxford (1939-41, 1945-46), MA; Treas., Oxford Union Society, 1941; served in Shropshire Yeo. (76th Medium Regt RA), 1942-45; Staff Captain, HQ 13th Corps, 1945 (despatches). Called to Bar, Gray's Inn, 1946; joined Oxford Circuit, 1947; QC 1962; Mem. Gen. Council of the Bar, 1961-65, 1968-69; Bencher, Gray's Inn, 1969-. Recorder of: Shrewsbury, 1964-66; Wolverhampton, 1966-71; the Crown Court, 1972; Dep. Chm., Herefordshire QS, 1961-71; a Circuit Judge, 1972-73. *Recreations*: theatre, opera, boats. *Address*: Royal Courts of Justice, Strand, WC2A 2LL.

JONES, Air Vice-Marshal Laurence Alfred, AFC 1971; Senior Air Staff Officer, Strike Command, since 1982; *b* 18 Jan. 1933; *s* of Benjamin Howel and Irene Dorothy Jones; *m* 1956, Brenda Ann; two *d*. *Educ*: Trinity Sch., Croydon; RAF College, Cranwell. Entry to RAF Coll., 1951, graduated 1953; served as Jun. Officer Pilot with 208 Sqdn in Middle East, 1954-57; Fighter Weapons Sch., 74 Sqdn, until 1961; commanded: No 8 Sqdn, Aden, 1961-63; No 19 Sqdn, RAF Germany, 1967-70; Station Comdr, RAF Wittering, 1975-76; RCDS 1977; Director of Operations (Air Support), MoD, 1978-81. *Recreations*: golf, skiing. *Address*: Headquarters, Strike Command, RAF High Wycombe, Bucks. *Club*: Royal Air Force.

JONES, Maj.-Gen. Leonard Hamilton H.; see Howard-Jones.

JONES, Leonard Ivan S.; see Stranger-Jones.

JONES, Leslie, MA; JP; Secretary for Welsh Education, Welsh Office and Department of Education and Science, 1970-77; *b* Tumble, Carms, 27 April 1917; *y s* of late William Jones, ME and Joanna (*née* Peregrine); *m* 1948, Glenys, *d* of late D. R. Davies, Swansea; one *s* one *d*. *Educ*: Gwendraeth Valley Grammar Sch.; Univ. of Wales. Served with RN, 1940-46 (Lieut RNVR). UC Swansea, 1937-40 and 1946-47 (1st cl. hons Econs); Lectr in Econs, Univ. of Liverpool, 1947-51; Lectr and Sen. Lectr in Econs, UC Cardiff, 1952-65; Dir, Dept of Extra-Mural Studies, UC Cardiff, 1965-69. Hon. Lectr, Dept of Educn, UC Cardiff, 1977-. Member: Ancient Monuments Bd for Wales, 1970-77; Council, UWIST, 1978-; Council, St David's University Coll., 1978-; Court, Univ. of Wales, 1979-; Court, Nat. Library of Wales, 1978-; Court, Nat. Mus. of Wales, 1978-; Council, Dr Barnardo's, 1978-. Hon. Fellow, UC Cardiff, 1971. JP Cardiff 1966. *Publications*: The British Shipbuilding Industry, 1958; articles on maritime, coal, iron and steel industries; industrial economics generally. *Recreations*: walking, gardening. *Address*: 43 Cyncoed Road, Cardiff. *Club*: Naval.

JONES, Lewis C.; see Carter-Jones.

JONES, Lilian Pauline N.; see Neville-Jones.

JONES, Maude Elizabeth, CBE 1973; Deputy Director-General, British Red Cross Society, 1970-77; *b* 14 Jan. 1921; 2nd *d* of late E. W. Jones, Dolben, Ruthin, North Wales. *Educ*: Brynhyfryd Sch. for Girls, Ruthin. Joined Foreign Relations Dept, Jt War Organisation BRCS and OStJ, 1940; Dep. Dir, Jun. Red Cross, BRCS, 1949; Dir, Jun. Red Cross, 1960; Dep. Dir-Gen. for Branch Affairs, BRCS, 1966. Member: Jt Cttee (and Finance and Gen. Purposes Sub-Cttee) OStJ and BRCS, 1966-77; Council of Nat. Council of Social Service; Council of FANY, 1966-77. Governor, St David's Sch., Ashford, Mddx. SSStJ 1959. *Recreations*: music, gardening, reading. *Address*: Dolben, Ruthin, Clwyd, North Wales. *T*: Ruthin 2443. *Club*: VAD.

JONES, Mervyn; see Jones, Thomas Mervyn.

JONES, Mervyn; author; *b* 27 Feb. 1922; *s* of Ernest Jones and Katharine (*née* Jokl); *m* 1948, Jeanne Urquhart; one *s* two *d*. *Educ*: Abbotsholme School; New

York University. Assistant Editor: Tribune, 1955-59; New Statesman, 1966-68; Drama Critic, Tribune, 1959-67. *Publications:* No Time to be Young, 1952; The New Town, 1953; The Last Barricade, 1953; Helen Blake, 1955; On the Last Day, 1958; Potbank, 1961; Big Two, 1962; A Set of Wives, 1965; Two Ears of Corn, 1965; John and Mary, 1966; A Survivor, 1968; Joseph, 1970; Mr Armitage isn't back yet, 1971; Life on the Dole, 1972; Holding On, 1973; The Revolving Door, 1973; Strangers, 1974; Lord Richard's Passion, 1974; The Pursuit of Happiness, 1975; Scenes from Bourgeois Life, 1976; Nobody's Fault, 1977; Today The Struggle, 1978; The Beautiful Words, 1979; A Short Time to Live, 1980; Two Women and their Man, 1982. *Address:* 10 Waterside Place, NW1. *T:* 01-586 4404.

JONES, Nigel John L; *see* Inglis-Jones.

JONES, Norman Stewart C.; *see* Carey Jones.

JONES, Norman William, TD 1962; FIB; Director since 1976, and Group Chief Executive since 1978, Lloyds Bank plc; *b* 5 Nov. 1923; *s* of late James William Jones and Mabel Jones; *m* 1950, Evelyn June Hall; two *s. Educ:* Gravesend Grammar Sch. FIB 1972. Served War, Army, 1942-47: commnd Beds and Herts Regt, 1943; with Airborne Forces, 1944-47; TA, 1947-64. Entered Lloyds Bank, 1940; Gen. Man., 1973; Asst Chief Gen. Man., 1975; Dep. Group Chief Exec., 1976. Director: Lloyds Bank California, 1974-; National Bank of New Zealand, 1978-. *Recreations:* sailing, photography, DIY. *Address:* Rowans, 21 College Avenue, Grays, Essex. *T:* Grays Thurrock 73101. *Clubs:* Naval and Military, Overseas Bankers.

JONES, Norvela, (Mrs Michael Jones); *see* Forster, N.

JONES, Sir (Owen) Trevor, Kt 1981; Leader, Liverpool City Council; Member, Merseyside Development Corporation, since 1981; *b* 1927; *s* of Owen and Ada Jones, Dyserth. Mem., Liverpool City Council, 1968, Liverpool District Council, 1973-. Pres., Liberal Party, 1972-73; contested (L) Liverpool, Toxteth, Feb. and Oct. 1974. *Address:* Town Hall, Liverpool L2 3SW.

JONES, Penry; Chief Assistant (Television) (formerly Deputy Head of Programme Services), IBA (formerly ITA), since 1971; *b* 18 Aug. 1922; *s* of Joseph William and Edith Jones; *m* Beryl Joan Priestley; two *s. Educ:* Rock Ferry High Sch.; Liverpool Univ. Gen. Sec., YMCA, Altrincham, 1940; Sec., SCM, Southern Univs, 1945; Industrial Sec., Iona Community, 1948; Religious Programmes Producer, ABC Television, 1958; Religious Programmes Officer of ITA, 1964; Head of Religious Broadcasting, BBC, 1967. *Recreations:* hill-walking, swimming, watching Rugby football. *Address:* 36 Queens Gate, SW7. *T:* 01-584 8029. *Club:* Reform.

JONES, Brig. Percival de Courcy, OBE 1953; Chief Secretary, The Royal Life Saving Society, 1965-75; *b* 9 Oct. 1913; *s* of P. de C. Jones, Barnsley; *m* 1st, 1947, Anne Hollins (marr. diss., 1951); one *s*; 2nd, 1962, Elaine Garnett. *Educ:* Oundle; RMC, Sandhurst. Commissioned KSLI 1933; Staff Coll., 1942; comd Northamptons, Burma, 1944-45; Staff Coll. Instructor, 1949-50; AA & QMG, 11th Armoured Div., 1951-53; comd 1st KSLI, 1953-55; AQMG, War Office, 1955-58; NATO Defence Coll., 1958-59; Bde Comdr, 1959-62; retd 1962. Mem., Aylesbury Vale DC, 1976-79. *Recreation:* gardening. *Address:* c/o Midland Bank, 2 Walton Road, Aylesbury, Bucks.

JONES, Peter Benjamin Gurner; Under Secretary; Director of Data Processing, Board of Inland Revenue, since 1981; *b* 25 Dec. 1932; *s* of Gurner Prince Jones and Irene Louise Jones (*née* Myall); *m* 1962, Diana Margaret Henly; one *s* one *d. Educ:* Bancroft's Sch.; St Catherine's Society, Oxford (BA (Hons) English Language and Literature). Inspector of Taxes, 1957; Inspector (Higher Grade), 1963; Sen. Inspector, 1969; Principal Inspector, 1975; Sen. Principal Inspector, 1980. *Recreations:* Rugby, books, canal cruising. *Address:* 106 Vale Road, Ash Vale, Aldershot, Hants GU12 5HS. *Clubs:* Hampshire Rugby Union, Swanage and Wareham RFC.

JONES, Peter Derek; Secretary: Council of Civil Service Unions, since 1980; Civil Service National Whitley Council (Trade Union Side), since 1963; *b* 21 May 1932; *s* of Richard Morgan Jones and Phyllis Irene (*née* Lloyd); *m* 1962, Noreen Elizabeth (*née* Kemp). *Educ:* Wembley County Grammar School. National Service and TA, Green Jackets/Parachute Regt, 1950-56; Civil Service, Nat. Assistance Bd, 1952-59; Asst Sec., Civil Service Nat. Whitley Council, 1959-63. Vice Chm., Civil Service Housing Assoc. Ltd, 1981- (Dir, 1963-81); Dir, Civil Service Building Soc., 1963-; Mem. Exec. Council, RIPA, 1981-. Editor, Whitley Bulletin, 1963-. *Publications:* articles in RIPA and personnel management jls. *Recreations:* relaxing, reading, agriculture (amateur). *Address:* Highlands Farm, Cross in Hand, East Sussex TN21 0SX. *T:* Heathfield 3577. *Clubs:* Wig and Pen, Belfry; Middlesex CCC.

JONES, Peter Eldon, FRIBA, FRTPI; Director of Architecture and Superintending Architect of Metropolitan Buildings, Greater London Council, since 1982; *b* 11 Oct. 1927; *s* of Wilfrid Eldon Jones and Jessie Meikle (*née* Buchanan); *m* 1954, Gisela Marie von Arnswaldt; two *s* one *d. Educ:* Surbiton County Grammar Sch.; Kingston Polytechnic; University College London. DipTP. Private practice, 1950-54; joined LCC Architects Dept, 1954; Dep. Schools Architect, LCC, 1960-65; Town Development Architect/Planner, 1965-71; Technical Policy Architect, GLC, 1971-74;

Education Architect, ILEA, 1974-82; Acting Director of Architecture, GLC, 1980-82. Junior Vice Pres., Soc. of Chief Architects of Local Authorities, 1982-83. *Publications:* articles and papers on town development, educn building and housing design. *Recreations:* building, photography. *Address:* The Pleasance, 2 Upper Brighton Road, Surbiton, Surrey KT6 6JY. *T:* 01-399 0552.

JONES, Peter Ferry, MA, MChir, FRCS, FRCSE; Surgeon to the Queen in Scotland, since 1977; Consultant Surgeon, Woodend Hospital and Royal Aberdeen Children's Hospital, Aberdeen, since 1958; Clinical Reader in Surgical Paediatrics, University of Aberdeen, since 1965; *b* 29 Feb. 1920; *s* of Ernest and Winifred Jones; *m* 1950, Margaret Thomson; two *s* two *d. Educ:* Emmanuel Coll., Cambridge (MA); St Bartholomew's Hosp. Med. Sch., London (MB, MChir). FRCS 1948; FRCSE 1964. Served War, RAMC, 1944-46, Captain. House Surgeon, St Bartholomew's Hosp., 1943; Surg. Registrar, N Middlesex Hosp., 1948-51; Surg. Tutor, St Bartholomew's Hosp., 1951-53; Sen. Surg. Registrar, Central Middlesex Hosp. and the Middlesex Hosp., London, 1953-57. *Publications:* Abdominal Access and Exposure (with H. A. F. Dudley), 1965; Emergency Abdominal Surgery in Infancy, Childhood and Adult Life, 1974; papers on paediatric and gen. surgery in Brit. Jl of Surg., BMJ, Lancet, etc. *Recreations:* dinghy sailing, hill walking. *Address:* 7 Park Road, Cults, Aberdeen AB1 9HR. *T:* Aberdeen 867702.

JONES, Peter George Edward Fitzgerald; Director, Atomic Weapons Research Establishment, since 1982; *b* 7 June 1925; *s* of John Christopher Jones and Isobel (*née* Howell); *m* 1st; two *s*; 2nd, Jacqueline Angela (*née* Gilbert); two *s* one *d. Educ:* various schs; Dulwich Coll.; London Univ. (BSc (Special) Physics 1st Cl. Hons 1951). FInstP. Served RAF, flying duties, 1943-47. GEC Res. Labs, 1951-54; AWRE and Pacific Test Site, 1955-63; Asst Dir of Res., London Communications Security, 1963; Atomic Weapons Research Establishment: Supt, Electronics Res., 1964; Head, Electronics Div., 1966; Head, Special Projs, 1971; Chief, Warhead Develt, 1974; Principal Dep. Dir, 1980. *Recreations:* flying, motoring. *Address:* 38 Oakley Lane, Basingstoke, Hants RG23 7JY. *T:* Basingstoke 780706.

JONES, Peter Llewellyn G.; *see* Gwynn-Jones.

JONES, Peter Trevor S.; *see* Simpson-Jones.

JONES, Philip; *see* Jones, T. P.

JONES, Sir Philip (Frederick), Kt 1971; Director: The Herald and Weekly Times Limited, Melbourne, Australia, since 1957 (Vice-Chairman, 1966-70; General Manager, 1953-63, retired); Advertiser Newspapers Ltd, since 1975; *b* 14 Aug. 1912; British; *s* of J. F. Jones, Napier, NZ; *m* 1942, Josephine N., *d* of H. Kirschlager; no *c. Educ:* Barker's Coll., Hornsby, NSW, Australia. Dept of Treasury to 1951; Sec., The Herald and Weekly Times Ltd, 1951-53. ACA, AASA. *Recreation:* golf. *Address:* 546 Toorak Road, Toorak, Victoria, 3142, Australia. *Clubs:* Melbourne, Athenæum, Metropolitan Golf, VRC, VATC, Moonee Valley Racing (all in Melbourne).

JONES, Philip Graham, CEng, MIChemE; HM Chief Inspector of Explosives, since 1981; *b* 3 June 1937; *s* of Sidney and Olive Jones; *m* 1961, Janet Ann Collins; one *s* three *d. Educ:* Univ. of Aston in Birmingham (BSc). Professional position in UK explosives industry, 1961-68 and 1972-76; service with Australian Public Service, 1969-71, with UK Civil Service, 1976-. *Publications:* articles in The Chemical Engineer. *Recreations:* bridge, chess, reading. *Address:* HSE Explosives Inspectorate, Baynards House, 1 Chepstow Place, W2. *T:* 01-229 3456.

JONES, Philip (Mark), OBE 1977; Founder and Director, Philip Jones Brass Ensemble, since 1951; *b* 12 March 1928. *Educ:* Royal College of Music (ARCM). Principal Trumpet with Royal Opera House, Royal Philharmonic, London Philharmonic, Philharmonia, New Philharmonia and BBC Symphony Orchestras; Head of Dept of Wind and Percussion, Royal Northern Coll. of Music, 1975-77. FRNCM. *Publications:* Joint Editor, Just Brass series (for Chester Music London). *Recreations:* ski-ing, mountain walking. *Address:* 14 Hamilton Terrace, NW8 9UG. *T:* 01-286 9155.

JONES, Mrs Rachel (Marianne); *b* 4 Aug. 1908; *d* of John Powell Jones Powell, solicitor, Brecon, and Kathleen Mamie Powell; *m* 1935, Very Rev. William Edward Jones (*d* 1974); one *s* three *d. Educ:* Princess Helena Coll.; Bedford Coll., University of London. Subwarden, Time and Talents Settlement, Bermondsey, 1931-32; Member: Bd of Governors, Fairbridge Farm Sch., Western Australia, 1945-49; Council for Wales and Mon, 1959-66; Nat. Governor for Wales of BBC and Chm. of Broadcasting Council for Wales, 1960-65. Member: Governing Body of the Church in Wales, 1953-78; Court and Council of Nat. Museum of Wales, 1962-78; St Fagan's Welsh Folk Museum Cttee, 1978-; Pres., St David's Diocesan Mothers' Union, 1965-70. *Recreations:* music, gardening. *Address:* 59 Sopwell Lane, St Albans, Herts. *T:* St Albans 69810.

JONES, Raymond Edgar; HM Diplomatic Service, retired; *b* 6 June 1919; *s* of Edgar George Jones, Portsmouth; *m* 1942, Joan Mildred Clark; one *s* two *d. Educ:* Portsmouth Northern Grammar Sch. Entered Admiralty service as Clerical Officer, 1936; joined RAF, 1941; commissioned, 1943; returned to Admty as Exec. Officer, 1946; transf. to Foreign Service, 1948; Singapore,

1949; Second Sec., Rome, 1950; Bahrain, 1952; Rio de Janeiro, 1955; Consul, Philadelphia, 1958; FO, 1961; First Sec., Copenhagen, 1963; Consul, Milan, 1965; Toronto (Dir of British Week), 1966; Dep. High Comr, Adelaide, 1967-71; FCO, 1971-76; Consul-Gen., Genoa, 1976-79. *Recreations:* music, gardening. *Address:* 156 Harestone Valley Road, Caterham, Surrey.

JONES, Reginald Ernest, MBE 1942; Chief Scientific Officer, Ministry of Technology, 1965-69, retired; *b* 16 Jan. 1904; *m* 1933, Edith Ernestine Kressig; one *s* one *d. Educ:* Marylebone Gram. Sch.; Imperial Coll. of Science and Technology. MSc, DIC, FIEE. International Standard Electric Corp., 1926-33; GPO, 1933-65 (Asst Engr-in-Chief, 1957). Bronze Star (US), 1943. *Recreations:* music, gardening, walking. *Address:* 22 Links Road, Epsom, Surrey. *T:* Epsom 23625.

JONES, Reginald Victor, CB 1946; CBE 1942; FRS 1965; Professor of Natural Philosophy, University of Aberdeen, 1946-81, now Emeritus; *b* 29 Sept. 1911; *s* of Harold Victor and Alice Margaret Jones; *m* 1940, Vera, *d* of late Charles and Amelia Cain; one *s* two *d. Educ:* Alleyn's; Wadham Coll., Oxford (Exhibitioner; MA, DPhil, 1934; Hon. Fellow, 1968); Balliol Coll., Oxford (Skynner Senior Student in Astronomy, 1934-36; Hon. Fellow 1981). Air Ministry: Scientific Officer, 1936 (seconded to Admiralty, 1938-39); Air Staff, 1939; Asst Dir of Intelligence, 1941, Dir, 1946; Dir of Scientific Intelligence, MoD, 1952-53; Mem., Carriers Panel, 1962-63; Chm., Air Defence Working Party, 1963-64; Scientific Adv. Council, War Office, 1963-66. Chairman: Infra-Red Cttee, Mins of Supply and Aviation, 1950-64; British Transport Commn Res. Adv. Council, 1954-55; Safety in Mines Res. Advisory Bd, 1956-60 (Mem., 1950-56); Electronics Res. Council, Mins of Aviation and Technol., 1964-70. Royal Society: Chm., Paul Fund Cttee, 1962-; a Vice-Pres., 1971-72; Chairman: Inst. of Physics Cttee on Univ. Physics, 1961-63; British Nat. Cttee for History of Science, Medicine and Technol., 1970-78 (Chm., Org. Cttee, Internat. Congress, 1977); President: Crabtree Foundation, 1948; Sect. A, British Assoc., 1971. Also a mem., various cttees on electronics, scientific res., measurement, defence and educn. Rapporteur, European Convention on Human Rights, 1970. Jt Editor, Notes and Records of the Royal Society, 1969-. Hon. Fellow: College of Preceptors, 1978; IREE, 1982. Hon. DSc: Strathclyde, 1969; Kent, 1980; DUniv: York, 1976; Open, 1978; Surrey, 1979; Hon. LLD Bristol, 1979. Baillie of Benachie, 1980. US Medal of Freedom with Silver Palm, 1946; US Medal for Merit, 1947; BOIMA Prize, Inst. of Physics, 1934; Duddell Medal, Physical Soc., 1960; Parsons Medal, 1967; Hartley Medal, Inst. of Measurement and Control, 1972; Mexican Min. of Telecommunications Medal, 1973; Rutherford Medal, USSR, 1977; R. G. Mitchell Medal, 1979; Old Crows Medal, 1980; Hon. Mem., US Air Force, 1982. *Publications:* Most Secret War (The Wizard War, USA, La Guerre Ultra Secrète, France), 1978; Future Conflict and New Technology, 1981; lectures and papers on scientific subjects, defence, educn, engrg, history of science and policy. *Address:* Natural Philosophy Department, University of Aberdeen, Aberdeen AB9 2UE. *T:* Aberdeen 40241; 8 Queens Terrace, Aberdeen AB1 1XL. *T:* Aberdeen 648184. *Clubs:* Athenæum, Special Forces; Royal Northern (Aberdeen).

JONES, Rhona Mary; Chief Nursing Officer, St Bartholomew's Hospital, 1969-74, retired; *b* 7 July 1921; *d* of late Thomas Henry Jones and late Margaret Evelyn King; single. *Educ:* Liverpool; Alder Hey Children's Hosp.; St Mary's Hosp., Paddington. RSCN 1943; SRN 1945; SCM 1948. Post-Registration Training, and Staff Nurse, Queen Charlotte's Hosp., 1946-48; Ward Sister, 1948-50, Departmental Sister, 1950-52, St Mary's Hosp., Paddington; General Duty Nurse, Canada, 1952-53; Asst Matron, Gen. Infirmary, Leeds, 1953-57; Dep. Matron, Royal Free Hosp., London, 1957-59; Matron, Bristol Royal Hosp., 1959-67; Matron and Superintendent of Nursing, St Bartholomew's Hosp., 1968-69. Chm., Bristol Branch, Royal Coll. of Nursing, 1962-65; Member: Standing Nursing Adv. Cttee, Central Health Services Council, 1963-74; Exec. Cttee, Assoc. Nurse Administrators (formerly Assoc. Hosp. Matrons for England and Wales), 1963-74; Area Nurse Trng Cttee, SW Region, 1965-67; NE Metropolitan Area Nurse Training Cttee, 1969-74; E London Group Hosp. Management Cttee, 1969-74. Vice-Pres., Bristol Royal Hosp. Nurses League. *Recreations:* reading, gardening, travel. *Address:* 26 Seaton Drive, Bedford MK40 3BG. *T:* Bedford 65868.

JONES, Air Vice-Marshal Richard Ian, CB 1960; AFC 1948; psa; pfc; *m* 1940, Margaret Elizabeth Wright. *Educ:* Berkhamsted Sch.; Cranwell. Group Captain, 1955; Air Commodore, 1960; Air Vice-Marshal, 1965. Senior Air Staff Officer, Royal Air Force, Germany (Second Tactical Air Force), Command Headquarters, 1959-63; Dir of Flying Training, 1963-64; AOC No 25 Group, RAF Flying Training Command, 1964-67; SASO, Fighter Command, 1967-68; AOC No 11 (Fighter) Gp, Strike Command, 1969-70; retired 1970. *Recreations:* golf, ski-ing. *Club:* Royal Air Force.

JONES, Maj.-Gen. Richard K.; see Keith-Jones.

JONES, (Robert) Gerallt; writer; Staff Tutor, Extra-Mural Department, University College of Wales, Aberystwyth, since 1979; *b* 11 Sept. 1934; *s* of Rev. R. E. Jones and Elizabeth Jones, Nefyn, Wales; *m* 1962, Susan Lloyd Griffith; two *s* one *d. Educ:* Denstone; University of Wales (University Student Pres., 1956-57). Sen. English Master, Sir Thomas Jones Sch., Amlwch, 1957-60; Lectr in Educn, University Coll., Aberystwyth, 1961-65; Prin., Mandeville Teachers' Coll., Jamaica, 1965-67; Warden and Headmaster, Llandovery Coll., 1967-76; Fellow in Creative Writing, Univ. of Wales, 1976-77. Dir, Sgrîn 82, 1981-. Member Gov. Body, Church in Wales, 1959-;

Welsh Acad. (Yr Academi Gymreig), 1959- (Vice-Chm., 1981; Chm., 1982-); Broadcasting Council for Wales; Welsh Arts Council; Univ. Council, Aberystwyth. FRSA. Editor of Impact (the Church in Wales quarterly). *Publications:* Ymysg Y Drain, 1959; Y Foel Fawr, 1960; Cwlwm, 1962; Yn Frawd I'r Eos, 1962; (ed) Fy Nghymru I, 1962; Nadolig Gwyn, 1963; Gwared Y Gwirion, 1966; The Welsh Literary Revival, 1966; Jamaican Landscape, 1969; Cysgodion, 1973; Jamaica, Y Flwyddyn Gyntaf, 1974; (ed) Poetry of Wales 1930-1970, 1975; Bardsey, 1976; Jamaican Interlude, 1977; Triptych, 1978; Teithiau Gerallt, 1978; Pererindota, 1978; Cafflogion, 1979; Murmur Llawer Man, 1980; Dyfal Gerddwyr y Maes (poems), 1981; T. S. Eliot (critisism), 1981. *Recreations:* freelance TV interviewing, cricket, journalism, writing. *Address:* Lerry Dale, Dolybont, Borth, Aberystwyth, Wales.

JONES, Robert Gwilym L.; see Lewis-Jones.

JONES, Robert Hefin, CVO 1969; PhD; Under Secretary, Education Department, Welsh Office, since 1980; *b* 30 June 1932; *s* of late Owen Henry and Elizabeth Jones, Blaenau Ffestiniog. *Educ:* Ysgol Sir Ffestiniog; University Coll. of Wales, Aberystwyth (BSc); University of London (PhD). Asst Master, Whitgift Sch., 1957-63; HM Inspector of Schools (Wales), 1963; seconded to Welsh Office as Sec., Prince of Wales Investiture Cttee, and Personal Asst to the Earl Marshal, 1967; Principal, Welsh Office, 1969, Asst Sec. 1972. *Recreations:* music, reading, cooking. *Address:* 34 The Grange, Llandaff, Cardiff. *T:* Cardiff 564573. *Club:* East India, Devonshire, Sports and Public Schools.

JONES, Brig. Robert Llewellyn J.; see Jephson-Jones.

JONES, Rev. (Robert William) Hugh; Minister, United Reformed Church, Foleshill Road, Coventry, 1978-81, retired; Moderator of the West Midland Province of the United Reformed Church (formerly of the Congregational Church in England and Wales), 1970-78; *b* 6 May 1911; *s* of Evan Hugh Jones and Sarah Elizabeth Salmon; *m* 1st, 1939, Gaynor Eluned Evans (*d* 1974); one *s* one *d* ; 2nd, 1979, Mary Charlotte Pulsford, *widow* of H. E. Pulsford, FIEE. *Educ:* Chester Grammar Sch.; Univs of Wales and Manchester; Lancashire Independent College. BA Wales, History and Philosophy. Ordained, 1939; Congregational Church: Welholme, Grimsby, 1939-45; Muswell Hill, London, 1945-49; Warwick Road, Coventry, 1949-61; Petts Wood, Orpington, 1961-69; President, Congregational Church in England and Wales, 1969-70. Frequent broadcaster, radio and TV; Mem., BBC/ITA Central Religious Adv. Cttee, 1971-75. Guest preacher, USA. *Recreations:* painting, photography. *Address:* 36 Almond Avenue, Leamington Spa, Warwicks. *T:* Leamington Spa 30509.

JONES, Robin Francis McN.; see McNab Jones.

JONES, R(obin) Huws, CBE 1969; Associate Director, Joseph Rowntree Memorial Trust, 1972-76 (Consultant, 1976-78); *b* 1 May 1909; *m* 1944, Enid Mary Horton; one *s* two *d. Educ:* Liverpool Univ. Frances Wood Prizeman, Royal Statistical Society. Lectr, Social Science Dept, Liverpool Univ., 1937-39; Staff Tutor (City of Lincoln) Oxford Univ. Extra-mural Delegacy, 1939-47; Dir of Social Science Courses, University Coll., Swansea, 1948-61; Principal, Nat. Inst. for Social Work Training, 1961-72. Visiting Prof., University of Minnesota, 1964; Heath Clark Lectr, University of London, 1969; Neely Memorial Lectr, Cleveland, O, 1969. Member: Minister of Health's Long Term Study Group, 1965-69; Cttee on Local Authority and Allied Personal Social Services, 1965-68; NE Metropolitan Reg. Hosp. Bd, 1967-72; Central Council for Educn and Training in Social Work, 1971-72; Cttee, King's Fund Centre, 1970-75; Chief Scientist's Cttee, DHSS, 1971-77; Scientific Advr to DHSS and to Welsh Office, 1977-. Mem., Ciba Foundn Cttee on Compensation in Biomedical Research, 1979-80. Chm., Consultative Cttee, The Family Fund; Pres., Internat. Assoc. of Schools of Social Work, 1976 (Hon. Treasurer, 1970-74). Chm., W Cumbria SDP, 1981-. Hon. Fellow, Inst. of Social Welfare. Council Mem., Policy Studies Inst. Vice-Pres., Beacon Hostels. Hon. LLD Wales, 1982. *Publications:* The Doctor and the Social Services, 1971; contributions to journals. *Recreation:* gardening. *Address:* Lambfold, High Lorton, Cockermouth, Cumbria. *T:* Lorton 619.

JONES, Brigadier Ronald M.; see Montague-Jones.

JONES, Group Captain Royden Anthony; RAF retired; Regional Chairman of Industrial Tribunals, London (Central) Region, since 1975; *b* 11 June 1925; *s* of Daniel Richard Glyndwr Jones and Hilda Margaret Jones (*née* Carruthers); *m* 1st, 1948, Krystyna Emilia Kumor (decd); one *s* ; 2nd, 1955, Peggy Elizabeth Martin; one *s. Educ:* Torquay Grammar Sch. Trooper, Household Cavalry, 1943; RMC, Sandhurst, 1944; Captain, Arab Legion armoured car squadron, 1945-48. Qualified as solicitor, 1949; joined RAF Legal Services as prosecuting officer, 1950; RAF Staff Coll., 1961; served as Dep. Dir of Legal Services (RAF), in Cyprus and Germany, retiring as Gp Captain, 1975. *Publication:* Manual of Law for Kenya Armed Forces, 1971. *Recreations:* country pursuits, reading, house maintenance, photography. *Address:* The Ferrers, 130 The Avenue, Sunbury-on-Thames, Middx. *T:* Sunbury 83484. *Club:* Royal Air Force.

JONES, Sir Samuel (Owen), Kt 1966; FIREE (Aust.); FIE Aust.; Chairman, Standard Telephones & Cables Pty Ltd, 1968-76 (Managing Director, 1961-69); Chairman: Concrete Industries (Monier) Ltd, 1969-76; Austral Standard Cables Pty Ltd, 1967-69 and 1972-75; Export Finance and Insurance

Corporation, 1975-77; Director, Overseas Corporation (Australia) Ltd, 1969-75; *b* 20 Aug. 1905; *s* of late John Henry Jones and Eliza Jones (*née* Davies); *m* 1932, Jean, *d* of late J. W. Sinclair; two *d*. *Educ:* Warracknabeal High Sch.; University of Melbourne. Engineering Branch, PMG's Dept, 1927-39. Lt-Col comdg Divisional Signal Unit, AIF abroad, 1939-41; CSO Aust. Home Forces, 1941-42; Dir, Radio and Signal Supplies, Min. of Munitions, 1942-45. Technical Manager, Philips Electrical Industries Pty Ltd, 1945-50, Tech. Dir, 1950-61; Chairman: Telecommunication Co. of Aust., 1956-61; Australian Telecommunications Develt Assoc., 1967-70 (Mem., 1963-75); Consultative Council, Export Payments Insurance Corp, 1970-75; Director: Television Equipment Pty Ltd, 1960-61; Cannon Electric (Australia) Pty Ltd, 1964-68. National Pres., Aust. Inst. of Management, 1968-70; Councillor, Chamber of Manufactures of NSW, 1968-72; Member: Govt's Electronics and Telecommunications Industry Adv. Cttee, 1955-72; Export Develt Council, 1969-74; Council, Macquarie Univ., 1969-74; Council, Nat. Library of Australia, 1971-74; Australian Univs Commn, 1972-75. *Publications:* several technical articles. *Recreations:* bowls, fishing. *Address:* Apartment 11, 321 Edgecliff Road, Woollahra, NSW 2025, Australia; Mummuga Lodge, Dalmeny, NSW 2546. *Clubs:* Union (Sydney); Naval and Military (Melbourne).

JONES, Sir Simon (Warley Frederick) Benton, 4th Bt *cr* 1919; *b* 11 Sept. 1941; *o s* of Sir Peter Fawcett Benton Jones, 3rd Bt, OBE, and Nancy (*d* 1974), *d* of late Warley Pickering; *S* father, 1972; *m* 1966, Margaret Fiona, *d* of David Rutherford Dickson; three *s* two *d*. *Educ:* Eton; Trinity College, Cambridge (MA). JP for Lincolnshire (parts of Kesteven), 1971; High Sheriff, Lincs, 1977. *Heir: s* James Peter Martin Benton Jones, *b* 1 Jan. 1973. *Address:* Irnham Hall, Grantham, Lincs. *T:* Corby Glen 212; Sopley, Christchurch, Dorset.

JONES, Stephen Barry; BSc (Econ); MP (Lab) Flint East, since 1970; *b* 1938; *s* of Stephen Jones and late Grace Jones, Mancot, Flintshire; *m* Janet Jones (*née* Davies); one *s* PPS to Rt Hon. Denis Healey, 1972-74; Parly Under-Sec. of State for Wales, 1974-79; Opposition spokesman on employment, 1980-. *Address:* 30 Paper Mill Lane, Oakenholt, Flint. *T:* Flint 3430; 105 Hawkins House, Dolphin Square, SW1V 3NS. *T:* 01-834 7786. *Club:* Connah's Quay Labour Party.

JONES, S(tuart) Lloyd; *b* 26 Aug. 1917; *s* of Hugh and Edna Lloyd Jones, Liverpool; *m* 1942, Pamela Mary Hamilton-Williams, Heswall; one *s* three *d*. *Educ:* Rydal Sch.; Univ. of Liverpool. Solicitor, 1940; Dep. Town Clerk, Nottingham, 1950-53; Town Clerk of Plymouth, 1953-70; Chief Exec. Officer and Town Clerk of Cardiff, 1970-74; Chm., Welsh Health Technical Services Orgn, 1973-76. Chief Counting Officer, Welsh Referendum, 1979. US State Dept Foreign Leader Scholarship, 1962. One of Advisers to Minister of Housing and Local Govt on Amalgamation of London Boroughs, 1962; Indep. Inspector, extension of Stevenage New Town, 1964; Member: Adv. Cttee on Urban Transport Manpower, 1967-69; Cttee on Public Participation in Planning, 1969; PM's Cttee on Local Govt Rules of Conduct, 1973-74. Pres., Soc. of Town Clerks, 1972. Chm. of Governors, Plymouth Polytechnic. Distinguished Services Award, Internat. City Management Assoc., 1976. Pres., Dittisham United FC, 1979-. *Recreations:* sailing, bookbinding. *Address:* High Dolphin, Dittisham, South Devon. *Club:* Royal Western Yacht Club of England (Plymouth).

JONES, Sydney, CBE 1971; PhD; FEng; Chairman, Conformable Wheel Co., since 1981; independent consultant; Member of Board, British Railways, 1965-76, part-time, 1975-76 (Director of Research, BR Board, 1962-65); Chairman, Computer Systems and Electronics Requirement Board, Department of Industry, 1975-78; *b* 18 June 1911; *s* of John Daniel Jones and Margaret Ann (*née* Evans); *m* 1938, Winifred Mary (*née* Boulton); two *s* one *d*. *Educ:* Cyfarthfa Castle Grammar Sch.; Cardiff Technical Coll.; Cardiff Univ. Coll.; Birmingham Univ. BSc 1st cl. hons (London) 1932; PhD (London) 1951. General Electric Co., Witton, 1933-36; teaching in Birmingham, 1936-40; Scientific Civil Service at HQ, RRE, Malvern, and RAE, Farnborough, 1940-58; Dir of Applications Research, Central Electricity Generating Board, 1958-61; Technical Dir, R. B. Pullin, Ltd 1961-62. Chm., SIRA Inst. Ltd, 1970-78. Chm., Transport Adv. Cttee, Transport and Road Res. Lab., 1972-77; Independent Consultant, Ground Transport Technology, 1978. FIEE 1960; FIMechE 1965; FCIT 1971; Fellow, Fellowship of Engineering, 1977. Hon. DSc City, 1977. *Publications:* Introductory Applied Science, 1942; papers on automatic control. *Recreations:* gardening, wine, photography, house design. *Address:* Cornerstones, Back Lane, Malvern, Worcs WR14 2HJ. *T:* Malvern 2566. *Club:* Athenæum.

JONES, Sydney T.; *see* Tapper-Jones.

JONES, Terence Leavesley; Under-Secretary, Department of the Environment, since 1974; *b* 24 May 1926; *s* of late Reginald Arthur Jones and Grace Jones; *m* 1966, Barbara Hall; one *s*. *Educ:* Nottingham High Sch.; Jesus Coll., Cambridge (MA). RNVR, 1944-46 (Sub-Lt). Asst Inspector of Ancient Monuments, Min. of Works, 1949; Principal, 1957; Sec., Historic Buildings Council for England, 1961-67; Asst Sec., 1967; on loan to Housing Corp., 1979-81. *Recreations:* music, archæology. *Address:* 6 Broughton Gardens, Highgate, N6 5RS. *T:* 01-348 3144. *Club:* Athenæum.

JONES, Thomas; *see* Jones, Tom.

JONES, Thomas E.; *see* Elder-Jones.

JONES, Thomas Glanville; a Recorder of the Crown Court, since 1972; *b* 10 May 1931; *s* of late Evan James and Margaret Olive Jones; Welsh; *m* 1964, Valma Shirley Jones; three *s*. *Educ:* St Clement Dane's Grammar Sch.; University Coll., London (LLB). Called to Bar, 1958. Sec., Swansea Law Library Assoc., 1963; Exec. Mem., Swansea Festival of Music and the Arts, 1967; Chm., Guild for Promotion of Welsh Music, 1970; Chm., Jt Professional Cttees of Swansea Local Bar and Swansea Law Soc. and W. Wales Law Soc.; Mem., Grand Theatre Trust. *Recreations:* Welsh culture, Rugby, reading, music, poetry, gardening. *Address:* Angel Chambers, 94 Walter Road, Swansea SA1 5QA. *T:* Swansea 56123/4; Gelligron, 12 Eastcliff, Southgate, Swansea SA3 2AS. *T:* Bishopston 3118. *Club:* Ffynone (Swansea).

JONES, (Thomas) Mervyn, CBE 1961; Chairman, Civic Trust for Wales, since 1964; *b* 2 March 1910; *s* of late Rev. Dr Richard Jones and Violet Jones, Llandinam; *m* 1st (marr. diss. 1960); one *s* one *d* ; 2nd, 1960, Margaret, *d* of Ernest E. Cashmore, Newport; one *s* one *d*. *Educ:* Newtown Co. Sch.; University Coll. of Wales, Aberystwyth (LLB); Trinity Hall, Cambridge (MA, LLM). Pres. Trinity Hall Law Soc., 1950. Asst Solicitor, Newport Corporation, Town Clerk, 1948; Chairman: Wales Gas Bd, 1948-70; Wales Tourist Bd, 1970-76; Wales Cttee, European Architectural Heritage Year (EAHY), 1975; Trustee, Welsh National Opera Company; Member: Ashby Cttee on Adult Education, 1953-54; Tucker Cttee on Proceedings before Examining Justices, 1957-58. Member: Council, University of Wales; Council, UWIST; Bd of Governors, Christ Coll., Brecon. Pres., Industrial Assoc., Wales and Mon, 1959-60. FBIM; Hon. FSIAD. *Publications:* Planning Law and the Use of Property; Requisitioned Land and War Works Act, 1945; various titles and articles in Local Govt books and journals. *Recreations:* playing at golf, helping to keep Wales beautiful. *Address:* Erw Hir, 38 Fairwater Road, Llandaff, Cardiff. *T:* Cardiff 562070. *Clubs:* United Oxford & Cambridge University; Cardiff and County (Cardiff).

JONES, (Thomas) Philip, CB 1978; Deputy Secretary, Department of Energy, since 1976; *b* 13 July 1931; *s* of William Ernest Jones and Mary Elizabeth Jones; *m* 1955, Mary Phillips; two *s*. *Educ:* Cowbridge Grammar Sch.; Jesus Coll., Oxford (BA). 2nd Lieut, Royal Artillery, 1953-55; Asst Principal, Min. of Supply, 1955; Principal Min. of Aviation, 1959; on loan to HM Treasury, 1964-66; Principal Private Sec. to Minister of Aviation, 1966-67; Asst Sec., Min. of Technology, subseq. Min. of Aviation Supply, 1967-71; Under Secretary, DTI, 1971; Under Sec., Dept of Energy, 1974. Mem., British Nat. Oil Corpn, 1980-. *Recreations:* squash, reading. *Address:* 12 Broomwater West, Teddington, Middx. *T:* 01-977 6336.

JONES, Tom, CBE 1974 (OBE 1962); JP; Regional Secretary for Wales, Transport and General Workers' Union, 1969-73, retired (N Wales and Border Counties, 1953); Chairman, Appeals Tribunal North Wales, NHS Staff Commission, 1974-81; Member of Industrial Tribunal for North Wales and North West England, 1975-81; *b* 13 Oct. 1908; Welsh parents, father coalminer; *m* 1942, Rosa Jones (*née* Thomas); two *s* two *d*. *Educ:* Elem. Sch., Rhos, Wrexham; WEA Studies, Summer Schools. Coalminer, 1922-36 (having left sch. aged 14). Soldier, Spanish Republican Army (Internat. Bde), 1937-38 (captured by Franco Forces, 1938; PoW, 1940; sentenced to death by Franco Authorities, sentence commuted to 30 years imprisonment; released following representations by British Govt which involved a Trade Agreement; Knight of Order of Loyalty, Spanish Republic (Spanish Govt in Exile) 1974). Worked in Chem. Industry, 1941-44; became full-time Union Official of T&GWU, 1945; Hon. Sec., RAC of N Wales (TUC) for 20 years, retired. Member: Welsh Economic Council; Welsh Council, to 1979 (former Vice-Chm.); Merseyside and N Wales Electricity Bd, 1976-80; Court of Governors, Univ. of Wales; Prince of Wales Cttee; Treasurer, N Wales WEA; Governor, Coleg Harlech (Vice-Chm., 1980-); Past Member: Welsh Industrial Estates Corp.; Welsh Bd for Industry. JP Flint, 1955. *Recreations:* reading, do-it-yourself hobbies, extra-mural activities. *Address:* 2 Blackbrook Avenue, Hawarden, Deeside, Clwyd. *T:* Hawarden 532365.

JONES, Tom, OBE 1978; FRICS; JP; Senior Partner/Consultant, Tom Parry & Co., Chartered Surveyors, Portmadoc, since 1976 (Principal, 1963-76); *b* 4 Sept. 1910; *m* 1934, Ethel Jane Edwards; three *s* two *d*. *Educ:* Bala Grammar Sch. FRICS 1963. Merioneth County Sec., NFU, 1946-53; Gen. Man., Farmers Marts Ltd, 1953-63. Member: Merioneth CC, 1953-74 (Chm., 1965-66); Gwynedd CC, 1974- (Chm., 1975-76). JP Gwynedd, 1953; Chm., Bala Bench of Magistrates, 1972-80. Chm., Welsh Counties Cttee, 1977-78; Pres., Welsh Agric. Organisation Soc., 1978-. Conductor, Godre'r Aran Male Choir (Pres., 1949-74). Hon. MA Wales, 1978. *Recreation:* music. *Address:* Godre'r Aran, Llanuwchllyn, Bala, Gwynedd LL23 7UB. *T:* Llanuwchllyn 687. *Club:* Farmers'.

JONES, Sir Trevor; *see* Jones, Sir O. T.

JONES, Rt. Hon. (Trevor) Alec; PC 1979; MP (Lab) Rhondda, since 1974 (Rhondda West, March 1967-1974); *b* 12 Aug. 1924; *m* 1950, Mildred M. Evans; one *s*. *Educ:* Porth County Grammar Sch.; Bangor Normal Training Coll. Schoolteacher from 1949. PPS to Minister of Defence for Equipment, 1968-70, to Minister of State, DHSS, 1974; Parliamentary Under-Secretary of State: DHSS, 1974-75; Welsh Office, 1975-79; Labour Party Front Bench Spokesman on Welsh Affairs, 1979-. Sponsored Divorce Reform Act, 1969.

Address: 58 Kenry Street, Tonypandy, Rhondda, Wales. *T:* Tonypandy 433472. *Club:* Ystrad Labour (Rhondda).

JONES, Vera June, (Mrs Ernest Brynmor Jones); *see* Di Palma, V. J.

JONES, Wilfred, CMG 1982; HM Diplomatic Service; High Commissioner to Botswana, since 1981; *b* 29 Nov. 1926. Joined Foreign Office, 1949; served in Tamsui, Jedda, Brussels, Athens and FCO, 1950-66; First Sec. (Admin), Canberra, 1966-68; FCO, 1968-71; Copenhagen, 1971-74, Blantyre, 1974-75; Lilongwe, 1975-77; FCO, 1977-81. *Address:* c/o Foreign and Commonwealth Office, SW1.

JONES, William Armand Thomas Tristan G.; *see* Garel-Jones.

JONES, Sir (William) Elwyn (Edwards), Kt 1978; *b* 1904; *s* of the Rev. Robert William Jones and Elizabeth Jane Jones, Welsh Methodist Minister; *m* 1936, Dydd, *d* of Rev. E. Tegla Davies; one *s* two *d*. *Educ:* Bootle Secondary Sch.; Festiniog County Sch.; University of Wales. BA (Wales), LLB (London). Admitted Solicitor, 1927; Clerk to the Justices, Bangor Div., Caernarvonshire, 1934. Town Clerk, Bangor, 1939-69. MP (Lab) Conway Div. of Caernarvonshire, 1950-51. Member: Nat. Parks Commn, 1966-68, Countryside Commn, 1968-71; Council and Court of Governors (Vice-Pres.), and Treasurer, University Coll. of N Wales; Court of Governors, Univ. of Wales. Hon. LLD Wales, 1979. CC Caernarvonshire, 1948-69. *Publications:* Press articles in Welsh and English. *Recreation:* walking. *Address:* 23 Glyngarth Court, Glyngarth, Menai Bridge, Gwynedd, N Wales. *T:* Menai Bridge 913422.

JONES, Sir (William) Emrys, Kt 1971; BSc; Principal, Royal Agricultural College, Cirencester, 1973-78, now Principal Emeritus; *b* 6 July 1915; *s* of late William Jones and Mary Ann (*née* Morgan); *m* 1938, Megan Ann Morgan (marr. diss., 1966); three *s*; *m* 1967, Gwyneth George. *Educ:* Llandovery Gram. Sch.; University Coll. of Wales, Aberystwyth. Agricultural Instr, Gloucester CC, 1940-46; Provincial Grassland Adv. Officer, NAAS, Bristol, 1946-50; County Agricultural Officer, Gloucester, 1950-54; Dep. Dir, 1954-57, Dir 1957-59, NAAS, Wales; Sen. Advisory Officer, NAAS, 1959-61; Dir, 1961-66; Dir-Gen., Agricultural Develt and Adv. Service (formerly Chief Agricl Advr), MAFF, 1967-73. Mem., Adv. Council for Agriculture and Horticulture in England and Wales, 1973-79. Independent Chm., Nat. Cattle Breeders' Assoc., 1976-79. Dir, North and East Midlands Reg. Bd, Lloyds Bank, 1978-. Hon. LLD Wales, 1973; Hon. DSc Bath, 1975. *Recreations:* golf, shooting. *Address:* The Draey, 18 St Mary's Park, Louth, Lincs. *Club:* Farmers'.

JONES, Sir William Lloyd M.; *see* Mars-Jones.

JONES, Wyn; *see* Jones, G. W.

JONES, Wynn Normington H., *see* Hugh-Jones.

JONES-PARRY, Sir Ernest, Kt 1978; *b* 16 July 1908; *o s* of late John Parry and Charlotte Jones, Rhuddlan; *m* 1938, Mary Powell; two *s*. *Educ:* St Asaph; University of Wales; University of London. MA (Wales) 1932; PhD (London) 1934; FRHistS. Lecturer in History, University Coll. of Wales, 1935-40; Ministry of Food, 1941; Treasury, 1946-47; Asst Sec., Ministry of Food, 1948-57; Under Sec., 1957; Dir of Establishments, Ministry of Agriculture, Fisheries and Food, 1957-61. Exec. Director: Internat. Sugar Council, 1965-68; Internat. Sugar Orgn, 1969-78. *Publications:* The Spanish Marriages, 1841-46, 1936; The Correspondence of Lord Aberdeen and Princess Lieven, 1832-1854 (2 vols), 1938-39; articles and reviews in History and English Historical Review. *Recreations:* reading, watching cricket. *Address:* 3 Sussex Mansions, Old Brompton Road, SW7. *T:* 01-589 7979. *Club:* Athenæum.

JONES-WILLIAMS, Dafydd Wyn, OBE 1970; MC 1942; TD 1954; DL; Commissioner for Local Administration for Wales (Local Ombudsman), 1974-79; *b* 13 July 1916; *s* of late J. Jones-Williams, Dolgellau; *m* 1945, Rosemary Sally, *e d* of late A. E. Councell, Blaenau Hall, Rhydymain; two *d*. *Educ:* Dolgellau Grammar Sch.; UCW Aberystwyth (LLB). Served 1939-45 with HAC and X Royal Hussars (Western Desert). Formerly comdg 446 (Royal Welch) AB, LAA Regt, RA (TA). Solicitor, 1939. Clerk of County Council, Clerk of Peace, and Clerk to Lieutenancy, Merioneth, 1954-70; Circuit Administrator, Wales and Chester Circuit, 1970-74. Member: Hughes-Parry Cttee on Legal Status of Welsh Language, 1963-65; Lord Chancellor's Adv. Cttee on Trng of Magistrates, 1974-81; Council on Tribunals, 1980-; BBC Gen. Adv. Council, 1979-. Formerly: Mem., Nature Conservancy (Chm., Cttee for Wales); Mem., Nat. Broadcasting Council for Wales; Chm., Merioneth and Montgomeryshire T&AFA. DL Merioneth, 1958. *Recreation:* golf. *Address:* Bryncoedifor, Rhydymain, near Dolgellau, Gwynedd. *T:* Rhydymain 635. *Clubs:* Army and Navy; Royal St Davids Golf.

JONZEN, Mrs Karin, FRBS; sculptor; *b* London (Swedish parents), 22 Dec. 1914; *d* of U. Löwenadler and G. Munck av Fulkila; *m* 1944, Basil Jonzen (*d* 1967); one *s*; *m* 1972, Åke Sucksdorff. Studied Slade Sch., 1933; Slade Dipl. and Scholarship, 1937; studied Royal Academy, Stockholm, 1939. Mem. Accad. delle Arte e Lavore, Italy, 1980 (Gold Medal, 1980); Diploma of Merit, Università delle Arti, 1982. *Works in municipal museums and art galleries:*

V&A Museum, Bradford, Brighton, Glasgow, Southend, Liverpool, Melbourne, Andrew White Museum, Cornell Univ., USA. *Works commissioned by:* Arts Council (reclining figure), 1950; Festival of Britain for sports pavilion (standing figure), 1950; Modern Schs in Leics and Hertford, 1953 and Cardiff, 1954 (animals and figures in terracotta and stone); Selwyn Coll. Chapel, Cambridge (over-life size ascension group, bronze), 1956; St Michael's Church, Golders Green (carving on exterior), 1959; Guildford Cathedral (carving on exterior), 1961; WHO HQ, New Delhi (life size bronze torso), 1963 (gift of British Govt); St Mary le Bow, Cheapside (Madonna and child), 1969; City of London Corp. for London Wall site (life size bronze figure), 1971; Guildhall Forecourt (over-life size bronze group), 1972; Swedish Church, Marylebone (three-quarter life size Pietà, bronze resin), 1975; Action Research (annual trophy), 1979; Cadogan Estate (figure of young girl for Sloane Gardens), 1981. *Works exhibited by invitation:* Battersea Park open air exhibns, 1948-51; Tate Gall., 1957-59; City of London Festival, 1968; (one man exhibn) Fieldbourne Gall., London, 1974. Lecturer Camden Arts Centre, 1968-72; extra mural lectures in art appreciation, London Univ., 1965-71. *Portrait busts include:* Sir Alan Herbert, Lord Constantine, Dame Ninette de Valois (purchased by V&A Mus., 1980), Sir Hugh Casson, Donald Tretford, Sir Monty Finniston. *Relevant publication:* Karin Jonzen: sculptor, introd. Carel Weight, foreword by Norman St John-Stevas, 1976. *Recreation:* music. *Address:* The Studio, 6A Gunter Grove, SW10.

JOOSTE, Gerhardus Petrus; retired; South African Secretary for External Affairs, 1956-66 (Secretary for Foreign Affairs, 1961); retired, 1966; Special Adviser (part-time) on Foreign Affairs to Prime Minister and Minister of Foreign Affairs, 1966-68; Chairman, State Procurement Board, 1968-71; *b* 5 May 1904; *s* of Nicolaas Jooste and Sofie Jooste (*née* Visser); *m* 1st, 1934, Anna van Zyl van der Merwe (*d* 1974); one *s* one *d*; 2nd, 1981, Jemima Neveling (*née* Steyn). *Educ:* Primary and Secondary Schs, Winburg and Kroonstad; Rondebosch Boys High; Grey Coll., Bloemfontein; Pretoria Univ. Entered Union Public Service, 1924; Priv. Sec. to Hon. N. C. Havenga, Minister of Finance, 1929; Dept of External Affairs, 1934; Legation Sec. and Chargé d'Affaires ad interim, Brussels, 1937-40; Chargé d'Affaires to Belgian Government-in-Exile, 1940-41; transf. to Dept of External Affairs, Pretoria, as Head of Economic Div., 1941-46; Head of Political and Diplomatic Div. of the Dept, 1946-49; Ambassador to US and Permanent Delegate to UN, 1949-54; High Commissioner of the Union of South Africa in London, 1954-56. Mem., Commn of Enquiry regarding Water Matters, 1966-; Mem. (ex officio), Atomic Energy Bd, 1956-66. Mem., South African Acad. of Science and Arts. *Recreation:* bowls. *Address:* 851 Government Avenue, Arcadia, Pretoria, South Africa.

JOPE, Prof. Edward Martyn, FBA 1965; FSA 1946; MRIA 1973; Professor of Archæology, The Queen's University of Belfast, 1963-81; Visiting Professor in Archaeological Sciences, University of Bradford, 1974-81; *b* 28 Dec. 1915; *s* of Edward Mallet Jope and Frances Margaret (née Chapman); *m* 1941, Margaret Halliday; no *c*. *Educ:* Kingswood Sch., Bath; Oriel Coll., Oxford. Staff of Royal Commission on Ancient Monuments (Wales), 1938; Biochemist, Nuffield and MRC Grants, 1940; Queen's Univ., Belfast: Lectr in Archæology, 1949; Reader, 1954. Member: Ancient Monuments Adv. Coun. (NI), 1950; Royal Commission on Ancient Monuments (Wales), 1963-; Sci.-based Archaeology Cttee, SRC, 1976-; Ancient Monuments Bd (England), 1980-; Pres. Section H, British Assoc., 1965. Rhys Res. Fellow and Vis. Sen. Res. Fellow, Jesus Coll., Oxford, 1977-78. Hon. DSc Bradford, 1980. *Publications:* Early Celtic Art in the British Isles, 1977; (ed) Studies in Building History, 1961; (ed and contrib.) Archaeological Survey of Co. Down, 1966; papers in Biochem. Jl, Proc. RSocMed, Phil. Trans Royal Soc., Spectrochemica Acta, Trans Faraday Soc., Proc. Prehistoric Soc., Antiquaries' Jl, Medieval Archæology, Oxoniensia, Ulster Jl of Archæology, Proc. Soc. of Antiquaries of Scotland, etc. *Recreations:* music, travel. *Address:* 1 Chalfont Road, Oxford.

JOPLING, Rt. Hon. (Thomas) Michael; PC 1979; MP (C) Westmorland since 1964; Parliamentary Secretary to HM Treasury, and Chief Whip, since 1979; farmer; *b* 10 Dec. 1930; *s* of Mark Bellerby Jopling, Masham, Yorks; *m* 1958, Gail, *d* of Ernest Dickinson, Harrogate; two *s*. *Educ:* Cheltenham Coll.; King's Coll., Newcastle upon Tyne (BSc Agric). Mem., Thirsk Rural District Council, 1958-64; contested Wakefield (C), 1959; Mem. National Council, National Farmers' Union, 1962-64. Jt Sec., Cons. Party Agric. Cttee, 1966-70; PPS to Minister of Agriculture, 1970-71; an Asst Govt Whip, 1971-73; a Lord Comr, HM Treasury, 1973-74; an Opposition Whip, March-June 1974; an opposition spokesman on agriculture, 1974-75, 1976-79; Shadow Minister of Agriculture, 1975-76. Mem., UK Exec., Commonwealth Parly Assoc., 1974- (Vice Chm., 1977-79). *Address:* Ainderby Hall, Thirsk, North Yorks. *T:* Thirsk 567224; Pine Rigg, Windermere, Cumbria. *T:* Windermere 2590. *Clubs:* Carlton, St Stephen's Constitutional, Beefsteak, Buck's.

JORDAN, David Harold, CMG 1975; MBE 1962; *b* Sunderland, 27 Oct. 1924; *er s* of late H. G. Jordan, OBE, and Gwendolyn Rees; *m* 1st, 1951, Lorna Mary Holland (marr. diss.), *er d* of late W. R. Harvey; three *s* one *d*; 2nd, 1971, Penelope Amanda, *d* of Lt-Col B. L. J. Davy, OBE, TD; one *d*. *Educ:* Roundhay Sch., Leeds; Berkhamsted; Magdalen Coll., Oxford (1st Cl. Chinese), MA 1956. 9th Gurkha Rifles, Indian Army, 1943-47. Colonial Administrative Service (Hong Kong), 1951; Asst Sec. for Chinese Affairs, 1952-55; Colonial Secretariat, 1956-68: Asst Sec., 1956-60; jssc 1960; Defence

Sec., 1961-66; Dep. Dir, Commerce and Industry, 1968-70; Dep. Economic Sec., 1970-71; Dep. Financial Sec., 1971-72; Dir of Commerce and Industry, later Trade, Industry and Customs, and MLC, Hong Kong, 1972-79. *Address:* The Lower Farm, Drayton Parslow, Milton Keynes, Bucks MK17 0JS. *T:* Mursley 688. *Clubs:* Hong Kong; Royal Hong Kong Jockey.

JORDAN, Douglas Arthur, CMG 1977; Commissioner of Customs and Controls, Trade, Industry and Customs Department, Hong Kong, since 1979 (Deputy Commissioner, 1977-79); *b* 28 Sept. 1918; *s* of late Arthur Jordan and Elizabeth Jordan; *m* 1st, 1940, Violet Nancy (*née* Houston); one *d* ; 2nd, 1970, Constance Dorothy (*née* Wallis). *Educ:* East Ham Grammar Sch., London. HM Customs and Excise: Officer, 1938; Surveyor, 1953; Inspector, 1960; Asst Collector, Manchester and London, 1962-68; Sen. Inspector, 1968-69; Chief Investigation Officer, 1969-77. Freeman, City of London, 1964. *Recreations:* golf, music. *Address:* Trade, Industry and Customs Department, Room 1401, 14th floor, Ocean Centre, Canton Road, Kowloon, Hong Kong; 10 Crouchmans Close, Sydenham Hill, SE26. *T:* 01-670 9638. *Clubs:* Wig and Pen, Press; World Trade Centre (Hong Kong), Hong Kong Cricket.

JORDAN, Henry; Under-Secretary, Department of Education and Science, 1973-75; *b* 1919; *s* of late Henry Jordan and Mary Ann Jordan (*née* Shields); *m* 1946, Huguette Yvonne Rayée; one *s. Educ:* St Patrick's High Sch., Dumbarton. Served War, RA, 1939-46. Home Civil Service, Post Office, 1936; Foreign Office, 1947; Central Land Board and War Damage Commn, 1949; Min. (later Dept) of Educn, 1957. *Address:* 72 Shearman Road, Lee Park, Blackheath, SE3 9HX. *T:* 01-318 0906.

JORDAN, Rev. Preb. Hugh; Curate of St James's, Hereford, and teaching at Hereford High School, 1969-72, retired; a Prebendary of St Paul's Cathedral, 1963-69, now Emeritus; *b* 29 Dec. 1906; *m* 1936, Elizabeth Hamilton Lamb, Dublin; two *s* one *d. Educ:* Trinity Coll., Dublin; Royal School, Cavan, Eire. School Teacher, 1924-29; Curate, St Kevin's Church, Dublin, 1932-34; Gen. Sec. City of Dublin YMCA, 1934-39; Vicar: St Luke's, Eccleston, St Helens, Lancs, 1939-45; Penn Fields, Wolverhampton, 1945-49; Redland, Bristol (and Lecturer and Tutor, Tyndale Hall, Bristol), 1949-56; Principal, London Coll. of Divinity, 1956-69. *Publication:* Born Under a Lucky Star, 1977. *Recreations:* formerly: hockey, soccer, cricket, tennis, athletics and boxing. *Address:* 4 Market Square, Newcastle Emlyn, Dyfed, West Wales. *T:* Newcastle Emlyn 710024.

JORDAN, Air Marshal Sir Richard Bowen, KCB 1956 (CB 1947); DFC 1941; psa; RAF retired; *b* 7 Feb. 1902; *s* of late A. O. Jordan, Besford Ct, Worcestershire; *m* 1932, F. M. M. Haines; one *d. Educ:* Marlborough Coll.; RAF Coll., Cranwell. Joined RAF, 1921. Late AOC the RAF in India and Pakistan; Air Officer Commanding RAF Gibraltar, 1948-49; Commandant of the Royal Observer Corps, 1949-51; ADC to the King, 1949-51; Air Officer Commanding No. 25 Group, 1951-53; Dir-Gen. of Organisation, Air Ministry, 1953-55; Air Officer Commanding-in-Chief, Maintenance Command, 1956-58, retd. *Address:* The Herons, Abbots Ann, near Andover, Hants.

JORDAN-MOSS, Norman, CB 1972; CMG 1965; Director: Crown Life Assurance Company Ltd, since 1980; Crown Life Pensions, since 1980; Crown Life Management Services, since 1980; 1928 Investment Trust Ltd, since 1981; Consultant to Hambros Bank Ltd, since 1980; *b* 5 Feb. 1920; *o s* of Arthur Moss and Ellen Jordan Round; *m* 1st, 1965, Kathleen Lusmore (*d* 1974); one *s* one *d* ; 2nd, 1976, Philippa Rands; one *d. Educ:* Manchester Gram. Sch.; St John's Coll., Cambridge (MA). Ministry of Economic Warfare, 1940-44; HM Treasury, 1944-71; Asst Representative of HM Treas. in Middle East, 1945-48; Principal, 1948; First Sec. (Econ.), Belgrade, 1952-55; Financial Counsellor, Washington, 1956-60; Counsellor, UK Permanent Delegation to OECD, Paris, 1963-66; Asst Sec., HM Treasury, 1956-68, Under-Sec., 1968-71, Dep. Sec., 1976-80; Dep. Under-Sec. of State, DHSS, 1971-76. *Recreations:* music, theatre. *Address:* Milton Way, Westcott, Dorking, Surrey. *Club:* Travellers'.

JORISCH, Mrs Robert; *see* Lofts, Norah.

JOSCELYNE, Richard Patrick; Controller, Overseas Division B, British Council, since 1980; *b* 19 June 1934; *s* of Patrick C. Joscelyne and Rosalind Whitcombe; *m* 1961, Vera Lucia Mello; one *s* one *d. Educ:* Bryanston; Queens' Coll., Cambridge. Teaching posts in France, Brazil and Britain, 1958-62. British Council: Montevideo, 1962; Moscow, 1967; Madrid, 1969; Director, North and Latin America Dept, 1973; Representative, Sri Lanka, 1977. *Address:* c/o British Council, 10 Spring Gardens, SW1A 2BN. *T:* 01-930 8466.

JOSEPH, Sir (Herbert) Leslie, Kt 1952; DL; Vice-Chairman, Trust Houses Forte Ltd, 1970-80; *b* 4 Jan. 1908; *s* of David Ernest and Florence Joseph; *m* 1934, Emily Irene, *d* of Dr Patrick Julian Murphy, Cwmbach, Aberdare; two *d. Educ:* The King's Sch. Canterbury. Commissioned RE, 1940-46. Pres., Assoc. Amusement Parks Proprietors of Great Britain; Chairman: National Amusements Council, 1950-51; Amusement Caterers' Assoc., 1953, 1954; Housing Production Board for Wales, 1952-53. High Sheriff, 1975-76, DL 1982, Mid Glamorgan. Governor, King's Sch., Canterbury, 1968-. *Recreations:* horticulture and ceramics. *Address:* Coedargraig, Newton, Porthcawl, Mid Glamorganshire. *T:* Porthcawl 2610.

JOSEPH, Rt. Hon. Sir Keith (Sinjohn), 2nd Bt, *cr* 1943; PC 1962; MP (C) Leeds North-East since Feb. 1956; Secretary of State for Education and Science, since 1981; *b* 17 Jan. 1918; *o c* of Sir Samuel George Joseph, 1st Baronet, and Edna Cicely (*d* 1981), *yr d* of late P. A. S. Phillips, Portland Place, W1; *S* father 1944; *m* 1951, Hellen Louise (separated 1978), *yr d* of Sigmar Guggenheimer, NY; one *s* three *d. Educ:* Harrow; Magdalen Coll., Oxford. War of 1939-45, served 1939-46; Captain RA; Italian campaign (wounded, despatches). Fellow All Souls Coll., Oxford, 1946-60, 1972-; barrister, Middle Temple, 1946. Contested (C) Baron's Court, General Election, 1955. PPS to Parly Under-Sec. of State, CRO, 1957-59; Parly Sec., Min. of Housing and Local Govt, 1959-61; Minister of State at Board of Trade, 1961-62; Minister of Housing and Local Govt and Minister for Welsh Affairs, 1962-64; Secretary of State: for Social Services, DHSS, 1970-74; for Industry, 1979-81. Co-Founder and first Chm., Foundation for Management Education, 1959; Founder and first Chm., Mulberry Housing Trust, 1965-69; Founder, and Chm. Management Cttee, Centre for Policy Studies Ltd, 1974-79. Chm., Bovis Ltd, 1958-59; Dep. Chm., Bovis Holdings Ltd, 1964-70 (Dir, 1951-59); Director: Gilbert-Ash Ltd, 1949-59; Drayton Premier Investment Trust Ltd, 1975-79. FIOB. Common councilman of City of London for Ward of Portsoken, 1946, Alderman, 1946-49. Liveryman, Vintners' Company. *Publications:* Reversing the Trend: a critical appraisal of Conservative economic and social policies, 1975; (with J. Sumption) Equality, 1979. *Heir: s* James Samuel Joseph, *b* 27 Jan. 1955. *Address:* 63 Limerston Street, Chelsea, SW10 0BL. *Club:* Carlton.

JOSEPH, Sir Leslie; *see* Joseph, Sir H. L.

JOSEPH, Leslie, QC 1978; *b* 13 Aug. 1925; *s* of Benjamin Francis Joseph and Sarah Edelman; *m* 1964, Ursula Mary Hamilton; one *s* two *d. Educ:* Haberdashers' Aske's, Hampstead; University Coll. London (LLB Hons). Called to the Bar, Middle Temple, 1953. *Recreations:* wine, toymaking. *Address:* 34 Upper Park Road, NW3 2UT. *T:* 01-722 3390.

JOSEPHS, Wilfred; composer; *b* 24 July 1927; *s* of Philip Josephs and Rachel (*née* Block); *m* 1956, Valerie Wisbey; two *d. Educ:* Rutherford Coll. Boys' Sch.; Univ. of Durham at Newcastle (now Newcastle Univ.) (BDS Dunelm). Qual. dentistry, 1951. Army service, 1951-53. Guildhall Sch. of Music (schol. in composition, prizes), 1954; Leverhulme Schol. to study musical comp. in Paris with Maîitre Max Deutsch, 1958-59; Harriet Cohen Commonwealth Medal (for 1st quartet) and prizes; First Prize, La Scala, Milan, for Requiem, 1963. Abandoned dentistry completely and has since been a full-time composer, writing many concert works (incl. nine symphonies), many film and television scores and themes, incl. music for: The Great War, I, Claudius, Disraeli, Cider with Rosie, All Creatures Great and Small, Sister Dora, Swallows and Amazons, The Brontë Series, The Somerset Maugham Series, Horizon, Chéri, A Place in Europe, The Inventing of America, The Norman Conquests, The Ghosts of Motley Hall, The House of Bernardo Alba, The Hunchback of Notre Dame, The Voyage of Charles Darwin, Enemy at the Door, People Like Us, Black Sun, The Uncanny, The Atom Spies, Churchill and the Generals, Pride and Prejudice, Strangled, A Walk in the Dark, Gift of Tongues, Miss Morison's Ghosts, The Human Race, Weekend Theatre, The Moles, The Home Front, also a television opera, The Appointment; one-act opera, Pathelin; children's opera, Through the Looking-glass and What Alice found there; children's musical, King of the Coast (Guardian/Arts Council Prize, 1969); Equus, the ballet (best ballet award, USA, 1980); Rebecca, 3-act opera. Vis. Prof. of Comp. and Composer-in-Residence at Univ. of Wisconsin-Milwaukee, 1970, at Roosevelt Univ., Chicago, 1972. Member: BAFTA; ISM; Council, Soc. for Promotion of New Music. Hon. DMus Newcastle, 1978. *Publications:* Requiem, Symphonies 1-9, various sonatas, quartets etc. *Recreations:* writing music, swimming, reading, opera, theatre, films. *Address:* c/o London Management, Regent House, 235 Regent Street, W1. *Club:* Savage.

JOSEPHSON, Prof. Brian David, FRS 1970; Professor of Physics, Cambridge University, since 1974; Fellow of Trinity College, Cambridge, since 1962; *b* 4 Jan. 1940; *s* of Abraham Josephson and Mimi Josephson; *m* 1976, Carol Anne Olivier; one *d. Educ:* Cardiff High School; Cambridge Univ. BA 1960, MA, PhD 1964, Cantab. FInstP. Asst Dir of Res. in Physics, 1967-72, Reader in Physics, 1972-74, Univ. of Cambridge. Vis. Faculty Mem., Maharishi European Res. Univ., 1975-. Hon. MIEEE, 1982; For. Hon. Mem., Amer. Acad. of Arts and Scis, 1974. Hon. DSc Wales, 1974. Awards: New Scientist, 1969; Research Corp., 1969; Fritz London, 1970; Nobel Prize for Physics, 1973. Medals: Guthrie, 1972; van der Pol, 1972; Elliott Cresson, 1972; Hughes, 1972; Holweck, 1973; Faraday, 1982. *Publications:* Consciousness and the Physical World, 1980 (ed jtly); research papers on physics and theory of intelligence. *Recreations:* mountain walking, ice skating. *Address:* Cavendish Laboratory, Madingley Road, Cambridge CB3 0HE. *T:* Cambridge 66477; telex 81292 CAVLAB G.

JOSLIN, Ivy Collin, BSc; late Headmistress, Francis Holland School, Clarence Gate, NW1; *b* 12 April 1900. *Educ:* Skinners' Company's Sch., London; University Coll. London. Science Mistress, Howell's Sch., Denbigh, 1922-24; Physics Mistress, Southend-on-Sea High Sch., 1924-29; Science Mistress, St Stephen's High Sch., Clewer, 1929-30; Mathematics Mistress, Dame Alice Owen's Sch., London, 1930-33; Headmistress, Derby High Sch., 1933-39; Headmistress, Newcastle on Tyne Church High Sch., 1943-45. *Publications:* Everyday Domestic Science (with P. M. Taylor), 1932; General Science, 1937;

The Air Around Us, 1961; Water in the World, 1962; Electricity in Use, 1964. *Recreations:* bridge, chess. *Club:* University Women's.

JOSLING, John Francis; writer on legal subjects; Principal Assistant Solicitor of Inland Revenue, 1965-71; *b* 26 May 1910; *s* of John Richard Josling, Hackney, London, and Florence Alice (*née* Robinson); *m* 1935, Bertha Frearson; two *s* two *d. Educ:* Leyton Co. High Sch. Entered a private Solicitor's office, 1927; articled, 1937; admitted as Solicitor, 1940. Served War of 1939-45 (war stars and medals): RA, 1940-45; JAG's Br, 1945-46. Entered office of Solicitor of Inland Revenue, 1946; Sen. Legal Asst, 1948; Asst Solicitor, 1952. Mem., Law Society. Coronation Medal, 1953. *Publications:* Oyez Practice Notes on Adoption of Children, 1947, 9th edn 1980; Execution of a Judgment, 1948, 5th edn 1974; (with C. Caplin) Apportionments for Executors and Trustees, 1948, 3rd edn 1963; Change of Name, 1948, 12th edn 1980; Naturalisation, 1949, 3rd edn 1965; Summary Judgment in the High Court, 1950, 4th edn 1974; Periods of Limitation, 1951, 5th edn 1981; (with L. Alexander) The Law of Clubs, 1964, 4th edn 1981; contribs to: Simon's Income Tax (2nd edn); Halsbury's Laws of England vol. 20 (3rd edn); Pollard's Social Welfare Law, 1977; (ed) Caplin's Powers of Attorney, 1954, 4th edn 1971; (ed) Wilkinson's Affiliation Law and Practice, 1971, 4th edn 1977; (ed) Summary Matrimonial and Guardianship Orders, 3rd edn 1973; many contribs to Solicitors' Jl and some other legal jls. *Recreations:* music and musical history; Victorian novels; Georgian children and Elizabethan grandchildren. *Address:* Proton, Farley Way, Fairlight, Sussex. *T:* Pett 2501.

JOSSET, Lawrence; RE 1951 (ARE 1936); ARCA; free-lance artist; *b* 2 Aug. 1910; *s* of Leon Antoine Hyppolite and Annie Mary Josset; *m* 1960, Beatrice, *d* of William Alford Taylor. *Educ:* Bromley County Sch. for Boys; Bromley and Beckenham Schs of Art; Royal College of Art (diploma). Engraver's Draughtsman at Waterlow and Son Ltd, Clifton Street, 1930-32; Art Master at Red Hill Sch., East Sutton, near Maidstone, Kent, 1935-36. Mem. of Art Workers' Guild. *Publications:* Mezzotint in colours; Flowers, after Fantin-Latour, 1937; The Trimmed Cock, after Ben Marshall, 1939; Brighton Beach and Spring, after Constable, 1947; Carting Timber and Milking Time, after Shayer, 1948; The Pursuit, and Love Letters, after Fragonard, 1949; Spring and Autumn, after Boucher, 1951; A Family, after Zoffany, 1953; Master James Sayer, 1954; HM The Queen after Annigoni, commissioned by the Times, 1956, and plates privately commissioned after de Lazlo, James Gunn and Oswald Birley. *Recreations:* outdoor sketching, cycling, etc. *Address:* The Cottage, Pilgrims Way, Detling, near Maidstone, Kent.

JOST, H. Peter, CBE 1969; DSc; CEng; FIMechE; Hon. FIProdE; Managing Director, since 1955, and Chairman, since 1973, K. S. Paul Products Ltd; Director, Stothert & Pitt Ltd, 1971; Director of overseas companies; *b* 25 Jan. 1921; *o s* of late Leo and Margot Jost; *m* 1948, Margaret Josephine, *o d* of late Michael and Mrs Sara Kadesh, Norfolk Is, S Pacific; two *d. Educ:* City of Liverpool Techn. Coll.; Manchester Coll. of Technology. Apprentice, Associated Metal Works, Glasgow and D. Napier & Son Ltd, Liverpool; Methods Engr, K & L Steelfounders and Engrs Ltd, 1943; Chief Planning Engr, Datim Machine Tool Co. Ltd, 1946; Gen. Man. 1949, Dir 1952, Trier Bros Ltd; Lubrication Consultant: Richard Thomas & Baldwins Ltd, 1960-65; August Thyssen Hütte AG 1963-66; Chairman: Bright Brazing Ltd, 1969-76; Peppermill Brass Foundry Ltd, 1970-76; Centralube Ltd, 1974-77 (Man. Dir, 1955-77); Associated Technology Gp Ltd, 1976-; Engineering & General Equipment Ltd, 1977-; Dir, Williams Hudson Ltd, 1967-75. Chairman: Lubrication Educn and Res. Working Gp, DES, 1964-65; Cttee on Tribology, DTI, 1966-74; Industrial Technologies Management Bd, DTI, 1972-74; Dep. Chm., Cttee for Industrial Technologies, DTI, 1972-74; Member: Adv. Council on Technology, 1968-70; Cttee on Terotechnology, 1971-72. Hon. Associate, Manchester Coll. of Science and Technology, 1962; Univ. of Salford: Privy Council's Nominee to Ct, 1970-; Mem. Council, 1974-. Mem. Council: IProdE, 1973- (Vice-Pres., 1975-77, Pres., 1977-78); Chm., Technical Policy Bd and Mem., Exec. Policy Cttee, 1974; Hon. Fellow, 1980; IMechE, 1974- (Member: Technical Bd, 1975; Finance Bd, 1979-; Disciplinary Bd, 1979-); Council of Engineering Institutions: Mem. Bd, 1977-; Mem. Exec., 1979- (Mem. External Affairs Cttee, 1974-80; Chm. Home Affairs Cttee, 1980-); Pres., Internat. Tribology Council, 1973-. Fellow, American Soc. Mechanical Engrs, 1970. Chm., Manchester Technology Assoc. in London, 1976-. Hon. MIPlantE, 1969; Hon. Member: Société Française de Tribologie, 1972; Gesellschaft für Tribologie, 1972; Amer. Soc. of Manufacturing Engrs, 1977. Rutherford Lectr, 1979; James Clayton Lectr, IMechE, 1981. Hon. DSc Salford, 1970. San Fernando Valley Engineers Council (USA) Internat. Achievement Award, 1978; State of California State Legislature Commendation, 1978; Georg Vagelpohl Insignia, Germany, 1979. Sir John Larking Medal 1944, Derby Medal 1955, Liverpool Engrg Soc.; Hutchinson Meml Medal 1952, Silver Medal for Best Paper 1952-53, 1st Nuffield Award 1981, IProdE. *Publications:* Lubrication (Tribology) Report of DES Cttee, 1966 (Jost Report); The Introduction of a New Technology, Report of DTI Cttee, 1973; various papers in Proc. IMechE, Proc.IProdE, technical jls, etc. *Recreations:* music, opera, gardening, riding. *Address:* Hill House, Wills Grove, Mill Hill, NW7. *T:* 01-959 3355. *Club:* Athenæum.

JOUGHIN, Michael, CBE 1971; JP; Chairman, North of Scotland Milk Marketing Board, since 1974; farmer since 1952; *b* 26 April 1926; *s* of John Clague Joughin and May Joughin; *m* 1948, Lesley Roy Petrie; one *s* one *d* ; *m* 1981, Anne Hutchison. *Educ:* Kelly Coll., Tavistock. Lieut, Royal Marines, 1944-52, RM pilot with Fleet Air Arm, 1946-49. Pres., NFU of Scotland, 1964-66. Chm. of Governors: N of Scotland Coll. of Agriculture, 1969-72;

Blairmore Prep. Sch., 1966-72; Chairman: N of Scotland Grassland Soc., 1970-71; Elgin Market Green Auction Co., 1969-70; Scottish Agricl Devlt Council, 1971-80; Governor: Rowett Research Inst., 1968-74; Scottish Plant Breeding Inst., 1969-74; Animal Diseases Research Assoc., Moredun Inst., 1969-74; Member: Intervention Bd for Agric. Produce, 1972-76; Econ. Devlt Council for Agriculture, 1967-70; Agric. Marketing Devlt Exec. Cttee, 1965-68; Scottish Constitutional Cttee, 1969-70; British Farm Produce Council, 1965-66. Contested (C) Highland and Islands, European Parly Elections, 1979. FRAgS 1975. FBIM 1979. JP Moray, 1965; DL Moray, 1974-80. *Recreation:* sailing. *Address:* Wester Manbeen, Elgin, Moray. *T:* Elgin 7082. *Clubs:* New (Edinburgh); Royal Naval Sailing Assoc., Royal Marines Sailing, Royal Findhorn Yacht, Goldfish.

JOWETT, Very Rev. Alfred, CBE 1972; Dean of Manchester since 1964; *b* 29 May 1914; *s* of Alfred Edmund Jowett; *m* 1939, Margaret, *d* of St Clair Benford; one *s* three *d. Educ:* High Storrs Grammar Sch., Sheffield; St Catharine's Coll., Cambridge; Lincoln Theological Coll. BA 1935; Certif. Educn 1936; MA 1959. Deacon 1944; Priest 1945. Curate of St John the Evangelist, Goole, 1944-47; Sec., Sheffield Anglican and Free Church Council and Marriage Guidance Council, 1947-51; Vicar of St George with St Stephen, Sheffield, 1951-60; Part-time Lecturer, Sheffield Univ. Dept of Education, 1950-60; Vicar of Doncaster, 1960-64; Hon. Canon of Sheffield Cathedral, 1960-64. Select Preacher, Oxford Univ., 1964 and 1979. Mem., Community Relations Commn, 1968-77 (Dep. Chm., 1972-77). A Church Comr, 1978-80. Hon. Fellow, Manchester Polytechnic, 1972. OStJ 1979. Hon. LittD Sheffield, 1982. *Publication:* (Part-author) The English Church: a New Look, 1966. *Recreations:* theatre, music, walking. *Address:* The Deanery, Prestwich, Manchester M25 8QF. *T:* 061-773 4301.

JOWETT, Ronald Edward, CBE 1969; MD, FRCS; Hon. Consultant Otolaryngologist, Sunderland and Durham Hospital Groups; *b* 5 March 1901; *s* of James and Emma Jowett, Halifax, Yorks; *m* 1929, Lilian Waring, Halifax; two *s. Educ:* Heath Sch., Halifax; Leeds Univ.; Leeds Med. Sch. MB, ChB (Hons) Leeds, 1922; Scattergood and Hardwick Prizes; MD Leeds, 1923; DLO, RCP&S London, 1925, MRCP 1933; FRCS 1966. Otolaryngologist, Sunderland Hosp. Gp, 1925-71; Surgeon, Newcastle upon Tyne Throat, Nose and Ear Hosp., 1937-50. President: Regional Hospitals' Consultants and Specialists Assoc., 1951-53 and 1964-65; Newcastle upon Tyne and Northern Counties Med. Soc., 1955; N of England Otolaryngological Soc., 1955. Mem., Newcastle Regional Hosp. Bd, 1947-69 (Chm. of its Med. Adv. Cttee, 1953-69); Vice-Chm. of the Bd, 1967-69). FRSM. *Publications:* The Injured Workman (with G. F. Walker), 1933; contribs to: Med. Press and Circular, BMJ, Proc. Roy. Soc. Med., Jl of Mental Science, Jl of Laryngology and Otology, Den Norske Turistforenning. *Recreations:* making music, fishing. *Address:* 18 Brookfield, Westfield, Gosforth, Newcastle upon Tyne NE3 4YB. *T:* Gosforth 853551.

JOWITT, Edwin Frank, QC 1969; His Honour Judge Jowitt; a Circuit Judge, since 1980; *b* 1 Oct. 1929; *s* of Frank and Winifred Jowitt; *m* 1959, Anne Barbara Dyson; three *s* two *d. Educ:* Swanwick Hall Grammar Sch.; London Sch. of Economics. LLB London 1950. Called to Bar, Middle Temple, 1951, Bencher 1977; Member Midland and Oxford Circuit. Dep. Chm. Quarter Sessions: Rutland, 1967-71; Derbyshire, 1970-71; a Recorder of the Crown Court, 1972-80. *Recreation:* fell walking. *Address:* Church House, Desborough, Northants NN14 2NP.

JOWITT, Juliet Diana Margaret, (Mrs Thomas Jowitt); Member, Independent Broadcasting Authority, since 1981; *b* 24 Aug. 1940; *yr d* of late Lt-Col Robert Henry Langton Brackenbury, OBE and Eleanor Trewlove (*née* Springman); *m* 1963, Frederick Thomas Benson Jowitt; one *s* one *d. Educ:* Hatherop Castle; Switzerland and Spain. Associate Shopping Editor, House and Garden and Vogue, 1966-69; Proprietor, Colour Go Round (Interior Design), 1971-. JP North Yorkshire, 1973; Mem. Combined Juvenile Court sitting at Thirsk, 1976-. *Address:* Sharow Close, Ripon, N Yorkshire; 11 St George's Square, SW1.

JOY, David, HM Diplomatic Service; Counsellor and Head of British Interests Section, Buenos Aires, since 1982; *b* 9 Dec. 1932; *s* of Harold Oliver Joy and late Doris Kate Buxton; *m* 1957, Montserrat Morancho Saumench, *o d* of Angel Morancho Garreta and Josefa Saumench Castells, Zaragoza, Spain; one *s* one *d. Educ:* Hulme Grammar Sch., Oldham, Lancs; St Catharine's Coll., Cambridge (MA); Member of Gray's Inn. FBIM. HMOCS, Northern Rhodesia, 1956-64 (Principal, Exec. Council Office, 1962-64); Zambia, 1964-70: Cabinet Office, 1964; Asst Sec., 1966, Under Sec. (Cabinet), 1968; seconded as Town Clerk, Lusaka City Council, 1969; Under Sec., Min. of Commerce and Industry, 1970; Ashridge Management Coll., 1970; joined HM Diplomatic Service, 1971; FCO, 1971-73; First Sec. (Inf.), Caracas, 1973-75; Head of Chancery, Caracas, 1975-77; Asst Head, Mexican and Caribbean Dept, FCO, 1977-78; Counsellor and Head of Chancery, Warsaw, 1978-82. *Recreations:* family-life, reading, tennis, golf. *Address:* c/o Foreign and Commonwealth Office, SW1A 2AH; Flat 6, 9 Beaufort Gardens, SW3 1PT. *T:* 01-589 6170. *Club:* United Oxford & Cambridge University.

JOY, Michael Gerard Laurie, CMG 1965; MC 1945; *b* 27 Oct. 1916; *s* of late Frank Douglas Howarth Joy, Bentley, Hants; *m* 1951, Ann Félise Jacomb; one *s* three *d. Educ:* Winchester; New Coll., Oxford. Served RA, 1940-46 (MC, wounded). Foreign Office, 1947; Private Sec. to Permanent Under Sec. of State, 1948-50; Saigon, 1950-53; Washington, 1953-55; IDC, 1956; Foreign

Office, 1957-59; Counsellor, 1959; Addis Ababa, 1959-62; Stockholm, 1962-64; seconded to Cabinet Office, 1964-66; Foreign Office, 1966-68. *Recreation:* shooting. *Address:* Marelands, Bentley, Hants. *T:* Bentley 23288.

JOY, Peter, OBE 1969; HM Diplomatic Service; Counsellor, Foreign and Commonwealth Office, since 1980; *b* 16 Jan. 1926; *s* of late Neville Holt Joy and Marguerite Mary Duff Beith; *m* 1953, Rosemary Joan Hebden; two *s* two *d. Educ:* Downhouse Sch., Pembridge; New Coll., Oxford. Served with RAF, 1944-47. Entered Foreign (subseq. Diplomatic) Service, 1952; 1st Sec., Ankara, 1959; 1st Sec., New Delhi, 1962; FO, 1965; 1st Sec., Beirut, 1968; FCO, 1973; Counsellor, Kuala Lumpur, 1979-80. *Recreations:* shooting, fishing. *Address:* The Old Rectory, Stoke Bliss, near Tenbury, Worcs. *T:* Kyre 342; Carrick House, Eday, Orkney. *Club:* Travellers'.

JOY, Thomas Alfred, MVO 1979; Managing Director, Hatchards Ltd, since 1965; *b* 30 Dec. 1904; *s* of Alfred Joy and Annie Carpenter; *m* 1932, Edith Ellis. *Educ:* privately; Bedford House Sch., Oxford. Jun. Assistant, Bodleian Library, Oxford, 1919; indentured apprentice, 1919-25, buyer and cataloguer, 1925-35, J. Thornton & Son, University Booksellers, Oxford; Manager, Circulating Library, 1935-45, and Manager, Book Dept, 1942-45, Harrods; Army & Navy Stores: Manager, Book Dept, and founder of Library, 1945-56; Merchandise Manager, 1956; Dep. Managing Dir, 1956-65. Began Authors of the Year parties, 1966. Employers' rep., Bookselling and Stationery Trade Wages Council, 1946-79, leader of employers' side, 1957; Member: Nat. Chamber of Trade, 1946-51; Wholesale Trades Adv. Cttee, 1946-51; 1948 Book Trade Cttee; Arts Council working party on obscene pubns, 1968-69, and sub-cttee on Public Lending Rights, 1970. President: Booksellers Assoc. of GB and Ire, 1957-58; Book Trade Charity, Book Trade Benevolent Soc., 1974-. Inaugurated Nat. Book Sale (first Chm. of Cttee, 1954-65). Hon. Life Mem., Soc. of Bookmen. FRSA 1967. Jubilee Medal, 1977. *Publications:* The Right Way to Run a Library Business, 1949; Bookselling, 1953; The Truth about Bookselling, 1964; Mostly Joy (autobiog.), 1971; The Bookselling Business, 1974; contribs to Bookseller and other trade jls. *Recreations:* reading, fishing, walking, motoring. *Address:* 13 Cole Park Gardens, Twickenham, Middlesex TW1 1JB. *T:* 01-892 5660.

JOYCE, Eileen Alannah, CMG 1981; concert pianist; *b* Zeehan, Tasmania; *d* of Joseph and Alice Joyce, Western Australia. *Educ:* Loreto Convent, Perth, Western Australia; Leipzig Conservatoire. Studied in Germany under Teichmuller, and later, Schnabel. Concert début in London at Promenade Concerts under Sir Henry Wood. Numerous concert tours, radio performances and gramophone recordings. During War of 1939-45, played in association with London Philharmonic Orchestra, especially in blitzed towns and cities throughout Great Britain. Concerts with: all principal orchestras of the UK; Berlin Philharmonic Orchestra in Berlin; Conservatoire and National Orchestras, France; Concertgebouw Orchestra, Holland; La Scala Orchestra, Italy; Philadelphia Orchestra, Carnegie Hall, New York. Concert tours in: Australia, 1948; SA, 1950; Scandinavia and Holland, 1951; S Amer., Scandinavia and Finland, 1952; Jugoslavia, 1955; NZ, 1958; USSR, 1961; India, 1962; also performed harpsichord in several concerts Royal Albert Hall and Royal Festival Hall. Has contributed to sound tracks of films including: The Seventh Veil, Brief Encounter, Man of Two Worlds, Quartet, Trent's Last Case; appeared in films: Battle for Music, Girl in a Million, Wherever She Goes (biographical). Hon. DMus Cantab, 1971; Hon. DMus Univ. of Western Australia, 1979. *Address:* Chartwell Farm, Westerham, Kent.

JOYCE, William R., Jr, lawyer, since 1951; Director and Secretary-Treasurer, Battle of Britain Museum Foundation (USA), since 1976; *b* 18 May 1921; *s* of William R. Joyce and Winifred Lowery; *m* 1956, Mary-Hoyt Sherman; one *s* two *d. Educ:* Loyola Univ. (BA); New York and Harvard Law Schs. JD. Lawyer, in private practice, New York City and Washington, DC; member of firm, Vance & Joyce, 1977-; Consul General *ad hon.,* Republic of Bolivia (Washington, DC), 1963-. Kt 1973, Kt Comdr (pro Merito Melitensi), 1976; Kt Comdr of Grace, Order of Malta, 1977; Kt, Equestrian Order of Holy Sepulchre, Jerusalem, 1976; Kt Comdr of Grace, Order of Constantine and S George (Borbon-Two Sicilies), Naples, 1977; Order of Condor of the Andes, Bolivia, 1978. *Recreations:* sailing, golf. *Address:* (residence) 4339 Garfield Street NW, Washington, DC 20007, USA. *T:* 202/244-7648; (office) 1701 Pennsylvania Avenue NW, Washington, DC 20006. *T:* 202/298-7133. *Clubs:* Squash Racquets Association, Middlesex CCC; The Brook, India House, Union, New York Yacht (New York City); Metropolitan, Chevy Chase (Washington); Cooperstown Country (New York); Conanicut Yacht (RI).

JOYNSON-HICKS, family name of **Viscount Brentford.**

JOYNT, Evelyn Gertrude, MBE 1967; Major (retired) WRAC; Director, World Bureau of World Association of Girl Guides and Girl Scouts, 1971-79; *b* 5 Sept. 1919; 2nd *d* of late Rev. George Joynt, Dublin. *Educ:* Collegiate Sch., Enniskillen; Banbridge Academy. Joined ATS, 1942; transf. to WRAC, 1952; jsc, WRAC Staff Coll., 1954; served Middle East and Far East; OC Drivers and Clerks Training Wing, WRAC; DAQMG, Eastern Comd; retired 1967; Nat. Gen. Sec., YWCA of GB, 1968-71. *Address:* Bowden House, West Street, Alresford, Hants.

JUDD, Clifford Harold Alfred; Under Secretary, HM Treasury, since 1981; *b* 27 June 1927; *s* of Alfred Ernest and Florence Louisa Judd; *m* 1951, Elizabeth Margaret Holmes; two *d. Educ:* Christ's Hospital; Keble Coll., Oxford.

National Service, RA, 1946-48 (to 2/Lt). HM Treasury: Executive Officer, 1948, through ranks to Principal, 1964, Sen. Prin., 1969, Asst Sec., 1973. *Recreations:* cricket, do-it-yourself. *Address:* 4 Colets Orchard, Otford, Kent TN4 5RA. *T:* Otford 2398. *Clubs:* Sevenoaks Vine; Otford Casuals CC.

JUDD, Eric Campbell, CBE 1974; MVO 1956; Chairman, West Africa Committee, since 1976; *b* St Thomas, Ont, 10 Aug. 1918; *s* of Frederick William Judd, PhmB (Canada), and Marjorie Katherine (*née* Bell); *m* 1947, Janet Creswell (*née* Fish); two *s* one *d. Educ:* Wellington, Canada; St Thomas Collegiate; Toronto Univ. Trainee Manager, Cities Service Oil Co., Canada, 1937-40. RCAF and RAF, 1940-45: Canada, N Atlantic Ferry Comd, Europe, Malta, Middle East, Far East, W Indies; retd Sqdn Ldr RCAF Reserve, 1945. Joined Unilever Ltd, 1946; United Africa Co. Ltd, Nigeria, 1946-60, Chm., 1957-60; Dir, UAC Ltd London, 1960, Man. Dir, 1968; Dep. Chm. and Jt Man. Dir, UAC International, 1969-77. Mem. House of Assembly, Western Nigeria, 1955-56; Chm., BNEC Africa, 1969-72; Chm., Adv. Gp Africa BOTB, 1972-74; Vice-Chm., West Africa Cttee, London, 1963-76. Mem. Council and Exec. Cttee, Royal African Soc., 1975-. *Recreations:* golf, tennis, theatre, music, reading. *Address:* Amberway, 23 Townsend Lane, Harpenden, Herts AL5 2PY. *T:* Harpenden 2617. *Clubs:* Pathfinder, MCC; Mid-Herts Golf.

JUDD, Frank Ashcroft; Director, Voluntary Services Overseas, since 1980; *b* 28 March 1935; *s* of Charles and Helen Judd; *m* 1961, Christine Elizabeth Willington; two *d. Educ:* City of London Sch.; London Sch. of Economics. Sec.-Gen., IVS, 1960-66. Contested (Lab): Sutton and Cheam, 1959; Portsmouth West, 1964; MP (Lab) Portsmouth W, 1966-74, Portsmouth N, 1974-79; PPS: to Minister of Housing, 1967-70; to the Leader of the Opposition, 1970-72; Mem., Opposition's Front Bench Defence Team, 1972-74; Parliamentary Under-Secretary of State: for Defence (Navy), MoD, 1974-76; ODM 1976; Minister of State: for Overseas Develt, 1976-77; FCO, 1977-79; Mem., British Parly Delegn to Council of Europe and WEU, 1970-73. Indep. Advr to UK Delegn to UN Special Session on Disarmament, 1982. Associate Dir, Internat. Defence Aid Fund for Southern Africa, 1979-80. Chm., Centre for World Development Educn, 1980-. Member: Council, NACRO; Council, Overseas Development Inst.; RIIA; ASTMS; Fabian Soc. Executive. Governor, LSE, 1982-. *Publications:* (jtly) Radical Future, 1967; Fabian International Essays, 1970; Purpose in Socialism, 1973; various papers and articles on current affairs. *Recreations:* walking, family holidays. *Address:* 42 The Crescent, Belmont, Sutton, Surrey.

JUDD, John Basil Thomas; HM Consul-General at Zagreb, 1961-65; retired; re-employed in the Foreign Office, 1966-69; *b* 12 May 1909; *s* of John Matthews Judd and Helena Beatrice Jenkins; *m* 1939, Cynthia Margaret Georgina, *yr d* of Sir Henry White-Smith, CBE; two *s* one *d. Educ:* The Leys; Downing Coll., Cambridge; Inner Temple (called to the Bar, 1931). Entered Levant Consular Service, 1932; Vice-Consul and 3rd Sec. at Jedda, 1936; Vice-Consul at Casablanca and Tangier, 1939-43; Consul at Tunis and Marseilles, 1943-46; Consul and 1st Sec. at Paris, 1946; Consul at Jerusalem, 1949; Foreign Office, 1951; Consul-Gen. at Valparaiso, 1953; Consul-Gen. and Counsellor, Cairo, 1955-57; Consul-Gen. at Basra, 1957-61. *Recreations:* fishing, theatre and opera. *Address:* 77 Siren Street, Senglea, Malta. *Clubs:* Brooks's; Union, Sports (Malta).

JUDD, Nadine; *see* Nerina, Nadia.

JUDGE, Edward Thomas, MA Cantab; Director: ETJ Consultancy Services; Zenith Electric Co. Ltd; Weldall Engineering Ltd; Cleveland Scientific Institution; *b* 20 Nov. 1908; *o s* of late Thomas Oliver and Florence Judge (*née* Gravestock); *m* 1934, Alice Gertrude Matthews; two *s. Educ:* Worcester Royal Grammar Sch.; St John's Coll., Cambridge. Joined Dorman Long, 1930, and held various appts, becoming Chief Technical Engr, 1937; Special Dir, 1944; Chief Engr, 1945; Dir, 1947; Asst Man. Dir, Dorman Long (Steel) Ltd, 1959; Jt Man. Dir, 1960; Chm. and Gen. Man. Dir, Dorman Long & Co. Ltd, 1961-67; Dir, Dorman Long Vaderbijl (SA), 1959-79. Chairman: Reyrolle Parsons Ltd, 1969-74 (Dep. Chm., 1968); A. Reyrolle & Co. Ltd, 1969-73; C. A. Parsons & Co. Ltd, 1969-73; Director: BPB Industries, 1967-79; Pilkington Bros, 1968-79; Fibreglass, 1968-79. Mem. Exec. and Develt Cttees of Brit. Iron & Steel Fedn; Rep. of Minister of Transport on Tees Conservancy Commn., 1951-66; part-time Mem. N Eastern Electricity Bd, 1952-62; Vice-Pres., Iron & Steel Inst., 1958. President: British Iron & Steel Federation, 1965, 1966, 1967; British Electrical Allied Manufacturers' Assoc. Ltd, 1970-71 (Dep. Pres., 1969-70). Bessemer Gold Medal, Iron and Steel Inst., 1967. *Publications:* technical papers. *Recreation:* fishing. *Address:* Wood Place, Aspley Guise, Milton Keynes MK17 8EP.

JUDGE, Harry George, MA Oxon, PhD London; Director, University of Oxford Department of Educational Studies, since 1973; Fellow of Brasenose College, since 1973, and Tutor for Admissions, since 1980; *b* 1 Aug. 1928; *s* of George Arthur and Winifred Mary Judge; *m* 1956, Elizabeth Mary Patrick; one *s* two *d. Educ:* Cardiff High Sch.; Brasenose Coll., Oxford. Asst Master, Emanuel Sch. and Wallington County Grammar Sch., 1954-59; Dir of Studies, Cumberland Lodge, Windsor, 1959-62; Head Master, Banbury Grammar Sch., 1962-67; Principal, Banbury Sch., 1967-73. Vis. Prof., MIT, 1977 and 1980-82. Member: Public Schools Commission, 1966-70; James Cttee of Inquiry into Teacher Training, 1971-72; Educn Sub-Cttee, UGC, 1976-80; Oxon Educn Cttee. Chm., School Broadcasting Council, 1977-81. Member Governing Body: Grad. Schs of Educn in US, 1982; Bartholomew Sch.,

Eynsham; Wycombe Abbey Sch. *Publications:* Louis XIV, 1965; School Is Not Yet Dead, 1974; contribs on educational and historical subjects to collective works and learned jls. *Recreation:* canals. *Address:* 2 Upland Park Road, Oxford.

JUDGE, Igor, QC 1979; a Recorder of the Crown Court, since 1976; *b* 19 May 1941; *s* of Raymond and Rosa Judge; *m* 1965, Judith Mary Robinson; one *s* two *d. Educ:* Oratory Sch., Woodcote; Magdalene Coll., Cambridge (Exhbnr, MA). Harmsworth Exhbn and Astbury Scholar, Middle Temple. Called to the Bar, Middle Temple, 1963. Prosecuting Counsel to Inland Revenue, Midland and Oxford Circuit, 1977-79. *Recreations:* history, music, cricket. *Address:* The Homestead, Crick, Northampton. *T:* Crick 822333.

JUKES, Rt. Rev. John, OFMConv; STL; an Auxiliary Bishop in Southwark, (RC), since 1980; Titular Bishop of Strathearn, since 1980; *b* 7 Aug. 1923; *s* of Francis Bernard Jukes and Florence Jukes (*née* Stampton). *Educ:* Blackheath; Rome. Professed in Order of Friars Minor Conventual, 1948; Priest, 1952. Lectr in Canon Law, Franciscan Study Centre, Univ. of Kent at Canterbury; Minister Provincial, English Province, 1979. Episcopal Vicar for Religious, Southwark; Area Bishop with special responsibility for Deaneries of Canterbury, Chatham, Dover, Gravesend, Ramsgate and Tunbridge Wells, 1980-. *Publications:* contribs to Misc. Francescana, Studia Canonica, New Life, Clergy Rev., etc. *Recreation:* mountain walking and climbing. *Address:* The Hermitage, More Park, West Malling, Kent ME19 6HN.

JUKES, John Andrew, CB 1968; Member, Central Electricity Generating Board, 1977-80; *b* 19 May 1917; *s* of Captain A. M. Jukes, MD, IMS, and Mrs Gertrude E. Jukes (*née* King); *m* 1943, Muriel Child; two *s* two *d. Educ:* Shrewsbury Sch.; St John's Coll., Cambridge; London Sch. of Economics. MA in physics Cambridge, BSc (Econ.) London. FInstHE 1977. Cavendish Laboratory, Cambridge, 1939; Radar and Operational Research, 1939-46; Research Dept, LMS Railway, 1946-48; Economic Adviser, Cabinet Office and Treasury, 1948-54; British Embassy, Washington, DC, 1949-51; Economic Adviser to UK Atomic Energy Authority, 1954-64 and Principal Economics and Programming Office, UKAEA, 1957-64; appointed to Dept Economic Affairs as Dep. Dir Gen., 1964; Dep. Under-Sec. of State, Dept of Economic Affairs, 1967; Dir Gen., Research and Economic Planning, MoT, 1969-70; Dir Gen., Economics and Resources, DoE, 1970-72; Dep. Sec. (Environmental Protection), DoE, 1972-74; Chm., Steering Gp on Water Authority Econ. and Financial Objectives, 1973-74; Dir-Gen., Highways, DoE, 1974-76, Dept of Transport, 1976-77. *Recreations:* orienteering, travelling, gardening. *Address:* 38 Albion Road, Sutton, Surrey. *T:* 01-642 5018.

JUKES, Richard Starr, CBE 1969; FCA; Director, BPB Industries Ltd, 1943-76 (Chairman, 1965-73); *b* 6 Dec. 1906; *s* of late Rev. Arthur Starr Jukes and Mrs Annie Florance Jukes; *m* 1935, Ruth Mary Wilmot; one *s* two *d. Educ:* St Edmund's, Canterbury. Mem. Inst. of Chartered Accountants, 1929. Gyproc Products Ltd: Sec./Accountant, 1934; Dir, 1939; The British Plaster Board (Holdings) Ltd: Dir, 1943; Jt Man. Dir, 1947; Man. Dir, 1954; Dep. Chm., 1962; Chm., 1965 (since Aug. 1965 the company has been known as BPB Industries). *Recreation:* golf. *Address:* White House, Watford Road, Northwood, Mddx. *T:* Northwood 24125. *Clubs:* Island Sailing; Sandy Lodge Golf; Hillside Golf (Zimbabwe).

JUMA, Sa'ad; *b* Tafila, Jordan, 21 March 1916; *s* of Mohammed Juma; *m* 1959, Salwa Ghanem, Beirut; two *s* one *d. Educ:* Damascus Univ. (L'Essence in Law). Chief of Protocol, Min. of For. Affairs, 1949; Dir of Press, 1950; Sec. to Prime Minister's Office, 1950-54; Under-Sec., Min. of Interior, 1954-57; Governor of Amman, 1957-58; Under-Sec., Min. of For. Affairs, 1958-59; Ambassador: to Iran, 1959-61; to Syria, 1961-62; to USA, 1962-65; Minister of the Royal Court, 1965-67; Prime Minister, 1967; Ambassador to United Kingdom, 1969-70; Senator, 1970-75. Orders of El Nahda (1st Class) and Star of Jordan (1st Class); decorations from Syria, Lebanon, China, Italy, Libya, Malaysia and Ethiopia. *Publications:* Conspiracy and the Battle of Destiny, 1968; Hostile Society, 1970; God or Destruction, 1973; Sons of Snakes, 1973. *Recreations:* reading, music, bridge. *Address:* Jebel Amman, 4th Circle, Amman, Jordan. *T:* Amman 44111. *Clubs:* Travellers', Hurlingham.

JUNGIUS, Vice-Adm. Sir James (George), KBE 1977; DL; farmer; Supreme Allied Commander Atlantic's Representative in Europe, 1978-80, retired; *b* 15 Nov. 1923; *s* of Major E. J. T. Jungius, MC; *m* 1949, Rosemary Frances Turquand Matthey; three *s. Educ:* RNC, Dartmouth. Served War of 1939-45: Midshipman, Sub-Lt and Lt, in Atlantic and Mediterranean; Commando Ops in Adriatic (despatches). Specialised in Navigation in 1946, followed by series of appts as Navigating Officer at sea and instructing ashore. Comdr, Dec. 1955; CO, HMS Wizard, 1956-57; Admlty, 1958-59; Exec. Officer, HMS Centaur, 1960-61; Captain, 1963; Naval Staff, 1964-65; CO, HMS Lynx, 1966-67; Asst Naval Attaché, Washington, DC, 1968-70; CO, HMS Albion, 1971-72; Rear-Adm., 1972; Asst Chief of Naval Staff (Operational Requirements), 1972-74; Vice-Adm., 1974; Dep. Supreme Allied Comdr Atlantic, 1975-77. CBIM. DL Cornwall, 1982. *Recreation:* fishing. *Address:* c/o National Westminster Bank, Wadebridge, Cornwall. *Clubs:* Naval and Military; RN Club of 1765 and 1785; Pilgrims; Chesapeake (Norfolk, Va).

JUNOR, Sir John, Kt 1980; Editor, Sunday Express, since 1954; Chairman, Sunday Express, 1968; Director: Express Newspapers; Fleet Holdings; *b* 15 Jan.

1919; *s* of Alexander Junor, Black Isle, Ross and Cromarty; *m* 1942, Pamela Mary Welsh; one *s* one *d. Educ:* Glasgow Univ. (MA Hons English). Lt (A) RNVR, 1939-45. Contested (L) Kincardine and West Aberdeen, 1945, East Edinburgh, 1948, Dundee West, 1951; Asst Editor, Daily Express, 1951-53; Dep. Editor, Evening Standard, 1953-54; Dir, Beaverbrook (later Express) Newspapers, 1960. Hon. LLD New Brunswick, 1973. *Publication:* The Best of JJ, 1981. *Recreations:* golf, tennis, sailing. *Address:* c/o Sunday Express, Fleet Street, EC4Y 2NJ. *Clubs:* Royal Southern Yacht; Royal and Ancient; Walton Heath.

JUPE, George Percival; Under Secretary, Ministry of Agriculture, Fisheries and Food, Food Standards and Emergency Planning Group, since 1979; *b* 6 April 1930; *s* of Frederick Stuart Jupe and Elizabeth (*née* Clayton); unmarried. *Educ:* Sandown Grammar Sch., IoW; Hertford Coll., Oxford. Ministry of Agriculture, Fisheries and Food: Asst Principal, 1955; Principal, 1960; Asst Sec., 1970-79: Eggs and Poultry, and Potatoes Divs, 1970-74; Internat. Fisheries Div., 1975-78. *Recreations:* hill walking, gardening, music. *Address:* c/o Ministry of Agriculture, Fisheries and Food, Whitehall Place, SW1A 2HH.

JUPP, Clifford Norman, CMG 1966; *b* 24 Sept. 1919; *s* of Albert Leonard Jupp and Marguerite Isabel (*née* Day Winter); *m* 1945, Brenda (*née* Babbs); one *s* two *d. Educ:* Perse Sch., Cambridge; Trinity Hall, Cambridge. Armed Forces, 1940-46. Mem. of HM Foreign and Diplomatic Service, 1946-70; served in: Foreign Office, 1946; Beirut, 1947-49; New York, 1949-51; Foreign Office, 1951-53; Cairo, 1953-56; Kabul, 1956-59; Foreign Office, 1959-61; Brussels, 1961-63; Belgrade, 1963-66; seconded to BoT and Min. of Technology, 1967-70. With Burton Gp Ltd, 1970-72; Dir, British Textile Confedn, 1972-76. *Address:* Tigh nan Croitean, Kildalton, Isle of Islay, Argyll, Scotland.

JUPP, Hon. Sir Kenneth Graham, Kt 1975; MC 1943; **Hon. Mr Justice Jupp;** a Judge of the High Court, Queen's Bench Division, since 1975; *b* 2 June 1917; *s* of Albert Leonard and Marguerite Isabel Jupp; *m* 1947, Kathleen Elizabeth (*née* Richards); two *s* two *d. Educ:* Perse Sch., Cambridge; University Coll., Oxford (Sen. Class. Schol., 1936; 1st Cl. Hon. Mods 1938); Lincoln's Inn (Cholmeley Schol., 1939; Cassel Schol., 1946). Regimental Service in France, Belgium, N Africa and Italy, 1939-43; War Office Selection Board, 1943-46. Called to Bar, Lincoln's Inn, 1945, Bencher, 1973; QC 1966; Dep. Chm., Cambridge and Isle of Ely QS, 1965-71; a Recorder of the Crown Court, 1972-75; Presiding Judge, NE Circuit, 1977-81. Chm., Independent Schs Tribunal, 1964-67; conducted MAFF inquiry into Wool Marketing Scheme, 1965; Chm., Public Inquiry into Fire at Fairfield Home, Nottingham, 1975. *Recreations:* music (DIY), language. *Address:* Royal Courts of Justice, Strand, WC2. *Club:* Garrick.

JURINAC, (Srebrenka) Sena; opera singer; Member of Vienna State Opera since 1944; *b* Travnik, Yugoslavia, 24 Oct. 1921; *d* of Ludwig Jurinac, MD, and Christine Cerv. *Educ:* High Sch.; Musical Academy. Made first appearance on stage as Mimi in Zagreb Opera, 1942. Frequent appearances at Glyndebourne Festivals, 1949-56, as well as at the Salzburg Festivals. Guest appearances at La Scala, Covent Garden, San Francisco, Teatro Colón. Principal parts include: Donna Anna and Donna Elvira in Don Giovanni; Elisabeth in Tannhauser; Tosca; Jenufa; Marie in Wozzeck; Marschallin in Der Rosenkavalier; Composer in Ariadne auf Naxos; Elisabeth in Don Carlos; Desdemona in Othello. *Film:* Der Rosenkavalier, 1962. Kammersängerin award, 1951; Ehrenkreuz für Wissenschaft und Kunst, 1961; Grosses Ehrenzeichen für Verdienste um die Republik Oesterreich, 1967. *Address:* c/o Vienna State Opera, Austria.

JURY, Archibald George, CBE 1961; FRIBA; FRIAS; City Architect, Glasgow, 1951-72, retired; *b* 23 June 1907; *s* of late George John Jury and Mabel Sophie Jury (*née* Fisher); *m* 1931, Amy Beatrice Maw; one *d. Educ:* Mount Radford, Exeter; SW School of Art. Architect to Council, Taunton, 1938-40, and 1945. Served War, 1940-45, with Corps of Royal Engineers (rank of Major). Chief Housing Architect, Liverpool, 1946-49; Dir of Housing, Glasgow, 1949-51; Dir of Planning, Glasgow, 1951-66. Organised the building of 100,000 houses, 100,000 school places and numerous civic buildings; responsible for the Glasgow Devpt Plan, 1960-80, and implementation of urban renewal programme and official architecture. Several Saltire Soc. awards for best-designed flats in Scotland. Chairman: Technical Panel, Scottish Local Authorities Special Housing Group, 1965-72; Technical Panel, Clyde Valley Planning Adv. Cttee, 1960-70; Pres., Glasgow Inst. of Architects, 1970-72. *Publications:* contrib. professional and technical journals. *Recreations:* fishing, gardening, painting. *Address:* West Acres, Lockerbie, Dumfriesshire.

K

KABERRY, Sir Donald, 1st Bt, cr 1960; TD 1946; DL; MP (C) North-West Division of Leeds since 1950; b 18 Aug. 1907; m 1940, Lily Margaret Scott; three s. Educ: Leeds Grammar Sch. Solicitor (Mem. of Council of The Law Society, 1950-55). Served War of 1939-45, in RA (despatches twice). Mem. Leeds City Council for 20 years, now Hon. Alderman. Asst Government Whip, 1951-April 1955; Parliamentary Sec., Board of Trade, April-Oct. 1955; Vice-Chm., Conservative Party, Oct. 1955-61; Mem., Select Cttee Nationalised Industries, 1961-79 (Chm. Sub-Cttee C, 1974-79); Chm., Select Cttee on Industry and Trade, 1979-; Mem., Speaker's Panel of Chairmen, 1974-. Chairman: Yorkshire Chemicals Ltd, 1964-77; W. H. Baxter Ltd; Pres., Yorks Area Council of Conservative Party, 1966- (Chm. 1952-56; Dep. Pres. 1956-65); Chm., Assoc. of Conservative Clubs, 1961-; Chairman: Bd of Governors, United Leeds Hosps, 1961-74; Leeds Teaching Hosps Special Trustee, 1974-; Pres., Headingly Branch, Royal British Legion; Hon. Legal Adviser, National Dunkirk Veterans Assoc. (Founder and Pres., Leeds Branch, 1973-); Treasurer, Leeds Poppy Day Appeal Fund, 1947-73. Pres., Incorporated Leeds Law Soc., 1952. DL York and West Yorks, 1974. Heir: s Christopher Donald Kaberry [b 14 March 1943; m 1967, Gaenor Elizabeth Vowe, yr d of C. V. Peake; two s one d. Educ: Repton Sch.]. Address: Beckfield, East Keswick, Leeds LS17 9DB. T: Collingham Bridge 73257. Clubs: Carlton, St Stephen's Constitutional; Leeds.

KADOORIE, family name of Baron Kadoorie.

KADOORIE, Baron cr 1981 (Life Peer), of Kowloon in Hong Kong and of the City of Westminster; **Lawrence Kadoorie**; Kt 1974; OBE 1970; JP (Hong Kong); Partner, Sir Elly Kadoorie & Sons; Chairman: Sir Elly Kadoorie Successors Ltd; St George's Building Ltd; Director, Sir Elly Kadoorie Continuation Ltd; also chairman and director of many other companies; b Hong Kong, 2 June 1899; s of Sir Elly Kadoorie, KBE, and Laura Kadoorie (née Mocatta); m 1938, Muriel, d of David Gubbay, Hong Kong; one s one d. Educ: Cathedral Sch., Shanghai; Ascham St Vincents, Eastbourne; Clifton Coll., Bristol; Lincoln's Inn. With his brother, Horace, founded New Territories Benevolent Soc. Is also Chairman: China Light & Power Co., Ltd, Schroders & Chartered Ltd, Hong Kong Carpet Manufacturers Ltd, Nanyang Cotton Mill Ltd and others. Mem. Council and Court, Univ. of Hong Kong. Fellow, Mem., Patron, Governor, Chm., etc, of numerous other assocs, cttees, etc. JP Hong Kong 1936; MEC 1954, MLC 1950, 1951, 1954, Hong Kong. Hon. LLD Univ. of Hong Kong, 1961; FInstD (London). KStJ (A) (UK) 1972. Solomon Schechter Award (USA), 1959; Ramon Magsaysay Award (Philippines), 1962; Officier de l'Ordre de Léopold (Belgium), 1966; Comdr, Légion d'Honneur (France), 1982 (Officier, 1975). Recreations: sports cars (Life Mem. Hong Kong AA), photography, Chinese works of art. Address: St George's Building, 24th floor, 2 Ice House Street, Hong Kong. T: 5-249221. Clubs: Royal Automobile; Hong Kong, Hong Kong Country, Royal Hong Kong Jockey, Jewish Recreation, American (Hong Kong); Travellers' Century (USA).

KADRI, Sibghat Ullah; barrister-at-law; President, Standing Conference of Pakistani Organisations in UK, since 1978 (Secretary General, 1975-78); Chairman, Society of Afro-Asian and Caribbean Lawyers, UK, since 1979; b 23 April 1937; s of Haji Maulana Firasat Ullah Kadri and Begum Tanwir Fatima Kadri; m 1963, Carita Elisabeth Idman; one s one d. Educ: S. M. Coll., Karachi; Karachi Univ. Called to the Bar, Inner Temple, 1969. Sec. Gen., Karachi Univ. Students Union, 1957-58; jailed without trial, for opposing military regime of Ayub Khan, 1958-59; triple winner, All Pakistan Students Debates, 1960; Gen. Sec., Pakistan Students' Fedn in Britain, 1961-62, Vice Pres., 1962-63; Pres., Inner Temple Students Assoc., 1969-70. Producer and broadcaster, BBC Ext. Urdu Service, 1965-68, and Presenter, BBC Home Service Asian Prog., 1968-70. In practice at the Bar, 1969- (Head of Chambers, 11 King's Bench Walk). Vis. Lectr in Urdu, Holborn Coll., London, 1967-70. Org. Pakistani Def. Cttees during wave of 'Paki-bashing', 1970; active in immigrant and race-relations activities, 1970-; led Asian delegn to Prime Minister, June 1976; attended UN Conf., Migrant Workers in Europe, Geneva, 1975; led Pakistan delegn to 3rd Internat. Conf., Migrant Workers in Europe, Turin, 1977. Gen. Sec., Pakistan Action Cttee, 1973; Convenor, Asian Action Cttee, 1976. Vice Chm., All Party Jt Cttee Against Racism, 1978-80. Publisher, Scopo News, London. Publications: articles in ethnic minority press on immigration and race relations. Recreations: family and reading. Address: 11 King's Bench Walk, Temple, EC4Y 7EQ. T: 01-353 4931/2.

KAGAN, family name of Baron Kagan.

KAGAN, Baron cr 1976 (Life Peer), of Elland, W Yorks; **Joseph Kagan;** b 6 June 1915; s of Benjamin and Miriam Kagan; m 1943, Margaret Stromas; two s one d. Educ: High School, Kaunas, Lithuania; Leeds University. BCom hons (Textiles). Founder of 'Gannex'-Kagan Textiles Limited, 1951, thereafter Chairman and Managing Director. Recreation: chess. Address: Barkisland Hall, Barkisland, near Halifax, West Yorks.

KAHN, family name of Baron Kahn.

KAHN, Baron, cr 1965 (Life Peer), of Hampstead; **Richard Ferdinand Kahn**, CBE 1946; FBA 1960; MA; Professor of Economics, Cambridge University,

1951-72; Fellow of King's College, Cambridge; b 10 Aug. 1905; s of late Augustus Kahn. Educ: St Paul's Sch. (Scholar); King's College, Cambridge (Scholar). Temporary Civil Servant in various Govt Depts, 1939-46. Publications: Selected Essays on Employment and Growth, 1973; articles on economic subjects. Address: King's College, Cambridge CB2 1ST. T: Cambridge 350411. Club: United Oxford & Cambridge University.

KAHN-ACKERMANN, Georg; Secretary General, Council of Europe, 1974-79; b 4 Jan. 1918; m 1945, Rosmarie Müller-Diefenbach; one s three d. Educ: in Germany and Switzerland. Served in Armed Forces, 1939-45. Press Reporter and Editor from 1946; Commentator with Radio Bavaria and wrote for newspaper, Abendzeitung, 1950. Author of several books, a publisher's reader, and mem. Exec. Cttee of Bavarian Assoc. of Journalists. Dir, VG WORT, Munich, 1972-74; Vice-Chm., Bd of Deutschlandfunk (Cologne). Mem., Social Democratic Party (SDP), from 1946, and of the German Federal Parliament, 1953-57, 1962-69 and 1970-74. Previous appts include: Vice-Pres., Western European Union Assembly, 1967-70; Chm., Political Commn of Western European Union, 1971-74; Vice-Pres., Consultative Assembly of Council of Europe until elected Secretary General in 1974. Recreations: horse-riding, ski-ing. Address: Sterzenweg 3, 8193 Ammerland, Bayern, Germany.

KAHURANANGA, Most Rev. Musa; see Tanzania, Archbishop of.

KAISER, Philip M.; political and economic consultant; b 12 July 1913; s of Morris Kaiser and Temma Kaiser (née Sloven); m 1939, Hannah Greeley; three s. Educ: University of Wisconsin; Balliol Coll., Oxford (Rhodes Scholar). Economist, Bd of Governors, Fed. Reserve System, 1939-42; Chief, Project Ops Staff, also Chief, Planning Staff, Bd Economic Warfare and Foreign Econ. Admin., 1942-46; Expert on Internat. Organization Affairs, US State Dept., 1946; Exec. Asst to Asst Sec. of Labor in charge of internat. labor affairs, US Dept of Labor, 1947-49; Asst Sec. of Labor for Internat. Labor Affairs, 1949-53; mem., US Govt Bd of Foreign Service, Dept of State, 1948-53; US Govt mem., Governing Body of ILO, 1948-53; Chief, US delegn to ILO Confs, 1949-53; Special Asst to Governor of New York, 1954-58; Prof. of Internat. Relations and Dir, Program for Overseas Labor and Industrial Relations, Sch. of Internat. Service, American Univ., 1958-61; US Ambassador, Republic of Senegal and Islamic Republic of Mauritania, 1961-64; Minister, Amer. Embassy, London, 1964-69. Chm., Encyclopaedia Britannica International Ltd, 1969-75; Dir, Guinness Mahon Holdings Ltd, 1975-77. US Ambassador to Hungary, 1977-80, to Austria, 1980-81. Member: US Govt Interdepartmental Cttee on Marshall Plan, 1947-48; Interdepartmental Cttee on Greek-Turkish aid and Point 4 Technical Assistance progs, 1947-49. Recreations: tennis, swimming, music. Address: 2101 Connecticut Avenue NW, Washington, DC 20008, USA.

KALDOR, family name of Baron Kaldor.

KALDOR, Baron cr 1974 (Life Peer), of Newnham in the City of Cambridge; **Nicholas Kaldor**, MA; FBA 1963; Professor of Economics in the University of Cambridge, 1966-75, now Emeritus (Reader in Economics, 1952-65); Fellow of King's College, Cambridge, since 1949; b Budapest, 12 May 1908; s of late Dr Julius Kaldor; m 1934, Clarissa Elisabeth Goldschmidt; four d. Educ: Model Gymnasium, Budapest; London Sch. of Economics. BSc (Econ.). 1st Class hons, 1930. Asst Lecturer, Lecturer and Reader in Economics, London Sch. of Economics, 1932-47; Rockefeller travelling Fellowship in US, 1935-36; Research Associate (part-time), Nat. Inst. of Economic and Social Research, 1943-45; Chief of Economic Planning Staff, US Strategic Bombing Survey, 1945; Dir, Research and Planning Division, Economic Commission for Europe, Geneva, 1947-49; Mem. of UN group of experts on international measures for full employment, 1949; Mem. of Royal Commission on Taxation of Profits and Income, 1951-55; Adviser on tax reform, Government of India, 1956; Economic Adviser, Economic Commission for Latin America, Santiago, Chile, 1956; Fiscal Adviser, Govt of Ceylon, 1958; Ford Visiting Research Prof., University of Calif., 1959-60; Fiscal Adviser, Government of Mexico, 1960; Economic Adviser, Govt of Ghana, 1961; Fiscal Adviser, Govt of British Guiana, 1961, of Turkey, 1962, of Iran, 1966, of Venezuela, 1976; Visiting Economist, Reserve Bank of Australia, Sydney, 1963. Special Adviser to the Chancellor of the Exchequer, 1964-68 and 1974-76. Pres., Section F, British Assoc. for Advancement of Science, 1970. Hon. Member: Amer. Acad. of Arts and Scis; Amer. Econ. Assoc.; Royal Econ. Soc. of Belgium; Hungarian Acad. of Scis, 1979. Hon. Fellow, LSE, 1970. Pres., REconS, 1974-76. Hon. doctorates, Dijon and Frankfurt. Publications: Quantitative Aspects of the Full Employment Problem in Britain (in Beveridge's Full Employment in a Free Soc.), 1944; (jointly) Statistical Analysis of Advertising Expenditure and Revenue of the Press, 1948; (part author) National and International Measures for Full Employment, 1950; An Expenditure Tax, 1955; Indian Tax Reform, 1956; Essays in Economic Stability and Growth, 1960; Essays in Value and Distribution, 1960; Capital Accumulation and Economic Growth (in The Theory of Capital), 1961; Ensayos sobre Desarrollo Económico (Mexico), 1961; Essays on Economic Policy, Vols I, II, 1964; Causes of the Slow Rate of Growth of the United Kingdom, 1966; Conflicts in Policy Objectives, 1971; Further Essays on Economic Theory, 1978; Further Essays on Applied Economics, 1978; Reports on Taxation, Vols I, II, 1980; Origins of the New Monetarism, 1981; The Scourge of Monetarism, 1982; papers in various economic jls. Address: King's College, Cambridge CB2 1ST; 2 Adams Road, Cambridge CB3 9AD. T: Cambridge 59282. Club:

Reform.
See also M. J. Stewart.

KAMBA, Prof. Walter Joseph; Principal and Vice-Chancellor, since 1981 (Vice-Principal, 1980-81), Professor of Law, since 1980, University of Zimbabwe; *b* 6 Sept. 1931; *s* of Joseph Mafara and Hilda Kamba; *m* 1960, Angeline Saziso Dube; three *s. Educ:* University of Cape Town (BA, LLB); Yale Law School (LLM). Attorney of the High Court of Rhodesia (now Zimbabwe), 1963-66; Research Fellow, Institute of Advanced Legal Studies, London Univ., 1967-68; Lecturer, then Sen. Lectr, in Comparative Law and Jurisprudence, 1969-80, Dean of the Faculty of Law, 1977-80, Univ. of Dundee. Vice-Chm., Bd of Governors, Zimbabwe Broadcasting Corp., 1980-; Member: Public Service Professional Qualifications Panel, Harare, 1981-; Council, ACU, 1981-; Standing Cttee on student mobility within Commonwealth, 1982-. Legal Adviser, ZANU (Patriotic Front), 1977-80. Trustee: Zimbabwe Mass Media Trust, 1981-; Conservation Trust of Zimbabwe, 1981-. Mem. Council, Univ. for Peace, Costa Rica, 1981-; Governor, Ranche House Coll., Harare, 1980-. Hon. LLD Dundee, 1982. *Publications:* articles in Internat. and Comparative Law Quarterly, Juridical Review. *Recreation:* tennis. *Address:* University of Zimbabwe, PO Box MP 167, Mount Pleasant, Harare, Zimbabwe. *T:* Harare 303211.

KAN, Prof. Yuet Wai, FRS 1981; Professor of Medicine, since 1977, and Investigator (formerly Director), Howard Hughes Medical Institute Laboratory, since 1976, University of California, San Francisco; *b* 11 June 1936; *s* of Kan Tong Po and Kan Li Lai Wan; *m* 1964, Alvera L. Limauro; two *d. Educ:* Univ. of Hong Kong (MB, BS, DSc). Research Associate, Children's Hosp. Medical Center, Dept of Pediatrics, Harvard Medical Sch., Boston, Mass; Asst Prof. of Pediatrics, Harvard Medical Sch., 1970-72; Associate Prof. of Medicine, Depts of Medicine and Laboratory Medicine, Univ. of California, San Francisco, 1972-77; Chief, Hematology Service, San Francisco General Hospital, 1972-79. Hon. MD, Univ. of Caglieri, Sardinia, 1981. *Publications:* contribs to: Nature, Proc. of Nat. Academy of Sciences, Jl of Clinical Investigation, Blood, British Jl of Haematology, and others. *Recreations:* tennis, skiing. *Address:* 1504 HSE, University of California San Francisco, San Francisco, California 94143, USA. *T:* (415) 666-5841.
See also Sir Kan Yuet-Keung.

KAN YUET-KEUNG, Sir, GBE 1979 (CBE 1967; OBE 1959); Kt 1972; JP; Chairman, Hong Kong Trade Development Council, since 1979; Chairman, Bank of East Asia Ltd, since 1963; *b* 26 July 1913; *s* of late Kan Tong Po, JP; *m* 1940, Ida; two *s* one *d. Educ:* Hong Kong Univ.; London Univ. BA Hong Kong 1934. Solicitor. Pro-Chancellor and Chm. of Council, Chinese Univ. of Hong Kong, 1973-. Hon. Fellow, LSE, 1980. Hon. LLD: Chinese Univ. of Hong Kong, 1968; Univ. of Hong Kong, 1973. Order of Sacred Treasure, 3rd Class, Japan; Officier de l'Ordre National du Mérite (France), 1978. *Recreations:* tennis, swimming, golf. *Address:* Swire House, 11th Floor, Chater Road, Hong Kong. *T:* Hong Kong 238181.
See also Yuet Wai Kan.

KANE, Professor George; FBA 1968; William Rand Kenan Jr Professor of English in the University of North Carolina at Chapel Hill, since 1976, Chairman of the Division of the Humanities, since 1980; *b* 4 July 1916; *o s* of George Michael and Clara Kane; *m* 1946, Katherine Bridget, *o d* of Lt-Col R. V. Montgomery, MC; one *s* one *d. Educ:* St Peter's Coll.; British Columbia University; Toronto Univ.; University Coll., London (Fellow 1971). BA (University of BC), 1936; Research Fellow, University of Toronto, 1936-37; MA (Toronto), 1937; Research Fellow, Northwestern Univ., 1937-38; IODE Schol., for BC, 1938-39. Served War of 1939-45: Artists' Rifles, 1939-40; Rifle Bde, 1940-46 (despatches). PhD (London), 1946; Asst Lecturer in English, University Coll., London, 1946, Lecturer, 1948, Reader in English, 1953; Prof. of English Language and Literature and Head of English Dept, Royal Holloway College, London Univ., 1955-65; Prof. of English Language and Medieval Literature, 1965-76 and Head of English Dept, 1968-76, King's College, London, Prof. Emeritus, 1976, Fellow, 1976. Vis. Prof., Medieval Acad. of America, 1970, 1982, Corresp. Fellow, 1975, Fellow, 1978; Fellow, Amer. Acad. of Arts and Scis, 1977; Sen. Fellow, Southeastern Inst. of Medieval and Renaissance Studies, 1978. Member: Council, Early English Text Soc., 1969; Governing Body, SOAS, 1970-76; Council, British Acad., 1974-76; Governing Body, Univ. of N Carolina Press, 1979. Sir Israel Gollancz Memorial Prize, British Acad., 1963; Haskins Medallist, Med. Acad. of Amer., 1978. Chambers Meml Lectr, University Coll. London, 1965; British Academy Lectr, Accademia Nazionale dei Lincei, Rome, 1976; John Coffin Meml Lectr, Univ. of London, 1979; Public Orator, Univ. of London, 1962-66; Annual Chaucer Lectr, New Chaucer Soc., 1980. Gen. editor of London Edn of Piers Plowman. *Publications:* Middle English Literature, 1951; Piers Plowman, the A Version, 1960; Piers Plowman: The Evidence for Authorship, 1965; Piers Plowman: the B version, 1975; articles and reviews. *Recreation:* fishing. *Address:* Greenlaw Hall, Chapel Hill, North Carolina, USA. *Clubs:* Athenæum, Flyfishers'.

KANE, Jack, OBE 1969; DL; JP; Chairman, Consultative Council, South of Scotland Electricity Board, 1977-81; Lord Provost of the City of Edinburgh and Lord Lieutenant of the County of the City of Edinburgh, 1972-75; *b* 1 April 1911; *m* 1940, Anne Murphy; one *s* two *d. Educ:* Bathgate Academy. Served War, 1940-46. Librarian, 1936-55; SE of Scotland Dist Sec., Workers' Educational Assoc., 1955-76. Chm., Board of Trustees for Nat. Galls of Scotland, 1975-80; Mem., South of Scotland Electricity Bd, 1975-81. JP

Edinburgh, 1945; DL City of Edinburgh, 1976. Dr *hc* Edinburgh, 1976. Grand Officer, Order of the Oaken Crown (Luxembourg), 1972; Grand Cross of Merit (W Germany). *Recreations:* reading, walking. *Address:* 88 Thirlestane Road, Edinburgh EH9 1AS. *T:* 031-447 7757. *Club:* Newcraighall Miners' Welfare Inst.

KANTOROVICH, Prof. Leonid Vitaljevich; Head of Department, Institute of Systems Research, Moscow, USSR, since 1976; mathematician, economist; *b* Leningrad, 19 Jan. 1912; *m* 1938, Natalja Vladimirovna Iljana; one *s* one *d. Educ:* Univ. of Leningrad, 1930. Instructor, Leningrad Inst. of Industrial Construction Engineering, 1930-34; Professor, 1934-39; Instructor, Leningrad Univ., 1932-34; Professor, 1934-41, 1945-60, Mathem. Inst., Acad. of Sciences (Leningrad Filial) (Head of Dept, 1945-60); Dep. Dir, Mathem. Inst., Siberian Branch, Acad. of Sciences of the USSR, 1960-71; Prof., Novosibirsk State Univ., 1960-70; Head of Research Lab., Inst. of Nat. Economy Control, Moscow, 1971-76. Corr. Mem., Acad. of Sciences of the USSR, 1958-64; Mem., 1964-. Foreign Member: Hungarian Acad. of Sciences, 1967; Acad. of Arts and Science, Boston, USA, 1969; Mexican Engrg Acad., 1976; Yugoslavian Acad. of Sciences and Arts, 1979. Dr *hc:* Glasgow, 1966; Grenoble, 1967; Nice, 1969; Helsinki, 1970; Sorbonne, Paris, 1975; Vysoka Scola Econ. i Plan., Warsaw, 1975; Cambridge, 1976; Pennsylvania, 1976; Indian Statistical Inst., Calcutta, 1978. State Prize, USSR, 1949; Lenin Prize, USSR, 1965; Nobel Prize for Economics, 1975. Order Sign of Honour, 1944; Order of Labour Red banner, 1949, 1950, 1975; Order of Lenin, 1967, 1982. *Publications:* Variatsionnoe iscislenie (Calculus of Variations), 1933; Priblizhennye metody vysshego analiza (Approximate Methods of Higher Analysis), 1936; Matematicheskie metody organizatsii i planirvaniya proizvodstva (Mathematical Methods of Organizing and Planning Production), 1939; Funktsional'nyi analiz v poluuporyadochennyh prosranstvah (Functional Analysis in Semiordered Spaces), 1950; Rascet ratsional'nogo raskroya promyschlennyh materialov (Calculation of Rational Cutting of Industrial Materials), 1951; Ekonomichesky rascet nailuchschego ispolzovaniya resursov (Economical Calculation of the Best Use of Resources), 1959; Funktsional'nyi analiz y normirovannyh prostranstvah (Functional Analysis in Normed Spaces), 1959; Optimal'nye rescheniya v ekonomike (Optimal Decisions in Economy), 1972; Essays in Optimal Planning, 1976; Funktsional'nyi Analiz (Functional Analysis), 1977. *Recreations:* swimming, chess. *Address:* Akademia Nauk, Leninsky Prospekt, 14, Moscow, USSR.

KANTOROWICH, Prof. Roy Herman, BArch (Witwatersrand), MA (Manchester), RIBA, FRTPI; Professor of Town and Country Planning, University of Manchester, since 1961; Dean of the Faculty of Arts, 1975-76; *b* Johannesburg, 24 Nov. 1916; *s* of George Kantorowich and Deborah (*née* Baranov); *m* 1943, Petronella Sophie Wissema (violinist, as Nella Wissema); one *s* two *d. Educ:* King Edward VII Sch., Johannesburg; University of Witwatersrand. BArch 1939; ARIBA 1940; MTPI 1965 (AMTPI 1946). Post-grad. studies in Housing and Planning, MIT and Columbia Univ., 1939-41; Planning Officer: Vanderbijl Park New Town, 1942-45; directing Cape Town Foreshore Scheme, 1945-48; private practice in Cape Town, in architecture and town planning, 1948-61. Pres., S African Inst. Town and Regional Planners, 1960. Formerly Town Planning Consultant to Cape Provincial Admin., and for many cities and towns in S Africa incl. Durban, Pretoria and Port Elizabeth; Cons. for New Town of Ashkelon, Israel, 1950-56. Member: NW Econ. Planning Coun. 1965-79; Council (Chm., Educn Cttee), TPI, 1965-70; Planning Cttee, SSRC, 1969-73; Construction and Environment Bd, and Chm., Town Planning Panel, CNAA, 1971-75; Natal Building Soc. Fellowship, 1980. Buildings include: Civic Centre, Welkom, OFS; Baxter Hall, University of Cape Town; Sea Point Telephone Exchange (Cape Province Inst. of Architects Bronze Medal Award); Architecture and Planning Building, Univ. of Manchester. FRSA 1972. *Publications:* Cape Town Foreshore Plan, 1948; (with Lord Holford) Durban 1985, a plan for central Durban in its Regional Setting, 1968; Three Perspectives on planning for the 'eighties, 1981; contribs to SAArch. Record, Jl RTPI and other professional jls. *Recreations:* music, tennis. *Address:* 3 Winster Avenue, Manchester M20 8YA. *T:* 061-445 9417. *Club:* Northern Lawn Tennis.

KAPITZA, Peter Leonidovich, FRS 1929; PhD Cantab; FInstP; Director of Institute for Physical Problems of Academy of Sciences of the USSR; Editor, Journal of Experimental and Theoretical Physics of Academy of Sciences, USSR; late Royal Society Messel Research Professor; late Director of the Royal Society Mond Laboratory; *b* Kronstadt, Russia, 26 June (old style) 1894; *s* of late Gen. Leonid Kapitza and Olga, *d* of Gen. J. Stebnitskiy; *m* 1st, late Nadejda, *d* of Cyril Tschernosvitoff; 2nd, Anna, *d* of Professor A. N. Kryloff; two *s. Educ:* Secondary Sch., Kronstadt; Petrograd Politechnical Inst. (Faculty of Electrical Engrg). Lecturer, Petrograd Politechnical Inst., 1919-21; Clerk Maxwell Student, Cambridge Univ., 1923-26; Fellow, Trinity Coll., 1925 (Hon. Fellow, 1966). Asst Dir of Magnetic Research, Cavendish Laboratory, Cambridge, 1924-32; Cor. Mem. Acad. of Science of USSR, 1929; Mem. Acad. of Science, USSR, 1939; Hon. Member: Société des Naturalistes de Moscou, 1935; European Physical Soc., 1981; Fellow, Amer. Physical Soc., 1937; Hon. MInst. Met., 1943; Hon. Mem. and Franklin Medal of Franklin Inst., USA, 1944; Foreign Member: Council, French Physical Soc., 1935; Royal Acad. of Science, Sweden, 1966; Royal Netherlands Acad. of Sciences, 1969; Serbian Acad. of Sciences and Arts, 1971; Finnish Acad. of Science and Letters, 1974; Czechoslovak Acad. of Sciences, 1980; For. Hon. Mem., Amer. Acad. of Arts and Sciences, 1968. Numerous Hon. Doctorates,

Fellowships, etc, 1944-. Rutherford Memorial Lectr, 1969. Medal Liege Univ., 1934; State prize for Physics, 1941 and 1943; Faraday Medal of Electr. Engrs, 1942; Sir Devaprasad Sarbadhikari Gold Medal, Calcutta Univ., 1955; Kothenius Gold Medal of German Acad. of Naturalists, 1959; Lomonosov Gold Medal, Acad. of Sciences, USSR, 1959; Great Gold Medal, Exhibn of Economic Achievements USSR, 1962; International Niels Bohr Gold Medal of Dansk Ingeniørvorening, 1964; Rutherford Medal of Inst. of Physics and Physical Soc., England, 1966; Kamerlingh Onnes Gold Medal of Netherlands Soc. for Refrigeration, 1968; Simon Prize, Inst. Physics, 1973; (jtly) Nobel Prize for Physics, 1978; Helmholtz Medal, Akad. der Wissenschaften, DDR, 1981. Order of Lenin, 1943, 1944, 1945, 1964, 1971, 1974; Moscow Defence Medal, 1944; Hero of Socialist Labour, 1945, 1974; Order of the Red Banner of Labour, 1954; Order of Yugoslav Banner with Ribbon, 1967. *Publications:* Collected Papers, 3 vols, 1964-67; Experiment, Theory, Practice, 1980; various publications on physics, mainly on magnetism, cryogenics and high temperature plasma in scientific journals. *Recreation:* chess. *Address:* The Institute for Physical Problems, ul. Kosygina 2, Moscow GSP1, 117973, USSR.

KAPLAN, Prof. Joseph; Professor of Physics, University of California at Los Angeles (UCLA), 1940-70, now Professor Emeritus; *b* 8 Sept. 1902; *s* of Henry and Rosa Kaplan, Tapolcza, Hungary; *m* 1933, Katherine Elizabeth Feraud; no *c. Educ:* Johns Hopkins University, Baltimore, Md, PhD 1927; National Research Fellow, Princeton Univ., 1927-28. University of Calif. at Los Angeles: Asst Prof. of Physics, 1928-35; Associate Prof., 1935-40; Prof., 1940-. Chief, Operations Analysis Section, Second Air Force, 1943-45 (Exceptional Civilian Service Medal, US Air Corps, 1947). Chm., US Nat. Cttee for Internat. Geophysical Year, 1953-64. Fellow: Inst. of Aeronautical Sciences, 1957; Amer. Meteorological Soc., 1970 (Pres., 1963-67). Mem. Nat. Acad. of Sciences, 1957; Hon. Mem., Amer. Meteorological Soc., 1967; Vice-Pres., International Union of Geodesy and Geophysics, 1960-63, Pres., 1963-; Hon. Governor, Hebrew Univ. of Jerusalem, 1968. Hon. DSc: Notre Dame, 1957; Carleton Coll., 1957; Hon. LHD: Yeshiva Univ. and Hebrew Union Coll., 1958; Univ. of Judaism, 1959. Exceptional Civilian Service Medal (USAF), 1960; Hodgkins Prize and Medal, 1965. Exceptional Civilian Service Medal, 1969; John A. Fleming Medal, Amer. Geophysical Union, 1970; Commemorative Medal, 50th Anniversary, Amer. Meteorological Soc., 1970; Special Award, UCLA Alumni Assoc., 1970. *Publications:* Across the Space Frontier, 1950; Physics and Medicine of the Upper Atmosphere, 1952; (co-author) Great Men of Physics, 1969; publications in Physical Review, Nature, Proc. Nat. Acad. of Sciences, Jl Chemical Physics. *Recreations:* golf, ice-skating, walking. *Address:* 1565 Kelton Avenue, Los Angeles, Calif 90024, USA. *T:* Granite 38839. *Club:* Cosmos (Washington, DC).

KAPPEL, Frederick R.; retired as Chairman of Boards, American Telephone & Telegraph Company and International Paper Company; Chairman, Board of Governors, US Postal Service; *b* Albert Lea, Minnesota, 14 Jan. 1902; *s* of Fred A. Kappel and Gertrude M. Towle Kappel; *m* 1st, 1927, Ruth Carolyn Ihm (decd); two *d* ; 2nd, 1978, Alice McW. Harris. *Educ:* University of Minnesota (BSE). Northwestern Bell Telephone Company: various positions in Minnesota, 1924-33; Plant Engineer, Nebraska, S Dakota, 1934. Plant Operations Supervisor (Exec.) Gen. Staff, Omaha, Nebraska, 1937, Asst Vice-Pres. Operations, 1939, Vice-Pres. Operations and Dir, 1942. Amer. Telephone & Telegraph Co., NY: Asst Vice-Pres. (O & E), Vice-Pres. (Long Lines), Vice Pres. (O & E), 1949. Pres. Western Electric Co., 1954-56; Chm. and Chief Exec. Officer, Amer. Tel. & Tel. Co., 1956-67, Chm. Exec. Cttee, 1967-69; Chm. Bd, International Paper Co., 1969-71, Chm. Exec. Cttee 1971-74. Director: Amer. Telephone & Telegraph Co., 1956-70; Chase Manhattan Bank, 1956-72; Metropolitan Life Insurance Co., 1958-75; General Foods Corporation, 1961-73; Standard Oil Co. (NJ), 1966-70; Whirlpool Corp., 1967-72; Chase Manhattan Corp., 1969-72; Boys' Club of America; Acad. of Polit. Sciences, 1963-71; Member: Business Council (Chm., 1963-64); Advisory Board of Salvation Army, 1957-73; US Chamber of Commerce; various societies. Trustee: Presbyterian Hospital, 1949-74; Grand Central Art Galleries, Inc., 1957-70; Aerospace Corp., 1967-74; Tax Foundation, 1960-72. Trustee, University of Minnesota Foundation. Holds numerous hon. doctorates and awards, including: Cross of Comdr of Postal Award, France, 1962; Presidential Medal of Freedom, 1964. *Publications:* Vitality in a Business Enterprise, 1960; Business Purpose and Performance. *Recreation:* golf. *Address:* Apt 1101, 435 S Gulfstream Avenue, Sarasota, Fla 33577, USA. *Clubs:* Triangle, University, Economic (New York); International (Washington); Bird Key Yacht, Sarabay Country (Sarasota, Fla).

KARACHI, Archbishop of, (RC), since 1958; **His Eminence Cardinal Joseph Cordeiro;** *b* Bombay, India, 19 Jan. 1918. *Educ:* St Patrick's High School; DJ College, Karachi; Papal Seminary, Kandy, Ceylon. Priest, 1946; Asst Chaplain, St Francis Xavier's, Hyderabad, Sind, 1947; Asst Principal, St Patrick's High School, Karachi, 1948; Student at Oxford, 1948; Asst Principal, St Patrick's High Sch., 1950; Principal, Grammar Sch., and Rector, Diocesan Seminary, Quetta, 1952. Cardinal, 1973. *Address:* St Patrick's Cathedral, Karachi 3, Pakistan. *T:* 515870.

KARAJAN, Herbert von; *see* Von Karajan.

KARANJA, Dr Josphat Njuguna; Chairman, General Accident Insurance Co. (Kenya) Ltd, since 1980; *b* 5 Feb. 1931; *s* of Josphat Njuguna; *m* 1966, Beatrice Nyindombi, Fort Portal, Uganda; one *s* two *d. Educ:* Alliance High Sch., Kikuyu, Kenya; Makerere Coll., Kampala, Uganda; University of Delhi,

India; Princeton Univ., New Jersey, USA (PhD). Lecturer in African Studies, Farleigh Dickinson Univ., New Jersey, 1961-62; Lecturer in African and Modern European History, University College, Nairobi, Kenya, 1962-63; High Comr for Kenya in London, 1963-70; Vice-Chancellor, Univ. of Nairobi, 1970-79. *Recreations:* golf, tennis. *Address:* General Accident Insurance Co. (Kenya) Ltd, Icea Building, Kenyatta Avenue, PO Box 42166, Nairobi, Kenya.

KARASEK, Franz, DL; Austrian international administrator; Secretary-General, Council of Europe, since 1979; *b* 22 April 1924; *m* 1951, Gertrud Hnolik; one *s* one *d. Educ:* Vienna Univ. and Paris. Official, Ministry for Foreign Affairs, 1950-52; Private Sec. to Fed. Chancellor, 1952-56; Counsellor, Austrian Embassy, Paris 1956-60 and Moscow 1960-64; Prin. Private Sec. to Fed. Chancellor, 1964-66; Dir-Gen. for Foreign Cultural Relations at Fed. Min. of Educn, 1966-70; Mem. Nat. Council (lower house of Parlt), 1970-79; substitute Mem., Austrian delegn to Parly Assembly of Council of Europe, 1970-72, Rep. in Austrian delegn 1972-79; Vice-Pres., Parly Assembly of CE, 1973-74; Mem. Austrian delegn to UN Gen. Assembly, 1970-79; Austrian Mem., Council of IPU, 1972-79. Grosses Goldenes Ehrenzeichen, Austria; Chevalier, Ordre Léopold II, Belgium; Chevalier, Ordre Couronne de Chêne, Luxembourg; Knight of St Sylvester, Vatican; Commandeur, Ordre de la Couronne Belge; Commander of Order of Nat. Merit, Italy; Commandeur de la Légion d'honneur. *Publications:* articles in international reviews. *Recreation:* horse-riding. *Address:* Council of Europe, avenue de l'Europe, F-67006 Strasbourg Cedex, France. *T:* 61-49-61.

KARIMJEE, Sir Tayabali Hassanali Alibhoy, Kt 1955; Brilliant Star of Zanzibar (3rd Class); Jubilee Medal of Sultan of Zanzibar; *b* 7 Nov. 1897; *s* of Hassanali A. Karimjee and Zenubbai H. A. Karimjee; *m* 1917, Sugrabai Mohamedali Karimjee; one *d. Educ:* Zanzibar and Karachi. Pres., Indian National Association, Zanzibar, 1930 and 1942; Pres. Chamber of Commerce, Zanzibar, 1940 1941, 1942; Mem. Fighter Fund Cttee, 1940-43; Mem. Red Cross Cttee, 1940-45; MLC, Zanzibar, 1933-45. Chm. Board of Directors, Karimjee Jivanjee & Co. Ltd, Karimjee Jivanjee Estates Ltd, Karimjee J. Properties Ltd, International Motor Mart Ltd (Tanganyika); Director, Karimjee Jivanjee & Co. (UK) Ltd, London. King George V Jubilee Medal, 1935; Coronation Medals, 1937 and 1953. *Address:* 234 E. I. Lines, Aziz Bhatti (NH) Road, Karachi 4, Pakistan. *Clubs:* Royal Commonwealth Society, Royal Over-Seas League; Karachi (Karachi); WIAA (Bombay).

KARK, (Arthur) Leslie; MA (Oxon); FRSA; Author, Barrister; Chairman: Lucie Clayton Secretarial College; Lucie Clayton Ltd; *b* 12 July 1910; *s* of Victor and Helena Kark, Johannesburg; *m* 1st, 1935, Joan Tetley (marr. diss., 1956); two *d* ; 2nd, 1956, Evelyn Gordine (see E. F. Kark); one *s* one *d. Educ:* Clayesmore; St John's Coll., Oxford. Called to Bar, Inner Temple, 1932; Features Editor of World's Press News, 1933; Editor of Photography, 1934; Public Relations Officer to Advertising Association, 1935; Features Editor News Review, 1936-39; London Theatre Critic, New York Herald Tribune; News Editor, Ministry of Information, 1940. Served War of 1939-45, RAF, 1940-46; Air-gunner; Wing Commander in Command of Public Relations (Overseas) Unit; author, Air Ministry's official book on Air War, Far East. Short stories and novels translated into French. Swedish, German, Polish, etc. *Publications:* The Fire Was Bright, 1944; Red Rain, 1946; An Owl in the Sun, 1948; Wings of the Phœnix, 1949; On the Haycock, 1957. *Recreations:* fly-fishing, golf. *Address:* 9 Clareville Grove, SW7. *T:* 01-373 2621; Roche House, Sheep Street, Burford, Oxon. *T:* Burford 3007. *Club:* Savage.

KARK, Austen Steven; Deputy Managing Director, External Broadcasting, BBC, since 1981; *b* 20 Oct. 1926; *s* of Major Norman Kark and late Ethel Kark, Eaton Place, London, and Johannesburg; *m* 1st, 1949, Margaret Solomon (marr. diss. 1954); two *d* ; 2nd, 1954, Nina Mary Bawden, *qv* ; one *d* two step *s. Educ:* Upper Canada Coll., Toronto; Nautical Coll., Pangbourne; RNC; Magdalen Coll., Oxford (MA). Served RN and RIN, 1943-46. Directed first prodn in UK of Sartre's The Flies, Oxford, 1948; trained in journalism, Belfast Telegraph, L'Illustré, Zofingen, Switzerland; Courier, Bandwagon, London Mystery Magazine; free-lance journalist and broadcaster, London and New York, 1952-54; joined BBC, 1954, as scriptwriter, European productions; Producer, External Services; travelled widely from Senegal to S Africa; Head of S European Service, 1964; Head of E European (and Russian) Service, 1972; Editor, World Service, 1973; Controller, English Services, and Editor, World Service, 1974; advised Lord Soames on election broadcasting, Rhodesia, and chaired, for Prime Minister Mugabe, enquiry into future of radio and television in Zimbabwe, 1980; Chairman, UK Alumni, Salzburg Seminar in American Studies, 1979-. *Recreations:* Real tennis, mosaics, croquet. *Address:* 22 Noel Road, N1 8HA. *T:* 01-226 2839. *Clubs:* MCC, Royal Tennis Court, Lansdowne, Bushmen (ex-Chairman), Royal Institute of International Affairs.

KARK, Mrs Evelyn Florence, (nom de plume **Lucie Clayton**); Director; *b* 5 Dec. 1928; *d* of Emily and William Gordine; *m* 1956 (Arthur) Leslie Kark, *qv* ; one *s* one *d. Educ:* privately and inconspicuously. Asst to Editor, Courier Magazine, 1950; became Head of model school and agency (assuming name of Lucie Clayton), 1952; founded Lucie Clayton Sch. of Fashion Design and Dressmaking, 1961, and Lucie Clayton Secretarial College, 1966. *Publication:* The World of Modelling, 1968. *Recreations:* talking, tapestry, cooking. *Address:* 9 Clareville Grove, SW7. *T:* 01-373 2621; Roche House, Burford, Oxfordshire. *T:* Burford 3007.

KARK, Leslie; see Kark, A. L.

KARK, Mrs Nina Mary; see Bawden, N. M.

KARMEL, His Honour Alexander D., QC 1954; an Additional Judge, Central Criminal Court, later a Circuit Judge, 1968-79; *b* 16 May 1904; *s* of Elias Karmel and Adeline (*née* Freedman); *m* 1937, Mary, *widow* of Arthur Lee and *d* of Newman Lipton; one *s. Educ:* Newcastle upon Tyne Royal Grammar Sch. Barrister-at-law, Middle Temple, 1932; Master of the Bench, 1962; Leader of Northern Circuit, 1966; Comr of Assize, Stafford, summer 1967; Recorder of Bolton, 1962-68. Mem., Bar Council, 1950-53, 1961-64. *Recreations:* croquet, golf. *Address:* 171 Rivermead Court, Ranelagh Gardens, SW6 3SF. *T:* 01-736 4609. *Clubs:* Royal Automobile, Hurlingham.

KARMEL, Emeritus Prof. Peter Henry, AC 1976; CBE 1967; Vice-Chancellor, Australian National University, since 1982; *b* 9 May 1922; *s* of Simeon Karmel; *m* 1946, Lena Garrett; one *s* five *d. Educ:* Caulfield Grammar Sch.; Univ. of Melbourne (BA); Trinity Coll., Cambridge (PhD). Research Officer, Commonwealth Bureau of Census and Statistics, 1943-45; Lectr in Econs, Univ. of Melbourne, 1946; Rouse Ball Res. Student, Trinity Coll., Cambridge, 1947-48; Sen. Lectr in Econs, Univ. of Melbourne, 1949; Prof. of Econs, 1950-62, Emeritus, 1965, Univ. of Adelaide; Principal-designate, Univ. of Adelaide at Bedford Park (subseq. Flinders Univ. of SA), 1961-66; Vice-Chancellor, Flinders Univ. of SA, 1966-71; Chancellor, Univ. of Papua and New Guinea, 1969-70 (Chm., Interim Council, 1965-69); Chairman: Univs Commn, 1971-77; Commonwealth Tertiary Educn Commn, 1977-82. Mem., SSRC, 1952-71; Mem. Council, Univ. of Adelaide, 1955-69; Vis. Prof. of Econs, Queen's Univ., Belfast, 1957-58; Mem. Commonwealth Cttee: on Future of Tertiary Educn, 1961-65; of Economic Enquiry, 1963-65; Member: Australian Council for Educnl Research, 1968- (Pres., 1979-); Cttee of Enquiry into Educn in SA, 1969-70 (Chm.); Adv. Cttee of Cities Commn, 1972-74; Interim Cttee for Aust. Schools Commn, 1972-73 (Chm.); Cttee of Enquiry on Med. Schs, 1972-73 (Chm.); Cttee of Enquiry on Open Univ., 1973-74 (Chm.); CSIRO Adv. Council, 1979-82. Chairman: Australia Council, 1974-77; Cttee on Post-Secondary Educn in Tasmania, 1975-76. Leader, OECD Review of US Educn Policy, 1978-79 and NZ Educn Policy, 1982. FACE 1969; FASSA 1971. Hon. LLD: Univ. of Papua and New Guinea, 1970; Univ. of Melbourne, 1975; Hon. LittD Flinders Univ. of SA, 1971; Hon. DLit, Murdoch Univ., 1975; DU Newcastle, NSW, 1978. *Publications:* Applied Statistics for Economists, 1957, 1962 (1970 edn with M. Polasek, 4th edn 1977), Portuguese edn, 1972; (with M. Brunt) Structure of the Australian Economy, 1962, repr. 1963, 1966; (with G. C. Harcourt and R. H. Wallace) Economic Activity, 1967 (Italian edn 1969); articles in Economic Record, Population Studies, Jl Royal Statistical Assoc., and other learned jls. *Address:* Australian National University, PO Box 4, Canberra, ACT 2600, Australia. *T:* 062-495111.

KARP, David; novelist; *b* New York City, 5 May 1922; *s* of Abraham Karp and Rebecca Levin; *m* 1944, Lillian Klass; two *s. Educ:* College of The City of New York. US Army, 1943-46, S Pacific, Japan; College, 1946-48; Continuity Dir, Station WNYC, New York, 1948-49; free-lance motion picture-television writer and motion picture producer, 1949-; President: Tela Productions Inc., 1968-; Television-Radio Branch, Writers Guild of America West, 1969-71; Member: Editorial Bd, Television Quarterly, 1966-72, 1971-77; Council, Writers Guild of America, 1966-73; Bd of Trustees, Producer-Writers Guild of America Pension Plan, 1968- (Chm., 1978); Bd of Trustees, Writers Guild-Industry Health Fund, 1973- (Chm., 1980). Guggenheim Fellow, 1956-57. *Publications:* One, 1953; The Day of the Monkey, 1955; All Honorable Men, 1956; Leave Me Alone, 1957; The Sleepwalkers, 1960; Vice-President in Charge of Revolution (with Murray D. Lincoln), 1960; The Last Believers, 1964; short stories in Saturday Eve. Post, Collier's, Esquire, Argosy, The American, etc; articles and reviews in NY Times, Los Angeles Times, Saturday Review, Nation, etc. *Recreations:* photography, reading. *Address:* 1116 Corsica Drive, Pacific Palisades, Calif 90272, USA. *T:* 459-1623. *Club:* PEN (New York).

KARSH, Yousuf, OC 1968; Portrait Photographer since 1932; *b* Mardin, Armenia-in-Turkey, 23 Dec. 1908; parents Armenian; Canadian Citizen; *m* 1939, Solange Gauthier (*d* 1961); *m* 1962, Estrellita Maria Nachbar. *Educ:* Sherbrooke, PQ Canada; studied photography in Boston, Mass., USA. Portrayed Winston Churchill in Canada's Houses of Parliament, 1941; King George VI, 1943; HM Queen (then Princess) Elizabeth and the Duke of Edinburgh, 1951; HH Pope Pius XII, 1951; also portrayed, among many others: Shaw, Wells, Einstein, Sibelius, Somerset Maugham, Picasso, Eden, Eisenhower, Tito, Eleanor Roosevelt, Thomas Mann, Bertrand Russell, Attlee, Nehru, Ingrid Bergmann, Lord Mountbatten of Burma, Augustus John, Pope John Paul II; nine portraits used on postage stamps of eleven countries. One man exhibns: Men Who Make our World, Pav. of Canada, Expo. 67; Montreal Mus. of Fine Arts, 1968; Boston Mus. of Fine Arts, 1968; Corning Mus., 1968; Detroit Inst. of Arts, 1969; Corcoran Gall. of Art, Washington, 1969; Macdonald House, London, 1969; Seattle Art Museum; Japan (country-wide), and Honolulu, 1970; Men Who Make our World, Europe and USA, 1971, 1972, 1973, 1974, 1975, 1976, 1977, 1978, 1979, 1980; exhibn acquired in toto by: Museum of Modern Art, Tokyo; Nat. Gall. of Australia; Province of Alberta, Canada, 1975-76; numerous exhibns throughout US, 1971-75, 1976-77; Ulrich Museum, Wichita, Kansas, 1978; Museum of Science and Industry, Chicago, 1978; Evansville Museum, Ind.,

1979; Palm Springs Desert Museum, 1980. Visiting Professor: Ohio Univ., 1967-69; Emerson Coll., Boston, 1972-73, 1973-74; Photographic Advisor, Internat. Exhibn, Expo '70, Osaka, Japan. Trustee, Photographic Arts and Scis Foundn, 1970. FRPS; Fellow Rochester Sci. Mus. RCA 1975. Holds fifteen hon. degrees. Canada Council Medal, 1965; Centennial Medal, 1967; Master of Photographic Arts, Prof. Photogrs of Canada, 1970; First Gold Medal, Nat. Assoc. Photog. Art, 1974; Life Achievement Award, Encyclopaedia Britannica, 1980. *Publications:* Faces of Destiny, 1947; (co-author) This is the Mass, 1958; Portraits of Greatness, 1959; (co-author) This is Rome, 1960; (co-author) This is the Holy Land, 1961; (autobiog.) In Search of Greatness, 1962; (co-author) These are the Sacraments, 1963; (co-author) The Warren Court; Karsh Portfolio, 1967; Faces of our Time, 1971; Karsh Portraits, 1976; Karsh Canadians, 1979. *Recreations:* tennis, bird-watching, archæology, music. *Address:* (business) Chateau Laurier Hotel, Suite 660, Ottawa, Canada. *T:* AC 613-236-7181. *Clubs:* Garrick; Rideau (Ottawa); Century, Dutch Treat (NY).

KASER, Michael Charles, MA; Reader in Economics, University of Oxford, and Professorial Fellow of St Antony's College since 1972; *b* 2 May 1926; *er s* of Charles Joseph Kaser and Mabel Blunden; *m* 1954, Elisabeth Anne Mary, *er d* of Cyril Gascoigne Piggford; four *s* one *d. Educ:* King's Coll., Cambridge (Exhibr). Foreign Service, London and Moscow, 1947-51; UN Secretariat, Econ. Commn for Europe, Geneva, 1951-63; Faculty Fellow, St Antony's Coll., Oxford, 1963-72. Vis. Prof. of Econs, Univ. of Michigan, 1966; Vis. Lectr, Cambridge Univ., 1967-68, 1977-78 and 1978-79; Vis. Lectr, INSEAD, Fontainebleau, 1959-. Oxford Univ. Latin Preacher, 1982. Convenor/Chm., Nat. Assoc. for Soviet and East European Studies, 1965-73, Chm., Jt Cttee with BUAS, 1980-; Dep. Treas., Internat. Econ. Assoc.; Vice-Chm., Internat. Activities Cttee (formerly Vice-Chm., Area Studies Panel), SSRC; Sec., Co-ordinating Council, Area Studies Assocs. Governor, Plater Coll., Oxford. Member: Council, Royal Econ. Soc.; Council, RIIA; Internat. Soc. Sci. Council, UNESCO; Council, SSEES; Editorial Boards: Soviet Studies, Energy Economics, Jl Industrial Economics, Oxford Rev. of Educn, CUP East European Monograph Series; Steering Cttee, Königswinter Anglo-German Confs (Chm., Oxford Organizing Cttee, 1975-78). *Publications:* Comecon: Integration Problems of the Planned Economies, 1965, 2nd edn 1967; (ed) Economic Development for Eastern Europe, 1968; (with J. Zieliński) Planning in East Europe, 1970; Soviet Economics, 1970; (ed, with R. Portes) Planning and Market Relations, 1971; (ed, with H. Höhmann and K. Thalheim) The New Economic Systems of Eastern Europe, 1975; (ed, with A. Brown) The Soviet Union since the Fall of Khrushchev, 1975, 2nd edn 1978; Health Care in the Soviet Union and Eastern Europe, 1976; (ed, with E. A. Radice) The Economic History of Eastern Europe 1919-1975, Vols I and II (1919-49), 1982; (ed with A. Brown) Soviet Policy for the 1980s, 1982; (ed jtly) The Cambridge Encyclopaedia of Russia and the Soviet Union, 1982; papers in economic jls and symposia. *Address:* 7 Chadlington Road, Oxford. *T:* Oxford 55581. *Club:* Reform.

KASSANIS, Basil, OBE 1977; DSc (London), FRS 1966; retired; Senior Principal Scientific Officer, Department of Plant Pathology, Rothamsted Experimental Station, Harpenden, Herts, 1961-77; *b* 16 Oct. 1911; *s* of Zacharias and Helen Kassanis; *m* 1952, Jean Eleanor Matthews; one *s* one *d. Educ:* University of Thessaloniki, Greece. Came to Rothamsted Experimental Station as British Council scholar, 1938; appointed to staff, 1943. Hon. DSc Aristotelian Univ. of Thessaloniki. Research Medal, Royal Agricultural Soc., 1965. *Publications:* scientific papers in various jls. *Recreation:* sculpture (local exhibns). *Address:* 3 Rosebery Avenue, Harpenden, Herts AL5 2QT. *T:* 5739.

KASTLER, Alfred; French physicist; retired; *b* 3 May 1902; *s* of Frédéric Kastler and Anna (*née* Frey); *m* 1924, Elise Cosset; two *s* one *d. Educ:* Lycée Bartholdi, Colmar; Ecole Normale Supérieure. Taught in Lycées, Mulhouse, Colmar, Bordeaux, 1926-31; Asst at Faculty of Sciences, Bordeaux, 1931-36; Lecturer, Faculty of Science, University of Clermont-Ferrand, 1936-38; Prof., Faculty of Sciences, Bordeaux, 1938-41; Prof. of Physics: Ecole Normale Supérieure, and Univ. of Paris, 1941-68; University of Louvain, Belgium, 1953-54; Dir, Atomic Clock Lab., Centre national de la Recherche Scientifique, 1958-72. Member: Institut de France; Académie Royale Flamande; Polish Acad. of Science; Deutsche Akademie der Wissenschaften zu Berlin; Akademie Leopoldina; Indian Acad. of Science; Royal Acad. of the Netherlands; Hungarian Acad. of Science. Hon. Member: Société Française de Physique; Optical Soc. of America; Polish Soc. of Physics. Hon. Doctorates: Louvain, Pisa, Oxford, Edinburgh, Laval and Sherbrooke (Quebec), Jerusalem, Belgrade, Bucharest, Nottingham. Holweck Medal and Prize, Phys. Soc., 1954; Nobel Prize for Physics, 1966. Commandeur de la Légion d'Honneur; Grand Officier de l'Ordre National du Mérite. *Address:* 1 Rue du Val-de-Grâce, 75005 Paris, France.

KASTNER, Prof. Leslie James, MA, ScD Cantab, FIMechE; Professor of Mechanical Engineering, King's College, University of London, 1955-76; Dean of Faculty of Engineering, University of London, 1974-76; *b* 10 Dec. 1911; *o s* of late Professor Leon E. Kastner, sometime Prof. of French Language and Literature, University of Manchester, and of Elsie E. Kastner; *m* 1958, Joyce, *o d* of Lt-Col Edward Lillington, DSO, Belstone, Devon. *Educ:* Dreghorn Castle Sch.; Colinton, Midlothian; Highgate Sch.; Clare Coll., Cambridge (Mechanical Science Tripos). Apprenticeship with Davies and Metcalfe, Ltd, Locomotive Engineers, of Romiley, Stockport, 1930-31 and 1934-36; Development Engineer, 1936-38; Osborne Reynolds Research

Fellowship, University of Manchester, 1938; Lectr in Engineering, University of Manchester, 1941-46; Senior Lectr, 1946-48; Prof. of Engineering, University Coll. of Swansea, University of Wales, 1948-55. Mem. of Council, Institution of Mechanical Engineers, 1954. FKC 1974. Graduates' Prize, InstMechE, 1939; Herbert Ackroyd Stuart Prize, 1943; Dugald Clerk Prize, 1956. *Publications:* various research papers in applied thermodynamics and fluid flow. *Address:* 37 St Anne's Road, Eastbourne. *Club:* National Liberal.

KATCHALSKI-KATZIR, Prof. Ephraim; *see* Katzir, Prof. E.

KATENGA-KAUNDA, Reid Willie; Malaŵi Independence Medal, 1964; Malaŵi Republic Medal, 1966; business executive; *b* 20 Aug. 1929; *s* of Gibson Amon Katenga Kaunda and Maggie Talengeske Nyabanda; *m* 1952, Elicy Nyabanda; one *s* three *d* (and one *s* one *d* decd). *Educ:* Ndola Govt Sch., Zambia; Inst. of Public Administration, Malaŵi; Trinity Coll., Oxford; Administrative Staff Coll., Henley. Sec., Nkhota Kota Rice Co-op. Soc. Ltd, 1952-62; Dist. Comr, Karonga, Malaŵi, 1964-65; Sen. Asst Sec., Min. of External Affairs, Zomba, Malaŵi, 1966; MP and Parly Sec., Office of the President and Cabinet, Malaŵi, 1966-68; Dep. Regional Chm., MCP, Northern Region, 1967-68; Under Sec., Office of the President and Cabinet, 1968-69; High Comr in London, 1969-70; Perm. Sec., Min. of Trade, Industry and Tourism, 1971-72; High Comr in London, 1972-73, and concurrently to the Holy See, Portugal, Belgium, Holland and France. Dep. Chm., Ncheu and Mchinji Inquiry Commn, 1967. *Recreations:* reading, walking, cinema, Association football. *Address:* c/o PO Box 511, Blantyre, Malaŵi.

KATIN, Peter Roy; Concert Pianist; *b* 14 Nov. 1930; *m* 1954, Eva Zweig; two *s. Educ:* Henry Thornton Sch.; Westminster Abbey; Royal Academy of Music. First London appearance at Wigmore Hall, 1948. A leading Chopin interpreter. Performances abroad include most European countries, West and East, S and E Africa, Japan, Canada, USA, Hong Kong, India, New Zealand, Singapore, Malaysia. Recordings, Decca, Everest, Unicorn, HMV, Philips, Lyrita, MFP, Pickwick International. Currently writing book about Chopin. Vis. Prof. in piano, Univ. of Western Ontario, 1978-. Mem. Incorporated Soc. of Musicians (ISM). FRAM, ARCM. Chopin Arts Award, NY, 1977. *Recreations:* reading, writing, fishing, tape recording, photography. *Address:* c/o John Higham International Ltd, 16 Lauriston Road, SW19 4TQ. *T:* 01-946 0467; c/o Direction Arts, Box 7275 Station A, Toronto, Canada M5W 1X9. *T:* 416 766 2397.

KATO, Tadao; Counsellor in Japan to John Swire & Sons, Imperial Chemicals, Sumitomo Metals, Suntory, Long-Term Credit Bank, since 1980; *b* 13 May 1916; *m* 1946, Yoko; two *s. Educ:* Tokyo Univ.; Cambridge Univ. Joined Japanese Diplomatic Service 1939; Singapore, 1952; London, 1953; Counsellor, Economic Affairs Bureau, Min. of Foreign Affairs, 1956-69; Counsellor, Washington, 1959-63 (Vis. Fellow, Harvard, 1959-60); Dep. Dir, Econ. Affairs Bureau, Min. of Foreign Affairs, 1963-66, Dir, 1966-67; Ambassador to OECD, 1967-70, to Mexico, 1970-74, to UK, 1975-79. 1st Class Order of Aztec Star, Mexico, 1972. *Recreations:* golf, goh. *Address:* 3-10-22, Shimo-Ochiai, Shinjuku-Ku, Tokyo, Japan. *Clubs:* Koganei Golf, Abiko Golf (Japan).

KATRITZKY, Prof. Alan Roy, DPhil, PhD, ScD; FRS 1980; FRSC; Kenan Professor of Chemistry, University of Florida, since 1980; *b* 18 Aug. 1928; *s* of Frederick Charles Katritzky and Emily Catherine (*née* Lane); *m* 1952, Agnes Juliane Dietlinde Kilian; one *s* three *d. Educ:* Oxford Univ. (BA, BSc, MA, DPhil); Cambridge Univ. (PhD, ScD). FRIC 1963. Lectr, Cambridge Univ., 1958-63; Fellow of Churchill Coll., Cambridge, 1960-63; Prof. of Chemistry, Univ. of E Anglia, 1963-80, Dean, Sch. of Chem. Sciences, UEA, 1963-70 and 1976-80. Tilden Medal, Chem. Soc., 1975-76. Cavaliere ufficiale, Order Al Merito Della Repubblica Italiana, 1975. *Publications:* (ed) Advances in Heterocyclic Chemistry, Vols 1-25, 1963-80; (ed) Physical Methods in Heterocyclic Chemistry, Vols 1-6, 1963-72; Principles of Heterocyclic Chemistry, 1968 (trans. into French, German, Italian, Japanese, Russian, Polish and Spanish); Chemistry of Heterocyclic N-Oxides (monograph), 1970; Heteroaromatic Tautomerism (monograph), 1975; scientific papers in Heterocyclic Chem. *Recreations:* walking, travel. *Address:* Department of Chemistry, University of Florida, Gainesville, Fla 32611, USA.

KATZ, Sir Bernard, Kt 1969; FRS 1952; Professor and Head of Biophysics Department, University College, London, 1952-78, now Emeritus, Hon. Research Fellow, 1978; *b* Leipzig, 26 March 1911; *s* of M. N. Katz; *m* 1945, Marguerite, *d* of W. Penly, Sydney, Australia; two *s. Educ:* University of Leipzig (MD 1934). Biophysical research, University Coll., London, 1935-39; PhD London, and Beit Memorial Research Fellow, 1938; Carnegie Research Fellow, Sydney Hospital, Sydney, 1939-42; DSc London, 1943. Served War of 1939-45 in Pacific with RAAF, 1942-45; Flt-Lt, 1943. Asst Dir of Research, Biophysics Research Unit, University Coll., London, and Henry Head Research Fellow (Royal Society), 1946-50; Reader in Physiology, 1950-51. Lectures: Herter, Johns Hopkins Univ., 1958; Dunham, Harvard Coll., 1961; Croonian, Royal Society, 1961; Sherrington, Liverpool Univ., 1967. A Vice-Pres., Royal Society, 1965, Biological Secretary and Vice-President, 1968-76. Mem., Agric. Research Coun., 1967-77. Fellow of University Coll., London. FRCP, 1968. Hon. FIBiol, 1978. Hon. DSc: Southampton, 1971; Melbourne, 1971; Cambridge, 1980; Hon. PhD Weizmann Inst., Israel, 1979. Feldberg Foundation Award, 1965; Baly Medal, RCP, 1967; Copley Medal, Royal Society, 1967; Nobel Prize (jtly) for Physiology and Medicine, 1970.

For. Member: Royal Danish Academy Science and Letters, 1968; Accad. Naz. Lincei, 1968; Amer. Acad. of Arts and Sciences, 1969; For. Assoc., Nat. Acad. of Scis, USA, 1976; Hon. Mem., Japanese Pharmacol. Soc., 1977; Assoc. Mem., European Molecular Biol. Orgn, 1978. *Publications:* Electric Excitation of Nerve, 1939; Nerve, Muscle and Synapse, 1966; The Release of Neural Transmitter Substances, 1969; papers on nerve and muscle physiology in Jl of Physiol., Proc. Royal Society, etc. *Address:* University College, WC1E 6BT.

KATZ, Milton; Director, International Legal Studies, and Henry L. Stimson Professor of Law, Harvard University, 1954-78, now Emeritus; Distinguished Professor of Law, Suffolk University Law School, Boston, Mass, since 1978; *b* 29 Nov. 1907; *m* 1933, Vivian Greenberg; three *s. Educ:* Harvard Univ. AB 1927; JD 1931. Anthropological Expedition across Central Africa for Peabody Museum, Harvard, 1927-28; Mem. of Bar since 1932; various official posts, US Government, 1932-39; Prof. of Law, Harvard Univ., 1940-50; served War of 1939-45, with War Production Board and as US Executive Officer, Combined Production and Resources Board, 1941-43, thereafter Lt-Comdr, USNR, until end of war; Dep. US Special Representative in Europe with rank of Ambassador, 1949-50; Chief US Delegation, Economic Commission for Europe, and US Mem., Defense Financial and Economic Cttee under North Atlantic Treaty, 1950-51; Ambassador of the United States and US Special Representative in Europe for ECA, 1950-51; Associate Dir, Ford Foundation, 1951-54, and Consultant, 1954-66. Dir, Internat. Program in Taxation, 1961-63. Consultant, US Office of Technology Assessment, 1974-; Chm., Energy Adv. Cttee, 1975-. Pres., Amer. Acad. of Arts and Sciences, 1979-; Trustee: Carnegie Endowment for Internat. Peace (Chm. Bd, 1970-78); World Peace Foundation (Exec. Cttee); Citizens Research Foundation (Pres., 1969-78); Brandeis Univ.; Case Western Reserve Univ., 1967-80; International Legal Center (Chm. Bd, 1971-78); Director, Internat. Friendship League; Member: Corp., Boston Museum of Science; Cttee on Foreign Affairs Personnel, 1961-63; Case Inst. of Technology Western Reserve Univ. Study Commn, 1966-67; Panel on Technology Assessment, Nat. Acad. of Sciences, 1968-69; Cttee on Life Sciences and Social Policy, Nat. Research Council, 1968-75 (Chm.); Vis. Cttee for Humanities, MIT, 1970-73; Adv. Bd Energy Laboratory, MIT, 1974-; Co-Chm., ABA-AAAS Cttee on Science and Law, 1978-. Sherman Fairchild Dist. Schol., Cal. Tech., 1974. John Danz Lectr, Univ. of Washington, 1974, Phi Beta Kappa Nat. Vis. Scholar, 1977-78. Hon LLD Brandeis, 1972. Legion of Merit (US Army), 1945; Commendation Ribbon (US Navy), 1945. Order of Merit, Fed. Rep. of Germany, 1968. *Publications:* Cases and Materials on Administrative Law, 1947; Government under Law and the Individual (co-author and editor), 1957; The Law of International Transactions and Relations (with Kingman Brewster, Jr), 1960; The Things That are Caesar's, 1966; The Relevance of International Adjudication, 1968; The Modern Foundation: its dual nature, public and private, 1968; Man's Impact on the Global Environment (contrib, with others), 1970; (ed) Federal Regulation of Campaign Finance, 1972; Assessing Biomedical Technologies (with others), 1975; Technology, Trade and the US Economy (with others), 1978; articles in legal, business and other jls. *Address:* (business) Harvard Law Sch., Cambridge, Mass, USA; (home) 6 Berkeley Street, Cambridge, Mass, USA.

KATZIN, Olga, Journalist; Pen-name Sagittarius; *b* London, 9 July 1896; *d* of John and Mathilde Katzin; *m* 1921, Hugh Miller, actor; two *s* one *d. Educ:* Privately. *Publications:* Troubadours, 1925; A Little Pilgrim's Peeps at Parnassus, 1927; Sagittarius Rhyming, 1940; London Watches, 1941; Targets, 1943; Quiver's Choice, 1945; Let Cowards Flinch, 1947; Pipes of Peace, 1949; Up the Poll, 1950; Strasbourg Geese and Other Verses, 1953; Unaida (with Michael Barsley), play, 1957; The Perpetual Pessimist (with Daniel George), 1963. *Address:* 28 St Ann's Terrace, NW8.

KATZIR, Prof. Ephraim, PhD; Institute Professor, Weizmann Institute of Science, since 1978; University Professor, Tel Aviv University, since 1978; President, State of Israel, 1973-78; *b* Kiev, Ukraine, 16 May 1916; *s* of Yehuda Katchalski and Tsila Katchalski; *m* 1938, Nina Gotlieb; one *s* one *d. Educ:* Rehavia High Sch., Jerusalem; Hebrew Univ., Jerusalem (chemistry, botany, zool., bacteriol.; MSc *summa cum laude* 1937; PhD 1941). Settled in Israel with parents, 1922; involved in Labour youth movement; Inf. Comdr, Jewish Self-Defence Forces (Hagana). Asst, Dept of Theoretical and Macromolecular Chem., Hebrew Univ., 1941-45; Res. Fellow, Polytechnic Inst., and Columbia Univ., NY, 1946-48; Actg Head, Dept of Biophys., Weizmann Inst. of Science, Rehovot, Israel, 1949-51, Head 1951-73 (mem. founding faculty of Inst.); Chief Scientist, Israel Def. Min., 1966-68. Vis. Prof. of Biophys., Hebrew Univ., 1953-61; Guest Scientist, Harvard Univ., 1957-59; Vis. Prof., Rockefeller Univ., NY, and Univ. of Mich, Ann Arbor, 1961-65; Sen. Foreign Scientist Fellowship, UCLA, 1964; Battelle Seattle Res. Center, Washington, 1971; Regents Prof., Univ. of Calif., San Diego, 1979; First Herman F. Mark Chair in Polymer Sci., Poly. Inst., NY, 1979. Member: Biochem. Soc. of Israel; Israel Acad. of Sciences and Humanities; Israel Chem. Soc.; Council, Internat. Union of Biochem.; Scientific Adv. Panel, Ciba Foundn; AAAS; Assoc. of Harvard Chemists; Leopoldina Acad. of Science, Germany; World Acad. of Art and Science; New York Acad. of Science (Life Mem.). Centennial Foreign Fellow, Amer. Chem. Soc.; For. Associate, Nat. Acad. of Sciences of USA. For. Member: Royal Soc.; Amer. Philosoph. Soc. Hon. Member: Amer. Acad. of Arts and Sciences; Amer. Soc. of Biol Chemists; Harvey Soc. Hon. Prof., Polytechnic Inst. of New York, 1975. Hon. Dr: Hebrew Univ., 1973; Brandeis Univ., Univ. of Mich, and Hebrew Union Coll., 1975; Weizmann Inst. of Science, 1976; Northwestern Univ., Evanston,

1978; Harvard, 1978; McGill, 1980; ETH Zurich, 1980; Thomas Jefferson, 1981; Oxford, 1981. Tchernikhovski Prize, 1948; Weizmann Prize, 1950; Israel Prize in Nat. Sciences, 1959; Rothschild Prize in Nat. Sciences, 1961; Linderstrøm Lang Gold Medal, 1969; Hans Krebs Medal, 1972. Ephraim Katzir Chair of Biophysics, Bar Ilan Univ., Israel, founded 1976; Alpha Omega Achievement Medal, 1979. Adv. Editor: (series) Progress in Surface and Membrane Science; Jl of Life Sciences; TIT Jl of Life Scis; Hon. Editor, Jl of Applied Biochem. Mem. Editorial Board: Biopolymers; (series) Applied Biochem. and Bioengrg; (series) Advances in Exper. Medicine and Biol. *Address:* Weizmann Institute of Science, PO Box 26, Rehovot, Israel.

KAUFFMANN, C. Michael, MA, PhD; Keeper, Department of Prints & Drawings and Paintings, Victoria and Albert Museum, since 1975; *b* 5 Feb. 1931; *s* of Arthur and late Tamara Kauffmann; *m* 1954, Dorothea (née Hill); two *s*. *Educ*: St Paul's Sch.; Merton Coll., Oxford (Postmaster); Warburg Inst., London Univ. (Jun. Research Fellow). Asst Curator, Photographic Collection, Warburg Inst., 1957-58; Keeper, Manchester City Art Gall., 1958-60; Asst Keeper, Dept of Prints & Drawings and Paintings, Victoria and Albert Museum, 1960-75, and Asst to the Director, 1963-66; Visiting Associate Prof., Univ. of Chicago, 1969. *Publications:* The Baths of Pozzuoli: medieval illuminations of Peter of Eboli's poem, 1959; The Legend of St Ursula, 1964; An Altar-piece of the Apocalypse, 1968; Victoria & Albert Museum: catalogue of foreign paintings, 1973; British Romanesque Manuscripts 1066-1190, 1975; exhibn catalogues; articles in art historical jls. *Address:* 53 Twyford Avenue, W3 9PZ. *T:* 01-992 6050.

KAUFMAN, Rt. Hon. Gerald (Bernard); PC 1978; MP (Lab) Manchester, Ardwick, since 1970; *b* 21 June 1930; *s* of Louis and Jane Kaufman. *Educ*: Leeds Grammar Sch.; The Queen's Coll., Oxford. Asst Gen.-Sec., Fabian Soc., 1954-55; Political Staff, Daily Mirror, 1955-64; Political Correspondent, New Statesman, 1964-65; Parly Press Liaison Officer, Labour Party, 1965-70. Parly Under-Sec. of State, DoE, 1974-75, Dept of Industry, 1975; Minister of State, Dept of Industry, 1975-79; Parly Cttee of PLP, 1980-. *Publications:* (jtly) How to Live Under Labour, 1964; (ed) The Left, 1966; To Build the Promised Land, 1973; How to be a Minister, 1980. *Recreations:* travel, going to the pictures. *Address:* 87 Charlbert Court, Eamont Street, NW8. *T:* 01-722 6264.

KAUL, Mahendra Nath, OBE 1975; Managing Director: G. L. Restaurants Ltd, since 1982; Gaylord Restaurants (Midlands) Ltd, since 1982; Gaylord Caterers Ltd, since 1982; Viceroy of India (Restaurants) Ltd, since 1982; Vice Chairman, Harilela (London) Ltd, since 1981; Managing Editor and Director, South Asia Times, since 1982; *b* 28 July 1922; *s* of Dina Nath Kaul and Gauri Kaul; *m* 1955, Rajni Kapur, MA, MLS; one *d*. *Educ*: Univ. of the Punjab, India (BA). Joined Radio Kashmir of All India Radio, as news reader, actor and producer of dramas, 1949; appeared in two feature films and assisted in producing several documentaries, 1950-52; news reader and actor in three languages, also drama producer, All India Radio, New Delhi, 1952-55; joined Indian service of Voice of America, Washington DC, 1955, later becoming Editor of the service; joined external service of BBC, as newscaster, producer and dir of radio plays; producer/presenter, BBC TV prog. for Asian Viewers in UK, 1966-82. OBE awarded for services to race relations in Gt Britain. Received The Green Pennant from HRH The Duke of Edinburgh, awarded by Commonwealth Expedition (COMEX 10), 1980. *Recreations:* golf, cooking, boating, classical and light classical music, reading political works. *Address:* 50 Grove Court, Grove End Road, St John's Wood, NW8. *T:* 01-286 8131.

KAULBACK, Ronald John Henry, OBE 1946; *b* 23 July 1909; *er s* of late Lieutenant-Colonel Henry Albert Kaulback, OBE, and Alice Mary, *d* of late Rev. A. J. Townend, CF; *m* 1940, Audrey Elizabeth, 3rd *d* of late Major H. R. M. Howard-Sneyd, OBE; two *s* two *d*. *Educ*: Rugby; Pembroke Coll., Cambridge. In 1933 journeyed through Assam and Eastern Tibet with Kingdon Ward; returned to Tibet, 1935, accompanied by John Hanbury-Tracy, spending eighteen months there in an attempt to discover source of Salween River; 1938 spent eighteen months in Upper Burma hunting and collecting zoological specimens for the British Museum (Natural History); Murchison Grant of Royal Geog. Society, 1937. *Publications:* Tibetan Trek, 1934; Salween, 1938. *Recreations:* fishing, schnorkeling. *Address:* Altbough, Hoarwithy, Hereford. *T:* Carey 676. *Club:* Special Forces.

KAUNDA, David Kenneth; President of Zambia, since Oct. 1964 (Prime Minister, N Rhodesia, Jan.-Oct. 1964); Chancellor of the University of Zambia since 1966; *b* 28 April 1924; *s* of late David Julizgia and Hellen Kaunda, Missionaries; *m* 1946, Betty Banda; seven *s* two *d*. *Educ*: Lubwa Training Sch.; Munali Secondary Sch. Teacher, Lubwa Training Sch., 1943-44, Headmaster, 1944-47; Boarding Master, Mufulira Upper Sch., 1948-49. African National Congress: District Sec., 1950-52; Provincial Organising Sec., 1952-53; Sec.-Gen., 1953-58; Nat. Pres., Zambia African Nat. Congress, 1958-59; Nat. Pres., United Nat. Independence Party, 1960; Chm., Pan-African Freedom Movement for East, Central and South Africa, 1962; Minister of Local Government and Social Welfare, N Rhodesia, 1962-63. Chairman: Organization of African Unity, 1970; Non-aligned Countries, 1970. Hon. Doctor of Laws: Fordham Univ., USA, 1963; Dublin Univ., 1964; University of Sussex, 1965; Windsor Univ., Canada, 1966; University of Chile, 1966; Univ. of Zambia, 1974; Univ. of Humboldt, 1980; DUniv York, 1966. *Publications:* Black Government, 1961; Zambia Shall Be Free, 1962; Humanist in Africa, 1966; Humanism in Zambia and its implementation, 1967;

Letter to My Children; Kaunda on Violence, ——— *ecreations:* golf, music, table tennis, football, draughts, gardening and reading. *Address:* State House, PO Box 135, Lusaka, Zambia.

KAUNDA, Reid Willie K.; *see* Katenga-Kaunda.

KAUNTZE, Ralph, MBE 1944; MD; FRCP; Physician to Guy's Hospital, 1948-71, Consultant Physician Emeritus since 1971; *b* 5 June 1911; *s* of Charles Kauntze and Edith, *d* of Ralph Bagley; *m* 1935, Katharine Margaret, *yr d* of late Ramsay Moodie; two *s* one *d*. *Educ*: Canford Sch.; Emmanuel Coll., Cambridge; St George's Hosp., London. William Brown Sen. Schol., St George's Hosp. 1932; MRCS, LRCP 1935; MA, MB, BCh Cantab 1937; MRCP 1939; MD Cantab 1946; FRCP 1950. Served, 1939-45, RAMC, chiefly Mediterranean area, Lt-Col O i/c Med. Div. Asst Dir of Dept of Med., Guy's Hosp., 1947-48, Physician to Cardiac Dept, 1956-71; Cons. Phys. to High Wycombe War Memorial Hosp., 1948-50; Dir Asthma Clinic, 1948-52, and of Dept of Student Health, 1950-63, Guy's Hosp.; Physician to Royal Masonic Hospital, 1963-76. Former Senior Cons. Phys. to: Commercial Union Assurance Co. Ltd; British & European Assurance Co.; European Assurance Co. Ltd. Hon. Vis. Phys., Johns Hopkins Hosp., Baltimore, 1958. Examiner in Medicine: RCP; London Univ. Mem. Brit. Cardiac Soc.; Mem. Assoc. of Physicians. *Publications:* contrib. med. jls. *Recreations:* farming, walking. *Address:* Blewbury Manor, near Didcot, Oxon. *T:* Blewbury 850246.

KAVANAGH, P. J., (Patrick Joseph Gregory Kavanagh); writer; *b* 6 Jan. 1931; *s* of H. E. (Ted) Kavanagh and Agnes O'Keefe; *m* 1st, 1956, Sally Philipps (*d* 1958); 2nd, 1965, Catherine Ward; two *s*. *Educ*: Douai Sch.; Lycee Jaccard, Lausanne; Merton Coll., Oxford (MA). British Council, 1957-59. Actor, 1959-70. *Publications: poems:* One and One, 1960; On the Way to the Depot, 1967; About Time, 1970; Edward Thomas in Heaven, 1974; Life before Death, 1979; Selected Poems, 1982; *novels:* A Song and Dance, 1968 (Guardian Fiction Prize, 1968); A Happy Man, 1972; People and Weather, 1979; *autobiog.:* The Perfect Stranger, 1966 (Richard Hillary Prize, 1966); *for children:* Scarf Jack, 1978; Rebel for Good, 1980; (ed) Collected Poems of Ivor Gurney, 1982. *Recreation:* walking. *Address:* Sparrowthorn, Elkstone, Cheltenham, Glos.

KAVANAGH, Patrick Bernard, CBE 1977; QPM 1974; Deputy Commissioner, Metropolitan Police, 1977-83; *b* 18 March 1923; *s* of late Michael Kavanagh and late Violet Kavanagh (née Duncan); *m* Beryl, *er d* of late Lt-Comdr Richard Owen Williams, RNR and Annie (née McShiells); one *s* two *d*. *Educ*: St Aloysius Coll., Glasgow. Rifle Bde, 1941-43; Para. Regt, 1943-46 (Lieut). Manchester City Police (Constable to Supt), 1946-64; Asst Chief Constable, Cardiff City Police, 1964-69; Asst and Dep. Chief Constable, S Wales Constabulary, 1969-73; Asst Comr (Traffic), Metropolitan Police, 1974-77. Attended Administrative Staff Coll., Henley-on-Thames, 1961. *Recreations:* cricket, swimming, music, crosswords. *Address:* c/o Barclays Bank Ltd, Greyfriars Road, Cardiff.

KAY, Sir Andrew Watt, Kt 1973; retired; Regius Professor of Surgery, University of Glasgow, 1964-81; part-time Chief Scientist, Scottish Home and Health Department, 1973-81; *b* 14 Aug. 1916; of Scottish parentage; *m* 1943, Janetta M. Roxburgh; two *s* two *d*. *Educ*: Ayr Academy; Glasgow Univ. MB, ChB (Hons) with Brunton Memorial Prize, 1939; FRCSEd 1942; FRFPSG 1956 (Pres. 1972-); FRCS 1960; FRCSGlas 1967; FRSE 1971; MD (Hons) with Bellahouston Gold Medal, 1944; Major Royal Army Medical Corps i/c Surgical Div., Millbank Military Hospital, 1946-48; ChM (Hons) 1949; Consultant Surgeon in charge of Wards, Western Infirmary, Glasgow, 1956-58; Asst to Regius Prof. of Surgery, Glasgow Univ., 1942-56; Prof. of Surgery, University of Sheffield, 1958-64. Sims Travelling Prof., Australasia, 1969; McLaughlin Foundn Edward Gallie Vis. Prof., Canada, 1970. Rock Carling Fellowship, 1977. Pres., Surgical Research Soc., 1969-71. Member: Royal Commission on Medical Education, 1965-68; MRC, 1967-71; Hon. Mem., The N Pacific Surgical Assoc. FRACS 1970; FRCSCan 1972; FCS (SoAf) 1972; Hon. Fellow: Norwegian Surgical Assoc., Belgian Surgical Soc.; Amer. Surg. Assoc., 1972; Hon. FÁCS, 1973; Hon. FRCSI, 1979. Hon. DSc: Leicester, 1973; Sheffield, 1975; Manchester, 1981; Nebraska, 1981; Hon. MD Edinburgh, 1981. Cecil Joll Prize, 1963, 1969; Gordon-Taylor Lectureship and Medal, 1970. *Publications:* (with R. A. Jamieson, FRCS) Textbook of Surgical Physiology, 1959 (2nd edn 1964); Research in Medicine: problems and prospects, 1977; several papers in medical and surgical jls on gastroenterological subjects. *Recreation:* gardening. *Address:* 14 North Campbell Avenue, Milngavie, Glasgow G62 7AA.

KAY, Bernard Hubert Gerard; HM Diplomatic Service, retired; *b* 7 July 1925; *s* of William and Alice Kay; *m* 1957, Teresa Jean Dyer; three *d*. *Educ*: St Bede's, Bradford; Wadham Coll., Oxford (MA, MLitt). Royal Navy, 1943-46. Foreign Office, 1955; served: Hong Kong, 1958-62; Singapore, 1964; Manila, 1965; New Delhi, 1967; Vientiane, 1968; Dacca, 1972; Ulan Bator, 1973; FCO, 1973-80. *Recreations:* Asia, books, mountains, the sea. *Address:* 6 Savona Close, Wimbledon, SW19. *Club:* United Oxford & Cambridge University.

KAY, Brian Wilfrid; Chief Inspector, Teacher Training and Research, Department of Education and Science, 1979-81, retired; *b* 30 July 1921; *s* of Wilfrid and Jessie Kay; *m* 1947, Dorothea Sheppard Lawson; two *d*. *Educ*: King's Sch., Chester; University Coll., Oxford (exhibnr). Classics Master, Birkenhead Sch., 1947-59; Head of Classics, Liverpool Collegiate Sch.,

1959-64; HM Inspector of Schs (Wales), 1964-71; Staff Inspector, Classics, Secondary Educn, 1971-74; Head of Assessment of Performance Unit, DES, 1974-77; Chief Inspector, Res. and Planning, DES, 1977-79. *Recreations:* gardening, music, architecture. *Address:* Pond Cottage, Botolph Claydon, Buckingham MK18 2NG. *T:* Winslow 3477.

KAY, Air Vice-Marshal Cyril Eyton, CB 1958; CBE 1947; DFC 1940; retired as Chief of Air Staff, with the rank of Air Vice-Marshal, RNZAF (1956-58); *b* 25 June 1902; *s* of David Kay and Mary, *d* of Edward Drury Butts; *m* 1932, Florence, *d* of Frank Armfield; two *d. Educ:* Auckland, NZ. Joined RAF, 1926, 5 years Short Service Commn; joined RNZAF, 1935, Permanent Commn. As Flying Officer: flew London-Sydney in Desoutter Light aeroplane, 1930 (with Flying Off. H. L. Piper as Co-pilot); first New Zealanders to accomplish this flight; also, as Flying Off. flew a De Havilland-Dragon Rapide (with Sqdn Ldr J. Hewett) in London-Melbourne Centenary Air Race, 1934; then continued over Tasman Sea to New Zealand (first direct flight England-New Zealand). Comdg Officer No 75 (NZ) Sqdn "Wellington" Bombers stationed Feltwell, Norfolk, England, 1940; Air Board Mem. for Supply, RNZAF, 1947; AOC, RNZAF, London HQ, 1950; Air Board Mem. for Personnel, 1953. *Publication:* The Restless Sky, 1964. *Recreation:* golf. *Clubs:* Royal Air Force; Officers' (Wellington, NZ).

KAY, Ernest, FRGS; Director-General, International Biographical Center, New York, since 1976; *b* 21 June 1915; *s* of Harold and Florence Kay; *m* 1941, Marjorie Peover; two *s* one *d. Educ:* Spring Bank Central Sch., Darwen, Lancs. Reporter, Darwen News, 1931-34; Ashton-under-Lyne Reporter, 1934-38; Industrial Corresp., Manchester Guardian and Evening News, 1938-41; The Star, London, 1941-47; London Editor, Wolverhampton Express and Star, 1947-52, Managing Editor, 1952-54; Managing Editor, London Evening News, 1954-57; Editor and Publisher, John O'London's, 1957-61; Managing Editor, Time and Tide, 1961-67; Founder of Internat. Biographical Centre, Cambridge, and Dir-Gen., 1967-. Chairman: Kay Sons and Daughter Ltd, 1967-77; Dartmouth Chronicle Group Ltd, 1968-77; Cambridge and Newmarket Radio Ltd, 1981-; Pres., Melrose Press Ltd, 1970-77. Chm., Cambridge Symphony Orchestra Trust, 1979-. FRSA 1967; FRGS 1975. Hon. DLitt Karachi, 1967; Hon. PhD Hong Kong, 1976. Emperor Haile Selassie Gold Medal, 1971. Key to City of: Las Vegas, 1972; New York, 1975; Miami, 1978; New Orleans (and Hon. Citizen), 1978; Beverly Hills, 1981; LA, 1981. Staff Col and ADC to Governor of Louisiana, 1979. Gold Medal, Ordre Supreme Imperial Orthodoxe Constantinian de Saint-Georges (Greece), 1977. *Publications:* Great Men of Britain, 1956, 2nd edn 1960; Isles of Flowers: the story of the Isles of Scilly, 1956, 3rd edn 1977; Pragmatic Premier: an intimate portrait of Harold Wilson, 1967; The Wit of Harold Wilson, 1967; Editor, Dictionary of International Biography, 1967-; Dictionary of Caribbean Biography, 1970-; Dictionary of African Biography, 1970-; Dictionary of Scandinavian Biography, 1972-; International Who's Who in Poetry, 1970-; World Who's Who of Women, 1973-; International Who's Who in Music, 1975-; International Authors and Writers Who's Who, 1976-; Women in Education, 1977-; Who's Who in Education, 1978-; International Youth in Achievement, 1981-. *Recreations:* reading, writing, music, watching cricket, travel. *Address:* Orcheston, 11 Madingley Road, Cambridge CB3 0EG. *T:* Cambridge 63893. *Clubs:* Surrey CCC; Derbyshire CCC; National Arts (New York City).

KAY, Dr Harry, CBE 1981; PhD; Vice-Chancellor, University of Exeter, since 1973; *b* 22 March 1919; *s* of late Williamson T. Kay; *m* 1941, Gwendolen Diana, *d* of Charles Edward Maude; one *s* one *d. Educ:* Rotherham Grammar Sch.; Trinity Hall, Cambridge (1938-39, 1946-51). Served War of 1939-45 with Royal Artillery. Research with Nuffield Unit into Problems of Ageing, Cambridge, 1948-51; Psychologist of Naval Arctic Expedition, 1949. Lecturer in Experimental Psychology, Univ. of Oxford, 1951-59; Prof. of Psychology, Univ. of Sheffield, 1960-73. Visiting Scientist, National Institutes of Health, Washington, DC, 1957-58. Pro-Vice-Chancellor, University of Sheffield, 1967-71. Pres., British Psychological Soc., 1971-72. Hon. Director: MRC Unit, Dept of Psychology, Sheffield; Nat. Centre of Programmed Instruction for Industry, Sheffield. Member: SSRC, 1970-73; MRC, 1975-77 (Chm., Environmental Medicine Res. Policy Cttee, 1975-77); CNAA, 1974-79; Open Univ. Acad. Adv. Cttee; BBC Continuing Educn Adv. Cttee; Southern Univs Jt Bd (Chm., 1978-80); UCCA (Chm., 1978-); Oakes Cttee on Management of Higher Educn, 1977-78; NATO Human Factors Panel, 1972-75. Chairman: Central Council for Educn and Trng in Social Work, 1980-; Bd of Management, Northcott Theatre, 1973-. Hon. DSc Sheffield, 1981. Vernon Prize, 1962. *Publication:* (with B. Dodd and M. Sime) Teaching Machines and Programmed Instruction, 1968. *Address:* The University, Exeter, Devon EX4 4QJ. *Club:* Athenæum.

KAY, Prof. Humphrey Edward Melville, MD, FRCP, FRCPath; Haematologist, Royal Marsden Hospital, since 1956; Professor of Haematology, University of London; *b* 10 Oct. 1923; *s* of late Rev. Arnold Innes and Winifred Julia Kay; *m* 1950, April Grace Lavinia Powlett; one *s* two *d. Educ:* Bryanston Sch.; St Thomas's Hospital. MB, BS 1945. RAFVR, 1947-49; junior appts at St Thomas's Hosp., 1950-56. Sec., MRC Cttee on Leukaemia, 1968-; Dean, Inst. of Cancer Research, 1970-72. Editor, Jl Clinical Pathology, 1972-80. *Publications:* papers and chapters on blood diseases, etc. *Recreation:* natural history including gardening. *Address:* 15 Earls Court Gardens, SW5.

KAY, John Menzies, MA, PhD; CEng, FIMechE, FIChemE; Director, GSK Steel Developments Ltd, since 1976; *b* 4 Sept. 1920; *s* of John Aiton Kay and Isabel Kay (*née* Menzies). *Educ:* Sherborne Sch.; Trinity Hall Cambridge. University Demonstrator in Chemical Engineering, Cambridge University, 1948; Chief Technical Engineer, Division of Atomic Energy Production, Risley, 1952; Prof. of Nuclear Power, Imperial Coll. of Science and Technology, University of London, 1956; Dir of Engineering Development, Tube Investments Ltd, 1961; Chief Engineer, Richard Thomas & Baldwins Ltd, 1965; Dir-in-charge, Planning Div., BSC, 1968-70; Dir of Engrng, Strip Mills Div., BSC, 1970-76. Mem., Nuclear Safety Adv. Cttee, 1960-76; Chm., Radioactive Waste Study Gp, 1974-81; Mem., Adv. Cttee on Safety of Nuclear Installations, 1980-. *Publications:* Fluid Mechanics and Heat Transfer, 1963; contribs to Proc. of Institution of Mechanical Engineers. *Recreations:* hill-walking, gardening, music. *Address:* Church Farm, St Briavels, near Lydney, Glos. *Clubs:* Alpine, United Oxford & Cambridge University.

KAY, Jolyon Christopher; HM Diplomatic Service; Commercial (formerly Science) Counsellor, Paris, since 1980; *b* 19 Sept. 1930; *s* of Colin Mardall Kay and Gertrude Fanny Kay; *m* 1956, Shirley Mary Clarke; two *s* two *d. Educ:* Charterhouse; St John's Coll., Cambridge (BA). Chemical Engr, Albright and Wilson, 1954; UKAEA, Harwell, 1958; Battelle Inst., Geneva, 1961; Foreign Office, London, 1964; MECAS, 1965; British Interests Section, Swiss Embassy, Algiers, 1967; Head of Chancery and Information Adviser, Political Residency, Bahrain, 1968; FCO, 1970; Economic Counsellor, Jedda, 1974-77; Consul-Gen., Casablanca, 1977-80. *Recreations:* acting, skiing, croquet. *Address:* c/o Foreign and Commonwealth Office, SW1; Double Doors, Blewbury, Oxfordshire. *T:* Blewbury 850640. *Clubs:* National Liberal; Harwell Croquet.

KAY, Neil Vincent; Director of Social Services, Sheffield, since 1979 (Deputy Director, 1971-79); *b* 24 May 1936; *s* of Charles Vincent Kay and Emma Kay; *m* 1961, Maureen (*née* Flemons); one *s* two *d. Educ:* Woodhouse Grammar Sch.; Downing Coll., Cambridge (MA); Birmingham Univ. (Prof. Social Work Qual.). Social Worker (Child Care), Oxford CC, and Sheffield CC, 1960-66; Lectr and Tutor in Social Work, Extramural Dept, Sheffield Univ., 1966-71. *Address:* 22 Westwood Road, Sheffield S11 7EY. *T:* Sheffield 301934.

KAY, Maj.-Gen. Patrick Richard, CB 1972; MBE 1945; RM retired; *b* 1 Aug. 1921; *y s* of late Dr and Mrs A. R. Kay, Blakeney, Norfolk; *m* 1944, Muriel Austen Smith; three *s* one *d. Educ:* Eastbourne Coll. Commissioned in Royal Marines, 1940; HMS Renown, 1941-43; 4 Commando Bde, 1944-45; Combined Ops HQ, 1945-48; Staff of Commandant-Gen., Royal Marines, 1948-50 and 1952-54; Staff Coll., Camberley, 1951; 40 Commando, RM, 1954-57; Joint Services Amphibious Warfare Centre, 1957-59; Plans Div., Naval Staff, 1959-62; CO, 43 Commando, RM, 1963-65; CO, Amphibious Training Unit, RM, 1965-66; Asst Dir (Jt Warfare) Naval Staff, 1966-67; Asst Chief of Staff to Comdt-Gen. RM, 1968; IDC, 1969; C of S to Comdt-Gen., RM, 1970-74, retired 1974. Dir of Naval Security, 1974-81. *Recreations:* gardening, golf. *Address:* Halfway, Church Lane, Ewshot, Farnham, Surrey.

KAY-SHUTTLEWORTH, family name of **Baron Shuttleworth.**

KAYE, Danny, (Daniel Kominski); Actor (Stage, Film, TV, and Radio); Comedian; Baseball Executive; conductor; *b* New York, NY, 18 Jan.; *s* of Jacob Kominski and Clara Nemorovsky; *m* 1940, Sylvia Fine, producer, lyricist and composer; one *d.* Official Permanent Ambassador-at-Large for UNICEF (first award for Internat. Distinguished Service). Scopus Laureate, 1977. Founder, managing limited partner, Seattle Mariners baseball team, 1976. Jean Hersholt Humanitarian Award, 1982; George Foster Peabody Award, 1982. *Stage:* Straw Hat Review, Ambassador Theatre, New York City, 1939; Lady in the Dark, 1940; Let's Face It, 1941; appeared London Palladium, also provincial tour, Great Britain, 1949; London Palladium, 1955. *Television:* annual 'Look In' for Children, Metropolitan Opera, NYC (founder), 1975-; Pinocchio, 1976; Skokie, 1981. *Films include:* Up In Arms, 1943; Wonder Man, 1944; Kid from Brooklyn, 1945; The Secret Life of Walter Mitty, 1946; That's Life, 1947; A Song is Born, 1949; The Inspector-General, 1950; On the Riviera, 1951; Hans Christian Andersen, 1952; Knock on Wood, 1954; White Christmas, 1954; The Court Jester, 1956; Merry Andrew, 1957; Me And The Colonel, 1958; Five Pennies, 1959; On the Double, 1960; The Man from The Diner's Club, 1963; The Madwoman of Chaillot, 1969; *Play:* Two by Two, NY, 1970; *Television includes:* weekly show (CBS), 1963-67; The Danny Kaye Show (Special Acad. award, 1954; Emmy award, 1963; George Foster Peabody award, 1963; Best Children's Special award, 1975). *Address:* Box 750, Beverly Hills, Calif, USA.

KAYE, Col Douglas Robert Beaumont, DSO 1942 (Bar 1945); DL; JP; *b* 18 Nov. 1909; *s* of late Robert Walter Kaye, JP, Great Glenn Manor, Leics; *m* 1946, Florence Audrey Emma, *d* of late Henry Archibald Bellville, Tedstone Court, Bromyard, Herefordshire; one *s* one *d. Educ:* Harrow. 2nd Lieut Leicestershire Yeo., 1928; 2nd Lieut 10th Royal Hussars, 1931. Served War of 1939-45: Jerusalem, 1939-41; Cairo and HQ 30 Corps, 1941-42; Lieut-Col comdg 10th Royal Hussars, Africa and Italy, 1943-46 (despatches twice). Bde Major, 30 Lowland Armd Bde (TA), 1947-49; Lieut-Col comdg 16th/5th Queen's Royal Lancers, 1949-51; AA & QMG 56 London Armd Div. (TA), 1952-54; Col Comdt and Chief Instructor, Gunnery Sch., RAC Centre, 1954-56; retd 1956. Master of Newmarket and Thurlow Foxhounds,

1957-59. DL 1963, JP 1961, High Sheriff 1971, Cambridgeshire and Isle of Ely. Mem., Newmarket RDC, 1959-74 (Chm., 1972-74), E Cambridgeshire DC, 1974. *Recreations:* hunting, shooting. *Address:* Brinkley Hall, near Newmarket, Suffolk. *T:* Stetchworth 202. *Club:* Cavalry and Guards.

KAYE, Elaine Hilda; Headmistress, Oxford High School, GPDST, 1972-81; *b* 21 Jan. 1930; *d* of late Rev. Harold Sutcliffe Kaye and Kathleen Mary (*née* White). *Educ:* Bradford Girls' Grammar Sch.; Milton Mount Coll.; St Anne's Coll., Oxford. Assistant Mistress: Leyton County High Sch., 1952-54; Queen's Coll., Harley Street, 1954-59; South Hampstead High Sch., GPDST, 1959-65; Part-time Tutor, Westminster Tutors, 1965-67; Dep. Warden, Missenden Abbey Adult Coll., 1967-72. *Publications:* History of the King's Weigh House Church, 1968; History of Queen's College, Harley St, 1972; Short History of Missenden Abbey, 1973. *Recreations:* music, walking, conversation. *Address:* 20 Rowland Close, Wolvercote, Oxford OX2 8PW. *T:* Oxford 53917.

KAYE, Sir Emmanuel, Kt 1974; CBE 1967; Founder and Chairman of The Kaye Organisation Ltd, since 1966; Joint Founder and Governing Director (with J. R. Sharp, died 1965), of Lansing Bagnall Ltd, since 1943; *b* 29 Nov. 1914; *m* 1946, Elizabeth Cutler; one *s* two *d. Educ:* Richmond Hill Sch.; Twickenham Technical Coll. Founded J. E. Shay Ltd, Precision Gauge, Tool and Instrument Makers, and took over Lansing Bagnall & Co. of Isleworth, 1943; then founded Lansing Bagnall Ltd (all with late J. R. Sharp). Transf. to Basingstoke, 1949 (from being smallest manufr of electric lift trucks, became largest in Europe). Royal Warrant as supplier of Industrial Trucks to Royal Household, 1971; Queen's Awards for Export Achievement in 1969, 1970, 1971 and 1979 and only co. to win Queen's Awards for both Export Achievement and Technological Innovation, 1972; Design Council Award, 1974; winners of Gold and other Continental Awards. Chairmanships include: Industrial Modernisation Ltd, 1953-76; Lansing Bagnall International Ltd, Switzerland, 1957-; Fork Truck Rentals, 1961-77; Lansing Leasing Ltd, 1962-; Elvetham Hall Ltd, 1965-; Lansing Bagnall AG, Switzerland, 1966-; Lansing GmbH, Germany, 1966-; Pool & Sons (Hartley Wintney) Ltd, 1967-; Hubbard Bros Ltd, 1969-78; Regentruck Ltd, 1969-77; Hawkington Ltd, 1972-; L. B. Components, 1973-77; Wigan Engineering Ltd, 1973-78; Hadley Contract Hire Ltd, 1973-; Lansing Bagnall (Northern) Ltd, 1974-78; Lansing Bagnall Inc., 1974-; Henley Forklift Gp, 1976-; Lansing Henley Ltd, 1977-; Lansing Ltd, 1977-80; Bonser Engineering Ltd, 1978-; Kaye Steel Stockholders, 1978-. Worshipful Co. of Farriers, 1953; Freeman of City of London, 1954. Founded Unquoted Companies' Gp, 1968; Member: CBI Taxation Cttee, 1970-77; Council of Industry for Management Educn, 1970-; Export Guarantees Adv. Council, 1971-74; Inflation Accounting Cttee, 1974-75; CBI Wealth Tax Panel, 1974-77; Queen's Award Review Cttee, 1975; CBI President's Cttee, 1976-; CBI Council, 1976-; Reviewing Cttee on Export of Works of Art, 1977-80. Visiting Fellow, Univ. of Lancaster, 1970-. Governor: Girls' High Sch., Basingstoke, 1955-70; Queen Mary's Coll., Basingstoke, 1971-75. Trustee, Glyndebourne, 1977-. Fellow, Psionic Medical Soc., 1977-. FBIM 1975; FRSA 1978. *Recreations:* art, chess, music, ski-ing. *Address:* The Croft, Hartley Wintney, Hampshire RG27 8HT; 25 St James's Place, SW1 1NP. *Club:* Brooks's.

KAYE, Geoffrey John; *b* 14 Aug. 1935; *s* of Michael and Golda Kaye; two *d. Educ:* Christ College, Finchley. Started with Pricerite Ltd when business was a small private company controlling six shops, 1951; apptd Manager (aged 18) of one of Pricerite Ltd stores, 1953; Supervisor, Pricerite Ltd, 1955; Controller of all stores in Pricerite Ltd Gp, 1958; Director, 1963; Chairman and Man. Dir, 1966-73. Mem. Cttee, British Assoc. Monte Carlo. *Recreations:* football, golf. *Address:* L'Estoril, Avenue Princesse Grace, Monte Carlo, Monaco. *Club:* Monte Carlo Yacht.

KAYE, Sir John Phillip Lister L.; *see* Lister-Kaye.

KAYE, Mary Margaret, (Mrs G. J. Hamilton), FRSL; authoress and illustrator; *d* of late Sir Cecil Kaye, CSI, CIE, CBE, and Lady Kaye; *m* Maj.-Gen. G. J. Hamilton, *qv* ; two *d. Publications: historical novels:* Six Bars at Seven, 1940; Trade Wind, 1963, revd edn 1981; The Far Pavilions, 1978; Shadow of the Moon, 1979; *detective novels:* Death Walked in Kashmir, 1953; Death Walked in Berlin, 1955; Death Walked in Cyprus, 1956; Later Than You Think, 1958; The House of Shade, 1959; Night on the Island, 1960; *for children:* The Potter Pinner Books (series), 1937-41; The Ordinary Princess, 1980; *edited:* The Golden Calm, 1980; *illustrated:* The Story of St Francis; Children of Galilee; Adventures in a Caravan. *Recreation:* painting. *Club:* Army and Navy.

KAYE, Michael; Arts Director, Greater London Council, and General Administrator, South Bank Concert Halls, since 1980; *b* 27 Feb. 1925; *s* of Harry Kaye and Annie Steinberg; *m* 1st, 1950, Muriel Greenberg (marr. diss. 1959); one *d* ; 2nd, 1962, Fay Bercovitch. *Educ:* Malmesbury Road, Bow; Cave Road, Plaistow; Water Lane, Stratford; West Ham Secondary Sch., E15. Served in Army, REME and Intelligence Corps, 1943-47. Journalism and Public Relations, 1947-53; Marketing and Public Relations in tobacco industry, 1953-61; PR Manager, later PR Director, Carreras-Rothmans, 1961-76; Director, Peter Stuyvesant Foundation, 1963-76; General Administrator, Rupert Foundn, 1972-76; Man. Dir, London Symphony Orchestra, 1976-80. Trustee: Whitechapel Art Gallery, 1964-75; Youth & Music, 1970-78. *Recreations:* photography, music (clarinet). *Address:* 3 Coppice Way, E18 2DU. *T:* 01-989 1281.

KAYE, Sir Stephen Henry Gordon, 3rd Bt, *cr* 1923; *b* 24 March 1917; *s* of Sir Henry Gordon Kaye, 2nd Bt and Winifred (*d* 1971), *d* of late Walter H. Scales, Verwood, Bradford; *S* father 1956. *Educ:* Stowe; Trinity Coll., Cambridge. Heir: *brother* David Alexander Gordon Kaye [*b* 26 July 1919; *m* 1st, 1942, Elizabeth (marr. diss. 1950), *o d* of Capt. Malcolm Hurtley, Baynards Manor, Horsham, Sussex; 2nd, 1955, Adelle, *d* of Denis Thomas, Brisbane, Queensland; two *s* four *d*]. *Address:* Mortimore's, New Buildings, Sandford, near Crediton, Devon EX17 4PP.

KAYLL, Wing Commander Joseph Robert, DSO 1940; OBE 1946; DFC 1940; DL; JP; *b* 12 April 1914; *s* of late J. P. Kayll, MBE, The Elms, Sunderland; *m* 1940, Annette Lindsay Nisbet; two *s. Educ:* Aysgarth; Stowe. Timber trader; joined 607 Sqdn AAF, 1934; mobilised Sept. 1939; Commanding Officer 615 Squadron, 1940; (prisoner) 1941; OC 607 Sqdn AAF 1946. DL Durham, 1956; JP Sunderland, 1962. Mem., Wear Boating Assoc. *Recreation:* yachting. *Address:* Hillside House, Hillside, Sunderland, Tyne and Wear. *T:* 283282. *Clubs:* Royal Ocean Racing; Sunderland Yacht; Royal Northumberland Yacht.

KAYSEN, Prof. Carl; David W. Skinner Professor of Political Economy, since 1977, and Director of Program in Science, Technology and Society, since 1981, Massachusetts Institute of Technology; *b* 5 March 1920; *s* of Samuel and Elizabeth Kaysen; *m* 1940, Annette Neutra; two *d. Educ:* Philadelphia Public Schs; Overbrook High Sch., Philadelphia; Pennsylvania, Columbia and Harvard Univs. AB Pa 1940; MA 1947, PhD 1954, Harvard. Nat. Bureau of Economic Research, 1940-42; Office of Strategic Services, Washington, 1942-43; Intelligence Officer, US Army Air Force, 1943-45; State Dept, Washington, 1945. Dep. Special Asst to President, 1961-63. Harvard University, 1947-66: Teaching Fellow in Econs, 1947; Asst Prof. of Economics, 1950-55; Assoc. Prof. of Economics 1955-57; Prof. of Economics, 1957-66; Assoc. Dean, Graduate Sch. of Public Administration, 1960-66; Lucius N. Littauer Prof. of Political Economy, 1964-66; Jr Fellow, Soc. of Fellows, 1947-50, Actg Sen. Fellow, 1957-58, 1964-65; Syndic, Harvard Univ. Press, 1964-66; Dir, Inst. for Advanced Study, Princeton, NJ, 1966-76, Dir Emeritus, 1976; Vice Chm., and Dir of Research, Sloan Commn on Govt and Higher Educn, 1977-79. Sen. Fulbright Res. Schol., LSE, 1955-56. Trustee: Pennsylvania Univ., 1967-; German Marshall Fund Foundn; Russell Sage Foundn. *Publications:* United States v United Shoe Machinery Corporation, an Economic Analysis of an Anti-Trust Case, 1956; The American Business Creed (with others), 1956; Anti-Trust Policy (with D. F. Turner), 1959; The Demand for Electricity in the United States (with F. M. Fisher), 1962; The Higher Learning, The Universities, and The Public, 1969; (contrib.) Nuclear Energy Issues and Choices, 1979; A Program for Renewed Partnership (Sloan Commn on Govt and Higher Educn Report), 1980; numerous articles on economic theory, applied economics, higher education, military strategy and arms control. *Address:* E51-110D, Massachusetts Institute of Technology, Cambridge, Mass. 02139, USA.

KAZAN, Elia; author; independent producer and director of plays and films; *b* Constantinople, 7 Sept. 1909; *s* of George Kazan and Athena Sismanoglou; *m* 1st, 1932, Molly Thacher (*d* 1963); two *s* two *d* ; 2nd, 1967, Barbara Loden (*d* 1980). *Educ:* Williams Coll. (AB); 2 years postgraduate work in Drama at Yale. Actor, Group Theatre, 1932-39; first London appearance as Eddie Fuseli in Golden Boy, St James, 1938. Directed *plays:* Skin of Our Teeth, 1942; All My Sons, A Streetcar Named Desire, 1947; Death of a Salesman, 1949; Camino Real, Tea and Sympathy, 1953; Cat on a Hot Tin Roof, 1955; Dark at Top of the Stairs, JB, 1958; Sweet Bird of Youth, 1959; After the Fall, 1964; But For Whom Charlie, 1964; The Changeling, 1964; Four times won best stage Director of Year, 1942, 1947, 1948, 1949. Directed *films:* Streetcar named Desire, 1951; Viva Zapata, 1952; Pinky, 1949; Gentleman's Agreement, 1948 (won Oscar, best Dir); Boomerang, 1947; A Tree Grows in Brooklyn, 1945; On the Waterfront, 1954 (won Oscar, best Dir); East of Eden, 1954; Baby Doll, 1956; A Face in the Crowd, 1957; Wild River, 1960; Splendour in the Grass, 1962; America, America, 1964; The Arrangement, 1969; The Visitors, 1972; The Last Tycoon, 1977. Three times won Best Picture of Year from New York Film Critics, 1948, 1952, 1955. *Publications:* America, America (novel), 1963; The Arrangement (novel), 1967; The Assassins, 1972; The Understudy, 1974; Acts of Love, 1978; The Anatolian, 1982; magazine articles in New York Times, Theatre Arts, etc. *Recreation:* tennis. *Address:* 22 West 68th Street, New York City, NY 10023, USA.

KEAL, Dr Edwin Ernest Frederick, FRCP; Consultant Physician: Brompton Hospital, London, since 1966; St Mary's Hospital, London, since 1977; Kensington Chest Clinic, since 1963; Dean, Cardiothoracic Institute, since 1979; Consultant in Chest Diseases to the Army, since 1979; Chief Medical Officer, Eagle Star Insurance Co., since 1968; *b* 21 Aug. 1921; *s* of Frederick Archibald Keal and Mabel Orange Keal; *m* 1945, Constance Mary Gilliams; one *s. Educ:* Kingston High Sch., Hull; London Hospital Med. Coll. MB BS London 1952, DCH 1954, MD London 1971; FRCP 1973 (MRCP 1957). Service in RNVR (Lieut), 1939-46. Junior hosp. posts, London Hosp., 1952-59; Sen. Medical Registrar, Brompton Hosp., 1959-63; Cons. Physician, St Charles Hosp., London, 1963-77; Sen. Lectr, Cardiothoracic Inst., 1972-77. Member: Bd of Governors, National Heart and Chest Hosps, 1975-; Cttee of Management, Cardiothoracic Inst., 1978-. *Publications:* chapters in various books, and articles, mainly related to diseases of the chest. *Address:* 12 Dorchester Drive, Herne Hill, SE24 0DQ. *T:* 01-733 1766.

KEAN, Arnold Wilfred Geoffrey, CBE 1977; FRAeS; Member, UN Administrative Tribunal, since 1980; *b* 29 Sept. 1914; *s* of late Martin Kean; *m* 1939, Sonja Irene, *d* of late Josef Andersson, Copenhagen; two *d. Educ:* Blackpool Gram. Sch.; Queens' Coll., Cambridge (Schol.). 1st cl. 1st div. Law Tripos, Pts I and II; Pres., Cambridge Union, 1935; Wallenberg (Scandinavian) Prize; Commonwealth Fund Fellow, Harvard Law Sch.; Yarborough-Anderson Schol., Inner Temple. Called to the Bar (studentship, certif. of honour, 1939). Wartime service on legal staff of British Purchasing Commn and UK Treas. Delegn in N America. HM Treasury Solicitor's Dept, 1945; Princ. Asst Solicitor, 1964–72; Sec. and Legal Adviser, CAA, 1972–79. Member: Legal Cttee, Internat. Civil Aviation Organisation, 1954– (Chm., 1978–); Air Travel Reserve Fund Agency, 1975–79; UK Deleg. at internat. confs on maritime, railway, atomic energy and air law. Tutor in Law, Civil Service Coll., 1963–; Vis. Lectr, Univ. of Auckland, NZ, 1980. Air Law Editor, Jl of Business Law, 1970–. King Christian X Liberation Medal (Denmark), 1945. *Publications:* (ed) Essays in Air Law, 1982; articles in legal periodicals. *Recreations:* music, stamps, gardening. *Address:* Tall Trees, South Hill Avenue, Harrow HA1 3NU. *T:* 01-422 5791.

KEANE, Desmond St John, QC 1981; a Recorder of the Crown Court, since 1979; *b* 21 Aug. 1941; *er s* of late Henry Keane, MB, BCh, and of Patricia Keane; *m* 1968, Susan Mary Little; two *s* one *d. Educ:* Downside Sch.; Wadham Coll., Oxford (MA Mod. Hist.). Called to the Bar, Middle Temple, 1964 (Harmsworth Scholar); called to the Irish Bar, King's Inns, 1975. *Recreations:* cricket, lawn tennis, golf. *Address:* 2 Mitre Court Buildings, Temple, EC4Y 7BX. *T:* 01-583 1355. *Clubs:* Travellers'; Kildare Street and University (Dublin).

KEANE, Mary Nesta, (Mrs Robert Keane); *(nom de plume:* **M. J. Farrell**); *b* 20 July 1905; *d* of Walter Clarmont Skrine and Agnes Shakespeare Higginson; *m* 1938, Robert Lumley Keane; two *d. Educ:* privately. Author of plays: (with John Perry) Spring Meeting (play perf. Ambassadors Theatre and New York, 1938); Ducks and Drakes (play perf. Apollo Theatre, 1941); Guardian Angel (play perf. Gate Theatre, Dublin, 1944); Treasure Hunt (play perf. Apollo Theatre, 1949). *Publications:* as *M. J. Farrell:* Young Entry; Taking Chances; Mad Puppetstown; Conversation Piece; Devoted Ladies; Full House; The Rising Tide; Two Days in Aragon, 1941; Loving Without Tears (novel), 1951; Treasure Hunt, 1952; *as Molly Keane:* Good Behaviour, 1981. *Address:* Dysert, Ardmore, Co. Waterford, Ireland. *TA:* Ardmore. *T:* Youghal 4225.

KEANE, Major Sir Richard (Michael), 6th Bt *cr* 1801; farmer; *b* 29 Jan. 1909; *s* of Sir John Keane, 5th Bart, DSO, and Lady Eleanor Hicks-Beach (*d* 1960), *e d* of 1st Earl St Aldwyn; *S* father, 1956; *m* 1939, Olivia Dorothy Hawkshaw; two *s* one *d. Educ:* Sherborne Sch.; Christ Church, Oxford. Diplomatic Correspondent to Reuters 1935–37; Diplomatic Corresp. and Asst to Editor, Sunday Times, 1937–39. Served with County of London Yeomanry and 10th Royal Hussars, 1939–44; Liaison Officer (Major) with HQ Vojvodina, Yugoslav Partisans, 1944; attached British Military Mission, Belgrade, 1944–45. Publicity Consultant to Imperial Chemical Industries Ltd, 1950–62. *Publications:* Germany: What Next?, (Penguin Special), 1939; Modern Marvels of Science (editor), 1961. *Recreation:* fishing. *Heir:* *s* John Charles Keane, *b* 16 Sept. 1941. *Address:* Cappoquin House, Cappoquin, County Waterford, Ireland. *T:* 058-54004.

KEAR, Graham Francis; Under-Secretary, Energy Policy Division, Department of Energy, retired 1980; *b* 9 Oct. 1928; *s* of Richard Walter Kear and Eva Davies; *m* 1978, Joyce Eileen Parks. *Educ:* Newport (St Julian's) High Sch., Mon; Balliol Coll., Oxford (BA). Min. of Supply, 1951–52 and 1954–57; UK Delegn to ECSC, 1953–54; Min. of Aviation, 1957–59 and 1960–63; NATO Maintenance Supply Agency, Paris, 1959–60; MoD, 1963–65; Cabinet Office, 1968–71; Min. of Aviation Supply/DTI, 1971–72; Fellow, Harvard Univ. Center for Internat. Affairs, 1972–73; Under-Sec., Dept of Energy, 1974–80. *Recreation:* music. *Address:* 8 Branstone Court, Kew Road, Richmond, Surrey TW9 3LE. *T:* 01-940 7341.

KEARLEY, family name of **Viscount Devonport.**

KEARNEY, Sheriff Brian; Sheriff of Glasgow and Strathkelvin, since 1977; *b* 25 Aug. 1935; *s* of late James Samuel and Agnes Olive Kearney; *m* 1965, Elizabeth Mary Chambers; three *s* one *d. Educ:* Largs Higher Grade; Greenock Academy; Glasgow Univ. (MA, LLB). Qualified solicitor, 1960; Partner, Biggart, Lumsden & Co., Solicitors, Glasgow, 1965. Sheriff of N Strathclyde at Dumbarton, 1974–77. Sometime tutor in Jurisprudence, and external examnr in legal subjects, Glasgow Univ.; Pres., Glasgow Juridical Soc., 1964–65; Chm., Glasgow Marriage Guidance Council, 1977–. *Publications:* An Introduction to Ordinary Civil Procedure in the Sheriff Court, 1982; articles in legal jls. *Recreations:* cutting sandwiches for family picnics, listening to music, reading, writing and resting. *Address:* Sheriff's Chambers, Sheriff Court House, 149 Ingram Street, Glasgow G1 1EJ.

KEARNEY, Hon. Sir William (John Francis), Kt 1982; CBE 1976; Judge of the Supreme Court of the Northern Territory, since 1982; Aboriginal Land Commissioner, since 1982; *b* 8 Jan. 1935; *s* of William John Kilbeg Kearney and Gertrude Ivylene Kearney; *m* 1959, Jessie Alice Elizabeth Yung; three *d. Educ:* Univ. of Sydney (BA, LLB); University Coll. London (LLM). Legal Service of Papua New Guinea, 1963–75; Sec. for Law, 1972–75; dormant Commn as Administrator, 1972–73, and as High Comr, 1973–75; Judge,

Supreme Ct of PNG, 1976–80; Dep. Chief Justice, 1980–82. *Recreations:* travelling, literature. *Address:* Judges' Chambers, Supreme Court, Darwin, NT 5794, Australia.

KEARNS, Sir Frederick (Matthias), KCB 1975 (CB 1970); MC 1944; Consultant and policy adviser to Rank Hovis MacDougall Ltd, since 1981; *b* 21 Feb. 1921; *er s* of G. H. and Ivy Kearns, Burnley; *m* 1946, Betty Broadbent; one *d. Educ:* Burnley Gram. Sch.; Brasenose Coll., Oxford; RMC Sandhurst. BA (Hons) 1941; MA 1947, Oxon. Commissioned Royal Fusiliers, 1942. Served 8th and 5th Armies, N Africa and Italy, 1942–46; Brigade Major, 167th Inf. Brigade, Trieste, 1946. Asst Principal, Ministry of Agriculture, 1948, Principal 1950; Asst Sec., Min. of Agriculture, Fisheries and Food, 1957; Regional Controller, Northern Region, 1957–60; Head of Finance Division, 1960–63; Head of External Relations Div., 1963–64; Under-Sec., External Relations, 1964–68; Meat and Livestock Group 1968–69; Deputy Secretary, 1969–73; on special assignment to UK Delegn for EEC Negotiations, 1970–72; Second Permanent Sec., MAFF, 1973–78. *Recreations:* fishing, poetry. *Address:* 26 Brookway, Blackheath, SE3. *T:* 01-852 0747. *Club:* Reform.

KEARNS, Prof. Howard George Henry, OBE 1954; Professor of Agricultural and Horticultural Science, Bristol University 1957–67, now Emeritus; Dir, Long Ashton Research Station, 1957–67; *b* 13 May 1902; *s* of Henry Kearns and Elizabeth Anne Baker; *m* 1930, Molly Yvonne Cousins. *Educ:* St Paul's Sch., West Kensington; Downing Coll., Cambridge; Wye Coll., University of London. Lecturer in Zoology (Entomology), Bristol Univ., 1926–31; Advisory Entomologist, Long Ashton Research Station, 1931–32; Research Entomologist, 1933–; Reader in Entomology, Bristol Univ., 1950. Particular interests in applied biology, spray techniques and design of spray machinery for temperate and tropical crops. *Publications:* contrib. to: Insecticides and Colonial Agricultural Development, 1954; Science and Fruit, 1953; Modern Commercial Fruitgrowing, 1956; articles in learned jls on various aspects of plant protection. *Recreations:* engineering, natural history, photography. *Address:* Clive Weare House, Clewer, Wedmore, Som. *T:* Cheddar 742165.

KEARTON, family name of **Baron Kearton.**

KEARTON, Baron *cr* 1970 (Life Peer), of Whitchurch, Bucks; **Christopher Frank Kearton;** Kt 1966; OBE 1945; FRS 1961; Chancellor, University of Bath, since 1980; *b* 17 Feb. 1911; *s* of Christopher John Kearton and Lilian Hancock; *m* 1936, Agnes Kathleen Brander; two *s* two *d. Educ:* Hanley High Sch.; St John's Coll., Oxford. Joined ICI, Billingham Division, 1933. Worked in Atomic Energy Project, UK and USA, 1940–45. Joined Courtaulds Ltd, i/c of Chemical Engineering, 1946; Dir 1952; Dep. Chm., 1961–64; Chm., 1964–75; Chm. and Chief Exec., British Nat. Oil Corp., 1976–79. Part-time Member: UKAEA, 1955–81; CEGB, 1974–80. Dir, Hill Samuel Gp, 1970–81; Chm., British Printing Corp., 1981. Visitor, DSIR, 1955–61, 1963–68. Chairman: Industrial Reorganisation Corp., 1966–68; Electricity Supply Res. Council, 1960–77 (Mem., 1954–77); Tropical Products Inst. Cttee, 1958–79; East European Trade Council, 1975–77. Member: Windscale Accident Cttee, 1957; Special Advisory Group, British Transport Commn, 1960; Adv. Council on Technology, 1964–70; Council, RIIA, 1964–75; NEDC, 1965–71; Adv. Cttee, Industrial Expansion Bill, 1968–70 (Chm.); Central Adv. Council for Science and Technology; Cttee of Enquiry into Structure of Electricity Supply Industry, 1974–75; Offshore Energy Technology Bd, 1976–79; Energy Commn, 1977–79; Council, Royal Soc., 1970; Pres., Soc. of Chemical Industry, 1972–74 (Chm., Heavy Organic Chemical Section, 1961–62). President: RoSPA, 1973–80; BAAS, 1978–79; Pres., Aslib, 1980–82. Fellow, Imperial Coll. London, 1976; Hon. Fellow: St John's Coll., Oxford, 1965; Manchester Coll. of Sci. and Techn., 1966; Soc. of Dyers and Colourists, 1974. Comp. TI, 1965; Hon. MIChemE 1968; Hon. LLD: Leeds, 1966; Strathclyde, 1981; Hon. DSc: Bath, 1966; Aston in Birmingham, 1970; Reading, 1970; Keele, 1973; Ulster, 1975; Hon. DCL Oxon, 1978; DUniv Heriot-Watt, 1979. FRSA 1970; CBIM 1980. Grande Ufficiale, Order of Merit (Italy), 1977. *Address:* The Old House, Whitchurch, near Aylesbury, Bucks HP22 4JS. *T:* Whitchurch 232.

KEATING, Donald Norman, QC 1972; FCIArb; a Recorder of the Crown Court, since 1972; *b* 24 June 1924; *s* of late Thomas Archer Keating and late Anne Keating; *m* 1st, 1945, Betty Katharine (*d* 1975); two *s* one *d* ; 2nd, 1978, Kay Rosamond, *d* of Geoffrey and Avis Blundell Jones and *widow* of Edmund Deighton; one *s* one step *d. Educ:* Roan Sch.; King's Coll., London. BA History, 1948. RAFVR, 1943–46 (Flt Lt). Called to Bar, Lincoln's Inn, 1950; Bencher, 1979. *Publications:* Building Contracts, edns 1955, 1963, 1969, 1978 and supp. 1982; Guide to RIBA Forms, 1959; various articles in legal and other jls. *Recreations:* theatre, music, travel, walking. *Address:* 11 King's Bench Walk, Temple, EC4Y 7EQ. *T:* 01-353 9281.

KEATING, Frank; Sports Columnist, The Guardian, since 1976; *b* 4 Oct. 1937; *s* of Bryan Keating and Monica Marsh; *m* 1975, Sally Head (separated 1981). *Educ:* Belmont Abbey; Douai. Stroud News, 1956–58; Hereford Times, 1958–60; Evening World, Bristol, 1960–62; Editor, Outside Broadcasts, Rediffusion Television, 1963–67; Editor, Features, and Head of Special Projs, Thames Television, 1968–72; The Guardian, 1972–. Astroturf Sportswriter of the Year, 1978; 'What the Papers Say' Sportswriter of the Year, 1979. *Television series:* Maestro, BBC, 1981, 1982. *Publications:* Caught by Keating, 1979; Bowled Over, 1980; Another Bloody Day in Paradise, 1981; contrib. Punch, New Statesman, Spectator, BBC. *Recreations:* bad village cricket, worse golf. *Address:* 57 Holland Park, W11. *T:* 01-727 0269; Hyde Cottage, Lower Chute, Wilts SP10 1BD. *T:* Chute Standen 365. *Clubs:* Chelsea Arts; Chute (Wilts); Jolly Rogers Cricket (Home Counties touring).

KEATING, Henry Reymond Fitzwalter; author; *b* 31 Oct. 1926; *s* of John Hervey Keating and Muriel Marguerita Keating (*née* Clews); *m* 1953, Sheila Mary Mitchell; three *s* one *d. Educ:* Merchant Taylors' Sch.; Trinity Coll., Dublin. Journalism, 1952-60; Crime Reviewer for The Times, 1967-. Chm. Crime Writers' Assoc., 1970-71. *Publications:* Death and the Visiting Firemen, 1959; Zen there was Murder, 1960; A Rush on the Ultimate, 1961; The Dog it was that Died, 1962; Death of a Fat God, 1963; The Perfect Murder, 1964; Is Skin-Deep, Is Fatal, 1965; Inspector Ghote's Good Crusade, 1966; Inspector Ghote Caught in Meshes, 1967; Inspector Ghote Hunts the Peacock, 1968; Inspector Ghote Plays a Joker, 1969; Inspector Ghote Breaks an Egg, 1970; Inspector Ghote goes by Train, 1971; The Strong Man, 1971; (ed) Blood on My Mind, 1972; Inspector Ghote Trusts the Heart, 1972; The Underside, 1974; Bats Fly Up for Inspector Ghote, 1974; A Remarkable Case of Burglary, 1975; Filmi, Filmi, Inspector Ghote, 1976; Murder Must Appetize, 1976; (ed) Agatha Christie: First Lady of Crime, 1977; A Long Walk to Wimbledon, 1978; Inspector Ghote Draws a Line, 1979; Sherlock Holmes: the man and his world, 1979; The Murder of the Maharajah, 1980; Go West, Inspector Ghote, 1981; (ed) Whodunit, 1982; The Lucky Alphonse, 1982. *Recreation:* popping round to the post. *Address:* 35 Northumberland Place, W2 5AS. *T:* 01-229 1100.

KEATINGE, Sir Edgar (Mayne), Kt 1960; CBE 1954; *b* 3 Feb. 1905; *s* of late Gerald Francis Keatinge, CIE; *m* 1930, Katharine Lucile Burrell; one *s* one *d. Educ:* Rugby Sch.; School of Agriculture, S Africa. Diploma in Agriculture, 1925. S African Dept of Agriculture, 1926-29. Served War of 1939-45 with RA. Resigned with rank of Lieut-Col. West African Frontier Force, 1941-43; Commandant Sch. of Artillery, West Africa, 1942-43; CC West Suffolk, 1933-45. Parliamentary Candidate, Isle of Ely, 1938-44; MP (C) Bury St Edmunds, 1944-45; JP Wilts 1946; Chm. Wessex Area Nat. Union of Conservative Assocs, 1950-53; Mem. Panel, Land Tribunal, SW Area. Director: St Madeleine Sugar Co., 1944-62; Caromi Ltd, 1962-66. Governor, Sherborne Sch., 1951-74. Mem. Council, Royal African Soc., 1970-80. *Recreations:* travel, shooting. *Address:* Teffont, Salisbury, Wilts SP3 5RG. *T:* Teffont 224. *Clubs:* Carlton, Boodle's.
See also Prof. W. R. Keatinge.

KEATINGE, Prof. William Richard; MA; MB, BChir; PhD; Professor of Physiology, London Hospital Medical College, since 1971; *b* 18 May 1931; *s* of Sir Edgar Keatinge, *qv; m* 1955, M. E. Annette Hegarty; one *s* two *d. Educ:* Upper Canada Coll.; Rugby Sch.; Cambridge Univ.; St Thomas's Hospital. House Phys., St Thomas's Hospital, 1955-56; Surg.-Lt RN (Nat. Service), 1956-58; Jun. Research Fellow and Dir of Studies in Medicine, Pembroke Coll., Cambridge, 1958-60; Fellow, Cardiovascular Research Inst., San Francisco, 1960-61; MRC appt Radcliffe Infirmary, Oxford, 1961-68; Fellow of Pembroke Coll., Oxford, 1965-68; Reader in Physiology, London Hosp. Med. Coll., 1968. *Publications:* Survival in Cold Water, 1969; Local Mechanisms Controlling Blood Vessels, 1980; chapters in textbooks of physiology and medicine; papers in physiological and medical jls on temperature regulation and on control of blood vessels. *Recreations:* ski-ing, archaeology. *Address:* London Hospital Medical College, Turner Street, E1 2AD.

KEAY, Ronald William John, CBE 1977 (OBE 1966); DPhil; FIBiol; Executive Secretary, The Royal Society, since 1977; *b* 20 May 1920; *s* of Harold John Keay and Marion Lucy (*née* Flick); *m* 1944, Joan Mary Walden; one *s* two *d. Educ:* King's College Sch., Wimbledon; St John's Coll., Oxford (BSc, MA, DPhil). Colonial Forest Service, Nigeria, 1942-62. Seconded to Royal Botanic Gardens, Kew, 1951-57; Dir, Federal Dept of Forest Research, Nigeria, 1960-62; Dep. Exec. Sec., The Royal Society, 1962-77. Pres., Science Assoc. of Nigeria, 1961-62; Vice-Pres., Linnean Soc., 1965-67, 1971-73, 1974-76; Pres., African Studies Assoc., 1971-72. Chm., Finance Cttee. Internat. Biological Programme, 1964-74; Treasurer, Scientific Cttee for Problems of the Environment, 1976-77; Mem., Lawes Agricl Trust Cttee, 1978-. Mem. Court, Brunel Univ., 1978-. Church Warden, St Martin-in-the-Fields, 1981-. *Publications:* Flora of West Tropical Africa, Vol. 1, 1954-58; Nigerian Trees, 1960-64; papers on tropical African plant ecology and taxonomy, and science policy. *Recreations:* gardening, walking, natural history. *Address:* Flat 1 (Private), 6 Carlton House Terrace, SW1Y 5AG. *T:* 01-839 5260. *Club:* Athenæum.

KEDOURIE, Prof. Elie, FBA 1975; Professor of Politics in the University of London, since 1965; Editor, Middle Eastern Studies, since 1964; *b* 25 Jan. 1926; *er s* of A. Kedourie and L. Dangour, Baghdad; *m* 1950, Sylvia, *d* of Gourgi Haim, Baghdad; two *s* one *d. Educ:* College A-D Sasson and Shamash Sch., Baghdad; London Sch. of Economics; St Antony's Coll., Oxford (Sen. Scholar). BSc(Econ). Has taught at the London Sch. of Economics, 1953-. Visiting Lecturer: Univ. of California, Los Angeles, 1959; Univ. of Paris, 1959; Visiting Prof.: Princeton Univ., 1960-61; Monash Univ., Melb., 1967; Harvard Univ., 1968-69; Tel Aviv Univ., 1969. Fellow, Netherlands Inst. for Advanced Study, 1980-81. *Publications:* England and the Middle East, 1956; Nationalism, 1960; Afghani and 'Abduh, 1966; The Chatham House Version, 1970; Nationalism in Asia and Africa, 1971; Arabic Political Memoirs, 1974; In the Anglo-Arab Labyrinth, 1976; (ed) The Middle Eastern Economy, 1977; (ed) The Jewish World, 1979; (ed jtly) Modern Egypt, 1980; Islam in the Modern World, 1980; (ed jtly) Towards a Modern Iran, 1980; (ed jtly) Palestine and Israel in the Nineteenth and Twentieth Centuries, 1982; (ed jtly) Zionism and Arabism in Palestine and Israel, 1982. *Address:* London School of Economics, Houghton Street, Aldwych, WC2A 2AE. *T:* 01-405 7686.

KEE, Robert; author and broadcaster; *b* 5 Oct. 1919; *s* of late Robert and Dorothy Kee; *m* 1st, 1948, Janetta, *d* of Rev. G. H. Woolley, VC; one *d*; 2nd, 1960, Cynthia, *d* of Edward Judah; one *s* one *d* (and one *s* decd). *Educ:* Stowe Sch.; Magdalen Coll., Oxford (Exhibr, MA). RAF, 1940-46. Atlantic Award for Literature, 1946. Picture Post, 1948-51; Picture Editor, WHO, 1953; Special Corresp., Observer, 1956-57; Literary Editor, Spectator, 1957; Special Corresp., Sunday Times, 1957-58; BBC TV (Panorama, etc), 1958-62; Television Reporters International, 1963-64; ITV (Rediffusion, Thames, London Week-End, ITN, Yorkshire), 1964-78; BBC, 1978-82; Presenter, Panorama, BBC1, 1982. *Television series:* Ireland: a television history (13 parts), 1981. Alistair Horne Research Fellow, St Antony's Coll., Oxford, 1972-73. BAFTA Richard Dimbleby Award, 1976. *Publications:* A Crowd Is Not Company, 1947, repr. 1982; The Impossible Shore, 1949; A Sign of the Times, 1955; Broadstrop In Season, 1959; Refugee World, 1961; The Green Flag, 1972; Ireland: a history, 1980; many translations from German. *Recreations:* swimming, bicycling, listening to music. *Address:* c/o Lloyds Bank, 112 Kensington High Street, W8.
See also William Kee.

KEE, William; His Honour Judge Kee; a Circuit Judge, since 1972; *b* 15 Oct. 1921; *yr s* of Robert and Dorothy Kee; *m* 1953, Helga Wessel Eckhoff; one *s* three *d. Educ:* Rottingdean Sch.; Stowe Sch. Served War, Army, 1941-46: attached 9th Gurkha Rifles, Dehra Dun, 1943; Staff Captain, Bde HQ, 1945-46. Called to Bar, Inner Temple, 1948. Jt Chm., Independent Schools' Tribunal, 1971-72. *Publications:* (jt) Divorce Case Book, 1950; contributor to: titles in Atkin's Encyclopaedia of Court Forms; Halsbury's Laws of England. *Recreations:* listening to music, walking. *Address:* Oak Hill Cottage, Oak Hill Road, Sevenoaks, Kent TN13 1NP. *T:* 52737.
See also Robert Kee.

KEEBLE, Sir (Herbert Ben) Curtis, GCMG 1982 (KCMG 1978; CMG 1970); HM Diplomatic Service, retired; Ambassador at Moscow, 1978-82; *b* 18 Sept. 1922; *s* of Herbert Keeble and Gertrude Keeble, BEM; *m* 1947, Margaret Fraser; three *d. Educ:* Clacton County High Sch.; London University. Served HM Forces, 1942-47. Entered HM Foreign (subsequently Diplomatic) Service, 1947; served in Djakarta, 1947-49; Foreign Office, 1949-51; Berlin, 1951-54; Washington, 1954-58; Foreign Office, 1958-63; Counsellor and Head of European Economic Organisations Dept, 1963-65; Counsellor (Commercial), Berne, 1965-68; Minister, Canberra, 1968-71; Asst Under-Sec. of State, FCO, 1971-73; HM Ambassador, German Democratic Republic, 1974-76; Dep. Under Sec. of State (Chief Clerk), FCO, 1976-78. *Recreations:* sailing, skiing. *Address:* c/o Foreign and Commonwealth Office, SW1. *Club:* Travellers'.

KEEBLE, Major Robert, DSO 1940; MC 1945; TD 1946; Director: Associated Portland Cement Manufacturers Ltd, 1970-74; Aberthaw & Bristol Channel Portland Cement Co. Ltd, 1970-74; engaged in cement manufacture; Manager, Hull Savings Bank; *b* 20 Feb. 1911; *s* of late Edwin Percy and Alice Elizabeth Keeble; unmarried. *Educ:* King Henry VIII's Sch., Coventry. Commanded Royal Engineer Field Company; Territorial Army Commission, passed Staff Coll., Camberley, 1939; Freeman of City of London and Liveryman of Company of Fanmakers; served in War of 1939-45 (despatches twice, twice wounded, DSO, MC, 1939-45 Star, African Star, France-Germany Star and Defence Medal, TD). Mem., Inst. Quarrying. Governor, Hull Univ. Hon. Brother, Hull Trinity House. *Recreations:* fired in rifle team winning Lord Wakefield Shield for TA, 1939; sailing. *Address:* 15 Fernhill Close, Kenilworth CV8 1AN. *T:* Kenilworth 55668. *Club:* Army and Navy.

KEEBLE, Thomas Whitfield; HM Diplomatic Service, retired 1976; Senior Clerk (Acting), Committee Office, House of Commons, since 1976; *b* 10 Feb. 1918; *m* 1945, Ursula Scott Morris; two *s. Educ:* Sir John Deane's Grammar Sch., Cheshire; St John's Coll., Cambridge (MA); King's Coll., London (PhD). Served, 1940-45, in India, Persia, Iraq and Burma in RA (seconded to Indian Artillery), Captain. Asst Principal, Commonwealth Relations Office, 1948; Private Sec. to Parliamentary Under Sec. of State; Principal, 1949; First Sec., UK High Commn in Pakistan, 1950-53, in Lahore, Peshawar and Karachi; seconded to Foreign Service and posted to UK Mission to the United Nations in New York, 1955-59; Counsellor, 1958; Head of Defence and Western Dept, CRO, 1959-60; British Dep. High Comr in Ghana, 1960-63; Head of Econ. Gen. Dept, CRO, 1963-66; Minister (Commercial), British Embassy, Buenos Aires, 1966-67; Hon. Research Associate, Inst. of Latin American Studies, Univ. of London, 1967-68; Minister, British Embassy, Madrid, 1969-71; Head of UN (Econ. and Social) Dept, FCO, 1971-72, of UN Dept, 1972-74; Sen. Directing Staff (Civil), Nat. Defence Coll., Latimer, 1974-76. *Publications:* British Overseas Territories and South America, 1806-1914, 1970; articles in Hispanic reviews. *Recreations:* golf, Spanish literature, bird watching. *Address:* 715 Willoughby House, Barbican, EC2Y 8BN. *Club:* United Oxford & Cambridge University.

KEEFFE, Barrie Colin; dramatist; *b* 31 Oct. 1945; *s* of Edward Thomas Keeffe and Constance Beatrice Keeffe (*née* Marsh); *m* 1st, 1969, Dee Sarah Truman (marr. diss. 1979); 2nd, 1981, Verity Eileen Proud (*née* Bargate) (*d* 1981); Guardian of her two *s. Educ:* East Ham Grammar School. Formerly actor with

Nat. Youth Theatre; began writing career as journalist; Thames Television Award writer-in-residence, Shaw Theatre, 1977; Resident playwright, Royal Shakespeare Co., 1978; Mem. Board of Directors, Soho Theatre Co., 1978-. *Theatre plays:* Only a Game, 1973; A Sight of Glory, 1975; Scribes, 1975; My Girl, 1975; Here Comes the Sun, 1976; Gimme Shelter, 1977; A Mad World My Masters, 1977; Barbarians, 1977; Frozen Assets, 1978; Sus, 1979; Bastard Angel, 1980; She's So Modern, 1980; Black Lear, 1980; Chorus Girls, 1981; *television plays:* Substitute, 1972; Not Quite Cricket, 1977; Gotcha, 1977; Nipper, 1977; Champions, 1978; Hanging Around, 1978; Waterloo Sunset, 1979; *film:* The Long Good Friday, 1981; also radio plays. French Critics Prix Revelation, 1978; Giles Cooper Best Radio Plays, 1980. *Publications: novel:* Gadabout, 1969; *plays:* Gimme Shelter, 1977; A Mad World My Masters, 1977; Barbarians, 1977; Here Comes the Sun, 1978; Frozen Assets, 1978; Sus, 1979; Bastard Angel, 1980. *Recreations:* friends, gardening. *Address:* 24 Pottery Lane, W11. *T:* 01-727 1346. *Club:* Soho Poly Theatre.

KEEGAN, Denis Michael; Barrister; General Manager, Mercantile Credit Co. Ltd; Director, Barclays Mercantile Industrial Finance Ltd; Deputy Chairman, HP Information PLC; *b* 26 Jan. 1924; *o s* of Denis Francis Keegan and Mrs Duncan Campbell; *m* 1st, 1951, Pamela Barbara (marr. diss.), *yr d* of late Percy Bryan, Purley, Surrey; one *s*; 2nd, 1961, Marie Patricia (marr. diss.), *yr d* of late Harold Jennings; one *s*; 3rd, 1972, Ann Irene, *d* of Norman Morris. *Educ:* Oundle Sch.; Queen's University, Kingston, Ontario, Canada (BA). Served RN Fleet Air Arm, 1944-46 (petty officer pilot). Called to Bar, Gray's Inn, 1950. Mem. Nottingham City Council, 1953-55, resigned. MP (C) Nottingham Sth, 1955-Sept. 1959. Formerly Dir, Radio and Television Retailers' Assoc. *Recreations:* reading, talking, music. *Address:* 95 Clare Court, Judd Street, WC1. *T:* 01-242 1234.

KEEGAN, (Joseph) Kevin, OBE 1982; professional footballer; *b* 14 Feb. 1951; *s* of late Joseph Keegan; *m* 1974, Jean Woodhouse; two *d.* Professional footballer with: Scunthorpe Utd, 1966-71; Liverpool, 1971-77; Hamburg, 1977-80; Southampton, 1980-82; Newcastle Utd, 1982-. Internat. appearances for England, 1973-82, Captain, 1976-82. Winners' medals: League Championships, 1973, 1976; UEFA Cup, 1973; FA Cup, 1974; European Cup, 1977. European Footballer of the Year, 1978, 1979. *Publications:* Kevin Keegan, 1978; Against the World: playing for England, 1979. *Address:* c/o Newcastle United Football Club, St James Park, Newcastle upon Tyne.

KEELE, Prof. Cyril Arthur; Emeritus Professor of Pharmacology, University of London; *b* 23 Nov. 1905; 2nd *s* of Dr David and Jessie Keele; *m* 1942, Joan Ainslie, *er d* of Lieut-Col G. A. Kempthorne; three *s. Educ:* Epsom Coll.; Middlesex Hospital Medical Sch. MRCS, LRCP 1927; MB, BS (London) 1928; MRCP 1929; MD London 1930; FRCP 1948; FFARCS 1958. Medical Registrar, Middlesex Hosp., 1930-32; Demonstrator and Lectr in Physiology, 1933-38; Lectr in Pharmacology, 1938-49; Reader in Pharmacology and Therapeutics, 1949-52, at Middlesex Hospital Medical Sch.; Prof. of Pharmacology and Therapeutics, Univ. of London, 1952-68; Dir, Rheumatology Res. Dept, Middlesex Hosp. Med. Sch., 1968-73. Hon. Mem., Internat. Assoc. for the Study of Pain, 1975. *Publications:* Recent Advances in Pharmacology (with Prof. J. M. Robson), 1956; Samson Wright's Applied Physiology, 13th edn (with Prof. E. Neil and Prof. N. Joels); (with Dr D. Armstrong) Substances producing Pain and Itch, 1964. Papers in scientific journals on the control of sweating, analgesic drugs and chemical factors producing pain. *Address:* 25 Letchmore Road, Radlett, Herts WD7 8HU.

KEELEY, Thomas Clews, CBE 1944; MA; physicist; Fellow of Wadham College, Oxford, 1924-61, now Emeritus Fellow; Sub-Warden, 1947-61, retired; *b* 16 Feb. 1894; *s* of T. F. Keeley, Erdington, Birmingham. *Educ:* King Edward's School, Birmingham; St John's Coll., Cambridge (Scholar). Royal Aircraft Establishment, 1917-19. Oxford from 1919. Fellow of the Institute of Physics. *Recreations:* photography, travel. *Address:* Wadham College, Oxford. *T:* 42564. *Club:* English-Speaking Union.

KEELING, Surgeon Rear-Adm. John, CBE 1978; QHP 1977; Director of Medical Policy and Plans, Ministry of Defence, since 1980; Chairman, NATO Joint Civil/Military Medical Group, since 1981; *b* 28 Oct. 1921; *s* of John and Grace Keeling; *m* 1948, Olwen Anne Dix; one *s* (and one *s* decd). *Educ:* Queen Elizabeth's Sch., Hartlebury; Birmingham Univ. MRCS, LRCP; MFOM. Entered RN as Surg. Lieut, 1946; served with Fleet Air Arm, 1947-75: Pres., Central Air Med. Bd, 1954-56 and 1960-63; SMO, HMS Albion, 1956-57, HMS Victorious, 1965-67, and several Royal Naval Air Stns; Staff MO to Flag Officer Sea Trng, 1970-73; Dir of Environmental Medicine and Dep. MO i/c Inst. of Naval Medicine, 1975-77; Dep. Med. Dir-Gen. (Naval), 1977-80. Surg. Captain 1970, Surg. Cdre 1977, Surg. Rear-Adm. 1980. *Recreations:* music, gardening, micro-computing, caravanning. *Address:* Merlin Cottage, Brockhampton, Hereford HR1 4TQ. *T:* How Caple 649. *Club:* Army and Navy.

KEELING, Robert William Maynard; a Recorder of the Crown Court, since 1980; Consultant with Monier Williams Keeling & Dehn; *b* 16 Dec. 1917; *s* of Dr George Sydney Keeling, MD, and Florence Amy Keeling (*née* Maynard); *m* 1942, Kathleen Busill Jones; one *s* two *d. Educ:* Uppingham; Corpus Christi Coll., Cambridge (BA 1939). Served War, RASC, 1939-46: Western Desert, Italy, Greece (despatches 1944), Burma. FO, 1946-47. Solicitor 1950; Partner in Monier Williams & Keeling, 1956-80; Solicitor to Vintners Company, 1953-79. Director, Sherry Producers Committee Ltd, 1957-80, Chairman 1980-. Knight Comdr, Order of Civil Merit (Spain), 1967.

Recreations: growing English wine, travel, painting, music. *Address:* Hembury Knoll, Hook Heath, Woking, Surrey GU22 0QE.

KEELY, Eric Philipps, CBE 1950; Director, National Sulphuric Acid Association Ltd, 1959-67; *b* 11 Aug. 1899; *s* of late Erasmus Middleton Keely, Nottingham; *m* 1942, Enid Betty Curtis; two *d. Educ:* Highgate Sch. Served European War, 1917-18, Lancashire Fusiliers; Ministry of Agriculture and Fisheries, 1930; Food (Defence Plans) Dept, Board of Trade 1937; Ministry of Food, 1939; seconded to Govt of India, 1943-44; Under-Sec., Ministry of Food, 1952; Under-Sec., Ministry of Agriculture, Fisheries and Food, 1955-59. *Address:* Queen's Cottage, Horsham Road, Findon, West Sussex. *T:* Findon 2677.

KEEN, Patrick John, CMG 1968; MBE 1944; retired; *b* 30 June 1911; *s* of Brig. P. H. Keen, CB; *m* 1st, 1940, Joyce (*d* 1954), *d* of E. Seth-Ward; two *s* one *d* (and one *s* decd); 2nd, 1958, Anne Cunitia, *d* of Capt. J. A. A. Morris, RN. *Educ:* Haileybury Coll.; RMC Sandhurst. Hampshire Regt, 1931; Indian Political Service, 1936-47; served with 2/13th FF Rifles, 1939-43; HM Diplomatic Service, 1948-68; served in Afghanistan, Pakistan, Cyprus and British Guiana; retd, 1968. *Address:* Saxted House, Emsworth, Hants. *T:* Emsworth 2302.

KEENE, Air Vice-Marshal Allan L. A. P.; *see* Perry-Keene.

KEENE, David Wolfe, QC 1980; *b* 15 April 1941; *s* of Edward Henry Wolfe Keene and Lillian Marjorie Keene; *m* 1965, Gillian Margaret Lawrance; one *s* one *d. Educ:* Hampton Grammar Sch.; Balliol Coll., Oxford (Winter Williams Prizewinner, 1962; BA 1st Cl. Hons Law, 1962; BCL 1963). Called to the Bar, Inner Temple, 1964; Eldon Law Scholar, 1965. Chm. of Panel, Cumbria Structure Plan Examination in Public, 1980. Contested (Lab) Taunton, Feb. 1974, and Croydon S, Oct. 1974. *Recreations:* walking, opera, listening to jazz. *Address:* 17 Belsize Lane, NW3 5AD. *T:* 01-794 3570; 4 and 5, Gray's Inn Square, Gray's Inn, WC1R 5AY. *T:* 01-404 5252. *Clubs:* Athenæum, Wig and Pen.

KEENE, John Robert R.; *see* Ruck Keene.

KEENLEYSIDE, Hugh Llewellyn, CC (Canada) 1969; consultant; *b* 7 July 1898; *s* of Ellis William Keenleyside and Margaret Louise Irvine; *m* 1924, Katherine Hall Pillsbury, BA, BSc; one *s* three *d. Educ:* Langara School and Public Schools, Vancouver, BC; University of British Columbia (BA); Clark University (MA, PhD). Holds several hon. degrees in Law, Science. Instructor and Special Lecturer in History, Brown University, Syracuse Univ., and University of British Columbia, 1923-27; Third Sec., Dept of External Affairs, 1928; Second Sec., 1929; First Sec. and First Chargé d'Affaires, Canadian Legation, Tokyo, 1929; Dept of External Affairs and Prime Minister's Office, 1936; Chm, Board of Review to Investigate charges of illegal entry on the Pacific Coast, 1938; Sec., Cttee in charge of Royal Visit to Canada, 1938-39; Counsellor, 1940; Asst Under-Sec. of State for External Affairs, 1941-44; Mem. and Sec., Canadian Section, Canada-United States Permanent Jt Bd on Defence, 1940-44, Acting Chm., 1944-45; Member: North-West Territories Council, 1941-45; Canada-United States Joint Economic Cttees, 1941-44; Special Cttee on Orientals in BC; Canadian Shipping Board, 1939-41; War Scientific and Technical Development Cttee, 1940-45; Canadian Ambassador to Mexico, 1944-47; Deputy Minister of Resources and Development and Comr of Northwest Territories, 1947-50; Head of UN Mission of Technical Assistance to Bolivia, 1950; Dir-Gen., UN Technical Assistance Administration, 1950-58; Under-Sec. Gen. for Public Administration, UN, 1959. Chairman: BC Power Commn, 1959-62; BC Hydro and Power Authy, 1962-69. Vice-Pres. National Council of the YMCAs of Canada, 1941-45; Vice-Chm., Canadian Youth Commission, 1943-45; Head of Canadian Deleg. to UN Scientific Conf. on Conservation and Utilization of Resources, 1949. Life Mem., Asiatic Soc. of Japan; one of founders and mem. of first Board of Governors of Arctic Institute of North America; Vice-Chm., Board of Governors, Carleton Coll., 1943-50; Pres. Assoc. of Canadian Clubs, 1948-50; Mem. Bd of Trustees, Clark Univ., 1953-56; Mem. Senate, University of British Columbia, 1963-69. Hon. Life Mem., Canadian Association for Adult Education; Mem. Board of Governors, Canadian Welfare Council, 1955-69; Member: Canadian National Cttee of World Power Conference; Adv. Bd (BC), Canada Permanent Co.; Hon. Bd of Dirs, Resources for the Future; Dir, Toronto-Dominion Bank, 1960-70. Assoc. Comr General, UN Conf. on Human Settlements, 1975-76 (Hon. Chm. Canadian Nat. Cttee, 1974-77). Chancellor, Notre Dame Univ., Nelson, BC, 1969-76. Dir and Fellow, Royal Canadian Geographic Soc. Haldane Medal, Royal Inst. of Public Administration, 1954; first recipient, Vanier Medal, Inst. of Public Administration of Canada, 1962. *Publications:* Canada and the United States, 1929, revised edn 1952; History of Japanese Education (with A. F. Thomas), 1937; International Aid: a summary, 1966; various magazine articles. *Recreations:* reading, outdoor sports, cooking, poker. *Address:* 3470 Mayfair Drive, Victoria, BC V8P 1P8, Canada. *T:* 592-9331.

KEENLYSIDE, Francis Hugh; *b* 7 July 1911; *s* of late Capt. Cecil A. H. Keenlyside and Gladys Mary (*née* Milne); *m* 1st, 1935, Margaret Joan, *d* of late E. L. K. Ellis; two *s* two *d*; 2nd, 1962, Joan Winifred (*née* Collins); one *d. Educ:* Charterhouse; Trinity Coll., Oxford. 1st class Hons in Philosophy, Politics and Economics, 1933, Whitehead Travelling Student. Entered Administrative Class, Home Civil Service, 1934; Principal Private Sec. to four successive Ministers of Shipping and War Transport, 1939-43; Asst Sec. in charge of Shipping Policy Div., 1943; Asst Manager, Union Castle, 1947; Dep. Leader, British delegation to Danube Conf., Belgrade, 1948; Gen. Manager, Union Castle, 1953; Asst Managing Dir, Union-Castle, 1956-60; Shipping Adviser, Suez Canal Users Assoc., 1957. Mem., Gen. Council of Chamber of Shipping, 1953-60; Editor, Alpine Journal, 1953-62. Chevalier (1st Cl.) of Order of St Olav (Norway), 1948; Officer of Order of George I (Greece), 1950; King Christian X Liberty Medal (Denmark), 1946. *Publications:* Peaks and Pioneers, 1975; contrib. to mountaineering jls, etc. *Recreation:* mountaineering. *Address:* c/o Credit Andorra, La Massana, Principality of Andorra. *Clubs:* Alpine; Salisbury.

KEENS, Philip Francis, CBE 1973 (OBE 1966); Director, TSB Unit Trust Managers (Channel Islands) Ltd, since 1972; Chairman, TSB Gilt Fund Ltd, since 1978; *b* 18 June 1903; *s* of Sir Thomas Keens; *m* 1st, 1930, Sylvia Irene Robinson (*d* 1970); one *s* one *d* ; 2nd, 1974, Mrs Margaret Faith Warne. *Educ:* Tettenhall Coll., Staffs. Incorporated Accountant, 1925; Chartered Accountant, 1957. Partner, Keens, Shay, Keens & Co., London, 1926-67; Trustee, Luton Trustee Savings Bank, 1934 (Chairman, 1949-64); Dep. Chm., Trustee Savings Bank Assoc., 1966-76 (Chm. Southern Area, 1967-76); Chm., London South Eastern Trustee Savings Bank, 1964-76 (Vice-Chm., 1958-64); Chairman: Trustee Savings Bank Trust Co. Ltd, 1967-79; Central Trustee Savings Bank Ltd, 1972-79; Trustee Savings Bank, South East, 1975-78, Pres., 1978; Mem., Trustee Savings Bank Central Bd, 1976-79. Past Master, Worshipful Co. of Feltmakers. *Recreation:* golf. *Address:* 15 Links Court, Grouville, Jersey, CI. *T:* Jersey 53719. *Club:* Victoria (Jersey).

KEEP, Charles Reuben; Chairman: Towergate Securities Ltd, since 1978; Tozer Kemsley & Millbourn Trading Ltd; Director, Manufacturers Hanover Credit Corporation; President, France Motors sa Paris, since 1974; *b* 1932; *m* ; one *d. Educ:* HCS, Hampstead. Joined Lloyds & Scottish Finance Ltd, 1956, Director, 1969; Man. Dir, International Factors Ltd, 1970; Group Man. Dir, Tozer Kemsley & Millbourn (Holdings) Ltd, 1973. *Address:* The Oaks, 20 Forest Lane, Chigwell, Essex IG7 5AE. *T:* 01-504 3897. *Clubs:* Gresham; Chigwell Golf.

KEEPING, Charles William James; artist, book designer and Fine Art Lecturer since 1952; Visiting Lecturer in Art, Croydon College of Art, since 1963; *b* 22 Sept. 1924; *s* of Charles Keeping and Eliza Ann Trodd; *m* 1952, Renate Meyer; three *s* one *d. Educ:* Frank Bryant Sch., Kennington; Polytechnic, Regent Street. Apprenticed to printing trade, 1938; served as telegraphist, RN, 1942-46; studied for Nat. Diploma of Design at Polytechnic, London, 1946-52; Vis. Lectr in Art, Polytechnic, 1956-63. Illustrated over 100 books, drawings for wall murals, television and advertising. MSIA. Certificate of Merit (for illustrations to The God Beneath the Sea) 1970, Library Assoc.; Certificate, Highly Commended, for Hans Andersen Medal, Rio de Janeiro, Internat. Bd on Books for Young People, 1974. *Publications:* Black Dolly, 1966; Shaun and the Carthorse, 1966; Charley Charlotte and the Golden Canary, 1967 (Kate Greenaway Medal); Alfie and the Ferryboat, 1968; Tinker Tailor, 1968 (a Francis Williams Meml Bequest prize-winner, 1972); Joseph's Yard, 1969 (Honour Book award) (also filmed for TV); Through the Window, 1970 (also filmed for TV); Spider's Web, 1973 (Bratislava cert.); Richard, 1973; Railway Passage, 1974 (Golden Apple, Bienalle Illustration Bratislava, 1975); Wasteground Circus, 1975; Cockney Ding Dong, 1975; The Wildman, 1976 (a Francis Williams prize-winner, 1977); Inter-City, 1977; River, 1978; Miss Emily and the Bird of Make-believe, 1978; Willie's Fire-Engine, 1980; *Illustrations for:* The Highwayman, by Alfred Noyes, 1981 (Kate Greenaway Medal, 1982); The Pickwick Papers and Great Expectations, by Charles Dickens, 1981; Beowulf, 1982. *Recreations:* talking, walking, driving ponies. *Address:* 16 Church Road, Shortlands, Bromley BR2 0HP. *T:* 01-460 7679. *Club:* Nash House.

KEETON, George Williams, FBA 1964; Barrister-at-law; Principal, London Institute of World Affairs, 1938-52, President, since 1952; Leverhulme Fellow, 1971; *b* 22 May 1902; *o s* of John William and Mary Keeton; *m* 1st, 1924, Gladys Edith Calthorpe; two *s* ; 2nd, Kathleen Marian Willard. *Educ:* Gonville and Caius Coll., Cambridge (Foundation Scholar in Law); Gray's Inn (Bacon Scholar). BA, LLB, with first class hons, 1923; MA, LLM, 1927; LLD 1932. Called to Bar, 1928; Editor, The Cambridge Review, 1924; Reader in Law and Politics, Hong Kong Univ., 1924-27; Senior Lecturer in Law, Manchester Univ., 1928-31; Reader in English Law, 1931-37, Prof. of English Law, 1937-69, Dean, Faculty of Laws, 1939-54, Vice-Provost, 1966-69, University Coll., London; Professor of English Law, Univ. of Notre Dame, 1969-77; Professor Associate, Brunel Univ., 1969-77. Distinguished Vis. Prof., Miami Univ., 1971-73. Mem. Exec. Cttee, American Judicature Soc., 1974-77. Hon. LLD: Sheffield 1966; Hong Kong 1972; DUniv Brunel, 1977. *Publications:* The Development of Extraterritoriality in China, 1928; The Austinian Theories of Law and Sovereignty (with R. A. Eastwood, LLD), 1929; The Elementary Principles of Jurisprudence, 1930, 2nd edn 1949; Shakespeare and his Legal Problems, 1930; The Problem of the Moscow Trial, 1933; The Law of Trusts, 1st edn 1934, 10th edn 1974; An Introduction to Equity, 1st edn 1938, 8th edn 1976; National Sovereignty and International Order, 1939; Making International Law Work (with G. Schwarzenberger, PhD), 1st edn 1939, 2nd edn 1946; The Speedy Return (novel), 1938; Mutiny in the Caribbean (novel), 1940; The Case for an International University, 1941; Russia and Her Western Neighbours (with R. Schlesinger), 1942; China, the Far East, and the Future, 1st edn 1942, 2nd edn 1949; A Liberal Attorney-General, 1949; The Passing of Parliament, 1952; Social Change in the Law of Trusts, 1958; Case Book on Equity and Trusts, 1958, 2nd edn 1974;

Trial for Treason, 1959; Trial by Tribunal, 1960; Guilty but Insane, 1961; The Modern Law of Charities, 1962, 2nd edn 1971; The Investment and Taxation of Trust Funds, 1964; Lord Chancellor Jeffreys, 1964; The Norman Conquest and the Common Law, 1966; Shakespeare's Legal and Political Background, 1967; (with L. Sheridan) Equity, 1970; Government in Action, 1970; Modern Developments in the Law of Trusts, 1971; The Football Revolution, 1972; English Law: the judicial contribution, 1974; (with S. N. Frommel) British Industry and European Law, 1974; Keeping the Peace, 1976; (with L. A. Sheridan) Trusts in the Commonwealth, 1977; Harvey the Hasty, 1978; numerous contributions to periodicals. *Address:* Picts Close, Picts Lane, Princes Risborough, Bucks. *T:* 94.

KEEWATIN, Bishop of, since 1974; **Rt. Rev. Hugh James Pearson Allan,** DD; *b* 7 Aug. 1928; *s* of Hugh Blomfield Allan and Agnes Dorothy (*née* Pearson); *m* 1955, Beverley Edith Baker; one *s* three *d. Educ:* St John's Coll., Univ. of Manitoba (LTh 1955, BA 1957). Deacon 1954, priest 1955; Assistant: St Aidan's, Winnipeg, 1954; All Saints, Winnipeg, 1955; Missionary, Peguis Indian Reserve, 1956-60; Rector, St Mark's, Winnipeg, 1960-68; Hon. Canon, Diocese of Rupert's Land, 1967; Rector, St Stephen's Swift Current, Sask., 1968-70; Rural Dean of Cypress, 1968-70; Dean of Qu'Appelle and Rector of St Paul's Cathedral, Regina, Sask., 1970-74. Hon. DD, St John's Coll., Univ. of Manitoba, 1974. *Recreations:* ornithology, boating. *Address:* Bishopstowe, 15 Sylvan Street, Kenora, Ont. P9N 3W7. *T:* (home) 468-5655, (office) 468-7011.

KEGGIN, Air Vice-Marshal Harold, CB 1967; CBE 1962; LDS; Director of Dental Services, Royal Air Force, 1964-69, retired; *b* 25 Feb. 1909; *y s* of John and Margaret Keggin, Port Erin, Isle of Man; *m* 1935, Margaret Joy (*née* Campbell); one *s* two *d. Educ:* Douglas High Sch.; University of Liverpool. Dental Officer, RAF, commissioned, 1932; Flt Lieut 1934; Sqdn Ldr 1939; Wing Comdr 1942; Gp Capt. 1954; Air Cdre 1958; Air Vice-Marshal 1964. QHDS 1958-69. *Recreations:* golf, fishing. *Address:* Rosecroft, 7 Cotlands, Sidmouth, Devon EX10 8SP. *T:* Sidmouth 4790.

KEGIE, James, OBE 1967; FRTPI, FRICS, AIAS; Town Planning Consultant, and retired from local government, 1974; *b* 30 Sept. 1913; *s* of Henry Kegie and Mary Ann (May) Kegie; *m* 1st, 1939, Doreen (*d* 1969), *d* of Rev. Nicholas Martin Cuthbert and Mary Ann Cuthbert; two *s* ; 2nd, 1974, Helen Ruth, *d* of Alfred Quinton Barton and Amy Elizabeth Barton. *Educ:* Gateshead-upon-Tyne Grammar Sch.; Coll. of Estate Management. Planning appts in private practice and local govt in Durham, W Sussex, Cheshire and Monmouthshire, 1929-45; County Planning Officer, Monmouthshire CC, 1945-74. Member: Exec. Council, Co. Planning Officers' Soc. 1948-74 (Pres., 1968-69); Bd of Housing Corp., 1974-; Countryside Commn, 1974-82; Welsh Cttee of Countryside Commn, 1974-82 (Chm., 1981-82); Bd of Welsh Develt Agency, 1976-79; Management Cttee, Sch. of Advanced Urban Studies, Bristol Univ., 1974-80; Consultant to Nat. Trust on Structure Plans in Wales, 1974-; Member: European Architectural Heritage Cttee for Wales, 1972-74; Bi-lingual Signs Cttee, Wales, 1971-72; Working Parties and Research Gps on Town and Country Planning, 1960-77; Bd of Civic Trust for Wales, 1970-; Tech. Unit on Structure Plans (Chm.), Sports Council for Wales, 1977-81. Knight of Mark Twain. *Publications:* County of Monmouth Development Plan, 1953; Minority Report, Bilingual Signs Cttee, 1972; contrib. Jl of RICS. *Recreations:* river and sea fishing, caravanning, motoring, walking, gardening; conservation of the countryside and built environment. *Address:* High Meadow, Christchurch, near Newport, Gwent NP6 1JJ. *T:* Caerleon 422141.

KEIGHLY-PEACH, Captain Charles Lindsey, DSO 1940; OBE 1941; RN retired; *b* 6 April 1902; *s* of late Admiral C. W. Keighly-Peach, DSO; *m* 1st, V. B. Cumbers; one *s* one *d* ; *m* 2nd, Beatrice Mary Harrison (*d* 1974). *Educ:* RN Colleges, Osborne and Dartmouth. Midshipman, 1919; Sub-Lieut 1922; Lieut 1924; 3 Squadron, RAF, 1926; HMS Eagle (402 Sqdn), 1927; H/M S/M M2, 1929; HMS Centaur, 1930; Lieut-Cdr 1932; HMS Glorious (802 Sqdn), 1932; RN Staff Coll., Greenwich, 1934; SOO to RA Destroyers, 1935; HMS London, 1937; Commander, 1938; RN Air Station Lee-on-Solent, 1939; HMS Eagle, 1940-41; Naval Assistant (Air) to 2nd Sea Lord, 1941-44; Capt. 1943; RN Air Station, Yeovilton, 1944-45; Comdg HMS Sultan, Singapore, 1945-47; in command HMS Troubridge and 3rd Destroyer Flot. Med., 1947-49; Dir Captain, Senior Officer's War Course, RN, 1949-51; Asst Chief Naval Staff (Air) on loan to Royal Canadian Navy, 1951-53. *Recreations:* golf, gardening. *Address:* Hatteras, Hall Road, Brockdish, Diss, Norfolk IP21 5JY. *T:* Harleston 853136.

KEIGHTLEY, Maj.-Gen. Richard Charles; Commander Western District, since 1982; *b* 2 July 1933; *s* of General Sir Charles Keightley, GCB, GBE, DSO, and Lady (Joan) Keightley (*née* Smyth-Osbourne); *m* 1958, Caroline Rosemary Butler, *er d* of Sir Thomas Butler, Bt, *qv* ; three *d. Educ:* Marlborough Coll.; RMA, Sandhurst. Commissioned into 5th Royal Inniskilling Dragoon Guards, 1953; served Canal Zone, BAOR, N Africa, Singapore, Cyprus; sc Camberley, 1963; comd 5th Royal Inniskilling Dragoon Guards, 1972-75; Task Force Comdr, 3 Armd Div., 1978-79; RCDS 1980; Brigadier General Staff HQ UKLF, 1981. *Recreations:* field sports, cricket, polo. *Address:* c/o Lloyds Bank plc, 39 Piccadilly, W1. *Club:* Cavalry and Guards.

KEIR, James Dewar, QC 1980; Joint Secretary, Unilever plc and Unilever NV, since 1976; *b* 30 Nov. 1921; *s* of David Robert Keir and Elizabeth Lunan (née Ross); *m* 1948, Jean Mary, *e d* of Rev. and Mrs E. P. Orr; two *s* two *d. Educ:* Edinburgh Acad.; Christ Church, Oxford (MA 1948). Served War, 1941-46: ME, Italy; Captain, The Black Watch (RHR). Called to the Bar, Inner Temple, 1949; Yarborough-Anderson Scholar, Inner Temple, 1950. Legal Adviser, United Africa Co. Ltd, 1954-66, Sec., 1966; Dep. Head of Legal Services, Unilever Ltd, 1973; Dir, UAC Internat. Ltd, 1973-77. Chm., Bar Assoc. for Commerce, Finance and Industry, 1969-72; Member: Bar Council, 1971-73; Senate of Inns of Ct and Bar, 1973-78; Pres., Bar Assoc. for Commerce, Finance and Industry, 1980-82. *Recreations:* ski-ing, Rugby, opera, reading. *Address:* Crossways, High Street, Dormansland, Surrey. *T:* Lingfield 834621. *Club:* Caledonian.

KEIR, Thelma C.; *see* Cazalet-Keir.

KEITH, family name of **Barons Keith of Castleacre** and **Keith of Kinkel** and of **Earl of Kintore.**

KEITH OF CASTLEACRE, Baron *cr* 1980 (Life Peer), of Swaffham in the County of Norfolk; **Kenneth Alexander Keith;** Kt 1969; merchant banker and industrialist; Vice-Chairman, Beecham Group Ltd, since 1970 (Director, since 1949); *b* 30 Aug. 1916; *er s* of late Edward Charles Keith, Swanton Morley House, Norfolk; *m* 1st, 1946, Lady Ariel Olivia Winifred Baird (marr. diss., 1958), 2nd *d* of 1st Viscount Stonehaven, PC, GCMG, DSO, and Countess of Kintore; one *s* one *d* : 2nd, 1962, Mrs Nancy Hayward (marr. diss. 1972), Manhasset, New York; 3rd, 1973, Mrs Marie Hanbury, Burley-on-the-Hill, Rutland. *Educ:* Rugby Sch. Trained as a Chartered Accountant. 2nd Lt Welsh Guards, 1939; Lt-Col 1945; served with North Africa, Italy, France and Germany (despatches, Croix de Guerre with Silver Star). Asst to Dir Gen. Political Intelligence Dept, Foreign Office, 1945-46. Chm., Philip Hill Investment Trust Ltd; Vice-Chm., BEA, 1964-71; Chm., Hill Samuel Group Ltd, 1970-80; Chm. and Chief Exec., Rolls Royce Ltd, 1972-80; Director: British Airways, 1971-72; Times Newspapers Ltd, 1967-81; Standard Telephones and Cables Ltd; Bank of Nova Scotia Ltd. Member: NEDC, 1964-71; CBI/NEDC Liaison Cttee, 1974-78. Chairman: Economic Planning Council for East Anglia, 1965-70; Governor, Nat. Inst. of Economic and Social Research. Council Mem. and Dir, Manchester Business Sch. FBIM; Hon. Companion, RAeS. *Recreations:* farming, shooting, golf. *Address:* 80 Eaton Square, SW1W 9AP. *T:* 01-730 4000; The Wicken House, Castle Acre, Norfolk. *T:* Castle Acre 225. *Clubs:* White's, Pratt's; Racquet and Tennis (New York).

KEITH OF KINKEL, Baron *cr* 1977 (Life Peer), of Strathtummel; **Henry Shanks Keith,** PC 1976; a Lord of Appeal in Ordinary, since 1977; *b* 7 Feb. 1922; *s* of late Baron Keith of Avonholm, PC (Life Peer); *m* 1955, Alison Hope Alan Brown; four *s* (including twin *s*) one *d. Educ:* Edinburgh Academy; Magdalen Coll., Oxford (MA; Hon. Fellow 1977); Edinburgh Univ. (LLB). War of 1939-45 (despatches); commnd Scots Guards, Nov. 1941; served N Africa and Italy, 1943-45; released, 1945 (Capt.). Advocate, Scottish Bar, 1950; Barrister, Gray's Inn, 1951, Bencher 1976; QC (Scotland), 1962. Standing Counsel to Dept of Health for Scotland, 1957-62; Sheriff Principal of Roxburgh, Berwick and Selkirk, 1970-71; Senator of Coll. of Justice in Scotland, 1971-77. Chairman: Scottish Valuation Adv. Coun., 1972-76 (Mem., 1957-70); Cttee on Powers of Revenue Depts, 1980-; Dep. Chm., Parly Boundary Commn for Scotland, 1976; Member: Law Reform Cttee for Scotland, 1964-70; Cttee on Law of Defamation, 1971-74; Mem. Panel of Arbiters: European Fisheries Convention, 1964-71; Convention for Settlement of Investment Disputes, 1968-71. *Address:* House of Lords, SW1; Strathtummel, by Pitlochry, Perthshire. *T:* Tummel Bridge 255.

KEITH, David; *see* Steegmuller, Francis.

KEITH, John Lucien, CBE 1951 (OBE 1943); *b* 22 May 1895; 2nd *s* of George Keith, Director of Cable Companies; unmarried. *Educ:* Ecole Closelet, Lausanne; Hertford Coll., Oxford (MA). British South Africa Co., N Rhodesia, 1918-25; District Officer, Colonial Service, N Rhodesia, 1925-38; Acting Dir of African Education, N Rhodesia, 1930-31; African Research Survey, Chatham House, 1938-39; Colonial Office, 1939; Dir of Colonial Scholars and head of Student Dept, Colonial Office, 1941-56. Adviser on Students' Affairs, W Nigeria Office, London, 1957-62; London Rep. of Univ. of Ife, Nigeria, 1962-72. Official missions to British West Africa, 1947, BWI, 1947, Malaya and Hong Kong, 1948, British East Africa and Mauritius, 1951, North America and British West Indies, 1954, British East and Central Africa, 1955, Ghana, 1957, Nigeria, 1960, and Zambia, 1964, for Independence celebrations. *Recreations:* travelling, talking books for the blind. *Address:* 49A Sea Road, Bexhill-on-Sea, East Sussex. *T:* Bexhill-on-Sea 215463. *Club:* Royal Commonwealth Society.

KEITH, Penelope Anne Constance, (Mrs Rodney Timson); *b* 2 April; *d* of Frederick A. W. Hatfield and Constance Mary Keith; *m* 1978, Rodney Timson. *Educ:* Annecy Convent, Seaford, Sussex; Webber Douglas Sch., London. First prof. appearance, Civic Theatre, Chesterfield, 1959; repertory, Lincoln, Salisbury and Manchester, 1960-63; RSC, Stratford, 1963, and Aldwych, 1965; rep., Cheltenham, 1967; Maggie Howard in Suddenly at Home, Fortune Theatre, 1971; Sarah in The Norman Conquests, Greenwich, then Globe Theatre, 1974; Lady Driver in Donkey's Years, 1976; Orinthia in The Apple Cart, Chichester, then Phoenix Theatre, 1977; Epifania in The Millionairess, Haymarket, 1978; Sarah in Moving, Queen's Theatre, 1981; Maggie in Hobson's Choice, Haymarket, 1982; Lady Cicely Waynflete in

Captain Brassbound's Conversion, Haymarket, 1982; *film:* The Priest of Love, 1980. Television appearances incl.: The Good Life, 1974-77; Amanda in Private Lives, 1976; Sarah in The Norman Conquests, 1977; Audrey Fforbes Hamilton in To the Manor Born, 1979, 1980 and 1981; Maria in On Approval, 1980. *Recreations:* gardening, theatre-going. *Address:* c/o Howes & Prior, 66 Berkeley House, Hay Hill, W1X 7LH. *T:* 01-493 7570.

KEITH, Robert Farquharson, CB 1973; OBE 1948; Chief Registrar of Trade Unions and Employers' Associations from 1971 until repeal of Industrial Relations Act 1971 in 1974; *b* 22 June 1912; *s* of Dr Robert Donald Keith and Mary Lindsay (née Duncan), Turriff, Aberdeenshire; *m* 1958, Jean Abernethy (née Fisher); one *s. Educ:* Fettes; Caius Coll., Cambridge (Classical Scholar). Indian Civil Service, 1937-47; Dep. Comr, Upper Sind Frontier, 1945-47; Home Civil Service, Min. of Labour, later Dept of Employment, 1948; Under-Sec., Employment Services and Estabs Divs, 1965-71. *Address:* Parkhead, Auchattie, Banchory, Kincardineshire. *T:* Banchory 2166. *Club:* Caledonian.

KEITH, Trevor; Charity Commissioner, 1972-81; *b* 3 Sept. 1921. *Educ:* Isleworth County Grammar School. Called to Bar, Lincoln's Inn, 1951. Entered Civil Service, Air Min., 1938; RAF, 1941-45; Air Min., 1946-48; Inland Revenue, Estate Duty Office, 1948-52; Charity Commn, 1952-81. *Recreations:* cricket, travel, gastronomy. *Address:* 7 Lucastes Road, Haywards Heath, Sussex RH16 1JJ.

KEITH-JONES, Maj.-Gen. Richard, CB 1968; MBE 1947; MC 1944; Manager, Management Development, Mardon Packaging International Ltd, 1969-75; *b* 6 Dec. 1913; *o s* of late Brig. Frederick Theodore Jones, CIE, MVO, VD; *m* 1938, Margaret Ridley Harrison; three *d. Educ:* Clifton Coll.; Royal Military Academy Woolwich. Commissioned into Royal Artillery, 1934; served in UK, 1934-42; 1st Airborne Div., 1943-44; War Office, 1944-47; Palestine and Egypt, 1st Regt RHA, 1947-49; Instructor Staff Coll., Camberley, 1949-52; Military Asst to F-M Montgomery, 1953-55; CO 4th Regt, RHA, 1955-57; Senior Army Instructor, JSSC, 1957-59; Dep. Comdt 17 Gurkha Div., Malaya, 1959-61; Student, Imperial Defence Coll., 1962-63; Military Adviser, High Comr, Canada, 1963-64; GOC 50 (Northumbrian) Div. (TA), 1964-66; Comdt, Jt Warfare Establishment, 1966-68; retd 1969. Col Comdt RA, 1970-78; Hon. Col, 266 (Glos Vol. Artillery) Batt., RA, T&AVR, 1975-. *Recreations:* fishing, shooting, golf. *Address:* The White House, Brockley, Backwell, Bristol BS19 3AU. *Clubs:* Army and Navy, MCC.

KEITH-LUCAS, Prof. Bryan; Professor of Government, University of Kent at Canterbury, 1965-77, now Emeritus (Master of Darwin College, 1970-74); part-time Assistant Master, King's School, Canterbury, since 1978; *b* 1 Aug. 1912; *y s* of late Keith Lucas, ScD, FRS, and Alys (née Hubbard); *m* 1946, Mary Hardwicke (MBE 1982; Sheriff of Canterbury, 1971); one *s* two *d. Educ:* Gresham's Sch., Holt; Pembroke Coll., Cambridge. MA Cantab 1937, MA Oxon 1948; DLitt Kent, 1980. Solicitor, 1937. Asst Solicitor: Kensington Council, 1938-46; Nottingham, 1946-48. Served 1939-45 in Buffs and Sherwood Foresters, N Africa and Italy (Major, despatches); DAAG Cyprus, 1945-46. Sen. Lectr in Local Govt, Oxford, 1948-65; Faculty Fellow of Nuffield Coll., 1950-65, Domestic Bursar, 1957-65. Chm., Commn on Electoral System, Sierra Leone, 1954; Commn on local govt elections, Mauritius, 1955-56. Member: Roberts Cttee on Public Libraries, 1957-59; Commn on Administration of Lagos, 1963; Mallaby Cttee on Staffing of Local Govt, 1964-67; Local Govt Commn for England, 1965-66; Royal Commn on Elections in Fiji, 1975. Vice-Chm., Hansard Soc., 1976-80. Chairman: Nat. Assoc. of Parish Councils, 1964-70 (Vice-Pres., 1970-; Pres., Kent Assoc., 1972-81); Canterbury Soc., 1972-75; Pres., Kent Fedn of Amenity Socs, 1976-81. City Councillor, Oxford, 1950-65. Hon. Fellow, Inst. of Local Govt Studies, Birmingham Univ., 1973. *Publications:* The English Local Government Franchise, 1952; The Mayor, Aldermen and Councillors, 1961; English Local Government in the 19th and 20th Centuries, 1977; (with P. G. Richards) A History of Local Government in the 20th Century, 1978; The Unreformed Local Government System, 1980; various articles on local govt. *Address:* 7 Church Street, Wye, Kent. *T:* Wye 812621. *Club:* National Liberal. *See also* David Keith-Lucas.

KEITH-LUCAS, Prof. David, CBE 1973; MA; FEng, FIMechE, FRAeS; Chairman, Airworthiness Requirements Board, 1972-82; *b* 25 March 1911; *s* of late Keith Lucas, ScD, FRS, and Alys (née Hubbard); *m* 1942, Dorothy De Bauduy Robertson (*d* 1979); two *s* one *d* ; *m* 1981, Phyllis Marion Everard (née Whurr). *Educ:* Gresham's Sch., Holt; Gonville and Caius Coll., Cambridge. BA (Mech Sci Tripos, 2nd Class Hons) 1933; MA 1956; FRAeS 1948, Hon. FRAeS, 1979; FIMechE 1949; FAIAA 1973, Hon. FAIAA 1974; FEng 1978. Apprenticed 1933-35, design team 1935-39, C. A. Parsons & Co. Ltd; Chief Aerodynamicist, Short Bros Ltd, 1940-49; Short Bros & Harland Ltd: Chief Designer, 1949-58; Technical Dir, 1958-64; Dir of Research, 1964-65; Dir, John Brown & Co., 1970-77; Cranfield Inst. of Technology (formerly Coll. of Aeronautics): Prof. of Aircraft Design, 1965-72; Pro-Vice-Chancellor, 1970-73; Prof. of Aeronautics and Chm. College of Aeronautics, 1972-76, now Emeritus Prof. Member: Senate, Queen's Univ., Belfast, 1955-65; Council, Air Registration Board, 1967-; Commn on Third London Airport, 1968-70; Civil Aviation Authority, 1972-80. President: RAeS, 1968; Engrg Section, British Assoc. for the Advancement of Science, 1972. Hon. DSc: Queen's Univ., Belfast, 1968; Cranfield Inst. of Technology, 1975. Gold Medal, RAeS, 1975. *Publications:* The Shape of Wings to Come, 1952; The

Challenge of Vertical Take-Off (lects IMechE), 1961-62; The Role of Jet Lift (lect. RAeS), 1962; papers on aircraft design, vertical take-off, engrg economics, in engrg jls. *Recreations:* youth organisations, small boats. *Address:* Manor Close, Emberton, Olney, Bucks MK46 5BX. *T:* Bedford 711552. *Club:* Naval and Military.
See also B. Keith-Lucas.

KEKWICK, Prof. Ralph Ambrose, FRS 1966; Professor of Biophysics, University of London, 1966-71, now Emeritus; Member Staff, Lister Institute, 1940-71 (Head, Division of Biophysics, 1943-71); *b* 11 Nov. 1908; 2nd *s* of late Oliver A. and Mary Kekwick; *m* 1st, 1933, Barbara (*d* 1973), 3rd *d* of W. S. Stone, DD, New York; one *d*; 2nd, 1974, Dr Margaret Mackay (*d* 1982), *er d* of J. G. Mackay, MB, BS, Adelaide, Australia. *Educ:* Leyton County High Sch.; University Coll., London (Fellow, 1971). BSc 1928; MSc 1936; DSc 1941. Bayliss-Starling Scholar, University Coll. London, 1930-31. Commonwealth Fund Fellow, New York and Princeton Univs, 1931-33. Lectr in Biochemistry University Coll. London, 1933-37. Rockefeller Fellow, University of Uppsala, Sweden, 1935; MRC Fellow, Lister Inst., 1937-40. Reader in Chemical Biophysics, University of London, 1954-66. Oliver Memorial Award for Blood Transfusion, 1957. *Publications:* MRC Special Report "Separation of protein fractions from human plasma" (with M. E. Mackay), 1954. Papers on physical biochemistry and hæmatology, mostly in Biochemical Jl and Brit. Jl of Hæmatology. *Recreations:* music, gardening and bird watching. *Address:* 31 Woodside Road, Woodford Wells, Essex IG8 0TW. *T:* 01-504 4264.

KELBIE, Sheriff David; Sheriff of North Strathclyde, since 1979; *b* 28 Feb. 1945; *s* of Robert Kelbie and Monica Eileen Pearn; *m* 1966, Helen Mary Smith; one *s* one *d*. *Educ:* Inverurie Acad.; Aberdeen Univ. (LLB Hons). Advocate; called to the Scottish Bar, 1968. Associate Lectr, Heriot-Watt Univ., 1971-75; Hon. Sec., Scottish Congregational Coll., 1975-82. *Publications:* articles in legal jls. *Recreations:* sailing, hill-walking, reading, listening to jazz and folk music. *Address:* 52 Abercromby Crescent, Helensburgh, Dunbartonshire G84 9DX. *T:* Helensburgh 4690.

KELBURN, Viscount of; Patrick Robin Archibald Boyle; television director/producer; *b* 30 July 1939; *s* and heir of 9th Earl of Glasgow, *qv*; *m* 1975, Isabel Mary James; one *s* one *d*. *Educ:* Eton; Paris Univ. National Service in Navy; Sub-Lt, RNR, 1959-60. Worked in Associated Rediffusion Television, 1961, since when has worked at various times for Woodfall Film Productions; Asst on Film Productions, 1962-64; Asst Dir in film industry, 1962-67; producer/director of documentary films, Yorkshire TV, 1968-70; freelance film producer, 1971-, making network television documentaries for BBC, Yorkshire Television, ATV and Scottish Television. Formed Kelburn Country Centre, May 1977, opening Kelburn estate and gardens in Ayrshire to the public. *Recreations:* ski-ing, theatre. *Heir:* s Hon. David Michael Douglas Boyle, *b* 15 Oct. 1978. *Address:* 93 Hereford Road, W2. *T:* 01-727 9725; South Offices, Kelburn Estate, Fairlie, Ayrshire.

KELL, Joseph; see Burgess, Anthony.

KELLAR, Alexander James, CMG 1961; OBE 1948; *b* 26 June 1905; *er s* of James Dodds Ballantyne Kellar and Florence Maud Kellar (*née* Coveney). *Educ:* George Watson's Coll.; Edinburgh Univ. (MA, LLB). Sen. Pres., Students' Representative Council; Pres., Nat. Union of Scottish Students, 1929-30; Commonwealth Fund Fellow, Yale (Mem. Elizabethan Club) and Columbia (AM Internat. Law and Relations); called to Bar, Middle Temple, 1936. Asst Sec., Brit. Employers' Confedn, 1938-41; Employers' (Substitute) Delegate, Governing Body of ILO, 1940. Mem. Army Officers' Emergency Reserve, 1938. Attached War Office, 1941-65; ODM, 1970-73; English Tourist Bd, 1970-73. *Recreations:* riding, travel. *Address:* 5 Sheffield Terrace, W8; Grey Walls, Friston, Sussex. *Club:* Travellers'.

KELLAS, Arthur Roy Handasyde, CMG 1964; HM Diplomatic Service, retired; High Commissioner in Tanzania, 1972-74; *b* 6 May 1915; *s* of Henry Kellas and Mary Kellas (*née* Brown); *m* 1952, Katharine Bridget, *d* of Sir John Le Rougetel, KCMG, MC; two *s* one *d*. *Educ:* Aberdeen Grammar Sch.; Aberdeen Univ.; Oxford Univ.; Ecole des Sciences Politiques. Passed into Diplomatic Service, Sept. 1939. Commissioned into Border Regt, Nov. 1939. War of 1939-45: Active Service with 1st Bn Parachute Regt and Special Ops, Af. and Gr, 1941-44 (despatches twice). Third Sec. at HM Embassy, Tehran, 1944-47; First Sec. at HM Legation, Helsingfors, 1948-50; First Sec. (press) at HM Embassy, Cairo, 1951-52; First Sec. at HM Embassy, Baghdad, 1954-58; Counsellor, HM Embassy, Tehran, 1958-62; Imperial Defence Coll., 1963-64; Counsellor, HM Embassy and Consul-Gen., Tel Aviv, 1964-65; Ambassador to Nepal, 1966-70, to Democratic Yemen, 1970-72. Pres., Britain-Nepal Soc., 1975-79. *Recreations:* reading, riding, boxing. *Address:* Inverockle, Achateny, Ardnamurchan, Argyll PH36 4LG. *T:* Kilchoan 265. *Club:* United Oxford & Cambridge University.

KELLAWAY, (Charles) William; Secretary and Librarian, Institute of Historical Research, University of London, since 1971; *b* 9 March 1926; *s* of late Charles Halliley Kellaway, FRS; *m* 1952, Deborah, *d* of late Sir Hibbert Alan Stephen Newton; one *s* two *d*. *Educ:* Geelong Grammar Sch.; Lincoln Coll., Oxford. BA Modern History, 1949, MA 1955. FLA, FRHistS, FSA. Asst Librarian, Guildhall Library, 1950-60; Sub-Librarian, Inst. of Historical Research, 1960-71. Hon. General Editor, London Record Society, 1964-. *Publications:* The New England Company, 1649-1776, 1961; (Joint Editor)

Studies in London History, 1969; Bibliography of Historical Works Issued in UK, 1957-70, 3 vols, 1962, 1967, 1972; (ed jtly) The London Assize of Nuisance 1301-1431, 1973. *Address:* 2 Grove Terrace, NW5. *T:* 01-485 1741.

KELLEHER, Dame Joan, DBE 1965; Hon. ADC to the Queen, 1964-67; Director, Women's Royal Army Corps, 1964-67; *b* 24 Dec. 1915; *d* of late Kenneth George Henderson, Stonehaven; *m* 1970, Brig. M. F. H. Kelleher, OBE, MC, late RAMC. *Educ:* privately at home and abroad. Joined ATS, 1941; commissioned ATS, 1941; WRAC, 1949. *Recreations:* golf and gardening. *Address:* c/o Midland Bank, 123 Chancery Lane, WC2.

KELLER, Prof. Andrew, FRS 1972; Research Professor in Polymer Science, Department of Physics, University of Bristol, since 1969; *b* 22 Aug. 1925; *s* of Imre Keller and Margit Klein; *m* 1951, Eva Bulhack; one *s* one *d*. *Educ:* Budapest Univ. (BSc); Bristol Univ. (PhD). FInstP. Techn. Officer, ICI Ltd, Manchester, 1948-55; Bristol Univ.: Min. of Supply res. appt, 1955-57; Res. Asst, 1957-63; Lectr, 1963-65; Reader, 1965-69. High Polymer Prize, Amer. Phys. Soc., 1964; Swinburne Award, Plastics Inst., 1974. *Publications:* numerous papers in Jl Polymer Science, Progress Reports in Physics, Proc. Royal Soc., Macromol. Chem., etc. *Recreations:* outdoor sports, mountain walking, concerts. *Address:* 41 Westbury Road, Bristol BS9 3AU. *T:* Bristol 629767.

KELLER, René; Ambassador of Switzerland to Austria, 1976-79, retired; *b* 19 May 1914; *s* of Jacques Keller and Marie (*née* Geiser); *m* 1942, Marion (*née* Werder); one *s* two *d*. *Educ:* Geneva; Trinity Coll., Cambridge. Vice-Consul, Prague, 1941-45; 2nd Sec. of Legation, The Hague, 1947-50; 1st Sec., London, 1950-54; Head of News Dept, Berne, 1954-56; 1st Counsellor, Swiss Embassy, Paris, 1957-60; Ambassador to Ghana, Guinea, Liberia, Mali and Togo, 1960-62; Ambassador to Turkey, 1962-65; Head of Perm. Mission of Switzerland to Office of UN and Internat. Organisations, Geneva, 1966-68; Ambassador of Switzerland to UK, 1968-71; Head of Direction for International Organisation, Foreign Ministry of Switzerland, 1971-75. *Recreations:* golf, sailing. *Address:* 1 Promenade du Pin, CH-1204 Geneva, Switzerland. *Club:* Travellers'.

KELLER, Prof. Rudolf Ernst, MA Manchester; DrPhil Zürich; Professor of German Language and Medieval German Literature, University of Manchester, 1960-82, now Emeritus; *b* 3 Feb. 1920; *m* 1947, Ivy Sparrow; two *d*. *Educ:* Kantonsschule Winterthur, Switzerland; University of Zürich. Teacher at Kantonsschule Winterthur, 1944-46; Asst, 1946-47, Asst Lecturer, 1947-49, University of Manchester; Lecturer in German, Royal Holloway College, University of London, 1949-52; Sen. Lecturer, 1952-59, Reader in German, 1959-60, Dean of Faculty of Arts, 1968-70, Pro-Vice-Chancellor, 1976-79, University of Manchester. Corresp. Mem., Inst. für deutsche Sprache, 1969; Goethe Medal, 1981. *Publications:* Die Ellipse in der neuenglischen Sprache als semantisch-syntaktisches Problem, 1944; Die Sprachen der Welt, 1955 (trans. Bodmer: The Loom of Language); German Dialects, Phonology and Morphology with Selected Texts, 1961; The German Language, 1978; articles in learned periodicals. *Recreations:* reading, travel. *Address:* 11a Rathen Road, Manchester M20 9QJ. *T:* 061-445 6952.

KELLETT, Alfred Henry, CBE 1965; Chairman, South Western Areas, National Coal Board, 1967-69, retired; *b* 2 Aug. 1904; British; *m* 1934, Astrid Elizabeth (*née* Hunter); one *s* three *d*. *Educ:* Rossall Sch.; Universities of Cambridge and Birmingham. Man. Dir, Washington Coal Co. Ltd, 1940-47; Area Gen. Man., NCB Durham Div., 1950-59; Dep. Chm., Durham Div., 1960; Chm., South Western Div., NCB, 1961-67. CStJ. *Recreation:* travel. *Address:* Pent House, Benenden, Cranbrook, Kent.

KELLETT, Sir Brian (Smith), Kt 1979; Chairman, TI Group plc (formerly Tube Investments Ltd), since 1976 (a Managing Director, 1968-82); Director: Unigate Ltd, since 1974; National Westminster Bank Ltd, since 1981; *b* 8 May 1922; *s* of late Harold Lamb Kellett and Amy Elizabeth Kellett (*née* Smith); *m* 1947, Janet Lesly Street; three *d*. *Educ:* Manchester Grammar Sch.; Trinity Coll., Cambridge (MA). Wrangler and Sen. Scholar, 1942. Exper. Officer, Admty, 1942-46; Asst Principal, Min. of Transport, 1946-48; Sir Robert Watson-Watt & Partners, 1948-49; Pilkington Bros Ltd, 1949-55; joined Tube Investments Ltd, 1955, Dir 1965, Dep. Chm. and Chief Exec., 1974; Chm., British Aluminium Co. Ltd, 1972-79. Member: Royal Commn on Standards of Conduct in Public Life, 1974-76; PO Review Cttee, 1976-77; Council, Industrial Soc., 1981-. A Vice-Pres., Engineering Employers' Fedn, 1976-. Governor: London Business Sch., 1976-; Imperial Coll., 1979-. *Address:* 14 South Street, W1Y 5PJ.

KELLETT, Sir Stanley Everard, 6th Bt *cr* 1801; *b* 1911; *s* of Francis Stanley Kellett (*d* 1955) (2nd *s* of 3rd Bt); *S* kinsman, Sir Henry de Castres Kellett, 5th Bt, 1966; *m* 1938, Audrey Margaret Phillips; one *s* one *d*. *Heir:* s Stanley Charles Kellett [*b* 5 March 1940; *m* 1st, 1962, Lorraine May (marr. diss. 1968), *d* of F. Winspear; 2nd, 1968, Margaret Ann, *d* of J. Bofinger]. *Address:* 33 Caroma Avenue, Kyeemagh, New South Wales 2216, Australia.

KELLETT-BOWMAN, Edward Thomas, JP; Member (C) Lancashire East, European Parliament, since 1979; *b* 25 Feb. 1931; *s* of late R. E. Bowman and of M. Bowman (*née* Mathers); *m* 1st, 1960, Margaret Patricia Blakemore (*d* 1970); three *s* one *d*; 2nd, 1971, (Mary) Elaine Kellett (*see* M. E. Kellett-Bowman). *Educ:* Reed's Sch.; Cranfield Inst. of Technol. MBA, DMS, FBIM.

Technical and management trng in textiles, 1951-53; textile management, 1953-55; pharmaceutical man., 1955-72; business and man. consultant in private practice, 1974-. Liveryman, Worshipful Co. of Wheelwrights, 1979; Freeman, City of London, 1978; Hon. Citizen, New Orleans, 1960. JP Mddx, 1966. *Recreations:* shooting, tennis, swimming. *Address:* Park Farm, Gressenhall, Norfolk. *T:* Dereham 860245; 42 Schoolhouse Lane, Halton, Lancaster; 33D Curzon Street, W1.

KELLETT-BOWMAN, (Mary) Elaine, MA; MP (C) Lancaster, since 1970; Member (C) European Parliament, since 1975, elected for Cumbria, 1979; *b* 8 July 1924; *d* of late Walter Kay; *m* 1st, 1945, Charles Norman Kellett (decd); three *s* one *d*; 2nd, 1971, Edward Thomas Kellett-Bowman, *qv. Educ:* Queen Mary Sch., Lytham; The Mount, York; St Anne's Coll., Oxford (postgraduate distinction in welfare diploma). Contested (C): Nelson and Colne, 1955; South-West Norfolk, March and Oct. 1959; Buckingham, 1964, 1966. Mem. Social Affairs and Regional Policy Cttees, 1975-79). Camden Borough Council: Alderman, 1968-74; Vice-Chm., Housing Cttee, 1968; Chm., Welfare Cttee, 1969. Called to Bar, Middle Temple, 1964. Lay Mem., Press Council, 1964-68. Governor, Culford Sch., 1963; Mem. Union European Women, 1956; Delegate to Luxemburg, 1958. No 1 Country Housewife, 1960; Christal MacMillan Law Prize, 1963. *Recreations:* gardening, collecting and repairing Morris Minors. *Address:* House of Commons, SW1; 42 Schoolhouse Lane, Halton, Lancaster. *Club:* English-Speaking Union.

KELLEY, Joan; Under Secretary, HM Treasury, since 1979; *b* 8 Dec. 1926; *er d* of late George William Kelley and Dora Kelley. *Educ:* Whalley Range High Sch. for Girls, Manchester; London Sch. of Econs and Polit. Science (BScEcon 1947). Europa Publications Ltd, 1948; Pritchard, Wood & Partners Ltd, 1949; joined Civil Service as Econ. Asst in Cabinet Office, 1949; admin. work in Treasury, 1954; Principal, 1956; Asst Sec., 1968; Under Sec., 1979; on secondment to NI Office, 1979-81. *Recreations:* gardening, map reading, drinking wine, foreign travel. *Address:* 21 Langland Gardens, NW3 6QE.

KELLEY, Mrs Joanna Elizabeth, OBE 1973; Assistant Director of Prisons (Women), 1967-74; *b* 23 May 1910; *d* of late Lt-Col William Beadon, 51st Sikhs; *m* 1934, Harper Kelley (*d* 1962); no *c. Educ:* Hayes Court; Girton Coll., Cambridge (MA). Souschargé, Dept of Pre-History, Musée de l'Homme, Paris, 1934-39; Mixed Youth Club Leader, YWCA, 1939-42; Welfare Officer, Admiralty, Bath, 1942-47; Prison Service, 1947-74; Governor of HM Prison, Holloway, 1959-66. Member: Council, St George's House, Windsor, 1971-77; Redundant Churches Cttee, 1974-79; Scott Holland Trust, 1978-; Sponsor, YWCA of GB, 1979-. FSA. Hon. Fellow Girton Coll., Cambridge, 1968. Hon. LLD Hull Univ., 1960. *Publications:* When the Gates Shut, 1967; Who Casts the First Stone, 1978. *Recreation:* reading. *Address:* c/o Lloyds Bank Ltd, 6 Pall Mall, SW1V 4AQ.

KELLEY, Richard; *b* 24 July 1904; *m* 1924; four *s* three *d. Educ:* Elementary Sch. Councillor, West Riding of Yorks County Council, 1949-59; a Trade Union Secretary for ten years. MP (Lab) Don Valley, W Yorks, 1959-79. Mem. of the National Union of Mineworkers. *Address:* 23 St Lawrence Road, Dunscroft, Doncaster, S Yorks DN7 4AS.

KELLGREN, Prof. Jonas Henrik, FRCS, FRCP; Professor of Rheumatology, University of Manchester, 1953-76, now Emeritus; Dean, 1970-73; *b* 11 Sept. 1911; *s* of Dr Harry Kellgren and Vera (*née* Dumelunksen); *m* 1942, Thelma Marian Reynolds; four *d. Educ:* Bedales Sch.; University Coll., London. MB, BS, 1934; FRCS 1936; FRCP 1951. Junior clinical appointments, University Coll. Hosp., 1934-42 (Beit Memorial Fellow 1938-39); served War, 1942-46, as surgical and orthopædic specialist, RAMC; Mem. Scientific Staff, Med. Research Council, Wingfield Morris Orthopædic Hosp., Oxford, Chronic Rheumatism, University of Manchester, 1947. Pres. Heberden Soc., 1958-59. *Publications:* numerous articles in medical and scientific jls. *Recreation:* landscape painting. *Address:* Beckside Cottage, Rusland, Ulverston, Cumbria LA12 8J4. *T:* Ulverton 84244.

KELLIHER, Sir Henry (Joseph), Kt 1963; Founder-President, Dominion Breweries Ltd; *b* March 1896; *s* of Michael Joseph Kelliher; *m* 1917, Evelyn J., *d* of R. S. Sproule; one *s* four *d. Educ:* Clyde Sch. Dir, Bank of New Zealand, 1936-42. Founded League of Health of NZ Youth, 1934 (objective, Free milk scheme for NZ children, in which it succeeded); purchased Puketutu Island, 1938; established Puketutu Ayrshire Stud, 1940, Aberdeen Angus Stud, 1942, Suffolk Stud, 1946; Thoroughbred and Standard Bred Studs, 1969. Founded: Kelliher Art Trust, 1961; Kelliher Charitable Trust, 1963. KStJ 1960. *Publications:* New Zealand at the Cross Roads, 1936; Why your £ buys Less and Less, 1954. *Recreations:* gardening, riding. *Address:* Puketutu Island, Manukau Harbour, Auckland, New Zealand. *T:* 543733.

KELLOCK, Jane Ursula, JP; Member, Police Complaints Board, since 1977; *b* 21 Oct. 1925; *d* of late Arthur George Symonds and late Gertrude Frances Symonds; *m* 1967, Thomas Oslaf Kellock, *qv. Educ:* Priors Field Sch., Godalming. WRNS, 1943-45. Sec., Africa Bureau, London, 1957-67; Editor, Africa Digest, 1957-75; Board Member, Commonwealth Development Corporation, 1965-73. Former Mem., S Metropolitan Conciliation Cttee, Race Relations Bd. JP: Inner London, 1968-77; Nottingham City Bench, 1977. *Recreation:* travel. *Address:* 8 Huntingdon Drive, The Park, Nottingham NG7 1BW; 8 King's Bench Walk, EC4.

KELLOCK, Thomas Oslaf, QC 1965; **His Honour Judge Kellock;** a Circuit Judge, since 1976; *b* 4 July 1923; *s* of late Thomas Herbert Kellock, MA, MD, MCh Cambridge, FRCS LRCP; *m* 1967, Jane Ursula Kellock, *qv. Educ:* Rugby; Clare Coll., Cambridge. Sub-Lieut (Special Branch), RNVR, 1944-46. Called to the Bar, Inner Temple, 1949, Bencher, 1973. Admitted: Gold Coast (Ghana) Roll of Legal Practitioners, 1955; N Rhodesia (Zambia) Bar, 1956; Nigeria Bar, 1957; Ceylon (Sri Lanka) Roll of Advocates, 1960; Sierra Leone Bar, 1960; Malayan Bar, 1967; Fiji Bar, 1975. Has also appeared in courts of Kenya, Malawi, Pakistan, Jammu and Kashmir, Sarawak. Dir, Legal Div., Commonwealth Secretariat, 1969-72; a Recorder of the Crown Court, 1974-76. Constitutional Advr to HH Sultan of Brunei, 1975-76. Chm., Anti-Apartheid Movement, 1963-65; Contested (L) Torquay, 1949, S Kensington, 1966 and March 1968, Harwich, Oct. 1974. *Recreation:* travelling. *Address:* 8 Huntingdon Drive, The Park, Nottingham NG7 1BW. *T:* Nottingham 48304; 8 King's Bench Walk, Temple, EC4. *T:* 01-353 6997. *Club:* Reform.

KELLOW, Kathleen; *see* Hibbert, Eleanor.

KELLY, Dr Anthony, FRS 1973; FEng; Vice-Chancellor, University of Surrey, since 1975; *s* of late Group Captain Vincent Gerald French and Mrs Violet Kelly; *m* 1956, Christina Margaret Dunleavie, BA; three *s* one *d. Educ:* Presentation Coll., Reading; Univs of Reading (Schol.) and Cambridge. BSc Reading 1949; PhD 1953, ScD 1968, Cantab. Research Assoc., Univ. of Illinois, 1953-55; ICI Fellow, Univ. of Birmingham, 1955; Asst, Associate Prof., Northwestern Univ., 1956-59; Univ. Lectr, Cambridge, 1959-67; Founding Fellow, Churchill Coll., 1960; Dir of Studies, Churchill Coll., 1960-67; Supt, Div. of Inorganic and Metallic Structure, 1967-69, Dep. Dir, 1969-75, Nat. Physical Lab. (seconded to ICI, 1973-75). Director: Teddington Developments Ltd, 1981-; Johnson Wax Ltd, 1981-. Vis. Fellow, Univ. of Göttingen, 1960; Vis. Prof., Carnegie Inst. of Technol., 1967; Prof. invité, Ecole Polytechnique Fédérale de Lausanne, 1977. Member: SRC Cttee, 1967-72; Council, Inst. of Metals, 1969-74; Council, British Non-Ferrous Metals Res. Assoc., 1970-73; Engrg Materials Requirements Bd, DoI, 1973-75 (Chm., 1976-80); Adv. Cttee, Community Ref. Bureau of EEC, 1973-75. William Hopkins Prize, 1967; Beilby Medal, 1967; A. A. Griffith Medal, 1974. *Publications:* Strong Solids, 1966, 2nd edn 1973; (with G. W. Groves) Crystallography and Crystal Defects, 1970; many papers in jls of physical sciences. *Recreations:* science of materials, sailing. *Address:* Yardfield, Church Lane, Worplesdon, Surrey. *Club:* Hardway Sailing (Gosport).

KELLY, Sir Arthur (John), Kt 1961; CBE 1950; *b* 17 Nov. 1898; *yr s* of John Kelly, Hodge Bower, Shropshire; *m* 1928, Florence Mary Smyth, *yr d* of John Smyth, Belfast. *Educ:* Bridgnorth; Shrewsbury. Served European War, 1917-19: RFC 12 Sqdn and RAF Army of Occupation, Germany. Temp. Asst, Min. of Labour, Whitehall, 1919-22; Asst Principal, Min. of Labour, N Ireland, 1922; Principal, Cabinet Offices, N Ireland, 1940; Asst Sec., 1941; seconded as N Ireland Govt Liaison Officer at Home Office, Whitehall, 1943; Permanent Sec., Min. of Labour N Ireland, 1956; Sec. to the Cabinet and Clerk of the Privy Council of Northern Ireland, 1957-63, retd. *Recreation:* golf. *Address:* 6 Cherryhill, Beechlands, Malone Road, Belfast. *Club:* Malone Golf (Belfast).

KELLY, Basil; *see* Kelly, J. W. B.

KELLY, Brian; *see* Kelly, H. B.

KELLY, Charles Henry, QPM 1978; DL; Chief Constable of Staffordshire, since 1977; *b* 15 July 1930; *s* of Charles Henry Kelly and Phoebe Jane Kelly; *m* 1952, Doris (*née* Kewley); one *s* one *d. Educ:* Douglas High Sch. for Boys, IOM; London Univ. LLB (Hons). Asst Chief Constable of Essex, 1972; Dep. Chief Constable of Staffordshire, 1976. Pres., Staffordshire Small Bore Rifle Assoc.; Chm., Staffordshire Police St John Special Centre. DL Stafford, 1979. OStJ 1979. *Recreations:* cricket, reading, walking. *Address:* Chief Constable's Office, Cannock Road, Stafford ST17 0QG. *T:* Stafford 57717; 55530. *Club:* Special Forces.

KELLY, Edward Ronald; Overseas Controller, Central Office of Information, since 1978; *b* 14 Oct. 1928; *s* of late William Walter Kelly and of Millicent Kelly; *m* 1954, Storm Massada. *Educ:* Honiton Sch. Journalist: Bath Evening Chronicle, 1952; East African Standard, 1953; Sunday Post, Kenya, 1954; Reuters, 1956; Central Office of Information, 1958-: Editor in Chief, Overseas Press Services Div., 1964; Asst Overseas Controller, 1968; Dir, Publications and Design Services Div., 1970; Home Controller, 1976. *Recreations:* fishing, fly-tying, carpentry. *Address:* The Coach House, Willinghurst, Shamley Green, near Guildford, Surrey GU5 0SU. *T:* Cranleigh 5461. *Club:* Flyfishers'.

KELLY, Graham; *see* Kelly, R. H. G.

KELLY, Air Vice-Marshal (Herbert) Brian, MVO 1960; QHS 1978; MD, FRCP; Senior Consultant to the RAF, since 1979 (Consultant Adviser in Medicine, since 1974); *b* 12 Aug. 1921; *s* of late Surg. Captain James Cecil Kelly and of Meta Matheson (*née* Fraser). *Educ:* Epsom Coll.; St Thomas' Hosp. (MB, BS 1943, MD 1948). MRCP 1945, FRCP 1968; DCH 1966. House appts, St Thomas' Hosp., and St Luke's Hosp., Guildford, 1943-45; RNVR, Med. Specialist, RNH Hong Kong, 1945-48; Med. Registrar and Lectr in Medicine, St Thomas' Hosp., 1948-53; joined RAF Medical Br., 1953;

Consultant in Medicine at RAF Hosps, Aden, Ely, Nocton Hall, Singapore, Cyprus, Germany, 1953-; Consultant to CAA, 1974-. FRSocMed; Fellow, Med. Soc. London; Mem., British Cardiac Soc. Liveryman, Worshipful Soc. of Apothecaries, 1978; Freeman, City of London, 1978. *Publications:* papers in BMJ, Lancet, Brit. Heart Jl, and Internat. Jl of Epidemiology. *Recreation:* choir singing. *Address:* 32 Chiswick Quay, Hartington Road, W4. *T:* 01-995 5042. *Club:* Royal Air Force.

KELLY, Rev. Canon John Norman Davidson, DD; FBA 1965; Principal of St Edmund Hall, Oxford, 1951-79, Honorary Fellow 1979; Vice-Chancellor, Oxford University, Sept.-Oct. 1966 (Pro-Vice-Chancellor, 1964-66, 1972-79); *b* 13 April 1909; *s* of John and Ann Davidson Kelly. *Educ:* privately; Glasgow Univ.; The Queen's Coll., Oxford (Ferguson Scholar; Hertford Scholar; 1st Cl. Hon. Mods, Greats and Theology; Hon. Fellow, 1963); St Stephen's House. Deacon, 1934; priest, 1935; Curate, St Lawrence's, Northampton, 1934; Chaplain, St Edmund Hall, Oxford, 1935; Vice-Principal and Trustee, 1937. Select Preacher (Oxford), 1944-46, 1959, 1961, 1962; Speaker's Lectr in Biblical Studies, 1945-48; University Lecturer in Patristic Studies, 1948-76; Select Preacher (Cambridge), 1953; Chm. Cttee of Second Internat. Conf. on Patristic Studies, Oxford, 1955; Proctor in Convocation of Canterbury representing Oxford University, 1958-64; Chm. Archbishop's Commn on Roman Catholic Relations, 1964-68; accompanied Archbishop of Canterbury on his visit to Pope Paul VI, 1966; Mem., Academic Council, Ecumenical Theological Inst., Jerusalem, 1966-. In the War of 1939-45 did part-time work at Chatham House and collaborated in organizing the Oxford Leave Courses for United States, Allied, and Dominions Forces. Canon of Chichester and Prebendary of Wightring, 1948, Highleigh, 1964. Took lead in obtaining Royal Charter, new statutes and full collegiate status for St Edmund Hall, 1957. Mem. Governing Body: Royal Holloway Coll., London, 1959-69; King's Sch., Canterbury. Lectures: Paddock, General Theological Seminary, NY, 1963; Birkbeck, Cambridge, 1973; Hensley Henson, Oxford, 1979-80. Hon. DD: Glasgow, 1958; Wales, 1971. Dean of Degrees, St Edmund Hall, 1982-. *Publications:* Early Christian Creeds, 1950, 3rd edn 1972; Rufinus, a Commentary on the Apostles' Creed, 1955; Early Christian Doctrines, 1958, 5th edn 1977; The Pastoral Epistles, 1963; The Athanasian Creed, 1964; The Epistles of Peter and of Jude, 1969; Aspects of the Passion, 1970; Jerome, 1975. *Recreations:* motoring, gardening, travel. *Address:* 7 Crick Road, Oxford OX2 6QJ. *T:* Oxford 512907. *Clubs:* Athenæum; Vincent's, Gridiron (Oxford).

KELLY, Rt. Hon. (John William) Basil, PC (NI) 1969; **Rt. Hon. Mr Justice Kelly;** Judge of the High Court of Justice in Northern Ireland, since 1973; *b* 10 May 1920; *o s* of late Thomas William Kelly and late Emily Frances (*née* Donaldson); *m* 1957, Pamela, *o d* of late Thomas Colmer and Marjorie Colthurst. *Educ:* Methodist Coll., Belfast; Trinity Coll., Dublin. BA (Mod.) Legal Science, 1943; LLB (Hons) 1944. Called to Bar: of Northern Ireland, 1944; Middle Temple, 1970; QC (N Ireland) 1958. Senior Crown Counsel: Co. Fermanagh, 1965-66; Co. Tyrone, 1966-67; Co. Armagh, 1967-68; MP (U) Mid-Down, Parliament of Northern Ireland, 1964-72; Attorney-Gen. for Northern Ireland, 1968-72. *Recreations:* golf, music. *Address:* Chatelar, Circular Road East, Cultra, Co. Down. *T:* Holywood 4742. *Club:* Ulster Reform (Belfast).

KELLY, Kenneth Linden; Secretary-General of the Automobile Association, 1954-63; *b* 5 Dec. 1913; *s* of Herbert Linden Kelly and Alice Maud Gray; *m* 1939, Betty Joan Roe; two *d. Educ:* Kingston Grammar School. Served War of 1939-45 in RAOC, Europe and Middle East; Actg Dep. Dir of OS Middle East Forces, 1945 (Col.). Chm., Governors of Kingston Grammar School, 1957-72. FRSA 1955. *Address:* 37 Henly House, Lynwood, Sunninghill, Ascot, Berks. *Clubs:* Kingston Rowing (Vice-Pres.); Remenham (Henley).

KELLY, Laurence Charles Kevin; Deputy Chairman, Helical Bar Ltd, since 1981 (Director, since 1972); Chairman, Queenborough Steel Co., since 1980; Member, Monopolies and Mergers Commission, since 1982; Vice Chairman, British Iron and Steel Consumers' Council, since 1976; *b* 11 April 1933; *s* of late Sir David Kelly, GCMG, MC, and Lady Kelly (*née* Jourda de Vaux); *m* 1963, Alison Linda McNair Scott; one *s* two *d. Educ:* Downside Sch.; New Coll., Oxford (Beresford Hope Schol.; MA Hons); Harvard Business Sch. Lieut, The Life Guards, 1949-52; served (temp.) Foreign Office, 1955-56; Guest, Keen and Nettlefolds, 1956-72; Director, GKN International Trading Ltd, 1972. Member, Northern Ireland Development Agency, 1972-78; Chairman, Opera da Camera Ltd (charity), 1981-. FRGS. *Publications:* Lermontov, Tragedy in the Caucasus, 1978 (Cheltenham Literary Prize, 1979); St Petersburg, a Travellers' Anthology, 1981; reviews, TLS, etc. *Recreations:* skiing, shooting. *Address:* 44 Ladbroke Grove, W11 2PA. *T:* 01-727 4663. *Clubs:* Beefsteak, Brooks's, Turf; Kildare Street and University (Dublin).

KELLY, Dr Michael, JP; Lord Provost of Glasgow, since 1980; *b* 1 Nov. 1940; *s* of David and Marguerite Kelly; *m* 1965, Zita Harkins; one *s* two *d. Educ:* Univ. of Strathclyde (BSc(Econ), PhD). Asst Lectr in Economics, Univ. of Aberdeen, 1965-67; Lectr in Economics, Univ. of Strathclyde, 1967-. Councillor: Anderston Ward Corp. of Glasgow, 1971-75 (Convener, Schools and Sch. Welfare; Vice-Convener, Transport); Hillington Ward, Glasgow Dist, 1977- (Chairman: General Purposes Cttee; Buildings and Property Cttee). Hon. Mem., Clan Donald, USA; Hon. Mayor, Tombstone, Ariz. JP Glasgow 1973. Founding Editor, Jl Economic Studies. *Publication:* Studies in the British Coal Industry, 1970. *Recreations:* photography, football, philately. *Address:* City Chambers, Glasgow G2 1DU. *T:* 041-221 9600.

KELLY, Peter (John); Under-Secretary for Atomic Energy, United Kingdom Department of Energy, since 1980; *b* 26 Nov. 1922; *s* of Thomas and Lucy Kelly; *m* 1949, Gudrun Kelly (*née* Falck); two *s* three *d* (and one *s* decd). *Educ:* Downside; Oxford Univ. (BA). RNVR, 1942-46. 3rd Secretary, Moscow Embassy, 1948-49; journalism, 1950; rejoined public service, 1956; posts in Foreign Office, Defence Dept, Dept of Trade and Industry; Asst Secretary for Internat. Atomic Affairs, 1969-71; Counsellor, Office of UK Permanent Representative to the European Communities, Brussels, 1972-75; Director, Internat. Energy Agency, 1976-79. *Recreations:* walking, music. *Address:* 73 Ottways Lane, Ashtead, Surrey KT21 2PS. *T:* Ashtead 72177.

KELLY, Richard Denis Lucien, MC 1944; a Recorder of the Crown Court, 1972-80; *b* 31 Jan. 1916; *e s* of late Richard Cecil Kelly, OBE and Joan Maisie Kelly, Hyde Manor, Kingston, Sussex; *m* 1945, Anne Marie (marr. diss. 1954), *o d* of late James Stuart Anderson, Hinton House, Christchurch; one *d. Educ:* Marlborough Coll.; Balliol Coll., Oxford. Served Surrey and Sussex Yeomanry, 1939-40; Indian Mountain Artillery, India and Burma, 1941-45; Hon. Major, retd. Called to Bar, in absentia, Middle Temple, 1942; Midland and Oxford Circuit; Bencher, 1976. Blackstone Pupillage Prize, 1947; Harmsworth Law Scholar, 1948. Dep. Chm., Kesteven QS, and Dep. Recorder of Bedford, 1968. Alternate Chm., Burnham Cttee, 1973-. *Publications:* (abridgement) The Second World War, by Sir Winston Churchill, 1959; (with R. MacLeod) The Ironside Diaries 1939-40, 1962. *Recreations:* walking, history. *Address:* 3 Temple Gardens, Temple, EC4Y 9AU. *T:* 01-353 4949. *Club:* Garrick.

KELLY, (Robert Henry) Graham, FCIS; Secretary of the Football League, since 1979; *b* 23 Dec. 1945; *s* of Thomas John Kelly and Emmie Kelly; *m* 1970, Elizabeth Anne Wilkinson; one *s* one *d. Educ:* Baines Grammar Sch., Poulton-le-Fylde. FCIS 1973. Barclays Bank, 1964-68; Football League, 1968-. *Address:* The Football League, Lytham St Annes, Lancs FY8 1JG. *T:* St Annes 729421.

KELLY, Rosaline; publishing and industrial relations consultant; part-time Lecturer in Journalism, London College of Printing; *b* 27 Nov. 1922; *d* of Laurence Kelly and Ellen (*née* Fogarty), Drogheda, Co. Louth, Eire. *Educ:* St Louis Convent, Carrickmacross; University Coll., Dublin, NUI. Journalist with Woman magazine, 1958-77; local management, IPC Magazines Ltd, 1977-80. Active for 23 yrs in NUJ: Mem., National Exec. Council, 1972-78; first woman Pres., 1975-77; Membership of Honour, 1979; Member: NUJ Appeals Tribunal, 1978-; NUJ Standing Orders Cttee, 1978-; Trustee, Widow and Orphan Fund, 1977-80, Chairperson Management Cttee,1980-. Mem., Press Council, 1977-80 (first woman to represent Press side). *Recreations:* language and languages, music, compulsive reader. *Address:* 2 Elmar Court, Fulham Road, SW6 5SQ. *T:* 01-736 4290.

KELLY, Sir Theo, (William Theodore), Kt 1966; OBE 1958; JP; Chairman, Woolworths Ltd, Australia, 1963-80, retired (Managing Director, 1945-71), and its subsidiary and associated companies; Chairman: Woolworths (NZ) Ltd, 1963-79 (Director and General Manager, 1934-71); Woolworths Properties Limited, 1963-80; retired 1980; *b* 27 June 1907; *s* of W. T. Kelly; *m* 1944, Nancy Margaret, *d* of W. E. Williams, NZ; two *s* two *d.* War of 1939-45; RAAF, 1942-44, Wing Comdr. Chm., RAAF Canteen Services Bd, 1944-59. General Manager: Woolworths Ltd (NZ), 1932; Woolworths (Australia and NZ), 1945. Mem. Board, Reserve Bank of Australia, 1961-75; Dep. Chm., Australian Mutual Provident Soc., 1972-79 (Dir, 1967-79); Chm., Aust. Mutual Provident Fire and Gen. Insurance Pty Ltd, 1967-79. Life Governor, Royal Life Saving Soc.; Vice-Pres., Royal Hort. Soc., NSW; Trustee, National Parks and Wildlife Foundn, 1969-. Mem. Board, Royal North Shore Hosp., 1969-77. Fellow, Univ. of Sydney Senate, 1968-75. FRSA 1971; FAIM 1967. JP NSW, 1946. *Recreations:* golf, boating. *Address:* 8/73 Yarranabbe Road, Darling Point, Sydney, NSW 2027, Australia. *Clubs:* Sydney Rotary, Royal Motor Yacht, American National, Royal Sydney Golf, White City Tennis (Sydney).

KELLY, Sir William Theodore; *see* Kelly, Sir Theo.

KELSALL, William, OBE 1971; QPM 1969; DL; Chief Constable of Cheshire, 1974-77; retired; *b* 10 Jan. 1914. DL Cheshire, 1979. OStJ 1978. *Address:* Three Keys Cottage, Quarry Bank, Utkinton, Tarporley, Cheshire.

KELSEY, Mrs Denys E. R.; *see* Grant, Joan.

KELSEY, Emanuel; Solicitor and Parliamentary Officer to the Greater London Council, 1964-70; *b* 16 Feb. 1905; *s* of late Emanuel and Margaret Kelsey, Blyth, Northumberland; *m* 1934, Dorothy, *d* of late Alexander Mitchell-Smith, Bathgate, Scotland; one *s* one *d. Educ:* King Edward VI School, Morpeth. Legal Asst, Min. of Agric. and Fisheries, and Commissioners of Crown Lands, 1929; Sen. Asst, Parly Dept, LCC, 1931; Dep. Solicitor and Parly. Officer, LCC, 1962; Solicitor and Parly Officer, LCC, 1964. Hon. Solicitor to Royal Society for the Prevention of Accidents, 1964-70. *Address:* 26 Clifton Road, Wimbledon, SW19 4QT. *T:* 01-946 2564.

KELSEY, Maj.-Gen. John, CBE 1968; Director, Wild Heerbrugg (UK) Ltd, since 1978; Director of Military Survey, 1972-77; *b* 1 Nov. 1920; *s* of Benjamin Richard Kelsey and Daisy (*née* Powell); *m* 1944, Phyllis Margaret, *d* of Henry Ernest Smith, Chingford; one *s* one *d. Educ:* Royal Masonic Sch.;

Emmanuel Coll., Cambridge; Royal Mil. Coll. of Science. BSc. Commnd in RE, 1940; war service in N Africa and Europe; Lt-Col 1961; Col 1965; Dep. Dir Mil. Survey; Brig. Dir Field Survey, Ordnance Survey, 1968; Dir of Mil. Survey, Brig. 1972; Maj.-Gen. 1974. *Recreations:* Rugby football (played for Cambridge Univ., Richmond, Dorset, Wilts; Mem. RFU, 1965-66); sailing. *Address:* 33 Courtenay Place, Lymington, Hants. *T:* Lymington 73649.

KELSEY, Julian George, CB 1982; Deputy Secretary (Fisheries and Food), Ministry of Agriculture, Fisheries and Food, 1980-82; *b* 1922; *s* of William and Charlotte Kelsey, Dulwich; *m* 1944, Joan (*née* Singerton); one *d.* Lord Chancellor's Dept, 1939; War Service, 1941-46: Captain, Lancs Fusiliers and RAC; SOE and Force 136; Comdg No 11 Searcher Party Team, Burma; Exec. Officer, Central Land Board, 1948; Asst Principal, MAFF, 1951; Under Sec., 1969; Dir of Establishments, 1971-76; Fisheries Sec., 1976-80. *Address:* Shaston House, St James, Shaftesbury, Dorset. *Club:* Special Forces.

KELSICK, Osmund Randolph, DFC 1944; Chairman and Managing Director of Carib Holdings Ltd (owning and operating The Blue Waters Beach Hotel); Antigua Land Development Co. Ltd; Director: Caribbean Consultants Ltd; Vigie Beach Hotel Ltd (St Lucia); T. H. Kelsick Ltd (Montserrat); Caribbean Hotel Association; *b* 21 July 1922; *s* of T. H. Kelsick; *m* 1950, Doreen Avis Hodge; one *s* (and one *s* decd); two step *d. Educ:* private preparatory sch.; Montserrat Grammar Sch.; Oxford Univ. (Devonshire Course). RAF, Fighter Pilot, 1940-46. ADC and Personal Sec. to Governor of the Leeward Islands, 1946-47; District Commissioner, Carriacou, 1947-51; Asst Chief Sec., Governor's Office, Grenada, 1951-52; Asst Administrator and Administrator, St Vincent, 1952-57. In 1956 seconded for short periods as Asst Trade Commissioner for British West Indies, British Guiana and British Honduras in UK, and Executive Sec. of Regional Economic Cttee in Barbados. Chief Sec., Leeward Islands, 1957-60. Past Pres., Caribbean Hotel Assoc. FRSA 1973. *Recreations:* fishing, gardening, tennis. *Address:* Blue Waters Beach Hotel, Antigua, Leeward Islands, West Indies. *Clubs:* Royal Commonwealth Society (West Indian); New (Antigua); Celebrity (Toronto).

KELWAY, Colonel George Trevor, CBE 1963; TD 1941; DL; JP; District Registrar, HM High Court of Justice in Pembrokeshire and Carmarthenshire, 1940-62; *b* 30 March 1899; *yr s* of late George Stuart Kelway, Milford Haven, Ch. de la Légion d'Honneur, Ch. de l'Ordre de Léopold, &c.; *m* 1931, Gwladys, *d* of late Joseph Rolfe, Goodig, Burry Port, Carm., formerly High Sheriff of Carmarthenshire; one *d. Educ:* Warminster; St Edmund Hall, Oxford. Served European War, 1914-18, and War of 1939-45; Comdg Pembrokeshire Hy. Regt RA (TA), 1927-35; formerly Hon. Col. Pembs Coast Regt, 424 and 425 (Pembs.) Regts RA (TA), and The Pembroke Yeomanry, 1943-58; Chm. Pembs T&AFA, 1945-60. Admitted a Solicitor, 1922. Dep. Chm., Pembs QS, 1960-71. Chm. Pembs Conservative Assoc., 1950-60; Pres. Wales & Mon Cons. Party, 1957 and 1961; Mem. Lloyd's, 1942-; an original Mem. Milford Haven Conservancy Bd, 1958-. DL 1948, JP 1957, Pembrokeshire; High Sheriff, 1958. Provincial Grand Master, S Wales (Western Div.). *Recreation:* golf. *Address:* Cottesmore, near Haverfordwest, Dyfed. *T:* Haverfordwest 2282. *Club:* Pembrokeshire County (Haverfordwest).

KEM, (pseudonym of Kimon Evan Marengo); Political Cartoonist and Journalist; *b* Zifta, Egypt, 4 Feb. 1906; 2nd *s* of Evangelo Tr. Marengo and Aristea, *d* of Capt. John Raftopoulo, Lemnos; *m* 1954, Una O'Connor (*d* 1979); two *s. Educ:* privately, publicly and personally and from time to time attended such seats of learning as the Ecole des Sciences Politiques, Paris, Exeter Coll., Oxford, etc. Edited and Illustrated Maalèsh, a political weekly published simultaneously in Cairo and Alexandria, 1923-31; in summer of 1928 represented a group of Newspapers at International Press Conference, Cologne; has travelled extensively; a fluent linguist, has command of English, French, Greek, Italian, and Arabic and understands a few other languages. *Publications:* In French: Oua Riglak! 1926; Gare les Pattes! 1929; Alexandrie, Reine de la Méditerranée, 1928. In English: Toy Titans, International politics in verse and pictures, 1937; Lines of Attack, 1944. In Arabic: Adolf and his donkey Benito, 1940; now a free-lance, contributing to newspapers and periodicals all over the world. *Recreations:* swimming, riding, drawing, and castigating politicians. *Address:* 40 Grand Avenue, Southbourne, Bournemouth, Dorset BH6 3TA.

KEMBALL, Prof. Charles, MA, ScD Cantab; FRS 1965; FRSC; MRIA; FRSE; Professor of Chemistry, Edinburgh University, since 1966; Dean of the Faculty of Science, 1975-78; *b* 27 March 1923; *s* of late Charles Henry and of Janet Kemball; *m* 1956, Kathleen Purvis, *o d* of late Dr and Mrs W. S. Lynd, Alsager, Cheshire; one *s* two *d. Educ:* Edinburgh Academy; Trinity Coll., Cambridge (Sen. Schol.). First Class Hons in Natural Sciences Tripos, Pt I, 1942, Pt II, 1943. Employed by Ministry of Aircraft Production in Dept of Colloid Science, University of Cambridge, 1943-46; Commonwealth Fund Fellow, Princeton Univ., 1946-47; Fellow of Trinity Coll., Cambridge, 1946-54 (Junior Bursar, 1949-51; Asst Lectr, 1951-54); Univ. Demonstrator in Physical Chemistry, 1951-54; Professor of Physical Chemistry, Queen's Univ., Belfast, 1954-66 (Dean of the Faculty of Science, 1957-60, Vice-Pres., 1962-65). President: RIC, 1974-76 (Vice-Pres., 1959-61; Chm., Publications Bd, Chem. Soc./RSC, 1973-81); British Assoc. Section B (Chem.), 1976-77; Vice President: Faraday Soc., 1970-73; RSE, 1971-74. Hon. DSc Heriot-Watt, 1980. Meldola Medal, 1951, Royal Inst. of Chemistry; Corday-Morgan Medal, 1958, Tilden Lectr, 1960, Surface and Colloid Chem. Award, 1972,

Chemical Soc.; Ipatieff Prize, American Chemical Soc., 1962; Gunning Victoria Jubilee Prize, RSE, 1981. *Publications:* contributions to various scientific jls. *Recreation:* hill walking. *Address:* 5 Hermitage Drive, Edinburgh EH10 6DE. *Club:* English-Speaking Union.

KEMBALL, Brig. Humphrey Gurdon, CBE 1971 (OBE 1966); MC 1940; *b* 6 Nov. 1919; *s* of late Brig.-Gen. Alick Gurdon Kemball (late IA) and late Evelyn Mary (*née* Synge); *m* 1945, Ella Margery Emmeline (*née* Bickham); no *c. Educ:* Trinity Coll., Glenalmond; RMC, Sandhurst. Commissioned 1939, 1st Bn The Prince of Wales's Volunteers. Served War of 1939-45 (MC); Staff Coll., 1943. JSSC, 1956; commanded 1st Bn The Lancashire Regt (PWV), 1961-63; i/c Administration, HQ Federal Regular Army, Aden, 1964-66; Asst Dir, MoD, 1966-68; Mil. Attaché, Moscow, 1968-71; HQ British Forces, Near East, 1971-73; Dep. Comdr, SW District, 1973-74, retired. *Recreations:* fishing, travelling. *Address:* c/o Grindlay's Bank Ltd, 13 St James's Square, SW1. *Club:* Naval and Military.

KEMBALL-COOK, Brian Hartley, MA Oxon; Headmaster, Bedford Modern School, 1965-77; *b* 12 Dec. 1912; *s* of Sir Basil Alfred Kemball-Cook, KCMG, CB, and Lady Nancy Annie Kemball-Cook (*née* Pavitt); *m* 1947, Marian, *d* of R. C. R. Richards, OBE; three *s* one *d. Educ:* Shrewsbury Sch. (Sidney Gold Medal for Classics); Balliol Coll., Oxford (Scholar). First Class Classical Honour Mods, 1933; First Class, Litt. Hum., 1935. Sixth Form Classics Master, Repton Sch., 1936-40. Intelligence Corps, 1940-46 (despatches); Regional Intelligence Officer and Political Adviser to Regional Comr, Hanover, 1946; Principal, Min. of Transport, 1946-47. Sen. Classics Master, Repton Sch., 1947-56; Headmaster, Queen Elizabeth's Grammar Sch., Blackburn, 1956-65. Chm., Bedfordshire Musical Festival, 1967-77. Croix de Guerre with Palm, 1946. *Publications:* Ed. Shakespeare's Coriolanus, 1954; (contrib.) Education: Threatened Standards, 1972. *Recreations:* mountaineering, music, translating Homer. *Address:* 23 Grosvenor Road, East Grinstead, West Sussex RH19 1HS. *T:* East Grinstead 23360. *Club:* Climbers.

KEMBER, Anthony Joseph, MA; Administrator, South West Thames Regional Health Authority, since 1978; *b* 1 Nov. 1931; *s* of Thomas Kingsley Kember and May Lena (*née* Pryor); *m* 1957, Drusilla Mary (*née* Boyce); one *s* two *d. Educ:* St Edmund Hall, Oxford (MA). Associate, Inst. of Health Service Administrators (AHA). Deputy House Governor and Secretary to Bd of Governors, Westminster Hospital, 1961-69; Gp Secretary, Hillingdon Gp Hospital Management Cttee, 1969-73; Area Administrator, Kensington and Chelsea and Westminster Area Health Authority (Teaching), 1973-78. *Publications:* various articles for professional jls. *Recreations:* painting, tennis, golf. *Address:* 16 Orchard Rise, Richmond, Surrey TW10 5BX.

KEMBER, William Percy, FCA; FCT; Chief Accountant, British Telecommunications, since 1981; *b* 12 May 1932; *s* of late Percy Kember, Purley, and Mrs Q. A. Kember, Oxted, Surrey; *m* 1982, Lynn Kirkham. *Educ:* Uppingham. Chartered Accountant; Corporate Treasurer. Various posts with Royal Dutch/Shell Group in Venezuela, 1958-63; British Oxygen Co., 1963-67; Coopers & Lybrand, 1967-72; Post Office (Telecommunications), 1972-81. Visitor, Royal Institution, 1977, Chm., 1979. *Recreations:* golf, ski-ing. *Address:* 83 Hillway, N6 6AB. *T:* 01-341 2300. *Clubs:* Royal Automobile, Highgate Golf, Ski Club of Great Britain.

KEMMER, Prof. Nicholas, FRS 1956; FRSE 1954; MA Cantab, DrPhil Zürich; Tait Professor of Mathematical Physics, University of Edinburgh, 1953-79, now Professor Emeritus; *b* 7 Dec. 1911; *o s* of late Nicholas P. Kemmer and of late Barbara Kemmer (*née* Stutzer; later Mrs Barbara Classen); *m* 1947, Margaret, *o d* of late George Wragg and late Nellie (who *m* 2nd, C. Rodway); two *s* one *d. Educ:* Bismarckschule, Hanover; Universities of Göttingen and Zürich. DrPhil Zürich, 1935; Imperial Coll., London: Beit Scientific Research Fellow, 1936-38; Demonstrator, 1938; Fellow 1971. Mem. of UK Govt Atomic Energy Research teams in Cambridge and Montreal, 1940-46; University Lecturer in Mathematics, Cambridge, 1946-53 (Stokes Lecturer since 1950). Hughes Medal, Royal Society, 1966. J. Robert Oppenheimer Meml Prize (Univ. of Miami), 1975. *Publications:* The Theory of Space, Time and Gravitation, 1959 (trans. from the Russian of V. Fock, 1955); What is Relativity?, 1960 (trans from the Russian, What is the theory of Relativity?, by Prof. L. D. Landau and Prof. G. B. Rumer, 1959); Vector Analysis, 1977; papers in scientific jls on theory of nuclear forces and elementary particles. *Address:* 35 Salisbury Road, Edinburgh EH16 5AA. *T:* 031-667 2893.

KEMP, family name of **Viscount Rochdale.**

KEMP, Arnold; Editor, Glasgow Herald, since 1981; *b* 15 Feb. 1939; *s* of Robert Kemp and Meta Strachan; *m* 1963, Sandra Elizabeth Shand; two *d. Educ:* Edinburgh Academy; Edinburgh Univ. (MA). Sub-Editor: Scotsman, 1959-62; Guardian, 1963-66; Production Editor, 1966-71, London Editor, 1971-73, Dep. Editor, 1973-81, Scotsman. *Recreations:* music, reading, theatre. *Address:* 4 Kensington Road, Glasgow G12 9LF. *T:* 041-339 7685. *Club:* Caledonian.

KEMP, Athole Stephen Horsford, OBE 1958 (MBE 1950); Secretary-General, Royal Commonwealth Society, 1967-82; *b* 21 Oct. 1917; *o s* of late Sir Joseph Horsford Kemp, CBE, KC, LLD, and Mary Kemp; *m* 1940, Alison, *yr d* of late Geoffrey Bostock, FCA; two *s* one *d. Educ:* Westminster Sch.;

Christ Church, Oxford (MA). War service, RA, 1939-46; POW Far East (Thailand-Burma Railway). Malayan CS, 1940-64. *Recreations:* gardening, walking rights of way, wine. *Address:* Lockey House, Langford, near Lechlade, Glos. *T:* Filkins 239.

KEMP, Charles, CMG 1957; CBE 1951; retired as UK Senior Trade Commissioner and Economic Adviser to UK High Commissioner in South Africa (1953-58); *b* Whitstable, Kent, 25 Oct. 1897; *e s* of late Capt. Alfred and Elizabeth Kemp; *m* 1924, Helen Beatrice Stowe (*d* 1957); one *s. Educ:* Christ's Hospital; London University. HM Office of Works, 1915; served European War (wounded 1917); rejoined HM Office of Works, 1917; Dept of Overseas Trade, 1918; Asst to UK Trade Comr in E Africa, 1920; Trade Comr Grade III, 1931; Winnipeg, 1935; Cape Town, 1937; Trade Comr, Grade II, 1942, Grade I and transferred to Johannesburg, 1946. *Address:* 57 Hedge Row, Brighton Beach, Durban, South Africa. *Clubs:* Royal Commonwealth Society; Durban (Durban).

KEMP, Charles Edward; retired as Headmaster of Reading School; *b* 18 Nov. 1901; *e s* of Frederick Kemp, Salford, Lancs; *m* 1927, Catherine Mildred (*d* 1980), *e d* of W. H. Taggart, IOM; two *s. Educ:* Manchester Grammar School (Foundation Scholar); Corpus Christi Coll., Oxford (open Scholar), Goldsmith Exhibitioner, 1922; 1st Class Maths, 1923. Master, Manchester Grammar Sch., 1923-30; Master, Royal Naval Coll., Dartmouth, 1930-34; Headmaster: Chesterfield Sch., 1934-39; Reading Sch., 1939-66. *Address:* The Coombe House, Streatley, Reading, Berks RG8 9QL.

KEMP, Rear-Adm. Cuthbert Francis, CB 1967; ADC 1965; Chief Service Manager, Westland Helicopters, 1968-69; *b* 15 Sept. 1913; *s* of A. E. Kemp, Willingdon; *m* 1947, Margaret Law, *d* of L. S. Law, New York; two *s. Educ:* Victoria Coll., Jersey. Joined RN, 1931; RN Engrg Coll., 1936. Served in HMS Ajax and Hood; Pilot, 1939. Served War of 1939-45: carriers and air stations at home and abroad; Naval Staff, Washington, 1945-47; Fleet Engr Officer, E Indies, 1950-52; qual. Staff Coll., 1956; Admty, 1957-59; qual. Canadian Nat. Defence Coll., 1962; Supt RN Aircraft Yard, Belfast, 1962-65; Rear-Adm., Engineering, Staff of Flag Officer, Naval Air Command, 1965, retd 1967. *Recreations:* cricket, squash, shooting. *Address:* Beech House, Marston Magna, Som. *T:* Marston Magna 850563. *Clubs:* Army and Navy; Royal Naval and Royal Albert Yacht (Portsmouth).

KEMP, David Ashton McIntyre, QC 1973; a Recorder of the Crown Court, since 1976; *b* 14 Oct. 1921; *s* of late Sir Kenneth McIntyre Kemp and Margaret Caroline Clare Kemp; *m* 1st, 1949, Margaret Sylvia Jones (*d* 1971); 2nd, 1972, Maureen Ann Frances Stevens, widow. *Educ:* Winchester Coll.; Corpus Christi Coll., Cambridge. 1st cl. hons Law Cantab. Called to Bar, Inner Temple, 1948, Bencher, 1980. *Publications:* (with M. S. Kemp) The Quantum of Damages, Personal Injuries Claims, 1954 (4th edn 1975); (with M. S. Kemp) The Quantum of Damages, Fatal Accident Claims, 1956 (4th edn 1975). *Recreations:* ski-ing, tennis, gardening. *Address:* 63 Brixton Water Lane, SW2. *T:* 01-733 9735. *Clubs:* Hurlingham, Ski Club of Great Britain; Kandahar Ski.

KEMP, Edward Peter; Under Secretary, HM Treasury, since 1978; *b* 10 Oct. 1934; *s* of late Thomas Kemp and Nancie (*née* Sargent); *m* 1961, Enid van Popta; three *s* one *d. Educ:* Millfield Sch.; Royal Naval Coll., Dartmouth. FCA (ACA 1959). Professional work in this country and overseas, 1959-67. Principal, later Asst Sec., Min. of Transport, 1967-73; HM Treasury, 1973-. *Recreation:* reading. *Address:* 2 Longton Avenue, SE26 6QJ. *T:* 01-778 7310.

KEMP, Rt. Rev. Eric Waldram; see Chichester, Bishop of.

KEMP, Air Vice-Marshal George John, CB 1976; *b* 14 July 1921; *m* 1943, Elspeth Beatrice Peacock; one *s* two *d.* Commnd RAF, 1941; served in night fighter sqdns with spell on ferrying aircraft to Middle East; served in Iraq, 1953-54 and Far East, 1960-61; Stn Comdr RAF Upwood, 1968-69; Dir of Manning RAF, 1970-71; Dir of Personnel (Policy and Plans) RAF, 1972; Dir-Gen. of Personnel Management, RAF, 1973-75. *Recreations:* many and various. *Address:* Courts Cottage, Forge Hill, Acrise, Folkestone, Kent CT18 8LJ. *T:* Hawkinge 3188. *Club:* Royal Air Force.

KEMP, Hubert Bond Stafford, MS; FRCS, FRCSE; Consultant Orthopaedic Surgeon, Royal National Orthopaedic Hospital, London and Stanmore, since 1974; Hon. Consultant Orthopaedic Surgeon, St Luke's Hospital for the Clergy, since 1975; University Teacher in Orthopaedics; *b* 25 March 1925; *s* of John Stafford Kemp and Cecilia Isabel (*née* Bond); *m* 1947, Moyra Ann Margaret Odgers; three *d. Educ:* Cardiff High Sch.; Univ. of South Wales; St Thomas' Hosp., Univ. of London (MB, BS 1949; MS 1969); MRCS, LRCP 1947; FRCSE 1960; FRCS 1970. Robert Jones Gold Medal and Assoc. Prize, 1969 (Proxime Accessit, 1964); Hunterian Prof., RCS, 1969; Hon. Consultant, Royal Nat. Orthopaedic Hosp., London and Stanmore, 1965-74; Sen. Lectr, Inst. of Orthopaedics, 1965-74, Hon. Sen. Lectr, 1974-. Vis. Professor, VII Congress of Soc. Latino Amer. de Orthopedia y Traumatologica, 1971. Mem., MRC Working Party on Tuberculosis of the Spine, 1974-. Fellow, Brit. Orthopaedic Assoc., 1972-; Member: Brit. Orthopaedic Research Soc., 1967-; Internat. Skeletal Soc., 1977-. *Publications:* papers on diseases of the spine, the hip, metal sensitivity, bone scanning and haemophilia. *Recreations:* fishing, painting (walls and canvasses). *Address:* 55 Loom Lane, Radlett, Herts WD7 8NX. *T:* Radlett 4265; 107 Harley Street,

W1N 1DG. *T:* 01-935 2776.
See also G. D. W. Odgers.

KEMP, Prof. Kenneth Oliver; Chadwick Professor of Civil Engineering and Head of Civil Engineering Department, University College London, since 1970; *b* 19 Oct. 1926; *s* of Eric Austen Kemp; *m* 1952, Josephine Gloria (*née* Donovan); no *c. Educ:* University College London. BSc(Eng), PhD, FICE, FIStructE. Surveyor, Directorate of Colonial Surveys, 1947-49; Asst Engr, Collins and Mason, Consulting Engrs, 1949-54. University College London: Lectr, Sen. Lectr, Dept of Civil Engrg, 1954-69; Reader in Structural Engrg, 1969-70. *Publications:* papers in: Proc. Instn of Civil Engrs; The Structural Engr; Magazine of Concrete Research; Internat. Assoc. of Bridge and Structural Engrg. *Recreation:* Norfolk. *Address:* Frenchmans, Duck Street, Wendens Ambo, Essex CB11 4JU. *T:* Saffron Walden 40966.

KEMP, Sir Leslie (Charles), KBE 1957 (CBE 1948); BScEng; FICE, MIEE, ACGI; Vice-Chairman, General Development Corporation, Athens, since 1960; *b* 22 April 1890; *s* of John Charles Kemp, London; *m* 1st, 1918, Millicent Constance (marr. diss., 1959), *d* of late Thomas Maitland; two *s*; 2nd, 1961, Melina Enriquez. *Educ:* Forest Hill House School; London Univ. BScEng 1st Cl. Hons, 1910. Engineer with Fraser and Chalmers, Erith, 1910-14. Served as captain in RGA, France, 1914-19. Contract Engineer, English Electric Co., 1919-23; Technical Adviser, Power and Traction Finance Co., 1923-25; Midlands Branch Manager, English Electric Co., 1924-26; Man. Dir, Athens Piraeus Electricity Co., 1926-41; Manager, Asmara War (land plane repair) base, Asmara, Eritrea, 1942-43; Dep. Regional Dir, Middle East, BOAC, 1943-44; Vice-Chm and Managing Director, Athens Piraeus Electricity Co., 1944-55; Vice-Chm., Société Générale Héllenique, 1957-72. Citizen (Feltmaker) and Freedom of City of London, 1956. Cross of Commander of Royal Order of George I of Greece, 1951. *Recreations:* yachting and golf. *Address:* 12 Queen Amalia Avenue, Athens, Greece. *Clubs:* Carlton, Royal Thames Yacht; Royal Yacht Squadron (Cowes); Royal Corinthian Yacht (Burnham-on-Crouch); Royal Hellenic Yacht (Greece).

KEMP, Leslie Charles, CBE 1982; FCIArb, FBIM; Chairman: Construction Industry Training Board, since 1976; Griffiths McGee Ltd, Demolition Contractors, since 1982; Deputy Chairman, Peterborough Development Corporation, since 1974; Proprietor, Leslie Kemp Associates, since 1976; *b* 10 Oct. 1920; *s* of Thomas and Violet Kemp. *Educ:* Hawkhurst Moor Boys' School. Apprentice blacksmith, 1934-39; served War, 1939-46: Infantry, N Africa and Italy. Civil Engrg Equipment Operator, 1947-51; District Organiser, 1951-57, Regional Organiser, 1958-63, Nat. Sec. (Construction), TGWU, 1973-76. Jt Registrar, 1975-76, Dep. Chm., 1976-81, Demolition and Dismantling Industry Registration Council. Member, Nat. Jt Council for Building Industry, 1957-76; Operatives Sec., Civil Engrg Construction Conciliation Bd for GB, 1963-76; Member: Construction Industry Trng Bd, 1964-73, Dep. Chm., 1973-76 (Chm., Civil Engrg Cttee, 1964-76); EDC for Civil Engrg, 1964-76; Construction Ind. Liaison Gp, 1974-76; Construction Ind. Manpower Bd, 1976-; Bragg Adv. Cttee on Falsework, 1973-75; Vice-Pres., Construction Health and Safety Gp. Chm., Corby Develt Corp., 1976-80. Member, Outward Bound Trust, 1977-. Construction News Man of the Year Award, 1973; in recognition of services to trng, Leslie Kemp Europ. Prize for Civil Engrg trainees to study in France, instituted 1973. CompICE. *Recreations:* golf, walking, fishing. *Address:* 3rd Floor, Radnor House, 1272 London Road, Norbury, SW16 4EL. *T:* 01-764 3552. *Club:* Lighthouse.

KEMP, Oliver, CMG 1969; OBE 1960; *b* 12 Sept. 1916; *s* of Walter Kemp; *m* 1940, Henrietta Taylor; two *s. Educ:* Wakefield Grammar Sch.; Queen's Coll., Oxford. MA Oxon (Lit. Hum.), 1939. Served in HM Forces, 1939-45. Apptd Officer in HM Foreign Service, 1945; served in Moscow, Egypt, Indonesia, Yemen, Laos and Foreign Office, 1946-62. HM Chargé d'Affaires in Yemen, 1957-58; First Secretary and Head of Chancery in Laos, 1958-60. HM Ambassador to Togo (and Consul-General), 1962-65; Deputy Head of the United Kingdom Delegation to the European Communities, Luxembourg, 1965-67; Ambassador to Mongolia, 1967-68; FCO, 1968-70 and 1971-73 (European affairs). Dir, BSC Office, Brussels, 1973-81. *Recreations:* music, reading, languages, golf, gardening, travel. *Address:* 10 Manor Gardens, Hunmanby, Filey, N Yorks YO14 0PT. *T:* Scarborough 890051.

KEMP, Lt-Comdr Peter Kemp, OBE 1963; RN (retd); FSA, FRHistS; Head of Naval Historical Branch and Naval Librarian, Ministry of Defence, 1950-68; Editor of Journal of Royal United Service Institution, 1957-68; *b* 11 Feb. 1904; *e s* of Henry and Isabel Kemp; *m* 1st, 1930, Joyce, *d* of Fleming Kemp; 2nd, 1949, Eleanore, *d* of Frederick Rothwell; two *d* (and one *s* decd). *Educ:* Royal Naval Colleges, Osborne and Dartmouth. Served in submarines till 1928 (invalided); Naval Intelligence Division, 1939-45. Asst Editor, Sporting and Dramatic, 1933-36; Member: Editorial Staff, The Times, 1936-39 and 1945-50; Council of Navy Records Society; Editorial Adv. Board of Military Affairs (US). *Publications:* Prize Money, 1946; Nine Vanguards, 1951; HM Submarines, 1952; Fleet Air Arm, 1954; Boys' Book of the Navy, 1954; HM Destroyers, 1956; Famous Ships of the World, 1956; Victory at Sea, 1958; Famous Harbours of the World, 1958; (with Prof. C. Lloyd) Brethren of the Coast, 1960; History of the Royal Navy, 1969; The British Sailor: a social history of the lower deck, 1970; Escape of the Scharnhorst and Gneisenau, 1975; A History of Ships, 1978; Merchant Ships, 1982. Regimental Histories of: Staffordshire Yeomanry; Royal Norfolk Regiment; Middlesex Regiment; King's Shropshire Light Infantry; Royal Welch Fusiliers. Books on sailing. Children's novels. Edited: Hundred Years of Sea Stories; Letters of Admiral Boscawen (NRS); Fisher's First Sea Lord Papers, Vol. I (NRS), 1960, Vol. II (NRS), 1964; Oxford Companion to Ships and the Sea, 1976; Encyclopædia of Ships and Seafaring, 1980. *Recreations:* sailing, golf. *Address:* 53 Market Hill, Maldon, Essex. *T:* Maldon 52609. *Clubs:* West Mersea Yacht, Maldon Golf.

KEMP, Robert Thayer; Head of Project Underwriting Group, Export Credits Guarantee Department, since 1981; *b* 18 June 1928; *s* of Robert Kemp and Ada Kemp (*née* Thayer); *m* 1951, Gwendolyn Mabel Minty; three *s*. *Educ:* Bromley Grammar Sch.; London Univ. (BA (Hons) Medieval and Mod. History). Asst Secretary, Export Credits Guarantee Dept, 1970, Under-Sec., 1975. *Recreations:* cricket, music, theatre. *Address:* c/o Export Credits Guarantee Department, Aldermanbury House, Aldermanbury, EC2P 2EL. *T:* 01-606 6699. *Club:* Overseas Bankers.

KEMP, Thomas Arthur, MD; FRCP; Physician, St Mary's Hospital, 1947-75, Paddington General Hospital 1950-75; *b* 12 Aug. 1915; *s* of late Fred Kemp and Edith Peters; *m* 1942, Ruth May Scott-Keat; one *s* one *d. Educ:* Denstone Coll.; St Catharine's Coll., Cambridge (Exhibitioner); St Mary's Hospital, London (Scholar). MB, BChir 1940; MRCP 1941; FRCP 1949; MD 1953. Examiner in Medicine, Universities of London and Glasgow. FRSM (Jt Hon. Sec., 1961-67). Served in Middle East, 1944-47; Lt-Col RAMC Officer i/c Medical Division; Hon. Cons. Physician to the Army, 1972-75. Pres. Brit. Student Health Assoc., 1962-63; Chm. Brit. Student Tuberculosis Foundation, 1963-65. Fellow, Midland Div., Woodard Schs, 1962; Commonwealth Travelling Fellowship, 1967. *Publications:* papers in medical journals. *Recreations:* games, especially Rugby football (played for Cambridge (1936), England (Captain 1948); President: Rugby Football Union, 1971-72; Students' RFU, 1980-). *Address:* 2 Woodside Road, Northwood, Mddx. *T:* Northwood 21068. *Club:* Hawk's (Cambridge).

KEMPE, John William Rolfe, CVO 1980; Headmaster of Gordonstoun, 1968-78; *b* 29 Oct. 1917; *s* of late William Alfred Kempe and Kunigunda Neville-Rolfe; *m* 1957, Barbara Nan Stephen, *d* of late Dr C. R. Huxtable, MC, FRCS and Mrs Huxtable, Sydney, Australia; two *s* one *d. Educ:* Stowe; Clare Coll., Cambridge (Exhibitioner in Mathematics). Served war of 1939-45, RAFVR Training and Fighter Command; CO 153 and 255 Night Fighter Squadrons. Board of Trade, 1945; Firth-Brown (Overseas) Ltd, 1946-47; Head of Maths Dept, Gordonstoun, 1948-51; Principal, Hyderabad Public Sch., Deccan, India, 1951-54; Headmaster, Corby Grammar School, Northants, 1955-67. Chm., Round Square Internat. Service Cttee; Vice Chm., The European Atlantic Movement. Exploration and mountaineering, Himalayas, Peru, 1952-56; Member: Cttee, Mount Everest Foundation, 1956-62; Cttee, Brathay Exploration Group, 1964-73. FRGS. *Publications:* articles in Alpine Jl, Geographical Jl, Sociological Review. *Address:* Two Gates, Old North Road, Wansford, near Peterborough. *Club:* Alpine.

KEMPFF, Wilhelm Walter Friedrich; pianist and composer; *b* Jüterbog, Berlin, 25 Nov. 1895. *Educ:* Viktoria Gymnasium, Potsdam; Berlin University and Conservatoire (studied under H. Barth and Robert Kahn). Professor and Director of Stuttgart Staatliche Hochschule für Musik, 1924-29, has made concert tours throughout the world since then. Has made numerous recordings. Mem. of Prussian Academy of Arts. Mendelssohn Prize, 1917; Swedish Artibus et Litteris Medal, etc. Hon. RAM, 1980; Hon. Mem., Bayerische Akad. der schönen Künste, 1980. *Compositions* include: two symphonies; four operas; piano and violin concertos; chamber, vocal and choral works. *Publications:* Unter dem Zimbelstern, Das Werden eines Musikers (autobiog.), 1951; Was ich hörte, was ich sah: Reisebilder eines Pianisten, 1981. *Address:* Wallgraben 14, D-8193 Ammerland-Münsing 2, Germany; c/o Ibbs & Tillett, 450-452 Edgware Road, W2 1EG.

KEMPNER, Prof. Thomas; Principal, Administrative Staff College, Henley-on-Thames, and Professor and Director of Business Studies, Brunel University, since 1972; *b* 28 Feb. 1930; *s* of late Martin and Rosa Kempner; *m* 1st, 1958, June Maton (*d* 1980); three *d*; 2nd, 1981, Mrs Veronica Ann Vere-Sharp. *Educ:* University Coll. London (BSc (Econ)). Asst Administrator, Hyelm Youth Hostels, 1948-49, and part-time, 1951-55; Research Officer, Administrative Staff Coll., Henley, 1954-59; Lectr (later Sen. Tutor) in Business Studies, Sheffield Univ., 1959-63; Prof. of Management Studies, Founder, and Dir of Management Centre, Univ. of Bradford, 1963-72. Member of various cttees, including: Social Studies and Business Management Cttees of University Grants Cttee, 1966-76; Management, Education and Training Cttee of NEDO, 1969- (Chm. of its Student Grants Sub-Cttee); Chm., Food Industry Manpower Cttee of NEDO, 1968-71; Jt Chm., Conf. of Univ. Management Schools, 1973-75. CBIM (FBIM 1971). Hon. DSc Cranfield, 1976. Burnham Gold Medal, 1970. *Publications:* editor, author, and contributor to several books, including: Bradford Exercises in Management (with G. Wills), 1966; Is Corporate Planning Necessary? (with J. Hewkin), 1968; A Guide to the Study of Management, 1969; Management Thinkers (with J. Tillet and G. Wills), 1970; Handbook of Management, 1971; (with K. Macmillan and K. H. Hawkins) Business and Society, 1974; Models for Participation, 1976; numerous articles in Management jls. *Recreation:* travel. *Address:* Administrative Staff College, Henley-on-Thames, Oxon. *T:* Hambleden 454.

KEMPSON, Rachel, (Lady Redgrave); actress; *b* Devon, 28 May 1910; *d* of Eric William Edward Kempson and Beatrice Hanitton Kempson; *m* 1935, Sir Michael Redgrave, *qv*; one *s* two *d. Educ:* St Agnes Convent, East

Grinstead; Colchester County High Sch.; Oaklea, Buckhurst Hill; RADA. First stage appearance in Much Ado About Nothing, Stratford, 1933; first London appearance in The Lady from Alfaqueque, Westminster, 1933. Stratford season, 1934; Liverpool Playhouse, 1935-36; Love's Labour's Lost, Old Vic, 1936; Volpone, Westminster, 1937; Twelfth Night, Oxford, 1937; The School for Scandal, Queen's, 1937; The Shoemaker's Holiday, Playhouse, 1938; Under One Roof, Richmond, 1940; The Wingless Victory, Phoenix, 1943; Uncle Harry, Garrick, 1944; Jacobowsky and the Colonel, Piccadilly, 1945; Fatal Curiosity, Arts, 1946; The Paragon, Fortune, 1948; The Return of the Prodigal, Globe, 1948; Candida, Oxford, 1949; Venus Observed, Top of the Ladder, St James's, 1950; The Happy Time, St James's, 1952; Shakespeare Meml Theatre Co., 1953; English Stage Co., 1956. Recent stage appearances include: The Seagull, St Joan of the Stockyards, Queen's, 1964; Samson Agonistes, Lionel and Clarissa, Guildford, 1965; A Sense of Detachment, Royal Court, 1972; The Freeway, National Theatre, 1974; A Family and a Fortune, Apollo, 1975; The Old Country, Queen's, 1977. Films include: The Captive Heart, 1945; Georgy Girl; The Jokers; Charge of the Light Brigade; The Virgin Soldiers; Jane Eyre. Frequent television appearances include series: Elizabeth R, Jennie, Love for Lydia, The Jewel in the Crown; plays: Winter Ladies, Sweet Wine of Youth, 1979; Kate, the Good Neighbour, Getting On, The Best of Everything, and Jude, 1980; Blunt Instrument, Bosom Friends, The Box wallah, and The Bell, 1981. *Recreations:* gardening, letter writing. *Address:* Hutton Management Ltd, 194 Old Brompton Road, SW5 0AS.
See also Lynn Redgrave, Vanessa Redgrave.

KEMPSTER, Hon. Michael Edmund Ivor; Hon. Mr Justice Kempster; a Judge of the Supreme Court of Hong Kong, since 1982; *b* 21 June 1923; *s* of late Rev. Ivor T. Kempster, DSO; *m* 1949, Sheila, *d* of late Dr T. Chalmers, KiH, Inverness; two *s* two *d. Educ:* Mill Hill Sch.; Brasenose Coll., Oxford (Scholar, MA, BCL). Royal Signals, 1943-46; commissioned in India, served 14th Army. Called to Bar, Inner Temple, 1949; Profumo Prize; Bencher 1977. QC 1969; a Recorder of the Crown Court, 1972-81. Mem., Govt Cttee on Privacy, 1971. Chm., Bd of Governors, Mill Hill School, 1979-82. *Recreations:* skiing, fishing, hare-hunting. *Address:* 2801A Tregunter Mansions, Hong Kong. *Clubs:* Travellers'; Hong Kong (Hong Kong).

KEMSLEY, 2nd Viscount *cr* 1945, of Dropmore; **(Geoffrey) Lionel Berry,** DL; Bt 1928; Baron 1936; *b* 29 June 1909; *e s* of 1st Viscount Kemsley, GBE and Mary Lilian (*d* 1928), *d* of Horace George Holmes; *S* father, 1968; *m* 1933, Lady Helen Hay, DStJ, *e d* of 11th Marquess of Tweeddale; four *s. Educ:* Marlborough; Magdalen Coll., Oxford. Served War of 1939-45. Capt. Grenadier Guards; invalided out of Army, 1942. MP (C) Buckingham Div. of Bucks, 1943-45. Dep. Chm., Kemsley Newspapers Ltd, 1938-59. Chm., St Andrew's Hospital, Northampton; Pres., Assoc. of Independent Hospitals. Mem. Chapter General, Order of St John. Master of Spectacle Makers' Co., 1949-51, 1959-61. CC Northants, 1964-70; High Sheriff of Leicestershire, 1967, DL 1972. FRSA; KStJ. *Heir:* *b* Hon. Denis Gomer Berry, TD [*b* 11 July 1911; *m* 1st, 1934, Rosemary Leonora de Rothschild (marr. diss., 1942); two *d*; 2nd, 1947, Mrs Pamela Grant, *d* of late Lord Richard Wellesley; one *s* one *d*]. *Address:* Thorpe Lubenham, Market Harborough, Leics. *T:* Market Harborough 62816. *Clubs:* Turf, Pratt's.
See also Hon. A. G. Berry, G. N. Mobbs.

KEMSLEY, Col Sir Alfred Newcombe, KBE 1980 (CBE 1960); CMG 1973; MSM 1916; ED 1947; FIA; business consultant; *b* Prospect, SA, 29 March 1896; *s* of Alfred Kemsley; *m* 1st, 1921, Glydus Logg (decd); one *s* (killed, RAAF, 1941); 2nd, 1925, Jean Oldfield (decd); one *s* one *d*; 3rd, 1972, Anne Copsey. *Educ:* Adelaide Business Training Academy. Lands Dept, Adelaide, 1911-15; served War, AIF, 1915-18 (Private to Staff Captain; MSM); BHP Co., 1920-23; Sec., Melbourne Metrop. Town Planning Commn, 1923-29; Sec., Liquor Trades Defence Union, 1930-34; Gen. Manager, 3UZ Melbourne, 1934-44; Vice-Pres., Aust. Fedn of Commercial Broadcasting Stations, 1935-36, Trustee, 1938-40; War of 1939-45 (Captain to Colonel): DADOS, 4th Div.; Dir of Organisation and Recruiting, Army HQ, 1941-43; Business Adviser and Army Rep., Bd of Administration, 1943-46; Mem., Mil. Bd, 1946; R of O. Dir, United Services Publicity, later USP Needham Pty Ltd, 1945-65 (Chm., 1960-64), Consultant Dir, 1965-. Director: Fire Fighting Equipment Pty Ltd, 1959-62; Ponsford Newman and Benson, 1964-69; Aust. Inhibitor Paper Pty Ltd, 1965-73; Consultant, TraveLodge Aust. Ltd, 1966-75. Member: Town and Country Planning Bd, 1945-68 (Mem. Aust. Planning Inst.; Sir James Barnett Meml Medal for Town Planning, 1964); Council, Melb. Chamber of Commerce, 1947-76; Inst. of Public Affairs, 1950-69; Aust. Inst. of Management, 1956-64; Aust. Nat. Travel Assoc., 1956-68 (Dep. Chm., 1967-68); Inst. of Directors, 1958-. Trustee, Melb. Nat. War Meml, 1938- (Chm., 1978); Founder Mem., Bd of Governors, Corps of Commissionaires, 1946- (Vice-Chm., 1964); Founder Mem., Field Marshal Sir Thomas Blamey Meml Cttee, 1954- (Chm., 1978); Member: War Nurses Meml Cttee, 1945-80; Discharged Servicemen's Employment Bd, 1969-74; Fourth University Cttee, 1970-71. *Address:* 41 Bay Street, Brighton, Victoria 3186, Australia. *Clubs:* Melbourne Legacy (Founder Mem., 1923; Pres., 1932); Australian (Melbourne); Melbourne Cricket.

KENDAL, Felicity; actress; with the National Theatre, since 1979; *d* of Geoffrey and Laura Kendal; *m* (marr. diss.); one *s. Educ:* six convents in India. First appeared on stage in 1947, at age of 9 months, when carried on as the Changeling boy in A Midsummer Night's Dream; grew up touring India and Far East with parents' theatre co., playing pageboys at age of eight and graduating through Puck, at nine, to parts such as Viola in Twelfth Night,

Jessica in The Merchant of Venice, and Ophelia in Hamlet; returned to England, 1965; made London debut, Carla in Minor Murder, Savoy, 1967; Katherine in Henry V, and Lika in The Promise, Leicester, 1968; Amaryllis in Back to Methuselah, Nat. Theatre, 1969; Hermia in A Midsummer Night's Dream, and Hero in Much Ado About Nothing, Regent's Park, 1970; Anne Danby in Kean, Oxford, 1970, London, 1971; Romeo and Juliet, 'Tis Pity She's A Whore, and The Three Arrows, 1972; The Norman Conquests, London, 1974; Viktosha in Once Upon a Time, Bristol, 1976; Arms and The Man, Greenwich, 1978; Mara in Clouds, London, 1978; National Theatre, 1979–: Constance Mozart in Amadeus; Desdemona in Othello; Christopher in On the Razzle; Paula in The Second Mrs Tanqueray. *Television:* four series of The Good Life, 1975–77; Viola in Twelfth Night, 1979; Solo, 1980; plays and serials. *Films:* Shakespeare Wallah, 1965; Valentino, 1976. Variety Club Most Promising Newcomer, 1974, Best Actress, 1979; Clarence Derwent Award, 1980. *Recreation:* golf. *Address:* c/o Chatto & Linnit, Globe Theatre, W1. *T:* 01-439 4371.

KENDALL, Prof. David George, DSc; FRS 1964; Professor of Mathematical Statistics, University of Cambridge, and Fellow of Churchill College, since Oct. 1962; *b* 15 Jan. 1918; *s* of Fritz Ernest Kendall and Emmie Taylor, Ripon, Yorks; *m* 1952, Diana Louise Fletcher; two *s* four *d. Educ:* Ripon GS; Queen's Coll., Oxford (MA, DSc). Fellow Magdalen Coll., Oxford, and Lectr in Mathematics, 1946-62. Vis. Lectr, Princeton Univ., USA, 1952-53 (Wilks Prize, 1980). Larmor Lectr, Cambridge Philos. Soc., 1980. Mem. Internat. Statistical Inst.; Mem. Council, Royal Society, 1968-69; President: London Mathematical Soc., 1972-74; Internat. Assoc. Statist. in Phys. Sci., 1973-75; Bernoulli Soc. for Mathematical Stats and Probability, 1975; Section A (Math.) and Section P (Physics), BAAS, 1982. Chm. Parish Reg. Sect., Yorks Archaeol. Soc., 1974-79. Hon. D. de l'U. Paris (René Descartes), 1976. Guy Medal in Silver, Royal Statistical Soc., 1955; Weldon Meml Prize and Medal for Biometric Science, 1974; Sylvester Medal, Royal Soc., 1976; Whitehead Prize, London Math. Soc., 1980; Guy Medal in Gold, Royal Statistical Soc., 1981. *Publications:* (jt ed) Mathematics in the Archaeological and Historical Sciences, 1971; (jt ed) Stochastic Analysis, 1973; (jt ed) Stochastic Geometry, 1974. *Address:* Churchill College, Cambridge.

KENDALL, Denis; *see* Kendall, W. D.

KENDALL, Henry Walter George, OBE 1979; Director, British Printing Industries Federation, 1972-81; *b* 21 Dec. 1916; *s* of Henry Kendall and Beatrice (Kerry) Kendall; *m* 1945, Audrey Alison Woodward; two *s* one *d. Educ:* Archbishop Temple's Sch., Lambeth. FCMA, AMBIM. Training with Blades, East & Blades Ltd, 1933-40. War service, RAOC; special duties, War Office, London, 1941; Mil. Coll. of Science, Inspecting Ordnance Officer Western Comd, HQ Allied Land Forces SE Asia, 1940-46. Cost accountant, British Fedn of Master Printers, 1947-55; Chief Cost Accountant, 1955; Head of Management Services, 1967. Mem. Council: CBI, 1972-81; Printing Industry Research Assoc., 1972-81; Inst. of Printing, 1972-81. *Recreations:* theatre, gardening, travel. *Address:* 28 Foxgrove Avenue, Beckenham, Kent BR3 2BA. *Clubs:* Royal Automobile, Press.

KENDALL, Sir Maurice (George), Kt 1974; MA, ScD; FBA 1970; Director, World Fertility Survey, 1972-80; Chairman, Scientific Control Systems (Holdings), 1971-72; Fellow: American Statistical Association; Econometric Society; Institute of Mathematical Statistics; London Graduate School of Business Studies; *b* 6 Sept. 1907; *s* of late John Roughton Kendall and Georgina Kendall; *m* 1st, 1933, Sheila Frances Holland Lester; two *s* one *d* ; 2nd, 1947, Kathleen Ruth Audrey Whitfield; one *s. Educ:* Central Sch., Derby; St John's Coll., Cambridge (Wrangler 1929). Entered Administrative Class, Civil Service, 1930; Ministry of Agriculture, 1930-41; Statistician, Chamber of Shipping, 1941-49 and Jt Asst Gen. Manager, 1947-49; Professor of Statistics in the University of London 1949-61. Chm., Scientific Control Systems Ltd, 1967-71. Fellow, British Computer Soc.; ex-President: Royal Statistical Soc.; Operational Research Soc.; Inst. of Statisticians; Hon. Member: Market Research Soc.; Internat. Statistical Inst., 1979. Hon. Fellow, LSE, 1975. Gold Medal, Royal Statistical Society, 1968; United Nations Peace Medal, 1980. DUniv: Essex, 1968; Lancaster, 1975. *Publications:* (with G. Udny Yule) An Introduction to the Theory of Statistics, 14th edn, 1950; (with Alan Stuart) The Advanced Theory of Statistics, vol. I, 1958, 4th edn 1977; vol. II, 1961, 4th edn 1979; vol. III, 1966, 3rd edn 1975; Contributions to Study of Oscillatory Time-Series, 1947; Rank Correlation Methods, 1948, 4th edn 1970; (ed) The Sources and Nature of the Statistics of the United Kingdom, vol. 1, 1952, vol. 2, 1957; Exercises in Theoretical Statistics, 1954, 3rd edn 1968; (with W. R. Buckland) A Dictionary of Statistical Terms, 1955, 3rd edn 1971; A Course in Multivariate Analysis, 1957; A Course in the Geometry of n Dimensions, 1961; (with Alison G. Doig) A Bibliography of Statistical Literature, vol. 1, 1962, vol. 2, 1965, vol. 3, 1968; (with P. A. Moran) Geometrical Probability, 1963; (ed) Mathematical Model Building in Economics and Industry, first series, 1968, second series, 1970; (ed, with E. S. Pearson) Studies in the History of Probability and Statistics, 1970; (ed) Cost-benefit Analysis, 1971; (ed, with Alan Stuart) Selected Papers of George Udny Yule, 1971; Time-Series, 1973; Multivariate Analysis, 1975; (ed, with R. L. Plackett) Second Series of Studies in the History of Probability and Statistics, 1977; various papers on theory of statistics and applications to economics and psychology. *Recreations:* chess, gardening. *Address:* 1 Frank Dixon Close, SE21. *T:* 01-693 6076.

KENDALL, (William) Denis, PhD; FRSA; FIMechE; MIAE; Chartered Engineer; *b* Halifax Yorks, 27 May 1903; *yr s* of J. W. Kendall, Marton, Blackpool; *m* 1952, Margaret Hilda Irene Burden. *Educ:* Trinity Sch.; Halifax Technical Coll. MP (Ind.) Grantham Division of Kesteven and Rutland, 1942-50; Mem., War Cabinet Gun Bd, 1941-45 (decorated). Cadet in Royal Fleet Auxiliary; Asst to Chief Inspector, Budd Manufacturing Corp., Philadelphia, Pa, 1923; Dir of Manufacturing, Citroen Motor Car Co., Paris, 1929-38; Managing Director, British Manufacture and Research Co., Grantham, England (manufacturers of aircraft cannon and shells), 1938-45, and Consultant to Pentagon, Washington, on high velocity small arms. Executive Vice-Pres., Brunswick Ordnance Corp., New Brunswick, NJ, 1952-55 (also Dir and Vice-Pres. Ops, Mack Truck Corp.); President and Director: American MARC, Inc., 1955-61 (manufacturers of Diesel Engines, who developed and produced the world's first Diesel outboard engine, and also electric generators, etc), Inglewood, Calif; Dynapower Systems Corp. (Manufacturers of Electro-Medical equipment), Santa Monica, Calif, 1961-73; Pres., Kendall Medical International, Los Angeles, Calif, 1973–. Mem. President's Council, American Management Assoc. Mem. Worshipful Co. of Clockmakers, Freeman City of London, 1943; Governor of King's Sch., Grantham, 1942-52. Chevalier de l'Ordre du Ouissam Alouite Cherifien. Mason. Religious Society of Friends (Quakers). *Address:* 1319 North Doheny Drive, Los Angeles, Calif 90069, USA. *T:* 5508963; 159 Abbotts Road, Mitcham, Surrey. *Clubs:* Riviera Country, United British Services (Los Angeles, Calif).

KENDALL, William Leslie; Secretary General, Council of Civil Service Unions (formerly Civil Service National Whitley Council, Staff Side), since 1976; *b* 10 March 1923; *m* 1943, Irene Canham; one *s* one *d.* Clerk Insurance Cttee, 1937-41. RAF 1941-46. Entered Civil Service, 1947; Civil Service Clerical Association: held hon. posts; Asst Sec., 1952; Dep. Gen. Sec., 1963; Gen. Sec., CPSA (formerly CSCA), 1967-76. Sec., Civil Service Alliance, 1967; Governor, Ruskin Coll., 1967-76. Member: CS Nat. Whitley Council (Chm. Staff Side, 1973-75); Advisory Council, Civil Service Coll., 1976–; Civil Service Pay Bd, 1978-81; Employment Appeal Tribunal, 1976–. Vice Pres., Civil Service Council Further Educn, 1978–. Dir, Civil Service Building Soc., 1980–. *Recreations:* reading, music. *Address:* (home) 87 Christian Fields, SW16 3JU. *T:* 01-764 7735; (office) 19 Rochester Row, SW1. *T:* 01-828 2727.

KENDALL-CARPENTER, John MacGregor Kendall; Headmaster, Wellington School, since 1973; *b* 25 Sept. 1925; *s* of late C. E. Kendall-Carpenter and F. F. B. Kendall-Carpenter (*née* Rogers); *m* 1955, Iris Anson; three *s* two *d. Educ:* Truro Sch.; Exeter Coll., Oxford. Fleet Air Arm, Pilot RNVR, 1943-46. Oxford, 1947-51; Asst Master, Clifton Coll., 1951-61, and Housemaster, 1957-61; Headmaster: Cranbrook School, Kent, 1961-70; Eastbourne Coll., 1970-73. Member: Air Cadet Council, 1965-70; Air League Council, 1963-70; Chm., Boarding Schools Assoc., 1981-May 1983; Pres., Rugby Football Union, 1980-81 (Member or Captain: Oxford Univ. Rugby XV, 1948-50, England Rugby XV, 1948-54); Hon. Manager Australasian Team, Rugby Football Schools' Union, 1979, Chm. RFSU, 1981-. Bard of the Gorsedd of Cornwall, 1981–. *Recreations:* outdoor activities, church architecture. *Address:* Headmaster's House, South Street, Wellington, Som; 1 Coulson's Terrace, Penzance, Cornwall. *Clubs:* East India, Devonshire, Sports and Public Schools; Vincent's (Oxford).

KENDON, Donald Henry, CBE 1961; FIEE, FIMechE; Chairman Merseyside and North Wales Electricity Board, 1954-62, retired; *b* 9 Aug. 1895; *s* of Samuel and Ellen Susan Kendon; *m* 1923, Katharine Grace Honess (*d* 1978); five *s. Educ:* Goudhurst, Kent; King's Coll., University of London. BSc (Eng.) Hons. Served European War, 1914-19, in RE and RAF. Electrical Engineer with Edmundson's Electricity Corp., Ltd, 1921-34; General Manager: Cornwall Electric Power Co., 1934-39; Shropshire, Worcestershire and Staffordshire Electric Power Co., 1939-48; Dep. Chairman, Midlands Electricity Board, 1948-54; formerly Member: Central Electricity Authority, 1956, 1957; Electricity Council. *Address:* Quedley, Flimwell, via Wadhurst, East Sussex.

KENDREW, Maj.-Gen. Sir Douglas (Anthony), KCMG 1963; CB 1958; CBE 1944; DSO 1943 (Bar 1944, 2nd Bar 1944, 3rd Bar 1953); Governor of Western Australia, 1963-73; *b* 22 July 1910; *er s* of Alexander John Kendrew, MC, MD, Barnstaple, North Devon; *m* 1936, Nora Elizabeth, *d* of John Harvey, Malin Hall, County Donegal; one *s* one *d. Educ:* Uppingham Sch. 2nd Lieut Royal Leicestershire Regt, 1931; Capt. 1939; Major 1941; served War of 1939-45: Bde Major, N Africa, 1942; comd 6th Bn York and Lancaster Regt. N Africa and Italy, 1943; Bde Comd. Italy, Middle East and Greece, 1944-46; Commandant, Sch. of Infantry, Rhine Army, 1946-48; Commandant Army Apprentice Sch., Harrogate, 1948-50; Chief of Staff, NID, 1950-52; Bde Comd. 29 Brit. Inf. Bde, Korea, 1952-53; idc 1954; Brig. Administration HQ Northern Comd, 1955; GOC Cyprus Dist, and Dir of Ops, 1956-58; Dir of Infantry, War Office, 1958-60; Head of British Defence Liaison Staff, Australia, 1961-63. Col, Royal Leicestershire Regt, 1963-64. Hon. Col, SAS Regt, RWAR Australia, 1965. Pres., Knights of the Round Table, 1975. Comr, Royal Hospital, Chelsea, 1974-80. Hon. LLD Univ. of WA, 1969. KStJ 1964. *Recreations:* Rugby football (played for England 10 times, Capt. 1935; toured NZ and Australia, 1930; Army XV, 1932-36); golf and fishing. *Address:* The Manor House, Islip, Northants. *T:* Thrapston 2325. *Club:* Army and Navy.

KENDREW, Sir John (Cowdery), Kt 1974; CBE 1963; ScD; FRS 1960; President of St John's College, Oxford, since 1982; b 24 March 1917; s of late Wilfrid George Kendrew, MA, and Evelyn May Graham Sandberg. *Educ:* Dragon Sch., Oxford; Clifton Coll., Bristol; Trinity Coll., Cambridge (Hon. Fellow, 1972). Scholar of Trinity Coll., Cambridge, 1936; BA 1939; MA 1943; PhD 1949; ScD 1962. Min. of Aircraft Production, 1940–45; Hon. Wing Comdr, RAF, 1944. Fellow, Peterhouse, Cambridge, 1947–75 (Hon. Fellow, 1975); Dep. Chm., MRC Lab. for Molecular Biology, Cambridge, 1946–75; Dir Gen., European Molecular Biology Lab., 1975–82. Reader at Davy-Faraday Laboratory at Royal Instn, London, 1954–68. Mem., Council for Scientific Policy, 1965–72 (Dep. Chm., 1970–72); Sec.–Gen., European Molecular Biology Conf., 1970–74. Chm., Defence Scientific Adv. Council, 1971–74; Pres., British Assoc. for Advancement of Science, 1973–74; Trustee, British Museum, 1974–79. Pres., Internat. Union for Pure and Applied Biophysics, 1969–72; Sec. Gen. Internat. Council of Scientific Unions, 1974–80; Trustee, Internat. Foundn for Science, 1975–78; Mem. Council, UN Univ., 1980–. Hon. MRIA 1981; Hon. Member: American Soc. of Biological Chemists, 1962; RIA, 1981; Foreign Hon. Mem., Amer. Acad. of Arts and Sciences, 1964; Leopoldina Academy, 1965; Foreign Assoc., Amer. Nat. Acad. of Sciences, 1972; Hon. Fellow: Inst. of Biology, 1966; Weizmann Inst., 1970; Corresp. Mem., Heidelberg Acad. of Scis, 1978; Foreign Mem., Bulgarian Acad. of Scis, 1979. Lectures: Herbert Spencer, Univ. of Oxford, 1965; Crookshank, Faculty of Radiologists, 1967; Procter, Internat. Soc. of Leather Chemists, 1969; Fison Meml, Guy's Hosp., 1971; Mgr de Brún, Univ. Coll. of Galway, 1979; Saha Meml, Univ. of Calcutta, 1980. Hon. Prof., Univ. of Heidelberg, 1982. Hon. DSc: Univ. of Reading, 1968; Univ. of Keele, 1968; Exeter, 1982; DUniv Stirling, 1974; Dr *honoris causa* Pécs, Hungary, 1975. (Jointly) Nobel Prize for Chemistry, 1962; Royal Medal of Royal Society, 1965; Order of Madara Horseman, 1st degree, Bulgaria, 1980. Editor in Chief, Jl of Molecular Biology, 1959–. *Publications:* The Thread of Life, 1966; scientific papers in Proceedings of Royal Society, etc. *Address:* President's Lodgings, St John's College, Oxford OX1 3JP. *T:* Oxford 247671; The Guildhall, 4 Church Lane, Linton, Cambridge CB1 6JX. *T:* Cambridge 891545. *Club:* Athenæum.

KENDRICK, John Bebbington Bernard; Chief Inspector of Audit, Ministry of Housing and Local Government, 1958–65, retired; b 12 March 1905; 3rd s of late John Baker Kendrick and Lenora Teague, Leominster, Herefordshire; m 1932, Amelia Ruth, 4th d of late James Kendall, Grange-over-Sands; two s. *Educ:* Leominster Grammar Sch.; King's Sch., Chester; Queen's Coll., Oxford (MA). Called to Bar, Middle Temple. Asst District Auditor, 1926; Deputy District Auditor, 1946; District Auditor, 1953; Deputy Chief Inspector of Audit, 1958. *Recreation:* fell walking. *Address:* Green Acres, Old Hall Road, Troutbeck Bridge, Windermere, Cumbria LA23 1HF. *T:* Windermere 3705.

KENEALLY, Thomas Michael; author; b 7 Oct. 1935; s of Edmond Thomas Keneally; m 1965, Judith Mary Martin; two d. Studied for NSW Bar. Schoolteacher until 1965; Commonwealth Literary Fellowship, 1966, 1968, 1972; Lectr in Drama, Univ. of New England, 1968–69. FRSL 1973. *Publications:* The Place at Whitton, 1964; The Fear, 1965, 2nd edn 1973; Bring Larks and Heroes, 1967, 2nd edn 1973; Three Cheers for the Paraclete, 1968; The Survivor, 1969; A Dutiful Daughter, 1971; The Chant of Jimmie Blacksmith, 1972 (filmed 1978); Blood Red, Sister Rose, 1974; Gossip from the Forest, 1975 (TV film, 1979); The Lawgiver, 1975; Season in Purgatory, 1976; A Victim of the Aurora, 1977; Ned Kelly and the City of the Bees, 1978; Passenger, 1979; Confederates, 1979; Schindler's Ark, 1982. *Recreations:* swimming, sailing, hiking. *Address:* c/o Hope Leresche & Sayle, 11 Jubilee Place, SW3 3TE.

KENILOREA, Rt. Hon. Sir Peter (Kauona Keninaraiso'ona), KBE 1982; PC 1979; MP (formerly MLA) Solomon Islands, since 1976; Leader of the Opposition, since 1981; b Takataka, Malaita, 23 May 1943; m 1971, Margaret Kwanairara; two s two d. *Educ:* Univ. and Teachers' Coll., NZ (Dip. Ed.). Teacher, King George VI Secondary Sch., 1968–70. Asst Sec., Finance, 1971; Admin. Officer, Dist Admin, 1971–73; Lands Officer, 1973–74; Dep. Sec. to Cabinet and to Chief Minister, 1974–75; Dist Comr, Eastern Solomon Is, 1975–76; Chief Minister, 1976–78; Prime Minister, 1978–81. Queen's Silver Jubilee Medal, 1977. *Publications:* political and scientific, numerous articles. *Address:* c/o Legislative Assembly, Honiara, Guadalcanal, Solomon Islands.

KENILWORTH, 4th Baron cr 1937, of Kenilworth; **(John) Randle Siddeley;** Managing Director, Siddeley Landscapes, since 1976; Director, John Siddeley International Ltd; b 16 June 1954; s of John Tennant Davenport Siddeley (3rd Baron Kenilworth) and of Jacqueline Paulette, d of late Robert Gelpi; S father, 1981. *Educ:* Northease Manor, near Lewes, Sussex; West Dean College (studied Restoration of Antique Furniture); London College of Furniture. Worked at John Siddeley International as Interior Designer/Draughtsman, 1975; formed own company, Siddeley Landscapes, as Landscape Gardener, 1976. *Recreation:* ski-ing. *Address:* 4 Harriet Street, SW1X 9QT. *T:* 01-235 9321. *Clubs:* St James's; Annabel's.

KENNABY, Very Rev. Noel Martin; b 22 Dec. 1905; s of Martin and Margaret Agnes Kennaby; m 1st, 1933, Margaret Honess Elliman; 2nd, 1937, Mary Elizabeth Berry. *Educ:* Queens' Coll., Cambridge; Westcott House, Cambridge. BA 1928; MA 1932. Deacon 1929, priest 1930, Diocese of Guildford; Curate of Epsom, 1929–32; in charge of Christ Church, Scarborough, 1932–36; Vicar of St Andrew's, Handsworth, 1936–42;

Tynemouth, 1942–47; Surrogate from 1942; Rural Dean of Tynemouth, 1943–47; Provost and Vicar of Newcastle upon Tyne, 1947–61; Rural Dean of Newcastle upon Tyne, 1947–61; Senior Chaplain to the Archbishop of Canterbury, 1962–64; Hon. Canon, Newcastle Cathedral, 1962–64; Dean of St Albans and Rector of the Abbey Church, 1964–73, Dean Emeritus, 1973. Commissary, Jamaica, 1950–67. *Publication:* To Start You Praying, 1951. *Address:* 60 Alexandra Road, Bridport, Dorset.

KENNAN, Prof. George Frost; Professor, Institute for Advanced Study, Princeton, NJ, 1956–74, now Professor Emeritus; b 16 Feb. 1904; m 1931, Annelise Sorensen; one s three d. *Educ:* Princeton Univ. (AB); Seminary for Oriental Languages, Berlin. Foreign Service of the USA; many posts from 1926–52; US Ambassador to the USSR, 1952–53; Institute for Advanced Study, Princeton, 1953–61; US Ambassador to Yugoslavia, 1961–63. George Eastman Vis. Prof., Oxford, 1957–58; Reith Lectr, BBC, 1957; Prof., Princeton Univ., 1963 and 1964. Hon. LLD: Dartmouth and Yale, 1950; Colgate, 1951; Notre Dame, 1953; Kenyon Coll., 1954; New School for Social Research, 1955; Princeton, 1956; University of Michigan and Northwestern, 1957; Brandeis, 1958; Wisconsin, 1963; Harvard, 1963; Denison, 1966; Rutgers, 1966; Marquette, 1972; Catholic Univ. of America, 1976; Duke, 1977; Ripon Coll., 1978; Dickinson Coll., 1979; Hon. DCL Oxford, 1969. Benjamin Franklin Fellow, RSA, 1968. President: Nat. Inst. of Arts and Letters, 1965–68; Amer. Acad. of Arts and Letters, 1968–72. Pour le Mérite (Germany), 1976. Albert Einstein Peace Prize, Albert Einstein Peace Prize Foundn of Chicago, 1981; Grenville Clark Prize, Grenville Clark Fund at Dartmouth Coll., Inc., 1981. *Publications:* American Diplomacy, 1900-50, 1951 (US); Realities of American Foreign Policy, 1954 (US); Amerikanisch Russische Verhältnis, 1954 (Germany); Soviet-American Relations, 1917-20; Vol. I, Russia Leaves the War, 1956 (National Book Award; Pulitzer Prize 1957); Vol. II, The Decision to Intervene, 1958; Russia, the Atom and the West, 1958; Soviet Foreign Policy, 1917-1941, 1960; Russia and the West under Lenin and Stalin, 1961; On Dealing with the Communist World, 1964; Memoirs, vol. 1, 1925-1950, 1967 (National Book Award 1968; Pulitzer Prize 1968); Memoirs, vol. 2, 1950-1963, 1973; From Prague after Munich: Diplomatic Papers 1938-1940, 1968; Democracy and the Student Left, 1968; The Marquis de Custine and his 'Russie en 1839', 1972; The Cloud of Danger, 1977; (jtly) Encounters with Kennan: the Great Debate, 1979; The Decline of Bismarck's European Order, 1979. *Club:* Century (New York City).

KENNARD, Sir George Arnold Ford, 3rd Bt cr 1891; Midland Representative for Cement Marketing Co.; b 27 April 1915; s of Sir Coleridge Kennard, 1st Bt; S brother, 1967; m 1st, 1940, Cecilia Violet Cokayne Maunsel (marr. diss. 1958); one d; 2nd, 1958, Jesse Rudd Miskin (marr. diss. 1974), d of Hugh Wyllie. *Educ:* Eton. Commissioned 4th Queen's Own Hussars, 1939; served War of 1939-45 (despatches twice), Egypt, Greece (POW Greece); comd Regt, 1955-58; retired, 1958. Joined Cement Marketing Co., 1967. *Recreations:* hunting, shooting, fishing. *Heir:* none. *Address:* Gogwell, Tiverton, Devon. *T:* Tiverton 2154. *Club:* Cavalry and Guards.

KENNAWAY, Prof. Alexander, MA; CEng, FIMechE, FPRI; consulting engineer, since 1966; Director, Thomas Jourdan Ltd, since 1976; Board Member, Civil Aviation Authority, since 1979; b 14 Aug. 1923; s of late Dr and Mrs Barou; m 1st, 1947, Xenia Rebel (marr. diss. 1970); two s one d; 2nd, 1973, Jean Simpson. *Educ:* Downsend Sch., Leatherhead; St Paul's Sch., London; Pembroke Coll., Cambridge (MA). CEng, FIMechE 1962; FPRI 1968. Engr Officer, RN: active list, 1942-47; reserve, 1970. Imperial Chemical Industries Ltd, 1947-58; Metal Box Co., 1958-60; Director: BTR Industries, 1960-66; Allied Polymer Gp, 1972-78; Hon. medical engrg consultant, various hosps and charities, 1950-. Mem., Standing Adv. Cttee on artificial limbs, DHSS, 1964-70. Vis. Prof. of Chem. Engrg, Imp. Coll. of Science and Technology, 1976-. *Publications:* (contrib.) Advances in Surgical Materials, 1956; (contrib.) Polythene—technology and uses, 1958, 2nd edn 1960; (contrib.) Engineers in Industry, 1981; (contrib.) The British Malaise, 1982; some 30 papers on biomechanics, technology of use and production of rubbers and plastics, and on design of specific aids for disabled living. *Recreations:* sailing, chess, music, loving à la Russe culturally and in cuisine, enlarging the limits imposed by an insular and specialist education. *Address:* 12 Fairholme Crescent, Ashtead, Surrey KT21 2HN. *T:* Ashtead 77678. *Clubs:* Reform, Central YMCA Chess; Royal Naval Sailing Association (Portsmouth).
See also L. Archibald.

KENNAWAY, Sir John (Lawrence), 5th Bt, cr 1791; b 7 Sept. 1933; s of Sir John Kennaway, 4th Bt and Mary Felicity, yr d of late Rev. Chancellor Ponsonby; S father 1956; m 1961, Christina Veronica Urszenyi, MB, ChB (Cape Town); one s two d. *Educ:* Harrow; Trinity Coll., Cambridge. *Heir:* s John Michael Kennaway, b 17 Feb. 1962. *Address:* Escot, Ottery St Mary, Devon EX11 1LU.

KENNEDY, family name of **Marquess of Ailsa.**

KENNEDY, Sir Albert (Henry), Kt 1965; KPM 1947; Chairman, Securicor (Ulster) Ltd; Director, Securicor Main Board. Held various ranks in Royal Ulster Constabulary, incl. Inspector General, 1961-69. *Address:* Richmond, 41 Sheridan Drive, Helen's Bay, Co. Down, Northern Ireland BT19 1LB. *T:* Helen's Bay 853208. *Club:* Royal Belfast Golf (Ulster).

KENNEDY, A(lfred) James, CBE 1979; DSc (London), PhD (London), FEng, MIEE, FIMM, FIM, FInstP; Deputy Director, Technical Change

Centre, since 1981; a Director, BL Technology Ltd, since 1979; *b* 6 Nov. 1921; *m* 1950, Anna Jordan; no *c. Educ:* Haberdashers' Aske's Hatcham Sch.; University Coll., London (Fellow 1976). BSc (Physics) 1943. Commissioned R Signals, 1944; Staff Major (Telecommunications) Central Comd, Agra, India, 1945-46 and at Northern Comd, Rawalpindi, 1946-47; Asst Lectr in Physics, UCL 1947-50; Res. Fellow, Davy-Faraday Lab. of Royal Institution, London, 1950-51; Royal Society, Armourers' and Brasiers' Research Fellow in Metallurgy (at Royal Institution), 1951-54; Head of Metal Physics Sect., BISRA, 1954-57; Prof. of Materials and Head of Dept. of Materials, Coll. of Aeronautics, Cranfield, 1957-66; Dir, British Non-Ferrous Metals Res. Assoc., later BNF Metals Technol. Centre, Wantage, 1966-78; Dir of Research, Delta Metal Co., and Man. Dir, Delta Material Research Ltd, 1978-81. Vis. Prof. in Metallurgy, Imperial Coll. of Science and Technol., London, 1981. Institution of Metallurgists: Pres., 1976-77; a Vice Pres., 1971-74, 1975-76; Mem. Council, 1968-74, 1975-. President: Inst. of Metals, 1970-71 (Mem. Council, 1968-73; Fellow, 1973); Engrg Section, BAAS, 1983; Member: Metallurgy Cttee, CNAA, 1965-71; ARC, 1967-70, 1971-74, 1977-80 (also Mem., ARC cttees); Adv. Council on Materials, 1970-71; Council, The Metals Soc., 1974- (Platinum Medallist, 1977); Inst. of Physics, 1968-71; SRC, 1974-78; Metall. and Mat. Cttee, SRC, 1970-75 (Chm. 1973-74); Engrg Bd, 1973-78; Council of Env. Sci. and Eng., 1973-78; Adv. Council for Applied R&D, 1976-80; Mat. and Chem. Res. Requirements Bd, DoI, 1981- (Chm., Non-Ferrous Metals Cttee). Fellow, Amer. Soc. Met., 1972. Pres., Brit. Soc. of Rheology, 1964-66; a Governor, Nat. Inst. for Agric. Engrg, 1966-74. Hon. DSc Aston, 1980. *Publications:* Processes of Creep and Fatigue in Metals, 1962; The Materials Background to Space Technology, 1964; Creep and Stress Relaxation in Metals (English edn), 1965; (ed) High Temperature Materials, 1968; research papers and articles, mainly on physical aspects of deformation and fracture in crystalline materials, particularly metals. *Recreations:* music, painting. *Address:* Woodhill, Milton under Wychwood, Oxon. *T:* Shipton under Wychwood 830334. *Club:* Athenæum.

KENNEDY, Archibald E. C.; *see* Clark-Kennedy.

KENNEDY, Brig. Archibald Gordon M.; *see* Mackenzie-Kennedy.

KENNEDY, Prof. Arthur Colville, FRCPE, FRCPGlas, FRCP; Muirhead Professor of Medicine, Glasgow University, since 1978; *b* 23 Oct. 1922; *s* of Thomas and Johanna Kennedy; *m* 1947, Agnes White Taylor; two *d* (one *s* decd). *Educ:* Whitehill Sch., Glasgow; Univ. of Glasgow. MB ChB 1945, MD 1956. FRCPE 1960, FRCPGlas 1964, FRCP 1977. Hon. Consultant in Medicine, Royal Infirmary, Glasgow, 1959-; Titular Professor, Univ. of Glasgow, 1969-78. *Publications:* various papers on renal disease. *Recreations:* gardening, walking, reading. *Address:* 16 Boclair Crescent, Bearsden, Glasgow G61 2AG. *T:* 041-942 5326. *Club:* Athenæum.

KENNEDY, Sir Clyde (David Allen), Kt 1973; Chairman of Sydney (New South Wales) Turf Club, 1972-77 and since 1980 (Vice-Chairman, 1967-72); company director; Member, NSW Totalisator Agency Board; Chairman, Spinal Research Foundation. *Address:* 13A/23 Thornton Street, Darling Point, NSW 2027, Australia. *Clubs:* Australian Jockey, Sydney Turf; Rugby, Tattersalls (all NSW).

KENNEDY, David Matthew; American Banker; Special Representative of the First Presidency of The Church of Jesus Christ of Latter-day Saints; *b* Randolph, Utah, 21 July 1905; *s* of George Kennedy and Katherine Kennedy (*née* Johnson); *m* 1925, Lenora Bingham; four *d. Educ:* Weber Coll., Ogden, Utah (AB); George Washington Univ., Washington, DC (MA, LLB); Stonier Grad. Sch. of Banking, Rutgers Univ. (grad.). Technical Asst to Chm. of Bd, Federal Reserve System, 1930-46; Vice-Pres. in charge of bond dept, Continental Illinois Bank and Trust Co., Chicago, 1946-53, full Vice-Pres., 1951, Pres., 1956-58, Chm. Bd and Chief Exec. Officer, 1959- (temp. resigned, Oct. 1953-Dec. 1954, to act as special Asst to Sec. of Treas., in Republican Admin.); after return to Continental Illinois Bank, still advised Treasury (also under Democrat Admin). Chm. of a Commission: (apptd by President Johnson) to improve drafting of Federal budget, 1967; (apptd by Mayor of Chicago) for Economic and Cultural Develt of Chicago, 1967. Again in Govt, when nominated to Nixon Cabinet, Dec. 1968; Secretary of the Treasury, 1969-70; Ambassador-at-large, USA, and Mem. President Nixon's Cabinet, 1970-73; US Ambassador to NATO, 1972. Director (past or present) of many corporations and companies including: Internat. Harvester Corp.; Abbott Laboratories; Swift & Co.; Pullman Co.; Nauvoo Restoration Inc.; Member of numerous organizations; Trustee: Univ. of Chicago; George Washington Univ.; Brookings Instn, etc. Holds hon. doctorates. *Address:* 3793 Parkview Drive, Salt Lake City, Utah 84117, USA. *Clubs:* Union League, Commercial Executives (Chicago); Old Elm Country (Fort Sheridan, Ill); Glenview Country, etc.

KENNEDY, Douglas Neil, OBE 1952 (MBE); Vice-President, English Folk Dance and Song Society; President, Folk Lore Society, 1964-65; *b* Edinburgh, 1893; *s* of John Henderson Kennedy and Patricia Grieve Thomson, *g s* of David Kennedy the Scottish singer; *m* 1st, 1914, Helen May Karpeles; two *s* ; 2nd, 1976, Elizabeth Ann Ogden. *Educ:* George Watson's Coll., Edinburgh; Imperial College of Science. Served London Scottish prior to and during European War, 1914-18, and received his commission in that regiment; MBE for War services, and retired with the rank of Captain; served War of 1939-45, RAF, 1940-45. Demonstrator in the Department of Botany, Imperial Coll., 1919-24; Organising Dir, English Folk Dance Society (on the death of its

founder Cecil J. Sharp), 1924. *Publications:* England's Dances, 1950; English Folk-dancing Today and Yesterday, 1964; other works relating to traditional dance and song. *Address:* Deck House, Waldringfield, Woodbridge, Suffolk.

KENNEDY, Eamon, MA, PhD; Irish Ambassador to the Court of St James's, since 1978; *b* 13 Dec. 1921; *s* of Luke William Kennedy and Ellen (*née* Stafford); *m* 1960, Barbara Jane Black, New York; one *s* one *d. Educ:* O'Connell Schools, Dublin; University Coll., Dublin, National University of Ireland (PhD 1970). Entered Irish Diplomatic Service, 1943; 2nd Sec., Ottawa, 1947-49; 1st Sec., Washington, 1949-50; 1st Sec., Paris, 1950-54; Chief of Protocol, Dublin, 1954-56; Counsellor, UN Mission, New York, 1956-61; Ambassador to: Nigeria, 1961-64; Federal Republic of Germany, 1964-70; France, OECD and UNESCO, 1970-74; UN, 1974-78. Grand Cross: German Order of Merit, 1970; French Order of Merit, 1974. *Recreations:* golf, theatre, music. *Address:* Irish Embassy, 17 Grosvenor Place, SW1X 7HR. *T:* 01-235 2171. *Clubs:* Garrick, Irish; Royal Wimbledon Golf.

KENNEDY, Edward Arthur Gilbert; Senior Director, Office of the Northern Ireland Ombudsman, since 1973; *b* Dublin, 5 May 1920; *s* of Captain Edward H. N. Kennedy, RN, and Frances A. Gosling, Bermuda; *m* 1944, Margarita Dagmara Hofstra; two *s* two *d. Educ:* Oundle; Pembroke Coll., Cambridge (BA Mod Langs). Served War, RNVR, 1941-46. Joined Northern Ireland Civil Service, 1947; served mainly in Dept of Commerce until 1970, when seconded to Ombudsman's office. Vice-Chm., Music Cttee, N Ireland Arts Council, 1978-; Hon. Pres., Belfast Ballet Club, 1970-82; Chm., Belfast Picture Borrowing Gp, 1970-. *Recreation:* interest in the arts. *Address:* 29 Tweskard Park, Belfast BT4 2JZ. *T:* Belfast 63638.

KENNEDY, Edward Moore; US Senator (Democrat) from Massachusetts, since 1963; *b* Boston, Mass, 22 Feb. 1932; *y s* of late Joseph Patrick Kennedy and of Rose Kennedy (*née* Fitzgerald); *m* ; two *s* one *d. Educ:* Milton Acad.; Harvard Univ. (BA 1954); Internat. Law Inst., The Hague; Univ. of Virginia Law Sch. (LLB 1959). Served US Army, 1951-53. Called to Massachusetts Bar, 1959; Asst Dist Attorney, Suffolk County, Mass, 1961-62. Senate majority whip, 1969-71; Chm., Judiciary Cttee, 1979-81; Ranking Democrat, Labor and Human Resources Cttee, 1981-. Pres., Joseph P. Kennedy Jr Foundn, 1961-; Trustee: John F. Kennedy Library; John F. Kennedy Center for the Performing Arts; Robert F. Kennedy Meml Foundn. Holds numerous hon. degrees and foreign decorations. *Publications:* Decisions for a Decade, 1968; In Critical Condition, 1972; (with Senator Mark Hatfield) Freeze: how you can help prevent nuclear war, 1982. *Address:* United States Senate, Washington, DC 20510, USA.

KENNEDY, Francis, CBE 1977 (MBE 1958); HM Diplomatic Service; Ambassador to Angola, since 1981; *b* 9 May 1926; *s* of late James and Alice Kennedy; *m* 1957, Anne O'Malley; two *s* two *d. Educ:* Univs of Manchester and London. HM Colonial Service, Nigeria, 1953-63; HM Diplomatic Service, 1964-; served Dar-es-Salaam, Kuching and Istanbul; Consul-Gen., Atlanta, 1973-77; Counsellor, 1978, Minister, 1979-81, Lagos. *Address:* c/o Foreign and Commonwealth Office, SW1. *Club:* Brooks's.

KENNEDY, (George) Michael (Sinclair), OBE 1981; Northern Editor, The Daily Telegraph, since 1960, and Northern Music Critic since 1950; *b* 19 Feb. 1926; *s* of Hew Gilbert Kennedy and Marian Florence Sinclair; *m* 1947, Eslyn Durdle; no *c. Educ:* Berkhamsted School. Joined Daily Telegraph, Manchester, 1941; served Royal Navy (BPF), 1943-46; rejoined Daily Telegraph, Manchester, serving in various capacities on editorial staff; Asst Northern Editor, 1958. Mem. Council, Royal Northern Coll. of Music; Mem. Cttee, Vaughan Williams Trust, 1965- (Chm., 1977-); Trustee: Barbirolli Memorial Foundn, 1971; Elgar Foundn and Birthplace Trust, 1975; Civic Trust for the North West, 1978. Hon. Mem., Royal Manchester Coll. of Music, 1971. Hon. MA Manchester, 1975. FJI 1967; FRNCM 1981. *Publications:* The Hallé Tradition, 1960; The Works of Ralph Vaughan Williams, 1964, 2nd edn 1980; Portrait of Elgar, 1968, 2nd rev. edn, 1982; Portrait of Manchester, 1970; Elgar Orchestral Works, 1970; History of Royal Manchester College of Music, 1971; Barbirolli: Conductor Laureate, 1971; (ed) The Autobiography of Charles Hallé, 1973; Mahler, 1974 (Japanese edn 1978); Richard Strauss, 1976; (ed) Concise Oxford Dictionary of Music, 3rd edn, 1980; Britten, 1981; scripts for BBC, contrib. musical jls. *Recreations:* listening to music, watching cricket. *Address:* 3 Moorwood Drive, Sale, Cheshire M33 4QA. *T:* 061-973 7225. *Club:* Portico Library (Manchester).

KENNEDY, Lt-Col Sir (George) Ronald (Derrick), 7th Bt *cr* 1836; OBE 1975; Administrator, World Pheasant Association; *b* 19 Nov. 1927; *s* of Sir Derrick Edward de Vere Kennedy, 6th Bt, and of Phyllis Victoria Levine, *d* of late Gordon Fowler; *S* father, 1976; *m* 1949, Noelle Mona, *d* of Charles Henry Green; one *s* one *d. Educ:* Clifton College. Regimental service in RA, 1947-58; Staff Coll., Camberley, 1959; staff duties, Aden, 1960-63; regimental duty, 1963-66; staff duties, MoD and HQ BAOR, 1966-71; Defence Attaché, Mexico City, Havana and El Salvador, 1971-74; GSO 1, UK Delegn to Live Oak, SHAPE, 1974-77; HQ Dhekelia Garrison, 1977; retired 1979. *Recreations:* foreign travel, military history. *Heir:* *s* Michael Edward Kennedy, *b* 12 April 1956. *Address:* Harraton Square, Church Lane, Exning, near Newmarket, Suffolk.

KENNEDY, Horas Tristram, OBE 1966; HM Diplomatic Service, retired; *b* 29 May 1917; *s* of George Lawrence Kennedy and Mary Dow; *m* 1953, Maureen Beatrice Jeanne Holmes (formerly Stevens) (*d* 1976); three *d* (one *s* decd). *Educ:* Oundle; King's Coll., Cambridge. History and Mod Langs, MA. Entered HM Consular Service, 1939; Vice-Consul, Valparaiso, Chile, 1939-46; Foreign Office, 1946-48; 1st Secretary: Belgrade, 1949-52; Buenos Aires, 1952-56; Berne, 1956-61; Santiago de Chile, 1961-67; Commercial Counsellor, Warsaw, 1967-70; Consul-Gen., Barcelona, 1971-73. *Recreations:* country walking, landscape painting. *Address:* Borea Farm, Nancledra, Penzance, Cornwall. *T:* Penzance 2722.

KENNEDY, Ian McColl; Reader in English Law, and Director, Centre of Law, Medicine and Ethics, King's College, London, since 1978; *b* 14 Sept. 1941; *s* of Robert Charles Kennedy and Dorothy Elizabeth Kennedy; *m* 1980, Andrea, *d* of Frederick and Barbara Gage, Oceanside, Calif. *Educ:* King Edward VI Sch., Stourbridge; University Coll. London (1st Cl. Hons LLB); Univ. of Calif, Berkeley (LLM). Called to the Bar, Inner Temple, 1974. Fulbright Fellow, 1963-65; Lectr in Law, UCL, 1965-71; Ford Foundn Fellow, Yale Univ. and Univ. of Mexico, 1966-67; Vis. Prof., Univ. of Calif, LA, 1971-72; Lectr in Law, King's Coll., London, 1973-78; British Acad. Res. Fellow, 1978. Member: Editorial Bd, Jl of Medical Ethics, 1978-; Council, Open Section, RSM, 1978- (Vice-Pres., 1981-). Reith Lectr, 1980. *Publication:* The Unmasking of Medicine, 1981. *Address:* 5 Estelle Road, NW3. *T:* 01-485 6656.

KENNEDY, James Cowie; *b* 27 Dec. 1914; *e s* of Robert and Elizabeth Kennedy; *m* 1st, 1939, Eleanor Colman (*d* 1970); one *s* one *d* ; 2nd, 1972, Joan G. Cooper, Bristol. *Educ:* Bishops Stortford Coll.; Northern Polytechnic, London. Joined LCC, 1947; Chief Officer, GLC Parks Dept, 1970-79. Mem. Council, SPCK, 1980. *Recreations:* playing with children; enjoying food and drink; working for the Church. *Address:* 174 Clarence Gate Gardens, NW1 6AR.

KENNEDY, John Norman; Commissioner for Forest and Estate Management, Forestry Commission, since 1980; *b* 3 March 1927; *e s* of late James Domoné Kennedy, MBE, and late Margaret Henderson Lawrie; *m* 1953, Margaret Rose Johnston; one *s* one *d*. *Educ:* Hawick High Sch.; Edinburgh Univ. (BSc 1952). MIFor. Served RAF, 1945-48. Forestry Commission: Dist Officer, 1952; Asst Conservator, 1965; Conservator, N Wales, 1973; Dir, Forest Management Div., 1977. *Recreations:* gardening, photography, music. *Address:* 1 Marchfield Park, Edinburgh EH4 5BW.
See also Air Marshal Sir Thomas Kennedy.

KENNEDY, Prof. John (Stodart), FRS 1965; Deputy Chief Scientific Officer, Agricultural Research Council, 1967-77, and Professor of Animal Behaviour in the University of London, Imperial College at Silwood Park, Ascot, 1968-77, now Professor Emeritus and Senior Research Fellow; *b* 19 May 1912; *s* of James John Stodart Kennedy, MICE, and Edith Roberts Kennedy (*née* Lammers); *m* 1st, 1936, Dorothy Violet Bartholomew (divorced, 1946); one *s* ; 2nd, 1950, Claude Jacqueline Bloch (widow, *née* Raphäel); one step *s*, one *s* one *d*. *Educ:* Westminster Sch.; University Coll. London. BSc (London) 1933; DSc (London) 1956. Locust investigator for Imperial Inst. of Entomology, University of Birmingham, 1934-36, Anglo-Egyptian Sudan, 1936-37; MSc (London) 1936; London Sch. of Hygiene and Trop. Med., 1937-38; PhD (Birmingham) 1938; Rockefeller Malaria Res. Lab., Tirana, Albania, 1938-39; Wellcome Entomolog. Field Labs, Esher, Surrey, 1939-42; Res. Officer, Middle East Anti-Locust Unit, 1942-44; Chem. Defence Exptl Station, Porton, Wilts, 1944-45; ARC Unit of Insect Physiology, Cambridge, 1946-67. Pres. Royal Entomological Society, 1967-69 (Hon. Fellow, 1974). Fellow: University (now Wolfson) Coll., Cambridge, 1966; University Coll., London, 1967; Imperial Coll., London, 1982. *Publications:* numerous research papers and review articles on the biology of locusts, mosquitos, moths and greenfly, and insect behaviour generally. *Address:* 3 The Glade, Woodend Drive, South Ascot, Berks SL5 9BE. *T:* Ascot 20633.

KENNEDY, Ludovic Henry Coverley; writer and broadcaster; *b* Edinburgh, 3 Nov. 1919; *o s* of Captain E. C. Kennedy, RN (killed in action, 1939, while commanding HMS Rawalpindi against German battle-cruisers Scharnhorst and Gneisenau), and Rosalind, *d* of Sir Ludovic Grant, 11th Bt of Dalvey; *m* 1950, Moira Shearer King (*see* Shearer); one *s* three *d*. *Educ:* Eton; Christ Church, Oxford (MA). Served War, 1939-46: Midshipman, Sub-Lieut, Lieut, RNVR. Priv. Sec. and ADC to Gov. of Newfoundland, 1943-44. Librarian, Ashridge (Adult Education) Coll., 1949; Rockefeller Foundation Atlantic Award in Literature, 1950; Winner, Open Finals Contest, English Festival of Spoken Poetry, 1953; Editor, feature, First Reading (BBC Third Prog.), 1953-54; Lecturer for British Council, Sweden, Finland and Denmark, 1955; Belgium and Luxembourg, 1956; Mem. Council, Navy Records Soc., 1957-60. Contested (L) Rochdale, by-elec., 1958 and Gen. elec., 1959; Pres., Nat. League of Young Liberals, 1959-61; Mem., Lib. Party Council, 1965-67. Pres., Sir Walter Scott Club, Edinburgh, 1968-69. FRSA 1974-76. Columnist: Newsweek International, 1974-75; Sunday Standard, 1981-82. Chm., Royal Lyceum Theatre Co. of Edinburgh, 1977-. Cross, First Class, Order of Merit, Fed. Repub. of Germany, 1979. *TV and radio:* Introd. Profile, ATV, 1955-56; Newscaster, Independent Television News, 1956-58. Introducer of AR's feature On Stage, 1957; Introducer of AR's, This Week, 1958-59; Chm. BBC features: Your Verdict, 1962; Your Witness, 1967-70; Commentator: BBC's Panorama, 1960-63; Television Reporters Internat., 1963-64 (also Prod.).

Introducer, BBC's Time Out, 1964-65, World at One, 1965-66; Presenter: Lib. Party's Gen. Election Television Broadcasts, 1966; The Middle Years, ABC, 1967; The Nature of Prejudice, ATV, 1968; Face the Press, Tyne-Tees, 1968-69, 1970-72; Against the Tide, Yorkshire TV, 1969; Living and Growing, Grampian TV, 1969-70; 24 Hours, BBC, 1969-72; Ad Lib, BBC, 1970-72; Midweek, BBC, 1973-75; Newsday, BBC, 1975-76; Interviewer, Tonight, BBC, 1976-78; Presenter: A Life with Crime, BBC, 1979; Change of Direction, BBC, 1979; Lord Mountbatten Remembers, 1980; Did You See?, 1980-. *Films include:* The Sleeping Ballerina; The Singers and the Songs; Scapa Flow; Battleship Bismarck; Life and Death of the Scharnhorst; U-Boat War; Target Tirpitz; The Rise of the Red Navy; Lord Haw-Haw; Great Railway Journeys of the World. *Publications:* Sub-Lieutenant, 1942; Nelson's Band of Brothers, 1951; One Man's Meat, 1953; Murder Story (play, with essay on Capital Punishment), 1956; play: Murder Story (Cambridge Theatre), 1954; Ten Rillington Place, 1961; The Trial of Stephen Ward, 1964; Very Lovely People, 1969; Pursuit: the chase and sinking of the Bismarck, 1974; A Presumption of Innocence: the Amazing Case of Patrick Meehan, 1975; Menace: the life and death of the Tirpitz, 1979; The Portland Spy Case, 1979; Wicked Beyond Belief, 1980; (ed) A Book of Railway Journeys, 1980; (ed) A Book of Sea Journeys, 1981; (ed) A Book of Air Journeys, 1982; Gen. Editor, The British at War, 1973-77. *Address:* c/o A.D. Peters, 10 Buckingham Street, WC2. *Clubs:* Brooks's, Army and Navy, MCC; Puffins (Edinburgh).

KENNEDY, Michael; *see* Kennedy, G. M. S.

KENNEDY, Moira, (Mrs L. Kennedy); *see* Shearer, M.

KENNEDY, Nigel Paul; solo concert violinist; *b* 28 Dec. 1956; *s* of John Kennedy and Scylla Stoner; *m* 1980, Joanna Phillips. *Educ:* Yehudi Menuhin School; Juilliard School of Performing Arts, NY. ARCM. Début at Festival Hall with Philharmonia Orch., 1977; regular appearances with London and provincial orchestras, 1978-; Berlin début with Berlin Philharmonic, 1980; Henry Wood Promenade début, 1981; tour of Hong Kong and Australia, with Hallé Orch., 1981; foreign tours, 1978-: India, Japan, S Korea, Turkey, USA; many appearances as jazz violinist with Stephane Grappelli, incl. Edinburgh Fest., 1974 and Carnegie Hall, 1976; many TV and radio appearances, incl. Coming Along Nicely, BBC TV documentary on early life, 1973-78. *Recreations:* golf, football (watching and playing), cricket. *Address:* 26 College Crescent, NW3. *T:* 01-586 8666.

KENNEDY, Paul Joseph Morrow, QC 1973; a Recorder of the Crown Court, since 1972; *b* 12 June 1935; *o s* of Dr J. M. Kennedy, Sheffield; *m* 1965, Virginia, twin *d* of Baron Devlin, *qv* ; two *s* two *d*. *Educ:* Ampleforth Coll.; Gonville and Caius Coll., Cambridge (MA, LLB). Called to Bar, 1960. *Address:* Rydal, 11A Kent Road, Harrogate HG1 2LE. *T:* Harrogate 502704.

KENNEDY, Sir Ronald; *see* Kennedy, Sir G. R. D.

KENNEDY, Thomas Alexander; Visiting Fellow, Clare Hall, Cambridge, 1981-82; *b* 11 July 1920; *s* of late Rt Hon. Thomas Kennedy, PC, and Annie S. Kennedy (*née* Michie); *m* 1947, Audrey (*née* Plunkett); one *s* two *d*. *Educ:* Alleyn's Sch., Dulwich; Durham Univ. (BA). Economist: Bd of Trade, 1950-52; Colonial Office, 1952-55; Lecturer in Economics at Makerere Coll., Uganda, 1955-61; Economist: Treasury, Foreign Office, DEA, 1961-67; Economic Director, NEDO, 1967-70; Under-Sec.: DTI, 1970-74; Dept of Energy, 1974-80, resigned. Chief Tech. Adviser (Economist Planner), Min. of Petroleum and Mineral Resources, Bangladesh, 1980-81. *Address:* 31 Greys Close, Cavendish, Suffolk. *T:* Glemsford 280754.

KENNEDY, Air Marshal Sir Thomas (Lawrie), KCB 1980 (CB 1978); AFC 1953 and Bar 1960; C-in-C, RAF Germany, and Commander, Second Allied Tactical Air Force, since 1981; *b* 19 May 1928; *s* of James Domoné Kennedy and Margaret Henderson Lawrie; *m* 1959, Margaret Ann Parker; one *s* two *d*. *Educ:* Hawick High Sch. RAF Coll., Cranwell, 1946-49; commissioned, 1949. Sqdn service, 1949-53; exchange service, RAAF, 1953-55; returned to UK, 1955; 27 Sqdn (Canberra), 1955-57; Radar Research Estabt, 1957-60; RAF Coll. Selection Bd, 1960-62; RN Staff Coll., Greenwich, 1962; HQ Middle East, 1962-64; CO, No 99 (Britannia) Sqdn, 1965-67; HQ Air Support Comd, 1967-69; CO, RAF Brize Norton, 1970-71; Dep. Comdt, RAF Staff Coll., 1971-73; Dir of Ops (AS) MoD, 1973-75; Royal Coll. of Defence Studies, 1976; Comdr, Northern Maritime Air Region, 1977-79; Deputy C-in-C, RAF Strike Command, 1979-81. *Recreations:* golf, sailing. *Address:* HQ RAF Germany, BFPO 40. *Club:* Royal Air Force.
See also J. N. Kennedy.

KENNERLEY, Prof. (James) Anthony (Machell), CEng, MIMechE; Director, Strathclyde Business School, since 1973; *b* 24 Oct. 1933; *s* of William James Kennerley and Vida May (*née* Machell); *m* 1978, Dorothy Mary (*née* Simpson); one *s* one *d* (twins). *Educ:* Universities of Manchester (BSc) and London (MSc). AFIMA, AFRAeS. Engineer, A. V. Roe, Manchester, 1955-58; Aerodynamicist, Pratt & Whitney, Montreal, Canada, 1958-59; Jet Pilot, RCAF, 1959-62; Asst Professor of Mathematics, Univ. of New Brunswick, Canada, 1962-67; Director of Graduate Studies, Manchester Business Sch., 1967-69; Associate Professor of Business Studies, Columbia Univ., New York, 1969-70; Director, Executive Programme, London Business Sch., 1970-73.

Chairman: Management Res. Gp, Scotland, 1981-82; Scottish Milk Marketing Scheme Arbitration Panel, 1981-. Member: South of Scotland Electricity Bd, 1977-; Management Studies Bd, CNAA, 1977-; Arbitrator, ACAS, 1976-. Founder Mem., Bridgegate Trust, Glasgow. *Publications:* articles, papers on business studies and on applied mathematics. *Recreations:* flying, travelling. *Address:* Strathclyde Business School, 130 Rottenrow, Glasgow. *T:* 041-552 7141; 12 Yeomans Mews, Whittondene, Isleworth, Mddx. *T:* 01-898 0799. *Clubs:* Reform, Caledonian.

KENNET, 2nd Baron *cr* 1935; **Wayland Hilton Young;** author and politician; *b* 2 Aug. 1923; *s* of 1st Baron Kennet, PC, GBE, DSO, DSC, and of Kathleen (who *m* 1st, Captain Robert Falcon Scott, CVO, RN, and died 1947); *S* father 1960; *m* 1948, Elizabeth Ann, *d* of late Captain Bryan Fullerton Adams, DSO, RN; one *s* five *d. Educ:* Stowe; Trinity Coll., Cambridge; Perugia; Harvard. Served in RN, 1942-45. Foreign Office, 1946-47, and 1949-51. Deleg., Parliamentary Assemblies, WEU and Council of Europe, 1962-65; Parly Sec., Min. of Housing and Local Govt, 1966-70; Opposition Spokesman on Foreign Affairs and Science Policy, 1971-74; SDP Chief Whip in H of L, 1981-. Chairman: Adv. Cttee on Oil Pollution of the Sea, 1970-74; CPRE, 1971-72; Internat. Parly Confs on the Environment, 1972-78; Dir, Europe Plus Thirty, 1974-75; Mem., European Parlt, 1978-79. Mem., Redundant Churches Fund, 1978-81 (Mem., Cathedrals Adv. Cttee, 1978-81). Hon. FRIBA 1970. Editor of Disarmament and Arms Control, 1962-65. *Publications:* (as Wayland Young): The Italian Left, 1949; The Deadweight, 1952; Now or Never, 1953; Old London Churches (with Elizabeth Young), 1956; The Montesi Scandal, 1957; Still Alive Tomorrow, 1958; Strategy for Survival, 1959; The Profumo Affair, 1963; Eros Denied, 1965; Thirty-Four Articles, 1965; (as Wayland Kennet) Preservation, 1972; The Futures of Europe, 1976; (ed) Existing Mechanisms of Arms Control, 1965; Fabian pamphlets on defence, disarmament, environment, multinational companies, etc. *Heir: s* Hon. William Aldus Thoby Young, *b* 24 May 1957. *Address:* 100 Bayswater Road, W2.

KENNEY, Prof. Edward John, FBA 1968; Kennedy Professor of Latin, University of Cambridge, 1974-82; Fellow of Peterhouse, Cambridge, since 1953; *b* 29 Feb. 1924; *s* of George Kenney and Emmie Carlina Elfrida Schwenke; *m* 1955, Gwyneth Anne, *d* of late Henry Albert Harris. *Educ:* Christ's Hospital; Trinity Coll., Cambridge. BA 1949, MA 1953. Served War of 1939-45: Royal Signals, UK and India, 1943-46; commissioned 1944, Lieut 1945. Porson Schol., 1948; Craven Schol., 1949; Craven Student, 1949; Chancellor's Medallist, 1950. Asst Lectr, Univ. of Leeds, 1951-52; University of Cambridge: Research Fellow, Trinity Coll., 1952-53; Asst Lectr, 1955-60, Lectr, 1966-70; Reader in Latin Literature and Textual Criticism, 1970-74; Peterhouse: Director of Studies in Classics, 1953-74; Librarian, 1953-82; Tutor, 1956-62; Senior Tutor, 1962-65. Jt Editor, Classical Quarterly, 1959-65. James C. Loeb Fellow in Classical Philology, Harvard Univ., 1967-68; Sather Prof. of Classical Literature, Univ. of California, Berkeley, 1968; Carl Newell Jackson Lectr, Harvard Univ., 1980. President: Jt Assoc. of Classical Teachers, 1977-79; Classical Assoc., 1982-83. For. Mem., Royal Netherlands Acad. of Arts and Scis, 1976. *Publications:* P. Ouidi Nasonis Amores etc (ed), 1961; (with Mrs P. E. Easterling) Ovidiana Graeca (ed), 1965; (with W. V. Clausen, F. R. D. Goodyear, J. A. Richmond) Appendix Vergiliana (ed), 1966; Lucretius, De Rerum Natura III (ed), 1971; The Classical Text, 1974; (with W. V. Clausen) Latin Literature (ed and contrib.) (Cambridge History of Classical Literature II), 1982; articles and reviews in classical jls. *Recreations:* cats and books. *Address:* Peterhouse, Cambridge CB2 1RD. *T:* Cambridge 350256.

KENNEY, Reginald; Principal, Harper Adams Agricultural College, 1962-77; *b* 24 Aug. 1912; *m* 1946, Sheila Fay De Sa; two *d. Educ:* King Edward VII School, Lytham St Anne's; Leeds Univ.; West of Scotland Agric. Coll. Warden and Lectr, Staffordshire Farm Inst. (now Staffordshire Coll. of Agriculture), 1937-38; Asst County Agric. Educn Officer, Beds CC, 1938-42 (seconded Beds WAEC, 1939-42); Lectr in Farm Management and Animal Husbandry, University of Reading, 1942-48; Principal, Dorset Farm Inst. (now Dorset Coll. of Agriculture), 1948-62. Hon. FRAgS. *Publication:* Dairy Husbandry, 1957. *Recreations:* travel, mountains. *Address:* Ashridge, Ragleth Road, Church Stretton, Shropshire. *T:* Church Stretton 723138. *Club:* Farmers'.

KENNEY, (William) John; United States lawyer; Partner, Squire, Sanders & Dempsey; *b* Oklahoma, 16 June 1904; *s* of Franklin R. Kenney and Nelle Kenney (*née* Torrence); *m* 1931, Elinor Craig; two *s* two *d. Educ:* Lawrenceville Sch., New Jersey; Stanford Univ (AB); Harvard Law Sch. (LLB). Practised law in San Francisco, 1929-36; Head of oil and gas unit, Securities and Exchange Commission, 1936-38; practised law in Los Angeles, 1938-41; Special Asst to Under-Sec. of the Navy; Chm. Navy Price Adjustment Board, General Counsel, 1941-46; Asst Sec. of the Navy, 1946-47; Under-Sec. of the Navy, 1947-49; Minister in charge of Economic Cooperation Administration Mission to the UK, 1949-50; Deputy Dir for Mutual Security, resigned 1952. Chairman: Democratic Central Cttee of DC, 1960-64; DC Chapter, American Red Cross, 1968-71. Director: Riggs National Bank, 1959-81; Merchants Fund Inc.; Porter International; Trustee, George C. Marshall Foundn, Lexington, Va. *Address:* 2700 Calvert Street, NW, Washington, DC 20008; (office) 1201 Pennsylvania Avenue, NW, Washington, DC 20004, USA. *Clubs:* California (Los Angeles); Alibi, Metropolitan, Chevy Chase (Washington).

KENNON, Vice-Adm. James Edward Campbell, CBE 1974 (OBE 1962); Chief of Fleet Support, since 1981; *b* 26 Nov. 1925; *s* of late Robert Kennon, MC, FRCS, and Ethel Kennon, OBE; *m* 1950, Anne, *e d* of Captain Sir Stuart Paton, RN retd, *qv*; two *s* one *d. Educ:* Stowe School. Special entry to RN, 1943; Military Assistant to CDS, 1959-62; Supply Officer, HMS Kent, 1963-65; Secretary: to VCNS, 1965-67; to C-in-C Fleet, 1968-70; Admiralty Interview Bd, 1970; Sec. to First Sea Lord, 1971-74; NATO Defence Coll., 1974; Captain, HMS Pembroke, 1974-76; Dir, Naval Administrative Planning, 1976-78; Asst Chief of Naval Staff (Policy), 1978-79; Chief Naval Supply Officer, 1979-81, and Port Adm., Rosyth, 1980-81. *Recreations:* walking, languages, photography. *Address:* 43 Tonsley Hill, SW18. *Club:* Army and Navy.

KENNY, Dr Anthony John Patrick, FRSE 1979; FBA 1974; Master of Balliol College, Oxford, since 1978 (Fellow, 1964-78; Senior Tutor, 1971-72 and 1976-78); *b* Liverpool, 16 March 1931; *s* of John Kenny and Margaret Jones; *m* 1966, Nancy Caroline, *d* of Henry T. Gayley, Jr, Swarthmore, Pa; two *s. Educ:* Gregorian Univ., Rome (STL); St Benet's Hall, Oxford; DPhil 1961, DLitt 1980. Ordained priest, Rome, 1955; Curate in Liverpool, 1959-63; returned to lay state, 1963. Asst Lectr, Univ. of Liverpool, 1961-63; Lectr in Philosophy, Exeter and Trinity Colls, Oxford, 1963-64; Lectr, Oxford, 1965-78. Wilde Lectr in Natural and Comparative Religion, Oxford, 1969-72; jt Gifford Lectr, Univ. of Edinburgh, 1972-73; Speaker's Lectureship in Biblical Studies, Univ. of Oxford, 1980-; Stanton Lectr, Univ. of Cambridge, 1980-. Visiting Professor: Univs of Chicago, Washington, Michigan, and Cornell, Stanford and Rockefeller Univs. Editor, The Oxford Magazine, 1972-73. *Publications:* Action, Emotion and Will, 1963; Responsa Alumnorum of English College, Rome, 2 vols, 1963; Descartes, 1968; The Five Ways, 1969; Wittgenstein, 1973; The Anatomy of the Soul, 1974; Will, Freedom and Power, 1975; The Aristotelian Ethics, 1978; Freewill and Responsibility, 1978; Aristotle's Theory of the Will, 1979; The God of the Philosophers, 1979; Aquinas, 1980. *Address:* Balliol College, Oxford. *T:* Oxford 48766. *Clubs:* Athenæum, United Oxford & Cambridge University.

KENNY, Anthony Marriott; a Recorder of the Crown Court, since 1980; *b* 24 May 1939; *o s* of late Noel Edgar Edward Marriott Kenny, OBE, and Cynthia Margaret Seton Kenny (*née* Melville); *m* 1969, Monica Grant Mackenzie, *yr d* of H. B. Grant Mackenzie, Pretoria; two *s. Educ:* St Andrew's Coll., Grahamstown, Cape Province; Christ's Coll., Cambridge (MA). Called to the Bar, Gray's Inn, 1963; South Eastern Circuit. *Recreations:* music, reading, golf. *Address:* Melbury Place, Wentworth, Surrey GU25 4LB; 12 King's Bench Walk, Temple, EC4. *T:* 01-583 0811.

KENNY, Arthur William, CBE 1977; CChem, FRSC; Director in the Directorate General of Environmental Protection of the Department of the Environment, 1974-79; *b* 31 May 1918; *s* of Ernest James Kenny and Gladys Margaret Kenny; *m* 1947, Olive Edna West; one *s. Educ:* Canton High Sch., Cardiff; Jesus Coll., Oxford (schol.). BA (1st Cl. Hons Natural Sci.), MA, BSc, Oxon. Min. of Supply, 1941; Min. of Health, 1950; Min. of Housing and Local Govt, 1951; DoE, 1971. *Publications:* papers on disposal of radioactive and toxic wastes and on quality of drinking water. *Address:* 134 Manor Green Road, Epsom, Surrey KT19 8LL. *T:* Epsom 24850.

KENNY, Maj.-Gen. Brian Leslie Graham, CBE 1979; Commander 1st Armoured Division, since 1982; *b* 18 June 1934; *s* of late Brig. James Wolfenden Kenny, CBE, and of Aileen Anne Georgina Kenny (*née* Swan); *m* 1958, Diana Catherine Jane Mathew; two *s. Educ:* Canford School. Commissioned into 4th Hussars (later Queen's Royal Irish Hussars), 1954; served BAOR, Aden, Malaya and Borneo; Pilot's course, 1961; Comd 16 Recce Flt QRIH; psc 1965; MA/VCGS, MoD, 1966-68; Instructor, Staff Coll., 1971-73; CO QRIH, BAOR and UN Cyprus, 1974-76; Col GS 4 Armd Div., 1977-78; Comd 12 Armd Bde (Task Force D), 1979-80; RCDS 1981. *Recreations:* skiing, cricket, shooting, racing, moving house. *Address:* c/o Lloyds Bank plc, Camberley, Surrey. *Clubs:* MCC, I Zingari, Free Foresters.

KENNY, David John; Regional Administrator, North West Thames Regional Health Authority, since 1982; *b* 2 Dec. 1940; *s* of late Gerald Henry Kenny and Ellen Veronica (*née* Crosse); *m* 1964, Elisabeth Ann, *d* of late Robert and of Jean Ferris; three *s. Educ:* Royal Belfast Academical Instn; Queen's Univ., Belfast (LLB). AHA. Dep. House Governor, Bd of Governors, London Hosp., 1972; Dist Administrator, Tower Hamlets Health Dist, 1974; Area Administrator, Kensington, Chelsea and Westminster AHA, 1978. Mem. Nat. Council, Inst. of Health Service Administrators, 1975- (Pres. 1981-82); Chm., Data Protection Working Gp, Internat. Med. Informatics Assoc., 1979-. *Publications:* (jtly) Data Protection in Health Information Systems, 1980; articles on management topics and data protection. *Recreations:* theatre, athletics, Rugby football. *Address:* 131 Maze Hill, SE3 7UB. *T:* 01-858 1545.

KENNY, Douglas Timothy, MA, PhD; President of the University of British Columbia, since 1975; Professor of Psychology, since 1965; *b* Victoria, BC, 1923; *m* ; one *s* one *c. Educ:* Univ. of British Columbia (BA 1945, MA 1947); Univ. of Washington (PhD). Dept of Psychology, Univ. of British Columbia, 1950, Head of Dept 1965-69; Dean of Faculty of Arts, 1970-75 (Acting Dean, 1969-70). Pres., Faculty Assoc., 1962. Pres., BC Psychological Assoc., 1961. Member: Canada Council, 1975-78; Bd of Trustees, Vancouver Gen. Hosp.,

1976-78; Social Scis and Humanities Res. Council, 1978-. *Publications:* articles in Canadian and US jls. *Address:* University of British Columbia, Vancouver, BC V6T 1W5, Canada.

KENNY, Michael, ARA 1976; Sculptor and Lecturer at University of London, Goldsmiths' College and Slade School of Fine Art; *b* 10 June 1941; *s* of James Kenny and Helen (*née* Gordon); *m* ; one *s* one *d* and one step *d* ; *m* Angela Kenny (*née* Smith); two step *s* one step *d. Educ:* St Francis Xavier's Coll., Liverpool; Liverpool Coll. of Art; Slade Sch. of Fine Art (DFA London). Works in public collections of: Tate Gallery; Arts Council of GB; London Borough of Camden; pub. collections in W Germany, etc, and private collections in England, Europe and America. Exhibited extensively in Gt Britain, Europe, S America, Canada and Australia. Chairman, Faculty of Sculpture, British School at Rome, 1982-. *Relevant publications:* Contemporary Artists, 1977; Contemporary British Artists, 1979. *Recreation:* ornithology. *Address:* c/o Juda Rowan Gallery Ltd, Tottenham Mews, W1. *Club:* Chelsea Arts.

KENNY, Sir Patrick (John), Kt 1976; FRCS, FRACS; Consultant Emeritus Surgeon, St Vincent's Hospital and Lewisham Hospital, Sydney; *b* 12 Jan. 1914; *s* of Patrick John Kenny and Agnes Margaret Carberry; *m* 1942, Beatrice Ella Hammond; two *s. Educ:* Marcellin Coll., Sydney; Sydney Univ. (MB, BS 1936, MS 1946). FRCS 1940; FRACS 1944. War Service, AIF, UK, ME and SWPA, 1940-46. Hon. Surgeon: St Vincent's Hosp., 1946-79; Lewisham Hosp., Sydney, 1946-76. Anderson Stuart Memorial Res. Fellow, Sydney Univ., 1938, Lectr in Surg. Anat., 1949-55. Royal Australasian Coll. of Surgeons: Councillor, 1959; Vice Pres., 1967-69; Pres., 1969-71; Mem., Ct of Honour, 1979-. Pres., NSW Med. Bd, 1974-79. FRCPS(Hon.) 1970. *Publications:* surgical treatises. *Recreation:* gardening. *Address:* 13 David Street, Mosman, Sydney, NSW 2088, Australia. *T:* 960-2820. *Club:* Australian.

KENSINGTON, 8th Baron *cr* 1776 (Ire.); **Hugh Ivor Edwardes;** Baron Kensington (UK) 1886; *b* 24 Nov. 1933; *s* of Hon. Hugh Owen Edwardes (*d* 1937) (2nd *s* of 6th Baron) and of Angela Dorothea (who *m* 1951, Lt Comdr John Hamilton, RN retd), *d* of late Lt-Col Eustace Shearman, 10th Hussars; *S* uncle, 1981; *m* 1961, Juliet Elizabeth Massy Anderson; two *s* one *d. Educ:* Eton. *Heir: s* Hon. William Owen Alexander Edwardes, *b* 21 July 1964. *Address:* Ringwood Farm, PO Box 114, Hillcrest, Natal, 3650, S Africa. *T:* (031) 752763. *Clubs:* Boodle's; Durban (Durban).

KENSINGTON, Area Bishop of, since 1981; **Rt. Rev. Mark Santer,** MA; *b* 29 Dec. 1936; *s* of late Rev. Canon Eric Arthur Robert Santer and Phyllis Clare Barlow; *m* 1964, Henriette Cornelia Weststrate; one *s* two *d. Educ:* Marlborough Coll.; Queens' Coll., Cambridge; Westcott House, Cambridge. Deacon, 1963; priest 1964; Asst Curate, Cuddesdon, 1963-67; Tutor, Cuddesdon Theological Coll., 1963-67; Fellow and Dean of Clare Coll., Cambridge, 1967-72 (and Tutor, 1968-72); Univ. Asst Lectr in Divinity, 1968-72; Principal of Westcott House, Cambridge, 1973-81; Hon. Canon of Winchester Cathedral, 1978-81. *Publications:* (contrib.) The Phenomenon of Christian Belief, 1970; (with M. F. Wiles) Documents in Early Christian Thought, 1975; articles in: Jl of Theological Studies; New Testament Studies; Theology. *Address:* 19 Campden Hill Square, W8 7JY. *T:* 01-727 9818.

KENSWOOD, 2nd Baron, *cr* 1951; **John Michael Howard Whitfield;** *b* 6 April 1930; *o s* of 1st Baron Kenswood; *S* father, 1963; *m* 1951, Deirdre Anna Louise, *d* of Colin Malcolm Methven, Errol, Perthshire; four *s* one *d. Educ:* Trinity Coll. Sch., Ontario; Harrow; Grenoble Univ.; Emmanuel Coll., Cambridge (BA). *Heir: s* Hon. Michael Christopher Whitfield, *b* 3 July 1955. *Address:* Domaine de la Forêt, 31340 Villemur sur Tarn, France. *T:* (61) 09 22 90.

KENT, Arthur William, CMG 1966; OBE 1950; Chairman, United Transport Overseas Ltd, 1980-82 (Deputy Chairman, 1978-80, Joint Managing Director, 1977-80); Managing Director, United Transport Co., 1980-82; *b* 22 March 1913; *s* of Howard and Eliza Kent; *m* 1st, 1944, Doris Jane (*née* Crowe; marr. diss., 1958); one *s* one *d* ; 2nd, 1958, Mary (*née* Martin). Deputy City Treasurer, Nairobi, 1946-48, City Treasurer, 1948-65. Chief Executive: United Transport Overseas Ltd, Nairobi, 1966-69; Transport Holdings of Zambia Ltd, 1969-71; Chief Exec., United Transport Holdings (Pty) Ltd, Johannesburg, 1971-76; Dir of a number of cos owned by United Transport Overseas Ltd and other BET cos. IPFA; FCA; FCIT. *Address:* (home) Muthaiga, Beechwood Road, Combe Down, Bath, Avon. *Clubs:* East India, Naval and Military; Rand (Johannesburg).

KENT, Very Rev. Mgr. Bruce; General Secretary, Campaign for Nuclear Disarmament, since 1980; *b* 22 June 1929; *s* of Kenneth Kent and Rosemary Kent (*née* Marion). *Educ:* Lower Canada Coll., Montreal; Stonyhurst Coll.; Brasenose Coll., Univ. of Oxford. LLB. Ordination, Westminster, 1958; Curate, Kensington, North and South, 1958-63; Sec., Archbishop's House, Westminster, 1963-64; Chm., Diocesan Schools Commn, 1964-66; Catholic Chaplain to Univ. of London, 1966-74; Chaplain, Pax Christi, 1974-77; Parish Priest, Somers Town, NW1, 1977-80. *Publications:* essays and pamphlets on disarmament, Christians and peace. *Recreations:* friends, hill walking. *Address:* c/o Campaign for Nuclear Disarmament, 11 Goodwin Street, N4. *T:* 01-263 0977.

KENT, Rear-Adm. Derrick George, CB 1971; retired 1971; *b* May 1920; *s* of Eric William Kent and Doris Elizabeth Osborn; *m* 1943, Estelle Clare Firkins; two *d. Educ:* St Lawrence College, Ramsgate. Joined RN 1938; Midshipman, HMS Cumberland, 1939-40; Submarine Service, 1940; Comdr, HM Submarine Spark, in Far East, 1943-45; Captain, 1960; Commanded: HMS Diana, 1963; HMS Plymouth; 22nd Escort Squadron, Far East, 1963-64; Imperial Defence Coll., 1965; Captain (SM), Third Submarine Sqdn, HMS Maidstone, 1966-67; Comdr, Clyde Submarine Base, and HMS Neptune, 1967-68; Commodore, 1968; Comdr, Clyde, and Supt Clyde Submarine Base, 1968-69; Rear-Adm., 1969; Flag Officer, Malta, and NATO Commander, SE Mediterranean, 1969-71. *Address:* 73 Exeter House, Putney Heath, SW15.

KENT, Dorothy Miriam; Under-Secretary, Department of Employment, 1973-80; *d* of Donald Roy Thom, CBE, and Elsie Miriam Thom (*née* Rundell); *m* 1948, Eric Nelson Kent; one *s* two *d. Educ:* North London Collegiate Sch.; Somerville Coll., Oxford (Scholar). MA Hons History. Temp. wartime civil service posts, 1941-46; entered Min. of Labour, 1946; Principal, 1950; Asst Sec., 1964; Under-Sec., 1973; retired, 1980. *Address:* 45 Lytton Grove, SW15 2HD. *T:* 01-788 0214.

KENT, Geoffrey Charles; Director, since 1975, Chairman and Chief Executive, since 1981, Imperial Group plc; *b* 2 Feb. 1922; *s* of late Percy Whitehead and Madge Kent; *m* 1955, Brenda Georgine Conisbee. *Educ:* Blackpool Grammar Sch. CBIM 1976; FInstM 1977. Served RAF, 1939-46; Flt Lieut Coastal Comd. Advertising and marketing appts with Colman, Prentis & Varley, Mentor, and Johnson & Johnson, 1947-58; John Player & Son: Advertising Manager, 1958; Marketing Dir, 1964; Asst Man. Dir, 1969; Chm. and Man. Dir, 1975; Chm. and Chief Exec., Courage Ltd, 1978-81. Director: Team Lotus Internat., 1974-; Lloyds Bank Ltd, 1978-; Lloyds Bank Property Co. Ltd, 1980-81; Brewers' Soc., 1978-. *Recreations:* flying, ski-ing. *Address:* Hill House, Gonalston, Nottingham NG14 7JA. *Club:* Army and Navy.

KENT, Sir Harold Simcox, GCB 1963 (KCB 1954; CB 1946); QC 1973; Commissary to Dean and Chapter of St Paul's Cathedral, since 1976; *b* 11 Nov. 1903; *s* of late P. H. B. Kent, OBE, MC; *m* 1930, Zillah Lloyd; one *s* (one *d* decd). *Educ:* Rugby School; Merton Coll., Oxford. Barrister-at-law, 1928; Parliamentary Counsel to the Treasury, 1940-53; HM Procurator-General and Treasury Solicitor, 1953-63; Standing Counsel to Church Assembly and General Synod, 1964-72; Vicar-General of the Province of Canterbury, 1971-76; Dean of the Arches Court of Canterbury and Auditor of the Chancery Court of York, 1972-76. Mem., Departmental Cttee to examine operation of Section 2 of Official Secrets Act, 1911-72. DCL Lambeth, 1977. *Publication:* In On the Act, 1979. *Address:* Alderley, Calf Lane, Chipping Campden, Glos. *T:* Evesham 840421. *Club:* United Oxford & Cambridge University.

KENT, Paul Welberry, DSc; FRSC; JP; Student Emeritus of Christ Church, Oxford; *b* Doncaster, 19 April 1923; *s* of Thomas William Kent and Marion (*née* Cox); *m* 1952, Rosemary Elizabeth Boutflower, *y d* of Major C. H. B. Shepherd, RE; three *s* one *d. Educ:* Doncaster Grammar Sch.; Birmingham Univ.; Jesus Coll., Oxford. BSc 1944, PhD 1947, Birmingham; MA 1952, DPhil 1953, DSc 1966, Oxon. Asst Lectr, subseq. ICI Fellow, Birmingham Univ., 1946-50; Vis. Fellow, Princeton Univ., 1948-49; Univ. Demonstrator in Biochem., Oxford, 1950-72; Lectr, subseq. Student, Tutor and Dr Lees Reader in Chem., Christ Church, 1955-72; Master of Van Mildert Coll. and Dir, Glycoprotein Res. Unit, Durham Univ., 1972-82. Research Assoc., Harvard, 1967; Vis. Prof., Windsor Univ., Ont, 1971, 1980. Mem., Oxford City Council, 1964-72; Governor, Oxford Coll. of Technology, subseq. Oxford Polytechnic, 1964-72, Vice-Chm. 1966-69, Chm. 1969-70; Member: Cttee, Biochemical Soc., 1963-67; Chemical Council, 1965-70; Res. Adv. Cttee, Cystic Fibrosis Res. Trust, 1977-; Commn on Religious Educn in School. Sec., Foster and Wills Scholarships Bd, 1960-72; Pres., Soc. for Maintenance of the Faith, 1975-. JP Oxford, 1972. Hon. DLitt Drury Coll., 1972. Hon. Fellow, Canterbury Coll., Ont, 1976. Rolleston Prize, 1952; Medal of Société de Chemie Biologique, 1969; Verdienstkreuz (Bundesrepublik), 1970. *Publications:* Biochemistry of Amino-sugars, 1955; (ed) Membrane-Mediation Information, Vols I and II, 1972; (ed) International Aspects of the Provision of Medical Care, 1976; (ed) New Approaches to Genetics, 1978; (ed) Resources, Environment and the Future, 1982; articles in sci. and other jls. *Recreations:* music, travel. *Address:* 18 Arnolds Way, Cumnor Hill, Oxford OX2 9JB. *T:* Oxford 862087; Briscoe Gate, Cotherstone, Barnard Castle, Co. Durham. *Club:* Athenæum.

KENT, Sir Percy Edward, (Sir Peter Kent), Kt 1973; DSc, PhD; FRS 1966; FGS; consultant geologist; Member, Natural Environment Research Council, 1973-80 (Chairman, 1973-77); Director, London and Scottish Marine Oil, since 1977; *b* 18 March 1913; *s* of Edward Louis Kent and Annie Kate (*née* Woodward); *m* 1940, Margaret Betty Hood, JP (*d* 1974); two *d* ; *m* 1976, Lorna Ogilvie Scott, BA. *Educ:* West Bridgford Gram. Sch.; Nottingham Univ. 1st cl. hons BSc London 1934; PhD 1941; DSc 1959. RAFVR, 1941-46 (despatches, 1944). Legion of Merit (USA), 1946. Geologist to E African Archæological Expedn (L. S. B. Leakey), 1934-35. Joined Anglo Iranian Oil (later BP), 1936; responsible for geological survey work in UK, Iran, E Africa, Papua, Canada and Alaska, for BP, 1946-60; managerial duties in BP, 1960-65; Chief Geologist, BP Co. Ltd, 1966-71, Exploration Manager, 1971-73. Pres. Yorks Geol Soc., 1964-66; Chm., Petroleum Exploration Soc. of Great Britain, 1966-68; Member: Council, Royal Soc., 1968-70; Council for Science

Policy, 1968-72; Adv. Bd for Res. Councils, 1972-77; Pres., Geological Soc., 1974-76. Adrian Vis. Fellow, Univ. of Leicester, 1967-70. Hon. DSc: Leicester, 1972; Durham, 1974; Bristol, 1977; Hull, 1981; Hon. LLD: Glasgow, 1977; Aberdeen, 1978; Hon. ScD Cambridge, 1979. Murchison Medal, Geological Soc. of London, 1969; (jt) MacRobert Award, 1970; Royal Medal, Royal Soc., 1971; Sorby Medal, Yorkshire Geol. Soc., 1973. *Publications:* British Regional Geology, Eastern England, 1980; Minerals from the Marine Environment, 1980; many papers on stratigraphy and structural geology, Britain and abroad. *Recreations:* walking, gardening, landscape painting, choral singing. *Address:* 38 Rodney Road, West Bridgford, Nottingham. *T:* Nottingham 23-13-55. *Club:* Geological Society Club.

KENT, Ronald Clive, CB 1965; Consultant and Council Secretary, Institution of Civil Engineers, since 1980 (Director (Administration), 1976-79); *b* 3 Aug. 1916; *s* of Dr Hugh Braund Kent and Margaret Mary Kent; *m* 1965, Mary Moyles Havell; one step-*s* one step-*d. Educ:* Rugby Sch.; Brasenose Coll., Oxford. Air Ministry, 1939; Royal Artillery, 1940-45; Air Ministry, 1945-58; Asst Under-Sec. of State, Air Min., 1958-63, MoD, 1963-67; Dep. Under-Sec. of State, MoD, 1967-76. *Address:* Seafields, 106 Littlestone Road, Littlestone-on-Sea, New Romney, Kent TN28 8NH.

KENT, Brig. Sidney Harcourt, OBE 1944; *b* 22 April 1915; *s* of Major Geoffrey Harcourt Kent, Hindhead; *m* 1945, Nina Ruth, *d* of Gen. Sir Geoffry Scoones, KCB, KBE, CSI, DSO, MC; one *s* one *d. Educ:* Wellington Coll.; RMC Sandhurst. 2nd Lieut KOYLI, 1935; Lt-Col 1944; Brig. 1944; GSO1 Eighth Army, 1944; BGS Allied Land Forces, SE Asia, 1944. Comd 128 Inf. Bde (TA), 1960-63. Manager and Sec., Turf Board, 1965; Gen. Manager, 1969, Chief Executive, 1973-76, The Jockey Club. Racing Adviser, Royal Horse Soc., Iran, 1978. *Recreations:* farming, travel. *Address:* The Old Vicarage, Kingsey, Aylesbury, Bucks. *T:* Haddenham 291411.

KENT, Thomas George, CBE 1979; CEng, MIMechE, MRAeS; Group Deputy Chief Executive, British Aerospace Dynamics Group, since 1980; Board Member, British Aerospace, since 1981; *b* 13 Aug. 1925. *Educ:* Borden Grammar School; Medway College of Technology. Joined English Electric Co., 1951; Special Director, British Aircraft Corp., 1967; Dep. Managing Director, 1974. Director, Hatfield/Lostock Division and Stevenage/Bristol Div. of Dynamics Group, British Aerospace, 1977-79. *Address:* Mereworth, 5 Deards Wood, Knebworth, Herts. *T:* Stevenage 812057; British Aerospace, Dynamics Group, Stevenage, Herts. *T:* Stevenage 2422.

KENTNER, Louis Philip, CBE 1978; Concert Pianist and Composer; *b* Silesia, 19 July 1905; *s* of Julius and Gisela Kentner; *m* 1931, Ilona Kabos (marr. diss. 1945); *m* 1946, Griselda Gould, *d* of late Evelyn Suart; no *c. Educ:* Budapest, Royal Academy of Music (at age of 6) under Arnold Szekely, Leo Weiner, Zoltan Kodaly. Concert début Budapest at age of 15; awarded a Chopin prize, Warsaw, a Liszt prize, Budapest. Has given concerts in most European countries; toured South Africa, Far East, New Zealand, Australia, S America; 6 tours of USA; three tours of USSR. First world performance, Bartok 2nd Piano Concerto, Budapest, and first European performance, Bartok 3rd Piano Concerto, London, 1946; many first performances of Kodaly and Weiner's Piano works. Came to England, 1935; naturalised British, 1946; since residence in England played much modern British music. Played numerous troop concerts during the War of 1939-45. Has made many gramophone recordings. President: Liszt Society, 1965-; European Piano Teachers Assoc., 1978-. Hon. RAM 1970. *Publications:* Three Sonatinas for Piano, 1939; two essays in Liszt Symposium, 1967; The Piano, 1976. *Recreations:* reading, chess playing. *Address:* 1 Mallord Street, Chelsea, SW3.

KENWARD, Michael; Editor, New Scientist, since 1979; *b* 12 July 1945; *s* of Ronald Kenward and Phyllis Kenward; *m* 1969, Elizabeth Rice. *Educ:* Wolverstone Hall; Sussex Univ. Res. scientist, UKAEA, Culham Laboratory, 1966-68; Technical editor, Scientific Instrument Res. Assoc., 1969; various editorial posts, New Scientist, 1969-79. *Publications:* Potential Energy, 1976; articles on science and technology and energy in particular. *Recreations:* photography, collecting 'middle-aged' books. *Address:* Grange Cottage, Staplefield, W Sussex.

KENWORTHY, family name of **Baron Strabolgi.**

KENWORTHY, Cecil; Registrar of Family Division (formerly Probate and Divorce Division), of High Court of Justice, since 1968; *b* 22 Jan. 1918; *s* of John T. and Lucy Kenworthy; *m* 1944, Beryl Joan Willis; no *c. Educ:* Manchester and Bristol Grammar Schools. Entered Principal Probate Registry, 1936. *Publications:* (co-editor) supplements to Rayden on Divorce, 1967, 1968; (co-editor) Tolstoy on Divorce, 7th edn, 1971. *Address:* 526 Ben Jonson House, Barbican, EC2.

KENWORTHY, Joan Margaret, BLitt, MA; Principal, St Mary's College, University of Durham, since 1977; *b* Oldham, Lancs, 10 Dec. 1933; *o d* of Albert Kenworthy and late Amy (*née* Cobbold). *Educ:* Girls Grammar Sch., Barrow-in-Furness; St Hilda's Coll., Oxford (BLitt, MA). Henry Oliver Beckit Prize, Oxford, 1955; Leverhulme Overseas Res. Scholar, Makerere Coll., Uganda, and E African Agriculture and Forestry Res. Org., Kenya, 1956-58; Actg Tutor, St Hugh's Coll., Oxford, 1958-59; Tutorial Res. Fellow, Bedford Coll., London, 1959-60; Univ. of Liverpool: Asst Lectr in Geography, 1960-63; Lectr, 1963-73; Sen. Lectr, 1973-77; Warden of

Salisbury Hall, 1966-77 and of Morton House, 1974-77. IUC short-term Vis. Lectr, Univ. of Sierra Leone, 1975. Member: Council, African Studies Assoc. of UK, 1969-71; Council, Inst. of Brit. Geographers, 1976-78; Cttee, Merseyside Conf. for Overseas Students Ltd, 1976-77; Council, RMetS, 1980-83; Treasurer, Assoc. of Brit. Climatologists, 1976-79; Northern Chm., Durham Univ. Soc., 1979-82. *Publications:* (contrib.) Geographers and the Tropics, ed R. W. Steel and R. M. Prothero, 1964; (contrib.) Oxford Regional Economic Atlas for Africa, 1965; (contrib.) Studies in East African Geography and Development, ed S. Ominde, 1971; (contrib.) An Advanced Geography of Africa, ed J. I. Clarke, 1975; (contrib.) Rangeland Management and Ecology in East Africa, ed D. J. Pratt and M. D. Gwynne, 1977; articles in jls and encycs. *Address:* 1 Elvet Garth, South Road, Durham DH1 3TP. *T:* Durham 43865. *Club:* Royal Commonwealth Society.

KENWORTHY-BROWNE, (Bernard) Peter (Francis); Registrar of the High Court (Family Division), since 1982; *b* 11 May 1930; *s* of late Bernard Edelyn Kenworthy-Browne and of Margaret Sibylla Kenworthy-Browne; *m* 1975, Jane Elizabeth Arthur. *Educ:* Ampleforth; Oriel Coll., Oxford. MA. Called to the Bar, Lincoln's Inn, 1955; Oxford Circuit, 1957-; a Recorder of the Crown Court, 1981-82. *Recreations:* music, hunting, shooting. *Address:* 45 Oakley Road, N1. *T:* 01-226 6184; (chambers) Goldsmith Building, Temple, EC4. *T:* 01-353 7881.

KENYA, Archbishop of, since 1980; **Most Rev. Manasses Kuria;** Bishop of Nairobi, since 1980; *b* 22 July 1927; *s* of John Njoroge Kuria; *m* 1947, Mary Kuria; two *s* four *d. Educ:* locally. Teaching, 1944-53; Deacon, 1955; ordained Priest, 1957; Archdeacon of Eldoret, 1965-70; Asst Bishop of Nakuru, 1970-75; Bishop of Naburn, 1976-79. *Publication:* Uwakili Katika Kristo (Stewardship of Christ), 1969. *Address:* PO Box 40502, Nairobi, Kenya. *T:* 721838/723394/28146.

KENYON, family name of **Baron Kenyon.**

KENYON, 5th Baron, *cr* 1788; **Lloyd Tyrell-Kenyon,** CBE 1972; FSA; DL; Bt 1784; Baron of Gredington, 1788; Captain late Royal Artillery, TA; *b* 13 Sept. 1917; *o s* of 4th Baron and Gwladys Julia (*d* 1965), *d* of late Col H R. Lloyd Howard, CB; *S* father, 1927; *m* 1946, Leila Mary, *d* of Comdr J. W. Cookson, RN, Strand Hill, Winchelsea, and widow of Lt Hugo Peel, Welsh Guards; three *s* one *d. Educ:* Eton; Magdalene Coll., Cambridge. BA (Cambridge), 1950. 2nd Lt Shropshire Yeo. 1937; Lt RA, TA, retired (ill-health) 1943 with hon. rank of Captain. Dir, Lloyds Bank Ltd, 1962- (Chm. North West Bd); President: University Coll. of N Wales, Bangor, 1947-; Nat. Museum of Wales, 1952-57. Trustee, Nat. Portrait Gall., 1953-, Chm., 1966-; Chairman: Wrexham Powys and Mawddach Hosp. Management Cttee, 1960-74; Clwyd AHA, 1974-78; Friends of the Nat. Libraries, 1962-; Flint Agricultural Exec. Cttee, 1964-73. Member: Standing Commn on Museums and Galleries, 1953-60; Welsh Regional Hosp. Bd, 1958-63; Council for Professions Supplementary to Medicine, 1961-65; Royal Commn on Historical MSS, 1966-; Ancient Monuments Bd for Wales, 1979-; Bd of Governors, Welbeck Coll. Chief Comr for Wales, Boy Scouts' Assoc., 1948-65. DL Co. Flint, 1948; CC Flint, 1946 (Chm., 1954-55). Hon. LLD Wales, 1958. *Heir: s* Hon. Lloyd Tyrell-Kenyon, [*b* 13 July 1947; *m* 1971, Sally Carolyn, *e d* of J. F. P. Matthews; two *s*]. *Address:* Cumbers House, Gredington, Whitchurch, Salop SY13 3DH. *TA:* Hanmer 330. *T:* Hanmer 330. *Clubs:* Brooks's, Cavalry and Guards, Beefsteak.

KENYON, Clifford, CBE 1966; JP; farmer; *b* 11 Aug. 1896; *m* 1922, Doris Muriel Lewis, Herne Hill, London; three *s* two *d. Educ:* Brighton Grove Coll., Manchester; Manchester Univ. Joined Labour Party, 1922; Mem. Rawtenstall Council, 1923; Mayor, 1938-42, resigned from Council, 1945. MP (Lab) Chorley Div. of Lancs, 1945-70. JP Lancs, 1941. *Address:* Scarr Barn Farm, Crawshawbooth, Rossendale, Lancs. *T:* Rossendale 5703.

KENYON, Sir George (Henry), Kt 1976; DL; JP; LLD; Chairman, since 1978, and Director, since 1972, Williams & Glyn's Bank plc; *b* 10 July 1912; *s* of George Henry Kenyon and Edith (*née* Hill); *m* 1938, Christine Dorey (*née* Brentnall); two *s* one *d. Educ:* Radley; Manchester Univ. Director: Will[?]am Kenyon & Sons Ltd, 1942- (Chm., 1961-82); Tootal Ltd, 1971-79 (C[?], 1976-79); Manchester Ship Canal, 1972; Royal Bank of Scotland, 19[?]. Gen. Comr, Inland Revenue, 1957-73. Manchester University: Chm. Bldgs Cttee, 1962-70; Treas., 1970-72, 1980-; Chm. Council, 1972-80. Hon. Treas., Civic Trust, NW, 1962-78. Vice Pres., 1978; Member: NW Adv. Cttee, Civil Aviation, 1967-72; Manchester Reg. Hosp. Bd, 1962-68; NW Reg. Econ. Planning Council, 1970-73. JP Cheshire, 1959; Chm., S Tameside Bench, 1974-82; DL Chester, 1969; High Sheriff, Cheshire, 1973-74. Hon. LLD Manchester, 1980. *Recreations:* reading, talking, travel. *Address:* Limefield House, Hyde, Cheshire. *T:* 061-368 2012.

KENYON, Prof. John Philipps, FBA 1981; Professor of Modern History, University of St Andrews, since 1981; *b* 18 June 1927; *s* of William Houston Kenyon and Edna Grace Philipps; *m* 1962, Angela Jane Ewert (*née* Venables); one *s* two *d. Educ:* King Edward VII Sch., Sheffield; Univ. of Sheffield (BA; Hon. LittD, 1980); Christ's Coll., Cambridge (PhD). Fellow of Christ's Coll., Cambridge, 1954-62; Lectr in Hist., Cambridge, 1955-62; G. F. Grant Prof. of History, Univ. of Hull, 1962-81. Visiting Prof., Columbia Univ., New York, 1959-60; Junior Proctor, Cambridge, 1961-62; John U. Nef Lectr, Univ. of Chicago, 1972; Ford's Lectr in English Hist., Oxford, 1975-76. *Publications:* Robert Spencer Earl of Sunderland, 1958; The Stuarts, 1958, 2nd edn 1970; The Stuart Constitution, 1966; The Popish Plot, 1972; Revolution Principles, 1977; Stuart England, 1978; contribs to various learned jls. *Recreation:* bridge. *Address:* 82 Hepburn Gardens, St Andrews, Fife KY16 9LN. *T:* St Andrews 73356.

KEOGH, Charles Alfred, FRCS; Hon. Consulting Surgeon, Ear, Nose and Throat Department, The London Hospital and Medical Coll. *Educ:* London Hosp. Comdr of Royal Norwegian Order of St Olaf, 1943. *Address:* 139 Harley Street, W1.

KEOHANE, Dr Kevin William, CBE 1976; Rector, Roehampton Institute of Higher Education, since 1976; *b* 28 Feb. 1923; *s* of William Patrick and Mabel Margaret Keohane; *m* 1949, Mary Margaret (Patricia) Ashford; one *s* three *d. Educ:* Borden Grammar Sch., Sittingbourne, Kent; Univ. of Bristol (BSc; PhD). FInstP. War service, RAF, Radar Br. Research appts and Lectr in Anatomy, Univ. of Bristol, 1947-59; Chelsea College, London: Reader in Biophysics, 1959; Prof. of Physics and Head of Dept of Physics, 1965; Prof. of Science Educn and Dir, Centre for Science Educn, 1967-76; Vice-Principal, 1966-76. Royal Society Leverhulme Prof., Fed. Univ. of Bahia, Brazil, 1971; Vis. Prof., Chelsea College, 1977-. Member: Academic Adv. Cttee, Open Univ., 1970- (Chm., 1978-); Court, Univ. of Bristol, 1968-76; Court, Univ. of Surrey, 1982-; University of London: Member: Academic Council, 1974-76; Extra-Mural Council, 1974-76; School Examinations Council, 1975-76. Dir, Nuffield Foundn Science Projects, 1966-79; Chairman: DES Study Gp on Cert. of Extended Educn, 1978-79; Education Cttee, Commonwealth Inst., 1978-; Nuffield-Chelsea Curriculum Trust, 1979-; Member: Nat. Programme Cttee for Computers in Educn, 1974-78; Royal Society/Inst. of Physics Educn Cttee, 1970-73; SSRC Educn Bd, 1971-74; BBC Further Educn Adv. Cttee, 1972-75; TEAC, RAF, 1977-79; Gen. Optical Council, 1979; Bd of Educn, Royal Coll. of Nursing, 1980-. Manager, Royal Instn, 1972-75. Chairman, Formation Cttees: City of London Polytechnic, 1974-75; Goldsmiths' Coll., 1975-. Mem. Delegacy, Goldsmiths' Coll., 1974-; Chm. of Governors, Garnett Coll., 1974-78; Governor: Philippa Fawcett and Digby Stuart Colls, 1973-76; Ursuline Convent Sch., Wimbledon, 1967-; Heythrop Coll., Univ. of London, 1977-; Wimbledon Coll., 1982-. Numerous overseas consultancies and visiting professorships; Academic Mem., British Assoc. of Science Writers, 1971-; Editor, Jl of Physics Educn, 1966-69; Mem., Editorial Bd, Jl Curriculum Studies, and Studies in Sci. Educn. *Recreations:* Rugby (spectator), railways, bee-keeping. *Address:* Roehampton Institute, Grove House, Roehampton Lane, SW15 5PJ. *T:* 01-878 5751; 3 Thetford Road, New Malden, Surrey. *T:* 01-942 6861. *Club:* Athenæum.

KEPPEL, family name of **Earl of Albemarle.**

KEPPEL-COMPTON, Robert Herbert, CMG 1953; *b* 11 Dec. 1900; *s* of late J. H. Keppel-Compton, Southampton; *m* 1930, Marjorie, *yr d* of late Rev. W. B. Preston; one *s* one *d. Educ:* Oakham Sch.; Sidney Sussex Coll., Cambridge. BA, LLB Cantab. Entered Colonial Administrative Service, 1923. Dep. Provincial Commissioner, 1945; Development Sec., 1946; Provincial Commissioner, Nyasaland, 1949-55; retired from Colonial Service, 1955. *Address:* April Cottage, Churchstow, Kingsbridge, Devon.

KER; *see* Innes-Ker, family name of **Duke of Roxburghe.**

KER, K(eith) R(eginald) Welbore, OBE 1964; HM Diplomatic Service, retired; Director, Anglo-German Association, 1971-73; *b* 8 Aug. 1913; *s* of late Reginald Arthur Ker and Morna, *d* of Welbore MacCarthy, sometime Bishop of Grantham; *m* 1954, Marisa (*née* Ummarino), formerly Lo Bianco; three *s* two *d* (one step *s* one step *d*). *Educ:* Malvern Coll. Business, 1932-39. Served in HM Army, 1939-46, Major 1945 (despatches). Apptd British Consul, Bolzano, 1946; Second Sec., Rio de Janeiro, 1948; transf. to Stockholm, 1950; to Singapore, 1951; acting Consul, Hanoi, 1952; First Sec., Belgrade, 1953-55; transf. to Rangoon, 1956; to Saigon, 1957; to FO, 1957; to Hamburg, 1958; to Bonn, 1959; HM Consul-Gen., Hanover, 1961-64; First Sec., 1965-67, Counsellor, 1967-69, Lisbon; Consul-General, Cape Town, 1970-73. *Recreations:* walking, travel, collecting water-colour drawings. *Address:* Beckington Abbey, near Bath, Somerset BA3 6TD. *T:* Frome 830695.

KERANS, Comdr John Simon, DSO 1949; RN retired; *b* 30 June 1915; *m* 1946, Stephanie Campbell Shires; two *d. Educ:* RN Coll., Dartmouth. Cadet and Midshipman, HMS Rodney, Home Fleet, 1932-33; Midshipman and Sub-Lt HMS Cornwall, 1933-35; RN Coll., Greenwich, 1935-37; China Station, 1937-39. Served War of 1939-45: Staff, Chief of Intelligence Staff, Far East, Hong Kong and Singapore, 1939; HMS Naiad, Home and Medit. Stations, 1940-42; Staff Officer (Intelligence), Staff C-in-C, Medit. and Levant, 1942-43; 1st Lt, HMS Icarus, N Atlantic, 1943-44; Staff, C-in-C, Portsmouth, 1944; i/c HMS Blackmore (Lt-Comdr) 1944; Security Intelligence, Hong Kong, 1947; on loan to Malayan Police, Kuala Lumpur, 1948; Asst Naval Attaché, Nanking, 1949, joined frigate Amethyst after her attack by Communist forces (DSO), 1949; Comdr Dec. 1949; RN Staff Course, Greenwich, 1950; Head Far East Section, Naval Intelligence Admiralty, 1950-52; i/c HMS Rinaldo, 1953-54; Brit. Naval Attaché, Bangkok, Phnom Penh, Ventiane, Saigon and Rangoon, 1954-55; Sen. Officers' Technical Course Portsmouth, 1957; retired RN, 1958. MP (C) The Hartlepools, 1959-64; Civil Servant, Pensions Appeal Tribunals, 1969-80. *Address:* 44 Gordons Way, Oxted, Surrey RH8 0LW. *T:* Oxted 2751. *Clubs:* Littlehampton Sailing; Oxted Cricket.

KEREMA, Archbishop of, (RC), since 1976; **Most Rev. Virgil Copas,** KBE 1982; DD; Member of Religious Order of Missionaries of Sacred Heart (MSC); *b* 19 March 1915; *s* of Cornelius Copas and Kathleen (*née* Daly). *Educ:* St Mary's Coll. and Downlands Coll., Toowoomba, Queensland. Sec. to Bp L. Scharmach, Rabaul, New Britain, New Guinea, 1945-51; Religious Superior, Dio. of Darwin, Australia, 1954-60; Bishop of Port Moresby, 1960-66; Archbishop of Port Moresby, 1966-76, resigned in favour of a national archbishop. *Address:* Catholic Church, Box 90, PO Kerema, Gulf Province, Papua New Guinea, Oceania. *T:* Kerema 681079.

KERENSKY, Dr Oleg Alexander, CBE 1964; FRS 1970; FEng; Consultant, Freeman Fox & Partners, Consulting Engineers, since 1975 (Partner, 1955-75); *b* 16 April 1905; *s* of late Alexander F. Kerensky and Olga (*née* Baronovsky); *m* 1928, Nathalie (*d* 1969); one *s* ; *m* 1971, Mrs Dorothy Harvey. *Educ:* Russia, later small private sch. in England; Northampton Engrg Coll. (now The City Univ.). FICE; FIStructE; FIHE; FWeldI; Fellow, Fellowship of Engineering 1976. Jun. Asst, Oxford CC, 1926; Dorman Long & Co.: Asst Engr, Bridge Design Office, 1927-30, construction of Lambeth Bridge, 1930-32; Sen. Design Engr, Bridge Dept, 1932-37; Chief Engr and Sub-Agent: on construction of Wandsworth Bridge, Holloway Bros (London) Ltd, 1937-40; on Avonmouth Oil Jetty, 1940-43; Chief Engr, Mulberry Harbours, N Wales, 1943-45; Sen. Designer, Holloway Bros (London) Ltd, 1945-46; Principal Bridge Designer, Freeman Fox & Partners, 1946-55. Chm., Bridge Cttee, BSI; Pres., CIRIA, 1978-. Mem. Council, City Univ. President: IStructE, 1970-71; IHE, 1971-72. Hon. Fellow, Concrete Soc. Hon. Dr of Science, City Univ., 1967. Gold Medal, IStructE, 1977; Internat. Award of Merit in Structural Engrg, Internat. Assoc. for Bridge and Structural Engrg, 1979. *Publications:* numerous papers in learned jls. *Recreations:* bridge, croquet. *Address:* 27 Pont Street, SW1. *T:* 01-235 7173. *Clubs:* Athenæum, Hurlingham.

KERLE, Rt. Rev. Ronald Clive; Rector of St Swithun's Pymble, Diocese of Sydney, since 1976; *b* 28 Dec. 1915; *s* of William Alfred Ronald Kerle and Isabel Ada (*née* Turner); *m* 1940, Helen Marshall Jackson; one *s* one *d. Educ:* Univ. of Sydney (BA); Moore Theological Coll., Sydney. Sydney ACT, ThL 1937; BA 1942. Deacon 1939; Priest, 1940; Curate, St Paul's, Sydney, 1939; St Anne, Ryde, 1939-41; Rector, Kangaroo Valley, 1941-43; St Stephen, Port Kembla, 1943-47; Chaplain, AIF, 1945-47; Gen. Sec., NSW Branch, Church Missionary Society, 1947-54; Rector of Summer Hill, 1954-56; Archdeacon of Cumberland, 1954-60; Bishop Co-adjutor of Sydney, 1956-65; Bishop of Armidale, 1965-76. *Address:* Rectory, 11 Merrivale Road, Pymble, NSW 2073, Australia.

KERMACK, Stuart Ogilvy; Sheriff of Tayside, Central and Fife at Forfar and Arbroath, since 1971; *b* 9 July 1934; *s* of late Stuart Grace Kermack, CBE and of Nell P., *y d* of Thomas White, SSC; *m* 1961, Barbara Mackenzie, BSc; three *s* one *d. Educ:* Glasgow Academy; Jesus Coll., Oxford; Glasgow Univ.; Edinburgh Univ. BA Oxon (Jurisprudence), 1956; LLB Glasgow, 1959. Elected to Scots Bar, 1959. Sheriff Substitute of Inverness, Moray, Nairn and Ross, at Elgin and Nairn, 1965-71. *Publications:* articles in legal journals. *Address:* 7 Little Causeway, Forfar, Angus. *T:* Forfar 64691.

KERMAN, Prof. Joseph Wilfred; Professor of Music, University of California at Berkeley, since 1974; *b* 3 April 1924; *m* 1945, Vivian Shaviro; two *s* one *d. Educ:* New York Univ. (AB); Princeton Univ. (PhD). Dir of Graduate Studies, Westminster Choir Coll., Princeton, NJ, USA, 1949-51; Music Faculty, Univ. of California at Berkeley, 1951-72 (Dep. Chm., 1960-63); Heather Prof. of Music, Oxford Univ., and Fellow of Wadham Coll., Oxford, 1972-74. Co-editor, 19th Century Music, 1977-. Guggenheim and Fulbright Fellowships; Visiting Fellow: All Souls Coll., Oxford, 1966; Society for the Humanities, Cornell Univ., USA, 1970; Clare Hall, Cambridge, 1971. Fellow, American Academy of Arts and Sciences. Hon. FRAM. Hon. DHL Fairfield Univ., 1970. *Publications:* Opera as Drama, 1956; The Elizabethan Madrigal, 1962; The Beethoven Quartets, 1967; A History of Art and Music (with H. W. Janson), 1968; (ed) Ludwig van Beethoven: Autograph Miscellany, 1786-99 (Kafka Sketchbook), 2 vols, 1970 (Kinkeldey Award); Listen, 1972; The Masses and Motets of William Byrd, 1981 (Deems Taylor Award); (co-ed) Beethoven Studies, vol 1 1973, vol 2 1977, vol. 3 1982; essays, in music criticism and musicology, in: Hudson Review, New York Review, San Francisco Chronicle, etc. *Address:* Music Department, University of California, Berkeley, Calif 94720, USA; 107 Southampton Avenue, Berkeley, Calif 94707.

KERMODE, Prof. (John) Frank, MA; FBA 1973; Julian Clarence Levi Professor, Columbia University, New York, since 1982; Fellow of King's College, Cambridge, since 1974; *b* 29 Nov. 1919; *s* of late John Pritchard Kermode and late Doris Pearl Kermode; *m* 1st, 1947, Maureen Eccles (marr. diss. 1970); twin *s* and *d* ; 2nd, 1976, Anita Van Vactor. *Educ:* Douglas High Sch.; Liverpool Univ. BA 1940; War Service (Navy), 1940-46; MA 1947; Lecturer, King's Coll., Newcastle, in the University of Durham, 1947-49; Lecturer in the University of Reading, 1949-58; John Edward Taylor Prof. of English Literature in the University of Manchester, 1958-65; Winterstoke Prof. of English in the University of Bristol, 1965-67; Lord Northcliffe Prof. of Modern English Lit., UCL, 1967-74; King Edward VII Prof. of English Literature, Cambridge Univ., 1974-82. Charles Eliot Norton Prof. of Poetry at Harvard, 1977-78. Co-editor, Encounter, 1966-67. Editor, Fontana Masterguides series, 1982-. FRSL 1958. Mem. Arts Council, 1968-71; Chm., Poetry Book Soc., 1968-76. For. Hon. Mem., Amer. Acad. of Arts and Scis.

Hon. DHL Chicago, 1975; Hon. DLitt Liverpool, 1981. Officier de l'Ordre des Arts et des Sciences. *Publications:* (ed) Shakespeare, The Tempest (Arden Edition), 1954; Romantic Image, 1957; John Donne, 1957; The Living Milton, 1960; Wallace Stevens, 1960; Puzzles & Epiphanies, 1962; The Sense of an Ending, 1967; Continuities, 1968; Shakespeare, Spenser, Donne, 1971; Modern Essays, 1971; Lawrence, 1973; (ed, with John Hollander) Oxford Anthology of English Literature, 1973; The Classic, 1975; (ed) Selected Prose of T. S. Eliot, 1975; The Genesis of Secrecy, 1979; Essays on Fiction, 1971-82, 1982; contrib. Review of Eng. Studies, Partisan Review, New York Review, New Statesman, London Rev. of Books, etc. *Address:* King's College, Cambridge CB2 1ST. *T:* Cambridge 350411; 27 Luard Road, Cambridge. *T:* Cambridge 247398; Department of English and Comparative Literature, Columbia University, New York, NY 10027, USA.

KERN, Karl-Heinz; Ambassador of German Democratic Republic to the Court of St James's, 1973-80; *b* 18 Feb. 1930; *m* 1952, Ursula Bennmann; one *s. Educ:* King George Gymnasium, Dresden; Techn. Coll., Dresden (chem. engrg); Acad. for Polit. Science and Law (Dipl. jur., post-grad. History). Leading posts in diff. regional authorities of GDR until 1959; foreign policy, GDR, 1959-62; Head of GDR Mission in Ghana, 1962-66; Head of African Dept, Min. of For. Affairs, 1966-71; Minister and Chargé d'Affaires, Gt Britain, 1973. Holds Order of Merit of the Fatherland, etc. *Recreations:* sport, reading, music. *Address:* Ministry of Foreign Affairs, 102 Berlin, Marx Engels Platz, German Democratic Republic.

KERNOHAN, Thomas Hugh, CBE 1978 (OBE 1955); Parliamentary Commissioner for Administration and Commissioner for Complaints, Northern Ireland, since 1980; *b* 11 May 1922; *s* of Thomas Watson Kernohan and Caroline Kernohan; *m* 1948, Margaret Moore; one *s* one *d. Educ:* Carrickfergus Model Sch.; Carrickfergus Technical Sch. On staff (admin), Harland & Wolff Ltd, Belfast, 1940-44; Engineering Employers' NI Association: Asst Sec., 1945; Sec., 1953; Dir, 1966-80; Founder, 1959, and Chm., 1961-80, family joinery and plastic firm, Kernohans Joinery Works Ltd. *Recreations:* Rugby (management now), boating, fishing. *Address:* Beach House, Island Park, Greenisland, Carrickfergus, N Ireland. *T:* Whiteabbey 62030.

KERR, family name of **Marquess of Lothian** and **Baron Teviot.**

KERR, Andrew Stevenson, CBE 1976; arbitrator in industrial relations disputes; *b* 28 Aug. 1918; *s* of John S. Kerr and Helen L. Kerr; *m* 1946, Helen Reid Bryden; two *s* two *d. Educ:* Spiers' Sch., Beith, Ayrshire; Glasgow Univ. MA (Hons). Served Army, 1940-46. Entered Min. of Labour, 1947; general employment work in the Ministry, in Scotland, 1947-63; Industrial Relns Officer for Scotland, Min. of Labour, 1964-66; Dep. Chief Conciliation Officer, Min. of Labour, 1966-68; Chief Conciliation Officer, Dept of Employment, 1968-71; Controller (Scotland), Dept of Employment, 1972-74; Chief Conciliation Officer, ACAS, 1974-80. *Recreations:* golf, history. *Address:* 11 Forest Way, Tunbridge Wells, Kent TN2 5HA. *T:* Tunbridge Wells 24858.

KERR, Archibald Brown, CBE 1968 (OBE 1945); TD; Hon. Consulting Surgeon, Western Infirmary, Glasgow (Surgeon, 1954-72); Member of Court, University of Glasgow; *b* 17 Feb. 1907; *s* of late Robert Kerr and Janet Harvey Brown; *m* 1940, Jean Margaret, *d* of late John Cowan, MBE; one *d. Educ:* High Sch. and University of Glasgow. BSc 1927; MB, ChB 1929; Hon. LLD, 1973; FRFPSGlas. 1933; FRCSEd 1934; FRCSGlas. 1962. Asst to Prof. Path. Glasgow Univ., 1931-33; Surg. to Out-Patients, West. Infirm. Glasgow, 1932-39. Served in 156 (Lowland) Field Amb. and as Surgical Specialist, Officer in Charge of Surgical Div. and Col Comdg No. 23 (Scottish) Gen. Hosp., 1939-45. Surg. to Royal Alexandra Infirmary, Paisley, 1946-54; Asst Surg., West. Infirm., Glasgow, 1945-54. Lectr in Clinical Surgery, Univ. of Glasgow, 1946-72. Pres. 1951-52, Hon. Mem. 1971, Royal Medico-Chirurgical Society of Glasgow; Pres., Royal College of Physicians and Surgeons of Glasgow, 1964-66. Mem., Western Regional Hosp. Bd. Periods on Council of RCPS Glasgow and RCS Edinburgh. *Publications:* The Western Infirmary 1874-1974, 1974; contrib to Med. and Surg. Jls. *Recreation:* golf. *Address:* 10 Iain Road, Bearsden, Glasgow G61 4LX. *T:* 041-942 0424. *Clubs:* College (University of Glasgow), Royal Scottish Automobile.

KERR, Clark; educator; *b* 17 May 1911; *s* of Samuel W. and Caroline Clark Kerr; *m* 1934, Catherine Spaulding; two *s* one *d. Educ:* Swarthmore Coll. (AB); Stanford Univ. (MA); Univ. of Calif., Berkeley (PhD). Actg Asst Prof., Stanford Univ., 1939-40; Asst Prof., later Assoc. Prof., Univ. of Washington, 1940-45; Prof., Dir, Inst. of Industrial Relations, Univ. of Calif, Berkeley, 1945-52; Chancellor, Univ. of Calif at Berkeley, 1952-58; Pres., Univ. of Calif, 1958-67, now Emeritus President. Chairman: Carnegie Commn on Higher Educn, 1967-74; Carnegie Council on Policy Studies in Higher Educn, 1974-80. Govt service with US War Labor Board, 1942-45. Mem. Pres. Eisenhower's Commn on Nat. Goals, President Kennedy and President Johnson Cttee on Labor-Management Policy; Contract Arbitrator for: Boeing Aircraft Co. and Internat. Assoc. of Machinists, 1944-45; Armour & Co. and United Packinghouse Workers, 1945-47, 1949-52; Waterfront Employers' Assoc. and Internat. Longshoremen's and Warehousemen's Union, 1946-47, etc. Member: Amer. Acad. of Arts and Sciences; Royal Economic Society; Amer. Econ. Assoc.; Nat. Acad. of Arbitrators, etc. Phi Beta Kappa, Kappa Sigma. Trustee, Rockefeller Foundation, 1960-75; Chm., Armour

Automation Cttee, 1959-. Hon Fellow, LSE, 1977. Hon. LLD: Swarthmore, 1952; Harvard, 1958; Princeton, 1959; Notre Dame, 1964; Chinese Univ. of Hong Kong, 1964; Rochester, 1967; Hon. DLitt, Strathclyde, 1965; Hon. DHC, Bordeaux, 1962, etc. *Publications:* Unions, Management and the Public (jt), 1948 (rev. edns 1960, 1967); (jtly) Industrialism and Industrial Man, 1960 (rev. edns 1964, 1973); The Uses of the University, 1963 (rev. edn 1972, 1982); Labor and Management in Industrial Society, 1964 (rev. edn 1972); Marshall, Marx and Modern Times, 1969; (jtly) Industrialism and Industrial Man Reconsidered, 1975; Labor Markets and Wage Determination, 1977; Education and National Development, 1979; contribs to American Economic Review, Review of Economics and Statistics, Quarterly Jl of Economics, etc. *Recreation:* gardening. *Address:* 8300 Buckingham Drive, El Cerrito, Calif 94530, USA. *T:* 5291910.

KERR, Dr David Leigh; Chief Executive, Manor House Hospital, London NW11, since 1982; *b* 25 March 1923; *s* of Myer Woolf Kerr and Paula (*née* Horowitz); *m* 1st, 1944, Aileen Saddington (marr. diss. 1969); two *s* one *d*; 2nd, 1970, Margaret Dunlop; one *s* two *d. Educ:* Whitgift Sch., Croydon; Middlesex Hosp. Med. Sch., London. Hon. Sec., Socialist Medical Assoc., 1957-63; Hon. Vice-Pres., 1963-72. LCC (Wandsworth, Central), 1958-65, and Coun., London Borough of Wandsworth, 1964-68. Contested (Lab) Wandsworth, Streatham (for Parlt), 1959; MP (Lab) Wandsworth Central, 1964-70. Vis. Lectr in Medicine, Chelsea Coll., 1972-82. War on Want: Dir, 1970-77; Vice-Chm., 1973-74; Chm., 1974-77. Family Doctor, Tooting, 1946-82. Member: Royal Society of Medicine; Inter-departmental Cttee on Death Certification and Coroners. Governor, British Film Inst., 1966-71. *Recreations:* gardening, photography, squash. *Address:* 222 Norbury Avenue, Thornton Heath, Surrey CR4 8AJ. *T:* 01-764 7654.

KERR, Deborah Jane, (Deborah Kerr Viertel); Actress; *b* 30 Sept. 1921; *d* of Capt. Arthur Kerr-Trimmer; *m* 1st, 1945, Sqdn Ldr A. C. Bartley (marr. diss., 1959); two *d*; 2nd, 1960, Peter Viertel. *Educ:* Northumberland House, Clifton, Bristol. Open Air Theatre, Regent's Park, 1939, Oxford Repertory, 1939-40; after an interval of acting in films, appeared on West End Stage; Ellie Dunn in Heartbreak House, Cambridge Theatre, 1943; went to France, Belgium, and Holland for ENSA, playing in Gaslight, 1945. *Films:* Major Barbara, 1940; Love on the Dole, 1940-41; Penn of Pennsylvania, 1941; Hatter's Castle, 1942; The Day Will Dawn, 1942; Life and Death of Colonel Blimp, 1942-43; Perfect Strangers, 1944; I See a Dark Stranger, 1945; Black Narcissus, 1946; The Hucksters and If Winter Comes, 1947 (MGM, Hollywood); Edward My Son, 1948; Please Believe Me, 1949 (MGM, Hollywood); King Solomon's Mines, 1950; Quo Vadis, 1952; Prisoner of Zenda, Julius Caesar, Dream Wife, Young Bess (MGM), 1952; From Here to Eternity, 1953; The End of the Affair, 1955; The Proud and Profane, The King and I, 1956; Heaven Knows, Mr Allison, An Affair to Remember, Tea and Sympathy, 1957; Bonjour Tristesse, 1958; Separate Tables, The Journey, Count Your Blessings, 1959; The Sundowners, The Grass is Greener, The Naked Edge, The Innocents, 1961; The Chalk Garden, The Night of the Iguana, 1964; Casino Royale, 1967; Eye of the Devil, Prudence and the Pill, 1968; The Arrangement, 1970. *Stage:* Tea and Sympathy, NY, 1953; The Day After the Fair, London, 1972, tour of US, 1973-74; Seascape, NY, 1975; Candida, London, 1977; The Last of Mrs Cheyney, tour of US, 1978-79; The Day After the Fair, Melbourne and Sydney, 1979; Overheard, Haymarket, 1981. *Address:* Klosters, 7250 Grisons, Switzerland.

KERR, Desmond Moore, OBE 1970; HM Diplomatic Service; High Commissioner, Swaziland, since 1979; *b* 23 Jan. 1930; *s* of late Robert John Kerr and Mary Elizabeth Kerr; *m* 1956, Evelyn Patricia South; one *s* two *d. Educ:* Methodist Coll., Belfast; Queen's Univ., Belfast. BA Hons (Classics and Ancient History). CRO, 1952; British High Commn, Karachi, 1956-59, Lagos, 1959-62; Second Sec., 1960; Commonwealth Office, 1962-66; First Sec., 1965; Dep. British Govt Rep., West Indies Associated States, 1966-70; FCO, 1970-76; Dep. High Comr, Dacca, 1976-79. *Address:* c/o Foreign and Commonwealth Office, SW1.
See also E. Kerr.

KERR, Donald Frederick, CVO 1961; OBE 1960; Manager, Government Press Centre, Foreign and Commonwealth Office, 1976-77, retired; *b* 20 April 1915; *s* of Dr David Kerr, Cheshire; *m* 1942, Elizabeth Hayward (*d* 1978); two *s* one *d. Educ:* Sydney High Sch.; University of Sydney (BEcon). Served RAF (Navigator), SEAC, 1942-46. Deputy Director: British Information Services, New Delhi, 1947-53; UK Information Service, Ottawa, 1953-55; UK Information Service, Toronto, 1955-56; Dir, UK Information Service in Canada, Ottawa, 1956-59; Dir, British Information Services in India, New Delhi, 1959-63; Controller (Overseas), COI, 1963-76; on secondment, Dir of Information, Commonwealth Secretariat, Sept. 1969-Sept. 1970. *Recreation:* golf. *Address:* 4 Southdown House, 11 Lansdowne Road, Wimbledon, SW20. *Clubs:* Royal Commonwealth Society; Royal Wimbledon Golf.

KERR, Dr Edwin; Chief Officer, Council for National Academic Awards, since 1972; *b* 1 July 1926; *e s* of late Robert John Kerr and Mary Elizabeth Kerr (*née* Ferguson); *m* 1949, Gertrude Elizabeth (*née* Turbitt); one *s* two *d. Educ:* Royal Belfast Academical Instn; Queen's Univ., Belfast (BSc, PhD). FIMA, FBCS. Asst Lectr in Maths, QUB, 1948-52; Lectr in Maths, Coll. of Technology, Birmingham (now Univ. of Aston in Birmingham), 1952-55; Lectr in Maths, Coll. of Science and Technology, Manchester (now Univ. of Manchester Inst. of Science and Technology), 1956-58; Head of Maths Dept, Royal Coll. of Advanced Technology, Salford (now Univ. of Salford),

1958–66; Principal, Paisley Coll. of Technology, 1966–72. Member: Adv. Cttee on Supply and Training of Teachers, 1973–78; Adv. Cttee on Supply and Educn of Teachers, 1980–; Bd for Local Authority Higher Educn, 1982–. President: Soc. for Res. into Higher Educn, 1974–77; The Mathematical Assoc., 1976–77. Hon. DUniv Open, 1977. *Publications:* (with R. Butler) An Introduction to Numerical Methods, 1962; various mathematical and educational. *Recreation:* gardening. *Address:* The Coppice, Kingfisher Lure, Loudwater, Chorleywood, Herts. *T:* Rickmansworth 77187.
  See also D. M. Kerr.

KERR, Francis Robert Newsam, OBE 1962; MC 1940; JP; farmer since 1949; Vice Lieutenant of Berwickshire since 1970; *b* 12 Sept. 1916; *s* of late Henry Francis Hobart Kerr and Gertrude Mary Kerr (*née* Anthony); *m* 1941, Anne Frederica Kitson; two *s* one *d. Educ:* Ampleforth College. Regular Officer, The Royal Scots, 1937–49; TA 1952–63; retired as Lt-Col. Member: Berwickshire County Council, 1964–75; SE Scotland Regional Hosp. Bd, 1971–74; Borders Area Health Bd, 1973–81 (Vice-Chm.); Borders Reg. Council, 1974–78; Post Office Users Nat. Council, 1972–73; Whitley Council, 1970–81; Council, Multiple Sclerosis Soc., 1973–. Sheriff of Berwick upon Tweed, 1974. *Recreations:* country pursuits. *Address:* Blanerne, Duns, Berwickshire. *T:* Cumledge 222. *Club:* Farmers'.

KERR, James, QPM 1979; Chief Constable, Lincolnshire Police, since 1977; *b* 19 Nov. 1928; *s* of William and Margaret Jane Kerr; *m* 1952, Jean Coupland; one *d. Educ:* Carlisle Grammar School. Cadet and Navigating Officer, Merchant Navy, 1945–52 (Union Castle Line, 1949–52). Carlisle City Police and Cumbria Constabulary, 1952–74; Asst Director of Command Courses, Police Staff Coll., Bramshill, 1974; Asst Chief Constable (Operations), North Yorkshire Police, 1975; Deputy Chief Constable, Lincs, 1976. FBIM. Officer Brother, OStJ, 1980. *Recreations:* music, squash. *Address:* Monk Bretton, Burton, Lincoln LN1 2RD. *T:* Lincoln 26898. *Clubs:* London, Special Forces, Rotary (Lincoln).

KERR, John Olav; HM Diplomatic Service; Principal Private Secretary to the Chancellor of the Exchequer, since 1981; *b* 22 Feb. 1942; *s* of Dr and Mrs J. D. O. Kerr; *m* 1965, Elizabeth, *d* of W. G. Kalaugher; two *s* three *d. Educ:* Glasgow Academy; Pembroke Coll., Oxford. Entered Diplomatic Service, 1966; served FO, Moscow, Rawalpindi, FCO; Private Sec. to Permanent Under Secretary, FCO, 1974–79; Head of DM1 Division, HM Treasury, 1979–81. *Address:* 60 Abbey Road, NW8 0QH.

KERR, Rt. Hon. Sir John Robert, AK 1976 (AC 1975); GCMG 1976 (KCMG 1974; CMG 1966); GCVO 1977; PC 1977; Governor-General of Australia, 1974–77; *b* 24 Sept. 1914; *s* of late H. Kerr, Sydney; *m* 1st, 1938, Alison (*d* 1974), *d* of F. Worstead, Sydney; one *s* two *d*; 2nd, 1975, Mrs Anne Robson, *d* of J. Taggart. *Educ:* Fort Street Boys' High Sch.; Sydney Univ. (LLB). Admitted NSW Bar, 1938. Served War of 1939–45: 2nd AIF, 1942–46; Col, 1945–46. First Princ., Australian Sch. of Pacific Admin., 1946–48; Organising Sec., S Pacific Commn, 1946–47; QC (NSW) 1953; Mem. NSW Bar Coun., 1960–64; Vice-Pres., 1962–63, Pres., 1964, NSW Bar Assoc.; Vice-Pres., 1962–64, Pres., 1964–66, Law Coun. of Australia; Judge of Commonwealth Industrial Court and Judge of Supreme Court of ACT, 1966–72; Judge of Courts of Marine Inquiry, 1967–72; Chief Justice, Supreme Court, NSW, 1972–74; Lieutenant Governor, NSW, 1973–74. Chairman: Commonwealth Cttee on Review of Admin. Decisions, 1968–72; Commonwealth Cttee on Review of Pay for Armed Services, 1970; Deputy President: Trades Practices Tribunal, 1966–72; Copyright Tribunal, 1969–72; presided at 3rd Commonwealth and Empire Law Conf., Sydney, 1965; Pres., Industrial Relations Soc. of Australia, 1964–66; Pres., NSW Marriage Guidance Coun., 1961–62; Mem. Bd of Coun. on New Guinea Affairs, 1964–71; Mem. Med. Bd of NSW, 1963–66; Pres., Law Assoc. for Asia and Western Pacific, 1966–70. Hon. Life Mem., Law Soc. of England and Wales, 1965; Hon. Mem., Amer. Bar Assoc., 1967–. KStJ 1974. *Publications:* Matters for Judgment, 1979; various papers and articles on industrial relations, New Guinea affairs, organisation of legal profession, etc. *Address:* c/o Australia House, The Strand, WC2B 4LA. *Clubs:* Carlton; Union (Sydney).

KERR, Rt. Hon. Sir Michael (Robert Emanuel), Kt 1972; PC 1981; **Rt. Hon. Lord Justice Kerr**; a Lord Justice of Appeal, since 1981; *b* 1 March 1921; *s* of Alfred Kerr; *m* 1952, Julia, *d* of Joseph Braddock; two *s* one *d. Educ:* Aldenham Sch.; Clare Coll., Cambridge. Served War, 1941–45 (Pilot; Flt-Lt). BA Cantab (1st cl. Hons Law) 1947, MA 1952; called to Bar, Lincoln's Inn, 1948, Bencher 1968; QC 1961. Member: Bar Council, 1968–72; Senate, 1969–72. Dep. Chm., Hants QS, 1961–71; Mem. Vehicle and General Enquiry Tribunal, 1971–72; a Judge of the High Court of Justice, Queen's Bench Div., and of the Commercial and Admiralty Cts, 1972–78; Chm., Law Commn of England and Wales, 1978–81. Mem. Council of Management: British Inst. of Internat. and Comparative Law, 1973–; Inst. of Advanced Legal Studies, 1979–; Chairman: Lord Chancellor's inter-deptl cttee on Foreign Judgments, 1974–; Cttee of Management, Centre of Commercial Law Studies, QMC, 1980–; Supreme Court Procedure Cttee, 1982–. Vice-Pres., British Maritime Law Assoc., 1977–. Hon. Life Mem., Amer. and Canadian Bar Assocs, 1976. Chorley Lectr, LSE, 1977. Governor, Aldenham Sch., 1959–. *Publications:* McNair's Law of the Air, 1953, 1965; articles and lectures on commercial law and arbitration. *Recreations:* travel, ski-ing, tennis, music. *Address:* c/o Royal Courts of Justice, Strand, WC2. *Club:* Garrick.

KERR, Robert Reid, TD; MA, LLB; Sheriff of Tayside, Central and Fife (formerly Stirling, Dumbarton and Clackmannan) at Falkirk, since 1969; *b* 7 May 1914; *s* of James Reid Kerr, sugar refiner, and Olive Rodger; *m* 1942, Mona Kerr; three *d. Educ:* Cargilfield; Trinity Coll., Glenalmond; Oxford Univ.; Glasgow Univ. Sheriff-Substitute: of Inverness, Moray, Nairn and Ross and Cromarty at Fort William, 1952–61; of Aberdeen, Kincardine and Banff at Banff, 1961–69. OStJ. *Address:* Bagatelle, 11 Majors Place, Falkirk FK1 5QS.

KERR, Russell (Whiston); MP (Lab) Hounslow, Feltham and Heston, since 1974 (Middlesex, Feltham, 1966–74); Air Charter Executive; *b* 1 Feb. 1921; *s* of Ivo W. and Constance Kerr, Australia; *m* 1st, 1946, Shirley W. N. Huie; one *s* one *d*; 2nd, 1960, Anne P. Clark (*née* Bersey) (*d* 1973); no *c. Educ:* Shore Sch., Sydney; University of Sydney. BEcon 1941. RAAF Aircrew, 1942–46; operational service with Bomber Comd Pathfinder Force, flying Lancaster Bombers over Germany (Flying Officer/Navigator). Returned to England to live, 1948. Contested (Lab): Horsham, Sussex, 1951; Merton and Morden, 1959; Preston North, 1964. Dir (unpaid), Tribune, 1969–; Chairman: Tribune group of MPs, 1969–70; Labour Aviation Gp, 1974–79. Nat. Exec. Mem., ASTMS, 1964–76 (Chm., Aerospace Cttee, 1970–80); Chm., Select Cttee on nationalised industries, 1974–79. Chm., Internat. Commn on human rights in Iran, 1978. *Publications:* articles in various radical and TU jls. *Recreations:* cricket, golf, walking, talking. *Address:* c/o House of Commons, SW1. *Clubs:* Feltham Ex-Servicemen's, Feltham Labour, Royal Mid-Surrey Golf.

KERR, Thomas Henry; Director, Royal Aircraft Establishment, since 1980; *b* 18 June 1924; *s* of late Albert Edward Kerr and Mrs Francis Jane Kerr (*née* Simpson); *m* 1946, Myrnie Evelyn Martin Hughes; two *d. Educ:* Magnus Grammar, Newark; University Coll., Durham Univ. BSc 1949; FRAeS; Diplôme Paul Tissendier 1957. RAFVR pilot, 1942–46. Aero Flight, RAE, 1949–55; Head of Supersonic Flight Group, 1955–59; Scientific Adviser to C-in-C Bomber Comd, High Wycombe, 1960–64; Head of Assessment Div., Weapons Dept, RAE, 1964–66; Dep. Dir and Dir of Defence Operational Analysis Estabt, 1966–70; Head of Weapons Research Gp, Weapons Dept, RAE, 1970–72; Dir Gen. Establishments Resources Programmes (C), MoD (PE), 1972–74; Dir, Nat. Gas Turbine Estabt, 1974–80. Mem. Council, RAeS, 1979. FRSA 1980. *Publications:* reports and memoranda of Aeronautical Research Council, lectures to RAeS and RUSI. *Recreations:* bridge, water ski-ing, tennis, badminton. *Address:* Bundu, 013 Kingsley Avenue, Camberley, Surrey GU15 2NA. *T:* Camberley 25961.

KERR, Sir William Alexander B., (Sir Alastair); *see* Blair-Kerr.

KERR, William Francis Kennedy, PhD, CEng, FIMechE; Principal, Belfast College of Technology, since 1969; *b* 1 Aug. 1923; *m* 1953, H. Adams; two *s. Educ:* Portadown Technical Coll. and Queen's Univ., Belfast. BSc (Hons) in Mech. Engineering, MSc, PhD. Teacher of Mathematics, Portadown Techn. Coll., 1947–48; Teacher and Sen. Lectr in Mech. Eng, Coll. of Techn., Belfast, 1948–55; Lectr and Adviser of Studies in Mech. Eng, Queen's Univ. of Belfast, 1955–62; Head of Dept of Mech., Civil, and Prod. Eng, Dundee Coll. of Techn., 1962–67; Vice-Principal, Coll. of Techn., Belfast, 1967–69. Member: Belfast Educn and Library Bd, 1977–81; NI Council for Educnl Develt, 1980–81; NI Manpower Adv. Council, 1981–; Chm., Assoc. of Principals of Colleges (NI Branch), 1982; Governor, Royal Belfast Academical Instn, 1969–. *Publications:* contribs on environmental testing of metals, etc. *Recreations:* golf, motoring, reading. *Address:* 27 Maxwell Road, Bangor, Co. Down BT20 3SG, Northern Ireland. *T:* Bangor 65303.

KERR-DINEEN, Ven. Frederick George; Archdeacon of Horsham, since 1975; Rector of Stopham with Hardham, since 1973; *b* 26 Aug. 1915; second *s* of late Mr and Mrs Henry John Dineen and adopted *s* of late Prebendary Colin Kerr; added Kerr to family name in 1938; *m* 1951, Hermione Iris, *er d* of late Major John Norman MacDonald (KEH) and Mrs MacDonald; four *s* one *d. Educ:* Tyndale Hall, Clifton; St John's Coll., Durham. MA, LTh. Ordained, 1941; Curate: St Paul's, Portman Square, 1941–44; St John's, Weymouth, 1945–46; Vicar: St Michael's, Blackheath Park, 1946–53; Lindfield, 1953–62; Holy Trinity, Eastbourne, 1962–73; Archdeacon of Chichester, and Canon Residentiary of Chichester Cathedral, 1973–75; Proctor in Convocation, 1970–74. *Address:* The Rectory, Stopham, Pulborough, West Sussex. *T:* Fittleworth 333.

KERRIN, Very Rev. Richard Elual, MA; Dean of Aberdeen and Orkney, 1956–69; Rector of St John's Episcopal Church, Aberdeen, 1954–70, retired; *b* 4 July 1898; *s* of Rev. Daniel Kerrin and Margaret Kerrin; *m* 1925, Florence Alexandra, *d* of Captain J. Reid; one *s. Educ:* Robert Gordon's Coll., Aberdeen; University of Aberdeen (MA); Edinburgh Theological Coll. (Luscombe Scholar). Ordained deacon, 1922; priest, 1923. Curate, Old St Paul, Edinburgh, 1922–25; Rector, Inverurie, 1925–37; Rector, Holy Trinity, Stirling, 1937–47; Rector, Fraserburgh, 1947–54; Canon of Aberdeen, 1954–56. *Address:* Elora, St Bryde's Road, Kemnay, Aberdeenshire AB5 9NB. *T:* Kemnay 2480.

KERRUISH, Sir (Henry) Charles, Kt 1979; OBE 1964; Speaker of the House of Keys, Isle of Man, since 1962; *b* 23 July 1917; *m* 1st, 1944, Margaret Gell; one *s* three *d*; 2nd, 1975, Kay Warriner. *Educ:* Ramsey Grammar Sch. Farmer. Member, House of Keys, 1946–. Regional Councillor for British Isles and Mediterranean, CPA, 1975–77. Mem. Court, Liverpool Univ., 1974–.

Recreations: light horse breeding, motor cycling. *Address:* Ballafayle, Maughold, Isle of Man. *T:* Ramsey (IOM) 812293. *Club:* Farmers'.

KERRY, Knight of; *see* FitzGerald, Sir G. P. M.

KERRY, Michael James, CB 1976; HM Procurator General and Treasury Solicitor, since 1980; *b* 5 Aug. 1923; *s* of Russell Kerry and Marjorie (*née* Kensington); *m* 1951, Sidney Rosetta Elizabeth (*née* Foster); one *s* two *d. Educ:* Rugby Sch.; St John's Coll., Oxford (MA). Served with RAF, 1942-46. Called to Bar, Lincoln's Inn, 1949. Joined BoT as Legal Asst, 1951; Sen. Legal Asst, 1959; Asst Solicitor, 1964; Principal Asst Solicitor, Dept of Trade and Industry, 1972, Solicitor, 1973-80. *Recreations:* golf, tennis, gardening. *Address:* South Bedales, Lewes Road, Haywards Heath, W Sussex. *T:* Scaynes Hill 303. *Club:* Piltdown Golf.

KERSH, Cyril; Assistant Editor (Features), Sunday Mirror, since 1979; *b* 24 Feb. 1925; *s* of Hyman and Leah Kersh; *m* 1956, Suzanne Fajner. *Educ:* Westcliff High Sch., Essex. Served War, RN, 1943-47. Worked variously for newsagent, baker, woollen merchant and toy manufr, 1939-43; Reporter, then News and Features Editor, The People, 1943-54; Features Editor, Illustrated, 1954-59; Features staff, London Evening Standard, 1959-60; Editor, Men Only, 1960-63; Daily Express (one day), 1963; Features Editor, then Sen. Features Exec., Sunday Mirror, 1963-76; Editor, Reveille, 1976-79 (Fleet Street's 1st photocomposition editor). *Publications:* The Aggravations of Minnie Ashe, 1970; The Diabolical Liberties of Uncle Max, 1973; The Soho Summer of Mr Green, 1974; The Shepherd's Bush Connection, 1975; Minnie Ashe at War, 1979. *Recreations:* talking, walking, reading, writing. *Address:* 14 Ossington Street, W2 4LZ. *T:* 01-229 6582. *Club:* Our Society.

KERSHAW, family name of **Baron Kershaw.**

KERSHAW, 4th Baron, *cr* 1947; **Edward John Kershaw;** Chartered Accountant; Partner in Kidsons, Chartered Accountants, 3 Beaufort Buildings, Spa Road, Gloucester; *b* 12 May 1936; *s* of 3rd Baron and Katharine Dorothea Kershaw (*née* Staines); *S* father, 1962; *m* 1963, Rosalind Lilian Rutherford; one *s* two *d. Educ:* Selhurst Grammar Sch., Surrey. Entered RAF Nov. 1955, demobilised Nov. 1957. Admitted to Inst. of Chartered Accountants in England and Wales, Oct. 1964. *Heir: s* Hon. John Charles Edward Kershaw, *b* 23 Dec. 1971.

KERSHAW, Sir Anthony; *see* Kershaw, Sir J. A.

KERSHAW, Henry Aidan; His Honour Judge Henry Kershaw; a Circuit Judge, since 1976; *b* 11 May 1927; *s* of late Rev. H. Kershaw, Bolton; *m* 1960, Daphne Patricia, *widow* of Dr. C. R. Cowan; four *s. Educ:* St John's, Leatherhead; Brasenose Coll., Oxford (BA). Served RN, 1946-48. Called to Bar, Inner Temple, 1953. Councillor, Bolton CBC, 1954-57. Asst Recorder of Oldham, 1970-71; a Recorder of the Crown Court, 1972-76. Dep. Chm., Agricultural Land Tribunal, 1972-76. Chm., Lancs Schs Golf Assoc. *Recreations:* golf, ski-ing, oil-painting. *Address:* Broadhaven, St Andrew's Road, Lostock, Bolton, Lancs. *T:* Bolton 47088. *Club:* Bolton Golf.

KERSHAW, Sir (John) Anthony, Kt 1981; MC 1943; MP (C) Stroud Division of Gloucestershire, since 1955; Barrister-at-Law; *b* 14 Dec. 1915; *s* of Judge J. F. Kershaw, Cairo and London, and of Anne Kershaw, Kentucky, USA; *m* 1939, Barbara, *d* of Harry Crookenden; two *s* two *d. Educ:* Eton; Balliol Coll., Oxford (BA). Called to the Bar 1939. Served War, 1940-46: 16th/5th Lancers. Mem. LCC, 1946-49; Westminster City Council, 1947-48. Parly Sec., Min. of Public Building and Works, June-Oct. 1970; Parliamentary Under-Secretary of State: FCO, 1970-73; for Defence (RAF), 1973-74; Chm., H of C Select Cttee on Foreign Affairs, 1979-. Vice-Chm., British Council, 1974-. *Address:* The Tithe Barn, Didmarton, Badminton, Glos. *Club:* White's.

KERSHAW, Joseph Anthony; independent management consultant, since 1975; Associate Director, Foote, Cone & Belding Ltd, since 1979; Director, John Stork & Partners Ltd, since 1980; *b* 26 Nov. 1935; *s* of Henry and Catherine Kershaw, Preston; *m* 1959, Ann Whittle; three *s* two *d. Educ:* Ushaw Coll., Durham; Preston Catholic Coll., SJ. Short service commn, RAOC, 1955-58; Unilever Ltd, 1958-67; Gp Marketing Manager, CWS, 1967-69; Managing Director: Underline Ltd, 1969-71; Merchant Div., Reed International Ltd, 1971-73; Head of Marketing, Non-Foods, CWS, 1973-74; (first) Director, Nat. Consumer Council, 1975. *Recreations:* fishing, flying, shooting, cooking; CPRE. *Address:* Westmead, Meins Road, Blackburn, Lancs BB2 6QF. *T:* Blackburn 55915. *Club:* Institute of Directors.

KERSHAW, Michael; *see* Kershaw, P. M.

KERSHAW, Philip Charles Stones; His Honour Judge Kershaw; a Circuit Judge (formerly Deputy Chairman, Lancashire Quarter Sessions), since 1961; *b* 9 April 1910; *s* of Joseph Harry and Ethel Kershaw; *m* 1935, Michaela Raffael; one *s* one *d. Educ:* Stonyhurst Coll.; Merton Coll., Oxford. Called to the Bar, Gray's Inn, 1933; practised Northern Circuit until Aug. 1939. Served in Army, 1939-45 (Major). Resumed practice, 1945-61. *Address:* Fountain House, East Beach, Lytham, Lancs. *T:* Lytham 736072. *Club:* Portico Library (Manchester).
See also P. M. Kershaw.

KERSHAW, (Philip) Michael, QC 1980; a Recorder of the Crown Court, since 1980; *b* 23 April 1941; *s* of His Honour Judge Kershaw, *qv*; *m* 1980, Anne (*née* Williams). *Educ:* Ampleforth Coll.; St John's Coll., Oxford (MA). Called to the Bar, Gray's Inn, 1963; in practice, 1963-. *Address:* 5 Essex Court, Temple, EC4Y 9AH. *Clubs:* Reform; Portico (Manchester).

KERSHAW, Mrs W. J. S.; *see* Paling, Helen Elizabeth.

KERSHAW, Prof. William Edgar, CMG 1971; VRD; Professor of Biology, University of Salford, 1966-76, now Emeritus Professor; Advisor in Tropical Medicine to Manchester Area Health Authority, since 1976. *Educ:* Manchester University. MB, ChB, 1935; MRCS, LRCP, 1936; DTM&H Eng. 1946; MD 1949; DSc 1956. Chalmers Memorial Gold Medal, Royal Society of Tropical Medicine and Hygiene, 1955. Formerly: Surgeon Captain, RNR; Demonstrator in Morbid Anatomy, Manchester Univ.; Leverhulme Senior Lectr in Med. Parasitology, Liverpool Sch. of Trop. Med. and Liverpool Univ.; Walter Myers and Everett Dutton Prof. of Parasitology and Entomology, Liverpool Univ., 1958-66. Hon. Lectr, Dept of Bacteriology, Univ. of Manchester, 1977-. *Address:* Mill Farm, Hesketh Bank, Preston PR4 6RA. *T:* Hesketh Bank 4299.

KERWIN, Prof. Larkin, CC 1980 (OC 1977); FRSC; President, National Research Council of Canada, since 1980; *b* 22 June 1924; *s* of T. J. Kerwin and Catherine Lonergan-Kerwin; *m* 1950, Maria Guadaloupe Turcot; five *s* three *d. Educ:* St Francis Xavier Univ. (BSc 1944); MIT (MSc 1946); Université Laval (DSc 1949). Laval University: Dir, Dept of Physics, 1961-67; Vice-Dean, Faculty of Sciences, 1967-68; Vice-Rector, Academic, 1969-72; Rector, 1972-77. Sec.-Gen., IUPAP, 1972-. Pres., Royal Soc. of Canada, 1976-77. Hon. LLD: St Francis Xavier, 1970; Toronto, 1973; Concordia, 1976; Hon. DSc: British Columbia, 1973; McGill, 1974; Memorial, 1978; Royal Military Coll., Canada, 1982; Hon. DCL Bishop's, 1978. Médaille du Centenaire, 1967; Médaille de l'Assoc. Canadienne des Physiciens, 1969; Médaille Pariseau, 1965; Medal of Centenary of Roumania, 1977; Jubilee Medal, 1977. Kt Comdr with star, Holy Sepulchre of Jerusalem, 1974. *Publications:* Atomic Physics, 1963 (trans. French, 1964, Spanish, 1970); papers in jls. *Recreation:* sailing. *Address:* 2166 Parc Bourbonnière, Sillery, Quebec G1T 1B4, Canada. *T:* (613) 993-2024. *Club:* Cercle Universitaire (Quebec).

KESSEL, Prof. Lipmann, MBE (mil.) 1946; MC 1946; FRCS; Emeritus Professor of Orthopaedics, University of London; Director of Clinical Studies, Institute of Orthopaedics, and Hon. Consultant Surgeon, Royal National Orthopaedic Hospital, since 1974; Hon. Consultant Orthopaedic Surgeon, Charing Cross Hospital, since 1966; *m* 1st, Mary (*née* Morgan); 2nd, Peggy (*née* Oughton); two *s*; 3rd, Beryl (*née* Tilley); two *d. Educ:* Pretoria High Sch.; Univ. of the Witwatersrand; St Mary's Hosp., London (qual. 1938). FRCS 1947. Served War, RAMC: Surgeon i/c 1 Parachute Surg. Team; POW Holland, escaped. Jun. hosp. appts; Sen. Registrar Orthopaedics, St Mary's Hosp., London, 1946; Clin. Res. Asst, Inst. of Orthops, 1947; Cons. Orthopaedic Surgeon: Fulham, St Mary Abbots, and Charing Cross Hosps.; Prof. of Orthopaedics, Inst. of Orthopaedics, Univ. of London, 1976-80. Samuel Camp Vis. Prof., Harvard Med. Sch., 1967. *Publications:* Surgeon at Arms, 1956 (2nd edn 1977); (contrib.) Clinical Surgery, 1967; (contrib.) Watson-Jones, Fractures and Joint Injuries, 1977; (contrib.) Triumphs of Medicine, 1977; Colour Atlas of Clinical Orthopaedics, 1980; Clinical Disorders of the Shoulder, 1981; articles on orthop. surg. in jls. *Recreations:* theatre, games of chance. *Address:* 36 Menelik Road, NW2 3RH. *T:* 01-794 3221. *Clubs:* Garrick, Sportsman.

KESSEL, Prof. William Ivor Neil, MD; FRCP, FRCPE, FRCPsych; Professor of Psychiatry, since 1965 and Dean of Postgraduate Studies, Faculty of Medicine, since 1982, University of Manchester; *b* 10 Feb. 1925; *s* of Barney Kessel and Rachel Isabel Kessel; *m* 1958, Pamela Veronica Joyce (*née* Boswell); one *s* one *d. Educ:* Highgate Sch.; Trinity Coll., Cambridge (MA, MD); UCH Med. Sch.; Inst. of Psychiatry. MSc Manchester. FRCP 1967; FRCPE 1968; FRCPsych 1972. Staff, Inst. of Psych., 1960; scientific staff, MRC Unit for Epidemiol. of Psych. Illness, 1961, Asst Dir 1963; Hon. Sen. Lectr, Edinburgh Univ., 1964; Dean, Faculty of Med., Univ. of Manchester, 1974-76. Member: NW RHA, 1974-77; GMC, 1974-; Adv. Council on Misuse of Drugs, 1972-80; Health Educn Council, 1979-; Chm., Adv. Cttee on Alcoholism, DHSS, 1975-78; Cons. Adviser on alcoholism to DHSS, 1972-81. *Publications:* Alcoholism (with Prof. H. J. Walton), 1965, 3rd edn 1975; articles on suicide and self-poisoning, alcoholism, psych. in gen. practice, psychosomatic disorders, psych. epidemiol. *Address:* Department of Psychiatry, University Hospital of South Manchester, West Didsbury, Manchester M20 8LR. *T:* 061-455 8111, ext. 2616. *Club:* Athenæum.

KESWICK, Henry Neville Lindley; Chairman: Matheson & Co. Ltd, since 1975; Jardine Matheson Insurance Brokers Management Ltd, since 1979; Member, London Advisory Committee, Hongkong and Shanghai Banking Corporation, since 1975; *b* 29 Sept. 1938; *e s* of Sir William Keswick, *qv. Educ:* Eton Coll.; Trinity Coll., Cambridge. BA Hons Econs and Law. Commnd Scots Guards, Nat. Service, 1956-58. Dir, Jardine, Matheson & Co. Ltd, Hong Kong, 1967 (Chairman, 1972-75); Director: Sun Alliance and London Insurance, 1975-; Robert Fleming Holdings Ltd; United Race Courses. Proprietor, The Spectator, 1975-81. *Recreation:* country pursuits. *Address:* 10 Egerton Place, SW3 2EF. *Clubs:* White's, Turf; Third Guards.

KESWICK, Sir William (Johnston), Kt 1972; Director, Matheson & Co. Ltd, 1943–75 (Chairman, 1949–66); *b* 6 Dec. 1903; *s* of late Major Henry Keswick of Cowhill Tower, Dumfries, Scotland; *m* 1937, Mary, *d* of late Rt Hon. Sir Francis Lindley, PC, GCMG; three *s* one *d. Educ:* Winchester Coll.; Trinity Coll., Cambridge. Director: Hudson's Bay Co., 1943–72 (Governor 1952–65); Bank of England, 1955–73; British Petroleum Co. Ltd, 1950–73; Jardine, Matheson & Co. Ltd (Hong Kong and Far East); Chm. of various public companies in Far East; Chm., Shanghai Municipal Council of late International Settlement; Mem., Royal Commission on Taxation of Profits and Income; Brigadier Staff Duties 21 Army Gp; Mem., Royal Company of Archers. Trustee, National Gallery 1964–71. *Recreations:* shooting, fishing. *Address:* Theydon Priory, Theydon Bois, Essex. *T:* Theydon Bois 2256; Glenkiln, Shawhead, Dumfries, Scotland. *Club:* White's.
See also H. N. L. *Keswick.*

KETTLE, Captain Alan Stafford Howard; Royal Navy (retired); General Manager, HM Dockyard, Chatham, since 1977; *b* 6 Aug. 1925; *s* of Arthur Stafford Kettle and Marjorie Constance (*née* Clough); *m* 1952, Patricia Rosemary (*née* Gander); two *s. Educ:* Rugby School. CEng, FIMechE. Joined RN, 1943; Comdr, Dec. 1959; Captain, Dec. 1968; retired, Sept. 1977. Entered Civil Service as Asst Under-Sec., Sept. 1977. *Address:* High Timbers, Sutton Street, Bearsted, near Maidstone, Kent ME14 4HP. *T:* Maidstone 38330.

KETTLEWELL, Comdt Dame Marion M., DBE 1970 (CBE 1964); General Secretary, Girls' Friendly Society, 1971–78; *b* 20 Feb. 1914; *d* of late George Wildman Kettlewell, Bramling, Virginia Water, Surrey, and of Mildred Frances (*née* Atkinson), Belford, Northumberland. *Educ:* Godolphin Sch., Salisbury; St Christopher's Coll., Blackheath. Worked for Fellowship of Maple Leaf, Alta, Canada, 1935–38; worked for Local Council, 1939–41; joined WRNS as MT driver, 1941; commnd as Third Officer WRNS, 1942; Supt WRNS on Staff of Flag Officer Air (Home), 1961–64; Supt WRNS Training and Drafting, 1964–67; Director, WRNS, 1967–70. Pres., Assoc. of Wrens, 1981–. *Recreations:* needlework, walking, and country life. *Address:* c/o Lloyds Bank Ltd, 263 Tottenham Court Road, W1P 0AT.
See also R. W. *Kettlewell.*

KETTLEWELL, Richard Wildman, CMG 1955; Colonial Service, retired 1962; *b* 12 Feb. 1910; *s* of late George Wildman Kettlewell and of Mildred Frances Atkinson; *m* 1935, Margaret Jessie Palmer; one *s* one *d. Educ:* Clifton Coll.; Reading and Cambridge Univs. BSc 1931; Dip. Agric. Cantab 1932; Associate of Imperial Coll. of Tropical Agriculture (AICTA), 1933. Entered Colonial Agricultural Service, 1934; appointed to Nyasaland. Served War of 1939–45 (despatches) with 2nd Bn King's African Rifles, 1939–43; rank of Major. Recalled to agricultural duties in Nyasaland, 1943; Dir of Agriculture, 1951–59; Sec. for Natural Resources, 1959–61; Minister for Lands and Surveys, 1961–62. Consultant to Hunting Technical Services, 1963–79. *Address:* Orchard Close, Over Norton, Chipping Norton, Oxon. *T:* Chipping Norton 2407.
See also Comdt Dame M. M. *Kettlewell.*

KEVILL-DAVIES, Christopher Evelyn, CBE 1973; JP; DL; *b* 12 July 1913; 3rd *s* of William A. S. H. Kevill-Davies, JP, Croft Castle, Herefordshire; *m* 1938, Virginia, *d* of Adm. Ronald A. Hopwood, CB; one *s* one *d. Educ:* Radley College. Served with Suffolk Yeomanry, 1939–43 and Grenadier Gds, 1943–45, France, Belgium and Germany. Mem., Gt Yarmouth Borough Council, 1946–53; Chm., Norfolk Mental Deficiency HMC, 1950–69; Mem., East Anglian Regional Hosp. Bd, 1962 (Vice-Chm. 1967); Vice-Chm., E Anglian RHA, 1974–. JP 1954, DL 1974, Norfolk; High Sheriff of Norfolk, 1965. *Address:* 11 Hale House, 34 De Vere Gardens, Kensington, W8. *T:* 01-937 5066. *Clubs:* Cavalry and Guards; Norfolk (Norwich).

KEVILLE, Sir (William) Errington, Kt 1962; CBE 1947; *b* 3 Jan. 1901; *s* of William Edwin Keville; *m* 1928, Ailsa Sherwood, *d* of late Captain John McMillan; three *s* two *d. Educ:* Merchant Taylors'. Pres., Chamber of Shipping, 1961 (Vice-Pres. 1960, Mem. of Council, 1940–); Chairman: Gen. Coun. of British Shipping, 1961; International Chamber of Shipping, 1963–68; Cttee of European Shipowners, 1963–65; Member: Executive Council of Shipping Federation Ltd, 1936–68; Board of PLA, 1943–59; National Maritime Board, 1945–68; Mem. of Cttee of Lloyd's Register of Shipping, 1957–68; Director: Shaw Savill & Albion Co. Ltd, 1941–68 (former Dep. Chm.); National Bank of New Zealand Ltd, 1946–75; Economic Insurance Co. Ltd, 1949–68 (Chm., 1962–68); National Mortgage & Agency Co. of NZ Ltd, 1950–68; British Maritime Trust Ltd, 1959–72 (Chm. 1962–68); Furness Withy & Co. Ltd, 1950–68 (Chm., 1962–68); Chm., Air Holdings Ltd, 1968–69. *Recreations:* walking, history. *Address:* Stroud Close, Grayswood, Haslemere, Surrey GU27 2DJ. *T:* Haslemere 3653.

KEWISH, John Douglas, CB 1958; TD 1944; DL; Registrar, Westminster County Court, 1971–73; *b* 4 May 1907; *s* of late John James Kewish, Birkenhead; *m* 1934, Marjorie Phyllis, *d* of late Dr Joseph Harvey, Wimbledon; one *s* one *d. Educ:* Birkenhead Sch. Admitted a Solicitor, 1931. Served TA, 1928–45; served 1939–44, with 4th Bn Cheshire Regt (UK, France and Belgium); commanded 4th Bn, 1940–44; commanded depots, The Cheshire Regt and The Manchester Regt and 24 Machine Gun Training Centre, 1944–45. Hon. Col 4th Bn Cheshire Regt, 1947–62. Chm., Cheshire T & AFA, 1951–59. Head of County Courts Branch in Lord Chancellor's Dept, 1960–71; Mem. Civil Judicial Statistics Cttee, 1966–68. Chm., Liverpool

Shipwreck and Humane Soc., 1953–60. DL Cheshire, 1952. *Address:* 41 Peel Park Avenue, Clitheroe, Lancs. *T:* Clitheroe 23052.

KEY, Maj.-Gen. Berthold Wells, CB 1947; DSO; MC; psc; IA (retired); *b* 19 Dec. 1895; *s* of late Dr J. M. Key; *m* 1917, Aileen Leslie (*d* 1951), *d* of late Col E. L. Dunsterville, RE; (one *s* killed in action in Italy) two *d. Educ:* Dulwich Coll. Joined 45th Rattrays Sikhs, IA, 1914; European War, 1914–19. Mesopotamia (wounded, MC); Afghanistan, 1919; NWF of India, 1930 (despatches); NWF Waziristan, 1936–37 (despatches, DSO); SE Asia, 1941–45; Comd, 2nd (Royal) Bn The Sikh Regt; Comd, 8 Ind. Bde, 1940–41; Comd 11 Ind. Div. 1942; ADC to the King, 1945–47; Comd, Rawalpindi Dist, 1946; Comd, Lahore Dist, 1947; Col, The Sikh Regt, 1947–62. *Recreation:* golf. *Address:* Naini, St George's Road, Sandwich, Kent.

KEY, Brian Michael; Member (Lab) Yorkshire South, European Parliament, since 1979; *b* 20 Sept. 1947; *s* of Leslie Granville Key and Nora Alice (*née* Haylett); *m* 1974, Lynn Joyce Ambler. *Educ:* Darfield County Primary Sch.; Wath upon Dearne Grammar Sch.; Liverpool Univ. (BA Hons). Careers Officer, West Riding County Council, 1970–73; Sen. Administrative Officer, South Yorkshire CC, 1973–79. *Address:* 25 Cliff Road, Darfield, Barnsley S73 9HL. *Clubs:* Darfield Working Men's; Trades and Labour (Doncaster).

KEY, Maj.-Gen. Clement Denis, MBE 1945; late RAOC; Clerk to the Governors, Tudor Hall School, Banbury, since 1976; *b* 6 June 1915; *s* of late William Clement Key, Harborne, Birmingham; *m* 1941, Molly, *d* of late F. Monk, Kettering, Northants; two *s. Educ:* Seaford Coll. Commnd in RAOC, 1940; served in: England, 1940–44; France, Belgium, Burma, Singapore, 1944–48; Staff Coll., Camberley, 1945; England, 1948–51; USA, 1951–54; England, 1954–59; jssc 1954; Belgium, 1959–61; War Office, 1961–64; Dep. Dir of Ordnance Services, War Office, 1964–67; Dep. Dir of Ordnance Services, Southern Comd, 1967; Comdr, UK Base Organisation, RAOC, 1968–70; retd, 1970. Hon. Col, RAOC (T&AVR), 1968–71; Col Comdt, RAOC, 1972–75. Bursar, Tudor Hall Sch., Banbury, 1971–76. *Recreations:* rowing, gardening, bee-keeping. *Address:* 104 Maidenhead Road, Stratford-upon-Avon, Warwicks. *T:* Stratford-upon-Avon 4345.

KEY, Rt. Rev. John Maurice, DD Lambeth, 1960; MA; an Assistant Bishop, Diocese of Exeter, since 1975; *b* 4 June 1905; *s* of late Preb. Frederick John Key, Lichfield, and Winifred Mary Head, Hexham, Northumberland; *m* 1935, Agnes Joan Dence (JP 1946-), *d* of late Rev. A. T. Dence, Abbotskerswell, Devon; three *s* one *d. Educ:* Rossall Sch.; Pembroke Coll., Cambridge; Westcott House, Cambridge. Assistant Curate, S. Mary's, Portsea, 1928–32; Vicar of Aylesbeare, Exeter, 1932–34; Rector of Highweek with S. Mary's, Newton Abbot, 1934–40; Rector of Stoke Damerel with S. Bartholomew's and S. Luke's. Devonport, 1940–47; Rural Dean of the Three Towns (Plymouth), 1944–47; Bishop Suffragan of Sherborne, 1947–59; Bishop of Truro, 1959–73. *Recreations:* music, gardening and country. *Address:* Donkeys, Stover, Newton Abbot, Devon. *T:* Newton Abbot 3997.

KEYES, family name of Baron Keyes.

KEYES, 2nd Baron, *cr* 1943, of Zeebrugge and of Dover; **Roger George Bowlby Keyes;** Bt, *cr* 1919; RN, retired; *b* 14 March 1919; 2nd *s* of Admiral of the Fleet Baron Keyes, GCB, KCVO, CMG, DSO and Eva Mary Salvin Bowlby (*d* 1973), Red Cross Order of Queen Elisabeth of Belgium, *d* of late Edward Salvin Bowlby, DL, of Gilston Park, Herts, and Knoydart, Inverness-shire; *S* father 1945; *m* 1947, Grizelda Mary, 2nd *d* of late Lieut-Col William Packe, DSO; three *s* two *d. Educ:* King's Mead Sch., Seaford; RNC, Dartmouth. *Publication:* Outrageous Fortune, 1982. *Heir: s* Hon. Charles William Packe Keyes [*b* 8 Dec. 1951; *m* 1978, Sadiye Yasmin Coskun, *e d* of late Mahir Coskun, Istanbul]. *Address:* Elmscroft, Charlton Lane, West Farleigh, near Maidstone, Kent. *T:* Maidstone 812477.

KEYNES, Prof. Richard Darwin, MA, PhD, ScD Cantab; FRS 1959; Professor of Physiology, University of Cambridge, since 1973; Fellow of Churchill College, since 1961; *b* 14 Aug. 1919; *e s* of Sir Geoffrey Keynes, MD, FRCP, FRCS, FRCOG, and late Margaret Elizabeth, *d* of Sir George Darwin, KCB; *m* 1945, Anne Pinsent Adrian, *e d* of 1st Baron Adrian, OM, FRS, and Dame Hester Agnes Adrian, DBE, *o d* of Hume C. and Dame Ellen Pinsent, DBE; three *s* (and one *s* decd). *Educ:* Oundle Sch. (Scholar); Trinity Coll., Cambridge (Scholar). Temporary experimental officer, HM Anti-Submarine Establishment and Admiralty Signals Establishment, 1940–45. 1st Class, Nat. Sci. Tripos Part II, 1946; Michael Foster and G. H. Lewes Studentships, 1946; Research Fellow of Trinity Coll., 1948–52; Gedge Prize, 1948; Rolleston Memorial Prize, 1950. Demonstrator in Physiology, University of Cambridge, 1949–53; Lecturer, 1953–60; Fellow of Peterhouse, 1952–60; Head of Physiology Dept and Dep. Dir, 1960–64, Dir, 1965–73, ARC Inst. of Animal Physiology. Sec.-Gen., Internat. Union for Pure and Applied Biophysics, 1972–78, Vice-Pres., 1978–81, Pres., 1981–. A Vice-Pres., Royal Society, 1965–68. Fellow of Eton, 1963–78. For. Member: Royal Danish Acad., 1971; American Philosophical Soc., 1977; Amer. Acad. of Arts and Scis, 1978. Dr *hc* Univ. of Brazil, 1968. *Publications:* The Beagle Record, 1979; (with D. J. Aidley) Nerve and Muscle, 1981; papers in Journal of Physiology, Proceedings of Royal Soc., etc. *Recreations:* sailing, gardening. *Address:* 4 Herschel Road, Cambridge. *T:* Cambridge 353107; Primrose Farm, Wiveton, Norfolk. *T:* Cley 740317.
See also S. J. *Keynes.*

KEYNES, Stephen John; Director: The English Association Group Ltd and subsidiaries, since 1980; Sun Life Assurance Society Ltd; Premier Consolidated Oilfields Ltd; *b* 19 Oct. 1927; 4th *s* of Sir Geoffrey Keynes, MD, FRCP, FRCS, FRCOG, and late Margaret Elizabeth, *d* of Sir George Darwin, KCB; *m* 1955, Mary, *o d* of late Senator the Hon. Adrian Knatchbull-Hugessen, QC (Canada), and late Margaret, *o d* of G. H. Duggan; three *s* two *d*. *Educ:* Oundle Sch.; King's Coll., Cambridge (Foundn Scholar; MA). Royal Artillery, 1949-51. Partner, J. F. Thomasson & Co., Private Bankers, 1961-65; Director: Charterhouse Japhet Ltd and Charterhouse Finance Corp., 1965-72; Arbuthnot Latham Holdings Ltd, 1973-80. Member: IBA (formerly ITA), 1969-74; Cttee and Treas., Islington and North London Family Service Unit, 1956-68; Adv. Cttee, Geffrye Museum; Trustee: Centerprise Community Project, 1971-75; William Blake Trust; Chm. of Trustees, Whitechapel Art Gallery. *Recreations:* medieval manuscripts, painting, gardening, travelling. *Address:* 16 Canonbury Park South, Islington, N1. *T:* 01-226 8170; White Hart Cottage, Brinkley, Newmarket, Suffolk. *T:* Stetchworth 223; Gunnerside, near Richmond, Yorks. *Clubs:* City of London, Cranium, Roxburghe.
See also R. D. Keynes.

KEYS, Sir (Alexander George) William, Kt 1980; OBE 1969; MC 1951; National President, Returned Services League of Australia, since 1978; Deputy Chairman, Canberra Permanent Building Society, since 1980; *b* 2 Feb. 1923; *s* of John Alexander Binnie Keys and Irene Daisy Keys; *m* 1950, Dulcie Beryl (*née* Stinton); three *d*. *Educ:* Hurlstone Agricultural High Sch. National Secretary, RSL, 1961-78; Nat. President, Korea and SE Asia Forces Assoc. of Australia, 1964-; World Pres., Internat. Fedn of Korean War Veterans Assoc., 1978-; Mem. Nat. Exec., Royal Australian Regt Assoc., 1967-; Nat. Chm., Australian Forces Overseas Fund, 1978-, Legatee, 1955-; Mem. Bd of Trustees, Aust. War Memorial, 1975-; Mem., Administrative Review Council, 1978-; Pres., ACT Br., Churchill Fellows Assoc. Korean Order of National Security and Merit, 1980. *Address:* Glenlee, Post Office Box 455, Queanbeyan, NSW 2620, Australia. *T:* (home) 97 5440; (office) 48 7199. *Clubs:* Commonwealth, National Press (Canberra); Imperial Services (Sydney); Returned Services League (Queanbeyan).

KEYS, Prof. Ivor Christopher Banfield, CBE 1976; MA, DMus Oxon; FRCO; Hon. RAM; Professor of Music, University of Birmingham, since 1968; *b* 8 March 1919; *er s* of Christopher Richard Keys, Littlehampton, Sussex; *m* 1944, Margaret Anne Layzell; two *s* two *d*. *Educ:* Christ's Hospital, Horsham; Christ Church, Oxford. FRCO 1935; music scholar and asst organist, Christ Church Cathedral, Oxford, 1938-40 and 1946-47. Served with Royal Pioneer Corps, 1940-46. Lecturer in Music, Queen's University of Belfast, 1947, Reader, 1950, Sir Hamilton Harty Professor of Music, QUB, 1951-54; Prof. of Music, Nottingham Univ., 1954-68. Pres., RCO, 1968-70. Hon. DMus QUB, 1972. *Publications:* The Texture of Music: Purcell to Brahms, 1961; Brahms Chamber Music, 1974; Mozart, 1980; *compositions:* Sonata for Violoncello and Pianoforte; Completion of Schubert's unfinished song Gretchens Bitte; Concerto for Clarinet and Strings; Prayer for Pentecostal Fire (choir and organ); The Road to the Stable (3 Christmas songs with piano); Magnificat and Nunc Dimittis (choir and organ); editions of music; reviews of music, in Music and Letters, and of books, in Musical Times. *Recreation:* bridge. *Address:* Barber Institute of Fine Arts (Department of Music), PO Box 363, Birmingham B15 2TS.

KEYS, Sir William; *see* Keys, Sir A. G. W.

KEYS, William Herbert; Joint General Secretary, Society of Graphical and Allied Trades 1982, since 1982 (General Secretary, SOGAT, from 1974 until amalgamation with NATSOPA in 1982); *b* 1 Jan. 1923; *s* of George William and Jessie Keys; *m* 1941, Enid Gledhill; two *s*. *Educ:* Grammar Sch., South London. Served Army, 1939-46. National Organiser, Printing, Bookbinding and Paper Workers Union, 1953-61; Secretary, London, 1961-70. Society of Graphical and Allied Trades (SOGAT): General President, 1970-74. Member, General Council, TUC, 1974-; Chairman: TUC Printing Industries Committee, 1974-; TUC Media Cttee, 1977-; Equal Rights Cttee, TUC, 1974-; Race Relations Cttee, TUC, 1974-; TUC Employment Policy and Organisation Cttee (Mem., 1976-); Member: Central Arbitration Cttee, 1977-; Commission for Racial Equality, 1977-81; Manpower Services Commn, 1979-; Joint Chairman, Pulp and Paper Division, Internat. Chemical Federation, 1976-. Member: Inst. of Manpower Studies, 1979-; European Social Fund, 1979-. *Recreation:* music. *Address:* 274-288 London Road, Hadleigh, Essex. *T:* Southend-on-Sea 553131.

KHAN, Vice-Adm. Afzal Rahman, HQA 1961 (SQA 1958); HPk 1964; HJ 1965; Chairman, ARK International, since 1970; *b* 20 March 1921; *s* of late Abdur Rahman Khan, landlord, Gurdaspur District; *m* 1944, Hameeda Khan; one *s* two *d*. *Educ:* Baring High Sch., Batala; Govt Coll., Lahore. Joined Indian Mercantile Marine Trng Ship Dufferin, 1936; entered Royal Indian Navy, 1938; Actg Sub-Lieut 1940; Lieut 1942; Lieut-Comdr 1947; Comdr 1950; Captain 1953; Cdre 1958; Rear-Adm. 1959; Vice-Adm. 1961. War of 1939-45: active service, HM Ships in Atlantic, Mediterranean and N Sea and in Royal Indian Navy ships in Indian Ocean and Burma Coast. After Independence in 1947, comd various ships and shore estabs of Pakistan Navy and held other sen. appts; Specialist in Gunnery; psc, jssc; C-in-C, Pakistan Navy, 1959; retd from Navy, 1966. Minister for Defence, and for Home Affairs, Pakistan, 1966-69; Minister in charge of Ports and Shipping, 1967-69. Order of Humayun (Iran), 1961; Legion of Merit (US), 1960 and 1964.

Recreations: shooting, deep-sea fishing, tennis, golf, study of naval history. *Address:* The Anchorage, 27b South Central Avenue, 8th South Street, Defence Housing Society, Karachi, Pakistan. *T:* 541550. *Clubs:* Royal Overseas League; Sind, Rawalpindi; Golf, Gymkhana (Karachi).

KHAN, Sir Muhammad Zafrulla; *see* Zafrulla Khan.

KHORANA, Prof. Har Gobind; Sloan Professor of Chemistry and Biology, Massachusetts Institute of Technology, since 1970; *b* Raipur, India, 9 Jan. 1922; *s* of Shri Ganpat Rai and Shrimata Krishna (Devi); *m* 1952, Esther Elizabeth Sibler; one *s* two *d*. *Educ:* Punjab Univ. (BSc, MSc); Liverpool Univ. (PhD, Govt of India Student). Post-doctoral Fellow of Govt of India, Federal Inst. of Techn., Zurich, 1948-49; Nuffield Fellow, Cambridge Univ., 1950-52; Head, Organic Chemistry Group, BC Research Council, 1952-60. Univ. of Wisconsin: Co-Dir, Inst. for Enzyme Research, 1960-70; Prof., Dept of Chemistry, 1962-70; Conrad A. Elvehjem Prof. in the Life Sciences, 1964-70. Visiting Professor: Rockefeller Inst., NY, 1958-60; Stanford Univ., 1964; Harvard Med. Sch., 1966. Has given special or memorial lectures in USA, Poland, Canada, Switzerland, UK and Japan. Fellow: Chem. Inst. of Canada; Amer. Assoc. for Advancement of Science; Amer. Acad. of Arts and Sciences; Overseas Fellow, Churchill Coll., Cambridge; Member: Nat. Acad. of Sciences; Deutsche Akademie der Naturforscher Leopoldina; Foreign Mem., Royal Society, 1978. Hon. Dr Science, Chicago, 1967. Merck Award, Chem. Inst. Canada, 1958; Gold Medal for 1960, Professional Inst. of Public Service of Canada; Dannie-Heinneman Preiz, Germany, 1967; Remsen Award, Johns Hopkins Univ., ACS Award for Creative Work in Synthetic Organic Chemistry, Louisa Gross Horwitz Award, Lasker Foundn Award for Basic Med. Research, Nobel Prize for Medicine (jtly), 1968. *Publications:* Some Recent Developments in the Chemistry of Phosphate Esters of Biological Interest, 1961; numerous papers in Biochemistry, Jl Amer. Chem. Soc., etc. *Recreations:* hiking, swimming. *Address:* Department of Biology, Massachusetts Institute of Technology, Cambridge, Mass 02139, USA.

KIBBEY, Sidney Basil; Under-Secretary, Department of Health and Social Security, 1971-76; *b* 3 Dec. 1916; *y s* of late Percy Edwin Kibbey and Winifred Kibbey, Mickleover, Derby; *m* 1939, Violet Gertrude Eyre; (twin) *s* and *d*. *Educ:* Derby Sch. Executive Officer, Min. of Health, 1936; Principal, Min. of National Insurance, 1951; Sec., Nat. Insurance Adv. Cttee, 1960-62; Asst Sec., Min. of Pensions and Nat. Insurance, 1962. *Address:* 29 Beaulieu Close, Datchet, Berks. *T:* Slough 49101.

KIBBLE, Prof. Thomas Walter Bannerman, PhD; FRS 1980; Professor of Theoretical Physics, Imperial College, London, since 1970; *b* 1932; *s* of Walter Frederick Kibble and Janet Cowan Watson (*née* Bannerman); *m* 1957, Anne Richmond Allan; one *s* two *d*. *Educ:* Melville Coll., Edinburgh; Univ. of Edinburgh (MA, BSc, PhD). Commonwealth Fund Fellow, California Inst. of Technology, 1958-59; Imperial College, London: NATO Fellow, 1959-60; Lecturer, 1961; Sen. Lectr, 1965; Reader in Theoretical Physics, 1966. Sen. Visiting Research Associate, Univ. of Rochester, New York, 1967-68. *Publications:* Classical Mechanics, 1966, 2nd edn 1973; papers in Phys. Rev., Proc. Royal Soc., Nuclear Physics, Nuovo Cimento, Jl Physics, and others. *Recreations:* cycling, destructive gardening. *Address:* Blackett Laboratory, Imperial College, Prince Consort Road, SW7 2BZ. *T:* 01-589 5111.

KIDD, Dame Margaret (Henderson), (Dame Margaret Macdonald), DBE 1975; QC (Scotland), 1948; Sheriff Principal of Perth and Angus, 1966-74 (of Dumfries and Galloway, 1960-66); *b* 14 March 1900; *e d* of James Kidd, Solicitor, Linlithgow (sometime MP (U) for W Lothian), and late J. G. Kidd (*née* Turnbull); *m* 1930, Donald Somerled Macdonald (*d* 1958), WS Edinburgh; one *d*. *Educ:* Linlithgow Acad.; Edinburgh Univ. Admitted to the Scottish Bar, 1923; contested (U) West Lothian, 1928. Keeper of the Advocates' Library, 1956-69; Editor Court of Session Reports in Scots Law Times, 1942-76; Vice-Pres. British Federation of University Women, Ltd. *Address:* 5 India Street, Edinburgh EH3 6HA. *T:* 031-225 3867.

KIDD, Sir Robert (Hill), KBE 1979; CB 1975; Director, since 1979, and Chairman, Northern Ireland Local Board, since 1980, Allied Irish Banks Ltd; Head of Northern Ireland Civil Service, 1976-79; *b* 3 Feb. 1918; *s* of Andrew Kidd and Florence Hill, Belfast; *m* 1942, Harriet Moore Williamson; three *s* two *d*. *Educ:* Royal Belfast Academical Instn; Trinity Coll., Dublin. BA 1940, BLitt 1941. Army, 1941-46: commnd 1942, Royal Ulster Rifles, later seconded to Intell. Corps. Entered Northern Ireland Civil Service, 1947; Second Sec., Dept of Finance, NI, 1969-76. Governor, Royal Belfast Academical Inst., 1967-76, 1979-; a Pro-Chancellor and Chm. Council, New Univ. of Ulster, 1980-; Pres., TCD Assoc. of NI, 1981-83; Trustee: Scotch-Irish Trust of Ulster, 1980-; Ulster Historical Foundn, 1981-. *Recreations:* gardening, caravanning, photography. *Address:* 24 Massey Court, Belfast BT4 3GJ. *T:* Belfast 768693.

KIDD, Ronald Alexander; HM Diplomatic Service, retired; consultant on Japan; *b* 19 June 1926; *s* of Alexander and Jean Kidd; *m* 1954, Agnes Japp Harrower; two *d*. *Educ:* Robert Gordon's College, Aberdeen; Queens' College, Cambridge; BA Hons 1951, MA 1956. Royal Air Force, 1944-48; Foreign Office, 1951; served at Singapore, Djakarta, Osaka and Macau, 1952-56; FO, 1956-60; Second, later First Sec., Seoul, 1961-62; Djakarta, 1962-63; Tokyo, 1964-68; Dar Es Salaam, 1971-72; Tokyo, 1972-77; Counsellor, FCO, 1977-81. Jubilee Medal, 1977. *Recreations:* golf and most sports. *Address:* Kellwood Cottage, Wilksby, Revesby, Boston,

Lincs. *T:* Mareham-le-Fen 321. *Clubs:* Royal Air Force; Ecurie Ecosse (Edinburgh).

KIDMAN, Thomas Walter, ERD 1954; Regional Administrator, East Anglian Regional Health Authority, 1973-75, retired; *b* 28 Aug. 1915; *s* of Walter James Kidman and Elizabeth Alice Kidman (*née* Littlejohns); *m* 1939, Lilian Rose Souton; one *s* two *d. Educ:* Cambridge Central Sch.; Cambs Techn. Coll. FHA. War service, 1939-46: Warrant Officer, RAMC, BEF France, 1940; Major, Suffolk Regt, seconded Corps of Mil. Police, MEF Egypt and Palestine, 1943-46; served in TA/AER, 1939-67. Local Govt Officer, Health and Educn, Cambridgeshire CC, 1930-48; East Anglian Regional Hosp. Bd: Admin. Officer, 1948; Asst Sec., 1952; Dep. Sec., 1957; Sec. of Bd, 1972. Mem., NHS Advisory Service, 1976-; Chm., Cambs Mental Welfare Assoc., 1977-. *Recreations:* photography, walking, gardening, golf. *Address:* Alwoodley, 225 Arbury Road, Cambridge CB4 2JJ. *T:* Cambridge 357384.

KIDRON, Abraham; Ambassador of Israel to Australia, since 1979; *b* 19 Nov. 1919; *m* 1946, Shoshanna; two *d. Educ:* Hebrew Univ. of Jerusalem (BA). Captain, Israel Def. Forces, 1948. Min. of Foreign Affairs, 1949-50; Attaché, Embassy of Israel, Rome, 1950-52; Min. of Foreign Affairs, 1953-54; Consul, Cyprus, 1954-56; First Sec. (Press), Embassy of Israel, London, 1957-59; Head of Res. Dept and Spokesman for Min. of Foreign Affairs, 1959-63; Minister, Israel Legation, Yugoslavia, 1963-65; Ambassador to the Phillipines, 1965-67; Asst Dir Gen., Min. of Foreign Affairs, 1969-71, Dep. Dir Gen., 1972-73, Dir Gen., 1973-76; Ambassador: to the Netherlands, 1976-77; to the Court of St James's, 1977-79. *Recreation:* golf. *Address:* c/o Embassy of Israel, Canberra, ACT 2600, Australia.

KIDU, Hon. Sir Buri (William), Kt 1980; Chief Justice of Papua New Guinea, since 1980; *b* 8 Aug. 1945; *s* of Kidu Gaudi and Dobi Vagi; *m* 1969, Carol Anne Kidu; three *s* two *d. Educ:* Univ. of Queensland, Australia (LLB). Barrister-at-Law of Supreme Courts of Queensland and Papua New Guinea. Legal Officer, Dept of Law, 1971; Crown Prosecutor, 1972; Deputy Crown Solicitor, 1973-74; Crown Solicitor, 1974-77; Secretary for Justice, 1977-79; Secretary of Prime Minister's Dept, 1979-80. Chancellor, Univ. of Papua New Guinea, 1981-. *Recreations:* reading, swimming. *Address:* Supreme Court, PO Box 7018, Boroko, Port Moresby, Papua New Guinea. *T:* 25 7099.

KIDWELL, Raymond Incledon, QC 1968; a Recorder, since 1972; *b* 8 Aug. 1926; *s* of Montague and late Dorothy Kidwell; *m* 1st, 1951, Enid Rowe (marr. diss. 1975); two *s* ; 2nd, 1976, Carol Evelyn Beryl Maddison, *d* of late Warren G. Hopkins, Ontario. *Educ:* Whitgift Sch.; Magdalen Coll., Oxford. RAFVR, 1944-48. BA (Law) 1st cl. 1950; MA 1951; BCL 1st cl. 1951; Vinerian Law Schol., 1951; Eldon Law Schol., 1951; Arden Law Schol., Gray's Inn, 1952; Birkenhead Law Schol., Gray's Inn, 1955. Called to Bar, 1951; Bencher, 1978. Lectr in Law, Oriel Coll., Oxford, 1952-55; Mem., Winn Commn on Personal Injuries, 1966-68. Member: Bar Council, 1967-71; Senate, 1981-. *Address:* Sanderstead House, Rectory Park, Sanderstead, Surrey. *T:* 01-657 4161; Burrows Farm West, Croyde, North Devon. *T:* Croyde 890576; 2 Crown Office Row, Temple, EC4. *T:* 01-353 9337. *Club:* United Oxford & Cambridge University.

KIELY, Dr David George; Under Secretary; Director, Naval Surface Weapons Projects, Admiralty Surface Weapons Establishment, Procurement Executive, Ministry of Defence, since 1978; Chairman, R&D Policy Committee of the General Lights Authorities of the UK and Eire, since 1974; *b* 23 July 1925; *o s* of late George Thomas and Susan Kiely, Ballynahinch, Co. Down; *m* 1956, Dr Ann Wilhelmina (*née* Kilpatrick), MB, BCh, BAO, DCH, DPH, MFCM, Hillsborough, Co. Down; one *s* one *d. Educ:* Down High Sch., Downpatrick; Queen's Univ., Belfast (BSc, MSc); Sorbonne (DSci). CEng, FIEE, FInstP; psc 1961. Appts in RN Scientific Service from 1944; Naval Staff Coll., 1961-62; Head of Electronic Warfare Div., ASWE, 1965-68; Head of Communications and Sensor Dept, ASWE, 1968-72; Dir-Gen., Telecommunications, 1972-74, Dir-Gen., Strategic Electronic Systems, 1974-76, Dir-Gen., Electronics Res., 1976-78, Exec. Officer, Electronics Research Council, 1976-78, MoD, PE. Governor, Portsmouth Coll. of Technology, 1965-69. Mem. Council, Electronic Cathedral, 1982-. *Publications:* Dielectric Aerials, 1953; chapter: in Progress in Dielectrics, 1961; in Fundamentals of Microwave Electronics, 1963; papers in Proc. IEE and other learned jls, etc. *Recreations:* fly fishing, gardening, World Pheasant Assoc. *Address:* Cranleigh, Havant Road, Emsworth, Hants. *T:* Emsworth 2250. *Club:* Naval and Military.

KIER, Olaf, CBE 1970; Director of J. L. Kier & Co. Ltd, 1934-76; Life President, French Kier Holdings Ltd; *b* Copenhagen, 4 Sept. 1899; *s* of Hector Kier, Cdre Royal Danish Navy; naturalized British subject, 1947; *m* 1st, 1924 (marr. diss.); two *d* (one *s* decd); 2nd, 1963, Bente Gudrun Tummler; one *s. Educ:* Copenhagen Univ. MSc Civil Engrg. FICE 1955. Resident in UK from 1922. Founded J. L. Kier & Co. Ltd, Civil Engrg Contractors, 1932 (became a public company, 1963). Underwriting Member of Lloyds, 1948. Comdr, Order of Dannebrog, 1966. *Address:* Abbotsbury Manor, Barley, Royston, Herts. *T:* Barkway 427.

KIESINGER, Kurt Georg; Member of Bundestag, 1949-58 and 1969-80; Chancellor of the Federal Republic of Germany, 1966-69; *b* 6 April 1904; *m* Marie-Luise Schneider; one *s* one *d. Educ:* Tübingen Univ.; Berlin Univ. Lawyer. Minister-Pres., Baden-Württemberg 1958-66; Pres., Bundesrat, 1962-

63. Chm., Christian Democratic Group, 1958. Member: Consultative Assembly, Council of Europe, 1958 (Vice-Pres.); WEU Assembly, 1958; Central Cttee, Christian Democratic Party (Chm., 1967-71). Dluris *hc:* Univ. of Cologne, 1965; New Delhi, 1967; Maryland, 1968; Coimbra, 1968. Grand Cross, Order of Merit, German Federal Republic; Grand Cross, Order of Merit, Italian Republic; Grand Officier de la Légion d'Honneur, Palmes Academiques. *Address:* Tübingen, Engelfriedshalde 48, West Germany.

KIKI, Hon. Sir (Albert) Maori, KBE 1975; Chairman of the Constitutional Commission, since 1976; *b* 21 Sept. 1931; *s* of Erevu Kiki and Eau Ulamare; *m* 1957, Elizabeth Hariai Miro; two *s* three *d. Educ:* London Missionary Soc. Sch.; Sogeri Central Sch., Papua New Guinea; Fiji Sch. of Med. (Pathology); Papua New Guinea Admin. Coll. Medical Orderly, Kerema, Gulf Province, 1948; Teacher Trng, Sogeri, CP, 1950; Central Med. Sch., Fiji, 1951; Dept of Public Health, Port Moresby, 1954. Formed first trade union in Papua New Guinea and Pres., Council of Trade Unions; Welfare Officer, CP, Land Claims work amongst Koiari people, 1964; studied at Admin. Coll., 1964-65; Foundn Mem. and first Gen. Sec. of Pangu Pati (PNG's 1st Political League); Mem., Port Moresby CC, 1971. MP for Port Moresby, 1972; Minister for Lands, Papua New Guinea, 1972; Deputy Prime Minister and Minister for Defence, Foreign Affairs and Trade, 1975-77. Chairman of Directors, 1977-: Nat. Shipping Corp.; New Guinea Motors Pty Ltd; Credit Corp. (PNG) Ltd; Kwila Insurance Corp. Ltd; Ovameveo Develts Pty Ltd (Property Developers); Maruka Pty Ltd; On Pty Ltd; Maho Investments Ltd; Consultants Pty Ltd. Hon. Dr Laws Kyung Hee Univ., South Korea, 1976. *Publications:* Ten Thousand Years in a Lifetime (autobiog.), 1970; (with Ulli Beier) HoHao: art and culture of the Orokolo people, 1972. *Recreations:* care of farm; formerly Rugby (patron and founder of PNG Rugby Union). *Address:* PO Box 1739, Boroko, Papua New Guinea; (private) Granville Farm, 8 Mile, Port Moresby, PNG.

KILBRACKEN, 3rd Baron, *cr* 1909, of Killegar; **John Raymond Godley;** journalist and author; *b* 17 Oct. 1920; *er s* of 2nd Baron, CB, KC, and Elizabeth Helen Monteith, *d* of Vereker Monteith Hamilton and *widow* of Wing Commander N. F. Usborne, RNAS; *S* father 1950; *m* 1st, 1943, Penelope Anne (marr. diss., 1949), *y d* of Rear-Adm. Sir C. N. Reyne, KBE; one *s* (and one *s* decd); 2nd, 1981, Susan Lee, *yr d* of N. F. Heazlewood, Melbourne, Australia; one *s. Educ:* Eton; Balliol Coll., Oxford (MA). Served in RNVR (Fleet Air Arm), as air pilot, 1940-46 (DSC 1945); entered as naval airman, commissioned 1941; Lieut-Comdr 1944; commanded Nos 835 and 714 Naval Air Sqdns. A reporter for many UK, US and foreign journals, 1947-; mainly as foreign corresp., 1960-74; major assignments in Cuba, China, Yemen, Mozambique, Angola, Kurdistan, Aden; cameraman (TV and stills), 1962-. Joined Parly Liberal Party, 1960; transferred to Labour, 1966. Hon. Sec., Connacht Hereford Breeders' Assoc., 1973-76. Pres., British-Kurdish Friendship Soc., 1975-. *Publications:* Even For An Hour (poems), 1940; Tell Me The Next One, 1950; The Master Forger, 1951; Living Like a Lord, 1955; A Peer behind the Curtain, 1959; Shamrocks and Unicorns, 1962; Van Meegeren, 1967; Bring Back My Stringbag, 1979; The Easy Way to Bird Recognition, 1982; (ed) Letters from Early New Zealand, 1951. TV documentaries: The Yemen, 1964; Morgan's Treasure, 1965; Kurdistan, 1966. *Recreation:* bird-watching. *Heir: s* Hon. Christopher John Godley [*b* 1 Jan. 1945; *m* 1969, Gillian Christine, *yr d* of Lt-Comdr S. W. Birse, RN retd; Alverstoke; one *s* one *d. Educ:* Rugby; Reading Univ. (BSc Agric.)]. *Address:* Killegar, Cavan, Ireland. *T:* Cavan 34309.
See also Hon. W. A. H. Godley.

KILBRANDON, Baron *cr* 1971 (Life Peer), of Kilbrandon, Argyll; **Charles James Dalrymple Shaw,** PC 1971; a Lord of Appeal in Ordinary, 1971-76; *b* 15 Aug. 1906; *s* of James Edward Shaw, DL, County Clerk of Ayrshire, and Gladys Elizabeth Lester; *m* 1937, Ruth Caroline Grant; two *s* three *d. Educ:* Charterhouse; Balliol Coll., Oxford; Edinburgh Univ. Admitted to Faculty of Advocates, 1932, Dean of Faculty, 1957; KC 1949; Sheriff of Ayr and Bute, 1954-57; Sheriff of Perth and Angus, 1957; Senator of Coll. of Justice in Scotland and Lord of Session, 1959-71. Chairman: Standing Consultative Council on Youth Service in Scotland, 1960-68; Departmental Cttee on Treatment of Children and Young Persons, 1964; Scottish Law Commn, 1965-71; Commn on the Constitution, 1972-73 (Mem., 1969-72); Bd of Management, Royal Infirmary, Edinburgh, 1960-68. Hon. LLD Aberdeen, 1965; Hon. DSc (Soc. Sci.) Edinburgh, 1970. Hon. Fellow, Balliol Coll., Oxford, 1969, Visitor, 1974-; Hon. Bencher, Gray's Inn, 1971. *Address:* Kilbrandon House, Balvicar, by Oban. *T:* Balvicar 239. *Clubs:* New, Royal Highland Yacht (Oban).

KILBURN, Prof. Tom, CBE 1973; FRS 1965; Professor of Computer Science, University of Manchester, 1964-81, now Emeritus; *b* 11 Aug. 1921; *o s* of John W. and Ivy Kilburn, Dewsbury; *m* 1943, Irene (*née* Marsden); one *s* one *d. Educ:* Wheelwright Grammar Sch., Dewsbury; Sidney Sussex Coll., Cambridge; Manchester Univ. MA Cambridge 1944. Telecommunications Research Estab., Malvern, 1942-46. Manchester Univ., 1947-81; PhD 1948; Lecturer, 1949; Senior Lecturer, 1951; DSc 1953; Reader in Electronics, 1955; Prof. of Computer Engineering, 1960. FIEE; FBCS 1970. Royal Medal, Royal Society, 1978. *Publications:* papers in Jl of Instn of Electrical Engineers, etc. *Address:* 11 Carlton Crescent, Urmston, Lancs. *T:* Urmston 3846.

KILDARE, Marquess of; Maurice FitzGerald; landscape and contract gardener; *b* 7 April 1948; *s* and *heir* of 8th Duke of Leinster, *qv* ; *m* 1972,

Fiona Mary Francesca, *d* of Harry Hollick; one *s* two *d*. *Educ:* Millfield School. Pres., Oxfordshire Dyslexia Assoc. *Heir: s* Earl of Offaly, *qv*. *Address:* 7 Littleworth Hill, Wantage, Oxon.

KILDARE AND LEIGHLIN, Bishop of, (RC), since 1967; **Most Rev. Patrick Lennon,** DD; *b* Borris, Co. Carlow, 1914. *Educ:* Rockwell Coll., Cashel; St Patrick's Coll., Maynooth. BSc 1934; DD 1940. Prof. of Moral Theology, St Patrick's Coll., Carlow, 1940; Pres., St Patrick's Coll., 1956–66; Auxiliary Bishop and Parish Priest of Mountmellick, 1966–67. *Address:* Bishop's House, Carlow. *T:* Carlow 31102.

KILÉNYI, Edward A.; Professor of Music, Florida State University; *b* 7 May 1911; *s* of Edward Kilényi and Ethel Frater; *m* 1945, Kathleen Mary Jones; two *d*. *Educ:* Budapest; since childhood studied piano with Ernő Dohnányi; Theory and conducting Royal Academy of Music. First concert tour with Dohnányi (Schubert Centenary Festivals), 1928; concert tours, recitals, and soloist with Principal Symphony Orchestras, 1930–39, in Holland, Germany, Hungary, Roumania, France, Scandinavia, North Africa, Portugal, Belgium; English debut, 1935, with Sir Thomas Beecham in Liverpool, Manchester, London; tours 1940–42, and 1946–, US, Canada, Cuba. Columbia and Remington Recordings internationally distributed. Served War of 1939–45, Capt. US Army, European theatre of operations. *Address:* c/o Florida State University, Tallahassee, Fla 32306, USA.

KILFEDDER, James Alexander; MP North Down since 1970; Leader, Ulster Popular Unionist Party, since 1980; Barrister-at-law; *b* 16 July 1928; *yr s* of late Robert and Elizabeth Kilfedder; unmarried. *Educ:* Model Sch. and Portora Royal Sch., Enniskillen, NI; Trinity Coll., Dublin (BA); King's Inn, Dublin. Called to English Bar, Gray's Inn, 1958. MP (UU) Belfast West, 1964–66, North Down, 1970–80. Mem. (Official Unionist), N Down, NI Assembly, 1973–75; Mem. (UUUC) N Down, NI Constitutional Convention, 1975–76; Former Chief Whip and Hon. Sec., Ulster Unionist Parly Party; Mem., Trustee Savings Banks Parly Cttee. *Recreation:* walking in the country. *Address:* Eastonville, Donaghadee Road, Millisle, NI. *T:* Donaghadee 883222; House of Commons, SW1. *T:* 01-219 3563.

KILFOIL, Geoffrey Everard; a Recorder of the Crown Court, since 1980; *b* 15 March 1939; *s* of Thomas Albert Kilfoil and Hilda Alice Kilfoil; *m* 1962, Llinos Mai Morris; one *s* one *d*. *Educ:* Acrefair Primary Sch.; Ruabon Grammar Sch.; Jesus Coll., Oxford (Weldon Law prizeman, 1958, and Viscount Sankey Foundn Bar Schol., 1960; BA Hons (Jurisprudence), MA). Gray's Inn Holker schol., 1966, and called to Bar, 1966; practised Wales and Chester Circuit, 1966–; Dep. Circuit Judge, 1976; Circuit Junior, 1979–80. Member: Cefn Parish Council, Wrexham RDC and Denbighshire CC, 1961–67; adopted prospective parly candidate (Lab), Ludlow constituency, 1966 General Election. *Recreations:* listening to and making music; extolling to unconverted foreigners the unchallengeable virtues of Wales and her people. *Address:* (chambers) 40 King Street, Chester. *T:* Chester 49591; 5 Essex Court, Temple, EC4. *T:* 01-353 2440; (home) Clayton Court, Mold, Clwyd. *T:* Mold 3859.

KILGOUR, Dr John Lowell; Director of Coordination, The World Health Organisation, since 1978; *b* 26 July 1924; *s* of Ormonde John Lowell Kilgour and Catherine (*née* MacInnes); *m* 1955, Daphne (*née* Tully); two *s*. *Educ:* St Christopher's Prep. Sch., Hove; Aberdeen Grammar Sch.; Aberdeen Univ. MB, ChB 1947, MRCGP, FFCM. Joined RAMC, 1948; served in: Korea, 1950–52; Cyprus, 1956; Suez, 1956; Singapore, 1961–64 (Brunei, Sarawak); comd 23 Para. Field Amb., 1954–57; psc 1959; ADMS HQ FARELF, 1961–64; jssc 1964. Joined Min. of Health, 1968, Med. Manpower and Postgrad. Educn Divs; Head of Internat. Health Div., DHSS, 1971–78; Under-Sec. and Chief Med. Advr, Min. of Overseas Develt, 1973–78; UK Deleg. to WHO and to Council of Europe Public Health Cttees; Chm., European Public Health Cttee, 1976; Mem. WHO Expert Panel on Communicable Diseases, 1972–; Chm., Cttee for Internat. Surveillance of Communicable Diseases, 1976. Vis. Lectr, LSHTM, 1976–. Mem. Governing Council, Liverpool Sch. of Tropical Medicine. Winner, Cons. Constituency Speakers' Competition for London and the SE, 1968. *Publications:* chapter in, Migration of Medical Manpower, 1971; contrib. The Lancet, Hospital Medicine, Health Trends and other med. jls. *Recreations:* reading, gardening, one dachshund, travel. *Address:* c/o The World Health Organisation, 1211 Geneva 27, Switzerland. *T:* 010-4122 346061; 29 Napier Court, Hurlingham, SW6. *T:* 01-731 3881. *Clubs:* Athenæum, Hurlingham; Royal Windsor Racing.

KILLALOE, Bishop of, (RC), since 1967; **Most Rev. Michael Harty;** *b* Feb. 1922; *s* of Patrick Harty, Lismore, Toomevara, Co. Tipperary, Ireland. *Educ:* St Flannan's Coll., Ennis, Ire.; St Patrick's Coll., Maynooth, Ire.; University Coll., Galway. Priest, 1946; Prof., St Flannan's Coll., Ennis, 1948; Dean, St Patrick's Coll., Maynooth, 1949, 1955–67; Asst Priest, dio. Los Angeles, 1954. BA, BD, LCL, DD (Hon.); HDiplEduc. *Address:* Westbourne, Ennis, Co. Clare, Ireland. *T:* Ennis 21638.

KILLANIN, 3rd Baron, *cr* 1900; **Michael Morris,** Bt, *cr* 1885; MBE 1945; TD 1945; MA; Author, Film Producer; President, International Olympic Committee, 1972–80, now Honorary Life President; *b* 30 July 1914; *o s* of late Lieut-Col Hon. George Henry Morris, Irish Guards, 2nd *s* of 1st Baron, and

Dora Maryan [who *m* 2nd, 1918, Lieut-Col Gerard Tharp, Rifle Brigade (*d* 1934)], *d* of late James Wesley Hall, Melbourne, Australia; *S* uncle, 1927; *m* 1945, Mary Sheila Cathcart, MBE 1946, *o d* of late Rev. Canon Douglas L. C. Dunlop, MA, Kilcummin, Galway; three *s* one *d*. *Educ:* Eton; Sorbonne, Paris; Magdalene Coll., Cambridge. BA 1935; MA 1939; formerly on Editorial Staff, Daily Express; Daily Mail, 1935–39; Special Daily Mail War Correspondent Japanese-Chinese War, 1937-38. Political Columnist Sunday Dispatch, 1938-39. Served War of 1939–45 (MBE, TD), KRRC (Queen's Westminsters); Brigade Maj. 30 Armd Bde, 1943–45. Director: Irish Shell Ltd; Chubb (Ireland) Ltd; Syntex Ireland Ltd; Ulster Bank Ltd; Ulster Investment Ltd (Chm.); Lombard and Ulster Banking (Ireland) Ltd (Chm.); Northern Telecom (Ireland) Ltd (Chm.); Life Assoc. Ireland Ltd (Chm.); Gallahers (Dublin) Ltd (Chm.); Beamish & Crawford Ltd; Fitzwilton Ltd. Member of Lloyd's. International Olympic Committee: Mem., 1952; Mem., Exec. Bd, 1967; Vice-Pres., 1968–72; President: Olympic Council of Ireland, 1950–73; Incorporated Sales Managers' Association (Ireland), 1955–58; Galway Chamber of Commerce, 1952–53; Chm. of the Dublin Theatre Festival, 1958–70. Member: Council Irish Red Cross Soc., 1947–72; Cttee RNLI (a Vice-Pres.); Cultural Adv. Cttee to Minister for External Affairs, 1947–72; Nat. Monuments of Ireland Advisory Council, 1947– (Chm., 1961–65); RIA, 1952; Irish Nat. Sports Council, 1970–72; Irish Turf Club (Steward 1971–73, 1981–); National Hunt Steeplechase Cttee; first President, Irish Club, London, 1947–65; Hon. Life Mem., Royal Dublin Soc., 1982; Trustee, Irish Sailors and Soldiers Land Trust, 1947–; Hon. Consul-General for Monaco, in Ireland, 1961–. Hon. LLD NUI, 1975; Hon. DLitt New Univ. of Ulster, 1977. Mem., French Acad. of Sport, 1974. Grand Cross, Order of Civil Merit (Spain), 1976; Grand Officer, Order of Merit of Rep. of Italy, 1973; Grand Officer, Order of Republic (Tunis), 1976; Grand Officer, Order of the Phoenix of Greece, 1976; Knight of Honour and Devotion, Sovereign Order of Malta, 1943; Commander's Cross, Order of Polonia Restituta (Poland), 1979; Commander, Order of Olympic Merit (Finland), 1951; Commander, Order of the Grimaldis, 1961; Grand Cross, German Federal Republic, 1972 (Commander); Star of the Sacred Treasure (Second Class) (Japan), 1972; Order of the Madara Rider (Bulgaria); Commander, Order of Sports Merit (Ivory Coast), 1977; Commander of Legion of Honour (France), 1980; Chevalier, Order of Duarte Sanchez y Mella (Dominican Rep.), 1977; Star of Solidarity 1st Class (Italy), 1957; Medal Miroslav Tyrš (Czechoslovakia), 1970; Olympic Order of Merit (gold), 1980; decorations from Africa, Austria, Brazil, China, Columbia, USSR etc. *Films:* (with John Ford) The Rising of the Moon; Gideon's Day; Young Cassidy; Playboy of the Western World; Alfred the Great; Connemara and its Pony (scriptwriter). *Publications:* contributions to British, American and European Press; (ed and contrib.) Four Days; Sir Godfrey Kneller; Shell Guide to Ireland, 1975 (with Prof. M. V. Duignan); (ed with J. Rodda) The Olympic Games, 1976; Olympic Games Moscow–Lake Placid, 1979; My Olympic Days, 1982. *Heir: s* Hon. (George) Redmond (Fitzpatrick) Morris [*b* 26 Jan. 1947; *m* 1972, Pauline, *o d* of Geoffrey Horton, Dublin; one *s* one *d*. *Educ:* Ampleforth; Trinity Coll., Dublin]. *Address:* 30 Lansdowne Road, Dublin 4. *T:* 6017780; St Annins, Spiddal, County Galway. *T:* Galway 83103. *Clubs:* Garrick, Beefsteak; Stephen's Green (Dublin); County (Galway).

See also W. C. R. Bryden.

KILLEARN, 2nd Baron, *cr* 1943; **Graham Curtis Lampson;** 4th Bt *cr* 1866; *b* 28 Oct. 1919; *er s* of 1st Baron Killearn, PC, GCMG, CB, MVO, and his 1st wife (*née* Rachel Mary Hele Phipps) (*d* 1930), *d* of W. W. Phipps; *S* father as 2nd Baron, 1964, and kinsman as 4th Bt, 1971; *m* 1946, Nadine Marie Cathryn, *o d* of late Vice-Adm. Cecil Horace Pilcher, DSO; two *d*. *Educ:* Eton Coll.; Magdalen Coll., Oxford (MA). Served war of 1939–45, Scots Guards (Major). US Bronze Star. *Heir:* half-*b* Hon. Victor Miles George Aldous Lampson, Captain RARO, Scots Guards [*b* 9 Sept. 1941; *m* 1971, Melita Amaryllis Pamela Astrid, *d* of Rear-Adm. M. C. Morgan-Giles, *qv*; one *s* two *d*]. *Address:* 6 Trevor Street, SW7. *T:* 01-584 7700. *Club:* MCC.

See also Sir N. C. Bonsor, Bt, Lord Eliot.

KILLEN, Hon. Sir Denis James, KCMG 1982; LLB; MP (Lib) for Moreton, Queensland, since 1955; Vice-President of the Executive Council and Leader of the House of Representatives, Commonwealth of Australia, since 1982; *b* 23 Nov. 1925; *s* of James W. Killen, Melbourne; *m* 1949, Joyce Claire; three *d*. *Educ:* Brisbane Grammar Sch.; Univ. of Queensland. Barrister-at-Law. Jackaroo; RAAF (Flight Serjeant); Mem. staff, Rheem (Aust.) Pty Ltd. Minister for the Navy, 1969–71; Opposition Spokesman: on Educn, 1973–74; on Defence, 1975; Minister for Defence, 1975–82. Foundn Pres., Young Liberals Movement (Qld); Vice-Pres., Lib. Party, Qld Div., 1953-56. *Recreations:* horseracing, golf. *Address:* Parliament House, Canberra, ACT 2600, Australia. *T:* 733955. *Clubs:* Johnsonian, Tattersall's, Irish Association, QTC (Brisbane), Brisbane Cricket.

KILLIAN, James Rhyne, Jr; Chairman of Corporation, 1959–71, Hon. Chairman of Corporation, 1971–79, Massachusetts Institute of Technology, USA; *b* 24 July 1904; *s* of James R. and Jeannette R. Killian; *m* 1929, Elizabeth Parks; one *s* one *d*. *Educ:* Trinity Coll. (Duke Univ.), Durham, North Carolina; Mass Institute of Technology, Cambridge, Mass (BS). Asst Managing Editor, The Technology Review, MIT, 1926–27; Managing Editor, 1927–30; Editor, 1930–39; Exec. Asst to Pres., MIT, 1939–43; Exec. Vice-Pres., MIT, 1943–45; Vice-Pres., MIT, 1945–48; 10th Pres. of MIT, 1948–59 (on leave 1957–59). Special Asst to Pres. of United States for Science and Technology, 1957–59; Mem., 1957–61, Chm. 1957-59, Consultant-at-large, 1961–73, President's Science Advisory Cttee; Mem., President's Bd of

Consultants on Foreign Intelligence Activities, 1956-59 (Chm., 1956-57); Mem. of President's Commission on National Goals, 1960; Chm., President's Foreign Intelligence Advisory Board, 1961-63. Mem., Bd of Trustees, Mitre Corporation, 1960-81; Pres. Bd of Trustees, Atoms for Peace Awards, Inc., 1959-69; Mem., Bd of Visitors, Tulane Univ., 1960-69; Trustee: Institute for Defense Analyses, Inc., 1959-69 (Chm., 1956-57, 1959-61); Mount Holyoke Coll., 1962-72; Alfred P. Sloan Foundn, 1954-77; Boston Museum of Science; Boston Museum of Fine Arts, 1966-79; Chairman: Carnegie Commn on Educl TV, 1965-67; Corp. for Public Broadcasting, 1973-74 (Dir, 1968-75); Director: Polaroid Corp.; former Director: Amer. Tel. & Tel. Co.; Cabot Corp.; General Motors Corp.; IBM; Ingersoll-Rand Co. Fellow Amer. Acad. of Arts and Sciences; Hon. Mem., Amer. Soc. for Engrg Educn; Mem., Nat. Acad. of Engineering; Moderator, Amer. Unitarian Assoc., 1960-61; President's Certificate of Merit, 1948; Certificate of Appreciation, 1953, and Exceptional Civilian Service Award, 1957, Dept of the Army; Public Welfare Medal of the Nat. Acad. of Sciences, 1957; Officier Légion d'Honneur (France), 1957. Gold Medal Award, Nat. Inst. of Social Sciences, 1958; World Brotherhood Award, Nat. Conf. of Christians and Jews, 1958; Award of Merit, Amer. Inst. of Cons. Engineers, 1958; Washington Award, Western Soc. of Engineers, 1959; Distinguished Achievement Award, Holland Soc. of NY, 1959; Gold Medal of Internat. Benjamin Franklin Soc., 1960; Good Govt Award, Crosscup-Pishon Post, American Legion, 1960; Hoover Medal, 1963; George Foster Peabody Award, 1968 and 1976; first Marconi Internat. Fellowship, 1975; Sylvanus Thayer Award, 1978; Vannevar Bush Award, Nat. Science Foundn, 1980. Hon. degrees: ScD: Middlebury Coll., 1945; Bates Coll., 1950; University of Havana, 1953; University of Notre Dame, Lowell Technological Inst., 1954; Columbia Univ., Coll. of Wooster, Ohio, Oberlin Coll., 1958; University of Akron, 1959; Worcester Polytechnic Inst., 1960; University of Maine, 1963; DEng: Drexel Inst. of Tech., 1948; University of Ill., 1960; University of Mass., 1961; LLD: Union Coll., 1947; Bowdoin Coll., Northeastern Univ., Duke Univ., 1949; Boston Univ., Harvard Univ., 1950; Williams Coll., Lehigh Univ., University of Pa, 1951; University of Chattanooga, 1954; Tufts Univ., 1955; University of Calif. and Amherst Coll., 1956; College of William and Mary, 1957; Brandeis Univ., 1958; Johns Hopkins Univ., New York Univ., 1959; Providence Coll., Temple Univ. 1960; University of S Carolina, 1961; Meadville Theological Sch., 1962; DAppl Sci., University of Montreal, 1958; EdD, Rhode Island Coll., 1962; HHD, Rollins Coll., 1964; DPS, Detroit Inst. of Technology, 1972. *Publications:* Sputnik, Scientists, and Eisenhower, 1977; Moments of Vision (with Harold E. Edgerton), 1979. *Address:* 77 Massachusetts Avenue, Cambridge, Mass 02139, USA. *Clubs:* St Botolph (Boston); The Century, University (New York).

KILLICK, Sir John (Edward), GCMG 1979 (KCMG 1971; CMG 1966); HM Diplomatic Service, retired; Director, Dunlop, South Africa, since 1980; *b* 18 Nov. 1919; *s* of late Edward William James Killick and Doris Marjorie (*née* Stokes); *m* 1949, Lynette du Preez (*née* Leach); no *c. Educ:* Latymer Upper Sch.; University Coll., London, Fellow 1973; Bonn Univ. Served with HM Forces, 1939-46: Suffolk Regt, W Africa Force and Airborne Forces. Foreign Office, 1946-48; Control Commn and High Commn for Germany (Berlin, Frankfurt and Bonn), 1948-51; Private Sec. to Parly Under-Sec., Foreign Office, 1951-54; British Embassy, Addis Ababa, 1954-57; Canadian Nat. Def. Coll., 1957-58; Western Dept, Foreign Office, 1958-62; Imp. Def. Coll., 1962; Counsellor and Head of Chancery, British Embassy, Washington, 1963-68; Asst Under-Sec. of State, FCO, 1968-71; Ambassador to USSR, 1971-73; Dep. Under-Sec. of State, FCO and Permanent Rep. on Council of WEU, 1973-75; Ambassador and UK Permanent Rep. to NATO, 1975-79. *Recreations:* golf, tennis, sailing. *Address:* Highcliff, Box 122, Wilderness, 6560, South Africa. *Clubs:* East India, Devonshire, Sports and Public Schools, Brooks's.

KILLICK, Paul Victor St John, OBE 1969; HM Diplomatic Service, retired; Ambassador to the Dominican Republic, 1972-75; *b* 8 Jan. 1916; *s* of C. St John Killick and Beatrice (*née* Simpson); *m* 1947, Sylva Augusta Leva; one *s* two *d. Educ:* St Paul's School. Served with Army, N Africa and Italy, 1939-46 (despatches 1944). Diplomatic Service: Singapore, 1946-47; Tokyo, 1947-49; Katmandu, 1950-53; FO, 1953-55; Oslo, 1955-58; San Francisco, 1958-60; Djakarta, 1960-61; Rome, 1962-66; Pretoria/Cape Town, 1966-70; Tangier, 1971-72. *Recreation:* walking. *Address:* Rose Cottage, Bexley Hill, Lodsworth, Petworth, W Sussex GU28 9EA.

KILMAINE, 7th Baron *cr* 1789; **John David Henry Browne;** Bt 1636; Director of Fusion (Bickenhill) Ltd, since 1969; Director of Whale Tankers Ltd, since 1974; *b* 2 April 1948; *s* of 6th Baron Kilmaine, CBE, and of Wilhelmina Phyllis, *o d* of Scott Arnott, Brasted, Kent; *S* father, 1978; *m* 1982, Linda, *yr d* of Dennis Robinson. *Educ:* Eton. *Heir: kinsman* Peter Kilmaine Browne [*b* 1920; *m* 1948, Grace Dorothy Robson; two *d*]. *Address:* Ravenshaw Hall, Ravenshaw Lane, Solihull, West Midlands.

KILMANY, Baron, *cr* 1966 (Life Peer), of Kilmany; **William John St Clair Anstruther-Gray;** 1st Bt, *cr* 1956; PC 1962; MC 1943; Lord-Lieutenant of Fife, 1975-80; *b* 1905; *o s* of late Col W. Anstruther-Gray, MP, DL, JP, of Kilmany; *m* 1934, Monica Helen, OBE 1946, JP, *o c* of late Geoffrey Lambton, 2nd *s* of 4th Earl of Durham; two *d. Educ:* Eton; Christ Church, Oxford, MA (Hons). Lieut, Coldstream Guards, 1926-30; served Shanghai Defence Force, 1927-28; rejoined Sept. 1939 and served N Africa, France, Germany, etc with Coldstream Guards and Lothians and Border Horse; Major, 1942; MP (U) for North Lanark, 1931-45; up to Sept. 1939 Parly Private Sec. to Rt Hon. Sir John Colville, MP, Sec. of State for Scotland, and previously

to the Financial Sec. to the Treasury, and to Sec. for Overseas Trade; Asst Postmaster-Gen., May-July 1945; Crown nominee for Scotland on Gen. Medical Council, 1952-65. Contested (U) Berwick and East Lothian, Feb. 1950; MP (U) Berwick and East Lothian, 1951-66. Chm. of Ways and Means and Dep. Speaker, House of Commons, 1962-64 (Dep. Chm., 1959-62); Chm. Conservative Members' 1922 Cttee, 1964-66. Elected Mem. National Hunt Cttee, 1948; Mem., Horserace Betting Levy Bd, 1966-74. DL Fife, 1953. *Address:* Kilmany, Cupar, Fife. *T:* Gauldry 247. *Clubs:* Pratt's, Brooks's, Cavalry and Guards, Turf, Jockey; New (Edinburgh); Royal and Ancient (St Andrews).

See also J. C. Macnab of Macnab.

KILMARNOCK, 7th Baron *cr* 1831; **Alastair Ivor Gilbert Boyd;** Chief of the Clan Boyd; *b* 11 May 1927; *s* of 6th Baron Kilmarnock, MBE, TD, and Hon. Rosemary Guest (*d* 1971), *er d* of 1st Viscount Wimborne; *S* father, 1975; *m* 1st, 1954, Diana Mary (marr. diss. 1970, she *d* 1975), *o d* of D. Grant Gibson; 2nd, 1977, Hilary Ann, *yr d* of Leonard Sidney and Margery Bardwell; one *s. Educ:* Bradfield; King's Coll., Cambridge. Lieutenant, Irish Guards, 1946; served Palestine, 1947-48. Mem. SDP, 1981-. Vice-Pres., Inst. of Sales and Marketing Management, 1981-. *Publications:* Sabbatical Year, 1958; The Road from Ronda, 1969; The Companion Guide to Madrid and Central Spain, 1974. *Heir: b* Dr the Hon. Robin Jordan Boyd, MB BS, MRCP, MRCPEd, DCH, *b* 6 June 1941. *Address:* 1 Bridge Street, Thornborough, Bucks MK18 2DN. *Club:* Pratt's.

KILMARTIN, Terence Kevin; Literary Editor, The Observer, since 1952; *b* 10 Jan. 1922; *s* of Ambrose Joseph Kilmartin and Eve (*née* Hyland); *m* 1952, Joanna (*née* Pearce); one *s* one *d. Educ:* Xaverian Coll., Mayfield, Sussex. Private tutor, France, 1938-39; Special Operations Executive, 1940-45; Asst Editor, World Review, 1946-47; freelance journalist, Middle East, 1947-48; Asst Editor, Observer Foreign News Service, 1949-50; Asst Literary Editor, 1950-52. *Publications:* translations of Henry de Montherlant: The Bachelors, 1960; The Dream, 1962; Chaos and Night, 1964; The Girls, 1968; The Boys, 1974; André Malraux: Anti-Memoirs, 1968; Lazarus, 1977; Charles de Gaulle: Memoirs of Hope, 1971; Marcel Proust: rev. trans. of Remembrance of Things Past, 1981. *Address:* 20 Cheyne Row, SW3. *T:* 01-352 2375.

KILMISTER, Prof. Clive William; Professor of Mathematics, King's College, London, since 1966; *b* 3 Jan. 1924; *s* of William and Doris Kilmister; *m* 1955, Peggy Joyce Hutchins; one *s* two *d. Educ:* Queen Mary Coll., Univ. of London. BSc 1944, MSc 1948, PhD 1950. King's Coll. London: Asst Lectr, 1950; Lectr, 1953; Reader, 1959. Gresham Prof. of Geometry, 1972-. President: British Soc. for History of Mathematics, 1973-76; Mathematical Assoc., 1979-80; British Soc. for Philos. of Science, 1981-83. *Publications:* Special Relativity for Physicists (with G. Stephenson), 1958; Eddington's Statistical Theory (with B. O. J. Tupper), 1962; Hamiltonian Dynamics, 1964; The Environment in Modern Physics, 1965; Rational Mechanics (with J. E. Reeve), 1966; Men of Physics: Sir Arthur Eddington, 1966; Language, Logic and Mathematics, 1967; Lagrangian Dynamics, 1967; Special Theory of Relativity, 1970; The Nature of the Universe, 1972; General Theory of Relativity, 1973. *Recreation:* opera going. *Address:* 11 Vanbrugh Hill, Blackheath, SE3 7UE. *T:* 01-858 0675.

KILMORE, Bishop of, (RC), since 1972; **Most Rev. Francis J. McKiernan,** DD; *b* 3 Feb. 1926; *s* of Joseph McKiernan and Ellen McTague. *Educ:* Aughawillan National School; St Patrick's Coll., Cavan; University College, Dublin; St Patrick's Coll., Maynooth. BA, BD, HDE. St. Malachy's Coll., Belfast, 1951-52; St Patrick's Coll., Cavan, 1952-53; University Coll., Dublin, 1953-54; St Patrick's Coll., Cavan, 1954-62; Pres., St Felim's Coll., Ballinamore, Co. Leitrim, 1962-72. Editor of Breifne (Journal of Breifne Historical Society), 1958-72. *Address:* Bishop's House, Cullies, Cavan. *T:* 049-31496.

KILMOREY, 6th Earl of; *see* Needham, Richard Francis.

KILMUIR, Countess of; *see* De La Warr, Countess.

KILNER, Cyril; Assistant Editor, Doncaster Gazette, 1952-75, retired; *b* 5 Sept. 1910; *s* of Bernard Kilner and Edith Annie (*née* Booker); *m* 1949, Joan Siddons; one *s* one *d. Educ:* Mexborough Grammar School. Army War Service in Royal Tank Regt, 1940-45. Reporter, Barnsley Independent, 1927-30; Reporter, Sports Editor, Sub-Editor, Barnsley Chronicle, 1931-47; Reporter, Sub-Editor, Yorkshire Evening News (Doncaster edn), 1947-52. Member: The Press Council, 1968-74; Nat. Exec. Council, NUJ, 1958-72 (Pres., 1969, Mem. of Honour, 1976). Hon. Gen. Treasurer, Internat. Fedn. of Journalists, 1972-76. *Recreations:* watching (sports, TV etc.), reading, motoring, travelling. *Address:* Cranford, 159 Boothferry Road, Goole, N Humberside. *T:* Goole 60192.

KILNER BROWN, Hon. Sir Ralph; *see* Brown.

KILPATRICK, Rev. George Dunbar; Dean Ireland's Professor of Exegesis of Holy Scripture, Oxford, 1949-77; Fellow of the Queen's College, Oxford, 1949-77; Fellow of University College, London, since 1967; *b* Coal Creek, Fernie, BC, Canada, 15 Sept. 1910; *o c* of late Wallace Henry and Bessie Kilpatrick; *m* 1943, Marion, *d* of Harold Laver and Dorothy Madeline Woodhouse; one *s* three *d. Educ:* Ellis Sch., BC; St Dunstan's Coll.; University Coll., London; Oriel Coll., Oxford (Scholar); University of

London, Granville Scholar, 1931; BA Classics (1st Class), 1932; University of Oxford, BA Lit. Hum. (2nd Class), 1934, Theology (2nd Class), 1936, Junior Greek Testament Prize, 1936, Senior Greek Testament Prize, 1937, Junior Denyer and Johnson Scholarship, 1938, BD 1944; Grinfield Lecturer, 1945-49; DD 1948; Schweich Lecturer, 1951. Deacon 1936; Priest 1937; Asst Curate of Horsell, 1936; Tutor, Queen's Coll., Birmingham, 1939; Asst Curate of Selly Oak, 1940; Acting Warden of Coll. of the Ascension, Birmingham, 1941; Rector of Wishaw, Warwicks, and Lecturer at Lichfield Theological Coll., 1942; Head of Dept of Theology and Reader in Christian Theology, University Coll., Nottingham, 1946. Vice-Pres., British and Foreign Bible Soc., 1958. *Publications:* The Origins of the Gospel according to St Matthew, 1946; The Trial of Jesus, 1953; Remaking the Liturgy, 1967. Editor: The New Testament in Greek, British and Foreign Bible Society's 2nd edn, 1958; contributions to periodicals. *Recreation:* reading. *Address:* 27 Lathbury Road, Oxford. *T:* Oxford 58909.

KILPATRICK, Prof. Robert, CBE 1979; Dean, Faculty of Medicine, and Professor and Head of Department of Clinical Pharmacology and Therapeutics, University of Leicester, since 1975; *b* 29 July 1926; *s* of Robert Kilpatrick and Catherine Sharp Glover; *m* 1950, Elizabeth Gibson Page Forbes; two *s* one *d*. *Educ:* Buckhaven High Sch.; Edinburgh Univ. MB, ChB (Hons) 1949; Ettles Schol.; Leslie Gold Medallist; MD 1960; FRCP(Ed) 1963; FRCP 1975. Med. Registrar, Edinburgh, 1951-54; Lectr, Univ. of Sheffield, 1955-66; Rockefeller Trav. Fellowship, MRC, Harvard Univ., 1961-62; Commonwealth Trav. Fellowship, 1962; Prof. of Clin. Pharmacology and Therapeutics, Univ. of Sheffield, 1966-75; Dean, Faculty of Medicine, Univ. of Sheffield, 1970-73. Chm., Adv. Cttee on Pesticides, 1975-; Chm., Soc. of Endocrinology, 1975-78; Mem., GMC, 1972-76 and 1979-. *Publications:* articles in med. and sci. jls. *Recreations:* golf, sailing. *Address:* The Barn, Smeeton Westerby, Leics LE8 0QL. *T:* Kibworth 2202. *Club:* Royal and Ancient (St Andrews).

KILPATRICK, Sir William (John), KBE 1965 (CBE 1958); Chairman: Mulford Holdings Ltd; Kilpatrick Holdings Ltd; Director, Guardian Assurance Group; *b* 27 Dec. 1906; *s* of late James Park Scott Kilpatrick, Scotland; *m* 1932, Alice Margaret Strachan; one *s* three *d*. *Educ:* Wollongong, NSW. Sqdn Ldr, RAAF, 1942-45. Pastoral interests, Victoria. Mem., Melbourne City Council, 1958-64. Chm. Cancer Service Cttee, Anti-Cancer Coun. of Vic., 1958-; Dep. Nat. Pres., Nat. Heart Foundn of Aust., 1960-64; Chm., Finance Cttee, Nat. Heart Foundn of Aust., 1960-; Pres. Aust. Cancer Soc., 1961-64, 1974-; World Chm., Finance Cttee, Internat. Union Against Cancer, 1961-; Ldr Aust. Delegn to 8th Internat. Cancer Congr, Moscow, 1962. Nat. Chm. Winston Churchill Mem. Trust, 1965; Chm., Drug Educn Sub-Cttee, Commonwealth Govt, 1970; Chm., Plastic and Reconstructive Surgery Foundn, 1970. *Recreations:* golf, swimming. *Address:* 23 Hopetoun Road, Toorak, Victoria 3142, Australia. *T:* 20 5206. *Clubs:* Naval and Military, Victorian Golf, VRC, VATC (all Melbourne); Commonwealth (Canberra).

KILROY, Dame Alix; *see* Meynell, Dame Alix.

KILROY-SILK, Robert; MP (Lab) Ormskirk since Feb. 1974; *b* 19 May 1942; *m* 1963, Jan Beech; one *s* one *d*. *Educ:* Saltley Grammar Sch., Birmingham; LSE (BScEcon). Lectr, Dept of Political Theory and Institutions, Liverpool Univ., 1966-74. PPS to Minister for the Arts, 1974-75; Vice-Chairman: Merseyside Gp of MPs, 1974-75; PLP Home Affairs Gp, 1976-; Chairman: Parly All-Party Penal Affairs Gp, 1979-; PLP Civil Liberties Gp, 1979-; Parly Alcohol Policy and Services Group, 1982-; Member: Home Affairs Select Cttee, 1979-; Council, Howard League for Penal Reform, 1979-; Sponsor, Radical Alternatives to Prison, 1977-; Patron, APEX Trust. Governor, National Heart and Chest Hospital, 1974-77. *Publications:* Socialism since Marx, 1972; (contrib.) The Role of Commissions in Policy Making, 1973; articles in Political Studies, Manchester School of Economic and Social Science, Political Quarterly, Industrial and Labor Relations Review, Parliamentary Affairs, etc. *Recreations:* skin diving, gardening. *Address:* House of Commons, SW1A 0AA.

KILVINGTON, Frank Ian; Headmaster of St Albans School since 1964; *b* West Hartlepool, 26 June 1924; *e s* of H. H. Kilvington; *m* 1949, Jane Mary, *d* of late Very Rev. Michael Clarke and of Katharine Beryl (*née* Girling); one *s* one *d*. *Educ:* Repton (entrance and foundn scholar); Corpus Christi, Oxford (open class. scholar). 2nd cl. Lit Hum, 1948; MA 1950. Served War of 1939-45: RNVR, 1943-46 (Lt); West Africa Station, 1943-45; RN Intelligence, Germany, 1945-46. Westminster School: Asst Master, 1949-58; Housemaster of Rigaud's House, 1957-64. Chairman: St Albans Marriage Guidance Council, 1968-74; St Albans CAB, 1981-; Pres., St Albans and Herts Architectural and Archæological Soc., 1974-77. E-SU Page Scholar, 1976-77. *Publication:* A Short History of St Albans School, 1970. *Recreations:* music, local history. *Address:* Abbey Gateway, St Albans, Herts AL3 4HB. *T:* St Albans 55702. *Club:* East India, Devonshire, Sports and Public Schools.

KIMBALL, Sir Marcus (Richard), Kt 1981; MP (C) Gainsborough Division of Lincolnshire since Feb. 1956; *b* 18 Oct. 1928; *s* of late Major Lawrence Kimball; *m* 1956, June Mary Fenwick; two *d*. *Educ:* Eton; Trinity Coll., Cambridge. Contested Derby South, Gen. Election, 1955. Privy Council Rep., Council of RCVS, 1969. Jt Master and Huntsman: Fitzwilliam Hounds, 1950-51 and 1951-52; Cottesmore Hounds, 1952-53, 1953-54, 1955-56 (Jt Master, 1956-58). Chm., British Field Sports Soc., 1966-82. Lt Leics Yeo.

(TA), 1947; Capt., 1951. Mem. Rutland CC, 1955. *Address:* Great Easton Manor, Market Harborough, Leics LE16 8TB. *T:* Rockingham 770333; Altnaharra, Lairg, Sutherland IV27 4AE. *T:* Altnaharra 224; 70 Cranmer Court, Sloane Avenue, SW3. *T:* 01-589 3257. *Clubs:* White's, Pratt's.

KIMBER, Sir Charles Dixon, 3rd Bt, *cr* 1904; *b* 7 Jan. 1912; *o surv. s* of Sir Henry Dixon Kimber, 2nd Bt, and Lucy Ellen, *y d* of late G. W. Crookes; *S* father 1950; *m* 1st, 1933, Ursula (marr. diss., 1949; she *d* 1981), *er d* of late Ernest Roy Bird, MP; three *s*; 2nd, 1950, Margaret Bonham (marr. diss., 1965), writer; one *d* (and one *s* decd). *Educ:* Eton; Balliol Coll., Oxford (BA). *Heir:* *s* Timothy Roy Henry Kimber [*b* 3 June 1936; *m* 1960, Antonia Kathleen Brenda (marr. diss. 1974), *d* of Sir Francis Williams, Bt, *qv*; two *s*; *m* 1979, Susan, *widow* of Richard North, Newton Hall, near Carnforth]. *Address:* No 2 Duxford, Hinton Waldrist, near Faringdon, Oxon. *T:* Longworth 820004.

KIMBER, Derek Barton, OBE 1945; FEng; Chairman: Austin & Pickersgill Ltd, since 1973; Sunderland Shipbuilders Ltd, since 1980; Govan Shipbuilders Ltd, since 1980; Smith's Dock Co. Ltd, since 1980; Director: Equity Capital for Industry Ltd, since 1977; London & Overseas Freighters Ltd, since 1979; *b* 2 May 1917; *s* of George Kimber and Marion Kimber (*née* Barton); *m* 1943, Gwendoline Margaret Maude Brotherton; two *s* two *d*. *Educ:* Bedford Sch.; Imperial Coll., London Univ; Royal Naval Coll., Greenwich. MSc(Eng), FCGI, DIC; FEng, FRINA, FIMechE, FIMarE, MNECInst, FWeldI, FRSA. Royal Corps of Naval Constructors, 1939-49; Consultant, Urwick, Orr & Partners Ltd, 1950-54; Fairfield Shipbuilding & Engineering Co. Ltd: Manager, 1954; Dir, 1961; Dep. Man. Dir, 1963-65; Dir, Harland & Wolff Ltd, 1966-69; Dir Gen., Chemical Industries Assoc., 1970-73; Director: A. & P. Appledore International Ltd, 1974-77; British Ship Research Assoc. (Trustees) Ltd, 1973-81; R. S. Dalgliesh Ltd, 1978-80. Dir, Glasgow Chamber of Commerce, 1962-65. Chm., C. & G. Jt Adv. Cttee for Shipbuilding, 1968-70; Pres., Clyde Shipbuilders Assoc., 1964-65; Member: Shipbuilding Industry Trng Bd, 1964-69; Scottish Cttee, Lloyds Register of Shipping, 1964-65, Gen. Cttee, 1973-, Technical Cttee, 1976-80, Exec. Bd, 1978-; Research Council, British Ship Res. Assoc., 1973-81; Brit. Tech. Cttee, Amer. Bureau of Shipping, 1976-; Standing Cttee, Assoc. of W European Shipbuilders, 1976- (Vice-Chm., 1982); Chm., Management Bd, Shipbuilders & Repairers Nat. Assoc., 1974-76, Vice-Pres., 1976-77; Mem., Jt Industry Cons. Cttee, (SRNA/CSEU), 1966-76. Member: EDC for Chem. Industry, 1970-72; Process Plant Working Party (NEDO), 1970-72; CBI Central Council, 1970-72, 1975-; CBI Northern Reg. Council, 1973-80 (Chm. 1975-77). Member: Council, RINA, 1961- (Chm., 1973-75, Pres. RINA 1977-81); Council, Welding Inst., 1959-74, 1976-82; Bd, CEI, 1977-81, Exec. Cttee, 1978-80; C. & G. Senior Awards Cttee, 1970-81; Vice Pres., NE Coast Inst. of Engrs and Shipbuilders, 1978-. Liveryman, Worshipful Co. of Shipwrights, 1967 (Asst to Court 1974-, Warden, 1982-). Governor, Imperial Coll., London Univ., 1967-. FEng 1976. Hon. FRINA 1981. RINA Gold Medallist, 1977. *Publications:* papers on shipbuilding subjects in learned soc. Trans. *Recreations:* shipbuilding, DIY, golf, rough gardening. *Address:* Broughton, Monk's Road, Virginia Water, Surrey. *T:* Wentworth 4274. *Clubs:* Brooks's, Caledonian, City Livery, MCC; Anchorites; Den Norske Klub; Yacht Club of Greece.

KIMBER, Herbert Frederick Sidney; Director, Southern Newspapers Ltd, since 1975; *b* 3 April 1917; *s* of H. G. Kimber; *m* Patricia Boulton (*née* Forfar); one *s*. *Educ:* elementary sch., Southampton. Southern Newspapers Ltd, office boy, 1931. Served War, Royal Navy, 1939-46: commissioned Lieut RNVR, 1941. Manager, Dorset Evening Echo, 1960; Advertisement Manager-in-Chief, Southern Newspapers Ltd, 1961; then Dep. Gen. and Advertisement Manager, 1972; Gen. Manager, 1974. *Recreations:* reading, travel, gardening under protest. *Address:* 11 Purbeck Heights, Belle Vue Road, Durlston, Swanage, Dorset. *Clubs:* Royal Naval; Royal Southampton Yacht.

KIMBERLEY, 4th Earl of, *cr* 1866; **John Wodehouse;** Bt, 1611; Baron Wodehouse, 1797; Lt Grenadier Guards; *b* 12 May 1924; *o s* of 3rd Earl and Margaret (*d* 1950), *d* of late Col Leonard Howard Irby; *S* father 1941; *m* 1st, 1945; 2nd, 1949; one *s*; 3rd, 1953; two *s*; 4th, 1961; one *s*; 5th, 1970; 6th, 1982, Jane Consett. *Educ:* Eton; Cambridge. Lieut, Grenadier Guards, 1942-45; Active Service NW Europe. Member: House of Lords All Party Defence Study Gp, 1976- (Sec., 1978-); House of Lords All Party UFO Study Gp, 1979-; former Liberal Spokesman on: aviation and aerospace; defence; voluntary community services; left Liberal Party, May 1979, joined Cons. Party. Member: Electoral Reform Soc., 1978; Cons. Action for Electoral Reform, 1979; Exec. Cttee, Assoc. of Cons. Peers; Council, The Air League; Council, British Maritime League; Foreign Affairs Club; RUSI; IISS; British Atlantic Cttee. Delegate to N Atlantic Assembly, 1981-. Vice-Pres., World Council on Alcoholism; Chm., Nat. Council on Alcoholism, 1982-. Mem., British Bobsleigh Team, 1949-58. ARAeS 1977. *Recreations:* shooting, big game fishing, all field sports, gardening. *Heir:* *s* Lord Wodehouse, *qv*. *Address:* House of Lords, Westminster, SW1; Hailstone House, Cricklade, Swindon, Wilts. *T:* Swindon 750344. *Clubs:* Cavalry and Guards, Naval and Military, MCC; House of Lords' Yacht; Royal Cornwall Yacht, Falmouth Shark Angling (Pres.), Shark Angling of Great Britain.

KIMBLE, Dr David (Bryant), OBE 1962; Vice-Chancellor of the University of Malaŵi, since 1977; *b* 12 May 1921; *s* of John H. and Minnie Jane Kimble; *m* 1st, 1948, Helen Rankin (marr. diss.); four *d*; 2nd, 1977, Margareta Westin. *Educ:* Eastbourne Grammar Sch.; Reading Univ. (BA 1942, DipEd 1943,

Pres. Students Union, 1942-43); London Univ. (PhD 1961). Lieut RNVR, 1943-46. Oxford Univ. Staff Tutor in Berks, 1946-48, and Resident Tutor in the Gold Coast, 1948-49; Dir, Inst. of Extra-Mural Studies, Univ. of Ghana, 1949-62, and Master of Akuafo Hall, 1960-62; Prof. of Political Science, Univ. Coll., Dar es Salaam, Univ. of E Africa, and Dir, Inst. of Public Admin, Tanzania, 1962-68; Research Advr in Public Admin and Social Sciences, Centre africain de formation et de recherche administratives pour le développement, Tanger, Morocco, 1968-70, and Dir of Research, 1970-71; Prof. of Govt and Admin, Univ. of Botswana, Lesotho, and Swaziland, 1971-75, and Nat. Univ. of Lesotho, 1975-77; Prof. Emeritus, Nat. Univ. of Lesotho, 1978. Founder and Joint Editor (with Helen Kimble), West African Affairs, 1949-51, Penguin African Series, 1953-61, and Jl of Modern African Studies, 1963-71; Editor, Jl of Modern African Studies, 1972-. *Publications:* The Machinery of Self-Government, 1953; (with Helen Kimble) Adult Education in a Changing Africa, 1955; A Political History of Ghana, Vol. I, The Rise of Nationalism in the Gold Coast, 1850-1928, 1963. *Recreations:* cricket, editing. *Address:* PO Box 278, Zomba, Malaŵi.
See also G. H. T. Kimble.

KIMBLE, George (Herbert Tinley), PhD; retired; *b* 2 Aug. 1908; *s* of John H. and Minnie Jane Kimble; *m* 1935, Dorothy Stevens Berry; one *s* one *d*. *Educ:* Eastbourne Grammar Sch.; King's Coll., London (MA); University of Montreal (PhD). Asst Lecturer in Geography, University of Hull, 1931-36; Lecturer in Geography, University of Reading, 1936-39. Served War as Lt and Lt-Comdr, British Naval Meteorological Service, 1939-44. Prof. of Geography and Chm. Dept of Geography, McGill Univ., 1945-50; Sec.-Treasurer, Internat. Geographical Union, 1949-56; Chm., Commn on Humid Tropics, Internat. Geog. Union, 1956-61. Dir, Amer. Geog. Soc., 1950-53; Dir, Survey of Tropical Africa, Twentieth Century Fund, NY, 1953-60. Chm., Dept of Geography, Indiana Univ., 1957-62; Prof. of Geography, Indiana Univ., 1957-66; Research Dir, US Geography Project, Twentieth Century Fund, 1962-68. Rushton Lecturer, 1952; Borah Lecturer, University of Idaho, 1956; Haynes Foundn Lectr, University of Redlands, 1966; Visiting Prof., University of Calif. (Berkeley), 1948-49; Stanford Univ., 1961; Stockholm Sch. of Economics, 1961. Governor, Eastbourne Sixth Form Coll., 1980-81. Hon. Mem., Inst. British Geographers. *Publications:* Geography in the Middle Ages, 1938; The World's Open Spaces, 1939; The Shepherd of Banbury, 1941; (co-author) The Weather, 1943 (Eng.), 1946 (Amer.), (author) 2nd (Eng.) edn, 1951; Military Geography of Canada, 1949; The Way of the World, 1953; Our American Weather, 1955; Le Temps, 1957; Tropical Africa (2 vols), 1960; Tropical Africa (abridged edition), 1962; (with Ronald Steel) Tropical Africa Today, 1966; Man and his World, 1972; From the Four Winds, 1974; (ed for Hakluyt Soc.) Esmeraldo de Situ Orbis, 1937; (ed for American Geographical Soc. with Dorothy Good) Geography of the Northlands, 1955; articles in: Geog. Jl, Magazine, Review; Canadian Geog. Jl; Bulletin Amer. Meteorological Soc.; The Reporter; Los Angeles Times; The New York Times Magazine. *Recreations:* music, gardening. *Address:* 2 Dymock's Manor, Ditchling, E Sussex BN6 8SX.
See also Dr D. B. Kimble.

KIMMANCE, Peter Frederick, CB 1981; Chief Inspector of Audit, Department of the Environment, since 1979; *b* 14 Dec. 1922; *s* of Frederick Edward Kimmance, BEM, and Louisa Kimmance; *m* 1944, Helen Mary Mercer Cooke. *Educ:* Raines Foundation, Stepney; University of London. Post Office Engineering Dept, 1939; served Royal Signals, 1943; District Audit Service, 1949; District Auditor, 1973; Controller (Finance), British Council, 1973-75; Dep. Chief Inspector of Audit, DoE, 1978. Mem. Council, CIPFA, 1979; Hon. Mem., British Council, 1975. *Recreations:* sailing, books, music. *Address:* Herons, School Road, Saltwood, Hythe, Kent CT21 4PP. *T:* Hythe 67921. *Clubs:* Royal Over-Seas League; Medway Yacht (Lower Upnor).

KIMMINS, Simon Edward Anthony, VRD 1967; Lt-Comdr RNR; *b* 26 May 1930; *s* of late Captain Anthony Kimmins, OBE, RN, and of Mrs Elizabeth Kimmins; *m* 1976, Jonkvrouwe Irma de Jonge; one *s* one *d*. *Educ:* Horris Hill; Charterhouse. Man. Dir, London American Finance Corpn Ltd (originally BOECC Ltd), 1957-73; Dir (non-exec.), Balfour Williamson, 1971-74; Chief Exec., Thomas Cook Gp, 1973-75; Director: Debenhams Ltd, 1972-; TKM International Trade Finance, 1978-80; Chairman: Ardil SA, Geneva, 1980-; Associated Retail Develt Internat. Ltd, 1981-. Vice-Pres., British Export Houses Assoc., 1974- (Chm., 1970-72). Governor, Royal Shakespeare Theatre, 1975-. *Recreations:* cricket (played for Kent), golf, shooting. *Address:* 37 Chemin de Grange Canal, Geneva 1208, Switzerland. *T:* Geneva 35 6657. *Clubs:* Garrick, MCC, The Pilgrims; Haagseclub.

KINAHAN, Charles Henry Grierson, CBE 1972; JP; DL; retired 1977; Director, Bass Ireland Ltd, Belfast, and subsidiary companies, 1956-77; *b* 10 July 1915; *e s* of Henry Kinahan, Belfast, and Ula, *d* of late Rt Rev. C. T. P. Grierson, Bishop of Down and Connor and Dromore; *m* 1946, Kathleen Blanche McClintock, MB, BS, *e d* of Rev. E. L. L. McClintock; three *s*. *Educ:* Stowe School. Singapore Volunteer Corps, 1939-45, POW Singapore, 1942-45. Commerce, London, 1933-38 and Malaya, 1938-56. Dir, Dunlop Malayan Estates Ltd, 1952-56; Man. Dir, Lyle and Kinahan Ltd, Belfast, 1956-63. Mem. (Alliance) Antrim S, NI Constitutional Convention, 1975-76; contested (Alliance) Antrim S, gen. election 1979. Belfast Harbour Comr, 1966-80; Chm., 1969-73, Pres., 1975, NI Marriage Guidance Council; Mem. Senate, QUB, 1968-; Chairman: NI Historic Buildings Council, 1973-; Ulster '71 Exhibn, 1971; NI Mountain Rescue Working Party; Trustee, Nat. Heritage Memorial Fund, 1980-. JP 1961, High Sheriff 1971, DL 1977, Co. Antrim; Mem., Antrim District Council (Alliance Party), 1977-81. *Recreations:* mountain trekking, farming, classical music. *Address:* Clady Cottage, Dunadry, Antrim. *T:* Templepatrick 32379. *Club:* Royal Over-Seas League.
See also Sir R. G. C. Kinahan, D. McClintock.

KINAHAN, Maj.-Gen. Oliver John, CB 1981; Paymaster-in-Chief and Inspector of Army Pay Services, since 1979; *b* 17 Nov. 1923; *s* of late James Edward and Mary Kinahan (*née* McGoldrick); *m* 1950, Margery Ellis Fisher (*née* Hill); one *s* two *d*. *Educ:* St Mary's ICBS; Queen's University, Belfast. Commissioned Royal Irish Fusiliers, 1942; served with Nigeria Regt, RWAFF, Sierra Leone, Nigeria, India, Burma, 1943-46; Instr, Sch. of Signals, 1947-49, Sch. of Infantry, 1950-51; transf. to RAPC, 1951; Japan and Korea, 1952-53; psc 1957; Staff Pmr, Hong Kong, 1961-64, Berlin, 1964-66; Chief Instr, RAPC Trng Centre, 1968-71; Comd Pmr, BAOR, Station Comdr, Moenchengladbach, 1972-73; Comdt, RAPC Trng Centre, 1974-75; Chief Pmr, HQ UKLF, 1975-76; Dep. Paymaster-in-Chief (Army), 1977-78. FBIM. *Recreations:* country pursuits, golf. *Address:* c/o Williams and Glyn's Bank Ltd, Kirkland House, Whitehall, SW1. *Club:* Naval and Military.

KINAHAN, Sir Robert (George Caldwell), (Sir Robin Kinahan), Kt 1961; ERD 1946; JP; Vice Lord-Lieutenant, County Borough of Belfast, since 1976; Chairman: Inglis & Co. Ltd, 1962-82; E. T. Green Ltd, 1964-82; Director: National Westminster Bank Ltd, 1973-82; Ulster Bank Ltd, since 1963 (Chairman, 1970-82); Gallaher Ltd, since 1967; Abbey Life (Ireland) Ltd, 1981; Standard Telephones and Cables (Northern Ireland) Ltd, 1974; *b* 24 Sept. 1916; *s* of Henry Kinahan, Lowwood, Belfast; *m* 1950, Coralie I., *d* of late Capt. C. de Burgh, DSO, RN; two *s* three *d*. *Educ:* Stowe Sch., Buckingham. Vintners' Scholar (London), 1937. Served Royal Artillery, 1939-45, Capt. Councillor, Belfast Corporation, 1948; JP Co. Antrim, 1950, DL 1962; High Sheriff: Belfast, 1956; Co. Antrim, 1969. Mem. N Ireland Adv. Commn, 1972-73. MP (N Ireland), Clifton constituency, 1958-59. Lord Mayor of Belfast, 1959-61. Hon. LLD (Belfast) 1962. *Recreations:* gardening, family life. *Address:* Castle Upton, Templepatrick, Co. Antrim. *T:* Templepatrick 32466. *Clubs:* Ulster (Belfast); Kildare Street and University (Dublin).
See also C. H. G. Kinahan, Sir A. T. C. Neave, Bt.

KINCADE, James, MA, PhD; Headmaster, Methodist College, Belfast, since 1974; *b* 4 Jan. 1925; *s* of George and Rebecca Jane Kincade; *m* 1952, Elizabeth Fay, 2nd *d* of J. Anderson Piggot, OBE, DL, JP; one *s* one *d*. *Educ:* Foyle Coll.; Magee University Coll.; Trinity Coll. Dublin (Schol. and Gold Medallist, MA, Stein Research Prize); Oriel Coll., Oxford (MA, BLitt); Edinburgh Univ. (PhD). Served RAF, India and Burma, 1943-47 (commnd, 1944). Senior English Master, Merchiston Castle Sch., 1952-61; Vis. Professor of Philosophy, Indiana Univ., 1959; Headmaster, Royal Sch., Dungannon, 1961-74. Chairman, Schools Cttee Ulster Savings, 1973-; President, Ulster Headmasters' Assoc., 1975-77; Chm., Joint Five, 1980-. *Publications:* An Interpretation of Christian Ethics, 1980; articles in Mind, Hermathena, Jl of Religion. *Recreations:* gardening, reading. *Address:* 23 Adelaide Park, Belfast BT9 6FX.

KINCH, Anthony Alec; Head of Division for Foodstuffs, Commission of the European Communities, since 1973; *b* 13 Dec. 1926; *s* of E. A. Kinch, OBE, retd Polit. Adviser, Iraq Petroleum Co. Ltd, and C. T. Kinch (*née* Cassidy); *m* 1952, Barbara Patricia (*née* Paton Walsh); four *s* two *d*. *Educ:* Ampleforth; Christ Church, Oxford (MA). Practised at Bar, 1951-57; Contracts Man., Electronics Div., Plessey Co. Ltd, 1957-60; Legal Adviser and Insce Consultant, R. & H. Green and Silley Weir Ltd, 1960-66; Dir, Fedn of Bakers, 1966-73. KCHS. Chevalier du Fourquet. *Recreation:* living. *Address:* Commission of the European Communities, 200 Rue de la Loi, 1049 Brussels, Belgium. *T:* (02) 2351531.

KINCHIN SMITH, Michael; Lay Assistant to the Archbishop of Canterbury, since 1979; *b* 8 May 1921; *s* of Francis John Kinchin Smith, Lectr in Classics, Inst. of Educn, London, and Dione Jean Elizabeth, *d* of Sir Francis Henry May, GCMG, sometime Governor of Hong Kong; *m* 1947, Rachel Frances, *er d* of Rt Hon. Sir Henry Urmston Willink, Bt, MC, QC, Master of Magdalene Coll., Cambridge; four *s* two *d*. *Educ:* Westminster Sch. (King's Schol.); Christ Church, Oxford (Schol.). 1st cl. hons Mod. History; Pres. Oxford Union, 1941. Served with 2nd and 3rd Bns, Coldstream Guards in Italian Campaign (Captain; despatches). Commercial and Admin. Trainee, ICI Ltd, 1947; admin. posts with BBC, 1950-78: Asst. Staff Admin, 1950; Admin Officer, Talks (Sound), 1954; Asst Estabt Officer, TV, 1955; Estabt Officer, Programmes, TV, 1961; Staff Admin Officer, 1962; Asst Controller, Staff Admin, 1964; Controller, Staff Admin, 1967; Controller, Development, Personnel, 1976. Chm. Exec. Council, RIPA, 1975-77; CIPM; Vice Pres. (Pay and Employment Conditions), IPM, 1978-80; Lay Selector, ACCM, 1963-73 (Mem. Candidates Cttee, 1966-69); Lay Chm., Richmond and Barnes Deanery Synod, 1970-76; Mem. General Synod, C of E, 1975-78. 1st Chm., Mortlake with East Sheen Soc., 1969-71; Chm., Assoc. of Amenity Societies in Richmond-upon-Thames, 1973-77. *Publication:* (jtly) Forward from Victory, 1943. *Recreations:* walking, local history. *Address:* The Old Bakery, Epwell, Banbury, Oxon OX15 6LA. *T:* Swalcliffe 773; 85 Shuttleworth Road, SW11 3DJ. *T:* 01-228 4979. *Club:* United Oxford & Cambridge University.

KINCRAIG, Hon. Lord; Robert Smith Johnston; a Senator of the College of Justice in Scotland, since 1972; *b* 10 Oct. 1918; *s* of W. T. Johnston, iron merchant, Glasgow; *m* 1943, Joan, *d* of late Col A. G. Graham, Glasgow; one *s* one *d. Educ:* Strathallan, Perthshire; St John's Coll., Cambridge; Glasgow Univ. BA (Hons) Cantab, 1939; LLB (with distinction) Glasgow, 1942. Mem. of Faculty of Advocates, 1942; Advocate-Depute, Crown Office, 1953-55; QC (Scotland) 1955; Home Advocate Depute, 1959-62; Sheriff of Roxburgh, Berwick and Selkirk, 1964-70; Dean of the Faculty of Advocates of Scotland, 1970-72. Contested (U) Stirling and Falkirk Burghs General Election, 1959. *Recreations:* golf, curling, gardening. *Address:* Westwood, Longniddry, East Lothian. *T:* Longniddry 52197. *Club:* Hon. Company of Edinburgh Golfers (Edinburgh).
    See also A. G. Johnston.

KINDERSLEY, family name of **Baron Kindersley.**

KINDERSLEY, 3rd Baron *cr* 1941; **Robert Hugh Molesworth Kindersley;** Chairman, Commonwealth Development Corporation, since 1980; a Vice-Chairman, Lazard Bros & Co. Ltd, since 1981 (Executive Director, since 1960); *b* 18 Aug. 1929; *s* of 2nd Baron Kindersley, CBE, MC, and Nancy Farnsworth (*d* 1977), *d* of Dr Geoffrey Boyd, Toronto; *S* father, 1976; *m* 1954, Venice Marigold (Rosie), *d* of late Captain Lord (Arthur) Francis Henry Hill; three *s* one *d. Educ:* Eton; Trinity Coll., Oxford; Harvard Business Sch., USA. Lt Scots Guards; served Malaya, 1948-49. Director: London Assurance, 1957-; Witan Investment Co. Ltd, 1958-; Steel Company of Wales, 1959-67; Marconi Co. Ltd, 1963-68; Sun Alliance & London Insurance Gp, 1965-; English Electric Co. Ltd, 1966-68; Gen. Electric Co. Ltd, 1968-70; British Match Corp. Ltd, 1969-73; Swedish Match Co., 1973-; Financial Adviser to Export Gp for the Constructional Industries, 1961-; Mem., Adv. Panel, Overseas Projects Gp, 1975-77; Dep. Chm., Export Guarantees Adv. Council, 1975-80; Chm., Exec. Cttee, BBA, 1976-78; Pres., Anglo-Taiwan Trade Cttee, 1976-. Hon. Treasurer, YWCA, 1965-76. Member: Institut International d'Etudes Bancaires, 1971-; Ct, Fishmongers' Co, 1973-. *Recreations:* all sports, including farming and gardening. *Heir: s* Hon. Rupert John Molesworth Kindersley [*b* 11 March 1955; *m* 1975, Sarah, *d* of late John D. Warde]. *Address:* Ramhurst Manor, near Tonbridge, Kent. *T:* Hildenborough 832174. *Clubs:* Pratt's, MCC, All England Lawn Tennis and Croquet, Queen's.

KINDERSLEY, Lt-Col Claude Richard Henry, DSO 1944; MC 1943; DL; Vice Lord-Lieutenant, Isle of Wight, since 1980; *b* 11 Dec. 1911; *s* of late Lt-Col Archibald Ogilvie Lyttelton Kindersley, CMG, and Edith Mary Kindersley (*née* Craven); *m* 1938, Vivien Mary, *d* of late Charles John Wharton Darwin, Elston Hall, Notts; three *d. Educ:* Wellington Coll.; Trinity Coll., Cambridge. MA. Commissioned HLI, 1933; served with 2nd Bn HLI, NW Frontier, Palestine and Middle East, 1936-43, and with 1st Bn HLI, France and Germany, 1944-45; commanded 1st Bn HLI, 1945; comd Infantry Boys' Batt., 1953-54; retd 1955. DL: Hants, 1962-74; Isle of Wight, 1974; High Sheriff, Isle of Wight, 1974-75. President: Country Landowners' Assoc. (IoW Branch), 1978-; Isle of Wight Scout Assoc., 1966-. *Recreation:* yachting. *Address:* Hamstead Grange, Yarmouth, Isle of Wight. *T:* Yarmouth 760230. *Clubs:* Royal Yacht Squadron, Royal London Yacht (Cowes); Royal Solent (Yarmouth).

KINDERSLEY, David Guy, MBE 1979; stone-carver and designer of alphabets (self-employed); *b* 11 June 1915; *s* of Guy Molesworth Kindersley and Kathleen Elton; *m* 1957, Barbara Pym Eyre Petrie; two *s* one *d. Educ:* St Cyprian's, Eastbourne (prep. sch.); Marlborough Coll., Wilts. Apprenticed to Eric Gill, ARA, 1933-36. Taught at Cambridge Coll. of Arts and Technology, 1946-57; one-time adviser to MoT on street-name alphabets; adviser to Shell Film Unit on design of titles, 1949-58; consultant to Letraset Internat., 1964-; Sen. Research Fellow, William Andrews Clark Memorial Library, Univ. of California, Los Angeles, 1967. Chm., Wynkyn de Worde Soc., 1976. *Publications:* Optical Letter Spacing and its Mechanical Application, 1966 (rev. and repub. by Wynkyn de Worde Soc., 1976); Mr Eric Gill, 1967, new edn (Eric Gill—Further Thoughts by an Apprentice), 1982; Graphic Variations, 1979; (with L. L. Cardozo) Letters Slate Cut, 1981; contribs to Printing Technology, Penrose Annual, Visible Language. Limited edns: Variations on the Theme of 26 Letters, edn 50, 1969; Graphic Sayings, edn 130, 1973. *Recreation:* archaeology. *Address:* 45 Highworth Avenue, Cambridge CB4 2BQ. *T:* Cambridge 57349. *Clubs:* Arts, Double Crown; (Hon. Mem.) Rounce and Coffin (Los Angeles).

KING, family name of **Earl of Lovelace.**

KING; *see* Maybray-King.

KING, Sir Albert, Kt 1974; OBE 1958; Leader, Labour Group, Leeds Metropolitan District Council, 1975-78, retired (Leader of the Council with one break, 1958-75); *b* 20 Aug. 1905; *s* of George and Ann King; *m* 1928, Pauline Riley; one *d. Educ:* Primrose Hill, Leeds. Full-time officer, engrg, 1942-70, retd. Hon. Freedom of the City of Leeds, 1976. *Recreations:* walking, reading. *Address:* 25 Brook Hill Avenue, Leeds LS17 8QA. *T:* Leeds 684684. *Clubs:* Beeston Working Men's, East Leeds Labour (Leeds).

KING, Albert Leslie, MBE 1945; *b* 28 Aug. 1911; *s* of late William John King and late Elizabeth Mary Amelia King; *m* 1938, Constance Eileen Stroud; two *d. Educ:* University Coll. Sch., Hampstead. Joined Shell-Mex and BP Statistical Dept, 1928. Joined Territorial Army, 1939; Major, RA, 1944.

Manager, Secretariat, Petroleum Board, 1947; Manager, Trade Relations Dept, Shell-Mex and BP Ltd, 1948; Gen. Manager: Administration, 1954; Sales, 1957; Operations, 1961; apptd Dir, 1962, Managing Dir, 1963-66. Dep. Dir-Gen., BIM, 1966-68. FCCA; FSS; CBIM; Hon. JDipMA. Barrister (Called to the Bar 1980). *Address:* Highlands, 50 Waggon Road, Hadley Wood, Barnet, Herts. *T:* 01-449 6424. *Clubs:* MCC; Surrey CCC, Saracens.

KING, Alexander, CMG 1975; CBE 1948; Chairman, International Federation of Institutes for Advanced Study, since 1974; *b* Glasgow, 26 Jan. 1909; *s* of J. M. King; *m* 1933, Sarah Maskell Thompson; three *d. Educ:* Highgate Sch.; Royal College of Science, London (DSc); University of Munich. Demonstrator, 1932, and later Senior Lecturer, until 1940, in physical chemistry, Imperial Coll. of Science; Dep. Scientific Adviser, Min. of Production, 1942; Head of UK Scientific Mission, Washington, and Scientific Attaché, British Embassy 1943-47; Head of Lord President's Scientific Secretariat, 1947-50; Chief Scientific Officer, Dept of Scientific and Industrial Research, 1950-56; Dep. Dir, European Productivity Agency, 1956-61; Dir for Scientific Affairs, OECD, 1961-68, Dir-Gen., 1968-74. Adviser, Govt of Ontario. Assoc. Fellow, Center for the Study of Democratic Institutions, Santa Barbara, Calif; Vis. Professor: Brandeis Univ., 1978; Univ. of Montréal, 1979. Leader Imperial Coll. Expedition to Jan Mayen, 1938; Harrison Prize of Chemical Soc., 1938; Gill Memorial Prize, Royal Geographical Society, 1938, Mem. Council, 1939-41; Hon. Sec. Chemical Soc., 1948-50; Founder and Exec. Mem., Club of Rome. DSc (hc) Ireland, 1974; DUniv Open, 1976; Hon. LLD Strathclyde, 1982. *Publications:* The International Stimulus, 1974; The State of the Planet, 1980; various chemistry textbooks, and papers in Journal of The Chemical Soc., Faraday Soc.; numerous articles on education, science policy and management. *Address:* 168 Rue de Grenelle, Paris 75007, France. *Club:* Athenæum.

KING, Alexander Hyatt; musical scholar; a Deputy Keeper, Department of Printed Books, British Museum, 1959-76, retired; *b* 18 July 1911; *s* of Thomas Hyatt King and Mabel Jessie (*née* Brayne); *m* 1943, Evelyn Mary Davies; two *s. Educ:* Dulwich Coll.; King's Coll., Cambridge (schol.; MA). Entered Dept of Printed Books, British Museum, 1934; Dep. Keeper, 1959-76; Supt of Music Room, 1944-73; Music Librarian, Ref. Div., British Library, 1973-76. Hon. Sec., British Union Catalogue of Early Music, 1948-57; Mem. Council, Royal Musical Assoc., 1949-, Editor, Proc. of the assoc., 1952-57, Pres., 1974-78; Pres., Internat. Assoc. of Music Libraries, 1955-59 (Hon. Mem., 1968), Pres., UK Br., 1953-68, Vice-Chm. jt cttee, Internat. Musicological Soc. and IAML, for Internat. Inventory of Musical Sources, 1961-76; Chm., exec. cttee, Brit. Inst. of Recorded Sound, 1951-62. Sandars Reader in Bibliography, Univ. of Cambridge, 1962; Vice-Chm., exec. cttee, Grove's Dictionary of Music, 1970-74; Trustee, Hinrichsen Foundn, 1976-; Hon. Librarian, Royal Philharmonic Soc., 1970-82. Mem., Zentralinst. für Mozartforschung, 1953. DUniv York, 1978; Hon. DMus St Andrews, 1981. *Publications:* Chamber Music, 1948; (jtly) catalogue: Music in the Hirsch Library, 1951; catalogue: Exhibition of Handel's Messiah, 1951; Mozart in Retrospect, 1955, 3rd edn 1976; Mozart in the British Museum, 1956, repr. 1975; exhibn catalogue: Henry Purcell—G. F. Handel, 1959; Some British Collectors of Music, 1963; 400 Years of Music Printing, 1964, 2nd edn 1968; Handel and his Autographs, 1967; Mozart Chamber Music, 1968, 2nd edn 1970; Mozart String and Wind Concertos, 1978; Printed Music in the British Museum: an account of the collections, the catalogues, and their formation, up to 1920, 1979; A Wealth of Music in the various collections of the British Library (Reference Division) and the British Museum, 1983; *edited:* (jtly) Mozart's Duet Sonata in C K19d, 1953; illustr. edn of Alfred Einstein's Short History of Music, 1953; P. K. Hoffmann's Cadenzas and elaborated slow movements to 6 Mozart piano concertos, 1959; (jtly) 2nd edn of Emily Anderson's Letters of Mozart and his Family, 1966; Concert Goer's Companion series, 1970-; Auction catalogues of Music, 1973-; *contribs to:* Year's Work in Music, 1947-51; Schubert, a symposium, 1947; Music, Libraries and Instruments, 1961; Deutsch Festschrift, 1963; Essays in honour of Victor Scholderer, 1970; Grasberger Festschrift, 1975; Essays in honour of Sir Jack Westrup, 1976; The New Grove, 1980; various articles; *relevant publication* (ed by Oliver Neighbour) Music and Bibliography: Essays in honour of Alec Hyatt King, 1980. *Recreations:* watching cricket, opera, exploring Suffolk. *Address:* 29 Lauradale Road, N2 9LT. *T:* 01-883 1623. *Club:* MCC.

KING, Alison, OBE 1978; Co-ordinator Properties, Women's Royal Voluntary Service, 1974-78; Director, WRVS Office Premises Board, since 1969; Member, WRVS Housing Association Committee, since 1973. Flight-Capt., Operations, Air Transport Auxiliary, 1940-45. Dir, Women's Junior Air Corps, 1952-58; Gen. Sec., NFWI, 1959-69. Chm., British Women Pilots' Assoc., 1956-64. *Publication:* Golden Wings, 1956 (repr. 1975). *Recreations:* writing, painting in oils. *Address:* 4 Chagford House, Chagford Street, NW1. *T:* 01-262 4631. *Club:* University Women's.

KING, Prof. Anthony Stephen; Professor of Government, University of Essex, since 1969; *b* 17 Nov. 1934; *o s* of late Harold and of Marjorie King; *m* 1st, 1965, Vera Korte (*d* 1971); 2nd, 1980, Jan Reece. *Educ:* Queen's Univ., Kingston Ont. (1st Cl. Hons, Hist. 1956); Magdalen Coll., Oxford (Rhodes Schol.; 1st Cl. Hons, PPE, 1958). Student, Nuffield Coll., Oxford, 1958-61; DPhil (Oxon) 1962. Fellow of Magdalen Coll., Oxford, 1961-65; Amer. Council of Learned Societies Fellow, Columbia Univ., NY, 1962-63; Vis. Prof., Univ. of Wisconsin, 1967; Fellow, Center for Advanced Study in the Behavioral Scis, Stanford, Calif., 1977-78. Elections Commentator, BBC and

Observer; Univ. of Essex: Sen. Lectr, 1966-68; Reader, 1968-69. Editor, British Jl of Political Science, 1972-77. *Publications:* (with D. E. Butler) The British General Election of 1964, 1965; (with D. E. Butler) The British General Election of 1966, 1966; (ed) British Politics: People, Parties and Parliament, 1966; (ed) The British Prime Minister, 1969; (with Anne Sloman) Westminster and Beyond, 1973; British Members of Parliament: a self-portrait, 1974; (ed) Why is Britain becoming Harder to Govern?, 1976; Britain Says Yes: the 1975 referendum on the Common Market, 1977; (ed) The New American Political System, 1978; frequent contributor to British and American jls and periodicals. *Recreations:* music, theatre, holidays, walking. *Address:* Department of Government, University of Essex, Wivenhoe Park, Colchester, Essex CO4 3SQ. *T:* Colchester 862286; The Mill House, Middle Green, Wakes Colne, Colchester, Essex CO6 2BP. *T:* Earls Colne 2497.

KING, Prof. Basil Charles; Professor of Geology, Bedford College, University of London, 1956-77, now Emeritus; *b* 1 June 1915; *s* of Charles William Argent King; *m* 1939, Dorothy Margaret Wells; two *s* one *d* (and one *d* decd). *Educ:* King Edward VI Sch., Bury St Edmunds; Durham Univ.; London Univ. Demonstrator, Bedford Coll., London, 1936-38; Chemist and Petrologist, Geological Survey of Uganda, 1938-46; Mineralogist, Geological Survey of Nigeria, 1946-48; Senior Lecturer, University of Glasgow, 1948-56. FRSE 1950; FRSA 1978. Bigsby Medal, Geological Soc., 1959; André Dumont Medal, Société Géologique de Belgique, 1967; Murchison Medal, Geological Soc., 1971; Clough Medal, Geol Soc. of Edinburgh, 1978. *Publications:* geological publications on E Africa, Nigeria, Botswana and Scotland. *Address:* 1 Catacol, Lochranza, Isle of Arran, Scotland KA27 8HN. *T:* Lochranza 658.

KING, Billie Jean; tennis player; Publisher, womenSports, since 1973; Commissioner, US Team Tennis, since 1981; *b* 22 Nov. 1943; *d* of Willard J. Moffitt; *m* 1965, Larry King. *Educ:* Los Cerritos Sch.; Long Beach High Sch.; Los Angeles State Coll. Played first tennis match at age of eleven; won first championship, Southern California, 1958; coached by Clyde Walker, Alice Marble, Frank Brennan and Mervyn Rose; won first All England Championship, 1966, and five times subseq., and in 1979 achieved record of 20 Wimbledon titles (six Singles, ten Doubles, four Mixed Doubles); has won all other major titles inc. US Singles and Doubles Championships on all four surfaces, and 24 US national titles in all. Pres., Women's Tennis Assoc., 1980-81. *Publications:* Tennis to Win, 1970; Billie Jean, 1974; (with Joe Hyams) Secrets of Winning Tennis, 1975; Tennis Love (illus. Charles Schulz), 1978; (with Frank Deford) Billie Jean King (Misfit, in USA), 1982. *Address:* Future, Inc., 1801 Avenue of the Stars, Suite 325, Los Angeles, Calif 90067, USA.

KING, Dr Brian Edmund; Director, since 1967, and Chief Executive, since 1977, Wira (formerly Wool Industries Research Association); *b* 25 May 1928; *s* of Albert Theodore King and Gladys Johnson; *m* 1952 (marr. diss.); two *s*; *m* 1972, Eunice Wolstenholme; one *d*. *Educ:* Pocklington Sch.; Leeds Univ. TMM (Research) Ltd, 1952-57; British Oxygen, 1957-67. *Recreations:* bridge, swimming, tennis. *Address:* 2 Slant Gate, Kirkburton, Huddersfield, W Yorks HD8 0QL. *T:* Huddersfield 604613.

KING, Cecil (Harmsworth); *b* 20 Feb. 1901; *e* surv. *s* of Sir Lucas White King, CSI, and Geraldine Adelaide Hamilton, *d* of Alfred Harmsworth, barrister of the Middle Temple; *m* 1st, 1923, Agnes Margaret, *d* of the Rev. Canon G. A. Cooke, DD, Regius Prof. of Hebrew, Oxford, and Canon of Christ Church; one *s* one *d* (and two *s* decd). 2nd, 1962, Dame Ruth Railton, *qv. Educ:* Winchester; Christ Church, Oxford (2nd class hons history, MA). Dir, Daily Mirror, 1929; Dep. Chm., Sunday Pictorial, 1942; Chairman: Daily Mirror Newspapers Ltd and Sunday Pictorial Newspapers Ltd, 1951-1963; International Publishing Corp., 1963-68; The Reed Paper Group, 1963-68; Wall Paper Manufacturers, 1965-67; British Film Institute, 1948-52; Newspaper Proprietors' Assoc., 1961-68; Nigerian Printing & Publishing Co., 1948-68; Butterworth & Co. Ltd, 1968. Director: Reuters, 1953-59; Bank of England, 1965-68. Part-time Mem., National Coal Board, 1966-69. Mem., National Parks Commn, later Countryside Commn, 1966-69. Gold Badge for services to City of Warsaw; Gold Medal for services to British paper trade. Hon. DLitt Boston, 1974. *Publications:* The Future of the Press, 1967; Strictly Personal, 1969; With Malice Towards None: a war diary, 1970; Without Fear or Favour, 1971; The Cecil King Diary 1965-70, 1972; On Ireland, 1973; The Cecil King Diary 1970-74, 1975; Cecil King's Commonplace Book, 1981. *Recreation:* reading. *Address:* 23 Greenfield Park, Dublin 4, Ireland. *T:* Dublin 695870.

See also Sir G. V. K. Burton.

KING, Charles Andrew Buchanan, CMG 1961; MBE 1944; HM Diplomatic Service, retired; Chairman, Premier Sauna Ltd, to 1981; *b* 25 July 1915; *s* of late Major Andrew Buchanan King, 7th Argyll and Sutherland Highlanders and of Evelyn Nina (née Sharpe). *Educ:* Wellington Coll.; Magdalene Coll., Cambridge (MA). Vice-Consul: Zürich, 1940, Geneva, 1941; Attaché, HM Legation, Berne, 1942; transf. to FO, 1946; 2nd Sec., Vienna, 1950; transf. to FO 1953; to Hong Kong, 1958; to FO 1961; retired, 1967; Head of W European Div., Overseas Dept, London Chamber of Commerce, 1968-70. *Recreation:* travel. *Address:* 19 Archery Close, W2. *Club:* Naval and Military.

KING, Charles Martin M. ; *see* Meade-King.

KING, Colin Sainthill Wallis-; *see* Wallis-King.

KING, Prof. David Anthony, FRSC, MInstP; Brunner Professor of Physical Chemistry, University of Liverpool, since 1974; *b* 12 Aug. 1939; *s* of Arnold King and Patricia (née Vardy), Durban; *m* 1971, Anne Julia (née Donat); two *s. Educ:* St John's Coll., Johannesburg; Univ. of the Witwatersrand, Johannesburg. BSc, PhD (Rand), ScD (E Anglia). Shell Scholar, Imperial Coll., 1963-66; Lectr in Chemical Physics, Univ. of E Anglia, Norwich, 1966-74. Member: Comité de Direction of Centre de Cinétique Physique et Chimique, Nancy, 1974-81; Nat. Exec., Assoc. of Univ. Teachers, 1970-78 (Nat. Pres., 1976-77); British Vacuum Council, 1978-; Internat. Union for Vacuum Science and Technology, 1978-; Faraday Div., Council, Chem. Soc., 1979-; Scientific Adv. Panel, Daresbury Lab., 1980-82; Res. Adv. Cttee, Leverhulme Trust, 1980-; Beirat, Fritz Haber Inst., West Berlin, 1981-. Mem. Editorial Bd, Jl of Physics C, 1977-80. Chem. Soc. Award for surface and colloid chemistry, 1978. *Publications:* papers on the physics and chemistry of solid surfaces in: Proc. Royal Soc., Surface Science, Jl Chem. Soc., Jl of Physics, etc. *Recreations:* photography, reading, squash. *Address:* 27 Mount Street, Liverpool L1 9HD. *T:* (home) 051-709 8871, (office) 051-709 6022 (ext. 2560).

KING, (Denys) Michael (Gwilym), CEng, FICE, MIMechE; Director, Heathrow Airport, since 1977; Member (full-time), British Airports Authority, since 1980; *b* 29 May 1929; *s* of William James King, FCIS, and Hilda May King; *m* 1956, Monica Helen (marr. diss. 1973), *d* of David and Constance Murray; three *d. Educ:* St Edmund's Sch., Canterbury; Simon Langton Sch., Canterbury; Battersea Polytechnic, London (BScEng Hons London, 1949). MIMechE 1966; FICE 1977. Engr, J. Laing Construction Ltd, 1961-71, Dir, 1971-74; Engrg Dir, BAA, 1974-77 (also at other cos). *Recreations:* yachting, squash, golf. *Address:* c/o British Airports Authority, D'Albiac House, Heathrow, Hounslow, Mddx. *T:* 01-759 7241. *Clubs:* Foxhills Country (Ottershaw); Cobbs Quay Yacht (Poole); Mid Surrey Squash (Stoneleigh).

KING, Douglas James Edward, FRICS; Senior Partner, King & Co., Chartered Surveyors, since 1960; Chairman, Hearts of Oak and Enfield Building Society, since 1975; *b* 12 April 1919; *s* of Herbert James King, OBE, FRICS and Gertrude Carney; *m* 1941, Betty Alice Martin; two *s* one *d. Educ:* Hillcrest Prep. Sch., Frinton-on-Sea; Taunton Sch. FRICS 1952. Served War, TA, 1939-46, Captain RA. Vice Pres., London Chamber of Commerce and Industry, 1980- (Chm., 1978-80); Chm., London Court of Internat. Arbitration, 1981-82; Gen. Comr of Income Tax, City of London, 1978-. Governor, Queenswood Sch., 1980-. *Recreation:* lives and writings of Johnson, Boswell and Pepys. *Address:* Monkswood Cottage, 73a Camlet Way, Hadley Wood, Herts EN4 0NL. *T:* 01-236 3000. *Clubs:* Carlton, City Livery.

KING, Prof. Edmund James, MA, PhD, DLit; Professor of Education, University of London King's College, 1975-79, now Emeritus Professor; *b* 19 June 1914; *s* of James and Mary Alice King; *m* 1939, Margaret Mary Breakell; one *s* three *d. Educ:* Univ. of Manchester (BA, MA); Univ. of London (PhD, DLit). Taught in grammar schs, 1936-47; Asst, then Sen. Asst to Dir of Extra-Mural Studies, Univ. of London, 1947-53; Lectr, subseq. Reader, Univ. of London King's Coll., 1953-75, also Dir, Comparative Research Unit, King's Coll., 1970-73. Visiting appts at Amer. and Can. univs; also in Melbourne, Tokyo, Tehran, etc; lecturing and adv. assignments in many countries. Editor, Comparative Education, 1978-. *Publications:* Other Schools and Ours, 1958, 5th edn 1979; World Perspectives in Education, 1962, 2nd edn 1965; (ed) Communist Education, 1963; Society, Schools and Progress in the USA, 1965; Education and Social Change, 1966; Comparative Studies and Educational Decision, 1968; Education and Development in Western Europe, 1969; (ed) The Teacher and the Needs of Society, 1970; The Education of Teachers: a comparative analysis, 1970; (with W. Boyd) A History of Western Education, 1972; Post-compulsory Education, vol. I: a new analysis in Western Europe, 1974; vol. II: the way ahead, 1975 (both with C. H. Moor and J. A. Mundy); (ed) Reorganizing Education, 1977; (ed) Education for Uncertainty, 1979. *Recreations:* gardening, music, writing. *Address:* 40 Alexandra Road, Epsom, Surrey.

KING, Very Rev. Edward Laurie; Dean of Cape Town since 1958; *b* 30 Jan. 1920; *s* of William Henry and Norah Alice King; *m* 1950, Helen Stuart Mathers, MB, BCh, MMed; one *s* three *d. Educ:* King's Coll., Taunton; University of Wales (BA). Deacon, 1945; priest, 1946, Monmouth; Associate in Theology (S Af.). Curate of Risca, 1945-48; Diocese of Johannesburg, 1948-50; Rector of Robertson, Cape, 1950-53; Rector of Stellenbosch, 1953-58. *Recreations:* cricket, reading. *Address:* The Deanery, Upper Orange Street, Cape Town, South Africa. *T:* 45-2609. *Club:* City and Civil Service.

KING, Evelyn Mansfield, MA; *b* 30 May 1907; *s* of Harry Percy King and Winifred Elizabeth Paulet; *m* 1935, Hermione Edith, *d* of late Arthur Felton Crutchley, DSO; one *s* two *d. Educ:* Cheltenham Coll.; King's Coll., Cambridge; Inner Temple. Cambridge Univ. Correspondent to the Sunday Times, 1928-30; Asst Master Bedford Sch., 1930; Headmaster and Warden, Claysmore Sch., 1935-50; Gloucestershire Regt 1940; Acting Lt-Col 1941. MP (Lab) Penryn and Falmouth Div. of Cornwall, 1945-50; Parly Sec., Min. of Town and Country Planning, 1947-50. Resigned from Labour Party, 1951, and joined Conservative Party; contested (C) Southampton (Itchen), 1959;

MP (C) Dorset S, 1964–79. Member of Parly delegations: Bermuda and Washington, 1946; Tokyo, 1947; Cairo and ME, 1967; Jordan and Persian Gulf, 1968; Kenya and Seychelles, 1969; Malta, 1970 (leader); Malawi, 1971 (leader); Mem. Select Cttee on Overseas Aid, 1971; Chm. Food Cttee, 1971–73. *Publications:* (with J. C. Trewin) Printer to the House, Biography of Luke Hansard, 1952. *Recreations:* boats, riding. *Address:* Embley Manor, near Romsey, Hants. *T:* Romsey 512342; 11 Barton Street, SW1. *T:* 01-222 4525. *Clubs:* Carlton, Little Ship; Royal Dorset Yacht (Weymouth).
See also Sir R. G. Cooke.

KING, Francis Henry, OBE 1979; FRSL; Author; *b* 4 March 1923; *o s* of Eustace Arthur Cecil King and Faith Mina Read. *Educ:* Shrewsbury; Balliol Coll., Oxford. Drama critic, Sunday Telegraph. Chm., Soc. of Authors, 1975–77; Pres., English PEN, 1978– (Vice-Pres., 1977). *Publications:* novels: To the Dark Tower, 1946; Never Again, 1947; An Air That Kills, 1948; The Dividing Stream, 1951 (Somerset Maugham Award, 1952); The Dark Glasses, 1954; The Widow, 1957; The Man on the Rock, 1957; So Hurt and Humiliated (short stories), 1959; The Custom House, 1961; The Japanese Umbrella (short stories), 1964 (Katherine Mansfield Short Story Prize, 1965); The Last of the Pleasure Gardens, 1965; The Waves Behind the Boat, 1967; The Brighton Belle (short stories), 1968; A Domestic Animal, 1970; Flights (two short novels), 1973; A Game of Patience, 1974; The Needle, 1975; Hard Feelings (short stories), 1976; Danny Hill, 1977; The Action, 1978; Indirect Method (short stories), 1980; *poetry:* Rod of Incantation, 1952; *biography:* E. M. Forster and His World, 1978; *general* (ed): Introducing Greece, 1956; Japan, 1970. *Address:* 19 Gordon Place, W8 4JE. *T:* 01-937 5715. *Club:* PEN.

KING, Gen. Sir Frank (Douglas), GCB 1976 (KCB 1972; CB 1971); MBE 1953; Chairman: John Taylor Trust, since 1978; Assets Protection International Ltd, since 1981; Director, since 1978: John Taylor Ltd; John Taylor (Worksop); Leicester Frozen Foods; Kilton Properties; Springthorpe Property Co.; PLAZA Fish Ltd; Military Adviser to Short Brothers Ltd, Belfast, since 1979; Director, Control Risks Ltd, since 1979; *b* 9 March 1919; *s* of Arthur King, Farmer, and Kate Eliza (*née* Sheard), Brightwell, Berks; *m* 1947, Joy Emily Ellen Taylor-Lane; one *s* two *d.* Educ: Wallingford Gram. Sch. Joined Army, 1939; commnd into Royal Fusiliers, 1940; Parachute Regt, 1943; dropped Arnhem, Sept. 1944; Royal Military College of Science (ptsc), 1946; Staff Coll., Camberley (psc), 1950; comd 2 Parachute Bn, Middle East, 1960–62; comd 11 Infantry Bde Gp, Germany, 1963–64; Military Adviser (Overseas Equipment), 1965–66; Dir, Land/Air Warfare, MoD, 1967–68; Dir, Military Assistance Overseas, MoD, 1968–69; Comdt, RMCS, 1969–71; GOC-in-C, Army Strategic Comd, 1971–72; Dep. C-in-C UK Land Forces, 1972–73; GOC and Dir of Ops, N Ireland, 1973–75; Comdr, Northern Army Gp, and C-in-C BAOR, 1976–78; ADC Gen. to the Queen, 1977–78. Col Comdt, Army Air Corps, 1974–79. Trustee, Airborne Forces Security Trust, 1981–; Mem. Council, Air League, 1982–. Kermit Roosevelt Lectr, 1977. *Recreations:* golf, gardening, flying. *Address:* c/o Williams & Glyn's Bank, Columbia House, 69 Aldwych, WC2. *Clubs:* Army and Navy; Berkshire Golf.

KING, Frank Gordon, QC 1970; *b* 10 March 1915; *s* of late Lt-Col Frank King, DSO, OBE; *m* 1937, Monica Beatrice, *d* of late Arthur Collins; two *s* one *d.* Educ: Charterhouse, Godalming; Christ's Coll., Cambridge (BA 1936, LLB 1938). Served War of 1939–45; RA 1939–46, Major 1943. Called to the Bar, Gray's Inn, 1946. A Church Commissioner, 1973–81. *Address:* 24 Old Buildings, Lincoln's Inn, WC2. *T:* 01-405 1124; Red Chimneys, Warren Drive, Kingswood, Surrey. *Club:* Walton Heath Golf.

KING, Frederick Ernest, FRS 1954; MA, DPhil, DSc Oxon; PhD London; Scientific Adviser to British Petroleum Co. Ltd, 1959–71, retired; *er s* of late Frederick and Elizabeth King, Bexhill, Sussex. *Educ:* Bancroft's Sch.; University of London; Oriel Coll., Oxford. Ramsay Memorial Fellow, 1930–31; Demonstrator, Dyson Perrins Laboratory, 1931–34; University Lecturer and Demonstrator in Chemistry, Oxford Univ., 1934–48, and sometime lecturer in Organic Chemistry, Magdalen Coll. and Balliol Coll.; Sir Jesse Boot Prof. of Chemistry, University of Nottingham, 1948–55; Dir in charge of research, British Celanese Ltd, 1955–59. Fellow Queen Mary Coll., 1955. *Publications:* scientific papers mainly in Jl of Chem. Soc. *Recreation:* gardening. *Address:* Glyde's Farm, Ashburnham, East Sussex TN33 9PB; 360 The Water Gardens, W2. *Club:* Athenæum.

KING, Hilary William, CBE 1964; HM Diplomatic Service, retired; *b* 10 March 1919; *s* of Dr W. H. King, Fowey, Cornwall; *m* 1947, Dr Margaret Helen Grierson Borrowman; one *s* three *d.* Educ: Sherborne; Corpus Christi Coll. Cambridge. Served War of 1939–45; Signals Officer, mission to Yugoslav Partizan GHQ, 1943–45 (MBE 1944). Apptd Mem. Foreign (subseq. Diplomatic) Service, Nov. 1946. A Vice-Consul in Yugoslavia, 1947–48; transferred to Foreign Office, 1949; promoted 1st Sec., 1950; transf. to Vienna as a Russian Sec., 1951; Washington, 1953; transf. Foreign Office, 1958; Commercial Counsellor, Moscow, 1959; acted as Chargé d'Affaires, 1960; Ambassador (and Consul-Gen.) to Guinea, 1962–65; St Antony's Coll., Oxford, Oct. 1965–June 1966; Counsellor of Embassy, Warsaw, 1966–67; Head of UN (Economic and Social) Dept, FCO, 1968–71; Consul-Gen., Hamburg, 1971–74. *Recreation:* sailing. *Address:* Fuaim an Sruth, South Cuan, Oban, Argyll PA34 4TU. *Club:* Clyde Cruising.

KING, Prof. Hubert John, CBE 1976; FEng, FIME, FIMM; *b* 5 May 1915; *s* of Hubert and Emmeline Elizabeth King; *m* 1940, Ceridwen Richards; one *s* two *d.* Educ: Porth County Sch.; University Coll., Cardiff (PhD London); Glamorgan Polytechnic. Underground worker, S Wales Coalfield, 1931–36; served HM Forces, 1939–45; successively, Lecturer, Reader and Head of Mining and Mineral Sciences Dept, Univ. of Leeds, 1947–67; Univ. of Nottingham: Professor and Head, Mining Engineering Dept, 1967–77, Emeritus Prof., 1977; Dean, Faculty of Applied Science, 1973–76. President, Instn of Mining Engineers, 1974 (Institution Medal, 1980); Member and Chairman, Safety in Mines Research Adv. Cttee, 1967–79; Mem., Internat. Cttee for World Mining Congresses, 1967–77. *Publications:* various research papers in fields of surveying, rock mechanics and mineral economics. *Recreation:* golf. *Address:* Leewood, Oakham Road, Nottingham NG11 6LT. *T:* Nottingham 211091.

KING, Isobel Wilson; *see* Buchanan, I. W.

KING, Ivor Edward, CB 1961; CBE 1943; CEng, FRINA; Royal Corps of Naval Constructors; Director of Dockyards, Admiralty, 1958–61; *b* 1899; *s* of John and Minnie Elizabeth King, Pembroke Dock; *m* 1923, Doris, *d* of John and Catherine Hill, Lee, SE; three *d.* Educ: Royal Naval College, Greenwich. Formerly Manager, HM Dockyards, Portsmouth, Malta, Sheerness and Bermuda. Constructor Capt. to Commander-in-Chief, Mediterranean, 1942–44. Served War, 1942–44 (CBE). Hon. Vice-Pres., Royal Institution of Naval Architects. *Recreation:* golf. *Address:* 10 Combe Park, Bath BA1 3NP. *T:* Bath 23047.
See also G. R. Serjeant.

KING, Sir James Granville Le Neve, 3rd Bt, *cr* 1888; TD; *b* 17 Sept. 1898; *s* of Sir John Westall King, 2nd Bt, and Frances Rosa (*d* 1942), *d* of John Neve, Oaken, Staffs; *S* father 1940; *m* 1928, Penelope Charlotte, *d* of late Capt. E. Cooper-Key, CB, MVO, RN; one *s* two *d.* Educ: Eton; King's Coll., Cambridge. Heir: *s* John Christopher King [*b* 31 March 1933; *m* 1958, Patricia Monica (marr. diss. 1972), *o d* of late Lt-Col Kingsley Foster and of Mrs Foster, Hampton Court Palace; one *s* one *d*]. *Address:* Church Farm House, Chilbolton, Hants.

KING, Prof. James Lawrence; Regius Professor of Engineering, University of Edinburgh, since 1968; *b* 14 Feb. 1922; *s* of Lawrence Anderson King and Wilhelmina Young McLeish; *m* 1951, Pamela Mary Ward Hitchcock; one *s* one *d.* Educ: Latymer Upper Sch.; Jesus Coll., Cambridge; Imperial Coll., London. Min. of Defence (Navy), 1942–68. *Recreation:* walking. *Address:* 2 Arboretum Road, Edinburgh EH3 5PD. *T:* 031-552 3854.

KING, Prof. Jeffrey William Hitchen, MSc, CEng, FICE, FIStructE; Professor of Civil Engineering, Queen Mary College, University of London, 1953–72, now Emeritus Professor; *b* 28 Sept. 1906; *s* of Alfred George and Edith King, Wigan; *m* 1930, Phyllis Morfydd Harris (*d* 1977), *d* of Rev. W. Harris; one *s* one *d.* Educ: Ashton-in-Makerfield Grammar Sch.; Manchester Univ. Engineer and Agent to Cementation Co. Ltd, British Isles, Spain and Egypt, 1927–36; Research Engineer, Michelin Tyre Co. 1936–37; Lecturer in Civil Engineering, University Coll., Nottingham, 1937–47; Reader in Civil Engineering, Queen Mary Coll., London, 1947–53. Governor, Queen Mary Coll., 1962–65; formerly Mem., Academic Board and Vice-Chm., Civil Engineering Cttee of Regional Advisory Council for Higher Technological Education; formerly mem., Research Cttee, formerly Chm., Concrete Specification Cttee and Cttee on Accelerated Testing of Concrete, Instn of Civil Engineers; formerly Mem. BSI Cttees, CEB/4/4, CEB/21. *Publications:* papers in Journals of Instn of Civil Engineers, Instn of Structural Engineers, and Inst. of Mine Surveyors, and in various technical periodicals. *Recreations:* many and varied. *Address:* The Nook, Crayke Road, Easingwold, York YO6 3PN. *T:* Easingwold 21151.

KING, John Edward; Principal Establishment Officer and Under Secretary, Welsh Office, since 1977; *b* 30 May 1922; *s* of late Albert Edward and of Margaret King; *m* 1st, 1948, Pamela White (marr. diss.); one *d*; 2nd, 1956, Mary Margaret Beaton; two *d.* Educ: Penarth County Sch.; Sch. of Oriental and African Studies, London Univ. Served with Rifle Bde, RWF and Nigeria Regt, 1941–47; Chindit campaign, Burma, with 77 Bde (despatches). Cadet, Colonial Admin. Service, N Nigeria, 1947; Permanent Sec., Fed. Govt of Nigeria, 1960; retired from HMOCS, 1963. Principal, CRO, 1963; Navy Dept, MoD, 1966–69; Private Sec. to Sec. of State for Wales, 1969–71; Asst Sec., Welsh Office, 1971–77. *Recreations:* books, photography, swimming, tennis. *Address:* Fairfields, Fairwater Road, Llandaff, Cardiff CF5 2LF. *T:* Cardiff 562825. *Clubs:* Civil Service; Cardiff Lawn Tennis.

KING, John George Maydon, CMG 1959; OBE 1953 (MBE 1945); retired from Colonial Agricultural Service; *b* 26 Jan. 1908; *s* of late Harold Edwin and Elizabeth Lindsay King, Durban, Natal, SA; *m* 1st, 1938, Françoise Charlotte de Rham (*d* 1966), Lausanne; two *s*; 2nd, 1970, Violet, *widow of* Colin MacPherson, late of Tanganyika Administration Service. *Educ:* University Coll. Sch. (Preparatory); Oundle Sch.; London Univ. (Wye Coll.); Cambridge Univ. (Colonial Office Schol., Cambridge Univ. and Imperial Coll. of Tropical Agric.). Appointed to Colonial Agricultural Service as Agricultural Officer, Tanganyika, 1932–46; seconded to Cambridge Univ. as Lecturer in Tropical Agric. to Colonial Services Courses, 1946–48; Dir of livestock and Agricultural Services, Basutoland, 1948–54; Dir of Agriculture, Uganda, 1954–60, Swaziland, 1960–63; Regional Manager, Lower Indus

Project, Hyderabad-Sind, 1964–66. *Recreations:* walking, photography. *Address:* Brockley House, Nailsworth, near Stroud, Glos GL6 0AR. *T:* Nailsworth 2407. *Club:* Farmers'.

KING, Sir John (Leonard), Kt 1979; Chairman: Babcock International plc (formerly Babcock & Wilcox Ltd), since 1972; British Airways, since 1981; *yr s* of Albert John King and Kathleen King; *m* 1st, 1941, Lorna Kathleen Sykes (*d* 1969); three *s* one *d* ; 2nd, 1970, Hon. Isabel Monckton, *y d* of 8th Viscount Galway. Founded Whitehouse Industries Ltd, 1945 and Ferrybridge Industries Ltd, subseq. Pollard Ball & Roller Bearing Co. Ltd (Man. Dir 1945, Chm. 1961–69); Chm., Dennis Motor Hldgs Ltd, 1970–72; Chairman: Babcock International Inc.; British Nuclear Associates Ltd; SKF (UK) Ltd, 1976–; R. J. Dick Inc. (USA); Dick Corp. (USA); Director: First Union Corp. (USA); 1928 Investment Trust Ltd; Dep. Chm., Nat. Nuclear Corp. Chm., Macmillan Appeal for Continuing Care, 1977–78; Vice Pres., Nat. Soc. for Cancer Relief. Dep. Chm., NEB, 1979–81. Member: NEDC Cttee on Finance for Investment, 1976–78; Review Bd for Govt Contracts, 1975–78; Chairman: City and Industrial Liaison Council; British Olympic Appeals Cttee, 1975–78; Alexandra Rose Day, 1980–. MFH Badsworth Foxhounds, 1949–58; MFH Duke of Rutland's Foxhounds (Belvoir), 1958–72. Hon. Dr Hum. Gardner-Webb Coll., USA, 1980. ARAeS 1982. FCIT 1982; FBIM. *Recreations:* hunting, field sports, racing. *Address:* Cleveland House, St James's Square, SW1Y 4LN. *T:* 01-930 9766. *Clubs:* White's; Brook (New York).

KING, Prof. John Oliver Letts, FRCVS; FIBiol; Professor of Animal Husbandry, University of Liverpool, 1969– 30 Sept. 1982; *b* 21 Dec. 1914; *s* of Richard Oliver King and Helen Mary (*née* Letts); *m* 1942, Helen Marion Gudgin; one *s* one *d. Educ:* Berkhamsted Grammar Sch.; Royal Veterinary Coll. (MVSc, MRCVS); Univ. of Reading (BScAgric); Univ. of Liverpool (MVSc, PhD); FRCVS 1969. Assistant in veterinary practice, 1937; Ho. Surg., Royal Veterinary Coll., 1938; Lectr in Animal Husbandry, 1941, Sen. Lectr 1948, Reader 1961, Univ. of Liverpool. Mem. Council, British Veterinary Assoc., 1953–68; Chairman: Council, N of England Zoological Soc., 1972–; British Council Vet. Adv. Panel, 1978–; Member: Medicines Commn, 1969–71; Horserace Anti-Doping Cttee, 1973–; Farm Animal Welfare Council, 1979–; President: Assoc. of Veterinary Teachers and Research Workers, 1961; Lancashire Veterinary Assoc., 1967; British Veterinary Zoological Soc., 1971–74; Royal Coll. of Veterinary Surgeons, 1980. Dalrymple-Champneys Cup, 1976. *Publications:* Veterinary Dietetics, 1961; An Introduction to Animal Husbandry, 1978; papers on animal husbandry in various scientific pubns. *Recreation:* gardening. *Address:* Arnside, Hooton Road, Willaston, South Wirral L64 1SL. *T:* 051-327 4850. *Club:* Athenæum.

KING, Dr John William Beaufoy; Chief Scientific Officer, ARC Animal Breeding Research Organisation; *b* 28 June 1927; *s* of late John Victor Beaufoy and Gwendoleen Freda King; *m* 1951, Pauline Margaret Coldicott; four *s. Educ:* Marling Sch., Stroud; St Catharine's Coll., Cambridge; Edinburgh Univ. BA Cantab 1947, MA Cantab 1952; PhD Edinburgh 1951; FIBiol 1974; FRSE 1975. ARC Animal Breeding Res. Organisation, 1951–. Kellogg Foundn Schol. to USA, 1954; Genetics Cons. to Pig Industry Develt Authority, 1959; David Black Award (services to pig industry), 1966; Nuffield Foundn Fellowship to Canada, 1970; Vis. Lectr, Göttingen Univ., 1973. *Publications:* papers in scientific jls. *Recreations:* gardening, shooting, dog training. *Address:* Cottage Farm, West Linton, Peeblesshire EH46 7AS. *T:* West Linton 448. *Club:* Farmers'.

KING, Joseph, OBE 1971; JP; Group Industrial Relations Advisor, Smith and Nephew Associated Cos Ltd, 1978–82; *b* 28 Nov. 1914; *s* of John King, coal miner, and Catherine King (*née* Thompson); *m* 1939, Lily King (*née* Pendlebury); one *s* five *d. Educ:* St James' RC Sch., Atherton, Lancashire. Left school at age of 14 and commenced work in cotton mill, 1929. Took active part in Union of Textile and Allied Workers from early years in industry. Elected, 1949: Labour Councillor, Tyldesley; Trades Union Organiser; Dist. Sec., NE Lancs. Gen. Sec., Nat. Union of Textile and Allied Workers, 1962–75; Jt Gen. Sec., Amalgamated Textile Workers' Union, 1974; Mem., TUC Gen. Council, 1972–75; Member, many cttees in Textile Industry. Industrial Advr ACAS NW Reg., 1975–78. Created Accrington Pakistan Friendship Association, 1961 (Pres.). JP Accrington, 1955. *Recreations:* pleasure is in domestic work in the home and family and in trade union and political field. *Address:* 44 Southwood Drive, Baxenden, Accrington, Lancs. *T:* Accrington 394551.

KING, Hon. Leonard James; Hon. Mr Justice King; Chief Justice of South Australia, since 1978; *b* 1 May 1925; *s* of Michael Owen and Mary Ann King; *m* 1953, Sheila Therese (*née* Keane); two *s* three *d. Educ:* Marist Brothers Sch., Norwood, S Aust; Univ. of Adelaide, S Aust (LLB). Admitted to Bar, 1950; QC 1967. Member, House of Assembly, Parlt of S Australia, 1970; Attorney-General and Minister of Community Welfare, 1970; additionally, Minister of Prices and Consumer Affairs, 1972. Judge of Supreme Court of S Aust, 1975. *Address:* c/o Chief Justice's Chambers, Supreme Court House, Victoria Square, Adelaide, South Australia 5000, Australia. *T:* 217 0451.

KING, Michael; *see* King, D. M. G.

KING, Michael Gardner; His Honour Judge King; a Circuit Judge since 1972; *b* 4 Dec. 1920; *s* of late David Thomson King and late Winifred Mary King, Bournemouth; *m* 1951, Yvonne Mary Lilian, *d* of late Lt-Col M. J. Ambler; two *s* one *d. Educ:* Sherborne Sch.; Wadham Coll., Oxford (MA).

Served in RN, Lieut RNVR, 1940–46. Called to Bar, Gray's Inn, 1949. Dep. Chm., IoW QS, 1966–72; Dep. Chm., Hants QS, 1968–72. *Recreations:* sailing, shooting, golf. *Address:* Oak Cottage, East End, Lymington, Hants. *Clubs:* Hampshire (Winchester); Royal Naval Sailing Association, Royal Lymington Yacht, Bar Yacht; Brokenhurst Manor Golf.

KING, Phillip, CBE 1975; ARA 1977; sculptor; *b* 1 May 1934; *s* of Thomas John King and of Gabrielle (*née* Liautard); *m* 1957, Lilian Odelle; one *s. Educ:* Mill Hill Sch.; Christ's Coll., Cambridge Univ. (languages); St Martin's Sch. of Art (sculpture). Teacher at St Martin's Sch. of Art, 1959–; Asst to Henry Moore, 1959–60. Trustee, Tate Gallery, 1967–69; Mem. Art Panel, Arts Council, 1977–. *One-man Exhibitions include:* British Pavilion, Venice Biennale, 1968; European Mus. Tour, 1974–75 (Kroller-Muller Nat. Mus., Holland; Kunsthalle, Düsseldorf; Kunsthalle, Bern; Musée Galliera, Paris; Ulster Mus., Belfast); UK Touring Exhib., 1975–76 (Sheffield, Cumbria, Aberdeen, Glasgow, Newcastle, Portsmouth); Hayward Gall. (retrospective), 1981. First Prize, Socha Piestanskych Parkov, Piestany, Czechoslovakia, 1969. *Address:* c/o Juda Rowan Gallery, 11 Tottenham Mews, W1P 9PJ. *T:* 01-637 5517.

KING, Ralph Malcolm MacDonald, OBE 1968; Colonial Service, retired; *b* 8 Feb. 1911; *s* of Dr James Malcolm King and Mrs Norah King; *m* 1948, Rita Elizabeth Herring; two *s* one *d. Educ:* Tonbridge Sch. Solicitor (Hons) 1934. Asst to Johnson, Stokes and Master, Solicitors, Hong Kong, 1936–41. Commissioned Middx Regt, 1941; prisoner of war, 1941–45; demobilised, 1946. Colonial Legal Service, 1947; Legal Officer, Somaliland, 1947; Crown Counsel, Somaliland, 1950. Called to Bar, Gray's Inn, 1950. Solicitor-General, Nyasaland, 1953; Attorney-General, Nyasaland, 1957–61. Disbarred at his own request and since restored to Roll of Solicitors, in April 1961. Legal Draftsman to Government of Northern Nigeria, 1963–67, and to Northern States of Nigeria, 1967–73; Dir, Legislative Drafting Courses, Commonwealth Secretariat, Jamaica, 1974–75, Trinidad, 1976, and Barbados, 1977. *Recreations:* watching cricket, walking. *Address:* 36 Mill View Close, Woodbridge, Suffolk.

KING, Sir Richard (Brian Meredith), KCB 1976 (CB 1969); MC 1944; Senior Adviser to S. G. Warburg & Co. Ltd, since 1980; *b* 2 Aug. 1920; *s* of late Bernard and Dorothy King; *m* 1944, Blanche Phyllis Roberts; two *s* one *d. Educ:* King's Coll. Sch., Wimbledon. Air Ministry, 1939; Min. of Aircraft Prod., 1940. Army 1940–46: Major, N Irish Horse; N Af. and Ital. campaigns (MC, Cassino). Min. of Supply, 1946; Asst Principal, Ministry of Works, 1948; Principal, 1949; Asst Regional Dir (Leeds), 1949–52; seconded Treas., 1953–54; Prin. Priv. Sec. to Minister of Works, 1956–57; Asst Sec., 1957; seconded Cabinet Off., 1958 (Sec. of Commonwealth Educn. Conf. (Oxford), 1959; Constitutional Confs: Kenya, 1960; N Rhodesia, Nyasaland and Fed. Review, 1960; WI Fedn, 1961); Dept of Tech. Co-op., on its formation, 1961; Min. of Overseas Develt, on its formation, 1964: Under-Sec., 1964; Dep. Sec., 1968; Permanent Sec., 1973–76; Exec. Sec., IMF/World Bank Develt Cttee, 1976–80. *Publications:* The Planning of the British Aid Programme, 1971; Criteria for Europe's Development Policy to the Third World, 1974. *Recreations:* music, lawn tennis, gardening, doing-it-himself. *Address:* Woodlands Farm House, Woodlands Lane, Stoke D'Abernon, Cobham, Surrey. *T:* Oxshott 3491. *Club:* All England Lawn Tennis.

KING, Maj.-Gen. Robert Charles Moss, CB 1955; DSO 1945; OBE 1944; retired; *b* 6 June 1904; *s* of Robert Henry Curzon Moss King, ICS and Mrs King; *m* 1940, Elizabeth Stuart Mackay (*d* 1966); two *d. Educ:* Clifton Coll.; RMC, Camberley. 2nd Lieut, W Yorks Regt, 1924; Capt. 1935. Served War of 1939–45: India, Malaya, Java, Assam and Burma (despatches). Maj.-Gen. 1955. GOC Home Counties District and 44th (HC) Infantry Division TA, Deputy Constable Dover Castle, 1954–56; Dir of Quartering, War Office, 1957–58. *Recreations:* shooting and fishing. *Address:* c/o Willow Hey Cottage, Ovington, Alresford, Hampshire.

KING, Robert Shirley; Secretary, Working Party on Role and Tasks of Social Workers, National Institute for Social Work, 1980–82, retired; *b* 12 July 1920; *s* of Rev. William Henry King, MC, TD, MA, and late Dorothy King (*née* Sharpe); *m* 1st, 1947, Margaret Siddall (*d* 1956); two *d* ; 2nd, 1958, Mary Rowell; one *s* two *d. Educ:* Alexandra Road Sch., Oldham; Manchester Grammar Sch.; Trinity Coll., Cambridge (Schol., MA). Served War, RAF, 1940–45. Colonial Service, Tanganyika, 1949–62 (Dist Comr, Geita, 1959–62); Home Office: Principal, 1962–69 (seconded to Civil Service Dept, 1968–69); Asst Sec., 1969–70; transf., with Children's Dept, to DHSS, 1971; DHSS, Asst Sec., 1971–76, Under Sec., 1976–80. Governor, Cheshunt Foundn, 1976–. *Recreations:* walking, gardening, African affairs. *Address:* 3 Nightingale Avenue, Cambridge. *T:* Cambridge 248965.

KING, Dame Ruth; *see* Railton, Dame R.

KING, Sir Sydney (Percy), Kt 1975; OBE 1965; JP; District Organiser, National Union of Agricultural and Allied Workers, 1946–80; Chairman, Trent Regional Health Authority, 1973–82; *b* 20 Sept. 1916; *s* of James Edwin King and Florence Emily King; *m* 1944, Millicent Angela Prendergast; two *d. Educ:* Brockley Central School. Member: N Midland Regional Board for Industry (Vice-Chm. 1949); Sheffield Regional Hosp. Bd, 1963–73 (Chm, 1969–73); E Midland Economic Planning Council, 1965–; E Midlands Gas Board, 1970; MAFF E Midland Regional Panel, 1972– (Chm., 1977). JP 1956, Alderman 1967, Kesteven. Hon. LLD: Leicester, 1980; Nottingham, 1981.

Recreations: reading, music, talking. *Address:* 49 Robertson Drive, Sleaford, Lincs. *T:* Sleaford 302056.

KING, Prof. Thea, (Mrs T. Thurston), FRCM; freelance musician; Professor of Clarinet, Royal College of Music, since 1961; *b* 26 Dec. 1925; *m* Jan. 1953, Frederick John Thurston (*d* Dec. 1953). *Educ:* Bedford High Sch.; Royal College of Music (FRCM 1975; ARCM 1944 and 1947). Sadler's Wells Orchestra, 1950-52; Portia Wind Ensemble, 1955-68; Member: English Chamber Orchestra, London Mozart Players, Melos Ensemble of London, Vesuvius Ensemble, Robles Ensemble. Frequent soloist, broadcaster, recitalist; recordings include Mozart, Spohr, Finzi, Bruch, Mendelssohn, Stanford and 20th Century British music. *Publications:* clarinet solos, Chester Woodwind series, 1977; arrangement of J. S. Bach, Duets for 2 Clarinets, 1979. *Recreations:* cows, drawing, painting, travel. *Address:* 16 Milverton Road, NW6 7AS. *T:* 01-459 3453.

KING, Rt. Hon. Thomas Jeremy, (Tom); PC 1979; MP (C) Bridgwater since March 1970; Minister for Local Government and Environmental Services, Department of the Environment, since 1979; *b* 13 June 1933; *s* of late J. H. King, JP; *m* 1960, Jane, *d* of late Brig. Robert Tilney, CBE, DSO, TD; one *s* one *d. Educ:* Rugby; Emmanuel Coll., Cambridge (MA). National service, 1951-53: commnd Somerset Light Inf., 1952; seconded to KAR; served Tanganyika and Kenya; Actg Captain 1953. Cambridge, 1953-56. Joined E.S. & A. Robinson Ltd, Bristol, 1956; various positions up to Divisional Gen. Man., 1964-69; Chm., Sale, Tilney Co Ltd, 1971-79 (Dir 1965-79). PPS to: Minister for Posts and Telecommunications, 1970-72; Minister for Industrial Develt, 1972-74; Front Bench spokesman for: Industry, 1975-76; Energy, 1976-79. Vice-Chm., Cons. Parly Industry Cttee, 1974. *Recreations:* cricket, ski-ing. *Address:* House of Commons, SW1.

KING, Air Vice-Marshal Walter MacIan, CB 1961; CBE 1957; retired, 1967; *b* 10 March 1910; *s* of Alexander King, MB, ChB, DPH, and Hughberta Blannin King (*née* Pearson); *m* 1946, Anne Clare Hicks; two *s. Educ:* St Mary's Coll., Castries, St Lucia, BWI; Blundell's Sch., Tiverton, Devon. Aircraft Engineering (Messers Westland Aircraft Ltd, Handley-Page Ltd, Saunders-Roe Ltd), 1927-33; joined Royal Air Force, 1934; Overseas Service: No 8 Sqdn, Aden, 1935-37; South-east Asia, 1945-47; Middle East (Egypt and Cyprus), 1955-57. Student: RAF Staff Coll., 1944; Joint Services Staff Coll., 1947; IDC, 1954. Directing Staff, RAF Staff Coll., 1957-58; Comdt, No 16 MU, Stafford, 1958-60; Dir of Equipment (B), Air Ministry, 1961-64; Air Cdre Ops (Supply), HQ's Maintenance Command, during 1964; Senior Air Staff Officer, RAF Maintenance Command, 1964-67. Joined Hooker Craigmyle & Co. Ltd, 1967; Gen. Manager, Hooker Craigmyle (Scotland) Ltd, 1969-72; Dir, Craigmyle & Co. (Scotland) Ltd, 1972-76. *Recreations:* swimming (rep. RAF in inter-services competition, 1934); gardening. *Address:* 24 Arthur's Avenue, Harrogate HG2 0DX.

KING, Sir Wayne Alexander, 8th Bt *cr* 1815; *b* 2 Feb. 1962; *s* of Sir Peter Alexander King, 7th Bt, and of Jean Margaret (who *m* 2nd, 1978, Rev. Richard Graham Mackenzie), *d* of Christopher Thomas Cavell, Deal; *S* father, 1973. *Address:* 365 London Road, Upper Deal, Deal, Kent; Church View, Herne Street, Herne, Herne Bay, Kent.

KING-HAMILTON, His Honour (Myer) Alan (Barry), QC 1954; an additional Judge of the Central Criminal Court, later a Circuit Judge, 1964-79; *b* 9 Dec. 1904; *o s* of Alfred King-Hamilton; *m* 1935, Rosalind Irene Ellis; two *d. Educ:* Bishop's Stortford Grammar Sch.; Trinity Hall, Cambridge (BA 1927, MA 1929; Pres. Cambridge Union Soc., 1927). Called to Bar, Middle Temple, 1929; served War of 1939-45, RAF, finishing with rank of Squadron Leader; served on Finchley Borough Council, 1938-39 and 1945-50. Recorder of Hereford, 1955-56; Recorder of Gloucester, 1956-61; Recorder of Wolverhampton, 1961-64; Dep. Chm. Oxford County Quarter Sessions, 1955-64, 1966-71; Leader of Oxford Circuit, 1961-64. Elected Bencher, Middle Temple, 1961. Elected to General Council of Bar, 1958. President: West London Reform Synagogue, 1967-75, 1977-; Westlon Housing Assoc., 1975-; Vice-Pres., World Congress of Faiths, 1967-. Freeman of City of London; Master, Needlemakers Co., 1969. *Publication:* And Nothing but the Truth (autobiog.), 1982. *Recreations:* cricket, gardening, the theatre. *Clubs:* Royal Air Force, MCC.

KING-HELE, Desmond George, FRS 1966; Deputy Chief Scientific Officer, Space Department, Royal Aircraft Establishment, Farnborough, since 1968; *b* 3 Nov. 1927; *s* of late S. G. and of B. King-Hele, Seaford, Sussex; *m* 1954, Marie Thérèse Newman; two *d. Educ:* Epsom Coll.; Trinity Coll., Cambridge. BA (1st cl. hons Mathematics) 1948; MA 1952. At RAE, Farnborough, from 1948, working on space research from 1955. Mem., International Academy of Astronautics, 1961; FIMA; FRAS. Hon. DSc Aston, 1979. Eddington Medal, RAS, 1971; Charles Chree Medal, Inst. of Physics, 1971; Lagrange Prize, Acad. Royale de Belgique, 1972. Lectures: Symons, RMetS, 1967; Duke of Edinburgh's, Royal Inst. of Navigation, 1964; Jeffreys, RAS, 1971; Halley, Oxford, 1974; Bakerian, Royal Soc., 1974; Sydenham, Soc. of Apothecaries, 1981; H. L. Welsh, Univ. of Toronto, 1982. *Publications:* Shelley: His Thought and Work, 1960, 2nd edn 1971; Satellites and Scientific Research, 1960; Erasmus Darwin, 1963; Theory of Satellite Orbits in an Atmosphere, 1964; (ed) Space Research V, 1965; Observing Earth Satellites, 1966; (ed) Essential Writings of Erasmus Darwin, 1968; The End of the Twentieth Century?, 1970; Poems and Trixies, 1972; Doctor of Revolution, 1977; (ed) The Letters of Erasmus Darwin, 1981; The RAE Table

of Earth Satellites, 1981; *radio drama scripts:* A Mind of Universal Sympathy, 1973; The Lunaticks, 1978; numerous papers in Proc. Royal Society, Nature, Keats-Shelley Memor. Bull., New Scientist, Planetary and Space Science, and other scientific and literary jls. *Recreations:* tennis, walking, reading. *Address:* 3 Tor Road, Farnham, Surrey. *T:* Farnham 714755.

KING-MARTIN, Brig. John Douglas, CBE 1966; DSO 1957; MC 1953; Deputy Commander, HQ Eastern District, 1968-70, retired; *b* 9 March 1915; *s* of late Lewis King-Martin, Imperial Forest Service; *m* 1940, Jeannie Jemima Sheffield Hollins, *d* of late S. T. Hollins, CIE; one *s* one *d. Educ:* Allhallows Sch.; RMC Sandhurst. Commnd 1935; 3rd Royal Bn 12 Frontier Force Regt, IA, 1936; Waziristan Ops, 1936-37; Eritrea, Western Desert, 1940-42; Staff Coll., Quetta, 1944; Bde Maj., 1944-46, India, Java; GSO 2, Indian Inf. Div., Malaya, 1946-47; transf. to RA, 1948; Battery Comdr, 1948-50, 1951-54; Korea, 1952-53; CO, 50 Medium Regt, RA, 1956-57; Suez, Cyprus, 1956-57; Coll. Comdr, RMA Sandhurst, 1958-60; Dep. Comdr and CRA, 17 Gurkha Div., 1961-62; Comdr, 17 Gurkha Div., 1962-64; Comdr, Rhine Area, 1964-67. Lieut-Col 1956; Brig. 1961. ADC to The Queen, 1968-70. *Recreations:* golf, painting, photography. *Address:* White House Farm, Polstead, Suffolk. *T:* Boxford 210327. *Clubs:* East India, Devonshire, Sports and Public Schools.

KING MURRAY, Ronald; *see* Murray.

KING-REYNOLDS, Guy Edwin, JP; Head Master, Dauntsey's School, West Lavington, since Sept. 1969; *b* 9 July 1923; *er s* of late Dr H. E. King Reynolds, York; *m* 1st, 1947, Norma Lansdowne Russell (*d* 1949); 2nd, 1950, Jeanne Nancy Perris Rhodes; one *d. Educ:* St Peter's Sch., Yorks; Emmanuel Coll., Cambridge (1944-47). Served RAF, 1942-44. BA 1946, MA 1951. Asst Master, Glenhow Prep. Sch., 1947-48; Head of Geography Dept, Solihull Sch., Warwickshire, 1948-54; family business, 1954-55; Head of Geography, Portsmouth Grammar Sch., 1955-57; Solihull School: Housemaster, 1957-63, Second Master, 1963-69. Part-time Lecturer in International Affairs, Extra-Mural Dept, Birmingham Univ.; Chm., Solihull WEA. LRAM (speech and drama) 1968. Chm., Devizes Bench, 1982-. JP Solihull, 1965-69, Wiltshire, 1970-. *Recreations:* drama (director and actor); travel. *Address:* Head Master's House, Dauntsey's School, West Lavington, Wilts SN10 4HE. *T:* Lavington 3382; Sandpipers, 12 Rectory Road, Llangwm, near Haverfordwest, Dyfed. *Club:* East India, Devonshire, Sports and Public Schools.

KING-TENISON, family name of **Earl of Kingston.**

KINGDOM, Thomas Doyle, CB 1959; Controller, Government Social Survey Department, 1967-70, retired; *b* 30 Oct. 1910; *er s* of late Thomas Kingdom; *m* 1937, Elsie Margaret, *d* of late L. C. Scott, MBE, Northwood; two *d. Educ:* Rugby; King's Coll., Cambridge (MA). Entered Civil Service as Asst Principal, Inland Revenue, 1933; transferred to Unemployment Assistance Bd, 1934; seconded to HM Treasury as Dep. Dir, Organisation and Methods, 1945-49; Under Sec., 1955. Chm., Exec. Council, Royal Inst. of Public Administration, 1965-66. Chm. West London Suppl. Benefit Appeal Tribunal, 1971-. *Address:* 2 Grosvenor Road, Northwood, Mddx HA6 3HJ. *T:* Northwood 22006.

KINGHAM, James Frederick; His Honour Judge Kingham; a Circuit Judge, since 1973; *b* 9 Aug. 1925; *s* of Charles William and Eileen Eda Kingham; *m* 1958, Vivienne Valerie Tyrrell Brown; two *s* two *d. Educ:* Wycliffe Coll.; Queens' Coll., Cambridge (MA); Graz Univ., Austria. Served with RN, 1943-47. Called to Bar, Gray's Inn, 1951; Mem. Gen. Council of Bar, 1954-58; Mem. Bar Council Sub-Cttee on Sentencing and Penology. A Recorder, 1972-73. Dep. County Comr, Herts Scouts, 1971-80, formerly Asst County Comr for Venture Scouts; Venture Scout Leader, Harpenden, 1975-. *Recreations:* mountain activities, squash, ski-ing, youth work, history, gardening, football. *Address:* Copelands, Blackmore Way, Blackmore End, Wheathampstead, Herts. *T:* Kimpton 832308. *Clubs:* Northampton and County (Northampton); Union (Cambridge).

KINGHORN, Squadron Leader Ernest; *b* 1 Nov. 1907; *s* of A. Kinghorn, Leeds; *m* 1942, Eileen Mary Lambert Russell (*d* 1980); one *s* (and one *s* one *d* decd). *Educ:* Leeds, Basel and Lille Universities. Languages Master Ashville Coll., Doncaster Grammar Sch. and Roundhay Sch., Leeds. Served in Intelligence Branch, RAF. British Officer for Control of Manpower, SHAEF, and Staff Officer CCG. MP (Lab) Yarmouth Division of Norfolk, 1950-51, Great Yarmouth, 1945-50. *Address:* 59 Queens Avenue, Hanworth, Middx.

KINGHORN, William Oliver; Chief Agricultural Officer, Department of Agriculture and Fisheries for Scotland, 1971-75; *b* 17 May 1913; *s* of Thomas Kinghorn, Duns, and Elizabeth Oliver; *m* 1943, Edith Johnstone; one *s* two *d. Educ:* Berwickshire High Sch.; Edinburgh Univ. BSc (Agr) Hons, BSc Hons. Senior Inspector, 1946; Technical Develt Officer, 1959; Chief Inspector, 1970. SBStJ. *Publication:* contrib. Annals of Applied Biology, 1936. *Recreation:* golf. *Address:* 23 Cumlodden Avenue, Edinburgh EH12 6DR. *T:* 031-337 1435.

KINGMAN, Prof. John Frank Charles, FRS 1971; Chairman, Science and Engineering Research Council, since 1981; Professor of Mathematics in the University of Oxford, since 1969; Fellow, St Anne's College, Oxford, since 1978; *b* 28 Aug. 1939; *er s* of Frank Edwin Thomas Kingman and Maud Elsie

Harley; *m* 1964, Valerie Cromwell; one *s* one *d. Educ:* Christ's Coll., Finchley; Pembroke Coll., Cambridge. MA, ScD Cantab; Smith's Prize, 1962. Fellow of Pembroke Coll., Cambridge, 1961-65. Asst Lectr in Mathematics, 1962-64, Lectr, 1964-65, Univ. of Cambridge; Reader in Mathematics and Statistics, 1965-66, Prof. 1966-69, Univ. of Sussex. Visiting appointments: Univ. of Western Australia, 1963, 1974; Stanford Univ., USA, 1968; ANU, 1978. Wald Meml Lectr, Inst. of Math. Stats, 1977; Rouse Ball Lectr, Cambridge Univ., 1978. Mem., Brighton Co. Borough Council, 1968-71; Chm., Regency Soc. of Brighton and Hove, 1975-81. Chm., 1973-76, Vice-Pres., 1976-, Inst. of Statisticians; Vice-Pres., Royal Statistical Soc., 1977-79 (Guy Medal in Silver, 1981); Chm., Science Bd, SRC, 1979-81. *Publications:* Introduction to Measure and Probability (with S. J. Taylor), 1966; The Algebra of Queues, 1966; Regenerative Phenomena, 1972; Mathematics of Genetic Diversity, 1980; papers in mathematical and statistical jls. *Address:* Science and Engineering Research Council, Polaris House, North Star Avenue, Swindon SN2 1ET.

KINGS NORTON, Baron *cr* 1965, of Wotton Underwood (Life Peer); **Harold Roxbee Cox,** Kt 1953; PhD, DIC, FIMechE, Hon. FRAeS; Chairman: Landspeed Ltd, since 1975; Submarine Products, since 1978; President: Royal Institution, 1969-76; Campden Food Preservation Research Association, since 1961; British UFO Research Association, since 1980; British Balloon Museum and Library, since 1980; Chancellor, Cranfield Institute of Technology, since 1969; *b* 6 June 1902; *s* of late William John Roxbee Cox, Birmingham, and Amelia Stern; *m* 1927, Marjorie (*d* 1980), *e d* of late E. E. Withers, Northwood; two *s*; *m* 1982, Mrs Joan R. Pascoe. *Educ:* Kings Norton Grammar Sch.; Imperial Coll. of Science and Technology (Schol.). Engineer on construction of Airship R101, 1924-29; Chief Technical Officer, Royal Airship Works, 1931; Investigations in wing flutter and stability of structures, RAE, 1931-35; Lectr in Aircraft Structures, Imperial Coll., 1932-38; Principal Scientific Officer. Aerodynamics Dept, RAE, 1935-36; Head of Air Defence Dept, RAE, 1936-38; Chief Technical Officer, Air Registration Board, 1938-39; Supt of Scientific Research, RAE, 1939-40; Dep. Dir of Scientific Research, Ministry of Aircraft Production, 1940-43; Dir of Special Projects Ministry of Aircraft Production, 1943-44; Chm. and Man. Dir Power Jets (Research and Development) Ltd, 1944-46; Dir National Gas Turbine Establishment, 1946-48; Chief Scientist, Min. of Fuel and Power, 1948-54. Chairman: Metal Box Co., 1961-67 (Dir, 1957-67, Dep. Chm., 1959-60); Berger Jenson & Nicholson Ltd, 1967-75; Applied Photophysics, 1974-81; Withers Estates, 1976-81; Director: Ricardo & Co. (Engrs) 1927 Ltd, 1965-77; Dowty Rotol, 1968-75; British Printing Corp., 1968-77; Hoechst UK, 1970-75. Chm. Gas Turbine Collaboration Cttee, 1941-44, 1946-48; Mem. Aeronautical Research Council, 1944-48, 1958-60; Chairman: Coun. for Scientific and Industrial Research, 1961-65; Council for National Academic Awards, 1964-71; Air Registration Bd, 1966-72; Past Pres. Royal Aeronautical Soc. Fellow of Imperial Coll. of Science and Technology, 1960; FCGI 1976. Membre Correspondant, Faculté Polytechnique de Mons, 1946. R38 Memorial Prize, 1928; Busk Memorial Prize, 1934; Wilbur Wright Lecturer, 1940; Wright Brothers Lecturer (USA), 1945; Hawksley Lecturer, 1951; James Clayton Prize, 1952; Thornton Lectr, 1954; Parsons Memorial Lectr, 1955; Handley Page Memorial Lectr, 1969. Hon. DSc: Birmingham, 1954; Cranfield Inst. of Technology, 1970; Hon. DTech Brunel, 1966; Hon. LLD CNAA, 1969. Bronze Medal, Univ. of Louvain, 1946; Medal of Freedom with Silver Palm, USA, 1947. *Publications:* numerous papers on theory of structures, wing flutter, gas turbines, civil aviation and airships. *Address:* Westcote House, Chipping Campden, Glos. *T:* Evesham 840 440. *Clubs:* Athenæum, Turf.

KINGSALE, 35th Baron *cr* 1223 (by some reckonings 30th Baron); **John de Courcy;** Baron Courcy and Baron of Ringrone; Premier Baron of Ireland; Chairman, Strand Publications Ltd, since 1971; Director, D'Olier, Grantmesnil & Courcy Acquisitions Ltd, since 1970; Chairman, National Association for Service to the Realm; *b* 27 Jan. 1941; *s* of Lieutenant-Commander the Hon. Michael John Rancé de Courcy, RN (killed on active service, 1940), and Joan (*d* 1967), *d* of Robert Reid; *S* grandfather, 1969. *Educ:* Stowe; Universities of Paris and Salzburg. Short service commission, Irish Guards, 1962-65. At various times before and since: law student, property developer, film extra, white hunter, bingo caller, etc. *Recreations:* shooting, food and drink, palaeontology, self deception. *Heir: cousin* Nevinson Russell de Courcy [*b* 21 July 1920; *m* 1954, Nora Lydia, *yr d* of James Arnold Plint; one *s* one *d*]. *Address:* Orchard Villa, Upton Noble, Somerset. *Club:* Cavalry and Guards'.

KINGSBOROUGH, Viscount; Robert Charles Henry King-Tenison; *b* 20 March 1969; *s* and *heir* of 11th Earl of Kingston, *qv.*

KINGSHOTT, (Albert) Leonard; Director, Lloyds Bank International, responsible for the European Division, since 1980; *b* 16 Sept. 1930; *s* of A. L. Kingshott and Mrs K. Kingshott; *m* 1958, Valerie Simpson; two *s* one *d. Educ:* London Sch. of Economics (BSc); ACIS 1958. Flying Officer, RAF, 1952-55; Economist, British Petroleum, 1955-60; Economist, British Nylon Spinners, 1960-62; Financial Manager, Iraq Petroleum Co., 1963-65; Chief Economist, Ford of Britain, 1965; Treas., Ford of Britain, 1966-67; Treas., Ford of Europe, 1968-70; Finance Dir, Whitbread & Co., 1972; Man. Dir, Finance, BSC, 1972-77; Dir, Lloyds Bank International, responsible for Merchant Banking activities, 1977-80. Director: Alexander Fund, SA; Bank of London and South America Ltd; Lloyds Bank International (Belgium) SA; Lloyds Bank (Cannes) SA. Associate Mem. of Faculty, 1978, Governor, 1980-,

Ashridge Management Coll. *Publication:* Investment Appraisal, 1967. *Recreations:* golf, chess. *Address:* The White House, Great Warley, Brentwood, Essex. *T:* Brentwood 210671.

KINGSHOTT, Air Vice-Marshal Kenneth, CBE 1972; DFC 1953; Royal Air Force, retired 1980; *b* 8 July 1924; *s* of Walter James Kingshott and Eliza Ann Kingshott; *m* 1948, Dorrie Marie (*née* Dent) (*d* 1978); two *s.* Joined RAF, 1943; served: Singapore and Korea, 1950; Aden, 1960; Malta, 1965; MoD, London, 1968; OC RAF Cottesmore, 1971; HQ 2 Allied Tactical Air Force, 1973; HQ Strike Command, 1975; Dep. Chief of Staff Operations and Intelligence, HQ Allied Air Forces Central Europe, 1977-79. *Recreations:* golf, tennis, music. *Address:* Tall Trees, Manor Road, Penn, Bucks. *Club:* Royal Air Force.

KINGSHOTT, Leonard; *see* Kingshott, A. L.

KINGSLAND, Sir Richard, Kt 1978; CBE 1967; DFC 1940; idc; psa; Secretary to Department of Veterans' Affairs, Canberra, 1976-81; *b* Moree, NSW, 19 Oct. 1916; *m* 1943, Kathleen Jewel, *d* of late R. B. Adams; one *s* two *d. Educ:* Sydney High Sch., NSW. Served War: No 10 Sqdn, Eng., 1939-41; commanded: No 11 Sqdn, New Guinea, 1941-42; RAAF Stn, Rathmines, NSW, 1942-43; Gp Captain 1943; Dir, Intell., RAAF, 1944-45. Director: Trng, 1946; Org. RAAF HQ, 1946-48; SA Reg. 1950-51, NT Reg. 1951-52, Dept of Civil Aviation; Chief Admin. Asst to CAS, RAAF, 1952-53; IDC 1955. Asst Sec., Dept of Air, Melb., 1954-58; First Asst Sec., Dept of Defence, 1958-63; Secretary: Dept of Interior, 1963-70; Dept of Repatriation, 1970-74; Repatriation and Compensation, 1974-76. Chairman: Repatriation Commn, 1970-81; ACT Arts Develt Bd (first Chm.), 1981-; Commonwealth Films Bd of Review, 1982-; Uranium Adv. Council, 1982-. Hon. Nat. Sec., Nat. Heart Foundn, 1976-. A Dir, Arts Council of Aust., 1970-72; Chm. Council: Canberra Sch. of Music, 1970-74; Canberra Sch. of Art, 1976-; Mem. Bd of Trustees, Aust. War Meml, Canberra, 1966-76. *Recreations:* music, looking at paintings, swimming. *Address:* 36 Vasey Crescent, Campbell, ACT 2601, Australia. *Club:* Commonwealth (Canberra).

KINGSLEY, Ben; actor; *b* 31 Dec. 1943; *s* of Rahimtulla Harji Bhanji and Anna Leina Mary Bhanji; *m* 1978, Gillian Alison Macaulay Sutcliffe; one *s. Educ:* Manchester Grammar Sch. Associate artist, Royal Shakespeare Co.; work with RSC, 1970-80, includes: Peter Brook's Midsummer Night's Dream, Stratford, London, Broadway, NY; Gramsci in Occupations; Ariel in The Tempest; title role, Hamlet; Ford in Merry Wives of Windsor; title role, Baal; Squeers and Mr Wagstaff in Nicholas Nickleby; National Theatre, 1977-78: Mosca in Volpone; Trofimov in The Cherry Orchard; Sparkish in The Country Wife; Vukhov in Judgement; additional theatre work, 1973-81, includes: Johnny in Hello and Goodbye (Fugard), King's Head; Errol Philander in Statements After An Arrest (Fugard), Royal Court; Edmund Kean, Harrogate Th.; title role, Dr Faustus, Manchester Royal Exchange; *television* 1974-82, includes: Rossetti, The Love School; Silas Marner; Thank You Comrades; Ivanov, EGBDF; Edmund Kean; *films:* 1980-82: title role, Gandhi; Robert in Betrayal. *Recreations:* music, gardening. *Address:* c/o ICM Ltd, 388/396 Oxford Street, W1.

KINGSLEY, David John; consultant in communications, since 1975; Director: King Publications Ltd, since 1975; Francis Kyle Gallery Ltd, since 1978; *b* 10 July 1929; *s* of Walter John Kingsley and Marjorie Kingsley; *m* 1st, 1954, Enid Sophia Jones; two *d* ; 2nd, 1968, Gillian Leech; two *s. Educ:* Southend High Sch.; London School of Economics (BScEcon). Pres., Students' Union, LSE, 1952; Vice-Pres., Nat. Union of Students, 1953. FIPA. Served RAF, Personnel Selection, commnd 1948. Prospective Parly Candidate (Lab) E Grinstead, 1952-54; founded Kingsley, Manton and Palmer, advertising agency, 1964; Chm., Guinness Morison Internat. Communications Gp, 1977-79; Publicity Advisor to Labour Party and Govt, 1962-70; Publicity and Election advisor to President of Republic of Zambia, 1974-; Election and Broadcasting advisor to Govt of Mauritius, 1976-; Publicity advisor to SDP, 1981-. Mem. Boards, Council for Nat. Academic Awards, 1970-82; Mem., Central Religious Adv. Cttee for BBC and IBA, 1974-82; Governor, LSE, 1966-; Advisor to UK Cttee, Internat. Year of the Child, 1979; Trustee: Inter-Action Trust, 1971-; Young Musicians Symphony Orch., 1978-82; Vice-Chm., Royal Philharmonic Orch., 1972-77. FRSA; ASIAD. *Publications:* Albion in China, 1979; contribs to learned jls; various articles. *Recreations:* politics, music, travel, art and any books. *Address:* 99 Hemingford Road, N1 1BY. *Clubs:* Reform, Royal Automobile.

KINGSLEY, Sir Patrick (Graham Toler), KCVO 1962 (CVO 1950); Secretary and Keeper of the Records of the Duchy of Cornwall, 1954-72 (Assistant Secretary, 1930-54); *b* 1908; *s* of late Gerald Kingsley; *m* 1947, Priscilla Rosemary, *o d* of late Capt. Archibald A. Lovett Cameron, RN; three *s* one *d. Educ:* Winchester; New Coll., Oxford. OUCC 1928-30 (Capt. 1930), OUAFC 1927 and 1929. Served War of 1939-45 with Queen's Royal Regt. *Address:* West Hill Farm, West Knoyle, Warminster, Wilts.

KINGSLEY, Roger James, FEng, FIChemE; Deputy Chairman, Diamond Shamrock Europe Ltd; General Manager, Duolite International Worldwide; *b* 2 Feb. 1922; *s* of Felix and Helene Loewenstein; changed name to Kingsley, 1942; *m* 1949, Valerie Marguerite Mary (*née* Hanna); one *s* two *d. Educ:* Manchester Grammar Sch.; Faculty of Technol., Manchester Univ. (BScTech); Harvard Business Sch. (Internat. Sen. Managers Program). Served War, Royal Fusiliers, 1940-46; Commando service, 1942-45; Captain; mentioned in despatches, 1946. Chemical Engr, Petrocarbon Ltd, 1949-51; technical appts, ultimately Tech. Dir, Lankro Chemicals Ltd, 1952-62; gen. management appts, Lankro Chemicals Group Ltd, 1962-77; Man. Dir, Lankro Chemicals Group Ltd, 1972-77; Director: ICI-Lankro Plasticisers Ltd, 1972-77; Fallek-Lankro Corp., Tuscaloosa, Ala, 1976-77. Pres., IChemE, 1974-75 (Vice-Pres., 1969-71 and 1973-74). Member: Court of Governors, Univ. of Manchester Inst. of Science and Technol., 1969-79; Adv. Cttee for Chem. Engrg and Fuel Technol., Univ. of Sheffield, 1977-80. *Publications:* contrib. Chem. Engr, and Proc. IMechE. *Recreations:* skiing, riding, music. *Address:* Fallows End, Wicker Lane, Hale Barns, Cheshire WA15 0HQ. *T:* 061-980 6253. *Club:* Anglo-Belgian.

KINGSTON, 11th Earl of, *cr* 1768; **Barclay Robert Edwin King-Tenison,** Bt 1682; Baron Kingston, 1764; Viscount Kingsborough, 1766; Baron Erris, 1800; Viscount Lorton, 1806; formerly Lieutenant, Royal Scots Greys; *b* 23 Sept. 1943; *o s* of 10th Earl of Kingston and Gwyneth, *d* of William Howard Evans (who *m* 1951, Brig. E. M. Tyler, DSO, MC, late RA; she *m* 1963, Robert Woodford); *S* father 1948; *m* 1st, 1965, Patricia Mary (marr. diss. 1974), *o d* of E. C. Killip, Llanfairfechan, N Wales; one *s* one *d* ; 2nd, 1974, Victoria (marr. diss. 1979), *d* of D. C. Edmonds. *Educ:* Winchester. *Heir: s* Viscount Kingsborough, *qv. Address:* c/o Midland Bank Ltd, 47 Ludgate Hill, EC4. *Club:* Cavalry and Guards.

KINGSTON-UPON-THAMES, Bishop Suffragan of, since 1978; **Rt. Rev. Keith Norman Sutton;** *b* 23 June 1934; *s* of Norman and Irene Sutton; *m* 1963, Edith Mary Jean Geldard; three *s* one *d. Educ:* Jesus College, Cambridge (MA 1959). Curate, St Andrew's, Plymouth, 1959-62; Chaplain, St John's Coll., Cambridge, 1962-67; Tutor and Chaplain, Bishop Tucker Coll., Mukono, Uganda, 1968-73; Principal of Ridley Hall, Cambridge, 1973-78. *Recreations:* walking, music. *Address:* 173 Kew Road, Richmond, Surrey TW9 2BB.

KINGSTON-UPON-THAMES, Archdeacon of; *see* Jacob, Ven. B. V.

KININMONTH, Sir William (Hardie), Kt 1972; PPRSA, FRIBA, FRIAS; Architectural Consultant, formerly Senior Partner, Sir Rowand Anderson, Kininmonth and Paul, architects, Edinburgh; *b* 8 Nov. 1904; *s* of John Kininmonth and Isabella McLean Hardie; *m* 1934, Caroline Eleanor Newsam Sutherland (*d* 1978); one *d. Educ:* George Watson's Coll., Edinburgh. Architectural training in Edinburgh Coll. of Art, and in offices of Sir Edwin Lutyens, Sir Rowand Anderson and Paul, and Wm N. Thomson; entered partnership Rowand Anderson and Paul, 1933; served War of 1939-45: RE 1940, North Africa, Sicily and Italy; resumed architectural practice, 1945; buildings for Edinburgh Univ., Renfrew Air Port and Naval Air Station, Edinburgh Dental Hospital, Town Hall, churches, banks, hospitals, schools, housing, etc. Saltire and Civic Trust Awards. Appointed: 1955, Adviser to City of Edinburgh, for development of Princes Street; 1964, to design new Festival Theatre and Festival Centre. Pres., Royal Scottish Academy, 1969-73 (formerly Treas. and then Sec.); Pres. Edinburgh Architectural Association, 1951-53; Member: Royal Fine Arts Commn for Scotland, 1952-65; Council RIBA, 1951-53; Council Royal Incorp. of Architects in Scot., 1951-53; Board, Edinburgh Coll. of Art, 1951-, Board Merchant Co. of Edinburgh, 1950-52. Edinburgh Dean of Guild Court, 1953-69. Hon. LLD Dundee, 1975; Hon. RA; Hon. RSW. *Address:* The Lane House, 46a Dick Place, Edinburgh EH9 2JB. *T:* 031-667 2724. *Clubs:* Scottish Arts, New (Edinburgh).

KINLOCH, Sir Alexander (Davenport), 12th Bt of Gilmerton, *cr* 1685; Major Special Reserve Grenadier Guards, retired 1952; *b* 17 Sept. 1902; *s* of Brig.-Gen. Sir David Kinloch, 11th Bt, and Elinor Lucy (*d* 1943), *d* of Col Bromley Davenport of Capesthorne, Cheshire; *S* father 1944; *m* 1st, 1929, Alexandra (marr. diss., 1945), *d* of Frederick Y. Dalziel, New York; two *d* ; 2nd, 1946, Anna (marr. diss., 1965), *d* of late Thomas Walker, Edinburgh; three *s* three *d* ; 3rd, 1965, Ann, *d* of late Group Capt. F. L. White and of Mrs H. R. White, London; one *s. Educ:* Eton. Mem. of Queen's Body Guard for Scotland (Royal Company of Archers). *Heir: s* David Kinloch, *b* 5 Aug. 1951. *Address:* Gilmerton House, North Berwick, East Lothian. *Clubs:* White's; New (Edinburgh).
See also Hon. H. W. Astor, Baron Brownlow, Baron Grantley.

KINLOCH, Henry; Deputy Managing Director, Liberty Life Assurance Co. Ltd, since 1980; *b* 7 June 1937; *s* of William Shearer Kinloch and Alexina Alice Quartermaine Kinloch; *m* 1966, Gillian Anne Ashley (marr. diss. 1979); one *s* one *d. Educ:* Queen's Park Sch., Glasgow; Univs of Strathclyde, Birmingham and Glasgow. MSc, PhD, ARCST, CEng, FIMechE. Lecturer in Engineering: Univ. of Strathclyde, 1962-65; Univ. of Liverpool, 1966; Vis. Associate Prof. of Engrg, MIT, 1967; Sen. Design Engr, CEGB, 1968-70; PA Management Consultants, 1970-73; Chief Exec., Antony Gibbs (PFP) Ltd, 1973-74; Chm. and Chief Exec., Antony Gibbs Financial Services Ltd, 1975-77; Man. Dir, British Shipbuilders, 1978-80. *Publications:* many publications on theoretical and applied mechanics, financial and business studies. *Recreations:* music, political biography, golf. *Address:* 1 Palace Court Gardens, Muswell Hill, N10 2LB. *T:* 01-883 1019. *Clubs:* Athenæum, Caledonian; Wentworth; Royal Liverpool Golf.

KINLOCH, Sir John, 4th Bt, of Kinloch, *cr* 1873; *b* 1 Nov. 1907; *e s* of Sir George Kinloch, 3rd Bt, OBE, and Ethel May (*d* 1959), *y d* of late Major J. Hawkins; *S* father 1948; *m* 1934, Doris Ellaline, *e d* of C. J. Head, London; one *s* two *d. Educ:* Charterhouse; Magdalene Coll., Cambridge. Served with

British Ministry of War Transport as their repr. at Abadan, Persia, and also in London. Employed by Butterfield & Swire in China and Hong Kong, 1931-63, and by John Swire & Sons Ltd, London, 1964-73. *Recreations:* shooting, golf. *Heir: s* David Oliphant Kinloch, CA [*b* 15 Jan. 1942; *m* 1968, Susan Minette (marr. diss. 1979), *y d* of Maj.-Gen. R. E. Urquhart, *qv* ; one *s* three *d*]. *Address:* Aldie Cottage, Kinross, Kinross-shire KY13 7QH. *T:* Fossoway 305. *Club:* New (Edinburgh).

KINLOSS, Lady (12th in line, of the Lordship *cr* 1602); **Beatrice Mary Grenville Freeman-Grenville** (surname changed by Lord Lyon King of Arms, 1950); *b* 1922; *e d* of late Rev. Hon. Luis Chandos Francis Temple Morgan-Grenville, Master of Kinloss; *S* grandmother, 1944; *m* 1950, Dr Greville Stewart Parker Freeman-Grenville, FSA, FRAS (name changed from Freeman by Lord Lyon King of Arms, 1950), Capt. late Royal Berks Regt, *er s* of late Rev. E. C. Freeman; one *s* two *d. Heir: s* Master of Kinloss, *qv. Address:* North View House, Sheriff Hutton, York YO6 1PT. *T:* Sheriff Hutton 447. *Club:* Royal Commonwealth Society.

KINLOSS, Master of; Hon. Bevil David Stewart Chandos Freeman-Grenville; *b* 20 June 1953; *s* of Dr Greville Stewart Parker Freeman-Grenville, FSA, Capt. late Royal Berks Regt, and of Lady Kinloss, *qv. Educ:* Redrice Sch. *Address:* North View House, Sheriff Hutton, York YO6 1PT.

KINNAIRD, family name of **Lord Kinnaird.**

KINNAIRD, 13th Lord *cr* 1682, of Inchture; **Graham Charles Kinnaird;** Baron Kinnaird of Rossie (UK), 1860; Flying Officer RAFVR; *b* 15 Sept. 1912; *e s* of 12th Lord Kinnaird, KT, KBE, and Frances Victoria (*d* 1960), *y d* of late T. H. Clifton, Lytham Hall, Lancs; *S* father, 1972; *m* 1st, 1938, Nadia (who obtained a decree of divorce, 1940), *o c* of H. A. Fortington, Isle of Jethou, Channel Islands; 2nd, 1940, Diana, *yr d* of R. S. Copeman, Roydon Hall, Diss, Norfolk; four *d* (one *s* decd). *Educ:* Eton. Demobilised RAF, 1945. *Address:* Rossie Priory, Inchture, Perthshire. *T:* Inchture 246; Durham House, Durham Place, SW3. *Clubs:* Brooks's, Carlton, Pratt's; New (Edinburgh).

KINNEAR, Ian Albert Clark, CMG 1974; HM Diplomatic Service, retired; Consul-General, San Francisco, 1977-82; *b* 23 Dec. 1924; *s* of late George Kinnear, CBE and Georgina Lilian (*née* Stephenson), Nairobi; *m* 1966, Rosemary, *d* of Dr K. W. D. Hartley, Cobham; two *d. Educ:* Marlborough Coll.; Lincoln Coll., Oxford (MA). HM Forces, 1938-42 (1st E Africa Reconnaissance Regt). Colonial Service (later HMOCS): Malayan Civil Service, 1951-56: District Officer, Bentong, then Alor Gajah, Asst Sec. Econ. Planning Unit; Kenya, 1956-63: Asst Sec., then Sen. Asst Sec., Min. of Commerce and Industry; 1st Sec., CRO, later Commonwealth Office, 1963-66; 1st Sec. (Commercial), British Embassy, Djakarta, 1966-68; 1st Sec. and Head of Chancery, British High Commn, Dar-es-Salaam, 1969-71; Chief Sec., later Dep. Governor, Bermuda, 1971-74; Senior British Trade Comr, Hong Kong, 1974-77. *Recreations:* painting, golf. *Address:* c/o Foreign and Commonwealth Office, SW1A 2AH. *Club:* Royal Commonwealth Society.

KINNEAR, Nigel Alexander, FRCSI; Surgeon to Federated Dublin Voluntary Hospitals until 1974, retired; *b* 3 April 1907; *s* of James and Margaret Kinnear; *m* 1947, Frances Gardner; one *d. Educ:* Mill Hill Sch.; Trinity Coll., Dublin (MA, MB). Surgeon to Adelaide Hosp., Dublin, 1936; Regius Prof. of Surgery, TCD, 1967-72. President: RCSI, 1961; Royal Academy of Medicine of Ireland, 1968; James IV Surgical Assoc. Hon. FRCSGlas. *Publications:* articles in surgical jls. *Recreations:* salmon fishing, gardening. *Address:* Summerseat Cottage, Clonee, Co. Meath. *T:* Dunboyne 255353. *Clubs:* Old Millhillian; Kildare Street and University (Dublin).

KINNOCK, Neil Gordon; MP (Lab) Bedwellty, since 1970; *b* 28 March 1942; *s* of Gordon Kinnock, Labourer, and Mary Kinnock (*née* Howells), Nurse; *m* 1967, Glenys Elizabeth Parry; one *s* one *d. Educ:* Lewis Sch., Pengam; University Coll., Cardiff. BA in Industrial Relations and History, UC, Cardiff (Chm. Socialist Soc., 1962-65; Pres. Students' Union, 1965-66). Tutor Organiser in Industrial and Trade Union Studies, WEA, 1966-70; Mem., Welsh Hosp. Bd, 1969-71. PPS to Sec. of State for Employment, 1974-75. Member: Nat. Exec. Cttee, Labour Party, 1978-; Parly Cttee of PLP, 1979-; Chief Opposition spokesman on educn, 1979-. Director (unpaid): Tribune Publications, 1974-82; Fair Play for Children, 1979-; 7:84 Theatre Co. (England) Ltd, 1979-; Member: Editorial Bd, Labour Research Dept, 1974-; Socialist Educational Assoc., 1975-; Pres., Assoc. of Liberal Educn, 1980-82. *Publications:* Wales and the Common Market, 1971; contribs to Tribune, Guardian, New Statesman, etc. *Recreations:* male voice choral music, reading, children; Rugby Union and Association football. *Address:* House of Commons, SW1.

KINNOULL, 15th Earl of, *cr* 1633; **Arthur William George Patrick Hay;** Viscount Dupplin and Lord Hay, 1627, 1633, 1697; Baron Hay (Great Britain), 1711; *b* 26 March 1935; *o surv. s* of 14th Earl and Mary Ethel Isobel Meyrick (*d* 1938); *S* father 1938; *m* 1961, Gay Ann, *er d* of Sir Denys Lowson, 1st Bt; one *s* three *d. Educ:* Eton. Chartered Land Agent, 1960; Mem., Agricultural Valuers' Assoc., 1962. Fellow, Chartered Land Agents' Soc., 1964. Pres., National Council on Inland Transport, 1964-76. Mem. of Queen's Body Guard for Scotland (Royal Company of Archers), 1965. Junior Cons. Whip, House of Lords, 1966-68; Cons. Opposition Spokesman on Aviation,

House of Lords, 1968-70. Chm., Property Owners' Building Soc., 1976- (Dir, 1971-). Mem., Air League Council, 1972; Council Mem., Deep Sea Fishermen's Mission, 1977. Vice-Pres., Nat. Assoc. of Local Councils (formerly Nat. Assoc. of Parish Councils), 1979-. FRICS 1970. *Heir: s* Viscount Dupplin, *qv. Address:* 15 Carlyle Square, SW3; Pier House, Seaview, Isle of Wight. *Clubs:* Turf, Pratt's, White's, MCC.

KINROSS, 4th Baron *cr* 1902; **David Andrew Balfour,** OBE 1968; TD; DL; Writer to the Signet, retired 1981; *b* 29 March 1906; second *s* of 2nd Baron Kinross and Caroline Elsie (*d* 1969), *d* of A. H. Johnstone Douglas, DL; *S* brother, 1976; *m* 1st, 1936, Araminta Peel (marr. diss. 1941); one *d*; 2nd, 1948, Helen (*d* 1969), *d* of late A. W. Hog, Edinburgh; one *s*; 3rd, 1972, Ruth Beverley, *d* of late W. H. Mill, SSC, and formerly wife of K. W. B. Middleton. *Educ:* Sherborne; Edinburgh Univ. Qualified Solicitor, 1931; joined WS Society, 1931. Commissioned RA (TA), 1926; served War of 1939-45, Europe and Burma; Lt-Col 78 LAA Regt RA, 1942, 56 Anti-Tank Regt RA, 1944; Hon. Col 278 (Lowland) Field Regt RA (TA), 1964-67. Member Queen's Body Guard for Scotland (Royal Company of Archers). National Chairman, British Legion, Scotland, 1965-68; Chm., Astley Ainslie, Edenhall and Associated Hospitals, Edinburgh, 1957-74. DL Edinburgh, 1966. *Recreations:* shooting, gardening and travel. *Heir: s* Hon. Christopher Patrick Balfour [*b* 1 Oct. 1949; *m* 1974, Susan, *d* of I. R. Pitman, WS; two *s*]. *Address:* 58 India Street, Edinburgh EH3 6HD. *T:* 031-225 2651; The Forge Cottage, Humbie, East Lothian. *T:* Humbie 277. *Clubs:* Army and Navy; New (Edinburgh); Hon. Co. of Edinburgh Golfers.

KINROSS, John Blythe, CBE 1967 (OBE 1958); *b* 31 Jan. 1904; *s* of late John Kinross, RSA, architect, and late Mary Louisa Margaret Hall; *m* 1st, 1930; one *s* two *d*; 2nd, 1943, Mary Elizabeth Connon; one *s* two *d. Educ:* George Watson's Coll., Edinburgh. Manager Issue Dept, Gresham Trust, until 1933 when started business on own account as Cheviot Trust (first Issuing House to undertake small issues). Joined Industrial & Commercial Finance Corp. Ltd at inception, 1945; Gen. Man., 1948; Exec. Dir, 1961; Dep. Chm., 1964-74. Mem. Finance Cttee, Royal College of Surgeons, 1956-79; Hon. Financial Adviser to Royal Scottish Academy, 1950-. Founded Mary Kinross Charitable Trust, 1957 (includes Good Companions Workshops Ltd, Student Homes Ltd and various med. res. projects). Chairman: Imperial Investments (Grosvenor) Ltd; Estate Duties Investment Trust Ltd, 1973-76; Director: Equity Income Trust Ltd; House of Fraser Ltd, 1966-72; London Atlantic Investment Trust Ltd; Scottish Ontario Investment, 1961-79; Investment Trust of Guernsey Ltd and other companies. Hon. RSA, 1957; Hon. FFARCS, 1961. *Publication:* Fifty Years in the City, 1982. *Recreation:* farming. *Address:* 23 Cumberland Terrace, NW1. *T:* 01-935 8979; (office) 01-928 7822. *Club:* Athenæum.

KINSELLA, Thomas; poet; Professor of English, Temple University, Philadelphia, since 1970; *b* 4 May 1928; *m* 1955, Eleanor Walsh; one *s* two *d.* Entered Irish Civil Service, 1946; resigned from Dept of Finance, 1965. Artist-in-residence, 1965-67, Prof. of English, 1967-70, Southern Illinois Univ. Elected to Irish Academy of Letters, 1965. J. S. Guggenheim Meml Fellow, 1968-69, 1971-72. *Publications: poetry:* Poems, 1956; Another September, 1958; Downstream, 1962; Nightwalker and other poems, 1968; Notes from the Land of the Dead, 1972; Butcher's Dozen, 1972; A Selected Life, 1972; Finistère, 1972; New Poems, 1973; Selected Poems 1956 to 1968, 1973; Vertical Man and The Good Fight, 1973; One, 1974; A Technical Supplement, 1976; Song of the Night and Other Poems, 1978; The Messenger, 1978; Fifteen Dead, 1979; One and Other Poems, 1979; Poems 1956-73, 1980; Peppercanister Poems 1956-73, 1980; (trans.) The Táin, 1969; An Duanaire— Poems of the Dispossessed (trans. Gaelic poetry, 1600-1900), 1981; contrib. essay in Davis, Mangan, Ferguson, 1970; (ed) Selected Poems of Austin Clarke, 1976; (ed) Our Musical Heritage: lectures on Irish traditional music by Seán O Riada. *Address:* 47 Percy Place, Dublin, Ireland.

KINSEY, Joseph Ronald, JP; Chairman, West Midland Traffic Users Consultative Committee, since 1981; *b* 28 Aug. 1921; *s* of Walter and Florence Annie Kinsey; *m* 1953, Joan Elizabeth Walters; one *d. Educ:* Birmingham elementary and C of E schools. Shop management trng; served RAF ground staff, 1940-47; GPO telephone engr, 1947-57; started own business, florists, horticultural and fruit shop, 1957. MP (C) Birmingham, Perry Barr, 1970-Feb. 1974; contested (C) Birmingham, Perry Barr, Oct. 1974, 1979. JP Birmingham, 1962. *Address:* 147 Grange Road, Birmingham B24 0ES. *T:* 021-373 4606.

KINSLEY, Rev. Prof. James, MA, PhD, DLitt; FBA 1971; Professor of English Studies and Head of Department of English Studies, University of Nottingham, since 1961; *b* Borthwick, Midlothian, 17 April 1922; *s* of late Louis Morrison Kinsley, Gorebridge; *m* 1949, Helen, 2nd *d* of late C. C. Dawson, Dewsbury; two *s* one *d. Educ:* Royal High Sch., Edinburgh; Edinburgh Univ.; Oriel Coll., Oxford. MA Edinburgh and James Boswell Scholar, 1943; BA Oxford (1st cl. Hons Sch. of Eng. Lang. and Lit.), 1947; PhD Edinburgh, 1951; MA Oxford, 1952; DLitt Edinburgh, 1959. Served with RA, 1943-45 (Captain). Lectr in English, University Coll. of Wales, 1947-54; Prof. of English Language and Literature in Univ. of Wales (at Swansea), 1954-61; Dean, Faculty of Arts, Univ. of Nottingham, 1967-70. Lectures: William Will Meml, 1960, 1975; Gregynog, Aberystwyth, 1963; Warton, British Acad., 1974. Editor, Renaissance and Modern Studies, Nottingham Miscellany, 1961-68; Gen. Editor: Oxford English Novels, 1967-77; Oxford English Memoirs and Travels, 1969-77; (with Kathleen Tillotson) The Clarendon Dickens, 1977-. Vice-President: Tennyson Soc.,

1963-; Scottish Text Soc., 1971-79. Ordained deacon 1962, priest 1963; Public Preacher, Southwell Diocese, 1964; Mem., C of E Liturgical Commn, 1976-80. FRSL 1959; FRHistS 1961. *Publications:* (ed) Lindsay, Ane Satyre of the Thrie Estaits, 1954; Scottish Poetry: A Critical Survey, 1955; (ed) W. Dunbar: Poems, 1958; (ed) John Dryden: Poems, 4 vols, 1958; (ed) Lindsay, Squyer Meldrum, 1959; (ed) Robert Burns: Poems and Songs, 1959; (ed) Dryden, The Works of Virgil, 1961; (ed with Helen Kinsley) Dryden, Absalom and Achitophel, 1961; (ed) John Dryden: Poetical Works, 1962; (ed) John Dryden: Selected Poems, 1963; (with J. T. Boulton) English Satiric Poetry: Dryden to Byron, 1966; (ed) J. Galt, Annals of the Parish, 1967; (ed) Robert Burns: Poems and Songs, 3 vols, 1968; (ed) The Oxford Book of Ballads, 1969; (textual editor) The Novels of Jane Austen, 5 vols, 1970-71; (ed with George Parfitt) Dryden's Criticism, 1970; (with Helen Kinsley) Dryden: The Critical Heritage, 1971; (ed) Alexander Carlyle of Inveresk: Anecdotes and Characters, 1973; Poems of W. Dunbar, 1979. Contribs to Encyclopædia Britannica, Review of English Studies, Medium Aevum, Modern Language Review, etc. *Recreations:* carpentry, gardening, folk-song. *Address:* 17 Elm Avenue, Beeston, Nottingham NG9 1BU. *T:* Nottingham 257438.

KINSMAN, Surgeon Rear-Adm. Francis Michael, CBE 1982 (OBE 1972); Surgeon Rear Admiral (Ships and Establishments), 1980-82; *b* 5 May 1925; *s* of Oscar Edward Kinsman and Margaret Vera Kinsman; *m* 1st, 1949, Catherine Forsyth Barr; one *s*; 2nd, 1955, Margaret Emily Hillier; two *s. Educ:* Rydal Sch., Colwyn Bay; St Bartholomew's Hosp. MRCS, LRCP, MFCM; DA. Joined RN, 1952; served, 1952-66: HMS Comus, HMS Tamar, HMS Centaur; RN Hosp. Malta, RN Air Med. Sch., RNAS Lossiemouth; Pres., Central Air Med. Bd, 1966-69; Jt Services Staff Coll., 1969; Staff, Med. Dir Gen. (Naval), 1970-73; Dir, Naval Med. Staff Trng, 1973-76; Comd MO to C-in-C Naval Home Comd, 1976-79; MO i/c RN Hosp. Gibraltar, 1979-80. QHP 1980-82. OStJ 1977. *Recreations:* music, painting, fishing, woodwork. *Address:* Pound House, Meonstoke, Southampton, Hants.

KINTORE, 12th Earl of, *cr* 1677; **James Ian Keith;** Lord Keith of Inverurie, 1677 (Scot.); Bt 1897; Baron 1925; Viscount Stonehaven 1938; CEng; AIStructE; Major, RM, Royal Marine Engineers; Member Royal Company of Archers; *b* 25 July 1908; *er s* of John Lawrence Baird, 1st Viscount Stonehaven, PC, GCMG, DSO, and Lady Ethel Sydney Keith-Falconer (later Countess of Kintore, 11th in line), *e d* of 9th Earl of Kintore; name changed from Baird to Keith, 1967; *S* to Viscountcy of Stonehaven, 1941, and to Earldom of Kintore, 1974; *m* 1935, Delia Virginia, *d* of William Loyd; two *s* one *d. Educ:* Eton; Royal School of Mines, London. UK Delegate to Council of Europe and Western European Union, 1954-64. Councillor, Grampian Region (Chm., Water Services Cttee), 1974-78. DL Kincardineshire, 1959; Vice-Lieut, 1965-76. *Heir: s* Master of Kintore, Lord Inverurie, *qv. Address:* Glenton House, Rickarton, near Stonehaven, Kincardineshire. *T:* Stonehaven 63071. *Clubs:* Beefsteak; Rand (Johannesburg).

KIPARSKY, Prof. Valentin Julius Alexander, MA, PhD; Finnish writer and Professor, Helsinki, retired 1974; Member of the Finnish Academy, 1977; *b* St Petersburg, 4 July 1904; *s* of Professor René Kiparsky and Hedwig (*née* Sturtzel); *m* 1940, Aina Dagmar, MagPhil, *d* of Rev. Matti Jaatinen and Olga (*née* Jungmann); one *s. Educ:* St Annen-Schule, St Petersburg; St Alexis Sch., Perkjärvi, Finland; Finnish Commercial Sch., Viipuri, Finland; Helsinki Univ.; Prague Univ.; and research work in different countries. Helsinki University: Junior Lectr, 1933, Sen. Lectr, 1938, actg Prof., 1946, Prof., 1947 and again, 1963. Visiting Prof., Indiana Univ., Bloomington, USA, 1952, Minnesota Univ., USA, 1961-62; Prof. of Russian Language and Literature, University of Birmingham, 1952-55, when he returned to Finland; Prof. of Slavonic Philology, Freie Univ., Berlin, 1958-63. Co-Editor: Slavistische Veröffentlichungen (W Berlin), 1958-; Scando-Slavica (Copenhagen), 1983-. Lt Finnish Army, 1939-40, 1941-42; Translator and Interpreter to Finnish Govt, 1942-44; Director: Finnish Govtl Inst. for studies of USSR, 1948-50; Osteuropa-Institut, W Berlin, 1958-63. Pres., Societas Scientiarum Fennica; Mem., Finn. Acad.; Corresp. Member: Akad. der Wissenschaften und der Literatur, Mainz; Internat. Cttee of Slavists. Dr *hc* Poznań, 1973; Stockholm 1975. Comdr of the Finnish Lion, 1954; Order Zasługi, Poland, 1974. *Publications:* Die gemeinslavischen Lehnwörter aus dem Germanischen, 1934; Fremdes im Baltendeutsch, 1936; Die Kurenfrage, 1939; Suomi Venäjän Kirjallisuudessa, 1943 and 1945; Venäjän Runotav, 1946; Norden i den Ryska Skönlitteraturen, 1947; Wortakzent der russischen Schriftsprache, 1962; Russische historische Grammatik I, 1963; English and American Characters in Russian Fiction, 1964; Russische historische Grammatik II, 1967, III, 1974; numerous articles in various languages in learned jls. *Recreation:* cycling. *Address:* Maurinkatu 8-12 C 37, Helsinki, Finland.

KIRALFY, Prof. Albert Kenneth Roland; Professor of Law, King's College, London, 1964-81, now Emeritus Professor; *b* Toronto, 5 Dec. 1915; *s* of Bolossy Kiralfy, Theatrical Impresario, and Helen Dawnay; *m* 1960, Roberta Ann Routledge. *Educ:* Streatham Grammar Sch.; King's Coll., London Univ. LLB 1935, LLM 1936, PhD 1949. Served War of 1939-45. Called to the Bar, Gray's Inn, 1947. King's Coll., London: Asst Lectr, 1937-39 and 1947-48; Lectr, 1948-51; Reader, 1951-64; Dean of College Law Faculty, 1974-77; FKC 1971. Chm., Bd of Studies in Laws, London Univ., 1971-74; Dean of Univ. Law Faculty, 1980-81. Vis. Prof., Osgoode Hall Law Sch., Toronto, 1961-62; Exchange Scholar, Leningrad Law Sch., Spring 1964, Moscow Law Sch., April 1970; Prague Acad. of Sciences, April 1975. Dir, Comparative Law Course,

Luxembourg, Aug. 1968. Chm., Council of Hughes Parry Hall, London Univ., 1970-. Editor, Journal of Legal History, 1980-; Mem. Editorial Bd, Internat. and Comparative Law Quarterly, 1956-; Reviser, English trans., Polish Civil Code, 1981. *Publications:* The Action on the Case, 1951; The English Legal System, 1954 (and later edns; 6th edn 1978); A Source Book of English Law, 1957; Potter's Historical Introduction to English Law, (4th edn) 1958; (with Prof. G. Jones) Guide to Selden Society Publications, 1960; Translation of Russian Civil Codes, 1966; chapter, English Law, in Derrett, Introduction to Legal Systems, 1968; (with Miss R. A. Routledge) Guide to Additional MSS at Gray's Inn Library, 1971; General Editor, Comparative Law of Matrimonial Property, 1972; contributed: Encyclopædia of Soviet Law (Leiden), 1973; Contemporary Soviet Law, 1974; East-West Business Transactions, 1974; Common Law, Encyclopædia Britannica, 1974; Russian Law: Historical Perspectives, 1977; Review of Socialist Laws, 1979; Le Nuove Frontiere del Diritto, 1979; Journal of Legal History, 1980; *Rapporteur,* The Child without Family Ties, Congress of Jean Bodin Soc., Strasbourg, 1972. *Recreations:* travel, reading, languages. *Address:* 25 Woodhayes Road, Wimbledon, SW19 4RF.

KIRBY, Sir Arthur (Frank), GBE 1969 (KBE 1957); CMG 1945; FCIT; *b* Slough, 13 July 1899; *s* of George and Lily Maria Kirby; *m* 1935, Winifred Kate, *d* of Fred Bradley, Waterloo Park, Liverpool; one *d. Educ:* Sir William Borlase's Sch., Marlow; London Sch. of Economics. Entered Service GWR 1917; returned 1919 after serving with London Rifle Brigade and 2nd Rifle Brigade; special training for six years with GWR; entered Colonial Service, Asst Sec., Takoradi Harbour, Gold Coast, 1928; Traffic Manager, Gold Coast Railway, 1936; Asst Supt of the Line, Kenya and Uganda Railways and Harbours, 1938; Gen. Man., Palestine Railways and Ports Authority and Dir Gen. Hejaz Railway, 1942-48; Supt of the Line, E African Railways and Harbours, 1949-50; Asst Comr for Transport, E Africa High Commn, 1951-52; Actg Comr for Transport, 1952-53; Gen. Manager, East African Railways and Harbours 1953-57; Commissioner for East Africa, London, 1958-63; Chairman: British Transport Docks Board, 1963-67; Nat. Ports Council, 1967-71; Pres., Shipping and Forwarding Agents Inst., 1966. Vice-Pres., Royal Commonwealth Society (Dep. Chm., 1965-68); Dep. Chm., Gt Ormond Street Children's Hosp., 1963-69; Governor, National Hosp. for Nervous Diseases, 1966-69; Mem. Council, Royal Society of Arts, 1966-71. Chm., Palestine Assoc.; Vice-Pres., British Inst. in Eastern Africa. OStJ. Liveryman, Worshipful Co. of Barber Surgeons, 1977-. *Address:* 6 Baltimore Court, The Drive, Hove, E Sussex BN3 3PR.

KIRBY, David Donald; Director, London and South East, and General Manager, Southern Region, British Rail, since 1982; *b* 12 May 1933; *s* of Walter Donald Kirby and Margaret Irene (*née* Halstead); *m* 1955, Joan Florence (*née* Dickins); one *s* one *d. Educ:* Royal Grammar Sch., High Wycombe; Jesus Coll., Oxford (MA). FCIT. British Rail and its subsidiaries: Divisional Shipping Manager, Dover, 1964; Operations Manager, Shipping and Continental, 1965; Asst Gen. Man., Shipping and International Services, 1966; Continental Traffic Man., BR, 1968; Gen. Man., Shipping and Internat. Services, 1974; Man. Dir, Sealink UK Ltd, 1979. *Recreations:* messing about in boats, choral singing. *Address:* Waterloo Station, SE1 8SE.

KIRBY, Dennis, MVO 1961; MBE 1955; Directeur Adjoint, European Investment Bank, since 1974; *b* 5 April 1923; *s* of William Ewart Kirby and Hannah Kirby; *m* 1943, Mary Elizabeth Kilby; one *d. Educ:* Hull Grammar Sch.; RNC Greenwich; Queen's Coll., Cambridge. Lt (A) RNVR (fighter pilot), 1940-46. Colonial Service, Sierra Leone, 1946-62 (District Comr, 1950; Perm. Sec., 1961-62); 1st Sec., UK Diplomatic Service, 1962; General Manager: East Kilbride Development Corp., 1963-68; Irvine Development Corp., 1967-72; Industrial Dir, Scotland, DTI, 1972-74. MBIM. *Publication:* Careers in New Town Building, 1970. *Recreations:* shooting, fishing, ski-ing, golf, squash. *Address:* European Investment Bank, 100 Boulevard Konrad Adenauer, Luxembourg; Monkton Hall, Southwood, Troon, Ayrshire. *Clubs:* United Oxford & Cambridge University; RNVR (Scotland) (Glasgow).

KIRBY, Prof. Gordon William, ScD, PhD; FRSC; FRSE; Regius Professor of Chemistry, University of Glasgow, since 1972; *b* 20 June 1934; *s* of William Admiral Kirby and Frances Teresa Kirby (*née* Townson); *m* 1964, Audrey Jean Rusbridge, *d* of Col C. E. Rusbridge; two *s. Educ:* Liverpool Inst. High Sch.; Gonville and Caius Coll., Cambridge (Schuldham Plate 1956; MA, PhD, ScD); FRIC 1972; FRSE 1975. 1851 Exhibn Senior Student, 1958-60, Asst Lectr, 1960-61, Lectr, 1961-67, Imperial Coll. of Science and Technology; Prof. of Organic Chemistry, Univ. of Technology, Loughborough, 1967-72; Mem., Chem. Cttee, SRC, 1971-75. Corday-Morgan Medal, Chem. Soc., 1969; Tilden Lectr, Chem. Soc., 1974-75. *Publications:* Co-editor: Elucidation of Organic Structures by Physical and Chemical Methods, vol. IV, parts I, II, and III, 1972; Fortschritte der Chemie organischer Naturstoffe, 1971-; contributor to Jl Chem. Soc., etc. *Address:* Chemistry Department, The University, Glasgow G12 8QQ.

KIRBY, Gwendolen Maud, MVO; Matron, The Hospital for Sick Children, Great Ormond Street, 1951-69; *b* 17 Dec. 1911; 3rd *d* of late Frank M. Kirby, Gravesend, Kent. *Educ:* St Mary's Sch., Calne, Wilts. State Registered Nurse: trained at Nightingale Training Sch., St Thomas' Hosp., SE1. 1933-36; The Mothercraft Training Soc., Cromwell House, Highgate, 1936; State Certified Midwife: trained at General Lying-in Hosp., York Road, Lambeth, 1938-39; Registered Sick Children's Nurse: trained at the Hospital for Sick Children, Great Ormond Street, WC1, 1942-44. Awarded Nightingale Fund Travelling

Scholarship, 1948-49, and spent 1 year in Canada and United States. Mem. of Gen. Nursing Council, 1955-65. *Address:* Brackenfield, Winsford, Minehead, Som.

KIRBY, Jack Howard, CBE 1972; Chairman, International Tanker Owners Pollution Federation, 1968-73; Chairman, Shell Tankers (UK) Ltd, 1963-72; Managing Director, Shell International Marine Ltd, 1959-72; Director, Shell International Petroleum Co. Ltd, 1969-72; *b* 1 Feb. 1913; *s* of late Group Captain Frank Howard Kirby, VC, CBE and late Kate Kirby; *m* 1940, Emily Colton; one *s. Educ:* Sir Roger Manwood's Sch., Sandwich. Joined Shell, 1930, retired 1972; in USA with Shell, 1937-52, incl. secondment to British Shipping Mission and British Petroleum Mission, Washington, DC, 1940-46. Chm., Lights Adv. Cttee, 1958-78. Pres., Chamber of Shipping of the UK, 1971-72. Chevalier 1st Class, Order of St Olav, 1968. *Recreations:* golf, fishing, gardening, bridge. *Address:* September Song, West Drive, Sunningdale, Ascot, Berks SL5 0LF. *T:* Wentworth 4154. *Clubs:* Berkshire Golf, Royal and Ancient Golf.

KIRBY, Louis; Editor, The Standard, since 1980; *b* 30 Nov. 1928; 2nd *s* of late William Kirby and Anne Kirby; *m* 1st, 1952, Marcia Teresa Lloyd (marr. diss. 1976); two *s* three *d*; 2nd, 1976, Heather Veronica (*née* Nicholson); one *s* one *d. Educ:* Our Lady Immaculate, Liverpool; Coalbrookdale High Sch. Daily Mail: Gen. Reporter, subseq. Courts Corresp., and Polit. Corresp., 1953-62; Daily Sketch: Chief Reporter, subseq. Leader Writer and Polit. Editor, Asst Editor, Exec. Editor, and, Actg Editor, 1962-71; Daily Mail (when relaunched): Dep. Editor, 1971-74; Editor, Evening News, 1974-80; Vice-Chm., Evening News Ltd, 1975-80; Dir, Evening Standard Co., 1980-. *Recreations:* tennis, theatre, reading. *Address:* The Standard, Fleet Street, EC4. *Club:* Savile.

KIRBY, Maj.-Gen. Norman George, OBE 1971; FRCS; Consultant Casualty Surgeon, Guys Hospital; *b* 19 Dec. 1926; *s* of George William Kirby and Laura Kirby; *m* 1949, Cynthia Bradley; one *s* one *d. Educ:* King Henry VIII Sch., Coventry; Univ. of Birmingham (MB, ChB). FRCS 1964, FRCSE 1980; FICS 1980. Surgical Registrar: Plastic Surg. Unit, Stoke Mandeville Hosp., 1950-51; Birmingham Accident Hosp., 1953-55; Postgraduate Med. Sch., Hammersmith, 1964. Regt MO 10 Parachute Regt, 1950-51; OC 5 Parachute Surgical Team, 1956-59 (Suez Landing, 5 Nov. 1956); Officer i/c Surg. Div., BMH Rinteln, 1959-60; OC and Surg. Specialist, BMH Tripoli, 1960-62; OC and Consultant Surgeon, BMH Dhekelia, 1967-70; Chief Cons. Surgeon, Cambridge Mil. Hosp., 1970-72; Cons. Surg. HQ BAOR, 1973-78; Dir of Army Surgery, Cons. Surg. to the Army and Hon. Surgeon to the Queen, 1978-82; Hon. Cons. Surgeon, Westminster Hosp., 1979-82. Chm., Army Medicine Dept Working Party Surgical Support for BAOR, 1978-80; Mem., Med. Cttee, Defence Scientific Adv. Council, 1979-82. Member: Council Internat. Coll. of Surgeons; Airborne Med. Soc.; Casualty Surgeons Assoc., 1981-; Vice-Pres., British Assoc. of Trauma in Sport, 1982. Yeoman, Soc. of Apothecaries of London, 1979-. McCombe Lectr, RCSE, 1979. Mem., Editl Bd, Brit. Jl Surg. and Injury, 1979-82. Mem., Surgical Travellers Club, 1979-. FMS London 1981. OStJ 1977. *Publications:* (ed) Field Surgery Pocket Book, 1981; contrib. Brit. Jl Surg. and Proc. RSocMed. *Recreations:* travel, motoring, reading, archaeology. *Address:* 12 Woodsyre, Sydenham Hill, Dulwich, SE26 6SS. *T:* 01-670 5327.

KIRBY, Hon. Sir Richard (Clarence), Kt 1961; Chairman, Advertising Standards Council, since 1973; *b* 22 Sept. 1904; *s* of Samuel Enoch Kirby and Agnes Mary Kirby, N Queensland; *m* 1937, Hilda Marie Ryan; two *d. Educ:* The King's Sch., Parramatta; University of Sydney (LLB). Solicitor, NSW, 1928; called to Bar, 1933; served AIF, 1942-44; Mem. Adult Educl Council to NSW Govt, 1944-46; Judge, Dist Court, NSW, 1944-47; Mem. Austr. War Crimes Commn, 1945, visiting New Guinea, Morotai, Singapore, taking evidence on war crimes; Australia Rep. on War Crimes, Lord Mountbatten's HQ, Ceylon, 1945; Royal Commissioner on various occasions for Federal, NSW and Tasmanian Govts, 1945-47; Acting Judge Supreme Court of NSW, 1947; Chief Judge, Commonwealth Court of Conciliation and Arbitration, 1956-73; Austr. Rep., UN Security Council's Cttee on Good Offices on Indonesian Question, 1947-48, participating in Security Council Debates, Lake Success, USA; Chm. Stevedoring Industry Commn, 1947-49; (first) Pres., Commonwealth Conciliation and Arbitration Commn, 1956-73. Chm., Nat. Stevedoring Conf., 1976-77. Pres., H. V. Evatt Meml Foundn, 1979-. Mem. Council, Wollongong Univ., 1979-. *Recreations:* horse racing and breeding. *Address:* The White House, Berrara, NSW 2540, Australia. *T:* Nowra 412171. *Clubs:* Athenæum, Victoria Racing, Victoria Amateur Turf, Moonee Valley Racing and Mornington Racing, Victoria Golf (Melbourne).

KIRCHEIS, John Reinhardt; Regional Executive, Mobil South, 1976-77; *b* 14 April 1916; *s* of J. R. Kircheis III and Thelba Deibeet; *m* 1940, Jean Ohme; two *d. Educ:* Buena Vista College. Teacher and Prin., Bode Public Schools, 1937; Account Analyst, General Motors Corp., 1940; Lt-Comdr, USNR, 1942; various assignments, Mobil Oil Corp., 1946; Vice-Pres. and Area Manager, Mobil Europe Inc., 1966; Man. Dir, Mobil Oil Co. Ltd, 1968; Chm., Mobil Oil Co. Ltd and Mobil Holdings Group, 1969-75. *Recreations:* golf, fishing, music. *Clubs:* Royal Automobile, New Century.

KIRCHNER, Peter James, MBE 1970; HM Diplomatic Service, retired; Consul General, Berlin, 1978-79; *b* 17 Sept. 1920; *s* of late William John Kirchner and Winifred Emily Homer (*née* Adams); *m* 1952, Barbro Sarah

Margaretha (née Klockhoff); one s two d. Educ: St Brendan's Coll., Clifton, Bristol. Served War, RA, 1939-41. Timber production, UK and Germany, 1941-48; FO, Germany, 1948; Home Office Immigration Dept, 1952-64; Head of UK Refugee Missions in Europe, 1960-63; FCO (formerly FO): Barbados, 1965; Nairobi, 1968; Ankara, 1970; Vienna, 1973; Jerusalem, 1976. Freeman, City of London, 1963. Recreations: chatty golf, 18th-19th century Europe, discovering European backwaters, trying to write. Address: St John's House, Susan Wood, Chislehurst, Kent. T: 01-467 5058; Neulinggasse 48, Vienna 3, Austria. Clubs: Rotary in several countries; Chislehurst Golf.

KIRK, Prof. Geoffrey Stephen, DSC 1945; LittD; FBA 1959; Regius Professor of Greek, University of Cambridge, since 1974; Fellow of Trinity College, Cambridge, since 1974; b 3 Dec. 1921; s of Frederic Tilzey Kirk, MC, and Enid Hilda (née Pentecost); m 1st, 1950, Barbara Helen Traill (marr. diss. 1975); one d; 2nd, 1975, Kirsten Jensen (Ricks). Educ: Rossall Sch.; Clare Coll., Cambridge. LittD Cambridge, 1965. Served War in Royal Navy, 1941-45; commissioned 1942; Temp. Lt, RNVR, 1945. Took Degree at Cambridge, 1946; Research Fellow, Trinity Hall, 1946-49; Student, Brit. Sch. at Athens, 1947; Commonwealth Fund Fellow, Harvard Univ., 1949-50; Fellow, Trinity Hall, 1950-70; Cambridge University: Asst Lecturer in Classics, 1951; Lecturer in Classics, 1952-61; Reader in Greek, 1961-65; Prof. of Classics, Yale Univ., 1965-70; Prof. of Classics, Bristol Univ., 1971-73. Visiting Lecturer, Harvard Univ., 1958; Sather Prof. of Classical Literature, University of California, Berkeley, 1968-69; Mellon Prof., Tulane Univ., 1979. Pres., Soc. for Promotion of Hellenic Studies, 1977-80. MA (Yale) 1965. Publications: Heraclitus, the Cosmic Fragments, 1954; (with J. E. Raven) The Presocratic Philosophers, 1958; The Songs of Homer, 1962 (abbrev., as Homer and the Epic, 1965); Euripides, Bacchae, 1970; Myth, 1970; The Nature of Greek Myths, 1974; Homer and the Oral Tradition, 1977; articles in classical, archæological and philosophical journals. Recreation: sailing. Address: Trinity College, Cambridge; Burkitt House, Chapel Street, Woodbridge, Suffolk.

KIRK, Grayson Louis; President Emeritus, Columbia University; b 12 Oct. 1903; s of Traine Caldwell Kirk and Nora Eichelberger; m 1925, Marion Louise Sands; one s. Educ: Miami Univ. (AB); Clark Univ. (AM); Ecole Libre des Sciences Politiques, Paris, 1928-29. PhD University of Wisconsin, 1930. Prof. of History, Lamar Coll., Beaumont, Tex, 1925-27; Social Science Research Coun. Fellowship (chiefly spent at London Sch. of Economics), 1936-37; Instructor in Political Science, 1929-30, Asst Prof., 1930-36, Associate Prof., 1936-38, Prof., 1938-40, University of Wisconsin; Associate Prof. of Government, Columbia Univ., 1940-43; Head, Security Section, Div. of Political Studies, US Dept of State, 1942-43; Mem. US Delegn Staff, Dumbarton Oaks, 1944; Exec. Officer, Third Commn, San Francisco Conf., 1945. Research Associate, Yale Inst. of Internat. Studies, 1943-44; Prof. of Government, Columbia Univ., 1943-47; Prof. of Internat. Relations, Acting Dir of Sch. of Internat. Affairs, and Dir of European Inst., 1947-49. Appointed Provost in Nov. 1949, and also Vice-Pres in July 1950; became acting head of Columbia in President Eisenhower's absence on leave, March 1951; Pres. and Trustee of Columbia Univ., 1953-68; Bryce Prof. of History of Internat. Relations, Columbia, 1959-72, Emeritus Prof., 1972. Trustee Emeritus, The Asia Foundation; Trustee: French Inst.; Lycée Français of NY; Academy of Political Science (Chm. and Dir); American Philosophical Soc.; Pilgrims of the US (Vice-Pres.); Council on Foreign Relations; Amer. Acad. of Arts and Sciences; Amer. Soc. of French Legion of Honour (Chm.). Director: Monthly Income Shares Inc.; Money Shares Inc.; Bullock Fund Ltd; Bullock Tax-Free Shares Inc.; Dividend Shares Inc.; High Income Shares; Nation-Wide Securities Co. Inc.; France-America Soc.; Mem. Adv. Bd, International Business Machines Corp. Hon. LLD: Miami, 1950; Waynesburg Coll., Brown Univ., Union Coll, 1951; Puerto Rico, Clark, Princeton, New York, Wisconsin, Columbia, Jewish Theol. Seminary of America, 1953; Syracuse, Williams Coll., Pennsylvania, Harvard, Washington, St Louis, Central Univ., Caracas, Univ. of the Andes, Merida, Venezuela, Univ. of Zulia, Maracaibo, Venezuela, Univ. of Delhi, India, Thamasset Univ., Bangkok, 1954; Johns Hopkins Univ., Baltimore, Amherst, 1956; Dartmouth Coll., Northwestern Univ., 1958; Tennessee, 1960; St Lawrence, 1963; Denver, Notre Dame, Bates Coll., 1964; Waseda (Japan), Michigan, 1965; Sussex, 1966; Hon. LHD N Dakota, 1958; Hon. PhD Bologna, 1951; Dr of Civil Law King's Coll., Halifax, Nova Scotia, 1958. Associate KStJ 1959. Comdr, Order of Orange-Nassau, 1952; Hon. KBE, 1955; Grand Officer, Order of Merit, of the Republic, Italy, 1956; Grand Officier Légion d'Honneur, France, 1973. Medal of the Order of Taj, Iran, 1961; Grand Cross, Order of George I (Greece), 1965; Order of the Sacred Treasure, 1st Class (Japan), 1965; Comdr, Ordre des Palmes Académiques (France), 1966. Publications: Philippine Independence, 1936; Contemporary International Politics (with W. R. Sharp), 1940; (with R. P. Stebbins) War and National Policy, 1941; The Study of International Relations in American Colleges and Universities, 1947. Address: Columbia University, 225 Broadway, New York, NY 10007, USA. T: 227-3300. Clubs: Century, University (New York); Bohemian (San Francisco).

KIRK, Rt. Hon. Herbert Victor, PC (N Ireland) 1962; Member (U) for South Belfast, Northern Ireland Assembly, 1973-75; b 5 June 1912; s of Alexander and Mary A. Kirk; m 1944, Gladys A. Dunn; three s. Educ: Queen's Univ., Belfast (BComSc). MP Windsor Div. of Belfast, NI Parlt, 1956-72; Minister of Labour and Nat. Insce, Govt of N Ireland, 1962-64; Minister of Education, 1964-65; Minister of Finance, 1965-72, Jan.-May 1974, resigned. FCA 1940. JP Co. Borough Belfast. Recreation: golf. Address: 38 Massey

Avenue, Belfast BT4 2JT, Northern Ireland. Clubs: Royal Portrush Golf, Belvoir Park Golf (Pres.).

KIRK, James Balfour, CMG 1941; MB, ChB; FRCP; DPH; DTM and H; retired; b 7 April 1893; s of John A. G. Kirk, Falkirk, and Jessie Y. Rintoul, also of Falkirk; m 1917, Jane C., d of Hume Purdie, LDS, Edinburgh; three d. Educ: Falkirk High Sch.; George Watson's Coll., Edinburgh; Edinburgh Univ. (Vans Dunlop Scholar). Private, 9th Bn Royal Scots, Aug.-Dec. 1914; 2nd Lt, RFA 1914-16; Lt RAMC, 1917-20 (1914-15 Star, Victory and General Service Medals); Medical Officer of Health, Port Louis, Mauritius, 1922-26; Acting Dir, Medical and Health Dept, Mauritius, 1926-27; Dir, Medical and Health Dept, Mauritius, 1927-41; Dir of Medical Services, Gold Coast, 1941-44; Dir, Health Div. Greece Mission, UNRRA, 1945; Chief Medical Officer, Central Headquarters, Displaced Persons Operation UNRRA, Germany, Aug. 1945-Feb. 1946; Temp. MO, Min. of Health, 1946-62. Publications: Public Health Practice in the Tropics, 1928; Hints on Equipment and Health for Intending Residents in the Tropics, 1926; Practical Tropical Sanitation, 1936; numerous articles on public health and medical subjects. Recreations: gardening, photography. Address: 16 Brook Lane, Haywards Heath, West Sussex RH16 1SG. T: Lindfield 2185.

KIRK, John Henry, CBE 1957; Emeritus Professor of Marketing (with special reference to horticulture), University of London; b 11 April 1907; s of William Kirk, solicitor; m 1946, Wilfrida Margaret Booth; two s. Educ: Durban High Sch., S Africa; Universities of S Africa, Cambridge, North Carolina and Chicago. Ministry of Agriculture (from 1934, as economist and administrator); Under-Sec., 1959-65; Prof. of Marketing, Wye Coll., 1965-72. Publications: Economic Aspects of Native Segregation, 1929; Agriculture and the Trade Cycle, 1933. Contributions to Journals of Sociology, Economics and Agricultural Economics. Recreation: gardening. Address: Burrington, Cherry Gardens, Wye, Ashford, Kent. T: Wye 812640.

KIRK, Dame (Lucy) Ruth, DBE 1975; Patron, Society for the Protection of the Unborn Child; m 1941, Norman Eric Kirk (later, Rt Hon. Norman Kirk, PC, Prime Minister of New Zealand; d 1974); three s two d. Awarded title, Dame of the Order of the British Empire, for public services. Address: 7 Rimu Vale Street, Rotorua, New Zealand.

KIRK, Dame Ruth; see Kirk, Dame L. R.

KIRKALDY, Prof. John Francis, DSc (London); FGS; Emeritus Professor of Geology, University of London, since 1974; b 14 May 1908; o s of late James and Rose Edith Kirkaldy, Sutton, Surrey; m 1935, Dora Muriel, e d of late Grimshaw Heyes Berry, Enfield, Middlesex; four d. Educ: Felsted Sch.; King's Coll., London. 1st Cl. Special Hons BSc (Geol.) 1929; MSc 1932; DSc 1946. Demonstrator in Geology, King's Coll., 1929-33; Asst Lectr in Geology, University Coll., London, 1933-36; Lectr in Geology, King's Coll., London, 1936-47. War Service with Meteorological Branch, RAF, Sqdn Ldr, 1939-45. Reader in Geology and Head of Dept, Queen Mary Coll., 1947-62; Prof. of Geology and Head of Dept, QMC, 1962-74. FKC 1970; Fellow, Queen Mary College, 1976. Daniel Pidgeon Fund, Geol. Soc., 1935; Foulerton Award, Geologists' Assoc., 1947. Publications: Outline of Historical Geology (with A. K. Wells), 1948 (and subseq. edns); General Principles of Geology, 1954 (and subseq. edns); Rocks and Minerals in Colour, 1963. Papers in Quart. Jl Geol. Soc.; Proc. Geol. Assoc., Geol. Mag., etc. Recreation: gardening. Address: Stone House, Byfield Road, Chipping Warden, Banbury, Oxon. T: Chipping Warden 689. Club: Geological Society's.

KIRKE, Rear-Adm. David Walter, CB 1967; CBE 1962 (OBE 1945); Director: Brim Exports Ltd, since 1970; Sudan British Development Co. Ltd; GRP Technical Services Ltd; Mercantile Airship Transportation Ltd; Thermo-Skyship Ltd; Airship Industries Ltd; Airship Development Ltd; Consultant, Coverdale Training Ltd; b 13 March 1915; s of late Percy St George Kirke and late Alice Gertrude, d of Sir James Gibson Craig, 3rd Bt; m 1st, 1936, Tessa O'Connor (marr. diss., 1950); one s; 2nd, 1956, Marion Margaret Gibb; one s one d. Educ: RN Coll., Dartmouth. China Station, 1933-35; Pilot Training, 1937; served War of 1939-45, Russian Convoys, Fighter Sqdns; loaned RAN, 1949-50; Chief of Naval Aviation, Indian Navy, New Delhi, 1959-62; Rear-Adm. 1965; Flag Officer, Naval Flying Training, 1965-68; retired, 1968. MBIM 1967. Recreation: golf. Address: Lismore House, Pluckley, Kent. T: Pluckley 439. Clubs: Army and Navy, Royal Commonwealth Society.

KIRKHAM, Rt. Rev. John Dudley Galtrey; see Sherborne, Bishop Suffragan of.

KIRKHILL, Baron cr 1975 (Life Peer), of Kirkhill, Aberdeen; **John Farquharson Smith;** Chairman, North of Scotland Hydro-Electric Board, since 1979; b 7 May 1930; s of Alexander F. Smith and Ann T. Farquharson; m 1965, Frances Mary Walker Reid; one step-d. Educ: Robert Gordon's Colleges, Aberdeen. Lord Provost of the City and Royal Burgh of Aberdeen, 1971-75. Minister of State, Scottish Office, 1975-78. Hon. LLD Aberdeen, 1974. Recreation: golf. Address: 3 Rubislaw Den North, Aberdeen. T: Aberdeen 34167.

KIRKLAND, Joseph Lane; President, American Federation of Labor & Congress of Industrial Organizations, since 1979; b Camden, SC, 12 March 1922; s of Randolph Withers Kirkland and Louise Richardson; m Irena

Neuman; five d. *Educ:* US Merchant Marine Academy, Kings Point, NY (grad. 1942); Georgetown Univ. Sch. of Foreign Service (BS 1948). Deck officer, various merchant ships, 1942-45; Staff Scientist, US Navy Hydrographic Office, 1945-48; Staff Representative, AFL-CIO, 1948-58; Research and Information Dir, Internat. Union of Operating Engrs, 1958-60; Exec. Asst to President, AFL-CIO, 1960-69; Sec.-Treasurer, AFL-CIO, 1969-79. Member: US Delegn, ILO Confs, Geneva, 1958, 1969, 1970, 1975, 1976, 1980, 1981; Blue Ribbon Defense Panel, 1969-70; Commn on CIA Activities Within the US, 1975; Commn on Foundns and Private Philanthropy, 1969-70; Gen. Adv. Cttee on Arms Control and Disarmament, 1974-78; Nat. Commn on Productivity, 1971-74; Presidential Commn on Financial Structure and Regulation, 1970-72; President's Maritime Adv. Cttee, 1964-66; President's Missile Sites Labor Commn (Alternate), 1961-67; Commn on Exec., Legislative and Judicial Salaries; Cttee on Selection of Fed. Judicial Officers. Director: Amer. Council on Germany; Amer. Arbitration Assoc.; Afr.-Amer. Labor Center; Asian-Amer. Free Labor Inst.; Nat. Urban League; Rockefeller Foundn; Amer. Inst. for Free Labor Develt; Council on For. Relns, Inc.; Nat. Planning Assoc. Mem., Internat. Org. of Masters, Mates and Pilots; FAAAS. *Recreation:* archaeology. *Address:* (office) 815 16th Street NW, Washington, DC 20006, USA. *T:* (202) 637-5000.

KIRKLEY, Sir (Howard) Leslie, Kt 1977; CBE 1966; Chief Executive, Voluntary and Christian Service Trust, since 1979; Member, Advisory Panel of Experts, United Nations Disaster Relief Organisation, since 1976; *b* Manchester, 1911; *m* 1st, Elsie May, (*née* Rothwell) (*d* 1956); 2nd, Constance Nina Mary, (*née* Bannister-Jones); three *s* two *d. Educ:* Manchester Central High Sch. Associate of the Chartered Inst. of Secretaries (ACIS). Worked in local government in Manchester until War of 1939-45 (during which he was engaged in relief work in Europe). Founder and Hon. Sec. of the Leeds and District European Relief Cttee; Gen. Sec., Oxford Cttee for Famine Relief, 1951-61; Dir, Oxfam, 1961-74. Mem., Bd of Crown Agents, 1974-80. Pres., Gen. Conf., Internat. Council of Voluntary Agencies, 1968-71, Chm., Governing Board, 1972-76; Vice-Chm., 1974-77, Chm., 1977-81, Disasters Emergency Cttee. Chairman: Standing Conf. on Refugees, 1974-81 (Vice-Chm., 1969-74); UK Standing Conf. on 2nd UN Develt Decade, 1975-76; Chairperson, British Volunteer Programme, 1981-; Vice-Chairman: Voluntary Cttee for Overseas Aid and Develt, 1973-76; British Refugee Council, 1981-. Hon. MA: Oxford, 1969; Leeds, 1970; Bradford, 1974. Fellow, Manchester Polytechnic, 1971. Knight Comdr of the Order of St Sylvester (conferred by HH the Pope), 1963; holds other foreign decorations. *Address:* 25 Capel Close, Oxford. *T:* Oxford 53167; (office) 01-236 2701. *Club:* Royal Commonwealth Society.

KIRKMAN, Gen. Sir Sidney Chevalier, GCB 1951 (KCB 1949; CB 1944); KBE 1945 (CBE 1943; OBE 1941); MC; retired; *b* 29 July 1895; *s* of late J. P. Kirkman, Bedford; *m* 1932, Amy Caroline Erskine Clarke; two *s. Educ:* Bedford Sch.; RMA, Woolwich. Served European War, 1914-18 (wounded twice, MC, despatches). Staff Coll. Camberley, 1931-32. Served War of 1939-45: Brig. RA, 8th Army, 1942; Comd 50 (N) Div., 1943; Comd British 13th Corps in Italy, 1944; GOC-in-C Southern Comd 1945; Comd 1 Corps BLA, 1945; Dep. Chief of Imperial Gen. Staff, 1945-47; Quartermaster-Gen. to the Forces, 1947-50; Mem. of Army Council, 1945-50; Col Comdt RA, 1947-57; Special Financial Representative in Germany, 1951-52; Dir Gen. of Civil Defence, 1954-60; Chm. Central Fire Brigades Advisory Council for England and Wales, 1957-60. Comdr, Legion of Merit (USA); Officier Légion d'Honneur, Croix de Guerre (France). *Address:* 8 Courtenay Place, Lymington, Hants SO4 9NQ.

KIRKMAN, William Patrick; Secretary, University of Cambridge Appointments Board, since 1968; Fellow, Wolfson College, Cambridge (formerly University College); *b* 23 Oct. 1932; *s* of late Geoffrey Charles Aylward Kirkman and Bertha Winifred Kirkman; *m* 1959, Anne Teasdale Fawcett; two *s* one *d. Educ:* Churcher's Coll., Petersfield, Hants; Oriel Coll., Oxford. 2nd cl. hons. mod. langs, 1955; MA 1959; MA (Cantab) by incorporation, 1968. National Service, 1950-52, RASC (L/Cpl). Editorial staff: Express & Star, Wolverhampton, 1955-57; The Times, 1957-64 (Commonwealth staff, 1960-64, Africa Correspondent, 1962-64). Asst Sec., Oxford Univ. Appointments Cttee, 1964-68. Chm., Standing Conf. of University Appointments Services, 1971-73; Mem., Management Cttee, Central Services Unit for Univ. Careers and Appointments Services, 1971-74. Vice-Pres., Wolfson Coll., 1980- (Mem. Council, 1969-73, 1976-80). Churchwarden, St Mary and All Saints Willingham, 1978-. Trustee: Sir Halley Stewart Trust, 1970- (Hon. Sec., 1978-); Willingham British Sch. Trust, 1974-; Homerton Coll., 1980-; Mem. Cttee, Cambridge Soc., 1979-. *Publications:* Unscrambling an Empire, 1966; contributor to: Commonwealth, International Affairs, Africa Contemporary Record, Financial Times, BBC, etc. *Recreations:* broadcasting, gardening, church activities, writing. *Address:* 19 High Street, Willingham, Cambridge CB4 5ES. *T:* Willingham 60393. *Club:* Royal Commonwealth Society.

KIRKNESS, Donald James, CB 1980; Deputy Secretary, Overseas Development Administration, 1977-80; *b* 29 Sept 1919; *s* of Charles Stephen and Elsie Winifred Kirkness; *m* 1947, Monica Mary Douch; one *d. Educ:* Harvey Grammar Sch., Folkestone. Exchequer and Audit Dept, 1938. Served War: RA and Royal Berkshire Regt, 1939-46. Colonial Office, 1947 (Asst Principal); Financial and Economic Adviser, Windward I, 1955-57; Asst Secretary: Colonial Office, 1962; Dept of Economic Affairs, 1966; Under-Secretary, 1969; Civil Service Dept, 1970-73; DTI, 1973; ODA/ODM, 1973.

UK Governor, Internat. Fund for Agricultural Develt, 1977-; Mem., Exec. Bd, UNESCO, 1978-. *Address:* 113 Blackheath Park, SE3.

KIRKPATRICK, Sir Ivone Elliott, 11th Bt, *cr* 1685; *b* 1 Oct. 1942; *s* of Sir James Alexander Kirkpatrick, 10th Bt and Ellen Gertrude, *o d* of Captain R. P. Elliott, late RNR; *S* father 1954. *Educ:* Wellington Coll., Berks; St Mark's Coll., University of Adelaide. *Heir: b* Robin Alexander Kirkpatrick, *b* 19 March 1944. *Address:* c/o ANZ Bank, 75 King William Street, Adelaide, SA 5000, Australia.

KIRKPATRICK, John Lister, CBE 1981; Chairman and Senior Partner, Thomson McLintock & Co., Chartered Accountants, Glasgow and Edinburgh, since 1980; Joint Chairman, Thomson McLintock & Co., UK, since 1974; Chairman and Managing Partner, KMG (Klynveld Main Goerdeler), Europe, Africa, Middle East, India, etc, since 1979; *b* 27 June 1927; *s* of late Henry Joseph Rodway Kirkpatrick and Nora (*née* Lister); *m* 1977, Gay Elmslie (*née* Goudielock); one *s* one *d* of former marriage. *Educ:* Inverness Royal Acad. CA. Served RNVR, 1944-47. Thomson McLintock & Co.: apprentice, 1948; qual. CA 1952; Partner, 1958; Joint Senior Partner, 1974-80. Member: BoT Accountants' Adv. Cttee, 1967-72; Internat. Accounting Standards Cttee, 1978-. Vice-Pres., Inst. of Chartered Accountants of Scotland, 1975-77, Pres., 1977-78. *Publications:* various papers. *Recreations:* fishing, gardening, sailing. *Address:* 1 Letham Drive, Glasgow G43 2SL. *T:* 041-633 1407. *Clubs:* Caledonian; Western (Glasgow); New (Edinburgh).

KIRKPATRICK, William Brown; Director and Manager, Finance for Shipping Limited (a subsidiary of FFI), since 1976; Director, H. Clarkson Holdings, since 1981; *b* 27 April 1934; *s* of late Joseph Kirkpatrick and Mary Laidlaw Kirkpatrick (*née* Brown), Thornhill, Dumfries-shire. *Educ:* Morton Acad., Thornhill; George Watson's Coll., Edinburgh; Univ. of Strathclyde (BScEcon); Columbia Business Sch., NY (MS and McKinsey Scholar); Stanford Business Sch. After two years in manufacturing industry in Glasgow, Dundee and London, joined ICFC (now subsid. of FFI), 1960; held various posts in the City, 1960-64 and 1972-74, and in Scotland, 1964-72, inc. Scottish Man., 1969-72, and a number of directorships; Industrial Dir, Industrial Develt Divn, Scottish Office, 1974-76 (on secondment). *Recreations:* the countryside, current affairs, collecting paintings. *Address:* 20 Abbotsbury House, Abbotsbury Road, W14 8EN. *T:* 01-603 3087; Kirkpatrick Hill, Closeburn, Dumfriesshire. *Club:* Caledonian.

KIRKUP, James; travel writer, poet, novelist, playwright, translator, broadcaster; *b* 23 April 1923; *o s* of James Harold Kirkup and Mary Johnston. *Educ:* South Shields High Sch.; Durham Univ. (BA). FRSL 1962. Atlantic Award in Literature (Rockefeller Foundation), 1950; Keats Prize for Poetry, 1974; Gregory Fellow in Poetry, University of Leeds, 1950-52. Visiting Poet and Head of English Dept, Bath Academy of Art, Corsham Court, Wilts, 1953-56; Lectr in English, Swedish Ministry of Education, Stockholm, 1956-57; Prof. of Eng. Lang. and Lit., University of Salamanca, 1957-58, of English, Tohoku Univ., Sendai, Japan, 1958-61; Lecturer in English Literature, University of Malaya in Kuala Lumpur, 1961-62; Literary Editor, Orient/West Magazine, Tokyo, 1963-64; Prof., Japan Women's Univ., 1964-; Poet in Residence and Visiting Prof., Amherst Coll., Mass, 1968-; Prof. of English Literature, Nagoya Univ., 1969-72. Arts Council Fellowship in Creative Writing, Univ. of Sheffield, 1974-75; Morton Vis. Prof. of Internat. Literature, Ohio Univ., 1975-76; Playwright in Residence, Sherman Theatre, University Coll., Cardiff, 1976-77; Prof. of English Lit., Kyoto Univ. of Foreign Studies, Kyoto, Japan, 1977-. President: Poets' Soc. of Japan, 1969; Blackmore Soc., 1970; Inst. of Pyschophysical Res., 1970. Mabel Batchelder Award, 1968. *Plays performed:* Upon this Rock (perf. Peterborough Cathedral), 1955; Masque, The Triumph of Harmony (perf. Albert Hall), 1955; The True Mistery of the Nativity, 1957; Dürrenmatt, The Physicists (Eng. trans.), 1963; Dürrenmatt, The Meteor (Eng. trans.); Dürrenmatt, Play Strindberg (Eng. trans.), 1972; The Magic Drum, children's play, 1972, children's musical, 1977; Dürrenmatt, Portrait of a Planet, 1972; Dürrenmatt, The Conformer, 1974; Schiller, Don Carlos, 1975; Cyrano de Bergerac, 1975; *operas:* An Actor's Revenge, 1979; Friends in Arms, 1980; The Damask Drum, 1982; *television plays performed:* The Peach Garden, Two Pigeons Flying High, etc. Contributor to BBC, The Listener, The Spectator, Times Literary Supplement, Time and Tide, New Yorker, Botteghe Oscure, London Magazine, Japan Qly, English Teachers' Magazine (Tokyo), etc. *Publications:* The Drowned Sailor, 1948; The Cosmic Shape, 1947; The Creation, 1950; The Submerged Village, 1951; A Correct Compassion, 1952; A Spring Journey, 1954; Upon This Rock, 1955; Camara Laye, The Dark Child (Eng. trans.), 1955; Ancestral Voices (Eng. trans.), 1956; Camara Laye, The Radiance of the King (Eng. trans.), 1956; The True Mistery of the Nativity, 1957; The Descent into the Cave, 1957; The Only Child (autobiog.), 1957; Simone de Beauvoir, Memoirs of a Dutiful Daughter (Eng. trans.), 1958; The Girl from Nowhere (Eng. trans.), 1958; Sorrows, Passions and Alarms, 1959; The Prodigal Son (poems), 1959; It Began in Babel (Eng. trans.), 1961; The Captive (Eng. trans.), 1962; Sins of the Fathers (Eng. trans.), 1962; The Gates of Paradise (Eng. trans.), 1962; These Horned Islands, A Journal of Japan, 1962; frères Gréban, The True Mistery of the Passion, 1962; The Love of Others (novel), 1962; Refusal to Conform, 1963; Tropic Temper: a Memoir of Malaya, 1963; The Heavenly Mandate (Eng. trans.), 1964; Daily Life of the Etruscans (Eng. trans.), 1964; Erich Kästner, The Little Man (Eng. trans.), 1966; Erich Kästner, The Little Man and The Little Miss (Eng. trans.), 1969; Heinrich von Kleist, The Tales of Hoffmann (Eng. trans.), 1966; Michael Kohlhaas (Eng. trans.), 1966; Japan Industrial, 1964-65 (2 vols); Daily Life in the French Revolution,

1964; Tokyo, 1965; England, Now, 1965; Japan, Now, 1966; Camara Laye, A Dream of Africa (Eng. trans.), 1967; Frankly Speaking, I-II, 1968; Paper Windows: Poems from Japan, 1968; Bangkok, 1968; One Man's Russia, 1968; Filipinescas, 1968; Streets of Asia, 1969; Japan Physical, 1969; Aspects of the Short Story, 1969; Shepherding Winds (anthol.), 1969; Songs and Dreams (anthol.), 1970; White Shadows, Black Shadows: Poems of Peace and War, 1970; Hong Kong, 1970; Japan Behind the Fan, 1970; The Eternal Virgin (Eng. trans of Valéry's La Jeune Parque), 1970; The Body Servant; poems of exile, 1971; Insect Summer (novel for children), 1971; A Bewick Bestiary (poems), 1971; (trans., with C. Fry) The Oxford Ibsen, vol III, Brand and Peer Gynt, 1972; (trans.) Selected Poems of Takagi Kyozo, 1973; The Magic Drum (children's novel), 1973; Heaven, Hell and Hara-Kiri, 1974; (with Birgit Skiöld) Zen Gardens, 1974; Scenes from Sesshu, 1977; Anthology of Contemporary Japanese Poetry, 1978; Zen Contemplations, 1979; (with Birgit Skiöld) The Tao of Water, 1980; Camara Laye, The Guardian of the Word (trans.), 1980; Eibungaku Saiken (essays), 1980; Dengonban Messages (one-line poems), 1980; Cold Mountain Poems (trans. Han Shan), 1980; To the Unknown God (trans.), 1982; Ecce Homo: My Pasolini (poems and trans.), 1982; No More Hiroshimas (poems and trans.), 1982; Folktales Japanesque, 1982; An African in Greenland (trans.), 1982; The Bush Toads (trans.), 1982; The Damask Drum (opera), 1982; I Am Count Dracula, 1982. *Recreation:* standing in shafts of moonlight. *Address:* BM-Box 2780, London WC1N 3XX.

KIRKWOOD, family name of **Baron Kirkwood**.

KIRKWOOD, 3rd Baron *cr* 1951, of Bearsden; **David Harvie Kirkwood;** Senior Lecturer in Metallurgy, Sheffield University, since 1976; *b* 24 Nov. 1931; *s* of 2nd Baron Kirkwood and Eileen Grace, *d* of Thomas Henry Boalch; *S* father, 1970; *m* 1965, Judith Rosalie, *d* of late John Hunt; three *d*. *Educ:* Rugby; Trinity Hall, Cambridge (MA, PhD); CEng. Lectr in Metallurgy, Sheffield Univ., 1962; Warden of Stephenson Hall, Sheffield Univ., 1974-80. *Heir: b* Hon. James Stuart Kirkwood [*b* 19 June 1937; *m* 1965, Alexandra Mary, *d* of late Alec Dyson; two *d*]. *Address:* 56 Endcliffe Hall Avenue, Sheffield S10 3EL. *T:* Sheffield 663107.

KIRKWOOD, Ian Candlish, QC (Scot.) 1970; *b* 8 June 1932; *o s* of late John Brown Kirkwood, OBE, and of Mrs Constance Kirkwood, Edinburgh; *m* 1970, Jill Ingram Scott; two *s*. *Educ:* George Watson's Boys' Coll., Edinburgh; Edinburgh Univ.; Univ. of Michigan, USA. MA (Edin) 1952; LLB (Edin) 1954; LLM (Mich) 1956. Called to Scottish Bar, 1957; apptd Standing Junior Counsel to Scottish Home and Health Dept, 1963; Mem. Rules Council (Court of Session). Pres., Wireless Telegraphy Appeal Tribunal in Scotland. Chm., Med. Appeal Tribunal in Scotland. Contested (C) Dunfermline Burghs, 1964, 1966, 1970. *Recreations:* fishing, golf, chess. *Address:* 58 Murrayfield Avenue, Edinburgh EH12 6AY. *T:* 031-337 3468; Low Kirkland, Kirkcudbright.

KIRKWOOD, Prof. Kenneth, MA; Rhodes Professor of Race Relations, University of Oxford, since 1954; Fellow of St Antony's College, since 1954, and Sub-Warden, 1968-71; *b* Benoni, Transvaal, 1919; *s* of late Thomas Dorman Kirkwood and Lily Kirkwood (*née* Bewley); *m* 1942, Deborah Burton, *d* of late Burton Ireland Collings and Emily Frances Collings (*née* Loram); three *s* three *d*. BA; BSc Rand. Captain, South African Engineer Corps, War of 1939-45; served in East Africa, North Africa and Italy (despatches). Lecturer, University of the Witwatersrand, 1947; Lecturer, University of Natal, 1948-51; Fellowship, University of London (Inst. of Commonwealth Studies), 1952; Carnegie Travelling Fellowship, USA, 1953; Senior Research Officer, Inst. of Colonial Studies, Oxford Univ., 1953; Organiser of Institute for Social Research, University of Natal, 1954. Chm. Regional Cttee, S African Inst. of Race Relations in Natal, 1954; UK Rep. SA Inst. of Race Relations, 1955. Investigation on behalf UNESCO into trends in race relations in British Non-Self-Governing Territories of Africa, 1958; Visiting Prof. of Race Relations (UNESCO), University Coll. of Rhodesia and Nyasaland, 1964; composed memorandum on meaning, and procedure for further study of 'racial discrimination,' for UN Div. of Human Rights, 1966-67; Mem., Africa Educational Trust, Oxfam, etc, 1955-. *Publications:* The Proposed Federation of the Central African Territories, 1952; other booklets and articles on race relations and international affairs; contributions to revision of Lord Hailey's An African Survey, 1957, and 2nd edn, Vol. VIII, Cambridge History of the British Empire, 1963; Britain and Africa, 1965; Editor, St Antony's Papers: African Affairs, number 1, 1961; number 2, 1963; number 3, 1969. *Address:* St Antony's College, Oxford. *T:* Oxford 55867.

KIRKWOOD, Sir Robert (Lucien Morrison), OJ 1974; KCMG 1972; Kt 1959; Chairman, Sugar Manufacturers' Association of Jamaica, 1945-74; Chairman: West Indies Sugar Association, 1946-74; Citrus Growers Association, 1944-60; *b* Yeo, Fairy Cross, N Devon, 9 Jan. 1904; *e s* of late Major John Hendley Morrison Kirkwood, DSO, sometime MP for Southend Div. of Essex, and Gertrude Agnes, *e d* of Sir Robert Park Lyle, 1st and last Bt, Eaton Place, SW1; *m* 1925, Sybil Attenborough (*d* 1977), Hartford House, Nottingham; one *s* two *d*. *Educ:* Wixenford; Harrow; Le Rosey (Switzerland). Joined Tate & Lyle, 1922; Managing Dir, The United Sugar Company, 1929-36; Dir Yorks Sugar Co., 1928-36 and Central Sugar Co. (Peterborough), 1929-36; joined Board of Tate & Lyle, 1935; Man. Dir, West Indies Sugar Co., Jamaica, 1937; Dir, Caroni Ltd, Trinidad, 1937. MLC Jamaica, 1942-62. Rep. Jamaica on Colonial Sugar Cttee, 1937-. Rep. West Indies at Internat. Sugar Confs, 1953, 1956, 1958, 1961, 1965, 1968, 1973. Pres. Sugar Club of New York, 1965-66; Chm. International Sugar Council, 1966. Mem. various Govt Bds and Cttees in Jamaica. Liveryman, Grocers' Co., 1935-. *Publication:* A Farm Production Policy for Jamaica, 1967. *Recreations:* gardening, golf and good food. *Address:* Three Kings, Sandwich, Kent. *T:* Sandwich 612221. *Clubs:* White's, Queen's; St George's (Sandwich); The Brook (New York).

KIRSOP, Arthur Michael Benjamin; Chairman, Forth Thyme Ltd, since 1976; Chairman and Managing Director, Ollerenshaw Threads Ltd, since 1981; *b* 28 Jan. 1931; *s* of Arthur Kirsop and Sarah (*née* Cauthery); *m* 1957, Patricia (*née* Cooper); two *s*. *Educ:* St Paul's Sch., Brazil; Glasgow Academy; Univ. of Oxford (BA). Joined English Sewing Cotton Co. Ltd, 1955; Area Sales Man., 1957; Export Sales Man., 1961; Man. Dir, Thread Div., 1964; Dir, English Sewing Cotton Co. Ltd, 1967 (later English Calico Ltd, then Tootal Ltd); Jt Man. Dir, 1973-76; Chief Exec., 1974-76; Chm., Tootal Ltd, 1975-76. Hon. Consul for the Netherlands, 1971-80. CBIM (FBIM 1973). *Recreations:* gardening, sport. *Address:* Peel House, 5 Planetree Road, Hale, Cheshire WA15 9JJ. *T:* 061-980 5173. *Clubs:* St James's (Manchester); Albany (Halifax); Lancs CC.

KIRSTEIN, Lincoln Edward; Director: School of American Ballet; New York City Ballet Company; *b* Rochester, NY, 4 May 1907; *s* of Louis E. Kirstein and Rose Stein; *m* 1941, Fidelma Cadmus; no *c*. *Educ:* Harvard Coll.; BS 1930. Edited Hound & Horn, 1927-34; founded School of American Ballet, 1934; founded and directed American Ballet Caravan, 1936-41; Third US Army (Arts, Monuments and Archives Section), 1943-45. Editor, The Dance Index, 1941-47. Benjamin Franklin Medal, RSA, 1981. *Publications:* Flesh is Heir, 1932, repr. 1975; Dance, A Short History of Theatrical Dancing, 1935; Blast at Ballet, 1938; Ballet Alphabet, 1940; Drawings of Pavel Tchelitchew, 1947; Elie Nadelman Drawings, 1949; The Dry Points of Elie Nadelman, 1952; What Ballet is About, 1959; Three Pamphlets Collected, 1967; The Hampton Institute Album, 1968; Movement and Metaphor: four centuries of ballet, 1970; Lay This Laurel, 1974; Nijinsky, Dancing, 1975; *verse:* Rhymes of a PFC (Private First Class), 1964; *monographs:* Gaston Lachaise, 1935; Walker Evans, 1938; Latin American Art, 1942; American Battle Art, 1945; Henri Cartier-Bresson, 1946; Dr William Rimmer, 1946; Elie Nadelman, 1948; Pavel Tchelitchew, 1964; W. Eugene Smith, 1970; *edited:* The Classic Dance, Technique and Terminology, 1951; William Shakespeare: A Catalogue of the Works of Art in the American Shakespeare Festival Theater, 1964; Elie Nadelman, 1973; New York City Ballet, 1973; Nijinsky Dancing, 1975; Thirty Years: the New York City Ballet, 1978. *Address:* School of American Ballet, 144 West 66th Street, New York, NY 10023, USA. *T:* 877-0600.

KIRTON, Col Hugh, TD 1952; Vice Lord-Lieutenant, County Durham, since 1978; *b* Plawsworth, Co. Durham, 7 Aug. 1910; 2nd *s* of late Hugh Kirton and Margaretta Kirton (*née* Darling). *Educ:* Durham Sch. Chartered Accountant, 1933. Army Service: commnd in Tyne Electrical Engrs (TA), 1937; RE(TA), 1937-40; RA(TA), 1940-45 and 1951-56, Lt Col 1945; Dep. Comdr, 31A Bde(TA), 1959-61, Col 1959; Hon. Col 439 (Tyne) Lt AD Regt RA(TA), 1961-67. With Procter & Gamble Ltd, Newcastle upon Tyne, 1934-70, Dir, 1963-70; retired 1970. Mem., North Regional Health Authority, 1973-76; General Comr of Taxes (Newcastle upon Tyne), 1965-. Mem. Council, Inst. of Chartered Accountants in England and Wales, 1966-70; Pres., Northern Soc. of Chartered Accountants, 1968-69. Mem., St John Council for Co. Durham, 1970-, Chm., 1974-. DL: Northumberland 1961; Durham 1974; High Sheriff Co. Durham 1973-74. CStJ 1980. *Recreations:* golf, gardening. *Address:* Plawsworth House, Plawsworth, Chester-le-Street, Co. Durham DH2 3LD. *T:* Durham 710261. *Clubs:* Army and Navy; Northern Counties (Newcastle upon Tyne), County (Durham); Brancepeth Castle Golf (Captain 1969-71).

KIRTON, Robert James, CBE 1963; MA, FIA; Director, Equity and Law Life Assurance Society, Ltd, 1944-77 (General Manager, 1939-66; Actuary, 1947-66); Chairman, Equity and Law Unit Trust Managers Ltd, 1969-77; *b* 13 July 1901; *er s* of late Albert William Kirton, Ealing, Middlesex; *m* 1931, Isabel Susan, *y d* of late Henry Hosegood, JP, Bristol; two *s* two d. *Educ:* Merchant Taylors' Sch.; Peterhouse, Cambridge. Scottish Widows' Fund and Life Assurance Soc., 1923-32; Scottish Amicable Life Assce Soc., 1932-38; Equity and Law Life Assce Soc. Ltd, 1938-77. Chairman: Life Offices' Assoc., 1945-47; Royal UK Beneficent Assoc., 1958-74 (Vice-Pres., 1981-); Nat. Council of Social Service: Hon. Treas., 1962-72; Vice-Pres., 1972-80; Trustee, Charities Official Investment Fund, 1962-77; Governor, London Sch. of Economics, 1963-; Vice-Chm., St Peter's Hosp., 1967-75; Mem. Council, Bath Univ., 1967-75; Mem., Buitengewoon Lid, Actuarial Genootschap, Holland, 1949. Silver Medal, Institute of Actuaries, 1966. *Publications:* contrib. Jl Inst. Actuaries, Trans. Faculty of Actuaries (with A. T. Haynes). *Recreations:* walking, ski-ing and squash rackets. *Address:* Byron Cottage, North End Avenue, NW3 7HP. *T:* 01-455 0464. *Club:* Athenæum.

KIRWAN, Sir (Archibald) Laurence (Patrick), KCMG 1972 (CMG 1958); TD; MLitt Oxon; Hon. Vice-President, Royal Geographical Society, since 1981 (Director and Secretary, 1945-75); *b* 1907; 2nd *s* of Patrick Kirwan, Cregg, County Galway, Ireland, and Mabel Norton; *m* 1st, 1932, Joan Elizabeth Chetwynd; one *d*; 2nd, 1949, Stella Mary Monck. *Educ:* Wimbledon Sch.; Merton Coll., Oxford. Asst Dir of the Archaeological Survey of Nubia, Egyptian Dept of Antiquities, 1929-34; Field Dir, Oxford

Univ. Expeditions to Sudan, 1934-37; Tweedie Fellowship in Archæology and Anthropology, Edinburgh Univ., 1937-39. Boston and Philadelphia Museums, 1937; Exploratory journeys, Eastern Sudan and Aden Protectorate, 1938-39. TARO Capt., General Staff, 1939; Major, 1941; Lieut-Col 1943; Joint Staffs, Offices of Cabinet and Ministry of Defence, 1942-45; Hon. Lt-Col, 1957. Editor, Geographical Journal, 1945-78; Pres., Brit. Inst. in Eastern Africa, 1961-81, Hon. Pres. and Hon. Mem., 1981. Pres. (Section E), British Assoc. for the Advancement of Science, 1961-62; Member: Court of Arbitration, Argentine-Chile Frontier Case, 1965-68 (Leader, Field Mission, 1966); Sec. of State for Transport's Adv. Cttee on Landscape Treatment of Trunk Roads, 1968-81 (Dep. Chm., 1970-); UN Register of fact-finding experts, 1968-; Court, Exeter Univ., 1969-80; a Governor, Imperial Coll. of Science and Technology, 1962-81; British Academy/Leverhulme Vis. Prof., Cairo, 1976; Mortimer Wheeler Lectr, Brit. Acad., 1977. Fellow: University Coll. London; Imperial College of Science and Technology; Hon. Fellow, SOAS. Hon. Member: Geographical Societies of Paris, Vienna, Washington; Royal Inst. of Navigation; Institut d'Egypte; Hon. Fellow, American Geographical Soc. Founder's Medal, RGS, 1975. Knight Cross of the Order of St Olav, Norway; Jubilee Medal, 1977. *Publications:* Excavations and Survey between Wadi-es-Sebua and Adindan, 1935 (with W. B. Emery); Oxford University Excavations at Firka, 1938; The White Road (polar exploration), 1959; papers on archæology, historical and political geography, exploration, in scientific and other publications. *Recreation:* travelling. *Address:* c/o Royal Geographical Society, SW7. *Club:* Geographical.

KIRWAN, Sir Laurence; see Kirwan, Sir A. L. P.

KISCH, (Alastair) Royalton; Conductor of Symphony Concerts; Artistic Director, Cork Street Art Gallery; *b* London, 20 Jan. 1919; *s* of late E. Royalton Kisch, MC and Pamela Kisch; *m* 1940, Aline, *d* of late Bruce Hylton Stewart and M. F. (Molly) Hylton Stewart; one *s* two *d. Educ:* Wellington Coll., Berks; Clare Coll., Cambridge. War service, Captain, KRRC (60th Rifles), 1940-46. Has conducted Royal Festival Hall concerts with London Philharmonic Orchestra, London Symphony Orchestra, Philharmonia Orchestra, Royal Philharmonic Orchestra, etc. Guest conductor to Hallé Orchestra, Birmingham Symphony Orchestra, etc. Has also conducted concerts in Europe with Paris Conservatoire Orchestra, Palestine Symphony Orchestra, Florence Philharmonic Orchestra, Athens State Symphony Orchestra, Pasdeloup Orchestra of Paris, Royal Opera House Orchestra of Rome, San Carlo Symphony Orchestra of Naples, Vienna Symphony Orchestra, etc. Has broadcast on BBC with London Symphony Orchestra, Royal Philharmonic Orchestra, and Philharmonia Orchestra. Gramophone recordings for Decca. Specialist in English and French paintings of 20th century. Mem., Friends of Tate Gallery. *Recreations:* good food and wine. *Address:* 2 Edwardes Square, Kensington, W8. *T:* 01-602 6655. *Clubs:* Athenæum, Hurlingham.

KISCH, John Marcus, CMG 1965; Planning Inspector, Department of the Environment, 1972-79; *b* 27 May 1916; *s* of late Sir Cecil Kisch, KCIE, CB, and late Myra Kisch; *m* 1951, Gillian Poyser; four *d. Educ:* Rugby Sch.; King's Coll., Cambridge. Asst Principal, Board of Inland Revenue, 1938; Asst Principal, Colonial Office, 1939. Served Royal Corps of Signals, 1939-45. Principal, Colonial Office, 1945; seconded E Africa High Commission, 1951; Kenya Govt 1952; Asst Sec., Colonial Office, 1956; seconded CRO, 1964; transferred Min. of Defence, 1965; Asst Sec., MoD (Navy Dept), 1965-68; Asst Sec., ODM, later ODA, 1968-72. *Recreations:* chess, croquet. *Address:* Hatchford Corner, Cobham, Surrey. *T:* Cobham 2138; 21 Pembroke Square, W8. *T:* 01-937 8590.

KISCH, Royalton; see Kisch, A. R.

KISSIN, family name of **Baron Kissin.**

KISSIN, Baron *cr* 1974 (Life Peer), of Camden in Greater London; **Harry Kissin;** President, Guinness Peat Group, since 1979 (Chairman, Lewis & Peat Ltd, 1961-72, Guinness Peat Group, 1973-79); Chairman: Linfood Holdings, 1974-81; Esperanza International Services plc, since 1970, and Director of other public and private companies in the City of London, since 1934; *b* 23 Aug. 1912; *s* of Israel Kissin and Reusi Kissin (*née* Model), both of Russian nationality; *m* 1935, Ruth Deborah Samuel, London; one *s* one *d. Educ:* Danzig and Switzerland. Dr of Law, Basle. Swiss lawyer until 1933. Dir, Royal Opera Hse, Covent Gdn, 1973-; Mem., Royal Opera House Trust, 1974- (Chm., 1974-80). Chm. Council, ICA, 1968-75. Governor: Bezalel Acad. of Arts and Design, 1975-; Haifa Univ., 1976-; Hebrew Univ. of Jerusalem, 1980; Mem. Bd of Governors, Ben Gurian Univ. of the Neger, 1979-. Comdr, Ordem Nacional do Cruzeiro do Sul (Brazil), 1977; Légion d'honneur, 1981. *Address:* c/o House of Lords, SW1. *Clubs:* Reform, East India, Devonshire, Sports and Public Schools.

KISSINGER, Henry Alfred; Bronze Star (US); University Professor of Diplomacy, School of Foreign Service, Georgetown University, since 1977; Counselor to Center for Strategic and International Studies, Georgetown University, since 1977; Special Consultant for World Affairs, NBC, since 1977; Senior Fellow, Aspen Institute, since 1977; *b* 27 May 1923; *s* of late Louis Kissinger and Paula (*née* Stern); *m* 1st, 1949, Anne Fleischer (marr. diss. 1964); one *s* one *d* ; 2nd, 1974, Nancy Maginnes. *Educ:* George Washington High Sch., NYC; Harvard Univ., Cambridge, Mass (AB, MA, PhD). Teaching Fellow, Harvard Univ., 1950-54; Study Director: Council on

Foreign Relations, 1955-56: Rockefeller Bros Fund, 1956-58; Associate Professor of Govt, Harvard Univ., 1958-62, Prof. of Govt, 1962-71, and Faculty Mem., Center for Internat. Affairs, Harvard; Director: Harvard Internat. Seminar, 1951-71; Harvard Defense Studies Program, 1958-71; Asst to US President for Nat. Security Affairs, 1969-75; Secretary of State, USA, 1973-77. Consultant to various government agencies. Mem., Internat. Adv. Cttee, Chase Manhattan Bank, 1977-; Chm., Internat. House, 1977-. Dir, Foreign Policy Assoc., 1977-; Mem., Council on Foreign Relations, 1977-81. Trustee, Rockefeller Brothers Fund, 1977-. (Jtly) Nobel Peace Prize, 1973; Presidential Medal of Freedom, 1977. *Publications:* A World Restored: Castlereagh, Metternich and the Restoration of Peace, 1957; Nuclear Weapons and Foreign Policy, 1957 (Woodrow Wilson Prize, 1958; citation, Overseas Press Club, 1958); The Necessity for Choice: Prospects of American Foreign Policy, 1961; The Troubled Partnership: a reappraisal of the Atlantic Alliance, 1965; Problems of National Strategy: A Book of Readings (ed), 1965; American Foreign Policy: three essays, 1969, 3rd edn 1977; White House Years (memoirs), 1979; For the Record, 1981; Years of Upheaval (memoirs), 1982; articles in Foreign Affairs, Harper's Magazine, The Reporter, New York Times Sunday Magazine, etc. *Address:* Suite 400, 1800 K Street, NW, Washington, DC 20006, USA. *Clubs:* Century (New York); Cosmos, Federal City, Metropolitan (Washington).

KISTIAKOWSKY, Prof. Emeritus George Bogdan; Professor of Chemistry, Harvard University, 1938-71 (Chairman, 1947-50), Emeritus since 1971; Special Assistant to the President of the USA for Science and Technology, 1959-61; Vice-President, National Academy of Sciences, 1965-72; *b* Kiev, Ukraine, 18 Nov. 1900; *s* of Bogdan Kistiakowsky and Mary Berenstam; came to USA, 1926; naturalized citizen, 1933; *m* 1st, 1926, Hildegard Moebius (marr. diss. 1942); one *d* ; 2nd, 1945, Irma E. Shuler (marr. diss. 1962); 3rd, 1962, Elaine Mahoney. *Educ:* University of Berlin (DPhil). Fellow and Staff Mem. Chem. Dept, Princeton, 1926-30; Asst Prof., 1930-33, Associate Prof., 1933-38, Harvard. On leave from Harvard to: Nat. Defense Research Cttee, 1941-43; Los Alamos Lab., 1944-46. Asst to the President for Sci. and Technol., 1959-61; Member: President's Science Adv. Cttee, 1957-64; Gen. Adv. Cttee to US Arms Control and Disarmament Agency, 1962-68. Mem. National Acad. of Sciences, etc; Hon. Fellow, Chem. Soc., London; Foreign Mem. Royal Society, London, 1959. Hon. DSc: Harvard Univ., 1955; Williams Coll., 1958; Oxford Univ., 1959; University of Pennsylvania, 1960; University of Rochester, 1960; Carnegie Inst. of Technology, 1961; Princeton Univ., 1962; Case Institute, 1962; Columbia Univ., 1967. Medal for Merit, USA, 1946; King's Medal for Services in the Cause of Freedom, 1948; Willard Gibbs Medal, 1960; Medal of Freedom (awarded by Pres. Eisenhower), 1961; George Ledlie Prize, Harvard Univ., 1961; Nat. Medal of Science (awarded by Pres. Johnson), 1967; Peter Debye Award, 1968; Theodore William Richards, 1968; Priestley Medal, 1972, and several other awards. *Publications:* Photochemical Processes, 1929; A Scientist at the White House, 1976; numerous articles. *Address:* 12 Oxford Street, Cambridge, Mass 02138, USA. *T:* University 617-495-4083.

KITAJ, R. B.; artist; *b* Ohio, 1932; *m* (wife decd); two *c. Educ:* Ruskin Sch. of Art, Oxford; RCA (ARCA). Lives in London. One-man Exhibitions: Marlborough New London Gall., 1963, 1970; Marlborough Gall., NY, 1965, 1974; Los Angeles County Museum of Art, 1965; Stedelijk Mus., Amsterdam, 1967; Mus. of Art, Cleveland, 1967; Univ. of Calif, Berkeley, 1967; Galerie Mikro, Berlin, 1969; Kestner Gesellschaft, Hanover, 1970; Boymans-van-Beuningen Mus., Rotterdam, 1970; (with Jim Dine) Cincinnati Art Mus., Ohio, 1973; Marlborough Fine Art, 1977, 1980; Retrospective Exhibitions: Hirshhorn Museum, Washington, 1981; Cleveland Museum of Art, Ohio, 1981; Kunsthalle, Düsseldorf, 1982. Member: US Inst. of Arts and Letters, NY, 1982; Nat. Acad. of Design, NY, 1982. *Address:* c/o Marlborough Fine Art (London) Ltd, 6 Albemarle Street, W1.

KITCATT, Peter Julian; Under Secretary, HM Treasury, since 1973; *b* 5 Dec. 1927; *s* of late Horace Wilfred Kitcatt of and Ellen Louise Kitcatt (*née* Julian); *m* 1952, Audrey Marian Aylen; three *s* two *d. Educ:* Borden Grammar Sch., Sittingbourne; King's Coll., Cambridge. RASC (2nd Lt) 1948. Asst Principal, Colonial Office, 1950-53; Asst Private Sec. to Sec. of State for the Colonies, 1953-54; Principal, Colonial Office, 1954-60; Sec. to HRH The Princess Royal on Caribbean Tour, 1960; Sec., E African Econ. and Fiscal Commn, 1960; HM Treasury: Principal, 1964; Asst Sec., 1966; RCDS, 1972; Under Sec., 1973, seconded to DHSS, 1975-78. *Recreation:* golf. *Address:* 20 Winchelsey Rise, South Croydon, Surrey. *T:* 01-688 7990. *Club:* Croham Hurst Golf (Croydon).

KITCHEN, Frederick Bruford, CBE 1975; *b* Melbourne, 15 July 1912; *o s* of F. W. Kitchen, Malvern, Vic, Australia; *m* 1936, Una Bernice Sloss; two *s* one *d. Educ:* Melbourne Grammar Sch.; Melbourne Univ. (BSc). Joined family firm (in Melb.), J. Kitchen and Sons Pty Ltd, which had become a Unilever soap co., 1934. Sales Dir, Lever Bros Ltd, Canada, 1946. Came to England, 1949, as Chm., Crosfields (CWG) Ltd; Chm., Lever Bros Ltd, 1957; Marketing Dir, Lever Bros & Associates Ltd, 1960; Chm., Van den Berghs & Jurgens Ltd, 1962-74; Mem., Price Commn, 1973-75. Past Pres.: Incorp. Soc. of British Advertisers; Internat. Fedn of Margarine Assocs; Margarine and Shortening Manufacturers' Assoc. Associate, Royal Australian Chemical Inst. *Recreation:* gardening. *Address:* Southdown, Yal Yal Road, Merricks, Victoria 3916, Australia. *T:* 059-898411. *Club:* Australian (Melbourne).

KITCHEN, Stanley, FCA; Partner, Touche Ross & Co., Chartered Accountants, Birmingham, 1948-81; *b* 23 Aug. 1913; *s* of late Percy Inman Kitchen and Elizabeth Kitchen; *m* 1941, Jean Craig; two *d. Educ:* Rugby Sch. ACA 1937, FCA 1953. Army, 1939-46: Major, RASC. Sec., British Rollmakers Corp. Ltd, Wolverhampton, 1946-48; Partner, Foster & Stephens, Birmingham, 1948-81 (merged with Touche Ross & Co., 1965). Chm., STEP Management Services Ltd, 1978-. Birmingham and West Midlands Soc. of Chartered Accountants: Mem. Cttee, 1951-81; Sec., 1953-55; Pres., 1957-58; Inst. of Chartered Accountants in England and Wales: Mem. Council, 1966-81; Vice-Pres., 1974-75; Dep. Pres., 1975-76; Pres., 1976-77. *Publications:* Learning to Live with Taxes on Capital Gains, 1967; Important Aspects of Professional Partnerships, 1974. *Recreations:* gardening, golf. *Address:* 1194 Warwick Road, Knowle, Solihull, West Midlands B93 9LL. *T:* Knowle 2360. *Clubs:* Lansdowne; Birmingham, Chamber of Commerce (Birmingham).

KITCHENER OF KHARTOUM, and of Broome; 3rd Earl, *cr* 1914; **Henry Herbert Kitchener,** TD; DL; Viscount, *cr* 1902, of Khartoum; of the Vaal, Transvaal, and Aspall, Suffolk; Viscount Broome, *cr* 1914, of Broome, Kent; Baron Denton, *cr* 1914, of Denton, Kent; late Major, Royal Corps of Signals; *b* 24 Feb. 1919; *er s* of Viscount Broome (*d* 1928) and Adela Mary Evelyn, *e d* of late J. H. Monins, Ringwould House, near Dover; *S* grandfather, 1937. *Educ:* Sandroyd Sch.; Winchester Coll.; Trinity Coll., Cambridge. DL Cheshire 1972. *Heir: cousin* Henry Hamilton Kitchener [*b* 10 Sept. 1890; *m* 1st, 1916, Winifred Esther Everest Bluck (*d* 1959); two *d*; 2nd, 1961, Mrs Gwynneth Champion]. *Address:* Westergate Wood, Chichester, W Sussex PO20 6SB. *T:* Eastergate 3061. *Club:* Brooks's.

KITCHIN, Prof. Laurence Tyson; university teacher, translator and critic; *b* 21 July 1913; *s* of James Tyson Kitchin, MD Edin, and Eliza Amelia Kitchin (*née* Hopps); *m* 1955, Hilary Owen, artist. *Educ:* Bootham Sch.; King's Coll., London Univ. (BA 1934); Central Sch. of Drama. Served War, RAMC and briefly, RAEC, 1941-46. Mem., univ. debates team, 1933; acted in Housemaster on stage and screen, 1936, and in films, incl. Pimpernel Smith; wrote extensively for BBC Third Prog., 1948-55; The Times corresp. and drama critic, 1956-62; numerous BBC talks on literature and drama, 1962-66; UK rep., Théâtre dans le Monde, UNESCO, 1961-66; Lectr, Bristol Univ. and Tufts, London, 1966-70; Vis. Prof. of Drama, Stanford Univ., Calif, 1970-72; Vis. Prof. of Liberal Arts, City Univ. of NY, 1972-73, Prof., 1973-76; Vis. Prof. of Shakespeare Studies, Simon Fraser Univ., Canada, 1976-77. Renaissance verse translations from Italian, French and Spanish, BBC, 1978-79. Selected as one of Outstanding Educators of America, 1973. *Publications:* Len Hutton, 1953; Three on Trial, 1959; Mid-Century Drama, 1960, 2nd edn 1962; Drama in the Sixties, 1966; radio scripts, incl.: The Trial of Lord Byron, 1948, Canada 1978; The Trial of Machiavelli, 1957; The Court Lady (trans. from Castiglione), 1954; The Elizabethan, Canada 1978; The Flaming Heart (Crashaw), 1981; contrib. Shakespeare Survey, Mod. Lang. Rev., TLS, Encounter, Observer, and Listener. *Recreations:* tennis, televised soccer. *Address: c/o* National Westminster Bank, 33 St James's Square, SW1Y 4JT. *Club:* Athenæum.

KITCHING, Maj.-Gen. George, CBE 1945; DSO 1943; Canadian Military Forces, retired; Co-ordinator, Duke of Edinburgh's Award in Canada, 1967-76, President, British Columbia and Yukon Division, since 1979; *b* 1910; *m* 1946, Audrey Calhoun; one *s* one *d. Educ:* Cranleigh; Royal Military College. 2nd Lieut Glos Regt, 1930. Served War of 1939-45 with Royal Canadian Regt, in Sicily, Italy and North-West Europe; commanding Canadian Infantry Brigade, 1943; actg Maj.-Gen. comdg an armoured div., 1944 (despatches, DSO, CBE). Subseq. Vice-Chief of General Staff at Army Headquarters, Ottawa; Chairman of the Canadian Joint Staff in London, 1958-62; GOC Central Command, Canada, 1962-65, retd. Col Comdt of Infantry, 1974-78. Comr, Ont Pavilion, Osaka, Japan, for Expo 1970; Chief Comr, Liquor Control Bd of Ont, 1970-76. Chm. and Patron, Gurkha Welfare Appeal (Canada), 1974-; Patron: United World Colls, 1970 (Exec. Dir, Canadian Nat. Cttee, 1968-70); Sir Edmund Hillary Foundn (Canada), 1976-; Old Fort York, Toronto, 1975-. Trustee and Dir, Art Gallery of Greater Victoria. Commander: Order of Orange Nassau (Netherlands); Military Order of Italy; Order of Merit (US). *Address:* 3434 Bonair Place, Victoria, BC V8P 4V4, Canada.

KITCHING, John Alwyne, OBE 1947; FRS 1960; ScD (Cambridge); PhD (London); Professor of Biology, University of East Anglia, 1963-74, now Emeritus Professor; Dean of School of Biological Sciences, 1967-70; Leverhulme Fellowship, 1974; *b* 24 Oct. 1908; *s* of John Nainby Kitching; *m* 1933, Evelyn Mary Oliver; one *s* three *d. Educ:* Cheltenham Coll.; Trinity Coll., Cambridge. BA 1930, MA 1934, ScD 1956; PhD London. Lecturer: Birkbeck Coll., London, 1931; Edinburgh Univ., 1936; Bristol Univ., 1937; Rockefeller Fellow, Princeton Univ., 1938; Research in aviation-medical problems under Canadian Nat. Research Council, 1939-45; Reader in Zoology, University of Bristol, 1948-63. *Publications:* contrib. Jl of Experimental Biol., Jl of Ecology, Jl of Animal Ecology, etc. *Recreations:* travel, gardening. *Address:* University of East Anglia, University Plain, Norwich NR4 7TJ; 29 Newfound Drive, Cringleford, Norwich NR4 7RY.

KITSON, family name of **Baron Airedale.**

KITSON, Alexander Harper, JP; Deputy General Secretary, Transport and General Workers Union, since 1980; *b* 21 Oct. 1921; *m* 1942, Ann Brown McLeod; two *d. Educ:* Kirknewton Sch., Midlothian, Scotland. Lorry Driver, 1935-45; Trade Union official, 1945-. Mem., Freight Integration Council, 1969-78. Mem. Nat. Exec. Cttee of Labour Party, 1968-; Chm., Labour Party, 1980-81. *Address:* Transport and General Workers Union, Transport House, Smith Square, SW1P 3JB. *T:* 01-828 7788.

KITSON, Gen. Sir Frank (Edward), KCB 1980; CBE (mil.) 1972 (OBE 1968; MBE 1959); MC 1955 and Bar 1958; C-in-C, United Kingdom Land Forces, since 1982; *b* 15 Dec. 1926; *s* of late Vice-Adm. Sir Henry Kitson, KBE, CB and of Lady (Marjorie) Kitson (*née* de Pass); *m* 1962, Elizabeth Janet, *d* of Col C. R. Spencer, OBE; three *d. Educ:* Stowe. 2nd Lt Rifle Bde, 1946; served BAOR, 1946-53; Kenya, 1953-55; Malaya, 1957; Cyprus, 1962-64; CO 1st Bn, Royal Green Jackets, 1967-69; Defence Fellow, University Coll., Oxford, 1969-70; Comdr, 39 Inf. Bde, NI, 1970-72 (CBE for gallantry); Comdt, Sch. of Infantry, 1972-74; RCDS, 1975; GOC 2nd Division, later 2nd Armoured Division, 1976-78; Comdt, Staff College, 1978-80; Dep. C-in-C, UKLF, and Inspector-Gen., TA, 1980-82. Col Comdt, 2nd Bn The Royal Green Jackets, 1979-; Hon. Col, Oxford Univ. OTC, 1982-. *Publications:* Gangs and Counter Gangs, 1960; Low Intensity Operations, 1971; Bunch of Five, 1977. *Recreations:* horses, wildlife, books. *Address: c/o* Lloyds Bank, Farnham, Surrey. *Club:* Boodle's.

KITSON, George McCullough; Principal, Central School of Speech and Drama, London, since 1978; *b* Castlegore, Ireland, 18 May 1922; *s* of George Kitson and Anna May McCullough-Kitson; *m* 1951, Jean Evelyn Tyte; four *s. Educ:* early educn in Ireland; London Univ. (Dip. in Child Develt, 1947); Trent Park Coll. (Teachers' Cert., 1949). Associate, Cambridge Inst. of Educn, 1956; MEd Leicester, 1960. Served War, RAF, 1940-45; Navigator, Coastal Comd. Asst Master, schs in Herts, 1949-54; Dep. Headmaster, Broadfield Sch., Hemel Hempstead, Herts, 1954-56; Lectr in Educn, Leicester Coll. of Educn, 1956-66; Tutor i/c Annexe for Mature Teachers, Northampton, 1966-71; Dep. Principal, Furzedown Coll., London, 1971-76; Vice-Principal, Philippa Fawcett and Furzedown Coll., 1976-78. Mem., Nat. Council of Drama Trng, 1978-; Chm., Conference of Drama Schs, 1980-. *Publications:* (contrib.) Map of Educational Research, 1969; articles on educn, social psychol., and interprofessionalism in Forum, New Era, Educn for Teaching, and Brit. Jl of Educnl Psychol. *Recreations:* book collecting (first editions), sailing, walking, music, theatre. *Address:* 56 Woodbourne Avenue, SW16 1BU. *T:* 01-769 7621.

KITSON, Sir Timothy (Peter Geoffrey), Kt 1974; MP (C) Richmond, Yorkshire, since 1959; *b* 28 Jan. 1931; *s* of late Geoffrey H. and of Kathleen Kitson; *m* 1959, Diana Mary Fattorini; one *s* two *d. Educ:* Charterhouse; Royal Agricultural College, Cirencester. Farmed in Australia, 1949-51. Member: Thirsk RDC, 1954-57; N Riding CC, 1957-61. PPS to Parly Sec. to Minister of Agriculture, 1960-64; an Opposition Whip, 1967-70; PPS to the Prime Minister, 1970-74, to Leader of the Opposition, 1974-75. Chm., Defence Select Cttee, 1982-. *Recreations:* shooting, hunting, racing. *Address:* Leases Hall, Leeming Bar, Northallerton, North Yorks. *T:* Bedale 2180.

KITTO, Rt. Hon. Sir Frank (Walters), PC 1963; KBE 1955; Chancellor, University of New England, 1970-81; Chairman, Australian Press Council, 1976-82; *b* 30 July 1903; *s* of late James W. Kitto, OBE, Austinmer, New South Wales; *m* 1928, Eleanor, *d* of late Rev. W. H. Howard; four *d. Educ:* North Sydney High Sch.; Sydney Univ. BA 1924; Wigram Allen Scholar, G. and M. Harris Scholar and Pitt Cobbett Prizes in Faculty of Law, and LLB first class hons, 1927; called to Bar of NSW, 1927. KC (NSW), 1942. Challis Lecturer in Bankruptcy and Probate, Sydney Univ., 1930-33; Justice of the High Court of Australia, 1950-70. Mem. Council, University of New England, 1967-, Deputy Chancellor, 1968-70. Hon. DLitt New England, 1982. *Address:* 11 Werrina Crescent, Armidale, NSW 2350, Australia. *T:* Armidale 72-1189. *Club:* Australian (Sydney).

KITZINGER, Sheila Helena Elizabeth, MBE 1982; Course Team Chairman, Open University, since 1981; *b* 29 March 1929; *d* of Alec and Clare Webster; *m* 1952, Uwe Kitzinger, *qv*; five *d. Educ:* Bishop Fox's Girls' Sch., Taunton; Ruskin Coll., Oxford; St Hugh's Coll., Oxford; motherhood; educn continuing. Res. Asst, Dept of Anthropology, Univ. of Edinburgh, 1952-53 (MLitt 1954; thesis on race relations in Britain). Mem., Panel of Advisers, National Childbirth Trust of GB; Consultant, Internat. Childbirth Educn Assoc. MRSocMed. Joost de Blank Award, to do research on problems facing West Indian mothers in Britain, 1971-73. *Publications:* The Experience of Childbirth, 1962, 4th edn 1978; Giving Birth, 1971, rev. and expanded edn 1979; Education and Counselling for Childbirth, 1977; Women as Mothers, 1978; (ed with John Davis) The Place of Birth, 1978; The Good Birth Guide, 1979; The Experience of Breastfeeding, 1979; Pregnancy and Childbirth, 1980; Sheila Kitzinger's Birth Book, 1981; (with Rhiannon Walters) Some Women's Experiences of Episiotomy, 1981; Episiotomy: physical and emotional aspects, 1981; The New Good Birth Guide, 1982; Birth over Thirty, 1982; (contrib.) Ethnography of Fertility and Birth, 1982. *Recreations:* painting, cooking, talking. *Address:* The Manor, Standlake, Oxfordshire OX8 7RH. *T:* Standlake 266.
See also David Webster.

KITZINGER, Uwe, CBE 1980; Director, Oxford Centre for Management Studies, since 1980; *b* 12 April 1928; *o s* of late Dr G. Kitzinger and Mrs L.

Kitzinger, Abbots Langley, Herts; *m* 1952, Sheila Helena Elizabeth Webster (*see* S. H. E. Kitzinger); five *d*. *Educ:* Watford Grammar Sch.; Balliol Coll. and New Coll. (Foundn Schol.), Oxford. 1st in Philosophy, Politics and Economics, MA, MLitt; Pres., Oxford Union, 1950. Economic Section, Council of Europe, Strasbourg, 1951-58; Nuffield College, Oxford: Research Fellow, 1956-62, Official Fellow, 1962-66; Acting Investment Bursar, 1962-64; Investment Bursar, 1964-76; Ford Fellow in European Politics, 1966-76; Emeritus Fellow, 1976-. Assessor of Oxford University, 1967-68. Visiting Prof.: of Internat. Relations, Univ. of the West Indies, 1964-65; of Government, at Harvard, 1969-70; at Univ. of Paris (VIII), 1970-73. Leave of absence as Adviser to Sir Christopher (now Lord) Soames, Vice-Pres. of the Commn of the European Communities, Brussels, 1973-75; Dean, INSEAD (European Inst. of Business Admin), Fontainebleau, 1976-80 (Mem. Board, 1976-). Consultant to various nat. and internat. orgns. Member: ODM Cttee for University Secondment, 1966-68; British Universities Cttee of Encyclopædia Britannica, 1967-73; Adv. Bd, Pace Univ., NY, 1982-; Chairman: Cttee on Atlantic Studies, 1967-70; Major Projects Assoc., 1981-. Directly elected Mem., Nat. Council of European Movement, 1974-76. Dir, Internat. Schs of Business Management, London, 1977-80. Trustee: European Foundn for Management Educn, Brussels, 1978-80; Oxfam, 1981-. *Publications:* German Electoral Politics, 1960, German edn, 1960; The Challenge of the Common Market, 1961 (Amer. edn, The Politics and Economics of European Integration, 1963, et al); Britain, Europe and Beyond, 1964; The Background to Jamaica's Foreign Policy, 1965; The European Common Market and Community, 1967; Commitment and Identity, 1968; The Second Try, 1968; Diplomacy and Persuasion, 1973, French edn, 1974; Europe's Wider Horizons, 1975; (with D. E. Butler) The 1975 Referendum, 1976. Founding Editor, Jl of Common Market Studies, 1962-. *Recreations:* sailing, travel, old buildings. *Address:* Oxford Centre for Management Studies, Kennington Road, Kennington, Oxford. *T:* Oxford 735422; Standlake Manor, near Witney, Oxon. *T:* Standlake 266; La Rivière, 11100 Bages, France. *T:* (68) 32 47 55. *Clubs:* Reform; Royal Solent (Yarmouth, IoW).

KLARE, Hugh John, CBE 1967; columnist in Justice of the Peace on crime and penology; *b* Berndorf, Austria, 22 June 1916; *yr s* of F. A. Klare; *m* 1946, Eveline Alice Maria, *d* of Lieut-Col J. D. Rankin, MBE. *Educ:* privately. Came to England, 1932. Served war in Middle East and Europe; Major. Dep. Dir, Economic Organisation Br., Brit. Control Commn for Germany, 1946-48; Sec., Howard League for Penal Reform, 1950-71; seconded to Coun. of Europe as Dep. Head, Div. of Crime Problems, 1959-61; Head of Div., 1971-72; Member of Council: Internat. Soc. of Criminology, 1960-66; Inst. for Study and Treatment of Delinquency, 1964-66; Nat. Assoc. for Care and Resettlement of Offenders, 1966-71. Chm. Planning Cttee, Brit. Congress on Crime, 1966. Member: Bd of Visitors, Long Lartin Prison, 1972-76; Gloucestershire Probation and Aftercare Cttee, 1972-; Parole Board, 1972-74. A Governor, British Inst. of Human Rights, 1974-80. *Publications:* Anatomy of Prison, 1960; (ed and introd) Changing Concepts of Crime and its Treatment, 1966; (ed jtly) Frontiers of Criminology, 1967; People in Prison, 1972. *Address:* 28 Pittville Court, Albert Road, Cheltenham GL52 3JA. *T:* Cheltenham 34224.

KLEEMAN, Harry; Chairman, Kleeman Plastics group of companies, since 1968; *b* 2 Mar. 1928; *s* of Max Kleeman and Lottie Bernstein; *m* 1955, Avril Lees; two *s* two *d*. *Educ:* Westminster Sch.; Trinity Coll., Cambridge. Director, O. & M. Kleemann Ltd, 1951-65. President, British Plastics Fedn, 1979-80; Chairman: Polymer Engineering Directorate of Science and Engineering Research Council, 1980-; Plastics Processing Sector Working Party, NEDO, 1980-. FPRI 1980. Member: Zoological Soc., 1950-; Royal Society of Arts, 1978-; Worshipful Co. of Horners, 1954-. *Recreations:* horse riding, amateur radio. *Address:* 41 Frognal, NW3 6YD. *T:* 01-794 3366. *Club:* City Livery.

KLEFFENS, Eelco Nicolaas van; Netherlands Minister of State (life), 1950; *b* Heerenveen (Netherlands), 17 Nov. 1894; *m* 1935, Margaret Helen Horstman. *Educ:* University of Leyden. Adjusted shipping questions arising out of European War for Netherlands, 1919; Mem. Secretariat League of Nations, 1919-21; Sec. to directorate of Royal Dutch Petroleum Co., 1921-23; deputy-chief of legal section, Netherlands Ministry for Foreign Affairs, 1923-27; deputy-chief of diplomatic section, 1927-29; chief of diplomatic section, 1929-39; appointed Minister to Switzerland and Netherlands representative with League of Nations, 1939; Minister for Foreign Affairs of the Netherlands, 1939-46; Minister without portfolio and Netherlands representative on Security Council and Economic and Social Council of UN, 1946-47; Netherlands Ambassador to the United States of America, 1947-50; Minister to Portugal, 1950-56; Permanent Representative of Netherlands on NATO Council and OEEC (Paris), 1956-58; Chief Representative in UK of High Authority of European Coal and Steel Community, 1958-67; Pres., IX Session United Nations General Assembly. Pres., Arbitral Tribunal established under Bonn-Paris Agreements, 1952-54, by France, Germany, UK, USA, 1957-70. Holds several hon. degrees; Corresponding Mem., Netherlands and Portuguese Academy of Sciences; Mem. of Curatorium, Hague Academy of International Law, 1947-68; Hon. Member, Amer. Soc. of Internat. Law. Grand Cross: Orange-Nassau (Netherl.); Legion of Honour (France); St Gregory (Holy See); Christ (Portugal), *et al*. *Publications:* The Relations between the Netherlands and Japan in the Light of International Law, 1605-1919, 1919; The Rape of the Netherlands, 1940; Sovereignty in International Law, 1953; Hispanic Law until the end of the Middle Ages, 1968;

Belevenissen (Experiences), vol. I, 1980; articles in periodicals. *Address:* Casal de Santa Filomena, Almoçagême, Colares, Portugal. *Clubs:* Haagsche (The Hague); Eça de Queiroz (Lisbon); Century (New York).

KLEIN, Bernat, CBE 1973; FSIAD 1974; Chairman and Managing Director, Bernat Klein Ltd, since 1973; *b* 6 Nov. 1922; *s* of Lipot Klein and Serena Weiner; *m* 1951, Margaret Soper; one *s* two *d*. *Educ:* Senta, Yugoslavia; Bezalel Sch. of Arts and Crafts, Jerusalem; Leeds Univ. Designer to: Tootal, Broadhurst, Lee, 1948-49; Munrospun, Edinburgh, 1949-51; Chm. and Man. Dir, Colourcraft, 1952-62; Man. Dir of Bernat Klein Ltd, 1962-66; Chm. and Man. Dir, Bernat Klein Design Ltd, 1966-81. Member: Council of Industrial Design, Scottish Cttee, 1965-71; Royal Fine Art Commn for Scotland, 1980-. Exhibitions of paintings: E-SU, 1965; Alwyn Gall., 1967; O'Hana Gall., 1969; Assoc. of Arts Gall., Capetown, Goodman Gall., Johannesburg, and O'Hana Gall., 1972; Laing Art Gall., Newcastle upon Tyne, 1977; Manchester Polytechnic, 1977. *Publications:* Eye for Colour, 1965; Design Matters, 1976. *Recreations:* reading, tennis, walking. *Address:* High Sunderland, Galashiels, Selkirkshire. *T:* Selkirk 20730.

KLEIN, Prof. Lawrence Robert; economist; Benjamin Franklin Professor, University of Pennsylvania, since 1968; *b* Omaha, 14 Sept. 1920; *s* of Leo Byron Klein and Blanche Monheit; *m* 1947, Sonia Adelson; one *s* three *d*. *Educ:* Univ. of Calif at Berkeley (BA); MIT (PhD 1944); Lincoln Coll., Oxford (MA 1957). Chicago Univ., 1944-47; Nat. Bureau of Econ. Res., Mass, 1948-50; Michigan Univ., 1949-54; Oxford Inst. of Stats, 1954-58; Prof., 1958, University Prof., 1964, Univ. of Pennsylvania. Consultant: UNCTAD, 1966, 1967, 1975; UNIDO, 1973-75; Congressional Budget Office, 1977-; Council of Econ. Advisers, 1977-. Mem., Commn on Prices, Fed. Res. Bd, 1968-70. Member: Adv. Bd, Strategic Studies Center, Stanford Res. Inst., 1974-76; Adv. Council, Inst. for Advanced Studies, Vienna, 1977-. Fellow: Econometric Soc. (past Pres.); Amer. Acad. of Arts and Scis; Mem., Nat. Acad. of Scis. William F. Butler Award, NY Assoc. of Business Economists, 1975; Nobel Prize for Economics, 1980. *Publications:* The Keynesian Revolution, 1947; Textbook of Econometrics, 1953; An Econometric Model of the United States 1929-52, 1955; Wharton Econometric Forecasting Model, 1967; Essay on the Theory of Economic Prediction, 1968; (ed) Econometric Model Performance, 1976. *Address:* 1317 Medford Road, Wynnewood, Pa 19096, USA; University of Pennsylvania, Philadelphia, Pa 19104, USA.

KLEIN, Prof. Rudolf Ewald; Professor of Social Policy, University of Bath, since 1978; *b* 26 Aug. 1930; *o s* of Robert and Martha Klein; *m* 1957, Josephine Parfitt; one *d*. *Educ:* Bristol Grammar Sch.; Merton Coll., Oxford (Postmaster) (Gibbs Schol. 1950; MA). Leader Writer, London Evening Standard, 1952-62; Editor, 'The Week', Leader Writer, Home Affairs Editor, The Observer, 1962-72; Research Associate, Organisation of Medical Care Unit, London Sch. of Hygiene and Tropical Medicine, 1972-73; Sen. Fellow, Centre for Studies in Social Policy, 1973-78. Member: Wiltshire AHA, 1980-82; Bath DHA, 1982-. Jt Editor, Political Quarterly, 1981-. *Publications:* Complaints Against Doctors, 1973; (ed) Social Policy and Public Expenditure, 1974; (ed) Inflation and Priorities, 1975; (with Janet Lewis) The Politics of Consumer Representation, 1976; The Politics of the NHS, 1983; papers on public policy, health policy and public expenditure in various jls. *Recreations:* opera, cooking, football. *Address:* 3 Macaulay Buildings, Widcombe Hill, Bath BA2 6AS. *T:* Bath 310774. *Club:* United Oxford & Cambridge University.

KLEINDIENST, Richard Gordon; attorney; *b* 5 Aug. 1923; *s* of Alfred R. Kleindienst and late Gladys Love, Massachusetts; *m* 1948, Margaret Dunbar; two *s* two *d*. *Educ:* Harvard Coll. (*Phi Beta Kappa, magna cum laude*); Harvard Law Sch. Associate and Partner of Jennings, Strouss, Salmon & Trask, Phoenix, Arizona, 1950-57; Sen. Partner of Shimmel, Hill, Kleindienst & Bishop, 1958-Jan. 1969. Dep. Attorney-Gen. of the US, Jan. 1969-Feb. 1972; Actg Attorney-Gen. of the US, Feb. 1972-June 1972; Attorney-Gen. of the US, 1972-73, resigned 1973; private practice of law, Washington DC, 1973-75. Pres., Federal Bar Assoc., US, 1972- (was Pres. elect, Oct. 1971-72); Mem. Amer. Bar Assoc., Labor Section. Hon. Dr of Laws, Susquehanna Univ., 1973. *Recreations:* golf, chess, classical music, art. *Address:* (home) 6138 W Miramar, Tucson, Arizona 85715, USA. *T:* 602-885-3150.

KLEINPOPPEN, Prof. Hans Johann Willi; Professor of Experimental Physics, University of Stirling, since 1968 (Head of Physics Department, 1970-73); Director of Institute of Atomic Physics, University of Stirling, since 1975; *b* Duisburg, Germany, 30 Sept. 1928; *m* 1958, Renate Schröder. *Educ:* Univ. of Giessen (Dipl. Physics); Univ. of Tübingen. Dr re.nat. 1961. Habilitation, Tübingen, 1966; Vis. Fellow, Univ. Colorado, 1967-68; Vis. Associate Prof., Columbia Univ., 1968; Fellow, Center for Theoretical Studies, Univ. of Miami, 1972-73; Guest Prof., Bielefeld Univ.; Vis. Fellow, Zentrum für interdisziplinäre Forschung, Bielefeld Univ., 1979-80. Chairman: Internat. Symposium on Physics of One- and Two-Electron Atoms (Arnold Sommerfeld Centennial Meml Meeting, Munich 1968); Internat. Symposium on Electron and Photon Interactions with Atoms, in honour of Ugo Fano, Stirling, 1974; Internat. Workshop on Coherence and Correlation in Atomic Collisions, University Coll., London, 1978; Internat. Symp. on Amplitudes and State Parameters in Atomic Collisions, Kyoto, 1979; Co-Dir, Internat. Summer Sch. on Fundamental Processes in Energetic Atomic Collisions, Maratea, Italy, 1982. FInstP 1969; Fellow Amer. Physical Soc. 1969; FRAS 1974. *Publications:* (ed with F. Bopp) Physics of the One- and Two-Electron Atoms, 1969; (ed with M. R. C. McDowell) Electron and Photon Interactions with Atoms, 1976; (ed with W. Hanle) Progress in Atomic Spectroscop, Vol. I 1978, Vol. II 1979; (ed with J. F. Williams) Coherence and Correlations in Atomic Collisions, 1980; (ed jtly) Inner-Shell and X-Ray Physics of Atoms and Solids; (with P. G. Burke) series editor, Physics of Atoms and Molecules; papers in Zeitschr. f. Physik, Z. f. Naturf., Z. f. Angew Physik, Physikalische Blätter, Physical Review, Jl of Physics, Physics Letters, Internat. Jl of Quantum Chemistry; Physics Reports, Advances of Atomic and Molecular Physics, Applied Physics. *Address:* Dunvegan Lodge, 10 Upper Glen Road, Bridge of Allan, Stirlingshire. *T:* Bridge of Allan 832067.

KLEINWORT, Sir Alexander Santiago, 2nd Bt, *cr* 1909; *b* 31 Oct. 1892; *e s* of Sir Alexander D. Kleinwort, 1st Bt; *S* father, 1935; *m* 1938, Yvonne, *d* of late John Bloch. *Educ:* St John's Coll., Oxford. *Heir: nephew* Kenneth Drake Kleinwort [*b* 28 May 1935; *m* 1st, 1959, Lady Davina Rose Pepys (*d* 1973) *d* of 7th Earl of Cottenham; one *s* one *d* ; 2nd, 1973, Madeleine Hamilton, *e d* of Ralph Taylor; two *s* one *d*]. *Address:* 1 Third Avenue, Hove, East Sussex. *T:* Hove 71752.

KLEVAN, Rodney Conrad; a Recorder of the Crown Court, since 1980; *b* 23 May 1940; *s* of Sidney Leopold Klevan and late Florence Klevan (*née* Eaton); *m* 1968, Susan Rebecca (*née* Lighthill); two *s* one *d. Educ:* Temple Primary School; Manchester Central Grammar School; Birmingham Univ. (LLB Hons 1962). Pres., Birmingham Univ. Guild of Undergraduates, 1962-63. Called to the Bar, Gray's Inn, 1966; Deputy Circuit Judge, 1977. *Recreations:* theatre and television. *Address:* Beech House, 45 Manor Road, Bramhall, Stockport, Cheshire. *T:* 061-485 1847.

KLIBANSKY, Raymond, MA, PhD; Frothingham Professor of Logic and Metaphysics, McGill University, Montreal, 1946-75, now Emeritus Professor; Extraordinary Fellow of Wolfson College, Oxford, since 1981; *b* Paris, 15 Oct. 1905; *s* of late Hermann Klibansky. *Educ:* Paris; Odenwald Sch.; Univs of Kiel, Hamburg, Heidelberg. PhD, 1929; MA Oxon by decree, 1936. Asst, Heidelberg Acad., 1927-33; Lecturer in Philosophy: Heidelberg Univ., 1931-33; King's Coll., London, 1934-36; Oriel Coll., Oxford, 1936-48; Forwood Lectr in Philosophy of Religion, Univ. of Liverpool, 1938-39. Political Intelligence Dept, FO, 1941-46. Dir of Studies, Warburg Inst., Univ. of London, 1947-48. Vis. Prof. of History of Philosophy, Université de Montréal, 1947-68; Mahlon Powell Prof., Indiana Univ., 1950; Cardinal Mercier Prof. of Philosophy, Univ. of Louvain, 1956; Vis. Prof. of Philosophy, Univ. of Rome, 1961, Univ. of Genoa, 1964, Univ. of Tokyo, 1971; Prof. Emeritus, Heidelberg Univ., 1975-. President: Inst. Internat. de Philosophie, Paris, 1966-69 (Hon. Pres. 1969-); Société Internationale pour l'étude de la Philos. Médiévale, Louvain, 1968-72 (Hon. Pres., 1972-); Canadian Soc. for History and Philosophy of Science, 1959-72 (Pres. Emeritus, 1972-); Internat. Cttee for Anselm Studies, 1970-. FRSC; FRHistS; Fellow: Accademia Nazionale dei Lincei, Rome; Acad. of Athens; Académie Internationale d'Histoire des Sciences, Paris; Iranian Acad. of Philosophy, Teheran; Corresponding Fellow: Mediaeval Acad. of America; Heidelberg Acad. of Scis. Hon. Member: Allgemeine Gesellsch. für Philosophie in Deutschland; Assoc. des Scientifiques de Roumanie, Bucarest. Hon. Fellow: Oriel Coll., Oxford; Warburg Inst., Univ. of London; Accad. Ligure delle Scienze, Genoa. Guggenheim Foundation Fellow, 1954 and 1965; Vis. Fellow, Wolfson Coll., Oxford, 1976-78. Dir, Canadian Academic Centre in Italy, Rome, 1980. Mem. Exec. Council, Union Académique Internationale, 1978-80. Comité Directeur, Fedn Internat. des Socs de Philosophie, 1958-. DPhil *hc* Ottawa. Gen. Editor, Corpus Platonicum Medii Aevi, Union Académique Internat., 1937-; Joint Editor: Magistri Eckardi Opera Latina, 1933-36; Philosophy and History, 1936; Mediaeval and Renaissance Studies, 1941-68; Editor: Philosophical Texts, 1951-62; Philosophy and World Community, 1957-81; Philosophy in the Mid-Century, 1958-59; Contemporary Philosophy, 1968-71. *Publications:* Ein Proklos-Fund und seine Bedeutung, 1929; Heidelberg Acad. edn of Opera Nicolai de Cusa, 5 vols, 1929-82; The Continuity of the Platonic Tradition, 1939, enlarged edn incl. Plato's Parmenides in the Middle Ages and the Renaissance, 1981; (with E. Panofsky and F. Saxl) Saturn and Melancholy, 1964; articles in Jahresberichte d. Heidelberger Akademie, Proceedings of British Acad., Enciclopedia Italiana, and elsewhere. *Address:* McGill University, Montreal, Canada; Wolfson College, Oxford OX2 6UD.

KLIEN, Walter; musician (concert pianist); soloist with leading conductors and orchestras; *b* 27 Nov. 1928. *Educ:* Frankfurt-am-Main; Vienna. Concert tours in: Europe, USA, Canada, South America, South Africa, Far East. Many recordings, which include complete solo-works by Mozart and Brahms, also the complete Schubert Sonatas. *Address:* c/o Harold Holt Ltd, 122 Wigmore Street, W1.

KLUG, Aaron, PhD (Cantab); FRS 1969; Joint Head, Division of Structural Studies, Medical Research Council Laboratory of Molecular Biology, Cambridge, since 1978 (member of staff, since 1962); Fellow of Peterhouse, since 1962; *b* 11 Aug. 1926; *s* of Lazar Klug and Bella Silin; *m* 1948, Liebe Bobrow, Cape Town, SA; two *s. Educ:* Durban High Sch.; Univ. of the Witwatersrand (BSc); Univ. of Cape Town (MSc). Junior Lecturer, 1947-48; Research Student, Cavendish Laboratory, Cambridge, 1949-52; Rouse-Ball Research Studentship, Trinity Coll., Cambridge, 1949-52; Colloid Science Dept, Cambridge, 1953; Nuffield Research Fellow, Birkbeck Coll., London, 1954-57; Dir, Virus Structure Research Group, Birkbeck Coll., 1958-61. Lectures: Leeuwenhoek, Royal Soc., 1973; Dunham, Harvard Medical Sch., 1975; Harvey, NY, 1979. Hon. DSc: Chicago, 1978; Columbia Univ., 1978;

Dr *hc* Strasbourg, 1978; Hon. Dr Fil. Stockholm, 1980. Foreign Hon. Mem., Amer. Acad. of Arts and Sciences, 1969. Heineken Prize, Royal Netherlands Acad. of Science, 1979; Louisa Gross Horwitz Prize, Columbia Univ., 1981; Nobel Prize in Chemistry, 1982. *Publications:* papers in scientific jls. *Recreations:* reading, gardening. *Address:* 70 Cavendish Avenue, Cambridge. *T:* 248959.

KLYNE, Barbara Evelyn, (Mrs William Klyne); *see* Clayton, B. E.

KNAGGS, Kenneth James, CMG 1971; OBE 1959; Consultant, Commonwealth Development Corporation, since 1974; *b* 3 July 1920; *e s* of late James Henry Knaggs and Elsie Knaggs (*née* Walton); *m* 1945, Barbara, *d* of late Ernest James Page; two *s. Educ:* St Paul's Sch., London. Served War, 1939-46 (Major). Northern Rhodesia Civil Service, 1946; Sec. to Govt Seychelles, 1955; Northern Rhodesia: Asst Sec., 1960; Under Sec., 1961; Permanent Sec., Min. of Finance and subseq. the same in Zambia, 1964; retd 1970. European Rep. and Manager, Zambia Airways, 1970-72. *Recreations:* walking, gardening, languages, cooking. *Address:* High House Farm, Earl Soham, near Framlingham, Suffolk IP13 7SN. *T:* Earl Soham 416.

KNAPMAN, Dr Paul Anthony; HM Coroner for Westminster, since 1980 (Jurisdiction of Inner West London); *b* 5 Nov. 1944; *s* of Mr and Mrs F. E. Knapman; *m* 1970, Penelope Jane Cox; one *s* three *d. Educ:* Epsom Coll.; King's Coll., London; St George's Hosp. Med. Sch. (MB, BS 1968). MRCS, LRCP 1968; DMJ 1975. Called to the Bar, Gray's Inn, 1972. Dep. Coroner for Inner W London, 1975-80. Hon. Lectr in Med. Jurisprudence: St George's Hosp. Med. Sch., 1978-; St Thomas's Hosp. Med. Sch., 1980-; Westminster Hosp. Med. Sch., 1981-; Middlesex Hosp. Med. Sch., 1981-; St Mary's Hosp. Med. Sch., 1981-. Pres., S Eastern England Coroners' Soc., 1980. Yeoman, Worshipful Soc. of Apothecaries, 1980. *Publications:* papers on medico-legal subjects. *Recreations:* squash, sailing. *Address:* Westminster Coroner's Court, Horseferry Road, SW1P 2ED. *T:* 01-834 6515. *Clubs:* Athenæum; Royal Torbay Yacht.

KNAPP, David; *see* Knapp, J. D.

KNAPP, Edward Ronald, CBE 1979; Managing Director, Timken Europe, since 1973; *b* 10 May 1919; *s* of Percy Charles and Elsie Maria Knapp; *m* 1942, Vera Mary Stephenson; two *s* two *d. Educ:* Cardiff High Sch.; St Catharine's Coll., Cambridge (MA 1940); Harvard Business Sch. (AMP 1954). Served RNVR, Special Branch, Lt-Comdr, 1940-46: HMS Aurora, 1941-44; US Naval Research, Anacostia, 1944-46. Joined British Timken, 1946, Man. Dir, 1969; Dir, Timken Co., USA, 1976. Technical and Management Educnl Governor, Nene Coll., 1953-; Vice-Chm., Regional Adv. Council for Organisation of Further Educn, 1978-. *Recreations:* gardening, golf; played Rugby for Wales, 1940, Captain of Cambridge Univ. 1940 and Northampton RFC, 1948. *Address:* The Elms, 1 Millway, Duston, Northampton NN5 6ER. *T:* Northampton 584737. *Clubs:* East India, Devonshire, Sports and Public Schools, Naval; Northampton and County; Hawks (Cambridge).

KNAPP, (John) David; Director of Conservative Political Centre, since 1975; an Assistant Director, Conservative Research Department, since 1979; *b* 27 Oct. 1926; *s* of late Eldred Arthur Knapp and Elizabeth Jane Knapp; *m* 1st, 1954, Dorothy Ellen May (*née* Squires) (marr. diss.); one *s* ; 2nd, 1980, Daphne Monard, OBE, *widow* of Major S. H. Monard. *Educ:* Dauntsey's Sch., Wilts; King's Coll., London (BA Hons). Vice-Chm., Fedn of University Conservative and Unionist Assoc., 1948-49; Conservative Agent, Rochester and Chatham, 1951-52; Conservative Publicity and Political Educn Officer, Northern Area, 1952-56; Political Educn Officer, NW Area, 1956-61, and Home Counties N Area, 1961; Dep. Dir, Conservative Political Centre, 1962-75. *Recreations:* philately, listening to classical music. *Address:* 71 Kirby Road, Portsmouth, Hants PO2 0PF. *T:* Portsmouth 663709. *Club:* St Stephen's Constitutional.

KNAPP-FISHER, Rt. Rev. and Ven. Edward George; Sub-Dean since 1982, and Archdeacon since 1975, of Westminster; Canon of Westminster since 1975; an Assistant Bishop, Diocese of Southwark, since 1975, also Diocese of London, since 1976; *b* 8 Jan. 1915; *s* of late Rev. George Edwin Knapp-Fisher and of Agatha Knapp-Fisher; *m* 1965, Joan, *d* of late R. V. Bradley. *Educ:* King's School, Worcester; Trinity College, Oxford. Assistant Curate of Brighouse, Yorks, 1939; Chaplain, RNVR, 1942; Chaplain of Cuddesdon College, 1946; Chaplain of St John's College, Cambridge, 1949; Vicar of Cuddesdon and Principal of Cuddesdon Theological College, 1952-60; Bishop of Pretoria, 1960-75. Member, Anglican Roman-Catholic Preparatory Commission, 1967-68; Member, Anglican-Roman Catholic Internat. Commn, 1969-81. *Publications:* The Churchman's Heritage, 1952; Belief and Prayer, 1964; To be or not to be, 1968; Where the Truth is Found, 1975; (ed jtly and contrib.) Towards Unity in Truth, 1981. *Recreations:* walking, travel. *Address:* 1 Little Cloister, Westminster Abbey, SW1. *T:* 01-222 4027.

KNARESBOROUGH, Bishop Suffragan of, since 1979; **Rt. Rev. John Dennis;** Diocesan Director of Ordinands, Diocese of Ripon, since 1980; Episcopal Guardian of Anglican Focolarini, since 1981; *b* 19 June 1931; *s* of Hubert Ronald and Evelyn Dennis; *m* 1956, Dorothy Mary (*née* Hinnels); two *s. Educ:* Rutlish School, Merton; St Catharine's Coll., Cambridge (BA 1954; MA 1959); Cuddesdon Coll., Oxford (1954-56). RAF, 1950-51. Curate, St Bartholomew's, Armley, Leeds, 1956-60; Curate of Kettering, 1960-62;

Vicar of the Isle of Dogs, 1962-71; Vicar of John Keble, Mill Hill, 1971-79; Area Dean of West Barnet, 1973-79; Prebendary of St Paul's Cathedral, 1977-79. *Recreations:* walking, gardening, wood working. *Address:* 16 Shaftesbury Avenue, Leeds LS8 1DT. *T:* Leeds 664800.

KNATCHBULL, family name of **Baron Brabourne** and **Countess Mountbatten of Burma**.

KNEALE, (Robert) Bryan (Charles), RA 1974 (ARA 1970); sculptor; *b* 19 June 1930; *m* 1956, Doreen Lister; one *s* one *d. Educ:* Douglas High Sch.; Douglas Sch. of Art, IOM; Royal Academy Schools: Rome prize, 1949-51; RA diploma. Tutor, RCA Sculpture Sch., 1964-; Head of Sculpture Sch., Hornsey, 1967; Assoc. Lectr, Chelsea Sch. of Art, 1970. Fellow RCA, 1972, Senior Tutor, RCA, 1980-; Master of Sculpture, RA, 1982-. Member: Fine Art Panels, NCAD, 1964-71, Arts Council, 1971-73, CNAA, 1974-82; Chm., Air and Space, 1972-73. *Organised:* Sculpture '72, RA, 1972; Battersea Park Silver Jubilee Sculpture, 1977 (also exhibited); Sade Exhbn, Cork, 1982. *Exhibitions:* at Redfern Gallery, 1954, 1956, 1958, 1960, 1962, 1964, 1967, 1970, 1976, 1978, 1981; John Moores, 1961; Sixth Congress of Internat. Union of Architects, 1961; Art Aujourd'hui, Paris, 1963; Battersea Park Sculpture, 1963, 1966; Profile III Bochum, 1964; British Sculpture in the Sixties, Tate Gall., 1965; Whitechapel Gall. 1966 (Retrospective), 1981; Structure, Cardiff Metamorphis Coventry, 1966; New British Painting and Sculpture, 1967-68; City of London Festival, 1968; Holland Park, Sculpture in the Cities, Southampton, and British Sculptors, RA, 1972; Holland Park, 1973; Royal Exchange Sculpture Exhibition, 1974; New Art, Hayward Gallery, 1975; Sculpture at Worksop, 1976; Taranman Gall., 1977, 1981; Serpentine Gall., 1978; Monumental Sculpture for Manx Millenium, Ronaldsway, Isle of Man, 1979; Compass Gall., Glasgow, 1981; 51 Gall., Edinburgh, 1981; Bath Art Fair, 1981. Arts Council Tours, 1966-71. *Collections:* Arts Council of Gt Britain; Contemp. Art Soc.; Manx Museum; Leics Educn Authority; Nat. Galls of Victoria, S Australia and New Zealand; City Art Galls, York, Nottingham, Manchester, Bradford and Leicester; Tate Gall.; Beaverbrook Foundn, Fredericton; Museum of Modern Art, Sao Paulo, Brazil; Bahia Museum, Brazil; Oriel Coll., Oxford; Museum of Modern Art, New York; City Galleries, Middlesbrough, Birmingham, Wakefield; Fitzwilliam Museum, Cambridge; W Riding Educn Authority; Unilever House Collection. *Address:* 7 Winthorpe Road, SW15. *T:* 01-788 0869.

KNEALE, Prof. William Calvert, FBA 1950; White's Professor of Moral Philosophy, University of Oxford, and Fellow of Corpus Christi College, 1960-66; *b* 22 June 1906; *s* of late William Kneale; *m* 1938, Martha Hurst, Fellow of Lady Margaret Hall, Oxford; one *s* one *d. Educ:* Liverpool Institute; Brasenose Coll., Oxford (Classical Scholar). Senior Hulme Scholar, Brasenose Coll., 1927, studied in Freiburg and Paris; Asst in Mental Philosophy, University of Aberdeen, 1929; Asst Lecturer in Philosophy, Armstrong Coll., Newcastle upon Tyne, 1931; Lecturer in Philosophy, Exeter Coll., Oxford, 1932; Fellow, 1933-60; Senior Tutor, 1945-50; Emeritus Fellow, 1960. War of 1939-45, temp. Civil Servant, Ministry of Shipping (later War Transport). Vice-Pres., British Acad., 1971-72. Hon. Fellow, Brasenose Coll., Oxford, 1962, and Corpus Christi Coll., Oxford, 1966. Hon. LLD Aberdeen, 1960; Hon. DLitt: Durham, 1966; St Andrews, 1973. *Publications:* Probability and Induction, 1949; (with M. Kneale) The Development of Logic, 1962; On Having a Mind, 1962; articles in Mind, Proceedings of Aristotelian Society, etc. *Address:* 4 Bridge End, Grassington, near Skipton, North Yorks. *T:* Grassington 752710.

KNEBWORTH, Viscount; John Peter Michael Scawen Lytton; *b* 7 June 1950; *s* and *heir* of 4th Earl of Lytton, *qv*; *m* 1980, Ursula Alexandra (*née* Komoly). *Educ:* Downside; Reading Univ. (BSc, Estate Management). ARICS 1976. *Address:* Lillycombe, Porlock, Somerset. *T:* Porlock 862353.

KNEIPP, Hon. Sir (Joseph Patrick) George, Kt 1982; a Judge of the Supreme Court of Queensland, since 1969; Chancellor, James Cook University of North Queensland, since 1974; *b* 13 Nov. 1922; *s* of A. G. Kneipp and K. B. McHugh; *m* 1948, Ada Joan Crawford Cattermole; two *s* one *d. Educ:* Downlands Coll., Toowoomba; Univ. of Queensland (LLB). Called to the Queensland Bar, 1950; in practice as Barrister-at-Law, 1950-69. *Recreations:* reading, gardening. *Address:* 20 Kenilworth Avenue, Hyde Park, Townsville, Qld 4812, Australia. *T:* 794652. *Clubs:* North Queensland, James Cook University, Townsville Turf, North Queensland Amateur, Townsville Golf (Queensland).

KNELL, Rt. Rev. Eric Henry, MA Oxon; *b* 1 April 1903; *s* of Edward Henry and Edith Helen Knell; unmarried. *Educ:* Trinity College, Oxford. Assistant Curate of St Barnabas, Southfields, 1928; Domestic Chaplain to Bishop of Lincoln, 1933; in charge of Trinity College, Oxford, Mission in Stratford, E15, 1936; Vicar of Emmanuel, Forest Gate, 1941; Vicar of Christ Church, Reading, 1945; Archdeacon of Berkshire, 1955-67; Suffragan Bishop of Reading, 1955-72; Assistant Bishop, Diocese of Oxford, 1972-75. *Address:* College of St Barnabas, Lingfield, Surrey.

KNIGHT, Sir Allan Walton, Kt 1970; CMG 1960; FIE (Aust.); Commissioner, The Hydro-Electric Commission, Tasmania, 1946-77; Chief Commissioner, Tasman Bridge Restoration Commission, 1975-80; *b* 26 Feb. 1910; *s* of late Mr and Mrs G. W. Knight, Lindisfarne, Tasmania; *m* 1936, Margaret Janet Buchanan; two *s* one *d. Educ:* Hobart Technical Coll.; University of Tasmania. Diploma of Applied Science, 1929; BSc 1932; ME

1935; BCom 1946. Chief Engineer, Public Works Dept, Tasmania, 1937-46. Member: Australian Univs Commn, 1966-74; Council, Tasmanian Coll. of Advanced Education, 1968-75. Peter Nicol Russell Medal, Instn of Engrs of Australia, 1963; William Kernot Medal, Univ. of Melbourne, 1963; Wilfred Chapman Award, Inst. of Welding, Australia, 1974; John Storey Medal, Inst. of Management, Australia, 1975. *Recreation:* royal tennis. *Address:* 64 Waimea Avenue, Hobart, Tasmania 7005, Australia. *T:* Hobart 251498. *Club:* Tasmanian (Hobart).

KNIGHT, Andrew Stephen Bower; Editor, The Economist, since 1974; *b* 1 Nov. 1939; *s* of M. W. B. Knight and S. E. F. Knight; *m* 1st, 1966, Victoria Catherine Brittain (marr. diss.); one *s* (Casimir); 2nd, 1975, Begum Sabiha Rumani Malik; two *d. Educ:* Ampleforth Coll.; Balliol Coll., Oxford. Joined J. Henry Schroder Wagg & Co., 1961; Investors Chronicle, 1964; The Economist, 1966. Member: Council, Chatham House, 1976-; Core Cttee, British exec. of IPI, 1978-; Steering Cttee, Bilderberg meetings, 1980-. Governor: Imp. Coll. of Science and Technology, 1977-; Ditchley Foundn, 1981-. *Address:* 25 St James's Street, SW1. *Clubs:* Brooks's, Royal Automobile.

KNIGHT, Sir Arthur (William), Kt 1975; Chairman, National Enterprise Board, 1979-80; Chairman, Courtaulds Ltd, 1975-79; *b* 29 March 1917; *s* of Arthur Frederick Knight and Emily Scott; *m* 1st, 1945, Beatrice Joan Osborne (*née* Oppenheim) (*d* 1968); one *s* three *d*; 2nd, 1972, Sheila Elsie Whiteman. *Educ:* Tottenham County Sch.; London Sch. of Economics (evening student) (BCom). J. Sainsbury, Blackfriars, 1933-38; LSE, Dept of Business Admin (Leverhulme Studentship), 1938-39; Courtaulds, 1939. Served War, Army, 1940-46. Courtaulds, 1946-: apptd Dir, 1958; Finance Dir, 1961. Non-exec. Director: Pye Holdings, 1972-75; Rolls-Royce (1971), 1973-78; Richard Thomas & Baldwin, 1966-67; Dunlop Holdings, 1981-. Member: Council of Manchester Business Sch., 1964-71; Cttee for Arts and Social Studies of Council for Nat. Academic Awards, 1965-71; Commn of Enquiry into siting of Third London Airport, 1968-70; Council of Industry for Management Educn, 1970-73; Finance Cttee, RIIA, 1971-75; Council, RIIA, 1975-; Court of Governors, London Sch. of Economics, 1971-; Economic Cttee, CBI, 1965-72; Cairncross (Channel Tunnel) Cttee, 1974-75; NIESR Exec. Cttee, 1976-; BOTB, 1978-79. *Publications:* Private Enterprise and Public Intervention: the Courtauld experience, 1974; various papers. *Recreations:* walking, sailing, music, reading. *Address:* Charlton End, Singleton, West Sussex PO18 0HX. *Club:* Reform.

KNIGHT, Brian Joseph; QC 1981; practising barrister, since 1966; *b* 5 May 1941; *s* of Joseph Knight and Vera Lorraine Knight (*née* Docksey); *m* 1967, Cristina Karen Wang Nobrega de Lima. *Educ:* Colbayns High Sch., Clacton; University Coll. London. LLB 1962, LLM 1963. Called to the Bar, Gray's Inn, 1964; ad eundem Lincoln's Inn, 1979; called to the Bar of Hong Kong, 1978, of Northern Ireland, 1979. *Address:* 22 Old Buildings, Lincoln's Inn, WC2A 3UJ. *T:* 01-405 2072. *Club:* Carlton.

KNIGHT, Charles, RWS 1935 (VPRWS 1961-64; ARWS 1933); ROI 1933; Landscape Painter and Designer; Vice-Principal, Brighton College of Art and Crafts, 1959-67, retired; *b* 27 Aug. 1901; *s* of Charles and Evelyn Mary Knight; *m* 1934, Leonora Vasey (*d* 1970); one *s*. Art training, Brighton Coll. of Art; Royal Academy Schools, London (Turner Gold Medal); works in permanent collections, London, British Museum, Victoria and Albert Museum, Sheffield, Leeds, Hull, Oxford, Brighton, Hove, Eastbourne, Preston, etc; regular exhibitor RA, 1924-65. Illustrated monograph by Michael Brockway, 1952. *Address:* Chettles, 34 Beacon Road, Ditchling, Sussex. *T:* Hassocks 3998.

KNIGHT, Edmund Alan; European Affairs Adviser to British-American Tobacco Company Ltd, since 1978; *b* 17 June 1919; *s* of Arthur Philip and Charlotte Knight; *m* 1953, Annette Ros Grimmitt; one *d. Educ:* Drayton Manor Sch.; London Sch. of Economics. Entered Exchequer and Audit Dept, 1938; HM Customs and Excise, 1948; Asst Sec., 1957; Sec. to Cttee on Turnover Taxation, 1963-64; seconded to Inland Revenue, 1969-71; Comr of Customs and Excise, 1971-77. Member: SITPRO Bd, 1971-76; EDC for Internat. Freight Movement, 1971-76; Taxation and Trade Cttee, Tobacco Adv. Council, 1978-. *Recreation:* gardening. *Address:* 40 Park Avenue North, Harpenden, Herts. *Club:* Royal Commonwealth Society.

KNIGHT, Eric John Percy Crawford L.; see Lombard Knight.

KNIGHT, Esmond Pennington; actor; *b* 4 May 1906; 3rd *s* of Francis and Bertha Knight; *m* 1st, 1929, Frances Clare (marr. diss.); one *d*; 2nd, 1946, Nora Swinburne, *qv. Educ:* Willington Prep. Sch.; Westminster. Made first appearance on stage at Pax Robertson's salon in Ibsen's Wild Duck, 1925; Old Vic., 1925-27; Birmingham Repertory Co., 1927-28; Contraband, Prince's Theatre; To What Red Hell, Wyndham's, 1928; The Children's Theatre; Fashion, Kingsway; Maya, Studio des Théâtres des Champs-Elysées, Paris, 1929; Art and Mrs Bottle, Royalty; Hamlet, Queen's, 1930; Salome, Gate; Waltzes from Vienna, Alhambra, 1931; Wild Violets, Drury Lane, 1932; Three Sisters, Drury Lane; Streamline, Palace, 1934; Wise Tomorrow, Lyric; Van Gogh, Arts Theatre Club; Night Must Fall, Cambridge Theatre, 1936; The Insect Play, Little; The King and Mistress Shore, Little, 1937; Crest of the Wave, Tour; Twelfth Night, Phœnix, 1938; in management with Wilson Barrett, King's, Hammersmith and Edinburgh, 1939; Peaceful Inn, Duke of York's; Midsummer Night's Dream, Open Air, 1940. Joined RNVR (HMS

King Alfred, Drake, Excellent, Prince of Wales); discharged from Navy as a result of being blinded in HMS Prince of Wales during action with Bismarck, 1941. Returned to stage in Crisis in Heaven, March 1945; shared lead with Evelyn Laye in The Three Waltzes, Princes. Season of plays with travelling Repertory Theatre, King's, Hammersmith, 1946; The Relapse, 1947; Memorial Theatre, Stratford-on-Avon, 1948-49; Caroline (by Maugham), Arts Theatre Club; Old Vic Co., Edinburgh Festival, 1950, in Bartholomew Fair by Ben Jonson; Who is Sylvia, Criterion, 1950; Sir Laurence Olivier's Festival Season, St James's Theatre, 1951; Heloise, Duke of York's; Montserrat, Lyric; Bermuda Festival (Bermuda); Emperor's Clothes (New York); Age of Consent; Bell, Book and Candle, Phœnix, 1955; The Caine Mutiny, Hippodrome, 1956; The Country Wife, Adelphi, 1957; The Russian, Lyric, Hammersmith, 1958; A Piece of Silver (Cheltenham), 1960; The Lady from the Sea, Queen's, 1961; Becket, Taming of the Shrew, Aldwych, 1961; Two Stars for Comfort, Garrick, 1962; Last Old Vic Season, 1962-63; Season, Mermaid, 1965; Edinburgh Festival: Winter's Tale, and Trojan Women 1966; Getting Married, Strand, 1967; Greenwich Theatre: Martin Luther King, 1969; Spithead, 1969; The Servants and the Snow, 1970; Mister, Duchess, 1971; Family Reunion, '69 Theatre Co., Manchester, 1973, Vaudeville, 1979; The Cocktail Party, '69 Theatre Co., Manchester, 1975; Loves Old Sweet Song, Greenwich, 1976; Three Sisters, Cambridge, 1976; Henry V and Agincourt, The Archer's Tale, Open Air Theatre, 1976; Crime and Punishment, Royal Exchange, Manchester, and City of Munster Fest., 1978; Family Reunion, Royal Exchange, Manchester, The Round House and Vaudeville, 1979; Hamlet, Young Vic, 1982. *Films:* Romany Love, 77 Park Lane, The Ringer, Pagliacci, Waltzes from Vienna, Black Roses (Ufa, Berlin), What Men Live By, The Bermondsey Kid, The Blue Squadron, Girls Will Be Boys, Dandy Dick, Someday, Crime Unlimited, Contraband, The Silver Fleet, Half-Way House, King Henry V, A Canterbury Tale, Black Narcissus, Hamlet, Red Shoes, Gone to Earth, The River, 1950, Helen of Troy (Rome), 1954, The Dark Avenger, Ratcliffe in Olivier's Richard III, The Sleeping Prince, On Secret Service, Battle of the V1; Sink the Bismarck; The Spy Who Came in From the Cold; Anne of the Thousand Days; Where's Jack, 1968; The Boy who turned Yellow; The Yellow Dog; Robin and Marian, 1975. Assisted in making several Natural History films. *Television:* has appeared frequently on BBC and Independent Television, notably in Dickens and Ibsen; Dr Finlay's Casebook; Elizabeth I; The Pallisers; Fall of Eagles; History of the English-speaking Peoples; Shades of Greene; Ballet Shoes; Quiller; I Claudius; 1900: Voices from the Past; Kilvert's Diaries; Supernatural; Romeo and Juliet; Rebecca; Nelson; The Borgias; Troilus and Cressida; My Cousin Rachel; Drake's Venture, and other plays. Also tours with his one man show: Agincourt—The Archer's Tale. *Publications:* Seeking the Bubble (Autobiography), 1943; Story in Blackwood's, Jan. 1942; various articles in daily and weekly Press. *Recreation:* painting. *Address:* c/o Norman Boyack, 9 Cork Street, W1X 1PD. *T:* 01-734 2858. *Club:* Savage.

KNIGHT, Geoffrey Cureton, MB, BS London; FRCS; FRCPsych; Consulting Neurological Surgeon in London, since 1935; Hon. Consultant Neurosurgeon: West End Hospital for Neurology and Neurosurgery; SE Metropolitan Regional Neurosurgical Centre; Royal Postgraduate Medical School of London; Teacher of Surgery, University of London; *b* 4 Oct. 1906; *s* of Cureton Overbeck Knight; *m* 1933, Betty, *d* of Francis Cooper Havell, London; two *s. Educ:* Brighton Coll.; St Bartholomew's Hosp. Medical Sch. Brackenbury Surgical Schol. St Bart's Hosp., 1930. Ho. Surg. and Chief Asst, Surgical Professorial Unit at St Bart's Hosp.; Demonstrator in Physiology, St Bart's Hosp. Medical Sch.; Leverhulme Research Scholar, Royal College of Surgeons, 1933-35; Mackenzie Mackinnon Research Scholar, 1936-38; Bernard Baron Research Scholar, 1938; Hunterian Prof., 1935-36 and 1963. FRSocMed; Fellow Soc. Brit. Neurological Surgeons; Fellow Med. Soc. London; Vice-Pres., Internat. Soc. for Psychosurgery. Neurological Surg. Armed Forces of Czecho-Slovakia, 1941; Hon. Fellow, Czecho-Slovak Med. Soc., Prague, 1946; Officer, Order of the White Lion of Czecho-Slovakia, 1946. *Publications:* contrib. med. jls on aetiology and surgical treatment of diseases of the spine and nervous system and the surgical treatment of mental illness. *Recreations:* gardening, swimming. *Address:* 7 Aubrey Road, Campden Hill, W8. *T:* 01-727 7719 (Sec., 01-935 7549). *Club:* Hurlingham.

KNIGHT, Geoffrey Egerton, CBE 1970; Director, Guinness Peat Group plc, since 1976; Chairman: Guinness Peat Aviation Ltd, since 1977; St Mary at Hill Properties Ltd, since 1979; Fenchurch Insurance Holdings Ltd, since 1980; Director, Trafalgar House Public Limited Company, since 1980; *b* 25 Feb. 1921; *s* of Arthur Egerton Knight and Florence Gladys Knight (née Clarke); *m* 1947, Evelyn Bugle; two *d. Educ:* Stubbington House; Brighton Coll. Royal Marines, 1939-46. Joined British Aeroplane Co. 1952; Dir, Bristol Aircraft Ltd, 1956; Dir, BAC Ltd, 1964-77, Vice Chm., 1972-76. *Publication:* Concorde: the inside story, 1976. *Address:* 33 Smith Terrace, SW3. *T:* 01-352 5391. *Club:* Boodle's.

KNIGHT, Dr Geoffrey Wilfred; retired; Regional Medical Officer, North West Thames Regional Health Authority, 1973-76; *b* 10 Jan. 1920; *s* of Wilfred Knight and Ida Knight; *m* 1944, Christina Marion Collins Scott; one *s* one *d. Educ:* Leeds Univ. Med. Sch. MB, ChB, MD, DPH (Chadwick Gold Medal). County Med. Officer of Health, Herts, 1962-73. Formerly: Governor, Nat. Inst. of Social Work; Member: Personal Social Services Council; Central Midwives Bd; Exec. Cttee, Child Health Bureau; Adv. Panel, Soc. for Health Educn; formerly Mem., Govt Techn. and Sci. Cttee on Disposal of Toxic

Wastes. *Recreations:* painting, golf. *Address:* 4947 197A Street, Langley, BC V3A 6W1, Canada.

KNIGHT, Prof. (George Richard) Wilson, CBE 1968; MA Oxon; FRSL; FIAL; Professor of English Literature, Leeds University, 1956-62, now Emeritus (Reader in English Literature, Leeds University, 1946-56); *b* 19 Sept. 1897; *s* of George Knight and Caroline L. Jackson; brother of late W. F. Jackson Knight; unmarried. *Educ:* Dulwich Coll.; St Edmund Hall, Oxford. Served European War, Middle East; Master at Seaford House, Littlehampton, 1920, and St Peter's, Seaford, 1921; St Edmund Hall, 1922-23; Honour Sch. of English Language and Literature, 1923; Chess, Oxford *v* Cambridge, 1923; Master at Hawtreys, Westgate-on-Sea, 1923-25, and Dean Close Sch., Cheltenham, 1925-31; Chancellors' Prof. of English, Trinity Coll., University of Toronto, 1931-40; Master at Stowe, Buckingham, 1941-46. Stage: Shakespearian productions at Hart House Theatre, Toronto, 1932-40; produced and acted in: Hamlet, Rudolf Steiner Hall, London, 1935; This Sceptred Isle, Westminster Theatre, London, 1941; productions (Agamemnon, Athalie, Timon of Athens) and performances (Timon, Lear, Othello, Shylock) at Leeds Univ., 1946-60; Shakespeare's Dramatic Challenge, Northcott Theatre, Exeter, 1975 and 1976, and various other centres, 1976-82; including World Shakespeare Congress, Washington, 1976, Video-tape Yeovil Coll., 1979, and Indiana Univ., 1982. Lectures and lecture recitals since 1951: Cambridge (Clark Lectures), London, Nottingham (Byron Foundn Lecture), Canada, S Africa, USA and W Indies. BBC talks and readings on Shakespeare and Byron, 1963-64 and tape recordings (USA); joint-petitioner, Byron Memorial (Westminster Abbey, 1969); shareholder, Byron Soc. Jl, 1972. Sculpted by Robert Russin, USA, 1975, Kenneth Carter, Exeter, 1975 and Peter Thursby, Exeter, 1980. Mem., Internat. Adv. Cttee, World Shakespeare Congress, Vancouver, 1971; Powys Centenary, Cambridge, 1972. Pres., Devonshire Assoc., 1971; Hon. Vice-Pres., Spiritualist Assoc. of Great Britain, 1955; Hon. Life Pres., Dulwich Coll. Literary Soc., 1971; President: Powys Soc., 1981–; Interdiscipline Soc. (USA), 1981- (Hon. Pres., 1980). Hon. Fellow St Edmund Hall, Oxford, 1965; Hon. LittD Sheffield, 1966; Hon. DLitt Exon, 1968. Hon. Mem., Mark Twain Soc., 1976–, Hon. Chm., 1980–. *Publications:* Myth and Miracle, 1929; The Wheel of Fire, 1930; The Imperial Theme, 1931; The Shakespearian Tempest, 1932; The Christian Renaissance, 1933; Principles of Shakespearian Production, 1936; Atlantic Crossing, 1936; The Burning Oracle, 1939; This Sceptred Isle, 1940; The Starlit Dome, 1941; Chariot of Wrath, 1942; The Olive and the Sword, 1944; The Dynasty of Stowe, 1945; Hiroshima, 1946; The Crown of Life, 1947; Christ and Nietzsche, 1948; Lord Byron: Christian Virtues, 1952; Laureate of Peace, 1954; The Last of the Incas, 1954 (play, first prod. Sheffield, 1954; BBC 1974); The Mutual Flame, 1955; Lord Byron's Marriage, 1957; The Sovereign Flower, 1958; The Golden Labyrinth, 1962; Ibsen, 1962; Shakespearian Production, 1964; The Saturnian Quest, 1965; Byron and Shakespeare, 1966; Shakespeare and Religion, 1967; Poets of Action, 1967; Gold-Dust, 1968; Neglected Powers, 1971; (ed) W. F. Jackson Knight, Elysion, 1970; Jackson Knight: a biography, 1975; Vergil and Shakespeare, 1977; Shakespeare's Dramatic Challenge, 1977; Symbol of Man, 1979; also contribs to: John Masefield, OM, ed G. Handley-Taylor, 1960; Powys to Knight (letters, ed Robert Blackmore), 1982; Times Literary Supplement, The Yorkshire Post, Review of English Studies, Essays in Criticism, Contemporary Review, etc. *Address:* Caroline House, Streatham Rise, Exeter EX4 4PE.

KNIGHT, Air Vice-Marshal Glen Albyn Martin, CB 1961; CBE 1956; *b* 10 Sept. 1903; *e s* of Lt-Col G. A. Knight, OBE, VD, Melbourne, Australia; *m* 1933, Janet Elizabeth Warnock (*d* 1982), *o d* of Peter Crawford, Dargavel, Dumfriesshire; two *d. Educ:* Scotch Coll., Melbourne, Australia; Melbourne Univ. MB, BS, 1927; Diploma in Laryngology and Otology (RCP & S), 1937. House Surgeon and Physician, Alfred and Children's Hospitals, Melbourne; joined Medical Branch, RAF, 1932. War Service: South Africa, Malta (despatches), Italy; PMO Desert Air Force. Principal Medical Officer, 2nd Tactical Air Force, 1956-57; Dep. Dir-Gen. of Medical Services, Royal Air Force, 1958-61, retired, 1961. QHS, 1959-61. *Recreation:* golf. *Address:* 7 Mount Pleasant, Kirkcudbright.

KNIGHT, Sir Harold Murray, KBE 1980; DSC 1945; Governor and Chairman of Board, Reserve Bank of Australia, since 1975; *b* 13 Aug. 1919; *s* of W. H. P. Knight, Melbourne; *m* 1951, Gwenyth Catherine Pennington; four *s* one *d. Educ:* Scotch Coll., Melbourne; Melbourne Univ. Commonwealth Bank of Australia, 1936-40. AIF (Lieut), 1940-43; RANVR (Lieut), 1943-45. Commonwealth Bank of Australia, 1946-55; Asst Chief, Statistics Div., Internat. Monetary Fund, 1957-59; Reserve Bank of Australia: Research Economist, 1960-62; Asst Manager, Investment Dept, 1962-64, Manager, 1964-68; Dep. Governor and Dep. Chm. of Board, 1968-75. *Publication:* Introduccion al Analisis Monetario (Spanish), 1959. *Address:* (office) Reserve Bank of Australia, 65 Martin Place, Sydney, NSW 2000, Australia.

KNIGHT, Henry Lougher; HM Lieutenant, Mid-Glamorgan, 1974-82; *b* 7 Aug. 1907; *e s* of Robert Lougher Knight; *m* 1932, Pamela, *d* of E. Colville Lyons; three *s. Educ:* Radley; Exeter Coll., Oxford. Regular Army, RA and RHA, invalided 1934. Chartered Land Agent, 1939; Chartered Surveyor, 1970. Pres., Chartered Land Agents Soc., 1964. JP Glam 1946; DL Glam 1957. *Address:* Tythegston Court, Bridgend, Mid-Glamorgan. *T:* Porthcawl 3379. *Clubs:* Naval and Military, MCC; Cardiff and County (Cardiff).

KNIGHT, Jeffrey Russell, FCA; Chief Executive, The Stock Exchange, since 1982; *b* 1 Oct. 1936; *s* of Thomas Edgar Knight and Ivy Cissie Knight (*née* Russell); *m* 1959, Judith Marion Delver Podger; four *d. Educ:* Bristol Cathedral Sch.; St Peter's Hall, Oxford (MA). Chartered Accountant, 1966; The Stock Exchange, 1967–: Head of Quotations Dept, 1973; Dep. Chief Executive, 1975. Member: City Company Law Cttee, 1974–80; Dept of Trade Panel on Company Law Revision, 1980–; Special Adviser to Dept of Trade, 1975–; Adviser to Council for the Securities Industry, 1978–; UK Delegate: to EEC Working Parties; to Internat. Fedn of Stock Exchanges, 1973–. *Recreations:* cricket, music. *Address:* 18 Boxgrove Road, Guildford, Surrey GU1 2NF. *T:* Guildford 76518.

KNIGHT, Joan Christabel Jill, (Mrs Jill Knight), MBE 1964; MP (C) Edgbaston since 1966; *m* 1947, Montague Knight; two *s. Educ:* Fairfield Sch., Bristol; King Edward Grammar Sch., Birmingham. Mem., Northampton County Borough Council, 1956–66. Member: Parly Select Cttee on Race Relations and Immigration, 1969–72; Council of Europe, 1977–; WEU, 1977–; Select Cttee for Home Affairs, 1980–; Pres., West Midlands Conservative Political Centre, 1980–. Kentucky Colonel, USA, 1973; Nebraska Admiral, USA, 1980. *Recreations:* music, reading, tapestry work, theatre-going, antique-hunting. *Address:* House of Commons, SW1.

KNIGHT, Very Rev. Marcus; Dean of Exeter, 1960–72; *b* 11 Sept. 1903; *e s* of late Mark Knight, Insurance Manager; *m* 1931, Claire L. Hewett, MA, *o d* of late Charles H. Hewett, Bank Dir; two *s. Educ:* Christ's Hosp.; University of London; Birkbeck Coll. (BA Hons); King's Coll. (BD Hons); Fellow of King's Coll.; Union Theological Seminary, New York; STM 1930. Curacies at Stoke Newington and Ealing; Priest-Vicar of Exeter Cathedral; Vicar of Cockington, 1936–40; Vicar of Nuneaton; RD of Atherstone, 1940–44; Examining Chaplain to Bishop of Coventry, 1944; Canon of St Paul's, 1944–60, Precentor, 1944–54, Chancellor, 1954–60. Hon. Sec. Church of England Council for Education, 1949–58; Chapter Treas., St Paul's, 1950–60; Church Commissioner, 1968–72. Hon. LLD Exeter, 1973. *Publications:* Spiritualism, Reincarnation, and Immortality, 1950; (part author) There's an Answer Somewhere, 1953; many papers and reviews. *Recreations:* reading, TV, walking. *Address:* 1 Execliff, Trefusis Terrace, Exmouth, Devon. *T:* Exmouth 71153.

KNIGHT, Air Vice-Marshal Michael William Patrick, CB 1980; AFC 1964; Air Officer Commanding No 1 Group, RAF Strike Command, since 1980; *b* 23 Nov. 1932; *s* of William and Dorothy Knight; *m* 1967, Patricia Ann (*née* Davies); one *s* two *d. Educ:* Leek High Sch.; Univ. of Liverpool (BA Hons 1954). MBIM 1977. Univ. of Liverpool Air Sqdn, RAFVR, 1951–54; commnd RAF, 1954; served in Transport and Bomber Comds, and in Middle and Near East Air Forces, 1956–63; Comd No 32 Sqdn, RAF Akrotiri, 1961–63; Min. of Aviation, 1965–66; Comd Far East Strike Wing, RAF Tengah, 1966–68; Head of Secretariat, HQ STC, 1969–70; Mil. Asst to Chm., NATO Mil. Cttee, 1970–73; Comd RAF Laarbruch, 1973–74; RCDS, 1975; Dir of Ops (Air Support), MoD, 1975–77; SASO, HQ Strike Command, 1977–80. ADC to the Queen, 1973–74. Chairman: RAF Rugby Union, 1975–78; Combined Services RFC, 1977–79; Mem., RFU Cttee, 1977–. *Recreations:* Rugby football, lesser sports, music, writing. *Address:* HQ No 1 Group, RAF Bawtry, Doncaster, South Yorks DN10 6JS. *Club:* Royal Air Force.

KNIGHT, Richard James, MA; JP; *b* 19 July 1915; *s* of Richard William Knight; *m* 1953, Hilary Marian, *d* of Rev. F. W. Argyle; two *s* one *d. Educ:* Dulwich Coll. (Scholar); Trinity Coll., Cambridge (Scholar). 1st class Hons Classical Tripos Pt I, 1936, Part II, 1937. Asst Master, Fettes Coll., Edinburgh, 1938–39. Served War of 1939–45 in Gordon Highlanders, Capt. Asst Master and Housemaster, Marlborough Coll., 1945–56; Headmaster of Oundle Sch., 1956–68, of Monkton Combe Sch., 1968–78. Lay Reader, Dio. Bath and Wells. JP Bath, 1970, Avon, 1974. *Recreations:* cricket and other games. *Address:* 123 Midford Road, Bath.

KNIGHT, Warburton Richard; Director of Educational Services, Bradford Metropolitan District Council, since 1974; *b* 2 July 1932; *s* of Warburton Henry Johnston and Alice Gweneth Knight; *m* 1961, Pamela Ann (*née* Hearmon); two *s* one *d. Educ:* Trinity Coll., Cambridge (MA). Teaching in Secondary Modern and Grammar Schs in Middlesex and Huddersfield, 1956–62; joined West Riding in junior capacity, 1962; Asst Dir for Secondary Schs, Leics, 1967; Asst Educn Officer for Sec. Schs and later for Special and Social Educn in WR, 1970. Mem., DES Review Gp on the Youth Service, 1981–. Pres., Soc. of Educn Officers, 1983. *Recreations:* choral music, beekeeping, general cultural interests. *Address:* Thorner Grange, Sandhills, Thorner, Leeds LS14 3EB. *T:* Leeds 892356.

KNIGHT, William Arnold, CMG 1966; OBE 1954; Controller and Auditor-General of Uganda, 1962–68, retired; *b* 14 June 1915; *e s* of late William Knight, Llanfairfechan, and of Clara Knight; *m* 1939, Bronwen Parry; one *s* one *d. Educ:* Friars' Sch., Bangor; University Coll. of North Wales (BA Hons). Entered Colonial Audit Dept as an Asst Auditor, 1938; service in Kenya, 1938–46; Mauritius, 1946–49; Sierra Leone, 1949–52; British Guiana, 1952–57; Uganda, 1957–68; Commissioner, inquiry into economy and efficiency, Uganda, 1969–70. *Recreations:* fishing and gardening. *Address:* Neopardy Mills, near Crediton, Devon. *T:* Crediton 2513. *Club:* East India.

KNIGHT, Wilson; *see* Knight, G. W.

KNIGHTLEY; *see* Finch-Knightley.

KNIGHTON, William Myles, CB 1981; Deputy Secretary, Department of Trade, since 1978; *b* 8 Sept. 1931; *s* of late George Harry Knighton, OBE, and Ella Knighton (*née* Stroud); *m* 1957, Brigid Helen Carrothers; one *s* one *d. Educ:* Bedford School; Peterhouse, Cambridge (BA). Asst Principal, Min. of Supply, 1954; Principal, Min. of Aviation, 1959; Cabinet Office, 1962–64; Principal Private Sec. to Minister of Technology, 1966–68; Asst Sec., Min. of Technology, subseq. Dept of Trade and Industry and Dept of Trade, 1967–74; Under Sec., Dept of Trade, 1974–78. *Recreations:* gardening, hill-walking, painting. *Address:* 115 Dacre Park, SE13 5BZ. *T:* 01-852 8267. *Club:* United Oxford & Cambridge University.

KNIGHTS, Lionel Charles, MA, PhD; King Edward VII Professor of English Literature, University of Cambridge, 1965–73, now Emeritus Professor; Fellow, Queens' College, Cambridge, 1965–73; *b* 15 May 1906; *s* of C. E. and Lois M. Knights; *m* 1936, Elizabeth M. Barnes; one *s* one *d. Educ:* grammar schs; Selwyn Coll. (Hon. Fellow, 1974), and Christ's Coll., Cambridge Univ.; Charles Oldham Shakespeare Scholar, 1928; Members' Prize, 1929. Lecturer in English Literature, Manchester Univ., 1933–34, 1935–47; Prof. of English Lit., Univ. of Sheffield, 1947–52; Winterstoke Prof. of English, Bristol Univ., 1953–64; Andrew Mellon Vis. Prof., Univ. of Pittsburgh, 1961–62 and 1966; Mrs W. Beckman Vis. Prof., Berkeley, 1970. Mem. of editorial board of Scrutiny, a Quarterly Review, 1932–53. For. Hon. Mem., Amer. Acad. of Arts and Sciences, 1981. Docteur (*hc*) de l'Univ. de Bordeaux, 1964; Hon. DUniv York, 1969; Hon. DLitt: Manchester, 1974; Sheffield, 1978; Warwick, 1979. *Publications:* Drama and Society in the Age of Jonson, 1937; Explorations: Essays in Literary Criticism, 1946; Shakespeare's Politics, Shakespeare Lecture, British Academy, 1957; Some Shakespearean Themes, 1959; An Approach to Hamlet, 1960; (ed with Basil Cottle), Metaphor and Symbol, 1961; Further Explorations, 1965; Public Voices: literature and politics (Clark Lectures), 1971; Explorations 3, 1976; Hamlet and other Shakespeare Essays, 1979; Selected Essays in Criticism, 1981. *Address:* 57 Jesus Lane, Cambridge. *Club:* Royal Commonwealth Society.

KNIGHTS, Sir Philip (Douglas), Kt 1980; CBE 1976 (OBE 1971); QPM (Dist. Service) 1964; Chief Constable, West Midlands Police, since 1975; *b* 3 Oct. 1920; *s* of Thomas James Knights and Ethel Knights; *m* 1945, Jean Burman. *Educ:* King's Sch., Grantham. Lincolnshire Constabulary: Police Cadet, 1938–40; Constable, 1940. Served War, RAF, 1943–45. Sergeant, Lincs Constab., 1946; seconded to Home Office, 1946–50; Inspector, Lincs Constab., 1953, Supt 1955, Chief Supt 1957. Asst Chief Constable, Birmingham City Police, 1959; seconded to Home Office, Dep. Comdt, Police Coll., 1962–66; Dep. Chief Constable, Birmingham City Police, 1970; Chief Constable, Sheffield and Rotherham Constab., 1972–74; Chief Constable, South Yorks Police, 1974–75. Winner of Queen's Police Gold Medal Essay Competition, 1965. Mem. Lord Devlin's Cttee on Identification Procedures, 1974–75. Pres., Assoc. of Chief Police Officers, 1978–79. CBIM. *Recreations:* sport, gardening. *Address:* West Midlands Police Headquarters, PO Box 52, Lloyd House, Colmore Circus Queensway, Birmingham B4 6NQ. *T:* 021-236 5000.

KNILL, Sir John Kenelm Stuart, 4th Bt *cr* 1893, of The Grove, Blackheath; Civil Servant, Ministry of Defence, 1963–77; *b* 8 April 1913; *s* of Sir John Stuart Knill, 3rd Bt and Lucy Emmeline (*d* 1952), *o d* of Captain Thomas Willis, MN, FRGS; *S* father, 1973; *m* 1950, Violette Maud Florence Martin Barnes; two *s. Educ:* St Gregory's School, Downside. Gas industry apprenticeship, 1932–39; industrial management trainee, 1945–48; canal transport proprietor, 1948–54; pig farmer, 1954–63. Served as Lieut, RNVR, 1940–45 (Atlantic Star, Italy, France and Germany Stars). *Recreations:* canal and railway restoration (Member of Kennet and Avon Canal Trust, Great Western Soc., Inland Waterways Assoc.); scouting. *Heir: s* Thomas John Pugin Bartholomew Knill [*b* 24 Aug. 1952; *m* 1977, Kathleen Muszynski]. *Address:* Canal Cottage, Bathampton, Somerset. *T.:* Bath 63603. *Club:* Victory Services.

KNILL, Prof. John Lawrence, PhD, DSc; FICE; Professor of Engineering Geology since 1973, Head of Department of Geology since 1979, and Dean of Royal School of Mines since 1980, Imperial College of Science and Technology, University of London; *b* 22 Nov. 1934; *s* of William Cuthbert Knill and Mary (*née* Dempsey); *m* 1957, Diane Constance Judge; one *s* one *d. Educ:* Whitgift Sch.; Imperial Coll. of Science and Technol. (BSc, ARCS 1955; PhD, DIC 1957; DSc 1981). MIGeol 1977; FICE 1981. Geologist, Sir Alexander Gibb & Partners, 1957; Asst Lectr 1957, Lectr 1959, Reader in Engrg Geology 1965, Imperial Coll. of Science and Technol. President: Instn of Geologists, 1981–; Geologists' Assoc., 1982–. Membre Correspondant, Société Geologique de Belgique, 1976. Whitaker Medal, IWES, 1969. *Publications:* Industrial Geology, 1978; articles on geology of Scotland and engrg geology. *Recreation:* viticulture. *Address:* Highwood Farm, Shaw-cum-Donnington, Newbury, Berks RG16 9LB. *Clubs:* Athenæum, Chaps.

KNIPE, Sir Leslie Francis, Kt 1980; MBE; farmer; *b* Pontypool, 1913. *Educ:* West Monmouth School, Pontypool. Served War of 1939–45, Burma; RASC, attained rank of Major. President: Conservative Party in Wales (Chairman, 1972–77); Monmouth Conservative and Unionist Assoc. *Address:* Brook Acre, Llanvihangel, Crucorney, Abergavenny, Gwent NP7 8DH.

KNOLLYS, family name of **Viscount Knollys.**

KNOLLYS, 3rd Viscount, of Caversham, *cr* 1911; **David Francis Dudley Knollys**; Baron *cr* 1902; *b* 12 June 1931; *s* of 2nd Viscount Knollys, GCMG, MBE, DFC, and Margaret, *o d* of Sir Stuart Coats, 2nd Bt; *S* father 1966; *m* 1959, Hon. Sheelin Virginia Maxwell (granted, 1959, title, rank and precedence of a baron's *d*, which would have been hers had her father survived to succeed to barony of Farnham), *d* of late Lt-Col Hon. Somerset Maxwell, MP and late Mrs Remington Hobbs; three *s* one *d*. *Educ:* Eton. Lt, Scots Guards, 1951. *Heir: s* Hon. Patrick Nicholas Mark Knollys, *b* 11 March 1962. *Address:* Bramerton Grange, Norwich NR14 7HF. *T:* Surlingham 266.

KNOPF, Alfred A.; publisher; Founding Chairman, Alfred A. Knopf, Inc., 1957–72, now Chairman Emeritus; *b* 12 Sept. 1892; *s* of Samuel Knopf and Ida Japhe; *m* 1st, 1916, Blanche Wolf (*d* 1966); one *s*; 2nd, 1967, Helen Norcross Hedrick. *Educ:* Mackenzie Sch.; Columbia Coll. AB (Columbia), 1912; Pres., Alfred A. Knopf, Inc., NYC, 1918–57 (Chm. of the Board, 1957, now Emeritus). Fellow, Amer. Acad. of Arts and Scis, 1976. Gold Medal, Amer. Inst. of Graphic Arts, 1950; C. A. Pugsley Gold Medal for conservation and preservation, 1960; Alexander Hamilton Medal, Columbia Coll., 1966; Francis Parkman Silver Medal, Soc. of Amer. Historians, 1974; Distinguished Service Award, Assoc. of Amer. Univ. Presses, 1975; Distinguished Achievement Awards: Drexel Univ. Library Sch. Alumni Assoc., 1975; Nat. Book Awards Cttee, 1975; Notable Achievement Award, Brandeis, 1977; Machado de Assis Medal, Brazilian Acad. of Letters, 1978; Gold Medal, Nat. Cowboy Hall of Fame, 1981; Annual Award for distinguished service to the arts, Amer. Acad. and Inst. of Arts and Letters, 1982. Hon. LHD: Yale, 1958; Columbia, 1959; Bucknell, 1959; William and Mary, 1960; Lehigh, 1960; Michigan, 1969; Bates Coll., 1971; Univ. of Arizona, 1979; Hon. LLD (Brandeis), 1963; Hon. DLitt: Adelphi, 1966; Chattanooga, 1966; C. W. Post Center, Long Island Univ., 1973. *Address:* (home) Purchase, NY 10577, USA. *TA:* KSP KNOPF.

KNORPEL, Henry, CB 1982; Solicitor to the Department of Health and Social Security, and to the Office of Population Censuses and Surveys, and the General Register Office, since 1978; *b* 18 Aug. 1924; 2nd *s* of late Hyman Knorpel and Dora Knorpel; *m* 1953, Brenda Sterling; two *d*. *Educ:* City of London Sch.; Magdalen Coll., Oxford. BA 1945, BCL 1946, MA 1949. Called to Bar, Inner Temple, 1947, Entrance Scholar, 1947–50; practised 1947–52; entered Legal Civil Service as Legal Asst, Min. of Nat. Insce, 1952; Sen. Legal Asst, Min. of Pensions and Nat. Insce, 1958; Law Commn, 1965; Min. of Social Security, 1967; Asst Solicitor, Dept of Health and Social Security, 1968; Principal Asst Solicitor (Under-Sec.), 1971. Vis. Lecturer: Kennington Coll. of Commerce and Law, 1950–58; Holborn Coll. of Law, Languages and Commerce, 1958–70; Polytechnic of Central London, 1970–. *Publications:* articles on community law. *Recreation:* relaxing. *Address:* Conway, 32 Sunnybank, Epsom, Surrey KT18 7DX. *T:* Epsom 21394.

KNOTT, Sir John Laurence, AC 1981; Kt 1971; CBE 1960; Director: Australian Consolidated Industries Ltd; Equity Trustees Co. Ltd; World Airways Inc., California; Chairman: Jennings Industries Ltd (Australian); ACTA (Australian) Pty; SAAB/Scania (Australian) Pty Ltd; Wm Drummond Ltd; Australian Fibreglass Ltd; Associated Broadcasting Services Ltd; *b* 6 July 1910; *s* of J. Knott, Kyneton, Victoria; *m* 1935, Jean R., *d* of C. W. Milnes; three *s* one *d*. *Educ:* Cobram State Sch.; Melbourne Univ. (Dip Com). Private Sec. to Minister for Trade Treaties, 1935–38; Sec., Aust. Delegn, Eastern Gp Supply Council, New Delhi, 1940; Exec. Officer, Secondary Industries Commn, 1943–45; Mem. Jt War Production Cttee; Dir, Defence Prod. Planning Br., Dept of Supply, 1950–52; Sec., Dept of Defence Prod., 1957–58; Mem., Aust. Defence Mission to US, 1957; Sec., Dept of Supply, Melb., 1959–65; Leader, Aust. Mission to ELDO Confs: London, 1961; Paris, 1965, 1966; Rome, 1967; Vice-Pres., ELDO Council, 1967–69. Dep. High Comr for Australia, London, 1966–68; Dir-Gen., Australian PO, 1968–72. Mem. Council, Melbourne Univ., 1973–76. Pres., ESU (Victoria); Chairman: Australian Accounting Res. Foundn; Victoria Conservation Trust. Freeman, City of London. AASA, FCIS, AFAIM, LCA; idc. *Recreations:* bowls (Vice-Pres., Royal Victorian Bowling Assoc., 1957–58; Chm., World Bowls (1980) Ltd), golf, gardening. *Address:* 3 Fenwick Street, Kew, Victoria 3101, Australia. *T:* 86 7777. *Clubs:* East India, Devonshire, Sports and Public Schools; Melbourne, West Brighton (Melbourne); Union (Sydney).

KNOTT, Air Vice-Marshal Ronald George, CB 1967; DSO 1944; DFC 1943; AFC 1955; retired 1972; *b* 19 Dec. 1917; *s* of late George Knott and of Edith Rose Knott; *m* 1941, Hermione Violet (*née* Phayre); three *s* one *d*. *Educ:* Borden Grammar Sch., Sittingbourne, Kent. No 20 Sqdn RAF, 1938–40; No 5 Flight IAFVR, 1940–41; HQ Coast Defence Wing, Bombay, 1942; No 179 Sqdn, 1943–44; No 524 Sqdn, 1944–45; RAF, Gatow (Ops), 1949–50; OC, RAF Eindhoven, 1950–51; HQ 2nd TAF, 1951–52; RAF Staff Coll., 1952; Flying Trng Comd, 1953–55; Chief Flying Instructor, Central Flying Sch., 1956–58; Air Plans, Air Min., 1959; OC, RAF Gutersloh, 1959–61; ACOS Plans, 2 ATAF, 1962–63; Defence Res. Policy Staff Min. of Def. 1963; DOR2 (RAF), Min. of Def., 1963–67; SASO, HQ NEAF Cyprus, 1967–70; AOA, HQ Air Support Comd, RAF, 1970–72. *Recreations:* squash, gardening, painting, building. *Address:* Pilgrims Cottage, Charing, Kent. *T:* Charing 2723.

KNOWELDEN, Prof. John, MD, FRCP, FFCM, DPH, JP; Professor of Community Medicine (formerly of Preventive Medicine and Public Health),

University of Sheffield, since 1960; Academic Registrar, Faculty of Community Medicine, since 1977; *b* 19 April 1919; *s* of Clarence Arthur Knowelden; *m* 1946, Mary Sweet; two *s*. *Educ:* Colfe's Grammar Sch., Lewisham; St George's Hosp. Med. Sch.; London Sch. of Hygiene and Trop. Med.; Johns Hopkins Sch. of Public Health, Baltimore. Surg. Lt, RNVR, 1942–46. Rockefeller Fellowship in Preventive Med., 1947–49; Lectr in Med. Statistics and Mem., MRC Statistical Research Unit, 1949–60. Civil Consultant in Community Medicine to Royal Navy, 1977–. Editor, Brit. Jl of Preventive and Social Medicine, 1959–69 and 1973–76. Formerly Hon. Sec., Sect. of Epidemiology, Royal Society Medicine and Chm., Soc. for Social Medicine; Mem., WHO Expert Advisory Panel on Health Statistics. *Publications:* (with Ian Taylor) Principles of Epidemiology, 2nd edn, 1964; papers on clinical and prophylactic trials and epidemiological topics. *Recreations:* photography, gardening. *Address:* 2 St Helen's Croft, Grindleford, Sheffield S30 1JG. *T:* Hope Valley 30014.

KNOWLES, Sir Charles (Francis), 7th Bt *cr* 1765; *b* 20 Dec. 1951; *s* of Sir Francis Gerald William Knowles, 6th Bt, FRS, and of Ruth Jessie, *d* of late Rev. Arthur Brooke-Smith; *S* father, 1974; *m* 1979, Amanda Louise Margaret, *d* of Lance Bromley, *qv*. *Educ:* Marlborough Coll.; Oxford Sch. of Architecture (BA 1974; DipArch 1977; RIBA 1979). *Recreations:* shooting, travel. *Heir: cousin* Peter Cosby Knowles. *Address:* Merlin Haven House, Wootton Under Edge, Glos.

KNOWLES, Colin George; company director; *b* 11 April 1939; *s* of late George William Knowles, Tarleton, Lancs; *m* 1st, 1961, Mary B. D. Wickliffe, *e d* of William Wickliffe, Co. Antrim, NI; two *d*, 2nd, 1971, Mrs (Marjorie) Alison Taylor (marr. diss. 1980), *y d* of late Major R. Balfour Kerr, TD, DL, JP, Haddington, East Lothian; three step *d*; 3rd, 1981, Mrs Carla Johannes, *d* of Roland Stansfield Stamp, Blantyre, Malaŵi. *Educ:* King George V Grammar Sch., Southport; CEDEP, Fontainebleau. MInstM 1966; MIPR 1970; BAIE 1972; FBIM 1972. Joined John Player & Sons, 1960; sales and marketing management appts; Head of Public Relations, 1971–73; joined Imperial Tobacco Ltd, 1973; Hd of Public Affairs, 1973–80; Company Sec., 1979–80; Chm., Griffin Associates Ltd, 1980–. Mem. Council, Tobacco Trade Benevolent Assoc., 1975–80. Director: Nottingham Festival Assoc. Ltd, 1969–71; English Sinfonia Orchestra, 1972–80; Midland Sinfonia Concert Soc. Ltd, 1972–80; (also co-Founder) Assoc. for Business Sponsorship of The Arts Ltd, 1975– (Chm., 1975–80); Bristol Hippodrome Trust Ltd, 1977–81; Bath Archaeological Trust Ltd, 1978–81; The Palladian Trust Ltd, 1979–; Mem., Chancellor of Duchy of Lancaster's Cttee of Honour on Business and the Arts, 1980–81. Arts sponsorship initiatives include responsibility for: Internat. Cello Competition (with Tortelier), Bristol, 1975 and 1977; Internat. Conductors Awards, 1978; Pompeii Exhibn, RA, 1976–77; new prodns at Royal Opera House, Covent Garden, at Glyndebourne, and at National Theatre. Governor: Manning Grammar Sch., Nottingham, 1972–73; Clayesmore Sch., Dorset, 1975–. Liveryman, Worshipful Co of Tobacco Pipe Makers and Tobacco Blenders; Freeman, City of London. FRSA 1975; FRCSoc 1976. OStJ 1977. *Publications:* papers, articles and documentary film treatments on the arts, sponsorship, and tobacco industry topics. *Recreations:* country pursuits, the Arts. *Address:* PO Box 60, Douglas, Isle of Man. *Clubs:* Carlton, MCC.

KNOWLES, George Peter; Registrar of the Province and Diocese of York, and Archbishop of York's Legal Secretary, since 1968; *b* 30 Dec. 1919; *s* of Geoffrey Knowles and Mabel Bowman; *m* 1948, Elizabeth Margaret Scott; one *s* two *d*. *Educ:* Clifton Coll., Bristol; Queens' Coll., Cambridge. MA, LLB. Served war, Royal Artillery, 1939–46 (Lieut). Admitted a solicitor, 1948; Chm., York Area Rent Tribunal, 1959; Mem., Mental Health Review Tribunal for Yorkshire Regional Health Authority Area, 1960. *Recreations:* fishing, wildlife. *Address:* The Old Rectory, Skelton, York YO3 6XY. *T:* York 470301. *Clubs:* Royal Automobile; Yorkshire (York).

KNOWLES, Prof. Jeremy Randall, FRS 1977; Amory Houghton Professor of Chemistry, Harvard University, since 1974; *b* 28 April 1935; *s* of Kenneth Guy Jack Charles Knowles and Dorothy Helen Swingler; *m* 1960, Jane Sheldon Davis; three *s*. *Educ:* Magdalen College Sch.; Balliol Coll., Merton Coll. and Christ Church, Oxford (MA, DPhil). Sir Louis Stuart Exhibr, Balliol Coll., Oxford, 1955–59; Harmsworth Schol., Merton Coll., Oxford, and Research Lectr, Christ Church, Oxford, 1960–62; Research Associate, Calif. Inst. of Technology, 1961–62; Fellow of Wadham Coll., Oxf., 1962–74; Univ. Lectr, Univ. of Oxford, 1966–74. Visiting Prof., Yale Univ., 1969, 1971; Sloan Vis. Prof., Harvard Univ., 1973; Newton-Abraham Vis. Prof., Oxford Univ., 1983–84. Fellow, Amer. Acad. of Arts and Scis, 1982. Charmian Medal, RSC, 1980. *Publications:* research papers and reviews in learned jls. *Address:* 44 Coolidge Avenue, Cambridge, Mass 02138, USA. *T:* (617) 876-8469.

KNOWLES, Hon. Sir Leonard Joseph, Kt 1974; CBE 1963; Chief Justice of the Bahamas, 1973–78; *b* Nassau, 15 March 1916; *s* of late Samuel Joseph Knowles; *m* 1939, Harriet Hansen, *d* of John Hughes, Liverpool; two *s*. *Educ:* Queen's Coll., Nassau, Bahamas; Faculty of Laws, King's Coll., Univ. of London (LLB); first Bahamian student to take and pass Higher Sch. Certif. in Bahamas, 1934; LLB Hons 1937, Cert. of Honour in Final Bar Examinations. Called to the Bar, Gray's Inn, London, 1939; Lord Justice Holker Scholar, Gray's Inn, 1940; practised law in Liverpool for some years. Served War of 1939–45, Royal Air Force (radar). Returned to Nassau, 1948, and was called to local Bar; Attorney-at-Law and Actg Attorney-Gen. of the Bahamas, 1949; Registrar-Gen., 1949–50. Past Stipendiary and Circuit

Magistrate. Chm., Labour Board, Bahamas, 1953-63; MLC (Upper House of Legislature), 1960-63; President, Senate; 1964; re-elected, 1967, 1968, and continued to hold that office until 1972. Has always been an active lay preacher. *Publications:* Elements of Bahamian Law; Financial Relief in Matrimonial Cases. *Recreations:* music, motion photography, swimming. *Address:* PO Box SS 6378, Nassau, Bahamas. *Club:* Royal Commonwealth Society.

KNOWLES, Maurice Baxendale, CBE 1952; late Government Actuary's Department; retired 1953; *b* 6 Nov. 1893; *m* 1919, Lilla Shepherdson (decd); one *s* one *d. Educ:* Bridlington Sch. Served European War, 1914-18, in 3 London Regt and RFC. *Address:* Janvier, Moor Road, Langham, Colchester, Essex CO4 5NR.

KNOWLES, Wyn; Editor, Woman's Hour, BBC, since 1971; *b* 30 July 1923; *d* of Frederick Knowles and Dorothy Ellen Knowles (*née* Harrison). *Educ:* St Teresa's Convent, Effingham; Convents of FCJ in Ware and Switzerland; Polytechnic Sch. of Art, London. Cypher Clerk, War Office, 1941-45. Secretarial work, 1948-57; joined BBC, 1951; Asst Producer, Drama Dept, 1957-60; Woman's Hour: Producer, Talks Dept, 1960-65; Asst Editor, 1965-67; Dep. Editor, 1967-71. *Publication:* (ed with Kay Evans) The Woman's Hour Book, 1981. *Recreations:* travel, cooking, writing, painting, being owned by cats. *Address:* 80A Parkway, Regent's Park, NW1 7AN. *T:* 01-485 8258.

KNOX, family name of **Earl of Ranfurly**.

KNOX, Bryce Harry; Commissioner (and Secretary), HM Customs and Excise, since 1975; *b* 21 Feb. 1929; *e s* of Brice Henry Knox and Rose Hetty Knox; *m* 1957, Norma, *d* of late George Thomas and of Rose Thomas; one *s. Educ:* Stratford Grammar Sch.; Nottingham Univ. BA(Econ). Asst Principal, HM Customs and Excise, 1953; Principal, 1958; on loan to HM Treasury, 1963-65; Asst Sec., HM Customs and Excise, 1966; seconded to HM Diplomatic Service, Counsellor, Office of UK Perm. Rep. to European Communities, 1972-74; Under-Sec., HM Customs and Excise, 1974. *Address:* 9 Manor Way, Blackheath, SE3 9EF. *T:* 01-852 9404. *Clubs:* Reform; MCC.

KNOX, Col Bryce Muir, MC 1944 and Bar, 1944; TD 1947; Lord-Lieutenant of Ayr and Arran (formerly County of Ayr), since 1974 (Vice-Lieutenant, 1970-74); Vice-Chairman, Lindustries Ltd, 1979 (Director, 1953-79); *b* 4 April 1916; *s* of late James Knox, Kilbirnie; *m* 1948, Patricia Mary Dunsmuir; one *s* one *d. Educ:* Stowe; Trinity Coll., Cambridge. Served with Ayrshire (ECO) Yeomanry, 1939-45, N Africa and Italy; CO, 1953-56; Hon. Col, 1969-71; Hon. Col, The Ayrshire Yeomanry Sqdn, Queen's Own Yeomanry, T&AVR, 1971-77; Pres., Lowlands TA&VRA, 1978. Member, Queen's Body Guard for Scotland, Royal Company of Archers. CStJ. *Recreation:* country sports. *Address:* Martnaham Lodge, By Ayr KA6 6ES. *T:* Dalrymple 204. *Club:* Cavalry and Guards.

KNOX, David Laidlaw; MP (C) Leek Division of Staffordshire since 1970; *b* 30 May 1933; *s* of late J. M. Knox, Lockerbie and Mrs C. H. C. Knox (*née* Laidlaw); *m* 1980, Mrs Margaret Eva Maxwell, *d* of late A. McKenzie. *Educ:* Lockerbie Academy; Dumfries Academy; London Univ. (BSc (Econ) Hons). Management Trainee, 1953-56; Printing Executive, 1956-62; O&M Consultant, 1962-70. Contested (C): Stechford, Birmingham, 1964 and 1966; Nuneaton, March 1967. PPS to Ian Gilmour, Minister of State for Defence, 1973, Sec. of State for Defence, 1974. Secretary: Cons. Finance Cttee, 1972-73; Cons. Trade Cttee, 1974; Vice-Chm., Cons. Employment Cttee, 1979-80; Chairman: W Midlands Area Young Conservatives, 1963-64; W Midlands Area Cons. Political Centre, 1966-69; a Vice-Chm., Cons. Party Organisation, 1974-75. Editor, Young Conservatives National Policy Group, 1963-64. *Recreations:* watching association football, reading. *Address:* House of Commons, SW1.

KNOX, Prof. Henry Macdonald; Professor of Education, The Queen's University of Belfast, 1951-82; *b* 26 Nov. 1916; *e s* of Rev. R. M. Knox, Edinburgh, and J. E. Church; *m* 1945, Marian, *yr d* of N. Starkie, Todmorden; one *s* one *d. Educ:* George Watson's Coll., Edinburgh; University of Edinburgh. MA 1938; MEd 1940; PhD 1949. Served as Captain, Intelligence Corps, commanding a wireless intelligence section, Arakan sector of Burma, and as instructor, War Office special wireless training wing, 1940-46. Lecturer in Education, University Coll. of Hull, 1946; Lecturer in Education, University of St Andrews, 1949; former Dean of Faculty of Education, QUB. Sometime Examiner in Educn, Universities of Durham, Leeds, Sheffield, Aberdeen, Glasgow, Wales and Ireland (National); occasional Examiner, Universities of Edinburgh, Dublin and Bristol. Formerly: Chm., N Ireland Council for Educnl Research; Member: Governing Body, Stranmillis and St Joseph's Colls of Educn, Belfast; Adv. Cttee on Supply and Training of Teachers for NI. Formerly Member: Advisory Council on Educn for N Ireland; Senior Certificate Examination Cttee for N Ireland; Adv. Bd for Postgraduate Studentships in Arts Subjects, Ministry of Educn for N Ireland. *Publications:* Two Hundred and Fifty Years of Scottish Education, 1696-1946, 1953; John Dury's Reformed School, 1958; Introduction to Educational Method, 1961; Schools in Europe (ed W. Schultze): Northern Ireland, 1969; numerous articles in educational journals. *Address:* 69 Maryville Park, Belfast BT9 6LQ. *T:* 665588.

KNOX, Henry Murray Owen, OBE 1944; Senior Partner, Oxley, Knox & Co., Stock-jobbers, retired, 1965; *b* 5 March 1909; *yr s* of late Brig.-Gen. and Mrs H. O. Knox; *m* 1932, Violet Isabel (*d* 1962), *yr d* of late Mr and Mrs Frank Weare, The Dell, Tunbridge Wells, Kent; two *s*; *m* 1963, Mrs E. M. Davidson. *Educ:* Charterhouse; Trinity Coll., Oxford (MA Hons Law). Joined Oxley, Knox & Co., 1930; Partner, 1931. Served War of 1939-45, Queen's Own Royal West Kent Regt (despatches, wounded, OBE); various appts. Staff, ending in Col "A" Organisation, HQ 21 Army Group. Master, Skinners' Company, 1951-52 and 1972-73. Stock Exchange Council, 1948-64; Dep. Chm., Stock Exchange, 1958-64, Actg Chm., 1963-64. Governor: Tonbridge Sch.; Charterhouse Sch.; Sutton's Hosp. in Charterhouse (Chm.). *Recreations:* golf, gardening. *Address:* Brooklands, Manwood Road, Sandwich, Kent.

KNOX, His Eminence Cardinal James Robert, DD, DCL; President of the Pontifical Council for the Family, since 1981; President, Permanent Committee for International Eucharistic Congresses, since 1973; *b* 2 March 1914; *s* of John Knox and Emily (*née* Walsh). *Educ:* St Ildephonsus Coll., New Norcia, Australia; Pontifical Urban College de Propaganda Fide, Rome. Priest, 1941; Vice-Rector, Pontifical Urban College de Propaganda Fide, Rome, 1945-48; attached to Secretariat of State of HH Pope Pius XII, 1948-50; Sec. of Apostolic Internunciature in Tokyo, Japan, 1950-53; Titular Archbishop of Melitene, 1953; Apostolic Delegate to British East and West Africa, 1953-57; Apostolic Internuncio in India, 1957-67; Archbishop of Melbourne, 1967-74; Prefect of the Sacred Congregation for the discipline of the Sacraments and of the Sacred Congregation for Divine Worship, 1974-75, Prefect of the Sacred Congregation for the Sacraments and Divine Worship, 1975-81. Member Sacred Congregation for: Evangelization of Peoples, 1973-; Oriental Churches, 1974-; Catholic Education, 1974-; Bishops, 1974-; Mem., Council for Public Affairs of the Church, 1974-; Member Pontifical Commission for: Revision of Code of Oriental Canon Law, 1974-; Revision of Code of Canon Law, 1974-; Interpretation of Decrees of 2nd Vatican Council, 1978 ; Cardinal, 1973. *Publication:* De Necessitudine Deiparam Inter et Eucharistia , 1949. *Address:* Vatican City State, Europe.

KNOX, Mrs J n M.; *see* Swaythling, Lady.

KNOX, John; Under-Secretary, Department of Trade and Industry, retired, 1974; Head of Research Contractors Division, 1972-74; *b* 11 March 1913; *s* of William Knox and May Ferguson; *m* 1942, Mary Blackwood Johnston; one *s* one *d. Educ:* Lenzie Acad.; Glasgow Univ. (Kitchener's Schol.; MA). Business Management Trng, 1935-39; joined RAE, 1939; Op. Research with RAF, 1939-45; Asst Chief Scientific Adviser, Min. of Works, 1945-50; Dep. Dir and Dir, Intelligence Div., DSIR, 1950-58; Dep. Dir (Industry), DSIR, 1958-64; Min. of Technology, later DTI: Asst Controller, 1964-65; CSO, Head of External Research and Materials Div., 1965-68; Head of Materials Div., 1968-71; Head of Res. Div., 1971-73. *Publications:* occasional articles on management of research, development and industrial innovation. *Recreation:* golf. *Address:* Traquair, 11 Haylings Grove, Leiston, Suffolk IP16 4DU. *T:* Leiston 831115.

KNOX, John, RSA 1979 (ARSA 1972); RGI 1980; Head of Painting Studios, School of Drawing and Painting, Glasgow School of Art, since 1981; *b* 16 Dec. 1936; *s* of Alexander and Jean Knox; *m* 1960, Margaret Kyle Sutherland; one *s* one *d. Educ:* Lenzie Acad.; Glasgow Sch. of Art (DA). On the Drawing and Painting Staff at Duncan of Jordanstone Coll. of Art, Dundee, 1965-81. Work in permanent collections: Scottish Nat. Gallery of Modern Art; Arts Council; Contemporary Arts Soc.; Scottish Arts Council; Otis Art Inst., Los Angeles; Olinda Museum, São Paulo; Aberdeen, Dundee and Manchester art galleries; Hunterian Museum, Glasgow. Member: Scottish Arts Council, 1974-7 ; Trustees Cttee, Scottish Nat. Gallery of Modern Art, 1975-; Bd of Trustees, Nat. Galls of Scotland, 1982-; Bd of Governors, Duncan of Jordanstone Coll. of Art, Dundee, 1980-82. *Address:* 31 North Erskine Park, Bearsden, Glasgow.

KNOX, John Leonard, QC 1979; *b* 6 April 1925; *s* of Leonard Needham Knox and Berthe Hélène Knox; *m* 1953, Anne Jacqueline Mackintosh; one *s* three *d. Educ:* Radley Coll.; Worcester Coll., Oxford (Hon. Mods, 1st Cl.; Jurisprudence, 1st Cl.). Called to the Bar, Lincoln's Inn, 1953, Bencher, 1977; Member, Senate of the Inns of Court, 1975-78; Junior Treasury Counsel: in *bona vacantia*, 1971-79; in probate, 1978-79. Member: Lord Chancellor's Law Reform Cttee, 1978-; Council of Legal Educn, 1975-79. *Address:* Clementsfield Farm, Witney, Oxon. *T:* Witney 2336.

KNOX, Prof. Joseph Alan Cruden; Professor of Physiology in the University of London, at Queen Elizabeth College, 1954-74, now Emeritus; *b* 23 March 1911; *s* of Dr Joseph Knox; *m* 1945, Elsa Margaret Henry; one *d. Educ:* Aberdeen Grammar Sch.; Glasgow High Sch.; Glasgow Univ. MB, ChB (Glasgow) 1935; MD (Hons) 1948; House Surgeon and Physician, Glasgow Royal Infirmary, 1935-36; Asst to Prof. of Physiology, Glasgow Univ., 1936-40; Lecturer in Physiology: Glasgow Univ., 1940-44; King's Coll., London, 1944-48; Senior Lecturer, King's Coll., 1948-54. Mem. of Physiological Soc., 1941. *Publications:* papers in Jl of Physiology, British Heart Jl, etc. *Recreations:* reading, gramophone, railways. *Address:* 129 Northumberland Road, North Harrow, Harrow, Middlesex HA2 7RB. *T:* 01-866 6778.

KNOX, Robert, MA, MD, FRCP, FRCPath; Emeritus Professor of Bacteriology, University of London (Professor of Bacteriology, Guy's Hospital Medical School, 1949-69); *b* 29 May 1904; *s* of Dr Robert Knox, radiologist; *m* 1936, Bessie Lynda Crust; three *d*. *Educ:* Highgate; Balliol Coll., Oxford (Classical Scholar); St Bartholomew's Hosp. 1st Class Hon. Mods, 1924, 2nd Class Lit Hum, 1926; BA Oxford, 1927; MB, BS London, 1932; MD 1934; MRCS 1932; LRCP 1932, MRCP 1934, FRCP 1953; FCPath, 1964. House Physician and Chief Asst St Bartholomew's Hosp., 1932-35; MA Cambridge 1935; Demonstrator in Pathology, University of Cambridge, 1935-37; Mem. of Scientific Staff, Imperial Cancer Research Fund, 1937-39; Dir of Public Health Laboratories (Med. Research Council) at Stamford, 1939, Leicester 1940, and Oxford, 1945; MA Oxford, 1945. Fellow Royal Society Medicine; Member: Pathological Soc.; Soc. of Gen. Microbiology; Assoc. of Clinical Pathologists. *Publications:* on bacteriological subjects in medical and scientific journals. *Recreations:* coxed Oxford Univ., 1925; golf. *Address:* Oakhurst, Warren Drive, Kingswood, Surrey. *Club:* Athenæum.

KNOX, Hon. Sir William Edward, Kt 1979; FCIT, FAIM; MLA (Lib), Nundah, since 1957; Minister for Employment and Labour Relations, Queensland, since 1980; *b* 14 Dec. 1927; *s* of E. Knox, Turramurra; *m* 1956, Doris Ross; two *s* two *d*. *Educ:* Melbourne High School. State Pres., Qld Young Liberals, 1953-56; Vice-Pres., Qld Div., Liberal Party, 1956-57, Mem. Exec., 1953-58, 1962-65; Sec., Parly Lib. Party, 1960-65. Minister for Transport, Qld, 1965-72; Minister for Justice and Attorney-Gen., Qld, 1971-76; Dep. Premier and Treasurer of Qld, 1976-78; Leader, State Parly Liberal Party, 1976-78; Minister for Health, Queensland, 1978-80. Chm., Qld Road Safety Council and Mem., Aust. Transport Adv. Council, 1965-72. Mem., Nat. Exec. Aust. Jnr Chamber of Commerce, 1961-62; Senator Jnr Chamber Internat., 1962-; State Pres., Father and Son Movement, 1965. *Address:* 1621 Sandgate Road, Nundah, Queensland 4012, Australia.

KNOX-JOHNSTON, Robin, (William Robert Patrick Knox-Johnston), CBE 1969; Marina Consultant since 1974; Chairman, Knox-Johnston Marine Ltd, since 1976; *b* 17 March 1939; *s* of late David Robert Knox-Johnston and Elizabeth Mary Knox-Johnston (*née* Cree); *m* 1962, Suzanne (*née* Singer); one *d*. *Educ:* Berkhamsted School. Master Mariner; FRGS. Merchant Navy, 1957-67. First person to sail single-handed non-stop Around the World 14 June 1968 to 22 April 1969, in yacht Suhaili; won Sunday Times Golden Globe, 1969; won Round Britain Race, Ocean Spirit, 1970; won round Britain Race, British Oxygen, 1974. Man. Dir, St Katharine's Yacht Haven Ltd, 1975-76; Director: Mercury Yacht Harbours Ltd, 1976; Rank Marine International, 1973-75; Hoo Marina Ltd, 1974-; Hogg Robinson Knox-Johnston (Yacht Brokers), 1976-; Troon Marina Ltd, 1976; National Yacht Racing Centre Ltd, 1979-. Pres., British Olympic Yachting Appeal, 1977-; Mem. Exec. Cttee, RNLI, 1973-; Mem. Bd of Governors, Ocean Youth Club, 1979-. Freeman, Borough of Bromley, Kent, 1969; Younger Brother, Trinity House, 1973. Mem., Co. of Master Mariners, 1975. Lt-Comdr RNR 1971. Yachtsman of the Year, 1969. *Publications:* A World of my Own, 1969; Sailing, 1975; Twilight of Sail, 1978; Last but not Least, 1978; Bunkside Companion, 1982. *Recreation:* sailing. *Address:* 24 Ottoline Drive, Troon, Ayrshire. *Clubs:* Savage, Naval, Royal Ocean Racing.

KNOX-MAWER, Ronald; a Metropolitan Stipendiary Magistrate, since 1975; *b* 3 Aug. 1925; *s* of George Robert Knox-Mawer and Clare Roberts; *m* 1951, June Ellis; one *s* one *d*. *Educ:* Grove Park Sch.; Emmanuel Coll., Cambridge (MA). Royal Artillery, 1943-47. Called to Bar, Middle Temple; Wales and Chester Circuit, 1947-52; Chief Magistrate and Actg Chief Justice, Aden, 1952-58; Chief Magistrate, Puisne Judge and Actg Chief Justice, Fiji, and conjointly Chief Justice, Nauru and Tonga, 1958-70; Northern Circuit, 1970-75. *Publications:* ed, Aden and Fiji Law Reports 1937-1966; short stories in Punch, Cornhill, Argosy, Times, etc; various papers in legal jls. *Recreation:* countryside. *Address:* c/o Oriel Chambers, 14 Water Street, Liverpool L2 8TD. *T:* 051-236 7191. *Club:* Royal Commonwealth Society.

KNUDSEN, Semon Emil; retired; Chairman and Chief Executive, White Motor Corporation, 1971-80; *b* 2 Oct. 1912; *o s* of William S. and Clara Euler Knudsen; *m* 1938, Florence Anne McConnell; one *s* three *d*. *Educ:* Dartmouth Coll.; Mass Inst. of Technology. Joined General Motors, 1939; series of supervisory posts; Gen. Man., Detroit Diesel Div., 1955; Gen. Man., Pontiac Motor Div., 1956; Gen. Man., Chevrolet Motor Div., 1961; Dir of General Motors and Gp Vice-Pres. i/c of all Canadian and overseas activities, 1965; Exec. Vice-Pres. with added responsibility for domestic non-automotive divs, 1966, also defense activities, 1967; resigned from Gen. Motors Corp., 1968; Pres., Ford Motor Co., 1968-69. Director: UAL Inc.; United Airlines; Cowles Communications; Michigan National Bank; Michigan National Corp.; First National Bank in Palm Beach; Armada Corp. Mem., MIT Corp. Mem. Bd of Dirs, Boys Clubs of Amer.; Trustee, Oakland (Mich) Univ. Foundn and Cleveland Clinic Fund. *Recreations:* golf, tennis, deepsea fishing, hunting. *Address:* 1700 N Woodward, Suite E, Bloomfield Hills, Mich 48013, USA. *Clubs:* Detroit Athletic (Detroit); Bloomfield Hills Country (Mich); Pepper Pike (Ohio); Union (Cleveland); Everglades, Seminole (Fla); Augusta National (Ga).

KNUTSFORD, 5th Viscount *cr* 1895; **Julian Thurstan Holland-Hibbert;** CBE 1957; Bt 1853; Baron 1888; JP; *b* 3 May 1920; *o s* of 4th Viscount Knutsford, and Viola Mary (*d* 1964), *d* of Thomas Meadows Clutterbuck; *S* father, 1976. *Educ:* Eton; Trinity Coll., Cambridge. Served War of 1939-45,

Coldstream Guards. JP Herts, 1953. OStJ. *Heir: cousin* Michael Holland-Hibbert [*b* 27 Dec. 1926; *m* 1951, Hon. Sheila Constance, *er d* of 5th Viscount Portman; two *s* one *d*]. *Address:* Munden, Watford, Herts. *T:* Garston 72002.

KNUTTON, Maj.-Gen. Harry, CB 1975; MSc, CEng, FIEE, CBIM; Director-General, City and Guilds of London Institute, since 1976; *b* Rawmarsh, Yorks, 26 April 1921; *m* 1958, Pamela Brackley, E Sheen, London; three *s* one *d*. *Educ:* Wath-upon-Dearne Grammar Sch.; RMCS. Commnd RA, 1943; served with 15th Scottish and 1st Airborne Divs, NW Europe, 1944-45; India, 1945-47; Instructor in Gunnery, 1946-49; Project Officer, Min. of Supply, 1949-51; served Middle East, 1953-55; Directing Staff, RMCS, 1955-58; jssc 1958; various staff appts, MoD, 1958-60, 1962-64, 1966-67; Comdr Missile Regt, BAOR, 1964-66; Comdr Air Defence Bde, 1967-69; Fellow, Loughborough Univ. of Technology, 1969-70; Dir-Gen. Weapons (Army), 1970-73; Dir, Royal Ordnance Factories and Dep. Master-Gen. of Ordnance, 1973-75; retd. Col Comdt, RA, 1977-. Teacher, Whitgift Foundn, 1975-76. Member: Associated Examining Bd, 1976-; Council, British Assoc. of Commercial and Indust. Educn, 1977-; Nat. Exams Bd of Supervisory Studies, 1979-; Exec. Cttee, Standing Conf. on Schools' Science and Technology, 1979-. Governor, Imperial Coll. of Science and Technology, 1976-. *Recreations:* golf, sailing. *Address:* 43 Essendene Road, Caterham, Surrey. *T:* Caterham 47278.

KOECHLIN, Patricia Rosemary, OBE 1956; President, British Show Jumping Association, since 1983; Member of British Show Jumping Team, 1947-64; *b* 22 Nov. 1928; *d* of late Capt. Eric Hamilton Smythe, MC, Légion d'Honneur, and late Frances Monica Smythe (*née* Curtoys); *m* 1963, Samuel Koechlin, Switzerland; two *d*. *Educ:* St Michael's Sch., Cirencester; Talbot Heath, Bournemouth. Show Jumping: first went abroad with British Team, 1947; Leading Show Jumper of the Year, 1949, 1958 (with T. Edgar), and 1962; European Ladies' Championship: Spa, 1957; Deauville, 1961; Madrid, 1962; Hickstead, 1963; Harringay: BSJA Spurs, 1949, 1951, 1952, 1954 (Victor Ludorum Championship), 1953 and 1954; Harringay Spurs, 1953; Grand Prix, Brussels, 1949, 1952 and 1956. Ladies' record for high jump (2 m. 10 cm.) Paris, 1950; won in Madrid, 1951. White City: 1951 (Country Life Cup); 1953 (Selby Cup). Was Leading Rider and won Prix du Champion, Paris, 1952; Leading Rider, etc, Marseilles, 1953; Individual Championship, etc, Harrisburg, Penn, USA, 1953; Pres. of Mexico Championship, New York, 1953; Toronto (in team winning Nations Cup), 1953; Lisbon (won 2 events), Grand Prix, Madrid, and Championship, Vichy, 1954; Grand Prix de Paris and 3 other events, 1954; Bruxelles Puissance and new ladies' record for high jump (2m. 20 cm.), Leading Rider of Show, 1954; BHS Medal of Honour, Algiers Puissance and Grand Prix, 4 events in Paris, 4 events at White City including the Championship, 1955; Grand Prix and Leading Rider of Show and 4 other events, Brussels, 1956; Grand Prix Militaire and Puissance, Lucerne; Mem. British Equestrian Olympic Team, Stockholm (Show Jumping Bronze Medal), 1956; IHS National Championship, White City; Leading Rider and other events, Palermo, 1956; won 2 Puissance events, Paris, 1957; BSJA, 1957; Ladies' National Championship in 1954-59 and 1961 and 1962 (8 times); Daily Mail Cup, White City, 1955, 1957, 1960, 1962; Mem. winning British Team, White City: 1952, 1953, 1956, 1957; Amazon Prize, Aachen, 1958; Queen's Cup, Royal Internat. Horse Show, White City, 1958; Preis von Parsenn, Davos, 1957, 1958, 1959; Championship Cup, Brussels Internat. Horse Show, 1958; Lisbon Grand Prix, 1959; Olympic Trial, British Timken Show, and Prix de la Banque de Bruxelles at Brussels, 1959. Lucerne Grand Prix; Prince Hal Stakes, Country Life and Riding Cup, White City; Pembroke Stakes, Horse Show Cttee Cup, and Leading Rider, Dublin (all in 1960). Mem. British Olympic Team in Rome, 1960. Copenhagen Grand Prix; Amazon Prize, Aachen; John Player Trophy, White City; St Gall Ladies Championship (all in 1961); Saddle of Honour and Loriners' Cup, White City, 1962; British Jumping Derby, Hickstead, 1962. Hon. Freeman, Worshipful Co. of Farriers, 1955; Freeman of the City of London, 1956; Hon. Freeman, Worshipful Company of Loriners, 1962; Yeoman, Worshipful Company of Saddlers, 1963. *Publications:* (as Pat Smythe): Jump for Joy; Pat Smythe's Story, 1954; Pat Smythe's Book of Horses, 1955; One Jump Ahead, 1956; Jacqueline rides for a Fall, 1957; Three Jays against the Clock, 1957; Three Jays on Holiday, 1958; Three Jays go to Town, 1959; Horses and Places, 1959; Three Jays over the Border, 1960; Three Jays go to Rome, 1960; Three Jays Lend a Hand, 1961; Jumping Round the World, 1962; Florian's Farmyard, 1962; Flanagan My Friend, 1963; Bred to Jump, 1965; Show Jumping, 1967; (with Fiona Hughes) A Pony for Pleasure, 1969; A Swiss Adventure, 1970; (with Fiona Hughes) Pony Problems, 1971; A Spanish Adventure, 1971; A Cotswold Adventure, 1972. *Recreations:* tennis, swimming, music, ski-ing, sailing, all sports, languages. *Address:* Sudgrove House, Miserden, near Stroud, Glos. *T:* Miserden 360; Im Steinacker, 4117 Burg-im-Leimental, BE, Switzerland. *T:* Basle 751411.

KOENIGSBERGER, Prof. Helmut Georg, MA, PhD; Professor of History, King's College London, since 1973; *b* 24 Oct. 1918; *s* of late Georg Felix Koenigsberger, chief architect, borough of Treptow, Berlin, Germany, and of late Käthe Koenigsberger (*née* Born); *m* 1961, Dorothy M. Romano; two *d* (twins). *Educ:* Adams' Grammar Sch., Newport, Shropshire; Gonville and Caius Coll., Cambridge. Asst Master: Brentwood Sch., Essex, 1941-42; Bedford Sch., 1942-44. Served War of 1939-45, Royal Navy, 1944-45. Lecturer in Economic History, QUB, 1948-51; Senior Lecturer in Economic History, University of Manchester, 1951-60; Prof. of Modern History, University of Nottingham, 1960-66; Prof. of Early Modern European

History, Cornell, 1966-73. Visiting Lecturer: Brooklyn Coll., New York, 1957; University of Wisconsin, 1958; Columbia University, 1962; Cambridge Univ., 1963; Washington Univ., St Louis, 1964. Sec., 1955-75, Vice-Pres., 1975-80, Pres., 1980-, Internat. Commn for the History of Representative and Parliamentary Institutions; Vice-Pres., RHistS, 1982-. *Publications:* The Government of Sicily under Philip II of Spain, 1951, new edn, as The Practice of Empire, 1969; The Empire of Charles V in Europe (in New Cambridge Modern History II), 1958; Western Europe and the Power of Spain (in New Cambridge Modern History III), 1968; Europe in the Sixteenth Century (with G. L. Mosse), 1968; Estates and Revolutions, 1971; The Habsburgs and Europe, 1516-1660, 1971; (ed) Luther: a profile, 1972; contrib. to historical journals. *Recreations:* playing chamber music, sailing, travel. *Address:* King's College London, Strand, WC2.

KOESTLER, Arthur, CBE 1972; CLit 1974; FRSL; FRAS; author; *b* Budapest, Hungary, 5 Sept. 1905; *o s* of Henrik and Adela Koestler; *m* 1935, Dorothy Asher, Zürich; divorced 1950; no *c*; *m* 1950, Mamaine Paget; divorced 1953; no *c*; *m* 1965, Cynthia Jefferies. *Educ:* University of Vienna. Foreign Correspondent in Middle East, Paris, Berlin, 1926-31; Mem. of Graf Zeppelin Arctic Expedition, 1931; travels in Russia and Soviet Central Asia, 1932-33; covering the Spanish Civil War for News Chronicle, London, 1936-37; imprisoned by General Franco; served 1939-40 in French Foreign Legion and 1941-42 in British Pioneer Corps. Fellow, Centre for Advanced Study in the Behavioural Sciences, Stanford, 1964-65. Hon. Mem., AAIL. Hon. LLD Queen's Univ., Kingston, Ont, 1968; Hon. DLitt Leeds, 1977; Dr *hc* Liège, 1979; Hon. DSc Manchester, 1981. Sonning Prize, 1968. *Publications:* Spanish Testament, 1938; The Gladiators, 1939; Darkness at Noon, 1940; Scum of the Earth, 1941; Arrival and Departure, 1943; The Yogi and the Commissar, 1945; Twilight Bar, 1945; Thieves in the Night, 1946; Insight and Outlook, 1948; The God that Failed (with others), 1949; Promise and Fulfilment, 1949; The Age of Longing, 1950; Arrow in the Blue, 1952; The Invisible Writing, 1954; The Trail of the Dinosaur, 1955; Reflections on Hanging, 1956; The Sleepwalkers, 1959; The Lotus and the Robot, 1960; Suicide of a Nation? (ed), 1963; The Act of Creation, 1964; The Ghost in the Machine, 1967; Drinkers of Infinity, 1968; (ed with J. R. Smythies) Beyond Reductionism — New Perspectives in the Life Sciences: The Alpbach Symposium 1968, 1969; The Case of the Midwife Toad, 1971; The Roots of Coincidence, 1972; The Call-Girls, 1972; (with others) The Challenge of Chance, 1973; The Heel of Achilles, Essays 1968-1973, 1974; The Thirteenth Tribe, 1976; (with others) Life After Death, 1976; Janus: a summing-up, 1978; Bricks to Babel, 1980; Kaleidoscope, 1981; contribs: Encyclopaedia of Philosophy, 1967; Encyclopaedia Britannica, 1974; *relevant publications:* Arthur Koestler, by John Atkins, 1956; Arthur Koestler, Das Literarische Werk, by Peter Alfred Huber, Zürich, 1962; Arthur Koestler, Cahiers de l'Herne, 1975; Astride the Two Cultures: Arthur Koestler at Seventy, ed Harold Harris, 1975; Arthur Koestler, by Sidney A. Pearson Jr, 1978. *Recreations:* chess, good wine. *Address:* c/o A. D. Peters, 10 Buckingham Street, WC2.

KOGAN, Prof. Maurice; Professor of Government and Social Administration, Brunel University, since 1969; *b* 10 April 1930; *s* of Barnett and Hetty Kogan; *m* 1960, Ulla Svensson; two *s. Educ:* Stratford Grammar Sch.; Christ's Coll., Cambridge (MA). Entered Civil Service, admin. cl. (1st in open examinations), 1953. Secretary: Secondary Sch. Exams Council, 1961; Central Advisory Council for Educn (England), 1963-66; Harkness Fellow of Commonwealth Fund, 1960-61. Asst Sec., DES, 1966. Member: Educn Sub-Cttee, Univ. Grants Cttee, 1972-75; SSRC, 1975-77; Davies Cttee on Hosp. Complaints' Procedure, 1971; Houghton Cttee on Teachers' Pay, 1974; Genetic Manipulation Adv. Gp, 1979-; Head of School, Sch. of Social Sciences, Brunel Univ., 1971-74. George A. Miller Vis. Prof., Univ. of Illinois, 1976; Vis. Scholar, Univ. of Calif, Berkeley, 1981. *Publications:* The Organisation of a Social Services Department, 1971; Working Relationships within the British Hospital Service, 1971; The Government of Education, 1971; The Politics of Education, 1971; (ed) The Challenge of Change, 1973; County Hall, 1973; Advisory Councils and Committees in Education, 1974; Educational Policy-Making, 1975; The Politics of Educational Change, 1978; The Working of the National Health Service, 1978; (with T. Becher) Process and Structure in Higher Education, 1980; The Government's Commissioning of Research, 1980; (with T. Bush) Directors of Education, 1982; (with D. Kogan) The Battle for the Labour Party, 1982; contribs to TES, THES, Jl of Social Policy. *Recreations:* reading, listening to music. *Address:* 48 Duncan Terrace, Islington, N1 8AL. *T:* 01-226 0038.

KOHL, Helmut; Chancellor, Federal Republic of Germany, since 1982; Chairman, Christian Democratic Union of Western Germany, since 1973; *b* 3 April 1930; *s* of Hans and Cecilie Kohl; *m* 1960, Hannelore Renner; two *s. Educ:* Frankfurt Univ.; Heidelberg Univ. (Dr phil 1958 Heidelberg). Adv. Mem., Management Group for chemical industries, Rheinland-Pfalz, 1959; Dir, ZDF, 1970. President: Rheinland-Pfalz CDU, 1965; Parly CDU of Landtag, Rheinland-Pfalz, 1959; Mem., Central Cttee, 1964, Vice-Chm., 1970-73, CDU of W Germany; Minister-Pres. for Rheinland-Pfalz, 1969-76; Mem. Bundesrat, 1969-76; Leader of the Opposition, Bundestag, 1976-82. *Publications:* Hausputz hinter den Fassaden, 1971; Zwischen Ideologie und Pragmatismus, 1973. *Address:* Bundeskanzleramt, Adenauerallee 139, 53 Bonn 1, West Germany; 6700 Ludwigshafen/Rhein, Marbacher Strasse 11, W Germany. *T:* 680019.

KOHLER, Foy David; Associate, Advanced International Studies Institute; consultant; *b* 15 Feb. 1908; *s* of Leander David Kohler and Myrtle McClure; *m* 1935, Phyllis Penn. *Educ:* Toledo and Ohio State Univs, Ohio. US Foreign Service: posts include (1932-): Amer. Emb., London, 1944; Adviser to US Mem., 2nd Session of Council of UN Relief and Rehabilitation Admin., Montreal, Can., Sept. 1944; 1st Sec. Amer. Emb., Moscow, 1947; Counselor, 1948; Minister, Oct. 1948; Chief, Internat. Broadcasting Div., Dept of State, 1949; VOA 1949; Asst Administr, Internat. Information Admin, 1952; Policy Planning Staff, Dept of State, 1952; Counselor, Amer. Emb., Ankara, Turkey, 1953-56; detailed ICA, 1956-58; Deputy Asst Sec. of State for European Affairs, 1958-59; Asst Sec. of State, 1959-62; US Ambassador to USSR, 1962-66; Deputy Under-Sec. of State for Political Affairs, United States, 1966-67; Career Ambassador, USA, 1966-67 (Career Minister, Foreign Service of USA, 1959). Prof., Univ. of Miami, 1968-80. Editor, Soviet World Outlook, 1976-. Holds honorary doctorates. *Publications:* Understanding the Russians: a citizen's primer, 1970; (jtly) Soviet Strategy for the Seventies: from Cold War to peaceful coexistence, 1973; (jtly) The Role of Nuclear Forces in Current Soviet Strategy, 1974; (jtly) The Soviet Union: yesterday, today, tomorrow, 1975; Custine's Eternal Russia, 1976; Salt II: how not to negotiate with the Russians, 1979. *Recreations:* golf, swimming. *Address:* 215 Golf Club Circle, Village of Tequesta, Jupiter, Fla 33458, USA.

KOHLER, Irene; pianist; Professor, Trinity College of Music, London, 1952-79; *b* London; *m* 1950, Dr Harry Waters, medical practitioner. *Educ:* Royal College of Music. Studied with Arthur Benjamin (Challen Medal, Danreuther Prize, etc); travelling scholarship to Vienna; studied there with Edward Steuermann and Egon Wellesz. BMus; Hon. FTCL, GRSM, LRAM, ARCM. First professional engagement, Bournemouth, 1933, resulting in engagement by BBC; played at first night of 40th Promenade Season, 1934. First foreign tour (recitals and broadcasts), Holland, 1938. During War of 1939-45 gave concerts for the Forces in this country and toured France and Belgium, also India and Burma, under auspices of ENSA; subsequently played in many countries of Europe and made tours. Eugene Goossens selected her for first European performance of his Phantasy Concerto; broadcast 1st performance of Sonata by Gunilla Lowenstein, Stockholm. She gave 3 concerts at the Festival Hall in Festival of Britain Year, 1951. Canadian American Tour, 1953; World Tour, 1955-56; African Tour, 1958; 2nd African Tour, 1959; Bulgarian Tour, 1959; 2nd World Tour, 1962; Czechoslovakian Tour, 1963; Scandinavian Tour, 1970; Far and Middle East Tour, 1972; recitals and master classes, Japan, 1979, 1981; Polish Tour, 1980. Film appearances include: Train of Events, Odette, Secret People, Lease of Life, and a documentary for the Ministry of Information. *Address:* 28 Castelnau, SW13 9RU. *T:* 01-748 5512.

KOHNSTAM, George, PhD; Principal of the Graduate Society, University of Durham, since 1981 (Deputy Principal, 1972-81); Reader in Physical Chemistry, University of Durham, since 1962; *b* 25 Dec. 1920; *s* of Emil and Margaret Kohnstam; *m* 1953, Patricia Elizabeth, *d* of Rev. A. W. G. Duffield and Margaret Duffield; one *s* three *d. Educ:* Royal Grammar Sch., High Wycombe; University Coll. London (BSc 1940, PhD 1948). Tuffnel Scholar, Univ. of London, 1940 (postponed); applied chemical res., 1941-45; Temp. Asst Lectr in Chemistry, UCL, 1948-50; Lectr in Phys. Chem., Univ. of Durham, 1950-59, Sen. Lectr, 1959-62. *Publications:* papers and review articles in chemical jls. *Recreations:* dinghy sailing, gardening, bridge, travel. *Address:* 67 Hallgarth Street, Durham City DH1 3AY. *T:* Durham 42018.

KOHNSTAMM, Max, Comdr of the Order of the House of Orange Nassau; Principal, European University Institute of Florence, 1975-81; *b* 22 May 1914; *s* of Dr Philip Abraham Kohnstamm and Johanna Hermana Kessler; *m* 1944, Kathleen Sillem; two *s* three *d. Educ:* Univ. of Amsterdam (Hist. Drs); American Univ., Washington. Private Sec. to Queen Wilhelmina, 1945-48; subseq. Head of German Bureau, then Dir of European Affairs, Netherlands FO; Sec. of High Authority, 1952-56; 1st Rep. of High Authority, London, 1956; Sec.-Gen. (later Vice-Pres.), Action Cttee for United States of Europe, 1956-75; Pres., European Community Inst. for Univ. Studies, 1958-75. Co-Chm., Cttee on Soc. Develt and Peace, World Council of Churches and Pontifical Commn for Justice and Peace, 1967-75; European Pres., Trilateral Commn, 1973-75. *Publications:* The European Community and its Role in the World, 1963; (ed jtly) A Nation Writ Large?, 1972. *Recreations:* tennis, walking. *Address:* 5421 Ciergnon-Fenffe, Namur, Belgium. *T:* (84) 37 71 83.

KOHOBAN-WICKREME, Alfred Silva, CVO 1954; Member Ceylon Civil Service; Secretary to the Cabinet, 1968-70; *b* 2 Nov. 1914; *m* 1941, Mona Estelle Kohoban-Wickreme. *Educ:* Trinity Coll., Kandy; University Coll., Colombo. BA (Hons) London, 1935. Cadet, Ceylon Civil Service, 1938; served as Magistrate, District Judge, Asst Govt Agent etc, until 1948; Chief Admin. Officer, Ceylon Govt Rly, 1948; Asst Sec., Min. of Home Affairs, 1951; attached to Ceylon High Commissioner's Office in UK, May-July, 1953; Dir of Social Services and Commissioner for Workmen's Compensation, Ceylon, 1953; Conservator of Forests, Ceylon, 1958; Port Commissioner, Ceylon, 1959; Postmaster General and Dir of Telecommunications, Dec. 1962; Permanent Sec., Ministry of: Local Govt and Home Affairs, April 1964; Cultural Affairs and Social Services, June 1964; Ministry of Communications, 1965. Organised the Queen's Tour in Ceylon, April 1954 (CVO). *Recreations:* sports activities, particularly Rugby football, tennis and cricket. *Address:* 6 Kalinga Place, Jawatta Road, Colombo 5, Sri Lanka. *T:* (residence) 86385.

KOHT, Paul; Ambassador of Norway to Denmark, 1975-82; *b* 7 Dec. 1913; *s* of Dr Halvdan Koht and Karen Elisabeth (*née* Grude); *m* 1938, Grete Sverdrup; two *s* one *d. Educ:* University of Oslo. Law degree, 1937. Entered Norwegian Foreign Service, 1938; held posts in: Bucharest, 1938-39; London, 1940-41; Tokyo, 1941-42; New York, 1942-46; Lisbon, 1950-51; Mem. Norwegian Delegn to OEEC and NATO, Paris, and Perm. Rep. to Coun. of Europe, 1951-53; Dir General of Dept for Econ. Affairs, Min. of For. Affairs, Oslo, 1953-56; Chargé d'Affaires, Copenhagen, 1956-58; Ambassador to USA, 1958-63; Ambassador to Fed. Republic of Germany, 1963-68; Ambassador to the Court of St James's, 1968-75. Comdr, Order of St Olav; Grand Cross, Order of Dannebrog; Grand Cross, Order of Merit (Federal Republic of Germany). *Address:* Lille Frogner Allé 4b, Oslo 2, Norway.

KOLAKOWSKI, Leszek, PhD, FBA 1980; Senior Research Fellow, All Souls College, Oxford, since 1970; *b* 23 Oct. 1927; *s* of Jerzy and Lucyna (*née* Pietrusiewicz); *m* 1949, Dr Tamara Kolakowska (*née* Dynenson); one *d. Educ:* Lódź Univ., Poland 1945-50; Warsaw Univ. (PhD 1953). Asst in Philosophy: Lódź Univ., 1947-49; Warsaw Univ., 1950-59; Prof. and Chm., Section of History of Philosophy, Warsaw Univ., 1959-68, expelled by authorities for political reasons; Visiting Professor: McGill Univ., 1968-69; Univ. of California, Berkeley, 1969-70; Yale Univ., Conn, 1975. Mem. Internat. Inst. of Philosophy; Foreign Mem., Amer. Academy of Arts and Science; Mem.-correspondent, Bayerische Akademie des Künste. Friedenspreis des Deutschen Buchhandels, 1977; Jurzykowski Foundn award, 1968; Charles Veillou Prix Européen d'Essai, 1980. *Publications:* about 25 books, some of them only in Polish; trans. of various books in 14 languages; *in English:* Marxism and Beyond, 1968; Conversations with the Devil, 1972; Positivist Philosophy, 1972; Husserl and the Search for Certitude, 1975; Main Currents of Marxism, 3 vols, 1978; Religion, 1982; *in French:* Chrétiens sans Eglise, 1969; *in German:* Traktat über die Sterblichkeit der Vernunft, 1967; Geist und Ungeist christlicher Traditionen, 1971; Die Gegenwärtigkeit des Mythos, 1973; Der revolutionäre Geist, 1972; Leben trotz Geschichte Lesebuch, 1977; Zweifel und die Methode, 1977. *Address:* 77 Hamilton Road, Oxford OX2 7QA. *T:* Oxford 58790.

KOLBUSZEWSKI, Prof. Janusz, DSc (Eng), PhD, DIC, Dipl.Ing; FICE; FCIT; Professor of Transportation and Environmental Planning and Head of Department, University of Birmingham, 1965-81, now Emeritus Professor (Professor of Highway and Traffic Engineering, 1959-64, of Transportation, 1964-65); *b* 18 Feb. 1915; *s* of Jan Alexander and Bronislawa Kolbuszewski; *m* 1946, Marie-Louise Jasinska; one *s* one *d. Educ:* Technical University of Lwow, Poland (Dipl.Ing); Imperial Coll. of Science and Technology, University of London. PhDEng, London, 1948; DIC 1948; DSc(Eng), London, 1968. Lecturer, Technical Univ. of Lwow, Poland, until 1939. Served War of 1939-45: Polish, French and British Armies. Imperial Coll. Science and Technology, London, 1945-48; Prof., Dir of Studies, Polish University Coll., London, 1948-50; Lecturer, Sen. Lecturer, Reader, in charge of Graduate Schs in Foundation Engrg and in Highway and Traffic Engineering, University of Birmingham, 1951-59. Lectr of Honour, Inst. Traffic Sci., Japan, 1972; James Forrest Lectr, ICE, 1972. Member: Civil Engrg and Aero Cttee, SRC, 1967; Research Cttee, ICE, 1966; Transport Bd, CNAA, 1974; Chm., Bd of the Inst. of Transportation Safety, USA, 1980-. Governor, Birmingham Coll. of Arts. Hon. Mem., Midlands Soc. for Soil Mechanics and Foundn Engrg. Lister Prize, Midland Branch of IStructE, 1953; Nusey Prize, Soc. of Engineers, London, 1967; Certificate of Merit, Inst. of Highway Engineers, 1977. *Publications:* various scientific papers on Geometry, Perspective, Soil Mechanics, Foundations and Highway Engineering, Transportation and Planning. *Recreations:* travelling, oil painting. *Address:* Passy, Star Lane, All Stretton, Shropshire. *T:* Church Stretton 3149.

KOLHAPUR, Maharaja of; Maj.-Gen. HH Sir Shahaji Chhatrapati, (adopted these names in lieu of those of Vikramsinharao Puar, on succeeding to Kolhapur Gadi, 1947); GCSI, 1947 (KCSI, 1941); *b* 4 April 1910. Formerly Maharaja of Dewas (Senior Branch); State merged with Bombay, 1949. Appointed Major and Hon. ADC to HM King Emperor George VI, 1946; Hon. Maj.-Gen. Indian Army, 1962. *Address:* New Palace, Kolhapur, Maharashtra, India.

KOLO, Sule; Chairman, Alheri Enterprises; Executive Director, Rainone-Washik Construction Co.; Consultant, Knight Frank & Rutley (Nigeria); High Commissioner for Nigeria in London, 1970-75; *b* 1926; *m* 1957, Helen Patricia Kolo; one *s* three *d.* BSc (Econ); attended Imperial Defence College. Counsellor, Nigerian High Commn in London, 1962; Perm. Sec., Nigerian Min. of Defence, 1963; Perm. Sec., Nigerian Min. of Trade, 1966; Nigeria's Perm. Representative to European Office of UN and Ambassador to Switzerland, 1966; Chm. of GATT, 1969. FR.EconS; FRSA 1973. Franklin Peace Medal, 1969. *Recreations:* swimming, tennis. *Address:* PO Box 917, Jos, Nigeria. *Clubs:* Travellers'; Island (Lagos).

KOLTAI, Ralph; freelance stage designer; designer for Drama, Opera and Dance, since 1950; Associate Designer, Royal Shakespeare Company, 1963-66 and since 1976; *b* 31 July 1924; Hungarian-German; *s* of Dr(med) Alfred Koltai and Charlotte Koltai (*née* Weinstein); *m* 1956, Annena Stubbs. *Educ:* Central Sch. of Art and Design (Dip. with Dist.). Early work entirely in field of opera. First production, Angelique, for London Opera Club, Fortune Theatre, 1950. Designs for The Royal Opera House, Sadler's Wells, Scottish Opera, National Welsh Opera, The English Opera Group. First of 7 ballets for Ballet Rambert, Two Brothers, 1958. *Productions:* RSC: The Caucasian

Chalk Circle, 1962; The Representative, 1963; The Birthday Party; Endgame; The Jew of Malta, 1964; The Merchant of Venice; Timon of Athens, 1965; Little Murders, 1967; Major Barbara, 1970; Too True To Be Good, 1975; Old World, 1976; Wild Oats, 1977; The Tempest, Love's Labour's Lost, 1978; Hippolytus, Baal, 1979; Romeo and Juliet, Hamlet, 1980; The Love Girl and the Innocent, 1981 (London Drama Critics Award); Much Ado About Nothing, 1982; for National Theatre: an "all male" As You Like It, 1967; Back to Methuselah, 1969; State of Revolution, 1977; Brand (Soc. of West End Theatres Award), The Guardsman, 1978; Richard III, The Wild Duck, 1979; Man and Superman, 1981; has worked in most countries in Western Europe, also Bulgaria, Argentine, USA, Canada, Australia; *other notable productions include:* for Sadler's Wells/English National Opera: The Rise and Fall of the City of Mahagonny, 1963; From the House of the Dead, 1965; Bluebeard's Castle, 1972; Wagner's (complete) Ring Cycle, 1973; Seven Deadly Sins, 1978; Anna Karenina, 1981; for The Royal Opera House: Taverner, 1972; The Ice Break, 1977; for Sydney Opera House: Tannhauser, 1973; for Netherlands Opera: Wozzeck, 1973; Billy, Drury Lane, 1974; Fidelio, Munich, 1974; Verdi's Macbeth, Edinburgh Festival, 1976; for Aalborg Theatre, Denmark: Threepenny Opera, 1979; The Love Girl and the Innocent, 1980; Terra Nova, 1981; The Carmelites, 1981. London Drama Critics Award, Designer of the Year, 1967 (for Little Murders and As You Like It); (jtly) Gold Medal, Internat. Exhibn of Stage Design, Prague Quadriennale, 1975, 1979. *Recreation:* wildlife photography. *Address:* c/o Macnaughton Lowe Representation Ltd, 194 Old Brompton Road, SW5 0AS. *T:* 01-373 1161.

KOMINSKI, Daniel; *see* Kaye, Danny.

KONSTANT, Rt. Rev. David Every; Auxiliary Bishop of Westminster (Bishop in Central London) (RC), and Titular Bishop of Betagbara, since 1977; *b* 16 June 1930; *s* of Antoine Konstant and Dulcie Marion Beresford Konstant (*née* Leggatt). *Educ:* St Edmund's College, Old Hall Green, Ware; Christ's College, Cambridge (MA); Univ. of London Inst. of Education (PGCE). Priest, dio. Westminster, 1954; Cardinal Vaughan School, Kensington, 1959; Diocesan Adviser on Religious Education, 1966; St Michael's School, Stevenage, 1968; Director, Westminster Religious Education Centre, 1970. *Publications:* various books on religious education and liturgy. *Recreation:* music. *Address:* 31 Holland Park Gardens, W14 8EA. *T:* 01-603 7409.

KOO, Vi Kyuin Wellington; Judge of International Court of Justice, 1957-67 (Vice-President, 1964-67); Senior Adviser to the President of the Republic of China in USA, since 1975; *b* 1888; *m* Juliana Yen. *Educ:* Columbia Univ. (Doctor of Philosophy). Sec. to Pres. of China; Councillor in Foreign Office; Minister to USA, 1915; attended Peace Conference as China's Plenipotentiary, and later as Head of the Chinese Delegation, 1919; Chinese delegate to the Assembly and China's representative on the Council of the League of Nations at Geneva, 1920-22; Chinese Minister to Great Britain, 1921; Plenipotentiary to Washington Conference, 1921-22; Minister of Foreign Affairs, Peking, 1922-24; Finance Minister, 1926; Prime Minister and Minister of Foreign Affairs, 1926-27; Mem. on the International Court of Arbitration at The Hague, 1927-57; Minister of Foreign Affairs, China, 1931; Chinese Assessor to the Commission of Inquiry of the League of Nations, 1932; Chinese Minister to France, 1932-35; Chinese Ambassador to France, 1936-41; in London, 1941-46; Chinese representative on the Council of the League of Nations at Geneva, 1932-34; Delegate 13th and 14th Assemblies of League of Nations and to the Special Assembly of the League of Nations, 1932-33; Delegate to the World Monetary and Economic Conference, London, 1933; Delegate to Conference for Reduction and Limitation of Armaments, at Geneva, 1933; Chief Delegate to Assemblies of League of Nations, 1935-36 and 1938; Special Envoy to Accession of Leopold to throne of Belgium, 1938; Delegate to sessions of League Coun., 1937-39 (Pres. 96th); Chief Deleg. to Brussels Conference, Nov. 1937; Special Envoy to coronation of His Holiness Pius XII; Ambassador Extraordinary to 800th Anniversary of Foundation of Portugal, 1940; Chief Delegate to Dumbarton Oaks Conf.; Rep. on War Crimes Commn, London; Delegate and Actg Chief Delegate to San Francisco Conf. to draft UN charter; Chinese Ambassador in Washington, 1946-56; Delegate to UNRRA and FAO, 1946-49; Mem., Far Eastern Commn, 1946-49; Senior Advisor to General Chiang Kai-Shek, 1956-57, 1967-74. *Publications:* Status of Aliens in China, 1912; Memorandum presented to Lytton Commission (3 volumes), 1932. Hon. degrees: LLD: Columbia, Yale, St John's, Birmingham, Aberdeen, Manchester; LHD, Rollins Coll.; DCL, Miami. *Recreations:* tennis, golf, fishing, skiing. *Address:* 1185 Park Avenue, New York, NY 10028, USA.

KOOPMANS, Prof. Tjalling Charles; Alfred Cowles Professor Emeritus of Economics, Yale University (Professor of Economics, Yale, 1955-80, Alfred Cowles Professor, 1967-80); *b* Holland, 28 Aug. 1910; *m* 1936, Truus Wanningen; one *s* two *d. Educ:* Univ. of Utrecht (MA, Phys. and Maths); Univ. of Leiden (PhD, Math. Statistics). Lectr, Netherlands Sch. of Economics, Rotterdam, 1936-38; Economist, Financial Section, League of Nations, Geneva, 1938-40; Special Lectr, Sch. of Business, New York Univ., 1940-41; Research Associate, Princeton Univ., 1940-41; Economist, Penn Mutual Life Ins. Co., 1941-42; Statistician, Combined Shipping Adjustment Bd, Washington, 1942-44; Research Associate, Cowles Commn for Research in Economics, Univ. of Chicago, 1944-54; Associate Prof. of Economics, 1946-48, Prof. of Economics, 1948-55, Univ. of Chicago; Dir of Research, Cowles Commn, 1948-54; Frank W. Taussig Prof. of Economics, Harvard

Univ., 1960–61; Dir, Cowles Foundn, 1961–67. Member: Econometric Soc. (Mem. 1934–, Fellow, 1940–, Vice-Pres. 1949, Pres. 1950, Council Mem. 1949–55, 1966–71, 1973–78); American Economic Assoc., 1941– (Distinguished Fellow, 1971, Pres., 1978); (Corresp.) Royal Netherlands Acad. of Arts and Scis, 1950–; Amer. Math. Soc., 1952–; Inst. of Management Scis, 1954–; Ops Research Soc. of Amer., 1954–; Amer. Acad. of Arts and Scis, 1960–; Nat. Acad. of Scis, 1969–. Nobel Prize for Economics (jt), 1975; Honours and Awards from Belgium, Netherlands and USA. *Publications:* Linear Regression Analysis of Economic Time Series (PhD Thesis), 1936; Tanker Freight Rates and Tankship Building, 1939; Three Essays on the State of Economic Science: Allocation of Resources and the Price System, The Construction of Economic Knowledge, The Interaction of Tools and Problems in Economics, 1957; ed and contrib. Cowles Commn Monographs Nos 10 and 13, 1950 and 1951; Co-ed and contrib. No 14, 1953; contrib. Studies in the Economics of Transportation (by Beckmann, McGuire and Winsten), 1956; Selected Scientific Papers, 1934–67, repr. 1970; numerous articles to economic and other professional jls, reviews, annals, proc. confs and papers. *Address:* (office) Cowles Foundation, Box 2125 Yale Station, New Haven 06520, USA. *T:* (203) 436 2578; (home) 459 Ridge Road, Hamden, Connecticut 06517, USA. *T:* (203) 248 5872.

KOOTENAY, Bishop of, since 1971; **Rt. Rev. Robert Edward Fraser Berry;** *b* Ottawa, Ont; *s* of Samuel Berry and Claire Hartley; *m* 1951, Margaret Joan Trevorrow Baillie; one *s* one *d*. *Educ:* Sir George Williams Coll., Montreal; McGill Univ., Montreal; Montreal Diocesan Theological Coll. Assistant, Christ Church Cathedral, Victoria, BC, 1953–55; Rector: St Margaret's, Hamilton, Ont, 1955–61; St Mark's, Orangeville, Ont, 1961–63; St Luke's, Winnipeg, Manitoba, 1963–67; St Michael and All Angels, Kelowna, BC, 1967–71. Hon. DD, Montreal Diocesan Theol Coll., 1973. *Address:* (home) 1857 Maple Street, Kelowna, BC, Canada. *T:* (604) 762-2923; (office) Box 549, Kelowna, BC V1Y 7P2, Canada. *T:* (604) 762-3306.

KOPAL, Prof. Zdeněk; Professor of Astronomy, University of Manchester, 1951–81, now Emeritus; *b* 4 April 1914; 2nd *s* of Prof. Joseph Kopal, of Charles University, Prague, and Ludmila (*née* Lelek); *m* 1938, Alena, *o d* of late Judge B. Muldner; three *d*. *Educ:* Charles University, Prague; University of Cambridge, England; Harvard Univ., USA. Agassiz Research Fellow, Harvard Observatory, 1938–40; Research Associate in Astronomy, Harvard Univ., 1940–46; Lecturer in Astronomy, Harvard Univ., 1948; Associate Prof., Mass Institute of Technology, 1947–51. Pres., Foundation Internationale du Pic-du-Midi; Mem. Internat. Acad. of Astronautical Sciences, New York Acad. of Sciences; Chm., Cttee for Lunar and Planetary Exploration, Brit. Nat. Cttee for Space Research; Mem. Lunar-Planetary Cttee, US Nat. Space Bd. Editor-in-Chief, Astrophysics and Space Science, 1968–; Founding Editor: Icarus (internat. jl of solar system); The Moon (internat. jl of lunar studies), 1969–. Pahlavi Lectr, Iran, 1977. Gold Medal, Czechoslovak Acad. of Sciences, 1969; Copernicus Medal, Krakow Univ., 1974. For. Mem., Greek Nat. Acad. of Athens, 1976; DSc (*hc*) Krakow, 1974; Hon. Citizen of Delphi, 1978. *Publications:* An Introduction to the Study of Eclipsing Variables, 1946 (US); The Computation of Elements of Eclipsing Binary Systems, 1950 (US); Tables of Supersonic Flow of Air Around Cones, 3 vols, 1947–49 (US); Numerical Analysis (London), 1955; Astronomical Optics (Amsterdam), 1956; Close Binary Systems, 1959; Figures of Equilibrium of Celestial Bodies, 1960; The Moon, 1960; Physics and Astronomy of the Moon, 1962, 2nd edn 1971; Photographic Atlas of the Moon, 1965; An Introduction to the Study of the Moon, 1966; The Measure of the Moon, 1967; (ed) Advances in Astronomy and Astrophysics, 1968; Telescopes in Space, 1968; Exploration of the Moon by Spacecraft, 1968; Widening Horizons, 1970; A New Photographic Atlas of the Moon, 1971; Man and His Universe, 1972; The Solar System, 1973; Mapping of the Moon, 1974; The Moon in the Post-Apollo Stage, 1974; Dynamics of Close Binary Systems, 1978; The Realm of Terrestrial Planets, 1978; Language of the Stars, 1979; over 320 original papers on astronomy, aerodynamics, and applied mathematics in publications of Harvard Observatory, Astrophysical Journal, Astronomical Journal, Astronomische Nachrichten, Monthly Notices of Royal Astronomical Society, Proc. Amer. Phil. Soc., Proc. Nat. Acad. Sci. (US), Zeitschrift für Astrophysik, etc. *Recreation:* mountaineering. *Address:* Greenfield, Parkway, Wilmslow, Cheshire. *T:* Wilmslow 22470. *Club:* Explorers' (NY).

KORNBERG, Prof. Arthur; Professor of Biochemistry, Stanford University, since 1959; *b* Brooklyn, 3 March 1918; *m*; three *s*. *Educ:* College of the City of New York (BSc 1937); University of Rochester, NY (MD 1941). Strong Memorial Hospital, Rochester, 1941–42; National Insts of Health, Bethesda, Md, 1942–52; Professor of Microbiology, Washington Univ., and Head of Dept of Microbiology, 1953–59; Head of Dept of Biochemistry, Stanford Univ., 1959–69. MNAS; MAAS; Mem. Amer. Phil Soc. Foreign Mem., Royal Soc., 1970. Many honours and awards, including: Paul Lewis Award in Enzyme Chemistry, 1951; Nobel Prize (joint) in Medicine, 1959. *Publications:* articles in scientific jls. *Address:* Stanford University Medical Center, Palo Alto, Calif 94305, USA.

KORNBERG, Prof. Sir Hans (Leo), Kt 1978; MA, DSc Oxon, ScD Cantab, PhD Sheffield; FRS 1965; FIBiol 1965; Sir William Dunn Professor of Biochemistry, University of Cambridge, and Fellow of Christ's College, since 1975; *b* 14 Jan. 1928; *o s* of Max Kornberg and Margarete Kornberg (*née* Silberbach); *m* 1956, Monica Mary (*née* King); twin *s* two *d*. *Educ:* Queen Elizabeth Grammar Sch., Wakefield; University of Sheffield (BSc). Commonwealth Fund Fellow of Harkness Foundation, at Yale University and Public Health Research Inst., New York, 1953–55; Mem. of scientific staff, MRC Cell Metabolism Res. Unit, University of Oxford, 1955–60; Lectr, Worcester Coll., Oxford, 1958–61 (Hon. Fellow 1980); Prof. of Biochemistry, Univ. of Leicester, 1960–75; Res. Associate of University of Calif, Berkeley, 1954, of Harvard Med. Sch., Boston, 1958; Visiting Instructor, Marine Biological Lab., Woods Hole, Mass, 1964–66, 1981, 1982; Visiting Professor: Univ. of Miami, 1970–; Univ. of Cincinnati, 1974; Lectures: CIBA, Rutgers, NJ, 1968; Life Sciences, Univ. of Calif. at Davis, California, 1971; Leeuwenhoek, Royal Soc., 1972; Australian Biochem. Soc., 1973; Japan Acad., 1978; Weizmann Meml, Israel, 1975; Fedn European Biochem. Socs Springer, 1975; Griffith Meml, Soc. General Microbiology, 1976; Barton-Wright, Inst. Biol., 1977; Leverhulme Meml, Liverpool, 1977; David Henderson Meml, MRE Porton, 1979; Penn, Univ. of Pennsylvania, 1979; Sir Henry Tizard Meml, Westminster, 1981; Redfearn Meml, Leicester, 1981; Lansdowne, Univ. of Victoria, BC, 1982. Member: SRC, 1967–72 (Chm., Science Bd, 1969–72); ARC, 1980–; Adv. Council for Applied R&D, 1982–; UGC Biol. Sci. Cttee, 1967–77; NATO Adv. Study Inst. Panel, 1970–76 (Chm., 1974–75); Kuratorium, Max-Planck Inst., Dortmund, 1979– (Chm., Sci. Adv. Cttee); BP Venture Res. Council, 1981–; Vice-Chm., EMBO, 1978–81; Scientific Counsellor, Inst. Cytol., Valencia, 1978–; Chm., Royal Commn on Environmental Pollution, 1976–81. A Managing Trustee, Nuffield Foundn, 1973–; Alternate Governor, Hebrew Univ. of Jerusalem, 1976–; Governor, Weizmann Inst., 1980–; Mem. Council, Epsom Coll., 1981–. Vice-Pres., Inst. of Biol., 1971–73. FRSA 1972. Hon. Member: Amer. Soc. Biol Chem., 1972–; Biochem. Soc. FRG, 1973–; Japanese Biochem. Soc., 1981–. Hon. ScD Cincinnati, 1974; Hon. DSc: Warwick, 1975; Leicester, 1979; Sheffield, 1979; Bath, 1980; DUniv Essex, 1979. Colworth Medal of Biochemical Soc., 1965; Otto Warburg Medal, Biochem. Soc. of Federal Republic of Germany, 1973. *Publications:* (with Sir Hans Krebs) Energy Transformations in Living Matter, 1957; articles in scientific jls. *Recreations:* cooking and conversation. *Address:* Pine Trees, 111 Glebe Road, Cambridge CB1 4TE; Christ's College, Cambridge CB2 3BU.

KÖRNER, Prof. Stephan, JurDr, PhD; FBA 1967; Professor of Philosophy, Bristol University, 1952–79, and Yale University, since 1970; *b* Ostrava, Czechoslovakia, 26 Sept. 1913; *o s* of Emil Körner and Erna (*née* Maier); *m* 1944, Edith Laner, BSc, JP; one *s* one *d*. *Educ:* Classical Gymnasium; Charles' Univ., Prague; Trinity Hall, Cambridge. Army Service, 1936–39, 1943–46. University of Bristol: Lectr in Philosophy, 1946; Dean, Faculty of Arts, 1965–66; Pro-Vice-Chancellor, 1968–71; Visiting Prof. of Philosophy: Brown Univ., 1957; Yale Univ., 1960; Texas Univ., 1964; Indiana Univ., 1967; Graz Univ., 1980 (Hon. Prof., 1982). President: Brit. Soc. for Philosophy of Science, 1965; Aristotelian Soc., 1967; Internat. Union of History and Philosophy of Science, 1969; Mind Assoc., 1973. Editor, Ratio, 1961–80. Hon. DLitt Belfast, 1981. *Publications:* Kant, 1955; Conceptual Thinking, 1955; The Philosophy of Mathematics, 1960; Experience and Theory, 1966; Kant's Conception of Freedom (British Acad. Lecture), 1967; What is Philosophy?, 1969; Categorial Frameworks, 1970; Abstraction in Science and Morals (Eddington Meml Lecture), 1971; (ed) Practical Reason, 1974; (ed) Observation and Interpretation, 1957; (ed) Explanation, 1976; Experience and Conduct, 1976; contribs to philosophical periodicals. *Recreation:* walking. *Address:* 10 Belgrave Road, Bristol BS8 2AB.

KOSINSKI, Jerzy Nikodem; author; *b* Lodz, Poland, 14 June 1933; naturalised US citizen, 1965; *s* of Mieczyslaw and Elzbieta (Liniecka) Kosinski; *m* 1962, Mary H. Weir (*d* 1968). *Educ:* Univ. of Lodz (MA (Polit. Sci.) 1953; MA (Hist.) 1955); Univ. of Columbia (Ford Foundn Fellow, 1958–60). Asst Prof., Inst. Sociology and Cultural Hist., Polish Acad. of Scis, Warsaw, 1955–57; Guggenheim Lit. Fellow, 1967; Fellow, Center for Advanced Studies, Wesleyan Univ., 1968–69; Sen. Fellow, Council of Humanities. Vis. Lectr in English, Princeton, 1969–70; Vis Prof. in English Prose, Sch. of Drama, Yale, also resident Fellow, Davenport Coll., 1970–73. Member: PEN (Pres., 1973–75); Bd, Nat. Writers Club; Bd, Internat. League for Human Rights; Amer. Civil Liberties Union (Chm., Artists and Writers Cttee; Mem., Nat. Adv. Council); Authors Guild. Film début as Zimoviev in Reds, 1982. Literature Award, Amer. Acad. Arts and Letters, 1970; Brith Sholom Humanitarian Freedom Award, 1974. *Publications:* The Future is Ours, Comrade, 1960; No Third Path, 1962; The Painted Bird, 1965 (Best Foreign Book Award, Paris, 1966); Steps, 1968 (Nat. Book Award, 1969); Being There, 1971 (filmed, 1978; Best Screenplay Awards, Writers Guild of Amer., 1979, and BAFTA, 1980); The Devil Tree, 1973, rev. and enlarged edn 1981; Cockpit, 1975; Blind Date, 1977; Passion Play, 1979; Pinball, 1982. *Address:* 60 W 57th Street, New York, NY 10019, USA. *Club:* Century Association (NY).

KOSSOFF, David; actor; designer-illustrator; *b* 24 Nov. 1919; *s* of Louis and Anne Kossoff, both Russian; *m* 1947, Margaret (Jennie) Jenkins; two *s*. *Educ:* elementary sch.; Northern Polytechnic. Commercial Artist, 1937; Draughtsman, 1937–38; Furniture Designer, 1938–39; Technical Illustrator, 1939–45. Began acting, 1943; working as actor and illustrator, 1945–52, as actor and designer, 1952–. BBC Repertory Company, 1945–51. Took over part of Colonel Alexander Ikonenko in the Love of Four Colonels, Wyndham's, 1952; Sam Tager in The Shrike, Prince's, 1953; Morry in The Bespoke Overcoat, and Tobit in Tobias and the Angel, Arts, 1953; Prof. Lodegger in No Sign of the Dove, Savoy, 1953; Nathan in The Boychik, Embassy, 1954 (and again Morry in The Bespoke Overcoat); Mendele in The World of Sholom Aleichem, Embassy, 1955, and Johannesburg, 1957; one-man show, One Eyebrow Up, The Arts, 1957; Man on Trial, Lyric, 1959; Stars in Your Eyes, Palladium, 1960; The Tenth Man, Comedy, 1961; Come Blow Your Horn, Prince of Wales, 1962; one-man show, Kossoff at the Prince Charles, 1963, later called A Funny Kind of Evening (many countries); Enter Solly Gold, Mermaid, 1970; Cinderella, Palladium, 1971; Bunny, Criterion, 1972; own Bible storytelling programmes on radio and TV, as writer and teller, 1964-66; solo performance (stage), 'As According to Kossoff', 1970-. Has appeared in many films. Won British Acad. Award, 1956. Elected MSIA 1958. FRSA 1969. *Play:* Big Night for Shylock, 1968. *Publications:* Bible Stories retold by David Kossoff, 1968; The Book of Witnesses, 1971; The Three Donkeys, 1972; The Voices of Masada, 1973; The Little Book of Sylvanus, 1975; You Have a Minute, Lord?, 1977; A Small Town is a World, 1979. *Recreations:* conversation, watching other actors work. *Address:* 45 Roe Green Close, Hatfield, Herts.

KOSTERLITZ, Hans Walter, MD, PhD, DSc; FRCPE 1981; FRS 1978; FRSE 1951; Director, Unit for Research on Addictive Drugs, University of Aberdeen, since 1973; Fogarty Scholar-in-Residence, US National Institutes of Health, since 1982; *b* 27 April 1903; *s* of Bernhard and Selma Kosterlitz; *m* 1937, Johanna Maria Katherina Gresshöner; one *s. Educ:* Univs of Heidelberg, Freiburg and Berlin. MD Berlin 1929; PhD 1936, DSc 1944, Hon. LLD 1979, Aberdeen. Assistant, 1st Medical Dept, Univ. of Berlin, 1928-33; University of Aberdeen: Research Worker in Physiology, 1934-36; Asst and Carnegie Teaching Fellow, 1936-39; Lectr, 1939-45; Sen. Lectr, 1945-55; Reader in Physiology, 1955-68; Prof. of Pharmacology and Chm., 1968-73. Visiting Lecturer: in Pharmacology, Harvard Med. Sch., 1953-54; in Biology, Brown Univ., 1953; Vis. Prof. of Pharmacology, Harvard Med. Sch., 1977; Lectures: J. Y. Dent Meml, 1970; Otto Krayer, 1977; Scheele, 1977; Gen. Session, Fedn Amer. Socs for Experimental Biol., 1978; Sutcliffe Kerr, 1978; Charnock Bradley Meml, 1979; Arnold H. Maloney, 1979; Lister, 1980; Lita Annenberg Hazen, 1980; Lilly, 1980; Sherrington Meml, RSocMed, 1982; N. J. Giarmen Meml, Yale Univ. Sch. of Med., 1982. Dr *hc* Liège, 1978; Hon. DSc St Andrews, 1982. Schmiedeberg Plakette, German Pharmacol Soc., 1976; Pacesetter Award, US Nat. Inst. on Drug Abuse, 1977; Nathan B. Eddy Award, US Cttee on Problems of Drug Dependence, 1978; (jtly) Albert Lasker Prize, 1978; Baly Medal, RCP, 1979; Royal Medal, 1979, Wellcome Foundn Prize, 1982, Royal Soc.; MacDougall-Brisbane Medal, RSE, 1980; Thudicum Medal, Biochem. Soc., 1980; Feldberg Foundn Prize, 1981; Harvey Prize, Technion, 1981. *Publications:* (joint editor): Agonist and Antagonist Actions of Narcotic Analgesic Drugs, 1972; The Opiate Narcotics, 1975; Opiates and Endogenous Opioid Peptides, 1976; Pain and Society, 1980; articles in Nature, Jl of Physiol, Brit. Jl of Pharmacol. *Recreations:* music, walking, travelling. *Address:* Unit for Research on Addictive Drugs, University of Aberdeen, Aberdeen AB9 1AS. *T:* Aberdeen 40241; 16 Glendee Terrace, Cults, Aberdeen AB1 9HX. *T:* Aberdeen 867366.

KOTCH, Laurie, (Mrs J. K. Kotch); *see* Purden, R. L.

KOTSOKOANE, Hon. Joseph Riffat Larry; *b* 19 Oct. 1922; *s* of Basotho parents, living in Johannesburg, South Africa; *m* 1947, Elizabeth (*née* Molise); two *s* three *d.* BSc (SA); BSc Hons (Witwatersrand); Cert. Agric. (London). Development Officer, Dept of Agric., Basutoland, 1951-54; Agric. Educn Officer i/c of Agric. Sch. for junior field staff, 1955-62; Agric. Extension Officer i/c of all field staff of Min. of Agric., 1962-63; Prin. Agric. Off. (Dep. Dir), Min. of Agric., 1964-66; High Comr for Lesotho, in London, 1966-69; Ambassador to Germany, Holy See, Rome, France, and Austria, 1968-69; Permanent Sec. and Hd of Diplomatic Service, Lesotho, 1969-70; Permanent Sec. for Health, Educn and Social Welfare, Lesotho, 1970-71; High Comr for Lesotho in East Africa, Nigeria and Ghana, 1972-74; Minister: of Foreign Affairs, Lesotho, 1974-75; of Education, 1975-76; of Agriculture, 1976-78; Perm. Rep. to UN, 1978-79. Guest of Min. of Agric., Netherlands, 1955; studied agric. educn, USA (financed by Carnegie Corp. of NY and Ford Foundn), 1960-61; FAO confs in Tunisia, Tanganyika and Uganda, 1962 and 1963; Mem. Lesotho delegn to 24th World Health Assembly, 1971; travelled extensively to study and observe methods of agric. administration, 1964; meetings on nutrition, Berlin and Hamburg, 1966; diplomatic trainee, Brit. Embassy, Bonn, 1966. *Recreations:* swimming, tennis, amateur dramatics, photography, debating, reading, travelling. *Address:* c/o Ministry of Foreign Affairs, PO Box MS 527, Maseru, Lesotho, Southern Africa.

KOVACEVICH, Stephen B.; *see* Bishop-Kovacevich.

KRABBÉ, Col Clarence Brehmer, OBE 1918; DL; *b* 16 Jan. 1886; *s* of Charles Krabbé, Buenos Aires; *m* 1915, Joan Alison (*d* 1968), *d* of Col A. Evans-Gordon, IA; one *s* (killed 1940) one *d. Educ:* Dulwich Coll.; Trinity Coll., Oxford. Served European War, 1914-19, with Berks Yeomanry and RFC, Gallipoli and France (despatches). Col Berks Home Guard, 1943-45. Chm., Royal Berks Hosp., 1942-48; Chm., S Berks Conservative Assoc., 1946-52; Vice-Chm., Berks T & AF Assoc., 1950-54; Mem., Oxford Regional Hosp. Bd, 1947-62 (Vice-Chm. 1951-62). Mem., Board of Governors, Oxford United Hosps, 1953-57; Mem. of Reading and District Hosp. Management Cttee (Chm., 1948-50), 1948-66; Mem. St Birinus Hosp. Management Cttee, 1962-66. DL Berks, 1946. High Sheriff of Berks, 1952-53. *Recreation:* gardening. *Address:* Calcot Green, near Reading, Berks. *T:* Reading 27428.

KRAFT, Rt. Rev. Richard Austin; *see* Pretoria, Bishop of.

KRAMER, Prof. Ivor Robert Horton, MDS; FDSRCS, FFDRCSI, Hon. FRACDS, FRCPath; Professor of Oral Pathology, Institute of Dental Surgery, University of London, since 1962, and Dean and Director of Studies of the Institute, since 1970; Head of Department of Pathology, Eastman Dental Hospital, since 1950; *b* 20 June 1923; *yr s* of late Alfred Bertie and Agnes Maud Kramer; *m* 1st, 1946, Elisabeth Dalley; one *s*; 2nd, 1979, Mrs Dorothy Toller. *Educ:* Royal Dental Hosp. of London Sch. of Dental Surgery; MDS 1955; FDSRCS 1960 (LDSRCS 1944); FRCPath 1970 (MCRPath 1964); FFDRCSI 1973. Asst to Pathologist, Princess Louise (Kensington) Hosp. for Children, 1944-48; Wright Fleming Inst. of Microbiol., 1948-49; Instr in Dental Histology, Royal Dental Hosp. Sch. of Dental Surgery, 1944-50; Asst Pathologist, Royal Dental Hosp., 1950-56; Institute of Dental Surgery: Lectr in Dental Path., 1949-50, Sen. Lectr, 1950-57; Reader in Oral Path., 1957-62; Sub-dean, 1950-70; Civilian Cons. in Dental Path., RN, 1967-. Member: WHO Expert Adv. Panel on Dental Health, 1975-; Bd of Faculty of Dental Surgery, RCS, 1964-80, Council, RCS, 1977-80; Mem. Council for Postgrad. Med. Educn in Eng. and Wales, 1972-77 (Chm., Dental Cttee, 1972-77); Pres., Odontological Section, RSocMed, 1973-74; Pres., British Div., Internat. Assoc. for Dental Res., 1974-77. Hon. Pres. of the Assoc., 1974-75. Editor, Archives of Oral Biology, 1959-69. Lectures: Wilkinson, Manchester, 1962; Charles Tomes, 1969, Webb Johnson, 1981, RCS; Holme, UCH, 1969; Elwood Meml, QUB, 1970; Hutchinson, Edinburgh, 1971. Hon. FRACDS 1978. Howard Mummery Prize, BDA, 1966; Maurice Down Award, Brit. Assoc. of Oral Surgeons, 1974. *Publications:* (with R. B. Lucas) Bacteriology for Students of Dental Surgery, 1954, 3rd edn 1966; (with J. J. Pindborg and H. Torloni) World Health Organization International Histological Classification of Tumours: Odontogenic Tumours, Jaw Cysts and Allied Lesions, 1972; (with B. Cohen) Scientific Foundations of Dentistry, 1976; numerous papers in med. and dental jls. *Address:* c/o Institute of Dental Surgery, Gray's Inn Road, WC1X 8LD. *T:* 01-837 3646; 33 Sandy Lodge Road, Rickmansworth, Herts WD3 1LP. *T:* Northwood 25012.

KRAMRISCH, Stella, PhD; Professor of Indian Art, Institute of Fine Arts, New York University, since 1964; Curator of Indian Art, Philadelphia Museum of Art, since 1954; *d* of Jacques Kramrisch, scientist, and Berta Kramrisch; *m* 1929, Laszlo Neményi (*d* 1950). *Educ:* Vienna University. Prof. of Indian Art, Univ. of Calcutta, 1923-50; Prof. in the Art of South Asia, Univ. of Pennsylvania, 1950-69; Lectr on Indian Art, Courtauld Inst. of Art, Univ. of London, 1937-41. Public lectures in USA, Canada, India, Nepal, W Germany. Editor: Jl Indian Soc. of Oriental Art, 1932-50; Artibus Asiae, 1959-. Hon. DLit Visva Bharati Univ., 1974. Cross of Honour for Science and Art, Austria. *Publications:* Principles of Indian Art, 1924; Vishnudharmottara, 1924; History of Indian Art, 1929; Indian Sculpture, 1932; Asian Miniature Painting, 1932; A Survey of Painting in the Deccan, 1937; Indian Terracottas, 1939; Kantha, 1939; The Hindu Temple, 1946, repr. 1976; Arts and Crafts of Travancore, 1948; Dravida and Kerala, 1953; Art of India, 1954; Indian Sculpture in the Philadelphia Museum of Art, 1960; The Triple Structure of Creation, 1962; The Art of Nepal, 1964; Unknown India: Ritual Art in Tribe and Village, 1968; The Presence of Siva, 1981; Manifestations of Shiva, 1981; various articles. *Address:* Philadelphia Museum of Art, PO Box 7646, Philadelphia, Pa 19101, USA; University of New York, Institute of Fine Arts, 1 East 78th Street, New York, NY 10021, USA.

KREISEL, Prof. Georg, FRS 1966; Professor of Logic and the Foundations of Mathematics, Stanford University, Stanford, California, USA; *b* 15 Sept. 1923. *Address:* Department of Philosophy, Stanford University, Stanford, California 94305, USA.

KREMER, Michael, MD; FRCP; Emeritus Neurologist, Middlesex Hospital, W1; Honorary Consulting Neurologist, National Hospital, Queen Square, WC1; Hon. Consultant Neurologist to St Dunstan's, since 1966; Hon. Consultant in Neurology to the Army, since 1969; *b* 27 Nov. 1907; *s* of W. and S. Kremer; *m* 1933, Lilian Frances (*née* Washbourn); one *s* two *d. Educ:* Middlesex Hosp. Medical Sch. BSc 1927; MD 1932; FRCP 1943. *Recreations:* music, reading, photography. *Address:* 121 Harley Street, W1. *T:* 01-935 4545.

KRESTIN, David, MD (London), BS, MRCP; Consulting Physician, London Jewish Hospital; Medical Specialist, Ministries of Pensions and of National Insurance; late Physician with charge of Out-Patients, Dreadnought Hospital; Medical Registrar, Prince of Wales' Hospital; Lecturer in Medicine, N-E London Post-Graduate Medical College; *b* London; *s* of Dr S. Krestin; *m* Ruth Fisher; one *s. Educ:* University of London; London Hosp. Medical Coll.; University of Pennsylvania. Anatomy prize, London Hosp.; MRCS, LRCP 1922; MB, BS London 1923, Hons Medicine and Surgery; MD London 1926, MRCP 1926. Clinical Asst, House Surg., House Physician, Medical Registrar and First Asst, London Hosp.; Rockefeller Medical Fellowship, 1928-29; Fellow in Pathology, Henry Phipps Institute, University Penna; Yarrow Research Fellow, London Hosp. *Publications:* Pulsation in Superficial Veins, Lancet, 1927; The Seborrhœic facies in Post-Encephalitic Parkinsonism, Quart. Jour. Med., 1927; Congenital Dextrocardia and Auric. Fibrillation, Brit. Med. Jour., 1927; Latent Pulmonary Tuberculosis, Quart. Journ. Med., 1929; Glandular Fever, Clinical Journal, 1931 and other medical papers. *Recreation:* fishing. *Address:* 14 Spaniards End, NW3. *T:* 01-455 1500.

KRETZMER, Herbert; television critic, Daily Mail, since 1979; feature writer and lyric writer; *b* Kroonstad, OFS, S Africa, 5 Oct. 1925; *s* of William and

Tilly Kretzmer; *m* 1961, Elisabeth Margaret Wilson (marr. diss., 1973); one *s* one *d*. *Educ:* Kroonstad High Sch.; Rhodes Univ., Grahamstown. Entered journalism, 1946, writing weekly cinema newsreel commentaries and documentary films for African Film Productions, Johannesburg. Reporter and entertainment columnist, Sunday Express, Johannesburg, 1951-54; feature writer and columnist, Daily Sketch, London, 1954-59; Columnist, Sunday Dispatch, London, 1959-61; theatre critic, Daily Express, 1962-78. TV Critic of the Year, Philips Industries Award, 1980; commended in British Press Awards, 1981. As lyric writer, contributed weekly songs to: That Was The Week . ., Not So Much A Programme . ., BBC 3, That's Life. Wrote lyrics for Ivor Novello Award song Goodness Gracious Me, 1960, and ASCAP award song Yesterday When I was Young, 1969; Gold record for She, 1974; Our Man Crichton, Shaftesbury Theatre, 1964 (book and lyrics); The Four Musketeers, Drury Lane, 1967 (lyrics); *film:* Can Heironymus Merkin Ever Forget Mercy Humppe And Find True Happiness?, 1969 (lyrics); has also written lyrics for other films, and for TV programmes. *Publications:* Our Man Crichton, 1965; (jointly) Every Home Should Have One, 1970. *Address:* 55 Lincoln House, Basil Street, SW3. *T:* 01-589 2541. *Club:* Royal Automobile.

KRIKLER, Dennis Michael, MD; FRCP; Consultant Cardiologist, Hammersmith and Ealing Hospitals, and Senior Lecturer in Cardiology, Royal Postgraduate Medical School, since 1973; *b* 10 Dec. 1928; *s* of Barnet and Eva Krikler; *m* 1955, Anne (*née* Winterstein); one *s* one *d*. *Educ:* Muizenberg High Sch.; Univ. of Cape Town, S Africa. Ho. Phys. and Registrar, Groote Schuur Hosp., 1952-55; Fellow, Lahey Clinic, Boston, 1956; Sen. Registrar, Groote Schuur Hosp., 1957-58; Consultant Physician: Salisbury Central Hosp., Rhodesia, 1958-66; Prince of Wales's Hosp., London, 1966-73. Member, British Cardiac Soc., 1971- (Treasurer, 1976-81); Hon. Mem., Soc. Française de Cardiologie, 1981-; Editor, British Heart Journal, 1981-. FRSM; FACC 1971. *Publications:* Cardiac Arrhythmias (with J. F. Goodwin), 1975; papers on cardiology in British, American and French jls. *Recreations:* reading, especially history; photography. *Address:* 81 Harley Street, W1N 1DE. *T:* 01-935 2098.

KRIKLER, Leonard Gideon; a Recorder of the Crown Court, since 1980; *b* 23 May 1929; *s* of late Major James Harold Krikler, OBE, ED, and Tilly Krikler; *m* 1st, 1955, Dr Thilla Krikler (*d* 1973); four *s*; 2nd, 1975, Lily Appleson; one *s*, and one step *s* two step *d*. *Educ:* Milton Sch., Bulawayo, S Rhodesia (Zimbabwe). Called to Bar, Middle Temple, 1953. *Recreations:* painting, music, chess. *Address:* Lamb Building, Temple, EC4. *T:* 01-353 0774.

KRIKORIAN, Gregory, CB 1973; Solicitor for the Customs and Excise, 1971-78; *b* 23 Sept. 1913; *s* of late Kevork and late Christine Krikorian; *m* 1943, Seta Mary, *d* of Souren Djirdjirian; one *d*. *Educ:* Polytechnic Secondary Sch.; Lincoln Coll., Oxford (BA). Called to Bar, Middle Temple, 1939; practised at Bar, 1939; BBC Overseas Intell. Dept, 1940; served in RAF as Intell. Officer, Fighter Comd, 1940-45 (despatches); practised at Bar, 1945-51, Junior Oxford Circuit, 1947; joined Solicitor's Office, HM Customs and Excise, 1951. *Publication:* (jtly) Customs and Excise, in Halsbury's Laws of England, 1975. *Recreations:* gardening, bird-watching. *Address:* The Coach House, Hawkchurch, Axminster, Devon. *T:* Hawkchurch 414. *Clubs:* Reform, Civil Service, MCC.

KRISH, Tanya, (Mrs Felix Krish); see Moiseiwitsch, T.

KRISHNA, Sri, CIE 1942; DSc (London), PhD, FRSC, FNA; late Scientific Adviser to High Commission of India and Scientific Liaison Officer, London; Deputy Director, Council of Scientific and Industrial Research, New Delhi, India, 1952; Vice-Pres. and Director of Research, Forest Research Institute, Dehra Dun, UP, India, 1950; Biochemist since 1928; *b* 6 July 1896; *s* of M. Mohan; *m* 1st, 1925, Usha Khanna (*d* 1929); (one *s* decd); 2nd, 1972, Olga Hellerman. *Educ:* Forman Coll., Lahore; Government Coll., Lahore; Queen Mary Coll., London; King's Coll., London. Prof. of Chemistry, University of the Punjab, Lahore, 1925-28. *Publications:* numerous scientific. *Recreations:* tennis, etc. *Address:* 62 Perryn Road, Acton, W3 7LX; 88 Rajpur Road, Dehra Dun, UP, India.

KRISHNAMURTI, Jiddu; philosopher and religious teacher; *b* 13 May 1895; *s* of Jiddu Narianiah and Jiddu Sanjeevamma. *Educ:* privately in England. Adopted by Mrs Annie Besant, 1910; made Head of Order of the Star in the East, an offshoot of Theosophy, 1912 (Order proclaimed the Coming of the World Teacher who would occupy the body of Krishnamurti); dissolved Order, 1929; since then, has travelled the world speaking as a philosopher and religious teacher. *Publications:* The First and Last Freedom, 1954; Education and the Significance of Life, 1955; Commentaries on Living: 1st Series, 1956; 2nd Series, 1959; 3rd Series, 1960; Life Ahead, 1963; This Matter of Culture, 1964; Freedom From The Known, 1969; The Only Revolution, 1970; Penguin Krishnamurti Reader, 1970; The Urgency of Change, 1971; The Impossible Question, 1972; Tradition and Revolution, 1972; Beyond Violence, 1973; The Awakening of Intelligence, 1973; The Second Penguin Krishnamurti Reader, 1973; Krishnamurti on Education, 1974; Beginnings of Learning, 1975; Krishnamurti's Notebook, 1976; Truth & Actuality, 1977; The Wholeness of Life, 1978; Beginnings of Learning, 1978; The Impossible Question, 1978; Exploration into Insight, 1979; Meditations, 1979; Poems and Parables, 1981; Krishnamurti's Letters to the Schools, 1981; Krishnamurti's Journal, 1982; Questions & Answers, 1982; series of books, mainly of talks,

1933-67; many booklets on education, philosophy and religion, 1910-. *Address:* Brockwood Park, Bramdean, near Alresford, Hants SO24 0LQ. *T:* Bramdean 228.

KRISTENSEN, Prof. Thorkil; Director, Institute for Development Research, Copenhagen, 1969-72; Secretary-General, Organisation for Economic Co-operation and Development, 1960-69; *b* Denmark, 9 Oct. 1899; *m* 1931, Ellen Christine Nielsen; one *s* one *d*. *Educ:* School of Commerce; People's Coll., Askov; University of Copenhagen (Cand. polit.). Dipl. Polit. and Econ. Sciences, 1927. Lectr in High Sch. of Commerce, Aarhus, and in University of Copenhagen, 1927-38; Prof. of Commercial and Industrial Economics: University of Aarhus, 1938-47; Sch. of Advanced Commercial Studies, Copenhagen, 1947-60. Mem., Danish Parliament, 1945-60; Minister of Finance, 1945-47 and 1950-53; Mem. Finance Cttee, 1947-49 and 1953-60; Mem. Consultative Assembly of Council of Europe, 1949-50; Mem. Foreign Affairs Cttee, 1953-60; Mem. Nordic Council, 1953-60; Mem. Acad. of Technical Sciences; Pres. Foreign Policy Soc., 1948-60; Pres. Nat. Anti-Unemployment Fedn, 1956-60; Mem. Assurance Council, 1958-60; Mem. Institute of History and Economics. DrSc Pol *hc* (Ankara), 1962. *Publications:* several, on finance, 1930-39; The Food Problem of Developing Countries, 1968. Editor of: De europaeiske markedsplaner (European Markets-Plans and Prospects), 1958; The Economic World Balance, 1960; Development in Rich and Poor Countries, 1974; Inflation and Unemployment in the Modern Society, 1981, etc. *Address:* Odinsvej 18, 3460 Birkerød, Denmark.

KRISTIANSEN, Erling (Engelbrecht), Grand Cross, Order of Dannebrog; Hon. GCVO 1974; Director: East Asiatic Co., since 1978; S. G. Warburg & Co. International Holdings Ltd, since 1980, and other companies; *b* 31 Dec. 1912; *s* of Kristian Engelbrecht Kristiansen, Chartered Surveyor, and Andrea Kirstine (*née* Madsen); *m* 1938, Annemarie Selinko, novelist. *Educ:* Herning Gymnasium; University of Copenhagen (degree awarded equiv. of MÅ Econ). Postgraduate Studies, Economics and Internat. Relations, Geneva, Paris, London, 1935-37. Sec.-Gen., 1935, Pres. 1936, of the Fédération Universitaire Internationale pour la Société des Nations. Danish Civil Servant, 1941; served with: Free Danish Missions, Stockholm, 1943; Washington, 1944; London, 1945; joined Danish Diplomatic Service and stayed in London until 1947; Danish Foreign Ministry, 1947-48; Head of Denmark's Mission to OEEC, Paris, 1948-50; Sec. to Economic Cttee of Cabinet, 1950-51; Asst Under-Sec. of State, 1951; Dep. Under-Sec. of State (Economic Affairs), Danish For. Min., 1954-64; Ambassador to UK, 1964-77, retired. Chm. of Bd, Nordic Investment Bank, 1978-80. Grand Officier, Légion d'Honneur; Kt Comdr: Order of St Olav; Order of White Rose of Finland; Star of Ethiopia; Knight Grand Cross, Icelandic Falcon; Comdr, Order of Northern Star of Sweden. *Publication:* Folkeforbundet (The League of Nations), 1938. *Recreations:* ski-ing, fishing and other out-door sports, modern languages. *Address:* 4 Granhøjen, Dk-2900, Hellerup, Denmark. *Clubs:* MCC; Special Forces *et al.*

KROHN, Dr Peter Leslie, FRS 1963; Professor of Endocrinology, University of Birmingham, 1962-66; *b* 8 Jan. 1916; *s* of Eric Leslie Krohn and Doris Ellen Krohn (*née* Wade); *m* 1941, Joanna Mary French; two *s*. *Educ:* Sedbergh; Balliol Coll., Oxford. BA 1st Cl. Hons Animal Physiol, 1937; BM, BCh Oxon, 1940. Wartime Research work for Min. of Home Security, 1940-45; Lectr, then Reader in Endocrinology, University of Birmingham, 1946-53; Nuffield Sen. Gerontological Research Fellow and Hon. Prof. in University, 1953-62. *Publications:* contrib. to scientific jls on physiology of reproduction, transplantation immunity and ageing. *Recreations:* ski-ing, mountain walking. *Address:* La Forêt, St Mary, Jersey, Channel Islands. *T:* Jersey 62158.

KROLL, Natasha, RDI, FSIAD; freelance television and film designer; *b* Moscow, 20 May 1914; *d* of Dr (phil.) Hermann Kroll and Sophie (*née* Rabinovich). *Educ:* Berlin. Teacher of window display, Reimann Sch. of Art, London, 1936-40; Display Manager: Messrs Rowntrees, Scarborough and York, 1940-42; Simpson Piccadilly Ltd, 1942-55; Sen. Designer, BBC TV, 1955-66; programmes include: Monitor, Panorama, science programmes, Lower Depths, Death of Danton, The Duel, Ring Round the Moon, La Traviata, Day by the Sea, The Sponge Room and many others; freelance designer, 1966-; TV designs include: The Seagull, 1966; Family Reunion, 1966; Eugene Onegin, 1967; The Soldier's Tale, 1968; La Vida Breve, 1968; Mary Stuart, 1968; Doll's House, 1969; Three Sisters, Cherry Orchard, Rasputin, Wild Duck, 1971; Summer and Smoke, Hedda Gabler, 1972; The Common, 1973; Lady from the Sea, 1974; Love's Labour's Lust, 1975; Very Like a Whale, 1980; production-designer of: The Music Lovers, 1970; The Hireling, 1973 (FTA Film award for best Art Direction); Summer Rag-time, 1976; Absolution, 1978. RDI 1966. *Publication:* Window Display, 1954. *Recreations:* painting, family, entertaining. *Address:* 5 Ruvigny Gardens, SW15 1JR. *T:* 01-788 9867.

KROLL, Dss Dr Una (Margaret Patricia); Deaconess Doctor; Clinical Medical Officer, Hastings Health District, since 1981; licensed deaconess to St Clements and All Saints, Hastings, since 1981; worker deaconess, since 1970; writer and broadcaster, since 1970; *b* 15 Dec. 1925; *d* of George Hill, CBE, DSO, MC, and Hilda Hill; *m* 1957, Leopold Kroll; one *s* three *d*. *Educ:* St Paul's Girls' Sch.; Malvern Girls' Coll.; Girton Coll., Cambridge; The London Hosp. MB, BChir (Cantab) 1951; MA 1969. MRCGP 1967. House Officer, 1951-53; Overseas service (Africa), 1953-60; General Practice, 1960-81. Theological trng, 1967-70; political work as a feminist, with particular ref.

to status of women in the churches in England and internationally, 1970-; Member: Christian Med. Commn, WCC, 1979-; Churches' Religious Adv. Cttee, BBC, 1980-; Churches Council for Health and Healing, 1980-. *Publications:* Transcendental Meditation: a signpost to the world, 1974; Flesh of My Flesh: a Christian view on sexism, 1975; Lament for a Lost Enemy: study of reconciliation, 1976; Sexual Counselling, 1980; contrib. Cervical Cytology (BMJ), 1969. *Recreations:* gardening, reading, sitting. *Address:* Datcha, Clinton Way, Fairlight Cove, E Sussex TN35 4DL. *T:* Pett 3241.

KRUGER, Prudence Margaret; *see* Leith, P.M.

KRUSIN, Sir Stanley (Marks), Kt 1973; CB 1963; Second Parliamentary Counsel, 1970-73; *b* 8 June 1908; *m* 1st, 1937 (she *d* 1972); one *s* one *d* ; 2nd, 1976. *Educ:* St Paul's Sch.; Balliol Coll., Oxford. Called to the Bar, Middle Temple, 1932. Served RAFVR, Wing Comdr, 1944. Dep. Sec., British Tabulating Machine Co. Ltd, 1945-47. Entered Parliamentary Counsel Office, 1947; Parliamentary Counsel, 1953-69. *Address:* 5 Coleridge Walk, NW11. *T:* 01-458 1340. *Club:* Royal Air Force.

KUBELIK, Rafael; conductor and composer; Chief Conductor of Bayerischer Rundfunk, München, 1961-79; *b* Bychory, Bohemia, 29 June 1914; *s* of Jan Kubelik, violinist, and Marianne (*née* Szell); *m* 1942, Ludmila Bertlova, (*decd*), violinist; one *s* ; *m* 1963, Elsie Morison, singer. *Educ:* Prague Conservatoire. Conductor, Czech Philharmonic Society, Prague, 1936-39; Musical Director of Opera, Brno, Czechoslovakia, 1939-41; Musical Dir, Czech Philharmonic Orchestra, 1941-48; Musical Dir, Chicago Symphony Orchestra, 1950-53; Musical Dir of the Covent Garden Opera Company, 1955-58; Music Dir, Metropolitan Opera, New York, 1973-74. Compositions include: 5 operas; 2 symphonies with chorus; a third symphony (in one movement); Orphikon, symphony for orch.; Sequences for orch.; 6 string quartets; 1 violin concerto; 1 cello concerto; 1 cantata; cantata without words for chorus and orch.; Requiems: Pro Memoria Uxoris; Libera Nos; Quattro Forme per Archi; songs; piano and violin music. *Address:* Kastanienbaum, Haus im Sand, Switzerland.

KUBRICK, Stanley; producer, director, script writer; *b* 26 July 1928; *s* of Dr Jacques L. Kubrick and Gertrude Kubrick; *m* 1958, Suzanne Christiane Harlan; three *d. Educ:* William Howard Taft High Sch.; City Coll. of City of New York. Joined Look Magazine, 1946. At age of 21 made Documentary, Day of the Fight; made Short for RKO, Flying Padre. *Feature Films:* Fear and Desire, 1953 (at age of 24); Killer's Kiss, 1954; The Killing, 1956; Paths of Glory, 1957; Spartacus, 1960; Lolita, 1962; Dr Strangelove or How I Learned to Stop Worrying and Love the Bomb, 1964; 2001: A Space Odyssey, 1968; A Clockwork Orange, 1971; Barry Lyndon, 1975; The Shining, 1978. *Recreations:* literature, music, public affairs. *Address:* c/o Loeb & Loeb, 10100 Santa Monica Boulevard, Suite 2200, Los Angeles, Calif 90067, USA.

KUENSSBERG, Ekkehard von, CBE 1969; FRCGP, 1967; FRCOG (*ae*) 1981; FRCPEd 1981; President, Royal College of General Practitioners, 1976-79; *b* 1913; *s* of Prof. Eberhard von Kuenssberg; *m* 1941, Dr Constance Ferrar Hardy; two *s* two *d. Educ:* Schloss Schule, Salem; Univs of Innsbruck, Heidelberg and Edinburgh. MB, ChB 1939. Gen. practice throughout (Edin.). RAMC, 1944-46 (Lt-Col, DADMS E Africa Comd). Mem., Safety of Drugs Cttee, 1964-71; Chm., Gen. Med. Services Cttee, Scotland; Mem., GMSC, UK, 1960-68; RCGP: Chm. Council, 1970-73; Hon. Treas., Research Foundn Bd, 1960-77; Mackenzie Lectr, 1970; Wolfson Travelling Prof., 1974. Mem., Lothian Area Health Bd, 1974-; Member: Council, Queen's Nursing Inst., 1972-76; Court, Edinburgh Univ., 1971-79. Foundation Council Award, RCGP, 1967; Hippocrates Medal, 1974 (SIMG). FRSocMed. *Publications:* The Team in General Practice, 1966; An Opportunity to Learn, 1977. *Recreations:* skiing, forestry. *Address:* Little Letham, Haddington, East Lothian. *T:* Haddington 2529.

KUHN, Heinrich Gerhard, FRS 1954; DPhil, MA; Reader in Physics, Oxford University, 1955-71, now Emeritus; Fellow of Balliol College 1950-71, now Emeritus; *b* 10 March 1904; *s* of Wilhelm Felix and Martha Kuhn; *m* 1931, Marie Bertha Nohl; two *s. Educ:* High Sch., Lueben (Silesia); Universities of Greifswald and Goettingen. Lecturer in Physics, Goettingen Univ., 1931; Research at Clarendon Laboratory, Oxford, 1933; Lecturer, University Coll., Oxford, 1938; work for atomic energy project, 1941-45; University Demonstrator, Oxford, 1945-55. Dr *hc* Aix-Marseille, 1958. Holweck Prize, 1967. *Publications:* Atomspektren, 1934 (Akad. Verl. Ges., Leipzig); Atomic Spectra, 1962, 2nd edn 1970; articles on molecular and atomic spectra and on interferometry. *Address:* 25 Victoria Road, Oxford OX2 7QF. *T:* 55308.

KUIPERS, John Melles; Chairman: Huntleigh Group PLC; Hymatic Engineering Co. Ltd; Director: Huntleigh Medical Ltd; Micro-image Technology Ltd; Consultant, Gowrings Ltd; *b* 7 July 1918; *s* of late Joh Kuipers and Anna (*née* Knoester); *m* 1947, Joan Lilian Morgan-Edwards; one *s* three *d. Educ:* Royal Masonic Sch., Bushey. Served RA, 1939-46 (Lt-Col). Ford Motor Co. Ltd, 1947-51; Treasurer, Canadian Chemical Co. Ltd, Montreal, 1951-55; Gp Manager, Halewood, and Dir, Stamping and Assembly Gp, Ford Motor Co. Ltd, 1955-67; EMI Ltd, 1967-80: Chief Exec. Electronic and Industrial Ops, 1969-72; Chm. and Chief Exec., EMI (Australia) Ltd, 1974-77; Man. Dir and Vice-Chm., 1977-79. Dir, Thames TV Ltd, 1977-81. FBIM. *Recreations:* golf, home-making. *Address:* Marsh Mills Stable, Wargrave Road, Henley-on-Thames, Oxon. *T:* Henley-on-Thames 4760.

KULUKUNDIS, Eddie, (Elias George); Chairman, Knightsbridge Theatrical Productions Ltd, since 1970; Director: Rethymnis & Kulukundis Ltd, since 1964; London & Overseas Freighters plc, since 1980; Member of Lloyd's, since 1964, and Baltic Exchange, since 1959; *b* 20 April 1932; *s* of late George Elias Kulukundis and of Eugenie (*née* Diacakis); *m* 1981, Susan Hampshire, *qv. Educ:* Collegiate Sch., New York; Salisbury Sch., Connecticut; Yale Univ. Governor: Greenwich Theatre Ltd; Mermaid Theatre Trust Ltd; The Raymond Mander and Joe Mitchenson Theatre Collection Ltd; Royal Shakespeare Theatre; Sports Aid Foundn Ltd. Director: Apollo Soc. Ltd; Hampstead Theatre Ltd; Pioneer Theatres Ltd. Member, Councils of Management: Round House Trust Ltd; Royal Shakespeare Theatre; Royal Shakespeare Theatre Trust; Traverse Theatre Club. Mem. Exec. Council, SWET. Trustee: Hammersmith Riverside Arts Trust Ltd; Theatres Trust. FRSA. As Theatrical Producer, London prodns incl. (some jtly): Enemy, 1969; The Happy Apple, Poor Horace, The Friends, How the Other Half Loves, Tea Party and The Basement (double bill), The Wild Duck, 1970; After Haggerty, Hamlet, Charley's Aunt, Straight Up, 1971; London Assurance, Journey's End, 1972; Small Craft Warnings, A Private Matter, Dandy Dick, 1973; The Waltz of the Toreadors, Life Class, Pygmalion, Play Mas, The Gentle Hook, 1974; A Little Night Music, Entertaining Mr Sloane, The Gay Lord Quex, What the Butler Saw, Travesties, Lies, The Sea Gull, A Month in the Country, A Room With a View, Too True to Be Good, The Bed Before Yesterday, 1975; Dimetos, Banana Ridge, Wild Oats, 1976; Candida, Man and Superman, Once A Catholic, 1977; Privates on Parade, Gloo Joo, 1978; Bent, Outside Edge, Last of the Red Hot Lovers, 1979; Beecham, Born in the Gardens, 1980; Tonight At 8.30, Steaming, Arms and the Man, 1981. New York prodns (jtly): How the Other Half Loves, 1971; Sherlock Holmes, London Assurance, 1974; Travesties, 1975; The Merchant, 1977; Players, 1978; Once a Catholic, 1979. *Address:* c/o Rethymnis & Kulukundis, Ltd, 30-33 Minories, EC3N 1DT. *T:* 01-480 5611; c/o Knightsbridge Theatrical Productions, Ltd, 2 Goodwin's Court, St Martin's Lane, WC2N 4LL. *T:* 01-240 2196. *Club:* Garrick.

KUNCEWICZ, Eileen, (Mrs Witold Kuncewicz); *see* Herlie, E.

KUNERALP, Zeki, Hon. GCVO 1971; *b* Istanbul, 5 Oct. 1914; *s* of Ali Kemal and Sabiha, *d* of Mustafa Zeki Pasha; *m* 1943, Necla Ozdilci (*d* 1978); two *s. Educ:* Univ. of Berne. DrIuris 1938. Entered Diplomatic Service, 1940: served Bucharest, Prague, Paris, Nato Delegn and at Min. of Foreign Affairs, Ankara; Asst Sec.-Gen. 1957; Sec.-Gen. 1960; Ambassador to Berne, 1960, to Court of St James's, 1964-66; Sec.-Gen. at Min. of Foreign Affairs, Ankara, 1966-69; Ambassador to Court of St James's, 1969-72, to Spain, 1972-79, retired. Mem., Hon. Soc. of Knights of the Round Table. Holds German, Greek, Italian, Papal, Jordanian, Iranian and National Chinese orders. *Publication:* Memoirs, 1981. *Recreations:* reading, ballet. *Address:* Fenerbahçe Cad. 85/B, D4, Kiziltoprak, Istanbul, Turkey.

KÜNG, Prof. Dr Hans; Ordinary Professor of Ecumenical Theology, since 1980 and Director of Institute for Ecumenical Research, since 1963, University of Tübingen; *b* Sursee, Lucerne, 19 March 1928. *Educ:* schools in Sursee and Lucerne; Papal Gregorian Univ., Rome (LPhil, LTh); Sorbonne; Inst. Catholique, Paris. DTheol 1957. Further studies in Amsterdam, Berlin, Madrid, London. Ordained priest, 1954. Pastoral work, Hofkirche, Lucerne, 1957-59; Asst for dogmatic theol., Univ. of Münster, 1959-60; Ord. Prof. of fundamental theol., 1960-63, Ord. Prof. of dogmatic and ecumenical theol., 1963-80, Univ. of Tübingen. Official theol. consultant (peritus) to 2nd Vatican Council, 1962; Visiting Professor: Union Theol. Seminary, NYC, 1968; Univ. of Basle, 1969; guest lectures at univs in Europe, America, Asia and Australia. Editor series, Theologische Meditationen; co-Editor series, Ökumenische Forschungen; Associate Editor: Tübingen Theologische Quartalschrift, 1960-80; Jl of Ecum. Studies; Mem. Exec. Editorial Cttee, Concilium. Mem., Amer. and German Pen Clubs. Holds hon. doctorates. *Publications:* (first publication in German) The Council and Reunion, 1961; That the World may Believe, 1963; The Living Church, 1963; The Changing Church, 1965; Justification: the doctrine of Karl Barth and a Catholic reflection, 1965; Structures of the Church, 1965; The Church, 1967; Truthfulness: the future of the Church, 1968; Infallible? an enquiry, 1971 (paperback 1972); Why Priests?, 1972; 20 Thesen zum Christein, 1975; On Being a Christian, 1976 (abridged as The Christian Challenge, 1979); Was ist Firmung?, 1976; Jesus im Widerstreit: ein jüdisch-christlicher Dialog (with Pinchas Lapide), 1976; Signposts for the Future, 1978; Does God Exist?, 1979; Freud and the Problem of God, 1979; The Church—Maintained in Truth?, 1980; contribs to Theologische Meditationen, and to Christian Revelation and World Religions, ed J. Neuner, 1967. American edns of the above books and also of contribs to Theol. Med., etc, the latter under one title, Freedom Today, 1966. *Address:* D-74 Tübingen, Waldhäuserstrasse 23, SW Germany.

KURIA, Most Rev. Manasses; *see* Kenya, Archbishop of.

KUROSAWA, Akira; Japanese film director; *b* 1910. *Educ:* Keika Middle School. Assistant Director, Toho Film Co., 1936. Mem. Jury, Internat. Film Fest. of India, 1977. Directed first film, Sugata Sanshiro, 1943. *Films include:* Sugata Sanshiro, Ichiban Utsukushiku, Torano Owofumu Otokotachi, Rashomon (1st Prize, Venice Film Festival), Hakuchi, Ikiru, The Seven Samurai, Living, Kakushi Toride no San Akunin, The Hidden Fortress, Throne of Blood, Yojimbo, The Bad Sleep Well, Tsubaki Sanjuro, Tengoku To Jigoku, Red Beard, 1965; Dodeska-Den, 1970; Dersu Uzala (Oscar Award), 1975; Barkerousse, 1977; Kagemusha (Golden Palm Award, Cannes

Film Festival), 1980. *Publication:* Something like an Autobiography (trans. Audie Bock), 1982.

KURTI, Prof. Nicholas, CBE 1973; FRS 1956; MA Oxon; DrPhil (Berlin); FInstP; Emeritus Professor of Physics, University of Oxford; Vice-President, Royal Society, 1965-67; *b* 14 May 1908; *s* of late Charles Kürti and Margaret Pintér, Budapest; *m* 1946, Georgiana, *d* of late Brig.-Gen. and Mrs C. T. Shipley; two *d. Educ:* Minta-Gymnasium, Budapest; University of Paris (Licence ès sci. phys.); University of Berlin (DrPhil). Asst, Techn Hochschule Breslau, 1931-33; Research Position, Clarendon Laboratory, Oxford, 1933-40; UK Atomic Bomb Project, 1940-45; University Demonstrator in Physics, Oxford, 1945-60; Reader in Physics, Oxford, 1960-67; Prof. of Physics, Oxford, 1967-75; Senior Research Fellow, Brasenose Coll., 1947-67; Professorial Fellow, 1967-75, Emeritus Fellow, 1975-. Buell G. Gallagher Visiting Prof., City Coll., New York, 1963; Vis. Prof., Univ. of Calif, Berkeley, 1964; Dist. Vis. Prof., Amherst Coll., 1979. A Governor, College of Aeronautics, Cranfield, 1953-69. Member: Electricity Supply Research Council, 1960-79; Advisory Cttee for Scientific and Technical Information, 1966-68; Chairman: Adv. Cttee for Research on Measurement and Standards, DTI, 1969-73; Jt Cttee on Scientific and Technol Records, Royal Soc./Royal Commn on Historical MSS, 1970-76. Member: Council, Royal Soc., 1964-67; Council, Soc. Française de Physique, 1957-60, 1970-73; Council, Inst. of Physics and Physical Soc., 1969-73; Treasurer, CODATA (Cttee on data for sci. and technol., ICSU), 1973-80; Chm., Cttee of Management, Science Policy Foundn, 1970-75. Foreign Hon. Mem., Amer. Acad. Arts and Sciences, 1968; Hon. Member: Hungarian Acad. of Sciences, 1970; Société Française de Physique, 1974; Fachverband deutscher Köche, 1978; Foreign Member: Finnish Acad. of Sciences and Letters, 1974; Akad. der Wissenschaften der DDR, 1976. Holweck Prize (British and French Physical Socs), 1955; Fritz London Award, 1957; Hughes Medal, Royal Soc., 1969. Chevalier de la Légion d'Honneur, 1976. *Publications:* (jointly) Low Temperature Physics, 1952. Papers on cryophysics, magnetism, energy and culinary physics; articles in the New Chambers's Encyclopædia. *Recreations:* cooking, enjoying its results and judiciously applying physics to the noble art of cookery. *Address:* 38 Blandford Avenue, Oxford OX2 8DZ. *T:* 56176; Department of Engineering Science, Parks Road, Oxford OX1 3PJ. *T:* 59988. *Club:* Athenæum.

KUSCH, Prof. Polykarp; Professor Emeritus, Department of Physics, The University of Texas at Dallas; *b* Germany, 26 Jan. 1911; *s* of John Matthias Kusch and Henrietta van der Haas; *m* 1935, Edith Starr McRoberts (*d* 1959); three *d* ; *m* 1960, Betty Jane Pezzoni; two *d. Educ:* Case Inst. of Technology, Cleveland, O (BS); Univ. of Illinois, Urbana, Ill. (MS, PhD). Asst, Univ. of Illinois, 1931-36; Research Asst, Univ. of Minnesota, 1936-37; Instr in Physics, Columbia Univ., 1937-41; Engr, Westinghouse Electric Corp., 1941-42; Mem. Tech. Staff, Div. of Govt Aided Research, Columbia Univ., 1942-44; Mem. Tech. Staff, Bell Telephone Laboratories, 1944-46; Columbia University: Associate Prof. of Physics, 1946-49; Prof. of Physics, 1949-72; Exec. Officer, Dept of Physics, 1949-52, Chm. 1960-63; Exec. Dir, Columbia Radiation Laboratory, 1952-60; Vice-Pres. and Dean of Faculties, 1969-70; Exec. Vice-Pres. and Provost, 1970-71. Member: Nat. Acad. of Sciences, US; American Philosophical Soc.; Amer. Acad. of Arts and Scis. Phi Beta Kappa. Hon. DSc: Case Inst. of Tech., 1956; Ohio State Univ., 1959; Colby Coll., 1961; Univ. of Illinois, 1961; Gustavus Adolphus Coll., 1963; Yeshiva Univ., 1976; Incarnate Word Coll., 1980. (Jointly) Nobel Prize in Physics, 1955. *Publications:* technical articles in Physical Review and other jls. *Address:* University of Texas at Dallas, Department of Physics, PO Box 688, Richardson, Texas 75080, USA; 7241 Paldao, Dallas, Texas 75240, USA. *T:* (214)661-1247.

KUSTOW, Michael David; Commissioning Editor for Arts Programmes, Channel Four Television, since 1981; writer, stage director, exhibition organiser; *b* 18 Nov. 1939; *m* 1973, Orna, *d* of Jacob and Rivka Spector, Haifa, Israel. *Educ:* Haberdashers' Aske's; Wadham Coll., Oxford (BA Hons English). Festivals Organiser, Centre 42, 1962-63; Royal Shakespeare Theatre Company: Dir, RSC Club, Founder of Theatreground, Editor of Flourish, 1963-67; Dir, Inst. of Contemporary Arts, 1967-70; Associate Dir, National Theatre, 1973-81. Lectr in Dramatic Arts, Harvard Univ., 1980-82. *Productions:* Punch and Judas, Trafalgar Square, 1963; I Wonder, ICA, 1968; Nicholas Tomalin Reporting, 1975; Brecht Poetry and Songs, 1976; Larkinland, Groucho Letters, Robert Lowell, Audience, 1977-78; Miss South Africa, Catullus, A Nosegay of Light Verse, The Voice of Babel, Anatol, 1979; Iris Murdoch's Art and Eros, Shakespeare's Sonnets, Stravinsky's Soldier's Tale, 1980; Charles Wood's Has Washington Legs, Harold Pinter's Family Voices, 1981. *Exhibitions:* Tout Terriblement Guillaume Apollinaire, ICA, 1968; AAARGH! A Celebration of Comics, ICA, 1971. *Publications:* Punch and Judas, 1964; The Book of US, 1968; Tank: an autobiographical fiction, 1975. *Recreations:* painting, jazz. *Address:* c/o Channel Four Television, 60 Charlotte Street, W1.

KUTSCHER, Hans, Dr Jur; President, Court of Justice of the European Communities, 1976-80 (Judge of Court, 1970-80), retired 1980; *b* Hamburg, 14 Dec. 1911, *m* 1946, Irmgard Schroeder; two step *d. Educ:* Univ. of Graz, Austria; Univ. of Freiburg-im-Breisgau, Berlin. Started career as civil servant; Ministry of: Commerce and Industry, Berlin, 1939; Transport, Baden Württemberg, 1946-51; Foreign Affairs, Bonn, 1951; Sec., Legal Cttee and Conf. Cttee of Bundesrat, 1951-55; Judge, Federal Constitutional Court, 1955-70. Hon. Prof., Univ. of Heidelberg, 1965. Hon. Bencher: Middle Temple, 1976; King's Inns, Dublin, 1977. Awarded Grand Cross Verdienstorden of Federal Republic of Germany, 1980. *Publications:* Die Enteignung, 1938; Bonner Vertrag mit Zusatzvereinbarungen, 1952; various contribs to professional jls. *Recreations:* literature, history. *Address:* Viertelstr. 10, D-7506, Bad Herrenalb, W Germany.

KUZNETS, Prof. Simon, MA, PhD; Economist and Statistician, USA; Professor Emeritus of Economics, Harvard University; *b* Kharkov, Ukraine, 30 April 1901; *s* of Abraham Kuznets and Pauline (*née* Friedman); *m* 1929, Edith Handler; one *s* one *d. Educ:* Columbia Univ., USA. BA 1923, MA 1924, PhD 1926. Nat. Bureau of Economic Research, New York, 1927- (Mem. staff); Asst Prof. Economics and Statistics, Univ. of Pennsylvania, 1930-54; Associate Dir, Bureau of Planning and Statistics, WPB, Washington, DC, 1942-44; Economic Adviser, Nat. Resources Commn of China, 1946; Adviser, Nat. Income Cttee of India, 1950-51; Prof. of Political Economy, Johns Hopkins Univ., 1954-60; Prof. of Economics, Harvard Univ., 1960-71. Marshall Lectures, Cambridge Univ., delivered 1969; Nobel Prize in Economics, 1971. Hon. Fellow, Royal Statistical Soc. (England); FAAAS; Fell. Amer. Statistical Assoc.; Member: Internat. Statistical Inst.; Amer. Philosophical Soc.; Econometric Soc.; Royal Acad. of Sciences, Sweden, etc. Hon. ScD: Princeton; Pennsylvania; Harvard; Hon. DHL: Columbia; Brandeis, 1975; PhD Hebrew Univ. of Jerusalem. *Publications:* Cyclical Fluctuations in Retail and Wholesale Trade, 1926; Secular Movements in Production and Prices, 1930; Seasonal Variations in Industry and Trade, 1934; Commodity Flow and Capital Formation, 1938; National Income and its Composition (2 vols, 1919-38), 1941; National Product since 1869, 1946; Upper Income Shares, 1953; Economic Change, 1954; Six Lectures on Economic Growth, 1959; Capital in the American Economy, 1961; Modern Economic Growth, 1966; Economic Growth of Nations: Total Output and Production Structure, 1971; Population, Capital and Growth, 1974. *Address:* Department of Economics, Harvard University, Cambridge, Mass 02138, USA; 67 Francis Avenue, Cambridge, Mass 02138, USA.

KWAKYE, Dr Emmanuel Bamfo; Vice-Chancellor, University of Science and Technology, Kumasi, Ghana, since 1974; *b* 19 March 1933; *s* of Rev. W. H. Kwakye and F. E. A. Kwakye; *m* 1964, Gloria E. (*née* Mensah); two *d. Educ:* a Presbyterian sch., Ghana; Achimota Secondary Sch., Ghana; Technical Univ., Stuttgart, West Germany (DipIng, DrIng). Development Engr, Siemens & Halske, Munich, W Germany, 1960-62; Univ. of Science and Technology, Kumasi: Lectr, 1963; Sen. Lectr, 1964; Associate Prof., 1966; Head of Dept, 1970; Dean of Faculty, 1971; Pro Vice-Chancellor, 1971. *Publications* : design and research reports on digital equipment. *Recreations:* tennis, indoor games, opera and operette. *Address:* University of Science and Technology, Kumasi, Ghana. *T:* Kumasi 5351 (ext. 200).

KWAN SAI KHEONG; Singapore Ambassador to the Philippines, since 1980; *b* 11 Sept. 1920; *s* of F. H. Kwan; *m* 1945, Sim Poh Geok; one *s* one *d. Educ:* Raffles Instn, Singapore; Raffles Coll., Singapore; Royal College of Art, London. BA Hons, ARCA. Teacher, 1946-53; various appts in Min. of Educn; Permanent Sec. and Dir of Educn, Singapore, 1966-75; concurrently Chm., Singapore Nat. Commn for UNESCO, 1968-75; Vice-Chancellor, Univ. of Singapore, 1975-80. Hon. DLitt, Singapore, 1973; Hon. DEd, Chulalongkorn Univ., Bangkok, 1977. Public Administration Medal (Gold, Singapore Govt award), 1963; Meritorious Service Medal (Singapore Govt), 1968; L'Ordre des Palmes Académiques (French Govt), 1977. *Recreations:* painting, inventing. *Address:* 34-N Mount Elizabeth, Singapore 0922. *T:* 2351272. *Clubs:* Pyramid, American, Island Country (all in Singapore).

KWAPONG, Alexander Adum, MA, PhD Cantab; Vice-Rector for Planning and Development, United Nations University, since 1976; *b* Akropong, Akwapim, 8 March 1927; *s* of E. A. Kwapong and Theophilia Kwapong; *m* 1956, Evelyn Teiko Caesar, Ada; six *d. Educ:* Presbyterian junior and middle schools, Akropong; Achimota Coll.; King's Coll., Cambridge (Exhibr, Minor Schol. and Foundn Schol.). BA 1951, MA 1954, PhD 1957, Cantab. 1st cl. prelims, Pts I and II, Classical Tripos, 1951; Sandys Res. Student, Cambridge Univ.; Richards Prize, Rann Kennedy Travel Fellowship, King's Coll., Cambridge. Lectr in Classics, UC Gold Coast, 1953, Sen. Lectr in Classics 1960; Vis. Prof., Princeton Univ., 1961-62; Prof. of Classics, Univ. of Ghana, 1962; Dean of Arts, Pro-Vice-Chancellor, Univ. of Ghana, 1963-65, Vice-Chancellor 1966-75. Chairman: Educn Review Cttee, Ghana Govt, 1966-67; Smithsonian Instn 3rd Internat. Symposium, 1969; Assoc. of Commonwealth Univs, 1971. Member: Admin. Bd, Internat. Assoc. Univs, Paris; Exec. Bd, Assoc. African Univs, 1967-74; Bd of Trustees, Internat. Council for Educnl Develt, NY; Aspen Inst. for Humanistic Studies; Bd of Dirs, Internat. Assoc. for Cultural Freedom, Paris, 1967-75. Fellow, Ghana Academy of Arts and Sciences. Hon. DLitt: Warwick; Ife; Hon. LLD Princeton. Order of Volta, Ghana. *Publications:* Higher Education and Development in Africa Today: a reappraisal, 1979; Underdevelopment and the Challenges of the 1980's: the role of knowledge, 1980; The Relevance of the African Universities to the Development Needs of Africa, 1980; *contribs to:* Grecs et Barbars, 1962; Dawn of African History (ed R. Oliver); Man and Beast: Comparative Social Behaviour (ed J. F. Eisenberg and W. S. Dillon), 1971; various articles in classical jls, especially on Ancient and Greco-Roman Africa; various addresses and lectures on internat. higher educn in ICED pubns. *Recreations:* tennis, billiards, music and piano-playing. *Address:* The United Nations University, 29th Floor, Toho Seimei Building, 15-1, Shibuya 2-chome, Shibuya-ku, Tokyo 150, Japan. *T:* 03-499-2811. *Club:* Athenæum.

KYLE, Air Chief Marshal Sir Wallace (Hart), GCB 1966 (KCB 1960; CB 1953); KCVO 1977; CBE 1945; DSO 1944; DFC 1941; Governor of Western Australia, 1975–80; *b* 22 Jan. 1910; *s* of A. Kyle, Kalgoorlie, Western Australia; *m* 1941, Molly Rimington (*née* Wilkinson); three *s* one *d. Educ:* Guildford Sch., WA; RAF Coll., Cranwell. 17 Sqdn, 1930-31; Fleet Air Arm, 1931-34; Flying Instructor, 1934–39; served War of 1939-45; Bomber Command, 1940–45; Staff Coll., 1945–47; Middle East, 1948-50; ADC to King George VI, 1949; Asst Commandant, RAF Coll., Cranwell, 1950-52; Dir of Operational Requirements, Air Ministry, 1952-54; AOC Malaya, 1955-57; ACAS (Op. Req.), 1957-59. AOC-in-C Technical Training Command, 1959-62; VCAS, 1962-65; AOC-in-C, Bomber Command, 1965-68, Strike Command, 1968; retired. ADC to the Queen, 1952-56. Air Marshal, 1961; Air Chief Marshal, 1964; Air ADC to the Queen, 1966-68. Hon. DTech W Australia Inst. of Technology, 1979; Hon. LLD Univ. of Western Australia, 1980. KStJ 1976. *Recreations:* cricket, golf. *Address:* Kingswood, Tiptoe, near Lymington, Hants. *Club:* Royal Air Force.

KYME, Rt. Rev. Brian Robert; an Assistant Bishop of Perth, Western Australia, since 1982; *b* 22 June 1935; *s* of John Robert Kyme and Ida Eileen Benson; *m* 1961, Doreen Muriel Williams; one *s* one *d. Educ:* Melbourne High School; Ridley Theological Coll., Melbourne (ThL, DipRE). Deacon, 1958; priest, 1960; Curate: St John's, E Malvern, 1958-60; Glenroy and Broadmeadows, 1960-61; Morwell, 1961-63; Vicar, St Matthew's, Ashburton, 1963-69; Dean, Holy Cross Cathedral, Geraldton, WA, 1969-74; Rector, Christ Church, Claremont, Perth, 1974-82; Archdeacon of Stirling, 1977-82. *Recreations:* golf, reading. *Address:* 52 Swan Street, Guildford, Western Australia. *T:* (office) (09)325.7455, (home) (09)279.7790. *Club:* Rotary.

KYNASTON, Nicolas; freelance organist, since 1971; *b* 10 Dec. 1941; *s* of Roger Tewkesbury Kynaston and Jessie Dearn Caecilia Kynaston (*née* Parkes); *m* 1961, Judith Felicity Heron; two *s* two *d. Educ:* Westminster Cathedral Choir Sch.; Downside; Accademia Musicale Chigiana, Siena; Conservatorio San Cecilia, Rome; Royal Coll. of Music. Organist of Westminster Cathedral, 1961-71; concert career, 1971-, travelling throughout Europe, North America, Asia and Africa. Début recital, Royal Festival Hall, 1966; Recording début, 1968. Artistic Dir, J. W. Walker & Sons Ltd, 1978-. Jury member: Grand Prix de Chartres, 1971; St Albans Internat. Organ Festival, 1975. Hon. FRCO 1976. Records incl. 5 nominated Critic's Choice; EMI/CFP Sales Award, 1974; MTA nomination Solo Instrumental Record of the Year, 1977; Deutscher Schallplattenpreis, 1978. *Recreations:* walking, church architecture. *Address:* 35 Back Hill, Ely, Cambs.

KYNCH, Prof. George James, ARCS, DIC, PhD (London); FIMA; Professor of Mathematics at the Institute of Science and Technology and in the University of Manchester, 1957-78, now Emeritus; Dean, Faculty of Technology, 1973-75; *b* 26 Oct. 1915; *s* of Vincent Kynch; *m* 1944, Eve, *d* of Edward A. Robinson; one *s* two *d. Educ:* Selhurst Grammar Sch.; Imperial Coll. of Science, London. BSc in physics, 1935, and mathematics, 1936; PhD 1939; Sir John Lubbock Memorial Prize, 1936; Hon. MScTech Manchester, 1960. Demonstrator at Imperial Coll., 1937; Lecturer at Birmingham Univ., 1942-52; Prof. of Applied Mathematics, University Coll. of Wales, Aberystwyth, 1952-57. Founder Mem., Council of Inst. of Mathematics and its Applications, 1963-66; President: Northenden Civic Soc., 1966-80; Manchester Literary and Philosophical Soc., 1971-73. *Publications:* Mathematics for the Chemist, 1955; articles in scientific jls. *Recreations:* lecturing, caravanning, dry stone wall-building. *Address:* Rectory Cottage, Ford Lane, Northenden, Manchester M22 4NQ.

KYNNAIRD, Viscount; Prince Don Filippo Giambattista Francesco Aldo Maria Rospigliosi; *b* 4 July 1942; *s* and *heir* of 11th Earl of Newburgh, *qv*; *m* 1972, Baronessa Donna Luisa, *d* of Count Annibale Caccia Dominioni; one *d. Address:* Via San Vittore, 16 Milan, Italy.

KYPRIANOU, Spyros; Grand Cross of the Order of George I of Greece, 1962; President of the Republic of Cyprus, since 1977; *b* Limassol, 1932; *s* of Achilleas and Maria Kyprianou; *m* Mimi Kyprianou; two *s. Educ:* Greek Gymnasium, Limassol; City of London Coll. Called to the Bar, Gray's Inn, 1954. Dip. Comparative Law. Founded Cypriot Students' Union in England (first Pres. 1952-54). Sec. of Archbp Makarios, in London, 1952; Sec. of Cyprus Ethnarchy in London, 1954; left Britain for Greece, 1956, to work for world projection of Cyprus case; later in 1956, rep. Cyprus Ethnarchy, New York, until 1957; resumed London post until signing of Zürich and London Agreements, returning to Cyprus with the Archbp in 1959. On declaration of Independence, 16 Aug. 1960, following brief appt as Minister of Justice, became Foreign Minister, accompanying the Pres. on visits to countries world-wide, 1961-71; rep. Cyprus at UN Security Council and Gen. Assembly sessions, notably during debates on the Cyprus question; signed Agreement in Moscow for Soviet Military Aid to Cyprus, 1964; had several consultations with Greek Govt on Cyprus matter. Mem. Cttee of Ministers of Council of Europe at meetings in Strasburg and Paris (Pres. Cttee, April-Dec. 1967). Resigned post of Foreign Minister, 1972, after dispute with military régime in Athens. Practised law, withdrawing from politics until the coup and Turkish invasion of Cyprus, 1974; travelled between Athens, London and New York, where he led Cyprus delegn during debate on Cyprus in Gen. Assembly of UN, 1974; participated in talks between Greek Govt and Pres. Makarios, 1974; an *ad hoc* member of Cyprus delegn at Security meeting in New York, 1975. Announced estabt of Democratic Party in Cyprus, 1976, becoming Pres. of House of Reps on the party's victory in parly elections.

On death of Archbp Makarios, Aug. 1977, became Actg Pres. of Republic, until elected Pres. in same month; re-elected Pres., unopposed, in Feb. 1978 for a full five-year term. Holds numerous foreign decorations. *Recreations:* literature, music, sport. *Address:* The Presidential Palace, Nicosia, Cyprus.

KYRLE POPE, Rear-Adm. Michael Donald, CB 1969; MBE 1946; *b* 1 Oct. 1916; *e s* of late Comdr R. K. C. Pope, DSO, OBE, RN retd, and of Mrs A. J. Pope (*née* Macdonald); *m* 1947, Angela Suzanne Layton; one *s* one *d. Educ:* Wellington Coll., Berks. Joined RN, 1934; Sen. Naval Off., Persian Gulf, 1962-64; MoD (Naval Intell.), 1965-67; Chief of Staff to C-in-C Far East, 1967-69; retd 1970. Comdr 1951; Capt. 1958; Rear-Adm. 1967. Gen. Manager, Middle East Navigation Aids Service, Bahrain, 1971-77. Dean's Administrator, St Alban's Cathedral, 1977-80. *Recreations:* country pursuits, sailing. *Address:* Hopfields, Westmill, Buntingford, Herts. *T:* Royston 71835. *Club:* Army and Navy.
See also Sir J. E. Pope.

L

LABOUCHERE, Sir George (Peter), GBE 1964; KCMG 1955 (CMG 1951); *b* 2 Dec. 1905; *s* of late F. A. Labouchere; *m* 1943, Rachel Katherine, *d* of Hon. Eustace Hamilton-Russell. *Educ:* Charterhouse Sch.; Sorbonne, Paris. Entered Diplomatic Service, 1929. Served in Madrid, Cairo, Rio de Janeiro, Stockholm, Nanking, Buenos Aires. UK Deputy-Commissioner for Austria, 1951-53; HM Minister, Hungary, 1953-55; Ambassador to Belgium, 1955-60; Ambassador to Spain, 1960-66. Retired, 1966. Member of Council, Friends of the Tate Gallery; Pres., Shropshire Br., CPRE; Mem., Dilettanti Society; FRSA. *Recreations:* shooting, fishing, Chinese ceramics, contemporary painting and sculpture. *Address:* Dudmaston, Bridgnorth, Salop. *Clubs:* Brooks's, Pratt's, Beefsteak.

LABOUISSE, Henry (Richardson); consultant on organisation and development matters; lawyer, US; *b* New Orleans, La., 11 Feb. 1904; *s* of Henry Richardson Labouisse; *m* 1935, Elizabeth Scriven Clark (*d* 1945); one *d*; *m* 1954, Eve Curie, *qv. Educ:* Princeton Univ. (AB); Harvard Univ. (LLB). Attorney-at-Law, NYC, 1929-41. Joined US State Dept, 1941; Minister Economic Affairs, US Embassy, Paris, 1945; Chief, Special Mission to France of Economic Co-operation Administration, 1951-54; Director, UN Relief and Works Agency for Palestine Refugees, 1954-58; Consultant, International Bank for Reconstruction and Development, 1959-61 (Head of IBRD Mission to Venezuela, 1959); Director, International Co-operation Admin., 1961-62; US Ambassador to Greece, 1962-65; Exec. Dir, United Nations Children's Fund (UNICEF), 1965-79. Hon. LLD: University of Bridgeport, 1961; Princeton Univ., 1965; Lafayette Coll., 1966; Tulane Univ., 1967. Holds several decorations and hon. awards, incl. Woodrow Wilson Award, Princeton Univ., 1978. *Recreations:* swimming, golf, reading. *Address:* 1 Sutton Place South, NY 10022, USA. *Clubs:* Century Association, Piping Rock (NY); Metropolitan, Chevy Chase (Washington).

LABOUISSE, Mrs H. R.; *see* Curie, Eve.

LACEY, Daniel; *see* Lacey, W. D.

LACEY, Frank; Director, Metrication Board, 1976-79, retired; *b* 4 Feb. 1919; *s* of Frank Krauter and Maud Krauter (*née* Lacey); *m* 1944, Maggie Tyrrell; one *s* one *d. Educ:* St Ignatius Coll., N7. Served War, 1939-46, RAFVR. Tax Officer, Inland Revenue, 1936; joined Board of Trade, 1946, Regional Dir, E Region, 1967-70; Counsellor (Commercial), UK Mission, Geneva, 1973-76. Hon. Advr on Metrication to Commonwealth Secretariat, 1979-. *Recreation:* ski-ing. *Address:* Alma Cottage, Whistley Green, Hurst, Berks RG10 0EH. *T:* Twyford 340880.

LACEY, George William Brian; Keeper, Department of Transport, Science Museum, London, since 1971; *b* 15 Nov. 1926; *m* 1956, Lynette (*née* Hogg); two *s. Educ:* Brighton, Hove and Sussex Grammar Sch., 1938-44; Brighton Technical Coll., 1944-47. BSc(Eng) 2nd Cl. Hons (External, London). National Service, REME, 1947-49. Rolls-Royce Ltd, Derby: Grad. Apprentice, Tech. Asst, Mechanical Develt and Performance Analysis, 1949-54. Asst Keeper, Science Museum, London, SW7, 1954. Chairman: Historical Gp, Royal Aeronautical Soc., 1971-78; Assoc. British Transport Museums, 1973-; Exec. Cttee, Transport Trust, 1980-; Mem. Council, Transport Trust, 1978-. *Recreation:* golf. *Address:* 7 Wilmington Close, Hassocks, W Sussex BN6 8QB. *T:* Hassocks 3231.

LACEY, Janet, CBE 1960; Director, Christian Aid Department, British Council of Churches, 1952-May 1968, retired; *b* 25 Oct. 1903; *d* of Joseph Lacey, Property Agent, and Elizabeth Lacey. *Educ:* various schools, Sunderland; Drama Sch., Durham. YWCA, Kendal, 1926; General Secretary, YMCA/YWCA Community Centre, Dagenham, 1932; YMCA Education Secretary, BAOR, Germany, 1945; Youth Secretary, British Council of Churches, 1947. Dir, Family Welfare Assoc., 1969-73; Consultant to Churches' Council for Health and Healing, 1973-77. Hon. DD Lambeth, 1975.

Publications: A Cup of Water, 1970; series booklets, Refugees, Aid to Developing Countries, Meeting Human Need with Christian Aid, 1956-64. *Recreations:* theatre, music, reading, crosswords. *Address:* Flat 8, Lesley Court, Strutton Ground, SW1. *T:* 01-222 4573. *Club:* Nikaean.

LACEY, (William) Daniel, CB 1978; CBE 1961; Director-General, Design Services, Department of the Environment, Property Services Agency, since 1975; *b* 8 Jan. 1923; *s* of Ivor Ewart and Mary Lacey; *m* 1946, Julie Ellen (*née* Chandler); no *c. Educ:* Bishop Gore's Grammar Sch., Swansea. FRIBA 1967; MRTPI. Assistant Architect, Herts County Council, 1946-55; Assistant County Architect, Notts County Council, 1955-58; County Architect, Notts County Council, 1958-64; Chief Architect, 1964-69, Head of Architects and Building Br., 1969-75, DES. RIBA: Hon. Sec., 1967-69; Vice-Pres., 1971-72. Awarded Gran Premio Con Menzione Speciale at Milan Triennale Exhibition, 1960. *Publications:* various papers in Architectural Journals. *Recreation:* gardening. *Address:* c/o Department of the Environment, 2 Marsham Street, SW1. *Club:* Reform.

LACHMANN, Prof. Peter Julius, FRCP; FRCPath 1981; FRS 1982; Sheila Joan Smith Professor of Tumour Immunology, University of Cambridge, since 1977; Honorary Director of MRC Mechanisms in Tumour Immunity Unit, since 1980 (Head, MRC Group on Mechanisms in Tumour Immunity, 1976-77, Honorary Head, 1977-80); Hon. Clinical Immunologist, Addenbrooke's Hospital, since 1976; Fellow, Christ's College, Cambridge, since 1976; *b* 23 Dec. 1931; *s* of late Heinz Lachmann and Thea (*née* Heller); *m* 1962, Sylvia Mary, *d* of Alan Stephenson; two *s* one *d. Educ:* Christ's Coll., Finchley; Trinity Coll., Cambridge; University College Hosp. MA, MB BChir, PhD, ScD (Cantab). John Lucas Walker Student, Dept of Pathology, Cambridge, 1958-60; Vis. Investigator, Rockefeller Univ., New York, 1960-61; Empire Rheumatism Council Res. Fellow, Dept of Pathology, Cambridge, 1962-64; Asst Dir of Res. in Pathology, Univ. of Cambridge, 1964-71; Fellow, Christ's Coll., Cambridge, 1962-71; Prof. of Immunology, Royal Postgraduate Med. Sch., 1971-75. Member: Systems Bd, MRC, 1982; Hammersmith Special Health Auth., 1982. Vis. Investigator, Scripps Clinic and Research Foundn, La Jolla, 1966, 1975 and 1980; Vis. Scientist, Basel Inst. of Immunology, 1971. *Publications:* co-ed, Clinical Aspects of Immunology, 3rd edn 1975, 4th edn 1982; papers in sci. jls on complement and immunopathology. *Recreations:* walking in mountains, keeping bees. *Address:* Conduit Head, 36 Conduit Head Road, Cambridge CB3 0EY. *T:* Cambridge 354433.

LACHS, Henry Lazarus; His Honour Judge Lachs; a Circuit Judge, since 1979; *b* 31 Dec. 1927; *s* of Samuel and Mania Lachs; *m* 1959, Edith Bergel; four *d. Educ:* Liverpool Institute High Sch.; Pembroke Coll., Cambridge (MA, LLB). Called to Bar, Middle Temple, 1951. A Recorder of the Crown Court, 1972-79. Chm., Merseyside Mental Health Review Tribunal, 1968-79. Chm. of Governors, King David High Sch., Liverpool, 1971-. *Address:* 41 Menlove Gardens West, Liverpool L18 2ET. *T:* 051-722 5936.

LACHS, Manfred; Judge, International Court of Justice, since 1967 (President, 1973-76); *b* 21 April 1914; *m* Halina Kirst. *Educ:* Univs of Cracow, Vienna, London and Cambridge; Univ. of Cracow, Poland (LLM 1936, Dr jur 1937); Univ. of Nancy, France (Dr); Univ. of Moscow (DSc Law). Legal Adviser, Polish Ministry Internat. Affairs, 1947-66 (Ambassador, 1960-66). Prof., Acad. Polit. Sci., Warsaw, 1949-52; Prof. Internat. Law, Univ. of Warsaw, 1952; Dir, Inst. Legal Scis, Polish Academy of Sciences, 1961-67. Chm., Legal Cttee, UN Gen. Assemblies, 1949, 1951, 1955; Rep. of Poland, UN Disarmament Cttee, 1962-63. Rapporteur, Gen. Colloque. Internat. Assoc. Juridical Sciences, UNESCO, Rome, 1948; Internat. Law Commn, UN, 1962; Chm., Legal Cttee UN Peaceful Uses of Outer Space, 1962-66; Hon. Sen. Fellow, UNITAR. Member: Inst. of Internat. Law; Curatorium, Hague Acad. of Internat. Law (Vice-Pres.); Acad. of Bologna; Polish Acad. of Sciences. Hon. Mem., Amer. Soc. Internat. Law; Corr. Mem., Institut de France; Foreign Mem., Dutch Soc. of Scis, 1982. LLD (Hon.): Univs of: Budapest 1967; Algiers 1969; Delhi 1969; Nice 1972; Halifax, 1973; Bruxelles, 1973; Bucarest, 1974; New York, 1974; Southampton, 1975; Howard (Washington), 1975; Sofia, 1975; Vancouver, 1976; London, 1976; Helsinki, 1980. Gold medal for outstanding contribs devel. rule of law outer space, 1966; World Jurist Award for enormous contrib. to improvement of justice, Washington, 1975; Netherland's Wateler Peace Prize, 1976; also other awards. *Publications:* War Crimes, 1945; The Geneva Agreements on Indochina, 1954; Multilateral Treaties, 1958; The Law of Outer Space, 1964; Polish-German Frontier, 1964; The Law of Outer Space—an experience in law making, 1972; Teachings and Teaching of International Law, 1977; The Teacher in International Law, 1982; numerous essays and articles in eleven languages. *Address:* International Court of Justice, Peace Palace, The Hague, Holland. *T:* 92-44-41.

LACK, Victor John Frederick, FRCP, FRCS; FRCOG; retired. *Educ:* London Hospital. Examiner: Universities of Oxford and Cambridge and Central Midwives' Board; Midwifery and Diseases of Women Conjoint Board, London; late Lectr in Midwifery and Diseases of Women, Birmingham Univ.; Asst Obst. Queen Elizabeth Hosp., Birmingham; Obst. Regist., Ho. Surg. and Ho. Phys. London Hosp. Obstetrical and Gynæcological Surgeon, London Hospital; Cons. Obstetrican Greenwich Borough Council Maternity Home; Gynæcologist King George's Hosp., Ilford; Obst. and Gyn. Surgeon, Royal Bucks Hosp., Aylesbury. FRSM (Mem. Obst. Sect.); a Vice-Pres., RCOG, 1955-. *Publications:* (jointly) Ten Teachers of Midwifery and Diseases of Women. Contrib. to medical jls. *Address:* 82 Bradwell Road, Loughton, Milton Keynes, Bucks MK8 0AL. *T:* Shenley Church End 243.

LACKEY, Rt. Rev. Edwin Keith; *see* Ottawa, Bishop of.

LACKEY, Mary Josephine, OBE 1966; Under Secretary, Department of Trade, since 1974; *b* 11 Aug. 1925; *d* of William and Winifred Lackey. *Educ:* King Edward VI High Sch., Birmingham; Lady Margaret Hall, Oxford (MA). Board of Trade, 1946; Asst Principal, Central Land Bd, 1947-50; BoT, 1950-61; UK Delegn to EFTA and GATT, 1961-66; BoT, subseq. DTI and Dept of Trade, 1966-; Asst Sec., 1968. *Club:* United Oxford & Cambridge University.

LACOME, Myer; Principal, Duncan of Jordanstone College of Art, Dundee, since 1978; *b* 13 Nov. 1927; *s* of Colman Lacome and Sara (*née* Sholl); *m* 1954, Jacci Edgar; one *s* two *d. Educ:* Regional Coll. of Art, Liverpool. MSIAD, MSTD, MInstPkg; FRSA. National Service, RAF, 1946-48. Post-grad. course, 1948-49; designer, New York, 1949-51; consultant designer, London, 1951-59; Head of Sch. of Design, Duncan of Jordanstone Coll. of Art, Dundee, 1962-77. Vis. Fellow, Royal Melbourne Inst. of Technol., 1979. Member: Senate, Univ. of Dundee; Council and Three Dimensional Design Bd, CNAA. *Publications:* papers on crafts in Scotland and on Scandinavian design and crafts. *Recreations:* the man-made environment, travel, swimming, fishing. *Address:* 72 Tay Street, Newport-on-Tay, Fife, DD6 8AP. *T:* Newport-on-Tay 3230.

LACON, Sir Edmund (Vere), 8th Bt *cr* 1818; General Manager, Abdul Aziz Al-Babtain, Kuwait, since 1980; *b* 3 May 1936; *s* of Sir George Vere Francis Lacon, 7th Bt, and of Hilary Blanche (now Mrs J. D. Turner), *d* of late C. J. Scott, Adyar, Walberswick; *S* father, 1980; *m* 1963, Gillian, *d* of J. H. Middleditch, Wrentham, Suffolk; one *s* one *d. Educ:* Taverham Hall, Norfolk; Woodbridge School, Suffolk. RAF Regiment, 1955-59. Career in sales management and marketing, 1959-. *Recreations:* golf, water-skiing, go-karting. *Heir:* *s* (Edmund) Richard (Vere) Lacon, *b* 2 Oct. 1967. *Address:* c/o Abdul Aziz Al-Babtain, PO Box 599, Kuwait. *T:* Kuwait 412730; Milbrook, Holton St Peter, Halesworth, Suffolk. *T:* Halesworth 2536.

LACOSTE, Paul, OC 1977; DU Paris; Rector, Université de Montréal, since 1975; *b* 24 April 1923; *s* of Emile Lacoste and Juliette Boucher Lacoste; *m* 1973, Louise Marcil; one *s* one *d. Educ:* Univ. de Montréal (BA, MA, LPh, LLL). DUP 1948. Fellow, Univ. of Chicago, 1946-47; Univ. de Montréal: Prof., Faculty of Philosophy, 1948; Full Prof., 1958; Vice-Rector, 1968-75. Practising lawyer, 1964-66. Pres., Assoc. des universités partiellement ou entièrement de langue française, 1978-81. Hon. LLD: McGill, 1975; Toronto, 1978. *Publications:* (jtly) Justice et paix scolaire, 1962; A Place of Liberty, 1964; Le Canada au seuil du siècle de l'abondance, 1969; Principes de gestion universitaire, 1970; (jtly) Education permanente et potentiel universitaire, 1977. *Address:* Université de Montréal, PO Box 6128, Montréal H3C 3J7, Canada. *T:* 343-6776; 2900 boulevard Edouard-Montpetit, Montréal. *Club:* St-Denis (Montréal).

LA COUR, Leonard Francis, OBE 1973 (MBE 1952); FRS 1970; Professor, University of East Anglia, 1973-78; *b* 28 July 1907; *o* *c* of Francis La Cour and Maud (*née* Coomber); *m* 1935, Anne Wilkes; no *c. Educ:* Merton Sch., Surrey. John Innes Institute: Sen. Exper. Officer 1948, Chief Exper. Officer 1956, Senior Principal Scientific Officer, 1970, retired 1972. Hon. MSc East Anglia, 1969, DSc, 1977. *Publications:* (with C. D. Darlington) The Handling of Chromosomes, 6th edn 1976; various research articles in scientific jls. *Recreation:* gardening. *Address:* 4 Greencroft, Trinity Place, Eastbourne, E Sussex BN21 3DA.

LACRETELLE, J. de; *see* de Lacretelle.

LACY, Sir Hugh Maurice Pierce, 3rd Bt, *cr* 1921; *b* 3 Sept 1943; *s* of Sir Maurice John Pierce Lacy, 2nd Bt, and of his 2nd wife, Nansi Jean, *d* of late Myrddin Evans, Bangor, Caernarvonshire; *S* father, 1965; *m* 1968, Deanna, *d* of Howard Bailey. *Educ:* Aiglon Coll., Switzerland. *Heir:* *b* Patrick Bryan Finucane Lacy [*b* 18 April 1948; *m* 1971, Phyllis Victoria, *d* of E. P. H. James; one *s* one *d*].

LADAS, Mrs Diana Margaret, *b* 8 Feb. 1913; *er* *d* of late Bertram Hambro and late Mrs Charles Boyle; *m* 1945, Alexis Christopher Ladas (marr. diss. 1955); one *s. Educ:* Downe House Sch.; Girton Coll., Cambridge. Before the war, Sec. in Geneva, Malta and London. During War of 1939-45, worked as temp. asst Principal in Min. of Economic Warfare, Board of Trade and Political Warfare executive in Cairo. Transferred to UNRRA, worked in Athens, Washington and London; on the staff of British Information Services, in New York, 1948-50. Began teaching at Westminster Tutors, 1955; joined staff of Heathfield Sch., 1958; Dep. Head of Moira House Sch., 1959, Head Mistress, 1960; Vice-Principal of Queen's Gate Sch., 1962-65; Head Mistress, Heathfield Sch., 1965-72. *Recreations:* gardening and travelling. *Address:* Prospect Place, 154 Peckham Rye, SE22.

LADDIE, Hugh Ian Lang; Junior Counsel to the Treasury in Patent Matters, since 1981; *b* 15 April 1946; *s* of Bertie Daniel Laddie and Rachel Laddie; *m* 1970, Stecia Elizabeth (*née* Zamet); two *s* one *d. Educ:* Aldenham Sch.; St Catharine's Coll., Cambridge (MA). Called to the Bar, Middle Temple, 1969. *Publications:* (jtly) Patent Law of Europe and the United Kingdom, 1978;

(jtly) The Modern Law of Copyright, 1980. *Recreations:* music, gardening, fishing. *Address:* 34 Manor House Drive, NW6 7DE. *T:* 01-459 3804.

LAFITTE, Prof. François; Professor of Social Policy and Administration, University of Birmingham, 1959-80; *b* 3 Aug. 1913; *s* of Françoise Lafitte and adopted *s* of late Havelock Ellis; *m* 1938, Eileen (*née* Saville); (one *s* decd). *Educ:* Collège Municipal, Maubeuge; George Green's Sch., Poplar; St Olave's Grammar Sch., Southwark; Worcester Coll., Oxford. Research and translating for Miners' Internat. Fed., 1936-37; on research staff, and subseq. Dep. Sec., PEP, 1938-43; on editorial staff of The Times, as special writer on social questions, 1943-59; Chm. of PEP research groups on health services, 1943-46, on housing policy, 1948-51. Dean of Faculty of Commerce and Social Science, Birmingham, Univ., 1965-68. Member: Home Office Advisory Council on the Treatment of Offenders, 1961-64; Adv. Cttees Social Science Research Council, 1966-69; Redditch New Town Corp., 1964-75; Chm., British Pregnancy Adv. Service, 1968-. *Publications:* The Internment of Aliens, 1940; Britain's Way to Social Security, 1945; Family Planning in the Sixties, 1964; (part author) Socially Deprived Families in Britain, 1970; many PEP Planning monographs; many papers on abortion and related issues; contributed to British Journal of Delinquency, Eugenics Review, Chambers's Encyclopædia. etc. *Address:* 77 Oakfield Road, Birmingham B29 7HL. *T:* 021-472 2709. *Clubs:* Royal Society of Medicine (London); University (Birmingham).

LAGACOS, Eustace P.; Greek Ambassador to the Court of St James's, 1979-82; *b* 4 June 1921; one *d. Educ:* Univ. of Athens (Graduate of Law). Embassy Attaché, 1949; served Athens, Paris, Istanbul, Nicosia, London; Minister, 1969; Foreign Ministry, Athens, 1970; Ambassador to Nicosia, 1972; Dir Gen., Economic Affairs, Foreign Ministry, Athens, 1974; Permanent Representative to NATO, Brussels, 1976. Grand Officer of Order of the Phoenix, Greece; Commander of Order of George I, Greece; Grand Cordon of Order of Manuel Amadoi Guerrero, Panama; Commander of Legion of Honour, France; Kt Commander of Order of Queen Isabella I, Spain; Grand Officer of Order of the Republic, Egypt. *Address:* Ministry of Foreign Affairs, Athens, Greece.

LAGDEN, Godfrey William; *b* 12 April 1906; *s* of Augustine William and Annie Lagden; *m* 1935, Dorothy Blanche Wheeler. *Educ:* Richmond Hill Sch., Richmond, Surrey. Sun Insurance Office, London, 1931-34; IBM (United Kingdom) Ltd, 1934-. MP (C) Hornchurch, 1955-66. Pres., Harold Wood Hosp. League of Friends. *Recreations:* cricket, water polo, boxing, and dog breeding. *Address:* St Austell, 187 Southend Arterial Road, Hornchurch, Essex. *T:* Ingrebourne 42770. *Clubs:* St Stephen's Constitutional, Wig and Pen, Spanish.

LAGESEN, Air Marshal Sir Philip (Jacobus), KCB 1979 (CB 1974); DFC 1945; AFC 1959; FBIM; *b* 25 Aug. 1923; *s* of late Philip J. Lagesen, Johannesburg, South Africa; *m* 1944, Dulcie, *d* of late H. McPherson, Amanzimtoti, Natal, S Africa; one *s* one *d. Educ:* Jeppe, Johannesburg. Served War, 1939-45, South African Air Force. Joined RAF, 1951; Flying Instructor, Rhodesia Air Trng Gp, 1952-53; Kenya, 1953-55; No 50 Squadron, 1955-57; Staff, RAF Flying Coll., Manby, 1957-59; PSO, C-in-C Middle East, 1959-61; Comdr, No 12 (B) Sqdn, 1961-64; Wing Comdr Ops, No 1 (B) Group 1964-66; CO, RAF Tengah, Singapore, 1966-69; SPSO, Strike Comd, 1969-70; Dir Ops (S), RAF, MoD, 1970-72; SASO, HQ Strike Comd, 1972-73; Dep. Comdr, RAF Germany, 1973-75; AOC 1 Group, 1975-78; AOC 18 Group, 1978-80. *Recreations:* golf, motoring. *Address:* c/o Lloyds Bank, 6 Pall Mall, SW1. *Club:* Royal Air Force.

LAGHZAOUI, Mohammed; Ouissam El Ouala (1st class) and Commander of the Order of the Crown, Morocco; Moroccan Ambassador to France, 1971-72; *b* Fez, Morocco, 27 Sept. 1906; *m* 1940, Kenza Bouayad; three *s* three *d. Educ:* Moulay Idriss Coll., Fez. Founded many commercial and industrial companies; Chm., Société marocaine des Transports Laghzaoui. During French Protectorate over Morocco, he was Mem. Government's Council (many times Chm.); one of principal Signatories to Act of Independence, 1944; Dir-Gen. of Nat. Security (apptd by late Mohammed V), 1956-60. Then, as Dir-Gen. of Office chérifien des Phosphates (first nat. mining concern) he promoted production and export; later, he was responsible for Office marocain des Phosphates, and Coordinator of Nat. Mining and Industrial Cos. In charge of four ministries: Industry, Mining, Tourism and Handicraft, and was Pres. of Afro-Asiatic Assoc. for Economic Development, 1966-69; Moroccan Ambassador to UK, 1969-71. Holds foreign orders. *Recreations:* bridge, football. *Address:* Résidence Laghzaoui, Route de Suissi, Rabat, Morocco.

LAGOS, Archbishop of, (RC), since 1973 (and Metropolitan); **Most Rev. Anthony Olubunmi Okogie,** DD; *b* Lagos, 16 June 1936. *Educ:* St Gregory's Coll., Lagos; St Peter and St Paul's Seminary, Ibadan; Urban Univ., Rome. Priest, 1966; appointments include: Acting Parish Priest, St Patrick's Church, Idumagbo; Asst Priest, Holy Cross Cathedral, Lagos; Religious Instructor, King's Coll., Lagos; Director of Vocations, Archdiocese of Lagos; Manager, Holy Cross Group of Schools, Lagos; Master of Ceremonies, Holy Cross Cathedral; Auxiliary Bishop of Oyo, 1971-72; Auxiliary Bishop to Apostolic Administrator, Archdiocese of Lagos, 1972-73. Roman Catholic Trustee of CAN. *Address:* Holy Cross Cathedral, PO Box 8, Lagos, Nigeria. *T:* 635729 and 633841.

LAHNSTEIN, Manfred; *b* 20 Dec. 1937; *s* of Walter and Hertha Lahnstein; one *s. Educ:* Cologne Univ. (Dipl. Kfin). German Trade Union Fedn, Dusseldorf, 1962-64; European Trade Union Office, Brussels, 1965-67; European Commn, 1967-73; German Govt service, 1973-: served in Finance Min. and as Head of Chancellor's Office; Minister of Finance, April-Oct. 1982. *Publications:* various articles. *Recreation:* classical music. *Address:* c/o Bonn, Graurheindorfer Strasse 108, Federal Republic of Germany. *T:* 6824200.

LAIDLAW, Sir Christophor (Charles Fraser), Kt 1982; Chairman, ICL, since 1981; Director: Commercial Union Assurance, since 1978; Barclays Bank International, since 1980; Barclays Bank Ltd, since 1981; *b* 9 Aug. 1922; *m* 1952, Nina Mary Prichard; one *s* three *d. Educ:* Rugby Sch.; St John's Coll., Cambridge (MA). Served War of 1939-45: Europe and Far East, Major on Gen. Staff. Joined British Petroleum, 1948: BP Rep. in Hamburg, 1959-61; Gen. Manager, Marketing Dept, 1963-67; Dir, BP Trading, 1967; Dir (Ops), 1971-72; a Man. Dir, 1972-81, and Dep. Chm., BP, 1980-81; President, BP: Belgium, 1967-71; Italiana, 1972-73; Deutsche BP, 1972-83; Chairman: BP Oil, 1977-81; BP Oil Internat., 1981. *Recreation:* fishing. *Address:* Bridge House, Putney Bridge, Fulham, SW6 3JX. *Club:* Anglo-German.

LAIDLAW, William Allison, MA, LittD; Professor of Classics in the University of London, Queen Mary College, 1949-64, now Emeritus Professor; *b* 15 July 1898; *s* of James and Sarah A. Laidlaw. *Educ:* Wesley Coll., Dublin; Trinity Coll., University of Dublin. Classical Foundation Scholar, Vice-Chancellor's Medallist in Latin, Vice-Chancellor's Prize for Latin Prose; Senior Moderator in Classics and in Mental and Moral Science, 1922; Lecturer in Classics and Philosophy, University of W. Australia, 1923-28; Student of British Sch., Athens, 1929; Asst Lecturer in Classics, University Coll., Southampton, 1929-31; Lecturer in Latin, University of St Andrews, 1931-46; Reader in Classics, University of London, Queen Mary Coll., 1946-49; Ford Visiting Prof. of Classics, University of Ibadan, 1964-65. *Publications:* A History of Delos, 1933; The Prosody of Terence, 1938; Latin Literature, 1951; contribs to: Oxford Classical Dictionary, 1949; Fifty Years of Classical Scholarship, 1954, Chambers's Encyclopædia: articles, notes, reviews in various classical journals. *Recreation:* reading. *Address:* 4 Inverclyde Court, Nicholas Road, Blundellsands, Liverpool L23 6TS. *T:* 051-924 1279.

LAINE, Cleo, (Mrs Clementina Dinah Dankworth), OBE 1979; vocalist; *b* 28 Oct. 1927; British; *m* 1st, 1947, George Langridge (marr. diss. 1957); one *s*; 2nd, 1958, John Philip William Dankworth, *qv*; one *s* one *d*. Joined Dankworth Orchestra, 1953. Melody Maker and New Musical Express Top Girl Singer Award, 1956; Moscow Arts Theatre Award for acting role in Flesh to a Tiger, 1958; Top place in Internat. Critics Poll by Amer. Jazz magazine, Downbeat, 1965. Lead, in Seven Deadly Sins, Edinburgh Festival and Sadler's Wells, 1961; acting roles in Edin. Fest., 1966, 1967. Many appearances with symphony orchestras performing Façade (Walton) and other compositions; played Julie in Show Boat, Adelphi, 1971; title role in Colette, Comedy, 1980. Frequent TV appearances. Woman of the Year, 9th annual Golden Feather Awards, 1973; Edison Award, 1974; Variety Club of GB Show Business Personality Award (with John Dankworth), 1977; TV Times Viewers Award for Most Exciting Female Singer on TV, 1978. *Recreation:* painting. *Address:* International Artistes Representation, Regent House, 235 Regent Street, WC1. *T:* 01-439 8401.

LAING, Alastair Stuart, CBE 1980; MVO 1959; Deputy Director General, Commonwealth War Graves Commission, since 1975; *b* 17 June 1920; *s* of Captain Arthur Henry Laing and Clare May Laing (*née* Ashworth); *m* 1946, Audrey Stella Hobbs, MCSP, *d* of Dr Frederick Hobbs and Gladys Marion Hobbs (*née* George); one *s* decd. *Educ:* Sedbergh School. Served Indian Army, 10th Gurkha Rifles, 1940-46, Captain; seconded to Civil Administration, Bengal, 1944-46. Commonwealth War Graves Commission, 1947-. Chm., Vale of Aylesbury Hunt, 1981-. *Recreations:* gardening, foxhunting, fell walking, history. *Address:* Wagtails, Lower Wood End, Marlow, Bucks SL7 2HN. *T:* Marlow 4481.

LAING, Austen, CBE 1973; Director General, British Fishing Federation Ltd, since 1962; *b* 27 April 1923; *s* of William and Sarah Ann Laing; *m* 1945, Kathleen Pearson; one *s* one *d. Educ:* Bede Grammar Sch., Sunderland; Newcastle Univ. BA (Social Studies) and BA (Econs). Lectr, Univ. of Durham, 1950-56; Administrator, Distant Water Vessels Develt Scheme, 1956-61. Mem. Cttee of Inquiry into Veterinary Profession, 1971-75. *Publications:* numerous articles in British and foreign jls on fishing industry. *Address:* Boulder Cottage, Swanland, North Ferriby, North Humberside HU14 3PE. *Club:* Army and Navy.

LAING, Sir Hector, Kt 1978; Chairman, United Biscuits (Holdings) plc, since 1972 (Director, 1953; Managing Director, 1964); Director, Court of the Bank of England; *b* 12 May 1923; *s* of Hector Laing and Margaret Norris Grant; *m* 1950, Marian Clare, *d* of Maj.-Gen. Sir John Laurie, Bt, *qv*; three *s. Educ:* Loretto Sch., Musselborough, Scotland; Jesus Coll., Cambridge. Served War, Scots Guards, 1942-47 (American Bronze Star, despatches, 1944); final rank, Captain. McVitie & Price: Dir, 1947; Chm., 1963. Mem. Bd, Royal Insurance Co., 1970-78; Dir, Allied-Lyons, 1979-82. Chm., Food and Drink Industries Council, 1977-79. Mem. Council, Wycombe Abbey Sch., 1981-. Businessman of the Year Award, 1979; National Free Enterprise Award, 1980. *Recreations:*

gardening, walking, flying. *Address:* High Meadows, Windsor Road, Gerrards Cross, Bucks. *T:* Gerrards Cross 82437. *Club:* White's.

LAING, James Findlay; Under Secretary, Scottish Economic Planning Department, since 1979; *b* 7 Nov. 1933; *s* of Alexander Findlay Laing and Jessie Ross; *m* 1969, Christine Joy Canaway; one *s. Educ:* Nairn Academy; Edinburgh Univ. MA (Hons History). Nat. Service, Seaforth Highlanders, 1955-57. Asst Principal and Principal, Scottish Office, 1957-68; Principal, HM Treasury, 1968-71; Asst Sec., Scottish Office, 1972-79. *Recreations:* squash, chess. *Address:* 6 Barnton Park Place, Edinburgh EH4 6ET. *T:* 031-336 5951. *Clubs:* Royal Commonwealth Society; Edinburgh Sports.

LAING, Prof. John Archibald, PhD; MRCVS; Courtauld Professor of Animal Husbandry and Hygiene, at Royal Veterinary College, University of London, since 1959; *b* 27 April 1919; *s* of late John and Alexandra Laing; *m* 1946, June Margaret Lindsay Smith, *d* of Hugh Lindsay Smith, Downham Market; one *s* two *d. Educ:* Johnston Sch.; Royal (Dick) School of Veterinary Studies, Edinburgh University; Christ's Coll. Cambridge. BSc(Edinburgh); MRCVS; PhD Cantab. FIBiol. Aleen Cust Scholar, Royal Coll. of Veterinary Surgeons. Research Officer, 1943-46, Asst Veterinary Investigation Officer, 1946-49, Ministry of Agriculture; Lecturer in Veterinary Science, 1949-51, Senior Lecturer in Veterinary Medicine, 1951-57, Reader in Veterinary Science, 1957-59, Univ. of Bristol. Anglo-Danish Churchill Fellowship, Univ. of Copenhagen, 1954; Visiting Professor, Univs of: Munich, 1967; Mexico, 1967; Queensland, 1970 (and John Thompson Memorial Lectr); Ankara, 1977; Assiut, 1980; Consultant to FAO, UN, 1955-57; Representative of FAO in Dominican Republic, 1957-58; Consultant to UNESCO in Central America, 1963-65; Mem., British Agricultural Mission to Peru, 1970. Mem., EEC Veterinary Scientific Cttee, 1981-. Pres., Perm. Cttee. Internat. Congress on Animal Reproduction, 1980 (Sec., 1961-80); Member: Governing Body, Houghton Poultry Research Station, 1968-74; Council, Royal Veterinary Coll.; Vice-Pres., University Fedn for Animal Welfare (Treasurer, 1969-75; Chm., 1975-77). Hon. Fellow Veterinary Acad., Madrid. Editor, British Veterinary Journal. *Publications:* Fertility and Infertility in the Domestic Animals, 1955, 3rd edn 1979; papers on animal breeding and husbandry in various scientific journals. *Address:* Ayot St Lawrence, Herts. *T:* Stevenage 820413. *Club:* Athenæum.

LAING, Sir (John) Maurice, Kt 1965; Director, since 1939, and President, since 1982, John Laing plc (formerly John Laing & Son Ltd) (Deputy Chairman, 1952-77; Chairman, 1977-82); *b* 1 Feb. 1918; *s* of Sir John Laing, CBE, and late Beatrice Harland; *m* 1940, Hilda Violet Richards; one *s. Educ:* St Lawrence Coll., Ramsgate. RAF, 1941-45. Member: UK Trade Missions to Middle East, 1953, and to Egypt, Sudan and Ethiopia, 1955; Economic Planning Bd, 1961; Export Guarantees Adv. Council, 1959-63; Min. of Transport Cttee of Inquiry into Major Ports of Gt Brit. (Rochdale Cttee), 1961-62; NEDC, 1962-66; Dir, Bank of England, 1963-80. First Pres., CBI, 1965-66; President: British Employers Confederation, 1964-65; Export Group for the Constructional Industries, 1976-80; Fedn of Civil Engrg Contractors, 1977-80. Visiting Fellow, Nuffield Coll., 1965-70; A Governor: Administrative Staff Coll., 1966-72; Nat. Inst. of Economic and Social Research, 1964-82. Hon. LLD University of Strathclyde, 1967. Has keen interest in Church activities at home and abroad. *Recreations:* sailing, swimming. *Address:* Reculver, 63 Totteridge Village, N20 8AG. *Clubs:* Royal Yacht Squadron, Royal Ocean Racing (Commodore, 1973-75, Admiral, 1976-), Arts; Royal Burnham Yacht (Burnham-on-Crouch).

See also Sir W. K. Laing.

LAING, Sir Kirby; *see* Laing, Sir W. K.

LAING, Sir Maurice; *see* Laing, Sir J. M.

LAING, Peter Anthony Neville Pennethorne; *b* 12 March 1922; *s* of late Lt-Col Neville Ogilvie Laing, DSO, 4th QO Hussars, and of Zara Marcella (*née* Pennethorne), Fleet, Hants; *m* 1958, Penelope Lucinda, *d* of Sir William Pennington-Ramsden, Bt, *qv* ; one *s. Educ:* Paris Univ. Served War: volunteer, French Army, 1939-40, Free French Forces, 1942-44; Grenadier Guards, 1944-46. Attaché, British Embassy, Madrid, 1946; internat. marketing consultant in Western Europe, USA, Caribbean and Latin America; UN, 1975-: Dir of ITC proj. for UNDP in the Congo; Dir, Help the Aged internat. charity, 1976-82. *Recreations:* people, foreign travel, riding any horse, fine arts. *Address:* Northfields House, Turweston, near Brackley, Northants. *T:* Brackley 700049, 703498. *Club:* Turf.

LAING, Ronald David, MB, ChB, DPM; Chairman, Philadelphia Association Ltd, since 1964; *b* 7 Oct. 1927; *s* of D. P. M. and Amelia Laing. *Educ:* Glasgow Univ. Glasgow and West of Scotland Neurosurgical Unit, 1951; Central Army Psychiatric Unit, Netley, 1951-52; Psychiatric Unit, Mil. Hosp., Catterick, 1952-53; Dept of Psychological Med., Glasgow Univ., 1953-56; Tavistock Clinic, 1956-60; Tavistock Inst. of Human Relations, 1960-; Fellow, Foundns Fund for Research in Psychiatry, 1960-67; Dir, Langham Clinic for Psychotherapy, 1962-65; Fellow, Tavistock Inst. of Med. Psychology, 1963-64; Principal Investigator, Schizophrenia and Family Research Unit, Tavistock Inst. of Human Relations, 1964-67. *Publications:* The Divided Self, 1960 (London and New York) (Pelican edn, 1962, Penguin repr. 1971); The Self and Others, 1961 (London and New York) (rev. edn 1969, Penguin, 1971); (jtly) Reason and Violence (introd. by J. P. Sartre), 1964 (London and New York) (Pantheon, 1971); (jtly) Sanity, Madness and

the Family, 1965 (London and New York); The Politics of Experience and the Bird of Paradise (Penguin), 1967 (London, repr. 1971), (Pantheon, 1967, New York); Knots, 1970 (London), (Pantheon, 1970, New York), (Penguin, 1972); The Politics of the Family, 1971 (London); The Facts of Life, 1976 (Pantheon, New York); Do You Love Me, 1977 (London); Conversations with Children, 1978 (London); Sonnets, 1979 (London); The Voice of Experience, 1982 (London). *Address:* 2 Eton Road, NW3. *T:* 01-722 9448.

LAING, (William James) Scott; international trade and marketing consultant, New York City; *b* 14 April 1914; *er s* of late William Irvine Laing and Jessie C. M. Laing (*née* Scott); one *s. Educ:* George Watson's Coll., Edinburgh Univ. Appointed to Dept of Overseas Trade, 1937; Asst to Commercial Counsellor, British Embassy, Buenos Aires, 1938; Second Sec. (Commercial), Buenos Aires, 1944; First Sec. (Commercial), Helsinki, 1947; Consul, New York, 1950; Consul-Gen. (Commercial), New York, 1954; Counsellor (Commercial), Brussels and Luxembourg, 1955; Consultant to UN Secretariat, Financial Policies and Institutions Section, 1958, African Training Programme, 1960; Editor, UN Jl, 1964; Chief, Publications Sales Section, UN Secretariat, 1969-76. *Publications:* The US Market for Motor Vehicle Parts and Accessories, 1977; Concentration and Diversification of the Self-Propelled Heavy Machinery Industries in USA, 1979; (jtly) Financial Assessment of the US Automotive Industry, 1982. *Address:* PO Box 4207, Grand Central PO, New York, NY 10017, USA. *Club:* Caledonian.

LAING, Sir (William) Kirby, Kt 1968; JP; MA, FEng, FICE; DL; Chairman, Laing Properties plc, since 1978; *b* 21 July 1916; *s* of late Sir John Laing, CBE, and late Lady Laing (*née* Beatrice Harland); *m* 1939, Joan Dorothy Bratt (*d* 1981); three *s. Educ:* St Lawrence Coll., Ramsgate; Emmanuel Coll., Cambridge. Served with Royal Engineers, 1943-45. Dir John Laing plc (formerly John Laing & Son Ltd), 1939-80 (Chm., 1957-76). President: London Master Builders Assoc., 1957; Reinforced Concrete Assoc., 1960; Nat. Fedn of Building Trades Employers, 1965, 1967 (Hon. Mem., 1975); ICE, 1973-74 (a Vice-Pres., 1970-73); Chairman: Nat. Jt Council for Building Industry, 1968-74; Construction Industry Res. and Inf. Assoc., 1978-81; Member: Board of Governors, St Lawrence Coll (Pres., 1977-); Court of Governors, The Polytechnic of Central London, 1963-82; Council, Royal Albert Hall, 1970- (Pres., 1979-); Council, The Covenanter Union; Trustee, Inter-Varsity Fellowship; Hon. Mem., Amer. Assoc. of Civil Engineers. DL Greater London, 1978. *Publications:* papers in Proc. ICE and other jls concerned with construction. *Address:* Laing Properties plc, Watford, Herts WD1 1JL. *Club:* Naval and Military.

LAINSON, Prof. Ralph, FRS 1982; Director, Wellcome Parasitology Unit, Instituto Evandro Chagas, Belém, Pará, Brazil, since 1965; *b* 21 Feb. 1927; *s* of Charles Harry Lainson and Anne (*née* Woods); *m* 1st, 1957, Anne Patricia Russell; one *s* two *d* ; 2nd, 1974, Zeá Constante Lins. *Educ:* Steyning Grammar Sch., Sussex; London Univ. (BSc, PhD, DSc). Lecturer in Medical Protozoology, London Sch. of Hygiene and Tropical Medicine, London Univ., 1955-59; Officer-in-Charge, Dermal Leishmaniasis Unit, Baking-Pot, Cayo Dist, Belize, 1959-62; Attached Investigator, Dept of Medical Protozoology, London Sch. of Hygiene and Tropical Medicine, 1962-65. Career devoted to research in Medical Protozoology in the Tropics. Hon. Fellow, LSHTM, 1982; Hon. Professor, Federal Univ. of Pará, Brazil, 1982. Chalmer's Medal, Royal Soc. of Tropical Medicine and Hygiene, 1971; Oswaldo Cruz Medal, Conselho Estadual de Cultura do Pará, 1973. *Publications:* author, or co-author, of approximately 170 pubns in current scientific jls, on protozoal parasites of man and animals. *Recreations:* fishing, swimming, collecting South American Lepidoptera, music, philately. *Address:* Avenida Visconde de Souza Franco, 1237 (Edifício 'Visconti'), Apartamento 902, 66.000 Belém, Pará, Brazil. *T:* 223-2382 (Belém).

LAIRD, Edgar Ord, (Michael Laird), CMG 1969; MBE 1958; HM Diplomatic Service, retired; *b* 16 Nov. 1915; *s* of late Edgar Balfour Laird; *m* 1940, Heather Lonsdale Forrest; four *d. Educ:* Rossall; Emmanuel Coll., Cambridge. Surveyor, Uganda Protectorate, 1939. Served Army, 1939-46 (Major). Appointed to Malayan Civil Service, 1947; Sec. to Government, Federation of Malaya, 1953-55; Sec. for External Defence, Federation of Malaya, 1956; Sec., Federation of Malaya Constitutional Commission, 1956-57; Dep. Sec., Prime Minister's Dept, Federation of Malaya, 1957. Appointed to Commonwealth Relations Office, 1958; First Sec. (Finance), Office of British High Comr, Ottawa, Canada, 1960-63; High Comr in Brunei, 1963-65; Dep. High Comr, Kaduna, 1965-69; RNC Greenwich, 1969-70; Head of Hong Kong and Indian Ocean Dept, FCO, 1970-72; British Govt Rep., West Indies Associated States, 1972-75. *Recreations:* playing the piano, reading. *Address:* Greenhill, Lympstone, Devon. *Club:* Royal Commonwealth Society.

LAIRD, Gavin Harry; General Secretary, since 1982, Member, Executive Council, since 1975, Amalgamated Union of Engineering Workers; Director, British National Oil Corporation, since 1976; *b* 14 March 1933; *s* of James and Frances Laird; *m* 1956, Catherine Gillies Campbell; one *d. Educ:* Clydebank High School. Convener of Shop Stewards, Singer Manufacturing Co. Ltd, UK, 1964-71; full-time Trade Union Official, 1971-; Mem., TUC Gen. Council, 1979-82. Part-time Dir, Highlands and Islands Develt Bd, 1974-75; Mem., Industrial Develt Adv. Bd, 1980-. *Recreations:* hill walking, reading, bowls. *Address:* Flat 9, 270 Camphill Avenue, Langside, Glasgow G41 3AS. *Club:* AUEW Social Club (Clydebank).

LAIRD, John Robert, (Robin Laird), TD 1946; FRICS; chartered surveyor; Member, Lands Tribunal, England and Wales, 1956-76; retired; *b* Marlow, Bucks, 3 Sept. 1909; *o s* of late John Laird, JP, and Mary (*née* Wakelin); *m* 1st, 1940, Barbara Joyce Muir (marr. diss. 1965); one *s* one *d* ; 2nd, 1966, Betty Caroline McGregor (widow). *Educ:* Sir William Borlase's Sch., Marlow; Coll. of Estate Management, London. Partner, private practice, Lawrence, Son & Laird, Chartered Surveyors, Marlow, 1938-56. Served war: 2nd Lieut RA (TA), 1939; Staff Captain 35AA Bde, RA, 1941; Acting Lt-Col Eastern Comd, 1945. *Recreations:* hockey (Scottish International; 12 caps; Captain 1935), rowing, sailing, walking. *Address:* 8 Marine Square, Kemp Town, Brighton, E Sussex BN2 1DL. *T:* Brighton 602065. *Club:* Brighton Marina Yacht (Brighton).

LAIRD, Hon. Melvin R.; Senior Counsellor for National and International Affairs, Reader's Digest Association, since 1974; *b* 1 Sept. 1922; *s* of Melvin R. Laird and Helen Laird (*née* Connor); *m* 1945, Barbara Masters; two *s* one *d. Educ:* Carleton Coll., Northfield, Minn (BA 1944). Enlisted, US Navy, 1942, commissioned, 1944; served in Third Fleet and Task Force 58 (Purple Heart and other decorations). Elected: to Wisconsin State Senate, 1946 (re-elected, 1948); to US Congress, Nov. 1952 (83rd through 90th; Chm., House Republican Conf., 89th and 90th); Sec. of Defense, 1969-73; Counsellor to President of the US, 1973-74. Director: Chicago Pneumatic Tool Co.; Metropolitan Life Insurance Co.; Northwest Airlines; Communications Satellite Corp.; Investors Gp of Cos; Phillips Petroleum Co.; Science Applications, Inc.; Martin Harriett & Co. Member Board of Trustees: George Washington Univ.; Kennedy Center. Various awards from Assocs, etc (for med. research, polit. science, public health, nat. educn); many hon. memberships and hon. degrees. *Publications:* A House Divided: America's Strategy Gap, 1962; Editor: The Conservative Papers, 1964; Republican Papers, 1968. *Recreations:* golf, fishing. *Address:* Suite 212, 1730 Rhode Island Avenue NW, Washington, DC 20036, USA. *Club:* Burning Tree (Washington, DC).

LAIRD, Michael; *see* Laird, E. O.

LAIRD, Robin; *see* Laird, J. R.

LAISTER, Peter; Group Managing Director, THORN EMI, since 1980 (Thorn Electrical Industries Ltd, 1979); *b* 24 Jan. 1929; *s* of late Horace Laister and of Mrs I. L. Bates; *m* 1st, 1951, Barbara Cooke; one *s* one *d* ; 2nd, 1958, Eileen Alice Goodchild (*née* Town); one *d. Educ:* King Edward's Sch., Birmingham; Manchester Univ., Coll. of Technology (BSc Tech.). AMCT; FInstPet. Process Engr to Refining Co-ordinator, then Gen. Manager, Marketing Ops, Esso Petroleum Co. Ltd, 1951-66; British Oxygen Co. Ltd (BOC Intl Ltd): Chief Exec. Chemical Plant Div., 1966; Chief Exec., Gases Div., 1967-69; a Gp Man. Dir, 1969-73; Chm., BOC Financial Corp. (USA), 1974-75; Gp Man. Dir, Ellerman Lines Ltd, 1976-79; Chairman: Tollemache and Cobbold Breweries, 1978-79; London & Hull Insce Co., 1976-79. Industrial Society: Council Mem., 1971-; Mem. Exec. Cttee, 1976-; Mem., Industrial Develt Adv. Bd, 1981-. BUPA: Governor, Medical Centre, 1977-; Dir, Research Co., 1977-; Governor, 1980-. Chm., British Foundn for Age Res., 1982-. Mem., Council, UCL, 1978-. *Recreations:* private pilot, gardening, boating and angling, photography. *Address:* Thatches, 92 Staines Road, Wraysbury, Bucks.

LAITHWAITE, Prof. Eric Roberts; Professor of Heavy Electrical Engineering, Imperial College of Science and Technology, London, since 1964; *b* 14 June 1921 ; *s* of Herbert Laithwaite; *m* 1951, Sheila Margaret Gooddie; two *s* two *d. Educ:* Kirkham Gram. Sch.; Regent Street Polytechnic; Manchester Univ. RAF, 1941-46 (at RAE Farnborough, 1943-46). BSc 1949, MSc 1950. Manchester Univ.: Asst Lectr, 1950-53; Lectr, 1953-57; Sen. Lectr, 1957-64; PhD 1957; DSc 1964. Pres., Assoc. for Science Educn, 1970. S. G. Brown Award and Medal of Royal Society, 1966; Prof. of Royal Instn, 1967-76. *Publications:* Propulsion without Wheels, 1966; Induction Machines for Special Purposes, 1966; The Engineer in Wonderland, 1967; Linear Electric Motors, 1971; Exciting Electrical Machines, 1974; (with A. Watson and P. E. S. Whalley) The Dictionary of Butterflies and Moths, 1975; (ed) Transport without Wheels, 1977; (with M. W. Thring) How to Invent, 1977; Engineer through the Looking-Glass, 1980; (with L. L. Freris) Electric Energy: its Generation, Transmission and Use, 1980; many papers in Proc. IEE (7 premiums) and other learned jls. *Recreations:* entomology, gardening. *Address:* Department of Electrical Engineering, Imperial College, SW7 2BT. *T:* 01-589 5111. *Club:* Athenæum.

LAITHWAITE, John, FIMechE, FInstPet; Director, Capper Neill Ltd, since 1965 (Vice-Chairman, 1972-82); *b* 29 Nov. 1920; *s* of Tom Prescott Laithwaite and Mary Anne Laithwaite; *m* 1943, Jean Chateris; one *s* two *d. Educ:* Manchester Univ. (BSc Hons Mech. Eng). FIMechE 1974; FInstPet 1960; AMInstW 1950. Wm Neill & Son (St Helens) Ltd, 1942-43; Dartford Shipbuilding & Engineering Co., 1943-44; Dir, Wm Neill & Son (St Helens) Ltd, 1955-58; Man. Dir, 1958-64; Man. Dir, Capper Neill Ltd, 1968. Mem. Council, NW Regional Management Centre. Chm., Process Plant Assoc., 1975-77, Hon. Vice-Pres., 1980-. *Publications:* articles on process plant industry and pressure vessel standardisation. *Recreations:* shooting, golf. *Address:* Willow Croft, Golborne Dale, Newton-le-Willows, Merseyside. *Clubs:* Royal Automobile; Haydock Park.

LAITHWAITE, Sir (John) Gilbert, GCMG 1953 (KCMG 1948); KCB 1956; KCIE 1941 (CIE 1935); CSI 1938; Director, Inchcape Overseas Ltd, since 1969 (Deputy Chairman Inchcape & Co. Ltd, 1960-64; Director 1964-69); former Chairman: Bedford Life Assurance Co. Ltd; Bedford General Insurance Co. Ltd; UK Committee of Federation of Commonwealth Chambers of Commerce; *b* 5 July 1894; *e s* of late J. G. Laithwaite, formerly of the Post Office Survey. *Educ:* Clongowes; Trinity Coll., Oxford (Scholar). Hon. Fellow, Trinity Coll., Oxford, 1955. Served in France with 10th Lancs Fusiliers, 1917-18 (wounded); appointed to India Office, 1919; Principal, 1924; specially attached to Prime Minister (Mr Ramsay MacDonald) for 2nd Indian Round Table Conference, Sept.-Dec. 1931; Secretary, Indian Franchise (Lothian) Committee, Jan.-June 1932; Secretary, Indian Delimitation Cttee, Aug. 1935-Feb. 1936; Private Secretary to the Viceroy of India (Marquess of Linlithgow), 1936-43, and a Secretary to the Governor-General 1937-43; Assistant Under-Secretary of State for India, 1943; an Under-Secretary (Civil) of the War Cabinet, 1944-45; Deputy Under-Secretary of State for Burma, 1945-47, for India, 1947, for Commonwealth Relations, 1948-49; Ambassador, 1950-51 (United Kingdom Representative, 1949-50) to the Republic of Ireland; High Commissioner for the UK in Pakistan, 1951-54; Permanent Under-Secretary of State for Commonwealth Relations, 1955-59. Vice-Chm., Commonwealth Inst., 1963-66; Governor, Queen Mary Coll., Univ. of London, 1959-; Trustee, Hakluyt Soc., 1958- (Pres., 1964-69); Vice-Pres., Royal Central Asian Soc., 1967- (Chm. Council, 1964-67); Vice-Pres., RGS, 1969 (Pres., 1966-69); Mem. Standing Commn on Museums and Galleries, 1959-72. A Freeman of the City of London, 1960. Master, Tallowchandlers' Co., 1972-73. Hon. LLD Dublin, 1957. Kt of Malta, 1960. *Publications:* The Laithwaites, Some Records of a Lancashire Family, 1941, rev. edn 1961; Memories of an Infantry Officer, 1971; etc. *Address:* c/o Grindlay's Bank Ltd, 13 St James's Square, SW1. *Clubs:* Travellers', Oxford & Cambridge University, City of London.

LAJTHA, Prof. Laszlo George, MD, DPhil, FRCPE, FRCPath; Director of Paterson Laboratories, Christie Hospital and Holt Radium Institute, since 1962; Professor of Experimental Oncology, University of Manchester, since 1970; *b* 25 May 1920; *s* of Laszlo John Lajtha and Rose Stephanie Hollos; *m* 1954, Gillian Macpherson Henderson; two *s. Educ:* Presbyterian High School, Budapest; Medical School, Univ. of Budapest (MD 1944); Exeter Coll., Univ. of Oxford (DPhil 1950). FRCPath 1973; FRCPE 1980. Asst Prof., Dept of Physiology, Univ. of Budapest, 1944-47; Research Associate, Dept of Haematology, Radcliffe Infirmary, Oxford, 1947-50; Head, Radiobiology Laboratory, Churchill Hosp., Oxford, 1950-62; subseq. Research Fellow, Pharmacology, Yale Univ., New Haven, Conn., USA. Editor, British Jl of Cancer, 1972-. President: British Soc. of Cell Biology, 1977-80; European Orgn for Res. on Treatment of Cancer, 1979-. Hon. Citizen, Texas, USA; Hon. Member: Amer. Cancer Soc.; German, Italian and Hungarian Socs of Haematology. Dr *hc* Szeged Univ., Hungary, 1981. *Publications:* Isotopes in Haematology, 1961; over 200 articles in scientific (medical) jls. *Recreation:* alpine gardening. *Address:* 5 Carrwood Road, Wilmslow, Cheshire SK9 5DJ. *T:* Wilmslow 22338. *Club:* Athenæum.

LAKE, Sir (Atwell) Graham, 10th Bt *cr* 1711; Senior Technical Adviser, Ministry of Defence; *b* 6 Oct. 1923; *s* of Captain Sir Atwell Henry Lake, 9th Bt, CB, OBE, RN, and Kathleen Marion, *d* of late Alfred Morrison Turner; *S* father, 1972. *Educ:* Eton. British High Commission, Wellington, NZ, 1942; Gilbert and Ellice Military Forces, 1944; Colonial Administrative Service, 1945 (Secretary to Govt of Tonga, 1950-53); Norris Oakley Bros, 1957; Min. of Defence, 1959; British High Commission, New Delhi, 1966; attached Foreign and Commonwealth Office, 1969-72. *Recreations:* golf, bridge, chess, skiing. *Heir: b* Willoughby Alfred Lake [*b* 31 Aug. 1925; *m* 1952, Elizabeth Elsie Faith, *d* of Sir Rupert Turner Havelock Clarke, 2nd Bt; two *d*].

LAKEMAN, Miss Enid, OBE 1980; Editorial Consultant and a Vice-President, Electoral Reform Society, since 1979 (Director, 1960-79); *b* 28 Nov. 1903; *d* of Horace B. Lakeman and Evereld Simpson. *Educ:* Tunbridge Wells County Sch.; Bedford Coll., Univ. of London. Posts in chemical industry, 1926-41; WAAF, 1941-45; Electoral Reform Soc., 1945-. Parly candidate (L): St Albans, 1945; Brixton, 1950; Aldershot, 1955 and 1959. *Publications:* When Labour Fails, 1946; (with James D. Lambert) Voting in Democracies, 1955, (2nd edn 1959; 3rd and 4th edns, 1970 and 1974, as sole author, as How Democracies Vote); Nine Democracies, 1973 (3rd edn 1978); Power to Elect, 1982; pamphlets; articles in polit. jls. *Recreations:* travel, gardening. *Address:* 37 Culverden Avenue, Tunbridge Wells, Kent TN4 9RE. *T:* Tunbridge Wells 21674. *Club:* National Liberal.

LAKER, Sir Freddie, (Sir Frederick Alfred Laker), Kt 1978; Director, Sir Freddie Laker Ltd, since 1982; *b* 6 Aug. 1922; British. *Educ:* Simon Langton Sch., Canterbury. Short Brothers, Rochester, 1938-40; General Aircraft, 1940-41; Air Transport Auxiliary, 1941-46; Aviation Traders, 1946-65; British United Airways, 1960-65; Chm. and Man. Dir, Laker Airways Ltd, 1966-82; creator of Skytrain Air Passenger Service to USA. Hon. Fellow Univ. of Manchester Inst. of Science and Technol., 1978; Hon. DSc: City, 1979; Cranfield Inst. of Technol., 1980; Hon. LLD Manchester, 1981. *Recreations:* horse breeding, racing, sailing. *Address:* c/o Cheapside House, 138 Cheapside, EC2V 6BL. *T:* 01-606 9898. *Clubs:* Eccentric, Little Ship, Jockey.

LAKIN, Sir Michael, 4th Bt *cr* 1909; *b* 28 Oct. 1934; *s* of Sir Henry Lakin, 3rd Bt, and Bessie (*d* 1965), *d* of J. D. Anderson, Durban; *S* father, 1979; *m* 1965, Felicity Ann Murphy; one *s* one *d. Educ:* Stowe. *Heir: s* Richard

Anthony Lakin, *b* 26 Nov. 1968. *Address:* Torwood, PO Box 40, Rosetta, Natal, South Africa. *T:* Rosetta 1613.

LAKING, George Robert, CMG 1969; Chief Ombudsman, New Zealand, since 1977; *b* Auckland, NZ, 15 Oct. 1912; *s* of R. G. Laking; *m* 1940, Patricia, *d* of H. Hogg; one *s* one *d. Educ:* Auckland Grammar Sch.; Auckland Univ.; Victoria Univ. of Wellington (LLB). Prime Minister's and Ext. Affairs Depts, 1940–49; New Zealand Embassy, Washington: Counsellor, 1949–54; Minister, 1954–56. Dep. Sec. of Ext. Affairs, Wellington, NZ, 1956–58; Acting High Comr for NZ, London, 1958–61, and NZ Ambassador to European Economic Community, 1960–61; New Zealand Ambassador, Washington, 1961–67; Sec. of Foreign Affairs and Permanent Head, Prime Minister's Dept, NZ, 1967–72; Ombudsman, 1975–77; Privacy Comr, 1977–78. Member: Human Rights Commn, 1978–; Public and Administrative Law Reform Cttee, 1980–. Chm. NZ–US Educnl Foundn, 1976–78; Pres., NZ Inst. of Internat. Affairs. *Address:* 3 Wesley Road, Wellington 1, New Zealand. *T:* 728-454.

LAL, Prof. Devendra, PhD; FRS 1979; Director, Physical Research Laboratory, India, since 1972; Professor (part-time), Geological Research Division, Scripps Institution of Oceanography, University of California, La Jolla, since 1967; *b* 14 Feb. 1929; *s* of Radhekrishna Lal and Sita Devi; *m* 1955, Aruna L. Damany. *Educ:* Banaras Hindu Univ. (MSc); Univ. of Bombay (PhD). Fellow, Indian Acad. of Sciences, 1964. Tata Inst. of Fundamental Research, Bombay: Res. Student, 1949-50; Res. Asst, 1950-53; Res. Fellow, 1953-57; Fellow, 1957-60; Associate Prof., 1960-63; Prof., 1963-70; Sen. Prof., 1970-72. Res. Geophysicist, UCLA-IGPP, 1965-66. Foreign Associate, Nat. Acad. of Sciences, USA, 1975. *Publications:* contributed: Earth Science and Meteoritics, 1963; International Dictionary of Geophysics, 1968; The Encyclopedia of Earth Sciences: vol. IV, Geochemistry and Environmental Sciences, 1972; Future Advances in Lunar Research: Luna 16 and 20 samples, 1974; jt author of chapters in books; scientific papers to learned jls; proc. confs. *Recreations:* puzzles, painting, swimming. *Address:* Physical Research Laboratory, Navrangpura, Ahmedabad 380-009, India. *T:* (office) 448029, (home) 441451.

LAL, Shavax Ardeshir, CIE 1941; Advocate, High Court, Bombay; *b* 12 Nov. 1899; *s* of Ardeshir Edulji Lal, Nasik, Bombay Presidency; *m* 1933, Coomi, *d* of N. N. Master; three *d. Educ:* Fergusson College and Law College, Poona. Practised law, 1926-30; joined Bombay Judicial Service, 1930; transferred to Legal Department, Bombay, 1930; Assistant Secretary to Government of Bombay, Legal Department, 1932-36; nominated member and Secretary of Council of State, 1936-46; Secretary to Government of India, Ministry of Law, 1947-48; Secretary to Governor-General of India, 1948-50; Secretary to President of India, 1950-54. *Address:* Windcliffe, Pedder Road, Bombay, India.

LALANDI, Lina, OBE 1975; Festival Director, English Bach Festival, since 1962; *b* Athens; *d* of late Nikolas Kaloyeropoulos (former Dir of Byzantine Museum, Athens, and Dir of Beaux Arts, Min. of Educn, Athens) and Toula Gelekis. *Educ:* Athens Conservatoire (grad. with Hons in Music); privately, in England (harpsichord and singing studies). International career as harpsichordist in Concert, Radio and TV. Founded English Bach Festival Trust, 1962. Officier, l'Ordre des Arts et des Lettres, 1978. *Recreations:* cats, cooking, Flamenco. *Address:* 15 South Eaton Place, SW1W 9ER. *T:* 01-730 5925.

LALANNE, Bernard Michel L.; *see* Loustau-Lalanne.

LALOUETTE, Marie Joseph Gerard; retired; *b* 24 Jan. 1912; 3rd *s* of late Henri Lalouette and Mrs H. Lalouette; *m* 1942, Jeanne Marrier d'Unienville; four *s* two *d. Educ:* Royal Coll., Mauritius; Exeter Coll., Oxford; London School of Economics; Middle Temple. District Magistrate, Mauritius, 1944; Electoral Commissioner, 1956; Addl. Subst. Procureur-General, 1956; Master, and Registrar, Supreme Court, 1958; Assistant Attorney-General, 1959; Solicitor-General, 1960; Puisne Judge, 1961; Senior Puisne Judge, Supreme Court, Mauritius, 1967-70; Justice of Appeal, Seychelles, 1977-82. *Publications:* Digest of Decisions of Supreme Court of Mauritius, 1926-43; The Mauritius Digest to 1950; A First Supplement to the Mauritius Digest, 1951-55; A Second Supplement to the Mauritius Digest, 1956-60; The Seychelles Digest, 1982; contrib. Internat. Encyclopedia of Comparative Law. *Recreations:* music, gardening. *Address:* 419 Windermere Centre, Windermere Road, Durban, Republic of South Africa.

LAM, Martin Philip; Associate of Mackintosh Consultants, and others; *b* 10 March 1920; *m* 1953, Lisa Lorenz; one *s* one *d. Educ:* University College Sch.; Gonville and Caius Coll., Cambridge (Scholar). Served War of 1939-45, Royal Signals. Asst Principal, Board of Trade, 1947; Nuffield Fellowship (Latin America), 1952-53; Asst Sec., 1960; Counsellor, UK Delegn to OECD, 1963-65, Advr, Commercial Policy, 1970-74, Leader UNCTAD Delegn, 1972; Under-Sec. (Computer Systems and Electronics), DoI, 1974-78. *Address:* 22 The Avenue, Wembley, Middlesex HA9 9QJ. *T:* 01-904 2584.

LAMB, family name of **Baron Rochester.**

LAMB, Sir Albert; *see* Lamb, Sir Larry.

LAMB, Sir Albert Thomas, (Sir Archie), KBE 1979 (MBE 1953); CMG 1974; DFC 1945; HM Diplomatic Service, retired; Ambassador to Norway,

1978-80; *b* 23 Oct. 1921; *s* of R. S. Lamb and Violet Lamb (*née* Haynes); *m* 1944, Christina Betty Wilkinson; one *s* two *d. Educ:* Swansea Grammar Sch. Served RAF 1941-46. FO 1938-41; Embassy, Rome, 1947-50; Consulate-General, Genoa, 1950; Embassy, Bucharest, 1950-53; FO 1953-55; Middle East Centre for Arabic Studies, 1955-57; Political Residency, Bahrain, 1957-61; FO 1961-65; Embassy, Kuwait, 1965; Political Agent in Abu Dhabi, 1965-68; Inspector, 1968-70, Sen. Inspector, 1970-73, Asst Under-Sec. of State and Chief Inspector, FCO, 1973-74; Ambassador to Kuwait, 1974-77. Mem., BNOC, 1981-; Consultant to NEDC, 1981-. Dir, Samuel Montagu and Co. Ltd, 1981-. *Address:* East House, Wyke Hall, Gillingham, Dorset. *T:* Gillingham 3409. *Club:* Travellers'.

LAMB, Air Vice-Marshal George Colin, CB 1977; CBE 1966; AFC 1947; Chief Executive, Badminton Association of England, since 1978; *b* 23 July 1923; *s* of late George and Bessie Lamb, Hornby, Lancaster; *m* 1st, 1945, Nancy Mary Godsmark; two *s*; 2nd, 1981, Mrs Maureen Margaret Mepham. *Educ:* Lancaster Royal Grammar School. War of 1939-45: commissioned, RAF, 1942; flying duties, 1942-53; Staff Coll., 1953; Air Ministry, special duties, 1954-58; OC No 87 Sqdn, 1958-61; Dir Admin. Plans, MoD, 1961-64; Asst Comdt, RAF Coll., 1964-65; Dep. Comdr, Air Forces Borneo, 1965-66; Fighter Command, 1966; MoD (Dep. Command Structure Project Officer), 1967; HQ, Strike Command, 1967-69; OC, RAF Lyneham, 1969-71; RCDS, 1971-72; Dir of Control (Operations), NATS, 1972-74; Comdr, Southern Maritime Air Region, RAF Mount Batten, 1974-75; C of S, No 18 Gp Strike Comd, RAF, 1975-78. RAF Vice-Pres., Combined Cadet Forces Assoc., 1978-. Mem., RFU, 1973-. FBIM. *Recreation:* international Rugby football referee, cricket (former Pres., Adastrian Cricket Club). *Address:* Hambledon, 17 Meadway, Berkhamsted, HP4 2PN. *T:* Berkhamsted 2583. *Club:* Royal Air Force.

LAMB, Harold Norman, CBE 1978; Regional Administrator, South East Thames Regional Health Authority, 1973-81; *b* 21 July 1922; *s* of Harold Alexander and Amelia Lamb; *m* 1946, Joyce Marian Hawkyard; one *s* one *d. Educ:* Saltley Grammar School. FHA. House Governor, Birmingham Gen. Hosp., 1958; Dep. Sec., United Birmingham Hosps, and House Governor, Queen Elizabeth Hosp., 1961; Sec., SE Metrop. RHB, 1968. Mem. Exec. Council, Royal Inst. of Public Admin, 1970-78. *Recreations:* golf, music. *Address:* 40 Windmill Way, Reigate, Surrey RH2 0JB. *T:* Reigate 21846. *Club:* Walton Heath Golf.

LAMB, Prof. John; James Watt Professor of Electrical Engineering, since 1961, and Vice-Principal, 1977-80, University of Glasgow; *b* 26 Sept. 1922; *m* 1947, Margaret May Livesey; two *s* one *d. Educ:* Accrington Grammar Sch.; Manchester Univ. BSc (1st class Hons) Manchester Univ. 1943; Fairbairn Prizeman in Engineering; MSc 1944, PhD 1946, DSc 1957, Manchester. Ministry of Supply Extra-Mural Res., 1943-46. Assistant Lecturer, 1946-47, Lecturer, 1947-56, Reader, 1956-61, in Electrical Engineering at Imperial Coll. (London Univ.); Assistant Director, Department of Electrical Engineering, Imperial Coll., 1958-61. Pres., British Soc. of Rheology, 1970-72. Chm., Scottish Industry Univ. Liaison Cttee in Engrg, 1969-71; Member: Nat. Electronics Council, 1963-78; CNAA, 1964-70. MIEE 1967; FInstP 1960; Fellow, Acoustical Society of America, 1960; FRSE 1968; Hon. Fellow, Inst. of Acoustics, 1980. *Publications:* numerous in Proc. Royal Society, Trans Faraday Society, Proc. Instn Electrical Engineers, Proc. Physical Society, Journal Acoustical Society of America, Quarterly Reviews of Chem. Society, Nature, Phys. Review, Journal of Polymer Science; contrib.: (The Theory and Practice of Ultrasonic Propagation) to Principles and Practice of Non-destructive Testing (ed) J. H. Lamble), 1962; (Dispersion and Absorption of Sound by Molecular Processes) to Proc. International School of Physics "Enrico Fermi" Course XXVII (ed D. Sette), 1963; (Thermal Relaxation in Liquids) to Physical Acoustics, Vol. II (ed W. P. Mason), 1965; (Theory of Rheology) to Interdisciplinary Approach to Liquid Lubricant Technology (ed P. M. Ku), 1973; (Viscoelastic and Ultrasonic Relaxation Studies) to Molecular Motions in Liquids (ed J. Lascombe), 1974; (Motions in Low Molecular Weight Fluids and Glass forming Liquids) to Molecular Basis of Transitions and Relaxations (ed D. J. Meier), 1978; Shear Waves of Variable Frequency for Studying the Viscoelastic Relaxation Processes in Liquids and Polymer Melts (ed A. Kawski and A. Sliwinsky), 1979. *Recreations:* walking, wine-making, music. *Address:* Royston, 10 Crown Road North, Glasgow G12 9DH. *T:* 041-339 2101.

LAMB, Hon. Kenneth Henry Lowry; Secretary to the Church Commissioners, since 1980; *b* 23 Dec. 1923; *y s* of 1st Baron Rochester, CMG; *m* 1952, Elizabeth Anne Saul; one *s* two *d. Educ:* Harrow; Trinity Coll., Oxford (MA). President of the Union, Oxford, 1944. Instructor-Lieut, Royal Navy, 1944-46. Lecturer, then Senior Lecturer in History and English, Royal Naval Coll., Greenwich, 1946-53. Commonwealth Fund Fellow in United States, 1953-55. Joined BBC in 1955 as a Talks Producer (Radio); became a Television Talks Producer, 1957, and then Chief Assistant, Current Affairs, TV talks, 1959-63; Head of Religious Broadcasting, BBC, 1963-66; Secretary to the BBC, 1967-68; Dir, Public Affairs, BBC, 1969-77; Special Adviser (Broadcasting Research), BBC, 1977-80. *Recreations:* cricket, walking, golf. *Address:* Church Commissioners, 1 Millbank, SW1P 3JZ; 25 South Terrace, Thurloe Square, SW7. *T:* 01-584 7904. *Clubs:* MCC, National Liberal; Royal Fowey Yacht. *See also Baron Rochester.*

LAMB, Sir Larry, Kt 1980; Editor, The Australian, since 1982; *b* Fitzwilliam, Yorks, 15 July 1929; *m* Joan Mary Denise Grogan; two *s* one *d*. *Educ:* Rastrick Grammar Sch. Worked as journalist on Brighouse Echo, Shields Gazette, Newcastle Journal, London Evening Standard; Sub-Editor, Daily Mirror; Editor: (Manchester) Daily Mail, 1968-69; The Sun, 1969-72, 1975-81; Dir, 1970-81, Editorial Dir, 1971-81, News International Ltd; Dep. Chm., News Group, 1979-81; Dir, The News Corporation (Australia) Ltd, 1980-81; Dep. Chm. and Editor-in-Chief, Western Mail Ltd, Perth, Australia, 1981-82. *Recreations:* fell-walking, cricket, fishing. *Address:* Hoskins Barn, Buckland Road, Bampton, Oxfordshire OX8 2AA; Tara Penthouse, 3 Greenknowe Avenue, Potts Point, NSW 2011, Australia.

LAMB, Sir Lionel (Henry), KCMG 1953 (CMG 1948); OBE 1944; HM Diplomatic Service, retired; *b* 9 July 1900; *s* of late Sir Harry Lamb, GBE, KCMG; *m* 1927, Jean Fawcett (*née* MacDonald); one *s*. *Educ:* Winchester; Queen's Coll., Oxford. Appointed HM Consular Service in China, Dec. 1921; Consul (Gr. II), 1935; served Shanghai, 1935-37, Peking, 1937-40; Consul (Gr. I), 1938; Superintending Consul and Assistant Chinese Secretary, Shanghai, 1940; transferred to St Paul-Minneapolis, 1943; Chinese Counsellor, HM Embassy, Chungking, 1945; HM Minister, Nanking, 1947-49; Chargé d'Affaires, Peking, China, 1951-53; Ambassador to Switzerland, 1953-58, retired. *Address:* Roxford Barn, Hertingfordbury, Herts.

LAMB, Captain William John, CVO 1947; OBE 1944; RN retired; *b* 26 Dec. 1906; *s* of late Sir Richard Amphlett Lamb, KCSI,CIE, ICS, and Kathleen Maud Barry; *m* 1948, Bridget, widow of Lieut-Commander G. S. Salt, RN; two *d*. *Educ:* St Anthony's, Eastbourne; RNC Osborne and Dartmouth. Commander, 1941; Staff of C-in-C Mediterranean Fleet, 1940-42; Staff of C-in-C, Eastern Fleet, 1942-44; Executive Officer, HMS Vanguard, 1945-47; Deputy Director of Naval Ordnance, 1948-50; Comd HMS Widemouth Bay and Captain (D) 4th Training Flotilla, Rosyth, 1951-52; Commanding Admiralty Signal and Radar Establishment, 1952-54; Commanding HMS Cumberland, 1955-56. Hon. Life Mem., BIM, 1974. *Recreation:* sailing. *Address:* Westons, Bank, Lyndhurst, Hampshire. *T:* Lyndhurst 2620. *Clubs:* Naval and Military; Royal Cruising.

LAMB, Prof. Willis E(ugene), Jr; Professor of Physics and Optical Sciences, University of Arizona, since 1974; *b* Los Angeles, California, USA, 12 July 1913; *s* of Willis Eugene Lamb and Marie Helen Metcalf; *m* Ursula Schaefer. *Educ:* Los Angeles High Sch.; University of California (BS, PhD). Columbia Univ.: Instructor in Physics, 1938-43, Associate, 1943-45, Assistant Professor, 1945-47, Associate Professor, 1947-48, Professor of Physics, 1948-52; Professor of Physics, Stanford Univ., California, 1951-56; Wykeham Prof. of Physics and Fellow of New Coll., University of Oxford, 1956-62; Yale University: Ford Prof. of Physics, 1962-72; Gibbs Prof. of Physics, 1972-74. Morris Loeb Lectr, Harvard Univ., 1953-54; Lectr, University of Colorado, Summer, 1959; Shrum Lectr, Simon Fraser Univ., 1972; Visiting Professor, Tata Institute of Fundamental Research, Bombay, 1960; Guggenheim Fellow, 1960-61; Visiting Professor, Columbia Univ., 1961; Fulbright Lecturer, University of Grenoble, Summer, 1964. MNAS, 1954. Hon. DSc: Pennsylvania, 1954; Gustavus Adolphus Coll., 1975; MA (by decree), Oxford, 1956; Hon. MA Yale, 1961; Hon. LHD Yeshiva, 1965; Hon. Fellow: Institute of Physics and Physical Society, 1962; RSE, 1981; Res. Corp Award, 1954; Rumford Medal, American Academy of Arts and Sciences, 1953; (jointly) Nobel Prize in Physics, 1955; Guthrie Award, The Physical Society, 1958; Yeshiva University Award, 1962. *Publications:* (with M. Sargent and M. O. Scully) Laser Physics, 1974; contributions to The Physical Review, Physica, Science, Journal of Applied Physics, etc. *Address:* Department of Physics, University of Arizona, Tucson, Arizona 85721, USA.

LAMBART, family name of Earl of Cavan.

LAMBART, Sir Oliver Francis, 2nd Bt *cr* 1911; Lieut late RASC; *b* 6 April 1913; *s* of 1st Bt and Kathleen Moore-Brabazon; *S* father, 1926. Heir: none. *Address:* Beau Parc, Co. Meath. *Club:* Turf.

LAMBERT, family name of Viscount Lambert.

LAMBERT, 2nd Viscount, *cr* 1945, of South Molton; **George Lambert**, TD; *b* 27 Nov. 1909; *e s* of 1st Viscount Lambert, PC; *S* father, 1958; *m* 1939, Patricia Mary, *d* of J. F. Quinn; one *d* (two *s* decd). *Educ:* Harrow Sch.; New Coll., Oxford. War of 1939-45: TA, Lieut-Colonel 1942. MP (L-Nat) South Molton Division, Devon, July 1945-Feb. 1950. (Nat. L-C) Torrington Division, Devon, 1950-58. Chm., Devon and Exeter Savings Bank, 1958-70. Formerly Chm. Governors, Seale-Hayne Agricultural Coll., Newton Abbot, Devon. Pres., Young Farmers' Club, 1968-70; Life Vice-Pres., National Federation of Young Farmers' Clubs, 1970. DL Devon, 1969-70. *Recreation:* golf. Heir presumptive: *b* Hon. Michael John Lambert [*b* 29 Sept. 1912; *m* 1939, Florence Dolores, *d* of N. L. Macaskie; three *d*]. *Address:* Les Fougères, 1806 St-Légier, Switzerland. *T:* (021) 53 10 63. *Clubs:* Carlton, Army and Navy.

See also Hon. Margaret Lambert, P. W. Gibbings.

LAMBERT, Sir Anthony (Edward), KCMG 1964 (CMG 1955); HM Diplomatic Service, retired; *b* 7 March 1911; *o s* of late R. E. Lambert, Pensbury House, Shaftesbury, Dorset; *m* 1948, Ruth Mary, *d* of late Sir Arthur Fleming, CBE; two *d*. *Educ:* Harrow; Balliol Coll., Oxford (Scholar). Entered HM Foreign (subseq. Diplomatic) Service, 1934, and served in: Brussels, 1937; Ankara, 1940; Beirut and Damascus, 1942; Brussels, 1944; Stockholm, 1949; Athens, 1952; HM Minister to Bulgaria, 1958-60; HM Ambassador to: Tunisia, 1960-63; Finland, 1963-66; Portugal, 1966-70. *Address:* 28 Victoria Road, W8. *Club:* Travellers'.

LAMBERT, Ven. Charles Henry, MA; Archdeacon of Lancaster, 1959-66, Emeritus, 1966; Vicar of St Cuthbert's, Lytham, 1960-66; Senior Examining Chaplain to Bishop of Blackburn; *b* 13 Jan. 1894; *s* of Henry and Frances Ann Lambert; *m* 1920, Dorothy Ellen Birch; three *s* one *d*. *Educ:* Primary Schools; privately; Leeds Univ.; Cuddesdon Coll. BA 1916; MA 1932; deacon 1917; priest 1918; Curate of Redcar, 1917-20; of Guisborough, 1920-22; Rector of St Denys with St George, York, 1922-24; Vicar of Royston, Yorks, 1924-28; Rector of St Mary Bishophill Senior with St Clement, York, 1928-34; Warden of Whalley Abbey, 1934-45; Director of Religious Education, diocese of Blackburn, 1934-46; Canon, Blackburn, 1934-46; Archdeacon of Blackburn, 1946-59; Proctor, 1929-34, York, 1935-45, Blackburn. OCF 1941-44; Archbishops' Visitor to RAF, 1944-45; Rural Dean of Whalley, 1942-45. *Publications:* Go Ye, ... Teach, 1939; Whalley Abbey, Yesterday and To-Day, 1948. *Recreations:* reading, walking, keenly interested in all outdoor sports. *Address:* 19 Connaught Mansions, Great Pulteney Street, Bath. *T:* Bath 66429.

LAMBERT, David Arthur Charles; General Secretary, National Union of Hosiery and Knitwear Workers, 1975-82, General President, since 1982; *b* 2 Sept. 1933; *m* ; two *s* one *d*. *Educ:* Hitchin Boys' Grammar Sch., Herts. Employed as production worker for major hosiery manufr; active as lay official within NUHKW; full-time official, NUHKW, 1964-. Workpeople's Sec., Nat. Jt Industrial Council for Hosiery Trade, 1975-; Mem., Employment Appeal Tribunal, 1978-. *Address:* 55 New Walk, Leicester LE1 7EB.

LAMBERT, Sir Edward (Thomas), KBE 1958 (CBE 1953); CVO 1957; retired from Foreign Service, 1960; *b* 19 June 1901; *s* of late Brig. and Mrs T. S. Lambert; *m* 1936, Rhona Patricia Gilmore, *d* of late H. St G. Gilmore and Mrs J. H. Molyneux; one *s* one *d*. *Educ:* Charterhouse and Trinity Coll., Cambridge. Member of HM Diplomatic (formerly Foreign) Service. Entered Far Eastern Consular Service, 1926; served at Bangkok, Batavia, Medan, Curaçao, and The Hague. Consul-General, Geneva, 1949-53, Paris, 1953-59. Commandeur, Légion d'Honneur, 1957. *Recreations:* reading and travel. *Address:* Crag House, Aldeburgh, Suffolk. *T:* 2296.

LAMBERT, Eric Thomas Drummond, CMG 1969; OBE 1946; KPM 1943; retd, 1968; *b* 3 Nov. 1909; *s* of late Septimus Drummond Lambert. *Educ:* Royal Sch., Dungannon; Trinity Coll., Dublin. Indian (Imperial) Police, 1929-47: Political Officer for Brahmaputra-Chindwin Survey, 1935-36, and Tirap Frontier Tract, 1942; District Comr, Naga Hills, 1938. Served with Chinese Vth Army, Indo-Burma Front, 1942; Chief Civil Liaison Officer XIVth Army, 1944; FCO, 1947-68, with service in SE Asia, W Africa, S America, Nepal, Afghanistan. Pres., Republic of Ireland Br., Burma Star Assoc. Trustee, Nat. Library of Ireland. Chinese Armed Forces Distinguished Service, 1st Order, 1st class, 1943. *Publications:* Assam (jointly with Alban Ali), 1943; Carabobo 1821, 1974; Voluntarios Britanicos y Irlandeses en la Gesta Bolivariana, 1982; articles in jls of RGS and Royal Siam Soc.; Man in India; The Irish Sword. *Recreations:* golf, historical research, lecturing. *Address:* Drumkeen, Glenamuck Road, Dublin 18. *T:* 893169. *Club:* Stephen's Green (Dublin).

LAMBERT, Sir Greville Foley, 9th Bt, *cr* 1711; *b* 17 Aug. 1900; *s* of late Lionel Foley Lambert, 4th *s* of 6th Bt; *S* cousin (Sir John Foley Grey), 1938; *m* 1932, Edith Roma, *d* of Richard Batson; three *d*. *Educ:* Rugby Sch. Chartered Accountant. Heir: kinsman, Peter John Biddulph Lambert, archaeologist, Min. of Culture and Recreation and Historical Researches Branch, Govt of Ontario [*b* 5 April 1952. *Educ:* Upper Canada Coll.; Trent Univ.; Univ. of Manitoba. BSc(Hons), MA].

LAMBERT, Guy William, CB 1942; BA; *b* 1 Dec. 1889; 2nd *s* of late Col J. A. Lambert, Brookhill, Claremorris, Co. Mayo, and Grace, *e d* of late W. D. Fane, Fulbeck Hall, Lincs; *m* 1917, Nadine, *y d* of late Wilson Noble, Park Place, Henley-on-Thames; one *s* two *d*. *Educ:* Cheltenham Coll.; St John's Coll., Oxford. Higher Div. Clerk, War Office, 1913; Private Secretary to Sir C. Harris, KCB, Assistant Financial Secretary, 1915; Private Secretary to H. W. Forster, Financial Secretary, 1916; Chevalier, Légion d'Honneur, 1920; Principal Private Secretary to successive Secretaries of State for War, Rt Hon. Sir L. Worthington-Evans Bt, GBE, and Rt Hon. T. Shaw, CBE, 1926-29; Assistant Under-Secretary of State for War, 1938-51. President Society for Psychical Research, 1955-58. Fellow, Irish Genealogical Research Soc., 1970. Silver Jubilee Medal, 1935; Coronation Medal, 1937. *Clubs:* Athenæum, Leander, London Rowing.

See also Sir A. C. W. Drew.

LAMBERT, Harold George; *b* 8 April 1910; *s* of late Rev. David Lambert; *m* 1934, Winifred Marthe, *d* of late Rev. H. E. Anderson, Farnham, Surrey; two *s*. *Educ:* King Edward's Sch., Birmingham; Corpus Christi Coll., Cambridge (MA); Imperial College of Science, London. Entered Ministry of Agriculture and Fisheries, 1933; Private Secretary to Parliamentary Secretary, 1938-39; Sec., Agricultural Machinery Develt Bd, 1942-45; Assistant Secretary, 1948; Under-Sec., MAFF, 1964-70, retired. Mem., panel of indep. inspectors for local enquiries, DoE and DoT, 1971-80. *Recreations:* music, art, *travel. Address:* 25 Lenham Avenue, Rottingdean, Sussex. *Club:* Royal Commonwealth Society.

LAMBERT, Henry Uvedale Antrobus; Chairman, Barclays Bank International, since 1979; Deputy Chairman, Barclays Bank PLC, since 1979; Deputy Chairman, Agricultural Mortgage Corporation Ltd, since 1977; Vice-Chairman, Sun Alliance and London Insurance Group and other companies; *b* 9 Oct. 1925; *o s* of Roger Uvedale Lambert and late Muriel, *d* of Sir Reginald Antrobus, KCMG, CB; *m* 1951, Diana, *y d* of Captain H. E. Dumbell, Royal Fusiliers; two *s* one *d. Educ:* Winchester College (Scholar); New College, Oxford (Exhibitioner; MA). Served War of 1939-45, Royal Navy, in HM Ships Stockham and St Austell Bay in Western Approaches and Mediterranean, subseq. RNR; Lt-Comdr (retired). Entered Barclays Bank 1948; a Local Dir at Lombard Street, 1957, Southampton, 1959, Birmingham, 1969; Vice-Chm., Barclays Bank UK Ltd, 1972. Fellow, Winchester Coll., 1979. *Recreations:* fishing, gardening, golf, naval history. *Clubs:* Brooks's, MCC. *Address:* c/o Barclays Bank International Ltd, 54 Lombard Street, EC3P 3AH.

LAMBERT, Jack Walter, CBE 1970; DSC 1944; *b* 21 April 1917; *o s* of Walter and Ethel Lambert; *m* 1940, Catherine Margaret, Hon. RCM, *e d* of Alfred Read, CBE; one *s* two *d. Educ:* Tonbridge Sch. Served with Royal Navy in Atlantic, Arctic, North Sea, Channel (Light Coastal Forces), 1940-46, dispatches 1944 (Ordinary Seaman; Lieut-Commander). Joined Sunday Times as Assistant Literary Editor, 1948; Literary and Arts Editor, 1960-76; Associate Editor, 1976-81. Member: Nat. Council, British Drama League, 1968-72; Drama Adv. Cttee, British Council, 1963- (Chm. 1968-69); Bd of Management, British Theatre Assoc., 1972-; Council, RADA, 1972-; Mem., Arts Council of GB, 1968-76: Mem., Drama Panel, 1965-76 (Chm. 1968-76); Theatre Enquiry, 1967-69; Vice-Chm., New Activities Cttee, 1969-70; Chm., Computer Booking Working Party, 1969-72; Cttee, Royal Literary Fund; Member: Theatres Adv. Cttee, 1973-75; Cttee of Management, Soc. of Authors, Mem. Council, 1975-; Dir, Theatre Investment Fund, 1972-. Governor, British Inst. of Recorded Sound, 1966-69, 1977-82; Chairman: Old Vic Trust, 1978-79; Opera 80, 1979-81; Trustee, Phoenix Trust, 1975-. Officier de l'Ordre des arts et des lettres, 1975; Officier de l'Ordre National du Mérite, 1976. *Publications:* Penguin Guide to Cornwall, 1939; The Bodley Head Saki (ed), 1963; Drama in Britain, 1964-73, 1974; much occasional writing and broadcasting on literature, music and the theatre. *Recreation:* singing. *Address:* 30 Belsize Grove, NW3. *T:* 01-722 1668. *Clubs:* Garrick, Beefsteak.

LAMBERT, Sir John (Henry), KCVO 1980; CMG 1975; HM Diplomatic Service, retired; Director, Heritage of London Trust, since 1981; *b* 8 Jan. 1921; *s* of Col R. S. Lambert, MC, and Mrs H. J. F. Mills; *m* 1950, Jennifer Ann (*née* Urquhart); one *s* two *d. Educ:* Eton Coll.; Sorbonne; Trinity Coll., Cambridge. Grenadier Guards, 1940-45 (Captain). Appointed 3rd Secretary, HM Embassy, The Hague, 1945; Member of HM Foreign Service, 1947; FO, 1948; 2nd Secretary, Damascus, 1951; 1st Secretary, 1953; FO, 1954; Dep. to UK Representative on International Commn for Saar Referendum, 1955; Belgrade, 1956; Head of Chancery, Manila, 1958; UK Delegation to Disarmament Conference, Geneva, 1962; FO, 1963; Counsellor, Head of Chancery, Stockholm, 1964-67; Head of UN (Political) Dept, FCO, 1967-70; Commercial Counsellor and Consul-Gen. Vienna, 1971-74; Minister and Dep. Comdt, Berlin, 1974-77; Ambassador to Tunisia, 1977-81. *Recreations:* the arts, music, tennis, golf. *Address:* 103 Rivermead Court, SW6. *T:* 01-731 5007. *Clubs:* MCC; Hurlingham, Royal St George's Golf.

LAMBERT, Hon. Margaret (Barbara), CMG 1965; PhD; British Editor-in-Chief, German Foreign Office Documents, since 1951; *b* 7 Nov. 1906; *yr d* of 1st Viscount Lambert, PC. *Educ:* Lady Margaret Hall, Oxford; London School of Economics. BA 1930, PhD 1936. Served during War of 1939-45 in European Service of BBC. Assistant Editor British Documents on Foreign Policy, 1946-50; Lecturer in Modern History, University College of the South-West, 1950-51; Lecturer in Modern European History, St Andrews University, 1956-60. *Publications:* The Saar, 1934; When Victoria began to Reign, 1937; (with Enid Marx) English Popular and Traditional Art, 1946, and English Popular Art, 1952. *Address:* 39 Thornhill Road, Barnsbury Square, N1. *T:* 01-607 2286; 1 St Germans, Exeter.

LAMBERT, Olaf Francis; Director General, The Automobile Association, since 1977; *b* 13 Jan. 1925; *s* of late Walter Lambert and Edith (*née* Gladstone); *m* 1950, Lucy, *d* of late John Adshead, Macclesfield, and Helen Seymour (*née* Ridgway); two *s* two *d. Educ:* Caterham Sch.; RMA, Sandhurst (war time). Commnd Royal Tank Regt, 1944; retd with rank of Major, 1959. Joined Automobile Assoc., 1959; Man. Dir, 1973. Director: Drive Publications Ltd, 1974-; AA Travel Services Ltd, 1977-; AA Insurance Services Ltd, 1974-; AA Leasing Ltd, 1979-; Mercantile Credit Co. Ltd, 1980-. Member: Council, Inst. of Advanced Motorists, 1968-; Exec. Cttee, British Road Fedn, 1977-; Management Cttee, Alliance Internationale de Tourisme, 1976- (Chm., Public Policy Commn); Inst. of Motor Industry, 1977. CBIM 1980. Freeman, City of London, 1978; Liveryman, Worshipful Co. of Coachmakers and Coach Harness Makers, 1978. *Recreations:* hunting, skiing, mountain walking, travelling, music. *Address:* Elm Farm, Baybridge, Owslebury, Hants. *Club:* Army and Navy.

LAMBERT, Patricia, OBE 1981; Chairman, Consumer Standards Advisory Committee, British Standards Institution, since 1981; *b* 16 March 1926; *d* of

Frederick and Elsie Burrows; *m* 1949, George Richard Lambert; one *s* one *d. Educ:* Malet Lambert High Sch., Hull; West Bridgford Grammar Sch., Nottingham; Nottingham and Dist Technical Coll. Served Royal Signals, Germany, 1944-46; medical technician, 1946-49. Fedn Chm., Notts WI, 1974-78; Member: BSI, 1972-; National Consumer Council, 1977-82; National House Bldg Council, 1981-; Cttee on Electrical Safety, Dept of Trade, 1981-; Adv. Panel, Unit Trust Assoc., 1981-. Mem. Council: British Electrotechnical Approvals Bd, 1981-; British Approvals Bd for Telecoms, 1982-. Local Govt Councillor, 1959-78. *Recreations:* driving (Mem., Inst. of Advanced Motorists), music, theatre, glass engraving. *Address:* 42 Tollerton Lane, Tollerton, Nottingham NG12 4FQ.

LAMBERT, Surgeon Rear Adm. Roger John William, QHP 1980; Surgeon Rear-Adm. (Ships and Establishments), since 1982; *b* 23 April 1928; *s* of Engr Rear Adm. C. W. Lambert, CB, and Muriel Nicholson; *m* 1952, Lois Barbara Kermode; one *s* one *d. Educ:* Oundle Sch.; Trinity Coll., Cambridge (MA 1952; MB, BChir 1953); Guy's Hosp. MRCS, LRCP 1952; DPH London, 1965; DIH 1966; MFCM 1974; MFOM 1980. Served HMS St Angelo, HMS Dolphin, HMS Dreadnought, HMS Maidstone, and Inst. of Naval Medicine, 1953-74; seconded US Naval Submarine Service, 1959; Dir of Health and Res. (Navy), 1975; MO i/c RN Hosp. Gibraltar, 1977. Surg. Comdr 1966, Surg. Captain 1974; Surgeon Rear Adm. (Inst. of Naval Medicine) and Dean of Naval Medicine, 1980-82. FRSM 1957; Member: BMA, 1952-; European Undersea Biomed. Soc., 1969-; Soc. of Occupational Medicine, 1976-. OStJ 1974. Erroll-Eldridge Prize, 1970. *Publications:* papers in fields of submarine medicine, submarine toxicology, and physiology of submarine escape. *Recreations:* painting, gardening, diving. *Address:* Royal William Yard, Plymouth PL1 3RP. *Club:* Army and Navy.

LAMBERT, Dr Royston James; writer; Director of the Reynolds Gallery, Plymouth; *b* 7 Dec. 1932; *s* of Albert Edward Lambert and Edith Alice Tyler; unmarried. *Educ:* Barking Abbey Sch.; Sidney Sussex Coll., Cambridge; Magdalen Coll., Oxford. Open Exhibitioner, Magdalen Coll., Oxford, 1951; Major Scholar, Sidney Sussex Coll., Cambridge, 1954; Hentsch Prize, 1954. 1st class Hist. Tripos Pt I (dist), 1954, 1st class Pt II 1955, MA 1959, PhD 1960, Cantab; BA Oxon, 1955. Bachelor Schol., Sidney Sussex Coll., Cambridge, 1956-58, Research Fellow, 1958-61; Nuffield Senior Sociological Schol., LSE, 1961-64; Ehrman Fellow, King's Coll., Cambridge, 1962-69; Headmaster, Dartington Hall Sch., 1969-73; Dir, Dartington Res. Unit, 1969-75; Advisor on Educn to Dartington Hall Trust, 1973-75. Founded and directed Research Unit into Boarding Education, 1964-68; directed research for Public Schools Commn, 1966-68; directed research for Home Office into Approved School system, 1968-. Founded Boarding Schools Assoc., 1966. *Publications:* Sir John Simon and English Social Administration, 1963; Nutrition in Britain 1950-1960, 1964; The State and Boarding Education, 1966; The Hothouse Society, 1968; New Wine in Old Bottles?: Studies in integration in the Public Schools, 1968; Manual to the Sociology of the School, 1970; Alternatives to School (W. B. Curry Meml Lecture), 1971; The Chance of a Lifetime?, 1975; Body and Soul, 1980; Beloved and God: the story of Hadrian and Antinous, 1982; contribs in: The Public Schools (G. Kalton, 1966); Religious Education (ed. P. Jebb, 1968); The Progressive School (ed. M. Ash, 1968); Education in the Seventies, 1971; Appendix to the First Report of the Public Schools Commission; pamphlets on education, and articles in learned journals on social and administrative history, art history, sociology and education. *Recreations:* restoring paintings; herbaceous borders; Bavarian Rococo; Victorian Gothic; Irish setters. *Address:* Island House, The Barbican, Plymouth. *T:* Plymouth 663318; 37 Lexham Gardens, W8. *T:* 01-370 2407.

LAMBERT, Prof. Thomas Howard; Professor since 1967, and Head of Department of Mechanical Engineering, since 1977, University College London; *b* 28 Feb. 1926; *s* of Henry Thomas Lambert and Kate Lambert. *Educ:* Emanuel Sch.; Univ. of London (BSc (Eng), PhD). FIMechE; FRINA. D. Napier & Sons: Graduate Apprentice, 1946-48; Develt Engr, 1948-51; University College London: Lectr, 1951-63; Sen. Lectr, 1963-65; Reader, 1965-67. Hon. RCNC. *Publications:* numerous articles in learned jls, principally in Stress Analysis, Medical Engrg and Automatic Control. *Recreations:* gardening, sailing, practical engineering. *Address:* Department of Mechanical Engineering, University College London, Gower Street, WC1. *T:* 01-387 7050.

LAMBERT, Verity Ann, (Mrs C. M. Bucksey); Director of Production, EMI Films, since 1982; Chief Executive, Euston Films, since 1979; *b* 27 Nov. 1935; *d* of Stanley Joseph Lambert and Ella Corona Goldburg; *m* 1973, Colin Michael Bucksey. *Educ:* Roedean; La Sorbonne, Paris. Joined BBC Television as drama producer, 1963; first producer of Dr Who; also produced: The Newcomers, Somerset Maugham Short Stories (BAFTA Award, 1969), Adam Adamant, Detective; joined LWT as drama producer, 1970: produced Budgie and Between the Wars; returned to BBC, 1973: produced and co-created Shoulder to Shoulder; joined Thames Television as Controller of Drama Dept, 1974 (Dir of Drama, 1981-82): resp. for: Rock Follies, Rooms, Rumpole of the Bailey, Edward and Mrs Simpson, The Naked Civil Servant (many awards), Last Summer, The Case of Cruelty to Prawns, No Mama No; made creatively resp. for Euston Films Ltd, 1976: developed series which included Out and Danger UXB; Euston Films: resp. for: Minder (three series), Quatermass, Fox, The Flame Trees of Thika, Reilly: ace of spies; single films include: Charlie Muffin, Stainless Steel and the Star Spies, The Sailor's Return, The Knowledge. Dir, Thames Television Ltd, 1982-. Governor, BFI, 1981-

(Chairperson, Prodn Bd, 1981-). *Recreations:* reading, cooking. *Address:* (office) 365 Euston Road, NW1 3AR. *T:* 01-387 0911.

LAMBIE, David; MP (Lab) Ayrshire Central since 1970; *b* 13 July 1925; *m* 1954, Netta May Merrie; one *s* four *d. Educ:* Kyleshill Primary Sch.; Ardrossan Academy; Glasgow University; Geneva University. BSc, DipEd. Teacher, Glasgow Corp., 1950-70. Chm., Glasgow Local Assoc., Educnl Inst. for Scotland, 1958-59; Chm., Scottish Labour Party, 1964; Chief Negotiator on behalf of Scottish Teachers in STSC, 1969-70. Chm., Select Cttee on Scottish Affairs, 1981-; Mem., Select Cttee for Parly Comr for Admin and Health Service. FEIS 1970. *Recreation:* watching football. *Address:* 11 Ivanhoe Drive, Saltcoats, Ayrshire, Scotland. *T:* Saltcoats 64843. *Clubs:* Bute and North Ayrshire Constituency Labour Social (Saltcoats); Irvine Trades Union Centre.

LAMBO, Prof. Thomas Adeoye, NNOM 1979; CON 1979; OBE 1962; MD, DPM; FRCPE; JP 1968; Deputy Director-General, World Health Organization, since 1973 (Assistant Director-General, 1971-73); *b* 29 March 1923; *s* of Chief D. B. Lambo, The Otunbade of Igbore, Abeokuta, and Madam F. B. Lambo, The Iyalode of Egba Christians; *m* 1945, Dinah Violet Adams; three *s. Educ:* Baptist Boys' High Sch., Abeokuta; Univs of Birmingham and London. From 1949, served as House Surg. and House Phys., Birmingham, England; Med. Officer, Lagos, Zaria and Gusau; Specialist, Western Region Min. of Health, 1957-60; Consultant Psychiatrist, UCH Ibadan, 1956-63; Sen. Specialist, Western Region Min. of Health, Neuro-Psychiatric Centre, 1960-63; Prof. of Psychiatry and Head of Dept of Psychiatry and Neurology, Univ. of Ibadan, 1963-71; Dean, Medical Faculty, Univ. of Ibadan, 1966-68; Vice-Chancellor, Univ. of Ibadan, 1968-71. Member: Scientific Council for Africa (Chm., 1965-70); Expert Adv. Panel on Mental Health, WHO, 1959-71; UN Perm. Adv. Cttee on Prevention of Crime and the Treatment of Offenders (Chm. 1968-71); Exec. Cttee, World Fedn for Mental Health, 1964-; Scientific Adv. Panel, Ciba Foundn, 1966-; WHO Adv. Cttee on Med. Research, 1970-71; Scientific Cttee on Advanced Study in Developmental Sciences, 1967-; Vice-Chm., UN Adv. Cttee on Application of Science and Technology to Development, 1970-71; Co-Chm., Internat. Soc. for Study of Human Development, 1968-; Chm., West African Examinations Council, 1969-71, etc. Mem. Pontifical Acad. of Sciences, 1974-. JP Western State, 1968. Hon. DSc Ahmadu Bello, 1967; Hon. LLD: Kent State, 1969; Birmingham 1971; hon. doctorates: Dahomey, 1973; Aix-Marseille, 1974; Long Island, NY, 1975; Louvain, 1976; Hon. DSc: McGill, 1978; Jos, Nigeria, 1979; Nigeria, Nsukka, 1979; Hacettepe, Ankara, 1980. Haile Sellassie African Res. Award, 1970. *Publications:* (jtly) Psychiatric Disorders Among the Yorubas, 1961; monographs, and contribs to medical and other scientific jls. *Recreation:* tennis. *Address:* World Health Organization, 1211 Geneva 27, Switzerland. *T:* 91 21 11; (home) Chemin des Châtaigniers 27, 1292 Chambésy-Genève, Switzerland. *T:* 58 19 42.

LAMBOLL, Alan Seymour, JP; Underwriting Member of Lloyd's; Director, Ellinger Heath Western (Underwriting Agencies), 1974-82; *b* 12 Oct. 1923; *s* of Frederick Seymour and Charlotte Emily Lamboll. *Educ:* Ascham St Vincents, Eastbourne (preparatory sch.); Marlborough Coll. BBC Engineering Staff, 1941-43. Served War: Royal Signals, East Africa Command (Captain), 1943-47. Dir, family firm of wine merchants, City of London, Slack & Lamboll, Ltd, 1947-54. Lloyd's Insurance Broker, Alexr Howden, Stewart Smith (Home), 1954-57; Past Director: Anglo-Portuguese Agencies Ltd (Insurance and Reinsurance Agents), 1957-62; Aga Dictating Machine Co. Ltd, 1962-70; Roger Grayson Ltd, Wine Merchants, 1971-74; London Investment Trust Ltd. JP Inner London, 1965; Dep. Chm., S Westminster PSD, 1980- (Chm., 1978-80); Dep. Chm., City of London Commn, 1979-. Mem. Council: City and Guilds of London Inst., 1965-79; Toynbee Hall, 1958-81 (Hon. Sec., 1968-71); Drama Centre London Ltd, 1974- (Chm. Council, 1975-). Dir, City Arts Trust Ltd, 1962-77; Member: Royal Gen. Theatrical Fund Assoc., 1963- (Vice-Chm., 1967-); Cttee, Industrial Sponsors, 1974-; Governor: Mermaid Theatre Trust, 1966-77; Christ's Hospital (Donation Governor, 1971-). Secretary: Ross McWhirter Foundation, 1980-; Dicey Trust, 1980-. Member Court of Assistants: Worshipful Co. of Distillers (Master, 1972-73, Tercentenary Year); Worshipful Co. of Parish Clerks (Master, 1975-76); Freedom of City of London, 1947; Common Council, Ward of Langbourn, 1949-70; Alderman, Ward of Castle Baynard, 1970-78; Sheriff, City of London, 1976-77 (Silver Jubilee Year). St John Council for London, 1971-; CStJ 1973. FRSA 1970. *Recreations:* theatre, music. *Address:* E4 Albany, Piccadilly, W1V 9RH. *T:* 01-734 0364. *Clubs:* Athenæum, Garrick, Pratt's.

LAMBTON, family name of **Earldom of Durham.**

LAMBTON, Prof. Ann Katharine Swynford, OBE 1942; FBA 1964; BA, PhD; Professor of Persian, University of London, 1953-79, now Emeritus; *b* 8 Feb. 1912; *d* of late Hon. George Lambton. PhD London, 1939; DLit London, 1953. Press Attaché, British Embassy (formerly Legation), Tehran, 1939-45; Senior Lecturer in Persian, School of Oriental and African Studies, 1945-48; Reader in Persian, University of London, 1948-53. Hon. DLit Durham, 1971; Hon. LittD Cambridge, 1973. *Publications:* Three Persian Dialects, 1938; Landlord and Peasant in Persia, 1953; Persian Grammar, 1953; Persian Vocabulary, 1964; The Persian Land Reform 1962-66, 1969; (ed, with others) The Cambridge History of Islam, vols 1-11, 1971; Theory and Practice in Medieval Persian Government, 1980; State and Government in Medieval Islam, 1981. *Address:* Gregory, Kirknewton, Wooler, Northumberland.

LAMBTON, Antony Claud Frederick, (Viscount Lambton, courtesy title by which he was known when his father was Earl of Durham); *b* 10 July 1922; *s* of 5th Earl of Durham (*d* 1970) (whose title he disclaimed), and Diana (*d* 1924), *o d* of Granville Farquhar; *m* 1942, Belinda, *d* of Major D. H. Blew-Jones, Westward Ho!, North Devonshire; one *s* five *d.* MP (C) Berwick upon Tweed Div. of Northumberland, 1951-73; Parly Under-Sec. of State, MoD, 1970-May 1973; PPS to the Foreign Secretary, 1955-57. *Heir to disclaimed peerages:* s Hon. Edward Richard Lambton (Baron Durham), *b* 19 Oct. 1961. *Address:* Garden House, Lambton Castle, Fence Houses, Co. Durham; Biddick Hall, Chester-le-Street, Co. Durham.

LAMBURN, Patricia, (Mrs Donald Derrick); Editorial Director, IPC Magazines Ltd, since 1981 (Director, since 1968); *er d* of Francis John Lamburn and Nell Winifred (*née* Kennedy); *m* 1949, Donald G. E. Douglas Derrick, DDS, LDSRCS, FACD, FICD; one *s* one *d. Educ:* Queen's Gate Sch., S Kensington. Amalgamated Press, 1943-49; Curtis Publishing Co., USA, 1949-50; joined George Newnes Ltd, 1950; during ensuing yrs, edited, developed and was associated creatively with wide range of women's and teenage magazines; Dir, George Newnes Ltd, 1966-68; IPC, 1968-: Gp Dir, Young Magazines Gp, 1968-71; Publishing Dir, Women's Magazines Gp, 1971-76, Asst Man. Dir (Editorial), 1976-81. Chm., Gen. Adv. Council, IBA, 1982- (Mem., 1980-82); Member: Health Educn Council, 1973-78; Information Cttee, British Nutrition Foundn, 1979-; Periodical Publishing Trng Cttee, PPITB, 1980-82; Public Relations Cttee, RCP, 1981-; Press Council, 1982-; Editorial Cttee, Periodical Publishers' Assoc., 1975-. *Recreations:* early mesoamerican civilisation, bird-watching. *Address:* (office) King's Reach Tower, Stamford Street, SE1 9LS; (home) Chelsea, London.

LAMERTON, Leonard Frederick, PhD, DSc, FInstP, FRCPath; Director, Institute of Cancer Research, London, 1977-80; Professor of Biophysics as Applied to Medicine, University of London, 1960-80; *b* 1 July 1915; *s* of Alfred Lamerton and Florence (*née* Mason); *m* 1965, Morag MacLeod. *Educ:* King Edward VI Sch., Southampton; University Coll., Southampton (PhD, DSc London). Staff member, Royal Cancer Hosp. and Inst. of Cancer Research, 1938-41 and 1946-80, Dean of the Inst., 1967-77; seconded to United Nations as a Scientific Sec. of First UN Conf. on Peaceful Uses of Atomic Energy, 1955. President: British Inst. of Radiology, 1957-58; Hosp. Physicists Assoc., 1961; Member: Bd of Governors, Royal Marsden Hosp., 1955-80; Bd of Governors, 1978-82, and Cttee of Management, 1978-, Cardiothoracic Hosp. and Inst. Roentgen Award, 1950, Barclay Medal, 1961, British Inst. of Radiology. *Publications:* various papers on medical physics, radiation hazard, cell kinetics, experimental cancer therapy. *Recreations:* reading, music, golf. *Address:* 10 Burgh Mount, Banstead, Surrey SM7 1ER. *T:* Burgh Heath 53697. *Club:* Athenæum.

LAMFORD, (Thomas) Gerald, OBE 1979; Commandant, Police Staff College, 1976-79; *b* Carmarthen, 3 April 1928; *s* of late Albert and Sarah Lamford; *m* 1952, Eira Hale; one *s* one *d. Educ:* Technical Coll., Swansea; London Univ. (LLB 1969); Police Coll. (Intermed. Comd Course, 1969; Sen. Comd Course, 1973). Radio Officer, Merchant Navy, 1945; Wireless Operator, RAF, 1946-48, Aden. Joined Carmarthenshire Constab. (now Dyfed Powys Police), 1949; reached rank of Chief Inspector, CID, Crime Squad; Force Trng Officer, 1965-69; Supt, Haverfordwest, 1970; Chief Supt, Llanelli, 1971-74; Asst Chief Constable, Greater Manchester Police, 1974-79. Vis. Prof. of Police Science, John Jay Coll. of Criminal Justice, City Univ. of New York, 1972; sometime Vis. Lecturer: Southern Police Inst., Univ. of Louisville, Ky; N Eastern Univ., Boston; NY Univ. Sch. of Law; Rutgers Univ., NJ; Mercy Coll., Detroit. County Comr, St John Amb. Bde, Pembrokeshire, 1970; SBStJ. Member: Consultative Cttee on Social Effects of Television, BBC, 1975-79; Bd of Governors, Police Coll., 1977-79. *Publications:* articles in Police Studies, Internat. Rev. of Police Develt, Police Rev., Bramshill Jl, World Police. *Recreations:* photography, antiques. *Address:* Nanteos, 11 Llwyn y Bryn, Parc Henri, Ammanford, Dyfed. *T:* Ammanford 3757.

LAMING, Rev. Canon Frank Fairbairn; Priest-in-Charge, St Ninian's, Glenurquhart, and Hon. Canon, Inverness Cathedral, since 1974; *b* 24 Aug. 1908; *s* of William John Laming and Maude Elizabeth (*née* Fairbairn); *m* 1939, Ruth Marion, *d* of Herbert William Pinder and Rose Marion (*née* Price). *Educ:* King Edward VI Sch., Retford; The Theological Coll., Edinburgh. In business, 1925-33; Edinburgh Theological Coll., 1933-36; Luscombe Scholar, 1936; Durham LTh, 1936. Deacon, 1936; Priest, 1937; Assistant Priest, Christ Church, Glasgow, 1936-39; Priest in Charge, St Margaret, Renfrew, 1939-44; Rector, Holy Trinity Church, Motherwell, 1944-53; Rector and Provost of St Mary's Cathedral, Glasgow, 1953-66; Provost of St Andrew's Cathedral, Inverness, 1966-74. Editor, Year Book and Directory of the Episcopal Church in Scotland, 1976-. *Recreations:* woodworking, gardening, fishing. *Address:* St Ninian's, Glenurquhart, Drumnadrochit, Inverness IV3 6TN. *T:* Glenurquhart 264.

LAMOND, James Alexander, JP; MP (Lab) Oldham East, since 1970; *b* Burrelton, Perthshire, 29 Nov. 1928; *s* of Alexander N. G. Lamond and Christina Lamond (*née* Craig); *m* 1954, June Rose Wellburn; three *d. Educ:* Burrelton Sch.; Coupar Angus Sch. Draughtsman, 1944-70. PPS to Minister of State: for NI, 1974-75; DHSS, 1975-76. Mem., Aberdeen City Council, 1959-71; Lord Provost of Aberdeen, 1970-71; Lord Lieutenant of the County of the City of Aberdeen, 1970-71. Mem., AUEW (TASS), 1944- (Chm., No 1 Divisional Council of DATA, 1965-70); Pres., Aberdeen Trades Council,

1969. Vice-Pres., World Peace Council; President: British Peace Assembly; Britain-GDR Soc. JP Aberdeen. *Recreations:* golf, travel, reading, thinking. *Address:* 15 Belvidere Street, Aberdeen AB2 4QS. *T:* Aberdeen 638074. *Clubs:* Labour, Irish (Oldham); Trades Council, Boilermaker's (Aberdeen).

LAMONT, Norman Stewart Hughson; MP (C) Kingston-upon-Thames since May 1972; Minister of State, Department of Industry, since 1981; *b* Lerwick, Shetland, 8 May 1942; *s* of late Daniel Lamont and of Helen Irene (*née* Hughson); *m* 1971, Alice Rosemary, *d* of Lt-Col Peter White; one *s* one *d. Educ:* Loretto Sch. (scholar); Fitzwilliam Coll., Cambridge (BA). Chm., Cambridge Univ. Conservative Assoc., 1963; Pres., Cambridge Union, 1964; Cambridge Union Debating tour of USA, 1965. PA to Rt Hon. Duncan Sandys, MP, 1965; Conservative Research Dept, 1966-68; Merchant Banker, N. M. Rothschild & Sons, 1968-79. Contested (C) East Hull, Gen. Election, 1970. PPS to Minister for the Arts, 1974; an Opposition Spokesman on: Prices and Consumer Affairs, 1975-76; Industry, 1976-79; Parly Under Sec. of State, Dept of Energy, 1979-81. Mem., Select Cttee on Procedure, 1976-79. Chairman: Coningsby Club, 1970-71; Bow Group, 1971-72. *Publications:* newspaper articles and various Bow Group memoranda. *Recreations:* reading, ornithology, following Association football and American politics. *Address:* House of Commons, SW1. *Club:* Carlton.

LAMONT, William Dawson, MA, DPhil; *b* Prince Edward Island, Canada, 3 Feb. 1901; 4th *s* of Rev. Murdoch Lamont, Rothiemurchus, Inverness-shire, and Euphemia Ann Hume; *m* 1930, Ann Fraser, *d* of Dr David Christie, Glasgow; no *c. Educ:* Glasgow Univ. (Edward Caird Medallist; First Class in Moral and Mental Philosophy 1924, Euing Fellow and Ferguson Scholar 1924); Balliol Coll., Oxford. Assistant in Moral Philosophy, University of Glasgow, 1926, and Lecturer, 1929; Professor of Philosophy, University of Cairo, 1942. Principal of Makerere Coll., East Africa, 1946-49. Served with Clyde River Patrol and as Naval Intelligence Liaison Officer, West Scotland, 1939-42. Hon. Secretary Anglo-Egyptian Union, 1944; Vice-Chairman Cairo Group of RIIA, 1944. FSA Scot. 1968. HonDLitt, University of East Africa, 1965. *Publications:* Introduction to Green's Moral Philosophy, 1934; Principles of Moral Judgement, 1946; The Value Judgement, 1955; The Early History of Islay, 1966; Ancient and Mediæval Sculptured Stones of Islay, 1968; Law and the Moral Order, 1981; articles (on philosophical subjects) in Mind, Proceedings of the Aristotelian Society, Philosophy; (on historical subjects) in Scottish Studies, Proceedings of the Royal Irish Academy and Scottish Historical Review. *Recreation:* walking. *Address:* 37 Kirklee Road, Glasgow G12 0SP. *T:* 041-339 5399.

LAMONTAGNE, Hon. (J.) Gilles, CD 1980; PC (Can.); MP (L) Langelier, Canada, since 1977; Minister of National Defence, since 1980; *b* 17 April 1919; *s* of Trefflé Lemontagne and Anna Kieffer; *m* 1949, Mary Katherine Schaefer; three *s* one *d. Educ:* Collège Jean-de-Brébeuf, Montréal, Québec (BA). Served RCAF, 1941-45. Businessman in Québec City, 1946-66. Alderman, Québec City, 1962-64, Mayor, 1965-78. Parly Sec. to Minister of Energy, Mines and Resources, 1977; Minister without Portfolio, Jan. 1978; Postmaster Gen., Feb. 1978; Actg Minister of Veterans Affairs, 1980. Dir, Québec City Chamber of Commerce and Industry; Member: Econ. Council of Canada; Br. 260, Royal Canadian Legion. Croix du Combattant de l'Europe. *Address:* 1040 Moncton Avenue, Québec, PQ E1S 2Y8, Canada. *Club:* Québec City Rotary (Pres.).

LAMPLUGH, Maj.-Gen. Stephen, CB 1954; CBE 1943; retired 1955; Past Director of Civil Defence, Northern Region (Newcastle upon Tyne), 1955-64; *b* 25 May 1900; *s* of late George William Lamplugh, FRS, Driffield, Yorks; *m* 1938, Mary Lewis, *d* of A. H. Vesey, Suddon Grange, Wincanton, Somerset; one *s* one *d. Educ:* St Albans; RMA, Woolwich. 2nd Lieut RE, 1919; Major, 1938; Lt-Col (temp.), 1940; Brigadier (temp.), 1942; Maj.-Gen. (temp.), 1945 and 1952; Colonel, 1945; Brigadier, 1947; Maj.-General, 1953. Served Near East, 1922-23; NW Frontier, 1930; France, 1939-40 (despatches); psc 1937. Commander Rhine District, BAOR, 1952-55, retired 1955. Chairman Joint War Office Treasury Cttee, 1955. *Recreations:* normal. *Address:* Amesbury Abbey, Amesbury, Wilts.

LAMPSON, family name of **Baron Killearn.**

LANCASTER, Bishop Suffragan of, since 1975; **Rt. Rev. Dennis Fountain Page;** *b* 1 Dec. 1919; *s* of Prebendary Martin Fountain Page and Lilla Fountain Page; *m* 1946, Margaret Bettine Clayton; two *s* one *d. Educ:* Shrewsbury Sch.; Gonville and Caius Coll., Cambridge (MA); Lincoln Theological Coll. Curate, Rugby Parish Church, 1943; Priest-in-Charge, St George's Church, Hillmorton, Rugby, 1945; Rector of Hockwold, Vicar of Wilton and Rector of Weeting, Norfolk, 1949; Archdeacon of Huntingdon and Vicar of Yaxley, 1965-75; Hon. Canon of Ely Cathedral, 1968. *Recreations:* music, carpentry, gardening. *Address:* Winmarleigh Vicarage, Preston PR3 0LA.

LANCASTER, Bishop of, (RC), since 1962; **Rt. Rev. Brian Charles Foley;** *b* Ilford, 25 May 1910. *Educ:* St Cuthbert's Coll., Ushaw; English College and Gregorian Univ., Rome. Priest, 1937; Assistant Priest, Shoeburyness; subseq. Assistant Priest, Romford; Parish Priest, Holy Redeemer, Harold Hill, and Holy Cross, Harlow. Canon of Brentwood Diocese, 1959. *Address:* Bishop's House, Cannon Hill, Lancaster.

LANCASTER, Archdeacon of; *see* Gibbons, Ven. K. H.

LANCASTER, Dame Jean, DBE 1963; *b* 11 Aug. 1909; *d* of late Richard C. Davies; *m* 1967, Roy Cavander Lancaster (*d* 1981). *Educ:* Merchant Taylors' Sch., Crosby, Lancashire. Director, Women's Royal Naval Service, 1961-64. *Address:* Greathed Manor, Dormansland, Lingfield, Surrey RH7 6PA.

LANCASTER, Joan Cadogan, CBE 1978; Director, India Office Library and Records, 1972-78; *b* 2 Aug. 1918; *yr d* of Cyril Cadogan Lancaster and Mary Ann Lancaster. *Educ:* Charles Edward Brooke Sch., London; Westfield Coll., Univ. of London. BA 1940, MA 1943; ALA 1943; FRHistS 1956; FSA 1960. Asst Librarian, University Coll., Leicester, and Asst Archivist, the Museum, Leicester, 1940-43. Served War, ATS, 1943-46. Archivist, City of Coventry, 1946-48; Asst Librarian, Inst. of Historical Research, Univ. of London, 1948-60; Asst Keeper, India Office Records, 1960-67; Dep. Librarian and Dep. Keeper, India Office Library and Records, 1968-72. Reviews Editor, Archives (Jl of British Records Assoc.), 1951-57, Editor, Archives, 1957-63. *Publications:* Guide to St Mary's Hall, Coventry, 1949, rev. edn 1981; Bibliography of historical works issued in the United Kingdom 1946-56 (Inst. of Historical Research), 1957; Guide to lists and catalogues of the India Office Records, 1966; Godiva of Coventry, 1967; India Office Records: Report for the years 1947-67 (FCO), 1970; contribs on Coventry to: Victoria County History, 1969; Historic Towns, vol. 2, 1974; Medieval Coventry—a city divided?, 1981; articles and reviews in Bulletin of Inst. of Historical Research, Archives, Asian Affairs, etc. *Recreations:* music, photography. *Address:* 43 Craignair Road, Tulse Hill, SW2 2DQ. *T:* 01-674 3451. *Club:* United Oxford & Cambridge University.

LANCASTER, Vice-Admiral Sir John (Strike), KBE 1961; CB 1958; retired 1962; *b* 26 June 1903; *s* of George Henry Lancaster; *m* 1927, Edith Laurie Jacobs (*d* 1980); two *d. Educ:* King Edward VI Sch., Southampton. Joined RN, 1921; Commander, 1940; Captain, 1951; Rear-Admiral, 1956; Vice-Admiral, 1959. Served War of 1939-45: HMS Gloucester; RN Barracks, Portsmouth; Persian Gulf; HMS Ocean. Rear-Admiral Personnel, Home Air Command, Lee-on-the-Solent, 1956; Director-General of Manpower, 1959-62; Chief Naval Supply and Secretariat Officer, 1959-62. *Recreation:* gardening. *Address:* Moorings, Western Way, Alverstoke, Hants. *Club:* Army and Navy.

See also P. M. Lancaster.

LANCASTER, Sir Osbert, Kt 1975; CBE 1953; RDI 1979; Artist and Writer; *b* 4 Aug. 1908; *o s* of late Robert Lancaster and Clare Bracebridge Manger; *m* 1933, Karen (*d* 1964), 2nd *d* of late Sir Austin Harris, KBE; one *s* one *d*; *m* 1967, Anne Scott-James, *qv. Educ:* Charterhouse; Lincoln Coll., Oxford (Hon. Fellow, 1979); Slade Sch. Hon. FRIBA. Cartoonist Daily Express since 1939; Foreign Office (News Dept), 1940; Attached to HM Embassy, Athens, 1944-46; Sydney Jones Lecturer in Art, Liverpool Univ., 1947. Adviser to GLC Historic Buildings Bd, 1969-. Governor King Edward VII Sch., King's Lynn. Hon. DLitt: Birmingham Univ., 1964; Newcastle-upon-Tyne, 1970; St Andrews, 1974; Oxon, 1975. Fellow, University College, London, 1967. Theatre Décors: Pineapple Poll, Sadler's Wells, 1951; Bonne Bouche, Covent Garden, 1952; Love in a Village, English Opera Group, 1952; High Spirits, Hippodrome, 1953; Rake's Progress, Edinburgh (for Glyndebourne), 1953; All's Well That Ends Well, Old Vic, 1953; Don Pasquale, Sadler's Wells, 1954; Coppelia, Covent Garden, 1954; Napoli, Festival Ballet, 1954; Falstaff, Edinburgh (for Glyndebourne), 1955; Hotel Paradiso, Winter Garden, 1956; Zuleika, Saville, 1957; L'Italiana in Algeri, Glyndebourne, 1957; Tiresias, English Opera Group, 1958; Candide, Saville, 1959; La Fille Mal Gardée, Covent Garden, 1960; She Stoops to Conquer, Old Vic, 1960; La Pietra del Paragone, Glyndebourne, 1964; Peter Grimes, Bulgarian National Opera, Sofia, 1964; L'Heure Espagnole, Glyndebourne, 1966; The Rising of the Moon, Glyndebourne, 1970; The Sorcerer, D'Oyly-Carte, 1971. *Publications:* Progress at Pelvis Bay, 1936; Our Sovereigns, 1936; Pillar to Post, 1938; Homes, Sweet Homes, 1939; Classical Landscape with Figures, 1947; The Saracen's Head, 1948; Drayneflete Revealed, 1949; Façades and Faces, 1950; Private Views, 1956; The Year of the Comet, 1957; Études, 1958; Here, of All Places, 1959, reissued as A Cartoon History of Architecture, 1976; Signs of the Times, 1961; All Done From Memory (Autobiog.), 1963; With an Eye to the Future (Autobiog.), 1967; Temporary Diversions, 1968; Sailing to Byzantium, 1969; Recorded Live, 1970; Meaningful Confrontations, 1971; Theatre in the Flat, 1972; The Littlehampton Bequest, 1973; (with Anne Scott-James) The Pleasure Garden, 1977; Scene Changes, 1978; Ominous Cracks, 1979; The Life and Times of Maudie Littlehampton, 1982. *Recreation:* topography. *Address:* 78 Cheyne Court, Royal Hospital Road, SW3. *Clubs:* Brooks's, Pratt's, Beefsteak, Garrick.

LANCASTER, Patricia Margaret; Headmistress, Wycombe Abbey School, since 1974; *b* 22 Feb. 1929; *d* of Vice-Adm. Sir John Lancaster, *qv. Educ:* Univs of London (BA) and Southampton (Certif. Educn). English Mistress, St Mary's Sch., Calne, 1951-58; Housemistress, St Swithun's Sch., Winchester, 1958-62; Headmistress, St Michael's, Burton Park, Petworth, 1962-73. Pres., Girls' Schools' Assoc., 1979-80. *Recreation:* theatre. *Address:* Wycombe Abbey School, High Wycombe, Bucks. *T:* High Wycombe 20381.

LANCE, Rev. Preb. John Du Boulay, MC 1945; MA; Prebendary of Henstridge in Wells Cathedral, since 1974; Assistant Curate, St Cuthbert, Wells, since 1981; *b* 14 March 1907; *s* of late Rev. Arthur Porcher Lance and Harriet Agatha Lance, Buckland St Mary, Somerset; *m* 1936, Lena Winifred Clifford; one *s. Educ:* Marlborough; Jesus Coll., Cambridge; Cuddesdon

Theological Coll. Assistant Curate, St Peter, Wolverhampton, 1930-34; Missioner, Trinity Coll., Oxford. Mission, Stratford, 1934-36; Vicar of Bishops Lydeard, 1936-47. Chaplain to the Forces, 1941-46 (despatches). Vicar of St Andrew's, Taunton, 1947-57; Preb. of Wells, 1951-63; Rector of Bathwick, Bath, 1957-63; Archdeacon of Wells and Canon of Wells Cathedral, 1963-73; Diocesan Dir of Ordinands, Wells, 1974-76. Proctor in Convocation, 1959-64; Diocesan Adviser in Christian Stewardship, 1961-67; Warden, Abbey Retreat House, Glastonbury, 1965-. *Address:* 14 Portway Avenue, Wells, Somerset BA5 2QF. *T:* Wells 72756. *Club:* Hawks (Cambridge).

LANCELYN GREEN, Roger G.; *see* Green, R. G. L.

LANCHBERY, John Arthur, FRAM; Conductor; *b* London, 15 May 1923; *s* of William Lanchbery and Violet (*née* Mewett); *m* 1951, Elaine Fifield (divorced 1960); one *d*. *Educ:* Alleyn's Sch., Dulwich; Royal Academy of Music. Henry Smart Composition Scholarship, 1942. Served, Royal Armoured Corps, 1943-45. Royal Academy of Music, 1945-47; Musical Director, Metropolitan Ballet, 1948-50; Sadler's Wells Theatre Ballet, 1951-57; Royal Ballet, 1957 (Principal Conductor, 1959); Musical Director: Australian Ballet, 1972; American Ballet Theatre, 1978. ARAM 1953; Bolshoi Theatre Medal, Moscow, 1961. *Publications:* Arrangements and Compositions of Ballets include: Pleasuredrome, 1949; Eve of St Agnes (BBC commission), 1950; House of Birds, 1955; La Fille Mal Gardée, 1960; The Dream, 1964; Don Quixote, 1966; Giselle, 1968; La Sylphide, 1970; Tales of Beatrix Potter, 1971; Tales of Hoffman, 1972; Merry Widow, 1975; Month in the Country, 1976; Mayerling, 1978; Rosalinda, 1978; Papillon, 1979; La Bayadère, 1980. *Recreations:* walking, reading. *Address:* c/o Roger Stone management, 132 Loudoun Road, NW8 0ND. *Club:* Garrick.

LANCHESTER, Elsa; Actress; *d* of James Sullivan and Edith Lanchester; *m* 1929, Charles Laughton (*d* 1962); became American Citizen, 1950. *Educ:* Privately. Started the Children's Theatre, Charlotte Street, Soho, 1918; first appearance on stage, 1922; afterwards played at Lyric, Hammersmith, in The Way of the World, 1924, in The Duenna, 1924 and in Riverside Nights, 1926; first appearance in New York at Lyceum Theatre, 1931; joined Old Vic-Sadler's Wells company, 1933; was Peter Pan, Palladium, 1936; was in They Walk Alone, New York, 1941; 10 years as star of Turnabout Theatre, Los Angeles, California; Turnabout Theatre, nightly continuously, from 1941. Acted in The Party, London, 1958. Has appeared in films including The Constant Nymph, Potiphar's Wife, The Private Life of Henry VIII, David Copperfield, Bride of Frankenstein, Naughty Marietta, The Ghost Goes West, Rembrandt, Vessel of Wrath, Ladies in Retirement, Son of Fury, Passport to Destiny, Lassie Come Home, Spiral Staircase, Razor's Edge, The Big Clock, The Inspector General, The Secret Garden, Come to the Stable, Buccaneer Girl, The Glass Slipper, Witness for the Prosecution, Bell, Book and Candle, Mary Poppins, That Darn Cat, Blackbeard's Ghost, Me Natalie, Rascal, My Dog, The Thief, Willard, Terror in the Wax Museum, Arnold, Murder by Death. Television series, The John Forsythe Show; talk shows: Jack Paar; David Frost; Dick Cavitt; Johnny Carson; Joey Bishop. *Publication:* Charles Laughton and I, 1938. *Recreation:* wild flowers. *Address:* 9405 Brighton Way, Beverly Hills, Calif 90210, USA.

LANCHIN, Gerald; Under Secretary, Consumer Affairs Division, Department of Trade, 1980-82; *b* 17 Oct. 1922; *o s* of late Samuel Lanchin, Kensington; *m* 1951, Valerie Sonia Lyons; one *s* two *d*. *Educ:* St Marylebone Grammar Sch.; London Sch. of Economics. BCom 1st cl. hons 1951; Leverhulme Schol. 1950-51. Min. of Labour, 1939-51; served with Army, RAOC and REME, 1942-46; Board of Trade (subseq. DTI and Dept of Trade): Asst Principal, 1952; Principal 1953; 1st Sec., UK Delegn to OEEC, Paris, 1955-59; Principal, Estabt and Commercial Relations and Exports Divs, 1959-66; Asst Sec., Finance and Civil Aviation Divs, 1966-71; Under-Sec., Tariff, Commercial Relations and Export, Shipping Policy, and General Divs, 1971-80. *Recreations:* reading, gardening, music. *Address:* Herrick, Doggetts Wood Close, Chalfont St Giles, Bucks. *T:* 02-404 2822. *Club:* Reform.

LAND, Edwin Herbert; US physicist and inventor; Founder Chairman of Board and Consulting Director of Basic Research, Polaroid Corporation, Cambridge, Massachusetts, retired 1982 (President, 1937-75; Chief Executive Officer and Director of Research, 1937-80); Fellow and Visiting Institute Professor, Massachusetts Institute of Technology, since 1956; *b* Bridgeport, Connecticut, 7 May 1909; *s* of Harry M. and Matha G. Land; *m* 1929, Helen Maislen; two *d*. *Educ:* Norwich Acad.; Harvard. Founded Polaroid Corporation, 1937. War of 1941-45, in charge of research into development of weapons and materials, and cons. on missiles to US Navy. Invented polarizer for light in form of extensive synthetic sheet; also camera which produces complete photograph immediately after exposure, 1947. Member: President's Science Adv. Cttee, 1957-59 (Consultant-at-large, 1960-73); President's Foreign Intelligence Adv. Bd, 1961-77; Nat. Commn on Technology, Automation, and Economic Progress, 1964-66; Carnegie Commn on Educational TV, 1966-67; President's Cttee, Nat. Medal of Science, 1968-72. Harvard University: Mem. Vis. Cttee, Dept of Physics, 1949-66, 1968; William James Lectr on Psychol., 1966-67; Morris Loeb Lectr on Physics, 1974. Trustee, Ford Foundn, 1967-75. Awards include: Hood Medal and Progress Medal, RPS; Cresson Medal and Potts Medal, Franklin Inst.; Scott Medal, Philadelphia City Trusts; Rumford Medal, Amer. Acad. of Arts and Sciences, 1945; Holley Medal, Amer. Soc. Mech. Engrs, 1948; Duddell Medal, British Physical Soc., 1949. Presidential Medal of Freedom,

1963; Nat. Medal of Science, 1967. Fellow: Photographic Soc. of America, 1950-; Amer. Acad. of Arts and Sciences, 1943- (Pres., 1951-53); Royal Photographic Society, 1958-; Nat. Acad. of Sciences, 1953-, etc. Hon. MRI, 1975; Hon. Mem., Soc. of Photographic Science and Technology, Japan, 1975; Hon. Fellow: Royal Microscopical Society, and many other American and foreign learned bodies. ScD (Hon.) Harvard Univ., 1957, and holds many other hon. doctorates in science and law. *Publications:* contributions Journal Opt. Soc. America, Amer. Scientist, Proceedings of Nat. Acad. of Science. *Recreations:* music, horseback riding. *Address:* 163 Brattle Street, Cambridge, Mass 02138, USA. *T:* Univ. 4-6000; 730 Main Street, Cambridge, Mass 02139. *Clubs:* Harvard (NY and Boston); Century Association (New York); St Botolph, Harvard Faculty (Boston); Cosmos (Washington, DC).

LAND, Prof. Frank William, MSc, PhD London; Professor of Education, University of Hull, 1961-77; *b* 9 Jan. 1911; *s* of Charles and Mary Land; *m* 1937, Nora Beatrice Channon; two *s* one *d*. *Educ:* King's Coll., University of London. Assistant Master, The Grammar School, Hampton-on-Thames, 1933-37; Mathematics Lecturer: College of St Mark and St John, Chelsea, 1937-39; Birkbeck Coll., London, 1939-40. Instructor Lieut, Royal Navy, 1940-46. Vice-Principal, College of St Mark and St John, Chelsea, 1946-49; Senior Lecturer, University of Liverpool, 1950-61. Chairman, Association of Teachers in Colleges and Departments of Education, 1956-57. *Publications:* Recruits to Teaching, 1960; The Language of Mathematics, 1961. *Recreation:* gardening. *Address:* Cremel Cwm, Church Lane, Gwernaffield, Mold, Clwyd CH7 5DT.
See also M. F. Land.

LAND, Gillian; *see* Lynne, Gillian.

LAND, Dr Michael Francis, FRS 1982; Reader in Biological Sciences, University of Sussex, since 1977; Senior Research Fellow, Australian National University, Canberra, since 1982; *b* 12 April 1942; *s* of Prof. Frank William Land, *qv*; *m* 1980, Rosemary (*née* Clarke); one *s* one *d*. *Educ:* Birkenhead Sch., Cheshire; Jesus Coll., Cambridge (MA); University Coll. London (PhD). Asst Lectr in Physiology, UCL, 1966-67; Miller Fellow, 1967-79, and Asst Prof. of Physiology-Anatomy, 1979-81, Univ. of Calif, Berkeley; Lectr in Biol Sciences, Univ. of Sussex, 1971-77. Vis. Prof., Univ. of Oregon, 1980. *Publications:* 42 papers on animal vision in learned jls. *Recreations:* photography, music. *Address:* 10 Cleve Terrace, Lewes, East Sussex BN7 1JJ. *T:* Lewes 6780.

LANDA, Hon. Abram, CMG 1968; LLB; Notary Public; Agent-General for New South Wales in London, 1965-70; *b* 10 Nov. 1902; *s* of late D. Landa, Belfast; *m* 1930, Perla (*d* 1976), *d* of late L. Levy; one *s* one *d*. *Educ:* Christian Brothers' Coll., Waverley, NSW; University of Sydney. Solicitor, 1927-. MLA for Bondi, NSW, 1930-32 and 1941-65; Minister for Labour and Industry, 1953-56; Minister for Housing and Co-operative Societies, 1956-65; Minister for Housing, NSW, 1956-65. Past Member Senate, University of Sydney; Past Trustee, NSW Public Library. *Recreations:* swimming, bowls. *Address:* 22 Coolong Road, Vaucluse, NSW, Australia. *Club:* Tattersall's (Sydney).

LANDA, Lynda, (Mrs Clive Landa); *see* Chalker, L.

LANDALE, Russell Talbot; HM Diplomatic Service, retired 1971; Consul-General, Amsterdam, 1969-71; *b* 25 Oct. 1911; 3rd *s* of late W. H. Landale and Ethel (*née* Talbot); *m* 1938, Margaret Myfanwy George; two *d* (one *s* decd). *Educ:* Berkhamsted Sch.; Wiesbaden Konservatorium; Rackows Kaufmännische Schule, Dresden; Institut de Touraine, Tours. British Tabulating Machine Co. (now ICL), 1933-39; HM Forces, 1940-46; Diplomatic Service, 1946-71. Chevalier de l'Ordre de Méduse, 1974. *Recreations:* viticulture, writing, music (compositions include Song of the Waves, Silver Jubilee Rag, Last Time We Met, Love has almost Gone, Meribel, Tulips of Holland, Let Our People Go, On Poets, Carol's Dance, Petit Nocturne Petite Valse, songs for children). *Address:* Fleur de France, Route de l'Ormée, 06140 Vence, France. *T:* Vence 580369.

LANDAU, Dennis Marcus; Chief Executive, Co-operative Wholesale Society Ltd, since 1980 (Deputy Chief Executive Officer, 1974-80); *b* 18 June 1927; *s* of late Michael Landau, metallurgist. *Educ:* Haberdashers' Aske's Hampstead Sch. Schweppes Ltd, 1952; Man. Dir, Schweppes (East Africa) Ltd, 1958-62; Chivers-Hartley: Prodn Dir, 1963; Man. Dir, 1966-69; Chm., Schweppes Foods Div., 1969; Dep. Chm. and Man. Dir, Cadbury Schweppes Foods, 1970; Controller, Food Div., Co-operative Wholesale Society Ltd, 1971. Director: C. W. S. Svineslagterier A/s; Co-operative Retail Services Ltd; Sorbie Cheese Ltd; CWS (NZ Hldgs) Ltd; CWS (India) Ltd; Co-operative Bank plc; Co-operative Insce Soc. Ltd. Member: Metrication Bd, 1972-80; Exec. Cttee, Food Manufacturers' Fedn Inc., 1972-. FIGD 1977 (Pres. 1982-); CBIM 1980. *Recreations:* Rugby, cricket, music. *Address:* 9 Grey Road, Altrincham, Cheshire WA14 4BT. *T:* 061-928 4116. *Club:* Lancashire CC.

LANDEN, Dinsdale (James); actor; *b* 4 Sept. 1932; *s* of Edward James Landen and Winifred Alice Landen; *m* 1959, Jennifer Daniel. *Educ:* King's Sch., Rochester; Hove County Grammar Sch. *Stage:* Dead Secret, Piccadilly, 1957; Auntie Mame, Adelphi; Provok'd Wife, Vaudeville; Philanthropist, May Fair, 1970; Alphabetical Order, May Fair, 1975; London Assurance, New, 1972; Bodies, Ambassadors; Taking Steps, Lyric, 1980; *National Theatre:* Plunder; The Philanderer; On the Razzle, 1981; Uncle Vanya, 1982; *television:* Great

Expectations, Mickey Dunne, The Spies, Glittering Prizes, Devenish, Two Sundays, Fathers and Families, Pig in the Middle. *Recreations:* walking, golf. *Address:* The Coach House, Larpent Avenue, SW15. *T:* 01-788 5273. *Club:* Stage Golfing Society.

LANDER, Donald Hartley; Managing Director, De Lorean Motor Cars Ltd, 1980-82; *b* 2 Aug. 1925; *s* of late Ralph Lander and of Ruby Lander; *m* 1946, Dorothy Marguerite (*née* Balmer); one *s* three *d*. *Educ:* Whitby High Sch., Ont, Canada; Univ. of BC (extension course). Sales and marketing, General Motors, 1945-59, Chrysler Corp., 1959-67; Vice-Pres., Parts Div., Chrysler Canada Ltd, 1967-68; Gen. Man., Import Vehicle Div., Chrysler Corp., 1968-69; Exec. Vice Pres., Chrysler Canada, 1969-70; Dep. Man. Dir, Chrysler UK Ltd, 1970-73, Man. Dir, 1973-76; Vice Pres., Europe, Chrysler Corp., and Pres., Chrysler Internat. SA, 1976-79; Pres. and Ch. Exec. Officer, Chrysler Canada Ltd, 1979; Gp Corporate Vice-Pres., Chrysler Corp., Detroit, 1980. *Recreations:* golf, skiing, water skiing.

LANDON, Alfred Mossman; Independent Oil Producer; *b* 9 Sept. 1887; *s* of John Manuel Landon and Anne Mossman; *m* 1915, Margaret Fleming (*d* 1918); one *d*; *m* 1930, Theo Cobb; one *s* one *d*. *Educ:* University of Kansas. Republican State Chm., 1928; Governor of Kansas, 1933-37; Republican nominee for Pres. of United States, 1936; Delegate to Eighth International Conference, Lima, Peru, 1938; Chm. Kansas Delegation Republican Nat. Convention, 1940, 1944, and 1948; Mem. Methodist Church; Member, Kansas Bar; Member, Phi Gamma Delta; Mason, Elks, Odd Fellows. Hon. LHD Kansas State, 1968; Hon. LLD Emporia Coll., 1969. Distinguished Citizenship Award: Washburn Univ., 1967; Baker Univ., 1975. *Recreations:* horseback riding, fishing, bridge. *Address:* PO Box 1280, Topeka, Kansas 66601, USA; Prospect Hills, Topeka, Kansas 66606, USA. *T:* 233-4136.

LANDON, Howard Chandler Robbins; author and music historian; *b* 6 March 1926; *s* of late William Grinnell Landon and Dorothea LeBaron Robbins; *m* 1957, Else Radant. *Educ:* Aiken Preparatory Sch.; Lenox Sch.; Swarthmore Coll.; Boston Univ., USA (BMus). European rep. of Intercollegiate Broadcasting System, 1947; founded Haydn Soc. (which recorded and printed music of Joseph Haydn), 1949; became a Special Correspondent of The Times, 1957 and contrib. to that newspaper until 1961. Visiting Prof., Queen's Coll., NYC, 1969; Regents Prof. of Music, Univ. of California (Davis), 1970, 1975, 1979; John Bird Prof. of Music, UC Cardiff, 1978-; Christian Johnson Prof. of Music, Middlebury Coll., Vermont, USA, 1980-. Hon. Professorial Fellow, University Coll., Cardiff, 1971-79; Hon. Fellow, Lady Margaret Hall, Oxford, 1979-. Hon. DMus: Boston Univ., 1969; Queen's Univ., Belfast, 1974; Bristol, 1982. Verdienstkreuz für Kunst und Wissenschaft from Austrian Govt, 1972. *Publications:* The Symphonies of Joseph Haydn, 1955 (London); The Mozart Companion (co-ed with Donald Mitchell), 1956 (London); The Collected Correspondence and London Notebooks of Joseph Haydn, 1959 (London); Essays on Eighteenth-Century Music, 1969 (London); Ludwig van Beethoven: a documentary study, 1970 (London); critical edn of the 107 Haydn Symphonies, (completed) 1968; five-vol. biog. of Haydn: vol. 3, Haydn in England, 1976; vol. 4, Haydn: The Years of The Creation, 1977; vol. 5, Haydn: The Late Years, 1977; vol. 1, Haydn: The Early Years, and vol. 2, Haydn in Eszterhaza, 1978-80; Haydn: a documentary study, 1981; The Masons Reveal'd: or Crowned Hope under Scrutiny, 1982; scholarly edns of eighteenth-century music (various European publishing houses). *Recreations:* swimming, cooking, walking. *Address:* Anton Frankgasse 3, Vienna 1180, Austria. *T:* 314205; Hirschbach 114 (Vitis), 3942 Austria. *T:* 02854/404; Castle House, 48 Bridge Street, Chepstow, Monmouthshire.

LANDRETH, Rev. Canon Derek; TD 1963; Priest-in-Charge of Icklesham, Diocese of Chichester, since 1982; Chaplain to the Queen, since 1980; *b* 7 June 1920; *s* of Rev. Norman Landreth and Muriel Landreth; *m* 1943, Myra Joan Brown; one *s* three *d*. *Educ:* Kingswood School, Bath; King's College, Cambridge (MA); Bishops' College, Cheshunt. Commissioned, Royal Artillery, 1942-46 (service India and Burma); CF (TA), 1951-67, (TAVR) 1967-70; Asst Curate, St George, Camberwell, 1948-53; Vicar, St Mark, Battersea Rise, 1953-59; Deputy Chaplain, HM Prison, Wandsworth, 1954-59; Vicar of Richmond, Surrey, and Chaplain, Star and Garter Home for Disabled Soldiers, Sailors and Airmen, 1959-70; Rector of Sanderstead, Surrey, 1970-77; Hon. Chaplain to Bishop of Southwark, 1962-80; Hon. Canon of Southwark Cathedral, 1968-77; Canon Residentiary and Librarian, Southwark Cathedral, 1977-82; Canon Emeritus, 1982-. Proctor in Convocation, 1980-. Indep. Mem., Richmond Borough Council, 1961-65. *Recreations:* gardening, fishing. *Address:* Icklesham Vicarage, Winchelsea, East Sussex TN36 6BH. *T:* Icklesham 207.

LANE, family name of **Baron Lane.**

LANE, Baron *cr* 1979 (Life Peer), of St Ippollitts; **Geoffrey Dawson Lane;** PC 1974; Kt 1966; AFC 1943; Lord Chief Justice of England, since 1980; *b* 17 July 1918; *s* of late Percy Albert Lane, Lincoln; *m* 1944, Jan, *d* of Donald Macdonald; one *s*. *Educ:* Shrewsbury; Trinity Coll., Cambridge (Hon. Fellow 1981). Served in RAF, 1939-45; Sqdn-Leader, 1942. Called to Bar, Gray's Inn, 1946; Bencher 1966. QC 1962. Dep. Chm., Beds. QS, 1960-66; Recorder of Bedford, 1963-66; a Judge of the High Court of Justice, Queen's Bench Div., 1966-74; a Lord Justice of Appeal, 1974-79; a Lord of Appeal in Ordinary, 1979-80. Mem., Parole Board, 1970-72 (Vice-Chm., 1972). Hon. Bencher, Inner Temple, 1980. *Address:* Royal Courts of Justice, Strand, WC2.

LANE, Dr Anthony John, FRCP, FFCM; Regional Medical Officer, North Western Regional Health Authority, since 1974; *b* 6 Feb. 1926; *s* of John Gill Lane and Marian (*née* Brumfield); *m* 1948, Hannah Holečkova; one *s* two *d*. *Educ:* St Christopher's Sch., Letchworth; Emmanuel Coll., Cambridge. MA,MB,BChir. House posts in surgery, medicine, obstetrics and paediatrics, 1949-51; MO with Methodist Missionary Soc., Andhra State, India, 1951-57; Registrar: Tropical Diseases, UCH, 1958; Gen. Med., St James' Hosp., Balham, 1958-61; Infectious Diseases, Western Hosp., Fulham, 1961-63; MO (Trainee), Leeds RHB, 1963-64; Asst Sen. MO, Leeds RHB, 1964-66; Principal Asst Sen. MO, Leeds RHB, 1966-70; Dep. Sen. Admin. MO, SW Metrop. RHB, 1970-71; Sen. Admin. MO, Manchester RHB, 1971-74. *Publications:* contrib. Positions, Movements and Directions in Health Services Research, 1974; contrib. Proc. Royal Soc. Med. *Recreations:* music, competitive indoor games, walking, gardening. *Address:* 4 Queens Road, Wilmslow, Cheshire, SK9 5HS. *T:* (office) 061-236 9456.

LANE, Anthony John; Under Secretary, Department of Trade, and Head of Shipping Policy Division, since 1980; *b* 30 May 1939; *s* of Eric Marshall Lane and Phyllis Mary Lane; *m* 1967, Judith Sheila (*née* Dodson); two *s* one *d*. *Educ:* Caterham Sch.; Balliol Coll., Oxford (BA PPE, MA). Investment Analyst, Joseph Sebag & Co., 1964-65; Asst Principal, Min. of Technology, 1965; Private Sec. to Parly Sec., 1968-69; Principal, 1969; Private Secretary: to Minister for Aerospace and Shipping, 1973-74; to Sec. of State for Prices and Consumer Protection, 1974-75; Asst Sec., Dept of Prices, 1975, Dept of Trade, 1979. *Recreations:* music, gardens, travel. *Address:* Foxbury, East Grinstead, Sussex RH19 3SS. *T:* East Grinstead 23293.

LANE, Dr Anthony Milner, FRS 1975; Deputy Chief Scientific Officer, Atomic Energy Research Establishment, Harwell, since 1976; *b* 27 July 1928; *s* of Herbert William Lane and Doris Ruby Lane (*née* Milner); *m* 1952, Anne Sophie Zissman (*d* 1980); two *s* one *d*. *Educ:* Trowbridge Boys' High Sch.; Selwyn Coll., Cambridge. BA Maths, PhD Theoretical Physics. Joined Harwell, 1953. *Publications:* Nuclear Theory, 1963; numerous research articles in Review of Modern Physics, Phys. Review, Nuclear Physics, etc. *Recreations:* gardening, bird-watching. *Address:* Nayles Bridge Cottage, Church Road, Blewbury, Didcot, Oxon OX11 9PY. *T:* Blewbury 850416.

LANE, David Neil; HM Diplomatic Service; High Commissioner in Trinidad and Tobago, since 1980; *b* 16 April 1928; *er s* of late Clive and Hilda Lane, Bath; *m* 1968, Sara, *d* of Cecil Nurcombe, MC; two *d*. *Educ:* Abbotsholme Sch.; Merton Coll., Oxford. Army, 1946-48; Foreign (later Foreign and Commonwealth) Office: 1951-53, 1955-58, 1963-68, 1972-74; British Embassy, Oslo, 1953-55; Ankara, 1959-61, 1975-78; Conakry, 1961-63; UK Mission to the United Nations, New York, 1968-72, 1979; Pres., UN Trusteeship Council, 1971-72; UK Delegate, Internat. Exhibns Bureau, 1973-74. *Recreations:* music, walking. *Address:* British High Commission, Port of Spain, Trinidad. *T:* 62-52861/6. *Club:* Travellers'.

LANE, Prof. David Stuart, PhD, DPhil; Professor of Sociology, University of Birmingham, since 1981; *b* Monmouthshire (now Gwent), 24 April 1933; *s* of Reginald and Mary Lane; *m* 1962, Christel Noritzsch; one *s* one *d*. *Educ:* Univ. of Birmingham (BSocSc); Univ. of Oxford (DPhil). PhD Cantab. Formerly engrg trainee, local authority employee, sch. teacher; univ. teacher, Birmingham, Essex and Cambridge Univs. *Publications:* Roots of Russian Communism, 1969, 2nd edn 1975; Politics and Society in the USSR, 1970, 2nd edn 1978; The End of Inequality?, 1971; (with G. Kolankiewicz) Social Groups in Polish Society, 1973; The Socialist Industrialist State, 1976; (with F. O'Dell) The Soviet Industrial Worker, 1978; The Work Needs of Mentally Handicapped Adults, 1980; Leninism: a sociological interpretation, 1981; The End of Social Inequality?: class status and power under state socialism, 1982. *Recreations:* soccer, squash, gardening, films, TV; active in numerous voluntary associations. *Address:* Department of Sociology, University of Birmingham, Birmingham B15 2TT. *T:* 021-472 1301.

LANE, David William Stennis Stuart; Chairman, National Association of Youth Clubs, since 1982; *b* 24 Sept. 1922; *s* of Hubert Samuel Lane, MC; *m* 1955, Lesley Anne Mary Clauson; two *s*. *Educ:* Eton; Trinity Coll., Cambridge; Yale Univ. Served War of 1939-45 (Navy). British Iron and Steel Federation, 1948 (Sec., 1956); Shell International Petroleum Co., 1959-67. Called to the Bar, Middle Temple, 1955. Chm., N Kensington Cons. Assoc., 1961-62. Contested (C) Lambeth (Vauxhall), 1964, Cambridge, 1966; MP (C) Cambridge, Sept. 1967-Nov. 1976; PPS to Sec. of State for Employment, 1970-72; Parly Under-Sec. of State, Home Office, 1972-74; Chm., Commn for Racial Equality, 1977-82. *Recreations:* walking, golf, cricket. *Address:* 5 Spinney Drive, Great Shelford, Cambridge. *Club:* MCC.

LANE, Dame Elizabeth (Kathleen), DBE 1965; a Judge of the High Court, Family Division (formerly Probate, Divorce and Admiralty Division), 1965-79; *b* 9 Aug. 1905; *o d* of late Edward Alexander Coulborn and late Kate May Coulborn (*née* Wilkinson); *m* 1926, Henry Jerrold Randall Lane, CBE (*d* 1975); one *s* decd. *Educ:* Malvern Girls Coll. and privately. Barrister, Inner Temple, 1940; Master of the Bench, 1965. Mem. of Home Office Committee on Depositions in Criminal Cases, 1948. An Asst Recorder of Birmingham, 1953-61; Chm. of Birmingham Region Mental Health Review Tribunal, 1960-62; Recorder of Derby, 1961-62; Commissioner of the Crown Court at Manchester, 1961-62; Judge of County Courts, 1962-65; Acting Dep. Chm., London Sessions, 1965. Chm., Cttee on the Working of the Abortion Act,

1971-73. *Recreations:* gardening, needlework. *Address:* Hillcrest, 60 Chilbolton Avenue, Winchester, Hants SO22 5HQ.

LANE, Frank Laurence, CBE 1961; Chairman, Elder Dempster Lines Ltd, 1963-72; *b* 1912; *s* of late Herbert Allardyce Lane, CIE, and late Hilda Gladys Duckle Lane (*née* Wraith); *m* 1938, Gwendolin Elizabeth Peterkin; one *s. Educ:* Wellington Coll., Berks; New Coll., Oxford. Mansfield & Co. Ltd, Singapore and Penang, 1934-42; BOAC, UK and USA, 1942-45; Mansfield & Co. Ltd, Singapore, 1945-61; Elder Dempster Lines Ltd, Liverpool, 1962-72. *Recreations:* golf, fishing. *Address:* Amberwood, Bisterne Close, Burley, Ringwood, Hampshire. *T:* Burley 3249.

LANE, John, CB 1981; Deputy Director, Central Statistical Office, 1978-81; retired; *b* 23 Oct. 1924; *e s* of R. J. I. and M. E. L. Lane; *m* 1954, Ruth Ann Crocker; one *s. Educ:* John Lyon Sch., Harrow; HMS Conway; Univ. of London (BSc(Econ)). Merchant Navy, 1943-47. Joined Ministry of Transport, 1950; Statistician, 1954; Asst Sec. to Council on Prices, Productivity and Incomes, 1959-61; Principal, MoT, 1962; Asst Sec., 1966; Under-Sec., DoE, 1972; Regional Dir, SE Region and Chm., SE Economic Planning Bd, 1973-76; Under Sec., Dept of Transport, 1976-78. *Address:* Broomfields, Lamberhurst, Kent. *T:* Lamberhurst 890427.

LANE, Kenneth Frederick; Consultant and Visiting Professor, Royal School of Mines; *b* 22 March 1928; British; *m* 1950, Kathleen Richards; one *s* two *d. Educ:* Emanuel Coll., Cambridge. Degree in Maths. Steel Industry in Sheffield, 1951-59; North America, 1959-61; Rio Tinto-Zinc Corp., 1961-65; Man. Dir, RTZ Consultants Ltd, 1965-70; Dir, RTZ Corp., 1970-75. Advisor on Civil Service Reform, 1970-74. *Recreations:* boat building, sailing. *Address:* Down House, Lezant, Launceston, Cornwall PL15 9PR. *T:* Stoke Climsland 70495.

LANE, Margaret; novelist, biographer, journalist; *b* 23 June 1907; *o d* of late H. G. Lane; *m* 1st, 1934, Bryan (marr. diss. 1939), *e s* of Edgar Wallace; 2nd, 1944, 15th Earl of Huntingdon, *qv* ; two *d. Educ:* St Stephen's, Folkestone; St Hugh's Coll., Oxford (MA). Reporter, Daily Express, 1928-31; special correspondent: in New York and for International News Service, USA, 1931-32: for Daily Mail, 1932-38. President: Women's Press Club, 1958-60; Dickens Fellowship, 1959-61, 1970; Johnson Soc., 1971; Brontë Soc., 1975-79. *Publications:* Faith, Hope, No Charity (awarded Prix Femina-Vie Heureuse), 1935; At Last the Island, 1937; Edgar Wallace: The Biography of a Phenomenon, 1938; Walk Into My Parlour, 1941; Where Helen Lies, 1944; The Tale of Beatrix Potter, 1946; The Brontë Story, 1953; A Crown of Convolvulus, 1954; A Calabash of Diamonds, 1961; Life With Ionides, 1963; A Night at Sea, 1964; A Smell of Burning, 1965; Purely for Pleasure, 1966; The Day of the Feast, 1968; Frances Wright and the Great Experiment, 1971; Samuel Johnson and his World, 1975; Flora Thompson, 1976; The Magic Years of Beatrix Potter, 1978; (ed) Flora Thompson's A Country Calendar and other writings, 1979; The Drug-Like Brontë Dream, 1980. *Address:* Blackbridge House, Beaulieu, Hants.

LANE, Hon. Mrs Miriam; *see* Rothschild, Hon. M. L.

LANE, Ronald Anthony Stuart, CMG 1977; MC 1945; Vice Chairman, Standard Chartered Bank Ltd, since 1977; Deputy Chairman, Chartered Trust Ltd, since 1979; *b* 8 Dec. 1917; 2nd *s* of late Wilmot Ernest Lane and F. E. Lane (*née* Blakey); *m* 1948, Anne Brenda, 2nd *d* of E. Walsh; one *s* one *d. Educ:* Lancing College. FIB. Served War, 1940-45, 7th Light Cavalry, Indian Army, India and Burma (Major). Joined Chartered Bank of India, Australia & China, 1937; served in Far East, 1939-60; Gen. Manager, 1961, Chief Gen. Manager, 1972, Man. Dir, 1973-77, Standard Chartered Bank Ltd. Mem., Export Guarantees Adv. Council, 1973-78 (Dep. Chm., 1977-78). *Recreations:* sailing, gardening. *Address:* West Hold, By the Church, West Mersea, Essex CO5 8QD. *T:* West Mersea 2563. *Clubs:* East India, MCC; West Mersea Yacht.

LANE, Prof. Ronald Epey, CBE 1957; Emeritus Nuffield Professor of Occupational Health, University of Manchester (Professor, 1945-65); *b* 2 July 1897; *s* of E. E. Lane; *m* 1924, Winifred E. Tickner (*d* 1981); one *s* (one *d* decd); *m* 1982, Ida, *widow* of Arnold Bailey. *Educ:* Simon Langton Sch. Canterbury; Guy's Hospital. Served European War, RFC, 1915-19. Guy's Hospital, 1919-24, qualified, 1923; General Medical practice, 1925-27; MRCP, 1925. Medical Officer, Chloride Elec. Storage Co. Ltd, 1928; Physician, Salford Royal Hospital, 1935; FRCP, 1938; Milroy Lecturer (Royal College of Physicians), 1947, McKenzie Lecturer, 1950. Mem. of various Govt Advisory Cttees. *Publications:* original papers on Lead Poisoning, Medical Education, Occupational Health and Universities, in Lancet, BMJ, Brit. Jl of Industrial Med., Jl of Industrial Hygiene and Toxicology, etc. *Recreations:* golf, fishing. *Address:* 3 Daylesford Road, Cheadle, Cheshire. *T:* 061-428 5738. *Club:* Athenæum.

LANE, Rear-Adm. Walter Frederick Boyt, CB 1960; DSC 1941; FIMechE; MIMarE; Director of Marine Engineering, Admiralty, 1958-61; *b* 7 Feb. 1909; *s* of W. H. Lane, Freshwater, IoW; *m* 1931, Anne Littlecott; one *s. Educ:* RN Engineering Coll., Devonport. Eng.-in-Chief, Admiralty, Bath, 1957; Rear-Adm., 1957; retired. Formerly Director, Fairfields (Eng.) Co., Glasgow. *Recreations:* tennis, painting. *Address:* Foxleaze, Limpley Stoke, Wilts. *T:* Limpley Stoke 3225.

LANE-FOX, Baroness *cr* 1981 (Life Peer), of Bramham in the County of West Yorkshire; **Felicity Lane-Fox,** OBE 1976; Vice-President, Royal Association for Disability and Rehabilitation, since 1963; Chairman of Patients' Association, Phipps Respiratory Unit, St Thomas' Hospital, since 1979; *b* 22 June 1918; *d* of late Edward Lane Fox and of Enid Maud Lane Fox. Acting Chief Billeting Officer, Wetherby RDC, 1939-42; Secretary, Marguerite Hepton Memorial Orthopaedic Hosp., Thorp Arch, Yorks, 1942-46; Jt Sec., Bramham Moor Hunt, 1946-50; Chm., Barkston Ash Women's Conservative Assoc., 1946-50; Assistant at Conservative Research Dept, 1960-65; Mem. Nat. Union Exec., Cons. and Unionist Assoc., 1963-66. Mem., Nuffield Orthopaedic Centre House Cttee, Oxford, 1958-66; Chm., Nat. Fund-Raising Cttee of Disablement Income Group, 1971-73; Vice-Pres., Yorks Assoc. for Disabled, 1958-80; Patron, Handicapped Adventure Playground Assoc., 1978-. Chm., IBA's London Local Radio Adv. Cttee, 1976-80. *Recreations:* drama, documentaries and sport on television, radio; watching racing, cricket and tennis. *Address:* 30 Marlborough Court, Pembroke Road, W8 6DE. *T:* 01-602 3734.

LANE FOX, Col Francis Gordon Ward; Vice-Lieutenant of West Riding of Yorkshire, 1968-74; Royal Horse Guards, 1919-46, retired; *b* 14 Oct. 1899; *s* of late C. Ward Jackson; assumed surname of Lane Fox in lieu of that of Jackson, by deed poll, 1937; *m* 1929, Hon. Marcia Agnes Mary (*d* 1980), *e d* of 1st and last Baron Bingley, PC (*d* 1947); two *s* one *d. Educ:* Eton; RMC, Sandhurst. West Riding of Yorkshire: JP 1948; DL 1952; CC 1949, CA 1955. KStJ 1965. Officer Order of the Crown, with Palm, and Croix de Guerre, with Palm (Belgium), 1946. *Address:* The Little House, Bramham Park, Wetherby, W Yorks LS23 6LS. *T:* Boston Spa 843220. *Clubs:* Cavalry and Guards; Yorkshire (York).

LANE FOX, Robin James, FRSL; Fellow, New College, Oxford, since 1977; University Lecturer in Ancient History, Oxford, since 1977; *b* 5 Oct. 1946; *s* of James Henry Lane Fox and Anne (*n* 1ee Loyd); *m* 1970, Louisa Caroline Mary, *d* of Charles and Lady Katherine Farrell; one *s* one *d. Educ:* Eton; Magdalen Coll., Oxford (Craven and de Paravicini scholarships, 1966; Passmore Edwards and Chancellors' Latin Verse Prize, 1968). FRSL 1974. Fellow by examination, Magdalen Coll., Oxford, 1970-73; Lectr in Classical Lang. and Lit., 1973-76, Res. Fellow, Classical and Islamic Studies, 1976-77, Worcester Coll., Oxford. Weekly gardening correspondent, Financial Times, 1970-. *Publications:* Alexander the Great, 1973, 3rd edn 1978 (James Tait Black, Duff Cooper, W. H. Heinemann Awards, 1973-74); Variations on a Garden, 1974; Search for Alexander, 1980; Better Gardening, 1982. *Recreations:* gardening, hunting, poetry, rough travel. *Address:* Old Manor House, Beckley, Oxon. *T:* Stanton St John 251. *Club:* Beefsteak.

LANESBOROUGH, 9th Earl of *cr* 1756; **Denis Anthony Brian Butler;** DL; Baron of Newtown-Butler, 1715; Viscount Lanesborough, 1728; Major, Leicestershire Yeomanry (RA); *b* 28 Oct. 1918; *er s* of 8th Earl and Grace Lilian, *d* of late Sir Anthony Abdy, 3rd Bt; *S* father 1950; *m* 1939, Bettyne Ione (marr. diss. 1950), *d* of late Sir Lindsay Everard; one *d* (and one *d* decd). *Educ:* Stowe. Leicestershire Yeomanry; Lieutenant, 1939; Major, RAC, TA (TD), 1945. Member: Nat. Gas Consumers' Council, 1973-78; Trent RHA, 1974-. Chm., Loughborough and District Housing Assoc., 1978-. DL 1962, JP 1967, Leicester. *Heir:* kinsman, Comdr Terence Brinsley John Danvers Butler, RN; *b* 7 March 1913. *Address:* Alton Lodge, Kegworth, Derby. *T:* Kegworth 2243.

LANG, Prof. Andrew Richard, FRS 1975; Professor of Physics, University of Bristol, since 1979; *b* 9 Sept. 1924; *s* of late Ernest F. S. Lang and late Susannah (*née* Gueterbock); unmarried. *Educ:* University College of South-West, Exeter, (BSc Lond. 1944; MSc Lond. 1947); Univ. of Cambridge (PhD 1953). Research Dept, Lever Bros, Port Sunlight, 1945-47; Research Asst, Cavendish Laboratory, 1947-48; North American Philips, Irvington-on-Hudson, NY, 1952-53; Instructor, Harvard Univ., 1953-54; Asst Professor, Harvard Univ., 1954-59; Lectr in Physics, 1960-66, Reader, 1966-79, Univ. of Bristol. MInstP, Mem. Geol Assoc.; Mem. Soc. Sigma Xi. Charles Vernon Boys Prize, Inst. of Physics, 1964. *Publications:* contribs to learned jls. *Address:* 1B Elton Road, Bristol BS8 1SJ. *T:* Bristol 739784.

LANG, Prof. David Marshall, MA, PhD, DLit, LittD; Professor of Caucasian Studies in the University of London since 1964; Warden of Connaught Hall, University of London, since 1955; *b* 6 May 1924; *s* of Dr David Marshall Lang, Medical Practitioner, Bath, and Mrs May Rena Lang; *m* 1956, Janet, *d* of late George Sugden, Leeds; one *s* two *d* (and one *s* decd). *Educ:* Monkton Combe Sch.; St John's Coll., Cambridge. Actg Vice-Consul, Tabriz, 1944-46; 3rd Sec., British Embassy, Tehran, 1946; Research Fellow, St John's Coll., Cambridge, 1946-52; Lectr in Georgian, School of Oriental and African Studies, University of London, 1949-58; Senior Fellow, Russian Inst., Columbia Univ., 1952-53; Reader in Caucasian Studies, University of London, 1958-64; Vis. Prof. of Caucasian Languages, University of California, Los Angeles, 1964-65. Hon. Sec., Royal Asiatic Society, 1962-64; Vice-Pres., Holborn Soc., 1973-; Pres., Georgian Cultural Circle, 1974-. Hon. Dr Philological Sciences, Tbilisi State Univ.; Prix Brémond, 1971. *Publications:* Studies in the Numismatic History of Georgia in Transcaucasia, 1955; Lives and Legends of the Georgian Saints, 1956; The Wisdom of Balahvar, 1957; The Last Years of the Georgian Monarchy, 1957; The First Russian Radical: Alexander Radishchev, 1959; A Modern History of Georgia, 1962; Catalogue of the Georgian Books in the British Museum, 1962; The Georgians, 1966; The Balavariani, 1966; Armenia, Cradle of Civilization, 1970, 3rd edn 1980; (with

C. Burney) The Peoples of the Hills, 1971; (ed) Guide to Eastern Literatures, 1971; The Bulgarians, 1976; (with C. Walker) The Armenians (Minority Rights Gp report), 1976; The Armenians: a people in exile, 1981; articles in Bulletin of School of Oriental and African Studies, Encyclopædia Britannica, etc. *Recreations:* music, foreign travel. *Address:* (office) School of Oriental and African Studies, University of London, WC1. *T:* (home) 01-387 6181. *Club:* Leander.

LANG, Lt-Gen. Sir Derek (Boileau), KCB 1967 (CB 1964); DSO 1944; MC 1941; DL; Associate Consultant, PA Management Consultants Ltd, since 1975; *b* 7 Oct. 1913; *s* of Lt-Col C. F. G. Lang and Mrs Lumsden Lang (*née* M. J. L. Forbes); *m* 1st, 1942, M. Massy Dawson (*d* 1953); one *s* one *d* ; 2nd, 1953, A. L. S. Shields (marr. diss. 1969); 3rd, 1969, Mrs E. H. Balfour (*d* 1982). *Educ:* Wellington Coll.; RMC Sandhurst. Commnd, The Queen's Own Cameron Highlanders, 1933; Adjutant, TA, 1938; Chief Instructor, Sch. of Infantry, 1943–44; Comdr, 5th Camerons, 1944–45; Comdt, Sch. of Infantry, BAOR, 1945–46; Directing Staff, Staff Coll., Camberley, 1947–48; Staff, Australia, 1949–51; GSO1, War Office, 1951–53; Chief Instructor, Sch. of Infantry Tactical Wing, 1953–55; AAG, War Office, 1955–57; NDC, 1957–58; Comd Infty Bde (153-TA), 1958–60; Chief of Staff, Scottish Comd, 1960; Gen. Officer Commanding, 51st Highland Div. and District, Perth, 1962–64; Dir of Army Training, 1964–66; GOC-in-C, Scottish Command, 1966–69; Governor of Edinburgh Castle, 1966–69; Sec., Univ. of Stirling, 1970–73; Hon. Col, 153 (Highland) Regt, RCT (Volunteers), T&AVR, 1970–76; Pres., Army Cadet Force Assoc. (Scotland). DL Edinburgh, 1978. OStJ. *Publication:* Return to St Valéry, 1974. *Recreations:* golf, fishing. *Address:* 4 Belford Place, Edinburgh EH4 3DH. *T:* 031-332 2364. *Clubs:* Army and Navy; New (Edinburgh); Senior Golfers' Society; Hon. Co. of Edinburgh Golfers (Muirfield).
See also J. M. Hunt.

LANG, Henry George, CB 1977; university teacher and company director, since 1977; *b* 3 March 1919; *s* of Robert and Anna Lang; *m* 1942, Octavia Gwendolin (*née* Turton); one *s* four *d.* *Educ:* Victoria Univ., Wellington. DPA, BA, BCom. Private enterprise, 1939–44; RNZAF, 1944–46. NZ government service: various economic appointments, 1946–55; Economic Advisor to High Comr in London, 1955–58; Treasury, 1958–77, Sec. to Treasury, 1968–77. Vis. Prof. of Economics, Victoria Univ. of Wellington, 1977–. *Publications:* (with J. V. T. Baker) Economic Policy and National Income, in, NZ Official Year Book, 1950; articles in learned journals. *Recreations:* skiing, swimming, reading. *Address:* 81 Hatton Street, Wellington, NZ. *T:* 768 788. *Clubs:* Wellington, Commonwealth (both Wellington, NZ).

LANG, Hugh Montgomerie, CBE 1978; Chairman: P-E International Ltd, since 1980; Redman Heenan International, since 1982 (Director, since 1981); *b* Glasgow, 7 Nov. 1932; *s* of John Montgomerie Lang and Janet Allan (*née* Smillie); *m* 1st, 1959, Marjorie Jean Armour (marr. diss. 1981); one *s* one *d* ; 2nd, 1981, Susan Lynn Hartley (*née* Russell). *Educ:* Shawlands Acad., Glasgow; Glasgow Univ. (BSc). ARCST 1953; CEng 1967; FIProdE 1976; FIMC 1970; CBIM 1980. Officer, REME, 1953–55 (National Service). Colvilles Ltd, 1955–56; Glacier Metal Co. Ltd, 1956–60; L. Sterne & Co. Ltd, 1960–61; P-E Consulting Group, 1961–: Manager for ME, 1965–68; Scottish Reg. Manager, 1968–72; Dir, 1972–; Man. Dir., 1974–77; Chief Exec., 1977–. Dir, Fairey Holdings Ltd, 1978–. Chairman: Food, Drink and Packaging Machinery Sector Working Party, 1976-81; Manufg Adv. Service Steering Cttee, 1982– (Mem., 1978–); Engineering Products Awards Panel, Design Council, 1982–; Member: Business Educn Council, 1980-81; CBI Industrial Policy Cttee, 1980–. *Recreations:* gardening, golf, reading. *Address:* Mount Hill Farm, Gerrards Cross, Bucks SL9 8SU. *T:* Fulmer 2406. *Clubs:* Caledonian; Denham Golf.

LANG, Ian Bruce; MP (C) Galloway, since 1979; an Assistant Government Whip, since 1981; *b* 27 June 1940; *y s* of James Fulton Lang, DSC, and Maude Margaret (*née* Stewart); *m* 1971, Sandra Caroline, *e d* of John Alastair Montgomerie, DSC; two *d. Educ:* Lathallan Sch., Kincardineshire; Rugby Sch.; Sidney Sussex Coll., Cambridge (BA 1962). Director: Hutchison & Craft Ltd, 1975-81; Hutchison & Craft (Underwriting Agents) Ltd, Lloyd's, 1976-81; P. MacCallum & Sons Ltd, 1976-81; Rose, Thomson, Young & Co. (Glasgow) Ltd, 1966-75. Member, Queen's Body Guard for Scotland (Royal Company of Archers), 1974–. Dir, Glasgow Chamber of Commerce, 1978-81; Trustee: Savings Bank of Glasgow, 1969-74; West of Scotland Trustee Savings Bank, 1974–. Contested (C): Central Ayrshire, 1970; Glasgow Pollok, Feb. 1974. Mem., Select Cttee on Scottish Affairs, 1979-81. Pres., Scottish Young Conservatives, 1982. OStJ 1974. *Recreations:* skiing, sailing, shooting, music. *Address:* Kersland, Monkton, Ayrshire KA9 2QU. *T:* Symington 830231. *Clubs:* Western (Glasgow); Prestwick Golf.

LANG, Sir John (Gerald), GCB 1954 (KCB 1947; CB 1946); *b* 20 Dec. 1896; *s* of late George and Rebecca Lang, Woolwich; *m* 1st, 1922, Emilie J. (*d* 1963), *d* of late Henry S. Goddard, Eastbourne; one *d* ; 2nd, 1970, Kathleen Winifred, widow of C. G. E. Edmeades, and *d* of late Henry S. Goddard. *Educ:* Aske's Haberdashers' Sch., Hatcham. Second Div. Clerk, Admiralty, 1914; Royal Marine Artillery, Lt, 1917-18; Returned to Admiralty: Asst Principal, 1930; Principal, 1935; Asst Sec., 1939; Principal Asst Sec., 1942; Under-Sec., 1946; Sec., Admiralty, SW1, 1947-61. Chm. Bettix Ltd, 1961-70. Principal Adviser on Sport to the Government, 1964-71, and Dep. Chm., Sports Council, 1965-71. Mem. Bd of Govs, Bethlem Royal Hosp. and Maudsley Hosp.,

1961-70; Treasurer, 1969-82, Hon. Vice Pres., 1977, RINA; Vice-Pres., Royal Naval Assoc. *Recreation:* gardening. *Address:* 2 Egmont Park House, Walton-on-the-Hill, Tadworth, Surrey. *T:* Tadworth 2200. *Club:* Samuel Pepys (Pres. 1965).

LANG, Very Rev. John Harley; Dean of Lichfield, since 1980; Chaplain to the Queen, 1976-80; *b* 27 Oct. 1927; *e s* of Frederick Henry Lang and Eileen Annie Lang (*née* Harley); *m* 1972, Frances Rosemary Widdowson; three *d. Educ:* Merchant Taylors' Sch.; King's Coll., London. MA Cantab, BD London, LRAM. Subaltern, XII Royal Lancers, 1951-52; Asst Curate, St Mary's Portsea, 1952-57; Priest Vicar, Southwark Cathedral, 1957-60; Chaplain, Emmanuel Coll., Cambridge, 1960-64; Asst Head of Religious Broadcasting, BBC, 1964-67; Head of Religious Programmes, Radio, 1967-71; Head of Religious Broadcasting, BBC, 1971-80. *Recreation:* music. *Address:* The Deanery, Lichfield, Staffs WS13 7LD.

LANG, John Russell, CBE 1963; Deputy Chairman, The Weir Group Ltd, 1968-73; *b* 8 Jan. 1902; *s* of Chas Russell Lang, CBE; *m* 1st, 1934, Jenny (*d* 1970), *d* of Sir John Train, MP, of Cathkin, Lanarkshire; four *d* (one *s* decd); 2nd, 1973, Gay Mackie (*d* 1979); 3rd, 1981, Kay, widow of Norman Macfie. *Educ:* Loretto Sch., Musselburgh; France and USA. Dir, G. & J. Weir Ltd, 1930-67. Chairman, Weir Housing Corp., 1946-66. President, Scottish Engineering Employers' Association, 1963-64. Mem., Toothill Cttee and EDC for Mec. Eng. Lt-Col 277 Field Regt, RA (TA), 1937. *Recreations:* hunting, shooting, golf. *Address:* The White House of Milliken, Brookfield, Renfrewshire PA5 8UN. *T:* Johnstone 20898. *Clubs:* Royal Scottish Automobile; Prestwick Golf.

LANG, Rear-Adm. William Duncan, CB 1981; Assistant Secretary, Ministry of Defence, since 1981; *b* 1 April 1925; *s* of James Hardie Lang and Elizabeth Foggo Paterson Lang (*née* Storie); *m* 1947, Joyce Rose Weeks; one *s* one *d. Educ:* Edinburgh Acad. FRAeS. Entered Royal Navy, 1943; trained as Pilot; served in 800, 816 and 825 Sqdns and as Flying Instr and Test Pilot; comd 802 Sqdn, 1958-59; Commander (Air): RNAS Culdrose, 1962-63; HMS Eagle, 1964-65; Fleet Aviation Officer, Far East Fleet, 1966-68; Captain 1969; comd RNAS Lossiemouth, 1970-72; Dep. Comdt, Jt Warfare Estabt, 1973-74; COS to Flag Officer, Naval Air Comd, 1975-76; Mil. Dep. to Hd of Defence Sales, 1978-81. Naval ADC to the Queen, 1978; Rear-Adm. 1978. *Recreation:* golf. *Address:* c/o Midland Bank, 19 High Street, Haslemere, Surrey GU27 2HQ. *Club:* Army and Navy.

LANG, William Marshall F.; see Farquharson-Lang.

LANGDALE, Simon John Bartholomew; Headmaster, Shrewsbury School, since 1981; *b* 26 Jan. 1937; *s* of G. R. Langdale and H. J. Langdale (*née* Bartholomew); *m* 1962, Diana Marjory Hall; two *s* one *d. Educ:* Tonbridge Sch.; St Catharine's Coll., Cambridge. Taught at Radley Coll., 1959-73 (Housemaster, 1968-73); Headmaster, Eastbourne Coll., 1973-81. *Recreations:* cricket, Rugby fives, real tennis, china fairings. *Address:* Headmaster's House, Shrewsbury School, Shrewsbury, Shropshire SY3 7BA. *Clubs:* Hawks (Cambridge); Free Foresters, Jesters.

LANGDON, Alfred Gordon, CMG 1967; CVO 1966; QPM 1961; Chairman, Security Specialists Ltd, Kingston, Jamaica; *b* 3 July 1915; *s* of Wilfred James Langdon and Norah (*née* Nixon); *m* 1947, Phyllis Elizabeth Pengelley; one *s* two *d. Educ:* Munro Coll., Jamaica. Berkhampstead Sch., Herts. Bank of Nova Scotia, Kingston, Jamaica, 1933-37; Jamaica Infantry Volunteers, 1937-39; Jamaica Constabulary Force, 1939-70: Asst Comr of Police, 1954-62; Dep. Comr, 1962-64; Comr, 1964-70, retd. Security Advisor, Min. of Home Affairs, Jamaica, 1970-72. *Recreations:* fishing, tennis, swimming. *Address:* 2637 Burntfork Drive, Clearwater, Fla 33519, USA. *Clubs:* Kingston Cricket; Countryside Country (Clearwater).

LANGDON, Anthony James; Assistant Under-Secretary of State, Home Office, since 1977; *b* 5 June 1935; *s* of Dr James Norman Langdon and Maud Winifred Langdon; *m* 1969, Helen Josephine Drabble, *y d* of His Honour J. F. Drabble, *qv* ; one *s* one *d. Educ:* Kingswood Sch., Bath; Christ's Coll., Cambridge. Entered Home Office, 1958; Office of Minister for Science, 1961-63; Treasury, 1967-69; Sec., Royal Commn on Standards of Conduct in Public Life, 1974-76. *Address:* c/o Home Office, SW1.

LANGDON, (Augustus) John; chartered surveyor and land agent; *b* 20 April 1913; *e s* of late Rev. Cecil Langdon, MA and Elizabeth Mercer Langdon, MBE; *m* ; two *d* ; *m* 1949, Doris Edna Clinard; one *s. Educ:* Berkhamsted Sch.; St John's Coll., Cambridge (Nat. Science Tripos; MA). FRICS (Chartered Land Agent); FRSA. Asst to J. Carter Jonas & Sons, Oxford, 1936-37, Partner 1945-48; Suptg Lands Officer, Admty, 1937-45; Regional Land Comr, Min. of Agriculture, 1948-65; Dep. Dir, Agric. Land Service, Min. of Agriculture, 1965-71; Chief Surveyor, Agricultural Develt and Advisory Service, MAFF, 1971-74; with the National Trust in London, 1974-76. Chm., Statutory Cttee on Agricultural Valuation; RICS: Mem., Gen. Council; Mem., Land Agency and Agricultural Divisional Council, 1971-75. *Publications:* contrib. Rural Estate Management (ed R. C. Walmsley), Fream's Elements of Agriculture, professional and agric. jls. *Recreations:* gardening, walking, collecting. *Address:* Thorn Bank, Long Street, Sherborne, Dorset DT9 3BS. *T:* Sherborne 2910. *Club:* United Oxford & Cambridge University.

LANGDON, David, FRSA; Cartoonist and Illustrator; Member of Punch Table; regular contributor to Punch since 1937, to The New Yorker since 1952; Cartoonist to Sunday Mirror, since 1948; *b* 24 Feb. 1914; *er s* of late Bennett and Bess Langdon; *m* 1955, April Sadler-Phillips; two *s* one *d. Educ:* Davenant Gram. Sch., London. Architect's Dept, LCC, 1931-39; Executive Officer, London Rescue Service, 1939-41; served in Royal Air Force, 1941-46; Squadron Leader, 1945. Editor, Royal Air Force Jl, 1945-46. Creator of Billy Brown of London Town for LPTB. Official Artist to Centre International Audio-Visuel d'Etudes et de Recherches, St Ghislain, Belgium. Exhibitions: Oxford, New York, London. *Publications:* Home Front Lines, 1941; All Buttoned Up, 1944; Meet Me Inside, 1946; Slipstream (with R. B. Raymond), 1946; The Way I See It, 1947; Hold Tight There!, 1949; Let's Face It, 1951; Wake Up and Die (with David Clayton), 1952; Look at You, 1952; All in Fun, 1953; Laugh with Me, 1954; More in Fun, 1955; Funnier Still, 1956; A Banger for a Monkey, 1957; Langdon At Large, 1958; I'm Only Joking, 1960; Punch with Wings, 1961; How to Play Golf and Stay Happy, 1964; David Langdon's Casebook, 1969; How To Talk Golf, 1975. *Recreations:* golf, non-League soccer. *Address:* South Copse, Nightingales Lane, Chalfont St Giles, Bucks HP8 4SF. *T:* Chalfont St Giles 2935. *Club:* RAF.

LANGDON, John; see Langdon, A. J.

LANGDON, Michael, CBE 1973; Principal Bass Soloist, Royal Opera House, Covent Garden, since 1951; Director, National Opera Studio, since 1978; *b* 12 Nov. 1920; *s* of Henry Langdon, Wednesfield Road, Wolverhampton; *m* 1947, Vera Duffield, Norwich; two *d. Educ:* Bushbury Hill Sch., Wolverhampton. First Principal Contract, Royal Opera House, Covent Garden, 1951; first Gala Performance, before Queen Elizabeth II (Gloriana), 1953; Grand Inquisitor in Visconti Production of Don Carlos, 1958; debut as Baron Ochs (Rosenkavalier), 1960; first International Engagement (Hamburg), 1961; first Glyndebourne Festival, 1961; since then, has appeared in international performances in Paris, Berlin, Aix-en-Provence, San Francisco and Los Angeles, 1962; Lausanne, Geneva, Vienna and Budapest, 1963; Zürich, New York, 1964; Geneva, Marseilles, 1965; Seattle, Buenos Aires; Houston, 1975; Gala Performances, 1967, 1969. *Recreations:* swimming, walking and Association football (now only as spectator). *Address:* 34 Warnham Court, Grand Avenue, Hove, East Sussex.

LANGDON, Richard Norman Darbey, FCA; Senior Partner, Spicer and Pegler, since 1978 (Managing Partner, 1971-82); *b* 19 June 1919; *s* of Norman Langdon and Dorothy Langdon; *m* 1944, June Dixon; two *s. Educ:* Shrewsbury Sch. Officer, RA, 1939-46. Admitted Mem. Inst. of Chartered Accountants in England and Wales, 1947; joined Spicer and Pegler, 1949, Partner 1953. Dep. Chm., First Nat. Finance Corp. Ltd; Chairman: Finlay Packaging Ltd; Hammond and Champness Ltd. Treasurer, CGLI, 1982-83. Liveryman, Co. of Chartered Accountants of England and Wales. *Recreations:* sailing, gardening, bricklaying. *Address:* Rough Hill House, Munstead, near Godalming, Surrey. *T:* Godalming 21507. *Clubs:* City of London; Old Salopian.

LANGDON-DOWN, Antony Turnbull; Clerk to Merchant Taylors Company, since 1980; *b* 31 Dec. 1922; *s* of Dr Reginald Langdon-Down and Ruth Langdon-Down (née Turnbull); *m* 1954, Jill Elizabeth Style (née Caruth); one *s* one *d. Educ:* Harrow School. Member of Lincoln's Inn, 1940-60, called to the Bar, 1948; enrolled as a solicitor, 1960; practised as solicitor, 1961-80. Pilot, Royal Air Force, 1942-47 (finally Flt Lieut). Master of Merchant Taylors Company, 1979-80. *Recreations:* sailing, tennis, bridge, music, art. *Address:* Tinley Lodge, Shipbourne, Tonbridge, Kent TN11 9QB. *T:* Plaxtol 810720. *Clubs:* Savile, MCC; Bough Beech Sailing, Law Society Yacht.

LANGDON-DOWN, Barbara; see Littlewood, Lady (Barbara).

LANGFORD, 9th Baron, *cr* 1800; **Colonel Geoffrey Alexander Rowley-Conwy,** OBE 1943; DL; RA, retired; Constable of Rhuddlan Castle and Lord of the Manor of Rhuddlan; *b* 8 March 1912; *s* of late Major Geoffrey Seymour Rowley-Conwy (killed in action, Gallipoli, 1915), Bodrhyddan, Flints, and of Bertha Gabrielle Rowley-Conwy, JP (now of Bodrhyddan), *d* of late Lieutenant Alexander Cochran, Royal Navy, Ashkirk, Selkirkshire; *S* kinsman 1953; *m* 1st, 1939, Ruth St John (marr. diss. 1956), *d* of late Albert St John Murphy, The Island House, Little Island, County Cork; 2nd, 1957, Grete (*d* 1973), *d* of late Col E. T. C. von Freiesleben, formerly Chief of the King's Adjutants Staff to the King of Denmark; three *s*; 3rd, 1959, Susan Winifred Denham, *d* of C. C. H. Denham, Chester; one *s* one *d. Educ:* Marlborough; RMA Woolwich. Served War of 1939-45, with RA; Singapore, (POW escaped) and with Indian Mountain Artillery in Burma, 1941-45 (despatches, OBE); Staff Coll., Quetta, 1945; Berlin Airlift, Fassberg, 1948-49; GSOI 42 Inf. Div., TA, 1949-52; Lt-Col 1945; retired 1957; Colonel (Hon.), 1967. DL Clwyd, 1977. *Heir: s* Hon. Owain Grenville Rowley-Conwy, *b* 27 Dec. 1958. *Address:* Bodrhyddan, Rhuddlan, Clwyd. *Club:* Army and Navy.

LANGFORD-HOLT, Sir John (Anthony), Kt 1962; Lieutenant-Commander RN (Retired); MP (C) Shrewsbury, since 1945; *b* 30 June 1916; *s* of late Ernest Langford-Holt; *m* 1953, Flora Evelyn Innes Stuart (marr. diss. 1969); one *s* one *d. Educ:* Shrewsbury Sch. Joined RN and Air Branch (FAA), 1939. Sec. of Conservative Parly Labour Cttee, 1945-50; Chm., Anglo-Austrian Soc., 1960-63, 1971-82; Member: CPA, 1945-; IPU, 1945-, and other Internat. Bodies; Parliamentary and Scientific Cttee, 1945-; Estimates Cttee, 1964-68; Expenditure Cttee, 1977-79. Chm., Select Cttee on Defence, 1979-81. Director: Authority Investments Ltd; Siebe Gorman Holdings Ltd. Freeman and Liveryman of City of London. Grand Decoration of Honour, in Silver with Star (Austria), 1980. *Address:* House of Commons, SW1. *Clubs:* White's, Carlton; Royal Yacht Squadron (Cowes).

LANGHAM, Sir James (Michael), 15th Bt *cr* 1660; TD 1965; *b* 24 May 1932; *s* of Sir John Charles Patrick Langham, 14th Bt, and of Rosamond Christabel (MBE 1969), *d* of late Arthur Rashleigh; *S* father, 1972; *m* 1959, Marion Audrey Eleanor, *d* of O. H. Barratt, Gararagua Estate, Tanzania; two *s* one *d. Educ:* Rossall School, Fleetwood. Served as Captain, North Irish Horse, 1953-67. *Recreations:* shooting, skin-diving. *Heir: s* John Stephen Langham, *b* 14 Dec. 1960. *Address:* Claranagh, Tempo, Co. Fermanagh. *T:* Tempo 247.

LANGHORNE, Richard Tristan Bailey; Fellow and Junior Bursar, St John's College, Cambridge, since 1974; *b* 6 May 1940; *s* of Eadward John Bailey Langhorne and Rosemary Scott-Foster; *m* 1971, Helen Logue, *o d* of William Donaldson, CB and Mary Donaldson; one *s* one *d. Educ:* St Edward's Sch., Oxford; St John's Coll., Cambridge (Exhibr). BA Hist. Tripos, 1962; Certif. in Hist. Studies, 1963; MA 1965. Tutor in History, Univ. of Exeter, 1963-64; Research Student, St John's Coll., Cambridge, 1964-66; Supervisor of Clare Coll., Cambridge, 1964-66; Lectr in History, 1966-74 and Master of Rutherford Coll., 1971-74, Univ. of Kent at Canterbury; Steward, St John's Coll., Cambridge, 1974-79. *Publications:* chapters in: The Twentieth Century Mind, 1971; British Foreign Policy under Sir Edward Grey, 1977; The Collapse of the Concert of Europe, 1890-1914, 1980; reviews and articles in Historical Jl and History. *Recreations:* music, railways. *Address:* St John's College, Cambridge; 15 Madingley Road, Cambridge. *Club:* Athenæum.

LANGLANDS, Prof. Robert Phelan, FRS 1981; Professor of Mathematics, Institute for Advanced Study, Princeton, New Jersey, since 1972; *b* 6 Oct. 1936; *s* of Robert Langlands and Kathleen Johanna (née Phelan); *m* 1956, Charlotte Lorraine Cheverie; two *s* two *d. Educ:* Univ. of British Columbia (BA 1957, MA 1958); Yale Univ. (PhD 1960). FRSC 1972. Princeton University: Instructor, 1960-61; Lectr, 1961-62; Asst Prof., 1962-64; Associate Prof., 1964-67; Prof., Yale Univ., 1967-72. Associate Prof., Ortadoğu Teknik Universitesi, 1967-68; Gast Prof., Universität Bonn, 1980-81. *Publications:* (with H. Jacquet) Automorphic Forms on GL(2), 1970; Euler Products, 1971; On the Functional Equations satisfied by Eisenstein Series, 1976; Base Change for GL(2), 1980; contrib. Canadian Jl Maths, Proc. Amer. Math. Soc. Symposia, Springer Lecture Notes. *Address:* Institute for Advanced Study, Princeton, New Jersey, USA. *T:* 609-734-8106.

LANGLEY, Brig. Charles Ardagh, CB 1962; CBE 1945; MC 1916 (Bar, 1918); Consultant, Kennedy & Donkin, 1974-81; *b* 23 Aug. 1897; *s* of late John Langley, CBE, Under Sec. of State, Egyptian Govt, 1922; *m* 1st, 1920, V. V. M. Sharp (*d* 1931); one *s* one *d* ; 2nd, 1936, M. J. Scott (*d* 1981); two *d. Educ:* Cheltenham Coll.; Royal Military Academy, Woolwich. Served Great War: commissioned Royal Engineers, 1915; France, 1916, served in field co. and as Adjutant to divisional engineers (MC and Bar; despatches three times). Subseq. took course of higher military engineer training, including one year at Cambridge Univ.; Railway Training Centre, Longmoor, 1922-27; seconded to Great Indian Peninsular Railway, 1927-33, in connection with electrification of Bombay-Poona main line, including construction of power station at Kalyan; Railway Trg Centre, Longmoor, 1933-38; various appointments, including Chief Instructor of Railways, War Office, 1938-40; War of 1939-45: responsible for initial transportation developments in Middle East; later formed Transportation Trg Centre for raising and training Docks and Inland Water Transport troops of Indian Engineers. Dep. Quartermaster-Gen. (Movements and Transportation), Allied Land Forces, South East Asia Command, 1943-45 (despatches, CBE); Commandant, Transportation Trg Centre, Longmoor, 1946. Inspecting Officer of Railways, 1946-58, Chief Inspecting Officer, 1958-63, Min. of Transport. Consultant: British Railways Bd, 1963-66; Transmark, 1972-73; Projects Manager, UKRAS (Consultants) Ltd, 1966-69, Man. Dir, 1969-72. Pres. Junior Institution of Engineers, 1961-62. FCIT. *Publications:* several military text books on transportation. *Recreation:* gardening. *Address:* Beeches, Little Austins, Farnham, Surrey GU9 8JR. *T:* Farnham 723212.

LANGLEY, Maj.-Gen. Henry Desmond Allen, MBE 1967; Commander, British Forces, Cyprus, from April 1983; *b* 16 May 1930; *s* of late Col Henry Langley, OBE, and Winsome Langley; *m* 1950, Felicity Joan, *d* of Lt-Col K. J. P. Oliphant, MC; one *s* one *d. Educ:* Eton; RMA Sandhurst. Commissioned The Life Guards, 1949; Adjt, Household Cavalry Regt, 1953-54; GSO3 HQ 10th Armoured Div., 1956-57; Regtl Adjt, Household Cavalry, 1959-60; psc 1961; GSO2(Ops) HQ Far East Land Forces, 1963-65; Bde Major, Household Bde, 1965-67; Comdg Officer, The Life Guards, 1969-71; Asst Sec., Chiefs of Staff Secretariat, 1971-72; Lt-Col Comdg Household Cavalry and Silver Stick-in-Waiting, 1972-75; Comdr 4th Guards Armoured Bde, 1976-77; RCDS 1978; BGS HQ UK Land Forces, 1979; GOC London District and Maj.-Gen. Comdg Household Div., 1979-83. *Address:* c/o RHQ Household Cavalry, Horse Guards, Whitehall, SW1.

LANGLEY MOORE, D.; see Moore, Doris L.

LANGMAN, Sir John Lyell, 3rd Bt, *cr* 1906; *b* 9 Sept. 1912; *o s* of Sir Archibald Langman, 2nd Bt, CMG, North Cadbury Court, Somerset, and late Eleanor Katherine, 2nd *d* of 1st Baron Lyell; *S* father 1949; *m* 1936, Pamela, *o d* of Capt. Spencer Kennard; two *d* (one *d* decd). *Educ*: Eton; Christ Church, Oxford. *Heir*: none. *Address*: Perrotts Brook Farm, near Cirencester, Glos. *T*: North Cerney 283.

LANGRIDGE, Philip Gordon; concert and opera singer, since 1964; *b* 16 Dec. 1939; *m* 1981, Ann Murray; one *s* two *d* by former marriage. *Educ*: Maidstone Grammar Sch.; Royal Academy of Music, London. ARAM 1977. Glyndebourne Festival début, 1964; BBC Promenade Concerts, 1970–; Edinburgh Fest., 1970–; Netherlands Opera, Scottish Opera and La Scala, annually 1979–: Rake's Progress, Wozzeck, Boris Godunov, Il Sosia; Frankfurt Opera: Castor and Pollux, Rigoletto, Die Entführung; Zurich Opera: Poppea, Lucio Silla; La Fenice: Janacek's Diary, L'Enfance du Christ; Palermo: Otello. Concerts with major, international orchestras and conductors; many first performances of works, some dedicated to and written for him. Has made over 40 records of early, baroque, classical, romantic and modern music. *Recreation*: collecting water colour paintings and Victorian postcards. *Address*: c/o Allied Artists Agency, 42 Montpellier Square, SW7 1JZ. *T*: 01-589 6243.

LANGRIDGE, Richard James; HM Diplomatic Service; Ambassador to Madagascar, since 1979; *b* 29 Oct. 1932; *m* 1965, Jeannine Louise Joosen; one *d*. HM Forces, 1951-53; joined FO 1953; served NY, Leopoldville, Athens, Dakar, Paris and FCO. *Address*: c/o Foreign and Commonwealth Office, SW1.

LANGRISHE, Sir Hercules (Ralph Hume), 7th Bt *cr* 1777; *b* 17 May 1927; *s* of Sir Terence Hume Langrishe, 6th Bt, and Joan Stuart (*d* 1976), *d* of late Major Ralph Stuart Grigg; *S* father, 1973; *m* 1955, Hon. Grania Sybil Enid Wingfield, *d* of 9th Viscount Powerscourt; one *s* three *d*. *Educ*: Summer Fields, St Leonards; Eton. 2nd Lieut, 9th Queen's Royal Lancers, 1947; Lieut, 1948; retd 1953. *Recreations*: shooting, fishing. *Heir*: *s* James Hercules Langrishe, *b* 3 March 1957. *Address*: Ringlestown House, Kilmessan, Co. Meath. *T*: Navan 25243. *Club*: Kildare Street and University (Dublin).

LANGSTONE, Rt. Rev. John Arthur William; *b* 30 Aug. 1913; *s* of Arthur James Langstone and Coullina Cook; *m* 1944, Alice Patricia Whitby; two *s*. *Educ*: Univ. of Toronto (BA); Trinity Coll., Toronto (LTh); Yale Univ. (MDiv). Asst Curate, St John Baptist, Toronto, 1938; Chaplain, Cdn Army, 1943; Exec. Officer, Dio. Toronto, 1947; Rector: Trinity Church, Port Credit, Toronto, 1950; St George's, Edmonton, 1958; St Faith's, Edmonton, 1969; Canon of All Saints' Cathedral, Edmonton, 1963; Archdeacon of Edmonton, 1965; Exec. Archdeacon, 1971; Bishop of Edmonton, 1976-79. Hon. DD Trinity Coll., Toronto, 1977. *Address*: 5112 109 Avenue, Edmonton, Alberta T6A 1S1, Canada. *T*: 465-4111.

LANGTON; *see* Temple-Gore-Langton, family name of Earl Temple of Stowe.

LANGTON, Sir Henry Algernon; *see under* Calley, Sir H. A.

LANGTON, Thomas Bennett, MC 1942; DL; Underwriting Member of Lloyd's, since 1946; *b* 6 March 1917; *s* of Leslie P. Langton and Mildred (*née* Holmwood); *m* 1st, 1943, Lucy Barbara Ettrick Welford (*d* 1978); three *d*; 2nd, 1980, Rosamonde Ann Clarke. *Educ*: Radley; Jesus Coll., Cambridge (MA). Called to Bar, Middle Temple, 1939. Served War of 1939-45: commnd Irish Guards, 1940; Special Boat Section (Middle East), 1942; 1st SAS Regt, 1943-45; Major. Chairman: Leslie Langton Holdings Ltd, 1972-77; Leslie Langton & Sons Ltd, 1953-80; Dir, Devitt Langton & Dawnay Day, 1965-80. Mem. Cttee of Lloyd's, 1968-71, 1973-76; Dep. Chm., of Lloyd's, 1973, 1974. Mem. Council, Radley Coll., 1958-73; Mem. Bd, Royal Merchant Navy Sch., Bearwood, 1975–; Trustee, Brendon Nursing Trust. Mem. Court of Skinners' Co., 1959–. Master 1964-65. DL Hants 1982. *Recreations*: sport, especially rowing (Steward, Henley Royal Regatta). *Address*: 40 St Cross Road, Winchester, Hants. *T*: Winchester 65345.

LA NIECE, Rear-Adm. Peter George, CB 1973; CBE 1967; Director in Astley & Pearce Group of Companies, since 1976; *b* 23 July 1920; *s* of George David Nelson La Niece and late Gwynneth Mary (*née* Morgan); *m* 1948, Evelyn Mary Wrixon Babington (*d* 1982); two *s* one *d*. *Educ*: Whitgift Sch., Croydon. Entered RN, 1937; served War of 1939-45 in battleships, cruisers and destroyers; Gunnery Specialist 1945; Comdr 1953; Captain 1961; comd HMS Rame Head, 1962; Senior UK Polaris Rep., Washington, 1963-66; comd HMS Triumph, 1966-68; Cdre Clyde in Comd Clyde Submarine Base, 1969-71; Rear-Adm. 1971; Flag Officer Spithead and Port Admiral, Portsmouth, 1971-73; retired 1973. *Recreation*: sailing. *Address*: Charltons, Yalding, Kent ME18 6DF. *T*: Maidstone 814161. *Club*: Army and Navy.

LANKESTER, Richard Shermer; Clerk of Select Committees, House of Commons, since 1979; Registrar of Members' Interests, since 1976; *b* 8 Feb. 1922; *s* of Richard Ward Lankester; *m* 1950, Dorothy, *d* of Raymond Jackson, Worsley; three *s* one *d*. *Educ*: Haberdashers' Aske's Hampstead Sch.; Jesus Coll., Oxford (MA). Served Royal Artillery, 1942-45. Entered Dept of Clerk of House of Commons, 1947; Clerk of Standing Cttees, 1973-75; Clerk of Expenditure Cttee, 1975-79. Co-Editor, The Table, 1962-67. *Address*: The

Old Farmhouse, The Green, Boughton Monchelsea, Maidstone, Kent. *T*: Maidstone 43749.

LANSBURY, Angela Brigid; actress; *b* London, England, 16 Oct. 1925; *d* of Edgar Lansbury and late Moyna MacGill (who *m* 1st, Reginald Denham); *m* 1st, Richard Cromwell; 2nd, 1949, Peter Shaw; one *s* one *d* and one step *s*; naturalized American citizen, 1951. *Educ*: South Hampstead High Sch. for Girls; Webber Douglas Sch. of Singing and Dramatic Art, Kensington; Feagin Sch. of Drama and Radio, New York. With Metro-Goldwyn-Mayer, 1943-50; films included: Gaslight, 1944; National Velvet, 1944; Dorian Gray, 1944; Harvey Girls, 1946; Till the Clouds Roll By, 1946; If Winter Comes, 1947; State of the Union, 1948; Samson and Delilah, 1949. As free lance, 1950–: films include: Kind Lady, 1951; The Court Jester, 1956; The Long Hot Summer, 1957; The Reluctant Debutante, 1958; Summer of the 17th Doll, 1959; A Breath of Scandal, 1959; Dark at the Top of the Stairs, 1960; Blue Hawaii, 1962; All Fall Down, 1962; The Manchurian Candidate, 1963; In the Cool of the Day, 1963; The World of Henry Orient, 1964; Out of Towners, 1964; Harlow, 1965; Bedknobs and Broomsticks, 1972; Black Flowers for the Bride, 1972; Death on the Nile, 1978; The Lady Vanishes, 1979; plays: appearances include: Hotel Paradiso (Broadway debut), 1957; Helen, in A Taste of Honey, Lyceum Theatre, New York, 1960; Anyone can Whistle (Broadway musical), 1964; Mame (Tony Award for best actress in a Broadway musical), Winter Garden, NYC, 1966-68; Dear World (Broadway), 1969 (Tony Award); Gypsy (Broadway Musical), Piccadilly, 1973, US tour, 1974 (Tony Award; Chicago, Sarah Siddons Award, 1974); Gertrude, in Hamlet, Nat. Theatre, 1975; Anna, in The King and I (Broadway), 1978; Mrs Lovett, in Sweeney Todd (Broadway), 1979 (Tony Award). *Address*: Suite 501, 1650 Broadway, New York City, NY 10019, USA.

LANSDOWN, Gillian Elizabeth, (Mrs Richard Lansdown); *see* Tindall, G. E.

LANSDOWNE, 8th Marquess of (GB), *cr* 1784; **George John Charles Mercer Nairne Petty-Fitzmaurice**; 29th Baron of Kerry and Lixnaw, 1181; Earl of Kerry, Viscount Clanmaurice, 1723; Viscount FitzMaurice and Baron Dunkeron, 1751; Earl of Shelburne, 1753; Baron Wycombe, 1760; Earl of Wycombe and Viscount Calne, 1784; PC 1964; *b* 27 Nov. 1912; *o s* of Major Lord Charles George Francis Mercer Nairne, MVO (killed in action, 1914; 2nd *s* of 5th Marquess), and Lady Violet Mary Elliot (she *m* 2nd, 1916, 1st Baron Astor of Hever), *d* of 4th Earl of Minto; *S* cousin, 1944; *m* 1st, 1938, Barbara, (*d* 1965), *d* of Harold Stuart Chase, Santa Barbara; two *s* one *d* (and one *d* decd); 2nd, 1969, Mrs Polly Carnegie (marr. diss. 1978), *d* of Viscount Eccles, *qv*; 3rd, 1978, Gillian Ann, *d* of Alured Morgan. *Educ*: Eton; Christ Church, Oxford. Sec. Junior Unionist League for E Scotland, 1939. Served War of 1939-45, Capt. Royal Scots Greys 1940, formerly 2nd Lt Scottish Horse (TA); Major 1944; served with Free French Forces (Croix de Guerre, Légion D'Honneur); Private Sec. to HM Ambassador in Paris (Rt Hon. A. Duff Cooper). 1944-45. Lord-in-Waiting to the Queen, 1957-58; Joint Parliamentary Under-Sec. of State, Foreign Office, 1958-62; Minister of State for Colonial Affairs, 1962-64, and for Commonwealth Relations, 1963-64. Mem. Royal Company of Archers (Queen's Body Guard for Scotland); JP, Perthshire, 1950; DL Wilts, 1952-73. Patron of two livings. Chm., Victoria League in Scotland, 1952-56; Inter-Governmental Cttee on Malaysia, 1962. Chm., Franco-British Soc., 1972–; Pres., Franco-Scottish Soc. Prime Warden, Fishmongers' Company, 1967-68. Comdr, Légion d'Honneur, 1979. *Heir*: *s* Earl of Shelburne, *qv*. *Address*: Meikleour House, Perthshire. *Clubs*: Turf; New (Edinburgh).
See also Lady Nairne.

LAPOINTE, Col Hon. Hugues, PC (Canada) 1949; QC; Barrister; *b* Rivière-du-Loup, Quebec, 3 March 1911; *s* of Rt Hon. Ernest Lapointe, PC, QC, Minister of Justice at Ottawa, and Emma Pratte; *m* 1938, Lucette, *d* of Dr and Mrs R. É. Valin, Ottawa. *Educ*: University of Ottawa (BA 1932); Laval Univ., Quebec (LLL 1935). Mem. of Quebec Bar, July 1935; KC 1949. Served War of 1939-45, Overseas, with Regt de la Chaudière. Elected (L) to House of Commons, Lotbinière County Constituency, 1940, 1945, 1949, 1953. Delegate to Gen. Assembly, UN: Paris, Sept. 1948; Lake Success, April 1949; Lake Success, Sept. 1950 (Vice-Chm. Canadian Delegation). Parliamentary Asst to Minister of National Defense, 1945, to Sec. of State for External Affairs, 1949; Solicitor-Gen. of Canada, 1949; Minister of Veterans Affairs, Aug. 1950; Postmaster-Gen., 1955; Agent-Gen. for Quebec in the United Kingdom, 1961-66; Lieut-Governor of Quebec, 1966-78. Hon. Col, Le Régiment de la Chaudière, 1970. Hon. LLD: University of Ottawa, 1954; Royal Military Coll. of Canada, 1967. Croix de Guerre avec palme. KStJ 1966; Kt Grand Cross, Sovereign and Milit. Order of Malta, 1966. Is a Roman Catholic. *Address*: 4262 Marie Victorin, St Antoine de Tilly, Co. Lotbinière, G0S 2C0, Canada. *Clubs*: Garrison (Quebec); Royal Quebec Golf (Boischatel).

LAPOTAIRE, Jane; actress; *b* 26 Dec. 1944; *d* of unknown father and Louise Elise Lapotaire; *m* 1st, 1965, Oliver Wood (marr. diss. 1967); 2nd, 1974, Roland Joffé (marr. diss. 1982); one *s*. *Educ*: Northgate Grammar Sch., Ipswich; Old Vic Theatre Sch., Bristol. Bristol Old Vic Co., 1965-67; Nat. Theatre Co., 1967-71; freelance films and TV, 1971-74; RSC, 1975-76; Prospect Theatre Co. in West End, 1975-76; freelance films and TV, 1976-78; RSC, 1978-81. TV Emmy nomination, 1976; Soc. of W End Theatre Award, 1979; London Critics Award, 1980; Variety Club Award, 1980; Broadway Tony Award, 1981. *Recreations*: water colours, cordon bleu cookery. *Address*:

c/o Hutton Management, 194 Old Brompton Road, SW5; c/o The Lantz Office Inc., 888 Fifth Avenue, New York, NY 10106, USA. *T:* (212) 586 0200.

LAPPER, Maj.-Gen. John; Director of Medical Services, Saudi Arabian National Guard, since 1981; *b* 24 July 1921; *s* of late Col Wilfred Mark Lapper, OBE, Legion of Merit (USA), late RE, and Agnes Lapper (*née* Powner); *m* 1948, Dorothy, *d* of late Roland John and Margaret Simpson (*née* Critchlow); three *s. Educ:* Wolverhampton Grammar Sch.; King Edward VI Sch., Birmingham; Birmingham Univ. MB, ChB 1946; DLO 1952. House appts, Queen Elizabeth and Children's Hosp., Birmingham, and Ronkswood Hosp. and Royal Infirm., Worcester; Registrar, Royal Berks Hosp., Reading. Commnd RAMC, 1950; ENT specialist, Mil. Hosps in UK, Libya, Egypt, Germany, Singapore, Malaya; CO 14 Field Amb., BAOR, 1958; CO BMH Rinteln, BAOR, 1964; Asst Comdt, Royal Army Med. Coll., 1965-68; ADMS Hong Kong, 1969-71; CO Queen Alexandra's Mil. Hosp., Millbank, 1971-73; ADMS 3 Div., 1973; DDMS HQ UKLF, 1974-77; Dir, Med. Supply, MoD, 1977; Dir, Med. Policy and Plans, MoD, 1978-80, retired; QHS 1977-80. Hudson-Evans Lectr, W Kent Medico-Chirurgical Soc., 1980; Mem. Sands Cox Med. Soc., Birmingham Univ. FFCM 1980; FBIM 1980; FRSocMed; FMedSoc London; Mem. BMA; Pres. Med. Soc., Hong Kong, 1970-71; Member: RUSI; Council, Yateley Industries for the Disabled. OStJ 1959. *Publications:* articles in professional jls. *Recreations:* gardening, travel, militaria. *Address:* Holmbush, Old School Lane, Yateley, Camberley, Surrey GU17 7NG. *T:* Yateley 874180. *Club:* Army and Navy.

LAPPERT, Prof. Michael Franz, FRS 1979; Professor of Chemistry, University of Sussex, since 1969; Science and Engineering Research Council Senior Research Fellow, since 1980; *b* 31 Dec. 1928; *s* of Julius Lappert and Kornelie Lappert (*née* Beran); *m* 1980, Lorna McKenzie. *Educ:* Wilson's Grammar School; Northern Polytechnic, London. BSc, PhD, DSc (London). FRIC. Northern Polytechnic, London: Asst Lecturer, 1952-53; Lecturer, 1953-55; Sen. Lectr, 1955-59. UMIST: Lectr, 1959-61; Sen. Lectr, 1961-64. Reader, Univ. of Sussex, 1964-69. First recipient of (London) Chemical Soc. Award in Main Group Metal Chemistry, 1970; Award in Organometallic Chemistry, 1978; Tilden Lectr, 1972-73; F. S. Kipping Award of American Chem. Soc., 1976. *Publications:* (jtly) Metal and Metalloid Amides, 1979; (ed jtly) Developments in Inorganic Polymer Chemistry, 1962; more than 300 papers in Jl Chem. Soc., etc. *Recreations:* golf, tennis, walking, theatre, opera. *Address:* 4 Varndean Gardens, Brighton BN1 6WL. *T:* Brighton 503661.

LAPPING, Anne Shirley Lucas; Producer, Channel Four politics programme; *b* 10 June 1941; *d* of late Frederick Stone and of Dr Freda Lucas Stone; *m* 1963, Brian Michael Lapping; three *d. Educ:* City of London Sch. for Girls; London Sch. of Econs (BScEcon). New Society, 1964-68; London Weekend TV, 1970-73; writer on The Economist, 1974-82. Other writing and broadcasting. Member: SSRC, 1977-79; Nat. Gas Consumers' Council, 1978-79. Mem., Fabian Soc. *Recreation:* housework. *Address:* 94 Highgate Hill, N6 5HE. *T:* 01-341 0523.

LAPSLEY, Air Marshal Sir John (Hugh), KBE 1969 (OBE 1944); CB 1966; DFC 1940; AFC 1950; *b* 24 Sept. 1916; *s* of late Edward John Lapsley, Bank of Bengal, Dacca, and Norah Gladis Lapsley; *m* 1st, 1942, Jean Margaret MacIvor (*d* 1979); one *s* one *d* ; 2nd, 1980, Millicent Rees (*née* Beadnell), widow of T. A. Rees. *Educ:* Wolverhampton Sch.; Royal Air Force Coll., Cranwell. Served in Fighter Squadrons in UK, Egypt and Europe, 1938-45; psc 1946; Air Ministry Directorate of Policy, 1946-48; Commander No 74 Fighter Squadron and Air Fighting Development Squadron, 1949-52; HQ Fighter Command Staff, 1952-54; 2nd TAF Germany, 1954-58; Ministry of Defence Joint Planning Staff, 1958-60; Deputy Chief of Staff Air, 2nd Allied TAF, 1960-62; IDC, 1963; Secretary to Chiefs of Staff Cttee and Director of Defence Operations Staff, Ministry of Defence, 1964-66; No 19 Group, RAF Coastal Comd, 1967-68; AOC-in-C, RAF Coastal Comd, 1968-69; Head of British Defence Staff and Defence Attaché, Washington, 1970-73. Mem. Council, Officers' Pension Soc., 1976-. Dir-Gen., Save the Children Fund, 1974-75. Dir, Falkland Is R&D Assoc. Ltd, 1978-; Councillor, Suffolk Coastal District Council, 1979-. Fellow RSPB. *Recreations:* golf, ornithology. *Address:* c/o Lloyds Bank, 6 Pall Mall, SW1. *Club:* Royal Air Force.

LAPUN, Sir Paul, Kt 1974; Member for South Bougainville, Papua New Guinea House of Assembly, since 1964; *b* 1923; *m* 1951, Lois, two *s* one *d. Educ:* Catholic Mission, Vunapope. Teacher, Catholic Mission, 1947-61. Under-Secretary for Forests, Papua and New Guinea, 1964-67. Founder, Pangu Party, 1967 (Leader, 1967-68; Dep. Parly Leader, 1968-); Minister: for Mines and Energy, 1972-75; for Health, 1975-77. Hon. Member, Internat. Mark Twain Soc., USA. *Address:* c/o House of Assembly, Port Moresby, Papua New Guinea.

LAQUEUR, Walter; Director, Institute of Contemporary History and Wiener Library, London, since 1964; *b* 26 May 1921; *s* of late Fritz Laqueur and late Else Laqueur; *m* 1941, Barbara (*née* Koch), *d* of Prof. Richard Koch and Maria Koch (*née* Rosenthal); two *d.* Agricultural labourer during War, 1939-44. Journalist, free lance author, 1944-55; Editor of Survey, 1955-65; Co-editor of Journal of Contemporary History, 1966-. Prof., History of Ideas, Brandeis Univ., 1967-71; Prof. of Contemporary History, Tel Aviv Univ., 1970-; Vis. Prof.: Chicago Univ.; Johns Hopkins Univ.; Harvard Univ. Chm., Res. Council, The Center for Strategic and Internat. Studies, Georgetown Univ., Washington. *Publications:* Communism and Nationalism in the

Middle East, 1956; Young Germany, 1961; Russia and Germany, 1965; The Road to War, 1968; Europe Since Hitler, 1970; Out of the Ruins of Europe, 1971; Zionism, a History, 1972; Confrontation: the Middle East War and World Politics, 1974; Weimar: a Cultural History, 1918-33, 1974; Guerrilla, 1976; Terrorism, 1977; The Missing Years, 1980; (ed jtly) A Reader's Guide to Contemporary History, 1972; (ed) Fascism: a reader's guide, 1978; The Terrible Secret, 1980; Farewell to Europe, 1981. *Recreations:* swimming, motor-boating. *Address:* 4 Devonshire Street, W1; 1800 K Street NW, Washington, DC, USA.

LARCOM, Sir (Charles) Christopher (Royde), 5th Bt, *cr* 1868; Partner in Grieveson, Grant & Co., Stockbrokers, since 1960; *b* 11 Sept. 1926; *s* of Sir Philip Larcom, 4th Bt, and Aileen Monica Royde (*née* Colbeck); *S* father, 1967; *m* 1956, Barbara Elizabeth, *d* of Balfour Bowen; four *d. Educ:* Radley; Clare Coll., Cambridge. (Wrangler, 1947; BA, 1947; MA, 1951). Served RN (Lieutenant), 1947-50. Articled to Messrs Spicer and Pegler (Chartered Accountants), 1950-53; ACA 1954; FCA 1965; joined Grieveson, Grant and Co., 1955; Member, The Stock Exchange, London, 1959 (Mem. Council, 1970-). *Recreations:* sailing, music. *Address:* Butlers, Hatfield Peverel, near Chelmsford, Essex. *T:* Chelmsford 380508.

LARDINOIS, Petrus Josephus; Chairman, Executive Board, Rabobank Nederland, since 1977; *b* Noorbeek, 13 Aug. 1924; *m* Maria Hubertina Gerardine Peeters; two *s* three *d. Educ:* Wageningen Agricultural Coll. Various agricultural posts until 1960; Agricultural Attaché, Dutch Embassy, London, 1960-63; Mem., Second Chamber, 1963-73 (Catholic People's Party); Mem., European Parliament, 1963-67; Minister of Agriculture and Fisheries, 1967-72; Comr for Agriculture, Commn of the European Communities, 1973-76. Pres., Brabant Farmers' Union, 1965-67. *Address:* Rabobank Nederland, Catharijnesinge 30, 3503 SE Utrecht, Netherlands.

LARGE, Prof. John Barry; Professor of Applied Acoustics, since 1969, and Director, since 1973, Institute of Sound and Vibration Research, University of Southampton; Dean of Faculty of Engineering and Applied Science, since 1982; *b* 10 Oct. 1930; *s* of Thomas and Ada Large; *m* 1958, Barbara Alicia Nelson; two *s. Educ:* Queen Mary Coll., London Univ.; Purdue Univ., USA. BScEng (Hons), MS. Group Engr, EMI Ltd, Feltham, Mddx, 1954-56; Sen. Systems Engr, Link Aviation, Binghampton, NY, USA, 1956-58; Chief Aircraft Noise Unit, Boeing Co., Seattle, USA, 1958-69. Mem., Noise Adv. Council, 1976-. Hon. Dep. Chief Scientific Officer, Royal Aircraft Estabt, 1974-; Adjunct Prof. of Mechanical Engrg, Univ. of Utah, USA, 1974-. *Publications:* contrib. (regarding aircraft noise, etc) to: Commn of European Communities, Eur 5398e, 1975; Proc. 5th Worlds' Airports Conf., Instn of CE, 1976; RSH Conf., Eastbourne, 1977; Proc. of Internoise 79, Warsaw, Internoise 80, Miami, Internoise 81, Amsterdam, Internoise 82, San Francisco; The Development of Criteria for Environmental Noise Control (Proc. Royal Instn, vol. 52), 1979. *Recreations:* skiing, gardening. *Address:* Chinook, Southdown Road, Shawford, Hants. *T:* Twyford 712307.

LARGE, Maj.-Gen. Stanley Eyre, MBE 1945; Director of Medical Services, King Edward VII Hospital, Midhurst, since 1978; *b* 11 Aug. 1917; *s* of late Brig. David Torquil Macleod Large and Constance Lucy Houston; *m* 1941, Janet Mary (*née* Brooks); three *s. Educ:* Edinburgh; Cheltenham Coll.; Caius Coll., Cambridge (MA,MD); St Thomas' Hosp. FRCP, FRCPE. Commnd in RAMC, 1942; war service in Tunisia, Italy, Austria, Greece, with field ambs and as Regimental MO; psc 1948; spec. medicine; served in hosps at home and overseas as med. specialist, later consultant in medicine, with particular interest in diseases of chest, 1950-65; various sen. admin. appts in Cyprus and BAOR, 1965-75; DMS, UKLF, 1975-78. QHP 1974-78. *Publications:* contrib. med. literature. *Recreations:* travel, ski-ing, golf, photography; formerly running (half blue, Cambridge v Oxford, mile, 1937). *Address:* Churt House, Churt, Farnham, Surrey GU10 2PX. *T:* Frensham 2642.

LARKIN, John Cuthbert, MA; Headmaster, Wyggeston School, Leicester, 1947-69, retired; *b* 15 Oct. 1906; *s* of J. W. Larkin; *m* 1933, Sylvia Elizabeth Pilsbury; one *s* three *d. Educ:* King Edward VI Sch., Nuneaton; Downing Coll., Cambridge. Assistant Master, Shrewsbury Sch., 1928-45; Headmaster, Chesterfield Grammar Sch., 1946-47. *Recreations:* cricket, gardening. *Address:* Groves Cottage, Summers Lane, Totland Bay, Isle of Wight. *T:* Freshwater 752506.

LARKIN, Philip (Arthur), CBE 1975; MA; CLit 1978; FRSL; poet and novelist; *b* 9 Aug. 1922; *o s* of late Sydney and Eva Emily Larkin. *Educ:* King Henry VIII Sch., Coventry; St John's Coll., Oxford (Hon. Fellow, 1973). Has held posts in different libraries since 1943. Jazz correspondent for the Daily Telegraph, 1961-71. Vis. Fellow, All Souls Coll., Oxford, 1970-71. Chm., Nat. Manuscript Collection of Contemporary Writers Cttee, 1972-79, Mem., Literature Panel, 1980-82, Arts Council of GB; Chm. Bd of Management, Poetry Book Soc., 1981-. Foreign Hon. Member, Amer. Acad. of Arts and Sciences, 1975. Coventry Award of Merit, 1978. Hon. FLA 1980. Hon. DLit Belfast, 1969; Hon. DLitt: Leicester, 1970; Warwick, 1973; St Andrews, 1974; Sussex, 1974. The Queen's Gold Medal for Poetry, 1965; Loines Award for Poetry, 1974; A. C. Benson Silver Medal, RSL, 1975; Shakespeare Prize, FVS Foundation of Hamburg, 1976. *Publications:* The North Ship (poems), 1945; Jill (novel), 1946 (rev. edn 1964); A Girl in Winter (novel), 1947; The Less Deceived (poems), 1955; The Whitsun Weddings (poems), 1964; All What Jazz (essays), 1970; (ed) The Oxford Book of Twentieth Century English

Verse, 1973; High Windows (poems), 1974. *Address:* c/o Faber & Faber Ltd, 3 Queen Square, WC1N 3AU.

LARMINIE, (Ferdinand) Geoffrey, OBE 1971; General Manager, Environmental Control Centre, British Petroleum Co. Ltd, since 1976; *b* 23 June 1929; *s* of late Ferdinand Samuel Larminie and of Mary Larminie (*née* Willis); *m* 1956, Helena Elizabeth Woodside Carson; one *s* one *d. Educ:* St Andrews Coll., Dublin; Trinity Coll., Dublin (BA 1954, MA 1972). Asst Lectr in Geology, Univ. of Glasgow, 1954-56; Lectr in Geology, Univ. of Sydney, 1956-60; joined British Petroleum Co. Ltd, 1960: Exploration Dept in Sudan, Greece, Canada, Libya, Kuwait, California, New York, Thailand and Alaska, 1960-74; Scientific Advr, Inf. Dept, London, 1974-75; Gen. Manager, Public Affairs and Inf. Dept, London, 1975-76. Mem., Royal Commn on Environmental Pollution, 1979-; Chm., Internat. Petrol. Industry Environmental Conservation Assoc., 1981-. Pres., Alaska Geol Soc., 1969; Council Mem., Soc. for Underwater Technology, 1976-; Trustee, Bermuda Biological Station 1978-; Mem. Bd of Management, Inst. of Offshore Engrg, Heriot-Watt Univ., 1981-. Mem., IBA Gen. Adv. Council, 1980-. Mem. of numerous scientific and professional socs. *Publications:* papers in scientific and technical jls on oil ind., and occasional reviews. *Recreations:* archaeology, natural history, reading, shooting. *Address:* Lane End, Lanes End, Tring, Herts. *T:* Wendover 624907.

LARMOUR, Sir Edward Noel, (Sir Nick Larmour), KCMG 1977 (CMG 1966); HM Diplomatic Service, retired; *b* 25 Dec. 1916; *s* of Edward and Maud Larmour, Belfast, N Ireland; *m* 1946, Nancy, 2nd *d* of Thomas Bill; one *s* two *d. Educ:* Royal Belfast Academical Institution (Kitchener Scholar); Trinity Coll., Dublin (Scholar) (1st Class Hons and University Studentship in Classics, 1939); Sydney Univ., NSW. Royal Inniskilling Fusiliers, 1940; Burma Civil Service, 1942; Indian Army, 1942-46 (Major); Dep. Secretary to Governor of Burma, 1947; Commonwealth Relations Office, 1948; served in New Zealand, Singapore, Australia and Nigeria, 1950-68; Asst Under-Secretary of State, 1964; Dep. Chief of Administration, FCO, 1968-70; High Comr, Jamaica, and non-resident Ambassador, Haiti, 1970-73; Asst Under Sec. of State, FCO, 1973-75; High Comr (non-resident) for New Hebrides, 1973-76; Dep. Under Sec. of State, FCO, 1975-76. Mem., Price Commn, 1977-80; Chm., Bermuda Constituency Boundaries Commn, 1979. *Recreations:* cricket, golf, music. *Address:* 68 Wood Vale, N10. *T:* 01-444 9744. *Clubs:* Royal Commonwealth Society; MCC.

LAROSIÈRE de CHAMPFEU, Jacques Martin Henri Marie de; *see* de Larosiére de Champfeu.

LARSON, Frederick H., DFM 1943; General Manager, Business Development, Alberta Opportunity Co., Edmonton, Alberta (Alberta Crown Corporation), since 1974; *b* 24 Nov. 1913; *s* of Herman B. and Martha C. Larson; *m* 1941, Dorothy A. Layng; one *s. Educ:* University of Saskatchewan. Observer, RCAF, 1941-43. Member for Kindersley, Parliament of Canada, 1949-53; Delegate to UN, Paris, 1952. Ten years in oil and gas business, production refining and sales, domestic and offshore; eight years in financial trust business, representing financial interests, Canada amd Jamaica; three years in construction and engineering; agricultural interests, Saskatchewan; Agent-Gen. for Province of Saskatchewan in London, 1967-73. *Recreation:* golf. *Address:* c/o Guaranty Trust Company, 10010 Jasper Avenue, Edmonton, Alberta, Canada. *Clubs:* Ranchmen's (Calgary); Mayfair Golf (Edmonton, Alta).

LARTIGUE, Sir Louis C.; *see* Cools-Lartigue.

LASCELLES, family name of **Earl of Harewood.**

LASCELLES, Viscount; David Henry George Lascelles; *b* 21 Oct. 1950; *s* and *heir* of 7th Earl of Harewood, *qv* ; *m* 1979, Margaret Rosalind Messenger; two *s* one *d. Educ:* The Hall Sch.; Westminster. *Address:* 2 Orme Square, W2.

LASCELLES, Daniel Richard, CBE 1962; *b* 18 Sept. 1908; 4th *s* of Councillor A. Lascelles, JP, Darlington; *m* 1941, Mildred Joyce Burr; two *s* one *d. Educ:* Durham Sch.; St John's Coll., Cambridge. Called to Bar, Inner Temple, 1930; Sarawak Administrative Service, 1932; Circuit Judge, Sarawak, 1948; Colonial Legal Service, 1951; Acting Puisne Judge, 1951; Puisne Judge of Supreme Court of Sarawak, North Borneo and Brunei, 1952-62. Legal Chairman Pensions Appeal Tribunals, 1964-74; Chairman, Medical Appeal Tribunals, 1967-74; Member, Mental Health Review Tribunal, 1967-74. *Recreations:* shooting, gardening, golf, tennis. *Address:* 39 13th Avenue, Edenvale, Johannesburg, 1610 South Africa.

LASCELLES, Maj.-Gen. Henry Anthony, CB 1967; CBE 1962 (OBE 1945); DSO 1944; Director-General, Winston Churchill Memorial Trust, 1967-80; *b* 10 Jan. 1912; *s* of Edward Lascelles and Leila Kennett-Barrington; *m* 1941, Ethne Hyde Ussher Charles. *Educ:* Winchester; Oriel Coll., Oxford (BA). Served War of 1939-45: Egypt, North Africa, Sicily and Italy, rising to second in command of an armoured brigade. Instructor, Staff Coll., Camberley, 1947-49; GSO 1, HQ 7th Armoured Div., BAOR, 1949-52; Comdg Officer 6th Royal Tank Regt, BAOR, 1952-55; Instructor NATO Defence Coll., 1955-56; Brigadier Royal Armoured Corps HQ 2nd Infantry Div., BAOR, 1956-57; National Defence Coll., Canada, 1958-59; BGS Military Operations, War Office, 1959-62; Chief of Staff, HQ Northern Ireland Command,

1962-63; Maj.-General, General Staff, Far East Land Forces, 1963-66. *Recreations:* squash, tennis, golf, music, gardening. *Address:* Manor Farm Cottage, Hedgerley Green, Bucks. *T:* Gerrards Cross 83582. *Club:* Naval and Military.

LASCELLES, Mary Madge, FBA 1962; Hon. Fellow, Somerville College, 1967; *b* 7 Feb. 1900; *d* of William Horace and Madeline Lascelles. *Educ:* Sherborne School for Girls; Lady Margaret Hall, Oxford. Research Studentship, Westfield Coll., 1923; Assistant Lecturer, Royal Holloway Coll., 1926; Somerville College: Tutor in English Language and Literature, 1931; Fellow, 1932-67; Vice-Principal, 1947-60; University Lecturer in English Literature, 1960-66; Reader, 1966-67. *Publications:* Jane Austen and her Art, 1939; Shakespeare's Measure for Measure, 1953; (ed) The Works of Samuel Johnson, vol. ix, A Journey to the Western Islands of Scotland, 1971; The Adversaries and Other Poems, 1971; Notions and Facts, 1973; The Story-Teller Retrieves the Past, 1980; contributions to learned journals, etc. *Address:* 3 Stratfield Road, Oxford OX2 7BG. *T:* Oxford 57817. *Club:* University Women's.

LASDUN, Sir Denys (Louis), Kt 1976; CBE 1965; FRIBA; architect in private practice with Alexander Redhouse and Peter Softley, since 1960; *b* 8 Sept. 1914; *s* of Norman Lasdun and Julie Abrahams; *m* 1954, Susan Bendit; two *s* one *d. Educ:* Rugby Sch.; Architectural Assoc. Served with Royal Engineers, 1939-45 (MBE). Practised with Wells Coates, Tecton and Drake. Hoffman Wood Professor of Architecture, University of Leeds, 1962-63. Assessor, Competitions for Belgrade Opera Hse, 1971, and new Parly Bldg, London, 1971-72. Mem., Mars Gp. Principal works: housing and schools for Bethnal Green and Paddington; London HQ, NSW Govt; flats at 26 St James's Place; Royal College of Physicians; Fitzwilliam College, and Christ's College extension, Cambridge; new University of East Anglia and work for the Universities of London (SOAS, Inst. of Educn, Law Inst., project for Courtauld Inst.), Leicester and Liverpool; National Theatre, South Bank; IBM Central London Marketing Centre, South Bank; new EEC HQ for European Investment Bank, Luxembourg; new design for Hurva Synagogue, Old City, Jerusalem; Cannock Community Hosp. Trustee, BM, 1975-; Member: V & A Adv. Cttee, 1973-; Slade Cttee, 1976-; Arts Panel, Arts Council of GB, 1980-. Hon. Fellow, American Institute of Architects, 1966; Hon. FRCP, 1975. Hon. DLitt: E Anglia, 1974; Sheffield, 1978; Hon. Diploma, First World Biennale of Architecture, Sofia, 1981. RIBA London Architecture Bronze Medallist, 1960 and 1964; RIBA Gold Medal, 1977; RIBA Architectural Award for London Region, 1978; Civic Trust Awards: Class I, 1967; Group A, 1969; Special Award, Sao Paulo Biennale, Brazil, 1969. *Publications:* A Language and a Theme, 1976; contributions to architectural and other papers incl. An Architects Approach to Architecture. Lectures given in UK, USA, Spain, Portugal, Norway, Denmark and Italy. *Address:* 50 Queen Anne Street, W1N 0DR. *T:* 01-486 4761.

LASH, Prof. Nicholas Langrishe Alleyne, DD; Norris-Hulse Professor of Divinity, since 1978, and Fellow of St Edmund's House, since 1969, University of Cambridge; *b* 6 April 1934; *s* of Henry Alleyne Lash and Joan Mary Lash (*née* Moore); *m* 1976, Janet Angela Chalmers; one *s. Educ:* Downside Sch.; Oscott Coll.; St Edmund's House, Cambridge. MA, PhD, BD, DD. Served RE, 1952-57. Oscott Coll., 1957-63; Asst Priest, Slough, 1963-68; Dean, St Edmund's House, Cambridge, 1971-75; Univ. Asst Lectr, Cambridge, 1974-78. *Publications:* His Presence in the World, 1968; Change in Focus, 1973; Newman on Development, 1975; Voices of Authority, 1976; Theology on Dover Beach, 1979; A Matter of Hope, 1982. *Address:* Faculty of Divinity, St John's Street, Cambridge CB2 1TW. *T:* Cambridge 358933.

LASH, Rt. Rev. William Quinlan; *b* 5 Feb. 1905; *s* of Nicholas Alleyne and Violet Maud Lash. *Educ:* Tonbridge Sch., Emmanuel Coll., Cambridge; Westcott House. BA 1927; MA 1932; Deacon, 1928; Priest, 1929; Curate, S Mary's Church, Portsea, 1928-32; Christa Seva Sangha, Poona, 1932; Acharya, Christa Prema Seva Sangha, Poona, 1934-49, 1953-61; Bishop of Bombay, 1947-61; Asst Bishop of Truro, Hon. Canon of St Mary's Cathedral, Truro, 1962-73; Vicar of St Clement, 1963-73. *Publications:* Approach to Christian Mysticism, 1947; The Temple of God's Wounds, 1951. *Address:* The Friary, Hilfield, Dorchester, Dorset DT2 7BE. *T:* Cerne Abbas 346.

LASKEY, Sir Denis (Seward), KCMG 1974 (CMG 1957); CVO 1958; HM Diplomatic Service, retired; *b* 18 Jan. 1916; *s* of F. S. Laskey; *m* 1947, Perronnelle Mary Gemma, *d* of late Col Sir Edward Le Breton, MVO; one *s* three *d. Educ:* Marlborough Coll.; Corpus Christi Coll., Oxford. 3rd Secretary, Diplomatic Service, 1939; FO, Sept. 1939-June 1940; served in Army, 1940-41; FO, 1941-46; Berlin, 1946-49; Member UK Delegation to UN, New York, 1949-53; FO, 1953-59; Private Secretary to Secretary of State for Foreign Affairs, 1956-59; Minister, HM Embassy, Rome, 1960-64; Under-Secretary, Cabinet Office, 1964-67; Minister, HM Embassy, Bonn, 1967-68; Ambassador to: Rumania, 1969-71; Austria, 1972-75. *Recreations:* ski-ing, fishing, golf. *Address:* Loders Mill, near Bridport, Dorset. *Club:* Leander (Henley-on-Thames).

LASKI, Marghanita; (Mrs J. E. Howard); *b* 24 Oct. 1915; *d* of late Neville J. Laski, QC; *m* 1937, John Eldred Howard; one *s* one *d. Educ:* Ladybarn House Sch., Manchester; Somerville Coll., Oxford. MA Oxon. Novelist, critic, journalist. Member: Annan Cttee of Inquiry into Future of Broadcasting, 1974-77; Arts Council, 1979- (Vice-Chm., Drama Adv. Panel, 1980- (Chm., 1980); Chm., Literature Adv. Panel, 1980-; Vice-Chm., 1982-).

Hon. Fellow, Manchester Polytechnic, 1971. F. D. Maurice Meml Lectures, 1974. *Publications:* Love on the Supertax (novel), 1944; The Patchwork Book (anthology), 1946; To Bed with Grand Music (pseudonymous novel), 1946; (ed) Stories of Adventure, 1947; (ed) Victorian Tales, 1948; Tory Heaven (novel), 1948; Little Boy Lost (novel), 1949; Mrs Ewing, Mrs Molesworth, Mrs Hodgson Burnett (criticism), 1950; The Village (novel), 1952; The Victorian Chaise-Longue (novel), 1953; The Offshore Island (play), 1959; Ecstasy: A study of some secular and religious experiences, 1961; Domestic Life in Edwardian England, 1964; (ed, with E.G. Battiscombe) A Chaplet for Charlotte Yonge, 1965; The Secular Responsibility (Conway Memorial Lecture), 1967; Jane Austen and her World, 1969; George Eliot and her World, 1973; Kipling's English History, 1974 (radio programme, 1973); Everyday Ecstasy, 1980; reviews. Radio and TV programmes. *Address:* c/o David Higham Associates, 5-8 Lower John Street, W1R 3PE.

LASKIN, Rt. Hon. Bora, PC(Can) 1973; FRSC; Chief Justice of Canada since Dec. 1973; *b* 5 Oct. 1912; *s* of late Max and Bluma Laskin; *m* 1938, Peggy Tenenbaum; one *s* one *d. Educ:* Univ. of Toronto (BA, MA, LLB); Osgoode Hall Law Sch.; Harvard Univ. (LLM). Lectr in Law, Univ. of Toronto, 1940-43; Asst Prof., 1943-45; Lectr, Osgoode Hall Law Sch., 1945-49; Prof. of Law, Univ. of Toronto, 1949-65; apptd: Justice, Ontario Court of Appeal, Aug. 1965; Justice, Supreme Court of Canada, March 1970. Hon. Bencher, Lincoln's Inn, 1974. Hon. LLD: Queen's; Edinburgh; Trent; Toronto; Alberta; Manitoba; York; Dalhousie; Law Soc. of Upper Canada; McGill; Ottawa; Simon Fraser; Ontario Inst. for Studies in Educn; Victoria; Carleton; Yeshiva; Harvard; British Columbia; Hon. DCL: New Brunswick; Windsor; W Ontario; NY Univ.; Hon. DPhil Hebrew Univ., Jerusalem; DHuL Hebrew Union Coll., Cincinnati. *Publications:* Canadian Constitutional Law (3rd edn), 1969; The British Tradition in Canadian Law, 1969. *Address:* Supreme Court Building, Wellington Street, Ottawa, Ontario K1A 0J1, Canada. *Club:* Rideau (Ottawa).

LASKO, Prof. Peter Erik, CBE 1981; FSA; FBA 1978; Professor of the History of Art, Courtauld Institute, University of London, since 1974; Director, Courtauld Institute, since 1974; *b* 5 March 1924; *s* of Leo Lasko and Wally Lasko (*née* Seifert); *m* 1948, Gwendoline Joan Norman; three *d. Educ:* Courtauld Institute, Univ. of London. BA Hons 1949. Asst Keeper, British Museum, 1950-65; Prof. of the Visual Arts, Univ. of East Anglia, 1965-73. *Publication:* Ars Sacra 800-1200 (Pelican History of Art), 1972. *Address:* Courtauld Institute, University of London, 20 Portman Square, W1. *T:* 01-935 9292. *Club:* Athenæum.

LASKY, Melvin Jonah, MA; Editor, Encounter Magazine, since 1958; *b* New York City, 15 Jan. 1920; *s* of Samuel Lasky and Esther Lasky (*née* Kantrowitz); *m* 1947, Brigitte Newiger (marr. diss. 1974); one *s* one *d. Educ:* City Coll. of New York (BSS); Univ. of Michigan (MA); Columbia Univ. Literary Editor, The New Leader (NY), 1942-43; US Combat Historian in France and Germany, 1944-45; Capt., US Army, 1946; Foreign Correspondent, 1946-48; Editor and Publisher, Der Monat (Berlin), 1948-58 and 1978-; Co-Editor, Encounter Magazine (London), 1958-; Editorial Director, Library Press, NY, 1970-; Publisher, Alcove Press, London, 1972-. Univ. of Michigan, Sesquicentennial Award, 1967; Distinguished Alumnus Award, City Univ., NY, 1978. *Publications:* Reisenotizen und Tagebücher, 1958; Africa for Beginners, 1962; Utopia and Revolution, 1976; contributor to: America and Europe, 1951; New Paths in American History, 1965; Sprache und Politik, 1969; Festschrift for Raymond Aron, 1971; (ed) The Hungarian Revolution, 1957. *Address:* c/o Encounter, 59 St Martins Lane, WC2N 4JS. *T:* 01-836 4194. *Club:* Garrick.

LASLETT, (Thomas) Peter (Ruffell), FBA 1979; Reader in Politics and the History of Social Structure, Cambridge University, since 1966; Director, Cambridge Group for the History of Population and Social Structure, since 1964; Fellow of Trinity College, Cambridge, since 1953; *b* 18 Dec. 1915; *s* of Rev. G. H. R. Laslett and E. E. Laslett (*née* Alden); *m* 1947, Janet Crockett Clark; two *s. Educ:* Watford Grammar Sch.; St John's Coll., Cambridge. Served War, Royal Navy, 1940-45: Lieut RNVR, Japanese Naval Intelligence. Producer, BBC, 3rd Programme Talks, 1946-49; Fellow: St John's Coll., Cambridge, 1948-51; Inst. for Advanced Study, Princeton, 1959; Founder (with E. A. Wrigley), Cambridge Gp for the History of Population and Social Structure, 1964; Member, Working Party on Foundn of Open Univ., 1965-. Visiting Professor: Collège de France, Paris, 1976; Yale Univ., 1977. DUniv. Open, 1980. *Publications:* Locke's Two Treatises of Government, 1960, 12th impr. 1978; The World We Have Lost, 1965, 15th Eng. Lang. impr. 1979; (with R. Wall) Household and Family in Past Time, 1972, 3rd impr. 1979; Family Life and Illicit Love in Earlier Generations, 1977, 3rd impr. 1979; (with R. M. Smith and others) Bastardy and its Comparative History, 1980. *Recreations:* book collecting, gardening. *Address:* Trinity College, Cambridge; 27 Trumpington Street, Cambridge. *T:* (Cambridge Group) Cambridge 354298.

LASOK, Prof. Dominik, QC 1982; PhD, LLD; Professor of European Law, since 1973, and Director of Centre for European Legal Studies, since 1972, University of Exeter; *b* 4 Jan. 1921; *s* of late Alojzy Lasok and Albina (*née* Przybyla); *m* 1952, Sheila May Corrigan; two *s* three *d. Educ:* secondary educn in Poland and Switzerland; Fribourg Univ. (Lic. en Droit); Univ. of Durham (LLM); Univ. of London (PhD, LLD); Universitas Polonorum in Exteris (Dr Juris). Called to the Bar, Middle Temple, 1954. Served Polish Army, Poland, France and Italy, 1939-46 (British, French and Polish mil.

decorations). Industry, 1948-51; commerce, 1954-58; academic career, 1958-: Prof. of Law, Univ. of Exeter, 1968. Vis. Professor: William and Mary, Williamsburg, Va, 1966-67 and 1977; McGill, Montreal, 1976-77; Rennes, 1980-81. *Publications:* Polish Family Law, 1968; (jtly, also ed) Polish Civil Law, 4 vols, 1973-75; (with J. W. Bridge) Introduction to the Law and Institutions of the European Communities, 1973, 3rd edn 1982; The Law of the Economy in the European Communities, 1980; (jtly, also ed) Les Communautés Européennes en Fonctionnement, 1981; over 100 articles in British and foreign legal jls. *Address:* Reed, Barley Lane, Exeter EX4 1TA. *T:* Exeter 72582.

LAST, John William; Special Duties Executive, The Littlewoods Organisation, Liverpool, since 1969; *b* 22 Jan. 1940; *s* of Jack Last (lately Dir of Finance, Metrop. Police) and late Freda Last (*née* Evans); *m* 1967, Susan Josephine, *er d* of John and Josephine Farmer; three *s. Educ:* Sutton Grammar Sch., Surrey; Trinity Coll., Oxford (MA 1965). Mem., Merseyside CC, 1973- (Chm., Arts Cttee, 1977-81); contested (C) Liverpool, West Derby, Feb. and Oct. 1974, Stockport N, 1979. Dir, Royal Liverpool Philharmonic Soc., 1973- (Chm., 1977-81); Chairman: NW Museum and Art Gall. Service, 1977-; Walker Art Gall., Liverpool, 1977-81; Empire Theatre Trust, Liverpool, 1979-81; Nat. Chm., Area Museums Councils of GB, 1979-. Member: Council, Museums Assoc., 1978-; Adv. Council, V&A Museum, 1979-; Arts Council of GB, 1980- (Chm., Housing the Arts Cttee, 1981-; Chm., Regional Cttee, 1980-); Council, Liverpool Univ., 1977-81; Lay Mem., Press Council, 1980-. Chm., Arts, Initiative and Money Cttee, Gulbenkian Foundn, 1980-. *Recreations:* swimming, music, Victoriana. *Address:* The Knoll, Meols Drive, Hoylake, Wirral, Merseyside L47 4AF. *T:* 051-632 4027. *Club:* Royal Automobile.

LAST, Prof. Raymond Jack, FRCS, FRACS; Professor of Applied Anatomy, and Warden, Royal College of Surgeons, 1949-70; *b* 26 May 1903; English. *Educ:* Adelaide High Sch., Australia. MB, BS (Adelaide), 1924; Medical practice S. Australia, 1927-38; arrived London, 1939; Surgeon, EMS, Northern Hospital, N21, 1939-40. OC Abyssinian Medical Unit, Hon. Surgeon to Emperor Haile Selassie I, also OC Haile Selassie Hospital, Surgeon to British Legation, Addis Ababa, 1941-44; returned to London, Lieut-Colonel, RAMC, 1945; ADMS, British Borneo, 1945-46. Anatomical Curator and Bland Sutton Scholar, RCS, 1946; FRCS 1947; Adviser to Central Government of Pakistan on organization and conduct of primary FRCS instruction, Colombo Plan, 1961. Vis. Prof. of Anatomy: UCLA, 1970-81; Mt Sinai Sch. of Medicine, NY, 1971-72. *Publications:* Anatomy, Regional and Applied, 6th edn 1978; Wolff's Anatomy of Eye and Orbit, 6th edn, 1968; Aids to Anatomy, 12th edn, 1962; contrib. to Journals of Surgery; various articles. *Address:* 52 Brougham Place, North Adelaide, South Australia 5006. *T:* (08) 2673480.

LATEY, Hon. Sir John (Brinsmead), Kt 1965; MBE 1943; **Hon. Mr Justice Latey;** Judge of the High Court of Justice, Family Division (formerly Probate, Divorce and Admiralty Division), since 1965; *b* 7 March 1914; *s* of late William Latey (CBE, QC, and of Anne Emily, *d* of late Horace G. Brinsmead; *m* 1938, Betty Margaret (*née* Beresford); one *s* one *d. Educ:* Westminster; Christ Church, Oxford. MA (Hon. Sch. Jurispr.). Called to the Bar, 1936; QC 1957. Served in Army during War, 1939-45, mainly in MEF (Lieut-Colonel, 1944-). General Council of the Bar, 1952-56, 1957-61 and 1964- (Hon. Treasurer, 1959-61). Master of the Bench of the Middle Temple, 1964. Chairman, Lord Chancellor's Cttee on Age of Majority, 1965-67. Dep. Chairman, Oxfordshire QS, 1966. *Publications:* (Asst Ed.) Latey on Divorce, 14th edn, 1952; Halsbury's Laws of England (Conflict of Laws: Husband and Wife), 1956. *Recreations:* golf, bridge, chess. *Address:* 16 Daylesford Avenue, Roehampton, SW15 5QR. *T:* 01-876 6436. *Club:* United Oxford & Cambridge University.

LATHAM, family name of **Baron Latham.**

LATHAM, 2nd Baron *cr* 1942, of Hendon; **Dominic Charles Latham;** Civil Engineer with Electricity Commission of New South Wales, since 1979; part-time post-graduate student of Civil Engineering, University of New South Wales; *b* 20 Sept. 1954; *s* of Hon. Francis Charles Allman Latham (*d* 1959) and of Gabrielle Monica, *d* of Dr S. M. O'Riordan; *S* grandfather, 1970. *Educ:* Univ. of New South Wales, Australia. Bachelor of Engineering (civil), 1977, Hons I; MEngSc 1981. *Recreations:* tennis, squash, snooker, electronics. *Heir: yr* twin *b* Anthony Michael Latham, *b* 20 Sept. 1954. *Address:* 6/226 Rainbow Street, Coogee, Sydney 2034, Australia.

LATHAM, Arthur Charles; *b* Leyton, 14 Aug. 1930; *m* 1951, Margaret Latham; one *s* one *d. Educ:* Romford Royal Liberty Sch.; Garnett Coll. of Educn. Lectr in Further Educn, Southgate Technical Coll., 1967-. Mem., Havering Council (formerly Romford Borough Council) 1952-78 (Alderman, 1962-78); Leader, Lab. Gp, Romford and Havering Councils, 1962-70. Contested (Lab): Woodford, 1959; Rushcliffe, Notts, 1964. Mem., NE Regional Metropolitan Hosp. Bd, 1966-72. MP (Lab) Paddington N, Oct. 1969-1974, City of Westminster, Paddington, 1974-79; Jt Chm., All Party Gp for Pensioners, 1971-79; Chairman: Tribune Gp, 1975-76 (Treasurer, 1977-79); Greater London Lab. Party, 1977-; Vice-Chm., Nat. Cttee, Labour League of Youth, 1949-53; Vice-President: Labour Action for Peace; AMA; Treasurer, Liberation (Movement for Colonial Freedom); Member: British Campaign for Peace in Vietnam; Campaign for Nuclear Disarmament. Vegetarian. *Recreations:* bridge, chess, cricket. *Address:* 17 Tudor Avenue, Gidea Park, Romford, RM2 5LB.

LATHAM, Cecil Thomas, OBE 1976; Stipendiary Magistrate, Greater Manchester (sitting at Salford), since 1976; *b* 11 March 1924; *s* of Cecil Frederick James Latham and Elsie Winifred Latham; *m* 1945, Ivy Frances (*née* Fowle); one *s* one *d. Educ:* Rochester Cathedral Choir Sch.; King's Sch., Rochester. Solicitor. War Service, 1942-45. Asst Clerk, Magistrates' Courts: Chatham, 1939-42; Maidstone, 1945; Leicester, 1948-54; Bromley, 1954-63; Dep. Justices' Clerk, Liverpool, 1963-65; Justices' Clerk, Manchester, 1965-76. Member: Royal Commn on Criminal Procedure, 1978-81; Criminal Law Revision Cttee, 1981-. *Publications:* (ed) Stone's Justices' Manual, 101st-109th edns; How Much?: determining maintenance in magistrates' courts, 1976; (ed) Family Law Reports, 1980-; contrib. Criminal Law Rev., Justice of Peace, Family Law. *Recreation:* music. *Address:* 19 Southdown Crescent, Cheadle Hulme, Cheshire SK8 6EQ. *T:* 061-485 1185.

LATHAM, Christopher George Arnot; Deputy Chairman, James Latham Ltd, since 1973; Trustee, Timber Trade Benevolent Society (Past President); *b* 4 June 1933; *s* of late Edward Bryan Latham, and of Anne Arnot Duncan; *m* 1963, Jacqueline Cabourdin; three *s. Educ:* Stowe Sch.; Clare Coll., Cambridge (MA). FCA. Articled Fitzpatrick Graham, chartered accountants, 1955; joined James Latham Ltd, timber importers, 1959, Dir 1963. A Forestry Comr, 1973-78. Chairman: Timber Res. and Develt Assoc., 1972-74; Commonwealth Forestry Assoc., 1975-77. Pres., Inst. of Wood Sci., 1977-79. *Recreations:* riding, sailing, tennis, collecting toby jugs. *Address:* Place Farm, Doddinghurst, Brentwood, Essex. *T:* Coxtie Green 73293.

LATHAM, Sir Joseph, Kt 1960; CBE 1950; Chairman, Ariel International Ltd, since 1977; Director, George Wimpey plc, since 1960; *b* 1 July 1905; *s* of John and Edith Latham, Prestwich, Lancs; *m* 1932, Phyllis Mary Fitton; one *s* one *d. Educ:* Stand Grammar Sch. Chartered Accountant, 1926; Liaison Officer, Lancashire Associated Collieries, 1935; Director and Secretary, Manchester Collieries Ltd, 1941; Director-General of Finance, National Coal Board, 1946-55; Finance Member, NCB, 1955-56; Deputy Chairman, NCB, 1956-60. Vice-Chm., AEI, 1964-65, Dep. Chm., 1965-68, Man. Dir, 1967-68. Mem., ECGD, Advisory Council, 1964-69; Chm., Economic Development Cttees, Food Processing and Chocolate & Sugar Confectionery Industries, 1965-66. *Address:* 25 Badingham Drive, Leatherhead, Surrey. *T:* Leatherhead 372433. *Club:* Effingham Golf.

LATHAM, Michael Anthony; MP (C) Melton since Feb. 1974; *b* 20 Nov. 1942; *s* of Wing-Comdr S. H. Latham, RAF and Mrs G. K. Ranoszek; *m* 1969, Caroline Terry; two *s. Educ:* Marlborough Coll.; King's Coll., Cambridge; Dept of Educn, Oxford. BA Cantab 1964, MA Cantab 1968, CertEd Oxon 1965. Housing and Local Govt Officer, Conservative Research Dept, 1965-67; Parly Liaison Officer, Nat. Fedn of Building Trades Employers, 1967-73; Dir, House-builders Fedn, 1971-73. Westminster City Councillor, 1968-71. Contested (C) Liverpool, West Derby, 1970. Vice-Chairman: Cons. Parly Housing Cttee, 1974-76; Cons. Parly Environment Cttee, 1979-; Member: House of Commons Expenditure Cttee, 1974-79; Jt Cttee on Statutory Instruments, 1974-75; Jt Ecclesiastical Cttee of both Houses of Parliament, 1974-; Select Cttee on Energy, 1979-. Sec., British-Gibraltar Parly Gp, 1981-; Chairman: British-Israel Parly Gp, 1981-; Cons. Friends of Israel, 1982-. Dir, Lovell Homes Ltd, 1975-. Mem. Bd of Management, Shelter, 1976-82. Vice-Pres., Building Socs Assoc., 1981-. CofE Deleg. to BCC, 1977-81. *Publications:* articles on housing, land, town planning and building. *Recreations:* gardening, fencing, listening to classical music, cricket. *Address:* House of Commons, SW1A 0AA. *Club:* Carlton.

LATHAM, Air Vice-Marshal Peter Anthony, CB 1980; AFC 1960; Principal, Oxford Air Training School, and Director, CSE Aviation Ltd, since 1982; *b* 18 June 1925; *s* of late Oscar Frederick Latham and Rhoda Latham; *m* 1953, Barbara Mary; two *s* six *d. Educ:* St Phillip's Grammar Sch., Birmingham; St Catharine's Coll., Cambridge. psa 1961. Joined RAF, 1944; 1946-69: served No 26, 263, 614, and 247 Sqdns; CFE; Air Min.; Comd No 111 Sqdn; RAF Formation Aerobatic Team (Leader of Black Arrows, 1959-60); MoD Jt Planning Staff; Comd NEAF Strike and PR Wing; Coll. of Air Warfare; Ops No 38 Gp; Comd RAF Tengah, 1969-71; MoD Central Staff, 1971-73; Comd Officer and Aircrew Selection Centre, Biggin Hill, 1973-74; SASO No 38 Gp, 1974-76; Dir Def. Ops, MoD Central Staff, 1976-77; AOC No 11 Group, 1977-81. Cdre, RAF Sailing Assoc., 1974-80; Pres., Assoc. of Service Yacht Clubs, 1978-81. *Recreations:* sailing, horology. *Address:* (office) C. S. E. Aviation, Oxford Airport, Kidlington, Oxford. *Club:* Royal Air Force.

LATHAM, Sir Richard Thomas Paul, 3rd Bt, *cr* 1919, of Crow Clump; *b* 15 April 1934; *s* of Sir (Herbert) Paul Latham, 2nd Bt, and Lady Patricia Doreen Moore (*d* 1947), *o d* of 10th Earl of Drogheda; *S* father, 1955; *m* 1958, Marie-Louise Patricia, *d* of Frederick H. Russell, Vancouver, BC; two *d. Educ:* Eton; Trinity Coll., Cambridge. *Address:* 830 Rockbridge Road, Santa Barbara, Calif 93108, USA.

LATHAM, Robert Clifford, CBE 1973; FBA 1982; Fellow and Pepys Librarian, Magdalene College, Cambridge, since 1972; *b* 11 March 1912; *s* of Edwin Latham, and Alice Latham, Audley, Staffs; *m* 1st, 1939, Eileen Frances Redding Ramsay (*d* 1969); one *s* one *d* ; 2nd, 1973, Rosalind Frances Birley. *Educ:* Wolstanton County Grammar Sch., Staffs; Queens' Coll., Cambridge (scholar). Hist. Tripos Pt I 1932, Pt II 1933; MA 1938. Asst Lectr in History, King's Coll., London, 1935; Lectr, 1939; University Reader in History, Royal Holloway Coll., London, 1947; Visiting Associate Prof., Univ. of Southern California, Los Angeles, 1955; Prof. of History, Univ. of Toronto, 1968; Research Fellow, Magdalene Coll., Cambridge, 1970. *Publications:* (ed) Bristol Charters, 1509-1899 (Bristol Rec. Soc., vol. xii), 1947; (ed) The Diary of Samuel Pepys, vols i-ix (with Prof. W. Matthews), 1970-76, vols x and xi, 1983; (ed) Catalogue of the Pepys Library at Magdalene College, Cambridge, Vol. I, 1978, vol. III, pt i, 1980; (ed) The Illustrated Pepys, 1978; articles and reviews in learned and other jls. *Recreations:* music, gossip. *Address:* Magdalene College, Cambridge CB3 0AG. *T:* Cambridge 61545.

LATHE, Prof. Grant Henry; Professor of Chemical Pathology, University of Leeds, 1957-77, now Emeritus Professor; *b* 27 July 1913; *s* of Frank Eugene and Annie Smith Lathe; *m* 1st, 1938, Margaret Eleanore Brown; one *s* ; 2nd, 1950, Joan Frances Hamlin; one *s* two *d. Educ:* McGill Univ.; Oxford Univ. ICI Research Fellow: Dept. of Biochemistry, Oxford Univ., 1946; Dept. of Chemical Pathology, Post Graduate Medical School of London, 1948; Lecturer in Chemical Pathology, Guy's Hospital Medical School, 1948; Biochemist, The Bernhard Baron Memorial Research Laboratories, Queen Charlotte's Maternity Hospital, London, 1949. John Scott Award (with C. R. J. Ruthven), 1971, for invention of gel filtration. *Publications:* papers in medical and biochemical journals. *Recreation:* listening to music. *Address:* 12A The Avenue, Leeds LS8 1EH. *T:* 661507.

LATIMER, Sir (Courtenay) Robert, Kt 1966; CBE 1958 (OBE 1948); *b* 13 July 1911; *er s* of late Sir Courtenay Latimer, KCIE, CSI; *m* 1944, Elizabeth Jane Gordon (*née* Smail); one *s* one *d. Educ:* Rugby; Christ Church, Oxford. ICS, 1934 (Punjab); IPS, 1939; Vice-Consul, Bushire, 1940-41; Sec. Foreign Publicity Office, Delhi, 1941-42; Sec. Indian Agency Gen., Chungking, 1944; in NW Frontier Prov., as Asst Political Agent N Waziristan, Dir of Civil Supplies, Sec. to Governor and District Comr, Bannu, 1942-43 and 1945-47. HM Overseas Service, 1948; served in Swaziland, 1948-49; Bechuanaland Protectorate, 1951-54; Office of High Comr for Basutoland, the Bechuanaland Protectorate and Swaziland, as Asst Sec., 1949-51; Sec. for Finance, 1954-60; Chief Sec., 1960-64; Minister, British Embassy, Pretoria, 1965-66; Registrar, Kingston Polytechnic, 1967-76. *Recreations:* golf, photography. *Address:* Benedicts, Old Avenue, Weybridge, Surrey.

LATIMER, Sir Graham (Stanley), KBE 1980; President, New Zealand Maori Council, since 1972 (Delegate, 1964; Vice-President, 1969-72); *b* Waiharara, N Auckland, 7 Feb. 1926; *s* of Graham Latimer and Lillian Edith Latimer (*née* Kenworthy); *m* 1948, Emily Patricia Moore; two *s* two *d. Educ:* Pukenui and Kaitaia District High School. Dairy farmer, 1961-. Member: Tai Tokerau Dist Maori Council, 1962- (Sec. 1966-75); Otamatea Maori Exec., 1959- (Sec. Treas. 1962-72, Chm. 1975-); Otamatea Maori Cttee, 1955-62; Arapaoa Maori Cttee, 1962- (Chm. 1962-69 and 1972-); N Auckland Power Bd, 1977-; Waitangi Tribunal, 1976-. Chm., since inception, Northland Community Coll.; Trustee, Maori Education Foundn; Member: Cttee, Nat. Art Gall. Museum and War Memorial; NZ Maori Arts and Crafts Inst., 1980-; Tourist Adv. Council; Northland Regional Develt Council, 1980-; Alcoholic Liquor Adv. Council, 1980-. Lay Canon, Auckland Anglican Cathedral, 1978; Mem. Gen. Synod. *Recreations:* Rugby football, tennis. *Address:* RD1, Taipuha, Northland, New Zealand. *T:* Taipuha 837.

LATIMER, Sir Robert; see Latimer, Sir C. R.

LATNER, Prof. Albert Louis; Professor of Clinical Biochemistry, University of Newcastle upon Tyne, 1963-78, now Emeritus Professor, and Director of Cancer Research Unit, 1967-78; Consultant Clinical Biochemist, Royal Victoria Infirmary, Newcastle upon Tyne, 1948-78, Hon. Consultant, since 1978; *b* 5 Dec. 1912; *s* of Harry Latner and Miriam Gordon; *m* 1936, Gertrude Franklin. *Educ:* Imperial College of Science and University College, London; University of Liverpool. ARCSc, 1931; MSc (London) 1933; DIC, 1934; MB, ChB (Liverpool) 1939; MD (Liverpool) 1948; FRIC 1953; MRCP 1956; DSc (Liverpool) 1958; FRCPath 1964; FRCP 1964. Lectr in Physiology, Univ. of Liverpool, 1933-36 and 1939-41; Pathologist in RAMC, 1941-46; Sen. Registrar, Postgrad. Medical Sch., 1946-47; Lectr in Chem. Pathol., King's Coll., Univ. of Durham, 1947-55; Reader in Medical Biochemistry, Univ. of Durham, 1955-61; Prof. of Clin. Chem., Univ. of Durham, 1961-63. Vis. Lectr, Amer. Assoc. Clinical Chemists, 1972. Chm. Assoc. of Clinical Biochemists, 1958-61 (Pres., 1961-63); Mem., Editorial Bd of Clinica Chimica Acta, 1960-68; Co-editor, Advances in Clinical Chemistry, 1971-. Titular Member, Section of Clinical Chemistry, International Union of Pure and Applied Chemistry, 1967-73; Hon. Fellow, American Nat. Acad. of Clinical Biochemistry, 1977-. Mem. Editorial Bd, Electrophoresis, 1980-. Wellcome Prize, 1976. *Publications:* (co-author) Isoenzymes in Biology and Medicine, 1968; Cantarow and Trumper Clinical Biochemistry, 7th edn, 1975; Chapter on Metabolic Aspects of Liver Disease in Metabolic Disturbances in Clinical Medicine (ed G. A. Smart), 1958; Chapters on Chemical Pathology and Clinical Biochemistry in British Encyclopædia of Med. Practice, Med. Progress (ed Lord Cohen of Birkenhead), 1961, 1962, 1964, 1966 and 1968; Chapter on Isoenzymes in Recent Advances in Clinical Pathology, Series IV, 1964; Section on Isoenzymes in Advances in Clinical Chemistry (ed C. P. Stewart), 1966; (ed with O. Bodansky and contrib. section on Isoelectric Focusing) Advances in Clinical Chemistry, 1975; contribs to Medical and Scientific Journals dealing with cancer, liver disease, pernicious anæmia, the serum proteins in disease and isoenzymes. *Recreations:* art, photography, gardening. *Address:* Ravenstones, Rectory Road, Gosforth, Newcastle upon Tyne NE3 1XP. *T:* Gosforth 858020. *Club:* Athenæum.

LATOUR-ADRIEN, Hon. Sir (Jean François) Maurice, Kt 1971; Chief Justice of Mauritius, 1970-77; Director, Mauritius Commercial Bank Ltd, since 1980; *b* 4 March 1915; 2nd *s* of late Louis Constant Emile Adrien and late Maria Ella Latour. *Educ:* Royal Coll., Mauritius; Univ. Coll., London; Middle Temple, London. LLB 1940. Called to the Bar, Middle Temple, 1940. Mauritius: Dist Magistrate, 1947; Crown Counsel, 1950; Additl Subst. Procureur and Advocate-Gen., 1954; Sen. Crown Counsel, 1958; Asst Attorney-Gen., 1960; Solicitor-Gen., 1961; Dir of Public Prosecutions, 1964; Puisne Judge, 1966. Pres., Mauritius Red Cross Soc., 1978-; Vice-Pres., Inst. Internat. de Droit d'Expression Française (IDEF). Dir, Mauritius Union Assurance Co. Ltd, 1978-. Vice-Pres., Mental Health Assoc., 1978-. KLJ 1969. *Address:* Vacoas, Mauritius.

LA TROBE-BATEMAN, Richard George Saumarez; furniture designer/maker; *b* 17 Oct. 1938; *s* of John La Trobe-Bateman and Margaret Schmid; *m* 1969, Mary Elizabeth Jolly; one *s* two *d*. *Educ:* Westminster Sch.; St Martin's Sch. of Art; Royal Coll. of Art (MDesRCA). Set up workshop, 1968. Mem., Council of Management, British Crafts Centre, 1975-; Crafts Council Index Selector, 1972-73; Chm., Index Selection Cttee, 1980-82. Official British Exhibitor: Kortrijk, 1979; Copenhagen, 1980; work in V&A Collection, 1979; work presented by Crafts Council to the Prince of Wales, 1982. *Publication:* article in Crafts. *Recreations:* listening to music, hill-walking. *Address:* Hillclose, Batcombe, Shepton Mallet, Somerset BA4 6AB. *T:* Upton Noble 442. *Club:* British Crafts Centre.

LATTER, Leslie William; Director General, Merseyside Passenger Transport Executive, since 1977; *b* 4 Nov. 1921; *s* of William Richard and Clara Maud Latter; *m* 1948, Pamela Jean Marsh; one *s*. *Educ:* Beckenham Grammar Sch., Kent. IPFA, FRVA, FCIT. Served Royal Air Force, 1940-46. London County Council, 1947-62; Chief Asst, Beckenham Borough Council, 1962-64; Asst Borough Treasurer, Bromley, 1964-68; Dep. Borough Treasurer, Greenwich, 1968-74; Dir of Finance and Administration, Merseyside PTE, 1974-77. *Recreations:* gardening, music. *Address:* Merseyside Passenger Transport Executive, 24 Hatton Garden, Liverpool L3 2AN. *T:* 051-227 5181. *Clubs:* Royal Commonwealth Society, Royal Over-Seas League; Skal (Liverpool).

LATTIMORE, Owen; Professor of Chinese Studies, Leeds University, 1963-70, now Professor Emeritus; Director, Page School of International Relations, 1938-50 and Lecturer in History to 1963, Johns Hopkins University, USA; *b* Washington, DC, 29 July 1900; *s* of David Lattimore and Margaret Barnes; *m* 1926, Eleanor, (*d* 1970), *d* of Dr T. F. Holgate, Evanston, Ill.; one *s*. *Educ:* St Bees Sch., Cumberland; Collège Classique Cantonal, Lausanne; Research Student at Harvard Univ., 1929. Early childhood in China; returned to China, 1919; engaged in business in Tientsin and Shanghai, 1920; Journalism in Tientsin, 1921; business in Tientsin and Peking with Arnhold and Co., 1922-25; travelled in Mongolia, 1926; in Chinese Turkestan, 1927; studied in America, 1928, 1929; travelled in Manchuria, as Fellow of Social Science Research Council, 1929-30; Research work in Peking, as Fellow of Harvard-Yenching Institute, 1930-31; Research Fellow, Guggenheim Foundation, Peking, 1931-33; travelled in Mongolia, 1932-33; editor, Pacific Affairs, 1934-41; research work in China and Mongolia, 1934-35, 1937; Political Adviser to Generalissimo Chiang Kai-Shek, 1941-42; Director, Pacific Operations, Office of War Information, San Francisco, 1943; accompanied Vice-President Wallace in Siberia and China, 1944; economic consultant, American Reparations Mission in Japan, 1945; UN Technical Aid Mission, Afghanistan, 1950; Visiting Lecturer: Ecole Pratique des Hautes Etudes, Sorbonne, 1958-59; University of Copenhagen, 1961. Travelled in Soviet Central Asia, 1960, Mongolia, 1961, 1964, 1966, 1969, 1970, 1971, 1972, 1973, 1974, 1975, 1976, 1978, 1979, China, 1972. Chichele Lecturer, Oxford, 1965; Vis. Prof., Rutgers Univ., 1979. Awarded Cuthbert Peek Grant by Royal Geographical Society for travels in Central Asia, 1930; gold medallist, Geographical Society of Philadelphia, 1933; Patron's Medal, Royal Geographical Society, 1942; Univ. of Indiana Medal, Perm. Internat. Altaistic Congress, 1974. FRGS; Fellow, Royal Asiatic Society; Member: Royal Soc. for Asian Affairs; American Historical Society; American Philosophical Society; For. Member, Academy of Sciences, Mongolian People's Republic; Hon. Member: American Geographical Society, Soc. Csoma Körösi, Hungary. Hon. DLitt Glasgow, 1964; Hon. PhD Copenhagen, 1972; Hon. Dr Law Brown Univ., 1974. Order of Golden Nail (Polar Star) (Mongolian People's Republic), 1979. *Publications:* The Desert Road to Turkestan, 1928; High Tartary, 1930; Manchuria: Cradle of Conflict, 1932; The Mongols of Manchuria, 1934; Inner Asian Frontiers of China, 1940; Mongol Journeys, 1941; Solution in Asia, 1945; China, A Short History (with Eleanor Lattimore), 1947; The Situation in Asia, 1949; Sinkiang, Pivot of Asia, 1950; Ordeal by Slander, 1950; Nationalism and Revolution in Mongolia, 1955; Nomads and Commissars, 1962; Studies in Asian Frontier History, 1962; Silks, Spices and Empire (with Eleanor Lattimore), 1968; contributor to periodicals. *Recreation:* cycling. *Address:* 3 Larchfield, Gough Way, Barton Road, Cambridge CB3 9LR; c/o Department of Chinese Studies, The University, Leeds LS2 9JT.

LATTIN, Francis Joseph, CMG 1953; Barrister-at-law; *b* 23 March 1905; *s* of John Lattin, Morland, Westmorland; *m* 1934, May Sadler, Harrogate; one *s* (and one *s* decd). *Educ:* Appleby Grammar Sch.; Durham Univ. (MA); Cambridge Univ.; called to Bar, Gray's Inn. Assistant District Officer, Colonial Administrative Service, Uganda, 1930; Deputy Controller of Prices and Military Contracts, Kenya, 1942; Development Comr, Uganda, 1949;

MLC 1949, MEC 1951, Uganda; Mem. East African Legislative Assembly, 1951; London Representative, Uganda Electricity Board, 1952. Bursar, Grey Coll., Durham, 1963-68. *Publications:* (jointly) Economic Survey of Western Uganda, 1951; articles on various aspects of colonial development. *Recreation:* interest in all outdoor sports. *Address:* The Green, Tirril, Penrith, Cumbria. *T:* Penrith 62960. *Club:* Royal Commonwealth Society.

LATTO, Dr Douglas; private medical practice; Chairman, British Safety Council, since 1971 (Vice-Chairman, 1968-71); *b* Dundee, Scotland, 13 Dec. 1913; *s* of late David Latto, Town Clerk of Dundee, and late Christina Latto; *m* 1945, Dr Edith Monica Druitt; one *s* three *d*. *Educ:* Dundee High Sch.; St Andrews Univ. MB, ChB (St And.) 1939; DObst, RCOG 1944, MRCOG 1949. During War: Ho. Surg., Dundee Royal Infirmary, 1939; Ho. Phys., Cornelia and East Dorset Hosp., Poole, 1940; Resident Obstetrician and Gynaecologist, Derbyshire Hosp. for Women, Derby, 1940; Res. Surgical Officer, Hereford Gen. Hosp., 1941; Res. Obst. and Gynaec., East End Maternity Hosp., London, 1942; Res. Obst. and Gynaec., City of London Maternity Hosp., 1943; Res. Surgical Officer, Birmingham Accident Hosp., 1944; Casualty Officer, Paddington Gen. Hosp., London, 1944; Asst Obst. and Gynaec., Mayday Hosp., Croydon, 1945. Res. Obst. and Gynaec., Southlands Hosp., Shoreham-by-Sea, Sussex, 1946-49; Asst, Nuffield Dept of Obstetrics and Gynaecology, Radcliffe Infirmary, Oxford, 1949-51. Member: BMA; Council, Soil Assoc.; Chm., Plantmilk Soc.; Vice-Pres., International Vegetarian Union; Governor, Internat. Inst. of Safety Management. Mem., Order of the Cross. FRSocMed; FRPSL 1975. Silver Jubilee Medal, 1977. *Publications:* Smoking and Lung Cancer: a report to all Members of Parliament for the British Safety Council, May 1969; contribs to BMJ; Proc. Royal Soc. Med.; Philatelic Jl; etc. *Recreations:* squash, travelling, gardening, philately (Internat. Stamp Exhibns: Large Gold Medal, London, 1970; Gold Medal, Brussels, 1972, Munich, 1973, Basle, 1974; Large Gold Medals: Paris 1975; Copenhagen, 1976 (and Prix d'Honneur); London, 1980 (and GB Philatelic Soc. Award); Vienna, 1981. *Address:* Lethnot Lodge, 4 Derby Road, Caversham, Reading, Berks RG4 0EY. *T:* Reading 472282; 59 Harley Street, W1N 1DD. *T:* 01-580 1070. *Club:* Royal Automobile.

LATYMER, 7th Baron, *cr* 1431; **Thomas Burdett Money-Coutts;** Member, 1948-80, Chairman, 1948-75, London Committee of Ottoman Bank; *b* 6 Aug. 1901; *e s* of 6th Baron and Hester Frances, 4th *d* of late Maj.-Gen. John Cecil Russell, CVO; *S* father 1949; *m* 1925, Patience (*d* 1982), *d* of late W. Courtenay-Thompson and Mrs Herbert Money; one *s* two *d*. *Educ:* Radley; Trinity Coll., Oxford. Served War of 1939-45. OStJ. *Heir: s* Hon. Hugo Neville Money-Coutts [*b* 1 March 1926; *m* 1st, 1951, Penelope Ann Clare (marr. diss., 1965), *yr d* of late T. A. Emmet and of Baroness Emmet of Amberley; two *s* one *d*; 2nd, 1965, Jinty, *d* of P. G. Calvert, London; one *s* two *d*]. *Address:* San Rebassa, Moscari, Mallorca. *Club:* MCC.

LAUCKE, Hon. Sir Condor (Louis), KCMG 1979; Lieutenant-Governor, State of South Australia, since 1982; *b* 9 Nov. 1914; *s* of Friedrich Laucke and Marie (*née* Jungfer); *m* 1942, Rose Hambour; one *s* one *d*. *Educ:* Immanuel Coll., Adelaide; South Australian School of Mines. Elected to S Australian House of Assembly, 1956, 1959, 1962; Government Whip, 1962-65; Member, Australian Senate for S Australia, 1967-81; Pres. Senate, Parlt of Commonwealth of Australia, 1976-81. Member, Liberal Party Executive, 1972-74. Joint President: CPA, 1976- (also Chm., Exec. Cttee, 1976-); IPU. *Address:* Bunawunda, Greenock, SA 5360, Australia. *T:* 085 628143.

LAUDER, Sir Piers Robert Dick-, 13th Bt *cr* 1688; *b* 3 Oct. 1947; *s* of Sir George Andrew Dick-Lauder, 12th Bt and of Hester Marguerite, *d* of late Lt-Col G. C. M. Sorell-Cameron, CBE, Gorthleck House, Inverness-shire; *S* father, 1981. *Heir: b* Mark Andrew Dick-Lauder [*b* 3 May 1951; *m* 1970, Jeanne Mullineaux; one *s*]. *Address:* Firth Mill House, near Roslin, Midlothian EH25 9QQ.

LAUDERDALE, 17th Earl of, *cr* 1624; **Patrick Francis Maitland;** Baron Maitland, 1590; Viscount Lauderdale, 1616; Viscount Maitland, Baron Thirlestane and Boltoun, 1624; Bt of Nova Scotia, 1680; Hereditary Bearer of the National Flag of Scotland, 1790 and 1952; *b* 17 March 1911; *s* of Reverend Hon. Sydney G. W. Maitland and Ella Frances (*née* Richards); *S* brother, 1968; *m* 1936, Stanka, *d* of Professor Milivoje Lozanitch, Belgrade Univ.; two *s* two *d*. *Educ:* Lancing Coll., Sussex; Brasenose Coll., Oxford. BA Hons Oxon, 1933; Journalist 1933-59. Appts include: Balkans and Danubian Corresp., The Times, 1939-41; Special Corresp. Washington, News Chronicle, 1941; War Corresp., Pacific, Australia, New Zealand, News Chronicle, 1941-43. Foreign Office, 1943-45. MP (U) for Lanark Div. of Lanarks, 1951-Sept. 1959 (except for period May-Dec. 1957 when Ind. C). Founder and Chairman, Expanding Commonwealth Group, House of Commons, 1955-59; re-elected Chairman, Nov. 1959. Chm., Sub-Cttee on Energy, Transport and Res., House of Lords Select Cttee on EEC Affairs, 1974-79. Director: Elf-Aquitaine (UK) Holdings; Harwich International Terminal (Holdings). Editor of The Fleet Street Letter Service, and of The Whitehall Letter, 1945-58. Mem., Coll. of Guardians of National Shrine of Our Lady of Walsingham, Norfolk, 1955-. President, The Church Union, 1956-61. FRGS. *Publications:* European Dateline, 1945; Task for Giants, 1957. *Heir: s* The Master of Lauderdale, Viscount Maitland, *qv*. *Address:* 10 Ovington Square, SW3. *T:* 01-589 7451; 12 St Vincent Street, Edinburgh. *T:* 031-556 5692. *Clubs:* New (Edinburgh); Royal Scottish Automobile (Glasgow).

LAUDERDALE, Master of; see Maitland, Viscount.

LAUGHARNE, Albert, QPM 1978; Chief Constable of Lancashire, since 1978; b 20 Oct. 1931; s of Reginald Stanley Laugharne and Jessica Simpson Laugharne; m 1954, Barbara Thirlwall; two d. Educ: Baines' Grammar Sch., Poulton-le-Fylde; Manchester Univ. Detective Inspector, Manchester City Police, 1952-66; Supt, Cumbria Constab., 1966-70; Chief Supt, W Yorks Constab., 1970-73; Asst Chief Constable, Cheshire Constab., 1973-76; Chief Constable, Warwicks, 1977-78. RCDS, 1975. Publication: Seaford House Papers, 1975. Recreations: gardening, painting. Address: The Laund, Saunders Lane, New Longton, Preston, Lancs. T: Longton 614444.

LAUGHLAND, (Graham Franklyn) Bruce, QC 1977; a Recorder of the Crown Court, since 1972; b 18 Aug. 1931; 3rd s of late Andrew and late Constance Laughland; m 1969, Victoria Nicola Christina Jarman; one s. Educ: King Edward's Sch., Birmingham; Christ Church, Oxford. Called to Bar, Inner Temple, 1958; Mem. Gen. Council of Bar, 1970; Dep. Chm., Bucks QS, 1971. Standing Counsel to the Queen's Proctor, 1968; First Prosecuting Counsel to the Inland Revenue (Midland and Oxford Circuit), 1973-77. Address: 4 King's Bench Walk, Temple, EC4 7DL. T: 01-353 3581; 30 Monmouth Road, W2. T: 01-229 5045.

LAUGHTON, Dr Anthony Seymour, FRS 1980; Director, Institute of Oceanographic Sciences, since 1978; b 29 April 1927; s of Sydney Thomas Laughton and Dorothy Laughton (née Chamberlain); m 1st, 1957, Juliet Ann Chapman (marr. diss. 1962); one s; 2nd, 1973, Barbara Clare Bosanquet; two d. Educ: Marlborough Coll.; King's Coll., Cambridge (MA, PhD). RNVR, 1945-48. John Murray Student, Columbia Univ., NY, 1954-55; Nat. Inst. of Oceanography, later Inst. of Oceanographic Sciences, 1955-: research in marine geophysics in Atlantic and Indian Oceans, esp. in underwater photography, submarine morphology, ocean basin evolution, midocean ridge tectonics; Principal Scientist of deep sea expedns. Mem., nat. and internat. cttees on oceanography and geophysics. Mem. Governing Body, Charterhouse Sch., 1981-. Silver Medal, RSA, 1958; Cuthbert Peek grant, RGS, 1967; Prince Albert 1er Monaco Gold Medal for Oceanography, 1980. Publications: papers on marine geophysics. Recreations: music, gardening, sailing. Address: Okelands, Pickhurst Road, Chiddingfold, Surrey. T: Wormley 3941. Club: Naval.

LAUGHTON, Prof. Eric; Firth Professor of Latin in the University of Sheffield, 1952-76, now Emeritus; b 4 Sept. 1911; 2nd s of Rev. G. W. Laughton; m 1938, Elizabeth Gibbons; one s one d. Educ: King Edward VII Sch., Sheffield; St John's Coll., Oxford (open classical scholar). Asst in Humanity Dept, University of Edinburgh, 1934-36; University of Sheffield: Asst Lecturer in Classics, 1939; Senior Lecturer, 1946; Public Orator, 1955-68; Pro-Vice-Chancellor, 1968-72. Service in Intelligence Corps, South East Asia, 1943-45. Publications: verse translation of Papyrus (17th-century Latin poem by J. Imberdis), 1952; The Participle in Cicero, 1964. Articles and reviews in various classical journals. Recreations: walking, music. Address: Forelane, Deerhurst, Glos. T: Tewkesbury 295437.

LAURENCE, Dan Hyman; Literary and Dramatic Advisor, Estate of George Bernard Shaw, since 1973; b 28 March 1920. Educ: New York City public schs; Hofstra Univ. (BA 1946); New York Univ. (MA 1950). First went on the stage as child actor, 1932; radar specialist with Fifth Air Force, USA, in S Pacific, 1942-45; wrote and performed for Armed Forces Radio Service in New Guinea and the Philippines during World War II, and subseq. for radio and television in USA and Australia; began teaching in 1950 as graduate asst, New York Univ.; Instr of English, Hofstra Univ., 1953-58; Editor, Readex Microprint Corp., 1959-60; Associate Prof. of English, New York Univ., 1962-67, Prof., 1967-70. Vis. Professor: Indiana Univ., 1969; Univ. of Texas at Austin, 1974-75; Tulane Univ., 1981 (Mellon Prof. in the Humanities); Vis. Fellow, Inst. for Arts and Humanistic Studies, Pennsylvania State Univ., 1976. John Simon Guggenheim Meml Fellow, 1960, 1961 and 1972. Phi Beta Kappa (hon.), 1967. Publications: Henry James: a bibliography (with Leon Edel), 1957 (3rd edn 1981); Robert Nathan: a bibliography, 1960; (ed) Collected Letters of Bernard Shaw, 1965-; (ed) Bernard Shaw, Collected Plays with their Prefaces, 1970-74; Shaw, Books, and Libraries, 1976; Shaw: an exhibit, 1977; (dramatization) The Black Girl in Search of God, 1977; (ed) Shaw's Music, 1981; Bernard Shaw: a bibliography, 1982; (Uncollected Writings of Shaw): How to Become a Musical Critic, 1960 (2nd edn 1978); Platform and Pulpit, 1961; (ed with David H. Greene) The Matter with Ireland, 1962; (ed with Daniel J. Leary) Flyleaves, 1977. Recreations: theatre-going, music, book-collecting, mountain climbing. Address: c/o The Society of Authors, 84 Drayton Gardens, SW10 9SD.

LAURENCE, Sir Peter (Harold), KCMG 1981 (CMG 1976); MC 1944; HM Diplomatic Service; Ambassador to Ankara, 1980-83; b 18 Feb. 1923; s of late Ven. George Laurence, MA, BD and late Alice (née Jackson); m 1948, Elizabeth Aïda Way; two s one d. Educ: Radley Coll.; Christ Church, Oxford. 60th Rifles, 1941-46 (Major). Entered Foreign Service, 1948; Western Dept, FO, 1948-50; Athens, 1950-53; Asst Political Adviser, Trieste, 1953-55; 1st Sec., Levant Dept, FO, 1955-57; Prague, 1957-60; Cairo, 1960-62; North and East African Dept, FO, 1962-65; Personnel Dept, DSAO, 1965-67; Counsellor, 1965; Political Adviser, Berlin, 1967-69; Visiting Fellow, All Souls Coll., 1969-70; Counsellor (Commercial), Paris, 1970-74; Chief Inspector, HM Diplomatic Service (Asst Under-Sec. of State), 1974-78. Address: Ley Marden, Yarnscombe, Barnstable, N Devon. Club: United Oxford & Cambridge University.

LAURENS, André; Editor-in-Chief of Le Monde, since 1982; b 7 Dec. 1934; unmarried. Journalist: L'Eclaireur méridional, Montpellier, 1953-55; l'Agence centrale de la presse, Paris, 1958-62; joined Le Monde, 1963; Home Affairs reporter, 1969; Associate Editor, Home Affairs, 1979. Vice-Pres., Société des Rédacteurs. Publications: Les nouveaux communistes, 1972; D'une France à l'autre, 1974; Le métier politique, 1980. Address: 34 rue de Clichy, 75009 Paris, France.

LAURIE, Maj.-Gen. Sir John Emilius, 6th Bt, cr 1834; CBE 1940; DSO 1916; b 12 Aug. 1892; S father 1936; m 1922, Evelyn Clare, o d of late Lt-Col L. J. Richardson-Gardner, 14th Hussars; one s two d. Served European War, 1914-18 (despatches 5 times, DSO and bar, Chevalier Légion d'Honneur); commanded 6th (Morayshire) Bn Seaforth Highlanders, 1918-19, and 2nd Bn Seaforth Highlanders, 1934-38; Comdr, Tientsin Area, British Troops in China, 1939-40 (despatches); 157 Inf. Bde., France, 1940 (CBE); 52nd (Lowland) Div., 1941-42; Combined Operations Training Centre, Inveraray; retired 1945; Col, Seaforth Highlanders, 1947-57. Heir: s Robert Bayley Emilius Laurie [b 8 March 1931; m 1968, Laurelie, er d of late Sir Reginald Williams, 7th Bt, MBE, ED; two d]. Address: Amesbury Abbey, Amesbury, Wilts. Clubs: Army and Navy, Caledonian, MCC.
See also Sir Hector Laing.

LAURISTON, Alexander Clifford, QC 1972; **His Honour Judge Lauriston;** a Circuit Judge, since 1976; b 2 Oct. 1927; s of Alexander Lauriston and Nellie Lauriston (née Ainsworth); m 1954, Inga Louise Cameron; two d. Educ: Coatham Sch., Redcar, Yorks; Trinity Coll., Cambridge (MA). National Service: Army, Green Howards and RAPC, 2nd Lieut, 1948-50. Called to Bar, Inner Temple, 1952. A Recorder of the Crown Court, 1972-76. Mem., Loriners' Co., 1969. Recreations: riding, motor sports, tennis, golf, painting, music. Address: 2 Harcourt Buildings, Temple, EC4. Club: Berkshire Golf.
See also R. B. Lauriston.

LAURISTON, Richard Basil; a Recorder of the Crown Court, since 1974; a Permanent Chairman of Industrial Tribunals, since 1976; formerly Senior Partner, Alex Lauriston & Son, Solicitors, Middlesbrough; b 26 Jan. 1917; s of Alexander Lauriston, MBE, and Nellie Lauriston; m 1944, Monica, d of Wilfred Leslie Deacon, BA, Tonbridge, and Dorothy Louise Deacon; three s. Educ: Sir William Turner's Sch., Redcar; St John's Coll., Cambridge (MA, LLB). Solicitor, 1948. Commnd and served in War of 1939-45, Royal Corps of Signals. Recreations: fishing, travelling. Address: 26 Easby Lane, Great Ayton, North Yorks TS9 6JZ. T: Great Ayton 2429.
See also A. C. Lauriston.

LAUTERPACHT, Elihu, QC 1970; Fellow of Trinity College, Cambridge, since 1953; Reader in International Law, University of Cambridge, since 1981; b 13 July 1928; o s of late Sir Hersch Lauterpacht, QC and Rachel Steinberg; m 1955, Judith Maria (d 1970), er d of Harold Hettinger; one s two d; m 1973, Catherine Daly; one s. Educ: Phillips Acad., Andover, Mass; Harrow; Trinity Coll., Cambridge (Entrance Schol.). 1st cl. Pt II of Law Tripos and LLB; Whewell Schol. in Internat. Law, 1950; Holt Schol. 1948 and Birkenhead Schol. 1950, Gray's Inn; called to Bar, 1950. Joint Sec., Interdepartmental Cttee on State Immunity, 1950-52; Asst Lectr in Law, Univ. of Cambridge, 1953, Lecturer, 1958-81; Sec., Internat. Law Fund, 1955; Dir of Research, Hague Academy of Internat. Law, 1959-60; Vis. Prof. of Internat. Law, Univ. of Delhi, 1960. Chm., East African Common Market Tribunal, 1972-; Consultant to Central Policy Review Staff, 1974-78, 1978-; Legal Adviser to Australian Dept of Foreign Affairs, 1975-77; Consultant on Internat. Law, UN Inst. for Training and Res., 1978-79; mem. arbitration panel, Internat. Centre for Settlement of Investment Disputes; Deputy Leader: Australian Delegn to UN Law of the Sea Conf., 1975-77; Australian Delegn to UN Gen. Assembly, 1975-77. Member: Social Services Adv. Cttee, UK Nat. Commn for Unesco, 1980-; World Bank Administrative Tribunal, 1980-; Panel of Arbitrators, Internat. Energy Agency Dispute Settlement Centre; Associate, Inst. of Internat. Law. Editor: British Practice in International Law, 1955-; International Law Reports, 1960-. Comdr, Order of Merit, Chile, 1969; awarded Annual Cert. of Merit, Amer. Soc. Internat. Law, 1972. Publications: Jerusalem and the Holy Places, 1968; (ed) International Law: the collected papers of Sir Hersch Lauterpacht, vol I, 1970, vol. II, 1975, vol. III, 1977, vol. IV, 1978; various articles on international law. Address: Trinity College, Cambridge. T: Cambridge 358201; 3 Essex Court, Temple, EC4. T: 01-353 2624; 7 Herschel Road, Cambridge. T: Cambridge 354707. Club: Athenæum.

LAUTI, Rt. Hon. Toaripi, PC 1979; MP; Leader of the Opposition, Tuvalu Parliament, since 1981; b Papua New Guinea, 1928; m; three s two d. Educ: Tuvalu; Fiji; St Andrew's Coll., Christchurch, NZ; Christchurch Teachers' Training Coll., NZ. Taught in Tarawa, Kiribati, 1953-62; engaged in Labour Relations, Nauru, Training Officer, British Phosphate Commn; returned to Tuvalu, 1974, and entered politics; elected unopposed to House of Assembly, May 1975; elected Chief Minister, Tuvalu, upon separation of Ellice Islands (Tuvalu) from Kiribati, Oct. 1975, re-elected Chief Minister in Sept. 1977; First Prime Minister, Tuvalu, 1978-81. Chm., 18th South Pacific Conference, Noumea, Oct. 1978. Address: Alapi, Funafuti Island, Tuvalu, South West Pacific.

LAVAN, Hon. Sir John Martin, Kt 1981; Senior Puisne Judge of the Supreme Court of Western Australia; *b* 5 Sept. 1911; *s* of late M. G. Lavan, KC; *m* 1939, Leith Harford; one *s* three *d. Educ:* Aquinas Coll., Perth; Xavier Coll., Melbourne. Barrister in private practice, 1934-69; a Judge of the Supreme Court of WA, 1969-. Chm., Parole Bd, WA, 1969-79. Mem., Barristers' Bd, WA, 1960-69; Pres., Law Soc. of WA, 1964-66. KStJ. *Address:* Supreme Court, Perth, Western Australia 6000; 165 Victoria Avenue, Dalkeith, WA 6009, Australia. *Club:* Weld (Perth).

LAVELLE, Roger Garnett; Under Secretary, HM Treasury, since 1975; *b* 23 Aug. 1932; *s* of Henry Allman Lavelle and Evelyn Alice Garnett; *m* 1956, Elsa Gunilla Odeberg; three *s* one *d. Educ:* Leighton Park; Trinity Hall, Cambridge (BA, LLB). Asst Principal, Min. of Health, 1955; Principal, HM Treasury, 1961; Special Assistant (Common Market) to Lord Privy Seal, 1961-63; Private Sec. to Chancellor of the Exchequer, 1965-68; Asst Secretary, HM Treasury, 1968. *Recreations:* music and gardening. *Address:* 36 Cholmeley Crescent, Highgate, N6. *T:* 01-340 4845.

LAVER, Frederick John Murray, CBE 1971; Member, Post Office Corporation, 1969-73, retired; *b* 11 March 1915; *er s* of late Clifton F. Laver and Elsie Elizabeth Palmer, Bridgwater; *m* 1948, Kathleen Amy Blythe; one *s* two *d. Educ:* Plymouth Coll. BSc London. Entered PO Engrg Dept, 1935; PO Research Stn, 1935-51; Radio Planning, 1951-57; Organization and Efficiency, 1957-63; Asst Sec., HM Treasury, 1963-65; Chief Scientific Officer, Min. of Technology, 1965-68; Director, National Data Processing Service, 1968-70; Mem., NRDC, 1974-80. Vis. Prof., Computing Lab., Univ. of Newcastle upon Tyne, 1975-79. Mem. Council: IEE, 1966-69, 1972-73; British Computer Soc., 1969-72; Nat. Computing Centre, 1966-68, 1970-73; IEE Electronic Divl Bd, 1966-69, 1970-73. Mem. Council, 1979-, Pro-Chancellor, 1981-, Exeter Univ. CEng, FIEE; Hon. FBCS. *Publications:* nine introductory books on physics and computing; several scientific papers. *Recreations:* reading, writing, and watching the sea. *Address:* Woodrising, Bickwell Valley, Sidmouth, Devon EX10 8RF. *T:* Sidmouth 5005.

LAVER, Patrick Martin; HM Diplomatic Service; Director of Research, Foreign and Commonwealth Office, since 1980; *b* 3 Feb. 1932; *s* of late James Laver, CBE, RE, FRSL, and late Veronica Turleigh; *m* 1st, 1966, Marianne Ford (marr. diss. 1973); one *d*; 2nd, 1979, Dr Elke Maria Schmitz, *d* of Thomas and Anneliese Schmitz. *Educ:* Ampleforth Coll., Yorks; New Coll., Oxford. Third Sec., Foreign Office, 1954; Second Sec., Djakarta, 1956; FO, 1957; Paris, 1958; Yaoundé, 1961; UK Delegn to Brussels Conf., 1962; First Sec., FO, 1963; UK Mission to UN, New York, 1964; Diplomatic Service Admin., 1965; Commercial Sec., Nairobi, 1968; FCO, 1970; Counsellor (Economic), Pretoria, 1973; UK Delegn to Conf. on Security and Co-operation in Europe, Geneva, 1974; Head of Rhodesia Dept, FCO, 1975-78; Counsellor, Paris, 1979-80. *Address:* c/o Foreign and Commonwealth Office, SW1; Flat 4, 10 The Glebe, SE3 9TG. *T:* 01-852 3905. *Club:* Athenæum.

LAVER, William Scott, CBE 1962; HM Diplomatic Service, retired; *b* 7 March 1909; *s* of Robert John Laver, Latchingdon, Essex, and Frances Lucy (*née* Pasmore), Windsor; *m* 1969, Marjorie Joan Hall, Chislehurst, Kent. *Educ:* St Dunstan's Coll., Catford; Downing Coll., Cambridge. Dept of Overseas Trade, 1932; Asst to Commercial Counsellor: Brussels, 1934, Rome, 1936; Commercial Sec., Rio de Janeiro, 1940; Commercial Sec., Cairo, 1946; Foreign Office, 1950-51; Financial Sec., Bahrain, 1951; Political Agent, Bahrain, 1951-52; Counsellor (Economic), Belgrade, 1954; Counsellor (Commercial), Oslo, 1958-62; Ambassador to Congo Republic, Gabon, Republic of Chad, and Central African Republic, 1962-66. *Address:* Flat 30, Mapledene, Kemnal Road, Chislehurst, Kent.

LAVERICK, Elizabeth, PhD, CEng, FIEE, FInstP, FIEEE (US); Deputy Secretary, Institution of Electrical Engineers, since 1971; *b* 25 Nov. 1925; *d* of William Rayner and Alice Garland; *m* 1946 (marr. diss. 1960); no *c. Educ:* Dr Challoner's Grammar Sch., Amersham; Durham Univ. Research at Durham Univ., 1946-50; Section Leader at GEC, 1950-53; Microwave Engineer at Elliott Bros, 1954; Head of Radar Research Laboratory of Elliott-Automation Radar Systems Ltd, 1959; Jt Gen. Manager, Elliott-Automation Radar Systems Ltd, 1968-69, Technical Dir, 1969-71. President, Women's Engineering Soc., 1967-69; Governor, Hatfield Polytechnic; Member: IEE Electronics Divisional Bd, 1967-70; Council IEE, 1969-70; Council, Inst. of Physics, 1970-73; DE Adv. Cttee on Women's Employment, 1970-; Hon. Fellow, UMIST, 1969. *Publications:* contribs to IEE and IEEE Jls. *Recreations:* music, gardening, careers talks, sailing. *Address:* Flat 4, Carlton Mansions, 16/17 York Buildings, WC2N 6LS.

LAVERS, Patricia Mae, (Mrs H. J. Lavers); Executive Director, Bond Street Association, 1961-76, and Regent Street Association, 1972-76; *b* 12 April 1919; *d* of Edric Allan Jordan and May Holdcraft; *m* 1st, 1945, Frederick Handel Hayward (*d* 1965); one *s*; 2nd, 1966, John Harold Ellen; 3rd, 1976, Lt-Comdr Herbert James Lavers. *Educ:* Sydenham High School. Clerk, Securities Dept, National Provincial Bank, 1938-45; Export Dir, Perth Radios, 1955-60. Alderman, St Pancras Council, 1960-66 (Libraries/Public Health). Elected to Executive of Westminster Chamber of Commerce, 1971, Chm. City Affairs Cttee, 1971-75. FZS. *Recreations:* swimming, collecting first editions, press books and Meissen china. *Clubs:* Arts, Naval and Military.

LAVIN, Deborah Margaret; Principal, Trevelyan College, University of Durham, since 1980; *b* 22 Sept. 1939. *Educ:* Roedean Sch., Johannesburg, SA; Rhodes Univ., Grahamstown, SA; Lady Margaret Hall, Oxford (MA, DipEd). Asst Lectr, Dept of History, Univ. of the Witwatersrand, 1962-64; Lectr, Dept of Mod. Hist., The Queen's Univ. of Belfast, 1965-78, Sen. Lectr, 1979. Senior Associate, St Antony's Coll., Oxford. *Publications:* South African Memories, 1979; articles in learned jls. *Recreations:* broadcasting; the arts; passionate but unsuccessful tennis player. *Address:* Trevelyan College, Elvet Hill Road, Durham DH1 3LN. *T:* Durham 61133; Hickmans Cottages, Cat Street, East Hendred, Oxon OX12 8JT. *T:* East Hendred 408. *Club:* Royal Commonwealth Society.

LAVIN, Mary, (Mrs M. MacDonald Scott); Writer; *b* East Walpole, Mass, USA, 11 June 1912; *m* 1st, 1942, William Walsh (*d* 1954), MA, NUI; three *d*; 2nd, 1969, Michael MacDonald Scott, MA, MSc. *Educ:* National Univ. of Ireland, Dublin (Graduate, MA; Hon DLitt, 1968). Mem. of Irish Academy of Letters, President, 1971. Guggenheim Fellow 1959, 1962 and 1972. Katherine Mansfield Prize, 1961; Ella Lynam Cabot Award, 1971; Eire Soc. Gold Medal, Boston, 1974; Arts Award, Royal Meath Assoc., 1975; Gregory Medal, Dublin, 1975; Amer. Irish Foundn Literary Award, 1979; Allied Irish Bank Award, 1981. Personality of the Year, Royal Meath Assoc., 1976. *Publications:* Tales from Bective Bridge (short stories, awarded James Tait Black Memorial Prize), 1942 (London, 1943); The Long Ago (short stories), 1944; The House in Clewe Street (novel), 1945; At Sally Gap (Boston), 1946; The Becker Wives, 1946; Mary O'Grady (novel), 1950; Patriot Son (short stories), 1956; A Single Lady (short stories); A Likely Story (short novel), 1957; Selected Stories, 1959 (New York); The Great Wave (short stories), 1961; Stories of Mary Lavin, 1964; In the Middle of the Fields (short stories), 1966; Happiness (short stories), 1969; Collected Stories, 1971; A Memory and other Stories, 1972; The Second Best Children in the World, 1972; The Stories of Mary Lavin, vol II, 1973; The Shrine and other stories, 1976. *Address:* The Abbey Farm, Bective, Co. Meath. *T:* 046 21243; Mews Eleven, Lad Lane, Rere Fitzwilliam Place, Dublin. *T:* 763031.

LAVINGTON, Cyril Michael, MBE 1946; JP; His Honour Judge Lavington; a Circuit Judge (formerly Judge of County Courts), since 1971; *b* 21 June 1912; *e s* of Cyril Claude Lavington, MB, BS of Bristol and Nora Vernon Lavington; *m* 1950, Frances Anne (marr. diss. 1968), *d* of Colston Wintle, MD, of Bristol; one *s*. Barrister-at-Law, Middle Temple, 1936; Western Circuit, Wilts QS. Joined Army, 1939; Major, DAA and QMG, 1 GRTD, N Africa, 1943; DAAG 37 Mil. Miss. to Yugoslav Army of Nat. Liberation, 1944; DAAG 3 Corps, Greece, 1945 (despatches twice, MBE). Returned to practice, 1946. Recorder of Barnstaple, 1964-71, Honorary Recorder, 1972-; Dep. Chm., Quarter Sessions: Dorset, 1962-71; Wiltshire, 1970-71; Hampshire, 1971. JP Cornwall, 1974. *Recreations:* sailing, gardening. *Address:* Stockadon Villa, St Mellion, Saltash, Cornwall. *T:* St Dominick 50259. *Clubs:* Royal Yachting Association; Bar Yacht.

LAVOIPIERRE, Jacques Joseph Maurice; Justice of Seychelles Court of Appeal, since 1977; *b* 4 April 1909; 3rd *s* of Antoine Lavoipierre and Elisa la Hausse de Lalouvière; *m* 1939, Pauline Koenig; two *s* one *d. Educ:* Royal Coll., Mauritius; King's Coll., London (LLB); Middle Temple. Magistrate, Mauritius, 1944; Civil Comr, 1946; Magistrate, Industrial Court, 1949; Master and Registrar, Supreme Court, 1952; Substitute Procureur and Advocate-Gen., 1954. QC (Mauritius), 1961; Judge of Supreme Court, Mauritius, 1956-60; Attorney-Gen., 1960-64; after new constitution, reverted to private practice, 1965-66; Legal Officer, La Trobe Univ., Aust., 1966-74. Coronation Medal, 1953. *Address:* 34 Hillcrest, Sir Winston Churchill Street, Curepipe, Mauritius. *Clubs:* Mauritius Turf, Grand Sable (Mauritius).

LAVRIN, Prof. Janko (John), MA; Professor of Slavonic Studies, University of Nottingham, 1923, Emeritus Professor since 1953; *b* 10 Feb. 1887; *s* of John Lavrin and Gertrude (*née* Golobich), both Slovene; *m* 1928, Nora (*née* Fry), artist; two *s. Educ:* Austria, Russia, and partly in Scandinavia. Began as journalist in Russia, 1910; Russian war correspondent, 1915-17. During War of 1939-45, attached to BBC (European service) as broadcaster and language superviser. Public lecturer. *Publications:* Aspects of Modernism, 1935; An Introduction to the Russian Novel, 1942 (repr. 1974); Dostoevsky, 1943 (repr. 1968); Tolstoy, 1944 (repr. 1968); Pushkin and Russian Literature, 1947 (repr. 1968); Nietzsche, 1948, new edn 1971; From Pushkin to Mayakovsky, 1948; Ibsen, 1950 (repr. 1968); Nikolai Gogol, 1951 (repr. 1968); Goncharov, 1954 (repr. 1968); Russian Writers, 1954; Lermontov, 1959; Tolstoy (in German), 1961; Dostojevsky (in German), 1963; Literature and the Spirit of the Age (in Slovene), 1968; Russia, Slavdom and the Western World, 1969; Nietzsche, 1971; A Panorama of Russian Literature, 1973 (some of these translated into several languages). *Recreation:* travels. *Address:* 28 Lower Addison Gardens, W14. *T:* 01-603 8347. *Club:* PEN.

LAW, family name of **Barons Coleraine** and **Ellenborough**.

LAW, Alfred Noel, CMG 1947; MC 1918; retired; *b* 1895; *s* of late Frank Law; *m* 1937, Kathleen, *d* of A. Fishkin, Newcastle upon Tyne; one *d. Educ:* Northampton Sch.; Hertford Coll., Oxford. Served European War, 1914-19, with 4th Battalion Northamptonshire Regiment. Entered Colonial Service (Palestine), 1920; District Commissioner, Haifa, Palestine, 1942-48; Chief Sec., British Administration, Somalia, 1948-50; Dep. Dir of Education (Administration), Uganda, 1950-53; Ministry of Education, Labour and

Lands, Nairobi, Kenya, 1954–57. *Address:* 23 The Sheraton, Oak Avenue, Kenilworth, 7700 South Africa.

LAW, Sir Eric (John Ewan), Kt 1979; **Hon. Mr Justice Law;** Judge of Appeal, Court of Appeal, Kenya, since 1977; *b* 10 June 1913; *er s* of late Sir Charles Ewan Law; *m* 1948, Patricia Constance Elizabeth, *d* of C. W. S. Seed, CBE; two *s* one *d. Educ:* Wrekin Coll.; St Catharine's Coll., Cambridge (Exhibitioner), MA (Hons). Called to Bar, Middle Temple, 1936. War Service, 1939–42: E Yorks Regt and KAR, Capt. Asst Judicial Adviser to Govt of Ethiopia, 1942–44; Crown Counsel, Nyasaland, 1944–53; Resident Magistrate, Tanganyika, 1953–55; Senior Resident Magistrate, 1955–56; Asst Judge, Zanzibar, 1956–58; Judge, Tanganyika, 1958–64; Justice of Appeal, Court of Appeal for E Africa, 1965–77 (Vice-Pres., 1975–77). *Recreations:* fishing, golf. *Address:* c/o Court of Appeal for Kenya, PO Box 30187, Nairobi, Kenya. *Clubs:* Nairobi, Muthaiga (Kenya).

LAW, Francis Stephen, (Frank Law), CBE 1981; Chairman: Varta Group UK, since 1971; IWKA Group UK, since 1971; CEAG Group UK, since 1971; Altana UK Group, since 1978; Deputy Chairman, National Freight Consortium, since 1982 (Director, Consortium and its predecessors, since 1969); *b* 31 Dec. 1916; *s* of Henry and Ann Law-Lowensberg; *m* 1959, Nicole Vigne (*née* Fesch); one *s* (one *d* by previous *m*). *Educ:* on the Continent. War service, 1939–45. Wills Law & Co., 1947; Truvox Engrg, 1960, subseq. Dir of Controls and Communications; Director: B. Elliott and Co. Ltd, 1968–; BMW (GB) Ltd, 1978–; Member: Org. Cttee, NFC, 1968; Economic and Social Council, EEC, 1978–. *Recreations:* music, reading, theatre, skiing, tennis, riding, swimming. *Address:* 61 Cadogan Square, SW1. *T:* 01-235 7879. *Clubs:* Boodle's, Hurlingham; Pilgrims.

LAW, Frank William, MA, MD, BChir Cantab, FRCS, LRCP; KStJ; Consulting Ophthalmic Surgeon, Guy's Hospital; Consulting Surgeon, Moorfields Eye Hospital; Hon. Visiting Ophthalmologist, Johns Hopkins Hospital, Baltimore; Treas. and Past Pres. Ophth. Soc. of UK; Councillor and late Master Oxford Ophth. Congress; Mem., Chapter General and Ophth. Hosp. Cttee, Order of St John; British Mem. Council, European Ophth. Soc.; Life Mem., Irish Ophth. Soc.; Membre d'Honneur, Soc. Belge d'Ophth.; Hon. Mem., Greek Ophth. Soc., Pan-American Medical Assoc. and American Acad. Ophth.; American Medical Assoc.; Canadian Ophth. Soc.; Past Master, Company of Spectacle Makers, and Freeman of the City of London; *b* Isleworth, 1898; *y s* of late Thomas Law and Emma Janet MacRae; *m* 1929, Brenda, *d* of Edwin Thomas; one *s* one *d. Educ:* St Paul's Sch.; St John's Coll., Cambridge; Middlesex Hosp. Served European War, France and Flanders, 1917–19, Royal Field Artillery; Capt. Lady Margaret Boat Club, 1922; Spare Man for Varsity Boat and Trial Cap, 1922; rowed 2 for Cambridge, 1923; Late Consultant to the Army in Ophthalmology and Surgeon to Queen Alexandra Military Hosp., Millbank; late Consulting Ophthalmic Surgeon, King Edward VII Hospital for Officers; Past Pres. and Councillor, Faculty of Ophthalmologists; Sec. Gen., International Ophth. Congress, 1950; Past Mem. International Ophthalmological Council. Hon. FBOA 1957. *Publications:* Ultra-Violet Therapy in Eye Disease, 1934; History of Moorfields Eye Hospital, 1975; History of the Worshipful Company of Spectacle Makers, 1979; History of the Ophthalmic Society of the UK, 1980; articles in Brit. Jl of Ophthalmology, Transactions of Ophthalmological Society, and other Med. Jls. *Recreations:* music, fishing, shooting. *Address:* Baldersby Cottage, Chipperfield, Herts WD4 9DB. *T:* Kings Langley 62905; Flat 14, 59 Weymouth Street, W1N 3LH. *T:* 01-935 7328. *Clubs:* Athenæum, MCC, Savage; Leander.

LAW, Harry Davis; President, Portsmouth Polytechnic, since 1982; *b* 10 Nov. 1930; *s* of late Harold and Edna Betina Law; *m* 1956, Hazel M. Harding; one *s* one *d. Educ:* King Edward VI Sch., Stafford; Keele Univ. (BA); Manchester Univ. (PhD). FRSC. Demonstrator, Keele Univ., 1957–58; Commonwealth Fund Fellow, Cornell Med. Sch., NY, 1958–59; ICI Research Fellow, Liverpool Univ., 1959–60; Head, Chemistry, Miles Labs, Stoke Poges, subseq. Head, Therapeutic Research Labs, 1960–65; Head Chemistry and Biol., Liverpool Reg. Coll. Technology, 1965–69; Head Chemistry and Chm., Faculty of Science, Liverpool Polytechnic, 1969–71; Dep. Dir, Glasgow Coll. of Technology, 1971–73; Dir, Preston Polytechnic, 1973–82. Chm., CNAA Bd of Food, Accommodation and Related Services (formerly Instnl and Domestic Science), 1975–81; Member: Lancs Educn Cttee, 1974–82; Hampshire CC Educn Cttee, 1982–; Technician Educn Council, 1977– (Vice-Chm., 1982–; Chm., Educn Cttee, 1979–); Sci. Bd, SRC, 1978–81. *Publications:* The Organic Chemistry of Peptides, 1970; numerous pubns in learned jls. *Recreation:* fishing. *Address:* Westcroft, 40 Clifton Drive, Fairhaven, Lytham St Annes, Lancs FY8 1AX. *T:* Lytham 738055.

LAW, Adm. Sir Horace (Rochfort), GCB 1972 (KCB 1967; CB 1963); OBE 1950; DSC 1941; retired 1972; Chairman, R. & W. Hawthorn Leslie & Co., 1973–81; *b* 23 June 1911; *s* of S. Horace Law, MD, FRCSI, and Sybil Mary (*née* Clay); *m* 1941, Heather Valerie Coryton; two *s* two *d. Educ:* Sherborne Sch. Entered Royal Navy, 1929; gunnery specialist, 1937. Served War of 1939–45 (DSC): AA Cruisers: Cairo, 1939; Coventry, 1940; Cruiser Nigeria, 1942; Comdr 1946; Capt. 1952; comd HMS Centaur, 1958 and Britannia, RN Coll., 1960; Rear-Adm. 1961; Vice-Adm. 1965; Flag Officer Sea Training, 1961–63; Flag Officer, Submarines, 1963–65; Controller of the Navy, 1965–70; C-in-C, Naval Home Comd, and Flag Officer, Portsmouth Area, 1970–72; First and Principal Naval Aide-de-Camp to the Queen, 1970–72. Mem., Security Commn, 1973–82. President: RINA, 1975–77;

Officers' Christian Union, 1976–; Chm., Church Army Bd, 1980–. *Recreations:* sailing, gardening. *Address:* West Harting, Petersfield, Hants. *Club:* Royal Ocean Racing.

LAW, Col Hugh Francis d'Assisi Stuart, DSO 1940; OBE 1956; MC 1917; TD; DL; *b* 29 Jan. 1897; *s* of late Hugh Alexander Law; *m* 1928, Susan Rosemary Dacre, *e d* of Sir George Clerk, 9th Bt of Penicuik; two *s* one *d. Educ:* Shrewsbury; RMC Sandhurst. 2nd Lt Irish Guards, 1915; with Irish Guards, France and Flanders, 1915–18; Acting Capt., 1916; attached General Headquarters, Intelligence, 1916; Capt., 1918 (wounded, MC); with Irish Guards Army of Occupation of Rhineland; ADC to GOC 22nd Army Corps, 1919; ADC Governor and C-in-C, Malta, 1921; with Irish Guards, Turkey, 1922–24; retired, 1931; Brevet Major, Irish Guards, Regular Army Reserve of Officers; Major 5th Bn Border Regt, 1932; Lt-Col, 1938; Col (Temp.) 1941; Commanding 5th Bn Border Regt, 1938–41; served France and Belgium, 1940 (DSO, despatches 1940) and in Middle East, 1943–45. Comdr Sub-District of South-West Scotland, 1941–43; Comdr Sub-Area of the Lebanon, 1943–45; Comdr Cyprus, 1945; Sec., Army Cadet Force in Scotland, 1948–65. DL Co. of Midlothian, 1965. *Recreations:* shooting, fishing, riding, gardening. *Address:* The Barony House, Lasswade, Midlothian. *T:* Lasswade 3217.

LAW, James, QC (Scot.) 1971; *b* 7 June 1926; *s* of late George Law, MA, and of Isabella Rebecca Lamb (or Law), MA; *m* 1956, Kathleen Margaret, *d* of Alexander Gibson; two *s* one *d. Educ:* Kilmarnock Academy; Girvan High Sch.; Univ. of Glasgow (MA 1948, LLB 1950). Admitted to Faculty of Advocates, 1951; Advocate-Depute, 1957–64. Mem., Criminal Injuries Compensation Bd, 1970–. *Address:* 7 Gloucester Place, Edinburgh EH3 6EE. *T:* 031-225 2974. *Clubs:* New, Caledonian (Edinburgh).

LAW, Phillip Garth, AO 1975; CBE 1961; MSc, FAIP, FTS, FAA; *b* 21 April 1912; *s* of Arthur James Law and Lillie Lena Chapman; *m* 1941, Nellie Isabel Allan; no *c. Educ:* Hamilton High Sch.; Ballarat Teachers' Coll.; Melbourne Univ. Science master, State secondary schs, Vic., 1933–38; Tutor in Physics, Newman Coll., Melbourne Univ., 1940–47; Lectr in Physics, 1943–48. Research Physicist and Asst Sec. of Scientific Instrument and Optical Panel of Austr. Min. of Munitions, 1940–45. Sen. Scientific Officer, ANARE, 1947–48; cosmic ray measurements in Antarctica and Japan, 1948; Dir, Antarctic Div., Dept of External Affairs, Aust., and Leader, ANARE, 1949–66; Expedition relief voyages to Heard I. and Macquarie I., 1949, 1951, 1952, 1954. Australian observer with Norwegian-British-Swedish Antarctic Exped., 1950; Leader of expedition: to establish first permanent Australian station in Antarctica at Mawson, MacRobertson Land, 1954; which established second continental station at Davis, Princess Elizabeth Land, 1957; which took over Wilkes station from USA, 1959; to relieve ANARE stations and to explore coast of Australian Antarctic Territory, annually, 1955–66. Chm., Australian Nat. Cttee for Antarctic Research, 1966–80. Exec. Vice-Pres., Victoria Inst. of Colls, 1966–77; Pres., Victorian Inst. of Marine Scis, 1978–80. Member: Council of Melbourne Univ., 1959–78; Council, La Trobe Univ., 1964–74; President: Royal Soc. of Victoria, 1967, 1968; Aust. and NZ Schs Exploring Soc., 1977–82. Dep. Pres., Science Museum of Victoria, Melbourne, 1979–82 (Trustee, 1968–). Pres., Grad. Union, Melbourne Univ., 1972–77. Fellow: Australian Acad. of Technological Sciences; Aust. Acad. of Sci.; ANZAAS. Hon. Fellow, Royal Melbourne Inst. of Technology. Hon. DAppSc (Melbourne); Hon. DEd (Victoria Inst. of Colls). Founder's Gold Medal, RGS, 1960. *Publications:* (with John Bechervaise) ANARE, 1957; chapters in: It's People that Matter, ed Donald McLean, 1969; Search for Human Understanding, ed M. Merbaum and G. Stricker, 1971; ed series of ANARE scientific reports; numerous papers on Antarctica and education. *Recreations:* tennis, ski-ing, skin diving, music, photography. *Address:* 16 Stanley Grove, Canterbury, Vic 3126, Australia. *Clubs:* Melbourne, Kelvin, Melbourne Cricket, Royal South Yarra Lawn Tennis (Melbourne).

LAW, Sylvia, OBE 1977; Group Planner, Greater London Council; *b* 29 March 1931; *d* of late Reginald Howard Law and late Dorothy Margaret Law. *Educ:* Lowther Coll.; Girton Coll., Cambridge (MA); Regent Street Polytechnic (DipTP). MRTPI. Teaching, Benenden Sch., 1952–55; market research, Unilever Ltd, 1955–58; town and country planning, Kent CC and GLC, 1959–. Royal Town Planning Institute: Mem. Council, 1965–78; Chm. of Educn Cttee, 1970–73; Vice-Pres., 1972–74; Pres., 1974–75. Mem. Planning Cttee, SSRC, 1977–79. *Publications:* (contrib.) Recreational Economics and Analysis, 1974; (ed) Planning and the Future, 1976; articles in RTPI Jl, Official Architecture and Planning, Planning Outlook, Town Planning Rev., Greater London Intelligence Qly, etc. *Recreations:* sailing, music, photography. *Address:* My Lady's Cottage, Cranbrook, Kent. *T:* Cranbrook 713807. *Club:* University Women's.

LAW-SMITH, Sir (Richard) Robert, Kt 1980; CBE 1965; AFC; Chairman: National Bank of Australasia, since 1978 (Vice-Chairman, 1968, Director, 1959); Chase—NBA Group Ltd, 1980; Australian National Airlines Commission, since 1979 (Vice-Chairman, 1975, Member, 1962); grazier; *b* Adelaide, 9 July 1914; *s* of W. Law-Smith; *m* 1941, Joan, *d* of Harold Gordon Darling; two *d. Educ:* St Edward's Sch., Oxford; Adelaide Univ. Served War, RAAF, 1940–46 (AFC), Sqdn Ldr. Director: Broken Hill Pty Co. Ltd, 1961–; Aust. Mutual Provident Soc. (Vic.) (Chm. 1977, Dir 1960); Commonwealth Aircraft Corp., 1965–; Blue Circle Southern Cement Ltd, 1974–. Director, Royal Flying Doctor Service, 1956–. *Address:* Bolobek, Macedon, Vic 3440, Australia. *Clubs:* Australian, Melbourne (Melbourne); Union (Sydney).

LAWDER, Rear-Adm. Keith Macleod, CB 1948; OBE 1919; Associate of the Chartered Institute of Secretaries; *b* 1893; *s* of F. E. Lawder; *m* 1918, Joyce Katharine Mary Watson (*d* 1980); two *d* (one *s* decd). *Educ:* Fettes Coll., Edinburgh. Joined Royal Navy, 1910; served European War, 1914-18 and War of 1939-45; retired, 1949. *Address:* Brook Cottage, South Zeal, Okehampton, Devon EX20 2QB. *T:* Whiddon Down 308. *Club:* Climbers'.

LAWLER, Sir Peter (James), Kt 1981; OBE 1965; Secretary, Department of Administrative Services, Canberra, since 1975; *b* 23 March 1921; *m* ; five *s* two *d*. *Educ:* Univ. of Sydney (BEc). Prime Minister's Dept, Canberra, 1949-68 (British Cabinet Office, London, 1952-53); Dep. Secretary: Dept of the Cabinet Office, 1968-71; Dept of the Prime Minister and Cabinet, 1972-73; Sec., Dept of the Special Minister of State, 1973-75. *Recreation:* farming. *Address:* 6 Tennyson Crescent, Forrest, ACT 2603, Australia. *Clubs:* Melbourne (Melbourne); University House (Canberra); Royal Canberra Golf.

LAWLEY, Dr Leonard Edward; Director of Kingston Polytechnic, 1969-82; *b* 13 March 1922; *yr s* of late Albert Lawley; *m* 1944, Dorothy Beryl Round; one *s* two *d*. *Educ:* King Edward VI Sch., Stourbridge; Univs of Wales and Newcastle upon Tyne. BSc, PhD, FInstP. Served with RAF, 1941-46; Lectr, Univ. of Newcastle upon Tyne, 1947-53; Sen. Lectr, The Polytechnic, Regent Street, 1953-57; Kingston Coll. of Technology: Head of Dept of Physics and Maths, 1957-64; Vice-Principal, 1960-64; Principal, 1964-69. *Publications:* various papers in scientific jls on transmission ultrasonic sound waves through gases and liquids and on acoustic methods for gas analysis. *Address:* Kingston Polytechnic, Penrhyn Road, Kingston upon Thames. *T:* 01-549 1366.

LAWLOR, Prof. John James, MA, DLitt, FSA; Professor of English Language and Literature, University of Keele, 1950-80, now Emeritus; *b* 5 Jan. 1918; *o s* of Albert John Lawlor, Chief Armourer, RN, and Teresa Anne Clare Lawlor, Plymouth; *m* 1941, Thelma Joan Weeks, singer (marr. diss. 1979); one *s* three *d*. *Educ:* Ryder's; Magdalen Coll., Oxford. BA Hons English Cl. I, 1939. Service in Devonshire Regt, 1940-45; Asst Chief Instructor, 163 Artists' Rifles OCTU, 1943-44; CMF, 1944-45; AMG Austria. Sen. Mackinnon Scholar, Magdalen Coll., 1946; Sen. Demy, 1947; Lectr in English, Brasenose and Trinity Colls, 1947-50; University Lectr in Eng. Lit., Oxford, 1949-50. Fellow of Folger Shakespeare Library, Washington, DC, 1962. Toured Australian and NZ Univs and visited Japan, 1964. Ziskind Visiting Prof., Brandeis Univ., Mass, 1966; Vis. Professor: Univ. of Hawaii, 1972; Univ. of Maryland, 1981-82. Sec.-Gen. and Treasurer, Internat. Assoc. of University Profs. of English; Contrib. Mem. Medieval Academy of America; Gov., Oswestry Sch.; Pres., N Staffs Drama Assoc.; Mem. Western Area Cttee, Brit. Drama League; Vice-Pres., The Navy League. *Publications:* The Tragic Sense in Shakespeare, 1960; Piers Plowman, an Essay in Criticism, 1962; The Chester Mystery Plays (with Rosemary Sisson), perf. Chester, 1962; The Vision of Piers Plowman, commnd, Malvern, 1964; (ed) Patterns of Love and Courtesy, 1966; (with W. H. Auden) To Nevill Coghill from Friends, 1966; Chaucer, 1968; (ed) The New University, 1968; (ed) Higher Education: patterns of change in the seventies, 1972; Elysium Revisited, 1978; (as James Dundonald): Letters to a Vice-Chancellor, 1962; La Vita Nuova, 1976; articles on medieval and modern literature in various journals and symposia. *Recreations:* travel, book-collecting, any sort of sea-faring. *Address:* c/o Magdalen Coll., Oxford. *T:* Oxford 41781; Penwithian, Higher Fore Street, Marazion, Cornwall. *T:* Penzance 711180. *Clubs:* Athenæum; Royal Fleet (Devonport).

LAWRANCE, Mrs June Cynthia; Headmistress of Harrogate College, since 1974; *b* 3 June 1933; *d* of Albert Isherwood and Ida Emmett; *m* 1957, Rev. David Lawrance, MA, BD; three *d*. *Educ:* St Anne's Coll., Oxford (MA). Teaching appts: Univ. of Paris, 1954-57; Cyprus, 1957-58; Jordan, 1958-61; Oldham, Lancs, 1962-70; Headmistress, Broughton High Sch., Salford, 1971-73. *Recreations:* music, French literature, chess. *Address:* Harrogate College, Clarence Drive, Harrogate, N Yorks. *T:* Harrogate 504543.

LAWRANCE, Keith Cantwell; Deputy Chairman, Civil Service Appeal Board, since 1981 (Member since 1980); Chairman, Civil Service Retirement Fellowship, since 1982; *b* 1 Feb. 1923; *s* of P. J. Lawrance; *m* 1952, Margaret Joan (*née* Scott); no *c*. *Educ:* Latymer Sch., N9. Clerical Officer, Admiralty, 1939. Served War, RNVR, 1942-46; Sub-Lt (A), 1945. Exec. Officer, Treasury, 1947; Asst Principal, Post Office, 1954; Principal, Post Office, 1959; Asst Sec., Dept of Economic Affairs, Dec. 1966; Under-Sec., Civil Service Dept, 1971-79. *Recreations:* model engineering, music. *Address:* 8 Clement Road, Wimbledon, SW19. *T:* 01-947 1676.

LAWRENCE, family name of **Baron Lawrence** and of **Baron Trevethin and Oaksey.**

LAWRENCE, 5th Baron *cr* 1869; **David John Downer Lawrence;** Bt 1858; *b* 4 Sept. 1937; *s* of 4th Baron Lawrence and Margaret Jean (*d* 1977), *d* of Arthur Downer, Kirdford, Sussex; *S* father, 1968. *Educ:* Bradfield College. *Address:* c/o Bird & Bird, 2 Gray's Inn Square, WC1.

LAWRENCE, Arnold Walter, MA; FSA; Professor of Archæology, University College of Ghana, and Director, National Museum of Ghana, 1951-57; Secretary and Conservator, Monuments and Relics Commission of Ghana, 1952-57; Laurence Professor of Classical Archæology, Cambridge University, 1944-51, and Fellow of Jesus College; *b* 2 May 1900; *s* of T. R.

Lawrence; *m* 1925, Barbara Thompson; one *d*. *Educ:* City of Oxford Sch.; New Coll., Oxford. Student, British Schs of Athens and Rome; Ur excavations, 1923; Craven Fellow, 1924-26; Reader in Classical Archæology, Cambridge Univ., 1930; Corr. Mem., German Archæological Institute; literary executor of T. E. Lawrence, 1935; Military Intelligence, Middle East, 1940; Scientific Officer, Coastal Command, RAF, 1942; Ministry of Economic Warfare, 1943; lectured in Latin America, 1948; Leverhulme Research Fellow, 1951. Hon. FBA 1982. *Publications:* Later Greek Sculpture and its Influence, 1927; Classical Sculpture, 1929; Herodotus, Rawlinson's translation revised and annotated, 1935; (ed) T. E. Lawrence by his Friends, 1937; Greek Architecture (Pelican History of Art), 1957, rev. edns 1967, and 1974;(ed) Letters to T. E. Lawrence, 1962; Trade Castles and Forts of West Africa, 1963, abr. as Fortified Trade Posts: the English in West Africa, 1968; Greek and Roman Sculpture, 1972; The Castle of Baghras, in The Armenian Kingdom of Cilicia (ed T. S. R. Boase), 1978; Greek Aims in Fortification, 1980. *Recreation:* going to and fro in the earth and walking up and down in it. *Address:* c/o Barclays Bank, 9 Gracechurch Street, EC3.

LAWRENCE, Bernard Edwin, CBE 1957; Chief Education Officer, County of Essex, 1939-65, retired; Dean of the College of Preceptors, 1958-68, Vice President, 1969-80; *b* 3 Jan. 1901; *s* of late Albert Edward and Emma Lawrence; *m* 1925, Dorothy Rosa Collings; two *s* one *d*. *Educ:* Sir Joseph Williamson's Sch., Rochester; Worcester Coll., Oxford. BA Oxon double first class Hons 1922; MA 1930; PhD, University Coll. London, 1934. Asst Master: George Green's Sch., 1923-25; Skinners' Sch., 1925-28; Lecturer: Goldsmiths' Coll., 1928-35; Birkbeck Coll., 1930-35; Asst Dir of Education, Essex, 1936-39; Chairman: Educational Commission to Uganda and Kenya, 1961; Nat. Inst. of Adult Educn, 1964-69. Pres. Assoc. of Chief Educn. Officers, 1957-58. Chevalier de la Légion d'Honneur, 1958. *Publications:* The Administration of Education in Britain, 1972; occasional contribs to Educational Jls and to Proceedings of London Mathematical Society and Mathematical Gazette. *Recreation:* gardening. *Address:* White Gable, Felsted, Great Dunmow, Essex.

LAWRENCE, Rt. Rev. Caleb James; *see* Moosonee, Bishop of.

LAWRENCE, Christopher Nigel; silversmith; industrial designer; *b* 23 Dec. 1936; *s* of late Rev. William W. Lawrence and of Millicent Lawrence; *m* 1958, Valerie Betty Bergman; two *s* two *d*. *Educ:* Westborough High Sch.; Central School of Arts and Crafts. Nat. Dip. Design, Full Technol. Cert. (City and Guilds of London). Apprenticed, C. J. Vander Ltd; started own workshops, 1968. *One man exhibitions:* Galerie Jean Renet, 1970, 1971; Hamburg, 1972; Goldsmiths' Hall, 1973; Ghent, 1975; Hasselt, 1977. Major commissions from British Govt, City Livery cos, banks, manufacturing cos. Judge and external assessor for leading art colleges; specialist in symbolic presentation pieces and limited edns of decorative pieces, eg silver mushrooms. Chm., Goldsmiths, Silversmiths and Jewellers Art Council, 1976-77; Liveryman, Goldsmiths' Co., 1978-; television and radio broadcaster. Jacques Cartier Meml award for Craftsman of the Year, 1960, 1963, 1967 (unique achievement). *Recreations:* cruising on family's narrow boat, archery, badminton, carpentry, pottery. *Address:* 20 St Vincent's Road, Westcliff-on-Sea, Essex SS0 7PR. *T:* Southend-on-Sea 44897; (business) Quintessence, 172 London Road, Southend-on-Sea, Essex SS1 1PH. *T:* Southend-on-Sea 44897.

LAWRENCE, Prof. Clifford Hugh; Professor of Medieval History, since 1970, and Head of the Department of History, Bedford College, University of London, since 1981; *b* 28 Dec. 1921; *s* of Ernest William Lawrence and Dorothy Estelle; *m* 1953, Helen Maud Curran; one *s* five *d*. *Educ:* Stationers' Co.'s Sch.; Lincoln Coll., Oxford. BA 1st Cl. Hons Mod. Hist. 1948, MA 1953, DPhil 1956; FRHistS. War service in RA and Beds and Herts: 2nd Lieut 1942, Captain 1944, Major 1945. Asst Archivist to Co. of Gloucester, 1949. Bedford Coll., London: Asst Lectr in History, 1951; Lectr, 1953-63; Reader in Med. History, 1963-70. External Examr, Univ. of Newcastle upon Tyne, 1972-74, Univ. of Bristol, 1975-77, Univ. of Reading, 1977-79; Chm., Bd of Examnrs in History, London Univ., 1981-. Member: Press Council, 1976-80; Governing Body, Heythrop Coll., Univ. of London. *Publications:* St Edmund of Abingdon, History and Hagiography, 1960; The English Church and the Papacy in the Middle Ages, 1965; (contrib.) Pre-Reformation English Spirituality, 1967; (contrib.) The Christian Community, 1971; articles and reviews in Eng. Hist. Review, History, Jl Eccles. Hist., Oxoniensia, Encycl. Brit., Lexicon für Theol u Kirche, etc. *Recreations:* gardening, painting. *Address:* 11 Durham Road, SW20 0QH. *T:* 01-946 3820.
See also G. C. Lawrence.

LAWRENCE, Sir David (Roland Walter), 3rd Bt, *cr* 1906; late Captain, Coldstream Guards, 1951; *b* 8 May 1929; *er s* of Sir Roland Lawrence, 2nd Bt, MC, and Susan, 3rd *d* of late Sir Charles Addis, KCMG; *S* father 1950; *m* 1955, Audrey, Duchess of Leeds, *yr d* of Brig. Desmond Young, OBE, MC. *Educ:* Radley; RMC Sandhurst. *Heir: b* Clive Wyndham Lawrence [*b* 6 Oct. 1939; *m* 1966, Sophia Annabel Stuart, *d* of Hervey Stuart Black, *qv*; three *s*]. *Address:* 28 High Town Road, Maidenhead, Berks. *Club:* Cavalry and Guards.

LAWRENCE, Dennis George Charles, OBE 1963; Director, 1978-82, Board Member, since 1981, Cooperative Development Agency; *b* 15 Aug. 1918; *s* of late George Herbert and Amy Frances Lawrence; *m* 1946, Alida Jantine, *d* of late Willem van den Berg, The Netherlands. *Educ:* Haberdashers' Aske's Hatcham School. Entered Civil Service as Clerical Officer, Min. of Transport,

1936; served RA, 1939-46; Exec. Officer 1946; Asst Principal, Central Land Board, 1947; Principal, 1949; GPO, 1953; Asst Sec. 1960; Sec., Cttee on Broadcasting, 1960-62; Asst Sec., GPO, 1962; Under-Secretary: GPO, 1969; Min. of Posts and Telecommunications, 1969-74; Dept of Industry, 1974-78. Chm., Working Group on a Cooperative Develt Agency, 1977. *Recreations:* walking, painting, travel. *Address:* Little London Farmhouse, Cann, Shaftesbury, Dorset. *T:* Shaftesbury 2252; 37 Aylesford Street, SW1.

LAWRENCE, Evelyn M., BSc (Econ.) London, PhD; **(Mrs Nathan Isaacs);** *b* 31 Dec. 1892; *d* of Samuel and Mary Lawrence, Walton-on-Thames; *m* 1950, Nathan Isaacs, OBE (*d* 1966). *Educ:* Tiffins Sch., Kingston-on-Thames; Stockwell Training Coll.; London Sch. of Economics, University of London. Teacher in LCC schs, 1913-24; BSc Econ. 1st cl. Hons 1923; Ratan Tata and Metcalfe scholar, London Sch. of Economics, 1924-26; on staff of Malting House Sch., Cambridge, 1926-28; Commonwealth Fund scholar, USA, 1929; Chief Social Worker, London Child Guidance Clinic, 1929-30; Lecturer in Education, National Training Coll. of Domestic Subjects, 1931-43. Dir, National Froebel Foundation, and Editor, Froebel Foundation Bulletin, 1943-63. Hon. Sec. British Psychological Soc., Education Section, 1931-34; Mem. of Council of Eugenics Soc., 1949-59. *Publications:* The Relation between Intelligence and Inheritance, 1931. Editor: Friedrich Froebel and English Education, 1952. *Recreations:* walking, gardening, music. *Address:* Grove Cottage, Owletts Lane, Ashurst Wood, East Grinstead, W Sussex. *T:* Forest Row 2728.

LAWRENCE, Geoffrey Charles, CMG 1963; OBE 1958; *b* 11 Nov. 1915; *s* of Ernest William Lawrence; *m* 1945, Joyce Acland Madge, MBE 1959, *d* of M. H. A. Madge, MC. *Educ:* Stationers' Company's Sch.; Brasenose Coll., Oxford. Served 1939-46, Middlesex Yeo. and Brit. Mil. Administration of Occupied Territories (Major). HM Overseas Civil Service (Colonial Administrative Service). Administrative Officer, Somaliland Protectorate, 1946; Asst Chief Sec., 1955; Financial Sec., 1956; Financial Sec., Zanzibar and Mem. of East African Currency Board, 1960-63; Colonial Office, 1964-66; ODM, later ODA, FCO, 1966-73; ODM, 1973-76. *Address:* c/o Barclays Bank Ltd, 42 Coombe Lane, SW20.
See also C. H. Lawrence.

LAWRENCE, Sir Guy Kempton, Kt 1976; DSO 1943; OBE 1945; DFC 1941; Chairman, Eggs Authority, 1978-81; *b* 5 Nov. 1914; *s* of Albert Edward and Bianca Lawrence; *m* 1947, Marcia Virginia Powell; two *s* one *d*. *Educ:* Marlborough Coll. FBIM, FIGD. RAFO, 1934-45; War of 1939-45: Bomber Pilot (48 sorties), Sqdn Comdr, 78 Sqdn, Gp Captain Trng, HQ Bomber Command (DFC DSO, despatches, OBE). Contested (L) Colne Valley, 1945. Man. Dir, Chartair Ltd-Airtech Ltd, 1945-48; Chairman: Glacier Foods Ltd, 1948-75; Findus (UK) Ltd, 1967-75; Dep. Chairman: J. Lyons & Co. Ltd, 1950-75; Spillers French Holdings Ltd, 1972-75; Vice-Chm., DCA Food Industries Inc., 1973-; Dir, Eagle Aircraft Services, 1977-81. Chm., Food and Drink Industries Council, 1973-77. Member of Stock Exchange, London, 1937-45. British Ski Team, FIS, 1937-38. *Recreations:* farming, carpentry, squash, tennis. *Address:* Courtlands, Kier Park, Ascot, Berks SL5 7DS. *T:* Ascot 21074. *Club:* Royal Air Force.

LAWRENCE, Ivan John, QC 1981; Barrister-at-law; MP (C) Burton, since Feb. 1974; *b* 24 Dec. 1936; *o s* of Leslie Lawrence, Brighton; *m* 1966, Gloria Hélène, *d* of Charles Crankshaw, Newcastle; one *d*. *Educ:* Brighton, Hove and Sussex Grammar Sch.; Christ Church, Oxford (MA). Nat. Service with RAF, 1955-57. Called to Bar, Inner Temple, 1962; S Eastern Circuit. Contested (C) Peckham (Camberwell), 1966 and 1970. Vice-Chm., Cons. Parly Legal Cttee, 1979-; Chm., All-party Parly Anti-Fluoridation Cttee; Sec., All-Party Parly Cttee for Release of Soviet Jewry; Member: Parly Expenditure Select Sub-Cttee, 1974-79 (reported on treatment of juvenile offenders, preventive medicine and anti-unemployment measures); Mem., Council of Justice and its Working Party on appeals in criminal cases. Vice-Pres., Fed. of Cons. Students, 1980-82. Pres., Nat. Assoc. of Approved Driving Instructors. *Publications:* pamphlets (jointly): Crisis in Crime and Punishment; The Conviction of the Guilty; Towards a New Nationality; Financing Strikes; newspaper articles on law and related topics. *Recreations:* piano, squash, football, travel. *Address:* 1 Essex Court, Temple, EC4Y 9AR. *T:* 01-583 7759; Dunally Cottage, Lower Halliford Green, Shepperton, Mddx. *T:* Walton-on-Thames 24692; Grove Farm, Drakelow, Burton-on-Trent. *T:* Burton-on-Trent 44360.

LAWRENCE, Air Vice-Marshal John Thornett, CB 1975; CBE (mil.) 1967 (OBE (mil.) 1961); AFC 1945; *b* 16 April 1920; *s* of late T. L. Lawrence, JP, and Mrs B. M. Lawrence; *m* 1951, Hilary Jean (*née* Owen); three *s* one *d*. *Educ:* The Crypt School, Gloucester. RAFVR 1938. Served War of 1939-45 in Coastal Command (235, 202 and 86 Squadrons); Directing staff, RAF Flying Coll., 1949-53; CO 14 Squadron, 1953-55; Group Captain Operations, HQ AFME, 1962-64; CO RAF Wittering, 1964-66; AOC, 3 Group, Bomber Command, 1967; Student, IDC, 1968; Dir of Organisation and Admin Plans (RAF), 1969-71; Dir-Gen. Personnel Management (RAF), 1971-73; Comdr N Maritime Air Region and AOC Scotland and NI, 1973-75, retired 1975. Mem. Council, Cheltenham Ladies' Coll., 1977-. Chm., Glos County SS&AFA, 1980. Order of Leopold II, Belgium, 1945; Croix de Guerre, Belgium, 1945. *Recreation:* golf. *Address:* Corinium House, Edge, Stroud, Gloucester. *Club:* Royal Air Force.

LAWRENCE, Sir John (Waldemar), 6th Bt, *cr* 1858; OBE 1945; Editor of Frontier, 1957-75; *b* 27 May 1907; *s* of Sir Alexander Waldemar Lawrence, 4th Bt, and Anne Elizabeth Le Poer (*née* Wynne); *S* brother, Sir Henry Eustace Waldemar Lawrence, 5th Bt, 1967; *m* 1948, Jacynth Mary (*née* Ellerton); no *c. Educ:* Eton; New Coll., Oxford (MA, Lit. Hum.). Personal Asst to Dir of German Jewish Aid Cttee, 1938-39; with BBC as European Intelligence Officer and European Services Organiser, 1939-42; Press Attaché, HM Embassy, USSR, 1942-45; became freelance writer, 1946. Chairman: Keston College (formerly Centre for Study of Religion and Communism), 1969-; GB USSR Assoc., 1970-. Officer, Order of Orange Nassau, 1950. *Publications:* Life in Russia, 1947; Russia in the Making, 1957; A History of Russia, 1960; The Hard Facts of Unity, 1961; Russia (Methuen's Outlines), 1965; Soviet Russia, 1967; Russians Observed, 1969; Take Hold of Change, 1976; The Journals of Honoria Lawrence, 1980. *Recreations:* travelling, reading in ten languages. *Heir: b* George Alexander Waldemar Lawrence [*b* 22 Sept. 1910; *m* 1949, Olga, *d* of late Peter Schilovsky; one *s* two *d*]. *Address:* 24 St Leonard's Terrace, SW3. *T:* 01-730 8033. *Club:* Athenæum.

LAWRENCE, Michael Hugh, CMG 1972; Head of the Administration Department, House of Commons, 1972-80; retired 1980; *b* 9 July 1920; *s* of late Hugh Moxon Lawrence and Mrs L. N. Lawrence; *m* 1948, Rachel Mary (MA Cantab), *d* of late Humphrey Gamon, Gt Barrow, Cheshire; one *s* two *d. Educ:* Highgate (Scholar); St Catharine's Coll., Cambridge (Exhibnr; MA). Served Indian Army, 1940-45. Indian Civil Service, 1945-46; Asst Clerk, House of Commons, 1947; Senior Clerk, 1948; Deputy Principal Clerk, 1962; Clerk of the Overseas Office, 1967-72; Clerk Administrator, of Services Cttee, 1972-76; Mem., Bd of Management, House of Commons, 1979-80. Sec., History of Parliament Trust, 1959-66. *Recreations:* beagling, lawn tennis, looking at churches. *Address:* 22 Stradbroke Road, Southwold, Suffolk. *T:* Southwold 722794.

LAWRENCE, Sir Robert (Leslie Edward), Kt 1980; CBE 1975 (OBE 1944); ERD 1952; FCIT; FRSA; CBIM; Member, British Railways Board, since 1971 (Vice-Chairman, 1975-81); Chairman, British Rail Property Board, since 1972; Director, National Freight Consortium, since 1982; *b* 29 Oct. 1915; *s* of late Robert Riach Lawrence; *m* 1940, Joyce Marjorie (*née* Ricketts); one *s* one *d. Educ:* Dulwich Coll. Served War of 1939-45 (despatches, 1942, 1945), RE; 2nd Lt; Col 1945; Hon. Col, 73 Movement Control Regt, RE, 1963-65; Col, Engr and Rly Staff Corps RE (TA); Hon. Col, 275 Rly Sqdn, RCT (TAVR), 1978-. Traffic Apprentice, LNER, 1934; Headquarters, LNER, 1938; appts in operating depts, 1946-59; London Midland Region: Divisional Man., 1959; Line Manager, 1961; Asst Gen. Manager, 1963-67; Chm. and Gen. Manager, 1968-71; Gen. Manager, Sundries Div., British Railways, 1967; Chairman: BR Hovercraft Ltd, 1971-72; British Rail Engineering, 1971-76; BRE Metro Ltd, 1971-78; Transmark Ltd, 1972-78; British Transport Hotels Ltd, 1978. Mem., 1969-82, Chm., 1979-82, Nat. Freight Corp., later Nat. Freight Co.; Chm., Nat. Freight Consortium, 1982; Bd Mem., Nat. Bus Co., 1982-; Dir, Mersey Docks and Harbour Bd, 1971-72. Mem., Energy Commn, 1977-79. Vice-Pres., Inst. of Transport, 1970-72 (Mem., Council, 1959-62); Chm., Centre for Physical Distribution Management, 1980-. Mem., Adv. Council, Science Mus., 1979-. Governor, Dulwich Coll., 1970, Dep. Chm. Bd, 1973-; Mem. Council, Westfield Coll., 1980-. Past Pres., Rly Students Assoc.; Vice-Chm., Movement Control Officers Club. Vice-Pres., London Cornish Assoc., 1979-. Chm., Railway Benevolent Inst., 1979-. Liveryman, Co. of Loriners. Freeman, City of London. CStJ 1982. Legion of Merit (US), 1945. *Publications:* various papers, Inst. of Transport. *Recreations:* swimming, Rugby football. *Address:* 37 Oakfield Gardens, SE19 1HQ. *T:* 01-670 7649; Clifford Cottage, St Levan, Cornwall. *T:* Sennen 297. *Clubs:* Army and Navy, MCC.

LAWRENCE, Air Vice-Marshal Thomas Albert, CB 1945; CD; RCAF, retired; *b* 1895; *s* of K. J. Lawrence; *m* 1921, Claudine Audrey Jamieson. AOC, 2 Training Comd, BCATP, 1942-44; AOC, NW Air Comd, Canada, 1944-47, retd. Comdr, Legion of Merit (USA), 1945. *Address:* 581 Avenue Road, Toronto, Ont M4V 2K4, Canada.

LAWRENCE, Sir William, 4th Bt, *cr* 1867; Sales Consultant, Long and Hambly Ltd (retired); Senior Executive, Wilmot Breeden, Ltd (retired); Major East Surrey Regiment; *b* 14 July 1913; *er s* of Sir William Matthew Trevor Lawrence, 3rd Bt, and Iris Eyre (*d* 1955), *y d* of late Brig.-Gen. E. M. S. Crabbe, CB; *S* father, 1934; *m* 1940, Zoë (marr. diss., 1945), *yr d* of H. S. S. Pether, Stowford, Headington, Oxford; *m* 1945, Pamela, *yr d* of J. E. Gordon, Beechbank, Bromborough, Cheshire; one *s* two *d. Educ:* Bradfield Coll. FRHS. Pres., W Warwickshire Scout Council; Vice-Pres., Stratford on Avon and S Warwickshire Cons. Assoc. *Recreation:* gardening. *Heir: s* William Fettiplace Lawrence, *b* 23 Aug. 1954. *Address:* The Knoll, Walcote, near Alcester, Warwicks. *T:* Great Alne 303.

LAWRENCE-JONES, Sir Christopher, 6th Bt *cr* 1831; Central Medical Adviser, Imperial Chemical Industries Ltd, Millbank, SW1, since 1979; *b* 19 Jan. 1940; *s* of Commander B. E. Jones, RN (*d* 1958) (*yr s* of Sir Lawrence Jones, 4th Bt), and Margaret Louise, *d* of late G. M. Cookson; *S* uncle, Sir Lawrence Jones, 5th Bt, MC, 1969; *m* 1967, Gail, *d* of C. A. Pittar, FRACS, Auckland, NZ; two *s. Educ:* Sherborne; Gonville and Caius Coll., Cambridge; St Thomas' Hospital. MA Cantab 1964; MB, BChir Cantab 1964; DIH Eng. 1968. MFOM 1979. Industrial Medical Adviser, 1967-: ICI Dyestuffs Div., 1967-70; BP Co. Ltd, 1970-73; Health and Safety Exec., 1973-75; ICI Paints Div., 1975-79. FRSocMed. *Recreation:* cruising under sail. *Heir: s* Mark

Christopher Lawrence-Jones, b 28 Dec. 1968. Address: Silwood House, London Road, Ascot, Berks. Clubs: United Oxford & Cambridge University; Royal Cruising.

LAWRENCE-WILSON, Harry Lawrence; Under-Secretary, Procurement Executive, Ministry of Defence, 1971-72; b 18 March 1920; s of late H. B. Wilson and of Mrs May Wilson, Biddenden, Kent; m 1945, Janet Mary Gillespie; two s one d. Educ: Cranbrook Sch.; Worcester Coll., Oxford. Served Indian Army, 1940-46. Colonial Office, 1946-47; MoD, 1947-66; Cabinet Office, 1967-69. Asst Principal, 1947; Principal, 1948; Assistant Secretary, 1956; Under-Secretary, 1961; Under-Secretary: Min. of Technology, 1969-70; DTI, 1970-71; CSD, 1971. Address: 22 Marlborough Crescent, Riverhead, Sevenoaks, Kent.

LAWRENSON, Prof. Peter John, DSc; FRS 1982; FEng, FIEE, FIEEE; Professor of Electrical Engineering since 1966, and Head of Department of Electrical and Electronic Engineering since 1974, Leeds University; b 12 March 1933; s of John Lawrenson and Emily (née Houghton); m 1958, Shirley Hannah Foster; one s three d. Educ: Prescot Grammar Sch.; Manchester Univ. (BSc, MSc; DSc 1971). FEng 1980; FIEE 1974; FIEEE 1975. Duddell Scholar, IEE, 1951-54; Res. Engr, Associated Electrical Industries, 1956-61; Univ. of Leeds: Lectr, 1961-65; Reader, 1965-66; Chm., Jt Faculties of Science and Applied Science, 1978-80; Chm., Shadow Faculty of Engrg, 1981. Science Research Council: Mem., Electrical and Systems Cttee, 1971-; Chm., Electrical Engrg Sub-Cttee, 1981-; Mem., Machines and Power Cttee, 1981-. Instn of Electrical Engineers: Mem. Council, 1966-69 and 1981-; Chm., Accreditation Cttee, 1979-. IEE Awards: Premia-Crompton, 1957 and 1967; John Hopkinson, 1965; The Instn, 1981. Publications: (with K. J. Binns) Analysis and Computation of Electromagnetic Field Problems, 1963, 2nd edn 1973; (with M. R. Harris and J. M. Stephenson) Per Unit Systems, 1970; papers and patents in areas of electromagnetism, electromechanics and control. Recreations: lawn tennis, squash, chess, bridge, jewelry making. Address: Spen Watch, 318 Spen Lane, Leeds LS16 5BA. T: Leeds 755849.

LAWREY, Keith, JP; Secretary-General, The Library Association, since 1978; b 21 Aug. 1940; s of George William Bishop Lawrey and Edna Muriel (née Gass); m 1969, Helen Jane Marriott; two s two d. Educ: Colfe's Sch. LLB London. Barrister-at-Law; called to Bar, Gray's Inn, 1972. Education Officer, Plastics and Rubber Inst., 1960-68; Lectr and Sen. Lectr, Bucks Coll. of Higher Educn, 1968-74; Head of Dept of Business Studies, Mid-Kent Coll. of Higher and Further Educn, 1974-78. ACP; FCIS. Mem., Worshipful Co. of Chartered Secretaries and Administrators. JP Inner London, 1974. Publications: papers in Jl, Coll. of Preceptors, Jl Assoc. of Law Teachers, Trans and Jl of Plastics Inst. Recreations: preaching, sailing, swimming, theatre, gardening. Address: 7 Ridgemount Street, WC1E 7AE. T: 01-636 7543. Club: Old Colfeians.

LAWS, Courtney Alexander, OD 1978; Director, Brixton Neighbourhood Community Association, since 1971; b Morant Bay, St Thomas, Jamaica, 16 June 1934; s of Ezekiel Laws and Agatha Laws; m 1955 Wilhel, (Rubie), Brown; one s two d. Educ: Morant Bay Elem. Sch.; Jones Pen and Rollington Town Elem. Sch.; Lincoln Coll.; Nat. Coll. for Youth Workers, Leicester; Cranfield Coll., Bedford. Member: Lambeth Council for Community Relations, 1964-; Consortium of Ethnic Minorities, Lambeth, 1978-; W Indian Standing Conf., 1959-; Campaign against Racial Discrimination, 1960-; NCCI, 1960-; Commn for Racial Equality, 1977-80; Central Cttee, British Caribbean Assoc. (Exec. Mem.), 1960-; Assoc. of Jamaicans (Founder Mem.), 1965; Geneva and Somerleyton Community Assoc., 1966-; Consultative Cttee, ILEA, Lambeth, 1975-; Consultative Council, City and E London Coll., 1975-; South Eastern Gas Consumers' Council, 1980-; Governor, Brixton Coll. of Further and Higher Educn, 1970-; Member: W Indian Sen. Citizens' Assoc. (Pres.), 1973-; St John's Interracial Club, 1958-; Brixton United Cricket Club, 1968- (Pres.); Brixton Domino Club (Chm.); Oasis Sports and Social Club, 1969-. Officer, Order of Distinction, Jamaica, 1978. Recreations: reading, music. Address: 164 Croxted Road, West Dulwich, SE21. T: 01-761 2614.

LAWS, Dr John William, CBE 1982; FRCP; FRCR; consultant radiologist; Director of Radiology, King's College Hospital, and Director of Radiological Studies, King's College Hospital Medical School, since 1967; b 25 Oct. 1921; s of Robert Montgomery Laws and Lucy Ibbotson; m 1945, Pamela King, MRCS, LRCP; one s one d. Educ: The Leys Sch., Cambridge; Sheffield Univ. Med. Sch. MB ChB 1944; DMRD 1952; MRCP 1951; FRCR (FFR 1955); FRCP 1967. Nat. service, 1947-49 (Captain RAMC). House Physician and House Surg., Royal Hosp., Sheffield, 1944-45; Res. Surgical Officer, Salisbury Gen. Infirmary, 1945-47; Med. Registrar, 1949-51, Registrar and Sen. Registrar, 1951-55, United Sheffield Hosps; Consultant Radiologist, Dep. Dir, Hammersmith Hosp., and Hon. Lectr, RPMS, 1955-67. Consultant Civilian Advr to Army, 1976-; Med. Dir, King's Centre for Assessment of Radiol Equipment, 1979-. Vis. Prof. and Lectr at academic institutions and congresses worldwide. Chm., Radiol Equipment Sub-Cttee, DHSS, 1972-81; Member: Central Adv. Cttee on Hosp. Med. Records, DHSS, 1969-74; Radiol Adv. Cttee, DHSS, 1972-; Consultant Advr in Radiol., DHSS, 1982-. Chm., British Delegn, XV Internat. Congress of Radiol., 1981. Royal College (formerly Faculty) of Radiologists: Mem. Fellowship Bd, 1966-71; Hon. Sec., 1974-75; Registrar, 1975-76; Warden of Fellowship, 1976-80; Pres., 1980-; Mem. Council, RCS. Member Editorial Board: Clin. Radiol., 1960-63; Gut, 1970-74; Gastrointestinal Radiol., 1975-; Asst, later Hon., Editor, British Jl

of Radiol., 1961-71. Hon. FACR 1973; Hon. FFR RCSI 1975; Hon. FRACR 1979. Barclay Prize, British Inst. of Radiol., 1964. Publications: (contrib.) Recent Advances in Radiology, 1979; (contrib.) Recent Advances in Surgery, 6th edn 1964; (contrib.) Textbook of Radiology, ed Sutton, 3rd edn 1980; numerous papers on various aspects of clinical radiology, particularly gastrointestinal and hepatic radiology and the radiology of pulmonary disease, in medical journals. Recreations: listening to music, golf. Address: 5 Frank Dixon Way, Dulwich, SE21 7BB. T: 01-693 4815.

LAWS, Richard Maitland, PhD; FRS 1980; Director, British Antarctic Survey, since 1973; b 23 April 1926; s of Percy Malcolm Laws and Florence May (née Heslop); m 1954, Maureen Isobel Winifred (née Holmes); three s. Educ: Dame Allan's Sch., Newcastle-on-Tyne; St Catharine's Coll., Cambridge (Open Scholar, 1944; Hon. Fellow, 1982). BA Cantab 1947, MA 1952, PhD 1953; FInstBiol 1973. Biologist and Base Leader, Falkland Is Dependencies Survey, 1947-53; Biologist and Whaling Inspector, F/F Balaena, 1953-54; Principal Sci. Officer, Nat. Inst. of Oceanography, 1954-61; Dir, Nuffield Unit of Tropical Animal Ecology, Uganda, 1961-67; Dir, Tsavo Research Project, Kenya, 1967-68; Smuts Meml Fund Fellowship, 1968-69; Leverhulme Research Fellowship, 1969; Head, Life Sciences Div., British Antarctic Survey, 1969-73. Dir, NERC Sea Mammal Res. Unit, 1977-; Convener, SCAR gp of specialists on seals, 1972-; Chm., SCAR Biology Working Gp, 1980-. Bruce Medal, RSE, 1954; Scientific Medal, Zool Soc. London, 1965; Polar Medal, 1977. Publications: (with I. S. C. Parker and R. C. B. Johnstone) Elephants and their Habitats, 1975; numerous papers in biol jls. Recreations: walking, photography, painting. Address: 3 The Footpath, Coton, Cambridge CB3 7PX. T: Madingley 210567.

LAWSON, family name of Baron Burnham.

LAWSON, His Honour Charles, QC 1961; a Circuit Judge, Central Criminal Court, 1972-82; b 23 Feb. 1916; 2nd s of late Barnet Lawson, London; m 1943, Olga Daphne Kay; three d. Educ: Grocers' Company Sch.; University College, London. LLB 1937. Served War of 1939-45: in Army, 1940-46; Major, Royal Artillery. Recorder: Burton-upon-Trent, 1965-68; Gloucester, 1968-71. Bencher, Inner Temple, 1968. Recreations: golf, music. Address: Mayes Green Cottage, Ockley, Surrey RH5 5PN.

LAWSON, Christopher Donald; Director of Marketing, Conservative and Unionist Party, since 1982; b 31 Oct. 1922; s of James Lawson and Ellen de Verrine; m 1945, Marjorie Bristow; two s one d. Educ: Magdalen Coll., Oxford. Served RAF, 1941-49: Pilot, Sqdn Leader. Thomas Hedley (Proctor and Gamble), 1949-57; Cooper McDougal Robertson, 1958-61; Managing Dir, TMC, 1961-63; Director: Mars Ltd, 1965-75; Mars Inc., USA, 1975-82; Pres., Mars Snackmaster, USA, 1977-82; Chm. and Man. Dir, Goodblue Ltd, 1981-82. Recreations: collecting antiques and new artists' work; all sport, particularly golf, cricket, hockey. Address: 16 Tufton Court, Tufton Street, SW1P 3QN. Clubs: Reform, Arts, MCC; Cotswold Hills Golf, Lillybrook Golf (Cheltenham); Doublegate Country (Ga, USA).

LAWSON, Prof. Donald Douglas; Professor of Veterinary Surgery, University of Glasgow, since 1974; b 25 May 1924; s of Alexander Lawson and Jessie Macnaughton; m 1949, Barbara Ness; two s two d. Educ: Whitehill Sch., Glasgow; Glasgow Veterinary Coll. MRCVS, BSc, DVR. Asst in Veterinary Practice, 1946-47; Asst, Surgery Dept, Glasgow Vet. Coll., 1947-49; Glasgow Univ.: Lectr, Vet. Surgery, 1949-57; Sen. Lectr, 1957-66; Reader, 1966-71; Titular Prof., 1971-74. Publications: many articles in Veterinary Record and Jl of Small Animal Practice. Recreations: gardening, motoring. Address: Burnbrae, Balfron, Glasgow G63 0NY. T: Balfron 40232.

LAWSON, Rear-Adm. Frederick Charles William, CB 1971; DSC 1942 and Bar, 1945; Chief Executive, Royal Dockyards, Ministry of Defence, 1972-75; b 20 April 1917; s of M. L. Lawson, formerly of Public Works Dept, Punjab, India; m 1945, Dorothy (née Norman), Eastbourne; one s three d. Educ: Eastbourne Coll.; RNEC. Joined RN, 1935; specialised in engrg; Cmdr 1949; Captain 1960; Cdre Supt Singapore, 1965-69; Rear-Adm. 1969; Flag Officer, Medway and Adm. Supt, HM Dockyard, Chatham, 1969-71, retired. Recreation: golf. Address: Weaverhoult, Woolley Street, Bradford-on-Avon, Wilts. Club: Army and Navy.

LAWSON, Frederick Henry, DCL 1947; FBA 1956; Part-time Professor of Law, University of Lancaster, 1964-77, now Emeritus; b Leeds, 14 July 1897; s of Frederick Henry Lawson and Mary Louisa Austerberry; m 1933, Elspeth, yr d of late Captain Alexander Webster, Kilmarnock; one s two d. Educ: Leeds Grammar Sch. Hastings Exhibitioner in Classics (Hon. Scholar), Queen's Coll., Oxford, 1915; Akroyd Scholar, 1915. Served European War, 1916-18. 1st Class, Final Hon. School of Modern History, 1921; 1st Class, Final Hon. School of Jurisprudence, 1922. Barrister-at-Law, Gray's Inn, 1923; Lecturer in Law, University Coll., Oxford, 1924-25, Christ Church, 1925-26, CCC, 1925-26 and 1927-30; Junior Research Fellow, Merton Coll., Oxford, 1925-30, official Fellow and Tutor in Law, 1930-48. Studied at Göttingen, 1926-27; University Lecturer in Byzantine Law, 1929-31; All Souls Reader in Roman Law, 1931-48; Temp. Principal in Ministry of Supply, 1943-45; Prof. of Comparative Law, and Fellow of Brasenose Coll., Oxford, 1948-64. Visiting Prof., Univ. of California, 1953; Thomas M. Cooley Lectr, Univ. of Michigan Law Sch., 1953; Joint Editor Journal of Comparative Legislation and International Law, 1948-52, of International and Comparative Law Quarterly,

1952-55; Senior Editor, Journal of Society of Public Teachers of Law, 1955-61; Member International Social Science Council, 1952-58; Lecturer in Roman Law, Council of Legal Education, 1954-58 (Reader, 1958-64); Visiting Lecturer, New York University School of Law, 1956, 1959, 1962, 1965; Visiting Professor, University of Pennsylvania Law School, 1959 (Spring Semester); University of Michigan Law School, 1959 (Fall Semester); University of Houston, 1967-68. Mem. Internat. Acad. of Comparative Law, 1958-; Sec.-Gen., Internat. Assoc. of Legal Science, 1964-69. Hon. Doctor: Louvain, 1958; Paris, 1964; Ghent, 1968; Hon. Dr jur. Frankfurt; Hon. LLD: Glasgow, 1960; Lancaster, 1977. *Publications:* (with Sir D. L. Keir) Cases in Constitutional Law, 1st edn 1928, 6th edn (with D. J. Bentley) 1979; Negligence in the Civil Law, 1950; The Rational Strength of English Law (Hamlyn Lectures), 1951; A Common Lawyer looks at the Civil Law (Thomas M. Cooley Lectures), 1955; An Introduction to the Law of Property, 1958; (with D. J. Bentley) Constitutional and Administrative Law, 1961; The Oxford Law School, 1850-1965, 1968; The Roman Law Reader, 1969; The Remedies of English Law, 1972; Selected Essays, 1977; much re-editing, including Buckland and McNair, Roman Law and Common Law, 2nd edn 1952. *Address:* 6 Thirsk Road, Stokesley, Middlesbrough, Cleveland TS9 5BW. *T:* Stokesley 710268.

LAWSON, Prof. Gerald Hartley; Professor of Business Finance, Manchester Business School, University of Manchester, since 1969; financial and economic consultant; *b* 6 July 1933; of English parents; *m* 1957, Helga Elisabeth Anna Heine; three *s. Educ:* King's Coll., Univ. of Durham. BA (Econ), MA (Econ) MBA Manchester; FCCA. Accountant in industry, 1957-59; Lectr in Accountancy and Applied Economics, Univ. of Sheffield, 1959-66; Prof. of Business Studies, Univ. of Liverpool, 1966-69. Prof., Univ. of Augsburg, Germany, 1971-72; Prof., Univ. of Texas, 1977, 1981; Prof., Ruhr Univ., Bochum, 1980; British Council Scholar, Hochschule für Welthandel, Vienna, 1967, and Univ. of Louvain, 1978. *Publications:* (with D. W. Windle): Tables for Discounted Cash Flow, etc, Calculations, 1965 (5th repr. 1978); Capital Budgeting in the Corporation Tax Regime, 1967; many articles and translations. *Recreations:* cricket, skiing. *Address:* Manchester Business School, Booth Street West, Manchester M15 6PB. *T:* 061-273 8228. *Club:* Manchester Business School.

LAWSON, Lt-Col Harold Andrew Balvaird, CVO 1971 (MVO 1963); Rothesay Herald Extraordinary, since 1981 (Rothesay Herald, 1939-81); Lyon Clerk and Keeper of the Records of the Court of the Lord Lyon, 1929-66; *b* 19 Oct. 1899; 2nd *s* of late Dr Charles Wilfrid Lawson, Edinburgh; *m* 1934, Kathleen Alice (*d* 1980), *o d* of Alexander Banks, of Banks & Co., Printers; one *d. Educ:* George Watson's Coll.; Edinburgh Univ. Joined RFA, 1916; 2nd Lieut, 1919; RA (TA), 1924; Major, 1936; Lieut-Colonel, 1939; Unicorn Pursuivant, 1929-39. OStJ 1968. *Address:* Lyon Office, HM Register House, Edinburgh.

LAWSON, Hugh McDowall, BScEng London; CEng, FIMunE; Director of Leisure Services, Nottingham City Council, 1973-76; *b* Leeds, 13 Feb. 1912; *s* of late John Lawson, Pharmaceutical Chemist; *m* 1937, Dorothy (*d* 1982), *d* of late Rev. T. H. Mallinson, BA; two *s. Educ:* Nottingham High Sch.; University Coll., Nottingham. Served in Royal Engineers, 1940-44. MP (Common Wealth) Skipton Div. of Yorks, 1944-45. Contested (Common Wealth) Harrow West Div., 1945; (Lab) Rushcliffe Div., 1950; (Lab) King's Lynn Div., 1955; joined SDP, 1981. Dep. City Engr, Nottingham, 1948-73. Mem. Council, ICE, 1972-75. *Address:* 45 Hazel Grove, Mapperley, Nottingham NG3 6DQ. *T:* 605241.

LAWSON, Air Vice-Marshal Ian Douglas Napier, CB 1965; CBE 1961; DFC 1941, Bar 1943; AE 1945; RAF, retired; *b* 11 Nov. 1917; *y s* of late J. L. Lawson and Ethel Mary Lawson (*née* Ludgate); *m* 1945, Dorothy Joyce Graham Nash; one *s* one *d. Educ:* Brondesbury Coll.; Polytechnic, Regent Street. Aircraft Industry, 1934-39. Joined RAFVR 1938. Served War of 1939-45 (despatches thrice): Bomber Comd, 1940-41; Middle East Comd, 1941-45. Permanent Commission, 1945. Bomber Comd, 1945-46; Staff Coll., 1946; Air Ministry, 1946-49; Transport Comd, 1949-50; Middle East Comd, 1950-52; JSSC, 1953; Ministry of Defence, 1953-56; Flying Coll., Manby, 1956-57; Transport Comd, 1957-62; Air Forces Middle East, 1962-64; Commandant, RAF Coll., Cranwell, 1964-67; Asst Chief Adviser (Personnel and Logistics), MoD, 1967-69. Joined BAC, 1969, Chief Sales Exec., Weybridge, Bristol Div., 1974-79; Gen. Marketing Manager (civil), BAe, 1979-81; non-exec. Dir, Glos Air (Holdings) Ltd, 1981-82. FBIM. US Legion of Merit. *Recreations:* gardening, motor sport. *Address:* Grove House, Lacock, Wilts. *T:* Lacock 307. *Club:* Royal Air Force.

LAWSON, John Alexander Reid, OBE 1979; FRCGP; General Medical Practitioner, since 1948; Regional Adviser in General Practice, Tayside Region, since 1972; *b* 30 Aug. 1920; *s* of Thomas Reid Lawson and Helen Scrimgour Lawson; *m* 1944, Pat Kirk; two *s* two *d. Educ:* High Sch. of Dundee; Univ. of St Andrews (MB, ChB). RAMC, 1944-47 (Major). Surgical Registrar, Royal Infirmary, Dundee, 1947-48. Royal College of General Practitioners: Mem., 1952; Fellow, 1967; Chm. Council, 1973-76. Mem. Cttee of Enquiry into Competence to Practice, 1974-76; Chairman: Jt Cttee on Postgraduate Training for General Practice, 1975-78; Armed Service Gen. Practice Approval Bd, 1979-. *Recreations:* shooting, fishing, golf, gardening. *Address:* The Ridges, 458 Perth Road, Dundee. *T:* Dundee 67408. *Clubs:* New (Edinburgh); Royal and Ancient Golf (St Andrews).

LAWSON, Col Sir John Charles Arthur Digby, 3rd Bt, *cr* 1900; DSO 1943; MC 1940; Lieutenant-Colonel 11th Hussars, retired; former Chairman, Fairbairn Lawson Ltd, Leeds; *b* 24 Oct. 1912; *e s* of Sir Digby Lawson, Bt, TD, JP, and late Mrs Gerald Wallis (*née* Iris Mary Fitzgerald); *S* father 1959; *m* 1st, 1945, Rose (marr. diss., 1950), *widow* of Pilot Officer William Fiske, RAF, and *er d* of late D. C. Bingham and late Lady Rosabelle Brand; 2nd, 1954, Tresilla Ann Eleanor (de Pret Roose), *d* of late Major E. Buller Leyborne Popham, MC; one *s. Educ:* Stowe; RMC, Sandhurst; commissioned 11th Hussars (PAO), 1933; Palestine, 1936-37; Transjordan Frontier Force, 1938; Western Desert, 1940-43 (despatches twice, MC, DSO); Armoured Adviser to Gen. Patton, N Africa, 1943; Staff Coll., 1943; US Marines Staff Course, 1944; Special Liaison Officer to Gen. Montgomery, NW Europe, 1944; Comd Inns of Court Regt, 1945-47; retired, 1947. Colonel, 11th Hussars (PAO), 1965-69; Col, The Royal Hussars (PWO), 1969-73. Legion of Merit (US). *Heir: s* Charles John Patrick Lawson [*b* 19 May 1959. *Educ:* Harrow; Royal Agricl Coll., Cirencester]. *Address:* Abbey Hill, Jervaulx, Ripon, N Yorks. *T:* Bedale 60209. *Clubs:* Army and Navy, MCC.

LAWSON, Hon. Sir Neil, Kt 1971; **Hon. Mr Justice Lawson;** Judge of High Court of Justice, Queen's Bench Division, since 1971; *b* 8 April 1908; *s* of late Robb Lawson and Edith Marion Lawson (*née* Usherwood); *m* 1933, Gweneth Clare (*née* Wilby); one *s* one *d.* Called to Bar, Inner Temple, 1929; QC 1955; Recorder of Folkestone, 1962-71; a Law Commissioner, 1965-71. RAFVR, 1940-45. Hon. Fellow, LSE, 1974. Foreign decorations: DK (Dato' Peduka Kerubat), 1959, DSN (Dato' Setia Negara), 1962, PSMB (Dato' Sri Mahota), 1969, Brunei. *Recreations:* literature, music, the country. *Address:* 30a Heath Drive, Hampstead, NW3.

LAWSON, Rt. Hon. Nigel, PC 1981; MP (C) Blaby, Leicestershire, since Feb. 1974; Secretary of State for Energy, since 1981; journalist; *b* 11 March 1932; *o s* of Ralph Lawson and Joan Elisabeth Lawson (*née* Davis); *m* 1st, 1955, Vanessa Salmon (marr. diss. 1980); one *s* three *d*; 2nd, 1980, Thérèse Mary Maclear; one *s* one *d. Educ:* Westminster; Christ Church, Oxford (Scholar). 1st class hons PPE, 1954. Served with Royal Navy (Sub-Lt RNVR), 1954-56. Mem. Editorial Staff, Financial Times, 1956-60; City Editor, Sunday Telegraph, 1961-63; Special Assistant to Prime Minister (Sir Alec Douglas-Home), 1963-64; Financial Times columnist and BBC broadcaster, 1965; Editor of the Spectator, 1966-70; regular contributor to: Sunday Times and Evening Standard, 1970-71; The Times, 1971-72; Fellow, Nuffield Coll., Oxford, 1972-73; Special Pol Advr, Cons. Party HQ, 1973-74. Contested (C), Eton and Slough, 1970. An Opposition Whip, 1976-77; an Opposition Spokesman on Treasury and Economic Affairs, 1977-79; Financial Sec. to the Treasury, 1979-81. Chm., Coningsby Club, 1963-64. Vice-Chm., Cons. Political Centre Nat. Adv. Cttee, 1972-75. *Publications:* (jtly) Britain and Canada, 1976; (with Jock Bruce-Gardyne) The Power Game, 1976; (jtly) The Coming Confrontation, 1978; The New Conservatism (pamphlet), 1980. *Address:* The Old Rectory, Stoney Stanton, Leics; 32 Sutherland Walk, SE17. *Clubs:* Garrick, Political Economy.

LAWSON, Gen. Sir Richard (George), KCB 1980; DSO 1962; OBE 1968; Commander-in-Chief, Allied Forces Northern Europe, since 1982; *b* 24 Nov. 1927; *s* of John Lawson and Florence Rebecca Lawson; *m* 1956, Ingrid Lawson; one *s. Educ:* St Alban's Sch.; Birmingham Univ. CO, Independent Squadron, RTR (Berlin), 1963-64; GSO2 MoD, 1965-66; CofS, South Arabian Army, 1967; CO, 5th RTR, 1968-69; Comdr, 20th Armoured Bde, 1972-73; Asst Military Deputy to Head of Defence Sales, 1975-77; GOC 1st Armoured Div., 1977-79; GOC Northern Ireland, 1980-82. Col Comdt, RTR, 1980-82. Leopold Cross (Belgium), 1963; Knight Commander, Order of St Sylvester (Vatican), 1964. *Publications:* Strange Soldiering, 1963; All the Queen's Men, 1967; Strictly Personal, 1972. *Address:* HQ Allied Forces Northern Europe, Oslo, BFPO 50. *Club:* Army and Navy.

LAWSON, Sir William (Howard), 5th Bt *cr* 1841; DL; *b* 15 July 1907; *s* of Sir Henry Joseph Lawson, 3rd Bt, and Ursula Mary (*d* 1960), *o c* of Philip John Canning Howard, Corby Castle, Carlisle; *S* brother, 1975; *m* 1933, Joan Eleanor, *d* of late Arthur Cowie Stamer, CBE; three *s* one *d. Educ:* Ampleforth College. DL Cumberland, 1963. *Recreations:* field sports. *Heir: s* John Philip Howard [*b* 6 June 1934; assumed surname and arms of Howard by Royal Licence, 1962; *m* 1960, Jean Veronica, *d* of late Col John Evelyn Marsh, DSO, OBE; two *s* one *d*]. *Address:* Wood House, Warwick Bridge, Carlisle. *T:* Wetheral 60330.

LAWSON DICK, Clare; OBE 1975; BBC Controller Radio 4, 1975-76; *b* 13 Oct. 1913; *d* of late John Lawson Dick, MD, FRCS, and Winifred Lawson Dick (*née* Duke). *Educ:* Channing Sch., Highgate; King's Coll., London (Dip. Journalism). Joined BBC, 1935. *Recreations:* enjoying the amenities of London; escaping from London into the country. *Address:* Flat 8, 92 Elm Park Gardens, SW10. *T:* 01-352 8395.

LAWSON JOHNSTON, family name of **Baron Luke.**

LAWSON JOHNSTON, Hon. Hugh de Beauchamp, TD 1951; DL; *b* 7 April 1914; *yr s* of 1st Baron Luke of Pavenham, KBE, and *b* of 2nd Baron Luke, *qv; m* 1946, Audrey Warren, *d* of late Colonel F. Warren Pearl and late Mrs A. L. Pearl; three *d. Educ:* Eton; Chillon Coll.; Corpus Christi, Cambridge. BA 1934, MA (Cantab), 1938. With Bovril Ltd, 1935-71, finally as Chm. Territorial Service with 5th Bn Beds and Herts Regt, 1935-; Captain, 1939, and throughout War. Chm., Tribune Investment Trust Ltd; Chm.,

Pitman Ltd, 1973-81. Chm. of Cttees, United Soc. for Christian Literature. High Sheriff of Bedfordshire, 1961-62; DL Beds, 1964. *Recreations:* walking, gardening, photography. *Address:* Flat 1, 28 Lennox Gardens, SW1. *T:* 01-584 1446; Melchbourne Park, Bedfordshire. *T:* Riseley 282.

LAWSON-TANCRED, Sir Henry, 10th Bt, *cr* 1662; JP; *b* 12 Feb. 1924; *e surv. s* of Major Sir Thomas Lawson-Tancred, 9th Bt, and Margery Elinor (*d* 1961), *d* of late A. S. Lawson, Aldborough Manor; *S* father, 1945; *m* 1st, 1950, Jean Veronica (*d* 1970), 4th and *y d* of late G. R. Foster, Stockeld Park, Wetherby, Yorks; five *s* one *d*; 2nd, 1978, Mrs Susan Drummond, *d* of Sir Kenelm Cayley, 10th Bt. *Educ:* Stowe; Jesus Coll., Cambridge. Served as Pilot in RAFVR, 1942-46. JP West Riding, 1967. *Heir: s* Andrew Peter Lawson-Tancred, *b* 18 Feb. 1952. *Address:* Aldborough Manor, Boroughbridge, Yorks YO5 9EP. *T:* Boroughbridge 2716.

LAWTHER, Prof. Patrick Joseph, CBE 1978; FRCP; Professor of Environmental and Preventive Medicine, University of London, at St Bartholomew's Hospital Medical College, since 1968, also at London Hospital Medical College, since 1976; Member, Medical Research Council Scientific Staff, since 1955; *b* 9 March 1921; *s* of Joseph and Winefride Lawther; *m* 1944, Kathleen May Wilkowski; two *s* one *d. Educ:* Carlisle and Morecambe Grammar Schs; King's Coll., London; St Bartholomew's Hosp. Med. Coll. MB BS 1950; DSc London 1971. FRCP 1963 (MRCP 1954). St Bartholomew's Hospital: Ho. Phys., Med. Professorial Unit, 1950; Cooper & Coventson Res. Schol., 1951-53; Associate Chief Asst, 1952-62; Hon. Cons. and Phys.-in-Charge, Dept of Envir. and Prev. Med., 1962-. Director, MRC Air Pollution Unit (later Envir. Hazards Unit), 1955-77; Head of Clinical Sect., MRC Toxicology Unit, 1977-. Cons. Expert, WHO, 1960-; Civilian Cons. in Envir. Medicine, RN, 1975-. RCP Marc Daniels Lectr, 1970; Sir Arthur Thomson Vis. Prof., Univ. of Birmingham, 1975-76; Guymer Meml Lectr, St Thomas' Hosp., 1979. RSA Silver Medal, 1964; Acad. Nat. de Médecine Bronze Medal, 1972; RCP Bissett Hawkins Medal, 1974; RSM Edwin Stevens Gold Medal, 1975. *Publications:* various papers and chapters in books relating to environmental and occupational medicine. *Recreations:* almost everything. *Address:* Apple Trees, Church Road, Purley, Surrey CR2 3QQ. *T:* 01-660 6398. *Clubs:* Surrey CCC; Middlesex CCC.

LAWTON, Alistair; *see* Lawton, J. A.

LAWTON, Frank Dickinson, CB 1972; FRES; a Consultant, British Institute of Management, since 1980; *b* 14 July 1915; *o s* of F. W. Lawton, CB, OBE, and Elizabeth Mary (*née* Savage); *m* 1943, Margaret Joan, *o d* of Frederick Norman Reed; one *s* two *d. Educ:* Epsom Coll.; Law Society's Sch. of Law. Solicitor (hons), 1937. Entered Solicitor's Dept, Ministry of Labour, 1939; seconded to Treasury, Solicitor's Dept, 1940; returned to Solicitor's Dept, Ministry of Labour, 1947; Assistant Solicitor, 1959; Solicitor, Min. of Labour (now Dept of Employment), 1967-76. Mem. Court of Assts, Scriveners' Co. (Master, 1970-71; Mem. Examination Cttee, 1967-76). *Publications:* occasional contribs about parasitic hymenoptera. *Recreations:* natural history, the arts. *Address:* Riversdale, Tarrant Monkton, Blandford Forum, Dorset. *T:* Tarrant Hinton 203. *Club:* Athenæum.

LAWTON, Prof. Sir Frank (Ewart), Kt 1981; DDS; FDSRCS; Professor of Operative Dental Surgery, University of Liverpool, 1956-80, now Emeritus Professor; *b* 23 Oct. 1915; *s* of Hubert Ralph Lawton and Agnes Elizabeth (*née* Heath); *m* 1943, Muriel Leonora Bacon; one *s* one *d. Educ:* Univ. of Liverpool (BDS 1st Cl. Hons 1937); Northwestern Univ., Chicago (DDS 1948). FDSRCS 1948. Lectr, 1939, and Dir of Dental Educn, 1957-80, Univ. of Liverpool. President: BDA, 1973-74; GDC, 1979-. Editor, Internat. Dental Jl, 1963-81. Hon. DDSc Newcastle, 1981; Hon. DDS Birmingham, 1982. *Publications:* (ed with Ed Farmer) Stones Oral and Dental Diseases, 1966; contrib. scientific and prof. jls. *Recreation:* music. *Address:* 55 Woolton Hill Road, Liverpool L25 6HU. *T:* 051-428 1323.

LAWTON, Rt. Hon. Sir Frederick (Horace), PC 1972; Kt 1961; **Rt. Hon. Lord Justice Lawton;** a Lord Justice of Appeal, since 1972; *b* 21 Dec. 1911; *o s* of William John Lawton; *m* 1937, Doreen (*née* Wilton) (*d* 1979); two *s. Educ:* Battersea Grammar Sch.; Corpus Christi Coll., Cambridge (Hon. Fellow, 1968). Barrister, Inner Temple, 1935; Bencher, 1961. Served with London Irish Rifles, 1939-41; invalided out of Army, 1941, and returned to practice at the Bar. QC 1957; Judge of the High Court of Justice, Queen's Bench Div., 1961-72. Recorder of City of Cambridge, 1957-61; Dep. Chm., Cornwall QS, 1968-71. Member: Bar Council, 1957-61; Departmental Cttee on Proceedings before Examining Justices, 1957-58; Standing Cttee on Criminal Law Revision, 1959- (Chm., 1977-); Inter-departmental Cttee on Court of Criminal Appeal, 1964-65; Chm., Adv. Cttee on Legal Educn, 1976-. Presiding Judge, Western Circuit, 1970-72. President, British Academy of Forensic Sciences, 1964. *Address:* 2 Harcourt Buildings, Temple, EC4Y 9DB. *T:* 01-353 3720; Mordryg, Stoptide, Rock, near Wadebridge, Cornwall. *T:* Trebetherick 3375. *Club:* Garrick.

LAWTON, Harold Walter, MA; Docteur de l'Université de Paris; Officier d'Académie; Emeritus Professor, University of Sheffield, since 1964; *b* Stoke-on-Trent, 27 July 1899; *y s* of late William T. C. and Alice Lawton; *m* 1933, Bessie, *y d* of T. C. Pate; two *s* one *d. Educ:* Middle Sch., Newcastle under Lyme; Rhyl Grammar Sch.; Universities of Wales and Paris. BA Hons (Wales) 1921; MA (Wales) 1923; Fellow University of Wales, 1923-26; Docteur de l'Univ. de Paris, 1926. University College, Southampton: Lecturer

in French, 1926-37; Professor of French, 1937-50; Dean of Faculty of Arts, 1945-49; first Warden of New, later Connaught, Hall, 1930-33; University of Sheffield: Professor of French, 1950-64; Warden of Ranmoor House, 1957-63; Deputy Pro-Vice-Chancellor, 1958-61; Pro-Vice-Chancellor, 1961-64. Médaille d'Argent de la Reconnaissance Française, 1946; Officier d'Académie, 1948. *Publications:* Térence en France au XVIe Siècle: éditions et traductions (Paris), 1926; repr. 1970; Handbook of French Renaissance Dramatic Theory, 1950, repr. 1972; J. du Bellay, Poems, selected with introduction and notes, 1961; Térence en France au XVIe Siècle: imitation et influence, 1972; articles and reviews to British and French periodicals. *Recreations:* walking, drawing. *Address:* Ranmoor, 4 Timber Bank, Vigo Village, Meopham, Kent DA13 0RZ. *T:* Fairseat 822712.

LAWTON, (John) Alistair, CBE 1981; with Sea Properties Ltd, since 1955; *b* 1 Oct. 1929; *s* of Richard Geoffrey Lawton and Emma Lawton; *m* 1952, Iris Lilian Barthorpe; one *s* two *d. Educ:* Crewkerne Sch., Somerset. Southern Rhodesia Govt, 1946-55. Chairman: Council of Local Education Authorities; Educn Cttee, ACC. Member: Deal Borough Council, 1956-74 (Mayor, 1966-68); Kent County Council, 1966- (Chm., 1977-79). Hon. DCL Kent, 1982. *Recreations:* cricket, Rugby (non-participating now). *Address:* 6 Archery Square, Walmer, Deal, Kent CT14 7HP. *T:* Deal 5060. *Club:* Savile.

LAWTON, Ven. John Arthur; Rector of Winwick since 1969; Archdeacon of Warrington, 1970-81; *b* 19 Jan. 1913; *s* of Arthur and Jennie Lawton; unmarried. *Educ:* Rugby; Fitzwilliam House, Cambridge (MA); Cuddesdon Theological College, Oxford. Curate, St Dunstan, Edgehill, Liverpool, 1937-40; Vicar of S Anne, Wigan, 1940-56; Vicar of St Luke, Southport, 1956-60; Vicar of Kirkby, Liverpool, 1960-69. *Address:* Winwick Rectory, Golborne Road, Winwick, Warrington WA2 8SZ. *T:* Warrington 32760.

LAWTON, Kenneth Keith Fullerton; His Honour Judge Lawton; a Circuit Judge since 1972; *b* 6 Aug. 1924; *o s* of late John William Lawton, MA, BSc, and Susan Fullerton; *m* 1st, 1959, Muriel Iris (*née* Parry) (*d* 1974); 2nd, 1975, Dorothy, *d* of Harold Rogers, Lancaster. *Educ:* Barrow Grammar Sch.; Trinity Hall, Cambridge (Exhibr, MA). Fleet Air Arm, 1943-45. Called to Bar, Middle Temple, 1947; practised Liverpool Bar, 1948-70; part-time Dep. Chm., Lancs QS, 1969 (full-time 1970). Member: Lancs SW Probation and After-Care Cttee, 1973-74; Parole Bd, 1981-. Contested (C) Barrow, 1951. JP Lancs, 1969. *Recreations:* gardening, reading. *Address:* 19 St Anne's Road, Liverpool L17 6BN. *T:* 051-427 3339. *Clubs:* United Oxford & Cambridge University; Athenæum, Artists (Liverpool).

LAWTON, Louis David, QC 1973; Barrister-at-Law; a Recorder of the Crown Court, since 1972; *b* 15 Oct. 1936; *m* 1959, Helen Margaret (*née* Gair); one *s* two *d. Educ:* Repton Sch.; Sidney Sussex Coll., Cambridge (MA). Called to Bar, Lincoln's Inn, 1959; Bencher, Lincoln's Inn, 1981. Mem. Criminal Injuries Compensation Bd, 1981-. *Address:* 2 Harcourt Buildings, Temple, EC4. *Club:* United Oxford & Cambridge University.

LAWTON, Philip Charles Fenner, CBE 1967; DFC 1941; Group Director and Chairman, BEA, 1972-73; Member: British Airways Board, 1972-73; Board, BOAC, 1972-73; Director, Stewart Wrightson (Aviation) Ltd, since 1974; *b* Highgate, London, 18 Sept. 1912; *o s* of late Charles Studdert Lawton and late Mabel Harriette Lawton; *m* 1941, Emma Letitia Gertrude, *y d* of late Lieut-Colonel Sir Henry Kenyon Stephenson, 1st Bt, DSO, and Frances, Hassop Hall, Bakewell, Derbyshire; one *s* one *d. Educ:* Westminster Sch. Solicitor, 1934-39. Joined AAF, 1935. Served War of 1939-45 (despatches twice, Group Captain): Pilot with 604 Aux. Sqdn (night fighters), 1939-41; Staff Officer HQ, Fighter Command, 1942; Station Commander, RAF Predannock; RAF Portreath; RAF Cranfield and Special Duties for Inspector-General, RAF, 1943-45. Joined BEA, 1946; Commercial and Sales Dir, 1947-71, Mem. Corporation 1964, Exec. Bd Member 1971; Chm., BEA Airtours, 1969-72. LLB Hons Degree, 1933; FCIT (MInstT 1955). *Address:* Adversane House, Billingshurst, West Sussex. *T:* Billingshurst 2559; 17 Pembroke Walk, W8. *T:* 01-937 3091. *Club:* RAF.

LAXNESS, Halldor Kiljan; Icelandic writer; *b* 23 April 1902; *s* of Gudjon Helgason and Sigridur Halldorsdottir, Iceland; *m* 1st, Ingibjörg Einarsdottir; one *s*; 2nd, Audur Sveinsdottir; two *d.* Awarded Nobel literary prize, 1955; Sonning Prize, 1969. *Publications:* (many of which have been translated into English): Undir Helgahnúk (Under the Holy Mountain), 1924; Vefarinn mikli frá Kasmir (The Great Weaver from Kashmir), 1927; Althydubókin (The Book of the People) (essays), 1929; Salka Valka, 1934 (first published as Thu vinvidur hreini, 1931, and Fuglinn i fjorunni, 1932); Sjálfstoett fólk (Independent People), 2 vols, 1934-35; Ljós heimsins, 1937, Holl sumarlandsins, 1938; Hus skaldsins, 1939, Fegurd himinsins, 1940 (these four republished as Heimsljos (The Light of the World), 2 vols, 1955); The Atom Station, 1948; Happy Warriors, 1952; Fish Can Sing, 1957; Paradise Reclaimed, 1960; Skaldatimi, 1963; Sjostafakverid, 1964; Kristnihald undir Jokli, 1968; Innansveitarkronika, 1970; Gudsgjafathula, 1972; I tuninu heima, 1975; Ungur eg var, 1976; Sjomeistarasagan, 1978; Grikklandsarid, 1980; translations into Icelandic include: Farewell to Arms by Ernest Hemingway; Candide by Voltaire. *Address:* PO Box 664, Reykjavik, Iceland.

LAYARD, Prof. Peter Richard Grenville; Professor of Economics, London School of Economics, since 1980, and Head, Centre for Labour Economics, since 1974; *b* 15 March 1934; *s* of Dr John Layard and Doris Layard. *Educ:*

Eton Coll.; King's Coll., Cambridge (BA); London School of Economics (MScEcon). History Master: Woodberry Down Sch., 1959-60; Forest Hill Sch., 1960-61; Senior Research Officer, Robbins Cttee on Higher Educn, 1961-63; London School of Economics: Dep. Director, Higher Educn Research Unit, 1964-74 (part-time from 1968); Lectr in Economics, 1968-75; Reader in the Economics of Labour, 1975-80. *Publications:* (jtly) The Causes of Educated Unemployment in India, 1969; (jtly) The Impact of Robbins: Expansion in Higher Education, 1969; (jtly) Qualified Manpower and Economic Performance: An Inter-Plant Study in the Electrical Engineering Industry, 1971; (ed) Cost-Benefit Analysis, 1973; (jtly) Microeconomic Theory, 1978; (jtly) The Causes of Poverty, 1978. *Recreations:* walking, the clarinet. *Address:* 18 Provost Road, NW3. *T:* 01-722 6347.

LAYE, Evelyn, CBE 1973; actress; singer; *b* London, 10 July 1900; *o d* of Gilbert Laye and Evelyn Froud; *m* 1st, 1926, Sonnie Hale (from whom she obtained a divorce, 1931); 2nd, 1934, Frank Lawton (*d* 1969). *Educ:* Folkestone; Brighton. Made first appearance on stage, Theatre Royal, Brighton, 1915, in Mr Wu. First London appearance in The Beauty Spot, Gaiety, 1918; first big success in title-role of The Merry Widow, Daly's, 1923; subsequently starred in London in Madame Pompadour, Daly's, 1923; The Dollar Princess, Daly's, 1925; Cleopatra, Daly's, 1925; Betty in Mayfair, Adelphi, 1925; Merely Molly, Adelphi, 1926; Princess Charming, Palace, 1927; Lilac Time, Daly's, 1927; Blue Eyes, Piccadilly, 1928; The New Moon, Drury Lane, 1929; Bitter Sweet, His Majesty's, 1930; Helen!, Adelphi, 1932; Give Me A Ring, Hippodrome, 1933; Paganini, Lyceum, 1937; Lights Up, Savoy, 1940; The Belle of New York, Coliseum, 1942; Sunny River, Piccadilly, 1943; Cinderella, His Majesty's, 1943; Three Waltzes, Prince's, 1945; Cinderella, Palladium, 1948; Two Dozen Red Roses, Lyric, 1949; Peter Pan, Scala, 1953; Wedding in Paris, Hippodrome, 1954-56; Silver Wedding, Cambridge, 1957; The Amorous Prawn, Saville/Piccadilly, 1959-62; Never Too Late, Prince of Wales, 1964; The Circle, Savoy, 1965; Strike A Light!, Piccadilly, 1966; Let's All Go Down the Strand, Phoenix, 1967; Charlie Girl, Adelphi, 1969; Phil the Fluter, Palace, 1969; No Sex, Please-We're British, Strand, 1971-73; A Little Night Music (revival), Exeter and on tour, 1979, Nottingham, 1980-81. First New York appearance in Bitter Sweet, Ziegfeld Theatre, 1929; subsequently on Broadway in Sweet Aloes, Booth, 1936; Between the Devil, Majestic, 1937. Film début in silent production, The Luck of the Navy, 1927. Films include: One Heavenly Night (Hollywood), 1932; Waltz Time, 1933; Princess Charming, 1934; Evensong, 1935; The Night is Young (Hollywood), 1936; Make Mine A Million, 1959; Theatre of Death, 1967; Within and Without, 1969; Say Hello to Yesterday, 1971. Numerous broadcasts and television appearances. *Publication:* Boo, to my Friends (autobiography), 1958. *Address:* c/o Jeremy Conway Ltd, 8 Cavendish Place, W1.

LAYFIELD, Sir Frank Henry Burland Willoughby, Kt 1976; QC 1967; a Recorder of the Crown Court, since 1979; *b* Toronto, 9 Aug. 1921; *s* of late H. D. Layfield; *m* 1965, Irene Patricia, *d* of late Captain J. D. Harvey, RN (retired); one *s* one *d. Educ:* Sevenoaks Sch. Army, 1940-46. Called to the Bar, Gray's Inn, 1954, Bencher, 1974. Chairman: Inquiry into Greater London Development Plan, 1970-73; Cttee of Inquiry into Local Government Finance, 1974-76. Associate, RICS, 1977; Hon. FSVA 1978. *Publications:* (with A. E. Telling) Planning Applications, Appeals and Inquiries, 1953; (with A. E. Telling) Applications for Planning Payments, 1955; Engineering Contracts, 1956. *Recreations:* walking, tennis. *Address:* 2 Mitre Court Buildings, Temple, EC4Y 7BX. *T:* 01-583 1355. *Clubs:* Garrick, United Oxford & Cambridge University.

LAYMAN, Captain Herbert Francis Hope, DSO and Bar, 1940; RN; *b* 23 March 1899; *s* of Major F. H. Layman, 11th Hussars; *m* 1934, Elizabeth, *o d* of Rear-Admiral A. P. Hughes; one *s* one *d. Educ:* Haileybury. Grand Fleet, 1918; Fleet Signal Officer, Home Fleet, 1933-36. Director of Radio Equipment, Admiralty, 1949-51; Commanded HMS Hotspur, 1939-41; HMS Rajah, 1945-46; Royal Naval Air Station, Culham, Oxon, 1947-48; Chief of Staff to Commander-in-Chief, The Nore, 1951-53; retired, 1953. Vice-Pres., Tennis and Rackets Association. *Publications:* articles on Rackets. *Address:* Cleve House, Blewbury, Didcot, Oxon.

LAYTON, family name of **Baron Layton.**

LAYTON, 2nd Baron *cr* 1947, of Danehill; **Michael John Layton;** Director: Wolff Steel Holdings Ltd, since 1977; Economist Newspaper Ltd, since 1973; *b* 28 Sept. 1912; *s* of Walter Thomas, 1st Baron Layton, and Eleanor Dorothea (*d* 1959), *d* of Francis B. P. Osmaston; *S* father, 1966; *m* 1938, Dorothy, *d* of Albert Luther Cross, Rugby; one *s* one *d. Educ:* St Paul's Sch.; Gonville and Caius Coll., Cambridge. BA Mech. Scis Cantab, 1934; CEng, FIMechE, FIM. Student Apprentice, British Thomson Houston Co. Ltd, Rugby (specialised in Industrial Admin), 1934-37; Student Engr, Goss Printing Co., Chicago, 1937-39; Works Man. and Production Engr, Ibbotson Bros & Co. Ltd, Sheffield, Manufacturing 25-pounder armour piercing shot, 1939-43; Gen. Man., two armoured car production plants, Rootes Ltd, Birmingham, 1943-46; Mem. Control Commn for Germany in Metallurgy Br. and latterly in Econ. Sub-Commn, assisting at formation of OEEC, 1946-48; Head of Internat. Relations Dept of British Iron and Steel Fedn, 1948-55; Sales Controller, 1956, Dir, 1960, Asst Man. Dir, 1965-67, Man. Dir, 1967, The Steel Co. of Wales Ltd; Exec. Board Mem., BSC, 1967-77. *Heir: s* Hon. Geoffrey Michael Layton [*b* 18 July 1947; *m* 1969, Viviane (marr. diss. 1970), *y d* of François Cracco, Belgium]. *Address:* 6 Old Palace Terrace, The Green,

Richmond, Surrey.
See also Hon. C. W. Layton.

LAYTON, Dr (Lt-Col) Basil Douglas Bailey, CD 1958; Principal Medical Officer, International Health, Department of National Health and Welfare, Canada, 1956-72; *b* 8 Aug. 1907; *s* of David Bailey Layton and Mary Eliza Merrick; *m* 1938, Marion Marie McDonald; three *s* one *d. Educ:* University of Toronto Medical Sch. (MD); Harvard University School of Public Health (MPH). Postgrad. medical study, 1931-36; medical practice, 1936-42. RCAMC, 1942-46: service in Canada, UK, and NW Europe. Dept of National Health and Welfare, 1946-72. Certified Specialist, Public Health, Royal Coll. of Phys and Surgs, Canada, 1951; postgrad. public health studies, Harvard School of Public Health, 1951-52. Canadian Army (Militia), RCAMC, 1949-58; retired Lt-Col, OC No 10 Medical Co., RCAMC(M). Mem. Canadian Delegn to 11th-24th World Health Assemblies, Head of Delegn to 15th, 16th; Pres., 25th World Health Assembly. Alternate to Canadian Mem., 1957-59, Mem. (Canada) 1962-65, 1968-71, Chm., 1963-64, of Exec. Board, WHO. Vice-President American Public Health Assoc., 1962-63; Vice-President, Harvard Public Health Alumni Assoc., 1961-63; President, 1963-64. Delta Omega (Beta Chapter) Hon. PH Fraternity, 1952. Fellow, American Public Health Assoc., 1957. France-Germany Star, Defence, Canada War Services and Victory Medals, 1946. *Publications:* scientific articles in Canadian Medical Assoc. Journal, Canadian Public Health Assoc. Journal, etc. *Address:* 1411 The Highlands, 515 St Laurent Boulevard, Ottawa, Ontario K1K 3X5. *T:* 749-5886.

LAYTON, Hon. Christopher Walter; Editor, Alliance, since 1982; *b* 31 Dec. 1929; *s* of 1st Baron Layton; *m* 1st, 1952, Anneliese Margaret, *d* of Joachim von Thadden, Hanover (marr. diss. 1957); one *s* one *d*; 2nd, 1961, Margaret Ann, *d* of Leslie Moon, Molesey, Surrey; three *d. Educ:* Oundle; King's Coll., Cambridge. Intelligence Corps, 1948-49; ICI Ltd, 1952; The Economist Intelligence Unit, 1953-62; Economic Adviser to Liberal Party, 1962-69; Dir, Centre for European Industrial Studies, Bath Univ., 1968-71; Commission of European Communities: Chef de Cabinet to Commissioner Spinelli, 1971-73; Dir, Computer Electronics, Telecomms and Air Transp. Equipment Manufg, Directorate-Gen. of Internal Market and Industrial Affairs, 1973-81; Hon. Director-General, EEC, and Special Adviser on Technology, 1981-. *Publications:* Transatlantic Investment, 1966; European Advanced Technology, 1968; Cross-frontier Mergers in Europe 1970; (jtly) Industry and Europe, 1971; (jtly) Ten Innovations: International Study on Development Technology and the Use of Qualified Scientists and Engineers in Ten Industries, 1972. *Address:* Orchard House, 3 Grange Road, SW13.
See also Baron Layton.

LAYTON, His Honour Paul Henry; a Circuit Judge (formerly Deputy Chairman, Inner London Quarter Sessions), 1965-79; *b* Walsall, 11 July 1905; *s* of Frank George Layton, MRCS, LRCP, and Dorothea Yonge; *m* 1950, Frances Evelyn Weekes, Ottawa; two *s. Educ:* Epsom Coll.; St John's Coll., Cambridge (MA). Called to Bar, Inner Temple, 1929; Joined Oxford Circuit, 1930; Recorder of Smethwick, 1952-64; Dep. Chm., Staffs QS, 1955-65; Chm., Agricultural Land Tribunal, W Midlands, 1955-65; Mem., Mental Health Review Tribunal, Birmingham Region, 1960-65; Recorder of Walsall, 1964-65. Served War of 1939-45, AAF and RAF. *Recreation:* gardening. *Address:* 70A Leopold Road, SW19 7JQ. *T:* 01-946 0865.

LAYTON, Thomas Arthur; writer on wine and food; editor; wine merchant; *b* 31 Dec. 1910; *s* of late T. B. Layton, DSO, FRCS, and Edney Sampson; *m* 1935, Eleanor de P. Marshall; one *s* one *d. Educ:* Bradfield Coll., Berks. Vintners' Co. Travelling Schol., 1929. Public Relations Officer, Wine Trade, 1951. Pres., Circle of Wine Tasters, 1936. Chevalier, Order of Civil Merit (Spain), 1971. *Publications:* Choose Your Wine, 1940 (rewritten, 1959); Table for Two, 1942; Restaurant Roundabout, 1944; Five to a Feast, 1948; Wine's my Line, 1955; Choose Your Cheese, 1957; Winecraft, 1959; Wines and Castles of Spain, 1959; Wines of Italy, 1961; Vignes et Vins de France (trans.), 1962; Choose Your Vegetables, 1963; Modern Wines, 1964; A Year at The Peacock, 1964; Cheese and Cheese Cookery, 1967; Wines and Chateaux of the Loire, 1967; Cognac and Other Brandies, 1968; Wines and People of Alsace, 1969; The Way of St James, 1976. Editor: Wine Magazine, 1958-60; Anglo-Spanish Journal (Quarterly), 1960-. *Recreations:* wine, travelling in Spain. *Address:* 3 Sussex Road, Hove, Sussex BN3 2WD. *T:* Brighton 738732.

LAZARUS, Peter Esmond, CB 1975; Permanent Secretary, Department of Transport, since 1982; *b* 2 April 1926; *er s* of late Kenneth M. Lazarus and Mary R. Lazarus (*née* Halsted); *m* 1950, Elizabeth Anne Marjorie Atwell, *e d* of late Leslie H. Atwell, OBE; three *s. Educ:* Westminster Sch.; Wadham Coll., Oxford (Open Exhibition). Served RA, 1945-48. Entered Ministry of Transport, 1949: Secretary, London and Home Counties Traffic Advisory Cttee, 1953-57; Private Secretary to Minister, 1961-62; Asst Sec., 1962; Under-Sec., 1968-70; Under-Sec., Treasury, 1970-72; Deputy Secretary: DoE, 1973-76; Dept of Transport, 1976-82. Chm., Assoc. of First Div. Civil Servants, 1969-71. Chm., Council, Liberal Jewish Synagogue, St John's Wood, 1972-75. FRSA 1981. *Recreations:* music, reading. *Address:* 28 Woodside Avenue, N6 4SS. *T:* 01-883 3186.

LAZARUS, Robert Stephen, QC; Social Security (formerly National Insurance) Commissioner, 1966-81; *b* 29 Oct. 1909; *s* of late Solomon and Mabel Lazarus; *m* 1938, Amelia (*née* Isaacs); two *d. Educ:* Marlborough Coll.;

Caius Coll., Cambridge. Called to the Bar, at Lincoln's Inn, 1933; QC 1958. Member: Bar Council, 1960-64; Legal Aid Cttee, 1961-66. Bencher, 1964. Served with RASC, 1940-46. *Recreations:* music, gardening. *Address:* 41 The Cliff, Roedean, Brighton, E Sussex BN2 5RF. *T:* Brighton 691162.

LAZELL, Henry George Leslie; Hon. President, Beecham Group Ltd (Chairman, 1958-68; President, 1968-70); Chairman, Beecham Incorporated, 1962-72; *b* 23 May 1903; *e s* of late Henry William Lazell and late Ada Louise Pickering; *m* 1928, Doris Beatrice Try; one *s*. *Educ:* LCC Elementary Sch. Left school at age of 13; various clerical employments until 1930; Accountant, Macleans Ltd, 1930; Secretary, 1930; Director and Secretary, 1936; Secretary, Beecham Group Ltd, 1939; Managing Director, Macleans Ltd, and Director, Beecham Group Ltd, 1940; Managing Director, Beecham Group Ltd, 1951; Director, ICI Ltd, 1966-68. Member of Association of Certified and Corporate Accountants, 1929, Fellow, 1965; Associate, Chartered Institute of Secretaries, 1930, Fellow, 1934. *Publication:* From Pills to Penicillin, 1975. *Recreations:* sailing, theatre-going, reading. *Address:* c/o Appleby, Spurling & Kempe, Reid Street, Bermuda; 3 Whaddon House, Williams Mews, SW1. *Clubs:* Thirty, Royal Bermuda Yacht.

LAZENBY, Prof. Alec, FTS, FIBiol; Vice-Chancellor, University of Tasmania, since 1982; *b* 4 March 1927; *s* of G. and E. Lazenby; *m* 1957, Ann Jennifer, *d* of R. A. Hayward; one *s* two *d*. *Educ:* Wath on Dearne Grammar Sch.; University Coll. of Wales, Aberystwyth. MSc (Wales), MA, PhD (Cantab). Scientific Officer, Welsh Plant Breeding Station, 1949-53; Demonstr in Agricultural Botany, 1953-58, Lectr in Agricultural Botany, 1958-65, Univ. of Cambridge; Fellow and Asst Tutor, Fitzwilliam Coll., Cambridge, 1962-65; Foundation Prof. of Agronomy, Univ. of New England, NSW, 1965-70, now Professor Emeritus; Vice-Chancellor, Univ. of New England, Armidale, NSW, 1970-77; Dir, Grassland Res. Inst., 1977-82. Vis. Prof., Reading Univ., 1978; Hon. Professorial Fellow, Univ. of Wales, 1979. Hon DRurSci New England, NSW, 1981. *Publications:* (jt Editor) Intensive Pasture Production, 1972; (jt Editor) Australian Field Crops, vol. I, 1975, vol. II, 1979; papers on: pasture plant breeding; agronomy; weed ecology, in various scientific jls. *Recreation:* golf. *Address:* University of Tasmania, Box 252C, GPO, Hobart, Tasmania 7001, Australia.

LEA, Christopher Gerald, MC; **His Honour Judge Christopher Lea;** a Circuit Judge, since 1972; *b* 27 Nov. 1917; *y s* of late George Percy Lea, Franche, Kidderminster, Worcs; *m* 1952, Susan Elizabeth Dorrien Smith, *d* of Major Edward Pendarves Dorrien Smith, Greatwood, Restronguet, Falmouth, Cornwall; two *s* one *d* (and one *d* deed). *Educ:* Charterhouse; RMC, Sandhurst. Commissioned into XX The Lancashire Fusiliers, 1937, and served with Regt in UK until 1939. Served War of 1939-45 (despatches, MC): with Lancashire Fusiliers, No 11 Special Air Service Commando, and Parachute Regt in France, Italy and Malaya. Post-war service in Indonesia, Austria and UK; retired, 1948. Called to Bar, Inner Temple, 1948; Oxford Circuit. Mem. Nat. Assistance Bd Appeal Tribunal (Oxford Area), 1961-63; Mem. Mental Health Review Tribunal (Oxford Region), 1962-68. A Metropolitan Magistrate, 1968-72; Dep. Chm., Berks QS, 1968-71. *Address:* Simms Farm House, Mortimer, Berks. *T:* Mortimer 332360. *Club:* English-Speaking Union.

See also Sir G. H. Lea.

LEA, David Edward, OBE 1978; Assistant General Secretary of the Trades Union Congress, since 1977; *b* 2 Nov. 1937; *s* of Edward Cunliffe Lea and Lilian May Lea. *Educ:* Farnham Grammar Sch.; Christ's Coll., Cambridge. Economist Intelligence Unit, 1961; Economic Dept, TUC, 1964, Asst Sec., 1967, Sec. 1970. Jt Sec., TUC-Labour Party Liaison Cttee, 1972-. Member: Royal Commn on the Distribution of Income and Wealth, 1974-79; Adv. Gp on Channel Tunnel and Cross-Channel Services, 1974-75; Cttee of Inquiry on Industrial Democracy, 1975-77; Energy Commn, 1977-79; Retail Prices Index Adv. Cttee, 1977-; EEC Expert Group on Economic and Social Concepts in the Community, 1977-79; NEDC Cttee on Finance for Investment, 1978-; Expert Adviser, UN Commn on Transnational Corporations, 1977-; Chairman: TUC Working Group on Employment and Technology, 1978-; Econ. Cttee, ETUC, 1980-. Mem., Franco-British Council, 1982-. Governor, NIESR, 1981-. *Publications:* Trade Unionism, 1966; contrib. The Multinational Enterprise, 1971; Industrial Democracy (TUC), 1974; Keynes Plus: a participatory economy (ETUC), 1979. *Address:* 17 Ormonde Mansions, 106 Southampton Row, WC1B 4BP. *T:* 01-405 6237.

LEA, Sir Frederick (Measham), Kt 1966; CB 1960; CBE 1952 (OBE 1944); DSc; FRSC; Hon. FRIBA; Hon. FIOB; Director of Building Research, Department of Scientific and Industrial Research, 1946-65; *b* 10 Feb. 1900; *s* of late Measham Lea, CIE, OBE; *m* 1938, Eleanor, *d* of Frank James. *Educ:* King Edward VI Sch., Birmingham; Univ. of Birmingham. Admiralty, 1922-25; Building Research Station, 1925-65; Guest Research Associate, Nat. Bureau of Standards, Washington, DC, USA, 1928-29; Mem. of Council, Royal Inst. of Chemistry, 1943-46, 1948-51; Chm., Concrete Cttee, Internat. Commn on Large Dams, 1953-59; Pres. Internat. Council for Building Research, 1955-57, 1959-62; Pres., Internat. Union of Testing and Res. Labs for Materials and Structures, 1957-58. Hon. Mem., Amer. Concrete Inst. Walter C. Voss Award, American Society for Testing and Materials, 1964. *Publications:* Chemistry of Cement and Concrete (3rd edn 1970); Science and Building, 1971; (with J. T. Crennel) Alkaline Accumulators, 1928; many papers in scientific and technical journals. *Address:* Sunnyridge, East Ogwell, Newton Abbot, Devon. *T:* Newton Abbot 3269.

LEA, Lt-Gen. Sir George (Harris), KCB 1967 (CB 1964); DSO 1957; MBE 1950; Lieutenant, HM Tower of London, 1972-75; *b* 28 Dec. 1912; *s* of late George Percy Lea, Franche, Kidderminster, Worcs; *m* 1948, Pamela Elizabeth, *d* of Brig. Guy Lovett-Tayleur; one *s* two *d*. *Educ:* Charterhouse; RMC, Sandhurst. Commnd into Lancashire Fusiliers, 1933, and served with Regt in UK, China and India until 1940. Served War of 1939-45 with Lancashire Fusiliers and Parachute Regt in India, N Africa, Italy and NW Europe. Post-war service: Regtl duty and on staff with Parachute Regt, Royal Marine Commando Bde and SAS Regt in UK, China and Malaya. Post-war staff appts in Allied Command Europe (SHAPE) and as Dep. Military Secretary (War Office); Comd 2nd Inf. Bde Group, 1957-60; GOC 42 (Lancs) Div. and North-West District, 1962-63; Comdr Forces, Northern Rhodesia and Nyasaland, 1963-64; Director of Borneo Operations and Commander Land Forces, Borneo, 1965-66; Head, British Defence Staff, Washington, 1967-70, retired. Col, The Lancashire Fusiliers, 1965-68; Col, The Royal Regt of Fusiliers, 1974-77 (Dep. Col for Lancashire, 1968-73). Brandt's Ltd, 1973-75; Man. Dir, Martin-Scott & Co. Ltd, 1975-82. Dato Seri Setia, Order of Paduka Stia Negara, Brunei, 1965. *Address:* Les Ruisseaux Lodge, St Brelade, Jersey, Channel Islands. *Clubs:* Army and Navy; Victoria, United (Jersey, CI).

See also C. G. Lea.

LEA, Vice-Adm. Sir John (Stuart Crosbie), KBE 1979; retired; Chairman, GEC Marine & Industrial Gears Ltd, since 1980; *b* 4 June 1923; *m* 1947, Patricia Anne Thoseby; one *s* two *d*. *Educ:* Boxgrove Sch., Guildford; Shrewsbury Sch.; RNEC, Keyham. Entered RN, 1941; Cruisers Sheffield and Glasgow, 1943; RNEC, 1942-45; HMS Birmingham, 1945; entered Submarines, 1946; HMS/Ms Talent, Tireless, Aurochs, Explorer; Sen. Engr, HMS Forth (Depot Ship), 1952-53; on Staff, RNEC; psc 1958; Sqdn Engr Officer, 2nd Destroyer Sqdn and HMS Daring, 1959-61; Staff of CinC Portsmouth, 1961-62; Naval Staff in Ops Div., 1963-65; Engr Officer, HMS Centaur, 1966; Staff of Flag Officer Submarines; Dep. Supt, Clyde Submarine Base, 1967-68; idc 1969; Dir of Naval Admin. Planning, 1970-71; Cdre HMS Nelson, 1972-75; Asst Chief of Fleet Support, 1976-77; Dir Gen., Naval Manpower and Trng, 1977-80. Comdr 1957; Captain 1966; Rear-Adm. 1976; Vice-Adm. 1978. *Recreations:* walking, gardening. *Address:* Springfield, Brights Lane, Hayling Island, Hants PO11 0JX.

LEA, Sir Thomas Claude Harris, 3rd Bt, *cr* 1892; *b* 13 April 1901; *s* of Sir Sydney Lea, 2nd Bt, and Mary Ophelia, *d* of Robert Woodward, of Arley Castle, Worcs; *S* father, 1946; *m* 1st, 1924, Barbara Katherine (*d* 1945), *d* of Albert Julian Pell, Wilburton Manor, Isle of Ely; one *s* four *d*; 2nd, 1950, Diana, *d* of Howard Thompson, Coton Hall, Bridgnorth, Salop. *Educ:* Lancing Coll.; Clare Coll., Cambridge. Served War of 1939-45: joined RNVR 1940 as Sub-Lieut; Lieut-Commander 1943; Commander, 1945; demobilised, 1946. *Recreations:* fishing, shooting, ornithology. *Heir:* s (Thomas) Julian Lea, [*b* 18 Nov. 1934; *m* 1970, Gerry Valerie, *d* of late Captain Gibson C. Fahnestock and of Mrs David Knightly, Brockenhurst, Hants; two *s* two *d*]. *Address:* Coneybury, Bayton, near Kidderminster, Worcs. *TA:* Bayton, Worcs. *T:* Clows Top 323.

LEACH, Archibald A.; *see* Grant, Cary.

LEACH, David; potter, designer, lecturer; *b* 7 May 1911; *e s* of Bernard Leach, CH, CBE, and Édith Muriel, *o d* of Dr William Evans Hoyle; *m* 1938, Mary Elizabeth Facey; three *s*. *Educ:* Prep. Sch., Bristol; Dauntsey's Sch., Wilts. At age of 19, began to work in his father's pottery at St Ives, Cornwall (tuition from him and associates); Manager and Partner, 1946-55; took Manager's course, N Staffs Technical Coll., Stoke-on-Trent, to 1937; taught pottery at Dartington Hall Progressive Sch., 1933. Served War, DCLI, 1941-45. Taught at Penzance Sch. of Art and St Ives, 1945. Designed and made David Leach Electric Kiln, 1950; helped to start a pottery in Norway, 1951; in charge of Ceramic Dept, and taught, at Loughborough Coll. of Art, 1953 (later Vis. Lectr). Started workshop at Bovey Tracey, 1956; researched into glazes and changed from slipware to stoneware, 1961; now makes a large percentage of porcelain. Late Mem. Council, Craftsmen Potters Assoc. of GB (Past Chm.), late Mem. Grants Cttee of the Crafts Adv. Commn; Mem. Council, Crafts Council, 1977; Adviser, Dartington Pottery Trng Workshop. Has exhibited in Europe, USA and Far East; first major one-man show, CPA, 1966; Internat. Ceramics Exhibn, 1972, and Craftsmen's Art, 1973, V&A Mus., 1973; major one-man show, NY, 1978; exhibitions in Germany at Darmstadt and Munich; Solus Exhibitions: NY, and lecture tour, USA, 1978; Washington DC, and 2nd lecture tour, USA, 1979; British Crafts Centre, London, 1979. Craft of the Potter, BBC, 1976. Gold Medal, Istanbul, 1967. *Publications:* David Leach: A Potter's Life, with Workshop Notes (introd. by Bernard Leach), 1977. *Address:* Lowerdown Pottery, Bovey Tracey, Devon. *T:* Bovey Tracey 833408.

LEACH, Prof. Sir Edmund Ronald, Kt 1975; FBA 1972; MA Cantab, PhD London; Provost of King's College, Cambridge, 1966-79; Professor of Social Anthropology, 1972-78 (University Reader, 1957-72); *b* 7 Nov. 1910; *s* of late William Edmund Leach; *m* 1940, Celia Joyce, *d* of late Henry Stephen Guy Buckmaster; one *s* one *d*. *Educ:* Marlborough Coll.; Clare Coll., Cambridge (Exhibnr). Served War of 1939-45, Burma Army. Commercial Asst, Butterfield & Swire, Shanghai, 1932-37; Graduate Student, LSE, 1938-39, 1946-47; Lectr, later Reader, in Social Anthrop., LSE, 1947-53 (Hon. Fellow, 1974); Lectr, Cambridge, 1953-57. Anthropological Field Research: Formosa, 1937; Kurdistan, 1938; Burma, 1939-45; Borneo, 1947; Ceylon, 1954, 1956. Fellow of King's Coll., Cambridge, 1960-66, 1979-; Fellow, Center for

Advanced Study in Behavioral Sciences, Stanford, 1961; Sen. Fellow, Eton Coll., 1966-79; Hon. Fellow, SOAS, 1974; Hinkley Vis. Prof., Johns Hopkins Univ., 1976. Hon. degrees: Chicago 1976, Brandeis 1976. Mem., Social Science Research Council, 1968-72; Trustee, British Museum, 1975-80. Royal Anthrop. Institute: Vice-Pres., 1964-66, 1968-70, Pres., 1971-75 (Curl Essay Prize, 1951, 1957; Rivers Medal, 1958; Henry Myers Lectr, 1966); Chm. Assoc. of Social Anthropologists, 1966-70; Pres. British Humanist Assoc., 1970-72; Lectures: Malinowski, 1959; Munro, 1963, 1977; Myers, 1966; Reith, 1967; Morgan, 1975; Radcliffe-Brown, 1976; Marett, 1977; Huxley, 1980; Frazer, 1982. Foreign Hon. Mem., Amer. Acad. of Arts and Sciences, 1968. *Publications:* Social and Economic Organization of the Rowanduz Kurds, 1940; Social Science Research in Sarawak, 1950; Political Systems of Highland Burma, 1954; Pul Eliya: A Village in Ceylon, 1961; Rethinking Anthropology, 1961; A Runaway World?, 1968; Genesis as Myth, 1970; Lévi-Strauss, 1970; Culture and Communication, 1976; Social Anthropology, 1982; Editor and contributor to various anthrop. symposia; numerous papers in Man, Journal of the Royal Anthropological Institute, American Anthropologist, South Western Journal of Anthropology, Daedalus, European Archives of Sociology, New Society, Current Anthropology, etc.; various articles in Encyclop. Britannica, Internat. Encyclop. of the Social Sciences. *Recreations:* ski-ing, travel. *Address:* 11 West Green, Barrington, Cambs. *T:* Cambridge 870675. *Club:* United Oxford & Cambridge University.

LEACH, Admiral of the Fleet Sir Henry (Conyers), GCB 1978 (KCB 1977); *b* 18 Nov. 1923; 3rd *s* of Captain John Catterall Leach, MVO, DSO, RN and Evelyn Burrell Leach (*née* Lee), Yarner, Bovey Tracey, Devon; *m* 1958, Mary Jean, *yr d* of Adm. Sir Henry McCall, KCVO, KBE, CB, DSO; two *d. Educ:* St Peter's Court, Broadstairs; RNC Dartmouth. Cadet 1937; served in: cruiser Mauritius, S Atlantic and Indian Ocean, 1941-42; battleship Duke of York, incl. Scharnhorst action, 1943-45; destroyers in Mediterranean, 1945-46; spec. Gunnery, 1947; various gunnery appts, 1948-51; Gunnery Officer, cruiser Newcastle, Far East, 1953-55; staff appts, 1955-59; comd destroyer Dunkirk, 1959-61; comd frigate Galatea as Captain (D) 27th Sqdn and Mediterranean, 1965-67; Dir of Naval Plans, 1968-70; comd Commando Ship Albion, 1970; Asst Chief of Naval Staff (Policy), 1971-73; Flag Officer First Flotilla, 1974-75; Vice-Chief of Defence Staff, 1976-77; C-in-C, Fleet, and Allied C-in-C, Channel and Eastern Atlantic, 1977-79; Chief of Naval Staff and First Sea Lord, 1979-82. First and Principal Naval ADC to the Queen, 1979-82. psc 1952; jssc 1961. *Recreations:* fishing, gardening. *Address:* Wonston Lodge, Wonston, Winchester, Hants.

LEACH, Norman, CMG 1964; Under-Secretary, Foreign and Commonwealth Office (Overseas Development Administration), 1970-72; *b* 8 March 1912; *s* of W. M. Leach. *Educ:* Ermysted's Gram. Sch., Skipton in Craven, Yorks; St Catharine's Coll., Cambridge (Scholar). 1st Class Hons, Pts I and II English Tripos, 1933 and 1934; Charles Oldham Shakespeare Schol., 1933. Asst Principal, Inland Revenue Dept, 1935; Under-Secretary: Ministry of Pensions and National Insurance, 1958-61; Dept of Technical Co-operation, 1961-64; ODM, 1964-70. *Address:* Low Bank, 81 Gargrave Road, Skipton in Craven, North Yorks. *T:* Skipton 3719.

LEACH, Paul Arthur; General Consultant to The Law Society, 1980-81, retired; *b* 10 July 1915; *s* of Rev. Edward Leach and Edith Swannell Leach; *m* 1st, 1949, Daphne Copeland (marr. diss. 1957); one *s* one *d* ; 2nd, 1958, Rachel Renée Lachmann. *Educ:* Marlborough Coll.; Keble Coll., Oxford (1st Cl. Hons BA Mod. Hist., 1937; MA 1945); Birmingham Univ. (2nd Cl. Hons LLB 1940). Law Soc. Finals, 1940; admitted Solicitor, 1946. Served War, RA, 1940-45: Staff Captain 1st AA Bde; attached SO II, RAEC, 1945-46. Private practice as solicitor, 1946-48; Talks Producer, BBC Home Talks, 1949; joined Law Soc. staff, 1950; Clerk and later Sec., Professional Purposes Cttee, 1950-71; Secretary: Future of the Profession Cttee, 1971-80; Internat. Relations Cttee, 1975-80; Dep. Sec.-Gen., 1975-80. Secretary: UK Delegn to Commn Consultative des Barreaux de la Communauté Européenne, 1975-81; Inter-Professional Gp, 1978-81; UK Vice-Pres., Union Internationale des Avocats, 1978-81. *Publications:* (ed) Guide to Professional Conduct of Solicitors, 1974; articles in Law Society's Gazette. *Recreations:* foreign travel, gardening, history, listening to classical music. *Address:* c/o 7 Litchfield Way, NW11; 5333 Myrtlewood Drive, The Meadows, Sarasota, Fla 33580, USA.

LEACH, Sir Ronald (George), GBE 1976 (CBE 1944); Kt 1970; FCA; Chairman, Standard Chartered Bank(CI), since 1980; Director: Jersey International Bank, since 1980; International Investment Trust of Jersey, since 1980; Ann Street Brewery Ltd, since 1981; *b* 21 Aug. 1907; *s* of William T. Leach, 14 Furze Croft, Hove; *m* Margaret Alice Binns. *Educ:* Alleyn's. Dep. Financial Sec. to Ministry of Food, Sept. 1939-June 1946. Member: Cttee on Coastal Flooding, 1953; Inquiry into Shipping, 1967-70; National Theatre Board, 1972-79; Chairman: Consumer Cttee for GB (Agricultural Marketing Acts, 1931-49), 1958-67; Accounting Standards Steering Cttee, 1970-76. Senior Partner in firm of Peat, Marwick, Mitchell & Co., Chartered Accountants, 1976-77; Dir, Samuel Montagu & Co., 1977-80. Pres. Inst. of Chartered Accountants in England and Wales, 1969-70. Hon. LLD Lancaster, 1977. *Address:* La Rosière, Mont de la Rosière, St Saviour, Jersey, CI. *T:* Jersey 77039 or 78427.

LEADBEATER, Howell; Controller of Supplies, 1968-76, and Board Member, Property Services Agency, Department of the Environment, 1972-

76, retired 1976; *b* 22 Oct. 1919; *s* of late Thomas and Mary Ann Leadbeater; *m* 1946, Mary Elizabeth Roberts; two *s* one *d. Educ:* Pontardawe Grammar Sch.; University College of Swansea. Army Service, 1940-46: Adjt 11th E African Divl Signals. Min. of Works, later MPBW and Dept of Environment: Asst Principal, 1948; Asst Sec., 1958; Under Sec., 1968; Under/Dep. Sec., 1973. Design Coordinator for Caernarfon Castle, Investiture of Prince of Wales, 1969. Mem., Crafts Adv. Cttee, 1978-80. *Address:* Milk Wood, Stokesheath Road, Oxshott, Surrey. *T:* 01-970 2614.

LEADBETTER, David Hulse, CB 1958; Assistant Under-Secretary of State, Department of Education and Science, 1964-68 (Under Secretary, Ministry of Education, 1953-64); *b* 14 Aug. 1908; *s* of late Harold Leadbetter; *m* 1933, Marion, *d* of late Horatio Ballantyne, FRIC, FCS; two *s* two *d* (and one *d* decd.). *Educ:* Whitgift; Merton Coll., Oxford. Entered Board of Education, 1933. *Address:* Old Mill House, Yetminster, Sherborne, Dorset. *T:* Yetminster 872216.

LEADBITTER, Edward; MP (Lab) The Hartlepools, since 1964; *b* 18 June 1919; *s* of Edward Leadbitter, Easington, Durham; *m* 1940, Phyllis Irene Mellin, Bristol; one *s* one *d. Educ:* State Schs; Teachers' Training Coll. Served War, 1939-45, with RA; commissioned 1943; War Office Instructor in Gunnery. Became a teacher. Joined Labour Party, 1938; Pres., Hartlepools Labour Party, 1958-62; Mem., West Hartlepool Borough Council, 1954-67 (sometime Mem., Town Planning, Finance, Housing, Industrial Develt, and Educn Cttees). Member: Estimates Cttee, 1966-69; Select Cttee on Science and Technology, 1970-80; Select Cttee on Energy, 1980-; Chairmens' Panel, House of Commons, 1980-; Chairman: Industrial Development Cttee; PLP Ports Cttee, 1975-; PLP Transport Gp, 1979-; Anglo-Tunisian Parly Group, 1974-. Mem. NUPE, 1963-. Organizer of Exhibition on History of Labour Movement, 1956. First Hon. Freeman, Co. Borough of Hartlepool, 1981. *Address:* 30 Hylton Road, Hartlepool, Cleveland. *T:* Hartlepool 63404.

LEADBITTER, Jasper Michael, OBE 1960; HM Diplomatic Service, retired 1973; Secretary, Royal Humane Society, 1974-78, Committee Member since 1978; *b* 25 Sept. 1912; *s* of late Francis John Graham Leadbitter, Warden, Northumberland, and Teresa del Riego Leadbitter; *m* 1942, Anna Lisa Hahne Johansson, Stockholm, Sweden; one *d. Educ:* Shrewsbury and Dresden. Asst Press Attaché, Stockholm, 1938-45, Press Attaché, 1945-47; established in Diplomatic Service, 1947; Foreign Office, 1947; Panama, 1948; Actg Consul-Gen., Detroit, 1952; First Sec. (Information), Buenos Aires, 1953 and Helsinki, 1956; Foreign Office, 1958; HM Consul and, later, 1st Sec. at Léopoldville, Congo, Dec. 1959 and at Brazzaville, 1961; Dep. Permanent UK Representative to Council of Europe and Consul at Strasbourg, March 1962; HM Consul-Gen., Berlin, Nov. 1963-66; Consul, Palermo, 1966-69; Consul-Gen., Hanover, 1969-73. Member: Cttee, Anglo-German Assoc.; Anglo-Swedish Soc. *Recreation:* travel. *Address:* Oak Lodge, Bayhall Road, Tunbridge Wells, Kent. *Club:* East India, Devonshire, Sports and Public Schools.

LEAHY, Sir John (Henry Gladstone), KCMG 1981 (CMG 1973); HM Diplomatic Service; Deputy Under-Secretary of State, Foreign and Commonwealth Office, since 1982; *b* 7 Feb. 1928; *s* of late William Henry Gladstone and late Ethel Leahy; *m* 1954, Elizabeth Anne, *d* of J. H. Pitchford, *qv* ; two *s* two *d. Educ:* Tonbridge Sch.; Clare Coll., Cambridge; Yale University. RAF, 1950-52; FO, 1952-54 (Asst Private Sec. to Minister of State, 1953-54); 3rd, later 2nd Sec., Singapore, 1955-57; FO, 1957-58; 2nd, later 1st Sec., Paris, 1958-62; FO, 1962-65; Head of Chancery, Tehran, 1965-68; Counsellor, FCO, 1969; Head of Personnel Services Dept, 1969-70; Head of News Dept, FCO, 1971-73; Counsellor and Head of Chancery, Paris, 1973-75; seconded as Under Sec., NI Office, 1975-76; Asst Under-Sec. of State, FCO, 1977-79; Ambassador to South Africa, 1979-82. Member of Livery, Skinners' Co., 1954. *Recreations:* golf, tennis. *Address:* c/o Personnel Records Section, Foreign and Commonwealth Office, SW1; 50 Stanford Road, W8 5PZ. *T:* 01-937 6948. *Clubs:* United Oxford & Cambridge University, Hurlingham.

LEAKE, Prof. Bernard Elgey, PhD, DSc, FRSE, FGS; Head of Department of Geology, and Keeper of Geological Collections in Hunterian Museum, University of Glasgow, since 1974; *b* 29 July 1932; *s* of late Norman Sidney Leake and Clare Evelyn (*née* Walgate); *m* 1955, Gillian Dorothy Dobinson; five *s. Educ:* Wirral Grammar Sch., Bebington, Cheshire; Liverpool Univ. (1st Cl. Hons BSc, PhD); Bristol Univ. (DSc 1974). Leverhulme post-doctoral Res. Fellow, Liverpool Univ., 1955-57; Asst Lectr, subseq. Lectr in Geology, Bristol Univ., 1957-68, Reader in Geol., 1968-74; Res. Associate, Berkeley, Calif, 1966. Sec., Cttee on amphibole nomenclature, Internat. Mineral Assoc., 1968-79; Member: NERC, 1978-; Council, Mineral Soc., 1965-68, 1978-80 (Vice-Pres., 1979-80); Council, Geol Soc., 1971-74, 1979- (Vice-Pres., 1980, Treasurer, 1981-; Lyell Medal, 1977); publication cttees, Mineral and Geol Socs, 1970-. FRSE 1978. Editor: Mineralogical Magazine, 1970-; Jl of Geol Soc., 1973 and 1974. *Publications:* A catalogue of analysed calciferous and sub-calciferous amphiboles together with 70 papers in geol, mineral and geochem. jls on geol. of Connemara, study of amphiboles, X-ray fluorescence anal. of rocks and use of geochem. in identifying origins of highly metamorphosed rocks; The geological map of Connemara. *Recreations:* walking, reading, theatre, gardening, museums, genealogy, study of railway and agricultural development. *Address:* Geology Department, The University, Glasgow G12 8QQ. *T:* 041-339 8855, ext. 7435; 2 Garngaber Avenue, Lenzie, Kirkintilloch, Dunbartonshire. *Club:* Geological Society.

LEAKEY, Maj.-Gen. Arundell Rea, CB 1967; DSO 1945; MC 1941 (Bar 1942); Director and Secretary, Wolfson Foundation, 1968-80; *b* 30 Dec. 1915; parents British; *m* 1950, Muriel Irene Le Poer Trench; two *s. Educ:* Weymouth Coll.; Royal Military Coll., Sandhurst. Command of 5th Royal Tank Regt, 1944; Instructor at Staff Coll., Camberley, 1951-52; Comdr, 1st Arab Legion Armoured Car Regt, 1954-56; Instructor (Col), Staff Coll., Camberley, 1958-60; Comdr, 7th Armoured Brigade, 1961-63; Dir-Gen. of Fighting Vehicles, 1964-66; GOC Troops in Malta and Libya, 1967-68; retired 1968. Czechoslovakian Military Cross, 1944. *Recreations:* squash, tennis. *Address:* c/o Williams & Glyn's Bank Ltd, Kirkland House, Whitehall, SW1. *Club:* Naval and Military.

LEAKEY, Prof. Felix William; Professor of French Language and Literature, Bedford College, London, since 1973; *b* 29 June 1922; *s* of Hugh Leakey and Kathleen Leakey (*née* March); *m* 1947, Daphne Joan Sleep (*née* Salter); one *s* two *d. Educ:* St Christopher Sch., Letchworth; Queen Mary Coll., London. BA, PhD (London). Asst Lectr, then Lectr in French, Univ. of Sheffield, 1948-54; Univ. of Glasgow: Lectr in French, 1954-64; Sen. Lectr, 1964-68; Reader, 1968-70; Prof. of French, Univ. of Reading, 1970-73. Carnegie Research Fellow, 1961-62; Leverhulme Research Fellow, 1971-72. Assoc. of University Profs of French: Hon. Sec., 1972-73; Jt Hon. Sec., 1973-75; Vice-Chm., 1975-76; Chm., 1976-77. *Publications:* Baudelaire and Nature, 1969; (ed, jtly) The French Renaissance and its Heritage: essays presented to Alan Boase, 1968; Sound and Sense in French Poetry (Inaugural Lecture, with readings on disc), 1975; (ed jtly) Samuel Beckett, Drunken Boat, 1977; contribs to: French Studies; Rev. d'hist. litt. de la France; Rev. de litt. comparée; Rev. des sciences humaines; Etudes baudelairiennes; etc. *Recreations:* foxhunting, beagling, riding, music, especially opera. *Address:* Department of French, Bedford College (University of London), Regent's Park, NW1 4NS. *T:* 01-486 4400.

LEAKEY, Mary Douglas, FBA 1973; Director, Olduvai Gorge Excavations; *b* 6 Feb. 1913; *d* of Erskine Edward Nicol and Cecilia Marion Frere; *m* 1936, Louis Seymour Bazett Leakey, FBA (*d* 1972); three *s. Educ:* privately. Hon. Mem., American Assoc. for Arts and Sciences, 1979-. Geological Soc. of London, Prestwich Medal and Nat. Geographic Soc. Hubbard Medal (jointly with late L. S. B. Leakey); Gold Medal, Soc. of Women Geographers, USA; Linneus Gold Medal, Roy. Swedish Acad., 1978. Elizabeth Blackwell Award, Mary Washington Coll., 1980; Bradford Washburn Award, Boston, 1980. Hon. DSc: Witwatersrand, 1968; Western Michigan, 1980; Chicago, 1981; Hon. DSSc Yale, 1976; Hon. DLitt Oxford, 1981. *Publications:* Olduvai Gorge, vol. 3, Excavation in Beds I and II, 1971; various papers in Nature and other scientific jls. *Recreations:* reading, game watching. *Address:* c/o National Museum, Box 30239, Nairobi, Kenya.
See also R. E. F. Leakey.

LEAKEY, Richard Erskine Frere; Director, National Museums of Kenya, since 1974 (Administrative Director, 1968-74); *b* 19 Dec. 1944; *s* of late Louis Seymour Bazett Leakey, FBA, and of Mary Leakey, *qv*; *m* 1970, Dr Meave (*née* Epps); three *d. Educ:* Nairobi Primary Sch.; Lenana (formerly Duke of York) Sch., Nairobi. Self employed tour guide and animal trapper, 1961-65; Dir, Photographic Safaris in E Africa, 1965-68. Co-leader, palaeontol expedn to Lake Natron, Tanzania, 1963-64; expedn to Lake Baringo, Kenya, in search of early man, 1966; Co-leader, Internation Omo River Expedn, Ethiopia, in search of early man, 1967; Leader, E Turkana (formerly E Rudolf) Res. Proj. (multi-nat., interdisciplinary sci. consortium investigation of Plio/Pleistocene, Kenya's northern Rift Valley), 1968-. Chairman: Wildlife Clubs of Kenya Assoc.; Foundn for Res. into Origin of Man (FROM); Vice-Chm., E African Wild Life Soc.; Trustee, Nat. Fund for the Disabled. Presenter, The Making of Mankind, BBC TV series, 1981. *Publications:* (contrib.) General History of Africa, vol. 1, 1976; (with R. Lewin) Origins, 1978; (with R. Lewin) People of the Lake, 1979; (with M. G. Leakey) Koobi Fora Research Project, vol. I, 1979; The Making of Mankind, 1981; Human Origins, 1982; One Life, 1982; articles on palaeontol. in Nature, Jl of World Hist., Science, Amer. Jl of Phys. and Anthropol. *Address:* PO Box 40658, Nairobi, Kenya.

LEAN, David, CBE 1953; film director; *b* 25 March 1908; *s* of late Francis William le Blount Lean and Helena Annie Tangye; *m* ; one *s* ; *m* 1949, Ann Todd, *qv* (marr. diss. 1957); *m* 1960, Mrs Leila Matkar (marr. diss. 1978). *Educ:* Leighton Park Sch., Reading. Entered film industry as number board boy, 1928; edited and did commentary for Gaumont Sound News and British Movietone News; then edited Escape Me Never, Pygmalion, 49th Parallel, etc. Co-directed, with Noel Coward, In Which We Serve. *Directed:* This Happy Breed, Blithe Spirit, Brief Encounter, Great Expectations, Oliver Twist, The Passionate Friends, Madeleine, The Sound Barrier (British Film Academy Award, 1952), Hobson's Choice, Summer Madness (Amer. title Summertime), The Bridge on the River Kwai (US Academy Award for Best Picture, 1957), Lawrence of Arabia (US Academy Award, 1963, Italian silver ribbon, 1964), Doctor Zhivago, Ryan's Daughter. Officier de l'Ordre des Arts et des Lettres, France, 1968.

LEANING, Ven. David; Archdeacon of Newark, since 1980. *Educ:* Lichfield Theological Coll. Deacon 1960, priest 1961, dio. Lincoln; Curate of Gainsborough, 1960-65; Rector of Warsop with Sookholme, 1965-76; Vicar of Kington and Rector of Huntington, Diocese of Hereford, 1976-80; RD of Kington and Weobley, 1976-80. *Address:* Eastfield House, Westgate, Southwell, Notts NG25 0JN. *T:* Southwell 812113.

LEAPER, Prof. Robert Anthony Bernard, CBE 1975; Professor of Social Administration, University of Exeter, since 1970; *b* 7 June 1921; *s* of William Bambrick Leaper and Gertrude Elizabeth (*née* Taylor); *m* 1950, Elizabeth Arno; two *s* one *d. Educ:* Ratcliffe Coll.; Leicester; St John's Coll., Cambridge (MA); Balliol Coll., Oxford (MA). Dipl. Public and Social Admin. (Oxon). Coal miner, 1941-44. Warden, St John Bosco Youth Centre, Stepney, 1945-47; Cadet officer, Civil Service, 1949-50; Co-operative Coll., Stanford Hall, 1950-56; Principal, Social Welfare Trng Centre, Zambia, 1956-59; Lectr, then Sen. Lectr, then Acting Dir, Social Admin., UC, Swansea, 1960-70. Exec., later Vice-Chm., Nat. Council of Social Service, 1964-80; Pres., European Region, Internat. Council on Social Welfare, 1971-79; Regional Chm., MSC Special Programmes, 1975-; Chm., Social Admin. Ctte, Jt Univ. Council, 1980-. Editor, Social Policy and Administration. Médaille de l'Ecole Nationale de Santé, France, 1975. *Publications:* Communities and Social Change, 1966; Community Work, 1969, 2nd edn 1972; Health, Wealth and Housing, 1980. *Recreations:* walking, railways, wine. *Address:* Birchcote, New North Road, Exeter. *T:* Exeter 72565. *Club:* University Staff (Exeter).

LEAR, Cyril James; Editorial Manager, News Group Newspapers Ltd, 1974-76 (Editor, News of the World, 1970-73); *b* 9 Sept. 1911; *s* of R. H. Lear, Plymouth; *m* Marie Chatterton; five *s* one *d. Educ:* Hoe Grammar Sch., Plymouth. Served War of 1939-45: Rifleman, Queen's Westminsters; Major, Royal Berks Regt. Western Morning News, 1928-32; Torquay Times, 1932-34; Daily Mail, 1934-38; Daily Telegraph, 1938-39; News of the World, 1946-70: Features Editor, Asst Editor, Dep. Editor. *Recreations:* fishing, shooting. *Address:* c/o News Group Newspapers Ltd, 30 Bouverie Street, EC4. *T:* 01-353 3030.

LEARMONT, Captain Percy Hewitt, CIE 1946; RIN retired; *b* 25 June 1894; *s* of late Capt. J. Learmont, OBE, DL, JP, Penrith and Skinburness, Cumberland; *m* 1926, Doris Orynthia, *e d* of E. G. Hartley, Dunoon, Argyll; one *s* one *d. Educ:* HMS Conway. Served European War, HMS Alsatian, 1914-17; HMS Ceres, 1917-19; joined RIN, 1919; Comdr, 1935; Extended Defence Officer, Calcutta, 1939-41; Capt. Superintendent, HMI Dockyard, Bombay, 1941-42; in command HMIS Bahadur, 1942-43; Capt., 1942; Naval Officer-in-Charge, Calcutta, 1943-45; in command HMIS Akbar, 1945; HMIS Kakauri, 1946; retired, 1946. *Address:* Crofters, Curry Rivel, Langport, Somerset. *T:* Langport 251317.

LEAROYD, Wing Comdr Roderick Alastair Brook, VC 1940; RAF; *b* 5 Feb. 1913; *s* of late Major Reginald Brook Learoyd and Marjorie Scott Boadle. *Educ:* Wellington Coll. *Address:* 5 Selsey Court, Chanctonbury Road, Rustington, W Sussex.

LEARY, Brian Leonard; QC 1978; *b* 1 Jan. 1929; *o s* of late A. T. Leary; *m* 1965, Myriam Ann Bannister, *d* of Kenneth Bannister, CBE, Mexico City. *Educ:* King's Sch. Canterbury; Wadham Coll., Oxford. MA Oxon. Called to the Bar, Middle Temple, 1953; Harmsworth Scholar. Senior Prosecuting Counsel to the Crown at Central Criminal Court, 1971-78. *Recreations:* travel, sailing, growing herbs. *Address:* The Old Rectory, Ightham, Kent. *T:* Borough Green 882608; 5 Paper Buildings, Temple, EC4. *T:* 01-353 7811.

LEARY, Leonard Poulter, CMG 1973; MC 1917; QC (New Zealand) 1952; retired; *b* 1891; *s* of Richard Leary and Florence Lucy Giesen; *m* ; three *s* two *d* (and one *d* decd). *Educ:* Palmerston North High Sch.; Wellington Coll.; Victoria and Auckland University Colleges (LLB). Called to the Bar, New Zealand, 1920. Served European War, 1914-18: Samoan Exped. Force (NZR), 1914; Special Reserve RFA Egypt and France, 1914-18 (Captain, MC); served War of 1939-45: NZ Home Forces; Lt-Col RNZA, Actg CRA, 1944. Mem., later Chm., Disciplinary Cttee of NZ Law Soc., 1948-74; Chm., Lake Weed Control Soc. *Publications:* New Zealanders in Samoa, 1918; Tutankhamen (musical play), 1923; Abbess of Whitby (musical play), 1924; Not Entirely Legal (autobiog.), 1977. *Recreations:* music, gardening, fishing. *Address:* RD4 Otaramarae, Rotorua, New Zealand. *T:* Okere Falls 635. *Clubs:* Northern, Officers' (Auckland).

LEASK, Lt-Gen. Sir Henry (Lowther Ewart Clark), KCB 1970 (CB 1967); DSO 1945; OBE 1957 (MBE 1945); GOC Scotland and Governor of Edinburgh Castle, 1969-72, retired; *b* 30 June 1913; *s* of Rev. James Leask, MA; *m* Zoë de Camborne, *d* of Col W. P. Paynter, DSO, RHA; one *s* two *d.* 2nd Lt Royal Scots Fusiliers, 1936. Served War of 1939-45 in Mediterranean and Italy; GSO 1942; Bde Major Inf. Bde 1943; 2nd in Comd and CO, 8 Bn Argyll and Sutherland Highlanders, 1944-45; Comd 1st Bn London Scottish, 1946-47; Gen. Staff Mil. Ops, WO, 1947-49; Instr Staff Coll., 1949-51; Comd 1st Bn The Parachute Regt, 1952-54; Asst Military Sec. to Sec. of State for War, 1955-57; Comdt, Tactical Wing Sch. of Inf., 1957-58; Comd Infantry Bde, 1958-61; idc 1961; Dep. Mil. Sec. to Sec. of State for War, 1962-64; GOC 52 Lowland Div., 1964-66; Dir of Army Training, MoD (Army), 1966-69. Brig. 1961, Maj.-Gen. 1964, Lt-Gen. 1969. Col of the Royal Highland Fusiliers, 1964-69; Col Comdt, Scottish Div. of Infantry, 1968-72. *Recreations:* shooting and fishing. *Address:* 9 Glenalmond House, Manor Fields, SW15. *Clubs:* Army and Navy, Hurlingham; New (Edinburgh).

LEASOR, (Thomas) James; author; *b* 20 Dec. 1923; *s* of late Richard and Christine Leasor, Erith, Kent; *m* 1951, Joan Margaret Bevan, Barrister-at-law, *o d* of late Roland S. Bevan, Crowcombe, Somerset; three *s. Educ:* City of London Sch.; Oriel Coll., Oxford. Kentish Times, 1941-42. Served in Army in Burma, India, Malaya, 1942-46, Capt. Royal Berks Regt. Oriel Coll., Oxford, 1946-48, BA 1948; MA 1952; edited The Isis. On staff Daily Express, London, 1948-55, as reporter, foreign correspondent, feature writer. Contrib. to many American and British magazines, newspapers and periodicals; scriptwriter for TV series The Michaels in Africa. FRSA. OStJ. *Publications: novels:* Not Such a Bad Day, 1946; The Strong Delusion, 1951; NTR-Nothing to Report, 1955; Passport to Oblivion, 1964; Spylight, 1966; Passport in Suspense, 1967; Passport for a Pilgrim, 1968; They Don't Make Them Like That Any More, 1969; A Week of Love, 1969; Never had a Spanner on Her, 1970; Love-all, 1971; Follow the Drum, 1972; Host of Extras, 1973; Mandarin Gold, 1973; The Chinese Widow, 1974; Jade Gate, 1976; Love and the Land Beyond, 1979; Open Secret, 1982; *non-fiction:* Author by Profession, The Monday Story, 1951; Wheels to Fortune, The Serjeant Major, 1954; The Red Fort; (with Kendal Burt) The One That Got Away, 1956; The Millionth Chance, 1957; War at the Top, 1959; (with Peter Eton) Conspiracy of Silence, 1959; Bring Out Your Dead, 1961; Rudolf Hess: The Uninvited Envoy, 1961; Singapore: The Battle that Changed the World, 1968; Green Beach, 1975; Boarding Party, 1977; The Unknown Warrior, 1980. *Recreation:* vintage cars. *Address:* Swallowcliffe Manor, Salisbury, Wilts; Casa do Zimbro, Praia da Luz, Lagos, Algarve, Portugal. *Club:* Garrick.

LEATHAM, Dr Aubrey (Gerald), FRCP; Physician: St George's Hospital since 1954; National Heart Hospital since 1956; Dean, Institute of Cardiology, 1962-69; *b* 23 Aug. 1920; *s* of Dr H. W. Leatham (*d* 1973), Godalming and Kathleen Pelham Burn (*d* 1971), Nosely Hall, Leicester; *m* 1954, Judith Augustine Savile Freer; one *s* three *d. Educ:* Charterhouse; Trinity Hall, Cambridge; St Thomas' Hospital. BA Cambridge 1941; MB, BChir 1944; MRCP 1945; FRCP 1957. House Phys., St Thomas' Hosp., 1944; RMO, Nat. Heart Hosp., 1945; Phys., RAMC, 1946-47; Sherbrook Research Fellow, Cardiac Dept, and Sen. Registrar, London Hosp., 1948-50; Asst Dir, Inst. of Cardiology, 1951-54. Goulstonian Lectr, RCP, 1958. R. T. Hall Travelling Prof., Australia and NZ, 1963. Member: Brit. Cardiac Soc.; Sociedad Peruana de Cardiologia, 1966; Sociedad Colombiana de Cardiologia, 1966. Royal Order of Bhutan, 1966. *Publications:* Auscultation of the Heart and Phonocardiography, 1970; articles in Lancet, British Heart Jl, etc, on auscultation of the heart and phonocardiography, artificial pacemakers, coronary artery disease, etc. *Recreations:* ski-ing and ski-touring, mountain walking, tennis, racquets, gardening, photography. *Address:* 75 Albert Drive, SW19 6LB. *T:* 01-788 5759; 45 Wimpole Street, W1M 7D9. *T:* 01-935 5295; Rookwood Lane House, West Wittering, Sussex.

LEATHART, Air Cdre James Anthony, CB 1960; DSO 1940; Manager, Machinery Division, Cleanacres Ltd; *b* 5 Jan. 1915; *s* of P. W. Leathart, BSc, MD, Ear, Nose and Throat Specialist, Liverpool; *m* 1939, E. L. Radcliffe, Birkenhead; two *s* one *d. Educ:* St Edward's, Oxford; Liverpool Univ. Joined Auxiliary Air Force (610 County of Chester Squadron), 1936; transferred RAF, 1937; Chief of Staff Headquarters, 12 Group, RAF, 1959-61; Dir of Operational Requirements, Air Ministry, 1961-62, retd. Oct. 1962. *Recreations:* fly-fishing, motoring, ornithology, gardening. *Address:* Wortley Farmhouse, Wotton-under-Edge, Glos. *T:* Wotton-under-Edge 2312.

LEATHEM, John Gaston, JP; Headmaster of Taunton School, 1945-66; *b* 14 May 1906; *s* of late J. G. Leathem, MA, ScD, fellow and senior bursar of St John's Coll., Cambridge, and Annie Muir (*née* McMullan), Belfast. *Educ:* Marlborough Coll.; St John's Coll., Cambridge. Pres. Cambridge Union, 1929. Housemaster St Lawrence Coll., Ramsgate, 1929; Asst Master, Marlborough Coll., 1932; Headmaster, King Edward VII Sch., King's Lynn, 1939; Marlborough Town Council, 1938; JP King's Lynn, 1941; Somerset Education Cttee, 1946-55; Somerset County Council, 1952-55. JP Somerset 1953; Chm. Juvenile Bench, 1959-68; Chm., Bench, 1968-76. *Recreations:* foreign travel, walking. *Address:* 8 Parkfield Road, Taunton, Somerset. *T:* Taunton 75385. *Clubs:* Royal Over-Seas League; Somerset County (Taunton); Jesters.

LEATHER, Sir Edwin (Hartley Cameron), KCMG 1974; KCVO 1975; Kt 1962; Governor and C-in-C of Bermuda, 1973-77; writer and broadcaster; *b* 22 May 1919; *s* of Harold H. Leather, MBE, Hamilton, Canada, and Grace C. Leather (*née* Holmes); *m* 1940, Sheila A. A. (CStJ), *d* of Major A. H. Greenlees, Hamilton; two *d. Educ:* Trinity College Sch., Canada; Royal Military Coll., Kingston, Canada. Served War of 1939-45 with Canadian Army, UK and in Europe, 1940-45. Contested (C) South Bristol, 1945; MP (C) N Somerset, 1950-64. Mem., Exec. Cttee, British Commonwealth Producers Organisation, 1960-63; Chairman: Bath Festival Soc., 1960-65; Horder Centres for Arthritics, 1962-65; Cons. and Unionist Assocs, 1969-70 (Mem. Nat. Exec. Cttee, 1963-70); Mem. Cons. Party Bd of Finance, 1963-67; Mem., Bd of Dirs, Yehudi Menuhin Sch., 1967-; Canadian Legion rep. on Exec. Cttee of Brit. Commonwealth Ex-Servicemen's League, 1954-63; Pres., Institute of Marketing, 1963-67. Lay reader, in Church of England. Mem. Council, Imp. Soc. of Knights Bachelor, 1969-. FRSA 1969; Hon. LLD Bath, 1975. KStJ 1974. Gold Medal, Nat. Inst. Social Sciences, NY, 1977; Hon. Citizen, Kansas City, USA. Medal of Merit, Royal Canadian Legion. *Publications:* The Vienna Elephant, 1977; The Mozart Score, 1979; The Duveen Letter, 1980. *Address:* PO Box 819, Hamilton, Bermuda. *Clubs:* Carlton; Hamilton (Canada); Canadian (NY); Royal Bermuda Yacht.

LEATHER, Ted; *see* Leather, Sir E. H. C.

LEATHERLAND, Baron, *cr* 1964, of Dunton (Life Peer); **Charles Edward Leatherland,** OBE 1951; Treasurer and Member of Council, University of Essex, from foundation until 1973; *b* 18 April 1898; *e s* of John Edward Leatherland, Churchover, Warwicks; *m* 1922, Mary Elizabeth, *d* of Joseph Henry Morgan, Shareshill, Staffs; one *s* one *d. Educ:* Harborne, Birmingham; University Extension Courses. Asst Editor, Daily Herald, until retirement, 1963. Served European War, 1914-19 (despatches, MSM); enlisted, 1914, aged 16; served in France, Belgium, Germany; Company Sgt Major, Royal Warwicks Regt; Essex TA Assoc., 1946-68, and E Anglian TA Assoc., 1968. Chm., Essex County Council, 1960-61 (Vice-Chm. 1952-55 and 1958-60); CA Essex, 1946-68. Dep. Chm., Epping Magistrates Bench. JP (Essex) 1944-70; DL Essex, 1963. Mem. Bd of Basildon Development Corporation, 1967-71. Addtl Mem., Monopolies Commn, to consider newspaper mergers, 1969. Chm., E Counties Regional Council of the Labour Party, 1950-66. DUniv. Essex, 1973. *Publications:* (part author) The Book of the Labour Party, 1925; Labour Party pamphlets; contribs on local govt affairs in Municipal Jl and general press; 4 Prince of Wales Gold Medals 1923 and 1924 for essays on: Measures that may be taken by other countries to promote an improvement in the economic condition of Czecho-Slovakia, 1923; The possibilities of the cinema in the development of commercial education, 1923; Difficulties attending the economic position of Czecho-Slovakia after the Peace Treaty, and the methods adopted to remove them, 1924; Home and foreign trade: their relative importance and interdependence, 1924. *Recreations:* formerly fox hunting, now walking. *Address:* 19 Starling Close, Buckhurst Hill, Essex. *T:* 01-504 3164.

LEATHERS, family name of **Viscount Leathers.**

LEATHERS, 2nd Viscount, *cr* 1954; **Frederick Alan Leathers;** Baron Leathers, 1941; Director: National Westminster Bank, Outer London Region; *b* 4 April 1908; *er s* of 1st Viscount Leathers, PC, CH, LLD; *S* father, 1965; *m* 1940, Elspeth Graeme, *yr d* of late Sir Thomas (Alexander) Stewart; two *s* two *d. Educ:* Brighton Coll.; Emmanuel Coll., Cambridge (MA (hons) in Economics). Mem. of Baltic Exchange. Director: Wm Cory & Son Ltd, 1929-72 (Chm.); Cory Mann George Ltd, 1941-72 (Chm.); Cory Ship Towage Ltd, 1941-72 (Chm.); Smit & Cory International Port Towage Ltd, 1970-72 (Chm.); Hull Blyth & Co. Ltd, 1949-72 (Chm.); Rea Ltd, 1941-72 (Chm.); St Denis Shipping Co. Ltd, 1957-72 (Chm.); Laporte Industries Ltd, 1959-71; Laporte Industries (Holdings) Ltd, 1959-71; Tunnel Cement Ltd, 1960-74; Guardian Cement Co. Ltd, 1963-71; New Zealand Cement Holdings Ltd, 1963-71. Member: Court of Worshipful Company of Shipwrights; Court of Watermen's and Lightermen's Company; Fellow Institute of Chartered Shipbrokers; FRPSL; FRSA; MInstPet. *Heir:* s Hon. Christopher Graeme Leathers [*b* 31 Aug. 1941; *m* 1964, Maria Philomena, *yr d* of Michael Merriman, Charlestown, Co. Mayo; one *s* one *d*]. *Address:* Huntsmore, Shackleford, Godalming, Surrey GU8 6AN. *T:* Guildford 810359. *Club:* Royal Automobile.

LEATHES, Maj.-Gen. Reginald Carteret de Mussenden, CB 1960; MVO 1947; OBE 1952; *b* 19 Sept. 1909; *s* of late Major Carteret de M. Leathes; *m* 1939, Marjorie Mary Elphinston; three *s* one *d. Educ:* Imperial Service Coll. 2nd Lt, Royal Marines, 1928; HMS Resolution, 1931-33; ADC to Governor of Queensland, 1935-37; 1st Bn Royal Marines, 1940-43; 42 Commando RM, 1943-44; GSO1 HQ, SACSEA, 1944-45; GSO1 HQ, Land Forces Hong Kong, 1945-46; HMS Vanguard, 1947; RN Staff Coll., 1947-49; 45 Commando RM, 1950-52; Comdt Amphibious Sch., RM, 1952-55; Col GS Staff Comdt Gen., RM, 1956; idc 1957, ADC to the Queen, 1957-58. Chief of Staff to Comdt Gen., RM, 1958-60; Maj.-Gen. Commanding Royal Marines, Portsmouth, 1961-62. Retired, 1962. Col Comdt, RM, 1971-74. Ski-ing representative, British Olympic Cttee, 1965-76. Officer Order of Phoenix (Greece), 1933; Chevalier Legion of Honour and Croix de Guerre (France), 1945; Officer Order of Cloud and Banner (China), 1945. *Recreations:* fishing, ski-ing.

LEAVER, Sir Christopher, GBE 1981; JP; Managing Director, Russell & McIver Group of Companies (Wine Merchants); Chairman: Strachan Motors Ltd; Metamid Ltd; Mechema Ltd; *b* 3 Nov. 1937; *s* of Dr Robert Leaver and Mrs Audrey Kerpen; *m* 1975, Helen Mireille Molyneux Benton; two *d. Educ:* Eastbourne Coll. FCIT 1980. Commissioned (Army), RAOC, 1956-58. Member, Retail Foods Trades Wages Council, 1963-64. JP Inner London, 1970; Member: Council, Royal Borough of Kensington and Chelsea, 1970-73; Court of Common Council (Ward of Dowgate), City of London, 1973; Alderman (Ward of Dowgate), City of London, 1974; Sheriff of the City of London, 1979-80; Lord Mayor of London, 1981-82; HM Lieutenant, City of London, 1982. Member: Ct of Assistants, Carmen's Company, 1973; Bd of Brixton Prison, 1975-78; Bd of Governors, City Univ., 1978- (Chancellor, 1981-82); Ct, Mary Rose Trust, 1982-; Trustee, Chichester Festival Theatre, 1982-; Vice-Pres., Bridewell Royal Hosp., 1982-; Governor: Christ's Hospital Sch., 1975; City of London Girls' Sch., 1975-78; City of London Freemen's Sch., 1980-81; Music Therapy Trust, 1981-; Chairman, Young Musicians' Symphony Orch. Trust, 1979-81; Hon. Mem., Guildhall Sch. of Music and Drama, 1982-. Church Warden, St Olave's, Hart Street, 1975-. Hon. Liveryman, Farmers' Company. Hon. DMus City, 1981. KStJ 1982; FCIT 1981; FRSA 1980. Order of Oman Class II. *Recreations:* gardening, music. *Address:* The Rectory, St Mary-at-Hill, EC3R 8EE. *T:* 01-283 3545. *Clubs:* City Livery, Guildhall.

LEAVETT, Alan; Member, Development Commission, since 1982; *b* 4 May 1924; *s* of George Leavett and Mabel Dorothy (*née* Witts); *m* 1948, Jean Mary, *d* of Arthur Wanford, ISO, Harwich; three *d. Educ:* Gosport County Sch.; UC, Southampton. BA Hons 1943. MAP (RAE), 1943; HM Customs and Excise, 1947; HM Foreign (subseq. Diplomatic) Service, 1949; 3rd Sec., Rio de Janeiro, 1950-53; 1st Sec., Bangkok, 1955-59; UK Perm. Delegate to ECAFE, 1958; Cabinet Office, 1961; Sec.-Gen., Uganda Constitutional Conf., 1961; Min. of Housing and Local Govt, 1963; Sec., Noise Adv. Council, 1970; Under-Sec., Civil Service Selection Bd, 1973, Dept of Environment, 1974-81. Vice-Chm., Avon Community Council, 1981-; Gen. Sec., Avon Wildlife Trust. *Publication:* Historic Sevenoaks, 1969. *Recreations:* book-collecting, music. *Address:* Darenth House, St Martins, Long Ashton, Bristol BS18 9HP. *T:* Long Ashton 2876. *Club:* Athenæum.

LEAVEY, John Anthony, BA; Director: Fläkt Ltd, since 1976; Wilson (Connolly) Holdings Ltd, since 1966 (Chairman, 1966-82); Chairman: Robert Moss Ltd, since 1981; Edward Barber & Co. Ltd, since 1982; *b* 3 March 1915; *s* of George Edwin Leavey and Marion Louise Warnock; *m* 1952, Lesley Doreen, *d* of Rt Hon. Sir Benjamin Ormerod. *Educ:* Mill Hill Sch.; Trinity Hall, Cambridge. Served War, 1939-46; 5th Royal Inniskilling Dragoon Guards. MP (C) Heywood and Royton Div. of Lancashire, 1955-64. *Recreation:* fishing. *Address:* 10 Alexander Place, SW7. *Club:* Army and Navy.

LE BAILLY, Vice-Adm. Sir Louis (Edward Stewart Holland), KBE 1972 (OBE 1952); CB 1969; DL; Director-General of Intelligence, Ministry of Defence, 1972-75; *b* 18 July 1915; *s* of Robert Francis Le Bailly and Ida Gaskell Le Bailly (*née* Holland); *m* 1946, Pamela Ruth Berthon; three *d. Educ:* RNC Dartmouth. HMS Hood, 1932; RNEC, 1933-37; HMS Hood, 1937-40; HMS Naiad, 1940-42; RNEC, 1942-44; HMS Duke of York, 1944-46; Admiralty, 1946-50; HMS Bermuda, 1950-52; RNEC, 1955-58; Admiralty: Staff Officer to Dartmouth Review Cttee, 1958; Asst Engineer-in-Chief, 1958-60; Naval Asst to Controller of the Navy, 1960-63; IDC, 1963; Dep. Dir of Marine Engineering, 1963-67; Naval Attaché, Washington, DC, and Comdr, British Navy Staff, 1967-69; Min. of Defence, 1970-72; Vice-Adm. 1970, retired 1972. Mem. Council, Inst. for Study of Conflict. Chm. of Governors, Rendcomb Coll., Cirencester, 1981-. DL Cornwall, 1982. FIMechE; FInstPet; MIMarE. *Address:* c/o Barclays Bank, Market Square, Chippenham, Wilts. *Club:* Boodle's.

LE BAS, Air Vice-Marshal Michael Henry, CB 1969; CBE 1966; DSO 1944; AFC 1954; retired; *b* 28 Sept. 1916; *s* of late R. W. O. Le Bas and Florence Marrs; *m* 1945, Moyra Benitz; one *s* one *d. Educ:* St George's Coll., Buenos Aires; Malvern Coll. Joined RAF, 1940; served in Fighter Command, Malta, Western Desert, and Italy, 1941-44; RAF Staff Coll., 1948-51; HQ 2 TAF and RAF Wildenrath, 1951-54; Sch. of Land Air Warfare, 1954-56; Suez, 1956; OC, RAF Coningsby, 1959-61; HQ Bomber Comd, 1961-63; SASO, Air Forces Middle East, 1963-66; AOC No. 1 Group, Bomber Command, 1966-68; AOC No. 1 (Bomber) Gp, Strike Comd, 1968; Dir Gen. of Personnel Services (RAF), MoD, 1969-71. *Recreations:* golf, shooting, photography. *Address:* c/o Midland Bank, Oakham, Leicestershire. *Club:* Royal Air Force.

LEBETER, Fred; Keeper, Department of Transport and Mining, Science Museum, 1953-67; *b* 27 Dec. 1903; *e s* of Arthur Lebeter, Mining Engineer, and Lucy Wilson; *m* 1926, Sybil Leah, *o d* of Henry Ward; one *d* decd. *Educ:* Rotherham and Bridgnorth Gram. Schs; Birmingham Univ. BSc 1925; MSc (Research on Classification of British Coals) 1926. Manager, Magnesite Mines and Works, Salem, S India, 1926-31; Lecturer in Mining, Heanor Mining Sch., 1931-33; Sen. Lectr in Mining, Chesterfield Tech. Coll., 1933-37; Asst Keeper, Science Museum, 1937-39; Dep. Chief Mining Supplies Officer, Min. of Fuel and Power, 1939-47; Asst Keeper, Science Museum, 1947-49, Dep. Keeper, 1949-53. Consultant on Mine Ventilation and Underground Transport, 1931-; Mem. Council Nat. Assoc. of Colliery Managers (Midland Br.), 1935-37; Adviser to Coal Commission, Germany, on Mining Supplies, 1944; UK rep. to European Coal Organisation, 1945-47. United Kingdom delegate to European Coal Organisation, Paris, 1946. Mem., Industrial Cttee, National Museum of Wales, 1959-67. Retired 1967. *Publications:* contributor of many technical articles to Colliery Engineering, Mine and Quarry Engineering, historical articles in Zeitschrift für Kunst und Kultur im Bergbau, etc. *Recreations:* sport and gardening. *Address:* The Lodge, 9a Southdown Road, Seaford, E Sussex BN25 4PA. *T:* Seaford 894751.

LEBLANC, Rt. Rev. Camille André; Chaplain at Caraquet Hospital; *b* Barachois, NB, 25 Aug. 1898. *Educ:* Collège Sainte-Anne, Church Point, NS; Grand Séminaire Halifax, NS. Priest, 1924; Subseq. Curé at Shemogue and the Cathedral of Nôtre Dame de l'Assomption, Moncton; Bishop of Bathurst, 1942-69. *Address:* c/o Caraquet Hospital, Caraquet, NB, Canada.

LEBLOND, Prof. C(harles) P(hilippe), OC 1977; MD, PhD, DSc; FRSC 1951; FRS 1965; Professor of Anatomy, McGill University, Canada, since 1948; *b* 5 Feb. 1910; *s* of Oscar Leblond and Jeanne Desmarchelier; *m* 1936, Gertrude Elinor Sternschuss; three *s* one *d. Educ:* Sch. St Joseph, Lille, France; Univs. of Lille, Nancy, Paris, Montreal. L-ès-S, Nancy 1932; MD Paris 1934; PhD Montreal 1942; DSc Sorbonne 1945. Asst in Histology, Med. School, Univ. of Paris, 1934-35; Rockefeller Fell., Sch. of Med., Yale Univ., 1936-37; Asst, Laboratoire de Synthèse Atomique, Paris, 1938-40; McGill Univ.: Lectr in Histology and Embryology, 1941-42; Asst Prof. of Anatomy, 1942-43;

Assoc. Prof. of Anatomy, 1946-48; Prof. of Anatomy, 1948-; Chm. of Dept of Anatomy, 1957-75. Mem. Amer. Assoc. of Anatomists; Fellow, Amer. Acad. of Arts and Scis. Hon. DSc: Acadia, 1972; McGill, 1982. *Publications:* over 300 articles in anatomical journals. *Recreation:* country. *Address:* (home) 68 Chesterfield Avenue, Westmount, Montreal, Quebec H3Y 2M5, Canada. *T:* 514- 486-4837; (office) Department of Anatomy, McGill University, 3640 University Street, Montreal, Quebec H3A 2B2, Canada. *T:* 514-392-4931.

LE BRETON, David Francis Battye, CBE 1978; HM Diplomatic Service; High Commissioner in The Gambia, since 1981; *b* 2 March 1931; *e s* of late Lt-Col F. H. Le Breton, MC, and Elisabeth Le Breton (*née* Trevor-Battye), Endebess, Kenya; *m* 1961, Patricia June Byrne; one *s* two *d. Educ:* Winchester; New Coll., Oxford. Colonial Administrative Service, Tanganyika, 1954; Private Sec. to Governor, 1959-60; Magistrate, 1962; Principal, CRO, 1963; HM Diplomatic Service, 1965; First Sec., Zanzibar, 1964; Lusaka, 1964-68; FCO, 1968-71; Head of Chancery, Budapest, 1971-74; HM Comr in Anguilla, 1974-78; Counsellor and Head of Chancery, Nairobi, 1978-81. *Recreations:* travel, African affairs. *Address:* c/o Foreign and Commonwealth Office, SW1; Brackenwood, Frenchstreet, near Westerham, Kent.

le BROCQUY, Louis, FSIA 1960; painter since 1939; *b* Dublin, 10 Nov. 1916; *s* of late Albert le Brocquy, MA, and late Sybil Staunton; *m* 1st, 1938, Jean Stoney (marr. diss., 1948); one *d*; 2nd, 1958, Anne Madden Simpson; two *s. Educ:* St Gerard's Sch., Wicklow, Ireland. Self-taught. Founder-mem. of Irish Exhibn of Living Art, 1943; Visiting Instructor, Central Sch. of Arts and Crafts, London, 1947-54; Visiting Tutor, Royal Coll. of Art, London, 1955-58. Member: Irish Council of Design, 1963-65; Council, Soc. of Designers in Ireland, 1974-75. Dir, Kilkenny Design Workshops, 1965-77. Represented Ireland, Venice Biennale (awarded internat. prize), 1956. Work exhibited in "50 Ans d'Art Moderne", Brussels, 1958. One Man Shows: Leicester Galleries, London, 1948; Gimpel Fils, London, 1947, 1949, 1951, 1955, 1956, 1957, 1959, 1961, 1966, 1968, 1971, 1974, 1978; Waddington, Dublin, 1951; Robles Gallery, Los Angeles, 1960; Gallery Lienhard, Zürich, 1961; Dawson Gallery, Dublin, 1962, 1966, 1969, 1971, 1973, 1974, 1975, 1981; Municipal Gallery of Modern Art, Dublin, 1966, 1978; Ulster Mus., Belfast (retrospective), 1966-67; Gimpel-Hanover, Zürich, 1969, 1978; Gimpel, NY, 1971, 1978; Foundation Maeght, 1973; Bussola, Turin, 1974; Arts Council, Belfast, 1975, 1978; Musée d'Art Moderne, Paris, 1976; Genoa, 1977; Waddington, Montreal, Toronto, 1978; Maeght, Barcelona, Madrid, Granada, 1978-79; Jeanne Bucher, Paris, 1979, 1982; NY State Mus., 1981; Palais des Beaux Arts, Charleroi, 1982. Public Collections possessing work include: Albright Museum, Buffalo; Arts Council, London; Carnegie Inst., Pittsburgh; Centre National d'Art Pompidou, Paris; Chicago Arts Club; Detroit Inst. of Art; Dublin Municipal Gallery; Fort Worth Center, Texas; J. H. Hirshhorn Foundation, Washington; Kunsthaus, Zürich; Fondation Maeght, St Paul; Leeds City Art Gallery; Musée d'Art Moderne, Paris; Foundation of Brazil Museum, Bahia; Tate Gallery; Uffizi, Florence; Ulster Museum, Belfast; V&A Museum. RHA 1950. Chevalier de la Légion d'Honneur, 1974. Hon. DLitt Dublin, 1962. Commandeur du Bontemps de Médoc et des Graves, 1969. *Illustrated work:* The Táin, trans. Thomas Kinsella, 1969; The Playboy of the Western World, Synge, 1970; The Gododdin, 1978. *Address:* c/o Gimpel Fils, 30 Davies Street, W1Y 1LG.

LE CARRÉ, John; see Cornwell, David John Moore.

LE CHEMINANT, Peter, CB 1976; Deputy Secretary, HM Treasury, since 1981 (Civil Service Department, 1981); *b* 29 April 1926; *s* of William Arthur Le Cheminant; *m* 1959, Suzanne Elisabeth Horny; three *s. Educ:* Holloway Sch.; London Sch. of Economics. Sub-Lt, RNVR, 1944-47. Min. of Power, 1949; Cabinet Office, 1950-52 and 1964-65; UK Delegn to ECSC, 1962-63; Private Sec. to Prime Minister, 1965-68; Min. of Power, later Min. of Technology, 1968-71; Under-Sec., DTI, 1971-74; Dep. Sec., Dept of Energy, 1974-77; Dep. Sec., Cabinet Office, 1978-81. *Recreations:* reading, walking, history. *Address:* c/o HM Treasury, Whitehall, SW1A 2AZ.

LE CHEMINANT, Air Chief Marshal Sir Peter (de Lacey), GBE 1978; KCB 1972 (CB 1968); DFC 1943, and Bar, 1951; Lieutenant-Governor and Commander-in-Chief of Guernsey, since 1980; *b* 17 June 1920; *s* of Lieut-Colonel Keith Le Cheminant and Blanche Etheldred Wake Le Cheminant (*née* Clark); *m* 1940, Sylvia, *d* of J. van Bodegom; one *s* two *d. Educ:* Elizabeth Coll., Guernsey; RAF Coll., Cranwell. Flying posts in France, UK, N Africa, Malta, Sicily and Italy, 1940-44; comd No 223 Squadron, 1943-44; Staff and Staff Coll. Instructor, 1945-48; Far East, 1949-53; comd No 209 Sqn, 1949-51; Jt Planning Staff, 1953-55; Wing Comdr, Flying, Kuala Lumpur, 1955-57; jssc 1958; Dep. Dir of Air Staff Plans, 1958-61; comd RAF Geilenkirchen, 1961-63; Dir of Air Staff Briefing, 1964-66; SASO, HQ FEAF, 1966-67, C of S, 1967-68; Comdt Joint Warfare Estabt, MoD, 1968-70; Asst Chief of Air Staff (Policy), MoD, 1971-72; UK Mem., Perm. Mil. Deputies Gp, CENTO, Ankara, 1972-73; Vice-Chief of Defence Staff, 1974-76; Dep. C-in-C, Allied Forces, Central Europe, 1976-79. KStJ 1980. *Recreations:* golf, sailing, reading. *Address:* Government House, Guernsey, CI. *Club:* Royal Air Force.

LECHIN-SUAREZ, Brigadier General Juan, Condor de los Andes, Guerrillero José Miguel Lanza, Mérito Aeronaútico, Mérito Naval (Bolivia); Chairman, National Advisory and Legislative Council, 1980; *b* 8 March 1921; *s* of Juan Alfredo Lechín and Julia Suárez; *m* 1947, Ruth Varela; one *s* three *d. Educ:* Bolivian Military College. Chief of Ops, Bolivian Army HQ,

1960-61; Military and Air Attaché, Bolivian Embassy, Bonn, 1962-63; Comdr. Bolivian Army Fifth Inf. Div., 1964; Pres., Bolivian State Mining Corp. (with rank of Minister of State), 1964-68; Comdr, Bolivian Army Third Inf. Div., 1969; Bolivian Ambassador to the UK and to the Netherlands, 1970-74; Minister for Planning and Co-ordination, 1974-78. Das Grosse Verdienstkreuz (Fed. Rep. Germany). *Recreations:* tennis, swimming. *Address:* Avenida Busch 2066, La Paz, Bolivia.

LECHMERE, Sir Berwick (Hungerford), 6th Bt, *cr* 1818; JP; Vice Lord-Lieutenant, Hereford and Worcester, since 1977; Land Agent; *b* 21 Sept. 1917; *s* of Sir Ronald Berwick Hungerford Lechmere, 5th Bt, and Constance Marguerite (*née* Long) (*d* 1981); *S* father, 1965; *m* 1954, Norah Garrett Elkington; no *c. Educ:* Charterhouse; Magdalene Coll., Cambridge. High Sheriff of Worcs, 1962, JP, 1966, DL 1972. FRICS. CStJ. *Heir: cousin* Reginald Anthony Hungerford Lechmere [*b* 24 Dec. 1920; *m* 1956, Anne Jennifer Dind; three *s* one *d*]. *Address:* Severn End, Hanley Castle, Worcester. *T:* Upton-on-Severn 2130.

LECKIE, John, CB 1955; *b* 2 Sept. 1911; *o s* of late Alexander M. Leckie; *m* 1937, Elizabeth Mary Murray Brown; two *s. Educ:* Hamilton Academy; Glasgow Univ. (MA, BSc). Entered Administrative Class, Home Civil Service, by competitive examination, 1934; Customs and Excise Dept, 1934; transferred to Board of Trade, 1940; Head of Board of Trade Delegation, Washington, USA, 1943-45; Adviser on Commercial Policy, 1950; Under-Sec., 1950-60, Second Sec., 1960-64, BoT; Deputy Secretary: Min. of Technology, 1964-70; DTI, 1970-72, retd 1972. *Address:* 1 The Wedges, West Chiltington Lane, Itchingfield, Horsham, Sussex RH13 7TA.

LECKONBY, William Douglas, CBE 1967; Collector of Customs and Excise, London Port, 1963-67, retired; *b* 23 April 1907; *m* 1933; one *d. Educ:* Hymers Coll., Hull. Entered Customs and Excise, 1928; subsequently held various posts in that department. *Address:* Ebor, Withyham Road, Groombridge, Sussex. *T:* Groombridge 481.

LECKY, Arthur Terence, CMG 1968; HM Diplomatic Service, retired; *b* 10 June 1919; *s* of late Lieut-Colonel M. D. Lecky, DSO, late RA, and late Bertha Lecky (*née* Goss); *m* 1946, Jacqualine (*d* 1974), *d* of late Dr A. G. Element; three *s. Educ:* Winchester Coll.; Clare Coll., Cambridge (1938-39). Served RA, 1939-46. FO (Control Commission for Germany), 1946-49; FO, 1950-54; Vice-Consul, Zürich, 1954-56; FO, 1957-61; First Secretary, The Hague, 1962-64, FCO (formerly FO), 1964-70, retired. Mem., Hants CC, 1981-. *Address:* Springfield, Mill End, Damerham, near Fordingbridge, Hants SP6 3HU. *T:* Rockbourne 595.

LECKY, Maj.-Gen. Samuel Knox, CB 1979; OBE 1967; BSc(Eng), CEng, FIMechE, FIAgrE, CBIM; Director-General, Agricultural Engineers Association, since 1980; *b* 10 Feb. 1926; *s* of late J. D. Lecky, Coleraine; *m* 1947, Sheila Jones; one *s* two *d. Educ:* Coleraine Acad.; Queen's Univ., Belfast (BSc). Commnd REME, 1946; served Egypt, 1951-52; Kenya, 1953-54; jssc 1964; AA&QMG HQ 1(BR) Corps, 1965-66; CREME 4 Div., 1966-68; Sec., Principal Personnel Officers, MoD, 1968-70; RCDS, 1971; Comdt, SEME, 1972-74; DEME, BAOR, 1975; Dir, Military Assistance Office, MoD, 1976-77; Minister (DS), British Embassy, Tehran, 1977-79. Hon. Col, QUB OTC, 1978-; Col Comdt, REME, 1980-. *Recreations:* fishing, shooting. *Address:* c/o Williams & Glyn's Bank, Victoria Road, Farnborough, Hants GU14 7PA. *Clubs:* Army and Navy, Caledonian.

LECLERC, Maj.-Gen. Pierre Edouard, CBE 1943; MM; ED; CD; *b* 20 Jan. 1893; *s* of late Pierre Leclerc, Civil Engineer, Montreal; *m* 1st, 1918, Esther (*d* 1956), *d* of Capt. Olsen Norlie, Bergen, and Arundal, Norway; one *d* ; 2nd, 1958, Germaine, *d* of late Robert Sarra-Bournet, Montreal. *Educ:* Mont St Louis Coll., Montreal; Methodist Institute, Westmount, PQ. Joined Canadian Expeditionary Force, 1915, as Sapper; commissioned, 1916; qualified Canadian Militia Staff Course, 1935; commanded 5th Canadian Infantry Bde, 1940 (overseas); Maj.-General, 1942; GOC 7th Canadian Div., 1942; GOC Canadian and Newfoundland Army Forces, Newfoundland, Oct. 1943; retired from Canadian Army, 1945. Mem., Sir Arthur Currie Branch, Montreal, Quebec, The Royal Canadian Legion, 1945. Hon. Colonel Le Regt de Joliette, 1955-; Hon. President Canadian Corps Association, 1956. *Address:* 2555 Benny Avenue, apt 1208, Montreal, P Que, H4B 2R6 Canada. *Clubs:* Canadian (Montreal); Royal Commonwealth Society (Montreal Branch).

LECONFIELD, Baron; *see* Egremont.

LECOURT, Robert; Commandeur, Legion of Honour; Croix de Guerre; Rosette de la Résistance; Member, Constitutional Council of the French Republic, since 1979; *b* 19 Sept. 1908; *s* of Léon Lecourt and Angéle Lépron; *m* 1932, Marguerite Chabrerie; one *d. Educ:* Rouen; Univ. de Caen (DenDroit). Advocate, Court of Appeal: Rouen, 1928; Paris, 1932. Served with French Air Force, 1939-40; Mem. Resistance Movt, 1942-44; Deputy for Paris, 1945-58 and for Hautes Alpes, 1958-61, National Assembly; Pres., MRP Party, 1945-48 and 1952-57; Minister of Justice, 1948-49 and 1957-58; Minister of State responsible for co-operation with Africa, 1958-61. Judge, Court of Justice, European Community, 1962, President 1967-76; Hon. Bencher, Gray's Inn, 1972; DUniv Exeter, 1975. Holds numerous foreign decorations. *Publications:* Nature juridique de l'action en réintégrande, 1931; Code pratique du travail, Responsabilité des architectes et entrepreneurs, etc, 1932-39; Le Juge devant le marché commun, 1970; L'Europe des juges, 1976;

Concorde sans concordat 1952-57, 1978; contrib. Le Monde, Figaro, Aurore, and other European jls. *Address:* 11 Boulevard Suchet, 75016 Paris, France. *T:* 504-27-95.

LEDERBERG, Prof. Joshua, PhD; President, Rockefeller University, since 1978; consultant, Cetus Cos, Berkeley, Calif., since 1972; *b* Montclair, NJ, USA, 23 May 1925; *s* of Zwi H. and Esther Lederberg (*née* Goldenbaum); *m* 1968, Marguerite Stein Kirsch, MD; one *d,* one step-*s. Educ:* Stuyvesant High Sch., NYC; Columbia Coll. (BA); Yale Univ. (PhD). Assistant Professor of Genetics, University of Wisconsin, 1947; Associate Professor, 1950; Professor, 1954; Prof. and Exec. Head, Dept of Genetics, Sch. of Medicine, Stanford Univ., 1959-78. Shared in discoveries concerning genetic re-combination, and organization of genetic material of bacteria, contributing to cancer research; discovered a method of artificially introducing new genes into bacteria in investigation of hereditary substance. Chm., President's Cancer Panel (US), 1980-81. Mem., National Academy of Sciences, United States, 1957. For. Mem., Royal Society, 1979. ScD (*hc*): Yale Univ.; Columbia Univ.; Univ. of Wisconsin; Mt Sinai Sch. of Medicine; Rutgers; MD (*hc*), Univ. of Turin; LittD (*hc*) Jewish Theol Seminary; LLD (*hc*) Univ. of Pennsylvania. (Jointly) Nobel Prize in Medicine, 1958. *Publications:* contribs to learned journals on genetics, bacteria and general biological problems. *Address:* Rockefeller University, 1230 York Avenue, New York, NY 10021, USA. *T:* 212.570.8080.

LEDGER, Sir Frank, (Joseph Francis), Kt 1963; Company Director (engineering etc); *b* 29 Oct. 1899; *s* of Edson and Annie Frances Ledger; *m* 1923, Gladys Muriel Lyons; one *s* two *d. Educ:* Perth Boys' Sch., Perth, WA. President: J. E. Ledger Cos; Mitchell Cotts Gp; Dir, Mitchell Cotts Australia; Governing Dir, Ledger Investments; Past Chm. of Dirs, S Australian Insurance Co.; Director: Chamber of Manufrs Insurance Co.; ARC Engineering Co.; Winget Moxey (WA) Pty Ltd; Lake View and Star Ltd; Member, Past Chairman: WA Branch of Inst. of Directors (London); WA Govt Industrial Develt Adv. Cttee; Pres., Royal Commonwealth Society (WA Branch); Past President: WA Chamber of Manufacturers; WA Employers Federation; Ironmasters Assoc. (WA); Metal Industries Assoc. (WA); Inst. of Foundrymen (WA); Past Vice-Pres., Associated Chamber of Manufacturers (Canberra). Pres., WA Trotting Assoc.; Vice-Pres., Australian Institute Traction Council. *Recreations:* golfing, sailing. *Address:* 2 The Esplanade, Peppermint Grove, Western Australia. *Clubs:* Weld, Perth, Royal Freshwater Bay Yacht, Cottesloe Golf; WA Turf, WA Cricket Association (all in Perth, WA).

LEDGER, Sir Joseph Francis; *see* Ledger, Sir Frank.

LEDGER, Philip (Stevens); Principal, Royal Scottish Academy of Music and Drama, since 1982; *b* 12 Dec. 1937; *s* of Walter Stephen Ledger and Winifred Kathleen (*née* Stevens); *m* 1963, Mary Erryl (*née* Wells); one *s* one *d. Educ:* Bexhill Grammar Sch.; King's Coll., Cambridge (Maj. Schol.). John Stewart of Rannoch Schol. in Sacred Music; 1st Cl. Hons in Pt I and Pt II, of Music Tripos; MA, MusB (Cantab). FRCO, Limpus and Read prizes, LRAM, ARCM. Master of the Music, Chelmsford Cathedral, 1962-65; Dir of Music, Univ. of East Anglia, 1965-73 (Dean of Sch. of Fine Arts and Music, 1968-71); Dir of Music and Organist, King's Coll., Cambridge, 1974-82; Conductor, CU Musical Soc., 1973-82. An Artistic Dir, Aldeburgh Festival of Music and the Arts, 1968-. *Publications:* (ed) Anthems for Choirs 2 and 3, 1973; (ed) The Oxford Book of English Madrigals, 1978; other edns of Byrd, Handel and Purcell; carol arrangements. *Recreations:* swimming, theatre, membership of Sette of Odd Volumes. *Address:* 322 Albert Drive, Pollokshields, Glasgow G41 5DZ. *T:* 041-429 0967. *Club:* Athenæum.

LEDGER, Ronald Joseph; Casino Proprietor and Manager; *b* 7 Nov. 1920; *s* of Arthur and Florence Ledger; *m* 1946, Madeleine Odette de Villeneuve; three *s* one *d. Educ:* Skinners Grammar Sch., Tunbridge Wells; Nottingham Univ. Toolroom Engineer, 1938-42. Served RAF, 1942-47, fitter, Leading Aircraftsman; India three years. Univ. of Nottingham, 1947-49 (Diploma in Social Science); Staff Training Officer, Enfield Highway Co-op. Society, 1949; Business Partner, 1950, Company Director, 1953, Employment Specialists. Mem. Herts CC, 1952-54. Contested (Lab) Rushcliffe Div. of Nottingham, 1951; MP (Lab and Co-op) Romford, 1955-70. Director: Enfield Electronics (CRT) Ltd, 1958; London Co-operative Society Ltd, 1961. Chairman, Hairdressing Council, 1966-79. *Recreations:* tennis, cricket, golf, snooker. *Address:* Pomona, Shanklin, Isle of Wight. *T:* Shanklin 2398. *Clubs:* Sandown and Shanklin Golf, Enfield Golf.

LEDINGHAM, John Gerard Garvin, DM; FRCP; May Reader in Medicine, University of Oxford, since 1974 (Director of Clinical Studies, 1977-82); Fellow of New College, Oxford, since 1974; *b* 1929; *s* of late John Ledingham, MB BCh, DPH, and late Una Ledingham, MD, FRCP, *d* of J. L. Garvin, CH, Editor of The Observer; *m* 1961, Élaine Mary, *d* of late R. G. Maliphant, MD, FRCOG, and of Dilys Maliphant, Cardiff; four *d. Educ:* Rugby Sch.; New Coll., Oxford; Middlesex Hosp. Med. Sch. (1st Cl. Physiol.; BM BCh; DM 1966). FRCP 1971 (MRCP 1959). Junior appts, Middlesex, London Chest, Whittington, and Westminster Hospitals, London, 1957-64; Travelling Fellow, British Postgraduate Med. Fedn, Columbia Univ., New York, 1965-66. Chairman, Medical Staff Council, United Oxford Hosps, 1970-72; Hon. Consultant Physician, Oxfordshire Health Authority, 1982- (Consultant Physician, Oxford AHA (T), 1966-82). Hon. Sec., Assoc. of Physicians of Gt Britain and Ireland, 1978-; Governing Trustee, Nuffield Provincial Hosps Trust, 1978-. *Publications:* contribs to med. books and scientific jls in the field of hypertension and renal diseases. *Recreations:* music, golf. *Address:* 22 Hid's Copse Road, Cumnor Hill, Oxford OX2 9JJ. *T:* Cumnor 2023. *Club:* Vincent's (Oxford).

LEDINGHAM, Prof. John Marshall, MD, FRCP; Consultant Physician, The London Hospital, 1954-81, now Consulting Physician; Professor of Medicine, University of London, at London Hospital Medical College, 1971-81, now Emeritus; *b* 1916; *s* of late Prof. Sir John C. G. Ledingham, CMG, FRS, of The Lister Institute, London, and late Lady Barbara Ledingham; *m* 1950, Josephine, *d* of late Matthew and Jane Metcalf, Temple Sowerby, Westmorland; two *s. Educ:* Whitgift Sch.; University College, London; The London Hospital. BSc (London) First Class Hons in Physics, 1936; MRCS, LRCP, 1942; MD (London) Gold Medal, 1951, FRCP, 1957. Service in RAMC as Graded Clinical and Experimental Pathologist, in UK, France, Middle and Far East, 1942-47. Lectr in Medicine, London Hosp. Med. Sch., 1948-53; Univ. Reader in Medicine, 1953-64; Prof. of Experimental Medicine, 1964-71, London Hosp. Med. Coll., London Univ. Editor, Dep. Chm. and Chm. Editorial Bd, Clinical Science, 1965-70. Past Pres., Section of Exptl Med. and Therapeutics, RSM. Bertram Louis Abrahams Lectr, RCP, 1970; Censor, RCP, 1975; Vis. Prof., Maiduguri Univ., Nigeria, 1982. *Publications:* numerous scientific, mainly in field of hypertension and renal disease, 1938-. *Address:* 11 Montpelier Walk, SW7. *T:* 01-584 7976.

LEDSOME, Neville Frank; Under Secretary, Establishment General Services Division, Department of Industry, since 1980; *b* 29 Nov. 1929; *s* of late Charles Percy Ledsome and Florence Ledsome; *m* 1953, Isabel Mary Lindsay; three *s. Educ:* Birkenhead Sch. Exec. Officer, BoT, 1948; Monopolies Commn, 1957; Higher Exec. Officer, BoT, 1961; Principal, 1964; DEA, 1967; HM Treasury, 1969; DTI, 1970; Asst Sec., 1973. *Recreations:* gardening, theatre. *Address:* 3 Homefield Close, Woodham, Weybridge, Surrey KT15 3QH. *T:* Byfleet 44330.

LEDWIDGE, Sir (William) Bernard (John), KCMG 1974 (CMG 1964); writer; HM Diplomatic Service, retired; Chairman, United Kingdom Committee for UNICEF, since 1976; *b* 9 Nov. 1915; *s* of late Charles Ledwidge and Eileen O'Sullivan; *m* 1st, 1948, Anne Kingsley (marr. diss. 1970); one *s* one *d*; 2nd, 1970, Flora Groult. *Educ:* Cardinal Vaughan Sch.; King's Coll., Cambridge; Princeton Univ., USA. Commonwealth Fund Fellow, 1937-39; served War of 1939-45: RA 1940; Indian Army, 1941-45. Private Secretary to Permanent Under-Secretary, India Office, 1946; Secretary, Frontier Areas Cttee of Enquiry, Burma, 1947; Foreign Office, 1947-49; British Consul, St Louis, USA, 1949-52; First Secretary, British Embassy, Kabul, 1952-56; Political Adviser British Military Govt, Berlin, 1956-61; Foreign Office, 1961-65; Minister, Paris, 1965-69; Ambassador to Finland, 1969-72; Ambassador to Israel, 1972-75. Mem., Police Complaints Bd, 1977-. *Publications:* Frontiers (novel), 1979; (jtly) Nouvelles de la Famille (short stories), 1980. *Recreations:* golf, bridge, chess. *Address:* 54 rue de Bourgogne, 75007 Paris, France. *T:* 705 8026; 19 Queen's Gate Terrace, SW7. *T:* 01-584 4132. *Clubs:* Travellers', MCC.

LEE, family name of **Baron Lee of Newton.**

LEE OF ASHERIDGE, Baroness *cr* 1970 (Life Peer), of the City of Westminster; **Janet Bevan, (Jennie Lee),** PC 1966; Director of Tribune; Member of Central Advisory Committee on Housing; Member, National Executive Committee, Labour Party, 1958-70 (Chairman, 1967-68); *b* 3 Nov. 1904; *d* of James Lee, Fifeshire miner; *m* 1934, Rt Hon. Aneurin Bevan, PC, MP (*d* 1960). *Educ:* Edinburgh Univ. MA, LLB. MP (Lab) North Lanark, 1929-31, Cannock, 1945-70. Parly Sec., Ministry of Public Building and Works, 1964-65; Parly Under-Sec. of State, Dept of Education and Science, 1965-67, Minister of State, 1967-70. Hon. Fellow, Royal Acad., 1981. Hon. LLD Cambridge, 1974. *Publications:* Tomorrow is a New Day, 1939; Our Ally, Russia, 1941; This Great Journey, 1963; My Life with Nye, 1980. *Address:* 67 Chester Row, SW1.

LEE OF NEWTON, Baron *cr* 1974 (Life Peer), of Newton, Merseyside; **Frederick Lee,** PC 1964; *b* 3 Aug. 1906; *s* of Joseph Wm and Margaret Lee; *m* 1938; one *d. Educ:* Langworthy Road Sch. Engineer. Chairman: Works Cttee, Metro-Vickers Ltd, Trafford Park, Manchester; National Cttee, Amal. Engineering Union, 1944-45; formerly Member Salford City Council. MP (Lab): Hulme, Manchester, 1945-50, Newton, Lancs, 1950-Feb. 1974; PPS to Chancellor of Exchequer, 1948; Parly Sec., Min. of Labour and Nat. Service, 1950-51; Minister of Power, 1964-66; Secretary of State for the Colonies, 1966-67; Chancellor of the Duchy of Lancaster, 1967-69. *Address:* Sunnyside, 52 Ashton Road, Newton-le-Willows, Merseyside WA12 0AE. *T:* Newton-le-Willows 5012.

LEE, Sir Arthur (James), KBE 1966 (CBE 1959); MC and Bar (1939-45); Company Director; National President, Returned Services League, Australia, 1960-74 (State President, 1954-60); *b* 30 July 1912; *s* of Arthur James and Kathleen Maud Lee; *m* 1945, Valerie Ann Scanlan; three *s* one *d. Educ:* Collegiate School of St Peter, Adelaide. Chairman: Regional Cttees Services Canteen Fund, S Australia, 1947-; Exec. Cttee, War Veterans Home, SA, 1967-. *Recreation:* golf. *Address:* 2 Arthur Street, Toorak Gardens, SA 5065, Australia. *T:* 35106. *Clubs:* Adelaide, Naval and Military, Royal Adelaide Golf (Adelaide).

LEE, Arthur James, CBE 1979; DSC (and Bar); Controller of Fisheries Research and Development, Ministry of Agriculture, Fisheries and Food, 1977-80; *b* 17 May 1920; *s* of Arthur Henry and Clara Lee; *m* 1953, Judith Graham; three *d. Educ:* City Boys' Sch., Leicester; St Catharine's Coll., Cambridge (MA). Served War of 1939-45 (DSC and Bar). Apptd: Scientific Officer at Fisheries Laboratory, Lowestoft, 1947; Dep. Dir of Fishery Research, 1965, Dir, 1974-77. *Publications:* (ed) Atlas of the Seas around the British Isles, 1981; contribs to various marine science jls. *Recreation:* gardening. *Address:* 191 Normanston Drive, Oulton Broad, Lowestoft, Suffolk NR32 2PY. *T:* Lowestoft 4707.

LEE, His Honour Arthur Michael, DSC 1941; QC 1961; DL; a Circuit Judge (formerly Judge of County Courts), 1962-77; *b* 22 Aug. 1913; *s* of Edward Cornwall Lee and Katherine Sybil Lee (*née* Wilberforce); *m* 1940, Valerie Burnett Georges Drake-Brockman; two *s. Educ:* Horris Hill Preparatory Sch.; Winchester Coll. (Scholar); Brasenose Coll. (Heath Harrison Schol.), Oxford. Honours Degree in Philosophy, Politics and Economics, 1935, in Law, 1936. Called to Bar, Middle Temple (Harmsworth Scholar), 1937. Served War of 1939-45, RNVR: served in destroyers, Atlantic convoys; Lieut, 1939; Lieut-Commander, 1943; Acting Commander, 1945. Returned to practice at the Bar, Jan. 1946; Recorder of Penzance, 1960-62; Dep. Chm., Hants QS, 1960-71. Chm., Hants Area Probation and After-Care Cttee, 1969-77. Chairman Governors, Horris Hill Sch., Newbury, 1964-70. DL Hants, 1975. *Publications:* ed Shawcross on Motor Insurance, 1947; ed Shaw on Evidence in Criminal Cases, 1950. *Recreation:* fishing. *Address:* The Manor Farm House, Easton, Winchester, Hants. *T:* Itchen Abbas 277.

LEE, Charles Guy V.; *see* Vaughan-Lee.

LEE, Christopher Frank Carandini; actor; entered film industry, 1947; *b* 27 May 1922; *s* of Geoffrey Trollope Lee (Lt-Col 60th KRRC), and Estelle Marie Carandini; *m* 1961, Birgit, *d* of Richard Emil Kroencke; one *d. Educ:* Wellington Coll. RAFVR, 1941-46 (Flt Lieut; mentioned in despatches, 1944). Films include: Moulin Rouge; Tale of Two Cities; Dracula; Rasputin; The Devil Rides Out; Private Life of Sherlock Holmes; The Wicker Man; The Three Musketeers; The Four Musketeers; The Man with the Golden Gun; To the Devil, a Daughter; Airport '77; The Passage; Bear Island; 1941; The Serial. Officier des Arts et des Lettres, France, 1973. *Publications:* Christopher Lee's 'X' Certificate, 1975 (2nd edn 1976); Christopher Lee's Archives of Evil, USA 1975 (2nd edn 1976); (autobiog.) Tall, Dark and Gruesome, 1977. *Recreations:* travel, opera, golf, cricket. *Address:* c/o Contemporary Korman Artists, 132 Lasky Drive, Beverly Hills, Calif 90210, USA. *Clubs:* Buck's, MCC; Honourable Company of Edinburgh Golfers; Travellers' (Paris); Bay Hill and Lodge (Orlando, Fla, USA); Bel-Air Country (Los Angeles, USA).

LEE, Air Chief Marshal Sir David (John Pryer), GBE 1969 (KBE 1965; CBE 1947; OBE 1943); CB 1953; retired, 1971; *b* 4 Sept. 1912; *s* of late John Lee, Byron Crescent, Bedford; *m* 1938, Denise, *d* of late Louis Hartoch; one *s* one *d. Educ:* Bedford Sch.; RAF Coll., Cranwell. NWFP, India, 1933-36; Central Flying Sch., Upavon, 1937; RAF Examining Officer, Supt. of Reserve, 1938-39; Bomber Command, Hemswell, 1939-40; RAF Staff Coll. (student), 1942; Deputy Director Plans, Air Ministry, 1943-44; OC 904 Fighter Wing, Batavia, Java, 1945-46; Directing Staff, RAF Staff Coll., 1948-50; Deputy Director Policy, Air Ministry, 1951-53; OC RAF Scampton, Lincs, 1953-55; Secretary, Chiefs of Staff Cttee, Ministry of Defence, 1956-59; AOC, AFME (Aden), 1959-61; Comdt, RAF Staff Coll., 1962-65; Air Member for Personnel, MoD, 1965-68; UK Military Rep. to NATO, 1968-71. Chairman: Grants Cttee, RAF Benevolent Fund, 1971-; Exec. Cttee, Nuffield Trust for Armed Forces, 1975-; Dir, Corps of Commissionaires, 1980-. *Publication:* Flight from the Middle East, 1981. *Address:* Danemore Cottage, South Godstone, Surrey. *T:* South Godstone 3162. *Club:* Royal Air Force.

LEE, Sir Desmond; *see* Lee, Sir H. D. P.

LEE, Rev. Donald Rathbone, MBE 1945; Methodist Minister, retired; President of the Methodist Conference, 1973; Moderator, Free Church Federal Council, 1975-76; *b* 28 March 1911; *s* of Thomas and Alice Lee, Stockport, Cheshire; *m* 1940, Nora Olive Fothergill, Greenock, Renfrewshire; two *s* three *d. Educ:* Stockport Grammar School; Handsworth College, Birmingham. BD (London). Methodist Circuit appointments in: Greenock, 1935; Runcorn, 1936; Edinburgh, 1937; Perth, 1940; Stockport, 1947; Upminster, 1951; Oxford, Wesley Memorial, 1952; Worcester, 1957; Sutton Coldfield, 1964-68; Chm., Southampton District, 1968-77; Supt, Jersey Methodist Circuit, 1977-82. Religious Adviser (Free Church): Southern Television, 1972-77; Channel Television, 1977-82. Chm., Adv. Cttee, Inter-Church Travel Ltd, 1976-; Pres., Jersey Council of Churches, 1978-80. Royal Army Chaplains' Dept, 1942-47 (Senior Chaplain, 1st Infantry Div., 1946). *Recreations:* music, gardening, ecumenical travel. *Address:* 12 Marshalwick Road, St Albans, Herts.

LEE, Edward, MSc, PhD; FInstP; Director, Admiralty Research Laboratory, Teddington, 1971-74, retired; *b* 2 March 1914; *s* of Thomas and Florence Lee; *m* 1942, Joan Pearson; three *d. Educ:* Consett Grammar Sch.; Manchester Univ.; Pembroke Coll., Cambridge. Admiralty Research Laboratory, 1939-46; Ministry of Defence, 1946-48; Dept of Physical Research, Admiralty, 1948-51; Admiralty Research Laboratory, 1951-55; Dir of Operational

Research, Admty, 1955-58; Dep. Dir, Nat. Physical Laboratory, 1958-60; Director, Stations and Industry Div., DSIR, 1960-65; Dep. Controller (R), Min. of Technology, 1965-70; Head of Res. Services, Dept of Trade and Industry, 1970-71. *Publications:* scientific papers. *Recreations:* golf, gardening. *Address:* 8 Courtlands Avenue, Hampton, Mddx. *T:* 01-979 1081.

LEE, (Edward) Stanley, FRCS; Consulting Surgeon Westminster Hospital; formerly Civilian Consultant in Surgery of Neoplastic Diseases, Queen Alexandra Military Hospital; Surgeon Emeritus, Guildford Radiotherapy Centre; *b* 1907. *Educ:* Westminster Hospital. MB, BS 1931; FRCS, 1933; MS London, 1936. Past Member of Court of Examiners, Royal College of Surgeons, England, 1953-59; Past Member: Grand Council British Empire Cancer Campaign; Internat. Union against Cancer; Assoc. of Head and Neck Oncologists of GB. FRSM; Sen. Fellow, Assoc. of Surgeons. Hon. Mem. Royal College of Radiologists. *Publications:* contributions to medical literature, etc. *Address:* Westminster Hospital, SW1; Little Gates, Benenden, Kent.

LEE, George Ranson, CVO 1980; HM Diplomatic Service; Counsellor, Berne, since 1978; *b* 26 Sept. 1925; *s* of late Wilfred Lee and Janet (*née* Ranson); *m* 1955, Anne Christine Black; one *d*. Served Indian Army, 6th Gurkha Rifles, NW Frontier Prov., 1945-47; TA, W Yorks Regt, 1948-53. Employed in Trng Dept, Min. of Food, 1948-53; joined CRO, 1954; Karachi, 1955-58; First Sec., Madras, 1959-63; CRO, 1964; Head of Chancery: Singapore, 1965-69; Santiago, 1969-72; FCO, 1972-74; Dep. UK Perm. Rep. to Council of Europe, Strasbourg, 1974-78. *Address:* c/o Foreign and Commonwealth Office, SW1. *Club:* Royal Commonwealth Society.

LEE, George Russell, CMG 1970; Acting Assistant Director, Ministry of Defence, 1967-78, retired; *b* 11 Nov. 1912; *s* of Ernest Harry Lee and Alice Mary Lee (*née* Russell); *m* 1947, Annabella Evelyn (*née* Dargie); one *s* one *d*. *Educ:* Birkenhead Sch., Cheshire. WO and MoD, 1940-78. *Address:* 13 Abberbury Road, Iffley, Oxford OX4 4ET.

LEE, Sir (George) Wilton, Kt 1964; TD 1940; President of Arthur Lee & Sons Ltd and Group of Companies, since 1976 (Chairman, 1949-76, Managing Director, 1949-68, Joint Managing Director, 1968-72); *b* 8 April 1904; *e s* of Percy W. Lee, Tapton Holt, Sheffield; *m* 1934, Bettina Stanley, *e d* of Colonel R. B. Haywood, TD; three *s*. *Educ:* Uppingham Sch.; Queens' Coll., Cambridge. Member Exec. Cttee, BISF, 1953-67 (Joint Vice-President, 1966-67); Founding Chm., British Independent Steel Producers' Assoc., 1967-69; Chairman: S Yorks Industrialists' Council; S Yorks Board of Eagle Star Insurance Co. Ltd, 1948-74. Master Cutler, 1950-51. Chm. City of Sheffield Cons. and Nat. Lib. Fedn., 1959-70. Town Trustee of the City of Sheffield; JP, 1950-64. *Recreations:* golf, shooting, fishing. *Address:* Thornfield, Lindrick Common, near Worksop, Nottinghamshire. *T:* Dinnington 562810. *Club:* Sheffield (Sheffield).

LEE, Gilbert Henry Clifton; Chairman, European Hotel Corporation NV, 1975-76; *b* 19 April 1911; *s* of Walter Lee and Sybil Townsend; *m* 1938, Kathleen Cooper; two *d*. *Educ:* Worksop College. FCIT. Joined Imperial Airways, 1931; served overseas India, E Africa, Pakistan; Gen. Man., West African Airways Corp., 1949-52; BOAC: Traffic Manager, 1953; Gen. Sales Man., 1955; Commercial Dir, 1959; Mem. Bd, BOAC, 1961-73; Chm., BOAC Associated Cos Ltd, 1964-73. *Recreation:* golf. *Address:* Dana, Callow Hill, Virginia Water, Surrey. *T:* Wentworth 2195. *Clubs:* Oriental; Wentworth (Virginia Water).

LEE, Sir (Henry) Desmond (Pritchard), Kt 1961; MA; President, Hughes Hall, Cambridge, 1973-78, Hon. Fellow 1978; *b* 30 Aug. 1908; *s* of Rev. Canon Henry Burgass Lee; *m* 1935, Elizabeth, *d* of late Colonel A. Crookenden, CBE, DSO; one *s* two *d*. *Educ:* Repton Sch. (George Denman Scholar); Corpus Christi Coll., Cambridge (Entrance Scholar). 1st Class Part 1 Classical Tripos, 1928; Foundation Scholar of the College; 1st Class Part 2 Classical Tripos, 1930; Charles Oldham Scholar; Fellow of Corpus Christi Coll., 1933, Life Fellow, 1948-78; Tutor, 1935-48; University Lecturer in Classics, 1937-48; Headmaster of Clifton Coll., 1948-54; Headmaster of Winchester Coll., 1954-68. Fellow, University Coll., later Wolfson Coll., Cambridge, 1968-73, Hon. Fellow, 1974. Regional Comr's Office, Cambridge, 1941-44; Mem. Council of the Senate, 1944-48. Mem. Anderson Cttee on Grants to Students, 1958-59; Chm., Headmasters' Conference, 1959-60, 1967. Hon. DLitt (Nottingham), 1963. *Publications:* Zeno of Elea: a Text and Notes in Cambridge Classical Studies), 1935; Aristotle, Meteorologica, 1952; Plato, Republic, 1955, rev. edn 1974; Plato, Timæus and Critias, 1971; Entry and Performance at Oxford and Cambridge, 1966-71, 1972; (ed) Wittgenstein's Lectures 1930-32, 1980. *Address:* 8 Barton Close, Cambridge.

LEE, Col Tun Sir Henry Hau Shik, SMN 1959 (Federation of Malaya); KBE 1957 (CBE 1948); JP; Chancellor of the Most Exalted Order of the Realm, Malaysia, since 1978; sole Proprietor, H. S. Lee Tin Mines, Malaya; Chairman: Development & Commercial Bank Ltd; China Press Ltd; Chartered Bank (M) Trustee Berhad; On Tai Development Sdn Berhad; D&C Nomura Merchant Bankers Berhad; D&C Finance Berhad; D&C Leasing Sdn Berhad; NEM (Malaysia) Sdn Berhad; Vice-Chairman: Golden Castle Finance Corp. Ltd; Institute Bank, Bank Malaysia, since 1977; *b* 19 Nov. 1901; *e s* of late K. L. Lee; *m* 1st, 1922 (wife *d* 1926); one *s*; 2nd, 1929, Choi Lin (*née* Kwan); three *s* one *d* (and two *s* one *d* decd). *Educ:* Queen's Coll., Hongkong; Univ. of

Cambridge. BA (Cantab) 1923. FREconS. War of 1939-45; Chief of Passive Defence Forces, Kuala Lumpur, 1941; Col in Allied Armed Forces, 1942-45. Member: Council of State, Selangor, 1946-47; Fed. Finance Cttee, 1946-56 (Chm., 1956-59); Fed. Legislative Council and Fed. Exec. Council, 1948-57; Dir, Ops Cttee, 1948-55; Minister of Transport, 1953-56, of Finance, 1956-59; Member: Merdeka Mission to London, 1956; Financial Mission to London, 1957; Cabinet, 1957-59. Co-founder, Alliance Party, 1949; Mem., Alliance Exec. Cttee and Nat. Council, 1953-59; Chm., MCA Standing Sub-Cttee, 1957-59. Member: KL Sanitary Bd, 1929-32, 1938-41, 1946-48; Council, FMS Chamber of Mines, 1929-55; War Damage Commn, 1946-56; Chinese Tin Mines Rehabilitation Loan Bd, 1946-59; Malayan Union Adv. Council, 1946-47; Tin Adv. Cttee, 1946-55; Malayan Tin Delegn, Internat. Tin Meetings, 1946-60. Chm., Bd of Governors, Lady Templer Hosp., KL. President: Selangor Chinese Chamber of Commerce, 1936-55; Kuen Cheng Girls' Sch., 1937-41, 1945-52; Miners Assoc. of Negeri Sembilan, Selangor and Pahang, 1938-55; All Malaya Chinese Mining Assoc., 1946-55; Associated Chinese Chambers of Commerce, 1947-55; United Lee's Assoc., 1949-59; Selangor Malaysian Chinese Assoc., 1949-56; Sen. Golfers Soc. of Malaya, 1957-58, 1960-63; Fedn of Malaya Red Cross Soc., 1957-62; Fedn of Malaya Olympic Council, 1957-59; Malaysian Golf Assoc., 1960-75 (Patron, 1975-); Oxford and Cambridge Soc., 1959-64; Royal Commonwealth Soc., 1969-73 (Vice Patron, 1973-); Selangor Miners Club, 1938-; All Malaya Kochow Assoc., 1949-; Fedn of Kwang Tung Assocs, 1962-; Selangor Kwan Tung Assoc., 1962-; Vice-Pres., Malaysian Zoo. Soc., 1965-. Hon. Pres., Wine and Food Soc., KL, 1970-; Hon. Vice-Pres., Selangor Chinese Recreation Club. Hon. Member, Clubs: KL Rotary, 1963-; KL Lake; Royal Selangor Golf; Selangor; Selangor Turf. JP Kuala Lumpur, 1938. *Recreations:* riding, golf, tennis. *Address:* 22 Jalan Langgak Golf, Kuala Lumpur 01-28, Malaysia. *Clubs:* Oriental, United Oxford & Cambridge University; Chinese (Hongkong); Royal and Ancient Golf (St Andrews); Royal Liverpool Golf (Hoylake); Singapore Island Country.

LEE, James Giles; Deputy Chairman and Chief Executive, Pearson Longman, since 1980; Deputy Chairman, Yorkshire Television, since 1982; *b* 23 Dec. 1942; *s* of John Lee, CBE and Muriel Giles; *m* 1966, Linn Macdonald; one *s* two *d*. *Educ:* Trinity Coll., Glenalmond; Glasgow Univ.; Harvard Univ., USA. Consultant, McKinsey & Co., 1969-80; Mem., Central Policy Review Staff, 1972. Chairman: Penguin Publishing Co., 1980-; Longman Gp, 1980-; Goldcrest Films and Television, 1981-; Dep. Chairman: Westminster Press, 1980-; Financial Times, 1980-; Dir, S. Pearson & Son, 1981-. *Publications:* Planning for the Social Services, 1978; The Investment Challenge, 1979. *Recreations:* photography, travelling, sailing. *Address:* Meadow Wood, Penshurst, Kent. *T:* Penshurst 870309. *Clubs:* Reform; Harvard (New York, USA).

LEE, John Michael Hubert; Barrister-at-Law; *b* 13 Aug. 1927; *s* of late Victor Lee, Wentworth, Surrey, and late Renee Lee; *m* 1960, Margaret Ann, *d* of James Russell, ICS, retired, and late Kathleen Russell; one *s* one *d*. *Educ:* Reading Sch.; Christ's Coll., Cambridge (Open Exhibnr Modern Hist.; 2nd Cl. Hons Pts I and II of Hist. Tripos; MA). Colonial Service: Administrative Officer, Ghana, 1951-58; Principal Assistant Secretary, Min. of Communications, Ghana, 1958. On staff of BBC, 1959-65. Called to the Bar, Middle Temple, 1960; practising, Midland and Oxford Circuit, 1966-; Dep. Circuit Judge, 1978-81; Assistant Recorder, 1981-. MP (Lab) Reading, 1966-70; MP (Lab) Birmingham, Handsworth, Feb. 1974-1979; Chm., W Midland Gp of Labour MPs, 1974-75. Mem., TGWU, 1959-. *Publications:* articles in Fabian Commonwealth magazine Venture and TGWU Jl Record; chapter in the Radical Future (ed Whitaker), 1967. *Recreations:* gardening, tennis, good conversation, walking. *Address:* 2 Dr Johnson's Buildings, EC4. *Club:* Royal Over-Seas League.

LEE, John Robert Louis; MP (C) Nelson and Colne, since 1979; *b* 21 June 1942; *s* of Basil and late Miriam Lee; *m* 1975, Anne Monique Bakirgian; two *d*. *Educ:* William Hulme's Grammar Sch., Manchester. FCA. Accountancy Articles, 1959-64; Henry Cooke, Lumsden & Co., Manchester, Stockbrokers, 1964-66; Founding Dir, Chancery Consolidated Ltd, Investment Bankers; Political Sec. to Rt Hon. Robert Carr (now Lord Carr of Hadley), 1974; contested (C) Manchester, Moss Side, Oct. 1974; Director Paterson Zochonis (UK) Ltd, 1975-76. Vice-Chm., NW Conciliation Cttee, Race Relations Bd, 1976-77; Chm. Council, Nat. Youth Bureau, 1980-. PPS to Minister of State for Industry, 1981-. Jt Sec., Conservative Back Benchers' Industry Cttee, 1979-80. *Recreations:* fly fishing, collecting. *Address:* 1 The Gateways, Whitehead's Grove, SW3. *T:* 01-589 6153. *Clubs:* Carlton; St James's (Manchester).

LEE, John (Thomas Cyril); His Honour Judge John Lee; Circuit Judge (attached Midland Oxford Circuit), since Sept. 1972; *b* 14 Jan. 1927; *s* of Cyril and Dorothy Lee; *m* 1956, Beryl Lee (*née* Haden); one *s* three *d*. *Educ:* Holly Lodge Grammar Sch., Staffs; Emmanuel Coll., Cambridge (MA, LLB). Called to Bar, Gray's Inn, 1952. Practised, Oxford Circuit, 1952-72. Chairman various Tribunals. *Recreation:* golf. *Address:* The Red House, Upper Colwall, Malvern, Worcs. *T:* Colwall 40645. *Clubs:* Union and County (Worcester); Worcester Golf and Country.

LEE KUAN YEW; Prime Minister, Singapore, since 1959; *b* 16 Sept. 1923; *s* of Lee Chin Koon and Chua Jim Neo; *m* 1950, Kwa Geok Choo; two *s* one *d*. *Educ:* Raffles Coll., Singapore; Fitzwilliam Coll., Cambridge, Hon Fellow, 1969. Double first Law Tripos, Star for special distinction. Called to Bar,

Middle Temple, 1950, Hon. Bencher, 1969. Advocate and Solicitor, Singapore, 1951. Formed People's Action Party, 1954, Sec.-Gen., 1954-. Fellow, Inst. of Politics, Harvard, 1968; Hoyt Fellow, Berkeley Coll., Yale, 1970. Hon. CH 1970; Hon. GCMG 1972. Hon. Bencher, Middle Temple, 1969; Hon. Fellow, Fitzwilliam Coll., Cambridge, 1969; Hon. FRACS, 1973; Hon. FRACP, 1974; Hon. LLD: Royal Univ. of Cambodia, 1965; Hong Kong, 1970; Liverpool, 1971; Sheffield 1971; Grand Cordon of Order of The Nile, 1962; Grand Cross of the Royal Order, Cambodia, 1966; First Class Order of the Rising Sun, 1967; Bintang Republik Indonesia Adi Pradana, 1973; Order of Sikatuna, The Philippines, 1974. *Recreations:* jogging, swimming. *Address:* Prime Minister's Office, St Andrew's Road, Singapore 0617. *T:* 3378191.

LEE, Laurie, MBE 1952; poet and author; *m* 1950, Catherine Francesca Polge; one *d. Educ:* Slad Village Sch.; Stroud Central Sch. Travelled Mediterranean, 1935-39; GPO Film Unit, 1939-40; Crown Film Unit, 1941-43; Publications Editor, Ministry of Information, 1944-46; Green Park Film Unit, 1946-47; Caption Writer-in-Chief, Festival of Britain, 1950-51. Freeman of City of London, 1982. *Publications:* The Sun My Monument (Poems), 1944; Land at War (HMSO), 1945; (with Ralph Keene) A Film in Cyprus, 1947; The Bloom of Candles (Poems), 1947; The Voyage of Magellan, 1948; My Many-Coated Man (Poems), 1955; A Rose for Winter, 1955; Cider With Rosie (autobiography), 1959; Pocket Poets (Selection), 1960; The Firstborn, 1964; As I Walked Out One Midsummer Morning (autobiography), 1969; I Can't Stay Long, 1975. *Recreations:* indoor sports, music, travel. *Address:* 9/40 Elm Park Gardens, SW10. *T:* 01-352 2197. *Clubs:* Chelsea Arts, Garrick.

LEE, Malcolm Kenneth; a Recorder of the Crown Court, since 1980; *b* 2 Jan. 1943; 2nd *s* of late Thomas Marston Lee, solicitor, Birmingham, and of Fiona Margaret Lee, JP (*née* Mackenzie); *m* 1970, Phyllis Anne Brunton Speed, *er d* of Andrew Watson Speed, Worcs; three *s* three *d* (and one *d* decd). *Educ:* King Edward's Sch., Birmingham (Foundation Schol.); Worcester Coll., Oxford (Schol.; MA Class. Hon. Mods and Lit.Hum.). Assistant Master: Marlborough Coll., 1965; King Edward's Sch., Birmingham, 1966; Major Schol., Inner Temple, 1967; called to the Bar, Inner Temple, 1967; practised on Midland Circuit, 1968-71, Midland and Oxford Circuit, 1972-. Dep. Chm., Agricl Land Tribunal, E Midland Area, 1979-82, Midland Area, 1982-; Prosecuting Counsel to DHSS, Midland and Oxford Circuit, 1979-. *Recreations:* squash, walking, reading. *Address:* (chambers) 4 Fountain Court, Steelhouse Lane, Birmingham B4 6DR. *T:* 021-236 3476; (home) 50 Wellington Road, Edgbaston, Birmingham B15 2EP. *T:* 021-440 1744.

LEE, Maj.-Gen. Patrick Herbert, CB 1982; MBE 1964; Director General, Electrical and Mechanical Engineering (Army), since 1979; *b* 15 March 1929; *s* of Percy Herbert and Mary Dorothea Lee; *m* 1952, Peggy Eveline Chapman; one *s* one *d. Educ:* King's Sch., Canterbury; London Univ. (BSc (Gen.), BSc (Special Physics)). Commnd RMA Sandhurst, 1948; Staff Coll., 1960; WO Staff Duties, 1961-63; CO, Parachute Workshop, 1964-65; JSSC, 1966; Military Asst to Master General of Ordnance, 1966-67; Directing Staff, Staff Coll., 1968-69; Commander, REME 2nd Div., 1970-71; Col AQ 1 British Corps, 1972-75; Dep. Comdt, Sch. of Electrical and Mechanical Engrg, 1975-77; Comdt, REME Trng Centre, 1977-79. *Recreations:* gardening, railways, Roman history, industrial archaeology. *Address:* c/o Williams and Glyn's Bank, Holts Branch, Farnborough, Hants. *Club:* Army and Navy.

LEE, Rt. Rev. Paul Chun Hwan; *see* Seoul (Korea), Bishop of.

LEE, Peter Gavin; Senior Partner, Strutt & Parker, since 1979; *b* 4 July 1934; *s* of Mr and Mrs J. G. Lee; *m* 1963, Caroline Green; two *s* one *d. Educ:* Midhurst Grammar School; College of Estate Management; Wye College. FRICS. Joined Strutt & Parker, 1957; became full partner, 1972. *Recreations:* vintage cars, clocks, shooting, squash. *Address:* Fanners, Great Waltham, Chelmsford, Essex. *T:* Chelmsford 360470. *Club:* Boodle's.

LEE, Rowland Thomas Lovell; a Recorder of the Crown Court, since 1979; Chairman, North Hertfordshire Health Authority (formerly Hertfordshire Area Health Authority), since 1977; *b* 7 March 1920; *s* of late Ronald Lovell Lee and of Jessie Maude Lee; *m* 1944, Marjorie Betty, *d* of late William Holmes and Clare Johnston Braid Holmes; two *d. Educ:* Bedford Modern School. Served Royal Navy, 1939-48. Bedfordshire Constabulary, 1948-52; Articles with E. A. S. Barnard, Dunstable, 1954; qualified as solicitor, 1957; Principal, Wynter Davies & Lee, Hertford, 1959-. Chairman, Medical Services Cttee, Hertfordshire Family Practitioners Cttee, 1970-77. *Address:* Culpepers, 5 Letty Green, Hertford, Herts SG14 2NZ. *T:* Hatfield 61445.

LEE, Stanley; *see* Lee, (Edward) S.

LEE, Tsung-Dao; Enrico Fermi Professor of Physics at Columbia University, USA, since 1964; *b* 25 Nov. 1926; 3rd *s* of C. K. and M. C. Lee; *m* 1950, Jeannette H. C. Chin; two *s. Educ:* National Chekiang Univ., Kweichow, China; National Southwest Associated Univ., Kunming, China; University of Chicago, USA. Research Associate: University of Chicago, 1950; University of California, 1950-51; Member, Inst. for Advanced Study, Princeton, 1951-53. Columbia University: Asst Professor, 1953-55; Associate Professor, 1955-56; Professor, 1956-60; Member, Institute for Advanced Study, Princeton, 1960-63; Columbia Univ.: Adjunct Professor, 1960-62; Visiting Professor, 1962-63; Professor, 1963-. Nobel Prize for the non-conservation of parity

(with C. N. Yang), 1957; Albert Einstein Award in Science, 1957; Member, National Academy of Sciences, 1964. Hon. Dr Science, Princeton Univ., 1958. *Publications:* Particle Physics: an introduction to field theory; papers mostly in Physical Review. *Address:* Department of Physics, Columbia University, New York, New York 10027, USA.

LEE, Sir William (Allison), Kt 1975; OBE 1945; TD 1948; DL; Chairman, Northern Regional Health Authority, 1973-78; *b* 31 May 1907; *s* of Samuel Percy and Florence Ada Lee, Darlington; *m* 1st, 1933, Elsa Norah (*d* 1966), *d* of late Thomas Hanning, Darlington; 2nd, 1967, Mollie Clifford, *d* of late Sir Cuthbert Whiteside, Knysna, S Africa; no *c. Educ:* Queen Elizabeth Grammar Sch., Darlington. Insurance Branch Manager, retd. Served R Signals, 1935-53; Dep. Comdr, 151 Inf. Bde (TA), 1953-58; County Comdt, Durham ACF, 1962-70. Mem., Darlington RDC, 1949-61, Chm. 1957-60. Chairman: Winterton HMC, 1967-70 (Mem., 1954-70); Newcastle Reg. Hosp. Bd, 1973-74 (Mem., 1956-74). President: Darlington Civic Soc.; Darlington Branch, SSAFA; Chm., Durham Co. Coordinating Cttee, Duke of Edinburgh's Award Scheme. DL County of Durham, 1965; High Sheriff, Durham, 1978. *Recreations:* beagling, fell walking, gardening. *Address:* The Woodlands, Woodland Road, Darlington, Co. Durham. *T:* Darlington 62318.

LEE, Sir Wilton; *see* Lee, Sir G. W.

LEE YONG LENG, Dr; Professor and Head of Department of Geography, University of Singapore, since 1977; *b* 26 March 1930; *m* Wong Loon Meng; one *d. Educ:* Univs of Oxford, Malaya and Singapore. BLitt (Oxon), MA (Malaya), PhD (Singapore). Research Asst, Univ. of Malaya, 1954-56; University Lectr/Sen. Lectr, Univ. of Singapore, 1956-70; Associate Prof., Univ. of Singapore, 1970-71; High Comr for Singapore in London, 1971-75; Ambassador to Denmark, 1974-75, and Ireland, 1975; Min. of Foreign Affairs, Singapore, 1975-76. Chm., Singapore Nat. Library Bd, 1978-80. *Publications:* North Borneo, 1965; Sarawak, 1970; Southeast Asia and the Law of the Sea, 1978; The Razor's Edge: boundaries and boundary disputes in Southeast Asia, 1980; Southeast Asia: essays in political geography, 1982; articles in: Population Studies; Geog. Jl; Erdkunde; Jl Trop. Geog., etc. *Recreations:* swimming, tennis, travelling, reading. *Address:* Department of Geography, National University of Singapore, Kent Ridge, Singapore 0511. *Club:* Explorers' (NY).

LEE-BARBER, Rear-Adm. John, CB 1959; DSO 1940 and Bar 1941; Admiral Superintendent, HM Dockyard, Malta, 1957-59, retired; *b* 16 April 1905; *s* of Richard Lee-Barber, Herringfleet, near Great Yarmouth; *m* 1939, Suzanne (*d* 1976), *d* of Colonel Le Gallais, ADC, MC, La Moye, Jersey, CI; two *d. Educ:* Royal Naval Colleges, Osborne and Dartmouth. Service in destroyers and in Yangtze gunboat until 1937; CO Witch, 1937-38; CO Griffin, 1939-40-41; Commander, 1941; CO Opportune, 1942-44; 2nd in Command, HMS King Alfred, 1945; CO, HMS St James, 1946-47; Captain, 1947; Senior Officer Reserve Fleet, Harwich, 1948-49; Naval Attaché, Chile, 1950-52; CO Agincourt and Captain D4, 1952-54; Commodore, Inshore Flotilla, 1954-56; Rear-Admiral, 1957. Polish Cross of Valour, 1940. *Recreation:* sailing. *Address:* Ferry House, The Quay, Wivenhoe, Essex. *T:* Wivenhoe 2592. *Club:* Royal Ocean Racing.

LEE-STEERE, Sir Ernest (Henry), KBE 1977 (CBE 1963); JP; Lord Mayor of Perth, Western Australia, 1972-78; company director, pastoralist and grazier; *b* Perth, 22 Dec. 1912; *s* of Sir Ernest Lee-Steere, JP, KStJ; *m* 1942, Jessica Margaret, *d* of Frank Venn; two *s* three *d. Educ:* Hale Sch., Perth; St Peter's Coll., Adelaide. Served War: Captain Army/Air Liaison Group, AIF; SW Pacific Area, 1944-45. President (for WA): Pastoralists and Graziers Assoc., 1959-72; Boy Scout Assoc., 1957-64; National Trust, 1969-72. Vice-Pres., Council of Royal Flying Doctor Service of WA, 1954-59 and 1962-74. Chairman: State Adv. Cttee, CSIRO, 1962-71 (Councillor, Fed. Adv. Council, 1960-71); WA Soil Conservation Adv. Cttee, 1955-72; Aust. Capital Cities Secretariat, 1975-76; WA Turf Club, 1963- (Vice-Chm., 1959-63). Member: Nat. Council of Aust. Boy Scouts Assoc., 1959-64; Exec. Cttee of WA State Cttee, Freedom from Hunger Campaign; WA State Adv. Cttee, Aust. Broadcasting Commn, 1961-64; Aust. Jubilee Cttee for the Queen's Silver Jubilee Appeal for Young Australians, 1977; Aust. Wool Industry Conf., 1971-74 (also Mem. Exec. Cttee). Councillor: Aust. Wool Growers and Graziers Council (Pres., 1972-73); St George's Coll., Univ. of WA, 1945-81. Chm. and dir of several cos. Leader, Trade Mission to India, 1962. JP Perth, 1965. *Recreation:* polo (played in WA Polo Team in Australasian Gold Cup). *Address:* Dardanup, 26 Odern Crescent, Swanbourne, WA 6010, Australia. *T:* 384-2929. *Club:* Weld (Perth).

LEECH, John, (Hans-Joachim Freiherr von Reitzenstein); Head of External Relations and Member of Management Board, Commonwealth Development Corporation, since 1981; *b* 21 April 1925; *s* of Hans-Joachim and Josefine von Reitzenstein; *m* 1st, 1949, Mair Eiluned Davies (marr. diss. 1958); one *d*; 2nd, 1963, Noretta Conci, concert pianist. *Educ:* Bismarck Gymnasium, Berlin; Whitgift, Croydon. L. G. Mouchel & Partners, Consulting Civil Engineers, 1942-52; Bird & Co. Ltd, Calcutta, 1953-57; Dir, Europe House, London, and Exec. Mem. Council, Britain in Europe Ltd, 1958-63; Pres., Internat. Fedn of Europe Houses, 1961-65; Dir, Joint Industrial Exports Ltd, 1963-65; with Commonwealth Develt Corp., London and overseas, 1965-; Co-ordinator, Interact Gp of European develt finance instns, 1973-. Asst Dir, NATO Parliamentarians' Conf., 1959-60. Vice-Chairman:

Indian Concrete Soc., 1953–57; Anglo-Ivory Coast Soc., 1981–; Member: National Council, European Movement, 1967–; Exec. Cttee, London Symphony Orch., 1979–; Overseas Panel PR Gp, Duke of Edinburgh's Award, 1980–. Liveryman, Worshipful Co. of Paviors, 1968–. FRSA. *Publications:* The NATO Parliamentarians' Conference 1955–59, 1960; Europe and the Commonwealth, 1961; Aid and the Community, 1972; contrib. to jls on aspects of overseas develt, European matters and arts subjects. *Recreations:* music, travel, Italy. *Address:* 8 Chester Square Mews, SW1W 9DS. *T:* 01-730 2307. *Club:* Travellers'.

LEECH, Robert Radcliffe; His Honour Judge Leech; a Circuit Judge (formerly Judge of County Courts), since 1970; *b* 5 Dec. 1919; *s* of late Edwin Radcliffe Leech; *m* 1951, Vivienne Ruth, *d* of A. J. Rickerby, Carlisle; two *d. Educ:* Monmouth Sch.; Worcester Coll., Oxford (Open Classics Exhibnr 1938). Served War, 1940–44, Border Regt (despatches twice). Called to Bar, Middle Temple, 1949 (Harmsworth Law Scholar); Dep. Chm., Cumberland QS, 1966–71. *Recreations:* sailing, golf. *Address:* Scaur House, Cavendish Terrace, Stanwix, Carlisle, Cumbria; Goldsmith Building, Temple, EC4. *Clubs:* Oriental; County and Border (Carlisle).

LEECH, William Charles, CBE 1980; Founder, 1932, President (since 1975) and Director (since 1940), William Leech Ltd; *b* 15 July 1900; *s* of Albert William Leech and Lucy Sophia Wright (*née* Slack); *m* 1947, Ellen Richards; two *d. Educ:* Westgate Road Council Sch., Newcastle upon Tyne. Apprentice Engineer, 1916–21; served RFC, 1916–19; window cleaning for eleven years; started building in own name, 1932; created limited company, 1940, public company, 1976. Hon. DCL Newcastle upon Tyne, 1975; Hon. Freeman, Borough of Wallsend, 1972; Order of Distinguished Auxiliary Service, Salvation Army, 1974. Mason (Doric Lodge). *Recreation:* inside gardening. *Address:* High House, Morpeth NE61 2YU. *T:* Morpeth 513364. *Club:* Heaton Rotary (Founder Mem. 1943).

LEECHMAN, Hon. Lord; James Graham Leechman; a Senator of the College of Justice in Scotland, 1965–76; *b* 6 Oct. 1906; *s* of late Walter Graham Leechman, solicitor, Glasgow, and late Barbara Louisa Leechman (*née* Neilson); *m* 1935, Margaret Helen Edgar; two *d. Educ:* High Sch. and Univ., Glasgow. MA 1927; BSc 1928; LLB 1930. Admitted to Membership of Faculty of Advocates, 1932; Advocate-Depute, 1947–49; KC 1949; Clerk of Justiciary, 1949–64; Solicitor-Gen. for Scotland, 1964–65. *Recreation:* golf. *Address:* 626 Queensferry Road, Edinburgh EH4 6AT. *T:* 031-339 6513.

LEECHMAN, Barclay, CMG 1952; OBE 1941; Executive Director, Tanganyika Sisal Growers' Assoc., 1959–66; Chairman, Transport Licensing Authority, Tanganyika, 1956–59; Member for Social Services, Tanganyika, 1948–55; retired from Colonial Service, 1956; *b* Eastbourne, 28 Sept. 1901; *e s* of late Alleyne Leechman, MA, FLS, FCS, Bexhill, and late of Colonial Civil Service and late Jean Macmaster Leechman; *m* 1933, Grace, 4th *d* of late Frederick William Coller, Cape Town, SA; no *c. Educ:* Oundle Sch. Cadet, Colonial Administrative Service, Tanganyika, 1925; Asst District Officer, 1928; District Officer, 1937; Dep. Provincial Commissioner, 1944; Labour Commissioner, 1946. Seconded as Sec. of East African Economic Council, Nairobi, 1940–41, and Dir of Economic Control, Aden, 1943–45. Pres. Fedn of Tanganyika Employers, 1964–66 (Vice-Pres., 1959–63). Fellow, Ancient Monuments Soc. *Recreations:* books and music. *Address:* c/o Grindlay's Bank, 13 St James's Square, SW1. *Clubs:* Reform, Farmers'; City (Cape Town).

LEECHMAN, James Graham; *see* Leechman, Hon. Lord.

LEEDALE, Harry Heath, CBE 1972; Controller of Surtax and Inspector of Foreign Dividends, 1968–74; *b* 23 June 1914; *s* of John Leedale and Amy Alice Leedale (*née* Heath), New Malden; *m* 1st, 1940, Audrey Beryl (*née* Platt) (*d* 1970); one *d* ; 2nd, 1971, Sheila Tyas Stephen. *Educ:* Henry Thornton Sch., Clapham, London. Served War, RAF, 1941–46. Entered Inland Revenue, 1933; Controller, Assessments Div., 1961; Asst Clerk to Special Commissioners of Income Tax, 1963; Controller, Superannuation Funds Office, 1964. *Recreations:* gardening, foreign travel. *Address:* Lavender Cottage, Rotherfield, Sussex. *T:* Rotherfield 2424.

LEEDS, Bishop of, (RC), since 1966; **Rt. Rev. William Gordon Wheeler,** MA Oxon; *b* 5 May 1910; *o s* of late Frederick Wheeler and Marjorie (*née* Upjohn). *Educ:* Manchester Gram. Sch.; University Coll. and St Stephen's House, Oxford; Beda Coll., Rome. Curate, St Bartholomew's, Brighton, 1933; Curate, St Mary and All Saints, Chesterfield, 1934; Asst Chaplain, Lancing Coll., 1935. Received into Roman Catholic Church at Downside, 1936; Beda Coll., Rome, 1936–40; ordained priest, 1940; Asst, St Edmund's, Lower Edmonton, 1940–44; Chaplain of Westminster Cathedral and Editor of Westminster Cathedral Chronicle, 1944–50; Chaplain to the Catholics in the University, London, 1950–54, and Ecclesiastical Adviser to the Union of Catholic Students, 1953–60; Privy Chamberlain to HH The Pope, 1952; Hon. Canon of Westminster, 1954, Administrator of Cathedral, 1954–64; Created Domestic Prelate to HH Pope Pius XII, 1955; Conventual Chaplain to the British Association of the Sovereign and Military Order of Malta, 1958; Coadjutor Bishop of Middlesbrough, 1964–66. *Publications:* Edited and contributed to Homage to Newman, 1945; Richard Challoner, 1947; The English Catholics, etc. Contribs to Dublin Review, The Tablet, etc. *Address:* Bishop's House, Eltofts, Carr Lane, Thorner, Leeds LS14 3HF. *T:* Leeds 892687. *Club:* Athenæum.

LEEDS, Archdeacon of; *see* Comber, Ven. A. J.

LEEDS, Sir George (Graham Mortimer), 7th Bt *cr* 1812; *b* 21 Aug. 1927; *s* of Sir Reginald Arthur St John Leeds, 6th Bt, and Winnaretta (*d* 1980), *d* of late Paris Eugene Singer; *S* father, 1970; *m* 1954, Nicola (marr. diss. 1965, she *d* 1972), *d* of Douglas Robertson McBean, MC; three *d. Educ:* Eton. Formerly Captain, Grenadier Guards. Chm., Clive Investments (Jersey), 1977–. *Heir: cousin* Christopher Anthony Leeds [*b* 31 Aug. 1935; *m* 1974, Elaine Joyce, *d* of late Sqdn Ldr C. H. A. Mullins]. *Address:* Le Vivier, St Martin, Jersey.

LEEMING, John Coates; Under Secretary, Department of Industry, since 1979; *b* 3 May 1927; *s* of late James Arthur Leeming and Harriet Leeming; *m* 1949 (marr. diss. 1974); two *s. Educ:* Chadderton Grammar Sch., Lancs; St John's Coll., Cambridge (Schol.). Teaching, Hyde Grammar Sch., Cheshire, 1948. Asst Principal, HM Customs and Excise, 1950 (Private Sec. to Chm.); Principal: HM Customs and Excise, 1954; HM Treasury, 1956; HM Customs and Excise, 1958; Asst Sec., HM Customs and Excise, 1965; IBRD (World Bank), Washington, DC, 1967; Asst Sec., 1970, Under Sec., 1972, CSD; a Comr of Customs and Excise, 1975–79. *Recreation:* golf. *Address:* 47 Pitt Place, Church Street, Epsom, Surrey. *T:* Epsom 25397. *Club:* Royal Automobile.

LEEPER, Richard Kevin; Life President of The Lep Group plc; *b* 14 July 1894; *s* of late William John Leeper of Leeperstown, Welchtown, Co. Donegal; *m* 1916, Elizabeth Mary Fenton (*d* 1975); two *s. Educ:* Sligo Gram. Sch.; London Univ. Served in Army, European War, 1914–18; Dir of Transport, MAP, 1940–45. Engaged in shipping and forwarding in Yugoslavia, 1920–32; British Vice Consul: Dubrovnik, 1922–25; Susak, 1926–32; Managing Dir of Lep Transport Ltd and Chief Executive of the Lep Group of Companies, 1932; Chm., The Lep Gp Ltd, 1956–72. FCIT; MIFF; FRSA. KCHS; Order of St Sava (Yugoslavia), 1930. *Address:* Holly Wood House, West Byfleet, Surrey. *T:* Byfleet 42537; Sunlight Wharf, Upper Thames Street, EC4. *T:* 01-236 5050.

LEES, Prof. Anthony David, FRS 1968; Senior Research Fellow, Imperial College at Silwood Park, since 1982; *b* 27 Feb. 1917; *s* of Alan Henry Lees, MA and Mary Hughes Bomford; *m* 1943, Annzella Pauline Wilson; one *d. Educ:* Clifton Coll., Bristol; Trinity Hall, Cambridge (Schol.). BA 1939; PhD (Cantab) 1943; ScD 1966. Mem., ARC Unit of Insect Physiology at Zoology Dept, Cambridge, 1945–67; Lalor Fellow, 1956; Vis. Prof., Adelaide Univ., 1966; Hon. Lectr, London Univ., 1968; DCSO and Prof. of Insect Physiology, ARC at Imperial Coll. Field Station, Ascot, now Prof. Emeritus. Pres., Royal Entomological Soc., 1973–75. *Publications:* scientific papers. *Recreations:* gardening, fossicking. *Address:* Wells Lane Corner, Sunninghill, Ascot, Berks.

LEES, Sir Antony; *see* Lees, Sir W. A. C.

LEES, C(harles) Norman; His Honour Judge Lees; a Circuit Judge since 1980; *b* 4 Oct. 1929; *s* of late Charles Lees, Bramhall, Cheshire; *m* 1961, Stella, *d* of late Hubert Swann, Stockport; one *d. Educ:* Stockport Sch.; Univ. of Leeds. LLB 1950. Called to Bar, Lincoln's Inn, 1951. Dep. Chm., Cumberland County QS, 1969–71; a Recorder of the Crown Court, 1972–80; Chm., Mental Health Review Tribunal, Manchester Region, 1977–80 (Mem., 1971–80). *Recreations:* squash rackets, music, history. *Address:* 1 Deans Court, Crown Square, Manchester M3 3JL. *T:* 061-834 4097. *Clubs:* Lansdowne; Northern Lawn Tennis.

LEES, David, CBE 1963; Rector, The High School of Glasgow, 1950–76; *b* 12 Aug. 1910; *s* of late David Lees and Margaret W. Lees, Airdrie; *m* 1935, Olive, *d* of Arthur and Alice Willington, Montreal; one *s* two *d. Educ:* Airdrie Academy; Glasgow, McGill and London Univs. MA (Hons) Glasgow, 1930; MA in Education, McGill, 1932; BA (Hons) London, 1945. Principal Teacher of Classics, Campbeltown Gram. Sch., 1933–46; Rector, Elgin Academy, 1946–49; Dir of Education, Roxburghshire, 1949–50. Hon. LLD Glasgow, 1970. *Recreation:* bridge. *Address:* Oaklea, 16 Larch Road, Glasgow G41 5DA. *T:* 041-427 0322. *Club:* St Andrew Bridge (Glasgow).

LEES, Prof. Dennis Samuel, CBE 1980; Professor of Industrial Economics, University of Nottingham, since 1968; *b* 20 July 1924; *s* of Samuel Lees and Evelyn Lees (*née* Withers), Borrowash, Derbyshire; *m* 1950, Elizabeth Bretisch, London; two *s* one *d. Educ:* Derby Technical Coll.; Nottingham Univ. BSc(Econ), PhD. Lecturer and Reader in Economics, Keele Univ., 1951–65; Prof. of Economics, University Coll., Swansea, 1965–67. Visiting Prof. of Economics: Univ. of Chicago, 1963–64; Univ. of California, Berkeley, 1971; Univ. of Sydney, 1975. Consultant, Economists' Advisory Gp Ltd, 1967–; Chairman: Nat. Ins. Advisory Committee, 1972–80; Industrial Injuries Advisory Council, 1973–78; Mem., Adv. Council, Inst. of Econ. Affairs, 1974–. Freeman, City of London, 1973. *Publications:* Local Expenditure and Exchequer Grants, 1956; Health Thru Choice, 1961; Economic Consequences of the Professions, 1966; Economics of Advertising, 1967; Financial Facilities for Small Firms, 1971; Impairment, Disability, Handicap, 1974; Economics of Personal Injury, 1976; Solicitors' Remuneration in Ireland, 1977; articles on industrial and social policy in: Economica, Jl of Political Economy, Amer. Econ. Rev., Jl of Law and Econ., Jl Industrial Econ., Jl Public Finance. *Recreations:* cricket and pottering.

Address: 8 Middleton Crescent, Beeston, Nottingham. *T:* Nottingham 258730.

LEES, Geoffrey William; Headmaster, St Bees School, 1963–80; *b* 1 July 1920; *o s* of late Mr F. T. Lees and of Mrs Lees, Manchester; *m* 1949, Joan Needham, *yr d* of late Mr and Mrs J. Needham, Moseley, Birmingham. *Educ:* King's Sch., Rochester; Downing Coll., Cambridge. Royal Signals, 1940–46 (despatches): commissioned 1941; served in NW Europe and Middle East, Captain. 2nd Class Hons English Tripos, Pt I, 1947; History Tripos, Part II, 1948; Asst Master, Brighton Coll., 1948–63. Leave of absence in Australia, Asst Master, Melbourne Church of England Gram. Sch., 1961–62. *Recreations:* reading, games, walking. *Address:* 10 Merlin Close, Upper Drive, Hove, Sussex BN3 6NU. *Clubs:* MCC; Hawks', Union (Cambridge).

LEES, Norman; *see* Lees, C. N.

LEES, Roland James, CB 1977; Director, Royal Signals and Radar Establishment, Malvern, 1976–77, retired; *b* 3 Dec. 1917; *s* of late Roland John Lees and late Ada Bell (*née* Jeavons), Stourbridge, Worcs; *m* 1948, Ésmé Joyce, *d* of late Alfred Thomas Hill, Malvern Link, Worcs; no *c. Educ:* King Edward's Sch., Stourbridge; St John's Coll., Cambridge. BA Cantab 1939; BSc London 1939; MA Cantab 1942. Dir, Scientific Research Electronics and Guided Weapons, Min. of Supply, 1955–56; Head of Airborne Radar Dept, RRE, 1957–58; Head of Instruments and Electrical Engrg Dept, RAE, 1959–62; Dir, Signals Research and Development Establishment, 1963–65; Dep. Dir (Equipment), RAE, 1966–72; Dir, RRE, 1972–76. Chm., Air Traffic Control Bd, 1978–81; Mem., PO Engineering Adv. Cttee, 1978–81. Assessor to Lord Mountbatten, Inquiry into Prison Security, 1966. *Address:* Fairoaks, 4 Frensham Vale, Lower Bourne, Farnham, Surrey GU10 3HN. *T:* Frensham 3146.

LEES, Air Marshal Sir Ronald Beresford, KCB 1961 (CB 1946); CBE 1943; DFC; retired as C-in-C, RAF, Germany, 1963–65; *b* 27 April 1910; *s* of John Thomas and Elizabeth Lees; *m* 1931, Rhoda Lillie Pank; one *s* one *d. Educ:* St Peter's Coll., Adelaide, Australia. Joined Royal Australian Air Force, 1930; transferred Royal Air Force, 1931. ADC to the Queen, 1952–53 (to King George VI, 1949–52); AOC No 83 Gp, 2nd TAF in Germany, 1952–55; Asst Chief of Air Staff (Operations), 1955–58; SASO, Fighter Command, 1958–60; Dep. Chief of the Air Staff, 1960–63; Air Marshal, 1961. *Address:* Jelbra, RMB 367, Albury, NSW 2640, Australia. *Club:* Commercial.

LEES, Sir Thomas (Edward), 4th Bt, *cr* 1897; landowner; *b* 31 Jan. 1925; 2nd *s* of Sir John Victor Elliott Lees, 3rd Bt, DSO, MC, and Madeline A. P. (*d* 1967), *d* of Sir Harold Pelly, 4th Bt; *S* father 1955; *m* 1949, Faith Justin, *d* of G. G. Jessiman, OBE, Great Durnford, Wilts; one *s* three *d. Educ:* Eton; Magdalene Coll., Cambridge. Served War in RAF; discharged 1945, after losing eye. Magdalene, Cambridge, 1945–47; BA Cantab 1947 (Agriculture). Since then has farmed at and managed South Lytchett estate. Chairman: Lytchett Minster Gospel Film Assoc. Ltd; Post Green Community Trust Ltd. Mem., General Synod of C of E, 1970–. JP 1951, CC 1952–74, High Sheriff 1960, Dorset. *Recreation:* sailing. *Heir: s* Christopher James Lees [*b* 4 Nov. 1952; *m* 1977, Jennifer, *d* of John Wyllie]. *Address:* Post Green, Lytchett Minster, Poole, Dorset. *T:* Lytchett Minster 622048. *Clubs:* Farmers', Royal Cruising.

LEES, Sir Thomas Harcourt Ivor, 8th Bt *cr* (UK) 1804, of Black Rock, County Dublin; *b* 6 Nov. 1941; *s* of Sir Charles Archibald Edward Ivor Lees, 7th Bt, and of Lily, *d* of Arthur Williams, Manchester; *S* father, 1963. *Heir: kinsman* John Cathcart d'Olier-Lees [*b* 12 Nov. 1927; *m* 1957, Wendy Garrold, *yr d* of late Brian Garrold Groom; two *s*].

LEES, Dr William, CBE 1970; TD 1962; FRCOG; Senior Principal Medical Officer, Department of Health and Social Security, 1977–81; *b* 18 May 1924; *s* of William Lees and Elizabeth Lees (*née* Massey); *m* 1947, Winifred Elizabeth (*née* Hanford); three *s. Educ:* Queen Elizabeth's, Blackburn; Victoria Univ., Manchester. MB ChB; LRCP; MRCS; MRCOG, FRCOG; DPH; MFCM. Obstetrics and Gynaecology, St Mary's Hosps, Manchester, 1947–58; Min. of Health, later DHSS, 1959–; Under Sec., 1977. QHP, 1969–72. Col, 10th, later no 257, Gen. Hosp., TAVR RAMC, 1966–71; Col Comdt, NW London Sector, ACF, 1971–76; Mem. for Greater London, TA&VRA, 1966–. OStJ 1967. *Publications:* numerous contribs on: intensive therapy, progressive patient care, perinatal mortality, day surgery, district general hospital. *Recreations:* music, golf, travel. *Address:* 13 Hall Park Hill, Berkhamsted, Herts. *T:* Berkhamsted 3010. *Clubs:* Athenæum; St John's.

LEES, Sir (William) Antony Clare, 3rd Bt *cr* 1937; *b* 14 June 1935; *s* of Sir (William) Hereward Clare Lees, 2nd Bt, and of Lady (Dorothy Gertrude) Lees, *d* of F. A. Lauder; *S* father, 1976. *Educ:* Eton; Magdalene Coll., Cambridge (MA). *Heir:* none. *Address:* Waterside Cottage, New Mill, Pewsey, Wilts SN9 5LD.

LEES-MILNE, James; *b* 6 Aug. 1908; *er s* of George Crompton Lees-Milne, Crompton Hall, Lancs and Wickhamford Manor, Worcs; *m* 1951, Alvilde, formerly wife of 3rd Viscount Chaplin and *d* of late Lt-Gen. Sir Tom Molesworth Bridges, KCB, KCMG, DSO; no *c. Educ:* Eton Coll.; Magdalen Coll., Oxford. Private Sec. to 1st Baron Lloyd, 1931–35; on staff, Reuters, 1935–36; on staff, National Trust, 1936–66; Adviser on Historic Buildings to National Trust, 1951–66. 2nd Lieut Irish Guards, 1940–41 (invalided). FRSL

1957; FSA 1974. *Publications:* The National Trust (ed), 1945; The Age of Adam, 1947; National Trust Guide: Buildings, 1948; Tudor Renaissance, 1951; The Age of Inigo Jones, 1953; Roman Mornings, 1956 (Heinemann Award, 1956); Baroque in Italy, 1959; Baroque in Spain and Portugal, 1960; Earls of Creation, 1962; Worcestershire: A Shell Guide, 1964; St Peter's, 1967; English Country Houses: Baroque 1685–1714, 1970; Another Self, 1970; Heretics in Love, 1973; Ancestral Voices, 1975; William Beckford, 1976; Prophesying Peace, 1977; Round the Clock, 1978; Harold Nicolson, vol. I, 1980, vol. II, 1981 (Heinemann Award, RSL, 1982); (with David Ford) Images of Bath, 1982. *Recreations:* walking, sightseeing. *Address:* Essex House, Badminton, Avon GL9 1DD. *T:* Badminton 288. *Club:* Brooks's.

LEES-SPALDING, Rear-Adm. Ian Jaffery, CB 1973; RN retd; Joint Editor, Macmillan and Silk Cut Nautical Almanac, since 1980; *b* London, 16 June 1920; *s* of Frank Souter Lees-Spalding and Joan (*née* Bodilly); *m* 1946, June Sandys Lyster Sparkes; two *d. Educ:* Blundells Sch.; RNEC. Served War of 1939–45 (King's Commendation for Bravery, 1941; Royal Lifesaving Inst. medal, 1942); served in HMS Sirius, HM S/Ms Trespasser, Teredo, Truculent and Andrew, HMS Cleopatra and Tiger; Chief of Staff to C-in-C Naval Home Comd, 1969; CSO (Technical) to C-in-C Fleet, 1971; retd 1974. Administrator, London Internat. Film Sch., 1975–79. *Recreations:* music, travelling. *Address:* St Olaf's, Wonston, Winchester, Hants S021 3LP. *T:* Sutton Scotney 249. *Club:* Army and Navy.

LEESE, Sir John Henry Vernon, 5th Bt *cr* 1908; *b* 7 Aug. 1901; *s* of Vernon Francis Leese, OBE (*d* 1927) and Edythe Gwendoline (*d* 1929), *d* of Charles Frederick Stevenson; *g s* of Sir Joseph Francis Leese, 1st Bt; *S* cousin, 1979. *Heir:* none.

LE FANU, George Victor Sheridan; Serjeant at Arms, House of Commons, since 1982; *b* 1925; *s* of late Maj.-Gen. Roland Le Fanu, DSO, MC, and Marguerite (*née* Lumsden); *m* 1956, Elizabeth, *d* of late Major Herbert Hall and Kitty (*née* Gauvain); three *s. Educ:* Shrewsbury School. Served Coldstream Guards, 1943–63; Asst-Adjt, Royal Military Academy, Sandhurst, 1949–52; Adjt 2nd Bn Coldstream Guards, 1952–55; sc Camberley, 1959; Staff Captain to Vice-Quartermaster-General to the Forces, War Office, 1960–61; GSO2, Headquarters London District, 1961–63; Dep. Asst Serjeant at Arms, House of Commons, 1963–76; Asst Serjeant at Arms, 1976–81; Deputy Serjeant at Arms, 1981–82. *Address:* Speaker's Court, House of Commons, SW1A 0AA.

LE FANU, Mark; General Secretary, The Society of Authors, since 1982; *b* 14 Nov. 1946; *s* of Admiral Sir Michael Le Fanu, GCB, DSC and Prudence, *d* of Admiral Sir Vaughan Morgan, KBE, CB, MVO, DSC; *m* 1976, Lucy Cowen; two *s. Educ:* Winchester; Univ. of Sussex. Admitted Solicitor, 1976. Served RN, 1964–73; McKenna & Co., 1973–78; The Society of Authors, 1979–. *Recreations:* canals, travel, washing up. *Address:* 25 St James's Gardens, W11 4RE. *Club:* PEN.

LE FANU, Mrs W. R.; *see* Maconchy, Elizabeth.

LEFEBVRE, Prof. Arthur Henry; Distinguished Reilly Professor of Combustion Engineering, School of Mechanical Engineering, Purdue University, since 1979 (Professor and Head of School, 1976–80); *b* 14 March 1923; *s* of Henri and May Lefebvre; *m* 1952, Elizabeth Marcella Betts; two *s* one *d. Educ:* Long Eaton Grammar Sch; Nottingham Univ.; Imperial Coll., London. DSc (Eng), DIC, PhD, CEng, FIMechE, FRAeS. Ericssons Telephones Ltd: Engrg apprentice, 1938–41; Prodn Engr, 1941–47; res. work on combustion and heat transfer in gas turbines, Rolls Royce, Derby, 1952–61; Prof. of Aircraft Propulsion, Coll. of Aeronautics, 1961–71; Prof. and Hd of Sch. of Mechanical Engrg, Cranfield Inst. of Technol., 1971–76. Mem., AGARD Combustion and Propulsion Panel, 1957–61; Mem., AGARD Propulsion and Energetics Panel, 1970–76; Chm., Combustion Cttee, Aeronautical Res. Council, 1970–74. *Publications:* papers on combustion and heat transfer in Proc. Royal Soc., internat. symposium vols on combustion, combustion and flame, combustion science and technology. *Recreations:* music, reading, golf. *Address:* 1741 Redwood Lane, Lafayette, Indiana 47905, USA. *T:* (317) 447-0117.

LEFEVER, Kenneth Ernest, CB 1974; Deputy Chairman, Civil Service Appeal Board, 1978–80 (Official Side Member, 1976–78); *b* 22 Feb. 1915; *s* of E. S. Lefever and Mrs E. E. Lefever; *m* 1939, Margaret Ellen Bowley; one *s* one *d. Educ:* County High Sch., Ilford. Board of Customs and Excise: joined Dept as Officer, 1935; War Service, 1942–46 (Captain, RE); Principal Inspector, 1966; Dep. Chief Inspector, 1969; Collector, London Port, 1971; Chief Inspector, 1972; Dir of Organisation and Chief Inspector, 1974; Comr, Bd of Customs and Excise, 1972–75, retd. *Recreations:* gardening, walking, cricket. *Address:* Trebarwith, 37 Surman Crescent, Hutton Burses, Brentwood, Essex. *T:* Brentwood 212110. *Clubs:* MCC, Civil Service.

LE FEVRE, Prof. Raymond James Wood, PhD, DSc London; FRS; FRSC; FRACI; FAA; Professor of Chemistry, 1946–71, now Emeritus, and Head of the School of Chemistry, 1948–71, in the University of Sydney; *b* 1 April 1905; *s* of Raymond James and Ethel May Le Fevre; *m* 1931, Catherine Gunn Tideman, DSc; one *d* (one *s* decd). *Educ:* Isleworth County Sch.; Queen Mary Coll., University of London. Lecturer in Organic Chemistry, University Coll., London, 1928; Reader, 1939; Chemical Adviser to RAF and RAAF in UK, Far East, and Australia, 1939–44; Asst Dir R & D (Armament Chemistry),

Ministry of Aircraft Production, London, 1944; Head, Chem. Dept, RAE Farnborough, 1944-46. Hon. Associate and Professorial Fellow, Macquarie Univ., NSW, 1971-. Trustee, Mitchell Library, Sydney, 1947; Mem., Development Council NSW University of Technology, 1948-50; Trustee, Museum of Applied Arts and Science, Sydney, 1947-75. Foundation Fellow, Austr. Acad. of Science, 1953. Liversidge Lecturer, 1960; Masson Lecturer, ANZAAS, 1967; Pres., Royal Society NSW, 1961. Pres. NSW Br., Royal Aust. Chem. Inst. Smith Medal, Royal Aust. Chem. Inst., 1952; Coronation Medal, 1953; Medal of Royal Soc. of NSW, 1969. Fellow, Queen Mary Coll., London, 1962. *Publications:* Dipole Moments, 3rd edn 1953; Molecular Polarizability and Refractivity, 1965; Establishment of Chemistry within Australian Science, 1968; about 450 papers on chemical research topics, mostly in Jl Chem. Soc., Trans. Faraday Soc., Austr. Jl Chem., etc. *Recreation:* pleasant work. *Address:* 6 Aubrey Road, Northbridge, Sydney, NSW 2063, Australia. *T:* 951018.

LEFF, Prof. Gordon; Professor of History, University of York, since 1969; *b* 9 May 1926; *m* 1953, Rosemary Kathleen (*née* Fox) (marr. diss. 1980); one *s. Educ:* Summerhill Sch.; King's Coll., Cambridge. BA 1st Cl. Hons, PhD, LittD. Fellow, King's Coll., Cambridge, 1955-59; Asst Lectr, Lectr, Sen. Lectr, in History, Manchester Univ., 1956-65; Reader in History, Univ. of York, 1965-69. Carlyle Vis. Lectr, Univ. of Oxford, 1983. *Publications:* Bradwardine and the Pelagians, 1957; Medieval Thought, 1958; Gregory of Rimini, 1961; The Tyranny of Concepts, 1961; Richard Fitzralph, 1963; Heresy in the Later Middle Ages, 2 vols, 1967; Paris and Oxford Universities in 13th and 14th Centuries, 1968; History and Social Theory, 1969; William of Ockham: the metamorphosis of scholastic discourse, 1975; The Dissolution of the Medieval Outlook, 1976. *Recreations:* walking, gardening, watching cricket, listening to music. *Address:* The Sycamores, 12 The Village, Strensall, York YO3 5XS. *T:* York 490358.

le FLEMING, Morris John; Chief Executive, Hertfordshire County Council, since 1979; *b* 19 Aug. 1932; *s* of late Morris Ralph le Fleming and Mabel le Fleming; *m* 1960, Jenny Rose Weeks; one *s* three *d. Educ:* Tonbridge Sch.; Magdalene Coll., Cambridge (BA). Admitted Solicitor, 1958. Junior Solicitor, Worcester CC, 1958-59; Asst Solicitor: Middlesex CC, 1959; Nottinghamshire CC, 1959-63; Asst Clerk, Lindsey (Lincolnshire) CC, 1963-69; Second Dep. Clerk, 1969-74, County Secretary, 1974-79, Hertfordshire CC. *Address:* 14 Swangleys Lane, Knebworth, Herts SG3 6AA. *T:* Stevenage 813152.

LE FLEMING, Peter Henry John; Regional Administrator, South East Thames Regional Health Authority, since 1981; *b* 25 Oct. 1923; *s* of late Edward Ralph Le Fleming and Irene Louise Le Fleming (*née* Adams); *m* 1949, Gudrun Svendsen (marr. diss. 1981); two *s. Educ:* Addison Gardens Sch., Hammersmith; Pembroke Coll., Cambridge. MA; FHA. Served 1942-47, RTR and Parachute Regt, MEF, CMF, Palestine; commnd 1943. Sudan Political Service, Equatoria, Kassala, Blue Nile Provinces, 1949-55; NHS, 1955-: Redevelt Sec., St Thomas's Hosp., London, 1955-57; Hosp. Sec., The London Hosp., 1957-61; Dep. Clerk to the Governors, Guy's Hosp., 1961-69; Gp Sec., Exeter and Mid Devon Hosp. Management Cttee, 1969-74; Area Administrator, Kent AHA, 1974-81. *Recreations:* long distance fell walking, breeding and showing elkhounds, trad jazz and serious music. *Address:* Kenmor, Paynesfield Road, Tatsfield, Westerham, Kent TN16 2BG. *T:* Tatsfield 845.

le FLEMING, Sir William Kelland, 11th Bt *cr* 1705; *b* 27 April 1922; *s* of Sir Frank Thomas le Fleming, 10th Bt, and of Isabel Annie Fraser, *d* of late James Craig, Manaia, NZ; *S* father, 1971; *m* 1948, Noveen Avis, *d* of C. C. Sharpe, Rukuhia, Hamilton, NZ; three *s* four *d. Heir: s* Quentin John le Fleming [*b* 27 June 1949; *m* 1971, Judith Ann, *d* of C. J. Peck, JP; one *s* one *d*]. *Address:* Kopane RD6, Palmerston North, New Zealand.

LE GALLAIS, Sir Richard (Lyle), Kt 1965; Regional Chairman, Industrial Tribunals (Bristol), since 1972; *b* 15 Nov. 1916; *s* of late William Le Gallais and Mrs Cory; *m* 1947, Juliette, *d* of late Lt-Col P. A. Forsythe, KRRC; two *s. Educ:* Victoria Coll., Jersey; Inns of Court Sch. of Law. Called to Bar, 1939. Served War of 1939-45, W Africa and Burma; Dep. Asst JAG (SEAC) 1945. Pres. War Crimes Tribunal, Singapore, 1946 (Lt-Col). Advocate, Royal Court, Jersey, 1947; Resident Magistrate, Kenya, 1949; Sen. Res. Magistrate and Acting Puisne Judge, N Rhodesia, 1958; Chief Justice, Aden, 1960-67. Mem. Panel of Chairmen, Industrial Tribunals for England and Wales, 1968-72. *Recreations:* gastronomy, music. *Address:* Bainly House, Gillingham, Dorset. *T:* Bourton 840373.

LE GALLIENNE, Eva; Theatrical Producer, Director and Actress; *b* London, England, 11 Jan. 1899; *d* of Richard Le Gallienne and Julie Norregaard. *Educ:* College Sévigné, Paris, France. Début Prince of Wales Theatre, London, in The Laughter of Fools, 1915; New York Début in The Melody of Youth, 1916; appeared in NY and on tour, in Mr Lazarus, season of 1916-17; with Ethel Barrymore in The Off Chance, 1917-18; Not So Long Ago, 1920-21; Liliom, 1921-22; The Swan, 1923; Hannele in The Assumption of Hannele, by Hauptmann, 1923; Jeanne d'Arc, by Mercedes de Acosta, 1925; The Call of Life, by Schnitzler, 1925; The Master Builder, by Henrik Ibsen, 1925-26. Founder and Director Civic Repertory Theatre, NY, 1926; played in Saturday Night, The Three Sisters, Cradle Song, 2x2-5, The First Stone, Improvisations in June, The Would-Be Gentleman, L'Invitation au Voyage, The Cherry Orchard, Peter Pan, On the High Road, The Lady from Alfaqueque, Katerina,

The Open Door, A Sunny Morning, The Master Builder, John Gabriel Borkman, La Locandiera, Twelfth Night, Inheritors, The Good Hope, Hedda Gabler, The Sea Gull, Mlle. Bourrat, The Living Corpse, Women Have Their Way, Romeo and Juliet, The Green Cockatoo, Siegfried, Allison's House, Camille, Liliom (revival), Dear Jane, Alice in Wonderland, L'Aiglon, 1934; Rosmersholm, 1935; Uncle Harry, 1942; Cherry Orchard, 1944; Thérèse, 1945; Elizabeth I in Schiller's Mary Stuart, Phœnix Theatre, NYC, 1958; toured in same, 1959-60; Elizabeth the Queen, 1961-62; The Sea Gull, 1963; Ring Round the Moon, 1963; The Mad Woman of Chaillot, 1964; The Trojan Women, 1964; Exit the King, 1967; All's Well That Ends Well, Amer. Shakespeare Theatre, 1970; Mrs Woodfin in The Dream Watcher, 1975; Fanny Cavendish in The Royal Family, NYC, 1976, tour, 1977; To Grandmother's House We Go, NYC, 1981; *film:* Resurrection, 1980. Man. Dir of Amer. Repertory Theatre, which did six classic revivals in repertory, NY, 1946 and 1947; Dir The Cherry Orchard, Lyceum Theatre, NY, 1967-68. MA (Tufts Coll.), 1927, and several honorary doctorates from 1930. Member Actors' Equity Assoc. and Managers' Protective Assoc. Has won various awards; Gold Medal, Soc. Arts and Sciences, 1926; Am. Acad. of Arts and Letters medal for good speech, 1945; Drama League Award, 1976; Handel Medallion, 1976; Anta Award, 1977. Cross of St Olav (Norway), 1961. *Publications:* At 33 (autobiography), 1934; Flossie and Bossy, (NY) 1949, (London) 1950; With A Quiet Heart, 1953; A Preface to Hedda Gabler, 1953; The Master Builder, a new translation with a Prefatory Study, 1955; trans. Six Plays by Henrik Ibsen, 1957 (NYC); trans. The Wild Duck and Other Plays by Henrik Ibsen, 1961 (NYC); The Mystic in the Theatre: Eleonora Duse, 1966 (NYC and London); trans. The Spider and Other Stories by Carl Evald, 1980; articles for New York Times, Theatre Arts Monthly, etc. *Recreations:* gardening, painting. *Address:* Weston, Conn 06880, USA.

LEGARD, Capt. Sir Thomas (Digby), 14th Bt, *cr* 1660; Captain Royal Artillery; *b* 16 Oct. 1905; *e s* of Sir D. A. H. Legard, 13th Bt; *S* father, 1961; *m* 1935, Mary Helen, *e d* of late Lt-Col E. G. S. L'Estrange Malone; three *s. Educ:* Lancing; Magdalene Coll., Cambridge. *Heir: s* Charles Thomas Legard [*b* 26 Oct. 1938; *m* 1962, Elizabeth, *d* of John M. Guthrie, High House, East Ayton, Scarborough; two *s* one *d*]. *Address:* Scampston Hall, Malton, North Yorks. *T:* Rillington 224. *Club:* MCC.

LÉGER, His Eminence Cardinal Paul Emile; *b* Valleyfield, Quebec, Canada, 26 April 1904; *s* of Ernest Léger and Alda Beauvais. *Educ:* Ste-Thérèse Seminary; Grand Seminary, Montreal. Seminary of Philosophy, Paris, 1930-31; Seminary of Theology, Paris, 1931-32; Asst Master of Novices, Paris, 1932-33; Superior Seminary of Fukuoka, Japan, 1933-39; Prof., Seminary of Philosophy, Montreal, 1939-40; Vicar-Gen., Diocese of Valleyfield, 1940-47; Rector, Canadian Coll., Rome, 1947-50; consecrated bishop in Rome and apptd to See of Montreal, 1950; elevated to Sacred Coll. of Cardinals and given titular Church of St Mary of the Angels, 1953; Archbishop of Montreal, 1950-67; resigned to work as a missionary in Africa; Parish Priest, St Madeleine Sophie Barat parish, Montreal, 1974-75. Variety Club award, 1976. Has several hon. doctorates both from Canada and abroad. Holds foreign decorations. *Address:* CP1500-Succursale A, Montréal, PQ H3C 2Z9, Canada.

LEGG, Allan Aubrey R.; *see* Rowan-Legg.

LEGG, Keith (Leonard Charles), OBE 1981; PhD, MSc, BSc (Eng); CEng, FIMechE, FRAeS, FCIT; FHKIE; JP; Director, Hong Kong Polytechnic, since 1975; *b* 24 Oct. 1924; *s* of E. H. J. Legg; *m* 1947, Joan, *d* of H. E. Green; two *s. Educ:* London Univ. (External); Cranfield Inst. of Technology. Engineering apprenticeship, 1940-45; Dep. Chief Research and Test Engr, Asst Chief Designer, Chief Project and Structural Engr, Short Bros & Harland Ltd, Belfast, 1942-56; Chief Designer and Prof., Brazilian Aeronautical Centre, São Paulo, 1956-60; Head of Dept and Prof., Loughborough Univ. of Technology, 1960-72 (Sen. Pro Vice-Chancellor, 1967-70); Dir, Lanchester Polytechnic, 1972-75. Chm., Internat. Directing Cttee, CERI/OECD Higher Educn Institutional Management, 1973-75; Member: Road Transport Industrial Trng Bd, 1966-75; Council, Royal Aeronautical Soc. (Chm., Hong Kong Br., RAeS); Hong Kong Management Assoc. Council; Bd of Educn; Environmental and Pollution Council of Hong Kong; Hong Kong Productivity Council. Adviser to OECD in Paris; Mem. various nat. and professional cttees. Fellow, Hong Kong Inst. Engrg. Hon. DTech Loughborough, 1982. *Publications:* numerous: on aerospace structures and design, transport systems, higher educn and educnl analytical models. *Recreations:* most sports, especially tennis, badminton and squash; aid to the handicapped. *Address:* Hong Kong Polytechnic, Hung Hom, Kowloon. *T:* Kowloon 638344; 19 Broom Park, Broom Road, Teddington, Middlesex. *T:* 01-977 8215.

LEGG, Thomas Stuart; Deputy Secretary, Lord Chancellor's Office, since 1982; *b* 13 Aug. 1935; *e s* of Stuart and Margaret Legg; *m* 1961, Patricia Irene, *d* of David Lincoln Dowie; two *d. Educ:* Frensham Heights Sch., Surrey; St John's Coll., Cambridge (MA, LLB). Served Royal Marines, 1953-55. Called to the Bar, Inner Temple, 1960; joined Lord Chancellor's Dept, 1962; Private Secretary to Lord Chancellor, 1965-68; Asst Solicitor, 1975; Under Sec., 1977-82; SE Circuit Administrator, 1980-82. *Recreations:* reading, walking. *Address:* 43 Inverness Street, NW1 7HB. *T:* 01-485 9962.

LEGGATE, John Mortimer, MB, ChB, FRCS; Dean of the Faculty of Medicine, University of Liverpool, 1953-69, retired; *b* 7 April 1904; *s* of late

Dr James Leggate, Liverpool; *m* 1936, Grace, *d* of late Rev. John Clark, Newport, Fife; one *s*. *Educ:* Liverpool Coll.; University of Liverpool. Gladstone Divinity Prize, 1923; Pres., Guild of Undergraduates, University of Liverpool, 1927-28; MB, ChB (Hons) 1929; MRCS, LRCP, 1929; FRCS, 1933; John Rankin Fellow in Anatomy, 1929-30. Resident Surgical Officer and Surgical Tutor, Liverpool Royal Infirmary, 1932; Prof. of Surgery, Moukden Med. Coll. (Manchuria), 1935-41 and 1946-49; Resident Asst Surgeon, David Lewis Northern Hosp., Liverpool, 1941-43. Served War of 1939-45, Major, RAMC, comdg Field Surgical Unit, D Day Landing, 1944 (despatches); OC Surgical Div. of a Gen. Hosp. in India, 1945-46; demobilised, 1946 (Hon. Lt-Col). Sen. Registrar in Neuro-Surgical Unit at Walton Hosp., Liverpool, 1950-51. *Address:* 19 Skipton Avenue, Banks Road, Southport, Merseyside. *T:* Southport 29171.

LEGGATT, Hon. Sir Andrew (Peter), Kt 1982; **Hon. Mr Justice Leggatt;** a Judge of the High Court of Justice, Queen's Bench Division, since 1982; *b* 8 Nov. 1930; *er s* of Captain William Ronald Christopher Leggatt, DSO, RN and Dorothea Joy Leggatt (*née* Dreyer); *m* 1953, Gillian Barbara Newton; one *s* one *d*. *Educ:* Eton; King's Coll., Cambridge (Exhibr). MA 1957. Commn in Rifle Bde, 1949-50; TA, 1950-59. Called to the Bar, Inner Temple, 1954, Bencher, 1976; QC 1972. A Recorder of the Crown Court, 1974-82. Mem., Bar Council, 1971-82; Mem. Senate, 1974-; Chm. of the Bar, 1981-82. Hon. Member: American Bar Assoc.; Canadian Bar Assoc.; Mem., Top Salaries Review Body, 1979-82. Inspector (for Dept of Trade), London & Counties Securities Group, 1975. *Recreations:* gardening, listening to music. *Address:* The Old Vicarage, Old Woking, Surrey GU22 9JF. *T:* Woking 63734; 3 Gray's Inn Place, WC1R 5EA. *T:* 01-831 8441. *Clubs:* MCC, Pilgrims.

LEGGATT, Hugh Frank John; Senior Partner, Leggatt Brothers (Fine Art Dealers); *b* 27 Feb. 1925; 2nd *s* of late Henry and Beatrice Leggatt; *m* 1953, Jennifer Mary Hepworth; two *s*. *Educ:* Eton; New Coll., Oxford. RAF, 1943-46. Joined Leggatt Bros, 1946; Partner, 1953; Senior Partner, 1962. Pres., Fine Art Trade Provident Instn, 1960-63; Chm., Soc. of London Art Dealers, 1966-70. Hon. Sec., Heritage in Danger, 1974-. *Publications:* contribs to newspapers and jls. *Address:* 3 Albert Place, W8. *T:* 01-937 3797. *Club:* White's.

LEGGE, family name of **Earl of Dartmouth.**

LEGGE, Prof. (Mary) Dominica, FBA 1974; Personal Professor of French (Anglo-Norman Studies), University of Edinburgh, 1968-73, Professor Emeritus, 1973; *b* 26 March 1905; 2nd *d* of late James Granville Legge and Josephine (*née* Makins). *Educ:* Liverpool Coll., Huyton; Somerville Coll., Oxford. BA Hon. Mod. Lang, BLitt, MA, DLitt. Editor, Selden Soc., 1928-34; Mary Somerville Res. Fellow, 1935-37; Asst Lectr, Royal Holloway Coll., 1938-42; Voluntary asst, BoT, 1942; Asst, Dundee Univ. Coll., 1942; Lectr, 1943, Reader, 1953, Univ. of Edinburgh. Hon. Fellow, Somerville Coll., 1968. FRHistS, FSAScot; Corresp. Fellow, Mediaeval Acad. of America. Officier des Palmes Académiques. *Publications:* (with Sir William Holdsworth) Year-Book of 10 Edward II, 1934-35; Anglo-Norman Letters and Petitions, 1941; (with E. Vinaver) Le Roman de Balain, 1942; Anglo-Norman in the Cloisters, 1950; Anglo-Norman Literature and its Background, 1963; (with R. J. Dean) The Rule of St Benedict, 1964; contribs to learned jls and volumes, British and foreign. *Recreations:* music, walking. *Address:* 191a Woodstock Road, Oxford OX2 7AB. *T:* Oxford 56455. *Clubs:* Royal Over-Seas League; University of Edinburgh Staff.

LEGGE, Rt. Rev. William Gordon, DD; *b* 20 Jan. 1913; *s* of Thomas Legge and Jane (*née* Gill); *m* 1941, Hyacinth Florence Richards; one *s* one *d*. *Educ:* Bishop Feild and Queen's Colls, St John's, Newfoundland. Deacon 1938, priest 1939; Curate, Channel, 1938-41; Incumbent of Botwood, 1941-44; Rector, Bell Island, 1944-55; Sec., Diocesan Synod, 1955-68; Archdeacon of Avalon, 1955-68; Canon of Cathedral, 1955-76; Diocesan Registrar, 1957-68; Suffragan Bishop, 1968; Bishop of Western Newfoundland, 1976-78. DD *hc*, Univ. of King's College, Halifax, NS, 1973. *Address:* 52 Glenhaven Boulevard, Corner Brook, Newfoundland A2H 4P6.

LEGGETT, Sir Clarence (Arthur Campbell), Kt 1980; MBE (mil.) 1943; FRACS, FACS; Surgeon, Queensland; *b* 24 July 1911; *s* of late A. J. Leggett; *m* 1939, Avril, *d* of R. L. Bailey; one *s* two *d*. *Educ:* Sydney Univ.; Queensland Univ. MB BS (Sydney); MS, MA (Queensland). RMO, Royal Prince Alfred Hosp., Sydney, 1927-38; Asst Dep. Med. Supt, 1939. Major, AAMC, 1941-46. Asst Surgeon, Royal Brisbane Hosp., 1941-51; Junior Surg., 1951-56; Senior Surg., Princess Alexandra Hosp., Brisbane, 1956-68; Hon. Cons. Surgeon, 1968-. University of Queensland: Hon. Demonstrator and Examiner, Anatomy Dept, 1941-47; Chief Asst, Dept of Surgery, 1947-51; Mem. Faculty Bd, 1947-51; Special Lectr, 1951-68. Member of Council: Queensland Inst. for Med. Research, 1948-65; RACS, 1966-75 (Chm. Court of Examiners, 1971-75; Junior Vice-Pres., 1973-75). *Address:* 217 Wickham Terrace, Brisbane, Queensland 4000, Australia.

LEGGETT, Douglas Malcolm Aufrère, MA, PhD, DSc; FRAeS; FIMA; Vice-Chancellor, University of Surrey, 1966-Sept. 1975; *b* 27 May 1912; *s* of George Malcolm Kent Leggett and Winifred Mabel Horsfall; *m* 1943, Enid Vida Southall; one *s* one *d*. *Educ:* Rugby Sch.; Edinburgh Univ.; Trinity Coll., Cambridge. Wrangler, 1934; Fellow of Trinity Coll., Cambridge, 1937; Queen Mary Coll., London, 1937-39; Royal Aircraft Establishment, 1939-45; Royal Aeronautical Society, 1945-50; King's Coll., London, 1950-60;

Principal, Battersea Coll. of Technology, 1960-66. FKC 1974; DUniv Surrey 1975. *Publications:* contrib. to scientific and technical jls. *Address:* Southlands, Fairoak Lane, Oxshott, Surrey. *T:* Oxshott 3061.

LEGGETT, Sir Frederick William, KBE 1951; Kt 1941; CB 1933; *b* 23 Dec. 1884; *s* of late F. J. Leggett and Frances Mary, *d* of William Murphy, Huntingdon; *m* 1st, Edith Guinevere (*d* 1949), *d* of Henry Kitson, Woodford; one *s* three *d*; 2nd, Beatrice Melville, *d* of Joseph Roe. *Educ:* City of London and Strand Schs; King's Coll., London. Entered Civil Service, 1900; Private Sec. to Parliamentary Sec., Board of Trade, 1915; to Minister of Labour, 1917; Asst Sec. Ministry of Labour, 1919; Under-Sec., 1939; Chief Industrial Commissioner, 1940-42; Mem. of Government Mission of Inquiry into Industrial Conditions in Canada and United States, 1926. Brit. Govt Member of Governing Body of ILO, 1932-44, Chm., 1937-38; Dep. Sec. Ministry of Labour and National Service, 1942-45. Member: British Reparations Mission, Moscow, 1945; Anglo-American Cttee of Inquiry into Palestine, 1946; Docks Emergency Cttee, 1949; Cttee on London Transport, 1956-57; Chairman: London and S-E Regional Board for Industry, 1947-48; London Docks Disputes Inquiry Cttee, 1950; Building Apprenticeship and Training Council, 1953; Bldg and Civil Engrg Holidays Management Bd, 1946-; Industrial Relations Adviser, Anglo-Iranian Oil Co., 1947-60. Vice-Pres. Royal Coll. of Nursing, 1948-. *Address:* Downside Lodge, Coastal Road, Angmering on Sea, Sussex. *T:* Rustington 6074. *Club:* Reform.

LEGGO, Sir Jack (Frederick), Kt 1982; DFC 1942, and Bar 1943; FAIM; company director; Chairman, Duke of Edinburgh's Award Scheme, Queensland, since 1982; *b* 21 April 1916; *s* of Frederick Henry Leggo and Leah Leggo; *m* 1947, Mary Patricia Best; one *s* two *d*. *Educ:* state schs, Orange and Newcastle, NSW. ABIA 1938; FAIM 1955. Served RAAF, 1940-45 (Dam Buster Raids, 1943). Commonwealth Bank, 1931-39; Managing Director: Hobourn Components (Aus.) Pty Ltd, 1950-62; Penn Elastic (Aus.) Pty Ltd, 1960-66; T. G. Cullum Pty Ltd, 1966-80; Chm., Pioneer Sugar Mills Ltd, 1978- (Dir, 1971-); Dir, ICL Holdings (Aus.) Pty Ltd, 1978-. Dep. Chm., Qld Br., Aust. Mutual Provident Soc., 1978- (Dir, 1968-); Mem. Council, Royal Automobile Club of Qld, 1968- (Pres., 1976-79). *Recreation:* boating. *Address:* 105 The Gardens, Alice Street, Brisbane, Qld 4000, Australia. *T:* 07-312059. *Clubs:* Queensland (Brisbane); Naval and Military (Melbourne); Southport Yacht (Southport, Qld).

LEGH, family name of **Baron Newton.**

LEGH, Charles Legh Shuldham Cornwall-, CBE 1977 (OBE 1971); DL; *b* 10 Feb. 1903; *er s* of late Charles Henry George Cornwall Legh, of High Legh Hall, Cheshire, and late Geraldine Maud, *d* of Lt-Col Arthur James Shuldham, Royal Inniskilling Fusiliers; *m* 1930, Dorothy, *er d* of late J. W. Scott, Seal, Sevenoaks; one *s* two *d*. Served 1939-45 with AAF and RAF. JP Cheshire, 1938-73; High Sheriff, 1939; DL, 1949; CC 1949-77. Chm., Cheshire Police Authority, 1957-74; Chm., New Cheshire CC, 1974-76 (Shadow Chm., 1973); Hon. Alderman, 1977. *Address:* High Legh House, Knutsford, Cheshire WA16 0QR. *T:* Lymm 2303. *Clubs:* Carlton, MCC.

LEGH, Major Hon. Sir Francis (Michael), KCVO 1968 (CVO 1967; MVO 1964); Major (retired), Grenadier Guards; Treasurer since 1962 (Private Secretary, 1959-71), to the Princess Margaret; also Equerry to Queen Elizabeth the Queen Mother, since 1956 (Assistant Private Secretary and Equerry, 1956-59); *b* 2 Aug. 1919; 3rd *s* of 3rd Baron Newton and Hon. Helen Winifred Meysey-Thompson (*d* 1958); *m* 1948, Ruadh Daphne (*d* 1973), *o c* of late Alan Holmes Watson; one *s* one *d*. *Educ:* Eton; Royal Military College, Sandhurst. Served War of 1939-45 (despatches); Italy, 1943-45; GSO2, Military Mission to Greece. *Recreations:* shooting, golf. *Address:* Orchard House, Littlestone-on-Sea, New Romney, Kent. *T:* New Romney 3167. *Clubs:* White's, Brooks's, Pratt's, Beefsteak, Cavalry and Guards.

LE GOY, Raymond Edgar Michel, FCIT; a Director General, Commission of the European Communities, since 1981; *b* 1919; *e s* of J. A. S. M. N. and May Le Goy; *m* 1960, Ernestine Burnett, Trelawny, Jamaica; two *s*. *Educ:* William Ellis Sch.; Gonville and Caius Coll., Cambridge (MA). 1st cl. hons Hist. Tripos, 1939, 1940. Sec. Cambridge Union. Served Army, 1940-46: Staff Captain, HQ E Africa, 1944; Actg Major, 1945. LPTB, 1947; Min. of Transport, 1947; UK Shipping Adviser, Japan, 1949-51; Far East and SE Asia, 1951; Dir, Goeland Co., 1952; Asst Secretary: MoT, 1958; Min. of Aviation, 1959; BoT, 1966; Under-Sec., 1968, BoT, later DTI; Dir Gen. for Transport, EEC, 1973-81. *Publication:* The Victorian Burletta, 1953. *Recreations:* theatre, music, race relations. *Address:* c/o Société Générale de Banque, 10 Rond Point Schumann, Brussels 1040, Belgium. *Clubs:* National Liberal, Players'.

LE GRICE, Very Rev. F(rederick) Edwin, MA; Dean of Ripon, since 1968; *b* 14 Dec. 1911; *s* of Frederick and Edith Le Grice; *m* 1940, Joyce Margaret Hildreth; one *s* two *d*. *Educ:* Paston Sch., North Walsham; Queens' Coll., Cambridge; Westcott House, Cambridge. BA (2nd class hons Mathematics, 2nd class hons Theology) 1934; MA 1946. Asst Curate: St Aidan's, Leeds, 1935-38; Paignton, 1938-46; Vicar of Totteridge, N20, 1946-58; Canon Residentiary and Sub-Dean of St Albans Cathedral, 1958-68; Examining Chaplain to the Bishop of St Albans, 1958-68. A Church Comr, 1973-. Mem., Church Commn on Crown Appts, 1977-82. *Address:* The Minster House, Ripon, North Yorks HG4 1PE. *T:* Ripon 3615.

LEHANE, Maureen, (Mrs Peter Wishart); concert and opera singer; *d* of Christopher Lehane and Honor Millar; *m* 1966, Peter Wishart, composer. *Educ:* Queen Elizabeth's Girls' Grammar Sch., Barnet; Guildhall Sch. of Music and Drama. Studied under Hermann Weissenborn, Berlin (teacher of Fischer Dieskau); also under John and Aida Dickens (Australian teachers of Joan Sutherland); gained Arts Council award to study in Berlin. Speciality is Handel; has sung numerous leading roles (operas inc. Ezio, Ariadne and Pharamondo) with Handel opera societies of England and America, in London, and in Carnegie Hall, New York, also in Poland, Sweden and Germany; gave a number of master classes on the interpretation of Handel's vocal music (notably at s'Hertogenbosch Festival, Holland, July 1972; invited to repeat them in 1973). Debut at Glyndebourne, 1967. Festival appearances include: Stravinsky Festival, Cologne; City of London; Aldeburgh; Cheltenham; Three Choirs; Bath; Oxford Bach; Göttingen Handel Festival, etc; has toured N America; also 3-month tour of Australia at invitation of ABC and 2-month tour of Far East and ME, 1971; sang in Holland, and for Belgian TV, 1978; visits also to Berlin, Lisbon, Poland and Rome, 1979-80, to Warsaw, 1981. Title rôle in: Handel's Ariodante, Sadler's Wells, 1974; (her husband's 4th opera) Clytemnaestra, London, 1974; Purcell's Dido and Aeneas, Netherlands Opera, 1976; castrato lead in J. C. Bach's Adriano in Siria, 1982. Cyrus in first complete recording of Handel's Belshazzar. Appears regularly on BBC; also in promenade concerts. Has made numerous recordings (Bach, Haydn, Mozart, Handel, etc). *Publication:* (ed with Peter Wishart) Songs of Purcell. *Recreations:* cooking, gardening, reading. *Address:* Bridge House, Great Elm, Frome, Somerset BA11 3NY.

LEHMAN, Prof. Meir Manny, PhD; FIEE, FBCS; Professor of Computing Science since 1972, and Head of the Department of Computing since 1979, Imperial College of Science and Technology, University of London; *b* 24 Jan. 1925; *s* of late Benno and of Theresa Lehman; *m* 1953, Chava Robinson; three *s* two *d*. *Educ:* Letchworth Grammar Sch.; Imperial Coll. of Science and Technol. (BSc Hons, PhD, ARCS, DIC). FIEE 1947; FBCS 1954; MACM 1955; SMIEEE. Murphy Radio, 1941-50; Imperial Coll., 1950-56; London Labs, Ferranti, 1956-57; Scientific Dept, Israeli Defence Min., 1957-64; Res. Div., IBM, 1964-72; Dept of Computing, Imperial Coll., 1972-. Mem. Bd, Imperial Software Technology Ltd, 1982-. Vice-Chm. of Exec., Kisharon Day Sch. for Special Educn, 1976-; Governor, Hasmonean Boys Sch., 1979-. *Publications:* over 80 refereed pubns and some 6 book chapters. *Recreations:* family, Talmudic studies, classical orchestral music, gardening, DIY. *Address:* 34 Ravenscroft Avenue, NW11 0RY. *T:* 01-589 5111; Department of Computing, Imperial College of Science and Technology, 180 Queen's Gate, SW7 2BZ.

LEHMANN, Andrew George; Director, Institute of European Studies, University of Hull, since 1978; *b* 1922; British; *m* 1942, Alastine Mary, *d* of late K. N. Bell; two *s* one *d*. *Educ:* Dulwich Coll.; The Queen's Coll., Oxford. MA, DPhil Oxon. Served with RCS and Indian Army, 6th Rajputana Rifles. Fenced for England (Sabre), 1939. Asst lecturer and lecturer, Manchester Univ., 1945-51; Prof. of French Studies, 1951-68, Dean of Faculty of Letters and Soc. Scis, Univ. of Reading, 1960-66. Vis. Prof. of Comparative Literature, Univ. of Mainz, 1956; Hon. Prof., Univ. of Warwick, 1968-78. Man. Dir, 1968 and Dep. Chm., 1970-77, Linguaphone Inst. Ltd (Westinghouse Electric Co.). Mem., Hale Cttee on University Teaching Methods, 1961-63; Chm., Industrial Council for Educnl and Trng Technology, 1974-76 (Pres., 1979-81, Vice-Pres., 1981-); Mem., Anglo-French Permanent Mixed Cultural Commission, 1963-68. Adviser: Chinese Univ. of Hong Kong, 1964; Haile Selassie I Univ., Ethiopia, 1965. Member: Hong Kong Univ. Grants Cttee, 1966-73; Academic Planning Board, New Univ. of Ulster, 1966; Court and Council, Bedford Coll., London Univ., 1971-78; British Library Adv. Cttee (Reference), 1975-78; Princeton Univ. Academic Adv. Council, 1975-81. Governor, Ealing Tech. Coll., 1974. *Publications:* The Symbolist Aesthetic in France, 1950 and 1967; Sainte-Beuve, a portrait of the Critic, 1962; articles in various periodicals and learned reviews. *Recreations:* music, travel, gardening. *Address:* Westway Cottage, West Adderbury, Banbury, Oxon. *T:* Banbury 810272. *Club:* Athenæum.

LEHMANN, Prof. Hermann, CBE 1980; MD, PhD, ScD, FRCP, FRCPath; FRS 1972, FRSC; Research Worker, University Department of Biochemistry, Cambridge; Professor of Clinical Biochemistry, Cambridge University, 1967-77, now Emeritus; University Biochemist to Addenbrooke's Hospital, Cambridge, 1963-77, now Hon. Consultant; Fellow of Christ's College, Cambridge, 1965-82, Hon. Fellow, since 1982; *b* 8 July 1910; *s* of Paul Lehmann, Publisher, and Bella Lehmann (*née* Apelt); *m* 1942, Benigna Norman-Butler; one *s* two *d* (and one *s* decd). *Educ:* Kreuzschule, Dresden; Universities of Freiburg-i-B, Frankfurt, Berlin, Heidelberg. MD Basle, 1934; PhD Cantab, 1938; FRCPath 1964, Hon. FRCPath 1983. Research Asst, Heidelberg, 1934-36; Research Student: Sch. of Biochem., also Christ's Coll., Cambridge, 1936-38; Beit Memorial Fellow for Med. Res., 1938-42. RAMC 1943-47. Colonial Med. Research Fellow for Malnutrition and Anæmia, Makerere Coll., Uganda, 1947-49; Cons. Pathologist, Pembury Hosp., Kent, 1949-51; Sen. Lectr, (Reader, 1959), Chem. Pathol. St Bart's Hosp., 1951-63. Hon. Dir, MRC Abnormal Haemoglobin Unit (WHO Ref. Centre for Abnormal Haemoglobins), 1963-75. Rockefeller Travelling Fellowship to USA, 1954. Pres., British Soc. for Haematology, 1975-76 (Hon. Fellow, 1979). Hon. Prof., University of Freiburg-i-B, 1964-; Praelector in Clinical Biochemistry, Univ. of Dundee, 1977; Vis. Prof., Univ. of Otago, Christchurch, NZ, 1980. Lectures: Ludwig Aschoff Meml, Freiburg Univ., 1964; Sydney Watson Smith, RCPE, 1965; Lord Horder Meml, St Bart's

Hosp. and Univ. of Malta, 1971. Mem., WHO Expert Adv. Panel on Human Genetics, 1971-; Chm., WHO Expert Cttee on Haemoglobins and Thalassaemia, 1972-79. Pres., Biomed. Sect., BAAS, 1978. Mem., Deutsche Akad. der Naturforscher Leopoldina, 1981. Corresp. Mem., Bayerische Akad. der Wissenschaften, 1982. Hon. Member: Haematology Socs of GB, Costa Rica, Europe, Germany, Italy, Netherlands, Switzerland, Turkey, USA, Venezuela; Pathology Soc. of Nigeria. Dr med *hc* Johann Wolfgang Goethe Universität, Frankfurt a/M, 1972. Rivers Medal, Royal Anthrop. Inst., 1963; Martin Luther King Prize, Southern Christian Fedn, USA, 1971; Conway Evans Prize, RCP and Royal Soc., 1976; Wellcome Prize, Assoc. of Clinical Biochemists, 1979; Ludwig Heilmeyer Medal, Univ. of Ulm, 1979. Officer, National Order (Ivory Coast), 1981. *Publications:* Man's Haemoglobins (with R. G. Huntsman), 1966, 2nd edn 1974; (ed with R. M. Schmidt and T. H. J. Huisman) The Detection of Hemoglobinopathics, 1974; (with P. A. M. Kynoch) Human Haemoglobin variants and their Characteristics, 1976; articles in sci. jls. *Address:* 22 Newton Road, Cambridge CB2 2AL. *Club:* Athenæum.

LEHMANN, John Frederick, CBE 1964; FRSL; Editor of the London Magazine from its foundation to 1961; Managing Director of John Lehmann Ltd from its foundation to 1952; Founder and Editor of New Writing and of Orpheus; *b* 2 June 1907; *s* of late Rudolph Chambers Lehmann and Alice Marie Davis. *Educ:* Eton (King's Scholar); Trinity Coll., Cambridge. Partner and Gen. Manager, The Hogarth Press, 1938-46; Advisory Editor, The Geographical Magazine, 1940-45. Editor, New Soundings (BBC Third Programme), 1952, The London Magazine, 1954. Chm., Editorial Advisory Panel, British Council, 1952-58; Mem., Anglo-Greek Mixed Commission, 1962-68; Pres., Royal Literary Fund, 1966-76. Vis. Professor: Univ. of Texas, and State Univ. of Calif at San Diego, 1970-72; Univ. of Calif at Berkeley, 1974; Emory Univ., Atlanta, 1977. Pres. Alliance Française in Great Britain, 1955-63. Hon. DLitt Birmingham, 1980. Officer, Gold Cross, Order of George I (Greece), 1954, Comdr, 1961; Officier Légion d'Honneur, 1958; Grand Officier, Etoile Noire, 1960; Officier, Ordre des Arts et des Lettres, 1965. Prix du Rayonnement Français, 1961. *Publications:* A Garden Revisited, 1931; The Noise of History, 1934; Prometheus and the Bolsheviks, 1937; Evil Was Abroad, 1938; Down River, 1939; New Writing in Europe, 1940; Forty Poems, 1942; The Sphere of Glass, 1944; Shelley in Italy, 1947; The Age of the Dragon, 1951; The Open Night, 1952; The Whispering Gallery (Autobiography I), 1955; I Am My Brother (Autobiography II), 1960; Ancestors and Friends, 1962; Collected Poems 1963; Christ the Hunter, 1965; The Ample Proposition (Autobiography III), 1966; A Nest of Tigers, 1968; In My Own Time (condensed one-volume autobiography), 1969 (USA); Holborn, 1970; The Reader at Night and other poems, 1974; Virginia Woolf and Her World, 1975; In the Purely Pagan Sense, 1976; Edward Lear and His World, 1977; Thrown to the Woolfs, 1978; Rupert Brooke: his life and his legend, 1980; English Poets of the First World War, 1981; Editor: Poems from New Writing, 1946, French Stories from New Writing, 1947, The Year's Work in Literature, 1949 and 1950, English Stories from New Writing, 1950, Pleasures of New Writing, 1952; The Chatto Book of Modern Poetry, 1956 (with C. Day Lewis); The Craft of Letters in England, 1956; Modern French Stories, 1956; Coming to London, 1957; Italian Stories of Today, 1959; Selected Poems of Edith Sitwell, 1965; (with Derek Parker) Edith Sitwell: selected letters, 1970. *Recreations:* gardening, swimming, reading. *Address:* 85 Cornwall Gardens, SW7. *Clubs:* Naval and Military, Eton Viking.

LEHMANN, Rosamond Nina, CBE 1982; 2nd *d* of R. C. Lehmann and Alice Davis; *m* 1928, Hon. Wogan Philipps (*see* 2nd Baron Milford); one *s* (and one *d* decd). *Educ:* privately; Girton Coll., Cambridge (scholar). *Publications:* Dusty Answer, 1927, repr. 1981; A Note in Music, 1930, repr. 1982; Invitation to the Waltz, 1932, repr. 1981; The Weather in the Streets, 1936, repr. 1981; No More Music (play), 1939; The Ballad and the Source, 1944; The Gypsy's Baby, 1946, repr. 1973; The Echoing Grove, 1953, repr. 1981; The Swan in the Evening, 1967; (with W. Tudor Pole) A Man Seen Afar, 1965; (with Cynthia, Baroness Sandys) Letters from Our Daughters, 2 vols, 1971; A Sea-Grape Tree, 1976. *Recreations:* reading, music. *Address:* 70 Eaton Square, SW1.

LEHRER, Thomas Andrew; writer of songs since 1943; *b* 9 April 1928; *s* of James Lehrer and Anna Lehrer (*née* Waller). *Educ:* Harvard Univ. (AB 1946, MA 1947); Columbia Univ.; Harvard Univ. Student (mathematics, especially probability and statistics) till 1953. Part-time teaching at Harvard, 1947-51. Theoretical physicist at Baird-Atomic, Inc., Cambridge, Massachusetts, 1953-54. Entertainer, 1953-55, 1957-60. US Army, 1955-57. Lecturer in Business Administration, Harvard Business Sch., 1961; Lecturer: in Education, Harvard Univ., 1963-66; in Psychology, Wellesley Coll., 1966; in Political Science, MIT, 1962-71; Vis. Lectr, Univ. of Calif, Santa Cruz, 1972-. *Publications:* Tom Lehrer Song Book, 1954; Tom Lehrer's Second Song Book, 1968; Too Many Songs by Tom Lehrer, 1981; contrib. to Annals of Mathematical Statistics, Journal of Soc. of Industrial and Applied Maths. *Recreation:* piano. *Address:* PO Box 121, Cambridge, Massachusetts 02138, USA. *T:* (617) 354-7708.

LEICESTER, 6th Earl of, *cr* 1837; **Anthony Louis Lovel Coke;** Viscount Coke 1837; farmer, since 1976; *b* 11 Sept. 1909; *s* of Hon. Arthur George Coke (killed in action, 1915) (2nd *s* of 3rd Earl) and of Phyllis Hermione (Lady Howard-Vyse), *d* of late Francis Saxham Elwes Drury; *S* cousin, 1976; *m* 1st, 1934, Moyra Joan (marr. diss. 1947), *d* of late Douglas Crossley; two *s* one *d* ; 2nd, 1947, Vera Haigh, Salisbury, Rhodesia. *Educ:* Gresham's School, Holt.

Served War of 1939–45 in RAF. Career spent ranching. *Recreations:* general. *Heir:* s Viscount Coke, *qv. Address:* Mhowani, PO Box 529, Plettenberg Bay, Cape Province, 6600, Republic of S Africa.

LEICESTER, Bishop of, since 1979; **Rt. Rev. Cecil Richard Rutt,** CBE 1973; MA; *b* 27 Aug. 1925; *s* of Cecil Rutt and Mary Hare Turner; *m* 1969, Joan Mary Ford. *Educ:* Huntingdon Grammar School; Kelham Theol. Coll.; Pembroke Coll., Cambridge. RNVR, 1943-46. Deacon, 1951; Priest, 1952. Asst Curate, St George's, Cambridge, 1951-54; Dio. of Korea, 1954; Parish Priest of Anjung, 1956-58; Warden of St Bede's House Univ. Centre, Seoul, 1959-64; Rector of St Michael's Seminary, Oryu Dong, Seoul, 1964-66; Archdeacon, West Kyonggi (Dio. Seoul), 1965-66; Asst Bishop of Taejon, 1966-68; Bishop of Taejon, 1968-74; Bishop Suffragan of St Germans, 1974-79; Hon. Canon, St Mary's Cathedral, Truro, 1974-79. Associate Gen. Sec., Korean Bible Soc., 1964-74; Episcopal Sec., Council of the Church of SE Asia, 1968-74; Commissary, Dio. Taejon, 1974-; Pres., Roy. Asiatic Soc., Korea Br., 1974. Chm., Adv. Council for Religious Communities, 1980. Interested in the Cornish language and Bard of the Gorsedd of Cornwall, Cornwhylen, 1976. ChStJ 1978. Tasan Cultural Award (for writings on Korea), 1964; Hon. DLitt, Confucian Univ., Seoul, 1974. Order of Civil Merit, Peony Class (Korea), 1974. *Publications:* (ed) Songgonghoe Songga (Korean Anglican Hymnal), 1961; Korean Works and Days, 1964; P'ungnyu Han'guk (in Korean), 1965; (trans.) An Anthology of Korean Sijo, 1970; The Bamboo Grove, an introduction to Korean Sijo poetry, 1971; James Scarth Gale and his History of the Korean People, 1972; Virtuous Women, three masterpieces of traditional Korean fiction, 1974; contribs on Korean classical poetry and history to Trans. Royal Asiatic Soc. (Korea Br.) and various Korean and liturgiological publications. *Address:* Bishop's Lodge, 10 Springfield Road, Leicester LE2 3BD. *T:* Leicester 708985. *Club:* United Oxford & Cambridge University.

LEICESTER, Provost of; *see* Warren, Very Rev. A. C.

LEICESTER, Archdeacon of; *see* Silk, Ven. R. D.

LEIGH, family name of **Baron Leigh.**

LEIGH, 5th Baron *cr* 1839; **John Piers Leigh;** *b* 11 Sept. 1935; *s* of 4th Baron Leigh, TD and Anne (*d* 1977), *d* of Ellis Hicks Beach; *S* father, 1979; *m* 1st, 1957, Cecilia Poppy (marr. diss. 1974), *y d* of late Robert Cecil Jackson; one *s* one *d* (and one *d* decd); 2nd, 1976, Susan (marr. diss. 1982), *d* of John Cleave, Whitnash, Leamington Spa; one *s. Educ:* Eton; Oxford and London Universities. *Recreations:* horses, hunting, racing, sport, country pursuits. *Heir: s* Hon. Christopher Dudley Piers Leigh, *b* 20 Oct. 1960. *Address:* Stoneleigh Abbey, Kenilworth, Warwickshire. *T:* Kenilworth 53981.

LEIGH, (Archibald) Denis, MD, FRCP; Consultant Physician, Bethlem Royal and Maudsley Hospitals, 1949-80, now Emeritus; Secretary-General, World Psychiatric Association, 1966-78; Hon. Consultant in Psychiatry to the British Army, 1969-80; Lecturer, Institute of Psychiatry; *b* 11 Oct. 1915; *o s* of Archibald Leigh and Rose Rushworth; *m* 1941, Pamela Parish; two *s* three *d. Educ:* Hulme Grammar Sch.; Manchester Univ.; University of Budapest. Manchester City Schol. in Medicine, 1932; BSc 1936; MB, ChB (1st class hons) 1939; Dauntesey Med. Sen. Schol., Prof. Tom Jones Exhibitioner in Anatomy; Sidney Renshaw Jun. Prize in Physiol.; Turner Med. Prize; John Henry Agnew Prize; Stephen Lewis Prize; Prize in Midwifery; MRCP 1941; MD (Manchester), 1947; FRCP, 1955. RAMC, 1940-45 (Lt-Col); Adviser in Neurology, Eastern Army, India. 1st Assistant, Dept of Neurology, London Hospital; Nuffield Fellow, 1947-48; Clinical Fellow, Harvard Univ., 1948. Recognised Clinical Teacher, London Univ.; Founder European Society of Psychosomatic Research; Editor-in-Chief and Founder, Journal of Psychosomatic Res.; Editorial Bd, Japanese Journal of Psychosomatic Medicine, Medicina Psychosomatica, Psychosomatic Medicine, Behaviour Therapy; Examiner in Psychological Med., Edinburgh Univ., 1958-65; Beattie Smith Lectr, Melbourne Univ., 1967. Governor, Bethlem Royal and Maudsley Hospitals, 1956-62; President Sect. of Psychiatry, Royal Society Med., 1967-68. Hon. Member: Deutschen Gesellschaft für Psychiatrie und Nervenheilkunde; Italian Psychosomatic Soc.; Assoc. Brasileira de Psiquiatria; Sociedad Argentina de Medicina Psicosomática; Polish Psychiatric Assoc.; Corresp. Mem., Pavlovian Soc. of N America; Hon. Corresp. Mem., Austn Acad. of Forensic Scis; Hon Fellow: Swedish Soc. of Med. Scis; Soc. Colombiana de Psiquiatría; Soviet Soc. of Neurologists and Psychiatrists; Czechoslovak Psychiatric Soc.; Finnish Psychiatric Soc. Distinguished Fellow, Amer. Psychiatric Assoc. *Publications:* (trans. from French) Psychosomatic Methods of Painless Childbirth, 1959; The Historical Development of British Psychiatry, Vol. I, 1961; Bronchial Asthma, 1967; A Concise Encyclopaedia of Psychiatry, 1977; chapters in various books; papers on neurology, psychiatry, history of psychiatry and psychosomatic medicine. *Recreations:* fishing, collecting. *Address:* 152 Harley Street, W1. *T:* 01-935 8868; The Grange, Otford, Kent. *T:* Otford 3427.

LEIGH, Sir John, 2nd Bt, *cr* 1918; *b* 24 March 1909; *s* of Sir John Leigh, 1st Bt, and Norah Marjorie, CBE (*d* 1954); *S* father 1959; *m* 1959, Ariane, *d* of late Joseph Wm Allen, Beverly Hills, California, and *widow* of Harold Wallace Ross, NYC. *Educ:* Eton; Balliol Coll., Oxford. *Heir:* nephew Richard Henry Leigh [*b* 11 Nov. 1936; *m* 1st, 1962, Barbro Anna Elizabeth (marr. diss. 1977), *e d* of late Stig Carl Sebastian Tham, Sweden; 2nd, 1977, Chérie Rosalind, *e d* of D. D. Dale and *widow* of A. Reece, RMS]. *Address:*

23 Quai du Mont Blanc, Geneva, Switzerland. *T:* 31 53 63. *Clubs:* Brooks's; Travellers' (Paris).

LEIGH, Mike; dramatist; theatre, television and film director; *b* 20 Feb. 1943; *s* of Alfred Abraham Leigh, LRCS, MRCP and Phyllis Pauline Leigh (*née* Cousin); *m* 1973, Alison Steadman; two *s. Educ:* North Grecian Street County Primary Sch.; Salford Grammar Sch.; RADA; Camberwell Sch. of Arts and Crafts; Central Sch. of Art and Design (Theatre Design Dept); London Film Sch. Sometime actor, incl. Victoria Theatre, Stoke-on-Trent, 1966; Assoc. Dir, Midlands Arts Centre for Young People, 1965-66; Asst Dir, RSC, 1967-68; Drama Lectr, Sedgley Park and De La Salle Colls, Manchester, 1968-69; Lectr, London Film Sch., 1970-73. Arts Council of GB: Member: Drama Panel, 1975-77; Dirs' Working Party and Specialist Allocations Bd, 1976-81; Member: Accreditation Panel, Nat. Council for Drama Trng, 1978-; Gen. Adv. Council, IBA, 1980-82. NFT Retrospective, 1979; George Devine Award, 1973. Productions of own plays and films evolved from scratch entirely by rehearsal through improvisation; *stage plays:* The Box Play, 1965, My Parents Have Gone To Carlisle, The Last Crusade Of The Five Little Nuns, 1966, Midlands Arts Centre; Nenaa, RSC Studio, Stratford-upon-Avon, 1967; Individual Fruit Pies, E15 Acting Sch., 1968; Down Here And Up There, Royal Ct Th. Upstairs, 1968; Big Basil, 1968, Glum Victoria And The Lad With Specs, Manchester Youth Theatre, 1969; Epilogue, Manchester, 1969; Bleak Moments, Open Space, 1970; A Rancid Pong, Basement, 1971; Wholesome Glory, Dick Whittington and his Cat, Royal Ct Th. Upstairs, 1973; The Jaws of Death, Traverse, Edinburgh Fest., 1973; Babies Grow Old, Other Place, 1974, ICA, 1975; The Silent Majority, Bush, 1974; Abigail's Party, Hampstead, 1977; Ecstasy, Hampstead, 1979; Goose-Pimples, Hampstead, Garrick, 1981 (Standard Best Comedy Award); *radio play:* Too Much Of A Good Thing (banned), *feature film:* Bleak Moments, 1971 (Golden Hugo, Chicago Film Fest., 1972; Golden Leopard, Locarno Film Fest., 1972); *BBC TV plays and films:* A Mug's Game, 1972; Hard Labour, 1973; The Permissive Society, Afternoon, A Light Snack, Probation, Old Chums, The Birth Of The 2001 FA Cup Final Goalie, 1975; Nuts in May, Knock For Knock, 1976; The Kiss Of Death, Abigail's Party, 1977; Who's Who, 1978; Grown-Ups, 1980; Home Sweet Home, 1982. Directed and designed orig. prodn of Halliwell's Little Malcolm And His Struggle Against The Eunuchs, Unity, 1965. *Address:* c/o A. D. Peters & Co. Ltd, 10 Buckingham Street, WC2N 6BU.

LEIGH, Sir Neville (Egerton), KCVO 1980 (CVO 1967); Clerk of the Privy Council since 1974; *b* 4 June 1922; *s* of late Cecil Egerton Leigh; *m* 1944, Denise Margaret Yvonne, *d* of late Cyril Denzil Branch, MC; two *s* one *d. Educ:* Charterhouse. RAFVR, 1942-47 (Flt-Lt). Called to Bar, Inner Temple, 1948. Legal Asst, Treasury Solicitors Dept, 1949-51; Senior Clerk, Privy Council Office, 1951-65; Deputy Clerk of Privy Council, 1965-74. *Address:* 11 The Crescent, Barnes, SW13 0NN. *T:* 01-876 4271. *Club:* Army and Navy.

LEIGH, Peter William John, FRICS; Director of Valuation and Estates, Greater London Council, since 1981; *b* 29 June 1929; *s* of John Charles Leigh and Dorothy Grace Leigh; *m* 1956, Mary Frances (*née* Smith); two *s* one *d. Educ:* Harrow Weald County Grammar Sch.; Coll. of Estate Management (ext.). National Service, Royal Signals, 1947-49. Private surveying practice, 1949-53; Valuation Asst, Mddx CC, 1953-60; Commercial Estates Officer, Bracknell Develt Corp., 1960-66; sen. appts, Valuation and Estates Dept, GLC, 1966-81. Exec. Mem., Assoc. of Local Authority Valuers and Estate Surveyors, 1981-; Member: Inland Revenue Valuation Liaison Gp, 1981-; Land Policy Cttee, RICS, 1981-. Chm., Old Wealden Assoc., 1978-. *Recreations:* sport, travel and caravanning, drawing, gardening (therapy). *Address:* 41 Sandy Lane, Wokingham, Berks RG11 4SS. *T:* Wokingham 782732.

LEIGH, Ralph Alexander, CBE 1977; FBA 1969; LittD; Professor of French, University of Cambridge, 1973-82; Professorial Fellow of Trinity College, Cambridge, since 1973 (Fellow, 1952, Prælector, since 1967, Senior Research Fellow, 1969); *b* London, 6 Jan. 1915; *m* 1945, Edith Helen Kern (*d* 1972); one *s* one *d. Educ:* Raine's Sch. for Boys, London; Queen Mary Coll., Univ. of London; Univ. of Paris (Sorbonne). BA London 1st class hons. 1936; Diplôme de l'Université de Paris, 1938. Served War, 1941-46: RASC and Staff; CCG; Lieut (ERE list) 1942; Major, 1944. Lectr, Dept of French, Univ. of Edinburgh, 1946; Lectr, 1952-69, Reader, 1969-73, Cambridge Univ. Vis. Prof., Sorbonne, 1973. Mem., Inst. for Adv. Studies, Princeton, 1967. Leverhulme Fellow, 1959-60, 1970, 1982-83. LittD (Cambridge) 1968. Docteur (*hc*) Univ. of Neuchâtel, 1978. Médaille de la Ville de Paris, 1978. Chevalier de la Légion d'Honneur, 1980. *Publications:* Correspondance Complète de Jean Jacques Rousseau, vols I-XL, 1965-82 (in progress); Rousseau and the Problem of Tolerance in the XVIIIth Century, 1979; (ed) Rousseau after 200 years, 1982; contrib to Revue de littérature comparée; Annales Rousseau; Revue d'Histoire littéraire; Modern Language Review; French Studies; Studies on Voltaire; The Library, etc. *Recreation:* book-collecting. *Address:* Trinity College, Cambridge. *Club:* United Oxford & Cambridge University.

LEIGH-PEMBERTON, John, AFC 1945; artist painter; *b* 18 Oct. 1911; *s* of Cyril Leigh-Pemberton and Mary Evelyn Megaw; *m* 1948, Doreen Beatrice Townshend-Webster. *Educ:* Eton. Studied Art, London, 1928-31. Past Member Royal Institute of Painters in Oils and other Societies. Served 1940-45 with RAF as Flying Instructor. Series of pictures for Coldstream

Guards, 1950. Festival Almanack, 1951, for Messrs Whitbread; Royal Progress, 1953, for Shell Mex & BP Ltd. Works in public and private collections, UK and America; decorations for ships: City of York, City of Exeter, Britannic, Caledonia, Corfu, Carthage, Kenya, Uganda. Many series of paintings, chiefly of natural history subjects, for Midland Bank Ltd. *Publications:* A Book of Garden Flowers, 1960; A Book of Butterflies, Moths and other Insects, 1963; British Wildlife, Rarities and Introductions, 1966; Garden Birds, 1967; Sea and Estuary Birds, 1967; Heath and Woodland Birds, 1968; Vanishing Wild Animals of the World, 1968; Pond and River Birds, 1969; African Mammals, 1969; Australian Mammals, 1970; North American Mammals, 1970; Birds of Prey, 1970; European Mammals, 1971; Asian Mammals, 1971; South American Mammals, 1972; Sea and Air Mammals, 1972; Wild Life in Britain, 1972; Disappearing Mammals, 1973; Ducks and Swans, 1973; Lions and Tigers, 1974; Baby Animals, 1974; Song Birds, 1974; Leaves, 1974; Big Animals, 1975; Apes and Monkeys, 1975; Reptiles, 1976; Seals and Whales, 1976; Butterflies and Moths, 1978; Hedges, 1979; Birds of Britain and Northern Europe, 1979; Bears and Pandas, 1979. *Address:* 5 Roehampton Gate, Roehampton, SW15. *T:* 01-876 3332.

LEIGH-PEMBERTON, Robert, (Robin Leigh-Pemberton); Lord-Lieutenant of Kent, since 1982 (Vice Lord-Lieutenant, 1972-82); Pro-Chancellor of University of Kent at Canterbury, since 1977; Chairman, National Westminster Bank Ltd, since 1977 (Director, 1972, Deputy Chairman, 1974); Director: Birmid Qualcast Ltd, since 1966 (Deputy Chairman, 1970; Chairman, 1975-77); University Life Assurance Society, 1967-78; Redland Ltd, since 1972; Equitable Life Assurance Society, since 1979 (Vice-President, since 1982); *b* 5 Jan. 1927; *e s* of late Robert Douglas Leigh-Pemberton, MBE, MC, Sittingbourne, Kent; *m* 1953, Rosemary Davina, *d* of late Lt-Col D. W. A. W. Forbes, MC, and the Dowager Marchioness of Exeter; five *s. Educ:* St Peter's Court, Broadstairs; Eton; Trinity Coll., Oxford (MA). Grenadier Guards, 1945-48. Called to Bar, Inner Temple, 1954; practised in London and SE Circuit until 1960. County Councillor (Chm. Council, 1972-75), 1961-77, C Ald. 1965, Kent. Member: SE Econ. Planning Council, 1972-74; Medway Ports Authority, 1974-76; NEDC, 1982-; Prime Minister's Cttee on Local Govt Rules of Conduct, 1973-74; Cttee of Enquiry into Teachers' Pay, 1974; Cttee on Police Pay, 1977-79. Chm., Cttee of London Clearing Bankers, 1982-. Trustee: Glyndebourne Arts Trust, 1978-; RA Trust, 1982-. Hon. Col, The Kent and County of London Yeomanry (Sharpshooters), 1979-. FRSA 1977; FBIM 1977. JP 1961-75, DL 1970, Kent. *Recreation:* country life. *Address:* Torry Hill, Sittingbourne, Kent ME9 0SP. *T:* Milstead 258; 66 Westminster Gardens, Marsham Street, SW1. *Clubs:* Brooks's, Cavalry and Guards, MCC, Leander; Union (New York).

LEIGH-WOOD, Roger, DL; *b* 16 Aug. 1906; *s* of Sir James Leigh-Wood, KBE, CB, CMG, and Joanna Elizabeth Turnbull; *m* 1936, Norah Elizabeth Holroyde; four *s. Educ:* Winchester Coll.; Trinity Coll., Oxford. Lt-Comdr RNVR, 1939-45. Brown Shipley & Co. Ltd, 1930-42; Eastern Bank Ltd, 1945, Chm. 1967-71; Chartered Bank, 1967-72 (Dep. Chm. 1971); Commercial Union Assce Co. Ltd, 1948-71; Dalgety Ltd, 1957-72; Chm., Scott & Bowne Ltd, 1964-78. High Sheriff of Hampshire, 1964-65; DL Hants, 1970. *Recreations:* yachting, gardening; formerly athletics (Pres. Oxford Univ. Athletic Club, 1929; British Olympic Team, 1928; Empire Games Team, 1930). *Address:* Summerley, Bentworth, Alton, Hants. *T:* Alton 62077. *Club:* Royal Yacht Squadron.

LEIGHTON OF ST MELLONS, 2nd Baron, *cr* 1962; **John Leighton Seager;** Bt 1952; *b* 11 Jan. 1922; *er s* of 1st Baron Leighton of St Mellons, CBE, JP, and of Marjorie, *d* of William Henry Gimson, Breconshire; *S* father, 1963; *m* 1953, Elizabeth Rosita, *o d* of late Henry Hopgood, Cardiff; two *s one d* (and one *d* decd). *Educ:* Caldicott Sch.; The Leys Sch., Cambridge. *Heir: s* Hon. Robert William Henry Leighton Seager, *b* 28 Sept. 1955. *Address:* 185 Lake Road West, Cardiff.

LEIGHTON, Clare, RE 1934; *b* 1899; *d* of late Marie Connor Leighton, and late Robert Leighton. *Educ:* privately; Brighton School of Art; Slade School. Elected Member of Society of Wood Engravers, 1928; First prize International Engraving Exhibition, Art Institute of Chicago, 1930; Fellow National Acad. of Design, New York; Member, Society of American Graphic Arts; Member, National Inst. of Arts and Letters, USA, 1951. Prints purchased for permanent collection of British Museum, Victoria and Albert Museum, National Gallery of Canada, Museums of Boston, Baltimore, New York, etc. Designed: 33 stained glass windows for St Paul's Cathedral, Worcester, Mass; 12 plates for Josiah Wedgwood & Sons Ltd. *Publications:* Illustrated with wood engravings the following books: Thomas Hardy's The Return of the Native, 1929; Thornton Wilder's The Bridge of San Luis Rey, 1930; The Sea and the Jungle, 1930; Wuthering Heights, 1931; E. Madox Roberts's The Time of Man, 1943; North Carolina Folk Lore, 1950; Woodcuts: examples of the Work of Clare Leighton, 1930; The Trumpet in the Dust, 1934; Writer: How to do Wood Engraving and Woodcuts, 1932; Wood Engraving of the 1930's, 1936; Tempestuous Petticoat, 1948; written and illustrated: The Musical Box, 1932; The Farmer's Year, 1933; The Wood That Came Back, 1934; Four Hedges, 1935; Country Matters, 1937; Sometime, Never, 1939; Southern Harvest, 1942; Give us this Day, 1943; Where Land meets Sea, 1954. *Address:* Woodbury, Conn 06798, USA.

LEIGHTON, Prof. Kenneth, MA, DMus; LRAM; composer; pianist; Reid Professor of Music, University of Edinburgh, since 1970; *b* 2 Oct. 1929; *s* of

Thomas Leighton; *m* 1st, 1953, Lydia Vignapiano; one *s one d* ; 2nd, 1981, Josephine Ann Prescott. *Educ:* Queen Elizabeth Grammar Sch., Wakefield; Queen's Coll., Oxford (schol.; MA 1955; DMus 1960); Petrassi, Rome. Prof. of Theory, RN Sch. of Music, 1952-53; Gregory Fellow in Music, Leeds Univ., 1953-56; Lectr in Music Composition, Edinburgh Univ., 1956-68; Lectr in Music, Oxford Univ., and Fellow of Worcester Coll., 1968-70. Hon. DMus St Andrews, 1977. *Compositions:* Concertos for: piano (3); violin; cello; viola and two pianos; symphony for string orchestra; two string quartets; piano quintet; sonatas for: violin and piano (2); piano (3); partita for cello and piano; orchestral works; Burlesque, Passacaglia, Chorale and Fugue; two symphonies; The Birds (chorus and strings); The Light Invisible (tenor, chorus and orch.), etc; Fantasia Contrappuntistica (piano); Columba (3 act opera); incidental music for radio and television drama; church, organ, and piano music. *Recreation:* walking. *Address:* Faculty of Music, University of Edinburgh, Alison House, Nicolson Square, Edinburgh EH8 9BH.

LEIGHTON, Leonard Horace; Under Secretary, Department of Energy, 1974-80; *b* 7 Oct. 1920; *e s* of Leonard and Pearl Leighton, Bermuda; *m* 1945, Mary Burrowes; two *s. Educ:* Rossall Sch.; Magdalen Coll., Oxford (MA). FInstF. Royal Engrs, 1940-46; Nat. Coal Bd, 1950-62; Min. of Power, 1962-67; Min. of Technology, 1967-70; Dept of Trade and Industry, 1970-74. *Publications:* papers in various technical jls. *Recreation:* gardening. *Address:* 19 McKay Road, Wimbledon, SW20 0HT. *T:* 01-946 4230.

LEIGHTON, Sir Michael (John Bryan), 11th Bt, *cr* 1693; *b* 8 March 1935; *o s* of Colonel Sir Richard Tihel Leighton, 10th Bt, and Kathleen Irene Linda, *o d* of Major A. E. Lees, Rowton Castle, Shrewsbury; *S* father 1957; *m* 1974 (marr. diss. 1980). *Educ:* Stowe; Tabley House Agricultural Sch.; Cirencester Coll. *Address:* Loton Park, Shrewsbury, Salop.

LEIGHTON, Ronald; MP (Lab) Newham North-East, since 1979; *b* 24 Jan. 1930; *s* of Charles Leighton and Edith (*née* Sleet); *m* 1951, Erika Wehking; two *s. Educ:* Monteagle and Bifrons Sch., Barking. Newspaper printer. Secretary, Labour Cttee for Safeguards on Common Market, 1967-70; Director, All-Party Common Market Safeguards Campaign, 1970-73; Editor, Resistance News, 1973-74; Secretary, Get Britain Out Campaign, 1974-75; National Organiser, National Referendum Campaign, which campaigned for 'No' vote in Referendum, 1975; Chairman, Labour Common Market Safeguards Cttee, 1975-. *Publications:* The Labour Case Against Entry to the Common Market; What Labour Should Do About the Common Market; also pamphlets (1963-). *Recreations:* reading, footpath walking. *Address:* 19 Woodlawn Road, Fulham, SW6. *T:* 01-385 7597.

LEIGHTON-BOYCE, Guy Gilbert; Accountant and Comptroller General, HM Customs and Excise, 1973-80; *b* 23 Oct. 1920; *s* of late Charles Edmund Victor and Eleanor Fannie Leighton-Boyce; *m* 1945, Adrienne Jean Elliott Samms; two *s two d. Educ:* Dulwich Coll. HM Customs and Excise, 1939. Served War, RAF, 1941-46. Asst Sec., 1960; Under Sec., 1973. *Publications:* Irish Setters, 1973; (with James Iliff) Tephrocactus, 1973; articles in Cactus and Succulent jls. *Recreations:* looking at pictures; dogs, plants. *Address:* 220 Leigham Court Road, Streatham, SW16 2RB. *T:* 01-769 4844. *Club:* Kennel.

LEINSDORF, Erich; orchestral and operatic conductor; *b* Vienna, 4 Feb. 1912; *s* of Ludwig Julius Leinsdorf and Charlotte (*née* Loebl); *m* 1st, 1939, Anne Frohnknecht (marr. diss. 1968); three *s two d* ; 2nd, 1968, Vera Graf. *Educ:* University of Vienna; State Academy of Music, Vienna (dipl.). Assistant conductor: Salzburg Festival, 1934-37; Metropolitan Opera, NY, 1937-39; Chief Conductor, German operas, 1939-43; Conductor, Rochester Philharmonic, 1947-56; Director, NYC Opera, 1956; Music Cons. Director, Metropolitan Opera, 1957-62; Music Director, Boston Symphony Orchestra, 1962-69. Director: Berkshire Music Center, Berkshire Music Festival, 1963-69; American Arts Alliance, 1979-. Guest appearances with virtually every major orchestra in the USA and Europe, incl. Philadelphia Orchestra, Los Angeles, St Louis, New Orleans, Minneapolis, Cleveland, New York, Concertgebouw Amsterdam, Israel Philharmonic, London Symphony, New Philharmonia, San Francisco Opera, Bayreuth, Holland and Prague Festivals, BBC. Records many symphonies and operas. Former Member Executive Cttee, John F. Kennedy Center for Performing Arts. Fellow, American Academy of Arts and Sciences. Holds hon. degrees. *Publications:* Cadenza (autobiog.), 1976; The Composer's Advocate, 1981; transcriptions of Brahms Chorale Preludes; contribs. to Atlantic Monthly, Saturday Review, New York Times, High Fidelity. *Address:* c/o Dodds, 209 East 56th Street, New York, NY 10022, USA.

LEINSTER, 8th Duke of, *cr* 1766; **Gerald FitzGerald;** Baron of Offaly, 1205; Earl of Kildare, 1316; Viscount Leinster (Great Britain), 1747; Marquess of Kildare, 1761; Earl of Offaly, 1761; Baron Kildare, 1870; Premier Duke, Marquess, and Earl, of Ireland; Major late 5th Royal Inniskilling Dragoon Guards; Chairman, CSE Aviation Group of Cos; *b* 27 May 1914; *o s* of 7th Duke of Leinster and May (*d* 1935), *d* of late Jesse Etheridge; *S* father, 1976; *m* 1st, 1936, Joane (who obtained a divorce, 1946), *e d* of late Major McMorrough Kavanagh, MC, Borris House, Co. Carlow; two *d* ; 2nd, 1946, Anne Eustace Smith; two *s. Educ:* Eton; Sandhurst. *Heir: s* Marquess of Kildare, *qv. Recreations:* flying, fishing, shooting. *Address:* Langston House, Chadlington, Oxford OX7 3LU. *T:* Chadlington 436.

LEISHMAN, Frederick John, CVO 1957; MBE 1944; *b* 21 Jan. 1919; *s* of Alexander Leishman and Freda Mabel (*née* Hood); *m* 1945, Frances Webb, Evanston, Illinois, USA; two *d. Educ:* Oundle; Corpus Christi, Cambridge. Served RE, 1940-46, and with Military Government, Germany, 1945-46; Regular Commission, 1945; resigned, 1946. Joined Foreign Service, 1946; FO, 1946-48; Copenhagen, 1948-51; Civil Service Selection Board, 1951; Assistant Private Secretary to the Foreign Secretary, 1951-53; First Secretary, Washington, 1953-58; First Secretary and Head of Chancery, Teheran, 1959-61; Counsellor, 1961; HM Consul-General, Hamburg, 1961-62; Foreign Office, 1962-63. Dir, Hill Samuel & Co. Ltd, 1965-80; Dep. Chm. and Chief Exec., Hill Samuel Gp (SA) Ltd, 1969-72; Partner and Chm., Hill Samuel & Co. ottG, Germany, 1975-77; Dir and Exec. Vice-Pres., Saehan Merchant Banking Corp., Seoul, 1977-80. FRSA. *Recreations:* golf, fishing. *Address:* Saltoun House, Cotherstone, Barnard Castle, Co. Durham DL12 9PF. *T:* Teesdale 50671. *Clubs:* Travellers'; London Scottish Rugby Football; Hawks, Cambridge University Rugby Union Football (Cambridge); Royal Ashdown Forest Golf.

LEITCH, David Alexander; Under Secretary, Local Government Finance, Scottish Office, since 1981; *b* 4 April 1931; *s* of Alexander and Eileen Leitch; *m* 1954, Marie (*née* Tain); two *s* one *d. Educ:* St Mungo's Acad., Glasgow. Min. of Supply, 1948-58; Dept of Agriculture and Fisheries for Scotland: Asst Principal, 1959; Principal, 1963; Asst Sec., 1971; Asst Sec., Local Govt Finance, Scottish Office (Central Services), 1976. *Recreations:* climbing, hill-walking. *Address:* 3 The Glebe, Cramond, Edinburgh EH4 6NW. *Clubs:* Royal Commonwealth Society; Deerhound.

LEITCH, Sir George, KCB 1975 (CB 1963); OBE 1945; Chairman, Short Brothers Ltd, since 1976; *b* 5 June 1915; *er s* of late James Simpson and Margaret Leitch; *m* 1942, Edith Marjorie Maughan; one *d. Educ:* Wallsend Grammar Sch.; King's Coll., University of Durham. Research and teaching in mathematics, 1937-39. War Service in Army (from TA), 1939-46 (despatches, OBE): Lieut-Colonel in charge of Operational Research in Eastern, then Fourteenth Army, 1943-45; Brigadier (Dep. Scientific Adviser, War Office), 1945-46; entered Civil Service, as Principal, 1947; Ministry of Supply, 1947-59 (Under-Secretary, 1959); War Office, 1959-64; Ministry of Defence: Asst Under-Secretary of State, 1964-65; Dep. Under-Sec. of State, 1965-72; Procurement Executive, MoD: Controller (Policy), 1971-72; Secretary, 1972-74; Chief Exec., 1974-75. Chm., Standing Adv. Cttee on Trunk Rd Assessment, 1977-80. Commonwealth Fund Fellow, 1953-54. Hon. DSc (Durham), 1946. *Recreations:* swimming, gardening. *Address:* 73 Princes Way, Wimbledon, SW19. *T:* 01-788 4658.

LEITCH, Isabella, OBE 1949; MA, DSc; retired as Director Commonwealth Bureau of Animal Nutrition (1940-60); *b* 13 Feb. 1890; 3rd *d* of John Leitch and Isabella McLennan. *Educ:* Peterhead Academy; Aberdeen Univ. MA (Hons Mathematics and Natural Philosophy), 1911; BSc, 1914; research in Genetics and Physiology at Copenhagen Univ., 1914-19; DSc 1919. Staff of Rowett Research Institute, 1923-29; Staff of Imperial (now Commonwealth) Bureau of Animal Nutrition, 1929. Hon. LLD (Aberdeen), 1965. *Publications:* (with Frank E. Hytten) The Physiology of Human Pregnancy, 1964; (with A. W. Boyne and G. F. Garton) Composition of British Feedingstuffs, 1976; also contributions on genetics, physiology, and nutrition in MRC Special Report Series and scientific journals, etc. *Recreation:* hill-climbing. *Address:* Rongai Farm, Old Koreelah, NSW 2476, Australia. *Clubs:* Farmers'; Strathcona (Bucksburn, Aberdeen).

LEITCH, William Andrew, CB 1963; Law Reform Consultant, Government of Northern Ireland, 1973-78; Examiner of Statutory Rules, Northern Ireland Assembly, 1974-78, retired; *b* 16 July 1915; *e s* of Andrew Leitch, MD, DPH, Castlederg, Co. Tyrone, and May, *d* of W. H. Todd, JP, Fyfin, Strabane, Co. Tyrone; *m* 1939, Edna Margaret, *d* of David McIlvennan, Solicitor, Belfast; one *s* two *d. Educ:* Methodist Coll., Belfast; Queen's Univ., Belfast; London Univ. (LLB). Admitted Solicitor, NI, 1937; Asst Solicitors Dept, Ministry of Finance, NI, 1937-43; Asst Parly Draftsman, 1944-56; First Parly Draftsman, 1956-74. Hon. LLM, Queen's Univ., Belfast, 1967. *Publications:* A Handbook on the Administration of Estates Act (NI), 1955, 1957; (jointly) A Commentary on the Interpretation Act (Northern Ireland) 1954, 1955; articles in various legal publications. *Recreations:* fishing, golf, reading. *Address:* 53 Kensington Road, Belfast BT5 6NL. *T:* Belfast 654784.

LEITH, family name of Baron Burgh.

LEITH, Sir Andrew George F.; *see* Forbes-Leith.

LEITH, Prudence Margaret, (Mrs Rayne Kruger); Managing Director, Prudence Leith Ltd (parent company of the Leith's Group), since 1972; Cookery Editor, The Guardian, since 1980; part-time Member, British Railways Board, since 1980; Director, British Transport Hotels, since 1977; *b* 18 Feb. 1940; *d* of late Sam Leith and of Margaret Inglis; *m* Rayne Kruger; one *s* one *d. Educ:* Hayward's Heath, Sussex; St Mary's, Johannesburg; Cape Town Univ.; Sorbonne, Paris; Cordon Bleu, London. French studies at Sorbonne, and preliminary cooking apprenticeship with French families; Cordon Bleu sch. course; small outside catering service from bedsitter in London, 1960-65; started Leith's Good Food (commercial catering co.), 1965, and Leith's (restaurant), 1969; Cookery Corresp., Daily Mail, 1969-73; opened Leith's Sch. of Food and Wine, 1975; added Leith's Farm, 1976; Cookery Corresp., Sunday Express, 1976– mid 1980. *Publications:* Leith's All-Party

Cook Book, 1969; Parkinson's Pie (in aid of World Wild Life Fund), 1972; Cooking For Friends, 1978; The Best of Prue Leith, 1979; (with J. B. Reynaud) Leith's Cookery Course (3-part paperback), 1979-80, (comp. hardback with C. Waldegrave), 1980; The Cook's Handbook, 1981. *Recreations:* riding, tennis, old cookbooks and kitchen antiques. *Address:* 94 Kensington Park Road, W11. *T:* 01-221 5282.

LEITH-BUCHANAN, Sir Charles (Alexander James), 7th Bt *cr* 1775; President, United Business Machines Inc., Alexandria, Va, since 1978; *b* 1 Sept. 1939; *s* of John Wellesley MacDonald Leith-Buchanan (*g s* of 4th Bt) (*d* 1956) and Jane Elizabeth McNicol (*d* 1955), *d* of Ronald McNicol; *S* cousin, 1973; *m* 1962, Mary Anne Kelly; one *s* one *d. Heir: s* Gordon Leith-Buchanan, *b* 18 Oct. 1974. *Address:* 10504 Adel Road, Oakton, Va 22124, USA.

LEITHEAD, James Douglas; *b* 4 Oct. 1911; *s* of late William Leithead, Berwick-on-Tweed; *m* 1936, Alice, *d* of late Thomas Wylie, Stirling, Scotland; one *s. Educ:* Bradford Grammar Sch. Accountant, 1927-32; ACA 1932; FCA 1960; Chartered Accountant, 1932-39. Lecturer Bradford Technical Coll., 1934-39; Secretarial Assistant, Midland (Amalgamated) District (Coal Mines) Scheme, 1939-42; Ministry of Supply, 1942-45; BoT, 1945-64; HM Diplomatic Service, 1965-68; BoT, later DTI, 1968-72, retired. British Trade Commissioner: Australia, 1950-63; New Zealand, 1963-67. Vice-Pres., W Australian Branch of Royal Commonwealth Soc., 1957-63. *Recreation:* chess. *Address:* 48 Eaton Road, Appleton, Oxon.

LEJEUNE, Maj.-Gen. Francis St David Benwell, CB 1949; CBE 1944; *b* 1 March 1899; *2nd s* of late J. F. P. Lejeune, Bedford; *m* 1927, Joyce Mary, *d* of late Charles E. Davies, Hampton Court; one *s* one *d. Educ:* Bedford; RMA, Woolwich. 2nd Lieut, RA, 1917; served European War, 1914-18, France and Belgium (despatches); seconded RAF, Somaliland and Iraq Operations, 1920-24; GSO 3 War Office, 1929; Asst Military Attaché, Washington, 1932-34; Special Mission in Spain, 1938-39. War of 1939-45 served in Italy and Burma (despatches); Maj.-General, 1944; Chief of Staff AA Command, Comdr AA Group, 1944; Director Technical Training, War Office, 1946; President Ordnance Board, 1947; retired, 1949; International Staff, NATO, 1952-62; psc; pac. *Address:* 68 South Cliff, Bexhill on Sea, East Sussex. *T:* Bexhill 211971.

LELOIR, Luis Federico; Director, Institute of Biochemical Research, Campomar, since 1947; Head of Department of Biochemistry, University of Buenos Aires, since 1962; *b* Paris, 6 Sept. 1906; *m* Amelie Zuberbuhler de Leloir; one *d. Educ:* Univ. of Buenos Aires. Engaged in research in Gt Britain, Argentina and USA; subseq. at Inst. of Biology and Experimental Med., Buenos Aires, 1946. Chm., Argentine Assoc. for Advancement of Science, 1958-59; Mem. Directorate, Nat. Research Council, 1958-64; Mem., Nat. Acad. of Med., 1961; Foreign Mem: Royal Society, 1972; Nat. Acad. of Sciences, USA; Amer. Acad. of Arts and Sciences; Amer. Philosophical Soc.; Nat. Acad. of Scis, France, 1978. Holds several hon. doctorates and has won numerous prizes, etc, inc. Nobel Prize for Chemistry, 1970. *Address:* Instituto de Investigaciones Bioquímicas, Fundación Campomar, Obligado 2490, 1428 Buenos Aires, Argentina. *T:* 783-2871.

LEMAIRE, Most Rev. Ishmael Samuel Mills, DD; Bishop of Accra, 1968-82; Archbishop of West Africa, 1981-82. Priest, Diocese of Accra, 1936-60; Canon of Accra, 1960-63; Archdeacon of Sekondi, 1961-63; Assistant Bishop of Accra, 1963-68. *Address:* c/o Bishopscourt, PO Box 8, Accra, Ghana.

LEMAN, Paul H.; Director, Alcan Aluminium Ltd; *b* 6 Aug. 1915; *s* of J. B. Beaudry Leman and Caroline Leman (*née* Beique); *m* 1939, Jeannine F. Prud'homme; two *s* three *d. Educ:* Collège Ste Marie, Montreal (BA); Univ. of Montreal (LL.L); Harvard Graduate School of Business Administration. Admitted to Quebec Bar, 1937; joined Aluminum Co. of Canada, Ltd, 1938: Asst Sec., 1943; Treas., 1949; Vice-Pres., 1952; Dir, 1963; Exec. Vice-Pres., 1964; Treas., Saguenay Power Co. Ltd, 1945; Alcan Aluminium Ltd: Dir, 1968; Exec. Vice-Pres., 1969; Pres., 1973; Vice-Chm., 1977-79. *Recreations:* golf, tennis, fishing. *Address:* 445 Ouest, Boulevard Saint Joseph, Apt 93, Outremont, Quebec H2V 2P8, Canada. *Clubs:* Mount Bruno Country, Mount Royal, University (Montreal).

LE MARCHANT, Sir Denis, 5th Bt, *cr* 1841; *b* 28 Feb. 1906; *er s* of Brigadier-General Sir Edward Thomas Le Marchant, 4th Bt, KCB, CBE, JP, DL, and Evelyn Brooks (*d* 1957), *er d* of late Robert Millington Knowles, JP, DL, Colston Bassett Hall, Nottinghamshire; *S* father, 1953; *m* 1933, Elizabeth Rowena, *y d* of late Arthur Hovenden Worth; one *s* one *d* (and one *s* decd). *Educ:* Radley. High Sheriff, Lincolnshire, 1958. *Heir: s* Francis Arthur Le Marchant, *b* 6 Oct. 1939. *Address:* Hungerton Hall, Grantham, Lincolnshire. *T:* Knipton 244.

LE MARCHANT, Spencer; MP (C) High Peak Division of Derbyshire since 1970; Comptroller of HM Household, and a Government Whip, 1979-81; *b* 15 Jan. 1931; *s* of Alfred Le Marchant and Turdis Le Marchant (*née* Mortensen); *m* 1955, Lucinda Gaye Leveson Gower; two *d. Educ:* Eton. National Service and Territorial Commissions, Sherwood Foresters. Mem., Stock Exchange, 1954-; Partner, L. Messel & Co., 1961-. Mem., Westminster City Council, 1956-71; contested (C) Vauxhall, 1966. PPS to Chief Sec., Financial Sec. and Minister of State, Treasury, 1972-74; PPS Dept of Energy, 1974; an Opposition Whip, 1974-79; PPS to Leader of Commons, 1981-82, to Sec. of State for Foreign and Commonwealth Affairs, 1982. *Address:* Breeze Mount, The Park, Buxton, Derbyshire; Rivermill, Grosvenor Road, SW1. *Clubs:* White's; Royal Yacht Squadron.

LE MASURIER, Sir Robert (Hugh), Kt 1966; DSC 1942; Bailiff of Jersey, 1962-74; *b* 29 Dec. 1913; *s* of William Smythe Le Masurier and Mabel Harriet Briard; *m* 1941, Helen Sophia Sheringham; one *s* two *d. Educ:* Victoria Coll., Jersey. MA 1935; BCL 1936. Sub-Lieut RNVR, 1939; Lieut RNVR, 1943; Lieut-Commander RNVR, 1944. Solicitor-General, Jersey, 1955; Attorney-General, Jersey, 1958. *Recreations:* sailing, carpentry. *Address:* La Ville-a-l'Evêque, Trinity, Jersey. *Clubs:* Royal Ocean Racing; St Helier Yacht, United (Jersey).

LEMIEUX, Most Rev. (M.) Joseph; *b* Quebec City, 10 May 1902; *s* of Joseph E. Lemieux and Eva (*née* Berlinguet). *Educ:* College of St Anne de la Pocatière; Dominican House of Studies, Ottawa; College of Angelico, Rome; Blackfriars, Oxford. Missionary to Japan, 1930; Parish Priest, Miyamaecho, Hakodate, Japan, 1931-36; First Bishop of Sendai, 1936; resigned, 1941; Administrator of Diocese of Gravelbourg, Sask., 1942; Bishop of Gravelbourg, 1944-53; Archbishop of Ottawa, 1953-66; Apostolic Nuncio to Haiti, 1966-69; Apostolic Pro-Nuncio in India, 1969-71; Delegate of St Peter's Basilica in Vatican, 1971-73. *Address:* 143 St Patrick, Ottawa, Ontario K1N 5J9, Canada.

LEMIEUX, Prof. Raymond Urgel, OC (Canada), 1968; FRS 1967; Professor of Organic Chemistry, University of Alberta, 1961-80, University Professor, since 1980; *b* 16 June 1920; *s* of Octave Lemieux; *m* 1948, Virginia Marie McConaghie; one *s* five *d* (and one *s* decd). *Educ:* Edmonton, Alberta. BSc Hons (Chem.) Alta, 1943; PhD (Chem.) McGill, 1946. Research Fellow, Ohio State Univ., 1947; Asst Professor, Saskatchewan Univ., 1948-49; Senior Research Officer, National Research Council, Canada, 1949-54, Member, 1976-81; Professor, Ottawa Univ., 1954-61. FRSC 1955. Hon. DSc: New Brunswick Univ., 1967; Laval Univ., 1970; Univ. de Provence, 1973; Univ. of Ottawa, 1975; Waterloo Univ., 1980; Meml Univ., Newfoundland, 1981; Hon. LLD Calgary, 1979. Chem. Inst. of Canada Medal, 1964; C. S. Hudson Award, Amer. Chem. Soc., 1966; W. N. Haworth Medal, Chem. Soc., 1978; Izaak Walton Killam Award, Canada Council, 1981; Diplôme d'Honneur, Groupe Français des Glucides, 1981; Sir Frederick Haultain Prize, Alberta, 1982. *Publications:* over 150 research papers mainly in area of carbohydrate chemistry in Canadian Journal of Chemistry, etc. *Recreations:* golf, curling, fishing. *Address:* 7602, 119th Street, Edmonton, Alberta, Canada. *T:* 436-5167. *Clubs:* University of Alberta Faculty (Edmonton); Lake Edith Golf (Jasper).

LEMKIN, James Anthony; a Senior Partner, Field Fisher & Martineau, Solicitors; Member for Hillingdon, Uxbridge, Greater London Council, since 1973 (Additional Member, 1970-73); *b* 21 Dec. 1926; *s* of William Lemkin, CBE, and Rachel Irene Lemkin; *m* 1960, Joan Dorothy Anne Casserley, FFARCS; two *s* two *s d. Educ:* Charterhouse; Merton Coll., Oxford (MA). Admitted solicitor, 1953; RN, 1945-47. Greater London Council: Additional Mem., 1970-73, elected Mem. for Hillingdon, Uxbridge, 1973-; Chm., Legal and Parly Cttee, 1977-78; Chm., Scrutiny Cttee, 1978-81; Cons. spokesman on police affairs, 1981-. Conservative and Nat. Liberal Party Candidate, Chesterfield, 1959; Liberal Cand., Cheltenham, 1964. Chm., Bow Gp, 1952, 1956, 1957 (Founder Chm., Crossbow, 1957-60); Mem. Exec. Cttee, Nat. Union of Cons. and Unionist Assocs, 1975-; Treasurer, Soc. of Cons. Lawyers, 1978 (Vice-Chm. Exec. Cttee, 1971-78). Member: N London Hosp. Management Cttee, 1971-74; NW Thames RHA, 1980-; Royal Marsden Hosp. SHA, 1982-; Appeal Cttee, Cancer Res. Campaign, 1967-81. Governor, Westfield Coll., London Univ., 1970-. Co-founder, Africa Confidential, 1960. *Publication:* (ed) Race and Power, 1956. *Recreations:* umpiring cricket, making soup. *Address:* 4 Frognal Close, NW3 6YB. *T:* 01-242 1250. *Club:* Carlton.

LEMMON, Cyril Whitefield, FRIBA, AIA; Architect, Honolulu, Hawaii (Private Practice), 1946-69; *b* Kent, 27 Oct. 1901; *s* of T. E. Lemmon and Catherine Whitefield; *m* 1st, 1921, Ethel Belinda Peters, artist (marr. diss., 1936); no *c*; 2nd, 1938, Rebecca Robson Ramsay; two *d. Educ:* University of Pennsylvania, Philadelphia, Pa. Fifth-year Studio Instructor and Lecturer in the School of Architecture, University of Liverpool, 1933-36; Consulting Architect to Government of India for Rebuilding of Quetta, 1936; Consulting Architect to MES for all military buildings in India, 1938. Lieut-Colonel, Royal Indian Engineers, 1941; Director of Civil Camouflage in India, 1943; GSO 1, GHQ, India and 11th Army Group, 1943-44. President, Hawaii Chapter, AIA, 1950. Exhibited paintings in Salon des Tuileries, Paris, 1933; travel in United States, Mexico, Europe, N Africa and Asia. Public Lectures on Architecture and Painting. *Publications:* contributions to professional journals on Architecture. *Recreations:* golf, swimming. *Address:* 4999 Kahala Avenue, Apartment 302, Honolulu, Hawaii 96816, USA. *Clubs:* Kiwanis, Oahu Country, etc. (Honolulu).

LEMNITZER, General Lyman L., DSM (US Army) (with 3 Oak Leaf Clusters); DSM (US Navy); DSM (US Air Force); Silver Star; Legion of Merit (Officer's Degree); Legion of Merit; Supreme Allied Commander, Europe, 1963-69; Commander-in-Chief, US European Command, 1962-69; *b* Pennsylvania, 29 Aug. 1899; *s* of late William L. Lemnitzer; *m* 1923, Katherine Mead Tryon; one *s* one *d. Educ:* Honesdale High Sch.; US Military Academy. Duty with troops, Instructor at Army Schools, etc., 1920-40; War

Plans Division, War Dept General Staff, 1941; Comdg General, 34th Anti-Aircraft Artillery Bde, and Allied Force HQ England, as Asst Chief of Staff for Plans and Ops, 1942 (2nd in Command, Secret Submarine Mission to contact friendly French Officials in N Africa); served in Europe and N Africa, 1942-45; with Joint Chiefs of Staff, 1945-47; Dep. Comdt National War Coll., 1947-49; Asst to Secretary of Defence, 1949-50; Head of US Delegn to Military Cttee of the Five (Brussels Pact) Powers. London; Student, Basic Airborne Course, Fort Benning, 1950; Comdg General 11th Airborne Div., 1951, 7th Infantry Div. (in Korea), 1951-52; DCS (Plans and Research), 1952-55; Comdg General Far East and 8th US Army, 1955; C-in-C, Far East and UN Commands, and Governor of Ryukyu Is, 1955-57; Vice-Chief of Staff, 1957-59, Chief of Staff, 1959-60, US Army; Chairman Joint Chiefs of Staff, 1960-62. Holds several hon. doctorates. Hon. CB and Hon. CBE (Great Britain); Grand Cross, Legion of Honour (France); Grand Cross, Order of Merit (Germany), 1969; and numerous other foreign Orders and decorations. *Recreations:* golf, fishing, photography, interested in baseball, correspondence with his many friends around the world. *Address:* 3286 Worthington Street, NW, Washington, DC 20015, USA.

LEMON, Sir (Richard) Dawnay, Kt 1970; CBE 1958; QPM 1964; Chief Constable of Kent, 1962-74; *b* 1912; *o s* of late Lieut-Colonel F. J. Lemon, CBE, DSO, and of Mrs Laura Lemon; *m* 1939, Sylvia Marie Kentish; one *s* one *d* (and one *d* decd). *Educ:* Uppingham Sch.; RMC, Sandhurst. Joined West Yorks Regt, 1932; retired 1934. Metropolitan Police, 1934-37; Leicestershire Constabulary, 1937-39; Chief Constable of East Riding of Yorkshire, 1939-42; Chief Constable of Hampshire and Isle of Wight, 1942-62. *Recreations:* cricket, golf, shooting. *Address:* West Coggers, St Margaret's Bay, Dover. *T:* Dover 852685. *Clubs:* Naval and Military, MCC; Royal Yacht Squadron (Cowes (hon.)).

LENDRUM, Prof. Alan Chalmers, MA, MD, BSc, ARPS; FRCPath; Professor of Pathology, University of Dundee, 1967-72, Professor Emeritus, 1972, Honorary Research Fellow, 1972; *b* 3 Nov. 1906; *yr s* of late Rev. Dr Robert Alexander Lendrum and Anna, *e d* of late James Guthrie of Pitforthie, Angus; *m* 1934, Elizabeth Bertram, *e d* of late Donald Currie, BA, LLB; two *s* one *d. Educ:* High Sch., Glasgow; Ardrossan Acad.; University of Glasgow. Asst to Sir Robert Muir, MD, FRS, 1933; Lecturer in Pathology, University of Glasgow; Prof. of Pathology, Univ. of St Andrews, 1947-67. Visiting Prof. of Pathology, Yale, 1960. Kettle Meml Lecture, RCPath, 1973. Hon. For. Mem. Argentine Soc. of Normal and Pathological Anatomy; Hon. Member: Pathol Soc. of GB and Ireland; Nederlandse Patholoog Anatomen Vereniging; Dialectic Soc., Glasgow Univ.; Forfarshire Medical Assoc.; Hon. Fellow, and ex-Pres., Inst. Med. Lab. Sci. Dean of Guildry of Brechin, 1971-73. Capt. RAMC (TA) retd. Sims Woodhead Medal, 1971. Chm. of Governors, Duncan of Jordanstone Coll. of Art, Dundee, 1975-77. *Publications:* (co-author) Recent Advances in Clinical Pathology, 1948; Trends in Clinical Pathology, 1969; publications in medical journals. *Address:* Invergowrie House, Dundee DD2 1UA. *T:* Dundee 66666.

LENG, Gen. Sir Peter (John Hall), KCB 1978 (CB 1975); MBE 1962; MC 1945; Master-General of the Ordnance, since 1981; *b* 9 May 1925; *s* of J. Leng; *m* 1st, Virginia Rosemary Pearson (marr. diss. 1981); three *s* two *d* ; 2nd, 1981, Mrs Flavia Tower. *Educ:* Bradfield Coll. Served War of 1939-45: commissioned in Scots Guards, 1944; Guards Armoured Div., Germany (MC). Various post-war appts; Guards Independent Parachute Company, 1949-51; commanded: 3rd Bn Royal Anglian Regt, in Berlin, United Kingdom and Aden, 1964-66; 24th Airportable Bde, 1968-70; Dep. Military Sec., Min. of Defence, 1971-73; Comdr Land Forces, N Ireland, 1973-75; Dir, Mil. Operations, MoD, 1975-77; Comdr 1 (Br) Corps, 1978-80. Colonel Commandant: RAVC, 1976-; RMP, 1976-. *Recreations:* fishing, shooting, painting. *Address:* c/o Barclays Bank, 1 Brompton Road, SW3 1EB. *Club:* Naval and Military.

LENIHAN, Brian Joseph; Teachta Dala (TD) for Dublin (West County), Parliament of Ireland, since 1977 (TD for Roscommon/Leitrim, 1961-73); *b* 17 Nov. 1930; *s* of Patrick Lenihan (TD Longford-Westmeath, 1965-70); *m* 1958, Ann Devine; four *s* one *d. Educ:* St Mary's Coll. (Marist Brothers), Athlone; University Coll., Dublin. Member: Roscommon CC, 1955-61; Seanad Eireann (FF), 1957-61 and (as Leader in Seanad, Fianna Fáil), 1973-77; Parly Sec. to Minister for Lands, 1961-64; Minister for: Justice, 1964-68; Educn, 1968-69; Transport and Power, 1969-73; Foreign Affairs, 1973; Fisheries and Forestry, 1977-79; Foreign Affairs, 1979-81. Mem., European Parlt, 1973-77. *Address:* 24 Park View, Castleknock, Co. Dublin, Ireland.

LENNARD, Rev. Sir Hugh Dacre B.; *see* Barrett-Lennard.

LENNIE, Douglas; *b* 30 March 1910; *e s* of Magnus S. Lennie; *m* 1941, Rhona Young Ponsonby; two *s. Educ:* Berkhamsted Sch.; Guy's Hospital, LDS, RCS, 1934; Northwestern University, Chicago, DDS, 1938. Served War of 1939-45, Temporary Surg. Lt-Comdr (D) RNVR; formerly Surgeon Dentist to Queen Mary. *Address:* 72 Chiltley Way, Liphook, Hants.

LENNON, Dennis, CBE 1968; MC 1942; Senior Partner, Dennis Lennon & Partners, since 1950; *b* 23 June 1918; British; *m* 1947, Else Bull-Andersen; three *s. Educ:* Merchant Taylors' Sch.; University Coll., London. Served Royal Engineers, 1939-45 (despatches): 1st, 7th, 6th Armd Divs; captured in France 1940, later escaped; 7th Armd Div., N Africa; 6th Armd Div., Italy. Dir, Rayon Industry Design Centre, 1948-50; private practice, 1950-. Main Work:

Jaeger shops; London Steak Houses; co-ordinator of interior, RMS Queen Elizabeth II; Chalcot Housing Estate, Hampstead; approved plans for Criterion site, Piccadilly Circus; Central Dining Room, Harrow Sch.; Arts Club. Work for stage: set for Capriccio, Glyndebourne; 9 state galas, Royal Opera House. FRIBA, FSIA, FRSA. *Recreations:* arts and design. *Address:* Hamper Mill, Watford, Herts. *T:* Watford 34445. *Clubs:* Savile; Royal Thames Yacht.

LENNON, Prof. (George) Gordon; retired gynæcologist; Professor Emeritus, University of Western Australia, Perth, 1974; *b* 7 Oct. 1911; *s* of late J. Lennon; *m* 1940, Barbara Brynhild (*née* Buckle); two *s. Educ:* Aberdeen Academy; Aberdeen Univ. MB, ChB Aberdeen, 1934; served in hospital posts in Aberdeen, Glasgow, London, Birmingham; MRCOG 1939; FRCOG 1952; MMSA 1943; ChM (Hons) Aberdeen, 1945. Served War of 1939-45, Sqdn-Ldr in charge of Surgical Div., RAFVR, 1942-46. First Asst, Nuffield Dept of Obstetrics and Gynæcology, Radcliffe Infirmary (University of Oxford), 1946-51; Prof. of Obstetrics and Gynæcology, Univ. of Bristol, 1951-67; Dean, Faculty of Med., Univ. of WA, Perth, 1967-74. Visiting Professor: Iraq and Turkey, 1956; South Africa and Uganda, 1958; Iran, 1965. *Publications:* Diagnosis in Clinical Obstetrics; articles in British Medical Journal, Proceedings of the Royal Society of Medicine, Journal of Obstetrics and Gynæcology of the British Empire, etc. *Recreation:* golf. *Address:* Mediaeval House, The Square, Axbridge, Somerset BS26 2BL.

LENNON, Most Rev. Patrick; *see* Kildare and Leighlin, Bishop of, (RC).

LENNOX; *see* Gordon-Lennox and Gordon Lennox.

LENNOX, Robert Smith, CBE 1978; JP; Lord Provost of Aberdeen, 1967-70 and 1975-77; *b* 8 June 1909; *m* 1963, Evelyn Margaret; no *c. Educ:* St Clement Sch., Aberdeen. Hon. LLD Aberdeen, 1970. JP Aberdeen. *Address:* 7 Gillespie Crescent, Ashgrove, Aberdeen. *T:* Aberdeen 43862.

LENNOX-BOYD, family name of **Viscount Boyd of Merton.**

LENNOX-BOYD, Hon. Mark Alexander; MP (C) Morecambe and Lonsdale, since 1979; barrister-at-law; *b* 4 May 1943; 3rd *s* of Viscount Boyd of Merton, *qv* ; *m* 1974, Arabella Lacloche; one *d. Educ:* Eton Coll.; Christ Church, Oxford. Called to the Bar, Inner Temple, 1968. PPS to Sec. of State for Energy, 1981-. *Recreation:* travel. *Address:* 3 Bloomfield Terrace, SW1W 8PG. *T:* 01-730 3754; Gresgarth Hall, Caton, Lancashire LA2 9NB. *T:* Caton 770313. *Clubs:* Pratt's, Beefsteak, Buck's.
    See also Hon. S. D. R. N. Lennox-Boyd.

LENNOX-BOYD, Hon. Simon (Donald Rupert Neville); Deputy Chairman, Arthur Guinness & Sons plc, since 1981; *b* 7 Dec. 1939; *e s* and *heir* of Viscount Boyd of Merton, *qv* ; *m* 1962, Alice Mary, *d* of late Major M. G. D. Clive and of Lady Mary Clive; two *s* two *d. Educ:* Eton; Christ Church, Oxford. Vice-Chm., Save the Children, 1979-82; Trustee, Guinness Trust, 1974-. *Address:* Wivelscombe, Saltash, Cornwall PL12 4QY. *T:* Saltash 2672; 9 Warwick Square, SW1V 2AA. *Clubs:* White's; Royal Yacht Squadron.

LENNY, Most Rev. Francis; Auxiliary Bishop of Armagh, (RC), and titular Bishop of Rotdon, since 1974; *b* 27 Sept. 1928; *s* of Francis Patrick Lenny and Mary Agnes O'Rourke. *Educ:* St Patrick's Coll., Armagh; St Patrick's Coll., Maynooth (BA, BD, LCL). Secretary to Cardinal D'Alton, 1955-63; Secretary to Cardinal Conway, 1963-72. *Address:* Parochial House, Mullavilly, Tandragee, Craigavon, Co. Armagh. *T:* Tandragee 840840.

LENTON, Aylmer Ingram, PhD; Managing Director, Bowater Corporation plc, since 1981; *b* 19 May 1927; *s* of Albert Lenton and Olive Lenton; *m* 1951, Ursula Kathleen King; one *s* two *d. Educ:* Leeds Grammar Sch.; Magdalen Coll., Oxford (MA); Leeds Univ. (PhD). Richard Haworth & Co. Ltd, 1951; British Nylon Spinners Ltd, 1956; Managing Director, S African Nylon Spinners Ltd, 1964; Director, ICI Fibres Ltd, 1966; Director, John Heathcoat & Co. Ltd, 1967, Man. Dir, 1971; Bowater Corporation Ltd: Chm., Bowater UK Paper Co., 1976; Chm., Bowater UK Ltd, 1979; Director, 1979. *Recreations:* golf, fencing, walking. *Address:* Bowater House, Knightsbridge, SW1X 7LR. *T:* 01-584 7070.

LEON, Sir John (Ronald), 4th Bt, *cr* 1911; Actor (stage name, John Standing); *b* 16 Aug. 1934; *er s* of 3rd Bt and late Kay Hammond; *S* father, 1964; *m* 1961, Jill (marr. diss. 1972), *d* of Jack Melford; one *s. Educ:* Eton. Late 2nd Lt, KRRC. *Plays include:* Darling Buds of May, Saville, 1959; leading man, season, Bristol Old Vic, 1960; The Irregular Verb to Love, Criterion, 1961; Norman, Duchess, 1963; So Much to Remember, Vaudeville, 1963; The Three Sisters, Oxford Playhouse, 1964; See How They Run, Vaudeville, 1964; Seasons at Chichester Theatre, 1966, 1967; The Importance of Being Earnest, Haymarket 1968; Ring Round the Moon, Haymarket, 1968; The Alchemist, and Arms and the Man, Chichester, 1970; Popkiss, Globe, 1972; A Sense of Detachment, Royal Court, 1972; Private Lives, Queen's and Globe, 1973, NY and tour of USA, 1974; Jingo, Aldwych, 1975; Plunder, The Philanderer, NT, 1978; Close of Play, NT, 1979; Tonight at 8.30, Lyric, 1981. *Films:* The Wild and the Willing, 1962; Iron Maiden, 1962; King Rat, 1964; Walk, Don't Run, 1965; Zee and Co., 1973; The Eagle has Landed, 1976; The Class of Miss MacMichael, 1977; The Legacy, 1977; The Elephant Man, 1979; The Sea Wolves, 1980. Television appearances incl. Arms and the Man; The

First Churchills; Charley's Aunt; Rogue Male; The Sinking of HMS Victoria; Home and Beauty; Tinker, Tailor, Soldier, Spy; The Other 'Arf. *Recreation:* painting. *Heir: s* Alexander John Leon, *b* 3 May 1965. *Address:* c/o William Morris, 147 Wardour Street, W1.

LEONARD, family name of **Baron Leonard.**

LEONARD, Baron *cr* 1978 (Life Peer), of the City of Cardiff in the County of S Glamorgan; **John Denis Leonard,** OBE 1976; Chairman, Cardiff Sheet Metal & Engineering Co. Ltd, since 1953; *b* 19 Oct. 1909; *s* of late Denis Leonard and Mary McDermott; *m* 1945, Glenys Evelyn Kenny; one *s* one *d. Educ:* Manorhamilton Boys' School, Republic of Ireland. Member: Cardiff City Council, 1970-76; S Glamorgan County Council, 1974-77 (Chairman, 1976-77). A Lord in Waiting (Govt Whip), 1978-79. Mem. Council, Univ. of Wales Inst. of Science and Technology, 1978. *Recreations:* Association football, golf and gardening. *Address:* 19 Queen Anne Square, Cardiff. *T:* Cardiff 387109.

LEONARD, Dick; *see* Leonard, Richard Lawrence.

LEONARD, Rt. Rev. and Rt. Hon. Graham Douglas; *see* London, Bishop of.

LEONARD, Hon. Sir (Hamilton) John, Kt 1981; Hon. Mr Justice Leonard; a Judge of the High Court, Queen's Bench Division, since 1981; *b* 28 April 1926; *s* of late Arthur and Jean Leonard, Poole, Dorset; *m* 1948, Doreen Enid, *yr d* of late Lt-Col Sidney James Parker, OBE, and May Florence Parker, Sanderstead, Surrey; one *s* one *d. Educ:* Dean Close Sch., Cheltenham; Brasenose Coll., Oxford (MA). Coldstream Guards (Captain), 1944-47. Called to Bar, Inner Temple, 1951; Master of the Bench, 1977; South-Eastern Circuit (Presiding Judge, 1982-). 2nd Junior Prosecuting Counsel to the Crown at Central Criminal Court, 1964-69; QC 1969; Dep. Chm., Surrey QS, 1969-71; Comr, CCC, 1969-71; a Recorder of the Crown Court, 1972-78; a Circuit Judge, 1978-81; Common Serjeant in the City of London, 1979-81. Member: General Council of the Bar, 1970-74, Senate, 1971-74, Senate of Four Inns and the Bar, 1974-77. Chm., Criminal Bar Assoc., 1975-77. Member: Home Sec.'s Adv. Bd on Restricted Patients, 1973-78; Dept'l Cttee to Review Laws on Obscenity, Indecency and Censorship, 1977-79; Judicial Studies Bd, 1979-. Mem. Council, Hurstpierpoint Coll., 1975-. Liveryman, Plaisterers' Co.; HM Lieutenant, City of London, 1980-81. *Recreations:* books, music, painting. *Address:* Royal Courts of Justice, WC2A 2LL. *Club:* Garrick.

LEONARD, Hugh, (John Keyes Byrne); playwright since 1959; Programme Director, Dublin Theatre Festival, since 1978; Literary Editor, Abbey Theatre, 1976-77; *b* 9 Nov. 1926; *m* 1955, Paule Jacquet; one *d. Educ:* Presentation College, Dun Laoghaire. Hon. DHL Rhode Island, 1980. *Stage plays:* The Big Birthday, 1956; A Leap in the Dark, 1957; Madigan's Lock, 1958; A Walk on the Water, 1960; The Passion of Peter Ginty, 1961; Stephen D, 1962; The Poker Session, and Dublin 1, 1963; The Saints Go Cycling In, 1965; Mick and Mick, 1966; The Quick and the Dead, 1967; The Au Pair Man, 1968; The Barracks, 1969; The Patrick Pearse Motel, 1971; Da, 1973; Thieves, 1973; Summer, 1974; Times of Wolves and Tigers, 1974; Irishmen, 1975; Time Was, 1976; A Life, 1977; Moving Days, 1981; Kill, 1982. *TV plays:* Silent Song (Italia Award, 1967); The Last Campaign, 1978; The Ring and the Rose, 1978. *TV serials:* Nicholas Nickleby, 1977; London Belongs to Me, 1977; Wuthering Heights, 1978; Strumpet City, 1979; The Little World of Don Camillo, 1980; Good Behaviour, 1982. *Film:* Herself Surprised, 1977. *Publication:* Home Before Night (autobiog.), 1979. *Recreations:* chess, travel, living. *Address:* Theros, Coliemore Road, Dalkey, Co. Dublin. *T:* Dublin 859856. *Clubs:* Dramatists'; PEN (Dublin); Players' (NY).

LEONARD, His Honour James Charles Beresford Whyte, MA Oxon; a Circuit Judge (formerly Deputy Chairman of Quarter Sessions, Inner London and Middlesex), 1965-79; Judge of the Mayor's and City of London Court, 1972-79; *b* 1905; *s* of Hon. J. W. Leonard, KC; *m* 1939, Barbara Helen, *d* of late Capt. William Incledon-Webber; two *s* one *d. Educ:* Clifton Coll.; Christ Church, Oxford. Called to the Bar, Inner Temple, 1928, Bencher 1961. Served 1940-45, with RAF (Sqdn Ldr). Recorder of Walsall, Staffs, 1951-64; Junior Counsel to Ministry of Agriculture, Fisheries and Food, Forestry Commission and Tithe Redemption Commission, 1959-64; Deputy Chairman of QS: Co. of London, 1964-65; Oxfordshire, 1962-71. Chairman: Disciplinary Cttee, Pharmaceutical Soc. of GB, 1960-64; Adv. Cttee dealing with internment under Civil Authorities (Special Powers) Act (NI) 1962, April-Nov. 1972; Comr under Terrorism (N Ireland) Order 1972, 1972-74; Dep. Chm., Appeal Tribunal, 1974-75. *Address:* Cross Trees, Sutton Courtenay, Oxon. *T:* Sutton Courtenay 230.
    See also Earl of Westmeath.

LEONARD, Hon. Sir John; *see* Leonard, Hon. Sir H. J.

LEONARD, Michael William, BSc(Eng), CEng, FICE, MIMechE, FCIArb; Secretary, The Fellowship of Engineering, since 1976; *b* 25 Dec. 1916; *e s* of late Frank Leonard and Marguerite Leonard (*née* Holborow); *m* 1945, Rosalinna Cushnir; three *s. Educ:* Haberdashers' Aske's; Pupilage in Mechanical Engineering, Messrs Fraser & Chalmers Ltd, Erith; University College London (Pres., Union Society, 1939). Civil Engineer, Mowlem Group of Companies, to 1968; Director: Soil Mechanics Ltd; Engineering

Laboratories Equipment Ltd. Mem., BSI Code of Practice on Site Investigations; Mem., later Chm., Tip Safety Cttee (post Aberfan); Sec., Council of Engineering Institutions, 1969-82; Chm., BSI Code of Practice Cttee on Foundations; Design Council Engineering Design Adv. Cttee; DoI Cttee for Industrial Technologies; Hon. Treasurer, Parly and Scientific Cttee; Vice-Pres., Fédération Européenne d'Associations Nationales d'Ingenieurs; Sec., Commonwealth Engineers' Council; Mem., Executive Cttee, World Fedn of Engineering Organizations. Hon. Prof., Sheffield Univ. *Publications:* papers and articles on Foundation and Geotechnical Engineering, and on Professional Engineering, for jls and confs. *Recreations:* touring, golf, fishing. *Address:* 5 Havelock Road, Croydon CR0 6QQ. *T:* 01-654 4493. *Club:* Athenæum.

LEONARD, Richard Lawrence, (Dick Leonard); Assistant Editor, The Economist, since 1974, based in Brussels since 1980; *b* 12 Dec. 1930; *s* of Cyril Leonard, Pinner, Mddx, and late Kate Leonard (*née* Whyte); *m* 1963, Irene, *d* of Dr Ernst Heidelberger, Colombes, France, and of Dr Gertrud Heidelberger, Bad Godesberg, Germany; one *s* one *d. Educ:* Ealing Grammar Sch.; Inst. of Education, London Univ.; Essex Univ. (MA). School teacher, 1953-55; Dep. Gen. Sec., Fabian Society, 1955-60; journalist and broadcaster, 1960-68; Sen. Research Fellow (Social Science Research Council), Essex Univ., 1968-70. Mem., Exec. Cttee, Fabian Soc., 1972-80 (Chm., 1977-78); Chm., Library Adv. Council, 1978-81. Trustee, Assoc. of London Housing Estates, 1973-78. Contested (Lab) Harrow W, 1955; MP (Lab) Romford, 1970-Feb. 1974; PPS to Rt Hon. Anthony Crosland, 1970-74; Mem., Speaker's Conf. on Electoral Law, 1972-74. Introduced Council Housing Bill, 1971; Life Peers Bill, 1973. *Publications:* Guide to the General Election, 1964; Elections in Britain, 1968; (ed jtly) The Backbencher and Parliament, 1972; Paying for Party Politics, 1975; BBC Guide to Parliament, 1979; (ed jtly) The Socialist Agenda, 1981; contrib.: Guardian, Sunday Times, Observer, New Society, Encounter, etc. *Recreations:* walking, neglecting the garden. *Address:* c/o The Economist, Rue Ducale 39, Bruxelles, Belgium.

LEONARD, Sir Walter McEllister, Kt 1977; DFC; Company Director; *b* Grafton, 22 Feb. 1915; *s* of W. Leonard, Grafton; *m* 1948, Yvonne M., *d* of J. V. Brady; two *s* three *d. Educ:* Cootamundra High Sch. Joined Ampol Petroleum Ltd, 1938; Chief Accountant, 1940; Sec., 1941. Served War, RAAF, Bomber Command, 1942-45 (DFC). Ampol Petroleum Ltd: Asst to Man. Dir, 1946-49; Gen. Manager, 1949-63; Dir, 1958; Man. Dir and Chief Exec., 1963-70; Chm. and Chief Exec., 1970-77; Chm., 1977-81; Ampol Exploration Ltd: Dir, 1954; Man. Dir and Chief Exec., 1967-70; Chm. and Chief Exec., 1970-77; Chm., 1977-81. Director: Australian Industry Develt Corp., 1971-; CRA Ltd, 1977-; Interscan Australia Pty Ltd, 1978-; Australian Liquid Assets Management Ltd, 1981-. *Address:* 51 Cutler Road, Clontarf, NSW 2093, Australia. *Clubs:* Australian (Sydney); Commonwealth (Canberra); Royal Sydney Yacht Squadron; American National; Elanora Country.

LEONARD-WILLIAMS, Air Vice-Marshal Harold Guy, CB 1966; CBE 1946; DL; retired; Chairman, Somerset County Council, since 1978; *b* 10 Sept. 1911; *s* of late Rev. B. G. Leonard-Williams; *m* 1937, Catherine Estelle, *d* of late G. A. M. Levett; one *d. Educ:* Lancing Coll.; RAF Coll., Cranwell. 58 Sqdn, 1932-33; 208 Sqdn, Middle East, 1933-36; No 17 Signals Course, 1936-37; Instructor, RAF Coll., 1937-38; Advanced Air Striking Force, France, 1939-40 (despatches, 1940); Air Min. (Signals), 1940-43; Chm., Brit. Jt Communications Bd, 1943-46; RAF Staff Coll., 1947; Dep. CSO, RAF Middle East, 1947-50; Jt Services Staff Coll., 1950-51; CO Radio Engrg Unit, 1951-53; Dep. Dir Signals, Air Min., 1953-56; Sen. Techn. Staff Off., 90 Signals Gp, 1956-57; Dir of Signals, Air Min., 1957-59; Comdt No 1 Radio Sch., 1959-61; Comd. Electronics Off., Fighter Comd., 1961-63; AOA, HQ Far East Air Force, and AOC, HQ Gp, 1963-65; Dir-Gen. of Manning (RAF), Air Force Dept, 1966-68. DL Somerset 1975. Officer, Legion of Merit (US), 1945. *Recreations:* gardening, do-it-yourself. *Address:* Open-barrow, Barrows Park, Cheddar, Somerset. *T:* Cheddar 742474. *Club:* Royal Air Force.

LEONTIEF, Prof. Wassily; Professor of Economics, since 1975, and Director, Institute for Economic Analysis, since 1978, New York University; *b* Leningrad, Russia, 5 Aug. 1906; *s* of Wassily Leontief and Eugenia Leontief (*née* Bekker); *m* 1932, Estelle Helena Marks; one *d. Educ:* Univ. of Leningrad (Learned Economist, 1925); Univ. of Berlin (PhD 1928). Research Associate, Univ. of Kiel, Germany, 1927-28; Economic Adviser to Chinese Govt, Nanking, 1929; Nat. Bureau of Econ. Res., NY, 1931; Instr Economics, Harvard Univ., 1931-33, Asst Prof., 1933-39, Associate Prof., 1939-46, Prof., 1946-75. Dir, Harvard Economic Research Project, 1948-72; Guggenheim Fellow, 1940, 1950; Chm., 1965-75, and Sen. Fellow, Soc. of Fellows, Harvard Univ. President: Amer. Econ. Assoc., 1970; Sect. F, BAAS, 1976; Mem., Nat. Acad. of Sciences, 1974; Corr. Mem., Institut de France, 1968; Corr. FBA, 1970; Hon. MRIA, 1976. Hon. PhD: Brussels, 1962; York, 1967; Dr *hc*: Louvain, 1971; Paris (Sorbonne), 1972; Pennsylvania, 1976; Lancaster, 1976; Toulouse, Louisville, Vermont, Long Island, 1980. Nobel Prize in Economic Science, 1973. Order of the Cherubim, Univ. of Pisa, 1953. Officier, Légion d'Honneur, 1968. *Publications:* Structure of the American Economy 1919-29, 1941, 2nd edn 1953; Studies in the Structure of the American Economy, 1953; Input-Output Economics, 1966; Essays in Economics, vol. I 1966, vol. II 1977; The Future of the World Economy, 1977; contribs to learned jls. *Recreation:* fly fishing. *Address:* Institute for Economic Analysis, 269 Mercer Street, 2nd floor, New York, NY 10003, USA.

LE POER TRENCH, family name of Earl of Clancarty.

LE POER TRENCH, Brinsley; see Clancarty, 8th Earl of.

LEPPARD, Captain Keith André, CBE 1977; RN; Secretary, Institute of Brewing, since 1977; Director Public Relations (Royal Navy), 1974-77; *b* 29 July 1924; *s* of Wilfred Ernest Leppard and Dora Gilmore Keith; *m* 1954, Betty Rachel Smith; one *s* one *d. Educ:* Purley Grammar Sch. MRAeS 1973; FBIM 1973. Entered RN, FAA pilot duties, 1943; Opnl Wartime Service, Fighter Pilot, N Atlantic/Indian Oceans, 1944-45; Fighter Pilot/Flying Instr, Aircraft Carriers and Air Stns, 1946-57; CO 807 Naval Air Sqdn (Aerobatic Display Team, Farnborough), 1958-59; Air Org./Flying Trng Staff appts, 1959-63; Comdr (Air), HMS Victorious, 1963-64; Jt Services Staff Coll., 1964-65; Dir, Naval Officer Appts (Air), 1965-67; Chief Staff Officer (Air), Flag Officer Naval Air Comd, 1967-69; Chief Staff Officer (Ops/Trng), Comdr Far East Fleet, 1969-71; CO, Royal Naval Air Stn, Yeovilton, and Flag Captain to Flag Officer Naval Air Comd, 1972-74. Naval ADC to the Queen, 1976-77. *Recreations:* country life, tennis, golf. *Address:* Little Holt, Kingsley Green, Haslemere, Surrey. *T:* Haslemere 2797. *Club:* Naval and Military.

LEPPARD, Raymond John; conductor, harpsichordist, composer; *b* 11 Aug. 1927; *s* of A. V. Leppard. *Educ:* Trinity Coll., Cambridge. Fellow of Trin. Coll., Cambridge, Univ. Lecturer in Music, 1958-68. Hon. Keeper of the Music, Fitzwilliam Museum, 1963. Conductor: Covent Garden, Sadler's Wells, Glyndebourne, and abroad; Principal Conductor, BBC Northern Symphony Orchestra, 1972-80. Commendatore al Merito della Repúbblica Italiana, 1974. *Publications:* realisations of Monteverdi: Il Ballo delle Ingrate, 1958; L'Incoronazione di Poppea, 1962; L'Orfeo, 1965; Il Ritorno d'Ulisse, 1972; realisations of Francesco Cavalli: Messa Concertata, 1966; L'Ormindo, 1967; La Calisto, 1969; Magnificat, 1970; L'Egisto, 1974; realisation of Rameau's Dardanus, 1980; British Academy Italian Lecture, 1969, Procs Royal Musical Assoc. *Recreations:* music, theatre, books, friends. *Address:* c/o Colbert Artists Management, 111 West 57th Street, New York, NY 10019, USA.

LE QUESNE, Sir (Charles) Martin, KCMG 1974 (CMG 1963); Member of the States of Jersey, since 1978 (Deputy for St Saviour's parish); HM Diplomatic Service, retired; *b* 10 June 1917; *s* of C. T. Le Quesne, QC; *m* 1948; three *s. Educ:* Shrewsbury; Exeter Coll., Oxford. Served in Royal Artillery, 1940-45. Apptd HM Foreign Service, 1946; 2nd Sec. at HM Embassy, Baghdad, 1947-48; 1st Secretary: Foreign Office, 1948-51, HM Political Residency, Bahrain, 1951-54; attended course at NATO Defence Coll., Paris, 1954-55; HM Embassy, Rome, 1955-58; Foreign Office, 1958-60; apptd HM Chargé d'Affaires, Republic of Mali, 1960, subsequently Ambassador there, 1961-64; Foreign Office, 1964-68; Ambassador to Algeria, 1968-71; Dep. Under-Sec. of State, FCO, 1971-74; High Comr in Nigeria, 1974-76. Dir and Chm., Barclaytrust International Ltd; Dir, Barclays Unicorn Gp Ltd. Mem. Council, Royal African Soc.; Trustee, Southern African Studies Trust, York Univ. *Recreations:* gardening, books. *Address:* Beau Désert, St Saviour's, Jersey, Channel Islands. *T:* Jersey-Central 22076. *Clubs:* Reform (Chairman 1973-74); United (Jersey); Royal Channel Islands Yacht.
See also Sir J. G. Le Quesne, L. P. Le Quesne.

LE QUESNE, Sir (John) Godfray, Kt 1980; QC 1962; Chairman, Monopolies and Mergers Commission, since 1975 (a part-time Member since Oct. 1974); Judge of Courts of Appeal of Jersey and Guernsey, since 1964; *a* 1924; since 1972; *b* 1924; 3rd *s* of late C. T. Le Quesne, QC; *m* 1963, Susan Mary Gill; two *s* one *d. Educ:* Shrewsbury Sch.; Exeter Coll., Oxford (MA). Pres. of Oxford Union, 1943. Called to bar, Inner Temple, 1947; Master of the Bench, Inner Temple, 1969; admitted to bar of St Helena, 1959. Dep. Chm., Lincs (Kesteven) QS, 1963-71. Chm. of Council, Regent's Park Coll., Oxford, 1958-. *Recreations:* music, walking. *Address:* 1 Crown Office Row, Temple, EC4. *T:* 01-583 9292.
See also Sir C. M. Le Quesne, L. P. Le Quesne.

LE QUESNE, Prof. Leslie Philip, DM, MCh, FRCS; Professor of Surgery, Middlesex Hospital Medical School and Director, Department of Surgical Studies, Middlesex Hospital, since 1963; Deputy Vice-Chancellor and Dean, Faculty of Medicine, University of London, since 1980; *b* 24 Aug. 1919; *s* of late C. T. Le Quesne, QC; *m* 1969, Pamela Margaret, *o d* of late Dr A. Fullerton, Batley, Yorks; two *s. Educ:* Rugby; Exeter Coll., Oxford; Middlesex Hosp. Med. Sch. Jun. Demonstrator, Path. and Anat., 1943-45; House Surgeon, Southend Hosp. and St Mark's Hosp., 1945-47; Appointments at Middlesex Hospital: Asst, Surgical Professorial Unit, 1947-52; Asst Dir, Dept of Surgical Studies, 1952-63; Surgeon, 1960-63. Sir Arthur Sims Commonwealth Travelling Prof., 1975. Mem. GMC, 1979-. Editor, Post Graduate Med. Jl, 1951-52. Arris and Gale Lectr, RCS, 1952; Baxter Lectr, Amer. Coll. Surgs, 1960. Examr in Surgery, Universities London, Glasgow, Birmingham, Malaya, Khartoum and Bristol; Mem., Ct of Examrs, RCS, 1971-77. Formerly Chm., Assoc. of Profs of Surgery; Pres., Surgical Res. Soc. Chm., The British Jl of Surgery. Hon. FRACS, 1975; Hon. FACS, 1982. Moynihan Medal, 1953. *Publications:* medical articles and contribs to text books; Fluid Balance in Surgical Practice, 2nd edn, 1957. *Recreations:* sailing, reading. *Address:* 8 Eton Villas, NW3 4SX.
See also Sir C. M. Le Quesne, Sir J. G. Le Quesne.

LE QUESNE, Sir Martin; see Le Quesne, Sir C. M.

LERMON, Norman, QC 1966; **His Honour Judge Lermon;** a Circuit Judge (formerly County Court Judge), since 1971; *b* 12 Dec. 1915; *s* of late Morris and Clara Lermon; *m* 1939, Sheila Veronica Gilks; one *d. Educ:* Clifton Coll.; Trinity Hall, Cambridge. Joined Royal Fusiliers, 1939; commnd into S Wales Borderers, 1940; served in 53 (W) and 11th Armoured Divs; Staff Officer Ops (Air) 8th Corps, France, Holland and Germany; Major, 1945; NW Europe 1946 (despatches). Called to the Bar, 1943. *Recreations:* golf, reading. *Address:* 2 Harcourt Buildings, Temple, EC4.

LERNER, Alan Jay; playwright; lyricist; *b* NYC, 31 Aug. 1918. *Educ:* Bedales Sch., Hants; Choate Sch., Wallingford, USA; Harvard Univ. Pres., Dramatists' Guild of America, 1958-63; Mem., Songwriter's Hall of Fame, 1971; Bd of Governors: Nat. Hosp. for Speech Disorders; NY Osteopathic Hosp. *Musical plays:* with F. Loewe: What's up, 1943; The Day before Spring, 1945; Brigadoon, 1947 (filmed 1954; NY Drama Critics' Circle Award, 1947; Christopher Award, 1954); Paint your Wagon, 1951 (filmed and produced, 1969); My Fair Lady, 1956 (filmed 1964; NY Drama Critics' Circle Award, Donaldson Award, Antoinette Perry Award, 1956); Camelot, 1960 (filmed 1968); with K. Weill, Love Life, 1948; with B. Lane, On a Clear Day you can see Forever, 1965 (filmed 1970; Grammy Award, 1966); with A. Previn, Coco, 1969; Gigi, 1973 (Antoinette Perry Award, 1973-74); with L. Bernstein, 1600 Pennsylvania Avenue, 1976; with Burton Lane, Carmelina, 1979; *films:* Royal Wedding, 1951; An American in Paris, 1951 (Academy Award, Screenwriters' Guild Award, 1951); Gigi, 1958 (two Academy Awards, Screenwriters' Guild Award, 1958); The Little Prince, 1975. *Publication:* The Street Where I Live, 1978. *Address:* 15th Floor, 21 E 40th Street, New York, NY 10016, USA. *Clubs:* Players, Lambs, Shaw Soc.

LERNER, Max; Author; Syndicated newspaper column appears New York Post, Los Angeles Times Syndicate and elsewhere; Professor of American Civilization and World Politics, Brandeis University, USA, 1949-73, now Emeritus; Professor of Human Behavior, Graduate School of Human Behavior, US International University, San Diego, since 1974; *b* 20 Dec. 1902; *s* of Benjamin Lerner and Bessie Podel; *m* 1st; two *d* (and one *d* decd); 2nd, 1941, Edna Albers; three *s. Educ:* Yale Univ. (BA); Washington Univ., St Louis (MA); Robert Brookings Graduate Sch. of Economics and Government (PhD). Encyclopædia of Social Sciences, 1927, managing editor; Sarah Lawrence Coll., 1932-36, Prof. of Social Science; Harvard, 1935-36, Prof. of Government; Prof. of Political Science, Williams Coll., 1938-43; Ford Foundation Prof. of Amer. Civilization, Sch. of Internat. Studies, University of Delhi, 1959-60; Ford Foundn res. project on European unity, 1963-64. Editor of the Nation, 1936-38; Editorial Director PM, 1943-48; Columnist for the New York Star, 1948-49. *Publications:* It is Later Than You Think, 1938, rev. edn, 1943; Ideas are Weapons, 1939; Ideas for the Ice Age, 1941; The Mind and Faith of Justice Holmes, 1943; Public Journal, 1945; The Third Battle for France, 1945; The World of the Great Powers, 1947; The Portable Veblen, 1948; Actions and Passions, 1949; America as a Civilization, 1957; The Unfinished Country, 1959; Education and a Radical Humanism, 1962; The Age of Overkill, 1962; Tocqueville and American Civilization, 1966; (ed) Essential Works of John Stuart Mill, 1961; (ed) Tocqueville, Democracy in America, 1966; Values in Education, 1976; Ted and the Kennedy Legend, 1980. *Address:* 25 East End Avenue, New York, NY 10028, USA; (office) New York Post, 210 South Street, New York, NY 10002, USA.

LeROY-LEWIS, David Henry, FCA; Deputy Chairman, Touche, Remnant & Co., since 1981 (Director, since 1974); Chairman: R. P. Martin plc, since 1981; Henry Ansbacher Holdings plc, since 1982; *b* 14 June 1918; *er s* of late Stuyvesant Henry LeRoy-Lewis and late Bettye LeRoy-Lewis; *m* 1953, Cynthia Madeleine, *er d* of Comdr John C. Boldero, DSC, RN (Retd); three *d. Educ:* Eton. FCA 1947. Chm., TR North America Trust PLC (formerly Continental Union Trust Ltd) 1974- (Dir, 1948-); Director: TR Industrial & General Trust PLC, 1967-; Akroyd & Smithers Ltd, 1970-81 (Chm., 1976-81); TR Trustees Corp. PLC, 1973-; TR Energy PLC, 1981-. Mem., 1961-81, a Dep. Chm., 1973-76, Stock Exchange Council. *Recreations:* shooting, fishing. *Address:* Bramlands, Woodmancote, Henfield, W Sussex BN5 9TQ. *T:* Henfield 493611. *Clubs:* Naval and Military, MCC.

LESLIE, family name of **Earl of Rothes.**

LESLIE, Lord; James Malcolm David Leslie; *b* 4 June 1958; *s* and *heir* of 21st Earl of Rothes, qv. *Educ:* Eton. *Address:* 25B Bolton Gardens, SW5. *T:* 01-370 6496.

LESLIE, Ann Elizabeth Mary, (Mrs Michael Fletcher); journalist and broadcaster; *b* Pakistan; *d* of Norman Leslie and Theodora McDonald; *m* 1969, Michael Fletcher; one *d. Educ:* Presentation Convent, Matlock, Derbyshire; Convent of the Holy Child, Mayfield, Sussex; Lady Margaret Hall, Oxford (BA). Daily Express, 1962-67; freelance, 1967-: regular contributor to Daily Mail; also contrib. various national newspapers and magazines, incl. Punch, Queen, Nova, Harper's and Playboy. Broadcasting includes Stop the Week, Any Questions, Kaleidoscope and Question Time. British Press Awards Commendation, 1980; Variety Club Women of the Year Award for journalism and broadcasting, 1981; British Press Awards Feature Writer of the Year, 1981. *Recreations:* motherhood, photography. *Address:* c/o Daily Mail, Northcliffe House, Tudor Street, EC4Y 0JA. *T:* 01-353 6000.

LESLIE, Prof. David Clement; Professor of Nuclear Engineering, University of London, since 1968 and Dean of the Faculty of Engineering, Queen Mary

College, since 1980; *b* Melbourne, 18 Dec. 1924; *o s* of Clement and Doris Leslie; *m* 1952, Dorothea Ann Wenborn; three *s* two *d. Educ:* Westminster; Leighton Park; Wadham Coll., Oxford (MA, DPhil). Royal Navy, 1944-47. Postgrad. research in physics, 1948-50; Sir W. G. Armstrong Whitworth Aircraft, Coventry, 1951-54; Guided Weapons Div., RAE Farnborough, 1954-58; UKAEA Harwell and Winfrith, 1958-68; Hd of Dept of Nuclear Engrg, QMC, 1968-80. Chm., Scientific and Technical Cttee, EEC, 1980-. *Publications:* Developments in the Theory of Turbulence, 1973; papers in Proc. Royal Soc., Jl of Fluid Mechanics, Nature, Nuclear Science and Engrg, etc. *Address:* 22 Piercing Hill, Theydon Bois, Essex. *T:* Theydon Bois 3249.

LESLIE, Mrs D. G.; *see* Erskine-Lindop, A. B. N.

LESLIE, Rt. Rev. (Ernest) Kenneth, OBE 1972; *b* 14 May 1911; *s* of Rev. Ernest Thomas Leslie and Margaret Jane Leslie; *m* 1941, Isabel Daisy Wilson; two *s* one *d* (and one *s* decd). *Educ:* Trinity Gram. Sch., Kew, Vict.; Trinity Coll., University of Melbourne (BA). Aust. Coll. of Theology. ThL, 2nd Cl. 1933, Th Schol. 1951, 2nd Cl. 1952. Deacon, 1934; Priest, 1935; Asst Curate, Holy Trinity, Coburg, 1934-37; Priest-in-Charge, Tennant Creek, Dio. Carpentaria, 1937-38; Alice Springs with Tennant Creek, 1938-40; Rector of Christ Church, Darwin, 1940-44; Chaplain, AIF, 1942-45; Rector of Alice Springs with Tennant Creek, 1945-46; Vice-Warden, St John's Coll., Morpeth, NSW, 1947-52; Chap. Geelong Church of Eng. Gram. Sch., Timbertop Branch, 1953-58; Bishop of Bathurst, 1959-81. *Recreations:* walking, woodwork, cycling. *Address:* 51 Asca Drive, Green Point, NSW 2250, Australia.

LESLIE, Rear-Adm. George Cunningham, CB 1970; OBE 1944; MA; Domestic Bursar and Fellow of St Edmund Hall, Oxford, since 1970; *b* 27 Oct. 1920; 4th *s* of Col A. S. Leslie, CMG, WS, and Mrs M. I. Leslie (*née* Horne); *m* 1953, Margaret Rose Leslie; one *s* three *d. Educ:* Uppingham. Entered RN, 1938; War service in HMS York, Harvester, Volunteer and Cassandra, 1939-45; comd HMS: Wrangler, 1950-51; Wilton, 1951; Surprise, 1954-55; Capt. Fishery Protection Sqdn, 1960-62; Cdre HMS Drake, 1964-65; comd HMS Devonshire, 1966-67; Flag Officer, Admiralty Interview Bd, 1967-68; NATO HQ, Brussels, 1968-70. Comdr 1952; Capt. 1958; Rear-Adm. 1967; retired 1970. *Recreations:* sailing, painting, country pursuits. *Address:* St Edmund Hall, Oxford.

LESLIE, His Honour Gilbert Frank; retired Circuit Judge (formerly Judge of County Courts); *b* 25 Aug. 1909; *e s* of late F. L. J. Leslie, JP and late M. A. Leslie (*née* Gilbert), Harrogate; *m* 1947, Mary Braithwaite, MD, JP, *e d* of late Col W. H. Braithwaite, MC, TD, DL and Mrs E. M. Braithwaite, Harrogate; three *d. Educ:* St Christopher Sch., Letchworth; King's Coll., Cambridge (MA). Called to the Bar, Inner Temple, 1932; joined North-Eastern Circuit. Served War of 1939-45; Private Sherwood Foresters, 1939; commissioned West Yorkshire Regt, 1940; on Judge-Advocate-General's staff from Nov. 1940; finally ADJAG, HQ BAOR; released Nov. 1945 (Lt-Col). Asst Recorder, Newcastle upon Tyne City Quarter Sessions, 1954-60; Sheffield City Quarter Sessions, 1956-60; Recorder of Pontefract, 1958-60; Recorder of Rotherham, 1960; Dep. Chm., West Riding Quarter Sessions, 1960-63; Judge of County Court Circuit 14, 1960; Circuit 46, 1960-63; Circuit 42 (Bloomsbury and Marylebone), 1963-80; Dep. Chm., Inner London Area Sessions, 1965-71. Dep. Chm., Agricultural Lands Tribunal (Yorkshire Area), 1958-60. Jt Pres., Council of HM Circuit Judges, 1978. Manager, 1974-77, 1980-, Vice-Pres., 1975-77, 1980-, Royal Institution. Mem. Board of Faculty of Law and Court of Governors, Sheffield Univ., 1958-61; Governor, 1964-, Chm. of Governors, 1974-, Parsons Mead Sch. for Girls. Liveryman, Worshipful Co. of Gardeners (Mem. Court of Assts, 1978-). *Recreations:* gardening, horticultural history. *Address:* Ottways, 26 Ottways Lane, Ashtead, Surrey. *T:* Ashtead 74191. *Club:* Reform.

LESLIE, Harald Robert; *see* Birsay, Hon. Lord.

LESLIE, Ian (William) Murray, CBE 1971 (OBE 1954); Editor of Building (formerly The Builder), 1948-70; Vice-Chairman, The Builder Ltd, 1970-75; *b* 13 March 1905; 2nd *s* of John Gordon Leslie, MB, CM, Black Isle, Inverness, and Agnes Macrae, Kintail, Wester Ross; *m* 1st, 1929, Josette (marr. diss. 1974), 2nd *d* of late André Délétraz, actor, Paris; one *s* ; 2nd, 1974, G. M. Vivian Williams, LLB, barrister, *d* of Evan Hughes, Tintagel, Cornwall. *Educ:* St Paul's (foundation scholar); Crown and Manor Boys' Club, Hoxton. Joined editorial staff of The Builder, 1926; Associate Editor, 1937. Mem. Council, National Assoc. of Boys' Clubs, 1944-54; Chm. London Federation of Boys' Clubs, 1945-50; Mem. Metropolitan Juvenile Courts panel, 1947-61. Founder-Pres., Internat. Assoc. of the Building and Construction Press (UK section), 1970-79; made survey (with J. B. Perks) of Canadian construction industry for The Builder, 1950; organized £1000 house architectural competition for The Builder, 1951; made survey of housing, South Africa and Rhodesia, for The Builder, 1954. Chm., Building Industry Youth Trust, 1975-81. Pres., Invalids Cricket Club, 1974-. Associate RICS; Hon. Mem. of Art Workers' Guild; Hon. FRIBA; Hon. FCIOB. *Recreations:* watching cricket; sleep. *Address:* 64 Hamilton Terrace, NW8 9UJ. *T:* 01-289 0178. *Clubs:* Savage, Architectural Association (Hon. Mem.), MCC.

LESLIE, James Bolton, MC 1944; Chairman, Qantas Airways Ltd, since 1980; Director: Capel CRT, since 1980; T and G Insurance, since 1980; Equity Trustees, since 1980; CIG Ltd, since 1981; *b* 27 Nov. 1922; *s* of Stuart Deacon

Leslie and Dorothy Clare (née Murphy); *m* 1955, Alison Baker; three *s* one *d*. *Educ:* Trinity Grammar Sch., Melbourne; Harvard Business Sch., Boston, USA. Served war, Australian Infantry, Pacific Theatre, Private to Major, 1941-46. Mobil Oil Australia Ltd: joined, 1946; Manager, Fiji, 1946-50; various postings, Australia, 1950-59; Mobil Corp., New York, 1959-61; Gen. Manager, New South Wales, 1961-66; Director, Mobil Australia, 1966-68; Chm. and Chief Exec., Mobil New Zealand, 1968-72; Chm., Mobil Australia and Pacific, 1972-80. Chairman: Internat. Culture Corp. of Australia, 1980-; Project Australia, 1980-. Vice-Chm., Inst. of Dirs in Australia. *Recreations:* farming, horse breeding. *Address:* 42 Grey Street, East Melbourne, Victoria 3002, Australia. *T:* 03 4196149. *Clubs:* Melbourne, Australian, Melbourne Cricket, Beefsteak (Melbourne).

LESLIE, Sir John (Norman Ide), 4th Bt *cr* 1876; *b* 6 Dec. 1916; *s* of Sir (John Randolph) Shane Leslie, 3rd Bt and Marjorie (*d* 1951), *y d* of Henry C. Ide, Vermont, USA; *S* father, 1971. *Educ:* Downside; Magdalene College, Cambridge (BA 1938). Captain, Irish Guards; served War of 1939-45 (prisoner-of-war). Kt of Honour and Devotion, SMO Malta, 1947; KCSG 1958. *Recreations:* ornithology, ecology. *Heir: b* Desmond Arthur Peter Leslie [*b* 29 June 1921; *m* 1st, 1945, Agnes Elizabeth, *o d* of late Rudolph Bernauer, Budapest; two *s* one *d* ; 2nd, 1970, Helen Jennifer, *d* of late Lt-Col E. I. E. Strong; two *d*]. *Address:* 19 Piazza in Piscinula, Trastevere, Rome, Italy. *Clubs:* Travellers'; Circolo della Caccia (Rome).

LESLIE, Hon. John Wayland; *b* 16 Dec. 1909; 2nd *s* of 19th Earl of Rothes; *m* 1932, Coral Angela, *d* of late G. H. Pinckard, JP, Combe Court, Chiddingfold, Surrey, and 9 Chesterfield Street, Mayfair; one *s* one *d*. *Educ:* Stowe Sch.; Corpus Christi Coll., Cambridge. Formerly Flt-Lieut, RAFVR; invalided 1943. Mem. of Royal Company of Archers (Queen's Body Guard for Scotland). Mem. Clothworkers' Co. *Recreations:* shooting, fishing. *Address:* Guildford House, Castle Hill, Farnham, Surrey GU9 7JG. *T:* Farnham 716975. *Club:* Carlton.

LESLIE, Rt. Rev. Kenneth; *see* Leslie, Rt Rev. E. K.

LESLIE, (Percy) Theodore; retired British Aerospace engineer; *b* 19 Nov. 1915; *s* of Frank Harvey Leslie (*d* 1965) (*g g s* of 4th Bt), Christ's Hospital, and Amelia Caroline (*d* 1918), *d* of Alexander Russon. *Educ:* London and privately. Freeman, City of London, 1978. *Recreations:* chess, gardening and visiting places of historic interest. *Address:* National Westminster Bank Ltd, 5 Market Place, Kingston upon Thames, Surrey.
   Succession to Leslie of Wardis and Findrassie baronetcy (*cr* 1625) as 10th Bt pending at time of going to press.

LESLIE, Theodore; *see* Leslie, P. T.

LESLIE MELVILLE, family name of **Earl of Leven and Melville.**

LESSER, Most Rev. Norman Alfred, CMG 1971; MA Cantab; ThD 1962; DD Lambeth 1963; *b* 16 March 1902; *s* of Albert Lesser, Liverpool; *m* 1930, Beatrice Barnes, Southport; one *d*. *Educ:* Liverpool Collegiate Sch.; Fitzwilliam Hall and Ridley Hall, Cambridge. Curate St Simon and St Jude, Anfield, Liverpool, 1925-26; Curate Holy Trinity, Formby, Lancs, 1926-29; Liverpool Cathedral, 1929-31; Vicar St John, Barrow-in-Furness, 1931-39; Rector and Sub-Dean, Nairobi Cathedral, 1939; Provost of Nairobi, 1942; Bishop of Waiapu, 1947-71; Primate and Archbishop of New Zealand, 1961-71. *Recreation:* model-making. *Address:* 4 Sealy Road, Napier, New Zealand. *T:* Napier 53509.

LESSER, Sidney Lewis; Vice-President, Royal Automobile Club, since 1979 (Executive Chairman, 1978-79); *b* 23 March 1912; *s* of Joseph and Rachel Lesser; *m* 1938, Nina Lowenthal; two *d*. Solicitor of Supreme Court of Judicature; Comr for Oaths. In sole practice, 1935-. *Recreations:* golf, travel, reading. *Address:* 37 Fairfax Place, Hampstead, NW6 4EJ. *T:* 01-328 2607. *Clubs:* Royal Automobile; Coombe Hill Golf; Propeller of the United States.

LESSING, Charlotte; Editor of Good Housekeeping since 1973; *b* 14 May; *m* 1948, Walter B. Lessing; three *d*. *Educ:* Henrietta Barnet Sch.; evening classes. Univ. of London Dipl. Eng. Lit. Journalism and public relations: New Statesman and Nation; Lilliput (Hulton Press); Royal Society of Medicine; Notley Public Relations; Good Housekeeping, 1964-. *Publications:* short stories, travel, wine and feature articles. *Recreations:* travel, wine. *Address:* 88 St George's Square, SW1.

LESSING, Mrs Doris (May); author; *b* Persia, 22 Oct. 1919; *d* of Captain Alfred Cook Tayler and Emily Maude McVeagh; lived in Southern Rhodesia, 1924-49; *m* 1st, 1939, Frank Charles Wisdom (marr. diss., 1943); one *s* one *d* ; 2nd, 1945, Gottfried Anton Nicholas Lessing (marr. diss., 1949); one *s*. Associate Member: AAAL, 1974; Nat. Inst. of Arts and Letters (US), 1974. Mem., Inst. for Cultural Res., 1974. Hon. Fellow, MLA (Amer.), 1974. Shakespeare Prize, 1982. *Publications:* The Grass is Singing, 1950 (filmed 1981); This Was the Old Chief's Country, 1951; Martha Quest, 1952; Five, 1953 (Somerset Maugham Award, Soc. of Authors, 1954); A Proper Marriage, 1954; Retreat to Innocence, 1956; Going Home, 1957; The Habit of Loving, 1957; A Ripple from the Storm, 1958; Fourteen Poems, 1959; In Pursuit of the English, 1960; The Golden Notebook, 1962 (Prix Médicis 1976 for French trans., Carnet d'or); A Man and Two Women (short stories), 1963; African

Stories, 1964; Landlocked, 1965; Particularly Cats, 1966; The Four-Gated City, 1969; Briefing for a Descent into Hell, 1971; The Story of a Non-Marrying Man, 1972; The Summer Before the Dark, 1973; The Memoirs of a Survivor, 1975 (filmed 1981); Collected Stories: Vol. I, To Room Nineteen, 1978; Vol. II, The Temptation of Jack Orkney, 1978; Re Planet 5, Shikasta, 1979; The Marriages Between Zones Three, Four and Five, 1980; The Sirian Experiments, 1981; The Making of the Representative for Planet 8, 1982; The Sentimental Agents, 1983; *play:* Play with a Tiger, 1962. *Address:* c/o Jonathan Clowes Ltd, 19 Jeffreys Place, NW1 9PP.

LESSOF, Prof. Maurice Hart, FRCP; Professor of Medicine, University of London at Guy's Hospital Medical School, since 1971; *b* 4 June 1924; *s* of Noah and Fanny Lessof; *m* 1960, Leila Liebster; one *s* two *d*. *Educ:* City of London Sch.; King's Coll., Cambridge. Appts on junior staff of Guy's Hosp., Canadian Red Cross Memorial Hosp., Johns Hopkins Hosp., etc.; Physician, Greenwich District Hosp., 1964; Clinical Immunologist and Physician, Guy's Hosp., 1967. Mem., N Southwark and Lewisham DHA, 1982-. President: Sect. of Medicine, RSocMed, 1977; British Soc. for Allergy, 1981-; Mem. Council, RCP, 1980-82. Mem. Senate, London Univ., 1981-. *Publications:* (ed) Immunological Aspects of Cardiovascular Diseases, 1981; (ed) Immunological and Clinical Aspects of Allergy, 1981; (ed) Clinical Reactions to Food, 1982. *Recreation:* painting. *Address:* 8 John Spencer Square, Canonbury, N1 2LZ. *T:* 01-226 0919. *Club:* Athenæum.

LESTANG, Sir M. C. E. C. N. de; *see* Nageon de Lestang.

LESTER, Anthony Paul, QC 1975; *b* 3 July 1936; *e s* of Harry and Kate Lester; *m* 1971, Catherine Elizabeth Debora Wassey; one *s* one *d*. *Educ:* City of London Sch.; Trinity Coll., Cambridge (Exhibnr) (BA); Harvard Law Sch. (Harkness Commonwealth Fund Fellowship) (LLM). Called to Bar, Lincoln's Inn, 1963 (Mansfield scholar). Served Royal Artillery, 1955-57. Special Adviser to: Home Secretary, 1974-76; Standing Adv. Commn on Human Rights, 1975-77. Vis. Prof., QMC, London, 1981-82. Member: Bd of Overseers, Univ. of Pennsylvania Law Sch., 1978-; Court of Governors, LSE. Chm., Social Democratic Lawyers Assoc., 1981-. Member: Council of Justice; Internat. Law Assoc. Cttees on Water Resources and on Human Rights; Trustee, Runnymede Trust. Governor, British Inst. of Human Rights. *Publications:* Justice in the American South, 1964 (Amnesty Internat.); (co-ed.) Shawcross and Beaumont on Air Law, 3rd edn, 1964; (co-author) Race and Law, 1972; contrib. to British Nationality, Immigration and Race Relations, in Halsbury's Laws of England, 4th edn, 1973. *Address:* 2 Hare Court, Temple, EC4. *T:* 01-353 0076. *Club:* Garrick.

LESTER, James Theodore; MP (C) Beeston, since Feb. 1974; Parliamentary Under Secretary of State, Department of Employment, 1979-81; *b* 23 May 1932; *s* of Arthur Ernest and Marjorie Lester; *m* ; two *s*. *Educ:* Nottingham High School. Mem. Notts CC, 1967-74. An Opposition Whip, 1976-79; Deleg. to Council of Europe and WEU, 1975-76. *Recreations:* reading, music, motor racing, travelling. *Address:* Flat 7, 37 Smith Square, SW1.

LESTER, Richard; Film Director; *b* 19 Jan. 1932; *s* of Elliott and Ella Young Lester; *m* 1956, Deirdre Vivian Smith; one *s* one *d*. *Educ:* Wm Penn Charter Sch.; University of Pennsylvania (BSc). Television Director: CBS (USA), 1951-54; AR (Dir TV Goon Shows), 1956. Directed The Running, Jumping and Standing Still Film (Acad. Award nomination; 1st prize San Francisco Festival, 1960). *Feature Films directed:* It's Trad, Dad, 1962; Mouse on the Moon, 1963; A Hard Day's Night, 1964; The Knack, 1964 (Grand Prix, Cannes Film Festival); Help, 1965 (Best Film Award and Best Dir Award, Rio de Janeiro Festival); A Funny Thing Happened on the Way to the Forum, 1966; How I won the War, 1967; Petulia, 1968; The Bed Sitting Room, 1969 (Gandhi Peace Prize, Berlin Film Festival); The Three Musketeers, 1973; Juggernaut, 1974 (Best Dir award, Teheran Film Fest.); The Four Musketeers, 1974; Royal Flash, 1975; Robin and Marian, 1976; The Ritz, 1976; Butch and Sundance: the early days, 1979; Cuba, 1979; Superman II, 1981. *Recreations:* composing, playing popular music. *Address:* Twickenham Film Studios, St Margaret's, Twickenham, Mddx.

LESTER SMITH, Ernest; *see* Smith, E. L.

LESTOR, Joan; MP (Lab) Eton and Slough since 1966; *b* Vancouver, British Columbia, Canada; one *s* one *d* (both adopted). *Educ:* Blaenavon Secondary Sch., Monmouth; William Morris Secondary Sch., Walthamstow; London Univ. Diploma in Sociology. Nursery Sch. Teacher, 1959-66. Member: Wandsworth Borough Council, 1958-68; LCC, 1962-64; Exec. Cttee of the London Labour Party, 1962-65; Nat. Exec., Labour Party, 1967-82 (Chm., 1977-78); Chm., Internat. Cttee, Labour Party, 1978-. Contested (Lab) Lewisham West, 1964. Parliamentary Under-Secretary: Dept of Educn and Science, Oct. 1969-June 1970; FCO, 1974-75; DES, 1975-76; resigned from Labour Govt on cuts policy, 1976. Chm. Council, Nat. Soc. of Children's Nurseries, 1969-70; Co-Chm., Jt Cttee against Racialism, 1978-. *Recreations:* theatre, reading, playing with children. *Address:* House of Commons, SW1.

L'ESTRANGE, Laurence Percy Farrer, OBE 1958; HM Diplomatic Service; retired; company director and consultant; *b* 10 Sept. 1912; *s* of late S. W. L'Estrange and Louie Knights L'Estrange (née Farrer); *m* 1933, Anne Catherine (née Whiteside); two *s*. *Educ:* Shoreham Grammar Sch., Shoreham, Sussex; Univ. of London. Employed at HM Embassy, Caracas, 1939, and

Acting Vice-Consul, 1941 and 1942. Resigned and joined RAF, 1943–46. HM Vice-Consul, Malaga, 1946; Second Sec., San Salvador, 1949; Chargé d'Affaires, 1952; Vice-Consul, Chicago, 1953; First Sec. (Commercial): Manila, 1954; Lima, 1958; Chargé d'Affaires, 1961; seconded to Western Hemisphere Exports Council, in charge of Latin American Div., 1962; HM Consul, Denver, 1963; Counsellor (Commercial), Lagos, 1967; Ambassador to Honduras, 1969–72. FRSA 1973. *Recreations:* golf, riding, sailing, fishing and shooting. *Address:* 154 Frog Grove Lane, Wood Street Village, Guildford, Surrey GU3 3HB. *Clubs:* Royal Automobile, Travellers'; Brighton Marina Yacht.

L'ETANG, Hugh Joseph Charles James; Editor of The Practitioner since 1973; *b* 23 Nov. 1917; *s* of late Dr J. G. L'Etang and Frances L'Etang; *m* 1951, Cecily Margaret Tinker, MD, MRCP; one *s* one *d. Educ:* Haileybury Coll.; St John's Coll., Oxford; St Bartholomew's Hosp.; Harvard Sch. of Public Health. BA 1939, BM, BCh 1942, DIH 1952. War Service, 1943–46, RMO 5th Bn Royal Berks Regt; TA from 1947, RAMC; Lt-Col 1953–56. Medical Adviser: North Thames Gas Bd, 1948–56; British European Airways, 1956–58; John Wyeth & Brother Ltd, 1958–69; Asst and Dep. Editor, The Practitioner, 1969–72. Hira S. Chouké Lectr, Coll. of Physicians of Philadelphia, 1972. Member: RUSI; IISS; Military Commentators' Circle (Hon. Sec.); Amer. Civil War Round Table, London; Sherlock Holmes Soc. *Publications:* The Pathology of Leadership, 1969; Fit to Lead?, 1980; articles in Practitioner, Jl RAMC, Army Qtly, Brassey's Annual, Navy Internat., NATO's Fifteen Nations. *Recreation:* medical aspects of military and foreign affairs. *Address:* 27 Sispara Gardens, SW18 1LG. *T:* 01-870 3836. *Club:* United Oxford & Cambridge University.

LETHBRIDGE, Sir Thomas (Periam Hector Noel), 7th Bt *cr* 1804; *b* 17 July 1950; *s* of Sir Hector Wroth Lethbridge, 6th Bt, and of Evelyn Diana, *d* of late Lt-Col Francis Arthur Gerard Noel, OBE; *S* father, 1978; *m* 1976, Susan Elizabeth Rocke; three *s* one *d. Educ:* Milton Abbey. Studied farming, Cirencester Agricultural Coll., 1969–70; Managing Director: Art Gallery, Dorset and London, 1972–77; Shirlstar Shipping Containers (Scotland) Ltd; now specialist in promoting wildlife and sporting artists and art valuations. *Recreations:* shooting, riding, walking. *Heir: s* John Francis Buckler Noel Lethbridge, *b* 10 March 1977. *Address:* Mains of Shiels, Sauchen, Aberdeenshire. *Club:* Farmers'.

LE TOCQ, Eric George, CMG 1975; HM Diplomatic Service, retired; British Government Representative in the West Indies Associated States, 1975–78; *b* 20 April 1918; *s* of Eugene Charles Le Tocq; *m* 1946, Betty Esdaile; two *s* one *d. Educ:* Elizabeth Coll., Guernsey; Exeter Coll., Oxford (MA). Served War of 1939–45: commissioned in Royal Engineers, 1939; North Africa, 1942–43; Italy, 1943; Austria and Greece; major. Taught Modern Languages and Mathematics at Monmouth Sch., 1946–48; Assistant Principal, Commonwealth Relations Office, 1948; Karachi, 1948–50; Principal, 1950; Dublin, 1953–55; Accra, 1957–59; Assistant Secretary, 1962; Adviser on Commonwealth and External Affairs, Entebbe, 1962; Deputy High Commissioner, Uganda, 1962–64; Counsellor, British High Commission, Canberra, 1964–67; Head of E African Dept, FCO, 1968–71; High Comr in Swaziland, 1972–75. *Recreations:* golf and gardening. *Address:* Maycroft, Tweed Lane, Boldre, Hants. *Club:* Royal Commonwealth Society.

LETSON, Major-General Harry Farnham Germaine, CB 1946; CBE 1944; MC; ED; CD; *b* Vancouver, BC, 26 Sept. 1896; *e s* of late J. M. K. Letson, Vancouver, BC; *m* 1928, Sally Lang Nichol; no *c. Educ:* McGill Univ.; University of British Columbia; University of London. BSc (UBC) 1919; PhD (Eng) London, 1923. Active Service Canadian Army, 1916–19; Associate Professor Mechanical and Electrical Engineering, University of BC, 1923–36; on Active Service Canadian Army, 1939–46; Adjt-General Canadian Army, 1942–44; Commander of Canadian Army Staff in Washington, 1944–46; Secretary to Governor-General of Canada, 1946–52; Adviser on Militia, Canadian Army, 1954–58, retired. Hon. Colonel British Columbia Regt, 1963. LLD (University of BC), 1945. *Recreation:* fishing. *Address:* 474 Lansdowne Road, Ottawa K1M 0X9, Canada. *Clubs:* Rideau (Ottawa); Vancouver (Vancouver, BC).

LETTS, Charles Trevor; Director, Greig Fester (Agencies) Ltd, since 1978; Underwriting Member of Lloyd's, since 1944; Deputy Chairman of Lloyd's, 1966 (entered Lloyd's, 1924; Member, 1941; Committee, 1964–67); *b* 2 July 1905; *o s* of late Charles Hubert and Gertrude Letts; *m* 1942, Mary R. (Judy), *o d* of late Sir Stanley and late Lady (Hilda) Woodwark; two *s* one *d. Educ:* Marlborough Coll. Served RNVR, Lieut-Commander, 1940–45. Member: Cttee, Lloyd's Underwriters' Assoc., 1960–70 (Chairman, 1963–64); Council, Lloyd's Register of Shipping, 1964–77 (Chairman, Yacht Sub-Cttee, 1967–75); Salvage Association, 1963–70. *Recreations:* sailing, golf. *Address:* Bearwood, Holtye, Edenbridge, Kent. *T:* Cowden 472. *Club:* Royal Ocean Racing.

LETWIN, Prof. William; Professor of Political Science, London School of Economics, since 1976; *b* 14 Dec. 1922; *s* of Lazar and Bessie Letwin; *m* 1944, Shirley Robin; one *s. Educ:* Univ. of Chicago (BA 1943, PhD 1951); London Sch. of Economics (1948–50). Served US Army, 1943–46. Postdoctoral Fellow, Economics Dept, Univ. of Chicago, 1951–52; Research Associate, Law Sch., Univ. of Chicago, 1953–55; Asst. Prof. of Industrial History, MIT, 1955–60; Associate Prof. of Economic History, MIT, 1960–67; Reader in Political Science, LSE, 1966–76. Chm., Bd of Studies in Economics, Univ. of London, 1971–73. *Publications:* (ed) Frank Knight, on The History and

Method of Economics, 1956; Sir Josiah Child, 1959; Documentary History of American Economic Policy, 1961, 2nd edn 1972; Origins of Scientific Economics 1660–1776, 1963; Law and Economic Policy in America, 1965; articles in learned jls. *Address:* 3 Kent Terrace, NW1 4RP. *T:* 01-262 2593.

LEUCHARS, Maj.-Gen. Peter Raymond, CBE 1966; Chief Commander, St John Ambulance, since 1980 (Commissioner-in-Chief, 1978–80); *b* 29 Oct. 1921; *s* of late Raymond Leuchars and Helen Inez Leuchars (*née* Copland-Griffiths); *m* 1953, Hon. Gillian Wightman Nivison, *d* of 2nd Baron Glendyne; one *s. Educ:* Bradfield College. Commnd in Welsh Guards, 1941; served in NW Europe and Italy, 1944–45; Adjt, 1st Bn Welsh Guards, Palestine, 1945–48; Bde Major, 4 Guards Bde, Germany, 1952–54; GSO1 (Instr.), Staff Coll., Camberley, 1956–59; GSO1 HQ 4 Div. BAOR, 1960–63; comd 1st Bn Welsh Guards, 1963–65; Principal Staff Off. to Dir of Ops, Borneo, 1965–66; comd 11 Armd Bde BAOR, 1966–68; comd Jt Operational Computer Projects Team, 1969–71; Dep. Comdt Staff Coll., Camberley, 1972–73; GOC Wales, 1973–76. Col, The Royal Welch Fusiliers, 1974–. Pres., Guards' Golfing Soc., 1977. KStJ 1978. Order of Istiqlal (Jordan), 1946. *Recreations:* golf, shooting, travel, photography. *Address:* 5 Chelsea Square, SW3 6LF. *T:* 01-352 6187. *Clubs:* Pratt's; Royal and Ancient Golf; Royal Mid-Surrey Golf; Sunningdale Golf (Captain 1975).

LEUCKERT, Jean Elizabeth, (Mrs Harry Leuckert); *see* Muir, J. E.

LEUTWILER, Fritz, PhD; Chairman of the Governing Board and Head of Department I, Swiss National Bank, Zurich, since 1974; Chairman of the Board of Directors and President, Bank for International Settlements, Basle, since 1982; *b* 30 July 1924; *m* 1951, Andrée Cottier; one *s* one *d. Educ:* Univ. of Zurich (PhD 1948). Sec., Assoc. for a Sound Currency, 1948–52; Swiss National Bank, Zurich: Econ. Scientist, 1952–59; Manager, 1959–66; Dep. Gen. Man., 1966–68; Mem., Governing Bd, and Head, Dept III, 1968–74. Hon. Dr Berne, 1978. *Recreations:* golf; collector of rare books (Helvetica, Economica). *Address:* Weizenacher 4, CH-8126 Zumikon, Switzerland. *T:* 01/918 03 36. *Club:* Golf and Country (Zumikon).

LEVEN, 14th Earl of, **AND MELVILLE,** 13th Earl of, *cr* 1641; **Alexander Robert Leslie Melville;** Baron Melville, 1616; Baron Balgonie, 1641; Earl of Melville, Viscount Kirkcaldie, 1690; Lord-Lieutenant of Nairn since 1969; *b* 13 May 1924; *e s* of 13th Earl and Lady Rosamund Sylvia Diana Mary Foljambe (*d* 1974), *d* of 1st Earl of Liverpool; *S* father, 1947; *m* 1953, Susan, *er d* of Lieut-Colonel R. Steuart-Menzies of Culdares, Arndilly House, Craigellachie, Banffshire; two *s* one *d. Educ:* Eton. ADC to Governor General of New Zealand, 1951–52. Formerly Capt. Coldstream Guards; retired, 1952. Vice-Pres., Highland Distr TA. Pres., British Ski Fedn, 1981–. DL, County of Nairn, 1961; Convener, Nairn CC, 1970–74. Chm. Governors, Gordonstoun Sch., 1971–. *Heir: s* Lord Balgonie, *qv. Address:* Glenferness House, Nairn. *T:* Glenferness 202. *Clubs:* Naval and Military, Pratt's.

LEVENE, Ben, ARA 1975; painter; *b* 23 Dec. 1938; *s* of Mark and Charlotte Levene. *Educ:* Slade School (DFA). Boise Scholarship, 1961; lived in Spain, 1961–62. First one-man show, 1973. *Address:* c/o Royal Academy of Arts, Piccadilly, W1.

LEVENTHAL, Colin David; Head of Programme Acquisition, Channel Four Television Co. Ltd, since 1982; *b* 2 Nov. 1946; *s* of Morris and Olga Leventhal. *Educ:* Carmel Coll., Wallingford, Berks; King's Coll., Univ. of London (BA Philosophy). Solicitor of Supreme Court of England and Wales. Admitted Solicitor, 1971; BBC, 1974–82: Asst Head of Programme Contracts, 1977; Head of Copyright, 1978. *Recreations:* theatre, film. *Address:* 60 Charlotte Street, W1. *T:* 01-631 4444.

LEVER, family name of **Baron Lever of Manchester** and of **Viscount Leverhulme.**

LEVER OF MANCHESTER, Baron *cr* 1979 (Life Peer), of Cheetham in the City of Manchester; **Harold Lever,** PC 1969; Director, The Guardian and Manchester Evening News, since 1979; *b* Manchester, 15 Jan. 1914; *s* of late Bernard and Bertha Lever; *m* 1962, Diane, *d* of Saleh Bashi; three *d* (and one *d* from late wife). *Educ:* Manchester Grammar Sch. Called to Bar, Middle Temple, 1935. MP (Lab) Manchester Exchange, 1945–50, Manchester, Cheetham, 1950–74, Manchester Central, 1974–79. Promoted Defamation Act, 1952, as a Private Member's Bill. Joint Parliamentary Under-Secretary, Dept of Economic Affairs, 1967; Financial Sec. to Treasury, Sept. 1967-69; Paymaster General, 1969–70; Chancellor of the Duchy of Lancaster, 1974–79. Chm., Public Accounts Cttee, 1970–73. Mem., Internat. Adv. Bd, Creditanstalt-Bankverein, 1982. Treasurer, Socialist International, 1971–73. Governor: LSE, 1971; E-SU, 1973; Trustee, Royal Opera House, 1974; Mem. Ct, Manchester Univ., 1975. Hon. Fellow, and Chm. Trustees, Royal Acad., 1981. Hon. doctorates in Law, Science, Literature and Technology. *Address:* House of Lords, SW1.

LEVER, Sir Christopher; *see* Lever, Sir T. C. A. L.

LEVER, Jeremy Frederick, QC 1972; *b* 23 June 1933; *s* of late A. Lever. *Educ:* Bradfield Coll.; University Coll., Oxford; Nuffield Coll., Oxford. Served RA, 1951–53. 1st cl. Jurisprudence, 1956, MA Oxon; Pres., Oxford Union Soc., 1957, Trustee, 1972–77. Fellow, All Souls Coll., Oxford, 1957- (Sub-

Warden, 1982-). Called to Bar, Gray's Inn, 1957. Dir, (non-exec.), Dunlop Holdings Ltd, 1973-80. *Publications:* The Law of Restrictive Practices, 1964; other legal works. *Recreations:* walking, music. *Address:* Avenue de Tervueren 27, 1040 Brussels, Belgium. *T:* Brussels (02) 733 73 02; (02) 735 93 54. *Club:* Garrick.

LEVER, John Michael, QC 1977; **His Honour Judge Lever;** a Circuit Judge, since 1981; *b* 12 Aug. 1928; *s* of late John Lever and Ida Donaldson Lever; *m* 1964, Elizabeth Marr; two *s. Educ:* Bolton Sch.; Gonville and Caius Coll., Cambridge (Schol.). BA (1st cl. hons Law Tripos), 1949. Flying Officer, RAF, 1950-52. Called to Bar, Middle Temple, 1951 (Blackstone Schol.); practised Northern Circuit from 1952; Asst Recorder, Salford, 1969-71; a Recorder of the Crown Court, 1972-81. Governor, Bolton Sch. *Recreations:* theatre, fell-walking. *Address:* Lakelands, Rivington, near Bolton, Lancs BL6 7RT.

LEVER, Sir (Tresham) Christopher (Arthur Lindsay), 3rd Bt *cr* 1911; *b* 9 Jan. 1932; *s* of Sir Tresham Joseph Philip Lever, 2nd Bt, and Frances Yowart Parker (*d* 1959), *d* of late Lindsay Hamilton Goodwin; *S* father, 1975; *m* 1st, 1970; 2nd, 1975, Linda Weightman McDowell, *d* of late James Jepson Goulden, Tennessee, USA. *Educ:* Eton; Trinity Coll., Cambridge (MA 1957). MBOU; FLS. Lieut, 17th/21st Lancers, 1950. Dir, John Barran & Sons Ltd, 1956-64. Trustee, Internat. Trust for Nature Conservation, 1980-. *Publications:* Goldsmiths and Silversmiths of England, 1975; The Naturalized Animals of the British Isles, 1977; contribs to various fine art, scientific and general publications. *Recreations:* golf, fishing, wildlife conservation. *Heir:* none. *Address:* Newell House, Winkfield, Windsor, Berks. *T:* Winkfield Row 882604. *Club:* Buck's.

LEVERHULME, 3rd Viscount, *cr* 1922, of the Western Isles; **Philip William Bryce Lever,** TD; Baron, *cr* 1917; Bt, *cr* 1911; Knight of Order of St John of Jerusalem; Major, Cheshire Yeomanry; Lord-Lieutenant of City and County of Chester since 1949; Advisory Director of Unilever Ltd; Chancellor of Liverpool University, since 1980; *b* 1 July 1915; *s* of 2nd Viscount and Marion, *d* of late Bryce Smith of Manchester; *S* father, 1949; *m* 1937, Margaret Ann (*d* 1973), *o c* of John Moon, Tiverton; three *d. Educ:* Eton; Trinity Coll., Cambridge. Hon. Air Commodore 663 Air OP Squadron, RAuxAF; Hon. Air Commodore 610 (County of Chester) Squadron, Royal Auxiliary Air Force; Dep. Hon. Col, Cheshire Yeomanry, T&AVR, 1971-72, Hon. Col, 1972-81; Hon. Col, The Queen's Own Yeomanry, 1979-81. Pres. Council, Liverpool Univ., 1957-63, Sen. Pro-Chancellor, 1963-66. Member: National Hunt Cttee, 1961 (Steward, 1965-68); Deputy Senior Steward, Jockey Club, 1970-73, Senior Steward, 1973-76; Council of King George's Jubilee Trust; Chairman, Exec. Cttee Animal Health Trust, 1964. Hon. FRCS 1970; Hon. ARCVS 1975. Hon. LLD Liverpool, 1967. *Recreations:* shooting, hunting. *Heir:* none. *Address:* Thornton Manor, Thornton Hough, Wirral, Merseyside; Badanloch, Kinbrace, Sutherland; 16 Clarendon Road, W11. *Clubs:* Boodle's, Jockey.

LEVERSEDGE, Leslie Frank, CMG 1955; MA Cantab; Economic Secretary to Northern Rhodesia Government, 1956-60, retired; *b* 29 May 1904; *s* of F. E. Leversedge, UP, India; *m* 1945, Eileen Melegueta Spencer Payne; two *s* three *d. Educ:* St Paul's Sch., Darjeeling, India; St Peter's Sch., York; St John's Coll., Cambridge; Inner Temple, London. Cadet in Colonial Administrative Service, Northern Rhodesia, Dec. 1926; District Officer, Dec. 1928; Provincial Commissioner, Jan. 1947; Senior Provincial Commissioner, Dec. 1948. Development Secretary to Northern Rhodesia Government, 1951-56. MLC 1951; MEC 1951. British Council Local Correspondent for Kent, 1963-75. FRSA 1973. *Recreations:* walking, overseas travelling. *Address:* Earley House, Petham, Canterbury, Kent CT4 5RY. *T:* Petham 285.

LEVERTON, Colin Allen H.; *see* Hart-Leverton.

LEVESON, Lord; Granville George Fergus Leveson Gower; *b* 10 Sept. 1959; *s* and *heir* of 5th Earl Granville, *qv.*

LEVESON GOWER, family name of **Earl Granville.**

LEVESQUE, Most Rev. Louis, ThD; *b* 27 May 1908; *s* of Philippe Levesque and Catherine Levesque (*née* Beaulieu); *Educ:* Laval Univ. Priest, 1932; Bishop of Hearst, Ontario, 1952-64; Archbishop of Rimouski, 1967-73. Chm., Canadian Cath. Conf., 1965-67; Mem. Congregation Bishops, Rome, 1968-73. *Address:* 57 rue Hôtel-de-Ville, Mont-Joli, PQ G5H 1W9, Canada.

LÉVESQUE, Hon. René; Premier of Province of Québec, Canada, since 1976; *b* 24 Aug. 1922; *s* of Dominique Lévesque and Diane Dionne; *m* 1st, 1947, Louise L'Heureux (marr. diss. 1978); two *s* one *d* ; 2nd, 1979, Corinne Cote. *Educ:* schs in New Carlisle and Gaspé; Québec Univ. (BA); Law Sch., Laval, Québec. Overseas duty as reporter with US Forces (attached to Office of War Information, Europe), 1944-45; reporter and commentator, Canadian Broadcasting Corp., 1946-59. Mem., Québec Nat. Assembly, 1960-70, 1976-; Minister, Public Works, Natural Resources and Social Welfare, 1960-66; Mem. Opposition, 1966-70; Pres., Parti Québécois, 1966-. Grand Médaille de Vermeil, 1977. Grand Officer, Legion of Honour, 1977. *Publications:* Option-Québec, 1968; La Passion du Québec, 1978; My Quebec, 1979; Oui, 1980. *Recreations:* tennis, swimming, skiing, reading, movies. *Address:* Government Buildings, Edifice J, Québec, Canada. *T:* 643-5321. *Club:* Cercle Universitaire (Québec).

LEVEY, Sir Michael (Vincent), Kt 1981; MVO 1965; MA Oxon and Cantab; FR.SL; Director of the National Gallery, since 1973 (Deputy Director, 1970-73); *b* 8 June 1927; *s* of O. L. H. Levey and Gladys Mary Milestone; *m* 1954, Brigid Brophy, *qv* ; one *d. Educ:* Oratory Sch.; Exeter Coll., Oxford, Hon. Fellow, 1973. Served with Army, 1945-48; commissioned, KSLI, 1946, and attached RAEC, Egypt. National Gallery: Asst Keeper, 1951-66, Dep. Keeper, 1966-68, Keeper, 1968-73. Slade Professor of Fine Art, Cambridge, 1963-64; Supernumerary Fellow, King's Coll., Cambridge, 1963-64. *Publications:* Six Great Painters, 1956; National Gallery Catalogues: 18th Century Italian Schools, 1956; The German School, 1959; Painting in 18th Century Venice, 1959, revd edn 1980; From Giotto to Cézanne, 1962; Dürer, 1964; The Later Italian Paintings in the Collection of HM The Queen, 1964; Canaletto Paintings in the Royal Collection, 1964; Tiepolo's Banquet of Cleopatra (Charlton Lecture, 1962), 1966; Rococo to Revolution, 1966; Bronzino (The Masters), 1967; Early Renaissance, 1967 (Hawthornden Prize, 1968); Fifty Works of English Literature We Could Do Without (co-author), 1967; Holbein's Christina of Denmark, Duchess of Milan, 1968; A History of Western Art, 1968; Painting at Court (Wrightsman Lectures), 1971; 17th and 18th Century Italian Schools (Nat. Gall. catalogue), 1971; The Life and Death of Mozart, 1971; The Nude: Themes and Painters in the National Gallery, 1972; (co-author) Art and Architecture in 18th Century France, 1972; The Venetian Scene (Themes and Painters Series), 1973; Botticelli (Themes and Painters Series), 1974; High Renaissance, 1975; The World of Ottoman Art, 1976; Jacob van Ruisdael (Themes and Painters Series), 1977; The Case of Walter Pater, 1978; Sir Thomas Lawrence (Nat. Portrait Gall. exhibn), 1979; The Painter Depicted (Neurath Lect.), 1981; Tempting Fate (fiction), 1982; contributions Burlington Magazine, etc. *Address:* 185 Old Brompton Road, SW5. *T:* 01-373 9335.

LEVI, Prof. Edward Hirsch; Glen A. Lloyd Distinguished Service Professor, University of Chicago, since 1977; *b* 26 June 1911; *s* of Gerson B. Levi and Elsa B. Levi (*née* Hirsch); *m* 1946, Kate Sulzberger; three *s. Educ:* Univ. of Chicago; Yale Univ. Law Sch. Univ. of Chicago: Asst Prof. of Law, 1936-40; Prof. of Law, 1945-75; Dean of the Law School, 1950-62; Provost, 1962-68; President, 1968-75; Pres. emeritus, 1975; Attorney-Gen. of US, 1975-77. Public Dir, Chicago Bd of Trade, 1977-80. Herman Phleger Vis. Prof., Stanford Law Soc., 1978. Special Asst to Attorney-Gen., Washington, DC, 1940-45; 1st Asst, War Div., Dept of Justice, 1943; 1st Asst, Anti-trust Div., 1944-45; Chm., Interdeptl Cttee on Monopolies and Cartels, 1944; Counsel, Subcttee on Monopoly Power Judiciary Cttee, 81st Congress, 1950; Member: White House Task Force on Educn, 1966-67; President's Task Force on Priorities in Higher Educn, 1969-70; White House Central Gp in Domestic Affairs, 1964; Citizens Commn on Graduate Medical Educn, 1963-66; Sloan Commn on Cable Communications, 1970-71; Nat. Commn on Productivity, 1970-75; Commn on Foundations and Private Philanthropy, 1969-70. Mem. Council, American Law Inst., 1965-; American Bar; Illinois Bar; Chicago Bar; Supreme Court, 1945-; Amer. Judicature Soc.; Council on Legal Educn for Profl. Responsibility, 1968-74; Order of Coif; Phi Beta Kappa; res. adv. bd, Commn Econ. Develt, 1951-54; bd Dirs, SSRC, 1959-62; Nat. Commn on Productivity, 1970-75; Nat. Council on the Humanities, 1974-75. Dir, MacArthur Foundn, 1979; Trustee: Internat. Legal Center; Museum of Science and Industry, 1971-75; Russell Sage Foundn, 1977-75; Aspen Inst. for Humanist Studies, 1970-75, 1977-79; Univ. Chicago, 1966; Woodrow Wilson Nat. Fellowship Foundn, 1972-75, 1977-79; Inst. Psycho-analysis, Chicago, 1961-75; Member Board of Trustees: Nat. Humanities Center, 1978- (Chm., 1979-); The Aerospace Corp., 1978-80; Trustee; William Benton Foundn, 1980-; Salzburg Seminar in Amer. Studies, 1980; Mem. Bd of Overseers, Univ. of Pennsylvania Law Sch., 1978-; Hon. Trustee: Inst. of Internat. Educn; Univ. of Chicago, 1975. Fellow: Amer. Bar Foundn; Amer. Acad. Arts and Scis; Amer. Philos. Soc. Chubb Fellow, Yale, 1977. Hon. degrees: LHD: Hebrew Union Coll.; Loyola Univ.; DePaul Univ.; Kenyon Coll.; Univ. of Chicago; Bard Coll.; Beloit Coll.; LLD: Univ. of Michigan; Univ. of California at Santa Cruz; Univ. of Iowa; Jewish Theological Seminary of America; Brandeis Univ.; Lake Forest Coll.; Univ. of Rochester; Univ. of Toronto; Yale Univ.; Notre Dame; Denison Univ., Nebraska Univ. Law Sch.; Univ. of Miami; Boston Coll.; Ben N. Cardozo Sch. of Law, Yeshiva Univ., NYC; Columbia Univ., Dropsie Univ., Pa; Univ. of Pa Law Sch.; Brigham Young Univ.; Duke Univ.; Ripon Coll.; DCL NY Univ. Legion of Honour (France); Chicago Bar Assoc. Centennial Award, 1975; Distinguished Citizen Award, Ill St. Andrews Soc., 1976; Herbert H. Lehman Ethics Medal, Jewish Theol. Seminary, 1976; Learned Hand Medal, Fedn Bar Council, NYC, 1976; Wallace Award, Amer.-Scottish, Foundn, 1976; Morris J. Kaplun Meml Prize, Dropsie, 1976; Fed. Bar Assoc. Award, 1977; Louis Stein Award, Fordham, 1977; Citation of Merit, Yale, 1977; Louis Dembitz Brandeis Award, 1978. *Publications:* Introduction to Legal Reasoning, 1949; Four Talks on Legal Education, 1952; Point of View, 1969; The Crisis in the Nature of Law, 1969; Elements of the Law (ed, with Roscoe Steffen), 1936; Gilbert's Collier on Bankruptcy (ed, with James W. Moore), 1936; Member, editorial board: Jl Legal Educn, 1956-68; Encyclopaedia Britannica, 1968-75. *Address:* (office) 1116 East 59th Street, Chicago, Illinois 60637, USA. *T:* (312) 962-8588; (home) 4950 Chicago Beach Drive, Chicago, Illinois 60615. *Clubs:* Quadrangle, Columbia Yacht, Mid-America (Chicago); Commercial, Century (New York); Chicago (DC).

LEVI, Peter Chad Tigar, FSA; Fellow of St Catherine's College, Oxford, since 1977; *b* 16 May 1931; *s* of Herbert Simon Levi and Edith Mary Tigar; *m* 1977, Deirdre, *o d* of Hon. Dennis Craig, MBE, and *widow* of Cyril Connolly, CBE, CLit. *Educ:* Beaumont; Oxford Univ. (MA). FSA 1976.

Society of Jesus, 1948–77: priest, 1964; resigned priesthood, 1977. Tutor and Lectr in Classics, Campion Hall, Oxford, 1965–77; student, Brit. Sch. of Archaeol., Athens, 1965–68; Lectr in Classics, Christ Church Coll., Oxford, 1979–82. The Times Archaeol Correspondent, 1977–78. Television films: Ruined Abbeys, 1966; Foxes have holes, 1967; Seven black years, 1975. *Publications: poetry:* The Gravel Ponds, 1960; Water, Rock and Sand, 1962; The Shearwaters, 1965; Fresh Water, Sea Water, 1966; Ruined Abbeys, 1968; Pancakes for the Queen of Babylon, 1968; Life is a Platform, 1971; Death is a Pulpit, 1971; Collected Poems, 1976; Five Ages, 1978; Private Ground, 1981; *prose:* Beaumont, 1961; Ο τόνος τῆς φωνῆς τοῦ Σεφέρη (Mr Seferis' Tone of Voice), 1970; The Lightgarden of the Angel King, 1973; The English Bible (1534–1859), 1974; In Memory of David Jones, 1975; John Clare and Thomas Hardy, 1975; The Noise made by Poems, 1976; The Head in the Soup, 1979; The Hill of Kronos, 1980; Atlas of the Greek World, 1980; *translations:* Yevtushenko, 1962; Pausanias, 1971; Pavlopoulos, The Cellar, 1976; The Psalms, 1976. *Recreations:* music, museums, architecture, country pursuits. *Address:* Austin's Farm, Stonesfield, Oxford. *T:* Stonesfield 726. *Club:* Beefsteak.

LÉVI-STRAUSS, Claude; Commandeur de la Légion d'Honneur, 1976; Commandeur, Ordre Nationale du Mérite, 1971; Member of French Academy, since 1973; Professor, Collège de France, 1959–82, Hon. Professor, since 1983; Director of Studies, Ecole pratique des hautes études, Paris, since 1950; *b* 28 Nov. 1908; *s* of Raymond Lévi-Strauss and Emma Lévy; *m* 1st, 1932, Dina Dreyfus; 2nd, 1946, Rose-Marie Ullmo; one *s*; 3rd, 1954, Monique Roman; one *s. Educ:* Lycée Janson-de-Sailly, Paris; Sorbonne. Prof., Univ. of São Paulo, Brazil, 1935–39; Vis. Prof., New School for Social Research, NY, 1941–45; Cultural Counsellor, French Embassy, Washington, 1946–47; Associate Curator, Musée de l'Homme, Paris, 1948–49. Corresp. Member: Royal Acad. of Netherlands; Norwegian Acad.; British Acad.; Nat. Acad. of Sciences, USA; Amer. Acad. and Inst. of Arts and Letters; Amer. Museum of Natural History; Amer. Philos. Soc.; Royal Anthrop. Inst. of Great Britain; London Sch. of African and Oriental Studies. Hon. Dr: Brussels, 1962; Oxford, 1964; Yale, 1965; Chicago, 1967; Columbia, 1971; Stirling, 1972; Univ. Nat. du Zaire, 1973; Uppsala, 1977; Johns Hopkins, 1978; Laval, 1979; Mexico, 1979; Visva Bharati, India, 1980. *Publications:* La Vie familiale et sociale des Indiens Nambikwara, 1948; Les Structures élémentaires de la parenté, 1949 (The Elementary Structures of Kinship, 1969); Race et histoire, 1952; Tristes Tropiques, 1955, complete edn, 1973 (A World on the Wane, 1961); Anthropologie structurale, Vol. 1, 1958, Vol. 2, 1973 (Structural Anthropology, Vol. 1, 1964, Vol. 2, 1977); Le Totémisme aujourd'hui, 1962 (Totemism, 1962); La Pensée sauvage, 1962 (The Savage Mind, 1966); Le Cru et le cuit, 1964 (The Raw and the Cooked, 1970); Du Miel aux cendres, 1967 (From Honey to Ashes, 1973); L'Origine des manières de table, 1968 (The Origin of Table Manners, 1978); L'Homme nu, 1971; La Voie des masques, 1975; *relevant publications:* Conversations with Lévi-Strauss (ed G. Charbonnier), 1969; by Octavio Paz: On Lévi-Strauss, 1970; Claude Lévi-Strauss: an introduction, 1972. *Address:* 2 rue des Marronniers, 75016 Paris, France. *T:* 288-34-71.

LEVICK, William Russell, FRS 1982; FAA; Professorial Fellow of Physiology, John Curtin School of Medical Research, Australian National University, since 1967; *b* 5 Dec. 1931; *s* of Russell L. S. Levick and Elsie E. I. (*née* Nance); *m* 1961, Patricia Jane Lathwell; two *s* one *d. Educ:* Univ. of Sydney (BSc 1st Cl. Hons, MSc, MB, BS 1st Cl. Hons). Registered Medical Practitioner, State of NSW. FAA 1973. RMO, Royal Prince Alfred Hosp., Sydney, 1957–58; National Health and Med. Res. Council Fellow, Univ. of Sydney, 1959–62; C. J. Martin Travelling Fellow, Cambridge Univ. and Univ. of Calif, Berkeley, 1963–64; Associate Res. Physiologist, Univ. of Calif, Berkeley, 1965–66; Sen. Lectr in Physiol., Univ. of Sydney, 1967. Fellow, Optical Soc. of America, 1977. *Publications:* articles on neurophysiology of the visual system in internat. scientific jls. *Address:* Department of Physiology, John Curtin School of Medical Research, Australian National University, Canberra, ACT 2601, Australia. *T:* (62)-49-2525.

LEVIN, (Henry) Bernard; journalist and author; *b* 19 Aug. 1928; *s* of late Phillip Levin and Rose (*née* Racklin). *Educ:* Christ's Hospital; LSE, Univ. of London. BSc (Econ.). Has written regularly or irregularly for many newspapers and magazines in Britain and abroad, 1953–, principally The Times, Sunday Times, Observer, Manchester Guardian, Truth, Spectator, Daily Express, Daily Mail, Newsweek, International Herald-Tribune; has written and broadcast for radio and television, 1952–, incl. BBC and most ITV cos. Various awards for journalism. Hon. Fellow, LSE, 1977–. Mem., Order of Polonia Restituta (by Polish Government-in-Exile), 1976. *Publications:* The Pendulum Years, 1971; Taking Sides, 1979; Conducted Tour, 1981; Speaking Up, 1982. *Address:* c/o Curtis Brown Ltd, 1 Craven Hill, W2.

LEVIN, Richard, OBE 1952; RDI 1971; photographer, since 1975; *b* 31 Dec. 1910; *s* of Henry Levin and Margaret Sanders; *m* 1st, 1932, Evelyn Alexander; two *d*; 2nd, 1960, Patricia Foy, Producer, BBC TV. *Educ:* Clayesmore; Slade, UC London. Assistant Art Director, Gaumont British, 1928; private practice; exhibition; graphic and industrial designer working for BBC, C. C. Wakefield Ltd, Bakelite Ltd, LEB, etc, 1931–39; Camouflage Officer, Air Ministry, 1940; MOI Exhibn Div.; Designer, British Army Exhibns, UK and Paris, 1943; private practice, 1946; Designer, Festival of Britain, Land Travelling Exhibn, 1951; Head of Design, BBC Television, 1953–71. FSIAD 1955. Silver Medal, Royal Television Soc., 1972. *Publications:* Television by Design, 1960; Design for Television (BBC lunch-time lecture), 1968.

Recreation: fishing. *Address:* Sandells House, West Amesbury, Wilts SP4 7BH. *T:* Amesbury 23857.

LEVINE, Sir Montague (Bernard), Kt 1979; general practitioner; Assistant Deputy Coroner, Inner South London, since 1974; Clinical Tutor in General Practice, St Thomas' Hospital, since 1972; *b* 15 May 1922; *s* of late Philip Levine and of Bessie Levine; *m* 1959, Dr Rose Gold; one *s* one *d. Educ:* Royal Coll. of Surgeons in Ireland (LRCSI); Royal Coll. of Physicians in Ireland (MRCPI, LRCPI, LM). DMJ Clin.; MRCGP. Licentiate of Rubber Industry, 1944. Industrial physicist, rubber industry, 1939–45; House Surgeon: Royal Victoria Hosp., Bournemouth, 1955; Meath Hosp., Dublin, 1955; Metrop. Police Surg., 1960–66. Royal Coll. of Surgeons in Ireland: Stoney Meml Gold Medal in Anatomy, 1951; Silver Medallist, Medicine, 1953, Pathology, 1953, and Medical Jurisprudence, 1954; Macnaughton Gold Medal in Obs and Gynae., 1955; Lectr in Anat., 1956. *Publication:* Inter-parental Violence and its Effect on Children, 1975. *Recreations:* fishing, photography, painting. *Address:* Gainsborough House, 120 Ferndene Road, Herne Hill, SE24 0AA. *T:* 01-274 5554. *Club:* Organon.

LEVINE, Sydney; a Recorder, North-Eastern Circuit, since 1975; *b* 4 Sept. 1923; *s* of Rev. Isaac Levine and Mrs Miriam Levine; *m* 1959, Cécile Rona Rubinstein; three *s* one *d. Educ:* Bradford Grammar Sch.; Univ. of Leeds (LLB). Called to the Bar, Inner Temple, 1952; Chambers in Bradford, 1953–. *Recreations:* music, gardening. *Address:* 1 Grove Road, Shipley, W Yorks. *T:* Shipley 581581.

LEVINGE, Major Sir Richard Vere Henry, 11th Bt, *cr* 1704; MBE 1941; TD 1977; President, The Salmon and Trout Association; *b* 30 April 1911; *o s* of 10th Bt and Irene Marguerite (who *m* 2nd, 1916, Major R. V. Buxton), *d* of late J. H. C. Pix of Bradford; *S* father, 1914; *m* 1st, 1935, Barbara Mary, 2nd *d* of late George J. Kidston, CMG; two *s* three *d*; 2nd, 1976, Jane Millward. *Educ:* Eton; Balliol Coll., Oxford (Domus Exhibition). Retired, 1976, as Dep. Man. Dir, Arthur Guinness Son & Co. Ltd. Chm. Cttee of Management, Salmon Res. Trust of Ireland, until 1977. War Service, 1939–45: Lovat Scouts and Staff (despatches Burma 1945). *Recreations:* shooting, fishing. *Heir: s* Richard George Robin Levinge [*b* 18 Dec. 1946; *m* 1st, 1969, Hilary Jane, *d* of Dr Derek Mark, Co. Wicklow; 2nd, 1978, Donna Maria d'Ardia Caracciolo, *d* of Prince Frederico Caracciolo, Grange Road, Rathfarnham, Ireland]. *Address:* Spindles, 27 The Grove, Radlett, Herts; Abbey Lodge, Rectory Lane, Itchen Abbas, Winchester, Hants. *Clubs:* Flyfishers'; Kildare Street and University (Dublin).

LEVIS, Maj.-Gen. Derek George, CB 1972; OBE 1951; DL; retired; *b* 24 Dec. 1911; *mr s* of late Dr George Levis, Lincoln; *m* 1938, Doris Constance Tall; one *d. Educ:* Stowe Sch.; Trinity Coll., Cambridge; St Thomas' Hospital, London. BA Cantab 1933; MRCS, LRCP 1936; MB, BChir (Cantab), 1937; DPH 1949. Commnd into RAMC, 1936; house appts, St Thomas' Hospital, 1936–37; served in: China, 1937–39; War of 1939–45 (1939–45 Star, Pacific Star, France and Germany Star, Defence and War Medal): Malaya and Java, 1939–42; Ceylon, 1942–43; NW Europe, 1944–45; qualified as specialist in Army Health, RAM Coll., 1949; Asst Director Army Health, HQ British Troops Egypt, 1949–51; Deputy Asst Dir Army Health, HQ British Commonwealth Forces, Korea, 1952–53 (Korean Co. Medal and UN Medal); Asst Dir Army Health: Malaya Comd, 1953–55 (Gen. Service Medal, Clasp Malaya, despatches); War Office, 1956–58; Deputy Director, Army Health, HQ, BAOR, 1958–62; Comdt Army School of Health, 1962–66; Director of Army Health, Australian Military Forces, Melbourne, 1966–68; Dep. Director Army Health, HQ Army Strategic Comd, 1968; Director of Army Health, MoD (Army), 1968–70; Dep. Dir, Medical Services, Southern Comd, 1970–71. QHP 1969–71. Col Comdt, RAMC, 1973–76. Co. Comr, St John's Ambulance Brigade, Lincs, 1972–. Mem., Faculty of Community Physicians, RCP, 1971. DL Lincs, 1976. CStJ 1979. *Publications:* contribs to journal RAMC and Proc. Royal Society Med. *Recreations:* fishing, gardening. *Address:* Sapperton Cottage, The Green, Welbourn, Lincoln LN5 0NJ. *T:* Loveden 72673.

LÉVIS MIREPOIX, Antoine, Duc de; Grand d'Espagne; Commandeur de la Légion d'Honneur, Croix de Guerre, Grand Croix de l'Ordre d'Adolphe de Nassau; author; Member of the French Academy since 1953; Mainteneur de l'Académie des Jeux floraux de Toulouse; Commandeur, Ordre des Palmes Académiques; *b* 1 Aug. 1884; *s* of Henri and Henriette de Chabannes La Palice; *m* 1911, Nicole de Chaponay; one *s. Educ:* Lycée de Toulouse; Sorbonne (Licencié en philosophie). Lecturer for the Alliance française; Mission Maria Chapdeleine, Canada; President, Cincinnati de France; President, Institut France-Canada. *Publications:* Le Seigneur Inconnu, 1922; Montségur, 1924; François 1er, 1931; Vieilles races et Temps nouveaux, 1934; Les Campagnes ardentes, 1934; Le Coeur secret de Saint-Simon, 1935; Le Siècle de Philippe le Bel, 1936; La Politesse (with M. de Vogüe), 1937; Sainte-Jeanne de France, fille de Louis XI, 1943; Les Trois Femmes de Philipe-Auguste, 1947; Les Guerres de religion, 1947; La France de la Renaissance (Grand Prix Gobert de l'Académie française), 1948; La Tragédie des Templiers, 1955; Aventure d'une famille française, 1955; Que signifie 'le Parti de Ducs', 1964; Le roi n'est mort qu'une fois, 1965; Le livre d'or des Maréchaux de France, 1970; L'Attentat d'Agnani, 1970; St Louis: Roi de France, 1970; Henri IV, 1971; Grandeur et misère de l'individualisme française, 1973; La France féodale (6 vols); Robespierre, 1978. *Heir: s* Charles Henri, Marquis de Lévis Mirepoix [*b* 4 Jan. 1912; *m* 1962, Mme Françoise Foucault; one *s* one *d*]. *Address:* 27

rue Daru, 75008 Paris, France; Léran, 09600 Laroque-d'Olmes, *Clubs:* Jockey (Vice-President), Union, Interallié (Paris).

LEVITT, Walter Montague, MD, FRCP, FRCR; Barrister-at-Law; Hon. Consulting Radiotherapist, St Bartholomew's Hospital, since 1945; *b* 1900; *e s* of Lewis and Caroline Levitt, Rathmines, Co. Dublin; *m* 1st, 1929, Sonia Esté Nivinsky (*d* 1977), BSc, MRCS, DPH; no *c* ; 2nd, 1977, Violet Irene Levitt (*née* Hirschland). *Educ:* High Sch., Dublin; University Coll., Dublin (Med. Schol. and 1st cl. Exhbnr); Cambridge (DMRE); Frankfurt. Called to the Bar, Lincoln's Inn, 1946. Demonstrator of anatomy, 1920-21, of pathology, 1921; formerly: Lectr in X-Ray Therapy for Dip. in Med. Radiol., Univ. Cambridge; Dir, Dept of Radiotherapy, London Clinic; Hon. Physician i/c, Dept of Radiotherapy, St George's Hosp.; MO i/c Radiotherapeutic Dept, St Bartholomew's Hosp. Member: Minister of Labour's Adv. Panel in Radiology; Clinical Res. Cttee, British Empire Cancer Campaign; Dep. Comr, 1967-69, Dep. Chm., 1969-73, Metropolitan Traffic Comrs. Hon. Assoc. Editor, British Jl of Radiology. Hon. Secretary: Section of Radiology, Internat. Cancer Conf., London, 1928; Radiology Section, BMA Centenary Meeting, London, 1932; Deleg. to Internat. Cancer Congress, Atlantic City, 1939. Foundn Fellow, Vice-Pres., Chm., Therapeutic Cttee, Faculty of Radiologists, 1940-43; Fellow, Vice-Pres., and Pres., Section of Radiology, RSM, 1945-46; formerly Hon. Med. Sec., BIR. Freeman, City of London; Liveryman, Apothecaries' Co., 1956. Gold Medallist, Mercers Hosp., 1922. *Publications:* Deep X-Ray Therapy in Malignant Disease (with Introduction by Lord Horder), 1930; completed and edited Knox's Text Book of X-Ray Therapeutics, 1932; Handbook of Radiotherapy for Senior and Post-graduate students, 1952; Short Encyclopædia of Medicine for Lawyers, 1966; Section on Diseases of the Blood in Paterson's Treatment of Malignant Disease by X-Rays and Radium, 1948; Section on X-Ray therapy in Bourne and Williams' Recent Advances in Gynæcology, 1952; Chapter on Reticulosis and Reticulosarcoma (with R. Bodley Scott) in British Practice in Radiotherapy, 1955; various articles on medico-legal subjects. *Address:* 17 Manor Court, Pinehurst, Cambridge CB3 9BE.

LEVY, Dennis Martyn, QC 1982; *b* 20 Feb. 1936; *s* of Conrad Levy and Tillie (*née* Swift); *m* 1967, Rachel Jonah; one *s* one *d. Educ:* Clifton Coll.; Gonville and Caius Coll., Cambridge (MA). Called to the Bar, Gray's Inn, 1960. Granada Group Ltd, 1960-63; Time Products Ltd, 1963-66; in practice at the Bar, 1966-. *Recreations:* reading, especially tall stories; visiting, especially the Barbican and South Bank; walking, especially on Hampstead Heath. *Address:* 4 Millfield Lane, N6 6JD. *T:* 01-348 5747.

LEVY, Sir (Enoch) Bruce, Kt 1953; OBE 1950; retired, 1951; *b* 19 Feb. 1892; *s* of William and Esther Ann Levy; *m* 1925, Phyllis R., *d* of G. H. Mason; no *c. Educ:* Primary Sch.; Banks Commercial Coll.; Victoria University College (BSc). Brought up on farm to age 18; appointed Dept Agriculture, 1911; agrostologist to 1937; charge seed-testing station. Ecological studies Grasslands and indigenous vegetative cover of NZ; transferred to DSIR, 1937, and appointed Director Grasslands Division; Director Green-keeping Research; Chairman NZ Institute for Turf Culture (Life Mem. 1957); Official Rep. International Grassland Conference, Great Britain, 1937, Netherlands, 1949; Lecture tour, Great Britain, 1949-50; Member: Rotary International; Grassland Assoc. (Life Mem. 1951); NZ Animal Production Society (Life Mem. 1961); Manawatu Catchment Board; Central Standing Cttee, Soil Conservation; Trustee, Grassland Memorial Trust (Chm. 1966-68). Life Member NZ Royal Agric. Society, 1956. Hon. Dr of Science, University of NZ; R. B. Bennett Empire Prize, 1951 (Royal Society of Arts, London). *Publications:* Grasslands of New Zealand, 1943 (revised and enlarged, 1951, 1955 and 1970); Construction, Renovation and Care of the Bowling Green, 1949; Construction, Renovation and Care of the Golf Course, 1950. 150 scientific papers in popular and scientific journals in NZ and overseas. *Recreations:* bowling, gardening. *Address:* Main Waihi Road, RDI, Tauranga, New Zealand. *T:* 64-522.

LEVY, Sir Ewart Maurice, 2nd Bt *cr* 1913; *b* 10 May 1897; *o s* of Sir Maurice Levy, 1st Bt; *S* father, 1933; *m* 1932, Hylda (*d* 1970), *e d* of late Sir Albert Levy; one *d. Educ:* Harrow. High Sheriff of Leicestershire, 1937; served, 1940-45, Royal Pioneer Corps, Lieut-Colonel, 1944; BLA, 1944-45 (despatches). JP Co. Leicester. *Heir:* none. *Address:* Welland House, Weston-by-Welland, Market Harborough, Leicestershire. *Club:* Reform.

LEVY, George Joseph; Chairman, H. Blairman & Sons Ltd, since 1965; *b* 21 May 1927; *s* of Percy and Maude Levy; *m* 1952, Wendy Yetta Blairman; one *s* three *d. Educ:* Oundle Sch. Joined H. Blairman & Sons Ltd (Antique Dealers), 1950, Dir, 1955. Pres., British Antique Dealers Assoc., 1974-76. Chairman: Grosvenor House Antiques Fair, 1978-79; Somerset Hse Art Treasures Exhibn, 1979; Burlington Hse Fair, 1980-. Chm., Friends of Kenwood, 1978-. *Recreations:* tennis, photography. *Address:* 27 Oakhill Avenue, NW3 7RD. *T:* 01-435 9528.

LEVY, Prof. John Court, CEng, FIMechE, MRAeS; Head of Department of Mechanical Engineering, The City University, London, since 1966; *b* London, 16 Feb. 1926; *s* of Alfred and Lily Levy; *m* 1952, Sheila Frances Krisman; two *s* one *d. Educ:* Owens Sch., London; Imperial Coll., Univ. of London (BScEng, ACGI, PhD); Univ. of Illinois, USA (MS). Stressman, Boulton-Paul Aircraft, 1945-47; Asst to Chief Engr, Fullers Ltd, 1947-51. Asst Lectr, Northampton Polytechnic, London, 1951-53; Fulbright Award to Univ. of Illinois, for research into metal fatigue, 1953-54; Lectr, Sen. Lectr, Reader,

Northampton Polytechnic (later Northampton Coll. of Advanced Technology), 1954-66; also a Recognised Teacher of the Univ. of London, 1958-66; Pro-Vice-Chancellor, City Univ., 1975-81. Member, Mechanical and Prodn Engrg Cttee, SRC, 1969-72; Chairman, 1st Panel on Marine Technology, SRC, 1971-73; Member: Metallurgical Engrg Cttee, Metals Soc., 1975-; Qualifications Bd, IMechE, 1975-; Court of Governors, City of London Polytechnic, 1976-82; Chm., Chartered Engr Section, Engineers Registration Bd, CEI, 1978-82. *Publications:* papers on metal fatigue, marine technology, engrg educn, IMechE, RAeS, etc. *Recreations:* theatre, chess, exploring cities. *Address:* 18 Woodberry Way, Finchley, N12 0HG. *T:* 01-445 5227. *Club:* Island Sailing (Cowes, IoW).

LEVY, Prof. Philip Marcus, PhD, FBPsS; Professor of Psychology, University of Lancaster, since 1972; *b* 4 Feb. 1934; *s* of late Rupert Hyam Levy and of Sarah Beatrice Levy; *m* 1958, Gillian Mary (*née* Harker); two *d. Educ:* Leeds Modern School; Univ. of Leeds (BA 1955); Univ. of Birmingham (PhD 1960). FBPsS. Res. Fellow, Birmingham Univ., 1955-59; Psychologist, RAF, 1959-62; Sen. Res. Fellow, Lectr, Sen. Lectr, Birmingham Univ., 1962-72. Hon. Vice-Pres., Assoc. for Teaching of Social Science, 1972-75; Chairman: Psychol. Cttee, SSRC, 1979-82 (Mem., 1976-82); Educn and Human Develt Cttee, SSRC, 1982-; Mem. Council 1973-80, Pres. 1978-79, BPsS. Editor, Brit. Jl of Mathematical and Statistical Psychology, 1975-80. *Publications:* numerous in psychol jls. *Address:* Department of Psychology, University of Lancaster, Lancaster LA1 4YF. *T:* Lancaster 65201.

LEWANDO, Sir Jan (Alfred), Kt 1974; CBE 1968; *b* 31 May 1909; *s* of Maurice Lewando and Eugenie Lewando (*née* Goldsmid); *m* 1948, Nora Slavouski; three *d. Educ:* Manchester Grammar Sch.; Manchester University. Served War of 1939-45, British Army: British Army Staff, Washington DC and British Min. of Supply Mission, 1941-45 (Lt-Col. 1943). Marks & Spencer Ltd, 1929-70 (Dir 1954); Chairman: Carrington Viyella Ltd, 1970-75; Consolidated Textile Mills Ltd, Canada, 1972-75; Pres., Carrington Viyella Inc. (USA), 1971-75; Director: Carrington Tesit (Italy), 1971-75; Heal and Son Holdings, 1975-82 (Dep. Chm., 1977-82); Bunzl Pulp & Paper Ltd, 1976-; W. A. Baxter & Sons Ltd, 1975-; Johnston Industries Inc. (USA), 1976-; Edgars Stores Ltd (South Africa), 1976-82; Royal Worcester Spode Ltd, 1978-79; Bunzl and Biach AG (Austria), 1979-80; Johnston Industries Ltd, 1980-; Chairman: Gelvenor Textiles Ltd, S Africa, 1973-75; Beaufort Engrg Co. Ltd, 1980-. Vice Chm., Clothing Export Council, 1976-70; Pres., British Textile Confedn, 1972-73; Vice Pres., Comitextil, Brussels, 1972-73; Member: British Overseas Trade Bd, 1972-77 (Mem., European Trade Cttee, 1973-); British Overseas Trade Adv. Council, 1975-77; BNEC, 1969-71 (Chm., Area Export Cttee for Israel, 1968-71); Export Council for Europe, 1965-69; European Steering Cttee, CBI, 1968-71; Grand Council, CBI, 1971-75. Vice-Pres., Transport Trust, 1973-. FBIM 1972; FRSA 1973. Companion, Textile Inst., 1972. Order of Legion of Merit (USA), 1946. *Address:* Davidge House, Knotty Green, Beaconsfield, Bucks. *T:* Beaconsfield 4987.

LEWEN, John Henry, CMG 1977; HM Diplomatic Service, retired; Ambassador to the People's Republic of Mozambique, 1975-79; *b* 6 July 1920; *s* of Carl Henry Lewen and Alice (*née* Mundy); *m* 1945, Emilienne Alette Julie Alida Galant; three *s. Educ:* Christ's Hospital; King's Coll., Cambridge. Royal Signals, 1940-45. HM Foreign (subseq. Diplomatic) Service, 1946; HM Embassy: Lisbon, 1947-50; Rangoon, 1950-53; FO, 1953-55; HM Embassy: Rio de Janeiro, 1955-59; Warsaw, 1959-61; FO, 1961-63; Head of Chancery, HM Embassy, Rabat, 1963-67; Consul-General, Jerusalem, 1967-70; Inspector of HM Diplomatic Estabts, 1970-73; Dir, Admin and Budget, Secretariat-Gen. of Council of Ministers of European Communities, 1973-75. OStJ 1969. *Recreations:* singing, sailing. *Address:* 1 Brimley Road, Cambridge CB4 2DQ. *Club:* Travellers'.

LEWERS, Very Rev. Benjamin Hugh; Provost of Derby, since 1981; *b* 25 March 1932; *s* of Hugh Bunnett Lewers and Coral Helen Lewers; *m* 1957, Sara Blagden; three *s. Educ:* Sherborne School; Selwyn Coll., Cambridge (MA); Lincoln Theological Coll. Employee, Dunlop Rubber Co., 1953-57. Curate: St Mary, Northampton, 1962-65; Priest-in-charge, Church of the Good Shepherd, Hounslow, 1965-68; Industrial Chaplain, Heathrow Airport, 1968-75; Vicar of Newark, 1975-80, Rector 1980-81. *Recreations:* cricket, music, gardening, wine and rug making. *Address:* The Provost's House, 9 Highfield Road, Derby DE3 1GX. *T:* Derby 42971.

LEWES, Suffragan Bishop of, since 1977; **Rt. Rev. Peter John Ball**, CGA; Prebendary of Chichester Cathedral, since 1978; *b* 14 Feb. 1932; *s* of Thomas James and Kathleen Obena Bradley Ball. *Educ:* Lancing; Queens' Coll., Cambridge; Wells Theological College. MA (Nat. Sci.). Ordained, 1956; Curate of Rottingdean, 1956-58; Co-founder and Brother of Monastic Community of the Glorious Ascension, 1960 (Prior, 1960-77). Fellow of Woodard Corporation, 1962-71; Member: Archbishops' Council of Evangelism, 1965-68; Midlands Religious Broadcasting Council of the BBC, 1967-69. *Recreations:* squash (Cambridge Blue, 1953) and music. *Address:* The Rectory, Litlington, Polegate, East Sussex BN26 5RB. *T:* Alfriston 870387.

See also Bishop of Jarrow.

LEWES, John Hext, OBE 1944; Lieutenant of Dyfed, 1974-78 (Lord Lieutenant of Cardiganshire, 1956-74); *b* 16 June 1903; *s* of late Colonel John Lewes, RA, and of Mrs Lewes (*née* Hext); *m* 1929, Nesta Cecil, *d* of late Captain H. Fitzroy Talbot, DSO, RN; one *s* two *d. Educ:* RN Colleges

Osborne and Dartmouth. Sub-Lieut, 1923, Lieut, 1925; specialised in Torpedoes, 1928; Commander, 1939; commanded: HMS Shikari, Intrepid, 1941–42 (despatches); Ameer, 1944–45 (despatches); retired 1947, with war service rank of Captain, RN. Now farming. FRAgSs 1972. KStJ 1964. *Address:* Llanllyr, near Lampeter, Dyfed. *T:* Aeron 470323.

LEWES AND HASTINGS, Archdeacon of; *see* Godden, Ven. M. L.

LEWIN, Captain (Edgar) Duncan (Goodenough), CB 1958; CBE 1953; DSO 1941; DSC 1939; Royal Navy, retired; Deputy Chairman, British Aerospace Dynamics Group, 1977–78; *b* 9 Aug. 1912; *s* of Captain G. E. Lewin, RN; *m* 1943, Nancy Emily Hallett, Tintinhull, Somerset; one *s* one *d. Educ:* RN Coll., Dartmouth. Cadet, HMS Royal Oak, 1930; specialized in flying, 1935. Served in HMS Ajax, River Plate action, 1939; Comd 808 Squadron in HMS Ark Royal, 1941; served staff of Admiral Vian in Mediterranean and Pacific, 1944–45. Comd HMS Glory, in Korean waters, 1952–53; Director of Air Warfare, Admiralty, 1953–54; Comd HMS Eagle, 1955; Director of Plans, Admiralty, 1956–57; retired from Navy and joined Board of Blackburn's, 1957; Sales Director, Hawker Siddeley Aviation Ltd, 1968–71; Man. Dir, Hawker Siddeley Dynamics, 1971–77, Chm., 1977. *Recreations:* croquet, gardening. *Address:* Hatching Green Lodge, Harpenden, Herts. *T:* Harpenden 62034.

LEWIN, (George) Ronald, FRSL, FRHistS; military historian; *b* 11 Oct. 1914; *s* of late Frank Lewin, Halifax; *m* 1938, Sylvia Lloyd Sturge; two *s* one *d* (and one *s* decd). *Educ:* Heath Sch., Halifax; The Queen's Coll., Oxford (Hastings Scholar, 1st Class Hon. Mods, 1st Class Lit. Hum., Goldsmiths' Exhibitioner). Editorial Assistant, Jonathan Cape Ltd, Publishers, 1937. Served in Royal Artillery, N Africa and NW Europe (wounded, despatches), 1939–45. Producer, BBC Home Talks Dept, 1946; Chief Asst, Home Service, 1954; Head, 1957; Chief, 1963. Retired 1965. Editor, Hutchinson Publishing Gp, 1966–69. Leverhulme Res. Fellow, 1973. FRSL 1977; FRHistS 1980. Chesney Gold Medal, RUSI, 1982. *Publications:* Rommel as Military Commander, 1968; (ed) Freedom's Battle, vol. 3, The War on Land 1939–45, 1969; Montgomery as Military Commander, 1971; Churchill as War Lord, 1973; Man of Armour: Lieut-General Vyvyan Pope and the development of armoured warfare, 1976; Slim the Standard-Bearer, the biography of Field Marshal the Viscount Slim, 1976 (W. H. Smith Award, 1977); The Life and Death of the Afrika Korps, 1977; Ultra goes to War, 1978; The Chief: Field Marshal Lord Wavell, Commander-in-Chief and Viceroy, 1980; The Other Ultra: codes, ciphers and the defeat of Japan, 1982; sundry introds to Time/Life Histories of the Second World War; numerous articles and reviews on military history. *Address:* Camilla House, Forest Road, East Horsley, Surrey. *T:* East Horsley 3779. *Club:* Army and Navy.

LEWIN, Admiral of the Fleet Sir Terence (Thornton), GCB 1976 (KCB 1973); MVO 1958; DSC 1942; Chief of the Defence Staff, 1979–82; *b* Dover, 19 Nov. 1920; *m* 1944, Jane Branch-Evans; two *s* one *d. Educ:* The Judd Sch., Tonbridge. Joined RN, 1939; War Service in Home and Mediterranean Fleets in HMS Valiant, HMS Ashanti in Malta Convoys, N Russian Convoys, invasion N Africa and Channel (despatches); comd HMS Corunna, 1955–56; Comdr HM Yacht Britannia, 1957–58; Captain (F) Dartmouth Training Squadron and HM Ships Urchin and Tenby, 1961–63; Director, Naval Tactical and Weapons Policy Division, MoD, 1964–65; comd HMS Hermes, 1966–67; Asst Chief of Naval Staff (Policy), 1968–69; Flag Officer, Second-in-Comd, Far East Fleet, 1969–70; Vice-Chief of the Naval Staff, 1971–73; C-in-C Fleet, 1973–75; C-in-C Naval Home Command, 1975–77; Chief of Naval Staff and First Sea Lord, 1977–79. Flag ADC to the Queen, 1975–77; First and Principal ADC to the Queen, 1977–79. Trustee, National Maritime Museum, 1981–. Elder Brother of Trinity House, 1975; Hon. Freeman: Skinners' Co., 1976; Shipwrights' Co., 1978. FRSA. Hon. DSc City, 1978. *Recreations:* golf; formerly athletics and Rugby football (rep. RN at both, 1947–48). *Address:* House of Lords, SW1A 0PW.

Created a Baron (Life Peer), 1982. See supplementary pages.

LEWIS, family name of **Barony of Merthyr.**

LEWIS, Maj.-Gen. Alfred George, CBE 1969; Company Secretary, Bus Manufacturers (Holdings), since 1980; Staff Director, BL plc, since 1981; *b* 23 July 1920; *s* of Louis Lewis; *m* 1946, Daye Neville, *d* of Neville Greaves Hunt; two *s* two *d. Educ:* St Dunstan's Coll.; King's Coll., London. Served War of 1939–45, India and Burma. Commanded 15th/19th Hussars, 1961–63; Dir, Defence Operational Requirements Staff, MoD, 1967–68; Dep. Comdt, Royal Mil. Coll. of Science, 1968–70; Dir Gen., Fighting Vehicles and Engineer Equipment, 1970–72, retired 1973. Man. Dir, 1973–80, Dep. Chm., 1980–81, Alvis Ltd; Dep. Chm., Self Changing Gears Ltd, 1976–81; Co. Sec., Leyland Vehicles, 1980–81. Hon. Col, Queen's Own Mercian Yeomanry, 1977–82. FIIM 1975. *Recreations:* shooting, golf, gardening. *Address:* c/o National Westminster Bank Ltd, Sydenham, SE26. *Club:* Cavalry and Guards.

LEWIS, Sir Allen (Montgomery), GCMG 1979; Kt 1968; (first) Governor-General of St Lucia, 1979–80 (Governor, 1974–79); *b* 26 Oct. 1909; *s* of George Ferdinand Montgomery Lewis and Ida Louisa (née Barton); *m* 1936, Edna Leofrida Theobalds; three *s* two *d. Educ:* St Mary's Coll., St Lucia. LLB Hons (external) London, 1941. Admitted to practice at Bar of Royal Court, St Lucia (later Supreme Court of Windward and Leeward Islands), 1931; called to English Bar, Middle Temple, 1946; in private practice, Windward Islands,

1931–59; Acting Magistrate, St Lucia, 1940–41; Acting Puisne Judge, Windward and Leeward Islands, 1955–56; QC 1956; Judge: of Federal Supreme Court, 1959–62; of British Caribbean Court of Appeal, 1962; of Court of Appeal, Jamaica, 1962–67; Acting President, Court of Appeal, 1966; Acting Chief Justice of Jamaica, 1966; Chief Justice, West Indies Associated States Supreme Court, 1967–72; Chm., Nat. Develt Corp., St Lucia, 1972–74. MLC, St Lucia, 1943–51; Member, Castries Town Council, 1942–56 (Chairman six times); President W Indies Senate, 1958–59. Served on numerous Government and other public cttees; Comr for reform and revision of laws of St Lucia, 1954–58; rep. St Lucia, Windward Islands, and W Indies at various Conferences. Director, St Lucia Branch, British Red Cross Society, 1955–59; President: Grenada Boy Scouts' Assoc., 1967–72; St John Council for St Lucia, 1975–80. Served as President and/or Cttee Member, cricket, football and athletic associations, St Lucia, 1936–59. Chancellor, Univ. of WI, 1975–; Hon. LLD Univ. of WI, 1974. Chief Scout, St Lucia, 1976–80. Coronation Medal, 1953; Silver Jubilee Medal, 1977. KStJ. *Publication:* Revised Edition of Laws of St Lucia, 1957. *Recreations:* gardening, swimming. *Address:* Beaver Lodge, The Morne, PO Box 1076, Castries, St Lucia. *T:* 2281. *Clubs:* Royal Commonwealth Society; St Lucia Golf.

LEWIS, (Alun) Kynric, QC 1978; a Recorder of the Crown Court, since 1979; *b* Harlech, 23 May 1928; 3rd *s* of Rev. Cadwaladr O. Lewis and late Ursula Lewis; *m* 1955, Bethan, *er d* of late Prof. Edgar Thomas, CBE, and Eurwen Thomas; one *s* two *d. Educ:* The Grammar School, Beaumaris; University Coll. of N Wales (BSc); London School of Economics (LLB). Barrister, Middle Temple, 1954; Gray's Inn, 1961. *Recreations:* walking, fishing. *Address:* Penrallt, Llys-faen, Caerdydd; Francis Taylor Building, Temple, EC4Y 7BY. *Club:* Reform.

LEWIS, Adm. Sir Andrew (Mackenzie), KCB 1971 (CB 1967); JP; Lord-Lieutenant and Custos Rotulorum of Essex, since 1978; Commander-in-Chief, Naval Home Command, and Flag Officer Portsmouth Area, 1972–74; Flag ADC to The Queen, 1972–74; *b* 24 Jan. 1918; *s* of late Rev. Cyril Lewis; *m* 1943, Rachel Elizabeth Leatham; two *s. Educ:* Haileybury. Director of Plans, Admiralty, 1961–63; in command of HMS Kent, 1964–65; Director-General, Weapons (Naval), 1965–68; Flag Officer, Flotillas, Western Fleet, 1968–69; Second Sea Lord and Chief of Naval Personnel, 1970–71. DL Essex 1975. KStJ 1978. *Address:* Coleman's Farm, Finchingfield, Braintree, Essex CM7 4PE. *Club:* Brooks's.

See also Sir Clive Rose.

LEWIS, Anthony; *see* Lewis, J. A.

LEWIS, Sir Anthony Carey, Kt 1972; CBE 1967; Principal of the Royal Academy of Music, 1968–82; *b* 1915; *s* of late Colonel Leonard Carey Lewis, OBE, and Katherine Barbara Lewis; *m* 1959, Lesley, *d* of Mr and Mrs Frank Lisle Smith. *Educ:* Wellington; Peterhouse, Cambridge (Organ Schol.). MA, MusB Cantab. Joined music staff of BBC, 1935; director Foundations of Music and similar programmes; responsible many revivals 16th-18th century music; War of 1939-45, served MEF; planned and supervised music in BBC Third Programme, 1946; Peyton-Barber Prof. of Music, Univ. of Birmingham, 1947–68, and Dean of the Faculty of Arts, 1961–64. Pres. RMA, 1963–69; Chairman: Music Adv. Panel, Arts Council of GB, 1954–65; Music Adv. Cttee, British Council, 1967–73; Founder and Gen. Editor, Musica Britannica; Chairman: Purcell Soc.; Purcell-Handel Festival, 1959; Dir, English Nat. Opera, 1974–78; Governor, Wellington Coll. Hon. RAM; FRCM; FRNCM; Hon. FTCL; Hon. GSM; FRSAMD. Hon. MusD Birmingham. *Compositions include:* Psalm 86 (Cambridge, 1935); A Choral Overture (Queen's Hall, 1937); City Dances for Orchestra (Jerusalem, 1944); Trumpet Concerto (Albert Hall, 1947); Three Invocations (Birmingham, 1949); A Tribute of Praise (Birmingham, 1951); Horn Concerto (London, 1956); Canzona for Orchestra, Homage to Purcell (Birmingham, 1959). Conductor many recordings, especially Purcell and Handel. *Publications:* research: A Restoration Suite (Purcell and others), 1937; Venus and Adonis (Blow), 1939; Matthew Locke, 1948; Libera me (Arne), 1950; Coronation Anthems (Blow), 1953; Apollo and Daphne (Handel), 1956; Odes and Cantatas (Purcell), 1957; Anthems (3 vols), (Purcell), 1959-62; Fairy Queen (Purcell), 1966; Athalia (Handel), 1967; Imeneo (Handel), 1977; Editor, English Songs Series; numerous contributions on musical subjects to various periodicals. *Address:* High Rising, Holdfast Lane, Haslemere, Surrey.

LEWIS, Sir Arthur; *see* Lewis, Sir W. A.

LEWIS, Arthur William John; MP (Lab) Newham North West, since 1974 (West Ham, Upton, 1945-50; West Ham North, 1950-74); Ex-Trade Union Official (National Union of General and Municipal Workers); *b* 21 Feb. 1917; *s* of late J. Lewis; *m* 1940, Lucy Ethel Clack; one *d. Educ:* Elementary Sch.; Borough Polytechnic. Shop steward of his Dept of City of London Corporation at 17; Vice-Chairman of TU branch (City of London NUGMW) at 18; full-time London district official NUGMW 1938-48; Member of London Trades Council and Holborn City Trades Council, various joint industrial councils, Government cttees, etc; Member: ASTMS; APEX; G&MWU. Mem., Expenditure Cttee. Formerly Member Exec. Cttee, London Labour Party; Chairman Eastern Regional Group of Labour MPs, 1950–; Member Eastern Regional Council of Labour Party and Exec. Cttee of that body, 1950–. Served in the Army. *Recreations:* swimming, motoring, boxing, general athletics. *Address:* 1 Doveridge Gardens, Palmers Green, N13.

LEWIS, Bernard, BA, PhD; FBA 1963; FRHistS; Cleveland E. Dodge Professor of Near Eastern Studies, Princeton University, and Long-term Member of School of Social Science, Institute for Advanced Study, since 1974; *b* London, 31 May 1916; *s* of H. Lewis, London; *m* 1947, Ruth Hélène (marr. diss. 1974), *d* of late Overretsagfører M. Oppenhejm, Copenhagen; one *s* one *d. Educ:* Wilson Coll.; The Polytechnic; Universities of London and Paris (Fellow UCL 1976). Derby Student, 1936. Asst Lecturer in Islamic History, Sch. of Oriental Studies, University of London, 1938; Prof. of History of Near and Middle East, SOAS, London Univ., 1949-74. Served RAC and Intelligence Corps, 1940-41; attached to Foreign Office, 1941-45. Visiting Prof. of History, University of Calif, Los Angeles, 1955-56, Columbia Univ., 1960 and Indiana Univ., 1963; Class of 1932 Lectr, Princeton Univ., 1964; Vis. Mem., Inst. for Advanced Study, Princeton, New Jersey, 1969; Gottesman Lectr, Yeshiva Univ., 1974; Vis. Prof., Collège de France, 1980. Membre Associé, Institut d'Egypte, Cairo, 1969; Hon. Fellow, Turkish Historical Soc., Ankara, 1972; Hon. Dr: Hebrew Univ., Jerusalem, 1974; Tel Aviv Univ., 1979. For. Mem., Amer. Philosophical Soc., 1973. Certificate of Merit for services to Turkish Culture, Turkish Govt, 1973. Harvey Prizewinner, 1978. *Publications:* The Origins of Isma'ilism, 1940; Turkey Today, 1940; British contributions to Arabic Studies, 1941; Handbook of Diplomatic and Political Arabic, 1947, 1956; (ed) Land of Enchanters, 1948; The Arabs in History, 1950 (5th rev. edn, 1970); Notes and Documents from the Turkish Archives, 1952; The Emergence of Modern Turkey, 1961 (rev. edn, 1968); The Kingly Crown (translated from Ibn Gabirol), 1961; co-ed. with P. M. Holt, Historians of the Middle East, 1962; Istanbul and the Civilization of the Ottoman Empire, 1963; The Middle East and the West, 1964; The Assassins, 1967; Race and Colour in Islam, 1971; Islam in History, 1973; Islam to 1453, 1974; co-ed., Encyclopædia of Islam, 1956-; (ed, with others) The Cambridge History of Islam, vols 1-11, 1971; Islam from the Prophet Muhammad to the Capture of Constantinople, 2 vols, 1974; History, Remembered, Recovered, Invented, 1975; (ed) The World of Islam: Faith, People, Culture, 1976; Studies in Classical and Ottoman Islam, 7th-16th centuries, 1976; (with Amnon Cohen) Population and Revenue in the Towns of Palestine in the Sixteenth Century, 1978; The Muslim Discovery of Europe, 1982; articles in learned journals. *Address:* Near Eastern Studies Department, Jones Hall, Princeton University, Princeton, NJ 08540, USA. *Club:* Athenæum.

LEWIS, His Honour Bernard; a Circuit Judge (formerly a County Court Judge), 1966-80; *b* 1 Feb. 1905; 3rd *s* of late Solomon and Jeannette Lewis, London; *m* 1934, Harriette, *d* of late I. A. Waine, Dublin, London and Nice; one *s. Educ:* Trinity Hall, Cambridge (MA). Called to the Bar, Lincoln's Inn, 1929. Mem. S-E Circuit. Hon. Mem., Central Criminal Court Bar Mess. *Recreations:* revolver shooting, bricklaying. *Address:* Trevelyan House, Arlington Road, St Margaret's, Middx. *Clubs:* Reform; Ham and Petersham Rifle and Pistol.

LEWIS, Cecil Arthur, MC; Author; *b* Birkenhead, 29 March 1898; *m* 1921 (marr. diss. 1940); one *s* one *d* ; *m* 1942 (marr. diss. 1950); no *c* ; *m* 1960. *Educ:* Dulwich Coll.; University Coll. Sch.; Oundle. Royal Flying Corps, 1915 (MC, despatches twice); Manager Civil Aviation, Vickers, Ltd, 1919; Flying Instructor to Chinese Government, Peking, 1920, 1921; one of four founders of BBC, Chm. of Programme Board, 1922-26; Varied Literary Activities: stage, screen (first two adaptations of Bernard Shaw's plays to screen, 1930-32), and television plays (Nativity, Crucifixion and Patience of Job, 1956-59) and production connected therewith. RAF, 1939-45. Sheep farming, South Africa, 1947-50. United Nations Secretariat, New York, radio and television, 1953-55. Commercial television, London, 1955-56. Daily Mail, 1956-66; retd. *Publications:* Broadcasting From Within, 1924; The Unknown Warrior, trans. from French of Paul Raynal, 1928; Sagittarius Rising, 1937; The Trumpet is Mine, 1938; Challenge to the Night, 1938; Self Portrait: Letters and Journals of the late Charles Ricketts, RA (Editor), 1939 (filmed for TV, 1979); Pathfinders, 1943; Yesterday's Evening, 1946; Farewell to Wings, 1964; Turn Right for Corfu, 1972; Never Look Back (autobiog.), 1974 (filmed for TV, 1978); A Way to Be, 1977. *Address:* c/o National Westminster Bank, 97 Strand, WC2.

LEWIS, Prof. Dan, PhD; DSc; FRS 1955; Quain Professor of Botany, London University, 1957-78, now Emeritus; Hon. Research Fellow, University College, London, since 1978; *b* 30 Dec. 1910; *s* of Ernest Albert and Edith J. Lewis; *m* 1933, Mary Phœbe Eleanor Burry; one *d. Educ:* High Sch., Newcastle-under-Lyme, Staffs; Reading University (BSc); PhD, DSc (London). Research Scholar, Reading Univ., 1935-36; Scientific Officer, Pomology Dept, John Innes Hort. Inst., 1935-48; Head of Genetics Dept, John Innes Horticultural Institution, Bayfordbury, Hertford, Herts, 1948-57. Rockefeller Foundation Special Fellowship, California Inst. of Technology, 1955-56; Visiting Prof. of Genetics, University of Calif, Berkeley, 1961-62; Royal Society Leverhulme Visiting Professor: University of Delhi, 1965-66; Singapore, 1970; Vis. Prof., QMC, 1978-. Pres., Genetical Soc., 1968-71; Mem., UGC, 1969-74. *Publications:* Sexual Incompatibility in Plants, 1979; Editor, Science Progress; scientific papers on Genetics and Plant Physiology. *Recreations:* swimming, gardening, music. *Address:* 56/57 Myddelton Square, EC1R 1YA. *T:* 01-278 6948.

LEWIS, David Courtenay M.; *see* Mansel Lewis.

LEWIS, David Henry L.; *see* LeRoy-Lewis.

LEWIS, David Malcolm, MA, PhD; FBA 1973; Tutor in Ancient History, Christ Church, Oxford, since 1955 (Student, 1956); University Lecturer in Greek Epigraphy, Oxford, since 1956; *b* London, 7 June 1928; *s* of William and Milly Lewis; *m* 1958, Barbara, *d* of Prof. Samson Wright, MD, FRCP; four *d. Educ:* City of London Sch.; Corpus Christi Coll., Oxford (MA); Princeton Univ. (PhD). National Service with RAEC, 1949-51. Mem., Inst. for Advanced Study, Princeton, 1951-52, 1964-65. Student, British Sch. at Athens, 1952-54; Junior Research Fellow, Corpus Christi Coll., Oxford, 1954-55. *Publications:* (with John Gould) Pickard-Cambridge: Dramatic Festivals of Athens (2nd edn), 1968; (with Russell Meiggs) Greek Historical Inscriptions, 1969; Sparta and Persia, 1977; Inscriptiones Graecae I, 1981; articles in learned jls. *Recreations:* opera, gardening. *Address:* Christ Church, Oxford. *T:* Oxford 42820.

LEWIS, David Thomas, CB 1963; Hon. Professorial Fellow, Department of Chemistry, University College of Wales, Aberystwyth, 1970-78; *b* 27 March 1909; *s* of Emmanuel Lewis and Mary (née Thomas), Breconshire, Wales; *m* 1st, 1934, Evelyn (née Smetham); one *d* ; 2nd, 1959, Mary (née Sadler). *Educ:* Brynmawr County Sch.; University Coll. of Wales, Aberystwyth. BSc (Wales), 1st Class Hons in Chemistry, 1930; PhD (Wales), 1933; DSc (Wales), 1958. Senior Chemistry Master, Quakers' Yard Secondary Sch., 1934-38; Asst Lecturer, University Coll., Cardiff, 1938-40. Various scientific posts finishing as Principal Scientific Officer, Ministry of Supply, Armaments Research Establishment, 1941-47, and as Senior Superintendent of Chemistry Div., Atomic Weapons Research Establishment. Aldermaston, 1947-60; Govt Chemist, 1960-70. FRIC 1940; FRSH 1964. Dawes Memorial Lectr, 1965. Scientific Governor, British Nutrition Foundn, 1967; Member: British National Cttee for Chemistry (Royal Society), 1961-70; British Pharmacopœia Commission, 1963-73. *Publications:* Ultimate Particles of Matter, 1959; Mountain Harvest (Poems), 1964. Analytical Research Investigations in learned jls; scientific articles in encyclopædias, scientific reviews, etc. *Recreations:* writing, fishing, shooting. *Address:* Green Trees, 24 Highdown Hill Road, Emmer Green, Reading, Berks. *T:* Reading 471653.

LEWIS, Donald Gordon; Director, National Exhibition Centre, since 1982; Chairman, West Midlands Metropolitan County Council, 1980-81; *b* 12 Sept. 1926; *s* of late Albert Francis Lewis and Nellie Elizabeth Lewis; *m* 1950, Doreen Mary (née Gardner); one *d. Educ:* King Edward's Sch., Birmingham; Liverpool Univ. Dairy Industry, 1947-: General Sales Manager, Birmingham Dairies, 1961-. Councillor (C) Birmingham CC, Selly Oak Ward, 1959, Alderman 1971-74; past Chairman, Transport and Airport Committees; West Midlands County Council: Mem., 1974-81; Chairman, Airport Cttee, 1974-80; Sec., Conservative Group, 1974-80; City of Birmingham District Council: Mem., 1982-; Chm., Nat. Exhibn Centre Cttee, 1982-. Chm., Selly Oak (Birmingham) Constituency Conservative Assoc., 1975-80, Pres., 1980-; Dep. Chm., Birmingham Cons. Assoc., 1982-; Chm., Birmingham S Euro-Constituency Cons. Assoc., 1982-. Governor, Dame Elizabeth Cadbury Sch., 1979-; Manager, St Mary's CofE Sch., 1966-. *Recreation:* eating out. *Address:* 6 Old Warwick Court, Old Warwick Road, Solihull, West Midlands B92 7JT. *T:* 021-707 1024. *Club:* Selly Oak (Birmingham) Conservative.

LEWIS, Ernest Gordon, (Toby), CMG 1972; OBE 1958; HM Diplomatic Service, retired; Chairman, Marine Chain Ltd, London, since 1977; *b* New Zealand, 26 Sept. 1918; *s* of George Henry Lewis; *m* 1949, Jean Margaret, *d* of late A. H. Smyth. *Educ:* Otago Boys' High Sch.; Otago Univ., NZ. Served War, Army, with 2nd NZ Div., Middle East, 1939-46 (Lt-Col; despatches, MBE). Joined Colonial Service, Nigeria, 1947; Administrator, Turks and Caicos Is, 1955-59; Permanent Sec., to Federal Govt of Nigeria, 1960-62; First Sec., Pakistan, 1963-66; Foreign and Commonwealth Office, 1966-69; Kuching, Sarawak, 1969-70; Governor and C-in-C, Falkland Islands, and High Comr, British Antarctic Territory, 1971-75; Head of Gibraltar and General Dept, FCO, 1975-77. *Recreation:* golf. *Address:* 5 Smith Street, Chelsea, SW3 4EE. *Club:* Army and Navy.

LEWIS, Esyr ap Gwilym, QC 1971; a Recorder of the Crown Court, since 1972; *b* 11 Jan. 1926; *s* of late Rev. T. W. Lewis, BA, and Mary Jane May Lewis (née Selway); *m* 1957, Elizabeth Anne Vidler Hoffmann, 2nd *d* of O. W. Hoffmann, Bassett, Southampton; four *d. Educ:* Salford Grammar Sch.; Mill Hill Sch.; Trinity Hall, Cambridge (MA, LLB). Served War in Intelligence Corps, 1944-47. Exhibitioner, 1944, Scholar, 1948, at Trinity Hall (Dr Cooper's Law Studentship, 1950); 1st cl. hons, Law Tripos II, 1949, 1st cl. LLB, 1950, Cambridge. Holker Sen. Schol., Gray's Inn, 1950; Called to Bar, Gray's Inn, 1951; Bencher, 1978. Law Supervisor, Trinity Hall, 1950-55; Law Lectr, Cambridgeshire Technical Coll., 1949-50. Member: Bar Council, 1965-68; Council of Legal Education, 1967-; Criminal Injuries Compensation Bd, 1977-. Leader, Wales and Chester Circuit, 1978-81. Contested (L) Llanelli, 1964. *Publication:* contributor to Newnes Family Lawyer, 1963. *Recreations:* reading, gardening, watching Rugby football. *Address:* 2 South Square, Gray's Inn, WC1. *T:* 01-405 5918; Farrar's Building, Temple, EC4Y 7BD. *T:* 01-583 9241. *Clubs:* Reform; Cardiff and County; Old Millhillians; Bristol Channel Yacht.

See also M. ap G. Lewis.

LEWIS, Dr Geoffrey Lewis, FBA 1979; Senior Lecturer in Turkish, University of Oxford, since 1964; Fellow of St Antony's College, Oxford, since 1961; *b* 19 June 1920; *s* of Ashley Lewis and Jeanne Muriel (née Sintrop); *m* 1941, Raphaela Rhoda Bale Seideman; one *s* (one *d* deed). *Educ:* University

Coll. Sch.; St John's Coll., Oxford (MA 1945, DPhil 1950; James Mew Arabic Scholar, 1947). Lectr in Turkish, 1950-54, and Sen. Lectr in Islamic Studies, 1954-64, Oxford Univ. Vis. Professor: Robert Coll., Istanbul, 1959-68; Princeton Univ., 1970-71, 1974; UCLA, 1975. Vice-Pres., Anglo-Turkish Soc., 1972-; Mem., British-Turkish Mixed Commn, 1975-; Pres., British Soc. for Middle Eastern Studies, 1981-. Corresp. Mem., Turkish Linguistic Inst., 1953-. Turkish Govt Cert. of Merit, 1973. *Publications:* Teach Yourself Turkish, 1953; Modern Turkey, 1955, 4th edn 1974; (trans., with annotations) Katib Chelebi, The Balance of Truth, 1957; (with Barbara Hodge) A Study in Education for International Misunderstanding (Cyprus School History Textbooks), 1966; Turkish Grammar, 1967; (with M. S. Spink) Albucasis on Surgery and Instruments, 1973; The Book of Dede Korkut, 1974; The Atatürk I Knew, 1981; articles on Turkish language, history and politics, and on Arab alchemy. *Recreations:* bodging, etymology. *Address:* Oriental Institute, Pusey Lane, Oxford. *T:* Oxford 59272; Springfield, Boar's Hill, Oxford. *T:* Oxford 735151; Le Bousset, 06500 Menton, France.

LEWIS, Gillian Marjorie; FIIC; Head of Conservation Department, since 1978, and Assistant Deputy Director, since 1982, National Maritime Museum; *b* 10 Oct. 1945; *d* of late William Lewis and of Marjorie Lewis (*née* Pargeter). *Educ:* Tiffin Sch., Kingston upon Thames; Univ. of Newcastle upon Tyne (BA 1967); DCP, Gateshead Tech. Coll., 1969; FIIC 1977. Shipley Art Gallery, Co. Durham, 1967-69; free-lance conservator, 1969-73; Nat. Maritime Mus., 1973-; Keeper of Conservation, 1978. Cttee mem., UK Inst. for Conservation, 1978-80. *Publications:* official publications of the National Maritime Museum. *Address:* c/o National Maritime Museum, SE10 9NF. *T:* 01-858 1167. *Clubs:* Arts; Civil Service Riding.

LEWIS, Gwynedd Margaret; a Recorder of the Crown Court, 1974-81; barrister-at-law; *b* 9 April 1911; *d* of late Samuel David Lewis and Margaret Emma Lewis. *Educ:* King Edward's High Sch., Birmingham; King's Coll., Univ. of London. BA. Called to Bar, Gray's Inn, 1939; Mem., Midland and Oxford Circuit; Dep. Stipendiary Magistrate for City of Birmingham, 1962-74. Legal Mem., Mental Health Review Tribunal for the W Midlands Region, 1972-. *Recreations:* archaeology, bird-watching. *Address:* 7 Heaton Drive, Edgbaston, Birmingham B15 3LW. *T:* 021-454 1514; Troutbeck, Leintwardine, Salop.

LEWIS, Henry Gethin, DL, JP; Chairman and Managing Director of private companies; *b* 31 Oct. 1899; *e s* of late Henry Gethin Lewis, LLD, JP, High Sheriff of Glamorgan, 1920-21, Porthkerry, Glamorgan; *m* 1925, Gwendolen Joan, 5th *d* of T. W. David, JP, Ely Rise, Cardiff; one *s* two *d. Educ:* Shrewsbury Sch.; Trinity Coll., Oxford (MA). Served European War 2nd Lt RFC with 48 Sqdn, 1918, BEF France (POW). Called to the Bar, Inner Temple, 1925. RAFVR, 1939-45, Sqdn-Ldr 1943. JP 1957, DL 1961, High Sheriff of Glamorgan, 1958. Chief Comr for Wales, St John Ambulance Bde, 1958-66; KStJ; Mem., Welsh Hosp. Bd, 1958-64, and Mem. Bd of Governors, United Cardiff Hosps, 1958-64. *Address:* Cliffside, Penarth, South Glamorgan. *T:* Penarth 707096. *Clubs:* Royal Air Force; Leander (Henley-on-Thames); Cardiff and County (Cardiff); Penarth Yacht.

LEWIS, Henry Nathan; Joint Managing Director, Marks & Spencer Ltd, since 1973, Joint Managing Director in charge of Food Division, since 1976; *b* 29 Jan. 1926; *m* 1953, Jenny Cohen; one *s* two *d. Educ:* Hollywood Park Council Sch., Stockport; Stockport Sch.; Manchester Univ. (BA Com); LSE. Served RAF (Flt Lt), 1944-48. Marks & Spencer Ltd, 1950; Dir, 1965. Industrial Governor, and Mem., Exec. Cttee, British Nutrition Foundn. Governor: Jerusalem Inst. of Management; Carmel Coll.; Vice Pres., British Friends of Israel War Disabled; Trustee, Jewish Educational Develt Trust; Member: Campaign and Finance Cttees, Joint Israel Appeal; Exec. Cttee, Bd of Deputies of British Jews; Yad Vashem Cttee; Holocaust Meml Cttee; Policy Adv. Gp, Inst. of Jewish Affairs; Council, British Industrial Biological Res. Assoc; Council, Anglo-Israel Chamber of Commerce. *Address:* Michael House, Baker Street, W1A 1DN.

LEWIS, H(erbert) J(ohn) Whitfield, CB 1968; *b* 9 April 1911; *s* of Herbert and Mary Lewis; *m* 1963, Pamela (*née* Leaford); one *s* three *d. Educ:* Monmouth Sch.; Welsh Sch. of Architecture. Associate with Norman & Dawbarn, Architects and Consulting Engineers; in charge of housing work, 1945-50; Principal Housing Architect, Architects Dept, London County Council, 1950-59; County Architect, Middlesex County Council, 1959-64; Chief Architect, Ministry of Housing and Local Govt, 1964-71. FRIBA; FRTPI, DisTP 1957. *Recreations:* music, electronics. *Address:* 8 St John's Wood Road, NW8. *Club:* Savile.

LEWIS, Rt. Rev. Hurtle John; *see* Queensland, North, Bishop of.

LEWIS, Prof. Hywel David, MA, BLitt; Professor of History and Philosophy of Religion, in the University of London, 1955-77; *b* 21 May 1910; *s* of Rev. David John and Rebecca Lewis, Waenfawr, Cærnarvon; *m* 1943, Megan Elias Jones, MA (*d* 1962), *d* of J. Elias Jones, Bangor; *m* 1965, K. A. Megan Pritchard, *d* of T. O. Pritchard, Pentrefoelas. *Educ:* University Coll., Bangor; Jesus Coll., Oxford. Lecturer in Philosophy, University Coll., Bangor, 1936; Senior Lecturer, 1947; Prof. of Philosophy, 1947-55; President: Mind Association, 1948-49, Aristotelian Soc., 1962-63; Chm. Council, Royal Inst. of Philosophy; Soc. for the Study of Theology, 1964-66; President: Oxford Soc. for Historical Theology, 1970-71; London Soc. for Study of Religion, 1970-72; Inst. of Religion and Theology, 1972-75; International Soc. for

Metaphysics, 1974-80. Editor, Muirhead Library of Philosophy, 1947-78; Editor, Religious Studies; Leverhulme Fellow, 1954-55; Visiting Professor: Brynmawr Coll., Pa, USA, 1958-59; Yale, 1964-65; University of Miami, 1968; Boston Univ., 1969; Kyoto Univ., 1976; Santiniketan Univ., 1977; Surrey Univ., 1977-83; Emory Univ., 1977-81; Jadavpur Univ., 1979; Vis. Professorial Fellow, UCW Aberystwyth, 1979-; Lectures: Robert McCahan, Presbyterian Coll., Belfast, 1960; Wilde, in Natural and Comparative Religion, Oxford, 1960-63; Edward Cadbury, Birmingham, 1962-63; Centre for the Study of World Religions, Harvard, 1963; Ker, McMaster Divinity Coll., Ont, 1964; Owen Evans, University Coll., Aberystwyth, 1964-65; Firth Meml, Nottingham, 1966; Gifford, Edinburgh, 1966-68; L. T. Hobhouse Meml, London, 1966-68; Elton, George Washington Univ., 1969; Otis Meml, Wheaton Coll., 1969; Drew, London, 1973-74; Laidlaw, Toronto, 1979. Commemoration Preacher, University of Southampton, 1958; Commemoration Lectr, Cheshunt Coll., Cambridge, 1960, and Westminster Coll., 1964. Fellow of King's Coll., London, 1963; Dean of the Faculty of Theology in the University of London, 1964-68; Dean of the Faculty of Arts, King's Coll., 1966-68, and Faculty of Theology, 1970-72. Warden, Guild of Graduates, University of Wales, 1974-77; Mem., Advisory Council for Education (Wales), 1964-67. Mem., Gorsedd of Bards. Hon. DD St Andrews, 1964; Hon. DLit Emory Univ., USA, 1978. *Publications:* Morals and the New Theology, 1947; Morals and Revelation, 1951; (ed) Contemporary British Philosophy, Vol. III, 1956, Vol. IV, 1976; Our Experience of God, 1959; Freedom and History, 1962; (ed) Clarity is not Enough, 1962; Teach yourself the Philosophy of Religion, 1965; World Religions (with R. L. Slater), 1966; Dreaming and Experience, 1968; The Elusive Mind, 1969; The Self and Immortality, 1973; (ed) Philosophy East and West, 1975; (ed with G. R. Damodaran) The Dynamics of Education, 1975; Persons and Life after Death, 1978; Jesus in the Faith of Christians, 1980; The Elusive Self, 1982; Gwerineth, 1940; Y Wladwriaeth a'i Hawdurdod (with Dr J. A. Thomas), 1943; Ebyrth, 1943; Diogelu Diwylliant, 1945; Crist a Heddwch, 1947; Dilyn Crist, 1951; Gwybod am Dduw, 1952; Hen a Newydd, 1972; Pwy yw Iesu Grist?, 1979; contributions to Mind, Proc. of Aristotelian Society, Philosophy, Ethics, Hibbert Jl, Philosophical Quarterly, Analysis, Efrydiau Athronyddol, Llenor, Traethodydd, etc. *Address:* 1 Normandy Park, Normandy, near Guildford, Surrey.

LEWIS, Sir Ian (Malcolm), Kt 1964; QC (Nigeria) 1961; LLD, MA Cantab, LLB; **His Honour Judge Sir Ian Lewis;** a Circuit Judge, since 1973; *b* 14 Dec. 1925; *s* of late Prof. Malcolm M. Lewis, MC, MA, LLB, and late Eileen (*née* O'Sullivan); *m* 1955, Marjorie, *d* of late W. G. Carrington; one *s. Educ:* Clifton Coll. (Governor, 1972-; Mem. Council, 1975-; Chm. Council, 1981-); Trinity Hall, Cambridge (Scholar, 1st cl. hons Law Tripos Pt 2, and LLB). Served with RAFVR, 1944-47. Called to Bar, Middle Temple, 1951; pupil of R. W. Goff (the late Rt Hon. Lord Justice Goff), 1951. Western Circuit, 1951; Crown Counsel, Nigeria, 1953; Northern Nigeria: Solicitor-Gen., 1958; Dir of Public Prosecutions, 1962; Attorney-Gen. and Minister in the Government of Northern Nigeria, 1962-66; Chancellor, Diocese of Northern Nigeria, 1964-66; a Justice, Supreme Court of Nigeria, 1966-72; Justice of Appeal, Anguilla, 1972-73; Comr in NI dealing with detention of terrorists, 1972-75; Mem., Detention Appeal Tribunal for NI, 1974-75; Adviser to Sec. of State for NI on Detention, 1975-; Liaison Judge for Wiltshire, 1973-81; Mem., Wilts Probation Cttee, 1973-; Hon. Vice-Pres., Magistrates Assoc., Wilts, 1973-. Mem. Council, Univ. of Bristol, 1979-. MEC, N Nigeria, 1962-66; Adv. Coun. on the Prerogative of Mercy, House of Assembly, 1962-66. Mem. of Nigerian Bar Council, 1962-66; Mem. of Nigerian Council of Legal Education, 1962-66; Assoc. Mem. Commonwealth Parly Assoc. Hon. LLD, Ahmadu Bello Univ., Nigeria, 1972. *Recreations:* swimming (Capt. Cambridge Univ. Swimming and Water Polo, 1949); bridge; sailing; trying to find chapels in Wales where Grandfather "Elfed" (late Rev. H. Elvet Lewis, CH, DD) had not preached. *Address:* Denehurst, 10 Southfield Road, Westbury-on-Trym, Bristol BS9 3BH. *Clubs:* Royal Commonwealth Society; Hawks (Cambridge); Savages, Constitutional (Bristol).

LEWIS, Prof. Sir Jack, Kt 1982; FRS 1973; FRSC; Professor of Chemistry, University of Cambridge, since 1970; Hon. Fellow of Sidney Sussex College (Fellow, 1970-77); (first) Warden of Robinson College, Cambridge, since 1975; *b* 13 Feb. 1928; *m* 1951, Elfreida Mabel (*née* Lamb); one *s* one *d. Educ:* Barrow Grammar Sch. BSc London 1949; PhD Nottingham 1951; DSc London 1961; MSc Manchester 1964; MA Cantab 1970; ScD Cantab 1977. Lecturer: Univ. of Sheffield, 1953-56; Imperial Coll., London, 1956-57; Lecturer-Reader, University Coll., London, 1957-62; Prof. of Chemistry: Univ. of Manchester, 1962-67; UCL, 1967-70. Firth Vis. Prof., Univ. of Sheffield, 1969; Lectures: Frontiers of Science, Case/Western Reserve, 1963; Tilden, RIC, 1966; Miller, Univ. of Illinois, 1966; Shell, Stanford Univ., 1968; Venables, Univ. of N Carolina, 1968; A. D. Little, MIT, 1970; Boomer, Univ. of Alberta, 1971; AM, Princeton, 1972; Baker, Cornell, 1974; Nyholm, Chem. Soc., 1974; Chini, Italian Chem. Soc., 1981; Bailar, Illinois, 1982. Member: CNAA Cttee, 1964-70; Exec. Cttee, Standing Cttee on Univ. Entry, 1966-76; Schs Council, 1966-76; SERC (formerly SRC): Polytechnics Cttee, 1973-; Chemistry Cttee (Chm., 1975-); Science Bd, 1975-; Council, 1980-; SERC/SSRC Jt Cttee, 1981-; UGC (Phy. Sci.), 1975-81. FNA 1980. Dr *hc* Rennes, 1980; DUniv Open, 1982. American Chem. Soc. Award in Inorganic Chemistry, 1970; Transition Metal Award, Chem. Soc., 1973. *Publications:* papers, mainly in Jl of Chem. Soc. *Address:* Chemistry Department, University Chemical Laboratory, Lensfield Road, Cambridge CB2 1EW. *Clubs:* Athenæum, United Oxford & Cambridge University.

LEWIS, John Elliott, MA; Head Master, Geelong Church of England Grammar School, Australia, since 1980; *b* 23 Feb. 1942; *s* of John Derek Lewis and Margaret Helen (*née* Shaw); *m* 1968, Vibeke Lewis (*née* Johansson). *Educ:* King's College, Auckland, NZ; Corpus Christi Coll., Cambridge (Girdlers' Company Schol.; MA Classics). Assistant Master, King's Coll., Auckland, 1964, 1966-70; Jun. Lecturer in Classics, Auckland Univ., 1965; Asst Master, 1971-80, Master in College, 1975-80, Eton College. *Address:* Geelong Church of England Grammar School, Corio, Victoria 3214, Australia. *T:* 052 (Geelong) 751142.

LEWIS, Maj.-Gen. (Retd) John Michael Hardwicke, CBE 1970 (OBE 1955); *b* 5 April 1919; *s* of Brig. Sir Clinton Lewis, OBE, and late Lilian Eyre (*née* Wace); *m* 1942, Barbara Dorothy (*née* Wright); three *s. Educ:* Oundle; RMA, Woolwich. Commissioned, 2nd Lieut, RE, 1939. Served War: in 18 Div. and Special Force (Chindits), in Far East, 1940-45. Staff Coll., Camberley, 1949; CRE, Gibraltar, 1959-61; Instr, JSSC, 1961-63; IDC, 1966; Asst Chief of Staff (Ops), HQ Northern Army Gp, 1967-69; Brig. GS (Intell.), MoD, 1970-72; ACOS (Intelligence), SHAPE, 1972-75. *Publications:* Michiel Marieschi: Venetian artist, 1967; J. F. Lewis, RA (1805-1876): a monograph, 1978. *Recreation:* English water-colours. *Address:* Bedford's Farm, Frimley Green, Surrey. *T:* Deepcut 5188.

LEWIS, Ven. John Wilfred; *b* 25 Sept. 1909; *e s* of Fritz and Ethel Mary Lewis; *m* 1938, Winifred Mary Griffin; one *s* two *d. Educ:* privately; Gonville and Caius Coll., Cambridge. History Tripos Pt I Cl. II, 1932; BA 1933; MA, 1937; Steel Studentship (University), 1933; Exhibitioner, 1933-34; Westcott House, 1934; Deacon, 1935; Priest, 1936; Asst Dir of London Diocesan Council for Youth, 1935-37; Head of Oxford House, 1937-40; Vicar of Kimbolton, 1940-46; Dir, Hereford Diocesan Council of Educn, 1943-63; Rector of Cradley, 1946-60; Archdeacon of Ludlow, 1960-70; Rector of Wistanstow, 1960-70; Archdeacon of Hereford and Canon Residentiary of Hereford Cathedral, 1970-76; Prebendary of Colwall in Hereford Cathedral, 1948-76; Archdeacon Emeritus, 1977. *Recreations:* walking, sailing. *Address:* 9 Claremont Hill, Shrewsbury. *T:* Shrewsbury 65685.

LEWIS, (Joseph) Anthony; Chief London Correspondent, New York Times, 1965-72, editorial columnist, since 1969; Lecturer in Law, Harvard Law School, since 1974; *b* 27 March 1927; *s* of Kassel Lewis and Sylvia Lewis (*née* Surut); NYC; *m* 1951, Linda, *d* of John Rannells, NYC; one *s* two *d. Educ:* Horace Mann Sch., NY; Harvard Coll. (BA). Sunday Dept, New York Times, 1948-52; Reporter, Washington Daily News, 1952-55; Legal Corresp., Washington Bureau, NY Times, 1955-64; Nieman Fellow, Harvard Law Sch., 1956-57. Governor, Ditchley Foundation, 1965-72. Pulitzer Prize for Nat. Correspondence, 1955 and 1963; Heywood Broun Award, 1955; Overseas Press Club Award, 1970. Hon. DLitt: Adelphi Univ. (NY), 1964; Rutgers Univ., NJ, 1973; NY Med. Coll., 1976; Williams Coll., Mass, 1978; Clark Univ., Mass, 1982; Hon. LlD Syracuse, 1979. *Publications:* Gideon's Trumpet, 1964; Portrait of a Decade: The Second American Revolution, 1964; articles in American law reviews. *Recreation:* dinghy sailing. *Address:* 84 State Street, Boston, Mass 02109, USA. *Clubs:* Garrick; Tavern (Boston).

LEWIS, Keith William, CB 1981; Director General and Engineer in Chief, Engineering and Water Supply Department, South Australia, since 1974; *b* 10 Nov. 1927; *s* of Ernest John and Aunda Myrtle Lewis; *m* 1958, Alison Bothwell Fleming; two *d. Educ:* Adelaide High Sch.; Univ. of Adelaide (BE Civil); Imperial Coll., Univ. of London (DIC). FIE(Aust); FAIM. Engineer for Water and Sewage Treatment, E and WS Dept, 1968-74. Chairman, S Australian Water Resources Council, 1974-; Member: State Planning Authority, 1974-; Electricity Trust of S Australia, 1974-; Environmental Protection Council, 1974-. Silver Jubilee Medal, 1977. *Recreations:* golf, skiing, tennis. *Address:* 24 Delamere Avenue, Netherby, SA 5062, Australia. *T:* (home) 793901; (office) 227 2022. *Clubs:* Adelaide, Kooyonga Golf (South Australia).

LEWIS, Kenneth; DL; MP (C) Rutland and Stamford since 1959; Chairman, Conservative Back Bench Labour Committee, 1963-64; *b* 1 July 1916; *s* of William and Agnes Lewis, Jarrow; *m* 1948, Jane, *d* of Samuel Pearson, of Adderstone Mains, Belford, Northumberland; one *s* one *d. Educ:* Jarrow; Edinburgh Univ. Served War of 1939-45. RAF, 1941-46; Flt Lt. Chm. Business and Holiday Travel Ltd. Contested (C) Newton-le-Willows, 1945 and 1950, Ashton-under-Lyne, 1951. CC Middx, 1949-51; Mem. NW Metropolitan Hosp. Management Cttee, 1949-62; Trustee: Uppingham Sch.; Oakham Sch. DL Rutland 1973. *Recreations:* music, travel. *Address:* 96 Green Lane, Northwood, Middx. *T:* Northwood 23354; Dale Cottage, Preston, Rutland. *Clubs:* Carlton, Pathfinder, St Stephen's Constitutional, Royal Air Force.

LEWIS, Maj.-Gen. Kenneth Frank Mackay, CB 1951; DSO 1944; MC 1918; retired; *b* 29 Jan. 1897; *s* of Frank Essex Lewis and Anne Florence Mackay; *m* 1930, Pamela Frank Menzies Pyne; two *s. Educ:* privately. Commissioned 2nd Lt RH & RFA, 1916; served with 9th Scottish Div., France and Belgium, 1916-18; ADC to GOC Lowland Div., 1921; ADC to GOC. Upper Silesia Force, 1922; Iraq Levies, 1923-25; Adjutant, Portsmouth and IOW, 1926-29; Royal West African Frontier Force, Nigeria Regt, 1929-30; Colchester, 1930-33; India, School of Artillery, 1933-37; Military Coll. of Science, UK, 1938; School of Artillery, Larkhill, 1939-41; CO 7th Survey Regt, 1942; CO 185 Field Regt, 1943; CRA 43 and 49 Divisions, 1944 and 1945 (despatches); CCRA Palestine, 1947 and 1948 (despatches); BRA Western Command, UK,

1948; GOC 4th Anti-Aircraft Group, 1949-50; Dir of Royal Artillery, War Office, Dec. 1950-54; retired, 1954; Col Comdt RA, 1957-62. OStJ 1955. Order of Leopold, Croix de Guerre (Belgium). *Recreations:* books and music. *Address:* 18 Beverley Road, Colchester CO3 3NG. *T:* Colchester 76507.

LEWIS, Kynric; *see* Lewis, A. K.

LEWIS, Leonard, QC 1969; *b* 11 May 1909; *e s* of Barnet Lewis; *m* 1939, Rita Jeanette Stone; two *s* one *d. Educ:* Grocer's Company Sch.; St John's Coll., Cambridge (Major Schol.). Wrangler, Wright's Prizeman, MA Cantab; BSc 1st class Hons London. Called to Bar, 1932 and started to practise. Served War of 1939-45, RAF. *Recreation:* tennis. *Address:* East Park House, Newchapel, near Lingfield, Surrey. *T:* Lingfield 114.

LEWIS, Prof. Leonard John, CMG 1969; BSc; DipEd; Principal and Vice-Chancellor, University of Zimbabwe, 1980-81; Professor of Education, with special reference to Education in Tropical Areas, in the University of London, 1958-73, now Emeritus; *b* 28 Aug. 1909; of Welsh-English parentage; *s* of Thomas James Lewis and Rhoda Lewis (*née* Gardiner); *m* 1940, Nora Brisdon (marr. diss. 1976); one *s* (and one *s* decd). *Educ:* Lewis Sch., Pengam; University Coll., of South Wales and Monmouth (BSc); University of London Institute of Education (DipEd). Lecturer, St Andrew's Coll., Oyo, Nigeria, 1935-36; Headmaster, CMS Gram. Sch., Lagos, Nigeria, 1936-41; Education Sec., CMS Yoruba Mission, 1941-44; Lectr, University of London Institute of Education, 1944-48; Editorial staff, Oxford Univ. Press, 1948-49; Prof. of Educn and Dir of Institute of Educn, University Coll. of Ghana, 1949-58. Nuffield Visiting Prof., University of Ibadan, 1966. Hon. Professorial Fellow, University Coll., Cardiff, 1973; Hon. FCP 1974. Coronation Medal, 1953; Zimbabwe Independence Medal, 1980. *Publications:* Equipping Africa, 1948; Henry Carr (Memoir), 1948; Education Policy and Practice in British Tropical Areas, 1954; (ed and contrib.) Perspectives in Mass Education and Community Development, 1957; Days of Learning, 1961; Education and Political Independence in Africa, 1962; Schools, Society and Progress in Nigeria, 1965; The Management of Education (with A. J. Loveridge), 1965. *Recreations:* music, walking. *Address:* Plas Pant-y-Berllan, Capel Isaac, Llandeilo, Dyfed. *T:* Dryslwyn 468.

LEWIS, Michael ap Gwilym, QC 1975; a Recorder of the Crown Court, since 1976; *b* 9 May 1930; *s* of Rev. Thomas William Lewis and Mary Jane May Selway; *m* ; three *s* one *d. Educ:* Mill Hill; Jesus Coll., Oxford (Scholar). MA (Mod. History). 2nd Royal Tank Regt, 1952. Called to Bar, Gray's Inn, 1956; Mem., Senate, 1979-; South Eastern Circuit. *Address:* Farrar's Building, Temple, EC4Y 7BD. *T:* 01-583 9241.
See also E. ap G. Lewis.

LEWIS, Norman; author; *s* of Richard and Louise Lewis. *Educ:* Enfield Grammar Sch. Served War of 1939-45, in Intelligence Corps. *Publications:* Sand and Sea in Arabia, 1938; Samara, 1949; Within the Labyrinth, 1950; A Dragon Apparent, 1951; Golden Earth, 1952; A Single Pilgrim, 1953; The Day of the Fox, 1955; The Volcanoes Above Us, 1957; The Changing Sky, 1959; Darkness Visible, 1960; The Tenth Year of the Ship, 1962; The Honoured Society, 1964; A Small War Made to Order, 1966; Every Man's Brother, 1967; Flight from a Dark Equator, 1972; The Sicilian Specialist, 1974; Naples '44, 1978; The German Company, 1979; Cuban Passage, 1982. *Address:* c/o Wm Collins Sons & Co. Ltd, 14 St James's Place, SW1.

LEWIS, Prof. Norman Bache, MA, PhD; retired; *b* 8 Nov. 1896; *o s* of G. D. and L. A. Lewis, Newcastle-under-Lyme; *m* 1928, Julia, *o d* of John and Catherine Wood, Riddlesden, Keighley; (one *s* one *d* decd). *Educ:* Boys' High Sch., Newcastle-under-Lyme (foundation scholar); University of Manchester (Jones scholar). Served European War in RFA, 1917-19. Manchester University: Hovell and Shuttleworth Prizes in History, 1919; BA in History Hons Cl I and graduate scholarship in History, 1921; Research Fellowship in History, 1922. University of Sheffield: Lecturer in Dept of Modern History, 1924; Senior Lecturer in Mediæval History, 1946; Reader in Mediæval History, 1955; Prof. of Mediæval History in the University of Sheffield, 1959-62, Emeritus Prof., 1962. *Publications:* articles in historical journals. *Recreations:* music, reading. *Address:* Sundial House, 79 Old Dover Road, Canterbury CT1 3DB.

LEWIS, Percival Cecil, QC; President of the Industrial Court, Antigua, since 1976; *b* St Vincent, 14 Aug. 1912; *s* of late Philip Owen Lewis; *m* 1936, Gladys Muriel Pool; one *s* one *d. Educ:* St Vincent Intermediate Sch.; St Vincent Gram. Sch. Called to Bar, Middle Temple, 1936. Practised in Uganda and St Vincent, 1936-40; Registrar and Additional Magistrate, St Lucia, 1940-43; Magistrate, Dominica, 1943-45; Crown Attorney, St Vincent, 1945-52; Crown Attorney, St Lucia, 1952-54; Attorney-Gen., Leeward Islands, 1954-56; Puisne Judge of Supreme Court of Windward and Leeward Islands, 1956-67; Justice of Appeal of the WI Assoc. States Supreme Court, 1967-75. *Recreations:* gardening and swimming. *Address:* c/o Industrial Court, PO Box 118, St Johns, Antigua, West Indies.

LEWIS, Peter Ronald; Director General, Bibliographic Services Division, British Library, since 1980; *b* 28 Sept. 1926; *s* of Charles Lewis and Florence Mary (*née* Kirk); *m* 1952, June Ashley; one *s* one *d. Educ:* Royal Masonic Sch.; Belfast Univ. (MA). FLA. Brighton, Plymouth, Chester public libraries, 1948-55; Head, Bibliographic Services, BoT Library, 1955-65; Lectr in Library Studies, QUB, 1965-69; Librarian: City Univ., 1969-72; Univ. of Sussex,

1972-80. Chm., Editorial Bd, Jl of Librarianship, 1972-79; Founder Editor, Catalogue & Index Qly, 1966-69. Mem., Library Adv. Council (England), 1976-78. Vice-Pres., 1979- and Hon. Treasurer, 1980-82, Library Assoc. (Chm., Bd of Fellowship, 1979-). *Publications:* The Literature of the Social Sciences, 1960; numerous papers on librarianship and bibliography, 1963-. *Recreation:* walking the South Downs Way. *Address:* 131 Western Road, Hurstpierpoint, W Sussex.

LEWIS, Peter Tyndale; Chairman, John Lewis Partnership, since 1972; *b* 26 Sept. 1929; *s* of Oswald Lewis and Frances Merriman Lewis (*née* Cooper); *m* 1961, Deborah Anne, *d* of late Sir William (Alexander Roy) Collins, CBE and Priscilla Marian, *d* of late S. J. Lloyd; one *s* one *d. Educ:* Eton; Christ Church, Oxford. National service, Coldstream Guards, 1948-49; MA (Oxford) 1953; called to Bar (Middle Temple) 1956; joined John Lewis Partnership, 1959. Member: Council, Industrial Soc., 1968-79; Design Council, 1971-74; Chm., Retail Distributors' Assoc., 1972. Governor, Windlesham Hse Sch., 1979-. CBIM. *Address:* John Lewis & Co. Ltd, Oxford Street, W1A 1AX.

LEWIS, Richard, CBE 1963; FRAM, FRMCM, LRAM; concert and opera singer, tenor; *b* of Welsh parents; *m* 1963, Elizabeth Robertson; one *s* (and one *s* by a previous *m*). *Educ:* Royal Manchester Coll. of Music (schol.; studied with Norman Allin); RAM. Well known boy soprano in N England. Served in RCS during war. English début in leading rôle of Britten's Opera The Rape of Lucretia at Glyndebourne, where he has sung every year since 1947; début, Teatro Colono, Buenos Aires, 1963; has sung at Edinburgh Fests, Covent Garden, San Francisco, Chicago, Vienna State Opera and Berlin Opera Houses, and toured America, Australia and NZ; has appeared with leading European and American orchs, incl. NY Philharmonic, Chicago Symphony, San Francisco Symphony and Philadelphia. Recitalist and oratorio singer, particularly of Handel, and in name part of Elgar's The Dream of Gerontius; has created parts: Troilus in Sir William Walton's Opera Troilus and Cressida; Mark in The Midsummer Marriage, and Achilles in King Priam, both operas by Michael Tippett; sang in first perf. of Stravinsky's Canticum Sacrum, under composer's direction, Venice Festival; sang Aaron in first British performance of Schoenberg's opera Moses and Aaron at Covent Garden; leading part in first American presentation of Cherubini's Opera, Medea, San Francisco, USA, 1958. Has made numerous recordings and appearances in films and on radio and television. Pres., ISM, 1975-76. *Recreations:* languages, golf, creative photography. *Address:* Combe House, 22 Church Street, Willington.

LEWIS, Maj.-Gen. (retd) Robert Stedman, CB 1946; OBE 1942; late IA; *b* 20 March 1898; *s* of Sidney Cooke Lewis, MInstCE, and Mary Anne Jane Lewis Lloyd; *m* 1925, Margaret Joan Hart (*d* 1980); one *s* one *d. Educ:* Amesbury Sch., Bickley Hall, Kent; Bradfield Coll., Berks; Royal Military Academy, Woolwich. 2nd Lt RFA 1915; Seconded to RFC in 1916 and 1917 and served as a pilot in France in 100 Squadron RFC; served in France with RFA, 1918; proceeded to India with RFA, 1919; Seconded to Indian Army Ordnance Corps, 1922, and permanently transferred to Indian Army, 1925, with promotion to Capt.; Major, 1933; Bt Lt-Col 1937; Lt-Col 1940; Col 1944; employed at General Headquarters, India, 1939; Dir of Ordnance Services (India), 1945; retired, 1948. High Sheriff of Radnorshire, 1951. *Address:* Y Neuadd, Rhayader, Powys. *T:* Rhayader 810227.

LEWIS, Captain Roger Curzon, DSO 1939; OBE 1944; RN retired; *b* 19 July 1909; *s* of late F. W. and K. M. Lewis; *m* 1944, Marguerite Christiane (*d* 1971), *e d* of late Captain A. D. M. Cherry, RN, retd; two *s. Educ:* Royal Naval Coll., Dartmouth. HMS Lowestoft, Africa Station, 1927-29; HMS Vivien and HMS Valentine, 6th Flotilla Home Fleet, 1930-32; Qualifying Lt T 1933; HMS Enterprise, East Indies Station, 1935-37; Staff of HMS Vernon, 1938-39; HMS Florentino, 1939-40; HMS Rodney, 1940-42; Staff of Comdr-in-Chief Mediterranean, 1942-45; Superintendent of Torpedo Experimental Establishment, Greenock, 1950-55; Capt. of the Dockyard and Queen's Harbourmaster, Chatham, 1955-58; retired, 1959. *Address:* 3 Albion Street, Shaldon, Teignmouth, Devon TQ14 0DF.

LEWIS, Roland Swaine, FRCS; Honorary Consultant Surgeon to the ENT Department, King's College Hospital, since 1973 (Consultant Surgeon, 1946-65, Senior Consultant Surgeon, 1965-73); Honorary Consultant ENT Surgeon: to Mount Vernon Hospital and The Radium Institute; to Norwood and District Hospital; *b* 23 Nov. 1908; *s* of Dr William James Lewis, MOH, and Constance Mary Lewis, Tyrwaun, Ystalyfera; *m* 1936, Mary Christianna Milne (Christianna Brand); one adopted *d. Educ:* Epsom Coll.; St John's Coll., Cambridge; St George's Hospital. BA Cantab 1929; FRCS 1934; MA Cantab 1945; MB BCh Cantab 1945. Surgical Chief Asst, St George's Hospital, 1935. Major, RAMC (ENT Specialist), 1939-45. *Publications:* papers to medical journals. *Recreations:* ornithology, fishing. *Address:* 88 Maida Vale, W9 1PR. *T:* 01-624 6253.

LEWIS, Ronald Howard; MP (Lab) Carlisle since 1964; *b* 16 July 1909; *s* of Oliver Lewis, coal miner; *m* 1937, Edna Cooke (*d* 1976); two *s. Educ:* Elementary Sch. and Cliff Methodist Coll. Left school at 14 years of age and worked in coal mines (Somerset; subseq. Derbyshire, 1930-36); then railways (LNER Sheds, Langwith Junction); left that employment on being elected to Parliament. Mem., Blackwell RDC, 1940-73 (twice Chm.); Derbyshire CC, 1949-74; Mem. Bd of Directors, Pleasley Co-operative Soc. Ltd, 1948-70 (Pres. 1952). Mem. NUR. Vice-Chm., House of Commons Trades Union Gp,

1979-82. Methodist Local Preacher. *Recreations:* walking, football, gardening. *Address:* 22 Alandale Avenue, Langwith Junction, Mansfield, Notts. *T:* Shirebrook 2460.

LEWIS, Saunders, MA; Welsh writer and dramatist; *b* 15 Oct. 1893; *s* of Rev. Lodwig Lewis and Mary Margaret Thomas; *m* 1924, Margaret Gilcriest; one *d. Educ:* privately; Liverpool Univ. *Publications:* plays: The Eve of St John, 1921; Gwaed yr Uchelwyr, 1922; Buchedd Garmon, 1937; Amlyn ac Amig, 1940; Blodeuwedd, 1948; Eisteddfod Bodran, 1952; Gan Bwyll, 1952; Siwan a Cherddi Eraill, 1956; Gymerwch Chi Sigaret?, 1956; Brad, 1958; Esther, 1960; Serch Yw'r Doctor (light opera libretto), 1960; Cymru Fydd, 1967; Problemau Prifysgol, 1968; Dwy Briodas Ann, 1973; Dramau'r Parlwr, 1975; Excelsior, 1981; *novels:* Monica, 1930; Merch Gwern Hywel, 1964; *poetry:* Mair Fadlen, 1937; Byd a Betws, 1941; *criticism:* A School of Welsh Augustans, 1924; Williams Pantycelyn, 1927; Ceiriog, 1929; Braslun o Hanes Llenyddiaeth Gymraeg Hyd 1535, 1932; Daniel Owen, 1936; Ysgrifau Dydd Mercher, 1945; Meistri'r Canrifoedd, 1973; *political and economic:* Canlyn Arthur, 1938; also many pamphlets in the Welsh language; *translations:* Molière, Doctor er ei Waethaf, 1924; Beckett, Wrth aros Godot, 1970; (ed with introd.) Ievan Glan Geirionydd, 1931; (ed with introd.) Straeon Glasynys, 1943; (ed) Crefft y Stori Fer (radio broadcasts), 1949. Translations of plays have been presented on stage and television in English, German, and Spanish. *Address:* 158 Westbourne Road, Penarth, South Glam.

LEWIS, Thomas Loftus Townshend, CBE 1979; FRCS; Consultant Obstetric and Gynæcological Surgeon at Guy's Hospital, Queen Charlotte's Maternity Hospital and Chelsea Hospital for Women, since 1948; Hon. Consultant in Obstetrics and Gynaecology, to the Army, since 1973; *b* 27 May 1918; *e s* of late Neville Lewis and his first wife, Theodosia Townshend; *m* 1946, Kathleen Alexandra Ponsonby Moore; five *s. Educ:* Diocesan Coll., Rondebosch, S Africa; St Paul's Sch.; Cambridge Univ.; Guy's Hospital. BA Cantab (hons in Nat. Sci. Tripos), 1939; MB, BChir Cantab, 1942. FRCS 1946; MRCOG 1948; FRCOG 1961. House Appointments Guy's Hospital, 1942-43; Gold Medal and Prize in Obstetrics, Guy's Hospital, 1942. Volunteered to join South African Medical Corps, 1944; seconded to RAMC and served as Capt. in Italy and Greece, 1944-45. Returned to Guy's Hospital: Registrar in Obstetrics and Gynæcology, 1946, Obstetric Surgeon, 1948; Surgeon, Chelsea Hosp. for Women, 1950; Surgeon, Queen Charlotte's Maternity Hosp., 1952. Examiner in Obstetrics and Gynæcology: University of Cambridge, 1950; University of London, 1954; Royal College of Obstetricians and Gynæcologists, 1952; London Soc. of Apothecaries, 1955; University of St Andrews, 1960. Hon. Sec. and Mem. Council, Royal College of Obstetricians and Gynæcologists, 1955-68, 1971-, Vice-Pres., 1976-78; Mem. Council Obstetric Section, Royal Society of Med., 1953- (Pres. 1981); co-opted Mem. Council, RCS, 1978-. Guest Prof. to Brisbane, Australia, Auckland, New Zealand, 1959, Johns Hopkins Hosp., Baltimore, 1966; Litchfield Lectr, University of Oxford, 1968; Sims-Black Prof. to Australia, NZ and Rhodesia, 1970. *Publications:* Progress in Clinical Obstetrics and Gynæcology, 2nd edn 1964; (ed jtly and contrib.) Obstetrics by Ten Teachers, 11th edn 1966 to 13th edn 1980; (jtly) Queen Charlotte's Textbook of Obstetrics, 12th edn 1970; (ed jtly and contrib.) Gynaecology by Ten Teachers, 12th edn 1970, 13th edn 1980; (jtly) French's Index of Differential Diagnosis, 10th edn 1973, 11th edn 1979; contributions to: Lancet, BMJ, Practitioner, Proc. Roy. Soc. Med., Encyclopædia Britannica Book of the Year (annual contrib.), etc. *Recreations:* ski-ing, sailing, tennis, golf, croquet, wind-surfing, underwater swimming, maculture on the Isle of Elba. *Address:* 109 Harley Street, W1. *T:* 01-935 5855; (home) 13 Copse Hill, Wimbledon, SW20. *T:* 01-946 5089. *Clubs:* Old Pauline; Royal Wimbledon Golf; Guy's Hospital Rugby Football (Pres.).

LEWIS, Trevor Oswin, JP; Deputy Chairman, Countryside Commission, since 1980; *b* 29 Nov. 1935; *s* of 3rd Baron Merthyr, PC, KBE, TD, and of Violet, *y d* of Brig.-Gen. Sir Frederick Charlton Meyrick, 2nd Bt, CB, CMG; *S* father, 1977, as 4th Baron Merthyr, but disclaimed his peerage for life; also as 4th Bt (*cr* 1896) but does not use the title; *m* 1964, Susan Jane, *yr d* of A. J. Birt-Llewellin; one *s* three *d. Educ:* Downs Sch.; Eton; Magdalen Coll., Oxford; Magdalene Coll., Cambridge. Mem. Countryside Commn, 1973-; Chm., Countryside Commn's Cttee for Wales, 1973-80. JP Dyfed, formerly Pembs, 1969. *Heir (to disclaimed peerage*): *s* David Trevor Lewis, *b* 21 Feb. 1977. *Address:* Hean Castle, Saundersfoot, Dyfed SA69 9AL. *T:* Saundersfoot 812222.

LEWIS, Dame Vera Margaret; *see* Lynn, Dame Vera.

LEWIS, Wilfrid Bennett, CC (Canada) 1967; CBE 1946; FRS 1945; FRSC 1952; MA; PhD; Senior Vice-President, Science, Atomic Energy of Canada Ltd, 1963-73, retired; Distinguished Professor of Science, Queen's University, since 1973; *b* 24 June 1908; *s* of Arthur Wilfrid Lewis and Isoline Maud Steavenson; unmarried. *Educ:* Haileybury Coll., Herts; Gonville and Caius Coll., Cambridge, Hon. Fellow 1971. Cavendish Laboratory, Cambridge, research in Radio-activity and Nuclear Physics, 1930-39; Research Fellowship, Gonville and Caius Coll., 1934-40; University Demonstrator in Physics, 1934; University Lecturer in Physics, 1937; lent to Air Ministry as Senior Scientific Officer, 1939; Chief Superintendent Telecommunications Research Establishment, Ministry of Aircraft Production, 1945-46; Dir of Division of Atomic Energy Research, National Research Council of Canada, 1946-52; Vice-Pres. Research and Development, Atomic Energy of Canada, Ltd, 1952-63. Canadian Representative United Nations Scientific Advisory

Cttee, 1955-. Fellow American Nuclear Soc., 1959 (Pres., 1961); For. Associate, Nat. Acad. of Engineering, USA, 1976; Hon. Fellow: IEE, 1974; UMIST, 1974. Hon. DSc: Queen's Univ., Kingston, Ontario, 1960; Saskatchewan, 1964; McMaster Univ., Hamilton, Ontario, 1965; Dartmouth Coll., New Hampshire, 1967; McGill Univ., Montreal, 1969; Royal Mil. Coll., Kingston, Ont, 1974; Laurentian, 1977; Birmingham, 1977; Hon. LLD: Dalhousie Univ., Halifax, Nova Scotia, 1960; Carleton Univ., Ottawa, 1962; Trent Univ., Peterborough, Ont, 1969; Toronto, 1972; Victoria, BC, 1975. Amer. Medal of Freedom, with Silver Palms, 1947. First Outstanding Achievement Award, Public Service of Canada, 1966; Atoms for Peace Award (shared), 1967; Can. Assoc. of Physicists 25th anniversary special Gold Medal, 1970; Royal Medal, Royal Soc., 1972; Gen. A. G. L. McNaughton Award and Medal, Canadian Region IEEE, 1981; Enrico Fermi Award and Medal, US Dept of Energy, 1982. *Publications:* Electrical Counting, 1942; (ed jtly) International Arrangements for Nuclear Fuel Reprocessing, 1977; articles in Wireless Engineer, 1929, 1932 and 1936; papers in Proc. Royal Society A. 1931, 1932, 1933, 1934, 1936, 1940; etc. *Recreation:* walking. *Address:* Box 189, 13 Beach Avenue, Deep River, Ontario K0J 1P0. *T:* 613-584-3561; Physics Department, Queen's University, Kingston, Ontario K7L 3N6. *T:* (office) 613-547-2869, (residence) 613-544-9667.

LEWIS, Sir (William) Arthur, Kt 1963; PhD, BCom (London); MA (Manchester); James S. McDonnell Distinguished University Professor of Economics and International Affairs, Princeton University, since 1982; *b* 23 Jan. 1915; 4th *s* of George F. and Ida Lewis, Castries, St Lucia; *m* 1947, Gladys Jacobs; two *d*. *Educ:* St Mary's Coll., St Lucia; London Sch. of Economics. Lecturer at London Sch. of Economics, 1938-47; Reader in Colonial Economics, University of London, 1947; Stanley Jevons Prof. of Political Economy, University of Manchester, 1948-58; Principal, University Coll. of the West Indies, 1959-62; Vice-Chancellor, University of the West Indies, 1962-63; Princeton University: Prof. of Public and International Affairs, 1963-68; James Madison Prof. of Political Economy, 1968-82. Pres., Caribbean Development Bank, 1970-73. Assigned by United Nations as Economic Adviser to the Prime Minister of Ghana, 1957-58; Dep. Man. Dir, UN Special Fund, 1959-60. Temp. Principal, Board of Trade, 1943, Colonial Office, 1944; Consultant to Caribbean Commn, 1949: Mem. UN Group of Experts on Under-developed Countries, 1951; Part-time Mem. Board of Colonial Development Corporation, 1951-53; Mem. Departmental Cttee on National Fuel Policy, 1951-52; Consultant to UN Economic Commission for Asia and the Far East, 1952; to Gold Coast Govt, 1953: to Govt of Western Nigeria, 1955. Mem. Council, Royal Economic Soc., 1949-58; Pres. Manchester Statistical Soc., 1955-56. Chancellor, Univ. of Guyana, 1966-73. Hon. LHD: Columbia, Boston Coll., Wooster Coll., DePaul, Brandeis; Hon. LLD: Toronto, Wales, Williams, Bristol, Dakar, Leicester, Rutgers, Brussels, Open Univ., Atlanta, Hartford, Bard; Hon. LittD: West Indies, Lagos, Northwestern; Hon. DSc, Manchester. Corresp. Fellow, British Acad., 1974; Hon. Fellow, LSE; For. Fellow Amer. Acad. of Arts and Sciences; Mem., Amer. Phil. Soc.; Hon. Fellow Weizmann Inst.; Distinguished Fellow, Amer. Economic Assoc., 1970. (Jtly) Nobel Prize for Economics, 1979. *Publications:* Economic Survey, 1918-1939, 1949; Overhead Costs, 1949; The Principles of Economic Planning, 1949; The Theory of Economic Growth, 1955; Politics in West Africa, 1965; Development Planning, 1966; Reflections on the Economic Growth of Nigeria, 1968; Some Aspects of Economic Development, 1969; Tropical Development 1880-1913, 1971; The Evolution of the International Economic Order, 1977; Growth and Fluctuations 1870-1913, 1978; articles in technical, economic and law jls. *Address:* Woodrow Wilson School, Princeton University, Princeton, NJ 08540, USA.

LEWIS, William Edmund Ames, OBE 1961; Charity Commissioner, 1962-72; *b* 21 Sept. 1912; *s* of late Ernest W. Lewis, FRCSE, Southport, Lancashire; *m* 1939, Mary Elizabeth, *e d* of late C. R. Ashbee; two *s* one *d*. *Educ:* Merchant Taylors', Great Crosby; Emmanuel Coll., Cambridge. Barrister-at-law, Inner Temple, 1935. Entered Charity Commission, 1939; Asst Commissioner, 1953-61; Sec., 1961-69. Served in RAF, 1941-46. *Recreations:* music, painting. *Address:* Watermans, Ewhurst Green, Robertsbridge, East Sussex. *T:* Staplecross 523. *Club:* United Oxford & Cambridge University.

LEWIS-BOWEN, Thomas Edward Ifor; His Honour Judge Lewis-Bowen; a Circuit Judge, since 1980; *b* 20 June 1933; *s* of Lt-Col J. W. Lewis-Bowen and late Mrs K. M. Lewis-Bowen (*née* Rice); *m* 1965, Gillian, *d* of Reginald Brett, Puckington, Som; one *s* two *d*. *Educ:* Ampleforth; St Edmund Hall, Oxford. Called to Bar, Middle Temple, 1958. A Recorder of the Crown Court, 1974-80. *Address:* 90 Eaton Crescent, Swansea, West Glamorgan. *T:* Swansea 473736. Clynfiew, Boncath, Dyfed.

LEWIS-JONES, Captain (Robert) Gwilym, CBE 1969; RN retired; JP; *b* 22 Feb. 1922; *s* of Captain David Lewis Jones and Olwen Lewis Jones (*née* Evans), Corris and Dolgellau; *m* 1946, Ann Mary, *d* of David and Margaret Owen, Dolgellau; two *s*. *Educ:* Tywyn Grammar Sch.; Gonville and Caius Coll., Cambridge. CEng, AFRAeS, FBIM. FAA Observers Course, 1942-43; 842 Sqdn in HM Ships Indefatigable, Furious and Fencer on Murmansk and Atlantic convoys, 1943-45; Long Air Communications Course, 1945-46; Long Air Electronics/Electrical Course, 1946-47; RRE Malvern, 1947-49; Long Ships Electrical Course, 1950; RAE Farnborough, 1950-53; Sen. Aircraft Engr Off., HMS Albion; 1953-56; Dep. Comd Engr Off., Staff of Flag Officer Naval Air Comd, 1956-58; Head of Air Electrical Comd, RN Air Stn Brawdy, 1958-61; Sqdn Weapons Off., HMS Caesar and 8th Destroyer Sqdn,

1961-63; Exec. Off. and 2nd in Comd, HMS Condor, 1963-65; Gen. Man., RN Aircraft Yard, Belfast, 1965-67; Dir of Aircraft Armament, MoD (N), 1967-68; Jt Services Planning and Co-ordinating Off. responsible for Armed Forces participation in Investiture of Prince of Wales, 1967-69; Sen. Officers War Course, RNC Greenwich, 1969-70; Staff of Dir Gen. Ships (Directorate Naval Ship Production), 1970-72; Dir, Fleet Management Services, 1973-75; Dir, Naval Management and Orgn, 1975-76. ADC 1976. Lt-Comdr 1952; Comdr 1958; Captain 1967. Mem. (C) for Carshalton, GLC, 1977-81. Mem., Snowdonia Nat. Park Cttee, 1982-. JP SE London, 1979-81. *Recreations:* golf, Association and Rugby football, choral music, and Welsh language. *Address:* Mansiriol, Dolgellau, Gwynedd. *T:* Dolgellau 422526.

LEWISHAM, Viscount; William Legge; Chartered Accountant; *b* 23 Sept. 1949; *e s* and heir of 9th Earl of Dartmouth, qv. *Educ:* Eton; Christ Church, Oxford; Harvard Business Sch. Secretary, Oxford Union Soc., 1969. Contested (C): Leigh, Lancs, Feb. 1974; Stockport South, Oct. 1974. *Recreations:* squash, watching American football. *Address:* The Manor House, Chipperfield, King's Langley, Herts. *Clubs:* Turf; Harvard (New York).

LEWISHAM, Archdeacon of; *see* Davies, Ven. Ivor Gordon.

LEWISOHN, Anthony Clive Leopold; His Honour Judge Lewisohn; a Circuit Judge, since 1974; *b* 1 Aug. 1925; *s* of John Lewisohn and Gladys (*née* Solomon); *m* 1957, Lone Ruthwen Jurgensen; two *s*. *Educ:* Stowe; Trinity Coll., Oxford (MA). Royal Marines, 1944-45; Lieut, Oxf. and Bucks LI, 1946-47. Called to Bar, Middle Temple, 1951; S Eastern Circuit.

LEWISOHN, Neville Joseph; Director of Dockyard Manpower and Productivity (Under Secretary), Ministry of Defence, 1979-82; *b* 28 May 1922; *s* of Victor and Ruth Lewisohn; *m* 1944, Patricia Zeffertt; two *d* (and one *d* decd). *Educ:* Sutton County Sch., Surrey. Entered Admiralty as Clerical Officer, 1939; promoted through intervening grades to Principal, 1964; Dir of Resources and Progs (Ships), 1972 (Asst Sec.); Head of Civilian Management (Specialists), 2 Div., 1976. *Recreations:* music, drama. *Address:* 46 Middle Stoke, Limpley Stoke, Bath BA3 6JG. *T:* Limpley Stoke 3357.

LEWISON, Peter George Hornby, CBE 1957; Chairman, National Dock Labour Board, 1969-77; Member, National Ports Council, 1972-77; *b* 5 July 1911; *s* of late George and Maud Elizabeth Lewison; *m* 1937, Lyndsay Sutton Rothwell; one *s* one *d*. *Educ:* Dulwich; Magdalen Coll., Oxford. Dunlop Rubber Co., Coventry, 1935-41; Min. of Supply (seconded), 1941-44; RNVR (Special Br.), 1944-46. Min. of Labour, 1946-47; Personnel Manager, British-American Tobacco Co. Ltd, 1947-68, retd. *Recreations:* music, cricket, maintaining a sense of curiosity. *Address:* Court Hill House, East Dean, Chichester, Sussex. *T:* Singleton 200. *Clubs:* MCC; Goodwood Golf.

LE WITT, Jan; painter, poet and designer; *b* 3 April 1907; *s* of Aaron Le Witt and Deborah (*née* Koblenz); *m* 1939, Alina Prusicka; one *s*. *Educ:* Czestochowa. Began artistic career as self-taught designer in Warsaw, 1927; first one-man exhibn of his graphic work, Soc. of Fine Arts, Warsaw, 1930. Co-author and illustrator of children's books, publ. several European langs. Settled in England, 1937; Brit. subject, 1947-; Member of Le Witt-Him partnership, 1933-54. During War of 1939-45 executed (in partnership) a series of murals for war factory canteens, posters for Min. of Inf., Home Office, GPO, etc. Co-designer of murals for Festival of Britain, 1951, and Festival Clock, Battersea Park. First one-man exhibn, Zwemmer Gall., London, 1947; subseq. Hanover Gall. London, 1951; in Rome, 1952; Zwemmer Gall., 1953; New York, 1954; Milan, 1957; Paris, 1960; Grosvenor Gall., London, 1961; Paris, 1963; Musée d'Antibes, 1965; Salon d'Automne, Paris, 1963; Salon de Mai, Paris, 1964; Warsaw (retrosp.), 1967; Venice (retrosp.) (organised by City of Venice), 1970; Paris, 1972. In 1955 when at top of his profession, he gave up graphic design to devote himself entirely to painting. *Works at:* Musee National d'Art Moderne, Paris; Nat. Museum, Jerusalem; Nat. Museum, Warsaw; Musée d'Antibes; Museum and Art Gall., Halifax; City Art Gall., Middlesbrough; British Council; Contemp. Art Soc., London; and in private collections. Represented in collective exhibns in Tate Gall., London, and many foreign galleries. Other artistic activities: décors and costumes for Sadler's Wells Ballet; glass sculptures Venice (Murano); tapestry designs, Aubusson. Gold Medal, Vienna, 1948; Gold Medal Triennale, Milan, 1954; Member: Alliance Graphique Internationale, 1948-60; Exec. Council, Société Européenne de Culture, Venice, 1961-; Nominated Member Italian Acad (with Gold Medal), 1980; Fellow, Internat. PEN, 1978. *Publications:* Vegetabull, 1956 (London and New York); A Necklace for Andromeda, 1976; contribs to Poetry Review; Temenos, Adam; Comprendre, Malahat Review, etc. *Relevant Publication:* Sir Herbert Read, Jean Cassou, Pierre Emmanuel and John Smith (jointly), Jan Le Witt, London 1971, Paris 1972, NY 1973. *Recreations:* music, swimming against the current. *Address:* The Studio, 117 Ladbroke Road, Holland Park, W11 3PR. *T:* 01-229 1570. *Club:* PEN.

LEWITTER, Prof. Lucjan Ryszard; Professor of Slavonic Studies, University of Cambridge, since 1968; *b* 1922. *Educ:* schools in Poland; Perse Sch., Cambridge; Christ's Coll., Cambridge. PhD 1951. Univ. Asst Lectr in Polish, 1948; Fellow of Christ's Coll., 1951; Dir of Studies in Modern Languages, 1951-64; Tutor, 1960-68; Vice-Master, 1977-80; Univ. Lectr in Slavonic Studies (Polish), 1953-68. *Publications:* articles in learned jls. *Address:* Department of Slavonic Studies, Sidgwick Avenue, Cambridge CB3 9DA. *T:* Cambridge 356411. *Club:* United Oxford & Cambridge University.

LEWTHWAITE, Brig. Rainald Gilfrid, CVO 1975; OBE 1974; MC 1943; *b* 21 July 1913; 2nd *s* of Sir William Lewthwaite, 2nd Bt of Broadgate, Cumberland, and Beryl Mary Stopford Hickman; *b* of Sir William Anthony Lewthwaite, 3rd Bt, *qv*; *m* 1936, Margaret Elizabeth Edmonds, MBE 1942, 2nd *d* of late Harry Edmonds and Florence Jane Moncrieffe Bolton, High Green, Redding, Conn, USA; two *s* one *d* (and one *d* decd). *Educ:* Rugby Sch.; Trinity Coll., Cambridge. BA (Hons) Law 1934. Joined Scots Guards, 1934. Served War of 1939-45 (MC, despatches twice). Retired as Defence and Military Attaché, British Embassy, Paris, 1968. Dir of Protocol, Hong Kong, 1969-76. French Croix-de-Guerre with Palm, 1945. *Recreation:* country life. *Address:* Broadgate, Millom, Cumbria LA18 5JZ. *T:* Broughton-in-Furness 295; 14 Edwardes Square, W8 6HE. *T:* 01-602 6323. *Clubs:* Cavalry and Guards, The Pilgrims.

LEWTHWAITE, Sir William Anthony, 3rd Bt, *cr* 1927; Solicitor of Supreme Court, 1937-75; *b* 26 Feb. 1912; *s* of Sir William Lewthwaite, 2nd Bt, JP, and Beryl Mary Stopford (*d* 1970), *o c* of late Major Stopford Cosby Hickman, JP, DL, of Fenloe, Co. Clare; *S* father, 1933; *m* 1936, Lois Mairi, *o c* of late Capt. Robertson Kerr Clark (brother of 1st Baron Inverchapel, PC, GCMG) and Lady Beatrice Minnie Ponsonby, *d* of 9th Earl of Drogheda (who *m* 2nd, 1941, 1st Baron Rankeillour, PC; she *d* 1966); two *d* (er adopted) (and one *d* decd). *Educ:* Rugby; Trinity Coll., Cambridge, BA. Signalman Royal Corps of Signals, 1942-43; Lt, Grenadier Guards, 1943-46. Mem. Council, Country Landowners Association, 1949-64. Mem. Cttee: Westminster Law Society, 1964-73; Brooks's Club, 1953-81. *Heir:* b Brig. Rainald Gilfrid Lewthwaite, *qv*. *Address:* 73 Dovehouse Street, SW3 6JZ. *T:* 01-352 7203.

LEWY, Casimir, FBA 1980; Fellow of Trinity College, Cambridge, since 1959; Reader in Philosophy, University of Cambridge, 1972-82, now Emeritus; *b* 26 Feb. 1919; *o c* of Ludwik Lewy and Izabela Lewy (*née* Rybier); *m* 1945, Eleanor Ford; three *s*. *Educ:* Mikolaj Rej Sch., Warsaw; Fitzwilliam House and Trinity Coll., Cambridge (BA 1939, MA 1943, PhD 1943). Stanton Student, Trinity Coll., Cambridge, 1939-41; Burney Student, Univ. of Cambridge, 1940-42; Sen. Rouse Ball Student, Trinity Coll., Cambridge, 1942-45; Lectr in Philosophy, Univ. of Liverpool, 1945-52; Univ. Lectr in Philosophy, Cambridge, 1952-72, Sidgwick Lectr, 1955-72. Visiting Professor of Philosophy: Univ. of Texas at Austin, 1967; Yale Univ., 1969. *Publications:* Meaning and Modality, 1976; *Editor:* G. E. Moore, Commonplace Book 1919-1953, 1962; G. E. Moore, Lectures on Philosophy, 1966; C. D. Broad, Leibniz, 1975; C. D. Broad, Kant, 1978; articles in philosophical jls. *Recreations:* reading, walking. *Address:* Trinity College, Cambridge. *T:* Cambridge 358201.

LEY, Arthur Harris, FRSA; FRIBA, AADip, FIStructE, MRAeS; former Partner, Ley Colbeck & Partners, Architects; *b* 24 Dec. 1903; *s* of late Algernon Sydney Richard Ley, FRIBA, and Esther Eliza Harris; *m* 1935, Ena Constance Riches; one *d*. *Educ:* Westminster City Sch.; AA Coll. of Architecture. Architect for: Principal London Office Barclays Bank DCO; Head Office Nat. Mutual Life Assce Soc.; Palmerston Hse, EC2; Baltic Hse, EC3; Bishops House, Bishopsgate; Broad Street House; Hqrs Marine Soc.; Hqrs SBAC; Hqrs RAeS; Hqrs Instn Struct. Engrs; York Hall, Windsor Gt Park; Aircraft Research Assoc. Estab., Bedford. Factories and Office Blocks for: Vickers Ltd, at Barrow, etc.; British Aircraft Corporation at Weybridge and Hurn; Wallpaper Manufrs Ltd; Sir Isaac Pitman & Sons; Decca Radar Ltd; Ever Ready Co.; also numerous office blocks in the City of London, Leeds, Inverness and Vancouver. Banks for: Hambro; Nat. Provincial; Barclays; Bank of Scandinavia; Head London office, Hongkong and Shanghai Bank. Central area develt, Watford and Ashford, Kent. Hospitals: Watford and Harrow. Schools: London, Hertfordshire, Barrow in Furness and Surrey. Mem. Council: Architects Registr. Coun. of UK, 1958-60; Instn Struct. Engrs, 1951-54; London Chamber of Commerce, 1955-79; Associated Owners of City Properties (Pres., 1971-77). Hosp. Bd, Ravenscourt Pk, 1972-. Governor, Bishopsgate Foundn; Mem. Court, City Univ.; Liveryman: Worshipful Co. of Paviors (Master, 1962), and of Upholders (Master, 1966); Freeman, City of London; Sheriff 1964-65, and Mem. Court of Common Council, City of London, 1964-80; Churchwarden of St Mary-le-Bow. Grand Officer of the Order of Merit (Chile). *Publications:* contributions to journals and technical press. *Address:* Weston House, 77 St John Street, EC1M 4HP. *T:* 01-253 5555; 14 Fox Close, off Queens Road, Weybridge, Surrey KT13 0AX. *T:* Weybridge 42701. *Clubs:* City Livery (Pres., 1968-69), Guildhall, United Wards (Pres., 1961), Bishopsgate Ward (Pres., 1966).

LEY, Sir Francis (Douglas), 4th Bt *cr* 1905; MBE 1961; TD; DL; JP; Director (formerly Chairman): Ley's Foundries and Engineering Ltd; Ley's Malleable Castings Co. Ltd; Ewart Chainbelt Co Ltd; W. Shaw & Co. Ltd; *b* 5 April 1907; *yr s* of Major Sir Gordon Ley, 2nd Bt (*d* 1944); *S* brother, 1980; *m* 1931, Violet Geraldine Johnson; one *s* one *d*. *Educ:* Eton; Magdalene Coll., Cambridge (MA). JP 1939, DL 1957, Derbyshire. High Sheriff of Derbyshire, 1956. *Heir:* s Ian Francis Ley [*b* 12 June 1934; *m* 1957, Caroline Margaret, *d* of Major George Henry Errington, MC; one *s* one *d*]. *Address:* Shirley House, Shirley, Derby DE6 3AZ. *T:* Brailsford 327.

LEYLAND, Sir V. E. N.; *see* Naylor-Leyland.

LEYTON, Dr (Robert) Nevil (Arthur); Consulting Physician, specialising in Migraine, since 1950; *s* of Prof. A. S. F. Leyton, MD, DSc, FRCP, and Mrs H. G. Leyton, MD; *m* 1943, Wendy (*d* 1960), *er d* of Tom and Dylis Cooper;

one *s*. *Educ:* private; Gonville and Caius Coll., Cambridge; Westminster Hospital (entrance Schol.). BA (Cantab) Double Hons Natural Sciences Tripos, 1932; MA 1938. Ho. Phys. and Surg., Westminster Hospital, 1937. Served with RAF, 1943-46, and with 601 Squadron RAuxAF, 1947-57; retired rank Squdn Leader. Registrar (Med.), St Stephen's Hospital, 1947-50; Hon. Cons. Physician to Migraine Clinic, Putney Health Centre, 1950-68; Hon. Cons. in migraine to Royal Air Forces Assoc., 1947-; Hon. Cons. Physician to Wendy Leyton Memorial Migraine Centre, Harley Street, 1961-; Sen. Medical Adviser, International Migraine Foundn, 1961-; Consulting Physician to Kingdom of Libya, 1968-69; MO, 1971-72, Chief MO, 1972-73, Gath's Mine Hosp., Mashaba, Rhodesia; Specialist Paediatrician, Estate Group Clinics, Lagos, Nigeria, 1975-76; Consultant Physician, County Hosp., Tralee, Eire, 1976-77. Late Medical Adviser, FA. President, 601 Squadron RAuxAF Old Comrades Assoc., 1963-. Air Force Efficiency Medal, 1954. Kt of Mark Twain, 1979. *Publications:* Migraine and Periodic Headache, 1952 (USA, 1954); Headaches, The Reason and the Relief, 1955 (USA); Migraine, 1962; Migraine, Modern Concepts and Preventative Treatment, 1964; contrib.: Lancet, British Medical Journal, Medical World and Journal, Lancet (USA), etc. *Recreations:* travel, riding, horse racing, lawn tennis (Cambridge Univ. Blue, 1933), squash racquets. *Address:* 49 Harrington Gardens, SW7. *Clubs:* Mashaba and British Lions; Hawks'.

LI, Choh-Ming, Hon. KBE 1973 (Hon. CBE 1967); Vice-Chancellor, The Chinese University of Hong Kong, 1964-78; *b* 17 Feb. 1912; *s* of Kanchi Li and Mewching Tsu; *m* 1938, Sylvia Chi-wan Lu; two *s* one *d*. *Educ:* Univ. of California at Berkeley (MA, PhD). Prof. of Economics, Nankai and Southwest Associated and Central Univs in China, 1937-43; Mem., China's special mission to USA, Canada and UK, 1943-45; Dep. Dir-Gen., Chinese Nat. Relief and Rehabilitation Admin. (CNRRA), 1945-47; China's chief deleg. to UN Relief and Rehabilitation Confs and to UN Econ. Commn for Asia and Far East, 1947-49; Chm., Board of Trustees for Rehabilitation Affairs, Nat. Govt of China, 1949-50; Expert on UN Population Commn and Statistical Commn, 1952-57; Lectr, Assoc. Prof., and Prof. of Business Admin., and sometime Dir of Center for Chinese Studies, Univ. of California (Berkeley), 1951-63, Prof. Emeritus, 1974-. Mem., Soc. of Berkeley Fellows, Univ. of Calif, 1981-. Hon. Dr of Laws: Hong Kong, 1967; Michigan, 1967; Marquette, 1969; Western Ontario, 1970; Chinese Univ. of Hong Kong, 1978; Hon. Dr Social Science, Pittsburgh, 1969. Hon. Mem., Internat. Mark Twain Soc. Elise and Walter A. Haas Internat. Award, 1974, Clark Kerr Award, 1979, Univ. of Calif; Soong Foundn Hall of Fame Award, 1980. *Publications:* Economic Development of Communist China, 1959; Statistical System of Communist China, 1962; (ed) Industrial Development in Communist China, 1964; (ed) Asian Workshop on Higher Education, 1969; The First Six Years, 1963-69, 1971; The Emerging University, 1970-74, 1975; New Era Begins 1975-78, 1979; C. M. Li's Chinese Dictionary, 1980 (Hong Kong edn 1980, Shanghai edn 1981). *Recreations:* tennis, calligraphy. *Address:* 81 Northampton Avenue, Berkeley, Calif 94707, USA. *Clubs:* American, Country (Hong Kong); Century, International Platform (USA).

LI, Fook Kow, CMG 1975; JP; Chairman, Public Service Commission, Hong Kong, since 1980; *b* 5 June 1922; *s* of Tse Fong Li; *m* 1946, Edith Kwong Li; four *c*. *Educ:* Massachusetts Inst. of Technology (BSc,MSc). Mem. Hong Kong Admin. Service; Teacher, 1948-54; Resettlement Officer, 1955-58; Labour Officer, 1959-60; various posts in Colonial Secretariat, incl. Asst Sec., Asst Financial Sec., Asst Estabt Officer, Dep. Financial Sec. and Estabt Officer, 1961-69; Dep. Dir of Commerce and Industry, 1970; Dep. Sec. for Home Affairs, 1971-72; Dir of Social Welfare, 1972; Sec. for Social Services, 1973; Sec. for Home Affairs, 1977-80. JP Hong Kong, 1959. *Address:* Government Secretariat, Hong Kong. *T:* H-95470. *Clubs:* Royal Hong Kong Jockey, Hong Kong Country, Chinese, Hong Kong (Hong Kong).

LI, Hon. Simon Fook Sean; Hon. Mr Justice Li; Justice of Appeal, Hong Kong, since 1980; *b* 19 April 1922; 2nd *s* of late Koon Chun Li and late Tam Doy Hing Li; *m* Marie Veronica Lillian Yang; four *s* one *d*. *Educ:* King's Coll., Hong Kong; Hong Kong Univ.; Nat. Kwangsi Univ.; University Coll., London Univ. (LLB 1950). Barrister-at-Law, Lincoln's Inn, 1951. Crown Counsel, Attorney-General's Chambers, Hong Kong, 1953; Senior Crown Counsel, 1962; District Judge, Hong Kong, 1966; Puisne Judge, Hong Kong, 1971-80. *Recreations:* hiking, swimming. *Address:* Appeal Courts Chambers, Courts of Justice, Hong Kong. *T:* 5-233994. *Clubs:* Royal Commonwealth Society; Hong Kong, Chinese (Hong Kong).

LIAO POON-HUAI, Hon. Donald, OBE 1972; Secretary for Housing, Hong Kong, since 1980; Member, Legislative Council, Hong Kong, since 1980; *b* 29 Oct. 1929; *s* of late Liao Huk-Koon and of Yeo Tsai-Hoon; *m* 1963, Christine Yuen Ching-Me; two *s* one *d*. *Educ:* Univ. of Hong Kong (BArch Hons); Univ. of Durham (Dip. Landscape Design). Architect, Hong Kong Housing Authority, 1960, Housing Architect, 1966; Commissioner for Housing and Member, Town Planning Board, 1968; Director of Housing and Vice-Chm., Hong Kong Housing Authority, 1973, Chm., 1980. Member, Hong Kong Inst. of Architects. Hon. FIH. *Recreations:* golf, skiing, riding. *Address:* (residence) 95A Kadoorie Avenue, Kowloon, Hong Kong. *T:* 3-7155822; (office) c/o Government Secretariat, Hong Kong. *T:* 5-95610. *Clubs:* Royal Hong Kong Golf, Royal Hong Kong Jockey (Hong Kong).

LIARDET, Maj.-Gen. Henry Maughan, CB 1960; CBE 1945 (OBE 1942); DSO 1945; DL; *b* 27 Oct. 1906; *s* of late Maj.-Gen. Sir Claude Liardet, KBE, CB, DSO, TD, DL; *m* 1933, Joan Sefton, *d* of Major G. S. Constable, MC,

JP; three s. *Educ:* Bedford School. 1st Commission for Territorial Army, 1924, Royal Artillery; Regular Commission, Royal Tank Corps, 1927; service UK, India, Egypt, 1927-38; Staff Coll., Camberley, 1939; War of 1939-45: War Office, 1939-41; active service in Egypt, N. Africa, Italy, 1941-45; General Staff appointments, command of Regiment and Brigade (despatches twice); Dep. Dir, Manpower Planning, War Office, 1950-52; Comdr, 23 Armd Bde, 1953-54; idc, 1955; Chief of Staff, British Joint Services Mission (Army Staff), Washington, DC, 1956-58; ADC to the Queen, 1956-58; Director-General of Fighting Vehicles, WO, 1958-61; Deputy Master-General of the Ordnance, War Office, 1961-64, retired. Colonel Comdt, Royal Tank Regt, 1961-67. Dir, British Sailors' Soc., 1961-78; Chm., SS&AFA W Sussex Crtee, 1966-82. DL, Sussex, 1964-74, W Sussex 1974-. Sussex CC, 1964-74; Alderman, 1970-74. Pres. Sussex Council, Royal British Legion, 1975-81. *Recreations:* shooting, gardening. *Address:* Warningcamp House, Arundel, West Sussex. *T:* Arundel 882533. *Clubs:* Army and Navy; Sussex.

LIBBERT, Laurence Joseph, QC 1980; *b* 22 June 1933; *s* of Arthur and Evelyn Libbert; *m* 1957, Margaret Low-Beer; one *s* one *d. Educ:* King Edward VII Sch., Lytham; Magdalen Coll., Oxford (BA 1st Cl. Hons 1953; BCL 1st Cl. Hons 1954; MA 1957; Vinerian Scholar, 1954). Gray's Inn: Bacon Scholar, 1954; Arden Scholar, 1955; called to the Bar, 1955. Law Lectr, Univ. of BC, Canada, 1957-58; Law Tutor, Christ Church, Oxford, 1958-63; Lectr, Council of Legal Educn, 1963-67. *Recreations:* art history, theatre, tennis. *Address:* 3 Paper Buildings, Temple, EC4Y 7EU. *T:* 01-353 3721; 30 Downshire Hill, NW3 1NT. *T:* 01-435 9286. *Club:* United Oxford & Cambridge University.

LIBBY, Donald Gerald, PhD; Under Secretary, Department of Education and Science, since 1980; *b* 2 July 1934; *s* of late Herbert Lionel Libby and of Minnie Libby; *m* 1st, 1961, Margaret Elizabeth Dunlop McLatchie (*d* 1979); one *d* ; 2nd, 1982, June Belcher. *Educ:* RMA, Sandhurst; London Univ. (BSc, PhD Physics). CEng, MIEE. Dept of Educn and Science: Principal Scientific Officer, 1967-72; Principal, 1972-74; Asst Sec., 1974-80; Under Sec., Planning and Internat. Relations Br., 1980-82, Architects, Bldg and Schs Br., 1982-. *Recreations:* music, rowing, tennis. *Address:* 10 Albany Close, East Sheen, SW14 7DX. *T:* 01-878 1546. *Club:* Roehampton.

LICHFIELD, 5th Earl of, *cr* 1831; **Thomas Patrick John Anson;** Viscount Anson and Baron Soberton, 1806; *b* 25 April 1939; *s* of Viscount Anson (Thomas William Arnold) (*d* 1958) and Princess Anne of Denmark (*née* Anne Fenella Ferelith Bowes-Lyon) (*d* 1980); *S* grandfather, 1960; *m* 1975, Lady Leonora Grosvenor, *d* of 5th Duke of Westminster, TD; one *s* two *d. Educ:* Harrow Sch.; RMA, Sandhurst. Joined Regular Army, Sept. 1957, as Officer Cadet; Grenadier Guards, 1959-62 (Lieut). Now Photographer. FRPS; FIIP. *Publications:* The Most Beautiful Women, 1981; Lichfield on Photography (also video cassettes), 1981; A Royal Album, 1982. *Heir:* s Viscount Anson, *qv. Address:* 20 Aubrey Walk, W8. *T:* 01-727 4468; (seat) Shugborough Hall, Stafford. *T:* Little Haywood 881454. *Club:* White's.

LICHFIELD, Bishop of, since 1975; **Rt. Rev. Kenneth John Fraser Skelton,** CBE 1972; *b* 16 May 1918; *s* of Henry Edmund and Kate Elizabeth Skelton; *m* 1945, Phyllis Barbara, *y d* of James Emerton; two *s* one *d. Educ:* Dulwich Coll.; Corpus Christi Coll., Cambridge; Wells Theological Coll. 1st Cl. Class. Tripos, Pt 1, 1939; 1st Cl. Theol. Tripos, Pt 1, 1940; BA 1940, MA 1944. Deacon, 1941; Priest, 1942; Curate: Normanton-by-Derby, 1941-43; Bakewell, 1943-45; Bolsover, 1945-46; Tutor, Wells Theol Coll., and Priest-Vicar, Wells Cathedral, 1946-50; Vicar of Howe Bridge, Atherton, 1950-55; Rector, Walton-on-the-Hill, Liverpool, 1955-62; Exam. Chap. to Bp of Liverpool, 1957-62; Bishop of Matabeleland, 1962-70; Asst Bishop, Dio. Durham, Rural Dean of Wearmouth and Rector of Bishopwearmouth, 1970-75. Select Preacher, Cambridge Univ., 1971, 1973. *Recreation:* music. *Address:* Bishop's House, The Close, Lichfield, Staffs WS13 7LG.

LICHFIELD, Dean of; *see* Lang, Very Rev. J. H.

LICHFIELD, Archdeacon of; *see* Ninis, Ven. R. B.

LICHFIELD, Prof. Nathaniel; Emeritus Professor of the Economics of Environmental Planning, University of London, since 1978; Senior Partner, Nathaniel Lichfield & Partners, Planning Development, Transportation and Economic Consultants, since 1962; Research Director, International Centre for Land Policy Studies, since 1980 (Executive Director, 1975-80); *b* 29 Feb. 1916; 2nd *s* of Hyman Lichman and Fanny (*née* Grecht); *m* 1st, 1942, Rachel Goulden (*d* 1969); two *d* ; 2nd, 1970, Dalia Kadury; one *s* one *d. Educ:* Raines Foundn Sch.; University of London. BSc (EstMan), PhD (Econ), PPRTPI, FRICS, CEng, MIMunE. From 1942 has worked continuously in urban and regional planning, specialising in econs of planning from 1950, with particular reference to social cost-benefit in planning and land policy; worked in local and central govt depts and private offices. Consultant commns in UK and abroad, incl. UN. Special Lectr, UCL, 1950; Prof. of Econs and Environmental Planning, UCL, 1966-79; Vis. Prof., Sch. of Architecture and Planning, UCL, 1979-. Vis. Prof., Univ. of California, Univ. of Tel Aviv, Hebrew Univ. Jerusalem, and Technion, Haifa. Director: Lichfield-Terp, BV, Holland, Consultants, 1978-; Lichfield Internat. Inc., Washington DC, Consultants, 1978-. *Publications:* Economics of Planned Development, 1956; Cost Benefit Analysis in Urban Redevelopment, 1962; Cost Benefit Analysis in Town Planning: A Case Study of Cambridge, 1966; Israel's New Towns: A Development Strategy, 1971; (with Prof. A. Proudlove) Conservation and

Traffic: a case study of York, 1975; (with Peter Kettle and Michael Whitbread) Evaluation in the Urban and Regional Planning Process, 1975; (with Haim Darin-Drabkin) Land Policy in Planning, 1980; papers in Urban Studies, Regional Studies, Land Economics, Town Planning Review. *Recreation:* finding out less and less about more and more. *Address:* 13 Chalcot Gardens, Englands Lane, NW3 4YB. *T:* 01-586 0461. *Club:* Reform.

LICHINE, Mme David; *see* Riabouchinska, Tatiana.

LICHTENSTEIN, Roy; American painter and sculptor; *b* 27 Oct. 1923; *s* of Milton Lichtenstein and Beatrice (*née* Werner); *m* 1st, 1949, Isabel Wilson (marr. diss.); two *s* ; 2nd, 1968, Dorothy Herzka. *Educ:* Art Students League, NY; Ohio State Univ. Cartographical draughtsman, US Army, 1943-46; Instructor, Fine Arts Dept, Ohio State Univ., 1946-51; product designer for various cos, Cleveland, 1951-57; Asst Prof., Fine Arts Dept, NY State Univ., 1957-60, Rutgers Univ., 1960-63. Works in Pop Art and other themes derived from comic strip techniques. One-man shows include: Carlebach Gall., NY, 1951; Leo Castelli Gall., NY, 1962, 1963, 1965, 1967, 1971-75, 1977, 1979; Galerie Illeana Sonnabend, Paris, 1963, 1965, 1970, 1975; Venice Biennale, 1966; Pasadena Art Museum, 1967; Walker Art Center, Minneapolis, 1967; Stedelijk Museum, Amsterdam, 1967; Tate Gall., London, 1967; Künsthalle, Berne, 1968; Guggenheim Museum, NY, 1969; Nelson Gall., Kansas City, 1969; Museum of Contemporary Art, Chicago, 1970; Galerie Beyeler, Basel, 1973; Centre Nat. d'Art Contemporain, Centre Beaubourg, Paris, 1975; Seattle Art Museum, 1976; Inst. of Contemp. Art, Boston, 1979; Portland Center for Visual Arts, 1980; St Louis Art Museum, 1981; Seattle Art Museum, 1981; Forth Worth Art Museum, 1981. Group exhibns include: Six Painters and the Object, Guggenheim Museum, 1963; Venice Biennale, 1966; US Pavilion Expo, (Montreal), 1967; São Paulo Biennale, 1968; 36th Biennial Exhibn of Contemp. Amer. Painting, Corcoran Gall., Washington, DC, 1979. Created outside wall for Circarama of NY State Pavilion, NY World's Fair, 1963; billboard for Expo 67. *Address:* PO Box 1369, Southampton, New York, NY 11968, USA.

LICKLEY, Robert Lang, CBE 1973; BSc; DIC; FRSE; FEng; FRAeS; FIProdE; consultant; *b* Dundee, 19 Jan. 1912. *Educ:* Dundee High Sch.; Edinburgh Univ. (Hon. DSc 1972); Imperial Coll. (Fellow, 1973); FCGI 1976. Formerly: Professor of Aircraft Design, College of Aeronautics, Cranfield; Managing Director, Fairey Aviation Ltd; Hawker Siddeley Aviation Ltd, 1960-76 (Asst Man. Dir, 1965-76); Head, Rolls Royce Support Staff, NEB, 1976-79. President: IMechE, 1971; IProdE, 1981-82. FRSE 1977. Hon. FIMechE 1982. *Recreation:* golf. *Address:* Forwood, Silverdale Avenue, Walton-on-Thames, Surrey KT12 1EQ.

LICKORISH, Leonard John, CBE 1975; Director General, British Tourist Authority, since 1970; *b* 10 Aug. 1921; *s* of Adrian J. and Josephine Lickorish; *m* 1945, Eileen Maris Wright; one *s. Educ:* St George's Coll., Weybridge; University Coll., London (BA). Served RAF, 1941-46. British Travel Association: Research Officer, 1946; Asst Dir Gen, 1955; Gen. Man., 1963. Officer of Crown of Belgium, 1967. *Publications:* The Travel Trade, 1955; The Statistics of Tourism, 1975; numerous for nat. and internat. organisations on internat. travel. *Recreation:* gardening. *Address:* 46 Hillway, Highgate, N6 6EP. *Clubs:* Royal Over-Seas League, Royal Automobile.

LIDBURY, Sir John (Towersey), Kt 1971; FRAeS; Vice-Chairman, Hawker Siddeley Group Ltd, since 1974 (Director, 1960; Deputy Managing Director, 1970-81); *b* 25 Nov. 1912; *m* 1939, Audrey Joyce (*née* Wigzell); one *s* two *d. Educ:* Owen's Sch. Joined Hawker Aircraft Ltd, 1940; Dir, 1951, Gen. Manager, 1953, Man. Dir, 1959, Chm., 1961; Jt Man. Dir, Hawker Siddeley Aviation Ltd, 1959, Dir and Chief Exec., 1961, Dep. Chm. and Man. Dir, 1963-77; Chairman: Hawker Siddeley Dynamics Ltd, 1971-77 (Dep. Chm., 1970); High Duty Alloys Ltd, 1978-79 (Dep. Chm., 1971); High Duty Alloys Castings Ltd, 1978-79; High Duty Alloys Extrusions Ltd, 1978-79; High Duty Alloys Forgings Ltd, 1978-79; Carlton Industries Ltd, 1981- (Dir, 1978-); Director: Hawker Siddeley International Ltd, 1963-; Smith Industries Ltd, 1978-; Invergordon Distillers (Hldgs) Ltd, 1978-. Dir, Hawker Siddeley Pensions Trustees Ltd, 1968- (Chm., 1975-). Pres., 1969-70, Mem. Council, 1959-77, Soc. of British Aerospace Companies Ltd. CBIM. JP Kingston-upon-Thames, 1952-62. *Address:* 18 St James's Square, SW1Y 4LJ. *T:* 01-930 6177.

LIDDELL, family name of **Baron Ravensworth.**

LIDDELL, Dr Donald Woollven; FRCP 1964; FRCPsych; Head of Department of Psychological Medicine, King's College Hospital, 1961-79; *b* 31 Dec. 1917; *m* 1954, Emily (*née* Horsfall) (marr. diss. 1977); one *s* one *d. Educ:* Aldenham Sch.; London Hospital. MRCP 1941; Neurological training as RMO, The National Hospital, Queen Square, 1942-45; Psychiatric training, Edinburgh and Maudsley Hospital. Medical Superintendent, St Francis Hospital, Haywards Heath, 1957-61; retired as Physician to Bethlem and Maudsley Hosps, 1968. Examr to RCP and RCPsych. Founder FRCPsych, 1971. *Publications:* contrib. Journal of Mental Science, Journal of Neurology, Psychiatry and Neuro-surgery, American Journal of Mental Diseases, Journal of Social Psychology. *Address:* 49 Bury Walk, SW3.

LIDDELL, (John) Robert; author; *b* 13 Oct. 1908; *e s* of late Major J. S. Liddell, CMG, DSO, and Anna Gertrude Morgan. *Educ:* Haileybury Coll.;

Corpus Christi Coll., Oxford. Lecturer in Universities of Cairo and Alexandria, 1942-51, and assistant professor of English, Cairo Univ., 1951; Head of English Dept, Athens Univ., 1963-68. FRSL. *Publications:* The Last Enchantments, 1948; The Rivers of Babylon, 1959; An Object for a Walk, 1966; The Deep End, 1968; Stepsons, 1969, and other novels; A Treatise on the Novel, 1947; Aegean Greece, 1954; The Novels of I. Compton-Burnett, 1955; Byzantium and Istanbul, 1956; The Morea, 1958; The Novels of Jane Austen, 1963; Mainland Greece, 1965; Cavafy: a critical biography, 1974; The Novels of George Eliot, 1977. *Address:* c/o Barclays Bank, High Street, Oxford.

LIDDELL, Laurence Ernest, CBE 1976; ERD, TD; retired; *b* Co. Durham, 27 Oct. 1916; *m* 1940, Alys Chapman, Askrigg, Yorks; two *s* one *d. Educ:* Yorebridge Grammar Sch.; Leeds Univ. (BA); Carnegie Coll. (DipPE). Reserve and Territorial Officer, The Royal Scots, 1939-59; served in France and Belgium (despatches), 1939-40; E Africa, 1944-45; Lectr in Educn, King's Coll., Durham Univ., 1946-59; Lt-Col comdg Univ. OTC, 1955-59; Dir, Dept of Physical Educn, Univ. of Edinburgh, 1959-80. First Pres./Chm., Scottish Orienteering Assoc., 1961-66; Chairman: Adv. Sports Council for Scotland, 1968-71; Main Stadium Cttee for 1970 Commonwealth Games in Edinburgh, 1967-70; Scottish Sports Council, 1971-75; Mem., UK Sports Councils, 1968-75. *Publications:* Batsmanship, 1958; (jtly) Orienteering, 1965. *Recreations:* golf; formerly: cricket (played for Univ., Army, 11 yrs Captain Northumberland, MCC, Captain English Minor Counties XI v NZ, 1958); Association football (played for Univ. and Yorks Amateurs); hockey (played for Northumberland and English Northern Counties). *Address:* 318 Gilmerton Road, Edinburgh EH17 7PR. *T:* 031-664 3710. *Clubs:* Lord's Taverners; Lowland Brigade (Edinburgh).

LIDDELL, Robert; *see* Liddell, J. R.

LIDDERDALE, Sir David (William Shuckburgh), KCB 1975 (CB 1963); Clerk of the House of Commons, 1974-76; *b* 30 Sept. 1910; *s* of late Edward Wadsworth and Florence Amy Lidderdale; *m* 1943, Lola, *d* of late Rev. Thomas Alexander Beckett, Tubbercurry and Ballinew; one *s. Educ:* Winchester; King's Coll., Cambridge (MA). Assistant Clerk, House of Commons, 1934. Served War of 1939-45, The Rifle Brigade (TA); active service, N Africa and Italy. Senior Clerk, 1946, Fourth Clerk at the Table, 1953, Second Clerk Assistant, 1959, Clerk Assistant, 1962, House of Commons. Joint Secretary, Assoc. of Secretaries-General of Parliaments (Inter-Parliamentary Union), 1946-54, Mem., 1954-76, Vice-Pres., 1973-76, Hon. Vice-Pres., 1976. *Publications:* The Parliament of France, 1951; (with Lord Campion) European Parliamentary Procedure, 1953; (ed) Erskine May's Parliamentary Practice, 19th edn, 1976. *Recreation:* walking. *Address:* 46 Cheyne Walk, SW3. *Clubs:* Travellers', MCC.

LIDDIARD, Richard England, CBE 1978; Chairman, Czarnikow Group Ltd, since 1974; *b* 21 Sept. 1917; *s* of late E. S. Liddiard, MBE, and M. A. Brooke; *m* 1943, Constance Lily, *d* of late Sir William J. Rook; one *s* three *d. Educ:* Oundle; Worcester Coll., Oxford (MA). Lt-Col, Royal Signals, 1939-46. Chairman: C. Czarnikow Ltd, 1958-74; Sugar Assoc. of London, 1960-78; British Fedn of Commodity Assocs, 1962-70, Vice-Chm., 1970-77; London Commodity Exchange, 1972-76; Mem., Cttee on Invisible Exports, 1966-70. Mem. Ct of Assts, Worshipful Co. of Haberdashers, 1958, Master 1978. FRSA. MC (Poland), 1941. *Recreation:* golf. *Address:* Oxford Lodge, 52 Parkside, Wimbledon, SW19. *T:* 01-946 3434. *Club:* Carlton.

LIDDIARD, Ronald; Director of Social Services, Birmingham, since 1974; *b* 26 July 1932; *s* of Tom and Gladys Liddiard; *m* 1957, June Alexandra (*née* Ford); two *d. Educ:* Canton High Sch., Cardiff; Colleges of Commerce and Technology, Cardiff. Dip. Municipal Admin, Certif. Social Work. Health Administrator, 1958-60; Social Worker, 1960-64; Sen. Welfare Administrator, 1964-70; Dir of Social Services, Bath, 1971-74. *Publications:* articles in social work and health jls. *Recreations:* private flying and wines. *Address:* Snow Hill House, 10-15 Livery Street, Birmingham B3 2PE. *T:* 021-235 2992.

LIDDLE, Sir Donald (Ross), Kt 1971; JP; Chairman, Cumbernauld Development Corporation, 1972-78; Vice-Lord-Lieutenant, City of Glasgow, Strathclyde Region, 1978-80; *b* 11 Oct. 1906; *s* of Thomas Liddle, Bonnington, Edinburgh; *m* 1933, May, *d* of R. Christie, Dennistoun, Glasgow; one *s* two *d. Educ:* Allen Glen's School, Glasgow. Served War of 1939-45 with RAOC, Burma and India; Major, 1944. DL, County of Glasgow, 1963; JP 1968; Lord Provost of Glasgow, 1969-72. Chm., Scottish Tourist Consultative Council, 1973-79. CStJ 1970. Hon. LLD Strathclyde, 1971. *Address:* 15 Riddrie Crescent, Riddrie Knowes, Glasgow G33 2QG. *Clubs:* Army and Navy; Conservative (Glasgow).

LIESNER, Hans Hubertus, CB 1980; Chief Economic Adviser, Departments of Industry and Trade (formerly also Prices and Consumer Protection), since 1976; *b* 30 March 1929; *s* of Curt Liesner, lawyer, and Edith L. (*née* Neumann); *m* 1968, Thelma Seward; one *s* one *d. Educ:* German grammar schs; Bristol Univ. (BA); Nuffield Coll., Oxford; MA Cantab. Asst Lectr, later Lectr, in Economics, London Sch. of Economics, 1955-59; Lectr in Economics, Univ. of Cambridge; Fellow, Dir of Studies in Economics and some time Asst Bursar, Emmanuel Coll., Cambridge, 1959-70; Under-Sec. (Economics), HM Treasury, 1970-76. *Publications:* The Import Dependence of Britain and Western Germany, 1957; Case Studies in European Economic Union: the mechanics of integration (with J. E. Meade and S. J. Wells), 1962;

Atlantic Harmonisation: making free trade work, 1968; Britain and the Common Market: the effect of entry on the pattern of manufacturing production (with S. S. Han), 1971; articles in jls, etc. *Recreations:* ski-ing, cine-photography. *Address:* 32 The Grove, Brookmans Park, Herts AL9 7RN. *T:* Potters Bar 53269. *Club:* Reform.

LIFAR, Serge; Dancer, Choreographer, Writer, Painter; Director, Université de Danse, since 1958; Professeur de Chorélogie, Sorbonne; Maître de Ballet, Théâtre National de l'Opéra, Paris, since 1968 (formerly Professeur); *b* Kieff, South Russia, 2 April 1905; *s* of Michel Lifar. Pupil of Bronislava Nijinska, 1921; joined Diaghileff company, Paris, 1923; studied under Cecchetti. Dir, Institut Chorégraphique, 1947-75. First London appearance, in Cimarosiana and Les Fâcheux, Coliseum, 1924. Choreographer (for first time) of Stravinsky's Renard, 1929; produced Prométhée, Opera House, Paris, 1929. Cochran's 1930 Revue, London Pavilion, 1930; returned to Paris, produced and danced in Bacchus and Ariadne, Le Spectre de la Rose, Giselle, and L'Après-midi d'un Faune, 1932; Icare, David Triomphant, Le Roi Nu, 1936; Alexandre le Grand, 1937; arranged season of Ballet at the Cambridge, London, 1946; Choreographer of Noces Fantastiques, Romeo et Juliette (Prokofiev), 1955. Paintings exhibited: Paris, 1972; Cannes, 1974; Monte Carlo, Florence, Venice, London. Prix de l'Académie Française; Corres. Mem., Institut de France. *Publications:* Traditional to Modern Ballet, 1938; Diaghilev, a biography, 1940; A History of Russian Ballet from its Origins to the Present Day (trans. 1954); The Three Graces, 1959; Ma Vie, 1965 (in Eng., 1969). *Address:* 89 quai d'Orsay, 75007 Paris, France.

LIFFORD, 8th Viscount *cr* 1781; **Alan William Wingfield Hewitt;** *b* 11 Dec. 1900; 2nd but *o* surv. *s* of Hon. George Wyldbore Hewitt (*d* 1924; 7th *s* of 4th Viscount Lifford) and Elizabeth Mary, *e d* of late Charles Rampini, DL, LLD, Advocate; *S kinsman* 1954; *m* 1935, Alison Mary Patricia, *d* of T. W. Ashton, The Cottage, Hursley, nr Winchester; one *s* three *d. Educ:* Winchester; RMC, Sandhurst. Lieut late Hampshire Regt. *Heir:* *s* Hon. Edward James Wingfield Hewitt [*b* 27 Jan. 1949; *m* 1976, Alison, *d* of Robert Law; one *s* one *d*]. *Address:* Field House, Hursley, Hants. *T:* Hursley 75203.

See also Sir Anthony Swann, Bt.

LIGGINS, Sir Edmund (Naylor), Kt 1976; TD 1947; Solicitor; *b* 21 July 1909; *s* of Arthur William and Hannah Louisa Liggins; *m* 1952, Celia Jean Lawrence (OBE 1982), *d* of William Henry and Millicent Lawrence; three *s* one *d. Educ:* King Henry VIII Sch., Coventry; Rydal Sch. Joined TA, 1936; commissioned 45th Bn (RWR), RE; served War: comd 399 Battery, RA, subseq. 498 LAA Battery, RA, 1942-45. Subseq. commanded 198 Indep. Battery, RA, 1948-51. Senior Partner, Liggins & Co., Solicitors, Coventry and Leamington Spa. Elected Mem. Council, Law Society, 1963, Vice-Pres., 1974-75, Pres., 1975-76 (Chm., Non-Contentious Business Cttee of Council, 1968-71; Chm., Educn and Trng Cttee, 1973-74); Chm., West Midland Legal Aid Area Cttee, 1963-64; Pres., Warwickshire Law Soc., 1969-70. Mem., Court of Univ. of Warwick. Hon. Mem., Amer. Bar Assoc. *Recreations:* cricket, rugby football, squash rackets; amateur theatre. *Address:* Hareway Cottage, Hareway Lane, Barford, Warwickshire CV35 8DB. *T:* Barford 624246. *Clubs:* Army and Navy, MCC, Forty, Eccentric; Coventry and North Warwickshire Cricket, Drapers' (Coventry).

LIGGINS, Prof. Graham Collingwood; FRCSE, FRACS, FRCOG; FRS 1980; FRSNZ 1976; Professor of Obstetrics and Gynaecological Endocrinology, University of Auckland, New Zealand, since 1968 (formerly Senior Lecturer); Consultant to National Women's Hospital, Auckland. *Educ:* Univ. of NZ. MB, ChB, Univ. NZ, 1949; PhD, Univ. of Auckland, 1969. MRCOG Lond. 1956; FRCSE 1958; FRACS 1960. Is distinguished for his work on the role of foetal hormones in the control of parturition. Hon. FAGS, 1976; Hon. FACOG, 1978. Hector Medal, RSNZ, 1980. *Publications:* over 100 published papers. *Recreations:* forestry, sailing, fishing. *Address:* Postgraduate School of Obstetrics and Gynaecology, National Women's Hospital, Claude Road, Auckland 3, New Zealand. *T:* 775-127; 3/38 Awatea Road, Parnell, Auckland 1, New Zealand.

LIGHT, (Sidney) David; a Civil Service Commissioner, 1978-79; *b* 9 Dec. 1919; *s* of late William Light; *m* Edna Margaret Honey; one *s. Educ:* King Edward VI Sch., Southampton. RAF, 1940-46. HM Customs and Excise, 1938; HM Treasury, 1948-68; Asst Sec., CS Commn, 1969-75; Under Sec., CSD, 1975-78. *Recreations:* watching cricket, travel. *Address:* Churchers, Upper Farringdon, near Alton, Hants GU34 3EG. *T:* Tisted 214. *Clubs:* Royal Commonwealth Society; Hampshire Cricket.

LIGHTBODY, Ian (Macdonald), CMG 1974; *b* 19 Aug. 1921; *s* of Thomas Paul Lightbody and Dorothy Marie Louise Lightbody (*née* Cooper); *m* 1954, Noreen, *d* of late Captain T. H. Wallace, Dromore, Co. Down; three *s* one *d. Educ:* Queens Park Sch., Glasgow; Glasgow Univ. (MA). War service, Indian Army, India and Far East, 1942-46 (Captain); Colonial Admin. Service, Hong Kong, 1945; various admin. posts; District Comr, New Territories, 1967-68; Defence Sec., 1968-69; Coordinator, Festival of Hong Kong, 1969; Comr for Resettlement, 1971; Sec. for Housing and Chm., Hong Kong Housing Authority, 1973-77; Sec. for Admin, Hong Kong, 1977-78; Chm., Public Services Commn, Hong Kong, 1978-80. MLC 1971; MEC 1977; retd from Hong Kong, 1980. *Recreation:* walking. *Address:* Two Stacks, Lake Lane, Barnham, Sussex. *Clubs:* Hong Kong, Royal Hong Kong Jockey.

LIGHTBOWN, Ronald William, MA, FSA, FRAS; Keeper of the Library, Victoria and Albert Museum, since 1976; *b* Darwen, Lancs, 2 June 1932; *s of* late Vincent Lightbown and Helen Anderson Lightbown (*née* Burness); *m* 1962, Mary Dorothy Webster; one *s. Educ:* St Catharine's Coll., Cambridge (MA). FSA, FRAS. Victoria and Albert Museum: Asst Keeper, Library, 1958-64; Asst Keeper, Dept of Metalwork, 1964-73; Dep. Keeper, Library, 1973-76. Fellow, Inst. for Res. in the Humanities, Wisconsin Univ., 1974. Sec., Soc. of Antiquaries, 1979-. *Publications:* Catalogue of Italian Sculpture (pt author), V&A Museum, 1964; Catalogue of Scandinavian and Baltic Silver, V&A Museum, 1975; French Secular Goldsmith's work of the Middle Ages, 1978; Sandro Botticelli, 1978; (with M. Corbett) The Comely Frontispiece, 1978; Catalogue of French Silver, V&A Museum, 1979; (ed and trans. with A. Caiger-Smith) Piccolpasso: the art of the potter, 1980; Donatello and Michelozzo, 1980; (with M. Archer) India Observed, V&A Museum, 1982; (ed and introd) series of source-books on 18th century British art, 14 vols, 1970-71; many articles in learned jls, incl. Burlington Magazine, Warburg Jl and Art Bulletin. *Recreations:* reading, travel, music, conversation. *Address:* Victoria and Albert Museum, Exhibition Road, SW7 2RL. *T:* 01-589 6371.

LIGHTHILL, Sir (Michael) James, Kt 1971; FRS 1953; FRAeS; Provost of University College London, since 1979, Hon. Fellow, 1982; *b* 23 Jan. 1924; *s of* E. B. Lighthill; *m* 1945, Nancy Alice Dumaresq; one *s* four *d. Educ:* Winchester Coll.; Trinity Coll., Cambridge. Aerodynamics Division, National Physical Laboratory, 1943-45; Fellow, Trinity Coll., Cambridge, 1945-49; Sen. Lectr in Maths, Univ. of Manchester, 1946-50; Beyer Prof. of Applied Mathematics, Univ. of Manchester, 1950-59; Dir, RAE, Farnborough, 1959-64; Royal Soc. Res. Prof., Imperial Coll., 1964-69; Lucasian Prof. of Mathematics, Univ. of Cambridge, 1969-79. Chm., Academic Adv. Cttee, Univ. of Surrey, 1964; Member: Adv. Council on Technology, 1964; NERC, 1965-70; Shipbuilding Inquiry Cttee, 1965; (part-time) Post Office Bd, 1972-74; First Pres., Inst. of Mathematics and its Applications, 1964-66; a Sec. and Vice-Pres., Royal Soc., 1965-69; Pres., Internat. Commn on Mathematical Instruction, 1971-74. FRAeS 1961. Foreign Member: American Academy of Arts and Sciences, 1958; American Philosophical Soc., 1970; US Nat. Acad. of Sciences, 1976; US Nat. Acad. of Engineering, 1977. Associate Mem., French Acad. of Sciences, 1976. Hon. Fellow American Inst. of Aeronautics and Astronautics, 1961. Hon. DSc: Liverpool, 1961; Leicester, 1965; Strathclyde, 1966; Essex, 1967; Princeton, 1967; East Anglia, 1968; Manchester, 1968; Bath, 1969; St Andrews, 1969; Surrey, 1969; Cranfield, 1974; Paris, 1975; Aachen, 1975; Rensselaer, 1980. Royal Medal, Royal Society, 1964; Gold Medal, Royal Aeronautical Society, 1965; Harvey Prize for Science and Technol., Israeli Inst. of Technol., 1981; Gold Medal, Inst. of Maths and Its Applications, 1982. Comdr Order of Léopold, 1963. *Publications:* Introduction to Fourier Analysis and Generalised Functions, 1958; Mathematical Biofluiddynamics, 1975; Newer Uses of Mathematics, 1977; Waves in Fluids, 1978; articles in Royal Soc. Proc. and Trans, Qly Jl of Mechanics and Applied Maths, Philosophical Magazine, Jl of Aeronautical Scis, Qly Jl of Maths, Aeronautical Qly, Communications on Pure and Applied Maths, Proc. Cambridge Philosophical Soc., Jl of Fluid Mechanics, Reports and Memoranda of ARC; contrib. to Modern Developments in Fluid Dynamics: High Speed Flow; High Speed Aerodynamics and Jet Propulsion; Surveys in Mechanics; Laminar Boundary Layers. *Recreations:* music and swimming. *Address:* University College London, Gower Street, WC1. *Club:* Athenæum.

LIGHTMAN, Gavin Anthony, QC 1980; *b* 20 Dec. 1939; *s of* Harold Lightman, *qv*; *m* 1965, Naomi Ann Claff; one *s* two *d. Educ:* Univ. of London (LLB); Univ. of Michigan (LLM). Called to the Bar, Lincoln's Inn, 1963. *Publication:* (with G. Battersby) Cases and Statutes on Real Property, 1965. *Recreations:* reading, walking, eating. *Address:* 5B Prince Arthur Road, Hampstead, NW3. *T:* 01-794 5180.

LIGHTMAN, Harold, QC 1955; Master of the Bench of Lincoln's Inn; *b* 4 April 1906; *s of* Louis Lightman, Leeds; *m* 1936, Gwendoline Joan, *d of* David Ostrer, London; three *s. Educ:* City of Leeds Sch.; privately. Accountant, 1927-29. Barrister, Lincoln's Inn, 1932. Home Guard, 1940-45. Defence Medal, 1946. Liveryman, Company of Glovers, 1960. *Recreation:* reading. *Address:* Stone Buildings, Lincoln's Inn, WC2. *T:* 01-242 3840. *Club:* Royal Automobile.
See also G. A. Lightman.

LIGHTMAN, Ivor Harry; Deputy Secretary, Welsh Office, since 1981; *b* 23 Aug. 1928; *s of* late Abraham Lightman, OBE and Mary (*née* Goldschneider); *m* 1950, Stella Doris Blend; one *s. Educ:* Abergele Grammar Sch. Clerical Officer, Min. of Food, 1946; Nat. Service, RAOC (Corp.), 1946-49; Officer of Customs and Excise, 1949-56; Asst Principal, Ministry of Works, 1957; Asst Private Sec. to successive Ministers, 1959-60; Principal, Ministry of Works, 1961-65; Sec., Banwell Cttee on Construction Contracts, 1962-64; Principal, HM Treasury, 1965-67; Asst Sec., MPBW, 1967-70; Asst Sec., CSD, 1970-73; Under Secretary: Price Commn, 1973-76; Dept of Prices and Consumer Protection, 1976-78; Dept of Industry, 1978-81. *Address:* c/o Welsh Office, Cathays Park, Cardiff.

LIGHTMAN, Lionel; Director of Competition Policy, Office of Fair Trading, since 1981; *b* 26 July 1928; *s of* late Abner Lightman and late Gitli Lightman (*née* Szmul); *m* 1952, Helen, *y d of* late Rev. A. Shechter and late Mrs Shechter; two *d. Educ:* City of London Sch.; Wadham Coll., Oxford (MA).

Nat. Service, RAEC, 1951-53 (Temp. Captain). Asst Principal, BoT, 1953; Private Sec. to Perm. Sec., 1957; Principal 1958; Trade Comr, Ottawa, 1960-64; Asst Sec. 1967; Asst Dir, Office of Fair Trading, 1973-75; Under Sec., Dept of Trade, 1975-78, DoI, 1978-81. *Address:* 55 The Pryors, East Heath Road, NW3 1BP. *T:* 01-435 3427.

LIGHTON, Sir Christopher Robert, 8th Bt, *cr* 1791; MBE 1945; *b* 30 June 1897; *o s of* 7th Bt and Helen (*d* 1927), *d of* late James Houldsworth, Coltness, Lanarkshire; *S* father, 1929; *m* 1st, 1926, Rachel Gwendoline (marr. diss. 1953), *yr d of* late Rear-Admiral W. S. Goodridge, CIE; two *d*; 2nd, 1953, Horatia Edith (*d* 1981), *d of* A. T. Powlett, Godminster Manor, Bruton, Somerset; one *s. Educ:* Eton Coll.; RMC. Late The King's Royal Rifle Corps; rejoined the Army in Aug. 1939 and served War of 1939-45. *Heir: s* Thomas Hamilton Lighton, *b* 4 Nov. 1954. *Address:* Heathers, Odiham, Hants.

LIGHTWOOD, Reginald, MD; FRCP; DPH; Consulting Physician to The Hospital for Sick Children, Great Ormond Street, London, and Consulting Paediatrician to St Mary's Hospital, London, since 1963; Teacher in Paediatrics at Norfolk and Norwich Hospital, since 1979; *b* 1898; *s of* late John M. Lightwood, Barrister-at-Law, and Gertrude (*née* Clench); *m* 1937, Monica Guise Bicknell, *d of* late Laurance G. Ray; two *s. Educ:* Monkton Combe Sch., Bath. Served European War in Royal Artillery, 1917-19. Jelf Medal and Alfred Hughes Memorial Prize, King's Coll., London, 1919; MD (London), 1924, FRCP 1936. Hon. Medical Staff: Westminster Hospital, 1933-39 (resigned); Hospital for Sick Children, Great Ormond Street, London, 1935-63; St Mary's Hospital, London, 1939-63; Prof. of Pediatrics, American University of Beirut, 1964 and 1965; Prof. of Paediatrics and Child Health, University Coll. of Rhodesia, 1966-69. Kenneth Blackfan Memorial Lecturer, Harvard Medical Sch., 1953; Visiting Prof. of Pediatrics: Boston Univ., 1966; Univ. of Calif, Los Angeles, 1969. Cons. Pædiatrician to Internat. Grenfell Assoc., Newfoundland, 1970-71. Pres., British Pædiatric Assoc., 1959-60; FRSM; Hon. Fellow, Amer. Acad. of Pediatrics; Mem., Irish Pædiatric Soc.; Hon. Member: Swedish Pædiatric Soc.; Portuguese Pædiatric Soc.; Mark Twain Soc. of America; corresp. Member: Société de Pédiatrie de Paris; Amer. Pediatric Soc. *Publications:* Textbooks: Pædiatrics for the Practitioner (ed jtly with Prof. W. Gaisford); Sick Children (with Dr F. S. W. Brimblecombe and Dr D. Barltrop); scientific papers and articles on pædiatrics in medical journals, textbooks, etc. *Address:* Grey Gables, Salhouse Road, Little Plumstead, Norwich NR13 5JJ.

LIKAKU, Victor Timothy; Assistant General Manager, The New Building Society, Blantyre, since 1979; Mayor of City of Blantyre, since 1981; *b* 15 Oct. 1934; *m* 1959, Hilda; one *s* two *d.* Malaŵi Civil Service, Min. of Finance, 1957-62; Malaŵi Govt Schol., St Steven's Coll., Univ. of Delhi, India, 1962 (BA Econ.); Dept of Customs and Excise, 1966; Customs and Admin. Courses, New Zealand, 1967, Vienna 1972; UN Fellowship, GATT, Geneva, 1973; Controller of Customs and Excise, Malaŵi Govt, 1973; High Comr for Malaŵi in London, 1976-78. *Recreations:* reading, soccer. *Address:* The New Building Society, Building Society House, Victoria Avenue, PO Box 466, Blantyre, Malaŵi. *T:* 634 753. *Clubs:* Hurlingham (Hon. Mem.), International Sporting, Penthouse.

LILEY, Sir (Albert) William, KCMG 1973 (CMG 1967); PhD; FRSNZ; FRCOG; Professor in Perinatal Physiology, New Zealand Medical Research Council Postgraduate School of Obstetrics and Gynæcology, University of Auckland; *b* 12 March 1929; *s of* Albert Harvey Liley; *m* 1953, Helen Margaret Irwin, *d of* William Irwin Hunt; two *s* three *d*, and one adopted *d. Educ:* Auckland Grammar Sch.; University of Auckland; University of Otago; Australian National Univ.; Columbia Univ. BMedSc 1952; MB, ChB (UNZ) 1954; PhD (ANU) 1957; Dip. Obst. (UA) 1962; FRSNZ 1964; FRCOG 1971. Research Schol. in Physiology, ANU, 1955-56. Sandoz Research Fellow in Obstetrics, Postgrad. Sch. of Obstetrics and Gynæcology, 1957-58; NZMRC Research Fellow in Obstetrics, 1959-. United States Public Health Service Internat. Research Fellowship, 1964-65. Mem., Pontifical Acad. of Scis, 1978. Hon. FACOG, 1975. Hon. DSc Victoria Univ., Wellington, 1971. *Publications:* numerous articles in physiological, obstetric and pædiatric journals. *Recreations:* farming, forestry. *Address:* 19 Pukenui Road, Epsom, Auckland 3, New Zealand. *T:* 656-433.

LILFORD, 7th Baron, *cr* 1797; **George Vernon Powys;** *b* 8 Jan. 1931; *s of* late Robert Horace Powys (*g g grandson* of 2nd Baron) and of Vera Grace Bryant, Rosebank, Cape, SA; *S* kinsman, 1949; *m* 1st, 1954, Mrs Eve Bird (marr. diss.); 2nd, 1957, Anuta Merritt (marr. diss., 1958); 3rd, 1958, Norma Yvonne Shell (marr. diss., 1961); 4th, 1961, Mrs Muriel Spottiswoode (marr. diss., 1969); two *d*; 5th, 1969, Margaret Penman; one *s* two *d. Educ:* St Aidan's Coll., Grahamstown, SA; Stonyhurst Coll. *Recreations:* boating, cricket. *Heir: s* Hon. Mark Vernon Powys, *b* 16 Nov. 1975. *Address:* PO Box 6733, Roggebaai, Cape, 8012, South Africa.

LILL, John Richard, OBE 1978; concert pianist; Professor at Royal College of Music; *b* 17 March 1944; *s of* George and Margery Lill. *Educ:* Leyton County High Sch.; Royal College of Music. FRCM; Hon. FTCL; FLCM. Gulbenkian Fellowship, 1967. First concert at age of 9; Royal Festival Hall debut, 1963; Promenade Concert debut, 1969. Numerous broadcasts on radio and TV; has appeared as soloist with all leading British orchestras. Recitals and concertos throughout Great Britain, Europe, USA, Canada, Scandinavia, USSR, Japan and Far East, Australia, New Zealand, etc. Overseas tours as soloist with many orchestras including London Symphony Orchestra and

London Philharmonic Orchestra. Complete recordings of Beethoven sonatas and concertos; complete Beethoven cycle, London, 1982. Chappell Gold Medal; Pauer Prize; 1st Prize, Royal Over-Seas League Music Competition, 1963; Dinu Lipatti Medal in Harriet Cohen Internat. Awards; 1st Prize, Internat. Tchaikowsky Competition, Moscow, 1970. Hon. DSc Aston, 1978; Hon. DMus Exeter, 1979. *Recreations:* amateur radio, chess, walking, avoiding news media. *Address:* c/o Harold Holt Ltd, 31 Sinclair Road, W14 0NS. *T:* 01-603 4600.

LILLEY, Prof. Geoffrey Michael, OBE 1981; CEng, FRSA, FRAeS, MIMechE, FIMA; Professor of Aeronautics and Astronautics, University of Southampton, since 1964; *b* Isleworth, Mddx, 16 Nov. 1919; *m* 1948, Leslie Marion Wheeler; *one s* two *d. Educ:* Isleworth Grammar Sch.; Battersea and Northampton Polytechnics; Imperial Coll. BSc(Eng) 1944, MSc(Eng) 1945, DIC 1945. Gen. engrg trg, Benham and Kodak, 1936-40; Drawing Office and Wind Tunnel Dept, Vickers Armstrong Ltd, Weybridge, 1940-46; Coll. of Aeronautics: Lectr, 1946-51; Sen. Lectr, 1951-55; Dep. Head of Dept of Aerodynamics, 1955, and Prof. of Experimental Fluid Mechanics, 1962-64. Vis. Prof., Stanford Univ., 1977-78. Past Member: Aeronautical Res. Council (Mem. Applied Aerodynamics Cttee; Chm., Noise Res. Cttee; past Mem. Council and Chm. Aerodynamics, Fluid Motion and Performance Cttees); formerly Mem., Noise Advisory Council (Chm., Noise from Air Traffic Working Group); Past Chm., Aerodynamics Cttee, Engrg Sci. Data Unit. Consultant to Rolls Royce; Past Consultant to AGARD and OECD. *Publications:* articles in reports and memoranda of: Aeronautical Research Council; Royal Aeronautical Soc., and other jls. *Recreations:* music, chess, walking. *Address:* Highbury, Pine Walk, Chilworth, Southampton SO1 7HQ. *T:* Southampton 769109.

LILLICRAP, Harry George, CBE 1976; Director, Telephone Rentals Ltd, since 1976; *b* 29 June 1913; *s* of late Herbert Percy Lillicrap; *m* 1938, Kathleen Mary Charnock; two *s. Educ:* Erith County Sch.; University College London. BSc (Eng) 1934. Post Office Telecommunications, 1936-72; Sen. Dir Planning, Sen. Dir Customer Services, 1967-72; Chm., Cable and Wireless, 1972-76. *Address:* Thornhurst, Felbridge, East Grinstead, West Sussex. *T:* East Grinstead 25811.

LILLIE, Beatrice, (Lady Peel); actress; *b* Toronto, 29 May 1894; *d* of John Lillie, Lisburn, Ireland, and Lucie Shaw; *m* 1920, Sir Robert Peel, 5th Bt (*d* 1934); (one *s,* Sir Robert Peel, 6th and last Bt, killed on active service 1942). *Educ:* St Agnes' Coll., Belleville, Ontario. First appearance, Alhambra, 1914; at the Vaudeville, Prince of Wales's etc., 1915-22; in The Nine O'Clock Revue, Little Theatre, 1922; first New York appearance, Times Square Theatre, in André Charlot's Revue, 1924; in Charlot's Revue at Prince of Wales's, 1925; in New York, 1925-26; at The Globe and The Palladium, 1928; This Year of Grace, New York, 1928; Charlot's Masquerade, at the Cambridge, London, 1930; New York; 1931-32; at the Savoy and London Palladium, 1933-34; New York, 1935; Queen's, London, 1939; Big Top, Adelphi, 1940; Troops: England, 1939-42; Africa, Italy, etc, 1942-45; Seven Lively Arts, Ziegfeld, New York, 1945; Better Late, Garrick, London, 1946; appeared in television and radio programmes, England and America, 1946-47; Inside USA, New York, 1948, subs. on tour for one year, USA; returned to London (cabaret), Café de Paris, 1950 and June 1951. Solo artiste at several Royal performances; appeared in NY television, 1951-52; produced one-woman show, Summer Theatre, 1952; subs. on tour and produced show in Broadway, Oct. 1952-June 1953. Radio and TV, London, July-Aug. 1953. Road tour in US of this production, Sept. 1953-June 1954; London, 1954-55. An Evening with Beatrice Lillie, Globe, AEWBL, Florida, Feb and March, 1956; 2nd one-woman show, Beasop's Fables, USA, June-Sept. 1956; Ziegfeld Follies, New York, 1957-58; Auntie Mame, Adelphi, London, 1958-59; High Spirits, Alvin Theatre, NYC, 1964-65. Appeared in films: Exit Smiling, 1927; Are You There, 1933; Doctor Rhythm, 1938; On Approval, 1944; Around the World in Eighty Days, 1956; Thoroughly Modern Millie, 1967. Free French Liberation Medal, N Africa, 1942, also African Star and George VI Medal, Donaldson Award, USA, 1945, also Antoinette Perry Award, New York, 1953, and many others. *Publication:* (with J. Philip and J. Brough) Every Other Inch a Lady (autobiog.), 1973. *Recreation:* painting. *Address:* Peel Fold, Mill Lane, Henley-on-Thames, Oxon.

LILLIE, Very Rev. Henry Alexander, MA; Dean of Armagh, and Keeper of Armagh Public Library, 1965-79; *b* 11 May 1911; *s* of David William Lillie and Alicia Lillie (*née* Morris), Carrick-on-Shannon; *m* 1942, Rebecca Isobel, *yr d* of Andrew C. Leitch, Homelea, Omagh, Co. Tyrone; one *d. Educ:* Sligo Grammar Sch.; Trinity Coll., Dublin. BA 1935, MA 1942. Junior Master, Grammar Schools: Elphin, 1932; Sligo, 1932-34. Deacon, 1936; Curate Asst, Portadown, 1936-41; Incumbent of: Milltown, 1941-47; Kilmore, 1947-52; Armagh, 1952-65; Armagh Cathedral: Prebendary of Tynan, 1952-60; Treas., 1960-61; Chancellor, 1961; Precentor, 1961-65. *Recreations:* reading, fishing, gardening. *Address:* 104 Drumman More Road, Armagh. *T:* Armagh 524926.

LILLIE, John Adam; QC; LLD; *b* 25 July 1884; *e s* of Thomas Lillie and Ellen Harper Tait. *Educ:* Brockley's Acad., Broughty Ferry; Aberdeen Grammar Sch.; University of Aberdeen (MA 1906); University of Edinburgh (LLB 1910). Admitted to Faculty of Advocates, 1912; called to English Bar, 1921; Lecturer on Mercantile Law, University of Edinburgh, 1928-47; KC (Scotland) 1931; Member Royal Commn on Workmen's Compensation, 1938; Sheriff of Fife and Kinross, 1941-71. Chairman for Scotland Board of

Referees under Income Tax Acts, 1942-55; Chairman for Scotland and NI of British Motor Trade Assoc. Price Protection Cttee, 1949-52; Legal Commissioner and Dep. Chairman, General Board of Control for Scotland, 1944-62; Convener of the sheriffs, 1960-65; Hon. LLD Aberdeen, 1967. *Publications:* The Mercantile Law of Scotland (6th edn, 1965); Articles in Green's Encyclopædia of the Law of Scotland on Company Law, and Sale of Goods; The Northern Lighthouses Service, 1965; Tradition and Environment in a Time of Change, 1970; An Essay on Speech Literacy, 1974; A Family History, 1976. *Address:* 85 Great King Street, Edinburgh. *T:* 031-556 1862. *Club:* Caledonian (Edinburgh).

LILLINGSTON, George David I. I.; *see* Inge-Innes-Lillingston.

LIM, Sir Han-Hoe, Kt 1946; CBE 1941; Hon. LLD (Malaya); MB, ChB (Edinburgh); JP; Pro-Chancellor, University of Malaya, 1949-59; *b* 27 April 1894; 2nd *s* of late Lim Cheng Sah, Singapore; *m* 1920, Chua Seng Neo; two *s* two *d. Educ:* St Andrew's Sch. and Raffles Institution; University of Edinburgh. RMO North Devon General Hospital, with charge of Military Auxiliary Hospital, 1919; Municipal Commissioner, Singapore, 1926-31; Member of Legislative Council, Straits Settlements, 1933-42, and its Finance Cttee, 1936-42; Member of Exec. Council, Straits Settlements, 1939-42; Member of Advisory Council, Singapore, 1946-48; Member of Exec. Council, Singapore, 1948-50. Member of Council, King Edward VII College of Medicine, Singapore, 1930-42; Mem. and Chm., Public Services Commission, Singapore, 1952-56. *Recreations:* tennis, chess. *Address:* 758 Mountbatten Road, Singapore 15. *T:* 40655. *Club:* Garden (Singapore).

LIMANN, Dr Hilla, Hon. GCMG 1981; President of Ghana, 1979-81; *b* 1934; *m* ; five *c. Educ:* Lawra Primary Boarding Sch.; Tamale Middle Boarding Sch.; Govt Teacher Trng Coll.; London Sch. of Economics (Hon. Fellow, 1982); Sorbonne; Univ. of London; Faculty of Law and Econ. Sciences, Univ. of Paris. BSc(Econ.) 1960; BA Hons (Hist.), 1964; PhD (Polit. Sci. and Law), 1965. Teacher, 1952-55; examiner for Civil Service grad. entry, W African Exams Council. Councillor, Tumu Dist Council, 1952 (Chm., 1953-55); contested (Indep.) Constituency, Party Elec., 1954. Head of Chancery and Official Sec., Ghana Embassy, Lomé, Togo, 1968-77; Mem., Constitutional Commn on 1969 Constitution for Ghana; Mem. Govt Delegns for opening of borders of Ghana with the Ivory Coast/Upper Volta; Mem./Sec. to Ghana delegns, OAU and Non-aligned States, Confs of ILO, WHO, Internat. Atomic Energy Agency. Leader, People's National Party.

LIMBU; *see* Rambahadur Limbu.

LIMENTANI, Prof. Uberto; Professor of Italian, University of Cambridge, 1962-81; Fellow of Magdalene College, Cambridge, since 1964; *b* Milan, 15 Dec. 1913; *er s* of Prof. Umberto Limentani and Elisa Levi; *m* 1946, Barbara Hoban; three *s. Educ:* University of Milan (Dr in Giurispr., Dr in Lettere); University of London (PhD); University of Cambridge (MA). Commentator and script-writer Italian Section, BBC European Service, 1939-45. Lector 1945, Assistant Lecturer, 1948, Lecturer, 1952, in Italian, University of Cambridge. Hon. Prof., Dept of Italian, Univ. of Hull, 1981-. Pres., MHRA, 1981. Corresp. Member Accademia Letteraria Ital. dell'Arcadia, 1964. Commendatore, Ordine al Merito della Repubblica Italiana, 1973. *Publications:* Stilistica e Metrica, 1936; Poesie e Lettere Inedite di Salvator Rosa, 1950; L'Attività Letteraria di Giuseppe Mazzini, 1950; La Satira nel Seicento, 1961; The Fortunes of Dante in Seventeenth Century Italy, 1964; (ed) The Mind of Dante, 1965; (ed) vol. xii (Scritti vari di critica storica e letteraria) of Edizione Nazionale of Works of U. Foscolo, 1978. Co-editor yearly review, Studi Secenteschi (founded 1960); an ed. of Italian Studies. Trans. E. R. Vincent's Ugo Foscolo Esule fra gli Inglesi, 1954. Several contrib. on Italian Literature to: Encyclopædia Britannica; Cassell's Encyclopædia of Literature; Italian Studies; La Bibliofilia; Giornale Storico della Letteratura Italiana; Amor di Libro; Studi Secenteschi; Il Pensiero Mazziniano; Bollettino della Domus Mazziniana; Il Ponte; Cambridge Review; Modern Language Review; Times Literary Supplement. *Recreation:* walking in the Alps. *Address:* 19A Victoria Street, Cambridge CB1 1JP. *T:* Cambridge 358198.

LIMERICK, 6th Earl of, *cr* 1803 (Ire.); **Patrick Edmund Pery,** MA, CA; Baron Glentworth, 1790 (Ire.); Viscount Limerick, 1800 (Ire.); Baron Foxford, 1815 (UK); Director: Kleinwort, Benson Ltd; Kleinwort, Benson, Lonsdale plc; Tanks Consolidated Investments plc and subsidiary cos; T. R. Pacific Basin Investment Trust plc; Brooke Bond Group plc; Vice-President, Association of British Chambers of Commerce, since 1977 (President, 1974-77); *b* 12 April 1930; *e s* of 5th Earl of Limerick, GBE, CH, KCB, DSO, TD, and Angela Olivia, Dowager Countess of Limerick, GBE, CH (*d* 1981); *S* father, 1967; *m* 1961, Sylvia Rosalind Lush (*see* Countess of Limerick); two *s* one *d. Educ:* Eton; New Coll., Oxford. CA 1957. Commercial Bank of Australia Ltd (London Adv. Bd), 1969-72. Parly Under-Sec. of State for Trade, Dept of Trade and Industry, 1972-74. Chm., BOTB, 1979-83; Member: Cttee for ME Trade, 1968-79 (Chm., 1975-79); Council, London Chamber of Commerce, 1968-79. Chm., Mallinson-Denny Ltd, 1979-81. Pres., Ski Club of Gt Britain, 1974-81; Vice-Pres., Alpine Ski Club, 1975-77. *Recreations:* skiing, mountaineering. *Heir: s* Viscount Glentworth, *qv. Address:* Chiddinglye, West Hoathly, East Grinstead, West Sussex. *T:* Sharpthorne 810214; 30 Victoria Road, W8 5RG. *T:* 01-937 0573.

LIMERICK, Countess of; Sylvia Rosalind Pery, MA; President, National Association for Maternal and Child Welfare, since 1973; Vice-Chairman,

Foundation for the Study of Infant Deaths, since 1971; Member, Maternity Services Advisory Committee, Department of Health and Social Security, since 1981; *b* 7 Dec. 1935; *e d* of Maurice Stanley Lush, *qv* ; *m* 1961, Viscount Glentworth (now 6th Earl of Limerick, *qv*); two *s* one *d. Educ:* St Swithun's, Winchester; Lady Margaret Hall, Oxford (MA). Research Asst, Foreign Office, 1959-62. Mem., Bd of Governors, St Bartholomew's Hosp., 1970-74; Vice-Chm., Community Health Council, S District of Kensington, Chelsea, Westminster Area, 1974-77; Mem., Kensington, Chelsea and Westminster AHA, 1977-82; a Vice-President: London Br. of British Red Cross Soc., 1972- (Nat. HQ Staff, 1962-66; Pres., Kensington and Chelsea Div., 1966-72); UK Cttee for UN Children's Fund (Pres., 1972-79); Invalid Children's Aid Assoc., 1976-; Health Visitors' Assoc., 1978-. Member: Cttee of Management, Inst. of Child Health, 1976-; Council and Cttee of Management, King Edward's Hospital Fund, 1977-81. *Recreations:* music, mountaineering, ski-ing. *Address:* 30 Victoria Road, W8 5RG. *T:* 01-937 0573; Chiddinglye, West Hoathly, East Grinstead, W Sussex RH19 4QT. *T:* Sharpthorne 810214.

LIMON, Donald William; Clerk of Financial Committees, House of Commons, since 1981; *b* 29 Oct. 1932; *s* of Arthur and late Dora Limon; unmarried. *Educ:* Durham Cathedral Chorister Sch.; Durham Sch.; Lincoln Coll., Oxford (MA). A Clerk in the House of Commons, 1956-; Sec. to House of Commons Commn, 1979-81. *Recreations:* cricket, golf, singing. *Address:* Wicket Gate, Churt, Farnham, Surrey GU10 2HY. *T:* Headley Down 714350.

LINACRE, John Gordon Seymour, CBE 1979; AFC 1943; DFM 1941; CBIM; Deputy Chairman and Joint Managing Director, United Newspapers Ltd, since 1981 (Director, since 1969); Managing Director, since 1965, Deputy Chairman, since 1981, Yorkshire Post Newspapers Ltd; *b* 23 Sept. 1920; *s* of John James Linacre and Beatrice Barber Linacre; *m* 1943, Irene Amy (*née* Gordon); two *d. Educ:* Firth Park Grammar Sch., Sheffield. CBIM (FBIM 1973). Served War, RAF, 1939-46, Sqdn Ldr. Journalistic appts, Sheffield Telegraph/Star, 1937-47; Kemsley News Service, 1947-50; Dep. Editor: Newcastle Journal, 1950-56; Newcastle Evening Chronicle, 1956-57; Editor: Sheffield Star, 1958-61; Asst Gen. Man., Sheffield Newspapers Ltd, 1961-63; Exec. Dir, Thomson Regional Newspapers Ltd, London, 1963-65. Chairman: Yorkshire Post & Evening Post, 1973-; East Yorkshire Printers Ltd, 1965-; Goole Times Printing & Publishing Co. Ltd, 1969-; The Reporter Ltd, 1970-; Doncaster Newspapers Ltd, 1981- (Man. Dir, 1966-81). Director: United Newspapers (Publications) Ltd, 1969-; Trident Television Ltd, 1970-; Yorkshire Television Ltd, 1967-. Dir, INCA/FIEJ Res. Assoc., Darmstadt, Germany, 1971-79 (Pres., 1974-77); Vice-Pres. and Mem. Exec. Cttee, FIEJ, 1971-. Member: Newspaper Soc. Council, 1966- (Pres., Newspaper Soc., 1978-79); Newspaper Soc. Indust. Relations Cttee, 1966-80; Press Assoc., 1967-74 (Chm., 1970-71); Reuters Ltd, 1970-74 (Trustee, 1974-); Evening Newspaper Advertising Bureau Ltd, 1966-78 (Chm., 1975-76); English National Opera, 1978-81; Opera North (formerly English National Opera North), 1978- (Chm.); N Eastern Postal Bd, 1974-80; Adv. Bd, Yorks and Lincs, BIM, 1973-75; Health Educn Council, 1973-77. Governor, Harrogate Festival of Arts and Sciences Ltd, 1973-. Trustee, Yorks and Lincs Trustee Savings Bank, 1972-78. Commendatore dell-ordine al Merito della Repubblica Italiana, 1973. *Recreations:* playing cricket, golf, squash; watching County cricket, Leeds United, and Leeds Rugby League Club; country walking, foreign travel. *Address:* White Windows, Staircase Lane, Bramhope, Leeds LS16 9JD. *T:* Arthington 842751. *Clubs:* Alwoodley Golf, Headingley Taverners (Leeds).

LINCOLN, Bishop of, since 1974; **Rt. Rev. Simon Wilton Phipps,** MC 1945; *b* 6 July 1921; *s* of late Captain William Duncan Phipps, CVO, RN, and late Pamela May Ross; *m* 1973, Mary, widow of Rev. Dr James Welch and *d* of late Sir Charles Eric Palmer. *Educ:* Eton; Trinity Coll., Cambridge; Westcott House, Cambridge. Joined Coldstream Guards, 1940; commnd. 1941; Capt., 1944; ADC to GOC-in-C Northern Comd India, Nov. 1945; Mil. Asst to Adjt Gen. to the Forces, War Office, 1946; Major, 1946. BA (History) Cantab, 1948; MA 1953; Pres., Cambridge Univ. Footlights Club, 1949. Ordained 1950. Asst Curate, Huddersfield Parish Church, 1950; Chaplain, Trinity Coll., Cambridge, 1953; Industrial Chaplain, Coventry Dio., 1958; Hon. Canon, Coventry Cath., 1965; Bishop Suffragan of Horsham, 1968-74. Member: Council, Industrial Soc.; Home Sec.'s Cttee of Inquiry into Liquor Licensing Laws, 1971-72. *Publication:* God on Monday, 1966. *Recreations:* walking, painting, cooking. *Address:* Bishop's House, Eastgate, Lincoln. *Club:* Army and Navy.

LINCOLN, Dean of; *see* Fiennes, Very Rev. Hon. O. W. T. -W.

LINCOLN, Archdeacon of; *see* Adie, Ven. M. E.

LINCOLN, Sir Anthony (Handley), KCMG 1965 (CMG 1958); CVO 1957; Ambassador to Venezuela, 1964-69; *b* 2 Jan. 1911; *s* of late J. B. Lincoln, OBE; *m* 1948, Lisette Marion Summers; no *c. Educ:* Mill Hill Sch.; Magdalene Coll., Cambridge (BA). Prince Consort and Gladstone Prizes, 1934. Appointed Asst Principal, Home Civil Service, 1934; subsequently transferred to Foreign Service; served in Foreign Office; on UK Delegation to Paris Peace Conf., 1946, and in Buenos Aires. Counsellor, and Head of a Dept of Foreign Office, 1950. Dept. Sec.-Gen., Council of Europe, Strasbourg, France, 1952-55; Counsellor, British Embassy, Copenhagen, 1955-58; British Ambassador to Laos, 1958-60; HM Minister to Bulgaria, 1960-63; Officer Order of Orange Nassau, 1950; Comdr Order of Dannebrog, 1957. *Publication:* Some Political

and Social Ideas of English Dissent, 1937. *Recreations:* country pursuits. *Clubs:* Brooks's, Reform.

LINCOLN, Hon. Sir Anthony (Leslie Julian), Kt 1979; **Hon. Mr Justice Lincoln;** a Judge of the High Court of Justice, Family Division, since 1979; a Judge of the Restrictive Practices Court, since 1980, President, since 1982; Writer and Broadcaster; *b* 7 April 1920; *s* of Samuel and Ruby Lincoln. *Educ:* Highgate; Queen's Coll., Oxford (Schol., MA). Served Somerset Light Inf. and RA, 1941-45. Called to Bar, 1949; QC 1968; Bencher, Lincoln's Inn, 1976; Mem. Senate of Inns of Court and the Bar, 1976-; Chm., Law Reform Cttee of Senate, 1979-81. A Recorder of the Crown Court, 1974-79. Chm., Justice Cttee on Freedom of Information, 1978; Pres., British Br., Internat. Law Assoc., 1981-. Vice-Princ., Working Men's Coll., 1955-60; Chm., Working Men's Coll. Corp., 1969-79; Chm. and Trustee, Harrison Homes for the Elderly, 1963-80. *Publications:* Wicked, Wicked Libels, 1972; (ed) Lord Eldon's Anecdote Book, 1960; regular contribs to Observer, Spectator and other jls. *Recreations:* fishing, swimming, walking. *Address:* Chelsea, SW3; Upper Woodford, Salisbury, Wilts. *Clubs:* Beefsteak, Lansdowne.

LINCOLN, F(redman) Ashe, QC 1947; MA, BCL; Captain RNVR; a Recorder, 1972-79 (Recorder of Gravesend, 1967-71); Master of the Bench, Inner Temple, since 1955; Master of the Moots, 1955-64, and 1968-70; *s* of Reuben and Fanny Lincoln; *m* 1933, Sybil Eileen Cohen; one *s* one *d. Educ:* Hoe Gram. Sch., Plymouth; Haberdashers' Aske's Sch.; Exeter Coll., Oxford, 1928; called to Bar, Inner Temple, Nov. 1929; joined RNV(S)R, 1937; served in Royal Navy (RNVR), Sept. 1939-May 1946: Admiralty, 1940-42; in parties to render mines safe, May 1940; rendered safe first type G magnetic mine (King's Commendation for bravery); Mediterranean, 1943, with commandos in Sicily and Italy at Salerno landings, 1943; assault crossing of Rhine, March 1945 (despatches twice). Dep. World Pres., Internat. Assoc. of Jewish Lawyers and Jurists, 1973-. Renter Warden of Worshipful Company of Plaisterers, 1946-47, Master, 1949-50; Freeman and Liveryman of City of London; fought general election 1945 (C) Harrow East Div. (Middx.); Chm. Administrative Law Cttee of Inns of Court Conservative Association, 1951; Mem. Exec., Gen. Council of the Bar, 1957-61. Associate MNI, 1976; Pres., RNR Officers' Club; Chm., London Devonian Assoc.; Mem., Exec., London Flotilla. KStJ 1980. *Publications:* The Starra, 1939; Secret Naval Investigator, 1961. *Recreations:* yachting, tennis. *Address:* 9 King's Bench Walk, Temple, EC4Y 7DX. *T:* 01-353 7202. *Clubs:* Athenæum, Royal Automobile, MCC, Naval; Royal Corinthian Yacht (Burnham-on-Crouch and Cowes); Bar Yacht; Royal Naval and Royal Albert Yacht (Portsmouth).

LIND, Per; Swedish Ambassador to the Court of St James's, 1979-82, retired; *b* 8 Jan. 1916; *s* of Erik and Elisabeth Lind; *m* 1942, Eva Sandström; two *s* two *d. Educ:* Univ. of Uppsala. LLB 1939. Entered Swedish Foreign Service as Attaché, 1939; served in Helsinki, 1939-41; Berlin, 1942-44; Second Sec., Stockholm Foreign Ministry, 1944-47; First Sec., Swedish Embassy, Washington, 1947-51; Personal Asst to Sec.-General of UN, 1953-56; re-posted to Swedish Foreign Ministry: Chief of Div. of Internat. Organisations, 1956-59; Dep. Political Affairs, 1959-64; Ambassador with special duties (*ie* disarmament questions) and actg Chm., Swedish Delegation in Geneva, 1964-66; Ambassador to Canada, 1966-69; Under-Sec. of State for Administration at Foreign Ministry, Stockholm, 1969-75; Chm. Special Political Cttee of 29th Session of Gen. Assembly of UN, 1974; Ambassador to Australia, 1975-79. *Recreation:* golf. *Address:* Strindbergsgatan 54, S-115 28 Stockholm, Sweden.

LINDARS, Rev. Prof. Frederick Chevallier, (Barnabas Lindars), SSF), DD; Rylands Professor of Biblical Criticism and Exegesis, University of Manchester, since 1978; Dean, Faculty of Theology, since 1982; *b* 11 June 1923; *s* of Walter St John Lindars and Rose Lindars. *Educ:* Altrincham Grammar Sch.; St John's Coll., Cambridge (Rogerson Scholar, 1941; BA 1945 (1st Cl. Oriental Langs Tripos, Pt I, 1943; 1st Cl. Theol Tripos, Pt I, 1946, 2nd Cl. Pt II, 1947); MA 1948, BD 1961, DD 1973). Served War, 1943-45. Westcott House, Cambridge, 1946-48; Deacon 1948, Priest 1949; Curate of St Luke's, Pallion, Sunderland, 1948-52; joined Soc. of St Francis (Anglican religious order), taking the name of Barnabas, 1952; Asst Lectr in Divinity, Cambridge Univ., 1961-66, Lectr, 1966-78; Fellow and Dean, Jesus Coll., Cambridge, 1976-78. Proctor for Northern Univs in Convocation of York and Gen. Synod of C of E, 1980-. T. W. Manson Meml Lectr, Manchester Univ., 1974. Canon Theologian (hon.), Leicester Cathedral, 1977-. Member: Studiorum Novi Testamenti Societas; Soc. for Old Testament Study. *Publications:* New Testament Apologetic, 1961 (2nd edn 1973); (ed and contrib.) Church without Walls, 1968; (ed with P. R. Ackroyd, and contrib.) Words and Meanings, 1968; Behind the Fourth Gospel, 1971 (also French edn 1974; Italian edn 1978); The Gospel of John, 1972 (2nd edn 1977); (ed with S. S. Smalley, and contrib.) Christ and Spirit in the New Testament, 1973; articles in Jl Theol Studies, New Testament Studies, Vetus Testamentum, and Theol. *Recreations:* walking, music. *Address:* Faculty of Theology, The University, Manchester M13 9PL. *T:* 061-273 3333.

LINDBERGH, Anne Spencer Morrow; author, United States; *b* 1906; *d* of Dwight Whitney Morrow and Elizabeth Reeve Morrow (*née* Cutter); *m* 1929, Col Charles Augustus Lindbergh, AFC, DFC (*d* 1974); three *s* two *d* (and one *s* decd). *Educ:* Miss Chapin's Sch., New York City; Smith Coll., Northampton, Mass (two prizes for literature). Received Cross of Honour of United States Flag Association for her part in survey of air route across Atlantic, 1933; received Hubbard Gold Medal of National Geographical Soc.

for work as co-pilot and radio operator in flight of 40,000 miles over five continents, 1934. Hon. MA, Smith Coll., Mass., 1935. *Publications:* North to the Orient, 1935; Listen, the Wind, 1938; The Wave of the Future, 1940; The Steep Ascent, 1944; Gift from the Sea, 1955; The Unicorn and other Poems, 1935-55, 1958; Dearly Beloved, 1963; Earth Shine, 1970; Bring Me a Unicorn (autobiog.), 1972; Hour of Gold, Hour of Lead (autobiog.), 1973; Locked Rooms and Open Doors: diaries and letters 1933-35, 1974; The Flower and the Nettle: diaries and letters 1936-39, 1976; War Within and Without: diaries and letters 1939-44, 1980.

LINDEN, Anya, (Lady Sainsbury); Ballerina, Royal Ballet, 1958-65; *b* 3 Jan. 1933; English; *d* of George Charles and Ada Dorothea Eltenton; *m* 1963, Sir John Sainsbury, *qv* ; two *s* one *d*. *Educ:* Berkeley, Calif; Sadler's Wells Sch. Entered Sadler's Wells Sch., 1947; promoted to 1st Company, 1951; became Soloist, 1952. Principal rôles in the ballets: Coppelia; Sylvia; Prince of Pagodas; Sleeping Beauty; Swan Lake; Giselle; Cinderella; Agon; Solitaire; Noctambules; Fête Etrange; Symphonic Variations; Invitation; Firebird; Lady and the Fool; Antigone; Seven Deadly Sins. Member: Council and Appeal Cttee, Nat. Council for One-Parent Families; Adv. Council, British Theatre Museum, 1975-; Drama and Dance Adv. Cttee, British Council, 1981-. Director: Ballet Rambert, 1975-; Royal Ballet Sch., 1977-; Young Vic, 1977-79. *Recreations:* drawing, gardening, filming. *Address:* c/o Stamford House, Stamford Street, SE1.

LINDESAY-BETHUNE, family name of **Earl of Lindsay.**

LINDISFARNE, Archdeacon of; *see* Smith, Ven. D. J.

LINDLEY, Sir Arnold (Lewis George), Kt 1964; DSc; CGIA; FEng, FIMechE, FIEE; Deputy-Chairman, Motherwell Bridge (Holdings) Ltd, 1965; *b* 13 Nov. 1902; *s* of George Dilnot Lindley; *m* 1927, Winifred May Cowling (*d* 1962); one *s* one *d* ; *m* 1963, Mrs Phyllis Rand. *Educ:* Woolwich Polytechnic. Chief Engineer BGEC, South Africa, 1933; Director: East Rand Engineering Co., 1943; BGEC, S Africa, 1945; Gen. Manager Erith Works, GEC, 1949; GEC England, 1953; Vice-Chm. 1959, Managing Dir, 1961-62, Chm., 1961-64, of GEC; retd. Chairman: BEAMA, 1963-64; Internat. Electrical Assoc., 1962-64; Engineering Industry Trng Bd, 1964-74. President, Instn of Mechanical Engineers, 1968-69; Chm., Council of Engineering Instns, 1972-73 (Vice-Chm., 1971-72); Member: Council, City Univ., 1969-; Design Council, 1971-. Appointed by Govt to advise on QE2 propulsion turbines, 1969; Associate Consultant, Thames Barrier. *Recreations:* sailing and golf. *Address:* Heathcote House, 18 Nab Lane, Shipley, W Yorks.

LINDLEY, Bryan Charles, CBE 1982; Director of Technology, Dunlop Holdings plc, since 1979; Director, Soil-Less Cultivation Systems Ltd, since 1980; Chairman and Director, Thermal Conversions (UK) Ltd, since 1982; *b* 30 Aug. 1932; *m* 1956; one *s* ; *m* 1980, Jennifer Kathryn Edwards. *Educ:* Reading Sch.; University Coll., London (Fellow 1979). BSc (Eng) 1954; PhD 1960; FIMechE 1968; FIEE 1968; FInstP 1968; FInstD 1968. National Gas Turbine Establishment, Pyestock, 1954-57; Hawker Siddeley Nuclear Power Co. Ltd, 1957-59; C. A. Parsons & Co. Ltd, Nuclear Research Centre, Newcastle upon Tyne, 1959-61; International Research and Development Co. Ltd, Newcastle upon Tyne, 1962-65; Man., R&D Div., C. A. Parsons & Co. Ltd, Newcastle upon Tyne, 1965-68; Electrical Research Assoc. Ltd: Dir, 1968-73; Chief Exec. and Man. Dir, ERA Technology Ltd, 1973-79; Dir, ERA Patents Ltd, 1968-79; Chm. and Man. Dir, ERA Autotrack Systems Ltd, 1971-79. Chm., Materials and Chemicals Requirements Bd, Dept of Industry, 1982-; Member: Nat. Electronics Council, 1969-79; Res. and Technol. Cttee, CBI, 1974-80; Design Council, 1980- (Mem., Design Adv. Cttee); Cttee of Inquiry into Engineering Profession, 1977-80; Adv. Council for Applied Research and Develt, 1980-. Chm., Sci. Educn and Management Div., IEE, 1974-75; Dep. Chm., Watt Cttee on Energy Ltd, 1976-80. *Publications:* articles on plasma physics, electrical and mechanical engineering, management science, impact of technological innovation, etc, in learned jls. *Recreations:* literature, ski-ing. *Address:* Apartment 1, Little Aston Hall, Streetly, West Midlands B74 3BH. *Club:* Institute of Directors.

LINDLEY, Prof. Dennis Victor; Professor and Head of Department of Statistics and Computer Science, University College London, 1967-77; *b* 25 July 1923; *s* of Albert Edward and Florence Louisa Lindley; *m* 1947, Joan Armitage; one *s* two *d*. *Educ:* Tiffin Boys' Sch., Kingston-on-Thames; Trinity Coll., Cambridge. MA Cantab 1948. Min. of Supply, 1943-45; Nat. Physical Lab., 1945-46 and 1947-48; Statistical Lab., Cambridge Univ., 1948-60 (Dir, 1957-60); Prof. and Head of Dept of Statistics, UCW, Aberystwyth, 1960-67, Hon. Professorial Fellow, 1978-. Hon. Prof., Univ. of Warwick, 1978-. Vis. Professor: Chicago and Stanford Univs, 1954-55; Harvard Business Sch., 1963; Univ. of Iowa, 1974-75; Univ. of Bath, 1978-. Guy Medal (Silver), Royal Statistical Soc., 1968. Fellow, Inst. Math. Statistics; Fellow, American Statistical Assoc.; Mem., Internat. Statistical Inst. *Publications:* (with J. C. P. Miller) Cambridge Elementary Statistical Tables, 1953; Introduction to Probability and Statistics (2 vols), 1965; Making Decisions, 1971; contribs to Royal Statistical Soc., Biometrika, Annals of Math. Statistics. *Address:* 2 Periton Lane, Minehead, Somerset TA24 8AQ. *T:* Minehead 5189.

LINDOP, Audrey Beatrice Noël E.; *see* Erskine-Lindop, A. B. N.

LINDOP, Sir Norman, Kt 1973; MSc, CChem, FRSC; Principal, British School of Osteopathy, since 1982; *b* 9 March 1921; *s* of Thomas Cox Lindop

and May Lindop, Stockport, Cheshire; *m* 1974, Jenny C. Quass; one *s*. *Educ:* Northgate Sch., Ipswich; Queen Mary Coll., Univ. of London (BSc, MSc). Various industrial posts, 1942-46; Lectr in Chemistry, Queen Mary Coll., 1946; Asst Dir of Examinations, Civil Service Commn, 1951; Sen. Lectr in Chemistry, Kingston Coll. of Technology, 1953; Head of Dept of Chemistry and Geology, Kingston Coll. of Technology, 1957; Principal: SW Essex Technical Coll. and Sch. of Art, 1963; Hatfield Coll. of Technology, 1966; Dir, Hatfield Polytechnic, 1969-82. Chairman: Cttee of Dirs of Polytechnics, 1972-74; Council for Professions Supplementary to Medicine, 1973-81; Home Office Data Protection Cttee, 1976-78; Member: CNAA, 1974-81; US-UK Educn (Fulbright) Commn, 1971-81; SRC, 1974-78; GMC, 1979-. Chm., Hatfield Philharmonic Soc., 1970. Fellow, QMC, 1976; FCP 1980; FRSA. Hon. DEd CNAA, 1982. *Recreations:* mountain walking, music (especially opera). *Address:* The British School of Osteopathy, 1-4 Suffolk Street, SW1Y 4HG. *T:* 01-930 9254-8. *Club:* Athenæum.

LINDOP, Prof. Patricia Joyce, (Mrs G. P. R. Esdale); Professor of Radiation Biology, University of London, since 1970; *b* 21 June 1930; 2nd *c* of Elliot D. Lindop and Dorothy Jones; *m* 1957, Gerald Paton Rivett Esdale; one *s* one *d*. *Educ:* Malvern Girls' Coll.; St Bartholomew's Hospital Med. Coll.; BSc (1st cl. Hons), MB, BS, PhD; DSc London 1974; MRCP 1956; FRCP 1977. Registered GP, 1954. Research and teaching in physiology and medical radiobiology at Med. Coll. of St Bartholomew's Hosp., 1955-. Hon. Mem., RCR, 1972. UK Mem., Continuing Cttee of Pugwash Confs on Science and World Affairs (Asst Sec. Gen., 1961-71); Mem., Royal Commn on Environmental Pollution, 1974-79; Mem. Council, St Bartholomew's Hospital Med. Coll. Chm. and Trustee, Soc. for Education in the Applications of Science, 1968-; Cttee 10 of ICRU, 1972-79. Member Council: Science and Society, 1975-; Soc. for Protection of Science and Learning, 1974-; formerly Mem. Council, British Inst. of Radiology; Chairman: Univ. of London Bd of Studies in Radiation Biology, 1979-81; Interdisciplinary Special Cttee for the Environment, 1979-81. *Publications:* in field of radiation effects. *Recreation:* watching events. *Address:* 58 Wildwood Road, NW11 6UP. *T:* 01-455 5860. *Club:* Royal Society of Medicine.

LINDSAY, family name of **Earl of Crawford** and **Baron Lindsay of Birker.**

LINDSAY, 14th Earl of, *cr* 1633; **William Tucker Lindsay-Bethune;** Lord Lindsay of The Byres, 1445; Baron Parbroath, 1633; Viscount Garnock; Baron Kilbirny, Kingsburne, and Drumry, 1703; Representative Peer, 1947-59; late Major, Scots Guards; Member of Queen's Body Guard for Scotland, Royal Company of Archers; *b* 28 April 1901; *s* of 13th Earl and Ethel (*d* 1942), *d* of W. Austin Tucker, Boston, USA; assumed addtl surname of Bethune, 1939; *S* father, 1943; *m* 1925, Marjory, DStJ, *d* of late Arthur J. G. Cross and Lady Hawke; two *s* two *d*. Served War of 1939-45 (wounded); retd pay, 1947. Hon. Col, Fife and Forfar Yeomanry/Scottish Horse, 1957-62. Zone Comr for Northern Civil Defence Zone of Scotland, 1963-69. Mem., Fife CC, 1956-64. Pres., Shipwrecked Fishermen and Mariners Royal Benevolent Soc., 1966-76. DL Co. of Fife. KStJ. *Heir:* s Viscount Garnock, *qv*. *Address:* Lahill, Upper Largo, Fife KY8 6JE. *T:* Upper Largo 251. *Clubs:* Cavalry and Guards; Leander (Henley).

LINDSAY OF BIRKER, 2nd Baron, *cr* 1945; **Michael Francis Morris Lindsay;** Professor Emeritus in School of International Service, The American University, Washington, DC; *b* 24 Feb. 1909; *e s* of 1st Baron Lindsay of Birker, CBE, LLD, and Erica Violet (*née* Storr) (*d* 1962); *S* father 1952; *m* 1941, Li Hsiao-li, *d* of Col Li Wen-chi of Lishih, Shansi; one *s* two *d*. *Educ:* Gresham's Sch., Holt; Balliol Coll., Oxford. Adult education and economic research work in S Wales, 1935-37; Tutor in Economics, Yenching Univ., Peking, 1938-41; Press Attaché, British Embassy, Chungking, 1940. Served War of 1939-45, with Chinese 18th Group Army, 1942-45. Vis. Lectr at Harvard Univ., 1946-47; Lectr in Econs, University Coll., Hull, 1948-51; Sen. Fellow of the Dept of Internat. Relations, ANU, Canberra, 1951-59 (Reader in internat. Relations, 1959); Prof. of Far Eastern Studies, Amer. Univ., Washington, 1959-74, Chm. of E Asia Programme, 1959-71. Visiting Professor: Yale Univ., 1958; Ball State Univ., Indiana, 1971-72. *Publications:* Educational Problems in Communist China, 1950; The New China, three views, 1950; China and the Cold War, 1955; Is Peaceful Co-existence Possible?, 1960; The Unknown War: North China 1937-45, 1975; Kung-ch'an-chu-i Ts' o-wu ts'ai Na-li, 1976; articles in learned journals. *Recreations:* wireless, tennis. *Heir:* s Hon. James Francis Lindsay, *b* 29 Jan. 1945. *Address:* 6812 Delaware Street, Chevy Chase, Md 20815, USA. *T:* (301)-656-4245.

LINDSAY, Maj.-Gen. Courtenay Traice David, CB 1963; Director-General of Artillery, War Office, 1961-64, retired; *b* 28 Sept. 1910; *s* of late Courtenay Traice Lindsay and Charlotte Editha (*née* Wetenhall); *m* 1934, Margaret Elizabeth, *d* of late William Pease Theakston, Huntingdon; two *s*. *Educ:* Rugby Sch.; RMA Woolwich. 2nd Lt RA, 1930. Mem., Ordnance Board (Col), 1952; Dir of Munitions, British Staff (Brig.), Washington, 1959; Maj.-Gen. 1961. *Address:* Huggits Farm, Stone-in-Oxney, Tenterden, Kent. *Club:* Rye Golf.

LINDSAY, Crawford Callum Douglas; barrister; a Recorder of the Crown Court, since 1982; *b* 5 Feb. 1939; *s* of Douglas Marshall Lindsay, FRCOG and Eileen Mary Lindsay; *m* 1963, Rosemary Gough; one *s* one *d*. *Educ:* Whitgift Sch., Croydon; St John's Coll., Oxford. Called to the Bar, Lincoln's

Inn, 1961. *Address:* 6 King's Bench Walk, Temple, EC4Y 7DR. *Club:* MCC.

LINDSAY, Donald Dunrod, CBE 1972; *b* 27 Sept. 1910; *s* of Dr Colin Dunrod Lindsay, Pres. BMA 1938, and Mrs Isabel Baynton Lindsay; *m* 1936, Violet Geraldine Fox; one *s* one *d. Educ:* Clifton Coll., Bristol; Trinity Coll., Oxford. Asst Master, Manchester Gram. Sch., 1932; Asst Master, Repton Sch., 1935; temp. seconded to Bristol Univ. Dept of Education as lecturer in History, 1938; Senior History Master, Repton Sch., 1938–42; Headmaster: Portsmouth Gram. Sch., 1942–53; Malvern Coll., 1953–71. Dir, Independent Schs Information Service, 1972–77. Chm., Headmasters' Conference, 1968. Governor, Harrow Sch., 1977–82. *Publications:* A Portrait of Britain Between the Exhibitions, 1952; A Portrait of Britain, 1688–1851, 1954; A Portrait of Britain Before 1066, 1962; Authority and Challenge, Europe 1300–1600, 1975; Europe and the World, 1979; Friends for Life: a portrait of Launcelot Fleming, 1981. *Recreations:* walking, theatre, music. *Address:* 34 Belgrave Road, Seaford, East Sussex.

LINDSAY, Maj.-Gen. Edward Stewart, CB 1956; CBE 1952 (OBE 1944); DSO 1945; Assistant Master General of Ordnance, 1961–64; Deputy Controller, Ministry of Supply, 1957–61; *b* 11 July 1905; *s* of Col M. E. Lindsay, DSO, DL, Craigfoodie, Dairsie, Fife; *m* 1933, Margaret, *d* of late Gen. Sir Norman Macmullen, GCB, CMG, CIE, DSO; two *d* (one *s* decd). *Educ:* Harrow Sch.; Edinburgh Univ. (BSc). 2nd Lt, RA 1926; served War of 1939–45, NW Europe (OBE, DSO); despatches, 1946; Col 1949; Brig. 1953; Maj.-Gen. 1955; Prin. Staff Officer to High Comr, Malaya, 1954–56; retired. Comdr Legion of Merit, USA, 1947. *Address:* Hill Cottage, Eversley, Hants. *T:* Eversley 3107. *Club:* Army and Navy.

LINDSAY, Rt. Rev. Hugh; *see* Hexham and Newcastle, Bishop of, (RC).

LINDSAY, Jack, AO 1981; author, *b* Melbourne, Australia, 1900; *s* of late Norman Lindsay; *m* 1958, Meta Waterdrinker; one *s* one *d. Educ:* Queensland Univ., BA, DLitt. FRSL. Soviet Badge of Honour, 1968. *Publications:* Fauns and Ladies (Poems); Marino Faliero (Verse Drama); Hereward (Verse drama); Helen Comes of Age (Three verse plays); Passionate Neatherd (Poems); William Blake, Creative Will and the Poetic Image, an Essay; Dionysos; The Romans; The Anatomy of Spirt; Mark Antony; John Bunyan; Short History of Culture; Handbook of Freedom; Song of a Falling World; Byzantium into Europe; Life of Dickens; Meredith; The Romans were Here; Arthur and his Times; A World Ahead; Daily Life in Roman Egypt; Leisure and Pleasure in Roman Egypt; Men and Gods on the Roman Nile; Origins of Alchemy; Origins of Astrology; Cleopatra; The Clashing Rocks; Helen of Troy; The Normans; translations of Lysistrata, Women in Parliament (Aristophanes), complete works of Petronius, Love Poems of Propertius, A Homage to Sappho, Theocritos, Heronadas, Catullus, Ausonius, Latin Medieval Poets, I am a Roman; Golden Ass; Edited Metamorphosis of Aiax (Sir John Harington, 1956); Loving Mad Tom (Bedlamite Verses); Parlement of Pratlers (J. Eliot, 1593); Blake's Poetical Sketches; Into Action (Dieppe), a poem; Russian Poetry, 1917–55 (selections and translations); Memoirs of J. Priestley; Blast-Power and Ballistics; Decay and Renewal: critical essays on twentieth century writing; *novels:* Cressida' First Lover; Rome for Sale; Cæsar is Dead, Storm at Sea; Last Days with Cleopatra; Despoiling Venus; The Wanderings of Wenamen; Come Home at Last; Shadow and Flame; Adam of a New World; Sue Verney; 1649; Lost Birthright; Hannibaal Takes a Hand; Brief Light; Light in Italy; The Stormy Violence; We Shall Return; Beyond Terror; Hullo Stranger; The Barriers are Down; Time to Live; The Subtle Knot; Men of Forty-Eight; Fires in Smithfield; Betrayed Spring; Rising Tide; Moment of Choice; The Great Oak; Arthur and His Times; The Revolt of the Sons; The Way the Ball Bounces; All on the Never-Never (filmed as Live Now-Pay Later); Masks and Faces; Choice of Times; Thunder Underground; *history:* 1764; The Writing on the Wall; The Crisis in Marxism, 1981; *autobiography;* Life Rarely Tells; The Roaring Twenties; Franfrolico and After; Meetings with Poets; *art-criticism;* The Death of the Hero; Life of Turner; Cézanne; Courbet; William Morris; The Troubadours; Hogarth; William Blake; Gainsborough. *Recreation:* anthropology. *Address:* Castle Hedingham, Halstead, Essex.

LINDSAY, Sir James Harvey Kincaid Stewart, Kt 1966; President, Institute of Cultural Affairs International, Brussels, since 1982; Chairman, Henley Training Ltd, since 1980; *b* 31 May 1915; *s* of Arthur Harvey Lindsay and Doris Kincaid Lindsay; *m* Marguerite Phyllis Boudville (one *s* one *d* by previous marriage). *Educ:* Highgate Sch. Joined Metal Box Co. Ltd, 1934; joined Metal Box Co. of India Ltd, 1937; Man. Dir, 1961; Chm., 1967–69; Dir of Internat. Programmes, Admin. Staff Coll., Henley-on-Thames, 1970–79. President: Bengal Chamber of Commerce and Industry; Associated Chambers of Commerce and Industry of India, 1965. Director: Indian Oxygen Co., 1966; Westinghouse, Saxon Farmer Ltd, Hindusthan Pilkington, 1966. Pres., Calcutta Management Association, 1964; Pres., All India Management Assoc., 1964–69; Mem. of Governing Body: Indian Inst. of Management, Calcutta, 1964; Administrative Staff Coll. of India, 1965; Indian Institutes of Technology, 1966; National Council of Applied Economic Research, 1966; All-India Board of Management Studies, 1964; Indian Inst. of Foreign Trade, 1965; Member: BoT, Central Adv. Council of Industries, Direct Taxes Adv. Cttee, 1966; National Council on Vocational and Allied Trades, 1963. Trustee, Inst. of Family and Environmental Research, 1971-. Dir, Nimbus International Business Development Ltd, 1975-. FInstM 1975; CBIM (FBIM 1971). *Recreations:* music, golf, riding, table tennis. *Address:* Christmas Cottage, Lower Shiplake, near Henley-on-Thames, Oxon. *T:* Wargrave 2859.

Clubs: East India, Devonshire, Sports and Public Schools; Delhi Gymkhana (New Delhi).

LINDSAY, Hon. James Louis; *b* 16 Dec. 1906; *yr s* of 27th Earl of Crawford and Balcarres; *m* 1933, Bronwen Mary, *d* of 8th Baron Howard de Walden; three *s* one *d. Educ:* Eton; Magdalen Coll., Oxford. Served 1939–45 war, Major KRRC. Contested (C) Bristol South-East, 1950 and 1951; MP (C) N Devon, 1955–Sept. 1959. *Address:* Spring Farm, Coleman's Hatch, Hartfield, East Sussex TN7 4EL. *T:* Forest Row 2414.

LINDSAY, John Edmund Fredric, QC 1981; *b* 16 Oct. 1935; *s* of late George Fredric Lindsay and Constance Mary Lindsay (*née* Wright); *m* 1967, Patricia Anne Bolton; three *d. Educ:* Ellesmere Coll.; Sidney Sussex Coll., Cambridge (BA 1959). Fleet Air Arm, 1954–56; Sub-Lt, RNVR. Called to the Bar, Middle Temple, 1961; joined Lincoln's Inn (*ad eundem*); Junior Treasury Counsel, *bona vacantia,* 1979–81. Mem., Senate of Inns of Court and Bar, 1979–82. *Address:* 7 Stone Buildings, Lincoln's Inn, WC2.

LINDSAY, (John) Maurice, CBE 1979; TD 1946; Director, The Scottish Civic Trust, since 1967; *b* 21 July 1918; *s* of Matthew Lindsay and Eileen Frances Brock; *m* 1946, Aileen Joyce Gordon; one *s* three *d. Educ:* Glasgow Acad.; Scottish National Acad. of Music (now Royal Scottish Acad. of Music, Glasgow). Drama Critic, Scottish Daily Mail, Edinburgh, 1946–47; Music Critic, The Bulletin, Glasgow, 1946–60; Prog. Controller, 1961–62, Prodn Controller, 1962–64, and Features Exec. and Chief Interviewer, 1964–67, Border Television, Carlisle. Atlantic-Rockefeller Award, 1946. Editor: Scots Review, 1949–50; The Scottish Review, 1975–. Mem., Historic Buildings Council for Scotland, 1976–; Trustee, National Heritage Meml Fund, 1980–. Hon. DLitt Glasgow, 1982. *Publications: poetry:* The Advancing Day, 1940; Perhaps To-morrow, 1941; Predicament, 1942; No Crown for Laughter: Poems, 1943; The Enemies of Love: Poems 1941–1945, 1946; Selected Poems, 1947; Hurlygush: Poems in Scots, 1948; At the Wood's Edge, 1950; Ode for St Andrews Night and Other Poems, 1951; The Exiled Heart: Poems 1941–1956, 1957; Snow Warning and Other Poems, 1962; One Later Day and Other Poems, 1964; This Business of Living, 1969; Comings and Goings: Poems, 1971; Selected Poems 1942–1972, 1973; Walking Without an Overcoat, Poems 1972–76, 1977; Collected Poems, 1979; A Net to Catch the Winds and Other Poems, 1981; *prose:* A Pocket Guide to Scottish Culture, 1947; The Scottish Renaissance, 1949; The Lowlands of Scotland: Glasgow and the North, 1953, 3rd edn, 1979; Robert Burns: The Man, His Work, The Legend, 3rd edn, 1980; Dunoon: The Gem of the Clyde Coast, 1954; The Lowlands of Scotland: Edinburgh and the South, 1956, 3rd edn, 1979; Clyde Waters: Variations and Diversions on a Theme of Pleasure, 1958; The Burns Encyclopedia, 1959, 3rd edn, 1980; Killochan Castle, 1960; By Yon Bonnie Banks: A Gallimaufry, 1961; Environment: A Basic Human Right, 1968; Portrait of Glasgow, 1972, rev. edn, 1981; Robin Philipson, 1977; History of Scottish Literature, 1977; Lowland Scottish Villages, 1980; Francis George Scott and the Scottish Renaissance, 1980; (with Anthony F. Kersting) The Buildings of Edinburgh, 1981; *editor:* Poetry Scotland One, Two, Three, 1943, 1945, 1946; Sailing Tomorrow's Seas: An Anthology of New Poems, 1944; Modern Scottish Poetry: An Anthology of the Scottish Renaissance 1920–1945, 1946, 3rd edn, 1977; (with Fred Urquhart) No Scottish Twilight: New Scottish Stories, 1947; Selected Poems of Sir Alexander Gray, 1948; Poems, by Sir David Lyndsay, 1948; (with Hugh MacDiarmid) Poetry Scotland Four, 1949; (with Helen Cruickshank) Selected Poems of Marion Angus, 1950; John Davidson: A Selection of His Poems, 1961; (with Edwin Morgan and George Bruce) Scottish Poetry One to Six 1966–72; (with Alexander Scott and Roderick Watson) Scottish Poetry Seven to Nine, 1974, 1976, 1977; A Book of Scottish Verse, 1967; The Discovery of Scotland: Based on Accounts of Foreign Travellers from the 13th to the 18th centuries, 1964, 2nd edn 1979; The Eye is Delighted: Some Romantic Travellers in Scotland, 1970; Scotland: An Anthology, 1974; As I Remember, 1979; Scottish Comic Verse 1425–1980, 1980. *Recreations:* enjoying and adding to gramophone record collection, walking. *Address:* 7 Milton Hill, Milton, Dumbarton G82 2TS. *T:* Dumbarton 61500.

LINDSAY, John Vliet; Mayor of New York City, 1965–73 (elected as Republican-Liberal, Nov. 1965, re-elected as Liberal-Independent, Nov. 1969); *b* 24 Nov. 1921; *s* of George Nelson and Eleanor (Vliet) Lindsay; *m* 1949, Mary Harrison; one *s* three *d. Educ:* St Paul's Sch., Concord, NH; Yale Univ. BA 1944; LLB 1948. Lt US Navy, 1943–46. Admitted to: NY Bar, 1949; Fed. Bar, Southern Dist NY, 1950; US Supreme Court, 1955; DC Bar, 1957. Mem., law firm of Webster, Sheffield, NYC, 1949–55, 1957–61, 1974-. Exec. Asst to US Attorney Gen., 1955–57; Mem., 86th-89th Congresses, 17th Dist, NY, 1959–65. Hon. LLD: Williams Coll., 1968; Harvard, 1969. *Publications:* Journey into Politics, 1967; The City, 1970; The Edge, 1976. *Address:* 1 Rockefeller Plaza, New York, NY 10020, USA.

LINDSAY, Kenneth; *b* 16 Sept. 1897; *s* of George Michael Lindsay and Anne Theresa Parmiter; unmarried. *Educ:* St Olave's; Worcester Coll., Oxford. Served European War, HAC, 1916–18; Pres., Oxford Union, 1922–23; Leader, First Debating Visit to Amer. Univs. Barnett Research Fellow, Toynbee Hall, 1923–26; Councillor and Guardian, Stepney, 1923–26; Dir of Voluntary Migration Societies, Dominions Office, 1929–31; First Gen. Sec. Political and Economic Planning, 1931–35; MP (Ind. Nat.) Kilmarnock Burghs, 1933–45; MP (Ind.) Combined English Universities, 1945–50; Civil Lord of the Admiralty, 1935–37; Parliamentary Sec., Board of Education, 1937–40; Founder of Youth Service, and of CEMA (now Arts Council); Mem.

Council, National Book League; a Vice-President: Educational Interchange Council (Ex-Chm.), 1968-73; Anglo-Israel Assoc. (Dir, 1962-73); Vis. Prof. at many Amer. Univs. Vice-Pres., Feathers Clubs Assoc. Contested Oxford, Harrow and Worcester. *Publications:* Social Progress and Educational Waste; English Education; Eldorado-An Agricultural Settlement: Towards a European Parliament; European Assemblies. *Recreations:* Association Football, Oxford University, 1921-22; Corinthians; cricket, Authentics. *Address:* 48 Basildon Court, Devonshire Street, W1. *T:* 01-486 2178. *Club:* Athenæum.

LINDSAY, Maurice; *see* Lindsay, J. M.

LINDSAY, Sir Ronald Alexander, 2nd Bt *cr* 1962, of Dowhill; Manager for UK of Ocaso SA Insurance Company of Madrid, since 1980; *b* 6 Dec. 1933; *er s* of Sir Martin Lindsay of Dowhill, 1st Bt, CBE, DSO, and of Joyce Lady Lindsay, *d* of late Major Hon. Robert Lindsay, Royal Scots Greys; *S* father, 1981; *m* 1968, Nicoletta, *yr d* of Captain Edgar Storich, Italian Navy, retd, and late Mrs Storich; three *s* one *d. Educ:* Eton College; Worcester Coll., Oxford (MA). National service in Grenadier Guards (Lieut), 1952-54; insurance executive, 1958-; Lloyd's underwriter, 1962-. FCII 1963. Member of Queen's Body Guard for Scotland (Royal Company of Archers). *Heir: s* James Martin Evelyn Lindsay, *b* 11 Oct. 1968. *Address:* Courleigh, Colley Lane, Reigate, Surrey RH2 9JJ. *T:* Reigate 43290. *Club:* White's.

LINDSAY, Sir William, Kt 1963; CBE 1956; DL; *b* 22 March 1907; *er s* of late James Robertson Lindsay, Tower of Lethendy, Meikleour, Perthshire, and late Barbara Coupar, *d* of late Sir Charles Barrie; *m* 1936, Anne Diana, *d* of late Arthur Morley, OBE, KC; one *s* two *d. Educ:* Trinity Coll., Glenalmond; Christ Church, Oxford. BA 1928, MA 1931; Barrister-at-Law, Inner Temple, 1931. Dir, Royal Caledonian Schs, 1934-; Admin Officer, HM Treas., 1940-45. Member: Cuckfield UD Council, 1946-67 (Chm. 1951-54); Mid-Sussex Water Bd, 1946-60 (Chm. 1952-60); E Sussex CC, 1949- (Ald. 1957, Chm. 1961-64); Nat. Health Exec. Coun. for E Sussex, 1954-66; Hailsham Hospital Management Cttee, 1956-68; National Parks Commn, 1961-68, Countryside Commn, 1968-72; Chairman: E Grinstead Conservative Assoc., 1948-51 and 1957-59; Sussex Co. Cons. Org., 1951-53 and 1958-59; Vice-Chm., 1951-54 and 1957-60 and Hon. Treas. 1960-69 of SE Area of Nat. Union of Cons. and Unionist Assocs.; Mem. Nat. Exec. Cttee of Conservative Party, 1952-54 and 1957-69. DL West Sussex, 1970-. Dir, Mid Sussex Water Co., 1961-79. *Address:* Wickham Farm, Haywards Heath, West Sussex. *T:* Haywards Heath 371. *Club:* Bath.

LINDSAY-FYNN, Sir Basil (Mortimer), Kt 1982; FCA; Director, Ward White Group Ltd, since 1934; President, St Marylebone Conservative Association, since 1980; President and Founder, Friends of Malta GC, since 1962; *b* 22 Dec. 1901; *s* of Newenham Wight Lindsay-Fynn and Annie Cecilia Victoria (*née* Lindsay); *m* 1932, Marion Audrey Ellen Chapman; two *s* one *d. Educ:* Wesley Coll., Dublin; Trinity Coll., Dublin, 1929; London Sch. of Econs and Pol. Science, Univ. of London, 1929-31 (BCom). Chartered Accountant, 1922; FCA 1929. Sen. Partner, Smallfield Lindsay-Fynn & Co., 1929-47; Chairman: Gossard Ltd, 1934-60; Lintafoam Industries Ltd, 1946-66; Crown Estate Paving Commn, 1958-81; Dir, Associated Weavers Ltd and its successor, AW Securities Ltd, 1936-77. President: Honiton Cons. Assoc., 1969-72; Holborn & St Pancras (S) Cons. Assoc., 1970-73. *Recreations:* walking, swimming, tennis, ballroom dancing; old paintings, silver, glass, objets d'art and old furniture. *Address:* 64 Avenue Road, NW8 6HU. *T:* 01-586 1104. *Club:* Buck's.

LINDSAY-HOGG, Sir William (Lindsay), 3rd Bt *cr* 1905; *b* 12 Aug. 1930; *s* of Sir Anthony Henry Lindsay-Hogg, 2nd Bt and Frances (*née* Doble; she *d* 1969); *S* father, 1968; *m* 1961, Victoria Pares (marr. diss. 1968); one *d. Educ:* Stowe. Man. Dir, Roebuck Air Charter Ltd, 1967-70, Chm. 1970-74. Hereditary Cavaliere d'Italia. *Recreations:* riding, skiing. *Heir: uncle* Edward William Lindsay-Hogg [*b* 23 May 1910; *m* 1st, 1936, Geraldine (marr. diss. 1946), *d* of E. M. Fitzgerald; one *s* ; 2nd, 1957, Kathleen Mary, *widow* of Captain Maurice Cadell, MC and *d* of James Cooney]. *Address:* Underwoods, Edgefield, Melton Constable, Norfolk NR24 2AR. *T:* Saxthorpe 590.

LINDSAY-SMITH, Iain-Mór; Executive Editor, The Observer, since 1977; *b* 18 Sept. 1934; *s* of Edward Duncanson Lindsay-Smith and Margaret Anderson; *m* 1960, Carol Sara (*née* Paxman); one *s. Educ:* High Sch. of Glasgow. Scottish Daily Record, 1951-57; Commissioned 1st Bn Cameronians (Scottish Rifles), 1953-55; Daily Mirror, 1957-60; Foreign Editor, subseq. Features Editor, Daily Mail, 1960-71; Dep. Editor, Yorkshire Post, 1971-74; Editor, Glasgow Herald, 1974-77. *Publication:* article in Electronics and Power. *Recreations:* Highland bagpipes, foreign affairs, outdoors, travel, shooting, gardening. *Address:* c/o The Observer, 8 St Andrew's Hill, EC4V 5JA. *Clubs:* Royal Automobile, Press.

LINDSEY, 14th Earl of, *cr* 1626, **AND ABINGDON,** 9th Earl of, *cr* 1682; **Richard Henry Rupert Bertie;** Baron Norreys, of Rycote, 1572; *b* 28 June 1931; *o s* of Hon. Arthur Michael Bertie, DSO, MC (*d* 1957) and Aline Rose (*d* 1948), *er d* of George Arbuthnot-Leslie, Warthill, Co. Aberdeen, and *widow* of Hon. Charles Fox Maule Ramsay, MC; *S* cousin, 1963; *m* 1957, Norah Elizabeth Farquhar-Oliver, *yr d* of Mark Oliver, OBE, Edgerston, Jedburgh, Roxburghshire; two *s* one *d. Educ:* Ampleforth. Lieut, Royal Norfolk Regt (Supplementary Reserve of Officers), 1951-52. Underwriting Member of Lloyd's, 1958-; company director; Chm., Anglo-Ivory-Coast Soc.,

1974-77. High Steward of Abingdon, 1963-. *Heir: s* Lord Norreys, *qv. Address:* Gilmilnscroft, Sorn, Mauchline, Ayrshire; 3 Westgate Terrace, SW10. *Club:* White's.

LINDSEY, Archdeacon of; *see* Dudman, Ven. R. W.

LINDT, Auguste Rudolph, LLD; retired as Swiss Ambassador; *b* Berne, Switzerland, 5 Aug. 1905. Studied law at Universities of Geneva and Berne. Special correspondent of several European newspapers, in Manchuria, Liberia, Palestine, Jordan, the Persian Gulf, Tunisia, Roumania and Finland, 1932-40. Served in Swiss Army, 1940-45. Special delegate of International Cttee of the Red Cross at Berlin, 1945-46. Press Attache, 1946, Counsellor, 1949, Swiss Legation in London. Switzerland's Permanent Observer to the United Nations (appointed 1953) and subseq. Minister plenipotentiary (1954); appointments connected with work of the United Nations: Chairman Exec. Board of UNICEF, 1953 and 1954; President, UN Opium Conference, 1953; Head of Swiss Delegation to Conference on Statute of International Atomic Energy Agency, held in New York, 1956. United Nations High Commissioner for Refugees (elected by acclamation), Dec. 1956-60; Swiss Ambassador to USA, 1960-63; Delegate, Swiss Fed. Council for Technical Co-operation, 1963-66; Swiss Amassador to Soviet Union and Mongolia, 1966-69, on leave as International Red Cross Comr-Gen. for Nigeria-Biafra relief operation, 1968-69; Swiss Ambassador to India and Nepal, 1969-70. Adviser to Pres. of Republic of Rwanda, 1973-75. Pres., Internat. Union for Child Welfare, Geneva, 1971-77. Hon. DrUniv Geneva, 1960; Hon. Dr, Coll. of Wilmington, Ohio, 1961. *Publication:* Special Correspondent with Bandits and Generals in Manchuria, 1933. *Address:* Jolimontstrasse 2, CH-3001 Berne, Switzerland.

LINE, Maurice Bernard, MA; FRSA; FLA, FIInfSc, FBIM; Director General, British Library Lending Division, since 1974 (Deputy Director General, 1973-74); *b* 21 June 1928; *s* of Bernard Cyril and Ruth Florence Line; *m* 1954, Joyce Gilchrist; one *s* one *d. Educ:* Bedford Sch.; Exeter Coll., Oxford (MA). Library Trainee, Bodleian Library, 1950-51; Library Asst, Glasgow Univ., 1951-53; Sub-Librarian, Southampton Univ., 1954-65; Dep. Librarian, Univ. of Newcastle upon Tyne, 1965-68; Librarian, Univ. of Bath, 1968-71; Librarian, Nat. Central Library, 1971-73; Project Head, DES Nat. Libraries ADP Study, 1970-71. Prof. Associate, Sheffield Univ., 1977-. Member: Library Adv. Council for England, 1972-75; British Library Board, 1974-. Hon. LittD Heriot Watt, 1980. FBIM. *Publications:* Bibliography of Russian Literature in English Translation to 1900, 1963; The College Student and the Library, 1965; Library Surveys, 1967, 2nd edn 1982; National Libraries, 1979; Universal Availability of Publications, 1982; contribs to: Jl of Documentation; Aslib Proc.; Jl of Librarianship, etc. *Recreations:* music, walking, other people. *Address:* 10 Blackthorn Lane, Burn Bridge, Harrogate, North Yorks HG3 1NZ. *T:* Harrogate 872984.

LINES, (Walter) Moray, CBE 1969; Chairman, Lines Brothers Ltd, 1962-71 (Joint Managing Director, 1962-70); *b* 26 Jan. 1922; *er s* of late Walter Lines; *m* 1955, Fiona Margaret Denton; three *s* one *d. Educ:* Gresham Sch. Joined Board of Lines Bros Ltd, 1946; Chm., British Toy Manufacturers Assoc., 1968-70. *Address:* The Old Rectory, Shirwell, near Barnstaple, N Devon. *T:* Shirwell 265.

LINFORD, Alan C.; *see* Carr Linford.

LING, Arthur George, FRIBA; PPRTPI; architect and town planner in practice with Arthur Ling and Associates; *b* 20 Sept. 1913; *s* of George Frederick Ling and Elsie Emily (*née* Wisbey); *m* 1939, Marjorie Tall; one *s* three *d. Educ:* Christ's Hospital; University College, London (Bartlett School of Architecture). BA (Architecture), London. Architect in Office of E. Maxwell Fry and Walter Gropius, 1937-39; Structural Engineer with Corporation of City of London (Air raid shelters and War debris clearance), 1939-41; Member town planning team responsible for preparation of County of London Plan, 1943, under direction of J. H. Forshaw and Sir Patrick Abercrombie, 1941-45; Chief Planning Officer, London County Council, 1945-55; Head of Department of Town Planning, University College, London Univ., 1947-48; Sen. Lecturer in Town Planning, 1948-55; City Architect and Planning Officer, Coventry, 1955-64; Prof. and Head of Dept of Architecture and Civic Planning, Univ. of Nottingham, 1964-69, Special Prof. of Environmental Design, 1969-72. Visiting Professor: University of Santiago, Chile, 1963; Univ. of NSW, Australia, 1969; Chancellor Lectures, Univ. of Wellington, NZ, 1969. Joint Architect for Development Plan for University of Warwick. Cons. Architect Planner, Runcorn New Town Corporation. UN (Habitat) Project Manager, Physical Perspective Plan, 1981-2000, Libyan Jamahiriya, 1977-. Former Chairman, Board of Chief Officers, Midlands Housing Consortium; Past Vice-Pres., RIBA; President: RTPI, 1968-69; Commonwealth Assoc. of Planners, 1968-76. Mem., Sports Council, 1968-71; Vice-Chm., E Midlands Sports Council, 1968-76. Pres., Heckington Village Trust. RIBA Dist. in Town Planning, 1956; Silver Medallist (Essay), 1937; Hunt Bursary, 1939. Fellow University College, London, 1967. *Publications:* Contrib. to professional journals on architecture and town planning. *Address:* The Old Rectory, Howell, Sleaford, Lincolnshire.

LING, Maj.-Gen. (Retd) Fergus Alan Humphrey, CB 1968; CBE 1964; DSO 1944; DL; Vice Lord-Lieutenant of Surrey, since 1975; Defence Services Consultant, Institute for the Study of Conflict, since 1970; *b* 5 Aug. 1914; 3rd *s* of John Richardson and Mabel Ling; *m* 1940, Sheelah Phyllis Sarel; two *s* three *d. Educ:* Stowe Sch.; Royal Military Coll., Sandhurst. Comd 2nd/5th Queen's, 1944; GSO 1 (Ops), GHQ, Middle East, 1945-46; British Liaison Officer, US Infantry Centre, 1948-50; Comd Regt Depot, Queen's Royal Regt, 1951; Directing Staff, Staff Coll., Camberley, 1951-53; comd 5th Queen's, 1954-57; Asst Military Secretary, War Office, 1957-58; comd 148 North Midland Brigade (TA), 1958-61; DAG, HQ, BAOR, 1961-65; GOC: 54 (East Anglian) Division/District, 1965-67; East Anglian District, 1967-68; Eastern District, 1968-69. Col, The Queen's Regt, 1973-77 (Dep. Col, 1969-73). Chairman: Surrey T&AVR Cttee, 1973-80; SE T&AVR Assoc., 1978-79. DL Surrey, 1970. *Recreations:* homes and gardens, country pursuits. *Address:* Tigbourne Cottage, Hambledon, Surrey. *T:* Wormley 2864. *Club:* Royal Commonwealth Society.

LING, Jeffrey; HM Diplomatic Service; Counsellor (Technology), Paris, since 1982; *b* 9 Sept. 1939; *s* of Frank Cecil Ling and Mary Irene Nixon; *m* 1967, Margaret Anne Tatton; one *s. Educ:* Bristol Univ. BSc (Hons); MInstP; FBIM. FCO, 1966-69; Private Sec. to HM Ambassador, Washington, 1969-71; First Sec., Washington, 1971-73; Perm. Delegn to OECD, Paris, 1973-77; FCO, 1977-79; on secondment as Special Adviser to HH the Sultan of Brunei, 1979-82. *Recreations:* travel, old cars. *Address:* c/o Foreign and Commonwealth Office, SW1A 2AH.

LING, John de Courcy; *see* de Courcy Ling.

LINGARD, Peter Anthony, CBE 1977; TD; County Director, Suffolk, St John Ambulance Association, since 1982; *b* 29 Feb. 1916; *s* of Herbert Arthur Lingard and Kate Augusta Burdett; *m* 1946, Enid Nora Argile; two *d. Educ:* Berkhamsted Sch.; London Univ. (BCom). Served RA, 1939-46; Major, 1941 (despatches twice). Co. of London Electric Supply Gp, 1936; Area Manager Lambeth and Camberwell, County Group, 1947; Commercial Officer, S Western Sub-Area, 1948, Chief Commercial Officer, 1959-62, London Electricity Board; Commercial and Development Adviser, Electricity Council, 1962-65; Mem., Electricity Council, 1965-77; Chm., E Midlands Electricity Bd, 1972-77. Member: CEGB, 1972-75; Directing Cttee, Internat. Union of Producers and Distributors of Electrical Energy, 1973-77. Dir Gen., St John Ambulance Assoc., 1978-82. Member until 1977: Ct of Governors, Admin. Staff Coll.; Council, IEE; Council of Industrial Soc.; E Midlands Econ. Planning Council; Mem. Nottingham Univ. Ct, 1975-77. CompIEE 1967. FBIM 1973. KStJ. *Recreations:* photography, sailing, walking, reading. *Address:* The Dumble, High Street, Orford, Woodbridge, Suffolk IP12 2NW. *T:* Orford 622. *Clubs:* Army and Navy; Aldeburgh Yacht.

LINGS, Dr Martin; Keeper Emeritus of Oriental Manuscripts and Printed Books, British Library; *b* 24 Jan. 1909; *e s* of late George Herbert Lings and late Gladys Mary Lings (*née* Greenhalgh), Burnage, Lancs; *m* 1944, Lesley, 3rd *d* of late Edgar Smalley. *Educ:* Clifton Coll.; Magdalen Coll., Oxford; Sch. of Oriental and African Studies, Univ. of London. Class. Mods 1930, BA English 1932, MA 1937, Oxon; BA Arabic 1954, PhD 1959, London. Lectr in Anglo-Saxon and Middle English, Univ. of Kaunas, 1935-39; Lectr in English Lit., Univ. of Cairo, 1940-51; Asst Keeper, Dept of Oriental Printed Books and Manuscripts, British Museum, 1955-70; Deputy Keeper, 1970; Keeper, 1971; seconded to the British Library, 1973. FRAS. *Publications:* The Book of Certainty, 1952; (with A. S. Fulton) Second Supplementary Catalogue of Arabic Printed Books in the British Museum, 1959; A Moslem Saint of the Twentieth Century, 1961 (trans. French 1967, Arabic 1972); Ancient Beliefs and Modern Superstitions, 1965; Shakespeare in the Light of Sacred Art, 1966; The Elements and Other Poems, 1967; The Heralds and Other Poems, 1970; A Sufi Saint of the Twentieth Century, 1971 (trans. Urdu, 1981, Persian, 1981, Spanish, 1982); What is Sufism?, (trans. French, 1977, Italian, 1978, Spanish, 1981, German, 1982); (with Y. H. Safadi) Third Supplementary Catalogue of Arabic Printed Books in the British Library, 1976; (with Y. H. Safadi) The Qur'an, Catalogue of an Exhibition at the British Library, 1976; The Quranic Art of Calligraphy and Illumination, 1977; Muhammad, 1982 (trans. French, 1983); articles in Encycl. Britannica, Encycl. Islam, Studies in Comparative Religion, etc. *Recreations:* walking, gardening, music. *Address:* 3 French Street, Westerham, Kent. *T:* Westerham 62855.

LINKLATER, Nelson Valdemar, CBE 1974 (OBE 1967); Drama Director, Arts Council of Great Britain, 1970-77; *b* 15 Aug. 1918; *s* of Captain Arthur David Linklater and Elsie May Linklater; *m* 1944, Margaret Lilian Boissard; two *s. Educ:* Imperial Service Coll.; RADA. RNVR, 1939-46 (final rank Lieut (S)). Professional theatre as actor and business manager, 1937-39. Documentary Films Manager, Army Kinema Corp., 1946-48; Arts Council of Great Britain: Asst Regional Dir (Nottingham), 1948-52; Asst and Dep. Drama Dir (London), 1952-70. Mem., Southern Arts Gen. Council and Exec. Cttee, 1978-. Chm., CPRE, Wallingford Area Cttee, 1977-80. Member: Bd, Anvil Productions (Oxford Playhouse), 1977-; Trent Polytechnic Theatre Design Adv. Cttee, 1980-. Governor: Central Sch. of Art and Design, London, 1978-; Wyvern Arts Trust (Swindon), 1978-; Trustee, Arts Council Trust for Special Funds, 1981-. *Publication:* (contrib.) The State and the Arts, 1980. *Recreations:* painting, reading, gardening. *Address:* 1 Church Close, East Hagbourne, Oxon OX11 9LP. *T:* Didcot 813340.

LINKS, Mary, (Mrs J. G. Links); *see* Lutyens, Mary.

LINLEY, Viscount; David Albert Charles Armstrong-Jones; *b* 3 Nov. 1961; *s* and *heir* of 1st Earl of Snowdon, *qv*, and *s* of HRH the Princess

Margaret. *Educ:* Bedales; Parnham School for Craftsmen in Wood. *See under Royal Family.*

LINLITHGOW, 3rd Marquess of, *cr* 1902; **Charles William Frederick Hope,** MC 1945; TD 1973; MA; Earl of Hopetoun, 1703; Viscount Aithrie, Baron Hope, 1703; Baron Hopetoun (UK) 1809; Baron Niddry (UK), 1814; Bt (Scotland), 1698; Captain (retired), 19th (Lothians and Border Horse) Armoured Car Company, Royal Tank Corps (Territorial Army); Lord-Lieutenant of West Lothian, since 1964; Director, Eagle Star Insurance Co. Ltd; *b* 7 April 1912; *er s* of 2nd Marquess of Linlithgow, KG, KT, PC and Doreen Maud, CI 1936, Kaisar-i-Hind Medal 1st Class (*d* 1965), 2nd *d* of Rt Hon. Sir F. Milner, 7th Bt; *S* father 1952; *m* 1st, 1939, Vivien (*d* 1963), *d* of Capt. R. O. R. Kenyon-Slaney, and of Lady Mary Gilmour; one *s* one *d*; 2nd, 1965, Judith, *widow* of Esmond Baring. *Educ:* Eton; Christ Church, Oxford. Lieut, Scots Guards R of O; served War of 1939-45 (prisoner, MC). *Heir: s* Earl of Hopetoun, *qv. Address:* Hopetoun House, South Queensferry, West Lothian EH30 9SL. *T:* 031-331 1169. *Club:* White's. *See also Baron Glendevon, Countess of Pembroke.*

LINNANE, Prof. Anthony William, FAA; FRS 1980; Professor of Biochemistry, Monash University, Australia, since 1965; *b* 17 July 1930; *s* of late W. Linnane, Sydney; *m* 1956, Judith Neil (marr. diss. 1980); one *s* one *d*; *m* 1980, Daryl, *d* of A. Skurrie. *Educ:* Sydney Boys' High School; Sydney Univ. (PhD, DSc); Univ. of Wisconsin, USA. Lecturer, then Senior Lectr, Sydney Univ., 1958-62; Reader, Monash Univ., Aust., 1962. Visiting Prof., Univ. of Wisconsin, 1967-68. President: Aust. Biochemical Soc., 1974-76; Fedn of Asian and Oceanic Biochemical Socs, 1975-77. Work concerned especially with the biogenesis and genetics of mitochondria. *Publications:* Autonomy and Biogenesis of Mitochondria and Chloroplasts, 1971; many contributions to learned journals. *Address:* Department of Biochemistry, Monash University, Clayton, Victoria 3168, Australia. *T:* Melbourne 541-3721. *Clubs:* VRC; VATC; Yarra Yarra Golf.

LINNELL, Prof. Wilfred Herbert, MSc, DSc, PhD, FRSC, FPS; retired as Dean of the School of Pharmacy, University of London (1956-62); Professor of Pharmaceutical Chemistry, 1944-62; Professor Emeritus, 1962; Fellow of School of Pharmacy, University of London, 1962; *b* Sandbach, Cheshire, 1894; *s* of John Goodman and Evelyn Pring Linnell; *m* 1927, Margery, *d* of R. H. Hughes, Streetly; one *s. Educ:* Stockport Grammar Sch.; University of Durham; Lincoln Coll., Oxford; Armstrong Coll., Durham Univ., 1919-23; awarded the Earl Grey Memorial Fellowship, which was held at Lincoln Coll., Oxford; Governor, Chelsea College of Science and Technology. Research Chemist at HM Fuel Research Station, 1924-26; Examiner to the Pharmaceutical Society for Statutory Examinations since 1927; Corresp. étranger de l'Acad. Royale de Médecine de Belgique; Corresp. étranger de l'Acad. de Pharmacie de France. *Publications:* original contribs to science, published in the Journal of the Chemical Society, Journal of Society of Chemical Industry, and Journal of Pharmacy and Pharmacology. *Address:* 7 South Drive, Ruislip, Middlesex.

LINNETT, Dr Michael Joseph, OBE 1975; FRCGP; general medical practitioner, since 1957; *b* 14 July 1926; *s* of Joseph Linnett and Dora Mary (*née* Eabry); *m* 1950, Marianne Patricia, *d* of Aubrey Dibdin, CIE; two *d* (and one *s* decd). *Educ:* Wyggeston Grammar School for Boys, Leicester; St Bartholomew's Hosp. Med. Coll., London (MB BS 1949; Wix Prize Essay 1947). FRCGP 1970 (MRCGP 1957). House Physician, 1949, Demonstrator in Pharmacology, 1954, Jun. Registrar, 1955, St Bartholomew's Hosp., London; Ho. Phys., Evelina Children's Hosp., 1950; RAF Medical Br., Sqdn Ldr, 1950-54. Chm. Council, RCGP, 1976-79; Member: Cttee on Safety of Medicines, 1970-75; Medicines Commn, 1976; Med. Adv. Panel, IBA, 1979-; Governor, National Hosp. for Nervous Diseases, 1974-82. Freeman, City of London, 1980; Chm., Livery Cttee, Worshipful Soc. of Apothecaries, 1982-. Chm., Editorial Bd, Prescribers' Jl, 1973-74. FRSocMed 1958. *Publications:* chapter, People with Epilepsy—the Burden of Epilepsy, in A Textbook of Epilepsy, ed Laidlaw & Richens, 1976; contrib. BMJ (jtly) Drug Treatment of Intractable Pain, 1960. *Recreation:* music. *Address:* 82 Sloane Street, SW1X 9PA. *T:* 01-245 9333; (home) 37 Ashcombe Street, SW6 3AW. *T:* 01-736 2487.

LINSTEAD, Sir Hugh (Nicholas), Kt 1953; OBE 1937; *b* 3 Feb. 1901; *e s* of late Edward Flatman Linstead and Florence Evelyn Hester; *m* 1928, Alice Winifred Freke (*d* 1978); two *d. Educ:* City of London Sch.; Pharmaceutical Society's Sch. (Jacob Bell Scholar); Birkbeck Coll. Pharmaceutical chemist; barrister, Middle Temple, 1929. MP (C) Putney Div. of Wandsworth, 1942-64. Chm., Macarthys Pharmaceuticals Ltd, 1964-80. Secretary: Pharmaceutical Society of Great Britain, 1926-64; Central Pharmaceutical War Cttee, 1938-46; Pres., Internat. Pharmaceutical Fedn, 1953-65; Member, Medical Research Council, 1956-64; Chairman and Vice-Chairman, Joint Negotiating Cttee (Hospital Staffs), 1946-48; Member Poisons Board (Home Office), 1935-57; Chairman: Wandsworth Group Hospital Cttee, 1948-53; Parliamentary and Scientific Cttee, 1955-57; Library Cttee, House of Commons, 1963-64; Franco-British Parliamentary Relations Cttee, 1955-60. Member: Central Health Services Council (Min. of Health), 1951-66; Departmental Cttee on Homosexual Offences and Prostitution; Departmental Cttee on Experiments on Animals. Parliamentary Charity Comr for England and Wales, 1956-60. First Chm., Farriers' Registration Council, 1976-79. Comr for Training Scout Officers, Boy Scouts' Assoc., 1932-41; Hon. LLD: British Columbia, 1956; Toronto, 1963; Hon. Member American and

Canadian Pharmaceutical Assocs, British Dental Assoc. and other societies; Corresponding Member Académie de Médecine de France and Académie de Pharmacie de Paris; Mem. Court, Farriers Co. (Master 1971-72). Commandeur de la Légion d'Honneur; Officier de la Santé Publique (France); Kt Comdr Al Merito Sanitario (Spain). *Address:* 15 Somerville House, Manor Fields, SW15 3LX. *Club:* Athenæum.

LINTON, Alan Henry Spencer, MVO 1969; HM Diplomatic Service, retired; Consul-General, Detroit, USA, 1976-79; *b* Nottingham, 24 July 1919; *s of* Rt Rev. James Henry Linton, DD and Alicia Pears (*née* Aldous); *m* 1959, Kaethe Krebs; four *d. Educ:* St Lawrence, Ramsgate; Magdalen Coll., Oxford (MA). Served War, RA, 1940-46. HM Overseas Civil Service, Tanganyika, 1947-62; FO, 1963-65; First Sec. (Inf.), Vienna, 1965-69; Head of Chancery, Lusaka, Zambia, 1970-73; First Sec. (Commercial), Kingston, Jamaica, 1973-75; Dep. High Comr, Kingston, 1975-76. *Recreations:* skiing, sailing, photography. *Address:* c/o Midland Bank, 47 Ludgate Hill, EC4M 7LA. *Club:* Royal Over-Seas League.

LINTOTT, Sir Henry, KCMG 1957 (CMG 1948); *b* 23 Sept. 1908; *s of* late Henry John Lintott, RSA, and of Edith Lunn; *m* 1949, Margaret Orpen; one *s* one *d. Educ:* Edinburgh Acad.; Edinburgh Univ.; King's Coll., Cambridge. Entered Customs and Excise Dept, 1932; Board of Trade, 1935-48; Dep. Secretary-General, OEEC, 1948-56. Dep. Under-Secretary of State, Commonwealth Relations Office, 1956-63; British High Commissioner in Canada, 1963-68. *Address:* 12 Willow Walk, Cambridge CB1 1LA. *T:* Cambridge 312410.

LIPFRIEND, Alan; His Honour Judge Lipfriend; Circuit Judge since 1974; *b* 6 Oct. 1916; 2nd *s of* I. and S. Lipfriend; *m* 1948, Adèle Burke; one *s. Educ:* Central Foundation Sch., London; Queen Mary Coll., London. BSc(Eng) (Hons) 1938. Design Staff, Hawker Aircraft Ltd, 1939-48. Called to Bar, Middle Temple, 1948; Pres., Appeal Tribunal, under Wireless and Telegraphy Act, 1949, apptd 1971; Mem. Parole Bd, 1978-81. A Governor, Queen Mary Coll., Univ. of London, 1981-. *Recreations:* theatre and all sport. *Address:* 10 Woodside Avenue, N6 4SS. *T:* 01-883 4420. *Club:* Royal Automobile.

LIPKIN, Miles Henry J.; *see* Jackson-Lipkin.

LIPMAN, Vivian David, CVO 1978; DPhil; FRHistS, FSA; Director of Ancient Monuments and Historic Buildings, Department of the Environment, 1972-78; *b* 27 Feb. 1921; *s of* late Samuel N. Lipman, MBE, and Cecelia (*née* Moses); *m* 1964, Sonia Lynette Senslive; one *s. Educ:* St. Paul's Sch.; Magdalen (Classical Demy) and Nuffield Colls, Oxford (MA). Served War, 1942-45, in Royal Signals and Intelligence Corps. Entered Civil Service as Asst Principal, 1947; Principal, 1950; Asst Sec., 1963; Under-Sec., 1972; Crown Estate Paving Commissioner, 1972. Mem., Redundant Churches Fund, 1979-. Hon. Research Fellow, University Coll. London, 1971-. Vice-Pres. (Pres., 1965-67), Jewish Historical Soc. of England, 1967-; Vice-Pres., Ancient Monuments Soc., 1978-. Member Council: Architectural Heritage Fund, 1978-; Textile Conservation Centre, 1978-; SPAB, 1978-. Esher Award, SPAB, 1979. Jt Editor, Littman Library, 1981-; British Editorial Co-ordinator, America Holy Land Proj., 1981-. *Publications:* Local Government Areas, 1949; Social History of the Jews in England, 1954; A Century of Social Service, 1959; (ed) Three Centuries of Anglo-Jewish History, 1961; The Jews of Medieval Norwich, 1967; (ed with S. L. Lipman) Jewish Life in Britain 1962-77, 1981. *Recreation:* reading detective stories. *Address:* 9 Rotherwick Road, NW11 9DG. *T:* 01-458 9792. *Club:* Athenæum.

LIPMANN, Fritz (Albert), MD, PhD; Professor of Biochemistry, Rockefeller University, since 1965 (Rockefeller Institute, 1957-65); Head of Biochemical Research Laboratory, Mass. General Hospital, 1941-57; Professor of Biological Chemistry, Harvard Medical School, 1949-57; *b* Koenigsberg, Germany, 12 June 1899; *s of* Leopold Lipmann and Gertrud Lachmanski; *m* 1931, Elfreda M. Hall; one *s. Educ:* Universities of Koenigsberg, Berlin, Munich. MD Berlin, 1924; PhD Koenigsberg, Berlin, 1927. Research Asst, Kaiser Wilhelm Inst., Berlin and Heidelberg, 1927-31; Research Fellow, Rockefeller Inst. for Medical Research, New York, 1931-32; Research Assoc., Biological Inst. of Carlsberg Foundation, Copenhagen, 1932-39; Res. Assoc., Dept of Biological Chem., Cornell University Med. Sch., NY, 1939-41; Res. Fellow in Surgery, 1941-43, and Associate in Biochemistry, 1943-49, Harvard Medical Sch.; Prof. of Biological Chemistry, Mass. General Hospital, 1949-57. Carl Neuberg Medal, 1948; Mead Johnson and Co. Award, 1948. Hon. MD: Marseilles, 1947; Copenhagen, 1972; Hon. DSc: Chicago, 1953; Sorbonne, 1966; Harvard, 1967; Rockefeller, 1971; Hon. Doc. Humane Letters: Brandeis, 1959; Albert Einstein College of Medicine of Yeshiva Univ., 1964; Nobel Prize in Medicine and Physiology, 1953; National Medal of Science, 1966. Member : National Academy of Sciences, American Association for Advancement of Science, American Chemical Society, Society of Biological Chemists, Harvey Society, Biochem. Society, Society of American Microbiologists; Hon. Life Mem., NY Acad. Scis, 1977; Fellow Danish Royal Academy of Sciences; Hon. Mem., Japanese Biochemical Soc., 1977; Foreign Member Royal Society, 1962. *Publications:* Wanderings of a Biochemist, 1971; articles in German, American and English journals. *Address:* (office) The Rockefeller University, New York, NY 10021, USA; (home) 201 East 17th Street, New York, NY 10003, USA.

LIPSCOMB, Air Vice-Marshal (retired) Frederick Elvy, CB 1958; CBE 1953; *b* 2 Sept. 1902; *s of* late Arthur Bossley Lipscomb, St Albans; *m* 1931,

Dorothy May (*d* 1964), *d* of Frederick Foskett, Berkhamsted, Herts; no *c. Educ:* Aldenham Sch.; Middlesex Hospital. MRCS LRCP 1927; DTM&H (Eng.), 1933; DPH (London) 1934. Commnd RAF 1927; psa 1946. Served Aden, Malta, Palestine; War of 1939-45, Mediterranean and West Africa (despatches thrice). Director of Hygiene and Research, Air Ministry, 1950; Principal Medical Officer, Far East Air Force, 1951-54; Dep. Director General RAF Medical Services, 1954-55; Principal Medical Officer, Home Command, 1955-57. KHP 1952; QHP 1952-57. CStJ 1952. *Publications:* Tropical Diseases section, Conybeare's Textbook of Medicine, 6th to 9th edns. Contributions to British Medical Journal, RAF Quarterly, etc. *Address:* 13 Lincoln Court, Charles Street, Berkhamsted, Herts HP4 3EN.

LIPSCOMB, Prof. William Nunn; Abbott and James Lawrence Professor of Chemistry, Harvard University, since 1971; Nobel Laureate in Chemistry, 1976; *b* 9 Dec. 1919; *s of* late William Nunn Lipscomb Sr, and of Edna Patterson Porter; *m* 1944, Mary Adele Sargent; one *s* one *d. Educ:* Univ. of Kentucky (BS); California Inst. of Technology (PhD). Univ. of Minnesota, Minneapolis: Asst Prof. of Physical Chem., 1946-50; Associate Prof., 1950-54; Actg Chief, Physical Chem. Div., 1952-54; Prof. and Chief of Physical Chem. Div., 1954-59; Harvard Univ.: Prof. of Chemistry, 1959-71 (Chm., Dept of Chem., 1962-65). MA (hon.) Harvard, 1959; Hon. DSc: Kentucky, 1963; Long Island, 1977; Rutgers, 1979; Gustavus Adolphus, 1980; Marietta, 1981; Dr *hc* Munich, 1976. Member: Amer. Chemical Soc. (Chm., Minneapolis Section, 1949); Amer. Acad. of Arts and Sciences, 1959-; Nat. Acad. of Sciences, USA, 1961-; Foreign Mem., Netherlands Acad. of Arts and Sciences, 1976. *Publications:* Boron Hydrides, 1963 (New York); (with G. R. Eaton) Nuclear Magnetic Resonance Studies of Boron and Related Compounds, 1969 (New York); contribs to scientific jls concerning structure and function of enzymes and natural products in inorganic chem. and theoretical chem. *Recreations:* tennis, chamber music. *Address:* Gibbs Chemical Laboratory, Harvard University, 12 Oxford Street, Cambridge, Mass 02138, USA. *T:* 617-495-4098.

LIPSEY, David Lawrence; Political Staff, Sunday Times, since 1980; *b* 21 April 1948; *s of* Lawrence and Penelope Lipsey; *m* 1970, Elizabeth Bray (marr. diss. 1979). *Educ:* Bryanston Sch.; Magdalen Coll., Oxford (1st Cl. Hons PPE). Research Asst, General and Municipal Workers' Union, 1970-72; Political Adviser to Anthony Crosland, MP, 1972-77 (Dept of the Environment, 1974-76; FCO, 1976-77); Prime Minister's Staff, 10 Downing Street, 1977-79; Journalist, New Society, 1979-80. Secretary, Streatham Labour Party, 1970-72; Chm., Fabian Soc., 1981-82. *Publications:* Labour and Land, 1972; (ed, with Dick Leonard) The Socialist Agenda: Crosland's Legacy, 1981; Making Government Work, 1982. *Recreations:* greyhound racing, opera, cooking and washing up. *Address:* 44 Drakefield Road, SW17 8RP. *T:* 01-767 3268.

LIPSEY, Prof. Richard George, FRSC; Sir Edward Peacock Professor of Economics, Queen's University, Kingston, Ontario, since 1970; *b* 28 Aug. 1928; *s of* R. A. Lipsey and F. T. Lipsey (*née* Ledingham); *m* 1960, Diana Louise Smart; one *s* two *d. Educ:* Univ. of British Columbia (BA 1st Cl. Hons 1950); Univ. of Toronto (MA 1953); LSE (PhD 1957). Dept of Trade and Industry, British Columbia Provincial Govt, 1950-53; LSE: Asst Lectr, 1955-58; Lectr, 1958-60; Reader, 1960-61; Prof. 1961-63; Univ. of Essex: Prof. of Economics, 1963-70; Dean of School of Social Studies, 1963-67. Vis. Prof., Univ. of California at Berkeley, 1963-64; Simeon Vis. Prof., Univ. of Manchester, 1973; Irving Fisher Vis. Prof., Yale Univ., 1979-80. Economic Consultant, NEDC, 1961-63; Member of Council: SSRC, 1966-69; Royal Economic Soc., 1968-71. Pres., Canadian Economics Assoc., 1980-81. Editor, Review of Economic Studies, 1960-64. Fellow, Econometric Soc., 1972. FRSC 1980. *Publications:* An Introduction to Positive Economics, 1963, 5th edn 1979; (with P. O. Steiner) Economics, 1966, 6th edn 1981; (with G. C. Archibald) An Introduction to a Mathematical Treatment of Economics, 1967, 3rd edn 1977; The Theory of Customs Unions: a general equilibrium analysis, 1971; (with G. C. Archibald) An Introduction to Mathematical Economics, 1975; articles in learned jls on many branches of theoretical and applied economics. *Recreations:* skiing, sailing, film making. *Address:* Department of Economics, Queen's University, Kingston, Ont K7L 3N6, Canada.

LIPSON, Prof. Henry Solomon, CBE 1976; FRS 1957; Professor of Physics, University of Manchester Institute of Science and Technology, 1954-77, now Emeritus; *b* 11 March 1910; *s of* Israel Lipson and Sarah (*née* Friedland); *m* 1937, Jane Rosenthal; one *s* two *d. Educ:* Hawarden Grammar Sch.; Liverpool Univ. BSc 1930, MSc 1931, DSc 1939 (Liverpool); MA Cambridge, 1942; MSc Tech., Manchester, 1958; Oliver Lodge Scholar, Liverpool, 1933; Senior DSIR Grant, Manchester, 1936. Junior Scientific Officer, National Physical Lab., 1937; Asst in Crystallography, Cambridge, 1938; Head of Physics Dept, Manchester College of Technology, 1945; Dean, Faculty of Technology, Manchester Univ., 1975. President Manchester Literary and Philosophical Society, 1960-62, 1977-79. Visiting Professor of Physics: University of Calcutta, 1963-64; Technion, Haifa, 1969. *Publications:* The Interpretation of X-ray Diffraction Photographs (with Drs Henry and Wooster), 1951; Determination of Crystal Structures (with Dr Cochran), 1953; Fourier Transforms and X-Ray Diffraction (with Prof. Taylor), 1958; Optical Transforms: Their Preparation and Application to X-ray Diffraction Problems (with Prof. Taylor), 1964; Optical Physics (with Prof. S. G. Lipson), 1968; The Great Experiments in Physics, 1968; Interpretation of X-ray Powder Diffraction Patterns (with Dr Steeple), 1970; Crystals and X-rays (with R. M. Lee), 1970; (ed) Optical Transforms, 1972; papers in Royal Society

Proceedings, Acta Crystallographica, etc. *Recreations:* table-tennis, D-I-Y, grandchildren. *Address:* 22 Cranmer Road, Manchester M20 0AW. *T:* 061-445 4517.

LIPSTEIN, Prof. Kurt; Professor of Comparative Law, Cambridge University, 1973-76; Fellow of Clare College, Cambridge, since 1956; *b* 19 March 1909; *e s* of Alfred Lipstein, MD and Hilda (*née* Sulzbach); *m* 1944, Gwyneth Mary Herford; two *d. Educ:* Goethe Gymnasium, Frankfurt on Main; Univs of Grenoble and Berlin; Trinity Coll., Cambridge. Gerichtsreferendar 1931; PhD Cantab 1936; LLD 1977. Called to Bar, Middle Temple, 1950, Hon. Bencher, 1966. Univ. Lectr, Cambridge, 1946; Reader in Conflict of Laws, Cambridge Univ., 1962-73. Dir of Research, Internat. Assoc. Legal Science, 1954-59. Vis. Professor: Univ. of Pennsylvania, 1962; Northwestern Univ., Chicago, 1966, 1968; Paris I, 1977. Humboldt Prize, 1981. *Publications:* The Law of the EEC, 1974; joint editor and contributor: Dicey's Conflict of Laws, 6th edn, 1948—8th edn, 1967; Leske-Loewenfeld, Das Eherecht der europäischen Staaten, 1963; International Encyclopaedia of Comparative Law, vol. Private International Law, 1972; Harmonization of Private International Law by the EEC, 1978; contrib. English and foreign legal periodicals. *Address:* Clare College, Cambridge. *T:* Cambridge 358681; 7 Barton Close, Cambridge. *T:* 357048; 13 Old Square, Lincoln's Inn, WC2A 3UA. *T:* 01-404 4800.

LIPWORTH, Maurice Sydney; Joint Managing Director, Hambro Life Assurance plc, since 1980 (Director, since 1971); *b* 13 May 1931; *s* of Isidore and Rae Lipworth; *m* 1957, Rosa Liwarek; two *s. Educ:* King Edward VII Sch., Johannesburg; Univ. of the Witwatersrand, Johannesburg (BCom, LLB). Admitted Solicitor, Johannesburg, 1955; called to the South African Bar, 1956. Barrister, Johannesburg, 1956-64; Non-Exec. Dir, Liberty Life Assoc. of Africa Ltd, 1956-64; Director: private trading/financial gps, 1965-67; Abbey Life Assurance Gp, 1968-70. Mem., Monopolies and Mergers Commn, 1981-. Governor, London Contemporary Dance Trust, 1981-. *Publications:* chapters and articles on investment, taxation, legal matters, life insurance and pensions. *Recreations:* tennis, music, theatre. *Address:* 7 Old Park Lane, W1Y 3LJ. *T:* 01-499 0031.

LISBURNE, 8th Earl of, *cr* 1776; **John David Malet Vaughan;** Viscount Lisburne and Lord Vaughan, 1695; barrister-at-law; *b* 1 Sept. 1918; *o s* of 7th Earl of Lisburne; *S* father, 1965; *m* 1943, Shelagh, *er d* of late T. A. Macauley, 1266 Redpath Crescent, Montreal, Canada; three *s. Educ:* Eton; Magdalen Coll., Oxford (BA, MA). Called to Bar, Inner Temple, 1947. Captain, Welsh Guards. Director: British Home Stores Ltd; S Wales Regional Bd, Lloyds Bank Ltd, 1978-. Chm., Council of Social Service for Wales, 1976-; Mem. Exec. Cttee, AA, 1981-. *Heir: s* Viscount Vaughan, *qv. Address:* 22 York House, Kensington Church Street, W8. *T:* 01-937 3043; Cruglas, Ystrad Meurig, Dyfed. *T:* Pontrhydfendigaid 230. *Clubs:* Buck's, Pratt's.

LISLE, 7th Baron, *cr* 1758; **John Nicholas Horace Lysaght;** *s* of late Hon. Horace G. Lysaght and Alice Elizabeth, *d* of Sir John Wrixon Becher, 3rd Bt; *b* 10 Aug. 1903; *S* grandfather, 1919; *m* 1st, 1928, Vivienne Brew (who obtained a divorce, 1939; she *died* 1948); 2nd, 1939, Mary Helen Purgold, Shropshire. *Heir: nephew* Patrick James Lysaght [*b* 1 May 1931; *m* 1957, Mrs Mary Louise Shaw-Stewart; two *s* one *d*].

LISLE, Aubrey Edwin O.; *see* Orchard-Lisle.

LISSMANN, Hans Werner, FRS 1954; Reader, Department of Zoology, Cambridge, 1966-77, now Emeritus, and Director, Sub-Department of Animal Behaviour, 1969-77; Fellow of Trinity College, Cambridge, since 1955; *b* 30 April 1909; *s* of Robert and Ebba Lissmann; *m* 1949, Corinne Foster-Barham; one *s. Educ:* Kargala and Hamburg. Dr.rer.nat., Hamburg, 1932; MA, Cantab, 1947. Asst Director of Research, Dept of Zoology, Cambridge, 1947-55; Lecturer, 1955-66. *Address:* 9 Bulstrode Gardens, Cambridge. *T:* 356126.

LISTER; *see* Cunliffe-Lister, family name of Earl of Swinton.

LISTER, Sir (Charles) Percy, Kt 1947; DL; *b* 15 July 1897; 3rd *s* of late Charles Ashton Lister, CBE; *m* 1953, Mrs Geraldine Bigger (*d* 1982), Portstewart, Ulster. *Educ:* Mill Hill; RMC, Sandhurst. 18th QMO Royal Hussars. Past Chairman and Managing Director: R. A. Lister and Co. Ltd, Dursley; United Kingdom Commercial Corp., 1940-45; Past Director: Sir W. G. Armstrong Whitworth (Engineers) Ltd; Hawker Siddeley Group Ltd. Member: Capital Issues Cttee, 1946-47; Dollar Exports Councils, 1949-64; Iron and Steel Board, 1953-58. DL County of Gloucester, 1960. *Recreations:* hunting, yachting, golf. *Address:* Stinchcombe Hill House, Dursley, Glos. *TA* and *T:* Dursley 2030. *Club:* Cavalry and Guards.

LISTER, Lt-Col (Bt Col) Harry Laidman, OBE 1946; TD 1943; JP; retired; Vice Lord-Lieutenant, County of Cleveland, 1974-77; *b* 25 Oct. 1902; *s* of John James Lister, JP, and Margaret Lister; *m* 1st, 1930, Janet McLaren; two *s* ; 2nd, 1971, Elizabeth Emmeline Walmsley. *Educ:* Durham School. Coal exporter and shipbroker (AICS), 1927-58; Welfare Officer, South Durham Steel & Iron Co., 1958-69. Joined TA, 1925, 55th (Northumbrian) Medium Bde RA TA; BEF, 1940, France and Belgium with 85th (Tees) HAA Regt RA, TA (despatches 1940); comd 53 City of London HAA Regt, RA TA, 1940; served in London, 1940-41, and India, 1942-45; comd 85 (City of London) Medium Regt, RA,, 1944-45; comd 6th Cadet Bn Durham LI, 1945;

raised and comd 654 LAA Regt RA, TA, 1946; comd 427 (M) HAA Regt RA, TA, 1948; Bt Col 1952; RofO 1952; comd 18th Bn Home Guard, 1953-56, when disbanded. Mem., Hartlepool Borough Council, 1945-48; Mem. Management Cttee, Hartlepool Gp of Hosps, 1958-74; Mem. T&AFA, Co. Durham, 1947-52 and 1953-68. Freeman, City of London, 1980. DL Co. Durham, 1956; JP Co. Durham and Hartlepool, 1958. *Recreation:* Rugby football (Captain 1926-27, Pres. 1969, Hartlepool Rovers FC; played for Durham County, 1923-28). *Address:* 10 Cliff Terrace, Hartlepool, Cleveland TS24 0PU. *T:* Hartlepool 66042.

LISTER, Very Rev. John Field, MA; *b* 19 Jan. 1916; *s* of Arthur and Florence Lister. *Educ:* King's Sch., Worcester; Keble Coll., Oxford; Cuddesdon Coll., Oxford. Asst Curate, St Nicholas, Radford, Coventry, 1939-44; Asst Curate, St John Baptist, Coventry, 1944-45; Vicar of St John's, Huddersfield, 1945-54; Asst Rural Dean of Halifax, 1955-61; Archdeacon of Halifax, 1961-72; Vicar of Brighouse, 1954-72; Provost of Wakefield, 1972-82. Examng Chaplain to Bishop of Wakefield, 1972-78. Hon. Canon of Wakefield Cathedral, 1961, Canon, 1968; RD of Wakefield, 1972-80. Chaplain to the Queen, 1966-72. *Address:* 5 Larkcliff Court, The Parade, Birchington, Kent CT7 9NB.

LISTER, Laurier, OBE 1976; Theatrical Director and Manager, since 1947; Consultant Director, Yvonne Arnaud Theatre, Guildford; *b* 22 April 1907; *s* of George Daniel Lister and Susie May Kooy. *Educ:* Dulwich Coll. Trained as actor at Royal Academy of Dramatic Art, 1925-26; appeared in Noël Coward's Easy Virtue, 1926; with Bristol Repertory Company, 1926-27; three seasons with Stratford-upon-Avon Festival Company, and also toured Canada and the USA with them, 1927-29; spent a year in S Africa with Olga Lindo's Company, 1930; Death Takes a Holiday, Savoy, 1931; The Lake, Westminster and Piccadilly, 1933; visited Finland with Sir Nigel Playfair's Company, 1933; Hervey House, His Majesty's, 1934; This Desirable Residence, Criterion, 1935; Parnell, New, 1936; People of our Class, New, 1938; The Flashing Stream, Lyric, 1938; also in New York, Biltmore, 1939. Served in RAF, 1940-45. Wrote, with Dorothy Massingham, The Soldier and the Gentlewoman, Vaudeville, 1933; with Hilda Vaughan, She Too Was Young, Wyndham's and New, 1938. Organized Poetry Recitals at the Lyric, Hammersmith, and Globe, 1946-47. Devised, directed and (except for the first two) presented under his own management, the following intimate revues: Tuppence Coloured, Lyric, Hammersmith, and Globe, 1947-48; Oranges and Lemons, Lyric, Hammersmith, and Globe, 1948-49; Penny Plain, St Martin's, 1951-52; Airs on a Shoestring, Royal Court, 1953-55; Joyce Grenfell Requests the Pleasure, Fortune and St Martin's, 1954-55, later, in New York, Bijou, 1955; Fresh Airs, Comedy, 1956. Directed plays in USA, 1957 and 1958; appointed Artistic Director to Sir Laurence Olivier's Company, 1959; Dear Liar (directed and presented) and The Art of Living (directed), Criterion, 1960; J. B., Phœnix, 1961 (directed and presented); Asst to Sir Laurence Olivier at Chichester Festivals, 1962, 1963; Director and Administrator, Yvonne Arnaud Theatre, Guildford, 1964-75. *Publications:* She Too Was Young, 1938; The Apollo Anthology, 1954. *Recreations:* gardening, travelling. *Address:* c/o National Westminster Bank Ltd, 57 Aldwych, WC2.

LISTER, (Margot) Ruth (Aline); Director, Child Poverty Action Group, since 1979; *b* 3 May 1949; *d* of Dr Werner Bernard Lister and Daphne (*née* Carter). *Educ:* Univ. of Essex (BA Hons Sociology); Univ. of Sussex (MA Multi-Racial Studies). Child Poverty Action Group: Legal Res. Officer, 1971-75; Asst Dir, 1975-77; Dep. Dir, 1977-79. *Publications:* Supplementary Benefit Rights, 1974; Welfare Benefits, 1981; chapters in: Justice, Discretion and Poverty, 1975; Labour and Equality, 1980; The Economics of Prosperity, 1980; Taxation and Social Policy, 1981; Families in Britain, 1982; pamphlets and articles on poverty and social security. *Recreations:* women's movement; relaxing—with friends, music, and through walking, meditation; reading. *Address:* 20 Ambler Road, N4 2QU. *T:* 01-359 9019.

LISTER, Sir Percy; *see* Lister, Sir C. P.

LISTER, Raymond (George), MA Cantab; President, Royal Society of Miniature Painters, Sculptors and Gravers, 1970-80; Chairman, Board of Governors, Federation of British Artists, 1970-80 (Governor, 1972-80); *b* 28 March 1919; *s* of late Horace Lister and Ellen Maud Mary Lister (*née* Arnold); *m* 1947, Pamela Helen, *d* of late Frank Bishop Brutnell; one *s* one *d. Educ:* St John's Coll. Choir Sch., Cambridge; Cambridge and County High Sch. for Boys. Served apprenticeship in family firm (architectural metalworking), 1934-39; specialised war service (engrg), 1939-45; Dir of family firm, 1941-; Man. Editor, Golden Head Press, 1952-72; Dir, John P. Gray and Son, craft bookbinders, 1978-82. Hon. Senior Mem., University Coll., now Wolfson Coll., Cambridge, 1971-75, Fellow, 1975-; a Syndic, Fitzwilliam Mus., Cambridge, 1981-. Liveryman, Blacksmiths' Co., 1957, Mem. Ct of Assistants, 1980-. Associate Mem. 1946, Mem. 1948, Royal Soc. of Miniature Painters; Pres., Private Libraries Assoc., 1971-74; Vice-Pres., Architectural Metalwork Assoc., 1970-75, Pres., 1975-77. *Publications:* Decorative Wrought Ironwork in Great Britain, 1957; Decorative Cast Ironwork in Great Britain, 1960; Edward Calvert, 1962; Beulah to Byzantium, 1965; Victorian Narrative Paintings, 1966; William Blake, 1968; Hammer and Hand, 1969; Samuel Palmer and his Etchings, 1969; A Title to Phoebe, 1972; British Romantic Art, 1973; Samuel Palmer: a biography, 1974; (ed) The Letters of Samuel Palmer, 1974; Infernal Methods: a Study of William Blake's art techniques, 1975; Apollo's Bird, 1975; For Love of Leda, 1977; Great Images of British Printmaking, 1978; (jtly) Samuel Palmer: a vision recaptured, 1978; Samuel

Palmer in Palmer Country, 1980; George Richmond, 1981; Bergomask, 1982; contrib. Climbers' Club Jl, The Irish Book, Blake Studies, Blake Newsletter, Gazette des Beaux-arts, Connoisseur, Studies in Romanticism, Book Collector and TLS. *Recreations:* mountaineering in the fens, merels. *Address:* Windmill House, Linton, Cambs CB1 6NS. *T:* Cambridge 891248. *Clubs:* Athenæum, City Livery, Sette of Odd Volumes (Pres. 1960, 1982).

LISTER, Ruth; *see* Lister, M. R. A.

LISTER, Thomas Liddell; Under Secretary, Scottish Development Department, since 1977; *b* 21 May 1922; *s* of David Lister and Margaret (*née* Liddell); *m* 1949, Isobel Wylie (*née* Winton); three *d. Educ:* Allan Glens, Glasgow; Glasgow Univ. DPA. Ministry of Labour, 1939; Scottish Office, 1951; seconded Scottish Council (Development and Industry) as Secretary, Cttee of Inquiry into Scottish Economy, 1959; Regional Development Div., 1961 and 1967; Private Sec. to Minister of State, 1962; Crofting and Estate Management, Dept of Agriculture and Fisheries for Scotland, 1965; Urban Renewal, 1974; Land Use Planning, 1977-. *Recreations:* hill walking, carpentry, music, dinghy sailing. *Address:* 29 Durham Road, Edinburgh EH15 1PB. *T:* 031-669 2170.

LISTER, Tom, CBE 1978; QFSM 1977; Chief Fire Officer, West Midlands County Council, 1975-81; *b* 14 May 1924; *s* of late T. Lister and of Mrs E. Lister; *m* 1954, Linda, *d* of late T. J. and Mrs H. Dodds; one *d. Educ:* Charter House, Hull. Hull Fire Service, 1947-60; divisional officer, Lancs, 1960-62; Asst Chief Fire Officer, Warwicks, 1962-68; Chief Fire Officer, Glos, 1968-71, Bristol and Avon, 1972-75.

LISTER, Dame Unity (Viola), DBE 1972 (OBE 1958); Member of Executive, European Union of Women, since 1971 (Vice-Chairman, 1963-69); Member: European Movement, since 1970; Conservative Group for Europe, since 1970; *b* 19 June 1913; *d* of Dr A. S. Webley; *m* 1940, Samuel William Lister. *Educ:* St Helen's, Blackheath; Sorbonne Univ. of Paris. Member, London County Council, 1949-65 (Dep.-Chm., 1963-64); Chairman: Women's Nat. Advisory Cttee, 1966-69; Nat. Union of Conservative and Unionist Assocs, 1970-71 (Mem. Exec); Mem., Inner London Adv. Cttee on Appt of Magistrates, 1966-. Vice-Chm., Horniman Museums (Chm., 1967-70); Governor: Royal Marsden Hosp., 1952-; various schools and colleges. *Recreations:* languages, travel, music, gardening, theatre, museums, reading, walking. *Address:* 32 The Court Yard, Eltham, SE9 5QE. *T:* 01-850 7038. *Club:* St Stephen's.

LISTER-KAYE, Sir John (Phillip Lister), 8th Bt *cr* 1812, of Grange, Yorks; Director of the Aigas Trust, since 1979; *b* 8 May 1946; *s* of Sir John Christopher Lister Lister-Kaye, 7th Bt and Audrey Helen (*d* 1979), *d* of E. J. Carter; *S* father, 1982; *m* 1972, Sorrel Deirdre, *d* of Count Henry Noel Bentinck; one *s* two *d. Educ:* Allhallows School. Naturalist, author, farmer, lecturer. Created first field studies centre in Highlands of Scotland, 1970; Founder Director of Scottish conservation charity, the Aigas Trust, 1979. *Publications:* The White Island, 1972; Seal Cull, 1979; The Seeing Eye, 1980. *Recreations:* breeding and showing pedigree highland cattle. *Heir:* *s* John Warwick Noel Lister-Kaye, *b* 10 Dec. 1974. *Address:* Aigas House, Beauly, Inverness-shire IV4 7AD. *T:* Beauly 782443. *Club:* Caledonian.

LISTON, David Joel, OBE 1975 (MBE (mil.) 1944); Visiting Professor, Polytechnic of Central London (Pro-Rector, 1972-79); Education Adviser to British Overseas Trade Board; Visiting Fellow, The Management College, Henley, since 1972; Development Adviser (Visiting Professor), European Business School, UK, since 1981; *b* 27 March 1914; *s* of Edward Lichtenstein and Hannah Davis, Manchester; *m* Eva Carole Kauffmann; one *s* two *d. Educ:* Manchester Grammar Sch.; Wadham Coll., Oxford (Open and Philip Wright Exhibr). MA (Lit. Hum.). FSS; FRSA. Joined Metal Box Co. 1937. TA, 1938; active service, 1939-46; 2nd in comd 8 Corps Sigs (Major, MBE, despatches). Rejoined Metal Box as Head, Information and Statistics Div., 1946; Gen. Man., Plastics Group, 1955; Man. Dir, Shorko-Metal Box, 1961; seconded as Asst Dir Manchester Business Sch., 1966. Member: British Nat. Cttee on Distribution, Internat. Chamber of Commerce, 1949-55; Council, British Plastics Fedn, 1956-69; Management Trng and Develt Cttee, Central Trng Council, 1967-69; NW Regional Council, BIM, 1966-69; CNAA, Cttee for Arts and Social Studies (Vice-Chm.), 1964-71; Econ. Develt Cttees for Food Manufrg and for Chemical Industries, 1969-72; Bd of Governors, English-Speaking Union, 1973-79 (Mem. Nat. Cttee for England and Wales, 1974-80, Current Affairs Cttee, 1981-); Council, London Regional Management Centre, 1976-79; Consultative Cttees on Adult Educn for Boroughs of Camden and Westminster, 1976-; Chairman: Camden Borough Small Firms Gp, 1979- (Co-opted Mem., Employment sub-cttee, 1979-); Liberal Party Industrial Policy Panel, 1975-. Industrial Adviser to Min. of Technology, 1969-70, to DTI, 1970-72. *Publications:* (editor) Hutchinson's Practical Business Management series, 1971; The Purpose and Practice of Management, 1971; Education and Training for Overseas Trade, BOTB, 1973; Liberal Enterprise: a fresh start for British Industry, 1977; Foreign Languages for Overseas Trade (BOTB Working Party), 1979. *Recreations:* travel, walking, current affairs. *Address:* Inglewood West, Sheiling Road, Crowborough, E Sussex. *T:* Crowborough 63582. *Clubs:* National Liberal, English-Speaking Union.

LISTON, James Malcolm, CMG 1958; Chief Medical Adviser, Foreign and Commonwealth Office, Overseas Development Administration, 1970-71; *b*

1909; *m* 1935, Isobel Prentice Meiklem, Edinburgh; one *s* one *d. Educ:* Glasgow High Sch.; Glasgow Univ. MB, ChB, Glasgow, 1932; DTM & H Eng., 1939; DPH University of London, 1947; FRCP Glasgow, 1963. Medical Officer, Kenya, 1935; Director of Medical and Health Services, Sarawak, 1947-52; Deputy Director of Medical Services, Hong Kong, 1952-55; Director of Medical Services, Tanganyika, 1955-59; Permanent Secretary to Ministry of Health, Tanganyika, 1959-60; Deputy Chief Medical Officer: Colonial Office, 1960-61; Dept of Tech. Co-op., 1961-62; Chief Medical Adviser, Dept of Tech. Co-op., 1962-64; Medical Adviser, Min. of Overseas Develt, 1964-70. *Address:* Honeybrae, Nine Mile Burn, Midlothian. *T:* West Linton 253.

LISTON-FOULIS, Sir Ian P., 13th Bt, *cr* 1634; Language Teacher, Madrid, since 1966; *b* 9 Aug. 1937; *s* of Lieut-Colonel James Alistair Liston-Foulis, Royal Artillery (killed on active service, 1942), and of Mrs Kathleen de la Hogue Moran; *S cousin,* Sir Archibald Charles Liston Foulis, 1961. *Educ:* Stonyhurst Coll.; Cannington Farm Inst., Somerset (Dip. Agr.); Madrid (Dip. in Spanish). National Service, 1957-59; Argyll and Sutherland Highlanders, Cyprus, 1958 (Gen. Service Medal). Language Teacher, Estremadura and Madrid, 1959-61; Trainee, Bank of London and South America, 1962; Trainee, Bank of London and Montreal (in Nassau, 1963, Guatemala City, 1963-64, Managua, Nicaragua, 1964-65); Toronto (Sales), 1965-66. Member: Spanish Soc. of the Friends of Castles; Friends of the St James Way. Cert. from Archbishop of Santiago de Compostela for pilgrimage on foot, Somport to Santiago, Jubilee Year, 1971. *Recreations:* long-distance running, swimming, walking, mountaineering, travelling, foreign languages and customs, reading, history. *Address:* Menéndez Pelayo 13, Piso 7, Izqda, Madrid 9, Spain.

LISTOWEL, 5th Earl of, *cr* 1822; **William Francis Hare,** PC 1946; GCMG 1957; Baron Ennismore, 1800; Viscount Ennismore, 1816; Baron Hare (UK), 1869; Chairman of Committees, House of Lords, 1965-76; *b* 28 Sept. 1906; *e s* of 4th Earl and Hon. Freda Vanden-Bempde-Johnstone (*d* 1968), *y d* of 2nd Baron Derwent; *S* father, 1931; *m* 1st, 1933, Judith (marr. diss., 1945), *o d* of R. de Marffy-Mantuano, Budapest; one *d* ; 2nd, 1958, Stephanie Sandra Yvonne Wise (marr. diss., 1963), Toronto; one *d* ; 3rd, 1963, Mrs Pamela Read; two *s* one *d. Educ:* Eton; Balliol Coll., Oxford. PhD London Univ. Lieut, Intelligence Corps; Whip of Labour Party in House of Lords, 1941-44; Parliamentary Under-Secretary of State, India Office, and Deputy Leader, House of Lords, 1944-45; Postmaster-General, 1945-47; Secretary of State for India, April-Aug. 1947; for Burma, 1947-Jan. 1948; Minister of State for Colonial Affairs, 1948-50; Joint Parliamentary Secretary, Ministry of Agriculture and Fisheries, 1950-51; Member (Lab) LCC for East Lewisham, 1937-46, for Battersea North, 1952-57. Governor-General of Ghana, 1957-60. Jt Patron, British Tunisian Soc.; President: British-Cameroon Soc.; Council for Aid to African Students; Jt Pres., Anti-Slavery Soc. for Protection of Human Rights; Vice-Pres., European-Atlantic Gp. *Publications:* The Values of Life, 1931; A Critical History of Modern Æsthetics, 1933 (2nd edn, as Modern Æsthetics: an Historical Introduction, 1967). *Heir:* *s* Viscount Ennismore, *qv. Address:* 7 Constable Close, Wildwood Road, NW11. *Club:* Athenæum.

See also Baron Grantley, Hon. A. V. Hare, Earl of Iveagh.

LITCHFIELD, Jack Watson, FRCP; Consulting Physician, St Mary's Hospital, since 1972 (Physician, 1946-72 and Physician i/c Cardiac Department, 1947-72); *b* 7 May 1909; *s* of H. L. Litchfield, Ipswich; *m* 1941, Nan, *d* of A. H. Hatherly, Shanghai; two *s* one *d. Educ:* Ipswich Sch.; Oriel Coll., Oxford (Scholar); St Mary's Hospital. Theodore Williams Schol. in Physiology, 1929, in Pathology, 1931; Radcliffe Schol. in Pharmacology, 1932; BA (2nd class hons) 1930; BM, BCh 1933; University schol. at St Mary's Hospital Medical Sch., 1931; MRCP 1936; FRCP 1947. Medical Registrar: St Mary's Hospital, 1936; Brompton Hospital, 1938; Physician, King Edward Memorial Hosp., W13, 1947-69. Served in RAMC in N Africa, Italy, etc (despatches), Lt-Col i/c Medical Div. Member Assoc. of Physicians of Great Britain and Ireland. *Publications:* papers on various subjects in medical journals. *Recreations:* gardening, walking. *Address:* Elm Green, Bradfield St Clare, Bury St Edmunds, Suffolk. *T:* Cockfield Green 399.

LITCHFIELD, Captain John Shirley Sandys, OBE 1943; RN; *b* 27 Aug. 1903; *e s* of late Rear-Admiral F. S. Litchfield-Speer, CMG, DSO, and late Cecilia Sandys; *m* 1939, Margaret, *d* of late Sir Bertram Portal, KCB, DSO, and late Hon. Lady Portal; one *s* two *d. Educ:* St Aubyns, Rottingdean; RN Colleges Osborne and Dartmouth. Midshipman and Lieut in HMS Renown during Royal Cruise to India and Japan, 1921-22 and to Australia and NZ, 1927; Yangtse river gunboat, 1929-31; RN Staff Coll., 1935; comd naval armoured trains and cars, Palestine, 1936 (despatches); Staff Officer (Ops) to C-in-C Mediterranean, 1936-38; comd HMS Walker, 1939, HMS Norfolk 1943, HMS Tyne, 1946-47 and HMS Vanguard, 1951-53; Naval SO, Supreme War Council, 1939, Joint Planning Staff, 1940; SO (O) Western Approaches, 1941; Russian Convoys and N. Africa landings, 1941-43; planning staff, Normandy ops, 1944; Combined Chiefs of Staff, Washington, 1945; National War College of US, 1947-48; Dep. Director Naval Intelligence, 1949-50; idc 1951; Director of Ops, Admiralty, 1953-54; retired 1955. CC Kent, 1955-58. MP (C) Chelsea, 1959-66. Mem. Lloyd's. Liveryman, Vintner's Company. *Address:* Snowfield, Bearsted, Kent. *Clubs:* Naval and Military, Royal Navy Club of 1765 and 1785; Bearsted Cricket (Pres.).

LITCHFIELD, Dame Ruby (Beatrice), DBE 1981 (OBE 1959); Member Board, Telethon Channel 9, since 1961; Director, Festival City Broadcasters

Ltd, since 1975; Trustee, Adelaide Festival Centre, since 1971 (first woman to be appointed to these positions); *b* 5 Sept. 1912; *d* of Alfred John Skinner and Eva Hannah Skinner; *m* 1940, Kenneth Lyle Litchfield (decd); one *d. Educ:* North Adelaide Primary Sch.; Presbyterian Girls' Coll., Glen Osmond. Bd Mem., Kidney Foundn, 1968–; Chairperson: Carclew Youth Performing Arts Centre, 1972–; Families and Cultural Cttee, S Aust. Jubilee 150th Bd, 1980; Women's Cttee, Nat. Heart Foundn. First woman Mem., Bd of S Aust. Housing Trust, 1962-70; Life Member: Queen Victoria Maternity Hosp., 1972 (Mem., Vice-Pres., 1953-72); Adelaide Rep. Th., 1967 (Bd Mem., 1951-68); Spastic Paralysis Welfare Assoc. Inc. Mayoress of Prospect, 1954-57; Pres., Sports Women's Assoc., 1969-74; Mem., Divl Council, Aust. Red Cross, S Aust. Div., 1955-71; Councillor, Royal Dist Bush Nursing Soc., 1956-66; Member: S Aust. Davis Cup Cttee, 1952, 1963, 1968; Aust. Cttee of Royal Acad. of Dancing, 1961-66; Bd of Governors, Adelaide Festival of Arts, 1966–; Sponsorship Cttee, Constitutional Mus., 1979–; Sudden Infant Death Res. Foundn Inc., 1979–; numerous charitable and med. appeal cttees; Bd Mem., Crippled Children's Assoc., 1976-80. Silver Jubilee Medal, 1977. *Recreations:* theatre, radio, tennis (S Aust. Hardcourt Champion, 1932-35, interstate lawn tennis player, 1936-39); charitable work. *Address:* 33 Hallett Road, Burnside, South Australia 5066. *Club:* Royal Commonwealth Society (Adelaide).

LITHERLAND, Prof. Albert Edward, FRS 1974; FRSC 1968; University Professor, since 1979 and Professor of Physics, since 1966, University of Toronto; *b* 12 March 1928; *e s* of Albert Litherland and Ethel Clement; *m* 1956, (Elizabeth) Anne Allen; two *d. Educ:* Wallasey Grammar Sch.; Univ. of Liverpool (BSc, PhD). State Scholar to Liverpool Univ., 1946; Rutherford Memorial Scholar to Atomic Energy of Canada, Chalk River, Canada, 1953; Scientific Officer at Atomic Energy of Canada, 1955-66. Canadian Assoc. of Physicists Gold Medal for Achievement in Physics, 1971; Rutherford Medal and Prize of Inst. of Physics (London), 1974; JARI Silver Medal, Pergamon Press, 1981. Izaac Walton Killam Memorial Scholarship, 1980. *Publications:* numerous, in scientific jls. *Address:* 3 Hawthorn Gardens, Toronto, Ontario M4W 1P4, Canada. *T:* 416-923-5616.

LITHERLAND, Robert Kenneth; MP (Lab) Manchester Central, since Sept. 1979; *b* 1930; *s* of Robert Litherland and Mary (*née* Parry); *m* 1953, Edna Litherland; one *s* one *d. Educ:* North Manchester High Sch. for Boys. Formerly sales representative for printing firm. Mem., Manchester City Council (Dep. Chm., Housing Cttee; former Chm., Manchester Direct Works Cttee); Dep. Chm., Public Works Cttee, Assoc. of Municipal Authorities. *Address:* House of Commons, SW1; 72 Ashdene Road, Manchester M20 9RZ.

LITHGOW, Sir William (James), 2nd Bt of Ormsary, *cr* 1925; DL; Master Shipbuilder and Farmer; Chairman: Lithgows (Holdings) Ltd (formerly Lithgows Ltd), since 1958; Campbeltown Shipyard Ltd, since 1970; Western Ferries (Argyll) Ltd, since 1972; Landcatch Ltd, since 1981; Director, Bank of Scotland, since 1962; *b* 10 May 1934; *o s* of Colonel Sir James Lithgow, 1st Bt of Ormsary, GBE, CB, MC, TD, DL, JP, LLD, and Gwendolyn Amy, *d* of late John Robinson Harrison of Scalesceugh, Cumberland; *S* father, 1952; *m* 1964, Valerie Helen (*d* 1964) 2nd *d* of late Denis Scott, CBE, and of Mrs Laura Scott; *m* 1967, Mary Claire, *d* of Colonel F. M. Hill, CBE; two *s* one *d. Educ:* Winchester Coll. Chm., Lithgow Drydocks Ltd, 1967-78; Vice-Chm., Scott Lithgow Ltd, 1968-78; Dir, Lithgows Pty Ltd, 1972–. Member: British Cttee, Det Norske Veritas, 1966–; Board of Nat. Ports Council, 1971-78; Exec. Cttee, Scottish Council Develt and Industry, 1969; Scottish Regional Council of CBI, 1969-76; Board, Clyde Port Authority, 1969-71; West Central Scotland Plan Steering Cttee, 1970-74; General Board, Nat. Physical Lab., 1963-66; Greenock Dist Hosp. Bd, 1961-66; Scottish Milk Marketing Bd, 1979–. Hon. President Students Assoc. and Member Court, University of Strathclyde, 1964-69. CEng, FRINA; FBIM; MIES, MInstPI. Member, Queen's Body Guard for Scotland (Royal Company of Archers), 1964. Chm., Iona Cathedral Trustees Management Bd, 1979–; Mem. Council, Winston Churchill Meml Trust, 1979–. DL Renfrewshire, 1970. Hon. LLD Strathclyde, 1979. *Publications:* (jtly) Oceanspan, 1970; sundry papers. *Recreations:* country pursuits, dealing with deadwood, invention, photography. *Heir: s* James Frank Lithgow, *b* 13 June 1970. *Address:* Drums, Langbank, Renfrewshire. *T:* Langbank 606; Ormsary House, Ormsary, By Lochgilphead, Argyllshire. *T:* Ormsary 252; (office) PO Box 2, Port Glasgow, Renfrewshire PA14 5JH. *T:* Langbank 692; (office) 8 Bell Street, Kewdale, WA 6105. *Clubs:* Oriental; Western, Royal Scottish Automobile (Glasgow).

LITTLE, Prof. Alan Neville, JP; Lewisham Professor of Social Administration, University of London, Goldsmiths' College, since 1978; *b* 12 July 1934; *s* of Charles Henry and Lilian Little; *m* 1955, Dr Valerie Hopkinson; one *s* two *d. Educ:* Northgate Grammar Sch., Ipswich; London Sch. of Economics (BSc (Sociology), PhD (Econs)); Univ. of Wisconsin. Lectr, LSE, 1959-66; Consultant, OECD, 1966-68; Director: Res. and Stats, ILEA, 1968-73; Community Relations Commn, 1973-78. Dep. Chm., Educn Res. Bd, 1972-74, and Chm., Sociol. and Social Admin Cttee, 1979-82, SSRC; Member: Educnl Adv. Council, IBA; BBC Consultative Cttee on Social Effects of TV; Council Mem., NACRO. Paul Lazarsfeld Lecture, 1979; The Goldsmiths' March Educn Conf. Lecture, 1980. JP Bromley, 1966–; Chm., Juvenile Panel, 1982–. *Publications:* Development of Secondary Education: trends and implications, 1969 (trans. in French); Strategies of Compensation, 1971 (trans. in French and Japanese); Homelessness and Unemployment, 1974; Urban Deprivation, Racial Inequality and Social Policy, 1977; Multi-Ethnic

Education: the way forward, 1981; Loading the Law, 1982; various articles in academic jls. *Address:* 28 West Oak, The Avenue, Beckenham, Kent. *T:* 01-650 3322.

LITTLE, His Honour David John, QC 1963; *er s* of late Rev. Dr James Little, MP for County Down (*er s* of Francis and Helen Little, Ouley House, Glascar, Co. Down), and Jeanie Graham Hastings, *d* of Rev. Hugh Hastings and Esther Hastings (*née* Larmor); *m* 1939, Nora Eileen Thomson; two *d. Educ:* Royal Belfast Academical Instn; St Andrew's Coll., Dublin; TCD. MA, LLB. Called to Bar 1938 and Inner Bar 1963, N Ireland. Crown Prosecutor for Co. Down and Belfast. MP (U) West Down, Parlt of NI, 1959-65. Recorder of Londonderry, and Judge for the County of Londonderry, 1965-79; Judge for North Antrim Div., 1979; retd 1980. *Recreations:* golf, reading, walking. *Address:* Seaforth, Whitehead, Co. Antrim. *T:* Whitehead 3722. *Club:* Royal Co. Down.

LITTLE, Hon. Sir Douglas (Macfarlan), Kt 1973; Justice of Supreme Court of Victoria, Australia, 1959-74; *b* 23 July 1904; *s* of John Little and Agnes Little (*née* Macfarlan); *m* 1931, Ida Margaret Chapple; one *d. Educ:* State Sch.; Scotch Coll.; Ormond Coll., Univ. of Melbourne (MA, LLM). QC (Aust.) 1954. Practised profession of the law in Melbourne since admission in 1929. Served War, with RAAF, 1942-45. *Recreations:* golf, lawn bowls. *Address:* 2 Lansell Crescent, Camberwell, Melbourne, Victoria 3124, Australia. *T:* 295361. *Clubs:* Australian (Melbourne); Metropolitan Golf; Glenferrie Hill Recreation.

LITTLE, Ian Malcolm David, AFC 1943; FBA 1973; *b* 18 Dec. 1918; *s* of Brig.-Gen. M. O. Little, CB, CBE, and Iris Hermione Little (*née* Brassey); *m* 1946, Doreen Hennessey; one *s* one *d. Educ:* Eton; New Coll., Oxford (MA, DPhil). RAF Officer, 1939-46. Fellow: All Souls Coll., Oxford, 1948-50; Trinity Coll., Oxford, 1950-52; Nuffield Coll., Oxford, 1952-76, Emeritus Fellow, 1976. Dep. Dir, Economic Section, Treasury, 1953-55; Mem., MIT Centre for Internat. Studies, India, 1958-59 and 1965; Vice-Pres., OECD Develt Centre, Paris, 1965-67; Prof. of Economics of Underdeveloped Countries, Oxford Univ., 1971-76. Dir, Investing in Success Ltd, 1960-65; Bd Mem., British Airports Authority, 1969-74. Dir, Gen. Funds Investment Trust, 1974-76; Special Adviser, IBRD, 1976-78. Hon. DSc(SocSci) Edinburgh, 1976. *Publications:* A Critique of Welfare Economics, 1950; The Price of Fuel, 1953; (jtly) Concentration in British Industry, 1960; Aid to Africa, 1964; (jtly) International Aid, 1965; (jtly) Higgledy-Piggledy Growth Again, 1966; (jtly) Manual of Industrial Project Analysis in Developing Countries, 1969; (jtly) Industry and Trade in Some Developing Countries, 1970; (jtly) Project Analysis and Planning, 1974; Economic Development: theory, policy and international relations; many articles in learned jls. *Address:* Lou Poulimas, 83310 La Garde Freinet, France.

LITTLE, John Eric Russell, OBE 1961 (MBE 1943); HM Diplomatic Service, retired; *b* 29 Aug. 1913; *s* of William Little and Beatrice Little (*née* Biffen); *m* 1945, Christine Holt; one *s* one *d. Educ:* Strand Sch. Served in FO, 1930-40, and in Army, 1940-41. Transferred to Minister of State's Office, Cairo, 1941, and seconded to Treasury. Returned to FO and appointed to British Middle East Office, 1946. Transferred to FO, 1948; Consul, Milan, 1950 (acting Consul-General, 1951, 1952); Bahrain as Asst Political Agent, 1952 (acting Political Agent, 1953, 1954, 1955); 1st Secretary, Paris, 1956; Asst Finance Officer, Foreign Office, 1958; HM Consul-General: Basra, 1962-65; Salonika, 1965-70; Counsellor, British Embassy, Brussels, 1970-72. *Recreations:* walking, reading, music. *Address:* Golna, Stonestile Lane, Hastings, East Sussex.

LITTLE, John Philip Brooke B.; *see* Brooke-Little.

LITTLE, Prof. Kenneth Lindsay; Professor of African Urban Studies, Edinburgh University, 1971-78, now Emeritus; *b* 19 Sept. 1908; *e s* of late H. Muir Little, Liverpool; *m* 1st, 1939, Birte Hoeck (marr. diss.); one *s* one *d*; 2nd, 1957, Iris May Cadogan (marr. diss. 1979). *Educ:* Liverpool Coll.; Selwyn Coll., Cambridge; Trinity Coll., Cambridge (William Wyse Student). MA Cantab 1944; PhD London 1945. Lectr in Anthropology, LSE, 1946; Reader in Social Anthropology, 1950-65, Professor, 1965-71, Edinburgh Univ. Frazer Lectr, Cambridge Univ., 1965. Leverhulme Res. Fellow, 1974-76. Vis. Prof., 1949-74, at Univs of New York, California, Washington, North Western, Fisk, Ghana and Khartoum. Chm., Adv. Cttee on Race Relations Research (Home Office), 1968-70. Pres., Sociology Section, British Assoc., 1968. *Publications:* Negroes in Britain, 1948 (rev. edn, 1972); The Mende of Sierra Leone, 1951 (rev. edn, 1967); Race and Society, 1952; West African Urbanization, 1967; African Women in Towns, 1973; Urbanization as a Social Process, 1974; The Sociology of Urban Women's Image in African Literature, 1980. *Recreation:* West African drumming and dancing. *Address:* 39 Dean Path, Edinburgh EH4 3AY. *Club:* Edinburgh University Staff.

LITTLE, Dr Robert Clement; Head of Chemistry Division, Agricultural Science Service, Ministry of Agriculture, Fisheries and Food, since 1979; *b* 8 Nov. 1925; *s* of Ernest William Little and Hannah Little; *m* 1950, Margaret Isobel Wilson; two *d. Educ:* Carlisle Grammar Sch.; Manchester Univ. (BScTech); Glasgow Univ. (PhD). W of Scotland Agricultural Coll., 1946-55; Agricultural Develt and Adv. Service (formerly National Agricl Adv. Service), MAFF, 1955–. *Recreations:* golf, gardening, fell walking. *Address:* 32 Ridge Avenue, Harpenden, Herts AL5 3LT. *T:* Harpenden 5613.

LITTLE, Most Rev. Thomas Francis; see Melbourne, Archbishop of, (RC).

LITTLE, William Morison, CBE 1972; BSc; MICE, MIEE, FCIT; Deputy Chairman, Scottish Transport Group, 1969-76, Managing Director, 1969-75; *b* Leith, 12 Oct. 1909; *s* of Wm J. S. Little and May Morison; *m* 1940, Constance Herries; one *s* one *d. Educ:* Melville Coll.; Edinburgh Univ. Manager of Corporation Transport at: St Helens, 1941; Reading, 1945; Edinburgh, 1948. Subseq. Chm. of Scottish Bus Gp and subsidiary cos, 1963; part-time Mem., Nat. Bus Co., 1968-75. President: Scottish Road Transport Assoc., 1951; Municipal Passenger Transport Assoc., 1963; CIT, 1974-. Mem. Council, Public Road Transport Assoc. (formerly Public Transport Assoc.; Chm. Council, 1965-66, 1966-67). *Publications:* contribs to technical press and Inst. of Transport (Henry Spurrier Memorial Lecture, 1970). *Recreation:* being retired. *Address:* Church Cottage, Ford, Midlothian EH37 5RE.

LITTLECHILD, Prof. Stephen Charles; Professor of Commerce and Head of Department of Industrial Economics and Business Studies, University of Birmingham, since 1975; *b* 27 Aug. 1943; *s* of Sidney F. Littlechild and Joyce M. Littlechild; *m* 1974, Kate Crombie; two *s* one *d. Educ:* Wisbech Grammar Sch.; Univ. of Birmingham (BCom); Univ. of Texas (PhD). Temp. Asst Lectr in Ind. Econs, Univ. of Birmingham, 1964-65; Harkness Fellow, Stanford Univ., 1965-66; Northwestern Univ., 1966-68; Univ. of Texas at Austin, 1968-69; ATT Post-doctoral Fellow, UCLA and Northwestern Univ., 1969; Sen. Res. Lectr in Econs, Graduate Centre for Management Studies, Birmingham, 1970-72; Prof. of Applied Econs and Head of Econs, Econometrics, Statistics and Marketing Subject Gp, Aston Management Centre, 1972-75; Vis. Scholar, Dept of Econs, Univ. of California at Los Angeles, 1975; Vis. Prof., New York, Stanford and Chicago Univs, and Virginia Polytechnic, 1979-80. *Publications:* Operational Research for Managers, 1977; The Fallacy of the Mixed Economy, 1978; Elements of Telecommunications Economics, 1979; Energy Strategies for the UK, 1982; numerous articles in econs and ops res. jls. *Recreations:* football, poker. *Address:* Faculty of Commerce and Social Science, University of Birmingham, Edgbaston, Birmingham B15 2TT. *T:* 021-472 1301.

LITTLEJOHN, Alan Morrison; Director: Shiprepairers and Shipbuilders Independent Association, since 1977; Association of High Pressure Water Jetting Contractors, since 1980; Secretary General, UK Land and Hydrographic Survey Association Limited, since 1980; Chairman, Catherine Place Personnel Services Ltd, since 1981; *b* 17 Oct. 1925; *s* of Frank Littlejohn and (Ethel) Lucy (*née* Main); *m* 1955, Joy Dorothy Margaret (*née* Till); one *d. Educ:* Dame Allan's Boys' Sch., Newcastle upon Tyne; King's Coll., Durham Univ. (BScAgric); Lincoln Coll. and Agricultural Economics Res. Inst., Oxford Univ. (BLitt, DipAgEcon). Asst Agric. Economist: King's Coll., Durham Univ., 1945-47; Wye Coll., London Univ., 1950-51; Agric. Chemical Div., Shell Internat. Chemical Co., London, 1951-67; Economist, Agric. Engineers Assoc., 1968-73; Dir Gen., Clay Pipe Develt Assoc., 1973-77. Mem., Chorleywood Parish Council, 1979-. *Recreations:* current affairs, gardening, photography. *Address:* 5 The Readings, Chorleywood, Herts. *T:* Chorleywood 4420.

LITTLEJOHN, William Hunter, RSA 1973 (ARSA 1966); Head of the Drawing and Painting Department, Gray's School of Art, Aberdeen, since 1970; *b* Arbroath, 16 April 1929; *s* of late William Littlejohn and of Alice Morton King. *Educ:* Arbroath High Sch.; Dundee Coll. of Art (DA). National Service, RAF, 1951-53; taught Art at Arbroath High Sch. until 1966, then Lectr, Gray's Sch. of Art, Aberdeen. *One man exhibitions:* The Scottish Gallery, Edinburgh, 1962, 1967, 1972, 1977. Exhibits in RA, RSA, SSA, etc. *Address:* 16 Colvill Place, Arbroath, Angus, Scotland. *T:* Arbroath 74402.

LITTLEJOHN COOK, George Steveni; HM Diplomatic Service, retired; *b* 29 Oct. 1919; *s* of late William Littlejohn Cook, OBE, and Xenia Steveni, BEM; *m* 1st, 1949, Marguerite Teresa Bonnaud; one *d* ; 2nd, 1964, Thereza Nunes Campos; one *s. Educ:* Wellington Coll.; Trinity Hall, Cambridge. Served with 2nd Bn Cameronians (Scottish Rifles), 1939-46, rank of Capt.; POW Germany; Political Intelligence Dept, Foreign Office, 1945-46. Entered Foreign Service, 1946; Third Secretary, Foreign Office, 1946-47; Second Secretary, Stockholm, 1947-49; Santiago, Chile, 1949-52; First Secretary, 1950; Foreign Office, 1952-53; Charge d'Affaires, Phnom-Penh, 1953-55; Berne, 1956-58; Director of British Information Service in Brazil, 1959-64; Head of Information Depts, FO (and FCO), 1964-69; Counsellor and Consul-General, Bangkok, 1969-71. *Recreations:* painting, sailing, ski-ing. *Address:* Quinta da Madrugada, Lagos, Algarve, Portugal. *Clubs:* Brooks's, Royal Automobile.

LITTLER, Sir Emile, Kt 1974; Theatrical Impresario, Producer, Author and Company Director; *b* Ramsgate, Kent, 9 Sept. 1903; *s* of F. R. and Agnes Littler; *m* 1933, Cora Goffin (actress); two *d. Educ:* Stratford-on-Avon. Served apprenticeship working on stage of the Theatre; was Asst Manager of Theatre in Southend, 1922; subsequently worked as Asst Stage Manager, Birmingham Rep. Theatre; in US, 1927-31; became Manager and Licensee of Birmingham Rep. Theatre for Sir Barry Jackson, Sept. 1931. Personally started in Management, Sept. 1934; theatrical productions include: Victoria Regina; 1066 and All That; Once in a Lifetime; The Maid of the Mountains, 1942, new production, Palace, 1972; The Night and the Music; Claudia; The Quaker Girl; Lilac Time; Song of Norway; Annie Get Your Gun; Zip Goes a Million; Blue for a Boy; Love from Judy; Affairs of State; Book of the Month; Hot Summer Night; Signpost to Murder; Kill Two Birds; The Right Honourable Gentleman; Latin Quarter; The Impossible Years; 110 in the Shade, Student Prince; Desert Song; Annual Pantomimes in London and big cities of British Isles totalling over 200. Dir, Theatres Mutual Insurance; Chm., London Entertainments Ltd (controlling Palace Theatre); Past Pres., Soc. of West End Theatre Managers, 1964-67, 1969-70; a Governor, Royal Shakespeare Theatre, Stratford-on-Avon. Prominent play-doctor and race-horse owner. *Publications:* (jointly): Cabbages and Kings; Too Young to Marry; Love Isn't Everything; and 100 Christmas Pantomimes. *Recreations:* tennis, swimming, racing. *Address:* Palace Theatre, Shaftesbury Avenue, W1. *T:* 01-734 9691/2; The Trees, Ditchling, Sussex. *Clubs:* Royal Automobile, Clermont.

LITTLER, (James) Geoffrey, CB 1981; Deputy Secretary, HM Treasury, since 1977; *b* 18 May 1930; *s* of late James Edward Littler and Evelyn Mary Littler (*née* Taylor); *m* 1958, Shirley Marsh (see Shirley Littler); one *s. Educ:* Manchester Grammar Sch.; Corpus Christi Coll., Cambridge (MA). Asst Principal, Colonial Office, 1952-54; transf. to Treasury, 1954; Principal 1957; Asst Sec. 1966; Under-Sec. 1972. Chm., EEC Monetary Cttee Deputies, 1974-77. *Recreation:* music. *Address:* 5 Earl's Court Gardens, SW5 0TD. *T:* 01-373 2911. *Club:* Reform.

LITTLER, Mrs Shirley; Assistant Under-Secretary of State, Home Office, since 1978; *b* 8 June 1932; *d* of late Sir Percy William Marsh, CSI, CIE, and late Joan Mary Beecroft; *m* 1958, James Geoffrey Littler, *qv* ; one *s. Educ:* Headington Sch., Oxford; Girton Coll., Cambridge (MA). Assistant Principal, HM Treasury, 1953; Principal: HM Treasury, 1960; Dept of Trade and Industry, 1964; HM Treasury, 1966; Asst Secretary, National Board for Prices and Incomes, 1969; Secretary, V&G Tribunal, 1971; transf. to Home Office, 1972. *Recreation:* reading. *Address:* 5 Earl's Court Gardens, SW5 0TD. *T:* 01-373 2911.

LITTLER, William Brian, CB 1959; MSc, PhD; *b* 8 May 1908; *s* of William Littler, Tarporley, Ches; *m* 1937, Pearl Davies, Wrexham; three *d. Educ:* Grove Park, Wrexham; Manchester Univ.; BSc (1st Class), Chemistry, 1929; MSc, 1930; PhD, 1932; Beyer Fellow, 1930-31. Joined Res. Dept, Woolwich, 1933; loaned by Min. of Supply to Defence Res. Bd, Canada; Chief Supt, Cdn Armament Research and Devel. Establishment, Valcartier, Quebec, 1947-49; Supt of Propellants Research, Explosives Research and Devel. Estab., Waltham Abbey, 1949-50; in industry (Glaxo Laboratories Ltd, Ulverston), 1950-52; Dir of Ordnance Factories (Explosives), Min. of Supply, 1952-55; Principal Dir of Scientific Research (Defence), Ministry of Supply, 1955-56; Dir-Gen. of Scientific Research (Munitions), Ministry of Supply, 1956-60; Dep. Chief Scientist, Min. of Defence (Army), 1960-65; Minister, and Head of Defence R&D Staff, British Embassy, Washington, DC, 1965-69; Chemist-in-Charge, Quality Assurance Directorate (Materials), Royal Ordnance Factory, Bridgwater, 1969-72. *Publications:* Papers on Flame and Combustion in Proc. Royal Society and Jour. Chem. Soc. *Recreations:* golf, swimming. *Address:* The Old School House, Catcott, near Bridgwater, Som. *T:* Chilton Polden 722412.
See also Philip Attenborough.

LITTLETON, family name of **Baron Hatherton.**

LITTLEWOOD, Lady (Barbara); Consultant with Barlows, Solicitors, of Guildford; *b* 7 Feb. 1909; *d* of Dr Percival Langdon-Down, Teddington; *m* 1934, Sir Sydney Littlewood (*d* 1967); one *s. Educ:* Summerleigh Sch., Teddington; King's Coll., London, (BSc). Admitted solicitor, 1936. Pres. West Surrey Law Soc., 1952-53; Mem. Home Office Departmental Committees on: the Summary Trial of Minor Offences, 1954-55; Matrimonial Proceedings in Magistrates' Courts, 1958-59; Financial Limits prescribed for Maintenance Orders made in Magistrates' Courts, 1966-68. Pres., Nat. Fedn of Business and Professional Women's Clubs of Gt Brit. and N Ire., 1958-60; Pres. Internat. Fedn of Business and Professional Women, 1965-68; Lay Member, Press Council, 1968-74. JP Middx, 1950-. *Recreation:* occasional golf. *Address:* 26 St Margarets, London Road, Guildford, Surrey. *T:* Guildford 504348.

LITTLEWOOD, Rear-Adm. Charles, CB 1954; OBE 1942; retired; *b* 1 Jan. 1902; *s* of Alfred Littlewood, Croydon, Surrey; *m* 1924, Doris Helen, *d* of William Mackean, London, SW16; no *c. Educ:* Falconbury Sch. (Preparatory), Purley; RN Colls Osborne and Dartmouth. Entered RN 1915; Midshipman, Emperor of India, 1918; Lt (E) RNEC Keyham, 1924; served in Ramillies, Concord, Erebus, Admiralty Experimental Station, 1924-32; Engineer Officer; HMS Ardent, 1932-34; HMS Apollo, 1934-36; Comdr (E) 1936; Flotilla Eng. Officer, HMS Kempenfelt, 1936-38; Manager Engineering Dept, Malta Dockyard, 1938-44; Actg Captain (E) 1942; Captain (E) 1945; Eng. Officer in HMS Howe, Brit. Pacific Fleet, served at Okinawa Operation, 1944-46; Asst Engineer in Chief, 1946-49; Manager Engineering Dept, Rosyth Dockyard, 1949-52; Rear-Admiral, 1952; Asst Dir of Dockyards, 1952-55, retd 1955. *Address:* Saddlers Mead, Sid Road, Sidmouth, Devon. *T:* Sidmouth 5482.

LITTLEWOOD, James, CB 1973; Director, Department for National Savings, 1972-81 (Deputy Secretary); *b* Royton, Lancashire, 21 Oct. 1922; *s* of late Thomas and Sarah Littlewood; *m* 1950, Barbara Shaw; two *s* one *d. Educ:* Manchester Grammar Sch.; St John's Coll., Cambridge (Scholar, MA). Army (Captain), 1942-46. HM Treasury, 1947-67; Civil Service Selection Bd,

1951-52; Sec. to Cttee on Administrative Tribunals and Enquiries, 1955-57; Colombo Plan Conf. Secretariat, 1955 and 1959; Dept for Nat. Savings, 1967-81. *Recreations:* golf, bridge. *Address:* 35 Ridings Avenue, N21 2EL. *Club:* United Oxford & Cambridge University.

LITTLEWOOD, Joan (Maud); theatre artist. *Educ:* London. Dir, Theatre of Action, Manchester (street theatre), 1931-37; founder, Theatre Union, Manchester, introducing individual work system, 1937-39; freelance writer, 1939-45 (banned from BBC and ENSA for political opinions); founded Theatre Workshop with Gerry Raffles, 1945; touring in GB, Germany, Norway, Sweden with original works, 1945-53; moved to Theatre Royal, Stratford, London, with classics, 1953; invited to Theatre of the Nations, Paris, 1955, then yearly (Best Production of the Year three times); Centre Culturel, Hammamet, Tunisia, 1965-67; Image India, Calcutta, 1968; creation of Children's Environments, Bubble Cities linked with Music Hall, around Theatre Royal, Stratford, 1968-75. Left England to work in France, 1975; Seminar Relais Culturel, Aix-en-Provence, 1976. Productions include: Lysistrata, 1958 (Gold Medal, East Berlin, 1958; Olympic Award, Taormina, 1959), transferred to London and Broadway from Stratford, 1960-61; Sparrers Can't Sing (film), 1962; O What a Lovely War (with Gerry Raffles and the Company), 1963. Mem., French Academy of Writers, 1964. Dr *hc,* Univ. of the Air, 1977. *Recreation:* theatre. *Address:* 1 Place Louis Revol, 38200 Vienne, France.

LITTMAN, Mark; QC 1961; resumed practice at Bar, Oct. 1979; Director: Rio Tinto-Zinc Corporation Ltd, since 1968; Amerada Hess Corp. (US), since 1973; Granada Group, since 1977; *b* 4 Sept. 1920; *s* of Jack and Lilian Littman; *m* 1965, Marguerite Lamkin, USA. *Educ:* Owen's Sch.; London Sch. of Economics; The Queen's Coll., Oxford. BScEcon. (first class hons) 1939; MA Oxon 1941. Served RN, Lieut, 1941-46. Called to Bar, Middle Temple, 1947, Bencher, 1970; practised, as Barrister-at-law, 1947-67; Member: General Council of the Bar, 1968-72; Senate of Inns of Court and the Bar, 1968-. Dep. Chm., BSC, 1970-79. Mem. Royal Commn on Legal Services, 1976-79. Director: Commercial Union Assurance Co. Ltd, 1970-81; British Enkalon Ltd, 1976-80; Envirotech Corp. (US), 1974-78. Mem., Ct of Governors, LSE. *Address:* 79 Chester Square, SW1. *Clubs:* Garrick, Reform; Century Association (New York).

LITTON, Peter Stafford; Under Secretary, Department of Education and Science, 1978-81; *b* 26 Oct. 1921; *s* of late Leonard Litton and Louisa (*née* Horn); *m* 1942, Josephine Peggy Bale; one *d. Educ:* Barnstaple Grammar School. Clerical Officer, Board of Education, 1938. Served in Royal Corps of Signals, 1941-46. Min. of Education, 1946; Jt Sec., Commonwealth Conf. on Teaching of Science in Schools, Univ. of Ceylon, 1963; Mem., British Delegn, Commonwealth Educn Conf., Ottawa, 1964; Principal Private Sec. to Secretary of State for Educn and Science, 1965-66. *Recreations:* gardening, armchair astronomy. *Address:* 61 Kingswood Road, Tadworth, Surrey KT20 5EF. *T:* Tadworth 2366.

LIU, Benjamin Tsz-Ming; Hon. Mr Justice Liu; a Judge of the High Court of the State of Brunei, since 1978, and of Hong Kong, since 1980; *b* 17 May 1931; *s* of Dr Y. T. Liu and Dorothy Liu; *m* 1954, Annemarie Marent; one *s* one *d. Educ:* Wah Yan College. Called to the Bar, Lincoln's Inn, 1957; QC (Hong Kong) 1973; District Judge, Hong Kong, 1973. *Address:* Supreme Court, Hong Kong. *T:* 5-238986. *Clubs:* Hong Kong, Chinese, Hong Kong Country (all in Hong Kong).

LIVELY, Penelope Margaret; writer; *b* 17 March 1933; *d* of Roger Low and Vera Greer; *m* 1957, Jack Lively; one *s* one *d. Educ:* St Anne's Coll., Oxford (BA Mod. History). *Publications:* Astercote, 1970; The Whispering Knights, 1971; The Wild Hunt of Hagworthy, 1971; The Driftway, 1972; The Ghost of Thomas Kempe, 1973 (Carnegie Medal); The House in Norham Gardens, 1974; Going Back, 1975; Boy Without a Name, 1975; A Stitch in Time, 1976 (Whitbread Award); The Stained Glass Window, 1976; Fanny's Sister, 1976; The Presence of the Past, 1976; The Road to Lichfield, 1977 (Short listed, Booker Prize); The Voyage of QV66, 1978; Nothing Missing but the Samovar and other stories, 1978 (Southern Arts Literature Prize); Treasures of Time, 1979 (National Book Award); Fanny and the Monsters, 1979; Judgement Day, 1980; Fanny and the Battle of Potter's Piece, 1980; The Revenge of Samuel Stokes, 1981; Next to Nature, Art, 1982; television and radio scripts. *Recreations:* gardening, landscape history, talking and listening. *Address:* Duck End, Great Rollright, Chipping Norton, Oxfordshire OX7 5SB. *T:* Hook Norton 737565.

LIVERMAN, John Gordon, CB 1973; OBE 1956; Consultant to Britoil, Danish Oil and National Gas Corporation; Member, Panel of Chairmen, Civil Service Selection Board; Specialist Adviser to Sub-Committee F (Energy, Transport, Technology and Research) of European Communities Committee of House of Lords; *b* London, 21 Oct. 1920; *s* of late George Gordon Liverman and of Hadassah Liverman. *Educ:* St Paul's Sch.; Trinity Coll., Cambridge (BA). Served with RA, 1940-46. Civil servant in various government departments, 1947-80; Dep. Sec., Dept of Energy, 1974-80. Mem., British Nat. Oil Corp., 1976-80. *Address:* 7 Martin Way, St John's, Woking, Surrey. *Club:* Royal Commonwealth Society.

LIVERMORE, Sir Harry, Kt 1973; Lord Mayor of Liverpool, 1958-59; *b* 17 Oct. 1908; *m* 1940, Esther Angelman; one *s* one *d. Educ:* Royal Grammar Sch., Newcastle upon Tyne; Durham Univ. Solicitor; qualified, 1930; practises

in Liverpool. Chm., Venture Housing Assoc. Ltd. Vice-President: Royal Liverpool Philharmonic Soc.; Liverpool Everyman Theatre, Ltd; Chm., Royal Court Theatre and Arts Trust Ltd. *Recreations:* music, theatre, swimming. *Address:* 18 Burnham Road, Liverpool L18 6JU.

LIVERPOOL, 5th Earl of, *cr* 1905 (2nd creation); **Edward Peter Bertram Savile Foljambe;** Baron Hawkesbury, 1893; Viscount Hawkesbury, 1905; Joint Chairman and Managing Director, Melbourns Brewery Ltd, since 1975; *b* posthumously, 14 Nov. 1944; *s* of Captain Peter George William Savile Foljambe (killed in action, 1944) and of Elizabeth Joan (who *m* 1947, Major Andrew Antony Gibbs, MBE, TD), *d* of late Major Eric Charles Montagu Flint, DSO; *S* great uncle, 1969; *m* 1970, Lady Juliana Noel, *e d* of Earl of Gainsborough, *qv* ; two *s. Educ:* Shrewsbury School; Univ. for Foreigners, Perugia. Director: Ellangee Holdings Ltd, 1973-; East Midlands Leisure Ltd, 1980-. *Heir: s* Viscount Hawkesbury, *qv. Address:* The Grange Farm, Exton, near Oakham, Leics; Flat 4, 27 Holland Park Avenue, W11. *Clubs:* Turf, Pratt's.

LIVERPOOL, Archbishop of, (RC), and Metropolitan of Northern Province with Suffragan Sees, Hallam, Hexham, Lancaster, Leeds, Middlesbrough and Salford, since 1976; **Most Rev. Derek John Harford Worlock;** *b* 4 Feb. 1920; 2nd *s* of Captain Harford Worlock and Dora (*née* Hoblyn). *Educ:* St Edmund's Coll., Ware, Herts. Ordained RC Priest, 1944. Curate, Our Lady of Victories, Kensington, 1944-45; Private Secretary to Archbishop of Westminster, 1945-64; Rector and Rural Dean, Church of SS Mary and Michael, London, E1, 1964-65; Bishop of Portsmouth, 1965-76. Privy Chamberlain to Pope Pius XII, 1949-53; Domestic Prelate of the Pope, 1953-65; Peritus at Vatican Council II, 1963-65; Consultor to Council of Laity, 1967-76; Episcopal Secretary to RC Bishops' Conference, 1967-76, Vice-Pres., 1979-. Member: Synod Council, 1976-77; Holy See's Laity Council, 1977- (formerly Mem., Cttee for the Family); English delegate to Internat. Synod of Bishops, 1974, 1977 and 1980. Chm., Nat. Pastoral Congress, 1980. Hon. LLD Liverpool, 1981. Knight Commander of Holy Sepulchre of Jerusalem, 1966. *Publications:* Seek Ye First (compiler), 1949; Take One at Bedtime (anthology), 1962; English Bishops at the Council, 1965; Turn and Turn Again, 1971; Give Me Your Hand, 1977. *Address:* Archbishop's House, 87 Green Lane, Liverpool L18 2EP. *T:* 051-722 2379.

LIVERPOOL, Bishop of, since 1975; **Rt. Rev. David Stuart Sheppard;** *b* 6 March 1929; *s* of Stuart Morton Winter Sheppard, Solicitor, and Barbara Sheppard; *m* 1957, Grace Isaac; one *d. Educ:* Sherborne; Trinity Hall, Cambridge (MA); Ridley Hall Theological Coll. Asst Curate, St Mary's, Islington, 1955-57; Warden, Mayflower Family Centre, Canning Town, E16, 1957-69; Bishop Suffragan of Woolwich, 1969-75. Cricket: Cambridge Univ., 1950-52 (Captain 1952); Sussex, 1947-62 (Captain 1953); England (played 22 times) 1950-63 (Captain 1954). Hon. LLD Liverpool, 1981. *Publications:* Parson's Pitch, 1964; Built as a City, 1974; Bias to the Poor, 1983. *Recreations:* family, reading, music, painting, theatre. *Address:* Bishop's Lodge, Woolton Park, Woolton, Liverpool L25 6DT.

LIVERPOOL, Auxiliary Bishops of, (RC); *see* Hitchen, Rt Rev. Anthony; O'Connor, Rt Rev. Kevin; Rawsthorne, Rt Rev. John.

LIVERPOOL, Dean of; *see* Walters, Very Rev. R. D. C.

LIVERPOOL, Archdeacon of; *see* Spiers, Ven. G. H. G.

LIVESEY, Ronald John Dearden, QC 1981; a Recorder of the Crown Court, since 1981; *b* 11 Sept. 1935; *s* of John William and Una Florence Livesey; *m* 1965, Elizabeth Jane Coutts; one *s* one *d. Educ:* Malvern Coll.; Lincoln Coll., Oxford (BA). Called to the Bar, Lincoln's Inn, 1962. *Recreation:* golf. *Address:* 46A Grosvenor Road, Birkdale, Southport L68 2ET. *T:* Southport 60561. *Clubs:* Athenæum (Liverpool); Union (Southport).

LIVINGS, Henry; *b* 20 Sept. 1929; *m* 1957, Judith Francis Carter; one *s* one *d. Educ:* Park View Primary Sch.; Stand Grammar Sch.; Liverpool Univ. Served in RAF. Joined Puritex, Leicester. Theatre Royal Leicester, then many Repertories; Theatre Workshop, 1956. 1st TV play, 1961; 1st stage play, 1961. *Publications:* contribs to Penguin New English Dramatists 5 and 6; Kelly's Eye and Other Plays, 1964; Eh?, 1965; Good Grief!, 1968; The Little Mrs Foster Show, 1969; Honour and Offer, 1969; Pongo Plays 1-6, 1971; This Jockey Drives Late Nights, 1972; The Ffinest Ffamily in the Land, 1973; Jonah, 1974; Six More Pongo Plays, 1975; That the Medals and the Baton be Put on View, 1975; Cinderella, 1976. *Recreations:* darts, dominoes, chess, clay pigeon shooting. *Address:* 33 Woods Lane, Dobcross, Oldham, Lancs. *T:* Saddleworth 2965. *Club:* Dobcross Band.

LIVINGSTON, James Barrett, CBE 1972; DSC 1942; formerly Consultant, Rockware Group Ltd (Director, retired 1970), Director, Rockware Glass Ltd, 1947-72 (Joint Managing Director, 1951-60; Managing Director, 1960-69; Vice-Chairman, 1967-69); *b* 13 Sept. 1906; *yr s* of late Capt. David Liddle Livingston and Ruth Livingston, Bombay and Aberdour; *m* 1933, Joyce Eileen, *fourth d* of late Arthur and Lilian Birkett, Clements Inn and Southwold; one *s* one *d. Educ:* HMS Worcester. Served War of 1939-45, RN: Staff Officer (Ops) 10th Cruiser Sqdn, Norwegian Campaign, North Russian and Malta Convoys (despatches 1943); Ops Div. Admiralty, 1943-45 (Comdr). Joined Rockware Group of Cos, 1945; Exec. Director, British

Hartford-Fairmont Ltd, 1947-50. Director: Portland Glass Co. Ltd, 1956-69; Jackson Bros (Knottingley) Ltd, 1968-69 (Chm.); Burwell, Reed & Kinghorn Ltd, 1962-71; Blewis & Shaw (Plastics) Ltd, 1960-70; Automotated Inspection Machinery Ltd, 1962-69; Garston Bottle Co. Ltd, 1966-69 (Chm.); Forsters Glass Co. Ltd, 1967-69; also other Glass and Associated Companies. Member: Bd of Govs, Charing Cross Hospital, 1956-73 (Chm., Medical School Council, 1967-73); Council, Glass Manufacturers' Fedn 1967 (Pres. 1970-71); Nat. Cttee, Assoc. of Glass Container Manufacturers, 1959-69 (Vice-Pres.); Nat. Jt Industrial Council 1959-69; Court of Ironmongers' Co., 1946 (Master, 1960-61); Adv. Cttee to Faculty of Materials Technology, Sheffield University, 1969-71; Council CBI, 1970-71; Furniture Develt Council, 1972-; Council, Royal College of Art, 1970-71. *Recreations:* golf, racket re-strings, gardening. *Address:* (home) Ferroners, Beaconsfield, Bucks. *T:* Beaconsfield 3853.

LIVINGSTON BOOTH, John Dick, OBE 1976; charity consultant, since 1981; President, International Standing Conference on Philanthropy, since 1975; Member of Lloyd's, since 1979; *b* 7 July 1918; *o s* of late Julian Livingston Booth and late Grace Marion (*née* Swainson); *m* 1st, 1941, Joan Ashley Tabrum (*d* 1976), *d* of Ashley Tabrum, OBE, LLM, MA; two *s* one *d* ; 2nd, 1979, Audrey Betty Hope Harvey, PhD, AcDipEd, DipHEd, DipSoc, SRN, *d* of Sqdn Leader John James Haslett, RAF. *Educ:* Melbourne Church of England Grammar Sch.; Sidney Sussex Coll., Cambridge (MA). Served War, 1940-43; T/Captain RA; RWAFF; Instructor, 121 HAC OCTU RHA. Nigerian Administrative Service, 1943-57; Perm. Sec., Min. of Local Govt, Eastern Nigeria, 1956-57; Dir, Charities Aid Foundn, 1957-81. Chm., Legislation Monitoring Service for Charities, 1981-; Member: Exec. Cttee, Nat. Council for Voluntary Organisations, 1974-81; Exec. Cttee, Christian Orgs Research and Adv. Trust, 1975-; Develt and Stewardship Cttee, Central Bd of Finance, 1977-80. FRGS. Lay Reader, Church of England, 1955-. *Publications:* Directory of Grant-Making Trusts, 1968, 7th edn 1981; Trusts and Foundations in Europe, 1971; Report on Foundation Activity, 1977; Charity Statistics (annual), 1978-81; articles and booklets on charity. *Recreations:* home-making, travel, philately. *Address:* Cedar House, Yalding, Maidstone, Kent ME18 6JD. *T:* Hunton 431. *Clubs:* Garrick, Royal Commonwealth Society.

LIVINGSTONE, James, CMG 1968; OBE 1951; *b* 4 April 1912; *e s* of late Angus Cook Livingstone, sometime Provost of Bo'ness, Scotland, and Mrs Jean Fraser Aitken Wilson Livingstone; *m* 1945, Dr Mair Eleri Morgan Thomas, MB, ChB, BSc, DPH, FRCPath, *e d* of late John Thomas, DSc, Harlech and Mrs O. M. Thomas, Llanddewi Brefi and Wilmslow; one *d* (one *s* decd). *Educ:* Bo'ness Acad.; Edinburgh Univ.; Moray House Trng Coll., Edinburgh. Adult Educn and School Posts, Scotland and Egypt, 1936-42; British Coun. Service, Egypt and Iran, 1942-45; Middle East Dept, 1945-46; Asst Rep., Palestine, 1946-48; Dep. Dir, Personnel Dept, 1949; Dir, Personnel Dept, 1956; Controller, Establishments Div., 1962; Controller, Overseas A Div. (Middle East and Africa), 1969-72, retired. *Recreations:* photography, exploring the West Highlands and Islands. *Address:* 21 Park Avenue, NW11 7SL. *T:* 01-455 7600; Tan-yr-allt, Llangeitho, Dyfed. *Clubs:* Royal Commonwealth Society, Travellers'.

LIVINGSTONE, James Livingstone, MD, FRCP; Retired; Consulting Physician: King's College Hospital; Brompton Hospital; St Dunstan's; *b* 8 May 1900; *m* 1935, Janet Muriel Rocke; two *s* one *d*. *Educ:* Worksop Coll., Notts; King's Coll., University of London; King's Coll. Hospital. MRCS, LRCP, 1922; MB, BS 1923; MRCP 1925; MD London 1925; FRCP 1933. RAF, 1918-19. Fellow of King's Coll., London. Member: Assoc. of Physicians of Gt Britain; Thoracic Soc. *Publications:* Bronchitis and Broncho-pneumonia in Brit. Encyc. of Med. Practice, 2nd edn; Modern Practice in Tuberculosis, 1952; jt editor contributions to medical journals. *Recreations:* golf, fishing. *Address:* 11 Chyngton Road, Seaford, East Sussex. *Club:* Seaford Golf.

LIVINGSTONE, Ken; Member for Paddington, since 1981, for Hackney North, 1973-81, and Leader, since 1981, Greater London Council; *b* 17 June 1945; *s* of Robert Moffat Livingstone and Ethel Ada Livingstone; *m* 1973, Christine Pamela Chapman (marr. diss. 1982). *Educ:* Tulse Hill Comprehensive Sch.; Philippa Fawcett Coll. of Educn (Teacher's Cert.). Technician, Chester Beatty Cancer Res. Inst., 1962-70. Joined Labour Party, 1968; Reg. Exec., Greater London Lab. Party, 1974-; Lambeth Borough Council: Councillor, 1971-78; Vice-Chm., Housing Cttee, 1971-73; Camden Borough Council: Councillor, 1978-82; Chm., Housing Cttee, 1978-80; Greater London Council: Lab. Transport spokesman, 1980-81; Leader, Lab. Gp, 1981-. Contested (Lab) Hampstead, gen. elec., 1979. Jt Editor, Labour Herald, 1981-. *Recreations:* snooker, cinema, science fiction. *Address:* 195 Randolph Avenue, W9 1DJ. *T:* 01-624 9174. *Club:* Paddington Labour.

LLANDAFF, Bishop of, since 1976; **Rt. Rev. John Richard Worthington Poole Hughes**; *b* 8 Aug. 1916; *s* of late Canon W. W. Poole Hughes, Warden of Llandovery College and late Bertha Cecil (*née* Rhys). *Educ:* Uppingham School; Hertford College, Oxford; Wells Theological College. BA (Lit. Hum.) 1939, MA 1945. Royal Artillery, 1939-45. Deacon, 1947; Priest, 1948; Curate St Michael and All Angels, Aberystwyth, 1947-50; UMCA Missionary, 1950-57; Staff, St Michael's College, Llandaff, 1957-59; Home Secretary, Universities' Mission to Central Africa, 1959-62; Bishop of South-West Tanganyika, 1962-74; Asst Bishop of Llandaff and Asst Curate, Llantwit Major, 1975. *Publication:* Asomaye na Afahamu (SPCK), 1959. *Recreation:*

writing. *Address:* Llys Esgob, The Cathedral Green, Llandaff, Cardiff, S. Glam CF5 2EB.

LLANDAFF, Dean of; *see* Davies, Very Rev. A. R.

LLEWELLYN, Bryan Henry; *b* 1 May 1927; *s* of Nora and Charles Llewellyn; *m* 1965, Pamela (*née* Pugh) (marr. diss.). *Educ:* Charterhouse; Clare Coll., Cambridge (BA). Commissioned, The Queen's, 1946. Research Asst, Dept of Estate Management, Cambridge, 1954; joined Fisons Ltd, 1955; Marketing Manager, Greaves & Thomas Ltd, 1960; Regional Marketing Controller, Thomson Regional Newspapers Ltd, 1962; Marketing Dir, TRN Ltd, 1966; Managing Director: Thomson Holidays Ltd, 1969; Thomson Travel Ltd, 1972 (Chm., 1977-78); Exec. Dir, Thomson Organisation Ltd, 1972-80; Man. Dir and Chief Exec., Thomson Publications Ltd, 1977-80. Non-Exec. Dir, Orion Insurance Ltd, 1976. *Address:* 18 Stockwell Park Road, SW9.

LLEWELLYN, Sir David (Treharne), Kt 1960; Captain, late Welsh Guards; *b* Aberdare, 17 Jan. 1916; 3rd *s* of Sir David Richard Llewellyn, 1st Bt, LLD, JP, and of Magdalene Anne (*d* 1966), *yr d* of late Rev. Henry Harries, DD, Porthcawl; *m* Joan Anne Williams, OBE, 2nd *d* of R. H. Williams, Bonvilston House, Bonvilston, near Cardiff; two *s* one *d*. *Educ:* Eton; Trinity Coll., Cambridge. BA 1938; MA 1979. Served War of 1939-45; enlisted Royal Fusiliers, serving in ranks; commissioned Welsh Guards; North-West Europe, 1944-45. Contested (Conservative) Aberavon Div. of Glamorgan, 1945. MP (C) Cardiff, North, 1950-Sept. 1959; Parliamentary Under-Sec. of State, Home Office, 1951-52 (resigned, ill-health). Journalist. *Publications:* Nye: The Beloved Patrician, 1961; The Adventures of Arthur Artfully, 1974. *Address:* Yattendon, Newbury, Berks.

LLEWELLYN, David Walter; Managing Director, Walter Llewellyn & Sons Ltd, and other Companies in the Llewellyn Group, since 1953; *b* 13 Jan. 1930; *s* of Eric Gilbert and Florence May Llewellyn; *m* 1955, Josephine Margaret Buxton; three *s*. *Educ:* Radley College. FCIOB. Commissioned Royal Engineers, 1952. Industrial Adviser to Minister of Housing and Local Govt, 1967-68; Mem., Housing Corp., 1975-77; Pres., Joinery and Timber Contractors' Assoc., 1976-77; Chm., Nat. Contractors' Gp of Nat. Fedn of Building Trades Employers, 1977; Chm., Building Regulations Adv. Cttee, 1977- (Mem. 1966-74); Dep. Chm., Nat. Building Agency, 1977-82 (Dir. 1968-82). Underwriting Member of Lloyds, 1978-. Governor, St Andrew's Sch., Eastbourne, 1966-78; Trustee, Queen Alexandra Cottage Homes, Eastbourne, 1973-. *Recreation:* the use, restoration and preservation of historic vehicles. *Address:* The Spinney, 20 Southdown Road, Willingdon, Eastbourne, East Sussex. *T:* Eastbourne 31717. *Clubs:* Reform, Steering Wheel; Devonshire (Eastbourne), Eastbourne.

LLEWELLYN, Dr Donald Rees; JP; Vice-Chancellor, University of Waikato, since 1964; *b* 20 Nov. 1919; *s* of late R. G. Llewellyn, Dursley; *m* 1943, Ruth Marian, *d* of late G. E. Blandford, Dursley; one *s* one *d*. *Educ:* Dursley Grammar Sch.; Univ. of Birmingham, 1939-41, BSc 1st cl. hons Chem. 1941, DSc 1957; Oxford 1941-44, DPhil 1943. Research Fellow, Cambridge Univ., 1944-46; Lectr in Chemistry, UC of N Wales, 1946-49; ICI Research Fellow, UCL, 1949-52; Lectr in Chemistry, UCL, 1952-57; Prof. of Chemistry and Dir of Labs, Univ. of Auckland, 1957-64; Asst Vice-Chancellor, Univ. of Auckland, 1962-64. Mem., NZ Atomic Energy Cttee, 1958-. Member: Council, Hamilton Teachers Coll., 1965-; Council, Waikato Tech. Inst., 1968-; Pres., NZ Nat. Field Days Soc., 1969-. JP Waikato, 1971. CChem, FRSC (FRIC 1952); FNZIC 1957; FRSA 1960. *Publications:* numerous papers on application of stable isotopes in Jl Chem. Soc. and others. *Recreations:* squash, tennis, showjumping (FEI Judge), photography, travel. *Address:* Hamilton RD3, New Zealand. *T:* 69-172. *Club:* Hamilton (NZ).

LLEWELLYN, Sir (Frederick) John, KCMG 1974; Director-General, British Council, 1972-80; *b* 29 April 1915; *er s* of late R. G. Llewellyn, Dursley, Glos.; *m* 1939, Joyce, *d* of late Ernest Barrett, Dursley; one *s* one *d*. *Educ:* Dursley Gram. Sch.; University of Birmingham. BSc, 1st Cl. Hons Chemistry, 1935; PhD, 1938; DSc, 1951 (Birmingham); FRIC, 1944, FNZIC, 1948; FRSA, 1952; FRSNZ, 1964. Lecturer in Chemistry, Birkbeck Coll., 1939-45; Dir, Min. of Supply Research Team, 1941-46; ICI Research Fellow, 1946-47; Prof. of Chemistry, Auckland Univ. Coll., 1947-55; Vice-Chancellor and Rector, University of Canterbury, Christchurch, NZ, 1956-61; Chairman: University Grants Cttee (NZ), 1961-66; N Zealand Broadcasting Corp., 1962-65; Vice-Chancellor, Exeter Univ., 1966-72. Mem. Senate, University of New Zealand, 1956-60; Mem. Council of Scientific and Industrial Research, 1957-61, 1962; Mem. NZ Atomic Energy Cttee, 1958; Mem. NZ Cttee on Technical Education, 1958-66; Chairman: NZ Council of Adult Educn, 1961-66; NZ Commonwealth Scholarships and Fellowships Cttee, 1961-66; Overall Review of Hong Kong Educn System, 1981-82; Member Council: Royal Society of NZ, 1961-63; Assoc. of Commonwealth Univs, 1967-72; Member: Inter-University Council for Higher Education Overseas, 1967-72; British Council Cttee for Commonwealth Univ. Interchange, 1968-72; Representative of UK Universities on Council of Univ. of Ahmado Bello, Nigeria, 1968-72. Chm., Northcott Theatre Bd of Management, 1966-72. Hon. LLD: Canterbury, 1962; Victoria Univ. of Wellington, 1966; Exeter, 1973; Birmingham, 1975; Hon. DSc Salford, 1975; DUniv Open, 1979. *Publications:* Crystallographic papers in Jl of Chemical Soc., London, and in Acta Crystallographica. *Recreations:* photography and travel. *Address:* 30 Lancaster Road, Wimbledon Village, SW19 5DD. *T:* 01-946 2754. *Club:*

Arts.
　See also D. R. Llewellyn.

LLEWELLYN, Col Sir Godfrey; see Llewellyn, Col Sir R. G.

LLEWELLYN, Sir Henry Morton, (Sir Harry Llewellyn), 3rd Bt cr 1922; Kt 1977; CBE 1953 (OBE 1944); MA; late Warwicks Yeomanry; President, Whitbread Wales Ltd, since 1972 (Chairman, 1958-72); Chairman: Davenco (Engineers) Ltd; Grid Management & Finance Ltd; Wales Board, Nationwide Building Society, since 1972; Director, Chepstow Racecourse Co. Ltd; Member, South Wales Regional Board, Lloyds Bank, since 1963; Vice-Chairman, Civic Trust for Wales, since 1960; b 18 July 1911; 2nd s of Sir David Llewellyn, 1st Bt, and Magdalene (d 1966), d of Dr H. Hiley Harries, DD, Porthcawl; S brother, 1978; m 1944, Hon. Christine Saumarez, 2nd d of 5th Baron de Saumarez; two s one d. Educ: Oundle; Trinity Coll., Cambridge (MA). Joined Warwickshire Yeo., Sept. 1939; Iraq-Syria Campaign, 1941; Middle East Staff Coll., Haifa, 1942; 8th Army from El Alamein to Tunis as GSO II Ops (Liaison) (despatches), 1942-43; Sicily, Italy (despatches), 1943; MA Chief of Staff HQ 21 Army Gp, 1943; NW Europe GSO I Ops (Liaison), 1943-44; OBE 1944; US Legion of Merit, 1945; Hon. Lt Col. Riding Ego, came 2nd in Grand National chase, 1936, 4th, 1937. Nat. Hunt Cttee, 1946-; The Jockey Club, 1969. Jt Master Monmouthshire Hounds, 1952-57, 1963-65; Captain winning Brit. Olympic Show-Jumping Team, Helsinki (riding Foxhunter), 1952; Chm., Brit. Show Jumping Assoc., 1967-69; Pres./Chm., British Equestrian Fedn, 1976-81. Chm., Welsh Sports Council, 1971-81; Mem., GB Sports Council, 1971-81. Pres., Inst. of Directors (Wales), 1963-65. Chm., Eagle Star Assurance Co. (Wales Bd), 1963-81; formerly Director: North's Navigation Colliery Ltd; TWW Ltd; Rhigos Colliery Ltd; C. L. Clay & Co. Ltd (Coal Exporters). Mem., Wales Tourist Board, 1969-75. DL Monmouthshire, 1952, JP 1954-68, High Sheriff 1966. Royal Humane Soc. Medal for Life-saving, 1956. Publications: Foxhunter in Pictures, 1952; Passports to Life, 1980. Recreations: hunting, all sports, wild life photography. Heir: s David St Vincent Llewellyn [b 2 April 1946; m 1980, Vanessa Mary Theresa, y d of Lieut-Comdr Peregrine and Lady Miriam Hubbard; one d. Educ: Eton]. Address: Llanvair Grange, near Abergavenny, Gwent. Club: Cavalry and Guards.

LLEWELLYN, Rear-Adm. Jack Rowbottom, CB 1974; Assistant Controller of the Navy, 1972-74; retired; b 14 Nov. 1919; s of Ernest and Harriet Llewellyn, Ashton under Lyne, Lancs; m 1944, Joan Isabel, d of Charles and Hilda Phillips, Yelverton, Devon; one s. Educ: Purley County Sch. Entered RN, 1938; RNEC, Keyham, 1939. Served War of 1939-45: HMS Bermuda, 1942; RNC, Greenwich, 1943; HMS Illustrious, 1945. Engr in Chief's Dept, Admlty, 1947; HMS Sluys, 1949; HMS Thunderer, 1951; HMS Diamond, 1953; Comdr, 1953; Asst Engr in Chief, on loan to Royal Canadian Navy, 1954; in charge Admty Fuel Experimental Station, Haslar, 1958; HMS Victorious, 1960; Asst Dir, Marine Engrg, MoD (N), 1963; Captain, 1963; in command, HMS Fisgard, 1966; Dep. Dir, Warship Design, MoD (N), 1969; Rear-Adm., 1972. Recreations: travel, gardening. Address: Bell Cottage, Pipehouse, Freshford, near Bath, Avon. T: Limpley Stoke 3580.

LLEWELLYN, Sir John; see Llewellyn, Sir F. J.

LLEWELLYN, His Honour John Charles, JP; a Circuit Judge (formerly a Judge of County Courts, and a Deputy Chairman, Inner London Area Sessions), 1965-82; b 11 Feb. 1908; o s of late J. E. Llewellyn, Letchworth, Herts; m 1937, Rae Marguerite Cabell Warrens, d of Lt-Col E. R. C. Warrens, DSO, Froxfield, Hants; one s two d. Educ: St Christopher Sch., Letchworth; Emmanuel Coll., Cambridge (MA, LLB). Barrister, Inner Temple, 1931; Master of the Bench, Inner Temple, 1963. Common Law Counsel to PO, 1960-65; Recorder of King's Lynn, 1961-65. Mem. Gen. Council of the Bar, 1956-60, and 1961-65; Chm. Jt Advisory Council, Carpet Industry of Gt Brit., 1958-79; Dep. Chm. Agric. Land Tribunal (Eastern Region), 1959-65; JP Greater London, 1965-. Recreation: riding. Address: 2 Temple Gardens, EC4. T: 01-353 7907; Bulford Mill, Braintree, Essex. T: Braintree 20616. Clubs: Athenæum, Boodle's.

LLEWELLYN, John Desmond Seys; His Honour Judge Seys Llewellyn; a Circuit Judge, (formerly a County Court Judge), since 1971; b 3 May 1912; s of Charles Ernest Llewellyn, FAI and Hannah Margretta Llewellyn, of Cardiff; m 1939, Elaine, d of H. Leonard Porcher, solicitor, and Mrs Hilda Porcher, JP, of Pontypridd; three s. Educ: Cardiff High School; Jesus College, Oxford; Exhibitioner, MA. Joined Inner Temple, 1936. War Service, RTR, 1940-46 (Captain). Called to the Bar, Inner Temple, in absentia OAS, 1945; Profumo Prizeman, 1947; practised on Wales and Chester Circuit, 1947-71; Local Insurance Appeal Tribunal, 1958-71; Dep. Chm., Cheshire QS, 1968-71; joined Gray's Inn, ad eundem, same day as youngest son, 1967. Contested Chester Constituency (L), 1955 and 1956. Recreations: languages, travel, archaeology, art galleries, music, two English Setters. Address: Chetwyn House, Gresford, Clwyd. T: Gresford 2419; Farrar's Building, Temple. Club: Athenæum (Liverpool).

LLEWELLYN, Rev. John Francis Morgan, MVO 1982; MA; Chaplain at the Chapel Royal of St Peter ad Vincula within HM Tower of London, since 1974; Chaplain, Order of St John of Jerusalem, since 1974; b 4 June 1921; s of late Canon D. L. J. Llewellyn; m 1955, Audrey Eileen (née Binks). Educ: King's College Sch., Wimbledon; Pembroke Coll., Cambridge (MA); Ely

Theological Coll. Served War, 1941-45, in Royal Welch Fusiliers and in India (Captain). Curate of Eltham, 1949-52; Chaplain and Asst Master, King's College Sch., Wimbledon, 1952-58; Headmaster, Cathedral Choir Sch., and Minor Canon of St Paul's Cathedral, 1958-74; Sacrist and Warden of College of Minor Canons, 1968-74; Dep. Priest-in-Ordinary to the Queen, 1968-70, 1974-, Priest-in-Ordinary, 1970-74. Sub-Chaplain, Order of St John of Jerusalem, 1970-74; Chaplain, City Solicitor's Co., 1975-. Publication: (contrib.) The Tower of London: Its Buildings and Institutions, 1978. Recreations: cricket, golf, fishing. Address: Chaplain's Residence, HM Tower of London, EC3N 4AB. T: 01-709 0765. Club: Hawks (Cambridge).

LLEWELLYN, Richard; see Lloyd, R. D. V. L.

LLEWELLYN, Col Sir (Robert) Godfrey, 1st Bt cr 1959; Kt 1953; CB 1950; CBE 1942 (OBE 1927); MC 1918; TD; DL; JP; Chairman Welsh Hospital Board, 1959-65; Director of Companies, including inception of Cambrian Air Services Ltd; Chairman of the Wales and Monmouthshire Conservative and Unionist Council, 1949-56, President, 1958, 1962, 1966, 1967, 1968, 1969; President, National Union of Conservative and Unionist Associations, 1962 (Vice-Chairman 1952-53, Chairman 1954-55); Chairman Glamorgan TA and AFA, 1953-58; b 13 May 1893; y s of Robert William Llewellyn, DL, JP, Cwrt-Colman, Bridgend and Baglan Hall, Briton-Ferry, Glamorgan; m 1920, Frances Doris (d 1969), d of Rowland S. Kennard, JP, Little Harrow, Christchurch, Hants; one s one d. Educ: Royal Naval Colls, Osborne and Dartmouth. Joined Royal Navy, 1906; Midshipman, 1910; Sub-Lt 1913; resigned, 1914; served European War, with Montgomeryshire Yeomanry Cavalry to 1917 when attached Royal Welch Fusiliers; commanded Brigade Signal Troop 6th Mounted Brigade, 1917-18; Captain 1918; 4th Cavalry Div. Signal Squadron, 1918 (despatches twice, MC); Commanded 53rd Div. Signals (TA), 1920-29; Major, 1920; Bt Lt-Col, 1924; Lt-Col 1925; Bt Col 1928; Dep. Chief Signal Officer, Western Command, 1929-37; retired, 1937; Hon. Col 53rd Div. Signals, Royal Corps Signals, 1929-33. Col i/c Administration, Home Guard and Home Guard Adviser, S Wales District, 1940-44; Hon. Col 38th Div. Royal Corps Signals, 1941-49; Col Commandant Glamorgan Army Cadet Force, 1943-49; formerly Hon. Col 16th (Welsh) Battalion The Parachute Regt, TA. JP Neath Borough, 1925. Pres. of the Bath and West Show, 1956; Chm. of Organising Cttee Empire and Commonwealth Games, 1958. DL Glamorgan, 1936-74, Gwent, 1974-; DL Mon, 1960; JP Glamorgan County, 1934; High Sheriff: of Glamorgan, 1947-48, of Monmouth, 1963-64. KStJ 1969. Recreations: yachting, shooting, fishing, racing. Heir: s Captain Michael Rowland Godfrey Llewellyn, Grenadier Guards R of O [b 15 June 1921; m 1st, 1946, Bronwen Mary (marr. diss. 1951), d of Sir (Owen) Watkin Williams-Wynn, 8th Bt; 2nd, 1956, Janet Prudence, y d of Lt-Col Charles Thomas Edmondes, DL, JP, Ewenny Priory, Bridgend, Glam; three d. Educ: Harrow; RMC Sandhurst]. Address: Tredilion Park, Abergavenny, Gwent NP7 8BD. T: 2178. Clubs: Carlton, Pratt's, Naval and Military, Royal Automobile, Institute of Directors; Royal Thames Yacht; Cardiff and County (Cardiff).

LLEWELLYN, Rt. Rev. William Somers; Assistant Curate of Tetbury with Beverston, since 1977; b 16 Aug. 1907; s of Owen John and Elizabeth Llewellyn; m 1947, Innis Mary, d of Major Arthur Dorrien-Smith, Tresco Abbey, Isles of Scilly; three s. Educ: Eton; Balliol and Wycliffe Hall, Oxford. BA 1929; diploma in Theology (with dist.) 1934; MA 1937. Priest, 1936; Curate of Chiswick, 1935-37; Vicar of Badminton, with Acton Turville, 1937-49. CF 1940-46; served with Royal Gloucestershire Hussars in Egypt and Western Desert, and as Senior Chaplain with 8th Army HQ, Canal Area and East Africa; Vicar of Tetbury with Beverston, 1949-61; Rural Dean of Tetbury, 1955-61; Archdeacon of Lynn, 1961-72; first Suffragan Bishop of Lynn, 1963-72; Priest-in-charge of Boxwell with Leighterton, 1973-77. Address: Scrubbetts, Kingscote, Tetbury, Glos. T: Leighterton 236.

LLEWELLYN-JONES, Frank; see Jones, F. Ll.

LLEWELLYN JONES, Ilston Percival; His Honour Judge Llewellyn Jones; a Circuit Judge, since 1978; b 15 June 1916; s of Rev. L. Cyril F. Jones and Gertrude Anne Jones; m 1963, Mary Evelyn; one s (by a former m). Educ: Baswich House and Fonthill prep. schs; St John's Sch., Leatherhead. Admitted Solicitor, Nov. 1938; practised privately until served Sussex Yeomanry RA and 23rd Field Regt RA (commnd), 1939-42; Solicitors Dept, Metropolitan Police, New Scotland Yard, 1942-48; private practice, Torquay, 1948-52; Devon County Prosecuting Solicitor, 1952-56; Clerk to N Devon Justices, 1956-62; private practice, 1962-77; a Recorder of the Crown Court, 1972-78. Recreations: now mainly golf; formerly Rugby football, tennis, squash, swimming, cross country running. Address: Little Beaney, Little Gaddesden, Berkhamsted, Herts HP4 1PE. T: Little Gaddesden 2302.

LLEWELLYN-SMITH, Elizabeth Marion; Deputy Director General, Office of Fair Trading, since 1982; b 17 Aug. 1934; d of John Clare Llewellyn Smith and Margaret Emily Frances (née Crawford). Educ: Christ's Hospital, Hertford; Girton Coll., Cambridge (BA). Joined Board of Trade, 1956; various appointments in Board of Trade, Cabinet Office, Dept of Trade and Industry, Dept of Prices and Consumer Protection, 1956-76; Royal Coll. of Defence Studies, 1977; Under Sec., Companies Div., Dept of Trade, 1978-82. Recreations: travel, books, entertaining. Address: 1 Charlwood Road, Putney, SW15 1PJ. T: 01-789 1572.
　See also M. J. Llewellyn Smith.

LLEWELLYN SMITH, Michael John; HM Diplomatic Service; Counsellor and Consul General, Athens, since 1980; *b* 25 April 1939; *s* of J. C. Llewellyn Smith and M. E. F. Crawford; *m* 1967, Colette Gaulier; one *s* one *d. Educ:* Wellington Coll.; New Coll., Oxford. BA, DPhil. FCO, 1970; Cultural Attaché, Moscow, 1973; Paris, 1976; Royal Coll. of Defence Studies, 1979. *Publications:* The Great Island: a study of Crete, 1965, 2nd edn 1973; Ionian Vision: Greece in Asia Minor 1919-22, 1973. *Recreations:* music, wine. *Address:* 25 Home Park Road, SW19. *Club:* Royal Commonwealth Society.

See also E. M. Llewellyn-Smith.

LLEWELLYN, Sir John Michael D. V.; see Venables-Llewelyn.

LLEWELLYN-DAVIES, family name of **Baroness Llewelyn-Davies of Hastoe.**

LLEWELLYN-DAVIES OF HASTOE, Baroness *cr* 1967, of Hastoe (Life Peer); **Patricia Llewelyn-Davies,** PC 1975; Opposition Chief Whip, House of Lords, 1973-74 and since 1979; *b* of Charles Percy Parry and Sarah Gertrude Parry (*née* Hamilton); *m* 1943, Richard Llewelyn-Davies (later Baron Llewelyn-Davies) (*d* 1981); three *d. Educ:* Liverpool Coll., Huyton; Girton Coll., Cambridge (Hon. Fellow, 1979). Civil Servant, 1940-51 (Min. of War Transp., FO, Air Min., CRO). Contested (Lab) Wolverhampton S-W, 1951, Wandsworth Cent., 1955, 1959. A Baroness-in-Waiting (Govt Whip), 1969-70; Dep. Opposition Chief Whip, House of Lords, 1972-73; Captain of the Gentlemen at Arms (Govt Chief Whip), 1974-79. Hon. Sec., Lab. Parly Assoc., 1960-69. Chm., Women's National Cancer Control Campaign, 1972-75; Member: Bd of Govs, Hosp. for Sick Children, Gt Ormond Street, 1955-67 (Chm. Bd, 1967-69); Court, Univ. of Sussex, 1967-69. Dir, Africa Educnl Trust, 1960-69. Co.-Chm., Women's Nat. Commn, 1976-79. *Address:* 36 Parkhill Road, NW3. *T:* 01-485 6576.

LLOYD, family name of **Barons Lloyd, Lloyd of Hampstead** and **Lloyd of Kilgerran.**

LLOYD, see Geoffrey-Lloyd.

LLOYD, 2nd Baron, *cr* 1925, of Dolobran; **Alexander David Frederick Lloyd,** MBE 1945; DL; Captain Welsh Guards (Reserve); Director: Lloyds Bank Ltd; Lloyds Bank International, 1974-78; Lloyds Bank Unit Trust Managers, 1974-81; Beehive Life Insurance, 1974-81; Grindlays Bank, 1961-74 (Vice-Chairman, 1970-74); Chairman: National Bank of New Zealand, 1970-77 (Vice-Chairman, 1969); London Board, National Bank of New Zealand Ltd, since 1978; *b* 30 Sept. 1912; *o s* of 1st Baron and Hon. Blanche (*d* 1969) (late Maid of Honour to Queen Alexandra), *d* of late Hon. F. C. Lascelles; *S* father, 1941; *m* 1942, Lady Victoria Jean Marjorie Mabel Ogilvy, *e d* of 11th Earl of Airlie; two *d* (one *s* decd). *Educ:* Eton; Cambridge (MA). Served in British Council prior to War of 1939-45; served War of 1939-45 in Palestine, Syria and NW Europe. Pres. Navy League, 1948-51; Mem. LCC, 1949-51. Lord in Waiting to King George VI, Oct. 1951-Feb. 1952, to the Queen until Dec. 1952; Jt Under-Sec. of State for Home Dept with responsibility for Welsh Affairs, Nov. 1952-Oct. 1954; Parliamentary Under-Sec. of State for the Colonies, Oct. 1954-Jan. 1957. Mem., White Fish Authority and Herring Bd, 1963-69. Pres. Commonwealth and British Empire Chambers of Commerce, 1957-61. Board of Governors, London Sch. of Hygiene and Tropical Medicine. DL Herts 1963. *Recreations:* shooting, fishing. *Address:* Clouds Hill, Offley, Hitchin, Herts. *T:* Offley 350. *Club:* White's.

LLOYD OF HAMPSTEAD, Baron *cr* 1965 (Life Peer); **Dennis Lloyd,** QC 1975; Quain Professor of Jurisprudence in the University of London (University College), 1956-82, now Emeritus; Hon. Research Fellow, University College London, since 1982; *b* 22 Oct. 1915; 2nd *s* of Isaac and Betty Lloyd; *m* 1940, Ruth Emma Cecilia Tulla; two *d. Educ:* University Coll. Sch.; University Coll., London; Gonville and Caius Coll., Cambridge. LLB (London) 1935; BA 1937, MA 1941, LLD 1956 (Cantab). Called to Bar, 1936; Yorke Prize, 1938; in practice in London, 1937-39 and 1946-. Served War of 1939-45 in RA and RAOC, Liaison Officer (DADOS) with Free French Forces in Syria and Lebanon, 1944-45. Reader in English Law, University Coll., London, 1947-56; Fellow of University Coll., London; Dean of Faculty of Laws, University of London, 1962-64; Head of Dept of Law, University Coll. Hon. Fellow, Ritsumeikan Univ., Kyoto, Japan, 1978. Member: Law Reform Cttee; Consolidation Bills Cttee, 1965-77; European Communities Cttee; Joint Cttee on Theatre Censorship; Joint Cttee on Broadcasting; Select Cttee on Bill of Rights; Interim Action Cttee on Film Industry; Conseil de la Fédération Britannique de l'Alliance Française, 1970-78; BAFTA; Chairman: Nat. Film Sch. Cttee; Planning for Nat. Film Sch.; Governors, Nat. Film School, 1970-; British Film Inst., 1973-76 (Governor, 1968-76); Chm. Council, University Coll. Sch., 1971-79. *Publications:* Unincorporated Associations, 1938; Rent Control, 1949, 2nd edition, 1955; Public Policy: A Comparative Study in English and French Law, 1953; United Kingdom: Development of its Laws and Constitution, 1955; Business Lettings, 1956; Introduction to Jurisprudence, 1959, 4th edn, 1979; The Idea of Law, 1964, 6 rev. imps, 1968-81, Japanese trans., 1969; Law (Concept Series), 1968; contrib. to periodicals. *Recreations:* painting, listening to music. *Address:* Faculty of Laws, University College London, 4-8 Endsleigh Gardens, WCIH 0EE. *T:* 01-387 7050. *Clubs:* Athenæum, Royal Automobile, PEN (Hon. Life Mem.).

LLOYD OF KILGERRAN, Baron *cr* 1973 (Life Peer), of Llanwenog, Cardigan; **Rhys Gerran Lloyd,** CBE 1953; QC 1961; JP; Barrister-at-law; *s* of late J. G. Lloyd, Kilgerran, Pembrokeshire; *m* Phyllis, *d* of late Ronald Shepherd, JP, Hants; two *d. Educ:* Sloane Sch.; Selwyn Coll., Cambridge (science scholar). MA Cantab; BSc London. Wartime service in scientific research Departments of Air Ministry and MAP, 1939-46. Royal Commn on Awards to Inventors, 1946. Contested (L) Anglesey, General Election, 1959. In practice at Patent Bar, 1946-68. Director: Strayfield Ltd; Morgan Marine Ltd. Chairman: Education Trust; Brantwood (John Ruskin) Trust. Mem., Sainsbury Cttee on NHS, 1965-67. Chm., Inst. of Sports Medicine, 1977-81. Vice-Chairman: Victoria League, 1975; Parly and Scientific Cttee, 1978-; House of Lords Select Cttee on Science and Technology, 1980-; European Communities Cttee, 1975-81; Parly Cttee on Information Technology, 1979-. Pres., Welsh Liberal Party, 1971-74; Pres., UK Liberal Party, 1973-74, Jt Treas., 1977-. Liberal Whip, and delegate, Council of Europe and WEU, 1973-75. Pres., Inst. of Patentees and Inventors, 1975-. Hon. Fellow, Selwyn Coll., Cambridge, 1967-. JP Surrey, 1954. *Publications:* Kerly on Trade Marks, 8th edn, 1960; Halsbury's Trade Marks and Designs, 3rd edn, 1962. *Address:* 15 Haymeads Drive, Esher, Surrey. *Clubs:* Reform, Royal Commonwealth, City Livery, National Liberal.

LLOYD, Rev. (Albert) Kingsley; President of the Conference of the Methodist Church, 1964; *b* 1903; *s* of Rev. Albert Lloyd; *m* 1926, Ida Marian (*née* Cartledge) (*d* 1969); one *s* one *d*; 2nd, 1972, Katharine G., *d* of A. G. L. Ives, *qv. Educ:* Kingswood Sch., Bath; Richmond Coll., Surrey (University of London). Methodist Circuit Minister: London, Bedford, Cambridge, 1926-52; Chm., London N Dist, 1951-53. Secretary, Dept of Connexional Funds of the Methodist Church, 1952-69. Wesley Historical Soc. Lectr, 1968. *Recreation:* gardening. *Address:* 13 High Street, Orwell, Royston, Herts.

LLOYD, Hon. Sir Anthony (John Leslie), Kt 1978; **Hon. Mr Justice Lloyd;** Judge of the High Court of Justice, Queen's Bench Division, since 1978; *b* 9 May 1929; *o s* of late Edward John Boydell Lloyd and Leslie Johnston Fleming; *m* 1960, Jane Helen Violet, *er d* of C. W. Shelford, Chailey Place, Lewes, Sussex. *Educ:* Eton (Schol.); Trinity Coll., Cambridge (Maj. Schol.). 1st cl. Classical Tripos Pt I; 1st cl. with distinction Law Tripos Pt II. National Service, 1st Bn Coldstream Guards, 1948. Montague Butler Prize, 1950; Sir William Browne Medal, 1951. Choate Fellow, Harvard, 1952; Fellow of Peterhouse, 1953 (Hon. Fellow of Peterhouse, 1981); Fellow of Eton, 1974. Called to Bar, Inner Temple, 1955; QC 1967; Bencher, 1976. Attorney-General to HRH The Prince of Wales, 1969-77. Mem., Criminal Law Revision Cttee, 1981-. Trustee: Crafts Centre of Great Britain, 1967-72; Smiths Charity, 1971; Glyndebourne Arts Trust, 1973- (Chm., 1975); Dir, RAM, 1979-; Member: Educn Cttee, ILEA, 1969-70; Top Salaries Review Body, 1971-77. Chm., Chichester Diocesan Bd of Finance, and Mem., Bishop's Council, 1972-76; Governor: West London Coll., 1970-74; Polytechnic of the South Bank, 1971-73. *Recreations:* music, carpentry; formerly running (ran for Cambridge in Mile, White City, 1950). *Address:* 68 Strand-on-the-Green, Chiswick, W4. *T:* 01-994 7790; Ludlay, Berwick, East Sussex. *T:* Alfriston 870204. *Club:* Brooks's.

LLOYD, Prof. Antony Charles; Professor of Philosophy, Liverpool University, since 1957; *b* 15 July 1916; *s* of Charles Mostyn Lloyd and Theodosia Harrison-Rowson. *Educ:* Shrewsbury Sch.; Balliol Coll., Oxford. Asst to Prof. of Logic and Metaphysics, Edinburgh Univ., 1938-39 and 1945; served in Army, 1940-45; Lecturer in Philosophy, St Andrews Univ., 1946-57. Vis. Prof., Kansas Univ., 1967. *Publications:* Form and Universal in Aristotle, 1981; chapters in Cambridge History of Later Ancient Philosophy, 1967; articles in philosophical journals. *Address:* The University, Liverpool L69 3BX.

LLOYD, Bernard Dean, FRVA; City Treasurer, Birmingham, 1980-82; *b* 23 March 1923; *s* of Stanley Lloyd and Eva Mary Lloyd; *m* 1955, Margaret Taylor; one *s* one *d. Educ:* Cardiff High Sch. CIPFA 1949; FRVA 1977. Served War, RN, 1942-46. City Treasurer's and Controller's Dept, Cardiff, 1940-42 and 1946-48; Accountancy Asst, Borough Treasurer's Dept, Ipswich, 1948-52; Technical Asst, Treasurer's Dept, Birmingham, 1952-72; Dep. Treasurer, Birmingham, 1972-80. Chm., LAMSAC Computer Panel, 1980-. *Publications:* articles in professional jls. *Recreations:* reading, gardening. *Address:* Blossomfield Road, Solihull, West Midlands B91 1TF. *T:* 021-705 5431.

LLOYD, Dr Brian Beynon; Chairman, Health Education Council, 1979-82 (Member, 1975-82); *b* 23 Sept. 1920; *s* of David John Lloyd, MA Oxon and Olwen (*née* Beynon); *m* 1949, Reinhild Johanna Engeroff; four *s* three *d* (inc. twin *s* and twin *d*). *Educ:* Newport High Sch.; Winchester Coll. (Schol.); Balliol Coll., Oxford (Domus and Frazer Schol.). Special Certif. for BA (War) Degree in Chem., 1940; took degrees BA and MA, 1946; Theodore Williams Schol. and cl. I in Physiology, 1948; DSc 1969. Joined Oxford Nutrition Survey after registration as conscientious objector, 1941; Pres., Jun. Common Room, Balliol, 1941-42; Chm., Undergraduate Rep. Coun., 1942; Biochemist: SHAEF Nutrition Survey Team, Leiden, 1945; Nutrition Survey Group, Düsseldorf, 1946. Fellow of Magdalen by exam. in Physiology, 1948-52, by special election, 1952-70; Senior Tutor, 1963-64; Vice-Pres., 1967 and 1968; Emeritus Fellow, 1970; Senior Research Officer, later Univ. Lectr, Univ. of Oxford, 1948-70; Senior Proctor, 1960-61; Dir, Oxford Polytechnic, 1970-80. Chm., CNAA Health and Med. Services Bd, 1975-80; Mem., Adv. Council on Misuse of Drugs, 1978-81. Vis. Physiologist, New York, 1963.

Pres., Section I, 1964–65, Section X, 1980, British Assoc. for the Advancement of Science. Chm. of Govs, Oxford Coll. of Technology, 1963–69; Chm. of Dirs, Oxford Gallery, 1967–. Chairman: Oxford–Bonn Soc., 1973–81; Oxford Management Club, 1979–80. *Publications:* Gas Analysis Apparatus, 1960; (jt ed) The Regulation of Human Respiration, 1962; Cerebrospinal Fluid and the Regulation of Respiration, 1965; articles in physiological and biochemical jls. *Recreations:* Klavarskribo, Correggio, haemoglobin, the analysis of running records, slide rules, ready reckoners. *Address:* High Wall, Pullen's Lane, Oxford OX3 0BX. *T:* Oxford 63353.
See also Sir J. P. D. Lloyd.

LLOYD, (Charles) Christopher; author, historian; *b* 2 Sept. 1906; *s* of E. S. Lloyd, CSI, and M. Young; *m* 1938, Katharine Brenda Sturge; one *s* one *d*. *Educ:* Marlborough; Lincoln Coll., Oxford. Lecturer: Bishop's Univ., Quebec, 1930–34; Royal Naval Coll., Dartmouth, 1934–45; Lectr, 1945–66, Prof. of History, 1962–66, Royal Naval College, Greenwich; retired, 1967. Editor, The Mariner's Mirror, 1970–79. *Publications:* The Navy and the Slave Trade, 1949; The Nation and the Navy, 1961; Medicine and the Navy, 1961; William Dampier, 1966; The British Seaman, 1968; Mr Barrow of the Admiralty, 1970; The Search for the Niger, 1973; The Nile Campaign: Nelson and Napoleon in Egypt, 1973; Nelson and Sea Power, 1973; Atlas of Maritime History, 1976; English Corsairs on the Barbary Coast, 1981, etc. *Address:* Lions Wood, Dern Lane, Heathfield, East Sussex. *T:* Horam Road 2702. *Club:* Travellers'.

LLOYD, Charles William, MA; JP; Master, Dulwich College, 1967–75; *b* 23 Sept. 1915; *s* of late Charles Lloyd and late Frances Ellen Lloyd, London; *m* 1939, Doris Ethel, *d* of late David Baker, Eastbourne; one *s* one *d* (and one *d* decd). *Educ:* St Olave's Sch.; Emmanuel Coll., Cambridge. Asst Master Buckhurst Hill Sch., 1938–40. War Service with RA, 1940–46 (despatches). Asst Master Gresham's Sch., Holt, 1946–51; Headmaster, Hutton Gram. Sch., near Preston, 1951–63; Headmaster, Alleyn's Sch., London, 1963–66. Trustee, Nat. Maritime Museum, 1974–. JP Inner London, 1970. *Recreations:* golf, gardening. *Address:* Stradbroke, 39 Upland Road, Eastbourne, Sussex. *T:* Eastbourne 20257.

LLOYD, Christopher; see Lloyd, Charles C.

LLOYD, Christopher, VMH 1979; MA, BSc (Hort.); writer on horticulture; regular gardening correspondent, Country Life, since 1963; *b* 2 March 1921; *s* of late Nathaniel Lloyd and Daisy (*née* Field). *Educ:* Wellesley House, Broadstairs, Kent; Rugby Sch.; King's Coll., Cambridge (MA Mod Langs); Wye Coll., Univ of London (BSc Hort.). Asst Lectr in Decorative Horticulture, Wye Coll., 1950–54. Then returned to family home at Great Dixter and started Nursery in clematis and uncommon plants. *Publications:* The Mixed Border, 1957; Clematis, 1965, rev. edn 1977; Shrubs and Trees for Small Gardens, 1965; Hardy Perennials, 1967; Gardening on Chalk and Lime, 1969; The Well-Tempered Garden, 1970; Foliage Plants, 1973; frequent contributor to gardening magazines, also to Jl of Royal Horticultural Soc. *Recreations:* walking, piano playing (mainly Brahms), canvas embroidery. *Address:* Great Dixter, Northiam, Rye, East Sussex TN31 6PH. *T:* Northiam 3107.

LLOYD, Clive Hubert; Captain; West Indies cricket team, 1974–78 and since 1979; Lancashire County Cricket Club, since 1981; *b* Georgetown, Guyana, 31 Aug. 1944; *er s* of late Arthur Christopher Lloyd and of Sylvia Thelma Lloyd; *m* 1971, Waveney Benjamin; two *d*. *Educ:* Chatham High Sch., Georgetown (schol.). Clerk, Georgetown Hosp., 1960–66. Began cricket career, Demarara CC, Georgetown, 1959; début for Guyana, 1963; first Test Match, 1966; played for Haslingden, Lancs League, 1967; joined Lancashire CCC, 1968, capped 1969; World Series Cricket in Australia, 1977–79. Made first 1st class century, 1966; passed total of 25,000 runs (incl. 69 centuries), 1981; captained WI teams which won World Cup, 1975, 1979. First Pres., WI Players' Assoc., 1973. Golden Arrow of Achievement (Guyana), 1975. *Publication:* (with Tony Cozier) Living for Cricket, 1980. *Address:* c/o Lancashire County Cricket Club, Warwick Road, Manchester M16 0PX.

LLOYD, Maj.-Gen. Cyril, CB 1948; CBE 1944 (OBE 1943); TD 1945 (2 bars); psc; Director-General, City and Guilds of London Institute, 1949–67, Consultant, since 1968; President, Associated Examining Board for General Certificate of Education, since 1976 (Chairman, 1970–76); *b* 1906; *s* of late A. H. Lloyd. *Educ:* Brighton Grammar Sch.; London and Cambridge Univs. First Class in Mathematics, Physics, Divinity. Fellow of Institute of Physics; FRGS; MRST; Lecturer and Teacher; Research Worker in Science; Sussex Territorials (RA), 1929–39; Major, 1939; BEF, 1939–40 (despatches); General Staff, Canadian Army, 1940–42 (despatches, OBE); served various overseas theatres; a Dep Chief of Staff, 21 Army Group, 1943–45; Invasion of Europe (despatches, CBE), 1944–45; Dir-Gen. of Army Education and Training, 1945–49; Member: Council of Boy Scouts Assoc., 1950–70; Council Assoc. of Techn. Institutions, 1961–64; Central Adv. Council for Educn (England) and Adv. Cttee on Educn in Colonies, 1949–53; Adv. Council on Sci. Policy (Jt Enquiry on Technicians, 1962–65; Bd, Internat. Centre for Advanced Technical and Vocational Trg (Turin); Council for Tech. Education and Training for Overseas Countries; Regional Adv. Council for Higher Technological Educn (London), 1950–67; Parly and Scientific Cttee; Nat. Adv. Council for Educn in Industry and Commerce, 1945–68; Southern Regional Council for Further Educn; Council, Instn of Environmental Studies; Vice-Pres. Brit. Assoc. for Commercial and Industrial Educn (Chm.

1955–58); Industrial Trg Council, 1958–64; Central Trg Council and its General Policy Cttee, 1964–68; Chm., Governing Body, National Institute of Agricultural Engineering, 1960–70; Schools Broadcasting Council for the UK, 1962–65; W Sussex Educn Cttee; Council Rural Industries Bureau, 1960–67; Pres., SASLIC, 1970–79; Pres., Soc. for Promotion of Vocational Trng and Educn, 1973; Chm., Cttee on Scientific Library Services; Chm. Governors, Crawley Coll. of Further Educn until 1978; Vice-Pres., Crawley Planning Gp, 1967–; Chief Officer, Commonwealth Tech. Trg Week, 1961; Treas., 1963 Campaign for Educn; Mem. Council for Educl Advance; Trustee: Edward James Foundn; Industrial Trg Foundn; Pres., Roffey Park Management Inst. Governor, Imperial Coll., 1950–70; Mem. Delegacy, City and Guilds Coll., 1950–70; Hon. Exec. Principal, West Dean Coll., 1969–72. Founder Life Mem., Cambridge Soc. Patron, Sussex Archaeological Museum. Liveryman, Goldsmiths' Co. and Freeman of City of London; FRSA. *Publications:* booklets: British Services Education, 1950; Human Resources and New Systems of Vocational Training and Apprenticeship, 1963; contrib. to jls. *Recreations:* the countryside, sailing, and traditional crafts. *Address:* The Pheasantry, Colgate, Horsham, Sussex RH13 6HU. *Club:* Athenæum.

LLOYD, Air Vice-Marshal Darrell Clive Arthur, CB 1980; Commander, Northern Maritime Air Region, since 1981; *b* 5 Nov. 1928; *s* of Cecil James Lloyd and Doris Frances Lloyd; *m* 1957, Pamela (*née* Woodside); two *s*. *Educ:* Stowe; RAF Coll., Cranwell. Commnd 1950; ADC to C-in-C, ME Air Force, 1955–57; Instr, Central Flying Sch., 1958–60; Personal Air Sec. to Sec. of State for Air, 1961–63; CO, RAF Bruggen, 1968–70; RCDS, 1972; Dir of Defence Policy, UK Strategy Div., 1973–75; Dep. Comdr, RAF Germany, 1976–78; ACAS (Ops), 1978–81. *Recreations:* travel, golf, painting. *Address:* c/o Lloyds Bank, 6 Pall Mall, SW1. *Club:* Royal Air Force.

LLOYD, Denis Thelwall; His Honour Judge Denis Lloyd; a Circuit Judge, since 1972; *b* 3 Jan. 1924; *s* of late Col Glyn Lloyd, DSO, FRCVS, Barrister-at-Law; *m* 1950, Margaret Sheila *d* (1976), *d* of Bernard Bushell, Wirral, Ches; one *s* two *d*. *Educ:* Wellington College. Enlisted KRRC, 1942; commnd KRRC Dec. 1942; Central Mediterranean Force, (Italy, S France, Greece) 1943–45; attached 1st York and Lancaster Regt and then joined Parachute Regt, 1944; Palestine, 1945–46; GSO3 (ops) HQ British Troops Austria, 1946; Staff Captain British Mil. Mission to Czechoslovakia, 1947. Called to the Bar, Gray's Inn, 1949; joined NE Circuit, 1950; an Asst Recorder, Leeds, 1961–67; Recorder of Pontefract, 1971; Dep. Chm., WR Yorks QS, 1968–71. Dep. Chm., Agricultural Land Tribunal, Yorks and Lancs, 1968. Contested (L): York, 1964; Hallam Div. of Sheffield, 1966. Czech War Cross, 1946. *Recreations:* gardening, fishing. *Address:* Bridge End Farm, Brough, Bradwell, Derbyshire. *T:* Hope Valley 20205.

LLOYD, Major Sir (Ernest) Guy (Richard), 1st Bt *cr* 1960; Kt 1953; DSO 1917; DL; late Administrator J. and P. Coats, Ltd, Glasgow (retired 1938); *b* 7 Aug. 1890; *e s* of late Major E. T. Lloyd, late Bengal Civil Service; *m* 1918, Helen Kynaston, *yr d* of late Col E. W. Greg, CB; one *s* two *d* (and two *d* decd). *Educ:* Rossall; Keble Coll., Oxford, MA. Served European War, 1914–18 (despatches, DSO); War of 1939–45, 1940. MP (U) East Renfrewshire, Scotland, 1940–Sept. 1959. DL, Dunbartonshire, 1953. *Recreations:* fishing and gardening. *Heir:* *s* Richard Ernest Butler Lloyd, *qv*. *Address:* Rhu Cottage, Carrick Castle, Lochgoilhead, Argyll.
See also Sir A. M. A. Denny, Bt, Sir Robert Green-Price, Bt.

LLOYD, Frederick John, CBE 1977; FIA; Chairman, Road Transport Industry Training Board, since 1978; *b* 22 Jan. 1913; *m* 1942, Catherine Johnson (*née* Parker); one *s* one *d*. *Educ:* Ackworth Sch., Yorks; Liverpool Univ. (BSc). FIA 1947; FIS 1949; FSS 1953; FCIT 1968. War Service, Operational Res., Bomber Comd, 1942–45. Royal Insurance Co., 1933–47; London Passenger Transport Bd, 1948–69: Staff Admin Officer, 1952; Divl Supt (South), 1957; Chief Operating Manager (Central Buses), 1961; Chief Commercial and Planning Officer, 1965–69; Dir Gen., West Midlands Passenger Transport Exec., 1969–78. *Publications:* contribs to actuarial and transport jls. *Recreations:* golf, photography and gardening. *Address:* 8 Cliveden Coppice, Sutton Coldfield, West Midlands B74 2RG. *T:* 021-308 5683. *Club:* Whittington Barracks Golf (Lichfield, Staffs).

LLOYD, (George) Peter, CMG 1965; Governor, Cayman Islands, since 1982; *b* 23 Sept. 1926; *er s* of late Sir Thomas Ingram Kynaston Lloyd, GCMG, KCB; *m* 1957, Margaret Harvey; two *s* one *d*. *Educ:* Stowe Sch.; King's Coll., Cambridge. Lieut, KRRC, 1945–48; ADC to Governor of Kenya, 1948; Cambridge, 1948–51 (MA; athletics blue); District Officer, Kenya, 1951–60; Principal, Colonial Office, 1960–61; Colonial Secretary, Seychelles, 1961–66; Chief Sec., Fiji, 1966–70; Defence Sec., Hong Kong, 1971–74; Dep. Governor, Bermuda, 1974–81. *Address:* Government House, Grand Cayman, Cayman Islands. *Clubs:* Royal Commonwealth Society; Royal Bermuda Yacht (Bermuda); Hong Kong (Hong Kong); Muthaiga (Nairobi, Kenya).

LLOYD, Major Sir Guy; see Lloyd, Major Sir E. G. R.

LLOYD, Very Rev. Henry Morgan, DSO 1941; OBE 1959; MA; *b* 9 June 1911; *y s* of late Rev. David Lloyd, Weston-super-Mare, Somerset; *m* 1962, Rachel Katharine, *d* of late J. R. Wharton, Hatfield, nr Ledbury; one *d*. *Educ:* Canford Sch.; Oriel Coll., Oxford; Cuddesdon Theological Coll. Deacon, 1935; priest, 1936; Curate of Hendon Parish Church, Middlesex, 1935–40. Served War as Chaplain RNVR, 1940–45. Principal of Old Rectory Coll., Hawarden, 1946–48; Secretary of Central Advisory Council of Training for the Ministry, 1948-50; Dean of Gibraltar, 1950-60; Dean of Truro and Rector of St Mary, Truro, 1960-81; Dean Emeritus, 1981. Hon. Burgess of the City of Truro, 1978. *Recreations:* walking and archæology. *Address:* 3 Hill House, The Avenue, Sherborne, Dorset. *T:* Sherborne 2037. *Club:* Royal Commonwealth Society (Fellow).

LLOYD, Humphrey John, QC 1979; *b* 16 Nov. 1939; *s* of Rees Lewis Lloyd of the Inner Temple, barrister-at-law, and Dorothy Margaret Ferry (*née* Gibson); *m* 1969, Ann Findlay; one *s* one *d. Educ:* Westminster; Trinity Coll., Dublin (BA (Mod), LLB; MA). Called to the Bar, Inner Temple, 1963. *Publications:* ed, *Building* Law Reports, 1977-. *Address:* 22 Old Buildings, Lincoln's Inn, WC2A 3UJ. *T:* 01-404 0102. *Club:* Reform.

LLOYD, Ian Stewart; MP (C) Havant and Waterloo, since 1974 (Portsmouth, Langstone, 1964-74); Economic Adviser, British and Commonwealth Shipping, since 1956 (Director of Research, 1956-64); *b* 30 May 1921; *s* of Walter John Lloyd and late Euphemia Craig Lloyd; *m* 1951, Frances Dorward Addison, *d* of late Hon. W. Addison, CMG, OBE, MC, DCM; three *s. Educ:* Michaelhouse; University of the Witwatersrand; King's Coll., Cambridge. President, Cambridge Union, and Leader, Cambridge tour of USA, 1947; MA 1951; MSc 1952. Econ. Adviser, Central Mining and Investment Corporation, 1949-52; Member, SA Board of Trade and Industries, 1952-55; Director, Acton Soc. Trust, 1956. Chairman, UK Cttee and Vice-Chairman, International Exec., International Cargo Handling Co-ordination Assoc., 1961-64. Chairman: Cons. Parly Shipping and Shipbuilding Cttee, 1974-77; Select Cttee on Sci. Sub-Cttee, 1975-77; Select Cttee on Sci. Sub-Cttee on Technological Innovation, 1977-; Select Cttee on Energy, 1979-; All-Party Cttee on Information Technology, 1979-. Member, UK Delegation, Council of Europe, Western European Union, 1968-72; UK rep., Internat. Parly Conf., Bucharest, 1975; Leader, UK Delegn, OECD Conf. on Energy, 1981. *Publications:* Rolls-Royce, 3 vols, 1978; contribs to SA Journal of Economics and Journal of Industrial Economics. *Recreations:* yachting, ski-ing, good music. *Address:* Bakers House, Priors Dean, Petersfield, Hants. *Clubs:* Brooks's, Army and Navy, Royal Yacht Squadron; Royal Cork Yacht.

LLOYD, His Honour Ifor Bowen, QC; a County Court Judge, later a Circuit Judge, 1959-76 (Judge of Wandsworth County Court, 1964-76); *b* 9 Sept. 1902; *er s* of late Rev. Thomas Davies Lloyd and Mrs Margaret Lloyd; *m* 1938, Naomi, *y d* of late George Pleydell Bancroft; one *s* one *d. Educ:* Winchester (Exhibitioner); Exeter Coll., Oxford (Scholar). BA Oxford (Mod. Hist.), 1924; called to Bar, Inner Temple, 1925, Bencher 1959, Treasurer 1981; Yarborough Anderson scholar, 1926; Midland Circuit; President, Hardwicke Society, 1929; KC 1951. Liberal Candidate, Burton Division of Staffordshire, 1929, Chertsey Division of Surrey, 1931. Member General Council of the Bar, 1950, 1957. *Address:* 1 Harcourt Buildings, Temple, EC4Y 9DA. *T:* 01-353 1484.

LLOYD, James Monteith, CD 1979; CMG 1961; Deputy Chairman, Industrial Disputes Tribunal, Jamaica, 1976-78; *b* 24 Nov. 1911; *s* of late Jethro and Frances Lloyd; *m* 1936, Mavis Anita Frankson; two *s* two *d. Educ:* Wolmer's High Sch., Jamaica. Called to Bar, Lincoln's Inn, 1948. Jamaica: entered Public Service as Asst, Registrar-General's Dept, 1931 (2nd Class Clerk, 1939, 1st Class Clerk, 1943, Asst Registrar-General, 1947); Asst Secretary, Secretariat, 1950; Principal Asst Secretary, Secretariat, 1953 (seconded to Grenada on special duty, Dec. 1955-May 1956); Permanent Secretary, Jamaica, 1956; Administrator, Grenada, 1957-62; Permanent Secretary, Jamaica, 1962-72; Chm., Ombudsman Working Party, Jamaica, 1972; retired from Civil Service, 1975. Chief Comr, Scouts, Jamaica, 1973-78. Coronation Medal, 1953; Jamaica Independence Medal, 1962. *Recreations:* cricket, tennis, golf. *Address:* 5 Melwood Avenue, Kingston 8, Jamaica. *Clubs:* Jamaica; Kingston CC; YMCA.

LLOYD, John Graham; Commercial Surveyor, Commission for the New Towns, Corby, since 1981; *b* Watford, 18 Feb. 1938; *s* of late Richard and Edith Lloyd; *m* 1960, Ann (*née* Plater); three *s. Educ:* City of London Sch.; College of Estate Management, London Univ. (BSc Estate Management). FRICS. In private practice, London, with: Chamberlain & Willows, 1959-62; Holcombe & Betts, 1962-65; Debenham Tewson & Chinnocks, 1965-68; Fuller Horsey Sons & Cassell, 1968-72; Associate Partner, Locke & England, Leamington Spa, 1972-75. Commercial and Industrial Manager, Hemel Hempstead, Commission for the New Towns, 1975-78, Manager, 1978-81. *Recreations:* soccer, motor racing, jazz and popular music, gardening. *Address:* 17 Woodfield Park, Amersham, Bucks HP6 5QH. *T:* Amersham 5149.

LLOYD, Sir (John) Peter (Daniel), Kt 1971; Chairman, Cadbury Fry Pascall Australia Ltd, 1953-71; Chancellor, University of Tasmania, since 1982; *b* 30 Aug. 1915; *s* of late David John Lloyd; *m* 1947, Gwendolen, *d* of late William Nassau Molesworth; two *s* four *d. Educ:* Rossall Sch.; Brasenose Coll., Oxford (MA). Royal Artillery, 1940-46 (despatches, Order of Leopold, Belgian Croix de Guerre). Member: Council, Univ. of Tasmania, 1957-; Council, Australian Admin. Staff Coll., 1959-71; Board, Commonwealth Banking Corp., 1967-; Board, Goliath Cement Holdings, 1969-; Board, Australian Mutual Provident Society, 1970-. Member: Australian Taxation Review Cttee, 1972-74; Cttee of Inquiry into Educn and Training, 1976-78. *Address:* Stonecrest, Sorell, Tasmania 7172, Australia. *Clubs:* Tasmanian (Hobart); Australian (Sydney).
See also B. B. Lloyd.

LLOYD, Prof. John Raymond; *see under* Lloyd, M. R.

LLOYD, Rev. Kingsley; *see* Lloyd, Rev. A. K.

LLOYD, Leslie, CBE 1981; FCIT; General Manager, Western Region, British Rail, since 1976; *b* 10 April 1924; *s* of Henry Lloyd and Lilian Wright; *m* 1953, Marie Snowden; one *s* two *d. Educ:* Hawarden Grammar Sch. RAF, 1943-47. British Rail: Management Trainee, Eastern Reg., 1949-52; Chief Controller, Manchester, 1953-56; Freight Officer, Sheffield, 1956-59; Modernisation Asst, King's Cross, 1959-61; Dist Manager, Marylebone, 1961-63; Movements Supt, Great Northern Line, 1963-64; Ops Officer, Eastern Reg., 1964-67; Man., Sundries Div., 1967; Movements Man., Western Reg., 1967-69; Chief Ops Man., British Rail HQ, 1969-76. *Recreations:* golf, gardening. *Address:* Headquarters, Western Region, British Rail, Paddington Station, W2. *T:* 01-723 7000, ext. 2819. *Club:* Burnham Beeches Golf (Burnham).

LLOYD, Martin, MA (Cantab); *b* 1908; 2nd *s* of late Thomas Zachary Lloyd, Edgbaston, Birmingham; *m* 1943, Kathleen Rosslyn, *y d* of late Colonel J. J. Robertson, DSO, Wick, Caithness; two *s* two *d. Educ:* Marlborough Coll.; Gonville and Caius Coll., Cambridge (1st Class Parts I and II Mod. Languages Tripos). Asst Master, Rugby Sch., 1930-40; on military service, 1940-44. Headmaster of Uppingham Sch., 1944-65; Warden, Missenden Abbey Adult Educn Coll., 1966-74. *Address:* Norton Cottage, Pitchcombe, Stroud, Glos GL6 6LU. *T:* Painswick 812329.

LLOYD, Prof. Michael Raymond; Senior Partner, Sinar Associates, Tunbridge Wells, since 1973; *b* 20 Aug. 1927; *s* of W. R. Lloyd; *m* 1957, Berit Hansen; one *s* two *d. Educ:* Wellington Sch., Somerset; AA School of Architecture. AA Dipl. 1953; ARIBA 1954; MNAL 1960. Private practice and Teacher, State School of Arts and Crafts, Oslo, 1955-60 and 1962-63; First Year Master, AA School of Architecture, 1960-62; Dean, Faculty of Arch., and Prof. of Arch., Kumasi Univ. of Science and Technology, 1963-66; Principal, AA Sch. of Architecture, 1966-71; Consultant, Land Use Consultants (Internat.) Lausanne, 1971-72; Consultant Head, Hull Sch. of Architecture, 1974-77. Leverhulme Sen. Res. Fellow, UCL, 1976-78. *Publications:* (as J. R. Lloyd) Tegning og Skissing; ed World Architecture, Vol. I Norway, Vol. III Ghana; Shelter in Society: Norwegian Laftehus. *Recreations:* sailing, ski-ing. *Address:* Studley Cottage, Bishops Down, Park Road, Tunbridge Wells, Kent.

LLOYD, Nicholas Markley, MA; Editor of the Sunday People, since 1982; *b* 9 June 1942; *s* of Walter and Sybil Lloyd; *m* 1st, 1968, Patricia Sholliker (marr. diss. 1978); two *s* one *d* ; 2nd, 1979, Eve Pollard; one *s. Educ:* Bedford Modern Sch.; St Edmund Hall, Oxford (MA Hons History). Reporter, Daily Mail, 1964; Educn Correspondent, Sunday Times, 1966; Dep. News Editor, Sunday Times, 1968; News Editor, The Sun, 1970; Asst Editor, News of the World, 1972; Asst Editor, The Sun, 1976; Dep. Editor, Sunday Mirror, 1980. *Recreations:* football, golf, reading. *Address:* Sunday People, 9 New Fetter Lane, EC4A 1AR. *T:* 01-353 0246.

LLOYD, Norman, FRSA, ROI, 1935; Landscape Painter; *b* 16 Oct. 1895; *s* of David Lloyd and Jane Ogilvie; *m* 1923, Edith Eyre-Powell (*d* 1971). *Educ:* Hamilton and Sydney Art School, Australia. Exhibitioner Royal Academy and Royal Institute of Oil Painters; Salon des Artistes Français, Paris; Laureat du Salon Mention Honorable, 1948; Silver Medal, Portrait Salon, Paris, 1956; Palmes, Acad. Française, 1957. Member Société des Artistes Français, Paysagistes; Member Internat. Assoc. of Plastic Arts, 1962. *Recreation:* travel. *Address:* c/o Dr J. A. Farrer, Hall Garth, Clapham, near Lancaster LA2 8DR.

LLOYD, Peter, CBE 1957; Director, Booth International Holdings Ltd, 1973-79 (Consultant, 1980); *b* 26 June 1907; *s* of late Godfrey I. H. Lloyd and late Constance L. A. Lloyd; *m* 1st, 1932, Nora K. E. Patten; one *s* one *d* ; 2nd, 1951, Joyce Evelyn Campbell. *Educ:* Gresham's Sch.; Trinity Coll., Cambridge (MA). Industrial Research in Gas Light and Coke Co., London, 1931-41; Royal Aircraft Establishment, 1941-44; Power Jets (Research and Development), 1944-46. National Gas Turbine Establishment, Pyestock, 1946-60, Deputy Director, 1950; Dir-Gen. Engine R&D, Mins of Aviation and Technology, 1961-69; Head of British Defence Research and Supply Staff, Canberra, 1969-72. Chm., Gas Turbine Collaboration Cttee, 1961-68. CEng, FRAeS, SFInstE. Pres., Cambridge Univ. Mountaineering Club, 1928-29; Chm., Mount Everest Foundn, 1982- (Vice Chm., 1980-82). Himalayan expeditions: Nanda Devi, 1936; Everest, 1938; Langtang Himal, 1949; Kulu, 1977. *Publications:* various papers in scientific and technical journals. *Recreations:* mountaineering, fishing, gardening. *Address:* Heath Hill, Old Park Lane, Farnham, Surrey. *T:* Farnham 714995. *Clubs:* Athenæum, Alpine (Vice-Pres., 1961-63, Pres., 1977-80).
See also T. A. Evans.

LLOYD, Peter; *see* Lloyd, G. P.

LLOYD, Sir Peter; *see* Lloyd, Sir J. P. D.

LLOYD, Peter Gordon, CBE 1976 (OBE 1965); retired; British Council Representative, Greece, 1976-80; *b* 20 Feb. 1920; *s* of Peter Gleave Lloyd and Ellen Swift; *m* 1952, Edith Florence (*née* Flurey); two *s* one *d. Educ:* Royal Grammar Sch., Newcastle upon Tyne; Balliol Coll., Oxford (Horsley Exhibnr, 1939; BA, MA 1948). RA (Light Anti-Aircraft), subseq. DLI, 1940-46, Captain. British Council, 1949-: Brit. Council, Belgium and Hon.

Lector in English, Brussels Univ., 1949-52; Reg. Dir, Mbale, Uganda, 1952-56; Dep. Dir Personnel, 1956-60; Representative: Ethiopia, 1960-68; Poland, 1969-72; Nigeria, 1972-76. *Publications:* (introd) Huysmans, A Rebours, 1940; The Story of British Democracy, 1959; critical essays on literature in periodicals. *Recreations:* literature, music, travel. *Address:* 25 Shenley Hill, Radlett, Herts. *T:* Radlett 7310. *Club:* United Oxford & Cambridge University.

LLOYD, Peter Robert Cable; MP (C) Fareham, since 1979; *b* 12 Nov. 1937; *s* of David and Stella Lloyd; *m* 1967, Hilary Creighton; one *s* one *d*. *Educ:* Tonbridge Sch.; Pembroke Coll., Cambridge (MA). Formerly Marketing Manager, United Biscuits Ltd. Sec., Cons. Parly Employment Cttee, 1979-81; Vice-Chm., Cons. European Affairs Cttee, 1980-81; PPS to Minister of State, NI Office, 1981-82. Chairman, Bow Group, 1972-73; Editor of Crossbow, 1974-76. *Recreations:* theatre, gardening, reading newspapers. *Address:* House of Commons, SW1A 0AA.

LLOYD, Richard Dafydd Vivian Llewellyn, (Richard Llewellyn); author; *b* Wales; *m* 1st, 1952, Nona Theresa Sonsteby (marr. diss., 1968), Chicago; 2nd, 1974, Susan Frances Heimann, MA, New York. *Educ:* St David's, Cardiff, London. Coalmining; studied hotel management in Italy; film writing and producing; Captain, The Welsh Guards, 1941-46. *Publications:* (as Richard Llewellyn) How Green Was My Valley, 1939; None But the Lonely Heart, 1943, new completed edn, 1968; A Few Flowers for Shiner, 1950; A Flame for Doubting Thomas, 1954; Sweet Witch, 1955; Mr Hamish Gleave, 1956; The Flame of Hercules, 1957; Warden of the Smoke and Bells, 1958; Chez Pavan, 1959; A Man in a Mirror, 1961; Up, Into the Singing Mountain, 1963; Sweet Morn of Judas' Day, 1964; Down Where the Moon is Small, 1966; The End of the Rug, 1968; But We Didn't Get the Fox, 1970; White Horse to Banbury Cross, 1972; The Night is a Child, 1972; Bride of Israel, My Love, 1973; A Hill of Many Dreams, 1974; Green, Green My Valley Now, 1975; At Sunrise, The Rough Music, 1976; Tell Me Now, and Again, 1977; A Night of Bright Stars, 1979; I Stand on a Quiet Shore, 1982; has also written for the younger reader. *Plays:* Poison Pen, 1937; Noose, 1947; The Scarlet Suit, 1962; Ecce!, 1974; Hat!, 1974; Oranges and Lemons, 1980 (for TV). *Recreations:* economics, anthropology, photography. *Address:* c/o Michael Joseph Ltd, 44 Bedford Square, WC1B 3DU. *Club:* Cavalry and Guards.

LLOYD, Richard Ernest Butler; Deputy Chairman, since 1978, Chief Executive, since 1980, Hill Samuel & Co. Ltd; *b* 6 Dec. 1928; *s* and *heir* of Major Sir (Ernest) Guy Richard Lloyd, Bt, *qv*; *m* 1955, Jennifer Susan Margaret, *e d* of Brigadier Ereld Cardiff, *qv*; three *s*. *Educ:* Wellington Coll.; Hertford Coll., Oxford (MA). Nat. Service (Captain, Black Watch), 1947-49. Joined Glyn, Mills & Co., 1952; Exec. Dir, 1964-70; Chief Executive, Williams & Glyn's Bank Ltd, 1970-78; non-exec. Dir, 1978-. Director: Australia & New Zealand Bank Ltd and Australia & New Zealand Banking Gp Ltd, 1961-75 (Dep. Chm. 1965-71); Legal & Gen. Assce Soc., 1966-; Vickers Ltd, 1978-. Member: London and SE Regional Council, CBI, 1966-72; Industrial Develt Adv. Bd, 1972-77; Nat. Econ. Develt Council, 1973-77; Cttee to Review the Functioning of Financial Institutions, 1977-80; CBI Council, 1978-. Member: Council, Inst. of Bankers, 1970-75; Council of Management, Ditchley Foundn, 1974-; Council, British Heart Foundn, 1977-. *Recreations:* walking, fishing, gardening. *Address:* Sundridge Place, Sundridge, Sevenoaks, Kent TN14 6DD. *T:* Westerham 63599. *Club:* Boodle's.

LLOYD, Maj.-Gen. Richard Eyre, CB 1959; CBE 1957 (OBE 1944); DSO 1945; late RE, retired, Sept. 1962; Arms Control and Disarmament Research Unit, Foreign and Commonwealth Office, 1966-73; *b* 7 Dec. 1906; *s* of late Lieut-Colonel W. E. Eyre Lloyd; *m* 1939, Gillian, *d* of late Rear-Adm. J. F. C. Patterson, OBE; one *s* two *d*. *Educ:* Eton; Pembroke Coll. (Cambridge). 2nd Lieut in Royal Engineers, 1927. Served War of 1939-45 on Staff, also with RE in North West Europe; Lieut-Colonel 1942; Colonel, 1951; Brigadier, 1955; Maj.-Gen., 1957. Chief of Staff, Middle East Land Forces, 1957-59; Director of Military Intelligence, 1959-62. Colonel Comdt, Intelligence Corps, 1964-69. *Recreation:* sailing. *Address:* Snooks Farm House, Walhampton, Lymington, Hants. *T:* Lymington 73569.

LLOYD, Richard Hey; Organist and Master of the Choristers, Durham Cathedral, since 1974; *b* 25 June 1933; *s* of Charles Yates Lloyd and Ann Lloyd; *m* 1962, Teresa Morwenna Willmott; four *d*. *Educ:* Lichfield Cathedral Choir Sch.; Rugby Sch. (Music Scholar); Jesus Coll., Cambridge (Organ Scholar). MA, FRCO, ARCM. Asst Organist, Salisbury Cath., 1957-66; Organist and Master of the Choristers, Hereford Cath., 1966-74; Conductor, Three Choirs Festival, 1966-74 (Chief Conductor 1967, 1970, 1973). Examiner, Associated Bd of Royal Schs of Music, 1967-. Member Council: Friends of Cathedral Music, 1968-; RCO, 1974-. Special Comr, RSCM, 1972-. *Publications:* church music. *Recreations:* cricket, theatre, travel, reading. *Address:* 6 The College, Durham. *T:* Durham 64766.

LLOYD, Prof. Seton Howard Frederick, CBE 1958 (OBE 1949); FBA 1955; Archæologist; Professor of Western Asiatic Archæology, University of London, 1962-69, now Emeritus; *b* 30 May 1902; *s* of John Eliot Howard Lloyd and Florence Louise Lloyd (*née* Armstrong); *m* 1944, Margery Ulrica Fitzwilliams Hyde; one *s* one *d*. *Educ:* Uppingham; Architectural Assoc. ARIBA 1926; Asst to Sir Edwin Lutyens, PRA, 1926-28; excavated with Egypt Exploration Society, 1928-30; excavated in Iraq for University of

Chicago Oriental Institute, 1930-37; excavated in Turkey for University of Liverpool, 1937-39; FSA 1938 (Vice-Pres., 1965-69); Technical Adviser, Government of Iraq; Directorate-General of Antiquities, 1939-49; Director British Institute of Archæology, Ankara, Turkey, 1949-61. Hon. MA (Edinburgh), 1960. Lawrence of Arabia Meml Medal, RCAS, 1971; Gertrude Bell Meml Medal, British Sch. of Archaeology in Iraq, 1979. *Publications:* Mesopotamia (London), 1936; Sennacherib's Aqueduct at Jerwan, (Chicago), 1935; The Gimilsin Temple (Chicago), 1940; Presargonid Temples (Chicago), 1942; Ruined Cities of Iraq (Oxford), 1942; Twin Rivers, (Oxford), 1942; Foundations in the Dust (London), 1947; Early Anatolia (Pelican), 1956; Art of the Ancient Near East (London), 1961; Mounds of the Ancient Near East (Edinburgh), 1963; Highland Peoples of Anatolia (London), 1967; Archaeology of Mesopotamia (London), 1978; Excavation Reports and many articles in journals. *Recreation:* travel. *Address:* Woolstone Lodge, Faringdon, Oxon. *T:* Uffington 248. *Club:* Chelsea Arts.

LLOYD DAVIES, John Robert; *see* Davies.

LLOYD-DAVIES, Oswald Vaughan; Surgeon Emeritus: Middlesex Hospital (Surgeon, 1950-81); St Mark's Hospital for diseases of the Colon and Rectum (Surgeon, 1935-81); Former Surgeon: Connaught Hospital; Hampstead General Hospital; *s* of late Rev. Samuel Lloyd-Davies, BA; *m* 1st, 1939, Menna (*d* 1968), *d* of late Canon D. J. Morgan, MA; one *s* one *d*; 2nd, 1970, Rosamund, *d* of late Rev. E. V. Bond, MA. *Educ:* Caterham Sch.; Middlesex Hospital Medical Sch., London Univ. MRCS, LRCP, 1929; MB, BS (London) 1930; FRCS 1932; MS (London) 1932. Fellow Royal Society of Med. (Past Pres. sect. of proctology); Fellow Assoc. of Surgeons of Great Britain and Ireland; Member, Harveian Society; Hon. Fellow, Amer. Soc. of Colon and Rectal Surgeons. *Publications:* various chapters in British Surgical Practice; articles on colon, rectal and liver surgery. *Recreations:* gardening, fishing. *Address:* Townsend Close, Ashwell, Herts. *T:* Ashwell 2386.

LLOYD DAVIES, Trevor Arthur, MD; FRCP; *b* 8 April 1909; *s* of Arthur Lloyd Davies and Grace Margret (*née* Bull); *m* 1936, Joan (*d* 1912), *d* of John Keily, Co. Dublin; one *d*; *m* 1975, Margaret, *d* of Halliday Gracey, Woodford. *Educ:* Woking Grammar Sch.; St Thomas' Hospital, SE1. MRCS, LRCP 1932; MB, BS London (gold medal and hons in surgery, forensic med., obst. and gynæc.); MRCP 1933; MD London 1934; FRCP 1952. Resident Asst Physician, St Thomas' Hospital, 1934-36; Prof. of Social Medicine, University of Malaya, 1953-61; Senior Medical Inspector of Factories, Min. of Labour and Dept of Employment and Productivity, 1961-70; Chief Med. Adviser, Dept of Employment, 1970-73. QHP 1968-71. *Publications:* The Practice of Industrial Medicine, 2nd edn, 1957; Respiratory Diseases in Foundrymen, 1971; Whither Occupational Medicine?, 1973; numerous papers on industrial and social medicine, in Lancet and Medical Journal of Malaya. *Recreations:* gardening, carpentry and bricklaying. *Address:* The Old Bakery, High Street, Elmdon, Saffron Walden, Essex CB11 4NL. *Club:* Athenæum.

LLOYD-ELEY, John, QC 1970; a Recorder of the Crown Court, since 1972; *b* 23 April 1923; *s* of Edward John Eley; *m* 1946, Una Fraser Smith; two *s*. *Educ:* Xaverian Coll., Brighton; Exeter Coll., Oxford (MA). Served War, 1942-46, Lieut 50th Royal Tank Regt and 7th Hussars, N Africa, Sicily and Italy. Barrister, Middle Temple, 1951; South-Eastern Circuit; Mem., Bar Council, 1969. *Recreations:* farming, travel. *Address:* 1 Hare Court, Temple, EC4Y 7BE. *T:* 01-353 5324; Luxfords Farm, East Grinstead. *T:* East Grinstead 21583.

LLOYD GEORGE, family name of **Earl Lloyd George of Dwyfor** and **Viscount Tenby.**

LLOYD GEORGE OF DWYFOR, 3rd Earl, *cr* 1945; **Owen Lloyd George;** Viscount Gwynedd, 1945; *b* 28 April 1924; *s* of 2nd Earl Lloyd George of Dwyfor, and Roberta Ida Freeman, 5th *d* of Sir Robert McAlpine, 1st Bt; *S* father, 1968; *m* 1st, 1949, Ruth Margaret (marr. diss. 1982), *o d* of Richard Coit; two *s* one *d*; 2nd, 1982, Cecily Josephine, *d* of Sir Alexander Gordon Cumming, 5th Bt, MC, and of Elizabeth Countess Cawdor, *widow* of 2nd Earl of Woolton and former wife of 3rd Baron Forres. *Educ:* Oundle. Welsh Guards, 1942-47. European War, 1944-45. Formerly Captain Welsh Guards. Director: Sedgwick Construction Services Ltd; Marchwiel Ltd; Sir Alfred McAlpine & Son (International) Ltd. An Underwriting Member of Lloyd's. Carried the Sword at Investiture of HRH the Prince of Wales, Caernarvon Castle, 1969. Mem., Historic Buildings Council for Wales, 1971. Mem. Court, Nat. Mus. of Wales, 1978. *Heir:* *s* Viscount Gwynedd, *qv*. *Recreation:* shooting. *Address:* 12 Lansdown Crescent, Bath, Avon BA1 5EX. *Clubs:* White's, City of London, Pratt's.

LLOYD-HUGHES, Sir Trevor Denby, Kt 1970; Chairman, Lloyd-Hughes Associates Ltd, International Consultants in Public Affairs; *b* 31 March 1922; *er s* of late Elwyn and Lucy Lloyd-Hughes, Bradford, Yorks; *m* 1st, 1950, Ethel Marguerite Durward (marr. diss., 1971), *o d* of late J. Ritchie, Dundee and Bradford; one *s* one *d*; 2nd, 1971, Marie-Jeanne, *d* of Marcel and Helene Moreillon, Geneva; one *d* (and one adopted *d*—a Thai girl). *Educ:* Woodhouse Grove Sch., Yorks; Jesus Coll., Oxford (MA). Commissioned RA, 1941; served with 75th (Shropshire Yeomanry) Medium Regt, RA, in Western Desert, Sicily and Italy, 1941-45. Asst Inspector of Taxes, 1948; freelance journalist, 1949; joined staff of Liverpool Daily Post, 1949; Political Corresp., Liverpool Echo, 1950, Liverpool Daily Post, 1951. Press Secretary to the Prime Minister, 1964-69; Chief Information Adviser to Govt, 1969-70. Dir, Liverpool Daily Post and Echo Ltd, 1978-. Member of Circle of Wine Writers, 1961, Chm., 1972-73. *Recreations:* yoga, playing the Spanish guitar, golf, walking, travel. *Address:* 33 Holly Grove, Peckham, SE15 5DF. *T:* 01-732 3394. *Clubs:* Reform, Belfry.

LLOYD-JOHNES, Herbert Johnes, OBE 1973; TD 1950; FSA; *b* 9 Dec. 1900; *e s* of Herbert Thomas Lloyd-Johnes, MC, and Georgina Mary Lloyd-Johnes, Dolaucothy, Co. Carmarthen; *m* 1942, Margaret Ruth Edgar (Lieut, FANY, War of 1939-45); two *d*. *Educ:* St Andrews, Eastbourne; Malvern. Spent much of his time in Poland, 1931-39; Member British Military Mission to Poland, 1939; a Senior British Liaison Officer to Polish Forces, 1940-46. Chairman: Historic Buildings Council for Wales, 1967-77 (Mem. 1955-77); Welsh Folk Museum Cttee, 1953-55; Rural Industries Cttee for Monmouth, Glamorgan and Radnor, 1955-66; Member: Council, Nat. Trust of GB, 1967-74; Court, Nat. Library of Wales, 1948- (Mem. Council, 1948-78); Nat. Museum of Wales, 1949; Court of Governors, University of Wales, 1952-78; Governor, University College of S Wales and Monmouth, Cardiff. Major RA, TA, Pembroke and Cardigan. Hon. LLD Wales, 1973. Cross For Valour (Poland), 1939. *Publications:* (with Sir Leonard Twiston-Davies) Welsh Furniture, 1950, repr. 1971; contributor to several learned journals. *Recreation:* reading. *Address:* Fosse Hill, Coates, near Cirencester, Glos. *T:* Kemble 279. *Club:* Boodle's.

LLOYD JONES, Charles Beynon; *see* Jones, C. B. L.

LLOYD JONES, David Elwyn, MC 1946; Under-Secretary, Department of Education and Science, 1969-80; *b* 20 Oct. 1920; *s* of late Daniel and Blodwen Lloyd Jones; *m* 1955, Mrs E. W. Gallie (widow of Ian Gallie), *d* of late Prof. Robert Peers, CBE, MC and late Mrs F. D. G. Peers; no *c* (one step *s*). *Educ:* Ardwyn Grammar Sch., Aberystwyth; University College of Wales, Aberystwyth (BA Hons). War Service, 1941-46, Indian Army; with 1st Bn, The Assam Regt, in Burma Campaign (Major, MC). Entered Ministry of Education, 1947. Principal Private Sec. to Chancellor of the Duchy of Lancaster, 1960-61; Asst Sec., Min. (later Dept) of Educn and Science, 1961-69. Mem., councils of Royal Acad. of Dancing, 1980-, Froebel Inst., 1980-, and RCM, 1981-. Hon. Sec., Assam Regt Assoc., 1948-. *Address:* 5 Playfair Mansions, Queen's Club Gardens, W14. *T:* 01-385 0586. *Clubs:* Royal Commonwealth Society, MCC, Roehampton.

LLOYD-JONES, David Trevor, VRD 1958; **His Honour Judge Lloyd-Jones;** a Circuit Judge, since 1972; *b* 16 March 1917; *s* of Trevor and Anne Lloyd-Jones, Holywell, Flints; *m* 1st, 1942, Mary Violet (*d* 1980), *d* of Frederick Barnardo, MD, London; one *d*; 2nd, 1958, Anstice Elizabeth, MB, BChir (*d* 1981), *d* of William Henry Perkins, Whitchurch; one *s* one *d*. *Educ:* Holywell Grammar School. Banking, 1934-39 and 1946-50. Called to the Bar, Gray's Inn, 1951; practised Wales and Chester Circuit, 1952-71; Prosecuting Counsel to Post Office (Wales and Chester Circuit), 1961-66; Dep. Chm., Caerns QS, 1966-70, Chm, 1970-71; Legal Mem., Mental Health Appeal Tribunal (Wales Area), 1960-72; Dep. Chm., Agricultural Land Tribunal (Wales Area), 1968-72. Served War of 1939-45, RNVR and RNR, Atlantic, Mediterranean and Pacific; Lt-Comdr, RNR, retd. *Recreations:* golf, music. *Address:* 29 Curzon Park North, Chester. *T:* Chester 675144. *Club:* Army and Navy.

LLOYD-JONES, Sir (Harry) Vincent, Kt 1960; a Judge of the High Court of Justice, Family Division (formerly Probate, Divorce and Admiralty Division), 1960-72; *b* 16 Oct. 1901; 3rd *s* of late Henry Lloyd-Jones; *m* 1933, Margaret Alwena, *d* of late G. H. Mathias; one *s* one *d*. *Educ:* St Marylebone Grammar Sch. (Old Philological); University Coll., London; Jesus Coll., Oxford. Exhibitioner English Language and Literature, Jesus Coll., Oxford, 1921; BA (Eng. Lang. and Lit.) 1923; BA (Jurisprudence) 1924; MA 1927. President Oxford Union Society, (Summer Term) 1925. Member Oxford Union Debating Team in USA, 1925. Called to Bar by Inner Temple, 1926, Master of the Bench, 1958; practised Common Law Bar; Wales and Chester Circuit; QC 1949. Recorder of Chester, 1952-58; Recorder of Cardiff, 1958-60. Hon. Fellow: Jesus Coll., Oxford, 1960; University Coll., London, 1962. *Recreations:* reading, walking. *Address:* 24 Vincent Square, SW1P 2NJ. *T:* 01-834 5109.

LLOYD-JONES, Prof. (Peter) Hugh (Jefferd); FBA 1966; Regius Professor of Greek in the University of Oxford and Student of Christ Church since 1960; *b* 21 Sept. 1922; *s* of Major W. Lloyd-Jones, DSO, and Norah Leila, *d* of F. H. Jefferd, Brent, Devon; *m* 1st, 1953, Frances Elisabeth Hedley (marr. diss. 1981); two *s* one *d*; 2nd, 1982, Mary Lefkowitz (Andrew W. Mellon Professor in the Humanities, Wellesley College, Mass), *d* of Harold and Mena Rosenthal, New York; *Educ:* Lycée Français du Royaume Uni, S. Kensington; Westminster Sch.; Christ Church, Oxford. Served War of 1939-45, 2nd Lieut, Intelligence Corps, India, 1942; Temp. Captain, 1944. 1st Cl. Classics (Mods), 1941; MA 1947; 1st Cl. LitHum, 1948; Chancellor's Prize for Latin Prose, 1947; Ireland and Craven Schol., 1947; Fellow of Jesus Coll., Cambridge, 1948-54; Asst Lecturer in Classics, University of Cambridge, 1950-52, Lecturer, 1952-54; Fellow and E. P. Warren Praelector in Classics, Corpus Christi Coll., Oxford, 1954-60; J. H. Gray Lecturer, University of Cambridge, 1961; Visiting Prof., Yale Univ., 1964-65, 1967-68; Sather Prof. of Classical Literature, Univ. of California at Berkeley, 1969-70; Alexander White Vis. Prof., Chicago, 1972; Vis. Prof., Harvard Univ., 1976-77. Fellow, Morse Coll., Yale Univ. Hon. Mem., Greek Humanistic Soc., 1968; Corres.

Mem., Acad. of Athens, 1978; Hon. Foreign Mem., Amer. Acad. of Arts and Scis, 1978. Hon. DHL Chicago, 1970. *Publications:* Appendix to Loeb Classical Library edn of Aeschylus, 1957; Menandri Dyscolus (Oxford Classical Text), 1960; Greek Studies in Modern Oxford, 1961; (trans.) Paul Maas, Greek Metre, 1962; (ed) The Greeks, 1962; Tacitus (in series The Great Historians), 1964; (trans.) Aeschylus: Agamemnon, The Libation-Bearers, and The Eumenides, 1970; The Justice of Zeus, 1971; (ed) Maurice Bowra, 1974; Females of the Species: Semonides of Amorgos on Women, 1975; (with Marcelle Quinton) Myths of the Zodiac, 1978; (with Marcelle Quinton) Imaginary Animals, 1979; Blood for the Ghosts, 1982; Classical Survivals, 1982; (with P. J. Parsons) Supplementum Hellenisticum, 1982; contributions to periodicals. *Recreations:* cats, watching cricket. *Address:* Christ Church, Oxford. *T:* Oxford 48737; 7 Norfolk Terrace, Wellesley, Mass 02181, USA. *T:* 617.237.2212.

LLOYD JONES, Richard Anthony, CB 1981; Deputy Secretary, Welsh Office, since 1978; *b* 1 Aug. 1933; *s* of Robert and Anne Lloyd Jones; *m* 1955, Patricia Avril Mary Richmond; two *d*. *Educ:* Long Dene Sch., Edenbridge; Nottingham High Sch.; Balliol Coll., Oxford (MA). Entered Admiralty, 1957; Asst Private Sec. to First Lord of the Admiralty, 1959-62; Private Sec. to Secretary of the Cabinet, 1969-70; Asst Sec., Min. of Defence, 1970-74; Under Sec., Welsh Office, 1974-78. *Recreations:* music, walking. *Address:* Penlan, 141 Heol Isaf, Radyr, Cardiff. *Club:* United Oxford & Cambridge University.

LLOYD-JONES, Robert; Director-General, Retail Consortium, since 1981; *b* 30 Jan. 1931; *s* of Robert and Edith Lloyd-Jones; *m* 1958, Morny Baggs-Thompson (marr. diss. 1977); two *s* one *d*. *Educ:* Wrekin Coll.; Queens' Coll., Univ. of Cambridge (MA Hons); Harvard Business School. Short Service Commission, RN, 1956; Shell International, 1959; BTR Industries Ltd, 1962; International Wool Secretariat, 1964; Schachenmayr, Germany, 1971; British Textile Employers Association, 1977-81. FRSA. *Recreations:* golf, squash, tennis, music, chess, art, and the general pursuit of pleasure. *Address:* Spurs Lodge, Sagars Road, Styal, Wilmslow, Cheshire SK9 4HE. *T:* Wilmslow 532892. *Clubs:* Lansdowne, Institute of Directors; Royal Birkdale Golf, Rye Golf, Formby Golf.

LLOYD-JONES, Sir Vincent; *see* Lloyd-Jones, Sir H. V.

LLOYD MEAD, William Howard; *see* Mead.

LLOYD-MOSTYN, family name of **Baron Mostyn.**

LLOYD OWEN, Maj.-Gen. David Lanyon, CB 1971; DSO 1945; OBE 1954; MC 1942; Chairman, British Foundation for Shooting and Conservation, since 1979; *b* 10 Oct. 1917; *s* of late Capt. Reginald Charles Lloyd Owen, OBE, RN; *m* 1947, Ursula Evelyn, *d* of late Evelyn Hugh Barclay, and of Hon. Mrs Barclay, MBE; three *s*. *Educ:* Winchester; RMC, Sandhurst. 2nd Lieut, The Queen's Royal Regt, 1938. Comdr, Long Range Desert Group, 1943-45. Military Asst to High Commissioner in Malaya, 1952-53; Comdg 1st Queen's, 1957-59; Comdr 24 Infantry Bde Group, 1962-64; GOC Cyprus District, 1966-68; GOC Near East Land Forces, 1968-69. Pres., Regular Commns Bd, 1969-72, retd. Kt of Cross of Merit, SMO Malta, 1946. *Publications:* The Desert My Dwelling Place, 1957; Providence Their Guide, 1980. *Address:* Violet Bank, Swainsthorpe, Norwich NR14 8PR. *T:* Swainsthorpe 470468. *Club:* Naval and Military.

LLOYD PHILLIPS, Ivan, CBE 1963 (OBE 1959); DPhil Oxon; *b* Cambridge, June 1910; *er s* of late Rev. A. Lloyd Phillips, formerly Vicar of Ware, Herts; *m* 1941, Faith Macleay, *o c* of late Brig.-Gen. G. M. Macarthur Onslow, CMG, DSO, Camden, New South Wales; one *s*. *Educ:* Worksop Coll.; Selwyn Coll., Cambridge; Balliol Coll., Oxford. Appointed Colonial Administrative Service, 1934; served in: Gold Coast, 1934-38; Palestine, 1938-47; District Commissioner, Gaza-Beersheba, 1946-47; Colonial Office, 1947-48; Cyprus, 1948-51; Commissioner, Nicosia-Kyrenia, 1950-51; Singapore, 1951-53; Commissioner-General's Office, 1951-52; Dep. Secretary for Defence, 1952-53; Malaya, 1953-62; Secretary to Chief Minister and Minister for Home Affairs, 1955-57; Secretary, Ministry of the Interior, 1957-62. Secretary, Oxford Preservation Trust, 1962-65; Inst. of Commonwealth Studies, Oxford Univ., 1965-70. Chairman, Oxfordshire Playing Fields Assoc., 1966-77, Pres., 1977-. Duke of Edinburgh's award for service to Nat. Playing Fields Movement, 1974. Commander, Order of Defender of the Realm (Malaysia), 1958. *Address:* Cranmer Cottage, Dorchester-on-Thames, Oxfordshire. *T:* Oxford 340026. *Clubs:* Travellers', MCC.

LLOYD-ROBERTS, George Charles, MChir; FRCS; Consultant Orthopædic Surgeon, St George's Hospital, since 1957; Consultant Orthopædic Surgeon, The Hospital for Sick Children, Great Ormond Street, since 1955; Consultant in Paediatric Orthopaedics to the RAF, since 1970 and RN, since 1972; *b* 23 Nov. 1918; *e s* of Griffith and Gwendoline Lloyd-Roberts; *m* 1st, 1947, Catherine Lansing Ray (marr. diss. 1967), widow of Edward Lansing Ray, St Louis, Missouri; one *s* two *d*; 2nd, 1980, Edome Broughton-Adderley. *Educ:* Eton Coll.; Magdalene Coll., Cambridge. BA, MB, BChir (Cantab), 1943, MChir (Cantab), 1946; FRCS, 1949. Graded Surgical Specialist, RAMC, 1944, Surgeon, Yugoslav and Italian Partisan Forces. Late 1st Assistant, Orthopædic Dept, St George's Hospital, 1954; Clinical Research Assistant, Royal National Orthopaedic Hospital, 1952;

Nuffield Fellow in Orthopædic Surgery, 1952. Mem. Council, RCS, 1976–; President: British Orthopædic Assoc., 1977–78; Orthopædic Section, RSM, 1976–77. Mem. Council, Game Conservancy, 1977–. Robert Jones Gold Medal of British Orthopædic Assoc., 1953. *Publications:* Orthopædics in Infancy and Childhood, 1972; The Hip Joint in Childhood, 1977; (ed) Orthopædic Surgery, 1968; articles on orthopædic subjects in medical journals. *Recreations:* fishing, shooting. *Address:* 9 Cheyne Place, SW3. *T:* 01-352 5622; (Private Consulting Room), Hospital for Sick Children, Great Ormond Street, WC1. *Club:* Boodle's.

LLOYD WEBBER, Andrew; composer; *b* 22 March 1948; *s* of William Southcombe Lloyd Webber, CBE; *m* 1971, Sarah Jane Tudor (*née* Hugill); one *s* one *d. Educ:* Westminster Sch. Composer (with lyrics by Timothy Rice): Joseph and the Amazing Technicolour Dreamcoat, 1968 (rev. 1973); Jesus Christ Superstar, 1970; Evita, 1976 (stage version, 1978); (with lyrics by Alan Ayckbourn) Jeeves, 1975; (with lyrics by Don Black) Tell Me on a Sunday, 1980; Cats, 1981 (based on poems by T. S. Eliot); (with lyrics by Don Black) Song and Dance, 1982. Film scores: Gumshoe, 1971; The Odessa File, 1974. Composed "Variations" (based on A minor Caprice No 24 by Paganini), 1977. *Publications:* (with Timothy Rice) Evita, 1978; (with Timothy Rice) Joseph and the Amazing Technicolour Dreamcoat, 1982. *Recreation:* architecture. *Address:* 11 West Eaton Place, SW1.
  See also J. Lloyd Webber.

LLOYD WEBBER, Julian; Professor of 'Cello, Guildhall School of Music, since 1978; *b* 14 April 1951; *s* of William Southcombe Lloyd Webber, CBE; *m* 1974, Celia Mary Ballantyne. *Educ:* University College Sch., London; Royal College of Music. ARCM. Studied 'cello with: Douglas Cameron, 1965–68; Pierre Fournier, Geneva, 1972. Début, Queen Elizabeth Hall, 1972; USA début, Lincoln Center, NY, 1980. Has performed with all major British orchestras; toured: USA, 1980; Germany, Holland, Africa, Bulgaria, S America, Spain, Belgium, France, Scandinavia, NZ, Portugal, Luxembourg. Has made first recordings of works by Benjamin Britten, Frank Bridge, Delius, Rodrigo, Holst, Vaughan Williams, Haydn. Awarded gold and silver discs for Variations, 1978. *Publications:* series, The Romantic 'Cello, 1978, The Classical 'Cello, 1980, The French 'Cello, 1981; (ed) Frank Bridge 'Cello Music, 1981; contribs to music jls and national Press in UK, US, Canada and Australia. *Recreations:* topography (especially British), keeping turtles, beer, Orient FC. *Address:* c/o Ibbs & Tillett Ltd, 450–452 Edgware Road, W2 1EG. *T:* 01-262 2864.
  See also A. Lloyd Webber.

LO, Kenneth Hsiao Chien; author, Chinese food critic and consultant; *b* 12 Sept. 1913; *s* of Lo Tsung Hsien and Wei Ying; *m* 1954, Anne Phillipe Brown; two *s* two *d. Educ:* Yenching Univ., Peking (BA); Cambridge Univ. (MA). Student-Consul for China, Liverpool, 1942–46; Vice-Consul for China, Manchester, 1946–49. Man. Director, Cathay Arts Ltd (Chinese Fine Art Publishers), 1951–66; Founder Director: Memories of China restaurant; Ken Lo's Kitchen, chinese cookery sch. Chm., Chinese Gourmet Club, London, 1975–. *Publications include:* Chinese Food, 1972; Peking Cooking, 1973; Chinese Vegetarian Cooking, 1974; Encyclopedia of Chinese Cookery, 1975; Quick and Easy Chinese Cooking, 1973; Cheap Chow, 1977; Love of Chinese Cooking, 1977; Chinese Provincial Cooking, 1979; Chinese Eating and Cooking for Health, 1979; Wok Cookbook, 1981; Chinese Regional Cooking, 1981. *Recreation:* tennis (Davis cup for China, 1946; Veteran Doubles Champion of Britain, 1976, 1979, 1981; First Single for UK in Britannia Cup, World Super Veteran Tennis Championship, 1981). *Address:* 249 Sandycombe Road, Kew, Surrey. *Clubs:* Hurlingham, Queen's.

LOACH, Kenneth; television and film director; *b* 17 June 1936. *Educ:* King Edward VI School, Nuneaton; St Peter's Hall, Oxford. BBC Trainee, Drama Dept, 1963. Television: Diary of a Young Man, 1964; 3 Clear Sundays, 1965; The End of Arthur's Marriage, 1965; Up The Junction, 1965; Coming Out Party, 1965; Cathy Come Home, 1966; In Two Minds, 1966; The Golden Vision, 1969; The Big Flame, 1969; After A Lifetime, 1971; The Rank and File, 1972; Days of Hope, 1975; The Price of Coal, 1977; The Gamekeeper, 1979; Auditions, 1980; A Question of Leadership, 1980. Films: Poor Cow, 1968; Kes, 1970; In Black and White, 1970; Family Life, 1972; Black Jack, 1979; Looks and Smiles, 1981. *Address:* c/o Central Independent Television, 46 Charlotte Street, W1.

LOANE, Most Rev. Marcus Lawrence, KBE 1976; DD; *b* 14 Oct. 1911; *s* of K. O. A. Loane; *m* 1937, Patricia Evelyn Jane Simpson Knox; two *s* two *d. Educ:* The King's School, Parramatta, NSW; Sydney University (MA). Moore Theological College, 1932–33; Australian College of Theology (ThL, 1st Class, 1933; Fellow, 1955). Ordained Deacon, 1935, Priest, 1936; Resident Tutor and Chaplain, Moore Theological College, 1935–38; Vice-Principal, 1939–53; Principal, 1954–59. Chaplain AIF, 1942–44. Canon, St Andrew's Cathedral, 1949–58; Bishop-Coadjutor, diocese of Sydney, 1958–66; Archbishop of Sydney and Metropolitan of Province of NSW, 1966–81; Primate of Australia, 1978–82. Hon. DD Wycliffe College, Toronto, 1958. *Publications:* Oxford and the Evangelical Succession, 1950; Cambridge and the Evangelical Succession, 1952; Masters of the English Reformation, 1955; Life of Archbishop Mowll, 1960; Makers of Religious Freedom, 1961; Pioneers of the Reformation in England, 1964; Makers of Our Heritage, 1966; The Hope of Glory, 1968; This Surpassing Excellence, 1969; They Were Pilgrims, 1970; They Overcame, 1971; By Faith We Stand, 1971; The King

is Here, 1973; This is My Son, 1977; The God Who Acts, 1978. *Address:* 18 Harrington Avenue, Warrawee, NSW 2074, Australia.

LOBB, Howard Leslie Vicars, CBE 1952; FRIBA, AIStructE, FRSA; architect; *b* 9 March 1909; *e s* of late Hedley Vicars Lobb and Mary Blanche (*née* Luscombe); *m* 1949, Charmian Isobel (*née* Reilly); three *s. Educ:* privately; Regent Street Polytechnic School of Architecture. Senior Partner, Howard Lobb Partnership, 1950–74. During War of 1939–45, Architect to various ministries: subseq. built numerous schools for County Authorities; HQ of City and Guilds of London Inst., W1; British Pavilion Brussels International Exhibition, 1958; Cons. Architect for Hunterston Nuclear Power Station, Ayrshire; Dungeness Nuclear Power Station; Newcastle Racecourse; Newmarket Rowley Mile, for Jockey Club; Car park, Savile Row, for City of Westminster; HQ for British Council, SW1; Calgary Exhbn and Stampede, Upper Alberta, Canada. Chairman Architectural Council, Festival of Britain, and later Controller (Constr.) South Bank Exhibition. Member RIBA Council and Executive, 1953–56; Life Vice-Pres. (formerly Chm.), London Group of Building Centres; Chm., Architects' Registr. Council, UK, 1957–60; Vice-Pres., Architects' Benevolent Society, 1980– (Hon. Sec., 1953–80). Freeman of City of London; Master, Worshipful Co. of Masons, 1974–75. Vice-Chm., Solent Protection Soc. *Publications:* contrib. various Arch. Journals, Reviews, etc. *Recreations:* sailing, gardening, colour photography, model railways. *Address:* 180 Tottenham Court Road, W1P 9LE. *T:* 01-636 6251; Black Hill, 18 Blackhills, Esher, Surrey. *T:* Esher 63092; 2 Admiral's Wharf, Cowes, Isle of Wight. *T:* Cowes 292414. *Clubs:* Arts; Royal Corinthian Yacht (Vice-Cdre 1960–63); Royal London Yacht; Island Sailing (Cowes); Tamesis (Teddington) (Cdre, 1954–57).

LOCH, family name of **Baron Loch.**

LOCH, 3rd Baron *cr* 1895, of Drylaw; **George Henry Compton Loch;** Major late 11th Hussars; Director and Proprietor, Lusitano Stud and Equitation Centre (dressage academy), since 1979; *b* 3 Feb. 1916; *s* of 2nd Baron and Lady Margaret Compton (*d* 1970), *o d* of 5th Marquess of Northampton; *S* father 1942; *m* 1st, 1942, Leila Mary Grace Isabel Hill Mackenzie (marr. diss., 1946); (one *d* decd) 2nd, 1946, Mrs Betty Castillon du Perron (marr. diss., 1952); 3rd, 1952, Joan Dorothy Hawthorn Binns (marr. diss.); 4th, 1975, Sylvia Barbara Beauchamp-Wilson, *o d* of A. G. Beauchamp Cameron; one *d. Educ:* Eton; RMC, Sandhurst. *Heir: b* Hon. Spencer Douglas Loch, MC 1945 [*b* 1920; *m* 1948, Hon. Rachel (*d* 1976), *yr d* of Group Captain H. L. Cooper, AFC, and of Baroness Lucas and Dingwall (Nan Ino Herbert-Cooper who *d* 1958); one *d* (and two *s* decd); *m* 1979, Davina Lady Boughey. *Educ:* Wellington Coll.; Trinity Coll., Cambridge. Major Grenadier Guards; called to Bar, 1948]. *Address:* Green Farm, Stoke-by-Clare, Suffolk. *T:* Clare 277266.

LOCK, Air Vice-Marshal Basil Goodhand, CB 1978; CBE 1969; AFC 1954; security consultant; *b* 25 June 1923; *s* of J. S. Lock; *m* 1944, Mona Rita; one *s*. Entered RAF from Durham Univ. Air Sqdn; commnd RAF, 1943; various operational sqdns, 1944–47; Exchange Sqdn posts, USA, 1947–48; Flying Instructor, RAF Coll., Cranwell, 1950–51; OC, HC Unit, 1951–54; HQ MEAF, 1954–57; Ops (O), Air Min., 1958–61; OC Flying, RAF Leeming, 1961–63; Plans (Cento), 1964–66; OC, RAF West Raynham, 1967–69; SDS (Air), JSSC, 1969–71; Dir of Ops (AS), MoD, 1971–73; Dir of Personal Services, MoD, 1974–75; Air Vice-Marshal 1975; Air Officer Scotland, 1975–77; Dir Gen. of Security (RAF), 1977–79. CBIM. *Recreations:* golf, gardening, music, motoring. *Address:* (home) Hereford House, Village Way, Little Chalfont, Bucks. *T:* Little Chalfont 2746. *Club:* Wellington.

LOCK, (Cecil) Max, FRIBA (Dist. TP), AADip, FRTPI; Head of Max Lock Group; *b* 29 June 1909; *s* of Cecil William Best Lock and Vivian Cecil Hassell. *Educ:* Berkhamsted Sch.; Architectural Assoc., London. Entered private practice, 1933; (firm established as Max Lock 1933, Max Lock Group 1944, Max Lock & Associates 1950, Max Lock & Partners 1954); retired 1972, remaining Consultant to partnership (now Max Lock, Easton, Perlston & King); formed Max Lock Group of Planning and Development Consultants, in partnership with Michael Theis, 1972; currently Max Lock Group Nigeria, as consultants to Govt of NE State Nigeria, engaged on surveys and master plans for Maiduguri, Nguru, Potiskum, Bauchi, Gombe, Yola-Jimeta and Mubi; retired 1976. Member Watford Borough Council, 1936–40; on staff of AA School of Architecture, 1937–39; Head of Hull School of Architecture, 1939; Leverhulme Research Schol. (carried out a Civic Diagnosis of Hull). Surveys and plans by Max Lock Group for: Middlesbrough, 1946; The Hartlepools, 1948; Portsmouth District, 1949; Bedford, 1951; by Max Lock and Partners, Surveys and Plans for Amman, Aqaba (Jordan), 1954–55; Town Plans for development of Iraq at Um Qasr, Margil and Basrah, 1954–56; New Towns at El Beida, Libya, 1956, and Sheikh Othman, Aden, 1960. Survey and plan for the Capital City and Territory of Kaduna for Government of Northern Nigeria, 1965–66. British Town Centre redevelopment plans, 1957–71, include: Sevenoaks; Thetford; Sutton Coldfield; Salisbury; Brentford; redevelopment of new central housing communities at Oldham; development of Woodley Airfield, Reading; a plan for Central Area of Beverley, Yorks. Visiting Professor: Dept of City Planning, Harvard Univ., 1957; University of Rio de Janeiro, 1960, 1968; Guest Chairman, 5th Australian National Planning Congress, 1960. Member Council, TPI, 1946–50 and 1961–63. Freeman of the City of London, 1978. *Publications:* The Middlesbrough Survey and Plan, 1946; The Hartlepools Survey and Plan, 1948; The Portsmouth and District Survey and Plan, 1949; Bedford by the

River, 1952; The New Basrah, 1956; Kaduna, 1917–1967–2017: A Survey and Plan of the Capital Territory for the Government of Northern Nigeria, 1967; contribs to RIBA Journal, TPI Journal, Town Planning Review, etc. *Recreations:* music, pianist. *Address:* 7 Victoria Square, SW1. *T:* 01-834 7071; Addicroft Mill, Plushabridge, Liskeard, Cornwall. *T:* Rilla Mill 62510. *Club:* Reform.

LOCK, Lt-Comdr Sir Duncan; see Lock, Lt-Comdr Sir J. D.

LOCK, (George) David; Managing Director, Private Patients Plan Ltd, since 1975; *b* 24 Sept. 1929; *s* of George Wilfred Lock and Phyllis Nita (*née* Hollingworth); *m* 1965, Ann Elizabeth Biggs; four *s* one *d. Educ:* Haileybury and ISC; Queens' Coll., Cambridge (MA). British Tabulating Machine Co. Ltd (now ICL), 1954–59; Save & Prosper Group Ltd, 1959–69; American Express, 1969–74; Private Patients Plan Ltd, 1974–. Director: Independent Hospital Gp, 1976–; Tillermound, 1979–; Priplan Investments Ltd, 1979–; Priplan Services Ltd, 1979–; PPP Medical Centre Ltd (incorp. Cavendish Medical Centre), 1981–; Trustee, Eynsham Trust, 1975–; Member: Nuffield Nursing Homes Trust, 1979–; Exec. Cttee, Assoc. of Independent Hosps, 1981–. Mem., RSocMed., 1979–. Freeman, Barbers' Co., 1982–. *Recreations:* bridge, music, family activities, entertaining. *Address:* (home) Buckhurst Place, Horsted Keynes, Sussex RH17 7AH. *T:* Danehill 790599; (business) Private Patients Plan Ltd, Eynsham House, Crescent Road, Tunbridge Wells, Kent TN1 2PL. *T:* Tunbridge Wells 40111.

LOCK, John Arthur, QPM 1975; Deputy Assistant Commissioner, Metropolitan Police, and National Co-ordinator, Regional Crime Squads of England and Wales, 1976–79; *b* 20 Oct. 1922; *s* of Sidney George Lock and Minnie Louise Lock; *m* 1950, Patricia Joyce Lambert; two *d. Educ:* George Palmer Central School, Reading. Royal Air Force, 1941–46; Wireless Operator/Air Gunner; Flying Officer. Joined Metropolitan Police, 1946. *Recreations:* Association football (Vice-Chm., Met. Police FC), tennis, sailing. *Address:* 11 Garden Way, Loughton, Essex. *Club:* Royal Air Force.

LOCK, Lt-Comdr Sir (John) Duncan, Kt 1978; RN; Chairman, Association of District Councils of England and Wales, 1974–79; *b* 5 Feb. 1918; *s* of Brig. Gen. F. R. E. Lock, DSO, and Mary Elizabeth Lock; *m* 1947, Alice Aileen Smith (*d* 1982); three *d. Educ:* Royal Naval Coll., Dartmouth. Served as regular officer in Royal Navy (retiring at his own request), 1931–58: specialised in navigation and navigated Battleships HMS King George V and Howe, the Cruiser Superb, destroyers and minesweepers. Served War of 1939–45: took part in Battle of Atlantic, Norwegian and N African campaigns, Pacific War and Normandy and Anzio landings. Farmed family estate in Somerset, 1958–61. Admty Compass Observatory as specialist in magnetic compasses, 1962–. Member of Lloyd's. Eton RDC, 1967–74; Chm., Bucks Br., RDC Assoc., 1969–74; Mem., S Bucks Dist Council, 1973–; Chm., Assoc. of Dist Councils of England and Wales Council and Policy Cttee, 1974–79 (Chm. Bucks Br., 1974–); Mem., Adv. Cttee on Local Govt Audit, 1979–82; British Rep., Council of Local and Reg. Authorities of Europe, 1979–; Chm., Local Authorities Management Services and Computer Cttee, 1981–. Chm., Beaconsfield Constituency Conservative Assoc., 1972–75. *Recreations:* gardening, shooting, bee-keeping. *Address:* Fen Court, Oval Way, Gerrards Cross, Bucks SL9 8QD. *T:* Gerrards Cross 82467.

LOCK, Max; see Lock, C. M.

LOCK, Stephen Penford, FRCP; MA; Editor, British Medical Journal, since 1975; *b* 8 April 1929; *er s* of Wallace Henry Lock, Romford, Essex; *m* 1955, Shirley Gillian Walker, *d* of E. W. Walker, Bridlington, Yorks; one *s* one *d. Educ:* City of London Sch.; Queens' Coll., Cambridge; St Bartholomew's Hosp., London. MA 1953; MB 1954; MRCP 1963; FRCP 1974. Ho. Phys., Bart's, Brompton, and Central Middlesex Hosps, and Med. Officer, RAF Bomber Comd, 1954–57; Jun. Registrar, London Hosp., London, 1958; Jun. Asst Editor, The Lancet, 1959; Registrar in Pathology, Hosp. for Sick Children, Gt Ormond St., London, 1959–61, and at Bart's, 1961–62; Sen. Registrar in Pathology, Lewisham Hosp., London, 1962–64; Asst Editor, British Med. Jl, 1964–69, Sen. Asst Editor, 1969–74, Dep. Editor, 1974–75. Med. Correspy., BBC Overseas Service, 1966–74. Chm., Internat. Gp on Medical Jl Style, 1978. Organiser and/or participant in 45 Postgrad. Courses in Med. Writing in Britain, Finland, Iraq, Iran, Eire, Canada, Australia, NZ, USA, 1971–; organiser BMJ/ELSE conf., Winchester, 1977, Bath, 1978, Salisbury, 1979, Oxford, 1980. Member: Council, ASH, 1975 (Chm., policy cttee, 1978); Council, Res. Defence Soc., 1976; Med. Adv. Cttee, British Council, 1976; Publications Cttee, King's Fund, 1977; Council, European Life Scis Editors, 1977 (Vice-Pres., 1979–82); Council, Med. Insurance Agency, 1978; RCP cttee on dietary fibre, 1978, on smoking, 1982; Med. Inf. Review Panel, 1979–; Managing Cttee, Bureau of Hygiene and Tropical Diseases, 1981–. Vice-Pres., Internat. Union of the Medical Press, 1976; Pres., European Assoc. of Sci. Editors, 1982–. Vis. Prof. in Medicine, McGill Univ., 1978; Visitor, Acad. Dept of Medicine, Monash Univ., 1982. Trustee, British Med. Students Trust, 1979–. Mem., 14 Editorial Bds of BMA jls. Donders Medal, Ned. Tijdsch. Geneesk, 1981; Internat. Medal, Finnish Med. Soc. Duodecim, 1981. Officer, first cl., White Rose of Finland, 1982. *Publications:* An Introduction to Clinical Pathology, 1965; Health Centres and Group Practices, 1966; The Enemies of Man, 1968; Better Medical Writing, 1970; Family Health Guide, 1972; Medical Risks of Life, 1976; Thorne's Better Medical Writing, 2nd edn 1977; (ed) Adverse Drug Reactions, 1977; (ed) Remembering Henry, 1977; articles on haematology and medical writing in

British, American, Swiss and Finnish jls. *Recreations:* as much opera as possible, hill walking, gardening. *Address:* 115 Dulwich Village, SE21 7BJ. *T:* 01-693 6317. *Club:* Athenæum.

LOCKE, Arthur D'Arcy, (Bobby Locke); professional golfer; Playing Professional at Observatory Golf Club, Johannesburg; *b* Germiston, Transvaal, 20 Nov. 1917; *s* of Charles James Locke; *m* 1943; one *d* ; *m* 1958, Mary Fenten, USA. *Educ:* Benoni High Sch. Won Open and Amateur South African Championships, 1935; won Irish, Dutch and New Zealand Open Championships, 1938; French Open Championship, 1952–53; British Open Championship, 1949, 1950, 1952, 1957; Canadian Open, 1947; Mexican Open, 1952; Egyptian Open, 1954; German Open, 1954; Swiss Open, 1954; Australian Open, 1955; Member Professional Golfers' Association (London). Served War of 1939–45, Middle East and Italy as Pilot, South African Air Force. *Publication:* Bobby Locke on Golf, 1953.

LOCKE, Bobby; see Locke, A. D'A.

LOCKE, John Howard; Director, Health and Safety Executive, since 1975; *b* 26 Dec. 1923; *s* of Percy Locke and Josephine Locke (*née* Marshfield); *m* 1948, Eirene Sylvia Sykes; two *d. Educ:* Hymers Coll., Hull; Queen's Coll., Oxford. Ministry of Agriculture, Fisheries and Food, 1945–65; Under-Secretary: Cabinet Office, 1965–66; MoT, 1966–68; Dept of Employment and Productivity, 1968–71; Dep. Sec., Dept of Employment, 1971–74. *Address:* 4 Old Palace Terrace, The Green, Richmond-on-Thames, Surrey. *T:* 01-940 1830; Old Box Trees, East Preston, Sussex.

LOCKETT, Reginald; His Honour Judge Lockett; a Circuit Judge, since 1981; *b* 24 June 1933; *s* of George Alfred Lockett and Emma (*née* Singleton); *m* 1959, Edna (*née* Lowe); one *s* one *d. Educ:* Ashton-in-Makerfield Grammar Sch.; Manchester Univ.; London Univ. (LLB 1954). Solicitor, 1955. Asst Coroner for Wigan, 1963; Dist Registrar and County Court Registrar, Manchester, 1970–81; a Recorder of the Crown Court, 1978–81. Pres., Manchester Law Students' Soc., 1975–77. Vice Pres., The Boys' Bde, 1978– (Dist Pres., NW Dist, 1973–). Reader, Anglican Church, 1970–. *Recreations:* music, photography. *Address:* 7 Blandford Rise, Lostock, Bolton BL6 4JH. *T:* Bolton 68591.

LOCKHART; see Bruce Lockhart.

LOCKHART, Brian Alexander; Sheriff in Glasgow and Strathkelvin, since 1981 (in North Strathclyde, 1979–81); *b* 1 Oct. 1942; *s* of John Arthur Hay Lockhart and Norah Lockhart; *m* 1967, Christine Ross Clark; two *s* two *d. Educ:* Glasgow Academy; Glasgow Univ. (BL). Qualified as solicitor, 1964; Partner in Robertson Chalmers & Auld, Solicitors, Glasgow, 1966–79. *Recreations:* fishing, golf, family. *Address:* 18 Hamilton Avenue, Glasgow G41 4JF. *T:* 041-427 1921.

LOCKHART, Sir Muir Edward S.; see Sinclair-Lockhart.

LOCKHART, Prof. Robert Douglas, MD, ChM; LLD; FSAScot, FRSE; Regius Professor of Anatomy, University of Aberdeen, 1938–65, now Emeritus Professor; concurrently Curator, Anthropological Museum (Hon. Curator, 1939–80, Consultant 1979–80); *b* 7 Jan. 1894; *s* of William Lockhart and Elizabeth Bogie. *Educ:* Robert Gordon's Coll., Aberdeen; University, Aberdeen (MB, ChB 1918). Ho. Surg. Aberdeen Royal Infirmary; Surgeon-Probationer, RNVR, 1916; Surgeon-Lt, RN 1918; Lecturer in Anatomy, Aberdeen Univ., 1919; Prof. of Anat., Birmingham Univ. 1931; Dean of Faculty of Medicine, Aberdeen, 1959–62. Past Pres., Anatomical Soc. of Great Britain and Ireland. LLD Aberdeen, 1965. *Publications:* Chapter, Ways of Living, in Man and Nature, 1926; Myology Section in Cunningham's Anatomy, 1964; Living Anatomy—photographic atlas, 1963, 7th edn 1974; Anatomy of the Human Body, 1969; contributor to Kodak Med. Film Library, 1933; Structure and Function of Muscle, 1960 (2nd rev. edn, vol. 1, ed Bourne, 1972). *Recreations:* roses and rhododendrons. *Address:* 25 Rubislaw Den North, Aberdeen AB2 4AL. *T:* Aberdeen 37833.

LOCKHART, Stephen Alexander, CMG 1960; OBE 1949; *b* 19 March 1905; *o s* of late Captain Murray Lockhart, RN, Milton Lockhart, and of Leonora Rynd; *m* 1944, Angela Watson; two *s* two *d. Educ:* Harrow; Jesus Coll., Cambridge. Served Lisbon, 1940–43; Ministry of Information, 1943; Press Attaché, Lisbon, 1944, Brussels, 1945; First Sec. (Information), Brussels, 1946–51; Foreign Office, 1951; First Sec., Buenos Aires, 1952–55; UK Rep., Trieste, 1955–57; HM Consul-Gen., Leopoldville, and in French Equatorial Africa, 1957–60; HM Consul-Gen., Zürich, 1960–62; HM Ambassador to Dominican Republic, 1962–65, retired; re-employed in FCO, 1965–70; Hon. Consul, Oporto, 1970–75. Chm. Exec. Cttee, Anglo-Portuguese Soc., 1977. *Address:* 10 Shelley Court, Tite Street, SW3; Casa Cardina, 8200 Albufeira, Portugal. *Club:* United Oxford & Cambridge University.

LOCKHART-MUMMERY, Sir Hugh (Evelyn), KCVO 1981; MD, MChir; FRCS; Serjeant-Surgeon to the Queen, since 1975 (Surgeon to HM Household, 1969–75, to the Queen, 1974–75); Consultant Surgeon: King Edward VII's Hospital for Officers since 1968; RAF since 1975; Consulting Surgeon: St Mark's Hospital; St Thomas' Hospital; *b* 28 April 1918; *s* of John Percy Lockhart-Mummery, FRCS; *m* 1946, Elizabeth Jean Crerar (*d* 1981), *d* of Sir James Crerar, KCSI, CIE; one *s. Educ:* Stowe Sch.; Trinity Coll., Cambridge; Westminster Hosp. Med. Sch. MB, BCh 1942; FRCS 1943;

MChir 1950; MD 1956. Served RAF, 1943–46. Examr in Surgery, Univ. of London, 1965; Pres., Sect. of Proctology, RSM, 1966. Dir, Med. Sickness Annuity & Life Assce Soc., 1973– (Chm., 1982-). Hon. Fellow, (French) Académie de Proctologie, 1961; Hon. Fellow, Amer. Soc. of Colon and Rectal Surgeons, 1974. *Publications:* chapters in surgical textbooks; articles on surgery of the colon and rectum in Brit. jls. *Recreations:* golf, fishing. *Address:* 5 Hereford Square, SW7 4TT. *T:* 01-373 3630; 149 Harley Street, W1N 2DE. *T:* 01-935 4444. *Club:* Royal Air Force.

LOCKLEY, Ven. Harold; Archdeacon of Loughborough, since 1963; Part-time Lecturer in Divinity, University of Leicester; *b* 16 July 1916; *s* of Harry and Sarah Elizabeth Lockley; *m* 1947, Ursula Margaret, JP, *d* of Rev. Dr H. Wedell and Mrs G. Wedell (*née* Bonhoeffer); three *s*. *Educ:* Loughborough Coll. (Hons Dip. Physical Education); London University; Westcott House, Cambridge. BA Hons 1937, BD Hons 1943, MTh 1949, London Univ.; PhD 1955, Nottingham Univ. Chaplain and Tutor, Loughborough Coll., 1946-51; Vicar of Glen Parva and South Wigston, 1951-58. OCF Royal Leics Regt, 1951-58; Chaplain, Leicester Royal Infirmary Maternity Hospital, 1967-74; Proctor in Convocation of Canterbury, 1960-80; Canon Chancellor of Leicester Cathedral, 1958-63, Vicar of All Saints, Leicester, 1963-78. Sen. Examining Chaplain to Bishop of Leicester, 1951-79. Mem., Leics Educn Cttee, 1973-. *Publications:* Editor, Leicester Cathedral Quarterly, 1960-63. *Recreations:* walking and foreign travel. *Address:* 1 Knighton Grange Road, Leicester. *T:* Leicester 707328. *Clubs:* English-Speaking Union, National Liberal; Leicestershire (Leicester).
See also Prof. E. A. O. G. Wedell.

LOCKLEY, Ronald Mathias; author and naturalist; *b* 8 Nov. 1903. Hon. MSc Wales, 1977. *Publications:* Dream Island, 1930; The Island Dwellers, 1932; Island Days, 1934; The Sea's a Thief, 1936; Birds of the Green Belt, 1936; I Know an Island, 1938; Early Morning Island, 1939; A Pot of Smoke, 1940; The Way to an Island, 1941; Shearwaters, 1942; Dream Island Days, 1943; Inland Farm, 1943; Islands Round Britain, 1945; Birds of the Sea, 1946; The Island Farmers, 1947; Letters from Skokholm, 1947; The Golden Year, 1948; The Cinnamon Bird, 1948; Birds of Pembrokeshire, 1949; The Charm of the Channel Islands, 1950; (with John Buxton) Island of Skomer, 1951; Travels with a Tent in Western Europe, 1953; Puffins, 1953; (with Rosemary Russell) Bird Ringing, 1953; The Seals and the Curragh, 1954; Gilbert White, 1954; (with James Fisher) Sea-Birds, 1954; Pembrokeshire, 1957; The Pan Book of Cage Birds, 1961; Britain in Colour, 1964; The Private Life of the Rabbit, 1964; Wales, 1966; Grey Seal, Common Seal, 1966; Animal Navigation, 1967; The Book of Bird-Watching, 1968; The Channel Islands, 1968, rev. edn, A Traveller's Guide to the Channel Islands, 1971; The Island, 1969; The Naturalist in Wales, 1970; Man Against Nature, 1970; Seal Woman, 1974; Ocean Wanderers, 1974; Orielton, 1977; Myself when Young, 1979; Whales, Dolphins & Porpoises, 1979; (with Noel Cusa) New Zealand Endangered Species, 1980; The House Above the Sea, 1980; Flight of the Storm Petrel, 1983; *edited:* Natural History of Selborne, by G. White, 1949, rev. edn 1976; Nature Lover's Anthology, 1951; The Bird-Lover's Bedside Book, 1958; *compiled:* In Praise of Islands, 1957. *Address:* 56 Baskerville, Malmesbury, Wilts.

LOCKSPEISER, Sir Ben, KCB 1950; Kt 1946; FRS 1949; FEng, FIMechE, FRAeS; *b* 9 March 1891; *s* of late Leon and Rose Lockspeiser, London; *m* 1920, Elsie Shuttleworth (*d* 1964); one *s* two *d*; *m* 1966, Mary Alice Heywood. *Educ:* Grocers' Sch.; Sidney Sussex Coll., Cambridge (Hon. Fellow); Royal School of Mines. MA; Hon. DSc Oxford; Hon. DEng Witwatersrand; Hon. DTech, Haifa; Aeronautical Research at Royal Aircraft Establishment, Farnborough, 1920-37; Head of Air Defence Dept, RAE, Farnborough, 1937-39; Asst Dir of Scientific Research, Air Ministry, 1939; Dep. Dir of Scientific Res., Armaments, Min. of Aircraft Production, 1941; Dir of Scientific Research, Ministry of Aircraft Production, 1943; Dir-Gen. of Scientific Research, Ministry of Aircraft Production, 1945; Chief Scientist to Ministry of Supply, 1946-49; Sec. to Cttee of Privy Council for Scientific and Industrial Research, 1949-56; retired 1956. President: Engineering Section of British Association, 1952; Johnson Soc., 1953-54; Council European Organization for Nuclear Research, 1955-57; Medal of Freedom (Silver Palms), 1946. *Recreations:* music, gardening. *Address:* Birchway, 15 Waverley Road, Farnborough, Hants. *T:* Farnborough, Hants, 543021. *Club:* Athenæum.

LOCKWOOD, Baroness *cr* 1978 (Life Peer), of Dewsbury, W Yorks; **Betty Lockwood;** Chairman, Equal Opportunities Commission, since 1975; *b* 22 Jan. 1924; *d* of Arthur Lockwood and Edith Alice Lockwood; *m* 1978, Lt-Col Cedric Hall. *Educ:* Eastborough Girls' Sch., Dewsbury; Ruskin Coll., Oxford. Asst Agent, Reading Labour Party, 1948-50; Sec./Agent, Gillingham Constituency Labour Party, 1950-52; Yorkshire Regional Women's Officer of Labour Party, 1952-67; Chief Woman Officer and Asst Nat. Agent of Labour Party, 1967-75. Secretary: Nat. Labour Women's Adv. Cttee, 1967-75; Nat. Jt Cttee, Working Women's Organisations, 1967-75; Vice-Chm., Internat. Council of Social Democratic Women, 1969-75; Chairman: Mary Macarthur Educnl Trust, 1971-; Mary Macarthur Holiday Homes, 1971-. Mem., Adv. Council on Energy Conservation, 1977-80. Hon. DLitt Bradford, 1981. Editor, Labour Woman, 1967-71. *Recreations:* walking and country pursuits, music. *Address:* 12 Fairdale Gardens, SW15; 6 Sycamore Drive, Addingham, Ilkley LS29 0NY. *Clubs:* Soroptomist, University Women's.

LOCKWOOD, Prof. David, FBA 1976; Professor of Sociology, University of Essex, since 1968; *b* 9 April 1929; *s* of Herbert Lockwood and Edith A. (*née* Lockwood); *m* 1954, Leonore Davidoff; three *s*. *Educ:* Honley Grammar Sch.; London Sch. of Economics. BSc(Econ) London, 1st Cl. Hons 1952; PhD London, 1957. Trainee, textile industry, 1944-47; Cpl, Intell. Corps, Austria, 1947-49. Asst Lectr and Lectr, London Sch. of Economics, 1953-60; Rockefeller Fellow, Univ. of California, Berkeley, 1958-59; Univ. Lectr, Faculty of Economics, and Fellow, St John's Coll., Cambridge, 1960-68. Visiting Professor: Dept of Sociology, Columbia Univ., 1966-67; Delhi Univ., 1975. Mem., SSRC (Chm., Sociol. and Soc. Admin Cttee), 1973-76. *Publications:* The Blackcoated Worker, 1958; The Affluent Worker in the Class Structure, 3 vols (with John H. Goldthorpe), 1968-69; numerous articles in learned jls and symposia. *Recreation:* cycling. *Address:* 82 High Street, Wivenhoe, Essex. *T:* Wivenhoe 3530.

LOCKWOOD, Lt-Col John Cutts, CBE 1960; TD; JP; *s* of late Colonel John Lockwood and Mrs Lockwood, Kingham, Oxon. Served European War, 1914-18, in Essex Regt and Coldstream Guards; War of 1939-45, with Essex Territorials; Staff Captain in JAG Dept; later Legal Officer to SHAEF Mission to Denmark, and with them in Copenhagen, 1945. MP (C) Central Hackney, 1931-35; Romford, 1950-55. Barrister, Middle Temple. Freeman of the City of London. Order of Dannebrog (Denmark). *Recreation:* gardening. *Address:* Bishops Hall, Lambourne End, Essex. *T:* 01-500 2016.

LOCKWOOD, Sir Joseph (Flawith), Kt 1960; Chairman, Royal Ballet, since 1971; *b* 14 Nov. 1904. Manager of flour mills in Chile, 1924-28; Technical Manager of Etablissements, Henry Simon Ltd, in Paris and Brussels, 1928-33; Director, 1933; Dir Henry Simon Ltd, Buenos Aires, Chm. Henry Simon (Australia) Ltd, Dir Henry Simon (Engineering Works) Ltd, etc, 1945, Chm. and Managing Dir, Henry Simon Ltd, 1950; Dir, NRDC, 1951-67; Chm., IRC, 1969-71 (Mem., 1966-71); Chm., EMI Ltd and subsidiaries, 1954-74 (Dir, 1954-79); Director: Smiths Industries Ltd, 1959-79; Hawker Siddeley Group, 1963-77; British Domestic Appliances Ltd, 1966-71 (Chm., 1966-70); The Beecham Group, 1966-75; Laird Group Ltd, 1970-. Member: Engineering Advisory Council, Board of Trade, 1959; Export Council for Europe, 1961-63; Export Credits Guarantee Adv. Council, 1963-67; Council Imperial Soc. of Knights Bach. Director: Sandown Park Ltd, 1969; Epsom Grandstand Assoc. Ltd, 1969; United Racecourses Ltd, 1969. Hon. Treasurer British Empire Cancer Campaign, 1962-67; Chairman: Royal Ballet Sch. Endowment Fund and Governors, Royal Ballet Sch., 1960-78; Young Vic Theatre Company, 1974-75; South Bank Theatre Bd, 1977- (Mem., 1968-); Vice-Pres., Central Sch. of Speech and Drama (Chm., Governors, 1965-68); Mem., Arts Council, 1967-70. CompIEE. *Publications:* Provender Milling-the Manufacture of Feeding Stuffs for Livestock, 1939; Flour Milling (trans. into various languages), 1945. *Address:* 33 Grosvenor Square, W1X 9LL. *Club:* Carlton.

LOCKWOOD, Margaret Mary, CBE 1981; Actress; *b* Karachi, India, 15 Sept. 1916; (*née* Margaret Lockwood); *m* Rupert W. Leon (marr. diss.); one *d*. *Educ:* Sydenham Girls' High Sch. Studied for Stage under Italia Conti and at Royal Academy of Dramatic Art. *Films:* Lorna Doone; Case of Gabriel Perry, 1934; Midshipman Easy; Jury's Evidence; Amateur Gentleman, 1935; Irish for Luck; Beloved Vagabond; Street Singer, 1936; Who's Your Lady Friend; Owd Bob; Bank Holiday, 1937; The Lady Vanishes; A Girl Must Live; Stars Look Down; Night Train to Munich, 1939; Quiet Wedding, 1940; Alibi; Man in Grey, 1942; Dear Octopus; Give Us The Moon; Love Story, 1943; Place of One's Own; I'll Be Your Sweetheart, 1944; Wicked Lady; Bedelia, 1945; Hungry Hill; Jassy, 1946; The White Unicorn, 1947; Look Before You Love, 1948; Cardboard Cavalier; Madness of the Heart, 1949; Highly Dangerous, 1950; Laughing Anne, 1952; Trent's Last Case, 1952; Trouble in the Glen, 1954; Cast A Dark Shadow, 1955; The Slipper and the Rose, 1976. Named top money-making Star in Britain by motion Picture Poll; Motion Picture Herald Fame Poll, 1945 and 1946; Winner Daily Mail Film Award, 1945-46, 1946-47 and 1947-48. *Stage:* tour in Private Lives, 1949; Peter Pan, 1949-50, 1950-51 and 1957-58; Pygmalion, 1951; Spider's Web, Savoy, 1954-56; Subway in the Sky, Savoy, 1957; And Suddenly It's Spring, Duke of York's, 1959-60; Signpost to Murder, Cambridge Theatre, 1962-63; Every Other Evening, Phœnix, 1964-65; An Ideal Husband, Strand, 1965 and Garrick, 1966; The Others, Strand, 1967; On a Foggy Day, St Martin's, 1969; Lady Frederick, Vaudeville, 1970; Relative Values (nat. tour), 1972, Westminster, 1973; Double Edge, Vaudeville, 1975-76; Quadrille (nat. tour), 1977; Suite in Two Keys (nat. tour), 1978; Motherdear Ambassadors, 1980. *Television:* BBC series (with daughter Julia) The Flying Swan, March-Sept. 1965; Yorkshire TV series, Justice, 1971, 1972-73, 1974. *Recreations:* crossword puzzles and swimming. *Address:* c/o Mrs H. de Leon, Flat 22, The Colonnades, Porchester Square, W2.

LOCKWOOD, Robert; Director of Planning and Development, General Motors Corporation, since 1982; *b* 14 April 1920; *s* of Joseph A. Lockwood and Sylvia Lockwood; *m* 1947, Phyllis M. Laing; one *s* one *d*. *Educ:* Columbia Univ. (AB); Columbia Law Sch. (LLB). Attorney, Bar of New York, 1941; US Dist of New York and US Supreme Court, 1952. Pilot, USAAF (8th Air Force), 1944-45. Attorney: Ehrich, Royall, Wheeler & Holland, New York, 1941 and 1946-47; Sullivan & Cromwell, New York, 1947-54; Sec. and Counsel, Cluett, Peabody & Co., Inc., New York, 1955-57; Man. Dir, Cluett, Peabody & Co., Ltd, London, 1957-59; General Motors: Overseas Ops, Planning and Develt, 1960-61; Asst to Man. Dir, GM Argentina, Buenos Aires, 1962; Asst to Man. Dir, and Manager, Parts, Power and Appliances, GM

Continental, Antwerp, 1964-66; Branch Man., Netherlands Br., GM Continental, Rotterdam, 1967-68; Man., Planning and Develt, GM Overseas Ops, New York, 1969-73; Vice Pres., GM Overseas Corp., and Gen. Man., Japan Br., 1974-76; Exec. Vice Pres., Isuzu Motors Ltd, Tokyo, 1976; Chm., GM European Adv. Council, 1977-82. *Recreations:* tennis, chess, reading. *Address:* General Motors Corporation, 3-263 General Motors Building, 3044 West Grand Boulevard, Detroit, Mich 48202, USA. *Clubs:* Hurlingham; Tokyo Lawn Tennis (Tokyo).

LOCKWOOD, Walter Sydney Douglas, CBE 1962 (OBE 1948); CEng; FRAeS; FInstProdE; *b* 4 Jan. 1895; *s* of Walter Lockwood, Thetford, Norfolk; *m* 1924, Constance Rose, *d* of T. F. Bayliss, Norwich. *Educ:* Thetford Sch.; Bristol Univ. Served European War, 1914-18: Gloucester Regt, France and Belgium (Belgian Croix de Guerre; despatches; wounded). Joined design staff of Sir W. G. Armstrong Whitworth Aircraft Ltd, 1921; became Works Man., 1944. Armstrong Whitworth Aircraft: Works Dir, 1950; Dir and Gen. Man., 1955; Man. Dir, 1960; Man. Dir, Whitworth Gloster Aircraft Ltd (when Armstrong Whitworth Aircraft and Gloster Aircraft Companies merged), 1961-63 (when Co. dissolved); Dir, Hawker Siddeley Aviation Ltd, 1961-64, retired. Mem. Coun., SBAC, 1960. *Address:* Wayside, Abbey Road, Leiston, Suffolk.

LOCKYER, Rear-Adm. (Alfred) Austin, MVO 1973; Chief Staff Officer (Engineering) to Commander-in-Chief Fleet, since 1982; *b* 4 March 1929; *s* of Austin Edmund Lockyer and Jane Russell (*née* Goldman); *m* 1965, Jennifer Ann Simmons; one *s.* *Educ:* Frome County School; Taunton School; Royal Naval Engineering College. Entered RN 1947; served in HM Ships Superb, Caledonia and Modeste, 1952-58; BRNC, Dartmouth, 1959-60; Area Schools Liaison Officer, 1961-62; HMS Bulwark, 1963-65; Staff of Commander Far East Fleet, 1965-67; Joint Services Staff Course, 1968-69; Ship Dept, 1969-71; HMY Britannia, 1971-73; Senior Officers War Course, 1973-74; Naval Ship Production Overseer, Scotland and NI, 1974-76; Dep. Dir, Fleet Maintenance, 1976-78; Dir, Naval Officers Appointing (Engrg), 1978-80; HMS Sultan in Comd, 1980-82; Rear-Adm. 1982. Governor: Forres School, Swanage; Sherborne School. *Recreations:* gardening, listening to good music and watching sport. *Address:* c/o Lloyds Bank Ltd, 8 Sycamore Road, Amersham, Bucks HP6 5DU.

LODER, family name of **Baron Wakehurst.**

LODER, Sir Giles Rolls, 3rd Bt, *cr* 1887; DL; *b* 10 Nov. 1914; *o s* of late Capt. Robert Egerton Loder, *s* of 2nd Bt, and late Muriel Rolls, *d* of J. Rolls-Hoare; *S* grandfather, 1920; *m* 1939, Marie, *o d* of late Captain Symons-Jeune, Runnymede House, Old Windsor; two *s.* *Educ:* Eton; Trinity Coll., Cambridge (MA). High Sheriff of Sussex, 1948-49; DL West Sussex, 1977. FLS. VMH. *Recreations:* sailing, horticulture. *Heir: s* Edmund Jeune Loder [*b* 26 June 1941; *m* 1966, Penelope Jane (marr. diss. 1971), *d* of Ivo Forde; one *d*]. *Address:* Ockenden House, Cuckfield, Haywards Heath, West Sussex. *T:* Haywards Heath 459433. *Club:* Royal Yacht Squadron.

LODGE, Prof. David John, MA, PhD; Professor of Modern English Literature, University of Birmingham, since 1976; *b* 28 Jan. 1935; *s* of William Frederick Lodge and Rosalie Marie Lodge (*née* Murphy); *m* 1959, Mary Frances Jacob; two *s* one *d.* *Educ:* St Joseph's Acad., Blackheath; University College, London (Fellow, 1982). BA hons, MA (London); PhD (Birm). National Service, RAC, 1955-57. British Council, London, 1959-60. Univ. of Birmingham: Asst Lectr in English, 1960-62; Lectr, 1963-71; Sen. Lectr, 1971-73; Reader in English, 1973-76. Harkness Commonwealth Fellow, 1964-65; Visiting Associate Prof., Univ. of California, Berkeley, 1969; Henfield Writing Fellow, Univ. of E Anglia, 1977. Yorkshire Post Fiction Prize, 1975; Hawthornden Prize, 1976; FRSL 1976. *Publications:* novels: The Picturegoers, 1960; Ginger, You're Barmy, 1962; The British Museum is Falling Down, 1965; Out of the Shelter, 1970; Changing Places, 1975; How Far Can You Go?, 1980 (Whitbread Book of the Year Award); *criticism:* Language of Fiction, 1966; The Novelist at the Crossroads, 1971; The Modes of Modern Writing, 1977; Working with Structuralism, 1981. *Recreations:* badminton, televised football, cinema. *Address:* Department of English, University of Birmingham, Birmingham B15 2TT. *T:* 021-472 1301.

LODGE, Prof. Geoffrey Arthur, BSc, PhD, FIBiol; Strathcona-Fordyce Professor of Agriculture, University of Aberdeen, and Principal of the North of Scotland College of Agriculture, since 1978. *Educ:* Durham University (BSc). PhD Aberdeen. Formerly Reader in Animal Production, Univ. of Nottingham School of Agriculture, and Principal Research Scientist, Animal Research Inst., Ottawa. *Publications:* (ed jointly) Growth and Development of Mammals, 1968; contribs to journals and books. *Address:* School of Agriculture, 581 King Street, Aberdeen AB9 1UD.

LODGE, Henry Cabot; Politician, US; President's Special Representative to the Vatican, 1970; *b* 5 July 1902; *s* of George Cabot Lodge and Mathilda Elizabeth Frelinghuysen Davis; *g s* of late Henry Cabot Lodge, Senator (US); *m* 1926, Emily Sears; two *s.* *Educ:* Middx Sch., Concord, Mass.; Harvard (AB *cum laude* ; LLD). Boston Transcript, New York Herald Tribune, 1923-32. Thrice elected US Senator from Massachusetts. Harvard Overseer. Senate author of the Lodge-Brown Act which created Hoover Commission; Chm., resolutions cttee, Republican National Convention, 1948; US Senate Foreign Relations Cttee. Campaign Manager of effort to win Republican nomination for Gen. Eisenhower, 1951-52; Mem. President's Cabinet and US Rep. to UN,

1953-60. Republican nominee for Vice-Pres., USA, 1960. Dir-Gen., Atlantic Inst., Paris, 1961-63; Ambassador to Vietnam, 1963-64, 1965-67, to Federal Republic of Germany, 1968-69. US Representative at Vietnam Peace Talks, Paris, Jan.-Nov. 1969. Had reached grade of reserve Captain when US entered war; served as Major United States Army, with first American tank detachment in Brit. 8th Army, Libya, 1942 (citation); resigned from Senate for further Army service (first Senator to do so since the Civil War); Italy, 1944; Lt-Col S France, Rhine and S Germany, 1944-45 (Bronze Star, US, 1944, Legion of Merit, 1945, Légion d'Honneur and Croix de Guerre with palm, France, 1945). Maj.-Gen., US Army Reserve. Has been awarded numerous Hon. Degrees; Sylvanus Thayer Medal, West Point; Theodore Roosevelt Assoc. Medal; Gold Medal from Pres. Eisenhower, 'for selfless and invaluable service to our nation'. Order of Polonia Restituta; Order of African Redemption, Liberia; Grand Cross of Merit, Order of Malta; National Order, Republic of Viet Nam. *Publications:* The Storm Has Many Eyes, 1973; As It Was, 1976; articles for Atlantic Monthly, Collier's, Life, Reader's Digest, Saturday Evening Post. *Address:* 275 Hale Street, Beverly, Mass 01915, USA. *T:* Beverly 617/922-0404. *Clubs:* Metropolitan, Myopia Hunt, Alfalfa (all Washington); Somerset, Tavern (both Boston).

LODGE, Oliver Raymond William Wynlayne; Regional Chairman of Industrial Tribunals, London (South), since 1980; *b* Painswick, Glos, 2 Sept. 1922; *e s* of Oliver William Foster Lodge and Winifred, (Wynlayne), *o d* of Sir William Nicholas Atkinson, ISO, LLD; *m* 1953, Charlotte, *o d* of Col Arthur Davidson Young, CMG; one *s* two *d.* *Educ:* Bryanston Sch.; King's Coll., Cambridge. BA 1943, MA 1947. Officer-cadet, Royal Fusiliers, 1942. Called to the Bar, Inner Temple, 1945; admitted *ad eundem,* Lincoln's Inn, 1949, Bencher, 1973; practised at Chancery Bar, 1945-74; Permanent Chairman of Industrial Tribunals, 1975-. Member: Bar Council, 1952-56, 1967-71; Supreme Court Rules Cttee, 1968-71. *Publications:* (ed) Rivington's Epitome of Snell's Equity, 3rd edn, 1948; (ed) Fraudulent and Voidable Conveyances, article in Halsbury's Laws of England, 3rd edn, 1956; contribs to legal periodicals. *Recreations:* walking, bell-ringing, reading history, formerly sailing. *Address:* Southridge House, Hindon, Salisbury, Wilts. *T:* Hindon 238; 33 The Little Boltons, SW10. *T:* 01-370 5265. *Clubs:* Garrick; Bar Yacht.

LODGE, Sir Thomas, Kt 1974; Consultant Radiologist, United Sheffield Hospitals, 1946-74, retired; Clinical Lecturer, Sheffield University, 1960-74; *b* 25 Nov. 1909; *s* of James Lodge and Margaret (*née* Lowery); *m* 1940, Aileen Corduff; one *s* one *d.* *Educ:* Univ. of Sheffield. MB, ChB 1934, FFR 1945, FRCP 1967, FRCS 1967. Asst Radiologist: Sheffield Radium Centre, 1936; Manchester Royal Infirmary, 1937-38; 1st Asst in Radiology, United Sheffield Hosps, 1938-46; Cons. Adviser in Radiology, DHSS, 1965-74. Hon. FRSocMed. Hon. FFR RCSI; Hon. FRACR 1963; Hon. FACR 1975; Hon. MSR 1975. Twining Medal, 1945, and Knox Lectr, 1962, Faculty of Radiologists. Hon. Editor, Clinical Radiology, 1954-59. *Publications:* Recent Advances in Radiology, 3rd edn 1955, 4th edn 1964, 5th edn 1975, 6th edn 1979; articles in Brit. Jl Radiology, Clinical Radiology, etc. *Recreation:* gardening. *Address:* 44 Sussex Square, Brighton, East Sussex BN2 1GE. *T:* Brighton 604242.

LODGE, Thomas C. S.; *see* Skeffington-Lodge.

LODGE, Tom Stewart, CBE 1967; Director of Research and Statistics, Home Office, 1969-73; retired; *b* 15 Dec. 1909; *s* of George Arthur and Emma Eliza Lodge, Batley, Yorks; *m* 1936, Joan McFadyean (*d* 1961); one *d.* *Educ:* Batley Grammar Sch.; Merton Coll., Oxford. BA Hons Maths 1931, MA 1934; FIA 1939. Prudential Assurance Co., 1931-43; Min. of Aircraft Production, 1943-46; Admty as Superintending Actuary, 1946-50; Statistical Adviser, Home Office, 1950; Statistical Adviser and Dir of Research, Home Office, 1957. Chm., Criminological Scientific Council, Council of Europe, 1975-77 (Mem., 1970-77). *Publications:* articles in British and French jls. *Address:* 16A The Avenue, Coulsdon, Surrey CR3 2BN. *T:* 01-660 3390. *Club:* Civil Service.

LOEHNIS, Anthony David; Executive Director, Bank of England, since 1981; *b* 12 March 1936; *s* of Sir Clive Loehnis, *qv* ; *m* 1965, Jennifer Forsyth Anderson; three *s.* *Educ:* New Coll., Oxford (BA); Harvard Sch. of Public Administration. HM Diplomatic Service, 1960-66; J. Henry Schroder Wagg & Co. Ltd, 1967-80 (on secondment to Bank of England, 1977-79); Associate Dir (Overseas), Bank of England, 1980-81. *Address:* c/o Bank of England, Threadneedle Street, EC2R 8AH. *Club:* Garrick.

LOEHNIS, Sir Clive, KCMG 1962 (CMG 1950); Commander RN (retired); *b* 24 Aug. 1902; *s* of H. W. Loehnis, Barrister-at-Law, Inner Temple; *m* 1929, Rosemary Beryl, *d* of late Major Hon. R. N. Dudley Ryder, 8th Hussars; one *s* one *d.* *Educ:* Royal Naval Colls, Osborne, Dartmouth and Greenwich. Midshipman, 1920; Lt, 1924; qualified in signal duties, 1928; Lt-Comdr, 1932; retired, 1935; AMIEE 1935. Re-employed in Signal Div. Admiralty, 1938; Comdr on retd List, 1942; Naval Intelligence Div., 1942; demobilised and entered Foreign Office, 1945; Dep. Dir, Government Communications Headquarters, 1952-60; Dir, Government Communications HQ, 1960-64. Dep. Chm., Civil Service Selection Bd, 1967-70. *Address:* 12 Eaton Place, SW1X 8AD. *T:* 01-235 6803. *Clubs:* White's, MCC.

See also A. D. Loehnis, Baron Remnant.

LOEWE, Frederick; composer; concert pianist; *b* Vienna, 10 June 1901; *s* of Edmund Loewe, actor. Began career as concert pianist playing with leading European orchestras; went to US, 1924; first musical, Salute to Spring, produced in St Louis, 1937; first Broadway production, Great Lady, 1938; began collaboration with Alan Jay Lerner, *qv*, in 1942, since when has written music for: Day Before Spring, 1945; Brigadoon, 1947 (1st musical to win Drama Critics' Award); Paint Your Wagon, 1951 (best score of year); My Fair Lady, 1956 (many awards); Gigi (film), 1958 (Oscar), (stage) 1974; Camelot, 1960; The Little Prince, 1975 (film). DMus *hc* Univ. of Redlands, Calif; Dr of Fine Arts *hc* Univ. of NYC. *Address:* c/o ASCAP, One Lincoln Plaza, New York, NY 10023, USA. *Clubs:* Players', Lambs (New York); Palm Springs Racquet.

LOEWEN, Gen. Sir Charles (Falkland), GCB 1957 (KCB 1954; CB 1945); KBE 1951 (CBE 1944); DSO 1945; late RA; *b* 17 Sept. 1900; *s* of late Charles J. Loewen, MA, Vancouver, Canada, and Edith Loewen; *m* 1928, Kathleen, *d* of late Maj.-Gen. J. M. Ross; two *s*. *Educ:* Haileybury Coll.; Royal Military College, Kingston, Canada. 2nd Lt RFA 1918; Capt. 1931; Bt Major, 1937; Major, 1938; Bt Lt-Col 1939; Col 1942; Maj.-Gen. 1944; Lt-Gen. 1950; Gen. 1954. Served War of 1939-45, in Norway (despatches) and in Italy (despatches); comd: 1st Inf. Div., 1944-45; 6th Armd Div., 1946; 1st Armd Div., 1947; Northumb. Dist and 50th (Inf.) Div. (TA), 1948-49; GOC-in-C Anti-Aircraft Command, 1950-53; GOC-in-C, Western Command, April-Sept. 1953; C-in-C Far East Land Forces, 1953-56; Adjutant-Gen. to the Forces, 1956-59; ADC Gen. to the Queen, 1956-59. Col Comdt, RA, 1953-63. Hon. DSc Mil., Roy. Mil. Coll. Canada, 1966. Comdr Legion of Merit (US), 1945. *Recreations:* fishing, gardening. *Address:* Boyne Mills House, Mansfield, Ontario LON 1MO, Canada.

LOEWENSTEIN-WERTHEIM-FREUDENBERG, Hubertus Friedrich, Prince of, Dr iur, LittD (*hc*); Commander's Cross of German Order of Merit, 1968; Special Adviser, German Government, Press and Information Office, 1960-71; Member of Parliament, 1953-57; *b* Schoenwoerth Castle, near Kufstein, Tirol, 14 Oct. 1906; *y s* of Prince Maximilian Loewenstein-Wertheim-Freudenberg and Constance, *y d* of 1st Baron Pirbright, PC; *m* 1929, Helga Maria Mathilde v. d. Schuylenburg; three *d*. *Educ:* Gymnasium at Gmunden and Klagenfurt, Austria; Universities at Munich, Hamburg, Geneva, and Berlin. Referendar Berlin Kammergericht, 1928, Doctor iuris utriusque, Hamburg, 1931; member of Catholic Centre Party, 1930; leader of Republican Students, and Republican Youth, Berlin, 1930; Prussian delegate to Munich, 1932; left Germany, 1933; returned 1946; Visiting Prof. of Hist. and Gov. to USA and Canada of the Carnegie Endowment for International Peace, 1937-46; Lecturer in History, University of Heidelberg, during 1947. Publisher and editor, Das Reich, Saarbrücken, 1934-35; Founder of American Guild for German Cultural Freedom, 1936; Founder and leader, German Action movement, 1949-. Southern German Editor, Die Zeit, 1952-53; Pres., Free German Authors' Assoc., 1973-. Hon. Mem., Exiles PEN Club, 1982. Hon. DLitt Hamline Univ., 1943. Grand Cross of Athos, 1966; Commendatore, Order of Merit (Italy), 1970; Saarland Order of Merit, 1980. *Publications:* The Tragedy of a Nation, 1934; After Hitler's Fall, Germany's Coming Reich, 1934; A Catholic in Republican Spain, 1937; Conquest of the Past, autobiography (till 1933), 1938; On Borrowed Peace, autobiography (1933 to 1942), 1942; The Germans in History, 1945; The Child and the Emperor: a Legend, 1945; The Lance of Longinus, 1946; The Eagle and the Cross, 1947; Deutsche Geschichte, 1950, 8th rev. edn, 1983; Stresemann, biography, 1953; Die römischen Tagebücher des Dr von Molitor, 1956; (co-author Volkmar von Zuehlsdorff) Das deutsche Schicksal 1945-1957, 1957; (same co-author) NATO, The Defence of the West, 1963; Towards The Further Shore (autobiography), 1968; Botschafter ohne Auftrag, 1970; Seneca: Kaiser ohne Purpur, 1975; Tiberius Imperator, 1977; Invitation to Capri, 1979; Rom, Reich ohne Ende, 1979; Trajanus, Optimus Princeps, 1981; contributions to (previous to 1933) Berliner Tageblatt, Vossische Zeitung, etc; (after 1933) Spectator, Nineteenth Century Review, Contemporary Review, American Mercury, Atlantic Monthly, New York Herald Tribune, Commonweal, American Scholar, Social Science, Die Tat, Die Zeit, Die Welt, etc. *Recreations:* swimming, riding. *Address:* c/o Mrs Milburne, Weeks Farm, Egerton, Kent; Lahnstrasse 50, 53 Bonn 2-Bad Godesberg, Federal Republic of Germany.

LOEWY, Raymond; Grand Officer, French Legion of Honour, 1980; Industrial Designer; Founder: Raymond Loewy International Inc., consultant designers to US and foreign Corporations; Compagnie de l'Esthétique Industrielle, Paris; Raymond Loewy Co., Lausanne; Lecturer: Massachusetts Institute of Technology; Harvard Graduate School of Business Administration; Institute of Design Technology, Moscow; *b* Paris, 5 Nov. 1893; *s* of Maximillian Loewy and Marie Labalme; naturalized citizen of US 1938; *m* 1948, Viola Erickson; one *d*. *Educ:* Chaptal Coll., Paris; Paris Univ.; Ecole de Lanneau (grad. eng.). Art Director, Westinghouse Electric Co. 1929; started private organization of Industrial Design, 1929. Served as Capt. Corps of Engineers attached to Gen. Staff, 5th Army, France, 1914-18; Liaison Officer, AEF (Officer Legion of Honour, Croix de Guerre, with 4 citations; Interallied Medal). Hon. RDI 1937; FRSA 1942; Fellow (Past Pres.), American Soc. of Industrial Designers; Lectr, Coll. of Arch., University of Calif. American Design Award, 1938; Indust. Designers Soc. of America Award of Recognition, 1978; Special Award of Recognition, Internat. Cttee of ICSID, Helsinki, 1981. California Design Award, LA, 1979. Hon. Doctor of Fine Arts, University of Cincinnati, 1956; Dr, Calif Coll. of Design, LA. Member: Society of Automotive Engineers; Amer. Soc. Mech. Engrs; Adv.

Board on Vocational Educn, Bd of Educn, NYC; Assoc. Mem. Soc. of Naval Arch. and Marine Engrs; Soc. of Space Medicine; Vice-Pres. French Chamber of Commerce of the US, 1958. Included in: Thousand Makers of Twentieth Century, Sunday Times, 1969; US Bicentennial List, 100 Events that shaped America 1776-1976, Smithsonian Institution, Washington. Fellow, Amer. Acad. of Achievement, 1970. Mem., President's Cttee on Employment of the Handicapped, 1965-; Habitability Consultant to NASA Apollo Saturn Application program, 1967-; Skylab and Space Shuttle Orbiter; Design Consultant to Soviet Union State Cttee for Science and Technology, 1973-. Exposition Raymond Loewy Designs, Smithsonian Institution, 1976. Citizen of Honour: France, 1954; New York City, 1966; Palm Springs; Chicago. Knight of Mark Twain. *Publications:* The Locomotive—its Esthetics, 1937; Never Leave Well Enough Alone (autobiography), 1951 (trans. various langs); RL Industrial Design Overlook (illustrated album, published in many countries); Industrial Design, 1980. *Address:* (office) 39 Avenue d'Iéna, Paris, France; Loewy International Ltd, 117b Fulham Road, Chelsea, SW3 6RL; Fribourg, Switzerland; (home) 2800 Haverill Road North, West Palm Beach, Fla, USA; 20 rue Boissiere, Paris XVI, France; L'Annonciade, Monte Carlo, Monaco. *Club:* NY Athletic.

LOFTHOUSE, Geoffrey; JP; MP (Lab) Pontefract and Castleford, since Oct. 1978; *b* 18 Dec. 1925; *s* of Ernest and Emma Lofthouse; *m* 1952, Sarah Lofthouse; one *d*. *Educ:* Featherstone Primary and Secondary Schs. Haulage hand in mining industry at age of 14. Personnel Manager, NCB Fryston, 1970-78. Member: Pontefract Borough Council, 1962-74 (Mayor, 1967-68); Wakefield Metropolitan District Council, 1974- (Chm., Housing Cttee). Mem., NUM, 1939-64, APEX, 1970-. JP Pontefract, 1970. *Recreations:* Rugby League; cricket. *Address:* 67 Carleton Crest, Pontefract, West Yorkshire.

LOFTHOUSE, John Alfred, (Jack), OBE 1967; Member, British National Oil Corporation, since 1980; Director, Imperial Chemical Industries Ltd, retired; *b* 30 Dec. 1917; *s* of John Duncan Lofthouse and Clara Margaret Smith; *m* 1950, Patricia Ninette Mann (*d* 1956); one *d*. *Educ:* Rutlish Sch., Merton; St Catharine's Coll., Cambridge (BA Hons, MA). Joined ICI Ltd as engr, 1939; Engrg Manager, Petrochemicals Div., 1958; Technical Dir, Nobel Div., 1961; Chm., Petrochems Div., 1967; Dir, Main Bd of ICI Ltd, 1970-80: responsibilities included Personnel Dir, Petrochems, Oil, and Explosives businesses, and Chm., ICI Americas Ltd. *Publications:* contrib. Geographical Jl and engrg jls. *Recreations:* gardening, hill-walking, music. *Address:* Little Paddocks, Streatley, Berks RG8 9RD.

LOFTHOUSE, Reginald George Alfred, FRICS; Adviser to the Nature Conservancy Council, since 1978; Convener, Standing Conference on Countryside Sports, since 1978; *b* Workington, 30 Dec. 1916; *m* 1939, Ann Bernardine Bannan; three *d*. *Educ:* Workington Secondary Sch.; with private land agent, Cockermouth. Chartered Surveyor and Land Agent (Talbot-Ponsonby Prizeman). Asst District Officer, Penrith, 1941-42; District Officer, Carlisle, for Cumberland War Agric. Exec. Cttee, 1942-43; Asst Land Comr, West Riding, 1943-46; Land Commissioner: N and E Ridings, 1946-48; Derbs, Leics, Rutland, Northants, 1948-50; Somerset and Dorset, 1950-52; Regional Land Comr, Hdqtrs, 1952-59, and SE Region, 1959-71; Regional Officer, SE Region, Agric., Develt and Adv. Service, 1971-73; Chief Surveyor, MAFF, 1973-76. Chairman: UK Jt Shelter Res. Cttee, 1958-71; Statutory Cttee on Agricl Valuations, 1973-76. Mem., Farming and Wildlife Adv. Gp, 1966-81. Adviser to: Lord Porchester's Exmoor Study, 1977; Council for Environmental Conservation, 1980-81. Vis. Lectr in Rural Estate Management and Forestry, Regent Street Polytechnic, 1954-62. Member: Bd of Governors, Coll. of Estate Management, 1963- (Chm., 1972-77; Chm., Centre for Advanced Land Use Studies, 1972-81); Court and Council, Reading Univ., 1973-; Adv. Cttee, Centre for Agricl Strategy, 1980-; Delegacy for Nat. Inst. for Res. in Dairying, Shinfield, 1974-80; Gen. Council, RICS, 1974-76; RICS Land Agency and Agric. Div. Council, 1974-77. Hon. Life Mem., Cambridge Univ. Land Soc.; Chm. Farm Bldgs Cttee 1973-80, Mem. Engrg and Bldgs Res. Bd 1973-80, Jt Consultative Organisation. Liveryman, Loriners' Co., 1976; Freeman, City of London, 1976. *Publications:* The Berwyn Mountains Area of Wales, 1979; contrib. professional, techn. and countryside jls. *Address:* c/o College of Estate Management, Whiteknights, Reading RG6 2AW. *Clubs:* Athenæum, MCC.

LOFTS, Norah, (Mrs Robert Jorisch); *b* 27 Aug. 1904; *d* of Isaac Robinson and Ethel (*née* Garner); *m* 1st, 1931, Geoffrey Lofts (decd); one *s*; 2nd, 1949, Dr Robert Jorisch. *Educ:* West Suffolk County Sch. *Publications:* I Met a Gypsy, 1935; White Hell of Pity, 1937; Out of This Nettle, 1939; Road to Revelation, 1941; Jassy, 1944; Silver Nutmeg, 1947; Women of the Old Testament, 1949; A Calf for Venus, 1949; The Luteplayer, 1951; Bless This House, 1954; Queen in Waiting, 1955; Afternoon of An Autocrat, 1956; Scent of Cloves, 1958; Heaven In Your Hand, 1959; The Town House, 1959; The House at Old Vine, 1961; The House at Sunset, 1963; The Concubine, 1964; How Far to Bethlehem?, 1965; (with M. Weiner) Eternal France, 1969; The Lost Ones, 1969; The King's Pleasure, 1970; Lovers All Untrue, 1970; A Rose For Virtue, 1971; Charlotte, 1972; Nethergate, 1973; Crown of Aloes, 1974; Knights Acre, 1974; The Homecoming, 1975; The Lonely Furrow, 1976; Domestic Life in England, 1976; Queens of Britain, 1977; Gad's Hall, 1977; Haunted House, 1978; Emma Hamilton, 1978; Day of the Butterfly (Georgette Heyer Historical Novel Prize), 1979; Anne Boleyn, 1979; A Wayside Tavern, 1980; The Claw, 1981. *As Peter Curtis:* You're Best Alone, 1939; Dead March in Three Keys, 1940; Lady Living Alone, 1944; The Devil's

Own, 1959. *Address:* Northgate House, Bury St Edmunds, Suffolk. *T:* Bury St Edmunds 2680.

LOFTUS, Viscount; Charles John Tottenham; Head of French Department, Strathcona-Tweedsmuir School, Calgary; *b* 2 Feb. 1943; *e s* and *heir* of 8th Marquess of Ely, *qv*; *m* 1969, Judith Marvelle, *d* of Dr J. J. Porter, FRS, Calgary, Alberta; one *s* one *d. Educ:* Trinity Coll. Sch., Port Hope, Ont; Ecole Internationale de Genève; Univ. of Toronto (MA). *Heir: s* Hon. Andrew John Tottenham, *b* 26 Feb. 1973. *Address:* 1424 Springfield Place SW, Calgary, Alberta T2W 0Y1, Canada.

LOFTUS, Col Ernest Achey, CBE 1975 (OBE (mil.) 1928); TD 1929; MA (TCD), BSc Econ. (London), LCP, FRGS, FRSA, MRST; Member RSL; DL; a pedagogue for 74 years and retired 1975 as the oldest civil servant in the World (see Guinness Book of Records); in service of Zambian Government 1963-75; *b* 11 Jan. 1884; *s* of Capt. William Loftus, Master Mariner, Kingston-upon-Hull; *m* 1916, Elsie (*d* 1979), *er d* of Allen Charles Cole, West Tilbury, Essex; two *s. Educ:* Archbishop Holgate's Gram. Sch., York; Trinity Coll., Dublin. Senior Geography Master, Palmer's Sch., Grays, Essex, 1906-19; Head of Junior Sch., Southend on Sea High Sch. for Boys, 1919-20; Asst Dir of Educn, Southend-on-Sea, 1920-22; Headmaster, Barking Abbey Sch., 1922-49; a select speaker, Conf. of World Educn Assocs, Oxford, 1935; coined term 'Health Science' and drew up first syllabus of work (London Univ.) in that subject, 1937; an Educn Officer in Kenya, 1953-60, in Nyasaland, 1960-63, in Zambia, 1963-75; formed two Cadet Corps and raised four Territl Units in Co. Essex; served with The Essex Regt 1910-29; European War in Gallipoli 1915, Egypt 1916, France 1918; Staff Officer for Educn 67th Div., Independent Force and Kent Force, 1917; a pioneer officer in what became RAEC; Lt-Col Commanding 6th Essex Regt, 1925-29; Mem. Essex Territorial Army Association 1925-29; Brevet Col, 1929; served in War of 1939—Pioneer Corps, 1939-42, commanding No 13 (Italian) Group in France and No 31 Group in London, etc.; Founder Hon. Sec. Essex County Playing Fields Association, 1925-29; Hon. Organiser or Sec. various Appeals, in Essex. Mem. Standing Cttee Convocation, London Univ., 1944-53, and Bedell of Convocation, 1946-53. A Chm. Nat. Assistance Board, 1949-53; Mem. Exec. Cttee Essex Playing Fields Assoc., 1925-53; Mem. Thurrock UDC 1946-53, Vice-Chm. 1951-52; Controller, Civil Defence, Thurrock area, 1951-53. Freeman, City of Kingston-upon-Hull, 1968. For some years a Governor, The Strand Sch. (Brixton); Palmer's Sch. (Grays), etc. A Selborne Lectr. DL Essex 1929-75, now inactive. Mason, 1915-; Rotarian (Pres., Barking, 1935), 1930-. *Publications:* Education and the Citizen; History of a Branch of the Cole Family; Growls and Grumbles; A History of Barking Abbey (with H. F. Chettle); A Visual History of Africa, 1953, 16 reprints, 2nd edn 1974; A Visual History of East Africa; and brochures for the East African Literature Bureau. Contributor of feature articles in London Daily and Weekly Press, etc. on Education; author of 8 scenes of Barking Pageant, 1931, and of Elizabethan scene in Ilford Pageant of Essex, 1932. *Recreations:* historical and genealogical research. *Address:* c/o Kingscote, Furze Hill, Kingswood, Surrey. *Club:* Royal Commonwealth Society.

LOGAN, Sir Donald (Arthur), KCMG 1977 (CMG 1965); HM Diplomatic Service, retired; Director, Great Britain/East Europe Centre, since 1980; *b* 25 Aug. 1917; *s* of late Arthur Alfred Logan and Louise Anne Bradley; *m* 1957, Irène Jocelyne Angèle, *d* of Robert Everts (Belgian Ambassador at Madrid, 1932-39) and Alexandra Comnène; one *s* two *d. Educ:* Solihull. Fellow, Chartered Insurance Institute, 1939. War of 1939-45: Major, RA; British Army Staff, Washington, 1942-43; Germany, 1945. Joined HM Foreign (subseq. Diplomatic) Service, Dec. 1945; Foreign Office, 1945-47; HM Embassy, Tehran, 1947-51; Foreign Office, 1951-53; Asst Political Agent, Kuwait, 1953-55; Asst Private Sec. to Sec. of State for Foreign Affairs, 1956-58; HM Embassy, Washington, 1958-60; HM Ambassador to Guinea, 1960-62; Foreign Office, 1962-64; Information Counsellor, British Embassy, Paris, 1964-70; Ambassador to Bulgaria, 1970-73; Dep. Permanent UK Rep. to NATO, 1973-75; Ambassador and Permanent Leader, UK Delegn to UN Conf. on Law of the Sea, 1976-77. Leader, UK delegn to Conf. on Marine Living Resources of Antarctica, Buenos Aires and Canberra, 1978-80. Vice-Pres., Internat. Exhibitions Bureau, Paris, 1963-67. *Address:* 6 Thurloe Street, SW7 2ST. *Clubs:* Brooks's, Royal Automobile.

LOGAN, Sir Douglas (William), Kt 1959; DPhil, MA, BCL; Principal of the University of London, 1948-75; President, British Universities Sports Board and Federation, 1953-75; Chairman, British Student Sports Federation, 1971-77; Consultant, Universities Superannuation Scheme Ltd (Chairman, 1974-77; Deputy Chairman, 1977-80); *b* Liverpool, 27 March 1910; *yr s* of Robert Logan and Euphemia Taylor Stevenson, Edinburgh; *m* 1st, 1940, Vaire Olive Wollaston (from whom he obtained a divorce); two *s*; 2nd, 1947, Christine Peggy Walker; one *s* one *d. Educ:* Liverpool Collegiate Sch.; University Coll., Oxford (Open Classical Scholar). First Classes: Hon. Mods 1930, Lit. Hum. 1932, Jurisprudence, 1933; Oxford Univ. Senior Studentship, 1933; Harmsworth Scholar, Middle Temple, 1933 (Hon. Bencher, 1965); Henry Fellowship Harvard Law Sch., 1935-36; Asst Lecturer, LSE, 1936-37; Barstow Scholarship, 1937; called to Bar, Middle Temple, 1937; Fellow of Trinity Coll., Cambridge, 1937-43; Principal, Ministry of Supply, 1940-44; Clerk of the Court, University of London, 1944-47. Rede Lecturer, 1963. Fellow: Wye Coll., 1970; Imperial Coll., 1974; School of Pharmacy, 1975. Vice-Chm., Association of Commonwealth Univs, 1961-67 (Chm. 1962-63); Hon. Treasurer, 1967-74; Dep. Hon. Treasurer, 1974-); Vice-Chm., Athlone Fellowship Cttee, 1959-71; Dep. Chm., Commonwealth Scholarships

Commn; Member: Marshall Scholarships Commn, 1961-67; Nat. Theatre Bd, 1962-68; a Governor, Old Vic, 1957-80 (Vice-Chm., 1972-80), and Bristol Old Vic; a Trustee, City Parochial Foundation, 1953-67; Member: Anderson Cttee on Grants to Students, 1958-60; Hale Cttee on Superannuation of Univ. Teachers, 1958-60; Northumberland Cttee on Recruitment to the Veterinary Profession, 1962-64; Maddex Working Party on the Superannuation of Univ. Teachers, 1965-68. Mem. British Delegation to 1st, 2nd, 3rd, and 4th Commonwealth Educn Confs, Oxford, 1959, Delhi, 1962, Ottawa, 1964, and Lagos, 1968; Commonwealth Medical Conf. Edinburgh, 1965. Hon. Mem., Pharmaceutical Soc. Hon. Fellow: LSE, 1962; University Coll., Oxford, 1973; University Coll. London, 1975. Hon. DCL Western Ontario; Hon. DLitt Rhodesia; Hon. LLD: Melbourne, Madras, British Columbia, Hong Kong, Liverpool, McGill, CNAA, London; Hon. FDSRCS; Hon. FRIBA. Chevalier de l'Ordre de la Légion d'Honneur. *Address:* Restalrig, Mountain Street, Chilham, Canterbury, Kent CT4 8DQ. *T:* Chilham 640. *Club:* Athenæum.

LOGAN, Lt-Col John, TD 1945; Vice-Lieutenant, Stirlingshire, 1965-79; *b* 25 May 1907; *s* of Crawford William Logan and Ada Kathleen Logan (*née* Kidston); *m* 1937, Rosaleen Muriel O'Hara (*d* 1967); one *s* one *d. Educ:* Eton Coll., Windsor. British American Tobacco Co. Ltd (China), 1928-32; Imperial Tobacco Co. (of Great Britain and Ireland) Ltd, 1932-39. POW in Germany, 1940-45 (Captain, 7th Argyll and Sutherland Hdrs; Co, 1949-50). Imperial Tobacco Co. (of Great Britain and Ireland) Ltd, 1946-67. DL Stirlingshire, 1956. *Publication:* China Old and New, 1981. *Recreation:* fishing. *Address:* Wester Craigend, Stirling. *T:* Stirling 5025.

LOGAN, Rt. Rev. Vincent; *see* Dunkeld, Bishop of, (RC).

LOGAN, William Philip Dowie, MD, PhD, BSc, DPH, FRCP; Director, Division of Health Statistics, WHO, 1961-74; *b* 2 Nov. 1914; *s* of late Frederick William Alexander Logan and late Elizabeth Jane Dowie; *m* 1st, Pearl (*née* Piper) (marr. diss.); four *s* two *d* (and one *s* decd); 2nd, Barbara (*née* Huneke). *Educ:* Queen's Park Sch., Glasgow; Universities of Glasgow and London. RAF Med. Branch, 1940-46 (Squadron Leader). Hospital appointments in Glasgow, 1939-40 and 1946. Gen. practice in Barking, Essex, 1947-48; General Register Office, 1948-60 (Chief Medical Statistician, Adviser on Statistics to Ministry of Health, Head of WHO Centre for Classification of Diseases, and Member, WHO panel of experts on Health Statistics). Epidemiological consultant to various nat. and internat. organisations. *Publications:* contribs on epidemiology, vital and health statistics in official reports and medical jls. *Address:* 10 chemin de la Tourelle, 1209 Geneva, Switzerland.

LOGUE, Christopher; *b* 23 Nov. 1926; *s* of John Logue and Molly Logue (*née* Chapman); unmarried. *Educ:* Prior Park Coll., Bath; Portsmouth Grammar Sch. Mem., Equity. *Publications: verse:* Wand & Quadrant, 1953; Devil, Maggot & Son, 1956; Songs, 1959; Patrocleia, 1962; ABC, 1966; Pax, 1967; New Numbers, 1969; Twelve Cards, 1972; The Crocodile (illus. Binette Schroeder), 1976; Abecedary (illus. Bert Kitchen), 1977; War Music, 1981; Ode to the Dodo, 1981; *anthology:* The Children's Book of Comic Verse, 1979; *plays:* The Trial of Cob & Leach, 1959; (with Harry Cookson) The Lilywhite Boys, 1959; (with Hugo Claus) Friday, 1971; *prose:* Ratsmagic (illus. Wayne Anderson), 1976; The Magic Circus (illus. Wayne Anderson), 1979; The Bumper Book of True Stories (illus. Bert Kitchen), 1980; contrib. Private Eye, The Times, The Sunday Times, etc; *as Count Palmiro Vicarion:* Lust, a pornographic novel, 1957; (ed) Count Palmiro Vicarion's Book of Limericks, 1957; (ed) Count Palmiro Vicarion's Book of Bawdy Ballads, 1957. *Screen plays:* Savage Messiah (dir Ken Russell), 1972. *Play:* The Story of Mary Frazer, 1962. *Recordings:* Red Bird (with Tony Kinsey and Bill Le Sage), 1960; Songs from The Establishment (singer Annie Ross), 1962; The Death of Patroclus (with Vanessa Redgrave, Alan Dobie and others), 1963. *Film roles:* Swinburne, in Ken Russell's Dante's Inferno, 1966; John Ball, in John Irvin's The Peasants' Revolt, 1969; Cardinal Richelieu, in Ken Russell's The Devils, 1970; TV and stage roles. *Address:* 18 Denbigh Close, W11.

LOISELLE, Gilles; Agent General for Quebec in London, with responsibility for Scandinavian countries, Iceland and Ireland, since 1977; *b* 20 May 1929; *s* of Arthur Loiselle and Antoinette Lethiecq; *m* 1962, Lorraine Benoit; one *s* one *d. Educ:* Sacred-Heart Coll., Sudbury, Ont. BA Laval. Tafari Makonnen Sch., Addis Ababa, 1951-53; Journalist, Le Droit, Ottawa, 1953-56; Haile Selassie First Day Sch., Addis Ababa, 1956-62; Dir, Behrane Zarie Néo Inst., Addis Ababa, 1958-62; Canadian Broadcasting Corporation: Editor, TV French Network, 1962-63; Quebec and Paris correspondent, French Radio and TV Network, 1963-67; Counsellor, Quebec House, Paris, 1967-72; Dir Gen. of Quebec Govt Communications, 1972-76; Pres., Intergovtl Deptl Cttee for Olympic Year, 1976; Dir, Interparly Relations, Quebec Nat. Assembly, 1977. Founder Mem., Assoc. France-Québec, 1969-72; Member: Council, Office franco-québécois pour la Jeunesse, 1973-76; Inst. of Public Admin; RIIA. *Recreations:* reading, gardening. *Address:* 12 Upper Grosvenor Street, W1. *T:* 01-629 4155; 6 Ilchester Place, W14. *T:* 01-602 2213. *Clubs:* Royal Automobile, Royal Commonwealth Society, East India, Devonshire, Sports and Public Schools.

LOKOLOKO, Sir Tore, GCMG 1977; OBE; Governor-General of Papua New Guinea, since 1977; *b* 21 Sept. 1930; *s* of Loko Loko Tore and Kevau Sarufa; *m* 1950, Lalahaia Meakoro; four *s* six *d. Educ:* Sogeri High Sch., PNG. Dip. in Cooperative, India. Chm., PNG Cooperative Fedn, 1965-68; MP,

1968-77 (two terms); Minister for Health, and Dep. Chm. of National Exec. Council, 1968-72. Rep. PNG: Co-op. Conf., Australia, 1951; S Pacific Conf., Lae, 1964; attended UN Gen. Assembly, 1969, and Trusteeship Council, 1971. KStJ 1979. *Address:* Government House, Port Moresby, Papua New Guinea. *T:* 21 4466.

LOMAS, Alfred; Member (Lab) London North East, European Parliament, since 1979; *b* 30 April 1928; *s* of Alfred and Florence Lomas; one *s* one *d. Educ:* St Paul's Elem. Sch., Stockport; various further educnl estabs. Solicitor's clerk, 1942-46; Radio Telephony Operator, RAF, 1946-49; various jobs, 1949-51; railway signalman, 1951-59; Labour Party Sec./Agent, 1959-65; Polit. Sec., London Co-op., 1965-79. *Publication:* The Common Market—why we should keep out, 1970. *Recreations:* chess, jogging, arts, sport. *Address:* 23 Hatcliffe Close, SE3 9UE. *T:* 01-852 5433. *Club:* Hackney Labour.

LOMAX, Sir John Garnett, KBE 1953 (MBE 1928); CMG 1944; MC 1917; HM Diplomatic Service, retired; *b* Liverpool, 27 Aug. 1896; *s* of Rev. Canon Edward Lomax and Bessie Garnett; *m* 1922, Feridah Yvette Krajewski; two *s. Educ:* Liverpool Coll.; Liverpool Univ. Served European War, France, Belgium, India, and Egypt; Driver, RFA (West Lancs), 1915, Lt 1916. HM Vice-Consul, New Orleans, 1920, Chicago, 1921; Vice-Consul and 2nd Sec. HM Legation, Bogota, 1926-30; 2nd Commercial Sec. HM Embassy, Rio de Janeiro, 1930; transferred to HM Embassy, Rome, 1935; HM Commercial Agent, Jerusalem, 1938; Commercial Counsellor, HM Embassy, Madrid, 1940; HM Legation, Berne, 1941; Commercial Counsellor at Angora, 1943; Minister (commercial), British Embassy, Buenos Aires, 1946-49; Ambassador to Bolivia, 1949-56. *Publication:* The Diplomatic Smuggler, 1965. *Address:* Tanterfyn, Llanelian, Anglesey, Gwynedd; 803 Nelson House, Dolphin Square, SW1. *Clubs:* Reform, Royal Automobile.

LOMBARD KNIGHT, Eric John Percy Crawford; Chairman: Kellock Factors Ltd; Prime Marketing Ltd; Director: Estates & General Investments Ltd; Sterling Credit Ltd; Kellock Holdings Ltd; *yr s* of late Herbert John Charles and Mary Henrietta Knight; *m* 1933, Peggy Julia (*née* Carter); one *s* one *d. Educ:* Ashford Grammar Sch. Served War of 1939-45, RAF. British Mercedes Benz; Bowmaker Ltd; established Lombard Banking, 1947; Chm. Lombank Ltd, 1951-71 (Man. Dir, 1951-68). *Address:* The White House, 18 Limpsfield Road, Sanderstead Village, Surrey. *T:* 01-657 2021. *Clubs:* Caledonian; Addington Golf.

LOMBE, Edward Christopher E.; *see* Evans-Lombe.

LOMER, Dennis Roy; Member, Central Electricity Generating Board, since 1977; *b* 5 Oct. 1923; *s* of Bertie Cecil Lomer and Agnes Ellen Coward; *m* 1949, Audrey May Bick; one *s* one *d.* With Consulting Engineers, 1948-50; joined Electricity Supply Industry, 1952; Project Engr, Transmission Div., 1961; Asst Chief Transmission Engr, 1965; Generation Construction Div. (secondment at Dir level), 1972; Dep. Dir-Gen. (Projects), 1973; Dir-Gen., Transmission Div., 1975. FIEE; CBIM. *Recreations:* golf, sailing. *Address:* Henley House, Heathfield Close, Woking, Surrey GU22 7JQ. *T:* Woking 64656. *Club:* West Hill Golf (Surrey).

LOMER, William Michael, PhD; Director, Culham Laboratory, United Kingdom Atomic Energy Authority, since 1981; *b* 2 March 1926; *s* of Frederick John Lomer and Dorothy Lomer; *m* 1952, Pamela Anne Wakelin; one *s* two *d. Educ:* St Austell County School; University College of the South West, Exeter (MSc London); Queens' College, Cambridge (MA, PhD). Research Scientist, UKAEA, 1952; AERE Harwell: Divison Head, Theory Div., 1958-62; Division Head, Solid State Physics, 1962-68; Research Director, 1968-81. Hon. Treasurer, Inst. of Physics, 1980-82. FInstP. *Publications:* papers in physics and metallurgical jls. *Recreations:* gardening, walking, painting. *Address:* 7 Hids Copse Road, Cumnor Hill, Oxford. *T:* Oxford 862173.

LONDESBOROUGH, 9th Baron, *cr* 1850; **Richard John Denison;** *b* 2 July 1959; *s* of John Albert Lister, 8th Baron Londesborough, TD, AMICE, and of Elizabeth Ann, *d* of late Edward Little Sale, ICS; *S* father, 1968. *Educ:* Wellington College; Exeter Univ.

LONDON, Bishop of, since 1981; **Rt. Rev. and Rt. Hon. Graham Douglas Leonard;** PC 1981; Dean of the Chapels Royal, since 1981; Prelate of the Order of the British Empire, since 1981; *b* 8 May 1921; *s* of late Rev. Douglas Leonard, MA; *m* 1943, Vivien Priscilla, *d* of late M. B. R. Swann, MD, Fellow of Gonville and Caius Coll., Cambridge; two *s. Educ:* Monkton Combe Sch.; Balliol Coll. Oxford. Hon. Sch. Nat. Science, shortened course. BA 1943, MA 1947. Served War, 1941-45; Captain, Oxford and Bucks Light Infantry; Army Operational Research Group (Ministry of Supply), 1944-45. Westcott House, Cambridge, 1946-47. Deacon 1947, Priest 1948; Vicar of Ardleigh, Essex, 1952-55; Director of Religious Education, Diocese of St Albans, 1955-58; Hon. Canon of St Albans, 1955-57; Canon Residentiary, 1957-58; Canon Emeritus, 1958; General Secretary, Nat. Society, and Secretary, C of E Schools Council, 1958-62; Archdeacon of Hampstead, Exam. Chaplain to Bishop of London, and Rector of St Andrew Undershaft *w* St Mary Axe, City of London, 1962-64; Bishop Suffragan of Willesden, 1964-73; Bishop of Truro, 1973-81. Chairman: C of E Cttee for Social Work and the Social Services, 1967-76; C of E Board for Social Responsibility, 1976-83; Churches Main Cttee, 1981-; C of E Board of Education, 1983-; Member: Churches Unity Commn, 1977-78; Consultant 1978; Churches Council for Covenanting,

1978-82. An Anglican Mem., Commn for Anglican Orthodox Jt Doctrinal Discussions, 1974-81; one of Archbp of Canterbury's Counsellors on Foreign Relations, 1974. Elected delegate, 5th Assembly WCC, Nairobi, 1975. Entered House of Lords, 1977. Select Preacher to University of Oxford, 1968. Freeman, City of London, 1970. President: Middlesex Assoc., 1970-73; Corporation of SS Mary and Nicholas (Woodard Schools), 1973-78, Hon. Fellow, 1978. Member Court and Council, City Univ., 1981-. DD (*hc*) Episcopal Seminary, Kentucky, 1974; Episcopal Canon of Jerusalem, 1982; Hon. Bencher, Middle Temple, 1982. *Publications:* Growing into Union (Jt author), 1970; The Gospel is for Everyone, 1971; God Alive: Priorities in Pastoral Theology, 1981; contrib. to: The Christian Religion Explained, 1960; Retreats Today, 1962; Communicating the Faith, 1969; A Critique of Eucharistic Agreement, 1975; Is Christianity Credible?, 1981. *Recreations:* reading, especially biographies; music. *Address:* London House, 8 Barton Street, Westminster, SW1P 3RX. *T:* 01-222 8661.
See also Baron Swann.

LONDON, Archdeacon of; *see* Harvey, Ven. F. W.

LONDON, CENTRAL, Bishop in, (RC); *see* Konstant, Rt Rev. David.

LONDON, EAST, Bishop in, (RC); *see* Guazzelli, Rt Rev. Victor.

LONDON, NORTH, Bishop in, (RC); *see* Harvey, Rt Rev. Philip.

LONDON, WEST, Bishop in, (RC); *see* Mahon, Rt Rev. Gerald Thomas.

LONDONDERRY, 9th Marquess of, *cr* 1816; **Alexander Charles Robert Vane-Tempest-Stewart;** Baron Londonderry, 1789; Viscount Castlereagh, 1795; Earl of Londonderry, 1796; Baron Stewart, 1814; Earl Vane, Viscount Seaham, 1823; *b* 7 Sept. 1937; *s* of 8th Marquess of Londonderry and Romaine (*d* 1951), *er d* of Major Boyce Combe, Great Holt, Dockenfield, Surrey; *S* father 1955; *m* 1st, 1958, Nicolette (marr. diss. 1971), *d* of Michael Harrison, Netherhampton, near Salisbury, Wilts; two *d* ; 2nd, 1972, Doreen Patricia Wells, *qv* ; two *s. Educ:* Eton. Heir: *s* Viscount Castlereagh, *qv. Address:* Wynyard Park, Billingham, Cleveland TS22 5NF. *T:* Wolviston 317.

LONDONDERRY, Marchioness of; *see* Wells, Doreen P.

LONG, family name of **Viscount Long.**

LONG, 4th Viscount, *cr* 1921, of Wraxall; **Richard Gerard Long;** a Lord in Waiting (Government Whip), since 1979; *b* 30 Jan. 1929; *s* of 3rd Viscount and Gwendolyn (*d* 1959), *d* of Thomas Reginald Hague Cook; *S* father, 1967; *m* 1957, Margaret Frances, *d* of late Ninian B. Frazer; one *s* two *d. Educ:* Harrow. Wilts Regt, 1947-49. Opposition Whip, 1974-79. Vice-Pres. and formerly Vice-Chm., Wilts Royal British Legion; Pres., Bath Gliding Club. Heir: *s* Hon. James Richard Long, *b* 31 Dec. 1960. *Address:* The Lodge, Coppice Hill, Bradford on Avon, Wilts. *Club:* Pratt's.

LONG, (Adrian) Douglas; Chief Executive, Mirror Group Newspapers Ltd, since 1980; Chairman, Syndication International Ltd, since 1975; *b* London, 9 Feb. 1925; *s* of late Harold Edgar Long and Kate Long; *m* 1949, Vera Barbara Wellstead; one *s. Educ:* Wandsworth Sch. MBIM. Served Indian Army, 1943-47: Royal Deccan Horse, 43rd Cavalry, Probyns Horse (Captain). Reporter/Feature Writer: Daily Graphic, 1947; Daily Record, Glasgow, 1948-54; Scottish Editor, Daily Herald, 1955-57; Chief News Editor/Features Editor, Daily Herald and Sun newspapers, 1958-68; Gen. Man., Odhams, 1969-71; Dep. Man. Dir/Dep. Chief Exec., Mirror Gp Newspapers Ltd, 1972-79. Director: Odhams Newspapers Ltd, 1976-; Mirror M&G Management Ltd, 1976-; Scottish Daily Record & Sunday Mail, 1977-; Reed Aviation Ltd, 1979-; Reed Publishing Pension Trustees Ltd, 1980-; Reed Publishing Holdings Ltd, 1981-. Member: President's Assoc.; Amer. Management Assoc. *Recreations:* theatre, cinema, tennis, swimming. *Address:* 3 Garbrand Walk, Ewell Village, Surrey KT17 1UQ. *T:* 01-394 1323.

LONG, Athelstan Charles Ethelwulf, CMG 1968; CBE 1964 (MBE 1959); Chairman and President, United Bank International, Cayman Islands, since 1975; Chairman, Cayman Airways Ltd, since 1979; Chairman, President and Director of some ten companies; Deputy Chairman, Public Service Commission, since 1976; *b* 2 Jan. 1919; *s* of Arthur Leonard Long and Gabrielle Margaret Campbell (historical writer and novelist, Marjorie Bowen); *m* 1948, Edit Majken Zadie Harriet Krantz, *d* of late Erik Krantz, Stockholm; two *s. Educ:* Westminster Sch.; Brasenose Coll., Oxford. Served War of 1939-45: commnd into RA, 1940; seconded 7th (Bengal) Battery, 22nd Mountain Regt, IA, 1940; served Malaya; POW as Capt., 1942-45. Cadet, Burma Civil Service, 1946-48; Colonial Admin. Service (N Nigeria), 1948; Sen. District Officer, 1958; Resident, Zaria Province, 1959; Perm. Sec., Min. of Animal Health and Forestry, 1959; started new Min. of Information as Perm. Sec., 1960; Swaziland: appointed Govt Sec., 1961; Chief Sec., 1964; Leader of Govt business in Legislative Council and MEC, 1964-67; HM Dep. Comr, 1967-68; Administrator, later Governor, of the Cayman Is, 1968-71; Temp. Comr of Anguilla, March-July 1972; Admin. Sec., Inter-University Council, 1972-73. Man. Dir, Anegada Corp. Ltd, 1973-74; Pres., Conagada Hotels Ltd, 1973-74. Chm. Governing Council, Waterford Sch., Swaziland, 1963-68. FRAS; FRGS. *Recreations:* travel, tropical farming, reading.

Address: Box 131, Savannah, Grand Cayman, Cayman Islands, West Indies.

LONG, Christopher William; HM Diplomatic Service; Counsellor and Deputy Permanent Representative, UK Mission, Geneva, since 1980; *b* 9 April 1938; *s* of Eric and May Long; *m* 1972, Patricia, *d* of Dennis and May Stanbridge; one *s* one *d. Educ:* King Edward's Sch., Birmingham; Balliol Coll., Oxford (Deakin Scholar); Univ. of Münster, W Germany. Served RN, 1956-58. HM Diplomatic Service, 1963-: FO, 1963-64; Jedda, 1965-67; Caracas, 1967-69; FCO, 1969-74; Budapest, 1974-77; Belgrade (CSCE), 1977; Counsellor, Damascus, 1978-80. *Address:* c/o Foreign and Commonwealth Office, King Charles Street, SW1A 2AH. *Club:* Travellers'.

LONG, Douglas; see Long, A. D.

LONG, Air Vice-Marshal Francis William, CB 1946; DL; *b* 10 Oct. 1899; *s* of Rev. F. P. Long, Oxford; *m* 1921, Doreen Langley, *d* of Rev. F. L. Appleford; one *d. Educ:* Lancing Coll. Joined RAF 1918; member Schneider Trophy Team, 1931. AOC No 23 Gp, Flying Training Command, 1952-53; retd, 1953. DL Herts, 1963. *Address:* 2 Cranford Court, Cranford Avenue, Exmouth, Devon. *T:* Exmouth 6320.

LONG, Gerald; Deputy Chairman, News International plc, since 1982; *b* 22 Aug. 1923; *o s* of Fred Harold Long and Sabina Long (*née* Walsh); *m* 1951, Anne Hamilton Walker; two *s* three *d. Educ:* St Peter's Sch., York; Emmanuel Coll., Cambridge. Army Service, 1943-47. Joined Reuters, 1948: served as Reuter correspondent in Germany, France and Turkey, 1950-60; Asst General Manager, 1960; Chief Exec., 1963-81 (Gen. Manager, 1963-73; Man. Dir, 1973-81); Man. Dir, Times Newspapers Ltd, 1981-82. Chairman: Visnews Ltd, 1968-79; Exec. Cttee, Internat. Inst. of Communications Ltd, 1973-78. FBIM 1978. Commander, Royal Order of the Phoenix, Greece, 1964; Grand Officer, Order of Merit, Italy, 1973; Commander, Order of the Lion of Finland, 1979. *Recreation:* cooking. *Address:* 38 Myddelton Square, EC1R 1YB. *T:* 01-278 9084.

LONG, Hubert Arthur, CBE 1970; Deputy Secretary, Exchequer and Audit Department, 1963-73; *b* 21 Jan. 1912; *s* of Arthur Albert Long; *m* 1937, Mary Louise Parker; three *s. Educ:* Taunton's Sch., Southampton. Entered Exchequer and Audit Department, 1930. *Address:* 48 Hayes Lane, Bromley, Kent. *T:* 01-460 4251.

LONG, Ven. John Sanderson, MA; Archdeacon of Ely, Hon. Canon of Ely and Rector of St Botolph's, Cambridge, 1970-81; Archdeacon Emeritus, 1981; *b* 21 July 1913; *s* of late Rev. Guy Stephenson Long and Ivy Marion Long; *m* 1948, Rosamond Mary, *d* of Arthur Temple Forman; one *s* three *d. Educ:* St Edmund's Sch., Canterbury; Queens' Coll.; Cuddesdon Theological Coll. Deacon, 1936; Priest, 1937; Curate, St Mary and St Eanswythe, Folkestone, 1936-41. Chaplain, RNVR, 1941-46. Curate, St Peter-in-Thanet, 1946; Domestic Chaplain to the Archbishop of Canterbury, 1946-53; Vicar of Bearsted, 1953-59; Petersfield with Sheet, 1959-70; Rural Dean of Petersfield, 1962-70. *Recreations:* walking, gardening. *Address:* 23 Thornton Road, Girton, Cambridge CB3 0NP. *T:* Cambridge 276421.

LONG, Olivier; Ambassador; Professor, Graduate Institute of International Studies, Geneva, since 1962; President, Graduate Institute of Public Administration, Lausanne, since 1981; *b* 1915; *s* of Dr Edouard Long and Dr Marie Landry; *m* 1946, Francine Roels; one *s* two *d. Educ:* Univ. de Paris, Faculté de Droit et Ecole des Sciences Politiques; Univ. de Genève. PhD Law, 1938; Rockefeller Foundn Fellow, 1938-39; PhD Pol. Sc., 1943. Swiss Armed Forces, 1939-43; International Red Cross, 1943-46; Swiss Foreign Affairs Dept, Berne, 1946-49; Washington Embassy, 1949-54; Govt Delegate for Trade Agreements, 1955-66; Head of Swiss Delegn to EFTA, 1960-66; Ambassador to UK and Malta, 1967-68; Dir-Gen., GATT, 1968-80. Mem., Internat. Red Cross Cttee, 1980-. *Publications:* several on political sciences and trade policies. *Address:* Graduate Institute of International Studies, 132 rue de Lausanne, 1211 Geneva, Switzerland.

LONG, Pamela Marjorie, (Mrs John Nichols); Metropolitan Stipendiary Magistrate, since 1978; *b* 12 Sept. 1930; *d* of late John Holywell Long, AMICE, and Emily McNaughton; *m* 1966, Kenneth John Heastey Nichols, *qv. Educ:* Carlisle High School for Girls. Admitted Solicitor of Supreme Court, 1959; private practice, 1959-63; Solicitor's Dept, New Scotland Yard, 1963-77. *Recreations:* music, riding, watching cricket. *Address:* Flat 1, 36 Buckingham Gate, SW1; Dolphin House, Porthgwarra, St Levan, Cornwall.

LONG, Sir Ronald, Kt 1964; Solicitor; *b* 5 Sept. 1902; *s* of Sydney Richard and Kate Long; *m* 1931, Muriel Annie Harper; one *s* two *d. Educ:* Earls Colne Grammar Sch.; The School, Stamford, Lincs. President, The Law Society, 1963-64. Chm., Stansted Airport Consultative Cttee, 1969-79. *Recreations:* fishing, gardening. *Address:* Ayletts Farm, Halstead, Essex. *T:* Halstead 472072.

LONG, Captain Rt. Hon. William Joseph, PC (N Ireland) 1966; JP; Minister of Education, Northern Ireland, 1969-72; MP (Unionist) Ards, Parliament of Northern Ireland, 1962-72; *b* 23 April 1922; *s* of James William Long and Frederica (Walker); *m* 1942, Dr Elizabeth Doreen Mercer; one *s. Educ:* Friends' Sch., Great Ayton, Yorks; Edinburgh Univ.; RMC, Sandhurst.

Served Royal Inniskilling Fusiliers, 1940-48. Secretary: NI Marriage Guidance Council, 1948-51; NI Chest and Heart Assoc., 1951-62. Parliamentary Secretary, Min. of Agriculture, NI, 1964-66; Sen. Parliamentary Secretary, Min. of Development, NI, Jan.-Oct. 1966; Minister of Educn, 1966-68; Minister of Home Affairs, Dec. 1968-March 1969; Minister of Develt, March 1969-May 1969. *Recreations:* cricket, horticulture, angling, sailing, model engineering, aviation. *Address:* Lisvarna, Warren Road, Donaghadee, Co. Down. *T:* Donaghadee 2538.

LONGAIR, Prof. Malcolm Sim, PhD; FRSE 1981; Astronomer Royal for Scotland, Regius Professor of Astronomy, University of Edinburgh, and Director of Royal Observatory, Edinburgh, since 1980; *b* 18 May 1941; *s* of James Sim Longair and Lily Malcolm; *m* 1975, Dr Deborah Janet Howard; one *s* one *d. Educ:* Morgan Acad., Dundee; Queen's Coll., Dundee, Univ. of St Andrews (BSc Electronic Physics, 1963); Cavendish Lab., Univ. of Cambridge (MA, PhD 1967). Res. Fellow, Royal Commn for Exhibn of 1851, 1966-68; Royal Soc. Exchange Fellow to USSR, 1968-69; Res. Fellow, 1967-71, and Official Fellow, 1971-80, Clare Hall, Cambridge; Univ. of Cambridge: Univ. Demonstrator in Phys., 1970-75; Univ. Lectr in Phys., 1975-80. Vis. Professor: of Radio Astronomy, Calif Inst. of Technol., 1972; of Astronomy, Inst. for Advanced Study, Princeton, 1978. Chairman: A II Cttee of Astronomy, Space and Radio Bd, SRC, 1979-80; Space Telescope Adv. Panel, 1977-. Mem. Committees: Eur. Space Agency Astronomy Wkg Gp, 1975-78; Eur. Space Agency Space Telescope Working Gp, 1977-; NASA Space Telescope Science Working Gp, 1977-. Editor, Monthly Notices of RAS, 1974-78. Hon. LLD Dundee, 1982. *Publications:* (ed) Confrontation of Cosmological Theories with Observational Data, 1974; (ed with J. Einasto) The Large-Scale Structure of the Universe, 1978; (with J. E. Gunn and M. J. Rees) Observational Cosmology, 1978; (ed with J. Warner) The Scientific Uses of the Space Telescope, 1980; High Energy Astrophysics: an informal introduction, 1980; (with R. A. Sunyaev) Matter and Radiation in the Universe, 1982; (ed with H. A. Brück and G. Coyne) Astrophysical Cosmology; over 100 papers, mostly in Monthly Notices of RAS. *Recreations:* music, esp. opera, 19th and 20th Century music and all piano music; art, architecture. *Address:* c/o Royal Observatory, Blackford Hill, Edinburgh EH9 3HJ. *T:* 031-667 3321.

LONGBOTHAM, Samuel; Lord-Lieutenant of the Western Isles, since 1975; *b* Elgin, Morayshire, 19 March 1908; *s* of George Longbotham and Elizabeth Longbotham (*née* Monks); *m* 1941, Elizabeth Rae, *d* of Donald Davidson, Glasgow; two *s* one *d. Educ:* Elgin. Served War, 1940-46: with RA and Intelligence Corps: commissioned, 1944. Major, Lovat Scouts TA (RA), 1952-60; Major, North Highland ACF, 1968-75. DL Ross and Cromarty, 1964. *Recreations:* angling, walking, reading, family life. *Address:* 25 Lewis Street, Stornoway, Isle of Lewis, Scotland. *T:* Stornoway 2519.

LONGBOTTOM, Charles Brooke; *b* 22 July 1930; *s* of late William Ewart Longbottom, Forest Hill, Worksop; *m* 1962, Anita, *d* of G. Trapani and Mrs Basil Mavroleon; two *d. Educ:* Uppingham. Contested (C) Stockton-on-Tees, 1955; MP (C) York, 1959-66; Parly Private Secretary to Mr Iain Macleod, Leader of the House, 1961-63. Barrister, Inner Temple, 1958; Chairman: Austin & Pickersgill, Shipbuilders, Sunderland, 1966-72; A&P Appledore International Ltd, 1970-79; Seascope Holdings Ltd, 1970-; Seascope Sale & Purchase, 1970-; Seascope Shipbrokers Ltd, 1972-; Seascope Offshore Ltd, 1978-; Director: Henry Ansbacher Holdings Ltd; Seascope Ltd, 1970-; Seascope Insurance Services Ltd, 1970-; Seascope Underwriting Agencies Ltd, 1976-. Chairman, Ariel Foundation, 1960-. Member: General Advisory Council, BBC, 1965-75; Community Relations Commn, 1968-70. Member of Lloyd's. *Recreations:* shooting, golf and racing. *Address:* 66 Kingston House North, Princes Gate, SW7. *Clubs:* White's, Carlton.

LONGDEN, Sir Gilbert (James Morley), Kt 1972; MBE 1944; MA (Cantab), LLB; *b* 16 April 1902; *e s* of late Lieut-Colonel James Morley Longden, Castle Eden, Co. Durham, and *d* of George Blacker Morgan, JP; unmarried. *Educ:* Haileybury; Emmanuel Coll., Cambridge. Secretary ICI (India) Ltd, 1930-36; travelled throughout Asia (Middle and Far East) and in North and South America. Student at University of Paris, 1937. Called up from AOER into DLI, 1940; served with 2nd and 36th Divisions in Burma campaigns (MBE (mil.)). Adopted Parliamentary Candidate for Morpeth, 1938; contested (C) Morpeth, 1945; MP (C) SW Herts, 1950-Feb. 1974. UK Representative to Council of Europe, 1953-54; United Kingdom Delegate to 12th and 13th Sessions of United Nations; Past Chairman: British Atlantic Cttee; Conservative Gp for Europe; Great Britain-East Europe Centre. Vice-Chm., British Council. *Publications:* A Conservative Philosophy, 1947; and (jointly): One Nation, 1950; Change is our Ally, 1954; A Responsible Society, 1959; One Europe, 1969. *Recreations:* reading, writing, gardening. *Address:* 89 Cornwall Gardens, SW7 4AX. *T:* 01-584 5666. *Clubs:* Brooks's, Hurlingham.

LONGDEN, Henry Alfred, FEng, FICE, FIMinE; FGS; Director, Trafalgar House Investments Ltd, 1970-76; *b* 8 Sept. 1909; *s* of late Geoffrey Appleby Longden and late Marjorie Mullins; *m* 1935, Ruth, *d* of Arthur Gilliat, Leeds; one *s* four *d. Educ:* Oundle; Birmingham Univ. (BSc Hons). Served in Glass Houghton and Pontefract Collieries, 1930; Asst Gen. Manager, Stanton Ironworks Co., 1935; Gen. Manager, Briggs Colliers Ltd, 1940; Director: Blackwell Colliery Co., 1940; Briggs Collieries Co., 1941; New Hucknell Colliery Co., 1941; Area Gen. Manager, 1947, and Production Dir, 1948, NE Div., NCB; Dir-Gen., Production, NCB, 1955; Chm., W Midlands Div.,

NCB, 1960; Chm. and Chief Exec., Cementation Co. Ltd, 1963-70 (Dep. Chm. and Chief Exec, 1961-63). President: Instn of Mining Engineers, 1958; Engineering Industries Assoc., 1965-71; Member: Engineering Industry Trg Bd, 1967-70; Confedn of British Industry, 1968. Fellow, Fellowship of Engineering, 1977. *Publication:* Cadman Memorial Lecture, 1958. *Recreations:* Rugby football, cricket, tennis, shooting, fishing, sailing. *Address:* Raeburn, Northdown Road, Woldingham, Surrey. *T:* Woldingham 2245.

LONGE, Desmond Evelyn, MC 1944; DL; President, later Chairman, Norwich Union Insurance Group, 1964-81; (Vice-President, 1963); Chairman: Norwich Union Life Insurance Society, 1964-81; Norwich Union Fire Insurance Society Ltd, 1964-81; Maritime Insurance Co. Ltd, 1964-81; Scottish Union and National Insurance Co., 1964-81; Director: East Coast Grain Ltd, since 1962; Napak Ltd, since 1969; D. E. Longe & Co. Ltd, since 1962; *b* 8 Aug. 1914; *y s* of late Rev. John Charles Longe, MA, Spixworth Park, Norfolk; *m* 1944, Isla (*née* Bell); one *s* one *d. Educ:* Woodbridge Sch., Suffolk. Director: Eastern Counties Group Ltd, to 1982; Eastern Counties Newspapers Ltd, 1977-82; Norwich Winterthur Holdings Ltd, 1977-81; Anglia TV Ltd. Member: BR Eastern Region Bd, 1969-70; BR London Midland Region Bd, 1971-74; (and Dep. Chm.) BR London and SE Region Bd, 1975-77; BR Property Bd, 1978-82. Mem., E Anglia Econ. Planning Council, 1965-68. A Church Commissioner, 1970-76. Chm., Royal Norfolk Agric. Assoc. (Pres., 1980). DL Norfolk, 1971; High Sheriff, Norfolk, 1975. Croix de Guerre avec Palme (French), 1944. *Recreations:* travel, hunting, fishing. *Address:* Woodton Grange, Bungay, Suffolk. *T:* Woodton 260. *Clubs:* Special Forces, MCC; Norfolk County (Norwich).

LONGFIELD, Dr Michael David; Director, Teesside Polytechnic, since 1980; *b* 28 April 1928; *s* of Edric Douglas Longfield and Dorothy Longfield (*née* Hennessey); *m* 1st, 1952, Ann McDonnell; two *s* two *d* ; 2nd, 1970, June Shirley, *d* of late Levi and of Esther Beman; two *s. Educ:* Prince Henry's Grammar Sch., Otley; Leeds Univ. BSc, PhD; CEng, MIMechE. Lectr in Mech. Engrg, Univ. of Leeds, 1960-68; Manager, Leeds Univ. Industrial Unit of Tribology, 1968-70; Head of Dept of Mech., Marine and Production Engrg, Liverpool Polytechnic, 1970-72; Asst Dir, Teesside Polytechnic, 1972-80. *Publications:* contribs to engineering and medical engineering journals. *Recreations:* music, gardening. *Address:* Plum Tree House, Thirlby, Thirsk, N Yorks YO7 2DJ.

LONGFORD, 7th Earl of, *cr* 1785, **Francis Aungier Pakenham,** KG 1971; PC 1948; Baron Longford, 1759; Baron Silchester (UK), 1821; Baron Pakenham (UK), 1945; *b* 5 Dec. 1905; 2nd *s* of 5th Earl of Longford, KP, MVO; *S* brother (6th Earl) 1961; *m* 1931, Elizabeth (*see* Countess of Longford); four *s* three *d* (and one *d* decd). *Educ:* Eton; New Coll., Oxford, MA. 1st Class in Modern Greats, 1927. Tutor, University Tutorial Courses, Stoke-on-Trent, 1929-31; Cons. Party Economic Res. Dept, 1930-32. Christ Church, Oxford: Lecturer in Politics, 1932; Student in Politics, 1934-46, and 1952-64. Prospective Parliamentary Labour Candidate for Oxford City, 1938. Enlisted Oxford and Bucks LI (TA), May 1939; resigned commission on account of ill-health, 1940. Personal assistant to Sir William Beveridge, 1941-44; a Lord-in-Waiting to the King, 1945-46; Parliamentary Under-Secretary of State, War Office, 1946-47; Chancellor of the Duchy of Lancaster, 1947-48; Minister of Civil Aviation, 1948-51; First Lord of the Admiralty, May-Oct. 1951; Lord Privy Seal, 1964-65; Secretary of State for the Colonies, 1965-66; Leader of the House of Lords, 1964-68; Lord Privy Seal, 1966-68; Chm., The National Bank Ltd, 1955-63; Dir, Sidgwick and Jackson (Chm., 1970-80). Chm., Nat. Youth Employment Council, 1968-71; Joint Founder: New Horizon Youth Centre, 1964; New Bridge for Ex-Prisoners, 1956. *Publications:* Peace by Ordeal (The Anglo-Irish Treaty of 1921), 1935 (repr. 1972); (autobiog.) Born to Believe, 1953; (with Roger Opie), Causes of Crime, 1958; The Idea of Punishment, 1961; (autobiog.) Five Lives, 1964; Humility, 1969; (with Thomas P. O'Neill) Eamon De Valera, 1970; (autobiog.) The Grain of Wheat, 1974; Abraham Lincoln, 1974; Jesus Christ, 1974; Kennedy, 1976; St Francis of Assisi, 1978; Nixon, 1980; (with Anne McHardy) Ulster, 1981; Pope John Paul II, 1982; Diary of a Year, 1982. *Heir:* s Thomas (Frank Dermot) Pakenham, qv. *Address:* Bernhurst, Hurst Green, East Sussex. *T:* Hurst Green 248; 18 Chesil Court, Chelsea Manor Street, SW3. *T:* 01-352 7794. *Club:* Garrick.
See also Lady Rachel Billington, Lady Antonia Fraser, A. D. Powell.

LONGFORD, Countess of; Elizabeth Pakenham, CBE 1974; *b* 30 Aug. 1906; *d* of late N. B. Harman, FRCS, 108 Harley Street, W1, and of Katherine (*née* Chamberlain); *m* 1931, Hon. F. A. Pakenham (*see* 7th Earl of Longford); four *s* three *d* (and one *d* decd). *Educ:* Headington Sch., Oxford; Lady Margaret Hall, Oxford (MA). Lectr for WEA and Univ. Extension Lectr, 1929-35. Contested (Lab) Cheltenham, 1935, Oxford, 1950; candidate for King's Norton, Birmingham, 1935-43. Mem., Rent Tribunal, Paddington and St Pancras, 1947-54; Trustee, National Portrait Gall., 1968-78; Member: Adv. Council, V&A Museum, 1969-75; Adv. Bd, British Library, 1976-80; Hon. Life Pres., Women Writers and Journalists, 1979. Hon. DLitt Sussex 1970. *Publications:* (as Elizabeth Pakenham): Points for Parents, 1956; Catholic Approaches (ed), 1959; Jameson's Raid, 1960; (as Elizabeth Longford) Victoria RI, 1964 (James Tait Black Memorial Prize for Non-Fiction, 1964); Wellington: Years of the Sword, 1969 (Yorkshire Post Prize); Wellington: Pillar of State, 1972; The Royal House of Windsor, 1974; Churchill, 1974; Byron's Greece, 1975; Life of Byron, 1976; A Pilgrimage of Passion: the life of Wilfrid Scawen Blunt, 1979; (ed) Louisa: Lady in Waiting, 1979; Images

of Chelsea, 1980; The Queen Mother, a biography, 1981; Eminent Victorian Women, 1981. *Recreations:* gardening, reading. *Address:* Bernhurst, Hurst Green, East Sussex. *T:* Hurst Green 248; 18 Chesil Court, Chelsea Manor Street, SW3. *T:* 01-352 7794.
See also Lady Rachel Billington, Lady Antonia Fraser, T. F. D. Pakenham.

LONGFORD, Elizabeth; *see* Longford, Countess of.

LONGLAND, Cedric James, MVO 1949; Surgeon, Glasgow Royal Infirmary, 1954-77; *b* 30 Sept. 1914; *s* of Frank Longland; *m* 1945, Helen Mary Cripps; three *d. Educ:* Monkton Combe Sch. MB, BS (Hons in Medicine) London, 1937; House Surgeon and Demonstrator of Pathology, St Bartholomew's Hosp.; FRCS, 1939; MS London, 1949. 1 Airborne Division; Lieut RAMC 1942, Temp. Major, RAMC, 1943; SMO Bermuda Command, 1945; First Assistant, Surgical Professorial Unit, St Bartholomew's Hospital, 1947; Assistant Surgical Professorial Unit, University College Hospital, 1951. Bronze Cross (Holland), 1945. *Publications:* articles in Lancet and British Journal of Surgery. *Address:* Malmesbury Lodge, Grittleton, near Chippenham, Wiltshire SN14 6AW. *T:* Castle Combe 782624.

LONGLAND, Sir David (Walter), Kt 1977; CMG 1973; Parliamentary Commissioner for Administrative Investigations, Queensland, 1974-79; *b* 1 June 1909; 2nd *s* of David Longland and Mary McGriskin; *m* 1935, Ada Elizabeth Bowness (*d* 1977); one *s* one *d. Educ:* Queensland Govt Primary and Secondary Schs. Queensland Educn Dept, High Sch. teaching, 1926. Appointed: to State Treasury Dept, 1938; Premier's Dept, 1939; (re-apptd) Treasury Dept, 1940; (re-apptd) Premier's Dept, 1942; Officer in Charge of Migration for Qld, 1946; Under-Sec., Dept of Works and Housing, 1957; Chm., Public Service Bd, Qld, 1969. Member: Australian Cerebral Palsy Assoc. (Nat. Pres., 1967-68); Queensland Spastic Welfare League, 1958- (Pres., 1962-); Exec. Dir, Queensland Art Gallery Foundn. FASA, FAIM, FRIPA. *Recreations:* tennis, surfing, reading, gardening. *Address:* 88 Lloyd Street, Camp Hill, Queensland 4152, Australia. *T:* 398-1152. *Club:* Rotary (Brisbane).

LONGLAND, Sir Jack, (Sir John Laurence Longland), Kt 1970; Director of Education, Derbyshire, 1949-70; *b* 26 June 1905; *e s* of late Rev. E. H. Longland and late Emily, *e d* of Sir James Crockett; *m* 1934, Margaret Lowrey, *y d* of late Arthur Harrison, Elvet Garth, Durham; two *s* two *d. Educ:* King's Sch., Worcester; Jesus Coll., Cambridge (Rustat Exhibitioner and Scholar). 2nd Class, 1st Part Classical Tripos, 1925; 1st Class, 1st Division, Historical Tripos, Part II, 1926; 1st Class with special distinction, English Tripos, 1927; Charles Kingsley Bye-Fellow at Magdalene Coll., Cambridge, 1927-29; Austausch-student, Königsberg Univ., 1929-30; Lectr in English at Durham Univ., 1930-36; Dir Community Service Council for Durham County, 1937-40; Regional Officer of Nat. Council of Social Service, 1939-40; Dep. Educn Officer, Herts, 1940-42; County Educn Officer, Dorset CC, 1942-49. Athletic Blue; Pres., Cambridge Univ. Mountaineering Club, 1926-27; Member: Mount Everest Expedn, 1933; British East Greenland Expedn, 1935; Pres., Climbers' Club, 1945-48 and Hon. Mem., 1964; Pres., Alpine Club, 1973-76 (Vice-Pres., 1960-61); Member: Colonial Office Social Welfare Adv. Cttee, 1942-48; Develt Commn, 1948-51; Nat. Adv. Cttee for Educn in RAF, 1950-57; Adv. Cttee for Educn in Germany, 1950-57; Central Adv. Council for Educn in England and Wales, 1948-51; Nat. Adv. Council on the Training and Supply of Teachers, 1951-; Children's Adv. Cttee of the ITA, 1956-60; Wolfenden Cttee on Sport, 1958-60; Outward Bound Trust Council, 1962-73; Central Council of Physical Recreation Council and Exec., 1961-72; Electricity Supply Industry Training Bd, 1965-66; Royal Commn on Local Govt, 1966-69; The Sports Council, 1966-74 (Vice-Chm. 1971-74); Countryside Commn, 1969-74; Commn on Mining and the Environment, 1971-72; Water Space Amenity Commn, 1973-76; President: Assoc. of Educn Officers, 1960-61; British Mountaineering Council, 1962-65; Chairman: Mountain Leadership Training Bd, 1964-80; Council for Environmental Educn, 1968-75. *Publications:* literary and mountaineering articles in various books and journals. *Recreations:* walking, books. *Address:* Bridgeway, Bakewell, Derbyshire. *T:* Bakewell 2252. *Clubs:* Savile, Alpine, Achilles.

LONGLAND, Sir John Laurence; *see* Longland, Sir Jack.

LONGLEY, Sir Norman, Kt 1966; CBE; DL; retired as Chairman, James Longley (Holdings) Ltd, Building and Civil Engineering Contractors, Crawley, Sussex; *b* 14 Oct. 1900; *s* of Charles John Longley and Anna Gibson Marchant; *m* 1925, Dorothy Lilian Baker; two *s* one *d. Educ:* Clifton. West Sussex County Council, 1945-61, Alderman 1957-61. President: National Federation of Building Trades Employers, 1950; International Federation of Building and Public Works Contractors, 1955-57. Hon. Fellow, Institute of Builders. DL West Sussex, 1975. Hon. DSc Heriot-Watt, 1968. Coronation Medal, 1953. *Recreation:* horticulture. *Address:* The Beeches, Crawley, Sussex. *T:* Crawley 20253.

LONGLEY-COOK, Vice-Adm. Eric William, CB 1950; CBE 1943; DSO 1945; *b* 6 Oct. 1898; *s* of late Herbert William Cook and late Alice Longley; *m* 1st, 1920, Helga Mayre Lowles (*d* 1962); one *d* ; 2nd, 1965, Elizabeth (*d* 1978), widow of Sir Ulick Temple Blake, 16th Baronet. *Educ:* Osborne and Dartmouth. Served at sea European War, 1914-18 (Dardanelles, 1915) and War of 1939-45 (Murmansk, N Africa, Sicily, Salerno, Aegean, E Indies, Okinawa; despatches thrice). Rear-Adm., 1948; Vice-Adm., 1951; Dir of

Naval Intelligence, 1948–51; retired, 1951. Formerly: Man. Dir, Fairfield Shipbuilding & Engineering Co., London; Dir, Lithgow Group; Member: Cttee, Lloyd's Register; Amer. Bureau of Ships; a Gen. Comr of Income Tax. Pres., Gallipoli Assoc., 1981 (Vice-Pres., 1975). Légion d'Honneur and Croix de Guerre, 1943. *Address:* Cordwainers, Titchfield, Hants. *Club:* Naval and Military.

LONGMORE, William James Maitland, CBE 1972; Director: Lloyds Bank International Ltd, 1971–75; Bank of London & South America Ltd, 1960–75; *b* 6 May 1919; 2nd *s* of late Air Chief Marshal Sir Arthur Murray Longmore, GCB, DSO; *m* 1941, Jean, *d* of 2nd Baron Forres of Glenogil; three *d. Educ:* Eton Coll. Royal Air Force, 1938–46 (Wing Comdr). Balfour, Williamson & Co. Ltd, 1946–75 (Chm., 1967–75). Vice-Chm., 1966–70, Chm., 1970–71, BNEC for Latin America. *Recreations:* shooting, sailing. *Address:* Strete End House, Bishop's Waltham, Hants SO3 1FS. *T:* Bishop's Waltham 2794. *Club:* Royal Yacht Squadron.

LONGRIGG, John Stephen, CMG 1973; OBE 1964; HM Diplomatic Service, retired; *b* 1 Oct. 1923; *s* of late Brig. Stephen Hemsley Longrigg, OBE; *m* 1st, 1953, Lydia Meynell (marr. diss. 1965); one *s* one *d*; 2nd, 1966, Ann O'Reilly; one *s. Educ:* Rugby Sch.; Magdalen Coll., Oxford (BA). War Service, Rifle Bde, 1942–45 (despatches). FO, 1948; Paris, 1948; Baghdad, 1951; FO, 1953; Berlin, 1955; Cabinet Office, 1957; FO, 1958; Dakar, 1960; Johannesburg, 1962; Pretoria, 1962; Washington, 1964; FO, 1965–67; Bahrain, 1967–69; FCO, 1969–73; seconded to HQ British Forces, Hong Kong, 1974–76; FCO, 1976–82. *Recreation:* golf. *Address:* 2 The Cedars, 3 Westcombe Park Road, Blackheath, SE3. *T:* 01-858 1604. *Clubs:* Reform; Royal Blackheath Golf.

See also R. E. Longrigg.

LONGRIGG, Roger Erskine; author; *b* 1 May 1929; *s* of Brig. S. H. Longrigg, OBE; *m* 1957, Jane Chichester; three *d. Educ:* Bryanston Sch.; Magdalen Coll., Oxford (BA Hons Mod. Hist.). *Publications:* A High Pitched Buzz, 1956; Switchboard, 1957; Wrong Number, 1959; Daughters of Mulberry, 1961; The Paper Boats, 1963; The Artless Gambler, 1964; Love among the Bottles, 1967; The Sun on the Water, 1969; The Desperate Criminals, 1971; The History of Horse Racing, 1972; The Jevington System, 1973; Their Pleasing Sport, 1975; The Turf, 1975; The History of Foxhunting, 1975; The Babe in the Wood, 1976; The English Squire and his Sport, 1977; Bad Bet, 1982. *Recreations:* trout fishing, racing. *Address:* Orchard House, Crookham, Hants. *T:* Aldershot 850333. *Clubs:* Brooks's, Pratt's.

See also J. S. Longrigg.

LONGSTRETH THOMPSON, Francis Michael; *see* Thompson, F. M. L.

LONGUET-HIGGINS, Prof. Hugh Christopher, FRS 1958; DPhil (Oxon); Royal Society Research Professor, University of Sussex, since 1974; *b* 11 April 1923; *e s* of late Rev. H. H. L. Longuet-Higgins. *Educ:* Winchester (schol.); Balliol Coll., Oxford (schol., MA). Research Fellow of Balliol Coll., 1946–48; Lecturer and Reader in Theoretical Chemistry, University of Manchester, 1949–52; Prof. of Theoretical Physics, King's Coll., University of London, 1952–54; FRSE; John Humphrey Plummer Professor of Theoretical Chemistry, University of Cambridge, 1954–67; Royal Soc. Res. Prof., Univ. of Edinburgh, 1968–74; Fellow of Corpus Christi Coll., 1954–67, Life Fellow 1968; Hon. Fellow: Balliol Coll., Oxford, 1969; Wolfson Coll., Cambridge, 1977. A Governor, BBC, 1979–. Warden, Leckhampton House, 1961–67; Harrison Memorial Prizeman (Chemical Society), 1950. Editor of Molecular Physics, 1958–61. Foreign Associate, US National Academy of Sciences, 1968. *Publications:* co-author, The Nature of Mind (Gifford Lectures), 1972; papers on theoretical physics, chemistry and biology in scientific journals. *Recreations:* music and arguing. *Address:* Centre for Research on Perception and Cognition, Laboratory of Experimental Psychology, University of Sussex, Falmer, Brighton BN1 9QY.

LONGUET-HIGGINS, Michael Selwyn, FRS 1963; Royal Society Research Professor, University of Cambridge, since 1969; *b* 8 Dec. 1925; *s* of late Henry Hugh Longuet and Albinia Cecil Longuet-Higgins; *m* 1958, Joan Redmayne Tattersall; two *s* two *d. Educ:* Winchester Coll. (Schol.); Trinity Coll., Cambridge (Schol.). (BA). Admiralty Research Lab., Teddington, 1945–48; Res. Student, Cambridge, 1948–51; PhD Cambridge, 1951; Rayleigh Prize, 1951; Commonwealth Fund Fellowship, 1951–52; Res. Fellow, Trinity Coll., Cambridge, 1951–55. Nat. Inst. of Oceanography, 1954–69. Visiting Professor: MIT, 1958; Institute of Geophysics, University of California, 1961–62; Univ. of Adelaide, 1964. Prof. of Oceanography, Oregon State Univ., 1967–69. Foreign Associate, US Nat. Acad. of Sci., 1979. Hon. DTech Tech. Univ. of Denmark, 1979; Hon. LLD Glasgow, 1979. *Publications:* papers in applied mathematics, esp. seismology and physical oceanography, dynamics of sea waves and currents, etc. *Recreations:* music, mathematical toys. *Address:* Gage Farm, Comberton, Cambridge CB3 7DH.

LONGWORTH, Ian Heaps, PhD; FSA; Keeper of Prehistoric and Romano-British Antiquities, British Museum, since 1973; *b* 29 Sept. 1935; *yr s* of late Joseph Longworth and Alice (*née* Heaps); *m* 1967, Clare Marian Titford; one *s* one *d. Educ:* King Edward VII, Lytham; Peterhouse, Cambridge. Open and Sen. Scholar, Matthew Wren Student, 1957, MA, PhD, Cantab. Temp. Asst Keeper, Nat. Museum of Antiquities of Scotland, 1962–63; Asst Keeper, Dept of British and Medieval Antiquities, Brit. Mus., 1963–69; Asst Keeper, Dept

of Prehistoric and Romano-British Antiquities, Brit. Mus., 1969–73. Mem., Ancient Monuments Bd for England, 1977–. Chm., Area Archaeol. Adv. Cttee for NW England, 1978–79. Hon. Sec., Prehistoric Soc., 1966–74, Vice-Pres., 1976–80; Sec., Soc. of Antiquaries of London, 1974–79. *Publications:* Yorkshire (Regional Archaeologies Series), 1965; (with G. J. Wainwright) Durrington Walls—excavations 1966–68, 1971; articles in various learned jls on topics of prehistory. *Address:* 2 Hurst View Road, South Croydon, Surrey CR2 7AG. *T:* 01-688 4960. *Club:* MCC.

LONGWORTH, Wilfred Roy, PhD; FRSC, FRACI, FACE; Director, Swinburne College of Technology Ltd, since 1970; *b* 13 Dec. 1923; *s* of Wilfred Arnold Longworth and Jessie Longworth; *m* 1951, Constance Elizabeth Dean; two *d. Educ:* Bolton Sch.; Manchester Univ. (BSc, MSc, PhD). FRIC 1963; FRACI 1970; FACE 1976. Works Manager and Chief Chemist, Blackburn & Oliver, 1948–56; postgrad. res., Univ. of Keele, 1956–59; Lectr in Physical Chemistry, Huddersfield Coll. of Technol., 1959–60; Sen. Lectr in Phys. Chem., Sunderland Technical Coll., 1960–64; Head, Dept of Chem. and Biol., Manchester Polytechnic, 1964–70. *Publications:* articles on cationic polymerisation in learned jls. *Recreations:* lawn bowls, gardening. *Address:* 35 Fairmont Avenue, Camberwell, Vic 3124, Australia. *T:* 299 1145. *Clubs:* Kelvin (Melbourne, Aust.); Hawthorn (Hawthorn, Aust.).

LONSDALE, 7th Earl of (UK), *cr* 1807; **James Hugh William Lowther,** Viscount and Baron Lowther, 1797; Bt 1764; *b* 3 Nov. 1922; *er s* of Anthony Edward, Viscount Lowther (*d* 1949), and Muriel Frances, Viscountess Lowther (*d* 1968), 2nd *d* of late Sir George Farrar, Bt, DSO, and Lady Farrar; *S* grandfather, 1953; *m* 1975, Caroline, *y d* of Sir Gerald Ley, 3rd Bt, TD; one *s* one *d* (and three *s* three *d* of previous marriages). *Educ:* Eton. Armed Forces, 1941–46; RAC and East Riding Yeo. (despatches, Capt.). Structural engineering, 1947–50. Farmer, forester, and director of associated and local companies in Cumbria; Chairman: Lakeland Investments Ltd and of nine subsid. or associated cos; Plan Invest Gp Ltd; Director: Cannon Assurance Ltd; Border TV; North Housing Assoc. Ltd. Chm., Northern Adv. Council for Sport and Recreation, 1966–71; Member: Northern Region Economic Planning Council, 1964–72; Sports Council, 1971–74; English Tourist Bd, 1971–75; TGO (Pres., 1971–73); Forestry Cttee for GB (Chm., 1974–76); President: NW Area British Legion, 1961–73; NW Div. YMCA, 1962–72; Cumberland and Westmorland NPFA; British Deer Soc., 1963–70; Lake District Naturalists' Trust, 1963–73; local agricultural societies. Master, Farmers' Co., 1973–74. CBIM. *Heir:* s Viscount Lowther, qv. *Address:* Askham Hall, Penrith, Cumbria. *T:* Hackthorpe 208. *Clubs:* Brooks's, Turf, National Sporting.

LONSDALE, Maj.-Gen. Errol Henry Gerrard, CB 1969; MBE 1942; Transport Officer-in-Chief (Army) 1966–69; *b* 26 Feb. 1913; 2nd *s* of Rev. W. H. M. Lonsdale, Arlaw Banks, Barnard Castle; *m* 1944, Muriel Allison, *d* of E. R. Payne, Mugswell, Chipstead; one *s* one *d. Educ:* Westminster Sch.; St Catharine's Coll., Cambridge (MA). 2nd Lt, RASC, 1934; Bt Lt-Col 1952; Col 1957; Brig. 1961; Maj.-Gen. 1966. Sudan Defence Force, 1938–43 (despatches); Chief Instr, RASC Officers Trng Centre, 1944–45; AQMG FARELF, 1945–47; CRASC 16 Airborne Div., 1947–48; GSOI, 1948–51; AA & QMG, War Office, 1951–53; Korea, 1953–54; Malaya, 1954–56 (despatches); Northern Army Group, 1957–60; DDST, 1st Corps, 1960–62; Comdt RASC Trng Centre, 1962–64; Inspector, RASC, 1964–65; ADC to the Queen, 1964–66; Inspector, RCT, 1965–66; psc; jssc. Col Comdt, RCT, 1969–74. Hon. Colonel: 160 Regt RCT(V), 1969–74; 562 Para Sqdn RCT(V), 1969–78. FCIT (MInstT) 1966. Vice-President: Transport Trust, 1974; Internat. Union for Modern Pentathlon and Biathlon, 1976–80; Pres., Modern Pentathlon Assoc. of Great Britain, 1977– (Chm., 1967); Chm., Inst. of Advanced Motorists, 1971–79, Vice-Pres., 1979. *Recreations:* modern pentathlon, photography, driving. *Address:* Stoke House, Stogursey, near Bridgwater, Somerset TA5 1TA. *T:* Nether Stowey 732763.

LOOKER, Sir Cecil (Thomas), Kt 1969; Chairman, Australian United Corporation Ltd; Principal Partner, Ian Potter & Co., Sharebrokers, 1967–76 (Partner, 1953); Director of various other companies; *b* 11 April 1913; *s* of Edward William and Martha Looker; *m* 1941, Jean Leslyn Withington; one *s* two *d. Educ:* Fort Street Boys' High Sch., Sydney; Sydney Univ. (BA). Apptd to Commonwealth Public Service, 1937; Private Sec. to Prime Minister (Rt Hon. later Sir Robert Menzies), 1939–41. War of 1939–45: RANVR, 1942–45. Resigned Commonwealth Public Service, 1946, and joined Ian Potter & Co. Chm., Stock Exchange of Melbourne, 1966–72 (Mem. 1962–78); Pres., Australian Associated Stock Exchanges, 1968–71. Apptd by Dept of Territories as Dir of Papua and New Guinea Development Bank, 1966. Chairman: Exec. Cttee, Duke of Edinburgh's Third Commonwealth Study Conf., Aust., 1966–68; Aust. Adv. Cttee, Duke of Edinburgh's Fifth Study Conf., Canada, 1980. *Recreation:* farming. *Address:* 26 Tormey Street, North Balwyn, Victoria 3104, Australia. *T:* 857-9316. *Clubs:* Australian, Royal Automobile Club of Victoria (Melbourne) (President).

LOOSLEY, Stanley George Henry, MC 1944; MA Cantab; JP Glos; Headmaster of Wycliffe College, 1947–67; *b* 18 July 1910; *s* of Harold D. and Edith M. Loosley; *m* 1938, Margaret Luker; two *s* one *d. Educ:* Wycliffe Coll.; St John's Coll., Cambridge. Asst Master, Wycliffe Coll., 1934–39; War of 1939–45, RA, Sept. 1939–Oct. 1945; Major OC 220 Field Battery, 1941 (despatches, MC); NW Europe Campaign, 1944; sc; Bde Major RA 43 Div., 1945; Senior Asst Master, Wycliffe Coll., 1945–47. A Vice-Pres.,

Gloucestershire Magistrates Assoc. *Publication:* Wycliffe College—The First Hundred Years, 1982. *Recreations:* travel, unskilled gardening, walking, looking, listening. *Address:* Brillings, Chalford Hill, Stroud, Glos. *T:* Brimscombe 883505. *Club:* Royal Over-Seas League.

LOPES, family name of **Baron Roborough.**

LORAINE, Dr John Alexander, FRCPEd; FRSE 1978; Senior Lecturer, Department of Community Medicine, University of Edinburgh, since 1979; *b* 14 May 1924; *s* of Lachlan Dempster Loraine and Ruth (*née* Jack); *m* 1974, Alison Blair. *Educ:* George Watson's Boys' Coll., Edinburgh; Univ. of Edinburgh. MB ChB (Hons) 1946, PhD 1949, DSc 1959; FRCPEd 1960. House Phys., Royal Infirmary, Edinburgh, under Prof. Sir Stanley Davidson, 1946; Mem., Scientific Staff, MRC Clinical Endocrinology Unit, Edinburgh, 1947-61; Dir of the Unit, 1961-72. Visiting Prof. of Endocrinology, Donner Laboratory and Donner Pavilion, Univ. of Calif., Berkeley, USA, 1964. Hon. Senior Lectr, Dept of Pharmacology, Univ. of Edinburgh, 1965-72; MRC Ext. Sci. Staff, 1972-79; Dir, Centre for Human Ecology, 1978-. Founder Chm., Doctors and Overpopulation Gp, 1972-; Vice-Chm., Conservation Soc., 1974-. Mem., Internat. Union for Scientific Study of Population, 1977-. FRSA. *Publications:* (co-author) Hormone Assays and their Clinical Application, 1958, (co-editor) 4th edn 1976; (co-author) Recent Research on Gonadotrophic Hormones, 1967; (co-author) Fertility and Contraception in the Human Female, 1968; Sex and the Population Crisis, 1970; The Death of Tomorrow, 1972; (ed) Reproductive Endocrinology and World Population, 1973; (ed) Environmental Medicine, 1973; (ed) Understanding Homosexuality: its biological and psychological bases, 1974; Syndromes of the 'Seventies, 1977; (ed) Here Today ..., 1979; Global Signposts to the 21st Century, 1979; (ed) Environmental Medicine, 2nd edn, 1980; Energy Policies Around the World, 1982; author and co-author of numerous scientific and popular pubns dealing with sex hormones, fertility, contraception, population and related issues, incl. women's rights, mineral resources, nuclear proliferation and environmental pollution. *Recreations:* reading modern history and political biography, music, bridge, golf. *Address:* 20 Buckingham Terrace, Edinburgh EH4 3AD. *T:* 031-332 3698. *Club:* University of Edinburgh Staff.

LORAM, Vice-Adm. Sir David (Anning), KCB 1979; MVO 1957; Deputy Supreme Allied Commander Atlantic, 1977-80, retired; Gentleman Usher to The Queen, since 1982; *b* 24 July 1924; *o surv. s* of late Mr and Mrs John A. Loram; *m* 1958, Fiona (marr. diss. 1981), *d* of late Vice-Adm. Sir William Beloe, KBE, CB, DSC; three *s. Educ:* Royal Naval Coll., Dartmouth (1938-41). Awarded King's Dirk. Served War: HMS Sheffield, Foresight, Anson, Zealous, 1941-45. ADC to Governor-Gen. of New Zealand, 1946-48; specialised in Signal Communications, 1949; served in HMS Chequers, 1951; Equerry to the Queen, 1954-57; qualified helicopter pilot, 1955; commanded HMS Loch Fada, 1957; Directing Staff, JSSC, 1959-60; served in HMS Belfast, 1961; Naval Attaché, Paris, 1964-67; commanded HMS Arethusa, 1967; Dir, Naval Ops and Trade, 1970-71; commanded HMS Antrim, 1971; ADC to The Queen, 1972-73; Comdr British Forces, FO Malta, and NATO Comdr SE Mediterranean, 1973-75; Comdt, Nat. Defence Coll., 1975-77. Mem., RN Cresta Team, 1954-59. *Recreations:* golf, squash, walking. *Address:* c/o Grindlay's Bank, 13 St James's Square, SW1. *Clubs:* Lansdowne; Chesapeake.

LORANT, Stefan; *b* 22 Feb. 1901; *m* 1963, Laurie Robertson (marr. diss. 1978); two *s. Educ:* Evangelical Gymnasium, Budapest; Academy of Economics, Budapest; Harvard Univ. (MA 1961). Editor: Das Magazin, Leipzig, 1925; Bilder Courier, Berlin, 1926; Muenchner Illustrierte Presse, 1927-33; Weekly Illustrated, 1934; Picture Post, 1938-40; Founder of Lilliput, Editor, 1937-40. Hon. LLD, Knox Coll., Galesburg, Ill., 1958. *Publications:* I Was Hitler's Prisoner, 1935; Lincoln, His Life in Photographs, 1941; The New World, 1946, rev. edn 1965; F.D.R., a pictorial biography, 1950; The Presidency, a pictorial history of presidential elections from Washington to Truman, 1951; Lincoln: a picture story of his life, 1952, rev. and enl. edns 1957, 1969; The Life of Abraham Lincoln, 1954; The Life and Times of Theodore Roosevelt, 1959; Pittsburgh, the story of an American city, 1964, rev. and enl. edns 1975, 1980; The Glorious Burden: the American Presidency, 1968, rev. and enl. edn, 1976; Sieg Heil: an illustrated history of Germany from Bismarck to Hitler, 1974; Pete: the story of Peter F. Flatery, 1978; My Years in England, fragments to an autobiography, 1982. *Address:* Farview, Lenox, Mass 01240, USA. *T:* Lenox 637-0666.

LORD, Sir Ackland (Archibald), Kt 1971; OBE 1970; Director of companies, Australia; Founder and Donor of A. A. Lord Homes for the Aged Inc., Hobart, Tasmania; Past Chairman (Founder): (A.A.) Lords Ltd, Wholesale Hardware and Steel Merchants, 1949-59 (Director to 1969); Lords Holdings Ltd, 1952-59 (Director, 1959-69); Director: Melbourne Builders Lime & Cement Co.; Big Ben Scaffolds Pty Ltd; U-Hire Pty Ltd; Melcann Holdings Ltd; *b* 11 June 1901; *s* of late J. Lord, Tasmania; *m* Ethel Dalton, MBE, *d* of late C. Dalton, Hobart. *Educ:* St Virgil's Coll., Hobart. Has given distinguished services to the community in Victoria and Tasmania. Past Chm. Galvanised Iron Merchants Assoc.; Council Mem., Ryder Cheshire Foundn (Vic.) for Internat. Centre, Dehra Dun, India; Past Member: Trotting Control Bd; Melbourne & Metropolitan Trotting Assoc. (Chm.); Life Governor: various Melb. Hosps; Royal Victoria Inst. for the Blind, etc. *Address:* Lawrenny, 3 Teringa Place, Toorak, Victoria 3142, Australia. *T:* 24-5283. *Clubs:* Hardware (Melbourne); Victoria Racing; Moonee Valley Racing.

LORD, Alan, CB 1972; Managing Director, Dunlop Holdings Ltd, since 1980; Director, Allied Breweries, since 1979; *b* 12 April 1929; *er s* of Frederick Lord and Anne Lord (*née* Whitworth), Rochdale; *m* 1953, Joan Ogden; two *d. Educ:* Rochdale; St John's Coll., Cambridge. Entered Inland Revenue, 1950; Private Sec. to Dep. Chm. and to Chm. of the Board, 1952-54; HM Treasury, 1959-62; Principal Private Sec. to First Secretary of State (then Rt Hon. R. A Butler), 1962-63; Comr of Inland Revenue, 1969-73, Dep. Chm. Bd, 1971-73; Principal Finance Officer to DTI, subseq. to Depts of Industry, Trade, and Prices and Consumer Protection, 1973-75; Second Permanent Sec. (Domestic Econ.), HM Treasury, 1975-77. Exec. Dir, Dunlop Hldgs, and Man. Dir, Dunlop Internat. Ltd, 1978-. Chm., CBI Taxation Cttee, 1979-81. Mem. Council of Management, Henley Centre for Forecasting. Governor, NIESR. *Publication:* A Strategy for Industry (Sir Ellis Hunter Meml Lecture, Univ. of York), 1976. *Recreations:* riding, gardening. *Address:* Mardens, Hildenborough, Tonbridge, Kent. *T:* Hildenborough 832268. *Club:* Reform.

LORD, Cyril, LLD (Hon.); Chairman and Managing Director, Cyril Lord Ltd, 1945-68; Director, numerous Companies in Great Britain, Northern Ireland, and South Africa, 1945-68; *b* 12 July 1911; *m* 1936, Bessie Greenwood (marr. diss. 1959); two *s* two *d ; m* 1974, Aileen Parnell, *widow* of Val Parnell. *Educ:* Central Sch., Manchester; Manchester Coll. of Technology (Associate), and University. Dir of Hodkin & Lord Ltd, 1939; Technical Adviser to the Cotton Board, England, 1941. Hon. LLD Florida Southern Coll., 1951. *Recreations:* yachting, tennis. *Clubs:* Royal Automobile, Naval and Military; Royal Corinthian (Cowes); Ballyholme Yacht (N Ire.).

LORD, Geoffrey; Secretary and Treasurer, Carnegie United Kingdom Trust, since 1977; *b* 24 Feb. 1928; *s* of Frank Lord and Edith Lord; *m* 1955, Jean; one *s* one *d. Educ:* Rochdale Grammar Sch.; Univ. of Bradford (MA Applied Social Studies). AIB. Midland Bank Ltd, 1946-58; Probation and After-Care Service, 1958-76: Dep. Chief Probation Officer, Greater Manchester, 1974-76. *Publication:* The Arts and Disabilities, 1981. *Recreations:* philately, walking, gardening, appreciation of the arts. *Address:* 9 Craigleith View, Ravelston, Edinburgh EH4 3JZ. *T:* 031-337 7623. *Club:* New (Edinburgh).

LORD, John Herent; His Honour Judge Lord; a Circuit Judge, since 1978; *b* 5 Nov. 1928; *s* of Sir Frank Lord, KBE; *m* 1959, June Ann, *d* of George Caladine, Rochdale; three *s. Educ:* Manchester Grammar Sch.; Merton Coll., Oxford (BA (Jurisprudence), MA). Half Blue, Oxford Univ. lacrosse XII, 1948 and 1949; represented Oxfordshire, 1949, and Middlesex 1950. Called to Bar, Inner Temple, 1951; The Junior of Northern Circuit, 1952; Asst Recorder of Burnley, 1971; a Recorder of the Crown Court, 1972-78. Governor, Bramcote Sch.; Trustee, Frank Lord Postgraduate Med. Centre. *Recreations:* photography, shooting. *Address:* Three Lanes, Greenfield, Oldham, Lancs. *T:* Saddleworth 2198. *Clubs:* St James's (Manchester); Leander.

LORD, William Burton Housley, CB 1979; Director, Royal Armament Research and Development Establishment, 1976-79; *b* 22 March 1919; *s* of Arthur James Lord and Elsie Lord (*née* Housley); *m* 1942, Helena Headon Jaques; two *d. Educ:* King George V Sch., Southport; Manchester Univ.; London Univ. (External MSc); Trinity Coll., Cambridge (MA). Enlisted Royal Fusiliers, wartime commn S Lancs Regt, 1941-46. Cambridge Univ., 1946. Entered Civil Service, 1949; joined Atomic Weapons Res. Estab., 1952; Head of Metallurgy Div., AWRE, 1958; moved to MoD, 1964; Asst Chief Scientific Adviser (Research), 1965; Dep. Chief Scientist (Army), 1968-71; Dir Gen., Establishments, Resources and Programmes (B), MoD, 1971-76. *Publications:* papers on metallurgy in learned jls. *Recreations:* amateur radio, walking, orienteering, water sports. *Address:* Fort Halstead, Sevenoaks, Kent TN14 7BP.

LOREN, Sophia; film actress; *b* 20 Sept. 1934; *d* of Ricardo Scicolone and Romilda Villani; *m* 1957, Carlo Ponti, film producer (marriage annulled in Juarez, Mexico, Sept. 1962; marriage in Paris, France, April 1966); two *s. Educ:* parochial sch. and Teachers' Institute, Naples. First leading role in Africa sotto i Mari, 1952; acted in many Italian films, 1952-55; subsequent films include: The Pride and the Passion; Boy on a Dolphin; Legend of the Lost; The Key; Desire under the Elms; Houseboat; The Black Orchid (Venice Film Festival Award, 1958); That Kind of Woman; It Started in Naples; Heller in Pink Tights; The Millionairess; Two Women (Cannes Film Festival Award, 1961); A Breath of Scandal; Madame sans Gêne; La Ciociara; El Cid; Boccaccio 70; Five Miles to Midnight; Yesterday, Today and Tomorrow; The Fall of the Roman Empire; Marriage, Italian Style; Operation Crossbow; Lady L; Judith; A Countess from Hong Kong; Arabesque; Sunflower; The Priest's Wife; The Man of La Mancha; The Verdict; The Voyage; Una Gionnata Particolare; Firepower; Blood Feud. *Publication:* Eat with Me, 1972; *relevant publication:* Sophia: living and loving, by A. E. Hotcher, 1979. *Address:* Chalet Daniel Burgenstock, Luzern, Switzerland.

LORENZ, Prof. Dr Konrad, MD, DPhil; Director, Department for Animal Sociology, Institute for Comparative Ethology, Austrian Academy of Sciences, since 1973; *b* 7 Nov. 1903; *s* of Prof. Dr Adolf Lorenz and Emma Lorenz (*née* Lecher); *m* 1927, Dr Margarethe Lorenz (*née* Gebhardt); one *s* two *d. Educ:* High Sch., Vienna; Columbia Univ., New York; Univ. of Vienna. Univ. Asst at Anatomical Inst. of University of Vienna (Prof. Hochstetter), 1928-35; Lectr in Comparative Anat. and Animal Psychol., University of Vienna, 1937-40; University Lectr, Vienna, 1940; Prof. of

Psychol. and Head of Dept, University of Königsberg, 1940; Head of Research Station for Physiology of Behaviour of the Max-Planck-Inst. for Marine Biol., 1951; Co-Director, Max-Planck-Inst. for Physiology of Behaviour, 1956-73. Hon. Prof., University of Münster, 1953 and München, 1957. Nobel Prize for Physiology or Medicine (jtly), 1973. Mem., Pour le Mérite for Arts and Science; Hon. Member: Assoc. for Study of Animal Behaviour, 1950; Amer. Ornithol. Union, 1951, etc; For. Mem., Royal Society, 1964. For. Assoc. Nat. Acad. of Sciences, USA, 1966. Hon. degrees: Leeds, 1962; Basel, 1966; Yale, 1967; Oxford, 1968; Chicago, 1970; Durham, 1972; Birmingham, 1974; Vienna, 1980. Gold Medal, Zoological Soc., New York, 1955; City Prize, Vienna, 1959; Gold Boelsche Medal, 1962; Austrian Distinction for Science and Art, 1964; Prix Mondial, Cino del Duca, 1969. Grosses Verdienstkreuz, 1974; Bayerischer Verdienstorden, 1974. *Publications*: King Solomon's Ring, 1952; Man Meets Dog, 1954; Evolution and Modification of Behaviour, 1965; On Aggression, 1966; Studies in Animal and Human Behaviour, 1970; (jtly) Man and Animal, 1972; Civilized Man's Eight Deadly Sins, 1974; Behind the Mirror, 1977; The World of the Greylag Goose, 1979; articles in Tierpsychologie, Behaviour, etc. *Address*: Institut für Vergleichende Verhaltensforschung, Abt. 4, Tiersoziologie, Adolf-Lorenzgasse 2, A-3422 Altenberg, Austria.

LORIMER, Hew Martin, RSA; FRBS; Sculptor; Representative in Fife of National Trust for Scotland; *b* 22 May 1907; 2nd *s* of late Sir Robert Stodart Lorimer, KBE, Hon. LLD, ARA, RSA, architect, and of Violet Alicia (*née* Wyld); *m* 1936, Mary McLeod Wylie (*d* 1970), 2nd *d* of H. M. Wylie, Edinburgh; two *s* one *d*. *Educ*: Loretto; Edinburgh Coll. of Art, Andrew Grant Scholarship, 1933 and Fellowship, 1934-35. National Library of Scotland, Edinburgh, sculptor of the 7 allegorical figures, 1952-55; Our Lady of the Isles, South Uist, 1955-57; St Francis, Dundee, 1957-59. *Recreations*: music, travel, home. *Address*: Kellie Castle, Pittenweem, Fife KY10 2RF. *T*: Arncroach 271. *Club*: Scottish Arts (Edinburgh).

LORIMER, Sir (Thomas) Desmond, Kt 1976; Chairman, Industrial Development Board for Northern Ireland, since 1982; *b* 20 Oct. 1925; *s* of Thomas Berry Lorimer and Sarah Ann Lorimer; *m* 1957, Patricia Doris Samways; two *d*. *Educ*: Belfast Technical High Sch. Chartered Accountant, 1948; Fellow, Inst. of Chartered Accountants in Ireland, 1957. Practised as chartered accountant, 1952-74; Sen. Partner, Harmood, Banner, Smylie & Co., Belfast, Chartered Accountants, 1960; Chairman: McCleery L'Amie Gp Ltd, 1970-; Lamont Holdings PLC, 1973-; Dir, Ruberoid PLC, 1972-. Pres., Inst. of Chartered Accountants in Ireland, 1968-69; Chairman: Ulster Soc. of Chartered Accountants, 1960; NI Housing Exec., 1971-75; Mem., Rev. Body on Local Govt in NI, 1970. *Recreations*: gardening and golf. *Address*: Windwhistle House, 6 Circular Road West, Cultra, Holywood, Co. Down BT18 0AT. *T*: Holywood 3323. *Clubs*: Carlton; Royal Belfast Golf, Royal Co. Down Golf (Co. Down).

LŐRINCZ-NAGY, János, Golden Grade of Order of Merit for Labour; Head of Department, Ministry of Foreign Affairs, Hungary, since 1981; *b* 19 Dec. 1931; *m* Ida Lőrincz-Nagy; one *d*. *Educ*: Foreign Affairs Acad., Budapest; Coll. of Polit. Sciences, Budapest. Entered Diplomatic Service, 1953; Press Attaché, Peking, 1953-55; 2nd Sec., Djakarta, 1957-61; Dep. Head of Personnel Dept, 1964-68; Ambassador to Ghana, 1968-72; Head of Press Dept, 1972-74; Ambassador, Head of Hungarian Delegn to Internat. Commn of Control and Supervision in Saigon, 1974; Ambassador: to Sweden, 1975-76; to the Court of St James's, 1976-81. *Recreations*: reading and walking. *Address*: Ministry of Foreign Affairs, II Bem József rakpart 47, H-1394 Budapest, Hungary.

LORING, James Adrian, CBE 1979; President, International Cerebral Palsy Society, since 1978; *b* 22 Nov. 1918; *s* of Francis and Ellen Elizabeth Loring; *m* 1971, Anita Susan Hunt; one *s* (and one *s* two *d* by previous marr.). *Educ*: Central Foundation Sch., London; London Univ. DipEcon; ACIS. Served War, Royal Air Force, 1940-46; CO No 200 Staging Post, Shanghai, 1946. Secretary, Culpeper House Gp of Companies, 1947-49; John Lewis Partnership, 1949-60: Central Merchandise Advisor (Food), 1949-55; Gen. Manager, Waitrose Gp, 1955-57; Mem., Central Management (specialising in financial matters), 1958-60. Asst Director, Services to Spastics, Spastics Soc., 1960-67; Director, 1967-80; Dir, Camphill Village Trust, 1981. *Publications*: ed, Learning Problems of the Cerebral Palsied, 1964; ed, Teaching the Cerebral Palsied Child, 1965; ed, The Spastic School Child and the Outside World, 1966; ed, The Subnormal Child, 1968; ed, Assessment of the Cerebral Palsied Child for Education, 1968. *Recreation*: country life. *Address*: 19 St Mary's Grove, Chiswick, W4 3LL. *T*: 01-995 5721.

LORNE, Marquess of; Torquhil Ian Campbell; *b* 29 May 1968; *s* and *heir* of 12th Duke of Argyll, *qv*. A Page of Honour to the Queen, 1981-.

LOSEY, Joseph; film director; *b* 14 Jan. 1909; *s* of Joseph Walton Losey and Ina Higbee; *m* ; two *s*. *Educ*: Dartmouth Coll., New Hampshire; Harvard Univ. Writer, producer and editor, radio and documentaries, 1936-43. Resident in England, 1953-74. Directed first Broadway play, 1932; subseq. productions include: (with Charles Laughton) Galileo Galilei, by Berthold Brecht, NY and Hollywood, 1947; (with Wilfrid Lawson) The Wooden Dish, London, 1954; Boris Godunov, Paris Opera, 1980. Films include: The Boy with Green Hair, 1948; The Dividing Line; The Prowler, 1950; Time Without Pity; Blind Date, 1959; The Criminal, 1960; The Damned, 1960; Eva, 1961; The Servant, 1963; King and Country, 1964; Modesty Blaise, 1965;

Accident, 1966; Boom, 1967; Secret Ceremony, 1968; Figures in a Landscape, 1969; The Go-Between (Golden Palm, Cannes Film Festival, 1971), 1970; The Assassination of Trotsky, 1971; A Doll's House, 1973; Galileo, 1974; The Romantic Englishwoman, 1974; Mr Klein, 1976; Les Routes du Sud, 1978; Don Giovanni, 1978; La Truite, 1982. Pres., Cannes Film Festival Jury, 1972. Guest Prof., 1970 and 1975, DLitHum, 1973, Dartmouth Coll., NH. Chevalier de l'Ordre des Arts et des Lettres, 1957. *Recreation*: work. *Address*: c/o Theo Cowan, 45 Poland Street, W1.

LOSINSKA, Kathleen Mary, (Kate); President, Civil and Public Services Association, 1979-82, a Vice-President, since 1982; *b* Croydon, Surrey, 5 Oct. 1924; *d* of late James Henry Conway and Dorothea Marguerite Hill; *m* 1942, Stanislaw Losinski (formerly serving Officer, Polish Air Force, subseq. 301 Bomber Sqdn, RAF, retd with rank of Sqdn Leader; awarded Polish Virtuti Militari Cross, Croix de Guerre, Cross of Lorraine, Yugoslav Cross of Valour, etc); one *s*. *Educ*: Selhurst Grammar Sch., Croydon (matriculation); university of life generally. Entered Civil Service, 1939; with Office of Population Censuses and Surveys. Delegate Mem., Council of Civil Service Unions (former Chm.). Has held all honorary positions, CPSA. Governor, Ruskin Coll., 1976, 1979-. Silver Jubilee Medal, 1977. *Recreations*: journalism, reading, music, history, travel; work for the Christian Trade Union and Moderate Trade Union Movements. *Address*: 45 Rectory Park, Sanderstead, South Croydon, Surrey. *T*: 01-657 4834. *Club*: Civil Service.

LOSS, Joshua Alexander, (Joe Loss), OBE 1978; band-leader; *b* 22 June 1909; *s* of Israel and Ada Loss; *m* 1938, Mildred Blanch Rose; one *s* one *d*. *Educ*: Jewish Free Sch., Spitalfields; Trinity Coll. of Music; London Coll. of Music. Played as silent film accompanist, Coliseum, Ilford and at Tower Ballroom, Blackpool, 1926; formed own orchestra at Astoria Ballroom, Charing Cross Road, 1930; first broadcast, 1934, then broadcast every week; was one of first West End bands to play in provinces in ballrooms and to top bill in variety theatres; toured through war inc. overseas; joined Mecca, 1959; became resident at Hammersmith Palais. Joined Regal Zonophone record co.; hit record, 1936, with Begin the Beguine (gold disc for sales of a million over 25 years); is now joint longest serving artiste on EMI label, has 50-year contract. First record with EMI I Only Have Eyes For You; hit singles inc. Wheels Cha Cha, The Maigret Theme, The Steptoe Theme; gold discs for long-playing albums inc. Joe Loss Plays Glenn Miller and All Time Party Hits. *Television*: Come Dancing, Bid for Fame, Home Town Saturday Night, and Holiday Parade; was featured in This Is Your Life, 1963 and 1980; panel member, New Faces. Awards: 15 Carl Alan Awards; Musical Express Top Big Band Award, 1963, 1964; Weekend Magazine Top Musical Personality Award, 1964; and Music Publishers' Assoc. Award as outstanding personality of 1976. Plays for dancing on QE2 world cruises, at Buckingham Palace and Windsor Castle on numerous occasions, and at pre-wedding balls for Princess Margaret, Princess Alexandra and Princess Anne, for Queen's 50th birthday celebrations and for Queen Mother's 80th birthday; Royal Variety Performance, 1980. Queen's Silver Jubilee Medal, 1978. Freeman, City of London, 1979. *Recreations*: motoring, watching television, collecting watches, playing with grandchildren. *Address*: Morley House, Regent Street, W1. *T*: 01-580 1212. *Club*: Middlesex County Cricket (Life Member).

LOSTY, Howard Harold Walter, FEng, FIEE; Secretary, Institution of Electrical Engineers, since 1980; *b* 1 Aug. 1926; *s* of Patrick J. Losty and Edith E. Wilson; *m* 1950, Rosemary L. Everritt; two *d*. *Educ*: Harvey Grammar Sch, Folkestone; Sir John Cass Coll., London. BSc. GEC Research Laboratories, 1942-53; GEC Nuclear Power Programme, 1953-66; Head of Engineering Div., GEC Research Centre, 1966-71; Dir, GEC Hirst Research Centre, 1971-77; Man. Dir, GEC Electronic Devices Ltd, 1977-80. *Publications*: (co-author) Nuclear Graphite, 1962; some forty technical papers. *Recreations*: walking, listening to music (opera), reading history. *Address*: Shandon, 14 Wyatts Road, Chorleywood, Herts WD3 5TE. *T*: Chorleywood 3568.

LOTEN, Alexander William, CEng, FIMechE; FCIBS; Under Secretary, Department of the Environment, and Director, Mechanical and Electrical Engineering Services, Property Services Agency, since 1981; *b* 11 Dec. 1925; *s* of late Alec Oliver Loten and of Alice Maud Loten; *m* 1954, Mary Diana Flint; one *s* one *d*. *Educ*: Church's Coll., Petersfield; Corpus Christi Coll., Cambridge Univ. (BA). CEng, FIMechE 1980; FCIBS 1970. Served War, RNVR, 1943-46 (Air Engr Officer). Engineer: Rolls-Royce Ltd, Derby, 1950-54; Benham & Sons, London, 1954-58; Air Min. Work Directorate, 1958-64; Sen. Engr, 1964-70; Superintending Engr (Mechanical Design), 1970-75, MPBW; Dir of Works, Civil Accommodation, PSA, 1975-81. Pres., CIBS, 1976-77. Major, Engr and Railway Staff Corps RE, T&AVR, 1979-. *Recreations*: walking, gardening. *Address*: Property Services Agency, Lunar House, Wellesley Road, Croydon CR9 2EL. *T*: 01-686 3499.

LOTH, David; Editor and Author; *b* St Louis, Missouri, 7 Dec. 1899; *s* of Albert Loth and Fanny Sunshine. *Educ*: University of Missouri. Staff of New York World, 1920-30; Editor and Publisher The Majorca Sun, 1931-34; NY Times, 1934-41; US Govt Information Services, 1941-45; Information Dir, Planned Parenthood Federation of America, 1946-51; Acting Nat. Dir, 1951; Information Dir, Columbia Univ. Bicentennial, 1953-54; Assoc. Nieman Fellow, Harvard Univ., 1957-58; Lecturer, Finch Coll., 1961-65. Senior Editor-Writer, High Sch. Geog. Project of Assoc. of Amer. Geographers, 1967-68. Consultant, Psychological Corp., 1969-76. Lectr, Univ. of Colorado, 1978-. Contributor to various English, American, and Australian publications.

Publications: The Brownings; Lorenzo the Magnificent; Charles II; Philip II; Public Plunder; Alexander Hamilton; Lafayette; Woodrow Wilson; Chief Justice; A Long Way Forward; Swope of GE; The Erotic in Literature; Pencoyd and the Roberts Family; Crime Lab.: How High is Up; The City Within a City; Crime in Suburbia; The Marriage Counselor; Gold Brick Cassie; Economic Miracle in Israel; The Tertelines: earth movers; Co-author: American Sexual Behaviour and the Kinsey Report; Report on the American Communist; For Better or Worse; Peter Freuchen's Book of the Seven Seas; The Frigid Wife; The Emotional Sex; Ivan Sanderson's Book of Great Jungles; The Taming of Technology; The Colorado Model for Conservation Education. *Address:* 2227 Canyon Boulevard, Boulder, Colo 80302, USA.

LOTHIAN, 12th Marquess of *cr* 1701; **Peter Francis Walter Kerr;** Lord Newbattle, 1591; Earl of Lothian, 1606; Baron Jedburgh, 1622; Earl of Ancram, Baron Kerr of Nisbet, Baron Long-Newton and Dolphinston, 1633; Viscount of Brien, Baron Kerr of Newbattle, 1701; Baron Ker (UK), 1821; DL; Lord Warden of the Stannaries and Keeper of the Privy Seal of the Duke of Cornwall, since 1977; *b* 8 Sept. 1922; *s* of late Captain Andrew William Kerr, RN, and Marie Constance Annabel, *d* of Capt. William Walter Raleigh Kerr; *S* cousin, 1940; *m* 1943, Antonella, *d* of late Maj.-Gen. Sir Foster Newland, KCMG, CB, and Mrs William Carr, Ditchingham Hall, Norfolk; two *s* four *d. Educ:* Ampleforth; Christ Church, Oxford. Lieut, Scots Guards, 1943. Mem. Brit. Delegation: UN Gen. Assembly, 1956-57; European Parliament, 1973; UK Delegate, Council of Europe and WEU, 1959. PPS to Foreign Sec., 1960-63; a Lord in Waiting (Govt Whip, House of Lords), 1962-63, 1972-73; Joint Parliamentary Sec., Min. of Health, April-Oct. 1964; Parly Under-Sec. of State, FCO, 1970-72. Chm., Scottish Council, British Red Cross Soc., 1976-. Mem., Queen's Body Guard for Scotland (Royal Company of Archers). Mem., Prince of Wales Council, 1976-. DL, Roxburgh, 1962. Kt, SMO Malta. *Heir: s* Earl of Ancram, *qv. Address:* Melbourne Hall, Derby. *T:* Melbourne 2163; Monteviot, Jedburgh, Roxburghshire. *T:* Ancrum 288; 54 Upper Cheyne Row, SW3. *Clubs:* Boodle's, Beefsteak; New (Edinburgh).
See also Col Sir D. H. Cameron of Lochiel, Earl of Dalkeith, Earl of Euston.

LOTHIAN, Andrew; Sheriff of Glasgow and Strathkelvin, since 1979; *b* 6 Feb. 1942; *s* of Andrew Lothian and Catriona Elizabeth (*née* Gillies); *m* 1st, 1969, Deidre Edith Shannon; two *s* ; 2nd, 1976, Susan Adiel Ogilvie Raeburn. *Educ:* Trinity Coll., Glenalmond; Univ. of St Andrews (MA); Univ. of Edinburgh (LLB). Kate's Fund, St Andrews Univ., 1964; Editor, Gambit, 1965-66. Admitted Advocate, 1968. Standing Junior Counsel to Highlands and Islands Development Bd, 1976-79. Member, Scottish Arts Council Publication Awards Cttee, 1970-73; President, Speculative Soc., 1971. *Publications:* So Many Kinds of Yes (with Alan Davidson), 1962; contrib. Times Educnl Supplement, Blackwood's Magazine, Jl of Law Soc. of Scotland. *Recreations:* ornithology, theatre. *Address:* 16 Clarendon Crescent, Edinburgh EH4 1PU. *Clubs:* Edinburgh University Staff, Scottish Arts.

LOTT, Dr Bernard Maurice, OBE 1966; Course Tutor, Open University, since 1979; *b* 13 Aug. 1922; *s* of late William Lott and of Margaret Lott (*née* Smith); *m* 1949, Helena, *d* of late Clarence Winkup; two *s* one *d. Educ:* Bancroft's Sch.; Keble Coll., Oxford (MA); Univ. of London (MA Distinction, PhD); Univ. of Edinburgh (Dip. in Applied Linguistics, Dist.). RN, 1942-46. Brit. Council Lectr in English, Ankara Univ. and Gazi Inst. of Educn, Turkey, 1949-55; Brit. Council Asst Rep., Finland, 1955-57; Prof. of Eng. and Head of Dept, Univ. of Indonesia, 1958-61; Dir of Studies, Indian Central Inst. of Eng., 1961-66; Dep. Controller, Educn Div., Brit. Council, 1966-72; Controller, Eng. Teaching Div., Brit. Council, 1972-75; Brit. Council Representative, Poland, 1975-77; English Language Teaching Develt Adviser, British Council, 1977-79. Hon. Res. Fellow, University Coll. London, 1980-. *Publications:* Gen. Editor, New Swan Shakespeare series, and edited: Macbeth, 1958, Twelfth Night, 1959, Merchant of Venice, 1962, Hamlet, 1968 (also Open Univ. edn 1970), King Lear, 1974; Much Ado About Nothing, 1977; contribs on teaching of English as foreign lang. to Times Educnl Supp. and Eng. Lang. Teaching Jl. *Recreations:* local studies, music. *Address:* 8 Meadway, NW11 7JT. *T:* 01-455 0918.

LOTT, Air Vice-Marshal Charles George, CB 1955; CBE 1944; DSO 1940; DFC 1940; Royal Air Force, retired; *b* 28 Oct. 1906; *s* of late Charles Lott, Sandown; *m* 1936, Evelyn Muriel Little; two *s* one *d. Educ:* Portsmouth Junior Technical Sch. Joined Royal Air Force as Aircraft Apprentice, 1922; learned to fly at Duxford in No 19 Squadron, 1927-28; Sergeant, 1928; Commissioned 1933 and posted to No 41 Squadron; Iraq, 1935-38; HQ No 11 Gp, 1938-39; Commanded No 43 Squadron, 1939-40 (DFC, wounded, DSO); Temp. Wing Comdr, 1941; HQ 13 Group, 1940-42; Sector Comdr, Fighter Command, 1952; Acting Group Capt. 1942; Temp. Group Captain 1944; RAF Delegation (USA), 1944-45; Group Captain 1947; Air Commodore, 1954; Air Vice-Marshal, 1956; Dir Air Defence, SHAPE, 1955-57; Commandant, Sch. of Land/Air Warfare, Old Sarum, Wilts, 1957-59. Retd 1959. *Club:* Royal Air Force.

LOTT, Felicity Ann, (Mrs R. M. Golding); soprano; *b* 8 May 1947; *d* of John Albert Lott and Whyla (*née* Williams); *m* 1973, Robin Mavesyn Golding. *Educ:* Pate's Grammar Sch. for Girls, Cheltenham; Royal Holloway Coll., Univ. of London (BA Hons French); Royal Acad. of Music (LRAM; ARAM 1976). Principal rôles with English National Opera, Glyndebourne, Welsh National Opera, Covent Garden, Scottish Opera; operatic rôles in France, Belgium, Germany; recitals, concerts and oratorio performances in UK, Belgium, Canada, France, Holland, Hong Kong, USA; several recordings. Founder Mem., The Songmakers' Almanac. *Recreations:* reading, dressmaking, cooking. *Address:* c/o Lies Askonas, 19A Air Street, W1. *T:* 01-734 0095.

LOTZ, Dr Kurt; German business executive; *b* 18 Sept. 1912; *m* Elizabeth Lony; two *s* one *d. Educ:* August-Vilmar-Schule, Homberg. Joined Police Service, 1932; Lieut 1934. Served Luftwaffe (Gen. Staff; Major), 1942-45. Employed by Brown Boveri & Cie, Dortmund, 1946; Head of Business Div., Mannheim, 1954; Dir 1957; Chm. 1958-67; Mem. Board of Directors in parent company, Baden, Switzerland, 1961; Managing Director, 1963-67. Dep. Chm., 1967-68, Chm., 1968-71, Volkswagenwerk AG. Member: Deutscher Rat für Landespflege. Chm., World Wildlife Fund, Germany, 1980. Mem., Rotary Internat. Hon. Senator, Heidelberg Univ., 1963; Hon. Prof., Technische Universität Carolo Wilhelmina, Brunswick, 1970. Dr rer. pol. *hc* Mannheim, 1963. *Publication:* Lebenserfahrungen: Worüber man in Wirtschaft und Politik auch sprechen sollte, 1978. *Recreations:* hiking, hunting, golf. *Address:* 69 Heidelberg, Ludolf-Krehl-Strasse 35, Germany.

LOUDON, John Hugo; Jonkheer (Netherlands title); Knight in the Order of the Netherlands Lion, 1953; Grand Officer, Order of Orange-Nassau, 1965; KBE (Hon.) (Gt Brit.), 1960; Officer, Légion d'Honneur, 1963; holds other decorations; Chairman: Board, Atlantic Institute, since 1969; European Advisory Committee, Ford Motor Company, since 1976; Institut Européen d'Administration des Affaires, since 1971; *b* 27 June 1905; *s* of Jonkheer Hugo Loudon and Anna Petronella Alida Loudon (*née* van Marken); *m* 1931, Baroness Marie Cornelie van Tuyll van Serooskerken; three *s* (and one *s* decd). *Educ:* Netherlands Lyceum, The Hague; Utrecht Univ., Holland. Doctor of Law, 1929. Joined Royal Dutch/Shell Group of Cos, 1930; served in USA, 1932-38; Venezuela, 1938-47 (Gen. Man., 1944-47); Man. Dir, 1947-52, Pres., 1952-65, Chm., 1965-76, Royal Dutch Petroleum Co.; former Chm., Shell Oil Co. (New York); Vice-Chm. Bd, Royal Netherlands Blast-furnaces & Steelworks, NV, 1971-76; Director: Orion Bank Ltd, 1971-81; Chase Manhattan Corp., 1971-76; Estel NV Hoesch-Hoogovens, 1972-76. Chm., Internat. Adv. Cttee, Chase Manhattan Bank, 1965-77. Mem. Bd Trustees, Ford Foundation, 1966-75; Internat. Pres., World Wildlife Fund, 1977-81. *Recreations:* golf, yachting. *Address:* 48 Lange Voorhout, 2514 EG The Hague, Holland. *T:* 453755; Koekoeksduin, 5 Vogelenzangseweg 2111 HP, Aerdenhout, Holland. *T:* Haarlem 245924. *Clubs:* White's; Royal Yacht Squadron.

LOUDOUN, Countess of (13th in line) *cr* 1633; **Barbara Huddleston Abney-Hastings;** Lady Campbell Baroness of Loudoun, 1601; Lady Tarrinzean and Mauchline, 1638; the 3 English baronies of Botreaux 1368, Stanley 1456, and Hastings 1461, which were held by the late Countess, are abeyant, the Countess and her sisters being *co-heiresses* ; *b* 3 July 1919; assumed by deed poll, 1955, the surname of Abney-Hastings in lieu of that of Griffiths; *S* mother, 1960; *m* 1st, 1939 (marr. diss., 1945), Capt. Walter Strickland Lord; one *s* ; 2nd, 1945, Capt. Gilbert Frederick Greenwood (*d* 1951); one *s* one *d* ; 3rd, 1954, Peter Griffiths (who assumed by deed poll the surname of Abney-Hastings in lieu of his patronymic, 1958); three *d. Heir: s* Lord Mauchline, *qv. Address:* Mount Walk, Ashby-de-la-Zouch, Leics. *T:* Ashby-de-la-Zouch 5844.

LOUDOUN, Maj.-Gen. Robert Beverley, CB 1973; OBE 1965; Director, Mental Health Foundation, since 1977; *b* 8 July 1922; *s* of Robert and Margaret Loudoun; *m* 1950, Audrey Stevens; two *s. Educ:* University College Sch., Hampstead. Served War of 1939-45 (despatches): enlisted Royal Marines, 1940; commissioned, 1941; 43 Commando, Central Mediterranean, 1943-45; 45 Commando, Hong Kong, Malta and Palestine, 1945-48. Instructor, RNC Greenwich, 1950-52; Staff of C-in-C America and West Indies, 1953-55; RN Staff Coll., 1956; Adjt, 40 Commando, Malta and Cyprus, 1958-59; USMC Sch., Quantico, Virginia, 1959-60; MoD, 1960-62; Second-in-Command, 42 Commando, Singapore and Borneo, 1963-64; CO, 40 Commando, Far East, 1967-69; Brig., UK Commandos, Plymouth, 1969-71; Maj.-Gen. RM Training Gp, Portsmouth, 1971-75, retired 1975. Col Comdt, RM, 1981-82; Representative Col Comdt, RM, 1983-. Chm., Jt Shooting Cttee for GB, 1977-82. Freeman, City of London, 1979. *Address:* 2 Warwick Drive, Putney, SW15 6LB. *Club:* Army and Navy.

LOUGH, Prof. John, FBA 1975; Professor of French, University of Durham (late Durham Colleges), 1952-78; *b* 19 Feb. 1913; *s* of Wilfrid Gordon and Mary Turnbull Lough, Newcastle upon Tyne; *m* 1939, Muriel Barker; one *d. Educ:* Newcastle upon Tyne Royal Grammar Sch.; St John's Coll., Cambridge; Sorbonne. Major Schol., St John's Coll., 1931; BA, First Cl. Hons Parts I and II Mod. and Medieval Langs Tripos, 1934; Esmond Schol. at British Inst. in Paris, 1935; Jebb Studentship, Cambridge, 1936; PhD 1937, MA 1938, Cambridge. Asst (later Lectr), Univ. of Aberdeen, 1937; Lectr in French, Cambridge, 1946. Leverhulme Res. Fellow, 1973. Hon. Dr, Univ. of Clermont, 1967; Hon. DLitt Newcastle, 1972. Officier de l'Ordre National du Mérite, 1973. *Publications:* Locke's Travels in France, 1953; (ed) selected Philosophical Writings of Diderot, 1953; (ed) The Encyclopédie of Diderot and d'Alembert: selected articles, 1954; An Introduction to Seventeenth Century France, 1954; Paris Theatre Audiences in the 17th and 18th centuries, 1957; An Introduction to Eighteenth Century France, 1960; Essays on the Encyclopédie of Diderot and D'Alembert, 1968; The Encyclopédie in 18th Century England and other studies, 1970; The Encyclopédie, 1971; The

Contributors to the Encyclopédie, 1973; (ed with J. Proust) Diderot: Œuvres complètes, vols V-VIII, 1977; (with M. Lough) An Introduction to Nineteenth Century France, 1978; Writer and Public in France, 1978; Seventeenth Century French Drama: the background, 1979; The Philosophes and Post-Revolutionary France, 1982; articles on French literature and ideas in 17th and 18th centuries in French and English learned jls. *Address:* 1 St Hild's Lane, Durham DH1 1QL. *T:* Durham 48034.

LOUGHBOROUGH, Archdeacon of; *see* Lockley, Ven. Harold.

LOUGHEED, Hon. (Edgar) Peter, QC (Can.); Premier of Alberta, Canada, since 1971; *b* Calgary, 26 July 1928; *s* of late Edgar Donald Lougheed and Edna Bauld; *m* 1952, Jeanne Estelle Rogers, Edmonton; two *s* two *d. Educ:* public and secondary schs, Calgary; Univ. of Alberta (BA, LLB); Harvard Grad. Sch. of Business (MBA). Read law with Calgary firm of lawyers; called to Bar of Alberta, 1955, and practised law with same firm, 1955-56. Joined Mannix Co. Ltd, as Sec., 1956 (Gen. Counsel, 1958, Vice-Pres., 1959, Dir, 1960). Entered private legal practice, 1962. Elected: Provincial Leader of Progressive Conservative Party of Alberta, also Member for Calgary West, 1965; Leader of the Official Opposition, 1967; Conservatives won Provincial Election, 1971, when he became Premier of Alberta (Conservatives re-elected 1975); re-elected as Premier, 1979. *Recreations:* all team sports (formerly football with Edmonton Eskimos). *Address:* (office) 307 Legislature Building, Edmonton, Alberta T5K 2B7, Canada.

LOUGHLIN, Charles William; trade union official; retired 1974; *b* 16 Feb. 1914; *s* of late Charles Loughlin, Grimsby; *m* 1945, May, *d* of David Arthur Dunderdale, Leeds; one *s* (one *d* decd). *Educ:* St Mary's Sch., Grimsby; National Council of Labour Colls. Area Organiser, Union of Shop, Distributive and Allied Workers, 1945-74. MP (Lab) Gloucestershire West, 1959-Sept. 1974; Parly Sec., Min. of Health, 1965-67; Jt Parly Sec., Min. of Social Security, then Dept of Health and Social Security, 1967-68; Parly Sec., Min. of Public Building and Works, 1968-70. *Address:* 22 Templenewsam View, Leeds LS15 0LW. *T:* Leeds 647354.

LOUGHRAN, James; Principal Conductor and Musical Adviser, Hallé Orchestra, since 1971; Chief Conductor, Bamberg Symphony Orchestra, from Sept. 1979; *b* 30 June 1931; *s* of James and Agnes Loughran; *m* 1961, Nancy (*née* Coggon); two *s. Educ:* St Aloysius' Coll., Glasgow; Bonn, Amsterdam and Milan. 1st Prize, Philharmonia Conducting Competition, 1961. Asst Conductor, Bournemouth Symphony Orchestra, 1962; Associate Conductor, Bournemouth Symphony Orchestra, 1964; Principal Conductor, BBC Scottish Symphony Orchestra, 1965-71. *Address:* Hallé Concerts Society, 30 Cross Street, Manchester M2 7BA.

LOUIS, John Jeffry, Jr; United States Ambassador to the Court of St James's, since 1981; *b* 10 June 1925; *s* of John Jeffry Louis and Henrietta Louis (*née* Johnson); *m* 1953, Josephine Peters; one *s* two *d. Educ:* Deerfield Academy, Mass; Northwestern Univ., 1943 and 1946; Williams Coll., Mass (BA 1947); Dartmouth Coll., New Hampshire (MBA 1949). Served with AUS, 1943-45. Account Executive, Needham, Louis & Brorby, Inc., Chicago, 1952-58; Director, International Marketing, Johnson's Wax, Wis, 1958-61; Chairman Board: KTAR Broadcasting Co., Ariz., 1961-68; Combined Communications Corp., Chicago, 1968-80; Chm., Exec. Cttee, Dir, Butler Internat., 1976-81; Director: Johnson's Wax, 1961-81; Atlanta LaSalle Corp., 1970-81; 1st Nat. Bank, Winnetka, Ill, 1973-81. Trustee: Northwestern Univ., 1967-81; Deerfield Acad., 1963-81; Foxcroft Sch., 1975-79; Williams Coll., 1979-81. Trustee, Evanston Hosp., 1959-81 (Chm., 1962-68). Hon. Master of The Bench, Middle Temple, 1981. *Recreations:* golf, tennis, skiing, shooting. *Address:* American Embassy, Grosvenor Square, W1. *T:* 01-499 9000. *Clubs:* Old Elm (Illinois); Pine Valley Golf (New Jersey); Augusta National Golf (Georgia); Gulfstream Golf (Florida).

LOUISY, Rt. Hon. Allan, PC 1981; Prime Minister of St Lucia, since 1979; Leader of St Lucia Labour Party; Minister of Finance, Home Affairs, Information and Tourism, 1979-. *Address:* Office of the Prime Minister, Castries, St Lucia, WI.

LOUSADA, Sir Anthony (Baruh), Kt 1975; Solicitor; Partner in Stephenson Harwood, 1935-73; Consultant, 1973-81; *b* 4 Nov. 1907; *s* of Julian George Lousada and Maude Reignier Conder; *m* 1st, 1937, Jocelyn (marr. diss. 1960), *d* of late Sir Alan Herbert, CH; one *s* three *d* ; 2nd, 1961, Patricia, *d* of late C. J. McBride, USA; one *s* one *d. Educ:* Westminster; New Coll., Oxford. Admitted Solicitor, 1933. Min. of Economic Warfare, 1939-44; Min. of Production and War Cabinet Office, 1944-45. Member: Council, Royal College of Art, 1952-79 (Hon. Fellow, 1957; Sen. Fellow, 1967; Vice-Chm., 1960-72; Treasurer, 1967-72; Chm., 1972-79; Hon. Dr 1977); Cttee, Contemp. Art Soc., 1955-71 (Vice-Chm., 1961-71); Fine Arts Cttee, British Council (visited Japan on behalf of Council, 1970, to set up exhibn of sculpture by Barbara Hepworth); GPO Adv. Cttee on Stamp Design, 1968-80; Council, Friends of Tate Gallery, 1958- (Hon. Treasurer, 1960-65, Chm., 1971-77); Chm., Adv. Cttee, Govt Art Collection; Trustee, Tate Gallery, 1962-69 (Vice-Chm., 1965-67; Chm., 1967-69). One-man exhibns of drawings, Covt Gdn Gall., 1977, 1981. Officer, Order of Belgian Crown, 1945. *Recreations:* painting, sailing. *Address:* The Tides, Chiswick Mall, W4. *T:* 01-994 2257. *Clubs:* Garrick; London Corinthian Sailing.

LOUSTAU-LALANNE, Bernard Michel; High Commissioner for Seychelles, in London, 1978-80; concurrently Seychelles Ambassador to USA, and Seychelles Permanent Representative to UN; *b* 20 June 1938; *s* of Joseph Antoine Michel Loustau-Lalanne, OBE, and Marie Therese Madeleine (*née* Boullé); *m* 1974, Debbie Elizabeth Temple-Brown; one *s* one *d. Educ:* Seychelles Coll.; St Mary's Coll., Southampton; Imperial Coll., London. Called to the Bar, Middle Temple, London, 1969. Assistant Inspector, Northern Rhodesia Police, 1962-64; Crown Counsel, Seychelles, 1970-72; Sen. State Counsel and Official Notary, 1972-76; Attorney-General, 1976-78. Internat. Representative, Performing Right Soc. Ltd. *Recreations:* windsurfing, tennis, swimming, scuba diving, reading. *Address:* 39 Montagu Square, W1. *T:* 01-262 4993. *Clubs:* Royal Commonwealth Society; Seychelles Yacht.

LOUTH, 16th Baron, *cr* 1541, **Otway Michael James Oliver Plunkett;** *b* 19 Aug. 1929; *o s* of Otway Randal Percy Oliver Plunkett, 15th Baron, and Ethel Molly, *d* of Walter John Gallichen, Jersey, Channel Islands; *S* father, 1950; *m* 1951, Angela Patricia Culinane, Jersey; three *s* two *d. Heir: s* Hon. Jonathan Oliver Plunkett, BSc [*b* 4 Nov. 1952; *m* 1981, Jennifer Hodgetts, Jersey]. *Address:* Les Sercles, La Grande Piece, St Peter, Jersey, Channel Islands.

LOUTIT, John Freeman, CBE 1957; FRS 1963; MA, DM, FRCP; External Scientific Staff Medical Research Council, 1969-75, Visitor at Radiobiology Unit since 1975; *b* 19 Feb. 1910; *s* of John Freeman Loutit, Perth, WA; *m* 1941, Thelma Salusbury; one *s* two *d. Educ:* C of E Grammar Sch., Guildford, W Australia; Univs of W Australia, Melbourne, Oxford, London. Rhodes Scholar (W Australia), 1930; BA Oxon 1933, BM, BCh Oxon 1935. Various appointments, London Hosp., 1935-39; MA (Oxon) 1938; Director, South London Blood Supply Depot, 1940-47; DM Oxon, 1946; Dir, Radiobiological Research Unit, AERE Harwell, 1947-69. FRCP 1955. VMD (*hc*) Stockholm, 1965. Officer, Order of Orange-Nassau (Netherlands) 1951. *Publications:* Irradiation of Mice and Men, 1962; Tissue Grafting and Radiation (jointly), 1966; articles in scientific journals. *Recreations:* cooking, gardening. *Address:* 22 Milton Lane, Steventon, Oxon. *T:* Abingdon 831279.

LOVAT, 17th Baron (S) *cr* before 1440 (*de facto* 15th Baron, 17th but for the Attainder); **Simon Christopher Joseph Fraser,** DSO 1942; MC; TD; JP; DL; Baron (UK) 1837; 24th Chief of Clan Fraser of Lovat; *b* 9 July 1911; *s* of 16th Baron and Hon. Laura Lister (*d* 1965), 2nd *d* of 4th Baron Ribblesdale; *S* father, 1933; *m* 1938, Rosamond, *o d* of Sir Delves Broughton, 11th Bt; four *s* two *d. Educ:* Ampleforth; Magdalen Coll., Oxford, BA. Lt, Scots Guards, 1932-37, retd. Served War of 1939-45: Capt. Lovat Scouts, 1939; Lt-Col 1942; Brig. Commandos, 1943 (wounded, MC, DSO, Order of Suvarov, Légion d'Honneur, Croix de Guerre avec palme; Norway Liberation Cross). Under-Sec. of State for Foreign Affairs, 1945. DL 1942, JP 1944, Inverness. Awarded LLD (Hon.) by Canadian universities. Order of St John of Jerusalem; Knight of Malta; Papal Order of St Gregory with Collar. *Publication:* March Past, 1978. *Heir: s* Master of Lovat, *qv. Address:* Balblair, Beauly, Inverness-shire. *Club:* Cavalry and Guards.
See also Earl of Eldon, Rt Hon. Sir Hugh Fraser, Sir Fitzroy Maclean of Dunconnel, Bt, Lord Reay.

LOVAT, Master of; Hon. Simon Augustine Fraser; *b* 28 Aug. 1939; *s* of 17th Baron Lovat, *qv* ; *m* 1972, Virginia, *d* of David Grose; one *s* one *d. Educ:* Ampleforth Coll. Lieut Scots Guards, 1960. *Address:* Beaufort Castle, Beauly, Inverness-shire.

LOVAT, Sheriff Leonard Scott; Sheriff of South Strathclyde, Dumfries and Galloway at Hamilton, since 1978; *b* 28 July 1926; *s* of late Charles Lovat and Alice (*née* Hunter); *m* 1960, Elinor Frances, *d* of late J. A. McAlister and Mary McAlister; one *s* one *d. Educ:* St Aloysius Coll., Glasgow; Glasgow Univ. (BL 1947). Solicitor, 1948; Partner, Jno. Shaughnessy and McColl, Solicitors, Glasgow, 1955-59. Asst to Prof. of Roman Law, Glasgow Univ., 1954-63; Cropwood Fellow, Inst. of Criminology, Univ. of Cambridge, 1971. Procurator Fiscal Depute, Glasgow, 1960; Sen. Asst Procurator Fiscal, Glasgow and Strathkelvin, 1976. *Publications:* Climbers' Guide to Glencoe and Ardgour, 2 vols, 1959, 1965; articles and reviews in legal jls. *Recreations:* music, mountaineering, bird-watching. *Address:* 25 Woodend Drive, Jordanhill, Glasgow G13 1QN. *T:* 041-959 3864. *Club:* Alpine.

LOVE, Prof. Philip Noel; Professor of Conveyancing and Professional Practice of Law, University of Aberdeen, since 1974 (Dean of Faculty of Law, 1979-82); *b* 25 Dec. 1939; *o s* of Thomas Isaac and Ethel Violet Love; *m* 1963, Isabel Leah, *yr d* of Innes Taylor and Leah Wallace Mearns; three *s. Educ:* Aberdeen Grammar Sch.; Aberdeen Univ. (MA 1961, LLB 1963). Admitted Solicitor in Scotland, 1963; Advocate in Aberdeen, 1963-; Partner, Campbell Connon & Co., Solicitors, Aberdeen, 1963-74. Consultant, 1974-. Law Society of Scotland: Mem. Council, 1975-; Examr, 1975- (Chm. Examrs, 1977-80); Vice-Pres., 1980-81; Pres., 1981-82; Local Chm., Rent Assessment Panel for Scotland, 1972-; Mem., Jt Standing Cttee on Legal Educn in Scotland, 1976- (Chm., 1976-80); Vice-Pres., Scottish Law Agents Soc., 1980; Mem., Rules Council, Court of Session, 1968-. Chairman: Aberdeen Home for Widowers' Children, 1971-; Exec. Cttee, Aberdeen Grammar Sch. Former Pupils' Club, 1982-. Hon. Sheriff of Grampian, Highland and Islands, 1978-. *Recreations:* formerly Rugby (player and thereafter selector, N and Midlands (Scotland)); now squash and golf. *Address:* 3A Rubislaw Den North, Aberdeen AB2 4AL. *T:* Aberdeen 33339. *Clubs:* New (Edinburgh); Royal Aberdeen Golf, Rotary of Aberdeen, Aberdeen Grammar School Former Pupils' Club Centre (Aberdeen).

LOVEDAY, Alan (Raymond); Solo Violinist; *b* 29 Feb. 1928; *s* of Leslie and Margaret Loveday; *m* 1952, Ruth Stanfield; one *s* one *d*. *Educ:* privately; Royal College of Music (prizewinner). Made debut at age of 4; debut in England, 1946; has given many concerts, broadcasts, and made TV appearances, in this country and abroad, playing with all leading conductors and orchestras; repertoire ranges from Bach (which he likes to play on an un-modernised violin), to contemporary music. Professor at RCM, 1955-72. Hon. ARCM 1961. *Recreations:* tennis, golf, chess, bridge.

LOVEDAY, Rt. Rev. David Goodwin, MA; Assistant Bishop, Diocese of Oxford, since 1971; *b* 13 April 1896; 6th *s* of late J. E. T. Loveday, JP, of Williamscote, near Banbury, Oxon; unmarried. *Educ:* Shrewsbury Sch. (Careswell Exhibitioner); Magdalene Coll., Cambridge (Sizar), 2nd cl. Class. Tripos, Part I, 2nd cl. Theol. Tripos, Part I. Deacon, 1923; Priest, 1924; Asst Master, Malvern Coll., 1917-19; Asst Master and Chaplain, Aldenham Sch.; 1922-25; Clifton Coll., 1925-31; Headmaster of Cranleigh Sch., 1931-54; Archdeacon of Dorking and Examining Chaplain, Guildford, 1954-57; Suffragan Bishop of Dorchester, 1957-71. Select Preacher: Cambridge 1933 and 1954, Dublin, 1951, Oxford, 1955 and 1957. *Address:* Wardington, Banbury, Oxon. *T:* Cropredy 219.

LOVEGROVE, Geoffrey David, QC 1969; **His Honour Judge Lovegrove;** a Circuit Judge (formerly County Court Judge), since 1971; *b* 22 Dec. 1919; *s* of late Gilbert Henry Lovegrove; *m* 1959, Janet, *d* of John Bourne; one *s* two *d*. *Educ:* Haileybury; New College, Oxford (MA). Army, 1940-46. Called to the Bar, Inner Temple, 1947; Dep. Chairman, W Sussex Quarter Sessions, 1965-71. Master, Innholders' Company, 1980-81. *Address:* 1 King's Bench Walk, Temple, EC4.

LOVELACE, 5th Earl of, *cr* 1838; **Peter Axel William Locke King;** Baron King and Ockham, 1725; Viscount Ockham, 1838; *b* 26 Nov. 1951; *s* of 4th Earl and of Manon Lis, *d* of Axel Sigurd Transo, Copenhagen, Denmark; *S* father, 1964. *Address:* Torridon House, Torridon, Ross-shire.

LOVELL, Sir (Alfred Charles) Bernard, Kt 1961; OBE 1946; FRS 1955; Director of Jodrell Bank Experimental Station, Cheshire, now Nuffield Radio Astronomy Laboratories, 1951-81; Professor of Radio Astronomy, University of Manchester, 1951-80, now Emeritus Professor; *b* 31 Aug. 1913; *s* of G. Lovell, Oldland Common, Gloucestershire; *m* 1937, Mary Joyce Chesterman; two *s* three *d*. *Educ:* Kingswood Grammar Sch., Bristol; University of Bristol. Asst Lectr in Physics, Univ. of Manchester, 1936-39; Telecommunication Res. Establishment, 1939-45; Physical Laboratories, Univ. of Manchester and Jodrell Bank Experimental Station, Cheshire; Lectr, 1945, Sen. Lectr, 1947, Reader, 1949, in Physics. Reith Lectr, 1958; Lectures: Condon, 1962; Guthrie, 1962; Halley, 1964; Queen's, Berlin, 1970; Brockington, Kingston, Ont, 1970; Bickley, Oxford, 1977; Crookshank, RCR, 1977; Angel Meml, Newfoundland, 1977. Vis. Montague Burton Prof. of Internat. Relations, Univ. of Edinburgh, 1973. Member: ARC, 1955-58; SRC, 1965-70; Amer. Philosophical Soc., 1974-. Pres., RAS, 1969-71; Vice-Pres., Internat. Astronomical Union, 1970-76; Pres., British Assocn, 1975-76. Pres., Inc. Guild of Church Musicians, 1976-. Hon. Freeman, City of Manchester, 1977. Hon. Fellow, Society of Engineers, 1964; Hon. Foreign Member American Academy of Arts and Sciences, 1955; Hon. Life Member, New York Academy, 1960; Hon. Member: Royal Swedish Academy, 1962; RNCM, 1981. Hon. LLD: Edinburgh, 1961; Calgary, 1966; Hon. DSc: Leicester, 1961; Leeds, 1966; London, 1967; Bath, 1967; Bristol, 1970; DUniv Stirling, 1974; DUniv Surrey, 1975; Hon. FIEE, 1967; Hon. FInstP, 1976. Duddell Medal, 1954; Royal Medal, 1960; Daniel and Florence Guggenheim International Astronautics Award, 1961; Ordre du Mérite pour la Recherche et l'Invention, 1962; Churchill Gold Medal, 1964; Maitland Lecturer and Silver Medallist, Institution of Structural Engineers, 1964; Second RSA American Exchange Lectr, Philadelphia, 1980; Benjamin Franklin Medal, RSA, 1980; Gold Medal, Royal Astronomical Soc., 1981. Commander's Order of Merit, Polish People's Republic, 1975. *Publications:* Science and Civilisation, 1939; World Power Resources and Social Development, 1945; Radio Astronomy, 1951; Meteor Astronomy, 1954; The Exploration of Space by Radio, 1957; The Individual and The Universe, (BBC Reith Lectures, 1958); The Exploration of Outer Space (Gregynog Lectures, 1961); Discovering the Universe, 1963; Our Present Knowledge of the Universe, 1967; (ed with T. Margerison) The Explosion of Science: The Physical Universe, 1967; The Story of Jodrell Bank, 1968; The Origins and International Economics of Space Exploration, 1973; Out of the Zenith, 1973; Man's Relation to the Universe, 1975; P. M. S. Blackett: a biographical memoir, 1976; In the Centre of Immensities, 1978; Emerging Cosmology, 1981; many publications in Physical and Astronomical journals. *Recreations:* cricket, gardening, music. *Address:* The Quinta, Swettenham, Cheshire. *T:* Lower Withington 71254. *Club:* Athenæum.

LOVELL, Arnold Henry; Under-Secretary, HM Treasury, since 1975; *b* 5 Aug. 1926; *s* of Alexander and Anita Lovell; *m* 1950, Joyce Harmer; one *s* one *d*. *Educ:* Hemsworth Grammar Sch., Yorks; London School of Economics (BScEcon, 1st Cl. Hons). HM Treasury: Asst Principal, 1952; Principal, 1956; Asst Financial Adviser to UK High Commn, New Delhi, India, 1962-65; re-joined HM Treasury, Monetary Policy Div., 1965-70; Asst Sec., 1967; Balance of Payments Div., 1970-75; Under-Sec., Fiscal Policy Div., 1975-80,

Industry and Agric. Gp, 1980-. *Recreations:* walking, Stafford bull terriers. *Address:* 12 Bromley Lane, Chislehurst, Kent BR7 5DY. *T:* 01-467 1116.

LOVELL, Kenneth Ernest Walter; Treasurer to the Greater London Council, 1977-80, retired; *b* 25 Oct. 1919; *s* of Ernest John and Alice Lovell; *m* 1946, Vera Mary Pithouse; one *s* two *d*. *Educ:* Ashford County Grammar School. Mem. Chartered Inst. of Public Finance and Accountancy. Middlesex County Council (Finance Dept): Computer Manager, 1961; Asst County Treasurer, 1963. Greater London Council: Asst Treasurer, 1965; Finance Officer, ILEA, 1972. *Recreations:* gardening, cricket, hockey, photography; study of social and economic development of British Isles; study of landscape of British Isles. *Address:* 15 Meadway Close, Staines, Mddx TW18 2PR. *T:* Staines 52806.

LOVELL, Stanley Hains, CMG 1972; ED; consultant surgeon; *b* 22 Sept. 1906; *er s* of late John Hains Lovell; *m* 1935, Eleanor, *o d* of late Dr Edgar Harold Young; three *d*. *Educ:* Fort Street Boys' High Sch.; St Andrew's Coll., Univ. of Sydney. MB, BS, MS Sydney; FRACS. Served War of 1939-45, Middle East and Pacific (despatches); Col, RAAMC. Hon. Consultant Surgeon, Royal Prince Alfred, Rachel Forster, Prince Henry, Prince of Wales and Eastern Suburbs Hosps. Fellow, Australian Medical Assoc.; Pres., NSW Medical Defence Union, 1958-. Formerly: Mem. Court of Examrs, and Chm., NSW State Cttee, RACS; Lectr in Clinical Surgery, Sydney Univ.; Examr in Surgery, Sydney Univ.; External Examr, Univ. of Queensland. *Publications:* contrib. various surgical jls. *Recreation:* gardening. *Address:* 229 Macquarie Street, Sydney, NSW 2000, Australia. *T:* 2321060. *Club:* Australian (Sydney).

LOVELL-DAVIS, family name of Baron Lovell-Davis.

LOVELL-DAVIS, Baron *cr* 1974 (Life Peer), of Highgate; **Peter Lovell Lovell-Davis;** Member: Commonwealth Development Corporation, since 1978; London Consortium, since 1978; *b* 8 July 1924; *s* of late William Lovell Davis and late Winifred Mary Davis; *m* 1950, Jean Graham; one *s* one *d*. *Educ:* Christ's Coll., Finchley; King Edward VI Sch., Stratford-upon-Avon; Jesus Coll., Oxford. BA Hons English, MA. Served War, RAF (Pilot), to Flt-Lt, 1943-47. Oxford, 1947-50. Managing Dir, Central Press Features Ltd, 1952-70; Dir, various newspaper and printing cos. Chm., Colour Features Ltd; Chairman: Davis & Harrison Ltd, 1970-73; Features Syndicate, 1971-74. A Lord in Waiting (Govt Whip), 1974-75; Parly Under-Sec. of State, Dept of Energy, 1975-76. Adviser to various Govt Cttees, Health Educn Council, Labour Party and Govt, on media. Vice-Pres., YHA, 1978-; UK Rep., Centre Européen de Co-opération International, 1980-; Trustee, Whittington Hosp. Academic Centre, 1980-. *Recreations:* industrial archaeology, inland waterways, bird-watching, walking, sketching—and flying kites. *Address:* 80 North Road, Highgate, N6 4AA. *T:* 01-348 3919.

LOVELOCK, Sir Douglas (Arthur), KCB 1979 (CB 1974); Chairman, Board of Customs and Excise, since 1977; *b* 7 Sept. 1923; *s* of late Walter and Irene Lovelock; *m* 1961, Valerie Margaret (née Lane); one *s* one *d*. *Educ:* Bec Sch., London. Entered Treasury, 1949; Min. of Supply, 1952; Private Sec. to Permanent Sec., 1953-54; Principal, 1954; Private Sec. to successive Ministers of Aviation (Rt Hon. Peter Thorneycroft and Rt Hon. Julian Amery), 1961-63; Asst Sec., 1963; Under-Sec. (Contracts), Min. of Technology, subseq. Min. of Aviation Supply, 1968-71; Asst Under-Sec. of State (Personnel), MoD, 1971-72; Dep. Sec., DTI, 1972-74, Depts of Trade, Industry, Prices and Consumer Protection, 1974-77. Chm., Civil Service Benevolent Fund, 1980-. *Recreations:* walking, gardening, outdoor activities generally. *Address:* The Old House, 91 Coulsdon Road, Old Coulsdon, Surrey. *T:* Downland 55211.

LOVELOCK, Prof. James Ephraim, FRS 1974; Independent Consultant since 1964; Visiting Professor, University of Reading, since 1967; *b* 26 July 1919; *s* of Tom Arthur Lovelock and Nellie Ann Elizabeth (née March); *m* 1942, Helen Mary Hyslop; two *s* two *d*. *Educ:* Strand Sch., London; Manchester and London Univs. BSc, PhD, DSc, ARIC. Staff Scientist, Nat. Inst. for Med. Research, 1941-61; Rockefeller Fellow, Harvard Univ., 1954-55; Yale Univ., 1958-59; Prof. of Chemistry, Baylor Univ. Coll. of Medicine, Texas, 1961-64. Mem. Sigma Xi, Yale Chapter, 1959. *Publications:* Gaia, 1979; numerous papers and patents. *Recreations:* walking, painting, computer programming, reading. *Address:* Coombe Mill, St Giles on the Heath, Launceston, Cornwall PL15 9RY. *T:* Launceston 84450.

LOVERIDGE, Joan Mary, OBE 1968; Matron and Superintendent of Nursing, St Bartholomew's Hospital, 1949-67; *b* 14 Aug. 1912; *d* of William Ernest Loveridge. *Educ:* Maidenhead, Berkshire. Commenced training, 1930, Royal National Orthopædic Hospital, W1; St Bartholomew's Hospital, 1933-37; Radcliffe Infirmary, Oxford, Midwifery Training, 1937-38; Night Sister, Ward Sister, Matron's Office Sister, Assistant Matron, St Bartholomew's Hospital. *Address:* 21 Witheby, Cotmaton Road, Sidmouth, Devon.

LOVERIDGE, Sir John (Henry), Kt 1975; CBE 1964 (MBE 1945); Bailiff of Guernsey, 1973-82; Barrister-at-Law; Judge of Appeal for Jersey, 1974-82; *b* 2 Aug. 1912; *e s* of late Henry Thomas and Vera Lilian Loveridge; *m* 1946, Madeleine Melanie, *o d* of late Eugene Joseph C. M. Tanguy; one *s* one *d*. *Educ:* Elizabeth Coll., Guernsey; Univ. of Caen. Called to Bar, Middle Temple, 1950. Advocate of Royal Court of Guernsey, 1951; HM Solicitor-General, Guernsey, 1954-60; HM Attorney-General, Guernsey, 1960-69;

Deputy Bailiff of Guernsey, 1969-73. RAFVR, 1954-59. KStJ 1980. *Recreations:* reading, swimming, sport. *Address:* Kinmount, Sausmarez Road, St Martin's, Guernsey. *T:* Guernsey 38038. *Club:* Royal Guernsey Golf.

LOVERIDGE, John Warren, JP; MP (C) Havering, Upminster, since 1974 (Hornchurch, 1970-74); Principal of St Godric's College since 1954; farmer; *b* 9 Sept. 1925; *s* of C. W. Loveridge and Emily (Mickie), *d* of John Malone; *m* 1954, Jean Marguerite, *d* of E. J. Chivers; three *s* two *d. Educ:* St John's Coll., Cambridge (MA). Contested (C) Aberavon, 1951, Brixton (LCC), 1952; Hampstead Borough Council, 1953-59. Former Mem., Parly Select Cttee on Expenditure (Mem. General Purposes Sub-Cttee); former Mem., Procedure Cttee; Chm., Cons. Smaller Business Cttee. Treasurer/Trustee, Hampstead Conservative Assoc., 1959-74. Pres., Axe Cliff Golf Club. JP West Central Division, 1963. FRAS; MRIIA. Liveryman, Girdlers' Co. *Recreations:* painting, historic houses and early furniture, shooting. *Address:* House of Commons, SW1A 0AA. *Clubs:* Carlton, Hurlingham.

LOVETT, Robert Abercrombie; Banker, United States; *b* 14 Sept. 1895; *s* of Robert Scott Lovett and Lavinia Chilton (*née* Abercrombie); *m* 1919, Adèle Quartley Brown; one *s* (one *d* decd). *Educ:* Yale Univ. (BA), 1918; law study, Harvard, 1919-20; course in business administration, Harvard Grad. Schools, 1920-21. Clerk, National Bank of Commerce, NY City, 1921-23; employee, Brown Brothers & Co., 1923; partner, 1926; continued in successor firm, Brown Brothers Harriman & Co. until 1940. Served as Special Asst to Secretary of War, and as Asst Secretary of War for Air in charge of Army Air Program, 1940-45. Under-Secretary of State, 1947-49; Deputy Secretary of Defence, 1950-51; Secretary of Defence, 1951-Jan. 1953. Readmitted Brown Brothers Harriman & Co., March 1953. Director: Union Pacific Railroad Co. and its leased lines, 1921-69 (Chm. Exec. Cttee and Chief Exec. Officer, 1953-67); Union Pacific Corp., 1969-78, retired; New York Life Insurance Co., 1949-68; CBS Inc., 1953-77; Freeport Minerals Co., 1953-70; North American Aviation Inc., 1953-69; Mem., NY Investment Cttee, Royal-Globe Insce Cos, 1953-75. Life Member Emeritus, Corp. of MIT. Holds hon. degrees. Served (pilot to Lieut-Commander) US Naval Air Service, March 1917-Dec. 1918 (Navy Cross, DSM). Grand Cross of the Order of Leopold II (Belgium), 1950; Presidential Medal of Freedom, USA, 1963. *Address:* Locust Valley, Long Island, NY 11560, USA. *Clubs:* Century, Yale, Links (New York); Creek (Locust Valley); Metropolitan (Washington, DC).

LOVICK, Albert Ernest Fred; Chairman, 1964-68, Director, 1950-68 and 1969-78, Co-operative Insurance Society Ltd; Chairman, Cumbrian Co-operative Society Ltd, Carlisle, since 1972; Director: CWS Ltd, 1949-78; Shoefayre Ltd, 1975-78; *b* 19 Feb. 1912; *s* of late Arthur Alfred Lovick and late Mary Lovick (*née* Sharland); *m* 1934, Florence Ena Jewell; no *c. Educ:* Elementary Sch., Eastleigh, Hants; Peter Symonds, Winchester. Hearne & Partner, rating surveyors, 1928; Eastleigh Co-operative Society, 1929-33; Harwich, Dovercourt and Parkeston CS, 1933-35; Managing Secretary, Basingstoke CS, 1935-49. During War of 1939-45, government cttees. Member, Basingstoke Borough Council, 1946-49. Former Chm., Centratours Ltd. Member: Export Credits Guarantees Advisory Council, 1968-73; Bristol Rent Assessment Cttee, 1973-; Bristol Rent Tribunal, 1973-. Fellow, Co-operative Secretaries Assoc.; FCIS; FCIArb. *Recreations:* golf, gardening. *Address:* 48 Botchergate, Carlisle CA1 1RG; Coedway, Bristol Road, Stonehouse, Glos GL10 2BQ. *T:* Stonehouse 3167. *Club:* Royal Commonwealth Society.

LOW, family name of **Baron Aldington.**

LOW, Sir Alan (Roberts), Kt 1977; Governor, Reserve Bank of New Zealand, 1967-77; *b* 11 Jan. 1916; 4th *s* of Benjamin H. Low and Sarah Low; *m* 1940, Kathleen Mary Harrow; one *s* two *d. Educ:* Timaru Main Sch.; Timaru Boys' High Sch.; Canterbury University College. MA 1937. Joined Reserve Bank of New Zealand, 1938; Economic Adviser, 1951; Asst Governor, 1960; Deputy Governor, 1962; Governor, 1967. Army Service, 1942-44; on loan to Economic Stabilisation Commission, 1944-46. Hon. Fellow, Bankers' Inst. of NZ, 1977. Hon. LLD Canterbury, 1977. *Publications:* contributions to many economic and financial jls. *Recreations:* gardening, music, reading. *Address:* 83 Penrose Street, Lower Hutt, New Zealand. *T:* 699-526. *Club:* Wellington (NZ).

LOW, Prof. Donald Anthony, DPhil; Smuts Professor of the History of British Commonwealth, University of Cambridge, since 1983; *b* 22 June 1927; *o s* of late Canon Donald Low and Winifred (*née* Edmunds); *m* 1952, Isobel Smails; one *s* two *d. Educ:* Haileybury and ISC; Univ. of Oxford (MA, DPhil). Open Scholar in Modern History, 1944 and Amelia Jackson Sen. Student, 1948, Exeter Coll., Oxford; Lectr, subseq. Sen. Lectr, Makerere Coll., University Coll. of E. Africa, 1951-58; Uganda corresp., The Times, 1952-58; Fellow, subseq. Sen. Fellow in History, Res. Sch. of Social Sciences, ANU, 1959-64; Founding Dean of Sch. of African and Asian Studies, and Prof. of Hist., Univ. of Sussex, 1964-72 (Dir, Graduates in Arts and Social Studies, 1970-71); Australian National University: Prof. of History, 1973-82; Dir, Res. Sch. of Pacific Studies, 1973-75; Vice Chancellor, 1975-82. Mem. Council, Univ. of Papua New Guinea, 1974-82; Chm., Educn Adv. Cttee, Aust. Develt Assistance Bureau, 1979-82; Mem. Exec., 1976-82, Dep. Chm., 1980, Aust. Vice-Chancellors' Cttee (Chm., Internat. Relations Cttee, 1979-82); Member: Standing Cttee, Aust. Univs Internat. Develt Program, 1975-82; Council, Assoc. of Commonwealth Univs, 1980-82; Bd of Trustees, Internat. Fedn of

Insts of Advanced Study, 1978-82. Sen. Visitor, Nuffield Coll., Oxford, 1956-57; Vis. Prof., Univ. of Calif, Berkeley, and Chicago Univ., 1967; Smuts Fellow and Vis. Fellow, Clare Hall, Cambridge, 1971-72; Vis. Academic, Nuffield Coll., Oxford, 1982-83; Hon. Fellow, Inst. of Develt Studies, UK, 1972; Kingsley Martin Meml Lectr, Cambridge, 1980. President: African Studies Assoc. of Aust. and Pacific, 1979-; Asian Studies Assoc. of Aust., 1980-82; FAHA 1973; FASSA 1975. *Publications:* Buganda and British Overrule, 1900-1955 (with R. C. Pratt), 1960; (ed) Soundings in Modern South Asian History, 1968; (with J. C. Iltis and M. D. Wainwright) Government Archives in South Asia: a guide to national and state archives in Ceylon, India and Pakistan, 1969; Buganda in Modern History, 1971; The Mind of Buganda, 1971; Lion Rampant: essays in the study of British imperialism, 1973; Congress and the Raj, facets of the Indian struggle, 1917-1947, 1977; Oxford History of East Africa: (contrib.) Vol. I, 1963 and Vol. II, 1965; (contrib. and ed jtly) Vol. III, 1976; articles on internat. history in jls. *Address:* Faculty of History, West Road, Cambridge.

LOW, Sir James (Richard) Morrison-, 3rd Bt, *cr* 1908; DL; DFH, CEng, MIEE; Director, Osborne & Hunter Ltd, Glasgow and Kirkcaldy, since 1956 (Electrical Engineer with firm, since 1952); *b* 3 Aug. 1925; *s* of Sir Walter John Morrison-Low, 2nd Bt and Dorothy Ruth de Quincey Quincey (*d* 1946); *S* father 1955; *m* 1953, Ann Rawson Gordon; one *s* three *d. Educ:* Ardvreck; Harrow; Merchiston. Served Royal Corps of Signals, 1943-47; demobilised with rank of Captain. Faraday House Engineering Coll., 1948-52. Chm., Scottish Cttee, Nat. Inspection Council for Electrical Installation Contracting, 1982-; Pres., Electrical Contractors Assoc. of Scotland, 1982-. Hon. Pipe-Major, Royal Scottish Pipers Soc., 1981-83. DL Fife, 1978. *Recreations:* shooting, piping. Heir: *s* Richard Walter Morrison-Low, *b* 4 Aug. 1959. *Address:* Kilmaron Castle, Cupar, Fife. *T:* Cupar 2248. *Clubs:* New, Royal Scottish Pipers Society (Edinburgh).

LOWE, Group Captain Cyril Nelson, MC, DFC; BA Cambridge; late OC, RAF Station, Amman, Trans Jordan; *b* 7 Oct. 1891; *s* of Rev. C. W. Nelson Lowe, MA; *m* Ethel Mary Watson; one *s* two *d. Educ:* Dulwich Coll.; Pembroke Coll., Cambridge. Rugby Blue at Cambridge, 1911-12-13; first played for England v S. Africa in 1913, and subsequently gained 25 International Caps; Commission Aug. 1914 in ASC, and qualified for 1914 Star; seconded to Royal Flying Corps, 1916; No. 11 Squadron RFC France, 1916-17; 24 Squadron RFC, France, 1918 (MC, DFC). *Address:* Little Brook, Burrow Hill, Chobham, Surrey.

LOWE, David Bruce Douglas; a Recorder of the Crown Court, since 1980; *b* 3 April 1935; *o s* of late Douglas Gordon Arthur Lowe, QC, and of Karen, *e d* of Surgeon Einar Thamsen; *m* 1978, Dagmar, *o d* of Horst and Anneliese Bosse; one *s* one *d* (and one *s* one *d* by a previous marriage). *Educ:* Winchester College; Pembroke Coll., Cambridge (MA). National service, RN, 1953-55. Profumo Scholar, Inner Temple. Called to the Bar, Inner Temple, 1960; Midland and Oxford Circuit (formerly Midland); Prosecuting Counsel to Dept of Trade, 1975-. *Recreations:* music, tennis, gardening (formerly rackets and real tennis). *Address:* 1 King's Bench Walk, Temple, EC4Y 7DB. *T:* 01-353 8436; 7 Cambridge Place, W8. *T:* 01-937 1583. *Club:* Hawks (Cambridge).

LOWE, David Nicoll, OBE 1946; MA, BSc; FRSE; Secretary, Carnegie United Kingdom Trust, 1954-70; *b* 9 Sept. 1909; *s* of George Black Lowe and Jane Nicoll, Arbroath, Angus; *m* 1939, Muriel Enid Bryer, CSP; one *s* three *d. Educ:* Arbroath High Sch.; St Andrews Univ. (Kitchener Scholar). MA 1931; BSc (1st Class Hons Botany) 1934; President Union, 1933-34; President Students' Representative Council, 1934-35; Founder President, University Mountaineering Club; Asst Secretary British Assoc. for the Advancement of Science, 1935-40, Secretary 1946-54. War Cabinet Secretariat, 1940-42 and 1945-46; Ministry of Production, 1942-45. Joint Hon. Secretary, Society of Visiting Scientists, 1952-54; Member Executive Cttee: Scottish Council of Social Service, 1953-71; Nat. Trust for Scotland, 1971-81; Member, Countryside Commn for Scotland, 1968-78. Chairman: Scottish Congregational Coll., 1961-68; Pollock Meml Missionary Trust, 1973-; Governor, Scottish Nat. Meml to David Livingstone, 1974-80. Contributor to Annual Register, 1947-59. Queen's Silver Jubilee Medal, 1977. *Recreations:* those of his family and gardening. *Address:* Caddam, Perth Road, Crieff, Perthshire.

LOWE, Hon. Douglas Ackley, MHA (ALP), for Franklin, Tasmania, 1969-82, re-elected as an Independent, 1982; *b* 15 May 1942; *s* of Ackley Reginald Lowe and Dulcie Mary Lowe (*née* Kean); *m* 1962, Pamela June (*née* Grant); two *s* two *d. Educ:* St Virgil's College, Hobart. Mem. Tasmanian House of Assembly, 1969; Minister for Housing, 1972; Chief Secretary, 1974; Deputy Premier, 1975-77; Chief Sec. and Minister for Planning and Reorganisation, 1975; Premier, 1977-81; Treasurer, 1980-81; Minister for: Industrial Relations, Planning and the Environment, 1976; Industrial Relations and Health, Aug. 1976; Industrial Relations and Manpower Planning, 1977-79; Economic Planning and Development, 1979-80; Energy, 1979-81. Australian Labor Party: State Sec. 1965-69, State Pres. 1974-75, Tasmanian Section. Tasmanian Deleg. to Aust. Constitutional Convention. Queen's Silver Jubilee Medal, 1977. *Address:* (home) 15 Tooma Avenue, Chigwell, Hobart, Tasmania; (office) Parliament House, Hobart, Tasmania. *T:* (002) 302218.

LOWE, Air Chief Marshal Sir Douglas (Charles), GCB 1977 (KCB 1974; CB 1971); DFC 1943; AFC 1946; Chief of Defence Procurement, Ministry of Defence, Sept. 1982-June 1983; Air ADC to the Queen, 1978-83; *b* 14 March 1922; *s* of John William Lowe; *m* 1944, Doreen Elizabeth (*née* Nichols); one *s* one *d. Educ:* Reading School. Joined RAF, 1940; No 75 (NZ) Sqdn, 1943; Bomber Comd Instructors' Sch., 1945; RAF Coll., Cranwell, 1947; Exam. Wing CFS, 1950; Air Min. Operational Requirements, 1955; OC No 148 Sqdn, 1959; Exchange Officer, HQ SAC, USAF, 1961; Stn Comdr Cranwell, 1963; idc 1966; DOR 2 (RAF), MoD (Air), 1967; SASO, NEAF, 1969-71; ACAS (Operational Requirements), 1971-73; AOC No 18 Group, RAF, 1973-75; Controller, Aircraft, MoD Procurement Executive, 1975-82. *Recreations:* gardening, domestic odd-jobbing, photography, theatre, music. *Address:* c/o Lloyds Bank Ltd, Byfleet, Surrey. *Club:* Royal Air Force.
See also Baron Glanusk.

LOWE, Air Vice-Marshal Sir Edgar (Noel), KBE 1962 (CBE 1945); CB 1947; Director General of Supply Co-ordination, Ministry of Defence, 1966-70, retired (Inspector General of Codification and Standardisation, 1964); *b* 1905; *s* of late Albert Henry Lowe, Church Stretton, Shropshire; *m* 1948, Mary McIlwraith, *o d* of George M. Lockhart, Stair House, Stair, Ayrshire; one *s* one *d.* Served India, 1934-38; psa 1939; served in France 1939-40 (despatches); Air Commodore, Director of Organisation (Forecasting and Planning), Air Ministry, 1945-47; idc 1949; ADC to the King, 1949-52, to the Queen, 1952-57; Directing Staff, RAF Staff Coll., Bracknell, 1950-51; Director of Organisation, Air Ministry, 1951-53; Deputy Asst Chief of Staff (Logistics), SHAPE, 1953-56; Senior Air Staff Officer, HQ No 41 Group, RAF, 1956-58; AOC No 40 Group, RAF, 1958-61; Director-General of Equipment, Air Ministry, 1961-64. *Address:* Wyndford, 97 Harestone Hill, Caterham, Surrey. *T:* Caterham 45757. *Club:* Royal Air Force.

LOWE, Sir Francis (Reginald Gordon), 3rd Bt *cr* 1918; *b* 8 Feb. 1931; *s* of Sir Francis Gordon Lowe, 2nd Bt, and Dorothy Honor, *d* of late Lt-Col H. S. Woolrych; *S* father, 1972; *m* 1st, 1961, Franziska Cornelia Steinkopf (marr. diss. 1971); two *s* ; 2nd, 1971, Helen Suzanne, *y d* of late Sandys Stuart Macaskie; one *s. Educ:* Stowe; Clare College, Cambridge (BA, LLB). Called to the Bar, Middle Temple, 1959; Western Circuit. *Recreations:* market gardening, cider making. *Heir: s* Thomas William Gordon Lowe, *b* 14 Aug. 1963. *Address:* Bagwich, Godshill, Isle of Wight. *T:* Godshill 252; 4 New Square, Lincoln's Inn, WC2A 3RJ. *T:* 01-242 8508.

LOWE, Geoffrey Colin; aviation consultant since 1980; *b* 7 Sept. 1920; *s* of late Colin Roderick and late Elsie Lowe; *m* 1948, Joan Stephen; one *d. Educ:* Reigate Grammar Sch. GPO, 1937; Exchequer and Audit Dept, 1939. Served War, RAFVR, 1941-46 (Flt-Lt). Asst Principal, Min. of Civil Aviation, 1947; Private Sec. to Permanent Sec., MCA, 1950; Principal, 1950; Colonial Office, 1954-57; Min. of Transport and Civil Aviation, 1957-61; Civil Air Attaché, SE Asia, 1961-64; Asst Sec., Overseas Policy Div., Min. of Aviation, 1964-68; Investment Grants Div., Bd of Trade, 1968-71; Counsellor (Civil Aviation), British Embassy, Washington, 1971-73, Counsellor (Civil Aviation and Shipping), Washington, 1973-74; Under Sec. (Management Services and Manpower), Depts of Industry and Trade, 1974-80. *Recreations:* theatre, crossword puzzles. *Address:* Starlings, 36a Monkhams Avenue, Woodford Green, Essex IG8 0EY. *T:* 01-504 7035.

LOWE, Dr John; Head, Country Educational Policy Reviews, Education and Training Division, OECD, since 1973; *b* 3 Aug. 1922; *s* of John Lowe and Ellen (*née* Webb); *m* 1949, Margaret James; two *s* one *d. Educ:* Univ. of Liverpool (BA Hons 1950); Univ. of London (CertEd 1951, PhD 1960). Lectr, subseq. Sen. Lectr, Univ. of Liverpool, 1955-63; Dir, Extra-Mural Studies, Univ. of Singapore, 1963-64; Dir, Dept of Adult Educn and Extra-Mural Studies, subsequently Head, Dept of Educnl Studies, Univ. of Edinburgh, 1964-72; OECD: Consultant in field, 1964-; Principal Administrator, 1973-. Sec./Treas., Internat. Congress of Univ. Adult Educn, 1972-76. *Publications:* Adult Education in England and Wales, 1970; (ed) Adult Education and Nation-Building, 1970; (ed) Education and Nation-Building in the Third World, 1971; The Education of Adults: a world perspective, 1975, rev. edn, 1982; articles in educnl and hist. jls. *Recreations:* reading, music, theatre, swimming. *Address:* 3 Rue Ribera, 75016 Paris, France. *T:* 520.2515. *Club:* National Liberal.

LOWE, John Eric Charles, MVO 1965; MBE 1937; *b* 11 Aug. 1907; 6th *s* of late John Frederick Lowe; *m* 1935, Trudy (*née* Maybury); one *s* two *d. Educ:* Burghley Road Sch., Highgate. Vice-Consul, Jibuti, 1930-37, Harar, 1940; Political Officer, Aden Protectorate, 1940; served in HM Forces, Somaliland and Ethiopia, 1941-46; Senior Asst. Foreign Office, 1947-49; Acting Consul, Suez, 1949; Vice-Consul, Beira, 1950; Vice-Consul, Hamburg, 1951 and Frankfurt, 1953; 2nd Secretary, Helsinki, 1953; Political Agent's Representative, Mina-Al-Ahmadi (Kuwait), 1956; Vice-Consul, Leopoldville, 1959; Consul, Khartoum, 1962; Consul-General, Basra, 1965-67; retired, Sept. 1967. Order of the Two Niles (Sudan), 1965. *Recreations:* gardening, golf, sailing. *Address:* Woodbine, Ewhurst Lane, Northiam, E Sussex. *T:* Northiam 2456.

LOWE, John Evelyn, MA, FSA, FRSA; cultural consultant and author, since 1978, foreign travel specialist, journalist and photographer; *b* 23 April 1928; *s* of late Arthur Holden Lowe; *m* 1956, Susan Helen Sanderson (marr. diss. 1981); two *s* one *d. Educ:* Wellington Coll., Berks; New Coll., Oxford.

Served in RAEC, 1947-49 (Sgt Instructor). Victoria and Albert Museum, Dept of Woodwork, 1953-56; Deputy Story Editor, Pinewood Studios, 1956-57; Victoria and Albert Museum: Dept of Ceramics, 1957-61; Assistant to the Director, 1961-64; Dir, City Museum and Art Gall., Birmingham, 1964-69; Dir, Weald and Downland Open Air Museum, 1969-74; Principal, West Dean College, Chichester, West Sussex, 1972-78. Member: Exec. Cttee, Midland Arts Centre for Young People, 1964-69; Council of the British School at Rome, 1968-70; Crafts Adv. Cttee, 1973-78. Vis. Prof. in British Cultural Studies, Doshisha Univ., Japan, 1979-81. *Publications:* Thomas Chippendale, 1955; major contribs to Encylopædia Britannica and OUP Children's Encyclopedia; articles on applied arts, foreign travel, social history and Japan. *Recreations:* Japan, music, reading, book-collecting, travel. *Address:* 302 Kamo Haitsu, 4 Nakagawara-cho, Shirnogamo, Sakyo-ku, Kyoto 606, Japan. *T:* 075.722.4546.

LOWE, Prof. Kenneth Gordon, CVO 1982; MD; FRCP, FRCPE, FRCPGlas; Physician to the Queen in Scotland, 1971-82; Formerly Consultant Physician, Royal Infirmary and Ninewells Hospital, Dundee; Hon. Professor of Medicine, Dundee University, since 1969; *b* 29 May 1917; *s* of Thomas J. Lowe, MA, BSc, Arbroath, and Flora MacDonald Gordon, Arbroath; *m* 1942, Nancy Young, MB, ChB, twin *d* of Stephen Young, Logie, Fife; two *s* one *d. Educ:* Arbroath High Sch.; St Andrews Univ. (MD Hons). Served with RAMC, 1942-46; Registrar, Hammersmith Hosp., Royal Postgrad. Med. Sch., 1947-52; Sen. Lectr in Medicine, St Andrews Univ., 1952-61. *Publications:* contribs to med. and scientific jls, mainly on renal, metabolic and cardiac disorders. *Recreations:* reading, fishing. *Address:* 36 Dundee Road, West Ferry, Dundee. *T:* Dundee 78787. *Club:* Flyfishers'.

LOWE, Dr Robert David; Dean, St George's Hospital Medical School, since 1971; Hon. Consultant to St George's Hospital; *b* 23 Feb. 1930; *s* of John Lowe and Hilda Althea Mead; *m* 1952, Betty Irene Wheeler; one *s* three *d. Educ:* Leighton Park Sch.; Emmanuel Coll., Cambridge; UCH Medical School. BCh, MB, MA, MD, PhD Cantab; FRCP, LMSSA. Medical Specialist, RAMC, 1955-59; Research Asst, UCH Med. Sch., 1959-61; St George's Hosp. Med. Sch.: MRC Res. Fellow, 1961-62; Wellcome Sen. Res. Fellow in Clinical Science, 1963-64; Sen. Lectr in Medicine, St Thomas' Hosp. Med. Sch., 1964-70; Hon. Consultant to St Thomas' Hosp., 1966-70. AUCAS: Exec. Mem., 1967-; Chm., 1972-78. *Publications:* (with B. F. Robinson) A Physiological Approach to Clinical Methods, 1970; papers on peripheral circulation, hypertension, adrenergic mechanisms, central action of angiotensin, control of cardiovascular system. *Recreations:* bridge, squash, hill-walking. *Address:* Brookfield, Tredington, near Shipston-on-Stour, Warwickshire. *T:* Shipston-on-Stour 62426.

LOWE, Robson; philatelist, publisher, editor, author, auctioneer; *b* 7 Jan. 1905; *s* of John Lowe and Gertrude Lee; *m* 1928, Winifred Marie Denne (*d* 1973); two *d. Educ:* Fulham Central Sch. Started own business, 1920; worked on PO Records, 1926; purchased control of Woods of Perth (Printers), 1964; formed Australian co., 1967; joined bd of Christie, Manson & Woods, 1968; formed Italian co., 1969 (founded Il Piccolo for Italian collectors). Chm., Expert Cttee of British Philatelic Assoc., 1941-61; Past Pres., British Philatelic Fedn, 1979-81; Co-founder, Postal History Soc., 1935; Founder: Soc. of Postal Historians, 1950; annual British Philatelic Exhibn, 1965; assoc. of four Eur. firms for extending auction business under title, The Uncommon Market, 1964. Mem. jury at internat. philatelic exhibns: first, Durban, 1928; Chm., Cape Town, 1979. Over 1000 lectures. Took over Philatelic Jl of GB, 1958 (still the publisher); Editor, The Philatelist, 1934-74 (centenary, 1966). *Publications:* Philatelic Encyclopaedia (ed), 1935; Handstruck Stamps of the Empire, 1937, 4th edn 1941; Sperati and his Craft, 1953; British Postage Stamps, 1968; (jtly) St Vincent, 1971; Encyclopaedia of Empire Stamps: Europe, 1947, 2nd edn 1951; Africa, 1949; Asia, 1951; Australia, 1962; North America, 1973; monographs (latest, De La Rue Key-plates, 1979); articles in philatelic pubns. *Recreations:* history, philately, study of forgers and forgery. *Address:* Robson Lowe, 10 King Street, SW1 6RA. *Clubs:* East India, Devonshire, Sports and Public Schools; Collectors (New York).

LOWENSTEIN, Prof. Otto Egon, FRS 1955; FRSE; DSc (Glasgow); PhD (Birmingham); DrPhil (Munich);Honorary Senior Research Fellow, Neurocommunications Research Unit, Birmingham University Medical School, since 1976 (Leverhulme Emeritus Research Fellow, 1974-76); *b* 24 Oct. 1906; *s* of Julius Lowenstein and Mathilde Heusinger; *m* 1st, Elsa Barbara, *d* of R. Ritter; two *s* ; 2nd, Gunilla Marika (*d* 1981), *d* of Prof. Gösta Dohlman; one step *s. Educ:* Neues Realgymnasium, Munich; Munich Univ. Asst, Munich Univ., 1931-33; Research Scholar, Birmingham Univ., 1933-37; Asst Lecturer, University College, Exeter, 1937-38; Senior Lecturer, Glasgow Univ., 1938-52; Mason Prof. of Zoology and Comparative Physiology, Birmingham Univ., 1952-74. President: Assoc. for the Study of Animal Behaviour, 1961-64; Section D, British Assoc., 1962; Institute of Biology, 1965-67; Member Council, Royal Society, 1968-69. *Publications:* Revision of 6th edn of A Textbook of Zoology (Parker and Haswell), Vol. I; The Senses, 1966; papers in various learned journals on Electrophysiology and Ultrastructure of Sense Organs, esp. inner ear of vertebrates. *Recreations:* music, golf, painting. *Address:* 22 Estria Road, Birmingham B15 2LQ. *T:* 021-440 2526.

LOWNIE, Ralph Hamilton; a Metropolitan Stipendiary Magistrate, since 1974; *b* 27 Sept. 1924; *yr s* of James H. W. Lownie and Jesse H. Aitken; *m* 1960, Claudine Therese, *o d* of Pierre Lecrocq, Reims; one *s* one *d. Educ:*

George Watson's Coll.; Edinburgh Univ. (MA,LLB). Royal Engineers, 1943-47, NW Europe. WS 1952; Mem. Faculty of Advocates 1959; called to Bar, Inner Temple, 1962. Judicial Dept, Kenya, 1954-63; Min. of Legal Affairs, Kenya, 1963-65; Admin of Justice Dept, Bermuda, 1965-72. *Recreations:* hill-walking, military heraldry. *Address:* Camberwell Magistrates Court, SE5. *Club:* Nairobi (Kenya).

LOWREY, Air Comdt Dame Alice, DBE 1960; RRC 1954; Matron-in-Chief, Princess Mary's Royal Air Force Nursing Service, 1959-63 (retired); *b* 8 April 1905; *d* of William John Lowrey and Agnes Lowrey (formerly Walters). *Educ:* Yorkshire; Training Sch., Sheffield Royal Hospital. Joined PMRAFNS, 1932; served in Iraq and Aden. Principal Matron: HQ, MEAF and FEAF, 1956-58; HQ, Home Command and Technical Training Command, 1958-59. Air Commandant, 1959. Officer Sister Order of St John, 1959. *Address:* Flat 4, The Homestead, South Green, Southwold, E Suffolk; c/o Midland Bank, St Nicholas Street, Scarborough, N Yorkshire YO11 2HN.

LOWRY, family name of **Baron Lowry.**

LOWRY, Baron *cr* 1979 (Life Peer), of Crossgar in the County of Down; **Robert Lynd Erskine Lowry;** PC 1974; PC (NI) 1971; Kt 1971; Lord Chief Justice of Northern Ireland, since 1971; *b* 30 Jan. 1919; *o s* of late William Lowry (Rt Hon. Mr Justice Lowry) and Catherine Hughes Lowry, 3rd *d* of Rev. R. J. Lynd, DD; *m* 1945, Mary Audrey, *o d* of John Martin, 43 Myrtlefield Park, Belfast; three *d*. *Educ:* Royal Belfast Academical Institution; Jesus Coll., Cambridge (Hon. Fellow 1977). Entrance Exhibn. (Classics); Scholar, 1939; 1st Class Classical Tripos, Part I, 1939, Part II 1940; MA 1944. Served HM Forces, 1940-46; Tunisia, 1942-43 with 38 Irish Inf. Bde; commissioned Royal Irish Fusiliers, 1941; Major, 1945; Hon. Colonel: 7th Bn Royal Irish Fusiliers, 1969-71 (5th Bn, 1967-68); 5th Bn Royal Irish Rangers, 1971-76. Called to the Bar of N Ireland, 1947; Bencher of the Inn of Court, 1955-; Hon. Bencher, Middle Temple, 1973; Hon. Bencher, King's Inns, Dublin, 1973; QC (N Ireland), 1956. Counsel to HM Attorney-General, 1948-56; Judge of the High Court of Justice (NI), 1964-71. Member Departmental Cttees on Charities, Legal Aid and Registration of Title; Dep. Chm., Boundaries Commn (NI) 1964-71; Chairman: Interim Boundary Commn (NI Constituencies), 1967; Permanent Boundary Commn, 1969-71; Dep. Chm., Lord Chancellor's Cttee on NI Supreme Court; Member, Jt Law Enforcement Commn, 1974; Chairman: N Ireland Constitutional Convention, 1975; Council of Legal Educn (NI), 1976-79. Governor, Royal Belfast Academical Instn, 1956-71, Chm., Richmond Lodge Sch., 1956-77; Chm. Governing Bodies Assoc. (NI), 1965. Hon. LLD QUB, 1980; Hon. DLitt NUU, 1981. *Recreations:* golf (Pres., Royal Portrush GC, 1974-); showjumping (Chm., SJAI Exec., 1970-72; Mem. Nat. Equestrian Fedn, 1969-78; Internat. Showjumping Judge, 1973-). *Address:* White Hill, Crossgar, Co. Down. *T:* Crossgar 830397. *Clubs:* Army and Navy, MCC; Royal and Ancient (St Andrews).

LOWRY, Hugh Avant, CB 1974; retired 1974; Comptroller and Auditor-General for Northern Ireland, 1971-74; *b* 23 May 1913; *s* of late Hugh George Lowry, HM Inspector of Taxes, and late Ellen Louisa Lowry (*née* Avant); *m* 1939, Marjorie Phyllis Mary (*née* Hale); two *d*. *Educ:* Watford Grammar Sch.; Gonville and Caius Coll., Cambridge. 1st Cl. Hons, both parts, Classical Tripos, 1932-35; MA; Apptd Asst Principal, Ministry of Labour for Northern Ireland, 1936. Served War, as Observer in Fleet Air Arm, RNVR, 1943-46. Served in various Ministries of Govt of N Ireland in various grades. Sec. to Nat. Assistance Bd for N Ireland, 1956-57; Second Sec. and Dir of Establishments, Min. of Finance for Northern Ireland, July 1970-June 1971. *Recreations:* bridge, bowls, watching games he used to play-Rugby football, cricket, tennis. *Address:* Woodridings, 7A Greenway Park, Chippenham, Wilts. *T:* Chippenham 3260. *Club:* Civil Service.

LOWRY, John Patrick, (Pat Lowry), CBE 1978; Chairman, Advisory, Conciliation and Arbitration Service, since 1981; *b* 31 March 1920; *s* of John McArdle and Edith Mary Lowry; *m* 1952, Sheilagh Mary Davies; one *s* one *d*. *Educ:* Wyggeston Grammar Sch., Leicester; London Sch. of Economics (evening student). BCom London; FIPM, CBIM. Statistical Clerk, Engineering Employers' Fedn, 1938; served Army, 1939-46; various posts in EEF, 1946-70, Dir 1965-70; Dir of Industrial Relations, British Leyland Motor Corp., 1970, Board Dir 1972; Dir of Personnel, 1975-77, of Personnel and Admin, British Leyland Ltd, 1977-78, of Personnel and External Affairs, 1978-81. Member: UK Employers' Delegn, ILO, 1962, 1963, 1967; Court of Inquiry, Barbican and Horseferry Road Building Disputes, 1967; Court of Inquiry, Grunwick Dispute, 1977. Pres., Inst. of Supervisory Management, 1972-74. *Recreations:* theatre, gardening, fishing. *Address:* Ashfield, Snowdenham Links Road, Bramley, Guildford, Surrey. *T:* Guildford 893289.

LOWRY, Mrs Noreen Margaret, (Nina); Her Honour Judge Lowry; a Circuit Judge, since 1976; *b* 6 Sept. 1925; *er d* of late John Collins, MC, and of Hilda Collins, Ham, Richmond, Surrey; *m* 1st, 1950, Edward Lucas Gardner, QC (marr. diss., 1962); one *s* one *d*; 2nd, 1963, Richard John Lowry, *qv*; one *d*. *Educ:* Bedford High Sch.; Birmingham Univ. LLB Birmingham, 1947. Called to the Bar, Gray's Inn, 1948. Criminal practice on S Eastern Circuit, Central Criminal Court, Inner London Sessions, etc., practising as Miss Nina Collins; Metropolitan Stipendiary Magistrate, 1967-76. Mem.

Criminal Law Revision Cttee, 1975-. *Recreations:* theatre, travel. *Address:* 3 Temple Gardens, EC4. *T:* 01-353 1662.

LOWRY, Pat; *see* Lowry, J. P.

LOWRY, Richard John, QC 1968; **His Honour Judge Richard Lowry;** a Circuit Judge, since 1977; *b* 23 June 1924; *s* of late Geoffrey Charles Lowry, OBE, TD, and late Margaret Spencer Lowry; *m* 1963, Noreen Margaret Lowry, *qv*; one *d*. *Educ:* St Edward's Sch.; University College, Oxford. RAF, 1943; qualified as pilot and commnd, 1944; No 228 Group Staff Officer, India, 1945; Flt-Lieut, 1946. University College, Oxford, 1942-43 and 1946-48; BA, 1948, MA 1949. Called to Bar, Inner Temple, 1949; Bencher 1977; Member, General Council of Bar, 1965-69. Dep. Chm., Herts QS, 1968; a Recorder, 1972-77. Mem., Home Office Adv. Council on Penal System, 1972-78. *Recreations:* theatre, swimming, fossicking; formerly rowing (Oxford Univ. wartime VIII, 1943). *Address:* Central Criminal Court, EC4M 7EH. *Clubs:* Garrick; Leander (Henley-on-Thames).

LOWRY-CORRY, family name of **Earl of Belmore.**

LOWSON, Sir Ian (Patrick), 2nd Bt *cr* 1951; *b* 4 Sept. 1944; *s* of Sir Denys Colquhoun Flowerdew Lowson, 1st Bt and of Patricia, OStJ, *yr d* of 1st Baron Strathcarron, PC, KC; *S* father, 1975; *m* 1979, Mrs Tanya Du Boulay, *d* of R. F. A. Joynson; one *s*. *Educ:* Eton; Duke Univ., USA. OStJ. *Heir: s* Henry William Lowson, *b* 10 Nov. 1980. *Address:* 23 Flood Street, SW3 5ST. *Clubs:* Boodle's, Pilgrims; Brook (NY).

LOWTHER, family name of **Earl of Lonsdale** and **Viscount Ullswater.**

LOWTHER, Viscount; Hugh Clayton Lowther, *b* 27 May 1949; *s* and *heir* of 7th Earl of Lonsdale, *qv*, and of Tuppina Cecily, *d* of late Captain G. H. Bennet; *m* 1971, Pamela Middleton.

LOWTHER, Major Sir Charles (Douglas), 6th Bt *cr* 1824; Queen's Royal Irish Hussars; *b* 22 Jan. 1946; *s* of Lt-Col Sir William Guy Lowther, 5th Bt, OBE, and of Grania Suzanne, *d* of late Major A. J. H. Douglas Campbell, OBE; *S* father, 1982; *m* 1975, Florence Rose, *y d* of Colonel Alexander James Henry Cramsie, O'Harabrook, Ballymoney, Co. Antrim; one *s* one *d*. *Educ:* Winchester College. Commissioned, Queen's Royal Irish Hussars, 1966; Regimental Duty UK and BAOR, including ADC to Chief of Defence Staff, 1974-76; Army Staff College, Camberley, 1978-79; Staff appointment, 1981. *Recreations:* polo, shooting, travel. *Heir: s* Patrick William Lowther, *b* 15 July 1977. *Address:* National Westminster Bank Ltd, 31 Lord Street, Wrexham, Clwyd L11 1LS. *Club:* Cavalry and Guards.

LOWTHIAN, George Henry, CBE 1963 (MBE 1949); General Secretary, Amalgamated Union of Building Trade Workers, 1951-73, retired; Part-time Member, British Transport Docks Board, 1963-77; *b* 30 Jan. 1908; *s* of Ernest and Margaret Lowthian; *m* 1933, Florence Hartley; one *s* one *d*. *Educ:* Creighton Sch., Carlisle. Branch Secretary, 1930-45; District Secretary, 1934-45; Exec. Council, 1940-45; Divisional Secretary, 1945-50; TUC General Council, 1951-73, Chairman, 1963-64; Chairman, Industrial Training Council, 1960-62; Chairman, Board of Directors, Industrial Training Service, 1965-. Mem., Workmen's Compensation and Pneumoconiosis, Byssinosis and Miscellaneous Diseases Benefit Bds, 1975-78. *Recreations:* photography, motoring. *Address:* 17 Holly Way, Mitcham, Surrey. *T:* 01-764 2200.

LOY, Francis David Lindley; Stipendiary Magistrate at Leeds since 1974; *b* 7 Oct. 1927; *s* of late Archibald Loy and late Sarah Eleanor Loy; *m* 1954, Brenda Elizabeth Walker; three *d*. *Educ:* Repton Sch.; Corpus Christi Coll., Cambridge. BA Hons (Law) 1950. Royal Navy, 1946-48. Called to the Bar, Middle Temple, 1952; practised North-Eastern Circuit, 1952-72; Recorder (Northern Circuit), 1972; Stipendiary Magistrate of Leeds, 1972-74. Hon. Sec., Soc. of Provincial Stipendiary Magistrates. *Recreations:* reading, English History, walking, wine making. *Address:* 4 Wedgewood Drive, Roundhay, Leeds LS8 1EF; The Red House, The Turning, Sheringham, Norfolk. *T:* Sheringham 822356. *Club:* Leeds (Leeds).

LOYD, Christopher Lewis, MC 1943; Landowner; *b* 1 June 1923; 3rd and *o surv. s* of late Arthur Thomas Loyd, OBE, JP, Lockinge, Wantage, Berks, and Dorothy, *d* of late Paul Ferdinand Willert, Headington, Oxford; *m* 1957, Joanna, *d* of Captain Arthur Turberville Smith-Bingham; Milburn Manor, Malmesbury, Wilts; two *s* one *d*. *Educ:* Eton; King's Coll., Cambridge (MA). Served 1942-46, with Coldstream Guards, Captain. ARICS 1952, FRICS 1955. Mem., Jockey Club. Trustee, Wallace Collection, 1973-. JP 1950, DL 1954, Oxfordshire (formerly Berks); High Sheriff of Berkshire, 1961. *Address:* Lockinge, Wantage, Oxfordshire OX12 8QL. *T:* East Hendred 265. *Clubs:* Boodle's, Buck's.

LOYD, Sir Francis Alfred, KCMG 1965 (CMG 1961); OBE 1954 (MBE 1951); *b* 5 Sept. 1916; *s* of Major A. W. K. Loyd, Royal Sussex Regt; *m* 1946, Katharine Layzell Layzell (*d* 1981); two *d*. *Educ:* Eton; Trinity Coll., Oxford (MA). District Officer, Kenya, 1939; Mil. Service, E Africa, 1940-42; Private Secretary to Governor of Kenya, 1942-45; HM Consul, Mega, Ethiopia, 1945; District Comdr, Kenya, 1947-55; Commonwealth Fund Fellowship to USA, 1953-54; Provincial Commissioner, 1956; Permanent Secretary, Governor's Office, 1962-63; HM Commissioner for Swaziland, 1964-68. Dir, London House for Overseas Graduates, 1969-79; Chm., Oxfam Africa Cttee, 1979-.

Recreations: golf, gardening. *Address:* 53 Park Road, Aldeburgh, Suffolk. *T:* Aldeburgh 2478. *Club:* Vincent's (Oxford).

LOYD, John Anthony Thomas, QC 1981; *b* 18 July 1933; *e s* of Leslie William Loyd and Joan Louisa Loyd; *m* 1963, Rosaleen Iona Ward; two *d*. *Educ:* Wycliffe Coll.; Gonville and Caius Coll., Cambridge (BA 1956, MA 1959). RAF Regt, 1951-53. Called to the Bar, Gray's Inn, 1958. *Recreations:* viticulture, sailing. *Address:* 603 Seddon House, Barbican, EC2; Segos, Le Boulvé, Lot, France.

LOYD, Julian St John, CVO 1979; FRICS; Land Agent to the Queen, Sandringham Estate, since 1964; *b* 25 May 1926; *s* of General Sir Charles Loyd, GCVO, KCB, DSO, MC and Lady Moyra Loyd; *m* 1964, Mary Emma, *d* of Sir Christopher Steel, GCMG, MVO and Lady Steel; one *s* two *d*. *Educ:* Eton Coll.; Magdalene Coll., Cambridge (MA). FRICS 1955. Partner in Savills, Norwich, 1955-64. *Recreation:* fishing. *Address:* Laycocks, Sandringham, King's Lynn P35 6EB. *Club:* Army and Navy.

LOYDEN, Edward; *b* 3 May 1923; *s* of Patrick and Mary Loyden; *m* 1944, Rose Ann; one *s* two *d* (and one *d* decd). *Educ:* Friary RC Elem. School. Shop boy, margarine factory, 1937; Able-Seaman, MN, 1938-46; Seaman Port Worker, Mersey Docks & Harbour Co., 1946-74. Member: Liverpool City Council, 1960; Liverpool District Council, 1973; Merseyside Met. CC, 1973; Liverpool Met. Dist Council (St Mary's Ward), 1980-. MP (Lab) Liverpool, Garston, Feb. 1974-1979. Shop Steward, TGWU, 1954, Branch Chm. 1959; Mem. District Cttee, Docks and Waterways, 1967; Mem. Nat. Cttee, TGWU, 1968; Pres., Liverpool Trades Council, 1967; Pres., Merseyside Trades Council, 1974. *Recreations:* full-time political. *Address:* 456 Queens Drive, Liverpool L4 8UA. *T:* 051-226 4478. *Clubs:* Gillmoss Labour, Woolton Labour.

LOYN, Prof. Henry Royston, DLitt; FSA, FRHistS; FBA 1979; Professor of History, since 1977, Vice-Principal, since 1980, Westfield College, University of London; *b* 16 June 1922; *s* of late Henry George Loyn and Violet Monica Loyn; *m* 1950, Patricia Beatrice, *d* of late R. S. Haskew; three *s*. *Educ:* Cardiff High Sch.; University Coll., Cardiff (MA 1949, DLitt 1968). FRHistS 1958; FSA 1968. Dept of History, University Coll., Cardiff: Asst Lectr, 1946; Lectr, 1949; Sen. Lectr, 1961; Reader, 1966; Prof. of Medieval Hist., 1969-77; Dean of Students, 1968-70 and 1975-76. President: Historical Assoc., 1976-79; Glam Hist. Soc., 1975-77; Cardiff Naturalists' Soc., 1975-76. Vice-Pres., Soc. for Medieval Archaeol., 1971-74. Mem., Ancient Monuments Commn for England, 1982-. *Publications:* Anglo-Saxon England and the Norman Conquest, 1962; Norman Conquest, 1965; Norman Britain, 1966; Alfred The Great, 1967; A Wulfstan MS, Cotton, Nero Ai, 1971; (ed with H. Hearder) British Government and Administration, 1974; (with J. Percival) The Reign of Charlemagne, 1975; The Vikings in Britain, 1977; (with Alan and Richard Sorrell) Medieval Britain, 1977; contribs to Eng. Hist. Rev., History, Antiquaries Jl, and Med. Archaeol. *Recreations:* natural history, gardening. *Address:* Westfield College, Kidderpore Avenue, NW3. *Club:* Athenæum.

LU, Dr Gwei-Djen; Associate Director, East Asian History of Science Library, Cambridge, since 1976; Fellow of Robinson College, Cambridge, 1979-80, Emeritus Fellow, since 1980; *b* 1 Sept. 1904; *d* of Mou-T'ing Lu and Hsiu-Ying Lu. *Educ:* Ming-Tê Sch., Nanking; Ginling Coll., Nanking (BA). PhD Cambridge. Trained as clin. pathologist, Peking Union Med. Coll.; Lectr in Physiology and Biochemistry, St John's Univ., Shanghai; Res. Fellow, Lester Inst. of Med. Research, Shanghai (nutritional biochemistry); research, Cambridge Biochemical Lab., 1937-39, followed by research at Univ. of Calif, Berkeley, Birmingham City Hosp., Alabama, and at Coll. of Physicians and Surgeons, Columbia Univ., NY; staff mem., Sino-British Science Co-operation Office, HM Embassy, Chungking, later Nanking; Prof. of Nutritional Science, Ginling Coll., Nanking, 1947; staff mem., Secretariat, UNESCO, Paris (i/c Nat. Sci. Div., Field Science Co-operation Offices); working with Dr Joseph Needham on Science and Civilisation in China proj., Cambridge, 1957-. *Publications:* Epicure in China, 1942; (with Dr J. Needham and others) Clerks and Craftsmen in China and the West, 1970; (with Dr J. Needham and others) Science and Civilisation in China, 1971-: Vol. 4, pt 3; Vol. 5, pts 2, 3, 4 and 5; Vol. 6, pts 1, 2 and 3; (with Dr J. Needham) Celestial Lancets: a history and rationale of acupuncture and moxa, 1980; papers in biochem. and historical jls. *Recreation:* reading, esp. history, economics, politics and sociology. *Address:* 28 Owlstone Road, Cambridge CB3 9JH. *T:* (home) Cambridge 356642, (office) 311545.

LUARD, (David) Evan (Trant); Fellow of St Antony's College, Oxford, since 1957; *b* 31 Oct. 1926; *s* of Colonel T. B. Luard, DSO, RM, Blackheath. *Educ:* Felsted; King's Coll., Cambridge (Maj. Schol.). Factory worker, 1949-50; HM Foreign Service, 1950-56; served in Hong Kong, Peking, London; resigned, 1956. Oxford City Councillor, 1958-61. Delegate, UN General Assembly, 1967-68. MP (Lab) Oxford, 1966-70 and Oct. 1974-1979; Parly Under-Sec. of State, FCO, 1969-70, 1976-79; now works for OXFAM. *Publications:* (part author) The Economic Development of Communist China, 1959 (2nd edn 1961); (part author) Britain and China, 1962; Nationality and Wealth, 1964; (ed) The Cold War, 1965; (ed) First Steps to Disarmament, 1966; (ed) The Evolution of International Organisations, 1967; Conflict and Peace in the Modern International System, 1968; (ed) The International Regulation of Frontier Disputes, 1970; (ed) The International Regulations of Civil Wars, 1972; The Control of the Sea-bed, 1974; Types of International Society, 1976; International Agencies, the Emerging Framework of Interdependence, 1977; The United Nations, 1978; Socialism

without the State, 1979; A History of the United Nations, vol I, 1982; articles in International Affairs, The China Quarterly, World Politics, World Today, The Annals. *Recreations:* music, painting. *Address:* St Antony's College, Oxford. *T:* 59651.

LUARD, Evan; *see* Luard, D. E. T.

LUBBOCK, family name of **Baron Avebury.**

LUBBOCK, Sir Alan, Kt 1963; MA, FSA; *b* 13 Jan. 1897; 6th *s* of Frederic Lubbock, Ide Hill, Kent; *m* 1918, Helen Mary, *d* of late John Bonham-Carter, Adhurst St Mary, Petersfield; two *s*. *Educ:* Eton; King's Coll., Cambridge. Served in Royal Artillery, 1915-19 and 1939-45. Fellow of King's, 1922-28. Hants County Council, 1932-74 (Alderman 1939, Vice-Chairman 1948, Chairman 1955-67); JP (Hants) 1935; DL; High Sheriff of Hants, 1949-; Member: National Parks Commission, 1954-61; Royal Commission on Common Land, 1955; War Works Commission, 1959-64. Chairman: Council, Southampton Univ., 1957-69 (Pro-Chancellor, 1967); County Councils Assoc., 1965-69 (Vice-Chairman 1963); Nat. Foundn for Educnl Research, 1967-73. Hon. LLD Southampton, 1969. *Publication:* The Character of John Dryden, 1925. *Address:* Adhurst St Mary, Petersfield, Hants. *T:* Petersfield 3043. *Clubs:* United Oxford & Cambridge University; Leander.

LUBBOCK, Christopher William Stuart; a Master of the Supreme Court (Queen's Bench Division), since 1970; *b* 4 Jan. 1920; 2nd *s* of late Captain Rupert Egerton Lubbock, Royal Navy; *m* 1947, Hazel Gordon, *d* of late Gordon Chapman; one *s* one *d*. *Educ:* Charterhouse; Brasenose Coll., Oxford. Served 1939-46, RNVR. Called to Bar, Inner Temple, 1947. *Recreation:* chatting to music publishers. *Address:* Great Horkesley, Essex. *Club:* Pratt's.

LUBBOCK, Roy; *b* 1 Oct. 1892; *s* of Frederic Lubbock and Catherine Gurney; *m* 1919, Yvonne Vernham; two *s*. *Educ:* Eton (Scholar); King's Coll., Cambridge (Exhibitioner, scholar); Fellow of Peterhouse, Cambridge and University Lecturer in Engineering, 1919-60; Bursar of Peterhouse, 1929-31 and 1940-45, Tutor, 1934-40. *Address:* Riding Oaks, Hildenborough, Tonbridge, Kent.

LUCAN, 7th Earl of, *cr* 1795; **Richard John Bingham;** Bt 1632; Baron Lucan, 1776; Baron Bingham (UK), 1934; *b* 18 Dec. 1934; *e s* of 6th Earl of Lucan, MC; *S* father, 1964; *m* 1963, Veronica, *d* of late Major C. M. Duncan, MC, and of Mrs J. D. Margrie; one *s* two *d*. *Educ:* Eton. Lieut (Res. of Officers) Coldstream Guards. Heir: *s* Lord Bingham, *qv*.

LUCAS, family name of **Baron Lucas of Chilworth.**

LUCAS; *see* Keith-Lucas.

LUCAS OF CHILWORTH, 2nd Baron *cr* 1946, of Chilworth; **Michael William George Lucas;** *b* 26 April 1926; *er s* of 1st Baron and Sonia (*d* 1979), *d* of Marcus Finkelstein, Libau, Latvia; *S* father, 1967; *m* 1955, Ann-Marie, *o d* of Ronald Buck, Southampton; two *s* one *d*. *Educ:* Peter Symond's Sch., Winchester. Served with Royal Tank Regt. TEng(CEI); FIMI (Mem. Council, 1972-76); FInstTA; President: Inst. HGV Instrs, 1972-78; League of Safe Drivers, 1976-80; Inst. of Transport Administration, 1980-; Vice-Pres., RoSPA, 1980; Mem., N Atlantic Assembly, 1981-. Heir: *s* Lieut Hon. Simon William Lucas, RE, *b* 6 Feb. 1957. *Address:* Constables, Knapp, Hants.
See also Hon. I. T. M. Lucas.

LUCAS OF CRUDWELL, Baroness (10th in line) *cr* 1663 **AND DINGWALL,** Lady (7th in line) *cr* 1609; **Anne Rosemary Palmer;** *b* 28 April 1919; *er d* of Group Captain Howard Lister Cooper, AFC, and Baroness Lucas and Dingwall; *S* mother, 1958; is a *co-heir* to Barony of Butler; *m* 1950, Major the Hon. Robert Jocelyn Palmer, MC, JP, late Coldstream Guards, 3rd and *e* surv. *s* of 3rd Earl of Selborne, PC, CH; two *s* one *d*. Heir: *er s* Hon. Ralph Matthew Palmer [*b* 7 June 1951; *m* 1978, Clarissa Marie, *d* of George Vivian Lockett, TD]. *Address:* The Old House, Wonston, Winchester, Hampshire.

LUCAS, (Charles) Vivian; Chief Executive, Devon County Council, 1974-79; solicitor; *b* 31 May 1914; *s* of Frank and Mary Renshaw Lucas, Malvern, Worcs; *m* 1941, Oonah Holderness; two *s* two *d*. *Educ:* Malvern Coll.; abroad; London Univ. (LLB). Clerk, Devon County Council, 1972-74; Clerk to the Lieutenancy of Devon, 1972-79. *Recreations:* sport, bridge. *Address:* Highfield Lodge, 7 Salterton Road, Exmouth EX8 2BR. *Club:* Golf and Country (Exeter).

LUCAS, Christopher Charles; Under Secretary, Community and International Policy Division, Department of Energy, 1977-80, retired; *b* 5 June 1920; *s* of Charles Edwin Lucas and Mabel Beatrice Read; *m* 1945, Beryl June Vincent; two *d*. *Educ:* Devonport High Sch.; Balliol Coll., Oxford (Newman Exhibnr). Min. of Fuel, 1946; Central Econ. Planning Staff, 1948; HM Treasury, 1950-70; Cabinet Office, 1970-72; Sec., NEDC, 1973-76; Under-Sec., Dept of Energy, 1976-. *Recreation:* riding. *Address:* Orchard Croft, Withycombe, near Minehead, Somerset. *T:* Dunster 551.

LUCAS, Colin Anderson, OBE 1972; BA Cantab; FRIBA; Architect; *b* London, 1906; 2nd *s* of late Ralph Lucas, Engineer, and late Mary Anderson Juler; *m* 1930, Dione Narona Margaris (marr. diss.), *d* of Henry Wilson; two *s*; *m* 1952, Pamela Margaret, *e d* of late Sir Gerald Campbell, GCMG; *Educ:* Cheltenham Coll.; Trinity Coll., Cambridge; Cambridge Univ. Sch. of Architecture. In practice in London, 1928–; Founder Mem. of Mars (Modern Architectural Research Group). *Publications:* works published in England, America and Continent. *Recreations:* sailing, ski-ing, travel. *Address:* 2 Queen's Grove Studios, Queen's Grove, NW8 6EP.

LUCAS, Sir Cyril (Edward), Kt 1976; CMG 1956; FRS 1966; Director of Fisheries Research, Scotland (Department of Agriculture and Fisheries for Scotland) and Director Marine Laboratory Aberdeen, 1948–70; *b* Hull, Yorks, 30 July 1909; *o s* of late Archibald and Edith Lucas, Hull; *m* 1934, Sarah Agnes (*d* 1974), *o d* of late Henry Alfred and Amy Rose; two *s* one *d*. *Educ:* Grammar Sch., Hull; University Coll., Hull. BSc (London) 1931, DSc (London) 1942. FRSE 1939; Vice-Pres., 1962–64; Neill Prize, 1960. Research Biologist, University Coll., Hull, 1931; Head of Dept of Oceanography, University Coll., Hull, 1942. UK Expert or Delegate to various internat. confs on Marine Fisheries and Conservation, 1948–, and Chm. of research cttees in connexion with these; Chm., Consultative and Liaison Cttees, Internat. Council for Exploration of Sea, 1962–67; Member: Adv. Cttee on Marine Resources Research, FAO, 1964–71 (Chm. 1966–71); Council for Scientific Policy, 1968–70; Nat. Environmental Res. Council, 1970–78. Hon. DSc Hull, 1975; Hon. LLD Aberdeen, 1977. *Publications:* various scientific, particularly on marine plankton and fisheries research in Bulletins of Marine Ecology (Joint Editor), Jl of Marine Biological Assoc., etc and various international jls. *Address:* 16 Albert Terrace, Aberdeen AB1 1XY. *T:* Aberdeen 25568.

LUCAS, Donald William; Fellow of King's College, Cambridge, 1929, and Director of Studies in Classics, 1935–65; University Lecturer in Classics, 1933–69; P. M. Laurence Reader in Classics, 1952–69; *b* 12 May 1905; *s* of Frank William Lucas and Ada Ruth Blackmur; *m* 1933, Mary Irene Cohen; one *s* one *d*. *Educ:* Colfe's Gram. Sch.; Rugby; King's Coll., Cambridge. War of 1939–45: FO, 1940–44. *Publications:* The Greek Tragic Poets, 1950; Aristotle Poetics, 1968; *translations* (from Euripides): Bacchae, 1930; Medea, 1949; Ion, 1949; Alcestis, 1951; Electra, 1951; Joint Editor, Classical Quarterly, 1953–59; articles and reviews in classical journals and Encyclopædia Britannica. *Recreations:* travel and reading. *Address:* 39 Bridle Way, Grantchester, Cambs. *T:* Cambridge 841108; Pwllymarch, Llanbedr, Gwynedd. *T:* Llanbedr 208.

LUCAS, Maj.-Gen. Geoffrey, CB 1957; CBE 1944; *b* 19 Oct. 1904; *s* of Henry Lucas, Mossley Hill, Liverpool; *m* 1927, Mabel Ellen, *d* of Dr George Henry Heald, Leeds; one *s* one *d*. *Educ:* Liverpool Institute; RMC, Sandhurst. Commissioned, 1925, in Royal Tank Corps; Staff Coll., Camberley, 1938; served War of 1939–45 in Italy and Greece; DQMG, BAOR, 1947–50; Dep. Dir Personnel Admin, War Office, 1950–53; Dep. Fortress Comd, Gibraltar, 1953–56; Chief Administrative Officer, Suez Operations, 1956; Maj.-Gen. i/c Admin, FARELF, 1957; retired, Hon. Maj.-Gen., 1958. *Address:* Newbold House, Linkway, Camberley, Surrey. *T:* Camberley 65544.

LUCAS, Ian Albert McKenzie, CBE 1977; Principal of Wye College, University of London, since 1977; *b* 10 July 1926; *s* of Percy John Lucas and Janie Inglis (*née* Hamilton); *m* 1950, Helen Louise Langerman; one *s* two *d*. *Educ:* Clayesmore Sch.; Reading Univ.; McGill Univ. BSc, MSc; FIBiol; FRAgS. Lectr, Harper Adams Agricl Coll., 1949–50; pig nutrition res., Rowett Res. Inst., Aberdeen, 1950–57 and 1958–61; Res. Fellow, Ruakura Res. Station, New Zealand, 1957–58; Prof. of Agriculture, UCNW, Bangor, 1961–77. *Publications:* scientific papers in Jl Agricl Science, Animal Production, Brit. Jl Nutrition and others. *Recreation:* sailing. *Address:* Court Lodge, Brook, Ashford, Kent TN25 5PF. *T:* Wye 812341. *Club:* Farmers'.

LUCAS, Hon. Ivor Thomas Mark, CMG 1980; HM Diplomatic Service; Ambassador to Syria, since 1981; *b* 25 July 1927; 2nd *s* of George William Lucas, 1st Baron Lucas of Chilworth, and Sonia Lucas (*née* Finkelstein); *m* 1954, Christine Mallorie Coleman; three *s*. *Educ:* St Edward's Sch., Oxford; Trinity Coll., Oxford (MA). Served in Royal Artillery, 1945–48 (Captain). BA Oxon 1951. Entered Diplomatic Service, 1951; Middle East Centre for Arabic Studies, Lebanon, 1952; 3rd, later 2nd Sec., Bahrain, Sharjah and Dubai, 1952–56; FO, 1956–59; 1st Sec., Karachi, 1959–62; 1st Sec. and Head of Chancery, Tripoli, 1962–66; FO, 1966–68; Counsellor, Aden, 1968–69 (Chargé d'Affaires, Aug. 1968–Feb. 1969); Dep. High Comr, Kaduna, Nigeria, 1969–71; Counsellor, Copenhagen, 1972–75; Head of Middle East Dept, FCO, 1975–79; Ambassador to Oman, 1979–81. *Recreations:* music, cricket, tennis. *Address:* c/o Foreign and Commonwealth Office, SW1. *Club:* Royal Commonwealth Society.

LUCAS, Ven. John Michael; Archdeacon of Totnes, 1976–81, now Archdeacon Emeritus; Vicar of Chudleigh Knighton, since 1976; *b* 13 June 1921; *s* of Rev. Stainforth John Chadwick Lucas and Dorothy Wybray Mary Lucas; *m* 1952, Catharina Madeleine Bartlett; three *s* (one *d* decd). *Educ:* Kelly Coll., Tavistock; Lichfield Theological Coll. Deacon 1944, priest 1945, dio. Exeter; Asst Curate: Parish of Wolborough, 1944; Parish of Ashburton, 1950; Rector of Weare Giffard with Landcross and Vicar of Monkleigh, 1952; Vicar of Northam, 1962. *Recreations:* family recreations, garden. *Address:* The Vicarage, Chudleigh Knighton, Newton Abbot, Devon. *T:* Chudleigh 853030.

LUCAS, Keith Stephen; Television Consultant, British Film Institute, since 1979; *b* 28 Aug. 1924; *m* 1969, Rona Stephanie Lucas (*née* Levy); two *s* one *d* (and two step *s*). *Educ:* Royal Coll. of Art (ARCA). London Press Exchange, 1956–64; Prof. of Film and Television, Royal Coll. of Art, 1964–72 (first holder of Chair); Dir, British Film Institute, 1972–78. Member: Nat. Panel for Film Festivals; Council, Children's Film Foundn; Governor: North East London Poly., 1971–72; Canterbury Sch. of Art, 1971–74, later Canterbury Coll. of Art, 1981–; Maidstone Coll. of Art, 1982–; Chm., Canterbury New Theatre Ltd, 1979–; Artistic Dir, Commonwealth Film and TV Festival and supporting arts programme, Cyprus, 1980; Vice-Pres., Centre Internat. de Liaison des Ecoles de Cinéma et de Télévision, 1970–72; Hon. Fellow, Royal Coll. of Art, 1972. *Recreations:* writing, painting. *Address:* 80 Valiant House, Vicarage Crescent, SW11. *T:* 01-228 5289. *Club:* Athenæum.

LUCAS, Percy Belgrave, CBE 1981; DSO 1943 and Bar 1945; DFC 1942; Chairman: GRA Property Trust Ltd, 1965–75 (Managing Director, 1957–65); John Jacobs Golf Consultants Ltd, since 1978; *b* Sandwich Bay, Kent, 2 Sept. 1915; *y s* of late Percy Montagu Lucas, Prince's, Sandwich, form. of Filby House, Filby, Norfolk; *m* 1946, Jill Doreen, *d* of Lt-Col A. M. Addison, Ascot; two *s* (and one *s* decd). *Educ:* Stowe; Pembroke Coll., Cambridge. Editorial Staff, Sunday Express, 1937–40. Joined RAFVR, 1939; Commanded: 249 (Fighter) Sqdn, Battle of Malta, 1942; 616 (Fighter) Sqdn, 1943; Coltishall Wing, Fighter Command, 1943; 613 Sqdn, North-West Europe, 1944–45; Fighter Command, HQ Staff, 1942; Air Defence of Great Britain HQ Staff, 1944; demobilised with rank of Wing Comdr, 1946. Contested (C) West Fulham, 1945; MP (C) Brentford and Chiswick, 1950–59. Capt. Cambridge Univ. Golf team, 1937; Pres. Hawks Club, Cambridge, 1937; English International Golf team, 1936, 1948, 1949 (Capt. 1949); British Walker Cup team, 1936, 1947, 1949 (Capt. 1949). President: Golf Foundation Ltd, 1963–66 (Mem. Council, 1966–); Nat. Golf Clubs Advisory Assoc., 1963–69 (Vice-Pres., 1969–); Assoc. of Golf Club Secretaries, 1968–74 (Vice-Pres., 1974–). Member: General Advisory Council, BBC, 1962–67; Council, National Greyhound Racing Soc. of Great Britain, 1957–72; Policy Cttee, Nat. Greyhound Racing Club Ltd, 1972–77; AAA Cttee of Inquiry, 1967; Exec. Cttee, General Purposes and Finance Cttee; Central Council of Physical Recreation; Management Cttee, Crystal Palace Nat. Sports Centre, 1961–73; Sports Council, 1971– (Chm., Finance Cttee, 1978–82; Chm., Sports Trade Adv. Panel, 1972–); Governor, Stowe Sch., 1964–79. Pres., Old Stoic Soc., 1979–81. Croix de Guerre avec Palmes, 1945. *Publications:* Five-Up (autobiography), 1978; The Sport of Prince's (reflections of a golfer), 1980; Flying Colours: the epic story of Douglas Bader, 1981. *Recreations:* golf, photography. *Address:* 11 Onslow Square, SW7 3NJ. *T:* 01-584 8373. *Clubs:* Naval and Military, Royal Air Force; Sandy Lodge Golf; Walton Heath Golf; Prince's Golf; Royal West Norfolk Golf.

LUCAS, Prof. Raleigh Barclay; Emeritus Professor of Oral Pathology, University of London; Consultant Pathologist, Royal Dental Hospital of London, 1950–79; *b* 3 June 1914; *s* of H. Lucas; *m* 1942, Violet Sorrell; one *d* (one *s* decd). *Educ:* George Watson's Coll.; Univ. of Edinburgh. MB, ChB (Edinburgh) 1937; DPH 1939; MD 1945; MRCP 1946; FRCPath 1963; FRCP 1974; FDS RCS 1974. Asst Bacteriologist, Edinburgh Royal Infirmary, 1939–40; Pathologist, Stoke Mandeville Hosp. and Royal Buckinghamshire Hospital, 1947–49; Reader in Pathology, University of London, 1950–54; Dean, Sch. of Dental Surgery, Royal Dental Hospital of London, 1958–73. Examiner in Pathology and Bacteriology for dental degrees, Univs of London, Glasgow, Birmingham, Sheffield, Liverpool and Wales. Served War of 1939–45, Major RAMC; FRSocMed; Fellow and Past Pres., Royal Medical Society; Mem. Pathological Soc. of Great Britain and Ireland; Mem. BMA. *Publications:* Bacteriology for Students of Dental Surgery (jointly), 1954; Pathology of Tumours of the Oral Tissues, 1964; various articles in medical and scientific journals. *Address:* Department of Pathology, Royal Dental Hospital of London, WC2. *T:* 01-930 8831.

LUCAS, Sir Thomas (Edward), 5th Bt *cr* 1887; MA; FBIM, MIMC; international scientific and technical business consultant; *b* 16 Sept. 1930; *s* of late Ralph John Scott Lucas (killed in action, 1941), and of Dorothy, *d* of late H. T. Timson, Tatchbury Mount, Hants; *S* cousin, 1980; *m* 1958, Charmian (*d* 1970), *d* of Col J. S. Powell; one *s*; *m* 1980, Ann Graham Moore. *Educ:* Wellington College; Trinity Hall, Cambridge. Bristol Cars Ltd, 1948–55; Director: Vacuum Research Ltd, 1959–62; Bourdon Tools Ltd, 1959–62; Board Mem., Vacuum Metallising Processes Inc.; Founded the Engineering Capacity Exchange, London, 1963 (Chairman); Director, Columbia Industrial Developments Ltd, 1969–72; Mem. Management Bd, Utopian Housing Soc. (Group One) Ltd, 1973–. *Publications:* Handbook of Vacuum Physics, Vol. 1, part 2, 1964; articles in scientific and technical jls. *Recreations:* winter sports, sailboarding, property restoration, fine wines. *Heir:* *s* Stephen Ralph James Lucas, *b* 11 Dec. 1963. *Address:* c/o Williams & Glyn's, 22 Whitehall, SW1.

LUCAS, Vivian; see Lucas, C. V.

LUCAS-TOOTH, Sir Hugh; see Munro-Lucas-Tooth.

LUCE, Mrs Henry Robinson, (Clare Boothe); playwright and author since 1933; *d* of William F. and Ann Snyder Boothe; *m* 1st, 1923, George Tuttle Brokaw; 2nd, 1935, Henry Robinson Luce (*d* 1967). *Educ:* St Mary's Sch., Garden City, Long Island; The Castle, Tarrytown, New York. Associate

Editor Vogue, 1930; Associate Editor Vanity Fair, 1931-32; Managing Editor Vanity Fair, 1933-34. Mem. of Congress from 4th District of Connecticut, 1943-47. United States Ambassador to Italy, 1953-57. Mem. Edit. Bd, Encyclopaedia Britannica, 1974-. Holds hon. doctorates. Dame of Magistral Grace, SMO Malta; Kt Gr. Cross, Order of Merit, Italy. *Publications:* Stuffed Shirts, 1933; Europe in the Spring (English Title-European Spring), 1940; (ed) Saints For Now, 1952; *plays:* Abide with Me, 1935; The Women, 1936; Kiss the Boys Goodbye, 1938; Margin for Error, 1939; Child of the Morning, 1952; articles to magazines. *Address:* Honolulu, Hawaii, USA.

LUCE, Richard Napier; MP (C) Shoreham, since 1974 (Arundel and Shoreham, Apr. 1971-1974); *b* 14 Oct. 1936; *s* of late Sir William Luce, GBE, KCMG, and of Margaret, *d* of late Adm. Sir Trevylyan Napier, KCB; *m* 1961, Rose, *d* of Sir Godfrey Nicholson, Bt, *qv*; two *s*. *Educ:* Wellington Coll.; Christ's Coll., Cambridge. 2nd cl. History. Nat. Service officer, 1955-57, served in Cyprus. Overseas Civil Service, served as District Officer, Kenya, 1960-62; Brand Manager, Gallaher Ltd, 1963-65; Marketing Manager, Spirella Co. of GB; Dir, National Innovations Centre, 1968-71; Chairman: IFA Consultants Ltd, 1972-79; Selanex Ltd, 1973-79; Courtenay Stewart International Ltd, 1975-79; Mem. European Adv. Bd, Corning Glass International, 1975-79. Contested (C) Hitchin, 1970. PPS to Minister for Trade and Consumer Affairs, 1972-74; an Opposition Whip, 1974-75; an Opposition spokesman on foreign and commonwealth affairs, 1977-79; Parly Under Sec. of State, 1979-81, Minister of State, 1981-82, FCO. *Recreations:* tennis, walking, reading, etc. *Address:* House of Commons, Westminster, SW1.

LUCET, Charles (Ernest); French Ambassador, retired; *b* Paris, 16 April 1910; *s* of Louis Lucet and Madeleine Lucet (*née* Zoegger); *m* 1931, Jacqueline Bardoux; one *s* one *d*. *Educ:* University of Paris. Degree in law, also degree of Ecole Libre des Sciences Politiques. French Embassy, Washington, 1935-Nov. 1942; then joined Free French movement and was apptd to its mission in Washington; attached to Foreign affairs Commissariat in Algiers, 1943; First Sec., Ankara, 1943-45; Asst Dir for Middle Eastern Affairs, Foreign Affairs Min., Paris, 1945-46; First Counsellor: Beirut, 1946; Cairo, 1949; Dept Head of Cultural Relations Div. of Foreign Affairs Min., Paris, 1950-53; rank of Minister Plenipotentiary, 1952; Mem. French Delegn to UN, serving as Dep. Permanent Rep. to UN and to Security Council, 1953-55; Minister Counsellor, French Embassy, Washington, 1955-59; Dir of Political Affairs, Foreign Affairs Min., Paris, 1959-65; Ambassador to USA, 1965-72; Ambassador to Italy, 1972-75. Commandeur de la Légion d'Honneur; Commandeur de l'Ordre National du Mérite; holds foreign decorations. *Address:* 9 rue de Thann, 75017 Paris, France. *T:* 622-5676.

LUCEY, Most Rev. Cornelius; *b* Windsor, Co. Cork. *Educ:* Maynooth; Innsbruck. Priest, 1927. Co-Founder and Pres., Christus Rex Soc. for priests; Founder and Superior, La Sociedad de Santo Toribio (missionary and welfare organisation for the barriadas of Peru). Bishop of Cork, 1952-80, and Ross, 1954-80. *Address:* Bishop's House, Farranferris, Cork, Eire.

LUCEY, Rear-Adm. Martin Noel, CB 1973; DSC 1944; RN retired; Director General, National Association of British and Irish Millers, since 1975; *b* 21 Jan. 1920; *s* of A. N. Lucey; *m* 1947, Barbara Mary Key; two *s* one *d*. *Educ:* Gresham's Sch., Holt. Entered RN, 1938. Served War of 1939-45: qualif. in navigation, 1944; "N" 10th Destroyer Sqdn, 1944. Comdr, 1953; Mem. NATO Defence Coll., 1954; Captain, 1961; Captain "F7" HMS Puma, 1964; Cdre, Sen. Naval Officer, West Indies, 1968; Rear-Adm., 1970; Adm. President, RNC Greenwich, 1970-72; Flag Officer, Scotland and NI, 1972-74. *Recreation:* painting. *Address:* Oldways, Houghton, Arundel, West Sussex.

LUCIE-SMITH, Edward; *see* Lucie-Smith, J. E. M.

LUCIE-SMITH, (John) Edward (McKenzie); poet and art critic; *b* Kingston, Jamaica, 27 Feb. 1933; *s* of John Dudley Lucie-Smith and Mary (*née* Lushington); unmarried. *Educ:* King's Sch., Canterbury; Merton Coll., Oxford (MA). Settled in England, 1946. Education Officer, RAF, 1954-56; subseq. worked in advertising and as free-lance journalist and broadcaster. FRSL. *Publications:* A Tropical Childhood and other poems, 1961 (jt winner, John Llewellyn Rhys Mem. Prize; winner, Arts Coun. Triennial Award); (ed, with Philip Hobsbaum) A Group Anthology, 1963; Confessions and Histories, 1964; (with Jack Clemo, George MacBeth) Penguin Modern Poets 6, 1964; (ed) Penguin Book of Elizabethan Verse, 1965; What is a Painting?, 1966; (ed) The Liverpool Scene, 1967; (ed) A Choice of Browning's Verse, 1967; (ed) Penguin Book of Satirical Verse, 1967; Thinking about Art, 1968; Towards Silence, 1968; Movements in Art since 1945, 1969; (ed) British Poetry Since 1945, 1970; (with Patricia White) Art in Britain 69-70, 1970; (ed) A Primer of Experimental Verse, 1971; (ed with S. W. Taylor) French Poetry: the last fifteen years, 1971; A Concise History of French Painting, 1971; Symbolist Art, 1972; Eroticism in Western Art, 1972; The First London Catalogue, 1974; The Well Wishers, 1974; The Burnt Child (autobiog.), 1975; The Invented Eye (early photography), 1975; World of the Makers, 1975; (with Celestine Dars) How the Rich Lived, 1976; Joan of Arc, 1976; (with Celestine Dars) Work and Struggle, 1977; Fantin-Latour, 1977; The Dark Pageant (novel), 1977; Art Today, 1977; A Concise History of Furniture, 1979; Super Realism, 1979; Cultural Calendar of the Twentieth Century, 1979; Art in the Seventies, 1980; The Story of Craft, 1981; The Body, 1981; contribs to Times, Sunday Times, Listener, Spectator, New Statesman, Evening Standard, Encounter, London Magazine, Illustrated London News, etc. *Recreations:* walking the

dog, malice. *Address:* c/o Deborah Rogers Ltd, 5-11 Mortimer Street, W1.

LUCKHOO, Hon. Sir Edward Victor, Kt 1970; QC (Guyana); Order of Roraima, 1979; High Commissioner for Guyana in India, since 1977; *b* Guyana (when Br. Guiana), 24 May 1912; *s* of late E. A. Luckhoo, OBE. *Educ:* New Amsterdam Scots Sch.; Queen's Coll., Guyana; St Catherine's Coll., Oxford (BA). Called to Bar, Middle Temple, 1936; QC Guyana 1965. Began career in magistracy as acting Magistrate, Essequibo District, 1943; Chancellor and President of Court of Appeal, Guyana, 1969-77. *Address:* 17 Lamaha Street, Georgetown, Guyana.

LUCKHOO, Hon. Sir Joseph (Alexander), Kt 1963; President, Bahamas Court of Appeal, since 1982 (Reserve Judge, 1978-81, Judge, 1981-82); Judge, Turks and Caicos Court of Appeal, since 1979; *b* 8 June 1917; *e s* of late Joseph Alexander Luckhoo, KC and Irene Luckhoo; *m* 1964, Leila Patricia Singh; three *s* one *d*. *Educ:* Queen's Coll., British Guiana; University Coll., London; Middle Temple. BSc London, 1939. Barrister, Middle Temple, 1944; practised at Bar, British Guiana. Crown Counsel, British Guiana, 1949; Legal Draftsman, 1953; acted as Solicitor Gen., British Guiana, 1952, 1954 and 1955; Puisne Judge, British Guiana, 1956; Acting Chief Justice, 1959; Chief Justice, 1960-66; Chief Justice Guyana, 1966; Judge, Court of Appeal, Jamaica, 1967-76; Acting Pres., Court of Appeal, Jamaica, 1972, 1973, and 1974-76. Chairman: Judicial Service Commission, 1961-66; Law Reform Cttee, Jamaica, 1973-76. *Publications:* Editor: Law Reports of British Guiana, 1956-58; British Guiana section of West Indian Reports, 1958-61, Jamaica section, 1970-72; Dominion Report Service (Canada), 1977-. *Recreations:* watching cricket and tennis; table tennis. *Address:* 31 Aldenham Crescent, Don Mills, North York, Ontario, Canada. *Club:* Royal Commonwealth Society (West Indian).

LUCKHOO, Sir Lionel (Alfred), KCMG 1969; Kt 1966; CBE 1962; QC (Guyana) 1954; *b* 2 March 1914; 2nd *s* of late Edward Alfred Luckhoo, OBE, Solicitor, and Evelyn Luckhoo; *m* Sheila Chamberlin; two *s* three *d*. *Educ:* Queen's Coll., Georgetown, Brit. Guiana; Middle Temple, London. MLC, 1949-51; Mem. State Coun., 1952-53; Minister without Portfolio, 1954-57; Mem. Georgetown Town Council, 1950-64; Mayor, City of Georgetown, 1954, 1955, 1960, 1964 (Dep. Mayor three times); High Comr in UK, for Guyana, May 1966-70; for Barbados, Nov. 1966-70; Ambassador of Guyana and Barbados, to Paris, Bonn and The Hague, 1967-70. Pres., MPCA Trade Union, Brit. Guiana, 1949-52; Pres. of several Unions; has served on Commns of Enquiry, Public Cttees, Statutory Bodies, Legal Cttees, Drafting Cttees, Disciplinary Cttees, etc. Head of Luckhoo & Luckhoo, Legal Practitioners. Chm., Red Cross Soc., 1978. Pres., Guyana Olympic Assoc., 1974-79. Mem. of the Magic Circle. Listed in the Guinness Book of Records as the world's most successful advocate with 242 successful defences in murder cases. Has travelled more than ½ million miles around the world speaking of Jesus. *Publications:* (jtly) The Fitzluck Theory of Breeding Racehorses, 1960; I Believe, 1968; God is Love, 1975; Life After Death, 1975; The Xmas Story, 1975; Sense of Values, 1975; Dear Atheist, 1977; Dear Boys and Girls, 1978; Dear Adults, 1979; God and Science, 1980; Dear Muslims, 1980. *Recreations:* cricket, horse-racing. *Address:* Lot 1, Croal Street, Georgetown, Guyana. *Club:* Royal Commonwealth Society (West Indian).

See also Hon. Sir E. V. Luckhoo, Hon. Sir Joseph A. Luckhoo.

LUCY, Sir Edmund J. W. H. C. R. F.; *see* Fairfax-Lucy.

LUDDINGTON, Sir Donald (Collin Cumyn), KBE 1976; CMG 1973; CVO 1974; retired; *b* 18 Aug. 1920; *s* of late F. Norman John Luddington, Ceylon Civil Service, and late M. Myrtle Amethyst Payne; *m* 1945, Garry Brodie Johnston; one *s* one *d*. *Educ:* Dover Coll.; St Andrews Univ. (MA). Served War, Army, 1940-46, KOYLI and RAC, Captain. Hong Kong Govt, 1949-73; Sec. for Home Affairs, 1971-73; Governor, Solomon Islands, 1973-76. Chm., Public Services Commn, Hong Kong, 1977-78; Comr, Indep. Commn against Corruption, Hong Kong, 1978-80. *Recreations:* walking, cycling. *Address:* The Firs, Little Lane, Easingwold, York. *Clubs:* Royal Commonwealth Society; Hong Kong (Hong Kong).

LUDER, (Harold) Owen, PRIBA; Chairman and Managing Director, Owen Luder partnership, since 1978; President, Royal Institute of British Architects, 1981-June 1983; Director, The Investment Co., since 1981; *b* London, 7 Aug. 1928; *s* of late Edward Charles and of Ellen Clara Luder; *m* 1951, Rose Dorothy (Doris) Broadstock; four *d* (one *s* decd). *Educ:* Deptford Park Primary Sch.; Peckham Central Sch.; Brixton Sch. of Building; Regent St Polytechnic Sch. of Architecture. ARIBA 1954, FRIBA 1967. Private practice in architecture, 1957-; Founder and Sen. Partner, Owen Luder partnership, 1958-78, when it became an unlimited co. Principal works in commercial and industrial architecture and environmental planning in UK and abroad. Royal Institute of British Architects: Mem. Council, 1967-80; Hon. Treasurer, 1975-78. Pres., Norwood Soc. Occasional radio and TV broadcaster, UK and USA. RIBA Architecture Bronze Medal, 1963; various Civic Trust and architectural awards and commendations. Arkansas Traveller, USA, 1971. *Publications:* contribs on architectural, planning and building matters to various jls. *Recreations:* writing, swimming, playing golf badly, supporting Arsenal FC avidly. *Address:* Woodlawn, 105 Dulwich Village, SE21. *Clubs:* Savage, Royal Automobile.

LUDLOW, Bishop Suffragan of, since 1981; **Rt. Rev. (Stanley) Mark Wood;** Archdeacon of Ludlow, since 1982; *b* 21 May 1919; *s* of Arthur Mark and Jane Wood; *m* 1947, Winifred Ruth, *d* of Edward James Toase; three *s* two *d. Educ:* Pontypridd County School; University College, Cardiff; College of the Resurrection, Mirfield. BA (2nd cl. Greek and Latin), Wales. Curate at St Mary's, Cardiff Docks, 1942-45; Curate, Sophiatown Mission, Johannesburg, 1945-47; Rector of Bloemhof, Transvaal, 1947-50; Priest in charge of St Cyprian's Mission, Johannesburg, 1950-55; Rector of Marandellas, Rhodesia, 1955-65; Dean of Salisbury, Rhodesia, 1965-70; Bishop of Matabeleland, 1971-77; Asst Bishop of Hereford, 1977-81. *Address:* Wistanstow Rectory, Craven Arms, Shropshire SY7 8DG. *T:* Craven Arms 3244.

LUDLOW, Archdeacon of; *see* Ludlow, Bishop Suffragan of.

LUDLOW, (Ernest John) Robin, TD 1979; Director of Directorship Appointments Ltd (Executive Search), since 1982; Vice-President, Boyden Inc., since 1981; Partner, Boyden International Ltd (Executive Search), since 1980; *b* 2 May 1931; *s* of late Donald Ernest Ludlow, Blandford, Dorset, and Buxted, Sussex; *m* 1970, Sonia Louise Hatfeild; one *s* one *d. Educ:* Framlingham Coll., Suffolk; RMA, Sandhurst. Regular Army: RMA Sandhurst, 1949-52; commissioned RASC, 1952; Staff, RMA Sandhurst, 1954-57; retd 1957. TA: Kent and County of London Yeomanry (Sharpshooters), 1959-68; The Queen's Regt, Major, 1971-78. Chm., Sharpshooters Yeomanry Assoc., 1973-; T&AVR: Mem., General Purposes and Finance Cttee, SE, 1973-; Mem., Nat. Recruiting and Publicity Cttee, 1976-. J. Lyons & Co. Ltd (Sales Management), 1957-60; The Economist (Sales Management and Marketing Promotion), 1960-72; Press Sec. to the Queen, 1972-73; Dep. Dir, Aims of Industry, 1973-77; Head of Publicity, Strutt and Parker, 1977; Managing Dir, Kiernan and Co. Ltd (Exec. Search), 1977-79. Governor, Clergy Orphan Corp., 1973-; Chm., The Yeomanry Benevolent Fund, 1981-. Fellow, Inst. of Sales Management, 1975; MIPR, 1972. *Recreations:* shooting, gardening, Territorial Army. *Address:* Grove Farm, Wingmore, Elham, near Canterbury, Kent. *T:* Elham 553. *Club:* Cavalry and Guards.

LUDWIG, Christa; singer; *b* Berlin, 16 March; *d* of Anton Ludwig, singer, stage director and opera general manager and Eugenie (*née* Besalla), singer; *m* 1st, 1957, Walter Berry (marr. diss. 1970), baritone; one *s* ; 2nd, 1972, Paul-Emile Deiber, actor and stage-director. *Educ:* Matura. Staedtische Buehnen, Frankfurt; Landestheater Darmstadt; Landestheater, Hannover; Vienna State Opera; guest appearances in New York, Chicago, London, Berlin, Munich, Tokyo, Milan, Rome, Lucerne, Salzburg, Epidauros, Zürich, Holland, Los Angeles, Cleveland, Saratoga, Bayreuth, Copenhagen, Gent, Montreal, Prague, Budapest and others. Kammersängerin, Austria, 1962; Grand Prix du Disque, 1966; Mozart Medal, Mozartgemeinde, Vienna, 1969; First Class Art and Science, Austria, 1969; Deutscher Schallplattenpreis, 1970; Orphée d'Or, 1970; Prix des Affaires Culturelles, 1972; Vienna Philharmonic Silver Rose, 1980; Hugo Wolf Medal, 1980; Gustav Mahler Medal, 1980; Ehrenring, Staatsoper Vienna, 1980, Hon. Mem., 1981. *Recreations:* listening to music, theatre, concerts, reading. *Address:* c/o Heidrun Artmüller, Goethegasse 1, A-1010 Wien, Austria; Fridolin-Hoferstrasse 17, CH-6045 Meggen, Switzerland.

LUFF, Rev. Alan Harold Frank; Precentor and Sacrist of Westminster Abbey, since 1979; *b* 6 Nov. 1928; *s* of Frank Luff and late Elsie Lilian Luff (*née* Down), Bristol; *m* 1956, Enid Meirion, *d* of late Robert Meirion Roberts and Daisy Harker Roberts; three *s* one *d. Educ:* Bristol Grammar School; University Coll., Oxford (BA 1951, Dip. Theol. 1952, MA 1954); Westcott House, Cambridge. ARCM 1977. Deacon, 1956; priest, 1957; Assistant Curate: St Mathew, Stretford, Manchester, 1956-59; St Peter, Swinton, Manchester (with charge of All Saints, Wardley), 1959-61; Precentor of Manchester Cathedral, 1961-68; Vicar of Dwygyfylchi (otherwise Penmaenmawr), Gwynedd, dio. Bangor, 1968-79. Hon. Sec., Hymn Soc. of Great Britain and Ireland, 1973-. *Publications:* Hymns and Psalms (composer and author), 1981; contribs to New Christian, Musical Times, Organist's Review, etc. *Recreations:* singing, conducting, cooking. *Address:* 7 Little Cloister, Westminster Abbey, SW1P 3PL. *T:* 01-222 1386.

LUFF, Richard William Peter, FRICS; FRSA; City Surveyor, Corporation of London, since 1975; *b* 11 June 1927; *s* of Victor and Clare Luff; *m* 1950, Betty Chamberlain; no *c. Educ:* Hurstpierpoint Coll., Sussex; Coll. of Estate Management. Service in RA, India and UK, 1945-48. Estates and Valuation Dept, MCC, 1949-65; Asst Valuer, GLC, 1968-75. Royal Institution of Chartered Surveyors: Mem., Gen. Practice Divl Council, 1973-; Chm., Valuation and Rating Cttee, 1974-79; Mem., Gen. Council, 1975-; Dep. Chm., Public Affairs Cttee, 1975-79; Pres., 1982-83; Pres., Assoc. of Local Authority Valuers and Estate Surveyors, 1978-79. Mem., Furniture History Soc. Mem. Ct of Assts, Chartered Surveyors' Co. *Publications:* Furniture in England—the age of the joiner (with S. W. Wolsey), 1968; articles and papers on compensation and allied property matters; nearly 50 articles on furniture history in Antique Collector, Country Life, and Connoisseur, 1961-73. *Recreations:* collecting antiquarian objects, writing and lecturing on English furniture. *Address:* Blossoms, Broomfield Park, Sunningdale, Ascot, Berks SL5 0JT. *T:* Ascot 23806. *Club:* Surrey County Cricket.

LUFT, Arthur Christian; His Honour Deemster Luft; HM's First Deemster, Clerk of the Rolls and Deputy Governor of the Isle of Man, since 1980; *b* 21 July 1915; *e s* of late Ernest Christian Luft and late Phoebe Luft; *m* 1950, Dorothy, *yr d* of late Francis Manley; two *s. Educ:* Bradbury Sch., Cheshire. Served Army, 1940-46. Admitted to Manx Bar, 1940; Attorney-Gen., IOM, 1972-74; Second Deemster, 1974-80. Chairman: IOM Criminal Injuries Compensation Tribunal, 1974-; Prevention of Fraud (Unit Trust) Tribunal, 1974-80; IOM Licensing Appeal Court, 1974-80; Wireless Telegraphy Appeal Bd for IOM, 1974-80; IOM Income Tax Appeal Comrs, 1980-. Pres., Manx Deaf Soc., 1975-. Pres., IOM Cricket Club, 1980. *Recreations:* theatre, watching cricket, gardening. *Address:* Leyton, Victoria Road, Douglas, Isle of Man. *T:* Douglas 21048. *Clubs:* Ellan Vannin, Manx Automobile (Douglas).

LUFT, Rev. Canon Hyam Mark, MA, MLitt; FRHistS; JP; Canon Theologian of Liverpool Cathedral, since 1979; *s* of I. M. Luft, Liverpool; *m* 1943, Frances, *er d* of F. Pilling, CBE; two *s* one *d. Educ:* Liverpool Institute; St John's Coll., University of Durham (Foundation Scholar). BA (1st Cl. Classics) 1934; Dip. TPT 1935; MA 1937; MLitt 1953. Deacon, 1937; Priest, 1938. Asst Priest, Liverpool Diocese, 1937-56; Asst Master, Merchant Taylors' Sch., Crosby, 1941-56; Headmaster, Blackpool Grammar Sch., 1956-64; Headmaster, Merchant Taylors' Sch., Crosby, 1964-79. Pres., Literary and Philosophical Soc. of Liverpool, 1953-54; Mem., Religious Education Commn, 1967-. Fellow-Commoner, Emmanuel Coll., Cambridge, 1968. JP Lancs, 1968-. *Publication:* History of Merchant Taylors' School, Crosby, 1620-1970, 1970. *Recreations:* gardening, foreign travel and lecturing. *Address:* 44 St Michael's Road, Liverpool L23 7UN. *T:* 051-924 6034. *Club:* East India, Devonshire, Sports and Public Schools.

LUKE, 2nd Baron *cr* 1929, of Pavenham; **Ian St John Lawson Johnston,** KCVO 1976; TD; DL; JP; *b* 7 June 1905; *e s* of 1st Baron and Hon. Edith Laura (*d* 1941), *d* of 16th Baron St John of Bletsoe; *S* father, 1943; *m* 1932, Barbara, *d* of Sir FitzRoy Hamilton Anstruther-Gough-Calthorpe, 1st Bt; four *s* one *d. Educ:* Eton; Trinity Coll., Cambridge, MA. Life President, Electrolux Ltd, 1978- (Chm., 1963-78); Chm., Gateway Building Society, 1978-; Dir, Ashanti Goldfields Corporation Ltd and other companies; Chm., Bovril Ltd, 1943-70. One of HM Lieutenants, City of London, 1953-. Hon. Col 5th Bn Beds Regt, 1947-62; OC 9th Bn Beds and Herts Regt, 1940-43; Chairman: Area Cttee for National Fitness in Herts and Beds, 1937-39; London Hospitals Street Collections Cen. Cttee, 1943-45; Beds TAA, 1943-46; Duke of Gloucester's Red Cross and St John Fund, 1943-46; Nat. Vice-Pres., Royal British Legion; Chm., National Playing Fields Assoc., 1950-76 (a Vice-Pres., 1977-); an Hon. Sec., Assoc. of British Chambers of Commerce, 1944-52; Mem. of Church Assembly (House of Laity), 1935; Lay Reader, St Alban's dio., 1933-; Mem., International Olympic Cttee, 1952-; President: Incorporated Sales Managers Assoc., 1953-56; Advertising Assoc., 1955-58; Outdoor Advertising Council, 1957; Operation Britain Organisation, 1957-62; London Chamber of Commerce, 1952-55; Inst. of Export, 1973-; Chm. Governors, Queen Mary Coll., Univ. of London, 1963-82, Fellow, 1980. MFH Oakley Hunt, 1947-49. CC, DL, JP, Bedfordshire. *Heir:* s Hon. Arthur Charles St John Lawson Johnston [*b* 13 Jan. 1933; *m* 1st, 1959, Silvia Maria (marr. diss. 1971), *yr d* of Don Honorio Roigt and Doña Dorothy Goodall de Roigt; one *s* two *d* ; 2nd, 1971, Sarah, *d* of Richard Hearne; one *s*]. *Address:* Odell Castle, Odell, Beds MK43 7BB. *T:* Bedford 720240. *Club:* Carlton.

See also Hon. H. de B. Lawson Johnston, Sir I. J. Pitman.

LUKE, Hon. Sir Emile Fashole, KBE 1969 (CBE 1959); Speaker of the House of Representatives, Sierra Leone, 1968-73; *b* 19 Oct. 1895; *s* of late Josiah Thomas Steven Luke and late Dorcas Evangeline Luke; *m* 1929, Sarah Christina Jones-Luke (decd); two *s* one *d. Educ:* Wesleyan Methodist High Sch.; Fourah Bay Coll.; Lincoln's Inn. Civil Servant, 1913-19; practised Law, 1926-44; City Councillor, Freetown, 1940-44; Asst Police Magistrate, 1944-45; Police Magistrate, 1945-51; Senior Police Magistrate, 1951; Actg Judge, Bathurst, Gambia, 1953; Actg Puisne Judge, 1951-54; Puisne Judge, Sierra Leone, 1954-59, retired; Acting Chief Justice, in Sierra Leone and Gambia, on various occasions between 1956 and 1968, and Appeal Court Justice on several occasions, 1960-68. Chief Scout, Scouts Assoc., Sierra Leone, 1969 (awarded the Silver Wolf); Bronze Wolf, World Bureau, 1971. DCL (hc) Univ. of Sierra Leone, 1976. Grand Cordon, Order of Cedar of Lebanon, 1971; Grand Cordon, Order of Menelik II, Ethiopia, 1972. *Recreations:* tennis and walking. *Address:* 85 Motor Road, Wilberforce, PO Box 228, Freetown, Sierra Leone. *T:* Freetown 30602. *Clubs:* Royal Commonwealth Society; Freetown Dinner (Freetown).

LUKE, Eric Howard Manley, CMG 1950; FRCSE 1922; FRACS 1932; retired; *b* 18 Aug. 1894; *s* of Sir Charles Luke; *m* 1923, Gladys Anne, *d* of Col J. J. Esson, CMG; one *s* two *d. Educ:* Wellington Coll.; Otago Univ.; Edinburgh Univ. MB, ChB, Otago Univ., NZ, 1920; senior surgeon, Wellington Hospital, NZ, 1925-50; Thoracic Surgeon, East Coast Hospitals, 1942-54; Chm. of Council, British Medical Association, NZ Branch, 1944-49; President BMA, NZ Branch, 1950. Has a citrus orchard. OStJ 1940. *Recreations:* formerly Rugby; now bowls and gardening. *Address:* Keri Keri, Bay of Islands, NZ. *Club:* Wellington (Wellington, NZ).

LUKE, Peter (Ambrose Cyprian), MC 1944; playwright and short story writer, freelance since 1967; *b* 12 Aug. 1919, *e s* of late Sir Harry Luke, KCMG, DLitt Oxon and Joyce Fremlin; *m* 1st, Carola Peyton-Jones (decd);

2nd, Lettice Crawshaw (marr. diss.); one s one d ; 3rd, June Tobin; two s three d. Educ: Eton; Byam Shaw Sch. of Art; Atelier André Lhote, Paris. Served War, 1939-46 with Rifle Bde in ME, Italy and NW Europe. Sub-Editor, Reuters News Desk, 1946-47; wine trade, 1947-57; Story Editor, ABC TV, 1958-62; Editor, The Bookman (ABC TV), 1962-63; Editor, Tempo (ABC TV Arts Programme), 1963-64; Drama Producer, BBC TV, 1963-67. Dir, Edwards-Mac Liammoir Dublin Gate Theatre Co., 1977-80; Directed, Gaiety Theatre, Dublin: Rings for a Spanish Lady, 1978. Author TV plays: Small Fish are Sweet, 1958; Pigs Ear with Flowers, 1960; Roll on Bloomin' Death, 1961; (with William Sansom) A Man on Her Back, 1965; Devil a Monk Wou'd Be, 1966. Produced, Silent Song, BBC TV (Prix Italia, 1967). Wrote and directed films: Anach Cuan (about Sean O Riada), BBC TV, 1967; Black Sound Deep Song (about Federico Garcia Lorca), BBC TV, 1968; wrote stage plays: Hadrian the Seventh, prod. Birmingham Rep. 1967, Mermaid 1968, Theatre Royal, Haymarket and Broadway, 1969 (Antoinette Perry Award nomination, 1968-69); Bloomsbury, Phoenix, 1974; Proxopera (adaptation), Dublin Gate Theatre, 1979. OStJ 1940. Publications: The Play of Hadrian VII, 1968; Sisyphus and Reilly, an autobiography, 1972; (ed) Enter Certain Players, Edwards-Mac Liammoir 1928-1978, 1978; Paquito and the Wolf (children), 1981; Telling Tales: selected short stories, 1981; translations from the Spanish: Yerma, by Federico Garcia Lorca, 1972; Rings for a Spanish Lady (Aniflos para Una Dama) by Antonio Gala, 1974; short stories in: Envoy, Cornhill, Pick of Today's Short Stories, Winter's Tales, Era, New Irish Writing, etc. Recreations: reading, writing, tauromachia. Address: Apartado 15, Jimena de la Frontera, Cádiz, Spain. Club: Kildare Street and University (Dublin).

LUKE, Sir Stephen (Elliot Vyvyan), KCMG 1953 (CMG 1946); b 26 Sept. 1905; o c of late Brigadier-General Thomas Mawe Luke, CBE, DSO; m 1st, 1929, Helen Margaret Reinold; two s ; 2nd, 1948, Margaret Stych; one d. Educ: St George's Sch., Harpenden; Wadham Coll., Oxford. Asst Clerk, House of Commons, 1930; Asst Principal, Colonial Office, 1930; Asst Private Sec. to successive Secs of State, 1933-35; seconded to Palestine Administration, 1936-37; Sec., Palestine Partition Commission, 1938; Under-Sec., Cabinet Office, 1947-50; Asst Under-Sec. of State, Colonial Office, 1950-53; Comptroller for Development and Welfare in the West Indies, and British Co-Chm. of Caribbean Commn, 1953-58; Comr for preparation of WI Federal Organisation, 1956-58; Senior Crown Agent for Oversea Governments and Administrations, 1959-68; Interim Comr for the West Indies, May 1962-68; Mem. Exec. Cttee, W India Cttee, 1969-72. Chm., Board of Governors, St George's Sch., Harpenden, 1963-68. Dir, Pirelli Ltd and other companies, 1968-76. First Class Order of Laila Jasa (PSLJ) (Brunei), 1966. Recreation: gardening. Address: Merryfields, Breamore, Fordingbridge, Hants. T: Downton 22389. Club: United Oxford & Cambridge University.

LUKE, William Edgell; Chairman, 1959-79 (Managing Director, 1949-73), Lindustries Ltd (formerly the Linen Thread Co. Ltd) and associated companies at home and abroad; Director: Powell Duffryn Ltd, 1966-79; Bankers Trust (Holdings) Ltd, 1975-78; b 9 June 1909; s of George Bingley Luke and Violet Edgell; m 1st, Muriel Aske Haley (marr. diss.); one s one d ; 2nd, Constance Anne Reid; two d. Educ: Old Hall, Wellington; Kelvinside Academy, Glasgow. Served War of 1939-45: Major, Intelligence Corps, S Africa and Central America. Mem. Grand Coun., FBI, 1947-73 (Chm. Scottish Council, 1957) (FBI is now CBI); Mem. Council, Aims of Industry, 1958-80; Chm. Industrial Advisers to the Blind Ltd, 1963-67; Pres., UK-S Africa Trade Assoc., 1977-79 (Chm., 1963-77); Mem., Brit. Nat. Export Council, and Chm., BNEC Southern Africa Cttee for Exports to Southern Africa, 1965-68; Mem., BOTB Adv. Council, 1975-78; Trustee, South Africa Foundation. FBIM. Master, Worshipful Company of Makers of Playing Cards, 1958. Mem. Lloyd's. Royal Order, Crown of Yugoslavia, 1944. Recreations: golf, music and travel. Address: Pickhurst Cottage, High Street Green, Chiddingfold, Surrey GU8 4YB. Clubs: Royal Thames Yacht, Travellers'.

LUMBY, Sir Henry, Kt 1973; CBE 1957; DL, JP; Chairman of Lancashire County Council, 1967-73; Chairman, Liverpool Diocesan Board of Finance, 1977-80; b 9 Jan. 1909; m 1936, Dorothy Pearl Watts; two s. Educ: Merchant Taylors' Sch., Crosby. Served War of 1939-45 (POW, 1942-45). Mem., Lancs CC, 1946; Alderman, 1956-74; Leader of Conservative Gp, Lancs CC, 1965-73; DL 1965, JP 1951, High Sheriff 1973, Lancashire. Recreation: gardening. Address: The Dawn, Dark Lane, Ormskirk, Lancs. T: Ormskirk 72030.

LUMET, Sidney; film director; b Philadelphia, 25 June 1924; o s of Baruch and Eugenia Lumet; m Rita Gam (marr. diss.); m 1956, Gloria Vanderbilt (marr. diss. 1963); m 1963, Gail Jones (marr. diss. 1978); two d. Educ: Professional Children's Sch., NY; Columbia Univ. Served US Army, SE Asia, 1942-46. Appeared as child actor: Dead End; The Eternal Road; Sunup to Sunday; Schoolhouse on the Lot; My Heart's in the Highlands; Dir, Summer Stock, 1947-49; taught acting, High Sch. of Professional Arts; Associate Dir, CBS, 1950, Dir, 1951-57. TV shows include: Danger; You Are There; Alcoa: The Sacco and Vanzetti Story; Goodyear Playhouse; Best of Broadway; Omnibus. Films directed include: Twelve Angry Men, 1957; Stage Struck, 1958; That Kind of Woman, 1959; The Fugitive Kind, 1960; A View from the Bridge, Long Day's Journey into Night, 1962; Fail Safe, 1964; The Pawnbroker, The Hill, 1965; The Group, 1966; The Deadly Affair, 1967; Bye Bye Braverman, Last of the Mobile Hot Shots, Child's Play, The Seagull, 1969; The Anderson Tapes, 1971; The Offence, 1973; Serpico, Murder on the Orient Express, 1974; Dog Day Afternoon, 1975; Network, 1977; Equus, 1977; The Wiz, 1979; Just Tell Me What You Want, 1979; Prince of the City, 1980; Deathtrap, 1981; The Verdict; Play: Caligula, 1960. Address: c/o 156 West 56 Street, New York, NY 10019, USA.

LUMLEY, family name of Earl of Scarbrough.

LUMLEY, Viscount; Richard Osbert Lumley; b 18 May 1973; s and heir of 12th Earl of Scarbrough, qv.

LUMLEY-SAVILE, family name of Baron Savile.

LUMSDEN, Dr David James; Principal, Royal Academy of Music, since 1982; b Newcastle upon Tyne, 19 March 1928; m 1951, Sheila Daniels; two s two d. Educ: Dame Allan's Sch., Newcastle upon Tyne; Selwyn Coll., Cambridge. Organ scholar, Selwyn Coll., Cambridge, 1948-51; BA Class I, 1950; MusB (Barclay Squire Prize) 1951; MA 1955; DPhil 1957. Asst Organist, St John's Coll., Cambridge, 1951-53; Res. Student, 1951-54; Organist and Choirmaster, St Mary's, Nottingham, 1954-56; Founder/Conductor, Nottingham Bach Soc., 1954-59; Rector Chori, Southwell Minster, 1956-59; Dir of Music, Keele, 1958-59; Prof. of Harmony, Royal Academy of Music, 1959-61; Fellow and Organist, New Coll., Oxford, and Lectr in the Faculty of Music, Oxford Univ., 1959-76; Principal, RSAMD, Glasgow, 1976-82. Conductor, Oxford Harmonic Soc., 1961-63; Organist, Sheldonian Theatre, 1964-76; Harpsichordist to London Virtuosi, 1972-75. Pres., Inc. Assoc. of Organists, 1966-68; Hugh Porter Lectr, Union Theological Seminary, NY, 1967; Vis. Prof., Yale Univ., 1974-75; Conductor, Oxford Sinfonia, 1967-70; Choragus, Oxford Univ., 1968-72. Hon. Editor, Church Music Soc., 1970-73. Hon. FRCO 1976; Hon. RAM 1978; FRCM 1980. Publications: An Anthology of English Lute Music, 1954; Thomas Robinson's Schoole of Musicke, 1603, 1971; Articles in: The Listener; The Score; Music and Letters: Galpin Soc. Jl; La Luth et sa Musique; La Musique de la Renaissance, etc. Recreations: reading, theatre, photography, travel, etc. Address: 47 York Terrace East, NW1; Royal Academy of Music, Marylebone Road, NW1 5HT.

LUMSDEN, James Alexander, MBE 1945; TD 1962; DL; Partner, Maclay, Murray & Spens, Solicitors, Glasgow, 1947-82; b 24 Jan. 1915; s of late Sir James Robert Lumsden and Lady (Henrietta) Lumsden (née Macfarlane Reid); m 1947, Sheila, d of late Malcolm Cross and Evelyn Cross (née Newlands); three s. Educ: Rugby Sch.; Corpus Christi Coll., Cambridge. BA Cantab, LLB. Director: Bank of Scotland, 1958-; Weir Group PLC, 1957-; William Baird PLC, 1959-; Murray Western Investment Trust PLC and other companies in Murray Johnstone Group, 1967- (Chm., 1971-); Scottish Provident Instn, 1968- (Chm., 1977-); and other companies; Dir, Burmah Oil Co. Ltd, 1957-76 (Chm., 1971-75). Mem. Jenkins Cttee on Company Law. DL Dunbartonshire, 1966. Recreations: shooting and other country pursuits. Address: Bannachra, Helensburgh, Dunbartonshire. T: Arden 653. Clubs: Caledonian; New (Edinburgh); Western (Glasgow).

LUNCH, John, CBE 1975; VRD 1965; FCA, FCIT; Director-General of the Port of London Authority, and Board Member, 1971-76; Chairman: Comprehensive Shipping Group, 1973-75; Transcontinental Air Ltd, 1973-75; b 11 Nov. 1919; s of late Percy Valentine Lunch and late Amy Lunch (née Somerville); m 1943, Joyce Barbara Clerke; two s. Educ: Roborough Sch., Eastbourne. Served War, Lt RNVR, Medit. and Home Fleets, 1939-46, subseq. Permanent RNVR, later RNR; Lt-Comdr RNR, retd list, 1969; Lt-Col RE (TA), Engr and Railway Staff Corps, 1971, Col, 1976. In business in City, 1946-48: Asst Man. Dir, Tokenhouse Securities Corp. Ltd, 1947, and dir several cos; British Transport Commn, 1948-61: road and rail transport and ancillary businesses; PLA, 1961; Dir of Finance, also Dir of Commerce, 1966; Asst Dir-Gen., responsible docks and harbour, 1969; Chairman: (and founder) PLA Port Users Consultative Cttee, 1966-71; Internat. Port Develt Cttee, Internat. Assoc. of Ports and Harbors, 1972-76; Pres., Inst. of Freight Forwarders, 1972-73; Member Council: Inst. of Chartered Accountants, 1970-77; Chartered Inst. of Transport, 1973-76. Mem. Cttee of Management, RNLI, 1977-; Chm. (and founder), RNLI Manhood Br., 1976-78, Pres., 1978-; Pres., RNLI Hayling Island Lifeboat Station, 1978-; Hon. Art Adviser, RNLI, 1981-. Hon. Life Mem. Internat. Assoc. of Airport and Seaport Police, 1974. CBIM (FBIM 1971); FInstM 1973; FRSA (Council nominee) 1976; HH 1979. Freeman: City of London, 1970; Watermen & Lightermen's Co. of River Thames, 1970 (Court Mem., 1976-80, Hon. Court Mem., 1980-). ADC to Governor of Louisiana, with rank Adm., 1971-. Publications: The Chartered Accountant in Top Management, 1965; A Plan for Britain's Ports, 1975. Recreations: sailing, art. Address: Twittens, Itchenor, Chichester, West Sussex PO20 7AN. T: Birdham 512105. Clubs: Army and Navy, Press; Itchenor Sailing (West Sussex).

LUND, John Walter Guerrier, CBE 1975; FRS 1963; DSc, PhD; Botanist, at Windermere Laboratory of Freshwater Biological Association, 1945-78; Deputy Chief Scientific Officer; b 27 Nov. 1912; s of George E. Lund and Kate Lund (née Hardwick); m 1949, Hilda M. Canter; one s one d. Educ: Sedbergh Sch.; Univs of Manchester and London. Demonstrator in Botany, Univ. of Manchester, also Queen Mary Coll. and Chelsea Polytechnic, Univ. of London, 1935-38; Temp. Lectr in Botany, Univ. of Sheffield, 1936; PhD (London) 1939; Staff Biologist, W Midland Forensic Science Laboratory, Birmingham, 1938-45; DSc (London) 1951. Publications: papers and articles in scientific jls, symposium vols, etc. Recreation: gardening. Address:

Ellerbeck, Ellerigg Road, Ambleside, Cumbria LA22 9EU. *T:* Ambleside 2369.

LUNKOV, Nikolai Mitrofanovich; Soviet Ambassador to Italy, since 1980; *b* Pavlovka, Ryazan Region, 7 Jan. 1919; *Educ:* Lomonosov Technical Inst., Moscow. Diplomatic Service, 1943–; Asst Minister of Foreign Affairs, 1951–52; Dep. Political Counsellor, Soviet Control Commn in Germany, 1952–54; Counsellor, Stockholm, 1954–57; Dep. Head, Dept of Internat. Organizations, Ministry of Foreign Affairs, 1957; 3rd European Dept, 1957–59; Head of Scandinavian Dept, Min. of Foreign Affairs, 1959–62; Ambassador to Norway, 1962–68; Head of Dept of Cultural Relations with Foreign Countries, 1968–71; Head of 2nd European Dept, 1971–73; Ambassador to the Court of St James's, 1973–80. Mem. of Collegium of Min. of Foreign Affairs, 1968–73. Awarded orders and medals. *Address:* Embassy of the USSR, Via Gaeta 5, Rome, Italy.

LUNN, Rt. Rev. David Ramsay; see Sheffield, Bishop of.

LUNN, Peter Northcote, CMG 1957; OBE 1951; HM Diplomatic Service, retired 1972; *b* 15 Nov. 1914; *e s* of late Sir Arnold Lunn; *m* 1939, Hon. (Eileen) Antoinette (*d* 1976), *d* of 15th Viscount Gormanston; three *s* three *d. Educ:* Eton. Joined RA, 1940; served 1940–46 (Malta, Italy and BAOR); entered FO, 1947; Vienna, 1948–50; Berne, 1950–53; Germany, 1953–56; London, 1956–57; Bonn, 1957–62; Beirut, 1962–67; FCO, 1967–72. Mem., Brit. International Ski team, 1931–37, Capt. 1934–37; Capt. British Olympic Ski team, 1936. *Publications:* High-Speed Skiing, 1935; Evil in High Places, 1947; A Skiing Primer, 1948, rev. edn 1951. *Club:* Ski Club of Great Britain.

LUNS, Dr Joseph Marie Antoine Hubert; Officer, Order of Orange-Nassau, 1947; Knight Grand Cross, Order of the Netherlands Lion, 1971; Hon. GCMG; Hon. CH 1971; Secretary-General of NATO, since 1971; *b* 28 Aug. 1911; *m* Baroness E. C. van Heemstra; one *s* one *d. Educ:* sec. schs, Amsterdam and Brussels; universities of Leyden, Amsterdam, London and Berlin. Attaché of Legation, 1938; 2nd Sec., 1942; 1st Sec., 1945; Counsellor, 1949. Served in: Min. for For. Affairs, 1938–40; Berne, 1940–41; Lisbon, 1941–43; London, at Netherlands Min. for For. Affairs, 1943–44, and at Netherlands Embassy, 1944–49; Netherlands Delegn to UN, NY, 1942–52; Minister of Foreign Affairs, The Netherlands, 1952–71. MP (Second Chamber, Netherlands), July–Oct. 1956 and March–June 1959. Hon. Fellow, London Sch. of Economics, 1969. Prix Charlemagne, Aachen, 1967; Gustav Stresemann Medal, 1968. Hon. DCL: Harvard, 1970; Oxon, 1972; Exeter, 1974; Dr Humanities, Hope Coll., USA, 1974. Holds numerous foreign orders. *Publications:* The Epic of The Royal Netherlands Navy; articles on Royal Netherlands Navy in Dutch and foreign jls, and articles on international affairs in International Affairs, La Revue Politique, and others. *Recreation:* swimming. *Address:* c/o North Atlantic Treaty Organisation, Brussels 39, Belgium. *Clubs:* Athenæum, Reform (Hon. Mem.); Haagsche, De Witte (Netherlands).

LUNT, Maj.-Gen. James Doiran, CBE 1964 (OBE 1958); MA (Oxon); FRGS; Domestic Bursar, and Fellow, Wadham College, Oxford, since Jan. 1973; *b* 13 Nov. 1917; *s* of late Brig. W. T. Lunt, MBE, Camberley, Surrey; *m* 1940, Muriel, *d* of late A. H. Byrt, CBE, Bournemouth; one *s* one *d. Educ:* King William's Coll., IOM; RMC, Sandhurst. 2nd Lieut, Duke of Wellington's Regt, 1937; served with 4th Bn Burma Rifles, 1939–41; Burma Campaign, 1942; transf. to 16/5th Queen's Royal Lancers, 1949; served with Arab Legion, 1952–55; comd 16/5th Queen's Royal Lancers, 1957–59; comd Fed. Regular Army, Aden, 1961–64; Dir of Admin. Planning (Army), MoD, 1964–66; Defence Adviser to British High Commissioner, India, 1966–68; Chief of Staff, Contingencies Planning, SHAPE, 1969–70; Vice-Adjt-Gen., MoD, 1970–72; Col, 16th/5th The Queen's Royal Lancers, 1975–80. Order of Independence (Jordan), 1956; Commander, Order of South Arabia, 1964. *Publications:* Charge to Glory, 1961; Scarlet Lancer, 1964; The Barren Rocks of Aden, 1966; Bokhara Burnes, 1969; From Sepoy to Subedar, 1970; The Duke of Wellington's Regiment, 1971; 16th/5th The Queen's Royal Lancers, 1973; John Burgoyne of Saratoga, 1975; Imperial Sunset, 1981. *Recreations:* golf, fishing, writing. *Address:* Hilltop House, Little Milton, Oxon. *T:* Great Milton 242. *Club:* Flyfishers'.

LUNT, Rev. Canon Ronald Geoffrey, MC 1943; MA, BD; Rector of Martley, 1974–78; Chief Master, King Edward's School, Birmingham, 1952–74; *b* 25 June 1913; *s* of late Rt Rev. G. C. L. Lunt, DD, Bishop of Salisbury; *m* 1945, Veslemoy Sopp Foss, Oslo, Norway; one *s* two *d. Educ:* Eton (King's Scholar); The Queen's Coll., Oxford (Scholar, 1st class Lit. Hum.); Westcott House, Cambridge. Assistant Master, St George's Sch., Harpenden, 1935; Haberdashers' Sch., Hampstead, 1936–37; Deacon, 1938; Priest, 1939; Master in Orders at Radley Coll., Abingdon, 1938–40; CF 1940–45; Middle East, 1941–44 (MC); CF 3rd class, SCF 1 Airborne Division, 1945; Headmaster, Liverpool Coll., 1945–52. Won Cromer Greek Prize, 1937; Page Scholar to USA, 1959; Select Preacher: University of Cambridge, 1948, 1960, Oxford, 1951–53, 1983. Chm., Birmingham Council of Churches, 1957–60; Hon. Canon, Birmingham Cathedral, 1969. Mem., Birmingham Educn Cttee, 1952–74. Life Governor, Queen's Coll., Birmingham, 1957; Trustee, 1954, Chm., 1971–74, E. W. Vincent Trust; Governor, 1952, Sen. Vice-Pres., 1971–72, Pres., 1973, Birmingham and Midland Inst. Pres., Incorporated Assoc. of Head Masters, 1962. Mem., Press Council, 1964–69. BD (Oxon), 1967. *Publications:* Edition of Marlowe's Dr Faustus, 1937, Edward II, 1938;

contrib. to Arts v. Science, 1967; articles in Theology, Expository Times, and other journals. *Address:* The Station House, Ledbury, Herefordshire. *T:* Ledbury 3174.

LUPTON, Prof. Thomas; Director, Manchester Business School, since 1977; Professor of Organisational Behaviour, University of Manchester, since 1966; *b* 4 Nov. 1918; *s* of Thomas Lupton, blacksmith, and Jane Lupton (*née* Vowell); *m* 1st, 1942, Thelma Chesney; one *d*; 2nd, 1963, Dr Constance Shirley Wilson; one *s* one *d. Educ:* Elem. and Central Sch.; Technical Coll.; Ruskin Coll.; Oriel Coll., Oxford; Univ. of Manchester. DipEconPolSci (Oxon), MA (Oxon), PhD (Manch.). Served War, HM Forces, 1939–41 and 1944–46; Marine Engr: 1932–39, 1941–44. Research Posts: Liverpool Univ., 1951–54; Manchester Univ., 1954–57; Lectr in Sociology, Manchester Univ., 1957–59; Head of Dept of Industrial Admin, Coll. of Advanced Techn., Birmingham, 1959–64; Montague Burton Prof. of Ind. Rel., Univ. of Leeds, 1964–66. Gen. Editor, Jl of Management Studies, 1966–76; Dir, Pirelli General Cables Ltd, 1970–77; Member: Civil Service Arbitration Tribunal, 1967–70; Arbitration Panel, Dept of Employment, 1969–; various official commns and tribunals, 1960–. *Publications:* On the Shop Floor, 1963; Industrial Behaviour and Personnel Management, 1964; Management and the Social Sciences, 1966 (rev. for Penguin, 1972); Selecting a Wage Payment System (with D. Gowler), 1969; Job and Pay Comparisons (with A. M. Bowey), 1973; Wages and Salaries (with A. M. Bowey), 1974; articles in Jl of Management Studies, Manchester Sch., Production Engineer, etc. *Recreations:* golf, Association Football. *Address:* 8 Old Broadway, Manchester M20 9DF. *T:* 061-445 3309.

LUPU, Radu; pianist; *b* 30 Nov. 1945; *s* of Mayer Lupu, lawyer, and Ana Gabor, teacher of languages; *m* 1971, Elizabeth Wilson. *Educ:* Moscow Conservatoire. Debut at age of twelve with complete programme of own music; studied with Florica Muzicescu, Cella Delavrancea, Heinrich Neuhaus and Stanislav Neuhaus. 1st prize: Van Cliburn Competition, 1966; Enescu Internat. Competition, 1967; Leeds Internat. Pianoforte Competition, 1969; Prix Academic Charles Gros, Paris, 1972. Numerous recordings include complete Mozart violin and piano sonatas, complete Beethoven Piano Concertos, 1979. *Recreations:* history, art, sport. *Address:* c/o Harrison/Parrott Ltd, 12 Penzance Place, W11 4PA. *T:* 01-229 9166.

LURGAN, 4th Baron *cr* 1839; **William George Edward Brownlow;** *b* 22 Feb. 1902; *o s* of 3rd Baron and Lady Emily Julia Cadogan (*d* 1909), *d* of 5th Earl Cadogan, KG; *S* father, 1937; *m* 1979, Florence May Cooper, *widow* of E. W. Cooper, Nottingham. *Educ:* Eton; Oxford. *Heir:* cousin John Desmond Cavendish Brownlow, OBE, *b* 29 June 1911. *Address:* c/o Messrs Lee & Pembertons, 45 Pont Street, SW1X 0BX. *Clubs:* Turf; Ulster (Belfast).

LURIA, Prof. Salvador Edward; Sedgwick Professor of Biology, Massachusetts Institute of Technology, 1964–70, Institute Professor since 1970; *b* 13 Aug. 1912; *s* of David Luria and Ester Sacerdote; *m* 1945, Zella Hurwitz; one *s. Educ:* Turin Univ. (MD 1935). Res. Fellow, Inst. of Radium, Paris, 1938–40; Res. Asst, Columbia Univ. Medical School, NY, 1940–42; Guggenheim Fellow, Vanderbilt and Princeton Univs, 1942–43; Instructor in Bacteriology, Indiana Univ., 1943–45, Asst Prof., 1944–47, Associate Prof. 1947–50; Prof. of Bacteriology, Illinois Univ., 1950–59; Prof. and Chm. of Dept of Microbiology, MIT, 1959–64. Fellow of Salk Inst. for Biol Studies, 1965–. Associate Editor, Jl Bacteriology, 1950–55; Editor: Virology, 1955–; Biological Abstracts, 1958–62; Member: Editorial Bd, Exptl Cell Res. Jl, 1948–; Advisory Bd, Jl Molecular Biology, 1958–64; Hon. Editorial Advisory Bd, Jl Photochemistry and Photobiology, 1961–. Lecturer: Univ. of Colorado, 1950; Jesup, Notre Dame, 1950; Nieuwand, Notre Dame 1959; Dyer, Nat. Insts of Health, 1963. Member: Amer. Phil Soc.; Amer. Soc. for Microbiology (Pres. 1967–68); Nat. Acad. of Scis; Amer. Acad. of Arts and Scis; AAAS; Soc. Genetic Microbiology; Genetics Soc. of America; Amer Assoc. Univ. Profs; Sigma Xi. Prizes: Lepetit, 1935; Lenghi, 1965; Louisa Gross Horowitz of Columbia University; Nobel Prize for Physiology or Medicine (jtly), 1969. Hon. ScD: Chicago, 1967; Rutgers, 1970; Indiana, 1970. *Recreation:* sculpting. *Address:* Department of Biology, Massachusetts Institute of Technology, Cambridge, Mass 02139, USA.

LUSAKA, Archbishop of, (RC), since 1969; **Most Rev. Emanuel Milingo;** *b* 13 June 1930; *s* of Yakobe Milingo Chilumbu and Tomaide Lumbiwe Miti. *Educ:* Kachebere Seminary, Malawi; Pastoral Inst., Rome; University Coll., Dublin. Curate: Minga Parish, Chipata Dio., 1958–60; St Mary's Parish, 1960–61; Chipata Cathedral, 1963–64; Parish Priest, Chipata Cathedral, 1964–65; Sec. for Communications at Catholic Secretariat, Lusaka, 1966–69. Founder, The Daughters of the Redeemer, Congregation for young ladies, 1971. *Publications:* Amake-Joni, 1972; To Die to Give Life, 1975; Summer Lectures for the Daughters of the Redeemer, 1976; Lukanko, 1977; My God is a Living God; Lord Jesus and My Saviour; The Demarcations. *Recreation:* music. *Address:* Archdiocese of Lusaka, PO Box 32754, Lusaka, Zambia. *T:* Lusaka 213188 or 217652.

LUSCOMBE, Rt. Rev. Lawrence Edward; see Brechin, Bishop of.

LUSH, Christopher Duncan; HM Diplomatic Service; Ambassador and UK Permanent Representative to the Council of Europe, Strasbourg, since 1982; *b* 4 June 1928; *s* of late Eric Duncan Thomas Lush and of Iris Leonora (*née* Greenfield); *m* 1967, Marguerite Lilian, *d* of Frederick Albert Bolden; one *s.*

Educ: Sedbergh; Magdalen Coll., Oxford. Called to Bar, Gray's Inn, 1953. Asst Legal Adviser, FO, 1959-62; Legal Adviser, Berlin, 1962-65, Dep. Political Adviser, Berlin, 1965-66; FO (later FCO), 1966-69; Head of Chancery, Amman, 1969-71; Head of Aviation and Telecommunications Dept, FCO, 1971-73; Canadian Nat. Defence Coll., 1973-74; Counsellor, Paris, 1974-78. Médaille de Vermeil, Société d'Encouragement au Progrès, 1978; Counsellor, Vienna, 1978-82. *Publications:* articles in Internat. and Compar. Law Qly, Connoisseur. *Address:* c/o Foreign and Commonwealth Office, SW1; Greywings, Fairlight, Sussex. *Club:* Travellers'.

LUSH, Hon. Sir George (Hermann), Kt 1979; Justice, Supreme Court of Victoria, since 1966; *b* 5 Oct. 1912; *s* of John Fullarton Lush and Dora Louise Emma Lush; *m* 1943, Winifred Betty Wragge; three *d. Educ:* Carey Grammar Sch.; Ormond Coll., Melbourne Univ. (LLM). Admitted, Victorian Bar, 1935; served War, Australian Imperial Forces, 1940-45; Lecturer, Mercantile Law, Melbourne Univ., 1947-55; QC: Victoria 1957, Tasmania 1958. Chairman, Victorian Bar Council, 1964-66; President: Medico-Legal Soc., Victoria, 1962-63; Australian Bar Assoc., 1964-66; Commissioner, Overseas Telecommunications Commn, 1961-66. Mem. Council, Monash Univ., 1969-74. *Recreations:* tennis, walking. *Address:* 37 Rochester Road, Canterbury, Victoria 3126, Australia. *Clubs:* Melbourne, Melbourne Cricket (Melbourne).

LUSH, Maurice Stanley, CB 1944; CBE 1942; MC 1916; *b* 23 Nov. 1896; *s* of late Hubert Stanley Lush; *m* 1930, Diana Ruth, *d* of late Charles Alexander Hill; one *s* two *d. Educ:* Tonbridge Sch.; RMA, Woolwich. European War, RA, 1915-19 (MC and Bar); Egyptian Army, 1919-22; Sudan Political Service from 1919; Secretary HM Legation, Addis Ababa, 1919-22; District Commissioner, Sudan, 1922-26; Assistant Civil Secretary Sudan Government, 1926-29; Private Secretary to Governor-General of Sudan, 1929-30; Dep. Governor, Sudan, 1930-35; Sudan Agent, Cairo, 1935-38; Governor, Northern Province, Sudan, 1938-41. War of 1939-45 recalled from RARO as Brig.; Chief Political Officer, Ethiopia, 1941-42; Military Administrator, Madagascar, 1942; Chief Civil Affairs Officer British Military Administration, Tripolitania, 1942-43; Executive Commissioner and Vice-President, Allied Commission, Italy, 1943-46; Resident representative for Germany and Austria of Intergovernmental Cttee on Refugees, 1946-47; Chief of Mission in Middle East, IRO, 1947-49; Special Representative for Middle East of IRO, 1949-51; Rep. Anglo-Saxon Petroleum Co. (Shell), Libya, 1952-56; Man. Dir, Pakistan Shell Oil Co. Ltd, 1956-59. Vice-Pres., British and Foreign Bible Soc. FRSA. FRGS. Order of the Nile, 3rd Class; Officer, Legion of Merit US, 1945; Comdr Order of Knights of Malta, 1945. *Recreation:* walking. *Address:* 3 Carlton Mansions, Holland Park Gardens, W14 8DW. *T:* 01-603 4425. *Club:* Athenæum.

See also Countess of Limerick.

LUSHINGTON, Sir Henry Edmund Castleman, 7th Bt *cr* 1791; *b* 2 May 1909; *s* of Sir Herbert Castleman Lushington, 6th Bt and Barbara Henrietta (*d* 1927), *d* of late Rev. William Greville Hazlerigg; *S* father, 1968; *m* 1937, Pamela Elizabeth Daphne, *er d* of Major Archer R. Hunter, Wokingham, Berks; one *s* two *d. Educ:* Dauntsey's Sch. Served War of 1939-45, Flt-Lieut, RAFVR. Metropolitan Police, 1935-58; retired as Superintendent. *Recreations:* gardening, golf. *Heir: s* John Richard Castleman Lushington [*b* 28 Aug. 1938; *m* 1966, Bridget Gillian Margaret, *d* of Colonel John Foster Longfield, Saunton, Devon; three *s*]. *Address:* Carfax, Crowthorne, Berkshire. *T:* Crowthorne 2819. *Clubs:* Royal Air Force; East Berks Golf.

LUSTIGER, Most Rev. Mgr. Jean-Marie; Archbishop of Paris, since 1981; *b* Paris, 1926. *Educ:* Carmelite Seminary; Institut Catholique de Paris, Sorbonne (LèsL, LenThéol). Converted to Catholicism, 1940; worked in factory, Decazeville, for one year; worked for Jeunesse Etudiante Chrétienne; ordained priest, 1954; Chaplain, Univ. Parish, Paris; Chaplain to students, Sorbonne; Dir, Centre d'étudiants Richelieu, Paris; Parish Priest, Sainte Jeanne de Chantal, Paris, 1969-79; Bishop of Orléans, 1979-81. *Publication:* Sermons d'un curé de Paris, 1978. *Address:* Maison diocésaine, 8 rue de la Ville l'Evêque, 75008 Paris, France.

LUSTY, Sir Robert (Frith), Kt 1969; *b* 7 June 1909; *o s* of late Frith Lusty; *m* 1st, 1939, Joan Christie (*d* 1962), *y d* of late Archibald Brownlie, Glasgow; 2nd, 1963, Eileen, widow of Dr Denis Carroll. *Educ:* Society of Friends' Co-educational Sch., Sidcot. Joined editorial staff The Kent Messenger, 1927; abandoned journalism for publishing and entered production and editorial departments Messrs Hutchinson and Company, 1928; appointed manager associated company, Messrs Selwyn & Blount, 1933; left in 1935 to join Michael Joseph Ltd, on its formation, resigned as Deputy Chairman, 1956, to become Man. Dir, Hutchinson Publishing Gp, until retirement in 1973; a Governor of the BBC, 1960-68 (Vice-Chairman, 1966-68); Member Council of Publishers' Assoc., 1955-61; Chairman: National Book League, 1949-51 and of its 1951 Festival Cttee; Soc. of Bookmen, 1962-65; Publication Panel, King Edward's Hosp. Fund for London. Liveryman Stationers' Co., 1945; Freeman of City of London. A Governor and Councillor, Bedford Coll., 1965-71. Hon. Mem., Eygalières Football Club. FRSA 1969. *Publication:* Bound to be Read (autobiog.), 1975. *Address:* The Old Silk Mill, Blockley, Moreton-in-Marsh, Glos. *T:* Blockley 700335. *Club:* Garrick.

LUTHER, Rt. Rev. Arthur William; Promotional Secretary of The Leprosy Mission, since 1980; *b* 21 March 1919; *s* of William and Monica Luther; *m* 1946, Dr Kamal Luther; one *s* two *d. Educ:* Nagpur University; India (MA,

BT); General Theological Seminary, New York (STD 1957). Deacon, 1943; Priest, 1944; in USA and Scotland for study and parish work, 1952-54; Chaplain to Bishop of Nagpur, 1954; Head Master, Bishop Cotton School, Nagpur, 1954-57; Bishop of Nasik, 1957-70; Bishop of Bombay, 1970-73; held charge of Kolhapur Diocese concurrently with Bombay Diocese, Dec. 1970-Feb. 1972; Bishop, Church of North India, and Reg. Sec. of the Leprosy Mission, 1973-80. *Address:* Leprosy Mission Hospital, Poladpur, Dist. Raigad, Maharashtra, India 402303. *T:* Poladpur 24.

LUTTRELL, Lt-Col Geoffrey Walter Fownes, MC 1945; JP; Lord-Lieutenant of Somerset, since 1978; *b* 2 Oct. 1919; *s* of late Geoffrey Fownes Luttrell of Dunster Castle, Somerset; *m* 1942, Hermione Hamilton, *er d* of late Capt. Cecil Gunston, MC, and of Lady Doris Gunston. *Educ:* Eton; Exeter Coll., Oxford. Served War of 1939-45, with 15th/19th King's Royal Hussars, 1940-46; North Somerset Yeomanry, 1952-57; Lt-Col 1955; Hon. Col, 6th Bn LI, TAVR, 1971-. Liaison Officer, Ministry of Agriculture, 1965-71. Regional Dir, Lloyds Bank, 1972-. Member: National Parks Commn, 1962-66; Wessex Regional Cttee, Nat. Trust, 1970-; SW Electricity Bd, 1969-78. DL Somerset, 1958-68, Vice Lord-Lieutenant, 1968-78; High Sheriff of Somerset, 1960; JP 1961. Hon. Col Somerset ACF, 1982-. KStJ. *Address:* Court House, East Quantoxhead, Bridgwater, Somerset. *T:* Holford 242. *Club:* Cavalry and Guards.

LUTYENS, (Agnes) Elisabeth, (Mrs Edward Clark), CBE 1969; musician, composer; *b* London, 9 July 1906; 3rd *d* of late Sir Edwin Landseer Lutyens, OM, KCIE, PRA, LLD and of late Lady Emily Lutyens; *m* 1st, 1933, Ian Herbert Campbell Glennie (marr. diss.); one *s* twin *d* ; 2nd, 1942, Edward Clark (*d* 1962); one *s. Compositions include:* The Pit, a dramatic scene (for tenor, bass, women's chorus, and orchestra); 3 Symphonic Preludes for orchestra; String Quartet No 6; O Saisons, O Châteaux! (Rimbaud) (for soprano and strings); String Trio; Viola Concerto; Four Chamber Concertos; Excerpta Tractatus-Logico Philosophici (Wittgenstein), Motet for unaccompanied chorus, 1952; Valediction for clarinet and piano, 1954; Infidelio, 1954; Four Nocturnes, 1954; 6 Tempi for 10 Instruments, 1957; Music for Orchestra, I, II, III; Quincunx for Orchestra, 1959; Wind Quintet, 1961; Symphonies for Solo Piano, Wind, Harps and Percussion, 1961; The Country of the Stars (cantata), 1963; Hymn of Man, 1965; The Valley of Hatsu-se, 1966; Akapotik Rose, 1966; And Suddenly It's Evening, 1967; The Numbered, opera, 1966; Time Off? Not a ghost of a chance, charade in 4 scenes and 3 interruptions, 1968; Isis and Osiris, lyric drama, 1969; Novenaria (for orchestra), 1969; The Tides of Time, 1969; Essence of our Happinesses (cantata), 1970; Oda a la tormenta (Neruda), 1971; The Tears of Night, 1972; Vision of Youth, 1972; Rape of the Moone, 1973; De Amore (cantata), 1973; The Waiting Game (music-theatre), 1973; Plenum I for solo piano, 1972; Plenum II for solo oboe and thirteen instrumentalists, 1973; Plenum III for string quartet, 1974; Plenum IV (What is the wind, what is it? . .) for organ duet, 1974; Winter of the World (for orchestras), commissioned by English Bach Festival, 1974; FOS, 1975; The Ring of Bone, 1975; Mare et Minutiae, 1976; Constants, 1976; O Absalom, 1977; Variations: Winter Series-Spring Sowing (song cycle), 1977; Elegy of the Flowers, 1978; Footfalls, 1978; Echoi, 1979; The Great Seas, 1979; Fleur du Silence, 1981; Reme de Gourment; also music for numerous films and radio features. City of London Midsummer Prize, 1969. Hon. DMus York, 1977. *Publication:* A Goldfish Bowl (autobiography), 1972. *Address:* 17 King Henry's Road, NW3. *T:* 01-722 8505; c/o Universal Edition (London) Ltd, 2/3 Fareham Street, Dean Street, W1V 4DU. *T:* 01-437 5203.

See also Mary Lutyens.

LUTYENS, Mary, (Mrs J. G. Links), FRSL; writer since 1929; *b* 31 July 1908; *y d* of late Sir Edwin Lutyens, OM, KCIE, PRA, and late Lady Emily Lutyens; *m* 1st, 1930, Anthony Sewell (marr. diss. 1945; decd); one *d* ; 2nd, 1945, J. G. Links, OBE. *Educ:* Queen's Coll., London; Sydney, Australia. FRSL 1976. *Publications: fiction:* Forthcoming Marriages, 1933; Perchance to Dream, 1935; Rose and Thorn, 1936; Spider's Silk, 1939; Family Colouring, 1940; A Path of Gold, 1941; Together and Alone, 1942; So Near to Heaven, 1943; And Now There is You, 1953; Week-End at Hurtmore, 1954; The Lucian Legend, 1955; Meeting in Venice, 1956; Cleo, 1973; *for children:* Julie and the Narrow Valley, 1944; *autobiography:* To Be Young, 1959; *edited:* Lady Lytton's Court Diary, 1961; (for Krishnamurti) Freedom from the Known, 1969; The Only Revolution, 1970; The Penguin Krishnamurti Reader, 1970; The Urgency of Change, 1971; *biography:* Effie in Venice, 1965; Millais and the Ruskins, 1967; The Ruskins and the Grays, 1972; Krishnamurti: the years of awakening, 1975; The Lyttons in India, 1979; Edwin Lutyens, 1980; Krishnamurti: the years of fulfilment, 1982; also numerous serials, afterwards published, under pseudonym of Esther Wyndham; contribs to Apollo, The Cornhill, The Walpole Soc. Jl. *Recreations:* reading, cinema-going. *Address:* 2 Hyde Park Street, W2. *T:* 01-262 0455.

See also Elisabeth Lutyens.

LUTZ, Marianne Christine; Headmistress, Sheffield High School for Girls (Girls' Public Day School Trust), since 1959; *b* 9 Dec. 1922; *d* of Dr H. Lutz; *m* 1981, Charles Alexander Whittington-Smith, LLM, FCA. *Educ:* Wimbledon High Sch., GPDST; Girton Coll., Cambridge (Schol.); University of London (DipEd, DipTh). Asst Mistress (History) at: Clergy Daughters' Sch., Bristol, 1946-47; South Hampstead High Sch., GPDST, 1947-59. Former Member: History Textbooks Panel for W Germany (under auspices of FO and Unesco); Professional Cttee, Univ. of Sheffield; Historical

Assoc.; Secondary Heads' Assoc.; Schnauzer Club of Great Britain. *Publications:* several in connection with Unesco work and Historical Assoc. *Recreations:* travel, crosswords, books, opera, art and theatre. *Address:* 36 Riverdale Road, Sheffield S10 3FB.

LUXON, Benjamin, FGSM; baritone; *b* Camborne, Cornwall, 1937; *m* 1969, Sheila Amit; two *s* one *d. Educ:* Truro Sch.; Westminster Trng Coll.; Guildhall Sch. of Music. Teacher of Physical Education until becoming professional singer, 1963. Repertoire includes lieder, folk music, Victorian songs and duets, oratorio (Russian, French and English song), and operatic rôles including: Aldeburgh: Tarquinius, The Rape of Lucretia, 1969; King Arthur, 1971; BBC TV, Owen Wingrave, 1970; Covent Garden: Owen Wingrave, 1972; Death, Taverner, 1972; Marcello, La Bohème, 1974; Wolfram, Tannhäuser, 1975; Diomede, Troilus and Cressida, 1976; Falke, Die Fledermaus, 1978; Glyndebourne: (tour) Eugène Onegin, 1971, 1975; Ulisse, Il ritorno d'Ulisse, 1972, 1973; Count, Le Nozze di Figaro, 1973; Gamekeeper, The Cunning Little Vixen, 1975; Ford, Falstaff, 1976, 1977; Don Giovanni, 1977; Papageno, Die Zauberflöte, 1978, 1980; English National Opera: Posa, Don Carlos, 1974; Paris Opera: Peter Grimes, 1981. Numerous recordings. Appointed Bard of the Cornish Gorsedd, 1974. Third prize, Munich Internat. Festival, 1961; Gold Medal GSM, 1963. FGSM 1970; Hon. RAM, 1980; Hon. DMus Exeter, 1980. *Recreations:* collecting English water-colours and drawings; tennis, swimming. *Address:* Bylands House, Dunstable Road, Redbourn, Herts.

LUXTON, William John, CBE 1962; Director, London Chamber of Commerce and Industry, 1964-74 (Secretary, 1958-74); *b* 18 March 1909; *s* of late John Luxton; *m* 1942, Megan, *d* of late John M. Harries; one *s* one *d. Educ:* Shebbear Coll., N Devon; London Univ. Wallace Brothers & Co. Ltd (merchant bankers), 1926-38. Called to the Bar, Lincoln's Inn, 1938; Chancery Bar, 1938-40. Served with Royal Armoured Corps, 1940-45. Legal Parliamentary Secretary, Association of British Chambers of Commerce, 1947-53 (Vice-Pres., 1974); Secretary Birmingham Chamber of Commerce, 1953-58; Dir, Fedn of Commonwealth Chambers of Commerce, 1958-74. *Address:* Abbots Lodge, Abbotswood, Guildford, Surrey. *T:* Guildford 63439.

LUYT, Sir Richard (Edmonds), GCMG 1966 (KCMG 1964; CMG 1960); KCVO 1966; DCM 1942; Vice-Chancellor and Principal, University of Cape Town, 1968-80; *b* 8 Nov. 1915; *m* 1st, 1948, Jean Mary Wilder (*d* 1951); one *d;* 2nd, 1956, Eileen Betty Reid; two *s. Educ:* Diocesan Coll., Rondebosch, Cape, SA; Univ. of Cape Town (BA); Trinity Coll., Oxford (MA). Rhodes Scholar from S Africa, 1937. Entered Colonial Service and posted to N Rhodesia, 1940; War Service, 1940-45: with Mission 101, in Ethiopia, 1941; remained in Ethiopia with British Military Mission, for remainder of War. Returned to N Rhodesia, Colonial Service, 1945; transferred to Kenya, 1953; Labour Commissioner, Kenya, 1954-57; Permanent Secretary to various Ministries of the Kenya Government, 1957-60; Secretary to the Cabinet, 1960-61; Chief Secretary, Northern Rhodesia, 1962-64; Governor and C-in-C, British Guiana, 1964-66, until Guyana Independence; Governor-General of Guyana, May-Oct. 1966. Hon. LLD: Natal, 1972; Witwatersrand, 1980; Hon. DAdmin Univ. of South Africa, 1980; Hon. DLitt Cape Town, 1982. *Recreations:* gardening, sport, particularly Rugby (Oxford Blue, 1938) and cricket (Oxford Captain 1940) (also played for Kenya at cricket). *Address:* Allandale, 64 Alma Road, Rosebank, Cape, 7700, South Africa. *T:* 666765. *Clubs:* Royal Commonwealth Society; Nairobi (Kenya); City and Civil Service (Cape Town).

LWOFF, Prof. André; Grand Officier de la Légion d'Honneur (Commandeur, 1966; Officier, 1960; Chevalier, 1947); Médaille de la Résistance, 1946; Directeur de l'Institut de Recherches Scientifiques sur le Cancer, 1968-72; Professor of Microbiology, Faculté des Sciences, Paris, 1959-68, and Head of Department of Microbial Physiology, Pasteur Institute, since 1938; *b* Ainay-le-Château, Allier, France, 8 May 1902; *m* 1925, Marguerite Bourdaleix. *Educ:* (Fac. des Sciences et de Méd.) Univ. of Paris. MD (Paris) 1927; DSc (Paris) 1932. With the Pasteur Institute, 1921-. Foreign Member of the Royal Society (London), 1958; also Hon. or Foreign Member of American Academies, etc; Pres., Internat. Assoc. of Societies of Microbiology, 1962. Vis. Prof., Albert Einstein Coll. of Medicine, New York, 1964. Pres., Mouvement Français pour le Planning Familial, 1970-. Holds hon. doctorates in science and law at British and other foreign univs. Awarded several prizes and medals from 1928 onwards, both French and foreign, for his work; Nobel Prize for Medicine (jointly), 1965; Einstein Award, 1967. *Publications:* L'Evolution physiologique, Collection de microbiologie, Hermann éd., 1944 (Paris); Problems of Morphogenesis in Ciliates, The Kinetosomes in Development, Reproduction and Evolution, 1950 (New York); Biological Order, 1962, MIT. *Recreation:* painting. *Address:* 69 avenue de Suffren, 75007 Paris, France. *T:* 783.27.82.

LYALL, Andrew Gardiner, CMG 1976; Under Secretary, International Transport, Department of Transport, since 1981; *b* 21 Dec. 1929; *s* of late William and Helen Lyall (*née* Gardiner); *m* 1953, Olive Leslie Gennoe White; one *s* one *d. Educ:* Kirkcaldy High Sch. Joined MoT, 1951; Asst Shipping Attaché, British Embassy, Washington, DC, 1961-64; Principal, Nationalised Industry Finance and Urban Transport Planning, 1965-70; Asst Sec., Railways Div., 1970-72; seconded to FCO as Counsellor, UK Representation to European Communities, 1972-75; Assistant Secretary: Land Use Planning, DoE, 1975-76; Central Unit on Environmental Pollution, 1976-77; Under

Sec., PSA, 1978-81. *Recreations:* walking, reading. *Address:* 5 Barrowfield, Cuckfield, Haywards Heath, West Sussex. *T:* Haywards Heath 454606. *Club:* Reform.

LYALL, Gavin Tudor; author; *b* 9 May 1932; *s* of J. T. and A. A. Lyall; *m* 1958, Katharine E. Whitehorn, *qv;* two *s. Educ:* King Edward VI Sch., Birmingham; Pembroke Coll., Cambridge (BA). RAF, 1951-53 (Pilot Officer, 1952). Journalist with: Picture Post, 1956-57; BBC, 1958-59; Sunday Times, 1959-63. Member: Air Transport Users' Cttee, CAA, 1979-; Air Travel Reserve Fund Agency, 1981-. *Publications:* The Wrong Side of the Sky, 1961; The Most Dangerous Game, 1964; Midnight Plus One, 1965; Shooting Script, 1966; Venus with Pistol, 1969; Blame the Dead, 1972; Judas Country, 1975; Operation Warboard, 1976; The Secret Servant, 1980; The Conduct of Major Maxim, 1982. (As Editor) Freedom's Battle: The RAF in World War II, 1968. *Recreations:* real beer, cooking, military history, model making. *Address:* 14 Provost Road, NW3 4ST. *T:* 01-722 2308. *Clubs:* Royal Air Force; Detection.

LYALL, Katharine Elizabeth; *see* Whitehorn, K.

LYALL, William Chalmers, MBE 1952; HM Diplomatic Service, retired; *b* 6 Aug. 1921; *s* of John Brown Lyall and Margaret Angus Leighton Stevenson Lyall; *m* 1948, Janet Lawson McKechnie; two *s* one *d. Educ:* Kelty Public and Beath Secondary schools. Min. of Labour, 1940-48; HM Forces, 1941-47; FO, 1948; Hankow, 1948-51; São Paulo, 1952-53; Manila, 1953-55; FO, 1955-57; Caracas, 1957-60; Bahrain, 1960-64; FO, 1964-65; DSAO, 1965-68; FCO, 1968-69; Consul-General, Genoa, 1969-73; FCO, 1973; Counsellor (Administration), Bonn, 1974-78. *Recreations:* music, photography. *Address:* 12 Fairway, Bexleyheath, Kent DA6 8LU.

LYALL GRANT, Maj.-Gen. Ian Hallam, MC 1944; Director General, Supply Co-ordination, Ministry of Defence, 1970-75; retired; *b* 4 June 1915; *s* of Col H. F. Lyall Grant, DSO; *m* 1951, Mary Jennifer Moore; one *s* two *d. Educ:* Cheltenham Coll.; RMA, Woolwich; Cambridge Univ. (MA). Regular Commission, RE, 1935; service in: India, Burma and Japan, 1938-46 (MC; twice mentioned in despatches); Cyprus and Egypt, 1951-52; Imperial Defence Coll., 1961; Aden, 1962-63; Comdt, Royal School of Mil. Engineering, 1965-67; Maj.-Gen. 1966; Dep. QMG, 1967-70, retired 1970. Col Comdt, RE, 1972-77. *Recreations:* sailing, fishing, paintings, gemmology. *Address:* Kingswear House, Kingswear, S Devon. *T:* Kingswear 359. *Club:* Naval and Military.

LYDDON, William Derek Collier; Chief Planning Officer, Scottish Development Department, since 1967; *b* 17 Nov. 1925; *s* of late A. J. Lyddon, CBE, and E. E. Lyddon; *m* 1949, Marian Louise Kaye Charlesworth, *d* of late Prof. J. K. Charlesworth, CBE; two *d. Educ:* Wrekin Coll.; University Coll., London. BA (Arch.) 1952; ARIBA 1953; DipTP 1954; AMTPI 1962; FRTPI 1973. Depute Chief Architect and Planning Officer, Cumbernauld Development Corp., 1962; Chief Architect and Planning Officer, Skelmersdale Development Corp., 1963-67. Pres., Internat. Soc. of City and Regional Planners, 1981-84. Hon. DLitt Heriot-Watt, 1981. *Recreations:* walking, reading. *Address:* 38 Dick Place, Edinburgh EH9 2JB. *T:* 031-667 2266.

LYELL, family name of **Baron Lyell.**

LYELL, 3rd Baron *cr* 1914, of Kinnordy; **Charles Lyell;** Bt, 1894; a Lord in Waiting (Government Whip), since 1979; *b* 27 March 1939; *s* of 2nd Baron, VC (killed in action, 1943), and Sophie, *d* of Major S. W. and Lady Betty Trafford; *S* father, 1943. *Educ:* Eton; Christ Church, Oxford. 2nd Lieut Scots Guards, 1957-59. CA Scotland. An Opposition Whip, 1975-79. Mem., Queen's Body Guard for Scotland (Royal Company of Archers). *Heir:* none. *Address:* Kinnordy House, Kirriemuir, Angus. *T:* Kirriemuir 2848; 20 Petersham Mews, SW7. *T:* 01-584 9419. *Clubs:* Turf, White's.

LYELL, Nicholas Walter; QC 1980; MP (C) Hemel Hempstead, since 1979; barrister-at-law; *b* 6 Dec. 1938; *s* of late Sir Maurice Legat Lyell and Veronica Mary Lyell; *m* 1967, Susanna Mary Fletcher; two *s* two *d. Educ:* Stowe Sch.; Christ Church, Oxford (BA Hons Mod. Hist.). National Service, commnd Royal Artillery, 1957-59; Walter Runciman & Co., 1962-64; called to the Bar, Inner Temple, 1965; private practice, London (Commercial and Industrial Law), 1965-. Jt Sec., Constitutional Cttee, 1979; PPS to the Attorney General, 1979-. *Recreations:* gardening, shooting, drawing. *Address:* Hill Farm, Markyate, St Albans, Herts. *T:* Luton 840783.

LYGO, Adm. Sir Raymond (Derek), KCB 1977; FRAeS; CBIM; Managing Director, British Aerospace, since 1983; Board Member, British Aerospace, since 1980; *b* 15 March 1924; *s* of late Edwin T. Lygo and of Ada E. Lygo; *m* 1950, Pepper Van Osten, USA; two *s* one *d. Educ:* Valentine's Sch., Ilford; Ilford County High Sch.; Clarke Coll., Bromley. The Times, 1940; Naval Airman, RN, 1942; CO, HMS Ark Royal, 1969-71; Vice Chief of Naval Staff, 1975-78. British Aerospace: Man. Dir, Hatfield/Lostock Div., 1978-79, Group Dep. Chm., 1980; Chm. and Chief Exec., Dynamics Gp, 1980-82. Dir, Boyle Industrial Gauging Systems Ltd, 1978-. *Recreations:* building, gardening, joinery. *Address:* British Aerospace, Six Hills Way, Stevenage, Herts SG1 2DA. *Club:* Royal Naval and Royal Albert Yacht (Portsmouth).

LYLE, Sir Gavin Archibald, 3rd Bt *cr* 1929; estate manager, farmer; company director; *b* 14 Oct. 1941; *s* of late Ian Archibald de Hoghton Lyle and of Hon. Lydia Yarde-Buller (who *m* 1947, as his 2nd wife, 13th Duke of Bedford; marr. diss. 1960; now Lydia Duchess of Bedford), *d* of 3rd Baron Churston; *S* grandfather, 1946; *m* 1967, Suzy Cooper; five *s* one *d*. *Heir: s* Ian Abram Lyle, *b* 25 Sept. 1968. *Address:* Glendelvine, Caputh, Perthshire PH1 4JN. *T:* Caputh 225.

LYLE, Thomas Keith, CBE 1949; MA, MD, MChir (Cantab); FRCP, FRCS; Consulting Ophthalmic Surgeon: King's College Hospital (Ophthalmic Surgeon, 1938-69); Moorfields Eye Hospital (Ophthalmic Surgeon, 1936-69); National Hospital, Queen Square (Ophthalmic Surgeon, 1936-69); Director, Orthoptic Department, Moorfields Eye Hospital, 1947-69; Dean of Institute of Ophthalmology, British Post-graduate Medical Federation of University of London, 1959-67; Teacher of Ophthalmology, University of London; *b* 26 Dec. 1903; *s* of late Herbert Willoughby Lyle, MD, FRCS, Fircliff, Portishead, Somerset; *m* 1949, Jane Bouverie, *e d* of late Major Nigel Maxwell, RA, and Mrs Maxwell, Great Davids, Kingwood, Henley-on-Thames; one *s* three *d*. *Educ:* Dulwich Coll.; Sidney Sussex Coll., Cambridge (Exhib.); King's College Hospital (Burney Yeo Schol.). Todd medal for Clinical Medicine; House Physician, House Surg., Sen. Surg. Registrar; First Asst Neurol. Dept, King's Coll. Hosp., 1929-33; House Surgeon, Royal Westminster Ophth. Hosp., 1934. Civilian Consultant in Ophth., RAF, 1948-; Mem., Flying Personnel Res. Cttee, RAF, Chm., Vision sub-cttee, 1975; Consultant in Ophth. Dept of Civil Aviation, Board of Trade; Hon. Consultant in Ophth., BALPA. Examiner in Ophthalmology: Bristol Univ., 1947-50; RCS, 1949-55; FRCS (Ophthalmology), 1958-66; FRCSE (Ophthalmology), 1960-70; Mem. Council, Faculty of Ophthalmologists, 1946-69, Pres., 1965-68, and Rep. on Council of RCS, 1958-63; Chm., Specialist Adv. Cttee in Ophthalmology, RCS; Past Mem., International Council of Ophthalmology; Mem. Court of Assts, Soc. of Apothecaries, Master, 1962-63. Order of St John: Deputy Hospitaller, 1960-69; Hospitaller, 1969-81; Chm., Hosp. Cttee; Member Council: Med. Protection Soc.; British Nat. Cttee for the Prevention of Blindness; Vice-Chm., Royal London Soc. for the Blind; Pres., St John Ambulance, Henley-on-Thames Div. Past Pres., Internat. Strabismological Assoc.; Member: Cttee of Management, Inst of Opthalmology; Ophth. Soc. UK, Pres. 1968-70; Orthoptists Bd, Council for Professions Supplementary to Medicine; Soc. Franc. d'Ophthalmologie; FRSocMed (Vice-Pres. Ophth. Section, Pres. United Services Section, 1964-66); Hon. Mem. Ophth. Socs of Australia, New Zealand and Greece. Chas H. May Memorial Lectr, New York, 1952; Doyne Memorial Lectr, Oxford, 1953; Alexander Welch Lectr, Edinburgh, 1965; Vis. Lectr, Blindness Res. Foundn, Univ. of the Witwatersrand, SA, 1974. Nettleship Medal, 1959; Richardson Cross Medal, 1972. Served RAFVR, 1939-46, Temp. Air Cdre Cons. in Ophth. RAF overseas (despatches). GCStJ 1980 (KStJ 1960; CStJ 1956); Kt, Order of Holy Sepulchre, 1970. *Publications:* (co-ed with Sylvia Jackson) Practical Orthoptics in the Treatment of Squint, 1937, 5th edn (co-ed with K. C. Wybar) 1967; (co-ed with Hon. G. J. O. Bridgeman) Worth's Squint by F. B. Chavasse, 9th edn 1959; (co-ed with A. G. Cross) May and Worth's Diseases of the Eye, 13th edn 1968; (co-ed with late H. Willoughby Lyle) Applied Physiology of the Eye, 1958; articles in British Jl Ophth., Lancet, BMJ, Med. Press and Circular, etc, chapters in Sorsby's Modern Trends in Ophthalmology, 1948, in Stallard's Modern Practice in Ophthalmology, 1949 and in Rob and Rodney Smith's Operative Surgery, 1958. *Recreations:* gardening, riding, ski-ing. *Address:* 18 Upper Wimpole Street, W1. *T:* 01-935 8851; Kingsley, Crowsley Road, Shiplake, near Henley-on-Thames, Oxon. *T:* Wargrave 2832. *Clubs:* Royal Air Force, Royal Automobile, Sloane, Ski Club of GB.

LYMBERY, Robert Davison, QC 1967; **His Honour Judge Lymbery;** a Circuit Judge (formerly Judge of County Courts), since 1971; *b* 14 Nov. 1920; *s* of late Robert Smith Lymbery and late Louise Lymbery; *m* 1952, Pauline Anne, *d* of John Reginald and Kathleen Tuckett; three *d*. *Educ:* Gresham's Sch.; Pembroke Coll., Cambridge. Served Army, 1940-46; commissioned 17/21 Lancers, 1941; Middle East, Italy, Greece (Royal Tank Regt), 1942-46, Major. Pembroke Coll., 1939-40, 1946-48 (MA, LLB 1st class hons). Foundation Exhibn. 1948; called to Bar, Middle Temple, 1949; Harmsworth Law Scholar, 1949; practice on Midland Circuit, 1949-71. Recorder of Grantham, 1965-71, now Honorary Recorder; Chairman: Rutland QS, 1966-71 (Dep. Chm., 1962-66); Bedfordshire QS, 1969-71 (Dep. Chm., 1961-69); Commissioner of Assize, 1971. *Recreations:* various. *Address:* Park Lodge, Knebworth, Herts. *T:* Stevenage 813308; 2 Crown Office Row, Temple, EC4. *T:* 01-353 1365. *Club:* Hawks (Cambridge).

LYMINGTON, Viscount; Oliver Kintzing Wallop; Lieut RNVR (retired); *b* 14 Jan. 1923; *s* and *heir* of 9th Earl of Portsmouth, *qv*; *m* 1st, 1952, Maureen (marr. diss. 1954), *o d* of Lt-Col Kenneth B. Stanley; 2nd, 1954, Ruth Violet (marr. diss. 1974; she *d* 1978), *yr d* of late Brig.-General G. C. Sladen, CB, CMG, DSO, MC; one *s* two *d*; 3rd, 1974, Julia Kirwan-Taylor (née Ogden), *d* of Graeme Ogden, DSC. *Educ:* Eton. *Address:* 11 Douro Place, W8. *Club:* Royal Automobile.

LYMPANY, Miss Moura, CBE 1979; FRAM 1948; concert pianist; *b* Saltash, Cornwall, 18 Aug. 1916; British; *d* of John and Beatrice Johnstone; *m* 1944, Lt-Col Colin Defries (marr. diss. 1950); *m* 1951, Bennet H. Korn, American Television Executive (marr. diss. 1961); one *s* decd. *Educ:* Belgium, Austria, England. First public performance at age of 12, 1929, at Harrogate, playing Mendelssohn G Minor Concerto. Won second prize out of 79 competitors at

Ysaye International Pianoforte Competition at Brussels, 1938. Has played in USA, Canada, South America, Australia, New Zealand, India, and all principal European countries. Records for HMV and Decca. Commander of the Order of the Crown, Belgium, 1980. *Recreations:* gardening, tapestry, reading. *Address:* c/o Ibbs & Tillett, 450/452 Edgware Road, W2.

LYNCH, Rev. Prebendary Donald MacLeod, CBE 1972; MA; Chaplain to the Queen, 1969-81; Priest-in-Charge of Seal, St Lawrence, in the diocese of Rochester, since 1974, also of Underriver, since 1980; Rural Dean of Sevenoaks, since 1979; *b* 2 July 1911; *s* of Herbert and Margaret Lynch; *m* 1st, 1941, Ailsa Leslie Leask; three *s* one *d*; 2nd, 1963, Jean Wileman. *Educ:* City of London Sch.; Pembroke Coll., Cambridge; Wycliffe Hall, Oxford. Curate, Christ Church, Chelsea, 1935; Tutor, Oak Hill Theological Coll., 1938; Curate, St Michael's, Stonebridge Park, 1940; Minister, All Saints, Queensbury, 1942; Vicar, St Luke's, Tunbridge Wells, 1950; Principal, Church Army Training Coll., 1953; Chief Sec., Church Army, 1960-76; Preb. of Twiford, St Paul's Cathedral, 1964-76, now Emeritus. *Publications:* Action Stations, 1981; Chariots of the Gospel, 1982. *Recreations:* reading and gardening. *Address:* St Lawrence Vicarage, Stone Street, near Sevenoaks, Kent TN15 0LQ. *T:* Sevenoaks 61766.

LYNCH, John; *b* 15 Aug. 1917; *y s* of Daniel Lynch and Norah O'Donoghue; *m* 1946, Mairin O'Connor. *Educ:* Christian Brothers' Schools, N Monastery, Cork; University College, Cork; King's Inns, Dublin. Entered Civil Service (Dept of Justice), 1936; called to Bar, 1945; resigned from Civil Service, became Mem. Munster Bar and commenced practice in Cork Circuit, 1945. Teachta Dala (TD) for Cork, Parlt of Ireland, 1948-81; Parly Sec. to Govt and to Minister for Lands, 1951-54; Minister for: Education, 1957-59; Industry and Commerce, 1959-65; Finance, 1965-66; Leader of Fianna Fail, 1966-79; Taoiseach (Head of Government of Ireland), 1966-73 and 1977-79. Alderman, Co. Borough of Cork, 1950-57; Mem. Cork Sanatoria Board and Cttee of Management, N Infirmary, Cork, 1950-51 and 1955-57; Mem. Cork Harbour Comrs, 1956-57; Vice-Pres., Consultative Assembly of Council of Europe, 1958; Pres., Internat. Labour Conf., 1962. Hon. LLD: Dublin, 1967; Nat. Univ. of Ireland, 1969; Rhode Island Coll., USA, 1980; Hon. DCL N Carolina, 1971. Grand Cross, Order of the Crown (Belgium), 1968. Robert Schumann Gold Medal, 1973. *Address:* 21 Garville Avenue, Rathgar, Dublin 6, Ireland.

LYNCH, Prof. John; Director of Institute of Latin American Studies since 1974 and Professor of Latin American History since 1970, University of London; *b* 11 Jan. 1927; *s* of late John P. Lynch and of Teresa M. Lynch, Boldon Colliery, Co. Durham; *m* 1960, Wendy Kathleen, *d* of late Frederick and of Kathleen Norman; two *s* three *d*. *Educ:* Corby Sch. Sunderland; Univ. of Edinburgh; University College, London. MA Edinburgh 1952; PhD London 1955. Army, 1945-48. Asst Lectr and Lectr in Modern History, Univ. of Liverpool, 1954-61; Lectr in Hispanic and Latin American History, University Coll., London, Reader 1964. Corresp. Mem., Academia Nacional de la Historia, Argentina, 1963, Venezuela, 1980; Academia Panameña de la Historia, 1981. Order of Andrés Bello, Venezuela, 1979. *Publications:* Spanish Colonial Administration 1782-1810, 1958; Spain under the Habsburgs, vol. 1 1964, vol. 2 1969; (with R. A. Humphreys) The Origins of the Latin American Revolutions, 1808-1826, 1965; The Spanish American Revolutions 1808-1826, 1973; Argentine Dictator: Juan Manuel de Rosas, 1829-52, 1981. *Address:* 8 Templars Crescent, N3 3QS. *T:* 01-346 1089.

LYNCH, Martin Patrick James; Under Secretary, Overseas Development Administration, Foreign and Commonwealth Office, since 1975; *b* 4 June 1924; 2nd *s* of late Frederick Lynch, DSM, and late Elizabeth Yeatman; *m* 1959, Anne, *d* of late Major Gerald McGorty, MC, RAMC; two *s* one *d* (and one *s* decd). *Educ:* London Oratory School. BA Hons London. RAF, 1942-49; Exec. Officer, HM Treasury, 1950; Asst Private Sec. to Financial Sec., 1953-54; Private Sec. to Minister Without Portfolio, 1954-55; Principal, 1958; Asst Sec., Min. of Overseas Develt, 1966 and 1971-75; Counsellor, UK Treasury and Supply Delegn, Washington, and UK Alternate Dir, World Bank, 1967-71. FRSA 1973; Chm., Assoc. for Latin Liturgy, 1976- (Mem. Council, 1973-76). *Address:* 29 Boileau Road, W5 3AP. *T:* 01-997 4004. *Club:* Reform.

LYNCH, Patrick, MA; MRIA; Joint Deputy Chairman, Allied Irish Banks, since 1976 (Director, since 1971); Professor of Political Economy (Applied Economics), University College, Dublin, 1975-80, now Emeritus; *b* 5 May 1917; *s* of Daniel and Brigid Lynch, Co. Tipperary and Dublin; *m* Mary Crotty (née Campbell), MA. *Educ:* Univ. Coll., Dublin. Fellow Commoner, Peterhouse, Cambridge, 1956. Entered Irish Civil Service, 1941; Asst Sec. to Govt, 1950; Univ. Lectr in Econs, UC Dublin, 1952, Associate Prof., 1966-75. Chm., Aer Lingus, 1954-75. Has acted as economic consultant to OECD, Council of Europe, Dept of Finance, Dublin, Gulbenkian Inst., Lisbon. Directed surveys sponsored by Irish Govt with OECD into long-term Irish educnl needs, 1965, and into requirements of Irish economy in respect of scientific res., develt and technology, 1966; estab. Science Policy Res. Centre in Dept of Applied Econs, UC Dublin, 1969. Mem., various Irish Govt Commns and Cttees, 1952-; Member: Club of Rome, 1973; EEC Economic and Monetary Union 1980 Group, 1974; Nat. Science Council, 1968-78; Exec. Cttee, Economic and Social Research Inst.; Nat. Economic and Social Council, 1973-76; European Science Foundn, 1974-77; Chairman: Medico-Social Research Board, 1966-72; Public Service Adv. Council, 1973-77; Mem., Higher Educn Authority, 1968-72; Chm. Editl Bd, Economic and

Social Review; Mem. Editorial Bd, University Review. Chm., Nat. Library of Ireland Soc., 1969-72; Chm., Irish Anti-Apartheid Movement, 1972; Member: Irish Assoc. for Civil Liberty; Movement for Peace in Ireland. Chm., Inst. of Public Administration, 1973-77. Member: Governing Body UC Dublin, 1963-75; Senate NUI, 1972-77; Treasurer, RIA, 1972-80. Hon. DUniv Brunel, 1976; Hon. LLD Dublin, 1979. *Publications:* Planning for Economic Development in Ireland, 1959; (with J. Vaizey) Guinness's Brewery in the Irish Economy, 1960; (jtly) Economics of Educational Costing, 1969; (with Brian Hillery) Ireland in the International Labour Organisation, 1969; (with B. Chubb) Economic Development Planning, 1969; Whither Science Policy, 1980; essays in various symposia, etc; articles in Administration, The Bell, Encycl. Britannica, Econ. History Review, Irish Hist. Studies, Irish Jl of Educn, Statist, Studies, University Review, etc. *Address:* 68 Marlborough Road, Dublin 4, Ireland.

LYNCH, Rt. Hon. Sir Phillip (Reginald), KCMG 1981; PC 1977; Minister for Industry and Commerce, Australia, 1977-82; MHR since 1966; *b* 27 July 1933; *m* 1958, Leah; three *s. Educ:* Xavier Coll., Melbourne; Melbourne Univ. (BA, DipEd). Management consultant; co. dir. Victorian State Pres., Young Liberal Movement; Nat. Pres., Aust. Jaycees, 1966. Minister for the Army, 1968-69; Minister for Immigration and Minister assisting the Treasurer, 1969-71; Minister for Labor, 1971-72; Dep. Opposition Leader, 1972-75; Treasurer of Australia, 1975-77, and Minister responsible for Dept of Finance, 1976-77. Dep. Leader, Federal Parly Liberal Party, 1973-82. Vice-Pres., Exec. Cttee of Commonwealth Parly Assoc., 1972-75; represented Australia at confs in Geneva, Hong Kong, Jakarta, Manila, Paris, Teheran, Barbados and Washington. Certificate of Merit, Royal Humane Soc., 1953. *Publications:* essays on Australian economy in jls and periodicals throughout Australia over past ten years. *Recreations:* sailing, swimming, reading. *Address:* Parliament House, Canberra, ACT 2600, Australia. *Clubs:* Naval & Military, Australian (Melbourne); Davey's Bay Yacht (Victoria).

LYNCH-BLOSSE, Captain Sir Richard Hely, 17th Bt *cr* 1622; RAMC; *b* 26 Aug. 1953; *s* of Sir David Edward Lynch-Blosse, 16th Bt, and of Elizabeth, *er d* of Thomas Harold Payne, Welwyn Garden City; *S* father, 1971; *m* 1976, Cara, *o d* of George Sutherland, St Ives, Cambs. *Educ:* Royal Free Hosp. Sch. of Medicine. Commnd RAMC, July 1975; LRCP MRCS 1978; MB BS 1979. *Heir: cousin* (Eric) Hugh Lynch-Blosse, OBE [*b* 30 July 1917; *m* 1946, Jean Evelyn, *d* of Commander Andrew Robertson Hair, RD, RNR; one *s* one *d* (and one *d* decd)]. *Address:* c/o National Westminster Bank, 13 Stonehills, Welwyn Garden City, Herts.

LYNCH-ROBINSON, Sir Niall (Bryan), 3rd Bt *cr* 1920; DSC 1941; late Lieut RNVR; one time Chairman, Leo Burnett Ltd, 1969-78; *b* 24 Feb. 1918; *s* of Sir Christopher Henry Lynch-Robinson, 2nd Bt and Dorothy (*d* 1970), *d* of Henry Warren, Carrickmines, Co. Dublin; *S* father 1958; *m* 1940, Rosemary Seaton, *e d* of Mrs M. Seaton Eller; one *s* one (adopted) *d. Educ:* Stowe. Sub-Lieut 1939, Lieut 1940, RNVR; served War of 1939-45 (DSC, Croix de Guerre). Mem. Exec. Cttee, Nat. Marriage Guidance Council. Chm. of Governors, Cranbourne Chase School. *Recreations:* fishing, gardening. *Heir: s* Dominick Christopher Lynch-Robinson, *b* 30 July 1948. *Address:* The Old Vicarage, Ampfield, Romsey, Hants SO5 9BQ.

LYNDEN-BELL, Prof. Donald, FRS 1978; Professor of Astrophysics, University of Cambridge, since 1972; Director, Institute of Astronomy, Cambridge, 1972-77 and since 1982; *b* 5 April 1935; *s* of Lt-Col L. A. Lynden-Bell, MC and M. R. Lynden-Bell (*née* Thring); *m* 1961, Ruth Marion Truscott, MA, PhD; one *s* one *d. Educ:* Marlborough; Clare Coll., Cambridge (MA, PhD). Harkness Fellow of the Commonwealth Fund, NY, at the California Inst. of Technology and Hale Observatories, 1960-62; Research Fellow and then Fellow and Dir of studies in mathematics, Clare Coll., Cambridge, 1960-65; Asst Lectr in applied mathematics, Univ. of Cambridge, 1962-65; Principal Scientific officer and later SPSO, Royal Greenwich Observatory, Herstmonceux, 1965-72. Visiting Associate, Calif. Inst. of Technology and Hale Observatories, 1969-70. *Publications:* contrib. to Monthly Notices of Royal Astronomical Soc. *Recreations:* hill walking, golf, squash racquets. *Address:* Institute of Astronomy, The Observatories, Madingley Road, Cambridge CB3 0HA. *T:* Cambridge 62204.

LYNE, Air Vice-Marshal Michael Dillon, CB 1968; AFC (two Bars); DL; *b* 23 March 1919; *s* of late Robert John Lyne, Winchester; *m* 1943, Avril Joy Buckley, *d* of late Lieut-Colonel Albert Buckley, CBE, DSO; two *s* two *d. Educ:* Imperial Service Coll.; RAF Coll., Cranwell. Fighter Comd and Middle East, 1939-46; Comdg No 54 Fighter Squadron, 1946-48; Comdg RAF Wildenrath, 1958-60; Air Attaché, Moscow, 1961-63; Commandant, Royal Air Force Coll., Cranwell, 1963-64; Air Officer Commanding No 23 Group, RAF Flying Training Command, 1965-67; Senior RAF Instructor, Imperial Defence Coll., 1968-69; Dir-Gen. Training, RAF, 1970-71; retired. Sec., Diocese of Lincoln, 1971-76. Vice-Chm. (Air), TAVR Assoc. for East Midlands, 1977-. Vice Chm., Governing Body, Bishop Grosseteste Coll., 1976-. Vice-President: RAF Gliding and Soaring Assoc.; RAF Motor Sport Assoc.; Old Cranwellian Assoc., 1982-. Founder and Chm., Lincs Microprocessor Soc., 1979-; Mem. Council, British Computer Soc., 1980-. President: Lincoln Branch, SCF, 1977-; Grantham Constituency Liberal Assoc., 1979-; No 54 Squadron Assoc., 1981-. DL Lincs, 1973. *Recreations:* sailing, gardening. *Address:* Far End, Far Lane, Coleby, Lincoln LN5 0AH. *T:* Lincoln 810468. *Clubs:* Royal Air Force; Royal Mersey Yacht.

LYNN, Bishop Suffragan of, since 1973; **Rt. Rev. William Aubrey Aitken;** also Archdeacon of Lynn, 1973-80; *b* 2 Aug. 1911; *s* of late Canon R. A. Aitken, Great Yarmouth; *m* 1937, Margaret Cunningham; three *s* two *d. Educ:* Norwich Grammar School; Trinity College, Oxford (MA Modern History, 2nd class Hons). Curate of: Tynemouth, 1934-37; Kingston, Jamaica, 1937-40; Rector of Kessingland, 1940-43; Vicar of: Sprowston, 1943-53; St Margaret's, King's Lynn, 1953-61; Archdeacon of Norwich, 1971-73. Proctor in Convocation, 1944-74; Hon. Canon of Norwich, 1958. *Recreations:* football, cricket, sailing. *Address:* Bishops House, Ranworth, Norwich. *T:* South Walsham 248.

LYNN, Archdeacon of; *see* Grobecker, Ven. G. F.

LYNN, Jonathan Adam; director, writer and actor; *b* 3 April 1943; *s* of Robin and Ruth Lynn; *m* 1967, Rita Merkelis; one *s. Educ:* Kingswood Sch., Bath; Pembroke Coll., Cambridge (MA). Acted in Cambridge Circus, New York, 1964; TV debut, Ed Sullivan Show, 1964; actor in repertory, Leicester, Edinburgh and Bristol Old Vic, and in London; performances include: Green Julia, 1965; Fiddler on the Roof, 1967-68; Blue Comedy, 1968; The Comedy of the Changing Years, 1969; When We Are Married, 1970; Dreyfus, 1982; actor in TV comedy programmes and plays, including: Barmitzvah Boy, 1975; The Knowledge, 1979. Artistic Dir, Cambridge Theatre Co., 1977-81 (dir. 19 prodns); director, London: The Plotters of Cabbage Patch Corner, 1970; The Glass Menagerie, 1977; The Gingerbread Man, 1977 and 1978; The Unvarnished Truth, 1978; The Matchmaker, 1978; Songbook, 1979 (Soc. of West End Theatre Award, Best Musical, 1979); Tonight at 8.30, 1981; Arms and the Man, 1981; Pass the Butler, 1982; director, RSC: Anna Christie, Stratford 1979, London 1980; director, Broadway: The Moony Shapiro Songbook, 1981; film director: Mick's People, 1982. TV scriptwriter: situation comedies, including: My Brother's Keeper, 2 series, 1974 and 1975 (also co-starred); Yes Minister, 3 series, 1980, 1981 and 1982; film scriptwriter: The Internecine Project, 1974. *Publications:* A Proper Man (novel), 1976; Yes Minister, The Diaries of a Cabinet Minister: Vol. I, 1981; Vol. II, 1982. *Recreations:* reading, music, going to the cinema. *Address:* c/o A. D. Peters & Co. Ltd, 10 Buckingham Street, WC2N 6BU.

LYNN, Prof. Richard; Professor of Psychology, New University of Ulster, since 1972; *b* 20 Feb. 1930; *s* of Richard and Ann Lynn; *m* 1956, Susan Maher (marr. diss. 1978); one *s* two *d. Educ:* Bristol Grammar Sch.; King's Coll., Cambridge. Lectr in Psychology, Univ. of Exeter, 1956-67; Prof. of Psychology, Dublin Economic and Social Res. Inst., 1967-71. *Publications:* Attention, Arousal and the Orientation Reaction, 1966; The Irish Braindrain, 1969; The Universities and the Business Community, 1969; Personality and National Character, 1971; An Introduction to the Study of Personality, 1972; (ed) The Entrepreneur, 1974; (ed) Dimensions of Personality, 1981; articles on personality and social psychology. *Recreation:* do-it-yourself house renovation. *Address:* Dundery House, Coleraine, Co. Londonderry. *Club:* Arts (Dublin).

LYNN, Stanley B.; *see* Balfour-Lynn.

LYNN, Dame Vera, (Dame Vera Margaret Lewis), DBE 1975 (OBE 1969); singer; *b* 20 March 1917; *d* of Bertram Samuel Welch and Annie Welch; *m* 1941, Harry Lewis; one *d. Educ:* Brampton Rd Sch., East Ham. First public appearance as singer, 1924; joined juvenile troupe, 1928; ran own dancing school, 1932; broadcast with Joe Loss and joined Charlie Kunz, 1935; singer with Ambrose Orch., 1937-40, then went solo; voted most popular singer, Daily Express comp., 1939, and named Forces Sweetheart; own radio show, Sincerely Yours, 1941-47; starred in Applesauce, London Palladium, 1941; sang to troops in Burma, etc, 1944; subseq. Big Show (radio), USA; London Laughs, Adelphi; appeared at Flamingo Hotel, Las Vegas, and many TV shows, USA and Britain, including own TV series on Rediffusion, 1955; BBC TV, 1956; BBC 2, 1970; also appearances in Holland, Denmark, Sweden, Norway, Germany, Canada, NZ and Australia; in seven Command Performances, also films and own shows on radio. Records include Auf Wiederseh'n (over 12 million copies sold), became first British artiste to top American Hit Parade. Pres., Printers' Charitable Corp., 1980. Hon. Citizen: Winnipeg, 1974; Nashville, Tennessee, 1977. Hon. LLD Memorial Univ. of Newfoundland, 1977 (founded Lynn Music Scholarship, first award, 1982). Freedom, City of London, 1978. FInstD. Comdr, Order of Orange-Nassau, Holland. *Publication:* Vocal Refrain (autobiog.), 1975. *Recreations:* gardening, painting, sewing, swimming.

LYNN, Wilfred; Director, National Westminster Bank Ltd (Outer London Board), 1969-73; *b* 19 May 1905; *s* of late Wilfred Crosland Lynn and Alice Lynn; *m* 1936, Valerie, *e d* of late B. M. A. Critchley; one *s* one *d* (twins). *Educ:* Hull Grammar School. Entered National Provincial Bank Ltd, 1921; Asst General Manager, 1952; Joint General Manager, 1953; Chief General Manager, 1961; Director, 1965-69; Dir, North Central Finance Ltd, 1962-70. FIB. *Recreation:* golf. *Address:* c/o National Westminster Bank Ltd, 15 Bishopsgate, EC2.

LYNNE, Gillian, (Mrs Peter Land); director, choreographer, dancer, actress; *d* of late Leslie Pyrke and late Barbara Pyrke (*née* Hart); *m* 1980, Peter Land, actor. *Educ:* Baston-Bromley, Kent; Arts Educnl School. Leading soloist, Sadlers Wells Ballet, 1944-51; star dancer, London Palladium, 1951, 1952, 1953; film, Master of Ballantrae, 1952; lead in Can-Can, London Coliseum, 1954-55; Becky Sharp in Vanity Fair, Windsor, 1956; guest principal dancer,

Covent Garden, Sadler's Wells, Aida, Samson and Delilah, 1957; Tannhauser, Covent Garden; ballerina in Chelsea at Nine, 1958; lead in New Cranks, 1959; Wanda, Rose Marie, Cinderella, Out of My Mind, lead in revue, 1960-61; staged revue England Our England, Princes, 1961; leading lady, 5 Past Eight Show, Edinburgh, 1962; choreographed first ballet Owl and the Pussycat, Western Theatre Ballet, 1962; Queen of the Cats, London Palladium, 1962-63; directed revue Round Leicester Square, 1963; conceived, directed, choreographed and starred in modern dance revue Collages, Edinburgh Fest., 1963, transf. to Savoy; chor. 1st film Wonderful Life, 1963-64; chor. musical films Every Day's a Holiday and Three Hats for Lisa, 1964; chor. musicals The Roar of the Greasepaint and Pickwick, Broadway, 1965; directed, chor. The Match Girls, Globe, 1966; chor. Flying Dutchman, Covent Garden, 1966; dir., chor. Bluebeard, Sadlers Wells Opera, 1966; chor. and staged musical nos in Half a Sixpence (film), 1966-67; How Now Dow Jones, Broadway, 1967; chor. Midsummer Marriage, 1968 and The Trojans, 1969, Covent Garden; chor. new ballet Breakaway, Scottish Theatre Ballet, 1969; Phil the Fluter, Palace, 1969; dir. new prod. Bluebeard, Sadler's Wells Opera, London Coliseum, 1969; dir. and chor. musical Love on the Dole, Nottingham Playhouse, 1970; dir. Tonight at Eight, Hampstead, 1970, and Fortune, 1971; staged 200 Motels (pop-opera film), 1971; dir. Lillywhite Lies, Nottingham, 1971; chor. Ambassador, Her Majesty's, 1971; chor. Man of La Mancha (film), 1972; dir and chor. Liberty Ranch, Greenwich, 1972; dir. and chor., Once Upon a Time, 1972; chor. The Card, Queen's, 1973; staged musical nos in Quilp (film), 1974; chor. Hans Andersen, 1975; staged A Comedy of Errors, Stratford, 1976 (TV musical, ATV, 1977); co-dir, A Midsummer Night's Dream, Stratford, 1977; staged musical As You Like It, Stratford, 1977; chor. The Trojans, Covt Gdn, 1977; Way of the World, Aldwych, 1978; dir and chor. Jasperina, Amsterdam, 1978; chor. My Fair Lady, nat. tour and Adelphi, 1979; chor. Parsifal, Covt Gdn, 1979; staged Songbook, Globe, 1979; staged Once in a Lifetime, Aldwych, 1979; new stage act for Tommy Steele, 1979; dir, Tomfoolery, Criterion, 1980; dir Jeeves Takes Charge, Fortune and Canada, 1980; dir To Those Born Later, New End, 1981; Associate Dir and chor., Cats, New London, 1981, Broadway, 1982; Additional Dir, La Ronde, RSC Aldwych, 1982; directed and appeared in Alone Plus One, Newcastle, 1982; staged wedding sequence in Yentyl (film), 1982; has also appeared in or choreographed TV shows inc. Peter and the Wolf, 1958 (narr. and mimed all 9 parts); Puck, Midsummer Night's Dream, 1958; Val Doonican Shows, 1970; Perry Como Special, 1971; At the Hawk's Well (ballet), 1975; There was a Girl, 1975; Nana Mouskouri Series, 1976; prod and devised TV Noël Coward and Cleo Laine Specials, 1968; four BBC TV Specials, 1975; Petula Clark Special, 1975; first colour special for ABC, with Australian Ballet and Sydney Symphony Orch., and stage prod. Sydney Opera House, The Fool on the Hill, 1975; Muppet Show Series, ATV, 1976, 1977, 1978, 1979, 1980; Perry Como Christmas Special, 1977; New Ice Dance for John Curry, 1977; three World of Music Specials, BBC, 1977; Harry Secombe Christmas Special, 1977; Secombe Special, 1978; Ray Charles Special, 1978; Mike Burstein Show series, Holland, 1979-80; Comedy Tonight, Thames, 1980; directed for TV: Mrs F's Friends, BBC, 1981; Easy Money, BBC, 1982. *Publications:* articles in Dancing Times. *Address:* 25 The Avenue, Bedford Park, Chiswick, W4. *Club:* Pickwick.

LYNTON, Norbert Caspar; Professor of the History of Art, University of Sussex, since 1975; *b* 22 Sept. 1927; *s* of Paul and Amalie Christiane Lynton; *m* 1st, 1949, Janet Irving; two *s*; 2nd, 1969, Sylvia Anne Towning; two *s*. *Educ:* Douai Sch.; Birkbeck Coll., Univ. of London (BA Gen.); Courtauld Inst., Univ. of London (BA Hons). Lectr in History of Art and Architecture, Leeds Coll. of Art, 1950-61; Sen. Lectr, then Head of Dept of Art History and Gen. Studies, Chelsea Sch. of Art, 1961-70. London Corresp. of Art International, 1961-66; Art Critic, The Guardian, 1965-70; Dir of Exhibitions, Arts Council of GB, 1970-75; Vis. Prof. of History of Art, Open Univ., 1975. *Publications:* (jtly) Simpson's History of Architectural Development, vol. 4 (Renaissance), 1962; Kenneth Armitage, 1962; Paul Klee, 1964; The Modern World, 1968; The Story of Modern Art, 1980; Looking at Art, 1981; articles in Burlington Mag., TLS, Studio International, Architectural Design, Art in America, Smithsonian, Leonardo, etc. *Recreations:* art, people, music, travel. *Address:* Haydon Lodge, 22 East Drive, Brighton BN2 2BQ. *T:* Brighton 680315.

LYON; see Bowes Lyon, family name of Earl of Strathmore.

LYON, Alexander Ward; MP (Lab) York since 1966; *b* 15 Oct. 1931. Contested (Lab) York, 1964. Addtl PPS to the Treasury Ministers, 1969; PPS to Paymaster General, 1969; Opposition Spokesman: on African Affairs, 1970; on Home Affairs, 1971; Min. of State, Home Office, 1974-76. Member: Younger Cttee on Intrusions into Privacy; Select Cttee on Home Affairs, 1979. Chairman: UK Immigrants Adv. Service, 1978-; Parly Labour Party Home Affairs Gp, 1979. *Address:* House of Commons, SW1. *T:* 01-219 4021.

LYON, (Colin) Stewart (Sinclair), FIA; FSA, FRNS; General Manager (Finance), Group Actuary and Director, Legal & General Group Plc, since 1980; Chief Actuary, Legal & General Assurance Society Ltd, since 1976; *b* 22 Nov. 1926; *s* of late Col Colin Sinclair Lyon, OBE, TD and Mrs Dorothy Winstanley Lyon (*née* Thomason); *m* 1958, Elizabeth Mary Fargus Richards; four *s* one *d*. *Educ:* Liverpool Coll.; Trinity Coll., Cambridge (MA). FIA 1954; FSA 1972; FRNS 1955. Chief Exec., Victory Insurance Co. Ltd, 1974-76. Mem., Occupational Pensions Bd, 1979-82. President: Inst. of Actuaries, 1982-; British Numismatic Soc., 1966-70 (Sanford Saltus Gold

Medal, 1974); Vice-Pres., Guildford Philharmonic Soc., 1974-. Trustee, Disablement Income Gp Charitable Trust, 1967-. *Publications:* papers on Anglo-Saxon coinage, particularly in British Numismatic Jl; contrib. Jl of Inst. of Actuaries and Trans Internat. Congress of Actuaries. *Recreations:* numismatics, music, short-wave radio. *Address:* Cuerdale, White Lane, Guildford, Surrey GU4 8PR. *T:* Guildford 573761. *Club:* Actuaries'.

LYON, Mary Frances, ScD; FRS 1973; Head of Genetics Section, Medical Research Council Radiobiology Unit, Harwell, since 1962; *b* 15 May 1925; *e d* of Clifford James Lyon and Louise Frances Lyon (*née* Kirby). *Educ:* King Edward's Sch., Birmingham; Woking Grammar Sch.; Girton Coll., Cambridge, ScD 1968; FIBiol. MRC Scientific Staff, Inst. of Animal Genetics, Edinburgh, 1950-55; MRC Radiobiology Unit, Harwell, 1955-. Clothworkers Visiting Research Fellow, Girton Coll., Cambridge, 1970-71. Foreign Hon. Mem., Amer. Acad. Arts and Scis, 1980 (Amory Prize, 1977). Foreign Associate, US Nat. Acad. of Scis, 1979. *Publications:* papers on genetics in scientific jls. *Address:* MRC Radiobiology Unit, Harwell, Oxon OX11 0RD. *T:* Abingdon 834393.

LYON, (Percy) Hugh (Beverley), MC, MA; *b* 14 Oct. 1893; *s* of late P. C. Lyon, CSI; *m* 1920, Nancy Elinor (*d* 1970), 3rd *d* of William Richardson, Guisborough and Sandsend; three *d*; *m* 1973, Elizabeth Knight (*née* Beater). *Educ:* Rugby Sch.; Oriel Coll., Oxford. Served with 6th Bn the Durham Light Infantry, 1914-19; Captain, 1917; MC 1917; wounded, 1918; prisoner of war, May 1918. Newdigate Prize Poem, 1919; BA and MA 1919; 1st class Final School Lit. Hum., 1921. Asst Master, Cheltenham Coll., 1921-26; Rector of the Edinburgh Academy, 1926-31; Headmaster of Rugby Sch., 1931-48; Chm., HMC, 1948; Director, Public Schools Appointments Bureau, 1950-61. *Publications:* Songs of Youth and War, 1917; Turn Fortune, 1923; The Discovery of Poetry, 1930. *Address:* Springhill, Amberley, Stroud, Glos. *T:* Amberley 2275.

LYON, Maj.-Gen. Robert, CB 1976; OBE 1964 (MBE 1960); Bursar, Loretto School, Musselburgh, since 1979; *b* Ayr, 24 Oct. 1923; *s* of David Murray Lyon and Bridget Lyon (*née* Smith); *m* 1951, Constance Margaret Gordon (*d* 1982); one *s* one *d*. *Educ:* Ayr Academy. Commissioned, Aug. 1943, Argyll and Sutherland Highlanders. Served Italy, Germany, Palestine, Greece; transf. to Regular Commn in RA, 1947; Regtl Service, 3 RHA in Libya and 19 Field in BAOR, 1948-56; Instr, Mons Officer Cadet Sch., 1953-55; Staff Coll., 1957; DAQMG, 3 Div., 1958-60; jssc, 1960; BC F (Sphinx) Bty 7 PARA, RHA, 1961-62 (Bt Lt-Col); GSO1, ASD2, MoD, 1962-65 (Lt-Col); CO 4 Lt Regt, RA, 1965-67, Borneo (despatches), UK and BAOR (Lt-Col); as Brig.: CRA 1 Div., 1967-69, BAOR; IDC, 1970; Dir Operational Requirements, MoD, 1971-73; DRA (Maj.-Gen.), 1973-75; GOC SW District, 1975-78; retired 1979. Pres., Army Hockey Assoc., 1974-76; Chm., Army Golf Assoc., 1977-78. Col Comdt RA. FBIM (MBIM 1978). *Recreations:* golf, fishing, ski-ing. *Address:* Woodside, Braemar, Aberdeenshire, Scotland. *T:* Braemar 667; Loretto School, Musselburgh, East Lothian EH21 7RE. *T:* 031-665 2380. *Club:* New (Edinburgh).

LYON, Stanley Douglas; Deputy Chairman, Imperial Chemical Industries Ltd, 1972-77 (Director, 1968-77); *b* 22 June 1917; *s* of Ernest Hutcheon Lyon and late Helen Wilson Lyon; *m* 1941, May Alexandra Jack; three *s*. *Educ:* George Heriot's Sch., Edinburgh; Edinburgh Univ. (BSc Hons Engrg). AMICE, FBIM. Major, Royal Engrs, 1939-46. ICI Ltd: Engr, Dyestuffs Div., 1946; Engrg Dir, Wilton Works, 1957; Prodn Dir, Agricl Div., 1962; Dep. Chm. 1964, Chm. 1966, Agric. Div. *Recreations:* golf, tennis, gardening, sculpture. *Address:* Bramble Carr, Danby, Whitby, N Yorks.

LYON, Hon. Sterling, QC (Canada) 1960; Premier, Province of Manitoba, 1977-82; *b* 30 Jan. 1927; *s* of David Rufus Lyon and Ella May (*née* Cuthbert); *m* 1953, Barbara Jean Mayers; two *s* three *d*. *Educ:* Portage Collegiate (Governor-General's Medal); United College (BA 1948); Univ. of Manitoba Law Sch. (LLB 1953). Crown Attorney, Manitoba, 1953-57; Member, Manitoba Legislative Assembly, and Executive Council, 1958-69; Attorney-General, 1958-63 and 1966-69; Minister of: Municipal Affairs, 1960-61; Public Utilities, 1961-63; Mines and Natural Resources, 1963-66; Tourism and Recreation, Commissioner of Northern Affairs, 1966-68; Govt House Leader, 1966-69. Director and General Counsel of National Corporation, 1969-72; Member, law firm Pitblado & Hoskin, from 1974. Leader, Progressive Conservative Party, from 1975; MLA 1976-; Leader of Opposition in Legislature, 1976-77; Premier of Manitoba and Minister of Dominion-Provincial Affairs, 1977-82. *Recreations:* hunting, fishing. *Address:* Legislative Building, Winnipeg, Manitoba R3C 0V8, Canada. *T:* (204) 944-3714. *Club:* Albany (Toronto).

LYON, Stewart; see Lyon, C. S. S.

LYON-DALBERG-ACTON, family name of **Baron Acton.**

LYONS, Bernard, CBE 1964; JP; DL; Chairman, UDS Group Ltd, 1972-82 (Joint Managing Director, 1966; Managing Director, 1972-79); *b* 30 March 1913; *m* 1938, Lucy Hurst; three *s* one *d*. *Educ:* Leeds Grammar Sch. Chm., Yorkshire and NE Conciliation Cttee, Race Relations Bd, 1968-70; Member: Leeds City Council, 1951-65; Community Relations Commn, 1970-72. Life Pres., Leeds Jewish Representative Council. JP Leeds, 1960; DL West Riding, Yorks, 1971. Hon. LLD Leeds, 1973. *Publication:* The Thread is Strong, 1981. *Recreation:* farming. *Address:* Upton Wood, Fulmer, Bucks. *T:* Fulmer 2404.

See also S. R. Lyons.

LYONS, Dennis John, CB 1972; CEng, FRAeS; Director General of Research, Department of the Environment, 1971-76; *b* 26 Aug. 1916; *s* of late John Sylvester Lyons and of Adela Maud Lyons; *m* 1939, Elisabeth, *d* of Arnold and Maria Friederika Müller Haefliger, Weggis, Switzerland; five *s* two *d. Educ:* Grocers' Company School; Queen Mary Coll., London Univ. (Fellow, 1969). Aerodynamics Dept, Royal Aircraft Estabt, 1937; RAFVR, 1935-41; Aerodynamics Flight Aero Dept, RAE, 1941-51; Head of Experimental Projects Div., Guided Missiles Dept, RAE, 1951; Head of Ballistic Missile Group, GW Dept, 1956; Head of Weapons Dept, RAE, 1962; Dir., Road Research Laboratory, 1965-72. Member: Adv. Board for Res. Councils, 1973-76; SRC, 1973-76; Engineering Bd, SRC, 1970-76; Natural Environment Res. Council, 1973-76. Pres. OECD Road Research Unit, 1968-72. Hon. Mem., Instn Highway Engineers. *Publications:* papers in scientific jls. *Recreations:* ski-ing, pottery-making, philately. *Address:* Summerhaven, Gough Road, Fleet, Hants. *T:* 4773.

LYONS, Edward, LLB, QC 1974; MP Bradford West, since 1974 (Bradford East, 1966-74) (Lab, 1966-81, SDP since 1981); a Recorder of the Crown Court, since 1972; *b* 17 May 1926; *s* of late A. Lyons and of Mrs S. Taylor; *m* 1955, Barbara, *d* of Alfred Katz; one *s* one *d. Educ:* Roundhay High Sch.; Leeds Univ. LLB (Hons) 1951. Served Royal Artillery, 1944-48; Combined Services Russian Course, Cambridge Univ., 1946; Interpreter in Russian, Brit. CCG, 1946-48. Called to Bar, Lincoln's Inn, 1952. Contested (Lab) Harrogate, 1964. PPS at Treasury, 1969-70; Chairman: Lab. Party Parly Legal and Judicial Gp, 1974-77; Lab. Party Parly Home Office Gp, 1974-79 (Dep. Chm., 1970-74); Mem., House of Commons Select Cttee on European Legislation, 1975-. Mem., Exec. of Justice, 1974-; SDP Parly Spokesman on Home and Legal Affairs; Mem., Amnesty. *Recreations:* history, opera. *Address:* House of Commons, SW1; 15 Old Square, Lincoln's Inn, WC2. *T:* 01-831 7517, 01-834 1960; 4 Primley Park Lane, Leeds LS17 7JR. *T:* Leeds 685351.

LYONS, Sir Edward Houghton, Kt 1977; Chairman, Katies Ltd (numerous subsidiaries); wholesaler and retailer of women's clothing, Australia. *Address:* Katies Ltd, Box 4259, GPO, Sydney 2001, NSW, Australia; 47 Kneale Street, Holland Park Heights, Brisbane, Queensland, Australia. *T:* 49 6461.

LYONS, Prof. Francis Stewart Leland, MA, PhD, LittD Dublin; FRHistS; FBA 1974; FRSL; MRIA; Professor of History in the University of Dublin, since 1981; *b* 11 Nov. 1923; *e s* of Stewart Lyons and Florence May Leland; *m* 1954, Jennifer Ann Stuart McAlister; two *s. Educ:* Dover Coll.; Trinity Coll., Dublin. Lecturer in History, University Coll., Hull, 1947-51; Fellow of Trinity Coll., Dublin, 1951-64, 1981-, Provost, 1974-81; Prof. of Modern History, Univ. of Kent, 1964-74. Master of Eliot Coll., Univ. of Kent, 1969-72. Ford's Lectr in English History, Univ. of Oxford, 1977-78. FRSL 1978. Hon. Fellow, Oriel Coll., Oxford, 1975. Hon. DLitt: Pennsylvania, 1975; Hull, 1978; Kent, 1978; NUU, 1980; Hon. DLit QUB, 1978; Hon. LLD St Andrew's, 1981. Wolfson Literary Award, 1980. *Publications:* The Irish Parliamentary Party, 1951; The Fall of Parnell, 1960; Internationalism in Europe, 1815-1914, 1963; John Dillon: a biography, 1968; Ireland since the Famine, 1971; Charles Stewart Parnell, 1977 (Heinemann award, 1978); Culture and Anarchy in Ireland 1890-1939, 1979 (Ewart-Biggs Meml Prize, 1980); (ed with R. A. J. Hawkins) Ireland under the Union: Varieties of Tension, essays in honour of T. W. Moody, 1980; articles and reviews in various historical jls. *Recreations:* walking, squash rackets. *Address:* Trinity College, Dublin. *T:* Dublin 772941. *Club:* Kildare Street and University (Dublin).

LYONS, Hamilton; Sheriff of North Strathclyde (formerly Renfrew and Argyll, and Ayr and Bute), since 1968; *b* 3 Aug. 1918; *s* of Richard Lyons and Annie Cathro Thomson; *m* 1943, Jean Cathro Blair; two *s. Educ:* Gourock High Sch.; Greenock High Sch.; Glasgow Univ. (BL 1940). Practised as Solicitor, Greenock, until 1966; Sheriff Substitute of Inverness, Moray, Nairn and Ross and Cromarty at Stornoway and Lochmaddy, 1966-68. Member: Coun. of Law Soc. of Scotland, 1950-66 (Vice-Pres., 1962-63); Law Reform Cttee for Scotland, 1954-64; Cttee of Inquiry on Children and Young Persons, 1961-64; Cttee of Inquiry on Sheriff Courts, 1963-67; Sheriff Court Rules Coun., 1952-66; Scottish Probation Adv. and Trng Coun., 1959-69. *Address:* 14 Cloch Road, Gourock, Inverclyde PA19 1AB. *T:* Gourock 32566.

LYONS, Sir (Isidore) Jack, Kt 1973; CBE 1967; Chairman, John David Ltd; Director of other companies; *b* 1 Feb. 1916; *s* of Samuel H. Lyons and Sophia Niman; *m* 1943, Roslyn Marion Rosenbaum; two *s* two *d. Educ:* Leeds Grammar Sch. Chm., Leeds Musical Festival, 1955-72, Vice-Pres., 1973; Chm., London Symphony Orchestra Trust, 1974 (Jt Chm., 1963-70), Trustee, 1970- (Hon. Mem., LSO, 1973); Jt Chm., Southwark Rehearsal Hall Trust, 1974-; Chm., Shakespeare Exhibn (quatercentenary celebrations Stratford-upon-Avon), 1964; Mem. Exec. Cttee, Royal Acad. of Dancing, 1964; Life Trustee, Shakespeare Birthplace Trust, 1967; Mem., Culture Adv. Cttee, UNESCO, 1973-, Dep. Chm., Fanfare for Europe, 1972-73; Chm., FCO US Bicentennial Cttee for the Arts, 1973-; Mem., Adv. Cttee of Honour, Britain's Salute to NY 1983 Bicentennial. Vice-Pres., Jt Israel Appeal, 1972 (Dep. Chm. 1957); Chm., Fedn of Jewish Relief Organisations, 1958. Member: Canadian Veterans' Assoc., 1964; Pilgrims, 1965. Patron, St Gemma's Hospice. Dep. Chm., Governors of Carmel Coll., 1961-69; Mem. Ct, York Univ., 1965. Hon. FRAM, 1973. DUniv York, 1975. *Recreations:* music, the arts and

swimming. *Address:* Blundell House, 2 Campden Hill, W8. *T:* 01-727 2750. *Club:* Carlton.

LYONS, James, OBE 1964; FDSRCSE; FFDRCSIre; retired as dental surgeon, 1974; Hon. Consultant Dental Surgeon to Northern Ireland Hospitals Authority, 1952; *b* 4 June 1887; *s* of Richard Lyons, Sligo; *m* 1916, Kathleen Arnold, *d* of George Myles, Crieff, Scotland; two *s* one *d. Educ:* Clevedon Sch., Somerset; Royal Coll. of Surgeons, Edinburgh. LDS 1912; FDS 1951, RCS Edinburgh; FFD 1963, RCS, Ireland. Hon. Dental Surgeon to Royal Victoria Hospital, Belfast, 1927-51; Lectr on Dental Materia Medica, at Dental Sch. of Queen's Univ., Belfast, 1935-52. Member: Dental Bd of UK, 1939-56; British Dental Assoc. (Pres. N Ireland Branch, 1939-41); N Ireland Health Services Bd, 1948-66; General Dental Council, 1956-61. Hon MDS QUB, 1971. *Recreations:* photography, motoring. *Address:* High Trees, 4 Kincraig Park, Newtownalley, Co. Antrim, NI.

LYONS, Sir James (Reginald), Kt 1969; JP; Chairman and Company Director, Park Lodge Property Company; Airport Manager, Cardiff Airport, 1955-75; *b* 15 March 1910; *s* of James Lyons; *m* 1937, Doreen Mary Fogg; one *s. Educ:* Howard Gardens High Sch.; Cardiff Technical Coll. Served War of 1939-45: Royal Tank Regt, 1940-46 (1939-45 Star, Africa Star, Italy Star, Defence Medal, War Medal of 1939-45). Civil Service, 1929-65: Post Office, Min. of Supply, Min. of Aviation. Mem., Wales Tourist Bd. Glamorgan CC, 1965-74; Cardiff City Council: Councillor, 1949-58; Alderman, 1958-74; Lord Mayor of Cardiff, 1968-69. Mem., BBC Broadcasting Council. Assessor under Race Relations Act, 1976. Life Vice Pres., Welsh Games Council. Trustee, Wales and Border Counties Trust. Governor: St Illtyds Coll.; De La Salle Prep. Sch. JP Cardiff, 1966-. OStJ; KCSG. *Recreations:* Rugby football, swimming, tennis. *Address:* 101 Minehead Avenue, Sully, S Glam. *T:* Sully 530403.

LYONS, Prof. John, FBA 1973; Professor of Linguistics, since 1976, and Pro-Vice-Chancellor, since 1981, University of Sussex; *b* 23 May 1932; *s* of Michael A. Lyons and Mary B. Lyons (*née* Sullivan); *m* 1959, Danielle J. Simonet; two *d. Educ:* St Bede's Coll., Manchester; Christ's Coll., Cambridge. MA; PhD 1961. Lecturer: in Comparative Linguistics, SOAS, 1957-61; in General Linguistics, Univ. of Cambridge, 1961-64; Prof. of General Linguistics, Edinburgh Univ., 1964-76. DesL (*hc*) Univ. Catholique de Louvain, 1980. *Publications:* Structural Semantics, 1964; Introduction to Theoretical Linguistics, 1968; New Horizons in Linguistics, 1970; Chomsky, 1970, 2nd edn 1977; Semantics, vols 1 and 2, 1977; Language and Linguistics, 1981; Language, Meaning and Context, 1981; articles and reviews in learned journals. *Address:* School of Social Sciences, University of Sussex, Falmer, Brighton BN1 9QN.

LYONS, John; General Secretary, Engineers' and Managers' Association (1977) and Electrical Power Engineers' Association, since 1973; *b* 19 May 1926; *s* of Joseph and Hetty Lyons; *m* 1954, Molly McCall; two *s* two *d. Educ:* St Paul's Sch.; Polytechnic, Regent Street; Cambridge Univ. (BA Econ). RN 1944-46. Asst. to Manager of Market Research Dept, Vacuum Oil Co., 1950; Research Officer: Bureau of Current Affairs, 1951; Post Office Engineering Union, 1952-57; Asst. Sec., Instn of Professional Civil Servants 1957-66, Dep. Gen. Sec. 1966-73. Member: Nat. Enterprise Bd, 1975-79; Exec. Cttee PEP, 1975-78; Council, PSI, 1978-80; Exec. Cttee, IPA, 1976-81; Adv. Council for Applied R&D, 1978-81; Engrg Council, 1982-; Mem., PO Bd, 1980-81, British Telecommunications Bd, 1981-; Sec., Employees' Nat. Cttee for Electricity Supply Industry, 1976-; Chm., NEDO Working Party on Industrial Trucks, 1977-80. Governor, Kingsbury High School, 1974-; Mem. Court of Governors, LSE, 1978-. FRSA. *Publications:* various papers and articles. *Recreation:* family. *Address:* Engineers' and Managers' Association, Station House, Fox Lane North, Chertsey, Surrey KT16 9HW. *T:* Chertsey 64131.

LYONS, His Honour Sir Rudolph, Kt 1976; QC 1953; a Circuit Judge, 1972-82; Honorary Recorder of Manchester, 1977-82; *b* 5 Jan. 1912; *er s* of late G. Lyons, Leeds; *m* 1936, Jeannette, *yr d* of late Philip Dante; one *s* two *d. Educ:* Leeds Grammar Sch.; Leeds Univ. (LLB). Called to Bar, Gray's Inn, 1934; Mem., Gen. Council of the Bar, 1958-70; Master of the Bench, Gray's Inn, 1961-. Recorder of: Sunderland, 1955-56; Newcastle upon Tyne, 1956-61; Sheffield, 1961-65; Leeds, 1965-70; Recorder and Judge of the Crown Ct of Liverpool, 1970-71; Hon. Recorder of Liverpool, 1972-77. Comr, Central Criminal Court, 1962-70; Comr of Assize, 1969; Leader of N Eastern Circuit, 1961-70; Solicitor-Gen., 1961-65, Attorney-Gen., 1965-70, County Palatine of Durham. Jt Pres., Council, HM Circuit Judges, 1974. Hon. Mem., Northern Circuit, 1979. Mem. Court, Univ. of Manchester, 1980-. Hon. LLD Leeds, 1982. *Recreations:* gardening, paintings, classical music. *Address:* 8 Brookside, Alwoodley, Leeds LS17 8TD. *T:* Leeds 683274. *Clubs:* Racquet (Liverpool); St James's (Manchester).

LYONS, Stuart Randolph; Managing Director, UDS Group plc, since 1979 (Director, since 1974); *b* 24 Oct. 1943; 3rd *s* of Bernard Lyons, *qv*; *m* 1969, Ellen Harriet Zion; two *s* one *d. Educ:* Rugby (Scholar); King's Coll., Cambridge (Major Scholar; 1st Cl. Hons Pt I Classical Tripos, Cl. II(I) Pt II Classical Tripos; BA 1965, MA 1969). Man. Dir, John Collier Tailoring Ltd, 1969-74. Member: Leeds CC, 1970-74; Yorkshire and Humberside Econ. Planning Council, 1972-75; Clothing EDC, 1976-79; Ordnance Survey Review Cttee, 1978-79; Monopolies and Mergers Commn, 1981-. Conservative Parly Candidate, Halifax, Feb. and Oct. 1974. *Recreations:*

Mandarin Chinese, squash. *Address:* 50 Seymour Walk, SW10 9NF. *T:* 01-352 3309. *Club:* Carlton.

LYONS, Terence Patrick; Executive Director (Personnel), Williams & Glyn's Bank Ltd, 1969-81, Director, 1981-82; Director: Industrial Services Ltd, since 1980; Robin Marlar and Associates Ltd, since 1981; *b* 2 Sept. 1919; *s* of Maurice Peter Lyons and Maude Mary Elizabeth Lyons (*née* O'Farrell); *m* 1945, Winifred Mary Normile; two *d. Educ:* Wimbledon Coll.; King's College, London; London Sch. of Economics. CompIPM, FIB. Indian Armd Corps, 1940-46. Unilever Ltd, 1948-54; Philips Electrical Industries Ltd, 1954-60; Ilford Ltd, 1960-66; Staveley Industries Ltd, 1966-69. Pres., Inst. of Personnel Management, 1971-73; Mem. Council, Inst. Bankers, 1975-81; Chairman: Manpower Services Adv. Panel, CBI, 1975-; Educn and Trng Cttee, CBI, 1976-77 (Vice-Chm., 1977-); Council, Fedn of London Clearing Bank Employers, 1976-78 (Mem., 1971-81). Member: Monopolies and Mergers Commn, 1975-81; MSC, 1981-82; EEC Vocational Trng Cttee, 1981-. Mem. Council, Open Univ., 1980-. *Publications:* The Personnel Function in a Changing Environment, 1971; contrib. personnel management and banking jls. *Recreations:* sailing, golf, tennis, music. *Address:* Winter Ride, 2 Rosefield, Kippington Road, Sevenoaks, Kent. *T:* Sevenoaks 456989. *Clubs:* Army and Navy; Wildernesse Golf; Chipstead Sailing.

LYONS, Thomas; MP (N Ireland) North Tyrone 1943-69, retired; farmer; *b* 18 Feb. 1896; *s* of late J. J. Lyons, JP, farmer, Newtownstewart, Co. Tyrone, and Elizabeth McFarland, Ballinamallaght, Donemana, Co. Tyrone; *m* 1927, Clarice E. Kiss, Croydon, Sydney, Australia; two *s* one *d. Educ:* Albert Agricultural Coll., Glasnevin, Dublin. Enlisted 1915, in N Irish Horse, served European War, France, with that Regt until transferred, 1917, to Royal Irish Fus. (wounded). Went to Australia, 1922; returned N Ireland, 1939; entered politics as result of by-election, Aug. 1943; Dep. Speaker and Chm. of Ways and Means, House of Commons, N Ireland, 1955-69. JP 1944, High Sheriff 1961, Co. Tyrone. *Address:* Riversdale, Newtownstewart, Co. Tyrone. *T:* Newtownstewart 253. *Club:* Tyrone County (Omagh).

LYONS, Sir William, Kt 1956; RDI 1954; President, Jaguar Cars Co. Ltd, since 1972; *b* 4th Sept. 1901, Blackpool; *s* of William Lyons; *m* 1924, Greta, *d* of Alfred Jenour Brown; two *d* (one *s* decd). *Educ:* Arnold Hse, Blackpool. Founded in partnership, Swallow Sidecar Co., 1922, which, after several changes in name, became Jaguar Cars Ltd (Chm. and Chief Exec., until 1972); formerly: Dep. Chm., British Leyland Motor Corp.; Chm. and Chief Exec., Daimler Co. Ltd; Chm., Coventry Climax Engines; Chm., Lanchester Motor Co. Ltd and other subsid. cos; retired 1972. Past President: Soc. of Motor Manufrs and Traders, 1950-51; Motor Industry Research Assoc., 1954; Motor Trades Benevolent Fund, 1954; Fellowship of the Motor Industry (FMI). FRSA 1964; Hon. AMIAE. Hon. DTech Loughborough, 1969. Coventry Award of Merit Gold Medal, 1970; Gold Medal, AA, 1972. *Recreation:* golf. *Address:* Wappenbury Hall, Wappenbury, near Leamington Spa, Warwickshire. *T:* Marton 632209.

LYSAGHT, family name of **Baron Lisle.**

LYTHALL, Basil Wilfrid, CB 1966; MA; *b* 15 May 1919; *s* of Frank Herbert Lythall and Winifred Mary (*née* Carver); *m* 1942, Mary Olwen Dando; one *s. Educ:* King Edward's Sch., Stourbridge; Christ Church, Oxford. Joined Royal Naval Scientific Service, 1940; Admiralty Signal and Radar Establishment, 1940-53; Admiralty Research Laboratory, 1954-57; Asst Dir of Physical Research, Admty, 1957-58; a Dep. Chief Scientist, Admty Signal and Radar Estabt (later Admty Surface Weapons Estabt), 1958-60; first Chief Scientist of Admty Underwater Weapons Estabt, Portland, 1960-64; Member of Admiralty Bd of Defence Council and Chief Scientist (RN), 1964-78; Dep. Controller, R&D Estab., Procurement Exec., 1971-78; Dir, SACLANT Anti-Submarine Warfare Res. Centre, La Spezia, Italy, 1978-81. Trustee, National Maritime Museum, 1974-80. *Publications:* occasional articles in learned jls. *Recreations:* walking, music. *Address:* 48 Grove Way, Esher, Surrey. *T:* 01-398 2958. *Club:* Athenæum.

LYTHGO, Wilbur Reginald, OBE 1964; HM Diplomatic Service, retired; *b* 7 June 1920; *yr s* of late Alfred and Marion Lythgo, Monkton, Ayrshire; *m* 1943, Patricia Frances Sylvia Smith; two *s. Educ:* Palmer's Sch., Grays, Essex. Joined Home Office, 1937. Served in RASC, 1939-41 and Indian Army, 1941-46. Rejoined Home Office, 1946; British Information Services, New Delhi, 1948-54; UK High Commn, New Delhi, 1956-59; British High Commn, Ottawa, 1962-66; Head of Office Services and Supply Dept, DSAO, 1966-68; Counsellor, British Embassy, and Consul-Gen., Washington DC, 1968-71; Consul-Gen., Cleveland, Ohio, 1971-73. Hon. Kentucky Col, 1971. *Recreations:* reading, gardening. *Address:* 200 Dovercourt Avenue, Ottawa, Ontario K1Z 7H2, Canada. *T:* (613) 722 3242.

LYTHGOE, Prof. Basil, FRS 1958; Professor of Organic Chemistry, Leeds University, 1953-78; *b* 18 Aug. 1913; 2nd *s* of Peter Whitaker and Agnes Lythgoe; *m* 1946, Kathleen Cameron, *er d* of H. J. Hallum, St Andrews; two *s. Educ:* Leigh Grammar Sch.; Manchester Univ. Asst Lectr, Manchester Univ., 1938; Univ. Lectr, Cambridge Univ., 1946. Fellow of King's Coll., Cambridge, 1950. *Publications:* papers on chemistry of natural products, in Jl of Chem. Soc. *Recreation:* mountaineering. *Address:* 113 Cookridge Lane, Leeds LS16 0JJ. *T:* Leeds 678837.

LYTHGOE, Ian Gordon, CB 1975; company director; *b* 30 Dec. 1914; *s* of John and Susan Lythgoe; *m* 1st, 1939, Marjory Elsie Fleming; three *s*; 2nd, 1971, Mary Margaret Pickard, CBE 1980. *Educ:* Southland Boys' High Sch., Invercargill; Victoria UC, Wellington. MComm (Hons); FCA(NZ). Private Sec., Ministers of Finance, 1944-53; Asst Sec., Treasury, 1960; State Services Commission: Mem., 1964-66; Dep. Chm., 1967-70; Chm., 1971-74. NZ Soc. of Accountants: Mem. Council, 1966-76; Vice-Pres., 1973-74; Pres., 1974-75. Mem. Council, Central Inst. of Technology (Vice Chm., 1978-80, Chm., 1980-; Chm., Finance Cttee, 1977-80). Mem., Commn of Enquiry into Rescue and Fire Safety at Internat. Airports (NZ). Director: Fletcher Challenge Corp. Ltd (formerly Challenge Corp. Ltd); Philips Electrical Industries of NZ Ltd. *Recreations:* gardening, reading. *Address:* Winara Avenue, Waikanae, New Zealand. *T:* 5113. *Club:* Wellington (Wellington, NZ).

LYTTELTON, family name of **Viscount Chandos** and of **Viscount Cobham.**

LYTTELTON, Humphrey Richard Adeane; musician; band-leader (specializing in Jazz); journalist; *b* Eton, Bucks, 23 May 1921; *s* of late Hon. George William Lyttelton; *m* 1st, 1948, Patricia Mary Braithwaite (marr. diss. 1952); one *d*; 2nd, 1952, Elizabeth Jill, *d* of Albert E. Richardson; two *s* one *d. Educ:* Sunningdale Sch.; Eton Coll.; self-taught as regards musical educn. Served War of 1939-45: Grenadier Guards, 1941-46. Camberwell Art Sch., 1947-48; Cartoonist, Daily Mail, 1949-53. Formed his own band, 1948; leader of Humphrey Lyttelton's Band, and free-lance journalist, 1953-. Numerous recordings and television appearances; recent jazz festival appearances, Bracknell, Zürich, Camden, Montreux, Newcastle, Warsaw, 1976. Compère, BBC Jazz programmes: Jazz Scene, Jazz Club, etc. *Publications:* I Play as I Please, 1954; Second Chorus, 1958; Take It from the Top (autobiog.), 1975; The Best of Jazz: Basin Street to Harlem, 1978; Humphrey Lyttelton's Jazz and Big Band Quiz, 1979; contributor: Melody Maker, 1954-; Reynolds News, 1955-62; Sunday Citizen, 1962-67; Harper's & Queen's; Punch. *Address:* BBC Light Music Department, Broadcasting House, Portland Place, W1A 4WW. *T:* 01-580 4468; (home) Alyn Close, Barnet Road, Arkley, Herts.

LYTTLE, James Brian Chambers; Under Secretary (formerly Deputy Secretary), Department of Commerce, Northern Ireland, since 1978; *b* 22 Aug. 1932; *s* of James Chambers Lyttle and Margaret Kirkwood Billingsley; *m* 1957, Mary Alma Davidson; four *d. Educ:* Bangor Grammar Sch.; Trinity Coll., Dublin (BA 1st Cl. Hons Classics). Entered NI Civil Service as Asst Principal, 1954; Private Sec. to Minister of Commerce, 1960-62; Chief Exec., Enterprise Ulster, 1972-75; Dir, Employment Service, Dept of Manpower Services, 1975-77; Dir, Industrial Develt Orgn, Dept of Commerce, 1977-81. *Recreations:* reading, walking. *Address:* Bayswater, 81 Princetown Road, Bangor, Co. Down BT20 3TD. *T:* Bangor 3209.

LYTTLETON, Prof. Raymond Arthur, FRS; MA, PhD; Emeritus Professor of Theoretical Astronomy, University of Cambridge; Fellow of St John's College, Cambridge; Member, Institute of Astronomy (formerly Institute of Theoretical Astronomy), University of Cambridge, since 1967; *o s* of William John Lyttleton and Agnes (*d* of Patrick Joseph Kelly), Warley Woods, near Birmingham, formerly of Ireland; *m* Meave Marguerite, *o d* of F. Hobden, Parkstone, formerly of Shanghai; no *c. Educ:* King Edward's Grammar Sch., Five Ways; King Edward's Sch., Birmingham; Clare Coll., Cambridge. Wrangler; Tyson Medal for Astronomy. Procter Visiting Fellowship, Princeton Univ., USA; Exptl Officer, Min. of Supply, 1940-42; Technical Asst to Scientific Adviser to the Army Council, War Office, 1943-45. Lectr in Mathematics, 1937-59, Stokes Lectr, 1954-59, Reader in Theoretical Astronomy, 1959-69 (resigned), Univ. of Cambridge. Jacob Siskind Vis. Prof., Brandeis Univ., USA, 1965-66; Vis. Prof., Brown Univ., USA, 1967-68; Halley Lectr, Oxford Univ., 1970; Milne Lectr, Oxford, 1978. Mem. of Council, Royal Society, 1959-61; Geophysical Sec. of Royal Astronomical Soc., 1949-60 and Mem. of Council, 1950-61, 1969-72; Fellow, 1934-; Pres., Milne Soc., 1977-. Hon. Mem., Mark Twain Soc., 1977. Hopkins Prize (for 1951) of Cambridge Philosophical Soc.; Gold Medallist of Royal Astronomical Soc., 1959; Royal Medallist of Royal Society, 1965. *Publications:* The Comets and their Origin, 1953; The Stability of Rotating Liquid Masses, 1953; The Modern Universe, 1956; Rival Theories of Cosmology, 1960; Man's View of the Universe, 1961; Mysteries of the Solar System, 1968; (Play) A Matter of Gravity (produced by BBC, 1968); Cambridge Encyclopædia of Astronomy (co-ed and contrib.), 1977; papers on astrophysics, cosmogony, cosmology, physics, dynamics, and geophysics in Proc. Royal Soc., Monthly Notices of Royal Astron. Soc., Proc. Camb. Phil Soc., etc. *Recreations:* golf, motoring, music; wondering about it all. *Address:* 165 Huntingdon Road, Cambridge. *T:* 354910; St John's College, Cambridge. *T:* 61621; Institute of Astronomy, Madingley Road, Cambridge. *T:* Cambridge 62204.

LYTTON, family name of **Earl of Lytton.**

LYTTON, 4th Earl of, *cr* 1880; **Noel Anthony Scawen Lytton,** OBE 1945; Viscount Knebworth, 1880; Baron Lytton, 1866; Baron Wentworth, 1529; Bt 1838; *b* 7 April 1900; *s* of 3rd Earl of Lytton, OBE, and 16th Baroness Wentworth (*d* 1957); *S* father, 1951; *m* 1946, Clarissa Mary, *er d* of late Brig.-Gen C. E. Palmer, CB, CMG, DSO, RA, and of Mrs Palmer, Christchurch, Hants; two *s* three *d. Educ:* Downside; RMC Sandhurst. Lieut, Rifle Bde, 1921, attached King's African Rifles, 1922-27; Administrator,

Samburu and Turkhana District, Kenya, 1924–25; Instructor (Economics), Sandhurst, 1931–35; Captain Rifle Bde, 1936; Staff Capt., War Office, 1937; Major, 1938; served War of 1939–45 (temp. Lt-Col) in N Africa, Italy, Greece and Austria; Administrator, Patras District, Greece, 1944; Chief Staff Officer, Mil. Government of Vienna, 1945–46; retd, 1946. Leader, Working Boys' Club, Bermondsey, 1937–39; formerly Member: Youth Adv. Council; Central Adv. Council for Educn (England). Farmer, 1959–; author; a crossbencher, House of Lords. Freeman: Missolonghi, Greece; Kismayu, Somalia. *Publications:* The Desert and the Green (autobiography), 1957; Wilfrid Scawen Blunt (biog.), 1961; Mickla Bendore (novel), 1962; Lucia in Taormina (novel), 1963; The Stolen Desert (history), 1966. *Heir:* s Viscount Knebworth, qv. *Address:* House of Lords, SW1A 0PW.

See also Baron Cobbold, Hon. C. M. Woodhouse.

LYVEDEN, 6th Baron cr 1859; **Ronald Cecil Vernon;** retired; b 10 April 1915; s of 5th Baron Lyveden and Ruby (*née* Shanley) (d 1932); S father, 1973; m 1938, Queenie Constance, d of Howard Ardern; three s. *Educ:* Te Aroha College. *Heir:* e s Hon. Jack Leslie Vernon [b 10 Nov. 1938; m 1961, Lynette June, d of William Herbert Lilley; one s two d]. *Address:* 20 Farmer Street, Te Aroha, New Zealand. *T:* 410. *Club:* RSA (Te Aroha).

M

MA LIN, PhD; Vice-Chancellor, The Chinese University of Hong Kong, since 1978; b 8 Feb. 1925; s of late Prof. Ma Kiam of and Sing-yu Cheng; m 1958, Dr Meng-Hua Chen; three d. *Educ:* West China Union Univ., China (BSc); Univ. of Leeds (PhD). Post-doctorate Fellow, University College Hosp. Med. Sch., London, and St James's Hosp., Leeds, 1955–56. Assistant Lectr, 1957–59, and Lectr, 1959–64, in Clinical Chemistry, Dept of Pathology, Univ. of Hong Kong; Chinese University of Hong Kong: part-time Lectr in Chemistry, 1964; Sen. Lectr, 1965–72, Reader, 1972–73, Prof., 1973–78, in Biochemistry; Dean of Faculty of Science, 1973–75. Visiting Biochemist, Hormone Research Laboratory, Univ. of California, San Francisco, 1969. *Publications:* various research papers in academic jls. *Recreations:* swimming, table-tennis. *Address:* The Vice-Chancellor's Residence, The Chinese University of Hong Kong, Shatin, New Territories, Hong Kong. *T:* 0–612581.

MAAN, Bashir Ahmed, JP; Councillor, City of Glasgow District; Chairman, Markets Committee; Bailie, City of Glasgow, since 1980; Judge, City of Glasgow District Courts; b Maan, Gujranwala, Pakistan, 22 Oct. 1926; s of Choudhry Sardar Khan Maan and late Mrs Hayat Begum Maan; m; one s three d. *Educ:* D. B. High Sch., Qila Didar Singh; Panjab Univ. Involved in struggle for creation of Pakistan, 1943–47; organised rehabilitation of refugees from India in Maan and surrounding areas, 1947–48; emigrated to UK and settled in Glasgow, 1953; Glasgow Sec., Pakistan Social and Cultural Soc., 1955–65, Pres., 1966–69; Vice-Chm., Glasgow Community Relations Council, 1970–75; Pres., Standing Conf. of Pakistani Orgns in UK, 1974–77; a Dep. Chm., Commn for Racial Equality, 1977–80. Councillor, Glasgow Corp., 1970–75; Magistrate, City of Glasgow, 1971–74; Vice-Chm. 1971–74, Chm. 1974–75, Police Cttee, Glasgow Corp.; Police Judge, City of Glasgow, 1974–75; Mem. Exec. Cttee, Glasgow City Labour Party, 1969–70. Contested (Lab) East Fife, Feb. 1974. Mem., BBC Immigrants Programme Adv. Cttee, 1972–80; Convener, Pakistan Bill Action Cttee, 1973; Member: Nat. Road Safety Cttee, 1971–75; Scottish Accident Prevention Cttee, 1971–75; Scottish Gas Consumers' Council, 1978–81; Greater Glasgow Health Bd, 1981–. JP Glasgow, 1968. *Publications:* articles, contrib. to press. *Recreations:* golf, reading. *Address:* 20 Sherbrooke Avenue, Glasgow G41 4PE. *T:* 041–427 4057. *Club:* Douglas Park Golf.

MAAZEL, Lorin; symphony conductor; b 6 March 1930; s of Lincoln Maazel and Marie Varencove; m 1st, 1952, Miriam Sandbank; two d ; 2nd, 1969, Israela Margalit; one s one d. *Educ:* Pittsburgh University. FRCM 1981. Début as a conductor at age of 9, as violinist a few years later; by 1941 had conducted foremost US Orchestras, including Toscanini's NBC; since 1952, over 500 concerts in Europe and performances at major festivals, including Edinburgh, Bayreuth, Salzburg and Lucerne; in USA: conducted Boston Symphony, New York Philharmonic, Philadelphia Orchestra, and at Metropolitan, 1960 and 1962; Covent Garden début, 1978. Several world tours, including Latin America, Australia, USSR and Japan. Artistic Director of Deutsche Oper Berlin, 1965–71; Music Director, Radio Symphony Orchestra, 1965–75; Associate Principal Conductor, Philharmonia (formerly New Philharmonia) Orchestra, 1970–72, Principal Guest Conductor, 1976–80; Music Director, Cleveland Orchestra, 1972–82, Conductor Emeritus, 1982–; Principal Guest Conductor, Orchestre National, 1977–; Director, Vienna State Opera, 1982–. Has made numerous recordings. Hon. Dr of Music Pittsburgh Univ., 1968; Hon. Dr of Humanities Beaver Coll., 1973; Hon. Dr of Fine Arts, Carnegie-Mellon Univ., Pennsylvania. Commander's Cross of Order of Merit, Federal Republic of Germany, 1977; Officier, Légion d'Honneur, France, 1981. *Address:* c/o Cleveland Orchestra, Severance Hall, Cleveland, Ohio, USA.

MABBOTT, John David, CMG 1946; President of St John's College, Oxford, 1963–69; b 18 Nov. 1898; s of late Walter John and Elizabeth Mabbott; m 1934, Doreen Roach (d 1975). *Educ:* Berwickshire High Sch.; Edinburgh Univ.; St John's Coll., Oxford. Asst Lectr in Classics, Reading Univ., 1922; Asst Lectr in Philosophy, Univ. Coll. of North Wales, 1923; John Locke Scholar, Univ. of Oxford, 1923; Fellow of St John's Coll., Oxford, 1924–63, Tutor, 1930–63, and Hon. Fellow, 1969. *Publications:* The State and the Citizen, 1948; An Introduction to Ethics, 1966; John Locke, 1973; contribs to Philosophy, Proc. Aristotelian Soc., Classical Quarterly, Mind. *Address:* Wing Cottage, Mill Lane, Islip, Oxon. *T:* Kidlington 2360.

MABBS, Alfred Walter, CB 1982; Keeper of Public Records, 1978–82; b 12 April 1921; e s of James and Amelia Mabbs; m 1942, Dorothy Lowley; one s. *Educ:* Hackney Downs Sch. Served War, RAF, 1941–46. Asst Keeper, Public Record Office, 1950–66; Principal Asst Keeper, 1967–69; Records Admin. Officer, 1970–73; Dep. Keeper of Public Records, 1973–78. Pres., Internat. Council on Archives, 1980–82. FRHistS 1954. FSA 1979. *Publications:* Guild Stewards Book of the Borough of Calne (vol. vii, Wilts Arch. and Record Soc.), 1953; The Records of the Cabinet Office to 1922, 1966; Guide to the Contents of the Public Record Office, vol. iii (main contributor), 1968; Exchequer of the Jews, vol. iv (jt contrib.), 1972; The Organisation of Intermediate Records Storage (with Guy Duboscq), 1974; articles and reviews in various jls. *Recreations:* golf, reading. *Address:* 14 Acorn Lane, Cuffley, Herts EN6 4DZ. *T:* Cuffley 3660.

MABON, Rt. Hon. (Jesse) Dickson, PC 1977; MP Greenock and Port Glasgow, since 1974 (Greenock, Dec. 1955–1974) (Lab and Co-op, 1955–81, SDP since 1981); Chairman, RGC (Offshore) plc, since 1979; b 1 Nov. 1925; s of Jesse Dickson Mabon and Isabel Simpson Montgomery; m 1970, Elizabeth, o d of William Zinn, qv ; one s. *Educ:* Possilpark, Cumbrae, North Kelvinside Schools. Worked in coalmining industry before Army service, 1944–48. MB, ChB (Glasgow); DHMSA; Visiting Physician, Manor House Hospital, London, 1958–64. President: Glasgow University Union, 1951–52; Scottish Union of Students, 1954–55; Chairman: Glasgow Univ. Labour Club, 1948–50; National Assoc. of Labour Students, 1949–50; contested: (Lab) Bute and N Ayrshire, Gen. Election, Oct. 1951; (Lab and Co-op) W Renfrewshire, Gen. Election, May 1955. Political columnist, Scottish Daily Record, 1955–64; studied under Dr Kissinger, Harvard, 1963. Joint Parly Under-Sec. of State for Scotland, 1964–67; Minister of State, Scottish Office, 1967–70; Dep. Opposition Spokesman on Scotland, 1970–72 (resigned over Labour's attitude to Common Mkt); Minister of State, Dept of Energy, 1976–79. Chairman: UK Labour Cttee for Europe, 1974–76; Scottish Parly Labour Party, 1972–73, 1975–76; Member: Council of Europe, 1970–72 and 1974–76; Assembly, WEU, 1970–72 and 1974–76; North Atlantic Assembly, 1980–82; Chm., European Movement, 1975–76, Dep. Chm., 1979–. Founder Chm., Manifesto Gp, Parly Lab. Party, 1974–76. Chm., Young Volunteer Force Foundn, 1974–76. Fellow: Inst. of Petroleum; Faculty of History of Medicine; Soc. of Apothecaries; FRSA. Freeman of City of London. *Recreations:* golf, theatre. *Address:* House of Commons, SW1.

MABY, (Alfred) Cedric, CBE 1962; HM Diplomatic Service, retired; b 6 April 1915; 4th s of late Joseph Maby, Penrose, Monmouthshire; m 1944, Anne-Charlotte, d of Envoyen Einar Mcdig, Stockholm; one s two d. *Educ:* Cheltenham; Keble Coll., Oxford. Joined HM Consular Service, 1939. Served at Peking, 1939, Chungking, 1940, Tsingtao, 1941, Istanbul, 1943, Angora, 1944, Buenos Aires, 1946, Caracas, 1949, Singapore, 1954; Counsellor and Consul-General, Peking, 1957–59 (Chargé d'Affaires, 1957 and 1958); Deputy Consul-General, New York, 1959–62; Counsellor (Commercial) at Vienna, 1962–64; Asst Sec., Min. of Overseas Development, 1964–67; Consul-General, Zürich and Liechtenstein, 1968–71; Dir, Trade Promotion for Switzerland, 1970–71. Member: Governing Body, Church in Wales, 1975–78; Church in Wales Adv. Commn on Church and Society, 1977–. High Sheriff of Gwynedd, 1976. *Publications:* contribs to Planet, Y Faner and other Welsh periodicals. *Address:* Cae Canol, Penrhyn-Deudraeth, Gwynedd LL48 6EN.

McADAM, Sir Ian (William James), Kt 1966; OBE 1957; FRCS, FRCSE; b 15 Feb. 1917; s of W. J. McAdam and Alice Culverwell; m 1st, 1939, Hrothgarde Gibson (marr. diss. 1961); one s two d ; 2nd, 1967, Lady (Pamela) Hunt, *née* Medawar. *Educ:* Plumtree Sch., S Rhodesia; Edinburgh Univ. MB, ChB. Cambridge Anatomy Sch., 1940; Dept of Surgery, Edinburgh, 1942; Wilkie Surgical Research Fellow, 1942; Clinical Tutor, Royal Infirmary, Edinburgh, 1942; Surgical Specialist, Uganda, 1946; Senior Consultant, Uganda, 1957; Prof. of Surgery, Makerere Univ., Univ. of E Africa, 1957–72, also Consultant Surgeon Uganda Govt and Kenyatta Hosp., Kenya; Consultant to Nat. Insts of Health, Bethesda, Md, 1973–74. *Publications:* various papers in medical jls. *Recreations:* golf, gardening. *Address:* Box 166, Plettenberg Bay, Cape Province, South Africa.

See also Sir Peter Medawar.

MACADAM, Sir Peter, Kt 1981; Chairman, BAT Industries plc, 1976–82; Director, NatWest Bank plc, since 1978; b 9 Sept. 1921; s of late Francis Macadam of and Marjorie Mary Macadam (*née* Browne); m 1949, Ann Musson; three d. *Educ:* Buenos Aires, Argentina; Stonyhurst Coll., Lancs. Served as Officer in Queen's Bays, 1941–46. Joined BAT Gp tobacco co., Argentina, 1946; Chm. and Gen. Man., gp co., Argentina, 1955–58; PA in London to Dir resp. for Africa, 1959–60 (travelled widely in Africa); Chm., BAT Hong Kong, 1960–62; BAT Main Bd, 1963 (resp. at times for interest in S and Central Africa, S and Central America and Caribbean); Mem., Chm.'s Policy Cttee with overall resp. for tobacco interests and special interest, USA, Canada and Mexico, 1970; Chm., Tobacco Div. Bd and Dir, Gp HQ Bd, 1973; Vice-Chm., 1975. Chm., British Nat. Cttee, ICC, 1978–; Mem. Exec. Cttee, ICC, Paris, 1982–. Hon. FBIM; FRSA 1975. *Recreations:* golf, shooting. *Address:* 34 Campden Hill Court, Campden Hill Road, W8 7HS. *T:* 01-937 1389. *Club:* Hurlingham.

McADAM CLARK, James; *see* Clark, James McAdam.

McADOO, Most Rev. Henry Robert; *see* Dublin, Archbishop of, and Primate of Ireland.

McALISKEY, (Josephine) Bernadette, (Mrs Micheal McAliskey); Chairman, Independent Socialist Party, Ireland; *b* 23 April 1947; *d* of late John James Devlin and Elizabeth Devlin; *m* 1973, Micheal McAliskey; three *c*. *Educ:* St Patrick's Girls' Acad., Dungannon; psychology student at Queen's Univ., Belfast, 1966-69. Youngest MP in House of Commons when elected at age of 21; MP (Ind. Unity) Mid Ulster, Apr. 1969-Feb. 1974. Founder Member and Mem. Exec., Irish Republican Socialist Party, 1975-76. Contested: (Ind) N Ireland, European Parlt, 1979; (People's Democracy), Dublin N Central, Dáil Eireann, 1982. *Publication:* The Price of my Soul (autobiog.), 1969. *Recreations:* walking, folk music, doing nothing, swimming.

McALISTER, Michael Ian, FCA; *b* Leeds, Yorkshire, 23 Aug. 1930; *s* of S. McAlister, CBE, and J. A. McAlister, (*née* Smith); *m* 1953, Patricia (*née* Evans); four *s* three *d*. *Educ:* Brazil; France; St John's Coll., Oxford (MA). Articled Clerk, Price Waterhouse, London, 1954-58; Private Sec. to the Duke of Windsor, 1959-61; Investment Manager, Ionian Bank Ltd, London, 1961-67; Managing Dir, Ionian Bank Trustee Co, London, 1967-68; Slater Walker Securities (Australia): Dep. Chm., 1969-70, Chm., 1970-72; Pres., Aust. Associated Stock Exchanges, 1972-74. *Recreations:* game fishing, archery, swimming.

McALISTER, Maj.-Gen. Ronald William Lorne, CB 1977; OBE 1968 (MBE 1959); Bursar, Wellesley House School, Broadstairs, since 1977; *b* 26 May 1923; *2nd s* of late Col R. J. F. McAlister, OBE and Mrs T. M. Collins, Bath; *m* 1964, Sally Ewart Marshall; two *d*. *Educ:* Dreghorn Castle Sch., Edinburgh; Sedbergh School. Commnd 3rd QAO Gurkha Rifles, 1942; Adjt 1/3 GR Burma, 1945 (despatches); Adjt 2/10 GR Malaya, 1950-52 (despatches); Instructor, Sch. of Infantry, 1953-55; psc 1956; Bde Major 99 Gurkha Bde, Malaya, 1957-59 (MBE); jssc 1961-62; Asst Sec., Chiefs of Staff Cttee, 1962-64; 2nd in comd and CO 10th PMO Gurkha Rifles, Borneo, 1964-66 (despatches); Internal Security Duties, Hong Kong, 1967-68 (OBE); Instructor, Jt Services Staff Coll., 1968; comd Berlin Inf. Bde, 1968-71; ndc, Canada, 1971-72; Exercise Controller UK Cs-in-C Cttee, 1972-75; Dep. Commander Land Forces Hong Kong and Maj.-Gen. Brigade of Gurkhas, 1975-77; retired 1977. Col, 10th Princess Mary's Own Gurkha Rifles, 1977–; Chm., Gurkha Brigade Assoc., 1980–. *Recreations:* golf, gardening. *Address:* The Chalet, 41 Callis Court Road, Broadstairs, Kent. *T:* Thanet 62351. *Club:* Army and Navy.

McALLISTER, John Brian; Under Secretary (formerly Deputy Secretary), Department of Finance, Northern Ireland since 1980; *b* 11 June 1941; *s* of late Thomas McAllister and of Jane (*née* McCloughan); *m* 1966, Margaret Lindsay Walker; two *d*. *Educ:* Royal Belfast Academical Instn; Queen's Univ., Belfast (BA Hons). Joined NI Civil Service as Asst Principal, Dept of Educn, 1964; Dep. Principal, Higher Educn Div., 1968; Principal: Secondary Schs Br., 1969; Re-Organisation of Local Govt Br., 1970; Department of Finance, 1971, Dept's Central Secretariat, 1972; Asst Sec. 1973, Sen. Asst Sec. 1976, Dep. Sec., 1978-80, Dept of Educn. *Recreations:* watching sport of all kinds, reading. *Address:* Department of Finance, Stormont, Belfast BT4 3SW.

McALLISTER, Sir Reginald (Basil), Kt 1973; CMG 1966; CVO 1963; FRGSA; JP; retired; Trustee: National Party of Australia, Queensland, since 1966; *b* 8 May 1900; *s* of Basil William and Beatrice Maud McAllister; *m* 1951, Joyce Isabel Roper; no *c*. *Educ:* Brisbane Primary and Secondary State Schools. Clerk, Railway Dept, Brisbane, 1916; secretarial duties, Parlt House, Brisbane, and Sec. to Speaker, 1924-26; reporter, State Reporting Bureau, Parlt House, 1926-33; Sec. to Premier of Queensland, 1933-37 (accompanied Premier on missions to: UK and Canada, 1934; UK and Europe, 1936; UK Internat. Sugar Conf., 1937); Asst Under-Sec., Premier and Chief Secretary's Dept, 1938; Official Sec., Qld Govt Offices, London, 1943-48 (actg Agent-Gen. on many occasions); resumed former duties in Brisbane, 1948; Clerk of Exec. Council of Qld, 1941-43, 1951-66; Under-Sec., Premier's Dept, and Chm., State Stores Board, 1962-66; acted as Sec. to Cabinet on many occasions; retd 1966; Executive Officer of five Premiers and four Governors, 1933-66. State Director, Royal Visits: HM Queen Elizabeth II and Prince Philip, 1963; TRH Duke and Duchess of Gloucester, 1965; HM King and Queen of Thailand, 1962; assisted with Royal Visits: HRH Duke of Gloucester, 1934; HM the Queen and Prince Philip, 1954; HM Queen Elizabeth the Queen Mother, 1958; HRH Princess Alexandra, 1959. Pres., Qld Br., Royal Commonwealth Soc.; Australian-Asian Soc.; Vice Patron, Australia-Japan Soc. (Pres., 1972); Exec. Ctree, Australian Red Cross Soc; Vice Patron and former Pres. Council, RGSA; Mem. State Council and Executive, Scout Assoc. of Australia. Dep. Chm., Bd of Dirs, Warana Spring Festival, 1965-. Liveryman, Farriers' Co.; Freeman, City of London; JP 1933. *Recreations:*

golf, fishing, gardening, politics. *Address:* 34 Scott Road, Herston, Brisbane, Queensland 4006, Australia. *T:* 356 5361. *Clubs:* Queensland Turf, Masonic, Tattersall's, Queensland Lawn Tennis, Royal Autobomile, Brisbane Cricket (all Queensland).

McALPINE, family name of **Baron McAlpine of Moffat.**

McALPINE OF MOFFAT, Baron *cr* 1980 (Life Peer), of Medmenham in the County of Buckinghamshire; **Robert Edwin McAlpine;** Kt 1963; Partner, Sir Robert McAlpine & Sons, since 1928; Deputy Chairman, British Nuclear Associates, since 1973; Chairman, Greycoat London Estates Ltd, since 1978; *b* 23 April 1907; *s* of William Hepburn McAlpine and Margaret Donnison; *m* 1930, Ella Mary Gardner Garnett; three *s* one *d*. *Educ:* Oundle. Joined Sir Robert McAlpine & Sons, 1925. *Recreations:* breeding race horses, farming, travel, golf, theatre. *Address:* Benhams, Fawley Green, Henley-on-Thames, Oxon. *T:* Hambleden 246. *Clubs:* Garrick, Buck's, Caledonian, Jockey. *See also* Hon. R. A. McAlpine, Sir T. G. B. McAlpine, Bt.

McALPINE, Hon. Alistair; *see* McAlpine, Hon. R. A.

McALPINE, Christopher; *see* McAlpine, R. D. C.

McALPINE, Hon. Sir John (Kenneth), KCMG 1977 (CMG 1970); Chairman, New Zealand Ports Authority, 1968-79; *b* 21 July 1906; *s* of Walter Kenneth and Gwendolin Marion McAlpine; *m* 1934, Lesley Ruth Hay; one *s* two *d*. *Educ:* Christ's Coll., Christchurch, New Zealand. MP Selwyn, NZ, 1946-66. Mem. Tawera CC, 1927-63; Pres. Canterbury Federated Farmers, 1945-47. Mem. Bd: Arthur's Pass National Park, 1942-79; Lyttleton Harbour, 1937-54 (Chm., 1942-45); Canterbury Univ., 1950-60; Canterbury Agricultural Univ., 1959-79 (Chm., 1967-73). Minister: Railways, Marine, and Printing, 1954-66; Mines, 1956-58; Transport and Civil Aviation, 1957-66; Labour, 1956-58. Mem., Exec., NZ Holiday Travel, etc, 1966-; Chairman: South Island, NZ, Promotion Bd, 1937-79; Canterbury Progress League, 1937-. *Recreations:* Rugby football, long distance running, gardening, skiing. *Address:* 50 McDougall Avenue, Christchurch 1, New Zealand. *Club:* Christchurch (NZ).

McALPINE, Hon. (Robert) Alistair; Hon. Treasurer, since 1975 (jointly since 1981), and Deputy Chairman, since 1979, Conservative and Unionist Party; Director, Sir Robert McAlpine & Sons Ltd, since 1963; *b* 14 May 1942; *s* of Lord McAlpine of Moffat, *qv* ; *m* 1964, Sarah Alexandra Baron (marr. diss. 1979); two *d* ; *m* 1980, Romilly, *o d* of A. T. Hobbs, Cranleigh, Surrey. *Educ:* Stowe. Joined Sir Robert McAlpine & Sons Ltd, 1958. Hon. Treasurer: Europ. Democratic Union, 1978-; Europ. League for Econ. Co-operation, 1974-75, Vice Pres., 1975-. Director: George Weidenfeld Holdings Ltd, 1975-; ICA, 1972-73. Mem., Arts Council of GB, 1981-82; Vice-President: Friends of Ashmolean Museum, 1969-; Greater London Arts Assoc., 1971-77; Vice-Chm., Contemporary Arts Soc., 1973-80. Pres., British Waterfowl Assoc., 1978-81, Patron 1981-. Member: Friends of V&A Museum, 1976-; Council, English Stage Co., 1973-75. Trustee, Royal Opera House Trust, 1974-80. Governor: Polytechnic of the South Bank, 1981-82; Stowe Sch., 1981-. *Recreations:* the arts, horticulture, aviculture, agriculture. *Address:* West Green House, Hartley Wintney, Basingstoke, Hants. *Clubs:* Garrick, Carlton.

McALPINE, Robert Douglas Christopher, CMG 1967; HM Diplomatic Service, retired; Director, 1969-79, Adviser, since 1979, Baring Brothers; Director, H. Clarkson (Holdings) Ltd, since 1980; *b* 14 June 1919; *s* of late Dr Douglas McAlpine, FRCP and late Elizabeth Meg Sidebottom; *m* 1943, Helen Margery Frances Cannan; two *s* one *d* (and one *d* deed). *Educ:* Winchester; New Coll., Oxford. RNVR, 1939-46. Entered Foreign Service, 1946. FO, 1946-47; Asst Private Sec. to Sec. of State, 1947-49; 2nd Sec. and later 1st Sec., UK High Commn at Bonn, 1949-52; FO, 1952-54; Lima, 1954-56; Moscow, 1956-59; FO, 1959-62; Dep. Consul-Gen. and Counsellor, New York, 1962-65; Counsellor, Mexico City, 1965-69. *Recreations:* sailing, tennis, fishing, photography. *Address:* 81 Dovehouse Street, SW3. *Club:* Hurlingham.

McALPINE, Sir Robin, Kt 1969; CBE 1957; Chairman: Sir Robert McAlpine & Sons Ltd, 1967-77; Newarthill Ltd, 1972-77; *b* 18 March 1906; *s* of late Sir (Thomas) Malcolm McAlpine, KBE, and late Lady (Maud) McAlpine; *m* 1st, 1939, Nora Constance (*d* 1966), *d* of F. H. Perse; 2nd, 1970, Mrs Philippa Nicolson, *d* of Sir Gervais Tennyson D'Eyncourt, 2nd Bt. *Educ:* Charterhouse. Pres., Federation of Civil Engineering Contractors, 1966-71. *Recreation:* owner and breeder of racehorses. *Address:* Aylesfield, Alton, Hants. *Club:* Jockey.

McALPINE, Sir Thomas (George Bishop), 4th Bt *cr* 1918; Director of Sir Robert McAlpine & Sons; *b* 23 Oct. 1901; *s* of William Hepburn McAlpine (2nd *s* of 1st Bt) and Margaret Donnison, *d* of T. G. Bishop; *S* kinsman, Sir (Alfred) Robert McAlpine, 3rd Bt, 1968; *m* 1st, 1934, Doris Frew (*d* 1964), *d* of late D. C. Campbell and *widow* of W. E. Woodeson; 2nd, 1965, Kathleen Mary, *d* of late Frederick Best and *widow* of Charles Bantock Blackshaw; no *c*. *Educ:* Warriston; Rossall Sch. Joined firm of Sir Robert McAlpine on leaving school; eventually became a partner and director; retired from the partnership, 1966. *Recreations:* farming, photography, travel. *Heir:* *b* Baron McAlpine of Moffat, *qv*. *Address:* The Manor House, Stanford-in-the-Vale,

Faringdon, Oxon. *Club:* Royal Automobile.
See also W. S. Blackshaw.

MacANDREW, family name of Baron MacAndrew.

MacANDREW, 2nd Baron *cr* 1959; **Colin Nevil Glen MacAndrew;** *b* 1 Aug. 1919; *s* of 1st Baron MacAndrew, PC, TD, and of Lilian Cathleen, *d* of James Prendergast Curran, St Andrews; *S* father, 1979; *m* 1943, Ursula Beatrice, *d* of Captain Joseph Steel; two *s* one *d*. *Educ:* Eton College; Trinity College, Cambridge. Served War, 1939-45. *Recreations:* hunting, racing, golf. *Heir:* *s* Hon. Christopher Anthony Colin MacAndrew [*b* 16 Feb. 1945; *m* 1975, Sarah, *o d* of Lt-Col P. H. Brazier; one *d*]. *Address:* Dilston House, Aldborough St John, Richmond, Yorks. *T:* Piercebridge 272.

MACARA, Sir (Charles) Douglas, 3rd Bt *cr* 1911; *b* 19 April 1904; *s* of 2nd Bt and Lillian Mary (*d* 1971), *d* of John Chapman, Boyton Court, East Sutton, Kent; *S* father, 1931; *m* 1926, Quenilda (marr. diss. 1945), *d* of late Herbert Whitworth, St Anne's-on-Sea; two *d* (one *s* decd). *Heir:* *b* Hugh Kenneth Macara, *b* 17 Jan. 1913.

McARDLE, Michael John Francis, MB, BS (Hons, London), FRCP; Consulting Physician Emeritus for Nervous Diseases, Guy's Hospital; Consulting Physician Emeritus, The National Hospital, Queen Square, WC1; Hon. Consulting Neurologist, Kingston Hospital and St Teresa's Maternity Hospital, Wimbledon, SW19; *b* 1909; *s* of Andrew McArdle; *m* 1955, Maureen MacClancy (*d* 1978). *Educ:* Wimbledon Coll.; Guy's Hospital; Paris. Entrance Scholarship, Arts, Guy's Hospital. Medical Registrar, Guy's Hospital; Asst Medical Officer, Maudsley Hospital. Rockefeller Travelling Fellow in Neurology, 1938. War of 1939-45, Temp. Lt-Col, RAMC and Adviser in Neurology, 21st Army Group. *Publications:* papers on neurological subjects in medical journals. *Recreation:* golf. *Address:* 3 Kingsdown, 115A The Ridgway, SW19 5RB. *T:* 01-946 4149.

McARDLE, Rear-Adm. Stanley Lawrence, CB 1975; MVO 1952; GM 1953; JP; Flag Officer, Portsmouth, and Port Admiral, Portsmouth, 1973-75; retired; *b* 1922; *s* of Theodore McArdle, Lochmaben, Dumfriesshire; *m* 1st, 1945, (Helen) Joyce, *d* of Owen Cummins, Wickham, Hants; one *d*; 2nd, 1962, Jennifer, *d* of Walter Talbot Goddard, Salisbury, Wilts; one *d*. *Educ:* Royal Hospital Sch., Holbrook, Suffolk. Joined RN, 1938; served War, 1939-45. Lieut 1945; Comdr 1956; Captain 1963. Directorate of Naval Operations and Trade, 1969; Comd HMS Glamorgan, 1970; Dir Naval Trng, Director General, Personal Services and Trng (Naval), 1971-73; Rear Admiral 1972. JP Wilts, 1977. *Address:* Barn Ridge Cottage, Farley, Salisbury, Wilts.

MACARTHUR, Rev. Arthur Leitch, OBE 1981; MA, MLitt; inducted, Christ Church, Marlow-on-Thames, 1980; *b* 9 Dec. 1913; *s* of Edwin Macarthur and Mary Macarthur (*née* Leitch); *m* 1950, Doreen Esmé Muir; three *s* one *d*. *Educ:* Rutherford Coll.; Armstrong Coll., Durham Univ. (MA, MLitt Dunelm); Westminster Coll., Cambridge. Ordained, 1937; inducted, Clayport, Alnwick, 1937; served with YMCA in France, 1940. Inducted: St Augustine's, New Barnet, 1944; St Columba's, North Shields, 1950. Gen. Sec., Presbyterian Church of England, 1960-72; Moderator, Presbyterian Church of England, 1971-72; Jt Gen.-Sec., URC, 1972-74; Moderator, URC, 1974-75; Gen. Sec., URC, 1975-80; Moderator, Free Church Federal Council, 1980-81. Vice-Pres., BCC, 1974-77 (Chm., Admin. Cttee, 1969-74). Director: Tavistock Court Ltd; URC Insurance Co., etc. *Recreations:* gardening, golf, walking. *Address:* Christ Church (United Reformed), Quoiting Square, Marlow, Bucks.

MacARTHUR, Brian; Joint Deputy Editor, The Sunday Times, since 1982; *b* 5 Feb. 1940; *o s* of late S. H. MacArthur and of Mrs M. MacArthur; *m* 1975, Bridget Trahair; two *d*. *Educ:* Brentwood Sch.; Helsby Grammar Sch.; Leeds Univ. (BA). Yorkshire Post, 1962-64; Daily Mail, 1964-66; The Guardian, 1966-67; The Times: Education Correspondent, 1967-70; Dep. Features Editor, 1970-71; Founder Editor, The Times Higher Educn Supplement, 1971-76; Home News Editor, 1976-78; Dep. Editor, Evening Standard, 1978-79; Chief Asst to the Editor, The Sunday Times, 1979-81; Exec. Editor (News), The Times, 1981-82. Hon. MA, Open Univ., 1976. *Publications:* several contribs to educnl and political symposia, incl. (jtly) The Struggle for Education (Nat. Union of Teachers' Centenary), 1970; (jtly) An Interim History of The Open University, in The Open University Opens, 1974. *Recreations:* reading, gardening, squash. *Address:* 50 Lanchester Road, N6. *T:* 01-883 1855. *Club:* Reform.

MacARTHUR, Mrs Charles; *see* Hayes, Helen.

MACARTHUR, Charles Ramsay, QC (Scot.) 1970; Sheriff of Tayside, Central and Fife, since 1981; *s* of late Alastair and late Joan Macarthur; *m* 1973, Rosemary Valda Morgan, Edinburgh. *Educ:* Glasgow Univ. (MA, LLB). Served War of 1939-45: joined Royal Navy, 1942; demobilised as Lieut, RNVR, 1946. Solicitor, 1952-59; admitted Scottish Bar, 1960; Standing Junior Counsel, Highlands and Islands Development Board, 1968-70; Sheriff of the Lothians and Borders, 1974-76. *Recreations:* travel, talking. *Clubs:* New (Edinburgh); RNVR (Scotland).

MacARTHUR, Ian; Director, British Textile Confederation, since 1977; *b* 17 May 1925; *yr s* of late Lt-Gen. Sir William MacArthur, KCB, DSO, MD,

DSc, FRCP; *m* 1957, Judith Mary, (RGN 1976), *d* of late Francis Gavin Douglas Miller; four *s* three *d*. *Educ:* Cheltenham Coll.; The Queen's Coll., Oxford (Scholar, MA). Contested (U), Greenock Gen. Election, May 1955, also by-election, Dec. 1955; MP (C) Perth and E Perthshire, 1959-Sept. 1974; Chm., Scottish Cons. Mems' Cttee, 1972-73. Introduced, as Private Member's Bills: Law Reform (Damages and Solatium) (Scotland) Act, 1962; Interest on Damages (Scotland) Act, 1971; Social Work (Scotland) Act, 1972; Domicile and Matrimonial Proceedings Act, 1973. An Asst Government Whip (unpaid), 1962-63; a Lord Comr of the Treasury and Govt Scottish Whip, 1963-64; Opposition Scottish Whip, 1964-65; an Opposition Spokesman on Scottish Affairs, 1965-70. Personal Asst to the Prime Minister, Rt Hon. Sir Alec Douglas-Home, Kinross and W Perthshire By-Election, Nov. 1963. Hon. Pres., Scottish Young Unionists, 1962-65; Vice-Chm., Cons. Party in Scotland, 1972-75. Formerly Dir of Administration, J. Walter Thompson Co. Ltd. Served War of 1939-45, with RN and RNVR, 1943-46 (Flag Lieut to C-in-C Portsmouth, 1946). Gold Cross of Merit, Polish Govt in Exile, 1971. *Address:* 15 Old Palace Lane, Richmond, Surrey. *Clubs:* Naval; Puffin's (Edinburgh).

McARTHUR, Col Sir Malcolm Hugh, Kt 1978; OBE; psc; Chairman of companies; farmer and grazier; Past Chairman, Australian Meat Board, 1970-77; *b* Armidale, NSW, 13 Dec. 1912; *s* of late Alex C. McArthur, Armidale; *m* 1949, Nancy, *d* of late A. Kellett; three *d*. *Educ:* Royal Military Coll., Duntroon, Aust. Aust. Staff Corps, and AIF, 1933-63. Served War of 1939-45: Australia, India, Middle East, Italy, Pacific Area, Japan (wounded, despatches). Chm., Aust. Egg Bd, 1967-70; Pres., Egg Marketing Authorities of Aust., 1960-70. Chairman: M H & N McArthur & Co. Pty Ltd; T L Kingston Pty Ltd; Russel Armstrong Pty Ltd; Mermargal Holdings Pty Ltd; Dep. Chm., Trans Otway Ltd; Councillor, Royal Agric. Soc. of Vic, 1959-. Breeder of Hereford cattle. Knighthood awarded for services to the meat industry. *Recreations:* racing, hunting, polo. *Address:* Melrose Farm, Wollert, Vic 3750, Australia. *Clubs:* Melbourne, Australian, Naval and Military (Melbourne); Union (Sydney); and all metropolitan racing (Melbourne); (Pres.) Findon Hunt.

MACARTHUR-ONSLOW, Maj.-Gen. Sir Denzil, Kt 1964; CBE 1951; DSO 1941; ED; *b* 5 March 1904; *s* of late F. A. Macarthur-Onslow; *m* 1st, 1927, Elinor Margaret (marr. diss. 1950), *d* of late Gordon Caldwell; three *s* one *d*; 2nd, 1950, Dorothy, *d* of W. D. Scott; one *s* one *d*. *Educ:* Tudor House Sch., Moss Vale; King's Sch., Parramatta, NSW. Commissioned Australian Field Artillery, 1924. Served War of 1939-45 in Middle East and New Guinea (despatches thrice, DSO). GOC 2nd Div. AMF, 1954-58; Citizen Forces Mem. of Australian Mil. Board, 1958-60. *Address:* Mount Gilead, Campbelltown, New South Wales; Camden Park, Menangle, NSW 2568, Australia. *Clubs:* Australian, Royal Sydney Golf, Australasian Pioneers (Sydney, NSW).

MACARTNEY, Sir John Barrington, 6th Bt *cr* 1799, of Lish, Co. Armagh; dairy farmer; *b* 21 Jan. 1917; *s* of John Barrington Macartney (3rd *s* of Sir John Macartney, 3rd Bt; he *d* 1951) and Selina Koch, Hampton, Mackay, Qld, Australia; *S* uncle, Sir Alexander Miller Macartney, 5th Bt, 1960; *m* 1944, Amy Isobel Reinke; one *s*. *Heir:* *s* John Ralph Macartney [*b* 24 July 1945; *m* 1966, Suzanne Marie Fowler; three *d*]. *Address:* 37 Meadow Street, North Mackay, Qld 4740, Australia.

MACAULAY, Sir Hamilton, Kt 1960; CBE 1956; *b* 1901; *s* of late Hugh Stevenson Macaulay, Glasgow; *m* 1930, Marjorie Slinger, *d* of late Francis Gill, Litton, Yorks. *Educ:* Calder HG Sch., Glasgow. Served War of 1939-45 (despatches), Lt-Col. Pres., Chittagong Chamber of Commerce, 1953-54, 1956-57 and 1959-60; Dep. Pres., Assoc. Chambers of Commerce of Pakistan, 1953-54. Chm., Chittagong Branch UK Assoc. of Pakistan, 1955-56 and 1959-60. *Recreation:* golf. *Address:* The Cottage, Harpers Road, Ash, Hants. *Club:* Oriental.

MACAULAY, Janet Stewart Alison, MA; Headmistress of St Leonards and St Katharines Schools, St Andrews, 1956-70; *b* 20 Dec. 1909; 3rd *d* of late Rev. Prof. A. B. Macaulay, DD, of Trinity Coll., Glasgow. *Educ:* Laurel Bank Sch., Glasgow; Glasgow Univ.; Somerville Coll., Oxford. BA Oxon 1932; BLitt Oxon 1934; MA Oxon 1936. Asst Mistress, Wycombe Abbey Sch., Bucks, 1933-36; Sutton High Sch. (GPDST), Sutton, Surrey, 1937-45; Headmistress, Blackheath High Sch. (GPDST), 1945-Dec. 1955. Hon. LLD St Andrews, 1977. *Address:* 3 Drummond Place, Edinburgh EH3 6PH; Grampian Cottage, Kincraig, Inverness-shire.

McAULAY, John Roy Vincent; QC 1978; a Recorder of the Crown Court, since 1975; Barrister-at-law, practising mainly in London and on Midland and Oxford Circuit; a legal assessor to General Medical Council and General Dental Council; *b* 9 Sept. 1933; *er s* of Dr John McAulay and Mrs Marty McAulay (*née* Hüni), West Wickham, Kent; *m* 1970, Ruth Hamilton Smith, Sundridge, Kent; one *s* one *d*. *Educ:* Whitgift Sch. (Victoria Scholar); Queens' Coll., Cambridge (MA Hons). National Service, Intelligence Corps, 1951-53. Called to Bar, Gray's Inn, 1957 (Lord Justice Holker Scholar); Recorder, Midland Circuit, 1965-67; Mem., Gen. Council of Bar, 1967-71. *Publications:* contrib. Halsbury's Laws of England, 3rd and 4th edns, and other legal pubns. *Recreations:* walking, swimming, animals, sport. *Address:* 1 Harcourt Buildings, Temple, EC4. *T:* 01-353 0375; Highcote House, Bromley Road, Shortlands, Bromley, Kent. *T:* 01-464 9877. *Clubs:* Caledonian; United Services (Nottingham).

McAVOY, Sir (Francis) Joseph, Kt 1976; CBE 1969; Chairman: Queensland Canegrowers Council, since 1963 (Member since 1952); Australian Canegrowers Council, since 1952; *b* 26 Feb. 1910; *s* of William Henry McAvoy and Hanorah Catherine McAvoy; *m* 1936, Mary Irene Doolan; four *s* (one *d* decd). *Educ:* Nudgee Coll., Brisbane; Sacred Heart Convent, Innisfail, Qld. Member: Goondi Mill Suppliers Cttee, 1946-79; Innisfail Canegrowers Exec., 1949-79; Metric Conversion Bd (Aust.), 1970-78; Exec. Council of Agriculture, 1963-79; Exec., Aust. Farmers Fedn, 1969-77. *Recreation:* lawn bowls. *Address:* Avoca, Daradgee, Qld 4860, Australia. *T:* 633224. *Clubs:* Rotary (Innisfail, Qld); United Services (Brisbane).

McBAIN, Ed; *see* Hunter, Evan.

MACBEATH, Prof. Alexander Murray, PhD (Princeton, NJ); MA (Cantab); Professor of Mathematics and Statistics, University of Pittsburgh, since 1979; *b* 30 June 1923; *s* of late Prof. Alexander Macbeath, CBE; *m* 1951, Julie Ormrod, Lytham St Anne's; two *s*. *Educ:* Royal Belfast Academical Inst.; Queen's Univ., Belfast; Clare Coll., Cambridge. Entrance Schol., Dixon Prize in Maths, Purser Studentship, 1st class hons in Maths, BA, QUB. Temp. post with Foreign Office, 1943-45. Cambridge, 1945-48; Maj. Entrance Schol., Wrangler Math. Tripos, Part II, dist. Part III, BA, Owst Prize. Commonwealth Fund Fellowship, Princeton, NJ, 1948-50; Smith's Prize, 1949; PhD Princeton, 1950. Research Fellow, Clare Coll., Cambridge, 1950-51; MA Cambridge, 1951. Lectr in Maths, Univ. Coll. of North Staffordshire, 1951-53; Prof. of Maths, Queen's Coll., Dundee, 1953-62; Mason Prof. of Pure Maths, Univ. of Birmingham, 1962-79. Visiting Professor: California Inst. of Technology, 1966-67; Univ. of Pittsburgh, 1974-75. *Publications:* Elementary Vector Algebra, 1964; papers in: Jl London Mathematical Soc.; Proc. London Math. Soc.; Proc. Cambridge Philosophical Soc.; Quarterly Jl of Mathematics; Annals of Mathematics; Canadian Jl of Mathematics. *Recreation:* Scottish country dancing. *Address:* 16 Highmeadow Road, Pittsburgh, Pa 15215, USA.

MacBETH, George Mann; writer; *b* Scotland, 1932; *s* of George MacBeth and Amelia Morton Mary Mann; *m* 1955, Elizabeth Browell Robson (marr. diss. 1975). *Educ:* New Coll., Oxford (read Classics and Philosophy). BBC, 1955-76: Producer, Overseas Talks Dept, 1957; Producer, Talks Dept, 1958; Editor: Poet's Voice, 1958-65; New Comment, 1959-64; Poetry Now, 1965-76. Sir Geoffrey Faber Memorial Award (jtly), 1964; Cholmondeley Award (jtly), 1977. *Publications: poems:* A Form of Words, 1954; The Broken Places, 1963; A Doomsday Book, 1965; The Colour of Blood, 1967; The Night of Stones, 1968; A War Quartet, 1969; The Burning Cone, 1970; Collected Poems 1958-1970, 1971; The Orlando Poems, 1971; Shrapnel, 1973; A Poet's Year, 1973; In The Hours Waiting For The Blood To Come, 1975; Buying a Heart, 1978; Poems of Love and Death, 1980; Poems from Oby, 1982; *prose poems:* My Scotland, 1973; *prose:* The Transformation, 1975; The Samurai, 1975; The Survivor, 1977; The Seven Witches, 1978; The Born Losers, 1981; A Kind of Treason, 1982; *anthologies:* The Penguin Book of Sick Verse, 1963; (with J. Clemo and E. Lucie-Smith) Penguin Modern Poets VI, 1964; The Penguin Book of Animal Verse, 1965; (with notes) Poetry, 1900-1965, 1967; The Penguin Book of Victorian Verse, 1968; The Falling Splendour, 1970; The Book of Cats, 1976; Poetry, 1900-1975, 1980; *children's books:* Jonah and the Lord, 1969; The Rectory Mice, 1982. *Recreation:* Japanese swords. *Address:* The Old Rectory, Oby, Thurne, Norfolk.

McBREARTY, Tony; Member for Enfield North, Greater London Council, since 1981; Chairman of the Housing Committee, Greater London Council, since 1982; *b* 26 April 1946; *s* of Patrick and Mary McBrearty; *m* 1969, Heather McGowan; one *s*. Councillor, London Bor. of Haringey, 1975-: Chm. of Personnel Cttee, 1976-79; Chm. of Housing Cttee, 1979-82. *Recreations:* politics, history. *Address:* 112 Inderwick Road, Hornsey, N8 9JY. *T:* 01-348 8159.

McBRIDE, Rt. Hon. Sir Philip Albert Martin, PC 1959; KCMG 1953; *b* 18 June 1892; *s* of late Albert J. McBride; *m* 1914, Rita I., *d* of late E. W. Crews, Kooringa, South Australia; two *s* (and one *s* decd). *Educ:* Burra Public Sch., South Australia; Prince Alfred Coll. MHR for Grey, South Australia, 1931-34; for Wakefield, S Australia, 1946-; Member of Senate for S Australia, 1937-43; Minister without Portfolio assisting Minister for Commerce, March-Aug. 1940; Minister: for the Army and for Repatriation, Aug.-Oct. 1940; for Supply and Development, Oct. 1940-June 1941; for Munitions, 1940-41; Mem. Australian Advisory War Council, Aug.-Oct. 1941; Mem. Economic Cabinet, 1939-40, and War Cabinet, 1940-41; Dep. Leader of Opposition in Senate, 1941-43; Minister for the Interior, 1949-50; Acting Minister for Defence, April-Oct. 1950; Minister: for Defence, 1950-58; for the Navy and for Air, May-July 1951; Leader of Australian Govt Delegn to Defence Conf., London, 1951; Federal Pres. of Liberal Party, 1960-65. *Address:* 30 Briar Avenue, Medindie, SA 5081, Australia. *Club:* Adelaide (Adelaide).

McBRIDE, Commandant (Sara) Vonla (Adair), CB 1979; Director, Central London Region, Lloyds Bank Ltd, since 1980; *b* 20 Jan. 1921; *d* of late Andrew Stewart McBride and Agnes McBride. *Educ:* Ballymena Acad., NI; TCD (Moderatorship in Mod. Lit; BA Hons). CBIM. Teacher of English and French, Ballymena Acad., 1942-45; Housemistress, Gardenhurst Sch., Burnham-on-Sea, Somerset, 1945-49. Dir, WRNS, 1976-79 (joined 1949); Hon. ADC to the Queen, 1976-79. Mem., Thames Water Authority, 1980-. Freeman, City of London, 1978. *Publication:* Never at Sea (autobiog.), 1966.

Recreations: golf, amateur dramatics, entertaining, continental travel. *Address:* Flat 11, 8 The Paragon, Blackheath, SE3. *T:* 01-852 8673. *Club:* Naval.

MacBRIDE, Seán; Senior Counsel, Irish Bar; Assistant Secretary-General, United Nations, and United Nations Commissioner for Namibia, 1973-77; *b* 26 Jan. 1904; *s* of late Major John MacBride and late Maud Gonne; *m* 1926, Catalina Bulfin; one *s* one *d*. *Educ:* St Louis de Gonzaque, Paris; Mount St Benedict, Gorey, Co. Wexford, Ireland. Was active in movement for Irish independence and suffered imprisonment in 1918, 1922 and 1930; was Sec. to Mr de Valera; decorated by Irish Govt for Military services in Ireland, 1938. Was a journalist for a number of years before being called to Irish Bar, 1937; Irish correspondent for Havas and some American and South African papers before War of 1939-45. Called to Bar, 1937; called to Inner Bar, 1943; holds record of having become a Senior Counsel in a shorter period of time than any other living member of the Bar; defended many sensational capital cases and had an extensive practice in High Court and Supreme Court. Founder, 1946, and Leader of political party, Clann na Poblachta (Republican Party). Member of Dail Eireann, 1947-58; Minister for External Affairs, Eire, 1948-51. Pres., Council of Foreign Ministers of Council of Europe, 1950; Vice-Pres., OEEC, 1948-51; declined ministerial portfolio, June 1954, on ground of inadequate parliamentary representation; delegate to Council of Europe from Ireland, 1954. Trustee, Internat. Prisoners of Conscience Fund; Mem. Exec., Pan-European Union; Consultant to late President K. N'Krumah in relation to forming OAU; Mem., European Round Table; Mem., Ghana Bar; International Congress of Jurists, New Delhi, 1958 and Rio de Janeiro, 1962; Chm., Irish Assoc. of Jurists; one of the founders of Amnesty International and Chm. Internat. Exec., 1961-75; President: Internat. Commn of Jurists (Sec.-Gen. of the Commn, 1963-70, Mem., 1971-); Internat. Peace Bureau, Geneva, 1972-; Internat. Commn for Study of Communication Problems, 1977. Elected to Internat. Gaelic Hall of Fame, 1974; Man of the Year, Irish United Socs, 1975. Nobel Peace Prize (jtly), 1974; Lenin Internat. Prize for Peace, 1977; Amer. Medal of Justice, 1978; Internat. Inst. of Human Rights Medal, 1978. LLD (hc): Coll. of St Thomas, Minnesota, 1975; Guelph Univ., Canada, 1977; TCD, 1978; Univ. of Cape Coast, 1978; DLitt (hc), Bradford Univ., 1977. *Publications:* Civil Liberty, 1948 (pamphlet); Our People—Our Money, 1951. *Recreation:* sailing. *Address:* Roebuck House, Clonskea, Dublin 14. *T:* Dublin 694225; United Nations, New York, NY 10017, USA; PO Box 3550, Lusaka, Zambia.

McBRIDE, Vonla; *see* McBride, S. V. A.

McBRIDE, William Griffith, AO 1977; CBE 1969; MD, FRCOG, FRACOG 1979; Consultant Obstetrician and Gynaecologist: The Women's Hospital, Sydney, since 1966; St George Hospital, Sydney, since 1957; *b* 25 May 1927; *s* of late John McBride, Sydney; *m* 1957, Patricia Mary, *d* of late Robert Louis Glover; two *s* two *d*. *Educ:* Canterbury High Sch., Sydney; Univ. of Sydney; Univ. of London. MB, BS Sydney 1950; MRCOG 1954; MD Sydney 1962; FRCOG 1968; FAGO 1972. Resident: St George Hosp., Sydney, 1950; Launceston Hosp., 1951; Med. Supt, Women's Hosp., Sydney, 1955-57; Cons. Gynaecologist, Bankstown Hosp., Sydney, 1957-66. Lectr in Obstetrics and Gynaecology, Univ. of Sydney, 1957-; Examr in Obstetrics and Gynaecology, Univ. of Sydney, 1960-; Medical Dir, Foundation 41 for the study of congenital abnormalities and mental retardation, 1972-. Vis. Prof. of Gynaecology, Univ. of Bangkok, 1968. Mem., WHO Sub-Cttee on safety of oral contraceptives, 1971-. Pres. Sect. of Obstetrics and Gynæcology, AMA, 1966-73. Fellow, Senate of Univ. of Sydney. Member: Faculty of Medicine, Univ. of NSW; Soc. of Reproductive Biology; Endocrine Soc.; Teratology Soc.; Soc. for Risk Analysis. BP Prize of Institut de la Vie, 1971 (for discovery of the teratogenic effects of the drug Thalidomide; first person to alert the world to the dangers of this drug and possibly other drugs). Member: Bd of Dirs, Australian Opera, 1979-82; Australian Opera Council, 1982-. *Publications:* Drugs, 1960-70; contrib. (on Teratogenic Effect of the Drug Thalidomide), Lancet 1961 (London); numerous papers in internat. med. jls and scientific jls. *Recreations:* tennis, swimming, riding, music, cattle breeding. *Address:* 183 Macquarie Street, Sydney, NSW 2000, Australia. *T:* 221-3898. *Clubs:* Union, Australian Jockey, American National, Royal Sydney Golf (all in Sydney).

McBURNEY, Air Vice-Marshal Ralph Edward, CBE 1945; CD; RCAF, retired; *b* Montreal, Quebec, 17 Aug. 1906; *s* of Irville Albert and Lilian McBurney, Saskatoon, Sask.; *m* 1931, Gertrude Elizabeth Bate, Saskatoon; two *s* one *d*. *Educ:* Univs of Saskatchewan and Manitoba. BSc (EE); Commenced flying training as a cadet in RCAF, 1924; Pilot Officer, 1926; employed on Forest Fire Patrols and photographic mapping; Course in RAF School of Army Co-operation and tour as Instructor in RCAF School of Army Co-operation, 1931; Course at RAF Wireless School, Cranwell, and tour as Signals Adviser at Air Force HQ, Ottawa, 1935-36; RAF Staff Coll., Andover, 1939; Dir of Signals, AFHQ, Ottawa, 1939-42; CO, RCAF Station, Trenton, Ont., 1943; CO, RCAF Station, Dishforth, Yorks, 1943; Air Cdre 1944; Base Comdr of 61 Training Base, and later, 64 Operational Base in No 6 (RCAF) Bomber Group of Bomber Comd; SASO of the Group, Dec. 1944; AOC RCAF Maintenance Comd, 1945-46; Senior Canadian Air Force Liaison Officer, London, 1946-48; AOC Air Materiel Comd, RCAF, Ottawa, 1948-52. Business Consultant, 1952-60; Chief, Technical Information Service, Nat. Research Council, Ottawa, 1960-72. Pres., Internat. Fedn for Documentation, 1968-72. *Address:* 2022 Sharon Avenue, Ottawa, Ontario K2A 1L8, Canada.

MacCABE, Brian Farmer, MC and Bar, 1942; Honorary President, Foote, Cone & Belding Ltd (London) (Chairman, 1948-78, President, 1978-80); Director and Senior Vice-President, Foote, Cone & Belding Communications Inc. (New York), 1953-80; *b* 9 Jan. 1914; *s* of late James MacCabe and Katherine MacCabe (*née* Harwood); *m* 1940, Eileen Elizabeth Noel Hunter; one *s. Educ:* Christ's Coll., Finchley. Executive, C. R. Casson Ltd, 1934-40. Major, RTR (Sqdn Comd, Alamein), 1940-45. World-wide Advertising Manager, BOAC, 1945-47; Chm., FCB International Inc. (NY), 1967-74. Mem. Council: Inst. of Practitioners in Advertising, 1951-80 (Pres., 1963-65); Advertising Assoc., 1952-69; Internat. Marketing Programme, 1965-80. Mem., Reith Commn on Advertising, 1962-66; Dir, American Chamber of Commerce, 1971-80; Member: Promotion Cttee, BNEC, 1965-68; Marketing Cttee, Ashridge Management Coll., 1965-78; Advertising Standards Authority, 1969-72; Appeals Cttee, Olympic and Commonwealth Games, 1952-; Management Cttee, British Sports Assoc. for the Disabled, 1962-65; Nat. Council, Brit. Polio Fellowship, 1959-65. Royal Humane Soc. Medal for saving life at sea, 1934; awards for services to advertising, 1957-. *Recreations:* finalist: (800 metres) Olympic Games, Berlin, 1936; (880 yards) British Commonwealth Games, Sydney, 1938; golf, fishing. *Address:* Somerford, Penn Road, Beaconsfield, Bucks. *T:* Beaconsfield 3365. *Clubs:* Boodle's; Wasps RFC; LAC (Vice-Pres.), Bucks AA (Vice-Pres.), Beaconsfield Golf, Denham Golf.

McCABE, John; professional musician; composer and pianist; *b* 21 April 1939; *s* of Frank and Elisabeth McCabe; *m* 1974, Monica Christine Smith. *Educ:* Liverpool Institute High Sch. for Boys; Manchester Univ. (MusBac); Royal Manchester Coll. of Music (ARMCM); Hochschule für Musik, Munich. Pianist-in-residence, University Coll., Cardiff, 1965-68; freelance musical criticism, 1966-71. Career as composer and pianist: many broadcasts and recordings as well as concert appearances in various countries. Prizewinner in Gaudeamus Competition for Interpreters of Contemporary Music, Holland, 1969. First European concert tour, 1971; first tour in USA and Canada, 1973. Recordings incl. 16-record set of complete piano music by Haydn; complete piano music of Nielsen (2 records). Awarded Special Citation by Koussevitsky Internat. Recording Foundn of USA, for recording of Symph. No 2 and Notturni ed Alba, 1974; Special Award by Composers' Guild of Gt Brit. (services to Brit. music), 1975; Ivor Novello Award (TV theme tune, Sam), 1977. Hon. FRMCM. *Publications:* many compositions, incl. three symphonies, two operas, ballets, concerti, orchestral works incl. The Chagall Windows and Hartmann Variations, Notturni ed Alba, for soprano and orch., chamber music, keyboard works, and vocal compositions. Rachmaninov (short biog.), 1974; Bartok's Orchestral Music (BBC Music Guide), 1974; reviews in Guardian, New Statesman, Records and Recordings, etc. *Recreations:* cricket, books, films. *Address:* 49 Burns Avenue, Southall, Mddx. *T:* 01-574 5039.

McCABE, Most Rev. Thomas, DD; *b* 30 June 1902; *s* of John Patrick and Elizabeth McCabe. *Educ:* St Augustine's School, Coffs Harbour, NSW; St Columba's College, Springwood, NSW; St Patrick's College, Manly, NSW; Propaganda College, Rome. Ordained Priest in Rome, 1925; Administrator of St Carthage's Cathedral, Lismore, NSW, 1931-39; Bishop of Port Augusta, 1939-52; Bishop of Wollongong, 1952-74; retired 1974. *Address:* Polding Villa, 2 Arcadia Avenue, Glebe Point, NSW 2037, Australia.

McCAFFREY, Sir Thos Daniel, (Sir Tom McCaffrey), Kt 1979; Chief Assistant to Rt Hon. Michael Foot, MP, since 1980; *b* 20 Feb. 1922; *s* of William P. and B. McCaffrey; *m* 1949, Agnes Campbell Douglas; two *s* four *d. Educ:* Hyndland Secondary Sch. and St Aloysius Coll., Glasgow. Served War, RAF, 1940-46. Scottish Office, 1948-61; Chief Information Officer, Home Office, 1966-71; Press Secretary, 10 Downing Street, 1971-72; Dir of Information Services, Home Office, 1972-74; Head of News Dept, FCO, 1974-76; Chief of Staff to Rt Hon. James Callaghan, MP, 1979-80 (his Chief Press Secretary, as Prime Minister, 1976-79). *Address:* Balmaha, The Park, Great Bookham, Surrey. *T:* Bookham 54171.

MacCAIG, Norman (Alexander), OBE 1979; MA; FRSL; *b* 14 Nov. 1910; *s* of Robert McCaig and Joan MacLeod; *m* 1940, Isabel Munro; one *s* one *d. Educ:* Edinburgh University. MA Hons Classics. Schoolteacher, 1932-67 and 1969-70; Fellow in Creative Writing, Univ. of Edinburgh, 1967-69; Lectr in English Studies, Univ. of Stirling, 1970-72, Reader in Poetry, 1972-77. Travelling Scholarship, Soc. of Authors, 1964; RSL Award (Heinemann Bequest), 1967; Cholmondeley Award, 1975; Scottish Arts Council Awards, 1954, 1966-67, 1970, 1971, 1978, 1980. DUniv Stirling, 1981. *Publications: poetry:* Far Cry, 1943; The Inward Eye, 1946; Riding Lights, 1955; The Sinai Sort, 1957; A Common Grace, 1960; A Round of Applause, 1962; Measures, 1965; Surroundings, 1966; Rings on a Tree, 1968; A Man in My Position, 1969; The White Bird, 1973; The World's Room, 1974; Tree of Strings, 1977; The Equal Skies, 1980; (ed anthology) Honour'd Shade, 1959; (with Alexander Scott, ed anthology) Contemporary Scottish Verse, 1970. *Recreations:* fishing, music. *Address:* 7 Leamington Terrace, Edinburgh EH10 4JW. *T:* 031-229 1809. *Club:* Scottish Arts (Edinburgh).

McCALL, Charles James, DA (Edinburgh); ROI 1949, NEAC 1957; artist-painter; *b* 24 Feb. 1907; *s* of late William McCall, Edinburgh; *m* 1945, Eloise Jerwood, *d* of late F. Ward, Bickley, Kent. *Educ:* Edinburgh Univ.; Edinburgh College of Art. RSA Travelling Schol., 1933; Edinburgh College of Art: Travelling Schol., 1936 (Fellow, 1938). Studied in many art galleries in Europe; also in studios in Paris. Returned to London in 1938, exhibiting

RA, NEAC, London Group, etc. Commissioned, RE 1940; at end of war taught drawing and painting at Formation College. Has exhibited regularly in London; one-man shows held at: Leicester Galleries, 1950 and 1953; Victor Waddington Galleries, Dublin, 1951; Duveen Graham Galleries, New York, 1955 and 1957; Crane Galleries, Manchester, 1955; Klinkhoff Gallery, Montreal, 1958 and 1960; Whibley Gallery, London, 1961; Federation of British Artists, 1965; Ash Barn Gallery, Stroud, 1965, 1969, 1973; Eaton's Gallery, Winnipeg, Canada, 1966; Nevill Gallery, Canterbury, 1972; Belgrave Gallery, 1975, 1977. BBC TV Programme on his life and work, 1975; profile in Artist magazine, 1981. Painter of portraits, landscapes, interiors with figures, and of contemporary life. Lord Mayor's Art Award, 1963, 1973, 1977. *Recreations:* music, literature, travel. *Address:* 1a Caroline Terrace, SW1W 8JS. *T:* 01-730 8737.

McCALL, Sir (Charles) Patrick (Home), Kt 1971; MBE 1944; TD 1946; solicitor; Clerk of the County Council, 1960-72, Clerk of the Peace, 1960-71, and Clerk of the Lieutenancy, Lancashire, 1960-74; *b* 22 Nov. 1910; *s* of late Charles and Dorothy McCall; *m* 1934, Anne, *d* of late Samuel Brown, Sedlescombe, Sussex; two *s* one *d. Educ:* St Edward's Sch., Oxford. Served 1939-45; Substantive Major TA. Hon. Lt-Col. Mem., Economic and Social Cttee, EEC, 1973-78. *Recreations:* travel, walking, swimming, gardening. *Address:* Auchenhay Lodge, Corsock, by Castle Douglas, Kirkcudbrightshire. *T:* Corsock 651.
See also R. H. McCall.

McCALL, Christopher Hugh; Junior Counsel to the Attorney General in charity matters, since 1981; *b* 3 March 1944; *yr s* of Robin Home McCall, *qv; m* 1981, Henrietta Francesca Sharpe. *Educ:* Winchester (Scholar); Magdalen Coll., Oxford (Demy; BA 1st Cl. Hons Maths, 1964; Eldon Law Scholar, 1966). Called to the Bar, Lincoln's Inn, 1966. Second Jun. Counsel to the Inland Revenue in chancery matters, 1977-. Member: Bar Council, 1973-76; Cttee of Management, Barristers Benevolent Assoc., 1977-81 (Jt Hon. Treasurer, 1981-). *Recreations:* music, travel, mountains, walking, dozing. *Address:* 7 New Square, Lincoln's Inn, WC2A 3QS. *T:* 01-405 1266. *Clubs:* Royal Automobile; Leander (Henley-on-Thames); Climbers.

McCALL, David Slesser; Director since 1970 and Chief Executive since 1976, Anglia Television Ltd; *b* 3 Dec. 1934; *s* of Patrick McCall and Florence Kate Mary Walker; *m* 1968, Lois Patricia Elder. *Educ:* Robert Gordon's Coll., Aberdeen. Mem., Inst. of Chartered Accountants of Scotland, 1958. National Service, 1959-61. Accountant, Grampian Television Ltd, 1961-68; Company Sec., Anglia Television Ltd, 1968-76. Director: Anglia Television Group plc, 1970-; ITN, 1978-; Ind. Television Publications Ltd, 1971-; Ind. Television Cos Assoc. Ltd, 1976-; Channel Four Television Co., 1981-; East Anglia Securities Holdings, 1974-; Sodastream Holdings Ltd, 1976-; Norwich City Football Club, 1979-. *Recreations:* sport, travel. *Address:* 168 St Clements Hill, Norwich NR3 4DG. *T:* Norwich 45911. *Club:* Norfolk (Norwich).

McCALL, John Armstrong Grice, CMG 1964; *b* 7 Jan. 1913; 2nd *s* of Rev. Canon J. G. McCall; *m* 1951, Kathleen Mary Clarke; no *c. Educ:* Glasgow Academy; Trinity Coll., Glenalmond; St Andrews Univ.; St John's Coll., Cambridge. MA 1st class hons Hist. St Andrews, 1935. Colonial Administrative Service (HMOCS), Nigeria, 1935-67; Cadet, 1936; Class I, 1956; Staff Grade, 1958. Chm., Mid-Western Nigeria Development Corp., Benin City, 1966-67, retired 1967. Asst Chief Admin. Officer, East Kilbride Develt Corp., 1967-76. Scottish Rep., Executive Cttee, Nigeria-British Chamber of Commerce, 1977-. Mem. 1969, Vice-Chm. 1971, S Lanarkshire Local Employment Cttee; Mem. Panel, Industrial Tribunals (Scotland), 1972-74; Gen. Sec., Scotland, Royal Over-Seas League, 1978-80. Sec., West Linton Community Council, 1980-. *Recreations:* golf, walking. *Address:* Burnside, West Linton, Peeblesshire. *T:* West Linton 60488. *Clubs:* Caledonian; Old Glenalmond (Chm., 1978-81); Royal and Ancient (St Andrews).

McCALL, John Donald; Director, Consolidated Gold Fields Ltd, 1959-81 (Chairman, 1969-76); *b* 1 Feb. 1911; *s* of late Gilbert Kerr McCall; *m* 1942, Vere Stewart Gardner; one *s* one *d. Educ:* Clifton Coll.; Edinburgh Univ. Gold Mining industry, S Africa, 1930-39. Served War of 1939-45: commissioned, Gordon Highlanders. Joined Consolidated Gold Fields Ltd, London, 1946 (Dir, 1959; Jt Dep. Chm., 1968). *Recreations:* gardening, golf. *Address:* 64 Pont Street, SW1. *Club:* Caledonian.

McCALL, Kenneth Murray, DL; Lord Lieutenant of Dumfriesshire, 1970-72; *b* 21 Dec. 1912; *s* of late Major William McCall, DL; *m* 1938, Christina Eve Laurie; two *s* two *d. Educ:* Merchiston Castle School. DL Dumfriesshire, 1973. *Recreations:* shooting, golf. *Address:* Caitloch, Moniaive, Thornhill, Dumfriesshire. *T:* Moniaive 211.

McCALL, Sir Patrick; see McCall, Sir C. P. H.

McCALL, Robin Home, CBE 1976 (OBE 1969); retired 1976; *b* 21 March 1912; *s* of late Charles and Dorothy McCall; *m* 1937, Joan Elizabeth Kingdon; two *s* one *d. Educ:* St Edward's Sch., Oxford. Solicitors Final (Hons), 1935. Served War, RAFVR Night Fighter Controller (Sqdn Ldr); D Day landing Normandy, in command of 15083 GCI, 1944. Asst Solicitor: Bexhill Corp., 1935-39; Hastings Corp., 1939-46; Bristol Corp., 1946-47; Dep. Town Clerk, Hastings, 1947-48; Town Clerk and Clerk of the Peace, Winchester, 1948-72; Sec., Assoc. of Municipal Corporations, later Assoc. of Metropolitan

Authorities, 1973-76. Hon. Sec., Non-County Boroughs Cttee for England and Wales, 1958-69; Member: Reading Cttee (Highway Law Consolidation); Morris Cttee (Jury Service); Kennett Preservation Gp (Historic Towns Conservation); Exec. Cttee, European Architectural Heritage Year, 1972-; UK delegn to ECLA (Council of Europe); North Hampshire Hosp. Cttee, 1969-72. Governor, St Swithin's Sch., Winchester, 1978-. Hon. Freeman, City of Winchester, 1973. *Publications:* contrib. Local Government, Halsbury's Laws, 4th edn, 1980; various articles and reviews on local govt. *Recreations:* gardening, mountains. *Address:* The Hospice, St Giles Hill, Winchester. *T:* Winchester 54101. *Club:* Alpine.

See also C. H. McCall, Sir C. P. H. McCall.

McCALL, William; General Secretary, Institution of Professional Civil Servants, since 1963; *b* 6 July 1929; *s* of Alexander McCall and Jean Corbet Cunningham; *m* 1955, Olga Helen Brunton; one *s* one *d. Educ:* Dumfries Academy; Ruskin College, Oxford. Civil Service, 1946-52; Social Insurance Dept, TUC, 1954-58; Asst Sec., Instn of Professional Civil Servants, 1958-63; Mem., Civil Service Nat. Whitley Council (Staff Side), 1963-, Chm. 1969-71. Mem., Management Cttee, Social Policy Research Ltd, 1976-; Hon. Treasurer, Parly Scientific Cttee, 1976-80; Part-time Mem., Eastern Electricity Board, 1977-; Member: Cttee of Inquiry into Engrg Profession, 1977-79; PO Arbitration Tribunal, 1980-. *Recreations:* reading, talking. *Address:* Bayston, Cross Oak Road, Berkhamsted, Herts. *T:* Berkhamsted 4974.

McCALLUM, Archibald Duncan Dugald, TD 1950; MA; Headmaster, Strathallan School, 1970-75; *b* 26 Nov. 1914; *s* of late Dr A. D. McCallum and Mrs A. D. McCallum; *m* 1950, Rosemary Constance, *widow* of Sqdn Ldr John Rhind, RAF, and *d* of William C. Thorne, OBE, Edinburgh; two *s* (one step *s*). *Educ:* Fettes Coll., Edinburgh; St John's Coll., Cambridge (Classical Sizar). Asst Master and Housemaster, Fettes Coll., 1937-39, 1945-51. Served War of 1939-45 (despatches): Home Forces, India, and Burma. Second Master, Strathallan Sch., 1951-56; Headmaster: Christ Coll., Brecon, 1956-62; Epsom Coll., 1962-70. FRSA 1969-75. *Recreations:* Rugby football, golf, reading. *Address:* 1 Church Row Cottages, Burnham Market, King's Lynn, Norfolk. *T:* Burnham Market 518.

McCALLUM, Brig. Frank, CIE 1947; OBE 1936; MC 1923; DL; *b* 11 March 1900; *s* of late Lt-Col D. McCallum, RASC, Edinburgh; *m* 1932, Sybilla Mary de Symons (OBE 1977; County Councillor for Kesteven, Lincs, 1964-74), *d* of late Gen. Sir George Barrow, GCB, KCMG; one *s* (and one *s* decd). *Educ:* George Watson's Coll.; RMC. Commissioned 1918; Brig. 1943. ADC to GOC-in-C Eastern Comd, India, 1928-29; Staff Coll., Quetta, 1934-35; Bde Major, Razmak, 1936-39; GSO2 Meerut Dist, 1940-41; served in Iraq, Persia, Western Desert, and Syria, 1941-46; GSO1, 8 Indian Div., 1941-43; Bde Comd, 1943-46; BGS Northern Comd, India, 1946-47; Dir Staff Duties, Army HQ, Pakistan, 1947. Served 3rd Afghan War, 1919; NWF, 1920-21 and 1923 (MC); NWF, 1936 (OBE) and 1937-39; despatches 7 times, 1936-46; retd 30 May 1948. Asst Regional Food Officer, North Midland Region, 1948-51; Regional Sec. Country Landowners Assoc. for Lincs, Notts, and Derbs, 1951-65; CC Kesteven, Lincolnshire, 1952-74, Alderman, 1964-74. DL Lincolnshire, 1965. Syrian Order of Merit, 1st Class, 1945-46. *Address:* Westborough Grange, near Newark, Notts NG23 5HH. *T:* Lovedon 81285.

McCALLUM, Googie; *see* Withers, Googie.

McCALLUM, Ian Stewart; Chairman, Association of District Councils, since 1979; Vice-Chairman, Sports Council, since 1980; Group Products Manager, Save & Prosper Group Ltd; *b* 24 Sept. 1936; *s* of John Blair McCallum and Margaret Stewart McCallum; *m* 1957, Pamela Mary (*née* Shave); one *s* two *d. Educ:* Kingston Grammar Sch. Eagle Star Insurance Co. Ltd, 1953-54; National Service, Highland Light Infantry, 1954-56; Eagle Star Insce Co. Ltd, 1956-58; F. E. Wright and Co., Insurance Brokers, 1958-63; H. Clarkson (Home) Ltd, Insurance Brokers, 1963-68; Save & Prosper Group Ltd, 1968-. Leader, Woking Borough Council, 1978-81, Dep. Leader, 1981-; Vice-Chairman: Standing Cttee on Local Authorities and Theatre, 1977-81; UK Steering Cttee on Local Authority Superannuation; Member: Consultative Council on Local Govt Finance; Local Authorities Conditions of Service Adv. Bd; Council for Business in the Community. *Recreations:* swimming, walking, reading. *Address:* 10 Queenswood Road, St John's, Woking, Surrey GU21 1XJ. *T:* Brookwood 2845. *Club:* St Stephen's and Constitutional.

McCALLUM, John, BSc, FEng, FRINA, FICE; consultant naval architect; Chief Ship Surveyor, Lloyd's Register of Shipping, 1970-81; *b* 13 Oct. 1920; *s* of Hugh McCallum and Agnes Falconer McCallum (*née* Walker); *m* 1948, Christine Peggy Sowden; two *s. Educ:* Allan Glen's Sch., Glasgow; Glasgow Univ. (BSc (First Cl. Hons Naval Architecture) 1943). Apprenticed John Brown & Co., Clydebank, 1938-43; Jun. Lectr, Naval Architecture, Glasgow Univ., 1943-44; Ship Surveyor, Lloyd's Register of Shipping, Newcastle upon Tyne, 1944, Glasgow, 1949, London, 1953; Naval Architect, John Brown & Co., 1961; Technical Dir, John Brown Shipbuilders, 1967, Upper Clyde Shipbuilders, 1969. FRINA (Mem. Council, 1970-; Chm., 1971-73; Vice-Pres., 1975-); FEng 1977; FICE 1978. Mem., IES, 1962- (past Mem. Council); Member: SNAME, 1970-81, Fellow, 1981-; Smeatonian Soc. of Civil Engrs, 1979-. Liveryman and Mem. Educn Cttee, Worshipful Co. of Shipwrights, 1975. *Publications:* various technical papers to Royal Soc., RINA, NE Coast IES, Assoc. Tech. Maritime et Aéronautique (1978 Medal), and other Europ. learned socs. *Recreations:* golf, piano, art, mathematics. *Address:* Dala,

Garvock Drive, Kippington, Sevenoaks, Kent TN13 2LT. *T:* Sevenoaks 455462. *Club:* Wildernesse (Sevenoaks).

McCALLUM, John Neil, CBE 1971; Chairman and Executive Producer, Fauna Films, Australia, since 1967, and John McCallum Productions, since 1976; actor and producer; *b* 14 March 1918; *s* of John Neil McCallum and Lilian Elsie (*née* Dyson); *m* 1948, Georgette Lizette Withers (*see* Googie Withers); one *s* two *d. Educ:* Oatlands Prep. Sch., Harrogate; Knox Grammar Sch., Sydney; C of E Grammar Sch., Brisbane; RADA. Served War, 2/5 Field Regt, AIF, 1941-45. Actor, English rep. theatres, 1937-39; Stratford-on-Avon Festival Theatre, 1939; Old Vic Theatre, 1940; British films and theatre, 1946-58; films include: It Always Rains On Sunday; Valley of Eagles; Miranda; London stage plays include: Roar Like a Dove; Janus; Waiting for Gillian; J. C. Williamson Theatres Ltd, Australia: Asst Man. Dir, 1958; Jt. Man. Dir, 1959-65; Man. Dir, 1966. Appeared in: (with Ingrid Bergman) The Constant Wife, London, 1973-74; (with Googie Withers) The Circle, London, 1976-77; (with Googie Withers) The Kingfisher, Australia, 1978-79; The Skin Game, The Cherry Orchard, and Dandy Dick, theatrical tour, England, 1981. Author of play, As It's Played Today, produced Melbourne, 1974. Produced television series, 1967-: Boney; Barrier Reef; Skippy; Bailey's Bird. Prod., Attack Force Z (feature film), 1980; Southern Cross (feature film), 1982. Pres., Aust. Film Council, 1971-72. *Publication:* Life with Googie, 1979. *Recreation:* golf. *Address:* 1740 Pittwater Road, Bayview, NSW 2104, Australia. *T:* Sydney 9976879. *Clubs:* Garrick, MCC; Melbourne (Melbourne); Australian, Elanora Country (Sydney).

MAC CANA, Prof. Proinsias; Professor of Early (including Medieval) Irish, University College, Dublin, since 1971; *b* 6 July 1926; *s* of George Mc Cann and Mary Catherine Mallon; *m* 1952, Réiltín (*née* Supple); one *s* one *d. Educ:* St Malachy's Coll., Belfast; The Queen's Univ., Belfast (BA, MA, PhD); Ecole des Hautes Etudes, Paris. Asst Lectr, Celtic Dept, QUB, 1951-54; University College Wales, Aberystwyth: Asst Lectr in Early Irish, 1955-57; Lectr, 1957-61; Prof., Sch. of Celtic Studies, Dublin Inst. for Advanced Studies, 1961-63; Prof. of Welsh, University Coll., Dublin, 1963-71. Co-editor, Eriu (RIA Jl of Irish Studies), 1973-; General editor, Medieval and Modern Welsh Series, Dublin Inst. for Advanced Studies, 1962-. Chm., Governing Bd, Sch. of Celtic Studies, Dublin Inst. for Advanced Studies, 1975-. PRIA, 1979-82. *Publications:* Scéalaíocht na Ríthe (collection of early Irish tales trans. into Modern Irish), 1956; Branwen Daughter of Llŷr: the second branch of the Mabinogi, 1958; Celtic Mythology, 1970; The Mabinogi, 1977; Regnum and Sacerdotium: notes on Irish Tradition (Rhys Meml Lecture, British Academy), 1979; The Learned Tales of Medieval Ireland, 1980. *Address:* 9 Silchester Road, Glenageary, Co. Dublin. *T:* Dublin 805062. *Club:* Kildare Street and University (Dublin).

McCANCE, Sir Andrew, Kt 1947; DSc; LLD; FRS 1943; DL; *b* 30 March 1889; *yr s* of John McCance; *m* 1936, Joya Harriett Gladys Burford (*d* 1969); two *d. Educ:* Morrison's Academy, Crieff; Allan Glen's Sch., Glasgow; Royal School of Mines, London. DSc London, 1916. Asst Armour Manager, W. Beardmore & Co., 1910-19; Founder and Man. Dir, Clyde Alloy Steel Co. Ltd, 1919-30, Pres. 1965-71; Formerly: Chm. and Man. Dir, later Hon. Pres., Colvilles Ltd. Past President: Iron and Steel Inst.; Glasgow and West of Scotland Iron and Steel Inst.; Inst. of Engineers and Shipbuilders in Scotland: President: British Iron and Steel Federation, 1957, 1958; Instn of Works Managers, 1964-67. Chm., Mechanical Engineering Research Board, DSIR, 1952-58. DL Lanarkshire. Hon. DSc Strathclyde, 1965. Bessemer Medallist, 1940. *Publications:* several papers in Technical Society jls. *Address:* Malin Court, Maidens, Girvan, Ayrshire KA26 9PB. *Clubs:* Athenæum; Scottish Automobile (Glasgow).

McCANCE, Robert Alexander, CBE 1953; FRS 1948; Professor of Experimental Medicine, Medical Research Council and University of Cambridge, 1945-66, now Emeritus; Director, MRC Infantile Malnutrition Research Unit, Mulago Hospital, Kampala, 1966-68; Fellow of Sidney Sussex College; *b* near Belfast, Northern Ireland, 9 Dec. 1898; *s* of Mary L. Bristow and J. S. F. McCance, linen merchant, Belfast; *m* 1922, Mary L. MacGregor (*d* 1965); one *s* one *d. Educ:* St Bees Sch., Cumberland; Sidney Sussex Coll., Cambridge. RN Air Service and RAF, 1917-18; BA (Cambridge), 1922; Biochemical Research, Cambridge, 1922-25; qualified in medicine King's Coll. Hosp., London, 1927; MD (Cambridge), 1929; Asst Physician i/c biochemical research, King's Coll. Hosp., London; FRCP 1935; Goulstonian Lectr, RCP, 1936; Humphrey Rolleston Lectr, RCP, 1953; Groningen Univ. Lectr, 1958; Leonard Parsons Lectr, Birmingham Univ., 1959; Lumleian Lectr, RCP, 1962. Reader in Medicine, Cambridge Univ., 1938; War of 1939-45, worked on medical problems of national importance; visited Spain and Portugal on behalf of British Council, 1943, South Africa, 1965; i/c Medical Research Council Unit, Germany, 1946-49. Hon. FRCOG; Hon. Member: Assoc. of American Physicians; American Pediatric Soc.; Swiss Nutrition Soc.; Brit. Pædiatric Assoc.; Nutrition Soc. Gold Medal, West London Medico-Chirurgical Soc., 1949. Conway Evans Prize, RCP and Royal Society, 1960; James Spence Medal, Brit. Pæd. Assoc., 1961. Hon. DSc Belfast, 1964. *Publications:* Medical Problems in Mineral Metabolism (Goulstonian Lectures), 1936; (jointly) The Chemical Composition of Foods; An Experimental Study of Rationing; (jointly) Breads White and Brown; numerous papers on the physiology of the newborn animal. *Recreations:* mountaineering, cycling, gardening. *Address:* 4 Kent House, Sussex Street, Cambridge CB1 1PH.

McCANN, Hugh James; Chairman, Cultural Relations Committee, Irish Department of Foreign Affairs and President, Ireland-France Economic Association, since 1981; *b* 8 Feb. 1916; *e s* of late District Justice Hugh Joseph McCann, BL, and late Sophie McCann, Dublin; *m* 1950, Mary Virginia Larkin, Washington, DC, USA; four *s* one *d. Educ:* Belvedere Coll., Dublin; London Sch. of Economics, Univ. of London. Served in Dept of Lands, Dublin, and in Dept of Industry and Commerce, Dublin; Commercial Sec., London, 1944-46; First Sec., Dept of External Affairs, Dublin, 1946-48; Counsellor, Irish Embassy, Washington, DC, 1948-54; Irish Minister to Switzerland and Austria, 1954-56; Asst Sec., Dept of External Affairs, Dublin, 1956-58; Irish Ambassador at the Court of St James's, 1958-62; Sec., Dept of Foreign Affairs, Dublin, 1963-74; Irish Ambassador to France, Perm. Rep. to OECD and to UNESCO, 1974-81, and concurrently Ambassador to Morocco, 1975-81. Grand Cross, Order of Leopold II, Belgium, 1968; Grand Officer, National Order of Merit, France, 1981. *Recreations:* golf, reading, swimming, and photography. *Address:* Frankfeld, Mart Lane, Foxrock, Co. Dublin. *Clubs:* Royal Dublin Society, Stephen's Green (Dublin), Woodbrook Golf.

McCANN, Most Rev. James, MA; PhD; DD; LLD; *b* Grantham, Lincs, 31 Oct. 1897; *s* of James W. and Agnes McCann; *m* 1924, Violet, *d* of James and Mary Henderson, Ballymena, Ireland; no *c. Educ:* Royal Belfast Academical Institution; Queen's University, Belfast (BA; Hon. LLD 1966); Trinity College, Dublin (MA, PhD, DD). Ecclesiastical History Prizeman (1st), 1917; Elrington Theological Prizeman (1st), 1930; ordained 1920; held curacies at Ballymena, Ballyclare, Cavan, Oldcastle; Rector of Donaghpatrick, 1930-36; St Mary's, Drogheda, 1936-45; Canon of St Patrick's Cathedral, Dublin, 1944-45; Bishop of Meath, 1945-59; Archbishop of Armagh and Primate of All Ireland, 1959-69. *Publication:* Asceticism: an historical study, 1944. *Recreations:* music, reading. *Address:* c/o Rev. H. A. McCann, The Rectory, Begbroke, Oxford. *T:* Kidlington 3253. *Club:* Kildare Street and University (Dublin).

McCANN, His Eminence Cardinal Owen; *see* Cape Town, Cardinal Archbishop of.

McCANN, Peter Toland McAree, CBE 1977; JP; DL; Lord Provost of the City of Glasgow and Lord-Lieutenant of the City of Glasgow, 1975-77; *b* 2 Aug. 1924; *s* of Peter McCann and Agnes (*née* Waddell); *m* 1958, Maura Eleanor (*née* Ferris); one *s. Educ:* St Mungo's Academy; Glasgow Univ. (BL). Solicitor and Notary Public. Pres., Glasgow Univ. Law Soc., 1946; Pres., St Thomas More Soc., 1959. Mem. Glasgow Corp., 1961. Chm., McCann Cttee (Secondary Educn for Physically Handicapped Children), 1971. DL Glasgow, 1978. OStJ 1977. *Recreations:* music, history, model aeroplane making. *Address:* 31 Queen Mary Avenue, Glasgow G42 8DS.

McCARRAHER, David, VRD 1964; Captain RNR retired; a Recorder of the Crown Court, since 1979; *b* 6 Nov. 1922; *s* of Colin McCarraher and Vera Mabel McCarraher (*née* Hickley); *m* 1950, Betty Johnson (*née* Haywood); one *s* three *d. Educ:* King Edward VI Sch., Southampton; Magdalene Coll., Cambridge (MA Law). RN, 1941-45. Called to the Bar, Lincoln's Inn, 1948; practised Western Circuit until 1952, disbarred at own request to be articled; admitted solicitor, 1955; Sen. Partner in private practice, 1960-. Mem. Panel, Dep. Circuit Judges, 1973-79. Founder Mem. and Past Pres., Southampton Junior Chamber of Commerce. Governor, King Edward VI Sch., Southampton, 1961-. Sub-Lieut, RNVR, 1943-45, RNVSR, 1946-52; served to Captain RNR, 1969; CO Solent Div., RNR, 1969-72; ADC to the Queen, 1972-73; retired 1975. Hon. Sec., RNR Benevolent Fund, 1973-. *Recreations:* family, golf, sailing. *Address:* 3 College Place, London Road, Southampton SO9 3RA. *T:* Southampton 32733. *Clubs:* Naval; Thames Rowing, Law Society's Yacht, Stoneham Golf (Southampton), Royal Southern Yacht (Hamble), Royal Naval Sailing Association (Portsmouth), Southampton Police (Hon. Mem.) (Southampton).

McCARTHY, family name of **Baron McCarthy.**

McCARTHY, Baron *cr* 1975 (Life Peer), of Headington; **William Edward John McCarthy,** DPhil; Fellow of Nuffield College and Oxford Management Centre; University Lecturer in Industrial Relations; engaged in Industrial Arbitration and Chairman of Committees of Inquiry and Investigation, since 1968; *b* 30 July 1925; *s* of E. and H. McCarthy; *m* Margaret McCarthy. *Educ:* Holloway County; Ruskin Coll.; Merton Coll.; Nuffield Coll. MA (Oxon), DPhil (Oxon). Trade Union Scholarship to Ruskin Coll., 1953; Research Fellow of Nuffield Coll., 1959; Research Dir, Royal Commn on Trade Unions and Employers' Assocs, 1965-68; Sen. Economic Adviser, Dept of Employment, 1968-71. Chm., Railway Staff Tribunal, 1973; Special Advisor on Industrial Relations to Sec. of State for Social Services, 1975-77; Member: Houghton Cttee on Aid to Political Parties, 1975-76; TUC Independent Review Cttee, 1976; Pres., British Univ. Industrial Relations Assoc., 1975-78; Special Comr, Equal Opportunities Commn, 1977-80; Dep. Chm., Teachers' Nat. Conciliation Cttee, 1979-. Chm., TUC Newspaper Feasibility Adv. Study Gp, 1981-. Mem., H of L Select Cttee on Unemployment, 1980-82; Opposition front bench spokesman on employment, 1980-. Dir, Harland & Wolff Ltd, 1976-. *Publications:* The Closed Shop in Britain, 1964; The Role of Shop Stewards in British Industrial Relations, 1966; (with V. L. Munns) Employers' Associations, 1967; (with A. I. Marsh) Disputes Procedures in Britain, 1968; The Reform of Collective Bargaining at Plant and Company Level, 1971; ed, Trade Unions, 1972; (with

A. I. Collier) Coming to Terms with Trade Unions, 1973; (with N. D. Ellis) Management by Agreement, 1973; (with J. F. O'Brien and V. E. Dowd) Wage Inflation and Wage Leadership, 1975; Making Whitley Work, 1977; (jtly) Change in Trade Unions, 1981; articles in: Brit. Jl of Industrial Relns; Industrial Relns Jl. *Recreations:* gardening, theatre, ballet. *Address:* 4 William Orchard Close, Old Headington, Oxford. *T:* Oxford 62016. *Club:* Reform.

McCARTHY, Adolf Charles; HM Diplomatic Service, retired; Consul-General, Stuttgart, 1977-82; *b* 19 July 1922; *s* of Herbert Charles McCarthy and Anna Schnorf; *m* 1949, Ursula Vera Grimm; one *s* two *d. Educ:* London Univ. (BScEcon). Served War, RN, 1942-46. Min. of Agriculture, Fisheries and Food, 1939-64; Min. of Overseas Develt, 1964-66; HM Diplomatic Service, 1966; First Secretary: (Economic), Pretoria, 1968-70; (Commercial), Wellington, 1971-74; Asst Head of Western European Dept, FCO, 1974-77. *Recreations:* music, modern political history. *Address:* Neufeldweg 5, 7880 Bad Saeckinge 13, Federal Republic of Germany. *Club:* Rotary (Stuttgart).

McCARTHY, Donal John, CMG 1969; HM Diplomatic Service, retired; *b* 31 March 1922; *s* of Daniel and Kathleen McCarthy; *m* 1951, Rosanna Parbury; three *s. Educ:* London Univ. Served Royal Navy, 1942-46. Foreign Office, 1946; Middle East Centre for Arab Studies, 1947-48; 3rd and 2nd Sec., Brit. Embassy, Jedda, 1948-51; 2nd Sec., Political Div., Brit. Middle East Office, 1951-55; 1st Sec., FO, 1955-58; Asst Polit. Agent, Kuwait, 1958-60; Brit. High Commn, Ottawa, 1960-63; FO, 1963-64; Counsellor, Brit. High Commn, Aden, and Polit. Adviser to C-in-C Middle East, 1964-67; Head of Aden Dept, FO, 1967-68, of Arabian Dept, FCO, 1968-70; IDC, 1970-71; Minister (Economic and Social Affairs), UK Mission to UN, 1971-73; Ambassador to United Arab Emirates, 1973-77; FCO, 1978-79. *Recreations:* music, skiing, being idle. *Address:* 23 Leighton Grove, NW5. *T:* 01-267 9169; Glenculloo Lodge, Killoscully, Newport, Tipperary, Ireland. *T:* Silvermines 21. *Clubs:* Travellers', Royal Automobile, Ski Club of Great Britain.

McCARTHY, Eugene Joseph; Writer, since 1971; *b* 29 March 1916; *s* of Michael J. and Anna Baden McCarthy; *m* 1945, Abigail Quigley McCarthy; one *s* three *d. Educ:* St John's Univ., Collegeville (BA); Univ. of Minnesota (MA). Teacher in public schools, 1935-40; Coll. Prof. of Econs and Sociology, and civilian techn. Asst in Mil. Intell. for War Dept, 1940-48; US Representative in Congress of 4th District, Minnesota, 1949-58; US Senator from Minnesota, 1959-70. Independent. Holds hon. degrees. *Publications:* Frontiers in American Democracy, 1960; Dictionary of American Politics, 1962; A Liberal Answer to the Conservative Challenge, 1964; The Limits of Power, 1967; The Year of the People, 1969; Other Things and the Aardvark (poetry), 1970; The Hard Years, 1975; (with James Kilpatrick) A Political Bestiary, 1977; Ground Fog and Night (poetry), 1978; The Ultimate Tyranny: the majority over the majority, 1979; contribs to Saturday Review, Commonweal, Harper's. *Address:* Box 22, Woodville, Va, USA.

McCARTHY, John Haydon, CB 1963; Controller, Central Office, Department of Health and Social Security, Newcastle upon Tyne, 1956-74; *b* 1914; 3rd *s* of late Lt-Comdr Jeremiah and Mrs Margaret McCarthy, Walton-on-Thames; *m* 1947, Mary, *e d* of Ebenezer Barclay, Lanark; three *s. Educ:* St Joseph's (de la Salle) Coll., London. Entered GPO, 1931; transferred Home Office, 1936; Min. of Nat. Insce, 1945; Under-Sec., 1956. *Recreation:* sea fishing. *Address:* 3 Front Street, Whitley Bay, Tyne and Wear. *T:* 520206.

McCARTHY, Mary, (Mrs James West); writer; *b* 21 June 1912; *m* 1933, Harold Johnsrud; *m* 1938, Edmund Wilson; one *s*; *m* 1946, Bowden Broadwater; *m* 1961, James Raymond West. *Educ:* Annie Wright Seminary; Vassar Coll. Theatre critic, Partisan Review, 1937-57, Editor, Covici Friede, 1937-38; Instructor, Bard Coll., 1945-46; Instructor, Sarah Lawrence Coll., 1948. Lectures and broadcasts, 1952-65. President's Distinguished Visitor, Vassar, 1982. Horizon award, 1948; Guggenheim Fellow, 1949-50, 1959-60; National Academy of Arts and Letters award, 1957. Hon. Dr Letters: Syracuse Univ., 1973; Bard, 1976; Hon. DLitt Hull, 1974; Hon. LLD Aberdeen, 1979; Hon. Dr Litt: Bowdoin, 1981; Maine, 1982. *Publications:* The Company She Keeps, 1942; The Oasis, 1949; Cast a Cold Eye, 1950; The Groves of Academe, 1952; A Charmed Life, 1955; Venice Observed, 1956; Sights and Spectacles, 1956; Memories of a Catholic Girlhood, 1957; The Stones of Florence, 1959; On the Contrary, 1962; The Group, 1963 (filmed 1966); Vietnam, 1967; Hanoi, 1968; The Writing on the Wall and Other Literary Essays, 1970; Birds of America, 1971; Medina, 1972; The Seventeenth Degree, 1974; The Mask of State: a gallery of Watergate portraits, 1974; Cannibals and Missionaries, 1979; Ideas and the Novel, 1980; essays, journalism, short stories and reviews in the New Yorker, Partisan Review, Horizon, The New York Review of Books, The Observer, etc. *Address:* 141 Rue de Rennes, Paris, France.

McCARTHY, Patrick Peter; Regional Chairman, Liverpool, Industrial Tribunals, since 1977; *b* 10 July 1919; *er s* of late William McCarthy and Mary McCarthy; *m* 1945, Isabel Mary, *y d* of late Dr Joseph Unsworth, St Helens; two *s* three *d. Educ:* St Francis Xavier's Coll., Liverpool; Liverpool Univ. LLB 1940, LLM 1942. Admitted Solicitor, 1942; in private practice until 1974. Part-time Chm., 1972-74, full-time Chm., 1975-, Industrial Tribunals; part-time Chm., Rent Assessment Cttee, 1972-74. JP Liverpool, 1968-74. *Address:*

19a Gloucester Road, Birkdale, Southport, Merseyside PR8 2AU. *T:* Southport 68061.

McCARTHY, Rt. Hon. Sir Thaddeus (Pearcey), PC 1968; KBE 1974; Kt 1964; Judge of the Court of Appeal of New Zealand, 1963-76, President, 1973-76; Chairman, New Zealand Press Council, since 1978; *b* 24 Aug. 1907; *s* of Walter McCarthy, Napier, merchant; *m* 1938, Joan Margaret Miller; one *s* two *d* (and one *d* decd). *Educ:* St Bede's Coll., Christchurch, New Zealand; Victoria Univ. Coll., Wellington. Master of Laws (1st Class Hons) 1931. Served War of 1939-45 in MEF with 22 Bn 2 NZEF, later as DJAG, 2 NZEF. Practised as Barrister and Solicitor until 1957 when appointed to Supreme Court. Chairman: Royal Commn on State Services, 1961-62; Winston Churchill Memorial Trust, 1966-76; Royal Commissions: on Salary and Wage Fixing Procedures in the State Services, 1968; on Social Security, 1969; on Horse Racing, Trotting and Dog Racing, 1969; on Salaries and Wages in the State Services, 1972; on Nuclear Power Generation, 1976-78; on Maori Land Courts, 1979-; Chm., Security Review Authority and Comr of Security Appeals, 1977-. Chm. Adv. Cttee, NZ Computer Centre, 1977-. Vice-Pres., NZ Sect., Internat. Commn of Jurists. Chm., Queen Elizabeth II Nat. Trust, 1978-. Hon. Bencher, Middle Temple, 1974. Hon. LLD Victoria Univ. of Wellington, 1978. *Recreations:* golf (Captain, Wellington Golf Club, 1952, Pres., 1973-77), fishing, sailing. *Address:* 383 Fergusson Drive, Heretaunga, New Zealand. *T:* 286322. *Club:* Wellington (Wellington, NZ) (Pres., 1976-78).

McCARTIE, Rt. Rev. Patrick Leo; Auxiliary Bishop of Birmingham, (RC), and Titular Bishop of Elmham, since 1977; *b* 5 Sept. 1925; *s* of Patrick Leo and Hannah McCartie. *Educ:* Cotton College; Oscott College. Priest, 1949; on staff of Cotton College, 1950-55; parish work, 1955-63; Director of Religious Education, 1963-68; Administrator of St Chad's Cathedral, Birmingham, 1968-77. Pres., Catholic Commn for Racial Justice, 1978-. *Recreations:* music, walking. *Address:* 84 St Bernard's Road, Olton, Solihull, W Midlands. *T:* 021-706 9721.

McCARTNEY, Gordon Arthur; Secretary, Association of District Councils, since 1981; *b* 29 April 1937; *s* of Arthur and Hannah McCartney; *m* 1960, Ceris Ysobel Davies; two *d*. *Educ:* Grove Park Grammar Sch., Wrexham. Articled to Philip J. Walters, MBE (Town Clerk, Wrexham), 1954-59; admitted solicitor, 1959. Asst Solicitor, Birkenhead County Bor. Council, 1959-61; Asst Solicitor, 1961-63, Sen. Asst Solicitor, 1963-65, Bootle County Bor. Council; Dep. Clerk, Wrexham RDC, 1965-73; Clerk, Holywell RDC, 1973-74; Chief Exec., Delyn Bor. Council, 1974-81. *Recreations:* squash, football, cricket, music. *Address:* 1 Kent Drive, Wrexham, Clwyd LL11 2UR. *T:* Wrexham 264355; 70 Eamont Court, Shannon Place, NW8. *T:* 01-586 9445. *Clubs:* Rotary of Erddig, Park View Squash (Wrexham); Middlesex CCC.

McCARTNEY, Hugh; MP (Lab) Dunbartonshire Central, since 1974 (Dunbartonshire East, 1970-74); *b* 3 Jan. 1920; *s* of John McCartney and Mary Wilson; *m* 1949, Margaret; one *s* two *d*. *Educ:* Royal Technical Coll., Glasgow; John Street Senior Secondary School. Apprentice in textile industry, 1934-39; entered aircraft engrg industry, Coventry, 1939; joined Rolls Royce, Glasgow, 1941; joined RAF as aero-engine fitter, 1942 and resumed employment with Rolls Royce, 1947; representative with company (now one of GKN group) specialising in manufacture of safety footwear, 1951. Joined Ind. Labour Party, 1934; joined Labour Party, 1936. Town Councillor, 1955-70 and Magistrate, 1965-70, Kirkintilloch; Mem., Dunbarton CC, 1965-70. Scottish Regional Whip, 1979-. *Recreation:* spectating at football matches and athletic meetings (political activities permitting). *Address:* 63g Townhead, Kirkintilloch, Glasgow G66 1NN.

McCARTNEY, (James) Paul, MBE 1965; musician, composer; *b* Allerton, Liverpool, 18 June 1942; *s* of James McCartney and late Mrs McCartney; *m* 1969, Linda Eastman; one *s* two *d*, and one step *d*. *Educ:* Liverpool Inst. Mem., sch. skiffle group, The Quarrymen, 1958; played with John Lennon and George Harrison as trio, The Moondogs, 1959; toured Scotland with them and Stu Sutcliffe as the Silver Beatles; made 1st official appearance as the Beatles at Litherland Town Hall, nr Liverpool, Dec. 1960; appeared as mem. of Beatles: Sweden, 1963; Royal Variety perf., London, 1963; Paris, Denmark, Hong Kong, Australia, NZ, 1964; TV appearances, USA, and later, coast-to-coast tour, 1964; France, Italy, Spain, USA, 1965; formed MPL group of cos, 1970, and own pop group, Wings, 1971; toured: GB, Europe, 1972-73; UK, Australia, 1975; Europe, USA, 1976. *Songs* (with John Lennon) include: Love Me Do; Please, Please Me; She Loves You; Can't Buy Me Love; I Want to Hold Your Hand; I Saw Her Standing There; Eight Days a Week; Yes It Is; This Boy; All My Loving; Help!; Ticket to Ride; I Feel Fine; I'm A Loser; A Hard Day's Night; No Reply; I'll Follow The Sun; Yesterday; Eleanor Rigby; Yellow Submarine; Penny Lane; All You Need Is Love; Lady Madonna; Hey Jude. *Albums* with The Beatles: Please, Please Me, 1963; With The Beatles, 1963; A Hard Day's Night, 1964; Beatles for Sale, 1965; Help!, 1965; Rubber Soul, 1966; Revolver, 1966; Sgt Pepper's Lonely Hearts Club Band, 1967; Magical Mystery Tour, 1967; The Beatles (White Album), 1968; Yellow Submarine, 1969; Abbey Road, 1969; Let it Be, 1970; subseq. *albums* include: McCartney, 1970; Ram, 1971; Wildlife, 1971; Red Rose Speedway, 1973; Band on the Run, 1973 (2 Grammy Awards); Venus and Mars, 1975; Wings at the Speed of Sound, 1976; Wings over America, 1976; London Town, 1978; Wings Greatest, 1978; Back to the Egg, 1979; McCartney II, 1980; Tug of War, 1982. *Films* (with Beatles): A Hard Day's Night, 1964;

Help!, 1965; Yellow Submarine, 1968; Let It Be, 1970; (with Wings) Rockshow, 1981. *Film scores:* The Family Way, 1967; James Paul McCartney, 1973; Live and Let Die, 1973; *TV score:* The Zoo Gang (series), 1973. Grammy Awards for best perf. by vocal group and best new artist of 1964 (with other Beatles), Nat. Acad. of Recording Arts and Scis, USA, 1965; Ivor Novello Special Award for Internat. Achievement, 1980; Music Achievement Award, Nat. Acad. of Popular Music, 1981; awards for arrangements and albums. *Address:* c/o MPL Communications Ltd, 1 Soho Square, W1V 6BQ. *T:* 01-439 6621.

McCAULEY, Air Marshal Sir John Patrick Joseph, KBE 1955 (CBE 1943); CB 1951; *b* 18 March 1899; *s* of late John and Sophia McCauley; *m* 1925, Murielle Mary, *d* of late John Burke, and of Maude Burke; one *s* two *d*. *Educ:* St Joseph's Coll., Sydney; RMC, Duntroon; Melbourne Univ. (BCom 1936). Grad. RMC 1919; Aust. Staff Corps, 1919-23; RAAF, 1924-; passed RAF Staff Coll., 1933; Flying Instructor's Course, Central Flying Sch., RAF, 1934; Dir Trg, RAAF HQ Melbourne, 1937-38; CO 1 Flying Trg Sch. 1939; CO 1 Eng. Sch., 1940; CO RAAF Stn Sembawang, Malaya, 1941-42; CO RAAF Stn, Palembang 11, Sumatra, 1942; SASO RAAF Darwin, 1942; DCAS, 1942-43; Air Cdre Ops, 2nd TAF France and Germany, 1944-45; DCAS, 1946-47; Chief of Staff, BCOF, Japan, 1947-49; AOC E Area, 1949-53; CAS, RAAF, 1954-57, retd. *Address:* 10 Onslow Gardens, Greenknowe Avenue, Elizabeth Bay, Sydney, NSW 2011, Australia.

McCAUSLAND, Lucius Perronet T.; see Thompson-McCausland.

McCAW, Hon. Sir Kenneth (Malcolm), Kt 1975; QC (Australia) 1972; Attorney-General of New South Wales, 1965-75, retired; *b* 8 Oct. 1907; *s* of Mark Malcolm and Jessie Alice McCaw; *m* 1968, Valma Marjorie Cherlin (*née* Stackpool); two *s* one *d*. *Educ:* matriculated evening college. Left school, 1919; farm and saw-mill hand; clerk, commercial offices and law office, 1922-28; articled law clerk, 1928-33; admitted Solicitor and founded city law firm, 1933; Attorney, Solicitor and Proctor, NSW Supreme Court, until 1965; admitted to NSW Bar, 1965. Councillor, NSW Law Soc., 1945-48. MLA (Lib.) for Lane Cove, NSW, 1947-75, retired. *Publication:* People Versus Power, 1978. *Recreations:* swimming, walking, Braille reading, music, elocution. *Address:* Woodrow House, Charlish Lane, Lane Cove, NSW 2066, Australia. *T:* 427-1900. *Clubs:* Sydney, Lane Cove Businessmen's, (Charter Mem.) Lane Cove Lions (all Sydney/Metropolitan).

McCLEAN, Prof. (John) David; Professor of Law, since 1973, Dean of Faculty of Law, 1978-81, University of Sheffield; *b* 4 July 1939; *s* of Major Harold McClean and Mrs Mabel McClean; *m* 1966, Pamela Ann Loader; one *s* one *d*. *Educ:* Queen Elizabeth's Grammar Sch., Blackburn; Magdalen Coll., Oxford (BCL, MA). Called to the Bar, Gray's Inn, 1963. Asst Lectr 1961, Lectr 1963, Sen. Lectr 1968, Univ. of Sheffield. Vis. Lectr in Law, Monash Univ., Melbourne, 1968, Vis Prof., 1978. Vice-Chm., C of E Bd for Social Responsibility, 1978-80. Member: Gen. Synod of C of E, 1970- (Vice-Chm., House of Laity, 1979-); Crown Appts Commn, 1977-. *Publications:* Criminal Justice and the Treatment of Offenders (jtly), 1969; (contrib.) Halsbury's Laws of England, 4th edn 1974; The Legal Context of Social Work, 1975, 2nd edn 1980; (jtly) Defendants in the Criminal Process, 1976; (ed jtly) Shawcross and Beaumont, Air Law, 4th edn 1977; (jtly) Recognition and Enforcement of Judgments, etc, within the Commonwealth, 1977; (ed jtly) Dicey and Morris, Conflict of Laws, 10th edn 1980. *Recreation:* detective fiction. *Address:* 6 Burnt Stones Close, Sheffield S10 5TS. *T:* Sheffield 305794. *Club:* Royal Commonwealth Society.

McCLEAN, Kathleen; see Hale, Kathleen.

McCLELLAN, John Forrest; Under Secretary, Scottish Economic Planning Department, since 1980; *b* 15 Aug. 1932; *s* of John McClellan and Hester (*née* Niven); *m* 1956, Eva Maria Pressel; three *s* one *d*. *Educ:* Ferryhill Primary Sch., Aberdeen; Aberdeen Grammar Sch.; Aberdeen Univ. (MA Hons Philosophy and Politics). Served Army, 2nd Lieut, Gordon Highlanders and Nigeria Regt, RWAFF, 1954-56. Entered Civil Service, 1956; Asst Principal, Scottish Educn Dept, 1956-59; Private Sec. to Perm. Under Sec. of State, Scottish Office, 1959-60; Principal, Scottish Educn Dept, 1960-68; Civil Service Fellow, Glasgow Univ., 1968-69; Asst Sec., Scottish Educn Dept, 1969-77; Asst Under Sec. of State, Scottish Office, 1977-80. *Recreations:* gardening, walking. *Address:* Grangeneuk, West Linton, Peeblesshire EH46 7HG. *T:* West Linton 502. *Club:* Royal Scots (Edinburgh).

McCLELLAND, George Ewart; Principal Assistant Solicitor, Department of Employment, since 1978; *b* 27 March 1927; *s* of George Ewart McClelland and Winifred (*née* Robinson); *m* 1956, Anne Penelope, *yr d* of late Judge Arthur Henry Armstrong; one *s* two *d*. *Educ:* Stonyhurst Coll.; Merton Coll., Oxford (Classical Scholar; MA). Called to the Bar, Middle Temple, 1952. Entered Solicitor's Dept, Min. of Labour, 1953; Asst Solicitor, 1969.

McCLELLAND, Prof. (William) Grigor; Chairman, Laws Stores Ltd, since 1966; Visiting Professor, Durham University Business School, since 1977; Chairman, Washington Development Corporation, since 1977; *b* 2 Jan. 1922; *o c* of Arthur and Jean McClelland, Gosforth, Newcastle upon Tyne; *m* 1946, Diana Avery Close; two *s* two *d*. *Educ:* Leighton Park; Balliol Coll., Oxford. First Class PPE, 1948. Friends' Ambulance Unit, 1941-46. Man. Dir, Laws Stores Ltd, 1949-65; Sen. Res. Fellow in Management Studies, Balliol Coll., 1962-65; Dir, Manchester Business Sch., 1965-77, and Prof. of Business

Administration, 1967-77, Univ. of Manchester; Dep. Chm., Nat. Computing Centre, 1966-68. Chm., EDC for the Distributive Trades, 1980- (Mem., 1965-70); Member: The Consumer Council, 1963-66; Economic Planning Council, Northern Region, 1965-66; IRC, 1966-71; NEDC, 1969-71; SSRC, 1971-74; Northern Industrial Develt Bd, 1977-; Trustee, Anglo-German Foundn for the Study of Industrial Soc., 1973-79; Governor: Nat. Inst. of Econ. and Social Research; Leighton Park Sch., 1952-60 and 1962-66; Trustee, 1956-, and Chm., 1965-78, Joseph Rowntree Charitable Trust. FBIM. *Publications:* Studies in Retailing, 1963; Costs and Competition in Retailing, 1966; And a New Earth, 1976; (ed) Quakers Visit China, 1957; Editor, Jl of Management Studies, 1963-65. *Recreation:* tennis. *Address:* 66 Elmfield Road, Gosforth, Newcastle upon Tyne NE3 4BD.

MACCLESFIELD, 8th Earl of cr 1721; **George Roger Alexander Thomas Parker;** Baron Parker, 1716; Viscount Parker, 1721; DL; b 6 May 1914; e s of 7th Earl of Macclesfield and Lilian Joanna Vere (d 1974), d of Major Charles Boyle; S father, 1975; m 1938, Hon. Valerie Mansfield, o d of 4th Baron Sandhurst, OBE; two s. DL Oxfordshire, 1965. *Heir:* s Viscount Parker, qv. *Address:* Shirburn, Watlington, Oxon.

MACCLESFIELD, Archdeacon of; *see* Simpson, Ven. Rennie.

McCLINTOCK, Surg. Rear-Adm. Cyril Lawson Tait, CB 1974; OBE 1964; Medical Officer in Charge, Royal Naval Hospital, Haslar and Command Medical Adviser on staff of Commander-in-Chief Naval Home Command, 1972-75; retired 1975; b 2 Aug. 1916; 2nd surv. s of late Lawson Tait McClintock, MB, ChB, Loddon, Norfolk; m 1966, Freda Margaret, o d of late Robert Jones, Caergwle, Denbighshire; two step s. *Educ:* St Michael's, Uckfield; Epsom; Guy's Hospital. MRCS, LRCP 1940; DLO 1955. Joined RN Medical Service, 1940; served War of 1939-45 in Western Approaches, N Africa, Eritrea, India and Singapore; Korea, 1950-51; ENT Specialist, RN Hosps, Port Edgar, Chatham, Hong Kong, Portland, Haslar, Malta and Russell Eve Building, Hamilton, Bermuda; MO i/c RN Hosp. Bighi, Malta, 1969; David Bruce RN Hosp. Mtarfa, Malta, 1970-71; Comd Med. Adviser to C-in-C Naval Forces Southern Europe, 1969-71. QHS 1971-75. FRSocMed 1948; MFCM 1974. CStJ 1973. *Recreations:* cricket, tennis, Rugby refereeing, history. *Address:* Blue Anchor, Paget, Bermuda. *Clubs:* Army and Navy, MCC.

McCLINTOCK, David, TD; writer, naturalist and horticulturist; b 4 July 1913; o s of Rev. E. L. L. McClintock, Glendaragh, Crumlin, Co. Antrim, and Margaret McClintock (née Buxton), Easneye, Ware, Herts; m Elizabeth Anne, d of Maj. V. J. Dawson, Miserden, Glos; two s two d. *Educ:* West Downs Sch., Winchester; Harrow Sch.; Trinity Coll., Cambridge. BA 1934, MA 1940. FCA 1938; FLS 1953. 2nd Lieut, Herts Yeomanry RA TA, 1938; HQ 54 Div., Captain, 1941; Intelligence Trng Centre, 1941-43; Major, 1942; Civil Affairs Trng Centre, 1943-44; Lt-Col, 1944; BAOR, 1944-45. K-H Newsletter, 1938-46; Commercial Manager, Air Contractors Ltd, 1946-47; Chief Accountant and Admin. Officer, Coal Utilisation Council, 1951-73. Member: Wild Flower Soc., 1934- (Chm., 1981-, Treasurer, 1978-); Council, Botanical Soc. of British Isles, 1954-64 (Pres., 1971-73); Council, Kent Trust for Nature Conservation, 1958-62 (Vice-Pres., 1963-); Council, Ray Soc., 1968-72, 1976-80 (Vice-Pres., 1972-76; Pres., 1980-); Council, Linnean Soc., 1970-78 (Vice-Pres., 1971-74; Editl Sec., 1974-78); Plant Variety Rights Adv. Panel for heathers, 1973-; Scientific and Publications Cttees, Royal Horticultural Soc.; Council, Internat. Dendrology Soc., 1979- (Ed., 1979-); Council, Nat. Trust, 1980-. Pres., Kent Field Club, 1978-80. Membre d'Honneur, Soc. Guernesiaise, 1968. Veitch Meml Medal in gold, 1981. *Publications:* Pocket Guide to Wild Flowers (with R.S.R. Fitter), 1956; Supplement to the Pocket Guide to Wild Flowers, 1987; (jtly) Natural History of the Garden of Buckingham Palace, 1964; Companion to Flowers, 1966; Guide to the Naming of Plants, 1969, 2nd edn 1980; Wild Flowers of Guernsey, 1975; (with J. Bichard) Wild Flowers of the Channel Islands, 1975; Joshua Gosselin of Guernsey, 1976; (with F. Perring and R. E. Randall) Picking Wild Flowers, 1977; (ed) H. J. van de Laar, The Heather Garden, 1978; Guernsey's Earliest Flora, 1982; contribs to several other books and numerous periodicals. *Recreations:* anything to do with wild life, music, formerly shooting, fishing, tennis etc. *Address:* Bracken Hill, Platt, Sevenoaks, Kent TN15 8JH. *T:* Borough Green 884102. *Clubs:* Horticultural, Linnean Dining.

See also C. H. G. Kinahan.

McCLINTOCK, Sir Eric (Paul), Kt 1981; Chairman, Woolworths Ltd, since 1980; b 13 Sept. 1918; s of Robert and Ada McClintock; m 1942, Eva Lawrence; two s one d. *Educ:* De La Salle Coll., Armidale; Sydney Univ. (DPA). Supply Dept, Dept of the Navy, Australia, 1935-47; served successively in Depts of Commerce, Agriculture, and Trade, in Washington, New York, Melbourne and Canberra, 1947-61 (1st Asst Sec. on resignation); investment banking, 1962-75. Chairman: Bestobell Australia Ltd; Australian Overseas Projects Corp.; Upper Hunter Newspapers Pty Ltd; Williams Bros Engineering Pty Ltd; Wilson Electric Transformer Co. Pty Ltd; G. S. Yuill & Co. Pty Ltd; Nedlloyd Australia Pty Ltd; Dep. Chm., Development Finance Corp. Ltd; Director: William Adams Ltd; Philips Industries Holdings Ltd; (Alternate), Brambles-Ruys Pty Ltd. *Recreations:* tennis, golf. *Address:* 16 O'Connell Street, Sydney, NSW, Australia. *T:* 233 5733. *Clubs:* Australian (Sydney); Commonwealth (Canberra).

McCLINTOCK, Nicholas Cole, CBE 1979; Secretary-General of the Order of St John, 1968-81 (Deputy Secretary-General, 1963-68); b 10 Sept. 1916; s of late Col Robert Singleton McClintock, DSO (3rd s of Adm. Sir Leopold McClintock), and Mary Howard, d of Sir Howard Elphinstone, VC; m 1953, Pamela Sylvia, d of late Major Rhys Mansel, Smedmore, Dorset; two s two d. *Educ:* Stowe Sch.; Trinity Coll., Cambridge (MA). Entered Colonial Admin. Service, N Nigeria, 1939 but went immediately on War Service with 18th and 28th Field Regts RA, Dunkirk 1940, India and Burma, 1942-45; commanded 1st Field Battery RA in final Burma campaign. Asst Principal, Appointments Dept, CO, Feb.-Oct. 1946; Asst Dist Officer, N Nigeria, 1946-49; Private Sec. to Governor (Sir John Macpherson), 1949-50; Clerk to Exec. Council and Clerk, Legislature, N Nigeria, 1951-53; Sen. Dist Officer and Actg Resident, Kano Province, 1955-59; Admin. Officer Grade 1 and Resident, Bornu Province, 1960-62; retd 1962 to allow for Africanisation of Service. KStJ 1968. *Address:* Lower Westport, Wareham, Dorset BH20 4PR. *T:* Wareham 2943. *Club:* Army and Navy.

McCLINTOCK-BUNBURY, family name of **Baron Rathdonnell.**

McCLOSKEY, Bernard Mary; Deputy Director of Public Prosecutions for Northern Ireland, since 1972; b 7 Aug. 1924; s of Felix and Josephine McCloskey; m 1952, Rosalie Donaghy; three s two d. *Educ:* St Malachy's Coll., Belfast; Queen's Univ., Belfast (LLB (Hons)). Admitted solicitor (Northern Ireland), 1947; private practice, 1947-72. Joint Solicitor to Scarman Tribunal of Enquiry, 1969-71. *Recreations:* swimming, golf. *Address:* Royal Courts of Justice, Chichester Street, Belfast, Northern Ireland BT1 3NX. *T:* Belfast 35111. *Club:* Fortwilliam Golf (Hon. Mem.).

McCLOY, John Jay, DSM, MF (US); Partner, Milbank Tweed, Hadley & McCloy, since 1963; Director and Chairman Executive Committee, Squibb Corporation; Hon. Chairman, Board of the Council on Foreign Relations, Inc.; b 31 March 1895; s of John Jay McCloy and Anna May Snader; m 1930, Ellen Zinsser; one s one d. *Educ:* Amherst Coll. (AB); Harvard Univ. (LLB). Admitted to New York Bar, 1921; mem. of law firm of Cravath, de Gersdorff Swaine & Wood, New York City, 1929-40; expert cons. to Sec. of War, 1940; The Asst Sec. of War, 1941-45; Chm. of The Combined Civil Affairs Cttee of Combined Chiefs of Staff; Mem. of law firm of Milbank, Tweed, Hope, Hadley & McCloy, NY City, 1945-47; Pres. International Bank for Reconstruction and Development, Washington, DC, 1947-49; US Military Governor and US High Comr for Germany, Frankfurt, Germany, 1949-52; Mem. State Dept Cttee on Atomic Energy, 1946-47; Counsel, Milbank, Tweed, Hope & Hadley, 1961; Adviser to President Kennedy on Disarmament, 1961; Chairman: Co-ordinating Cttee of the US on Cuban Crisis, 1962-63; Past Chm., Gen. Adv. Cttee on Arms Control and Disarmament; Mem. Exec. Cttee, The Salk Inst., La Jolla, Calif; Hon. Chairman: Atlantic Institute, 1966-68; Chm., Amer. Council on Germany Inc. Mem., President's Commn on the Assassination of President Kennedy; Mem., American and NY Bar Assocs; Mem., Bar Assoc. of City of New York. Director: Dreyfus Corp., NYC; Mercedes-Benz of N America, Inc. Past Chm. and Trustee, Ford Foundation. Chm. Public Oversight Bd, Sec. Practice Section, AICPA, 1978-. Retired Director: The Chase Manhattan Bank (Chm. 1953-60); Metropolitan Life Insurance Co.; Westinghouse Electric Corp.; American Telephone & Telegraph Co; Allied Chemical Corp. Trustee, John M. Olin Foundn. Hon. Trustee: Bd of Trustees, Amherst Coll., Mass (Chm.); Lenox Hill Hosp.; Johns Hopkins Univ.; Trustee, Amer. Sch. of Classical Studies, Athens; Mem., Bd of Overseers to visit Center for Internat. Studies, Harvard Univ. Capt. FA, AEF. Holds numerous hon. degrees both in US and abroad, also Civic Hons. US Presidential Medal of Freedom and Distinguished Service Medal; Grand Officer of Legion of Honour (France); Grand Officer of Order of Merit of the Republic (Italy); Grand Cross of Order of Merit (Federal Republic of Germany). *Publication:* The Challenge to American Foreign Policy, 1953. *Recreations:* tennis and fishing. *Address:* 1 Chase Manhattan Plaza, New York, NY 10005, USA. *Clubs:* Brook, Links, University, Century, Anglers, Recess, Ausable, Clove Valley Rod and Gun (NY); Metropolitan (Washington).

McCLUNE, Rear-Adm. (William) James, CB 1978; b Londonderry, 20 Nov. 1921; s of James McClune, MBE, Carrickmacross, Co. Monaghan, and Matilda (née Burns); m 1953, Elizabeth, yr d of A. E. D. Prideaux, LDS, Weymouth; one s one d. *Educ:* Model Sch. and Foyle Coll., Derry; QUB (BSc 1st Cl. Hons Elec. Eng. 1941); RN Staff Coll., Greenwich (1961); Univ. of Birmingham (Ratcliff Prizeman, MSc 1970); RN War Coll. (1971). Bronze Medal, CGLI, 1940; Belfast Assoc. of Engrs' Prize, 1940, 1941. CEng, MIEE; CBIM. Radar Officer, RNVR, 1941-47: HMS Howe and HMS Cleopatra; Staff of Vice-Adm. (Destroyers), Home Fleet; HMS Vanguard; Eng Dept, GPO, 1947-49; RN, 1949-78; HMS Euryalus and HMS Mermaid; Weapon Elec. Sch.; HMS Collingwood, HMS Barfleur, HMS Albion; ASRE; HMS Eastbourne; Exec. Officer, RNEC, Manadon; Weapons Dept; HMS London; Ship Dept; Defence Fellowship; Admiralty Interview Bd; Captain, HMS Collingwood; Dir, Naval Manning and Trng (Eng); CSO (Engrg) to C-in-C Fleet, 1976-78; Chm. Trustees, Royal Sailors Rests; Admty Governor, RN Benevolent Trust; RNLI Boat Cttee. Chm., South Western Electricity Consultative Council; Chm., Christian Alliance Trust Corp. Chm., Bd of Governors, Monkton Combe Sch. *Recreation:* sailing. *Address:* Harlam Lodge, Lansdown, Bath; 7 Theed Street, SE1. *Clubs:* Royal Commonwealth Society; Royal Naval and Royal Albert Yacht (Portsmouth).

McCLURE, David, RSA 1971 (ARSA 1963); RSW 1965; SSA 1951; Senior Lecturer in Drawing and Painting, Duncan of Jordanstone College of Art, Dundee, since 1971 (Lecturer, 1957); *b* 20 Feb. 1926; *s* of Robert McClure, MM, and Margaret Helena McClure (*née* Evans); *m* 1950, Joyce Dixon Flanigan; two *s* one *d*. *Educ:* Queen's Park Sch., Glasgow; Glasgow Univ., 1943-44; (coal-miner, 1944-47); Edinburgh Univ., 1947-49; Edinburgh Coll. of Art, 1947-52 (DA). Travelled in Spain and Italy, 1952-53; on staff of Edinburgh Coll. of Art, 1953-55; one year painting in Italy and Sicily, 1956-57. *One man exhibitions:* Palermo, 1957; Edinburgh, 1957, 1961, 1962, 1966, 1969; 14 Scottish Painters, London, 1964; Univ. of Birmingham, 1965; Thackeray Gall., London, 1978. *Work in public and private collections:* UK, USA, Canada, Italy. *Publication:* John Maxwell (monograph), 1976. *Recreations:* collecting Victorian china, gardening, the pianoforte, cooking. *Address:* 16 Strawberry Bank, Dundee, Scotland. *T:* Dundee 66959. *Club:* Scottish Arts (Edinburgh).

McCLURE, Joseph Robert; JP; Councillor, Tyne and Wear County Council, since 1974 (Chairman, 1977-78); *b* 23 Oct. 1923; *s* of Thomas Render McClure and Catherine Bridget McClure; *m* 1943, Evelyn Joice; one *d*. *Educ:* Prior Street Sch.; Oakwellgate Sch., Gateshead. Served War, Royal Marines, 1941-46. Elected Councillor, County Borough of Gateshead, 1964, Dep. Mayor, 1973-74. President, Gateshead Royal British Legion, 1976-. JP Gateshead and Blaydon 1979. *Recreation:* bowls. *Address:* 170 Rectory Road, Gateshead, Tyne and Wear. *T:* Gateshead 770709.

McCLUSKEY, family name of **Baron McCluskey.**

McCLUSKEY, Baron *cr* 1976 (Life Peer), of Churchhill in the District of the City of Edinburgh; **John Herbert McCluskey,** QC (Scotland) 1967; *b* 12 June 1929; *s* of Francis John McCluskey, Solicitor, and Margaret McCluskey (*née* Doonan); *m* 1956, Ruth Friedland; two *s* one *d*. *Educ:* St Bede's Grammar Sch., Manchester; Holy Cross Acad., Edinburgh; Edinburgh Univ. Harry Dalgety Bursary, 1948; Vans Dunlop Schol., 1949; Muirhead Prize, 1949; MA 1950; LLB 1952. Sword of Honour, RAF Spitalgate, 1953. Admitted Faculty of Advocates, 1955; Standing Jun. Counsel to Min. of Power (Scotland), 1963; Advocate-Depute, 1964-71; Sheriff Principal of Dumfries and Galloway, 1973-74; Solicitor General for Scotland, 1974-79. Chm., Medical Appeal Tribunals for Scotland, 1972-74. *Recreation:* tennis. *Address:* 11 Cluny Avenue, Edinburgh EH10 4RN. *T:* 031-447 3880. *Club:* Royal Air Force.

McCOLL, Colin Hugh Verel; Counsellor, Foreign and Commonwealth Office, since 1977; *b* 6 Sept. 1932; *s* of Dr Robert McColl and Julie McColl; *m* 1959, Shirley Curtis; two *s* two *d*. *Educ:* Shrewsbury School; The Queen's College, Oxford (BA). Foreign Office, 1956; Third Secretary, Bangkok, 1958, Vientiane, 1960; Second Secretary, FO, 1962; First Secretary, Warsaw, 1966; Consul and First Secretary (Disarmament), Geneva, 1973. *Recreations:* music, walks, cycling, tennis, flowers, classics. *Address:* c/o Foreign and Commonwealth Office, SW1. *Club:* Royal Commonwealth Society.

McCOLL, Ian; Chairman, Scottish Express Newspapers Ltd, 1975-82; *b* 22 Feb. 1915; *e s* of late John and Morag McColl, Glasgow and Bunessan, Isle of Mull; *m* 1948, Brenda, *e d* of late Thomas and Mary McKean, Glasgow; one *d*. *Educ:* Hillhead High Sch., Glasgow. Served in RAF, 1940-46 (despatches, 1945): Air Crew, Coastal Comd 202 Sqdn. Joined Scottish Daily Express as cub reporter, 1933; held various editorial executive posts; Editor, Scottish Daily Express, 1961-71; Editor, Daily Express, 1971-74; Dir, Express Newspapers Ltd, 1971-82. Contested (L): Dumfriesshire, 1945; Greenock, 1950. Mem., General Presbytery of Glasgow and Synod of Clydesdale, 1953-71; Mem., General Assembly Publications Cttee, until 1971; Session Clerk, Sandyford-Henderson Memorial Church of Scotland, Glasgow, 1953-71. Mem., Press Council, 1975-78; a Vice-Pres., Newspaper Press Fund, 1981-. Mem., Inst. of Journalists; Sec., Glasgow branch Nat. Union of Journalists, 1947-48. Mem., Saints and Sinners Club of Scotland, Chm., 1981-82. *Address:* 12 Newlands Road, Newlands, Glasgow G43 2JB. *T:* 041-632 0321.

McCOLL, Prof. Ian, MS, FRCS, FACS, FRCSE; Professor of Surgery, University of London at the United Medical Schools of Guy's and St Thomas' Hospitals; Director of the Surgical Unit and Consultant Surgeon to Guy's Hospital; Hon. Consultant Surgeon, King's College Hospital; Consultant Surgeon to Edenbridge District Memorial Hospital; *b* 6 Jan. 1933; *s* of Frederick George McColl, Dulwich; *m* 1960, Dr Jean Lennox, 2nd *d* of Arthur James McNair, FRCS, FRCOG; one *s* two *d*. *Educ:* Hutchesons' Grammar Sch., Glasgow; St Paul's Sch., London; Guy's Hosp., London. MB, BS 1957; FRCS 1962; FRCSE 1962; MS 1966; FACS 1975. Junior staff appts at St Bartholomew's, Putney, St Mark's, St Peter's, Great Ormond Street, Barnet, St Olave's and Guy's Hosps, 1957-67; Arris and Gale Lectr, RCS, 1964 and 1965; Research Fellow, Harvard Med. Sch., and Moynihan Fellowship, Assoc. of Surgeons, 1967; Reader in Surgery, St Bartholomew's Hosp. Med. Coll., 1967 (Sub dean, 1969). Visiting Professor: Univ. of South Carolina, 1974; Johns Hopkins Hosp., 1976. Hon. Consultant in Surgery to the Army, 1982-. Examiner: RCS, 1970-76; Queen's Univ. Belfast, 1972; Univ. of Newcastle, 1974; Univ. of London, 1976. Regional Advisor, RCS, 1975-80; Medical Advisor, BBC Television. Member: Central Health Services Council, 1972-74; Standing Medical Adv. Cttee, 1972-82; Management Cttee, King Edward VII Hospital Fund (Chm., R&D Cttee); Chm., King's Fund Centre Cttee, 1976-. Hon. Sec., British Soc. of Gastroenterology, 1970-74. *Publications:* (ed jtly) Intestinal Absorption in Man, 1975; med. articles, mainly on gastroenterology. *Recreations:* squash, forestry. *Address:* 10 Gilkes Crescent, Dulwich Village, SE21 7BS. *T:* 01-693 3084. *Club:* Athenæum.

McCOLOUGH, (Charles) Peter; Chairman, Xerox Corporation, since 1971; *b* 1 Aug. 1922; *s* of Reginald W. McColough and Barbara Martin McColough; *m* 1953, Mary Virginia White. *Educ:* Dalhousie Univ. (LLB); Harvard Grad. Sch. of Business Administration (MBA). Lehigh Coal & Navigation Co., Philadelphia, 1951-54; Xerox Corp.: Gen. Man., Reproduction Service Centers, 1954-56; Man. Marketing, 1957-59; Gen. Sales Man., 1959-60; Vice-Pres. Sales, 1960-63; Exec. Vice-Pres., Ops, 1963-66; Pres., 1966-68; Pres. and Chief Exec. Officer, 1968-71. Director: Citibank, NA; Citicorp; Fuji Xerox Co., Ltd; Internat. Executive Service Corps (Chm. Exec. Cttee); NY Stock Exchange; Union Carbide Corp.; Chamber of Commerce of USA; United Negro College Fund; Council on Foreign Relations; Jt Pres., Rank Xerox Ltd; Trustee: Eisenhower Exchange Fellowship; Univ. of Rochester; US Council of Internat. Chamber of Commerce; Asia Soc.; Member: Corp. of Greenwich Hospital Assoc. Inc.; Bd Governors, Fairfield Foundn of Diocese of Bridgeport; Develt Council; Industries Adv. Cttee of Advertising Council Inc.; Nat. Acad. of Engineering's Nat. Adv. Council on Minorities in Engrg; The Business Council; The Business Roundtable; Steering Cttee of Nat. Cttee for Full Employment; Adv. Council of Industrial Estates Ltd, Nova Scotia; Adv. Bd, Yale Univ. Sch. of Organization and Management. *Address:* Xerox Corporation, Stamford, Conn 06904, USA. *Clubs:* Harvard, River (New York); Country, Genesee Valley (Rochester); Belle Haven, Greenwich Country (Connecticut).

McCOMBS, Hon. Sir Terence (Henderson), Kt 1975; OBE 1971; ED 1943; retired; *b* 5 Sept. 1905. *Educ:* Christchurch and Waitaki Boys' High Schs, NZ; University of Canterbury, NZ (MSc(Hons)). CChem, MRSC; Hon. FNZIC. Teaching, 1931-35. MP (NZ), 1935-51; Parly Under-Sec. to Minister of Finance, 1945-47; Minister of Education and Sci. and Ind. Research, 1947-49. Teacher, 1951-55; Headmaster, Cashmere High Sch., Christchurch, 1956-72; High Commissioner for NZ in the UK and Ambassador for NZ in Ireland, 1973-75. Member: Christchurch City Council (Chm., Finance Cttee, 1951-57; Chm., Town Planning Cttee, 1977-); Lyttelton Harbour Bd; Bd of Governors, Canterbury Agric. Coll.; Chm., Christchurch Milk Co. Senate, Univ. of NZ, 1960-61; Chancellor, Univ. of Canterbury, NZ, 1969-73. Chm., Cttee on Secondary Educn, 1975-76. Trustee for NZ, Commonwealth Foundn (Chm., Conf. and Minor Grants Cttee). Freeman, City of London, 1973; Hon. Freeman, Worshipful Co. of Butchers, 1973. *Publications:* scientific papers in: Jl of Chem. Soc.; Science and Technology (NZ); NZ Foreign Policy (NZ); World Affairs (NZ). *Address:* 7 Freeman Street, Christchurch 8, New Zealand. *Clubs:* Rotary; University of Canterbury (Christchurch); Rotary (Christchurch South) (Governor, Dist 298, 1967-68).

McCONE, John A.; US business executive, retired; Chairman, Hendy International Co., 1969-75; *b* 4 Jan. 1902; *s* of Alexander J. McCone and Margaret McCone (*née* Enright); *m* 1938, Rosemary Cooper (*d* 1961); no *c*; *m* 1962, Mrs Theiline McGee Pigott (widow). *Educ:* Univ. of California, Coll. of Engineering. Began as construction engineer, Llewellyn Iron Works; supt Consolidated Steel Corp., 1929; Exec. Vice-Pres. and Dir, 1933-37; Pres. of Bechtel-McCone Corp., Los Angeles, 1937-45; Pres. and Dir, California Shipbuilding Corp., 1941-46; Joshua Hendy Corp., Joshua Hendy Iron Works, 1945-69; Mem. President's Air Policy Commn, 1947-48; Dep. to Sec. of Defense, March-Nov. 1948; Under Sec. of US Air Force, 1950-51. Chm., US Atomic Energy Commn, 1958-61; Dir, Central Intelligence Agency, 1961-65. Chm., Joshua Hendy Corp., 1961-69; holds hon. degrees from Univs and colls in the US. *Recreation:* golf. *Address:* (home) 1543 Riata Road, PO Box 1499, Pebble Beach, Calif 93953, USA. *T:* (408) 625 3266; Norcliffe, The Highlands, Seattle, Washington; PO Box 19, Rock Sound, Eleuthera, Bahamas. *Clubs:* California (Los Angeles); Los Angeles Country (Los Angeles); Pacific Union, Bohemian (San Francisco); Metropolitan, F Street (Washington, DC); The Links (NYC); Cypress Point (Pebble Beach, Calif); Seattle Golf, Ranier (Seattle).

McCONNELL, Albert Joseph, MA, ScD, Hon. DSc: Belfast; Ulster; Hon. ScD Columbia; Hon. LLD NUI; Hon. Fellow of Oriel College, Oxford; Provost of Trinity College, Dublin, 1952-74; Member of Council of State, Ireland, since 1973; *b* 19 Nov. 1903; *s* of Joseph McConnell; *m* 1934, Hilda (*d* 1966), *d* of late Francis McGuire. *Educ:* Ballymena Acad.; Trinity Coll., Dublin (Scholar, First Math. Moderator and Univ. Student); Univ. of Rome. Dr of Univ. of Rome, 1928; Mem. of Royal Irish Academy, 1929; ScD (Dublin), 1929; Fellow of Trinity Coll., Dublin, 1930-52; Chm., Governing Board of Sch. of Theoretical Physics, and Mem. Council of Dublin Inst. for Advanced Studies; Lectr in Maths, Trinity Coll., Dublin, 1927-30; Prof. of Natural Philosophy, Univ. of Dublin, 1930-57; Special Univ. Lectr, Univ. of London, 1949; Vis. Professor: Univ. of Alexandria, 1946-47; Univ. of Kuwait, 1970. *Publications:* Applications of the Absolute Differential Calculus, 1931; Applications of Tensor Analysis, 1957; papers on relativity, geometry and dynamics in various mathematical jls; Joint-editor of the Mathematical Papers of Sir W. R. Hamilton. *Address:* Seafield Lodge, Seafield Road, Killiney, Dublin. *Clubs:* Athenæum; Dublin University (Dublin).

McCONNELL, Comdr Sir Robert Melville Terence, 3rd Bt, *cr* 1900; VRD; RNVR (retired); *b* 7 Feb. 1902; *s* of Sir Joseph McConnell, 2nd Bt, and Lisa (*d* 1956), *d* of late Jackson McGown; *S* father, 1942; *m* 1st, 1928, Rosamond Mary Elizabeth (marr. diss., 1954), *d* of James Stewart Reade, Clonmore, Lisburn, Co. Antrim; three *s* one *d*; 2nd, 1967, Mrs Alice A. M. Hills. *Educ:*

Glenalmond; St John's Coll., Cambridge; College of Estate Management, London. Consultant with R. J. McConnell and Co., estate agents, Belfast. *Heir:* s Robert Shean McConnell, *b* 23 Nov. 1930. *Address:* Pigeon Hill, Island Road, Killyleagh, Co. Down, N Ireland.

McCONNELL, Rt. Hon. Robert William Brian, PC (N Ireland) 1964; Social Security (formerly National Insurance) Commissioner, Northern Ireland, since 1968; *b* 25 Nov. 1922; *s* of late Alfred E. McConnell, Belfast; *m* 1951, Sylvia Elizabeth Joyce Agnew; two *s* one *d. Educ:* Sedbergh Sch.; Queen's Univ., Belfast (BA, LLB). Called to Bar of Northern Ireland, 1948. MP (U) for South Antrim, NI Parlt, 1951-68; Dep. Chm. of Ways and Means, NI Parlt, 1962; Parly Sec. to Min. of Health and Local Govt for N Ireland, 1963; Minister of Home Affairs for Northern Ireland, 1964-66; Minister of State, Min. of Develt, 1966-67; Leader of the House of Commons, NI, 1967-68. Pres., Industrial Court of NI, 1968-81. *Recreation:* cattle breeding. *Address:* 50 Glenavy Road, Knocknadona, Lisburn, Co. Antrim, Northern Ireland. *T:* Lisburn 3432.

MacCONOCHIE, John Angus, MBE 1943; FCIT; Chairman: Furness Withy & Co. Ltd, 1968-72 (Director, 1964-73); Shaw Savill & Albion Co. Ltd, 1968-73 (Director, 1957-73); *b* 12 April 1908; *m* 1938, Peggy, *d* of late Robert Gunson Martindale, MA, Worthing, Sussex; one *s* one *d. Educ:* Royal Caledonian Schools, Bushey, Herts. Joined Shaw Savill Line, 1927. Seconded to Min. of War Transport, 1942; served on Staff of Resident Minister for W Africa, Accra; Min. of War Transport Rep. in Gold Coast (MBE); London, 1944; Min. HQ with 21 Army Group; subseq. Paris, Marseilles, Naples. Returned to Shaw Savill Line, 1945: New Zealand, 1949; subseq. Manager for Australia; Gen. Manager for New Zealand, 1953; returned to Britain, 1958; Dir, 1957. Chm., Royal Mail Lines, 1968-73; Director: Economic Insurance, 1967 (Chm. 1969-73); British Maritime Trust, 1966-73; Pacific Steam Navigation Co. Ltd, 1967-73; Pacific Maritime Services, 1967-73; Houlder Bros & Co. Ltd, 1967-73; Whitehall Insurance Co. Ltd, 1967-73; Manchester Liners Ltd, 1968-73; National Bank of New Zealand, 1970 (NZ Bd, 1973-78). Member: Council, Chamber of Shipping; Council of Management, Ocean Travel Development (past Chm.); Cttee, NZ Society (PP); Council Fedn of Commonwealth Chambers of Commerce (a NZ Rep.); British Ship Adoption Soc. (past Chm.); Pres., UK Chamber of Shipping, 1972-73 (Pres.-designate 1971). Patron, Auckland Maritime Soc. *Address:* 36 Barlow Place, Chatswood, Auckland 10, New Zealand. *Club:* Northern (Auckland).

McCONVILLE, Michael Anthony, MBE 1958; HM Diplomatic Service, retired; *b* 3 Jan. 1925; *s* of late Lt-Col James McConville, MC and late Winifred (*née* Hanley); *m* 1952, Beryl Anne (*née* Jerrett); two *s* four *d. Educ:* Mayfield Coll.; Trinity Coll., Dublin. Royal Marines, 1943-46. Malayan Civil Service, 1950-61: served in Perak, Johore, Trengganu, Negri Sembilam, Pahang and Kedah; retd as Chm., Border War Exec. Cttee. CRO (later HM Diplomatic Service), 1961: Colombo, 1963-64; Kingston, Jamaica, 1966-67; Ottawa, 1967-71; Consul-Gen., Zagreb, 1974-77. Kesatria Mankgu Negara (Malaya), 1962. *Publications:* (pseudonym Patrick Plum): articles and short stories in Blackwoods, etc. *Recreations:* walking, gardening, watching Rugby. *Address:* c/o Allied Irish Banks, Foster Place, Dublin, Ireland. *Clubs:* Royal Commonwealth Society; Kildare Street and University (Dublin).

McCORD, Brig. Mervyn Noel Samuel, CBE 1978 (OBE 1974); MC 1951; ADC 1981; *b* 25 Dec. 1929; *s* of Major G. McCord, MBE and Muriel King; *m* 1953, Annette Mary, *d* of C. R. W. Thomson; three *s. Educ:* Coleraine, NI; RMA Sandhurst. Commissioned Royal Ulster Rifles, 1949; Korea, 1950-51; School of Infantry, 1958-60; Staff Coll., Camberley, 1961-62; DAQMG, Eastern Command, Canada, 1963-65; BM, HQ 6 Infantry Brigade, 1967-69; JSSC, 1969; GSO1, HQNI, 1970-71; CO, 1st Bn The Royal Irish Rangers, 1971-74; Brig. 1975; Commander, Ulster Defence Regt, 1976-78; Dep. Comdr, Eastern Dist, 1978-81. Dep. Col, The Royal Irish Rangers, 1976-81. FBIM (MBIM 1978). *Recreations:* cricket, athletics, country sports, gardening. *Address:* c/o Williams & Glyn's Bank, Whitehall, SW1. *Club:* Army and Navy.

McCORKELL, Col Michael William, OBE 1964; TD 1954; Lord-Lieutenant, County Londonderry, since 1975; *b* 3 May 1925; *s* of late Captain B. F. McCorkell, Templeard, Culmore, Co. Londonderry and of Mrs E. M. McCorkell; *m* 1950, Aileen Allen, OBE 1975, 2nd *d* of late Lt-Col E. B. Booth, DSO, Darver Castle, Dundalk, Co. Louth, Eire; three *s* one *d. Educ:* Aldenham. Served with 16/5 Lancers, 1943-47; Major (TA) North Irish Horse, 1951; Lt-Col 1961; comd North Irish Horse (TA); retd, 1964. T&AVR Col, NI, 1971-74; Brevet Col, 1974; Pres., T&AVR, NI, 1977-; ADC to the Queen, 1972. Co. Londonderry: High Sheriff 1961, DL 1962. *Recreations:* fishing, shooting. *Address:* Ballyarnett, Londonderry, Northern Ireland. *T:* 51239. *Club:* Cavalry and Guards.

McCORMACK, Arthur Gerard; Director, Population and Development Office, Rome, since 1973; Consultant to United Nations Fund for Population Activities, since 1975; *b* 16 Aug. 1911; *s* of Francis McCormack and Elizabeth Ranard. *Educ:* St Francis Xavier Coll., Liverpool; Durham Univ. (MA Hons History and Econs). Ordained, 1936. Mill Hill Missionary, Africa, 1940-48 (invalided home, 1948); after lengthy illness and convalescence, hosp. chaplain and subseq. teacher-chaplain in secondary modern sch., Widnes; Adviser to Superior Gen., Mill Hill Missionaries, 1963; attended II Vatican Council as expert on population and develt of developing countries, 1963-65; part Founder, Vatican Commn, Justice and Peace (mem. staff for 7 yrs). Special

Adviser to Sec. Gen., World Population Conf., Bucharest, 1974. *Publications:* People, Space, Food, 1960; (ed) Christian Responsibility and World Poverty, 1963; World Poverty and the Christian, 1963; Poverty and Population, 1964; The Population Problem, 1970; The Population Explosion and Christian Concern, 1973; Multinational Investment: Boon or Burden for the Developing Countries, 1980; contrib. The Tablet, Population & Develt Rev., Populi, etc. *Recreations:* reading, driving scooter. *Address:* St Joseph's College, Lawrence Street, Mill Hill, NW7 4JX. *T:* 01-959 8493.

McCORMACK, Most Rev. John; *see* Meath, Bishop of, (RC).

McCORMACK, John P(atrick); Vice President, in charge of joint ventures and African operations, General Motors Corporation, since 1980; *b* New York, 23 Nov. 1923; *s* of John McCormack and Margaret (*née* Bannon); *m* 1952, Marian Martha Luhrs; two *s. Educ:* St John's Univ., Jamaica, NY (Bachelor of Business Admin); NY Univ., NYC (LLB). Joined General Motors, 1949; Gen. Clerk, Accounting Dept, NY, 1949, Sen. Clerk 1950, Sen. Accountant 1952; Asst to Treas., Djakarta Br., 1953; Asst Treas., Karachi Br., 1956; Asst Treas., Gen. Motors South African (Pty) Ltd, Port Elizabeth, 1958, Treas. 1961; Asst Finance Man., Overseas Div., NY, 1966; Treas., subseq. Man. Dir, Gen. Motors Continental, Antwerp, 1968; Finance Man., Adam Opel, 1970, Man. Dir and Chm. Bd, 1974; Gen. Dir, European Ops, Gen. Motors Overseas Corp., 1976. *Recreations:* golf, photography.

McCORMACK, Mark Hume; President and Chief Executive Officer, International Management Group; *b* 6 Nov. 1930; *s* of Ned Hume McCormack and Grace Wolfe McCormack; *m* 1954, Nancy Breckenridge McCormack; two *s* one *d. Educ:* Princeton Univ.; William and Mary Coll. (BA); Yale Univ. (LLB). Admitted to Ohio Bar, 1957; Associate in Arter, Hadden, Wykoff & Van Duzer, 1957-63; Partner, 1964-; started Internat. Management Gp, 1962. Commentator for televised golf, BBC. *Publications:* The World of Professional Golf, 1967, 9th edn 1975; Arnie: the evolution of a legend, 1967; The Wonderful World of Professional Golf, 1973. Publisher of Golf International (British golf paper), and of Tennis World (British tennis magazine). *Recreation:* golf. *Address:* No 1300, One Erieview Plaza, Cleveland, Ohio 44114, USA. *T:* 216/522-1200. *Clubs:* Wentworth (Virginia Water); Sunningdale Golf (Berkshire, England); Old Prestwick (Prestwick); Royal Dornoch (Dornoch); Country Club of Cleveland (Ohio).

MacCORMICK, Prof. Donald Neil; Regius Professor of Public Law, University of Edinburgh, since 1972, Dean of Faculty of Law, 1973-76; *b* 27 May 1941; *yr s* of J. M. MacCormick, MA, LLD (Glasgow) and Margaret I. Miller, MA, BSc (Glasgow); *m* 1965, Caroline Rona Barr, MA (Glasgow); three *d. Educ:* High School, Glasgow; Univ. of Glasgow (MA, 1st cl. Philos. and Eng. Lit.); Balliol Coll., Oxford (BA, 1st cl. Jurisprudence; MA). Called to the Bar, Inner Temple, 1971. Lecturer, St Andrew's Univ. (Queen's Coll., Dundee), 1965-67; Fellow and Tutor in Jurisprudence, Balliol Coll., Oxford, 1967-72, and CUF Lectr in Law, Oxford Univ., 1968-72; Pro-Proctor, Oxford Univ., 1971-72. Corry Lectr, Queen's Univ., Kingston, Ont, 1981; Vis. Prof., Univ. of Sydney, 1981; Dewey Lectr, NY Univ., 1982. Contested (SNP), Edinburgh North, 1979. Pres., Assoc. for Legal and Social Philosophy, 1974-76. Mem., Houghton Cttee on Financial Aid to Political Parties, 1975-76. *Publications:* (ed) The Scottish Debate: Essays on Scottish Nationalism, 1970; (ed) Lawyers in their Social Setting, 1976; Legal Reasoning and Legal Theory, 1978; H. L. A. Hart, 1981; Legal Right and Social Democracy: essays in legal and political philosophy, 1982; contribs to various symposia, jls on law, philosophy and politics. *Recreations:* hill walking, bagpiping, sailing. *Address:* The Old College, Edinburgh EH8 9YL.
See also I. S. MacD. MacCormick.

MacCORMICK, Iain Somerled MacDonald; Major Account Manager, British Telecommunications, since 1982; *b* 28 Sept. 1939; *er s* of John MacDonald MacCormick, MA, LLB, LLD and Margaret Isobel Miller, MA, BSc; *m* 1964, Micky Trefusis Elsom; two *s* three *d. Educ:* Glasgow High Sch.; Glasgow Univ. (MA). Queen's Own Lowland Yeomanry, 1957-67 (Captain). Contested (SNP) Argyll, 1970; MP (SNP) Argyll, Feb. 1974-1979. Joined SDP, 1981. Mem., Argyll and Bute District Council, 1979-80. *Recreations:* Rugby football, sailing, Scottish history. *Address:* Rahoy Lodge, Gallanach Road, Oban, Argyll PA34 4PD. *T:* Oban 62301.
See also Prof. D. N. MacCormick.

McCORMICK, Prof. James Stevenson, FRCPI, FRCGP; FFCM; Professor of Community Health, Trinity College Dublin, since 1973; *b* 9 May 1926; *s* of Victor Ormsby McCormick and Margaretta Tate (*née* Stevenson); *m* 1954, Elizabeth Ann Dimond; three *s* one *d. Educ:* The Leys Sch., Cambridge; Clare Coll., Cambridge (BA, MB); St Mary's Hospital, W2. Served RAMC, 1960-62; St Mary's Hosp., 1963; general practice, 1964-73. Chairman, Eastern Health Board, 1970. Dean of School of Physic, TCD, 1974-79. Hon. MCFP 1982. *Publications:* The Doctor—Father Figure or Plumber, 1979; papers, espec. on General Practice and Ischaemic Heart Disease. *Recreations:* open air, patients. *Address:* The Barn, Windgates, Bray, Co. Wicklow, Ireland. *T:* Dublin 874113.

McCORMICK, John Ormsby, CMG 1965; MC 1943; HM Diplomatic Service, retired; *b* Dublin, 7 Feb. 1916; *s* of Albert Victor McCormick and Sarah Beatty de Courcy; *m* 1955, Francine Guieu (*née* Pâris); one *d*, one step *s. Educ:* The Leys Sch., Cambridge; New Coll., Oxford. BA Hon. Mods and

Greats (Oxford), 1938. Passed Competitive Exam. for Consular Service, 1939, and appointed Asst Officer, Dept of Overseas Trade. Served War of 1939-45, in Royal Corps of Signals, Africa, Sicily, Germany, 1940-45. 2nd Sec. (Commercial), British Embassy, Athens, 1945-47; FO, London, 1948-50; 1st Sec., UK High Commn, Karachi, 1950-52; Consul, New York, 1952-54; transferred to Washington, 1954-55; NATO Defence Coll., 1955; Asst Head, SE Asia Dept, FO, 1956-59; Foreign Service Officer, Grade 6, 1959; Counsellor (Commercial), British Embassy, Djakarta, 1959-62; Corps of Inspectors, FO, 1962-64; Counsellor (Commercial), British Embassy, Ankara, 1965-67; Consul-General, Lyons, 1967-72. *Recreations:* golf, sailing, philosophy. *Address:* Oldfort, Newcastle, Co. Wicklow, Ireland.

McCORQUODALE, Mrs Barbara; *see* Cartland, Barbara H.

McCOWAN, Hon. Sir Anthony (James Denys), Kt 1981; **Hon. Mr Justice McCowan;** a Judge of the High Court, Queen's Bench Division, since 1981; *b* 12 Jan. 1928; *yr s* of John Haines Smith McCowan, MBE, and Marguerite McCowan, Georgetown, British Guiana; *m* 1961, Sue Hazel Anne, *d* of late Reginald Harvey and of Mrs Harvey, Braiseworth Hall, Tannington, Suffolk; two *s* one *d. Educ:* Epsom Coll.; (Open Hist. schol.) Brasenose Coll., Oxford (MA, BCL). Called to Bar, Gray's Inn, 1951, Atkin Scholar; Bencher, 1980. Dep. Chm., E Sussex QS, 1969-71; a Recorder of the Crown Court, 1972-81; QC 1972; Leader, SE Circuit, 1978-81. Mem., Parole Bd, 1982-. *Recreations:* sport, history, travel. *Address:* c/o Royal Courts of Justice, Strand, WC2A 2LL. *Club:* Hurlingham.
See also J. M. Archer.

McCOWAN, Sir Hew Cargill, 3rd Bt, *cr* 1934; *b* 26 July 1930; *s* of Sir David James Cargill McCowan, 2nd Bt and Muriel Emma Annie, *d* of W. C. Willmott; *S* father, 1965. *Heir: b* David William Cargill McCowan, *b* 28 Feb. 1934. *Address:* Vivenda Marbelo, Estrada da Lagoa Azul, Malveira da Serra, Cascais, Portugal.

McCOWEN, Alec, (Alexander Duncan McCowen), OBE 1972; actor; *b* 26 May 1925; *s* of Duncan McCowen and Hon. Mrs McCowen. *Educ:* Skinners' Sch., Tunbridge Wells; RADA, 1941. Repertory: York, Birmingham, etc, 1943-50; Escapade, St James's, 1952; The Matchmaker, Haymarket, 1954; The Count of Clérambard, Garrick, 1955; The Caine Mutiny Court Martial, Hippodrome, 1956; Look Back in Anger, Royal Court, 1956; The Elder Statesman, Cambridge, 1958; Old Vic Seasons, 1959-61: Touchstone, Ford, Richard II, Mercutio, Oberon, Malvolio; Dauphin in St Joan; Algy in The Importance of Being Earnest; Royal Shakespeare Company, 1962-63: Antipholus of Syracuse in The Comedy of Errors; Fool, in King Lear; Father Fontana in The Representative, Aldwych, 1963; Thark, Garrick, 1965; The Cavern, Strand, 1965; After the Rain, Duchess, 1967, Golden Theatre, NY, 1967; Hadrian VII, Birmingham, 1967, Mermaid, 1968, New York, 1969; Hamlet, Birmingham, 1970; The Philanthropist, Royal Court, 1970, NY, 1971; Butley, Criterion, 1972; The Misanthrope, National Theatre, 1973, 1975, NY 1975; Equus, National Theatre, 1973; Pygmalion, Albery, 1974; The Family Dance, Criterion, 1976; Antony and Cleopatra, Prospect Co., 1977; solo performance of St Mark's Gospel, Riverside Studios, Mermaid and Comedy, 1978, Globe, 1981; Tishoo, Wyndham's, 1979; The Browning Version, and A Harlequinade, National Theatre, 1980; The Portage to San Cristobal of A. H., Mermaid, 1982. Films include: Frenzy, 1971; Travels with My Aunt, 1972; Stevie, 1978. Evening Standard Drama Award, 1968, 1973; Stage Actor of the Year, Variety Club, 1970. *Publications:* Young Gemini (autobiog.), 1979; Double Bill (autobiog.), 1980. *Recreations:* music, gardening. *Address:* Flat 4, 2 Cresswell Gardens, SW5.

McCRAE, Alister Geddes, CBE 1973; Chairman: Clyde Port Authority, 1966-77; British Ports Association, 1972-74; *b* 7 Aug. 1909; *s* of Alexander McCrae; *m* 1st, 1938, Margaret Montgomery Reid (*d* 1977); one *s* ; 2nd, 1978, Norah Crawford Orr. *Educ:* Kelvinside Academy; High School of Glasgow. Joined: P. Henderson & Co., Shipowners, Glasgow, 1927; Irrawaddy Flotilla Co. Ltd (in Burma), 1933; Served War: Middle East and Burma, 1941-45; Lt-Col, Royal Indian Engrs (despatches). Irrawaddy Flotilla Co. Ltd, 1946-48 (Dep. Gen. Manager, in Burma); re-joined P. Henderson & Co., as Partner, 1948; Sen. Partner and Man. Dir, British & Burmese Steam Navigation Co. Ltd, 1966; retd 1972. Member: Nat. Dock Labour Bd, 1953-57; UK Chamber of Shipping Council, 1954-65; Clyde Navigation Trust, 1962-65; British Transport Docks Bd, 1963-65; Nat. Ports Council, 1967-71; Scottish Economic Council, 1969-74; Aldington/Jones Commn on Docks, 1972; Chm., Clyde Estuary Develt Gp, 1968-71; Dir, Hunterston Develt Co. Ltd, 1970-74. Chm., Glasgow Old People's Welfare Commn (Age Concern), 1969-79, Hon. Pres., 1979-. Freeman, City of London, 1959; Liveryman, Worshipful Co. of Shipwrights, 1959. FRSA. *Publications:* Irrawaddy Flotilla, 1978; (jtly) Tales of Burma, 1981. *Recreations:* country walking, the garden, fishing, the fine arts. *Address:* Belwood, Killearn, Stirlingshire G63 9LG. *Club:* Oriental.

McCRAITH, Col Patrick James Danvers, MC 1943; TD; DL; Solicitor and Notary Public; *b* 21 June 1916; *s* of late Sir Douglas McCraith; *m* 1946, Hon. Philippa Mary Ellis, *yr d* of 1st and last Baron Robins, KBE, DSO, of Rhodesia and Chelsea; one *s* one *d. Educ:* Harrow. 2nd Lieut, Sherwood Rangers Yeomanry, 1935; served War, 1939-45, N Africa and NW Europe (three times wounded); raised and commanded Yeomanry Patrol of Long Range Desert Group, 1940-41; commanded Sherwood Rangers Yeomanry, 1953-57; Bt Colonel, 1958. Hon. Col, B (Sherwood Rangers Yeomanry)

Squadron, The Royal Yeomanry, 1968-79. High Sheriff of Nottinghamshire, 1963; DL Notts, 1965. *Address:* Cranfield House, Southwell, Notts. *T:* Southwell 812129. *Clubs:* Special Forces; Nottingham, Notts United Services (both Nottingham).

McCRAY, Sir Lionel (Joseph), Kt 1978; FASA, FAIM; ACIS; full-time company director, since 1973; *b* 29 Aug. 1908; *s* of Joseph Burney McCray and Florence Mary McCray; *m* 1942, Phyllis Coralie Burbank; one *s* one *d. Educ:* Brisbane Grammar Sch. ACIS 1931; FASA 1930; FAIM 1950. Clerk: Eclipse Windmill Co. Ltd, 1923-24; State Govt Insurance Office, 1924-27; State Treasury, 1927-32; Accountancy Coach, Blennerhassetts Inst. of Accountancy, 1932-35; Sales Manager, Campbell Brothers Ltd, 1935-43, Man. Dir, 1943-56; Gen. Manager: Peters-Arctic Delicacy Co. Ltd, 1956-60; QUF Industries Ltd, 1960-73. Chairman: Australian United Foods; Sedgwick Pty Ltd (Qld Bd); Director: Campbell Brothers Ltd; Crusader Oil NL; Kennedy-Taylor Ltd; QUF Industries Ltd. Dep. Chancellor, Univ. of Qld, 1978- (Mem. Senate, 1972-). President: Industrial Management Assoc., 1948-50; Rotary Club of Fortitude Valley, 1949-50; Qld Chamber of Manufactures, 1950-53; Royal Qld Golf Club, 1963-66; Brisbane Club, 1970-71. Vice-President: Aust. Inst. of Management, 1950-56; Associated Chambers of Manufactures of Aust., 1951-53. Chm., State Govt Adv. Cttee on Youth Grants, 1967-81. Member: Manufg Industries Adv. Council, 1967-73; State Council, Inst. of Public Affairs, 1976-; State Cttee, the Queen's Silver Jubilee Appeal for Young Australians, 1977-78. Dist Governor, Rotary Internat. Dist 35, 1955-56. Trustee, Spina Bifida Assoc., 1972-. *Recreations:* golf, astronomy, travel. *Address:* 12 Blair Lane, Ascot, Qld 4007, Australia. *T:* 262 2095. *Clubs:* Brisbane, University of Queensland, Royal Queensland Golf, Royal Queensland Automobile (Brisbane); Rotary of Fortitude Valley.

McCREA, William Hunter, FRS 1952; MA; PhD; ScD (Cambridge); BSc (London); FRSE, FRAS, MRIA; Research Professor of Theoretical Astronomy, University of Sussex, 1966-72, now Emeritus; *b* Dublin, 13 Dec. 1904; *er s* of late Robert Hunter McCrea; *m* 1933, Marian Nicol Core, 2nd *d* of late Thomas Webster, JP, Burdiehouse, Edinburgh; one *s* two *d. Educ:* Chesterfield Grammar Sch.; Trinity Coll., Cambridge (Scholar); University of Göttingen. Wrangler, Rayleigh Prizeman, Sheepshanks Exhibitioner, and Isaac Newton Student, of Cambridge Univ.; Rouse Ball Travelling Student, and Rouse Ball Senior Student, of Trinity Coll.; Comyns Berkeley Bye-Fellow, Gonville and Caius Coll., Cambridge, 1952-53. Lecturer in Mathematics, Univ. of Edinburgh, 1930-32; Reader in Mathematics, Univ. of London, and Assistant Prof., Imperial Coll. of Science, 1932-36; Prof. of Mathematics: Queen's Univ., Belfast, 1936-44; Univ. of London (Royal Holloway Coll.), 1944-66. Visiting Prof. of Astronomy: Univ. of California, 1956; Case Inst. of Technology, 1964; Univ. of BC, Vancouver, 1975-76; Consulting Astronomer, Kitt Peak National Observatory, Arizona, 1965, 1975; Royal Society Exchange Visitor: to USSR, 1960, 1968; to Mexico, 1971; to Argentina, 1971; to India, 1976; to Egypt, 1981; For. Visiting Prof. of American Astronomical Soc. and Vis. Prof., Berkeley Astronomy Dept, 1967; first occupant, Chaire Georges Lemaître, Louvain Univ., 1969; Royal Soc. Leverhulme Vis. Prof. of Astronomy, Cairo Univ., 1973; Vis. Prof., Istanbul Univ., 1977, 1978; William Evans Vis. Prof., Otago Univ., 1979. Visiting Lecturer: Univ. of Liège, 1960; Technische Hochschule, Aachen, 1962; various universities in Greece and Turkey (British Council), 1971; York Univ., 1965; Lectures: Harland, Univ. of Exeter, 1970; Larmor, QUB, 1970; Halley, Oxford, 1975. Temp. Princ. Experimental Officer, Admty, 1943-45; Commnd RAFVR (Training Branch), 1941-45. Mem., Governing Board of School of Theoretical Physics, Dublin Institute for Advanced Studies, 1940-50; Governor: Royal Holloway Coll., 1946-49; Ottershaw Sch., 1947-52; Barclay Sch. for Partially Sighted Girls, 1949-66; Mem. Adv. Council, Chelsea Coll. of Aeronautical and Automobile Engineering, 1958-. Secretary of Section A of British Assoc., 1935-39, Pres. 1966; Pres., Mathematical Assoc., 1973-74. Joint Editor of The Observatory, 1935-37. Pres., Royal Astronomical Soc., 1961-63 (Sec., 1946-49; Foreign Correspondent, 1968-71; Treasurer, 1976-79). Fellow, Imperial Coll., 1967-; Leverhulme Emeritus Fellow, 1973-75. Mem., Akademie Leopoldina, 1972-. Keith Prize, RSE, 1939-41; Gold Medal, RAS, 1976. Hon. DSc: National Univ., Ireland, 1954; QUB, 1970; Sussex, 1978; Dr *hc* National Univ., Cordoba, Argentina, 1971; Hon. ScD Dublin, 1972. *Publications:* Relativity Physics, 1935; Analytical Geometry of Three Dimensions, 1942; Physics of the Sun and Stars, 1950; trans. A. Unsöld's The New Cosmos, 1969; Royal Greenwich Observatory, 1975; various papers and reviews in mathematical and astronomical journals. *Address:* 87 Houndean Rise, Lewes, East Sussex. *Club:* Athenæum.

McCREERY, Henry Edwin Lewis, QC 1965; **His Honour Judge McCreery;** a Circuit Judge (formerly Judge of County Courts), since 1971; *b* 26 July 1920; *s* of late Rev. William John McCreery, BD, and late Anne Cullen McCreery; *m* 1945, Margaret Elizabeth Booth; two *d. Educ:* St Andrew's Coll., Dublin; Trinity Coll., Dublin. RAF, 1942-47. Called: Irish Bar King's Inns, 1943; English Bar, Middle Temple, 1946 (Bencher, 1971). Dep. Chm., Quarter Sessions: Cornwall, 1966-71; Devon, 1967-71; Recorder of Salisbury, 1969-71. *Recreation:* gardening. *Clubs:* Royal Air Force; Hampshire (Winchester).

MacCRINDLE, Robert Alexander, QC 1963; commercial lawyer, Shearman and Sterling; *b* 27 Jan. 1928; *s* of F. R. MacCrindle; *m* 1959, Pauline Dilys, *d* of Mark S. Morgan; one *s* one *d. Educ:* Girvan High Sch.; King's Coll., London; Gonville and Caius Coll., Cambridge. LLB London, 1948. Served RAF, 1948-50, Flt-Lt. LLB Cantab, Chancellor's Medal, 1951. Called to Bar,

Gray's Inn, 1952 (Bencher, 1969); Junior Counsel to Board of Trade (Export Credits), 1961-63. Mem., Royal Commn on Civil Liability and Compensation for Personal Injury, 1973-78. Honorary Fellow: American Coll. of Trial Lawyers, 1974; Conseil Juridique (France). *Publication:* McNair's Law of the Air, 1953. *Recreation:* golf. *Address:* 4 Essex Court, Temple, EC4. *T:* 01-583 9191; 88 avenue de Breteuil, 75015 Paris, France. *T:* 567-1193. *Club:* University (New York).

McCRINDLE, Robert Arthur; MP (C) Brentwood and Ongar, since 1974 (Billericay, 1970-74); *b* 19 Sept. 1929; *o s* of Thomas Arthur and Isabella McCrindle; *m* 1953, Myra Anderson; two *s. Educ:* Allen Glen's Coll., Glasgow. Vice-Chm., Sausmarez, Carey & Harris, Financial Consultants, 1972-75; Director: Langham Life Assurance Co. Ltd, 1972-76; Worldmark Travel Ltd, 1978-82; Chm., Cometco Ltd, Commodity Brokers, 1972-78; Consultant, Hogg Robinson Travel Ltd. Contested: Dundee (East), 1959; Thurrock, 1964. PPS to Min. of State, Home Office, 1974; Mem., UK Delegn to N Atlantic Assembly, 1977- (Chm., Economic Cttee, 1980-); Parliamentary Consultant: British Transport Police Fedn; British Insurance Brokers' Assoc.; Guild of Business Travel Agents, 1975-78. Nat. Vice-Pres., Corp. of Mortgage Brokers, 1970-76. Fellow, Corp. of Insurance Brokers; AC11. *Address:* 26 Ashburnham Gardens, Upminster, Essex. *T:* Upminster 27152.

McCRINDLE, Susan; *see* Ertz, Susan.

McCRIRRICK, Thomas Bryce, FEng, FIEE, FIERE; Director of Engineering, BBC, since 1978; *b* 19 July 1927; *s* of late Alexander McCrirrick and Janet McCrirrick (*née* Tweedie); *m* 1953, Margaret Phyllis Yates; three *s. Educ:* Galashiels Academy; Heriot Watt Coll., Edinburgh; Regent Street Polytechnic, London. BBC Radio, Studio Centres in Edinburgh, Glasgow and London, 1943-46; served RAF, 1946-49; BBC Television, 1949; Engineer-in-Charge Television Studios, 1963; Head of Engineering Television Recording, and of Studio Planning and Installation Dept, 1969; Chief Engineer, Radio Broadcasting, 1970; Asst Dir of Engrg, 1971; Dep. Dir of Engrg, 1976. Chm., Management & Design Div., IEE, 1981-82. Vice-Pres., Soc. of Electronic and Radio Technicians, 1979-80, Pres., 1981-. FRTS 1980; FBKS 1982. *Recreations:* skiing, theatre. *Address:* Oakwood, Knightsbridge Road, Camberley, Surrey GU15 3TS. *T:* Camberley 65309.

McCRONE, Robert Gavin Loudon; Secretary of the Scottish Economic Planning Department, since 1980, and Chief Economic Adviser at the Scottish Office, since 1972; *b* 2 Feb. 1933; *s* of Robert Osborne Orr McCrone and Laura Margaret McCrone; *m* 1959, Alexandra Bruce Waddell; two *s* one *d. Educ:* Stowe Sch.; St Catharine's Coll., Cambridge (Economics Tripos); University Coll. of Wales, Aberystwyth (Milk Marketing Bd Research Schol. in agric economics); Univ. of Glasgow. Fisons Ltd, 1959-60; Lectr in Applied Economics, Glasgow Univ., 1960-65; Economic Consultant to UNESCO and Mem. Educl Planning Mission to Libya, 1964; Fellow of Brasenose Coll., Oxford, 1965-72; Chm., Oxford Univ. Economics Subfaculty, 1968-70; Mem. NEDC Working Party on Agricl Policy, 1967-68; Economic Adviser to House of Commons Select Cttee on Scottish Affairs, 1969-70; Special Economic Adviser to Sec. of State for Local Govt and Regional Planning, 1970; Sen. Economic Adviser and Head of Economics and Statistics Unit, 1970-72, Under-Sec. for Regional Develt, 1972-80, Scottish Office. Mem. Council, Royal Economic Soc., 1977-82. *Publications:* The Economics of Subsidising Agriculture, 1962; Scotland's Economic Progress 1951-60, 1963; Agricultural Integration in Western Europe, 1963; Regional Policy in Britain, 1969; Scotland's Future, 1969; contribs to various economic jls. *Recreations:* walking, music. *Address:* 28 Mansionhouse Road, Edinburgh EH9 2JD. *T:* 031-667 6687. *Club:* United Oxford & Cambridge University.

McCRORIE, Esther Linda, (Mrs Peter McCrorie); *see* Gray, E. L.

McCRUM, Michael William, MA; Master of Corpus Christi College, Cambridge, since 1980; *b* 23 May 1924; 3rd *s* of Captain C. R. McCrum, RN (retired) and of Ivy Hilda Constance (*née* Nicholson); *m* 1952, Christine Mary Kathleen, *d* of Sir Arthur fforde, *qv*; three *s* one *d. Educ:* Horris Hill, Newbury; Sherborne Sch.; Corpus Christi Coll., Cambridge. Entrance Scholar to CCC, Dec. 1942. Served RN, 1943-45 (Sub-Lt RNVR, Dec. 1943). CCC, Cambridge, 1946-48; Part I, Class. Tripos, First Class, 1947; Part II, First Class, with distinction, 1948. Asst Master, Rugby School, Sept. 1948-July 1950 (Lower Bench Master, 1949-50); Fellow CCC, Cambridge, 1949; Second Tutor, 1950-51; Tutor, 1951-62; Member, Council of the Senate, University of Cambridge, 1955-58, 1981-, General Board of Faculties, 1957-62; Headmaster, Tonbridge School, 1962-70; Head Master of Eton, 1970-80. Chm., HMC, 1974. Mem., Governing Body, Schools Council, 1969-76 (also mem., various cttees); Governor: Bradfield Coll., 1956-62; Eastbourne Coll., 1960-62; King's Sch., Canterbury, 1980-; Sherborne Sch., 1980-; Oakham Sch., 1981-; United World Coll. of the Atlantic, 1981-; Rugby Sch., 1982-. Dep. Chm., GBA, 1982. Hon. Freeman, Skinners' Co., 1980. *Publication:* (with A. G. Woodhead) Select Documents of the Principates of the Flavian Emperors AD 68-96, 1961. *Address:* The Master's Lodge, Corpus Christi College, Cambridge CB2 1RH. *T:* Cambridge 59418. *Clubs:* Athenæum, United Oxford & Cambridge University; Hawks (Cambridge).

MacCULLOCH, Dr Malcolm John, MD; DPM; FRCPsych; Medical Director, Park Lane Hospital, Liverpool, and Director of Special Hospitals Research Unit, since 1979; *b* 10 July 1936; *s* of William MacCulloch and Constance Martha MacCulloch; *m* 1962, Mary Louise Beton (marr. diss.

1975); one *s* one *d; m* 1975, Carolyn Mary Reid; two *d. Educ:* King Edward VII Sch., Macclesfield, Cheshire; Manchester Univ. (MB, ChB, DPM, MD). Consultant Child Psychiatrist, Cheshire Child Guidance Service, 1966-67; Director Univ. Dept, Child Psychiatry and Subnormality, Birmingham Univ., 1967-70; Sen. Lectr, Adult Psychiatry, Univ. of Liverpool, 1970-75; PMO, DHSS, 1975-78; SPMO, Mental Health Div., DHSS, 1979-80. *Publications:* Homosexual Behaviour: therapy and assessment, 1971; Human Sexual Behaviour, 1980; numerous med. papers on aspects of psychiatry. *Recreations:* inventing, playing music. *Address:* Park Lane Hospital, School Lane, Maghull, Liverpool L31 1HW. *T:* 051-520 2244. *Club:* Institute of Directors.

McCULLOCH, Ven. Nigel Simeon; Archdeacon of Sarum, since 1979; Rector of St Thomas' and St Edmund's, Salisbury, since 1978; *b* 17 Jan. 1942; *s* of late Pilot Officer Kenneth McCulloch, RAFVR, and of Audrey Muriel McCulloch; *m* 1974, Celia Hume Townshend, *d* of Canon H. L. H. Townshend; two *d. Educ:* Liverpool College; Selwyn Coll., Cambridge (Kitchener Schol., BA 1964, MA 1969); Cuddesdon Coll., Oxford. Ordained, 1966; Curate of Ellesmere Port, 1966-70; Chaplain of Christ's Coll., Cambridge, 1970-73; Director of Theological Studies, Christ's Coll., Cambridge, 1970-75; Diocesan Missioner for Norwich Diocese, 1973-78. *Recreations:* music, walking in the Lake District. *Address:* The Rectory, St Thomas' Square, Salisbury, Wilts. *T:* Salisbury 22537.

McCULLOUGH, Sir Charles; *see* McCullough, Sir I. C. R.

McCULLOUGH, Hon. Sir (Iain) Charles (Robert), Kt 1981; **Hon. Mr Justice McCullough;** a Judge of the High Court of Justice, Queen's Bench Division, since 1981; *b* 31 July 1931; *o s* of Thomas W. McCullough, *qv; m* 1965, Margaret Joyce, JP 1973, *o d* of late David H. Patey, MS, FRCS, of The Middlesex Hospital, W1; one *s* one *d. Educ:* Taunton Sch.; Trinity Hall, Cambridge. BA 1955; MA 1960. National Service, 1950-52, commnd Royal Artillery; RA (TA), 1952-54. Called to Bar, Middle Temple, 1956 (Harmsworth Law Schol.); Bencher, 1980. Midland and Oxford Circuit (formerly Midland Circuit), 1957-81; Dep. Chm., Notts QS, 1969-71; QC 1971; a Recorder of the Crown Court, 1972-81. Mem., Criminal Law Revision Cttee, 1973-. *Address:* Royal Courts of Justice, Strand, WC2. *Club:* Garrick.

McCULLOUGH, Thomas Warburton, CB 1962; OBE 1954; HM Chief Inspector of Factories, Ministry of Labour, 1958-63; *b* 13 March 1901; *o s* of late Robert McCullough and Emma Warburton, *d* of Thomas Rigby; *m* 1928, Lisette Hunter (*d* 1979), *d* of late Henry George Gannaway; one *s. Educ:* Ballymena Academy; Glasgow Univ.; Middle Temple. BSc 1925. Engineering training, Glasgow, 1917-25; Valuation Dept, Ministry of Finance, Belfast, 1925; joined Factory Dept, Home Office, 1926. Member Joint Advisory Cttee on Conditions in Iron Foundries, 1947; Hon. Adviser Scottish Industrial Groups Advisory Council, 1951-53; Chairman of numerous Joint Standing Cttees, 1950-56. Member: Home Office Inter-Departmental Cttee on Accidents in the Home, 1954-57; National Industrial Safety Cttee, 1954-57, Executive Cttee, 1958-63, Royal Society for Prevention of Accidents; Industrial Grants Cttee, Dept of Scientific and Industrial Research, 1958-63; Nuclear Safety Advisory Cttee, 1960-63; Technical Adviser (Safety), The United Steel Companies Ltd, 1963-67. Hon. Life Member, Royal Society for Prevention of Accidents, 1963; Hon. Fellow, Institution of Industrial Safety Officers, 1964; Hon. Adviser (Safety) British Steel Corp. (formerly British Iron and Steel Fedn), 1964-74; Pres., London Construction Safety Group, 1963-74. Silver Medal, L'Institut National de Sécurité, Paris, 1961; Industrial Safety Award, RoSPA, 1970. *Publications:* sundry contribs to literature of accident prevention in industry. *Recreation:* fly-fishing. *Address:* 69 Walsingham Road, Hove, East Sussex. *Club:* Flyfishers'.
See also Sir I. C. R. McCullough.

McCUNN, Peter Alexander, CBE 1980; Deputy Chairman, Cable & Wireless plc, since 1978; *b* 11 Nov. 1922; *m* 1943, Margaret Prescott; two *s* (and one *s* decd). *Educ:* Mexborough Grammar Sch.; Edinburgh University. Commnd W Yorks Regt, 1942; served in Normandy, Malta, Italy; left Army, Nov. 1946 (Captain). Joined Cable & Wireless, 1947; Director: Cable & Wireless/Western Union International Inc. of Puerto Rico, 1968-70; Cable & Wireless, 1969- (Exec. Dep. Chm., 1977); Nigerian External Telecommunications Ltd, 1969-72; Sierra Leone External Telecommunications Ltd, 1969-72; Trinidad and Tobago External Telecommunications Ltd, 1972-77; Jamaica International Telecommunications Ltd, 1972-77; Cable and Wireless (Hong Kong) Ltd, 1981-; Mercury Communications Ltd, 1981-. FBIM. *Recreations:* music, gardening, swimming, cricket, Association football (now non-active). *Address:* Wychelms, 14 Lime Walk, Pinkneys Green, Maidenhead, Berks. *T:* Maidenhead 24308, (office) 01-242 4433. *Clubs:* Royal Commonwealth Society; Exiles (Twickenham).

McCUSKER, (James) Harold; MP (UU) Armagh since 1974; Member (UU) Armagh, Northern Ireland Assembly, since 1982; *b* 7 Feb. 1940; *s* of James Harold McCusker and Lily McCusker; *m* 1965, Jennifer Leslie Mills; three *s. Educ:* Lurgan Coll.; Stranmillis Coll., Belfast. Teacher, 1961-68; Trng Officer, 1968-73; Production Man., 1973-74. Sec. and Whip, Ulster Unionist Party, Westminster, 1975-76. Chm., NI Gas Employers' Bd, 1977-81. *Address:* 33 Seagoe Road, Portadown, Craigavon BT63 5HW. *T:* Portadown 33876; 25 Vincent Square, SW1. *T:* 01-821 7036.

McCUTCHEON, Sir (Walter) Osborn, Kt 1966; LFRAIA, LFRAPI; Consultant (Partner, 1926-77), Bates, Smart & McCutcheon, Melbourne (Architects, Engineers and Town Planners); *b* 8 April 1899; *s* of W. B. McCutcheon, Solicitor, Melbourne; *m* 1928, Mary, *d* of A. A. Buley; two *s* one *d. Educ:* Wesley Coll., Melbourne; Univ. of Melbourne. Mem. Faculty, Melbourne Univ. School of Architecture; Director, Arch., Melbourne Technical Sch., 1930-39; Member Council, Royal Victorian Inst. of Architects, 1930-45 (Pres., 1940-42; Mem. Board of Arch. Educn, 1933-39, 1940-42, 1953-57); Pres., Building Indust. Congr. of Victoria, 1934-36; Member Council, RAIA, 1941-42; Chief Architect, Engineers HQ, US Army, SW Pacific Area, 1942-44; Controller of Planning etc to Australian Commonwealth Govt, 1944-46; resumed private practice, 1946. Mem. various cttees; assessor of sundry competitions. Mem., National Capital Planning Cttee, Nat. Capital Develt Commn, 1967-73; Chairman: Central City Consultative Cttee, 1976-79, Metropolitan Strategy Consultative Cttee, 1979-, Min. for Planning. Gold Medal, RAIA, 1965. Hon. LLD, Monash Univ., 1968. *Publications:* articles in Architecture in Australia, etc. *Recreations:* sailing, reading. *Address:* (office) 499 St Kilda Road, Melbourne, Vic 3004, Australia. *T:* Melbourne 267-5188; (home) 139 Baden Powell Drive, Mount Eliza, Vic 3930, Australia. *T:* Melbourne 787-1479. *Clubs:* Melbourne, Savage (Melbourne); Peninsula Country Golf, Davey's Bay Yacht, Mornington Yacht.

McCUTCHEON, Dr William Alan, FRGS, FSA; Director, Ulster Museum, Belfast, since 1977; *b* 2 March 1934; *s* of late William John and of Margaret Elizabeth McCutcheon; *m* 1956, Margaret Craig; three *s. Educ:* Royal Belfast Academical Instn; The Queen's University of Belfast (BA (Hons Geog.) 1955, MA 1958, PhD 1962). FRGS 1958; FSA 1970. School Teacher (Geography Specialist), Royal Belfast Academical Instn, 1956-62; Director, N Ireland Survey of Industrial Archaeology, 1962-68; Keeper of Technology and Local History, Ulster Museum, Belfast, 1968-77. Chairman: Historic Monuments Council (NI), 1980-; Jt Cttee on Industrial Archaeology (UK), 1981-; Member: Nat. Cttee for Archaeology (RIA), 1977-; Adv. Council to Reviewing Cttee on Export of Works of Art, 1977-; Nat. Cttee for the History and Philosophy of Science (RIA), 1980-; Industrial Archaeol. Cttee, Council for British Archaeol., 1981-; NI correspondent, Internat. Cttee for Conservation of Industrial Heritage, 1978-. Mem., Internat. Molinological Soc., 1973-. Member: Cttee of Management, Inst. of Irish Studies, QUB, 1977-; Bd of Governors, Belfast Coll. of Business Studies, 1981-. *Publications:* The Canals of the North of Ireland, 1965; Railway History in Pictures, Ireland: vol. 1 1970, vol. 2 1971; (contrib.) Travel and Transport in Ireland, 1973; (contrib.) Folk & Farm, 1976; Wheel and Spindle—Aspects of Irish Industrial History, 1977; The Industrial Archaeology of Northern Ireland, 1980; numerous papers. *Recreations:* reading, classical music, photography, etymology, hill walking, swimming. *Address:* 22 Moira Drive, Bangor, Co. Down, Northern Ireland BT20 4RN. *T:* Bangor 65005.

MacDERMOT, Brian (Charles), CBE 1966; MVO 1961; HM Diplomatic Service, retired; *b* 29 Jan. 1914; *m* 1949, Mary Arden Hunter; seven *s* two *d.* Probationer Vice-Consul, Peking, China, 1936; served at: Hankow, China, 1939-40; Kobe, Japan, 1940-41; Kunming, South China, 1942; Vice-Consul, Shiraz, Persia, 1943; Paris, 1944, promoted Consul, 1945; Foreign Office, 1946; Consul, Beirut, 1948; First Secretary, Belgrade, 1950; First Secretary, Berne, 1951, acted as Charge d'Affaires, 1951, 1952, 1953; transferred to Foreign Office, 1954; transferred to Holy See, 1955, acted as Chargé d'Affaires, 1958, 1959, 1960 and 1961; HM Consul-General, Oporto, 1962-68; Ambassador and Consul-Gen., Paraguay, 1968-72. *Address:* The Old Rectory, St James, Shaftesbury, Dorset SP7 8HG.

MacDERMOT, The, (Sir Dermot MacDermot), KCMG 1962 (CMG 1954); CBE 1947; styled Prince of Coolavin; *b* 14 June 1906; 2nd surv. *s* of late Charles Edward, The MacDermot, Prince of Coolavin; *S* brother, 1979; *m* 1934, Betty Steel; three *s. Educ:* Stonyhurst Coll.; Trinity Coll., Dublin, LLD *jure dignitatis,* 1964. Joined HM Consular Service in 1929 and served in Tokyo, Yokohama, Kobe and Osaka in Japan, Manila (Philippines), Tamsui (Formosa), New Orleans, and in the Foreign Office. Appointed a Counsellor in the Foreign Office, 1947; Inspector, HM Foreign Service, 1951; HM Minister to Roumania, 1954-56; HM Ambassador to Indonesia, 1956-59; Assistant Under-Secretary, Foreign Office, 1959-61; HM Ambassador to Thailand, 1961-65. *Recreation:* golf. *Heir: s* Niall Anthony MacDermot, *b* 25 April 1935. *Address:* Dunlavin, Co. Wicklow, Eire. *Club:* Kildare Street and University (Dublin).

MACDERMOT, Niall, OBE 1944; QC 1963; barrister-at-law; Secretary-General, International Commission of Jurists, since Dec. 1970; *b* 10 Sept. 1916; *s* of late Henry MacDermot, KC, Dublin; *m* 1940, Violet Denise Maxwell (marr. diss.); one *s; m* 1966, Ludmila Benvenuto. *Educ:* Rugby Sch.; Corpus Christi Coll., Cambridge; Balliol Coll., Oxford. Served in Intelligence Corps, 1939-46; GSO1 HQ 21 Army Group, 1944-45. MP (Lab) Lewisham North, Feb. 1957-59, Derby North, April 1962-1970; Mem. Exec., London Labour Party, 1958-62. Dep. Chm., Beds QS, 1961-64, 1969-72; Recorder of Newark-on-Trent, 1963-64; a Recorder of the Crown Court, 1972-74. Master of the Bench, Inner Temple, 1970-. Financial Sec., Treasury, 1964-67; Minister of State, Min. of Housing and Local Govt, 1967-68. Hon. Treasurer, Justice, 1968-70. Mem. Council, Internat. Inst. of Human Rights, Strasbourg, 1972-; Chm., Special NGO Cttee on Human Rights, Geneva, 1973-. Trustee of Tate Gall., 1969-76. *Address:* PO Box 120, 109 route de Chêne, 1224 Geneva, Switzerland. *T:* Geneva 49.35.45.

MacDERMOTT, Edmond Geoffrey; Metropolitan Stipendiary Magistrate since 1972. Called to Bar, Gray's Inn, 1935; Dept of Dir of Public Prosecutions, 1946-72; Asst Dir of Public Prosecutions, 1968-72. Dep. Circuit Judge, Inner London. *Address:* Horseferry Road Magistrates Court, 70 Horseferry Road, SW1P 2AX.

McDERMOTT, Sir Emmet; *see* McDermott, Sir L. E.

MacDERMOTT, Hon. John Clarke; Hon. Mr Justice MacDermott; Judge of the High Court of Northern Ireland, since 1973; *b* 1927; *s* of Baron MacDermott, PC, PC (NI), MC, and of Louise Palmer, *d* of Rev. J. C. Johnston, DD; *m* 1953, Margaret Helen, *d* of late Hugh Dales, Belfast; four *d. Educ:* Campbell Coll., Belfast; Trinity Hall, Cambridge (BA); QUB. Called to Bar, Inner Temple and Northern Ireland, 1949; QC (NI) 1964. *Address:* Royal Courts of Justice, Belfast, Northern Ireland; 6 Tarawood, Holywood, Co. Down.

McDERMOTT, Sir (Lawrence) Emmet, KBE 1972; Lord Mayor of Sydney, 1969-72; Alderman, Sydney, 1962-77; Dental Surgeon; *b* 6 Sept. 1911; *s* of O. J. McDermott; *m* 1939, Arline Beatrice Olga; one *s* one *d. Educ:* St Ignatius Coll., Sydney; Univ. of Sydney; Northwestern Univ., Chicago. MDS Sydney; DDS Northwestern; FICD, FRACDS, FACD. Hon. Consultant Dental Surgeon: Royal Prince Alfred Hosp., 1942-; Eastern Suburbs Hosp., 1945-; Pres., Bd of Control, United Dental Hosp., Sydney, 1967-79; Mem., NSW Dental Bd, 1967-79; Pres., Australian Dental Assoc. (NSW Br.), 1960-61; Councillor, Australian Dental Assoc., 1962-66. Mem., Liberal Party State Council, 1969; Councillor, Sydney County Council, 1973-80, Dep. Chm., 1975-77, Chm., 1977-78. Dir, City Mutual Life Assce Soc. Ltd, 1970-, Dep. Chm., 1976-; Member: Sydney Cove Redevelopment Authority, 1971-76; Convocation, Macquarie Univ., 1966-; Australia-Britain Soc. (NSW Br.), Vice-Pres., 1972-77. *Recreations:* golf, swimming (Sydney Univ. Blue), bowls. *Address:* T&G Tower, Hyde Park Square, Park & Elizabeth Streets, Sydney, NSW 2000, Australia. *T:* 264-3660; 20 Carnarvon Road, Roseville, NSW 2069. *T:* 46-2086. *Clubs:* Australian Jockey, Royal Sydney Golf, Elanora Country, Tattersall's, American National, Chatswood Bowling, City Bowling, Warrawee Bowling (all Sydney).

MACDONALD, family name of **Barons Macdonald** and **Macdonald of Gwaenysgor.**

MACDONALD, 8th Baron *cr* 1776; **Godfrey James Macdonald of Macdonald;** Chief of the Name and Arms of Macdonald; *b* 28 Nov. 1947; *s* of 7th Baron Macdonald, MBE, TD, and of Anne, *o d* of late Alfred Whitaker; *S* father, 1970; *m* 1969, Claire, *e d* of Captain T. N. Catlow, CBE, RN, Gabriel Cottage, Tunstall, Lancs; one *s* three *d. Heir: s* Hon. Godfrey Evan Hugo Thomas Macdonald of Macdonald, yr, *b* 24 Feb. 1982. *Address:* Ostaig House, Isle of Skye. *T:* Ardvasar 226. *Clubs:* Turf; New (Edinburgh).

McDONALD, Hon. Lord; Robert Howat McDonald, MC 1944; a Senator of the College of Justice in Scotland, since 1973; *b* 15 May 1916; *s* of Robert Glassford McDonald, and Roberta May Howat, Paisley, Renfrewshire; *m* 1949, Barbara Mackenzie, *d* of John Mackenzie, Badcaul, Ross-shire; no *c. Educ:* John Neilson Institution, Paisley. MA (Glasgow) 1935; LLB (Glasgow) 1937; admitted Faculty of Advocates, 1946; QC (Scot.) 1957. Served with KOSB, 1939-46 (despatches, 1945). Sheriff Principal of Ayr and Bute, 1966-71. Mem., Criminal Injuries Compensation Board, 1964-71; Pres., Industrial Tribunals for Scotland, 1972-73; Chm., Gen. Nursing Council for Scotland, 1970-73; Chm., Mental Welfare Commn for Scotland, 1965-; Mem., Employment Appeal Tribunal, 1976-. *Address:* Parliament House, Edinburgh. *Club:* New (Edinburgh).

MACDONALD OF GWAENYSGOR, 2nd Baron *cr* 1949, of Gwaenysgor, Flint; **Gordon Ramsay Macdonald;** business consultant; *b* 16 Oct. 1915; *er s* of 1st Baron Macdonald of Gwaenysgor, PC, KCMG; *S* father, 1966; *m* 1941, Leslie Margaret Taylor; three *d. Educ:* Manchester Univ. MA, Economics and Commerce. Served War, 1940-46; Army, Major, Artillery; GSO2 Operations and Intelligence (despatches, Burma). Board of Trade, 1946-53: Principal, 1946-47; UK Trade Comr, Canberra, ACT, 1947-53. With Tube Investments Ltd, and Man. Dir TI (Export) Ltd, 1953-64; Chief Exec., Telecommunications Group, Plessey Co., 1964-67; Chm., Hayek Engrg (UK) Ltd, 1967-76; Chm. and Chief Exec., Ferro Metal and Chemical Comp., and Satra Consultants (UK) Ltd, 1977. *Recreations:* golf, chess. *Heir: b* Hon. Kenneth Lewis Macdonald [*b* 3 Feb. 1921; *m* 1952, Maureen Margaret Watson-Allan; two *d*]. *Address:* Littleworth House, Littleworth Common, near Burnham, Bucks SL1 8PP.

MACDONALD of Sleat (Btcy); *see under* Bosville Macdonald.

MACDONALD, Alastair John Peter; Under Secretary, Information Technology Division, Department of Industry, since 1981; *b* 11 Aug. 1940; *s* of Ewen Macdonald and late Hettie Macdonald; *m* 1969, Jane, *d* of late T. R. Morris; one *s* two *d. Educ:* Wimbledon Coll.; Trinity Coll., Oxford. Editorial staff of Spectator, 1962; Financial Times, 1963-68: Washington DC, 1965-66; Features Editor, 1966-68; joined Home Civil Service as Asst Principal, 1968; Principal, 1971; Sec., Lord Devlin's Commn into Industrial and Commercial Representation, 1971-72; Asst Sec., 1975; RCDS, 1980.

Address: c/o Department of Industry, Ashdown House, 123 Victoria Street, SW1E 6RB.

McDONALD, Alex Gordon; Chief Scientific Officer, Department of Health and Social Security, since 1975; *b* 29 Jan. 1921; *m* 1st, 1942, P. Thomas; 2nd, 1950, J. James; two *d. Educ:* Tiffin Sch., Kingston upon Thames; Royal Coll. of Science (BSc, ARCS). Served RNVR, Lieut (A), Fleet Air Arm, 1939-46. Home Office, 1949; Chief of Staffs, MoD, 1956; Police Research and Develt Br., 1963; DHSS, 1970. Sometime Lectr at: Inst. of Criminology, Inst. of Advanced Legal Study, London Hosp. Sch. of Forensic Pathology, London Sch. of Hygiene and Trop. Med., and Univ. of Warwick Sch. of Business Studies. Member, Bd of Studies in Community Med., London. Hon. Prof. in Industrial and Business Studies, and Dir, Res. Centre on Mathematical Modelling of Clinical Trials, Univ. of Warwick. *Publications:* contrib. learned jls on OR and Systems Analysis. *Recreations:* Basset Hounds, Blood Hounds, needlework, reading. *Address:* 40 Wolsey Road, East Molesey, Surrey KT8 9EN. *Club:* Kennel.

McDONALD, Alexander Gordon; *see* McDonald, Alex G.

McDONALD, Prof. Alexander John, MA (Cantab), LLB, WS: Professor of Conveyancing, University of Dundee (formerly Queen's College), since 1955 (Dean of the Faculty of Law, 1958-62, 1965); *b* 15 March 1919; *o s* of late John McDonald, and Agnes Mary Stewart McDonald; *m* 1951, Doreen Mary, *o d* of late Frank Cook, OBE; two *s* two *d. Educ:* Cargilfield Sch.; Fettes Coll. (open scholar); Christ's Coll., Cambridge (Classical Exhibn, BA 1942); Edinburgh Univ. (Thow Schol. and John Robertson Prize in Conveyancing; LLB with dist., 1949). Admitted as Solicitor and Writer to the Signet, 1950; Lectr in Conveyancing, Edinburgh Univ., 1952-55; Registrar of the Diocese of Brechin, 1963-74. Sen. Partner, Thornton, Dickie & Brand, WS, Dundee DD2 1HY. *Address:* Hillside, 4 Forthill Road, Broughty Ferry, Dundee. *T:* Dundee 77301.

MACDONALD, Alistair; *b* 23 July 1912; 2nd *s* of late Reginald James Macdonald and Dorothy Bolden; *m* 1941, Myra Jones; one *s* six *d. Educ:* King's Sch., Bruton. Called to the Bar, Inner Temple, 1935. Worked with mentally handicapped children, Sunfield Childrens' Homes, Clent, 1936-40; served in RAF, 1940-45; Air Staff (Intelligence), 1943-45 (despatches). Legal Assistant, Law Officers Dept, 1948; Legal Sec. to Law Officers of the Crown, 1950-58; Secretary, The Council on Tribunals, 1958-70; Mem., Lord Chancellor's Dept: Consultant to: Royal Inst. of Public Admin, 1970-72; Emerson Coll., Forest Row, Sussex, 1973-. *Publication:* (with R. E. Wraith and P. G. Hutchesson) Administrative Tribunals, 1973. *Address:* Luxford's, Lewes Road, East Grinstead, W Sussex. *T:* East Grinstead 23365.

McDONALD, Alistair; Regional Director, North Western Region, Department of Industry, since 1979; *b* 13 March 1925; *e s* of late John Bell McDonald and Mary McDonald; *m* 1954, Isabel Margaret Milne; two *d. Educ:* Fraserburgh Academy; Aberdeen Univ. (BSc 1st Cl. Hons Natural Philosophy). Served RAF and Fleet Air Arm, 1943-46. Malayan Meteorological Service, 1950-56; ICI, 1956-66; Min. of Technology, 1966-70; Dept of Trade and Industry, 1970-74; Dept of Industry, 1974-77; Director, British Shipbuilders (on secondment), 1977-79. *Recreation:* golf. *Address:* Department of Industry, North West Regional Office, Sunley Building, Piccadilly Plaza, Manchester M1 4BA. *T:* 061-236 2171, ext. 664. *Club:* Caledonian.

MacDONALD, Alistair Archibald, MA, LLB; Sheriff of Grampian, Highland and Islands; at Lerwick and Kirkwall, since 1975; *b* 8 May 1927; *s* of James and Margaret MacDonald; *m* 1950, Jill Russell; one *s* one *d. Educ:* Broughton Sch.; Edinburgh Univ. Served in Army, 1944-48. Called to Scottish Bar, 1954. Formerly Sheriff Substitute, Caithness, Sutherland, Orkney and Zetland at Lerwick, 1961 and at Kirkwall, 1968. *Address:* West Hall, Shetland Islands; Hall Cottage, Burray, Orkney. *Club:* Royal Northern (Aberdeen).

MACDONALD, Alistair H.; *b* 18 May 1925. *Educ:* Dulwich Coll.; Enfield Technical Coll.; Corpus Christi Coll., Cambridge. MP (Lab) Chislehurst, 1966-70. Councillor, Chislehurst and Sidcup UDC, 1958-62; Alderman, 1964-68, Councillor, 1971-, London Borough of Bromley. *Address:* 79 Oakdene Avenue, Chislehurst, Kent BR7 6DZ. *T:* 01-857 8219.

McDONALD, Alistair Ian, CBE 1978; Director: Datastream Ltd, since 1981; Trust Union Ltd, 1981-82; Trans Oceanic Trust Ltd, since 1981; TR Industrial and General Trust PLC, since 1982; TR Trustees Corporation PLC, since 1982; *b* 12 Sept. 1921; *s* of late Angus McDonald and Blanche Elizabeth McDonald; *m* 1947, Olwen (*née* Evans); one *d. Educ:* Greenwich Sch. Served War, RAF, 1940-46. Church Comrs, 1947-81: Dep. Investments Sec., 1966-68; Investments Sec., 1968-81. Royal Coll. of Nursing: Investment Adviser, 1967-; Vice Pres., 1975-. Chm., Lampada Housing Assoc., 1975-. *Recreations:* golf, gardening, reading. *Address:* Newby, Tower Hill, Horsham, West Sussex. *T:* Horsham 2437. *Clubs:* Caledonian; West Sussex Golf.

MACDONALD, Allan Ronald, CMG 1953; *b* 21 Dec. 1906; *s* of Major Ronald Macdonald and Elizabeth Blair Macdonald (*née* Coats); *m* 1st, 1937, Katherine May Hodson; two *s* ; 2nd, 1954, Dr Mary Shaw (*d* 1956). *Educ:* Fettes Coll., Edinburgh; St John's Coll., Cambridge. Ceylon Civil Service, 1929-48; Establishment Sec., Uganda, 1948-51; Colonial Sec., Sierra Leone,

1951-56; Mem. of Lidbury Commn on Gold Coast Public Service, 1951; Chm., Public Service Commn: Kenya, 1956-64; Fedn of South Arabia, 1965-67. *Address:* c/o Hongkong and Shanghai Banking Corporation, PO Box 199, 99 Bishopsgate, EC2P 2LA. *Club:* United Oxford & Cambridge University.

McDONALD, Allan Stuart; Headmaster, George Heriot's School, Edinburgh, 1970-83; *b* 20 Aug. 1922; *s* of Allan McDonald and Clementina Peebles (*née* Stuart), both of Edinburgh; *m* 1948, Margaret Wilson, *d* of late James Adams, Paisley and Stranraer, and of Margaret Wilson (*née* Ferguson); one *s* two *d. Educ:* Royal High Sch., Edinburgh); Giffnock and Eastwood Schs, Renfrewshire; Glasgow Univ.; Sorbonne. MA Hons 1944; DipEd 1948. Commnd, Royal Corps of Signals (21st Army Group Signals), 1943-45. Asst Master: Johnstone High Sch., 1948-50; Eastwood Sch., 1950-54; Principal Teacher: Modern Languages, Fortrose Acad., 1954-59; German, George Heriot's Sch., 1959-67; Depute Headmaster, George Heriot's Sch., 1967-70. *Recreations:* formerly Rugby, cricket; now gardening, photography. *Address:* 34 Grange Road, Edinburgh, EH9 1UL. *T:* 031-667 6373.

MACDONALD, Angus Cameron; His Honour Judge Angus Macdonald; a Circuit Judge, since 1979; *b* 26 Aug. 1931; *o s* of Hugh Macdonald, OBE, and Margaret Cameron Macdonald (*née* Westley); *m* 1956, Deborah Anne, *d* of John Denny Inglis, DSO, MC, JP, and Deborah Margery Meiklem Inglis (*née* Thomson); three *d. Educ:* Bedford Sch.; Trinity Hall, Cambridge (BA 1954, MA 1960). Nat. service, 1950-51, commissioned, TA, 1951-57. Called to Bar, Gray's Inn, 1955; Resident Magistrate, then Crown Counsel, Nyasaland Govt, 1957-65; Sen. State Counsel, Malawi Govt, 1965-67; practised, NE Circuit, 1967-79; a Recorder of the Crown Court, 1974-79. *Recreations:* singing, fishing. *Address:* 21 Lindisfarne Road, Newcastle upon Tyne NE2 2HE. *T:* Newcastle upon Tyne 811695; Blaren, Kilninver, by Oban, Argyll. *T:* Kilmelford 246.

MACDONALD, Archibald J. F., JP; *s* of late Dr G. B. D. Macdonald, MB, ChM, and late Beatrice B. Macdonald; *m* 1945, Hon. Elspeth Ruth Shaw, *y d* of 2nd Baron Craigmyle; two *s. Educ:* Chatswood Grammar Sch., Australia; Royal Australian Naval Coll. Joint Chief Executive, Management Research Groups, London, 1937-40; Secretary, Paint Industry Export Group, 1940-47; Dir and Sec., Wartime Paint Manufacturers' Assoc., 1943-45; Dir, Robert Bowran & Co. Ltd, 1949-53; Vice-Chm., Joseph Freeman Sons & Co. Ltd, 1954-66. MP (L) Roxburgh and Selkirk, 1950-51. Member Bd of Visitors, Wormwood Scrubs and Pentonville Prisons. Councillor: Hampstead Borough Council, 1962-65; Camden Borough Council, 1971-76. JP County of London. *Recreations:* travel, people. *Address:* 22 Heath Drive, Hampstead, NW3 7SB. *T:* 01-435 2317. *Clubs:* Reform, Garrick.

MacDONALD, Gen. Sir Arthur (Leslie), KBE 1978 (OBE 1953); CB 1969; *b* 30 Jan. 1919; *s* of late Arthur Leslie MacDonald, Yaamba, Queensland; *m* 1940, Joan Bevington, *d* of late Sidney Brady, Brisbane, Queensland; one *d. Educ:* The Southport School, Southport, Queensland; Royal Military College, Duntroon, ACT. Regtl and Staff appts, Aust., ME and New Guinea, 1940-44; Instructor, Staff Coll., Camberley, 1944-45; CO 3rd Bn, The Royal Australian Regt, Korea, 1953-54; Dir of Mil. Ops, AHQ, 1955-56; Senior Aust. Planner, SEATO, Bangkok, 1957-58; Commandant, Jungle Training Centre, Canungra, 1959-60; Dir of Staff Duties, AHQ, 1960-61; Imperial Defence Coll., 1962; Dep. Commander, 1st Div., 1963-64; Commander, Papua New Guinea Comd, 1965-66; Dep. Chief of the General Staff, 1966-67; Commander Australian Force, Viet Nam, 1968-69; Adjutant-Gen., 1969-70; GOC Northern Comd, 1970-73; Chief of Operations, 1973; Vice Chief of Gen. Staff, 1973-75; CGS, 1975-77; Chief of Defence Force Staff, 1977-79, retired. Col Comdt, Royal Aust. Regt, 1981-. Dir, Carricks Ltd, 1980-. *Address:* 14 Meiers Road, Indooroopilly, Qld 4068, Australia. *Club:* Queensland (Brisbane).

McDONALD, Air Marshal Sir Arthur (William Baynes), KCB 1958 (CB 1949); AFC 1935; CEng, FRAeS 1959; DL; retired; *b* 14 June 1903; *s* of late Dr Will McDonald, OBE, Antigua, BWI; *m* 1928, Mary Julia Gray, Hindhead, Surrey; two *s* two *d. Educ:* Epsom Coll.; Peterhouse, Cambridge (MA). Joined RAF, 1924; served in Singapore, 1933-35; in Air Ministry, 1939-40; Fighter Command, 1941. Appointed Air Defence Commander, Ceylon, 1942; Air Officer Training, Air HQ, India, 1943-44; Air Officer Commanding No. 106 Group, 1945-46; Comdt RAF Staff Coll., Bulstrode and later Andover, 1947-48; Student Imperial Defence Coll., 1949; OC Aeroplane and Armament Experimental Establishment, under the Ministry of Supply, 1950-52; Director-General of Manning, Air Ministry, 1952-55; Commander-in-Chief, Royal Pakistan Air Force, 1955-57; AOC-in-C, RAF Technical Training Comd, 1958-59; Air Mem. for Personnel, Air Council, 1959-61, retired 1962. DL Hampshire, 1965. Britain in Olympic Games, 1948). *Address:* Five Oaks, Woodside, Lymington, Hants. *Clubs:* Royal Air Force; Royal Lymington Yacht; RAF Sailing Association (Adm.).

MACDONALD, Coll; Headmaster of Uppingham School, 1975-82; *b* 21 Jan. 1924; *s* of Coll Macdonald and Elizabeth (*née* Murray); *m* 1955, Hilary Constance Mowle; two *s. Educ:* Rugby Sch.; Christ's Coll., Cambridge (MA). Pilot, RAFVR, 1943-46. Lectr in Greek, Univ. of Sydney, 1949; Lectr in Classics, Univ. of Otago, 1950-51; Asst Master, Bradfield Coll., 1952-55; Asst Master, Sherborne Sch., 1955-60; Head Master: Maidenhead Grammar Sch., 1960-65; Portsmouth Grammar Sch., 1965-75. Research Fellow in Classical

Philology, Harvard Univ., 1972-73. *Publications*: (jtly) From Pericles to Cleophon, 1954; (jtly) Roman Politics 80-44 BC, 1960, 2nd edn 1965; (ed) Cicero: De Imperio Cn, Pompei, 1966, 2nd edn 1971; (ed) Cicero: Pro Murena, 1969; (ed) Cicero: De Provinciis Consularibus, 1971; (ed) Cicero: In Catilinam I-IV, Pro Murena, Pro Sulla, Pro Flacco (Loeb Classical Library), 1977; contrib. Greece and Rome, Classical Review, Classical Qly. *Recreations*: walking, swimming. *Address*: 11 Marine Court, Southsea, Hamphsire PO4 9QU. *T*: Portsmouth 756793.

MACDONALD, David Cameron; Chief Executive, Antony Gibbs Holdings Ltd, since 1980; Chairman: Antony Gibbs & Sons, since 1980; Bath and Portland Group, since 1982; Director: Coutts and Co., since 1980; Sears Holdings, since 1981; *b* 5 July 1936; *s* of James Fraser Macdonald, OBE, FRCS and Anne Sylvia Macdonald (*née* Hutcheson); *m* 1968, Melody Jane Coles (marr. diss. 1980); two *d*. *Educ*: St George's Sch., Harpenden; Newport Grammar Sch. Admitted a solicitor with Slaughter and May, 1962; joined Philip Hill Higginson Erlangers (now Hill Samuel & Co. Ltd), 1964: Dir, 1968; Dep. Chm., 1979-80; Dir, Hill Samuel Gp Ltd, 1979-80. Dir Gen., Panel on Takeovers and Mergers, 1977-79. Adviser to Govt on Upper Clyde Shipbuilders crisis, 1971. Chm., Issuing Houses Assoc., 1975-77. Mem., BTA, 1971-. *Recreations*: music, fishing. *Address*: Flat 4, 38 Tregunter Road, SW10. *T*: 01-373 0621.

McDONALD, David Wylie, CMG 1978; JP; DA, RIBA, ARIAS, HKIA; Secretary for Lands and Works, Hong Kong, since 1981; MLC Hong Kong, since 1974; *b* 9 Oct. 1927; *s* of William McDonald and Rebecca (*née* Wylie); *m* 1951, Eliza Roberts Steele; two *d*. *Educ*: Harris Acad., Dundee; School of Architecture, Dundee Coll. of Art (Lorimer Meml Prize, 1950; City Coronation Design Prize, 1953; DA 1953). Architect with Gauldie, Hardie, Wright and Needham, Chartered Architects, Dundee, 1953-55; Public Works Department, Hong Kong: Architect, 1955; Sen. Architect, 1964; Chief Architect, 1967; Govt Architect, 1970; Principal Govt Architect, 1972; Dir of Building Develt, 1973; Dir of Public Works, 1974: Member: Finance Cttee, Legislative Council, 1974-; Commonwealth Parly Assoc., 1974-. Director: Mass Transit Railway Corp., Hong Kong, 1975-; Ocean Park Ltd, Hong Kong, 1976-; Hong Kong Industrial Estate Corp., 1981-; Mem., Hong Kong Housing Auth., 1982-. Mem. Exec. Cttee: Girl Guides Assoc. (Hong Kong Br.), 1977-; Hong Kong Red Cross, 1981-. JP Hong Kong, 1972-. Silver Jubilee Medal, 1977. *Recreations*: swimming (Coach and Manager, Hong Kong Swimming Team at Commonwealth Games, Christchurch, NZ, 1974), drawing, painting and calligraphy. *Address*: 19 Severn Road, The Peak, Hong Kong. *T*: Hong Kong 96966; 12 Albert Road, West Ferry, Dundee, Scotland. *T*: Dundee 76810. *Clubs*: Hong Kong (Hong Kong) (Chairman, 1977); Royal Hong Kong Jockey (Hong Kong).

MACDONALD, Prof. Donald Farquhar; Professor of Modern Social and Economic History, University of Dundee, 1967-76 (University of St Andrews, 1955-67); *b* 3 June 1906; 3rd *s* of Donald Macdonald and Annabella Mackenzie; *m* Jeannette Eileen Bickle; one *s*. *Educ*: Dingwall Academy; Aberdeen Univ.; Balliol Coll., Oxford. University Lecturer, Aberdeeen Univ. and University Coll., Exeter, 1934-41; Ministry of Supply and Ministry of Labour and National Service, 1941-43; Secretary (later General Manager), National Assoc. of Port Employers, 1943-55. *Publications*: Scotland's Shifting Population, 1770-1850, 1937; The State and the Trade Unions, 1960, revised edn 1976; The Age of Transition, 1967, etc. *Address*: 11 Arnhall Drive, Dundee.

MACDONALD, Rev. Donald Farquhar Macleod, CBE 1979; Principal Clerk of General Assembly of the Church of Scotland, since 1972; *b* 1 May 1915; *s* of John Murchison Macdonald and Margaret Macleod; *m* 1948, Anne Jane Vance Sinclair; one *s* two *d*. *Educ*: North Kelvinside Secondary Sch.; Glasgow Univ. (MA, LLB). Ordained to Glasford Parish, 1948; Clerk to Presbytery of Hamilton, 1952-72; Dep. Clerk of General Assembly, 1955-71. *Publications*: (ed) Practice and Procedure in the Church of Scotland, 6th edn, 1977; (ed and comp.) Fasti Ecclesiae Scoticanae, vol. X, 1981. *Recreations*: chess, swimming, gardening. *Address*: 121 George Street, Edinburgh. *T*: 031-225 5722; 29 Auchingramont Road, Hamilton, Lanarkshire. *T*: Hamilton 423667; 1 Forth Crescent, Stirling. *Club*: Caledonian (Edinburgh).

MACDONALD, Donald Hardman, CMG 1974; *b* 16 May 1908; *s* of Archibald J. H. and Elizabeth Macdonald; *m* 1930, Simone Dumortier; one *s* one *d*. *Educ*: City of London Sch. Partner, Charles Fulton & Co., London, 1935-39; Bank of England, 1939-49; Chief, Allied Bank Commn, Frankfort, 1949-52; Adviser, Bank of England, 1953-54; Bank for International Settlements, Basle, 1954-73 (Head of Banking Dept, 1972-73). *Recreations*: reading, travel, gardening. *Address*: 3 rue Robert de Traz, 1206 Geneva, Switzerland. *T*: (022) 46.95.46.

MACDONALD, Air Vice-Marshal Donald Malcolm Thomas, CB 1952; RAF retired; *b* 15 Aug. 1909; *s* of late D. P. Macdonald, Tormore, Isle of Skye; *m* 1938, Kathleen Mary de Vere, *d* of late J. T. Hunt, Oxford; one *s* four *d*. *Educ*: Westminster School. Joined Royal Air Force, 1930. Dir-Gen. of Personal Services, Air Min., 1957-58; Dir-Gen. of Manning, Air Min., 1958-61, retd 1961. Mem. Crofters Commn, 1962-65. Chm., Royal British Legion, Scotland, 1977-81. *Address*: Torbeag, Clachan Seil, by Oban, Argyll. *T*: Balvicar 311.

MACDONALD, Hon. Donald (Stovel), PC (Canada) 1968; lawyer; Partner, McCarthy & McCarthy, since 1978; Director: Boise Cascade Corporation, since 1978; McDonnell Douglas Corporation, since 1978; Du Pont Canada Inc., since 1978; Manufacturers Life Insurance Co., since 1979; Bank of Nova Scotia, since 1980; Alberta Energy Co. Ltd, since 1981; Chairman, International Development Research Centre, Canada, since 1981; *b* 1 March 1932; *s* of Donald Angus Macdonald and Marjorie Stovel Macdonald; *m* 1961, Ruth Hutchison, Ottawa; four *d*. *Educ*: Univ. of Toronto (BA 1951); Osgoode Hall Law Sch. (1955); Harvard Law Sch. (LLM 1956); Cambridge Univ. (Dip. in Internat. Law, 1957). Called to Ont Bar, 1955; Prize in Insurance Law, Law Soc. of Upper Canada, 1955; Rowell Fellow, Canadian Inst. of Internat. Affairs, 1956; McCarthy & McCarthy, law firm, Toronto, 1957-62. Special Lectr, Univ. of Toronto Law Sch., 1978-. MP Rosedale, 1962-78; Parly Sec. to Ministers of Justice, Finance, Ext. Affairs, Industry, 1963-68; Minister without Portfolio, 1968; Pres., Queen's Privy Council, and Govt House Leader, 1968-70; Minister of National Defence, 1970-72; Minister of Energy, Mines and Resources, 1972-75; Minister of Finance, 1975-77. LLD (*hc*) St Lawrence Univ., 1974; Hon. DEng Colorado Sch. of Mines, 1976. *Recreations*: squash, cross-country skiing, tennis. *Address*: 29 Dunvegan Road, Toronto, Ont M4V 2P5, Canada. *T*: 960—1223; (office) PO Box 48, Toronto Dominion Tower, Toronto Dominion Center, Toronto, Ont M5K 1E6, Canada. *T*: 362-1812.

MacDONALD, Douglas George; Managing Director, John Menzies (Holdings) Ltd, since 1971; *b* 5 Aug. 1930; *s* of Colin Douglas MacDonald and Jane Grant Stewart; *m* Alexandra von Tschirschky und Boegendorf; one *s*. *Educ*: Morgan Acad., Dundee; Univ. of St Andrews (BSc). Queen's Own Cameron Highlanders, 1951-57. Potash Ltd, 1957-66; Man. Dir, Wyman Marshall Ltd, 1966-68. Member: National Freight Corp., 1973-80; Scottish Telecommunications Bd, 1973-76; Chm., East Lothian Conservative and Unionist Assoc., 1970-73; Director: Scottish Investment Trust Ltd, 1977-; William Muir (Bond 9) Ltd, 1981-; Robert Moss Ltd, 1981-; Scottish Life Assce Co. Ltd, 1982-; Royal Bank of Scotland, 1982-; Chm., Advent Technol. plc, 1981-. Chm., Scottish Council, Res. Inst. Ltd, 1975-. *Recreations*: golf, squash, politics. *Address*: Belton, Gullane, East Lothian EH31 2BE. *T*: Gullane 843189. *Clubs*: Royal Automobile; New (Edinburgh).

McDONALD, Duncan, CBE 1976; BSc, FH-WC, FRSE, FEng, FIEE, CBIM, SMIEEE; Chairman and Chief Executive, Northern Engineering Industries plc, since 1980 (Group Managing Director, 1977-80); *b* 20 Sept. 1921; *s* of Robert McDonald and Helen Orrick; *m* 1955, Jane Anne Guckian; three *s* one *d*. *Educ*: Inverkeithing Public Sch.; Dunfermline High Sch.; Edinburgh Univ. (BSc). Grad. App., BTH, Rugby, 1942-45; Transformer Design, Research and Develt, BTH, 1945-54. Bruce Peebles Industries Ltd: Chief Transformer Designer, 1954-59; Chief Engr, 1959; Dir and Chief Engr, 1960; Managing Dir, 1962; Chm. and Chief Exec. (and of A. Reyrolle & Co. Ltd), 1974; Reyrolle Parsons Ltd: Dir, 1973-77; Chief Exec., 1976-77. Member: Scottish Council Develt and Industry, 1967-76; Scottish Economic Council, 1975-. FH-WC 1962. Hon. DSc Heriot-Watt, 1982. *Publications*: various papers to learned socs, nat. and internat. *Recreation*: fishing. *Address*: 19 North Park Terrace, Edinburgh EH4 1DP. *T*: 031-332 5301; (office) Northern Engineering Industries plc, NEI House, Regent Centre, Newcastle upon Tyne NE3 3SB.

McDONALD, (Edward) Lawson, MA, MD Cantab; FRCP; FACC; Physician, National Heart Hospital, since 1961; Cardiologist, to King Edward VII's Hospital for Officers, London, since 1968, to King Edward VII Hospital, Midhurst, since 1970; Senior Lecturer (formerly Lecturer) to the Institute of Cardiology, since 1961; Hon. Consultant Cardiologist, Canadian Red Cross Memorial Hospital, Taplow, since 1960; *b* 1918; *s* of Charles Seaver McDonald, Belfast, NI; *m* 1953, Ellen Greig Rattray (marr. diss. 1972); one *s*. *Educ*: Felsted Sch.; Clare Coll., Cambridge; Middlesex Hospital; Harvard Univ. House appointments Middlesex Hospital, 1942-43. Temp. Surgeon-Lt, RNVR, 1943-46; served War of 1939-45, in N Atlantic and Normandy Campaigns. RMO, Nat. Heart Hosp., 1946-47; Asst Registrar, Inst. of Cardiology, 1947-48; Med. Registrar, Middlesex Hosp., 1948-49; studied in Stockholm, 1949; Asst to Prof. of Medicine, Middlesex Hosp., 1949-52; Rockefeller Travelling Fellow in Medicine, 1952-53; Asst in Medicine, Med. Dept, Peter Bent Brigham Hosp., Boston, Mass. and Research Fellow in Medicine, Harvard Univ., 1952-53; Clinical and Research Asst, Dept of Cardiology, Middlesex Hosp., 1953-55; Asst Dir, Inst. of Cardiology and Hon. Asst Physician, Nat. Heart Hosp., 1955-61; Physician, and Physician to Cardiac Dept, London Hosp., 1960-78. Member: Bd of Governors, National Heart and Chest Hosps, 1975-; Council, British Heart Foundn, 1975-. Visiting Lecturer: American Coll. of Cardiology; Univ. of Toronto, Queen's Univ., Kingston, Ont; Univ. of Bombay; University of Barcelona, Eliseo Migoya Inst. of Cardiology, Bilbao, Spain; Istanbul Univ. Turkey; Univs of Chicago, Cincinnati and Kansas; Harvard Univ.; Mayo Foundation, USA; Univs of Belgrade, Ljubljana and Zagreb, Yugoslavia; Nat. Univ. of Cordoba, Argentine; Univ. of Chile, and Catholic Univ., Santiago; Nat. Univ. of Colombia; Nat. Inst. of Cardiology, Mexico; Nat. Univ. of Mexico; University of San Marcos and University of Cayetano Heredia, Peru; Nat. Univ. of Venezuela. From 1961, has addressed numerous heart societies in Europe, Canada, USA, People's Republic of China, USSR, and South America; St Cyres Lecturer, 1966; First Charles A. Berns Meml Lectr, Albert Einstein Coll. of Medicine, NY, 1973; Vth World Congress of Cardiology Souvenir Orator and Lectr's Gold Medallist, 1977. Advisor to the Malaysian Govt on Cardiac Services. Member: British Cardiac Soc.; Assoc. of Physicians of Great Britain and Ireland, and other societies; FACC; Corresp. Mem. or Hon. Mem. of various socs of Cardiology or Angiology in S America. Hon. Fellow, Turkish Med. Soc.; Mem., Italian Soc. of Cardiology; Hon. Mem., Pakistan Cardiac Soc. Member, Most Honourable Order of the Crown of Johore, 1980. Editorial Bd, New Istanbul Contribution to Clinical Science. *Publications:* (ed) Pathogenesis and Treatment of Occlusive Arterial Disease, 1960; Medical and Surgical Cardiology, 1969; (ed) Very Early Recognition of Coronary Heart Disease, 1978; numerous contribs to learned jls; also papers and addresses. *Recreations:* ski-ing and sailing. *Address:* 9 Upper Wimpole Street, W1M 7TD. *T:* 01-935 7101; 9 Bentinck Mansions, Bentinck Street, W1M 5RJ. *T:* 01-935 0868; The Trippet, Old Bosham, near Chichester, West Sussex. *T:* Bosham 572373.

MacDONALD, Hon. Flora; MP (Progressive C) Kingston, Ontario, since 1972; *b* June 1926. *Educ:* schools in North Sydney, Nova Scotia; Empire Business Coll., Canadian Nat. Defence Coll. With Nat. HQ, Progressive Cons. Party, 1957-66 (Exec. Dir, 1961-66); Nat. Sec., Progressive Cons. Assoc. of Canada, 1966-69; Administrative Officer and Tutor, Dept of Political Studies, Queen's Univ., Kingston, 1966-72. Minister for External Affairs, Canada, 1979-80. Member: Canadian Inst. of Internat. Affairs; Canadian Civil Liberties Assoc.; Elizabeth Fry Soc., Kingston (former Pres.); Cttee for an Indep. Canada (former exec. dir); Canadian Political Science Assoc. (former dir). *Publications:* papers on political subjects. *Address:* House of Commons, Ottawa, Canada.

MacDONALD, George Alan; a Recorder of the Crown Court, 1972-81; *b* 21 April 1909; *s* of George John MacDonald, FIEE and Mabel Elizabeth Miriam (*née* Davies); *m* 1937, Frances Marguerite Davies; two *s* one *d. Educ:* St Joseph's, Totland Bay; Manor House, Havant; Hartley Univ. Coll., Southampton. Solicitor, 1931. RNVSR, 1938; Temp. Lt-Comdr RNVR, 1944. Pres., Hampshire Law Soc., 1959; Chairman: Southern Rent Tribunal, 1962-74; Mental Health Review Tribunal for Oxford and Wessex, 1968-81; Misuse of Drugs Act Tribunal, 1974-82; Isle of Wight Rent Tribunal, 1974-81; Mem. Council, Law Soc., 1970-79; Clerk of the Peace, Portsmouth, 1971; Pres., Southern Rent Assessment Panel, 1979-81. President: Portsmouth Harbour Racing and Sailing Assoc., 1964-64; Havant Hockey Club, 1973-77. *Publications:* occasional contrib. Law Society's Gazette. *Recreations:* hockey (Hampshire 1947-49), gardening, moorland walking, canal cruising, sound radio, cricket. *Address:* 8 King Street, Emsworth PO10 7AZ. *T:* Emsworth 4459; Whitehall House, Bideford, Devon EX39 5HF. *T:* Bideford 2532. *Clubs:* Royal Naval and Royal Albert Yacht (Portsmouth); Royal North Devon Golf.

MACDONALD, George Grant; His Honour Judge Macdonald; a Circuit Judge, since 1972; *b* 5 March 1921; *s* of late Patrick Macdonald, MA, Aberdeen, MB, ChB, Edinburgh, and Charlotte Primrose (*née* Rintoul); *m* 1967, Mary Dolores (*née* Gerrish), *widow* of G. G. Taylor; no *c. Educ:* Kelly Coll., Tavistock; Bristol Univ. (LLB (Hons)). Served War of 1939-45: in Royal Navy, Aug. 1941-July 1946, in Western Approaches, and Mine Sweeping, RNVR. Called to Bar, Gray's Inn, 1947; practised on Western Circuit, from Albion Chambers, Bristol; Dep.-Chm., Dorset QS, apptd 1969; Temp. Recorder of Barnstaple, Dec. 1971. *Recreations:* sailing, bridge, chess. *Address:* Hartfield, Wood Green, Fordingbridge, Hants. *T:* Downton 22248. *Club:* Clifton (Bristol).

MACDONALD, Sir Herbert (George deLorme), KBE 1967 (OBE 1948); JP (Jamaica); retired government officer (Jamaica); company director; sportsman; President Organising Committee, IX Central American and Caribbean Games, 1962, and 8th British Empire and Commonwealth Games, 1966 (compiled and edited history); Chairman, National Sports Ltd (a Government body owning and operating National Stadium and Sports Centre), 1960-67, now President (specially created post); Director: Prospect Beach Ltd; Macdonald Ltd; *b* Kingston, 23 May 1902; *s* of late Ronald Macdonald, JP, planter, and late Louise (*née* Alexander). *Educ:* Wolmer's Boys' Sch., Jamaica; Northeast High Sch., Philadelphia, USA. Clerical and planting activities, 1919-43. Published Sportsman Magazine (with late Sir Arthur Thelwell). Accompanied Jamaica's team to World Olympics, London, 1948, and (as Manager) to Helsinki, 1952, Melbourne, 1956; Chef de Mission, WI Olympic Team to Rome, 1960; Deleg., Tokyo, 1964. Chief Liaison Officer, BWI Central Lab. Org. (USA), 1943-55; Pres., Jamaica Olympic Assoc., 1940-44 and 1956-58; Pres., WI Olympic Assoc. (from inception), 1958-61 (when Polit. Fedn was broken up). Past Pres. etc, various Jamaican sporting assocs and boards; Mem. Exec. Cttee Pan American Sports Organisation which controls Pan American Games; Exec. Sec., Jamaica Tercentenary Celebrations Cttee, 1955. Mem. Bd of Trustees, Wolmer's Sch. Diploma of Merit, 1966 Internat. Olympic Cttee, 1968. Is an Anglican. *Recreations:* all sports; stamp collecting (athletic stamps); represented Jamaica in football and tennis *v* foreign teams, 1925-32. *Address:* 1 Liguanea Row, Kingston 6, Jamaica. *T:* 927-8213. *Clubs:* (Life Mem., past Hon. Sec.) Kingston Cricket (Kingston, Jamaica); Constant Spring Golf.

MACDONALD, Prof. Hugh Ian, OC 1977; Canada Centennial Medal, 1967; Silver Jubilee Medal, 1977; President, York University, Toronto, Ont., since 1974; Professor, Department of Economics and Faculty of Administrative Studies, since 1974; *b* Toronto, 27 June 1929; *s* of Hugh and Winnifred Macdonald; *m* 1960, Dorothy Marion Vernon; two *s* three *d. Educ:* public schs, Toronto; Univ. of Toronto; Oxford Univ. BCom (Toronto), MA (Oxon), BPhil (Oxon). Univ. of Toronto: Lectr in Economics, 1955; Dean

of Men, 1956; Asst Prof., Economics, 1961. Govt of Ontario: Chief Economist, 1965; Dep. Provincial Treas., 1967; Dep. Treas. and Dep. Minister of Economics, 1968; Dep. Treas. and Dep. Minister of Economics and Intergovernmental Affairs, 1972. Director: Canadian Gen. Electric Co.; Rockwell Internat. of Canada Ltd; the AGF Cos; CIBA-GEIGY Canada Ltd; Member: Bd of Dirs, Hockey Canada; Bd of Dirs, London House Assoc. of Canada; Bd of Governors, Inst. of Canadian Bankers; Bd of Advisors, Internat. Assoc. for Students of Economics and Commerce; Adv. Council, Niagara Inst.; Admin. Bd, Internat. Assoc. of Univs; Council and Exec. Cttee, Interamerican Org. for Higher Educn; Chm. Bd, Corp. to Promote Innovation Develt for Employment Advancement (Govt of Ontario). Member: Canadian Economics Assoc.; Amer. Economics Assoc.; Royal Economic Soc. (London); Canadian Assoc. for Club of Rome; Inst. of Public Admin of Canada; Lambda Alpha Fraternity (Land Economics); Amer. Soc. for Public Admin; Past President: Empire Club of Canada; Ticker Club; Couchiching Inst. Public Affairs; Past Chm., Toronto Men's Br. of CIIA; Past Mem., Attorney General's Cttee on Securities Legislation. Hon. LLD Toronto, 1974. *Recreations:* hockey, tennis; public service in various organizations. *Address:* 7 Whitney Avenue, Toronto, Ont. M4W 2A7, Canada. *T:* 921-2908; York University, 4700 Keele Street, Downsview, Ont. M3J 1P3, Canada. *T:* 667-2454.

MACDONALD, Iain Smith, MD; FRCPE, FFCM; Deputy Chief Medical Officer, Scottish Home and Health Department, since 1974; *b* 14 July 1927; *s* of Angus Macdonald, MA and Jabina Urie Smith; *m* 1958, Sheila Foster; one *s* one *d. Educ:* Univ. of Glasgow (MD, DPH). Lectr, Univ. of Glasgow, 1955; Deputy Medical Officer of Health: Bury, 1957; Bolton, 1959; joined Scottish Home and Health Dept, 1964. *Address:* 36 Dumyat Drive, Falkirk FK1 5PA. *T:* Falkirk 25100.

MacDONALD, Ian; see Mayfield, Hon. Lord.

MACDONALD, Prof. Ian Grant, FRS 1979; Professor of Pure Mathematics, Queen Mary College, University of London, since 1976; *b* 11 Oct. 1928; *s* of Douglas Grant Macdonald and Irene Alice Macdonald; *m* 1954, Margaretha Maria Lodewijk Van Goethem; two *s* three *d. Educ:* Winchester Coll.; Trinity Coll., Cambridge (MA). Asst Principal and Principal, Min. of Supply, 1952-57; Asst Lectr, Univ. of Manchester, 1957-60; Lectr, Univ. of Exeter, 1960-63; Fellow, Magdalen Coll., Oxford, 1963-72; Fielden Prof. of Pure Maths, Univ. of Manchester, 1972-76. *Publications:* Introduction to Commutative Algebra (with M. F. Atiyah), 1969; Algebraic Geometry, 1969; articles in math. jls. *Address:* 8 Blandford Avenue, Oxford. *T:* Oxford 55373.

MACDONALD, Ian Wilson, MA; DLitt; CA; Chairman, Scottish Hospitals Endowments Research Trust; *b* Old Cumnock, Ayrshire, 28 May 1907; *s* of late Rev. Alexander B. Macdonald, BD, PhD, Dron, Perthshire, and late Dr Mary B. W. Macdonald; *m* 1933, Helen Nicolson, MA; one *s* two *d. Educ:* Perth Academy; Edinburgh Academy. Prof. of Accountancy, Univ. of Glasgow, 1938-50. Partner in Kerr Macleod and Macfarlan, CA, Glasgow, 1933-53. Member: Cttee of Investigation into Port Transport Industry, 1945; Court of Inquiry into Omnibus Industry, 1946, Shipbuilding Industry, 1947, Railwaymen's Wages and Hours of Work, 1947; Arbitrator, Nigerian Railways Labour dispute, 1948; Mem. Gen. Claims Tribunal, 1943-58. Member: Cttee of Inquiry: Fishing Industry, 1957-60; Ports and Harbours, 1961-62; Member: S Scotland Electricity Board, 1956-61; National Ports Council, 1963-67; NRDC, 1959-73; CAA, 1972-75. Chairman: Lloyds and Scottish Ltd, 1959-78; Royal Bank of Scotland Ltd, 1969-72; Dir, Lloyds Bank Ltd, 1961-78; Dep. Chm., National and Commercial Banking Group Ltd, 1969-78. *Recreations:* shooting, fishing. *Address:* Seton Court, Gullane, East Lothian EH31 2BD. *Club:* Caledonian.

MacDONALD, Isabel Lillias, (Mrs J. G. MacDONALD); see Sinclair, I. L.

McDONALD, Iverach; Associate Editor, The Times, 1967-73; Director, The Times Ltd, 1968-73; *b* 23 Oct. 1908; *s* of Benjamin McDonald, Strathcool, Caithness, and Janet Seel; *m* 1935, Gwendoline, *o d* of late Captain Thomas R. Brown; one *s* one *d. Educ:* Leeds Gram. Sch. Asst Editor, Yorkshire Post, 1933; sub-editor, The Times, 1935; correspondent in Berlin, 1937; diplomatic correspondent 1938; Asst Editor, 1948; Foreign Editor, 1952; Managing Editor, 1965. War of 1939-45: Capt., Gen. Staff, 1939-40; travelled extensively in Soviet Union, Far East and America; reported all allied conferences after the war, including San Francisco, 1945, Paris, 1946 and 1947, Moscow, 1947, Colombo, 1950, and Bermuda, 1953. Sen. Associate Mem., St Antony's Coll., Oxford, 1976-. *Publications:* A Man of the Times, 1976; chapters in: Walter Lippmann and His Times, 1959; The Times History of our Times, 1971. *Address:* Whistlers, Beckley Common, Oxford. *T:* Stanton St John 226.

McDONALD, Sir James, KBE 1967 (CBE 1956; OBE 1948); British Consul (Hon.), Portland, Oregon USA, since 1938; President, McDonald Dock Co.; Managing Partner: Macdon & Co.; Kermac Investment Co.; Renfrew Associates; Director: Western Transportation Co.; Waterway Terminals Co.; *b* 23 July 1899; *s* of late James McDonald, Renfrew, Scotland; *m* 1933, Anne, *d* of late Peter Kerr, Portland, Ore, USA; one *s* two *d. Educ:* Allen Glen's Sch., Glasgow. Lt, RFC (later RAF), 1917-19. Partner McDonald Gattie & Co., 1927-67; Pres., Norpac Shipping Co., 1940-67. Trustee: Oregon Historical Soc.; Oregon Parks Foundn. *Recreations:* walking, farming.

Address: 11626 SW Military Lane, Portland, Ore, USA. *T:* 636-4775; Inchinnan Farm, Rt 1, Box 1405, Wilsonville, Ore, USA. *T:* 625-6914. *Clubs:* Boodle's, Royal Air Force; Arlington, University (Portland, Ore.).

MACDONALD, Prof. James Alexander, BSc (Agric.), PhD (Edinburgh), DSc (St Andrews); Professor of Botany, University of St Andrews, 1961-77, now Emeritus; *b* 17 June 1908; *s* of late James Alexander and Jessie Mary Macdonald; *m* 1935, Constance Mary Simmie; one *d. Educ:* Inverness Royal Academy; Edinburgh Univ.; Steven Scholarship in Agriculture, 1930; DSc with Sykes Gold Medal, 1947. Asst Lecturer in Botany, East of Scot. Coll. of Agriculture, 1932-35; St Andrews University: Lecturer in Botany, 1935-52; Senior Lecturer, 1952-60; Dean, Faculty of Science, 1967-69. Pres., Botanical Soc. of Edinburgh, 1955-57; FRSE 1940 (Council Mem., 1956-59); Vice-Pres. RSE, 1961-64. Fellow, Inst. Biology. Silver Jubilee Medal, 1977. *Publications:* Introduction to Mycology, 1951; scientific papers in Trans Brit. Mycol. Soc., Annals Applied Biol., Mycologia, Proc. and Trans Bot. Soc. Edinburgh, Proc. and Trans Royal Soc. Edinburgh. *Recreations:* golf, fishing, philately. *Address:* 17 Hepburn Gardens, St Andrews, Fife. *Club:* Royal and Ancient (St Andrews).

MACDONALD, John B(arfoot), DDS, MS, PhD; President and Chief Executive Officer, Addiction Research Foundation, since 1976; Executive Director, Council of Ontario Universities, since 1968; Professor of Higher Education, University of Toronto, since 1968; *b* 23 Feb. 1918; *s* of Arthur A. Macdonald and Gladys L. Barfoot; *m* ; two *s* one *d* ; *m* 1967, Liba Kucera; two *d. Educ:* Univ. of Toronto, University of Illinois, Columbia Univ. DDS (with hons) Toronto, 1942; MS (Bact) Ill, 1948; PhD (Bact) Columbia, 1953. Lectr, Prev. Dentistry, University of Toronto, and private practice, 1942-44. Canadian Dental Corps, 1944-46 (Capt.) Instr, Bacteriol, University of Toronto, and private practice, 1946-47; Res. Asst, Univ. of Illinois, 1947-48; Kellogg Fellow and Canadian Dental Assoc. Res. Student, Columbia Univ., 1948-49; University of Toronto: Asst Prof. of Bacteriol., 1949-53; Assoc. Prof. of Bacteriol., 1953-56; Chm., Div. of Dental Res., 1953-56; Prof. of Bacteriol., 1956; Cons. in Dental Educn, University of BC, 1955-56; Dir, Forsyth Dental Infirmary, 1956-62 (Cons. in Bacteriol., 1962); Prof. of Microbiol., Harvard Sch., of Dental Med., 1956-62 (Dir of Postdoctoral Studies, 1960-62); President, Univ. of British Columbia, 1962-67. Consultant: Dental Med. Section of Corporate Research Div. of Colgate-Palmolive Co., 1958-62; Donwood Foundn, Toronto, 1967- (Chm. of Bd, 1972-); Science Council of Canada, 1967-69; Addiction Research Foundn of Ontario, 1968- (Mem., 1974-). Chm., Commn on Pharmaceutical Services of the Canadian Pharmaceutical Assoc., 1967-; Consultant, Nat. Inst. of Health, 1968-; Mem., Dental Study Sect., Nat. Inst. of Health, 1961-65; Councillor-at-Large, Internat. Assoc. for Dental Research, 1963-, Pres. 1968-69. Fellow, Mem. or Chm. of numerous assocs. etc, both Canadian and international. FACD 1955; Hon. FICD 1965. Hon. AM, Harvard Univ., 1956; Hon. LLD: Univ. of Manitoba, 1962; Simon Fraser Univ., 1965; Hon DSc Univ. of British Columbia, 1967. *Publications:* Higher Education in British Columbia and a Plan for the Future, 1962, etc.; numerous contribs to learned jls. *Recreations:* golf, tennis. *Address:* Addiction Research Foundation, 33 Russell Street, Toronto, Ontario. *T:* 595-6000. *Clubs:* University, University of BC Faculty, Vancouver (Vancouver); Canadian, Faculty, University of Toronto (Toronto).

MACDONALD, Air Commodore John Charles, CB 1964; CBE 1957; DFC 1940 (Bar 1942); AFC 1941; Aviation Consultant; *b* 25 Dec. 1910; *s* of late Robert Macdonald; *m* 1952, Gladys Joan, *d* of John Hine, Beaminster, Dorset; two *s. Educ:* Berkhamsted Sch.; RAF Cadet Coll., Cranwell. Commissioned RAF, 1930. Served War of 1939-45 in Bomber Command; POW Stalag Luft III, 1942-45, escaped April 1945. Commanded RAF Akrotiri during Suez campaign; UK National Military Representative, SHAPE, 1959-61; Comdr RAF East Africa, 1961-64; Min. of Defence, 1964; retd, 1964. Chevalier, Légion d'Honneur, 1958; Croix de Guerre, 1958. *Recreations:* golf, sailing, shooting. *Address:* Woodbine Cottage, Osmington, Dorset. *T:* Preston 833259. *Club:* Royal Automobile.

McDONALD, Prof. John Corbett, MD; FRCP, FFCM, FFOM; Professor and Head, Institute of Occupational Health and Safety, McGill University, since 1981; *b* 20 April 1918; *s* of John Forbes McDonald and Sarah Mary McDonald; *m* 1942, Alison Dunstan Wells; one *s* three *d. Educ:* London Univ. (MD); Harvard Univ. (MS). DPH, DIH; FRCP (Canada) 1970; FRCP 1976; FFCM 1976; FFOM 1978. Served War, MO, RAMC, 1942-46. Epidemiologist, Public Health Lab. Service, 1951-64 (Dir, Epidemiol Res. Lab., 1960-64); Prof. and Head, Dept of Epidemiology and Health, McGill Univ., Montreal, 1964-76; Prof. of Occupational Health, LSHTM, Univ. of London, 1976-81; Dir, TUC Centenary Inst. of Occupational Health, 1976-81. *Publications:* (ed) Recent Advances in Occupational Health, 1981; papers on epidemiol subjects. *Recreations:* skiing, cycling. *Address:* 136 Pine Avenue West, Montreal, Quebec H2W 1S6, Canada. *Club:* Athenæum.

MACDONALD, John Reginald, QC 1976; barrister-at-law; *b* 26 Sept. 1931; *s* of Ranald Macdonald and Marion Olive (*née* Kirkby); *m* 1958; one *s* one *d. Educ:* St Edward's Sch., Oxford; Queens' Coll., Cambridge. Called to Bar, Lincoln's Inn, 1955. Contested (L) Wimbledon, 1966 and 1970 General Elections; prospective parly cand. (L), Folkestone and Hythe. Chm., Assoc. of Liberal Lawyers, 1973-78. *Recreation:* the theatre. *Address:* 12 New Square, Lincoln's Inn, WC2. *T:* 01-405 3808.

MACDONALD, Kenneth Carmichael; Deputy Under-Secretary of State (Policy), Procurement Executive, Ministry of Defence, since 1980; *b* 25 July 1930; *s* of William Thomas and Janet Millar Macdonald; *m* 1960, Ann Elisabeth (*née* Pauer); one *s* two *d. Educ:* Hutchesons' Grammar Sch.; Glasgow Univ. MA (Hons Classics). RAF, 1952-54. Asst Principal, Air Ministry, 1954; Asst Private Sec. to Sec. of State, 1956-57; Private Sec. to Permanent Sec., 1958-61; HM Treasury, 1962-65; MoD, 1965; Asst Sec., 1968; Counsellor (Defence), UK Delegn to NATO, 1973-75; Asst Under-Sec. of State, MoD, 1975-80. *Recreation:* golf. *Address:* 61 Park Avenue, Bromley, Kent BR1 4EG. *T:* 01-460 6262.

McDONALD, Lawson; *see* McDonald, E. L.

MACDONALD, Dame Margaret; *see* Kidd, Dame Margaret Henderson.

MacDONALD, Margo, (Mrs James Sillars); producer and presenter with Radio Forth, since 1981; *b* 19 April 1944; *d* of Robert and Jean Aitken; *m* 1st, 1965, Peter MacDonald (marr. diss. 1980); two *d* ; 2nd, 1981, James Sillars, *qv. Educ:* Hamilton Academy; Dunfermline Coll. (Diploma of Physical Educn). Contested (SNP) Paisley, Gen. Elec., 1970; MP (SNP) Glasgow (Govan), Nov. 1973-Feb. 1974; contested (SNP): Glasgow (Govan), Gen. Elec., Feb. 1974 and Oct. 1974; Hamilton, by-election, May 1978. Vice-Chm., Scottish National Party, 1972-79 (Senior Vice-Chm., 1974-78); Mem., SNP Nat. Exec., 1980-81; Chm., SNP '79 Group, 1978-81; Director of Shelter (Scotland), 1978-81. *Recreations:* family life, folk music, theatre, swimming, lazing. *Address:* Radio Forth, Forth Street, Edinburgh.

McDONALD, Dr Oonagh; MP (Lab) Thurrock, since July 1976; *b* Stockton-on-Tees, Co. Durham, 21 Feb. 1938; *d* of Dr H. D. McDonald. *Educ:* Roan Sch. for Girls, Greenwich; East Barnet Grammar Sch.; Univ. of London (BD Hons 1959; MTh 1962, PhD 1974, King's Coll.). Teacher, St Barnabas Sch., S Woodford, 1959-62; Lectr for Dip. in Sociology, Toynbee Hall, 1964-65; Teacher, Hornsey Grammar Sch. and Boreham Wood Sch., 1964-65; Lectr in Philosophy, Bristol Univ., 1965-76. Contested (Lab.), S Glos, Feb. and Oct. 1974. PPS to Chief Sec. to Treasury, 1977-79; Opposition front bench spokesman on defence, 1981-. Member: Public Accounts Cttee, 1977-78; Select Cttee on Employment, 1981. Member: ASTMS, 1972-; Industrial Policy sub-cttee, Labour Party NEC, 1976- (Finance and Economic Affairs sub-cttee, 1978-). Devised TV documentary, A Woman's Life. *Publications:* (jtly) The Economics of Prosperity, 1980; articles on taxation, child benefit, industrial strategy, etc. *Address:* House of Commons, Westminster, SW1A 0AA. *T:* 01-219 3415, 01-940 5563.

MACDONALD, Patrick Donald, CMG 1953; CVO 1963; *b* 21 July 1909; *s* of late Major E. W. Macdonald and Amy Beatrice Cavalier; *m* 1937, Delia Edith (marr. diss.), 5th *d* of Capt. R. W. Travers, RN (retired); twin *d* (and one *s* decd). *Educ:* Marlborough Coll.; St John's Coll., Cambridge. BA 1931. Cadet officer, Gilbert and Ellice Islands Colony, 1932; Administrative Officer, 1936; Sec. to Government, 1935-36 and 1938-39; Asst Sec., Western Pacific High Commission, 1940-42; Asst Colonial Sec., Trinidad and Tobago, 1942-45. Fiji: Administrative Officer, Grade II, 1946, Grade I, 1947; Asst Colonial Sec., 1946-49; Colonial Secretary, Governor's Deputy and Acting Governor: Leeward Islands, 1950-57; Colonial Sec. and Acting Governor, Fiji, 1957-66; Chm., Public and Police Service Commns, 1966-71. Actg Archivist, Western Pacific Archives, 1974, 1976 and 1978. *Recreations:* swimming and deep-sea fishing. *Address:* Flat 34, St Margarets, London Road, Guildford, Surrey GU1 1TJ. *T:* Guildford 75396.

MACDONALD, Sir Peter (George), Kt 1963; DL; Hon. Life President, United Biscuits Ltd (Chairman, 1948-67) and McVitie & Price Ltd (Chairman, 1947-64); former Director: Guardian Assurance Co. Ltd, London; Caledonian Insurance Co. and other companies; Senior Partner, W. & J. Burness, retired 1976, now Consultant; *b* 20 Feb. 1898; *s* of William Macdonald, Darnaway, Forres, and Annie Cameron; *m* 1929, Rachel Irene, *d* of Rev. Dr Robert Forgan; one *s* two *d. Educ:* Forres Academy; Edinburgh Univ. Served European War, 1914-18, with Scottish Horse, Black Watch, RGA, and Lovat Scouts. Served with Home Guard, 1940-45; Regional Deferment Officer, Bd of Trade, Edinburgh and SE Scotland; Mem., Edinburgh and dist local Emergency Reconstruction Panel (chm. Food Section); Staff Officer on Scottish Regional Comr's Staff: former Mem. London Council, Inst. of Directors (formerly Chm., Scottish Br.); WS 1927. JP Edinburgh, 1935. DL Edinburgh, 1966. *Recreations:* fishing, shooting, golf. *Address:* 18 Hermitage Drive, Edinburgh EH10 6BZ. *T:* 031-447 1256. *Clubs:* Caledonian (London); Conservative (Edinburgh).

MACDONALD OF CLANRANALD, Ranald Alexander; 24th Chief and Captain of Clanranald; Chairman and Managing Director, Tektura Ltd; *b* 27 March 1934; *s* of late Captain Kenneth Macdonald of Inchkenneth, DSO, and late Marjory Broad Smith, Basingstoke; *S* kinsman as Chief of Clanranald, 1944; *m* 1961, Jane Campbell-Davys, *d* of late I. E. Campbell-Davys, Llandovey, Carms; two *s* one *d. Educ:* Christ's Hospital. Founded: Fairfix Contracts Ltd, 1963; Tektura Wallcoverings, 1970. Chm., British Contract Furnishing Assoc., 1975-76. Lieut (TA) Cameron Highlanders, 1958-63. Mem., Standing Council of Scottish Chiefs, 1957-; Director, Highland Soc. of London, 1959-80; Vice Pres., Caledonian Catholic Assoc. of London. Chief Exec., Clan Donald Lands Trust, 1978-80; Chm., Museum of the Isles, 1981-. Knight of Malta. *Recreations:* sailing, fishing. *Heir: s* Ranald Og Angus

Macdonald, younger of Clanranald, *b* 17 Sept. 1963. *Address:* 74 Upper Street, N1. *T:* 01-226 3034. *Clubs:* Turf; New; Puffin's (Edinburgh).

McDONALD, Robert Howat; *see* McDonald, Hon. Lord.

MACDONALD, Vice-Adm. Sir Roderick (Douglas), KBE 1978 (CBE 1966); retired; artist, since 1979; *b* Java, 25 Feb. 1921; *s* of Douglas and Marjorie Macdonald; *m* 1st, 1943, Joan Willis (marr. diss. 1980); two *s* (and one *s* decd); 2nd, 1980, Mrs Pamela Bartosik. *Educ:* Fettes. Entered Royal Navy, 1939. Served War: Fleet and Convoy ops throughout 1939-45 (Atlantic, Norway, Mediterranean, Eastern Fleet, East Coast and Normandy). Commanded: HMS Leeds Castle, 1953, also HMS Essington; Sen. Officer, 104th Mine-Sweeping Sqdn and HMS Walkerton, 1957 (despatches, Cyprus); HMS Falmouth, 1961; Naval Forces, Borneo, 1965 (CBE); HMS Galatea; Captain (D): Londonderry Sqdn, 1968; First Frigate Sqdn, Far East, 1969; Captain of the Fleet, 1970; HMS Bristol, 1972; COS to C-in-C, Naval Home Command, 1973-76; ADC to the Queen, 1975; COS to Comdr, Allied Naval Forces Southern Europe, 1976-79. One-man exhibitions: Naples, 1978; Edinburgh, 1980; London, 1981; works purchased by, among others, Imperial War Mus., Submarine Mus., Fleet Air Arm Mus., BP, Queen's Dragoon Guards; painted HM Queen Mother presenting new guidons to 9th/12th Royal Lancers, 1979. Younger Brother of Trinity House; Vice-Pres. and Fellow, Nautical Inst. *Address:* Ollach, Braes, Isle of Skye. *Clubs:* Caledonian; Royal Scottish Pipers Society (Edinburgh); Royal Naval Sailing Assoc.

MACDONALD, Maj.-Gen. Ronald Clarence, CB 1965; DSO 1944 and Bar, 1945; OBE 1953; Director, Griffin Farms Ltd, Wilts; *b* 1 Aug. 1911; 2nd *s* of late Col C. R. Macdonald, CMG; *m* 1939, Jessie Ross Anderson; one *s* one *d*. *Educ:* Rugby; RMC, Sandhurst. Royal Warwicks Regt: Commissioned, 1931; Comdr 2nd Bn, 1945-46; Comdr 1st Bn, 1953-55; Bn Comdr, France, Germany Campaign, 1944-45; Mil. Asst to CIGS, 1946-49; GSO1, HQ, West Africa Comd, 1950-53; Col Gen. Staff, SHAPE, 1955-56; Comdr 10th Inf. Bde Gp, 1956-59; DDI, War Office, 1959-60; Chief of Staff, HQ Middle East Comd, 1960-62; Dep. Chief of Staff, Headquarters, Allied Land Forces, Central Europe, 1962-65; retired, 1965. Col Royal Warwicks Fusiliers, 1963-68; Dep. Col (Warwicks), The Royal Regt of Fusiliers, 1968-74. *Recreation:* golf. *Address:* Grassmead, Beanacre, near Melksham, Wilts. *Club:* Army and Navy.

MACDONALD, Ronald John, CEng, MIMechE; Director-General, Royal Ordnance Factories/Production, 1974-79, retired; *b* 2 Nov. 1919; *s* of Ronald Macdonald and Sarah Jane Macdonald; *m* 1944, Joan Margaret Crew; two *s*. *Educ:* Enfield Grammar Sch.; Enfield Technical Coll. Engrg apprenticeship at Royal Small Arms Factory, Enfield, 1936-40. Army service, REME, in India, China and Hong Kong, 1943-47 (Major). Established Civil Servant, Royal Small Arms Factory, 1948; Royal Ordnance Factory, Radway Green, 1949; ROF Headquarters, Mottingham, 1953; ROF, Blackburn, 1960; Director: ROF, Birtley, Co. Durham, 1964; Ordnance Factories/Ammunition, 1972. *Address:* 72 Lincoln Park, Amersham, Bucks HP7 0DQ. *T:* Amersham 7402. *Club:* Army and Navy.

MacDONALD, Prof. Simon Gavin George, FRSE; Professor of Physics, University of Dundee, since 1973; *b* 5 Sept. 1923; *s* of Simon MacDonald and Jean H. Thomson; *m* 1948, Eva Leonie Austerlitz; one *s* one *d*. *Educ:* George Heriot's Sch., Edinburgh; Edinburgh Univ. (MA (1st Cl. Hons) Maths and Nat. Phil); PhD (St Andrews). FIP 1958, FRSE 1972. Jun. Scientific Officer, RAE, Farnborough, 1943-46; Lectr, Univ. of St Andrews, 1948-57; Senior Lecturer: University Coll. of the West Indies, 1957-62; Univ. of St Andrews, 1962-67; Visiting Prof., Ohio Univ., 1963; University of Dundee: Sen. Lectr, then Prof., 1967-; Dean of Science, 1970-73; Vice-Principal, 1974-79. Convener, Scottish Univs Council on Entrance, 1977- (Dep. Convener, 1973-77); Mem. Exec. Cttee, UCCA, 1977- (Chm., Technical Subcttee, 1979-). Chm., Bd of Dirs, Dundee Rep. Th., 1975-; Chm., Fedn of Scottish Theatres, 1978-80. *Publications:* Problems and Solutions in General Physics, 1967; Physics for Biology and Premedical Students, 1970, 2nd edn 1975; Physics for the Life and Health Sciences, 1975; articles in physics jls. *Recreations:* bridge, golf, fiction writing. *Address:* 10 Westerton Avenue, Dundee DD5 3NJ. *T:* Dundee 78692. *Club:* Royal Commonwealth Society.

MACDONALD, Rt. Rev. Thomas Brian, OBE 1970; Coadjutor Bishop of Perth, Western Australia, 1964-79, retired; *b* 25 Jan. 1911; *s* of Thomas Joseph Macdonald, MD, and Alice Daisy Macdonald; *m* 1936, Audrey May Collins; three *d*. *Educ:* Mercers' Sch., Holborn, EC. Licentiate of Theology 1932, Aust. Coll. of Theol. Deacon 1934, priest 1935, Diocese of Ballarat, Vic.; Deacon in charge of All Saints, Ballarat, 1934; Priest in charge of Landsborough, 1935; Rector of Williams, Dio. of Bunbury, 1935-39; Rector of Manjimup, WA, 1939-40. Chaplain, Australian Imperial Forces, 1940-44 (despatches). Rector of Christ Church, Claremont, Dio. of Perth, 1944-50; Chaplain of Collegiate Sch. of St Peter, Adelaide, S Australia, 1950-58; Dean of Perth, Western Australia, 1959-61; Archdeacon of Perth, 1961-63. Administrator, Diocese of Perth during 1963 and 1969. *Address:* 33 Thomas Street, Nedlands, WA 6009, Australia. *Club:* Weld (Perth).

MACDONALD, Air Vice-Marshal Thomas Conchar, CB 1962; AFC 1942; MD (retired); *b* 6 Aug. 1909; *s* of John Macdonald, MA, BSc, and Mary Jane Conchar; *m* 1937, Katharine Cairns Frew. *Educ:* Hermitage Sch.; Glasgow High Sch.; University of Glasgow; MB, ChB 1932; MD 1940; DPH (London) 1949. Joined RAF Medical Br., 1933; served in Iraq, Egypt and England, before 1939. War service included RAF Inst. of Aviation Med., Farnborough, as Asst to Consultant in Applied Physiology, 1939-41; USA and Canada, 1941-42; DPMO (Flying) Fighter Command, 1942-45; Far East, 1945-46 (despatches, AFC). Post-war appts include: PMO 2nd TAF (Germany), 1951-53; Dir of Hygiene and Research, Air Min., 1953-56 (Chm. Aero-Medical Panel of Advisory Gp for Research and Develt (AGARD) of NATO); PMO, Bomber Command, 1956-58; PMO Middle East Air Force, 1958-61; PMO Technical Training Command, RAF, 1961-66. Air Vice-Marshal, 1961. QHP 1961-66; CStJ 1961. *Publications:* contributions to various med. jls. *Recreations:* sailing, fishing. *Address:* Wakeners Wood, Midhurst Road, Haslemere, Surrey. *T:* Haslemere 3685. *Club:* Royal Air Force.

McDONALD, William, CA; JP; Chamberlain since 1962, and Secretary since 1971, Company of Merchants of City of Edinburgh; *b* 9 Nov. 1929; yr *s* of late Joseph McDonald and Margaret Pringle (*née* Gibb); *m* 1956, Anne Kidd Laird Donald; one *s* one *d*. *Educ:* Perth Acad. Sec., South Mills and Grampian Investment, Dundee, 1957-62. Jt Sec., Scottish Council of Independent Schs, 1978-; Dep. Chief Comr for Scotland, Scout Assoc., 1977-79. *Recreations:* Scout Association, bridge, golf. *Address:* 4/5 West Grange Gardens, Edinburgh EH9 2RA. *T:* 031-668 1845. *Club:* New (Edinburgh).

McDONALD, Hon. Sir William (John Farquhar), Kt 1958; *b* 3 Oct. 1911; *s* of John Nicholson McDonald and Sarah McDonald (*née* McInnes); *m* 1935, Evelyn Margaret Koch; two *d*. *Educ:* Scotch Coll., Adelaide, South Australia. Served AIF, 1939-45, Capt. Councillor, Shire of Kowree, 1946-61. MLA, electorate of Dundas, Victoria, 1947-52, 1955-70; Speaker, Legislative Assembly, Victoria, 1955-67; Minister of Lands, Soldier Settlement, and for Conservation, 1967-70. Mem., Exec. Council, Victoria. Trustee, Shrine of Remembrance, 1955-70. Victoria State Pres., Poll Shorthorn Soc. of Aust., 1962-72; Trustee, Royal Agricultural Soc. of Victoria, 1968-. Trustee, Victoria Amateur Turf Club, 1969. *Address:* Brippick, 102 St Georges Road, Toorak, Vic. 3142, Australia. *T:* 241 5839. *Clubs:* Hamilton (Hamilton, Victoria); Australian, Naval and Military (Melbourne).

MACDONALD, Air Chief Marshal Sir William (Laurence Mary), GCB 1965 (KCB 1959; CB 1956); CBE 1946; DFC 1940; *b* 10 Aug. 1908; *s* of William Stephen Macdonald, Co. Cork; *m* 1939, Diana (*d* 1964), *d* of late Nicholas Challacombe; one *s* one *d*. *Educ:* Castleknock Coll., Eire. Joined RAF 1929; Group Capt., 1942; Air Commodore, 1944; Air Vice-Marshal, 1954; Air Marshal, 1960; Air Chief Marshal, 1963. Served War of 1939-45, France, Belgium, Holland, Germany (despatches twice, DFC, CBE). Comdt, Central Flying Sch., 1946-48; Exchange Officer with USAF, USA, 1948-50; Dep. Dir of Plans (Jt Planning), Air Min., 1952; AOC, RAF, Singapore, 1952-54; Asst Chief of Air Staff (Intelligence), 1954-58; Comdr-in-Chief, Middle East, Air Force, 1958-62, and Administrator of the Sovereign Base Areas of Akrotiri and Dhekelia, Cyprus, 1960-62; Air Sec., Ministry of Defence (formerly Air Ministry), 1962-66. Air ADC to the Queen, 1965-66. Vice-Pres., Oratory Sch. Chevalier, Legion of Honour; Croix de Guerre; Star of Jordan 1st Class. *Address:* Quarry House, Yateley, Camberley, Surrey. *T:* 873283. *Club:* East India, Devonshire, Sports and Public Schools.

MACDONALD, Prof. William Weir, PhD, DSc; FIBiol; Selwyn Lloyd Professor of Medical Entomology, Liverpool School of Tropical Medicine, since 1980; *b* 5 Dec. 1927; *s* of William Sutherland Macdonald and Ina Weir; *m* 1950, Margaret Lawrie; two *d*. *Educ:* Univ. of Glasgow (BSc 1948). MSc 1964, PhD 1965, Univ. of Liverpool; DSc 1973, Univ. of Glasgow; FIBiol 1966. Strang-Steel Scholar, Glasgow Univ., 1948; Colonial Office Res. Scholar, 1949-50; Entomologist, E African Fisheries Res. Org., Uganda, 1950-52; Res. Fellow, Inst. for Med. Res., Kuala Lumpur, 1953-60; Lectr, Sen. Lectr, and Reader, Liverpool Sch. of Trop. Medicine, 1960-76; Prof. of Med. Entomology, London Sch. of Hygiene and Trop. Medicine, 1977-80. Consultant: WHO; various overseas govts; Hon. Consultant on Entomology to the Army. Chalmers Medal, Royal Soc. of Trop. Medicine and Hygiene, 1972. *Publications:* papers on med. entomology in scientific jls. *Recreations:* golf, gardening. *Address:* 10 Headland Close, West Kirby, Merseyside L48 3JP. *T:* 051-625 7857. *Club:* Savage.

MacDONALD SCOTT, Mary, (Mrs Michael MacDonald Scott); *see* Lavin, Mary.

MACDONALD-SMITH, Maj.-Gen. Hugh, CB 1977; Director, Telecommunications Engineering and Manufacturing Association, since 1981 (Secretary to Council, 1979-80); *b* 8 Jan. 1923; *s* of Alexander and Ada Macdonald-Smith; *m* 1947, Désirée Violet (*née* Williamson); one *s* one *d* (and one *d* decd). *Educ:* Llanelli Grammar Sch.; Llandovery Coll.; Birmingham Univ. BSc. CEng, FIMechE, FIEE. Commissioned REME, 1944; served: India, 1945-47; Singapore, 1956-58; BAOR, 1961-63; Technical Staff Course, 1949-51; Staff Coll., Camberley, 1953; Lt-Col, 1963; Dir, Electrical and Mechanical Engineering, HQ Western Comd, 1963-65; Asst Mil. Sec., MoD, 1965-66; Comd REME, 1 (BR) Corps Troops, 1966-67; Technical Gp, REME, 1967-72; Col, 1967; Brig. 1970; Dep. Dir, Electrical and Mechanical Engineering (Eng. Pol.), (Army), 1972-75; Dir, later Dir Gen., Electrical and Mech. Engrg (Army), 1975-78; retired 1978. Col Comdt, REME, 1978-82; Rep. Col Comdt, REME, 1979-80. Mem., Cttee of Inquiry into Engrg

Profession, 1977-79. Mem. Council, IMechE, 1975-76. *Recreations:* golf, gardening, photography. *Address:* c/o Lloyds Bank Ltd, Llanelli.

MACDONALD-SMITH, Sydney, CMG 1956; retired; *b* 9 July 1908; *s* of late John Alfred Macdonald-Smith, MB, ChB, FRCSE; *m* 1st, 1935, Joyce (*d* 1966), *d* of Austen Whetham, Bridport, Dorset; one *s* one *d*; 2nd, 1968, Winifred Mary Atkinson, JP, *widow* of Captain T. K. W. Atkinson, RN. *Educ:* Nottingham High Sch.; New Coll., Oxford. Entered Colonial Administrative Service, Nigeria, 1931; Controller of Imports, 1945; Director of Supplies, 1947; Under-Sec., Gold Coast, 1949; Permanent Sec. Ministry of Communications and Works, 1950; Chief Regional Officer, Northern Territories, 1954-57; retired Nov. 1957. *Recreation:* gardening. *Address:* Woodman's, Westbourne, Emsworth, Hants. *T:* Emsworth 2943.

McDONAUGH, James, CBE 1970 (OBE 1965); retired 1973; reappointed 1973-75, Director North Europe Department, British Council; *b* 26 July 1912; *s* of late Edward McDonaugh and late Christina, *d* of William Bissell; *m* 1944, Mary-Eithné Mitchell, *d* of James Vyvyan Mitchell; three *s* two *d*. *Educ:* Royal Grammar Sch., Worcester; St Edmund Hall, Oxford (Exhibitioner, MA). Asst Master, Ampleforth Coll., 1935-40; War Service, 1940-45; Lecturer, Graz and Innsbruck Univs, 1947-50; Asst Rep., British Council, Austria, 1950-54; Representative, Malta, 1954-58; Dep. Counsellor (Cultural), Bonn, 1958-59; Dep. Rep., Germany, 1958-61; Dir Specialist Tours Dept, 1961-65; Asst Controller, Education Div., 1965; Rep., Germany, 1966-73. *Address:* Old Rectory Cottage, Whitestaunton, Chard, Somerset.

MacDONELL OF GLENGARRY, Air Cdre Aeneas Ranald Donald, CB 1964; DFC 1940; Hereditary 22nd Chief of Glengarry; *b* 15 Nov. 1913; *e s* of late Ranald MacDonell of Glengarry, CBE; *m* 1st, Diana Dorothy (*d* 1980), *yr d* of late Henry Keane, CBE; two *s* one *d*; 2nd, Lois Eirene Frances, *d* of Rev. Gerald Champion Streatfeild; one *s* one *d*. *Educ:* Hurstpierpoint Coll.; Royal Air Force Coll., Cranwell. No 54 Fighter Sqdn, 1934; Fleet Air Arm, 1935-37; Flying Instructor, 1938-39; Air Ministry, 1939-40; No 64 Fighter Sqdn, 1940-41; POW, 1941-45; Ministry of Defence, 1946-47; HQ Flying Training Command, 1947-49; Chief Flying Instructor, RAF Coll., Cranwell, 1949-51; Ministry of Defence, 1952-54; Senior RAF Instructor, Joint Services Staff Coll., 1954-56; Air Attaché, Moscow, 1956-58; Dir of Management and Work Study, Ministry of Defence, Air Force Dept, 1960-64, retd. *Recreations:* ciné photography, art, travel. *Address:* Elonbank, 23 Castle Street, Fortrose, Ross-shire IV10 8TH. *T:* Fortrose 20121. *Club:* Royal Air Force.

McDONNELL, family name of **Earl of Antrim.**

McDONNELL, Christopher Thomas; Assistant Under-Secretary of State, Ministry of Defence, since 1976; *b* 3 Sept. 1931; *s* of Christopher Patrick McDonnell and Jane McDonnell; *m* 1955, Patricia Anne (*née* Harvey) (*d* 1967); three *s* one *d*. *Educ:* St Francis Xavier's Coll., Liverpool; Corpus Christi Coll., Oxford (MA). WO, 1954; HM Treasury, 1966-68; RCDS, 1973. *Address:* 37 Dale Road, Purley, Surrey. *T:* 01-660 5040.

McDONNELL, Denis Lane, OBE 1945; **His Honour Judge McDonnell;** a Circuit Judge (formerly a County Court Judge), since 1967; *b* 2 March 1914; *o c* of late David McDonnell, LLD and Mary Nora (*née* Lane), Riversdale, Sundays Well, Cork and Fairy Hill, Monkstown, Co. Cork and *gs* of Denny Lane, poet and Young Irelander; *m* 1940, Florence Nina (Micky), *d* of late Lt-Col Hugh T. Ryan, DSO and Clare Emily (*née* Conry), Castle View, Ballincollig, Co. Cork; three *d* (and one *s* one *d* decd). *Educ:* Christian Brothers' Coll., Cork; Ampleforth Coll.; Sidney Sussex Coll., Cambridge (MA). Served in RAFVR, Equipment and Admin. and Special Duties Branches, 1940-45 in UK and with No. 84 Gp in NW Europe (Wing Comdr). Called to Bar, Middle Temple, 1936; Bencher, 1965. Practised at Bar, 1938-40 and 1946-67. Hon. Sec., Council of HM Circuit Judges, 1979-. *Publications:* Kerr on Fraud and Mistake (7th edn, with J. G. Monroe), 1952; titles on carriage in: Encyclopædias of Forms and Precedents and Court Forms and Precedents; Halsbury's Laws of England; articles in British Tax Review. *Recreations:* family life, listening to music, golf, gardening. *Address:* Westminster County Court, 82 St Martins Lane, WC2. *Clubs:* Piltdown Golf, Rye Golf, Woking Golf, Royal Cinque Ports Golf.

McDONNELL, John; Chair of Finance and General Purposes Committee, Greater London Council, since 1982; *b* 8 Sept. 1951; *s* of Robert and Elsie McDonnell; *m* 1971, Marilyn Jean Cooper; two *d*. *Educ:* Great Yarmouth Grammar Sch.; Burnley Technical Coll.; Brunel Univ. (BSc); Birkbeck Coll., Univ. of London (MSc Politics and Sociology). Prodn worker, 1968-72; Research Assistant: NUM, 1976-78; TUC, 1978-82; full-time GLC Councillor, Hayes and Harlington, 1982-. Housefather (pt-time) of family unit, children's home, 1972-. *Recreations:* gardening, reading, cycling; generally fermenting the overthrow of capitalism. *Address:* 15 Mulberry Parade, West Drayton, Mddx UB7 9AE. *T:* West Drayton 42775.

McDOUGALL, Archibald, MA, BCL; Attorney at Law and landowner, USA; *b* Hobart, 5 Aug. 1903; 2nd *s* of late Emeritus Prof. Dugald Gordon McDougall and Helen Ione Atkinson; *m* 1932, Corinne Margaret Cunningham Collins, artist (*d* 1977), Mobile, Alabama, and Washington, DC, USA. *Educ:* Hutchins Sch., Hobart; University of Tasmania; Balliol Coll., Oxford; Columbia Univ., New York. BA Tasmania, and Rhodes Scholar, 1924; 1st Class Final Honour Sch. of Jurisprudence, 1926; Proxime Accessit

Vinerian Law Scholarship, 1927; 2nd Class Examination for BCL 1927; Commonwealth Fund Fellowship, 1927-29; US Senate Legislative Counsel's Office, Washington, DC 1928; Harmsworth Law Scholarship, 1929; Lecturer in Law, Victoria Univ. of Manchester, 1931-35; called to Bar, Middle Temple, 1932; Mem. of Northern Circuit; practised in Chancery Div. of High Court and in Chancery of County Palatine of Lancaster, 1932-35; Examiner in Law, London Univ., 1934-35; 1936-40 Legal Adviser to Iraqi Ministry for Foreign Affairs, Baghdad, and Prof. of Int. Law at Iraqi Law Sch.; Delegate of Iraq at 17th Assembly of League of Nations, 1936; 1940 travelled extensively through India, Burma, Malaya, NEI, and Australia; Counsel, British Purchasing Commission, New York, 1940-41; Head, Non-Ferrous Metals Div., British Raw Materials Mission, Washington, DC, and UK Staff of Combined Raw Materials Board, 1941-43; Combined Production and Resources Board (UK Staff), Washington, DC, 1944-45; Head of UK Economic Group, US Dept of Commerce and British Embassy, Washington, DC, to Aug. 1946; Legal Counsellor, British Embassy, Cairo, 1946-49; Asst Legal Adviser, Foreign Office, 1949-50. Dep. Comr of Forfeited and Delinquent Lands, 1964-. Pres., Berkeley County Bar Assoc., 1964-65; Member: American Bar Assoc.; W Virginia State Bar; W Virginia Bar Assoc.; Sustaining Mem., Assoc., of Trial Lawyers, USA; admitted US Supreme Court Bar and Fourth Circuit Court of Appeals, 1973. Founder, Trial Lawyers for Public Justice, 1982; Governor, W Va Legal Services Plan, Inc., 1982. Mem. Emeritus, Amer. Soc. Internat. Law, 1978 (Mem., 1928-). Judge, Philip C. Jessup Internat. Law Moot Court Competition, Washington, DC, 1978-. Mem., Historic House Assoc. of America, 1980-, Owners' Gp, 1981-. *Publications:* Modern Conveyancing, 1936; and articles in British Year Book of International Law. *Recreation:* motoring. *Address:* Oban Hall, Gerrardstown, West Virginia 25420, USA. *T:* Area Code 304,229-5400.

MacDOUGALL OF MacDOUGALL, Madam; (Coline Helen Elizabeth); 30th Chief of Clan MacDougall, 1953; *b* 17 Aug. 1904; *e d* of Col Alexander J. MacDougall of MacDougall, 29th Chief, and Mrs Colina Edith MacDougall of MacDougall; *m* 1949, Leslie Grahame-Thomson (who assumed the surname of MacDougall, 1953), RSA, FRIBA, PPRIAS, FSAScot (*d* 1974); resumed surname of MacDougall of MacDougall on succession to Chiefship, 1953. *Educ:* St James's, West Malvern. Served WRNS (Second Officer), 1941-46. *Address:* Dunollie Castle, Oban, Argyll. *T:* Oban 2012.

MacDOUGALL, Brig. David Mercer, CMG 1946; MA; *b* 1904; *m* 1st, 1929, Catherine Crowther; one *d*; 2nd, 1951, Inez Weir, *o d* of late James Hislop Thompson; two *d*. *Educ:* St Andrews Univ. Cadet Hong Kong Administrative Service, 1928; seconded to Colonial Office as asst principal, Feb. 1937-March 1939; seconded Hong Kong Dept of Information and Sec. Far Eastern Bureau of British Ministry of Information, Oct. 1939; Colonial Office, 1942; British Embassy, Washington, DC, 1943; Dir British Political Warfare Mission, San Francisco, Dec. 1943; Colonial Office, 1944; Brig. Chief Civil Affairs Officer, Hong Kong, 1945; Colonial Sec., Hong Kong, 1946-49; retired, 1949; Order of the Brilliant Star (China), 1946. *Address:* Mercers, Finchingfield, Essex; Blackhill, By Aberfeldy, Perthshire.

MacDOUGALL, Sir (George) Donald (Alastair), Kt 1953; CBE 1945 (OBE 1942); FBA 1966; Chief Economic Adviser, Confederation of British Industry, since 1973; *b* 26 Oct. 1912; *s* of late Daniel Douglas MacDougall, Glasgow, and late Beatrice Amy Miller; *m* 1st, 1937, Bridget Christabel Bartrum (marr. diss. 1977); one *s* one *d*; 2nd, 1977, Margaret Hall (*see* L. M. MacDougall). *Educ:* Kelvinside Acad., Glasgow; Shrewsbury Sch.; Balliol Coll., Oxford. George Webb Medley Junior (1934) and Senior (1935) Scholarships in Political Economy; Asst Lecturer (later Lecturer) in Economics, University of Leeds, 1936-39; First Lord of the Admiralty's Statistical Branch, 1939-40; Prime Minister's Statistical Branch, 1940-45 (Chief Asst, 1942-45). Work on Reparations and German Industry, Moscow and Berlin, 1945; Mem. of Heavy Clothing Industry Working Party, 1946; Official Fellow of Wadham Coll., Oxford, 1945-50, Domestic Bursar, 1946-48, Hon. Fellow, 1964-; Econ. Dir, OEEC, Paris, 1948-49; Faculty Fellow, Nuffield Coll., 1947-50, Professorial Fellow, 1950-52, Official Fellow, 1952-64, First Bursar, 1958-64, Hon. Fellow, 1967-; Nuffield Reader in Internat. Economics, Oxford Univ., 1950-52; Chief Adviser, Prime Minister's Statistical Branch, 1951-53; Visiting Prof., Australian Nat. Univ., 1959; MIT Center for Internat. Studies, New Delhi, 1961; Dir, Investing in Success Equities, Ltd, 1959-62; Economic Dir, NEDC, 1962-64; Mem. Turnover Tax Cttee, 1963-64; Dir-Gen., Dept of Economic Affairs, 1964-68; Head of Govt Economic Service, and Chief Economic Adviser to the Treasury, 1969-73. Mem. Council, Royal Econ. Soc., 1950- (Hon. Sec., 1958-70; Vice-Pres., 1970-72, 1974-; Pres., 1972-74); Pres., Soc. for Long Range Planning, 1977-, Vice-Pres., 1968-77; Vice-Pres., Soc. of Business Economists, 1978-; Chm., Exec. Cttee NIESR, 1974-; Mem., EEC Study Gp on Economic and Monetary Union, 1974-75; Chm., EEC Study Gp on Role of Public Finance in European Economic Integration, 1975-77. Hon. LLD Strathclyde, 1968; Hon. LittD Leeds, 1971; Hon. DSc Aston in Birmingham, 1979. *Publications:* (part author) Measures for International Economic Stability, UN, 1951; The World Dollar Problem, 1957; (part author) The Fiscal System of Venezuela, 1959; The Dollar Problem: A Reappraisal, 1960; Studies in Political Economy (2 vols), 1975; contrib. to Britain in Recovery, 1938, Lessons of the British War Economy, 1951, and to various economic and statistical jls. *Address:* 86A Denbigh Street, Westminster, SW1V 2EX. *T:* 01-821 1998. *Club:* Reform.

MacDOUGALL, Air Cdre Ian Neil, CBE 1964; DFC 1942; Galt Glass Laminates Ltd, since 1977; b 11 June 1920; s of late Archibald MacDougall, Colonial Service, and Helen Grace (née Simpson); m 1944, Dorothy Eleanor, d of late John Frankland; one s one d. Educ: Morrison's Academy, Crieff; RAF Coll., Cranwell. Commnd Sept. 1939; served in Fighter Sqdns in Battle of Britain, Syrian and Western Desert Campaigns, Malta and in invasions of Sicily and Normandy; War Studies Lectr at RAF Coll., 1948-50 and USAF Academy, Colorado, 1956-58; Asst Air Attaché, Paris, 1950-53; Chief Flying Instructor, RAF Coll., 1953-56; Supt of Flying, Boscombe Down, 1959-62; comd RAF Fighter Stn, Binbrook, 1962-64; SASO 38 Gp, 1964-67; comd Zambian Expedn and Zambian Oil Lift, 1965-66; Air Attaché, Paris, 1967-69; jssc, psc, pfc, cfs; retd Dec. 1969. Mil. Liaison, Rolls Royce and Bristol Composite Materials Ltd, 1970-77. Recreation: fishing. Address: Batts Lane Cottage, East Grafton, Marlborough, Wilts SN8 3DB. T: Marlborough 810482. Club: Royal Air Force.

MacDOUGALL, Laura Margaret, (Lady MacDougall); Hon. Fellow of Somerville College, Oxford, since 1975; Consultant to National Economic Development Office; Economic Consultant to Distillers Co. Ltd; d of George E. Linfoot and Laura Edith Clayton; m 1932, Robert L. Hall (now Lord Roberthall) (marr. diss. 1968); two d ; m 1977, Sir Donald MacDougall, qv. Educ: Sheffield Girls' High Sch. and High Storrs Grammar Sch.; Somerville Coll., Oxford. Hon. Scholar, 1st Cl. Hons Philosophy, Politics and Economics; Jun. George Webb Medley Scholar. US Govt Office of Price Admin, 1941-44; UNNRA Planning Div., Washington, DC, Sydney and London, 1944-45; Lectr, Lincoln Coll., Oxford, 1946-47; Lectr, 1947-49, and Fellow and Tutor, 1949-75, Somerville Coll., Oxford; University Lectr in Economics, 1949-75. Member: Treasury Purchase Tax Cttee, 1954; Interdeptal Cttee on Economic and Social Research, 1957-58; Gaitskell Indep. Co-operative Commn, 1958; Min. of Ag. Cttee on the Remuneration of Milk Distributors in the UK, 1962; Reith Indep. Commn on Advertising, 1964; Covent Garden Market Authority Adv. Cttee, 1972; Distributive Trades Industrial Trng Bd's Research Cttee, 1972; EDC for Distributive Trades, 1963-75; Monopolies and Mergers Commn, 1973-76; Past Member: Retail Furnishing and Allied Trades Wages Council; Retail Newsagency, Confectioner and Tobacconist Wages Council. Visiting Prof. MIT, USA, 1961-62. Hon. LLD Nottingham, 1979. Publications: US Senate Cttee Print, Effect of War on British Retail Trade, 1943; Distributive Trading: an economic analysis, 1954; Distribution in Great Britain and North America (with Knapp and Winsten), 1961; contribs to: The British Economy, 1945-50, 1962; The British Economy in the 1950s, 1962; (Bolton Cttee, Research Report No 8) The Small Unit in Retail Trade, 1972; numerous contribs to various economic and statistical jls. Address: 86A Denbigh Street, Westminster, SW1V 2EX. T: 01-821 1998.

MACDOUGALL, Neil; Hon. Mr Justice Macdougall; a Judge of the High Court of Hong Kong, since 1980; b 13 March 1932; s of Norman Macdougall and Gladys Clare Kennerly. Educ: Aquinas Coll., Perth, WA; Univ. of Western Australia (LLB 1954). Admitted Barrister and Solicitor of Supreme Court, WA, 1957, and of High Court of Australia, 1958; Solicitor of Supreme Court of England, 1976, and of Supreme Court of Hong Kong, 1977. Crown Counsel, Hong Kong, 1965; Director of Public Prosecutions, Hong Kong, 1978. Recreations: classical music, study of natural history, long distance running. Address: 8B Severn Road, The Peak, Hong Kong. T: 5-97077. Clubs: Hong Kong, Australian, Jockey (all in Hong Kong).

McDOUGALL, Richard Sedgwick, CBE 1957; FCA; b 29 May 1904; o s of late R. E. C. McDougall and Evelyn Mary, d of Richard Sedgwick; m 1929, Margaret Sylvia (d 1976), d of late John Charles Denmead; two d. Educ: Haileybury Coll. County Treasurer, Hertfordshire County Council, 1939-57; General Manager, Stevenage Development Corporation, 1957-67. Member: Weeks Cttee on Army Works Services, 1956-57; Colonial Secretary's Advisory Cttee on Local Govt, 1950-; North West Metropolitan Regional Hosp. Bd, 1963-68; Chm., Building Research Station Steering Cttee, 1967-70. For British Govt, visited Sierra Leone, 1950, Nyasaland, 1954, Fiji Islands, 1957, and Kenya, 1967. Recreation: painting. Address: Firbank, 9 Moorside Road, West Moors, Wimborne, Dorset BH22 0EH.

McDOWALL, Dr David William; Director, Polytechnic of North London, since 1980 (Assistant Director, 1979); b 2 April 1930; o s of late William MacDowall and late Lilian May MacDowall (née Clarkson); m 1962, Mione Beryl, yr d of late Ernest Harold Lashmar and Dora Lashmar; two d. Educ: Liverpool Inst.; Corpus Christi Coll., Oxford; British Sch. at Rome. MA, DPhil; FSA, FRAS. Hugh Oldham Scholar 1947, Pelham Student in Roman History 1951; Barclay Head Prize for Ancient Numismatics, 1953 and 1956. 2nd Lieut Royal Signals, 1952. Asst Principal, Min. of Works, 1955; Asst Keeper, Dept of Coins and Medals, British Museum, 1956; Principal, Min. of Educn, 1960; Principal, Univ. Grants Cttee, 1965; Asst Sec. 1970; Master of Univ. Coll., Durham, 1973. Hon. Treas., Royal Numismatic Soc., 1966-73; Hon. Sec., Soc. for Afghan Studies, 1972-. Publications: Coin Collections, their preservation, classification and presentation, 1978; The Western Coinages of Nero, 1979; articles in Numismatic Chron., J Numismatic Soc. India, Schweizer Münzblätter, Acta Numismatica, S Asian Archaeology, Afghan Studies, Mithraic Studies, The Archaeology of Afghanistan, etc. Recreations: travel, antiquities, photography, natural history, gardening. Address: Admont, Dancers End, Tring, Herts. Club: Athenæum.

McDOWALL, Keith Desmond; Director of Information, Confederation of British Industry, since 1981; b 3 Oct. 1929; s of William Charteris McDowall and Edna Florence McDowall; m 1957, Shirley Margaret Russell Astbury; two d. Educ: Heath Clark Sch., Croydon, Surrey. Served RAF, National Service, 1947-49. South London Press, 1947-55; Daily Mail, 1955-67: Indust. Corresp., 1958; Indust. Editor, 1961-67; Man. Dir, Inca Construction (UK) Co. Ltd, 1967-69; Govt Information Service: successively Chief Inf. Officer, DEA, BoT, Min. of Housing and Local Govt, DoE, and Home Office, 1969-72; Dir of Inf., NI Office, 1972-74; Dir of Inf., Dept of Employment, 1974-78; Man. Dir Public Affairs, British Shipbuilders, 1978-80. Dir, Govan Shipbuilders Ltd, 1978-80. Publications: articles in newspapers and various pubns. Recreations: sailing, tennis, mingling. Address: Confederation of British Industry, Centre Point, 103 New Oxford Street, WC1A 1DU. Clubs: Reform; Medway Yacht (Rochester).

McDOWALL, Robert John Stewart, DSc, MD, MRCP; FRCPE; Professor Emeritus in the University of London since 1959; Professor of Physiology, 1923-59, and Dean of Faculty of Medicine and Fellow of King's College, London; Vice-Chairman Medical Advisory Committee and Founder Member, Asthma Research Council; Formerly Examiner for Universities of London, Leeds, Durham, Manchester, Aberdeen, St Andrews, Edinburgh, Sheffield, Bristol, West Indies, Nigeria, RCP, RCS, in India, Egypt, Australasia, and Eire; b 1892; s of Robert McDowall, Auchengaillie, Wigtonshire, and Fanny Grace Stewart; m 1st, 1921, Jessie (d 1963), yr d of Alexander Macbeth, JP, Pitlochry, Perthshire; two d ; 2nd, 1964, Dr Jean Rotherham, d of Col Ewan Rotherham, TD, DL (Warwickshire). Educ: Watson's Coll., Edinburgh; University of Edinburgh (Gold Medal for MD thesis). Assistant and Lecturer in Physiology, University of Edinburgh, 1919-21; Lectr, Experimental Physiology and Experimental Pharmacology, Univ. of Leeds, 1921-23; Lectr in Applied Physiology, London Sch. of Hygiene, 1927-29. Ellis prizeman, 1920; Parkin prizeman, RCP, Edinburgh, 1930; Gunning Victoria Jubilee Cullen Prize, RCP, Edinburgh, 1938; Arris and Gale Lectr, RCS, 1933; Oliver Sharpey Lectr, RCP, 1941; medal of honour, Univ. of Ghent, 1951; has given 3 lecture tours of America. Hon. Fellow: Amer. Acad. of Allergy, 1953; Soc. Française d'Allergie, 1957; European Acad. of Allergy; Finnish Acad. of Allergy. Pres. 4th European Congress of Allergy, 1959; Hon. Mem., British Soc. of Allergy; Extraordinary Mem., British Cardiac Soc. Has been Resident House Physician, Edinburgh Royal Infirmary, and Clinical Tutor in Medicine, Univ. of Edinburgh; served with RAMC, European War, 1914-18, also 1940-41; became DADMS for British Forces in Palestine, Syria, and Cilicia; President, Physiology Sect. British Assoc., 1936; Chairman Board of Intermediate Medical Studies and of Physiology, University of London. Publications: Clinical Physiology; The Science of Signs and Symptoms in relation to Modern Diagnosis and Treatment, 4 editions; Handbook of Physiology, 13 editions; The Control of the Circulation of the Blood, 1938, 1957; The Whiskies of Scotland, 1967, 3rd edn 1975 (Swedish, German, Spanish and American edns); Editor, The Mind, by various authors; Sane Psychology, 6 reprints; Anatomy and Physiology for students of Physiotherapy (with Smout) and numerous scientific papers. Recreations: chess, curling (1st President, Hampstead Curling Club; 1st President, London Watsonian Curling Club; former Pres. and Hon. Mem., Province of London; skipped England against Scotland, 1966 and 1969); golf (Ex-Captain, Life Mem. and Director, Hampstead Golf Club). Address: 34 Park Drive, NW11. T: 01-455 2858.

See also J. K. Rotherham.

McDOWALL, Robert William, CBE 1977 (OBE 1966); FSA (Lond.); Secretary, Royal Commission on Historical Monuments (England), 1973-79; b 13 May 1914; yr s of Rev. C. R. L. McDowall; m 1939, Avril Betty Everard Hannaford; three s one d. Educ: Eton; Magdalene Coll., Cambridge (MA). Investigator, Royal Commission on Historical Monuments (England), 1936. Served War, with Royal Engineers, 1939-45. Vis. Lectr, UCL, 1979. Mem., Ancient Monuments Bd for England, 1973-79; Pres., Surrey Archaeological Soc., 1975-80; Vice-Pres., Royal Archaeol Inst., 1980. Publications: contributor to: Monuments Threatened or Destroyed, 1963; Peterborough New Town, 1969; Shielings and Bastles, 1970; Recording Old Houses, 1980; County Inventories of RCHM; Archaeologia, Antiquaries Jl (and local archaeological jls). Address: Chandlers, Ballsdown, Chiddingfold, Surrey. T: Wormley 2995.

McDOWELL, Sir Frank (Schofield), Kt 1967; President, McDowells Holdings Ltd, 1971-72 (Chairman and Managing Director, McDowells Ltd, 1935-67, Chairman 1967); b 8 Aug. 1889; s of John McDowell; m 1912, Ethel Sophia Perrott; six s one d. Educ: Petersham Public School. Grand Master: United Grand Lodge of NSW Freemasons, 1947-49; Mark Master Masons NSW, 1946-48; Inspector General, 33rd Rose Croix SE Central District NSW, 1967-72. Recreations: bowls, garden, swimming. Address: Melrose, 157 Ewos Parade, Cronulla, Sydney, NSW 2230, Australia. T: 5235115. Clubs: (Hon. Mem.) All Nations, (Patron) Retailers, (Past Pres.) Sydney Rotary (Sydney); (Patron) South Cronulla Bowling.

McDOWELL, Sir Henry (McLorinan), KBE 1964 (CBE 1959); retired; b Johannesburg, S Africa, 10 Dec. 1910; s of John McDowell and Margaret Elizabeth Bingham; m 1939, Norah, d of Walter Slade Douthwaite; one s one d. Educ: Witwatersrand Univ.; Queen's Coll., Oxford; Yale Univ. Served War of 1939-45, 1 Bn Northern Rhodesia Regt, East Africa and South-East Asia, 1940-44. Entered HM Colonial Service (Cadet, Northern Rhodesia), 1938; Clerk, Legislative and Executive Councils, 1945; Assistant Secretary,

1950; Deputy Financial Secretary, 1952. Imperial Defence Coll., 1948; seconded Colonial Office, 1949. Economic and Financial Working Party, in preparation for federation of Rhodesias and Nyasaland, 1953; Federal Treasury, 1954; Secretary, Ministry of Transport, 1955; Secretary, Federal Treasury, 1959-63. Chm., Zimbabwe Board, Barclays Bank Internat. Ltd, 1969-79; Chm. or Dir, other cos in Zimbabwe, 1964-79. Chancellor, Univ. of Zimbabwe, 1971-81; Chm. or Mem., governing bodies, educational institutions, Zimbabwe, 1964-79. Hon. LLD Witwatersrand, 1971; Hon. DLitt Rhodesia, 1975. *Recreations:* walking, reading. *Address:* 2 Donne Court, Burbage Road, SE24. *Club:* Salisbury.

MACDUFF, Earl of; David Charles Carnegie; *b* 3 March 1961; *s* and *heir* of 3rd Duke of Fife, *qv.* BA Cantab 1982.

MacEACHEN, Hon. Allan Joseph, PC (Canada); MP (L) Cape Breton Highlands-Canso, Nova Scotia, since 1953; Deputy Prime Minister, 1977-79, and since 1980; Secretary of State for External Affairs, since 1982; *b* Inverness, Nova Scotia, 6 July 1921; *s* of Angus and Annie MacEachen. *Educ:* St Francis Xavier Univ. (BA 1944); Univ. of Toronto (MA 1946); Univ. of Chicago; MIT. Prof. of Economics, St Francis Xavier Univ., 1946-48; Head of Dept of Economics and Social Sciences; Special Asst and Consultant on Econ. Affairs to Hon. Lester Pearson, 1958; Minister: of Labour, 1963-65; of Nat. Health and Welfare, 1965-68; of Manpower and Immigration, 1968-70; of External Affairs, 1974-76; of Finance, 1980-82; Pres., Privy Council and Govt Leader in House of Commons, Canada, 1970-74 and 1976-79; Dep. Leader of the Opposition and Opposition House Leader, 1979-80. Hon. Degrees: St Francis Xavier Univ.; Acadia Univ.; Loyola Coll; St Mary's Univ.; Dalhousie Univ.; Wilfrid Laurier Univ. *Address:* Parliament Buildings, Ottawa, Ont, Canada.

McELDERRY, Samuel Burnside Boyd, CMG 1935; *b* 7 Oct. 1885; *s* of late Thomas McElderry and late Alice Knox of Ballymoney, Co. Antrim; *m* 1913, Mildred Mary Orme (*d* 1974); three *d. Educ:* Campbell Coll., Belfast; Trinity Coll., Dublin. Eastern Cadet, 1909; Hong Kong Administrative Service, 1909-28; Deputy Chief Secretary, Tanganyika, 1929-33; Chief Secretary, Zanzibar, 1933-40; retired 1940; attached to office of High Commissioner for Basutoland, Bechuanaland Protectorate and Swaziland (Pretoria and Cape Town), 1940-45; temporarily employed Colonial Office, 1945-46. Member of Council, Royal Commonwealth Society for Blind, 1951-70; Royal National Institute for Blind, 1958-70. *Address:* Fircroft, 19 Kivernell Road, Milford-on-Sea, Lymington, Hants.

See also W. Wenban-Smith.

McELENEY, Most Rev. John, SJ, DD; PhD; MA; Archbishop of Kingston (Jamaica), 1967-70; *b* 13 Nov. 1895; *s* of Charles McEleney and Bridget McEleney (*née* McGaffigan). *Educ:* Woburn Public Sch.; Weston Coll.; Boston Coll. Entered Soc. of Jesus at Yonkers, New York; classical studies at St Andrew on Hudson, 1920-21; Philosophy, Weston Coll. (MA), 1921-23. Teacher, Ateneo de Manila, 1923-27; Theology, 1927-31; formerly: Rector, Shadowbrook Jesuit Novitiate, Lenox, Mass; Rector, Prep. Sch., Fairfield, Conn; Tutor Ateneo de Manila Jesuit Coll., Manila; Provincial, New England Province Soc. of Jesus, 1944-50. Consecrated Bishop, 1950; Vicar Apostolic of Jamaica, 1950; Bishop of Kingston (Jamaica), 1956-67. Hon. Dr of Laws: Fairfield Univ., 1951; Boston Coll., 1968. *Address:* Boston College, Newton, Massachusetts 02167, USA. *T:* (617) 969-0100.

McELLIGOTT, Neil Martin; Metropolitan Magistrate at Great Marlborough Street Magistrates' Court, 1972-76 (at Old Street Magistrates' Court, 1961-72); *b* 21 March 1915; *s* of Judge E. J. McElligott, KC, Limerick; *m* 1939, Suzanne, *d* of late Air Chief Marshal Sir Arthur Barratt, KCB, CMG, MC, DL; one *d. Educ:* Ampleforth. Served in Royal Air Force, 1935-45. Called to Bar, Inner Temple, 1945, South Eastern Circuit, Recorder of King's Lynn, 1961. *Recreations:* hunting, racing, fishing, gardening. *Address:* Stone Cottage, Abthorpe, near Towcester, Northants. *T:* Silverstone 310.

McELROY, Roy Granville, CMG 1972; LLD, PhD; Pro-Chancellor of the University of Auckland, since 1968; *b* 2 April 1907; *s* of H. T. G. McElroy and Frances C. Hampton; *m* Joan H., *d* of R. O. H. Biss; two *d. Educ:* Auckland Univ.; Clare Coll., Cambridge. LLM NZ 1929; PhD Cantab 1934; LLD NZ 1936. Barrister. Lectr in Law, Auckland Univ., 1936-37. Mem., Auckland City Council, 1938-53; Dep. Mayor of Auckland, 1953, Mayor, 1965-68; Chm., Auckland Metro Planning Cttee, 1953; Mem., Auckland Regional Planning Authority, 1954-66; Chairman: Auckland Old People's Welfare Cttee, 1950-65; NZ Welfare of Aged Persons Distribution Cttee, 1962-75; Sunset Home Inc., 1972-82; Member: Bd of Trustees, NZ Retirement Life Care, 1972-82; Council, Dr Barnardo's in NZ; Auckland Medico-Legal Soc. Consular Agent of France in Auckland, 1948-72; Dean, Auckland Consular Corps, 1965 and 1971. Chm., NZ Section Internat. Commn of Jurists, 1965-72. Chm. Legal Research Foundn, Auckland Univ., 1968-72; Mem., Auckland Univ. Council, 1939-54 and 1960-78; Chm., Auckland Br., NZ Inst. of Internat. Affairs, 1970. FRSA 1971. Hon. DLitt Auckland Univ., 1976. Chevalier de l'Ordre National de la Légion d'Honneur, 1954. *Publications:* Law Reform Act 1936 NZ, 1937; Impossibility of Performance of Contracts, 1942; articles in Modern Law Review, NZ Law Jl, NZ Financial Times. *Recreation:* reading. *Address:* Highpoint, 119 St Stephens Avenue, Parnell, Auckland, New Zealand. *T:* 30-645. *Club:* Northern (Auckland).

McENERY, John Hartnett; author and conceptual analyst, since 1981; *b* 5 Sept. 1925; *y s* of late Maurice Joseph and Elizabeth Margaret McEnery (*née* Maccabe); *m* 1977, Lilian Wendy, *yr d* of late Reginald Gibbons and of Mrs L. Gibbons (*née* Cox). *Educ:* St Augustine's Sch., Coatbridge; St Aloysius Coll., Glasgow; Glasgow Univ. (MA(Hons)). Served War of 1939-45: RA, 1943-47; Staff Captain, Burma Command, 1946-47. Glasgow Univ., 1947-49. Asst Principal, Scottish Educn Dept, 1949; Principal, 1954; Cabinet Office, 1957; HM Treasury, 1959; Min. of Aviation, 1962; UK Delegn to NATO, 1964; Counsellor (Defence Supply), British Embassy, Bonn, 1966; Asst Sec., Min. of Technology, 1970; Dept of Trade and Industry, 1970-72; Under-Sec. and Regional Dir for Yorks and Humberside, DTI, 1972, Dept of Industry, 1974-76; Under Sec., Concorde and Nationalisation Compensation Div., Dept of Industry, 1977-81. *Publication:* Manufacturing Two Nations—the sociological trap created by the bias of British regional policy against service industry, 1981. *Recreations:* various games and sports, chess, travel. *Address:* 56 Lillian Road, SW13 9JF. *Club:* Hurlingham.

McENTEE, Peter Donovan, CMG 1978; OBE 1963; HM Diplomatic Service, retired; Governor and Commander-in-Chief of Belize, 1976-80; *b* 27 June 1920; *s* of Ewen Brooke McEntee and Caroline Laura Clare (*née* Bayley); *m* 1945, Mary Elisabeth Sherwood; two *d. Educ:* Haileybury Coll., Herts. Served War, HM Forces, 1939-45, KAR (Major). HM Overseas Civil Service, 1946-63: Dist Commissioner; retired as Principal of Kenya Inst. of Administration; First Secretary: Commonwealth Relations Office, 1963; Lagos, 1964-67; Commonwealth Office (later Foreign and Commonwealth Office), 1967-72; Consul-Gen., Karachi, 1972-75. *Recreations:* music, natural history, golf. *Address:* Woodlands, Church Lane, Danehill, Sussex. *Club:* Royal Over-Seas League.

MacENTEE, Seán; Member, Dáil Eireann for Dublin South (East), retired May 1969; Member, Council of State; Tánaiste (Deputy Prime Minister), 1959-65; Minister for Health, 1957-65 (of Social Welfare, 1958-61); a consulting electrical engineer, registered patent agent, company director, etc.; *b* 1889; *e s* of James MacEntee, TC, Belfast; *m* Margaret, *d* of late Maurice Browne, of Grange-Mockler, Co. Tipperary; one *s* two *d. Educ:* St Malachy's Coll., Belfast; Belfast College of Technology. Participated in Irish insurrection, 1916; tried by General Court-Martial, May 1916, and sentenced to death (sentence afterwards commuted to penal servitude for life); imprisoned in Dartmoor, Lewes and Portland prisons and released under General Amnesty, June 1917; MP (SF) South Monaghan, Dec. 1918; Member of National Executive Cttee of Irish Volunteers and Irish Republican Army, 1917-21; served with Irish Republican Army, 1916-21; contested County Dublin, Aug. 1923, Dec. 1924; TD (Representative Fianna Fail) Co. Dublin, June 1927; re-elected Sept. 1927, 1932, and 1933; TD Dublin Townships, 1937-48, and Dublin SE, 1948-69; Minister for Finance, Irish Free State, 1932-37, and Eire, 1937-39; Minister for Industry and Commerce, Eire, 1939-41; Minister for Local Government and Public Health, Eire, 1941-46; for Local Government, 1946-48; Minister for Finance, Republic of Ireland, 1951-54. LLD (*hc*) NUI. Kt Grand Cross, Pian Order. *Publications:* Poems (1918); Episode at Easter, 1966. *Address:* Montrose, Trimleston Avenue, Booterstown, Co. Dublin. *T:* 692441.

MACER, Dr Richard Charles Franklin, FIBiol; General Manager, The Plant Royalty Bureau Ltd, since 1981; *b* 21 Oct. 1928; *s* of Lionel William Macer and Adie Elizabeth Macer; *m* 1952, Vera Gwendoline Jeapes; three *d. Educ:* Worthing High Sch.; St John's Coll., Cambridge. MA, PhD. St John's Coll., Cambridge, 1949-55, Hutchinson Res. Student, 1952-53; Plant Pathologist, Plant Breeding Inst., Cambridge, 1955-66; Dir and Dir of Res., Rothwell Plant Breeders Ltd, Lincs, 1966-72; Prof. of Crop Production, Univ. of Edinburgh, 1972-76; Dir, Scottish Plant Breeding Station, 1976-81. *Publications:* papers on fungal diseases of cereals. *Recreations:* hill walking, archaeology, reading. *Address:* Cherry Trees, 61 Fleetwood, Ely, Cambs CB6 1BH. *T:* Ely 61395. *Club:* Farmers'.

McEVOY, David Dand; barrister-at-law; a Recorder of the Crown Court, since 1979; *b* 25 June 1938; *s* of David Dand McEvoy and Ann Elizabeth McEvoy (*née* Breslin); *m* 1974, Belinda Anne Robertson; two *d. Educ:* Mount St Mary's Coll.; Lincoln Coll., Oxford. BA (PPE). 2nd Lieut The Black Watch, RHR, 1958-59. Called to the Bar, Inner Temple, 1964. *Recreations:* golf, fishing. *Address:* Chambers Court, Longdon, Tewkesbury, Glos GL20 6AS. *T:* Birtsmorton 626. *Club:* Caledonian.

McEVOY, Air Chief Marshal Sir Theodore Newman, KCB 1956 (CB 1951); CBE 1945 (OBE 1941); *b* 21 Nov. 1904; *s* of late Rev. C. McEvoy, MA, Watford; *m* 1935, Marian, *d* of late W. A. E. Coxon, Cairo; one *s* one *d. Educ:* Haberdashers' School; RAF Coll., Cranwell. Served with Fighter Squadrons and in Iraq, 1925-36; psa 1937; Air Ministry, 1938-41; commanded Northolt, 1941; Group Captain Operations, HQ Fighter Command, 1942-43; SASO No 11 Group, 1943; SASO No 84 Group, 1944 (despatches); Air Ministry (DST), 1945-47; idc 1948; AOC No 61 Group, 1949-50; Assistant Chief of Air Staff (Training), 1950-53; RAF Instructor, Imperial Defence Coll., 1954-56; Chief of Staff, Allied Air Forces, Central Europe, 1956-59; Air Secretary, Air Ministry, 1959-62; Air ADC to the Queen, 1959-62; retired, 1962. Vice-President, British Gliding Assoc. Commander Order of Polonia Restituta (Poland), 1942. *Recreations:* gliding, golf. *Address:* 75A Boundstone Road, Rowledge, Farnham, Surrey GU10 4AT. *Club:* Royal Air Force.

McEWAN, Geraldine, (Mrs Hugh Cruttwell); actress; *b* 9 May 1932; *d* of Donald and Norah McKeown; *m* 1953, Hugh Cruttwell, *qv* ; one *s* one *d*. *Educ:* Windsor County Girls' School. Acted with Theatre Royal, Windsor, 1949-51; Who Goes There, 1951; Sweet Madness, 1952; For Better For Worse, 1953; Summertime, 1955; Love's Labour's Lost, Stratford-on-Avon, 1956; The Member of the Wedding, Royal Court Theatre, 1957; The Entertainer, Palace, 1957-58; Stratford-on-Avon, 1958: Pericles; Twelfth Night; Much Ado About Nothing; 1961: Much Ado About Nothing; Hamlet; Everything in the Garden, Arts and Duke of York's, 1962; School for Scandal, Haymarket, and USA, 1962; The Private Ear, and The Public Eye, USA, 1963; Loot, 1965; National Theatre, 1965-72: Armstrong's Last Goodnight; Love For Love; A Flea in Her Ear; The Dance of Death; Edward II; Home and Beauty; Rites; The Way of the World; The White Devil; Amphitryon 38; Dear Love, Comedy, 1973; Chez Nous, Globe, 1974; The Little Hut, Duke of York's, 1974; Oh Coward!, Criterion, 1975; On Approval, Haymarket, 1975; Look After Lulu, Chichester, and Haymarket, 1978; The Browning Version and A Harlequinade, National Theatre, 1980; The Provok'd Wife, National Theatre, 1980. *Television series:* The Prime of Miss Jean Brodie, 1978. *Address:* c/o Larry Dalzell Associates, 3 Goodwin's Court, WC2.

McEWAN, Ian Russell; author; *b* 21 June 1948; *s* of Major (retd) David McEwan and Rose Lilian Violet Moore. *Educ:* Woolverstone Hall Sch.; Univ. of Sussex (BA Hons Eng. Lit.); Univ. of East Anglia (MA Eng. Lit.). Began writing, 1970. *Film script:* The Ploughman's Lunch, 1983. *Publications:* First Love, Last Rites, 1975; In Between the Sheets, 1978; The Cement Garden, 1978; The Imitation Game, 1981; The Comfort of Strangers, 1981; Shall we Die? (oratorio), 1982. *Address:* c/o Jonathan Cape, 30 Bedford Square, WC1B 3EL.

McEWAN, Robin Gilmour, QC (Scot.) 1981; PhD; *b* 12 Dec. 1943; *s* of late Ian G. McEwan and of Mary McEwan, Paisley, Renfrewshire; *m* 1973, Sheena, *d* of late Stewart F. McIntyre and of Lillian McIntyre, Aberdour; one *d*. *Educ:* Paisley Grammar Sch.; Glasgow Univ. (1st Cl. Hons LLB; PhD). Faulds Fellow in Law, Glasgow Univ., 1965-68; admitted to Faculty of Advocates, 1967. Standing Jun. Counsel to Dept of Energy, 1974-76; Advocate Depute, 1976-79. *Publications:* Pleading in Court, 1980; (with Ann Paton) A Casebook on Damages, 1983. *Recreation:* golf. *Address:* 8 Ormelie Terrace, Edinburgh EH15 2EX. *T:* 031-669 3159. *Clubs:* New (Edinburgh); Honourable Company of Edinburgh Golfers.

MacEWEN, Ann Maitland, RIBA (DistTP), MRTPI; Planning Consultant; *b* 15 Aug. 1918; *d* of Dr Maitland Radford, MD, DPH, MOH St Pancras, and Dr Muriel Radford; *m* 1st, 1940, John Wheeler, ARIBA, AADip (Hons), Flt-Lt, RAF (killed on active service, 1945); two *d* ; 2nd, 1947, Malcolm MacEwen, *qv* ; one *d*. *Educ:* Howell's Sch., Denbigh, N Wales; Architectural Assoc. Sch. of Architecture (AA Dip., RIBA); Assoc. for Planning and Regional Reconstruction Sch. of Planning (SP Dip., MRTPI). Architectural Asst, 1945-46; Planning Asst, Hemel Hempstead New Town Master Plan, 1946-47; Architect-Planner with LCC, 1949-61; Mem., Colin Buchanan's Gp, Min. of Transport, which produced official report, Traffic in Towns, 1961-63; res. work, Transport Section, Civil Engineering Dept, Imperial Coll., 1963-64; Partner, Colin Buchanan and Partners, 1964-73, Consultant, 1973-. Senior Lectr, Bristol Univ. Sch. of Advanced Urban Studies, 1974-77; Hon. Res. Fellow, UCL, 1977-. Mem., Noise Adv. Council, 1971-73. RIBA Distinction in Town Planning, 1967. *Publication:* National Parks—Cosmetics or Conservation? (with M. MacEwen), 1982. *Recreations:* riding, swimming, cooking and entertaining. *Address:* Manor House, Wootton Courtenay, Minehead, Somerset. *T:* Timberscombe 325.

M'EWEN, Ewen, CBE 1975; MScEng; FRSE; CEng, FIMechE; FASME; Consulting Engineer, since 1980; *b* 13 Jan. 1916; *e s* of Clement M'Ewen and Doris Margaret Pierce-Hope; *m* 1938, Barbara Dorrien, *d* of W. F. Medhurst; two *s* one *d*. *Educ:* Merchiston; University Coll., London. BSc (Eng) 1st class Hons, 1935; MSc (Eng) 1948; Head Memorial Medallist and Prizeman, 1935; Graduate Apprentice David Brown & Sons (Huddersfield) Ltd, 1935-37; Research Engineer, 1937-40, Asst Works Manager, 1940-42; served War of 1939-45, 1942-46: Lt-Col 1943; Lt-Col (Hon. Col) REME (TA retd); Asst Dir, Dept of Tank Design, 1943-46; Asst Chief Engineer, Fighting Vehicles Design Dept, 1946-47; Prof. of Agricultural Engineering, King's Coll., Univ. of Durham, Newcastle upon Tyne, 1947-54, and Reader in Applied Mechanics, 1952-54; Dir Armament R and D Establishment, Fort Halstead, 1955-58; Dir of Engineering, Massey Ferguson Ltd, 1958-63; Dep. Man. Dir, 1963, Man. Dir, 1965-67, Hobourn Group Ltd; Vice-Chm. (Engrg), Joseph Lucas Ltd, 1967-80. Commanded REME 50 (N) Infantry Div. (TA), 1949-52. Hon. Col Durham Univ. OTC, 1955-60. Member: Council, Instn of Mech. Engs, 1961-81 (Vice-Pres., 1970-76; Pres., 1976-77); Design Council, 1971-77; Armed Forces Pay Review Body, 1971-; Chm., Metrology and Standards Requirements Bd, 1973-77. Chm., Lanchester Polytechnic, Coventry, 1970-73. Fellow, UCL, 1965; Visiting Professor: Imperial Coll., London, 1971-78; UCL, 1978-. Hon. DSc: Heriot-Watt, 1976; Newcastle, 1977. Liveryman, Glaziers Company; Hammerman, Glasgow. *Publications:* papers and articles in Technical Press. *Recreation:* sailing. *Address:* 45 Pearce Avenue, Poole, Dorset BH14 8EG. *T:* Parkstone 742067. *Clubs:* Army and Navy; Royal Thames Yacht; Parkstone Yacht.

McEWAN, Sir James (Francis Lindley), 4th Bt *cr* 1953; *b* 24 Aug. 1960; *s* of Sir Robert Lindley McEwan, 3rd Bt, of Marchmont and Bardrochat, and of Brigid Cecilia, *d* of late James Laver, CBE, and Veronica Turleigh; *S* father, 1980. *Educ:* Eton. *Recreations:* forestry, shooting, music. *Heir:* *b* John Roderick Hugh McEwen, *b* 4 Nov. 1965. *Address:* Marchmont, Greenlaw, Berwickshire. *T:* Duns 2321. *Club:* Turf.

McEWEN, Rev. Prof. James Stevenson, DD; Professor of Church History, University of Aberdeen, 1958-77; Master of Christ's College, Aberdeen, 1971-77; *b* 18 Feb. 1910; *s* of Rev. Thomas McEwen and Marjorie Bissett; *m* 1945, Martha M. Hunter, Auchendrane, Alexandria; two *s*. *Educ:* George Watson's Coll., Edinburgh Univ. Ordained Church of Scotland, 1940; held parishes at Rathen, Hawick and Invergowrie; Lecturer in Church History at University of Edinburgh, 1953. *Publication:* The Faith of John Knox, 1961. *Address:* 8 Westfield Terrace, Aberdeen AB2 4RU. *T:* Aberdeen 645413.

MacEWEN, Malcolm; journalist; *b* 24 Dec. 1911; *s* of late Sir Alexander MacEwen and of Lady (Mary Beatrice) MacEwen; *m* 1st, 1937, Barbara Mary Stebbing, BSc (*d* 1944); one *d* ; 2nd, 1947, Mrs Ann Maitland Wheeler (*see* Ann Maitland MacEwen); one *d* (and two step *d*). *Educ:* Edinburgh Univ. (MA, LLB). Member (Lab) Ross and Cromarty CC, 1938-40; wrote for Daily Worker, mainly as Parliamentary Correspondent, 1944-56; Asst Editor, Architects' Jl, 1956-60; Editor, RIBA Jl, 1964-71; RIBA: Head of Information Services, 1960-66; Publishing Services, 1966-70; Dir, Public Affairs, 1971-72. Leverhulme Res. Fellow, 1972-73; Res. Fellow, UCL, 1977-. Mem., Exmoor Nat. Park Cttee, 1973-81. Hon. Fellow, RIBA, 1974. *Publications:* Crisis in Architecture, 1974; (ed) Future Landscapes, 1976; (with Mrs A. M. MacEwen) National Parks—Cosmetics or Conservation?, 1982. *Address:* Manor House, Wootton Courtenay, Somerset. *T:* Timberscombe 325.

McEWIN, Hon. Sir (Alexander) Lyell, KBE 1954; *b* 29 May 1897; *s* of late A. L. McEwin; *m* 1921, Dora Winifred, *d* of late Mark Williams, Blyth; four *s* one *d*. *Educ:* State Sch.; Prince Alfred Coll., Adelaide. Engaged in farming at Hart, near Blyth, since 1912; Sec., Blyth Agric. Bureau, 1920-26, Pres., 1927-36; Life Mem. State Advisory Bd of Agric., 1930, Chm., 1935-37; Mem. Agric. Settlement Cttee, 1931; Mem. Debt Adjustment Cttee, 1933; Producers' representative for SA on Federal Advisory Cttee for Export Mutton and Beef, prior to appt of Australian Meat Bd, 1934. Entered Legislative Council of South Australian Parliament as Member for Northern District, 1934; Chief Secretary, Minister of Health, and Minister of Mines, 1939-65; Leader of Opposition in Legislative Council, 1965-67; Pres., Legislative Council, S Australia, 1967-75, retired. Councillor, Hart Ward of Hutt and Hill Rivers' District Council, 1932-35; transferred to Blyth Dist Council, 1935-53; retired. Member: South Australian Rifle Assoc., 1925 (Chairman, 1948-); Commonwealth Council, State Rifle Assocs, 1952-62 (Chm., 1959-62). Chief, Royal Caledonian Society (SA), 1959-68. *Recreation:* bowls. *Address:* 93 First Avenue, St Peters, SA 5069. *T:* 423698.

MACEY, Rear-Adm. David Edward; Deputy Assistant Chief of Staff (Operations), Staff of the Supreme Allied Commander, since 1981; *b* 15 June 1929; *s* of Frederick William Charles Macey and Florence May Macey; *m* 1st, 1958, Lorna Therese Verner (decd); one *s* one *d*, and one step *s* two step *d* ; 2nd, 1982, Fiona, *o d* of Vice-Adm. Sir William Beloe, KBE, CB, DSC; three step *s*. *Educ:* Sir Joseph Williamson's Mathematical Sch., Rochester; Royal Naval Coll., Dartmouth. Midshipman, 1948; Cruisers, Carriers, Destroyers, 1950-63; Comdr, 1963; Amer. Staff Coll., 1964; Comdr, RNC Dartmouth, 1970; Captain, 1972; Directorate Naval Plans, 1972-74; RCDS, 1975; Dir, RN Staff Coll., 1976-78; Dir, Naval Manpower, 1979-81; ADC to HM the Queen, 1981; Rear-Adm., 1981. *Recreations:* walking, cricket, cooking. *Address:* 7 Great Minister Street, Winchester, Hants SO23 9KA. *T:* Winchester 65906. *Clubs:* Anglo-Belgian, MCC.

MACEY, John Percival, CBE 1969; FRICS, FIHM; Chairman, Samuel Lewis Housing Trust, since 1974; Treasurer, Peabody Trust, since 1974; *b* 3 Dec. 1906; *s* of Edward Macey; *m* 1931, Jill, *d* of Joseph Gyngell; one *s* one *d*. *Educ:* Varndean Grammar Sch., Brighton. Entered LCC service, 1926; Principal Asst, Housing Dept, 1948-51; Dep. Housing Manager, City of Birmingham, 1951-54; Housing Manager, City of Birmingham, 1954-63; Director of Housing to LCC, later GLC, 1964-71. President: Inst. of Housing, 1957 and 1963; Inst. of Housing Managers, 1969; Vice-Pres., Surrey and Sussex Rent Assessment Panel, 1971-79. Served with Royal Engineers, 1939-45 (despatches); retired with rank of Major. *Publications:* Macey on the Housing Finance Act, 1972; The Housing Act, 1974; The Housing Rents and Subsidies Act, 1975; (joint author) Housing Management, 1965, 3rd edn 1978; papers to professional bodies on housing and allied subjects. *Recreations:* motoring, walking, gardening. *Address:* 7 Bath Court, Kings Esplanade, Hove, East Sussex BN3 1AB. *T:* Brighton 728104.

McFADDEN, Jean Alexandra, JP; Leader of Glasgow District Council, since 1980; Vice Lord Lieutenant of City of Glasgow, since 1980; Principal Teacher of Classics, St Patrick's High School, Coatbridge, since 1972; *b* 26 Nov. 1941; *d* of John and Elma Hogg; *m* 1966, John McFadden. *Educ:* Univ. of Glasgow (MA 1st Cl. Hons Classics). Teacher of Classics, Notre Dame High Sch. for Girls, 1964-70. Entered Local Govt as Mem. of Glasgow Corp. for Cowcaddens Ward, 1971; Chm., Manpower Cttee, 1974-77; Leader of Labour Group, 1977-. JP Glasgow, 1972; DL 1980. *Recreations:* cycling, theatre, dog walking, gliding, canoeing. *Address:* 16 Lansdowne Crescent, Glasgow G20 6NQ. *T:* 041-334 3522. *Club:* Tron Theatre (Glasgow).

McFADZEAN, family name of **Barons McFadzean** and **McFadzean of Kelvinside**.

McFADZEAN, Baron, *cr* 1966 (Life Peer); **William Hunter McFadzean,** KT 1976; Kt 1960; Director, Midland Bank, 1959-81 (Deputy Chairman, 1968-77); Hon. President, BICC Ltd, 1973 (Managing Director, 1954-61; Chairman, 1954-73); *b* Stranraer, 17 Dec. 1903; *s* of late Henry and of Agnes McFadzean, Stranraer; *m* 1933, Eileen, *e d* of Arthur Gordon, Blundellsands, Lancs.; one *s* one *d*, one adopted *d. Educ:* Stranraer Academy and High Sch.; Glasgow Univ. Served articles with McLay, McAllister & McGibbon, Chartered Accountants, Glasgow, 1922-27; qualified as Chartered Accountant, 1927; with Chalmers Wade & Co., 1927-32; joined British Insulated Cables Ltd, as Accountant, 1932 (Financial Secretary, 1937; Exec. Manager, 1942); on amalgamation of British Insulated Cables Ltd and Callender's Cable & Construction Co. Ltd, in 1945, appointed to Board of British Insulated Callender's Cables Ltd as Exec. Director (Dep. Chairman, 1947; Chief Exec. Director, 1950), retd 1973; Chairman: Standard Broadcasting Corp. (UK) Ltd, 1972-79; Home Oil (UK) Ltd, 1972-78; Scurry-Rainbow (UK) Ltd, 1974-78; Deputy Chairman: RTZ/BICC Aluminium Holdings Ltd, 1967-73; National Nuclear Corp., 1973-80; Canada Life Unit Trust Managers Ltd, 1982- (Chm., 1971-82); Director: Anglesey Aluminium Ltd, 1968-73; Midland Bank Executor and Trustee Co., 1959-67; English Electric Co., 1966-68; Steel Co. of Wales Ltd, 1966-67; Canadian Imperial Bank of Commerce, 1967-74; Canada Life Assurance Co., 1969-79; Canada Life Assurance Co. of GB (Dep. Chm., 1971-82); Home Oil Co. Ltd, 1972-77; Standard Broadcasting Corp. Ltd, 1976-79. Pres. FBI, 1959-61. Chairman: Council of Industrial Fedns of EFTA, 1960-63; Export Council for Europe, 1960-64 (Hon. Pres. 1964-71); Commonwealth Export Council, 1964-66; British Nat. Export Council, 1964-66 (Pres. 1966-68); President: Brit. Electrical Power Convention, 1961-62; Brit. Nuclear Forum, 1964-66; Coal Trade Benevolent Assoc., 1967-68; Electrical and Electronics Industries Benevolent Assoc., 1968-69. Vice-President: Middle East Assoc., 1965; City of London Soc., 1965-72; British/Swedish Chamber of Commerce, 1963-74. Member: Inst. of Directors, 1954-76 (Council, 1954-74); Min. of Labour Adv. Bd on Resettlement of Ex-Regulars, 1957-60; Bd of Trade Adv. Council on ME Trade, 1958-60; MoT Shipping Adv. Panel, 1962-64; Ct of British Shippers' Council, 1964-74 (Pres., 1968-71); Council, Foreign Bondholders, 1968-74; Anglo-Danish Soc., 1965-75 (Chm., 1969-75; Hon. Pres., 1975); Adv. Cttee, Queen's Award for Industry, 1965-67 (Chm., Review Cttee, 1970). CompIEE 1956. JDipMA 1965. Commander Order of Dannebrog (Denmark), 1964, Grand Commander, 1974; Grande Oficial da Ordem do Infante Dom Henrique, Portugal, 1972. *Address:* 114 Whitehall Court, SW1A 2EL. *T:* 01-930 3160; Garthland, Woldingham, Surrey CR3 7DH. *T:* Woldingham 3222. *Clubs:* Carlton, MCC.

McFADZEAN OF KELVINSIDE, Baron *cr* 1980 (Life Peer), of Kelvinside in the District of the City of Glasgow; **Francis Scott McFadzean;** Kt 1975; Chairman: Rolls Royce Ltd, 1980-April 1983; British Airways, 1976-79 (Director, 1975); *b* 26 Nov. 1915; *m* 1938, Isabel McKenzie Beattie; one *d. Educ:* Glasgow Univ.; London Sch. of Economics (Hon. Fellow, 1974). MA. BoT, 1938; Treasury, 1939; War Service, 1940-45; Malayan Govt, 1945; Colonial Develt Corp., 1949; Shell Petroleum Co. Ltd, 1952; Man. Dir, Royal Dutch/Shell Group of Companies, 1964-76; Dir, 1964-, Man. Dir 1971, Chm., 1972-76, "Shell" Transport and Trading Co. Ltd; Chairman: Shell International Marine Ltd, 1966-76; Shell Canada Ltd, 1970-76; Shell Petroleum Co. Ltd, 1972-76; Director: Shell Oil Co., 1972-76; Shell Petroleum Co. Ltd, 1964-; Beecham Group Ltd, 1974-; Coats Patons Ltd, 1979-; Chairman: Trade Policy Research Centre, 1971-82; Steering Bd, Strathclyde Div., Scottish Business Sch., 1970-76; Vis. Prof. of Economics, Strathclyde Univ., 1967-76. Hon. LLD Strathclyde, 1970. Comdr, Order of Oranje Nassau. *Publications:* Galbraith and the Planners, 1968; Energy in the Seventies, 1971; The Operation of a Multi-National Enterprise, 1971; The Economics of John Kenneth Galbraith: a study in fantasy, 1977; (jtly) Global Strategy for Growth: a report on North-South issues, 1981. *Address:* Shell Centre, SE1 7NA. *T:* 01-934 5116.
See also Baron Marsh.

McFALL, David (Bernard), RA 1963 (ARA 1955); Sculptor; Master of Sculpture, City and Guilds of London Art School, Lambeth, 1956-75; *b* 21 Dec. 1919; *s* of David McFall and Elizabeth McEvoy; *m* 1972, Alexandra Dane, actress; one *s* one *d. Educ:* Art Schools, Birmingham, Lambeth and Royal College of Art. Official Commissions: Unicorns (pair, 12 ft, gilt-bronze) mounted on roof of Bristol New Council House, known as The Bristol Unicorns, 1950; Finials (pair, carved, Portland stone, 10 ft), Zodiac Clock (8 ft, carved stone and cast aluminium), Bronze Portrait Bust (Alderman Frank Sheppard), 1955, same building; Festival of Britain, Boy and Foal (carved stone 5 ft), 1951, now at Missenden Abbey, Bucks. Pocahontas (bronze), 1956; Bust (bronze, Lord Methuen), 1956; Head of Ralph Vaughan Williams, OM (bronze) in Royal Festival Hall, 1957; 8 ft Statues of St Bride and St Paul in St Bride's Church, Fleet Street; Bronze Head of Sir Winston Churchill, in Grocers Hall, 1958; 8 ft 6 ins Bronze Figure of Sir Winston Churchill, 1959 (Woodford Green); Lord Balfour, House of Commons, 1962; Bust (bronze) Lord Brabazon of Tara (Royal Institution); Memorial to Sir Albert Richardson, PPRA, in Crypt of St Paul's Cathedral; Crucifixion (Portland stone), Church of Our Lady of Lourdes, Thames-Ditton; bust (bronze, Lord Ridley) for Univ., Newcastle upon Tyne; The Golden Gazelle, Abu Dhabi, Trucial States; bronze figure of Sir Winston Churchill, trophy for Dame Felicity Peake Essay Prize; The Black Horse for LTB Victoria Line, 1968; stone frieze on Wm Whitfield's extension to Inst. of Chartered Accountants, London, 1969; bust of Sir Thomas Holmes Sellors, Pres., RCS, 1971; Meml to Sir Gerald Kelly, St Paul's Cathedral Crypt, 1973; busts of:

Sir George Godber, for RCP; Prof. George Grenfell Baines, for Building Design Partnership, Preston; late Hugh Stenhouse, Glasgow, 1973-74; Oedipus and Jocasta (stone group), W Norwood Library, 1974; posthumous bust of Josiah Wedgwood, Barlaston, Stoke-on-Trent, 1974-75; portrait head of HRH Prince Charles, Duke of Cornwall, 1974-75; Meml to Lord Fraser of Lonsdale, Westminster Abbey, 1976; Official purchase: The Bullcalf (Chantrey Bequest), 1943. Has exhibited at Royal Academy yearly since 1943. *Recreations:* swimming, cycling. *Address:* 10 Fulham Park Gardens, SW6 4JX. *T:* 01-736 6532; Natura, Fairlight Cove, Sussex TN35 4DJ. *Club:* Hurlingham.

McFALL, Richard Graham; Chairman, Crossfriars Trust PLC, since 1980 (Director, since 1976); *b* 31 Jan. 1920; 3rd *s* of Henry Joseph Marshall and Sarah Gertrude McFall; *m* 1945, Clara Louise Debonnaire Mitford; one *s* one *d. Educ:* Holmwood Prep. Sch., Lancs; Clifton Coll., Bristol. Joined Pacol Ltd, 1938; Mil. Service, HAC, 1939-40; Colonial Office, 1941-45 (Asst Sec., then Sec., W African Produce Control Bd); Motor & Air Products Ltd, 1946-48; re-joined Pacol Ltd, 1949, Dir 1951; Chm., London Cocoa Terminal Market Assoc., 1954-55; Chm., Cocoa Assoc. of London, 1958-59; Dir 1962-82, Man. Dir 1965-74, Chm., 1970-76, Vice-Chm., 1976-78, Gill & Duffus Group PLC. *Recreation:* golf. *Address:* Springfold Cottage, Greendene, East Horsley, Surrey. *T:* East Horsley 3282. *Clubs:* Farmers'; Effingham Golf.

McFARLAND, Sir Basil (Alexander Talbot), 2nd Bt, *cr* 1914; CBE 1954; ERD 1954; HM Lieutenant for the City of Londonderry, 1939-75; *b* 18 Feb. 1898; *o c* of Sir John McFarland, 1st Bt, and Annie, 2nd *d* of late John Talbot, Terryglass, County Tipperary; *S* father, 1926; *m* 1st, 1924, Annie Kathleen (*d* 1952), 2nd *d* of late Andrew Henderson, JP, of Parkville, Whiteabbey, Belfast; one *s* (one *d* decd); 2nd, 1955, Mary Eleanor (*d* 1973), 2nd *d* of late William Dougan, Londonderry. *Educ:* Neuwied-on-Rhine, Germany; Brussels; Bedford Sch. High Sheriff, Londonderry, 1930, 1931, 1932, 1933, 1934, 1935, 1936, 1937, 1938 and 1952; Mayor of Londonderry, 1939, 1945, 1946, 1947, 1948, 1949, 1950. Formerly ADC (Additional) to The Queen. Member: Northern Ireland Air Advisory Council, 1946-65; Londonderry Port & Harbour Commissioners (Chairman, 1952-67); London Midland Area Board, British Transport Commission, 1955-61; Director, Belfast Banking Co. Ltd, 1930-70; Chairman: Lanes (Derry), Ltd; J. W. Corbett & Sons; A. Thompson & Co. Ltd; Lanes (Fuel Oils) Ltd; Lanes (Business Equipment) Ltd; Lanes (Patent Fuels) Ltd; J. & R. Waterson Ltd; R. C. Malseed & Co. Ltd; Holmes Coal Ltd; Trustee of Magee University College, 1962-65. Original Member, NI Unemployment Assistance Board, to 1939. Served War of 1914-18, Artists Rifles, 1918; War of 1939-45, Overseas with 9th Londonderry HAA Regt (despatches); Chm., T&AFA (Co. Londonderry), 1947-62; Hon. Col, 9th Londonderry HAA Regt RA (TA); Pres., NI TA&VR Assoc., 1968-71. Irish Rugby International, 1920-22. Hon. Freeman of City of Londonderry since 1944. CStJ. *Heir: s* John Talbot McFarland [*b* 3 Oct. 1927; *m* 1957, Mary Scott, *er d* of late Dr W. Scott Watson, Londonderry; two *s* two *d*]. *Address:* Aberfoyle, Londonderry. *T:* 62881. *Club:* Northern Counties (Londonderry).

McFARLANE OF LLANDAFF, Baroness *cr* 1979 (Life Peer), of Llandaff in the County of South Glamorgan; **Jean Kennedy McFarlane;** Professor and Head of Department of Nursing, University of Manchester, since 1974; *b* 1 April 1926; *d* of James and Elvina Alice McFarlane. *Educ:* Howell's Sch., Llandaff; Bedford and Birkbeck Colls, Univ. of London. MA, BSc(Soc); SRN, SCM, HV Tutor's Cert.; FRCN 1976; MSc (Manchester), 1979. Staff Nurse, St Bartholomew's Hosp., 1950-51; Health Visitor, Cardiff CC, 1953-59; Royal Coll. of Nursing: Organising Tutor, Integrated Course, Educn Div., London, 1960-62; Educn Officer, Birmingham, 1962-66; Res. Project Ldr (DHSS sponsored), London, 1967-69; Dir of Educn, Inst. of Advanced Nursing Educn, London, 1969-71; Univ. of Manchester: Sen. Lectr in Nursing, Dept of Social and Preventive Medicine, 1971-73; Sen. Lectr and Head of Dept of Nursing, 1973-74. Mem., Royal Commn on NHS, 1976-79. Chm., English Bd for Nursing, Midwifery and Health Visiting, 1980-. Hon. DSc Ulster, 1981. *Publications:* The Problems of Developing Criteria of Quality for Nursing Care (thesis), 1969; The Proper Study of the Nurse, 1970. *Recreations:* music, walking, travelling, photography. *Address:* Department of Nursing, University of Manchester, Stopford Building, Oxford Road, Manchester M13 9PT. *T:* 061-273 8241, ext. 182.

MacFARLANE, Prof. Alistair George James; Professor of Engineering, University of Cambridge, since 1974; Fellow since 1974, Vice-Master since 1980, Selwyn College, Cambridge; *b* 9 May 1931; *s* of George R. MacFarlane; *m* 1954, Nora Williams; one *s. Educ:* Hamilton Academy; Univ. of Glasgow. BSc 1953, DSc 1969, Glasgow; PhD London 1964; MSc Manchester 1973; MA 1974, ScD 1979, Cantab. Metropolitan-Vickers, Manchester, 1953-58; Lectr, Queen Mary Coll., Univ. of London, 1959-65, Reader 1965-66; Reader in Control Engrg, Univ. of Manchester Inst. of Sci. and Technology, 1966-69, Prof. 1969-74. Mem. Council, SERC, 1981-. *Publications:* Engineering Systems Analysis, 1964; Dynamical System Models, 1970; A Complex Variable Approach to the Analysis of Linear Multivariable Feedback Systems, 1979; Frequency-Response Methods in Control Systems, 1979; Complex Variable Methods for Linear Multivariable Feedback Systems, 1980. *Address:* 9 Dane Drive, Newnham, Cambridge CB3 9LP.

MACFARLANE, Rev. Alwyn James Cecil; Parish Minister of Newlands (South), Church of Scotland, since 1968; Chaplain to the Queen in Scotland, since 1977; *b* 14 June 1922; *s* of James Waddell Macfarlane and Ada Cecilia Rankin; *m* 1953, Joan Cowell Harris; one *s* one *d*. *Educ:* Cargilfield Sch.; Rugby Sch.; Oxford Univ. (MA); Edinburgh Univ. Served War: N Africa, Italy, Greece; Liaison Officer in Black Watch with 12th Bde, 1942-46. Ordained, 1951; served in parishes in Ross-shire, Edinburgh and Glasgow. *Recreations:* photography, walking. *Address:* 24 Monreith Road, Glasgow G43 2NY. *T:* 041-632 2588.

MACFARLANE, (David) Neil; MP (C) Sutton and Cheam, since Feb. 1974; Parliamentary Under Secretary of State (with special responsibility for Sport), Department of the Environment, since 1981; *b* 7 May 1936; *yr s* of Robert and Dulcie Macfarlane; *m* 1961, June Osmond King, Somerset; two *s* one *d*. *Educ:* St Aubyn's Prep. Sch.; Bancroft's, Woodford Green. Short Service Commission, Essex Regt, 1955-58; served TA, 265 LAA, RA, 1961-66. Joined Shell Mex and BP, 1959; contested (C): East Ham (North), 1970; Sutton and Cheam, by-election, 1972. Mem., All Party Select Cttee on Science and Technology; Secretary: Cons. Greater London Mems; Cons. Sports Cttee; Cons. Energy Cttee; Parly Under Sec. of State, DES, 1979-81. Mem., National Trust. *Recreations:* golf, swimming, cricket, cricket-watching. *Address:* 3 Collingwood House, Dolphin Square, SW1. *T:* 01-834 6307; 48 Benhill Avenue, Sutton, Surrey. *Clubs:* Caledonian, MCC; Surrey County Cricket; Huntercombe Golf.

MacFARLANE, Donald, CBE 1963; HM Diplomatic Service, retired; *b* 26 Oct. 1910; *s* of late Donald MacFarlane, CIE; *m* 1933, Jean Carmen, *d* of late Charles Young, Pitt Manor, Winchester; one *s* decd. *Educ:* Stowe; Queens' Coll., Cambridge. Lamson Paragon Supply Co. Ltd, 1932-39. Served in RA and Intelligence Corps, 1939-46 (despatches); North Africa, Sicily, Italy and France; Colonel, head of Anglo-Greek Information Services, Athens, 1945-46. First Secretary, Foreign Service, 1946; British Embassy, China, 1946-49; Foreign Office, 1949-52; British Embassy: Rio de Janeiro, 1952-55; Counsellor (Commercial), Washington, 1955-58; Lisbon, 1958-60; HM Consul-General, Frankfurt-am-Main, 1960-64; Naples, 1964-67; Head of Nationality and Treaty Dept, FCO, 1967-70. *Recreations:* fishing, ski-ing. *Address:* 27 Lennox Gardens, SW1. *Club:* Flyfishers'.

MACFARLANE, Sir George (Gray), Kt 1971; CB 1965; BSc; Dr Ing (Dresden); FEng; *b* 8 Jan. 1916; *s* of late John Macfarlane, Airdrie, Lanarks; *m* 1941, Barbara Grant, *d* of Thomas Thomson, Airdrie, Lanarks; one *s* one *d*. *Educ:* Airdrie Academy; Glasgow Univ.; Technische Hochschule, Dresden, Germany. On scientific staff, Air Ministry Research Establishment, Dundee and Swanage, 1939-41; Telecommunications Research Establishment (TRE), Malvern, 1941-60; Deputy Chief Scientific Officer (Individual Merit Post), 1954-60; Deputy Director, National Physical Laboratory, 1960-62; Director, Royal Radar Establishment, 1962-67; Controller (Research), Min. of Technology and Min. of Aviation Supply, 1967-71; Controller, Research and Develt Establishments and Research, MoD, 1971-75. Member: PO Review Cttee, 1976-77; PO Bd, 1977-81; British Telecom Bd, 1981-; NEB, 1980- and NRDC, 1981- (now British Technology Gp). Mem., Bd of Trustees, Imperial War Museum, 1978-. Deputy-Pres., IEE, 1970-74 (Vice-Pres., 1972-74); Hunter Meml Lecturer, IEE, 1966; Council Mem., Fellowship of Engrg, 1982-. Hon. LLD Glasgow. Glazebrook Medal and Prize, Inst. of Physics, 1978. *Publications:* papers in IEE, Proc. Phys. Society, Phys. Review. *Recreations:* walking, gardening. *Address:* Red Tiles, Orchard Way, Esher, Surrey. *T:* Esher 63778. *Club:* Athenæum.

McFARLANE, Prof. Ian Dalrymple, MBE 1946; FBA 1978; Professor of French Literature, Oxford, since 1971; *b* 7 Nov. 1915; *s* of James Blair McFarlane and Valérie Edith Liston Dalrymple; *m* 1939, Marjory Nan Hamilton; one *s* one *d*. *Educ:* Lycée St-Charles, Marseilles; Tormore Sch., Upper Deal, Kent; Westminster Sch.; St Andrews Univ. MA 1st class Hons, 1938; Carnegie Research Scholar, 1938-39. Served 1st Bn Black Watch, RHR, 1940-45. Apptd Lectr in French, Cambridge Univ., 1945; Gonville and Caius Coll.: elected Fellow, 1947; appointed Senior Tutor, 1956; Prof. of French Language and Literature, St Andrews, 1961-70. Member, Scottish Cert. of Educn Examination Board, 1964; Member Academic Planning Board, University of Stirling, 1964-67; Mem. Cttee on Research and Develt in Modern Languages, 1966. Doctor of Univ. of Paris, 1950; Hon. DLitt St Andrews, 1982. Officier des Palmes Académiques, 1971. *Publications:* critical edn of M. Scève's Délie, 1966; Renaissance France 1470-1589, 1974; Buchanan, 1981; The Entry of Henri II into Paris, 1549, 1982; various, in learned periodicals. *Recreations:* cricket, music. *Address:* Wadham College, Oxford.

McFARLANE, James Sinclair, MA, PhD; CEng, FIM; Director General, Engineering Employers' Federation, since 1982; *b* 8 Nov. 1925; *s* of John Mills McFarlane and Hannah McFarlane; *m* 1951, Ruth May Harden; three *d*. *Educ:* Manchester Grammar Sch.; Emmanuel Coll., Cambridge (MA, PhD). CEng, FIM 1961. ICI Ltd, 1949-53; Henry Wiggin & Co. Ltd, 1953-69; Chm. and Man. Dir, Smith-Clayton Forge Ltd (GKN Ltd), 1969-76; Man. Dir, Garringtons Ltd (GKN Ltd), 1976-77; Guest Keen & Nettlefolds Ltd: Gen. Man., Personnel, 1977-79; Exec. Dir, 1979-82. *Publications:* contrib. scientific and technical jls. *Recreation:* music. *Address:* The Court House, Atch Lench, Evesham, Worcs WR11 5SP. *T:* Evesham 870225. *Clubs:* Caledonian, United Oxford & Cambridge University.

McFARLANE, Prof. James Walter; Professor of European Literature, University of East Anglia, since 1964; *b* 12 Dec. 1920; *s* of James and Florence McFarlane; *m* 1944, Lillie Kathleen Crouch; two *s* one *d*. *Educ:* Bede Grammar Sch., Sunderland; St Catherine's Society, Univ. of Oxford. MA, BLitt 1948. War service, Intell. Corps, 1941-46 (Major); Oxford Soccer blue, 1947; Lectr and Sen. Lectr, Dept of German and Scandinavian Studies, King's Coll., Univ. of Durham, later Univ. of Newcastle upon Tyne, 1947-63; Dean of European Studies, Univ. of East Anglia, 1964-68; Public Orator, 1964-68, 1974-75, 1978-79; Pro-Vice-Chancellor, 1968-71. Vis. Prof., Univ. of Auckland, NZ, 1967. Mem., BBC Gen. Adv. Council, 1970-75; Chm., East Anglia Regional Adv. Council, 1970-75; Chm., Hunworth Crafts Trust, 1973-77; Mem. Exec., Eastern Arts Assoc., 1977-. Founder Trustee, Norwich Puppet Theatre, 1979. Editor, Scandinavica: an International Journal of Scandinavian Studies, 1975-. Leverhulme Faculty Fellow in European Studies, 1971-72; Brit. Acad. Wolfson Fellow. Fellow, Det Norske Videnskaps-Akademie, Oslo, 1977; Corresp. Mem., Svenska Litteratursällskapet i Finland, Helsinki, 1977. Commander's Cross, Royal Norwegian Order of St Olav, 1975. *Publications:* Ibsen and the Temper of Norwegian Literature, 1960; Discussions of Ibsen, 1962; Henrik Ibsen, 1970; (with Malcolm Bradbury) Modernism: European Literature 1890-1930, 1976; (editor and translator) The Oxford Ibsen, 1960-77: vol. 1, Early Plays, 1970; vol. 2, The Vikings at Helgeland, Love's Comedy, The Pretenders, 1962; vol. 3, Brand, Peer Gynt, 1972; vol. 4, The League of Youth, Emperor and Galilean, 1963; vol. 5, Pillars of Society, A Doll's House, Ghosts, 1961; vol. 6, An Enemy of the People, The Wild Duck, Rosmersholm, 1960; vol. 7, The Lady from the Sea, Hedda Gabler, The Master Builder, 1966; vol. 8, Little Eyolf, John Gabriel Borkman, When We Dead Awaken, 1977; (editor and translator with Janet Garton) Slaves of Love and other Norwegian short stories, 1982; *translations:* Hamsun's Pan, 1955; Hamsun's Wayfarers, 1980. *Recreation:* domestic odd-jobbery. *Address:* The Croft, Stody, Melton Constable, Norfolk NR24 2EE. *T:* Melton Constable 860505. *Club:* Athenæum.

MACFARLANE, Sir James (Wright), Kt 1973; PhD; FRSE; CEng, FIEE, FIMechE; JP; DL; Managing Director, Cathcart Investment Co. Ltd, since 1964; *b* 2 Oct. 1908; *s* of late James C. Macfarlane, OBE, MIEE, WhSch; *m* 1937, Claire Ross. *Educ:* Allan Glen's Sch.; Royal Technical Coll. (DRTC); Glasgow Univ. (PhD); London Univ. WhSch and WhSen.Sch. FIFire E. War of 1939-45: Home Guard (Major); Intell.; Lt-Col (TA) Comdg Renfrewshire Bn, Army Cadet Force. Apprentice, Engineer and Director, Macfarlane Engrg Co Ltd, 1926-; Chm., Macfarlane Engrg Co Ltd, Cathcart, 1967-69. Dir, National Building Agency, etc. Past Pres., Assoc. of County Councils in Scotland; Past Mem. various instns; Member: Royal Commn on the Police, 1960-62; Departmental Cttee on the Fire Service, 1968-70. JP 1940; entered local govt, 1944; DL 1962, Renfrewshire; Convener, County of Renfrew, 1967-73. Chm. of Governors, Paisley Coll. of Technology. *Publications:* numerous papers in IEE and IMechE Jls. *Recreations:* motor cycles and cars (vintage), sailing. *Address:* Cartbank, 45 Netherlee Road, Glasgow G44 3YU. *T:* 041-637 6135. *Clubs:* RNVR (Scotland); Royal Gourock Yacht (Gourock).

MACFARLANE, Neil; *see* Macfarlane, D. N.

MacFARLANE, Maj.-Gen. Robert Goudie, MBE 1952; FRCP; FRCPE; Deputy Secretary, Scottish Council for Postgraduate Medical Education, since 1975; *b* 1 March 1917; *s* of late Archibald Forsyth MacFarlane and Jessie Robertson Goudie; *m* 1945, Mary Campbell Martin; three *s*. *Educ:* Hillhead High Sch., Glasgow; Glasgow Univ. MB, ChB, 1940; MD 1955; FRCPE 1964; MRCP 1970; FRCP 1979. Served War: commissioned RAMC, 1941; in Madagascar, India, Burma, 1941-45. Specialist in Medicine and Consultant Physician, 1948-; CO, British Mil. Hosp., Iserlohn, 1968-70; Prof. of Mil. Med., Royal Army Medical Coll., 1970-71; Consulting Physician, BAOR, 1971-73. Dir. of Army Medicine and Consulting Physician to the Army, 1973-74. QHP 1973. *Recreation:* sailing. *Address:* 6 Redholm, Greenheads Road, North Berwick, East Lothian.

MACFARLANE, Robert Gwyn, CBE 1964; FRS 1956; MD; FRCP; retired; *b* 26 June 1907; *o c* of Robert Gray and Eileen Macfarlane; *m* 1936, Hilary, *o c* of H. A. H. and Maude Carson; four *s* one *d*. *Educ:* Highfield Sch., Liphook, Hants; Cheltenham Coll.; St Bartholomew's Hospital, London. MRCS, LRCP, 1933; MB, BS (London), 1933; MD (London), Gold Medal, 1938; MA (Oxford), 1948; FRCP 1960. Sir Halley Stewart Research Fellow, 1935; Asst Clinical Pathologist, Postgrad. Medical School, London, 1936; Asst Bacteriologist, Wellcome Physiological Research Lab., 1939. Major, RAMC, 1944, attached Mobile Bacteriological Research Unit, Normandy and NW Europe. Director, Medical Research Council Blood Coagulation Research Unit, Churchill Hospital, Oxford, 1959-67; Professor of Clinical Pathology, Oxford Univ., 1964-67, now Emeritus (Reader in Haematology, 1957-64); Fellow, All Souls Coll., Oxford, 1963-70, now Quondam Fellow; Clinical Pathologist, Radcliffe Infirmary, Oxford, 1941-67. Vice-Pres., Haemophilia Society, 1955, Pres., 1982. *Publications:* (with R. Biggs) Human Blood Coagulation and its Disorders (3rd edn, 1962); Howard Florey: the Making of a Great Scientist, 1979; papers, chapters in books and encyclopædias on haematological and pathological subjects. *Address:* Mallie's Cottage, Opinan, Laide, Ross-shire.

MACFARLANE, Hon. Sir Robert Mafeking, KCMG 1974 (CMG 1954); Speaker, New Zealand Parliament, 1957-60; *b* Christchurch, NZ, 17 May 1901; *m* 1932, Louisa E., *d* of T. F. Jacobs, Woolston. *Educ:* Christchurch, NZ. Secretary, Christchurch Labour Representation Cttee, 1929; MP (L) (NZ) for Christchurch S, 1936-46, for Christchurch Central, 1946-69;

formerly Sen. Opposition Whip. Member Christchurch City Council for many years (Mayor, 1938-41). Chairman Metropolitan Transport Licensing Authority. Served War of 1939-45 with Second New Zealand Expeditionary Force. *Address:* 71 Greenpark Street, Christchurch 2, New Zealand.

MACFARLANE, Maj.-Gen. William Thomson, CB 1981; Operations Director, Hong Kong Resort Co. Ltd, Hong Kong, since 1981; *b* Bath, 2 Dec. 1925; *s* of late James and Agnes Macfarlane; *m* 1955, Dr Helen D. Meredith; one *d.* Commissioned Royal Signals, 1947. Served Europe, Near East, ME, and Far East. Commanded 16th Parachute Bde Signal Squadron, 1961-63; Military Asst, Commander FARELF, 1964-66; Comd 1st Div. HQ and Signal Regt, BAOR, 1967-70; Services Mem., Cabinet Office Secretariat, 1970-72; Comd, Corps Royal Signals, 1972-73; Dir of Public Relations (Army), MoD, 1973-75; C of S, UKLF, 1976-78; Chief, Jt Services Liaison Organisation, Bonn, 1978-80. Col Comdt, Royal Corps of Signals, 1980-. jssc; psc. FBIM. *Recreations:* golf, music. *Address:* Aveley Lane, Farnham, Surrey. *Club:* Naval and Military.

MacFARQUHAR, Sir Alexander, KBE 1952; CIE 1945; Director of Personnel, United Nations, 1962-67; *b* 6 Nov. 1903; *s* of Roderick MacFarquhar; *m* 1929, Berenice Whitburn; one *s. Educ:* Aberdeen Univ. MA 1st class Hons Classics); Emmanuel Coll., Cambridge. Entered ICS 1926; Deputy Commissioner, Ferozepore, 1930; Deputy Commissioner, Amritsar, 1933; Settlement Officer, Amritsar, 1936; Deputy Secretary, Government of India, 1941; Deputy Director-General, Directorate-General of Supply, Government of India, 1943; Dir-Gen. Disposals, India, 1946; Commerce and Education Sec. Govt of Pakistan, 1947-51. Resident Rep. to Pakistan of UN Technical Assistance Board, 1952; Regional Rep. to Far East, of UN Technical Assistance Board, Bangkok, 1955; UN Secretary General's Special Adviser for Civilian Affairs in the Congo, 1960. Chm., Pakistan Soc., 1970-81. Hon. LLD Aberdeen, 1980. HQA, Pakistan, 1981. *Address:* Ottershaw, Beverley Lane, Coombe Hill, Kingston-upon-Thames, Surrey.
See also R. L. MacFarquhar.

MacFARQUHAR, Roderick Lemonde; Leverhulme Research Fellow, since 1980; *b* 2 Dec. 1930; *s* of Sir Alexander MacFarquhar, *qv; m* 1964, Emily Jane Cohen; one *s* one *d. Educ:* Fettes Coll.; Oxford Univ. (BA); Harvard Univ. (AM); LSE (PhD). Specialist on China, Daily Telegraph (and later Sunday Telegraph), 1955-61; Founding Editor, China Quarterly, 1959-68; Rockefeller Grantee, 1962; Reporter, BBC TV programme Panorama, 1963-64. Associate Fellow, St Antony's Coll., Oxford, 1965-68. Mem., Editorial Bd, New Statesman, 1965-69; Ford Foundation Grant, 1968; Senior Research Fellow, Columbia Univ., 1969; Senior Research Fellow, RIIA, 1971-74 (Mem. Council, 1978-); Co-presenter, BBC Gen. Overseas Services 24 Hours prog., 1972-74, 1979-80. Governor, SOAS, 1978-. Contested (Lab): Ealing South, 1966; Meriden, March 1968; MP (Lab) Belper, Feb. 1974-1979; PPS to Minister of State, FCO, March 1974; resignation accepted, April 1975; reappointed June 1975; PPS to Sec. of State, DHSS, 1976-78. Member: N Atlantic Assembly, 1974-79; Select Cttee for Sci. and Technology, 1976-79; Exec. Cttee, Trilateral Commn, 1976-; Exec. Cttee, Fabian Soc., 1976-80. Fellow, Woodrow Wilson Center, Smithsonian Instn, 1980-81; Vis. Prof. of Govt, Harvard, 1982. *Publications:* The Hundred Flowers, 1960; The Sino-Soviet Dispute, 1961; Chinese Ambitions and British Policy (Fabian Pamphlet), 1966; Sino-American Relations, 1949-71, 1972; The Forbidden City, 1972; The Origins of the Cultural Revolution: Vol. 1, Contradictions among the People 1956-1957, 1974; (ed) China under Mao, 1966; articles in Foreign Affairs, The World Today, Atlantic Monthly, Pacific Affairs, Commentary, etc. *Recreations:* reading, listening to music, travel. *Address:* 55 Campden Hill Road, W8. *Club:* Kilburn Miners' Welfare.

MacFEELY, Most Rev. Anthony C.; *b* 4 Feb. 1909. *Educ:* St Columb's Coll., Londonderry; St Patrick's Coll., Maynooth; Irish Coll., Rome. Priest, 1932; Prof., St Columb's Coll., Oct. 1934; Pres., St Columb's Coll., 1950; Parish Priest, Strabane, Co. Tyrone, 1959-65; Bishop of Raphoe, 1965-82. *Recreation:* walking. *Address:* Fernbank, Glebe, Letterkenny, Co. Donegal, Ireland. *T:* Letterkenny 074-21422.

McFEELY, Elizabeth Sarah Anne C.; *see* Craig McFeely.

McFETRICH, Cecil, OBE 1950; Director, Sunderland and Shields Building Society, since 1964; Partner, C. & K. M. McFetrich, since 1977; *b* 17 Jan. 1911; *y s* of Archibald B. and Hannah B. McFetrich; *m* 1937, Kathleen M. Proom; four *s. Educ:* Cowan Terrace Sch., Sunderland; Skerry's Coll., Newcastle upon Tyne. Qual. Chartered Accountant, 1933. After varied industrial and professional experience, joined Bartram & Sons Ltd, South Dock, Sunderland, as Sec., 1936; apptd a Dir, 1939; responsible for sales and marketing, 1945, Man. Dir, 1964-72; Jt Man. Dir, Austin & Pickersgill Ltd, 1968-69, Man. Dir 1969-72, Dep. Chm. and Chm., 1972-75; Founder Dir, A. & P. Appledore Internat. Ltd, 1970-74. Man. Dir, Ward & Davidson Ltd, 1946-75 (Chm. 1975-79); Chm., Sunderland Structural Steel Ltd, 1947-79. Mem., Sunderland Town Council, 1942-51 (Chm. Finance Cttee, 1943-44); Mem., River Wear Commn, 1943-45, 1949-72; served on various Nat. Savings Cttees, 1940-63; Chairman: Sunderland Savings Cttee, 1947-63; N Regional Industrial Savings Cttee, 1956-62. Life Governor, Nat. Children's Home, 1953-81 (Mem., Order of St Christopher, 1982); Pres., Bishopwearmouth Choral Soc., Sunderland, 1962-65. Liveryman, Worshipful Co. of Shipwrights. Freeman by redemption, City of London. Lord Mayor of London's Gold Medal for Export Achievement, 1963. *Recreations:* local history, antiques, champagne.

Address: 8 Belle Vue Drive, Sunderland, Tyne and Wear. *T:* Sunderland 226449. *Clubs:* MCC; Sunderland (Sunderland).

MACFIE, Maj.-Gen. John Mandeville, CB 1951; CBE 1946; MC 1917; OStJ 1945; *b* 13 Dec. 1891; *s* of Rev. W. G. Macfie, Mowbray, Cape Town; unmarried. *Educ:* S African College School; Glasgow High Sch.; Glasgow Univ. MB, ChB (with honours) Glasgow, 1915. FRCP Glasgow, 1964. Lieut, RAMC, 1915: Dep. Assistant Director of Pathology, India, 1926-29; Dep. Assistant Director-General of Army Medical Services, War Office, 1932-36; Dep. DGAMS War Office, 1943-46; DDMS, East Africa Command, 1946-48; DDMS, Scottish Command, 1949; Commandant RAM Coll., 1949-50; KHS 1950; Dep. Director of Medical Services, Western Command, UK, 1950-51; retired pay, Jan. 1952; Colonel Commandant RAMC, 1951-56. Commander Order Leopold II of Belgium, 1949. *Recreations:* golf, fishing. *Address:* Erskine Hospital, Bishopton, Renfrewshire PA7 5PU. *Club:* Glasgow Art.

McGAHERN, John; author; *b* 12 Nov. 1934; *s* of Francis McGahern and Susan McManus; *m* 1973, Madeline Green. Research Fellow, Univ. of Reading, 1968-71; O'Connor Prof., Colgate Univ., 1969, 1972 and 1977; British Northern Arts Fellow, 1974-76. AE Meml Award, 1962; McCauley Fellowship, 1964; British Arts Council Award, 1967; Soc. of Authors Award, 1975. *Publications:* The Barracks, 1963; The Dark, 1965; Nightlines, 1970; The Leavetaking, 1975; Getting Through, 1978; The Pornographer, 1979. *Address:* c/o Faber & Faber, 3 Queen Square, WC1N 3AU.

McGARRITY, J(ames) Forsyth, CB 1981; MA, MEd, BSc; HM Senior Chief Inspector of Schools (Scotland), 1973-81; *b* 16 April 1921; *s* of late James McGarrity and Margaret Davidson; *m* 1951, Violet S. G. Philp; one *s* one *d. Educ:* Bathgate Academy; Glasgow Univ. Schoolmaster, 1949-57; HM Inspector of Schools, 1957-68; HM Chief Inspector of Schools, 1968-73. *Recreations:* golf, gardening. *Address:* 30 Oatlands Park, Linlithgow, Scotland EH49 6AS. *T:* Linlithgow 3258.

McGEE, Prof. James Dwyer, OBE 1952; FRS 1966; MSc Sydney; PhD, ScD, Cantab; CEng; FIEE; FInstP; FRAS; Hon. ARCS; Professor of Applied Physics, 1954-71, now Emeritus, Senior Research Fellow, 1971-80, and Fellow, 1977, Imperial College of Science and Technology, University of London; *b* Canberra, ACT, 17 Dec. 1903; *s* of Francis and Mary McGee; *m* 1944, Hilda Mary, *d* of George Winstone, Takapuna, Auckland, NZ; no *c. Educ:* St Patrick's Coll., Goulburn, NSW; St John's Coll., Sydney Univ. (MSc); Clare Coll., Cambridge (PhD). 1851 Exhibition Scholar from Sydney Univ. to Cambridge. Nuclear physics research, Cavendish Laboratory, Cambridge, 1928-31; Research physicist, Electric and Musical Industries Research Laboratories, Hayes, Middx. Engaged on research on photo-electricity and electronic problems of Television, 1932-39; research on electronic problems in connection with military operations, in particular the use of infra-red light, 1939-45; returned to work on photo-electronic devices for television and other scientific purposes, 1945-54. Awarded Research Fellowship, Carnegie Inst., Washington, 1960; Hon. Research Associate, Carnegie Inst., 1960, 1962, 1966. Hon. Life Mem. IREE(Aust.), 1939. Hon. DSc Salford, 1972; Hon. DTech Brunel, 1978. Awarded prize of Worshipful Company of Instrument Makers, 1968; Callendar Medal, Inst. of Measurement and Control, for contribs to opto-electronics, 1975. *Publications:* chap. on Electronic Generation of Television Signals in Electronics (ed B. Lovell), 1947; ed Vols XII, XVI, XXII, XXVIII, XXXIII, Advances in Electronics: Symposia on Photoelectronic Devices, 1960, 1962, 1966, 1969, 1972; technical papers in Engineering, Physical and Technical Jls. *Recreations:* gardening, music. *Address:* 3E/10 Hilltop Crescent, Fairlight, NSW 2094, Australia. *T:* 949 3723. *Club:* Athenæum.

McGEE, Prof. James O'Donnell; Professor of Morbid Anatomy, University of Oxford, Fellow of Linacre College, Oxford, since Oct. 1975; *b* 27 July 1939; *s* of Michael and Bridget McGee; *m* 1961, Anne Lee; one *s* two *d. Educ:* Univ. of Glasgow. MB, ChB, PhD, MD, MRCPath; MA (Oxon). Various appts in Univ. Dept of Pathology, Royal Infirmary, Glasgow, 1962-69; Roche Inst. of Molecular Biology, Nutley, NJ: MRC Fellow 1969-70; Vis. Scientist 1970-71; Dept of Pathology, Royal Infirmary, Glasgow: Lectr 1971-74; Sen. Lectr, 1974-75. Mem., Scientific Cttee, Cancer Res. Campaign, 1978-. Kettle Meml Lectr, RCPath, 1980. *Publications:* Liver Biopsy Review, 1980; papers on collagen metabolism and liver disease in Proc. Nat. Acad. Sci., Gut, etc. *Recreations:* squash, swimming. *Address:* Nuffield Department of Pathology, Level 1, John Radcliffe Hospital, Headington, Oxford OX3 9DU.

McGEE, Rt. Rev. Joseph; *b* 13 Dec. 1904; *s* of Denis McGee and Sarah McGlinchey. *Educ:* St Dominic's Sch. and Morrison's Academy, Crieff; Blair's Coll., Aberdeen; Royal Scots Coll., Valladolid. Formerly Vicar-General and Canon (Penitentiary) of Dunkeld. Bishop of Galloway, 1952-81. *Address:* c/o Candida Casa, 8 Corsehill Road, Ayr. *T:* Ayr 66750.

McGEOCH, Vice-Adm. Sir Ian (Lachlan Mackay), KCB 1969 (CB 1966); DSO 1943; DSC 1943; Director, Wm McGeoch & Co. Ltd; Chairman, Midar (Marine Systems) Ltd; Editorial Director, Naval Forces, since 1980; *b* 26 March 1914; 3rd *s* of L. A. McGeoch of Dalmuir; *m* 1937, Eleanor Somers, *d* of Rev. Canon Hugh Farrie; two *s* two *d. Educ:* Pangbourne Coll. Joined RN, 1932. Comd HM Submarine Splendid, 1942-43; Staff Officer (Ops) 4th Cruiser Sqdn, 1944-45; Comd: HMS Fernie, 1946-47; 4th Submarine Squadron, 1949-51; 3rd Submarine Squadron, 1956-57; Dir of Undersurface

Warfare, Admiralty, 1959; IDC 1961; Comd HMS Lion 1962-64; Admiral Pres., RNC, Greenwich, 1964-65; Flag Officer Submarines, 1966-67; Flag Officer, Scotland and Northern Ireland, 1968-70. Trustee, Imperial War Museum, 1977-. Pres., RNVR Club (Scotland), 1981-. Mem., The Queen's Body Guard for Scotland, Royal Co. of Archers, 1969-. MPhil Edinburgh, 1975. *Publication:* (jtly) The Third World War: a future history, 1978. *Recreations:* sailing, music. *Address:* Southerns, Castle Hedingham, Essex. *Clubs:* Army and Navy; Royal Yacht Squadron, Royal Naval Sailing Association (Cdre 1968-70), Royal Cruising, Royal Northern and Clyde Yacht.

McGHEE, George Crews, Legion of Merit; businessman; former diplomat; Director: Mobil Oil Co., since 1969; Procter and Gamble Co., since 1969; American Security & Trust Co., since 1969; Trans World Airlines, since 1976; *b* Waco, Texas, 10 March 1912; *s* of George Summers McGhee and Magnolia (*née* Spruce); *m* 1938, Cicilia Jeanne DeGolyer; two *s* four *d. Educ:* Southern Methodist Univ., Dallas; Univ. of Oklahoma; Oxford Univ. (Rhodes Schol.); Univ. of London. BS (Oklahoma) 1933; DPhil (Oxon) 1937. Served with US Navy, 1943-45 (Asiatic ribbon with three battle stars). Geologist and geophysicist, 1930-40; Oil producer, sole owner, McGhee Production Co., 1940-. Special Asst to Under-Sec of State for Economic Affairs, 1946; Coordinator for Aid to Greece and Turkey, 1947; Asst Sec. of State for Near Eastern, South Asian and African Affairs, 1949; US Ambassador to Turkey, 1951; Consultant, Nat. Security Council, 1958; Mem. President's Cttee to Study Mil. Asst Program, 1958; Counselor of Dept of State and Chm. of State Dept Policy Planning Council, 1961; Under-Sec. of State for Political Affairs, 1961; Bd, Panama Canal Co., 1962; US Ambassador to the Federal Republic of Germany, 1963-68; Ambassador-at-Large, 1968-69. Chairman: English Speaking Union of US, 1969-74; Business Council for Internat. Understanding, 1969-73; Trustee: Salzburg Seminar, 1969-; Internat. Civil Service League, 1969-; Member Board: Geo. Cttee, Marshall Res. Fund, 1972-; Amer. Council on Germany, 1969-; Resources for Future, 1977-; Asia Foundn, 1974-; Atlantic Council, 1977-; Atlantic Inst. for Internat. Affairs, 1977-; Smithsonian Nat. Associates, 1971- (Chm., 1975-76); Population Crisis Cttee, 1969-. Trustee: Duke Univ.; Cttee for Economic Development, 1957-; Aspen Institute for Humanistic Studies, 1958-. Chm., Saturday Review World, 1974-77. Hon. Fellow, Queen's Coll., Oxford, 1969. Distinguished Service Citation, Univ. of Oklahoma, 1952; Hon. DCL, Southern Methodist Univ., 1953; Hon. LLD: Tulane Univ., 1957; Univ. of Maryland, 1965; Hon. DSc, Univ. of Tampa, 1969. Ouissam Alaouite Cherifien, Govt Morocco, 1950; Hon. Citizen, Ankara, Turkey, 1954. *Publications:* contribs to Foreign Affairs, Gewerkschaftliche Rundschau, Werk und Wir, Europa Archiv, Universitas, Ruperto-Carola Weltraumfahrt-Raketentechnik, Europa, Washington Post, New York Times, etc. *Recreations:* hunting, tennis, photography. *Address:* 2808 N Street, NW, Washington, DC 20007, USA; Farmers' Delight, Middleburg, Va, USA. *Clubs:* Metropolitan (Washington, DC); Brook, Century Association (New York); City Tavern Association (Georgetown, DC).

McGHIE, James Ironside, CMG 1973; HM Diplomatic Service, retired; *b* 12 Oct. 1915; *s* of William I. McGhie and Annie E. Ratcliffe; *m* 1946, Ellen-Johanne Gran, *d* of Maj. T. Gran, MC, Norway, and Ingeborg Gran (*née* Meinich); two *s* one *d. Educ:* King Henry VIII Sch., Coventry. Journalist, 1933-39. Army, 1940-46, attached Royal Norwegian Army, 1943-46. Entered Foreign Service, 1946; served: Stockholm, Helsinki, FO, Tokyo, FO, Singapore; Dir, British Information Services, Saigon; Head of Chancery, Bucharest; Consul-General, Seattle; Counsellor, Commercial, Stockholm; Minister (Commercial and Econ.), Tokyo; retired, 1975. Special Advr on Japanese market to BOTB, 1975-77; Co-Chm., Japan Task Force, 1976-77. Order of the Rising Sun (Japan) 3rd class, 1975. *Recreations:* Scandinavian studies and translations. *Address:* 10 Tylney Avenue, SE19 1LN. *Clubs:* Travellers', Royal Commonwealth Society.

McGHIE, Maj.-Gen. (retd) John, CB 1976; MD; FRCPsych; DPM; consultant psychiatrist to GLC and ILEA, since 1976; President, Ministry of Defence (Army) Medical Board, since 1976; *b* Larkhall, Scotland; *s* of Henry and Agnes McGhie; *m* 1940, Hilda Lilian Owen; two *s. Educ:* Hamilton Academy; Glasgow University. Medical Officer: Glasgow Western Infirmary, 1936-37; Bellshill Maternity Hosp., 1937; Captain, RAMC, 1938; MO, British Mil. Hosp. Rawalpindi, 1939; Major, 2nd in Comd Field Ambulance, 1939-43; Lt-Col, OC Field Amb., 1943-45; Comd Psychiatrist: Scottish Comd, 1948; Far East, 1949-52; OC, Royal Victoria Hosp., Netley, 1956-61; Dir of Army Psychiatry, 1961-67; DDMS, Malaya and Western Comd, 1967-70; Dir, Army Psychiatry and Consultant in Psychiatry to Army, 1970-76. *Recreations:* golf, motoring. *Address:* Mandavara, 9 Ross Road, South Norwood, SE25. *T:* 01-653 7488.

McGILL, Maj.-Gen. Allan, CB 1969; CBE 1964 (OBE 1945; MBE 1943); Director of Electrical and Mechanical Engineering (Army), 1966-69; *b* 1914; *s* of William McGill; *m* 1945, Kathleen German. *Educ:* George Heriot's, Edinburgh; Heriot-Watt Coll. (now Heriot-Watt Univ.). Served War of 1939-45 (despatches, 1943). Dir, Electrical and Mechanical Engineering, British Army of the Rhine, 1965-66. Brig., 1961; Maj.-Gen., 1966. Col Comdt, REME, 1969-74. CEng, MIMechE. *Recreations:* motor rallying, ski-ing. *Address:* Tudor House, Vicarage Gardens, Bray, Berks SL6 2AE. *Club:* Army and Navy.

MacGILL, George Roy Buchanan, CBE 1965; General Manager, Cumbernauld Development Corporation, 1956-70; Deputy Chairman, Scottish Special Housing Association, 1971-76; *b* 20 Dec. 1905; *s* of George Buchanan MacGill; *m* 1934, Jean Ferguson Anderson; two *d. Educ:* Glasgow High Sch. Chartered Accountant, 1928. FIMTA 1938. Town Chamberlain, Airdrie, 1932; Burgh Chamberlain, Dunfermline, 1947. *Recreations:* golf, music. *Address:* 28 Roman Court, Bearsden, Glasgow.

McGILL, Maj.-Gen. Nigel Harry Duncan, CB 1966; Chief of Staff to Commandant-General, Royal Marines, 1967-68, retired, 1968; *b* 15 Oct. 1916; *s* of Lt-Col H. R. McGill; *m* 1944, Margaret Constance Killen; two *s* one *d. Educ:* Victoria Coll., Jersey. Commissioned 2nd Lt RM 1934; Maj.-Gen. 1964; Comdr, Portsmouth Group, RM, 1964-67. Representative Col Comdt RM, 1977-78. Exec., Rolls Royce Ltd, 1968-78. *Recreations:* cricket, golf. *Address:* Alderwood, Manor Farm Road, Fordingbridge, Hants. *Club:* Army and Navy.

McGILL, Rt. Rev. Stephen; see Paisley, Bishop of, (RC).

McGILLIGAN, Denis Brian; Assistant Solicitor, Ministry of Agriculture, Fisheries and Food, since 1973; *b* 26 June 1921; *s* of Michael McGilligan, SC, and Mary Georgina McGilligan (*née* Musgrave); *m* 1952, Hazel Patricia Pakenham Keady; one *s* two *d. Educ:* St Gerard's, Bray, Co. Wicklow; Trinity Coll., Dublin (BA). Practised at Irish Bar, 1945-52; Crown Counsel, Sarawak, and Dep. Legal Adviser, Brunei, 1952-58; Senior Magistrate, Sarawak, 1958-59; Acting Puisne Judge, Combined Judiciary, 1959-60; Senior Magistrate, Sarawak, 1960-63; Puisne Judge, Combined Judiciary of Sarawak, North Borneo and Brunei, March, 1963; Judge of the High Court in Borneo, Malaysia, 1963-66. Called to the Bar, Gray's Inn, 1966. *Recreations:* hockey, swimming, walking, reading. *Address:* Lulworth Cottage, Tubs Hill, Sevenoaks, Kent. *T:* Sevenoaks 53622.

MacGILLIVRAY, Barron Bruce, FRCP; Consultant in Clinical Neurophysiology and Neurology, since 1964, and Dean, School of Medicine, since 1975, Royal Free Hospital; Consultant in Clinical Neurophysiology, National Hospital for Nervous Diseases, since 1971; *b* 21 Aug. 1927; *s* of late John MacGillivray and of Doreene (*née* Eastwood), S Africa; *m* 1955, Ruth Valentine; two *s* one *d. Educ:* King Edward VII Sch., Johannesburg; Univ. of Witwatersrand (BSc Hons 1949); Univ. of Manchester; Univ. of London (MB, BS 1962). FRCP 1973. House Surg., House Phys., Manchester Royal Infirm., 1955-56; RMO, Stockport and Stepping Hill Hosp., 1957-59; Registrar, subseq. Sen. Registrar, Nat. Hosp. for Nervous Diseases, Queen Sq., London, 1959-64; Res. Fellow, UCLA, 1964-65; Cons., Clin. Neurophysiol., Nat. Hosp. for Nervous Diseases, 1971. Member: NE Thames Regional Health Authority; Senate, Collegiate Council, Univ. of London; Univ. rep., Council, Sch. of Pharmacy and British Postgraduate Med. Fedn; Examr and Teacher, Univ. of London. Pres., Electrophys. Technicians Assoc., 1976-82. FRSocMed. *Publications:* papers in sci. jls on cerebral electrophysiol., epilepsy, computing and cerebral death. *Recreations:* PPL, photography, D-I-Y. *Address:* Rosslyn Tower, 18 St John's Avenue, Putney, SW15 2AA. *T:* 01-788 5213.

MacGILLIVRAY, Prof. Ian, MD, FRCP; FRCOG; Regius Professor of Obstetrics and Gynæcology, University of Aberdeen, since 1965 (Dean of Medical Faculty, 1976-79); *b* 25 Oct. 1920; *yr s* of W. and A. MacGillivray; *m* 1950, Edith Mary Margaret Cook; one *s* twin *d. Educ:* Vale of Leven Academy, Alexandria; University of Glasgow (MB, ChB 1944; MD 1953); MRCOG 1949, FRCOG 1959; FRCPGlas 1973. Gardiner Research Schol., 1949-51, Lectr in Midwifery, 1951-53, Univ. of Glasgow; Senior Lecturer: in Obstetrics and Gynæcology, Univ. of Bristol, 1953-55; in Midwifery and Gynæcology, Univ. of Aberdeen, 1955-61; Prof. of Obstetrics and Gynæcology, University of London, at St Mary's Hospital Medical Sch., 1961-65. Mem., GMC, 1979-. Founder Pres., Internat. Soc. for Study of Hypertension in Pregnancy, 1976-; Pres., Internat. Soc. for Twin Studies, 1980-; Mem. Council, RCOG, 1974-80. *Publications:* Outline of Human Reproduction, 1963; Combined Textbook of Obstetrics and Gynaecology, 1976; Human Multiple Reproduction, 1976; contrib. to: British Medical Journal, Lancet, Journal of Obstetrics and Gynæcology of the British Empire; Clinical Science. *Address:* 45 Woodburn Avenue, Aberdeen. *T:* Aberdeen 34681.

McGILLIVRAY, Hon. William Alexander; Chief Justice of Alberta, Canada, since Dec. 1974; *b* 14 Oct. 1918; *s* of Alexander A. and Margaret L. G. McGillivray; *m* 1950, Kathleen A. Bell; two *s* two *d. Educ:* Univ. of Alberta, Edmonton, Alta (BA,LLB). Graduated in Law, 1941; admitted to practice, 1942. Bencher, 1958-69, Pres., 1969-70, Law Society of Alberta. *Recreations:* shooting, fishing, golf, bridge. *Address:* The Court House, 611-4th Street, SW, Calgary, Alberta, T2P 1T5, Canada. *T:* 261-7434. *Clubs:* Ranchmen's, Calgary Golf and Country, Glencoe (Calgary).

McGINNIS, (Edward) Brian; Under Secretary, Department of Health and Social Security, since 1979; *b* 29 May 1938; *s* of Edward Patrick McGinnis and Florence (*née* Riddoch). *Educ:* Whitgift Sch.; Magdalene Coll., Cambridge (BA). Joined Min. of Pensions and National Insurance, 1959. Interests are Sunday School, youth work, disablement. *Address:* 31 Woodmere Avenue, Shirley, Croydon CR0 7PG. *T:* 01-654 6190.

MacGINNIS, Francis Robert, CMG 1979; HM Diplomatic Service; Minister and Deputy Commandant, British Military Government, Berlin, since 1977; *b* 6 March 1924; *s* of late Dr Patrick MacGinnis, Murray House, Chesterfield; *m* 1955, Carolyn, *d* of late Col D. W. McEnery, USA; three *s* two *d. Educ:* Stonyhurst; Merton Coll., Oxford (MA). Served with Rifle Bde, 1942-47 (Temp. Captain). Joined HM Foreign (subseq. Diplomatic) Service, 1949; served in London, Washington, Paris and Warsaw; Dir-Gen., British Information Services, New York, 1968-72; Counsellor, Bonn, 1972-76; RCDS, 1976. *Address:* c/o Foreign and Commonwealth Office, SW1. *Club:* Travellers'.

McGIRR, Prof. Edward McCombie, CBE 1978; BSc, MD Glasgow; FRCP, FRCPE, FRCPGlas; FACP (Hon.); FFCM; FRSE; Professor of Administrative Medicine, 1978-81, Dean, 1974-81, and Administrative Dean, 1978-81, Faculty of Medicine, University of Glasgow; Physician, Glasgow Royal Infirmary, 1952-81; Honorary Consultant Physician to the Army in Scotland, 1975-81; *b* 15 June 1916; *yr s* of William and Ann McGirr, Hamilton, Lanarkshire; *m* 1949, Diane Curzon, *y c* of Alexander Woods, MBE, TD, DL, and Edith E. C. Woods, Birmingham and London; one *s* three *d. Educ:* Hamilton Academy; Glasgow Univ. BSc 1937; MB, ChB (Hons) Glasgow, 1940; MD (Hons) and Bellahouston Medal, 1960. Served RAMC, 1941-46, in UK, India, Burma, Siam, Indo-China; Medical Specialist; demobilised with hon. rank of Major. Glasgow University: various appointments incl. Lectr and Sen. Lectr in Medicine, at Royal Infirmary, Glasgow, 1947-61; Muirhead Prof. of Medicine, 1961-78. External Examiner in Medicine for BDS Edinburgh Univ., 1957-60, MB ChB, Edinburgh Univ. 1962-65, Birmingham Univ., 1966-69, Aberdeen Univ., 1967-69, Hong Kong Univ., 1968, Univ. of W Indies, 1972; Examiner for MRCP Edinburgh, Glasgow and London. Visitor, Royal Coll. of Physicians and Surgeons of Glasgow, 1968-70, President 1970-72. Former West of Scotland Cttee for Postgrad. Med. Educn; Scottish Cttee for Hosp. Med. Services; West of Scotland Cttee for Hosp. Med. Services; Member: Medical Appeals Tribunals, 1961-; Nat. Radiological Protection Bd, 1976-; Scottish Health Services Planning Council, 1977- (Chm., 1978-); Nat. Med. Consultative Cttee, 1977-81; Med. Sub-Cttee, UGC, 1977-81; GNC for Scotland, 1978-; Greater Glasgow Health Bd, 1979-; Nat. Bd for Nursing, Midwifery and Health Visiting for Scotland, 1980-; Chm., Scottish Council for Postgrad. Med. Educn, 1979-. Member: Assoc. of Physicians of Gt Britain and Ireland (mem. of editorial panel, Quarterly Journal of Medicine, 1968-76; Mem. Council, 1972-76); Scottish Soc. of Physicians; Scottish Soc. for Experimental Med. (Treas., 1960-66); Pres., Harveian Soc. of Edin., 1979; Corresp. Member: Amer. Thyroid Assoc.; Medical Research Soc. (mem. of council, 1967-69); Royal Medico-Chirurgical Soc. of Glasgow (Pres., 1965-66). *Publications:* chiefly in relation to thyroid gland dysfunction, nuclear medicine and medical education. *Recreations:* family life, medical work, detective fiction, curling. *Address:* Anchorage House, Bothwell, by Glasgow G71 8NF. *T:* Bothwell 852194. *Club:* Royal Scottish Automobile.

McGLASHAN, John Reid Curtis, CBE 1974; HM Diplomatic Service, retired 1979; *b* 12 Dec. 1921; *s* of John Adamson McGlashan and Emma Rose May McGlashan; *m* 1947, Dilys Bagnall (*née* Buxton Knight); one *s* two *d. Educ:* Fettes; Christ Church, Oxford (Rugger Blue, 1945). RAF (Bomber Command), 1940-45 (POW, 1941-45). Entered Foreign Service, 1953; Baghdad, 1955; Tripoli, 1963; Madrid, 1968; Counsellor, FCO, 1970-79. *Recreations:* gardening, golf, reading, tennis. *Address:* The Bakehouse, Kingsley Green, Haslemere, Surrey GU27 3LH. *Club:* Vincent's (Oxford).

MacGLASHAN, Maureen Elizabeth; HM Diplomatic Service; seconded to Home Civil Service, since 1977; *b* 7 Jan. 1938; *d* of Kenneth and Elizabeth MacGlashan. *Educ:* Luton High Sch.; Girton Coll., Cambridge (MA, LLB). Joined FO, 1961; 2nd Sec., Tel Aviv, 1964-67; FCO, 1967-72; Head of Chancery, East Berlin, 1973-75; UK Representation to EEC, 1975-77.

McGLASHAN, Prof. Maxwell Len, FRSC; Professor of Chemistry and Head of the Department of Chemistry, University College London, since 1974; *b* 1 April 1924; *s* of Margaret Cordelia McGlashan and late Leonard Day McGlashan; *m* 1947, Susan Jane, *d* of late Col H. E. Crosse, MC, OBE, and late Mrs D. Crosse, Patoka Station, Hawkes Bay, NZ. *Educ:* Greymouth, NZ; Canterbury Univ. Coll., Christchurch, NZ; Univ. of Reading. MSc (NZ) 1946, PhD (Reading) 1951, DSc (Reading) 1962. Asst Lectr, 1946-48, Lectr, 1948-53, Sen. Lectr, 1953, in Chemistry, at Canterbury Univ. Coll., Christchurch, NZ. Sims Empire Scholar, 1949-52; Lectr in Chem., Univ. of Reading, 1954-61; Reader in Chem., Univ. of Reading, 1962-64; Prof. of Physical Chem., Univ. of Exeter, 1964-74 (Dean, Faculty of Science, 1973-74). Mem., 1963-65, Vice-Chm., 1965-67, Chm., 1967-71, Commn on Physicochemical Symbols, Terminology, and Units. Chm., Interdivl Cttee on Nomenclature and Symbols, Internat. Union of Pure and Applied Chem., 1971-76; Member: Royal Society Symbols Cttee, 1963-; BSI's Tech. Cttee on physical quantities and units, 1963- (Chm., 1978-); Council, Faraday Soc., 1965-67; Metrication Bd, 1969-80; Comité Consultatif des Unités (Metre Convention), 1969-; Council, Chem. Soc., 1970-73; SRC Chem. Cttee, 1974-76; Data Compilation Cttee, 1974-77; Res. Cttee, British Gas Corp., 1979-; Trustee, Ramsay Meml Fellowships Trust, 1982- (Chm. Adv. Council, 1975-). Editor, Jl of Chemical Thermodynamics, 1969-. *Publications:* Physicochemical Quantities and Units, 1968 (Royal Inst. of Chem.), 2nd edn, 1971; Chemical Thermodynamics, 1979; papers on chemical thermodynamics and statistical mechanics in Proc. Roy. Soc., Trans Faraday Soc., Jl Chem. Thermodynamics, etc. *Recreations:* climbing in the Alps, the theatre. *Address:*

9 Camden Square, NW1 9UY. *T:* 01-267 1583; Department of Chemistry, University College London, 20 Gordon Street, WC1H 0AJ. *T:* 01-387 7050. *Club:* Athenæum.

McGONAGLE, Stephen; Chairman, Northern Ireland Police Complaints Board, since 1977; *b* 17 Nov. 1914; *m* ; five *s* one *d. Educ:* Christian Brothers', Derry. Chairman, NI Cttee, Irish Congress of Trade Unions, 1959; Vice-Chm., Derry Develt Commn, 1969-71; Pres., Irish Congress of Trade Unions, 1972-73; Mem., NI Economic Council, Indust. Tribunal, Indust. Ct, until 1973; Dist Sec., Irish Transport and General Workers' Union, Dec. 1973; NI Parly Comr For Admin, and Comr for Complaints, 1974-79. *Recreations:* fishing, boating, reading. *Address:* (office) Windsor House, 9-15 Bedford Street, Belfast, Northern Ireland. *T:* Belfast 44821; (home) 10 Kingsfort Park, Derry.

MACGOUGAN, John; Member, Central Arbitration Committee, since 1977; *b* 21 Aug. 1913; *m* 1941, Lizzie Faulkner; three *s* one *d. Educ:* various Northern Ireland Schs; Technical Sch.; Correspondence courses. Accountancy profession, 1930-45. Irish Officer, NUTGW, in charge of all Irish affairs, 1945-69; Gen. Sec., NUTGW, 1969-79. Contested (Irish Labour) N Ireland Parly Elections, Oldpark 1938, Falls Div. 1951; Westminster Parly Election, South Down 1950; Member: Belfast Corporation, 1949-58; Executive, Irish TUC, 1950-69 (Pres. 1957-58 and 1963-64); TUC Gen. Council, 1970-79; MSC, 1977-79; Economic and Social Cttee, EEC, 1978-80. *Recreations:* proletarian pastimes, greyhound racing (owner). *Address:* 96 Whalley Drive, Bletchley, Milton Keynes, Bucks MK3 6HU. *T:* Milton Keynes 72174.

McGOUGH, Roger; poet; *b* 9 Nov. 1937; *s* of Roger Francis and Mary Agnes McGough; *m* 1970 (marr. diss. 1980); two *s. Educ:* St Mary's Coll., Crosby, Liverpool; Hull Univ. (BA, Grad. Cert. Ed.). Fellow of Poetry, Univ. of Loughborough, 1973-75. *Publications:* Watchwords, 1969; After The Merrymaking, 1971; Out of Sequence, 1972; Gig, 1972; Sporting Relations, 1974; In The Glassroom, 1976; Mr Noselighter, 1977; Summer with Monika, 1978; Holiday on Death Row, 1979; Unlucky For Some, 1981; Waving at Trains, 1982; The Great Smile Robbery, 1982; contrib. Oxford Book of 20th Century Verse; contrib. Penguin Modern Poets, No 10; (ed) Strictly Private, 1981. *Address:* c/o A. D. Peters, 10 Buckingham Street, WC2N 6BU. *T:* 01-839 2556. *Club:* Chelsea Arts.

McGOVERN, George Stanley; Chairman, Americans for Common Sense; *b* Avon, S Dakota, 19 July 1922; *s* of Rev. Joseph C. McGovern and Francis (*née* McLean); *m* 1943, Eleanor Faye Stegeberg; one *s* four *d. Educ:* Dakota Wesleyan Univ. (BA); Northwestern Univ. (MA, PhD). Served World War II, USAAF (DFC). Teacher, Northwestern Univ., 1948-50; Prof. of History and Govt, Dakota Wesleyan Univ., 1950-53. Exec. Sec., S Dakota Democratic Party, 1953-56; Mem., 1st Dist, S Dakota, US House of Reps, 1957-61; Dir, Food for Peace Programme, 1961-62; Senator from South Dakota, 1963-81. Democratic Candidate for US Presidential nomination, 1972. Vis. Prof., University Coll., Dublin, 1982. Mem., Amer. Hist. Assoc. *Publications:* The Colorado Coal Strike, 1913-14, 1953; War Against Want, 1964; Agricultural Thought in the Twentieth Century, 1967; A Time of War, A Time of Peace, 1968; (with Leonard F. Guttridge) The Great Coalfield War, 1972; An American Journey, 1974; Grassroots, an Autobiography, 1978. *Address:* 1825 Connecticut Avenue NW, Suite 213, Washington, DC 20009, USA.

McGOWAN, family name of **Baron McGowan.**

McGOWAN, 3rd Baron, *cr* 1937; **Harry Duncan Cory McGowan;** Partner, Panmure, Gordon & Co., since 1971; *b* 20 July 1938; *e s* of Harry Wilson McGowan, 2nd Baron McGowan, and Carmen, *d* of Sir (James) Herbert Cory, 1st Bt; *S* father, 1966; *m* 1962, Lady Gillian Angela Pepys, *d* of 7th Earl of Cottenham; one *s* two *d. Educ:* Eton. *Heir: s* Hon. Harry John Charles McGowan, *b* 23 June 1971. *Address:* House of Lords, Westminster, SW1; Highway House, Lower Froyle, Alton, Hants. *T:* Bentley 2104; 12 Stanhope Mews East, SW7. *T:* 01-370 2346. *Club:* Boodle's.

McGOWAN, Alan Patrick, PhD; Head of Department of Ships, National Maritime Museum, since 1971; *b* 16 Nov. 1928; *s* of Hugh McGowan and Alice Chilton; *m* 1958, Betty Eileen, *e d* of Mr and Mrs F. L. MacDougall, Ontario; three *s. Educ:* Spring Grove Grammar Sch.; Borough Road Coll.; Univ. of Western Ontario (BA, MA); Univ. of London (PhD). Associate RINA 1980. Served RASC (Air Freight), 1947-49. Asst Master (History), 1953-63; Lectr, Univ. of Western Ont Summer Sch., 1964; Canada Council Fellow, 1964-66; Asst Keeper, Dept of Ships, National Maritime Museum, 1967-71; Associate Prof. of History, Univ. of Western Ont Summer Sch., 1977. Member: Council, Navy Records Soc., 1968-; Adv. Council on Export of Works of Art, 1972-; Victory Adv. Technical Cttee, 1974-; Mary Rose Adv. Cttee, 1974-78; Ships Cttee, Maritime Trust, 1977-; Council, Soc. for Nautical Res., 1981-; Cttee, Falkland Islands Foundn, 1981-. *Publications:* (ed) Jacobean Commissions of Enquiry, 1608 and 1618, vol. 113 of Navy Records Society, 1971; Royal Yachts, 1975; (with J. Fabb) The Victorian and Edwardian Navy in Photographs, 1976; (ed and prefaced) Steel's Naval Architecture, 1976; Sailor, 1977; (ed and prefaced) Steel's Rigging and Seamanship, 1978; The Century before Steam, 1980; Tiller and Whipstaff, 1981; articles in jls of history and in encyclopaedia. *Recreations:* golf, reading, music. *Address:* c/o National Maritime Museum, Greenwich, SE10 9NF.

McGOWAN, Bruce Henry, MA; FRSA; Headmaster, Haberdashers' Aske's School, since 1973; b 27 June 1924; er s of late Rt Rev. Henry McGowan, sometime Bishop of Wakefield, and Nora Heath McGowan (née Godwin); m 1947, Beryl McKenzie (née Liggitt); one s three d. Educ: King Edward's Sch., Birmingham; Jesus Coll., Cambridge. War service, Royal Artillery, 1943-46. Asst Master, King's Sch., Rochester, 1949-53; Senior History Master, Wallasey Gram. Sch., 1953-57; Headmaster: De Aston Sch., Market Rasen, Lincs, 1957-64; Solihull Sch., 1964-73. Page Scholar of the English-Speaking Union, 1961. Member: Church Assembly, 1963-70; Public Schools Commn, 1968-70; Chairman: Boarding Schools Assoc., 1967-69; London Division of HMC, 1977; HMC Community Service Cttee, 1975-80; HMC Political and Public Relations Cttee, 1981-. Recreations: foreign travel, mountain-walking, music, the theatre. Address: Haberdashers' Aske's School, Elstree, Herts WD6 3AF.

McGRADY, Edward Kevin; Partner, M. B. McGrady & Co., chartered accountants and insurance brokers; Member (SDLP) South Down, Northern Ireland Assembly, since 1982; b 3 June 1935; y s of late Michael McGrady and late Lilian Leatham; m 1959, Patricia, d of Wm Swail and Margaret Breen; two s one d. Educ: St Patrick's High Sch., Downpatrick. ACA 1957, FCA 1962. Councillor, Downpatrick UDC, 1961; Chm. of UDC, 1964-73; Vice-Chm., Down District Council, 1973, 1975-76, 1977, Chm. 1974, 1976, 1978, 1981, 1982. 1st Chm. of SDLP, 1971-73; 1st Chm. of SDLP Assembly Party. Mem. (SDLP), S Down, NI Assembly, 1973-75, NI Constitutional Convention, 1975-76; Head of Office of Executive Planning and Co-ordination (Minister for Co-ordination, Jan.-May 1974); contested (SDLP) Down S, gen. election, 1979. Recreations: golf, badminton, choral work. Address: Cois Na Cille, Saul Brae, Downpatrick, Co. Down BT30 6NL. T: Downpatrick 2307.

McGRAIL, Dr Sean Francis, FSA; Chief Archaeologist and Head of Archaeological Research Centre, National Maritime Museum, since 1976; b 1928; m 1955, Ursula Anne Yates; one s three d. Educ: Royal Navy (Master Mariner); Univ. of Bristol (BA); Univ. of London (PhD). FSA 1981. Served RN, 1946-68: Seaman Officer; awarded Wings, 1952; comd 849 Sqdn, FAA, 1962-63 (pilot). Undergrad., Univ. of Bristol, 1968-71 (Harry Crook Scholar, 1969-71); Postgrad. Student, Inst. of Archaeology, London, 1972-73; Postgrad. Student (pt-time), UCL, 1973-78; National Maritime Museum, 1972-. Publications: Building and Trials of a Replica of an Ancient Boat, 1974; (ed) Sources and Techniques in Boat Archaeology, 1977; Logboats of England and Wales, 1978; (ed) Medieval Ships and Harbours, 1979; (ed) Paul Johnstone, Seacraft of Prehistory, 1980; (ed) Brigg'raft' and her Prehistoric Environment, 1981; Rafts, Boats and Ships, 1981; (ed) Woodworking Techniques before 1500, 1982; articles in archaeological and maritime jls. Recreations: rearing geese, real ale specialist. Address: c/o National Maritime Museum, Greenwich, SE10 9NF. T: 01-858 5265.

McGRATH, Sir Charles (Gullan), AC 1981; Kt 1968; OBE 1964; Chairman, Nylex Corporation Ltd, since 1970; b Ballarat, 22 Nov. 1910; s of David Charles McGrath and Elizabeth McGrath; m 1934, Madge Louise, d of Andrew McLaren; one s four d. Educ: Ballarat High Sch. Chairman: Repco Ltd, 1957-80; Petersville Australia Ltd, 1971-81; Premier's Economic Adv. Panel, Victoria, 1978-82; Director: Capel Court Corp.; Aust. Foundation Invest. Co. Ltd. Life Governor, Royal Melbourne Inst. of Technol., 1973. Hon. DEng Monash, 1978. Aust. Manufacturers Export Council Award for outstanding personal contrib. to Australia's export, 1969. Recreation: farming. Address: 46 Lansell Road, Toorak, Vic. 3142, Australia. Clubs: Australian, Athenæum, Melbourne, West Brighton (Melbourne).

McGRATH, John Cornelius, CBE 1971; FCA; FCIT 1970; Financial Adviser to British Airports Authority; full-time Board Member and Founder Financial Controller of British Airports Authority, 1966-71; s of Patrick and Johanna McGrath; bachelor. Educ: Jesuit Coll. of St Ignatius; Univ. of London. Schoolmaster, 1925-27; Asst to Public Auditor, 1927-34; Lectr in Accountancy and Finance, 1928-39; appointed Public Auditor by HM Treasury, 1934; qual. as Chartered Accountant, 1938; Dep. Man. of Audit Dept, CWS, 1938-66; Chief Accountant and Financial Adviser to LCS, 1947-66. Bd Mem. for Finance of Post Office, 1968-69. Mem., Worshipful Co. of Inn-holders, 1951; Freeman, City of London, 1951. Recreations: music, motor racing, travel, swimming. Address: 8 River Court, Surbiton, Surrey. T: 01-546 3833. Clubs: Reform, Royal Automobile, MCC.

McGRATH, John Peter; writer; Artistic Director, 7:84 Theatre Companies, since 1971; b 1 June 1935; s of John Francis McGrath and Margaret McGrath; m 1962, Elizabeth Maclennan; two s one d. Educ: Alun Grammar Sch., Mold; St John's Coll., Oxford. Theatre (playwright), 1958-61; BBC Television, 1960-65; film (screenwriting) and theatre (writing and directing), 1965-70; theatre, with regular forays into television and film, as writer and director, 1970-; founded 7:84 Theatre Co., 1971. Publications: plays: Events While Guarding the Bofors Gun, 1966; Random Happenings in the Hebrides, 1972; Bakke's Night of Fame, 1973; The Cheviot, The Stag and The Black Black Oil, 1974, 2nd edn 1981; The Game's A Bogey, 1974; Fish in the Sea, 1977; Little Red Hen, 1977; Yobbo Newt, 1978; Joe's Drum, 1979; Blood Red Roses, and Swings and Roundabouts, 1981; general: A Good Night Out, 1981. Address: 33A Pembroke Square, W8.

McGRATH, Dr Patrick Gerard, CB 1981; CBE 1971; Senior Consultant Psychiatrist and Physician Superintendent, Broadmoor Hospital, 1956-81,

now Physician Superintendent Emeritus; b 10 June 1916; s of late Patrick McGrath and Mary (née Murray), Glasgow; m 1949, Helen Patricia O'Brien; three s one d. Educ: St Aloysius Coll., Glasgow; Glasgow and Edinburgh Univs. MB, ChB Glasgow 1939; DipPsych Edinburgh 1955; FRCPsych (Vice-Pres., 1978-80), Hon. FRCPsych 1981; FRSocMed. RAMC, 1939-46 (Hon. Lt-Col); various trng posts in psychiatry, Glasgow, London and Colchester, 1946-51; Psychiatrist, Ayrshire, 1951-56. Member: Parole Board, 1982-; Adv. Council, Inst. of Criminology, Univ. of Cambridge, 1982-. Publications: chapter in Psychopathic Disorder, 1966; Mentally Abnormal Offender, 1968; contrib. Jl of RSH, Cropwood publications, etc. Recreation: golf (purely social). Address: 18 Heathermount Drive, Crowthorne, Berks. Club: East Berks Golf.

McGRATH, Peter William; UK Operations Director, Stone International Ltd, since 1982; Deputy Chairman, Swifts of Exmouth Ltd, since 1982; b 19 Nov. 1931; s of Major W. P. McGrath and Winifred Clara (née Fill); m 1954, Margaret Irene Page; one s three d. Educ: Boroughmuir Sch.; Royal Liberty Sch.; Univ. of London (Dip. in Econs). Sen. managerial positions in finance and prodn, Ford of Britain and Ford of Germany, 1962-69; Controller of Corporate Finance, BR Bd, 1969-72; Dir of Finance, NFC, 1972-77; Dir of Finance and Systems, Truck and Bus Div., British Leyland, 1977; Man. Dir, British Leyland Internat., 1977-78; Chm. and Man. Dir, BL Components Ltd, 1978-79; Group Man. Dir, Concord Rotaflex, 1980-82. Member of Lloyd's. Recreations: sailing, military history, opera. Address: De Fontenay, Chalk Lane, Hyde Heath, Amersham, Bucks. Club: Medway Yacht (Rochester).

McGREGOR, family name of **Baron McGregor of Durris.**

McGREGOR OF DURRIS, Baron cr 1978 (Life Peer), of Hampstead; **Oliver Ross McGregor;** Professor of Social Institutions in the University of London since 1964; Head of Department of Sociology, at Bedford College, 1964-77; Joint Director Rowntree Legal Research Unit, since 1966; Chairman, Advertising Standards Authority, since 1980; b 25 Aug. 1921; s of late William McGregor and late Anne Olivia Ross; m 1944, Nellie Weate; three s. Educ: Worksop Coll.; University of Aberdeen; London School of Economics (Hon. Fellow 1977). Temp. civil servant, War Office and Ministry of Agriculture, 1940-44. Asst Lecturer and Lecturer in Economic History, University of Hull, 1945-47; Lecturer, Bedford Coll., 1947-60, Reader in University of London, 1960-64; Simon Senior Research Fellow, University of Manchester, 1959-60. Fellow of Wolfson Coll., Oxford, 1972-75; Dir, Centre for Socio-Legal Studies, Univ. of Oxford, 1972-75. Member: Cttee on Enforcement of Judgment Debts, 1965; Cttee on Statutory Maintenance Limits, 1966; Cttee on Land Use (Recreation and Leisure), 1967; National Parks Commission, 1966-68; Independent Television Authority's General Advisory Council, 1967-73; Countryside Commission, 1968-80; Legal Aid Adv. Cttee, 1969-78; Cttee on One-Parent Families, 1969-74; Chm., Royal Commn on Press, 1975-77 (Mem., 1974). President: Nat. Council for One Parent Families, 1975-; Nat. Assoc. of Citizens' Advice Bureaux, 1981-. Lectures: Fawcett Meml, 1966; James Seth Meml, 1968; Hobhouse Meml, 1971; Maccabaean in Jurisprudence, 1973; Hamlyn, 1979; Eleanor Rathbone Meml, 1979; Ian Gulland, 1980. Publications: Divorce in England, 1957; ed, Lord Ernle, English Farming Past and Present, 6th edn, 1960; Bibliography of the National Association for the Promotion of Social Science, 1960; (jtly) Separated Spouses, 1970; Social History and Law Reform, 1981; various papers in British Journal of Sociology and other journals. Address: Far End, Wyldes Close, NW11 7JB. T: 01-458 2856. Club: Garrick.

MacGREGOR, Air Vice-Marshal Andrew, CB 1949; CBE 1945; DFC 1918; retired; b 25 Oct. 1897; s of late Andrew MacGregor, Glen Gyle, Crieff; m 1939, Isobel Jane, d of Gordon Eadie, Crieff; three d. Educ: Morrison's Acad., Crieff. Commissioned Argyll and Sutherland Highlanders and attached RFC, 1917. Served in Egypt and Iraq, 1919-27; graduated RAF Staff Coll., 1928; served in Sudan and Palestine, 1932-37; Dep. Directorate Organisation, Air Ministry, 1940; Senior Air Staff Officer, HQ, No. 4 Group, 1940-42; Air Officer Administrative, N Africa, 1942-44; Asst Commandant, Staff Coll., 1944; Air Officer comdg No 28 Group, 1945-46; Air Officer Administrative, HQ Fighter Command, 1946-49. Comdr Legion of Honour, 1944; Comdr Order of Crown of Belgium, 1948; Officer of Legion of Merit (USA), 1944; Croix de Guerre. Address: Glen Gyle, Crieff, Perthshire, Scotland. T: Crieff 2583.

McGREGOR, Dr Angus; Regional Medical Officer, West Midlands Regional Health Authority, since 1979; b 26 Dec. 1926; s of Dr William Hector Scott McGregor and Dr Olwen May Richards; m 1951, May Burke; one d. Educ: Solihull Sch.; St John's Coll., Cambridge. MA, MD; FFCM; DPH. Junior hospital posts, 1950; Army service, RAMC, 1951-52; general practice, 1953; Asst MOH, Chester, 1954-56; Deputy Medical Officer of Health: Swindon, 1957-58; Hull, 1958-65; MOH and Port MO, Southampton, 1965-74; District Community Physician, East Dorset, 1974-79. Publications: contrib. papers to medical journals. Recreation: piano. Address: (home) 68 Gillhurst Road, Birmingham B17 8PB. T: 021-427 2450; (office) 146 Hagley Road, Birmingham B16 9PA. T: 021-454 4828.

MacGREGOR, Duncan; Convenor of the Council of Fellows in Dental Surgery, Royal College of Surgeons of Edinburgh, 1965-67; President Odonto-Chirurgical Society of Scotland, 1956-57; President, British Dental Association, 1960-61 (now Vice-President); b 17 Feb. 1892; s of A. D. MacGregor and Jessie Steel Proudfoot; m 1921, Elizabeth Ruth Doig; one s one d. Educ: George Heriot's Sch.; Royal Coll. of Surgeons and Edinburgh Dental Hospital and Sch. LDS, RCS Edinburgh 1916; Surgeon Probationer, RNVR 1915-17; Surg. Lt (D) RNVR 1917-19; Surg. Lt-Comdr (D) RNVR, retd 1937. Hon. Dental Surg., Edinburgh Dental Hosp. and Sch., 1921-48; Consultant Dental Surg., Edinburgh Dental Hosp., 1948-61; Member: Dental Board of the UK 1946-56; Gen. Dental Council, 1956-66. Fellowship in Dental Surgery, Royal Coll. of Surgeons, Edinburgh, 1951. Publications: contributions to dental journals. Recreations: sketching, gardening. Address: 8 Seton Place, Edinburgh EH9 2JT. T: 031-667 5071. Club: Caledonian (Edinburgh).

MacGREGOR, Edward Ian Roy, CMG 1966; HM Diplomatic Service, retired; b 4 March 1911; s of late John MacGregor and late Georgina Agnes MacGregor (née Barbor); m 1944, Lilianne, d of William Swindlehurst, Washington, DC, USA; one s one d. Educ: Methodist Coll., Belfast; Queen's Univ., Belfast (MSc). Wing Comdr RAF, 1936-47. Asst Civil Air Attaché, Washington, 1948-52; Ministry of Transport and Civil Aviation, 1952-59; Civil Air Attaché, Washington, 1959-65; Asst Sec., BoT, 1965-67; Counsellor, FO, 1967-68; Consul-Gen., Detroit, 1968-71. Address: Spinneys, Brock Way, Virginia Water, Surrey. T: Wentworth 3612.

MACGREGOR, Sir Edwin (Robert), 7th Bt cr 1828; Assistant Deputy Minister, Ministry of Energy, Mines and Petroleum Resources, Province of British Columbia, Victoria, BC; b 4 Dec. 1931; e s of Sir Robert McConnell Macgregor, 6th Bt, and of Annie Mary Lane; S father, 1963; m 1952, (Margaret Alice) Jean Peake (marr. diss. 1981); one s two d (and one s decd). Educ: University of British Columbia. BASc 1955, MASc 1957, Metallurgical Engineering. Member: Assoc. of Professional Engrs, Province of British Columbia; Canadian Inst. of Mining and Metallurgy. Publications: contribs to Trans Amer. Inst. of Mining, Metallurgical and Petroleum Engrg, Jl Amer. Chem. Soc. Recreations: reading; participation in several outdoor sports such as golf, swimming, fishing, etc.; music. Heir: s Ian Grant Macgregor, b 22 Feb. 1959. Address: 6136 Kirby Road, RR3, Sooke, BC V0S 1N0, Canada.

MacGREGOR, Geddes; see MacGregor, J. G.

McGREGOR, Dr Gordon Peter; Principal, College of Ripon and York St John, since 1980; b Aldershot, Hants, 13 June 1932; 2nd s of William A. K. McGregor and Mary A. McGregor (née O'Brien); m 1957, Jean Olga Lewis; three d. Educ: Bishop Road Jun. Sch., Bristol; St Brendan's Coll., Bristol; Univ. of Bristol (BA Hons); Univ. of East Africa (MEd); Univ. of Sussex (DPhil); Dip. Coll. of Teachers of the Blind. Educn Officer, RAF, 1953-56; Asst Master, Worcester Coll. for the Blind, 1956-59; Asst Master, King's Coll., Budo, Uganda, 1959-62; Lecturer in English Language, Makerere Univ. Coll., Uganda 1963-66; Univ. of Zambia: Sen Lecturer in Educn, 1966-68; Reader and Head of Dept of Education, 1968-70; Prof. of Educn, 1970; Principal, Bishop Otter Coll., Chichester, 1970-80. FRSA (invited) 1976. Publications: King's College, Budo, The First Sixty Years, 1967; Educating the Handicapped, 1967; Education for Education?, 1968; Teaching English as a Second Language (with J. A. Bright), 1970; English in Africa, (UNESCO), 1971; Bishop Otter College and Policy for Teacher Education 1839-1980, 1981; contrib. Univs Qly, Times Higher Educn Supplement, PNEU Jl. Recreations: music, literature, theatre, travel, swimming. Address: Principal's House, College of Ripon and York St John, Lord Mayor's Walk, York. T: York 56771.

MacGREGOR OF MacGREGOR, Brig. Sir Gregor, 6th Bt, cr 1795; ADC 1979; 23rd Chief of Clan Gregor; b 22 Dec. 1925; o s of Capt. Sir Malcolm MacGregor of MacGregor, 5th Bt, CB, CMG, and Hon. Gylla Lady MacGregor of MacGregor, OBE (d 1980); S father 1958; m 1958, Fanny, o d of C. H. A. Butler, Shortgrove, Newport, Essex; two s. Educ: Eton. Commissioned Scots Guards, 1944; served War of 1939-45. Served in Palestine, 1947-48; Malaya, 1950-51; Borneo, 1965. Staff Coll. Course, 1960; Brigade Major, 16th Parachute Bde Gp, 1961-63; Joint Services Staff Coll., 1965; commanding 1st Bn Scots Guards, 1966-69; GSO1 (BLO) Fort Benning, USA, 1969-71; Col Recruiting, HQ Scotland, 1971; Lt-Col commanding Scots Guards, 1971-74; Defence and Mil. Attaché, British Embassy, Athens, 1975-78; Comdr, Lowlands, 1978-80. Dir, MacGregor Centrex Ltd. Mem. of the Royal Company of Archers (Queen's Body Guard for Scotland). Heir: s Malcolm Gregor Charles MacGregor of MacGregor, Scots Guards, b 23 March 1959. Address: Bannatyne House, Newtyle, Blairgowrie, Perthshire. T: Newtyle 314. Clubs: Buck's, Pratt's; New (Edinburgh).

McGREGOR, Harvey, QC 1978; Fellow of New College, Oxford, since 1972; b 25 Feb. 1926; s of William Guthrie Robertson McGregor and late Agnes (née Reid). Educ: Inverurie Acad.; Scarborough Boys' High Sch.; Queen's Coll., Oxford (Hastings Scholar; BA 1951, BCL 1952, MA 1955). Dr of Juridical Science, Harvard, 1962. Called to the Bar, Inner Temple, 1955. Flying Officer, RAF, 1946-48. Bigelow Teaching Fellow, Univ. of Chicago, 1950-51; Vis. Prof., New York Univ. and Rutgers Univ., 1963-69 (various times). Consultant to Law Commn 1966-73. Pres., Harvard Law Sch. Assoc. of UK, 1981-. Dep. Independent Chm., London Theatre Council, 1971-; Trustee, Oxford Union Soc., 1977-. Mem. Editorial Cttee, Modern Law Review, 1967-. Publications: McGregor on Damages, 12th edn 1961- 14th edn 1980; (contrib.) International Encyclopedia of Comparative Law, 1972; articles in legal jls. Recreations: music, theatre, travel, sailing. Address: (chambers) 4 Paper Buildings, Temple, EC4Y 7EX. T: 01-353 3366;

(residence) Gray's Inn Chambers, Gray's Inn, WC1R 5JA. T: 01-242 4942. Club: Garrick.

MacGREGOR, Ian; Chairman and Chief Executive, British Steel Corporation, since 1980; b 21 Sept. 1912; m Sibyl Spencer; one s, one d. Educ: George Watson's Coll., Edinburgh; Hillhead High Sch., Glasgow; Univ. of Glasgow. BSc (1st cl. Hons). Chairman and Chief Executive, Amax Inc., 1966-77 (Hon. Chm., 1977-); Deputy Chairman, BL Ltd, 1977-80; Partner, Lazard Freres & Co., New York, 1978-. President of the International Chamber of Commerce, Paris, 1978. Hon. degrees from Univs. of Glasgow (LLD), Strathclyde (LLD), Denver (LLD), Montana State (DEng), Wyoming (LLD), and Tri-State Coll., Indiana (DSc). John Fritz Medal, 1981. Chevalier, Légion d'Honneur, 1972. Address: c/o British Steel Corporation, 9 Albert Embankment, SE1 7SN.

McGREGOR, Sir Ian (Alexander), Kt 1982; CBE 1968 (OBE 1959); FRS 1981; Member, External Staff, Medical Research Council and Professorial Fellow, Department of Tropical Medicine, Liverpool School of Tropical Medicine, since 1981; b 26 Aug. 1922; s of John McGregor and Isabella (née Taylor), Cambuslang, Lanarks; m 1954, Nancy Joan, d of Frederick Small, Mapledurham, Oxon; one s one d. Educ: Rutherglen Academy; St Mungo Coll., Glasgow. LRCPE, LRCSE, LRFPS(G) 1945; DTM&H 1949; MRCP 1962; FRCP 1967; FFCM 1972. Mil. Service, 1946-48 (despatches). Mem. Scientific Staff, Human Nutrition Research Unit, MRC, 1949-53; Dir, MRC Laboratory, The Gambia, 1954-74, 1978-80; Head of Laboratory of Trop. Community Studies, Nat. Inst. for Med. Research, Mill Hill, 1974-77; Member: WHO Adv. Panel on Malaria, 1961-; Malaria Cttee, MRC, 1962-71; Cttee on Nutrition Surveys, Internat. Union of Nutrition Sciences, 1971-75; Tropical Medicine Res. Bd, MRC, 1974-77, 1981-; Steering Cttee on Immunology of Malaria, WHO, 1978-. Pres., Royal Soc. of Trop. Medicine and Hygiene, from June 1983 (Vice-Pres., 1981-83). Chalmers Medal, Royal Soc. Trop. Med. and Hygiene, 1963; Stewart Prize, BMA, 1970; Darling Foundn Medal, WHO, 1974. Hon. Fellow Liverpool Sch. of Trop. Medicine, 1980. Publications: scientific papers on infections, nutrition, immunity, child health and community medicine in tropical environments. Recreations: ornithology, golf, fishing. Address: The Glebe House, Greenlooms, Hargrave, Cheshire CH3 7RX.

McGREGOR, James Reid, CBE 1948; CBE 1945; MC 1916; m 1933, Dorothy Janet, d of Mr and Mrs Comrie, Ayr; one s one d. Educ: Edinburgh Academy, RMC Sandhurst. Served European War, 1914-18, Gordon Highlanders, 1915-19 (despatches, wounded, MC); War of 1939-45, Director of Army contracts, 1940-44; Private Secretary to Sir James Grigg, Secretary of State for War, 1944-45; Director of Finance, War Office, 1945-59. Member, Public Health Laboratory Service Board, 1961-69. Address: Torphins, Burntwood Road, Sevenoaks, Kent.

McGREGOR, James Stalker; Chairman, Honeywell Ltd, since 1981; Managing Director, Honeywell Control Systems Ltd, since 1971; b 30 Oct. 1927; s of John McGregor and Jean McCabe; m 1953, Iris Millar Clark; one s. Educ: Dumfries Acad.; Royal Tech. Coll., Glasgow (ARTC); Glasgow Univ. BSc (Hons); CEng, MIMechE; CBIM. Production Engr, Rolls Royce Ltd, 1952-56; Sales Engr, Sandvik Swedish Steels, 1956-57; Honeywell Control Systems: Assembly Manager, later Production Control Manager and Admin Manager, 1957-65; Divl Dir, Temperature Controls Gp, 1965-71. Recreation: golf. Address: 19 Burgess Wood Road, Beaconsfield, Bucks. T: Beaconsfield 2187.

MacGREGOR, Prof. (John) Geddes, DèsL (Sorbonne), DPhil, DD Oxon, BD Edinburgh et Oxon, LLB Edinburgh; FRSL 1948; Distinguished Professor of Philosophy, University of Southern California, 1966-75, now Emeritus; Dean of Graduate School of Religion, 1960-66; first holder of Rufus Jones Chair of Philosophy and Religion, Bryn Mawr, USA, 1949-60; Canon Theologian of St Paul's Cathedral, Los Angeles, 1968-74; b 13 Nov. 1909; o s of late Thomas and Blanche Geddes MacGregor, Angus; m 1941, Elizabeth, e d of late Archibald McAllister, Edinburgh; one s one d. Educ: Universities of Edinburgh, Paris, Heidelberg; The Queen's Coll., Oxford. Senior Assistant to Dean of Chapel Royal in Scotland, at St Giles' Cathedral, Edinburgh, 1939-41; served in Civil Defence, War of 1939-45; Minister, Trinity Church, Glasgow, S1, 1941-49; Assistant to Prof. of Logic and Metaphysics, Edinburgh Univ., 1947-49; Examiner: Swarthmore Coll., USA, 1950, 1953, 1955-57; Hebrew Union Coll., USA, 1959, 1961; Occasional Lectr at many US and Canadian Univs. Visiting Professor: Univ. of British Columbia, 1963, 1966, 1973; Hebrew Union Coll., 1964-65; Univ. of Santa Clara, 1968; World Campus Afloat (Orient, 1974; Mediterranean, 1975); McGill Univ., Montreal, 1976; Inst. for Shipboard Educn (round-the-world-voyage), 1977; Univ. of Iowa, 1979; Univ. of Saskatchewan, 1979; Vis. Fellow, Dept of Religious Studies, Yale Univ., 1967-68; Vis. Lectr, Rikkyo Univ., Tokyo, 1981; Hon. Fellow, Emporia State Univ., 1982. Special Preacher: St Paul's Cathedral, London, 1969; Westminster Abbey, 1970. Regent, American-Scottish Foundation, Inc., NY. Hon. LHD Hebrew Union, 1978. Hon. Phi Kappa Phi, 1972 (Distinguished Award, 1982). California Literature Award (Gold Medal, non fiction), 1964. Publications: Aesthetic Experience in Religion, 1947; Christian Doubt, 1951; Les Frontières de la Morale et de la Religion, 1952; From a Christian Ghetto, 1954; The Vatican Revolution, 1957; The Tichborne Impostor, 1957; The Thundering Scot, 1957; Corpus Christi, 1959; Introduction to Religious Philosophy, 1959; The Bible in the Making, 1959; The Coming Reformation, 1960; The Hemlock and the Cross, 1963; God Beyond Doubt, 1966; A Literary History of the Bible, 1968; The Sense of Absence, 1968; So Help Me God, 1970; Philosophical Issues in Religious Thought, 1973; The Rhythm of God, 1974; He Who Lets Us Be, 1975; Reincarnation in Christianity, 1978; Gnosis, 1979; Scotland Forever Home, 1980; The Nicene Creed, 1981; Reincarnation as a Christian Hope, 1982; The Gospels as a Mandala of Wisdom, 1982. *Recreation:* manual labour. *Address:* 876 Victoria Avenue, Los Angeles, California 90005, USA. *T:* 213-938-4826. *Clubs:* Athenæum, English-Speaking Union, Royal Commonwealth Society; Caledonian (Edinburgh); Union Society (Oxford); Automobile (Los Angeles).

MacGREGOR, John Roddick Russell, OBE 1971; MP (C) South Norfolk, since Feb. 1974; Parliamentary Under-Secretary of State, Department of Industry, since 1981; *b* 14 Feb. 1937; *s* of late Dr. N. S. R. MacGregor; *m* 1962, Jean Mary Elizabeth Dungey; one *s* two *d. Educ:* Merchiston Castle Sch., Edinburgh; St Andrews Univ. (MA, 1st cl. Hons); King's Coll., London (LLB). Univ. Administrator, 1961–62; Editorial Staff, New Society, 1962–63; Special Asst to Prime Minister, Sir Alec Douglas-Home, 1963–64; Conservative Research Dept, 1964–65; Head of Private Office of Rt Hon. Edward Heath, Leader of Opposition, 1965–68; an Opposition Whip, 1977–79; a Lord Comr of HM Treasury, 1979–81. Hill Samuel & Co. Ltd, 1968–79 (Dir, 1973–79). Chairman: Fedn of University Cons. and Unionist Assocs, 1959; Bow Group, 1963–64; 1st Pres., Conservative and Christian Democratic Youth Community, 1963–65; formerly Treasurer, Federal Trust for Educn and Research; formerly Trustee, European Educnl Research Trust; Governor, Langley Sch., Norfolk, 1976. *Publications:* contrib. The Conservative Opportunity; also pamphlets. *Recreations:* theatre, music, reading, travelling, gardening. *Address:* House of Commons, SW1A 0AA.

MACGREGOR, John Roy; His Honour Judge Macgregor; a Circuit Judge, since 1974; Honorary Recorder of Margate, 1972–79; *b* Brooklyn, NY, 9 Sept. 1913; 4th *s* of Charles George McGregor, of Jamaica and New York. *Educ:* Bedford School. Called to the Bar, Gray's Inn, 1939; Inner Temple (*ad eundem*), 1968. Served in Royal Artillery, 1939–46; RA (TA) and Special Air Service (TA), 1950–61. Dep. Chm., Cambridgeshire and Isle of Ely QS, 1967–71; a Recorder, 1972–74. Legal Assessor to Gen. Optical Council, 1972–74. *Address:* Nether Gaulrig, Yardley Hastings, Northampton NN7 1HD. *T:* Yardley Hastings 861. *Club:* Special Forces.

McGREGOR, Kenneth, CB 1963; CMG 1951; retired; *b* 11 Feb. 1903; *o c* of late James McGregor and Eugénie Lydia Johnson; *m* 1930, Dorothy Laura Roope, *o d* of late Judge R. Roope Reeve, QC; two *s. Educ:* Westminster (King's Scholar); New Coll., Oxford (Scholar). 1st class Hons; MA. Called to the Bar (Lincoln's Inn). Ministries of Health, Supply and Production; Board of Trade (Under-Secretary); the Senior British Trade Commissioner in Canada, 1958–62. Member of Quangos, and dir or consultant to Companies and Trade Assocs, 1963–73. Islington Borough Councillor, 1968–71. *Address:* 19 Emden House, Old Headington, Oxford OX3 9JU. *T:* Oxford 64897. *Club:* United Oxford & Cambridge University.

MacGREGOR, Neil; see MacGregor, R. N.

McGREGOR, Peter, CEng, FIEE; Industrial Director, National Economic Development Office, since 1981; *b* 20 May 1926; *s* of Peter McGregor and Margaret Thomson McGregor (*née* McAuslan); *m* 1954, Marion, *d* of H. T. Downer; one *s* one *d. Educ:* Cardiff High Sch.; Univ. of Birmingham; London Sch. of Economics (BSc (Econs)); CompIProdE; MInstM; FBIM. National Service, RE, 1946–48. Various appointments, Ferranti Ltd, incl. Works Manager, Distribution Transformer Dept, Sales Manager, Transformer Div., Gen. Manager, Power Div., 1950–74; Dir, Industrie Elettriche di Legnano (Italy), 1970–74; Dir, Oxford Univ. Business Summer Sch., 1972; first Sec. Gen., Anglo-German Foundn for Study of Industrial Soc., 1974–81. Industrial Advr to Liberal Party, 1960–73; Chm., Hazel Grove Liberal Assoc., 1971–74; contested (L) Ilford South, 1964. FRSA. *Publications:* various articles and pamphlets especially on industrial relations, company structure, market economy. *Recreations:* sailing, walking, reading, listening to music, writing, conversation. *Address:* Dacres, Troutstream Way, Loudwater, Rickmansworth, Herts WD3 4LA. *T:* Rickmansworth 76985. *Club:* Caledonian.

MacGREGOR, (Robert) Neil; Editor, The Burlington Magazine, since 1981; *b* 16 June 1946; *s* of Alexander Rankin MacGregor and Anna Fulton Scobie MacGregor (*née* Neil). *Educ:* Glasgow Acad.; New Coll., Oxford; Ecole Normale Supérieure, Paris; Univ. of Edinburgh; Courtauld Inst. of Art. Mem., Faculty of Advocates, Edinburgh, 1972. Lectr in History of Art and Architecture, Univ. of Reading, 1976. *Publications:* contribs to Apollo, The Burlington Magazine, Connoisseur, etc. *Address:* 10 Pembridge Crescent, W11.

McGRIGOR, Captain Sir Charles Edward, 5th Bt, *cr* 1831; Rifle Brigade, retired; Member Royal Company of Archers (HM Body Guard for Scotland); Exon, Queen's Bodyguard, Yeoman of the Guard, since 1970; *b* 5 Oct. 1922; *s* of Lieut-Colonel Sir Charles McGrigor, 4th Bt, OBE, and Lady McGrigor, *d* of Edward Lygon Somers Cocks, Bake, St Germans, Cornwall; *S* father, 1946; *m* 1948, Mary Bettine, *e d* of Sir Archibald Charles Edmonstone, 6th Bt; two *s* two *d. Educ:* Eton. War of 1939–45 (despatches); joined Army, 1941, from Eton; served with Rifle Bde, N. Africa, Italy, Austria. ADC to Duke of Gloucester, 1945–47, in Australia and England. Mem. Cttee of Management

and a Vice-Pres., RNLI and Convenor, Scottish Lifeboat Council. *Recreations:* fishing, gardening. *Heir:* *s* James Angus Rhoderick Neil McGrigor, *b* 19 Oct. 1949. *Address:* Upper Sonachan, Dalmally, Argyll. *Club:* Boodle's.

MacGUIGAN, Hon. Mark Rudolph, PC (Can.) 1980; PhD, JSD; MP for Windsor-Walkerville, Ont, since 1968; Minister of Justice, Government of Canada, since 1982; *b* 17 Feb. 1931; *s* of Hon. Mark R. MacGuigan and Agnes V. Trainor; *m* 1961, Maryellen Symons; two *s* one *d. Educ:* Queen Square Sch.; Prince of Wales (Jun.) Coll.; St Dunstan's Univ., Charlottetown (BA *summa cum laude*); Univ. of Toronto (MA, PhD); Osgoode Hall Law Sch.; Columbia Univ. (LLM, JSD). Admitted to Law Soc. of Upper Canada, 1958. Asst Prof. of Law, 1960–63, and Associate Prof. of Law, 1963–66, Univ. of Toronto; Prof. of Law, Osgoode Hall Law Sch., 1966–67; Dean, Faculty of Law, Univ. of Windsor, 1967–68. Parly Secretary: to Minister of Manpower and Immigration, 1972–74; to Minister of Labour, 1974–75; Opposition Critic of Solicitor Gen., 1979–80; Sec. of State for External Affairs, 1980–82. Chairman: House of Commons Special Cttee on Statutory Instruments, 1968–69; Standing Cttee on Justice and Legal Affairs, 1975–79; Sub-Cttee on Penitentiary System in Canada, 1976–77; Co-Chairman, Special Jt Cttee on Constitution of Canada, 1970–72 and 1978. Hon. LLD Univ. of PEI, 1971. *Publications:* Cases and Materials on Creditors' Rights, 2nd edn 1967; Jurisprudence: readings and cases, 2nd edn 1966. *Recreations:* running, tennis, skiing, swimming. *Address:* 2020 Willistead Crescent, Windsor, Ont N8Y 1K5, Canada. *Club:* Cercle universitaire (Ottawa).

McGUINNESS, James Henry, CB 1964; Chairman, Scottish Philharmonic Trust, since 1976; *b* 29 Sept. 1912; *s* of James Henry McGuinness, Scotstoun; *m* 1939, Annie Eveline Fordyce, Ayr; one *s* two *d. Educ:* St Aloysius Coll.; Univ. of Glasgow, 1st Cl. Hons Classics 1932, George Clark Fellow; Trinity Coll., Oxford (schol.), 1st cl. Hons Mods, 1934, 1st cl. Lit. Hum. Under-Secretary, Dept of Health for Scotland, 1959–62; Scottish Development Department, 1962–64; Asst Under-Sec. of State, Scottish Office and Chm., Scottish Economic Planning Bd, 1965–72; Sen. Res. Fellow in Politics, Univ. of Glasgow, 1973–74. Mem., Oil Develt Council for Scotland, 1973–75. Chairman: Scottish Baroque Ensemble, 1973–74; Scottish Philharmonic Society Ltd, 1974–78. Hon. MRTPI, 1978. *Address:* 10 Greenhill Terrace, Edinburgh EH10 4BS; Kendoon, Dalry, Kirkcudbrightshire. *Club:* Scottish Arts.

McGUINNESS, Rt. Rev. James Joseph; see Nottingham, Bishop of, (RC).

McGUIRE, Gerald, OBE 1974; Deputy National Secretary, Youth Hostels Association (England and Wales), 1974–82; *b* 12 July 1918; *s* of John Charles McGuire and late Adelaide Maud McGuire; *m* 1942, Eveline Mary Jenkins; one *s* one *d. Educ:* Trinity County Sch., Wood Green. Youth Hostels Association: Reg. Sec., N Yorks, 1944–64; National Countryside and Educn Officer, 1964–74. President: Ramblers Assoc., 1975–78 (Vice Pres., 1978–); Assoc. of National Park and Countryside Voluntary Wardens, 1978–80. Member: N York Moors Nat. Park Cttee, 1953–72; Exec. Cttee, CPRE, 1966–76, 1981–; Gosling Cttee on Footpaths, 1967–68; Countryside Commn, 1976–79; Commn on Energy and the Environment, 1978–81. Vice Pres., Commons, Open Spaces and Footpaths Preservation Soc., 1982– (Vice Chm. 1971–76); Vice Chairman: Standing Cttee on Nat. Parks, 1970–76; Council for Environmental Conservation, 1981–; Mem. and Trustee, Council for Nat. Parks, 1978–, Vice-Chm., 1981–. *Recreations:* reading, music, walking in the countryside. *Address:* c/o 14 Belmont, Kendal, Cumbria LA9 4JP.

McGUIRE, Michael Thomas Francis; MP (Lab) Ince since 1964; *b* 3 May 1926; *m* 1954, Marie T. Murphy; three *s* two *d. Educ:* Elementary Schools. Coal miner. Whole-time NUM Branch Secretary, 1957–64. Joined Lab. Party, 1951. PPS to Minister of Sport, 1974–77. Member: Council of Europe, 1977–; WEU, 1977–. *Recreations:* most out-door sports, especially Rugby League football; traditional music, especially Irish traditional music. *Address:* House of Commons, SW1.

McGUIRE, Robert Ely, CMG 1948; OBE 1943; Indian Civil Service (retired); *b* 22 Aug. 1901; *s* of late Major E. C. McGuire, 2nd Bn York and Lancaster Regt; *m* 1930, Barbara, *d* of late Sir Benjamin Heald, ICS, Judge of the High Court of Judicature, Rangoon; one *s* one *d. Educ:* High Sch., Dublin; Trinity Coll., Dublin. MA (Hons). Entered ICS, 1926; Warden, Burma Oilfields, 1932 and 1940–42; Dep. Commissioner, 1932–42. Secretary to Government of Burma (temp. in India), 1942–45. Dep. Director of Civil Affairs, with rank of Brigadier, British Military Administration in Burma, 1945. Divisional Comr, Burma, 1946–47; Secretary to Governor of Burma, 1947 to 4 Jan. 1948 (date of Independence of Burma). Secretary Cement Makers Federation, 1949–64. *Address:* Corofin, Rookery Way, Haywards Heath, West Sussex RH16 4RE. *T:* Haywards Heath 453692. *Club:* East India, Devonshire, Sports and Public Schools.

McGURK, Colin Thomas, OBE 1971 (MBE 1963); HM Diplomatic Service, retired; *b* 9 July 1922; *m* 1946, Ella Taylor; one *s. Educ:* St Mary's Coll., Middlesbrough. Served in Army, 1942–45. HM Foreign (subseq. Diplomatic) Service; served in British Embassies, Cairo, Addis Ababa, Ankara; 3rd Sec., HM Legation, Sofia, 1953–55; 2nd Sec. (Commercial), Athens, 1956–58; FO, 1958–62; HM Consul, Stanleyville, 1962; 1st Sec., Yaoundé, Brussels and Kuwait, 1962–70; Commercial Counsellor, Kuwait, 1971–72; Commercial

Inspector, FCO, 1972-75; Counsellor (Economic and Commercial), New Delhi, 1975-77 and Canberra, 1977-81. *Recreations:* painting, sailing. *Address:* 113 High Street, Burnham-on-Crouch, Essex CM0 8AH. *T:* Maldon 782467. *Club:* Royal Burnham Yacht.

McGUSTY, Victor William Tighe, CMG 1942; OBE 1937; OStJ; MB; DTM; *b* 20 June 1887; *m* 1st, 1912, Annie Bayliss; one *s* one *d*; 2nd, 1971, Joyce E. Johnston, Auckland, NZ. *Educ:* Coleraine (Ireland) Academical Institution; Trinity Coll., Dublin. Entered Colonial Medical Service, Fiji, 1912; retired, 1945; Director of Medical Services Colony of Fiji; also Director of Civil Defence and Secretary for Indian Affairs; held various other administrative posts as well as medical in the Colony. After retirement from Colonial Service, N London Postgrad. Med. Sch., 1945-46; GP in North Auckland, 1946-58. *Address:* 32 Hororata Road, Takapuna N2, New Zealand.
    See also Sir R. H. Garvey.

McHALE, Keith Michael; His Honour Judge McHale; a Circuit Judge, since 1980; *b* 26 March 1928; *s* of Cyril Michael McHale and Gladys McHale; *m* 1966, Rosemary Margaret Arthur; one *s* one *d*. Called to the Bar, Gray's Inn, 1951. *Address:* Oak Lodge, Albemarle Road, Beckenham, Kent.

McHARDY, Prof. William Duff; Regius Professor of Hebrew, Oxford University, and Student of Christ Church, 1960-78; *b* 25 May 1911; *o s* of late W. D. McHardy, Cullen, Banffshire; *m* 1941, Vera, *y d* of late T. Kemp, York; one *d. Educ:* Fordyce Academy; Universities of Aberdeen, Edinburgh, and Oxford (St John's College). MA, BD (Aberdeen), MA (Edinburgh), DPhil (Oxford). Research Fellow in Syriac, Selly Oak Colleges, Birmingham, 1942; Lecturer in Aramaic and Syriac, University of Oxford, 1945; Samuel Davidson Professor of Old Testament Studies in the University of London, 1948-60. Examiner, Universities of Aberdeen, Cambridge, Durham, Edinburgh, Leeds, London, Oxford and University Colleges of the Gold Coast/Ghana and Ibadan. Hon. Curator of Mingana Collection of Oriental Manuscripts, 1947. Grinfield Lecturer on the Septuagint, Oxford, 1959-61. Dir, New English Bible. Burgess, Royal Burgh of Cullen, 1975. Hon. DD Aberdeen, 1958. Hon. Fellow, Selly Oak Colleges, 1980. *Publications:* articles in journals. *Address:* 2 Ogilvie Park, Cullen, Banffshire. *T:* Cullen 41008.

McHENRY, Donald F.; University Research Professor of Diplomacy and International Affairs, Georgetown University, since 1981; *b* 13 Oct. 1936; *s* of Limas McHenry and Dora Lee Brooks; *m* Mary Williamson (marr. diss.); one *s* two *d. Educ:* Lincoln Senior High Sch., East St Louis, Ill; Illinois State Univ. (BS); Southern Illinois Univ. (MSc); Georgetown Univ. Taught at Howard Univ., Washington, 1959-62; joined Dept of State, 1963; Head of Dependent Areas Section, Office of UN Polit. Affairs, 1965-68; Asst to Sec. of State, US, 1969; Special Asst to Counsellor, Dept of State, 1969-71; Lectr, Sch. of Foreign Service, Georgetown Univ.; Guest Scholar, Brookings Inst., and Internat. Affairs Fellow, Council on Foreign Relations (on leave from State Dept), 1971-73; resigned from State Dept, 1973; Project Dir, Humanitarian Policy Studies, Carnegie Endowment for Internat. Peace, Washington, 1973-76; served in transition team of President Carter, 1976-77; Ambassador and Deputy Rep. of US to UN Security Council, 1977-79, Permanent Rep., 1979; US Ambassador to UN, 1979-81. Director: Internat. Paper Co.; First National Bank of Boston; First National Boston Corp.; Smith Kline Beckman Corp.; Coca-Cola; Inst. for Internat. Economics; American Ditchley Foundn. Governor, American Stock Exchange. Trustee: Mount Holyoke Coll.; Ford Foundn; Phelps-Stokes Fund. Member, Amer. Polit. Sci. Assoc. Hon. degrees: Dennison, Duke, Georgetown, Harvard, Illinois, Michigan, Princeton, Southern Illinois, and Washington Univs; Amherst, Boston and Williams Colleges. Superior Honor Award, Dept of State, 1966. Mem. Council on Foreign Relations and Editorial Bd, Foreign Policy Magazine. *Publication:* Micronesia: Trust Betrayed, 1975. *Address:* Georgetown University, 37th and O Streets, NW, Washington, DC 20057, USA.

MACHIN, Arnold, OBE 1965; RA 1956 (ARA 1947); sculptor, FRBS 1955; Master of Sculpture, Royal Academy School, 1958-67; Tutor, Royal College of Art, 1951-58; *b* 1911; *s* of William James Machin, Stoke-on-Trent; *m* 1949, Patricia, *d* of late Lt-Col Henry Newton; one *s. Educ:* Stoke School of Art; Derby School of Art; Royal College of Art. Silver Medal and Travelling Scholarship for Sculpture, 1940; two works in terracotta: St John the Baptist and The Annunciation, purchased by Tate Gallery, 1943; Spring terracotta purchased by President and Council of Royal Academy under terms of Chantrey Bequest, 1947; designed: new coin effigy, 1964, 1967 (decimal coinage); definitive issue of postage stamp, 1967; Silver Wedding commemorative crown, 1972; commemorative Silver Jubilee crown, 1977. *Recreations:* music, garden design. *Address:* 4 Sydney Close, SW3; Garmelow Manor, near Eccleshall, Staffordshire.

MACHIN, David; Managing Director of The Bodley Head Ltd, since 1982 (Joint Managing Director, 1981); *b* 25 April 1934; *s* of late Noel and Joan Machin; *m* 1963, Sarah Mary, *yr d* of late Col W. A. Chester-Master; two *d. Educ:* Eton (Oppidan Scholar); Trinity Coll., Cambridge. National Service, 1952-54 (2nd Lieut Welsh Guards). Editor, William Heinemann Ltd, 1957-66; Literary Agent, Gregson & Wigan Ltd and London International, 1966-68; Partner, A. P. Watt & Son, 1968-70; Director: Jonathan Cape Ltd, 1970-78; Chatto, Bodley Head and Jonathan Cape Ltd, 1977-78, 1981-; Gen. Sec., The Society of Authors, 1978-81; Mem., Nat. Trust Publishing Bd, 1981. FRSA

1981. *Publications:* (contrib.) Outlook, 1963; articles in The Author, The Bookseller. *Address:* 53 Westwick Gardens, W14 0BS. *T:* 01-603 4000. *Club:* Garrick.

MACHIN, Edward Anthony, QC 1973; a Recorder of the Crown Court, since 1976; *b* 28 June 1925; *s* of Edward Arthur Machin and Olive Muriel Smith; *m* 1953, Jean Margaret McKanna; two *s* one *d. Educ:* Christ's Coll., Finchley; New Coll., Oxford. MA 1950; BCL 1950; Vinerian Law Scholar, 1950; Tancred Student, 1950; Cassel Scholar, 1951. Called to Bar, Lincoln's Inn, 1951; Bencher, 1980. *Publications:* Redgrave's Factories Acts, 1962, 1966, 1972; Redgrave's Offices and Shops, 1965 and 1973; Redgrave's Health and Safety in Factories, 1976, 1982; Health and Safety at Work, 1980. *Recreations:* music, sailing, languages. *Address:* 11 Bedford Road, Moor Park, Herts. *T:* Northwood 24869. *Club:* Bar Yacht.

MACHIN, George; Secretary, Sheffield Trades and Labour Club, since 1981; *b* 30 Dec. 1922; *s* of Edwin and Ada Machin, Sheffield; *m* 1949, Margaret Ena (*née* Heard); one *s. Educ:* Marlcliffe Sch., Sheffield. Served RAF, 1943-47. Engineering Inspector. Shop Steward, and Mem., Sheffield District Cttee, AUEW. Sec., Sheffield Heeley Constituency Lab. Party, 1966-73. Mem., Sheffield City Council, 1967-74. MP (Lab) Dundee E, March 1973-Feb. 1974; contested (Lab) Dundee E, Oct. 1974. Governor, Granville Coll. of Further Educn, Sheffield, 1968-73. *Recreations:* swimming, walking. *Address:* 104 Norgreave Way, Sheffield S19 5TN.

MACHIN, Kenneth Arthur; QC 1977; a Recorder of the Crown Court, since 1979; *b* 13 July 1936; *o s* of Thomas Arthur Machin and Edith May Machin. *Educ:* St Albans School. Called to the Bar, Middle Temple, 1960; South Eastern Circuit. *Address:* 3 Hare Court, Temple, EC4. *T:* 01-353 7741; 69 Laurel Way, Totteridge, N20.

McHUGH, James, CEng; Member for Production and Supply, British Gas Corporation, since 1979; *b* 4 May 1930; *s* of late Edward McHugh and Martha (*née* Smith); *m* 1953, Sheila (*née* Cape); two *d. Educ:* Carlisle Grammar Sch.; various colls. MIGasE, AMBIM; FInstPet. Served Army, National Service. Entered Gas Industry, 1947; technical and managerial appts in Northern and E Midlands Gas Bds; Prodn Engr 1967, Dir of Engrg 1971, W Midlands Gas Bd; Dir of Ops, British Gas Corp., 1975. Mem., Meteorological Cttee, 1981-. *Recreations:* mountaineering, dinghy sailing. *Address:* 16 Miall Park Road, Solihull, W Midlands. *T:* 021-705 0836. *Club:* Royal Automobile.

McHUGH, Dr Mary Patricia; Coroner for Southern District of London, since 1965; *b* 5 June 1915; *d* of J. C. McHugh, MB, BS, BAO, Royal Univ., Dublin, and Madeleine Jeffroy Leblan, Brittany, France; *m* 1943, E. G. Murphy, FRCS (marr. diss., 1952); one *s* two *d. Educ:* Nymphenburg, Munich, Bavaria; Notre Dame, Clapham; Birmingham Univ. MB, ChB, 1942; PhD Fac. of Laws, London 1976. Birmingham House Physician and Anæsthetist, St Chad's Hospital, Birmingham, 1942-43; General Practice, London, 1944-65. Called to the Bar, Inner Temple, 1959. Past Chm., Whole Time Coroner's Assoc.; Mem., British Academy of Forensic Sciences, 1963; Founder Mem., RCGP; Associate, Inst. of Linguists, 1981. Medico Legal Columnist, Pulse, 1981-. *Publication:* Treasure Trove and the Law (Med. Sci. Law vol. 16 no 2), 1976. *Recreations:* cooking, languages. *Address:* 8 Hitherwood Drive, College Road, Dulwich, SE19. *T:* 01-681 2533, ext. 24, (home) 01-670 8400.

McILVENNA, Maj.-Gen. John Antony, CB 1980; Director of Army Legal Services, 1978-80; *b* 10 Dec. 1919; *s* of Joseph Henry McIlvenna and Dorothy (*née* Brown); *m* Dr Hildegard Paula Gertrud Overlack; one *s* one *d. Educ:* Royal Grammar School, Newcastle upon Tyne; Hymers Coll., Hull; Durham Univ. LLB 1940. Private, KOYLI; 2nd Lieut, DLI, 1941; despatches 1945; admitted Solicitor, 1947; Captain, Army Legal Services, 1950; served in Hong Kong, Aden, Egypt, Libya and BAOR; Maj.-Gen. and Dir, newly formed Army Legal Corps, 1978. Chm. and Dir, United Services Catholic Assoc., 1979-81, Vice-Pres., 1981-. *Recreations:* swimming, music, history. *Address:* 11 Aldenham Avenue, Radlett, Herts WD7 8HZ. *Club:* Army and Navy.

McILWAIN, Prof. Henry, DSc, PhD; Professor of Biochemistry in the University of London at Institute of Psychiatry, British Postgraduate Medical Federation, 1954-80, now Emeritus; Visiting Professor, Department of Biochemistry, St Thomas's Hospital Medical School, London, since 1980; *b* Newcastle upon Tyne, 20 Dec. 1912; *e s* of John McIlwain, Glasgow, and Louisa (*née* Widdowson), Old Whittington; *m* 1st, 1941, Valerie (*d* 1977), *d* of K. Durston, Bude, Cornwall; two *d*; 2nd, 1979, Marjorie Allan Crennell. *Educ:* King's Coll., Newcastle upon Tyne (University of Durham); The Queen's Coll., Oxford. Leverhulme Research Fellow and later Mem. of Scientific Staff, Medical Research Council, in Council's Dept of Bacterial Chemistry (Middlesex Hosp., London) and Unit for Research in Cell Metabolism (Univ. of Sheffield), 1937-47; Lectr in Biochemistry, Univ. of Sheffield, 1944-47; Senior Lectr (later Reader) in Biochemistry, Inst. of Psychiatry (British Postgraduate Medical Fedn), Univ. of London, 1948-54. Hon. Biochemist, Bethlem Royal Hosp. and Maudsley Hosp., 1948-80. Mem. Editorial Bd, Biochemical Jl, 1947-50; Research Associate, Univ. of Chicago, 1951; Visiting Lectr, Univ. of Otago, New Zealand, 1954; Lectr and Medallist, Univ. of Helsinki, 1973; Thudichum Lectr and Medallist, Biochemical Soc., 1975; Dr *hc* Univ. d'Aix-Marseille, 1974. *Publications:* Biochemistry and the Central Nervous System, 1955, 4th edn (with H. S. Bachelard), 1971; Chemotherapy and the Central Nervous System, 1957; (with R. Rodnight) Practical Neurochemistry, 1962; Chemical Exploration of the Brain, 1963;

(ed) Practical Neurochemistry, 1975; 250 papers in the Biochemical Journal and other scientific and medical publications. *Address:* 73 Court Lane, SE21 7EF. *T:* 01-693 5334.

McILWRAITH, Arthur Renwick; Sheriff of South Strathclyde, Dumfries and Galloway (formerly Lanark) at Airdrie since 1972; *b* 8 April 1914; *s* of Nicholas Renwick McIlwraith and Adaline Gowans McIlwraith; *m* 1950, Thelma Preston or Sargent; one *s* one *d*. *Educ:* High Sch. of Glasgow; Univ. of Glasgow (MA, LLB). Grad. 1938. Served War: Highland Light Infantry, 1939-45. Solicitor, 1945-72. *Recreation:* fishing. *Address:* 17 Bellshaugh Road, Glasgow G12 0SF. *T:* 041-339 6751. *Club:* Nomads (Glasgow).

McINDOE, William Ian, CB 1978; Deputy Secretary, Department of the Environment, since 1979; *b* 11 March 1929; *s* of John McIndoe, Leven, Fife and Agnes Scott; *m* 1st, 1954, Irene Armour Mudie (*d* 1966); one *s* two *d*; 2nd, 1971, Jamesanna Smart (*née* MacGregor). *Educ:* Sedbergh; Corpus Christi Coll., Oxford. 2nd Lieut 2 RHA, 1951-53; Asst Principal, CRO, 1953; 2nd Sec., Canberra, 1956-58; 1st Sec., Salisbury, 1958-62; Private Sec. to Commonwealth Sec., 1962-63; Private Sec. to Sec. of Cabinet, 1963-65; Assistant Secretary: Cabinet Office, 1965-66; Scottish Educn Dept, 1966-69; Scottish Develt Dept, 1969-71; Under-Secretary: Dept of Agriculture and Fisheries for Scotland, 1971-75; Scottish Economic Planning Dept, 1975-76; Dep. Sec., Cabinet Office, 1976-79. *Recreations:* ski-ing, golf. *Address:* 35 Fitzgerald Avenue, SW14 8SZ. *T:* 01-878 2626. *Club:* Royal Commonwealth Society.

McINERNEY, Hon. Sir Murray (Vincent), Kt 1978; Hon. Mr Justice **McInerney;** Judge of Supreme Court of Victoria, since 1965; *b* 11 Feb. 1911; *s* of Patrick McInerney and Kathleen Ierne (*née* Murray); *m* 1st, 1939, Manda Alice Franich (*d* 1973); two *s* five *d*; 2nd, 1975, Frances Mary Branagan (*née* O'Gorman). *Educ:* Christian Brothers' Coll., Pretoria; Xavier Coll., Melbourne; Newman Coll., Univ. of Melb. (MA, LLM). Served War, RANVR, 1942-45 (Lieut). Admitted as barrister and solicitor, 1934; practised at Victorian Bar, 1935-65; QC 1957. Sen. Law Tutor, Newman Coll., 1933-41; Lectr, Law of Evidence and Civil Procedure, Melb. Univ., 1949-62. Pres., Aust. Sect. of Lawasia, 1967-69; Vice-Pres., Law Council of Aust., 1964-65; Dep. Pres., Courts Martial Appeals Tribunal, 1958-65. Mem., Victorian Bar Council, 1952-65 (Chm., 1962, 1963). Chm., Council, State Coll. of Vic., 1973-81. Melb. Univ. Full Blue Athletics, and Aust. Univs Blue Athletics, 1933; Pres., Victorian Amateur Athletics Assoc., 1979-82; Mem., Lawn Tennis Assoc. of Vic. *Publications:* contrib. Aust. Law Jl and Melb. Univ. Law Review. *Recreations:* reading, watching cricket, tennis, athletics. *Address:* Judges' Chambers, Supreme Court of Victoria, Melbourne, Vic 3000, Australia. *T:* 60 0311; 7 Chatfield Avenue, Balwyn, Vic 3103. *T:* 80 5051. *Clubs:* Australian, Celtic, Melbourne Cricket, Royal Automobile of Victoria (Melbourne), West Brighton.

MacINNES, Archibald, CVO 1977; Consultant to HAT Group Ltd, since 1980; Ad Hoc Planning Inspector, Department of the Environment, since 1980; *b* 10 April 1919; *s* of Duncan and Catherine MacInnes; *m* 1950, Nancey Elisabeth Blyth (*d* 1976); one *s* two *d*. *Educ:* Kirkcudbright Academy; Royal Technical Coll., Glasgow. FIMechE. Scott's Shipbuilding and Engineering Co., Greenock, 1937-44; Colonial Service, Nigeria, 1945-59; War Office Works Organisation: Gibraltar, 1959-63; Southern Comd, Salisbury, Wilts, 1963-64; MPBW, Bristol, 1964-68; DoE, Germany, 1968-72; Dir, London Region, PSA, DoE, 1972-79. FBIM. Coronation Medal. *Recreations:* golf, shooting, fishing, gardening. *Address:* Lower Road, Homington, Salisbury, Wilts. *T:* Coombe Bissett 336.

MacINNES, Hamish, OBE 1979; BEM; Founder and Leader, Glencoe Mountain Rescue Team; author and film-maker (mountaineering); Hon. Director, Leishman Memorial Research Centre, Glencoe; *b* 7 July 1930. Dep. Leader, British Everest Expedition, 1975. Has served on Mountain Rescue Cttee for Scotland for 20 years (Past Sec.). Founder and Hon. Pres., Search and Rescue Dog Assoc.; Past Pres., Alpine Climbing Group. Designer of climbing equipment, incl. the first all metal ice axe, terrodactyl ice tools, the MacInnes stretchers, MacInnes Boxes for high altitude mountain camping. *Publications:* Climbing, 1964; Scottish Climbs, 2 vols, 1971; International Mountain Rescue Handbook, 1972; Call-Out: mountain rescue, 1973, new edn 1977; Climb to the Lost World, 1974; Death Reel (novel), 1976; West Highland Walks, vols 1 and 2, 1979; Look Behind the Ranges, 1979; Scottish Ice Climbs, 1980; High Drama (stories), 1980. *Address:* Achnacone, Glencoe, Argyll PA39 4LA.

MacINNES, Helen Clark; novelist; *b* 7 Oct. 1907; *d* of Donald McInnes and Jessica Cecilia Sutherland McDiarmid; *m* 1932, Prof. Gilbert Highet, DLitt (*d* 1978); one *s*. *Educ:* The Hermitage Sch., Helensburgh; The High School for Girls, Glasgow; Glasgow Univ. (MA); University College, London. *Publications:* Above Suspicion, 1941; Assignment in Brittany, 1942; The Unconquerable, 1944; Horizon, 1945; Friends and Lovers, 1947; Rest and Be Thankful, 1949; Neither Five Nor Three, 1951; I and My True Love, 1953; Pray for a Brave Heart, 1955; North from Rome, 1958; Decision at Delphi, 1961; The Venetian Affair, 1963; Home is the Hunter (play), 1964; The Double Image, 1966; The Salzburg Connection, 1968; Message from Málaga, 1972; The Snare of the Hunter, 1974; Agent in Place, 1976; Prelude to Terror, 1978; The Hidden Target, 1980. *Recreations:* two-piano duets; the American West. *Address:* 15 Jefferys Lane, East Hampton, NY 11937, USA.

McINNES, John Colin; Sheriff of Tayside Central and Fife, since 1974 (at Cupar and Perth); *b* 21 Nov. 1938; *s* of late Mr I. W. McInnes, WS, and of Mrs Lucy McInnes, Cupar, Fife; *m* 1966, Elisabeth Mabel Neilson; one *s* one *d*. *Educ:* Cargilfield Sch., Edinburgh; Merchiston Castle Sch., Edinburgh; Brasenose Coll., Oxford (BA); Edinburgh Univ. (LLB). 2nd Lieut 8th Royal Tank Regt, 1957-58; Lieut Fife and Forfar Yeomanry/Scottish Horse (TA), 1958-64. Advocate, 1963. In practice at Scottish Bar, 1963-73; Tutor, Faculty of Law, Edinburgh Univ., 1965-73; Sheriff of the Lothians and Peebles, 1973-74. Director: R. Mackness & Co. Ltd, 1963-70; Fios Group Ltd, 1970-72 (Chm., 1970-72). Contested (C) Aberdeen North, 1964. *Recreations:* shooting, fishing, gardening, photography. *Address:* Parkneuk, Blebo Craigs, Cupar, Fife KY15 5UG. *T:* Strathkinness 366.

MacINNES, Keith Gordon; HM Diplomatic Service; Head of Information Department, Foreign and Commonwealth Office, since 1980; *b* 17 July 1935; *s* of Kenneth MacInnes and Helen MacInnes (*née* Gordon); *m* 1966, Jennifer Anne Fennell (marr. diss. 1980); one *s* one *d*. *Educ:* Rugby; Trinity Coll., Cambridge (MA). HM Forces, 1953-55. FO, 1960; Third, later Second Secretary, Buenos Aires, 1961-64; FO, 1964 (Private Sec., 1965); Private Sec. to Permanent Under-Sec., Commonwealth Office, 1965-68; First Sec. (Information), Madrid, 1968-70; FCO, 1970-74; Counsellor and Head of Chancery: Prague, 1974-77; Dep. Perm. Rep., UK Mission, Geneva, 1977-80. *Recreations:* chess, bridge. *Address:* c/o Foreign and Commonwealth Office, SW1A 2AH.

McINTOSH, Andrew Robert; Member for Tottenham, Greater London Council, since 1973; Chairman, IFF Research Ltd, since 1981 (Managing Director, 1965-81); *b* 30 April 1933; *s* of Prof. A. W. McIntosh and Jenny (*née* Britton); *m* 1962, Naomi Ellen Sargant; two *s*. *Educ:* Haberdashers' Aske's Hampstead Sch.; Royal Grammar Sch., High Wycombe; Jesus Coll., Oxford (MA); Ohio State Univ. (Fellow in Econs, 1956-57). Gallup Poll, 1957-61; Hoover Ltd, 1961-63; Market Res. Manager, Osram (GEC) Ltd, 1963-65. Member: Hornsey Bor. Council, 1963-65; Haringey Bor. Council, 1964-68 (Chm., Develt Control); Greater London Council: Chm., NE Area Bd, 1973-74, W Area Bd, 1974-76, and Central Area Bd, 1976; Opposition Leader on Planning and Communications, 1977-80; Leader of the Opposition, 1980-81. Chairman: Market Res. Soc., 1972-73; Assoc. for Neighbourhood Councils, 1974-80; Member: Metrop. Water Bd, 1967-68; NEC, Fabian Soc., 1981-; Governor, Drayton Sch., Tottenham, 1967-. Editor, Jl of Market Res. Soc., 1963-67. *Publications:* Industry and Employment in the Inner City, 1979; (ed) Employment Policy in the UK and United States, 1980; Women and Work, 1981; jl articles on theory, practice and findings of survey res. *Recreations:* cooking, reading, music. *Address:* 4 Talbot Road, N6 4QR. *T:* 01-340 1496.

See also N. E. S. McIntosh.

McINTOSH, Prof. Angus, FRSE 1978; consultant on English language problems; Director, Middle English Dialect Atlas Project, since 1979; Forbes Professor of English Language, University of Edinburgh, 1964-79; *b* 10 Jan. 1914; *s* of late Kenneth and Mary McIntosh (*née* Thompson), Cleadon, Sunderland, Co. Durham; *m* 1939, Barbara, *d* of late Dr William Seaman and Mrs Bainbridge (*née* June Wheeler), New York City; two *s* one *d*. *Educ:* Ryhope Grammar Sch., Co. Durham; Oriel Coll., Oxford (BA, 1st Class Hons English Lang., and Lit., 1934); Merton Coll., Oxford (Harmsworth Scholar); (Dip. of Comparative Philology, University of Oxford, 1936); Harvard Univ. (Commonwealth Fund Fellow, AM, 1937). MA (Oxford) 1938. Lecturer, Dept of English, University College, Swansea, 1938-46. Served War of 1939-45, beginning as trooper in Tank Corps, finishing as Major in Intelligence Corps. University Lecturer in Mediæval English, Oxford, 1946-48; Lecturer in English, Christ Church, Oxford, 1946-47; Student of Christ Church, 1947-48; Prof. of English Language and General Linguistics, Univ. of Edinburgh, 1948-64; Rockefeller Foundation Fellowship, US, June-Sept. 1949. Pres., Scottish Text Soc., 1977. For. Mem., Finnish Acad. of Science and Letters, 1976. Hon. DPhil Poznan Univ., 1977; Hon. DLitt Durham, 1980. *Publications:* books, articles and reviews on subject of English language and related topics. *Recreations:* tennis, fishing, gardening, painting. *Address:* 32 Blacket Place, Edinburgh EH9 1RL. *T:* 031-667 5791.

McINTOSH, Prof. Frank Campbell; FRS 1954; FRSC 1956; J. M. Drake Professor of Physiology, McGill University, Montreal, Canada, 1949-78, Emeritus Professor since 1980; *b* 24 Dec. 1909; *s* of Rev. C. C. MacIntosh, DD, and Beenie MacIntosh (*née* Matheson); *m* 1938, Mary M. MacKay; two *s* three *d*. *Educ:* Dalhousie Univ., Halifax, NS (MA); McGill Univ. (PhD). Member of research staff, Medical Research Council of Great Britain, 1938. Hon. LLD: Alberta, 1964; Queen's, 1965; Dalhousie, 1976; Hon. MD Ottawa, 1974; Hon. DSc McGill, 1980. *Publications:* papers in physiological journals. *Address:* Department of Physiology, McGill University, 3655 Drummond Street, Montreal H3G 1Y6, Canada; 145 Wolseley Avenue, Montreal West, H4X 1V8, Canada. *T:* 481-7939.

McINTOSH, Rev. Canon Hugh; Rector of Christ Church, Lanark, since 1970; *b* 5 June 1914; *s* of Hugh Burns McIntosh and Mary (*née* Winter); *m* 1951, Ruth Georgina, er *d* of late Rev. William Skinner Wilson and Enid (*née* Sanders); two *s* one *d*. *Educ:* Hatfield Coll., Durham (Exhibr); Edinburgh Theological Coll. (Luscombe Schol.). LTh, 1941; BA (dist.), 1942; MA 1945. Deacon and Priest, 1942. Precentor and Senior Chaplain, St Paul's Cathedral, Dundee, 1942-46; Senior Chaplain, St Mary's Cathedral,

Edinburgh, 1946-49; Curate, St Salvador's, Edinburgh, 1949-51; Rector, St Adrian's, Gullane, 1951-54; Rector, St John's, Dumfries, 1954; Canon of St Mary's Cathedral, Glasgow, and Synod Clerk of Glasgow and Galloway, 1959; Provost of St Mary's Cathedral, Glasgow, 1966-70. *Recreations:* reading, writing, and (a little) arithmetic. *Address:* The Rectory, Lanark, Scotland. *T:* Lanark 3065.

McINTOSH, Vice-Admiral Sir Ian (Stewart), KBE 1973 (MBE 1941); CB 1970; DSO 1944; DSC 1942; Management Selection Consultant, 1973-78; *b* 11 Oct. 1919; *s* of late A. J. McIntosh, Melbourne, Australia; *m* 1943, Elizabeth Rosemary Rasmussen; three *s* (one *d* decd). *Educ:* Geelong Grammar Sch. Entered RN, 1938; comd HM Submarine: H44, 1942; Sceptre, 1943-44; Alderney, 1946-48; Aeneas, 1950-51; Exec. Officer, HMS Ark Royal, 1956-58; comd 2nd Submarine Sqn, 1961-63; comd HMS Victorious, 1966-68; Dir-Gen., Weapons (Naval), 1968-70; Dep. Chief of Defence Staff (Op. Req.), 1971-73, retd 1973. Captain, 1959; Rear-Adm., 1968; Vice-Adm., 1971. Chairman: Sea Cadet Assoc., 1973-; HMS Cavalier Trust, 1974-. *Recreations:* friends, reading, music. *Address:* 19 The Crescent, Alverstoke, Hants. *T:* Gosport 80510. *Club:* Royal Over-Seas League.

MACINTOSH, Joan, (Mrs I. G. Macintosh), CBE 1978; Chairman, Scottish Consumer Council, 1975-80; Vice-Chairman, National Consumer Council, since 1976; *b* 23 Nov. 1919; *d* of Leonard Burbidge and Edith Cockin; *m* 1952, Ian Gillies Macintosh; one *s* two *d* (and one *s* decd). *Educ:* Amer. and English schs; Oxford Univ. (MA Modern History). BBC, 1941-42; Amer. Div., Min. of Inf., 1942-45; HM Foreign Service, 1945-52: Washington; London; New Delhi; retd on marriage. Voluntary work in India, 1953-69; CAB Organiser, Glasgow, 1972-75. Member: Royal Commn on Legal Services in Scotland, 1975-80; Citizens rights prog., Radio Clyde; Chm. Council, Insurance Ombudsman Bureau, 1981-; Pres., Nat. Fed. of Consumer Gps, 1981-. Hon. LLD Dundee, 1982. *Publications:* Curiosity killed the Cat, 1946; Deadly Earnest, 1949; Villainy at Vespers, 1952; 18 educnl books, 1955-75. *Recreations:* writing, gardening. *Address:* Wynd End, Auchterarder, Perthshire PH3 1AD. *T:* Auchterarder 2499.

McINTOSH, Prof. Naomi Ellen Sargant; Senior Commissioning Editor, Channel Four Television Company Ltd, since 1981; *b* 10 Dec. 1933; *d* of Tom Sargant, *qv*, and Marie Cerny (*née* Hlouskova); *m* 1st, 1954, Peter Joseph Kelly; one *s*; 2nd, 1962, Andrew Robert McIntosh, *qv*; two *s*. *Educ:* Friends' Sch., Saffron Walden, Essex; Bedford Coll., London (BA Hons Sociology). Social Surveys (Gallup Poll) Ltd, 1955-67; Sen. Lectr in Market Res., Enfield Coll., of Technol., 1967-69; Open University: Sen. Lectr in Res. Methods, 1970-75; Reader in Survey Research, 1975-78; Head, Survey Res. Dept, Inst. of Educnl Technol., 1972-81; Pro Vice-Chancellor (Student Affairs), 1974-78; Prof. of Applied Social Research, 1978-81. Vis. Prof. in Higher Educn (part-time), Univ. of Mass, Amherst, 1974-75. Councillor, and Chm. Children's Cttee, London Bor. of Haringey, 1964-68; Vice-Chm., London Boroughs Trng Cttee (Social Services), 1966-68. Chm., National Gas Consumers' Council, 1977-80. Member: Council and Exec. Cttee, Social Work Adv. Council, 1966-68; Local Govt Trng Bd, 1967-68; Energy Commn, 1978-79; Commn on Energy and the Environment, 1978-81; Nat. Consumer Council, 1978-81; Adv. Council for Adult and Continuing Educn, 1977-; Council, Bedford Coll., Univ. of London, 1977-. Pres., Nat. Soc. for Clean Air, 1981-. *Publications:* A Degree of Difference, 1976 (New York 1977); (with A. Woodley) The Door Stood Open, 1980. *Recreation:* gardening. *Address:* 4 Talbot Road, N6 4QR. *T:* 01-340 1496.

McINTOSH, Neil Scott Wishart; Director, Shelter, the National Campaign for the Homeless, since 1976; *b* 24 July 1947; *s* of William Henderson McIntosh and Mary Catherine McIntosh; *m* 1971, Genista Mary Tandy; one *s* one *d*. *Educ:* Merchiston Castle Sch., Edinburgh; Univ. of York (BA Politics); London Sch. of Econs (MSc Industrial Relations). Res. Associate, PEP, 1969-73; Res. Dir. Southwark Community Develt Proj., 1973-76. Councillor, London Bor. of Camden, 1971-77; Chm., Housing Cttee, 1974-76. *Publication:* The Right to Manage?, 1971 (2nd edn 1976). *Recreations:* Rugby, hill walking, theatre. *Address:* 8 Lupton Street, NW5.

MACINTOSH, Sir Robert (Reynolds), Kt 1955; MA, DM, FRCSE, DA; FFARCS; Hon. Fellow: Faculties of Anæsthetists of Australasia, 1950, of Ireland, 1964, of England, 1968; Royal Society of Medicine, 1966; Pembroke College, Oxford, 1965; Nuffield Professor of Anæsthetics, Oxford University, 1937-65; former Hon. Consultant in Anæsthetics, Royal Air Force; *b* Timaru, New Zealand, 17 Oct. 1897; *s* of C. N. Macintosh. *Educ:* Waitaki, New Zealand; Guy's Hospital. Served European War (despatches), Spanish Civil War (Order of Military Merit); War of 1939-45 (Order of Liberty, Norway). Hon. FRCOG. Dr hc Univs of Buenos Aires, Aix-Marseilles and Poznan; Hon. DSc: Univ. of Wales; Med. Coll. of Ohio. *Publications:* Textbooks, Essentials of General Anæsthesia, Physics for the Anæsthetist, Lumbar Puncture and Spinal Analgesia, Local Anæsthesia, Brachial Plexus; various articles on anæsthesia in medical and dental journals. *Recreations:* golf, tennis. *Address:* 326 Woodstock Road, Oxford. *Clubs:* Bath, Royal Air Force.

McINTOSH, Sir Ronald (Robert Duncan), KCB 1975 (CB 1968); Chairman, APV Holdings plc, since 1982; Director: S. G. Warburg & Co.; Foseco Minsep; London & Manchester Assurance; *b* 26 Sept. 1919; *s* of late Thomas Steven McIntosh, MD, FRCP, FRCS, and late Christina Jane McIntosh; *m* 1951, Doreen Frances, *o d* of late Commander Andrew MacGinnity, Frinton-on-Sea. *Educ:* Charterhouse (Scholar); Balliol Coll.,

Oxford. Served in Merchant Navy, 1939-45; Second Mate, 1943-45. Assistant Principal, Board of Trade, 1947; General Manager, Dollar Exports Board, 1949-51; Commercial Counsellor, UK High Commn, New Delhi, 1957-61; attached to Lord President's Office for work on problems of NE England, 1963; Under-Secretary: BoT, 1963-64; DEA, 1964-66; Dep. Under-Sec. of State, Dept of Economic Affairs, 1966-68; Dep. Secretary, Cabinet Office, 1968-70; Dep. Under-Sec. of State, Dept of Employment, 1970-72; Dep. Sec., HM Treasury, 1972-73; Dir-Gen. Nat. Economic Development Office, and Mem. NEDC, 1973-77. Dir, Fisons Ltd, 1978-81. Member: British Overseas Trade Adv. Cttee, 1975-77; Council, CBI, 1980-; Member, Governing Bodies: St George's House, Windsor; BIM; Policy Studies Inst.; Centre for European Agricl Studies; NIESR. Lectures: Lubbock Meml, 1974; Mercantile Credit, 1976; Alfred Herbert Meml, 1977. CBIM; FRSA. Hon. DSc Aston, 1977. *Recreations:* sailing, travel. *Address:* 24 Ponsonby Terrace, SW1. *Club:* Royal Thames Yacht.

MacINTYRE, Prof. Alasdair Chalmers; W. Alton Jones Professor of Philosophy, Vanderbilt University, since 1982; *b* 12 Jan. 1929; *o s* of Eneas John MacIntyre, MD (Glasgow), and Margaret Emily Chalmers, MB, ChB (Glasgow); *m* 1st, 1953, Ann Peri (marr. diss. 1963); two *d*; 2nd, 1963, Susan Margery Willans (marr. diss. 1977); one *s* one *d*; 3rd, 1977, Lynn Sumida Joy. *Educ:* Epsom Coll. and privately; Queen Mary Coll., Univ. of London; Manchester Univ. BA (London); MA (Manchester); MA (Oxon). Lectr in Philosophy of Religion, Manchester Univ., 1951-55; Lectr in Philosophy, Leeds Univ., 1957-61; Research Fellow, Nuffield Coll., Oxford, 1961-62; Sen. Fellow, Council of Humanities, Princeton Univ., 1962-63; Fellow and Preceptor in Philosophy, University Coll., Oxford, 1963-66; Prof. of Sociology, Univ. of Essex, 1966-70; Prof. of History of Ideas, Brandeis Univ., 1970-72; Univ. Prof. in Philos. and Political Sci., Boston Univ., 1972-80; Luce Prof., Wellesley Coll., 1980-82. Riddell Lectr, Univ. of Newcastle upon Tyne, 1964; Bampton Lectr, Columbia Univ., USA, 1966; Carlyle Vis. Lectr, Univ. of Oxford, 1981-82. Mem. Nat. Coun. for Diplomas in Art and Design, 1969-70. Hon. Mem., Phi Beta Kappa, 1973; Metcalfe Prize, 1974. *Publications:* Marxism and Christianity, 1954 (revised, 1968); New Essays in Philosophical Theology (ed, with A. G. N. Flew), 1955; Metaphysical Beliefs (ed), 1956; The Unconscious: a conceptual analysis, 1958; A Short History of Ethics, 1965; Secularisation and Moral Change, 1967; Marcuse: an exposition and a polemic, 1970; Sociological Theory and Philosophical Analysis (ed with D. M. Emmet), 1971; Against the Self-Images of the Age, 1971; After Virtue, 1981; contributor to: Mind, Philosophy, Philosophical Review, Jl of Philosophy, Amer. Jl of Sociology, Brit. Jl of Sociology, Encounter, New York Review of Books. *Recreations:* walking, reading trash, cooking, sleeping. *Address:* Department of Philosophy, Vanderbilt University, Nashville, Tennessee 37235, USA.

MACINTYRE, Angus Donald, DPhil; Official Fellow and Tutor in Modern History, since 1963, Vice-President, since 1981, Magdalen College, Oxford (Senior Tutor, 1966-68); Editor, English Historical Review, since 1978; *b* 4 May 1935; *e s* of Major Francis Peter Macintyre, OBE, and Evelyn, *d* of Nicholas Synnott, JP, Furness, Naas, Co. Kildare, Eire; *m* 1958, Joanna Musgrave Harvey, *d* of Sir Richard Musgrave Harvey, 2nd Bt; two *s* one *d*. *Educ:* Wellington; Hertford Coll., Oxford (Baring Scholar); St Antony's Coll., Oxford (MA, DPhil). Coldstream Guards, 1953-55, 1956 (Lieut). Governor, Magdalen Coll. Sch., Brackley, 1965-77; Chm., Thomas Wall Trust, London, 1971-. Gen. Editor, Oxford Historical Monographs, 1971-79. FRHistS 1972. *Publications:* The Liberator: Daniel O'Connell and the Irish Parliamentary Party 1830-47, 1965; (ed with Kenneth Garlick) The Diary of Joseph Farington 1793-1821, vols I-II, 1978; vols III-IV, 1979; vols V-VI, 1980; (contrib.) Thank You Wodehouse by J. H. C. Morris, 1981. *Recreations:* cricket, bibliomania. *Address:* Magdalen College, Oxford OX1 4AU. *T:* Oxford 41781. *Club:* MCC.

McINTYRE, Donald Conroy, OBE 1977; opera singer, free-lance; *b* 22 Oct. 1934; *s* of George Douglas McIntyre and Mrs Hermyn McIntyre; *m* ; three *d*. *Educ:* Mount Albert Grammar Sch.; Auckland Teachers' Trng Coll.; Guildhall Sch. of Music. Debut in Britain, Welsh National Opera, 1959; Sadler's Wells Opera, many roles, 1960-67; Royal Opera, Covent Garden, from 1967; also Vienna, Bayreuth, La Scala, Milan and Metropolitan, NY. Principal roles: Barak, in Die Frau Ohne Schatten, Strauss; Wotan and Wanderer, in The Ring, Wagner; Hollander, Wagner; Heyst, in Victory, Richard Rodney Bennett; Macbeth, Verdi; Scarpia, in Tosca, Puccini; Count, in Figaro, Mozart. Bayreuth: Wotan, Wanderer, Hollander, Telramund, in Lohengrin, Klingsor and Amfortas in Parsifal. Films and television. *Recreations:* gardening, swimming, tennis. *Address:* 2 Roseneath Close, Orpington, Kent. *T:* Farnborough (Kent) 55368.

MacINTYRE, Rt. Hon. Duncan, PC (NZ) 1980; DSO; OBE; ED; MP (Nat., NZ), East Cape; Minister of Agriculture and Minister of Fisheries; Minister in charge of Rural Bank; Deputy Prime Minister of New Zealand, since 1981; *b* 1915; *s* of A. MacIntyre; *m* Diana, *d* of Percy Hunter. Farming, 1933-39; Served War, NZ Army, 1939-46; Territorial Force, 1949-60. MP Hastings, 1960-72, Bay of Plenty, 1975-78, East Cape, 1978-. Member, HB Catchment Bd, 1956. *Address:* Ministry of Agriculture and Fisheries, Wellington, New Zealand.

MacINTYRE, Prof. Iain; Professor of Chemical Pathology, University of London, and Director, Department of Chemical Pathology, Royal Postgraduate Medical School, since 1982; Chairman, Division of Biological

Chemistry, since 1974; Hon. Consultant Pathologist, Hammersmith Hospital, since 1960; b 30 Aug. 1924; s of John MacIntyre, Tobermory, and Margaret Fraser Shaw, Stratherick, Inverness-shire; m 1947, Mabel Wilson Jamieson, MA, y d of George Jamieson, Largs, Ayrshire; one d. Educ: Jordanhill Coll. Sch., Glasgow; Univ. of Glasgow. MB, ChB Glasgow 1947; PhD London 1960; MRCPath 1963 (Founder Mem.), FRCPath 1971; FRCP 1977 (MRCP 1969); DSc London 1970. Asst Clinical Pathologist, United Sheffield Hosps, and Hon. Demonstrator in Biochem., Sheffield Univ., 1948-52; Royal Postgraduate Medical School: Registrar in Chemical Pathology, 1952-54; Sir Jack Drummond Meml Fellow, 1954-56; Asst Lectr in Chem. Path., 1956-59; Reader in Chem. Path., 1963-67; Jt Dir and Dir, Endocrine Unit 1967-82; Chm., Audio Visual Aids Adv. Cttee, 1975-. Vis. Scientist, Nat. Insts of Health, Bethesda, 1960-61; Visiting Professor: San Francisco Medical Center, 1964; Melbourne Univ., 1979-80; Vis. Lectr, Insts of Molecular Biol. and Cytol., USSR Acad. of Scis, 1978. Chm. Organizing Cttee, Hammersmith Internat. Symposium on Molecular Endocrinology, 1967-79; Member: Orgng Cttee, Hormone and Cell Regulation Symposia, 1976-79; Adv. Council, Workshop on Vitamin D, 1977-79. Member: Cttee Soc. for Endocrinology, 1978-80; Biochem. Soc.; Bone and Tooth Soc.; European Soc. for Clinical Investigation; Royal Instn; NIH Alumni Assoc; Amer. Endocrine Soc.; Amer. Soc. for Bone and Mineral Res.; European Calcified Tissue Soc. Member Editorial Board: Clinical Endocrinology, 1975-79; Molecular and Cellular Endocrinology, 1975-80; Jl of Endocrinological Investigation; Jl of Mineral and Electrolyte Metabolism; Jl of Investigative and Cell Pathol.; Jl of Metabolic Bone Disease and Related Res. Gairdner Internat. Award, Toronto, 1967. Fellow RSM. Publications: articles in endocrinology. Recreations: tennis, squash, chess, music. Address: 76 Waterford Road, SW6 2DR. T: 01-731 2429. Clubs: Athenæum; Queen's, Hurlingham.

McINTYRE, Ian James; Controller, BBC Radio 3, since 1978; b Banchory, Kincardineshire, 9 Dec. 1931; y s of late Hector Harold McIntyre, Inverness, and late Annie Mary Michie, Ballater; m 1954, Leik Sommerfelt, 2nd d of late Benjamin Vogt, Kragerø, Norway; two s two d. Educ: Prescot Grammar Sch.; St John's Coll., Cambridge (Scholar; Med. and Mod. Langs Tripos, Pts I and II; BA 1953; MA); Coll. of Europe, Bruges. Pres., Cambridge Union, 1953. Commnd, Intelligence Corps, 1955-57. Current affairs talks producer, BBC, 1957; Editor, At Home and Abroad, 1959; Man. Trng Organiser, BBC Staff Trng Dept, 1960; Programme Services Officer, ITA, 1961; staff of Chm., Cons. Party in Scotland, 1962; Dir of Inf. and Res., Scottish Cons. Central Office, 1965; contested (C) Roxburgh, Selkirk and Peebles, 1966; long-term contract, writer and broadcaster, BBC, 1970-76; presenter and interviewer, Analysis, and other programmes on politics, for. affairs and the arts; travelled widely in Europe, N America, Africa, Asia and ME; Controller, BBC Radio 4, 1976-78. Publications: The Proud Doers: Israel after twenty years, 1968; (ed and contrib.) Words: reflections on the uses of language, 1975; articles in The Listener. Recreation: family life. Address: BBC, Broadcasting House, W1A 1AA. T: 01-580 4468. Clubs: Beefsteak; Union (Cambridge).

McINTYRE, James Gordon; see Sorn, Hon. Lord.

McINTYRE, Very Rev. Prof. John, DD, DLitt; FRSE; Professor of Divinity, University of Edinburgh, since 1956; Dean of the Order of the Thistle, since 1974; Chaplain to the Queen in Scotland, since 1975 (Extra Chaplain, 1974-75); Moderator of the General Assembly of the Church of Scotland (with designation Rt Rev.), May 1982-83; b 20 May 1916; s of late John C. McIntyre, Bathgate, Scotland, and Annie McIntyre; m 1945, Jessie B., d of late William Buick, Coupar Angus; two s one d. Educ: Bathgate Academy; University of Edinburgh; MA (1938); BD (1941); DLitt (1953). Ordained, 1941; Locum Tenens, Parish of Glenorchy and Inishail, 1941-43; Minister of Parish of Fenwick, Ayrshire, 1943-45; Hunter Baillie Prof. of Theology, St Andrew's Coll., University of Sydney, 1946-56; Principal of St Andrew's Coll., 1950-56; Principal Warden, Pollock Halls of Residence, Univ. of Edinburgh, 1960-71; actg Principal and Vice-Chancellor, Edinburgh Univ., 1973-74, 1979; Principal, New Coll., and Dean of Faculty of Divinity, 1968-74. FRSE 1977. DD hc Glasgow, 1961. Publications: St Anselm and His Critics, 1954; The Christian Doctrine of History, 1957; On the Love of God, 1962; The Shape of Christology, 1966; articles and reviews in various learned jls of Theology. Address: 11 Minto Street, Edinburgh EH9 1RG. T: 031-667 1203.

McINTYRE, Air Commodore Kenneth John, CB 1958; CBE 1951; JP; RAF retired; b 23 July 1908; s of late William Seymour McIntyre and Winifred May McIntyre, Clevedon, Somerset; m 1936, Betty Aveley, o d of late Lt-Col Percie C. Cooper, Dulwich. Educ: Blundell's Sch.; RMC Sandhurst. Commissioned Royal Tank Regt, 1928; served UK and India; seconded to RAF 1934; permanent commission RAF, 1945. Served War of 1939-45 in UK, France and Belgium. Dep. Dir of Organisation, Air Ministry, 1945-47; Joint Services Staff Coll., 1947-48; Group Capt. 1947; Group Capt. Operations, HQ MEAF, 1948-50; idc 1951; SHAPE (Paris), 1952-54; Air Commodore, 1955; Dir of Policy (Air Staff), Air Ministry, 1955-58. Mem., Dorset CC, 1967-, Chm., 1981-; JP Poole, 1967 (Supplementary list, 1978). Address: The East Penthouse, 57 Branksome Court, Canford Cliffs, Poole, Dorset BH13 7BD. T: Canford Cliffs 708250. Club: Royal Air Force.

McINTYRE, Robert Douglas, MB, ChB (Edinburgh), DPH (Glasgow); JP; Consultant Chest Physician; b Dec. 1913; 3rd s of Rev. John E. McIntyre and Catherine, d of Rev. William Morison, DD; m 1954, Letitia, d of Alexander Macleod; one s. Educ: Hamilton Acad.; Daniel Stewart's Coll.; University of

Edinburgh. MP (Scottish Nationalist), Motherwell and Wishaw, April-July 1945. Contested (SNP): Motherwell, 1950; Perth and E Perthshire, 1951, 1955, 1959, 1964; W Stirlingshire, 1966, 1970; Stirling, Falkirk and Grangemouth, by-election 1971, Feb. and Oct. 1974. Chm., 1948-56, Pres., 1958-80, Scottish National Party; Mem., Stirling Town Council (Hon. Treas., 1958-64, Provost, 1967-75); Chancellor's Assessor, Stirling Univ. Court, 1979-; Freeman, Royal Borough of Stirling, 1975. DUniv Stirling 1976. JP Co. Stirling. Publications: numerous articles on Scottish, political and medical subjects, including regular contribs to the Scots Independent. Recreation: yachting. Address: 8 Gladstone Place, Stirling. T: Stirling 3456. Clubs: Scottish Arts (Edinburgh); Stirling and County.

McINTYRE, Stuart Charles, MBE; FCIS; b 6 Feb. 1912; s of James and Eleanor McIntyre; m 1938, Edith Irene Walton; two d. Educ: Dulwich Coll. Served War, RAF, Wing Comdr, 1940-46. Joined Pearl Assurance Co. Ltd, 1930; Dir, 1952, Chm. 1972-77, Pres. 1977-80; Director: Arsenal Football Club Ltd, 1962-; The Charter Trust & Agency Ltd, 1962-82; The Cross Investment Trust Ltd, 1962-82; Property Holding & Investment Trust Ltd, 1965-82; Property Selection & Investment Trust Ltd, 1966-82; Property Selection Finance Ltd, 1966-82. Freeman, City of London; Past Master, Glass Sellers' Company. Recreation: Association football. Address: Barton, East Close, Middleton-on-Sea, Sussex. T: Middleton-on-Sea 3746. Clubs: Devonshire, Royal Air Force.

McINTYRE, Prof. William Ian Mackay, PhD; MRCVS; Professor of Veterinary Medicine, University of Glasgow, since 1961; b 7 July 1919; s of George John and Jane McIntyre; m 1948, Ruth Dick Galbraith; three s. Educ: Altnaharra Primary and Golspie Secondary Sch., Sutherland; Royal (Dick) Veterinary Coll. (MRCVS); University of Edinburgh (PhD). Clinical Asst, Royal (Dick) Veterinary Coll., 1944-48; Lectr, Vet. Med., Royal (Dick) Vet. Coll., 1948-51; Sen. Lectr, Vet. Med., University of Glasgow, 1951-61. Seconded to University of East Africa, University Coll., Nairobi, as Dean, Faculty of Veterinary Science, and Prof., Clinical Studies, 1963-67. Publications: various, on canine nephritis, parasitic diseases and vaccines, clinical communications, and African Trypanosomiasis. Address: University of Glasgow Veterinary Faculty, Bearsden Road, Bearsden, Glasgow G61 1QH. T: 041-942 2301.

McINTYRE, Surgeon Rear-Adm. William Percival Edwin, CB 1961; RN retired; b 21 Aug. 1903; s of George McIntyre, Rathgar, Dublin; m 1964, Mrs Eve Robertson-Rodger (d 1971), widow of P. J. Robertson-Rodger. Educ: St Andrews Coll.; Trinity Coll., Dublin. MB, BCh, BAO 1925; MA, MD 1929. Joined RN as Surg. Lt 1925; Surg.-Comdr 1937; Surg.-Captain 1949. Senior Medical Officer (Medical Sect.), RN Hospital, Chatham, 1950-52 and RN Hospital, Plymouth, 1956-58; Fleet Medical Officer, Home Fleet, 1952-54; Surgeon Rear-Adm. 1958; Dep. Medical Dir-Gen., RN, 1958-62. QHP 1958-62. OStJ 1950; CStJ 1960. Recreations: golf, tennis. Address: Chasmoor, 68 Terenure Road West, Dublin 6.

McIVOR, Rt. Hon. Basil; see McIvor, Rt Hon. W. B.

McIVOR, Frances Jill; Member, Independent Broadcasting Authority, since 1980; b 10 Aug. 1930; d of Cecil Reginald Johnston Anderson and Frances Ellen (née Henderson); m 1953, William Basil McIvor, qv ; two s one d. Educ: Methodist Coll.; Lurgan Coll.; Queen's Univ. of Belfast (LLB Hons). Called to Bar of Northern Ireland, 1980. Asst Librarian (Law), QUB, 1954-55; Tutor in Legal Res., Law Faculty, QUB, 1965-74; editorial staff, NI Legal Qtly, 1966-76; Librarian, Dept of Dir of Public Prosecutions, 1977-79. Member: Children's Community Holidays, 1975-; Lay Panel, Juvenile Court, 1976-77; Lagan Valley Regional Park Cttee, 1975-; GDC, 1979-; Exec., Belfast Voluntary Welfare Soc., 1981-. Publications: Irish Consultant (and contrib.), Manual of Law Librarianship, 1976; (ed) Elegantia Juris: selected writings of F. H. Newark, 1973; Chart of the English Reports (new edn), 1982. Recreations: gardening, bees. Address: Larkhill, 98 Spa Road, Ballynahinch, Co. Down. T: Ballynahinch 563534. Club: Royal Commonwealth Society.

McIVOR, Rt. Hon. (William) Basil, PC (NI) 1971; b 17 June 1928; 2nd s of Rev. Frederick McIvor, Methodist clergyman and Lilly McIvor; m 1953, Frances Jill Anderson (see F. J. McIvor); two s one d. Educ: Methodist Coll., Belfast; Queen's Univ., Belfast. LLB 1948. Called to NI Bar, 1950; Jun. Crown Counsel, Co. Down, Sept. 1974, Resident Magistrate, Dec. 1974. MP (UU) Larkfield, NI Parlt, 1969; Minister of Community Relations, NI, 1971-72; Member (UU) for S Belfast, NI Assembly, 1973-75; Minister of Education, NI, 1974. Governor, Campbell Coll., 1975-, Chm., 1983-; Chm., Lagan Coll., Belfast, 1981- (the first integrated RC and Protestant school in NI). Recreations: golf, music, gardening. Address: Larkhill, 98 Spa Road, Ballynahinch, Co Down. T: Ballynahinch 563534. Club: Royal Commonwealth Society.

MACK, Alan Frederick, JP; Director, Manchester Chamber of Commerce and Industry, 1971-81; b 5 Dec. 1920; s of late Stanley Mack and late Sarah Elizabeth Mack; m 1953, Ailsa Muriel Wells; two d. Educ: Manchester Grammar School. War Service, Royal Artillery, Middle East, Italy, 1940-46. Secretary, Textile Finishing Trade Assocs, 1946-68; Commercial Manager, British Textile Employers Assoc., 1968-70. Jt Hon. Sec., NW Industrial Develt Assoc., 1971-81; Hon. Sec., Manchester Post Office Adv. Cttee, 1971-81; Mem., NW Supplementary Benefits Tribunal, 1977-; Hon. Sec.,

Greater Manchester East County Scout Council, 1974–80; Pres., Manchester Jun. Ch. of Commerce, 1956–57. JP Manchester (Inner), 1974. *Recreations:* reading, gardening, historic buildings. *Address:* 8 Foxland Road, Gatley, Cheadle, Cheshire SK8 4QA. *T:* 061-428 6549. *Clubs:* St James's, Manchester (both Manchester).

MACK, Prof. Alan Osborne, MDS; FDS RCS; Professor of Dental Prosthetics, Institute of Dental Surgery, University of London, 1967–80, now Emeritus; Consultant Dental Surgeon, Eastman Dental Hospital; Civilian Consultant in Dental Prosthetics to the Royal Air Force since 1976; *b* 24 July 1918; *s* of Arthur Joseph Mack, Glos, and Florence Emily Mack (*née* Norris); *m* 1943, Marjorie Elizabeth (*née* Westacott); two *s* one *d. Educ:* Westbourne Park Sch.; London Univ. LDS RCS 1942; MDS Durham, 1958; FDS RCS 1971. House Surgeon, Royal Dental Hosp., Sch. of Dental Surgery, University of London, 1942–43; served in RAF Dental Branch, 1943–47; Demonstrator, Prosthetics Dept Royal Dental Hosp., 1948; successively Asst Dir, Prosthetics Dept, and Senior Lecturer, London Univ., Royal Dental Hosp., 1949–56; Prof. of Dental Prosthetics, Univ. of Newcastle upon Tyne (formerly King's Coll., Univ. of Durham), 1956–67; Examiner in Dental Prosthetics, Royal Coll. of Surgeons of England, 1956; Examiner, University of Manchester, 1959, Leeds, 1961, Glasgow, 1961, Liverpool, 1965, London, 1965, Edinburgh, 1968, Lagos, 1970, Singapore, Khartoum, 1977; Benghazi, 1978; Examination Visitor, GDC; Advisor, Univ. of Malaya. Mem. Board of Faculty, Royal College of Surgeons, 1959. Pres. British Soc. for Study of Prosthetic Dentistry (BSSPD), 1963. Hon. Consultant, Stoke Mandeville Hosp., 1976; part-time Consultant, John Radcliffe Hosp., 1980–. Vis. Prof., Univ. of Singapore, 1981–. Hon. Mem., Amer. Acad. of Implant Dentures, 1966. *Publications:* Full Dentures, 1971; articles in British Dental Jls. *Recreations:* gardening, pottering. *Address:* Home Farm, London Road, Aston Clinton, Bucks HP22 5HG.

MACK SMITH, Denis, FBA 1976; FRSL; Senior Research Fellow of All Souls College, Oxford, since 1962; *b* 3 March 1920; *s* of Wilfrid Mack Smith and Altiora Gauntlett; *m* 1963, Catharine Stevenson; two *d. Educ:* St Paul's Cathedral Choir Sch.; Haileybury Coll.; Peterhouse, Cambridge Univ. (organ and history schols). MA Cantab. MA Oxon. Asst Master, Clifton Coll., 1941–42; Cabinet Offices, 1942–46; Fellow of Peterhouse, Cambridge, 1947–62 (now Emeritus Fellow); Tutor of Peterhouse, 1948–58; Univ. Lectr, Cambridge, 1952–62. Commendatore dell'Ordine al Merito della Repubblica Italiana. For. Hon. Mem., Amer. Acad. of Arts and Sciences. Awards: Thirlwall, 1949; Serena, 1960; Elba, 1972; Villa di Chiesa, 1973; Mondello, 1975; Nove Muse, 1976; Duff Cooper Meml., 1977; Wolfson Literary, 1977. *Publications:* Cavour and Garibaldi 1860, 1954; Garibaldi, 1957; (jtly) British Interests in the Mediterranean and Middle East, 1958; Italy, a Modern History, 1959 (enlarged edn 1969); Medieval Sicily, 1968; Modern Sicily, 1968; Da Cavour a Mussolini, 1968; (ed) The Making of Italy 1796–1870, 1968; (ed) Garibaldi, 1969; (ed) E. Quinet, Le Rivoluzioni d'Italia, 1970; Victor Emanuel, Cavour and the Risorgimento, 1971; (ed) G. La Farina, Scritti Politici, 1972; Mussolini's Roman Empire, 1976; Un Monumento al Duce, 1976; Cento Anni di Vita Italiana attraverso il Corriere della Sera, 1978; L'Italia del Ventesimo Secolo, 1978; (ed) G. Bandi, I mille: da Genova a Capua, 1981; Mussolini, 1981; Jt Editor, Nelson History of England. *Address:* All Souls College, Oxford. *T:* Oxford 722251; White Lodge, Osler Road, Headington, Oxford. *T:* Oxford 62878.

McKAIG, Adm. Sir (John) Rae, KCB 1973; CBE 1966; Deputy Chairman and Chief Executive, Gray Mackenzie & Co., since 1980; Director, Inchcape plc, since 1981; *b* 24 April 1922; *s* of late Sir John McKaig, KCB, DSO, and Lady (Annie Wright) McKaig (*née* Lee); *m* 1945, Barbara Dawn, *d* of Dr F. K. Marriott, MC, Yoxford, Suffolk; two *s* one *d. Educ:* Loretto Sch. Joined RN as Special Entry Cadet, 1939; served in cruisers and destroyers in Home and Mediterranean Waters, 1940–43; in Amphibious Force S at invasion of Normandy, 1944; in coastal forces until 1945; qual. in Communications, 1945; Commander, 1952; Captain, 1959; served as Dep. to Chief Polaris Exec., 1963–66; comd HM Signal Sch., 1966–68; Rear-Adm., 1968; Asst Chief of Naval Staff (Operational Requirements), 1968–70; Vice-Adm., 1970; Flag Officer, Plymouth, and Port Admiral, Devonport, Comdr Central Sub Area, E Atlantic, and Comdr Plymouth Sub Area, Channel, 1970–73; Adm., 1973; UK Mil. Rep. to NATO, 1973–75. Mem., Royal Patriotic Fund Corp., 1978–. *Recreations:* offshore sailing, shooting, fishing. *Address:* Hill House, Hambledon, Hants. *Clubs:* Army and Navy; Royal Ocean Racing.

McKANE, Prof. William, FBA 1980; Professor of Hebrew and Oriental Languages, University of St Andrews, since 1968; *b* 18 Feb. 1921; *s* of Thomas McKane and Jemima Smith McKane; *m* 1952, Agnes Mathie Howie; three *s* two *d. Educ:* Univ. of St Andrews (MA 1949); Univ. of Glasgow (MA 1952, PhD 1956, DLitt 1980). RAF, 1941–45. University of Glasgow: Asst in Hebrew, 1953–56; Lectr in Hebrew, 1956–65; Sen. Lectr, 1965–68; Dean, Faculty of Divinity, St Andrews, 1973–77. Foreign Sec., Soc. for Old Testament Study (Pres., 1978); Chm., Peshitta project (Old Testament in Syriac), Internat. Org. for Study of Old Testament. *Publications:* Prophets and Wise Men, 1965; Proverbs: a new approach, 1970; Studies in the Patriarchal Narratives, 1979; articles and reviews in British and European learned jls. *Recreations:* a little indoor soccer (St Andrews association football blue, 1949), some club cricket, walking, including hill walking. *Address:* 51 Irvine Crescent, St Andrews, Fife KY16 8LJ. *T:* St Andrews 73797. *Club:* Royal and Ancient Golf (St Andrews).

MACKANESS, George Bellamy, MB, BS, DPhil; FRS 1976; President, Squibb Institute for Medical Research and Development, since 1976; *b* Sydney, Australia, 20 Aug. 1922; *s* of James V. Mackaness and Eleanor F. Mackaness; *m* 1945, Gwynneth Patterson; one *s. Educ:* Sydney Univ. (MB, BS Hons 1945); London Univ. (DCP 1948); Univ. of Oxford (Hon. MA 1949, DPhil 1953). Resident MO, Sydney Hosp., 1945–46; Resident Pathologist, Kanematsu Inst. of Pathology, Sydney Hosp., 1946–47; Dept of Path., Brit. Postgrad. Med. Sch., London Univ., 1947–48 (DCP); ANU Trav. Scholarship, Univ. of Oxford, 1948–51; Demonstrator and Tutor in Path., Sir William Dunn Sch. of Path., Oxford, 1949–53; Dept of Experimental Pathology, Australian National University: Sen. Fellow, 1954–58; Associate Prof. of Exp. Path., 1958–60; Professorial Fellow, 1960–63; Vis. Investigator, Rockefeller Univ., NY, 1959–60; Prof. of Microbiology, Univ. of Adelaide, 1963–65; Dir, Trudeau Inst. for Med. Res., NY, 1965–76; Adjunct Prof. of Path., NY Univ. Med. Center, 1969–. Member: Allergy and Immunol. Study Sect., Nat. Insts of Health, 1967–71; Bd of Sci. Counsellors, Nat. Inst. of Allergy and Infect. Diseases, 1971–75; Armed Forces Epidemicol Bd, 1967–73; Bd of Governors, W. Alton Jones Cell Science Center, 1970–72; Council, Tissue Culture Assoc., 1973–; Bd of Sci. Consultants, Sloan-Kettering Inst. Member: Amer. Assoc. of Immunologists; Amer. Assoc. for Advancement of Science; Reticuloendothelial Soc.; Lung Assoc.; Internat. Union Against Tuberculosis; Amer. Soc. of Microbiologists. Fellow, Amer. Acad. of Arts and Scis, 1978. Paul Ehrlich-Ludwig Darmstaedter Prize, 1975. *Address:* 1515 Rolling Green Road, Yardley, Pa 19067, USA. *T:* (215) 493-4229.

MACKAY, family name of Earl of Inchcape, Lord Reay and Barons Mackay of Clashfern and Tanlaw.

MACKAY OF CLASHFERN, Baron *cr* 1979 (Life Peer), of Eddrachillis in the District of Sutherland; **James Peter Hymers Mackay**; PC 1979; QC (Scotland) 1965; Lord Advocate, since 1979; *b* 2 July 1927; *s* of James Mackay and Janet Hymers; *m* 1958, Elizabeth Gunn Hymers; one *s* two *d. Educ:* George Heriot's Sch., Edinburgh. MA Hons Maths and Nat. Philosophy, Edinburgh Univ., 1948; Lectr in Mathematics, Univ. of St Andrews, 1948–50; Major Schol., Trinity Coll., Cambridge, in Mathematics, 1947, taken up 1950; Senior Schol. 1951; BA (Cantab) 1952; LLB Edinburgh (with Distinction) 1955. Admitted to Faculty of Advocates, 1955; Standing Junior Counsel to: Queen's and Lord Treasurer's Remembrancer; Scottish Home and Health Dept; Commissioners of Inland Revenue in Scotland; Sheriff Principal, Renfrew and Argyll, 1972–74; Vice-Dean, Faculty of Advocates, 1973–76; Dean, 1976–79. Part-time Mem., Scottish Law Commn, 1976–79. Hon. Master of the Bench, Inner Temple, 1979. Fellow: Internat. Acad. of Trial Lawyers, 1979; Inst. of Taxation, 1981. Dir, Stenhouse Holdings Ltd, 1976–77. Mem., Insurance Brokers' Registration Council, 1977–79. A Comr of Northern Lighthouses, 1975–. *Publication:* Armour on Valuation for Rating, 4th edn (with J. J. Clyde and J. A. D. Hope), 1971. *Recreation:* walking. *Address:* 34 Dick Place, Edinburgh. *T:* 031-667 5995. *Club:* New (Edinburgh).

MACKAY, Alastair, CMG 1966; *b* 27 Sept. 1911; *s* of late Alexander Mackay; *m* 1st, 1939, Janetta Brown Ramsay (*d* 1973); one *s* one *d*; 2nd, 1975, Edith Whicher. *Educ:* George Heriot's Sch.; Edinburgh Univ.; Berlin Univ. Entered HM Treasury, 1940. Member UK Treasury and Supply Delegation, Washington, 1951–54; seconded to Foreign Service Inspectorate, 1957–59; Financial Adviser to the British High Commissioner in India, 1963–66; Under-Sec., HM Treasury, 1967–71; Financial and Development Sec., Gibraltar, 1971–75. *Recreations:* golf, gardening. *Address:* 5 Darley Road, Eastbourne, Sussex. *T:* Eastbourne 22738.

McKAY, Sir Alex, (Sir Alick Benson McKay), KBE 1977 (CBE 1965); Director, News International Ltd (Deputy Chairman, 1969–78, Group Managing Director 1976–77); *b* Adelaide, S Australia, 5 Aug. 1909; *s* of George Hugh McKay, Master Mariner; *m* 1st, 1935, Muriel Frieda Searcy (decd); one *s* two *d*; 2nd, 1973, Beverley Hylton, widow of Jack Hylton. Joined News Ltd, Adelaide, 1933; Manager, News Ltd, Melbourne, 1939; Manager, News Ltd, Sydney, 1941; Dir and Gen. Man., Argus & Australasian Ltd, 1952; joined Daily Mirror Group, London, 1957, Dir, 1958. Dir, Internat. Publishing Corporation, 1963–69. Trustee, Reuters Ltd, 1975–. Chm. in London, Victorian Economic Develt Corp., Australia. *Address:* Ellingham, St Clements Road, Westgate-on-Sea, Kent. *Club:* Garrick.

McKAY, Maj.-Gen. Alexander Matthew, CB 1975; Secretary, Institution of Mechanical Engineers, since 1976; Vice-Chairman, Mechanical Engineering Publications Ltd, since 1976; Chairman, Stocklake Holdings Ltd, since 1976; Director, Northgate Publishing Co. Ltd, since 1978; *b* 14 Feb. 1921; *s* of Colin and Anne McKay; *m* 1949, Betty Margaret Lee; one *s* one *d* (and one *d* decd). *Educ:* Esplanade House Sch.; RN Dockyard Sch.; Portsmouth Polytechnic. CEng, FIEE, FIMechE, CBIM, psc, sm; Member: ASME; SAE (USA). Served War of 1939-45 (despatches twice); 2nd Lieut, 1943; Lieut 1944; Captain 1944; Major 1947; Lt-Col 1960; Col 1966; Brigadier 1968; Maj.-Gen. 1972. Served with 6th Airborne Div.; Staff Coll., Quetta, 1954; staff appts include GS02, DAA&QMG, DAQMG, AQMG; Dir, Elect. and Mech. Engrg, Army, 1972–75; Col Comdt, REME, 1974–80. Gen. Sec., IChemE, 1975–76. Mem. Council, IEE, 1973–76. Fellow, Inst. of Dirs. *Publications:* papers in Proceedings IMechE and REME Institution. *Recreations:* fly fishing, restoring antique furniture, outdoor sports. *Address:* Church Cottage, Martyr Worthy, near Winchester, Hants SO21 1DY. *Clubs:* Caledonian, Institute of Directors.

McKAY, Sir Alick Benson; see McKay, Sir Alex.

McKAY, Allen; JP; MP (Lab) Penistone, since July 1978; b 5 Feb. 1927; s of Fred and Martha Anne McKay; m 1949, June Simpson; one s. Educ: Hoyland Kirk Balk Secondary Modern School; extramural studies, Univ. of Sheffield. Clerical work, Steel Works, 1941-45; general mineworker, 1945-47; Mining Electrical Engineer, 1947-65; NCB Industrial Relations Trainee, 1965-66; Asst Manpower Officer, Barnsley Area, NCB, 1966-78. JP Barnsley, 1971. Recreation: reading. Address: House of Commons, SW1; 24 Springwood Road, Hoyland, Barnsley, South Yorks S74 0AZ. T: Barnsley 743418.

MacKAY, Andrew James; Partner, Jones MacKay & Croxford, Estate Agents, since 1974; b 27 Aug. 1949; s of Robert James MacKay and Olive Margaret MacKay; m 1975, Diana Joy (née Kinchin); one s one d. Educ: Solihull. Consultant, Birmingham Housing Industries Ltd, 1973-. MP (C) Birmingham, Stechford, Mar. 1977-1979; Mem., Conservative Party Nat. Exec., 1979-. Recreations: golf, squash, good food. Address: (office) 83 Edmund Street, Birmingham B3 2ET. T: 021-236 8600. Clubs: Birmingham (Birmingham); Olton Golf (Solihull); Aberdovey Golf (Wales); Washwood Heath Conservative (Birmingham).

McKAY, Archibald Charles; Sheriff of Glasgow and Strathkelvin, since 1979; b 18 Oct. 1929; s of Patrick McKay and Catherine (née McKinlay); m 1956, Ernestine Maria Tobia; one s three d. Educ: Knocknacarry, Co. Antrim; St Aloysius' Coll., Glasgow; Glasgow Univ. (MA, LLB 1954). National Service, 1955-56. Started practice in Glasgow as solicitor, 1957; estabd own firm of solicitors, 1961; apptd to the Bench, 1978. Recreations: flying, motor-cycling. Address: 18 Dargarvel Avenue, Dumbreck, Glasgow G41 5LU. T: 041-427 1525. Club: Western (Glasgow).

MACKAY, A(rthur) Stewart, ROI 1949; formerly Lecturer, Hammersmith College of Art; b 25 Feb. 1909; British. Educ: Wilson's Grammar Sch.; Regent Street Polytechnic School of Art. Art Master, Regent Street Polytechnic School of Art, 1936, Assistant Lecturer, 1936-60. Served War of 1939-45: enlisted Army, Jan. 1942; released with rank of Captain, 1946. Exhibitor: RA (43 pictures), Paris Salon, ROI, RBA, Leicester Galleries, Imperial War Museum; Royal Scottish Academy; New York. Publications: How to Make Lino Cuts, 1935; articles for Artist and Kent Life, 1953, 1963. Recreation: reading. Address: 4 Dog Kennel Hill, East Dulwich, SE22.

MACKAY, Charles, FIBiol; Chief Agricultural Officer, Department of Agriculture and Fisheries for Scotland, since 1975; b 12 Jan. 1927; s of Hugh and Eliza MacKay; m 1956, Marie A. K. MacKay (née Mitchell); one s one d. Educ: Strathmore Sch., Sutherland; Lairg Higher Grade Sch., Sutherland; Univ. of Aberdeen (BScAgric); Univ. of Kentucky (MSc). Department of Agriculture and Fisheries for Scotland: Temporary Inspector, 1947-48; Asst Inspector, 1948-54; Inspector, 1954-64; Sen. Inspector, 1964-70; Technical Develt Officer, 1970-73; Dep. Chief Agricl Officer, 1973-75. Hon. Order of Kentucky Colonels, 1960. Recreations: fishing, golf. Address: Dun Dornaig, 35 Boswall Road, Edinburgh EH5 3RP. T: 031-552 6063.

MacKAY, Prof. Donald Iain; Professor of Economics, Heriot-Watt University, Edinburgh, since 1976; Consultant to Secretary of State for Scotland, since 1971; b 27 Feb. 1937; s of William and Rhona MacKay; m 1961, Diana Marjory (née Raffan); one s two d. Educ: Dollar Academy; Univ. of Aberdeen (MA). English Electric Co., 1959-62; Lectr in Political Economy, Univ. of Aberdeen, 1962-65; Lectr in Applied Economics, Univ. of Glasgow, 1965-68, Sen. Lectr, 1968-71; Prof. of Political Economy, Univ. of Aberdeen, 1971-76. Lister Lectr, British Assoc. for the Advancement of Science, 1974. Sen. Partner, Planning, Economic and Industrial Development Advisors, 1975-; Man. Dir, Scottish Centre of Political Economy, 1979-; Dir, Lennox Oil Co., 1980-. Publications: Geographical Mobility and the Brain Drain, 1969; Local Labour Markets and Wage Structures, 1970; Labour Markets under Different Employment Conditions, 1971; The Political Economy of North Sea Oil, 1975; (ed) Scotland 1980: the economics of self-government, 1977; articles in Econ. Jl, Oxford Econ. Papers, Manch. Sch., Scottish Jl Polit. Econ., Jl Royal Stat. Soc. Recreations: tennis, chess, golf. Address: Newfield, 14 Gamekeeper's Road, Edinburgh EH4 6LU.

MacKAY, Prof. Donald MacCrimmon, BSc, PhD, FInstP; Professor Emeritus, University of Keele; Joint Editor, Biological Cybernetics; b 9 Aug. 1922; o s of Dr Henry MacKay; m 1955, Valerie Wood; two s three d. Educ: Wick High Sch.; St Andrews Univ. BSc (St Andrews) 1943; PhD (London) 1951. Radar research, Admiralty, 1943-46; Assistant Lecturer in Physics, 1946-48, Lecturer, 1948-59, Reader, 1959-60, King's Coll., London, FKC 1979; Research Prof. of Communication, Univ. of Keele, 1960-82. Rockefeller Fellow in USA, 1951. Vis. Prof., Univ. of California, 1969; Lectures: Fleming, 1961; Eddington, 1967; Herter, Johns Hopkins Univ., 1971; Foerster, Univ. of California, 1973; Drummond, Univ. of Stirling, 1975; Fremantle, Balliol Coll. Oxford, 1975; Riddell, Univ. of Newcastle, 1977; Pascal, Univ. of Waterloo, 1979. Publications: (with M. E. Fisher) Analogue Computing at Ultra-High Speed, 1962; (ed) Christianity in a Mechanistic Universe, 1965; Freedom of Action in a Mechanistic Universe, 1967; Information, Mechanism and Meaning, 1969; The Clockwork Image, 1974; Science, Chance and Providence, 1978; Human Science and Human Dignity, 1979; Brains, Machines and Persons, 1980; Science and the Quest for Meaning, 1982; Chapters in: Communication Theory, 1953; Information Theory, 1956, 1961; Sensory Communication, 1961; Man and his Future, 1963; Science in its Context, 1964; Information Processing in the Nervous System, 1964; Brain and Conscious Experience, 1966; Structure and Function of Inhibitory Neuronal Mechanisms, 1968; Evoked Brain Potentials, 1969; The Neurosciences, 1971; Non-Verbal Communication, 1972; Handbook of Sensory Physiology, 1973; Cybernetics and Bionics, 1974; Modifying Man: implications and ethics, 1978; Cerebral Correlates of Conscious Experience, 1978; Motivation, Motor and Sensory Processes of the Brain, 1980; Neural Communication and Control, 1981; scientific papers on electronic computing, information theory, experimental psychology, neurophysiology. Recreation: photography. Address: The Croft, Keele, Staffs ST5 5AN. T: Newcastle (Staffs) 627300.

McKAY, Hon. Sir Donald Norman, KCMG 1978; farmer and politician, New Zealand; b Waipu, NZ, 28 Nov. 1908; s of Angus John McKay; m 1934, Miriam Hilda, d of A. T. Stehr; two s one d. Educ: Whangarei High Sch.; Auckland Univ. MP, Marsden, NZ, 1954-72; Minister of Health and Social Security, and Minister in Charge of Child Welfare Div., 1962-72. Member: Marsden National Party; Waipu Centenary Celebrations Cttee; Caledonian Soc.; District High Sch. Cttee; Northland Harbour Bd (Chm.). Recreations: bowls, golf; (rep. Auckland Univ., Rugby football, 1928-30; N Auckland, cricket, 1932-36). Address: Waipu, Northland, New Zealand.

MACKAY, Eric Beattie; Editor of The Scotsman since 1972; b 31 Dec. 1922; s of Lewis Mackay and Agnes Johnstone; m 1954, Moya Margaret Myles Connolly (d 1981); three s one d. Educ: Aberdeen Grammar Sch.; Aberdeen Univ. (MA). Aberdeen Bon-Accord, 1948; Elgin Courant, 1949; The Scotsman, 1950; Daily Telegraph, 1952; The Scotsman, 1953: London Editor, 1957; Dep. Editor, 1961. Recreations: travel, golf, theatre. Address: 5 Strathearn Place, Edinburgh EH9 2AL. T: 031-447 7737. Club: Caledonian.

MACKAY, Maj.-Gen. Eric MacLachlan, CBE 1971 (MBE 1944); Managing Director, Galadari Cementation (Private) Ltc, since 1978; Regional Director Iraq, Engineering Services International, since 1981; b 26 Dec. 1921; s of Ian MacLachlan Mackay and Violet Aimée Scott-Smith; m 1954, Ruth Thérèse Roth; one s. Educ: Fettes Coll., Edinburgh. Served War: enlisted Royal Scots Fusiliers, 1940; commissioned Oct. 1941, Royal Engineers; 2/Lieut-Major, 1st Parachute Sqdn, RE, 1941-45, N Africa, Sicily, Italy, Arnhem, PoW (escaped) Norway. OC, Field Company, 20 Indian Div., French Indo-China, 1945-46; 2 i/c 23 Indian Div. Engrs, Java, 1946; OC, 35 Indian Field Company, Malaya, 1947; Supplementary Engrg Course, SME, 1948; GSO 2 Intell., Jt Intell. Bureau, 1949-50; Staff Coll., 1951; GSO 2, Org. and Equipment, HQ, ALFCE, 1952-53; Sen. Instructor Tactics, SME, 1954-55; OC, 33 Field Sqdn, RE, Cyprus, Suez, 1956-58; GSO 2, Wpns, MoD, 1958-60; JSSC, 1960; 2 i/c 2 Div. Engrs, 1961-62; Chief Engr, Malaysian Army, Borneo/Malaya, 1963-65; GSO 1, Co-ord., Master-Gen. of the Ordnance, 1966-67; Col, GS, RSME, 1968-69; Chief Engr (Brig.): Army Strategic Command, 1970-71; UK Land Forces, 1972; Maj.-Gen. 1973; Chief Engr, BAOR, 1973-76, retired. Man. Dir, Cementation Sico Oman Ltd, 1977. CEng 1976; MICE 1976. DSC (USA), 1944; Pingat Peringatan Malaysia (PPM), 1965. Recreations: motoring, skiing, photography. Address: c/o Galadari Cementation (Private) Ltd, Post Restante, Dubai, United Arab Emirates.

McKAY, Frederick; see McKay, J. F.

MACKAY, Sir (George Patrick) Gordon, Kt 1966; CBE 1962; Director, World Bank, 1975-78; Member, Board of Crown Agents, since 1980; b 12 Nov. 1914; s of Rev. Adam Mackay and Katie Forrest (née Lawrence); m 1954, Margaret Esmé Martin; one s two d. Educ: Gordon Sch., Huntly; Aberdeen Univ. Joined Kenya and Uganda Railways and Harbours (later East African Railways and Harbours), 1938; Chief Asst to Gen. Manager, 1948; Chief Operating Supt, 1954; Dep. General Manager, 1960, General Manager, 1961-64; with World Bank, 1965-78. FCIT (MInstT 1961). OStJ 1964. Recreation: golf. Address: Well Cottage, Sandhills, Brook, Surrey GU8 5UP. T: Wormley 2549. Club: Nairobi (Kenya).

MACKAY, Gillian Helen, (Mrs Walter Tallis); Public Relations Consultant; private pilot; b 20 Sept. 1923; er d of Stuart Mackay; m 1971, Walter John Tallis. Educ: Hunmanby Hall. WRNS, 1942-46. Dep. Press Officer, Conservative Central Office, 1947-52; BOAC, 1952-56. Executive Secretary, Guild of Air Pilots and Air Navigators, 1956-68 (Freeman; Liveryman, 1968); Press Officer to Liberal Party Leader, 1968-69; Campaign Manager, Health Education Council, 1969-71; Exec. Dir, Fluoridation Soc., 1971-74. Chm., British Women Pilots' Assoc., 1964-69, 1974-76; Mem., Charles Newton Meml Trust Cttee, 1968-; Gen. Sec., PR Consultants Assoc., 1974; Sec., Internat. Inst. of Human Nutrition, 1975-76; Member Council, Air League, 1966-71, 1972-76; Membership Sec., The Air League, 1976-79. Hon. Advr, Air Safety Gp, 1968-. Mem., Action Opportunities, 1976-. Companion, RAeS, 1960. Tissandier Diploma, Fédération Aéronautique Internat., 1966. MIPR 1974-82. Recreations: birdwatching, sailing, gardening. Address: The Stable House, Burcot, near Abingdon OX14 3DP. Clubs: Steering Wheel, Eagle Ski Club.

MACKAY, Sir Gordon; see Mackay, Sir G. P. G.

MACKAY, Ian Keith, CMG 1963; Consultant, since 1976; Assistant to Chairman, Papua New Guinea Broadcasting Commission, 1973-75; b 19 Oct. 1909; s of David and Margaret Mackay; m 1960, Lilian Adele Beatty; one s one d. *Educ:* Nelson Coll., New Zealand. New Zealand Broadcasting Service: Announcer, 1935-36; Sports Announcer, 1937; Station Manager, 1938-43; Senior Executive, Commercial Network, 1943-50; Australia: Asst Manager, Station 2GB, 1950-51; Production Manager, Macquarie Network, 1951-61; Director-General, Nigerian Broadcasting Corporation, 1961-64; Advisor on Mass Media to Minister and NBC Board of Governors, 1964-65; PRO, Papua and New Guinea Administration, 1966-68; Sen. Broadcast Officer, 1969-72, seconded Special Administrative duties in setting up the single broadcasting authority for Papua New Guinea, 1972-73. Member, Royal Society of Literature; Member, Society of Authors. *Publications:* Broadcasting in New Zealand, 1953; Broadcasting in Australia, 1957; Macquarie: The Story of a Network, 1960; Broadcasting in Nigeria, 1964; Presenting Papua and New Guinea, 1967; Broadcasting in Papua New Guinea, 1976; articles on social and historical aspects of broadcasting and articles on broadcasting in developing countries in numerous jls; also papers for UN agencies. *Recreations:* conchology, philately. *Address:* 405A Karori Road, Wellington 5, New Zealand.

McKAY, Very Rev. (James) Frederick, CMG 1972; OBE 1964 (MBE 1953); Associate Minister, St Stephen's Uniting (formerly Presbyterian) Church, Sydney, 1974-80; Chairman, Uniting Church Negotiators, NSW, 1976-80; recognised as a foundation minister of Uniting Church in Australia at time of Union, 1977; *b* 15 April 1907; father, Northern Ireland; mother, Australian; *m* 1938, Margaret Mary Robertson; one *s* three *d. Educ:* Thornburgh Coll., Charters Towers, Qld; Emmanuel Coll., Brisbane, Qld; University of Queensland. MA; BD. Ordained Minister, Presbyterian Church of Australia, 1935; Patrol Padre, Australian Inland Mission (working with Flynn of the Inland), 1935-41; Chaplain, RAAF, 1941-46; Command Chaplain, Middle East, 1943-45; Minister, Toowong Parish, Qld, 1946-50; Superintendent (succeeding Flynn of the Inland), Aust. Inland Mission, 1951-74, Archivist, 1974-75. Moderator, Presbyterian Church of NSW, 1965; Moderator-Gen., Presbyterian Church of Australia, 1970-73. Editor, Frontier News, 1951-74. Vocational Award, Sydney Rotary, 1972. *Address:* 65 Baroona Road, Northbridge, NSW 2063, Australia. *T:* Sydney 952757. *Club:* Australian (Sydney).

MACKAY, Sir James (Mackerron), KBE 1966; CB 1964; *b* 9 Aug. 1907; *o s* of Alexander and Annie Mackay; *m* 1938, Katherine, *d* of R. C. Hamilton; two *s. Educ:* Forres and Hamilton Academies; Glasgow and Oxford Universities. Glasgow Univ.: MA, 1929; Assistant in Greek, 1929-30. Balliol Coll., Oxford, 1930-34; Exhibitioner; Mods. and Greats. Lecturer in Humanity, Glasgow Univ., 1934-40. Entered Secretariat, Admiralty, 1940; Assistant Secretary, 1945; Under-Secretary, 1958; Deputy Secretary, 1961; Deputy Under Sec. of State, Min. of Defence, April 1964; Deputy Sec., Min. of Aviation, 1964-66; Deputy Under-Sec. of State, Home Office, 1966-67. Member: Scottish Tourist Bd, 1967-72; Highlands and Islands Develt Bd, 1967-72 (Dep. Chm., 1970-72); Countryside Commn for Scotland, 1967-72; Cttee of Enquiry into Future of Broadcasting, 1974-77. *Address:* Cluny, Drumnadrochit, Inverness. *T:* Drumnadrochit 268.

McKAY, Sir James (Wilson), Kt 1971; JP; DL; former Lord Provost of Edinburgh, and Lord Lieutenant of the County of the City of Edinburgh, 1969-72; *b* 12 March 1912; *s* of John McKay; *m* 1942, Janette Urquhart; three *d. Educ:* Dunfermline High Sch.; Portobello Secondary Sch., Edinburgh. Insurance Broker; Man. Dir, John McKay (Insurance) Ltd, Edinburgh; Director: George S. Murdoch & Partners Ltd, Aberdeen; Church of Scotland, Insurance Trust. Served with RN, 1941-46 (Lieut, RNVR). Hon. DLitt Heriot-Watt, 1972. JP Edinburgh, 1972; DL County and City of Edinburgh, 1972. Order of Cross of St Mark (Greek Orthodox Church), 1970; Knight, Order of Orange-Nassau, 1972. *Recreations:* walking, gardening, reading. *Address:* T'Windward, 11 Cammo Gardens, Edinburgh EH4 8EJ. *T:* 031-339 6755. *Clubs:* New (Edinburgh); RNVR (Glasgow); Caledonian (Hon. Mem.) (San Francisco).

MACKAY, John; Headmaster, Bristol Grammar School, 1960-75; *b* 23 June 1914; *s* of William Mackay, Nottingham, and Eliza Mackay; *m* 1952, Margaret Ogilvie; two *s* two *d. Educ:* Mundella Grammar Sch., Nottingham; University of Nottingham; Merton Coll., Oxford. BA London (External) 1st Class Hons (English), 1935; Cambridge Teacher's Certificate, 1936. On staff of SCM, 1936-38; English Lecturer, St John's Coll., York, 1938-40. Served War of 1939-45, in Royal Navy, 1940-46. Merton Coll., Oxford, 1946-48; DPhil (Oxon) 1953. English Master, Merchant Taylors' School, Crosby, Liverpool, 1948-54; Second Master, Cheltenham Coll., 1954-60. Chm., HMC, 1970, Treasurer, 1974-75. *Recreations:* literature, gardening, cricket, arguing. *Address:* The Old Post Office, Tormarton, Badminton, Avon GL9 1HU. *T:* Badminton 243.

MACKAY, John Alexander, MA, LittD, DD, LLD, LHD; President of Princeton Theological Seminary, 1936-59, President Emeritus, 1959; *b* Inverness, Scotland, 17 May 1889; *s* of Duncan Mackay and Isabella Macdonald; *m* 1916, Jane Logan Wells; one *s* three *d. Educ:* University of Aberdeen (MA 1912, 1st Cl. Hons in Philosophy); Princeton Theological Seminary (BD 1915). Studied at the University of Madrid, 1915-16, and University of Bonn, 1930. LittD, University of San Marcos, Lima, 1918; DD Princeton Univ., 1937, Aberdeen Univ., 1939, University of Debrecen, Hungary, 1939; LLD Ohio-Wesleyan, 1937, Lincoln Univ., 1953; LHD Boston, 1939; and Hon. Degrees from several colleges; Hon. Fellow, Leland Stanford Univ., 1941. Principal, Anglo-Peruvian Coll., Lima, Peru, 1916-25;

Prof. Philosophy, Univ. of San Marcos, Peru, 1925; Writer and Lecturer, South American Fedn YMCA, 1926-32; Pres. Bd Foreign Missions of Presbyterian Church, USA, 1945-51; Pres., World Presbyterian Alliance, 1954-59; Member: Central Cttee World Council of Churches, 1948-54 (Provl Cttee, 1946-48); Council on Theological Education, Presbyterian Church, USA, 1944-46 (Chairman); International Missionary Council, 1948-58 (Chairman); Joint Cttee World Council of Churches and International Missionary Council, 1949- (Chairman, 1949-54); Advisory Council, Dept of Philosophy, Princeton Univ., 1941-62; American Theological Soc.; Hon. For. Mem., British and Foreign Bible Soc.; Trustee of Mackenzie Univ., São Paulo, Brazil (Pres. Bd of Trustees, 1948). Special Lectr at many Univs and Colleges since 1932. Pres., American Assoc. of Theological Schs, 1948; Moderator, General Assembly of the Presbyterian Church in USA, 1953. Comendador, Palmas Magistrales (Peru), 1964. *Publications:* Mas Yo Os Digo, 1927; El Sentido de la Vida, 1931; The Other Spanish Christ, 1932; That Other America, 1935; A Preface to Christian Theology, 1941; Heritage and Destiny, 1943; Christianity on the Frontier, 1950; God's Order, 1953; The Presbyterian Way of Life, 1960; His Life and our Life, 1964; Ecumenics: The Science of the Church Universal, 1964; Christian Reality and Appearance, 1969; Realidad e Idolatria, 1970. Editor, Theology Today, 1944-51 (Chairman Editorial Council, Theology Today, 1951-59). *Recreations:* walking and motoring. *Address:* Meadow Lakes, Apartment 39-09, Hightstown, NJ 08520, USA. *Clubs:* Cosmos (Washington); Nassau (Princeton).
See also Rev. Prof. B. M. Metzger.

McKAY, Sir John (Andrew), Kt 1972; CBE 1966; QPM 1968; HM Chief Inspector of Constabulary for England and Wales, 1970-72; *b* 28 Nov. 1912; *s* of late Denis McKay, Blantyre, Lanarkshire; *m* 1st, 1947, Gertrude Gillespie Deighan (*d* 1971); two *d*; 2nd, 1976, Mildred Grace Kilday, *d* of Dr Emil Stern and late Grace Mildred Pleasants, San Francisco. *Educ:* Glasgow Univ. MA Glasgow, 1934. Joined Metropolitan Police, 1935; seconded to Army for service with Military Govt in Italy and Austria, 1943-47 (Lt-Col); Asst Chief Constable, then Deputy Chief Constable, Birmingham, 1953-58; Chief Constable of Manchester, 1959-66; HM Inspector of Constabulary, 1966-70. Mem., Panel of Chairmen, CS Selection Bd. Director: Securicor Ltd; Intertel Inc., USA; Chm., Cancer Res. Campaign, Tunbridge Wells. Freeman of City of London, 1972. OStJ 1963. Hon. MA, Manchester, 1966; Hon. Fellow, Manchester Polytechnic, 1971. *Address:* 1 Long Slip, Langton Green, Tunbridge Wells, Kent. *Club:* Royal Commonwealth Society.

MACKAY, John Jackson; MP (C) Argyll, since 1979; Parliamentary Under Secretary of State, Scottish Office, since 1982; *b* 15 Nov. 1938; *s* of Jackson and Jean Mackay; *m* 1961, Sheena Wagner; two *s* one *d. Educ:* Glasgow Univ. (BSc, DipEd). Formerly, Head of Maths Dept, Oban High Sch. *Recreations:* fishing, sailing. *Address:* Innishail, Polvinister Road, Oban, Argyll. *T:* Oban 62678.

MACKAY, Maj.-Gen. Kenneth, CB 1969; MBE 1943; idc, psc; GOC, Field Force Command Australia, Nov. 1973-Feb. 1974, retired; *b* 17 Feb. 1917; *m* 1943, Judith, *d* of F. Littler; two *s* one *d. Educ:* University High Sch., Melbourne; RMC Duntroon. Served War of 1939-45: Artillery, and Liaison Officer HQ 9th Australian Division, Middle East, 1940-41; ME Staff Sch., 1942; Bde Maj. 26 Bde, 1942-44; MO 12, War Office, 1944-45; Joint Sec., JCOSA, 1945-48; CO, 67 Inf. Bn, 1948; CO, 3 Bn Royal Aust. Regt, 1949; AHQ, 1949-52; Chief Instructor, Sch. of Tactics and Admin. 1952-55; Asst Aust. Defence Rep. UK, 1955-57; successively Dir of Maintenance, Personnel Admin., Quartering and Military Training, 1957-61; IDC, 1962; Dir Military Operations and Plans, Army HQ, Canberra, 1962-66; Comdr Aust. Force Vietnam, 1966; Commander 1st Division Australian Army, 1967-68; QMG AHQ, 1968-71; GOC Eastern Comd, 1971-73. *Recreations:* fishing, golf. *Address:* 3 Beauchamp Street, Deakin, ACT 2600, Australia. *Clubs:* Australian, Royal Canberra; New South Wales Golf.

McKAY, Mrs Margaret; Public Relations Consultant; *b* Jan. 1911. *Educ:* Elementary. Joined Labour Party 1932. Chief woman officer, TUC, 1951-62; Member of Co-operative Society, 1928-. Held administrative posts with Civil Service Clerical Association and Transport and General Workers' Union. MP (Lab) Clapham, 1964-70. Commander, Order of the Cedar of Lebanon. *Publications:* Generation in Revolt (pen name Margaret McCarthy), 1953; Women in Trade Union History (TUC), 1954; Arab Voices from the Past; Electronic Arabia, 1974; The Chainless Mind, 1974; Timeless Arabia, 1978; Who Goes Home?, 1979, reissued as part of Strangers in Israel, 1982; Gulf Saga, 1982. *Address:* PO Box 668, Abu Dhabi, Union of Arab Emirates.

McKAY, Rev. Roy; Hon. Canon, Chichester Cathedral, since 1957; *b* 4 Nov. 1900; *s* of William McKay and Sarah Evelyn (*née* Littlewood); *m* 1927, Mary Oldham Fraser; one *s* one *d. Educ:* Marlborough Coll.; Magdalen Coll., Oxford. Curate, S Paul's, Kingston Hill, 1926; Curate-in-charge and Vicar of St Mark's Londonderry, Smethwick, 1928; Vicar of Mountfield, Sussex, 1932; Chaplain of Christ's Chapel of Alleyn's College of God's Gift, Dulwich, 1937; Vicar of Goring-by-Sea, Sussex, 1943; Chaplain of Canford Sch., 1948; Head of Religious Broadcasting, 1955-63; Preacher to Lincoln's Inn, 1958-59; Rector of St James, Garlickhythe, EC4, 1965-70. *Publications:* Tell John (with Bishop G. F. Allen), 1932; The Pillar of Fire, 1933; Take Care of the Sense, 1964; John Leonard Wilson: Confessor for the Faith, 1973. *Address:* 64 Thomas More House, Barbican, EC2.

MACKAY, Sir William (Calder), Kt 1968; OBE 1957; MC 1918; JP; *b* 5 Aug. 1896; *s* of William Scoular Mackay and Anne Armstrong Henderson; *m* 1920, Constance May Harris; one *s. Educ:* Hillhead High Sch., Glasgow. Served European War, 1914-18, NZEF (Adjt), France; served War of 1939-45 as Hon. YMCA Comr i/c welfare work in military camps, Air Force stations and naval establishments, Auckland Province. Past Member Board, Auckland Provincial Patriotic Fund; Director, Christchurch YMCA, 1929-33; Director, Auckland YMCA, 1934-45; President, YMCA, 1939-45; Chairman, Campaign Cttee for new Auckland YMCA, 1954; Life Member, YMCA, 1966. Past Member: Council, Auckland Chamber of Commerce; Exec. Cttee, Auckland Provincial Retailers' Assoc.; Auckland City Council, 1948-54; Auckland Harbour Bridge Authority; Council, Auckland, War Memorial Museum (Hon. Life Member, 1962). President, Rotary Club of Auckland, 1944-45; District Gov., Rotary, 1948-49; Member Aims and Objects Cttee, Rotary International, 1949-50. Provincial Comr, Boy Scouts, 1958; Organising Comr for Pan-Pacific Boy Scouts Jamboree, 1959 (Medal of Merit). Patron, Crippled Children Soc. (Mem. Exec., 1935-66, past Vice-Pres., and Pres., 1958-66, Life Mem. 1974, Auckland Branch); Vice-President: NZ Crippled Children Soc., 1964; St John Amb. Assoc. Auckland Centre Trust Bd, 1970; Pres., Nat. Children's Med. Res. Foundn, 1974; Past Area Co-ordinator, Duke of Edinburgh Award for Auckland Province and Mem. NZ Council, 1963. Foundn Mem. Bd, St Andrews Presbyterian Hospital and Hostel for Aged. JP 1940. *Recreations:* fishing, outdoor bowls. *Address:* 416 Remuera Road, Auckland 5, New Zealand. *T:* 502 495. *Club:* Northern (Auckland).

MACKAY-TALLACK, Sir Hugh, Kt 1963; Chairman, Capital and National Trust Ltd; Deputy Chairman, The Standard & Chartered Bank Ltd until May 1983; Director: The London & Holyrood Trust Ltd; London & Provincial Trust Ltd; Assam Investments Ltd (formerly Chairman); *s* of E. H. Tallack and Deborah Lyle Mackay; unmarried. *Educ:* Kelly Coll., Devon; Heidelberg Univ. Served War of 1939-45, with 17th Dogra Regt, in Middle East and Burma; Private Sec. to C-in-C ALFSEA, and Mil. Sec. (Col) to Admiral Mountbatten, Supreme Allied Comdr, SEAC. Formerly: Chm., Macneill & Barry Ltd (Inchcape Gp) Calcutta; Governor of State Bank of India; Director numerous other cos in India; Chm., Indian Tea Assoc., 1954-55; Vice-Chairman, Tea Board of India, 1954-55; Member Government of India Tea Auction Cttee, 1954-55; Chairman, Ross Inst. of India, 1951-64; Pres., Bengal Chamber of Commerce and Industry and Associated Chambers of Commerce of India, 1962-63. Formerly Dir, Inchcape & Co. Ltd (Dep. Chm., 1964-77). Mem., Fedn, Commonwealth Chambers of Commerce. Governor: Nehru Meml Trust; Victoria League. *Recreation:* riding. *Address:* 47 South Street, Mayfair, W1. *T:* 01-493 5670. *Clubs:* White's, Oriental, City of London; Bengal, Tollygunge, Turf (all in Calcutta).

McKEAN, Douglas, CB 1977; Deputy Secretary, Central Board of Finance of Church of England, since 1978; Director, Agricultural Mortgage Corporation, since 1978; *b* 2 April 1917; *s* of late Alexander McKean, Enfield, Mddx; *m* 1942, Anne, *d* of late Roger Clayton, Riding Mill, Northumberland; two *s. Educ:* Merchant Taylors' Sch.; St John's Coll., Oxford. War Office, 1940; transferred to HM Treasury, 1949; Asst Sec., 1956; Under-Sec., 1962; on loan to Dept of the Environment, 1970-72; retired as Under Sec., HM Treasury, 1977. Dep. Sec., Central Bd of Finance, Church of England, 1978-82. Trustee, Irish Sailors and Soldiers Land Trust, 1980-. *Recreation:* mountain walking. *Address:* The Dower House, Forty Hill, Enfield, Middlesex EN2 9EJ. *T:* 01-363 2365. *Club:* United Oxford & Cambridge University.

McKEARNEY, Philip; HM Diplomatic Service; Consul-General, Boston, Massachusetts, since 1980; *b* 15 Nov. 1926; *s* of Philip McKearney, OBE; *m* 1950, Jean Pamela Walker; two *s. Educ:* City of London Sch.; Hertford Coll., Oxford. 4/7th Dragoon Guards, 1946-53; joined HM Diplomatic Service, 1953; 3rd Sec., British Embassy, Damascus, 1955-56; 1st Sec., British Legation, Bucharest, 1959-62; British Political Agent, Qatar, 1962-65; Counsellor and Consul-Gen., Baghdad, 1968-70; Counsellor, Belgrade, 1970-74; Inspector, FCO, 1975-77; Consul-Gen., Zagreb, 1977-80. *Address:* c/o Foreign and Commonwealth Office, SW1.

McKEE, Air Marshal Sir Andrew, KCB 1957 (CB 1951); CBE 1944; DSO 1942; DFC 1941; AFC 1938; *b* 1901; *s* of Samuel Hugh McKee, Eyredale, Oxford, Canterbury, NZ; *m* 1949, Cecelia Tarcille, *er d* of Michael Keating, NZ; two *d. Educ:* Christchurch Boys' High Sch., NZ. Joined RAF, 1927. AOC No 205 Group Mediterranean Allied Air Force, 1945-46; Senior Air Staff Officer, MEAF, 1946-47; Comdt OATS, 1947-49; First Comdt, RAF Flying Coll., 1949-51; Air Vice-Marshal, 1952; AOC No 21 Group, 1951-53; Senior Air Staff Officer, Bomber Command, 1953-55; Air Marshal, 1957; Air Officer Commanding-in-Chief, Transport Command, 1955-59, retired. *Address:* 27 Frederick Street, Palmerston North, New Zealand. *Club:* Royal Air Force.

McKEE, Major Sir Cecil; *see* McKee, Major Sir William Cecil.

McKEE, John, RD 1973; QC (NI) 1974; **His Honour Judge McKee;** a County Court Judge, Northern Ireland, since 1981; President: Industrial Tribunals (Northern Ireland), since 1981; Industrial Court (Northern Ireland), since 1982; *b* 18 May 1933; *s* of late Frank McKee and of Mollie A. McKee; *m* 1962, Annette S. Wilson; two *s* one *d. Educ:* Strathallan Sch., Scotland; Queen's Univ. of Belfast (BA Hons, LLB Hons). Called to the Bar of NI,

1960; Bar, Middle Temple, 1971; Sen. Bar, NI, 1974; Bar of Republic of Ireland (King's Inns), 1975. Chm., UK Delegn to CCBE, 1979-81. Served RNR; subseq. placed on Retd List with rank of Lt-Comdr RNR, 1952-73; *Publication:* (with Phyllis Bateson) Industrial Tribunals in Northern Ireland, 1981. *Recreation:* golf. *Clubs:* Ulster Reform (Belfast); Royal County Down Golf.

McKEE, Major Sir (William) Cecil, Kt 1959; ERD; JP; Estate Agent; *b* 13 April 1905; *s* of late W. B. McKee and M. G. B. Bulloch; *m* 1932, Florence Ethel Irene Gill; one *d. Educ:* Methodist Coll., Belfast; Queen's Univ., Belfast. Alderman, Belfast Corporation, 1934; High Sheriff, Belfast, 1946; Deputy Lord Mayor, 1947, Lord Mayor of Belfast, 1957-59. JP Belfast, 1957. Pres., NI Br., Inst. of Dirs, 1957-59. Served with Royal Artillery in War of 1939-45. KStJ. Hon. LLD Queen's Univ., Belfast, 1960. *Recreation:* golf. *Address:* 250 Malone Road, Belfast. *T:* Belfast 666979. *Clubs:* Ulster Reform (Belfast); Royal County Down Golf.

McKEE, Dr William James Ernest, MA, MD, FFCM; Regional Medical Officer, Wessex Regional Health Authority, since 1976; *b* 20 Feb. 1929; *s* of John Sloan McKee, MA, and Mrs Annie Emily McKee (*née* McKinley); *m* Josée Tucker; three *d. Educ:* Queen Elizabeth's, Wakefield; Trinity Coll., Cambridge; Queen's Coll., Oxford. MA, MD, BChir (Cantab); LRCP, MRCS, FFCM. Clinical trng and postgrad. clinical posts at Radcliffe Infirmary, Oxford, 1952-57; med. res., financed by Nuffield Provincial Hosps Trust, 1958-61; successive posts in community medicine with Metrop. Regional Hosp. Bds, 1961-69; Sen. Admin. Med. Officer, Liverpool Regional Hosp. Bd, 1970-74; Regional Med. Officer, Mersey RHA, 1974-76. *Publications:* papers on tonsillectomy and adenoidectomy in learned jls. *Address:* 22a Bereweeke Avenue, Winchester SO22 6BH. *T:* Winchester 61369.

MacKEIGAN, Hon. Ian Malcolm; Chief Justice of Nova Scotia and Chief Justice of Appeal Division of Supreme Court of Nova Scotia, since 1973; *b* 11 April 1915; *s* of Rev. Dr J. A. MacKeigan and Mabel (*née* McAvity); *m* 1942, Jean Catherine Geddes; two *s* one *d. Educ:* Univs of Saskatchewan, Dalhousie and Toronto. BA (Great Distinction) 1934, MA 1935, LLB 1938, Dalhousie; MA Toronto 1939. Member of Nova Scotia and Prince Edward Island Bars; QC (Nova Scotia) 1954. Dep. Enforcement Administrator, Wartime Prices and Trade Bd, Ottawa, 1942-46; Dep. Comr, Combines Investigation Commn, Ottawa, 1946-50; Partner, MacKeigan, Cox, Downie & Mitchell and predecessor firms, Halifax, NS, 1950-73; Chm., Atlantic Develt Bd, 1963-69; Dir, Gulf Oil (Canada) Ltd, 1968-73; Dir, John Labatt Ltd, 1971-73 and other companies. Hon. LLD Dalhousie, 1975. Centennial Medal, 1967; Jubilee Medal, 1977. *Publications:* articles in Can. Bar Review and Can. Jl Polit. Sci. and Econs. *Recreations:* fishing, golf. *Address:* 833 Marlborough Avenue, Halifax, NS B3H 3G7, Canada. *T:* 429-2291. *Clubs:* Halifax, Saraguay, Ashburn Golf (Halifax).

McKELL, Rt. Hon. Sir William John, GCMG 1951; PC 1948; *b* Pambula, NSW, 26 Sept. 1891; *m* 1920; one *s* two *d. Educ:* Public Sch., Surry Hills, Sydney. Served apprenticeship as boiler-maker, Morts' Dock and Engineering Co., Sydney; elected Financial Secretary, Boilermakers' Union; elected Member Legislative Assembly, NSW, at 25 years of age; Member, 1917-47; Minister of Justice (1920-22) at age of 28 years; Minister of Justice and Assistant Colonial Treasurer, 1925-27; visited London and New York on financial mission for State of New South Wales, 1927; Minister for Local Government, 1930; Minister of Justice, 1931-32; Leader of the Opposition, 1939-41; Premier and Colonial Treasurer of New South Wales, 1941-47; official visit to United States and Great Britain, 1945; Governor-General of Australia, 1947-53. Member Malayan Constitutional Commission, 1956-57. Barrister of Supreme Court of New South Wales, 1925; QC 1945. Chairman of Sydney Cricket Ground Trust, 1938. Hon. LLD, Sydney. *Recreations:* always active in football and boxing circles; played first-grade football and boxed in amateur championships. *Address:* 42/14 Leura Road, Double Bay, NSW 2028, Australia.

McKELLEN, Ian (Murray), CBE 1979; actor and director since 1961; *b* 25 May 1939; *s* of Denis Murray McKellen and Margery (*née* Sutcliffe). *Educ:* Wigan Grammar Sch.; Bolton Sch.; St Catharine's Coll., Cambridge (BA; Hon. Fellow, 1982). Pres., Marlowe Soc., 1960-61. Elected to Council of Equity, 1971-72. 1st appearance (stage): Belgrade Theatre, Coventry, in A Man for all Seasons, Sept. 1961. Arts Theatre, Ipswich, 1962-63; Nottingham Playhouse, 1963-64. 1st London appearance: A Scent of Flowers, 1964 (Clarence Derwent Award). National Theatre Co., 1965, Old Vic and Chichester Festival; A Lily in Little India; Man of Destiny/O'Flaherty VC, Mermaid Theatre, EC4; Their Very Own and Golden City, Royal Court, 1966; The Promise, Fortune and Broadway, 1967; White Lies/Black Comedy; Richard II, Prospect Theatre Co., 1968; Recruiting Officer, Chips with Everything, Cambridge Theatre Co., 1968; revived Richard II with Edward II, Edinburgh Festival; British and European Tour; Mermaid and Piccadilly Theatres, 1969-70; Hamlet, British and European Tours and Cambridge Theatre, WC2, 1971. Founder Mem., Actors' Company: Ruling the Roost, 'Tis Pity She's a Whore, Edin. Fest., 1972; Knots, Wood-Demon, Edin. Fest., 1973, and with King Lear, Brooklyn Acad. of Music, Wimbledon Theatre season, 1974; Royal Shakespeare Co.: Dr Faustus, Edin. Fest., 1974; Marquis of Keith, Aldwych, 1974-75; King John, Aldwych, 1975; Ashes, Young Vic, 1975; Too True to Be Good, Aldwych and Globe, 1975; Romeo and Juliet, The Winter's Tale, Macbeth (Plays and Players award, 1976), Stratford,

1976-77; Romeo and Juliet, Macbeth, Pillars of the Community (SWET Award, 1977), Days of the Commune, The Alchemist (SWET Award, 1978), Aldwych and RSC Warehouse, 1977-78; RSC touring company (also artistic dir), 1978: Twelfth Night; Three Sisters; Is There Honey Still for Tea?; solo recitals: Words, Words, Words, Edin. Fest. and Belfast Fest., 1976; repeated with Acting Shakespeare, Edin. and Belfast, 1977; Every Good Boy Deserves Favour, RFH, 1977 and Barbican Centre, 1982; Bent, Royal Court, Criterion, 1979 (SWET Award, 1979); Amadeus, Broadhurst, NY (Drama Desk, NY Drama League, Outer Critics' Circle, and Tony Awards), 1980-81; Acting Shakespeare tour, Israel, Norway, Denmark, Sweden, 1980; Tarnished Phoenix recital, Edin. Fest., 1980. Directed: Liverpool Playhouse, 1969; Watford and Leicester, 1972; A Private Matter, Vaudeville, 1973; The Clandestine Marriage, Savoy 1975. Films, 1968-: A Touch of Love, The Promise, Alfred the Great, Priest of Love, Walter, Scarlet Pimpernel. Has appeared on television, 1966-. *Address:* c/o Fraser and Dunlop Ltd, 91 Regent's Street, W1R 8RU. *T:* 01-734 7311.

McKELVEY, Air Cdre John Wesley, CB 1969; MBE 1944; CEng, MRAeS; RAF, retired; *b* 25 June 1914; *s* of late Captain John Wesley McKelvey, Enfield, Mddx; *m* 1938, Eileen Amy Carter, *d* of John Charles Carter, Enfield; two *s. Educ:* George Spicer Sch., Enfield. RAF Aircraft Apprentice, 1929; commnd 1941 (Eng Branch); served 1939-45, Egypt, Syria, Iraq and Bomber Comd (despatches, 1943); Group Captain 1960; Dep. Dir Intelligence (Tech.), 1962-64; Dir of Aircraft and Asst Attaché, Defence Research and Development, British Embassy, Washington, 1964-66; Air Officer Wales and CO, RAF St Athan, 1966-69; retd Aug. 1969. RAF Benevolent Fund: Sec. (Appeals), 1971-77; Legacies and Trusts Officer, 1977-79. *Recreations:* bowls, gardening, photography. *Address:* Inchmerle, 29 Manorway, Bush Hill Park, Enfield, Mddx EN1 2JD. *T:* 01-360 4054. *Club:* Royal Air Force.

McKELVEY, William; MP (Lab) Kilmarnock, since 1979; *b* Dundee, July 1934; *m* ; two *s. Educ:* Morgan Acad.; Dundee Coll. of Technology. Joined Labour Party, 1961; formerly Sec. Organiser, Lab. Party, and full-time union official. Mem., Dundee City Council. *Address:* House of Commons, SW1; 1 Rankin Court, Kilmarnock, Ayrshire.

MACKEN, Frederic Raymond, CMG 1964; *b* 23 Sept. 1903; *s* of Charles Alfred Macken and Ella (*née* Steadman); *m* 1929, Alma Doris (*née* Keesing); one *d. Educ:* Whangarei High Sch.; Auckland Univ., New Zealand. LLM (with Hons), 1927. Retired as Commissioner of Inland Revenue for New Zealand, 1964. *Recreations:* bowls, golf. *Address:* 9 Harley Grove, Lower Hutt, Wellington, New Zealand. *T:* 695205. *Club:* Civil Service (Wellington, NZ).

MacKENNA, Sir Bernard Joseph Maxwell, (Sir Brian MacKenna), Kt 1961; Judge of the High Court of Justice (Queen's Bench Division), 1961-77; *b* 12 Sept. 1905; unmarried. Called to the Bar, Inner Temple, Jan. 1932; Western Circuit; QC 1950; Master of the Bench of the Inner Temple, 1958. *Address:* 2 Paper Buildings, Temple, EC4. *T:* 01-353 2123. *Clubs:* Athenæum, Beefsteak.

MacKENNA, Sir Brian; see MacKenna, Sir Bernard Joseph Maxwell.

McKENNA, David, CBE 1967 (OBE 1946; MBE 1943); FCIT; Member, British Railways Board, 1968-76 (part-time Member, 1976-78); *b* 16 Feb. 1911; *s* of late Rt Hon. Reginald McKenna and Pamela Margaret McKenna (*née* Jekyll); *m* 1934, Lady Cecilia Elizabeth Keppel, *d* of 9th Earl of Albemarle, MC; three *d. Educ:* Eton; Trinity Coll., Cambridge. London Passenger Transport Board, 1934-39, and 1946-55; Asst General Manager, Southern Region of BR, 1955-61; Chief Commercial Officer, HQ, BR, 1962; General Manager, Southern Region of BR, and Chairman Southern Railway Board, 1963-68; Chairman, British Transport Advertising, 1968-81. Mem., Dover Harbour Bd, 1969-80. Dir, Isles of Scilly Steamship Co. War Service with Transportation Service of Royal Engineers, 1939-45; Iraq, Turkey, India and Burma; Lieut-Colonel. Pres., Chartered Inst. of Transport, 1972. Chairman of Governors, Sadler's Wells, 1962-76. Vice-Pres. and Hon. Secretary, Royal College of Music; Chairman of Bach Choir, 1964-76. FRCM. Commandeur de l'Ordre National du Mérite, 1974. *Publications:* various papers on transport subjects. *Recreations:* music, sailing. *Address:* Rosteague, Portscatho, Truro, Cornwall. *Clubs:* Brooks's; Royal Cornwall Yacht (Falmouth).

MacKENNA, Robert Merttins Bird, MA, MD, FRCP; Hon. Colonel RAMC, 1954; Dermatologist, King Edward VII's Hospital for Officers, 1946-72, now Consulting Dermatologist; Hon. Consultant in Dermatology to the British Army, 1946-64; Councillor Royal College of Physicians, 1956-59; President: Dermatological Section, Royal Society of Medicine, 1966-67; British Association of Dermatology, 1966-67; Physician in charge of the Department for Diseases of the Skin, St Bartholomew's Hospital, 1946-68, now Hon. Consultant in Dermatology; Hon. Member, British Association of Dermatologists, 1976; *b* 16 Nov. 1903; *s* of late R. W. MacKenna and Harriet A. S. Bird; *m* 1st, 1927, Helen, *e d* of Thomas Todrick; two *d* ; 2nd, 1943, Margaret, *d* of Rev. Christmas Hopkins and Eleanor Hopkins; two *s. Educ:* RN Colleges, Osborne and Dartmouth; Clare Coll., Cambridge Univ.; St Thomas' Hospital. Resigned from the Navy, 1919; studied at Liverpool Univ., 1920-21; Cambridge, 1921-24; BA (Nat. Sci. Tripos), 1924; MRCS, LRCP, 1926; MA, MB, BCh Cambridge, 1928; MRCP, 1928; MD Cambridge 1931; FRCP, 1941. Junior Asst MO Venereal Diseases Dept, and Clinical Asst,

Dermatological Dept, St Thomas' Hosp., 1927-28; Clinical Asst, St John's Hosp., for Diseases of the Skin, 1928; Hon. Asst Dermatologist Liverpool Radium Inst., 1929; Hon. Dermatologist, Liverpool Stanley Hosp., 1929-34; Hon. Dermatologist, Royal Liverpool United Hosp., (Royal Southern Hosp.), 1934-46; Dermatologist, Catterick Military Hosp., Oct. 1939; Comd Specialist in Dermatology, Northern Comd, 1940-41; Adviser in Dermatology and Asst Dir, Hygiene (c), War Office, 1941-43; Cons. Dermatologist to British Army, 1943-45. Malcolm Morris Meml Lectr, 1955; Watson Smith Lectr, 1957; Prosser White Orator, 1968. Hon. Fellow, Amer. Med. Assoc. Hon. Member: Dermatological Section, RSM; Dermatological Assoc. of Australia; Soc. for Investigative Dermatology; Canadian Dermatological Assoc.; NY Dermatolog. Soc.; Deutsche Dermatologische Gesellschaft; Sociedad Venezolana de Dermatologia; Alpha Omega Alpha Honor Med. Soc.; Corresp. Member: Amer. Dermatological Assoc.; Nederlandse Vereniging van Dermatologen; Societas Dermatologica Danica; Societas Dermatologica Austriaca; Societas Dermatologica Svecica; La Société Française de Dermatologie et de Syphiligraphie; Israeli Dermatological Soc. OStJ 1954. *Publications:* Aids to Dermatology, 1929, 1939, 1946, 1954, 1956; Diseases of the Skin, 1932, 1937, 1949 and 1952; Dermatology (jointly with E. L. Cohen), 1964. Joint Editor of The Medical History of Liverpool, 1936; Sections on Dermatology in Medical Annual, 1944-63; editor, Modern Trends in Dermatology, Series I, 1948, Series II, 1953, Series III, 1966; Associate Editor for Dermatological subjects British Encyclopædia of Medical Practice, 2nd Edition, 1950; short autobiog. in Jl of Amer. Acad. of Dermatology, vol. 6, 1982; various papers on dermatological subjects in medical journals. *Address:* 22 Hillbrow, Richmond Hill, Richmond, Surrey TW10 6BH. *T:* 01-940 3675.

MacKENNA, Robert Ogilvie, MA, ALA; University Librarian and Keeper of the Hunterian Books and MSS, Glasgow, 1951-78; *b* 21 March 1913; *s* of late Dr John G. MacKenna and Katherine Ogilvie; *m* 1942, Ray, *o d* of late Samuel Mullin, Glasgow. *Educ:* Paisley Grammar Sch.; Glasgow Univ. Assistant Librarian, Glasgow Univ., 1936; Sub-Librarian, Leeds Univ., 1946; Librarian, King's Coll., Newcastle upon Tyne (University of Durham), 1947. Served War as officer, RNVR, 1939-45. Trustee, National Library of Scotland, 1953-79. President, Scottish Library Association, 1966; Chairman, Standing Conference of National and University Libraries, 1967-69. President Scottish Cricket Union, 1968. Editor, The Philosophical Journal, 1976-77. *Publication:* Glasgow University Athletic Club: the story of the first hundred years, 1981. *Recreations:* cricket (played for Scotland, 1935-39 and 1946); hill-walking. *Address:* 2 Turnberry Avenue, Glasgow, G11 5AQ. *Club:* College (Glasgow).

McKENNA, Siobhán; actress; *b* Belfast, 24 May 1923; *d* of Prof. Owen McKenna and Margaret O'Reilly; *m* 1946, Denis O'Dea (*d* 1978); one *s. Educ:* St Louis Convent, Monaghan; Galway Univ. BA (1st cl. Hons, French, English and Irish Lit.). Holds 5 hon. doctorates in Literature and the Humanities, Apptd to Council of State, Republic of Ireland, by President Cearbhall O Dálaigh, 1975. First stage appearances with Irish trans of plays by Molière, O'Neill, O'Casey, Shaw, for Irish speaking theatre An Taibhdhearc, Galway, 1940-43; Abbey Theatre, Dublin, 1944-47 (first appearance in Le Bourgeois Gentilhomme). *Plays include:* The White Steed (first London appearance), Embassy and Whitehall, 1947; Fading Mansions, Duchess, 1949; Ghosts, Embassy; Berkeley Square, Queen's; Héloise and Abelard, Duke of York's; Shakespeare season, Stratford-upon-Avon, 1952; Saint Joan, Arts, 1954, St Martin's, 1955 (first Evening Standard Best Actress Award, 1955), European tour, NY, 1956; The Chalk Garden (first NY appearance), NY, 1955; The Rope-Dancers, NY, 1957; Hamlet (title role), NY, 1957; Shakespeare season, NY, Stratford, Canada, Cambridge Drama Fest.; Playboy of the Western World, Dublin, Edinburgh and Paris Festivals, then Piccadilly, 1960, European tour (Best Actress, Florence Festival); Captain Brassbound's Conversion, Dublin and Philadelphia, 1961; Saint Joan of the Stockyards, Dublin Festival, 1961, Queen's, 1964; Play with a Tiger, Comedy, 1962; The Cavern, Strand; Laurette, Dublin, 1964; Juno and the Paycock, Gaiety, Dublin, 1966, Toronto, 1973, Abbey, Dublin, 1979; The Loves of Cass Maguire, Abbey, 1967; The Cherry Orchard, Abbey, 1968; On a Foggy Day, St Martin's, 1969; Best of Friends, Strand, 1970; Here are Ladies (one woman show), Criterion, 1970, USA, Canada, Australia, Dublin, 1975; Fallen Angels, Gate, 1975; A Moon for the Misbegotten, Gate, 1976; Plough and the Stars, Abbey, 1977, US tour; Sons of Oedipus, Greenwich, 1977; Sarah Bernhardt in Memoir, Canada and Dublin, 1977, Ambassadors, 1978; Riders to the Sea, Greenwich Fest., 1978; Here are Ladies, Vienna, 1979; The Shadow of a Gunman, Vienna, 1980; Agrippina in Britannicus, Lyric, Hammersmith, 1981. *Plays directed:* St Joan (in Gaelic), Galway, 1943; Daughter from over the Water, Dublin; I must be getting out of this Kip, Dublin, 1968; Tinkers Wedding, Shadow of the Glen, Riders to the Sea, Dublin, 1973; Juno and the Paycock, Mermaid, 1973; Playboy of the Western World, USA, 1967, English tour and Hong Kong, 1977; Rising of the Moon; The Cat and the Moon, Purgatory and A Pot of Broth, Riders to the Sea, Greenwich, 1978; The Shadow of a Gunman, Vienna, 1980. *Films include:* Hungry Hill, Daughter of Darkness, The Lost People (Lejeune Gold Medal), The Adventurers, King of Kings, Doctor Zhivago, Playboy of the Western World, Philadelphia Here I Come, Of Human Bondage, Here are Ladies. Numerous television roles in UK, Europe, Canada and USA (UK work includes The Landlady by Roald Dahl, Juno and the Paycock, The Vicious Circle, The Diary of Brigid Hitler). *Publications:* trans. into Gaelic: Mary Rose; Saint Joan. *Recreations:* reading, swimming, theatre-going. *Address:* c/o Nick Legh-Heppel, Transcreative, 7A Sydney Place, SW7 3NL. *T:* 01-589 9984; c/o

Milton Goldman, ICM, 40 W 57th Street, New York, NY 10019, USA. *T:* (212) 556 5600.

MACKENZIE, family name of **Baron Amulree** and **Earl of Cromartie.**

MACKENZIE; *see* Montagu-Stuart-Wortley-Mackenzie, family name of Earl of Wharncliffe.

MACKENZIE of Gairloch; *see under* Inglis of Glencorse.

MACKENZIE, Dr Alastair Stewart, (Sandy); Regional Medical Officer, North West Thames Regional Health Authority, 1977-82; *b* 28 April 1930; *s* of late James S. Mackenzie, JP and Anne (*née* Evans). *Educ:* Gyfarthfa Castle Sch., Merthyr Tydfil; Bromsgrove Sch., Worcs; Jesus Coll., Cambridge (MA); University Coll. Hospital. MB, BChir; DMRT, FFCM. Captain and Specialist, RAMC, 1959. Sen. Admin. MO, NE Metrop. Regional Hosp. Bd, 1972; Regional MO, NE Thames RHA, 1974-77. Mem. Council (Section of Epidemiology), RSocMed, 1972; Mem. Council, British Cancer Council, 1972; a British Rep., Hosp. Cttee of EEC, 1974; Mem. Council, Queen's Nursing Inst., 1974; Mem. Bd of Governors, St John's Hosp. for Diseases of Skin, 1974; Mem. Ct of Governors, and Mem. Bd of Management, London Sch. of Hygiene and Trop. Medicine, 1975; Mem. Laboratory Develt Adv. Gp, 1975; Mem. Cttee of Management, Inst. of Child Health, 1976. Mem., London Health Planning Consortium, 1978; Health Dir designate, Emergency War Planning Region 5 (Gtr London), 1980. FRSocMed. *Publications:* various articles on epidemiology and med. care in med. jls. *Recreations:* music, gardening, Egyptology. *Address:* 22A Bolton Gardens, SW5 0AQ. *T:* 01-370 2480; Flat 11c, Sussex Square, Brighton, East Sussex. *T:* Brighton 600308.

McKENZIE, Sir Alexander, KBE 1962; Past Dominion President, New Zealand National Party (1951-62); *b* Invercargill, New Zealand, 1896; *m* 1935, Constance Mary Howard; two *s* two *d. Educ:* Isla Bank Primary Sch.; Southland Technical Coll.; Southland Boys' High Sch. Chm., Ponsonby Electorate, NZ Nat. Party, 1938-41; Chm., Auckland Div., NZ Nat. Party, 1941-51. Overseas Rep. for NZ Forest Products Ltd, 1925-29; engaged in Stock and Share Broking, 1929-; Mem. Auckland Stock Exchange; Dir, of companies covering finance, merchandising, manufacturing, etc. Mem. Anglican Church. *Recreations:* trout fishing, surfing, bowling, gardening. *Address:* 54 Wallace Street, Herne Bay, New Zealand. *Club:* Auckland (Auckland, NZ).

MACKENZIE, Sir Alexander Alwyne H. C. B. M.; *see* Muir Mackenzie.

MACKENZIE, Sir (Alexander George Anthony) Allan, 4th Bt, of Glen-Muick, *cr* 1890; CD 1957; retired; *b* 4 Jan. 1913; *s* of late Capt. Allan Keith Mackenzie (3rd *s* of 2nd Bt) and Hon. Louvima, *o d* of 1st Viscount Knollys (she *m* 2nd, 1922, Richard Henry Spencer Checkley); *S* uncle, 1944; *m* 1937, Marjorie McGuire, Vancouver, BC; four *d. Educ:* Stowe School. Page of Honour to King George V; Member Royal Canadian Mounted Police, 1932-37; served War of 1939-45, with Seaforth Highlanders of Canada (Captain), in Italy and in NW Europe. Subsequently Black Watch (RHR) of Canada (Regular Army). Canada Centennial Medal, 1967. *Heir:* cousin (James William) Guy Mackenzie [*b* 6 Oct. 1946; *m* 1972, Paulene Patricia Simpson; one *d*].

MACKENZIE, Sir Allan; *see* Mackenzie, Sir (Alexander George Anthony) Allan.

MACKENZIE, Archibald Robert Kerr, CBE 1967; HM Diplomatic Service, retired; *b* 22 Oct. 1915; *s* of James and Alexandrina Mackenzie; *m* 1963, Virginia Ruth Hutchison. *Educ:* Glasgow, Oxford, Chicago and Harvard Universities. Diplomatic Service, with duty at Washington, 1943-45; United Nations, 1946-49; Foreign Office, 1949-51; Bangkok, 1951-54; Cyprus, 1954; Foreign Office, 1955-57; OEEC, Paris, 1957-61; Commercial Counsellor, HM Embassy, Rangoon, 1961-65; Consul-General, Zagreb 1965-69; Ambassador, Tunisia, 1970-73; Minister (Econ. and Social Affairs), UK Mission to UN, 1973-75. Brandt Commission, 1978-80. *Recreation:* golf. *Address:* Strathcashel Cottage, Rowardennan, near Glasgow G63 0AW. *T:* Balmaha 262. *Clubs:* Royal Commonwealth Society; Royal Scottish Automobile (Glasgow).

MACKENZIE, Chalmers Jack, CC (Canada) 1967; CMG 1943; MC 1918; FRS 1946; FRSC; MEIC; Chancellor, Carleton University, 1954-68; Member Atomic Energy Control Board, 1946-61, and President, 1948-61; President, National Research Council of Canada, 1939-52; Member Defence Research Board, 1946-52; President Atomic Energy of Canada, Limited, 1952-53; Director: Canadian Patents and Development Ltd, 1947-61; Chemcell Ltd and Columbia Cellulose Co., 1954-68; Member, Army Technical Development Board, 1942; Chairman War Technical and Scientific Development Cttee, 1940; Inventions Board, 1940-46; *b* 10 July 1888; *s* of late James Mackenzie, St Stephen, NB; *m* 1st, 1916, Claire Rees (*d* 1922); one *s* ; 2nd, 1924, Geraldine Gallon (*d* 1976); two *d. Educ:* St Stephen, NB; Dalhousie Univ. (BE 1909); Harvard Univ. (MCE 1915). Engineering Firm, Maxwell & Mackenzie, 1912-16; Overseas 54th Canadian Infantry Bn, 1916-18 (MC); Prof. Civil Engineering, 1918-39, Dean of College of Engineering, 1921-39, University of Sask., President, Engineering Institute of Canada, 1941; Chairman Saskatoon City Planning Commission, 1928-39; Chairman Saskatoon City

Hospital Board, 1937-39. Dir Canadian Geographical Soc., 1937-60. Mem., Canada Council, 1963-69. Hon. LLD: Dalhousie, 1941, Western Ontario, 1943, Queen's, 1944, Saskatchewan, 1945; Carleton, 1969; DEng: Toronto, 1944; Nova Scotia Tech. Coll., 1950; Hon. DSc: McGill, 1941; Laval and Cambridge, 1946; UBC, 1947; Princeton, 1949; McMaster Univ., 1951; Univs of New Brunswick, Montreal, Manitoba, 1953; Ottawa, 1958; RMC, 1964; Hon. DCL Bishop's Univ., 1952. Hon. FRCP(C), 1947; Hon. Mem., Amer. Soc. Civil Engrs, 1952; Hon. FICE, 1968. US Medal for Merit, 1947; Chevalier de la Légion d'Honneur, 1947; Kelvin Medal, InstMechE, 1954; R. B. Bennett Empire Prize, RSA, 1954; Royal Bank Award, 1968. *Publications:* in scientific and technical press. *Recreations:* golf, curling. *Address:* 210 Buena Vista Road, Rockcliffe Park, Ottawa, Ontario K1M 0V7, Canada. *Club:* Rideau (Ottawa).

MACKENZIE, Colin Hercules, CMG 1946; *b* 5 Oct. 1898; *o s* of late Maj.-Gen. Sir Colin Mackenzie, KCB, and Ethel, *er d* of Hercules Ross, ICS; *m* 1940, Evelyn Clodagh, 2nd *d* of Charles and Lady Aileen Meade; one *d. Educ:* Summerfields; Eton (Schol.); King's Coll., Cambridge (1st Class Hons in Economics. Exhibitioner and Senior Scholar, also Chancellor's Medal for English Verse). Served France with 1st Bn Scots Guards in 1918 (wounded). Served in India and with South-East Asia Command, 1941-45, comd Force 136 (CMG, Officier de la Légion d'Honneur). British Economic Mission to Greece, 1946. Dir, J. and P. Coats Ltd, 1928-65. Chairman: Scottish Council, FBI, 1957-59; Scottish Cttee on Electricity, 1961-62; Scottish Arts Council, 1962-70; Inverness Conservative and Unionist Assoc., 1967-70. Hon. Sheriff Inverness-shire. Hon. LLD St Andrews, 1970. *Address:* Kyle House, Kyleakin, Isle of Skye. *T:* Kyle 4517. *Club:* Special Forces.

McKENZIE, Dan Peter, PhD; FRS 1976; Reader in Tectonics, Department of Earth Sciences, Cambridge University, since 1979; Fellow of King's College, Cambridge, 1965-73 and since 1977; *b* 21 Feb. 1942; *s* of William Stewart McKenzie and Nancy Mary McKenzie; *m* 1971, Indira Margaret (Misra); one *s. Educ:* Westminster Sch.; King's Coll., Cambridge (BA 1963, PhD 1966). Cambridge University: Sen. Asst in Res., 1969-75; Asst Dir of Res., 1975-79. Hon. MA Cambridge, 1966. *Publications:* papers in learned jls. *Recreation:* gardening. *Address:* 14 Humberstone Road, Cambridge CB4 1JE. *T:* Cambridge 59790.

MacKENZIE, David Alexander; General Secretary, Transport Salaried Staffs' Association, 1973-76; *b* 22 March 1922; *s* of David MacKenzie and Jeannie Ross; *m* 1945, Doreen Joyce Lucas; two *s* one *d. Educ:* Merkinch Public Sch.; Inverness High Sch. Entered London Midland Railway Service, 1936. Served in Royal Navy, 1941-45. Transport Salaried Staffs Assoc.: Divisional Sec., 1952-66; Sen. Asst Sec., 1966-68; Asst Gen. Sec., 1968. Mem., TUC Non-Manual Workers' Cttee; Mem., Air Transport and Travel Industry Trng Bd; former Mem., Hotel and Catering Industry Trng Bd. *Recreations:* golf, reading. *Address:* 10 Culverhouse Gardens, Streatham, SW16 2TX. *T:* 01-769 0711.

MACKENZIE, David James Masterton, CMG 1957; OBE 1947 (MBE 1944); FRCP; Hon. Research Associate, Department of Bacteriology, Medical School, University of Cape Town; Visiting Scientist, Malaria Eradication Program, Communicable Disease Center, Atlanta, Georgia, 1965-69; Director of Medical and Health Services in Hong Kong, 1958-64; Colonial Medical Service, retired; *b* 23 July 1905; *s* of John Henderson Mackenzie and Agnes Masterton; *m* 1934, Patricia Eleanor Margaret Bailey; two *d. Educ:* Rutherford College School; Edinburgh Univ. MB, ChB, Edinburgh, 1929; DPH (Edinburgh), 1948; MRCPE 1956, FRCPE 1959. Edinburgh Royal Infirmary, 1930-31. Joined Colonial Medical Service, 1934; DDMS Bechuanaland Protectorate, 1944, DMS 1946; DMS Nyasaland, 1949-55; DMS Northern Nigeria, 1955-57. *Recreations:* golf, fishing. *Address:* 8 Avondrust Avenue, Bergvliet, 7800, S Africa. *T:* 72-4541. *Clubs:* Royal Cape Golf; Royal Hong Kong Golf; Zomba Gymkhana (Malawi).

MACKENZIE, Rear-Adm. David John; Flag Officer and Port Admiral Gibraltar, Commander Gibraltar Mediterranean, 1981-83; *b* 3 Oct. 1929; *s* of late David Mackenzie and of Alison Walker Lawrie; *m* 1965, Ursula Sybil Balfour; two *s* one *d. Educ:* Cargilfield Sch., Barnton, Edinburgh; Royal Naval Coll., Eaton Hall, Cheshire. FNI. Cadet to Comdr, 1943-72: served in East Indies, Germany, Far East, Home and Mediterranean Fleets, and commanded: HMML 6011, HM Ships: Brinkley, Barrington, Hardy, Lincoln, Hermione; Captain 1972; Senior Officers War Course, 1972; commanded HMS Phoenix (NBCD School), 1972-74; Captain F8 in HMS Ajax, 1974-76; Director of Naval Equipment, 1976-78; Captain: HMS Blake, 1979; HMS Hermes, 1980; Rear Admiral 1981. Younger Brother of Trinity House, 1971-. Member, Queen's Body Guard for Scotland (Royal Company of Archers), 1976-. *Recreations:* shooting and fishing. *Address:* c/o Bank of Scotland, Haymarket Branch, SW1. *Clubs:* Naval and Military; Royal Naval Target Rifle (Bisley).

MacKENZIE, Rt. Hon. Gregor; *see* MacKenzie, Rt Hon. J. G.

MACKENZIE, Vice-Adm. Sir Hugh (Stirling), KCB 1966 (CB 1963); DSO 1942 and Bar 1943; DSC 1945; *b* 3 July 1913; *3rd s* of Dr and Mrs T. C. Mackenzie, Inverness; *m* 1946, Helen Maureen, *er d* of Major J. E. M. Bradish-Ellames; one *s* two *d. Educ:* Cargilfield Sch.; Royal Naval Coll., Dartmouth. Joined Royal Naval Coll., 1927; qualified in Submarines, 1935. Served throughout War of 1939-45 in Submarines, comdg HMS Thrasher,

1941–43; HMS Tantalus, 1943–45; Comdr 1946; Capt. 1951; Rear-Adm. 1961; Flag Officer, Submarines, 1961–63; Chief Polaris Executive, 1963–68; Vice-Adm. 1964; retired 1968. Chm., Navy League, 1969–74; Dir, Atlantic Salmon Research Trust Ltd, 1969–79 renamed Atlantic Salmon Trust, 1979, Chm., 1979–. Hon. Freeman, Borough of Shoreditch, 1942. FBIM. *Recreation:* the country. *Address:* Sylvan Lodge, Puttenham, near Guildford, Surrey. *Club:* Naval and Military.

MACKENZIE, Ian Clayton, CBE 1962; HM Diplomatic Service, retired; Ambassador to Korea, 1967–69; *b* 13 Jan. 1909; *m* 1948, Anne Helena Tylor; one *s* one *d. Educ:* Bedford Sch.; King's Coll., Cambridge. China Consular Service, 1932–41; Consul, Brazzaville, 1942–45, Foreign Office, 1945; 1st Sec., Commercial, Shanghai, 1946–49; Santiago, 1949–53; Commercial Counsellor: Oslo, 1953–58; Caracas, 1958–63; Stockholm, 1963–66. *Address:* Koryo, Armstrong Road, Brockenhurst, Hants SO4 7TA. *T:* Lymington 23453.

MACKENZIE, James, BSc; FIM, FICeram; Managing Director, BSC Plates, British Steel Corporation, since 1980; *b* 2 Nov. 1924; *s* of James Mackenzie and Isobel Mary Chalmers; *m* 1950, Elizabeth Mary Ruttle; one *s* one *d. Educ:* Queen's Park Sch., Glasgow; Royal Technical Coll., Glasgow (BSc). The United Steel Companies Ltd, Research and Develt Dept, 1944–67; British Steel Corporation, 1967–; Man. Dir (Technical), BSC, 1976–80. Pres., Inst. of Ceramics, 1965–67. *Address:* Westhaven, Beech Waye, Gerrards Cross, Bucks SL9 8BL. *T:* Gerrards Cross 86461. *Club:* Western (Glasgow).

MacKENZIE, James Alexander Mackintosh; Chief Road Engineer, Scottish Development Department, since 1976; *b* Inverness, 6 May 1928; *m* 1970, Pamela Dorothy Nixon; one *s* one *d. Educ:* Inverness Royal Acad. FEng, FICE, FIMunE, FIHE. Miscellaneous local govt appts, 1950–63; Chief Resident Engr, Durham County Council, 1963–67; Dep. Dir, 1967–71, Dir, 1971–76, North Eastern Road Construction Unit, MoT, later DoE. *Recreations:* golf, fishing. *Address:* Pendor, 2 Dean Park, Longniddry, East Lothian EH32 0QR. *T:* Longniddry 52643. *Club:* Royal Scottish Automobile (Glasgow).

MacKENZIE, Rt. Hon. (James) Gregor, PC 1977; MP (Lab) Rutherglen since May 1964; *b* 15 Nov. 1927; *o s* of James and Mary MacKenzie; *m* 1958, Joan Swan Provan; one *s* one *d. Educ:* Queen's Park Sch.; Royal Technical College; Glasgow Univ. (School of Social Studies). Joined Labour Party, 1944. Contested (Lab): East Aberdeenshire, 1950; Kinross and West Perthshire, 1959. Chm., Scottish Labour League, 1948; Mem. and Magistrate, Glasgow Corporation, 1952–55, 1956–64; PPS to Rt Hon. James Callaghan, MP, 1965–70; Opposition spokesman on Posts and Telecommunications, 1970–74; Parly Under-Sec. of State for Industry, 1974–75, Minister of State for Industry, 1975–76; Minister of State, Scottish Office, 1976–79. JP Glasgow, 1962. *Address:* 19 Stewarton Drive, Cambuslang, Glasgow G72 8DE. *T:* 041-641 3646; 7 Carrick Court, Kennington Park Road, SE11 4EE. *T:* 01-735 2957. *Club:* Reform.

MacKENZIE, James Sargent Porteous, OBE 1963; *b* 18 June 1916; *s* of late Roderick and Daisy W. MacKenzie; *m* 1944, Flora Paterson; three *s. Educ:* Portree High Sch.; Edinburgh Univ. (MA Hons 1939); Glasgow Univ. (Dip. Social Studies 1947). War Service, 1939–45: Captain RA (Combined Ops, Burma and Normandy). Scottish HQ, Min. of Labour, 1947–56; Labour Advr, UK High Commn, New Delhi, 1956–62 (First Sec., 1956, Counsellor, 1959); Ministry of Labour: Asst Controller, Scottish HQ, 1962–65; Dep. Controller, Yorks and Humberside Regional Office, 1965–67; Principal Dep. Controller, Scottish HQ, Dept of Employment, 1967–72; Asst Sec., 1970; Counsellor (Labour) British Embassy, Bonn, 1972–77, retired 1977. *Address:* 11 Baberton Park, Juniper Green, Edinburgh. *Club:* Royal Commonwealth Society.

McKENZIE, John, CMG 1970; MBE 1947; PhD; HM Diplomatic Service, retired; *b* 30 April 1915; *m* 1943, Sigridur Olafsdóttir; two *s* one *d. Educ:* Archbishop Holgate's Grammar Sch., York; Leeds Univ. Lectr, Univ. of Iceland, 1938–40; Second Sec. and Vice-Consul, Reykjavik, 1945; Consul, Helsinki, 1948; First Sec., 1949; Foreign Office, 1950; Sofia, 1953 (Chargé d'Affaires, 1954, 1955, 1956); Baghdad, 1956; Foreign Office, 1958; Counsellor, seconded to Cabinet Office, 1962; Helsinki, 1964 (Chargé d'Affaires, 1965, 1966); Dep. High Comr Calcutta, 1967–70; Ambassador to Iceland, 1970–75. *Address:* 60 Dome Hill, Caterham, Surrey CR3 6EB. *T:* Caterham 42546.

MACKENZIE, Brig. John Alexander, CBE 1955; DSO 1944 and Bar, 1944; MC 1940 and Bar, 1940; retired; *b* 9 March 1915; *s* of late Louis Robert Wilson Mackenzie; *m* 1952, Beryl Cathreen Culver; one *s. Educ:* Nautical Coll., Pangbourne; RMC, Sandhurst. 2nd Bn Gloucestershire Regt, 1935–43; Bn Comd, 2nd Bn Lancs Fusiliers, Tunisia, Sicily and Italy Campaigns, 1943–44 (despatches, 1944); Bde Comd: 11 Inf. Bde, Italy, 1944; 10 Inf. Bde, Greece, 1945–46; psc 1947; GSO1 HQ British Troops, Berlin, 1948–49; AAG (Organisation), HQ, BAOR, 1950; jssc 1951; GSO1 HQ Western Comd, 1951–54; Comd: Britcom Sub-area, N Korea, 1955; Inf. Trng Team, HQ Jordan Arab Army, 1956; Jt Concealment Centre, 1957–58; Small Arms Sch., Hythe, 1958–59; idc 1960; Comd: 1 Bde, Nigeria, 1961–63; 3 Bde, Congo, 1962; Actg GOC, Royal Nigerian Army, 1963; BGS Army Trng, MoD, 1964–67; ADC to the Queen, 1967–70; Comdt and Inspector of Intelligence, 1967–70; retired 1970. *Recreation:* gardening. *Address:* Slaybrook Hall, Sandling Road, Saltwood, Hythe, Kent.

McKENZIE, Rear-Adm. John Foster, CB 1977; CBE 1974 (OBE 1962); Member, Planning Tribunal, since 1979; *b* Waiuku, 28 June 1923; *s* of Dr J. C. McKenzie; *m* 1945, Doreen Elizabeth, *d* of Dr E. T. McElligott; one *s* one *d. Educ:* Timaru Boys' High Sch.; St Andrews Coll., Christchurch, NZ. Served War of 1939–45: Royal Navy; transferred to Royal New Zealand Navy, 1947; Head, Defence Liaison Staff, London, 1966–68; Imperial Defence Coll., 1969; Asst Chief of Defence Staff (Policy), Defence HQ, NZ, 1970–71; Deputy Chief of Naval Staff, 1972; Commodore, Auckland, 1973–75; Chief of Naval Staff, and Mem. Defence Council, 1975–77, retired 1977. ADC 1972–75. *Recreations:* gardening, fishing. *Address:* 64 Lohia Street, Khandallah, Wellington 4, New Zealand.

MACKENZIE of Mornish, John Hugh Munro; Chairman: London and Northern Group plc, since 1967; Pauling plc, since 1976; Scottish, English and European Textiles plc, since 1969; Tace plc, since 1967; *b* 29 Aug. 1925; *s* of Lt-Col John Munro Mackenzie of Mornish, DSO, JP, Mil. Kt of Windsor, Henry VIII Gateway, Windsor Castle, and Mrs E. H. M. Mackenzie (*née* Taaffe); *m* 1951, Eileen Louise Agate, *d* of Alexander Shanks, OBE, MC, and Mrs Shanks; five *s* one *d. Educ:* Edinburgh Acad.; Loretto Sch.; Trinity Coll., Oxford (MA (Hons)); Hague Acad. of Internat. Law; Inns of Court Law Schs; McGill Univ., Montreal. Served Army, 1945–49: Captain, The Royal Scots (Royal Regt); war service, Europe; 1st KOSB, A Company, 9th Brigade, 3rd Inf. Div. (despatches, certs of gallantry) and Far East HQ Allied Land Forces SE Asia and HQ Ceylon Army Comd, Staff Captain, A&MS; HM Guard of Honour, Balmoral, 1946; HQ 3rd Auto Aircraft Div., 1946–47, GSO III. Harmsworth Law Scholar, Middle Temple, 1950; called to the Bar, Middle Temple, 1950. United Dominions Trust Ltd, trainee, ICI Ltd, Legal Asst, Estates Dept, 1951; Hudson's Bay Scholar, 1952–53; ICI Ltd, Buyer Crop and misc. products, 1953–54; Trubenised (GB) Ltd and Associated Cos, Co. Sec. and Legal Advisor, 1955–56; Aspro-Nicholas Ltd, Gp Develt Officer, 1956–57; Knitmaster Holdings, 1957; formed: Grampian Holdings Ltd (Manager and Sec.), 1958, Man. Dir, 1960; London and Northern Gp Ltd (Dep. Chm. and Man. Dir), 1962; Tace plc, 1967 (Chm.); Scottish, English and European Textiles plc, 1969 (Chm.). Four Queen's Awards for Export won by Group Cos. FRSA, FBIM. *Recreations:* opera, bridge, shooting, fishing, all field sports. *Address:* Mortlake House, Vicarage Road, SW14 8RU; Scaliscro Lodge, Isle of Lewis, Outer Hebrides; Shellwood Manor, Leigh, Surrey RH2 8NX. *Clubs:* Royal Automobile; Royal Scots.

MACKENZIE, John Moncrieff Ord; *b* 1911; *s* of Kenneth Mackenzie, Dolphinton; *m* 1936, Delia Alice, *d* of late Wyndham Damer Clark, DL, JP, London, SW3; one *s* four *d. Educ:* Rugby; Corpus Christi Coll., Cambridge. WS, 1936. Captain, Lanarkshire Yeomanry (TA); served War of 1939–45 (despatches, Bronze Star Medal, US): GHQ, Liaison Regt. JP 1947, DL 1953, Peeblesshire. *Address:* Dolphinton House, Dolphinton, Peeblesshire. *T:* Dolphinton 286. *Club:* New (Edinburgh).

MacKENZIE, Keith Roderick Turing, MC; Secretary, Royal and Ancient Golf Club of St Andrews, Fife, Scotland, since 1967; *b* 19 Jan. 1921; *s* of Henry Roderick Turing Mackenzie and Betty Dalzell Mackenzie; *m* 1949, Barbara Kershaw Miles; two *s* two *d. Educ:* Uppingham Sch.; RMC, Sandhurst. Served War: Indian Army, 2/6th Gurkha Rifles, 1940–47 (MC, Italy, 1944). Burmah-Shell Oil Storage and Distributing Co. of India, 1947–65; Shell Company of Rhodesia, 1965–66. *Recreations:* gardening, golf. *Address:* Eden Hill, Kennedy Gardens, St Andrews, Fife KY16 9DJ. *T:* St Andrews 3581. *Clubs:* Royal Cinque Ports Golf (Deal); Royal Porthcawl Golf; Atlanta Athletic (Georgia); Royal Calcutta Golf (Calcutta); Royal Salisbury Golf (Rhodesia).

MacKENZIE, Kelvin Calder; Editor of The Sun, since 1981; *b* 22 Oct. 1946; *m* 1969, Jacqueline Mary Holland; two *s* one *d. Educ:* Alleyn's Sch., Dulwich. Sub-editor, The Sun, 1973, Asst Night Editor, 1976; Managing Editor, New York Post, 1978; Night Editor, The Sun, 1980; Night Editor, Daily Express, 1981. *Recreation:* squash. *Address:* The Sun, 30 Bouverie Street, EC4Y 8DE. *T:* 01-353 3030.

MACKENZIE, Kenneth Edward, CMG 1970; HM Diplomatic Service, retired; *b* 28 April 1910; *s* of late A. E. Mackenzie, Dundee, and late K. M. Mackenzie (*née* Foley); *m* 1935, Phyllis Edith Fawkes; one *s. Educ:* schools in India, Australia and in the UK; University Coll., London. Engineering industry, 1926–29; University Coll., London, 1929–32, BSc (Hons) in civil and mechanical engineering. Inst. of Civil Engineers, 1932–34; Dept of Overseas Trade, 1934–36; HM Embassy, Brussels, 1936–40; interned in Germany, 1940–41; HM Embassy, Tehran, 1942–45. Trade Commissioner: in India, 1945–48; in Malaya, 1949–54; Asst Sec., Bd of Trade, 1954–66; Counsellor (Commercial), HM Embassy, Stockholm, and Chargé d'Affaires ad interim, 1966–70; Counsellor (Investment), 1973; Counsellor (Investment), HM Embassy, Copenhagen, 1974–75. *Address:* Prestbury, Middle Hill, Englefield Green, Surrey TW20 0JP. *T:* Egham 37877. *Club:* Royal Commonwealth Society.

MACKENZIE, Kenneth Roderick, CB 1965; Clerk of Public Bills, House of Commons, 1959–73; *b* 19 April 1908; *s* of late Walter Mackenzie; *m* 1935, Mary Howard, *e d* of late Lt-Col C. H. Coode, RM; three *s* one *d. Educ:* Dulwich Coll.; New Coll., Oxford (scholar). 1st class Classical Moderations; 2nd class Literæ Humaniores. Asst clerk, House of Commons, 1930; Clerk of Standing Cttees, 1953. Mem., Cttee on Preparation of Legislation, 1973–74. Officer's Cross, Order of Polonia Restituta, 1964. *Publications:* The English

Parliament, 1950; Parliament, 1959; editions of Sir Bryan Fell's Guide to the Palace of Westminster, 1944-72; verse translations of: Slowacki's In Switzerland, 1953; Mickiewicz's Pan Tadeusz, 1964; Virgil's Georgics, 1969; Dante's Divine Comedy, 1979. *Recreations:* riding, gardening. *Address:* Woodnorton, Mayfield, East Sussex TN20 6EJ. *T:* Mayfield 872317.

MacKENZIE, Kenneth William Stewart, CMG 1958; CVO 1975; FRAI; a Director of Studies, Royal Institute of Public Administration (Overseas Unit), since 1976; *b* 30 July 1915; *s* of late W. S. MacKenzie and E. MacKenzie (*née* Johnson); *m* 1939, Kathleen Joyce Ingram; one *s* one *d. Educ:* Whitcliffe Mount Gram. Sch., Cleckheaton; Downing Coll., Cambridge. 1st Cl. Hist. Tripos, Part I, 1935; Class II, Div. I, 1936; 1st Cl. Arch. and Anthrop. Tripos, Section A, 1937, BA 1936, MA 1962. Cadet, Colonial Administrative Service, Basutoland, 1938; Asst Sec., Mauritius, 1944; Administrative Officer, Kenya, 1948; Asst Financial Sec., Kenya, 1950; HM Treasury, 1951-53; Dep. Sec., 1954 and Permanent Sec., 1955, Treasury, Kenya; Minister for Finance and Development and Financial Sec., Kenya, 1959-62. MLC Kenya, 1955-62; MLA East Africa, 1959-62. Retired, 1963 to facilitate constitutional change. Re-employed as Principal, Colonial Office, 1963; Principal, HM Treasury, 1966-70; Asst Sec., DoE, 1970-75. *Publication:* pamphlet, How Basutoland is Governed, 1944. *Recreations:* reading, gardening. *Address:* Beaumont, 28 Greenhurst Lane, Oxted, Surrey RH8 0LB. *T:* Oxted 3848. *Clubs:* Royal Over-Seas League; Achilles; Nairobi (Nairobi).

MACKENZIE, Maxwell Weir, OC 1972; CMG 1946; Director: Canadian Imperial Bank of Commerce, 1955-77, now Emeritus; Canron Ltd, 1961-77, now Hon. Director; International Multifoods Corp., 1964-77; Royal Trust, 1960-67; Imperial Life, 1962-75; *b* 30 June 1907; *s* of late Hugh Blair Mackenzie, Gen. Man., Bank of Montreal, Montreal, and Maude Marion Weir; *m* 1931, Jean Roger Fairbairn; two *s* two *d. Educ:* Lakefield Preparatory Sch., Lakefield, Ont.; Trinity Coll. School, Port Hope, Ont.; McGill Univ., Montreal (BCom 1928). Joined McDonald, Currie & Co., Chartered Accountants of Montreal, 1928; Mem. Soc. of Chartered Accountants of the Province of Quebec, 1929; Jr Partner, McDonald, Currie & Co., Montreal, 1935; on loan to Foreign Exchange Control Board, Ottawa, 1939-42; to Wartime Prices and Trade Board, Ottawa, 1942-44 (Dep. Chm. 1943-44); Mem., Royal Commission on Taxation of Annuities and Family Corporation, 1944; Dep. Minister of Trade and Commerce, 1945-51; Dep. Minister of Defence Production, Canada, 1951-52; Pres., Canadian Chemical & Cellulose Company, Ltd, 1954-59 (Exec. Vice-Pres., 1952-54). Mem., Economic Council of Canada, 1963-71. Dir, C. D. Howe Res. Inst., 1973-80, now Hon. Dir. Chairman: Royal Commission on Security, 1966; Federal Inquiry into Beef Marketing, 1975. Hon. LLD McGill, 1973. *Recreation:* ski-ing. *Address:* 383 Maple Lane, Rockcliffe Park, Ottawa K1M 1H7, Canada. *Clubs:* Rideau (Ottawa); Mount Royal (Montreal).

McKENZIE, Michael; Courts Administrator, Central Criminal Court, since 1979; Coordinator for Taxation of Crown Court Costs, South East Circuit, since 1979; *b* Hove, Sussex, 25 May 1943; *s* of Robert John McKenzie and Kitty Elizabeth McKenzie; *m* 1964, Peggy Dorothy, *d* of Thomas Edward William Russell and Dorothy Mabel Russell; three *s. Educ:* Varndean Grammar Sch., Brighton. Town Clerk's Dept, Brighton, 1961-63; Asst to Clerk of the Peace, Brighton Quarter Sessions, 1963-67; Sen. Clerk of the Court, 1967-70, Dep. Clerk of the Peace, 1970-71, Middlesex Quarter Sessions; Called to the Bar, Middle Temple, 1970; Deputy to Courts Administrator, Middlesex Crown Court, 1972-73; Courts Administrator (Newcastle), NE Circuit, 1974-79. *Recreations:* Northumbrian stick dressing, fell walking. *Address:* Central Criminal Court, Old Bailey, EC4. *T:* 01-248 3277.

MacKENZIE, Norman Archibald MacRae, CC (Canada) 1969; CMG 1946; MM and Bar, 1918; CD 1968; QC; BA, LLB (Dalhousie); LLM (Harvard); FRSC 1943; Hon. LLD (Mount Allison, New Brunswick, Toronto, Dalhousie, Ottawa, Bristol, Alberta, Glasgow, St Francis Xavier, McGill, Sydney, Rochester, Alaska, California, British Columbia, RMC (Cambridge); DCL (Saskatchewan, Whitman College); DSc Social, Laval; DLitt, Memorial University of Newfoundland; President Emeritus, Hon. Professor of International Law, University of British Columbia, Vancouver, since 1962; President of the University, 1944-62; appointed to The Senate of Canada, 1966, retired 1969; *b* Pugwash, Nova Scotia, Canada, 5 Jan. 1894; *s* of Rev. James A. MacKenzie and Elizabeth MacRae; *m* 1928, Margaret, *d* of A. W. and Helen Thomas; one *s* two *d. Educ:* Pictou Acad.; Dalhousie Univ. (BA 1921, LLB 1923); Harvard (LLM 1924); St John's Coll., Cambridge (Postgrad. Dipl., 1925); Grays' Inn, London. Read Law with McInnes, Jenks and Lovitt; called to Bar of Nova Scotia, 1926; KC 1942; Legal Adviser, ILO, Geneva, 1925-27; Assoc. Prof. of Law, 1927-33, Prof. of International and Canadian Constitutional Law, 1933-40, Toronto Univ.; Pres., University of New Brunswick, 1940-44; Pres., Nat. Council of Canadian Universities, 1946-48; Pres., Canadian Club of Toronto, 1939-40; Chm., Research Commission, Canadian Inst. of Internat. Affairs, 1929-40; Founding Mem. and Hon. Mem., National Council CIIA; Chm., Wartime Information Board, Canada, 1943-45; Chm., Reconstruction Commn, Province of New Brunswick, 1941-44; Pres., Toronto Branch, League of Nations Soc., 1932-36; Delegate to Institute of Pacific Relations Conferences, Shanghai 1931, Banff 1933, Yosemite 1936, Virginia Beach 1939, Mont Tremblant 1942; Delegate to British Commonwealth Conferences, Toronto, 1933, Sydney, Australia, 1938; Delegate to 7th Congress on Laws of Aviation, Lyons, France, 1925; War Record: Canadian Inf., 1914-19; 6th Canadian Mounted Rifles' 85th Bn,

Nova Scotia Highlanders (MM and Bar); Vice-Pres., National Council of Canadian YMCA's; Chm. Victory Loan Executive Cttee, Fredericton and York, New Brunswick, 1941-44; Mem., University Advisory Board, Dept of Labour; Mem., Advisory Cttee on University Training for Veterans, Dept of Veterans Affairs; Hon. Pres. Save the Children Fund, Canada; Mem., Legal Survey Cttee (Survey of Legal Profession of Canada), 1949-57; Chm., Consultative Cttee on Doukhobor Problems; Mem., Royal Commission on National Development in the Arts, Letters and Sciences, 1949-51; Dir, Bank of Nova Scotia, 1960-69; Mem. Vancouver Advisory Board, Canada Permanent Trust Company, 1962-; East African Commission on University Educn, 1962. Trustee: Teachers Insurance and Annuity Association of America, 1948-; Carnegie Foundation for the Advancement of Teaching, 1951- (Chm. Bd Trustees, 1959); Pres. Canadian Assoc. for Adult Education, 1957-59; Chm., University Grants Cttee, Prov. of NS, 1963-69; Mem. Royal Commission on Higher Educn, Prov. of PEI; Pres., Canadian Centenary Council; Dir, Centennial Commn (Canada); Dir, Fathers of Confedn Memorial Foundn; Pres., Nat. Assoc. of Canadian Clubs. Hon. Fellow: St John's Coll., Cambridge, 1964; LSE, 1980. John E. Read Medal for contributions to International Law, 1975. *Publications:* Legal Status of Aliens in Pacific Countries, 1937; Canada and Law of Nations (with L. H. Laing), 1938; Canada in World Affairs (with F. H. Soward, J. F. Parkinson, T. W. L. MacDermot), 1941; The Challenge to Education, 1953; First Principles, 1954; (with Jacob Austin) A Canadian View of Territorial Seas and Fisheries, 1956, etc. Contributor to: Canadian Bar Review, Law Journals, etc. *Recreations:* fishing, hunting, golf, tennis, badminton, ski-ing. *Address:* 4509 West 4th Avenue, Vancouver, BC V6R 1R4, Canada. *Clubs:* Vancouver, University, Faculty (Vancouver).

MACKENZIE, Sir Robert Evelyn, 12th Bt, *cr* 1673; *b* 15 Feb. 1906; *s* of 11th Bt and Evelyn Mary Montgomery (*d* 1908), *d* of Major-Gen. Sir Edward W. Ward; *S* father, 1935; *m* 1st, 1940, Mrs Jane Adams-Beck (*d* 1953); 2nd, 1963, Mrs Elizabeth Campbell. *Educ:* Eton; Trinity Coll., Cambridge. Mem. of Lloyd's, 1932-71. Intelligence Corps, 1939; British Embassy, Paris, 1944; Foreign Office, 1947; Washington, 1948; Foreign Office, 1951. *Heir:* kinsman Rev. Ramsay Malcolm Bolton Mackenzie [*b* Aug. 1893; *m* 1920, Margaret Cecilia (*d* 1965), *o d* of Rev. G. A. S. Metford; *m* 1971, Joan Mary Davey]. *Address:* 18 Melton Court, Old Brompton Road, SW7 3JQ.

MACKENZIE, Captain Sir Roderick (Edward François McQuhae), 11th Bt *cr* 1703, of Scatwell; CBE 1945; DSC 1916; RN retired; *b* 11 Dec. 1894; *s* of John Roderick Kenneth Mackenzie (*d* 1958) and Kathleen Elizabeth (*d* 1974), *d* of Captain Thomas Howard Blennerhasset Coulson, Royal Indian Marine; *S* cousin, 1981; *m* 1938, Marie Evelyn Campbell, *o c* of late William Ernest Parkinson; one *s* two *d. Educ:* RN Colls, Osborne and Dartmouth; RN Staff Coll., Greenwich. Served European War, 1914-18 (despatches): Midshipman, then Sub-Lieut, HMS Iron Duke, 1913-15; HMS Royalist, 1915-18; later served as Fleet Torpedo Officer, China Station, N America, W Indies and Home Fleet; also on staff, HMS Dolphin, as Torpedo Officer, Submarines; in comd HMS Sandwich, 1931-33; Admiralty, 1933-39; War of 1939-45, landings in Sicily, Naples, Anzio (despatches); Naval Officer i/c, Naples and Leghorn. Retired, 1946. American Medal of Freedom with silver palm, 1945. *Recreations:* golf, horse riding. *Heir:* s Roderick McQuhae Mackenzie, MB, BS, MRCP, DCH [*b* 17 April 1942; *m* 1970, Nadine, *d* of Georges Schlatter; one *s* one *d*]. *Address:* Finborough, 11 Morley Road, Farnham, Surrey. *T:* Farnham 716072. *Club:* Naval and Military.

MACKENZIE, Sandy; *see* Mackenzie, Dr A. S.

MACKENZIE, Wallace John, OBE 1974; Group Managing Director, Slough Estates plc, since 1975; *b* 2 July 1921; *s* of Wallace D. Mackenzie and Ethel F. Williamson; *m* 1951, Barbara D. Hopson; two *s* one *d. Educ:* Harrow Weald County Grammar Sch. Gen. Manager, Slough Estates Canada Ltd, 1952-72; Dep. Man. Dir, Slough Estates Ltd, 1972-75. Dir, Finance for Industry plc; Mem., Commn for New Towns. *Recreations:* golf, bridge. *Address:* Manitou, Spring Coppice, Lane End, High Wycombe, Bucks. *T:* High Wycombe 881032. *Club:* Arts.

MACKENZIE, Prof. William James Millar, CBE 1963; FBA 1968; Professor of Politics, Glasgow University, 1966-74, now Emeritus; *b* 8 April 1909; *s* of Laurence Millar Mackenzie, WS, Edinburgh; *m* 1943, Pamela Muriel Malyon; one *s* four *d. Educ:* Edinburgh Academy; Balliol Coll., Oxford (MA) (Ireland Schol. 1929); Edinburgh Univ. (LLB); Fellow of Magdalen Coll., Oxford, 1933-48; Temp. Civil Servant, Air Ministry, 1939-44; Official War Historian, SOE, 1945-48. Faculty Fellow, Nuffield Coll., 1948; Lecturer in Politics, Oxford Univ., 1948; Prof. of Government, Manchester Univ., 1949-66, Glasgow Univ., 1966-74; Special Comr, for Constitutional Development, Tanganyika, 1952; Co-opted Mem., Manchester City Educn Cttee, 1953-64; apptd Mem., British Wool Marketing Board, 1954-66; Mem. Royal Commn on Local Govt in Greater London, 1957; Constitutional Adviser, Kenya, 1959; Vice-Chm., Bridges Cttee on Training in Public Administration for Overseas Countries, 1962; Member: Maud Cttee on Management in Local Govt, 1964-66; Cttee on Remuneration of Ministers and Members of Parliament, 1963-64; North-West Regional Economic Planning Council, 1965-66; SSRC, 1965-69; Parry Cttee on University Libraries, 1964-67; Chm., Children's Panel Adv. Cttee, Glasgow City, 1973-75. Hon. LLD: Dundee, 1968; Lancaster, 1970; Manchester, 1975; Hon. DLitt Warwick, 1972; Hon. DSc (Econ) Hull, 1981. *Publications:* (in part) British Government since 1918, 1950; (jtly) Central Administration in Great

Britain, 1957; Free Elections, 1958; (ed with Prof. K. Robinson) Five Elections in Africa, 1959; Politics and Social Science, 1967; (jtly) Social Work in Scotland, 1969; Power, Violence, Decision, 1975; Explorations in Government, 1975; Political Identity, 1977; Biological Ideas in Politics, 1978; Power and Responsibility in Health Care, 1979. *Address:* 12 Kirklee Circus, Glasgow G12 0TW.

MACKENZIE CROOKS, Air Vice-Marshal Lewis, CBE 1963 (OBE 1950); Consultant Adviser in Orthopaedic Surgery, RAF, 1966-70, retired; Locum Consultant in Orthopaedic Surgery, Cornwall, since 1970; *b* 20 Jan. 1909; *s* of David Mackenzie Crooks and Mary (*née* McKechnie); *m* 1936, Mildred, *d* of A. J. Gwyther; two *s* one *d. Educ:* Epworth Coll.; Liverpool Univ. MB, ChB 1931; FRCS 1937; ChM (Liverpool) 1945. House Surgeon: Northern Hosp., Liverpool, 1931-32; Shropshire Orthop. Hosp., Oswestry, 1932-33; Sen. House Surgeon: Selly Oak Hosp., Birmingham, 1933-34; All Saints Hosp., London, 1934-35; commnd RAF, 1935; surgical hosp. appts in RAF, 1936-52; overseas service: Palestine, 1937-39; Iraq, 1939-42 (despatches 1941); Egypt, 1950-51. Clinical Tutor, Edinburgh Royal Infirmary, 1947; Cons. in Orthop. Surgery, 1952; Sen. Cons. in Orthop. Surgery, 1955. QHS, 1966-70. *Publication:* article on chondromalaca patellae in Jl of Bone and Joint Surgery. *Recreations:* golf, gardening. *Address:* Trelawney, Harlyn Bay, Padstow, Cornwall PL28 8SF. *T:* Padstow 520631. *Clubs:* Royal Air Force; Trevose Golf, Country (Constantine Bay, Cornwall).

McKENZIE JOHNSTON, Henry Butler, CB 1981; Vice-Chairman, Commission for Local Administration in England, since 1982 (Commissioner, since 1981); *b* 10 July 1921; *er s* of Colin Mackenzie Johnston and late Bernardine (*née* Fawcett Butler); *m* 1949, Marian Allardyce Middleton, *e d* of late Brig. A. A. Middleton and Winifred (*née* Salvesen); one *s* two *d. Educ:* Rugby. Served with Black Watch (RHR), 1940-46; Adjt 6th Bn, 1944-45; Temp. Major 1945. Staff of HM Embassy, Athens, 1946-47; entered Foreign (subseq. Diplomatic) Service, 1947; Paris, 1948-51; British High Commn, Germany, 1951-54; FO, 1954-56; 1st Sec. (Commercial), Montevideo, 1956-60; FO, 1960-63; Counsellor (Information), Mexico City, 1963-66; Dep. High Comr, Port of Spain, 1966-67; seconded to Min. of Overseas Develt, 1968-70; Consul-Gen., Munich, 1971-73; seconded to Office of Parly Comr, 1973-79, transferred permanently, 1979-81; Dep. Parly Comr for Admin, 1974-81. *Address:* 6 Pembroke Gardens, W8 6HS. *Clubs:* Athenæum, Hurlingham.

MACKENZIE-KENNEDY, Brig. Archibald Gordon, CBE 1952 (OBE 1949); DSO 1945; Brigadier late Royal Scots; *b* 1904; *s* of late Maj.-Gen. Sir Edward Charles William Mackenzie-Kennedy, KBE, CB; *m* 1937, Jean Katherine (*d* 1981), *d* of H. A. Law, Marble Hill, Ballymore, Co. Donegal. *Educ:* Marlborough; Royal Military College, Sandhurst. 2nd Lt Royal Scots, 1924. Served War of 1939-45: Burma, 1941-45 (DSO; despatches 1943); Lt-Col, 1943; Brig., 1947; Comdr Eritrea District, 1950-52; retd 1955. County Comdt, Ulster Special Constabulary, 1955. *Address:* Tarff Old Manse, Kirkcudbright. *T:* Ringford 219.

MACKENZIE STUART, Hon. Lord; Alexander John Mackenzie Stuart; Judge of the Court of Justice, European Communities at Luxembourg, since 1973; a Senator of the College of Justice in Scotland, 1972-73; *b* 18 Nov. 1924; *s* of late Prof. A. Mackenzie Stuart, KC, and Amy Margaret Dean, Aberdeen; *m* 1952, Anne Burtholme Millar, *d* of late J. S. L. Millar, ws, Edinburgh; four *d. Educ:* Fettes Coll., Edinburgh (open Schol.); Sidney Sussex Coll., Cambridge (schol. 1949, 1st cl. Pt II Law Tripos, BA 1949, Hon. Fellow, 1977); Edinburgh Univ. (LLB (dist.) 1951). Royal Engineers (Temp. Capt. 1946), 1942-47. Admitted Faculty of Advocates, 1951; QC (Scot.) 1963; Keeper of the Advocates Library, 1970-72. Standing Junior Counsel: to Scottish Home Dept, 1956-57; to Inland Revenue in Scotland, 1957-63. Sheriff-Principal of Aberdeen, Kincardine and Banff, 1971-72. Governor, Fettes College, 1962-72. Hon. Bencher, Middle Temple, 1978. Hon. Prof., Collège d'Europe, Bruges, 1974-77; DUniv. Stirling, 1973; Hon. LLD: Exeter, 1978; Edinburgh, 1978; Glasgow, 1981. *Publications:* Hamlyn Lectures: The European Communities and the Rule of Law, 1977; articles in legal publications. *Recreation:* collecting. *Address:* 48 rue de Wormeldange, Rodenbourg, Luxembourg. *T:* 77276; c/o Bank of Scotland, 64 George Street, Edinburgh. *Club:* New (Edinburgh).

MACKEOWN, John Ainslie, CIE 1942; Secretary, Arthur Guinness Son & Co. (Dublin) Ltd, 1962-67; retired; *b* 27 Oct. 1902; *s* of late Rev. William Mackeown; *m* 1935, Vivienne (marr. diss.), *d* of J. L. Musgrave, Hayfield House, Cork; two *s. Educ:* Radley; Worcester Coll., Oxford. Joined ICS, 1925; left India, 1947, after holding posts, Jt Sec. to Govt of India and Comr, Ambala Div. *Recreations:* golf, music, reading, bridge, sailing. *Address:* 83 Ardoyne House, Pembroke Park, Dublin 4. *T:* Dublin 601343.

McKEOWN, Prof. Patrick Arthur, MSc, CEng, FIProdE; FIQA; FIMechE; Professor of Precision Engineering since 1974, Director of Cranfield Unit for Precision Engineering since 1969, and Head of Department for Design of Machine Systems since 1975, Cranfield Institute of Technology; *b* 16 Aug. 1930; *s* of Robert Matthew McKeown and Augusta (*née* White); *m* 1954, Mary Patricia Heath; three *s. Educ:* Cambridge County High Sch. for Boys; Bristol Grammar Sch.; Cranfield Inst. of Technol. (MSc). CEng, MIMechE 1969; FIProdE 1971; FIQA 1973. National Service, RE, 1949-51; Suez Campaign, 1956: Captain RE; port maintenance. Student apprentice, Bristol Aircraft Co. Ltd, Bristol, 1951-54 (HNC National State Scholarship); Cranfield Inst. of Technol., 1954-56; Société Genevoise, Newport Pagnell and

Geneva, 1956-68 (Technical and Works Dir, 1965). Vice-Pres., Inst. of Qual. Assurance, 1976. Member: CIRP (Internat. Instn for Prodn Engrg Research); Evaluation Panel, National Bureau of Standards, Washington, USA; Mem., Metrology and Standards Requirements Bd, from July 1983. *Publications:* papers in CIRP Annals. *Recreations:* walking, travel, enjoyment of wine, good food, music, theatre. *Address:* 37 Church End, Biddenham, Bedford MK40 4AR. *T:* Bedford 67678.

McKEOWN, Prof. Thomas, BA British Columbia, PhD McGill, DPhil Oxon, MB, BS London, MD Birmingham, FRCP, FFCM; Professor of Social Medicine, 1945-77, and Pro-Vice-Chancellor, 1974-77, University of Birmingham; *b* 2 Nov. 1912; *s* of William McKeown; *m* 1940, Esmé Joan Bryan Widdowson; one *s* one *d. Educ:* Universities: British Columbia; McGill (National Research Council Schol.); Trinity Coll., Oxford (Rhodes Scholar); London (Guy's Hospital: Poulton Research Scholar). Demonstrator in biochemistry, McGill; demonstrator in physiology, Guy's Hosp. Lectures: Cutter, Harvard Sch. of Public Health, 1960; Lowell, Mass, General Hosp., 1963; British Council, Australia, 1963; De Frees, Univ. of Pennsylvania, 1969; Teale, RCP, 1969; BMA Winchester, 1970; Cecil and Ida Green, Univ. of BC, 1975; Osler, McGill, 1979; Alexander D. Langmuir, Center for Disease Control, Atlanta, 1980; James Seth, Univ. of Edinburgh, 1981. Rock Carling Fellow, Nuffield Provincial Hosps Trust, 1976. Jt Editor, Brit. Jl of Preventive and Social Medicine, 1950-58. Hon. FFCM Ireland, 1980; Hon. FACP, 1982; Hon. DSc McGill, 1981. *Publications:* A Balanced Teaching Hospital (jointly), 1965; Medicine in Modern Society, 1965; Introduction to Social Medicine (jt), 1966; Screening in Medical Care (jointly), 1968; Medical History and Medical Care (jt Ed.), 1971; The Modern Rise of Population, 1976; The Role of Medicine, 1976; contributions to scientific journals. *Address:* 23 Hintlesham Avenue, Edgbaston, Birmingham B15 2PH. *T:* 021-454 2810.

MACKEOWN, Thomas Frederick William; Administrator and Secretary, University College Hospital, London, 1946-63; *b* 3 Jan. 1904; *s* of Rev. William Mackeown, Rushbrooke, Co. Cork; *m* 1936, Lorraine, *d* of Major R. Hayes, Sherburn-in-Elmet, Yorks; one *d. Educ:* Felsted; Worcester Coll., Oxford (MA). Qualified as Chartered Accountant, 1927. Hospital Administrator: Liverpool Stanley Hospital, 1934-37; Clayton Hospital, Wakefield, 1937-45; Royal Infirmary, Sunderland, 1945-46; Hill Homes, Highgate (actg), 1966; King Edward VII Memorial Hospital, Bermuda, 1967; Vice-Chm., Management Cttee, Harefield and Northwoods Hosps, 1960-74; undertook Hosp. Domestic Staff Survey under aegis of King Edward's Hosp. Fund for London, 1968. Lay FRSocMed, 1974. *Address:* 4 Westhill Court, Millfield Lane, N6. *T:* 01-348 1952.

McKERN, Leo, (Reginald McKern); actor; *b* 16 March 1920; *s* of Norman Walton McKern and Vera (*née* Martin); *m* 1946, Joan Alice Southall, (Jane Holland); two *d. Educ:* Sydney Techn. High Sch. Engrg apprentice, 1935-37; artist, 1937-40; AIF (Corp., Engrs), 1940-42; actor, 1944; arrived England, 1946; CSEU tour, Germany; Arts Council tours, 1947; Old Vic, 1949-52; Shakespeare Meml Theatre, 1952-54; Old Vic last season, 1962-63; New Nottingham Playhouse, 1963-64; international films; *stage:* Toad of Toad Hall, Princes, 1954; Queen of the Rebels, Haymarket, 1955; Cat on a Hot Tin Roof, Aldwych, 1958; Brouhaha, Aldwych, 1958; Rollo, Strand, 1959; A Man for all Seasons, Globe, 1960; The Thwarting of Baron Bollegrew, RSC, Aldwych, 1965; Volpone, Garrick, 1967; The Wolf, Apollo, 1973; The Housekeeper, Apollo, 1982; *television:* Rumpole of the Bailey (series), 1977-. *Recreations:* sailing, swimming, photography, painting, ecology, environment preservation, model making, dolls' house and furniture construction. *Address:* 12 Summerhill Road, Summertown, Oxford OX2 7JY.

MACKERRAS, Sir (Alan) Charles (MacLaurin), Kt 1979; CBE 1974; Chief Conductor, Sydney Symphony Orchestra, Australian Broadcasting Commission, since 1982; Principal Guest Conductor, English National Opera, since 1979; Guest Conductor: Vienna State Opera; Geneva and Zurich Opera; Royal Opera House Covent Garden; San Francisco Opera; *b* 17 Nov. 1925; *s* of late Alan Patrick and Catherine Mackerras, Sydney, Australia; *m* 1947, Helena Judith (*née* Wilkins); two *d. Educ:* Sydney Grammar Sch. Principal Oboist, Sydney Symphony Orchestra, 1943-46; Staff Conductor, Sadler's Wells Opera, 1949-53; Principal Conductor BBC Concert Orchestra, 1954-56; freelance conductor with most British and many continental orchestras; concert tours in USSR, S Africa, USA, 1957-66; Conductor, Hamburg State Opera, 1966-69; Musical Dir, Sadler's Wells Opera, later ENO, 1970-77; Chief Guest Conductor, BBC SO, 1976-79; frequent radio and TV broadcasts; many commercial recordings, notably Handel series for DGG and Janáček operas for Decca; appearances at many internat. festivals and opera houses. Evening Standard Award for Opera, 1977; Janáček Medal, 1978; Gramophone Record of the Year Award, 1978 and 1980; Best Opera Recording, 1981. *Publications:* ballet arrangements of Pineapple Poll and of Lady and the Fool; articles in Opera Magazine, Music and Musicians and other musical jls. *Recreations:* languages, yachting. *Address:* 10 Hamilton Terrace, NW8 9UG. *T:* 01-286 4047. *Club:* Garrick.

MACKESON, Sir Rupert (Henry), 2nd Bt *cr* 1954; *b* 16 Nov. 1941; *s* of Brig. Sir Harry Ripley Mackeson, 1st Bt, and Alethea, Lady Mackeson (*d* 1979), *d* of late Comdr R. Talbot, RN; *S* father, 1964. *Educ:* Harrow; Trinity Coll., Dublin (MA). Captain, Royal Horse Guards, 1967, retd 1968. *Recreations:* art, racing. *Heir:* none.

MACKEY, Most Rev. John; *see* Auckland (NZ), Bishop of, (RC).

MACKEY, Prof. William Arthur, TD; St Mungo Professor of Surgery, University of Glasgow, 1953-72, now Emeritus; *b* 1 Oct. 1906; *s* of Arthur Edward Mackey, Schoolmaster, and Elizabeth Annie (*née* Carr); *m* 1939, Joan Margaret Sykes; two *s* two *d*. *Educ:* Ardrossan Academy; Univ. of Glasgow. MB, ChB (hons). Asst to Prof. of Pathology, Univ. of Glasgow, 1928; Asst to Regius Prof. of Surgery, University of Glasgow, 1931. Hon. FACS. *Recreations:* golf, gardening, repenting plans and pottering around bohemia. *Address:* 4 West Abercromby Street, Helensburgh, Dunbartonshire G84 9LJ. *T:* Helensburgh 3659. *Clubs:* Royal Scottish Automobile (Glasgow), Glasgow Golf.

MACKEY, William Gawen; Partner, Ernst & Whinney, since 1952; *b* 22 Sept. 1924; *s* of William Gawen Mackey and Jane Russell; *m* 1948, Margaret Reeves Vinycomb; two *s*. *Educ:* Dame Allan's Sch., Newcastle upon Tyne. Qualified Chartered Accountant, 1949. Served RN, 1942-45 (Sub-Lt). Joined Ernst & Whinney, 1952. Apptd Receiver: Airfix; British Tanners; Laker; Stone-Platt. Chm., Insolvency Services Sub Cttee, CCAB, 1973-82; Dir, Institute Corporate Insolvency Courses, 1974-80. *Publications:* articles on receivership. *Recreations:* opera, France, work. *Address:* 1 Lambeth Palace Road, SE1 7EU. *T:* 01-402 0198.

MACKIE; *see* John-Mackie.

MACKIE, family name of **Barons John-Mackie** and **Mackie of Benshie.**

MACKIE OF BENSHIE, Baron *cr* 1974 (Life Peer), of Kirriemuir; **George Yull Mackie,** CBE 1971; DSO 1944; DFC 1944; Chairman: Caithness Glass Ltd, since 1966; Caithness Pottery Co. Ltd; The Benshie Cattle Co. Ltd; Rector, Dundee University, since 1980; *b* 10 July 1919; *s* of late Maitland Mackie, OBE, Hon. LLD; *m* 1944, Lindsay Lyall Sharp, *y d* of late Alexander and Isabella Sharp, OBE, Aberdeen; three *d* (one *s* decd). *Educ:* Aberdeen Grammar Sch.; Aberdeen Univ. Served War of 1939-45, RAF; Bomber Command, (DSO, DFC); Air Staff, 1944. Farming at Ballinshoe, Kirriemuir, from 1945. Contested (L) South Angus, 1959; MP (L) Caithness and Sutherland, 1964-66; contested (L) Scotland NE, European Parliamentary election, 1979. Chm., Scottish Liberal Party, 1965-70. Member: EEC Scrutiny Cttee (D), House of Lords; Liberal Shadow Admin; Exec., Inter-Parly Union; Governing Body, GB/East Europe Centre; Liberal Spokesman, House of Lords: Devolution, Agriculture, Scotland, Industry. Chm., Mackie Yule & Co. Ltd, 1980-. Hon. LLD Dundee, 1982. *Publication:* Policy for Scottish Agriculture, 1963. *Address:* Ballinshoe, Kirriemuir, Angus. *T:* Kirriemuir 3466. *Clubs:* Garrick, Farmers', Royal Air Force.
See also Baron John-Mackie, Sir Maitland Mackie, A. G. Sharp.

MACKIE, Air Cdre (Retd) Alastair Cavendish Lindsay, CBE 1966; DFC 1943 and Bar 1944; Director General, Health Education Council, 1972-82; *b* 3 Aug. 1922; *s* of George Mackie, DSO, OBE, MD, Malvern, Worcs and May (*née* Cavendish); *m* 1944, Rachel Goodson; two *s*. *Educ:* Charterhouse. Royal Air Force, 1940-68; Under Treas., Middle Temple, 1968; Registrar, Architects' Registration Council, 1970; Sec., British Dental Assoc., 1971. *Recreation:* squash. *Address:* 4 Warwick Drive, SW15 6LB. *T:* 01-789 4544. *Club:* Royal Air Force.

MACKIE, Eric Dermott; Chief Executive and Managing Director, Govan Shipbuilders Ltd, since 1979; *b* 4 Dec. 1924; *s* of James Girvan and Ellen Dorothy Mackie; *m* 1950, Mary Victoria Christie; one *s* one *d*. *Educ:* Coll. of Technology, Belfast. CEng; MIMechE, MIMarE. 1st Class MoT Cert. (Steam and Diesel). Trained with James Mackie & Son (Textile Engrs), 1939-44; Design draughtsman, Harland & Wolff, Belfast, 1944-48; 2nd Engineer (sea-going) in both steam and diesel ships for Union Castle Mail Steamship Co., 1948-53; Harland & Wolff, Belfast, 1953-75: Test Engr; Manager, Shiprepair Dept; Gen. Manager i/c of Southampton branch; Gen. Manager i/c of ship prodn and shiprepair, Belfast; Man. Dir, James Brown Hamer, S Africa, 1975-79; Chief Exec. and Man. Dir of Shiprepair in UK, British Shipbuilders, 1979-81. *Publications:* articles for marine engrg instns on various subjects pertaining to marine engrg and gen. engrg. *Recreations:* golf, swimming, reading. *Address:* Middle Barton, Whittingham, near Alnwick, Northumberland. *T:* Whittingham 648. *Clubs:* Durban, Rand (Johannesburg, SA).

MACKIE, George, DFC 1944; RSW 1968; RDI 1973; freelance graphic artist and painter; Head of Design, Gray's School of Art, Aberdeen, 1958-80 (retd); *b* 17 July 1920; *s* of late David Mackie and late Kathleen Grantham; *m* 1952, Barbara Balmer, ARSA, RSW; two *d*. Served Royal Air Force, 1940-46. Consultant in book design to Edinburgh University Press, 1960-. *Publication:* Lynton Lamb: Illustrator, 1979. *Address:* 32 Broad Street, Stamford, Lincs. *T:* Stamford 53296; 37 Queensferry Street, Edinburgh. *T:* 031-226 5580. *Club:* Double Crown.

McKIE, Rt. Rev. John David; Assistant Bishop, Diocese of Coventry, 1960-80; Vicar of Great and Little Packington, 1966-80; *b* 14 May 1909; *s* of Rev. W. McKie, Melbourne, Vic; *m* 1952, Mary Lesley, *d* of late Brig. S. T. W. Goodwin, DSO and of Mrs Goodwin, Melbourne, Vic; four *d*. *Educ:* Melbourne Church of England Grammar Sch.; Trinity Coll., Melbourne Univ.; New Coll., Oxford. BA (Trinity Coll., Melbourne Univ.). 1931; MA (New Coll., Oxford), 1945; Deacon, 1932; Priest, 1934; Asst Chap. Melbourne

Church of England Grammar Sch., 1932-33; Chap. and lecturer, Trinity Coll., Melbourne, 1936-39; served War of 1939-45 (despatches): AIF, 1939-44; Asst CG; Vicar Christ Church, South Yarra, 1944-46; Coadjutor, Bishop of Melbourne (with title of Bishop of Geelong) and Archdeacon of Melbourne, 1946-60, Chaplain and Sub-Prelate, Order of St John of Jerusalem, 1949. *Address:* 2 Birdwood Avenue, Mornington, Victoria 3931, Australia.
See also Sir W. N. McKie.

MACKIE, Lily Edna Minerva; Head Mistress, City of London School for Girls, since 1972; *b* 14 April 1926; *d* of late Robert Wood Mackie and late Lilian Amelia Mackie (*née* Dennis). *Educ:* Plaistow Grammar Sch.; University Coll., London (BA); Lycée de Jeunes Filles, Limoges; Université de Poitiers. Asst Mistress: Ilford County High Sch. for Girls, 1950-59; City of London Sch. for Girls, 1960-64; Head Mistress: Wimbledon County Sch., 1964-69; Ricards Lodge High Sch., Wimbledon, 1969-72. FRSA. *Recreations:* theatre, music, gardening, travel, boating. *Address:* City of London School for Girls, Barbican, EC2Y 8BB. *T:* 01-628 0841.

MACKIE, Sir Maitland, Kt 1982; CBE 1965; JP; Lord-Lieutenant of Aberdeenshire, since 1975; farmer since 1932; *b* 16 Feb. 1912; *s* of late Dr Maitland Mackie, OBE and Mary (*née* Yull); *m* 1st, 1935, Isobel Ross (*d* 1960); two *s* four *d*; 2nd, 1963, Martha Pauline Turner. *Educ:* Aberdeen Grammar Sch.; Aberdeen Univ. (BSCAgric). FEIS 1972, FRAgSs 1974. County Councillor, Aberdeenshire, 1951-75 (Convener 1967-75); Chm., NE Develt Authority, 1969-75; Chairman: Jt Adv. Cttee, Scottish Farm Bldgs Investigation Unit, 1963-; Aberdeen Milk Marketing Bd, 1965-; Peterhead Bay Management Co., 1975; Member: Agric. Sub-Cttee, UGC, 1965-75; Bd, Scottish Council for Development and Industry, 1975- (Chm., Oil Policy Cttee, 1975-); Clayson Cttee on Drink Laws in Scotland. Director: Scottish Telecommunications, 1969; Hanover Housing Assoc., 1978; Highland Hydrocarbons Ltd, 1978. Governor: N of Scotland Coll. of Agriculture, 1968- (Vice-Chm., 1974-78); Rowett Inst., 1973. MInstM 1976. Burgess of Guild, Aberdeen, 1978. JP 1956. KStJ 1977. Hon. LLD Aberdeen, 1977. *Recreation:* travel. *Address:* Cramond House, 17 Rubislaw Den North, Aberdeen AB2 4AL. *T:* Aberdeen 33587. *Clubs:* Farmers'; Royal Northern (Aberdeen).
See also Barons John-Mackie and Mackie of Benshie.

McKIE, Sir William Neil, Kt 1953; MVO 1948; MA, Hon. DMus Oxon, Melbourne; FRSCM, FRCM, FRCO, FTCL, Hon. RAM; Hon. Secretary, Royal College of Organists, 1963-67; Hon. Fellow, Worcester College, Oxford, 1954; Organist and Master of the Choristers, Westminster Abbey, 1941-63 (on leave of absence, 1941-45, during war service, RAF, Volunteer Reserve); *b* Melbourne, Australia, 22 May 1901; *s* of Rev. William McKie; *m* 1956, Phyllis Ross, *widow* of Gerald Walker Birks, OBE, and *d* of John Wardrope Ross, Montreal. *Educ:* Melbourne Grammar Sch.; Royal Coll. of Music; Worcester Coll., Oxford. Organist St Agnes, Kennington Park, 1920-21; organ scholar, Worcester Coll., Oxford, 1921-24; asst music master, Radley Coll., 1923-26; Dir of Music, Clifton Coll., 1926-30; City Organist, Melbourne, 1931-38; Dir of Music, Geelong Grammar Sch., 1934-38; Organist and Instructor in Music, Magdalen Coll., Oxford, 1938-41; Organist at Sheldonian Theatre, 1939-41; Organ prof., Royal Acad. of Music, 1946-62; Hon. Associate Dir, Royal School of Church Music, 1947-52; Dir of Music, Coronation Service, 1953; President: Incorporated Association of Organists, 1950-52; Royal College of Organists, 1956-58; London Soc. of Organists, 1958-59; Incorporated Soc. of Musicians, 1959. Hon. Mem., American Guild of Organists; Hon. Fellow: Westminster Choir Coll., Princeton, NJ, 1965; Royal Canadian Coll. of Organists, 1965. Comdr with Star, Order of St Olav, Norway, 1964. *Address:* 10 Driveway, Ottawa, Ontario K2P 1C7, Canada. *Clubs:* Athenæum; Rideau (Ottawa).
See also Rt Rev. J. D. McKie.

McKIERNAN, Most Rev. Francis J.; *see* Kilmore, Bishop of, (RC).

MACKILLIGIN, David Patrick Robert; HM Diplomatic Service; Counsellor (Economic, Commercial and Aid), Jakarta, since 1980; *b* 29 June 1939; *s* of R. S. Mackilligin, CMG, OBE, MC and Patricia (*née* Waldegrave); *m* 1976, Gillian Margaret Zuill Walker; two *d*. *Educ:* St Mary's Coll., Winchester; Pembroke Coll., Oxford (2nd Cl. Hons PPE). Asst Principal, CRO, 1961-62; Third, later Second Sec., Jakarta, 1962-66; Asst Private Sec. to Sec. of State for Commonwealth Relations, 1966-68; Private Sec. to Minister Without Portfolio, 1968-69; Dep. Comr, Anguilla, 1969-71 (Actg Comr, July-Aug. 1970); First Sec., Ghana, 1971-73; First Sec., Head of Chancery and Consul, Cambodia, 1973-75 (Chargé d'Affaires at various times); FCO, 1975-80 (Asst Head of W African Dept, 1978-80). *Recreations:* walking and swimming in remote places, ruins, second-hand bookshops, theatre, literature, Arthurian romance. *Address:* c/o Foreign and Commonwealth Office, King Charles Street, SW1. *Clubs:* United Oxford & Cambridge University, Royal Commonwealth Society; Indonesia Petroleum (Jakarta).

McKILLOP, Edgar Ravenswood, CMG 1952; OBE 1942; Company Director; Commissioner of Works and Permanent Head, Ministry of Works, NZ, 1944-55, retired; *b* 26 July 1895; *s* of Alexander McKillop and Jean Cameron; *m* 1924, Marguerita Anne Mary Dennis. *Educ:* Canterbury Univ. Coll., New Zealand. Civil engineer, New Zealand Government engaged on developmental works; railway construction, irrigation and hydro-electric projects. Served 1914-18 with 1st NZEF overseas (twice wounded). Lt-Col NZ Eng. 2nd NZ Exp. Force, in Pacific, 1939-42; Dep. Comr Def. Constr.,

1942-44, in NZ and South Pacific. Past mem. Scientific and Industrial Research Council; FICE and past mem. of Council; FNZ Inst. of Engineers and past mem. of Council. *Recreation:* golf. *Address:* PO Box 3009, Raumati South, Paraparaumu, New Zealand.

MacKINLAY, Sir Bruce, Kt 1978; CBE 1970; company director; *b* 4 Oct. 1912; *s* of Daniel Robertson MacKinlay and Alice Victoria Rice; *m* 1943, Erica Ruth Fleming; two *s. Educ:* Scotch Coll. Served War, AASC, 1940-45 (Lieut). Director: J. Gadsden Australia Ltd, 1954-77; Whittakers Ltd, 1975-; Chm. Local Bd, Chamber of Manufactures Insurance Ltd, 1977-. President: WA Chamber of Manufactures, 1958-61; Confedn of WA Industry, 1976-78; WA Employers' Fedn, 1974-75; Fremantle Rotary Club, 1956; Vice-Pres., Associated Chambers of Manufactures of Aust., 1960. Chairman: WA Inst. of Dirs, 1975-77; WA Div., National Packaging Assoc., 1967-69; WA Finance Cttee for the Duke of Edinburgh's Third Commonwealth Study Conf., 1967-68; Mem., Commonwealth Manufg Industries Adv. Council, 1962-70. Leader: Aust. Trade Mission, E Africa, 1968; WA Trade Mission, Italy, 1970; Employers' Rep., Internat. Labour Conf., 1977; Comr, State Electricity Commn, 1961-74. Univ. of Western Australia: Mem. Senate, 1970-; Chm., Master of Business Admin Appeal, 1973. Life Governor, Scotch Coll. Council (Chm., 1969-74); Councillor: Organising Council of Commonwealth and Empire Games, 1962; Keep Australia Beautiful (WA), 1967- (Chm., 1981-); Aust. Council on Population and Ethnic Affairs, 1981-. *Recreations:* swimming, gardening. *Address:* 9B Melville Street, Claremont, WA 6010, Australia. *T:* 3832220. *Clubs:* Weld, WACA, Claremont Football (WA).

McKINLEY, Air Vice-Marshal David Cecil, CB 1966; CBE 1957; DFC 1940; AFC 1944, Bar 1945; RAF; *b* 18 Sept. 1913; *s* of David McKinley, Civil Engineer, and May McKinley (*née* Ward); *m* 1940, Brenda Alice (*née* Ridgway); three *s. Educ:* Bishop Foy Sch., Waterford; Trinity Coll., Dublin. Radio Engineering, Ferranti Ltd, 1935. Entered (regular) Royal Air Force, 1935; served continuously since that date; AOC Malta and Dep. C-in-C (Air), Allied Forces, Mediterranean, 1963-65; SASO, Transport Command, 1966, Air Support Command, 1967-68; retired 1968. Freeman, The Guild of Air Pilots and Air Navigators, 1959. FIN 1949. *Recreations:* sailing, fishing, water ski-ing, gardening. *Address:* Sundial Cottage, Fawley, Hants. *T:* Fawley 891031; Midland Bank, Bushey, Herts. *Club:* Royal Air Force.

McKINNEY, Mrs J. P.; see Wright, Judith.

McKINNEY, Sheila Mary Deirdre; Her Honour Judge McKinney; a Circuit Judge, since 1981; *b* 20 Oct. 1928; *d* of Patrick Peter McKinney and Mary Edith (*née* Conoley). *Educ:* Convent of the Cross, Boscombe, Bournemouth. Called to the Bar, Lincoln's Inn, 1951; a Recorder of the Crown Court, 1978-81. *Address:* 33 Granville Road, Boscombe, Bournemouth, Dorset. *T:* Bournemouth 423452.

MACKINNON, Angus, DSO 1945; MC 1940; TD; Director, Brown Shipley Holdings Ltd, since 1960; *b* 20 Feb. 1911; *s* of late William and Lucy Vere Mackinnon; *m* 1947, Beatrice Marsinah Neison; two *s. Educ:* Eton; Pembroke Coll., Oxford. Gray Dawes & Co., 1932; Mackinnon Mackenzie & Co, Calcutta, 1933-38. Joined Argyll and Sutherland Highlanders (TA), 1939; served BEF, MEF and BLA (despatches); comd 7th Bn A&SH, 1944-45, 51st Highland Div. Joined Brown Shipley & Co. Ltd, 1946, Chm., 1953-63, retired 1976; Chairman: Agricultural Credit Corp., 1959-75; Accepting Houses Cttee, 1967-70; Australia and New Zealand Banking Gp, 1975-77; Director: Australian Pastoral Co., 1955-71; P&O Steam Navigation Co., 1962-72; Guardian Royal Exchange Assurance, 1968-81; Inchcape & Co. Ltd. Chairman: Royal Nat. Orthopaedic Hosp., 1969-78; Governors, Keil Sch., Dumbarton, 1950-. An Underwriting Member of Lloyd's. *Recreations:* shooting, fishing, golf. *Address:* Hunton Manor, Sutton Scotney, Winchester, Hants SO21 3PT. *T:* Sutton Scotney 202. *Clubs:* White's, City.

MacKINNON, Prof. Donald MacKenzie, MA; FBA 1978; Norris-Hulse Professor of Divinity, Cambridge University, 1960-78; Fellow of Corpus Christi College, Cambridge, since 1960; *b* Oban, 27 Aug. 1913; *o s* of late D. M. MacKinnon, Procurator Fiscal, and late Grace Isabella Rhind; *m* 1939, Lois, *e d* of late Rev. Oliver Dryer; no *c. Educ:* Cargilfield Sch., Edinburgh; Winchester Coll. (scholar); New Coll., Oxford (scholar). Asst in Moral Philosophy (to late Prof. A. E. Taylor) at Edinburgh, 1936-37; Fellow and Tutor in Philosophy at Keble Coll., Oxford, 1937-47; Dir of Course for special courses in Philosophy for RN and RAF cadets at Oxford, 1942-45; Lectr in Philosophy at Balliol Coll., 1945-47; Wilde Lectr in Natural and Comparative Religion at Oxford, 1945-47; Regius Prof. of Moral Philosophy at Aberdeen, 1947-60. Lectures: Scott Holland, 1952; Hobhouse, 1953; Stanton, in the Philosophy of Religion, Cambridge, 1956-59; Gifford, Edinburgh, 1965-66; Prideaux, Exeter, 1966; Coffin, London, 1968; Riddell, Newcastle-upon-Tyne, 1970; D. Owen Evans, Aberystwyth, 1973; Drummond, Stirling, 1977; Martin Wight Meml, LSE, 1979; Boutwood, CCC Cambridge, 1981. *Publications:* Aristotelian Soc., 1976-77; Soc. for Study of Theol., 1981-82. Hon. DD Aberdeen, 1961. Mem. Labour Party. *Publications:* (ed) Christian Faith and Communist Faith, 1953; The Notion of a Philosophy of History, 1954; A Study in Ethical Theory, 1957; (with Prof. G. W. H. Lampe) The Resurrection, 1966; Borderlands of Theology and other papers, 1968; The Stripping of the Altars, 1969; The Problem of Metaphysics, 1974; Explorations in Theology 5, 1979; Creon and Antigone, 1981; articles, reviews, etc in periodicals and symposia in UK, France, Italy and Germany. *Recreations:* walking, cats, the cinema. *Address:* Dunbar

Cottage, 10 Dunbar Street, Old Aberdeen; Tigh Grianach, North Connel, Argyll.

MACKINNON, Duncan; *b* 18 Sept. 1909; *e s* of late Capt. William Mackinnon, Loup, Clachan, Argyll; *m* 1932, Pamela Rachel, 2nd *d* of late Capt. R. B. Brassey; one *s* one *d. Educ:* Eton; Magdalen, Oxford. Served War of 1939-45, Argyll and Sutherland Highlanders. Dep. Chm. Eagle Star Assurance Co. Ltd; Director: Smith St Aubyn & Co. (Holdings) Ltd; Hambros Investment Trust Ltd; Chm., Discount & General Securities Ltd. Chm., London Discount Market Assoc., 1959-61. JP Oxfordshire, 1945-56; High Sheriff of Oxfordshire, 1949-50. *Recreations:* fishing, shooting. *Address:* 100 Lancaster Gate, W2 3NY; Swinbrook House, Burford, Oxfordshire. *T:* Burford 2216. *Club:* White's.

McKINNON, Dr Kenneth Richard, FACE; Vice-Chancellor, University of Wollongong, Australia, since 1981; *b* 23 Feb. 1931; *s* of Charles and Grace McKinnon; *m* 1st, 1956 (marr. diss.); one *s*; 2nd, 1981, Suzanne Hopkin. *Educ:* Univ. of Adelaide (BA); Univ. of Queensland (BEd); Harvard Univ. (EdD). FACE 1972. Teacher, headmaster and administrator, 1957-65; Dir of Educn, Papua New Guinea, 1966-73; Mem., Australia Council, 1974-77 (Dep. Chm., 1976-77). Chm., Australian Schs Commn, 1973-81; Consultant in the Arts, Aust. Govt, 1981. *Publications:* Realistic Educational Planning, 1973; articles in jls and papers. *Recreations:* swimming, theatre, music, reading. *Address:* 2 Parrish Avenue, Mt Pleasant, Wollongong, NSW 2519, Australia. *T:* (042) 842-926. *Club:* Commonwealth (Canberra, Australia).

McKINNON, His Honour Neil Nairn, QC 1957; an Additional Judge, Central Criminal Court, 1968-82; *b* 19 Aug. 1909; *s* of late Neil Somerville and Christina McKinnon, Melbourne; *m* 1937, Janet, *d* of late Michael Lilley, Osterley; three *s* four *d. Educ:* Geelong Coll.; Trinity Hall, Cambridge (MA). Squadron Leader, RAFVR, Feb. 1940-Dec. 1945. Called to the Bar, Lincoln's Inn, 1937; Bencher, 1964. Recorder of Maidstone, 1961-68. *Recreation:* cricket. *Club:* Hawks (Cambridge).
See also S. N. McKinnon.

MACKINNON, Dame Patricia; see Mackinnon, Dame U. P.

MACKINNON, Peter Ralph, DSC 1942; Underwriting Member of Lloyd's, retired 1974; *b* 6 May 1911; *s* of Norman MacKinnon; *m* 1934, Jean Mary, *d* of G. N. Ogilvie; one *s* two *d. Educ:* Wellington Coll.; Jesus Coll., Cambridge. Entered Lloyd's, 1931; Underwriting Mem., 1932; Dep. Chm., 1964; Member: Cttee, Lloyd's Underwriters Assoc., 1958-73; Cttee of Lloyd's, 1961-64; Cttee Lloyd's Register of Shipping, 1958. Served War of 1939-45: RNVR, 1940; Combined Ops, Europe, N Africa, India, Malaya, Pacific (DSC, despatches twice); retd as Comdr RNVR, 1945. *Recreations:* golf, tennis. *Address:* Gorse Heath, Gerrards Cross, Bucks. *T:* Gerrards Cross 83451. *Clubs:* City University; All England Lawn Tennis; Denham Golf.

McKINNON, Stuart Neil, QC 1980; *b* 14 Aug. 1938; *s* of His Honour Neil Nairn McKinnon, *qv*; *m* 1966, Helena Jacoba Sara (*née* van Hoorn); two *d. Educ:* King's Coll. Sch., Wimbledon; Council of Legal Educn; Trinity Hall, Cambridge (LLB 1963, MA). Called to the Bar, Lincoln's Inn, 1960. *Recreations:* cricket, golf. *Address:* 1 The Ridgeway, Sanderstead, Surrey CR2 0LG. *T:* 01-657 4379. *Clubs:* Purley Cricket (Purley, Surrey); Croham Hurst Golf (South Croydon).

MACKINNON, Dame (Una) Patricia, DBE 1977 (CBE 1972); *b* Brisbane, 24 July 1911; *d* of Ernest T. and Pauline Bell; *m* 1936, Alistair Scobie Mackinnon; one *s* one *d. Educ:* Glennie School and St Margaret's School, Queensland. Member Cttee of Management, Royal Children's Hospital, Melbourne, 1948; Vice-President, 1958; President, 1965-79. *Recreations:* gardening, reading history and biographies. *Address:* 5 Moralla Road, Kooyong, Victoria 3144, Australia. *T:* 20-2733. *Club:* Alexandra (Melbourne).

McKINNON, Maj.-Gen. Walter Sneddon, CB 1966; CBE 1961 (OBE 1947); *b* 8 July 1910; *s* of Charles McKinnon and Janet Robertson McKinnon (*née* Sneddon); *m* 1937, Anna Bloomfield Plimmer; four *s* one *d. Educ:* Otago Boys High Sch., Dunedin, NZ; Otago Univ. (BSc); commissioned in NZ Army, 1935; various military courses, including Staff Coll., Camberley, England. Served War of 1939-45: Pacific, Italy (Lt-Col; despatches), Japan (occupation) (OBE); Brigadier, 1953; subsequent appointments: Comdr, Southern Mil. Dist (NZ), 1953; Head, NZ Joint Mil. Mission, Washington, DC, 1954-57; Comdr, Northern Military District, 1957-58; Adjutant-General, 1958-62; Quartermaster-General, 1963-65, Maj.-General, 1965; Chief of the General Staff, NZ Army, 1965-67; retired, 1967. Chm., NZ Broadcasting Corp., 1969-74. Member: Taupo Borough Council, 1977-80; Tongariro United Council, 1979-80. Pres., Taupo Regional Museum and Art Centre, 1975-79; Mem., Social Develt Council, New Zealand, 1976-79. *Recreations:* golf, fishing and gardening. *Address:* 43 Birch Street, Taupo, New Zealand. *Clubs:* Wellesley (Wellington); Taupo Golf.

MACKINTOSH, family name of Viscount Mackintosh of Halifax.

MACKINTOSH OF HALIFAX, 3rd Viscount *cr* 1957; **John Clive Mackintosh;** Bt 1935; Baron 1948; *b* 9 Sept. 1958; *s* of 2nd Viscount Mackintosh of Halifax, OBE, BEM; *S* father, 1980; *m* 1982, Elizabeth, *o d* of late David G. Lakin. *Educ:* The Leys School, Cambridge; Oriel College,

Oxford (BA in PPE). President, Oxford Univ. Conservative Assoc., 1979. *Recreations:* cricket, squash, hockey. *Heir: b* Hon. Graham Charles Mackintosh, *b* 12 March 1964. *Address:* House of Lords, SW1. *Clubs:* MCC, United Oxford & Cambridge University, East India, Coningsby.

MacKINTOSH, Sir Angus (MacKay), KCVO 1972; CMG 1958; HM Diplomatic Service, retired; British High Commissioner in Sri Lanka and Ambassador to the Republic of Maldives, 1969-73; *b* 23 July 1915; *s* of Angus MacKintosh, JP, Inverness; *m* 1947, Robina Marigold, *d* of J. A. Cochrane, MC; one *s* three *d. Educ:* Fettes Coll., Edinburgh; University College, Oxford (MA, BLitt). Agricultural Economics Research Institute, Oxford, 1938-41; Nuffield Colonial Research, Oxford, 1941-42. Served Army, 1942-46: Adjutant, 2nd Bn Queen's Own Cameron Highlanders; Major; despatches. Entered Colonial Office as Principal, 1946; Principal Private Secretary to Secretary of State, 1950; Assistant Secretary, 1952; seconded to Foreign Service as Dep. Commissioner-General for the UK in SE Asia, 1956-60; seconded to Cabinet Office, 1961-63; HM High Comr for Brunei, 1963-64; Asst Sec., Min. of Defence, 1964-65; Asst Under-Sec. of State, 1965-66; Senior Civilian Instructor, Imperial Defence Coll., 1966-68; Asst Under-Sec. of State, FCO, 1968-69. DK (Brunei), 1963; NSAIV (Maldives), 1972. *Address:* 9 Leven Terrace, Edinburgh EH3 9LW. *T:* 031-229 1091; Fenecreich, Gorthleck, Inverness IV1 2YS. *T:* Gorthleck 652. *Club:* Royal Commonwealth Society.

MACKINTOSH, David Forbes; Headmaster of Loretto, 1945-60; retired; *b* 7 May 1900; *s* of late Very Rev. Professor H. R. Mackintosh, DD; *m* 1930, Caroline Elisabeth, *o d* of Cyril Meade-King, Clifton, Bristol; three *s* one *d. Educ:* Merchiston; Oriel Coll., Oxford (MA); Princeton Univ., NJ (AM). Assistant Master at Clifton Coll., 1924-45; Housemaster, 1930-45. Conroy Fellow, St Paul's Sch., USA, 1960. Chm., Scottish Assoc. of Boys' Clubs, 1962-69. *Recreations:* gardening, bowls. *Address:* Bowling Green Cottage, Broadwell, by Lechlade, Glos GL7 3QS. *T:* Filkins 336.

MACKINTOSH, Duncan Robert, CBE 1969 (OBE 1948); *b* 4 Oct. 1902; *s* of Duncan H. Mackintosh; *m* 1937, Mary Isa Grant; one *s* three *d. Educ:* RN Colleges Osborne and Dartmouth; University Coll., London. Served with Royal Dutch Shell Group of Oil Cos, in China, Middle East and London, 1923-58. Mem. British Council. Chm. Exec. Cttee, Voluntary Service Overseas, (VSO), 1962-70. *Publications:* (with Alan Ayling): A Collection of Chinese Lyrics, 1965; A Further Collection of Chinese Lyrics, 1969; A Folding Screen, 1974. *Recreations:* bird-watching, gardening. *Address:* Apple Tree Cottage, Oaksey, Malmesbury, Wilts SN16 9TG. *T:* Crudwell 431. *Club:* Athenæum.

MACKINTOSH, (Hugh) Stewart, CBE 1956; Chairman, Scottish Sports Council, 1966-68; Chief Education Officer, Glasgow, 1944-68; *b* 1903; *s* of William Mackintosh, Helmsdale, Sutherland; *m* 1933, Mary, *d* of James Wilson. *Educ:* Helmsdale, Sutherland; Glasgow Univ. (MA, BSc, MEd); Aberdeen Univ. (PhD). Director of Education: Wigtownshire, 1931-37; Aberdeen, 1937-44; Glasgow, 1944. FEIS 1958; Hon. LLD Glasgow, 1969. *Address:* 12 Merrylee Road, Glasgow G43 2SH; Bayview, Helmsdale, Sutherland.

McKINTOSH, Ian; Partner, Lemon & Co., Swindon, since 1969; a Recorder of the Crown Court, since 1981; *b* 23 April 1938; *s* of Stanley and Gertrude McKintosh; *m* 1967, Alison Rosemary, *e d* of Kenneth Blayney Large and Margaret Wharton Large; two *s* one *d. Educ:* Leeds Grammar Sch.; Exeter Coll., Oxford (MA). Admitted Solicitor of the Supreme Court, 1966. Served RAF, 1957-59. Articled to Town Clerk, Chester and to Laces & Co., Liverpool, 1962-66; Dept of Solicitor to Metropolitan Police, New Scotland Yard, 1966-69. *Recreations:* cricket, sailing. *Address:* Whiteacre, Fyfield, Marlborough, Wilts SN8 1PX. *T:* Lockeridge 676. *Club:* XL.

MACKINTOSH, (John) Malcolm, CMG 1975; Assistant Secretary, Cabinet Office, since 1968; *b* 25 Dec. 1921; *s* of late James M. Mackintosh, MD, and Marjorie Mackintosh; *m* 1946, Elena Grafova; one *s* one *d* (and one *s* decd). *Educ:* Mill Hill; Edinburgh Academy; Glasgow Univ. MA (Hons) 1948. Served War, Middle East, Italy and Balkans, 1942-46; Allied Control Commn, Bulgaria, 1945-46. Glasgow Univ., 1946-48. Programme Organiser, BBC Overseas Service, 1948-60. Foreign Office, engaged on research, 1960-68. *Publications:* Strategy and Tactics of Soviet Foreign Policy, 1962, 2nd edn 1963; Juggernaut: a history of the Soviet armed forces, 1967. *Recreations:* walking, climbing. *Address:* 21 Ravensdale Avenue, N12 9HP. *T:* 01-445 9714. *Club:* Garrick.

MACKINTOSH OF MACKINTOSH, Lt-Comdr Lachlan Ronald Duncan, OBE 1972; 30th Chief of Clan Mackintosh; Vice-Lieutenant of Inverness-shire since 1971; Chairman, Highland Exhibitions Ltd, since 1964; *b* 27 June 1928; *o s* of Vice-Adm. Lachlan Donald Mackintosh of Mackintosh, CB, DSO, DSC (*d* 1957); *m* 1962, Mabel Cecilia Helen (Celia), *yr d* of Captain Hon. John Bernard Bruce, RN; one *s* two *d* (and one *d* decd). *Educ:* Elstree; RNC Dartmouth. Flag Lieut to First Sea Lord, 1951; spec. communications, 1954; served in HM Yacht Britannia, 1957; retd 1963. Vice-Pres., Scottish Conservative and Unionist Assoc., 1969-71. DL 1965, CC 1970-75, Inverness-shire; Regional Cllr, Highland Region, 1974-. *Heir: s* John Lachlan Mackintosh, younger of Mackintosh, *b* 2 Oct. 1969. *Address:* Moy Hall, Moy, Inverness-shire IV13 7YQ. *T:* Tomatin 211. *Club:* Naval and Military.

MACKINTOSH, Malcolm; *see* Mackintosh, J. M.

MACKINTOSH, Prof. Nicholas John, DPhil; Professor of Experimental Psychology, and Professorial Fellow of King's College, University of Cambridge, since 1981; *b* 9 July 1935; *s* of Dr Ian and Daphne Mackintosh; / *m* 1st, 1960, Janet Ann Scott; one *s* one *d* ; 2nd, 1978, Bundy Wilson; one *s. Educ:* Winchester; Magdalen Coll., Oxford. BA 1960, MA, DPhil 1963. Univ. Lectr, Univ. of Oxford, 1964-67; Res. Fellow, Lincoln Coll., Oxford, 1966-67; Res. Prof., Dalhousie Univ., 1967-73; Prof., Univ. of Sussex, 1973-81. Visiting Professor: Univ. of Pennsylvania, 1965-66; Univ. of Hawaii, 1972-73; Bryn Mawr Coll., 1977. Editor, Qly Jl of Experimental Psychology, 1977-. *Publications:* (ed with W. K. Honig) Fundamental Issues in Associative Learning, 1969; (with N. S. Sutherland) Mechanisms of Animal Discrimination Learning, 1971; The Psychology of Animal Learning, 1974; papers in psychological journals. *Address:* Department of Experimental Psychology, Downing Street, Cambridge CB2 3EB. *T:* Cambridge 51386.

MACKINTOSH, Stewart; *see* Mackintosh, H. S.

McKISSOCK, Sir Wylie, Kt 1971; OBE 1946; MS (London), FRCS; Consulting Neurological Surgeon in London, 1936-71, now retired; Neurological Surgeon, National Hospital for Nervous Diseases, Queen Square and Metropolitan Ear, Nose and Throat Hospital; Neurological Surgeon, Hospital for Sick Children, Great Ormond Street; Neurological Surgeon, St Andrew's Hospital, Northampton; Visiting Neurological Surgeon, Graylingwell Hospital, Chichester, St James's Hospital, Portsmouth, Belmont Hospital, Sutton, and Park Prewett Hospital, Basingstoke; Associate Neurological Surgeon, Royal Marsden Hospital; Director of Institute of Neurology, Queen Square; Surgeon in Charge, Department of Neuro-Surgery, Atkinson Morley Hospital branch of St George's Hospital; Hon. Civil Consultant in Neuro-Surgery to RAF; Hon. Neurological Surgeon, Welsh Regional Hospital Board; Teacher of Surgery, St George's Hospital Medical School (University of London); Member, Panel of Consultants, Royal Navy, British European Airways, British Overseas Airways Corporation; *b* 27 Oct. 1906; *s* of late Alexander Cathie McKissock; *m* 1934, Rachel, *d* of Leonard Marcus Jones, Beckenham, Kent; one *s* two *d. Educ:* King's Coll. and St George's Hospital, University of London. Junior University Schol., St George's Hospital, 1928; Laking Memorial Prize, 1932-33 and 1933-34; Rockefeller Schol. in Neuro-Surgery, 1937-38; Casualty Officer, House Surgeon, House Physician, House Surgeon to Ear, Nose, Throat and Eye Depts, Assistant Curator of Museum, Surgical Registrar, Surgical Chief Asst, St George's Hosp.; Surgical Registrar, Maida Vale Hosp. for Nervous Diseases, Hosp. for Sick Children, Great Ormond St, and Victoria Hospital for Children, Tite St. FRSM; Fellow, Society of British Neurological Surgeons (President), 1966); FRCR (Hon.) 1962; Corresponding Member, American Association of Neurological Surgeons, 1968. Hon. DSc, Newcastle upon Tyne, 1966. *Publications:* contributions to medical journals. *Recreations:* wine, food, gardening, ornithology, antagonism to Bureaucracy and the enjoyment of retirement. *Address:* Camus na Harry, Lechnaside, Gairloch, West Ross. *T:* Badachro 224.

MACKLEN, Victor Harry Burton, CB 1975; *b* 13 July 1919; *s* of H. Macklen and A. C. Macklen, Brighton, Sussex; *m* 1950, Ursula Irene Fellows; one *d. Educ:* Varndean Sch., Brighton; King's Coll., London. Air Defence Experimental Establishment, 1941; Operational Research Group, 1942; served Army, 1943-49; WO Scientific Staff, 1949-51; Head, Operational Research Section, BAOR, 1951-54; MoD Scientific Staff, 1954-60; Head, Technical Secretariat Reactor Group, UKAEA, 1960-64; Dep. Director, Technical Operations Reactor Group, UKAEA, 1966-67; Asst Chief Scientific Adviser (Studies and Nuclear), MoD, 1967-69; Dep. Chief Scientific Adviser (Projects and Nuclear), MoD, 1969-79. FRSA 1975. *Address:* Stepp House, Hartlip, near Sittingbourne, Kent. *T:* Newington 842591. *Club:* Army and Navy.

MACKLEY, Garnet Hercules, CMG 1938; *b* Port Chalmers, 9 Dec. 1883; *s* of John Charles Mackley and Esther Styles; *m* 1914, Isabel Robertson; one *s. Educ:* Grammar Sch., Invercargill. Cadet in clerical division, Traffic Branch, NZ. Government Railways Department, 1900; had varied experience in railway work in all parts of Dominion in executive capacity; promoted through various ranks of District Office and Head Office; Chief Clerk, Railways Head Office, Wellington, 1928; Assistant General Manager, 1931; General Manager, 1933-40. MP for Masterton, 1943-46; for Wairarapa, 1946-49; MLC, 1950. *Recreations:* fishing, racing, golf, swimming, field athletics. *Address:* Hillview Rest Home, Hospital Road, Tekuiti, King Country, New Zealand.

MACKLEY, George, Hon. Retired RE 1972 (RE 1961; ARE 1950); *b* 13 May 1900; *m* 1927, Caroline Toller, Hemingford Grey; no *c. Educ:* Judd Sch., Tonbridge. Art master, various schools in Kent and Surrey, 1921-45; Headmaster, Thames Ditton Primary Sch., 1945-53; Headmaster, Sutton East Secondary Sch. and Art Department, 1953-60. Hon. Mem., Soc. of Wood Engravers (Associate, 1946). Mem., 1948; Mem., Art Workers' Guild, 1959. Works in permanent collections: Victoria and Albert Museum; Ashmolean Museum; Fitzwilliam Museum; South London Art Gallery; Nat. Museum of Art, Stockholm; Hunt Botanical Library, Pittsburgh. *Publication:* Wood Engraving, 1948. *Recreations:* lurking by, and drawing, waterways and canal and river craft. *Address:* 7 Higham Lane, Tonbridge, Kent. *T:* Tonbridge 353968.

MACKLIN, Sir Bruce (Roy), Kt 1981; OBE 1970; FCA; company director; Chairman: South Australian Gas Company, since 1969; Robe River Ltd, since 1976; Onkaparinga Textiles Ltd, since 1982; *b* 23 April 1917; *s* of Hubert Vivian Macklin and Lillian Mabel Macklin; *m* 1944, Dorothy Potts, Tynemouth, England; two *s* one *d*. *Educ:* St Peter's Coll., Adelaide; St Mark's Coll., Univ. of Adelaide (AUA Commerce). Served RAAF (Aircrew), 1941-45. Practising chartered accountant, 1947-69. Director of eight major Aust. companies; Pres., Aust. Chamber of Commerce, 1967-69. Hon. Consul in S Aust. for Fed. Republic of Germany, 1968-; Leader, Aust. Govt Mission to Papua New Guinea, 1971. Mem. Council of Governors, St Peter's Coll., 1962-69; Mem. Council, Univ. of Adelaide, 1965-71. A Founder, Adelaide Festival of Arts, 1958, Chm. Bd of Governors, 1972-78; Dir, Queen Elizabeth II Silver Jubilee Trust for Young Australians. Silver Jubilee Medal 1977; Officer's Cross, Order of Merit of Fed. Republic of Germany, 1978. *Recreations:* tennis, gardening, music. *Address:* 45 Grenfell Street, Adelaide, SA 5000, Australia. *T:* 212-1533. *Clubs:* Adelaide, Naval, Military and Air Force (South Australia).

MACKLIN, David Drury; Chief Executive, Devon County Council, since 1979; *b* 1 Sept. 1928; *s* of Laurence Hilary Macklin and Alice Dumergue (*née* Tait); *m* 1955, Janet Smallwood; four *s*. *Educ:* Felsted Sch., Essex; St John's Coll., Cambridge. MA. Articled to Baileys Shaw & Gillett, Solicitors, 1951-54; Assistant Solicitor: Coward Chance & Co., 1954-56; Warwickshire CC, 1956-61; Devon CC, 1961-69; Dep. Clerk, Derbyshire CC, 1969-73; Chief Exec., Lincolnshire CC, 1973-79. *Recreations:* rowing, sailing, music, golf, theatre, walking. *Address:* County Hall, Exeter, Devon EX2 4QD. *T:* Exeter 77977.

MACKNIGHT, Dame Ella (Annie Noble), DBE 1969; Consultant Emeritus (Obstetrician and Gynaecologist), Queen Victoria Hospital, Melbourne, since 1964; *b* 7 Aug. 1904; 4th *d* of Dr Conway Macknight. *Educ:* Toorak Coll., Melbourne; Univ. of Melbourne, resident student, Janet Clarke Hall. MB, BS 1928; MD Melbourne 1931; DGO Melbourne 1936; MRCOG 1951; FRCOG 1958; FRACS 1971; FAGO 1973; FRACOG (FAustCOG 1978); Fellow AMA, 1976. Hon. Obstetrician and Gynaecologist, Queen Victoria Hosp., Melbourne, 1935-64; Pres., Queen Victoria Hosp., Melbourne, 1971-77 (Vice-Pres., 1965-71); Hon. Sec., 1963-67, Vice-Pres., 1967-70, Pres., 1970-72, Australian Council, RCOG. Hon. MD Monash, 1972. *Recreation:* golf. *Address:* 692 Toorak Road, Malvern, Victoria 3144, Australia. *Clubs:* Lyceum (Melbourne); Royal Melbourne Golf.

MACKSEY, Kenneth John, MC 1944; freelance author, since 1968; consultant to Canadian Armed Forces, since 1981; *b* 1 July 1923; *s* of Henry George Macksey and Alice Lilian (*née* Nightingall); *m* 1946, Catherine Angela Joan Little; one *s* one *d*. *Educ:* Goudhurst Sch.; Sandhurst; Army Staff Coll., Camberley. Served War, RAC: trooper, 1941-44; commnd 141st Regt RAC (The Buffs), 1944; Western Europe, 1944-45; Royal Tank Regt, 1946; served: India, 1947; Korea, 1950; Germany, 1957 and 1960-62; Singapore, 1958-60; retd, 1968. Dep. Editor, Purnell's History of the Second World War, and History of the First World War, 1968-70. Town Councillor, 1972-. *Publications:* To the Green Fields Beyond, 1965 (2nd edn 1977); The Shadow of Vimy Ridge, 1965; Armoured Crusader: the biography of Major-General Sir Percy Hobart, 1967; Afrika Korps, 1968 (4th edn 1976); Panzer Division, 1968 (4th edn 1976); Crucible of Power, 1969; Tank, 1970 (3rd edn 1975); Tank Force, 1970; Beda Fomm, 1971; Tank Warfare, 1971 (rev. edn 1976); Vimy Ridge, 1972; Guinness Book of Tank Facts and Feats, 1972 (3rd edn 1980); The Guinness History of Land Warfare, 1973 (2nd edn 1976); Battle, 1974; The Partisans of Europe, 1975; (jtly) The Guinness History of Sea Warfare, 1975; Guderian, Panzer General, 1975 (2nd edn 1976); (with Joan Macksey) The Guinness Guide to Feminine Achievements, 1975; (jtly) The Guinness History of Air Warfare, 1976; The Guinness Book of 1952, 1977; The Guinness Book of 1953, 1978; The Guinness Book of 1954, 1978; Kesselring: the making of the Luftwaffe, 1978; Rommel: battles and campaigns, 1979; The Tanks, vol. 3, 1979; Invasion, 1980; The Tank Pioneers, 1981; articles and reviews in RUSI Jl, Army Qly, Brit. Army Rev., and The Tank. *Recreations:* umpiring hockey, listening to music, living in Beaminster. *Address:* Whatley Mill, Beaminster, Dorset DT8 3EN. *T:* Beaminster 862321. *Clubs:* Savage; Social (Beaminster).

McKUEN, Rod; poet, composer, author, performer, columnist; *b* Oakland, Calif, 29 April 1933. Has appeared in numerous films, TV, concerts, nightclubs, and with symphony orchestras. Composer: modern classical music; scores for motion pictures and TV. President: Stanyan Records; Discus Records; New Gramophone Soc.; Mr Kelly Prodns; Montcalm Prodns; Stanyan Books; Cheval Books; Biplane Books; Rod McKuen Enterprises; Vice-Pres., Tamarack Books; Dir, Animal Concern. Member: Bd of Governors, Nat. Acad. of Recording Arts and Scis; Board of Directors: Amer. Nat. Theatre of Ballet; Amer. Dance Ensemble; Amer. Guild of Authors and Composers; Advisory Board: Market Theatre, Johannesburg; Internat. Platform Assoc.; Internat. Educn; Vice President: Amer. Guild of Variety Artists; Adv. Bd, Fund for Animals; ASCAP; Writers' Guild; AFTRA; MPA; AGVA. Has won numerous awards, including Grammy for best spoken word album, Lonesome Cities; nominated Pulitzer Prize in classical music for The City, 1973. *Publications:* And Autumn Came, 1954; Stanyan Street and Other Sorrows, 1966; Listen to the Warm, 1967; Lonesome Cities, 1968; Twelve Years of Christmas, 1968; In Someone's Shadow, 1969; A Man Alone, 1969; With Love, 1970; Caught in the Quiet, 1970; New Ballads, 1970; Fields of Wonder, 1971; The Carols of Christmas, 1971; And to Each Season, 1972;

Pastorale, 1972; Grand Tour, 1972; Beyond the Boardwalk, 1972; Come to Me in Silence, 1973; America: an Affirmation, 1974; Seasons in the Sun, 1974; Alone, Moment to Moment, 1974; The McKuen Omnibus, 1975; Alone, 1975; Celebrations of the Heart, 1975; The Sea Around Me, the Hills Above, 1976; Finding my Father: one man's search for identity, 1977; Hand in Hand, 1977; Coming Close to the Earth, 1978; We Touch the Sky, 1979; Love's Been Good to Me, 1979; Looking for a Friend, 1980; An Outstretched Hand, 1980; The Power Bright and Shining, 1980; Too Many Midnights, 1981; Rod McKuen's Book of Days, 1981; The Beautiful Strangers, 1981; *major classical works:* Symphony No One; Concerto for Guitar and Orchestra; Concerto for Four Harpsichords; Concerto for Cello and Orch.; Concerto for Bassoon and Orch.; Seascapes for Piano and Orchestra; Adagio for Harp and Strings; Piano Variations; various other classical commns; numerous lyrics; *film scores:* Joanna, 1968; The Prime of Miss Jean Brodie (Academy Award Nomination), 1969; Me, Natalie, 1969; A Boy Named Charlie Brown (Academy Award Nomination), 1970; Come to your Senses, 1971; Scandalous John, 1971; Wildflowers, 1971; The Borrowers, 1973; Lisa Bright and Dark, 1973; Emily, 1975; The Unknown War, 1979. *Address:* PO Box G, Beverly Hills, Calif 90213, USA; (business) 8440 Santa Monica Blvd, Los Angeles, Calif 90069.

MACKWORTH, Commander Sir David Arthur Geoffrey, 9th Bt, *cr* 1776; RN retired; Managing Director, South Coast Rod Rigging Company Ltd; *b* 13 July 1912; *o s* of late Vice-Admiral Geoffrey Mackworth, CMG, DSO, and Noel Mabel, *d* of late William I. Langford; *S* uncle, 1952; *m* 1st, 1941, Mary Alice (marr. diss. 1972), *d* of Thomas Henry Grylls; one *s*; 2nd, 1973, Beryl Joan, formerly wife of late Ernest Henry Sparkes, and 3rd *d* of late Pembroke Henry Cockayn Cross and of Jeanie Cross. *Educ:* Farnborough Sch., Hants; RNC Dartmouth. Joined RN 1926; served HMS Eagle, HMS Suffolk, 1939-45; Commander, 1948; Naval Adviser to Director of Guided Weapon Research and Development, Ministry of Supply, 1945-49; retired, 1956. MRIN. *Recreations:* sailing, cruising. Heir: *s* Digby John Mackworth [*b* 2 Nov. 1945; *m* 1971, Antoinette Francesca, *d* of Henry James McKenna, Ilford, Essex; one *d*. *Educ:* Wellington Coll. Served Australian Army Aviation Corps, Malaysia and Vietnam (Lieut). With British Airways Helicopters]. *Address:* 36 Wittering Road, Hayling Island, Hants. *Clubs:* Royal Ocean Racing; Royal Naval and Royal Albert Yacht (Portsmouth); Royal Corinthian Yacht; Royal Naval Sailing Association.

MACKWORTH-YOUNG, (Gerard) William; Chairman, Morgan Grenfell & Co. Ltd, since 1980 (Director since 1974); *b* 10 Oct. 1926; *s* of late Gerard Mackworth-Young, CIE and Natalie Hely-Hutchinson; *m* 1949, Lady Evelyn Leslie, *d* of 20th Earl of Rothes; four *d*. *Educ:* Eton College. Served Welsh Guards, 1945-48 (Lieut, RARO). Partner, Rowe & Pitman, stockbrokers, 1953-73; Vice-Chm., Morgan Grenfell Holdings Ltd; Dep. Chm. and Chief Exec., Morgan Grenfell & Co. Ltd, 1975-79; Director: Union Discount Co. of London plc; Willis Faber plc; London Bd, Halifax Building Soc; Lloyds Bank plc; Charter Consolidated plc; Chm., Industrial Develt Adv. Bd, 1980-. *Recreation:* deerstalking. *Address:* 21 St Petersburgh Place, W2 4LA. *T:* 01-229 4270; Barrs Lodge, Taynuilt, Argyll. *Clubs:* Boodle's, Pratt's; Union (Sydney); Links (NY).
See also Sir R. C. Mackworth-Young.

MACKWORTH-YOUNG, Sir Robert Christopher, (Sir Robin Mackworth-Young), KCVO 1975 (CVO 1968; MVO 1961); Librarian, Windsor Castle, and Assistant Keeper of The Queen's Archives, since 1958; *b* 12 Feb. 1920; *s* of late Gerard Mackworth-Young, CIE; *m* 1953, Rosemarie, *d* of W. C. R. Aue, Menton, France; one *s*. *Educ:* Eton; King's Coll., Cambridge. Pres., Cambridge Union Soc., 1948. Served in RAF, 1939-46. HM Foreign Service, 1948-55; Deputy Librarian, Windsor Castle, 1955-58. FSA; Hon. FLA. *Recreations:* music, electronics, ski-ing. *Address:* Garden House, Windsor Castle. *Club:* Roxburghe.
See also G. W. Mackworth-Young.

McLACHLAN, Angus Henry; journalist; *b* 29 March 1908; *s* of James H. and Mabel McLachlan; unmarried. *Educ:* Scotch Coll., Melbourne; University of Melbourne. Melbourne Herald, 1928-36; joined Sydney Morning Herald, 1936; News Editor, 1937-49; General Manager, John Fairfax & Sons Ltd (publishers of Sydney Morning Herald, Australian Financial Review, Sun), 1949-64, Dir, 1965-80 (Man. Dir, 1965-70). Jt Man. Dir, Australian Associated Press Pty Ltd, 1965- (Chairman, 1958-59, 1964-65, 1975-77); Director: Reuters Ltd, London, 1966-71 (Trustee, 1979-); Amalgamated Television Services Pty Ltd, 1955-; Macquarie Broadcasting Holdings Ltd, 1966-80; David Syme & Co. Ltd, Publishers of The Age, 1970-79; Federal Capital Press Ltd, Publishers of Canberra Times, 1970-79; Mem. Council, Library of NSW, 1966-75 (Dep. Pres., 1974-75); Mem., Library Council of NSW, 1975-78; Member, Sydney University Extension Board, 1960-. *Address:* Box 5303, GPO, Sydney, NSW 2001, Australia. *T:* 233-1550. *Clubs:* London Press; Australian, University, Union (Sydney); Royal Sydney Yacht Squadron.

McLACHLAN, Gordon, CBE 1967; BCom; FCA; Secretary, Nuffield Provincial Hospitals Trust, since 1956; *b* 12 June 1918; *s* of late Gordon and Mary McLachlan; *m* 1951, Monica Mary Griffin; two *d*. *Educ:* Leith Academy; Edinburgh Univ. Served with RNVR, 1939-46; Gunnery Specialist, 1943-46. Accountant, Edinburgh Corp., 1946-48; Dep. Treas., NW Met. Regional Hosps Bd, 1948-53; Accountant Nuffield Foundn, Nuffield Provincial Hosps Trust, Nat. Corp. for Care of Old People, 1953-56. Asst Dir, Nuffield Foundn, 1955-56. Henry Cohen Lectr, Univ. of Jerusalem, 1969.

Consultant, American Hospitals Assoc. and American Hospitals Research and Educational Trust, 1964–65; Member Council, American Hospitals Research and Educational Trust, 1965–74 (citation for meritorious service, AHA, 1976); Mem., Inst. of Medicine, Nat. Acad. of Sciences, Washington DC, 1974–. Parker B. Francis Foundn Distinguished Lectr, Amer. Coll. of Hosp. Admin, 1976. General Editor, Nuffield Provincial Hospitals Trust publications; Consulting Editor, Health Services Research Journal (US), 1966–74. Hon. FRCGP 1978. Hon. LLD Birmingham, 1977. *Publications:* editor of many publications on Nuffield Provincial Hospitals Trust list; contrib. to Lancet, Practitioner, Times, Twentieth Century, etc. *Recreations:* reading, watching ballet, theatre, Rugby football. *Address:* 3 Prince Albert Road, NW1. *T:* 01-485 6632. *Club:* Caledonian.

McLACHLAN, Air Vice-Marshal Ian Dougald, CB 1966; CBE 1954; DFC 1940; Consultant, Northrop Corporation; *b* Melbourne, 23 July 1911; *s* of Dougald McLachlan, author and teacher, and Bertha Frances (*née* Gilliam); *m* 1946, Margaret Helen Chrystal (marr. diss. 1968); one *d. Educ:* Melbourne High Sch.; Royal Military Coll., Duntroon. Imperial Defence Coll. 1954; Dir, Flying Trng, Air Min., London 1955–56; Dep. Chief of Air Staff, Australia, 1959–61; Australian Defence Adviser, Washington, 1962–63; Air Mem. for Supply and Equipment, Australian Air Bd, 1964–68. *Recreations:* tennis, squash, golf. *Address:* 2 Eastbourne Road, Darling Point, NSW 2027, Australia. *T:* 326-1860. *Clubs:* Australian (Sydney); Naval and Military (Melbourne); Melbourne Cricket, Royal Sydney Golf, Royal Canberra Golf.

McLACHLAN, Peter John; Secretary, Belfast Voluntary Welfare Society, since 1980; *b* 21 Aug. 1936; *s* of Herbert John McLachlan and Joan Dorothy McLachlan (*née* Hall); *m* 1965, Gillian Mavis Lowe; two *d. Educ:* Magdalen College Sch., Oxford; Queen's Coll., Oxford (schol.; BA Lit. Hum.; MA). Administrative trainee, Min. of Finance, NICS, 1959–62; Administrator, NYO of GB, 1962–65 and 1966–69; Personal Asst to Chm., IPC, 1965–66; Cons. Res. Dept, 1970–72; Exec. Dir, Warsaw & Powell Ltd, 1972–73; Mem. (Unionist) S Antrim, NI Assembly, 1973–75; Gen. Manager, S. H. Watterson Engineering, 1975–77; Jt Man. Dir, Ulster Metalspinners Ltd, 1976–77; Projects Manager, Peace By Peace Ltd, 1977–79; Sec., Peace People Charitable Trust, 1977–79; Chm., Community of The Peace People, 1978–80. Founder Chairman: NI Fedn of Housing Assocs, 1976–78; Belfast Improved Houses Ltd, 1975–81; Chairman: NI Adv. Cttee, Community Service Volunteers, 1979–; NI Peace Forum, 1980–; Vice-Chm., NI Hospice Ltd, 1981–; Member: Gulbenkian Adv. Cttee on Community Work, 1978–80; The Corrymeela Community; Minister's Adv. Cttee on Community Work, NI, 1982–; Administrative Council: Royal Jubilee Trusts, 1975–81; NI Projects Trust. *Recreations:* piano playing, mountain walking, fostering young offenders. *Address:* 79 Antrim Road, Lisburn, Co. Antrim, Northern Ireland. *T:* Lisburn 6339.

MACLAGAN, Michael, FSA; FRHistS; Richmond Herald of Arms, since 1980; *b* 14 April 1914; *s* of Sir Eric Robert Dalrymple Maclagan, KCVO, CBE, and Helen Elizabeth (*née* Lascelles); *m* 1st, 1939, Brenda Alexander (marr. diss. 1946); one *s* ; 2nd, 1949, Jean Elizabeth Brooksbank Garnett, *d* of late Lt-Col W. B. Garnett, DSO; one *s* two *d. Educ:* Winchester Coll.; Christ Church, Oxford (BA 1st Cl. Hons Modern History, MA). FSA 1948; FRHistS 1961; FSG 1970; FHS 1972. Lectr, Christ Church, Oxford, 1937–39; Fellow of Trinity Coll., 1939–81, Emeritus Fellow 1981, Sen. Proctor, 1954–55. 2/Lieut TA, 1938; served war, 1939–46: 16/5 Lancers; sc; Major, GSOII War Office. Slains Pursuivant, 1948–70; Portcullis Pursuivant, 1970–80. Vis. Professor, Univ. of S Carolina, 1974; Fellow of Winchester Coll. 1975; Sen. Librarian, Oxford Union, 1960–70; Trustee, Oxford Union, 1970. Councillor, Oxford CBC, 1964–74; Sheriff, 1964–65; Lord Mayor of Oxford, 1970–71. Chm., Oxford Dio. Adv. Cttee, 1961–. OStJ 1952. *Publications:* (ed) Bede: Ecclesiastical History I and II, 1949; Trinity College, 1955, rev. edn 1963; (jtly) The Colour of Heraldry, 1958; (ed) Richard de Bury: Philobiblon, 1960; 'Clemency' Canning, 1962 (Wheatley Gold Medal); City of Constantinople, 1968; (with J. Louda) Lines of Succession, 1981; articles in DNB, VCH, etc. *Recreations:* real tennis, wine, walking, travel. *Address:* 20 Northmoor Road, Oxford OX2 6UR. *T:* Oxford 58536; Trinity College, Oxford OX1 3BH. *T:* Oxford 41801; College of Arms, Queen Victoria Street, EC4V 4BT. *Clubs:* Cavalry and Guards, Pratt's, City Livery; Oxford Union (Oxford).

MACLAGAN, Noel Francis, DSc, MD, FRCP, FRIC; retired; formerly Professor of Chemical Pathology in University of London at Westminster Medical School; Chemical Pathologist, Westminster Hospital, 1947–70; *b* 1904; *y s* of late Oscar Frederick and Ada Maclagan, Newcastle and London; *m* 1933, Annemarie, *d* of Curt and Marie Herzog, London; one *s* one *d. Educ:* University Coll. Sch.; University Coll., London (First Cl. Hons BSc Chemistry, 1925); Middlesex Hosp. Medical School (MSc London in Biochemistry, 1933). DSc London, 1946; MD London, 1935; MRCP, 1933; FRIC 1944; FRCP 1952. Asst in Courtauld Inst. of Biochemistry, Middlesex Hosp., 1926–33; House Physician Middlesex Hosp., 1932; whole-time worker for Medical Research Council, 1933–34; Biochemist, Westminster Hosp., 1935–46; Pathologist, EMS, 1939–45; Chemical Pathologist at Westminster Hosp. Medical Sch., 1946–47. Chm., Nuffield Project on Clinical Chemistry Labs, 1976–79. Editor, Annals of Clinical Biochemistry, 1974–76. *Publications:* contributions to medical textbooks on various biochemical subjects and articles in scientific journals on thymol turbidity test, thyroid function, lipid

metabolism, etc. *Recreations:* music and chess. *Address:* 40 Temple Fortune Lane, NW11. *T:* 01-458 4032. *Clubs:* Athenæum, Savage.

McLAREN, family name of **Baron Aberconway.**

McLAREN, Dr Anne Laura, FRS 1975; Director, Medical Research Council's Mammalian Development Unit, since 1974; *b* 26 April 1927; *d* of 2nd Baron Aberconway; *m* 1952, Donald Michie (marr. diss.); one *s* two *d. Educ:* Univ. of Oxford (MA, DPhil). Post-doctoral research, UCL, 1952–55 and Royal Vet. Coll., London, 1955–59; joined staff of ARC Unit of Animal Genetics at Edinburgh Univ., 1959. Mem., ARC, 1978–. Mem., Cttee of Managers, Royal Instn, 1976–. Scientific Medal, Zool Soc. London, 1967. *Publications:* Mammalian Chimaeras, 1976; papers on reproductive biology, embryology, genetics and immunology in sci. jls. *Address:* 9 Steele's Road, NW3 4SG.

McLAREN, Digby Johns, PhD; FRS 1979; FRSC 1968; Senior Science Adviser, Department of Energy, Mines and Resources, Ottawa, since 1981; *b* 11 Dec. 1919; *s* of James McLaren and Louie Kinsey; *m* 1942, Phyllis Matkin; two *s* one *d. Educ:* Sedbergh Sch.; Queens' Coll., Cambridge (BA, MA); Univ. of Michigan (PhD). Served RA (Gunner to Captain), ME and Italy, 1940–46. Field Geologist, Geological Survey of Canada, in Alberta and British Columbia Rocky Mountains, District of Mackenzie, Yukon Territory, Arctic Islands, 1948–80; first Dir, Inst. of Sedimentary and Petroleum Geology, Calgary, Alberta, 1967–73; Dir Gen., Geological Survey of Canada, 1973–80. Pres., Commn on Stratigraphy, IUGS, 1972–76; Chm. of Bd, Internat. Geol Correlation Programme, UNESCO-IUGS, 1976–80; IUGS Deleg. to People's Republic of China to advise on participation in international science, 1977. Corresp. Mem., Geol Soc. of France, 1975; Foreign Associate, Nat. Acad. of Scis, USA, 1979. Hon. DSc Ottawa, 1980. *Publications:* 70 memoirs, bulletins, papers, geological maps, and scientific contribs to journals on regional geology, paleontology, geological time and correlation. *Recreations:* skiing, swimming, gardening, music. *Address:* 248 Marilyn Avenue, Ottawa, Ont K1V 7E5, Canada. *T:* (613) 737-4360.

MacLAREN, Sir Hamish (Duncan), KBE 1951; CB 1946; DFC; Director of Electrical Engineering, Admiralty, 1945–60; *b* 7 April 1898; *s* of Rev. Peter MacLaren, MA, and Constance Hamilton Simpson; *m* 1927, Lorna Cicely, *d* of late Dr R. P. N. B. Bluett, MC, Harrow; one *s* one *d. Educ:* Fordyce Academy, Banffshire; Edinburgh Univ. (BSc 1921). Served European war, 1914–18, in RNVR, RNAS and RAF (DFC and Bar, French Croix de Guerre with Palm). After completing degree at Edinburgh Univ. in 1921 joined British Thomson Houston Co., Rugby, as student apprentice. Awarded Bursary by Commission for Exhibition of 1851 for 1921–23; British Thomson Houston Fellowship to spend one year with the GE Co. of Schenectady, USA, 1923–24; on staff of British Thomson Houston, Rugby, 1924–26; joined Admiralty Service as Asst Electrical Engineer, 1926. In Admiralty Service at HM Dockyards, Chatham, Devonport, at Dir of Dockyards Dept, Admiralty, 1933–37, and in Ceylon, 1931–33; Superintending Electrical Engineer, HM Naval Base, Singapore, 1937–40; Asst Dir, Electrical Engineering Dept, Admiralty, 1940–45. Pres. Instn of Electrical Engineers, 1960–61. Hon. LLD St Andrews, 1954; Hon. DSc Bath, 1970. *Address:* 104 Heath Road, Petersfield, Hants. *T:* Petersfield 4562.

McLAREN, Prof. Hugh Cameron; Professor of Obstetrics and Gynæcology, University of Birmingham, 1951–78, now Emeritus; *b* 25 April 1913; *s* of John and Flora McLaren, Glasgow; *m* 1939, Lois Muirhead, Bridge of Weir, Scotland; one *s* six *d. Educ:* High Sch. of Glasgow; Univ. of Glasgow; postgraduate studies Glasgow and Aberdeen. MB, ChB Glasgow 1936; MD (Glasgow). Served RAMC, 1941–46; Surgical Specialist (Lt-Col). Univ. of Birmingham, 1946, Reader, 1949. FRCPGlas; FRCSE; FRCOG. Hon. Fellow, Societas Gynaecologica et Obstetrica Italica, 1979. Hon. Mem., Amer. Medical Assoc., 1969. Officer, Legion of Merit (Rhodesia), 1977. *Publications:* The Prevention of Cervical Cancer, 1963; contribs to Journal of Obstetrics and Gynæcology, Lancet, Brit. Med. Jl, etc. *Recreations:* golf, gardening. *Address:* 26 Ampton Road, Birmingham B15 2UP. *T:* 021-440 3223.

McLAREN, Robin John Taylor, CMG 1982; HM Diplomatic Service; Political Adviser, Hong Kong, since 1981; *b* 14 Aug. 1934; *s* of late Robert Taylor McLaren and of Marie Rose McLaren (*née* Simond); *m* 1964, Susan Ellen Hatherly; one *s* two *d. Educ:* Richmond and East Sheen County Grammar Sch. for Boys; Ardingly Coll.; St John's Coll., Cambridge (Schol.; MA). Royal Navy, 1953–55. Entered Foreign Service, 1958; language student, Hong Kong, 1959–60; Third Sec., Peking, 1960–61; FO, 1961–64; Asst Private Sec. to Lord Privy Seal (Mr Edward Heath), 1963–64; Second, later First Sec., Rome, 1964–68; seconded to Hong Kong Govt as Asst Political Adviser, 1968–69; First Sec., FCO, 1970–73; Dep. Head of Western Organisations Dept, 1974–75; Counsellor and Head of Chancery, Copenhagen, 1975–78; Head of Hong Kong and Gen. Dept, 1978–79, of Far Eastern Dept, 1979–81, FCO. *Recreations:* music, China, hill-walking. *Address:* c/o Foreign and Commonwealth Office, SW1A 2AH. *Clubs:* United Oxford & Cambridge University; Hong Kong (Hong Kong).

McLAUCHLAN, Madeline Margaret Nicholls; Head Mistress, North London Collegiate School, since 1965; *b* 4 June 1922; *o c* of late Robert and Gertrude McLauchlan, Birmingham. *Educ:* King Edward VI Grammar Sch. for Girls, Camp Hill, Birmingham; Royal Holloway College, University of

London. Asst Mistress: Shrewsbury High Sch., GPDST, 1944; Manchester High Sch., 1952. Senior Walter Hines Page Scholar, E-SU, 1955. Head Mistress, Henrietta Barnett Sch., 1958. Chm., Schoolboy and Schoolgirl Exchange Cttee, E-SU (Mem., Educn Cttee, 1966); Member: Exec. Cttee, Assoc. of Head Mistresses, 1966-76, Chm., 1974-76; Exec. Cttee, UCCA, 1968-; Direct Grant Cttee, GBGSA, 1972-; Assisted Places Cttee, ISJC, 1980-; Council, Westfield Coll., Univ. of London, 1975-78; Vice-Chm., Council, Nat. Youth Orchestra, 1981 (Mem., 1975-). Governor: Imperial Coll., 1968-; Bedford Coll., 1981-. *Recreations:* music, mountain walking, housekeeping. *Address:* North London Collegiate School, Canons, Edgware, Mddx. *T:* 01-952 0912. *Club:* English-Speaking Union.

McLAUCHLAN, Thomas Joseph, JP; Stipendiary Magistrate, 1966-82; *b* 15 May 1917; *s* of Alexander and Helen McLauchlan; *m* 1945, Rose Catherine Gray, MA. *Educ:* St Aloysius Coll., Glasgow; Univ. of Glasgow (BL). Law apprentice, 1936-39 and 1946-47. War service, Merchant Navy and RAF Y Section, Signals Intell., Wireless Officer, 1940-46. Legal Asst to Manager of large industrial insurance co., 1947-49; Clerk to Glasgow Police Courts, 1949-66. JP Scotland. *Recreations:* golf, bridge, travel. *Address:* 75 Clouston Street, Glasgow G20 8QW. *T:* 041-946 4222. *Clubs:* Centenary, College (Glasgow).

McLAUGHLAN, Rear-Adm. Ian David, CB 1970; DSC 1941 and Bar, 1953; Admiral Commanding Reserves and Director General, Naval Recruiting, 1970-72, retired; *b* 2 May 1919; *s* of Richard John and Margaret McLaughlan; *m* 1942, Charity Pomeroy Simonds; two *d. Educ:* St Paul's Sch. Entered Navy, 1937; served in destroyers, 1940-45 (despatches three times); comd HMS: Flint Castle, 1948-50; Concord, 1950-52; jssc 1952; Armed Forces Staff Coll., Norfolk, Va, 1953; HMS Jupiter, 1953-55; comd HMS: Chieftain, 1955; Chevron, 1955-56 (despatches); Staff of C-in-C, Portsmouth, 1957-59; Asst Dir of Plans, Admty, 1959-61; Capt. (F), 2nd Frigate Sqdn, 1961-62; idc 1963; Dir, Naval Ops and Trade, 1964-66; comd HMS Hampshire, 1966-67; Chief of Staff to Comdr Far East Fleet, 1967-70. Comdr 1951; Capt. 1958; Rear-Adm. 1968. Commendador d'Aviz, 1956. *Recreations:* gardening, house husbandry. *Address:* The Five Gables, Mayfield, East Sussex. *T:* Mayfield 2218.

McLAUGHLIN, Mrs (Florence) Patricia (Alice), OBE 1975; *b* 23 June 1916; *o d* of late Canon F. B. Aldwell; *m* 1937, Henry, *o s* of late Major W. McLaughlin, of McLaughlin & Harvey Ltd, London, Belfast and Dublin; one *s* two *d. Educ:* Ashleigh House, Belfast; Trinity Coll., Dublin. MP (UU) Belfast West, 1955-64; Past Chm., Unionist Soc.; Past Vice-Chm., Women's National Advisory Cttee of Cons. Party; Former Nat. Advisor on Women's Affairs to European Movement. Has been active in voluntary and consumer work for many years; Chairman: Steering Gp on Food Freshness, 1973-75; Housewife's Trust; Former Mem., Exec. Cttee, BSI. Vice-Pres., Royal Society for Prevention of Accidents. *Recreations:* talking and travelling. *Address:* 92 Iverna Court, W8; 5 Woodland Avenue, Helens Bay, Co. Down. *T:* Helens Bay 853333.

MacLAURIN, Ian Charter; Managing Director, TESCO Stores Holdings Ltd, since 1973 (Director, 1970); *b* 30 March 1937; *m* 1961, Ann Margaret (*née* Collar); one *s* two *d. Educ:* Malvern Coll., Worcs. Joined TESCO as trainee, 1960; Supermarket Manager, 1963; Exec. Dir, Supermarket Co., 1965; Managing Dir, TESCO Supermarkets, 1969. Liveryman, Carmen's Co., 1982-. *Recreations:* golf, cricket. *Address:* Longdene, Old Lane, Knebworth, Herts SG3 6AF. *T:* Stevenage 811259. *Clubs:* MCC; Lord's Taverners, XL; Band of Brothers.

MACLAY, family name of Baron Maclay and Viscount Muirshiel.

MACLAY, 3rd Baron *cr* 1922, of Glasgow; **Joseph Paton Maclay;** Bt 1914; Managing Director: Denholm Maclay Co. Ltd; Denholm Maclay (Offshore) Ltd; Triport Ferries (Management) Ltd; Deputy Managing Director, Denholm Ship Management Ltd, 1982; *b* 11 April 1942; *s* of 2nd Baron Maclay, KBE, and of Nancy Margaret, *d* of R. C. Greig, Hall of Caldwell, Uplawmoor, Renfrewshire; *S* father, 1969; *m* 1976, Elizabeth Anne, *o d* of G. M. Buchanan, Delamere, Pokataroo, NSW; two *s* one *d. Educ:* Winchester. Director: Milton Shipping Co. Ltd; Marine Shipping Mutual Insce Co., 1982-; Pres., Hanover Shipping Inc., 1982. Director: British Steamship Short Trades Assoc.; N of England Protection and Indemnity Assoc., 1976-. Chm., Scottish Br., British Sailors Soc., 1979-81; Vice-Chm., Glasgow Shipowners & Shipbrokers Benevolent Assoc., 1982. *Heir: s* Hon. Joseph Paton Maclay, *b* 6 March 1977. *Address:* Duchal, Kilmacolm, Renfrewshire.

MACLEAN, family name of Baron Maclean.

MACLEAN, Baron *cr* 1971 (Life Peer), of Duart and Morvern in the County of Argyll; **Charles Hector Fitzroy Maclean;** Bt 1631; KT 1969; PC 1971; GCVO 1971; KBE 1967; JP; 27th Chief of Clan Maclean; Lord Chamberlain of HM Household since 1971; Chancellor, Royal Victorian Order, since 1971; Scouts Guards, Major, retired; Lord Lieutenant of Argyll since 1954; Lieutenant, Royal Company of Archers (Queen's Body Guard for Scotland); President, Argyll T&AFA; *b* 5 May 1916; *e* surv. *s* of late Hector F. Maclean and Winifred Joan, *y d* of late J. H. Wilding; *S* grandfather, 1936; *m* 1941, Elizabeth, *er d* of late Frank Mann, Upper Farm House, Milton Lilbourne, Wilts; one *s* one *d. Educ:* Canford Sch., Wimborne. Served War of 1939-45 (despatches). Chief Commissioner for Scotland, Boy Scouts Assoc., 1954-59;

Chief Scout of the UK and Overseas Branches, 1959-71; Chief Scout of the Commonwealth, 1959-75. Patron: Coombe Trust Fund; Roland House; Argyll Div., Scottish Br., British Red Cross Soc.; Hon. Patron, Friends of World Scouting; Vice Patron: Argyll & Sutherland Highlanders Regimental Assoc.; President: T&AFA of Argyll; Argyll Br., Forces Help Soc. and Lord Robert's Workshops; Convenor, Standing Council of Scottish Chiefs; Hon. President: Argyll Co. Scout Council; Toc H; Scouts Friendly Soc.; Vice President: Highland Cattle Soc.; Scottish Br., Nat. Playing Fields Assoc.; (ex officio) Nat. Small-Bore Rifle Assoc.; Camping Club of GB; Trefoil Residential Sch. for Physically Handicapped Children; Casualties Union; Member of Council: Earl Haig Officers Meml Fund; Scottish Naval, Military and Air Forces Veteran Residences; Royal Zoological Soc.; Outward Bound Trust; Life Member: Highland and Agricultural Soc. of Scotland; Highland Cattle Soc.; Scottish Nat. Fatstock Club; Royal Agricultural Soc. of England. JP Argyll, 1955. *Publication:* Only (children's book), 1979. *Recreation:* travelling. *Heir:* (to Baronetcy only): *s* Hon. Lachlan Hector Charles Maclean, Major, Scots Guards, retired [*b* 25 Aug. 1942; *m* 1966, Mary Helen, *e d* of W. G. Gordon; two *s* two *d* (and one *d* decd)]. *Address:* St James's Palace, SW1. *T:* 01-930 4010; Duart Castle, Isle of Mull. *T:* Craignure 309. *Clubs:* Cavalry and Guards, Pratt's, Royal Commonwealth Society (Mem. Council); Royal Highland Yacht (Oban).
See also D. J. Graham-Campbell.

MACLEAN, Alistair; author; *b* Scotland, 1922. *Educ:* Glasgow Univ. *Publications:* HMS Ulysses, 1955; The Guns of Navarone, 1957 (filmed 1959); South by Java Head, 1958 (filmed 1959); The Last Frontier, 1959 (filmed 1960 as The Secret Ways); Night Without End, 1960; Fear Is the Key, 1961 (filmed 1972); The Golden Rendezvous, 1962 (filmed 1977); (for children) All About Lawrence of Arabia, 1962; Ice Station Zebra, 1963 (filmed 1968); When Eight Bells Toll, 1966 (filmed 1970); Where Eagles Dare, 1967 (filmed 1968); Force 10 From Navarone, 1968 (filmed 1978); Puppet on a Chain, 1969 (filmed 1970); Bear Island, 1971 (filmed 1979); Captain Cook, 1972; The Way to Dusty Death, 1973; (introd.) Alistair Maclean Introduces Scotland, ed, A. M. Dunnett, 1972; Breakheart Pass, 1974 (filmed 1975); Circus, 1975; The Golden Gate, 1976; Sea Witch, 1977; Goodbye California, 1977; Athabasca, 1980; River of Death, 1981; Partisans, 1982; *as Ian Stuart:* The Dark Crusader, 1961; The Satan Bug, 1962 (filmed 1965). *Screen plays:* Where Eagles Dare, Caravan to Vaccares, Puppet on a Chain, Breakheart Pass. *Film for TV:* Hostage Tower, 1980. *Address:* c/o Wm Collins Sons & Co. Ltd, 14 St James's Place, SW1.

McLEAN, Colin, CMG 1977; MBE 1964; HM Diplomatic Service; Head of Trade Relations and Export Department, Foreign and Commonwealth Office, since 1981; *b* 10 Aug. 1930; *s* of late Dr L. G. McLean and of H. I. McLean; *m* 1953, Huguette Marie Suzette Leclerc; one *s* one *d. Educ:* Fettes; St Catharine's Coll., Cambridge (MA). 2RHA, 1953-54. District Officer, Kenya, 1955-63; Vice-Principal, Kenya Inst. of Administration, 1963-64; HM Diplomatic Service, 1964; served Wellington, Bogotá and FCO, 1964-77; Counsellor, Oslo, 1977-81. *Recreation:* sailing. *Address:* c/o Foreign and Commonwealth Office, SW1.

McLEAN, Denis Bazeley Gordon; Secretary of Defence, New Zealand, since 1979; *b* Napier, NZ, 18 Aug. 1930; *s* of John Gordon McLean and Renée Maitland Smith; *m* 1958, Anne Davidson, Venado Tuerto, Argentina; two *s* one *d. Educ:* Nelson Coll., NZ; Victoria Univ. Coll., NZ (MSc); Rhodes Schol. 1954; University Coll., Oxford (MA). Jun. Lectr in Geology, Victoria UC, 1953-54; joined Dept of External Affairs of NZ Govt, London, 1957; served in: Wellington, 1958-60; Washington, 1960-63; Paris, 1963-66; Kuala Lumpur, 1966-68; Asst Sec. (Policy), MoD, Wellington, 1969-72; RCDS, 1972; Dep. High Comr, London, 1973-77; Dep. Sec. of Defence, NZ, 1977. *Recreations:* walking, modest mountaineering, geology. *Address:* 11 Dekka Street, Wellington, New Zealand. *Club:* Travellers'.

MacLEAN, Captain Donald Murdo, DSC 1944; RD 1940; RNR; Retired from Cunard Line, 1962; Commodore Captain Cunard Fleet and commanding RMS Queen Elizabeth, 1960-62; *b* 9 June, 1899; *s* of William MacLean and Isobel (*née* Graham); *m* 1929, Bernice Isobel Wellington; one *s* one *d. Educ:* The Nicholson Sch., Lewis Island. Apprenticed to Cunard Line, 1917-21; served, as Officer, 1921-39. Served War of 1939-45 (despatches): RNR, 1939-46; Trg Comdr RNC, Greenwich, 1941-43; Sen. Officer, 7th Escort Gp, Murmansk and Atlantic and Mediterranean Convoys; Staff Officer C-in-C Mediterranean, 1944-45. Returned to Cunard Line, 1946. ADC to Lord High Comr for Scotland, 1946. *Publications:* Queens' Company, 1965; Cachalots and Messmates, 1973. *Recreations:* sailing, fishing, travel. *Address:* Landfall, 99 Newtown Road, Warsash, Southampton. *T:* Locks Heath 3951. *Club:* Master Mariners (Southampton).

MACLEAN of Dunconnel, Sir Fitzroy Hew, 1st Bt, *cr* 1957; CBE 1944; 15th Hereditary Keeper and Captain of Dunconnel; *b* 11 March 1911; *s* of Major Charles Maclean, DSO; *m* 1946, Hon. Mrs Alan Phipps, 2nd *d* of 16th Baron Lovat, KT; two *s. Educ:* Eton; Cambridge. 3rd Sec., Foreign Office, 1933; transferred to Paris, 1934, and to Moscow, 1937; 2nd Sec., 1938; transferred to Foreign Office, 1939; resigned from Diplomatic Service, and enlisted as private in Cameron Highlanders; 2nd Lt Aug. 1941; joined 1st Special Air Service Regt Jan. 1942; Capt. Sept. 1942; Lt-Col 1943; Brig. Comdg British Military Mission to Jugoslav partisans, 1943-45. Lees Knowles Lecturer, Cambridge, 1953. MP (C) Lancaster, 1941-59, Bute and N Ayrshire, 1959-Feb. 1974; Parly Under-Sec. of State for War and Financial Sec. War

Office, Oct. 1954–Jan. 1957. Member: UK Delegn to North Atlantic Assembly, 1962–74; Council of Europe and WEU, 1972–74. Hon. LLD: Glasgow 1969; Dalhousie 1971; Hon. DLitt Acadia, 1970. French Croix de Guerre, 1943; Order of Kutusov, 1944; Partisan Star (First Class), 1945. *Publications:* Eastern Approaches, 1949; Disputed Barricade, 1957; A Person from England, 1958; Back to Bokhara, 1959; Jugoslavia, 1969; A Concise History of Scotland, 1970; The Battle of Neretva, 1970; To the Back of Beyond, 1974; To Caucasus, 1976; Take Nine Spies, 1978; Holy Russia, 1979; Tito, 1980. *Heir:* s Charles Maclean, yr of Dunconnel, b 31 Oct. 1946. *Address:* Strachur House, Argyll. *T:* Strachur 242. *Clubs:* White's, Pratt's; Puffin's (Edinburgh).

McLEAN, Sir Francis (Charles), Kt 1967; CBE 1953 (MBE 1945); b 6 Nov. 1904; s of Michael McLean; m 1930, Dorothy Mabel Blackstaffe; one s one d. *Educ:* University of Birmingham (BSc). Chief Engineer, Psychological Warfare Division, SHAEF, 1943–45. Dep. Chief Engineer, BBC, 1952–60; Dep. Dir of Engineering, BBC, 1960–63; Director, Engineering, BBC, 1963–68. Dir, Oxley Developments Ltd, 1961–. Chairman: BSI Telecommunications Industry Standards Cttee, 1960–77; Royal Commn on FM Broadcasting in Australia, 1974. Pres., Newbury Dist Field Club. FIEE. *Publications:* contrib. Journal of IEE. *Address:* Greenwood Copse, Tile Barn, Woolton Hill, Newbury, Berks. *T:* Newbury 253583.

MACLEAN, Vice-Adm. Sir Hector Charles Donald, KBE 1962; CB 1960; DSC 1941; JP; DL; b 7 Aug. 1908; s of late Captain D. C. H. Maclean, DSO, The Royal Scots; m 1933, Opre, d of late Captain Geoffrey Vyvyan, Royal Welch Fusiliers; one s two d. *Educ:* Wellington. Special Entry into Navy, 1926; Captain 1948; idc 1951; Comd HMS Saintes and 3rd Destroyer Sqdn, 1952–53; Dir of Plans, Admiralty, 1953–56; Comd HMS Eagle, 1956–57; Chief of Staff, Home Fleet, 1958–59; Chief of Allied Staff, Mediterranean, 1959–62; Vice-Adm. 1960; retired 1962. JP Norfolk, 1963; DL Norfolk, 1977. *Address:* Deepdale Old Rectory, Brancaster Staithe, King's Lynn, Norfolk. *T:* Brancaster 281. *Club:* Norfolk (Norwich).

MACLEAN, Hector Ronald; Sheriff of North Strathclyde (formerly Renfrew and Argyll) since 1968; b 6 Dec. 1931; s of Donald Beaton Maclean and Lucy McAlister; m 1967, Hilary Elizabeth Jenkins; three d. *Educ:* High Sch. of Glasgow; Glasgow Univ. Admitted to Faculty of Advocates, 1959. *Recreation:* golf. *Address:* Barrfield, Houston, Renfrewshire. *T:* Bridge of Weir 612449.

MACLEAN of Pennycross, Rear-Admiral Iain Gilleasbuig, CB 1954; OBE 1944; retired; b 25 Nov. 1902; s of late Norman H. Maclean; m 1st, 1931, Evelyn Marjorie, d of late R. A. and Mrs Winton Reid; one step d; 2nd, 1973, Nancy Margaret, widow of E. A. Barnard. *Educ:* Cargilfield; RN Colleges, Osborne and Dartmouth. Joined RN, 1916; Captain, 1945; Rear-Admiral, 1952; Served War of 1939–45: in Combined Operations, HMS Renown and Admiralty. Imperial Defence Coll., 1951; Dep. Engineer in Chief of the Fleet, 1952–55; retired, Nov. 1955. Director, Marine Development, Brush Group, 1956–60. Research Survey for National Ports Council, 1963–64. *Recreations:* fishing, gardening. *Address:* Pear Tree Cottage, Moorlands Drive, Pinkney's Green, Maidenhead, Berks. *T:* Maidenhead 30287.

MACLEAN, Ian Albert Druce; Director: Halifax Building Society, 1953–76 (Chairman, 1961–74); Fanhams Hall Services (Ware) Ltd; b 23 June 1902; s of Alick and Nina Maclean; m 1st, 1937, Diana, d of John and Gertrude Marsden-Smedley; twin s; 2nd, 1979, Heather Scott Thompson, d of Ronald and Dorothy Mackenzie. *Educ:* Marlborough; Pembroke Coll., Cambridge. Tobacco Industry, 1924; Cotton Industry, 1926; Carpet Industry, 1937; Halifax Building Society, 1953. Dir, Building Socs Training Coll. Ltd; Vice-Pres., Building Socs Assoc. Former Dir, Carpets International Ltd. *Recreations:* anything in the open air. *Address:* Bay Trees, 30 River Green, Hamble, Southampton SO3 5JA. *T:* Hamble 3403. *Clubs:* Lansdowne; Royal Southern Yacht (Southampton); Royal Windermere Yacht.

McLEAN, Ian Graeme; His Honour Judge McLean; a Circuit Judge since 1980; b Edinburgh, 7 Sept. 1928; s of Lt-Gen. Sir Kenneth McLean, qv; m 1957, Eleonore Maria Gmeiner, Bregenz, Austria; two d. *Educ:* Aldenham Sch.; Christ's Coll., Cambridge. BA Hons Law 1950; MA 1955. Intell. Corps, 1946–48. Called to Bar, Middle Temple, Nov. 1951; practised London and on Western Circuit, 1951–55; Crown Counsel, Northern Nigeria, 1955–59; Sen. Lectr and Head of Legal Dept of Inst. of Administration, Northern Nigeria, 1959–62; Native Courts Adviser, 1959–62; returned to English Bar, 1962; practised London and South Eastern Circuit, 1962–70; occasional Dep. Chm., Inner, NE, SW and Mddx Areas, London QS, 1968–70; occasional Dep. Recorder, Oxford, 1969–70; Adjudicator under Immigration Acts, 1969–70; Metropolitan Stipendiary Magistrate, 1970–80. *Publications:* Cumulative Index West African Court of Appeal Reports, 1958; (with Abubakar Sadiq) The Maliki Law of Homicide, 1959; (with Sir Lionel Brett) Criminal Law Procedure and Evidence of Lagos, Eastern and Western Nigeria, 1963; (with Cyprian Okonkwo) Cases on the Criminal Law, Procedure and Evidence of Nigeria, 1966; (with Peter Morrish) A Practical Guide to Appeals in Criminal Courts, 1970; (with Peter Morrish) The Crown Court, an index of common penalties, etc, 1972; (ed, with Peter Morrish) Harris's Criminal Law, 22nd edn, 1972; (with Peter Morrish) The Magistrates' Court, an index of common penalties, 1973; (with Peter Morrish) The Trial of Breathalyser Offences, 1975; A Practical Guide to Criminal Appeals, 1980; A Pattern of Sentencing, 1981; (with John Mulhern) The Industrial Tribunal: a practical guide to

employment law and tribunal procedure, 1982; contrib. Archbold's Criminal Pleadings, 38th edn, and Halsbury's Laws of England, 4th edn, title Criminal Law. *Recreations:* family, gardening, writing, languages.

MacLEAN, Dr John Alexander, CBE 1968; Chairman, Northern Regional Hospital Board (Scotland), 1971–74; b 12 Oct. 1903; s of Donald MacLean, Achiltibuie, Ross-shire; m 1935, Hilda M. L. Munro, BSc, Aberdeen; one s one d. *Educ:* Dingwall Academy; Aberdeen Univ. MA, LLB, PhD; FEIS. Aberdeen Educn Authority: Teacher, 1926–39; Asst Dir of Educn, 1939–43; Dir of Educn, Inverness-shire Educn Authority, 1943–68, retd. Member: Exec. Cttee, National Trust for Scotland, 1967–82; Scottish Council, Royal Over-Seas League, 1969–81; Scottish Arts Council, 1964–68; Sec. of State's Council for Care of Children; Council on School Broadcasting. *Publication:* Sources for History of the Highlands in the Seventeenth Century, 1939. *Recreation:* sport. *Address:* 12 Eriskay Road, Inverness IV2 3LX. *T:* Inverness 31566. *Club:* Royal Over-Seas House (Edinburgh).
See also R. N. M. *MacLean.*

McLEAN, John Alexander Lowry, QC 1974; Principal Secretary to Lord Chief Justice (formerly Permanent Secretary, Supreme Court of Northern Ireland) and Clerk of the Crown for Northern Ireland, since 1966; b 21 Feb. 1921; o s of John McLean and Phoebe Jane (née Bowditch); m 1950, Diana Elisabeth Campbell, e d of S. B. Boyd Campbell, MC, MD, FRCP, and Mary Isabella Ayre, St John's, Newfoundland; one s two d. *Educ:* Methodist Coll., Belfast; Queen's University Belfast. Served Intell. Corps, 1943–47. Called to Bar of Northern Ireland, 1949. Asst Sec., NI Supreme Court, and Private Sec. to Lord Chief Justice of NI 1956; Under Treas., Hon. Soc. of Inn of Court of NI, 1966; Clerk of Restrictive Practices Court in NI, 1957. Member: Jt Working Party on Enforcement of Judgments of NI Courts, 1963; Lord Chancellor's Cttee on NI Supreme Court, 1966; Lord Chancellor's Foreign Judgments Working Party, 1974–. *Publications:* contrib. legal periodicals. *Recreations:* not golf. *Address:* 24 Marlborough Park South, Belfast BT9 6HR. *T:* Belfast 667330; Lifeboat Cottage, Cloughey, Co. Down BT22 1HS. *T:* Portavogie 71313. *Club:* Royal Commonwealth Society.

MacLEAN, Hon. (John) Angus, PC 1957; DFC, CD; Premier of Prince Edward Island, since 1979; b 15 May 1914; s of George A. MacLean; m 1952, Gwendolyn Esther M. Burwash; two s two d. *Educ:* Mount Allison Academy; Summerside High Sch.; Univ. of British Columbia; Mount Allison Univ. BSc. Served War of 1939–45, RCAF: commanded Test and Development Estabt, 1943–45; Missing and Enquiry Unit, Europe, 1945–47, Wing Comdr (despatches). First elected to House of Commons by by-election, 1951, re-elected 1953, 1957, 1958, 1962, 1963, 1965, 1968, 1972, 1974; Minister of Fisheries in the Diefenbaker Cabinet, 1957–63; elected Leader of PC Party of PEI, 1976; first elected to PEI Legislature at by-election, 1976, re-elected 1978 and 1979. Mem. Royal Air Forces Escaping Soc. (Canadian Br.). Hon. LLD Mount Allison Univ., 1958. *Recreations:* genealogical research, bird watching. *Address:* (home) Lewes, RR3, Belle River, Prince Edward Island COA 1B0, Canada. *T:* (902) 962-2235, Murray River, PEI; (office) PO Box 2000, Charlottetown, PEI C1A 7N8. *T:* (902) 892-3535. *Clubs:* United Services, Charlottetown, RCAF Association, Masonic Lodge, AF and AM, Royal Canadian Legion, Charlottetown Chamber of Commerce, Canadian (PEI).

McLEAN, (John David) Ruari (McDowall Hardie), CBE 1973; DSC 1943; freelance typographer and author; b 10 June 1917; s of late John Thomson McLean and late Isabel Mary McLean (née Ireland); m 1945, Antonia Maxwell Carlisle; two s one d. *Educ:* Dragon Sch., Oxford; Eastbourne Coll. First studied printing under B. H. Newdigate at Shakespeare Head Press, Oxford, 1936. Industrial printing experience in Germany and England, 1936–38; with The Studio, 1938; Percy Lund Humphries, Bradford, 1939. Served Royal Navy, 1940–45. Penguin Books, 1945–46; Book Designer (freelance), 1946–53; Tutor in Typography, Royal College of Art, 1948–51; Typographic Adviser to Hulton Press, 1953; Founder Partner, Rainbird, McLean Ltd, 1951–58; Founder Editor, and Designer, Motif, 1958–67. Typographic Consultant to The Observer, 1960–64; Hon. Typographic Adviser to HM Stationery Office, 1966–80. Member: Nat. Council for Diplomas in Art and Design, 1971; Vis. Cttee of RCA, 1977–. Crown Trustee, Nat. Library of Scotland, 1981–. Croix de Guerre (French), 1942. *Publications:* George Cruikshank, 1948; Modern Book Design, 1958; Wood Engravings of Joan Hassall, 1960; Victorian Book Design, 1963, rev. edn 1972; Tschichold's Typographische Gestaltung (Trans.), 1967; (ed) The Reminiscences of Edmund Evans, 1967; Magazine Design, 1969; Victorian Publishers' Book-bindings in Cloth and Leather, 1973; Jan Tschichold, Typographer, 1975; Joseph Cundall, 1976; (ed) Edward Bawden: A Book of Cuts, 1979; Thames and Hudson Manual of Typography, 1980. *Recreations:* sailing, reading, acquiring books. *Address:* Pier Cottage, Carsaig, Pennyghael, Isle of Mull. *Clubs:* Double Crown; New (Edinburgh).

MACLEAN, Colonel John Francis, JP; Lord-Lieutenant of Hereford and Worcester, 1974–76 (Lord Lieutenant of Herefordshire, 1960–74); b 1 March 1901; s of late Montague Francis and Florence Maclean; m 1925, Vivienne A. M. Miesegaes (d 1969); two s. *Educ:* Eton Coll. Started in coal trade with Cannop Coal Co. Ltd, Forest of Dean, 1921; became a Director and Commercial Manager, in 1927, after being employed with United Collieries Ltd, Glasgow. Commnd Herefordshire Regt (TA), 1919–23. Coal Supplies Officer for Forest of Dean, 1939–40; commnd in Grenadier Guards, Sept. 1940, reaching rank of Major. Hon. Colonel, Herefordshire Light Infantry (TA), 1963–67; Pres., West Midland TAVR Assoc., 1970–76. Herefordshire: JP 1946, High Sheriff 1951, DL 1953–60. KStJ 1960. *Recreations:* golf, shooting; formerly lawn tennis and cricket (kept wicket for Worcestershire, 1922-24, and occasionally for Gloucestershire, 1929-30; toured Australia and New Zealand with MCC team, 1922-23). *Address:* Old School House, How Caple, Hereford HR1 4SY. *T:* How Caple 281.

McLEAN, Lieut-General Sir Kenneth Graeme, KCB 1954 (CB 1944); KBE 1951; US Legion of Merit, 1945; Officer, Legion of Honour (France); Croix de Guerre (France); *b* 11 Dec. 1896; *s* of late Arthur H. McLean, WS; *m* 1926, Daphne Winifred Ashburner Steele (*d* 1979); two *s. Educ:* Edinburgh Academy; RMA Woolwich. Commissioned RE 1918; served, in Ireland, 1919-20, and with KGO Bengal Sappers and Miners in India, 1923-29; Staff Coll., Quetta, 1930-31; on General Staff, AHQ, India, 1932-36; Assistant Secretary Cttee of Imperial Defence, 1938; Student at Imperial Defence Coll., 1939. Served France and Germany, 1944-45; Deputy Adjutant-General, GHQ, Far East, 1945-46; Dep. Adjutant-General, GHQ, Middle East, 1946; Vice-Adjutant-General, War Office, 1947-49; Chief of Staff, CCG, and Deputy Military Governor, British Zone in Germany, 1949; Military Secretary to the Secretary of State for War, 1949-51; Chief Staff Officer, Ministry of Defence, 1951-52; Special Duty, War Office, 1952-54. Retired, 1954. Colonel Comdt RE, 1956-61. *Address:* Greenways, Melrose, Roxburghshire.
See also I. G. McLean.

MacLEAN, Kenneth Smedley, MD, FRCP; Consultant Physician to Guy's Hospital, 1950-79, now Emeritus; *b* 22 Nov. 1914; *s* of Hugh MacLean and Ida Smedley; *m* 1939, Joan Hardaker; one *s* one *d* (and one *s* decd). *Educ:* Westminster; Clare Coll., Cambridge. MRCS, LRCP, 1939; House appts at Guy's, 1939; MB, BChir 1939. RNVR, 1939-46, Surg.-Lt and Surg.-Lt-Comdr. MRCP 1946; House Officer and Medical Registrar, Guy's Hosp., 1946-48; MD Cantab 1948; FRCP 1954; elected to Assoc. of Physicians of Great Britain and Ireland, 1956. Assistant Director, Dept of Medicine, Guy's Hospital Medical Sch., 1949, Director, 1961-63. Chm., University Hosps Assoc., 1975-78. *Publication:* Medical Treatment, 1957. *Recreation:* golf. *Address:* 7 Icehouse Wood, Oxted, Surrey. *T:* Oxted 6652.

MacLEAN, Murdo; Private Secretary to the Government Chief Whip, since 1979; *b* 21 Oct. 1943; *s* of Murdo MacLean and Johanna (*née* Martin). *Educ:* Glasgow. Temp. Clerk, Min. of Labour Employment Exchange, Govan, Glasgow, 1963-64; BoT, 1964-67; Prime Minister's Office, 1967-72; Dept of Industry, 1972-78. *Address:* c/o 12 Downing Street, SW1. *T:* 01-219 3595/4400.

McLEAN, Lt-Col Neil Loudon Desmond, DSO 1943; *b* 28 Nov. 1918; *s* of Neil McLean; *m* 1949, Daška Kennedy (*née* Ivanović-Banac), Dubrovnik, Jugoslavia. *Educ:* Eton; RMC, Sandhurst. Gazetted Royal Scots Greys, 1938; Palestine Campaign, 1939; served War of 1939-45, Middle East and Far East: Ethiopia under 101 Mission, 1941; Head of First Military Mission to Albania, 1942 and 1943; Lieut-Colonel, 1943; Far East, 1944-45. Contested (C) Preston South, 1950 and 1951; MP (C) Inverness, Dec. 1954-Sept. 1964. Member Highland and Islands Advisory Panel, 1955. Member of Queen's Body Guard for Scotland, Royal Company of Archers. Distinguished Military Medal of Haile Selassie I, 1941. *Publications:* contributions to Chatham House, Royal Central Asian Society Reviews. *Recreations:* travel, riding, shooting, underwater fishing. *Address:* 17 Eaton Square, SW1. *Clubs:* White's, Buck's, Cavalry and Guards, Pratt's; Highland (Inverness).

McLEAN, Peter Standley, OBE 1965; Minister and UK Permanent Representative to UN Food and Agriculture Organisation, since 1980; *b* 18 Jan. 1927; *s* of late William and Alice McLean; *m* 1954, Margaret Ann Minns; two *s* two *d. Educ:* King Edward's Sch., Birmingham; Wadham Coll., Oxford (MA). Served Army, 1944-48; Lieut, 15/19th King's Royal Hussars. Colonial Service, Uganda, 1951-65, retired from HMOCS as Permanent Sec., Min. of Planning and Economic Develt; Ministry of Overseas Development: Principal, 1965; Private Sec. to Minister for Overseas Develt, 1973; Head of Eastern and Southern Africa Dept, 1975; Head of Bilateral Aid and Rural Develt Dept, 1979. *Recreations:* watching sport, DIY, painting. *Address:* c/o Foreign and Commonwealth Office, SW1A 2AH. *T:* Rome 475-5441.

McLEAN, Philip Alexander; HM Diplomatic Service; Counsellor and Consul-General, Algiers, since 1981; *b* 24 Oct. 1938; *s* of late Wm Alexander McLean and of Doris McLean (*née* Campbell); *m* 1960, Dorothy Helen Kirkby; two *s* one *d. Educ:* King George V Sch., Southport; Keble Coll., Oxford (MA Hons). National Service, RAF, 1956-58. Industry, 1961-68; entered HM Diplomatic Service by Open Supplementary Competition, 1968; Second, later (1969) First, Secretary, FCO; La Paz, 1970-74: Head of Chancery, 1973; FCO, 1974-76; Dep. Director of British Trade Development Office and Head of Industrial Marketing, New York, 1976-80. *Recreations:* badminton, cricket, rural retreats, family life. *Address:* c/o Foreign and Commonwealth Office, SW1; Hill Cottage, Reading Road, Goring-on-Thames, near Reading RG8 0LH. *Club:* United Oxford & Cambridge University.

MacLEAN, Ranald Norman Munro, QC (Scot) 1977; *b* 18 Dec. 1938; *s* of John Alexander Maclean, *qv*; *m* 1963, Pamela Ross; two *s* one *d* (and one *s* decd). *Educ:* Inverness Royal Acad.; Fettes Coll.; Clare Coll., Cambridge Univ. (BA); Edinburgh Univ. (LLB); Yale Univ., USA (LLM). Called to the Scottish Bar, 1964. Advocate Depute, 1972-75, 1979-82, Senior Advocate Depute, 1979-82; Standing Jun. Counsel, Health and Safety Exec. (Scotland), 1975-77. Chm., Industrial Tribunals (Scotland), 1977-. Mem., Stewart Cttee

on Alternatives to Prosecution, 1977-. Trustee, Nat. Library of Scotland. Governor: Fettes Coll., 1977-; Cargilfield Sch., 1978-. *Publication:* (ed jtly) Gloag and Henderson, Introduction to the Law of Scotland, 7th edn 1968, 8th edn 1980. *Recreations:* hill walking, squash, tennis, birdwatching. *Address:* 12 Chalmers Crescent, Edinburgh EH9 1TS. *T:* 031-667 6217. *Clubs:* Scottish Arts, Edinburgh Sports (Edinburgh).

MACLEAN, Sir Robert (Alexander), KBE 1973; Kt 1955; DL; Chartered Accountant; Chairman, Stoddard Holdings Ltd; a Vice-President, Scottish Council (Development and Industry); Chairman, High School of Glasgow Educational Trust; *b* 11 April 1908; *s* of Andrew Johnston Maclean, JP, Cambuslang, Lanarkshire, and Mary Jane Cameron; *m* 1938, Vivienne Neville Bourke, *d* of Captain Bertram Walter Bourke, JP, Heathfield, Co. Mayo; two *s* two *d. Educ:* High Sch. of Glasgow. JDipMA. President: Glasgow Chamber of Commerce, 1956-58; Association British Chambers of Commerce, 1966-68; Chairman: Council of Scottish Chambers of Commerce, 1960-62; Scottish Cttee, Council of Industrial Design, 1949-58 (Mem., CoID, 1948-58); Council of Management, Scottish Industries Exhibns, 1949, 1954 and 1959; Scottish Exports Cttee, 1966-70; Scottish Industrial Estates Corp., 1955-72 (Mem., 1946-72); Pres., British Industrial Exhibn, Moscow, 1966; Vice-Chm., Scottish Bd for Industry, 1952-60; Member: Pigs and Bacon Marketing Commn, 1955-56; BNEC, 1966-70; Scottish Aerodromes Bd, 1950-61; Export Council for Europe, 1960-64; BoT Trade Exhbns Adv. Cttee, 1961-65; Nat. Freight Corp., 1969-72; Regional Controller (Scotland): Board of Trade, 1944-46; Factory and Storage Premises, 1941-44. Director: Scottish Union & Nat. Insce Co.; Scottish Adv. Bd, Norwich Union Insce Gp. Trustee, Clyde Navigational Trust, 1956-58; Pres., Scottish Youth Clubs, 1959-68. DL Renfrewshire, 1970. CStJ 1975. FRSA; CBIM. Hon. LLD Glasgow, 1970. *Recreations:* golf, fishing. *Address:* Woodend, Houston, Renfrewshire. *Clubs:* Carlton; Western (Glasgow).

McLEAN, Ruari; *see* McLean, J. D. R. McD. H.

McLEAN, Dr Thomas Pearson, FRSE, FInstP, CEng, FIEE; Under Secretary, Director General Air Weapons and Electronic Systems, Ministry of Defence, since 1980; *b* Paisley, 21 Aug. 1930; *s* of Norman Stewart McLean and Margaret Pearson McLean (*née* Ferguson); *m* 1957, Grace Campbell Nokes; two *d. Educ:* John Neilson Instn, Paisley; Glasgow Univ. (BSc, PhD); Birmingham Univ. Royal Radar Estabt (becoming Royal Signals and Radar Estabt, 1976), 1955-80: Head of Physics Gp, 1973-77; Dep. Dir, 1977-80. Member: Physics Cttee, SRC, 1968-73; Optoelectronics Cttee, Rank Prize Funds, 1972-81; Council, Inst. of Physics, 1980-. Hon. Prof. of Physics, Birmingham Univ., 1977-80. Dep. Editor, Jl of Physics C, 1976-77. *Publications:* papers in Physical Rev., Jl of Physics, etc. *Recreations:* music, Scottish country dancing. *Address:* Kinlochard, Purlieu Wood, Malvern, Worcs. *T:* Malvern 4061.

MacLEARY, Donald Whyte; principal male dancer with the Royal Ballet since 1959; Ballet Master to the Royal Ballet, since 1975; *b* Glasgow, 22 Aug. 1937; *s* of Donald Herbert MacLeary, MPS, and Jean Spiers (*née* Leslie). *Educ:* Inverness Royal Academy; The Royal Ballet School. *Classical Ballets:* (full length) Swan Lake, Giselle, 1958; Sleeping Beauty, Cinderella, Sylvia, 1959; Ondine, La Fille Mal Gardée, 1960; (centre male rôle) in Ashton's Symphonic Variations, 1962; Sonnet Pas de Trois, 1964; Romeo and Juliet, 1965; Eugene Onegin, Stuttgart, 1966; Apollo, 1966; Nutcracker, 1968; Swan Lake with N. Makarova, 1972. *Creations:* (1954-74): Solitaire, The Burrow, Danse Concertante, Antigone, Diversions, Le Baiser de la Fée, Jabez and the Devil, Raymonda Pas de Deux (for Frederick Ashton), two episodes in Images of Love; Song of the Earth; Lilac Garden (revival); Jazz Calendar; Raymonda (for Nureyeff); The Man in Kenneth MacMillan's Checkpoint; leading role in Concerto no 2 (Balanchine's Ballet Imperial, renamed); Elite Syncopations, 1974; Kenneth MacMillan's Four Seasons Symphony; the Prince in Cinderella. Toured Brazil with Royal Ballet, Spring 1973. Guest dancer, Scottish Ballet, 1979. *Recreations:* reading, theatre, records (all types); riding, fox hunting, swimming. *Address:* Bunyan Cottage, Wainwood, Preston, Herts. *Club:* Queen's.

McLEAY, Hon. Sir John, KCMG 1962; MM; retired as Speaker of the House of Representatives, Canberra, Australia (1956-66); Federal Member for Boothby, South Australia, 1949-66; *b* 19 Nov. 1893; *m* 1921, Eileen H. (*d* 1971), *d* of late H. Elden, Geelong; two *s* one *d.* Stretcher Bearer, 13 Field Ambulance, 1st AIF (awarded Military Medal); Life Member, Hindmarsh Ambulance. Formerly: Mayor of City of Unley; Lord Mayor of Adelaide; Member for Unley, House of Assembly, SA; Member Council of Governors, Adelaide Univ. and Scotch Coll., Adelaide. President or Past President various organisations; Hon. Member Town Planning Institute, SA, etc. *Address:* 7 Brae Road, St Georges, SA 5064, Australia.

MACLEHOSE, family name of **Baron MacLehose of Beoch.**

MACLEHOSE OF BEOCH, Baron *cr* 1982 (Life Peer), of Maybole in the District of Kyle and Carrick, and of Victoria in Hong Kong; **Crawford Murray MacLehose,** GBE 1976 (MBE 1946); KCMG 1971 (CMG 1964); KCVO 1975; HM Diplomatic Service, retired; Governor and Commander-in-Chief, Hong Kong, 1971-82; *b* 16 Oct. 1917; *s* of Hamish A. MacLehose and Margaret Bruce Black; *m* 1947, Margaret Noël Dunlop; two *d. Educ:* Rugby; Balliol Coll., Oxford. Served War of 1939-45, Lieut, RNVR. Joined Foreign Service, 1947; Acting Consul, 1947, Acting Consul-General, 1948, Hankow;

promoted First Secretary, 1949; transferred to Foreign Office, 1950; First Secretary (Commercial), and Consul, Prague, 1951; seconded to Commonwealth Relations Office, for service at Wellington, 1954; returned to Foreign Office and transferred to Paris, 1956; promoted Counsellor, 1959; seconded to Colonial Office and transferred to Hong Kong as Political Adviser; Counsellor, Foreign Office, 1963; Principal Private Secretary to Secretary of State, 1965-67; Ambassador: to Vietnam, 1967-69; to Denmark, 1969-71. KStJ 1972. *Recreations:* sailing, fishing. *Address:* Beoch, Maybole, Ayrshire. *Clubs:* Athenæum, Travellers'.

MacLELLAN, Maj.-Gen. Andrew Patrick Withy, CB 1981; MBE 1964; President, Regular Commissions Board, 1978-80; *b* 29 Nov. 1925; *y s of* Kenneth MacLellan and Rachel Madeline MacLellan (*née* Withy); *m* 1954, Kathleen Mary Bagnell; one *s* twin *d. Educ:* Uppingham. Commnd Coldstream Guards, 1944; served Palestine 1945-48, N Africa 1950-51, Egypt 1952-53, Germany 1955-56; psc 1957; DAA&QMG 4th Guards Brigade Group, 1958-59; Mil. Asst to Chief of Defence Staff, 1961-64; Instructor, Staff Coll., Camberley, 1964-66; GSO1 (Plans) Far East Comd, 1966-67; CO 1st Bn Coldstream Guards, 1968-70; Col GS Near East Land Forces, 1970-71; Comdr 8th Inf. Brigade, 1971-72; RCDS 1973; Dep. Comdr and COS, London District, 1974-77. Chevalier de la Légion d'Honneur, 1960. *Address:* c/o Bank of Scotland, 19 Roman Road, Bearsden, Glasgow. *Clubs:* White's, Pratt's.

McLELLAN, Prof. David; DPhil; Professor of Political Theory, University of Kent, since 1975; *b* 10 Feb. 1940; *s of* Robert Douglas McLellan and Olive May Bush; *m* 1967, Annie Brassart; two *d. Educ:* Merchant Taylors' Sch.; St John's Coll., Oxford (MA, DPhil). Lectr in Politics, Univ. of Kent, 1966-71; Vis. Prof., State Univ. of New York, 1969; Guest Fellow in Politics, Indian Inst. of Advanced Studies, Simla, 1970; Sen. Lectr in Politics, Univ. of Kent, 1972, Reader in Political Theory, 1973. *Publications:* The Young Hegelians and Karl Marx, 1969 (French, German, Italian, Spanish and Japanese edns); Marx before Marxism, 1970, 2nd edn 1972; Karl Marx: The Early Texts, 1971; Marx's Grundrisse, 1971, 2nd edn 1973; The Thought of Karl Marx, 1971 (Portuguese and Italian edns); Karl Marx: His Life and Thought, 1973, 22nd edn 1976 (German, Italian, Spanish, Japanese, Swedish and Dutch edns); Marx (Fontana Modern Masters), 1975; Engels, 1977; Marxism after Marx, 1979. *Recreations:* chess, Raymond Chandler, hill walking. *Address:* Eliot College, University of Kent, Canterbury, Kent CT2 7NS. *T:* Canterbury 63579.

McLELLAN, Eric Burns; His Honour Judge McLellan; a Circuit Judge (formerly County Court Judge), since 1970; *b* 9 April 1918; *s of* late Stanley Morgan McLellan, Christchurch, Newport, Mon; *m* 1949, Elsa Sarah, *d of* late Gustave Mustaki, Alexandria; one *s* one *d. Educ:* Newport High Sch.; New Coll., Oxford. BA 1939; MA 1967. Served RAF, 1940-46, N Africa, Italy, Egypt, 205 Group; Flt-Lt. Called to Bar, Inner Temple, 1947. Dep. Chm., IoW QS, 1967-72. Official Principal, Archdeaconry of Hackney, 1967-72; Dep. Chm., Workmen's Compensation Supplementation Bd and Pneumoconiosis, Byssinosis and Miscellaneous Diseases Benefit Bd, 1969-70; Mem., Dept of Health and Social Security Adv. Group on Use of Fetuses and Fetal Material for Research, 1970. Governor, Portsmouth Grammar Sch., 1980-. *Publications:* contribs to medico-legal jls. *Recreations:* heraldry and genealogy. *Address:* Lone Barn, Catherington, Hants PO8 0SF. *T:* Hambledon 436. *Clubs:* United Oxford & Cambridge University, Royal Air Force; Hampshire (Winchester).

MacLELLAN, Prof. George Douglas Stephen, MA, PhD (Cantab); CEng; FIMechE, FIEE; Professor and Head of Department of Engineering, University of Leicester, since 1965; *b* Glasgow, 1 Nov. 1922; *e s of* late Alexander Stephen MacLellan. *Educ:* Rugby Sch.; Pembroke Coll., Cambridge; Massachusetts Institute of Technology. Mech. Sci. Tripos, 1942. Dept of Colloid Science, Cambridge, and Callenders Cable and Construction Co. Ltd, 1942-44; Fellow, Pembroke Coll., 1944-59; Vickers-Armstrong Ltd, Newcastle upon Tyne, 1944-46; University Demonstrator and Lecturer in Engineering, Cambridge, 1947-59; Rankine Professor of Mechanical Engineering (Mechanics and Mechanism), University of Glasgow, 1959-65. Commonwealth Fund Fellow, MIT, 1948-49; Visiting Professor, Michigan State University, 1958; MIT, 1962. Pres. of the Soc. of Instrument Technology, 1964-65. Vice-Chm., United Kingdom Automation Council, 1961-64; Member: CNAA, 1970-80; Engrg Bd, SRC, 1971-74; Vis. Cttee, RCA, 1973-82; Council, IMechE, 1974-76; Council, Loughborough Univ. of Technology, 1979-. *Publications:* contribs to mech. and elec. jls. *Address:* Department of Engineering, The University, Leicester LE1 7RH. *T:* Leicester 554455. *Clubs:* Athenæum, Leander.

MacLELLAN, Sir (George) Robin (Perronet), Kt 1980; CBE 1969; JP; Chairman: Scottish Industrial and Trade Exhibitions Ltd, since 1981 (Director, 1975-79); Bield Housing Trust, Edinburgh, since 1982; Scottish Tourist Board, 1974-80; Director: Scottish National Trust Co. Ltd, since 1970; Nationwide Building Society, since 1971; British Tourist Authority, 1974-80; *b* 14 Nov. 1915; *e s of* George Aikman MacLellan, Glasgow, and Irene Dorothy Perronet Miller, Liverpool; *m* 1941, Margaret, *er d of* Dr Berkeley Robertson, Glasgow; one *s. Educ:* Ardvreck Sch., Crieff; Clifton Coll.; Ecole de Commerce, Lausanne. Chm., George MacLellan Hldgs Ltd, 1965-76; Dep. Chm., British Airports Authority, 1965-75; Pres., Glasgow Chamber of Commerce, 1970-71; Dir, Govan Shipbuilders Ltd, 1972-74; Mem., Scottish Industrial Develt Bd, 1972-74. Dir and Chm. of Governors, Ardvreck Sch. Ltd, 1970-; Governor, Clifton Coll.; Mem. Council, Scottish Business Sch.,

1972-75; Mem. Court, Strathclyde Univ., 1972-76. Member: West Central Scotland Plan Steering Cttee, 1970-75; Scottish Econ. Council, 1968-75; BNEC's Cttee for Exports to Canada, 1964-69; Council, Nat. Trust for Scotland, 1974- (Dep. Chm., 1980-); Gen. Adv. Council, IBA, 1976-79; BR Adv. Bd (Scottish), 1977-81. Chm., Soc. of Friends of Glasgow Cathedral, 1978-. A Vice-Pres., Assoc. British Chambers of Commerce, 1975-80; Pres., Inst. of Marketing (Scottish Branch). Hon. FRCPS Glas, 1979. JP Dunbartonshire, 1973. OStJ 1972. *Publications:* articles on travel, tourism, business matters and Scottish affairs. *Recreations:* swimming, angling, travelling, reading. *Address:* 11 Beechwood Court, Bearsden, Glasgow. *T:* 041-942 3876. *Clubs:* Caledonian; Western (Glasgow); RNVR (Scotland).

MacLELLAN, Sir Robin; *see* MacLellan, Sir G. R. P.

McLELLAND, Charles James; Deputy Managing Director, BBC Radio, since 1980; *b* 19 Nov. 1930; *s of* Charles John McLelland and Jessie Steele Barbour; *m* 1961, Philippa Mary Murphy; one *s* three *d. Educ:* Kilmarnock Acad.; Glasgow Acad.; Glasgow Univ. MA (Hons). Commissioned Royal Artillery, 1952-54. Sub-Editor, Leader Writer, Glasgow Herald, 1954-58; Scriptwriter, European Productions, BBC, 1958-61; Head of Programmes, Radio Sarawak, 1962-64; Indian Programme Organiser, BBC, 1964-67; Asst Head, Arabic Service, BBC, 1967-71; Head of Arabic Service, 1971-75; Controller, BBC Radio 2, 1976-80 (also Radio 1, 1976-78). *Recreations:* gardening, reading, flying. *Address:* c/o Broadcasting House, W1A 1AA. *Club:* Travellers'.

MacLENNAN, Maj.-Gen. Alastair, OBE 1945; Curator, Royal Army Medical Corps Historical Museum, Mytchett, Hants, 1969-Feb. 1977; *b* 16 Feb. 1912; *s of* Col. Farquhar MacLennan, DSO; *m* 1940, Constance Anne Cook; two *s* one *d. Educ:* Aberdeen Grammar Sch.; University of Aberdeen (MB, ChB). Commissioned Lieut, RAMC, 1934; Captain, 1935; Major, 1942; Lieut-Colonel, 1942; Colonel, 1952; Brigadier, 1964; Maj.-General, 1967; retired 1969. Appointments held include regimental, staff and Ministry of Defence in UK, Malta, NW Europe, India, Malaya, Korea, Egypt and Germany; ADGMS (Army), Min. of Defence, 1957-61; DDMS, HQ, BAOR, 1961-64; Inspector Army Medical Services, 1964-66; DDMS: 1 (Br) Corps, 1966-67; HQ Eastern Command, 1967-68; Dep. Dir-Gen., Army Med. Services, MoD, 1968-69; Col Comdt, RAMC, 1971-76. US Bronze Star Medal, 1952. OStJ, 1966. QHP, 1968-69. *Publications:* papers on history of military firearms and on Highland Regts in North America 1756-1783. *Recreations:* bird-watching, military history, collecting antique military firearms and swords, vintage motor-cars. *Address:* 56 Reigate Road, Ewell, Epsom, Surrey. *T:* 01-393 2132.

McLENNAN, Gordon; General Secretary, Communist Party of Great Britain, since 1975; *b* Glasgow, 12 May 1924; *s of* a shipyard worker; *m* ; four *c. Educ:* Hamilton Crescent Sch., Partick, Glasgow. Engineering apprentice, Albion Motors Ltd, Scotstoun, 1939, later engineering draughtsman. Elected Glasgow Organiser, Communist Party, 1949; Sec., Communist Party in Scotland, 1957; Nat. Organiser, Communist Party of GB, 1966. *Recreations:* golf and other sports; cultural interests. *Address:* 16 St John Street, EC1M 4AL.

MacLENNAN, Hugh; CC (Canada) 1967; Professor, English Literature, McGill University, 1967-79 (Associate Professor, 1951-67); now Professor Emeritus; *b* 20 March 1907; *s of* Dr Samuel John MacLennan and Katherine MacQuarrie; *m* 1st, 1936, Dorothy Duncan (*d* 1957); 2nd, 1959, Frances Aline, *d of* late Frank Earle Walker and Isabella Scott Benson. *Educ:* Dalhousie Univ.; Oriel Coll., Oxford; Graduate Coll., Princeton. Rhodes Schol. (Canada at large), 1928; PhD (Princeton) 1935. Classics Master, Lower Canada Coll., Montreal, 1935-45; writing, 1945-51. FRS Canada, 1953 (Gold Medal, 1951); FRSL, 1959. Governor-General's Award for Fiction, 1945, 1948, 1959; Governor-General's Award for non-fiction, 1949, 1954. Hon. DLitt: Waterloo Lutheran, 1961; Carleton Univ., 1967; Western Ontario, 1953, Manitoba, 1955; Hon. LLD: Dalhousie, 1956, Saskatchewan, 1959; McMaster, 1965; Toronto, 1966; Laurentian, 1966; Sherbrooke, 1967; British Columbia, 1968; St Mary's, 1968; Hon. DCL Bishop's, 1965. *Publications:* Oxyrhynchus: An Economic and Social Study, 1935; Barometer Rising, 1941; Two Solitudes, 1945; The Precipice, 1948; Cross Country (essays), 1949; Each Man's Son, 1951; Thirty and Three (essays), 1954; The Watch That Ends The Night, 1959; Scotchman's Return (essays), 1960; Return of the Sphinx, 1967; Rivers of Canada, 1974; Voices in Time, 1980. *Recreations:* walking, gardening. *Address:* 1535 Summerhill Avenue, Montreal, PQ, Canada. *T:* 932-0475. *Clubs:* Montreal Amateur Athletic Association, McGill Faculty (Montreal).

MACLENNAN, Sir Ian (Morrison Ross), KCMG 1957 (CMG 1951); HM Diplomatic Service, retired; *b* 30 Oct. 1909; *s of* late W. Maclennan, Glasgow; *m* 1936, Margherita Lucas, *d of* late F. Lucas Jarratt, Bedford; one *s* one *d. Educ:* Hymers Coll., Hull; Worcester Coll., Oxford. Appointed Colonial Office, 1933; Dominions Office, 1937; UK High Commissioner's Office, Ottawa, 1938; Pretoria, 1945; UK High Commissioner S Rhodesia, 1951-53; Federation of Rhodesia and Nyasaland, 1953-55; Assistant Under-Secretary of State, CRO, 1955-57; UK High Commissioner in Ghana, 1957-59; Ambassador to the Republic of Ireland, 1960-63; High Commissioner in New Zealand, 1964-69. Mem., Gen. Adv. Council, IBA, 1974-82 (Chm., 1979-82). *Address:* 26 Ham Street, Richmond, Surrey. *Club:* Travellers'.

McLENNAN, Sir Ian (Munro), KCMG 1979; KBE 1963 (CBE 1956); Chairman: Australia and New Zealand Banking Group Ltd, and Australia and New Zealand Group Holdings, 1977-82; Interscan Australia Pty Ltd, since 1978; Henry Jones (IXL) Ltd, since 1981; Elders IXL Ltd, since 1981; President, Australian Academy of Technological Sciences, since 1976; *b* 30 Nov. 1909; *s* of R. B. and C. O. McLennan; *m* 1937, Dora H., *d* of J. H. Robertson; two *s* two *d*. *Educ:* Scotch Coll., Melbourne; Melbourne Univ. Broken Hill Pty Co. Ltd: Cadet engineer, 1933; Asst Manager, Newcastle Steelworks of BHP Co. Ltd, 1943; Asst Gen. Man., BHP Co. Ltd, 1947; Gen. Man., 1950; Sen. Gen. Man., 1956; Chief Gen. Man., 1959; Man. Dir, 1967-71; Chm., 1971-77; Chairman: BHP-GKN Hldgs Ltd, 1970-78; Tubemakers of Australia Ltd, 1973-79; Bank of Adelaide, 1979-80; Dir, ICI Australia Ltd, 1976-79. Chairman: Defence (Industrial) Cttee, 1956-67; Ian Clunies Ross Meml Foundn; Australian Mineral Development Laboratories, 1959-67, Mem. Council, 1959-77; Dep. Chm., Immigration Planning Council, 1949-67. Former Dir, International Iron and Steel Inst.; Pres., Australia-Japan Business Co-operation Cttee, 1977-; Member: Internat. Council, Morgan Guaranty Trust Co. of NY, 1973-79; Australian Mining Industry Council, 1967-77; Australasian Inst. of Mining and Metallurgy (Pres., 1951, 1957 and 1972); Australian Mineral Industries Research Assoc. Ltd, 1958-77; General Motors Australian Adv. Council, 1978-; Adv. Council, CSIRO, 1979-. Chm., Queen Elizabeth II Jubilee Trust for Young Australians. For. Associate, Nat. Acad. of Engrg (USA), 1978. FIAM 1978; FAA 1980. *Recreations:* golf, gardening. *Address:* Apt 3, 112-120 Walsh Street, South Yarra, Victoria 3141, Australia. *Clubs:* Melbourne, Athenæum, Australian (all Melbourne); Union (Sydney); Newcastle (Newcastle); Commonwealth (Canberra); Royal Melbourne Golf; Melbourne Cricket.

MACLENNAN, Robert Adam Ross; MP Caithness and Sutherland since 1966 (Lab, 1966-81, SDP, since 1981); Barrister-at-Law; *b* 26 June 1936; *e s* of Sir Hector MacLennan, and late Isabel Margaret Adam; *m* 1968, Mrs Helen Noyes, *d* of Judge Ammi Cutter, Cambridge, Mass, and *widow* of Paul H. Noyes; one *s* one *d*, and one step *s*. *Educ:* Glasgow Academy; Balliol Coll., Oxford; Trinity Coll., Cambridge; Columbia Univ., New York City. Called to the Bar, Gray's Inn, 1962. Parliamentary Private Secretary: to Secretary of State for Commonwealth Affairs, 1967-69; to Minister without Portfolio, 1969-70; an Opposition Spokesman: on Scottish Affairs, 1970-71; on Defence, 1971-72; Parly Under-Sec. of State, Dept of Prices and Consumer Protection, 1974-79; opposition spokesman on foreign affairs, 1980-81. Member: House of Commons Estimates Cttee, 1967-69; House of Commons Select Cttee on Scottish Affairs, 1969-70; Public Accounts Cttee, 1979-; Latey Cttee on Age of Majority, 1968; National Steering and Policy Cttees of SDP. *Recreations:* theatre, music. *Address:* 74 Abingdon Villas, W8; Hollandmake, Barrock, Caithness.

MacLENNAN OF MacLENNAN, Ronald George; Chief of Clan MacLennan; teacher of and lecturer in physical education, 1949-82, retired; *b* 7 Feb. 1925; *s* of George Mitchell MacLennan and Helen Ames Thomson; recognised as Chief of Clan MacLennan, 1978; *m* 1970, Margaret, 2nd *d* of Donald and Jemima MacLennan; one *s* two *d*. *Educ:* Boroughmuir Secondary Sch., Edinburgh; Univ. of Copenhagen (Dip. in Physical Educn). Hon. Col, Oregon National Guard, 1981-; Hon. Ambassador of Scotland to Poland, London, 1981-; Hon. Brig.-Gen., Polish Armed Forces (in exile), 1982-. Kt, Order of St Lazarus of Jerusalem, 1976; Order of Virturi Militari, Poland, 1982. *Publication:* History of the MacLennans, 1978. *Recreations:* history, gardening, kayaking. *Heir: s* Ruairidh Donald George MacLennan, yr of MacLennan, *b* 22 April 1977. *Address:* The Old Mill, Dores, Inverness. *T:* Dores 228.

MacLEOD, family name of **Baron MacLeod of Fuinary.**

MACLEOD, family name of **Baroness Macleod of Borve.**

MACLEOD OF BORVE, Baroness *cr* 1971 (Life Peer), of Borve, Isle of Lewis; **Evelyn Hester Macleod,** JP; DL; *b* 19 Feb. 1915; *d* of Rev. Gervase Vanneck Blois (*d* 1961), and Hon. Hester Murray Pakington (*d* 1973), *y d* of 3rd Baron Hampton; *m* 1st, 1937, Mervyn Charles Mason (killed by enemy action, 1940); 2nd, 1941, Rt Hon. Iain Norman Macleod, MP (Minister of Health, 1952-55; Minister of Labour and Nat. Service, 1955-59; Secretary of State for the Colonies, 1959-61; Chancellor of the Duchy of Lancaster and Leader of the House of Commons, 1961-63; Chancellor of the Exchequer, June 1970) (*d* 1970), *e s* of late Norman A. Macleod, MD, Scaliscro, Isle of Lewis; one *s* one *d*. Chairman, Nat. Association of the Leagues of Hospital Friends; first Chm., Nat. Gas Consumers' Council, 1972-77; Member: IBA (formerly ITA), 1972-75; Energy Commn, 1977-78; Metrication Bd, 1978-80. Founder, Crisis at Christmas, 1967; Pres., Nat. Assoc. of Widows, 1976. Governor, Queenswood Sch., 1978-. JP Middlesex, 1955; DL Greater London, 1977. *Recreation:* my family. *Address:* House of Lords, SW1; Luckings Farm, Coleshill, Amersham, Bucks.

MacLEOD OF FUINARY, Baron, *cr* 1967 (Life Peer), of Fuinary in Morven; **Very Rev. George Fielden MacLeod,** Bt, 1924; MC; BA Oxford; DD (Glasgow); Moderator of the General Assembly of the Church of Scotland, May 1957-May 1958 (designation, Very Rev.); Founder of the Iona Community (Leader, 1938-67); one of Her Majesty's Chaplains in Scotland; *b* 17 June 1895; 2nd *s* of Sir John MacLeod, 1st Bt; *S* nephew, 1944; *m* 1948, Lorna Helen Janet, *er d* of late Rev. Donald Macleod, Balvonie of Inshes, Inverness; two *s* one *d*. *Educ:* Winchester; Oriel Coll., Oxford (Hon. Fellow

1969); Edinburgh Univ. Post Graduate Fellow, Union Theological Coll., New York, 1921; Missioner, British Columbia Lumber Camps, 1922; Collegiate Minister, St Cuthbert's Parish Church, Edinburgh, 1926-30; Minister of Govan Parish Church, Glasgow, 1930-38; served European War, 1914-18; Captain Argyll and Sutherland Highlanders (MC and Croix de Guerre); Warrack Lecturer on Preaching at Edinburgh and St Andrews Universities, 1936; Select Preacher, Cambridge Univ., 1943 and 1963; Cunningham Lecturer on Evangelism, 1954; first holder of Fosdick Professorship (Rockefeller Foundation), Union Theological Seminary, New York, 1954-55; Danforth Lecturer, USA Universities, 1960 and 1964. Rector of Glasgow Univ., 1968-71. Pres. and Chm. of Council of International Fellowship of Reconciliation, 1963. DLitt Muskingum Univ., USA; Dr of Laws, Iona Coll., New Rochelle, USA. *Publications:* Govan Calling: a book of Broadcast Sermons and Addresses, 1934; contributor to Way to God Series for the BBC; Speaking the Truth in Love: a book on Preaching, 1936; We Shall Rebuild (the principles of the Iona Community), 1944; Only One Way Left, 1956. *Heir* (to Baronetcy only): *s* Hon. John Maxwell Norman MacLeod, *b* 23 Feb. 1952. *Address:* 23 Learmonth Terrace, Edinburgh EH4 1PG. *T:* 031-332 3262.

MacLEOD, Angus, CBE 1967; Hon. Sheriff of Lothians and Peebles, since 1972; Procurator Fiscal of Edinburgh and Midlothian, 1955-71; *b* 2 April 1906; *s* of late Alexander MacLeod, Glendale, Skye; *m* 1936, Jane Winifred (*d* 1977), *d* of late Sir Robert Bryce Walker, CBE, LLD; three *s*. *Educ:* Hutchesons Grammar Sch.; Glasgow Univ. (MA, LLB). Solicitor, 1929; general practice, 1929-34; Depute Procurator Fiscal, Glasgow and Edinburgh, 1934-42; Procurator Fiscal of Dumfriesshire, 1942-52, of Aberdeenshire, 1952-55; Temp. Sheriff, Scotland, 1973-77. Part-time Chm., VAT Appeal Tribunals, 1973-77. *Recreations:* reading, walking, interested in sport. *Address:* 7 Oxford Terrace, Edinburgh EH4 1PX. *T:* 031-332 5466.

MacLEOD, Aubrey Seymour H.; *see* Halford-MacLeod.

McLEOD, Sir Charles Henry, 3rd Bt, *cr* 1925; *b* 7 Nov. 1924; *o surv. s* of Sir Murdoch Campbell McLeod, 2nd Bt, and Annette Susan Mary (*d* 1964), *d* of Henry Whitehead, JP, 26 Pelham Crescent, SW7; *S* father 1950; *m* 1957, Gillian (*d* 1978), *d* of Henry Bowlby, London; one *s* two *d*. *Educ:* Winchester. *Heir: s* James Roderick Charles McLeod, *b* 26 Sept. 1960.

MacLEOD, Donald Alexander; HM Diplomatic Service; Counsellor (Economic and Commercial), British High Commission, Singapore, since 1981; *b* 23 Jan. 1938; *er s* of late Col Colin S. MacLeod of Glendale, OBE, TD, and of Margaret Drysdale Robertson MacLeod; *m* 1963, Rosemary Lilian Abel (*née* Randle); two *s* two *d*. *Educ:* Edinburgh Academy; Pembroke Coll., Cambridge, 1958-61 (BA). National Service, Queen's Own Cameron Highlanders, 1956-58. HM Foreign Service, 1961; School of Oriental and African Studies, London, 1961-62; British Embassy, Rangoon, 1962-66; Private Sec. to Minister of State, Commonwealth Office, 1966-69; First Secretary, Ottawa, 1969-73; FCO, 1973-78; First Sec./Head of Chancery, Bucharest, 1978-80. *Address: c/o* Foreign and Commonwealth Office, SW1. *Club:* United Oxford & Cambridge University.

MacLEOD, Air Vice-Marshal Donald Francis Graham, CB 1977; Director of Royal Air Force Dental Services, 1973-77, retired; *b* Stornoway, Isle of Lewis, Scotland, 26 Aug. 1917; *s* of Alexander MacLeod; both parents from Isle of Lewis; *m* 1941, Marjorie Eileen (*née* Gracie); one *s* one *d*. *Educ:* Nicolson Inst., Stornoway, Isle of Lewis; St Andrews Univ.; Royal Coll. of Surgeons, Edinburgh. LDS St And. 1940; FDS RCSEd 1955. Qualif. in Dental Surgery, 1940; two years in private practice. Joined Royal Air Force Dental Branch, 1942; served in various parts of the world, mainly in hospitals doing oral surgery. QHDS, 1972. Royal Humane Society Resuscitation Certificate for life saving from the sea in the Western Isles, 1937. *Recreations:* golf, gardening; Captain of Soccer, St Andrews Univ., 1938 (full blue), Captain of Badminton, 1939 (half blue). *Address:* 20 Witchford Road, Ely, Cambs CB6 3DP. *T:* Ely 3164. *Club:* Royal Worlington Golf.

MacLEOD, Hugh Roderick; Chairman, Lloyd's Register of Shipping, from July 1983 (Chairman elect, Jan.-July 1983); part-time Board Member, British Railways, since 1980; Chairman, Scottish Board, British Railways, since 1980; *b* 20 Sept. 1929; *s* of Neil MacLeod and Ruth MacLeod (*née* Hill); *m* 1958, Josephine Seager Berry; two *s* one *d*. *Educ:* Bryanston Sch.; St John's Coll., Cambridge. Served 2nd Regt, RHA, 1948-50. Joined The Ben Line Steamers Limited, 1953, Jt Man. Dir, 1964-82; Partner, Wm Thomson & Co., 1959, Director, 1964; Chairman, Associated Container Transportation Ltd, 1975-78. Member, National Ports Council, 1977-80. *Recreations:* outdoor pursuits, music. *Address:* 33B Holland Park, W11.

MacLEOD, Sir John, Kt 1963; TD; *b* 23 Feb. 1913; *y s* of late Duncan MacLeod, CBE, Skeabost, Isle of Skye; *m* 1938, Rosemary Theodora Hamilton, *d* of late Frederick Noel Hamilton Wills, Miserden Park, Stroud, Glos; two *s* three *d*. *Educ:* Fettes Coll., Edinburgh. TA 1935. Served War of 1939-45, 51st Highland Division; France, 1940. MP (Nat. Liberal) Ross and Cromarty Div., 1945-64. *Address:* Bunkers Hill, Farmington, Northleach, Glos. *T:* Northleach 731. *Club:* Highland (Inverness).

McLEOD, Rev. John; Church of Scotland Minister, Livingston Ecumenical Team Ministry, since 1974; Chaplain to the Queen in Scotland, since 1978; *b* 8 April 1926; *s* of Angus McLeod and Catherine McDougall; *m* 1958, Sheila

McLeod; three *s* two *d. Educ:* Inverness Royal Academy; Edinburgh Univ. (MA); New Coll., Edinburgh. Farming until 1952; at university, 1952-58; ordained, Inverness, 1958. Missionary in India: Jalna, 1959-68; Poona, 1969-74; involved in rural development with special emphasis on development and conservation of water resource; also responsible for pastoral work in Church of N India, St Mary's, Poona, 1970-74; Warden of Nether Dechmont Farm Community Centre, 1977-81. *Recreations:* hill walking, gardening, swimming, music. *Address:* 53 Harburn Avenue, Deans, Livingston, West Lothian EH54 8NH. *T:* Livingston 412392.

MacLEOD OF MacLEOD, John; 29th Chief of MacLeod; *b* 10 Aug. 1935; second *s* of late Captain Robert Wolrige-Gordon, MC, and Joan, *d* of Hubert Walter and Dame Flora MacLeod of MacLeod, DBE; officially recognised in name of MacLeod of MacLeod by decree of Lyon Court, 1951; *S* grandmother, 1976; *m* 1973, Melita Kolin; one *s* one *d. Educ:* Eton. *Heir: s* Hugh Magnus MacLeod, younger of MacLeod. *Address:* Dunvegan Castle, Isle of Skye. *T:* Dunvegan 206.
See also P. Wolrige-Gordon.

MACLEOD, Joseph Todd Gordon; author and broadcaster; *b* 24 April 1903; *o* surv. *s* of late James Gordon Macleod; *m* 1st, 1928, Kate Macgregor (*d* 1953), *d* of late Robert Davis, Uddingston; 2nd, Maria Teresa, *d* of late Ing. Alfredo Foschini, Rome; one *s* one *d. Educ:* Rugby Sch.; Balliol Coll., Oxford. BA 1925; MA 1945; called to Bar, Inner Temple, 1928. Was book-reviewer, private tutor, actor, producer, lecturer on theatre-history. Directed the Festival Theatre, Cambridge, 1933-36; visited theatres in USSR, 1937; Secretary of Huntingdonshire Divisional Labour Party, 1937-38, also Parliamentary Candidate; announcer BBC, 1938-45. Managing Director, Scottish National Film Studios, Glasgow, 1946-47; Convener, Drama, Gœthe Festival Society, 1948-49; produced The Lady from the Sea, Festival of Britain, Aberdeen, 1951; Scottish Episcopal Church chronicle play St Mary's Cathedral, Edinburgh, 1952; toured Holland as guest of Dutch Ministry of Fine Arts, 1946; visited Soviet Union as guest of Moscow and Kiev Cultural Relations Societies, 1947; Silver Medal, Royal Society of Arts for paper on the Theatre in Soviet Culture, 1944. Hon. Member, British Actors' Equity. *Plays performed:* The Suppliants of Aeschylus translated with a verse sequel, 1933; A Woman Turned to Stone, 1934; Overture to Cambridge, 1934; A Miracle for St George, 1935; Leap in September (Arts Council Prize), 1952. *Publications:* Beauty and the Beast, 1927; The Ecliptic (poem), 1930; Foray of Centaurs (poem), 1931; Overture to Cambridge (novel), 1936; The New Soviet Theatre, 1943; Actors Cross the Volga, 1946; A Job at the BBC, 1947; A Soviet Theatre Sketchbook, 1951; The Passage of the Torch (poem), 1951; A Short History of the British Theatre (Italian edn), 1958; Abstractions, 1967; People of Florence, 1968; The Sisters D'Aranyi, 1969; An Old Olive Tree, 1971 (Arts Council Award); The Actor's Right to Act, 1981; poetry under *non-de-plume* Adam Drinan: The Cove, 1940; The Men of the Rocks, 1942; The Ghosts of the Strath, 1943; Women of the Happy Island, 1944; Script from Norway, 1953; contribution on Theatre history to Chambers's Encyclopædia. *Music:* The Kid from the City, 1941. *Recreations:* painting, music, bird-watching. *Address:* Via delle Ballodole 9/7, Trespiano, 50139 Firenze, Italy. *T:* Firenze 417056.

McLEOD, Keith Morrison, CBE 1975; Financial Controller, British Airports Authority, 1971-75; *b* 26 May 1920; *yr s* of John and Mary McLeod; *m* 1943, Patricia Carter; two *s* one *d. Educ:* Bancroft's School. FCIT. Asst Auditor, Exchequer and Audit Dept, 1939; served RAF, 1941-46; Asst Principal, Min. of Supply, 1948; Principal, 1950; BJSM, Washington, 1955-57; Asst Sec., Min. of Supply, 1957; Cabinet Office, 1962; Finance Dir, British Airports Authority, 1966. *Address:* 161 Banstead Road, Banstead, Surrey. *T:* 01-393 9005.

McLEOD, Malcolm Donald; Keeper of Ethnography, British Museum, since 1974; *b* 19 May 1941; *s* of Donald McLeod and Ellen (*née* Fairclough); *m* 1st, 1965, Jacqueline Wynborne (marr. diss. 1980); two *s* one *d*; 2nd, 1980, Iris Barry. *Educ:* Birkenhead Sch.; Hertford and Exeter Colls, Oxford. MA, BLitt. Lectr, Dept of Sociology, Univ. of Ghana, 1967-69; Asst Curator, Museum of Archaeology and Ethnology, Cambridge, 1969-74; Lectr, Girton Coll., Cambridge, 1969-74; Fellow, Magdalene Coll., Cambridge, 1972-74. Member: Hist. and Current Affairs Selection Cttee, Nat. Film Archive, 1978-; UK Unesco Cultural Adv. Cttee, 1980-. Hon. Lectr, Anthropology Dept, UCL, 1976-81. Marett Lectr, Exeter Coll., Oxford, 1982. *Publications:* The Asante, 1980; Treasures of African Art, 1980; articles and reviews in learned jls. *Address:* 6 Burlington Gardens, W1X 2EX.

MACLEOD, Nigel Ronald Buchanan, QC 1979; a Recorder of the Crown Court, since 1981; *b* 7 Feb. 1936; *s* of Donald Macleod, MB, ChB, and Katherine Ann Macleod; *m* 1966, Susan Margaret (*née* Buckley); one *s* one *d. Educ:* Wigan Grammar Sch.; Christ Church, Oxford (MA, BLC). Served RAF, 1954-56. Called to the Bar, Gray's Inn, 1961. Asst Comr, Boundary Commn for England, 1981-. *Publications:* contribs to legal jls. *Recreations:* sailing, walking. *Address:* Goyt Lodge, Marple, Cheshire. *T:* 061-427 2101; 87 Rennie Court, Kings Reach, Upper Ground, SE1. *T:* 01-633 9807.

MACLEOD, Norman Donald, MA, LLB; Advocate; Sheriff of Glasgow and Strathkelvin (formerly Lanarkshire at Glasgow), since 1967; *b* 6 March 1932; *s* of Rev. John MacLeod, Loch Carron, and late Catherine MacRitchie; *m* 1957, Ursula Jane, *y d* of George H. Bromley, Inveresk; two *s* two *d. Educ:* Mill Hill Sch.; George Watson's Boys' Coll., Edinburgh; Edinburgh Univ.;

Hertford Coll., Oxford. Passed Advocate, 1956. Colonial Administrative Service, Tanganyika: Dist. Officer, 1957-59; Crown Counsel, 1959-64; practised at Scots Bar, 1964-67. *Recreations:* sailing, gardening. *Address:* 27 Cleveden Drive, Glasgow G12 0SD. *T:* 041-339 1607.

MACLEOD-SMITH, Alastair Macleod, CMG 1956; Consultant, National Westminster Bank, since 1981; *b* 30 June 1916; *s* of late R. A. Smith, MIEE, and Mrs I. Macleod-Smith (*née* Kellner); *m* 1945, Ann (*née* Circuitt); one *s* one *d. Educ:* The Wells House, Malvern Wells, Worcs; Ellesmere Coll., Salop; The Queen's Coll., Oxford. BA Oxon 1938. Entered HM Oversea Service as administrative cadet, Nigeria, 1939; Asst Dist Officer, 1942, Dist Officer, Nigeria, 1949; seconded to Windward Islands as Financial and Economic Adviser, 1949-52; Financial Sec., Western Pacific High Commission, 1952-57; Financial Sec., Sierra Leone, 1957-61. Dir, Selection Trust Ltd, 1967-80. *Recreations:* golf, sailing. *Address:* Roughetts Lodge, Coldharbour Lane, Hildenborough, Kent. *Clubs:* United Oxford & Cambridge University; Knole Park Golf.

McLINTOCK, (Charles) Alan, CA; Joint Senior Partner, Thomson McLintock & Co., since 1982; Deputy Chairman, Woolwich Equitable Building Society, since 1980 (Director, since 1970); Chairman: Lake View Investment Trust, since 1975 (Director, since 1971); Stockholders Investment Trust, since 1978; Ecclesiastical Insurance Office, since 1981 (Director, since 1972); Director: National Westminster Bank Ltd, since 1979; M&G Group, since 1982; *b* 28 May 1925; *s* of late Charles Henry McLintock, OBE, and Alison McLintock; *m* 1955, Sylvia Mary Foster Taylor; one *s* three *d. Educ:* Rugby School. Served Royal Artillery, 1943-47; commnd 1945; Captain RHA 1946. With Thomson McLintock & Co., Chartered Accountants, 1948-; qualified, 1952; Partner, 1954. Chm., Grange Trust, 1973-81 (Dir, 1958-81); Dir, Trust Houses Ltd, 1967-71. Governor: Rugby Sch., 1973-; Westonbirt Sch., 1977-; Member: Clergy Orphan Corp. Cttee of Management, 1963-; Royal Alexandra and Albert Sch. Bd of Management, 1965-. *Recreations:* music, walking. *Address:* Burford House, Woodland Way, Kingswood, Tadworth, Surrey KT20 6NW. *T:* Mogador 832447.

McLINTOCK, Sir William Traven, 3rd Bt, *cr* 1934; *b* 4 Jan. 1931; *s* of Sir Thomas McLintock, 2nd Bt and Jean, *d* of R. T. D. Aitken, New Brunswick; *S* father 1953; *m* 1952, André (marr. diss.), *d* of Richard Lonsdale-Hands; three *s* ; *m* Heather, *d* of Philip Homfray-Davies; one step *s* one step *d. Educ:* Harrow. *Heir: s* Michael William McLintock, *b* 13 Aug. 1958.

MACLURE, Sir John (Robert Spencer), 4th Bt *cr* 1898; Headmaster, Croftinloan School, Pitlochry, Perthshire, since 1978; *b* 25 March 1934; *s* of Sir John William Spencer Maclure, 3rd Bt, OBE, and of Elspeth, *er d* of late Alexander King Clark; *S* father, 1980; *m* 1964, Jane Monica, *d* of late Rt Rev. T. J. Savage, Bishop of Zululand and Swaziland; four *s. Educ:* Winchester College. IAPS Diploma. 2nd Lt, 2nd Bn KRRC, 1953-55, BAOR; Lt, Royal Hampshire Airborne Regt, TA. Assistant Master: Horris Hill, 1955-66 and 1974-78; St George's, Wanganui, NZ, 1967-68; Sacred Heart Coll., Auckland, NZ, 1969-70; St Edmund's, Hindhead, Surrey, 1971-74. *Heir: s* John Mark Maclure, *b* 27 Aug. 1965. *Address:* Croftinloan School, Pitlochry, Perthshire PH16 5JR. *T:* Pitlochry 2837.

MACLURE, (John) Stuart, CBE 1982; Editor, Times Educational Supplement, since 1969; *b* 8 Aug. 1926; *s* of Hugh and Bertha Maclure, Highgate, N6; *m* 1951, Constance Mary Butler; one *s* two *d. Educ:* Highgate Sch.; Christ's Coll., Cambridge. MA. Joined The Times, 1950; The Times Educational Supplement, 1951; Editor, Education, 1954-69. Hon. Prof. of Educn, Keele Univ., 1981-. President: Br. Sect., Comparative Educn Soc. in Europe, 1979; Educnl Sect., BAAS, 1983; Member: Educnl Adv. Council, IBA, 1979-; Consultative Cttee, Assessment of Performance Unit, 1974-82. Regents' Lecturer, Univ. of California, Berkeley, 1980. Hon. Fellow, City of Sheffield Polytechnic, 1976. *Publications:* Joint Editor (with T. E. Utley) Documents on Modern Political Thought, 1956; Editor, Educational Documents, 1816-1963, 1965; A Hundred Years of London Education, 1970; (with Tony Becher) The Politics of Curriculum Change, 1978; (ed with Tony Becher) Accountability in Education, 1979; Education and Youth Employment in Great Britain, 1979. *Address:* 109 College Road, Dulwich, SE21. *Club:* MCC.

McLUSKEY, Rt. Rev. J(ames) Fraser, MC; MA, BD, DD; Minister at St Columba's Church of Scotland, Pont Street, London, since 1960; Moderator of the General Assembly of the Church of Scotland, May 1983-84 (designation subseq. Very Rev.); *b* 1914; *s* of James Fraser McLuskey and Margaret Keltie; *m* 1st, 1939, Irene (*d* 1959), *d* of Pastor Calaminus, Wuppertal; two *s* ; 2nd, 1966, Ruth Quartermaine (*née* Hunter), widow of Lt-Col Keith Briant. *Educ:* Aberdeen Grammar Sch.; Edinburgh Univ. Ordained Minister of Church of Scotland, 1938; Chaplain to Univ. of Glasgow, 1939-47. Service as Army Chaplain, 1943-46 (1st Special Air Service Regt, 1944-46); Sub Warden Royal Army Chaplains' Training Centre, 1947-50; Minister at Broughty Ferry East, 1950-55; Minister at New Kilpatrick, Bearsden, 1955-60. *Publication:* Parachute Padre, 1951. *Recreations:* walking, music, reading. *Address:* St Columba's Church of Scotland, Pont Street, SW1X 0BD. *T:* 01-584 2321. *Clubs:* Caledonian, Special Forces.

MacLYSAGHT, Edward Anthony, LLD, DLitt, MRIA; Member, Irish Manuscripts Commission, 1949-73 (Inspector, 1939-43; Chairman, 1956-73); Chief Herald and Genealogical Officer, Office of Arms, Dublin Castle,

1943-49; Keeper of Manuscripts, National Library of Ireland, 1949-55; *b* at sea, 1887 (bapt. Co. Clare); *m* 1st, 1915, Maureen Pattison; one *s* one *d* ; 2nd, 1936, Mary Frances Cunneen; three *s*. *Educ*: abroad; Nat. Univ. of Ireland (MA). Engaged in cattle-breeding and forestry since 1910; mem. of Irish Convention, 1917-18, Irish Senate, 1922-25; working in South Africa, 1929-30, 1936-38. Mem. Gov. Body, Sch. of Celtic Studies, Dublin Inst for Advanced Studies, 1942-76. *Publications*: The Gael, 1919, 2nd edn 1929; Cúrsaí Thomáis, 1927, new edn 1969; Toil Dé, 1933; Short Study of a Transplanted Family, 1935; Irish Life in the Seventeenth Century, 1939, 3rd edn 1969; (ed) The Kenmare Manuscripts, 1942, 2nd edn 1970; (ed) Analecta Hibernica (14 and 15), 1944; An Aifric Theas, 1947, East Clare (1916-21), 1954; Irish Families: Their Names, Arms and Origins, 1957, 4th edn 1978; More Irish Families, 1960, 2nd enlarged edn, inc. Supplement to Irish Families, 1982; The Surnames of Ireland, 1969, 5th edn 1980; (ed) Forth the Banners Go, reminiscences of William O'Brien, 1969; Leathanaigh óm' Dhialann, 1978; Changing Times, 1978. *Address*: Raheen, Tuamgraney, Co. Clare. *Club*: United Arts (Dublin).

McMAHON, Andrew, (Andy); MP (Lab) Glasgow, Govan, since 1979; *b* 18 March 1920; *s* of Andrew and Margaret McMahon; *m* 1944; one *s* one *d*. *Educ*: District School, Govan. Boilermaker, Govan shipyards, 1936; unemployed, 1971-79. First and only Boilermaker to enter House of Commons. Member, Glasgow Dist. Council, 1973-79. Chairman, Scottish Arab Friendship Assoc. *Recreations*: youth work, care and comfort for elderly. *Address*: House of Commons, SW1.

McMAHON, Sir Brian (Patrick), 8th Bt *cr* 1817; engineer; *b* 9 June 1942; *s* of Sir (William) Patrick McMahon, 7th Bt, and Ruth Stella, *yr d* of late Percy Robert Kenyon-Slaney; *S* father, 1977. *Educ*: Wellington. BSc, AIM. *Heir*: brother Shaun Desmond McMahon [*b* 29 Oct. 1945; *m* 1971, Antonia Noel Adie].

McMAHON, Christopher William; Deputy Governor, Bank of England, since 1980; *b* Melbourne, 10 July 1927; *s* of late Dr John Joseph McMahon and late Margaret Kate (*née* Brown); *m* 1st, 1956, Marion Kelso; two *s* ; 2nd, 1982, Barbara Alison Braimbridge, *d* of late Dr J. G. Cormie and Mrs B. E. Cormie. *Educ*: Melbourne Grammar Sch.; Univ. of Melbourne; Magdalen Coll., Oxford. 1st cl. hons PPE, 1953. Tutor in English Lit., Univ. of Melbourne, 1950; Econ. Asst, HM Treasury, 1953-57; Econ. Adviser, British Embassy, Washington, 1957-60; Fellow and Tutor in Econs, Magdalen Coll., Oxford, 1960-64 (Sen. Tutor, 1961-63); Tutor in Econs, Treasury Centre for Admin. Studies, 1963-64; Mem., Plowden Cttee on Aircraft Industry, 1964-65; entered Bank of England as Adviser, 1964; Adviser to the Governors, 1966-70; Exec. Dir, 1970-80. Mem., Steering Cttee, Gp of Thirty, 1978-; Chm., Working Party 3, OECD, 1980-. *Publications*: Sterling in the Sixties, 1964; (ed) Techniques of Economic Forecasting, 1965.

MacMAHON, Gerald John, CB 1962; CMG 1955; *b* 26 Sept. 1909; 2nd *s* of late Jeremiah MacMahon and Kathleen MacMahon (*née* Dodd); unmarried. *Educ*: Clongowes Wood Coll., Co. Kildare, Ireland; Emmanuel Coll., Cambridge (BA). Entered Board of Trade, 1933; Asst Sec., 1942. Imperial Defence Coll., 1949. Senior UK Trade Commissioner in India, 1952-58; Under-Sec., Board of Trade 1958-62 and 1964-70; Admiralty, Nov. 1962-64. *Recreation*: golf. *Address*: 19 Lower Park, Putney Hill, SW15. *Club*: Reform.

McMAHON, Rt. Rev. Thomas; *see* Brentwood, Bishop of, (R.C).

McMAHON, Rt. Hon. Sir William, GCMG 1977; CH 1972; PC 1966; MP for Lowe, NSW, 1949-82; Prime Minister of Australia, 1971-72; *b* 23 Feb. 1908; *s* of William Daniel McMahon; *m* 1965, Sonia R. Hopkins; one *s* two *d*. *Educ*: Sydney Grammar Sch.; St Paul's Coll., Univ. of Sydney (LLB, BEc). Practised as solicitor until 1939. Australian Army, 1940-45, Major. Elected to House of Representatives for Lowe, NSW, in gen. elections, 1949, 1951, 1954, 1955, 1958, 1961, 1963, 1966, 1969, 1972, 1974, 1975, 1977, 1980; Minister: for Navy, and for Air, 1951-54 (visited Korea and Japan in that capacity, 1952); for Social Services, 1954-56; for Primary Industry, 1956-58; for Labour and National Service, 1958-66; Treasurer, Commonwealth of Australia, 1966-69; Minister for External Affairs, later Foreign Affairs, 1969-71. Vice-Pres., Executive Council, 1964-66; Dep. Leader of Liberal Party, 1966-71, Leader, 1971-72; Acting Minister for Trade, Acting Minister for Labour and Nat. Service, Acting Minister in Charge, CSIRO, Acting Minister for National Development, Acting Minister for Territories, and Acting Attorney-Gen., for short periods, 1956-69; Leader of Aust. Delegation to Commonwealth Parliamentary Conf., New Delhi, Nov. 1957-Jan. 1958; Visiting Minister to ILO Conf., Geneva, June 1960 and June 1964; Pres., ILO Asian Regional Conf., Melbourne, Nov.-Dec., 1962; Mem., Bd of Governors, IMF and World Bank, 1966-69. Chm., Bd of Governors, Asian Development Bank, 1968-69. Led Australian delegns to Bangkok, Djakarta, Wellington, Tokyo, Manila and Saigon, 1970. As Prime Minister officially visited: USA, GB, 1971; Indonesia, Malaysia, Singapore, 1972. *Recreations*: golf, squash, farming. *Address*: 100 William Street, Sydney, NSW 2011, Australia. *Clubs*: Union, Royal Sydney, Australian, Australian Jockey (Sydney); Melbourne (Melbourne).

McMANNERS, Rev. Prof. John, DLitt; FBA 1978; Canon of Christ Church and Regius Professor of Ecclesiastical History, Oxford University, since 1972; *b* 25 Dec. 1916; *s* of Rev. Canon Joseph McManners and Mrs Ann McManners;

m 1951, Sarah Carruthers Errington; two *s* two *d*. *Educ*: St Edmund Hall, Oxford; Durham Univ. BA 1st cl. hons Mod. History Oxon, 1939; DipTheol Dunelm, 1947; DLitt Oxon 1980. Military Service, 1939-45 in Royal Northumberland Fusiliers (Major). Priest, 1948; St Edmund Hall, Oxford: Chaplain, 1948; Fellow, 1949; Dean, 1951; Prof., Univ. of Tasmania, 1956-59; Prof., Sydney Univ., 1959-66; Vis. Fellow, All Souls Coll., Oxford, 1965-66; Prof. of History, Univ. of Leicester, 1967-72. Birkbeck Lectr, Cambridge, 1976; John Coffin Meml Lectr, London Univ., 1982. Dir d'études associé, Ecole Pratique des Hautes Etudes, sect. IV, Paris, 1980-81. Mem., Doctrinal Commn of C of E, 1978-. Trustee, Nat. Portrait Gallery, 1970-78; Mem. Council, RHistS, 1971; Pres., Ecclesiastical Hist. Soc., 1977-78. FAHA 1970. Officer, Order of King George I of the Hellenes, 1945. *Publications*: French Ecclesiastical Society under the Ancien Régime: a study of Angers in the 18th Century, 1960; (ed) France, Government and Society, 1965, 2nd edn 1971; Lectures on European History 1789-1914: Men, Machines and Freedom, 1966; The French Revolution and the Church, 1969; Church and State in France 1870-1914, 1972; Death and the Enlightenment, 1981; contrib.: New Cambridge Modern History vols VI and VIII; Studies in Church History, vols XII and XV. *Recreations*: tennis, squash. *Address*: Christ Church, Oxford. *T*: Oxford 47047.

McMANUS, Francis Joseph; solicitor; *b* 16 Aug. 1942; *s* of Patrick and Celia McManus; *m* 1971, Carmel V. Doherty, Lisnaskea, Co. Fermanagh; one *s* one *d*. *Educ*: St Michael's Enniskillen; Queen's University, Belfast. BA 1965; Diploma in Education, 1966. Subsequently a Teacher. MP (Unity) Fermanagh and S Tyrone, 1970-Feb. 1974. Founder Mem. and Co-Chm., Irish Independence Party, 1977-. *Address*: Lissadell, Drumlin Heights, Enniskillen, Co. Fermanagh, N Ireland. *T*: Enniskillen 3401.

MacMANUS, John Leslie Edward, TD 1945; QC 1970; **His Honour Judge MacManus;** a Circuit Judge (formerly a Judge of County Courts), since 1971; *b* 7 April 1920; *o s* of E. H. MacManus and H. S. MacManus (*née* Colton); *m* 1942, Gertrude (Trudy) Mary Frances Koppenhagen; two *d*. *Educ*: Eastbourne College. Served 1939-45 with RA: Middle East, Italy, Crete, Yugoslavia; Captain 1942; Major 1945. Called to Bar, Middle Temple, 1947. Dep. Chm., East Sussex QS, 1964-71. *Recreations*: gardening, odd-jobbing, travel. *Address*: The Old Rectory, Twineham, Haywards Heath, West Sussex. *T*: Bolney 221; 1 Crown Office Row, Temple, EC4. *T*: 01-353 1801. *Club*: Sussex Martlets.

McMANUS, Maurice, CBE 1966; JP; DL; Lord Provost of Dundee and Lord Lieutenant of the County of the City of Dundee, 1960-67; *b* 17 Jan. 1906; *s* of Patrick and Ann McManus; *m* 1931, Lillian, *d* of James and Isobel Lindsay; three *s* two *d*. *Educ*: West Calder. Tutor at National Council of Labour Coll., 1945-. Chm. Dundee City Labour Party, 1950-56; Councillor, Tayside Region, 1974-. Member: Exec. Cttee, Scottish Council for Development and Industry; Scottish Advisory Cttee for Civil Aviation; Court of St Andrews Univ.; Council of Queen's Coll., Dundee; Dundee Univ., 1967; Chairman: Tayside Region Manpower Cttee, 1975-; Tay Road Bridge Jt Bd; Dundee Coll. of Art and Technology; Dundee & N Fife Local Employment Cttee, 1969. JP 1958, DL 1967, Dundee. Hon. LLD Dundee, 1969. *Recreation*: gardening. *Address*: 20 Merton Avenue, Dundee.

McMASTER, Brian John; General Administrator, Welsh National Opera, since 1976; *b* 9 May 1943; *s* of Brian John McMaster and Mary Leila Hawkins. *Educ*: Wellington Coll.; Bristol Univ. LLB. International Artists' Dept, EMI Ltd, 1968-73; Controller of Opera Planning, ENO, 1973-76. *Address*: 1 Cowper Court, Wordsworth Avenue, Cardiff. *T*: Cardiff 497694; 71 Breton House, Barbican, EC2. *T*: 01-638 4365.

McMASTER, Hughan James Michael, RIBA; Chief Architect and Director of Works, Home Office, since 1980; *b* 27 July 1927; *s* of William James Michael and Emly McMaster; *m* 1950, Heather Winifred Du Merton; one *s* two *d*. *Educ*: Christ's Coll., Finchley; Regent Street Polytechnic (DipArch). ARIBA 1951. Served RAF, India and Far East, 1946-48. T. P. Bennett and Son, 1951; Gollins Melvin Ward & Partners, 1955; joined Civil Service, 1961; Navy Works, 1961-69; Whitehall Development Gp, Directorate of Home Estate Management and Directorate of Civil Accommodation, 1969-76; Defence Works (PE and Overseas), 1976-80. Key contributions to: Polaris Programme, 1963-69; Crown Court Programme, 1972-76; also various Working Parties, incl. Higher Courts, Traffic in Parliament Square, Acoustic Conditions in Government Offices, Open Office Development. *Publications*: various articles in architectural jls. *Recreations*: music, swimming, hill walking, photography, trying to understand the universe. *Address*: c/o Home Office, St Vincent House, 30 Orange Street, WC2.

McMASTER, Stanley Raymond; *b* 23 Sept. 1926; *o s* of F. R. McMaster, Marlborough Park, Belfast, N Ireland; *m* 1959, Verda Ruth Tynan, SRN, Comber, Co Down, Northern Ireland; two *s* two *d* (and one *d* decd). *Educ*: Campbell Coll., Belfast; Trinity Coll., Dublin (MA, BComm). Called to the Bar, Lincoln's Inn, 1953. Lectr in Company Law, Polytechnic, Regent Street, 1954-59. Parliamentary and Legal Sec., to Finance and Taxation Cttee, Association of British Chambers of Commerce, 1958-59. MP (UU) Belfast E, March 1959-Feb. 1974; contested (UU) Belfast S, Oct. 1974. *Publications*: various articles in legal and commercial journals. *Recreations*: golf, rowing and shooting. *Address*: 31 Embercourt Road, Thames Ditton, Surrey. *Clubs*: Knock Golf, etc.

McMEEKIN, Lt-Gen. Sir Terence (Douglas Herbert), KCB 1973 (CB 1972); OBE 1960; Lieutenant, HM Tower of London, since 1981; Area Appeals Secretary (Avon, Gloucestershire and Wiltshire), Cancer Research Campaign, since 1976; b 27 Sept. 1918; e s of late Herbert William Porter McMeekin, Cogry, Co. Antrim, and Jean McMeekin, Elm Grove, Cirencester; m 1947, Averil Anne Spence Longstaff, 7th d of late Dr Tom Longstaff and Dora Longstaff (née Scott); one s two d. Educ: King William's Coll., IOM; RMA Woolwich. 2nd Lt RA, 1938; served War of 1939-45 (despatches); GSO2 (L) HQ 8th Army, 1943; Staff Coll., Haifa, 1943; GSO2 (Ops), HQ 3 Corps, 1944; Bde Major RA, 1 Airborne Div., 1945; Battery Comdr, 6 Airborne Div., Palestine, 1945-46; Instructor in Gunnery, 1947-48; GSO2 (Tactics), School of Artillery, Manorbier, 1949-50; DAQMG, HQ 1 (British) Corps, 1952-54; jssc 1955; Battery Comdr, 5 RHA, 1955-57; Bt Lt-Col, 1957; AA & QMG, HQ Land Forces, Hong Kong, 1958-60; comd 29 Field Regt, RA, 1960-62; converted Regt to Commando role, 1962; Col 1962; Chief Instructor (Tactics), School of Artillery, Larkhill, 1962-64; comd 28 Commonwealth Inf. Bde Gp, Malaya, 1964-66; Dir of Public Relations (Army), 1967-68; GOC 3rd Div., 1968-70; Comdt, Nat. Defence Coll. (formerly Jt Services Staff Coll.), 1970-72; GOC SE District, 1972-74, retd 1975. Col Comdt, RA, 1972-80; Hon. Col, 289 Commando Battery, RA, TAVR, 1978-. President: Army Cricket Assoc., 1969-72; Combined Services Cricket Assoc., 1971-72. Recreations: cricket, most field sports. Address: The Old Rectory, Beverston, near Tetbury, Glos. T: Tetbury 52735. Clubs: Army and Navy, MCC, Stragglers of Asia.

McMICHAEL, Sir John, Kt 1965; MD, FRCP, FRCPE; FRS 1957; Director, British Post-graduate Medical Federation, 1966-71; Emeritus Professor of Medicine, University of London; b 25 July 1904; s of James McMichael and Margaret Sproat; m 1942, Sybil E. Blake (d 1965); four s; m 1965, Sheila M. Howarth. Educ: Kirkcudbright Acad.; Edinburgh Univ. Ettles Scholar, 1927; Beit Memorial Fellow, 1930-34. MD (Gold Medal) Edinburgh 1933; MD Melbourne 1965; FRCPE 1940 (Hon. FRCPE 1981); FRCP 1946. Johnston and Lawrence Fellow, Royal Society, 1937-39; Univ. teaching appointments in Aberdeen, Edinburgh and London. Dir, Dept of Medicine, Post-grad. Med. Sch. of London, 1946-66; Mem. Medical Research Council, 1949-53. A Vice-Pres., Royal Soc., 1968-70. Pres., World Congress of Cardiology, 1970. Hon. Member: American Medical Association, 1947; Medical Soc., Copenhagen, 1953; Norwegian Medical Soc., 1954; Assoc. Amer. Physicians, 1959. For. Mem. Finnish Acad. of Science and Letters, 1963; For. Corresp., Acad. Roy. de Med. Belgique, 1971; For. Associate, Nat. Acad. Sci., Washington, 1974. Thayer Lectr, Johns Hopkins Hosp., 1948; Oliver Sharpey Lectr, 1952; Croonian Lectr, 1961, RCP; Watson Smith Lectr RCPEd, 1958. Cullen Prize, RCPEd, 1953. Jacobs Award, Dallas, 1958; Morgan Prof., Nashville, Tenn, 1964. Fellow, Royal Postgrad. Med. Sch., 1972. Moxon Medal, RCP, 1960; Gairdner Award, Toronto, 1960; Wihuri Internat. Prize, Finland, 1968. Harveian Orator, RCP, 1975. Krug Award of Excellence, 1980. Trustee, Wellcome Trust, 1960-77. Hon. FACP; Hon. LLD Edin.; Hon. DSc: Newcastle; Sheffield; Birmingham; Ohio; McGill; Wales; Hon. ScD Dublin. Publications: Pharmacology of the Failing Human Heart, 1951. Numerous papers on: Splenic Anaemia, 1931-35; Cardiac Output in Health and Disease, 1938-47; Lung Capacity in Man, 1938-39; Liver Circulation and Liver Disease, 1932-43. Recreation: gardening. Address: 2 North Square, NW11. T: 01-455 8731.

MacMICHAEL, Nicholas Hugh, FSA; Keeper of the Muniments of Westminster Abbey since 1967; b 2 Feb. 1933; o s of late Canon Arthur William MacMichael and of Elizabeth Helen Royale, o d of late Rev. Arthur William Newboult; unmarried. Educ: Eastbourne Coll.; Magdalene Coll., Cambridge. Asst Librarian and Asst Keeper of the Muniments of Westminster Abbey, 1956-66; Hon. Sec., 1961-64, Hon. Editor, 1964-70, Harleian Soc.; Member: Exec. Cttee, Soc. of Genealogists, 1963-67; Council: British Archaeological Assoc., 1960-62; Monumental Brass Soc., 1960-66; Kent Archaeological Soc., 1973-78. FSA 1962; FRHistS 1972; Fellow, Soc. of Genealogists, 1969. Publications: (ed) Westminster Abbey Official Guide, 1977; articles in learned jls. Recreations: genealogical and heraldic research; ecclesiology; watching cricket. Address: 2b Little Cloister, Westminster Abbey, SW1. T: 01-799 6893. Club: United Oxford & Cambridge University.

MACMILLAN, Alexander Daniel Alan; Chairman, Macmillan Publishers Ltd, since 1980; b Oswestry, Shropshire, 10 Oct. 1943; s of Rt Hon. Maurice Victor Macmillan, qv; m 1970, Hélène Birgitte, o d of late Alan D. C. Hamilton, Mitford, Northumberland; one s two d. Educ: Eton; Université de Paris; Strathclyde Univ. MBIM 1981. Sub-editor, Glasgow Herald, 1963-65; Reporter, Daily Telegraph, 1965-67, Foreign Correspondent, 1967-68; Chief European Correspondent, Sunday Telegraph, 1968-70; Dir, Macmillan and Co. Ltd, 1970-76; Dep. Chm., Macmillan Ltd, 1976-80. Director: Birch Grove Estates Ltd, 1969-; Wellbro Metals Ltd, 1972-; Counterpoint Productions (Cyprus) Ltd, 1973-; H. M. P. Jersey Ltd, 1974-; All News Radio Ltd, 1975-; Book Trade Benevolent Soc., 1976-; National Fedn of Industrial Assocs, 1981-82. Chm., Bookrest Appeal Cttee, 1978-; Mem., Lindemann Fellowship Cttee, 1979-. Hon. Sec., Carlton Club Political Cttee, 1975-. Governor: Archbishop Tenison's Grammar Sch. and Foundn, 1979-; Merchant Taylors' Sch., 1980-82; E-SU, 1980-. Liveryman: Worshipful Co. of Merchant Taylors, 1972; Worshipful Co. of Stationers and Newspaper Makers, 1973. Recreations: shooting, fishing, motor racing, conversation. Address: 51 Chelsea Square, SW3 6LH. T: 01-352 7596; Pooks, Chelwood Gate, near Haywards Heath, West Sussex RH17 7DG. T: Chelwood Gate 554. Clubs: Carlton, Beefsteak, Buck's.

MACMILLAN, Alexander Ross, FIBScot, CBIM; Director, Clydesdale Bank Ltd, since 1974 (Chief General Manager, 1971-82); b 25 March 1922; s of Donald and Johanna Macmillan; m 1961, Ursula Miriam Grayson; two s one d. Educ: Tain Royal Acad. FIBScot 1969; CBIM 1980. Served War, RAF, 1942-46 (despatches, King's Birthday Honours, 1945). Entered service of N of Scotland Bank Ltd, Tain, 1938; after War, returned to Tain, 1946; transf. to Supt's Dept, Aberdeen, and thereafter to Chief Accountant's Dept, Clydesdale Bank, Glasgow, 1950, on amalgamation with N of Scotland Bank; Chief London Office, 1952; Gen. Manager's Confidential Clerk, 1955; Manager, Piccadilly Circus Br., 1958; Supt of Branches, 1965; Gen. Manager's Asst, 1967; Asst Gen. Man., 1968. Freeman, Royal Burgh of Tain, 1975. Recreation: golf. Address: St Winnins, 16 Ledcameroch Road, Bearsden G61 4AB. T: 041-942 6455. Clubs: Overseas Bankers; Western (Glasgow); Glasgow Golf (Killermont).

McMILLAN, Col Donald, CB 1959; OBE 1945; Chairman, Cable & Wireless Ltd, and associated companies, 1967-72; b 22 Dec. 1906; s of Neil Munro McMillan and Isabella Jamieson; m 1946, Kathleen Ivy Bingham; one s. Educ: Sloane Sch., Chelsea; Battersea Polytechnic. Post Office Engineering Dept, 1925-54; Director External Telecommunications, Post Office External Telecommunications Executive, 1954-67. BSc Eng (London); FIEE. Publications: contribs to Institution Engineers Journal, Post Office Institution Engineers Journal. Recreations: golf and gardening. Address: 46 Gatehill Road, Northwood, Mddx. T: Northwood 22682. Club: Grim's Dyke Golf.

McMILLAN, Rt. Rev. Monsignor Donald Neil; Parish Priest, St Augustine's Church, Matson Lane, Gloucester, since 1981; b 21 May 1925; s of Daniel McMillan and Mary Cameron McMillan (née Farrell). Educ: St Brendan's Coll., Bristol; Prior Park Coll., Bath; Oscott Coll., Sutton Coldfield. Ordained Priest, Dio. Clifton, 1948; Curate: Bath, 1948-49; Gloucester, 1949-51; Taunton, 1951. Commissioned Army Chaplain, 1951; Served: BAOR, 1961-63, 1966-68, 1975-77; Middle East, 1956-59, 1968-70; Far East, 1952-55; Principal RC Chaplain and Vicar Gen. (Army), 1977-81. Apptd Prelate of Honour by Pope Paul VI, 1977. Recreations: reading, walking. Address: St Augustine's, 256 Painswick Road, Matson, Gloucester GL4 9BS. T: Gloucester 412702. Clubs: Army and Navy, Challoner.

McMILLAN, Prof. Duncan; John Orr Professor of French Language and Romance Linguistics, University of Edinburgh, 1955-80, now Emeritus; b London, 1914; o s of late Duncan McMillan and Martha (née Hastings); m 1945, Geneviève, er d of late M and Mme Robert Busse, Paris; one s. Educ: Holbeach Rd LCC; St Dunstan's Coll.; University Coll., London (Troughton Schol., Rothschild Prizeman, Univ. Postgrad. Student); Sorbonne, Paris (Clothworkers Schol., British Inst. in Paris). BA, PhD (London); Diplôme de l'Ecole des Hautes Etudes, Paris. Army, 1940-46. Lecteur d'anglais, Univ. of Paris, 1938-40; Lectr in French and Romance Philology, Univ. of Aberdeen, 1946-50, Univ. of Edinburgh, 1950-55. Founder Mem., Société Rencesvals, 1955, Pres., British Sect., 1956-59; Member Council: Société des anciens textes français, 1963- (Pres. elect.); Société de Linguistique romane, 1977-. Chevalier de la Légion d'Honneur, 1958; Médaille d'Honneur, Univ. of Liège, 1962. Publications: La Chanson de Guillaume (Société des anciens textes français), 2 vols, 1949-50; (in collaboration with Madame G. McMillan) An Anthology of the Contemporary French Novel, 1950; Le Charroi de Nîmes, 1972, 2nd edn 1978. Address: 11 rue des Prés Hauts, 92290 Châtenay Malabry, France. T: (1) 660 3713. Club: Scottish Arts (Edinburgh).

McMILLAN, Prof. Edwin Mattison; Professor of Physics, University of California, 1946-73, now Professor Emeritus; b Redondo Beach, Calif, 18 Sept. 1907; s of Edwin Harbaugh McMillan and Anna Marie (née Mattison); m 1941, Elsie Walford Blumer; two s one d. Educ: Calif Institute of Technology (MS); Princeton Univ. (PhD). Univ. of California: National Research Fellow, 1932-34; Research Assoc., 1934-35; Instructor, 1935-36; Asst Prof., 1936-41; Assoc. Prof., 1941-46. Leave of absence for war research, 1940-45. Mem. of staff of Radiation Laboratory, Univ. of Calif., 1934-; Assoc. Dir, 1954-58; Dir, 1958-71; Dir, Lawrence Berkeley Laboratory, 1971-73; Mem. General Advisory Cttee to Atomic Energy Commission, 1954-58. Member: Commission on High Energy Physics of International Union for Pure and Applied Physics (IUPAP), 1960-66; Scientific Policy Cttee of Stanford Linear Accelerator Center (SLAC), 1962-66; Physics Adv. Cttee, Nat. Accelerator Lab. (NAL), 1967-; Trustee, Univs Research Assoc., 1969-; Chm., Cl. I, Nat. Acad. of Sciences, 1968-71. Fellow Amer. Physical Soc. Member: Nat. Acad. of Sciences (USA); American Philosophical Soc.; Fellow, Amer. Acad. of Arts and Sciences. Research Corp. 1950 Scientific Award, 1951; (jtly) Nobel Prize in Chemistry, 1951; (jtly) Atoms for Peace Award, 1963; Alumni Dist. Service Award, Calif. Inst. of Tech., 1966; Centennial Citation, Univ. of California, Berkeley, 1968. Hon. DSc, Rensselaer Polytechnic Institute; Hon. DSc, Gustavus Adolphus Coll. Address: University of California, Berkeley, Calif 94720, USA.

MACMILLAN, Rev. Gilleasbuig Iain; Minister of St Giles', The High Kirk of Edinburgh, since 1973; Chaplain to the Queen in Scotland, since 1979; b 21 Dec. 1942; s of Rev. Kenneth M. Macmillan and Mrs Mary Macmillan; m 1965, Maureen Stewart Thomson; one d. Educ: Oban High School; Univ. of Edinburgh. MA, BD. Asst Minister, St Michael's Parish, Linlithgow,

1967-69; Minister of Portree Parish, Isle of Skye, 1969-73. Extra Chaplain to the Queen in Scotland, 1978-79. Hon. Chaplain: Royal Scottish Academy; Royal Coll. of Surgeons of Edinburgh; Soc. of High Constables of City of Edinburgh. *Recreations:* reading, friends, the country, America. *Address:* St Giles' Cathedral, Edinburgh EH1 1RE. *T:* 031-225 4363. *Club:* New (Edinburgh).

MacMILLAN OF MacMILLAN, Gen. Sir Gordon Holmes Alexander, of Knap, KCB 1949 (CB 1945); KCVO 1954; CBE 1943; DSO 1943; MC (two bars); Hereditary Chief of the Clan MacMillan; Colonel The Argyll and Sutherland Highlanders, 1945-58; Hon. Colonel The Argyll and Sutherland Highlanders of Canada, 1948-72; 402 (A. and S. H.) Lt Regt RA (TA), 1956-61; *b* 7 Jan. 1897; *s* of D. A. MacMillan and L. W. Allardice; *m* 1929, Marian Blakiston-Houston, OBE, CStJ, four *s* one *d. Educ:* St Edmund's Sch., Canterbury. RMC, Sandhurst, 1915; commissioned in Argyll and Sutherland Highdrs, 1915; served European War in 2nd Bn Argyll and Sutherland Highdrs, France, 1916-18 (MC and two bars): Adjutant, 1917-20; Staff Coll., Camberley, 1928-29; Staff Capt., War Office, 1930-32; GSO3, 1932-34; GSO2 RMC, Kingston, Ont., 1935-37; GSO2 WO and Eastern Command, 1937-40; GSO1, 1940-41; Brig. commanding Infantry Brigade, 1941; BGS UK and N Africa, 1941-43 (CBE); commanding Infantry Brigade, Sicily, 1943 (DSO); commanding 15th Scottish, 49 (WR) and 51st Highland Divs, 1943-45, UK, Normandy, Holland and Germany (CB); DWD War Office, 1945-46; GOC Palestine, 1947-48; Gen. Officer, C-in-C, Scottish Command, and Gov. of Edinburgh Castle, 1949-52; Gov. and C-in-C of Gibraltar, 1952-55, retd 1955. Chairman: Cumbernauld New Town Corporation, 1956-65; Greenock Harbour Trust, 1955-65; Erskine Hospital, 1955-80; Firth of Clyde Dry Dock, 1960-67. DL Renfrewshire, 1950, Vice-Lieutenant, 1955-72. Kt Grand Cross Order of Orange Nassau; KStJ. Mem. of The Queen's Body Guard for Scotland. Hon. LLD (Glasgow), 1964. *Address:* Finlaystone, Langbank, Renfrewshire PA14 6TJ. *T:* Langbank 235. *Club:* Caledonian.

MACMILLAN, Rt. Hon. Harold; *see* Macmillan, Rt Hon. M. H.

MACMILLAN, Iain Alexander, CBE 1978; LLD; Sheriff of South Strathclyde, Dumfries and Galloway at Hamilton, since 1981; *b* 14 Nov. 1923; *s* of John and Eva Macmillan; *m* 1954, Edith Janet (*née* MacAulay); two *s* one *d. Educ:* Oban High Sch.; Glasgow Univ. (BL). Served war, RAF, France, Germany, India, 1944-47. Glasgow Univ., 1947-50. Subseq. law practice; Sen. Partner, J. & J. Sturrock & Co., Kilmarnock, 1952-81. Temp. Sheriff, 1981. Member: Gen. Teaching Council for Scotland, 1978-; Ayrshire and Arran Health Bd, 1981-. Law Society of Scotland: Mem. Council, 1964-79; Vice-Pres., 1973; Pres., 1976-77. Pres., Rotary Club, Kilmarnock, 1979-80. Hon. LLD Aberdeen, 1975. *Publications:* contribs Jl Law Soc. of Scotland. *Recreations:* golf, sailing. *Address:* 2 Castle Drive, Kilmarnock. *T:* Kilmarnock 25864.

MacMILLAN, Jake; *see* MacMillan, John.

MacMILLAN, His Honour James; Judge of County Courts, 1950-65, retired; *b* Schoolhouse, Fisherton, Ayrshire, 18 April 1898; *s* of George Arthur MacMillan, MA, and Catherine, *d* of Alexander McQuiston; *m* 1931, Marjorie J. Triffitt, DSc (*d* 1957); one *d. Educ:* Troon Sch.; Ayr Acad.; Glasgow Univ. (MA, LLB). Royal Artillery, 1917-19, Lt. Called to Bar, Middle Temple, 1925, Midland Circuit; Legal Adviser, Ministry of Pensions, 1939-44. Mem. Bar Council, 1947-50; Mem. Supreme Court Rule Cttee, 1948-50; Dep. Chm. Beds Quarter Sessions, 1949-50; County Court Judge, Circuit 37, April-June 1950, Circuit 38, 1950-55, Circuit 39, 1955-65. *Recreation:* walking. *Address:* Cotswolds, 11 Lillington Avenue, Leamington Spa, Warwickshire CV32 5UL. *Club:* Reform.

MACMILLAN, Sir (James) Wilson, KBE 1976 (CBE 1962, OBE 1951); Governing Director, Macmillan Brothers Ltd; President, British Red Cross and Scout Association; *b* 1906; *m* Beatrice Woods. Served in Legislature for many years; formerly Minister of Education, Health and Housing. British Red Cross Badge of Honour, Class I, 1964. *Address:* 3 St Edward Street, Belize City, Belize.

McMILLAN, John, CBE 1969; *b* 29 Jan. 1915; *s* of late William McArthur McMillan, Sydney, NSW; *m* 1958, Lucy Mary, *d* of late Edward Moore, DSO; three *s* two *d. Educ:* Scots Coll., Sydney. Manager, Internat. Broadcasting Co. Ltd, London, 1936-38; Manager, EMI Ltd, developing the long-playing record, 1938-39. Served War: joined horsed cavalry as trooper, 1939; commissioned, S Wales Borderers, 1940; OC No 1 Field Broadcasting Unit, British Forces Network, and Telecommns Dir in interim NW German PO, 1945-46 (despatches). Asst, and later Chief Asst, to Controller, BBC Light Programme, 1946-53; USA television, 1954; Manager, Associated Broadcasting Develt Co., London, 1954-55; Controller of Programmes, later Gen. Man. and Dir Rediffusion Television Ltd, 1955-68; Director: Independent Television News Ltd, 1955-68; Global Television Services Ltd, 1960-68; Dir of Special Events and Sport, ITV, 1965-71; Sen. rep. of ITV cos at EBU (Geneva and Brussels), 1968-71. Member: ITA Programme Policy Cttee, 1960-68; Independent Television Standing Consultative Cttee, 1964-68; Independent Television Cos Assoc. (Chm., Finance and General Purposes Cttee), 1964-68; UK Consortium of Communications Satellite Cttee (INTELSAT), Washington DC, 1964-68. Dir, Theatre Royal Windsor Co., 1963-79; Man. Dir, Brompton Production Co. Ltd, 1971-77; Chm. and Man.

Dir, Sportsdata Ltd, 1978-80; Chm., Vernons Viewdata Services Ltd, 1978-80. *Recreations:* swimming, gardening, study of 1919-39 European history. *Address:* 10 rue du Cubert, 83230 Bormes-les-Mimosas, France. *T:* (94) 649211.

MacMILLAN, Prof. John, (Jake), PhD Glasgow; DSc Bristol; FRS 1978; CChem, ARIC; Professor of Organic Chemistry, University of Bristol, since 1978; *b* 13 Sept. 1924; *s* of John MacMillan and Barbara Lindsay; *m* 1952, Anne Levy; one *s* two *d. Educ:* Lanark Grammar Sch.; Glasgow Univ. Res. Chemist, Akers Res. Labs, ICI Ltd, 1949; Associate Res. Manager, Pharmaceuticals Div., ICI Ltd, 1962; Lectr in Org. Chemistry, Bristol Univ., 1963, Reader 1968. Pres., Internat. Plant Growth Substance Assoc., 1973-76. *Publications:* research papers in learned jls on natural organic products, esp. plant growth hormones. *Recreations:* golf, gardening, theatre, music. *Address:* 1 Rylestone Grove, Bristol BS9 3UT. *T:* Bristol 620535.

MacMILLAN, Kenneth; Principal Choreographer to the Royal Ballet, Covent Garden, since 1977; *b* 11 Dec. 1929; *m* 1974, Deborah Williams. *Educ:* Great Yarmouth Gram. Sch. Started as Dancer, Royal Ballet; became Choreographer, 1953; Dir of Ballet, Deutsche Oper, Berlin, 1966-69; Resident Choreographer, and Dir, Royal Ballet, 1970-77. First professional ballet, Danses Concertantes (Stravinsky-Georgiades). Principal ballets: The Burrow; Solitaire; Agon; The Invitation; Romeo and Juliet; Diversions; La Création du Monde; Images of Love; The Song of the Earth; Concerto; Anastasia; Cain and Abel; Olympiad; Triad; Ballade; The Poltroon; Manon; Pavanne; Elite Syncopations; The Four Seasons; Rituals; Requiem; Mayerling; My Brother, My Sisters; La Fin du Jour; Gloria; Isadora. Has devised ballets for: Ballet Rambert, American Ballet, Royal Ballet Sch., theatre, television, cinema, musical shows. Dr *hc* Edinburgh, 1976. Evening Standard Ballet Award, 1979; Ballet Award, SWET Managers, 1980. *Recreation:* cinema. *Address:* c/o Royal Opera House, Covent Garden, WC2.

MACMILLAN, Matthew, OBE 1977; Controller, English Language and Literature Division, British Council, since 1978; *b* 14 July 1926; *s* of David Craig Macmillan and Barbara Cruikshank Macmillan (*née* Gow); *m* 1949, Winifred (*née* Sagar); one *s* two *d. Educ:* Robert Gordon's Coll., Aberdeen; Aberdeen Univ. (MA Hons); Manchester Univ. (Teacher's Dip.). Served Royal Air Force, 1944-47. Schoolmaster, Chatham House Grammar Sch., Ramsgate, 1951-57; Sen. Lectr, Univ. of Science and Technology, Kumasi, Ghana, 1958-62; Associate Prof., University Coll. of Cape Coast, Ghana, 1962-64; Prof. of English, Univ. of Khartoum, The Sudan, 1965-70; British Council, London: Director, English-Teaching Information Centre, 1970-72; Dep. Controller, English Teaching Div., 1972-74; Asst Educn Adviser (English Studies), British Council, India, 1974-78. *Publications:* articles on the teaching of English as a second/foreign language. *Recreations:* gardening, walking. *Address:* Manor House Cottage, Old Road, Elham, Canterbury, Kent CT4 6UL. *T:* Elham 427. *Clubs:* Athenæum, Royal Commonwealth Society.

MACMILLAN, Rt. Hon. (Maurice) Harold, PC 1942; OM 1976; FRS 1962; Chancellor, University of Oxford, since 1960; President, Macmillan Ltd, since 1974 (Chairman, 1963-74; Chairman Macmillan & Co. and Macmillan (Journals), 1963-67). Prime Minister and First Lord of The Treasury, Jan. 1957-Oct. 1963; MP (C) Bromley, Nov. 1945-Sept. 1964; *b* 10 Feb. 1894; *s* of late Maurice Crawford Macmillan; *m* 1920, Lady Dorothy Evelyn Cavendish, GBE 1964 (*d* 1966), *d* of 9th Duke of Devonshire; one *s* two *d* (and one *d* decd). *Educ:* Eton (Scholar); Balliol Coll., Oxford (Exhibitioner). 1st Class Hon. Moderations, 1919; served during war, 1914-18, in Special Reserve Grenadier Guards (wounded 3 times); ADC to Gov.-Gen. of Canada, 1919-20; retired, 1920; MP (U) Stockton-on-Tees, 1924-29 and 1931-45; contested Stockton-on-Tees, 1923 and 1945; Parliamentary Sec., Ministry of Supply, 1940-42; Parliamentary Under-Sec. of State, Colonies, 1942; Minister Resident at Allied HQ in North-West Africa, 1942-45; Sec. for Air, 1945; Minister of Housing and Local Government, 1951-54; Minister of Defence, Oct. 1954-April 1955; Sec. of State for Foreign Affairs, April-Dec. 1955; Chancellor of the Exchequer, Dec. 1955-Jan. 1957. First Pres., Game Research Assoc., 1960-65. A Vice-Pres., Franco-British Soc., 1955; a Trustee, Historic Churches Preservation Fund, 1957-. Freeman of: City of London (Stationers' and Newspaper Makers' Company, 1957), 1957; Bromley, Kent, 1957; Hon. Freedom of City of London, 1961; Toronto, 1962; Stockton-on-Tees, 1968. Hon. Fellow Balliol Coll., Oxford, 1957; Hon. FBA, 1981. Hon. DCL Oxford, 1958; DCL Oxford (by diploma), 1960; LLD Cambridge, 1961, Sussex, 1963. Benjamin Franklin Medal, RSA, 1976; Olympia Prize, 1979. *Publications:* Industry and the State (jtly), 1927; Reconstruction: A Plea for a National Policy, 1933; Planning for Employment, 1935; The Next Five Years, 1935; The Middle Way, 1938 (re-issued 1966); Economic Aspects of Defence, 1939; Memoirs: Vol. I, Winds of Change, 1966; Vol. II, The Blast of War, 1967; Vol. III, Tides of Fortune, 1969; Vol. IV, Riding the Storm 1956-1959, 1971; Vol. V, Pointing the Way 1959-61, 1972; Vol. VI, At the end of the Day 1961-63, 1973; Past Masters, 1975. *Address:* Macmillan & Co. Ltd, 4 Little Essex Street, WC2; Birch Grove House, Chelwood Gate, Haywards Heath, West Sussex. *Clubs:* Carlton, Beefsteak, Buck's.
See also Rt Hon. Julian Amery, J. T. Faber, Rt Hon. M. V. Macmillan.

MACMILLAN, Rt. Hon. Maurice (Victor), PC 1972; MP (C) Farnham, since 1966; Group Chairman, Macmillan Ltd; Director, Yarrow and Co. Ltd; *b* 27 Jan. 1921; *s* of Rt Hon. Harold Macmillan, *qv* ; *m* 1942, Hon. Katharine Margaret Alice Ormsby-Gore, DBE 1974, 2nd *d* of 4th Baron Harlech, KG,

PC, GCMG; three s one d (and one s decd). *Educ:* Eton; Balliol Coll., Oxford. Served War of 1939-45 with Sussex Yeomanry, and after as Mil. Asst to Adjt-General. Mem. of Kensington Borough Council, 1949-53. Contested (C) Seaham Harbour, 1945, Lincoln, 1951, Wakefield, by-election, 1954; MP (C) Halifax, 1955-64; Economic Sec. to the Treasury, Oct. 1963-64; Chief Sec. to the Treasury, 1970-72; Sec. of State for Employment, 1972-73; Paymaster-General, 1973-74. Delegate: to Council of Europe, 1960-63 (Political Cttee rapporteur, 1962-63); to WEU, 1960-63; a Pres., UK Council of European Movement, 1961-63; Treasurer, British Section, European Movement, 1979. Chairman: Macmillan & Co. Ltd, 1967-70; Macmillan Journals Ltd, 1967-70; Macmillan & Cleaver Ltd, 1967-70; Macmillan (Publications) Ltd, 1974-77; Dep. Chm., Macmillan (Holdings) Ltd, 1966-70; formerly also Director: Monotype Corporation Ltd; Yorkshire Television Ltd; and Founder Chm., Wider Share Ownership Council. *Address:* 9 Warwick Square, SW1; Birch Grove House, Chelwood Gate, Haywards Heath, Sussex. *T:* Chelwoodgate 588. *Clubs:* Turf, Beefsteak, Pratt's, Garrick, Carlton.

See also Rt Hon. Julian Amery, J. T. Faber, A. D. A. Macmillan.

MACMILLAN, Prof. Robert Hugh; Professor of Vehicle Design and Head of School of Automotive Studies, 1977-82, Dean of Engineering, 1980-82, Cranfield Institute of Technology; *b* 27 June 1921; *s* of H. R. M. Macmillan and E. G. Macmillan (*née* Webb); *m* 1950, Anna Christina Roding, Amsterdam; one *s* two *d. Educ:* Felsted Sch.; Emmanuel Coll., Cambridge. Technical Branch, RAFVR, 1941; Dept of Engrg, Cambridge Univ., 1947; Prof. of Mech. Engrg, Swansea, 1956; Dir, Motor Industry Res. Assoc., 1964-77. Assoc. Prof., Warwick Univ., 1965-77. Mem. Council, Loughborough Univ., 1966-81; Chm. Council, Automobile Div., IMechE, 1976-77; Mem., Noise Adv. Council, 1970-77. FRSA; MIEE; FIMechE; FRPSL. *Publications:* Theory of Control, 1951; Automation, 1956; Geometric Symmetry, 1978. *Recreations:* music, philately, gardening. *Address:* 18 The Mount, Aspley Guise, Beds. *T:* Milton Keynes 584011. *Club:* Royal Air Force.

MACMILLAN, Wallace, CMG 1956; retired; *b* 16 Oct. 1913; *s* of late David Hutchen Macmillan and late Jean Wallace, Newburgh, Fife; *m* 1947, Betty Bryce, *d* of late G. R. Watson and of Mrs M. Y. Watson; three *s. Educ:* Bell-Baxter Sch.; University of St Andrews; Kiel Univ.; Corpus Christi Coll., Oxford. Administrative Officer, Tanganyika, 1937; District Officer, 1947; Administrator of Grenada, BWI, 1951-57. Acted as Governor, Windward Is, periods 1955. Federal Establishment Sec. (subsequently Permanent Sec., Min. of Estabts and Service Matters), Federation of Nigeria, 1957-61. Dir, Management Selection Ltd, 1961-78. *Recreations:* bridge, chess, golf. *Address:* Whiteside House, Kilrenny, Anstruther, Fife. *T:* Anstruther 310570.

MACMILLAN, Sir Wilson; see Macmillan, Sir J. W.

McMINN, Prof. Robert Matthew Hay; Conservator of the Hunterian Museum, Royal College of Surgeons of England, since 1970; *b* 20 Sept. 1923; *o s* of late Robert Martin McMinn, MB, ChB, Auchinleck and Brighton, and Elsie Selene Kent; *m* 1948, Margaret Grieve Kirkwood, MB, ChB, DA; one *s* one *d. Educ:* Brighton Coll. (Schol.); Univ. of Glasgow. MB, ChB 1947, MD (commendation) 1958, Glasgow; PhD Sheffield 1956; FRCS 1978. Hosp. posts and RAF Med. Service, 1947-50; Demonstrator in Anatomy, Glasgow Univ., 1950-52; Lectr in Anatomy, Sheffield Univ., 1952-60; Reader 1960-66, Prof. of Anatomy 1966-70, King's Coll., London Univ.; Sir William Collins Prof. of Human and Comparative Anatomy, RCS, and Prof. of Anatomy, Inst. of Basic Med. Scis, London Univ., 1970-82, prematurely retd. Examnr, RCP&S Glasgow; late Examnr to RCS and Univs of London, Cambridge, Edinburgh, Belfast, Singapore and Makerere. Arris and Gale Lectr, RCS, 1960; Arnott Demonstrator, RCS, 1970. Former Treas., Anatomical Soc. of Gt Britain and Ireland; Foundn Sec., British Assoc. of Clinical Anatomists; FRSocMed; Member: Amer. Assoc. of Anatomists; British Soc. of Gastroenterology; BMA; Trustee, Skin Res. Foundn. *Publications:* Tissue Repair, 1969; The Digestive System, 1974; The Human Gut, 1974; Colour Atlas of Human Anatomy, 1977; Colour Atlas of Head and Neck Anatomy, 1981; Colour Atlas of Ankle and Foot Anatomy, 1982; articles in various med. and sci. jls. *Recreations:* motoring, photography, archaeology, short-wave radio. *Address:* 74 Dorling Drive, Ewell, Epsom, Surrey. *T:* 01-393 6839.

McMINNIES, John Gordon, OBE 1965; HM Diplomatic Service, retired 1977; *b* 1 Oct. 1919; *s* of William Gordon McMinnies and Joyce Millicent McMinnies; *m* 1947, Mary (*née* Jackson) (*d* 1978), novelist. *Educ:* Bilton Grange; Rugby Sch.; Austria (language trng). Reporter: Western Mail, 1938; Reuters, 1939. Served War, Army, 1940-46: comd R Troop, RHA; retd, Major. HM Diplomatic Service (Athens, Warsaw, Bologna, Malaysia, Cyprus, Nairobi, Lusaka, New Delhi), 1946-77; retd, Counsellor. *Recreations:* crazy paving, crosswords, cricketology, the sea. *Address:* Villa Woodland, Avenue de Verdun, Ajaccio, Corsica.

McMORRAN, Helen Isabella, MA; Life Fellow, Girton College, Cambridge; *b* 26 July 1898; *d* of late Thomas McMorran and late Louise Maud White. *Educ:* Sutton High Sch., GPDST; Girton Coll., Cambridge. Assistant Librarian, Bedford Coll., London, 1921-28; Girton Coll., Cambridge; Librarian, 1930-62; Vice-Mistress, 1946-62; Registrar of the Roll, 1947-69. Member of Council, Girls' Public Day School Trust, 1952-69; Trustee, Homerton Coll., Cambridge, 1954-67. *Publications:* Editor, Girton Review, 1932-62; Joint Editor (with K. T. Butler) of Girton College Register,

1869-1946, 1948. *Address:* c/o Girton College, Cambridge. *T:* Cambridge 76219. *Club:* University Women's.

McMULLAN, Rt. Rev. Gordon; see Clogher, Bishop of.

McMULLAN, Henry Wallace, OBE 1967; Member of Independent Broadcasting Authority (formerly Independent Television Authority), 1971-74; *b* 20 Feb. 1909; *s* of William Muir McMullan and Euphemia McMullan; *m* 1934, Roberta Tener Gardiner; three *s. Educ:* King William's Coll., IOM. Worked on Belfast Telegraph and Belfast Newsletter; Producer and Commentator, BBC NI, 1930; Lt-Comdr RNVR, Map Room, Admty, 1939; Head of Programmes, BBC NI, 1945-69. *Recreations:* gardening, watching and listening to people, television and radio. *Address:* 119 Garner Crescent, Nanaimo, British Columbia, Canada. *Club:* Naval.

McMULLAN, Michael Brian; His Honour Judge McMullan; a Circuit Judge, since 1980; *b* 15 Nov. 1926; *s* of Joseph Patrick McMullan and Frances McMullan (*née* Burton); *m* 1960, Rosemary Jane Margaret, *d* of Stanley Halse deL. de Ville; one *s* two *d. Educ:* Manor Farm Road Sch.; Tauntons Sch., Southampton; The Queen's College, Oxford (MA). Called to the Bar, Gray's Inn, 1960. National Service, Army, 1946-48. Colonial Administrative Service: Gold Coast and Ghana, Political Administration Ashanti, Min. of Finance, Accra, Agricl Development Corp., 1949-60. In practice as Barrister, SE Circuit, 1961-80; a Recorder of the Crown Court, 1979. *Address:* 55 Meadway, NW11 6PP. *Club:* United Oxford & Cambridge University.

McMULLEN, Rear-Admiral Morrice Alexander, CB 1964; OBE 1944; Flag Officer, Admiralty Interview Board, HMS Sultan, Gosport, 1961-64, retired; Director, Civil Defence for London, 1965-68; *b* Hertford, 16 Feb. 1909; *m* 1st, 1946, Pamela (*née* May) (marr. diss. 1967), widow of Lt-Comdr J. Buckley, DSC, RN; two step *s*; 2nd, 1972, Peggy, widow of Comdr Richard Dakeyne, RN; two step *s* one step *d. Educ:* Oakley Hall, Cirencester; Cheltenham Coll. Entered Royal Navy, as Paymaster Cadet, HMS Erebus, 1927. Appts prewar included: S Africa Station, 1929-32; China Station, 1933-36; Asst Sec. to Lord Chatfield, First Sea Lord, 1936-38; Served War of 1939-45 (despatches, OBE); Atlantic, North Sea, Norwegian waters; served in HMS Prince of Wales (battle with Bismarck, and Atlantic Charter Meeting); HQ, Western Approaches, 1941-43; Member Allied Anti-Submarine Survey Board, 1943; served Mediterranean, 1944-45 (Anzio Landing, re-entry into Greece, invasion of S. France). Post-war appointments at home included Dep. Dir Manning (Suez operation), 1956-58, and Captain of Fleet to C-in-C Far East Station, Singapore, 1959-61. Chairman Royal Naval Ski Club, 1955-58. *Recreations:* fishing, sailing, ski-ing, shooting. *Address:* 3 The Crescent, Alverstoke, Hants. *T:* Gosport 82974. *Clubs:* Naval and Military, Royal Cruising, Royal Naval Sailing Association.

McMULLIN, Hon. Sir Alister (Maxwell), KCMG 1957; Chancellor, University of Newcastle, NSW, 1966-77; President of the Australian Senate, 1953-71; *b* Scone, NSW, Australia, 14 July 1900; *s* of W. G. McMullin, Aberdeen, NSW; *m* 1945, Thelma Louise (*née* Smith); one *d. Educ:* Public Sch., Australia. Elected to the Australian Senate, 1951, Senator to New South Wales. Chm., Gen. Council, Commonwealth Parly Assoc., 1959-60, 1969-70. Chm., Scott Memorial Hospital, Scone, NSW, 1934-40. Hon. DLitt Newcastle, NSW, 1966. *Address:* St Aubins, Scone, NSW 2337, Australia.

McMULLIN, Rt. Hon. Duncan Wallace, PC 1980; Rt. Hon. Mr Justice McMullin; Judge of Court of Appeal, New Zealand, since 1979; *b* 1 May 1927; *s* of Charles James McMullin and Kathleen Annie Shout; *m* 1955, Isobel Margaret, *d* of Robert Ronald Atkinson; two *s* two *d. Educ:* Auckland Grammar Sch.; Univ. of Auckland (LLB). Judge of Supreme Court, 1970. Chm., Royal Commn on Contraception, Sterilisation and Abortion in NZ, 1975-77. *Recreations:* boating, farming, squash. *Address:* 707 Remuera Road, Auckland, New Zealand. *T:* Auckland 546-583. *Club:* Wellington (Wellington, NZ).

McMURRAY, David Bruce, MA; Headmaster, Loretto School, since 1976; *b* 15 Dec. 1937; *s* of late James McMurray, CBE, and of Kathleen McMurray (*née* Goodwin); *m* 1962, Antonia Murray; three *d. Educ:* Loretto Sch.; Pembroke Coll., Cambridge (BA, MA). National service, Royal Scots, 1956-58, 2nd Lieut. Pembroke Coll., Cambridge, 1958-61; Asst Master, Stowe Sch., 1961-64; Fettes College: Asst Master, 1964-72; Housemaster, 1972-76. CCF Medal, 1976. *Recreations:* cricket, golf, sub-aqua diving, poetry, lecturing. *Address:* Pinkie House, Loretto School, Musselburgh, East Lothian, Scotland. *T:* 031-665 3108. *Clubs:* Free Foresters; Edinburgh Sports (Edinburgh).

MacMURRAY, Mary Bell McMillan, (Mrs Ian Mills); QC 1979; Barrister-at-Law; a Recorder of the Crown Court, since 1978; *d* of Samuel Bell MacMurray and Constance Mary MacMurray (*née* Goodman); *m* 1971, Ian Donald Mills. *Educ:* Queen Margaret's School, Escrick, York. Called to the Bar, Lincoln's Inn, 1954. Coronation Medal, 1953. *Recreation:* golf. *Address:* 1 Moor Court, Whitburn, Sunderland, Tyne and Wear. *T:* Whitburn 292152. *Clubs:* Durham County; Whitburn Golf; Boldon Golf.

McMURTRIE, Group Captain Richard Angus, DSO 1940; DFC 1940; Royal Air Force, retired; *b* 14 Feb. 1909; *s* of Radburn Angus and Ethel Maud McMurtrie; *m* 1st, 1931, Gwenyth Mary (*d* 1958), 3rd *d* of Rev. (Lt-Col) H. J. Philpott; no *c*; 2nd, 1963, Laura, 4th *d* of Wm H. Gerhardi. *Educ:* Royal

Grammar Sch., Newcastle on Tyne. First commissioned in Territorial Army (72nd Brigade, RA), 1927; transferred to Royal Air Force, 1929, as Pilot Officer; served in No 2 (AC) Squadron, 1931-32, and Fleet Air Arm (442 Flight, and 822 Squadron in HMS Furious), 1932-33; Cranwell, 1934-35; Flt-Lieut, 1935; Calshot and No. 201 (Flying Boat) Squadron, 1935-38; Squadron Leader, 1938, and commanded Recruits Sub-Depot, RAF, Linton-on-Ouse; served War of 1939-45 (despatches thrice, DFC, DSO); No 269 GR Squadron, 1939-41; Wing Commander, 1940; HQ No 18 Group RAF, 1941; Group Captain, commanding RAF Station, Sumburgh (Shetlands), 1942-43; HQ Coastal Command, 1943; RAF Staff Coll., Air Ministry, Whitehall, and HQ Transport Command, 1944; commanded RAF Station, Stoney Cross, Hants, 1945; and formed and commanded No. 61 Group (Reserve Command), 1946; Joint Services Mission, Washington, DC, 1946-49; commanded RAF Station, Cardington, 1949-52; HQ No 1 Group, RAF, 1952-54; Royal Naval College, Greenwich, 1954; HQ, Supreme Allied Commander, Atlantic (NATO), Norfolk, Virginia, USA, 1954-56; HQ, Coastal Command, RAF, Northwood, Mddx, 1957-59, now farming. *Recreations:* sailing, photography. *Address:* Rose in Vale Farm, Constantine, Falmouth, Cornwall TR11 5PU. *T:* Constantine 40338. *Clubs:* RAF Yacht (Hon. Life Mem.), Royal Cornwall Yacht.

MACNAB, Brigadier Sir Geoffrey (Alex Colin), KCMG 1962 (CMG 1955); CB 1951; retired; *b* 23 Dec. 1899; *s* of Brig.-General Colin Macnab, CMG; *m* 1930, Norah (*d* 1981), *d* of Captain H. A. Cramer-Roberts, Folkestone. *Educ:* Wellington Coll.; RMC Sandhurst. 1st Commission, 1919, Royal Sussex Regt; Instr., Small Arms Sch., Hythe, 1925-28; Captain, Argyll and Sutherland Highlanders, 1931; Staff Coll., Camberley, 1930-31; GSO 3, WO, 1933-35; BM 10 Infantry Bde, 1935-38; Military Attaché, Prague and Bucharest, 1938-40; served War of 1939-45, campaigns Western Desert, Greece, Crete; Brigadier, 1944; Military Mission, Hungary, 1945; DMI, Middle East, 1945-47; Military Attaché, Rome, 1947-49; Military Attaché, Paris, 1949-54; retired 1954. Service in Ireland, Germany, Far East, India, Middle East. Secretary, Government Hospitality Fund, 1957-68. *Address:* Stanford House, Stanford, Ashford, Kent. *T:* Sellindge 2118. *Clubs:* Army and Navy, MCC.

MACNAB OF MACNAB, James Charles; The Macnab; 23rd Chief of Clan Macnab; landowner since 1957; *b* 14 April 1926; *e s* of Lt-Col James Alexander Macnabb, OBE, TD (*de jure* 21st of Macnab), London, SW3, and late Mrs G. H. Walford, Wokingham, Berks; *S gt uncle,* Archibald Corrie Macnab, 22nd Chief, 1970; *m* 1959, Hon. Diana Mary, *er d* of Rt Hon. Lord Kilmany, *qv* ; two *s* two *d. Educ:* Cothill House; Radley Coll.; Ashbury Coll., Ottawa. Served in RAF and Scots Guards, 1944-45; Lieut, Seaforth Highldrs, 1945-48. Asst Supt, Fedn of Malaya Police Force, 1948; retd, 1957. CC, Perth and Kinross Jt County Council, 1964-75; Dist Councillor, 1961-64; Mem., Central Regional Council, 1978-82. Member, Royal Company of Archers, Queen's Body Guard in Scotland. JP 1968. *Recreations:* shooting, travel. *Heir: s* James William Archibald Macnab, younger of Macnab, *b* 22 March 1963. *Address:* Finlarig, Killin, Perthshire FK21 8TN. *T:* Killin 259. *Clubs:* New, Puffins (Edinburgh).

McNAB JONES, Robin Francis, FRCS; Surgeon: ENT Department, St Bartholomew's Hospital, since 1961; Royal National Throat, Nose and Ear Hospital, since 1962; *b* 22 Oct. 1922; *s* of E. C. H. Jones, CBE, and M. E. Jones, MBE; *m* 1950, Mary Garrett; one *s* three *d. Educ:* Manchester Grammar Sch.; Dulwich Coll.; Med. Coll., St Bartholomew's Hosp. (MB BS 1945); FRCS 1952. Ho. Surg., St Bart's, 1946-47; MO, RAF, 1947-50; Demonstrator of Anatomy, St Bart's, 1950-52; Registrar, Royal Nat. Throat, Nose and Ear Hosp., 1952-54; Sen. Registrar, ENT Dept, St Bart's, 1954-59; Lectr, Dept of Otolaryngology, Univ. of Manchester, 1959-61; Dean, Inst. of Laryngology and Otology, Univ. of London, 1971-76. Mem., Court of Examiners, RCS, 1972-78; External Examiner, RCSI, 1980-. Hon. Sec., Sect. of Otology, 1965-68, Pres., Sect. of Laryngology, 1981-82, RSocMed. *Publications:* various chapters in standard med. textbooks; contribs to med. jls. *Recreations:* tennis, ski-ing, golf, fishing, gardening. *Address:* 108 Harley Street, W1N 1AF. *T:* 01-935 7811; 52 Oakwood Avenue, Beckenham, Kent BR3 2PJ. *T:* 01-650 0217.

MACNAGHTEN, Sir Patrick (Alexander), 11th Bt *cr* 1836; Technical Manager, African Region, Cadbury Schweppes Ltd; *b* 24 Jan. 1927; *s* of Sir Antony Macnaghten, 10th Bt, and of Magdalene, *e d* of late Edmund Fisher; *S father,* 1972; *m* 1955, Marianne, *yr d* of Dr Erich Schaefer and Alice Schaefer, Cambridge; three *s. Educ:* Eton; Trinity Coll., Cambridge (BA Mechanical Sciences). Army (RE), 1945-48. Project Engineer, Cadbury Bros (later Cadbury Schweppes), 1950-69; in General Management, Cadbury-Schweppes Ltd, 1969-. *Recreations:* dinghy sailing, farming. *Heir: s* Malcolm Francis Macnaghten, *b* 21 Sept. 1956. *Address:* Cofton Crest, Cherry Hill Drive, Barnt Green, Birmingham B45 8JY. *T:* 021-445 2341; Dundarave, Bushmills, Co. Antrim, Northern Ireland. *T:* Bushmills 31215. *Club:* Barnt Green Sailing.

MACNAGHTEN, Robin Donnelly, MA; Headmaster of Sherborne, since 1974; *b* 3 Aug. 1927; 2nd *s* of late Sir Henry P. W. Macnaghten and of Lady Macnaghten; *m* 1961, Petronella, *er d* of late Lt-Col A. T. Card and Mrs Card; two *s* one *d. Educ:* Eton (Schol.); King's Coll., Cambridge (Schol.). 1st cl. Class. Tripos Pt I, 1947; 1st cl. with dist. Pt II, 1948; Browne Medallist; MA 1954. Travelled in Italy and Turkey, 1949. Asst, Mackinnon Mackenzie & Co., Bombay, 1949-54. Asst Master, Eton Coll., 1954, and Housemaster, 1965.

Publication: trans. Vita Romana (by U. E. Paoli), 1963. *Recreations:* numismatics (FRNS), walking, gardening. *Address:* Abbey Grange, Sherborne, Dorset DT9 3AP. *T:* Sherborne 2025. *Club:* Western India Turf (Bombay).

McNAIR, family name of **Baron McNair.**

McNAIR, 2nd Baron *cr* 1955, of Gleniffer; **Clement John McNair;** *b* 11 Jan. 1915; *s* of 1st Baron McNair, CBE, QC, and Marjorie (*d* 1971), *yr d* of late Sir Clement Meacher Bailhache; *S father,* 1975; *m* 1941, Vera, *d* of Theodore James Faithfull; two *s* one *d. Educ:* Shrewsbury; Balliol Coll., Oxford. Served War of 1939-45, Major, RA. Mem., Gen. Adv. Council, IBA, 1978-; Substitute Mem., Council of Europe and WEU, 1979-. *Publications:* Wagonload, 1971; A Place Called Marathon, 1976. *Heir: s* Hon. Duncan James McNair, *b* 26 June 1947. *Address:* House of Lords, SW1.

McNAIR, Archibald Alister Jourdan, (Archie); Chairman: Thomas Jourdan Group, since 1971; Mary Quant Group of Companies, since 1955; *b* 16 Dec. 1919; *s* of late Donald McNair and Janie (*née* Jourdan); *m* 1954, Catherine Alice Jane, *d* of late John and of Margaret Fleming; one *s* one *d. Educ:* Blundell's. Articled to Ford Simey & Ford, Solicitors, Exeter, 1938. Served War, 1939-45: River Thames Formation. Photographer, 1950-57; Co-founder, Mary Quant Gp of Cos, 1955; Founder, Thomas Jourdan Gp, 1971, incl. Simplon Interline (Queen's Award for Export Achievement, 1976). *Recreations:* fruit farming, wood-carving, tennis, reading. *Address:* c/o Thomas Jourdan plc, 28 Frances Road, Windsor, Berks SL4 3AD. *T:* Windsor 57951. *Club:* Turf.

McNAIR, Air Vice-Marshal James Jamieson; Principal Medical Officer, Headquarters Support Command, Royal Air Force, 1974-77; retired; *b* 15 June 1917; *s* of Gordon McNair and Barbara MacNaughton; *m* 1945, Zobell Pyper (*d* 1977). *Educ:* Kirkcudbright Academy; Huntly Gordon Sch.; Aberdeen Univ.; London Sch. of Hygiene and Tropical Medicine; Liverpool Sch. of Tropical Medicine. MB, ChB; FFCM; DPH; DTM&H. Sqdn Med. Officer, UK, N Africa, Sicily, Italy, 1942-45; OC, RAF Sch. of Hygiene at Home and Egypt, 1946-51; SMO, 66, 21 and 25 Gp HQ at Home, 1951-57; SMO Air HQ and OC RAF Hosp. Ceylon, 1957-59; OC RAF Inst. of Hygiene, 1959-62; DGMS Staff, Air Min., 1962-65; OC RAF Hosp. Changi, Singapore, 1965-67; PMO HQ's Fighter Comd, 1967-68; OC Jt Service Med. Rehabilitation Unit, 1968-71; Dir of Health and Research, MoD (Air), 1971-74; Dep. Dir GMS RAF, 1974; QHP 1974-77. CStJ. *Recreations:* golf, gardening, travel. *Address:* Wakenills Cottage, Hedgehog Lane, Haslemere, Surrey GU27 2PJ. *T:* Haslemere 51389. *Clubs:* Royal Air Force; Hankley Common Golf.

MACNAIR, Maurice John Peter; His Honour Judge Macnair; a Circuit Judge since 1972; *b* 27 Feb. 1919; *s* of late Brig. J. L. P. Macnair and Hon. Mrs J. L. P. Macnair; *m* 1952, Vickie Reynolds, *d* of Hugh Reynolds; one *s* two *d. Educ:* Bembridge Sch.; St Paul's Sch.; St Edmund Hall, Oxford. BA 1947. Served War of 1939-45, Captain, RA, 1944. Called to Bar, Gray's Inn, 1948. Dep. Chm., W Sussex QS, 1968-72. *Address:* 28 Rawlings Street, SW3 2LS.

McNAIR, Thomas Jaffrey, MD, FRCS, FRCSEd; Surgeon to the Queen in Scotland, since 1977; Consultant Surgeon, Royal Infirmary of Edinburgh, since 1961 (Member, Board of Management, 1970-72); *b* 1 March 1927; *s* of David McMillan McNair and Helen (*née* Rae); *m* 1951, Dr Sybil Monteith Dick Wood; one *s* one *d. Educ:* George Watson's Coll.; Univ. of Edinburgh (MB, ChB, MD). Ho. Surg., Registrar, Clinical Tutor, Royal Infirmary of Edin., 1949-60; MO, Marlu, Gold Coast, 1950. Served as Flt Lt, RAF, 1951-53. Lectr in Clin. Surgery, Univ. of Edin., 1960; Instr in Surgery, Univ. of Illinois, USA, 1960; Consultant Surgeon: Eastern Gen. Hosp., 1961-64; Chalmers Hosp., 1964-81. Vice-Pres., RCS, 1981-83; Mem. Pfizer Exec. Cttee, Edin., 1976-; Examr, RCSE, 1964-; Hon. Sen. Lectr in Clin. Surg., Univ. of Edin., 1976-. *Publications:* Emergency Surgery, 8th and 9th edns, 1967 and 1972; various, on surgical subjects. *Recreations:* golf, sailing. *Address:* 44 Cluny Drive, Edinburgh EH10 6DX. *T:* 031-447 1225; Easter Carrick, Chapel Green, Earlsferry, Fife. *Clubs:* New (Edinburgh); Golf House (Elie); Luffness New Golf (Aberlady).

McNAIR-WILSON, Michael; *see* McNair-Wilson, R. M. C.

McNAIR-WILSON, Patrick Michael Ernest David; MP (C) New Forest, since 1968 (Lewisham West, 1964-66); Consultant; *b* 28 May 1929; *s* of Dr Robert McNair-Wilson; *m* 1953, Diana Evelyn Kitty Campbell Methuen-Campbell, *d* of Hon. Laurence Methuen-Campbell; one *s* four *d. Educ:* Eton. Exec. in French Shipping Co., 1951-53; various appointments at Conservative Central Office, 1954-58; Staff of Conservative Political Centre, 1958-61; Director, London Municipal Society, 1961-63; Executive with The British Iron and Steel Federation, 1963-64. Opposition Front Bench Spokesman on fuel and power, 1965-66; Vice-Chm., Conservative Parly Power Cttee, 1969-70; PPS to Minister for Transport Industries, DoE, 1970-74; Opposition Front Bench Spokesman on Energy, 1974-76. Editor of The Londoner, 1961-63. *Recreations:* sailing, pottery. *Address:* House of Commons, SW1A 0AA.

See also R. M. C. McNair-Wilson.

McNAIR-WILSON, (Robert) Michael (Conal); MP (C) Newbury, since 1974 (Walthamstow East, 1969-74); *b* 12 Oct. 1930; *y s* of late Dr Robert McNair-Wilson and of Mrs Doris McNair-Wilson; *m* 1974, Mrs Deidre Granville; one *d. Educ:* Eton College. During national service, 1948-50, was commissioned in Royal Irish Fusiliers. Farmed in Hampshire, 1950-53. Journalist on various provincial newspapers, and did freelance work for BBC in Northern Ireland, 1953-55. Joined Sidney-Barton Ltd, internat. public relations consultants (Dir 1961-). Contested (C) Lincoln, Gen. Elec., 1964; PPS to Minister of Agriculture, 1979-. Mem. Council, Bow Group, 1965-66; Jt Secretary: UN Parly Gp, 1969-70; Cons. Greater London Members Gp, 1970-72; Sec., 1969-70, Vice-Chm., 1970-72, Chm., 1972-74, Cons. Aviation Cttee; Mem., Select Cttee on Nationalised Industries, 1973-79; Dep. Chm., Air Safety Gp, 1979-. Mem. Council, Air League, 1972-76. Mem. Ct, Reading Univ., 1979-. *Publications:* Blackshirt, a biography of Mussolini (jointly), 1959; No Tame or Minor Rule, (Bow Group pamphlet on the Common Market) (jointly), 1963. *Recreations:* golf, sailing, skiing, riding. *Address:* House of Commons, SW1.
   See also P. M. E. D. McNair-Wilson.

McNALLY, Tom; MP Stockport South, since 1979 (Lab 1979-81, SDP since 1981); *b* 20 Feb. 1943; *s* of John P. McNally and Elizabeth May (*née* McCarthy); *m* 1970, Eileen Powell. *Educ:* College of St Joseph, Blackpool; University Coll., London (BScEcon). President of Students' Union, UCL, 1965-66; Vice-Pres., Nat. Union of Students, 1966-67; Asst Gen. Sec. of Fabian Society, 1966-67; Labour Party researcher, 1967-68; Internat. Sec. of Labour Party, 1969-74; Political Adviser to: Foreign and Commonwealth Sec., 1974-76; Prime Minister, 1976-79. SDP Parly spokesman on educn and sport, 1981-. Mem., Select Cttee on Industry and Trade, 1979. *Recreations:* playing and watching sport, reading political biographies. *Address:* 5 Amroth Close, SE23. *T:* 01-699 3333.

McNAMARA, (Joseph) Kevin; MP (Lab) Kingston-upon-Hull Central, since 1974 (Kingston-upon-Hull North, Jan. 1966-1974); *b* 5 Sept. 1934; *s* of late Patrick and Agnes McNamara; *m* 1960, Nora (*née* Jones), Warrington; four *s* one *d. Educ:* various primary schools; St Mary's Coll., Crosby; Hull Univ. (LLB). Head of Dept of History, St Mary's Grammar Sch., Hull, 1958-64; Lecturer in Law, Hull Coll. of Commerce, 1964-66. Opposition spokesman on defence, 1982-. Mem., Select Cttee on For. Affairs (former Chm., Overseas Develt Sub-Cttee); former Chairman: Select Cttee on Overseas Develt; PLP NI Gp; Sec., Parly Gp, TGWU. Former Mem., UK Delegn to Council of Europe. Commendatore, Order Al Merito della Repubblica Italiana, 1977. *Recreations:* family and outdoor activities. *Address:* House of Commons, SW1; 128/130 Cranbrook Avenue, Hull HU6 7ST.

McNAMARA, Air Chief Marshal Sir Neville (Patrick), KBE 1981 (CBE 1972); AO 1976; AFC 1961; Chief of Defence Force Staff, Royal Australian Air Force, since 1982; *b* Toogoolawah, Qld, 17 April 1923; *s* of late P. F. McNamara; *m* 1950, Dorothy Joan Miller; two *d. Educ:* Christian Brothers Coll., Nudgee, Qld. Enlisted RAAF, 1941; commnd 1944; Fighter Pilot WWII with No 75 Sqdn, Halmaheras and Borneo; served with No 77 Sqdn in Japan on cessation of hostilities; Air Traffic Control duties, HQ NE Area, 1948; Flying Instructor, Central Flying Sch., 1951-53; operational tour with No 77 Sqdn in Korean War; Pilot Trng Officer, HQ Trng Comd, 1954-55; Staff Officer, Fighter Operations Dept Air, 1955-57; CO No 25 Sqdn W Australia, 1957-59; CO No 2 Operational Conversion Unit, 1959-61; CO and Sen. Air Staff Officer, RAAF Staff, London, 1961-63; Director of Personnel (Officers), Dept Air, 1964-66; OC RAAF Contingent, Thailand, 1966-67; Air Staff Officer, RAAF Richmond, 1967-69; Dir-Gen., Organisation Dept Air, 1969-71; Comdr RAAF Forces Vietnam, 1971-72; Aust. Air Attaché, Washington, 1972-75; Dep. Chief of Air Staff, 1975-79; Chief of Air Staff, 1979-82. RAAF sc, fs, jssc. *Recreations:* golf, fishing. *Address:* 19 Jukes Street, Hackett, Canberra, ACT 2602, Australia. *T:* 498196. *Clubs:* Canberra, Commonwealth, Yowani Golf (Canberra).

McNAMARA, Robert Strange; Medal of Freedom with Distinction; Director: Corning Glass Works, since 1981; TWA; Royal Dutch Petroleum; The Washington Post; Bank of America; *b* San Francisco, 9 June 1916; *s* of Robert James McNamara and Clara Nell (*née* Strange); *m* 1940, Margaret McKinstry Craig (decd); one *s* two *d. Educ:* University of California (AB); Harvard Univ. (Master of Business Administration); Asst Professor of Business Administration, Harvard, 1940-43. Served in USAAF, England, India, China, Pacific, 1943-46 (Legion of Merit); released as Lieut-Colonel. Joined Ford Motor Co., 1946; Executive, 1946-61; Controller, 1949-53; Asst General Manager, Ford Div., 1953-55; Vice-President, and General Manager, Ford Div., 1955-57; Director, and Group Vice-President of Car Divisions, 1957-61, President, 1960-61; Secretary of Defense, United States of America, 1961-68; Pres., The World Bank, 1968-81. Trustee: Ford Foundn; Brookings Instn. Holds several hon. doctorates; Phi Beta Kappa. Albert Pick Jr Award, Univ. of Chicago (first recipient), 1979. *Publications:* The Essence of Security, 1968; One Hundred Countries, Two Billion People: the dimensions of development, 1975; The McNamara Years at the World Bank, 1981. *Address:* 2412 Tracy Place, NW, Washington, DC 20008, USA.

McNAUGHT, John Graeme; a Recorder of the Crown Court, since 1981; *b* 21 Feb. 1941; *s* of Charles William McNaught and Isabella Mary McNaught; *m* 1966, Barbara Mary Smith; two *s* one *d. Educ:* King Edward VII Sch., Sheffield; The Queen's Coll., Oxford (BA Jurisprudence, 1962). Bacon

Scholar, Gray's Inn, 1962; called to the Bar, Gray's Inn, 1963. *Address:* Ryton House, Lechlade, Glos GL7 3AR. *T:* Faringdon 52286.

McNAUGHTON, Lt-Col Ian Kenneth Arnold; Chief Inspecting Officer of Railways, Department of Transport, 1974-82; *b* 30 June 1920; *er s* of late Brig. F. L. McNaughton, CBE, DSO and Betty, *d* of late Rev. Arnold Pinchard, OBE; *m* 1946, Arthea, *d* of late Carel Begeer, Voorschoten, Holland; two *d. Educ:* Loretto Sch.; RMA Woolwich; RMCS Shrivenham. BScEng, CEng, FIMechE, FCIT, FIRSE. 2nd Lieut RE, 1939; served War of 1939-45, NW Europe (Captain) (despatches); GHQ MELF, 1949 (Major); Cyprus, 1955; OC 8 Rly Sqdn, 1958; Port Comdt Southampton, 1959 (Lt-Col); SOI Transportation HQ BAOR, 1960; retd 1963. Inspecting Officer of Rlys, Min. of Transport, 1963. Chm., Rlys Industry Adv. Cttee, Health and Safety Commn, 1978-82. *Recreations:* gardening, foreign travel. *Address:* Chawton Glebe, Alton, Hants. *T:* Alton 83395.

McNEE, Sir David (Blackstock), Kt 1978; QPM 1975; Commissioner, Metropolitan Police, 1977-82; *b* 23 March 1925; *s* of John McNee, Glasgow, Lanarkshire; *m* 1952, Isabella Clayton Hopkins; one *d. Educ:* Woodside Senior Secondary Sch., Glasgow. Joined City of Glasgow Police, 1946. Apptd Dep. Chief Constable, Dunbartonshire Constabulary, 1968; Chief Constable: City of Glasgow Police, 1971-75; Strathclyde Police, 1975-77. Lectures: Basil Henriques, Bristol Univ., 1978; London, in Contemporary Christianity, 1979; Dallas, Glasgow, 1980; Peter le Neve Foster Meml, RSA, 1981. Hon. Vice-Pres., Boys' Bde, 1980; Vice-Pres., London Fedn of Boys Clubs, 1982; Governor and Dep. Chm., E-SU, 1982; Member: Lord's Taverners, 1981; Saints and Sinners Club of Scotland, 1982; Patron, Scottish Motor Neurone Assoc., 1982. Freeman of the City of London, 1977. FBIM 1977. CStJ 1978. *Recreations:* fishing, golf, music. *Clubs:* Caledonian, Naval (Hon. Mem.).

McNEE, Sir John (William), Kt 1951; DSO 1918; MD; DSc, FRCP (London, Edinburgh and Glasgow); FRS(E); Regius Professor of Practice of Medicine, Glasgow University, 1936-53; Professor Emeritus, 1953; Physician to the Queen in Scotland, 1952-54 (and to King George VI, 1937-52); Consulting Physician to Royal Navy, 1935-55; Consulting Physician to University College Hospital, London, and to the Western Infirmary, Glasgow; *b* 17 Dec. 1887; *o s* of late John McNee, Glasgow and Newcastle upon Tyne; *m* 1923, Geraldine Z. L., MSc (London) (*d* 1975), *o d* of late Cecil H. A. Le Bas, The Charterhouse, London. *Educ:* Royal Grammar Sch., Newcastle upon Tyne; Glasgow, Freiburg, and Johns Hopkins, USA, Universities. MB (Hons), 1909; MD (Hons) and Bellahouston Gold Medal, 1914; DSc 1920. Asst Professor of Medicine and Lecturer in Pathology, Glasgow University; Asst Professor of Medicine, and Associate Physician, Johns Hopkins Univ., USA; Consulting Physician UCH, London, and formerly Holme Lecturer in Clinical Medicine, UCH Medical Sch.; Rockefeller Fellow in Medicine, 1923; Lettsomian Lecturer, Medical Society of London, 1931; Croonian Lecturer, RCP, 1932; Anglo-Batavian Lectr, all Univs of Holland, 1936; Harveian Lecturer, Harveian Society, London, 1952; Vicary Lecturer, RCS, 1958. Examiner in Medicine, Universities of Cambridge, St Andrews, Sheffield, Glasgow, Aberdeen, Edinburgh, Leeds, National University of Ireland, and Conjoint Board; Inspector for GMC of all Univs in Gt Britain and Ireland and of Final Examinations in Medicine, 1954-56. Visiting Prof., Harvard Univ., USA (Brigham Hospital), 1949. President: Royal Medico-Chirurgical Society of Glasgow, 1950-51; Gastro-Enterological Society of Great Britain, 1950-51; Assoc. of Physicians, Great Britain and Ireland, 1951-52; BMA 1954-55. Original Mem., 1942 Club. Editor, Quarterly Journal of Medicine, 1929-48. Master of the Barber-Surgeons' Company of London, 1957-58; Served European War, Major, RAMC, 1914-19 (despatches, DSO, Comm. Military Order Avis). Served War of 1939-45, Surgeon Rear-Admiral RN, and Consulting Physician to the Navy in Scotland and Western Approaches, 1939-45. Hon. MD (NUI); LLD (Glasgow), LLD (Toronto). *Publications:* Diseases of the Liver-Gall-Bladder and Bile-Ducts (3rd edn, 1929, with Sir Humphrey Rolleston); Text-book of Medical Treatment (with Dunlop and Davidson), 1st edn 1939, and 6th edn 1955; numerous medical papers, especially on diseases of liver and spleen and various war diseases (Trench Fever, Gas Gangrene, War Nephritis, Immersion Foot (RN)), Rescue Ships (RN), New Internat. Med. Code for Ships. *Recreations:* country sports. *Address:* Barton Edge, Worthy Road, Winchester, Hants. *T:* Winchester 65444. *Clubs:* Athenæum, Fly-fishers'.

McNEICE, Sir (Thomas) Percy (Fergus), Kt 1956; CMG 1953; OBE 1947; *b* 16 Aug. 1901; *s* of late Canon W. G. McNeice, MA, and Mary Masterson; *m* 1947, Yuen Peng Loke, *d* of late Dr Loke Yew, CMG, LLD; one *s* one *d. Educ:* Bradford Grammar Sch.; Keble Coll., Oxford (MA). Malayan Civil Service, 1925; Captain, Straits Settlements Volunteer Force (Prisoner of War, 1942-45). MLC, Singapore, 1949; MEC 1949; President of the City Council, Singapore, 1949-56, retired. FZS. *Recreations:* bird watching, walking and swimming. *Address:* 1102 Cathay Apartments, Singapore 9. *Club:* Royal Commonwealth Society.

McNEIL, Anne, CBE 1950 (OBE 1946); retired; *d* of Archibald and Elizabeth McNeil, Thorganby, York. *Educ:* privately. Served WRNS, 1940-50; last appointment, Superintendent (training). *Address:* Birkwood, Thorganby, York YO4 6DH.

MACNEIL OF BARRA, Prof. Ian Roderick; The Macneil of Barra; 46th Chief of Clan Macneil and of that Ilk; Wigmore Professor of Law, Northwestern University, since 1980; *b* 20 June 1929; *s* of Robert Lister

Macneil of Barra and Kathleen, *d* of Orlando Paul Metcalf, NYC, USA; *m* 1952, Nancy, *e d* of James Tilton Wilson, Ottawa, Canada; two *s* one *d* (and one *s* decd). *Educ:* Univ. of Vermont (BA 1950); Harvard Univ. (JD 1955). Lieut, Infty, Army of US, 1951-53 (US Army Reserve, 1950-69, discharged honorably, rank of Major). Clerk, US Court of Appeals, 1955-56; law practice, Concord, NH, USA, 1956-59. Cornell Univ., USA: Asst Prof. of Law, 1959-62; Associate Prof., 1962-63; Prof. of Law, 1962-72 and 1974-76; Ingersoll Prof. of Law, 1976-80; Prof. of Law, Univ. of Virginia, 1972-74. Vis. Prof. of Law, Univ. of East Africa, Dar es Salaam, Tanzania, 1965-67; Guggenheim Fellow, 1978-79; Vis. Fellow, Wolfson Coll., Oxford, 1979. Hon. Vis. Fellow, Faculty of Law, Edinburgh Univ., 1979. Member: American Law Inst.; Standing Council of Scottish Chiefs. FSAScot. *Publications:* Bankruptcy Law in East Africa, 1966; (with R. B. Schlesinger, *et al*) Formation of Contracts: A Study of the Common Core of Legal Systems, 1968; Contracts: Instruments of Social Co-operation-East Africa, 1968; (with R. S. Morison) Students and Decision Making, 1970; Contracts: Exchange Transactions and Relations, 1971, 2nd edn 1978; The New Social Contract, 1980. *Heir: s* Roderick Wilson Macneil, Younger of Barra, *b* 22 Oct. 1954. *Address:* 3500 Lake Shore Drive, Chicago, Ill 60657, USA; Kisimul Castle, Isle of Barra, Scotland. *T:* Castlebay 300. *Clubs:* New, Puffin's (Edinburgh).

McNEIL, John Struthers, CBE 1967; Chief Road Engineer, Scottish Development Department, 1963-69; *b* 4 March 1907; *s* of R. H. McNeil, Troon; *m* 1931, Dorothea Yuille; two *s*. *Educ:* Ayr Academy; Glasgow Univ. BSc Hons, Civil Engineering, 1929; FICE 1955. Contracting and local government experience, 1929-35; joined Ministry of Transport as Asst Engineer, 1935; Divisional Road Engineer, NW Div. of England, 1952-55; Asst Chief Engineer, 1955-57; Dep. Chief Engineer, 1957-63. Telford Gold Medal, ICE. *Publications:* contribs. to technical journals. *Recreations:* fishing, gardening. *Address:* 306-250 Douglas Street, Victoria, BC V8V 2P4, Canada.

MacNEIL, Most Rev. Joseph Neil; *see* Edmonton (Alberta), Archbishop of, (RC).

McNEILE, Robert Arbuthnot, MBE 1943; Deputy Chairman, Arthur Guinness Son & Co. Ltd, 1978-81 (Managing Director, 1968-75; Co-Chairman, 1975-78); *b* 14 March 1913; *s* of A. M. McNeile, Housemaster at Eton College; *m* 1944, Pamela Rachel Paton (*née* Pollock); three *s* one *d*. *Educ:* Eton Coll.; King's Coll., Cambridge. Asst Master, Eton Coll., 1935; joined Arthur Guinness Son & Co. Ltd, 1936. Served War of 1939-45 in Royal Engineers, First Airborne Div., HQ 21st Army Group, Control Commn for Germany; Lt-Col. Chm., Brewers' Society, 1975-77 (Vice-Chm., 1974-75). *Recreations:* archaeology, ornithology, Tennis, ski-ing, shooting. *Address:* Broad Lane House, Brancaster, Norfolk. *T:* Brancaster 227.

McNEILL, Hon. Sir David (Bruce), Kt 1979; **Hon. Mr Justice McNeill**; a Judge of the High Court of Justice, Queen's Bench Division, since 1979; Member, Restrictive Practices Court, since 1981; *b* 6 June 1922; *s* of late Ferguson and Elizabeth Bruce McNeill; *m* 1949, Margaret Lewis; one *s* three *d*. *Educ:* Rydal Sch.; Merton Coll., Oxford. BCL, MA Oxon. 1947. Called to Bar, Lincoln's Inn, 1947 (Cassel Schol.); Bencher, 1974; Northern Circuit, Leader, 1974-78, Presiding Judge, 1980-. Lecturer in Law, Liverpool Univ., 1948-58. QC 1966; Recorder of Blackburn, 1969-71; Recorder of the Crown Court, 1972-78. Member: Bar Council, 1968-72; Senate of the Inns of Court and the Bar, 1975- (Vice-Chm., 1976-77; Chm., 1977-78). Hon. Member: American Bar Assoc.; Canadian Bar Assoc. Hon. LLD Liverpool, 1982. Commissioned into Reconnaissance Corps, 1943; served in N Africa, Sicily, Italy, Germany. *Address:* Ravelstone, Manley, Cheshire. *T:* Manley 379; Royal Courts of Justice, Strand, WC2A 2LL.

McNEILL, Sir James (Charles), Kt 1978; CBE 1972; FASA; FAIM; Chairman, The Broken Hill Proprietary Co. Ltd, since 1977; *b* 29 July 1916; *s* of Charles Arthur Henry McNeill and Una Beatrice Gould; *m* 1942, Audrey Evelyn Mathieson; one *s*. *Educ:* Newcastle Boys' High Sch., NSW. Joined Broken Hill Proprietary Co. Ltd, Junior Clerk, 1933; Gen. Manager Commercial, 1959; Exec. Gen. Manager Finance, 1967; Managing Dir, 1971. Chm., Tubemakers of Aust. Ltd; Deputy Chairman: Private Investment Co. for Asia; Woodside Petroleum Ltd. Mem., Commonwealth Govt Economic Adv. Gp. Hon. DSc Newcastle, NSW, 1981. *Recreations:* music, farming, gardening. *Address:* 104 Mont Albert Road, Canterbury, Victoria 3126, Australia. *T:* 836.4924. *Clubs:* Australian, Athenæum, Melbourne (all Melbourne); Frankston Golf.

McNEILL, Maj.-Gen. John Malcolm, CB 1963; CBE 1959 (MBE 1942); *b* 22 Feb. 1909; *s* of Brig.-General Angus McNeill, CB, CBE, DSO, TD, Seaforth Highlanders, and Lilian, *d* of Maj.-General Sir Harry Barron, KCVO; *m* 1939, Barbara, *d* of Colonel C. H. Marsh, DSO, Spilsby, Lincs; two *d*. *Educ:* Imperial Service Coll., Windsor; RMA, Woolwich. 2nd Lieut, RA, 1929. Served Western Desert, Sicily, Italy, N.W. Europe and Burma, 1939-45; Commanded 1st Regt RHA, 1948-51; Student Imperial Defence Coll., 1952; Dep. Secretary, Chiefs of Staff Cttee, Ministry of Defence, 1953-55; Comdr RA 2nd Div. 1955-58; Comdt School of Artillery, 1959-60; Commander, British Army Staff, and Military Attaché, Washington, DC, 1960-63; Col Comdt RA, 1964-74. Principal Staff Officer to Sec. of State for Commonwealth Relations, 1964-69. ADC to the Queen, 1958-60. *Address:*

Beales House, Pilton, Shepton Mallet, Som. *T:* Pilton 212. *Clubs:* Army and Navy, English-Speaking Union.

McNEILL, Peter Grant Brass, PhD; Sheriff of Glasgow and Strathkelvin (formerly Lanarkshire) at Glasgow, since 1965; *b* 3 March 1929; *s* of late William Arnot McNeill and late Lillias Philips Scrimgeour; *m* 1959, Matilda Farquhar Rose, *d* of Mrs Christina Rose; one *s* three *d*. *Educ:* Hillhead High Sch., Glasgow; Morrison's Academy, Crieff; Glasgow Univ. MA (Hons Hist.) 1951; LLB 1954; Law apprentice, Biggart Lumsden & Co., Glasgow, 1952-55; Carnegie Fellowship, 1955; Faulds Fellowship, 1956-59; Scottish Bar, 1956; PhD, 1961. Hon. Sheriff Substitute of Lanarkshire, and of Stirling, Clackmannan and Dumbarton, 1962; Standing Junior Counsel to Scottish Development Dept (Highways), 1964; Advocate Depute, 1964. Pres., Sheriffs' Assoc., 1982. *Publications:* (ed) Balfour's *Practicks* (Stair Society), 1962-63; (ed jtly) An Historical Atlas of Scotland *c* 400-*c* 1600, 1975; legal and historical articles in Juridical Review, Scots Law Times, Glasgow Herald, etc. *Recreations:* legal history, gardening, bookbinding. *Address:* Sheriffs' Library, County Buildings, PO Box 23, Glasgow G1 1SY. *T:* 041-552 3434.

McNEISH, Prof. Alexander Stewart, FRCP; Professor of Paediatrics and Child Health, and Director of the Institute of Child Health, University of Birmingham, since 1981; *b* 13 April 1938; *s* of Angus Stewart McNeish and Minnie Howieson (*née* Dickson); *m* 1963; Joan Ralston (*née* Hamilton); two *s* one *d*. *Educ:* Glasgow Acad.; Univ. of Glasgow (MB); Univ. of Birmingham (MSc). FRCP 1977. Sen. Lectr in Paediatrics and Child Health, Univ. of Birmingham, 1970-76; Foundn Prof. of Child Health, Univ. of Leicester, 1976-80. *Publications:* papers on paediatric gastroenterology in Lancet, BMJ and in Archives of Disease in Childhood. *Recreations:* golf, music. *Address:* 128 Westfield Road, Edgbaston, Birmingham B15 3JQ. *T:* 021-454 6081. *Clubs:* Royal Society of Medicine; Blackwell Golf.

McNICOL, David Williamson, CBE 1966; Australian Diplomatic Service, retired; *b* 20 June 1913; *s* of late Donald McNicol, Adelaide; *m* 1947, Elsa Margaret, *d* of N. J. Hargrave, Adelaide; one *s*. *Educ:* Carey Grammar Sch., Melbourne; Kings Coll., Adelaide; Adelaide Univ. (BA). RAAF, 1940-45, Pilot, 201 and 230 Sqdns RAF, Atlantic, Madagascar, Italy and Dodecanese. Australian Minister to Cambodia, Laos and Vietnam, 1955-56; idc 1957; Australian Comr to Singapore, 1958-60; Asst Sec., Dept of External Affairs, Australia, 1960-62; Australian High Comr to Pakistan, 1962-65 and to New Zealand, 1965-68; Australian Ambassador to Thailand, 1968-69; Australian High Comr to Canada, 1969-73; Dep. High Comr for Australia in London, 1973-75; Ambassador to S Africa, and High Comr to Botswana, Lesotho and Swaziland, 1975-77. *Recreations:* golf, gardening. *Address:* 18 Fishburn Street, Red Hill, ACT 2603, Australia. *Clubs:* Naval and Military (Melbourne); Royal Canberra Golf.

McNICOL, Prof. George Paul; Principal and Vice-Chancellor, University of Aberdeen, since 1981; *b* 24 Sept. 1929; *s* of Martin and Elizabeth McNicol; *m* 1959, Susan Ritchie; one *s* two *d*. *Educ:* Hillhead High Sch., Glasgow; Univ. of Glasgow. MD, PhD, FRCP, FRCPG, FRCPE, FRCPath. House Surg., Western Infirmary, Glasgow, 1952; House Phys., Stobhill Gen. Hosp., Glasgow, 1953; Regimental MO, RAMC, 1953-55; Asst, Dept Materia Medica and Therapeutics, Registrar, Univ. Med. Unit, Stobhill Gen. Hosp., 1955-57; Univ. Dept of Medicine, Royal Infirmary, Glasgow: Registrar, 1957-59; Hon. Sen. Registrar, 1961-65; Lectr in Medicine, 1963-65; Hon. Cons. Phys., 1966-71; Sen. Lectr in Medicine, 1966-70; Reader in Medicine, 1970-71; Prof. of Medicine and Hon. Cons. Phys., Leeds Gen. Infirmary, 1971-81; Chm., Bd of Faculty of Medicine, Leeds Univ., 1978-81. Harkness Fellow, Commonwealth Fund, Dept of Internal Medicine, Washington Univ., 1959-61; Hon. Clinical Lectr and Hon. Cons. Phys., Makerere UC Med. Sch. Extension, Kenyatta Nat. Hosp., Nairobi (on secondment from Glasgow Univ.), 1965-66. Former Mem., Adv. Council on Misuse of Drugs. Chm., Part I Examining Bd, Royal Colls of Physicians (UK). Hon. FACP. *Publications:* papers in sci. and med. jls on thrombosis and bleeding disorders. *Recreations:* gardening, skiing. *Address:* University Office, Regent Walk, Aberdeen AB9 1FX. *T:* Aberdeen 40241; Chanonry Lodge, 13 The Chanonry, Old Aberdeen AB2 1RP. *Clubs:* Athenæum, Caledonian; Royal Northern & University (Aberdeen).

See also A. H. Smallwood.

McNICOLL, Vice-Adm. Sir Alan (Wedel Ramsay), KBE 1966 (CBE 1954); CB 1965; GM 1941; Australian Ambassador to Turkey, 1968-73; *b* 3 April 1908; 2nd *s* of late Brig.-Gen. Sir Walter McNicoll and Lady McNicoll; *m* 1st, 1937; two *s* one *d*; 2nd, 1957, Frances, *d* of late J. Chadwick. *Educ:* Scotch Coll., Melbourne; Royal Australian Naval Coll. Joined Navy, 1922; Lieut, 1930; Captain, 1949; Rear-Admiral, 1958; Dep. Chief of Naval Staff, 1951-52; Commanded 10th Destroyer Flotilla, 1950; HMAS Australia, 1953-54; IDC, 1955; 2nd Naval Member, Commonwealth Naval Board, 1960-61; Commanded Australian Fleet, 1962-64; Vice-Admiral, 1965; Chief of Naval Staff, Australia, 1965-68. Comdr of Order of Orange Nassau, 1955. *Publications:* Sea Voices (verse), 1931; trans., Odes of Horace, 1979. *Recreations:* music, fly-fishing. *Address:* 6 Hutt Street, Yarralumla, ACT 2600, Australia.

See also Rev. Prof. H. Chadwick, Sir J. E. Chadwick, Prof. W. O. Chadwick.

MACNIE, William Alexander, CMG 1949; OBE 1941; *b* 1899. *Educ:* High Sch. and University, Glasgow. Served European War, 1914-18, Lieut, 1917-

20. Sub-Inspector, Police, British Guiana, 1921; District Inspector, 1925; seconded as additional Assistant Colonial Secretary, 1931; District Commissioner, 1932; Senior District Commissioner, 1936; Principal Assistant Colonial Secretary, 1945; seconded as Competent Authority and Controller of Supplies and Prices, British Guiana, 1939-45; Colonial Secretary, Leeward Islands, 1945-49. MLC, British Guiana, 1951.

McNISH, Althea Marjorie, (Althea McNish Weiss), CMT 1976; freelance textile designer, since 1957; *b* Trinidad; *d* of late J. Claude McNish, educnl reformer, and Margaret (*née* Bourne); *m* 1969, John Weiss. *Educ:* Port-of-Spain, by her father and others; London Coll. of Printing; Central School of Art and Crafts; Royal Coll. of Art. NDD, DesRCA; FSIAD (FSIA 1968, MSIA 1960). Painted throughout childhood; after design educn in London, freelance practice, with commns from Ascher and Liberty's, 1957; new techniques for laminate murals, for SS Oriana and hosp. and coll. in Trinidad; Govt of Trinidad and Tobago travelling schol., 1962; interior design (for Govt of Trinidad and Tobago) in NY, Washington and London, 1962. Cotton Bd trav. schol. to report on export potential for British printed cotton goods in Europe, 1963; textile designs in exhibn, Inprint, Manch. and London, 1964-71; collection of dress fabric designs for ICI and Tootal Thomson for promotion of Terylene Toile, 1966; special features for Daily Mail Ideal Home Exhibn, 1966-78; interior design for Sec.-Gen. of Commonwealth, 1975; bedlinen collection for Courtaulds, 1978; (with John Weiss) textile design develt for BRB, 1978-; textile hangings for BRB Euston offices, 1979-; banners for Design Centre, 1981; (with John Weiss) improvements to London office of High Comr for Trinidad and Tobago, 1981; exhibn design for Govt of Trinidad and Tobago, Commonwealth Inst., 1982. Member: Design Council selection panels for Design Awards and Design Index, 1968-; Design Council, 1974-81; Design Council's Jubilee Souvenir Selection Panel, 1976, Royal Wedding Souvenir Selection Panel, 1981; textile designs in exhibns of Design Council and BoT: USA, 1969; Sweden, 1969; London, 1970; London and USA, 1972; paintings and hangings in exhibns, London, 1954-, including one-man exhibn of hangings, Peoples Gall., 1982, Jamaica, 1975. (With John Weiss) exhibited textile designs, Amsterdam, 1972-74, Design Council, London, 1975-, Lille, 1981-; etched silver dishes, London, 1973-; hangings, Kilkenny, 1981; printed textiles, Commonwealth Fest. Art Exhibn, Brisbane, 1982. Research tours: Czechoslovakia, 1968; Yugoslavia, 1972; Tunisia, 1974; Caribbean and N America, 1976. Vis. Lectr, Central Sch. of Art and Crafts and other colls and polytechnics, 1960-; Advisory Tutor in Furnishing and Surface Design, London Coll. of Furniture, 1972-. External assessor for educnl and professional bodies, incl. SIAD and NCDAD/CNAA, 1966-; Mem. jury for Leverhulme schols, 1968; Judge: Portuguese textile design comp., Lisbon, 1973; 'Living' Design Awards, 1974-. Mem., London Local Adv. Cttee, IBA, 1981-. Vice-Pres., SIAD, 1977-78; Mem., Fashion and Textiles Design Bd, CNAA, 1975-78; Mem. Gov. Body, Portsmouth Coll. of Art, 1972-81. *BBC-TV:* studio setting for Caribbean edn of Full House, 1973. Has also appeared, with work, in films for COI and Gas Council. Chaconia Medal (Gold) (Trinidad and Tobago), 1976, for service to art and design. *Publications:* textile designs prod. in many countries, and published in Designers in Britain and design jls. *Recreations:* ski-ing, travelling, music, gardening. *Address:* 142 West Green Road, N15 5AD. *T:* 01-800 1686. *Club:* Soroptimist.

MACONCHY, Elizabeth, (Mrs W. R. Le Fanu), CBE 1977; ARCM; Hon. RAM; composer of serious music; *b* 19 March 1907; of Irish parentage; *d* of Gerald E. C. Maconchy, Lawyer, and Violet M. Poë; *m* 1930, William Richard Le Fanu (author of Bibliography of Edward Jenner, 1951, Betsy Sheridan's Journal, 1960, etc); two *d. Educ:* privately; Royal College of Music, London. Held Blumenthal Scholarship and won Sullivan Prize, Foli and other exhibitions, at RCM; pupil of Vaughan-Williams; travelled with Octavia Scholarship, 1929-30. First public performance: Piano Concerto with Prague Philharmonic Orchestra, 1930. Sir Henry Wood introduced "The Land", Promenade Concerts, 1930. Has had works performed at 3 Festivals of International Society for Contemporary Music (Prague, 1935; Paris, 1937; Copenhagen, 1947). Largest output has been in Chamber Music; String Quartets played as a series in BBC Third Programme, 1955, 1975. Chairman: Composers Guild of Great Britain, 1960; Soc. for Promotion of New Music, 1972-75 (Pres., 1977-). Hon. Fellow, St Hilda's Coll., Oxford, 1978. *Publications:* Suite for Orchestra, The Land; Nocturne, Overture, Proud Thames (LCC Coronation Prize, 1953); Dialogue for piano and orchestra; Serenata Concertante for violin and orchestra, 1963; Symphony for double string orchestra; Concertino for: bassoon and string orchestra; Piano and chamber orchestra; Concerto for oboe, bassoon and string orchestra; Variazioni Concertanti for oboe, clarinet, bassoon, horn and strings, 1965; Variations for String Orchestra; twelve String Quartets (No 5, Edwin Evans Prize; No 9, Radcliffe Award, 1969); Oboe Quintet (Daily Telegraph Prize); Violin Sonata; Cello Divertimento; Duo for 2 Violins; Duo for Violin and Cello; Variations for solo cello; Reflections, for oboe, clarinet, viola and harp (Gedok International Prize, 1961); Clarinet Quintet; Carol Cantata, A Christmas Morning; Samson and the Gates of Gaza for chorus and orchestra, 1964; 3 settings of Gerard Manley Hopkins for soprano and chamber orchestra; Sonatina for harpsichord and Notebook for harpsichord, 1965; Three Donne settings, 1965; Nocturnal for unaccompanied chorus, 1965; Music for brass and woodwind, 1966; An Essex Overture, 1966; 6 Miniatures for solo violin, 1966; Duo for piano duet, 1967; Extravaganza, The Birds, after Aristophanes, 1968; And Death shall have no Dominion for chorus and brass, 3 Choirs Festival, 1969; The Jesse Tree, masque for Dorchester Abbey, 1970; Music for double-bass and piano, 1971; Ariadne (C. Day Lewis), for soprano and orch.,

King's Lynn Festival, 1971; Faustus, scena for tenor and piano, 1971; Prayer Before Birth, for women's voices, 1971; 3 Bagatelles for oboe and harpsichord, 1972; oboe quartet, 1972; songs for voice and harp, 1974; The King of the Golden River, opera for children, 1975; Epyllion, for solo cello and strings, Cheltenham Festival, 1975; Sinfonietta, for Essex Youth Orch., 1976; Pied Beauty, and Heaven Haven (G. M. Hopkins), for choir and brass, Southern Cathedrals Fest., 1976; Morning, Noon and Night, for harp, Aldeburgh Fest., 1977; Sun, Moon and Stars (Traherne), song cycle for soprano and piano, 1977; Heloise and Abelard, for 3 soloists, chorus and orch., 1977-78; The Leaden Echo & the Golden Echo (Hopkins), for choir and 3 instruments, 1978; Contemplation, for cello and piano, 1978; Colloquy, for flute and piano, 1979; Romanza, for solo viola and 11 instruments, 1979; Creatures, for mixed voices, 1979; Fantasia, for clarinet and piano, 1980; Little Symphony, for Norfolk Youth Orch., 1980; 4 Miniatures for chorus, 1981; Trittico for 2 oboes, bassoon and harpsichord, 1981; Piccola Musica for string trio, 1981; My Dark Heart, for soprano and 6 instruments, for RCM cent., 1982; Wind Quintet, 1982. Songs, Piano Pieces, etc. Three One-Act Operas (The Sofa, The Three Strangers, The Departure). *Address:* Shottesbrook, Boreham, Chelmsford, Essex. *T:* Chelmsford 467 286.

MACOUN, Michael John, CMG 1964; OBE 1961; QPM 1954; Overseas Police Adviser, and Inspector-General of Police, Dependent Territories, Foreign and Commonwealth Office, 1967-79, retired; Police Training Adviser, Ministry of Overseas Development, 1967-79; *b* 27 Nov. 1914; *o s* of late John Horatio Macoun, Comr of Chinese Maritime Customs; *m* 1940, Geraldine Mabel, *o d* of late Brig.-Gen. G. C. Sladen, CB, CMG, DSO, MC; two *s. Educ:* Stowe Sch., Buckingham; Univ. of Oxford (MA). At Metropolitan Police Coll., 1938; Tanganyika Police, 1939-42, 1945-58; Inspector-Gen. of Police, Uganda, 1959-64; Directing Staff, Police Coll., Bramshill, 1965; Commonwealth Office, 1966. War Service, 1943-44. Colonial Police Medal, 1951; OStJ 1959. *Recreations:* travel, walking. *Address:* Furzedown, Rowledge, near Farnham, Surrey. *T:* Frensham 3196. *Club:* Royal Commonwealth Society.

McPETRIE, Sir James (Carnegie), KCMG 1966 (CMG 1961); OBE 1953; Honorary Fellow, Department of Public Law, Dundee University, since 1976; *b* 29 June 1911; *er s* of late James Duncan McPetrie and late Elizabeth Mary Carnegie; *m* 1941, Elizabeth, *e d* of late John Howie; one *d. Educ:* Madras Coll., St Andrews; Univ. of St Andrews; Jesus Coll., Oxford (Scholar), MA (St Andrews) 1933; BA Oxon 1937, MA 1972; Harmsworth Schol., Middle Temple, 1937; Barrister, Middle Temple, 1938. Served War of 1939-45, Royal Artillery and staff of JAG (India); commissioned, 1940; Major, 1944. Legal Asst, Commonwealth Relations Office and Colonial Office, 1946, Sen. Legal Asst, 1947, Asst Legal Adviser, 1952; Legal Adviser, Colonial Office, 1960, Commonwealth Office, 1966, FCO, 1968-71; retired from HM Diplomatic Service, 1971; temporary mem. Legal Staff, DoE, 1972-75. Chm., UNESCO Appeals Bd, 1973-79. *Address:* Nelson Cottage, Strathkinness, St Andrews, Fife KY16 9SA. *T:* Strathkinness 235. *Club:* United Oxford & Cambridge University.

McPETRIE, James Stuart, CB 1960; *b* 13 June 1902; *s* of John McPetrie and Mary (*née* Simpson); *m* 1st, 1931, Helen Noreen McGregor (*d* 1974); one *s* ; 2nd, 1975, Myra, widow of John F. Pullen. *Educ:* Robert Gordon's Coll., Aberdeen; Aberdeen Univ. National Physical Laboratory, 1925-43; Radio Physicist, British Supply Mission, Washington, DC, 1943-44; Research Superintendent, Signals Research and Development Establishment, Ministry of Supply, 1944-50; Head of Radio Dept, Royal Aircraft Establishment, 1950-58; Dir-Gen. of Electronics Research and Development at Ministry of Aviation, 1958-62; Consulting Electronic Engineer, 1962-; Dir, Racal Electronics, 1965-69. *Publications:* series of papers on various aspects of radio research to learned societies. *Address:* 8 Edenhurst Court, Torquay, Devon.

MACPHAIL, Sheriff Iain Duncan; Sheriff of Tayside, Central and Fife at Dunfermline and Alloa, since 1981; *b* 24 Jan. 1938; *o s* of Malcolm John Macphail and late Mary Corbett Duncan; *m* 1970, Rosslyn Graham Lillias, *o d* of E. J. C. Hewitt, MD, TD, Edinburgh; one *s* one *d. Educ:* George Watson's Coll.; Edinburgh and Glasgow Univs. MA Hons History Edinburgh 1959, LLB Glasgow 1962. Admitted to Faculty of Advocates, 1963; in practice at Scottish Bar, 1963-73; Faulds Fellow in Law, Glasgow Univ., 1963-65; Lectr in Evidence and Procedure, Strathclyde Univ., 1968-69 and Edinburgh Univ., 1969-72; Standing Jun. Counsel to Scottish Home and Health Dept and to Dept of Health and Social Security, 1971-73; Extra Advocate-Depute, 1973; Sheriff of Lanarks, later Glasgow and Strathkelvin, 1973-81. Examiner in legal subjects, Glasgow and Edinburgh Univs, 1979-. Chm., Scottish Assoc. for Study of Delinquency, 1978-81. *Publications:* Law of Evidence in Scotland (Scottish Law Commn), 1979; articles and reviews in legal jls. *Recreations:* music, theatre, reading and writing. *Address:* Sheriff Court, Dunfermline. *T:* Dunfermline 24666.

MACPHERSON, family name of **Barons Drumalbyn, Macpherson of Drumochter** and **Strathcarron.**

MACPHERSON OF DRUMOCHTER, 2nd Baron, *cr* 1951; **(James) Gordon Macpherson;** Chairman and Managing Director of Macpherson, Train & Co. Ltd, and Subsidiary and Associated Companies, since 1964; Chairman, A. J. Macpherson & Co. Ltd (Bankers), since 1973; *b* 22 Jan. 1924; *s* of 1st Baron (*d* 1965) and Lucy Lady Macpherson of Drumochter; *S* father,

1965; *m* 1st, 1947, Dorothy Ruth Coulter (*d* 1974); two *d* (one *s* decd); 2nd, 1975, Catherine, *d* of Dr C. D. MacCarthy; one *s* two *d. Educ:* Loretto; Wells House, Malvern. Served War of 1939-45, with RAF; 1939-45 Campaign medal, Burma Star, Pacific Star, Defence Medal, Victory Medal. Founder Chm. and Patron, British Importers Confedn, 1972-. Member: Council, London Chamber of Commerce, 1958-73; (Gen. Purposes Cttee, 1959-72); East European Trade Council, 1969-71; PLA, 1973-76; Exec. Cttee, W India Cttee, 1959- (Dep. Chm. and Treasurer, 1971, Chm. 1973-75). Freeman of City of London, 1969; Mem., Butchers' Co., 1969-75. Governor, Brentwood Sch. JP Essex, 1961-76; Dep. Chm., Brentwood Bench, 1972-76; Mem. Essex Magistrates Court Cttee, 1974-76. Hon. Game Warden for Sudan, 1974; Chief of Scottish Clans Assoc. of London, 1972-74. FRSA 1971; FRES 1940; FZS. *Recreations:* shooting, fishing, golf. *Heir: s* Hon. James Anthony Macpherson, *b* 27 Feb. 1979. *Address:* Kyllachy, Tomatin, Invernessshire. *T:* Tomatin 212. *Clubs:* Boodle's, East India, Devonshire, Sports and Public Schools, Skikar; Thorndon Park, House of Lords Yacht; Royal and Ancient (St Andrews); Nairn Golf.

MACPHERSON, Sheriff Alexander Calderwood; a Sheriff of South Strathclyde, Dumfries and Galloway, at Hamilton, since 1978; *b* 14 June 1939; *s* of Alexander and Jean Macpherson; *m* 1963, Christine Isobel Hutchison; two *s. Educ:* Glasgow Academy; Glasgow Univ. (MA 1959, LLB 1962). Qualified as solicitor, 1962; private practice, 1962-78; part-time Assistantship in Private Law at Glasgow Univ., 1962-69; Partner in West, Anderson & Co., Solicitors, Glasgow, 1968-78; Lectr in Evidence and Procedure at Strathclyde Univ., 1969-78. Chairman, Glasgow North and East Br., Multiple Sclerosis Soc., 1973-. *Recreations:* piping (especially Piobaireachd), fishing, fly tying, reading. *Address:* 3 Baird Drive, Bearsden, Glasgow G61 4BL. *T:* 041-942 3508. *Clubs:* Glasgow Highland, Glasgow Art, Royal Scottish Automobile, Bohemian (all Glasgow); Royal Scottish Pipers' Society (Edinburgh).

MACPHERSON, Rt. Rev. Colin; *see* Argyll and the Isles, Bishop of, (RC).

MACPHERSON, Colin, MA; CA; Senior Partner, Smith & Williamson, Chartered Accountants, since 1973 (Partner, since 1959); *b* 17 Feb. 1927; *s* of Ian Macpherson and Anna Elizabeth McLean; *m* 1st, 1951, Christian Elizabeth Randolph; two *s* one *d* ; 2nd, 1981, Judith Margaret Jackson, *widow* of Brig. Tom Jackson. *Educ:* Eton; Trinity Coll., Cambridge (MA). Director: Sun Life Assce, 1968-; Keystone Investment, 1975-. Dep. Chm., 1976-78, Chm., 1978-82, Commn for New Towns. Mem., Pilcher Cttee on Commercial Property Develt, 1975; Vice-Chm., Guide Dogs for the Blind, 1976-. *Recreations:* skiing, shooting. *Address:* Flat 3, 17 Redcliffe Square, SW10. *Clubs:* Oriental, City of London.

MacPHERSON, Donald, CIE 1946; *b* 22 March 1894; *s* of D. MacPherson, Edinburgh; *m* 1931, Marie Elizabeth, *d* of John Nicholson, Sydney, NSW; two *d. Educ:* Royal High Sch. and Univ., Edinburgh. Indian Civil Service; District Magistrate, Bengal, 1928; Commissioner of Excise, 1935; Commissioner of Division, 1944. Retired, 1948. *Address:* 11 Melville Place, Edinburgh EH3 7PR. *T:* 031-225 5716.

MACPHERSON, Sir Keith (Duncan), Kt 1981; company director; Chief Executive since 1975, and Chairman since 1977, The Herald and Weekly Times Ltd, Melbourne; *b* 12 June 1920; *m* 1946, Ena Forester McNair; three *s* two *d. Educ:* Scotch Coll., Melbourne. Joined The Herald and Weekly Times Ltd, 1938; Sec., 1959-64; Asst Gen. Man., 1965-67; Gen. Man., 1968-70; Dir., 1974. Chairman: Australian Newsprint Mills Holdings Ltd, 1978- (Vice-Chm., 1976-78); West Australian Newspapers Ltd, 1981- (Dir, 1970; Man. Dir, 1970-75); South Pacific Post Pty Ltd (New Guinea Newspapers), 1965-70; Dep. Chm., Queensland Press Ltd, 1981- (Dir, 1978). Director: Tasman Pulp & Paper Co. Ltd, 1977-78; Davies Bros Ltd, 1975-; New Nation Publishing Ltd, Singapore, 1974-81. Pres., Australian Newspapers Council, 1968-70; Chairman: Newspaper Proprietors' Assoc. of Melbourne, 1968-70; Media Council of Aust., 1969-70. *Recreations:* swimming, gardening. *Address:* Gleneagles, 24 Balwyn Road, Canterbury, Vic 3126, Australia. *T:* 836-8571. *Clubs:* Melbourne, Athenæum, Melbourne Cricket, Royal Automobile of Victoria, Victoria Racing, Victoria Amateur Turf, Moonee Valley Racing (Melbourne); American National (Sydney).

M'PHERSON, Prof. Philip Keith, CEng, FIMechE; Professor and Head of Department of Systems Science (Department of Production and Instrument Engineering, until 1971), since 1967 and Pro-Vice-Chancellor, since 1982, The City University; *b* 10 March 1927; *s* of Ven. Kenneth M'Pherson and Dulce M'Pherson; *m* 1975, Rosalie Margaret, *d* of Richard and Mary Fowler. *Educ:* Marlborough Coll.; Royal Naval Engineering Coll.; Royal Naval Coll., Greenwich; Massachusetts Inst. of Technology (SM); MA Oxon. Engineer Officer, Royal Navy, 1948-59; research in Admiralty Gunnery Establt, 1955-59, retired as Lt-Comdr, 1959. Head, Dynamics Gp, Atomic Energy Establt, UKAEA, 1959-65; SPSO, 1963; Fellow of St John's Coll., Oxford, 1965-67. Member: Executive Cttee, UK Automation Council, 1964-68; SRC Control Engrg Cttee, 1970-75; Chairman: IMechE Automatic Control Gp, 1967-69; IEE Systems Engrg Gp Cttee, 1966-69; IEE Control and Automation Div., 1967-69; Soc. for General Systems Research (UK), 1973-76. Vis. Scholar, Internat. Inst. of Applied Systems Analysis, Austria, 1976-77; Adjunct Prof., Xian Jiaotong Univ., China, 1980-. FRSA. *Publications:* many papers in the scientific literature. *Recreations:* life at home, walking in lonely places, history of naval technology, making things. *Address:* The City

University, Northampton Square, EC1V 0HB. *T:* 01-253 4399. *Club:* Royal Commonwealth Society.

MACPHERSON, Roderick Ewen; Registrary, University of Cambridge, 1969-Sept. 1983; *b* 17 July 1916; *s* of Ewen Macpherson, Chief Charity Commissioner, and Dorothy Mildred Hensley; *m* 1941, Sheila Joan Hooper, *d* of H. P. Hooper; two *s* two *d. Educ:* Eton College; King's College, Cambridge. Math. Tripos, Part II, Wrangler; Math. Tripos, Part III, Distinction; Smith's Prizeman, 1940. Served RAFVR, 1940-46, Navigator (Radio). Fellow, King's Coll., Cambridge, 1942-; Third Bursar, King's College, 1947-50, Second Bursar, 1950-51, First Bursar, 1951-62; University Treasurer, Univ. of Cambridge, 1962-69; Member: Council of the Senate, 1957-62; Financial Board, 1955-62. *Recreations:* gardening, hill-walking. *Address:* Orion, Coton Road, Grantchester, Cambridge CB3 9NX. *T:* Cambridge 840266.

MACPHERSON, Ronald Thomas Stewart, CBE 1968; MC 1943, Bars 1944 and 1945; TD 1960; DL; Chairman, Mallinson-Denny Group, 1980-82 (Chief Executive, 1967-82; Deputy Chairman, 1969-80); formerly Executive Director, Brooke Bond Group plc; Director: Birmid Qualcast; Scottish Mutual Assurance Society; Allstate Insurance Co.; *b* 4 Oct. 1920; 5th *s* of late Sir Thomas Stewart Macpherson, CIE, LLD, and Lady (Helen) Macpherson, K-i-H (*née* Cameron); *m* 1953, Jean Henrietta, *d* of late David Butler Wilson and Mrs Butler Wilson; two *s* one *d. Educ:* Cargilfield Sch.; Fettes Coll. (scholar); Trinity Coll., Oxford (1st open classical scholar; MA 1st Cl. Hons PPE). Athletics Blue and Scottish International; represented Oxford in rugby, football and hockey, 1946-47. Served War, 1939-45: commnd Queen's Own Cameron Highlanders TA, 1939; Scottish Commando, 1940; POW, 1941-43; Major 1943; served Special Forces with French and Italian Resistance. Consultant, Italo-Yugoslav Border Commn, 1946. Comd 1st Bn London Scottish TA, 1961-64; Col TA London Dist, 1964-67. Mem., Queen's Body Guard for Scotland (Royal Co. of Archers). Pres., Achilles Club. Chm. Council, London Chamber of Commerce, 1980-82. Member: Council, CBI (Chm., London and SE Reg., CBI, 1975-77); Scottish Council, London; Prices and Incomes Bd, 1968-69; Council, GBA; Council, Strathclyde Univ. Business Sch. Governor, Fettes Coll. FRSA, FBIM. DL Greater London, 1977. Chevalier, Légion d'Honneur, and Croix de Guerre with 2 palms, France; Medaglia d'Argento and Resistance Medal, Italy; Kt of St Mary of Bethlehem. *Recreations:* shooting, outdoor sport, modern languages. *Address:* 4 Somers Crescent, W2 2PN. *T:* 01-262 8487; Balavil, Kingussie, Inverness-shire. *T:* Kingussie 470. *Clubs:* Hurlingham, MCC.
See also Baron Drumalbyn.

MacPHERSON, Stewart Myles; Radio Commentator; Journalist; Variety Artist; Special Events Coordinator, Assiniboia Downs Racetrack, Winnipeg; *b* Winnipeg, Canada, 29 Oct. 1908; *m* 1937, Emily Comfort; one *s* one *d. Educ:* Canada. Started broadcasting, 1937, on ice hockey; War Correspondent. Commentator on national events and world championships. Question Master, Twenty Questions and Ignorance is Bliss. Compère, Royal Command Variety Performance, 1948; Dir of Programs, C-Jay Television, Winnipeg, 1960. *Publication:* The Mike and I, 1948; *relevant publication:* Highlights with Stewart MacPherson, by John Robertson, 1980. *Recreations:* golf, bridge, poker. *Address:* 709-3200 Portage Avenue, Winnipeg, Manitoba, Canada. *T:* (204) 889-0210.

MACPHERSON OF CLUNY (and Blairgowrie), William Alan, TD 1966; QC 1971; Cluny Macpherson; 27th Chief of Clan Macpherson; a Recorder of the Crown Court, since 1972; *b* 1 April 1926; *s* of Brig. Alan David Macpherson, DSO, MC, RA (*d* 1969) and late Catherine Richardson Macpherson; *m* 1962, Sheila McDonald Brodie; two *s* one *d. Educ:* Wellington Coll., Berkshire; Trinity Coll., Oxford (MA). Called to Bar, Inner Temple, 1952; Bencher, 1978. Served, 1944-47, in Scots Guards (Capt.). Commanded (Lt-Col) 21st Special Air Service Regt (TA), 1962-65, Hon. Col, 1983-; now Lt-Col, TARO. Mem., Queen's Body Guard for Scotland, Royal Co. of Archers, 1977-. *Recreations:* golf, fishing; Past Pres., London Scottish FC. *Heir: s* Alan Thomas Macpherson yr of Cluny and Blairgowrie. *Address:* Newton Castle, Blairgowrie, Perthshire; 2 Garden Court, Temple, EC4. *Club:* Caledonian.

MACPHERSON-GRANT, Sir Ewan (George), 6th Bt, *cr* 1838; TD; DL; Member Scottish Faculty of Advocates; Hon. Sheriff Substitute, Counties of Perth and Angus; *b* 29 Sept. 1907; *s* of late George Bertram Macpherson-Grant, OBE (2nd *s* of 3rd Bt) and of Dorothy Eleanor Kellie-MacCallum (*d* 1952); *S* cousin, 1951; *m* 1937, Evelyn Nancy Stopford, *yr d* of late Major Edward Spencer Dickin, Spenford House, Loppington, Salop; one *d. Educ:* Winchester; Christ Church, Oxford. DL, Co. Banff, 1952. Mem. of Royal Company of Archers. *Heir:* none. *Address:* Pitchroy Lodge, Ballindalloch, Banffshire. *T:* Ballindalloch 208; Craigo, by Montrose, Angus. *T:* Hillside 205. *Club:* Army and Navy.

McQUADE, John; MP (DUP) Belfast North, since 1979; *b* Shankill, Belfast, July 1912; *m* Hanna Williams. *Educ:* public elementary sch., Snugville, Belfast. Served War of 1939-45, with Chindits in Burma. Formerly professional boxer (as Jack Higgins), and docker. Member: Belfast, Woodvale, NI Parlt, 1965-72, resigned, and, later, NI Assembly, 1974-75, resigned; Belfast City Council, Court Ward and later Shankill Ward, to 1972, resigned. Contested (UUUP) Belfast W, Feb. and Oct. 1974. *Address:* House of Commons, SW1.

McQUAIL, Paul Christopher; Under Secretary, Department of the Environment, since 1977; *b* 22 April 1934; *s* of Christopher McQuail and Anne (*née* Mullan); *m* 1964, Susan Adler; one *s* one *d*. *Educ:* St Anselm's, Birkenhead; Sidney Sussex Coll., Cambridge. Min. of Housing and Local Govt, 1957; Principal, 1962; Asst Sec., 1969; DoE, 1970; Special Asst to Permanent Sec. and Sec. of State, 1972-73; Sec., Royal Commn on the Press, 1974-77. *Recreations:* harmless pleasures. *Address:* 158 Peckham Rye, SE22. *T:* 01-693 2865.

McQUARRIE, Albert; MP (C) Aberdeenshire East, since 1979; *b* 1 Jan. 1918; *s* of Algernon Stewart McQuarrie and Alice Maud Sharman; *m* 1945, Roseleen McCaffery; one *s*. *Educ:* Highlanders Acad., Greenock; Greenock High Sch.; Royal Coll. of Science and Technology. MSE, PEng. Served in HM Forces, 1939-45 (Officer in RE). Chm., A. McQuarrie & Son (Great Britain) Ltd, 1946-; Consultant, Bredero Homes Ltd, 1976-; Dir, Energy Explorations Ltd. Former Dean of Guild, Gourock Town Council; former Chm., Fyvie/Rothienorman/Monquhitter Community Council. Chm., British/Gibraltar All Party Gp; Vice Chm., Conservative Fisheries Sub Cttee; Mem., Select Cttee on Scottish Affairs. Member: Council, Soc. of Engineers, 1978-; Turriff Branch, British Legion. Hon Patron, North Eastern Junior Football Assoc.; Hon. Mem., Fraserburgh Junior Football Club. *Recreations:* golf, bridge, music, soccer. *Address:* Teuchar Lodge, Cuminestown, Aberdeenshire AB5 8HR. *T:* Cuminestown 441; 21 Sancroft Street, Kennington, SE11 5UG. *T:* 01-582 4345. *Clubs:* Royal Scottish Automobile (Mem. Council, 1978-); Turriff Golf.

MACQUARRIE, Rev. Prof. John, TD 1962; Lady Margaret Professor of Divinity, University of Oxford, and Canon of Christ Church, since 1970; *b* 27 June 1919; *s* of John Macquarrie and Robina Macquarrie (*née* McInnes); *m* 1949, Jenny Fallow (*née* Welsh); two *s* one *d*. *Educ:* Paisley Grammar Sch.; Univ. of Glasgow. MA 1940; BD 1943; PhD 1954; DLitt 1964; DD Oxon 1981. Royal Army Chaplains Dept, 1945-48; St Ninian's Church, Brechin, 1948-53; Lecturer, Univ. of Glasgow, 1953-62; Prof. of Systematic Theology, Union Theological Seminary, NY, 1962-70, and Chm., Theological Field, 1968-70. Consultant, Lambeth Conf., 1968 and 1978. Governor: St Stephen's Hse, Oxford, 1970-; Pusey House, Oxford, 1975-. Hon. degrees: STD: Univ. of the South, USA, 1967; General Theological Seminary, New York, 1968; DD: Univ. of Glasgow, 1969; Episcopal Seminary of SW, Austin, Texas, 1981; Virginia Theol Seminary, 1981. *Publications:* An Existentialist Theology, 1955; The Scope of Demythologising, 1960; Twentieth Century Religious Thought, 1963; Studies in Christian Existentialism, 1965; Principles of Christian Theology, 1966; God-Talk, 1967; God and Secularity, 1967; Martin Heidegger, 1968; Three Issues in Ethics, 1970; Existentialism, 1972; Paths in Spirituality, 1972; The Faith of the People of God, 1972; The Concept of Peace, 1973; Thinking about God, 1975; Christian Unity and Christian Diversity, 1975; The Humility of God, 1978; Christian Hope, 1978; In Search of Humanity, 1982. *Address:* Christ Church, Oxford OX1 1DP. *T:* Oxford 43588.

MACQUEEN, Angus, CMG 1977; Director, The British Bank of the Middle East, 1970-79 (Chairman, 1975-78); Member, London Advisory Committee, The Hongkong and Shanghai Banking Corporation, 1975-78; Chairman, Incotes Ltd, since 1975; *b* 7 April 1910; *s* of Donald Macqueen and Catherine Thomson; *m* 1st, 1940, Erica A. L. Sutherland (marr. diss.); one *d*; 2nd, 1950, Elizabeth Mary Barber; one *s* one *d*. *Educ:* Campbeltown Grammar Sch. Joined Union Bank of Scotland, 1927; Imperial Bank of Persia (now The British Bank of the Middle East), 1930; overseas service in Iraq, Iran, Kuwait, Aden, Lebanon, Morocco; Gen. Manager, 1965-70. Director: The British Bank of the Middle East (Morocco), 1961-70; The Bank of Iran and the Middle East, 1965-74; Bank of North Africa, 1965-70. Member: London Chamber of Commerce (Middle East Section), 1962-66; Council, Anglo-Arab Assoc., 1968-75; Corona (Overseas Students) Housing Assoc., 1969-81. AIB (Scot.). National Cedar Medal, Lebanon, 1960. *Recreations:* golf, walking, foreign travel. *Address:* 18 Montagu Square, W1H 1RD. *T:* 01-935 9015. *Clubs:* Oriental, Roehampton.

MacQUEEN, Prof. John; Professor of Scottish Literature and Oral Tradition, since 1972, and Director, School of Scottish Studies, since 1969, University of Edinburgh; *b* 13 Feb. 1929; *s* of William L. and Grace P. MacQueen; *m* 1953, Winifred W. McWalter; three *s*. *Educ:* Glasgow Univ.; Cambridge Univ. MA English Lang. and Lit., Greek, Glasgow; BA, MA Archaeology and Anthropology, Section B, Cambridge. RAF, 1954-56 (Flying Officer). Asst Prof. of English, Washington Univ., Missouri, 1956-59; Lectr in Medieval English and Scottish Literature, 1959-63, Masson Prof. of Medieval and Renaissance Literature, 1963-72, Univ. of Edinburgh. Barclay Acheson Vis. Prof. of Internat. Relations, Macalester Coll., Minnesota, 1967; Vis. Prof. in Medieval Studies, Australian Nat. Univ., 1971; Winegard Vis. Prof., Univ. of Guelph, Ont, 1981. Chairman: British Branch, Internat. Assoc. of Sound Archives, 1978-80; Exec. Cttee, Scottish Nat. Dictionary Assoc., 1978-; Mem., Scottish Film Council, 1981- (Chm., Archive Cttee, 1980-). *Publications:* St Nynia, 1961; (with T. Scott) The Oxford Book of Scottish Verse, 1966; Robert Henryson, 1967; Ballattis of Luve, 1970; Allegory, 1970; (ed with Winifred MacQueen) A Choice of Scottish Verse, 1470-1570, 1972; Progress and Poetry, 1982; articles and reviews in learned jls. *Recreations:* music, walking, archaeology. *Address:* 9 Learmonth Gardens, Edinburgh EH4 1HD. *T:* 031-332 1488; Slewdonan, Damnaglaur, Drummore, Stranraer DG9 9QN. *Clubs:* University Staff, Scottish Arts (Edinburgh).

McQUIGGAN, John, MBE 1955; Executive Director, United Kingdom-South Africa Trade Association Ltd, since 1978; retired at own request from HM Diplomatic Service; *b* 24 Nov. 1922; *s* of John and Sarah Elizabeth McQuiggan; *m* 1950, Doris Elsie Hadler; three *s* one *d*. *Educ:* St Edwards Coll., Liverpool. Served War, in RAF, 1942-47 (W Africa, Europe and Malta). Joined Dominions Office, 1940; Administration Officer, British High Commission, Canberra, Australia, 1950-54; Second Sec., Pakistan, Lahore and Dacca, 1954-57; First Sec. (Inf.), Lahore, 1957-58; Dep. Dir, UK Inf. Services, Australia (Canberra and Sydney), 1958-61; Dir, Brit. Inf. Services, Eastern Nigeria (Enugu), 1961-64; Dir, Brit. Inf. Services in Uganda, and concurrently First Sec., HM Embassy, Kigali, Rwanda, 1964-69; W African Dept, FCO, 1969-73; HM Consul, Chad, 1970-73 (London based); Dep. High Comr and Counsellor (Econ. and Commercial), Lusaka, Zambia, 1973-76. MIPR 1964; Mem., Internat. Public Relations Assoc., 1975. Fellow, Inst. of Dirs. *Publications:* pamphlets and contribs to trade and economic jls. *Recreations:* tennis, carpentry, craftwork. *Address:* 7 Meadowcroft, Bickley, Kent BR1 2JD. *T:* 01-467 0075; 45 Great Peter Street, SW1. *T:* 01-222 0781. *Clubs:* Royal Commonwealth Society, Institute of Directors.

McQUILLAN, William Rodger; HM Diplomatic Service; Ambassador to Iceland, since 1981; *b* 18 March 1930; *s* of late Albert McQuillan and of Isabella Glen McQuillan; *m* 1970, Sheriell May Fawcett; one *s* two *d*. *Educ:* Royal High Sch., Edinburgh; Edinburgh Univ.; Yale Univ. Served RAF, 1954-57. Asst Sec., Manchester Univ. Appointments Board, 1957-65; First Sec., CRO, 1965; Lusaka, 1968, Head of Chancery, 1969; First Sec. (Commercial), Santiago, Chile, 1970; Counsellor and HM Consul, Guatemala City, 1974; Head of Inf. Policy Dept, FCO, 1978-81. *Address:* c/o Foreign and Commonwealth Office, SW1A 2AH. *Club:* Royal Air Force.

MacQUITTY, James Lloyd, QC (NI) 1960; Chairman, Ulster Television Ltd, since 1977; Underwriting Member of Lloyd's; *b* 2 Nov. 1912; *s* of James MacQuitty and Henrietta Jane (*née* Little); *m* 1941, Irene Frances McDowell. *Educ:* Campbell Coll. and Methodist Coll., Belfast; St Catherine's Coll., Oxford (MA); Trinity Hall, Cambridge (MA, LLB). Vice-Pres., Cambridge Univ. Conservative Assoc., 1936. HG Instructor, 1940-43; HAA, 1943-44. Called to English Bar, 1938, to NI Bar, 1941. Chairman: Compensation Appeals Tribunal; Compensation Tribunal for Loss of Employment through Civil Unrest; NI Housing Exec. Appeals Bd, and six Wages Councils in NI; Arbitrator under the Industrial Courts Act 1919, 1958-78; Mem., Industrial Injuries Adv. Council. Before reorganisation in 1973 of Local Govt in NI, was Chm. of former Jt Adv. Bds for Local Authorities' Services, Municipal Clerks, Rural Dist Clerks and County Chief Educn Officers and County Surveyors. Vice-Chm., Management Cttee, Glenlola Collegiate Sch., 1964-75; Chm., Trustees of Ulster Folk and Transport Museum, 1976 (Vice-Chm., 1969-76). Freeman, City of London, 1967. Chevalier de l'Ordre de St Lazare, 1962. *Recreations:* swimming, sailing. *Address:* 10 Braemar Park, Bangor, Co. Down, Northern Ireland. *T:* Bangor 4420. *Clubs:* Carlton; Royal Ulster Yacht, Royal Belfast Golf.

MacRAE, (Alastair) Christopher (Donald Summerhayes); HM Diplomatic Service; Head of West Africa Department, Foreign and Commonwealth Office, since 1980, and Ambassador (non-resident) to Chad, since 1982; *b* 3 May 1937; *s* of Dr Alexander Murray MacRae and Dr Grace Maria Lynton Summerhayes MacRae; *m* 1963, Mette Willert; two *d*. *Educ:* Rugby; Lincoln Coll., Oxford (BA Hons English); Harvard (Henry Fellow in Internat. Relations). RN, 1956-58. CRO, 1962; 3rd, later 2nd Sec., Dar es Salaam, 1963-65; ME Centre for Arab Studies, Lebanon, 1965-67; 2nd Sec., Beirut, 1967-68; FCO, 1968-70; 1st Sec. and Head of Chancery: Baghdad, 1970-71; Brussels, 1972-76; attached European Commn, Brussels, on special unpaid leave from FCO, 1976-78; Ambassador to Gabon, 1978-80, and to Sao Tomé and Principé (non-resident), 1979-80. *Recreation:* trying to keep fit. *Address:* c/o Foreign and Commonwealth Office, King Charles Street, SW1A 2AH. *T:* 01-233 4576. *Club:* Royal Commonwealth Society.

MACRAE, Christopher, CBE 1956; MA, DPhil; Vice-President, Ashridge Management College, since 1969 (Principal, 1962-69); *b* 6 Jan. 1910; *s* of John Tait Macrae and Mary (*née* Mackenzie), Kintail, Ross-shire; *m* 1939, Mary Margaret Campbell Greig, *er d* of Robert Elliott, Glasgow; two *s* one *d* (*er d* decd in infancy). *Educ:* Dingwall Acad.; Glasgow Univ. (MA); New Coll., Oxford (DPhil). Civil Servant, 1937-46; Chief Exec. Scottish Counc. (Devel. and Industry), 1946-56; Prof. of Industrial Admin., The Royal Coll. of Science and Technology, Glasgow, and Head of Chesters Residential Management Educn Centre, 1956-62. *Publications:* various articles and papers. *Recreations:* reading, music, walking, climbing, sailing. *Address:* Cluain, Tomnacroich, by Aberfeldy, Perthshire PH15 2LJ. *T:* Kenmore 298.

MacRAE, Prof. Donald Gunn; Martin White Professor of Sociology, University of London, since 1978 (Professor of Sociology, University of London, since 1961); *b* 20 April 1921; *o s* of Donald MacRae and Elizabeth Maud Gunn; *m* 1948, Helen Grace McHardy; two *d*. *Educ:* various schools in Scotland; Glasgow High Sch.; Glasgow Univ.; Balliol Coll., Oxford. MA Glasgow 1942; BA 1945, MA 1949, Oxon. Asst Lectr, LSE, 1945; Univ. Lectr in Sociology, Oxford, 1949; Reader in Sociology, London Univ., 1954; Prof. of Sociology: UC Gold Coast, 1956; Univ. of California, Berkeley, 1959; Fellow, Center for Advanced Studies in Behavioral Sciences, Stanford, 1967. Vis. Prof., Univ. of the Witwatersrand, 1975. Member: Council, CNAA (Chm. Cttee for Arts and Social Studies, to 1978); Archbp of Canterbury's Gp on Divorce Law, 1964-66; Gaitskell Commn of Inquiry into Advertising,

1962-66; Internat. Council on the Future of the University, 1973-. Editor, British Jl of Sociology, from formation to 1965. *Publications:* Ideology and Society, 1960; (ed) The World of J. B. Priestley, 1967; (ed with intro.) The Man Versus the State, by Herbert Spencer, 1969; Ages and Stages, 1973; Max Weber, 1974. *Recreations:* talking, music, walking. *Address:* 17 Fitzwarren Gardens, N19. *T:* 01-272 4976; 33 Liverpool Road, Walmer, Kent. *Club:* Athenæum.

MACRAE, John Esmond Campbell, DPhil; HM Diplomatic Service; Head of Cultural Relations Department, Foreign and Commonwealth Office, since 1980; *b* 8 Dec. 1932; *s* of Col Archibald Campbell Macrae, IMS, and Euretta Margaret Skelton; *m* 1962, Anne Catherine Sarah Strain; four *s. Educ:* Sheikh Bagh Sch., Kashmir; Fettes Coll., Edinburgh; Christ Church Oxford (Open Scholar); Princeton, USA. DPhil, MA. Atomic Energy and Disarmament Dept, Foreign Office, 1959-60; 2nd Sec., British Embassy, Tel Aviv, 1961-64; 1st Secretary: Djakarta, 1964; Vientiane, 1964-66; FO, NE African Dept, 1966; Central Dept, 1967-69; Southern African Dept, 1970-72; UK Mission to the UN, New York (dealing with social affairs, population and outer space), 1972-75; Counsellor, Science and Technology, Paris, 1975-80. *Recreations:* swimming, travel, music. *Address:* 20 Thornhill Crescent, N1. *T:* 01-607 9457. *Club:* Royal Automobile.

MACRAE, Col Robert Andrew Alexander Scarth, MBE 1953; JP; Lord-Lieutenant of Orkney, since 1972 (Vice-Lieutenant, 1967-72); Farmer; *b* 14 April 1915; *s* of late Robert Scarth Farquhar Macrae, Grindelay House, Orphir, Orkney; *m* 1945, Violet Maud, *d* of late Walter Scott MacLellan; two *s. Educ:* Lancing; RMC Sandhurst. 2nd Lt Seaforth Highlanders, 1935; Captain 1939; Major 1948; Lt-Col 1958; Col 1963; retd 1968. Active Service: NW Europe, 1940-45 (despatches, 1945); Korea, 1952-53; E Africa, 1953-54. Member: Orkney CC, 1970-74; Orkney Islands Council, 1974-78; Vice-Chairman: Orkney Hospital Bd, 1971-74; Orkney Health Bd, 1974-79. Hon. Sheriff, Orkney, 1974. DL, Co. of Orkney, 1944; JP Orkney, 1975. *Recreations:* sailing, fishing. *Address:* Grindelay House, Orkney. *T:* Orphir 228. *Clubs:* Army and Navy; New, Puffin's (Edinburgh).

MACREADY, Sir Nevil (John Wilfrid), 3rd Bt *cr* 1923; Managing Director, Mobil Oil, since 1975; *b* 7 Sept. 1921; *s* of Lt-Gen. Sir Gordon (Nevil) Macready, 2nd Bt, KBE, CB, CMG, DSO, MC, and Elisabeth (*d* 1969), *d* of Duc de Noailles; *S* father 1956; *m* 1949, Mary, *d* of late Sir Donald Fergusson, GCB; one *s* three *d. Educ:* Cheltenham; St John's Coll., Oxford. Served in RA (Field), 1942-47 (despatches); Staff Captain, 1945. BBC European Service, 1947-50. Vice-Pres. and Gen. Manager, Mobil Oil Française, 1972-75. *Recreations:* racing, fishing, theatre. *Heir: s* Charles Nevil Macready, *b* 19 May 1955. *Address:* Langley House, Pirbright, Surrey. *T:* Brookwood 2172. *Clubs:* Boodle's, Naval and Military; Jockey (Paris).

MacRITCHIE, Prof. Farquhar, CBE 1968; MA, LLB (Aberdeen); Professor of Conveyancing at Aberdeen University, 1946-74; *b* 1 Nov. 1902; *s* of Donald MacRitchie, Isle of Lewis; *m* 1941, Isobel, *d* of William Ross, Aberdeen; one *s* decd. *Educ:* Aberdeen Univ. Asst Lecturer in Law, Aberdeen Univ., 1940-45; Lecturer in Mercantile Law, Aberdeen Univ., 1945-46. Hon. Sheriff Substitute in Aberdeen. Convener, Legal Education Cttee, Law Soc. of Scotland, 1955-70; Vice-Pres., Law Soc. of Scotland, 1963. Mem. of firm of Morice & Wilson, Advocates, Aberdeen, until 1979. Hon. LLD Edinburgh, 1965. *Recreation:* golf. *Address:* 60 Rubislaw Den North, Aberdeen. *T:* 35458. *Club:* University (Aberdeen).

McROBERT, Rosemary Dawn Teresa; Deputy Director, Consumers' Association, since 1980; *b* Maymyo, Burma, 29 Aug. 1927; *e d* of late Lt-Col Ronald McRobert, IMS, and Julie Rees. *Educ:* privately and at Gloucestershire College of Educn. Journalist and broadcaster on consumer subjects, 1957-63; Founder editor, Home Economics, 1954-63; Chief Information Officer, Consumer Council, 1965-70; Consumer Representation Officer, Consumers' Assoc., 1971-73; Adviser on consumer affairs in DTI and Dept of Prices and Consumer Protection, 1973-74; Dir, Retail Trading Standards Assoc., 1974-80. Member Council: Inst. of Consumer Ergonomics, 1974-81; Consumers' Assoc., 1974-79; Advertising Standards Authority, 1974-80; Member: Adv. Council on Energy Conservation, 1974-82; Design Council, 1975-; Post Office Review Cttee, 1976; Policyholders' Protection Bd, 1976-. Chm. Management Cttee, Camden Consumer Aid Centres, 1977-80. Liveryman, Worshipful Co. of Glovers. Freeman, City of London. *Address:* 57 Lawford Road, NW5 2LG.

MACRORY, Sir Patrick (Arthur), Kt 1972; Director, Rothman Carreras Ltd, 1971-82; Barrister-at-Law; *b* 21 March 1911; *s* of late Lt-Col F. S. N. Macrory, DSO, DL, and Rosie, *d* of Gen. Brabazon Pottinger; *m* 1939, Elisabeth, *d* of late Rev. J. F. O. Lewis and of Mrs Lewis; three *s* (one *d* decd). *Educ:* Cheltenham Coll.; Trinity Coll., Oxford (MA). Called to the Bar, Middle Temple, 1937. Served War, 1939-45, Army. Unilever Ltd: joined 1947; Secretary, 1956; Director, 1968-71, retd. Dir, Bank of Ireland Gp, 1971-79. Mem., Northern Ireland Development Council, 1956-64; Gen. Treasurer, British Assoc. for Advancement of Science, 1960-65; Chairman: Review Body on Local Govt in N Ireland, 1970; Confedn of Ulster Socs, 1974-79; Member: Commn of Inquiry into Industrial Representation, 1971-72; Cttee on the Preparation of Legislation, 1973. Mem. Council, Cheltenham Coll. (Dep. Pres., 1980-). *Publications:* Borderline, 1937; Signal Catastrophe—the retreat from Kabul, 1842, 1966; Lady Sale's Journal, 1969; The Siege of Derry, 1980. *Recreations:* golf, military history. *Address:*

Amberdene, Walton-on-the-Hill, Tadworth, Surrey. *T:* Tadworth 3086. *Clubs:* Athenæum, Army and Navy; Walton Heath Golf; Castlerock Golf (Co Londonderry).

McSHARRY, Deirdre; Editor of Cosmopolitan, since 1973; *b* 4 April 1932; *d* of late Dr John McSharry and of Mrs Mary McSharry. *Educ:* Dominican Convent, Wicklow; Trinity Coll., Dublin. Woman's Editor, Daily Express, 1962-66; Fashion Editor, The Sun, 1966-72. Editor of the Year, 1981. *Recreations:* the arts, travel, gardening. *Address:* c/o Cosmopolitan, National Magazine House, 72 Broadwick Street, W1V 2BP.

McSHINE, Hon. Sir Arthur Hugh, TC; Kt 1969; Chief Justice of Trinidad and Tobago, 1968-71; Acting Governor-General, Trinidad and Tobago, 1972; *b* 11 May 1906; *m* Dorothy Mary Vanier; one *s* one *d. Educ:* Queen's Royal Coll., Trinidad. Called to Bar, Middle Temple, 1931. Practised at Trinidad Bar for eleven years; Magistrate, 1942; Senior Magistrate, 1950; Puisne Judge, 1953; Justice of Appeal, 1962. Acting Governor-Gen., Trinidad and Tobago, 1970. *Recreations:* music and chess (Pres., Caribbean Chess Fedn and Trinidad Chess Assoc.); flying (holder of private pilot's licence). *Address:* 6 River Road, Maraval, Port-of-Spain, Trinidad. *Clubs:* Trinidad and Tobago Turf, Trinidad and Tobago Yacht.

MACTAGGART, Sir Ian (Auld), 3rd Bt *cr* 1938; Managing Director The Western Heritable Investment Company and Director of several Property and other Companies; *b* Glasgow, 19 April 1923; *e s* of Sir John (Jack) Mactaggart, 2nd Bt, Nassau, Bahamas; *S* father 1960; *m* 1946, Rosemary (marr. diss. 1969), *d* of Sir Herbert Williams, 1st Bt, MP; two *s* two *d. Educ:* Oundle; Clare Coll., Cambridge. Served with Royal Engineers in India, 1942-45. Contested (U) Gorbals div. of Glasgow, 1945; contested (C) Fulham, 1970. Mem. (C) London County Council, for Fulham, 1949-51. Chm., Soc. for Individual Freedom. *Heir: s* John Auld Mactaggart [*b* 21 Jan. 1951; *m* 1977, Patricia, *y d* of late Major Harry Alastair Gordon]. *Address:* 2A Westmoreland Terrace, SW1. *T:* 01-834 8062. *Club:* English-Speaking Union.

McTAGGART, Robert; MP (Lab) Glasgow Central, since June 1980; *b* 2 Nov. 1945; *s* of Robert and Mary McTaggart; *m* 1966, Elizabeth Jardine; one *s* two *d. Educ:* St Constantine's, St Bartholomew's and Holyrood. Apprentice Marine Plumber, 1962-67; Trigonometrical Calculator, 1968-72; Pipework Planner, 1972-80. EETPU Shop Steward, 1971-77. Joined Labour Party, 1969; Glasgow Corporation Councillor, 1974-75, District Councillor 1977-80; Parliamentary Election Agent, 1978-80. *Recreations:* watching football, athletics, playing draughts, snooker, reading. *Address:* 61 St Mungo Avenue, Townhead, Glasgow G4 0PL. *T:* 041-552 7346.

MACTAGGART, William Alexander, CBE 1964; JP; Chairman, 1960-70, and Managing Director, 1945-68, Pringle of Scotland Ltd, Knitwear Manufacturers, Hawick; *b* 17 Aug. 1906; *o s* of late William Alexander and Margaret Mactaggart, Woodgate, Hawick; *m* 1932, Marjorie Laing Innes; two *s* one *d. Educ:* Sedbergh Sch., Yorks. Joined Robert Pringle & Son Ltd (later Pringle of Scotland Ltd), 1925; Dir, 1932; Joint Managing Dir, 1933. Served War of 1939-45: Captain, RASC, Holland, Belgium, France, 1942-45. Elder of Lilliesleaf Parish Church. Pres. of Vertish Hill Sports; Chairman: Duke of Buccleuch's Hunt; Hawick Youth Centre. *Recreation:* hunting. *Address:* Bewlie House, Lilliesleaf, Melrose, Roxburghshire. *T:* Lilliesleaf 267.

MacTAGGART, Air Vice-Marshal William Keith, CBE 1976 (MBE 1956); CEng, FIMechE; FRAeS; FBIM; Deputy Chairman, Modern Precision Engineers Ltd, since 1980; *b* 15 Jan. 1929; *s* of Duncan MacTaggart and Marion (*née* Keith); *m* 1st, 1949, Christina Carnegie Geddes (marr. diss. 1977); one *s* two *d* ; 2nd, 1977, Barbara Smith Brown, *d* of Adm. Stirling P. Smith, late USN, and Mrs Smith; one step *d. Educ:* Aberdeen Grammar Sch.; Aberdeen Univ. (BScEng 1948). FIMechE 1973; FRAeS 1974; FBIM 1978. Commnd RAF, 1949; 1949-67: Engr Officer; Pilot; AWRE, Aldermaston (Montebello and Maralinga atomic trials); attended RAF Staff Coll., and Jt Services Staff Coll.; Def. Intell.; Systems Analyst, DOAE, West Byfleet, and MoD (Air); Head of Systems MDC, RAF Swanton Morley, 1968; OC RAF Newton, 1971 (Gp Captain); Dep. Comd Mech. Engr, HQ Strike Comd, 1973; Dir of Air Armament, MoD (PE), 1973 (Air Cdre); RCDS, 1977; Vice-Pres. (Air), Ordnance Bd, 1978 (Air Vice-Marshal), Pres., 1978-80. *Recreations:* music, travel. *Address:* 11 Rectory Meadow, Southfleet, Gravesend, Kent DA13 9NY. *T:* Southfleet 3962; Modern Precision Engineers Ltd, Brunswick Road, Cobbs Wood, Ashford, Kent TN23 1EB. *T:* Ashford 23404. *Club:* Royal Air Force.

MacTHOMAS OF FINEGAND, Andrew Patrick Clayhills; 19th Chief of Clan MacThomas (Mac Thomaidh Mhor); *b* 28 Aug. 1942; *o s* of late Captain Patrick Watt MacThomas of Finegand and of Elizabeth, *d* of late Becket Clayhills-Henderson, Invergowrie, Angus; *S* father 1970. *Educ:* St Edward's, Oxford. Sen. Exec., Barclaycard/Visa, Scotland, 1973-; Director, Scotworld Services Ltd, 1979-. FSA (Scot.) 1973. Pres., Clan MacThomas Soc., 1970-; Hon. Vice-Pres., Clan Chattan Assoc., 1970-. *Heir: sister* Elizabeth Gillian MacThomas, *b* 15 Feb. 1949. *Address:* c/o Clan MacThomas Society, 22 India Street, Edinburgh EH3 6HB. *T:* 031-225 3962. *Clubs:* New, Puffin's (Edinburgh).

MacTIER, Sir (Reginald) Stewart, Kt 1961; CBE 1946; Director: The Ocean Steam Ship Co. Ltd, 1955-67; Glen Line Ltd, London, 1939-67; *b* 9 Dec. 1905; *s* of late Major H. C. MacTier, Newton St Loe, Somerset, and of Mary Fitzroy

MacTier, *d* of Sir Charles Hobhouse, 3rd Bt; *m* 1941, Mary, *d* of Brig. C. G. Ling, CB, DSO, MC; two *s* one *d. Educ:* Eton; Magdalene Coll., Cambridge. Mansfield & Co. Ltd, Singapore, Shipping Agents, 1928-37; Dep. Dir and subseq. Dir of Port and Transit Control, Min. of War Transport, 1940-45. Chm. Liverpool Steam Ship Owners' Assoc. and Gen. Council of British Shipping, 1960-61; Pres., Inst. Marine Engineers, 1966-67. Comdr Order of Maritime Merit (French); Medal of Victory with silver palm (US). *Address:* Durris, Haulands Gap Road, Flinders Island, Tas 7255, Australia.

McTIERNAN, Rt. Hon. Sir Edward (Aloysius), PC 1963; KBE 1951; Justice of the High Court of Australia, 1930-76; *b* 16 Feb. 1892; *s* of Patrick and Isabella McTiernan; *m* 1948, Kathleen, *d* of Sidney and Ann Lloyd, Melbourne. *Educ:* Marist Brothers' High Sch., Sydney; Sydney Univ. (BA, LLB, 1st cl. Hons). Admitted to Bar, NSW, 1917; Lecturer in Law, Sydney Univ.; NSW Parliament, 1920-27; Attorney-Gen., 1920-22 and 1925-27; NSW Govt Representative in London, 1926; MHR for Parkes, Commonwealth Parl., 1928, Papal Chamberlain, 1927. *Address:* 36 Chilton Parade, Warrawee, Sydney, NSW 2074, Australia. *Club:* Australian (Sydney).

MacVICAR, Rev. Kenneth, MBE (mil.) 1968; DFC 1944; Chaplain in ordinary to the Queen in Scotland, since 1974; Minister of Kenmore and Lawers, Perthshire, since 1950; *b* 25 Aug. 1921; *s* of Rev. Angus John MacVicar, Southend, Kintyre; *m* 1946, Isobel Guild McKay; three *s* one *d. Educ:* Campbeltown Grammar Sch.; Edinburgh Univ.; St Andrews Univ. (MA); St Mary's Coll., St Andrews. Mem., Edinburgh Univ. Air Squadron, 1941; joined RAF, 1941: Pilot, 28 Sqdn, RAF, 1942-45, Flt Comdr, 1944-45 (despatches, 1945). Chaplain, Scottish Horse and Fife and Forfar Yeomanry/Scottish Horse, TA, 1953-65. Convener, Church of Scotland Cttee on Chaplains to HM Forces, 1968-73. Clerk to Presbytery of Dunkeld, 1955-. District Councillor, 1951-74. *Recreation:* golf. *Address:* Manse of Kenmore, Aberfeldy, Perthshire PH15 2HE. *T:* Kenmore 218.

MACVICAR, Neil, QC (Scotland) 1960; MA, LLB; Sheriff of Lothian and Borders (formerly the Lothians and Peebles), at Edinburgh, since 1968; *b* 16 May 1920; *s* of late Neil Macvicar, WS; *m* 1949, Maria, *d* of Count Spiridon Bulgari, Corfu; one *s* two *d. Educ:* Loretto Sch.; Oriel Coll., Oxford; Edinburgh Univ. Served RA, 1940-45. Called to Scottish Bar, 1948. Chancellor, Dio. of Edinburgh, 1961-74. *Address:* 39 Dick Place, Edinburgh EH9 2JA. *T:* 031-667 4793. *Club:* New (Edinburgh).

McVITTIE, Maj.-Gen. Charles Harold, CB 1962; CBE 1953; *b* 6 Aug. 1908; *s* of Col R. H. McVittie, CB, CMG, CBE; *m* 1939, Margaret Wark, *d* of Dr T. Divine, Huddersfield; two *s. Educ:* Haileybury; Brighton Coll.; Sandhurst. 2nd Lt Queen's Own Royal West Kent Regt, 1928; transferred to RAOC, 1935; Served War of 1939-45, ADOS Singapore Fortress, 1941-42; POW, 1942-45; comd Vehicle Organization, 1948-50; DOS, GHQ Farelf, 1951-53; comd Technical Stores Organization, 1953-56; comd RAOC Trg Centre, 1956-60; Comdr Stores Organization, RAOC, 1960-63. Hon. Col AER Units RAOC, 1961-64. Col Commandant, RAOC, 1965-69. *Recreation:* fencing (Blue, Sandhurst, 1928). *Address:* Clovers, Garelochhead, Dunbartonshire. *T:* Garelochhead 810266.

McVITTIE, George Cunliffe, OBE 1946; MA Edinburgh, PhD Cantab; Professor of Astronomy, University of Illinois, 1952-72, Emeritus Professor, 1972; Hon. Professor of Theoretical Astronomy, University of Kent at Canterbury, since 1972; *b* 5 June 1904; *e s* of Frank S. McVittie; *m* 1934, Mildred Bond, *d* of Prof. John Strong, CBE; no *c. Educ:* Edinburgh Univ.; Christ's Coll., Cambridge. Asst Lecturer, Leeds Univ., 1930-34; Lecturer in Applied Mathematics, Liverpool Univ., 1934-36; Reader in Mathematics, King's Coll., London, 1936-48; Prof. of Mathematics, Queen Mary Coll., London, 1948-52. War service with Meteorological Office, Air Ministry, and a Dept of the Foreign Office, 1939-45. FRS (Edinburgh), 1943. Mem. Sub-Cttee of Meteorological Research Cttee, 1948-52. Jt Editor of The Observatory, 1938-48. Jt Exec. Editor of Quarterly Journal of Mechanics and Applied Mathematics, 1947-51; Pres., Commn on Galaxies, Internat. Astronomical Union, 1967-70; Sec., American Astronomical Soc., 1961-69. *Publications:* Cosmological Theory, 1937; General Relativity and Cosmology, 1956, 2nd edn, 1965; Fact and Theory in Cosmology, 1961; (ed) Problems of Extra-galactic Research, 1962; papers on Relativity and its astronomical applications, classical mechanics, etc., Proc. Royal Soc. and other journals. *Address:* 74 Old Dover Road, Canterbury, Kent CT1 3AY. *Club:* Athenæum.

McWATTERS, George Edward; Chairman: Ward White Group Ltd (formerly John White Footwear Holdings Ltd), 1967-82; Avery & Co., since 1982; Vice-Chairman, HTV Ltd, since 1970; *b* India, 17 March 1922; *s* of Lt-Col George Alfred McWatters and Ellen Mary Christina McWatters (*née* Harvey); *m* 1st, 1946, Margery Robertson (*d* 1959); 2nd, 1960, Joyce Anne Matthews; one *s. Educ:* Clifton Coll., Bristol. Vintners' Scholar, 1947. Served War of 1939-45: enlisted ranks Royal Scots, 1940; commissioned 14th Punjab Regt, Indian Army, 1941-46. John Harvey & Sons (family wine co.): joined, 1947; Dir, 1951; Chm. 1956-66; estab. a holding co. (Harveys of Bristol Ltd), 1962, but Showerings took over, 1966, and he remained Chm. until resignation, Aug. 1966. Dir, Martins Bank, 1960-70; Local Adv. Dir (Peterborough), Barclays Bank, 1970-82; Local Dir (Northampton), Commercial Union Assce Co., 1969-82. Mem., CBI Grand Council, 1970-82. Mem. Cttee, Automobile Assoc., 1962-. Governor: Clifton Coll., 1958-;

Kimbolton Sch., 1970-82. City Councillor, Bristol, 1950-53; contested (C) Bristol South, elecs 1955 and 1959. JP, Bristol, 1960-67; JP, Marylebone, 1969-71; High Sheriff, Cambridgeshire, 1979. *Recreations:* tennis, swimming, walking. *Address:* Burrington House, Burrington, Bristol BS18 7AD. *T:* Blagdon 62291. *Club:* Buck's.

McWATTERS, Stephen John; Headmaster, The Pilgrims' School, since 1976; *b* 24 April 1921; *er s* of late Sir Arthur Cecil McWatters, CIE; *m* 1957, Mary Gillian, *o d* of late D. C. Wilkinson and Mrs G. A. Wilkinson; one *s* two *d. Educ:* Eton (Scholar); Trinity Coll., Oxford (Scholar, MA). 1st Cl. Class. Mods, 1941. Served in The King's Royal Rifle Corps, 1941-45. Distinction in Philosophy section of Litterae Humaniores, Oxford, 1946. Asst Master, Eton Coll., 1947-63 (Master in Coll., 1949-57, Housemaster, 1961-63); Headmaster, Clifton Coll., 1963-75. *Recreations:* music, bird-watching. *Address:* The Pilgrims' School, Winchester SO23 9LT. *T:* Winchester 4189.

McWEENY, Prof. Roy; Professor of Theoretical Chemistry, University of Pisa, since 1982; *b* 19 May 1924; *o s* of late Maurice and Vera McWeeny; *m* 1947, Patricia M. Healey (marr. diss. 1979); one *s* one *d. Educ:* Univ. of Leeds; University Coll., Oxford. BSc (Physics) Leeds 1945; DPhil Oxon. 1949. Lectr in Physical Chemistry, King's Coll., Univ. of Durham, 1948-57; Vis. Scientist, Physics Dept, MIT, USA, 1953-54; Lectr in Theoretical Chemistry, Univ. Coll. of N Staffs, 1957-62; Associate Dir, Quantum Chemistry Gp, Uppsala Univ., Sweden, 1960-61; Reader in Quantum Theory, 1962-64, Prof. of Theoretical Chemistry, 1964-66, Univ. of Keele; Prof. of Theoretical Chem., 1966-82, and Hd of Chemistry Dept, 1976-79, Sheffield Univ. Vis. Prof., America, Japan, Europe. *Publications:* Symmetry, an Introduction to Group Theory and its Applications, 1963; (with B. T. Sutcliffe) Methods of Molecular Quantum Mechanics, 1969; Spins in Chemistry, 1970; Quantum Mechanics: principles and formalism, 1972; Quantum Mechanics: methods and basic applications, 1973; Coulson's Valence, 3rd rev. edn 1979; contrib. sections in other books and encyclopædias; many research papers on quantum theory of atomic and molecular structure in Proc. Royal Soc., Proc. Phys. Soc., Phys. Rev., Revs. Mod. Phys., Jl Chem. Phys., etc. *Recreations:* drawing, sculpture, travel. *Address:* Via Pietro Giordano 16, Gello, Pisa, Italy.

McWHINNIE, Donald; Freelance Director, Stage and Television, since 1960; *b* 16 Oct. 1920; *s* of Herbert McWhinnie and Margaret Elizabeth (*née* Holland). *Educ:* Rotherham Gram. Sch.; Gonville and Caius Coll., Cambridge. MA Cantab 1941. Served War of 1939-45: RAF, 1941-46. Joined BBC, 1947; Asst Head of Drama (Sound), 1953-60, resigned. Theatrical productions include: Krapp's Last Tape, Royal Court, 1958; The Caretaker, Arts and Duchess, 1960, Lyceum, NY, 1961; The Duchess of Malfi, Aldwych, 1960; Three, Arts and Criterion, 1961; The Tenth Man, Comedy, 1961; A Passage to India, Ambassador, NY, 1962; Everything in the Garden, Arts and Duke of York's, 1962; Macbeth, Royal Shakespeare, 1962; Rattle of a Simple Man, Garrick, 1962, Booth, NY, 1963; Doctors of Philosophy, Arts, 1962; The Doctor's Dilemma, Haymarket, 1963; Alfie, Mermaid and Duchess, 1963; Out of the Crocodile, Phœnix, 1963; The Fourth of June, St Martin's, 1964; End Game, Aldwych, 1964; The Creeper, St Martin's, 1965; All in Good Time, Royale, NY, 1965; The Cavern, Strand, 1965; This Winter's Hobby, US Tour, 1966; The Astrakhan Coat, Helen Hayes, NY, 1967; Happy Family, St Martin's, 1967; Tinker's Curse, Nottingham Playhouse, 1968; Vacant Possession, Nottingham Playhouse, 1968; Hamlet, Covent Garden, 1969; No Quarter, Hampstead, 1969; There'll be Some Changes Made, Fortune, 1969; The Apple Cart, Mermaid, 1970; A Hearts and Minds Job, Hampstead, 1971; Meeting at Night, Duke of York's, 1971; Endgame, and Play and Other Plays, Royal Court, 1976; Translations, Hampstead and Nat. Theatre, Hedda Gabler, Cambridge, 1981; also numerous television productions for BBC and ITV. *Publication:* The Art of Radio, 1959. *Address:* 16 Chepstow Place, W2. *T:* 01-229 2120.

McWHIRTER, Norris Dewar, CBE 1980; author, publisher, broadcaster; Director, Guinness Superlatives Ltd, since 1954 (Managing Director, 1954-76); *b* 12 Aug. 1925; *er* (twin) *s* of William Allan McWhirter, Managing Director of Associated Newspapers and Northcliffe Newspapers Group, and Margaret Williamson; *m* 1957, Carole, *d* of George H. Eckert; one *s* one *d. Educ:* Marlborough; Trinity Coll., Oxford. BA (Internat. Rel. and Econs), MA (Contract Law). Served RN, 1943-46: Sub-Lt RNVR, 2nd Escort Gp, Atlantic; minesweeping Pacific. Dir, McWhirter Twins Ltd, 1950; Chm., Wm McWhirter & Sons, 1955-; co-founder, Redwood Press (Chm., 1966-72); Dir, Gieves Ltd, 1972-. Editor (with late Ross McWhirter till 1975) and compiler, Guinness Book of Records, 1955- (1st edn); by 1982 175 edns in 23 languages; over 45 million sales. Athletics Correspondent: Observer, 1951-67; Star, 1951-60; BBC TV Commentator, Olympic Games, 1960-72; What's In the Picture, 1957; The Record Breakers, 1972-82. Mem., Sports Council, 1970-73. Dep. Chm. Freedom Assoc., 1975-. Vice-Pres., Guinness Museums Inc., 1976-. Contested (C) Orpington, 1964, 1966. *Publications:* Get To Your Marks, 1951; (ed) Athletics World, 1952-56; Dunlop Book of Facts, 5 edns, 1964-73; Guinness Book of Answers, 1976, 4th edn 1982; Ross: story of a shared life, 1976; Guinness Book of Essential Facts (US), 1979. *Recreations:* ski-ing (water and snow), athletics (Oxford 100 yds, Scotland 1950-52, GB in Norway 1951); Rugby football (Mddx XV, 1950). *Address:* c/o 2 Cecil Court, London Road, Enfield EN2 6DJ. *T:* 01-367 4567. *Clubs:* Caledonian; Vincent's (Oxford); Achilles.

McWHIRTER, Prof. Robert, CBE 1963; FRCSEd; FRCPEd; FRCR; FRSE; Professor of Medical Radiology, Edinburgh University, 1946-70; Director of Radiotherapy, Royal Infirmary, Edinburgh, 1935-70; President, Medical and Dental Defence Union of Scotland, since 1959; *b* 8 Nov. 1904; *s* of Robert McWhirter and Janet Ramsay Gairdner; *m* 1937, Dr Susan Muir MacMurray; one *s. Educ:* Girvan Academy; Glasgow and Cambridge Universities. MB, ChB (High Commend), Glasgow, 1927; FRCS Edinburgh 1932; DMRE Cambridge, 1933; FFR 1939. Formerly: Student, Mayo Clinic; British Empire Cancer Campaign Research Student, Holt Radium Institute, Manchester; Chief Assistant, X-Ray Dept, St Bartholomew's Hospital, London. Member, British Institute of Radiology; Pres., Sect. of Radiology, RSM, 1956; Fellow Royal College of Radiologists (Twining Memorial Medal, 1943; Skinner Memorial Lecturer, 1956; Warden, 1961-66; Knox Memorial Lecturer, 1963, Pres. 1966-69); Past Pres., Internat. Radio Therapists Visiting Club; Hon. Member, American Radium Society; Membre Corresp. Etranger, Société Française d'Electro-Radiologie Médicale, 1967; Membro d'onore, Società Italiana della Radiologia Medica e Medicine Nucleare, 1968; Hon. Member: Sociedade Brasileira de Patologia Mamária, 1969; Nippon Societas Radiologica, 1970; Groupe Européen des Radiotherapeutes, 1971. Caldwell Memorial Lecturer, American Roentgen Ray Society, 1963; Hon. Fellow: Australasian College of Radiologists, 1954; American College of Radiology, 1965; Faculty of Radiologists, RCSI, 1967. *Publications:* contribs to medical journals. *Recreation:* golf. *Address:* 2 Orchard Brae, Edinburgh EH4 1NY. *T:* 031-332 5800. *Club:* University (Edinburgh).

McWIGGAN, Thomas Johnstone, CBE 1976; Secretary General, European Organisation for Civil Aviation Electronics, since 1979; *b* 26 May 1918; *s* of late Thomas and Esther McWiggan; *m* 1947, Eileen Joyce Moughton; two *d. Educ:* UC Nottingham. Pharmaceutical Chemist. FIEE, FRAeS, SMIEEE. Signals Officer (Radar), RAFVR, 1941-46. Civil Air Attaché (Telecommunications) Washington, 1962-65; Dir of Telecommunications (Plans), Min. of Aviation, 1965; Dir of Telecommunications (Air Traffic Services), BoT, 1967; Dir Gen. Telecommunications, Nat. Air Traffic Services, 1969-79 (CAA, 1972-79). *Publications:* various technical papers. *Recreations:* photography, cabinet-making, gardening. *Address:* The Squirrels, Liberty Rise, Addlestone, Weybridge, Surrey. *T:* Weybridge 43068. *Club:* St George's Hill Tennis.

McWILLIAM, (Frederick) Edward, CBE 1966; Sculptor; *b* 30 April 1909; *yr s* of Dr William Nicholson McWilliam, Banbridge, County Down, Ireland; *m* 1932, Elizabeth Marion Crowther; two *d. Educ:* Campbell Coll., Belfast; Slade School of Fine Art; Paris. Served War of 1939-45, RAF, UK and Far East. Member of Staff, Slade Sch. of Fine Art, London Univ., 1947-66. Mem. Art Panel, Arts Council, 1960-68. First one-man exhib., sculpture, London Gall., 1939; subsequently Hanover Gallery, 1949, 1952, 1956; Waddington Galleries, 1961, 1963, 1966, 1968, 1971, 1973, 1976, 1979; Dawson Gallery, Dublin; Felix Landau Gallery, Los Angeles; retrospective exhibitions: Belfast, Dublin, Londonderry, 1981; Warwick Arts Trust, 1982. Has exhibited in International Open-Air Exhibitions, London, Antwerp, Arnheim, Paris. Work included in British Council touring exhibitions USA, Canada, Germany, South America. Fellow, UCL, 1972. Hon. DLit Belfast, 1964. *Relevant Publication:* McWilliam, Sculptor, by Roland Penrose, 1964. *Address:* 8A Holland Villas Road, W14 8BP.

McWILLIAM, John David; MP (Lab) Blaydon, since 1979; *b* 16 May 1941; *s* of Alexander and Josephine McWilliam; *m* 1965, Lesley Mary Catling; two *d. Educ:* Leith Academy; Heriot Watt Coll.; Napier College of Science and Technology. Post Office Engineer, 1957-79. Councillor, Edinburgh CC, 1970-75 (last Treasurer of City of Edinburgh and only Labour one, 1974-75); Commissioner for Local Authority Accounts in Scotland, 1974-78. Member: Scottish Council for Technical Educn, 1973-; Select Cttee on Educn, Science and the Arts, 1980-. *Recreations:* reading, listening to music, angling. *Address:* 16 Farndale Close, Winlaton, Blaydon on Tyne. *T:* Blaydon 4424 88. *Clubs:* Bleach Green Labour (Blaydon); Chopwell Social, Chopwell RAOB (Chopwell); Dunston Social, Dunston Mechanics Institute (Dunston); Ryton Social (Ryton); Blackhall Mill Social (Blackhall Mill).

McWILLIAM, William Nicholson, CB 1960; *b* 26 Nov. 1897; *er s* of W. N. McWilliam, MD, Banbridge, Co. Down; *m* 1927, V. Maureen, *er d* of H. H. Mussen, Asst Chief Crown Solicitor; one *s* two *d. Educ:* Excelsior Academy, Banbridge; Campbell Coll., Belfast; Trinity Coll., Dublin. Served European War, 1916-18, Lieut, RGA, 1916-18. BA, BAI, 1921. Entered NI Civil Service, 1922; Asst Sec. to Cabinet, NI, 1945-57; Dep. Clerk of the Privy Council, NI, 1945-57; Permanent Sec., Min. of Labour and National Insurance, NI, 1957-62 (retired). Member Boundary Commn for NI, 1963-69. *Address:* Garryard, 34 Massey Avenue, Belfast BT4 2JT. *T:* Belfast 63179.

MADANG, Archbishop of, (RC), since 1976; **Most Rev. Leo Arkfeld,** CBE (Hon.) 1976; *b* 4 Feb. 1912; *s* of George Arkfeld and Mary Siemer. *Educ:* St Mary's Seminary, Techny, Ill., USA (BA). Bishop of Wewak, Papua New Guinea, 1948-76; Administrator Apostolic of Wewak, 1976. *Address:* Box 750, Madang, Papua New Guinea. *T:* 82-2707; Box 107, Wewak, PNG. *T:* Wewak 862573.

MADDEN, (Albert) Frederick (McCulloch), DPhil; Reader in Commonwealth Government, Oxford, since 1957; Fellow of Nuffield College since 1958; *b* 27 Feb. 1917; *s* of A. E. and G. McC. Madden; *m* 1941, Margaret, *d* of Dr R. D. Gifford; one *s* one *d. Educ:* privately, by mother;

Bishop Vesey's Grammar Sch.; Christ Church, Oxford. Boulter and Gladstone exhibns; BA 1938, BLitt 1939, DPhil 1950. Dep. Sup., Rhodes House Library, 1946-48; Beit Lectr, 1947-57; Sen. Tutor to Overseas Service Courses, 1950-; Dir, Inst. of Commonwealth Studies, 1961-68; Vice-Chm., History Bd, 1968-73. Canadian Vis. Fellow, 1970; Vis. Prof., Cape Town, 1973; Vis. Fellow, Res. Sch., ANU, 1974. Dir, Hong Kong admin. course, 1975-. Dir, Prospect Theatre, 1963-66. FRHistS 1952. *Publications:* (with V. Harlow) British Colonial Developments, 1774-1834, 1953; (with K. Robinson) Essays in Imperial Government, 1963; chapter in Cambridge History of British Empire III, 1959; Imperial Constitutional Documents, 1765-1965, 1966; (with W. Morris-Jones) Australia and Britain, 1980; (with D. K. Fieldhouse) Oxford and the Idea of Commonwealth, 1982; reviews in English Historical Review, etc. *Recreations:* acting; photographing islands and highlands, hill towns, country houses, churches; Renaissance art; writing music and listening. *Address:* Oak Apples, Shotover Hill, Oxford. *T:* Oxford 62972.

MADDEN, Admiral Sir Charles (Edward), 2nd Bt, *cr* 1919; GCB 1965 (KCB 1961; CB 1955); Vice Lord-Lieutenant of Greater London, 1969-81; *b* 15 June 1906; *s* of Admiral of the Fleet Sir Charles E. Madden, 1st Bart, GCB, OM, and Constance Winifred (*d* 1964), 3rd *d* of Sir Charles Cayzer, 1st Bart; *S* father, 1935; *m* 1942, Olive, *d* of late G. W. Robins, Caldy, Cheshire; one *d. Educ:* Royal Naval Coll., Osborne. ADC to the Queen, 1955. Commander, 1939; Captain, 1946; Rear-Admiral, 1955; Vice-Admiral, 1958; Admiral, 1961. Chief of Naval Staff, NZ, 1953-55; Dep. Chief of Naval Personnel, 1955-57; Flag Officer, Malta, 1957-59; Flag Officer, Flotillas, Home Fleet, 1959-60; C-in-C Plymouth, 1960-62; C-in-C Home Fleet and NATO C-in-C Eastern Atlantic Command, 1963-65; retired, 1965. Chairman, Royal National Mission to Deep Sea Fishermen, 1971-81 (Dep. Chm., 1966-71); Vice-Chairman, Sail Training Assoc., 1968-70. Trustee: National Maritime Museum, 1968- (Chm., 1972-77); Portsmouth Royal Naval Museum, 1973-77. Chm., Standing Council of the Baronetage, 1975-77. DL Greater London, 1969. Grand Cross of Prince Henry the Navigator, Portugal, 1960. *Recreation:* painting. *Heir: b* Lieut-Colonel John Wilmot Madden, MC, 1944, RA [*b* 1916; *m* 1941, Beatrice Catherine Sievewright; two *s* one *d*]. *Address:* 21 Eldon Road, W8. *Club:* Arts.

MADDEN, Rear-Admiral Colin Duncan, CB 1966; CBE 1964; MVO 1954; DSC 1940 and Bar, 1944; Registrar and Secretary, Order of the Bath, since 1979; *b* 19 Aug. 1915; *s* of late Archibald Maclean Madden, CMG, and Cecilia Catherine Moor; *m* 1943, Agnes Margaret, *d* of late H. K. Newcombe, OBE, Canada and London, and Eleanor Clare; two *d. Educ:* RN Coll., Dartmouth. During War of 1939-45, took part in blocking Ijmuiden harbour and Dutch evacuation; Navigating Officer of 7th Mine Sweeping Flotilla; HMS Arethusa; Assault Group J1 for invasion of Europe, and HMS Norfolk. Thence HMS Triumph. Commander, 1950; Comd HMS Crossbow, 1952; staff of Flag Officer Royal Yachts, SS Gothic and Comdr (N) HM Yacht Britannia, for Royal Commonwealth Tour, 1953-54; Captain, Naval Attaché, Rome; Captain D 7 in HMS Trafalgar; IDC. Comd HMS Albion, 1962; Rear-Admiral, 1965; Senior Naval Member Directing Staff, Imperial Defence Coll., 1965-67; retired, 1967. Dir, Nat. Trade Develt Assoc., 1967-69. Gentleman Usher of the Scarlet Rod to the Order of the Bath, 1968-79. Dir Gen., Brewers' Soc., 1969-80. *Recreations:* sailing, gardening, tapestry. *Address:* c/o Coutts & Co., 440 Strand, WC2R 0QS. *Clubs:* Army and Navy, Royal Cruising, Royal Ocean Racing.

MADDEN, Frederick; see Madden, A. F. McC.

MADDEN, Max; Director of Publicity, Labour Party, 1979-82; *b* 29 Oct. 1941; *s* of George Francis Leonard Madden and Rene Frances Madden; *m* 1972, Sheelagh Teresa Catherine Howard. *Educ:* Lascelles Secondary Modern Sch.; Pinner Grammar Sch. Journalist: East Essex Gazette; Tribune (political weekly); Sun, London; Scotsman, London; subseq. Press and Information Officer, British Gas Corp., London. MP (Lab) Sowerby, Feb. 1974-1979; formerly: Member: Trade and Industry Sub-Cttee, Select Cttee on Public Expenditure; Select Cttee on Conduct of Members; Chm., Parly Lab. Party Employment Gp. Prospective Parly Cand. (Lab), Bradford W, 1981-. *Recreation:* fishing. *Address:* 22 Hanson Close, SW12 9QA.

MADDISON, Vincent Albert, CMG 1961; TD 1953; *b* 10 Aug. 1915; *s* of late Vincent Maddison; *m* 1954, Jennifer Christian Bernard; two *s* one *d. Educ:* Wellingborough Sch.; Downing Coll., Cambridge (MA). Colonial Administrative Service, 1939. Served War of 1939-45: Ethiopian and Burma Campaigns. District Officer, Kenya, 1947; seconded to Secretariat, 1948; Director, Trade and Supplies, 1953; Secretary, 1954, Perm. Secretary, 1957-63, Min. of Commerce and Industry; retired from Kenya Government, 1963; Chairman: East African Power and Lighting Co. Ltd, 1965-70; Tana River Development Co. Ltd, 1965-70; The Kenya Power Co. Ltd 1965-70; Director: Nyali Ltd, 1966-70; Kisauni Ltd, 1966-70; East African Trust and Investment Co. Ltd, 1966-70; East African Engineering Consultants, 1966-70. *Recreations:* ski-ing, gardening, sailing. *Address:* Edifici la Neu, Arinsal, La Massana, Andorra. *Clubs:* East India, Devonshire, Sports and Public Schools; Muthaiga Country (Kenya).

MADDOCK, Rt. Rev. David Rokeby; *b* 30 May 1915; *s* of Walter Rokeby Maddock; *m* 1943, Mary Jesse Hoernle, widow of Edward Selwyn Hoernle, ICS and *d* of Rev. Selwyn Charles Freer; one *s* one *d. Educ:* Clifton Coll.; Bristol Univ.; St Catherine's, Oxford; Wycliffe Hall, Oxford. Curate, Chard, Somerset, 1939-43; Vicar, Wilton, Taunton, 1943-47; Rector, Wareham,

1947-61; Rector of Bradford Peverell and Stratton, 1961-66; Rector of West Stafford with Frome Billet, 1966-67. Rural Dean of Purbeck, 1948-61; Canon of Salisbury, 1956-67; Archdeacon of Sherborne, 1961-67; Bishop Suffragan of Dunwich, 1967-76; Archdeacon of Sudbury, 1968-70; Provost of St Edmundsbury, 1976-80. Hon. Chaplain Dorset Constabulary, 1964-67. *Address:* 3 Norfolk Court, East Street, Bridport, Dorset. *T:* Bridport 25338.

MADDOCK, Sir Ieuan, Kt 1975; CB 1968; OBE 1953; FRS 1967; FEng 1975; Chairman: Fulmer Research Institute, since 1978; Sira Institute, since 1978; Corporate Consulting Group, since 1979; Director, Chubb & Sons Ltd, since 1978; *b* 29 March 1917; British; *m* 1943, Eurfron May Davies; one *s. Educ:* Gowerton Grammar Sch., Glamorgan; University of Wales, Swansea. Entered Government service, Explosives Res. and Devel. 1940; Principal Scientific Officer, Armament Res. Dept, Fort Halstead, 1949; Head of Field Experiments Div., Atomic Weapons Research Establishment, 1960; directed UK Research programme for Nuclear Test Ban Treaty, 1957-66; Dep. Controller B, 1965-67, Controller (Industrial Technology) 1967-71, Min. of Technology; Chief Scientist: DTI, 1971-74; DoI, 1974-77; Dir, Nat. Physical Laboratory, 1976-77. Principal of St Edmund Hall, Oxford, 1979-82 (Hon. Fellow, 1982). Dir, Prutec, 1980-82. Sec., BAAS, 1977-81. Vis. Prof., Imperial Coll., London, 1977-79. Member: SRC, 1973-77; NERC, 1973-77; Science Cons. Cttee to BBC, 1969-80 (Chm., 1977-80); ABRC, 1973-77; Adv. Council for Applied R&D, 1977-80; Gen. Adv. Council, BBC, 1977-80; Ct, Brunel Univ., 1979-82; Ct, Cranfield Coll. of Technology, 1969-77; Court of Surrey Univ. President: IERE, 1973-75; IMGTechE, 1976; Dep. Chm., Nat. Electronics Council, 1977-80; Vice-Pres., ASLIB, 1977-. For. Mem., Royal Swedish Acad. of Engrg Science, 1975. Hon. FIQA. Hon. Fellow: Manchester Polytechnic, 1977; Polytechnic of Wales, 1982. Hon. DSc: Wales, 1970; Bath, 1978; Reading, 1980; Salford, 1980; Hon. DTech CNAA, 1980. *Publications:* in various scientific and technical jls. *Address:* 13 Darell Road, Caversham, Reading, Berks. *T:* Reading 474096.

MADDOCKS, Arthur Frederick, CMG 1974; HM Diplomatic Service, retired; Ambassador and UK Permanent Representative to OECD, Paris, 1977-82; *b* 20 May 1922; *s* of late Frederick William Maddocks and Celia Elizabeth Maddocks (*née* Beardwell); *m* 1945, Margaret Jean Crawford Holt; two *s* one *d. Educ:* Manchester Grammar Sch.; Corpus Christi Coll., Oxford. Army, 1942-46; Foreign (later Diplomatic) Service, 1946-: Washington, 1946-48; FO, 1949-51; Bonn, 1951-55; Bangkok, 1955-58; UK Delegn to OEEC, 1958-60; FO, 1960-64; UK Delegn to European Communities, Brussels, 1964-68; Political Adviser, Hong Kong, 1968-72; Dep. High Comr and Minister (Commercial), Ottawa, 1972-76. *Address:* Lynton House, 83 High Street, Wheatley, Oxford OX9 1XP. *Clubs:* Athenæum; Hong Kong (Hong Kong).

MADDOCKS, Sir Kenneth (Phipson), KCMG 1958 (CMG 1956); KCVO 1963; *b* 8 Feb. 1907; *s* of Arthur P. Maddocks, Haywards Heath, Sussex; *m* 1st, 1951, Elnor Radcliffe, CStJ (*d* 1976), *d* of late Sir E. John Russell, OBE, FRS; no *c*; 2nd, 1980, Patricia Josephine, *d* of Algernon and Irma Hare Duke and *widow* of Sir George Mooring, KCMG. *Educ:* Bromsgrove Sch.; Wadham Coll., Oxford. Colonial Administrative Service, Nigeria, 1929; Civil Secretary, Northern Region, Nigeria, 1955-57; Dep. Governor, 1957-58. Acting Governor, Northern Region, Nigeria, 1956 and 1957. Governor and Commander-in-Chief of Fiji, 1958-63; Dir and Secretary, E Africa and Mauritius Assoc., 1964-69. KStJ. *Recreations:* fishing, gardening. *Address:* 11 Lee Road, Aldeburgh, Suffolk. *T:* Aldeburgh 3443.

MADDOCKS, Rt. Rev. Morris Henry St John; *see* Selby, Bishop Suffragan of.

MADDOCKS, William Henry, MBE 1975; JP; General Secretary, National Union of Dyers, Bleachers and Textile Workers, since 1979; *b* 18 Feb. 1921; *m* 1944, Mary Holdsworth; one *d. Educ:* Eastwood Elem. Sch.; Holycroft Council Sch., Keighley. W of England full-time Organiser for National Union of Dyers, Bleachers and Textile Workers, 1946-79. JP Gloucestershire, 1968. *Address:* 61 Windermere Road, Great Horton, Bradford BD7 4RG. *T:* Bradford 575166. *Clubs:* Trades (Shipley, W Yorks); Yeadon Trades Hall (Yeadon, W Yorks).

MADDOX, Sir (John) Kempson, Kt 1964; VRD 1948; Hon. Consulting Physician: Royal Prince Alfred Hospital, Sydney; Royal Hospital for Women, Sydney; *b* Dunedin, NZ, 20 Sept. 1901; *s* of Sidney Harold Maddox and Mabel Kempson; *m* 1940, Madeleine Scott; one *s* one *d. Educ:* N Sydney Boys' High Sch.; Univ. of Sydney. MD, ChM (Sydney) 1924; MRCP 1928; FRACP 1935; FRCP 1958. Served War of 1939-45, Surgeon Comdr, RANR. President: BMA (NSW), 1950; Cardiac Soc. of Australia and NZ, 1958; Asian-Pacific Soc. of Cardiology, 1960-64; Internat. Soc. of Cardiology, 1966-70; Vice-Pres., Nat. Heart Foundation of Australia, 1960-64 (Pres. NSW Div.); FACC 1965; FACP 1968; Hon. Pres., Internat. Soc. of Cardiology, 1970-. Hon. AM (Singapore) 1963. Chevalier de l'Ordre de la Santé Publique, France, 1961; Comendador, Orden Hispolito Unanue (Peru), 1968. *Recreations:* golf, fishing, tennis. *Address:* 8 Annandale Street, Darling Point, Sydney, NSW 2027, Australia. *T:* 32-1707. *Clubs:* Australian (Sydney); Royal Sydney Golf.

MADDOX, John (Royden); writer and broadcaster; Editor, Nature, 1966-73 and since 1980; *b* 27 Nov. 1925; *s* of A. J. and M. E. Maddox, Swansea; *m*

1st, 1949, Nancy Fanning (*d* 1960); one *s* one *d*; 2nd, 1960, Brenda Power Murphy; one *s* one *d. Educ:* Gowerton Boys' County Sch.; Christ Church, Oxford; King's Coll., London. Asst Lecturer, then Lecturer, Theoretical Physics, Manchester Univ., 1949-55; Science Correspondent, Guardian, 1955-64; Affiliate, Rockefeller Institute, New York, 1962-63; Asst Director, Nuffield Foundation, and Co-ordinator, Nuffield Foundation Science Teaching Project, 1964-66; Man. Dir, Macmillan Journals Ltd, 1970-72; Dir, Macmillan & Co. Ltd, 1968-73; Chm., Maddox Editorial Ltd, 1972-74; Dir, Nuffield Foundn, 1975-80. Member: Royal Commn on Environmental Pollution, 1976-81; Genetic Manipulation Adv. Gp, 1976-80; British Library Adv. Council, 1976-81; Council on Internat. Develt, 1977-79; Chm. Council, Queen Elizabeth Coll., 1980-. *Publications:* (with Leonard Beaton) The Spread of Nuclear Weapons, 1962; Revolution in Biology, 1964; The Doomsday Syndrome, 1972; Beyond the Energy Crisis, 1975. *Address:* Macmillan Journals Ltd, 4 Little Essex Street, WC2; 9 Pitt Street, W8. *T:* 01-937 9750. *Club:* Athenæum.

MADDRELL, Dr Simon Hugh Piper, FRS 1981; Fellow of Gonville and Caius College, Cambridge, since 1964; Senior Principal Scientific Officer, Agricultural Research Council Unit of Invertebrate Chemistry and Physiology, Cambridge University, since 1968; *b* 11 Dec. 1937; *s* of Hugh Edmund Fisher Maddrell and Barbara Agnes Mary Maddrell; *m* 1961, Anna Myers; three *s* one *d. Educ:* Peter Symonds' Sch., Winchester; St Catharine's Coll., Cambridge. BA, MA, PhD 1964, ScD 1978. Res. Fellow, Dalhousie Univ., Canada, 1962-64; College Fellow and Lectr, Gonville and Caius Coll., Cambridge, 1968-. Scientific Medal, Zool Soc. of London, 1976. *Publication:* Neurosecretion, 1979. *Recreations:* cross-country running, golf, gardening, wine-tasting. *Address:* Gonville and Caius College, Cambridge; Ballamaddrell, Ballabeg, Arbory, Isle of Man. *T:* Castletown (IOM) 822787.

MADEL, William David; MP (C) South Bedfordshire since 1970; *b* 6 Aug. 1938; *s* of late William R. Madel and of Eileen Madel (*née* Nicholls); *m* 1971, Susan Catherine, *d* of late Lt-Comdr Hon. Peter Carew; one *s* one *d. Educ:* Uppingham Sch.; Keble Coll., Oxford. MA Oxon 1965. Graduate Management Trainee, 1963-64; Advertising Exec., Thomson Organisation, 1964-70. PPS to Parly Under-Sec. of State for Defence, 1973-74, to Minister of State for Defence, 1974. Vice-Chm., Cons. Backbench Employment Cttee, 1974-. *Recreations:* cricket, tennis, reading. *Address:* 120 Pickford Road, Markyate, Herts. *Clubs:* Carlton, Coningsby; Mid-Cheshire Pitt (Chester).

MADELUNG, Prof. Wilferd Willy Ferdinand; Laudian Professor of Arabic, University of Oxford, since 1978; *b* 26 Dec. 1930; *s* of Georg Madelung and Elisabeth (*née* Messerschmitt); *m* 1963, A. Margaret (*née* Arent); one *s. Educ:* Eberhard Ludwig Gymnasium, Stuttgart; Univs of Georgetown, Cairo, Hamburg. PhD (Hamburg). Cultural Attaché, W German Embassy, Baghdad, 1958-60. Vis. Professor, Univ. of Texas, Austin, 1963; Privatdozent, Univ. of Hamburg, 1963-64; University of Chicago: Asst Prof., 1964; Associate Prof., 1966; Prof. of Islamic History, 1969. Guggenheim Fellowship, 1972-73. Decoration of Republic of Sudan (4th cl.), 1962. *Publications:* Der Imam al-Qāsim ibn Ibrāhīm und die Glaubenslehre der Zaiditen, 1965; articles in learned jls and Encyc. of Islam. *Recreation:* travel. *Address:* The Oriental Institute, Pusey Lane, Oxford OX1 2LE. *T:* Oxford 59272.

MADEN, Margaret; Headmistress, Islington Green Comprehensive School, since 1975; *b* 16 April 1940; *d* of Clifford and Frances Maden. *Educ:* Arnold High Sch. for Girls, Blackpool; Leeds Univ. (BA Hons); Univ. of London Inst of Educn (PGCE). Asst Teacher of Geography, Stockwell Manor Comprehensive Sch., SW9, 1962-66; Lectr, Sidney Webb Coll. of Educn, 1966-71; Dep. Head, Bicester Comprehensive Sch., Oxon, 1971-75. *Publications:* contributions to: Dear Lord James, 1971; Teachers for Tomorrow (ed Calthrop and Owens), 1971; Education 2000 (ed Wilby and Pluckrose), 1979. *Recreations:* American painting, writing and films; politics, gardening. *Address:* 16 De Beauvoir Square, N1.

MADGE, Charles Henry; *b* 10 Oct. 1912; *s* of Lieut-Colonel C. A. Madge and Barbara (*née* Hylton Foster); *m* 1st, Kathleen Raine (marr. diss.); one *s* one *d*; 2nd, Inez Pearn (*d* 1976); one *s* one *d*; 3rd, Evelyn Brown. *Educ:* Winchester Coll. (Scholar); Magdalene Coll., Cambridge (Scholar). Reporter on Daily Mirror, 1935-36; founded Mass-Observation, 1937; directed survey of working-class saving and spending for National Institute of Economic and Social Research, 1940-42; Research staff of PEP, 1943; Director, Pilot Press, 1944; Social Development Officer, New Town of Stevenage, 1947; Prof. of Sociology, Univ. of Birmingham, 1950-70. Mission to Thailand on UN Technical Assistance, 1953-54. UNESCO Missions to India, 1957-58, to South-East Asia, 1959 and 1960 and Leader of Mission to Ghana for UN Economic Commission for Africa, 1963. *Publications:* The Disappearing Castle (poems), 1937; The Father Found (poems), 1941; part-author of Britain by Mass-Observation, 1938, and other books connected with this organisation; War-time Pattern of Saving and Spending, 1943; (ed) Pilot Papers: Social Essays and Documents, 1945-47; Society in the Mind, 1964; (with Barbara Weinberger) Art Students Observed, 1973; (with Peter Willmott) Inner City Poverty in Paris and London, 1981; contributions to Economic Journal, Town Planning Review, Human Relations, etc. *Address:* 28 Lynmouth Road, N2.

MADGE, James Richard, CB 1976; Deputy Secretary, Department of the Environment, on secondment as Chief Executive, Housing Corporation, since 1973; *b* 18 June 1924; *s* of James Henry Madge and Elisabeth May Madge; *m* 1955, Alice June Annette (*d* 1975), *d* of late Major Horace Reid, Jamaica; two *d. Educ:* Bexhill Co. Sch.; New Coll., Oxford. Pilot in RAFVR, 1942-46. Joined Min. of Civil Aviation, 1947; Principal Private Secretary: to Paymaster-General, 1950-51; to Minister of Transport, 1960-61; Asst Secretary, Min. of Transport, 1961-66; Under-Sec., Road Safety Gp, 1966-69; Head of Policy Planning, 1969-70; Under-Sec., Housing Directorate, DoE, 1971-73. *Recreations:* lawn tennis, swimming, furniture-making. *Address:* 56 Gordon Place, Kensington, W8. *T:* 01-937 1927.

MADIGAN, Sir Russel (Tullie), Kt 1981; OBE 1970; Deputy Chairman, CRA Ltd, since 1978; *b* 22 Nov. 1920; *s* of Dr Cecil T. Madigan and Wynnis K. Wollaston; *m* 1st, 1942, Margaret Symons (decd); four *s* one *d* ; 2nd, 1981, Satsuko Tamura. *Educ:* Univ. of Adelaide (BScEng 1941, BE 1946, ME 1954, LLB 1960). FSASM 1941; FTS. 1946-59: Ventilation Engr, Chief Mining Engr, Underground Manager, Zinc Corp. and New Broken Hill Consolidated Ltd; 1959-64: Gen. Manager, General Mining Div., CRA Ltd; Executive Director: Territory Enterprises Pty Ltd (Rum Jungle); Titanium and Zirconium Industries Pty Ltd; Herons Creek Timber Mills Pty Ltd; Mary Kathleen Uranium Ltd; Director: Western Mineral Sands Pty Ltd; Australian Fluorine Chemicals Pty Ltd; 1964-: Man. Dir and Chm., Hamersley Holdings Ltd; Chairman: Blair Athol Coal Pty Ltd; Interstate Oil Ltd; Dampier Salt Ltd; Atlas Steels (Australia) Pty Ltd; Conzinc Asia Holdings Pty Ltd; Director: CRA Ltd; Rio Tinto-Zinc Corp. Ltd; Australian Mining and Smelting Ltd; Comalco Ltd; Kembla Coal and Coke Pty Ltd; Queensland Alumina Ltd; RTZ (Japan) Ltd; Conzinc Riotinto Malaysia SB; PT Rio Tinto Indonesia; Kimberley Diamond Mines Pty Ltd; Commercial Union Assurance Co. of Aust. Ltd. Member: Australasian Inst. of Mining and Metallurgy (Pres., 1980); Amer. Inst. of Mining and Metallurgy. *Recreations:* flying, farming, music. *Address:* 60 Broadway, East Camberwell, Victoria 3126, Australia. *T:* 82 6152. *Clubs:* Athenæum, Melbourne, Royal Melbourne Golf, Returned Servicemen's League (all Melbourne).

MADOC, Maj.-Gen. Reginald William, CB 1959; DSO 1957; OBE 1951; Royal Marines, retired; *b* 15 Aug. 1907; *s* of late Lieut-Colonel H. W. Madoc, CBE, MVO, Garwick, Isle of Man; *m* 1938, Rosemary, *d* of late Dr Cyril Shepherd, Sydney, Australia; one *d. Educ:* King William's Coll., Isle of Man. 2nd Lieut, RM, 1926; HMS Rodney, 1929-31; HMS Royal Oak, 1932-34; ADC to Governor of Madras, 1934-38; HMS Furious, 1938-39; RM Mobile Naval Base Defence Org., UK, Egypt, Crete, 1940-41 (despatches twice, POW, 1941-45). Instructor, Officers' Sch., RM, 1946; Staff Coll., Camberley, 1947; Instructor, School of Combined Ops, 1948; HMS Vanguard, 1948-49; CO, 42 Commando, RM, Malaya, 1950-51 (despatches); CO Commando Sch., RM, 1952-53; Chief Instructor, School of Amphibious Warfare, 1953-55; Commanded 3rd Commando Bde, RM, Malta, Cyprus, Port Said, 1955-57; ADC to the Queen, 1955-57; Maj.-Gen., Plymouth Gp, RM, 1957-59; Maj.-Gen., Portsmouth Gp, RM, 1959-61; retired 1961. Col Comdt, RM, 1967-68; Rep. Col Comdt, RM, 1969-70. *Address:* The Malthouse, Meonstoke, by Southampton, SO3 1NH. *T:* Droxford 323. *Club:* Army and Navy.

MAEGRAITH, Brian Gilmore, CMG 1968; TD 1975; MA, MB, MSc, DPhil; FRCP, FRCPE, FRACP; Alfred Jones and Warrington Yorke Professor of Tropical Medicine, School of Tropical Medicine, Liverpool University, 1944-72, now Professor Emeritus; Hon. Senior Research Fellow, Department of Tropical Paediatrics, since 1978, and Dean, 1946-75, Vice-President, since 1975, Liverpool School of Tropical Medicine; *b* 26 Aug. 1907; *s* of late A. E. R. Maegraith, Adelaide, S Australia; *m* 1934, Lorna Langley, St Peters, Adelaide; one *s. Educ:* St Peter's and St Mark's Colleges, Adelaide University (MB 1930); Magdalen and Exeter Colleges, Oxford (Rhodes Scholar, Rolleston Memorial Prize). Beit Memorial Fellow, 1932-34; Medical Fellow, Exeter Coll., Oxford, 1934-40; University Lecturer and Demonstrator in Pathology, Dean of Faculty of Medicine, Oxford Univ., 1938-44; War of 1939-45, OC Army Malaria Research Unit. Med. Advisory Cttee ODM, 1963-72. Tropical Med. Research Board, MRC, 1960-65, 1966-69; Cttees on Malaria and Abnormal Haemoglobins, 1960-69; Hon. Consulting Physician, Liverpool Royal Infirmary; Hon. Consultant in Trop. Med., RAF (Consultant 1964-76); Hon. Malariologist, Army, 1967-73; Adviser: Council for Health in Socio-economic Developments, Thailand, 1964-; Faculty Tropical Medicine, Bangkok, 1959-; Reg. Trop. Medicine and Public Health Project, SE Asian Ministers of Educn Orgn. Sec.-Gen., Council of Institutes of Tropical Medicine, Europe and USSR, 1969-72 (Hon. Life Pres., 1972-); Pres., Royal Society Tropical Medicine, 1969-71 (Vice-Pres., 1949-51 and 1957-59; Chalmers Gold Medal, 1951); Vis. Prof., Univ. of Alexandria, 1956; Lectures: Lichfield, Oxford, 1955; Maurice Bloch, Glasgow, 1969; Heath Clark, London, 1970; Craig, US Soc. Trop. Med., 1976; Justus Ström, Stockholm, 1980. Membre d'Honneur: de Soc. Belg. de Méd. Tropicale; Soc. de Pathologie Exotique, Paris; Hon. Member American, Canadian and German Socs of Tropical Medicine and Hygiene, 1961. Hon. Fellow: St Mark's Coll., 1956; LSHTM, 1980. Hon. DSc Bangkok; MD (Emeritus) Athens, 1972. Le Prince Award and Medal, Soc. of Tropical Medicine, USA, 1954; Bernhard Nocht Medal (Hamburg), 1957; Mary Kingsley Medal, Liverpool Sch. of Trop. Med., 1973; Jubilee Medal, Swedish Med. Acad., 1980; Anniv. Plaque, Faculty of Trop. Medicine, Bangkok, 1980. KLJ 1977. *Publications:* Pathological Processes in Malaria and Blackwater Fever, 1948; Clinical Tropical Diseases, 5th edn, 1970 (with A. R. D. Adams), 7th edn

1980; Tropical Medicine for Nurses (with A. R. D. Adams), 1956, 5th edn (with H. M. Gilles), 1980; (with C. S. Leithead) Clinical Methods in Tropical Medicine, 1962; Exotic Diseases in Practice, 1965; (with H. M. Gilles) Management and Treatment of Diseases in the Tropics, 1970; One World, 1973; papers and articles in technical and scientific journals on various subjects. *Address:* 23 Eaton Road, Cressington Park, Liverpool L19 0PN. *T:* 051-427 1133; Department of Tropical Paediatrics, School of Tropical Medicine, Liverpool University, L3 5QA. *T:* 051-708 9393. *Clubs:* Athenæum; Athenæum (Liverpool).

MAELOR, Baron, *cr* 1966 (Life Peer), of Rhosllanerchrugog; **Thomas William Jones;** JP (Chairman Ruabon Bench); *b* 10 Feb. 1898; *s* of James Jones, Wrexham; *m* 1928, Flossy, *d* of Jonathan Thomas, Birkenhead; one *s* one *d. Educ:* Poncian Boys' Sch.; Bangor Normal Coll. Began working life as a miner; became pupil teacher and went to Bangor Coll. Welfare Officer and Education Officer for Merseyside and North Wales Electricity Board in North Wales. MP (Lab) Merioneth, 1951-66; Formerly: Chairman North Wales Labour Federation; Chairman Wrexham Trades Council. *Address:* Ger-y-Llyn, Poncian, Wrexham, Clwyd.

MAFFEY, family name of **Baron Rugby.**

MAGAREY, Sir (James) Rupert, Kt 1980; FRCS, FRACS: Senior Visiting Consultant Surgeon to Emergency Services, The Queen Elizabeth Hospital, Adelaide, since 1979; *b* 21 Feb. 1914; *s* of Dr Rupert Eric Magarey and Elsie Emily (*née* Cowell); *m* 1940, (Catherine) Mary Gilbert; one *s* two *d* (and one *d* decd). *Educ:* St Peter's Coll., Adelaide; St Mark's Coll., Univ. of Adelaide (MB, BS 1938; MS 1951). FRCS 1949; FRACS 1950. Served War, RAAMC, 1939-46: despatches, Syria, 1941; Captain, subseq. Major. Hon. Asst Surgeon, Royal Adelaide Hosp., 1950-58; Hon. Surgeon, 1958-70, and Sen. Vis. Surgeon, 1970-79, Queen Elizabeth Hosp., Adelaide. Pres., AMA, 1976-79 (Pres. SA Br., 1969-70); Mem. Ct of Examrs, RACS, 1960-; Hon. Fellow, Royal Aust. Coll. of Gen. Practitioners, 1978; Hon. Life Governor, Aust. Post-Grad. Fedn in Medicine, 1980. Silver Jubilee Medal, 1977. *Publications:* scientific articles in British Jl of Surgery and in Med. Jl of Australia. *Recreations:* music, the theatre, tennis, golf, rowing, beef cattle breeding. *Address:* 178 North Terrace, Adelaide, SA 5000, Australia. *T:* 51 5528. *Clubs:* Adelaide (Adelaide); Royal Adelaide Golf (Seaton, Adelaide).

MAGEE, Bryan; MP Leyton, since Feb. 1974 (Lab 1974-82, SDP since 1982); *b* 12 April 1930; *s* of Frederick Magee and Sheila (*née* Lynch); *m* 1954, Ingrid Söderlund (marr. diss.); one *d. Educ:* Christ's Hospital; Lycée Hôche, Versailles; Keble Coll., Oxford (Open Scholar). Pres., Oxford Union, 1953; MA 1956. Henry Fellow in Philosophy, Yale, 1955-56. Current Affairs Reporter on TV; Critic of the Arts on BBC Radio 3; own broadcast series include: Conversations with Philosophers, BBC Radio 3, 1970-71; Men of Ideas, BBC TV 2, 1978. Silver Medal, Royal Television Soc., 1978. Regular columnist, The Times, 1974-76. Contested (Lab): Mid-Bedfordshire, Gen. Elec., 1959; By-Elec., 1960. Theatre Critic of The Listener, 1966-67; elected to Critics' Circle (Drama and Music sections) 1970, Council Mem., 1975-, Trustee, 1979-. Judge for Evening Standard annual Opera Award, 1973-. Lectr in Philosophy, Balliol Coll., Oxford, 1970-71; Visiting Fellow of All Souls Coll., Oxford, 1973-74; Vis. Schol. in Philos., Harvard, 1974; Sydney Univ., 1982. Governor, Ditchley Foundn, 1979-. *Publications:* Crucifixion and Other Poems, 1951; Go West Young Man, 1958; To Live in Danger, 1960; The New Radicalism, 1962; The Democratic Revolution, 1964; Towards 2000, 1965; One in Twenty, 1966; The Television Interviewer, 1966; Aspects of Wagner, 1968; Modern British Philosophy, 1971; Popper, 1973; Facing Death, 1977; Men of Ideas, 1978; The Philosophy of Schopenhauer, 1983. *Recreations:* music, theatre, travel. *Address:* 12 Falkland House, Marloes Road, W8 5LF. *T:* 01-937 1210. *Clubs:* Beefsteak, Brooks's, Garrick.

MAGEE, Reginald Arthur Edward, FRCSI, FRCOG; Consultant Gynaecologist, Belfast; Active Administrative Medical Officer, Royal Group of Hospitals, North West District, Belfast; *b* 18 Aug. 1914; *s* of James and Ellen Magee; *m* 1945, Gwladys Susannah (*née* Chapman); two *d. Educ:* Campbell Coll., Belfast (Sen. Science Prizeman); Queen's Univ., Belfast (MB, BCh, BAO, 1937). FRCSI 1947; FRCOG 1963 (MRCOG 1947). Mem. Students' Rep. Council, QUB; Mem., Univ. Athletic Team; Prizeman, Diseases of Children, Royal Belfast Hosp. for Sick Children. Demonstr in Physiol., QUB; House Surgeon, later Resident Surg. Officer, Royal Victoria Hosp., Belfast; House Surg. and Asst in Plastic Surgery, N Staffs Royal Infirm.; House Surg., Royal Maternity Hosp., Belfast; Jun., later Sen. Tutor in Obs, QUB; Temp. Consultant Gen. Surgery, Belfast City Hosp.; Obstet. and Gynaecologist, Massereene Hosp., and Antrim and Newtownards Dist Hosp.; post-grad. studies, Radium Inst., Stockholm; Clin. Teacher in Obs and Gynae., Clin. Lectr and Examr, QUB; Sen. Obstet., Royal Maternity Hosp., Belfast, and Sen. Gynaecologist, Royal Victoria Hosp., Belfast, and Ulster Hosp., Belfast, 1948-79. Vis. Professor: Univ. of Basrah; Univ. of Baghdad; Vis. Lectr, Univ. of Cairo. Mem., NI Council for Post-grad. Med. Educn. Formerly: Chairman: Gp Med. Adv. Cttee, Royal Hosps, Belfast; Computer Cttee, Royal Victoria Hosp.; Member: Council, Jt Nurses and Midwives Council (also Lectr); Management Cttee, Ulster Hosp., Belfast; Royal Maternity Hosp. Cttee; Standing Cttee of Convocation, QUB. NI Hospitals Authority: formerly Chairman: Policy and Planning Cttee; Nurses and Midwives Cttee; Grading Cttee; Grading Appeals Cttee; formerly Mem., Exec. Cttee. Councillor: RCSI, 1974-; RCOG, 1972-78; Mem., Inst. of Obs and Gynae., Royal Coll. of Physicians of Ireland; Fellow, Ulster Med. Soc.

(formerly Mem. Council); Mem., Ulster Obstet. and Gynaecol Soc. (formerly Pres.). Chm., Unionist Party of NI; Official Unionist Mem. for S Belfast, NI Assembly, 1973: Mem., Cttee of Privileges, Cttee on Finance, and Cttee on Health and Social Services; Leader of Pro-Assembly Unionist Back Bench Cttee; Mem., Public Accounts Cttee, NI; Advisor, Sunningdale Conf., 1973. Mem. Senate, QUB, 1979-. Pres., Old Campbellian Soc., 1979. *Publications:* A Modern Record System of Obstetrics, 1963; A Computerised System of Obstetric Records, 1970; Royal Maternity Hospital Clinical Reports, and Ulster Hospital Clinical Reports, 1963-77; monographs on obstetric and gynaecological subjects; various hospital service reports. *Recreations:* riding, horse breeding, travel, photography. *Address:* Montpelier, 96 Malone Road, Belfast BT9 5HP. *T:* Belfast 666765. *Clubs:* Athenæum, Royal Over-Seas League, English-Speaking Union.

MAGGS, Air Vice-Marshal William Jack, CB 1967; OBE 1943; Fellow and Domestic Bursar, Keble College, Oxford, 1969-77, Emeritus Fellow since 1981; *b* 2 Feb. 1914; *s* of late Frederick Wilfrid Maggs, Bristol; *m* 1940, Margaret Grace, *d* of late Thomas Liddell Hetherington, West Hartlepool; one *s* one *d. Educ:* Bristol Grammar Sch.; St John's Coll., Oxford (MA). Management Trainee, 1936-38. Joined RAF, 1939; Unit and Training duties, 1939-42; Student, Staff Coll., 1942; Planning Staffs, and participated in, Algerian, Sicilian and Italian landings, 1942-44; SESO Desert Air Force, 1944; Jt Admin. Plans Staff, Cabinet Offices, Whitehall, 1945-48; Instructor, RAF Coll., Cranwell, 1948-50; comd No 9 Maintenance Unit, 1950-52; exchange officer at HQ, USAF Washington, 1952-54; Student Jt Services Staff Coll., 1954-55; No 3 Maintenance Unit, 1955-57; Dep. Director of Equipment, Air Ministry, 1958-59; SESO, HQ, NEAF, Cyprus, 1959-61; Student, Imperial Defence Coll., 1962; Director of Mech. Transport and Marine Craft, Air Ministry, 1963-64; Director of Equipment, Ministry of Defence (Air), 1964-67; SASO, RAF Maintenance Comd, 1967-69. Group Captain, 1958; Air Commodore, 1963; Air Vice-Marshal, 1967. Governor, Bristol Grammar Sch., 1980-. *Recreations:* golf, gardening. *Address:* Hillside, Noke, near Oxford OX3 9TT. *T:* Kidlington 3139. *Club:* Royal Air Force.

MAGILL, Air Vice-Marshal Graham Reese, CB 1966; CBE 1962 (OBE 1945); DFC 1941 and Bar, 1943; retired Jan. 1970; *b* 23 Jan. 1915; *s* of late Robert Wilson Magill and late Frances Elizabeth Magill, Te Aroha, NZ; *m* 1942, Blanche Marie Colson; two *s. Educ:* Te Aroha High Sch.; Hamilton Technical Coll., NZ. Joined Royal Air Force, 1936. Served War of 1939-45, Sudan, Egypt, UK, NW Europe; subsequently, UK, Egypt, France. Director of Operations (Bomber and Reconnaissance), Air Ministry, 1959-62; Commandant, RAF College of Air Warfare, Manby, Lincs, 1963-64; Director-General of Organisation (RAF), Ministry of Defence, 1964-67; AOC, 25 Group, RAF, 1967-68; AOC 22 Group, RAF, 1968-69. *Recreations:* generally interested in sport and gentle sailing. *Address:* Calle Guillermo Cifre de Colonia, 30, Pollensa, Majorca. *Club:* Royal Air Force.

MAGILL, Sir Ivan Whiteside, KCVO 1960 (CVO 1946); FRCS 1951; FFARCS; MB, BCh, Belfast, 1913; DA 1935; formerly Hon. Consulting Anæsthetist, Westminster, Brompton and St Andrew's, Dollis Hill, Hospitals; *b* Larne, 1888; *s* of Samuel Magill; *m* 1916, Edith (*d* 1973), *d* of Thomas Robinson Banbridge. *Educ:* Larne Grammar Sch.; Queen's Univ., Belfast. Formerly: Consultant Army, Navy, EMS; Senior Anæsthetist, Queen's Hospital, Sidcup; Anæsthetist, Seamens Hospital, Greenwich; Res. MO, Stanley Hospital, Liverpool; Examiner, DA; Robert Campbell Memorial Orator, Belfast, 1939; Bengué Memorial Lecturer, Royal Institute of Public Health, 1950; Hon. Member: Liverpool Medical Institution; American Society of Anæsthesiologists; New York State Society of Anæsthesiologists; British Assoc. of Plastic Surgeons; Canadian Society of Anæsthetists; Hon. Fellow: Royal Society of Medicine, 1956; Faculty of Anæsthetists, Royal College of Surgeons, 1958; Assoc. of Anæsthetists of Great Britain and Ireland, 1958; Hon. FFARCSI, 1961. Henry Hill Hickman Medal, 1938; John Snow Medal, 1958; Canadian Anæsthetists Society Medal, 1963; Medal, American Assoc. of Plastic Surgeons, 1965; Gillies Mem. Lecturer, British Assoc. of Plastic Surgeons, 1965; Ralph M. Waters Prize, Chicago, 1966. Hon. DSc, Belfast, 1945. Frederic Hewitt Lecturer for 1965. *Publications:* contributions and chapters in various medical journals. *Recreation:* trout fishing. *Address:* c/o Williams & Glyn's Bank, Holts Branch, Kirkland House, Whitehall, SW1.

MAGINNIS, John Edward, JP; *b* 7 March 1919; *s* of late Edward Maginnis, Mandeville Hall, Mullahead, Tanderagee; *m* 1944, Dorothy, *d* of late R. J. Rusk, JP, of Cavanaleck, Fivemiletown, Co. Tyrone; one *s* four *d. Educ:* Moyallon Sch., Co. Down; Portadown Technical Coll. Served War of 1939-45, Royal Ulster Constabulary. MP (UU) Armagh, Oct. 1959-Feb. 1974. JP, Co. Armagh, 1956. Group Secretary, North Armagh Group, Ulster Farmers' Union, 1956-59; Member, Co. Armagh Agricultural Society. *Recreations:* football, hunting, shooting. *Address:* Mandeville Hall, 68 Mullahead Road, Tandragee, Craigavon, Co. Armagh, N Ireland BT62 2LB. *T:* Tandragee 840260.

MAGNIAC, Rear-Admiral Vernon St Clair Lane, CB 1961; *b* 21 Dec. 1908; *s* of late Major Francis Arthur Magniac and of Mrs Beatrice Caroline Magniac (*née* Davison); *m* 1947, Eileen Eleanor (*née* Witney); one *s* one *d* (and one *d* deced). *Educ:* Clifton Coll. Cadet, RN, 1926; Served in HM Ships Courageous, Effingham, Resolution and Diamond, 1931-37; RN Engineering Coll., 1937-39; HMS Renown, 1940-43; Combined Ops, India, 1943-45; HM

Ships Fisgard, Gambia, and Nigeria, 1945-50; HM Dockyards Chatham, Malta and Devonport, 1950-62. *Recreations:* golf, fishing. *Address:* Marlborough, Down Park, Yelverton, Devon.

MAGNUS, Hilary Barrow, TD; QC 1957; Social Security (formerly National Insurance) Commissioner, 1964-82; *b* 3 March 1909; *yr s* of late Laurie Magnus, 34 Cambridge Square, W2; *b* and *heir-pres.* to Sir Philip Magnus-Allcroft, *qv; m* 1950, Rosemary, *d* of G. H. Masefield and *widow* of Quentin Hurst; one *s* one *d* and one step *s. Educ:* Westminster; Christ Church, Oxford. Barrister, Lincoln's Inn, 1933 (Bencher, 1963; Treasurer, 1982). Served War of 1939-45, Rifle Brigade TA (Lieut-Colonel). JP (Kent) 1948. *Recreations:* reading, gardening. *Address:* Cragmore House, Church Street, Wye, Ashford, Kent. *T:* Wye 812036; 3 Temple Gardens, EC4. *T:* 01-353 7884. *Clubs:* Garrick, Beefsteak.

MAGNUS, Philip; *see* Magnus-Allcroft, Sir Philip.

MAGNUS, Samuel Woolf; Justice of Appeal, Court of Appeal for Zambia, 1971; Commissioner, Foreign Compensation Commission, since 1977; *b* 30 Sept. 1910; *s* of late Samuel Woolf Magnus; *m* 1938, Anna Gertrude, *o d* of Adolph Shane, Cardiff; one *d. Educ:* University Coll., London. BA Hons, 1931. Called to Bar, Gray's Inn, 1937. Served War of 1939-45, Army. Practised in London, 1937-59. Treas., Assoc. of Liberal Lawyers, Mem. Council, London Liberal Party and Pres., N Hendon Liberal Assoc., until 1959. Contested (L) Central Hackney, 1945. Partner in legal firm, Northern Rhodesia, 1959-63; subseq. legal consultant. QC 1964, MLC 1962, MP Jan.-Oct. 1964, Northern Rhodesia; MP, Zambia, 1964-68. Puisne Judge, High Court for Zambia, 1968. Chm., Law, Parly and Gen. Purposes Cttee, Bd of Deputies of British Jews, 1979-. *Publications:* (with M. Estrin) Companies Act 1947, 1947; (with M. Estrin) Companies: Law and Practice, 1948, 5th edn 1978, and Supplement, 1981; (with A. M. Lyons) Advertisement Control, 1949; Magnus on Leasehold Property (Temporary Provisions) Act 1951, 1951; Magnus on Landlord and Tenant Act 1954, 1954; Magnus on Housing Repairs and Rents Act 1954, 1954; Magnus on the Rent Act 1957, 1957; (with F. E. Price) Knight's Annotated Housing Acts, 1958; (with Tovell) Magnus on Housing Finance, 1960; (with M. Estrin) Companies Act 1967, 1967; Magnus on the Rent Act 1968, 1969; Magnus on Business Tenancies, 1970; Magnus on the Rent Act 1977, 1978; contributor: Law Jl; Halsbury's Laws of England; Encycl. of Forms and Precedents; Atkin's Court Forms and Precedents. *Recreations:* writing, photography, enthusiastic spectator at all games, preferably on TV. *Address:* c/o Foreign Compensation Commission, Alexandra House, Kingsway, WC2B 6TT. *T:* 01-836 0701; 33 Apsley House, Finchley Road, St John's Wood, NW8. *T:* 01-586 1679. *Clubs:* National Liberal, MCC, Middlesex CC.

MAGNUS-ALLCROFT, Sir Philip, 2nd Bt, *cr* 1917; CBE 1971; MA; FRSL; FRHistS; author; *b* 8 Feb. 1906; *er s* of late Laurie Magnus and Dora, *e d* of late Sir I. Spielman, CMG; *S* grandfather, 1933; *m* 1943, Jewell Allcroft, Stokesay Court, Onibury, Shropshire, *d* of late Herbert Allcroft and of Mrs John Rotton. Formally assumed surname of Allcroft (in addition to that of Magnus), 1951. *Educ:* Westminster Sch.; Wadham Coll., Oxford. Civil Service, 1928-32 and 1946-50. Served War of 1939-45 in Royal Artillery and Intelligence Corps (Iceland and Italy); Major. CC 1952, CA 1968-74, Salop (Chairman, Planning Cttee, 1962-74; formerly: Chm., Records Cttee; Vice-Chm., Educn Cttee); Chairman of Governors, Attingham Coll.; JP Salop, 1953-71 (Chm., Juvenile Ct). Trustee, National Portrait Gall., 1970-77. Mem., Mercia Regional Cttee, Nat. Trust, 1973-81. Governor, Ludlow Grammar Sch., 1952-77. *Publications:* (as Philip Magnus): Life of Edmund Burke, 1939; Selected Prose of Edmund Burke (with Introduction), 1948; Sir Walter Raleigh, 1951 (revised edns, 1956, 1968); Gladstone—A Biography, 1954; Kitchener—Portrait of an Imperialist, 1958 (revised edn, 1968); King Edward the Seventh, 1964. *Recreations:* travel, gardening. *Heir: b* Hilary Barrow Magnus, *qv. Address:* Stokesay Court, Onibury, Craven Arms, Shropshire SY7 9BD. *T:* Bromfield 372 and 394. *Clubs:* Athenæum, Beefsteak, Brooks's, Pratt's.

MAGNUSSON, Magnus, MA (Oxon); FRSE 1980; writer and broadcaster; *b* 12 Oct. 1929; *s* of Sigursteinn Magnusson, Icelandic Consul-Gen. for Scotland, and Ingibjorg Sigurdardottir; *m* 1954, Mamie Baird; one *s* three *d* (and one *s* deced). *Educ:* Edinburgh Academy; Jesus Coll., Oxford (BA). Subseq. Asst Editor, Scottish Daily Express and Asst Editor, The Scotsman. Presenter, various television and radio programmes including: Chronicle; Mastermind; BC, The Archaeology of the Bible Lands; Tonight; Cause for Concern; All Things Considered; Living Legends; Vikings!; Scottish Television Personality of the Year, 1974. Editor: The Bodley Head Archaeologies; Popular Archaeology, 1979-80. Chairman: Ancient Monuments Bd for Scotland, 1981-; Stewards, York Archaeol Trust; Scottish Churches Architectural Heritage Trust; Scottish Youth Theatre, 1976-78; Hon. Vice-President: Age Concern Scotland; RSSPCC. Rector, Edinburgh Univ., 1975-78. FSAScot 1974. D *hc* Edinburgh, 1978; DUniv York, 1981. Knight of the Order of the Falcon (Iceland), 1975; Silver Jubilee Medal, 1977. *Publications:* Introducing Archaeology, 1972; Viking Expansion Westwards, 1973; The Clacken and the Slate (Edinburgh Academy, 1824-1974), 1974; Hammer of the North (Norse mythology), 1976; BC, The Archaeology of the Bible Lands, 1977; Landlord or Tenant? a view of Irish history, 1978; Iceland, 1979; Vikings!, 1980; Magnus on the Move, 1980; Treasures of Scotland, 1981; translations (all with Hermann Pálsson): Njal's Saga, 1960; The Vinland Sagas, 1965; King Harald's Saga, 1966; Laxdaela Saga, 1969; (all by

Halldor Laxness): The Atom Station, 1961; Paradise Reclaimed, 1962; The Fish Can Sing, 1966; World Light, 1969; Christianity Under Glacier, 1973; (by Samivel) Golden Iceland, 1967; contributor: The Glorious Privilege, 1967; The Future of the Highlands, 1968; Ancient China, 1974; Strange Stories, Amazing Facts, 1975; The National Trust for Scotland Guide, 1976; Pass the Port, 1976; Karluk, 1976; More Lives Than One?, 1976; Atlas of World Geography, 1977; Face to Face with the Turin Shroud, 1978; Book of Bricks, 1978; Chronicle, 1978; Modern Bible Atlas, 1979; Discovery of Lost Worlds, 1979; Living Legends, 1980; The Hammer and the Cross, 1980; Pass the Port Again, 1981; Household Guests, 1981; Great Books for Today, 1981; Second Book of Bricks, 1981; (introd.) Robert Burns: Bawdy Verse & Folksongs, 1982. *Recreations:* digging and delving. *Address:* Blairskaith House, Balmore-Torrance, Glasgow G64 4AX. *T:* Balmore 226. *Club:* New (Edinburgh).

MAGOR, Major (Edward) Walter (Moyle), CMG 1960; OBE 1956 (MBE 1947); DL; *b* 1 June 1911; *e s* of late Edward John Penberthy Magor, JP, Lamellen, St Tudy, Cornwall, and Gilian Sarah Magor, JP; *m* 1939, Daphne Davis (*d* 1972), *d* of late Hector Robert Lushington Graham, Summerhill, Thomastown, Co. Kilkenny; two *d. Educ:* Marlborough; Magdalen, Oxford; Magdalene, Cambridge. MA. Indian Army, 1934-47; RARO, 10th Hussars, 1949-61; Indian Political Service, 1937-39 and 1943-47; Colonial Administrative Service, 1947-61; Kenya: Asst Chief Secretary, 1953; Permanent Secretary, Ministry of Defence, 1954; Acting Minister for Defence, 1956; Secretary to the Cabinet, 1958. Home Civil Service, DTI, formerly BoT, 1961-71; Asst Secretary, 1964; retired 1971. Chm., St John Council for Cornwall, 1973-78. Asst Editor, RHS Rhododendron and Camellia Yearbook, 1974-; Chm., RHS Rhododendron and Camellia Gp, 1976-80. President: Cornwall Garden Soc., 1981-; Royal Cornwall Agricl Assoc., 1983. DL Cornwall, 1974; High Sheriff of Cornwall, 1981. CStJ 1978 (OStJ 1975). Médaille de La Belgique Reconnaissante, 1961. Lord of the Manor of Kellygreen. *Recreation:* gardening (Mem., Garden Soc.). *Address:* Lamellen, St Tudy, Cornwall PL30 3NR. *T:* Bodmin 850207. *Club:* Army and Navy.

MAGUINNESS, Prof. William Stuart; Professor of Latin Language and Literature, University of London, King's College, 1946-71; Senior Research Fellow, 1971-72; Head of Department of Classics, 1952-72; General Editor, Methuen's Classical Texts; Vice-President, Classical Association, Orbilian Society, Virgil Society and London Classical Society; *b* 12 Oct. 1903; *s* of George J. Maguinness, Belfast; *m* 1933, Olive D., *d* of George T. Y. Dickinson, Sheffield; one *d. Educ:* Royal Belfast Academical Institution; Trinity Coll., Dublin (Classical Sizarship, Classical Foundation Scholarship; Sen. Moderatorships with Gold Medals in Classics and Modern Literature (French and Italian) and Univ. Studentship in Classics 1926; MA 1929). FKC 1966. Asst Lecturer in Classics, University of Manchester, 1927-30; Lecturer in Classics, University of Sheffield, 1930-46; Administrative Officer, Admiralty, 1941-43; Visiting Lecturer in various Universities in France, Holland, Italy, Brazil, Poland and Greece. Hon. Fellow, Polish Acad. *Publications:* contributions on Classical subjects to the Oxford Classical Dictionary, Encyclopædia Britannica, Proc. Leeds Philosophical Society, Classical Review, Classical Quarterly, Revue de la France-ancienne, Wiener humanistische Blätter, Rivista di Cultura classica e medioevale, Phoenix, Aevum, Antiquité classique, Estudios Clásicos, Notes and Queries, Vita Latina, various Actes de Congrès, Hermathena and other journals, 1928-; Edition: of Racine's Bérénice, 1929 (2nd edn, 1956); of Virgil's Aeneid, Book XII, 1953 (3rd edn, 1973); 4th (revised) edn of Stobart's Grandeur that was Rome (in collaboration with H. H. Scullard), 1961; Index to the Speeches of Isaeus (in collaboration with the late W. A. Goligher), 1964; English translation of P. Grimal's La Civilisation romaine, 1963, and F. Chamoux' La Civilisation grecque, 1965; Chapter in volume on Lucretius, 1965. *Address:* 25 Hillway, Highgate, N6. *T:* 01-340 3064.

MAGUIRE, (Albert) Michael, MC 1945, MM 1943; QC 1967; *b* 30 Dec. 1922; *s* of late Richard Maguire and Ruth Maguire. *Educ:* Hutton Grammar Sch.; Trinity Hall, Cambridge (BA 1948). Served War of 1939-45, North Irish Horse (Captain), in Africa (MM) and Italy (MC). Inns of Court Regt, 1946. War Crimes Investigation Unit, 1946. Called to the Bar, Middle Temple, 1949 (Harmsworth Scholar); Bencher, 1973; Leader, Northern Circuit, 1980-. Last Recorder of Carlisle (1970-71). *Address:* Goldsmith Building, Temple, EC4Y 7BL; Chestnuts, Lower Bank Road, Fulwood, Preston, Lancs. *T:* Preston 719291. *Clubs:* United Oxford & Cambridge University; Racquet (Liverpool).

MAGUIRE, (Benjamin) Waldo, OBE 1973; *b* 31 May 1920; *s* of Benjamin Maguire and Elizabeth Ann Eldon; *m* 1944, Lilian Joan Martin; four *s. Educ:* Portadown Coll.; Trinity Coll., Dublin. BA 1st cl. hons Philosophy. Intell. Service, WO and FO, 1942-45; BBC Latin American Service, 1945; BBC Radio News, 1946-55; BBC TV News, 1955; Editor, BBC TV News, 1962-64; Controller, News and Public Affairs, NZ Broadcasting Corp., 1965-66; BBC Controller, NI, 1966-72; Head of Information Programmes, NZ TV2, 1975-76. *Recreations:* conversation, angling. *Address:* 116 Park Avenue, Ruislip, Mddx. *T:* Ruislip 35981.

MAGUIRE, Air Marshal Sir Harold John, KCB 1966 (CB 1958); DSO 1946; OBE 1949; Director, Commercial Union Assurance Co., 1975-82 (Political and Economic Adviser, 1972-79); *b* 12 April 1912; *s* of Michael Maguire, Maynooth, Ireland, and Harriett (*née* Warren), Kilkishen, Co. Clare, Ireland; *m* 1940, Mary Elisabeth Wild, Dublin; one *s* one *d. Educ:*

Wesley Coll., Dublin; Dublin Univ. Royal Air Force Commn, 1933; service in flying boats, 230 Sqdn, Egypt and Far East, 1935-38; commanded night fighter sqdn, UK, 1939-40 and day fighter sqdn, 1940; OC 266 (Fighter) Wing, Dutch E Indies, 1942; POW, Java, 1942; Staff Coll., 1947; Fighter Command Staff Duties, 1948-50; OC, RAF, Odiham, 1950-52; Senior Air Staff Officer, Malta, 1952-55; staff of CAS, Air Ministry, 1955-58; Senior Air Staff Officer, HQ No 11 Group, RAF, 1958-59; AOC No 13 Group, RAF, 1959-61; AOC No 11 Group, Fighter Command, 1961-62; SASO Far East Air Force, 1962-64; ACAS (Intelligence), 1964-65; Dep. Chief of Defence Staff (Intelligence), 1965-68; retired, 1968; Dir-Gen. of Intelligence, MoD, 1968-72. *Address:* c/o Lloyds Bank, 6 Pall Mall, SW1. *Club:* Royal Air Force.

MAGUIRE, Hugh, FRAM; violinist and conductor; Leader, Melos Ensemble, since 1972; Professor of Violin, Royal Academy of Music, since 1957; Director of Strings, Britten-Pears School for Advanced Music Studies, since 1978; *b* 2 Aug. 1927; *m* 1953, Suzanne Lewis, of International Ballet; two *s* three *d. Educ:* Belvedere Coll., SJ, Dublin; Royal Academy of Music, London (David Martin); Paris (Georges Enesco). Leader: Bournemouth Symphony Orchestra, 1952-56; London Symphony Orchestra, 1956-62; BBC Symphony Orchestra, 1962-67; Cremona String Quartet, 1966-68; Leader, Allegri String Quartet, 1968-76. Artistic Dir, Irish Youth Orch. String coach, European Commn Youth Orch. Mem., Irish Arts Council. Hon. MMus Hull, 1975. Harriet Cohen Internat. Award; Councils Gold Medal (Ireland), 1963; Cobbett Medal, Musicians' Co., 1982. *Address:* 84 Boston Place, NW1 6EX. *T:* 01-723 9969.

MAGUIRE, Mairead C.; *see* Corrigan-Maguire.

MAGUIRE, Michael; *see* Maguire, A. M.

MAGUIRE, Rt. Rev. Robert Kenneth, MA, DD; Assistant to the Primate, Anglican Church of Canada, since 1980; *b* 31 March 1923; *s* of late Robert Maguire and late Anne Crozier; unmarried. *Educ:* Trinity Coll., Dublin. BA 1945; Divinity Testimonium, 1947. Deacon, 1947; Priest, 1948. Curate of: St Mark, Armagh, 1947-49; St James the Apostle, Montreal, 1949-52; Dean of Residence, Trinity Coll., Dublin, 1952-60; Curate-in-charge of St Andrew's, Dublin, 1954-57; Minor Canon of St Patrick's Cathedral, Dublin, 1955-58; Dean and Rector of Christ Church Cathedral, Montreal, 1961-62; Bishop of Montreal, 1963-75. Co-ordinator: Canadian Conf., Theology '76, 1975-76; North American Consultation on the Future of Ministry, 1979-80. DD (*jure dig.*): Dublin Univ., 1963; Montreal Diocesan Theolog. Coll., 1963; DCL (*hc*), Bishop's Univ., Lennoxville, Qué., 1963. *Address:* 4875 Dundas Street West, Apt 304, Islington, Ontario M9A 1B3, Canada.

MAGUIRE, Waldo; *see* Maguire, B. W.

MAHER, Very Rev. William Francis, SJ; Provincial Superior of the English Province of the Society of Jesus, 1976-81; *b* 20 June 1916. *Educ:* St Ignatius' College, Stamford Hill; Heythrop College, Oxon. STL. Entered the Society of Jesus, 1935; ordained priest, 1948; Principal, Heythrop College, 1974-76. *Address:* 114 Mount Street, W1Y 6AH. *T:* 01-499 0285/6.

MAHLER, Dr Halfdan; Director-General, World Health Organization, since July 1973; *b* 21 April 1923; *m* 1957, Dr Ebba Fischer-Simonsen; two *s. Educ:* Univ. of Copenhagen (MD, EOPH). Planning Officer, Internat. Tuberculosis Campaign, Ecuador, 1950-51; Sen. WHO Med. Officer, Nat. TB Programme, India, 1951-61; Chief MO, Tuberculosis Unit, WHO/HQ, Geneva, 1961-69; Dir, Project Systems Analysis, WHO/HQ, Geneva, 1969-70; Asst Dir-Gen., WHO, 1970-73. Hon. FRSM 1976; Hon. Fellow: Indian Soc. for Malaria and other Communicable Diseases, Delhi; Faculty of Community Med., RCP, 1975; Hon. Member: Soc. médicale de Genève; Union internat. contre la Tuberculose; Hon. Life Mem., Uganda Medical Assoc., 1976; Assoc. Mem., Belgian Soc. of Trop. Med. FRCP 1981. Hon. LLD Nottingham, 1975; Hon. MD Karolinska Inst., 1977; Hon. Dr de l'Univ. Toulouse (Sciences Sociales), 1977; Hon. Dr Public Health, Seoul Nat. Univ., 1979; Hon. DSc Univ. of Lagos, 1979; Hon. Dr Med. Warsaw Med. Acad., 1980. Jana Evangelisty Purkyne Medal, Prague, 1974; Charles Univ. Medal, Prague, 1974; Comenius Univ. Gold Medal, Bratislava, 1974; Carlo Forlanini Gold Medal, 1975; Ernst Carlsens Foundn Prize, Copenhagen, 1980. *Publications:* papers etc on the epidemiology and control of tuberculosis, the political, social, economic and technological priority setting in the health sector, and the application of systems analysis to health care problems. *Recreations:* sailing, skiing. *Address:* (home) 12 chemin du Pont-Ceard, 1290 Versoix, Switzerland; (office) World Health Organization, Avenue Appia, 1211 Geneva 27, Switzerland.

MAHLER, Kurt, FAA 1965; FRS 1948; PhD, DSc; Professor Emeritus, Australian National University, since 1975; *b* 1903. *Educ:* Univs of Frankfurt and Göttingen. Research work at Univs of Göttingen, Groningen, and Manchester. Asst Lecturer at Manchester Univ., 1937-39, 1941-44; Lecturer, 1944-47; Senior Lecturer, 1948-49; Reader, 1949-52; Prof. of Mathematical Analysis, 1952-63; Prof. of Mathematics, Institute of Advanced Studies, ANU, 1963-68; Prof. of Mathematics, Ohio State Univ., USA, 1968-72. De Morgan Medal, 1971; Thomas Ranken Lyle Medal, 1977. *Publications:* Lectures on Diophantine Approximations, 1961; Introduction to p-adic Numbers and their Functions, 1973, 2nd edn 1980; Lectures on Transcendental Numbers, 1976; papers on different subjects in pure mathematics (Theory and Geometry of Numbers) in various journals, from 1928. *Recreations:* Chinese, photography.

Address: Mathematics Department, Institute of Advanced Studies, Australian National University, Canberra, ACT 2600, Australia.

MAHLER, Prof. Robert Frederick, FRCP, FRCPE; Consultant Physician, Clinical Research Centre, Northwick Park Hospital, Harrow, since 1979; *b* 31 Oct. 1924; *s* of Felix Mahler and Olga Lowy; *m* 1951, Maureen Calvert; two *s. Educ:* Edinburgh Academy; Edinburgh Univ. BSc; MB, ChB. Research fellowships and univ. posts in medicine, biochemistry and clinical pharmacology at various med. schs and univs: in Gt Britain: Royal Postgrad. Med. Sch., Guy's Hosp., Manchester, Dundee, Cardiff; in USA: Harvard Univ., Univ. of Indiana; in Sweden: Karolinska Inst., Stockholm; Prof. of Med., Univ. of Wales, 1970–79. Mem. MRC, 1977–81. *Publications:* contribs to British and Amer. med. and scientific jls. *Recreations:* moving to new places, winter sports, watching Rugby and rowing, music, theatre. *Address:* 14 Manley Street, NW1. *T:* 01–586 1198. *Club:* Royal Society of Medicine.

MAHMUD HUSAIN, Syed Abul Basher; Chief Justice of Bangladesh, 1975–78; *b* 1 Feb. 1916; *s* of late Syed Abdul Mutakabbir Abul Hasan, eminent scholar; *m* 1936, Sufia Begum; three *s* five *d. Educ:* Shaistagonj High Sch.; M. C. Coll., Sylhet; Dacca Univ. (BA,BL). Pleader, Judge's Court, Dacca, 1940–42; Hon. Supt, Darul-Ulum Govt-aided Sen., Madrassa, Dacca, 1937–42; Additional Govt Pleader, Habiganj, 1943–48; Advocate, Dacca High Ct Bar, 1948–51; Attorney, Fed. Ct of Pakistan, 1951, Advocate, 1953, Sen. Advocate, Supreme Ct of Pakistan, 1958; Asst Govt Pleader, High Ct of E Pakistan, 1952–56; Sen. Govt Pleader, 1956–65; Actg Advocate-Gen., E Pakistan for some time; Judge: High Ct of E Pakistan, 1965; High Ct of Bangladesh, 1972; Appellate Div. of High Ct of Bangladesh, Aug. 1972; Appellate Div. of Supreme Ct of Bangladesh, Dec. 1972. Mem. Bar Council, High Ct, Dacca, 1958–66; Chm., Enrolment Cttee, E Pakistan Bar Council, 1966–69; played important role in Muslim League and Pakistan Movement. Member: Coll. Rover Crew, 1933–34; Dacca Univ. OTC, 1935–39; Local Bd, Habiganj, 1944–50; Councillor: Assam Provincial Muslim League, 1944–47; All India Muslim League, 1945–47; All Pakistan Muslim League, 1947–55; Member: Constituent Assembly of Pakistan, 1949–54; Commonwealth Parly Assoc., 1950–54; Inter-Parly Union, 1950–54; Pakistan Tea Bd, 1951–54; Exec. Council, Univ. of Dacca, 1952–54; Local Adv. Cttee, East Bengal Rlwy, 1952–54; Dir, Pakistan Refugees Rehabilitation Finance Corp., 1953–54. Leader of Hajj Delegn of Bangladesh, 1975; attended Internat. Islamic Conf., London, 1976 (Chm., Third Session). *Address:* 56/1, Shah Saheb Lane, Narinda, Dacca, Bangladesh. *T:* 281986.

MAHON, Denis; *see* Mahon, J. D.

MAHON, Sir George Edward John, 6th Bt, *cr* 1819; *b* 22 June 1911; *s* of 5th Bt and late Hon. Edith Dillon, 2nd *d* of 4th Lord Clonbrock; *S* father, 1926; *m* 1st, 1938, Audrey Evelyn (*d* 1957), *o c* of late Dr Walter Jagger and late Mrs Maxwell Coote; two *s* one *d* ; 2nd, 1958, Suzanne, *d* of late Thomas Donnellan, Pirbright, Surrey, and late Mrs Donnellan; one *d.* Heir: *s* Lt Col William Walter Mahon, Irish Guards [*b* 4 Dec. 1940; *m* 1968, Rosemary Jane, *yr d* of Lt-Col M. E. Melvill, West Linton, Peebles-shire; one *s* two *d*]. *Address:* Greeninch, Enniskerry, Co. Wicklow.

MAHON, Rt. Rev. Gerald Thomas; Auxiliary Bishop of Westminster (Bishop in West London) (RC) and Titular Bishop of Eanach Duin since 1970; *b* 4 May 1922; *s* of George Elborne Mahon and Mary Elizabeth (*née* Dooley). *Educ:* Cardinal Vaughan Sch., Kensington; Christ's Coll., Cambridge. Priest, 1946. Teaching, St Peter's Coll., Freshfield, 1950–55; missionary work in Dio. of Kisumu, Kenya, 1955–63; Superior General of St Joseph's Missionary Society of Mill Hill, 1963–70. *Address:* 34 Whitehall Gardens, Acton, W3 9RD.

MAHON, (John) Denis, CBE 1967; MA Oxon; FBA 1964; Art Historian; Trustee of the National Gallery, 1957–64 and 1966–73; *b* 8 Nov. 1910; *s* of late John FitzGerald Mahon (4th *s* of Sir W. Mahon, 4th Bt) and Lady Alice Evelyn Browne (*d* 1970), *d* of 5th Marquess of Sligo. *Educ:* Eton; Christ Church, Oxford. Has specialised in the study of 17th-Century painting in Italy and has formed a collection of pictures of the period; is a member of the Cttee of the Biennial Exhibitions at Bologna, Italy; was awarded, 1957, Medal for Benemeriti della Cultura by Pres. of Italy for services to criticism and history of Italian art; Accademico d'Onore, Clementine Acad., Bologna, 1964; Serena Medal for Italian Studies, British Acad., 1972. Corresp. Fellow: Accad. Raffaello, Urbino, 1968; Deputazione di Storia Patria per le provincie di Romagna, 1969. Hon. DLitt, Newcastle, 1969. *Publications:* Studies in Seicento Art and Theory, 1947; Mostra dei Carracci, Catalogo critico dei Disegni, 1956 (1963); Poussiniana, 1962; Catalogues of the Mostra del Guercino (Dipinti, 1968; Disegni, 1969); contributed to: Actes of Colloque Poussin, 1960; Friedlaender Festschrift, 1965; Problemi Guardeschi, 1967; articles, including a number on Caravaggio and Poussin, in art-historical periodicals, *eg,* The Burlington Magazine, Apollo, The Art Bulletin, Journal of the Warburg and Courtauld Institutes, Bulletin of the Metropolitan Museum of New York, Gazette des Beaux-Arts, Art de France, Paragone, Commentari, Zeitschrift für Kunstwissenschaft; has collaborated in the compilation of catalogues raisonnés of exhibitions, *eg,* Artists in 17th Century Rome (London, 1955), Italian Art and Britain (Royal Academy, 1960), L'Ideale Classico del Seicento in Italia (Bologna, 1962), Omaggio al Guercino (Cento, 1967). *Address:* 33 Cadogan Square, SW1. *T:* 01–235 7311, 01–235 2530.

MAHON, Peter, JP; *b* 4 May 1909; *s* of late Alderman Simon Mahon, OBE, JP, Bootle, Liverpool; *m* 1935, Margaret Mahon (*née* Hannon). *Educ:* St James Elementary Sch.; St Edward's Coll. (Irish Christian Brothers). One of the longest serving Local Govt representatives in GB (42 years); Bootle Borough Council, 1933–70 (Mayor, 1954–55); Liverpool City Council, 1970–75; Liverpool DC, 1973–80 (Mem. (L) Old Swan Ward); Chm. or Dep. Chm. numerous cttees; Mem. Nat. Cttee of TGWU. Prospective Parly Candidate (Lab) Blackburn, 1952–54, contested (Lab) Preston, 1962–64; MP (Lab) Preston South, 1964–70; contested Liverpool Scotland, April 1971, as First Against Abortion candidate in UK; expelled from Labour Party; contested (L) Liverpool, Kirkdale, 1979. Talked out first Abortion Bill, House of Commons, 1966. *Recreations:* football and swimming enthusiast; fond of music. *Address:* Seahaven, Burbo Bank Road, Blundellsands, Liverpool L23 8TA.

MAHON, Simon; *b* 1914; *s* of late Alderman Simon Mahon, OBE, JP, Bootle, Liverpool; *m* 1941, Veronica Robertshaw. *Educ:* St James Elementary Sch.; St Joseph's Coll. Served War of 1939–45; commissioned Royal Engineers. Alderman of Bootle Borough Council; Mayor, 1962. MP (Lab) Bootle, 1955–1979; Opposition Whip, 1959–61. Trustee, Far Eastern Prisoners of War Fund. Freeman, Borough of Bootle, 1974. KCSG 1968; KHS 1977. *Address:* Greenrushes, 34 Princes Avenue, Great Crosby, Liverpool.

MAHONY, Francis Joseph, CB 1980; OBE 1972; President, Repatriation Review Tribunal, Australia, since 1979; *b* 15 March 1915; *s* of Cornelius J. Mahony and Angela M. Heagney; *m* 1939, Mary K. Sexton; seven *s* one *d. Educ:* De La Salle Coll., Armidale; Sydney Univ. (LLB 1940). Served War, CMF and AIF, 1942–44. Called to the Bar, Supreme Court of NSW, 1940; Commonwealth Crown Solicitor's Office, 1941; admitted Practitioner, High Ct of Australia, 1950; admitted Solicitor, Supreme Ct of NSW, 1952; Dep. Commonwealth Crown Solicitor, NSW, 1963–70; Dep. Sec., Attorney-Gen.'s Dept, Canberra, 1970–79. Leader, Aust. Delegn to Diplomatic Conf. on Humanitarian Law Applicable in Armed Conflicts, 1974–77. Chairman: Criminology Res. Council, 1972–79; Bd of Management, Aust. Inst. of Criminology, 1973–79; Mem. UN Cttee, Crime Prevention and Control, 1980–. *Recreation:* tennis. *Address:* 92 Cliff Avenue, Northbridge, NSW 2063, Australia. *T:* (02) 95 1853. *Clubs:* Tattersall's (Sydney); Sydney Cricket Ground.

MAHONY, Lt-Col John Keefer, VC 1944; *b* 30 June 1911; *s* of Joseph Jackson and Louise Mary Mahony; *m* 1950, Bonnie Johnston, Ottawa; two *d. Educ:* Duke of Connaught Sch., New Westminster, BC, Canada. On editorial staff of Vancouver Daily Province (newspaper) until outbreak of war of 1939–45; mem. Canadian Militia (equivalent of British Territorials) from 1936 until going on active service in Sept. 1939. Served War of 1939–45 (VC): (Canada, UK, Africa, Italy) Westminster Regt, Canadian Army; Major, 1943. Liaison Officer, US Dept of the Army, Washington, DC, 1954; retd as AA and QMG, Alberta Area, 1963. Exec. Dir, Junior Achievement of London, Inc. *Recreations:* swimming, lacrosse, baseball. *Address:* 657 Santa Monica Road, London, Ontario, Canada.

MAHTAB, Maharajadhiraja Bahadur Sir Uday Chand, of Burdwan, KCIE, 1945; *b* 1905; *s* of late Maharajadhiraja Bahadur Sir Bijay Chand Mahtab of Burdwan, GCIE, KCSI, IOM; *m* 1929, Radharani Devi, Amritsar, Punjab; three *s* three *d. Educ:* Presidency Coll., Calcutta; Calcutta Univ. (BA 1926). Pres. Non-Muslim block of Bengal Partition meeting, June 1947; Mem., Constituent Assembly. MLA Bengal, 1937–52; is a Zemindar; a Mem. of Damodar Canal Enquiry Cttee, 1938, and of Select Cttee on Calcutta Municipal (amendment) Bill, 1940; Chm. of Burdwan District Flood Relief and Bengal Central Flood Relief Cttees, 1943–44, of Indian Red Cross Appeal (Bengal), 1943–46, of Calcutta War Cttee, 1943–46, and of Damodar Flood Control Enquiry Cttee, 1944; a Mem. of Bengal Tanks Improvement Bill Select Cttee, 1944, of Advisory Cttee to examine cases of Terrorist Convicts in Bengal, 1944, of W Bengal Forest Denudation Enquiry Cttee, 1944, and of Select Cttee on Bengal Agricultural Income Tax Bill, 1944; Pres., British Indian Association; Mem., Central Jute Board, 1951–52; Dir of over 30 business firms and Chm. of several Boards. Mem. of Managing Body of several Government Organisations. Silver Jubilee (1935) and Coronation (1937) medals. *Address:* The Palace, Burdwan, India; Bijay Manzil, Alipore, Calcutta. *Clubs:* Calcutta (Calcutta); Aftab (Burdwan); Gymkhana (Darjeeling).

MAIDEN, Colin James, ME, DPhil; Vice-Chancellor, University of Auckland, New Zealand, since 1971; *b* 5 May 1933; *s* of Henry A. Maiden; *m* 1957, Jenefor Mary Rowe; one *s* three *d. Educ:* Auckland Grammar Sch.; Univ. of Auckland, NZ; Oxford Univ. ME(NZ), DPhil (Oxon). Post-doctorate research, Oxford Univ., Oxford, Eng. (supported by AERE, Harwell), 1957–58; Head of Hypersonic Physics Section, Canadian Armament Research and Develt Estabt, Quebec City, Canada, 1958–60; Sen. Lectr in Mechanical Engrg, Univ. of Auckland, 1960–61; Head of Material Sciences Laboratory, Gen. Motors Corp., Defense Research Laboratories, Santa Barbara, Calif, USA, 1961–66; Manager of Process Engineering, Gen. Motors Corp., Technl Centre, Warren, Michigan, USA, 1966–70. Director: Farmers Trading Co. Ltd, 1973–; Winstone Ltd, 1978–; Fisher & Paykel Ltd, 1978–. Chairman: NZ Energy R&D Cttee, 1974–81; Liquid Fuels Trust Bd, 1978–; NZ Synthetic Fuels Corp. Ltd, 1980–. NZ Agent for Joint NZ/US Sci. and Technol Agreement, 1974–81. *Publications:* numerous scientific and technical papers. *Recreations:* tennis, golf. *Address:* 1 Fern Avenue, Auckland, New Zealand. *T:* 685600. *Clubs:* Vincent's (Oxford); Northern, Rotary

(Auckland); Remuera Racquets, Eden Epsom Tennis, International Lawn Tennis of NZ, Auckland Golf.

MAIDMENT, Kenneth John, MA; *b* 29 Oct. 1910; *s* of Francis George Maidment and Jessie Louisa Taylor; *m* 1937, Isobel Felicity, *d* of Archibald Leitch; one *s* three *d. Educ:* Bristol Gram. Sch.; Merton Coll., Oxford (Emeritus Fellow, 1982). Hertford Scholar, 1929; First Class Classical Hon. Mods, 1930; Craven Scholar, 1930; First Class Litt. Hum., 1932; Junior Research Fellow, Merton Coll., 1932-34; Fellow and Classical Tutor, Jesus Coll. (Oxford), 1934-38; Fellow and Classical Tutor, Merton Coll., 1938-49; Oxford and Bucks Lt Infantry, 1940; seconded War Office, 1941; liaison duties in US, 1942-45, Lt-Col; University Lecturer in Greek Literature, 1947-49; Principal, Auckland Univ. Coll., 1950-57; Vice-Chancellor, Univ. of Auckland, 1957-71. Governor, Bristol Grammar Sch., 1972-79; Emeritus Fellow, Merton Coll., Oxford, 1982. Hon. LLD Auckland, 1970. *Publications:* critical edition and translation of Antiphon and Andocides (Loeb Library), 1940; contribs to classical journals. *Address:* 9 Highfield Avenue, Headington, Oxford.

MAIDSTONE, Viscount; Daniel James Hatfield Finch Hatton; *b* 7 Oct. 1967; *s* and *heir* of 16th Earl of Winchilsea, *qv.*

MAIDSTONE, Bishop Suffragan of, since 1980; **Rt. Rev. Robert Maynard Hardy;** *b* 5 Oct. 1936; *s* of Harold and Monica Mavie Hardy; *m* 1970, Isobel Mary, *d* of Charles and Ella Burch; two *s* one *d. Educ:* Queen Elizabeth Grammar School, Wakefield; Clare College, Cambridge (MA). Deacon 1962, priest 1963; Assistant Curate, All Saints and Martyrs, Langley, Manchester, 1962; Fellow and Chaplain, Selwyn College, Cambridge, 1965; Vicar of All Saints, Borehamwood, 1972; Priest-in-charge, Aspley Guise, 1975; Course Director, St Albans Diocese Ministerial Training Scheme, 1975; Incumbent of United Benefice of Aspley Guise with Husborne Crawley and Ridgmont, 1980. *Recreations:* walking, gardening, reading. *Address:* Bishop's House, Egerton, Ashford, Kent TN27 9DJ. *T:* Egerton 431.

MAIDSTONE, Archdeacon of; *see* Smith, Ven. A. M. P.

MAILER, Norman; *b* 31 Jan. 1923; *s* of Isaac Barnett Mailer and Fanny Schneider; *m* 1st, 1944, Beatrice Silverman (marr. diss., 1951); one *d*; 2nd, 1954, Adèle Morales (marr. diss., 1962); two *d*; 3rd, 1962, Lady Jeanne Campbell (marr. diss., 1963); one *d*; 4th, 1963, Beverly Bentley; two *s*; 5th, Carol Stevens; one *d*; 6th, Norris Church. *Educ:* Harvard. Infantryman, US Army, 1944-46. Co-founder of Village Voice, 1955; an Editor of Dissent, 1953-63. Democratic Candidate, Mayoral Primaries, New York City, 1969. Directed films: Wild 90, 1967; Beyond the Law, 1967; Maidstone, 1968. *Publications:* (American) The Naked and the Dead, 1948; Barbary Shore, 1951; The Deer Park, 1955 (dramatized, 1967); Advertisements for Myself, 1959; Deaths For The Ladies, 1962; The Presidential Papers, 1963; An American Dream, 1964; Cannibals and Christians, 1966; Why Are We In Vietnam?, 1967 (a novel); The Armies of the Night, 1968 (Pulitzer Prize, 1969); Miami and the Siege of Chicago, 1968 (National Book Award, 1969); Of a Fire on the Moon, 1970; The Prisoner of Sex, 1971; Existential Errands, 1972; St George and the Godfather, 1972; Marilyn, 1973; The Faith of Graffiti, 1974; The Fight, 1975; Some Honorable Men, 1976; Genius and Lust, 1976; A Transit to Narcissus, 1978; The Executioner's Song, 1979; The Essential Mailer, 1982. *Address:* c/o Molly Malone Cook, PO Box 338, Provincetown, Mass 02657, USA.

MAILLART, Ella (Kini); Explorer; *b* 20 Feb. 1903; Swiss father and Danish mother; unmarried. *Educ:* Geneva; and also while teaching French at two schools in England. Took to the seas at 20, cruising with 3 ton Perlette, 10 ton Bonita, 45 ton Atalante-all these manned by girls; then 120 ton Volunteer, 125 ton Insoumise; in Mediterranean, Biscay, Channel; sailed for Switzerland Olympic Games, Paris, 1924 single-handed competition; Hockey for Switzerland as captain in 1931; Ski-ed for Switzerland in the FIS races in 1931-34; went to Russia for 6 months, 1930; travelled in Russian Turkestan for 6 months 1932; went to Manchoukuo for Petit Parisien, 1934; returned overland accompanied by Peter Fleming, via Koko Nor; travelled overland to Iran and Afghanistan in 1937 and 1939, in South India, 1940-45, Nepal, 1951, Everest Base Camp, 1965. Fellow RGS, London; Member: Royal Soc. for Asian Affairs; Club des Explorateurs, Paris. Sir Percy Sykes Medal. *Publications:* Parmi la Jeunesse Russe, 1932; Des Monts Célestes aux Sables Rouges, 1934 (in English as Turkestan Solo, 1934); Oasis Interdites, 1937 (in English as Forbidden Journey, 1937); Gipsy Afloat, 1942; Cruises and Caravans, 1942; The Cruel Way, 1947; Ti-Puss, 1952; The Land of the Sherpas, 1955. *Recreations:* ski-ing, gardening. *Address:* c/o David Higham Associates Ltd, 5-8 Lower John Street, W1; 10 Avenue G. Vallette, Geneva, Switzerland. *T:* Geneva 46.46.57; Atchala, Chandolin sur Sierre, Switzerland. *Clubs:* Kandahar; (hon.) Ski Club de Dames Suisse; (hon.) Ski Club of Great Britain; (hon.) Alpine.

MAIN, Frank Fiddes, CB 1965; FRCPEd; Chief Medical Officer, Ministry of Health and Social Services, Northern Ireland, 1954-68, retired; *b* 9 June 1905; *s* of Frank and Mary Main, Edinburgh; *m* 1931, Minnie Roberta Paton; two *s* two *d. Educ:* Daniel Stewart's Coll., Edinburgh; Edinburgh Univ. MB, ChB 1927; DPH 1931; MRCPEd 1954; FRCPEd 1956. Medical Officer of Health, Perth, 1937-48; Senior Administrative Medical Officer, Eastern Regional Hosp. Bd (Scotland), 1948-54. Crown Mem., Gen. Med. Council,

1956-69. QHP 1956-59. *Recreation:* golf. *Address:* Bruce's Cottage, Kilconquhar, Elie, Fife KY9 1LG. *T:* Colinsburgh 312.

MAIN, John Roy, QC 1974; **His Honour Judge Main;** a Circuit Judge, since 1976; *b* 21 June 1930; *yr s* of late A. C. Main, MIMechE; *m* 1955, Angela de la Condamine Davies, *er d* of late R. W. H. Davies, ICS; two *s* one *d. Educ:* Portsmouth Grammar Sch.; Hotchkiss Sch., USA; Brasenose Coll., Oxford (MA). Called to Bar, Inner Temple, 1954; a Recorder of Crown Court, 1972-76. Mem. Special Panel, Transport Tribunal, 1970-76; Dep. Chm., IoW QS, 1971. *Recreations:* boating, gardening, music. *Address:* 4 Queen Anne Drive, Claygate, Surrey KT10 0PP. *T:* Esher 66380.

MAIN, Dr Peter Tester, ERD 1964; Chairman, The Boots Company Ltd, since 1982 (Director, since 1973); *b* 21 March 1925; *s* of late Peter Tester Main and Esther Paterson (*née* Lawson); *m* 1952, Dr Margaret Fimister, MB, ChB (*née* Tweddle); two *s* one *d. Educ:* Robert Gordon's Coll., Aberdeen; Univ. of Aberdeen (MB, ChB 1948, MD 1963). MRCPE 1981, FRCPE 1982. Captain, RAMC, 1949-51; MO with Commando Bde, Suez, 1956; Lt-Col RAMC (AER), retd 1964. House Surg., Aberdeen Royal Infirmary, 1948; House Physician, Woodend Hosp., Aberdeen, 1949; Demonstrator, Univ. of Durham, 1952; gen. practice, 1953-57; joined Res. Dept, Boots, 1957; Dir of Res., 1968; Man. Dir, Industrial Div., 1979-80; Vice-Chm., The Boots Co. Ltd, 1980-81. CBIM (FBIM 1978). *Publications:* contribs on therapeutics to learned jls. *Recreations:* fly fishing, shooting, Scottish music. *Address:* The Boots Co. Ltd, Nottingham NG2 3AA. *T:* Nottingham 56111. *Club:* Naval and Military.

MAINGARD de la VILLE ès OFFRANS, Sir (Louis Pierre) René, (Sir René Maingard), Kt 1982; CBE 1961; Chairman, Rogers & Co. Ltd, Mauritius, since 1956; *b* 9 July 1917; *s* of Joseph René Maingard de la Ville ès Offrans and Véronique Hugnin; *m* 1946, Marie Hélène Françoise Raffray; three *d. Educ:* St Joseph's Coll.; Royal Coll. of Mauritius; Business Training Corp., London. Clerk, Rogers & Co. Ltd, 1936, Man. Dir, 1948. Chairman: Colonial Steamships Co. Ltd, 1948-; Mauritius Steam Navigation Co. Ltd, 1964-; Mauritius Portland Cement Co. Ltd, 1960-. Director: Mauritius Commercial Bank Ltd, 1956-; New Mauritius Dock Co. Ltd, 1948-. Consul for Finland in Mauritius, 1957-. Chevalier 1st Cl., Order of the White Rose, Finland, 1973. *Recreations:* golf, fishing, boating. *Address:* Pereybere, Grand'Baie, Mauritius. *T:* 03 85 49; Rogers & Co. Ltd, PO Box 60, Port Louis. *T:* 08 68 01. *Clubs:* Royal Air Force; Dodo, Mauritius Naval & Military Gymkhana (Mauritius).

MAINI, Sir Amar (Nath), Kt 1957; CBE 1953 (OBE 1948); *b* Nairobi, 31 July 1911; *e s* of late Nauhria Ram Maini, Nairobi, Kenya, and Ludhiana, Punjab, India; *m* 1935, Ram Saheli Mehra, Ludhiana; two *s. Educ:* Govt Indian Sch., Nairobi; London Sch. of Economics (BCom, Hons 1932). Barrister-at-law, Middle Temple, London, 1933. Advocate of High Court of Kenya, and of High Court of Uganda. Sometime an actg MLC, Kenya, and Mem., Nairobi Municipal Council. From 1939 onwards, in Uganda; associated with family cotton business of Nauhria Ram & Sons (Uganda) Ltd. Formerly: Mem., Kampala Township Authority, Chm., Kampala Municipal Council, 1st Mayor of Kampala (1950-55); Dep. Chm., Uganda Electricity Board; Member: Uganda Development Corporation; Lint Marketing Board; Civil Defence Bd; Asian Manpower Cttee; Transport Bd; Supplies Bd; Immigration Advisory Bd; Advisory Bd of Health; Railway Advisory Council; Advisory Bd of Commerce; Rent Restriction Bd; Makerere Coll. Assembly, etc. Past Pres. Central Council of Indian Assocs in Uganda; Indian Assoc., Kampala; served on Cttees of Cotton Association. Formerly: Mem. Uganda Legislative and Exec. Councils; Development Council, Uganda; EA Legislative Assembly; EA Postal Advisory Bd; EA Transport Adv. Council; EA Air Adv Council, etc. Minister for Corporations and Regional Communications in the Government of Uganda, 1955-58; Minister of Commerce and Industry in Uganda, 1958-61; Speaker, E African Central Legislative Assembly, 1961-67; Mem., E African Common Market Tribunal, 1967-69. Dep. Chm. Kenya Broadcasting Corp., 1962-63. *Recreations:* walking, listening. *Address:* 55 Vicarage Road, East Sheen, SW14 8RY. *T:* 01-878 1497. *Clubs:* Reform; Nairobi.

MAINLAND, Prof. William Faulkner, MA; Professor of German, University of Sheffield, 1953-70; *b* 31 May 1905; *s* of late George Mainland and of Ada (*née* Froggatt); *m* 1930, Clarice Vowles, *d* of late A. E. Brewer; no *c. Educ:* George Heriot's Sch.; Univ. of Edinburgh. 1st Class Hons. Vans Dunlop Schol. in German; Postgrad. studies in London under late Prof. J. G. Robertson, and in Germany. Asst for French and German at London Sch. of Economics, 1929-30; thereafter attached to German Depts of Univs of: Manitoba, 1930; Manchester, 1935; London (UC, 1937, King's Coll., 1938, Birkbeck Coll., 1938); Sheffield, 1946; Leeds, 1947. Public Orator, Univ. of Sheffield, 1968-70. *Publications:* German for Students of Medicine, 1938; German Lyrics of the Seventeenth Century (with Prof. August Closs), 1941; E. T. A. Hoffmann, Der goldene Topf (Editor), 1942, 2nd edn, 1945; Schiller, Uber naive und sentimentalische Dichtung (Editor), 1951; Schiller and the Changing Past, 1957; Wilhelm Tell in metrical translation with commentary, 1972; chapters on Th. Storm, H. Sudermann, Fr. v. Unruh, H. Kasack, in German Men of Letters, 1961-66; Schiller, Jungfrau v. Orleans (Editor with Prof. E. J. Engel), 1963; Schiller, Wilhelm Tell (Editor), 1968. Reviews and articles on German and Dutch literature. *Recreations:* drawing, painting; Baltic language studies. *Address:* Apt 3, 46 Sale Hill, Sheffield S10 5BX. *T:* Sheffield 665759. *Club:* University Staff (Sheffield).

MAINWARING, Captain Maurice K. C.; *see* Cavenagh-Mainwaring.

MAIR, Prof. Alexander; FRSE 1980; Professor of Community and Occupational Medicine (formerly of Public Health and Social Medicine), University of Dundee, 1954-82; *m* 1945, Nancy Waddington; two *s* one *d. Educ:* Aberdeen Univ. MB, ChB, 1942, DPH, 1948, MD (Hons), 1952 (Aberdeen); DIH (London) 1955; FRCPE 1966; FFCM 1976; FFOM 1979. RAMC 1942-46. Lecturer, Univ. of Aberdeen, 1948-52; Senior Lecturer, Univ. of St Andrews, at Dundee, 1952-54. Formerly Founder and Dir, Scottish Occupational Health Laboratory Service, Ltd; Member: Steering Cttee, East of Scotland Occupational Health Service; Nat. Adv. Cttee for Employment of Disabled; Asbestos Adv. Cttee, 1976-; Adv. Cttee, Health and Safety Exec., 1976-; Industrial Injuries Adv. Council, 1977-; formerly Chm., Scottish Cttee for Welfare of Disabled and Sub-Cttee on Rehabilitation; Consultant, Occupational Health, to RN in Scotland. First Chm., British Soc. for Agriculture Labour Science. Occasional consultant to WHO, Geneva. *Publications:* Student Health Services in Great Britain and Northern Ireland, 1966; (jointly) Custom and Practice in Medical Care, 1968; Hospital and Community II, 1969; Sir James Mackenzie, MD, 1973 (Abercrombie Award); contrib.: Cerebral Palsy in Childhood and Adolescence, 1961; Further Studies in Hospital and Community, 1962; numerous publications on Researches into Occupational Diseases, especially Silicosis, Byssinosis, etc. *Address:* Tree Tops, Castle Roy, Broughty Ferry, Angus. *T:* 78727. *Club:* Caledonian.

MAIR, Alexander, MBE 1967; Chief Executive and Director, Grampian Television Ltd, since 1970; *b* 5 Nov. 1922; *s* of Charles Mair and Helen Dickie; *m* 1953, Margaret Isobel Gowans Rennie. *Educ:* Skene, Aberdeenshire; Webster's Business Coll., Aberdeen; Sch. of Accountancy, Glasgow. Associate, ICMA, 1953. Chief Accountant, Bayard Holdings Ltd, 1957-60; Company Sec., Grampian Television, 1961-70; apptd Dir, 1967; Dir, ITN, 1980-. Pres., Aberdeen Junior Chamber of Commerce, 1960-61; Hon. Manager, Aberdeen Savings Bank, 1973-; Chm., British Regional Television Assoc., 1973-75; Mem. Council, Aberdeen Chamber of Commerce, 1973. FRSA 1973. *Recreations:* golf, ski-ing, gardening. *Address:* Ravenswood, 66 Rubislaw Den South, Aberdeen AB2 6AX. *T:* Aberdeen 37619. *Clubs:* Caledonian; Royal Northern (Aberdeen).

MAIR, John Magnus; Director of Social Work, Edinburgh, 1969-75; Lecturer in Social Medicine, University of Edinburgh, 1959-75; *b* 29 Dec. 1912; *s* of Joseph Alexander Mair and Jane Anderson; *m* 1940, Isobelle Margaret Williamson (*d* 1969); three *s. Educ:* Anderson Inst., Lerwick; Univs of Aberdeen (MB, ChB) and Edinburgh (DPH). MFCM. Asst GP, Highlands and Islands Medical Service, 1937-40; RAMC, 1940-45; Edinburgh Public Health Dept (latterly Sen. Depute Medical Officer of Health), 1945-69. *Recreation:* golf. *Address:* 30 Honiton Gardens, Corby, Northants NN18 8BW. *Clubs:* Edinburgh University Staff; Grampian (Corby).

MAIR, Prof. Lucy Philip; Professor of Applied Anthropology, London School of Economics, 1963-68; *b* 28 Jan. 1901; *d* of David Beveridge Mair and Jessy Philip. *Educ:* St Paul's Girls' Sch.; Newnham Coll., Cambridge (Hon. Fellow, 1982). London Sch. of Economics: Asst Lectr, 1927; Lectr, 1932; Reader, 1946; Prof., 1963; Hon. Fellow 1975. Australian Land Headquarters Civil Affairs Sch., 1945-46; Lugard Memorial Lectr, Internat. African Inst., 1958; Gildersleeve Visiting Prof. Barnard Coll., Columbia Univ., 1965; Frazer Lecture, Cambridge, 1967; Hon. Prof. of Social Anthropology, Univ. of Kent, 1974-79. Vice-Pres., Royal Anthropological Inst., 1978-79 (Hon. Sec., 1974-78; Wellcome Medal 1936). Hon. DLitt: Durham, 1972; Kent, 1980. *Publications:* An African People in the Twentieth Century, 1934; Native Policies in Africa, 1936; Australia in New Guinea, 1948, 2nd edn 1971; Primitive Government, 1962; New Nations, 1963; An Introduction to Social Anthropology, 1966, 2nd edn 1972; The New Africa, 1967; Witchcraft, 1969; Marriage, 1971; African Societies, 1974; African Kingdoms, 1977; contribs to Africa, Cahiers d'Etudes Africaines, etc. *Recreations:* music, cooking. *Address:* 19 Hallgate, Blackheath Park, SE3. *T:* 01-852 8531.

MAIR, Prof. William Austyn, CBE 1969; MA; CEng; Francis Mond Professor of Aeronautical Engineering, University of Cambridge, since 1952; Head of Engineering Department, since 1973; Fellow of Downing College, Cambridge; *b* 24 Feb. 1917; *s* of William Mair, MD; *m* 1944, Mary Woodhouse Crofts; two *s. Educ:* Highgate Sch.; Clare Coll., Cambridge. Aerodynamics Dept, Royal Aircraft Establishment, Farnborough, 1940-46; Dir, Fluid Motion Laboratory, Univ. of Manchester, 1946-52. Mem. various cttees, Aeronautical Research Council, 1946-80. Dir, Hovercraft Development Ltd, 1962-81. Chm., Editorial Bd, Aeronautical Qly, 1975-81. FRAeS (Silver Medal 1975). *Publications:* papers on aerodynamics. *Address:* 74 Barton Road, Cambridge. *T:* Cambridge 350137. *Club:* United Oxford & Cambridge University.

MAIS, family name of Baron Mais.

MAIS, Baron, *cr* 1967 (Life Peer); **Alan Raymond Mais,** GBE 1973 (OBE (mil.) 1944); TD 1944; ERD 1958; DL; JP; Colonel; Director: Royal Bank of Scotland, 1969-81; Slag Reduction Co. Ltd; William Sindalls Ltd, 1969-81; Hay Consultants, 1969-81; Chairman, Peachey Property Corporation, 1977-81; *b* July 1911; *s* of late Capt. E. Mais, Mornington Court, Kensington; *m* 1936, Lorna Aline, *d* of late Stanley Aspinall Boardman, Addiscombe, Surrey; two *s* one *d. Educ:* Banister Court, Hants; Coll. of Estate Management,

London Univ. Commissioned RARO, Royal West Kent Regt, 1929; transf. RE 1931; Major 1939, Lt-Col 1941, Col 1944; served War of 1939-45; France, BEF 1939-40 (despatches); Special Forces, MEF, Iraq and Persia, 1941-43 (despatches); Normandy and NW Europe, 1944-46 (OBE, despatches), wounded; CRE 56 Armd Div., TA, 1947-50; CO 101 Field Engr Regt, 1947-50, Hon. Col, 1950-63; Comd Eng Gp, AER, 1951-54; DDES, AER, 1954-58. Worked for Richard Costain and other cos on Civil Engrg Works at home and abroad, 1931-38; Private Practice, A. R. Mais & Partners, Structural Engineers & Surveyors, 1938-39 and 1946-48. Dir Trollope & Colls Ltd, Bldg and Civil Engrg contractors and subsid. cos, 1948 (Asst Man. Dir, 1953; Man. Dir 1957; Dep.-Chm. 1961; Chm. and Man. Dir 1963; retired, 1968); Chairman: City of London Insurance Co. Ltd, 1970-77; Hay-MSL Consultants, 1971-78. Dir, Nat. Commercial Bank of Scotland, 1966-69. Pres., London Chamber of Commerce and Industry, 1975-78; Past Pres., London Master Builders' Assoc.; Member: Land Commn, 1967-69; House of Lords Select Cttee on EEC, 1974. Lord Mayor of London, 1972-73. Chancellor, 1972-73, Pro-Chancellor, 1979-, City Univ. Master: Worshipful Company of Paviors, 1975-76; Worshipful Company of Cutlers, 1968-69. Member: EDC Cttee for Constructional Industry, 1964-68; BNEC Cttee for Canada; Marshall Aid Commemoration Commn, 1964-74; Court and Council, City Univ.; Commonwealth Scholars Commn, 1978-80. Comr of Income Tax, 1972-. Treasurer, Royal Masonic Hosp., 1973-. Governor: Ewell Technical Coll., 1954-66; London Univ. Board of Studies, 1963-73; Hurstpierpoint Coll.; Hon. The Irish Soc., 1978-80. JP; DL Co. London (later Greater London), 1951-76; Lieut, City of London, 1963; Alderman, Ward of Walbrook, 1963; Sheriff, 1969-70; DL Kent, 1976. Vice-Pres. Emeritus, Inst. Quantity Surveyors; Treasurer, Fellowship of Engineering, 1977-81. FICE, FIStructE, MSocCE (France), FIArb, FRICS, KStJ 1973. Hon. BSc; Hon. DSc: City, 1972; Ulster, 1981. Hon. FICE 1975. Order of Patriotic War (1st class), USSR, 1942; Order of Aztec Eagle, Mexico, 1973; Order of Merit, Mexico, 1973. *Publications:* Yerbury Foundation Lecture, RIBA, 1960; Bossom Foundation Lecture, 1971. *Recreations:* family, Territorial Army. *Address:* Griffins, Sundridge Avenue, Bromley, Kent; Le Fontagnes, Roi Soleil, Antibes. *Clubs:* City Livery, Army and Navy, Special Forces, London Welsh.

MAIS, Francis Thomas; Permanent Secretary, Department of Manpower Services, Northern Ireland, since 1981; *b* 27 June 1927; *s* of Charles Edward Mais and Emma (*née* McLoughlin); *m* 1973, Margaret Edythe Evans; one *d. Educ:* Barnsley Grammar Sch.; Christ's Coll., Cambridge. Joined Ministry, later Dept, of Commerce, NI, 1951; Dep. Sec., 1973-79; Permanent Sec., 1979-81. *Address:* Department of Manpower Services, Netherleigh, Massey Avenue, Belfast BT4 2JP. *T:* Belfast 63244.

MAIS, Hon. Sir (Robert) Hugh, Kt 1971; Judge of the High Court of Justice, Queen's Bench Division, 1971-82; *b* 14 Sept. 1907; *s* of late Robert Stanley Oliver Mais, Chobham, Surrey; *m* 1938, Catherine, *d* of J. P. Pattinson; one *s. Educ:* Shrewsbury Sch.; Wadham Coll., Oxford (MA, 1948, Hon. Fellow, 1971). Called to the Bar, 1930, Bencher, Inner Temple, 1971; Mem. of Northern Circuit. Chancellor of the Diocese of: Manchester, 1948-71; Carlisle, 1950-71; Sheffield, 1950-71. Judge of County Courts: Circuit No 37 (West London), 1958-60; Circuit No 42 (Marylebone), 1960-71. Dep. Chm., Berkshire QS, 1964-71; Commissioner of Assize: SE Circuit, 1964, 1967; Oxford Circuit, 1968, 1969; NE Circuit, 1971. Mem., Winn Cttee on Personal Injuries Litigation. Served as Wing Comdr, RAF, 1940-44. *Recreations:* fishing, golf. *Address:* Ripton, Streatley-on-Thames, Berks. *T:* Goring 872397. *Club:* Athenæum.

MAISEY, Dr Michael Norman, FRCP; Consultant Physician in Endocrinology and Nuclear Medicine, Guy's Hospital, since 1973; *b* 10 June 1939; *s* of Harold Lionel Maisey and Kathleen Christine Maisey; *m* 1965, Irene Charlotte (*née* Askay); two *s. Educ:* Caterham Sch.; Guy's Hosp. Med. Sch. (BSc, MD). ABNM 1972; FRCP 1980. House appts, 1964-66; Registrar, Guy's Hosp., 1966-69; Fellow, Johns Hopkins Med. Instns, 1970-72; Sen. Registrar, Guy's Hosp., 1972-73. Hon. Consultant to the Army in Endocrinology and Nuclear Medicine, 1978-. *Publications:* Nuclear Medicine, 1980; Clinical Nuclear Medicine, 1982; papers on thyroid disease and nuclear medicine. *Recreations:* sailing, jazz appreciation. *Address:* Guy's Hospital, St Thomas Street, SE1 9RT. *T:* 01-407 7600.

MAISNER, Air Vice-Marshal Aleksander, CB 1977; CBE 1969; AFC 1955; *b* 26 July 1921; *s* of Henryk Maisner and Helene Anne (*née* Brosin); *m* 1946, Mary (*née* Coverley); one *s* one *d. Educ:* High Sch. and Lyceum, Czestochowa, Poland; Warsaw Univ. Labour Camps, USSR, 1940-41; Polish Artillery, 1941-42; Polish Air Force, 1943-46; joined RAF, 1946; Flying Trng Comd, 1946-49; No 70 Sqdn Suez Canal Zone, 1950-52; No 50 Sqdn RAF Binbrook, 1953-55; No 230 (Vulcan) OCU, RAF Waddington, 1955-59; psa 1960; OC Flying Wing, RNZAF Ohakea, 1961-62; Dirg Staff, RAF Staff Coll., Andover, 1963-65; DD Air Plans, MoD, 1965-68; CO, RAF Seletar, Singapore, 1969-71; Asst Comdt, RAF Coll., Cranwell, 1971-73; Dir, Personnel (Policy and Plans), MoD, 1973-75; Asst Air Sec., 1975; Dir-Gen. of Personnel Management, RAF, 1976. Personnel Exec., Reed Internat. Ltd, 1977-82. Governor, Shiplake Coll., 1978-. Pres., Polish Air Force Assoc., 1982-. *Recreations:* walking, gardening, reading. *Address:* 14 Orchard Close, Shiplake, Henley-on-Thames, Oxon RG9 4BU. *T:* Wargrave 2671. *Club:* Royal Air Force.

MAISONROUGE, Jacques Gaston; Senior Vice President, IBM Corporation, since 1972; Chairman, IBM World Trade Corporation, since 1976; *b* Cachan, Seine, 20 Sept. 1924; *s* of Paul Maisonrouge and Suzanne (*née* Cazas); *m* 1948, Françoise Andrée Féron; one *s* four *d. Educ:* Lycées Voltaire and Saint Louis, Paris. Studied engineering; gained dip. of Ecole Centrale des Arts et Manufactures, Chm., Bd of Trustees, 1977-. Engineer, 1948; various subseq. appts in IBM Corp., France; Chm. and Chief Exec. Officer, IBM World Trade Europe/ME/Africa Corp., 1974-81; Pres., IBM Europe, 1974-81. Philip Morris Inc. Dir, L'Air Liquide, 1964-. Councillor, French Chamber of Commerce, USA, 1964-. Chevalier, Ordre de la Légion d'Honneur; Comdr, Ordre National du Mérite; Commandeur des Palmes Académiques; Commander, Order of Merit of the Italian Republic; Commander, Order of Saint Sylvester; Kt of Malta; Commander, Order of Star of North (Sweden). *Recreations:* interested in sport (tennis, riding). *Address:* Old Orchard Road, Armonk, New York 10504, USA. *Club:* Automobile of France.

MAITLAND, family name of **Earl of Lauderdale.**

MAITLAND, Viscount; Master of Lauderdale; **Ian Maitland;** International Banking Division, National Westminster Bank Ltd, since 1975; *b* 4 Nov. 1937; *s* and *heir* of Earl of Lauderdale, *qv*; *m* 1963, Ann Paule, *d* of Geoffrey Clark; one *s* one *d. Educ:* Radley Coll., Abingdon; Brasenose Coll., Oxford (MA Modern History). Various appointments since 1960; with Hedderwick Borthwick & Co., 1970-75. Royal Naval Reserve (Lieutenant), 1963-73. Lay Reader, Church of England. *Recreations:* photography, sailing. *Heir: s* Master of Maitland, *qv. Address:* 150 Tachbrook Street, SW1.

MAITLAND, Master of; Hon. John Douglas Maitland; *b* 29 May 1965; *s* and *heir* of Viscount Maitland, *qv*.

MAITLAND, Alastair George, CBE 1966; Consul-General, Boston, 1971-75, retired; *b* 30 Jan. 1916; *s* of late Thomas Douglas Maitland, MBE, and Wilhelmina Sarah Dundas; *m* 1943, Betty Hamilton (*d* 1981); two *s* one *d. Educ:* George Watson's Coll., Edinburgh; Universities of Edinburgh (MA First Class Hons), Grenoble and Paris, Ecole des Sciences Politiques. Vice-Consul: New York, 1938; Chicago, 1939; New York, 1939; Los Angeles, 1940; apptd to staff of UK High Commissioner at Ottawa, 1942; apptd to Foreign Office, 1945; Brit. Middle East Office, Cairo, 1948; Foreign Office, 1952; UK Delegation to OEEC, Paris, 1954; Consul-General: at New Orleans, 1958-62; at Jerusalem, 1962-64; at Cleveland, 1964-68; Dir-Gen., British Trade Develt Office, NY, 1968-71. Hon. LLD Lake Erie Coll., Ohio, 1971. CStJ. *Recreations:* music, golf, gardening, reading. *Address:* Heath, Mass, USA.

MAITLAND, Sir Donald (James Dundas), GCMG 1977 (CMG 1967); Kt 1973; OBE 1960; Permanent Under-Secretary of State, Department of Energy, 1980-82; *b* 16 Aug. 1922; *s* of Thomas Douglas Maitland and Wilhelmina Sarah Dundas; *m* 1950, Jean Marie Young, *d* of Gordon Young; one *s* one *d. Educ:* George Watson's Coll.; Edinburgh Univ. Served India, Middle East, and SE Asia, 1941-47 (Royal Scots; Rajputana Rifles). Joined Foreign Service, 1947; Consul, Amara, 1950; British Embassy, Baghdad, 1950-53; Private Sec. to Minister of State, Foreign Office, 1954-56; Director, Middle East Centre for Arab Studies, Lebanon, 1956-60; Foreign Office, 1960-63; Counsellor, British Embassy, Cairo, 1963-65; Head of News Dept, Foreign Office, 1965-67; Principal Private Sec. to Foreign and Commonwealth Secretary, 1967-69; Ambassador to Libya, 1969-70; Chief Press Sec., 10 Downing St, 1970-73; UK Permanent Rep. to UN, 1973-74; Dep. Under-Sec. of State, FCO, 1974-75; UK Mem., Commonwealth Group on Trade, Aid and Develt, 1975; Ambassador and UK Perm. Rep. to EEC, 1975-79; Dep. to Perm. Under-Sec. of State, FCO, Dec. 1979-June 1980. *Recreations:* hill-walking, music. *Clubs:* Travellers'; New (Edinburgh).

MAITLAND, Air Vice-Marshal Percy Eric, CB 1945; CBE 1951; MVO 1935; AFC 1918; *b* 26 Oct. 1895; *s* of Surgeon-Captain P. E. Maitland, Royal Navy; *m* 1927, Alison Mary Kettlewell; six *s. Educ:* RN Coll., Osborne and Dartmouth. Royal Navy, 1908-18, attached RNAS 1915 for Airships (AFC); transferred to Royal Air Force 1918 as Captain; specialised in Navigation. Served in Egypt and Iraq; Navigator in Far East Flight to Australia, 1928-29; Staff Officer for Royal Review, 1935 (MVO); Singapore, 1937-39, promoted Group Captain; Flying Training Command, 1939-40; Bomber Command, 1940-43; Air Ministry, Director of Operational Training, 1943; AOC No 2 Group, BAOR, 1945; AOC, No 84 Group, BAOR, 1945-47; AOC No 22 Group; Technical Training Command, 1948-50; retired, 1950. JP Somerset, 1952. *Recreation:* fishing. *Address:* 60 Station Road, Wallingford OX10 0JZ. *T:* Wallingford 38921.

MAITLAND, Sir Richard John, 9th Bt, *cr* 1818; farmer; *b* 24 Nov. 1952; *s* of Sir Alexander Keith Maitland, 8th Bt, and of Lavender Mary Jex, *y d* of late Francis William Jex Jackson, Kirkbuddo, Forfar; *S* father, 1963; *m* 1981, Carine, *er d* of J. St G. Coldwell, Somerton, Oxford. *Educ:* Rugby; Exeter Univ. (BA Hons 1975); Edinburgh Sch. of Agriculture. *Heir: b* Robert Ramsay Maitland, *b* 14 July 1956. *Address:* Burnside, Forfar, Angus.

MAITLAND-MAKGILL-CRICHTON; *see* Crichton.

MAITLAND SMITH, Geoffrey; Chief Executive and Deputy Chairman, Sears Holdings plc, since 1978; chartered accountant; *b* 27 Feb. 1933; *s* of Philip John Maitland Smith and Kathleen (*née* Goff). *Educ:* University Coll. Sch., London. Partner, Thornton Baker & Co., Chartered Accountants, 1960-70;

Dir, Sears Holdings plc, 1971; Dep. Chairman: British Shoe Corp. Ltd, 1978-; Lewis's Investment Trust Ltd, 1978-; Selfridges Ltd, 1978-; Garrard & Co. Ltd, 1978-; Mappin & Webb Ltd, 1978-; Asprey & Co. plc, 1980-; Butler Shoe Corp. (USA), 1981-. Mem. Council, University Coll. Sch. Liveryman, Worshipful Co. of Gardeners. *Recreations:* opera, music. *Address:* (office) 40 Duke Street, W1A 2HP. *T:* 01-408 1180. *Club:* Cripplegate Ward.

MAJITHIA, Dr Sir Surendra Singh, Kt 1946; Industrialist; *b* 4 March 1895; *s* of late Hon. Sardar Bahadur Dr Sir Sundar Singh Majithia, CIE, DOL; *m* 1921, Lady Balbir Kaur (*d* 1977), *d* of late General Hazura Singh, Patiala. *Educ:* Khalsa Collegiate High Sch.; Khalsa Coll., Amritsar. Chairman, Saraya Sugar Mills Ltd, Sardarnagar; Senior Managing Partner, Saraya Surkhi Mill, Sardarnagar; Dir, Punjab & Sind Bank Ltd, Amritsar. Member: Khalsa College Council, Amritsar; Akal College Council, Gursagar; UP Fruit Development Board, Lucknow. President, Chairman, etc., of many educational foundations and social activities. Past member, various Advisory and Consultative Cttees. Chairman, Lady Parsan Kaur Charitable Trust (Éducnl Soc.), Sardarnagar; Patron: Wrestling Federation of India; UP Badminton Assoc.; Life Mem., Internal Soc. of Krishna Consciousness; Hon. Mem., Mark Twain Soc., USA; Member, Garden Advisory Cttee, Gorakhpur. Hon. DLitt Gorakhpur, 1970. *Address:* PO Sardarnagar, Dist Gorakhpur, Uttar Pradesh, India. *Clubs:* Gorakhpur, Nepal (Gorakhpur).

MAJOR; *see* Henniker-Major, family name of Baron Henniker.

MAJOR, John; MP (C) Huntingdonshire, since 1979; *b* 29 March 1943; *s* of Thomas Major and Gwendolyn Minny Coates; *m* 1970, Norma Christina Elizabeth (*née* Johnson); one *s* one *d. Educ:* Rutlish. AIB. Banker, Standard Chartered Bank: various executive posts in UK and overseas, 1965-79. Contested (C) St Pancras North (Camden), Feb. 1974 and Oct. 1974; PPS to Ministers of State at the Home Office, 1981-. Member, Lambeth Borough Council, 1968-71 (Chm. Housing Cttee, 1970-71). Jt Sec., Cons. Parly Party Environment Cttee, 1979-; Parly Consultant, Guild of Glass Engravers, 1979-. Mem. Bd, Warden Housing Assoc., 1975-. *Recreations:* opera, cricket. *Address:* Hemingford Grey, Huntingdon, Cambs.

MAJOR, Kathleen, FBA 1977; Professor (part-time) of History, University of Nottingham, 1966-71; Principal of St Hilda's College, Oxford, 1955-65; Hon. Fellow, St Hilda's College, 1965; *b* 10 April 1906; *er d* of late George Major and Gertrude Blow. *Educ:* various private schools; St Hilda's College, Oxford. Honour School of Modern History, 1928; BLitt 1931. Librarian, St Hilda's College, 1931. Archivist to the Bishop of Lincoln, 1936; Lecturer, 1945, subsequently Reader in Diplomatic in the University of Oxford, until July 1955. Hon. Secretary, Lincoln Record Society, 1935-56 and 1965-74, Hon. Gen. Editor, 1935-75. Member Academic Planning Board for the University of Lancaster, 1962, and of Academic Advisory Cttee, 1964-70. Trustee of the Oxford Preservation Trust, 1961-65; a Vice-Pres., RHistS, 1967-71, Hon. Vice-Pres., 1981-; Pres., Lincoln Civic Trust, 1980-. Hon. DLitt Nottingham, 1961. *Publications:* (joint editor with late Canon Foster) Registrum Antiquissimum of the Cathedral Church of Lincoln, vol. IV, 1938, (sole editor) vols V-X, 1940-73; *Acta Stephani Langton,* 1950; articles in English Hist. Review, Journal of Ecclesiastical Hist., etc. *Recreation:* reading. *Address:* 21 Queensway, Lincoln. *Club:* English-Speaking Union.

MAJURY, Maj.-Gen. James Herbert Samuel, CB 1974; MBE 1961; Senior Steward, National Greyhound Racing Club, since 1976; *b* 26 June 1921; *s* of Rev. Dr M. Majury, BA, DD, and Florence (*née* Stuart), Antrim, N Ireland; *m* 1948, Jeanetta Ann (*née* Le Fleming); two *s. Educ:* Royal Academical Institution, Belfast; Trinity College, Dublin. Royal Ulster Rifles, 1940; attached 15 Punjab Regt, 1942; seconded South Waziristan Scouts, 1943-47; Korean War, 1949 (Royal Ulster Rifles); Prisoner of War, Korea, 1950-53 (despatches 1954); Parachute Regiment, 1957-61; Comd Royal Irish Fusiliers, 1961-62; Comd 2nd Infantry Bde, 1965-67; GOC West Midland District, 1970-73. idc 1968. Col. Comdt, The King's Division, 1971-75, Col The Royal Irish Rangers, 1972-77; Hon. Col, 2nd Bn Mercian Volunteers, 1975-79. *Recreations:* golf, racing. *Address:* Hollybrook, Colemans Hatch, Hartfield, E Sussex TN7 4HH. *T:* Forest Row 2489. *Clubs:* Naval and Military, XL.

MAKEPEACE, John, FSIAD, FRSA: freelance furniture designer and maker, since 1961; Founder and Director, The Parnham Trust and The School for Craftsmen in Wood, since 1977; *b* 6 July 1939; *s* of Harold Alfred and Gladys Marjorie Smith; *m* 1964, Ann Sutton (marr. diss. 1979). *Educ:* Denstone Coll., Staffs. Trainee cabinet-maker with Keith Cooper, 1957-59; study tours of Scandinavia 1957, N America 1961, Italy 1968, W Africa 1972, N America 1974. Most work in private collections; exceptions incl. Oxford Centre for Management Studies, 1967; Attlee Room, Toynbee Hall, 1971; Keble College, Oxford, 1972-76; Reed Internat., 1980; British Caledonian Airways, 1981; RSA, 1981. *Museums:* Cardiff; Leeds; Fitzwilliam, Cambridge; Museum für Kunsthandwerk, Frankfurt; Victoria and Albert. Mounted exhibn, Twelve Designer Crafsmen, Coventry, 1963. *Exhibitions:* New Art Centre, London, 1971; Science Centre, Toronto, 1974; Mitsukoshi, Tokyo, 1975; Wohndesign, Dusseldorf, 1975; Fine Art Soc., London, 1977; Museum für Kunsthandwerk, Frankfurt, 1978; Interieur, Kortrijk, Belgium, 1978; Parnham at Nat. Theatre, 1980; Inscape, Barbican Centre, 1981; Parnham at Royal Show, 1981, 1982. *Consultancy/Lecture Tours:* develt of wood products in India, 1975 (EEC); furniture designs for Jammu and Kashmir Govt Industries, 1977 (Commonwealth Secretariat); design education, Belgrade Univ., 1978 (British

Council); Chm., Wood Programme, World Crafts Conf., Kyoto, Japan, 1979; Internat. Wood Turning Seminar at Parnham, 1980, 1982; Lecture tour of Australia, 1980 (Aust. Crafts Bd and Headmasters' Conf.); Selector for The Maker's Eye, 1982. Established workshops at Farnborough Barn, Banbury, 1964; moved to Parnham, 1976. Artist in Context, Study Day at V&A Mus., 1979. Mem., Crafts Adv. Cttee, 1972-77. *Television Films:* Made by Makepeace (dir, Sir Peter Hall), 1975; History of English Furniture, 1978; Heritage in Danger, 1979; First Edition (dir, Tony Palmer), 1980; Touch Wood (dir, John Read), 1982. Winner, Observer Kitchen Comp., 1971; Six Guild Marks, Worshipful Co. of Furniture Makers, 1977. *Address:* Parnham House, Beaminster, Dorset DT8 3NA. *T:* Beaminster 862204.

MAKGILL, family name of **Viscount of Oxfuird.**

MAKGILL CRICHTON MAITLAND, Major John David; Lord-Lieutenant of Renfrewshire, since 1980; *b* 10 Sept. 1925; *e s* of late Col Mark Edward Makgill Crichton Maitland, CVO, DSO, DL, JP, The Island House, Wilton, Salisbury, Wilts, and late Patience Irene Fleetwood Makgill Crichton Maitland (*née* Fuller); *m* 1954, Jean Patricia, *d* of late Maj.-Gen. Sir Michael Creagh, KBE, MC, Pigeon Hill, Homington, Salisbury; one *s* one *d. Educ:* Eton. Served War, 1944-45, Grenadier Guards. Continued serving until 1957 (temp. Major, 1952; retd 1957), rank Captain (Hon. Major). Governor, West of Scotland Agricl Coll.; Renfrew CC, 1961-75. DL Renfrewshire 1962, Vice-Lieutenant 1972-80. *Address:* Houston House, Houston, by Johnstone, Renfrewshire. *T:* Bridge of Weir 612545.

MAKHULU, Most Rev. Walter Paul Khotso; *see* Central Africa, Archbishop of.

MAKIN, Frank; Chief Inspector, Department of Education and Science, 1976-79; *b* 29 Oct. 1918; *s* of Tom Kay Makin and Phyllis H. Makin (*née* Taylor); *m* 1949, Marjorie Elizabeth Thomasson; three *d. Educ:* Bolton Municipal Secondary Sch.; Corpus Christi Coll., Cambridge (MA). Asst Master, Cheadle Hulme Sch., Burnley Grammar Sch., and Stretford Grammar Sch., 1941-56; Headmaster, South Hunsley Co. Secondary Sch., Yorks, 1956-62; HM Inspector of Schools, 1962-; Divisional Inspector, 1970-76. *Recreations:* languages, gardening. *Address:* 127 Hookfield, Epsom KT19 8JH. *T:* Epsom 40872.

MAKIN, Hon. Norman John Oswald; AO 1980; *b* Petersham, NSW, Australia, 31 March 1889; *s* of John Hulme Makin and Elizabeth Makin; *m* 1932, Ruby Florence Jennings; two *s. Educ:* Superior Public Sch., Broken Hill. Member Commonwealth Parliament for Hindmarsh, 1919-46; Member Joint Cttee Public Accounts, 1922-26; Member Select Cttee case ex-Gunner Yates; Temp. Chairman of Cttees, 1923-29; Speaker House of Representatives, Commonwealth of Australia, 1929-32; Member Advisory War Council, 1940; Ministry for Navy and Munitions, Australia, 1941-46; Minister for Aircraft Production, 1945-46. Australian Ambassador to United States, 1946-51. MP for Sturt, 1954-Nov. 1955, for Bonython Division, Dec. 1955-Nov. 1963, Commonwealth Parliament; retired. President Labour Party, 1936; Secretary Federal Parliamentary Labour Party, 1931; Member of Delegation to United Kingdom, King George V Jubilee in 1935 and to King George VI Coronation in 1937; 1st President of Security Council, Jan. 1946, and President, 1947; Leader, Australian Delegation to United Nations; Leader, Australian Delegation to ILO Conference, San Francisco. Alternate Governor, International Bank and International Monetary Fund; Member, Far Eastern Commn, 1947-48. Hon. Doctor of Laws, Univ. of Syracuse. *Publications:* A Progressive Democracy; Federal Labour Leaders, 1961. *Address:* Flat 219, 7 Raymond Grove, Glenelg, SA 5045, Australia.

MAKINS, family name of **Baron Sherfield.**

MAKINS, Sir Paul (Vivian), 4th Bt *cr* 1903; Company Director, 1962-73; *b* 12 Nov. 1913; *yr s* of Sir Paul Makins, 2nd Bt, and Gladys Marie (*d* 1919), *d* of William Vivian, Queen's Gate, London; *S* brother, 1969; *m* 1945, Maisie, *d* of Major Oswald Pedley and widow of Major C. L. J. Bowen, Irish Guards; no *c. Educ:* Eton Coll.; Trinity Coll. Cambridge (MA). Commissioned in Welsh Guards, 1935. Served War of 1939-45: France, 1940; Italy, 1944-45. Dir and Sec. Vitalba Co. Ltd (Gibraltar), 1962-73; Dir, Compañía Rentistica SA (Tangier), 1967-73. Kt of Magistral Grace, SMO Malta, 1955; JP Gibraltar, 1964-70. *Heir:* none. *Address:* Casas Cortijo 135, Sotogrande, Provincia de Cadiz, Spain. *Clubs:* Cavalry and Guards, Pratt's.
See also Archbishop of Southwark.

MAKINSON, William, CBE 1977; Director, the Grundy Group, since 1980; *b* 11 May 1915; *s* of Joshua Makinson and Martha (*née* Cunliffe); *m* 1952, Helen Elizabeth Parker; one *s* three *d. Educ:* Ashton-in-Makerfield Grammar Sch.; Manchester Univ. Asst Lecturer, Electronics, Manchester Univ., 1935-36; Education Officer, RAF Cranwell, 1936-39; RAE Farnborough, 1939-52; Hon. Squadron-Ldr, RAF, 1943-45; Superintendent, Blind Landing Experimental Unit, 1952-55; Defence Research Policy Staff, 1955-56; Managing Director, General Precision Systems Ltd, 1956-64; Group Jt Managing Director, Pullin, 1964-65; Mem., NRDC, 1967-80 (Man. Dir, 1974-80, Chief Exec., Engrg Dept, 1965-74). *Publications:* papers to Royal Aeronautical Society. *Recreation:* golf. *Address:* Ridings, Snows Paddock, Snows Ride, Windlesham, Surrey. *T:* Ascot 22431. *Clubs:* Athenæum, Directors.

MAKKAWI, Dr Khalil; Chevalier, Order of Cedars, Lebanon; Ambassador of Lebanon to the Court of St James's, since 1978 and to the Republic of Ireland, since 1979; *b* 15 Jan. 1930; *s* of Abdel Basset Makkawi and Rosa Makkawi; *m* 1958, Zahira Sibaei; one *s* one *d. Educ:* Amer. Univ. of Beirut (BA Polit. Science); Cairo Univ. (MA Polit. Science); Colombia Univ., NY, USA (PhD Internat. Relations). Joined Lebanese Min. of Foreign Affairs, 1957; UN Section at Min., 1957-59; Attaché to Perm. Mission of Lebanon to UN, New York, 1959, Dep. Perm. Rep., 1961-64; First Sec., Washington, 1964-66; Chief of Internat. Relations Dept, Min. of For. Affairs, Beirut, 1967-70; Counsellor, London, 1970-71; Minister Plenipotentiary, London, 1971-73; Ambassador to German Democratic Republic, 1973-78. Mem., Lebanese Delegn to UN Gen. Assembly Meetings, 14th-32nd Session. *Recreations:* sports, music. *Address:* 21 Kensington Palace Gardens, W8 4QM. *T:* 01-229 7265. *Clubs:* Travellers', Hurlingham, Royal Automobile.

MALAMUD, Bernard; Writer; Member, Division of Literature, Bennington College, since 1961; *b* 26 April 1914; *s* of Max and Bertha Malamud; *m* 1945, Ann de Chiara; one *s* one *d. Educ:* The City Coll., New York; Columbia Univ. Taught at Oregon State Coll., 1949-61, while writing first four books. Visiting Lecturer, Harvard Univ., 1966-68. Partisan Review Fiction Fellowship, 1956; Ford Foundation Fellowship, Humanities and Arts Program, 1959-60; Member: Amer. Acad. and Institute of Arts and Letters, 1964; American Academy of Arts and Sciences, 1967; Pres., Amer. PEN Center, 1979-81. Governor's Award for Excellence in The Arts, Vermont Council on the Arts, 1979; Creative Arts Award for Fiction, Brandeis Univ. *Publications:* The Natural, 1952; The Assistant, 1957 (Rosenthal Prize, Daroff Memorial Award, 1958); The Magic Barrel (short stories), 1958 (National Book Award, 1959); A New Life, 1961; Idiots First (short stories), 1963; The Fixer, 1966 (National Book Award and Pulitzer Prize for Fiction, 1967); Pictures of Fidelman, 1969; The Tenants, 1971; Rembrandt's Hat (short stories), 1973; Dubin's Lives, 1979. *Recreations:* reading, walking, music, poker, art galleries. *Address:* c/o Russell and Volkening, 551 Fifth Avenue, New York, NY 10017, USA.

MALAND, David; High Master, Manchester Grammar School, since 1978; *b* 6 Oct. 1929; *s* of Rev. Gordon Albert Maland and Florence Maud Maland (*née* Bosence); *m* 1953, Edna Foulsham; two *s. Educ:* Kingswood Sch.; Wadham Coll., Oxford. BA 2nd class Mod. Hist., 1951; MA 1957; Robert Herbert Meml Prize Essay, 1959. Nat. service commn RAF, 1951-53; Asst Master, Brighton Grammar Sch., 1953-56; Senior History Master, Stamford Sch., 1957-66; Headmaster: Cardiff High Sch., 1966-68; Denstone Coll., 1969-78. *Publications:* Europe in the Seventeenth Century, 1966; Culture and Society in Seventeenth Century France, 1970; (trans.) La Guerre de Trente Ans, by Pagès, 1971; Europe in the Sixteenth Century, 1973; Europe at War, 1600-1650, 1980; articles and reviews in History. *Address:* 143 Old Hall Lane, Fallowfield, Manchester M14 6HL. *Club:* East India, Devonshire, Sports and Public Schools.

MALCOLM, Lt-Col Arthur William Alexander, CVO 1954 (MVO 1949); *b* 31 May 1903; *s* of Major Charles Edward Malcolm, London; *m* 1928, Hester Mary, *d* of S. F. Mann, Lawrenny-Caramut, Victoria, Australia; two *s. Educ:* Repton. 2nd Lieut. Welsh Guards, 1924; psc 1938; served War of 1939-45 (POW); Lieut-Colonel, 1945; comd 3rd, 2nd and 1st Bn, Welsh Guards, 1945-49. ADC to Governor of Victoria, Australia, 1926-28. Asst Military Attaché, British Embassy, Paris, 1950-52; retired from Army, 1952. Private Secretary to Governor of South Australia, 1953-55; Queen's Foreign Service Messenger, 1955-68. *Recreations:* golf, shooting, fishing. *Address:* Faraway, Sandwich Bay, Kent. *T:* Sandwich 612054. *Clubs:* Army and Navy; Royal St George's Golf, Prince's Golf (Sandwich).

MALCOLM, Sir David (Peter Michael), 11th Bt *cr* 1665; *b* 7 July 1919; *s* of Sir Michael Albert James Malcolm, 10th Bt, and Hon. Geraldine Margot (*d* 1965), *d* of 10th Baron Digby; *S* father, 1976; *m* 1959, Hermione, *d* of Sir David Home, Bt, *qv*; one *d. Educ:* Eton; Magdalene Coll., Cambridge (BA). Served with Scots Guards, 1939-46 (Major). Mem., Inst. of Chartered Accountants of Scotland, 1949. Member: Stock Exchange, 1956-80; Stock Exchange Council, 1971-80. *Recreations:* shooting, golf. *Heir: cousin* Lt-Col Arthur William Alexander Malcolm, *qv. Address:* Whiteholm, Gullane, East Lothian EH31 2BD. *Clubs:* Pratt's, City of London; New (Edinburgh).

MALCOLM, Dugald, CMG 1966; CVO 1964; TD 1945; HM Diplomatic Service, retired; Minister to the Holy See, 1975-77; *b* 22 Dec. 1917; 2nd *s* of late Maj.-Gen. Sir Neill Malcolm, KCB, DSO, and Lady (Angela) Malcolm; *m* 1957, Patricia Anne Gilbert-Lodge (*d* 1976), *widow* of Captain Peter Atkinson-Clark; one *d* one *step d. Educ:* Eton; New Coll., Oxford. Served Argyll and Sutherland Highlanders, 1939-45; discharged wounded. Appointed Foreign Office, Oct. 1945; Served Lima, Bonn, Seoul; HM Vice-Marshal of the Diplomatic Corps, 1957-65; Ambassador: to Luxembourg, 1966-70; to Panama, 1970-74. Member Queen's Body Guard for Scotland (Royal Company of Archers). *Address:* White Court, Alfriston, near Polegate, East Sussex. *T:* Alfriston 870 404. *Club:* Travellers'.

MALCOLM, Ellen, RSA 1976 (ARSA 1968); *b* 28 Sept. 1923; *d* of John and Ellen Malcolm; *m* 1962, Gordon Stewart Cameron, *qv. Educ:* Aberdeen Acad.; Gray's Sch. of Art, Aberdeen. DA (Aberdeen) 1944. Teacher of Art, Aberdeen Grammar Sch. and Aberdeen Acad., 1945-62. Paintings in public galleries in Southend, Aberdeen, Perth, Milngavie, Edinburgh, and in private collections in Scotland, England, Wales, America, Switzerland, Sweden and

Australia. Chalmers-Jervise Prize, 1946; Guthrie Award, Royal Scottish Acad., 1952; David Cargill Award, Royal Glasgow Inst., 1973. *Recreation:* reading. *Address:* 7 Auburn Terrace, Invergowrie, Dundee DD2 5AB. *T:* Invergowrie 318.

MALCOLM, George (John), CBE 1965; musician; *b* London, 28 Feb. 1917; *o s* of George Hope Malcolm, Edinburgh, and Johanna Malcolm. *Educ:* Wimbledon Coll.; Balliol Coll., Oxford (Scholar); Royal College of Music (Scholar). MA, BMus (Oxon). Served in RAFVR, 1940–46. Master of the Cathedral Music, Westminster Cathedral, 1947–59, training unique boys' choir for which Benjamin Britten wrote Missa Brevis, Op. 63. Now mainly known as harpsichordist, pianist and conductor (making frequent concert tours). Cobbett Medal, Worshipful Company of Musicians, 1960; Hon. RAM, 1961; Hon. Fellow, Balliol Coll., Oxford, 1966; FRCM 1974; Hon. DMus, Sheffield, 1978. Papal Knight of the Order of St Gregory the Great, 1970. *Address:* 99 Wimbledon Hill Road, SW19 7QT. *T:* 01-947 6672.

MALCOLM, Gerald; *see* Malcolm, W. G.

MALCOLM, Prof. John Laurence; Regius Professor of Physiology, University of Aberdeen, 1959–75, retired; *b* 28 Aug. 1913; *s* of late Professor J. Malcolm, Dunedin, New Zealand; *m* 1st, 1940, Sylvia Bramston (*d* 1958), *d* of late Basil B. Hooper, Auckland, New Zealand; one *s* one *d* ; 2nd, 1961, Margaret Irvine Simpson (*d* 1967), *d* of late Colonel J. C. Simpson, Skene, Aberdeenshire. *Publications:* contributions to the Proceedings of Royal Society, Journal of Physiology, Journal of Neuro-physiology. *Address:* Heath Cottage, Crathie, Aberdeenshire AB3 5UP.

MALCOLM, Kenneth Robert, CBE 1964; *b* 17 Dec. 1908; 2nd *s* of Ronald Malcolm, Walton Manor, Walton-on-the Hill, Surrey; *m* 1950, Iris Lilian Knowles; two *s* one *d. Educ:* Eton; New College, Oxford. Indian Civil Service, 1932–47; Home Civil Service (Ministry of National Insurance, subseq. Dept of Health and Social Security), 1947–73; Under-Sec., 1969, retd 1973. *Address:* Ferndale, Dry Arch Road, Sunningdale, Ascot, Berks SL5 0DB. *T:* Ascot 22946. *Club:* Travellers'.

MALCOLM, (William) Gerald, CB 1976; MBE 1943; Member, Planning Appeals Commission (NI), since 1978; Permanent Secretary, Department of the Environment for Northern Ireland, 1974–76; *b* Stirling, 19 Dec. 1916; *s* of late John and Jane M. Malcolm; *m* 1949, Margaret Cashel. *Educ:* High Sch. of Stirling; Glasgow Univ. (MA) (Hons French and German, 1945); London Univ. (BA) (Hons French and German, 1945). Served War, Army, 1939–46: RASC and Intelligence Corps; Major, 1944; Africa and Italy Stars, 1939–45. Min. of Home Affairs for NI, Asst Principal, 1948; Min. of Agriculture for NI: Principal, 1956; Asst Sec., 1962; Sen. Asst Sec., 1966; Dep. Sec., 1970. *Recreations:* angling, swimming, ornithology, nature.

MALCOLMSON, Kenneth Forbes, MA, BMus (Oxon), FRCO; Precentor and Director of Music, Eton College, 1956–71; *b* 29 April 1911; *m* 1972, Mrs B. Dunhill. Organ Scholar, Exeter Coll., Oxford, 1931–35; Commissioner, Royal School of Church Music, 1935–36; Temporary Organist, St Alban's Cathedral, 1936–37; Organist, Halifax Parish Church, 1937–38; Organist and Master of the Music, Newcastle Cathedral, 1938–55. *Recreations:* gardening, swimming, walking. *Address:* The Lecturage, Newland, Coleford, Glos. *T:* Dean 32808.

MALDEN; *see* Scott-Malden.

MALDEN, Viscount; Frederick Paul de Vere Capell; Curriculum Co-ordinator, Skerton County Junior School, Lancaster, since 1981; *b* 29 May 1944; *s* and *heir* of 10th Earl of Essex, *qv. Educ:* Skerton Boys' School; Lancaster Royal Grammar School; Didsbury College of Education, Manchester; Northern School of Music. ACP, LLCM(TD). Assistant teacher, Marsh County Junior School, 1966–72; Deputy Head, 1972–75; Acting Head, 1975–77; Deputy Head Teacher, Marsh County Primary School, 1977–78; Head Teacher, Cockerham Parochial CE School, Cockerham, Lancaster, 1979–80. Chairman, Lancaster and District Schools' Music Festival. FRSA. *Recreations:* music, hi-fi. *Address:* 35 Pinewood Avenue, Brookhouse, Lancaster LA2 9NU.

MALE, Peter John Ellison, CMG 1967; MC 1945; HM Diplomatic Service, retired; Ambassador to Czechoslovakia, 1977–80; *b* 22 Aug. 1920; *s* of late H. J. G. Male and late Mrs E. A. Male; *m* 1947, Patricia Janet Payne; five *s* two *d. Educ:* Merchant Taylors' Sch.; Emmanuel Coll., Cambridge. HM Forces, 1940–45. HM Foreign Service (now HM Diplomatic Service), 1946; served in: Damascus, 1947–49; Wahnerheide, 1949–53; London, 1953–55; Guatemala City, 1955–57; Washington, 1957–60; London, 1960–62; Oslo, 1962–66; Bonn, 1966–70; New Delhi, 1970–74; Asst Under-Sec. of State, FCO, 1974–77. *Recreations:* gadgets, gardening. *Address:* Swinley Edge, Coronation Road, Ascot, Berks. *Club:* United Oxford & Cambridge University.

MALENKOV, Georgi Maximilianovich; Manager of Ust-Kamenogorsk Hydro-Electric Station, 1957–63, retired; *b* Orenburg, 1901; *m* 1st (marr. diss.); 2nd, Elena Khrushcheva. *Educ:* Moscow Higher Technical Coll. Member of the Communist Party, 1920–; Member of Organisation Bureau of Central Cttee of the Communist Party, 1934; Member Cttee for State Defence, 1941; Member Cttee for Economic Rehabilitation of Liberated Districts, 1946; Dep.-Chairman, Council of Ministers, 1946; Dep.-Chairman,

Council of Ministers of the Soviet Union, 1955–57 (Dep.-Chairman, 1946, Chairman, 1953–55); Minister of Electric Power Stations, 1955–57. Holds title Hero of Socialist Labour, Hammer and Sickle Gold Medal, Order of Lenin (twice).

MALET, Colonel Sir Edward William St Lo, 8th Bt, *cr* 1791; OBE 1953; 8th King's Royal Irish Hussars; retired; *b* 27 Nov. 1908; *o s* of Sir Harry Charles Malet, DSO, OBE, 7th Bt and Mildred Laura (*d* 1951), *d* of Captain H. S. Swiney, Gensing House, St Leonards; *S* father, 1931; *m* 1935, Baroness Benedicta Maasburg (*d* 1979), *e d* of Baron William von Maasburg; one *s* two *d. Educ:* Dover Coll.; Christ Church, Oxford. BA. Dep.-Chief Civil Affairs Officer, HQ, British Troops, Egypt, 1953–55. President Bridgwater Division, Conservative Assoc., 1959. High Sheriff of Somerset, 1966. *Heir: s* Harry Douglas St Lo Malet, late Lieut, The Queen's Royal Irish Hussars, now Special Reserve [*b* 26 Oct. 1936; *m* 1967, Julia Harper, Perth, WA; one *s. Educ:* Downside; Trinity Coll., Oxford]. *Address:* Chargot, Washford, Somerset. *Club:* Cavalry and Guards.

MALHERBE, Ernst G., MA, PhD; Hon. LLD Universities of: Cambridge, Queen's (Kingston, Ont), Melbourne, McGill, Capetown, Rhodes, Natal, Witwatersrand, St Andrews; Principal and Vice-Chancellor, University of Natal, Pietermaritzburg and Durban, 1945–65; *b* OFS, 8 Nov. 1895; *s* of late Rev. E. G. Malherbe, Villiersdorp, Cape Province, French Huguenot descent; *m* Janie A., *d* of Rev. Paul Nel, Moderator of Dutch Reformed Church, Transvaal; three *s* one *d. Educ:* Stellenbosch Univ., Stellenbosch, CP (BA, Hons, MA in Philosophy); Columbia Univ., New York (MA and PhD in Education). Union Government Scholarship for 2 years to study Education overseas; Oxford, The Hague, Amsterdam, Germany, etc.; 3 years in succession H. B. Webb Research Scholar for overseas Research in Educational Administration; Fellow of Teachers Coll., Columbia Univ., 1923–34; Chalmers Memorial Prize for Essay on Educational Administration, 1923; invited as special SA representative to Centenary meeting of British Assoc., London, 1931; teacher at Cape Town Training Coll.; Lecturer in Educational Psychology, University of Stellenbosch; Senior Lecturer in Education, University of Cape Town, 5 years; Chief Investigator Education Section Carnegie Poor White Commission of Research, 1928–32; Member of Government Commission to investigate Native Education in South Africa, 1935; Director, National Bureau of Educational and Social Research for SA, 1929–39; Sec. Government Commission on Medical Training in S Africa, 1938. Director of Census and Statistics for Union of South Africa, 1939–40; (Lieut-Col) Director of Military Intelligence, S African Army and Director Army Education Services, 1940–45. Member of Social and Economic Planning Council, 1946–50; of National Council for Social Research, 1945–50; Chairman National War Histories Cttee, 1945–49; President SA Assoc. for the Advancement of Science, 1950–51; President SA Institute of Race Relations, 1966–67; Mem., Govt Commn on Financial Relations between Central Govt and Provinces, 1960–64. Simon Biesheuvel Medal for Study of Man, 1969. *Publications:* Education in S Africa, 1652–1922, 1925; Chapters on S Africa in Year-books of Education, 1932–56; Education and the Poor White, 1929; articles in Chambers's Encyclopaedia, Standard Encyclopaedia for Southern Africa; numerous articles in Educational and Scientific Journals; Carnegie Commission's Poor White Report on Education, 1932; Education in a Changing Empire, 1932; Educational Adaptations in a Changing Society (Editor), 1937; Entrance Age of University Students in Relation to Success, 1938; Whither Matric?, 1938; Educational and Social Research in SA, 1939; The Bilingual School, 1943; Race Attitudes and Education, 1946; Our Universities and the Advancement of Science, 1951; The Autonomy of our Universities and Apartheid, 1957; Education for Leadership in Africa, 1960; Problems of School Medium in a Bilingual Country, 1962; Into the 70's: Education and the Development of South Africa's Human Resources, 1966; The Need for Dialogue, 1967; The Nemesis of Docility, 1968; Bantu Manpower and Education, 1969; Differing Values, 1973; Education in South Africa, 1923–1975, 1977; Never a Dull Moment, 1980. *Recreations:* swimming; Full Blue, Stellenbosch University; Half Blue, Capetown University; captained Hockey Team representing CP at inter-provincial tournament. *Address:* By-die-See, Salt Rock, Umhlali, Natal, South Africa. *Club:* Durban (Durban).

MALIK, Bidhubhusan; *b* 11 Jan. 1895; *s* of Raibahadur Chandrasekhar Malik, Chief Judge, Benares State; *m* 1916, Leelabati, *d* of Saratkumar Mitra, Calcutta; two *s. Educ:* Central Hindu Coll., Benares (graduated, 1917); Ewing Christian Coll. (MA in Economics, 1919); Allahabad Univ. (LLB 1919); LLD (*hc*), Saugur Univ. Vakil, Allahabad High Court, 1919; started practice in the civil courts in Benares; left for England in Sept. 1922; called to Bar, Lincoln's Inn, 1923; joined Allahabad High Court Bar, 1924; Member of Judicial Cttee of Benares State, 1941; Special Counsel for Income Tax Dept, 1943; Judge, Allahabad High Court, 1944; Chief Justice, High Court, Allahabad, Dec. 1947; thereafter Chief Justice, UP, from 26 July 1948–55, excepting 3 March–1 May 1949, when acted as Governor, Uttar Pradesh. Commissioner for Linguistic Minorities in India, 1957–62. Member: Constitutional Commission for the Federation of Malaya, 1956–57; Air Transport Council of India, 1955–62; National Integration Commn, India. Constitutional Adviser to Mr Jomo Kenyatta and the Kenya African National Union, Lancaster House Conference, London, 1961–62; Constitutional Expert for Republic of Congo appointed by UNO, Aug.–Oct. 1962; Constitutional Adviser to Kenya Government, Kenya Independence Conference, Lancaster House, Sept.–Oct. 1963; Adviser, Mauritius Constitutional Conference, London, Sept.–Nov. 1965. Vice-Chancellor, Calcutta Univ., 1962–68 (Life-Mem. Senate);

President: Jagat Taran Educn Soc., 1924–; Jagat Taran Degree Coll., 1924–; Jagat Taran Inter Coll., 1924–; Jagat Taran Golden Jubilee Eng. Med. Sch. and Hindi Med. Primary Sch., 1924–; Harijan Ashram Degree Coll., Allahabad, 1968–. Former Mem. Council, Ewing Christian Coll., Pres., Old Boys' Assoc., 1976–. Founder Mem., Lions Club, Allahabad, 1959-60; Rotary Club: Pres., Allahabad; Mem., Allahabad and Calcutta. Founder President: Golf Club, Allahabad, 1949-55; Allahabad Badminton Assoc., 1949-55. *Address:* 23 Muir Road, Allahabad, India.

MALIK, Sardar Hardit Singh, CIE 1941; OBE 1938; Indian Diplomat, retired, 1957; *b* 23 Nov. 1894; *s* of Malik Mohan Singh and Lajanwanti; *m* 1919, Prakash; one *s* two *d. Educ:* Eastbourne Coll.; Balliol Coll., Oxford, England. BA Hons in Mod. Hist., 1915. Served with French Army on Western Front, 1916. Fighter Pilot in RFC, 1917-18 (wounded in air combat over France, 1917); served in RAF, France, Italy and in home defence of UK. Entered ICS; Asst Commissioner, Punjab, 1922-23; Deputy Commissioner, Punjab, 1924-30; Dep. Trade Commissioner, London and Hamburg, 1931-34; Dep. Secretary Government of India, Commerce Dept, 1934-36; Joint Secretary, Government of India, Commerce Dept, 1937; Indian Government Trade Commissioner, New York, 1938; Delegate to International Cotton Conf., Washington, 1939, International Labour Office Conf., New York, 1940, UN Food Conf., Hotsprings, Virginia, 1943, and UN Relief Conf., Atlantic City, USA, 1943. Prime Minister, Patiala, 1944-47. Leader Indian States Industrial Delegation to UK and USA, 1945-46; represented Government of India at First and Second Sessions of Prep. Cttee of UN Conf. on Trade and Employment in London, Nov. 1946, and Geneva, April 1947, respectively. Leader Indian Delegation to UN Conf. on Trade and Employment, Havana, Nov. 1947; High Commissioner for India in Canada, 1947-49; Indian Ambassador to France, 1949-56, also Indian Minister to Norway, 1950-56. President, 3rd General Assembly of International Civil Aviation Organisation, Montreal, 1949; Leader of Indian Delegation to UN General Assembly, Paris, 1952. Grand Officier, Légion d'Honneur, 1954. *Recreations:* golf, cricket and tennis. *Address:* Palam Marg, Vasant Vihar, New Delhi, India. *Clubs:* Imperial Gymkhana (New Delhi); Delhi Golf; Pine Valley Golf (USA).

MALIM, Comdr David Wentworth, RN, retd; Director, Marconi Space & Defence Systems Ltd, retired 1982; *b* 28 April 1914; *s* of Frederick Blagden Malim and Amy Gertrude Malim; *m* 1939, Theodora Katharine Thackwell Lewis; one *s* two *d. Educ:* RNC, Dartmouth; RNEC, Keyham. Engineer Officer: HMS Cumberland, 1936-38; HMS Edinburgh, 1939-40; RNATE Torpoint, 1940-42; Ordnance Engineer Officer: HMS Warspite, 1943-44; HMS Excellent, 1944-46; Staff, BJSM, Washington, 1947-49; Naval Ordnance Dept, Admiralty, 1949-54; retd as Comdr (E) at own request. Laurence Scott & Electromotors Ltd, 1954-59; Manager, Lancashire Dynamo Co., 1959-61; Jt Man. Dir, Elliot Space & Weapon Automation Ltd, 1962-70; Chm., Marconi Space & Defence Systems Ltd, 1970-78. Pres., Electronic Engrg Assoc., 1975-76. *Recreation:* fishing. *Address:* Manor Mead, Great Chesterford, Saffron Walden, Essex CB10 1PL. *T:* Saffron Walden 30363. *See also* Hon. Sir Martin Nourse.

MALIM, Rear-Adm. Nigel Hugh, CB 1971; MVO 1960; FIMechE; FIMarE; *b* 5 April 1919; *s* of late John Malim, Pebmarsh, and Brenda Malim; *m* 1944, Moonyeen, *d* of late William and Winefride Maynard; two *s* one *d. Educ:* Weymouth Coll.; RNEC Keyham. Cadet, RN, 1936; HMS Manchester, 1940-41; HMS Norfolk, 1942; RNC Greenwich, 1943-45; HMS Jamaica, 1945-47; Staff of RNEC, 1948-50; Admty, 1951-54; HMS Triumph, 1954-56; Admty, 1956-58; HM Yacht Britannia, 1958-60; District Overseer, Scotland, 1960-62; Asst, and later Dep., Dir Marine Engrg, 1962-65; idc 1966; Captain, RNEC Manadon, 1967-69; Chief Staff Officer Technical to C-in-C, W Fleet, 1969-71, retd. *Recreations:* offshore racing and cruising. *Address:* The Old Vicarage, Caistor, Lincoln LN7 6UG. *Clubs:* Royal Ocean Racing, Royal Naval Sailing Association.

MALIN, Peter; *see* Conner, Rearden.

MALLABAR, Sir John (Frederick), Kt 1969; FCA; Senior Partner, J. F. Mallabar & Co., Chartered Accountants, 1929-80; *b* 19 July 1900; *e s* of Herbert John Mallabar and Gertrude Mallabar, *d* of Hugh Jones, Barrow; *m* 1st, 1931, Henrietta, *d* of George Goodwin-Norris; 2nd, 1949, Annie Emily (Pat), *d* of Charles Mealing, Princes Risborough, and *widow* of Richard Howard Ford, Bodweni, Merionethshire; no *c. Educ:* Sunbury House Sch.; King's Coll., London. Served European War, 1914-18: Inns of Court Regt and 5th KRRC, 1918-19. An Underwriting Member of Lloyd's. Chairman: Ruston & Hornby, 1964-66; Harland and Wolff Ltd, 1966-70. Chm., Cttee on Govt Industrial Establishments, 1968-70. *Recreations:* stalking, salmon fishing. *Address:* 39 Arlington House, St James's, SW1. *Clubs:* Carlton, Flyfishers'.

MALLABY, Christopher Leslie George, CMG 1982; HM Diplomatic Service; HM Minister, Bonn, since 1982; *b* 7 July 1936; *s* of late Brig. A. W. S. Mallaby, CIE, OBE, and Margaret Catherine Mallaby (née Jones); *m* 1961, Pascale Françoise Thierry-Mieg; one *s* three *d. Educ:* Eton; King's Coll., Cambridge. British Delegn to UN Gen. Assembly, 1960; 3rd Sec., British Embassy, Moscow, 1961-63; 2nd Sec., FO, 1963-66; 1st Sec., Berlin, 1966-69; 1st Sec., FCO, 1969-71; Harvard Business Sch., 1971; Dep. Dir, British Trade Develt Office, NY, 1971-74; Counsellor and Head of Chancery, Moscow, 1975-77; Head of Arms Control and Disarmament Dept, 1977-79, Head of

East European and Soviet Dept, 1979-80, Head of Planning Staff, 1980-82, FCO. *Recreations:* fishing, reading, travel. *Address:* c/o Foreign and Commonwealth Office, SW1A 2AH. *Club:* Beefsteak.

MALLE, Louis; Film Director; *b* 30 Oct. 1932; *s* of Pierre Malle and Françoise Béghin; one *s*; *m* 1980, Candice Bergen. *Educ:* Paris Univ.; Institut d'Etudes Politiques. Television, 1953; Asst to Comdt Cousteau on the Calypso, 1953-55. Films: Co-prod. Le Monde du Silence, 1955 (Palme d'Or, Cannes); Collab. techn of Robert Bresson for Un Condamné a mort s'est echappé, 1956; Author and Producer of: Ascenseur pour l'échafaud, 1957 (Prix Louis-Delluc, 1958); Les Amants, 1958 (Prix spécial du Jury du Festival de Venise, 1958); Zazie dans le métro, 1960; Vie privée, 1962; Le Feu Follet (again, Prix spécial, Venise, 1963); Viva Maria, 1965 (Grand Prix du Cinema français); Le Voleur, 1966; Histoires extraordinaires (sketch), 1968; Inde 68, 1968; Calcutta, 1969 (prix de la Fraternité; Phantom India, 1969; Le Souffle au Coeur, 1971 (nominated Best Screenplay, US Acad. Awards, 1972); Humain, trop Humain, 1972; Place de la République, 1973; Lacombe Lucien, 1974; Black Moon, 1975; Pretty Baby, 1977; Atlantic City, 1979 (Jt winner, Golden Lion, Venice Film Fest., 1980; Best Director, BAFTA awards, 1982; nominated Best Film and Best Director, US Acad. Awards, 1982); My Dinner With André, 1981. *Address:* c/o NEF, 15 rue du Louvre, 75001 Paris, France.

MALLET, Hooper Pelgué; Commodore P&OSN Company, 1960-61, retired; *b* 4 June 1901; *s* of Wesley John Mallet and Harriet Anley; *m* 1932, Ethel Margaret Stewart (*d* 1972), Launceston, Tasmania; no *c. Educ:* Oxenford House Sch., Jersey; HMS Worcester. Royal Naval Reserve, 1918-19; joined P&OSN Co., 1919. *Recreations:* chess, bowls. *Address:* 9 Selworthy Avenue, Melbourne, Vic 3167, Australia.

MALLET, Sir Ivo; *see* Mallet, Sir W. I.

MALLET, John Valentine Granville, FSA; FRSA; Keeper, Department of Ceramics, Victoria and Albert Museum, since 1976; *b* 15 Sept. 1930; *s* of Sir Victor Mallet, GCMG, CVO, and Lady Mallet (née Andreae); *m* 1958, Felicity Ann Basset; one *s. Educ:* Winchester Coll.; Balliol Coll., Oxford (BA Modern History). Mil. service in Army: commnd; held temp. rank of full Lieut in Intell. Corps, 1949-50. Messrs Sotheby & Co., London, 1955-62; Victoria and Albert Museum: Asst Keeper, Dept of Ceramics, 1962; Sec. to Adv. Council, 1967-73. Mem., Court of Assistants, Fishmongers' Co., 1970. *Publications:* articles on ceramics in Burlington Magazine, Apollo, Connoisseur, Trans English Ceramic Circle, and Faenza. *Recreation:* tennis. *Address:* Victoria and Albert Museum, South Kensington, SW7 2RL. *T:* 01-589 6371.
See also P. L. V. Mallet.

MALLET, Philip Louis Victor, CMG 1980; HM Diplomatic Service, retired; *b* 3 Feb. 1926; *e s* of late Sir Victor Mallet, GCMG, CVO and of Christiana Jean, *d* of Herman A. Andreae; *m* 1953, Mary Moyle Grenfell Borlase; three *s. Educ:* Winchester; Balliol Coll., Oxford. Army Service, 1944-47. Entered HM Foreign (subseq. Diplomatic) Service, 1949; served in: FO, 1949; Baghdad, 1950-53; FO, 1953-56; Cyprus, 1956-58; Aden, 1958; Bonn, 1958-62; FO, 1962-64; Tunis, 1964-66; FCO, 1967-69; Khartoum, 1969-73; Stockholm, 1973-76; Head of Republic of Ireland Dept, FCO, 1977-78; High Comr in Guyana and non-resident Ambassador to Suriname, 1978-82. *Address:* Wittersham House, Wittersham, Kent TN30 7ED. *Club:* Brooks's.
See also J. V. G. Mallet.

MALLET, Roger; Chairman, North Western Electricity Board, 1972-76, retired; *b* 7 June 1912; British; *m* 1942, Kathleen Els Walker; two *s* two *d. Educ:* Eastbourne Coll.; Trinity Hall, Cambridge. BA Mech. Sci. Tripos; CEng, FIEE. West Cambrian Power Co., S Wales, 1937-40; Buckrose Light & Power Co., Yorks, 1940-45; Shropshire, Worcestershire and Staffordshire Electric Power Co., 1945-47; Midlands Electricity Board, 1948-72. *Recreation:* golf. *Address:* 75 Carrwood, Hale Barns, Cheshire WA15 0ER. *T:* 061-980 3214.

MALLET, Sir (William) Ivo, GBE 1960; KCMG 1951 (CMG 1945); retired as Ambassador to Spain (1954-60); *b* 7 April 1900; *yr s* of late Sir Charles Mallet; *m* 1929, Marie-Angèle, *d* of Joseph Wierusz-Kowalski; two *s* one *d. Educ:* Harrow; Balliol Coll., Oxford. Entered Diplomatic Service, 1925. Served in Constantinople, Angora, London, Berlin, Rome; Asst Private Secretary to Secretary of State for Foreign Affairs, 1938-41; Acting Counsellor in FO, 1941; Counsellor, 1943; Consul-General, Tangier, 1946; Asst Under-Secretary, Foreign Office, 1949; HM Ambassador, Belgrade, 1951. *Address:* Chalet La Combe, Rossinière, Vaud, Switzerland.
See also R. A. Farquharson.

MALLETT, Edmund Stansfield; Director of Applications Programmes, European Space Agency, Paris, since 1981; *b* 21 April 1923; *s* of Cecil Finer Mallett and Elsie Stansfield; *m* 1953, Nancy Campbell; three *s. Educ:* Bradford Grammar Sch.; Leeds Univ. (BSc). CEng, MIEE, MInstMC. Gramophone Co., 1944; Fairey Aviation Co., 1948; Royal Aircraft Establishment: joined 1950; Head, Data Transmission and Processing Div., 1961; Supt, Central Unit for Scientific Photography, 1966; Head, Instrumentation Div., 1968; Head of Instruments Br., Min. of Technol., 1969; Head of Instrumentation and Ranges Dept, RAE, 1971; Director Space, DoI, 1976; Under Sec., and Head of Res. and Technol. Requirements and Space Div., DoI, 1978; Dir, Nat. Maritime

Inst., 1979. *Publications:* papers and articles on instrumentation and measurement. *Recreations:* music, art, genealogy, solving problems. *Address:* West End Farm House, Sandford Road, Aldershot, Hants GU11 3AQ. *T:* Aldershot 22968; 13 boulevard Henri IV, Paris 4, France. *Club:* Athenæum.

MALLETT, Francis Anthony; Chief Executive, South Yorkshire County Council, since 1973; Clerk of the Lieutenancy, South Yorkshire, since 1974; solicitor; *b* 13 March 1924; *s* of Francis Sidney and Marion Mallett; *m* 1956, Alison Shirley Melville, MA; *two s one d. Educ:* Mill Hill; London Univ. (LLB). Army, 1943-47: commissioned, Royal Hampshire Regt, 1944; served in Middle East, Italy and Germany. Staff Captain, 160 (South Wales) Infty Bde, 4th (Infty) Bde and 4th (Guards) Bde, successively, 1946 and 1947. Second Dep. Clerk, Hertfordshire CC, 1966-69; Dep. Clerk, West Riding CC, 1969-74. Chm., Assoc. of Local Authority Chief Execs, 1979-. *Recreations:* gardening, fishing, tennis. *Address:* Aketon Springs, Follifoot, Harrogate, N Yorks. *T:* Spofforth 395. *Club:* Lansdowne.

MALLETT, Ven. Peter, CB 1978; QHC 1973; AKC; Chaplain-General to the Forces, 1974-80; *b* 1925; *s* of Edwin and Beatrice Mallett; *m* 1958, Joan Margaret Bremer; *one s two d. Educ:* King's Coll., London; St Boniface Coll., Warminster, Wilts. Deacon, 1951, priest, 1952. Curate, St Oswald's, Norbury, S London, 1951-54. Joined Royal Army Chaplains' Dept (CF), 1954, and has served overseas in Far East, Aden, Germany (despatches, Malaya, 1957). Has been Senior Chaplain of Aden Brigade, and at RMA, Sandhurst; Dep. Asst Chaplain-General, Berlin, 1968, in N Ireland, 1972; Asst Chaplain-General, BAOR, 1973. Canon, dio. of Europe, 1982. OStJ 1976. Hon. DLitt Geneva Theol Coll., 1976. *Address:* Everleigh Cottage, The Hollow, Shrewton, near Salisbury, Wilts. *T:* Shrewton 620847. *Clubs:* Army and Navy, Naval and Military (Hon.).

MALLINSON, Dennis Hainsworth; Director, National Engineering Laboratory, East Kilbride, Department of Industry, 1974-80; *b* 22 Aug. 1921; *s* of David and Anne Mallinson; *m* 1945, Rowena Mary Brooke; *one s two d. Educ:* Leeds Univ. (BSc). RAE, 1942, early jet engines; Power Jets (R&D) Ltd, later Nat. Gas Turbine Estabt, 1944-63; Min. of Aviation and successors: Asst Dir, 1963; Dir, 1964; Dir–Gen., Engines, Procurement Exec., MoD, 1972-74. Vis. Prof., Strathclyde Univ., 1976-. Member Council: Instn Engrs and Shipbuilders in Scotland, 1977-80; Scottish Assoc. of Metals, 1976-78. *Address:* 19 Rossett Holt Close, Harrogate HG2 9AD.

MALLINSON, Sir Paul; *see* Mallinson, Sir W. P.

MALLINSON, William Arthur, CBE 1978; CBIM; Vice Chairman, Smiths Industries PLC, since 1978; *b* 12 June 1922; *s* of Arthur Mallinson and Nellie Jane Mallinson; *m* 1948, Muriel Ella Parker; *two d. Educ:* William Hulme's Grammar Sch., Manchester; Faculty of Technol., Manchester Univ. (BScTech 1st Cl. Hons). CEng, MIEE, MIMechE, MRAeS; FBIM 1976. Electrical Officer, Tech. Br., RAFVR, 1943-47; Elec. Designer, Electro-Hydraulics Ltd, 1947-51; Ferranti Ltd: Proj. Engr, GW Dept, 1951-55; Chief Engr, Aircraft Equipment Dept, 1955-68; Smiths Industries Ltd, 1968-: Technical Dir, then Gen. Man., Aviation Div.; Divl Man. Dir; Main Bd Dir; Corporate Man. Dir. Mem., Airworthiness Requirements Bd, CAA, 1981-. *Recreations:* music, horticulture. *Address:* Chestnut Cottage, Dukes Covert, Bagshot, Surrey GU19 5HU. *T:* Bagshot 72479.

MALLINSON, Sir (William) Paul, 3rd Bt, *cr* 1935; MA, BM, BCh, FRCP, FRCPsych; Hon. Consulting Psychiatrist to St George's Hospital, SW1; Civilian Consultant Emeritus in Psychiatry to Royal Navy; Chairman, Wm Mallinson & Denny Mott Ltd, 1962-73; *b* 6 July 1909; *s* of Sir William Mallinson, 2nd Bt, and Mabel (*d* 1948), *d* of J. W. Rush, Tunbridge Wells; *S* father, 1944; *m* 1st, 1940, Eila Mary (marr. diss. 1968), *d* of Roland Graeme Guy, Hastings, NZ; *one s two d*; 2nd, 1968, Margaret Cooper, BA, MB, BS, *d* of S. A. Bowden, Barnstaple, Devon. *Educ:* Westminster; Christ Church, Oxford; St Thomas's Hospital. Served RNVR, 1940-46, Surgeon Lieut-Commander. First class Order of the Family, Brunei, 1973. *Heir: s* William John Mallinson [*b* 8 Oct. 1942; *m* 1968, Rosalind Angela (marr. diss.), *o d* of Rollo Hoare, Dogmersfield, Hampshire; *one s one d*]. *Address:* 25 Wimpole Street, W1. *T:* 01-580 7919; Meadow Lea, Northclose Road, Bembridge, Isle of Wight. *T:* 2239. *Clubs:* Athenæum, MCC; Royal Thames Yacht.

MALLORIE, Air Vice-Marshal Paul Richard, CB 1979; AFC 1947; retired, 1980; *b* 8 March 1923; *s* of late Rev. W. T. Mallorie and Margaret Mallorie; *m* 1951, Ursula Joyce Greig; *three s one d. Educ:* King's Sch., Canterbury. Flying Instructor, 1945; India and Middle East, 1946-49; Air Ministry, 1951-53; Staff Coll., 1954; No 139 Sqdn, 1955-57; JSSC, 1960; UK Mil. Advisers' Rep., SEATO, Bangkok, 1963-66; OC RAF Wittering, 1967-68; IDC, 1969; Min. of Defence, 1974-76; Asst Chief of Staff (Info. Systems), SHAPE, 1976-79. Scientific Res. Fellow, NATO, 1981-82; consultant on information systems. *Recreations:* gardening, fishing. *Address:* c/o Barclays Bank, Framlingham, Woodbridge, Suffolk. *Club:* Royal Air Force.

MALLOWS, Surg. Rear-Adm. Harry Russell; Senior Medical Officer, Shell Centre, since 1977; *b* 1 July 1920; *s* of Harry Mallows and Amy Mallows (*née* Law); *m* 1942, Rhona Frances Wyndham-Smith; *one s two d. Educ:* Wrekin Coll.; Christ's Coll., Cambridge (MA, MD); UCH, London. FFCM, FFOM, DPH, DIH. SMO, HM Dockyards at Hong Kong, Sheerness,

Gibraltar and Singapore, 1951-67; Naval MO of Health, Scotland and NI Comd, and Far East Stn, 1964-68; Dir of Environmental Medicine, Inst. of Naval Medicine, 1970-73; Comd MO, Naval Home Comd, 1973-75; QHP, 1974-77; Surgeon Rear-Adm. (Ships and Estabts), 1975-77; retd 1977. *Publications:* articles in BMJ, Royal Naval Med. Service Jl, Proc. RSM. *Recreations:* music, travel. *Address:* 1 Shear Hill, Petersfield, Hants GU31 4BB. *T:* Petersfield 3116. *Club:* Naval.

MALMESBURY, 6th Earl of *cr* 1800; **William James Harris;** TD 1944 (2 Clasps); JP; Baron Malmesbury, 1788; Viscount FitzHarris, 1800; Official Verderer of the New Forest, 1966-74; Lord-Lieutenant and Custos Rotulorum of Hampshire, since 1973; served Royal Hampshire Regt, TA; *b* 18 Nov. 1907; *o s* of 5th Earl and Hon. Dorothy Gough-Calthorpe (*d* 1973), CBE (Lady of Grace, Order of St John of Jerusalem, Order of Mercy, with bar), *y d* of 6th Lord Calthorpe; *S* father 1950; *m* 1932, Hon. Diana Carleton, *e d* of 6th Baron Dorchester, OBE; *one s two d. Educ:* Eton; Trinity Coll., Cambridge (MA). Vice-Pres. of the Cambridge Univ. Conservative Association, 1930; Professional Associate of Surveyors Institution, 1937. Personal Liaison Officer to Min. of Agric., SE Region, 1958-64; Mem., Agric. and Forestry Cttee, RICS, 1953-69; Chm., Hants Agric. Exec. Cttee, 1959-67; Cttee which produced White Paper on the Growing Demand for Water, 1961. Dir, Mid-Southern Water Co., 1961-78. Chairman: Hants Br., Country Landowners Assoc., 1954-56; T&AFA, Hants and IoW, 1960-68; first Chm., Eastern Wessex TA&VRA, 1968-70 (Vice-Pres., 1973-78; Pres., 1978-80); Hon. Col, 65th (M) Signal Regt, R Sigs (TA), 1959-66; Hon. Col, 2nd Bn The Wessex Regt (V), 1970-73. Mem. Basingstoke RDC, 1946-52; County Councillor, Hants CC, 1952; Vice-Lt, Co. Southampton, 1960-73. Master, Worshipful Co. of Skinners, 1952-53. KStJ 1973. Coronation Medal, 1937, 1953; Silver Jubilee Medal, 1977. *Heir: s* Viscount FitzHarris, *qv. Address:* Greywell Hill, Basingstoke, Hants RG25 1DB. *T:* Odiham 2033. *Club:* Royal Yacht Squadron (Vice-Cdre, 1971-77).

MALMESBURY, Bishop Suffragan of, since 1973; **Rt. Rev. Frederick Stephen Temple;** *b* 24 Nov. 1916; *s* of Frederick Charles and Frances Temple; *m* 1947, Joan Catharine Webb; *one s one d* (and one *s* deceased). *Educ:* Rugby; Balliol Coll., Oxford; Trinity Hall, Cambridge; Westcott House, Cambridge. Deacon, 1947, Priest, 1948; Curate, St Mary's, Arnold, Notts, 1947-49; Curate, Newark Parish Church, 1949-51; Rector, St Agnes, Birch, Manchester, 1951-53; Dean of Hong Kong, 1953-59; Senior Chaplain to the Archbishop of Canterbury, 1959-61; Vicar of St Mary's, Portsea, 1961-70; Archdeacon of Swindon, 1970-73. Proctor, Canterbury Convocation, 1964; Hon. Canon, Portsmouth Cathedral, 1965. *Publication:* (ed) William Temple, Some Lambeth Letters, 1942-44, 1963. *Recreations:* gardening, reading. *Address:* Morwena, Mill Lane, Swindon, Wilts SN1 4HQ. *T:* Swindon 35798.

MALONE, Hon. Sir Denis (Eustace Gilbert), Kt 1977; **Hon. Mr Justice Malone;** Puisne Judge of the Commonwealth of the Bahamas, since 1979; *b* 24 Nov. 1922; *s* of Sir Clement Malone, OBE, QC, and Lady Malone; *m* 1963, Diana Malone (*née* Traynor). *Educ:* St Kitts-Nevis Grammar Sch.; Wycliffe Coll., Stonehouse, Glos; Lincoln Coll., Oxford (BA). Called to Bar, Middle Temple, 1950. Royal Air Force, Bomber Comd, 1942-46. Attorney General's Chambers, Barbados, WI, 1953-61, Solicitor-Gen., 1958-61; Puisne Judge: Belize, 1961-65; Trinidad and Tobago, 1966-74; Chief Justice of Belize, 1974-79. *Recreations:* tennis, swimming, walking, bridge, reading. *Address:* c/o The Supreme Court, PO Box N8167, Nassau, Bahamas.

MALONE, Denis George Withers, OBE 1967; retired as Governor, HM Prison, Dartmoor, (1960-66); lately, HM Prison Service; *b* 12 July 1906; *s* of Col William George Malone and Ida Katharine Withers; *m* 1935, Anita Cecilie Sophie Wolfermann. *Educ:* Douai Sch., Woolhampton, Berks. Asst Housemaster, Housemaster, Dep. Gov. (Gov. Cl. IV) and Gov. (Cl. III, II, I) Borstal and Prison Service of England and Wales, 1931-67; Seconded Foreign Office (German Section), Control Officer I sen. Control Officer, CCG Legal Div., Penal Branch, 1947-49; Seconded Colonial Office; Asst Commissioner, Prisons Dept, Kenya, 1950-54; Director of Prisons, Prisons Dept, Cyprus, 1958-60 (despatches). Vice-Pres., Kerikeri and Dist Beautifying Soc. *Recreations:* foreign travel and outdoor activities. *Address:* Kerikeri, Bay of Islands, Northland, New Zealand.

MALONEY, Michael John, JP; MA; Headmaster, Welbeck College, since 1972; *b* 26 July 1932; *s* of John William Maloney and Olive Lois Maloney; *m* 1960, Jancis Ann (*née* Ewing); *one s one d. Educ:* St Alban's Sch.; Trinity Coll., Oxford (MA). Nat. Service, 2nd Lieut RA, served with RWAFF, 1955-57. May & Baker Ltd, 1957-58; Asst Master, Shrewsbury Sch., 1958-66; Sen. Science Master, Housemaster, Dep. Headmaster, Eastbourne Coll., 1966-72. JP Worksop, 1975. *Publication:* (with D. E. P. Hughes) Advanced Theoretical Chemistry, 1964. *Recreations:* Rugby football, ornithology, cryptography. *Address:* Headmaster's House, Welbeck College, Worksop, Notts. *T:* Worksop 476581. *Club:* East India, Devonshire, Sports and Public Schools.

MALOTT, Deane Waldo; President Cornell University, Ithaca, NY, 1951-63, President Emeritus, 1963; Consultant, Association of American Colleges, 1963-70; *b* 10 July 1898; *s* of Michael Harvey Malott and Edith Gray Johnson; *m* 1925, Eleanor Sisson Thrum; *one s two d. Educ:* Univ. of Kansas (AB); Harvard Univ. (MBA). Asst Dean, Harvard Business Sch., 1923-29; Assoc. Prof. of Business, 1933-39; Vice-Pres., Hawaiian Pineapple Co., Honolulu, 1929-33; Chancellor, Univ. of Kansas, 1939-51. Educational Advisor, Ops

Analysis Div., US Army Air Corps, 1943-45; Mem., Business Council, Washington, DC, 1944-; Trustee: Corning Museum of Glass, 1952-73; Teagle Foundation, 1952-; William Allen White Foundation, 1952-; Kansas Univ. Endowment Assoc., 1952-; Pacific Tropical Botanical Garden, 1964-; Mem. Bd, Univ. of Kansas Alumni Assoc., 1974-; Director: General Mills, Inc., 1948-70; Citizens Bank, Abilene, Kans, 1944-73; Pitney-Bowes, Inc., 1951-71; First Nat. Bank, Ithaca, NY, 1951-69; Owens-Corning Fiberglas Corp., 1951-72; Lane Bryant, Inc., 1963-77; Servomation Corp., 1963-74; Hon. LLD: Washburn Univ., 1941; Bryant Coll., 1951; Hamilton Coll., 1951; Univ. of California 1954; Univ. of Liberia, 1962; Univ. of New Hampshire, 1963; Emory Univ., 1963; Juniata Coll., 1965; DCS, Univ. of Pittsburgh, 1957; Hon. DHL, Long Island Univ., 1967. Holds foreign Orders. Publications: Problems in Agricultural Marketing, 1938; (with Philip Cabot) Problems in Public Utility Management, 1927; (with J. C. Baker) Introduction to Corporate Finance, 1936; (with J. C. Baker and W. D. Kennedy) On Going into Business, 1936; (with B. F. Martin) The Agricultural Industries, 1939; Agriculture-the Great Dilemma (an essay in Business and Modern Society), 1951. Address: 322 Wait Avenue, Cornell University, Ithaca, NY 14850, USA. Clubs: University, Cornell (New York); Bohemian (San Francisco).

MALPAS, Prof. James Spencer, FRCP; Consultant Physician, St Bartholomew's Hospital, since 1973; Professor of Medical Oncology, since 1979, and Director, Imperial Cancer Research Fund Medical Oncology Unit, since 1976, St Bartholomew's Hospital; b 15 Sept. 1931; s of Tom Spencer Malpas, BSc, MICE and Hilda Chalstrey; m 1957, Joyce May Cathcart; two s. Educ: Sutton County Grammar Sch.; St Bartholomew's Hosp., London Univ. Schol. in Sci., 1951; BSc Hons, 1952; MB BS, 1955; DPhil, 1965; FRCP 1971. Junior appts in medicine, St Bartholomew's Hosp. and Royal Post-Grad. Med. Sch.; Nat. Service in RAF, 1957-61; Aylwen Bursar, St Bartholomew's Hosp., 1961; Lectr in Medicine, Oxford Univ., 1962-65; St Bartholomew's Hospital: Sen. Registrar in Medicine, 1966-68; Sen. Lectr in Medicine, 1968-72; Dean of Medical Coll., 1969-72. Cooper Res. Schol. in Med., 1966, 1967, 1968. Examr in Medicine, Univ. of Oxford, 1974. Asst Registrar, RCP, 1975-80; Lockyer Lectr, RCP, 1978. Publications: contrib. five medical textbooks; papers in BMJ, Brit. Jl Haematology, Jl Clinical Pathology, etc. Recreations: travel, history, painting. Address: 14 Carlisle Mansions, Carlisle Place, Westminster, SW1. T: 01-828 0042.

MALPAS, Robert, CBE 1975; a Managing Director, British Petroleum, since 1983; b 9 Aug. 1927; s of late Cheshyre Malpas and of Louise Marie Marcelle Malpas; m 1956, Josephine Dickenson. Educ: Taunton Sch.; St George's Coll., Buenos Aires; Durham Univ. BScMechEng (1st Cl. Hons); AMIMechE. Joined ICI Ltd, 1948; moved to Alcudia SA (48.5 per cent ICI), Spain, 1963; ICI Europa Ltd, Brussels, 1965; Chm., ICI Europa Ltd, 1973; ICI Main Board Dir, 1975-78; Pres., Halcon International Inc., 1978-82. Order of Civil Merit, Spain, 1967. Recreation: sport. Address: c/o BP Group of Companies, Britannic House, Moor Lane, EC2. Clubs: River (NY); Real Automóvil Club de España (Madrid).

MALTA, Archbishop of, (RC), since 1977; Most Rev. Joseph Mercieca, STD, JUD; b Victoria, Gozo, 11 Nov. 1928. Educ: Gozo Seminary; Univ. of London (BA); Gregorian Univ., Rome (STD); Lateran Univ., Rome (JUD). Priest, 1952; Rector of Gozo Seminary in late 1960s; Permanent Judge at Sacred Roman Rota and Commissioner to Congregation for the Sacraments and Congregation for the Doctrine of the Faith, 1969; Auxiliary Bishop of Malta, and Vicar-General, 1974-77. Address: Archbishop's Palace, Valletta, Malta.

MALTBY, Antony John, JP; MA; Headmaster of Trent College since 1968; b 15 May 1928; s of late G. C. Maltby and Mrs Maltby (née Kingsnorth); m 1959, Jillian Winifred (née Burt); four d. Educ: Clayesmore Sch., Dorset; St John's Coll., Cambridge. BA Hons (History) 1950; MA. Schoolmaster: Dover Coll., 1951-58; Pocklington Sch., 1958-68. JP Ilkeston, 1980. Recreations: squash, tennis, travel. Address: Westhorpe Drive, Long Eaton, Nottingham NG10 4AD. T: Long Eaton 2737. Clubs: East India, Devonshire, Sports and Public Schools; Hawks (Cambridge).

MALTBY, John Newcombe; Deputy Chairman, The Burmah Oil plc, since 1982; b 10 July 1928; s of Air Vice-Marshal Sir Paul Maltby, KCVO, KBE, CB, DSO, AFC, DL and Winifred Russell Paterson; m 1956, Lady Sylvia Veronica Anthea Harris, d of Earl of Malmesbury, qv; one s two d. Educ: Wellington Coll.; Clare Coll., Cambridge (MA Mech. Scis). Shell Internat. Petrolem, 1951-69; Founder and Man. Dir, Panocean Shipping & Terminals, 1969-75; Man. Dir, Panocean-Anco Ltd, 1975-79; Dir, The Burmah Oil Co. Ltd, 1980-82. Recreations: history, gardening, sailing. Address: Broadford House, Stratfield Turgis, Basingstoke, Hants RG27 0AS. Club: Naval and Military.

MALVERN, 3rd Viscount cr 1955, of Rhodesia and of Bexley, Kent; **Ashley Kevin Godfrey Huggins;** b 26 Oct. 1949; s of 2nd Viscount Malvern, and of Patricia Marjorie, d of Frank Renwick-Bower, Durban, S Africa; S father, 1978. Heir: uncle Hon. (Martin) James Huggins, b 13 Jan. 1928.

MAMBA, George Mbikwakhe; High Commissioner for the Kingdom of Swaziland to UK, since 1978; b 5 July 1932; s of Ndabazebelungu Mamba and Getrude Mthwalose Mamba, and g s of late Chief Bokweni Mamba; m 1960, Sophie Sidzandza Sibande; three s two d. Educ: Franson Christian High Sch.; Swazi National High Sch.; Morija Teacher Trng Coll.; Cambridge Inst. of

Educn; Nairobi Univ. Head Teacher, Makhonza Mission Sch., 1956-60; Teacher, Kwaluseni Central Sch., 1961-65; Head Teacher, Enkamheni Central Sch., 1966-67; Inspector of Schs, Manzini Dist, 1969-70; Welfare/Aftercare Officer, Prison Dept, 1971-72; Counsellor, Swaziland High Commn, Nairobi, 1972-77. Vice-Pres., Swaziland NUT, 1966-67. Field Comr, Swaziland Boy Scouts Assoc., 1967-68, Chief Comr, 1971-72. Publication: Children's Play, 1966. Recreations: scouting, reading. Address: Kingdom of Swaziland High Commission, 58 Pont Street, SW1. T: 01-589 7169.

MAMO, Sir Anthony (Joseph) Kt 1960; OBE 1955; b 9 Jan. 1909; s of late Joseph Mamo and late Carola (née Brincat); m 1939, Margaret Agius; one s two d. Educ: Royal Univ. of Malta. BA 1931; LLD 1934. Mem. Statute Law Revision Commn, 1936-42; Crown Counsel, 1942-51; Prof., Criminal Law, Malta Univ., 1943-57; Dep. Attorney-Gen., 1952-54, Attorney-Gen., 1955, Malta; Chief Justice and President, Court of Appeal, Malta, 1957-71; President, Constitutional Court, Malta, 1964-71; Governor-General, Malta, 1971-74; President, Republic of Malta, 1974-76. QC (Malta) 1957. Hon. DLitt Malta, 1969; Hon. LLD Libya, 1971. KStJ 1969. Publications: Lectures on Criminal Law and Criminal Procedure delivered at the University of Malta. Address: 49 Stella Maris Street, Sliema, Malta. T: 30708. Club: Casino (1852).

MAMOULIAN, Rouben; stage and screen director; producer; author; b 8 Oct. 1897; s of Zachary Mamoulian and Virginia Kalantarian; m Azadia Newman, Washington, DC. Educ: Lycée Montaigne, Paris; Gymnasium, Tiflis; Univ., Moscow. First English production, Beating on the Door, at St James's Theatre, London, Nov. 1922; arrived in Rochester, New York, Aug. 1923; from that date to summer of 1926 was Director of Production at the Eastman Theatre, producing Grand Operas, Operettas, Dramas, and stage presentations, among which were the following: Carmen, Faust, Boris Godounoff, Shanewis, Gilbert and Sullivan Operettas, Sister Beatrice, etc; also organised and was Director of the Eastman Theatre Sch.; came to New York at the end of 1926; started there as a Director of the Theatre Guild Sch.; first production of a play on Broadway, 10 Oct. 1927, Porgy, for the Theatre Guild; Porgy was followed by direction of the following plays on Broadway: Marco Millions, Congai, Wings over Europe, These Modern Women, RUR, The Game of Love and Death, A Month in the Country, A Farewell to Arms, and Solid South; also an opera at the Metropolitan Opera House, Hand of Fate, with L. Stokowski and the Philadelphia Orchestra; Opera Porgy and Bess (music by George Gershwin) for Theatre Guild, New York, 1935; in Los Angeles and San Francisco, 1938. Directed following motion pictures: Applause 1928; City Streets and Dr Jekyll and Mr Hyde, 1932; Love Me Tonight, and Song of Songs, 1933; Queen Christina, 1933 and We Live Again, 1934; Becky Sharp (Technicolor), 1935; The Gay Desperado, 1936; High, Wide and Handsome, 1937; Golden Boy, 1939; The Mark of Zorro, 1940; Blood and Sand (Technicolor), 1941; Rings on Her Fingers, 1942; Summer Holiday (technicolor musical, based on Eugene O'Neill's Ah Wilderness), 1947; Silk Stockings (musical film, cinemascope, color) 1957. Stage productions: Oklahoma!, 1943; Sadie Thompson, 1944, and Carousel, 1945, St Louis Woman, 1946, musical dramas in New York; Lost In The Stars (musical tragedy), 1949; Arms And The Girl (musical play), 1950, New York; Oklahoma! (for Berlin Arts Festival), 1951; Adolph Zukor's Golden Jubilee Celebration, Hollywood, 1953; Carousel (New Prod.), Los Angeles and San Francisco, 1953; Oklahoma!, new production for Paris, Rome, Milan, Naples and Venice, 1955. Co-Author (with Maxwell Anderson) of musical play The Devil's Hornpipe (made musical film Never Steal Anything Small), 1959. World Premiere Perf. of Shakespeare's Hamlet, A New Version, Lexington, Ky, 1966. Tributes and retrospective showings: NY, 1967, 1970, 1971; London, 1968; Montreal, Beverly Hills and Washington, 1970; Amer. Inst. for Advanced Studies, San Francisco, Toronto and Univs of Calif. at LA, S Florida and Yale, 1971; Hollywood, 1972; UCLA, Hollywood, Paris, San Sebastian, 1973; Washington DC, 1974; Univ. of California, Univ. of S California, 1975; Calif State Coll., 1976; Amer. Film Inst., 1976, 1977; Hollywood, N Carolina State Univ., 1977. Guest of Honour: Republics of Armenia and Georgia, 1971; Internat. Film Festivals, Moscow 1971, Iran 1974, Australia 1974, San Sebastian 1974, Boston 1976. Lectures, and appears on TV. Award of Excellence, Armenian Amer. Bicentennial Commemoration Cttee Inc., 1976. Publications: Abigayil, 1964; Hamlet Revised and Interpreted, 1965; contrib. Scoundrels and Scalawags, 1968; Ararat, 1969; Foreword to Chevalier, 1973. Recreations: swimming, horseback riding, and reading detective stories. Address: 1112 Schuyler Road, Beverly Hills, Calif 90210, USA.

MAN, Maj.-Gen. Christopher Mark Morrice, CB 1968; OBE 1958; MC 1945; retired; b 20 April 1914; s of late Rev. M. L. Man, MA, and late Evelyn Dora Man, Tenterden, Kent; m 1940, Georgina, d of late James Marr, Edinburgh; no c. Educ: Eastbourne Coll.; Emmanuel Coll., Cambridge. (MA). Lieut, Middlesex Regt, 1936; 1st Bn, The Middlesex Regt, 1937-45. Commanded Army Air Transport Training and Development Centre, 1953-55; GSO 1, WO, 1955-57; comdg Infantry Junior Leaders Battalion, 1957-59; comdg 125 Infantry Bde (TA), 1959-62; Head of Commonwealth Liaison Mission, UN Command, Korea and British Military Attaché, Seoul, 1962-64; GOC 49th Infantry Div. TA and N Midland District, 1964-67; Colonel, The Middlesex Regt, 1965-66; Pres., Regular Army Commn, 1967-69; Dep. Colonel The Queen's Regt, 1967-69, Hon. Colonel, 1970-71. Private, Atholl Highlanders, 1969. Address: The Clock Tower Flat, Blair Castle, Blair Atholl, Pitlochry, Perthshire PH18 5TL. T: Blair Atholl 452.

MAN, Morgan Charles Garnet, CMG 1961; DL; civil servant, employed by Ministry of Defence, since 1980; *b* 6 Aug. 1915; *s* of Henry Morgan Stoe Man and Nora Loeck; *m* 1st, 1941, Moira Farquharson Main (marr. diss.); two *d* ; 2nd, 1956, Patricia Mary (*née* Talbot) (marr. diss.). *Educ:* Cheltenham Coll.; Queen's Coll., Oxford. Joined HM Consular Service, 1937; Vice-Consul, Beirut, 1937-39; Assistant Oriental Secretary, HM Embassy, Bagdad, 1939; 2nd Secretary, HM Embassy, Jedda, 1943; Consul, Atlanta, Ga, USA, 1946; Consul, Kirkuk, 1948; First Secretary, HM Legation, Damascus, 1949; Oriental Secretary, HM Embassy, Bagdad, 1951; Assistant in American Dept, Foreign Office, Sept. 1953; Head of American Dept, 1954; Counsellor at HM Embassy, Oslo, Nov. 1956; Deputy Political Resident, Bahrain, 1959-62; Minister, HM Embassy, Ankara, 1962-64; HM Ambassador to Saudi Arabia, 1964-68; Senior Civilian Instructor, Imperial Defence Coll., 1968-69; retired, 1970. Director: Metallurgical Plantmakers' Fedn, 1970-80; British Metalworking Plantmakers' Assoc., 1970-80; Ironmaking and Steelmaking Plant Contractors' Assoc., 1970-80. DL Greater London, 1977. *Address:* 1 Boltons Court, 216 Old Brompton Road, SW5. *T:* 01-373 9396.

MANASSEH, Leonard Sulla, OBE 1982; RA 1979 (ARA 1976); FRIBA; Partner, Leonard Manasseh Partnership (formerly Leonard Manasseh & Partners), since 1950; *b* 21 May 1916; *s* of Alan Manasseh and Esther (*née* Elias); *m* 1st, 1947 (marr. diss. 1956); two *s* 2nd, 1957, Sarah Delaforce; two *s* one *d. Educ:* Cheltenham College; The Architectural Assoc. Sch. of Architecture (AA Dip.). ARIBA 1941, FRIBA 1964; FSIA 1965; RWA 1972. Asst Architect, CRE N London and Guy Morgan & Partners; teaching staff, AA and Kingston Sch. of Art, 1941-43; Fleet Air Arm, 1943-46; Asst Architect, Herts CC, 1946-48; Senior Architect, Stevenage New Town Develt Corp., 1948-50; won Festival of Britain restaurant competition, 1950; started private practice, 1950; teaching staff, AA Sch. of Architecture, 1951-59; opened office in Singapore and Malaysia with James Cubitt & Partners (Cubitt Manasseh & Partners), 1953-54. Member: Council, Architectural Assoc. 1959-66 (Pres., 1964-65); Council of Industrial Design, 1965-68; Council, RIBA 1968-70, 1976-82 (Hon. Sec., 1979-81); Council, National Trust, 1977-; Ancient Monuments Bd (England), 1978-. Pres., Franco-British Union of Architects, 1978-79. FRSA 1967. *Work includes:* houses, housing and schools; industrial work; conservation plan for Beaulieu Estate; Nat. Motor Museum, Beaulieu; Wellington Country Park, Stratfield Saye. *Publications:* Office Buildings (with 3rd Baron Cunliffe), 1962, Japanese edn 1964; Snowdon Summit Report (Countryside Commission), 1974; Eastbourne Harbour Study (Trustees, Chatsworth Settlement), 1976; (jtly) planning reports and studies. *Recreations:* photography, travel, sketching, watching aeroplanes, being optimistic. *Address:* 6 Bacon's Lane, Highgate, N6 6BL. *T:* 01-340 5528. *Club:* Athenæum.

MANBY, Mervyn Colet, CMG 1964; QPM 1961; retired; *b* 20 Feb. 1915; *s* of late Harold B. and Mary Manby (*née* Mills), late of Petistree, Suffolk; *m* 1949, Peggy Aronson, Eastern Cape, South Africa; one *s* one *d. Educ:* Bedford Sch., Bedford; Pembroke Coll., Oxford. Colonial Police Service, 1937; Malaya, 1938-47; Basutoland, 1947-54; Kenya, 1954-64. Dep. Inspector General, Kenya Police, 1961-64; retired, 1964. United Nations Technical Assistance Adviser to Government of Iran, 1965-70; UN Div. of Narcotic Drugs, 1971-75; special consultant, UN Fund for Drug Abuse Control, 1975. Mem. Council, Inst. for Study of Drug Dependence, 1975-78. *Address:* Old Well Cottage, Barham, Canterbury, Kent. *T:* Barham 369.

MANCE, Jonathan Hugh, QC 1982; barrister; *b* 6 June 1943; *e s* of late Sir Henry Stenhouse Mance and of Lady (Joan Erica Robertson) Mance; *m* 1973, Mary Howarth Arden; one *s* two *d. Educ:* Charterhouse; University Coll., Oxford (MA). Called to the Bar, Middle Temple, 1965. Worked in Germany, 1965. *Publications:* (asst editor) Chalmer's Sale of Goods, 1981; (ed jtly) Sale of Goods, Halsbury's Laws of England, 4th edn 1982. *Recreations:* tennis, languages, music. *Address:* 11 Frognal Lane, NW3 7DG. *T:* 01-794 8011. *Club:* Cumberland Lawn Tennis.

MANCHAM, James Richard Marie; KBE (Hon.) 1976; President, Republic of the Seychelles, 1976-77 (Prime Minister of Seychelles, 1975-76; Chief Minister, 1970-75); *b* 11 Aug. 1939; *e s* of late Richard Mancham and Evelyne Mancham (*née* Tirant); *m* 1963, Heather Jean Evans (marr. diss. 1974); one *s* one *d. Educ:* Seychelles Coll.; Wilson Coll., London. Called to Bar, Middle Temple, 1961. Auditeur Libre à la Faculté de Droit ès Sciences Economiques, Univ. of Paris, 1962; Internat. Inst. of Labour Studies Study Course, Spring 1968. Legal practice, Supreme Court of Seychelles. Seychelles Democratic Party (SDP), Pres. 1964; Mem. Seychelles Governing Council, 1967; Leader of Majority Party (SDP), 1967; Mem., Seychelles Legislative Assembly, 1970-76; led SDP to Seychelles Constitutional Conf., London, 1970 and 1976. Founder, Seychelles Weekly, 1962. Lecturer, 1981, on struggle for power in Indian Ocean, to US and Eur. univs and civic gps. Hon. Citizen: Dade County, Florida, 1963; New Orleans, 1965. FRSA 1968. Officier de la Légion d'Honneur, 1976; Grande Médaille de la Francophonie, 1976; Grande médaille vermeille, Paris, 1977; Quaid-i-Azam Medallion (Pakistan), 1976; Gold Medal for Tourism, Mexico, 1977; Gold Medal of Chamber of Commerce and Industries of France, 1977; Gold Medal des Excellences Européennes, 1977. *Publications:* Reflections and Echoes from Seychelles, 1972 (poetry); L'Air des Seychelles, 1974; Island Splendour, 1980. *Recreations:* travel, water sports, tennis, writing. *Address:* c/o Lloyds Bank Ltd, 81 Edgware Road, W2 2HY. *Clubs:* Annabel's, Les Ambassadeurs, Wig and Pen; El Morocco, Intrepids (NY); Régine (Paris); Griffin (Geneva).

MANCHESTER, 11th Duke of, *cr* 1719; **Sidney Arthur Robin George Drogo Montagu;** Baron Montagu, Viscount Mandeville, 1620; Earl of Manchester, 1626; *b* 5 Feb. 1929; *er s* of 10th Duke of Manchester, OBE, and Nell Vere (*d* 1966), *d* of Sidney Vere Stead, Melbourne; *S* father, 1977; *m* 1st, 1955, Adrienne Valerie (marr. diss. 1968), *d* of J. K. Christie; 2nd, 1978, Andrea Kent (*née* Joss). *Heir:* *b* lord Angus Charles Drogo Montagu [*b* 9 Oct. 1938; *m* 1961, Mary Eveleen (marr. diss. 1970), *d* of Walter Gillespie McClure; two *s* one *d*]. *Address:* PO Box 24667, Karen, Kenya. *Club:* Muthaiga (Nairobi, Kenya).

MANCHESTER, Bishop of, since 1979; **Rt. Rev. Stanley Eric Francis Booth-Clibborn;** *b* 20 Oct. 1924; *s* of Eric and Lucille Booth-Clibborn; *m* 1958, Anne Roxburgh Forrester, *d* of Rev. William Roxburgh Forrester, *qv* ; two *s* two *d. Educ:* Highgate School; Oriel Coll., Oxford (MA); Westcott House, Cambridge. Served RA, 1942-45; Royal Indian Artillery, 1945-47, Temp. Captain. Curate, Heeley Parish Church, Sheffield, 1952-54, The Attercliffe Parishes, Sheffield, 1954-56; Training Sec., Christian Council of Kenya, 1956-63; Editor-in-Chief, East African Venture Newspapers, Nairobi, 1963-67; Leader, Lincoln City Centre Team Ministry, 1967-70; Vicar, St Mary the Great, University Church, Cambridge, 1970-79. Hon. Canon, Ely Cathedral, 1976-79. Mem., Div. of Internat. Affairs, BCC, 1968-80. *Recreations:* photography, tennis, listening to music. *Address:* Bishopscourt, Bury New Road, Manchester M7 0LE. *T:* 061-792 2096/1779. *Club:* Royal Commonwealth Society.

MANCHESTER, Dean of; *see* Jowett, Very Rev. Alfred.

MANCHESTER, Archdeacon of; *see* Harris, Ven. R. B.

MANCHESTER, William; author; Purple Heart (US) 1945; Fellow, East College, since 1968, writer in residence since 1974, Adjunct Professor of History since 1979, Wesleyan University; *b* 1 April 1922; *s* of William Raymond Manchester and Sallie E. R. (*née* Thompson); *m* 1948, Julia Brown Marshall; one *s* two *d. Educ:* Springfield Classical High School; Univ. of Massachusetts; Dartmouth Coll., NH; Univ. of Missouri. Served US Marine Corps, 1942-45. Reporter, Daily Oklahoman, 1945-46; Reporter, foreign corresp., war corresp., Baltimore Sun, 1947-55; Man. editor, Wesleyan Univ. Publications, 1955-65; Fellow, Center for Advanced Studies, 1959-60, Lectr in English, 1968-69, Wesleyan Univ. Trustee, Friends of Univ. of Massachusetts Library, 1970-76, Pres., 1970-72. Guggenheim Fellow, 1959; Dr of Humane Letters: Univ. of Mass, 1965; Univ. of New Haven, 1979; Dag Hammarskjold Internat. Prize in Literature, 1967; Overseas Press Club (New York) Award for Best Book of the Year on Foreign Affairs, 1968; Univ. of Missouri Medal, 1969; Connecticut Book Award, 1974; President's Cabinet Award, Detroit Univ., 1981; Frederick S. Troy Medal, 1981; McConaughy Award, 1981. *Publications:* Disturber of the Peace, 1951 (publ. UK as The Sage of Baltimore, 1952); The City of Anger, 1953; Shadow of the Monsoon, 1956; Beard the Lion, 1958; A Rockefeller Family Portrait, 1959; The Long Gainer, 1961; Portrait of a President, 1962; The Death of a President, 1967; The Arms of Krupp, 1968; The Glory and the Dream, 1974; Controversy and other Essays in Journalism, 1976; American Caesar, 1978; Goodbye, Darkness, 1980; contrib. to Encyclopedia Britannica and to periodicals. *Recreation:* photography. *Address:* Wesleyan University, Middletown, Conn 06457, USA. *T:* 203-346-4789. *Clubs:* Century, Williams (New York).

MANCROFT, family name of Baron Mancroft.

MANCROFT, 2nd Baron, *cr* 1937, of Mancroft in the City of Norwich; Bt, *cr* 1932; **Stormont Mancroft Samuel Mancroft;** KBE 1959 (MBE 1945); TD 1950; MA; Chairman, British Greyhound Racing Board, since 1977; *b* 27 July 1914; *s* of 1st Baron and Phœbe (*d* 1969), 2nd *d* of Alfred Chune Fletcher, MRCS; *S* father, 1942; *m* 1951, Mrs Diana Elizabeth Quarry, *o d* of Lieut-Colonel Horace Lloyd; one *s* two *d. Educ:* Winchester; Christ Church, Oxford. Called to Bar, Inner Temple, 1938; Member of Bar Council, 1947-51; Member St Marylebone Borough Council, 1947-53; a Lord in Waiting to the Queen, 1952-54; Parliamentary Under-Secretary for Home Dept, Oct. 1954- Jan. 1957; Parliamentary Secretary, Min. of Defence, Jan.-June 1957; Minister without Portfolio, June 1957-Oct. 1958, resigned. Dir, GUS, 1958-66; Dep. Chm., Cunard Line Ltd, 1966-71; Chm., Horserace Totalisator Bd, 1972-76; Mem., Council on Tribunals, 1972-80; President: The Institute of Marketing, 1959-63; St Marylebone Conservative Assoc., 1961-67; London Tourist Board, 1963-73. Served RA (TA), 1939-46; Lieut-Colonel (despatches twice, MBE); commissioned TA, 1938; rejoined TA 1947-55. Hon. Col Comdt, RA, 1970-80. Croix de Guerre. *Publications:* Booking the Cooks (essays from Punch), 1969; A Chinaman in My Bath, 1974; Bees in some Bonnets, 1979. *Heir:* *s* Hon. Benjamin Lloyd Stormont Mancroft, *b* 16 May 1957. *Address:* 29 Margaretta Terrace, SW3 5NU. *T:* 01-352 7674. *Clubs:* Pratt's; West Ham Boys.

MANDELSTAM, Prof. Joel; FRS 1971; Iveagh Professor of Microbiology, University of Oxford, since 1966; *b* S Africa, 13 Nov. 1919; *s* of Leo and Fanny Mandelstam; *m* 1954, Dorothy Hillier; one *s* one *d* ; *m* 1975, Mary Maureen Dale. *Educ:* Jeppe High Sch., Johannesburg; University of Witwatersrand; Queen Elizabeth Coll., London. Lecturer, Medical Sch., Johannesburg, 1947; Scientific Staff, Nat. Institute for Med. Research, London, 1952-66. Fulbright Fellow, US, 1958-59; Vis. Prof., Univ. of Adelaide, 1971. Mem., ARC, 1973-. Leewenhoek Lectr, Royal Soc., 1975. Editorial Board, Biochemical Journal, 1960-66. *Publications:* Biochemistry of

Bacterial Growth (with K. McQuillen), 1968; articles in journals and books on microbial biochemistry. *Address:* Microbiology Unit, Department of Biochemistry, South Parks Road, Oxford. *T:* Oxford 511266.

MANDELSTAM, Prof. Stanley, FRS 1962; Professor of Physics, University of California. *Educ:* University of the Witwatersrand, Johannesburg, Transvaal, South Africa (BSc); Trinity Coll., Cambridge (BA). PhD, Birmingham. Formerly Professor of Math. Physics, University of Birmingham. *Publications:* (with W. Yourgrau) Variational Principles in Dynamics and Quantum Theory, 1955 (revised edn, 1956); papers in learned journals. *Address:* Department of Physics, University of California, Berkeley, California 94720, USA.

MANDER, Sir Charles (Marcus), 3rd Bt, *cr* 1911; Underwriting Member of Lloyd's; Director: Manders (Holdings) Ltd, Mander Brothers Ltd, until 1958; Arlington Securities Ltd; Headstaple Ltd; *b* 22 Sept. 1921; *o s* of Sir Charles Arthur Mander, 2nd Bart, and late Monica Claire Cotterill, *d* of G. H. Neame; *S* father, 1951; *m* 1945, Maria Dolores Beatrice, *d* of late Alfred Brodermann, Hamburg; two *s* one *d. Educ:* Eton Coll., Windsor; Trinity Coll., Cambridge. Commissioned Coldstream Guards, 1942; served War of 1939–45, Canal Zone, 1943; Italy, 1943, Germany, 1944; War Office (ADC to Lieut-General R. G. Stone, CB), 1945. High Sheriff of Staffordshire, 1962–63. *Recreations:* shooting, music. *Heir: s* Charles Nicholas Mander, [*b* 23 March 1950; *m* 1972, Karin Margareta, *d* of Arne Norin; three *s* one *d*]. *Address:* Little Barrow, Moreton-in-Marsh, Glos. *T:* Stow-on-the-Wold 30265; Greville House, Kinnerton Street, SW1. *T:* 01-235 1669. *Clubs:* Boodle's; Ski Club of Great Britain; Royal Thames Yacht.

MANDER, Noel Percy, MBE 1979; FSA; Managing Director, N. P. Mander Ltd, since 1946; *b* 19 May 1912; *s* of late Percy Mander and Emily Pike, Hoxne, Suffolk; *m* 1948, Enid Watson; three *s* two *d. Educ:* Haberdashers Aske's Sch., Hatcham. Organ building from 1930, interrupted by war service with RA (Hampshire Bde) in N Africa, Italy and Syria, 1940–46. FSA 1974. Mem., Nat. Council of Christians and Jews (former Chm., N London Council). Governor, Sir John Cass Foundn. Liveryman, Musicians' Co.; Past Master, Parish Clerks' Co. of City of London; Mem., Art Workers' Guild. Builder of Winston Churchill Meml Organ, Fulton, Missouri, and organs in many parts of world; organ builder to St Paul's Cathedral London and Canterbury Cathedral, and to HM Sultan of Oman. *Publications:* St Lawrence Jewry, A History of the Organs from the Earliest Times to the Present Day, 1956; St Vedast, Foster Lane, A History of the Organs from Earliest Times to the Present Day, 1961; St Vedast Foster Lane, in the City of London: a history of the 13 United Parishes, 1973; (with C. M. Houghton) St Botolph Aldgate: a history of the organs from the Restoration to the Twentieth Century, 1973. *Recreations:* archaeology, horology, reading. *Address:* St Peter's Organ Works, E2. *T:* 01-739 4747; Earl Soham, Woodbridge, Suffolk. *Club:* Savage.

MANDER, Raymond Josiah Gale; Joint Founder and Director, The Raymond Mander and Joe Mitchenson Theatre Collection, since 1939 (Theatre Collection Trust, since 1977); *b* 15 July; *s* of Albert Edwin Mander, MSA, LRIBA, FIAAS, and Edith Christina Gale. *Educ:* Battersea Grammar Sch. 1st professional appearance on stage, Bedford, 1934; acted in repertory, on tour and in London, until 1948. With Joe Mitchenson, founded Theatre Collection, 1939; during the War, resp. together for many BBC theatre gramophone progs; toured together in ENSA and in jt management, 1943; management of Collection became full-time occupation as authors and theatrical consultants; Collection subject of Aquarius programme, 1971; many TV appearances on theatrical subjects; many theatrical exhibns, incl. 50 Years of British Stage Design, for British Council, USSR, 1979. Archivist to: Sadler's Wells; Old Vic. Mem., Soc. of West End Theatre Awards Panel, 1976–78. *Publications:* with Joe Mitchenson: Hamlet Through the Ages, 1952 (2nd rev. edn 1955); Theatrical Companion to Shaw, 1954; Theatrical Companion to Maugham, 1955; The Artist and the Theatre, 1955; Theatrical Companion to Coward, 1957; A Picture History of British Theatre, 1957; (with J. C. Trewin) The Gay Twenties, 1958; (with Philip Hope-Wallace) A Picture History of Opera, 1959; (with J. C. Trewin) The Turbulent Thirties, 1960; The Theatres of London, 1961, illus. by Timothy Birdsall (2nd rev. edn, paperback, 1963; 3rd rev. edn 1975); A Picture History of Gilbert and Sullivan, 1962; British Music Hall: A Story in Pictures, 1965 (rev. and enlarged edn 1974); Lost Theatres of London, 1968 (2nd edn, rev. and enlarged, 1976); Musical Comedy: A Story in Pictures, 1969; Revue: A Story in Pictures, 1971; Pantomime: A Story in Pictures, 1973; The Wagner Companion, 1977; Victorian and Edwardian Entertainment from Old Photographs, 1978; Introd. to Plays, by Noël Coward (4 vols), 1979; Guide to the W. Somerset Maugham Theatrical Paintings, 1980; contribs to and revs in Encyc. Britannica, Theatre Notebook, and Books and Bookmen. *Recreations:* going to the theatre, gardening. *Address:* 5 Venner Road, Sydenham, SE26 5EQ. *T:* 01-778 6730.

MANDER, Lady (Rosalie), (R. Glynn Grylls), MA Oxon; Biographer; Lecturer; Cornish ancestry; *m* 1930, Sir Geoffrey Mander (*d* 1962), sometime MP for East Wolverhampton; one *d* (and one *s* decd). *Educ:* Queen's Coll., Harley Street, London; Lady Margaret Hall, Oxford. Lectures frequently in USA. *Publications:* Mary Shelley, 1936; Trelawny, 1950; Portrait of Rossetti, 1965; Mrs Browning, 1980. *Address:* Wightwick Manor, Wolverhampton, Staffs; 35 Buckingham Gate, SW1.

MANDI, Lt-Col Raja (Sir) Joginder Sen Bahadur of; KCSI 1931; *b* 20 Aug. 1904; *s* of late Mian Kishan Singh; *m* 1930, *d* of late Kanwar Prithiraj Sinhji, Rajpipla; two *s* two *d. Educ:* Queen Mary's Coll. and Aitchison Coll., Lahore. Ascended Gadi, 1913; full ruler, 1925. Visited various countries. Ambassador of Republic of India to Brazil, 1952–56; Member of Lok Sabha, 1957–62. Hon. Lt-Col 3rd/17th Dogra Regt and Bengal Sappers and Miners. *Address:* Bhawani Palace, Mandi, Mandi District (HP) 175001, India.

MANDUELL, John, CBE 1982; FRAM, FRCM, FRNCM, FRSAMD; composer; Principal, Royal Northern College of Music, since 1971; *b* 2 March 1928; *s* of Matthewman Donald Manduell, MC, MA, and Theodora (*née* Tharp); *m* 1955, Renna Kellaway; three *s* one *d. Educ:* Haileybury Coll.; Jesus Coll., Cambridge; Royal Acad. of Music. FRAM 1964; FRNCM 1974; FRCM 1980; Hon. FTCL 1973. BBC: music producer, 1956–61; Head of Music, Midlands and E Anglia, 1961–64; Chief Planner, The Music Programme, 1964–68; Univ. of Lancaster: Dir of Music, 1968–71; Mem. Court and Council, 1972–77, 1979–. Prog. Dir, Cheltenham Festival, 1969–. Arts Council: Mem. Council, 1976–78, 1980–; Mem. Music Panel, 1971–76, Dep. Chm., 1976–78, Chm., 1980–; Mem. Touring Cttee, 1975–80, Chm., 1976–78; Mem. Trng Cttee, 1973–77. Mem. Music Adv. Cttee, British Council, 1963–72, Chm., 1973–80; Chm. Music Panel, North West Arts, 1973–79; Gulbenkian Foundn Enquiry into Trng Musicians; Governor: Chetham's Sch., 1971–; National Youth Orch., 1964–73, 1978–; President: Lakeland Sinfonia, 1972–; Jubilate Choir, 1979–; Director: London Opera Centre, 1971–79; Associated Bd of Royal Schools of Music, 1971–; Northern Ballet Theatre, 1973–; Manchester Palace Theatre Trust, 1978–; London Orchestral Concert Bd, 1980–. Hon. Member: Roy. Soc. of Musicians, 1972; Chopin Soc. of Warsaw, 1973. Engagements and tours as composer, conductor and lectr in Canada, Europe, S Africa and USA. Chm., BBC TV Young Musicians of the Year, 1978, 1980; Chm. or mem., national and internat. music competition juries. FRSA 1981. First Leslie Boosey Award, Royal Phil. Soc. and PRS, 1980. *Publications:* (contrib.) The Symphony, ed Simpson, 1966; Cameos, 1981; *compositions:* Overture, Sunderland Point, 1969; Diversions for Orchestra, 1970; String Quartet, 1976. *Recreations:* cricket; travel; French life, language and literature. *Address:* Royal Northern College of Music, Oxford Road, Manchester M13 9RD. *T:* 061-273 6283.

MANGHAM, Maj.-Gen. William Desmond, CB 1978; Director, The Brewers' Society, since 1980; *b* 29 Aug. 1924; *s* of late Lt-Col William Patrick Mangham and Margaret Mary Mangham (*née* Donnachie); *m* 1960, Susan, *d* of late Col Henry Brabazon Humfrey; two *s* two *d. Educ:* Ampleforth College. 2nd Lieut RA, 1943; served India, Malaya, 1945–48; BMRA 1st Div. Egypt, 1955; Staff, HQ Middle East, Cyprus, 1956–58; Instructor, Staff Coll., Camberley and Canada, 1962–65; OC 3rd Regt Royal Horse Artillery, 1966–68; Comdr RA 2nd Div., 1969–70; Royal Coll. of Defence Studies, 1971; Chief of Staff, 1st British Corps, 1972–74; GOC 2nd Div., 1974–75; VQMG, MoD, 1976–79. Col Comdt RA, 1979–. *Recreations:* shooting, golf, tennis. *Address: c/o* Lloyds Bank Ltd, Cox's & King's Branch, 6 Pall Mall, SW1. *Club:* Army and Navy.

MANGO, Prof. Cyril Alexander, FBA 1976; Bywater and Sotheby Professor of Byzantine and Modern Greek, Oxford University, since 1973; *b* 14 April 1928; *s* of Alexander A. Mango and Adelaide Damonov; *m* 1st, 1953, Mabel Grover; one *d*; 2nd, 1964, Susan A. Gerstel; one *d*; 3rd, 1976, Maria C. Mundell. *Educ:* Univ. of St Andrews (MA); Univ. of Paris (Dr Univ Paris). From Jun. Fellow to Lectr in Byzantine Archaeology, Dumbarton Oaks Byzantine Center, Harvard Univ., 1951–63; Lectr in Fine Arts, Harvard Univ., 1957–58; Visiting Associate Prof. of Byzantine History, Univ. of California, Berkeley, 1960–61; Koraës Prof. of Modern Greek and of Byzantine History, Language and Literature, King's Coll., Univ. of London, 1963–68; Prof. of Byzantine Archaeology, Dumbarton Oaks Byzantine Center, 1968–73. FSA. *Publications:* The Homilies of Photius, 1958; The Brazen House, 1959; The Mosaics of St Sophia at Istanbul, 1962; The Art of the Byzantine Empire, Sources and Documents, 1972; Architettura bizantina, 1974; Byzantium, 1980. *Address:* Exeter College, Oxford.

MANGOLD, Thomas Cornelius; Reporter, BBC TV Panorama, since 1976; *b* 20 Aug. 1934; *s* of Fritz Mangold and Dorothea Mangold; *m* 1972, Valerie Ann Hare (*née* Dean); three *d. Educ:* Dorking Grammar Sch. Reporter, Croydon Advertiser, 1952. Served RA, 1952–54. Reporter: Croydon Advertiser, 1955–59; Sunday Pictorial, 1959–62; Daily Express, 1962–64; BBC TV News, 1964–70; BBC TV 24 Hours, later Midweek, 1970–76. *Publication:* (jtly) The File on the Tsar, 1976. *Recreations:* trampolining, playing Blues harp. *Address: c/o* BBC TV, Lime Grove, W12. *T:* 01-743 8000. *Club:* Wedgies.

MANGWAZU, Timon Sam, MA Oxon; Group Managing Director, Press (Holdings) Ltd, 1980 (Deputy Managing Director, 1978–80); Chairman, National Bank of Malaŵi, since 1980; *b* 12 Oct. 1933; *s* of Sam Isaac Mangwazu, Farmer; *m* 1958, Nelly Kathewera; three *s* three *d. Educ:* Ruskin Coll., Oxford; Brasenose Coll., Oxford (BA; MA 1976). Teacher at Methodist Sch., Hartley, S Rhodesia, 1955; Clerical Officer, Government Print, Agricultural Dept and Accountant General's Dept, 1956–62; Asst Registrar of Trade Unions, Ministry of Labour, 1962–63; Malaŵi Ambassador, West Germany, Norway, Sweden, Denmark, Netherlands, Belgium, Switzerland and Austria, 1964–67; High Comr in London for Republic of Malaŵi, and Ambassador to Belgium, Portugal, Netherlands and Holy See, 1967–69; Brasenose Coll., Oxford, 1969–72; Malaŵi Ambassador to EEC, Belgium and the Netherlands, 1973-78. Mem. Council, Univ. of Malaŵi; Chm., Bd of Governors, Malaŵi Polytechnic. *Recreation:* fishing. *Address:* Press (Holdings) Ltd, PO Box 30238, Capital City, Lilongwe 3, Malaŵi.

MANHOOD, Harold Alfred; Writer; *b* 6 May 1904; *m* 1937. *Educ:* Elementary Schooling. *Publications:* Nightseed, 1928; Gay Agony (novel), 1930; Apples by Night, 1932; Crack of Whips, 1934; Fierce and Gentle, 1935; Sunday Bugles, 1939; Lunatic Broth, 1944 (collections of short stories); Selected Stories, 1947; A Long View of Nothing (short stories), 1953. *Address:* Holmbush, near Henfield, W Sussex.

MANKIEWICZ, Joseph Leo; American writer and film director; *b* 11 Feb. 1909; *s* of Frank Mankiewicz and Johanna (*née* Blumenau); *m* 1939, Rosa Stradner (*d* 1958); two *s* (and one *s* by previous marriage); *m* 1962, Rosemary Matthews; one *d*. *Educ:* Columbia Univ. (AB 1928). Has written, directed and produced for the screen, 1929-. Received Screen Directors' Guild Award, 1949 and 1950; Screen Writers' Guild Award for best American comedy, 1949 and 1950; First Awards for direction and screen play, Motion Picture Academy, 1950, 1951. President, Screen Directors' Guild of America, 1950. Formed own company, Figaro Inc., 1953, dissolved, 1961. Order of Merit, Italy, 1965. Films include: Manhattan Melodrama, Fury, Three Comrades, Philadelphia Story, Woman of the Year, Keys of the Kingdom, A Letter to Three Wives, No Way Out, All About Eve, People Will Talk, Five Fingers, Julius Caesar, The Barefoot Contessa, Guys and Dolls; The Quiet American; Suddenly Last Summer; The Honey Pot; There Was a Crooked Man; Sleuth. Directed La Bohème for Metropolitan Opera, 1952. Fellow, Yale Univ., 1979-. Working on The Performing Woman: a history of when and how women came to perform the roles of women on the stages of the Western theatre. *Address:* Guard Hill Road, Bedford, NY 10506, USA.

MANKOWITZ, Wolf; author; Honorary Consul to the Republic of Panama in Dublin, 1971; *b* 7 Nov. 1924; *s* of Solomon and Rebecca Mankowitz; *m* 1944, Ann Margaret Seligmann; four *s*. *Educ:* East Ham Grammar Sch.; Downing Coll., Cambridge (MA, English Tripos). Adjunct Prof. of English, Univ. of New Mexico, 1982-83. *Publications:* novels: Make Me An Offer, 1952; A Kid for Two Farthings, 1953; Laugh Till You Cry, 1955 (USA); My Old Man's a Dustman, 1956; Cockatrice, 1963; The Biggest Pig in Barbados, 1965; Penguin Wolf Mankowitz, 1967; Raspberry Reich, 1979; ¡Abracadabra!, 1980; *short stories:* The Mendelman Fire, 1957; The Blue Arabian Nights, 1973; The Day of the Women and The Night of the Men (fables), 1977; *histories:* Wedgwood, 1953, 3rd repr. 1980; The Portland Vase, 1953; An Encyclopaedia of English Pottery and Porcelain, 1957; *biography:* Dickens of London, 1976; The Extraordinary Mr Poe, 1978; Mazeppa, 1982; *poetry:* 12 Poems, 1971; *plays:* The Bespoke Overcoat and Other Plays, 1955; Expresso Bongo (musical), 1958-59; Make Me An Offer (musical), 1959; Belle, 1961 (musical); Pickwick, 1963 (musical); Passion Flower Hotel (musical), 1965; The Samson Riddle, 1972; Stand and Deliver! (musical), 1972; The Irish Hebrew Lesson, 1978; Samson and Delilah, 1978; Casanova's Last Stand, 1980; Iron Butterflies, 1980; *films:* Make Me An Offer, 1954; A Kid for Two Farthings, 1954; The Bespoke Overcoat, 1955; Expresso Bongo, 1960; The Millionairess, 1960; The Long and The Short and The Tall, 1961; The Day the Earth Caught Fire, 1961; The Waltz of the Toreadors, 1962; Where The Spies Are, 1965; Casino Royale, 1967; The Assassination Bureau, 1969; Bloomfield, 1970; Black Beauty, 1971; Treasure Island, 1972; The Hebrew Lesson (wrote and dir.), 1972; The Hireling, 1973; *television:* Dickens of London, 1976. *Recreation:* sleeping. *Address:* The Bridge House, Ahakista, Co. Cork. *T:* Kilcrohane 11. *Club:* Savile.

MANKTELOW, Rt. Rev. Michael Richard John; *see* Basingstoke, Bishop Suffragan of.

MANLEY, Ivor Thomas; Deputy Secretary, Department of Energy, since 1981; *b* 4 March 1931; *s* of Frederick Stone and Louisa Manley; *m* 1952, Joan Waite; one *s* one *d*. *Educ:* Sutton High Sch., Plymouth. Entered Civil Service, 1951; Principal: Min. of Aviation, 1964-66; Min. of Technology, 1966-68; Private Secretary: to Rt Hon. Anthony Wedgwood Benn, 1968-70; to Rt Hon. Geoffrey Rippon, 1970; Principal Private Sec. to Rt Hon. John Davies, 1970-71; Asst Sec., DTI, 1971-74; Under-Sec., Principal Estabt Officer, 1974-78, Under Sec., Atomic Energy Div., 1978-81, Dept of Energy. UK Governor, IAEA, 1978-81; Mem., UKAEA, 1981-. *Recreations:* walking, badminton, squash, Russian literature. *Address:* 34 Rowhill Avenue, Aldershot, Hants GU11 3LS. *T:* Aldershot 22707.

MANLEY, Hon. Michael Norman; Leader of the Opposition, Jamaican Parliament, 1969-72, and since 1980; President, People's National Party, Jamaica since 1969 (Member, Executive, since 1952); MP for Central Kingston, Jamaica, since 1967; *b* St Andrew, Jamaica, 10 Dec. 1924; *s* of late Rt Excellent Norman W. Manley, QC, and of Edna Manley (*née* Swithenbank); *m* 1972, Beverly Anderson; one *d*; one *s* two *d* by previous marriages. *Educ:* Jamaica Coll.; London Sch. of Economics (BSc Econ Hons). Began as freelance journalist, working with BBC, 1950-51; returned to Jamaica, Dec. 1951, as Associate Editor of Public Opinion, 1952-53; Sugar Supervisor, Nat. Workers' Union, 1953-54; Island Supervisor and First Vice-Pres., 1955-72; Mem. Senate, 1962-67; Prime Minister of Jamaica, 1972-80. Has held various posts in Labour cttees and in Trade Union affairs; organised strike in sugar industry, 1959, which led to Goldenberg Commn of Inquiry. Vice-Pres., Socialist Internat., 1978. Hon. Doctor of Laws Morehouse Coll., Atlanta, 1973. UN Special Award for contrib. to struggle against

apartheid, 1978; Joliot Curie Medal, World Peace Council, 1979. Order of the Liberator, Venezuela, 1973; Order of Mexican Eagle, 1975; Order of Jose Marti, Cuba, 1975. *Publications:* The Politics of Change, 1974; A Voice at the Workplace, 1976; The Search for Solutions, 1977; Jamaica: Struggle in the Periphery, 1982. *Recreations:* sports, music, gardening, reading. *Address:* 89 Old Hope Road, Kingston 6, Jamaica.

MANN, Bruce Leslie Home D.; *see* Douglas-Mann.

MANN, Eric John; Controller, Capital Taxes Office, 1978-81; *b* 18 Dec. 1921; *s* of Percival John Mann and Marguerite Mann; *m* 1960, Gwendolen Margaret Salter; one *s* one *d*. *Educ:* University Coll. Sch., Hampstead; Univ. of London (LLB). Entered Inland Revenue, 1946; Dep. Controller, Capital Taxes Office, 1974. *Publications:* (ed jtly) Green's Death Duties, 5th-7th edns, 1962-71. *Address:* 74 Riddlesdown Road, Purley, Surrey.

MANN, Dr Felix Bernard; medical practitioner; *b* 10 April 1931; *s* of Leo and Caroline Mann. *Educ:* Shrewsbury Sch.; Malvern Coll.; Christ's Coll., Cambridge; Westminster Hosp. MB, BChir, LMCC. Practised medicine or studied acupuncture in England, Canada, Switzerland, France, Germany, Austria and China. *Publications:* Acupuncture: the ancient Chinese art of healing, 1962, 2nd edn 1971; The Treatment of Disease by Acupuncture, 1963; The Meridians of Acupuncture, 1964; Atlas of Acupuncture, 1966; Acupuncture: cure of many diseases, 1971; Scientific Aspects of Acupuncture, 1977; also edns in Italian, Spanish, Dutch, Finnish and Portuguese; contrib. various jls on acupuncture. *Recreations:* walking in the country and mountains. *Address:* 15 Devonshire Place, W1N 1PB. *T:* 01-935 7575. *Club:* Royal Society of Medicine.

MANN, Frederick (Francis) Alexander, CBE 1980; FBA 1974; LLD, DrJur; Solicitor of the Supreme Court, since 1946; Hon. Professor of Law in the University of Bonn, since 1960; *b* 11 Aug. 1907; *s* of Richard Mann and Ida (*née* Oppenheim); *m* 1933, Eleonore (*née* Ehrlich) (*d* 1980); one *s* two *d*. *Educ:* Univs of Geneva, Munich, Berlin (DrJur) and London (LLD). Asst, Faculty of Law, Univ. of Berlin, 1929-33; German lawyer, 1933; Internat. Law Consultant, London, 1933-46; Solicitor, 1946; Mem., Legal Div., Allied Control Council (British Element), Berlin, 1946; Partner, Herbert Smith & Co, 1957-. Member: Lord Chancellor's Standing Cttee for Reform of Private Internat. Law, 1952-64; numerous Working Parties of Law Commn. Member: Council, British Inst. of Internat. and Comparative Law; Rapporteur, 1952-73, Monetary Law Cttee, Internat. Law Assoc. Special Consultant, Cttee on Foreign Money Liabilities, Council of Europe, 1964-67; Chm., Cttee on Place of Payment, Council of Europe, 1968-71. Counsel for Belgium in Barcelona Traction Case, The Hague, 1969-70; Counsel for Federal Republic of Germany in Young Loan Case, Koblenz and Bonn, 1979-80. Mem., Editorial Cttee, British Year Book of International Law. Mem., Institut de Droit International. Lectures at Acad. of Internat. Law at The Hague, 1959, 1964 and 1971, and at numerous Univs in England, Austria, Belgium, Germany, Switzerland and USA. Blackstone Lectr, Oxford, 1978. Hon. Mem., Amer. Soc. of Internat. Law, 1980. Hon. DrJur Kiel. Grand Cross of Merit, Federal Republic of Germany, 1977, with Star, 1982. *Publications:* The Legal Aspect of Money, 1938, 4th edn 1982; Studies in International Law, 1973; numerous articles on international law, the conflict of laws, and monetary law in English and foreign legal pubns and periodicals. *Recreations:* music, walking. *Address:* Flat 4, 56 Manchester Street, W1. *T:* 01-487 4735. *Club:* Athenæum.

MANN, Rev. George Albert Douglas; General Secretary, Free Church Federal Council, 1970-79; *b* 17 April 1914; *er s* of George and Alice Mann; *m* 1940, Mabel Harwood; no *c*. *Educ:* Clifford Road Sch., Ipswich; Manchester Baptist Coll.; Manchester Univ. Minister, Mount Pleasant Baptist Church, Burnley, 1940-42. Chaplain to HM Forces, 1942-45 (now Hon. CF); Sen. Staff Chaplain, ALFSEA, 1945-46. Minister: Park Tabernacle Baptist Church, Great Yarmouth, 1947-52; Union Baptist Church, High Wycombe, 1952-58. Mem. Baptist Union Council, 1948-; Asst Sec., and Sec. of Hosp. Chaplaincy Bd, Free Church Federal Council, 1958-69. *Recreations:* gardening, philately. *Address:* 5 Gresham Close, Eastbourne, E Sussex BN21 1UW. *T:* Eastbourne 32540.

MANN, Dame Ida (Caroline), DBE 1980 (CBE 1950); MA Oxon, DSc London; MB, BS London; FRCS; FRACS; Cons. Surgeon, Royal London Ophthalmic (Moorfields) Hospital; late Member Expert Committee, WHO; late Cons. Ophthalmologist to Government of Western Australia; *b* London, 1893; *d* of F. W. Mann, MBE, and Ellen Packham; *m* 1944, William Ewart Gye, FRS, MD, FRCP (*d* 1952). *Educ:* University of London. Ophthalmic surgeon and research worker; late Research Student, Institute of Pathology, St Mary's Hospital; Henry George Plimmer Fellow of the Imperial College of Science and Technology; Assistant Surgeon, Central London Ophthalmic Hospital; Ophthalmic Surgeon, Royal Free Hospital and Elizabeth Garrett Anderson Hospital; Pathologist, Central London Ophthalmic Hospital; Senior Surgeon Oxford Eye Hospital; Margaret Ogilvie Reader, University of Oxford, 1941, Professor 1945-47; War Service as Head of Research Team for Ministry of Supply. Hon. MD Western Australia, 1977. Fellow of St Hugh's College; Gifford Edmonds Prize in Ophthalmology, 1926; Arris and Gale Lecturer, 1928; Doyne Memorial Lecturer, 1929; Montgomery Lecturer, 1935; Nettleship Prize, 1930; Mackenzie Memorial Medal, 1935; Howe Memorial Medal, 1958; Bowman Medal, 1961. Member: Ophthalmological Society of UK and other societies. *Publications:* The Development of the Human Eye; Developmental Abnormalities of the Eye; Culture, Race, Climate and Eye

Disease; and numerous papers in medical journals. *Recreation:* travel. *Address:* 56 Hobbs Avenue, Nedlands, Western Australia 6009, Australia.

MANN, John Frederick; Secretary, Schools Council for the Curriculum and Examinations, since 1978; *b* 4 June 1930; *e s* of Frederick Mann and Hilda G. (*née* Johnson); *m* 1966, Margaret (*née* Moore); one *s* one *d*. *Educ:* Poole and Tavistock Grammar Schs; Trinity Coll., Oxford (MA). Asst Master, Colchester Royal Grammar Sch., 1954–61; Admin. Asst, Leeds County Bor., 1962–65; Asst Educn Officer, Essex CC, 1965–67; Dep. Educn Officer, Sheffield County Bor., 1967–78. Member: Iron and Steel Industry Trng Bd, 1975–78; Exec., Soc. of Educn Officers, 1976–78; Sch. Broadcasting Council, 1979–; Council, British Educn Management and Admin Soc., 1979–. Hon. Fellow, Sheffield Polytechnic, 1980. FBIM; FRSA. *Publications:* Education, 1979; contrib. to Victoria County History of Essex, Local Govt Studies, and Educn. *Recreations:* travel, books, theatre, gardening. *Address:* 109 Chatsworth Road, NW2 4BH. *T:* 01-459 5419.

MANN, Julia de Lacy, MA; Principal, St Hilda's College, Oxford, 1928–July 1955; *o d* of James Saumarez Mann, MA, sometime Fellow of Trinity College, Oxford; *b* Aug. 1891. *Educ:* Bromley High Sch.; Somerville Coll., Oxford (Hon. Fellow, 1978). Classical Hon. Mods. 1912; Lit. Hum. 1914. Secretarial work, Admiralty and Foreign Office, 1915–19; Vice-Principal, St Hilda's Coll., 1923–28. Hon. Fellow, Merton Coll., Oxford, 1979. Hon. DLitt Oxon, 1973. *Publications:* (with A. P. Wadsworth), The Cotton Trade and Industrial Lancashire, 1600–1780, 1931, Ed. Documents illustrating the Wiltshire Textile Trades in the 18th Century (Wilts Arch. Society, Records Branch, Vol. XIX), 1964; The Cloth Industry in the West of England, 1640–1880, 1971. *Address:* The Cottage, Bower Hill, Melksham, Wilts. *Club:* University Women's.

MANN, Hon. Sir Michael, Kt 1982; **Hon. Mr Justice Mann;** a Judge of the High Court of Justice, Queen's Bench Division, since 1982; *b* 9 Dec. 1930; *s* of late Adrian Bernard Mann, CBE and of Mary Louise (*née* Keen); *m* 1957, Jean Marjorie (*née* Bennett), MRCVS; two *s*. *Educ:* Whitgift; King's Coll., London (LLB, PhD). Called to Bar, Gray's Inn, 1953, Bencher 1980; practised, 1955–82; Junior Counsel to the Land Commn (Common Law), 1967–71; QC 1972; a Recorder of the Crown Court, 1979–82. Asst Lectr 1954–57, Lectr 1957–64, in Law, LSE; part-time Legal Asst, FO, 1954–56. Inspector, Vale of Belvoir Coal Inquiry, 1979–80. *Publications:* (ed jtly) Dicey, Conflict of Laws, 7th edn, 1957; Dicey and Morris, Conflict of Laws, 8th edn 1967 to 10th edn, 1980. *Recreation:* making model aircraft. *Address:* The Royal Courts of Justice, WC2A 2LL.

MANN, Rt. Rev. Michael Ashley; Dean of Windsor, since 1976; Chairman, St George's House; Register, Order of the Garter, since 1976; Domestic Chaplain to the Queen, since 1976; *b* 25 May 1924; *s* of late H. G. Mann and F. M. Mann, Harrow; *m* 1949, Jill Joan Jacques; one *d* (and one *s* decd). *Educ:* Harrow Sch.; RMC Sandhurst; Wells Theological Coll.; Graduate School of Business Admin., Harvard Univ. Served War of 1939–45: RMC, Sandhurst, 1942–43; 1st King's Dragoon Guards, 1943–46 (Middle East, Italy, Palestine). Colonial Admin. Service, Nigeria, 1946–55. Wells Theological Coll., 1955–57; Asst Curate, Wolborough, Newton Abbot, 1957–59; Vicar: Sparkwell, Plymouth, 1959–62; Christ Church, Port Harcourt, Nigeria, 1962–67; Dean, Port Harcourt Social and Industrial Mission; Home Secretary, The Missions to Seamen, 1967–69; Residentiary Canon, 1969–74, Vice-Dean, 1972–74, Norwich Cathedral; Adviser to Bp of Norwich on Industry, 1969–74; Bishop Suffragan of Dudley, 1974–76. Church Comr, 1977–. Trustee, Imperial War Museum, 1980–. Governor: Harrow Sch. (Chm., 1980–); Wellington Sch., 1977–. CBIM; FRSA. *Recreations:* military history, philately, ornithology. *Address:* The Deanery, Windsor Castle, Berks SL4 1NJ. *T:* Windsor 65561. *Club:* Cavalry and Guards.

MANN, Murray G.; *see* Gell-Mann.

MANN, Rt. Rev. Peter Woodley; *see* Dunedin, Bishop of.

MANN, Ronald; Deputy Chairman, Grindlays Bank Ltd, 1964–77; Director, Grindlays Holdings Ltd, 1969–78; *b* 22 April 1908; *s* of Harry Ainsley Mann and Millicent (*née* Copplestone); *m* 1935, Beatrice Elinor Crüwell Wright; one *s* three *d*. *Educ:* Cranleigh Sch., Surrey. The Eastern Produce and Estates Co. Ltd: Asst, Ceylon, 1930–35; Man., Ceylon, 1935–46; Man. Dir, London, 1947–71; Chm., Eastern Produce Holdings Ltd, 1957–71. *Recreations:* golf, gardening. *Address:* Fernhurst Place, Fernhurst, near Haslemere, Surrey. *T:* Haslemere 52220. *Club:* Oriental.

MANN, Sir Rupert (Edward), 3rd Bt *cr* 1905; *b* 11 Nov. 1946; *s* of Major Edward Charles Mann, DSO, MC (*g s* of 1st Bt) (*d* 1959), and of Pamela Margaret, *o d* of late Major Frank Haultain Hornsby; *S* great uncle, 1971; *m* 1974, Mary Rose, *d* of Geoffrey Butler, Springhill, Saffron Walden; two *s*. *Educ:* Malvern. *Heir: s* Alexander Rupert Mann, *b* 6 April 1978. *Address:* Billingford Hall, Diss, Norfolk. *Clubs:* MCC; Norfolk.

MANN, Thaddeus Robert Rudolph, CBE 1962; FRS 1951; Biochemist; Professor of the Physiology of Reproduction, University of Cambridge, 1967–76, now Emeritus (Reader in Physiology of Animal Reproduction, 1953–67); Fellow of Trinity Hall, Cambridge, since 1961; Member of the Staff of Agricultural Research Council, 1944–76; *b* 1908; *s* of late William Mann and Emilia (*née* Quest); *m* 1934, Dr Cecilia Lutwak-Mann. *Educ:* Trin. Hall, Cambridge; MD Lwow 1935, PhD Cantab 1937, ScD Cantab 1950;

Rockefeller Research Fellow, 1935–37; Beit Mem. Research Fellow, 1937–44. Dir, ARC Unit of Reproductive Physiology and Biochemistry, Cambridge, 1954–76. Awarded Amory Prize of Amer. Academy of Arts and Sciences, 1955; Senior Lalor Fellow at Woods Hole, 1960; Vis. Prof. in Biology at Florida State Univ., 1962; Vis. Prof. in Biological Structure and Zoology, Univ. of Washington, 1968; Vis. Scientist, Reproduction Res. Br., Nat. Insts of Health, USA, 1978–82. Gregory Pincus Meml Lectr, 1969; Albert Tyler Meml Lectr, 1970. For. Member: Royal Belgian Acad. of Medicine, 1970; Polish Acad. of Science, 1980. Hon. doctorate: of Veterinary Medicine, Ghent, 1970, Hanover, 1977; of Natural Scis, Cracow, 1973. Cavaliere Ufficiale, Order of Merit (Italy), 1966. *Publications:* The Biochemistry of Semen, 1954; The Biochemistry of Semen and of the Male Reproductive Tract, 1964; (with C. Lutwak-Mann) Male Reproductive Function and Semen—Themes and Trends in Physiology, Biochemistry and Investigative Andrology, 1981; papers on Carbohydrate Metabolism of Muscle, Yeast and Moulds, on Metaloprotein Enzymes, and on Biochemistry of Reproduction. *Address:* Trinity Hall, Cambridge; 1 Courtney Way, Cambridge CB4 2EE.

MANN, William Neville, MD, FRCP; Consultant Physician Emeritus, Guy's Hospital, 1976; Physician, King Edward VII's Hospital for Officers, since 1965; *b* 4 April 1911; *s* of William Frank Mann and Clara, *d* of John Chadwick; *m* Pamela, *yr d* of late H. E. Chasteney; two *s* four *d*. *Educ:* Alleyn's Sch.; Guy's Hospital. MB, BS (London), 1935; MRCP 1937; MD (London), 1937; FRCP, 1947. House Physician, Demonstrator of Pathology and Medical Registrar, Guy's Hospital, 1935–39. Served, 1940–45, in RAMC in Middle East and Indian Ocean (Temp. Lt-Col). Physician, Guy's Hosp., 1946–76. Hon. Visiting Physician to Johns Hopkins Hosp., Baltimore, USA. Physician: to HM Household, 1954–64; to HM the Queen, 1964–70. Sen. Censor and Sen. Vice-Pres., RCP, 1969–70. *Publications:* Clinical Examination of Patients (jointly), 1950; The Medical Works of Hippocrates (jointly), 1950. Editor, Conybeare's Text-book of Medicine, 16th edn, 1975. *Address:* Keats' House, Guy's Hospital, SE1 9RT. *T:* 01-407 7600. *Clubs:* Athenæum, Garrick.

MANN, William Somervell; Radio Broadcaster on music since 1949; Associate Editor, Opera, since 1954; *b* 14 Feb. 1924; *s* of late Gerald and Joyce Mann; *m* 1948, Erika Charlotte Emilie Sohler; four *d*. *Educ:* Winchester Coll.; Magdalene Coll., Cambridge (BA, MusB). Music Critic, Cambridge Review, 1946–48; Asst Music Critic, The Times, 1948–60, Music Critic 1960–82. Member: ISM; CAMRA; Royal Musical Assoc.; The Critics' Circle (Pres., 1963–64). *Publications:* Introduction to the Music of J. S. Bach, 1950; (contrib. to symposium) Benjamin Britten, 1952; (contrib. to): The Concerto, 1952; The Record Guide, 1955; Chamber Music, 1957; The Analytical Concert Guide (English Editor), 1957; (contrib.) Music and Western Man, 1958; Let's Fake an Opera (with F. Reizenstein), 1958; Richard Strauss's Operas, 1964; Wagner's The Ring, Introduction and Translation, 1964; (contrib. to symposium) Michael Tippett, 1965; Wagner's Tristan, Introduction and Translation, 1968; The Operas of Mozart, 1977; (contrib.) Opera on Record, 1979; Music in Time, 1982; contributor: Musical Times, Opera, The Gramophone. *Recreations:* camping, winemaking, destructive gardening, phillumenism, interior decoration, food and drink, foreign languages, shove-halfpenny, Mah-Jong, making music. *Address:* 135 Cottenham Park Road, SW20 0DW. *T:* 01-946 0773.

MANNERS, family name of **Baron Manners,** and **Duke of Rutland.**

MANNERS, 5th Baron *cr* 1807; **John Robert Cecil Manners;** Partner, Osborne, Clarke & Co., Solicitors, Bristol; *b* 13 Feb. 1923; *s* of 4th Baron Manners, MC, and of Mary Edith, *d* of late Rt Rev. Lord William Cecil; *S* father, 1972; *m* 1949, Jennifer Selena, *d* of Ian Fairbairn; one *s* two *d*. *Educ:* Eton; Trinity College, Oxford. Served as Flt-Lieut, RAFVR, 1941–46. Solicitor to the Supreme Court, 1949. Official Receiver of the New Forest, 1983–. *Recreations:* hunting and shooting. *Heir: s* Hon. John Hugh Robert Manners, *b* 5 May 1956. *Address:* Wortley House, Wotton-under-Edge, Glos. *T:* Wotton-under-Edge 3174. *Clubs:* Brooks's; Constitutional (Bristol).

MANNERS, Elizabeth Maude, TD 1962; MA; Headmistress of Felixstowe College, Suffolk, 1967–79; Member, East Anglia Regional Health Authority, since 1982; *b* 20 July 1917; *d* of William George Manners and Anne Mary Manners (*née* Seed). *Educ:* Stockton-on-Tees Sec. Sch.; St Hild's Coll., Durham Univ. BA (Dunelm) 1938; MA 1941. Teacher of French at: Marton Grove Sch., Middlesbrough, 1939–40; Ramsey Gram. Sch., IOM, 1940–42; Consett Sec. Sch., Durham, 1942–44; Yarm Gram. Sch., Yorks, 1944–54; Deputy Head, Mexborough Gram. Sch., Yorks, 1954–59; Head Mistress, Central Gram. Sch. for Girls, Manchester, 1959–67. Vice-President: Girl Guides Assoc., Co. Manchester, 1959–67; Suffolk Agric. Assoc., 1967–82. Member: Educn Cttee, Brit. Fedn of Univ. Women, 1966–68; Council, Bible Reading Fellowship, 1973–81; Cttee, E Br., RSA, 1974–; Cttee, ISIS East, 1974–79. Mem., Suffolk CC, 1977– (Member: Educn Cttee, 1977–; Staff Joint and Personnel Cttees, 1981–); Vice-Chm., Secondary Educn Cttee, 1981–); Mem., Suffolk War Pensions Cttee, 1980–. Sponsor, the Responsible Society, 1982–. Enlisted ATS (TA), 1947; commissioned, 1949. FRSA 1972. Coronation Medal, 1953. *Publications:* The Vulnerable Generation, 1971; The Story of Felixstowe College, 1980. *Recreations:* foreign travel, theatre, motoring, good food and wine. *Address:* 6 Graham Court, Hamilton Gardens, Felixstowe, Suffolk. *Club:* East India, Devonshire, Sports and Public Schools.

MANNIN, Ethel, author; *e d* of Robert Mannin and Edith Gray; *b* London, 1900; *m* 1920, J. A. Porteous (*d* 1954); one *d*; *m* 1938, Reginald Reynolds (*d* 1958). *Educ:* Local Council Sch. Associate-Editor, theatrical paper, The Pelican, 1918; joined ILP 1932. *Publications:* Martha, 1923; Hunger of the Sea, 1924; Sounding Brass, 1925; Pilgrims, 1927; Green Willow, 1928; Crescendo, 1929; Children of the Earth, 1930; Confessions and Impressions, 1930; Ragged Banners, 1931; Commonsense and the Child, 1931; Green Figs (stories), 1931; Linda Shawn, 1932; All Experience (travel sketches), 1932; Venetian Blinds, 1933; Dryad (stories), 1933; Men are Unwise, 1934; Forever Wandering (travel sketches), 1934; Cactus, 1935; The Falconer's Voice (stories), 1935; The Pure Flame, 1936; South to Samarkand (travel), 1936; Women also Dream, 1937; Commonsense and the Adolescent, 1938; Women and the Revolution, 1938; Rose and Sylvie, 1938; Darkness my Bride, 1939; Privileged Spectator (sequel to Confessions), 1939; Julie, 1940; Rolling in the Dew, 1940; Christianity or Chaos: a Re-Statement of Religion, 1940; Red Rose: a Novel based on the Life of Emma Goldman, 1941; Commonsense and Morality, 1942; Captain Moonlight, 1942; The Blossoming Bough, 1943; No More Mimosa (stories), 1943; Proud Heaven, 1944; Bread and Roses, A Survey of and a Blue-Print for Utopia, 1944; Lucifer and the Child, 1945; The Dark Forest, 1946; Comrade, O Comrade, 1947; Late Have I Loved Thee, 1948; Connemara Journal (memoirs), 1948; German Journey (travel), 1948; Every Man a Stranger, 1949; Jungle Journey (travel), 1950; Bavarian Story, 1950; At Sundown, the Tiger . . ., 1951; The Fields at Evening, 1952; The Wild Swans (Tales from the Ancient Irish), 1952; This Was a Man (biography), 1952; Moroccan Mosaic (travel), 1953; Lover Under Another Name, 1953; Two Studies in Integrity (biography), 1954; So Tiberius (novella), 1954; Land of the Crested Lion (travel), 1955; The Living Lotus, 1956; Pity the Innocent, 1957; Country of the Sea (travel), 1957; A Scent of Hyacinths, 1958; Ann and Peter in Sweden (Children's book), 1958; Ann and Peter in Japan, 1960; Ann and Peter in Austria, 1961; The Blue-eyed Boy, 1959; Brief Voices (autobiography) 1959; The Flowery Sword (travel), 1960; Sabishisa, 1961; Curfew at Dawn, 1962; With Will Adams through Japan, 1962; A Lance for the Arabs (Travels in the Middle East), 1963; The Road to Beersheba (novel), 1963; Rebels' Ride, the Revolt of the Individual, 1964; Aspects of Egypt, some Travels in the United Arab Republic, 1964; The Burning Bush, 1965; The Lovely Land: the Hashemite Kingdom of Jordan, 1965; The Night and its Homing, 1966; Loneliness, A Study of the Human Condition, 1966; An American Journey, 1967; The Lady and the Mystic, 1967; England for a Change (travel), 1968; Bitter Babylon, 1968; The Saga of Sammy-Cat (children's story), 1969; The Midnight Street (novel), 1969; Practitioners of Love, Some Aspects of the Human Phenomenon, 1969; England at Large (travel), 1970; Free Pass to Nowhere (novel), 1970; Young in the Twenties (autobiography), 1971; My Cat Sammy, 1971; The Curious Adventure of Major Fosdick (novel), 1972; England My Adventure (travel), 1972; Mission to Beirut (novel), 1973; Stories from My Life (autobiog.), 1973; Kildoon (novel), 1974; An Italian Journey (travel), 1974; The Late Miss Guthrie (novel), 1976; Sunset over Dartmoor, A Final Chapter of Autobiography, 1977. *Recreation:* gardening. *Address:* Overhill, Shaldon, Teignmouth, Devon.

MANNING, Cecil Aubrey Gwynne; *b* 1892; *s* of Charles Walter Manning; *m* 1915, *d* of William Twitchett; two *s* two *d*; *m* 1940, *d* of William Green; one *s*. Rifleman, 1914-18, Queen's Westminsters and The Rangers (wounded in France, amputation of right arm); ARP and Civil Defence, and Invasion Defence Controller (Camberwell), 1939-44 (Defence Medal). Mem. LCC 1922-32 and 1937-49. Leader of Opposition, 1929-30, Dep. Chm., 1930-31; Member Metropolitan Borough Councils: Wandsworth, 1919-22; Camberwell, 1931-53 (Mayor, 1951-53); Mem., Shepton Mallet UDC, 1954-68 (Chm., 1967-68). MP (Lab) N Camberwell, 1944-50. JP 1927, DL 1931-82, Greater London (formerly Co. London). Coronation Medal 1953. *Address:* Woodstock, Norville Lane, Cheddar, Somerset.

MANNING, Frederick Allan, CVO 1954; ISO 1971; JP; Commissioner for Transport, Queensland, 1967-70, retired (Deputy Commissioner, 1960-67); *b* Gladstone, Qld, Australia, 27 Aug. 1904; British parentage; *m* 1934, Phyllis Maud Furlong; no *c*. *Educ:* Central Boys' State Sch. and Boys' Gram. Sch., Rockhampton, Qld. Entered Qld State Public Service as Clerk in Petty Sessions Office, Rockhampton, 1920; Clerk of Petty Sessions and Mining Registrar, 1923; Stipendiary Magistrate and Mining Warden, 1934; Petty Sessions Office, Brisbane, 1926; Relieving Clerk of Petty Sessions and Mining Registrar, 1931 (all parts of State); seconded to Commonwealth Govt for service in Qld Directorate of Rationing Commission, 1942; Asst Dep. Dir of Rationing, 1943. Dep. Dir, 1944, for Qld; returned to Qld Public Service, 1947; Sec., Dept of Transport, 1947-60; JP, Qld, 1925-. Coronation Medal, 1953; State Dir, Royal Visit to Queensland, 1954 (CVO). Exec. Vice-Chm., Qld Road Safety Coun., and Qld Rep. Aust. Road Safety Coun., 1962. Mem., Greyhound Racing Control Bd of Queensland, 1971-77. *Recreation:* bowls. *Address:* 126 Indooroopilly Road, Taringa, Brisbane, Qld 4068, Australia. *T:* 370-1936. *Club:* Tattersalls (Brisbane).

MANNING, Frederick Edwin Alfred, CBE 1954; MC 1919; TD 1937; BSc (Eng.); Hon. MA London; Hon. DEng NSTC; Hon. LLD RMC of Canada; Hon. DSc City; CEng; FIMechE; FIEE; FINucE; DPA (London); retired; *b* 6 April 1897; *s* of late Francis Alfred Manning and late Ellen Lavinia Manning; *m* 1927, Alice Beatrice Wistow, BSc; one *s* one *d* (and one *s* decd). *Educ:* Christ's Hospital; St Olave's; Univ. of London. Academic Diploma of Mil. Studies, Univ. of London; Certificate in Statistics, Univ. of Vienna. War Service, 1915-20 (Order of St Stanislas, 2nd Class; Order of St Vladimir, 4th

Class); RE (TA) 1920-38; Royal Signals (TA), 1938-52. Hon. Col, Univ. of London OTC, 1958-68, retired 1968, retaining rank of Col. Entered GPO 1925; late 1937; Home Office and Min. of Home Security, 1938-41; GPO, 1941; SHAEF, 1943-45; Asst Sec., Foreign Office (Allied Commission for Austria), 1945-47; GPO, 1947; Dir of the Post Office in Wales and Border Counties, 1950-59; Adviser on Athlone Fellowship Scheme, 1961-72; Chm. Boards for the CS Commn, 1961-68; Hon. Sen. Treas., Univ. of London Union, 1928-52, Chm. of Union Court, 1952-69, Chm., Sports Finance Cttee, 1969-74; Mem. of Senate, Univ. of London, 1952-74 (Chm. Military Educ. Cttee, 1952-55); First Chm. of Convocation, The City Univ., 1967-70; Vice-Pres., Univs in London Catholic Chaplaincy Assoc., 1970-. Metrop. Special Constabulary (Comdt, GPO Div.), 1931-41. KSG 1972. *Recreations:* gardening, Rotary (Pres. Shepperton, 1964-65). *Address:* 1 Range Way, Shepperton, TW17 9NW. *T:* Walton-on-Thames 23400. *Club:* Royal Commonwealth Society.

MANNING, Air Cdre Frederick John, CB 1954; CBE 1948; retired, 1967; *b* 5 May 1912; *s* of Frederick Manning; *m* 1937, Elizabeth Anwyl, *er d* of late Rev. Æ. C. Ruthven-Murray, BA, Bishop Burton, Beverley; four *d* (and one *s* decd). Cadet, P&OSN Co., 1928; Midshipman, RNR, 1929; Actg Sub-Lt, RNR, 1933; Pilot Officer, RAF, 1934; Flt Lt, 269 Squadron, 1938; Actg Group Capt., 1942; Dir of Organisation (Establishments), Air Ministry, 1944-45 (actg Air Commodore); commanding RAF Station Shaibah, Abu Sueir Shallufa, 1945-47 (acting Group Capt.); Group Capt., Organisation, HQ, RAF, Mediterranean and Middle East, 1947-48; Senior Air Adviser, and Dep. Head of Mission, British Services Mission, Burma, 1949-52; Senior Officer i/c Administration HQ Transport Command, 1952; Dep. Dir of Work Study, Air Ministry, 1956-59; Dir of Manning (2) Air Ministry, 1960-63; Air Officer Administration: HQ Near East Air Force, 1963-65; HQ Fighter Comd, 1965-67. *Address:* Myrtle Cottage, Eynsham, Oxford. *Club:* Royal Air Force.

MANNING, Dr Geoffrey; Director, Rutherford Appleton Laboratory, Science and Engineering Research Council, since 1981; *b* 31 Aug. 1929; *s* of Jack Manning and Ruby Frances Lambe; *m* 1951, Anita Jacqueline Davis; two *s* one *d*. *Educ:* Tottenham Grammar Sch.; Imperial Coll., London Univ. BSc, PhD; ARCS. Asst Lectr in Physics, Imperial Coll., 1953-55; Research worker: English Electric Co., 1955-56; Canadian Atomic Energy Co., 1956-58; Calif Inst. of Technol., 1958-59; AERE, 1960-65; Rutherford Laboratory, Science Research Council: Gp Leader, 1965-69; Dep. Dir, 1969-79; Head of High Energy Physics Div., 1969-75; Head of Atlas Div., 1975-79; Dir, Rutherford (Rutherford & Appleton Labs), 1979-81. *Recreations:* golf, squash, ski-ing. *Address:* 38 Sunningwell, Abingdon, Oxon OX13 6RB. *T:* Oxford 736123.

MANNING, Jane Marian; freelance concert and opera singer (soprano), since 1965; *b* 20 Sept. 1938; *d* of Gerald Manville Manning and Lily Manning (*née* Thompson); *m* 1966, Anthony Edward Payne, composer. *Educ:* Norwich High Sch.; Royal Academy of Music (LRAM 1958); Scuola di Canto, Cureglia, Switzerland. GRSM 1960, ARCM 1962. London début (Park Lane Group), 1964; first BBC broadcast, 1965; regular appearances in leading concert halls and festivals in UK and Europe, with leading orchestras and conductors. Specialist in contemporary music (over 200 world premières given); Warsaw Autumn Fest., 1975-78; début Henry Wood Promenade Concerts, 1972; Wexford Opera Fest., 1976; Scottish Opera, 1978; Brussels Opera, 1980. Canadian début, 1977; tours of Australia and New Zealand, 1978, 1980, 1982; tours of USA, 1981, 1983; many broadcasts and gramophone recordings, lectures and master classes. Lucie Stern Vis. Prof., Mills Coll., Oakland, 1981. Member, Internat. Jury, Gaudeamus Young Interpreters Competition, Holland, 1976, 1979. Hon. ARAM 1972; special award, Composers Guild of Gt Britain, 1973. *Publications:* chapter in How Music Works, 1981; articles in Composer, and Music and Musicians. *Recreations:* cooking, cinema, ornithology. *Address:* 2 Wilton Square, N1 3DL. *T:* 01-359 1593.

MANNING, Thomas Henry, OC 1974; zoologist; *b* 22 Dec. 1911; *s* of Thomas E. and Dorothy (*née* Randall) Manning, Shrublands, Dallington, Northampton; *m* 1938, Ella Wallace Jackson. *Educ:* Harrow; Cambridge. Winter journey across Lapland, 1932-33; Survey and Zoological work on Southampton Island, 1933-35; Leader, Brit. Canadian-Arctic Exped., 1936-41; Royal Canadian Navy, 1941-45; Geodetic Service of Canada, 1945-47; Leader Geographical Bureau Expedition to Prince Charles I. (Foxe Basin), 1949; Zoological and Geographical work in James Bay, 1950; Leader Defence Research Board Expeditions: Beaufort Sea, 1951; Banks Island, 1952, 1953; Nat. Mus. Canadian Expedition; King William Island, Adelaide Peninsula, 1957, Prince of Wales Island, 1958. FRGS (Patron's Gold Medal, 1948). Hon. LLD McMaster, 1979. Bruce Memorial Prize (Royal Society of Edinburgh, RPS, RSGS), 1944; Massey Medal, Royal Canadian Geographical Soc., 1977. Guggenheim Fellow, 1959. *Publications:* The Birds of North Western Ungava, 1949; Birds of the West James Bay and Southern Hudson Bay Coasts, 1952; Birds of Banks Island, 1956; Mammals of Banks Island, 1958; A Biological Investigation of Prince of Wales Island, 1961; articles in The Auk, Journal Mamm. and Geog. Journal, Canadian Geog. Jl., Canadian Field-Naturalist, Arctic, Nat. Mus. Can. Bull. *Recreations:* shooting, book-binding, cabinet-making, farming. *Address:* RR4, Merrickville, Ont., Canada. *T:* 269-4940.

MANNINGHAM-BULLER, family name of Viscount Dilhorne.

MANS, Maj.-Gen. Rowland Spencer Noel, CBE 1971 (OBE 1966, MBE 1956); Director, Military Assistance Office, 1973-76, retired; *b* 16 Jan. 1921; *s* of Thomas Frederick Mans and May Seigenberg; *m* 1945, Veeo Ellen Sutton; three *s*. *Educ:* Surbiton Grammar Sch.; RMC, Sandhurst; jssc, psc. Served War, Queen's Royal Regt and King's African Rifles, 1940-45. Regtl and Staff Duty, 1945-59; Instr, Staff Colleges, Camberley and Canada, 1959-63; Comd, 1st Tanganyika Rifles, 1963-64; Staff Duty, Far East and UK, 1964-68; Comd, Aldershot, 1969-72; DDPS (Army), 1967-73. Col, Queen's Regt, 1978- (Dep. Col (Surrey), 1973-77). Defence consultant and writer on defence and political affairs. *Recreations:* writing, reading, gardening. *Address:* Kirke House, Sway Road, Brockenhurst, Hants. *T:* Lymington 22291. *Club:* Army and Navy.

MANSAGER, Felix Norman, KBE (Hon.) 1976 (Hon. CBE 1973); Director and Member of Executive Committee, Hoover Co. USA (President-Chairman, Hoover Co. and Hoover World-wide Corporation, 1966-75); Director, Hoover Ltd UK (Chairman, 1966-75); *b* 30 Jan. 1911; *s* of Hoff Mansager and Alice (*née* Qualseth); *m* Geraldine (*née* Larson); one *s* two *d*. *Educ:* South Dakota High Sch., Colton. Joined Hoover Co. as Salesman, 1929; Vice-Pres., Sales, 1959; Exec. Vice-Pres. and Dir, 1961. Member: Council on Foreign Relations; Newcomen Soc. in N America; Trustee, Graduate Theological Union (Calif); The Pilgrims of the US; Assoc. of Ohio Commodores; Masonic Shrine (32nd degree Mason); Mem. and Governor, Ditchley Foundn; Member Board of Trustees: Ohio Foundn of Indep. Colls; Indep. Coll. Funds of America. Hon. Mem., World League of Norsemen. Marketing Award, British Inst. of Marketing, 1971. Executive Prof. of Business (Goodyear Chair), Univ. of Akron (Mem. Delta Sigma Pi; Hon. Mem., Beta Sigma Gamma). Hon. Fellow, UC Cardiff, 1973. Hon. Dr of Laws Capital Univ., 1967; Hon. LLD Strathclyde, 1970; Hon. DHL Malone Coll., Canton, Ohio, 1972; Hon. PhD Walsh Coll., Canton, 1974; Hon. Dr Humanities Wartburg Coll., Waverly, Iowa, 1976; Medal of Honor, Vassa Univ., Finland, 1973; Person of Year, Capital Univ. Chapter of Tau Pi Phi, 1981. Grand Officier, Dukes of Burgundy, 1968; Chevalier: Order of Leopold, 1969; Order of St Olav, Norway, 1971; Legion of Honour, France, 1973; Grande Officiale, Order Al Merito della Republica Italiana, 1975. *Recreation:* golf. *Address:* 3421 Lindel Court NW, Canton, Ohio 44718, USA. *Clubs:* Metropolitan (NYC); Congress Lake Country (Hartville, Ohio); Torske (Hon.) (Minneapolis).

MANSEL, Rev. Canon James Seymour Denis, KCVO 1979 (MVO 1972); Extra Chaplain to the Queen, since 1979; Sub-Dean of HM Chapels Royal, Deputy Clerk of the Closet, Sub-Almoner and Domestic Chaplain to the Queen, 1965-79; *b* 18 June 1907; *e s* of Edward Mansel, FRIBA, Leamington, and Muriel Louisa (*née* Denis Browne); *m* 1942, Ann Monica (*d* 1974), *e d* of Amyas Waterhouse, MD, Boars Hill, Oxford, and Ruth (*née* Gamlen); one *d*. *Educ:* Brighton Coll.; Exeter Coll., Oxford (MA); Westcott House. Asst Master, Dulwich Coll., 1934-39; Asst Master, Chaplain and House Master, Winchester Coll., 1939-65; Canon and Prebendary of Chichester Cathedral, 1971-81, Canon Emeritus, 1981. Mem., Winchester City Coun., 1950-56. JP: City of Winchester, 1964; Inner London Commn, 1972. FSA. ChStJ. *Address:* 15 Sandringham Court, Maida Vale, W9 1UA. *T:* 01-286 3052; Field House, Pitt, Winchester. *T:* Winchester 4812. *Club:* Athenæum.

MANSEL, Sir Philip, 15th Bt, *cr* 1621; FInstSM; Managing Director of Eden-Vale Engineering Co. Ltd; *b* 3 March 1943; *s* of Sir John Mansel, 14th Bt and Hannah, *d* of Ben Rees; *S* father, 1947; *m* 1968, Margaret, *o d* of Arthur Docker; one *s* one *d*. *Heir:* *s* John Philip Mansel, *b* 19 April 1982. *Address:* 4 Redhill Drive, Fellside Park, Whickham, Newcastle upon Tyne NE16 5TY.

MANSEL-JONES, David; Chairman, Huntingdon Research Centre, since 1978 (Vice-Chairman, 1974-78); *b* 8 Sept. 1926; *o s* of Rees Thomas Jones and Ceinwen Jones; *m* 1952, Mair Aeronwen Davies; one *s*. *Educ:* St Michael's Sch., Bryn; London Hospital. MB, BS 1950; MRCP 1973. Jun. Surgical Specialist, RAMC; Dep. Med. Dir, Wm R. Warner & Co. Ltd, 1957-59; Med. Dir, Richardson-Merrell Ltd, 1959-65; formerly PMO, SMO and MO, Cttee on Safety of Drugs; Med. Assessor, Cttee on Safety of Medicines, 1970-; Consultant to WHO; Senior PMO, Medicines Div., DHSS, 1971-74. Vis. Prof., Gulbenkian Science Inst., Portugal, 1981; Examiner, Dip. Pharm. Med., Royal Colls of Physicians, UK. *Publications:* papers related to safety of medicines. *Recreations:* music, painting. *Address:* 10 Pakenham Close, Cambridge CB4 1PW. *T:* Cambridge 358121; 9 Aldeburgh Lodge Gardens, Aldeburgh, Suffolk.

MANSEL LEWIS, David Courtenay; Lord-Lieutenant of Dyfed, since 1979 (Lieutenant, 1974-79; HM Lieutenant for Carmarthenshire, 1973-74); JP; *b* 25 Oct. 1927; *s* of late Charlie Ronald Mansel Lewis and Lillian Georgina Warner, *d* of Col Sir Courtenay Warner, 1st Bt, CB; *m* 1953, Lady Mary Rosemary Marie-Gabrielle Montagu-Stuart-Wortley, 4th *d* of 3rd Earl of Wharncliffe; one *s* two *d*. *Educ:* Eton; Keble Coll., Oxford (BA). Served in Welsh Guards, 1946-49; Lieut 1946, RARO. High Sheriff, Carmarthenshire, 1965; JP 1969; DL 1971. FRSA; KStJ. *Recreations:* music, sailing. *Address:* Stradey Castle, Llanelli, Dyfed. *T:* Llanelli 4626. *Clubs:* Lansdowne; Cruising Association.

MANSELL, Lt-Col George William, CBE 1959; DL; RA, retired; Chairman, new Dorset County Council, 1973-77; *b* 25 Dec. 1904; *s* of late Lt-Col Sir John H. Mansell, KBE, DL, RA (retd); *m* 1st, 1934, Joan (*d* 1940),

d of late Spencer Dawson, Stratton Hall, Levington, Ipswich; one *s* one *d*; 2nd, 1941, Mary Elizabeth, *d* of late Major C. L. Blew, Hafod, Trefnant, Denbigh. *Educ:* Wellington Coll., Berks; RMA Woolwich. Commnd into RA, 1924; wounded N Africa, 1942; invalided as a result, 1947. Dorset CC, 1950-77: Alderman, 1955-74; Vice-Chm., 1966; Chm., 1967-74; Hon. Alderman, 1977. DL Dorset, 1968. *Recreation:* fishing. *Address:* Kit Robins, Lytchett Matravers, Poole, Dorset. *T:* Morden (Dorset) 240.

MANSELL, Gerard Evelyn Herbert, CBE 1977; Managing Director, External Broadcasting, BBC, 1972-81; Deputy Director-General, BBC, 1977-81; retired; *b* 16 Feb. 1921; 2nd *s* of late Herbert and of Anne Mansell, Paris; *m* 1956, Diana Marion Sherar; two *s*. *Educ:* Lycée Hoche, Versailles; Lycée Buffon, Paris; Ecole des Sciences Politiques, Paris; Chelsea Sch. of Art. Joined HM Forces, 1940; served in Western Desert, Sicily and NW Europe, 1942-45 (despatches). Joined BBC European Service, 1951; Asst Head, Overseas Talks and Features Dept, 1958, Head, 1961; Controller, BBC Radio 4 (formerly Home Service), and Music Programme, 1965-69; Dir of Programmes, BBC, Radio, 1970. Chm., British Cttee, Journalists in Europe. Governor, English-Speaking Union, 1978-. FRSA 1979; CBIM 1980. French Croix de Guerre, 1945. *Publication:* Tragedy in Algeria, 1961. *Address:* 46 Southway, Hampstead, NW11.

MANSERGH, Vice-Adm. Sir (Cecil) Aubrey (Lawson), KBE 1953; CB 1950; DSC 1915; retired; *b* 7 Oct. 1898; *s* of Ernest Lawson Mansergh and Emma Cecilia Fisher Hogg; *m* 1st, 1928, Helen Raynor Scott (*d* 1967); one *s* (and one *s* decd); 2nd, 1969, Dora, widow of Comdr L. H. L. Clarke, RN. *Educ:* RN Colleges Osborne and Dartmouth. Served European War, 1914-18; Comdr, 1932; Captain, 1938; Commanded HMNZS Achilles, 1942 and HMNZS Leander, 1943, in Pacific; Commodore 1st Cl., Admiralty, 1944-46; Commanded HMS Implacable, 1946-47; Rear-Adm. 1948; Vice-Controller of Navy and Dir of Naval Equipment, 1948-50; Commanded 2nd Cruiser Squadron, 1950-52; Vice-Adm., 1951. Pres., Royal Naval Coll., Greenwich, 1952-54, retired Dec. 1954. *Address:* 102 High Street, Rottingdean, Sussex BN2 7HF. *T:* Brighton 32213.

MANSERGH, Prof. (Philip) Nicholas (Seton), OBE 1945; DPhil 1936; DLitt Oxon 1960; LittD Cantab 1970; FBA 1973; Master of St John's College, Cambridge, 1969-79, Fellow 1955-69 and since 1979; Editor-in-chief, India Office Records on the Transfer of Power, 1967-82 (11 volumes published); Hon. Fellow: Pembroke College, Oxford, 1954; Trinity College, Dublin, 1971; *b* 27 June 1910; *yr s* of late Philip St George Mansergh and late Mrs E. M. Mansergh, Grenane House, Tipperary; *m* 1939, Diana Mary, *d* of late G. H. Keeton, Headmaster's Lodge, Reading; three *s* two *d*. *Educ:* Abbey Sch., Tipperary; College of St Columba, Dublin; Pembroke Coll., Oxford. Sec. OU Politics Research Cttee and Tutor in Politics, 1937-40; Empire Div., Ministry of Information, 1941-46; Dir, 1944-46; Asst Sec., Dominions Office, 1946-47; Abe Bailey Research Prof. of British Commonwealth Relations, RIIA, 1947-53; Smuts Prof. of History of British Commonwealth, Univ. of Cambridge, 1953-April 1970, now Emeritus Professor. Visiting Professor: Nat. Univ. of Australia, 1951; Univ. of Toronto, 1953; Duke Univ., NC, 1957 and 1965 (W. K. Boyd Prof. of History); Indian Sch. of International Studies, New Delhi, 1958 and 1966; Jawaharlal Nehru Univ., 1980; Reid Lecturer, Acadia Univ., 1960; Smuts Meml Lectr, Cambridge Univ., 1976. Member: Editorial Board, Annual Register, 1947-73; Gen. Advisory Council, BBC, 1956-62; Adv. Council on Public Records, 1966-76; Councillor, RIIA, 1953-57; Chm. Faculty Board of History, 1960-62, Bd of Graduate Studies, 1970-73, Cambridge Univ. *Publications:* The Irish Free State: Its Government and Politics, 1934; The Government of Northern Ireland, 1936; Ireland in the Age of Reform and Revolution, 1940; Advisory Bodies (Jt Editor), 1941; Britain and Ireland, 1942, 2nd edn 1946; The Commonwealth and the Nations, 1948; The Coming of the First World War, 1949; Survey of British Commonwealth Affairs (2 vols), 1931-39, 1952 and 1939-52, 1958; Documents and Speeches on Commonwealth Affairs, 1931-62 (3 vols), 1953-63; The Multi-Racial Commonwealth, 1955; (jointly) Commonwealth Perspectives, 1958; South Africa, 1906-1961, 1962; The Irish Question, 1840-1921, 1965, 3rd edn 1975; The Commonwealth Experience, 1969, 2nd edn 1982; Prelude to Partition, 1978. *Recreation:* lawn tennis. *Address:* The Lodge, Little Shelford, Cambridge CB2 5EW. *Clubs:* Royal Commonwealth Society; Kildare Street and University (Dublin).

MANSFIELD, family name of **Baron Sandhurst.**

MANSFIELD AND MANSFIELD, 8th Earl of, *cr* 1776 and 1792 (GB); William David Mungo James Murray; JP, DL; Baron Scone, 1605; Viscount Stormont, 1621; Baron Balvaird, 1641; (Earl of Dunbar, Viscount Drumcairn, and Baron Halldykes in the Jacobite Peerage); Hereditary Keeper of Bruce's Castle of Lochmaben; Lieutenant The Scots Guards (RARO); Minister of State, Scottish Office, since 1979; *b* 7 July 1930; *o s* of 7th Earl of Mansfield and Mansfield, and of Dorothea Helena, *y d* of late Rt Hon. Sir Lancelot Carnegie, GCVO, KCMG; *S* father, 1971; *m* 1955, Pamela Joan, *o d* of W. N. Foster, CBE; two *s* one *d*. *Educ:* Eton; Christ Church, Oxford. Malayan campaign, 1949-50. Called to Bar, Inner Temple, 1958; Barrister, 1958-71. Mem., British Delegn to European Parlt, 1973-75; an opposition spokesman in the House of Lords, 1975-79. Mem., Tay Salmon Fisheries Bd, 1971-79. Dir, General Accident, Fire and Life Assurance Corp. Ltd, 1971-79. Ordinary Dir, Royal Highland and Agricl Soc., 1976-79. President: Fédn des Assocs de Chasse de l'Europe, 1977-79. Scottish Assoc. for Care and Resettlement of Offenders, 1974-79; Scottish Assoc. of Boys Clubs, 1976-79;

Royal Scottish Country Dance Soc., 1977; Chm., Scottish Branch, Historic Houses Assoc., 1976-79. Mem., Perth CC, 1971-75; Hon. Sheriff for Perthshire, 1974; JP 1975, DL 1980, Perth and Kinross. *Heir: s* Viscount Stormont, *qv. Address:* Scone Palace, Perthshire PH2 6BE; 16 Thorburn House, Kinnerton Street, SW1. *Clubs:* White's, Pratt's, Turf, Beefsteak.

MANSFIELD, Rear-Adm. David Parks, CB 1964; *b* 26 July 1912; *s* of Comdr D. Mansfield, RD, RNR; *m* 1939, Jean Craig Alexander; one *s* one *d. Educ:* RN Coll., Dartmouth; RN Engineering Coll., Keyham. Lt (E) 1934; HMS Nelson, 1934-36; Staff of C-in-C Med., 1936-39; HMS Mauritius, 1939-42; Lt-Comdr (E) 1942; HMS Kelvin, 1942-43; Chatham Dockyard, 1943-46; Comdr (E) 1945; Admty (Aircraft Maintenance Dept), 1946-49; Staff of FO Air (Home), 1949-51; HMS Kenya, 1951-53; RN Engrg Coll., 1953-55; Captain 1954; RNAS Anthorn (in command), 1955-57; RN Aircraft Yard, Fleetlands (Supt.), 1957-60; Admty Dir of Fleet Maintenance, 1960-62; Rear-Adm. 1963; Rear-Adm. Aircraft, on Staff of Flag Officer Naval Air Command, 1963-65. *Recreations:* reading, gardening. *Address:* The Outlook, Salisbury Road, St Margaret's Bay, Dover, Kent. *T:* Dover 852237. *Club:* Army and Navy.

MANSFIELD, Vice-Adm. Sir (Edward) Gerard (Napier), KBE 1974; CVO 1981; retired 1975; *b* 13 July 1921; *s* of late Vice-Adm. Sir John Mansfield, KCB, DSO, DSC, and Alice Talbot Mansfield; *m* 1943, Joan Worship Byron, *d* of late Comdr John Byron DSC and late Frances Byron; two *d. Educ:* RNC, Dartmouth. Entered Royal Navy, 1935. Served War of 1939-45 in destroyers and Combined Ops (despatches), taking part in landings in N Africa and Sicily. Comdr, 1953; comd HMS Mounts Bay, 1956-58; Captain 1959; SHAPE, 1960-62; Captain (F) 20th Frigate Sqdn, 1963-64; Dir of Defence Plans (Navy), 1965-67; Cdre Amphibious Forces, 1967-68; Senior Naval Member, Directing Staff, IDC, 1969-70; Flag Officer Sea Training, 1971-72; Dep. Supreme Allied Comdr, Atlantic, 1973-75. Chm., Assoc. of RN Officers, 1975-. Chm., Crondall Parish Council, 1977-81. Mem. Admin. Council, Royal Jubilee Trusts, 1978-81. *Recreations:* tennis, golf, gardening. *Address:* White Gate House, Ewshot, Farnham, Surrey GU10 5AH. *T:* Aldershot 850325. *Club:* Army and Navy.

MANSFIELD, Eric Harold, ScD; FRS 1971; Chief Scientific Officer (individual merit), Royal Aircraft Establishment, since 1980; *b* 24 May 1923; *s* of Harold Goldsmith Mansfield and Grace Phundt; *m* 1st, 1947, Mary Ola Purves Douglas (marr. diss. 1973); two *s* one *d*; 2nd, 1974, Eunice Lily Kathleen Shuttleworth-Parker. *Educ:* St Lawrence Coll., Ramsgate; Trinity Hall, Cambridge. MA, ScD, FRS, FEng, FRAeS, FIMA. Research in Structures Department, Royal Aircraft Establishment, Farnborough, Hants: Jun. Scientific Officer, 1943; Scientific Officer, 1948; Sen. Scientific Officer, 1950; Principal Scientific Officer, 1954; Sen. Principal Scientific Officer, 1959; DCSO, 1967. Mem. Council, Royal Soc., 1977-78. *Publications:* The Bending and Stretching of Plates, 1964; contribs to: Proc. Roy. Soc., Phil. Trans., Quarterly Jl Mech. Applied Math., Aero Quarterly, Aero Research Coun. reports and memos, and to technical press. *Recreations:* bridge, palaeontology, snorkling. *Address:* Evergreens, Tudor Way, Church Crookham, Aldershot, Hampshire. *T:* Fleet 28438.

MANSFIELD, Sir Gerard; *see* Mansfield, Sir E. G. N.

MANSFIELD, Philip (Robert Aked), CMG 1973; HM Diplomatic Service; Ambassador to the Netherlands, since 1981; *b* 9 May 1926; *s* of Philip Theodore Mansfield, CSI, CIE; *m* 1953, Elinor Russell MacHatton; two *s. Educ:* Winchester; Pembroke Coll., Cambridge. Grenadier Guards, 1944-47. Sudan Political Service, 1950-54. Entered HM Diplomatic Service, 1955; served in: Addis Ababa, Singapore, Paris, Buenos Aires; Counsellor and Head of Rhodesia Dept, FCO, 1969-72; RCDS, 1973; Counsellor and Head of Chancery, 1974-75; Dep. High Comr, 1976, Nairobi; Asst Under Sec. of State, FCO, and Comr for British Indian Ocean Territory, 1976-79; Ambassador and Dep. Perm. Representative to UN, 1979-81. *Recreations:* sailing, bird watching, gardening. *Address:* c/o Foreign and Commonwealth Office, SW1. *Clubs:* Royal Commonwealth Society; Aberdare Country (Kenya).

MANSFIELD COOPER, Prof. Sir William, Kt 1963; LLM; Professor of Industrial Law, University of Manchester, 1949-70, now Professor Emeritus; Vice-Chancellor of the University, 1956-70; *b* Newton Heath, Manchester, 20 Feb. 1903; *s* of William and Georgina C. Cooper; *m* 1936, Edna Mabel, *o c* of Herbert and Elizabeth Baker; one *s. Educ:* Elementary Sch.; Ruskin Coll., 1931-33; Manchester Univ., 1933-36 (LLB, Dauntesey Jun. Law Schol., Dauntesey Special Prizeman in International Law). Grad. Res. Schol., 1936-37; Lecturer WEA (LLM 1938). University of Manchester: Asst Lecturer, 1938; Lecturer, 1942; Asst to Vice-Chancellor, 1944; Registrar and Senior Lecturer in Law, 1945; Professor of Industrial and Commercial Law, 1949, continuing as Joint Registrar until 1952; Acting Vice-Chancellor, Nov. 1953-May 1954 and July 1954-Oct. 1954. Called to the Bar (Gray's Inn), 1940. Chairman John Rylands Library, 1956-70; Chairman Cttee of Vice-Chancellors and Principals, 1961-64; President, Council of Europe Cttee on Higher Education and Research, 1966-67; Vice-President, Standing Conference of European Rectors and Vice-Chancellors, 1964-69. Dep. Chm., Cttee of Inquiry into London Univ., 1970-72. Hon. Mem., Manchester Royal Coll. Music, 1971. Hon. LLD: Manitoba, 1964; Liverpool, 1970; Manchester, 1970; Hon. DLitt Keele, 1967; Hon. DSc Kharkov, 1970; Hon. DHL Rochester, 1970. Hon. Fellow, Manchester Inst. Science and Technology, 1972. *Publications:* Outlines of Industrial Law, 1947, 6th edn by John C.

Wood, 1972; papers and reviews in learned journals. *Recreations:* gardening, bird-watching. *Address:* Fieldgate Cottage, Meldreth, Royston, Herts. *Club:* Athenæum.

MANT, Prof. Arthur Keith, MD; FRCP; FRCPath; Professor of Forensic Medicine, since 1974, and Head of Department since 1972, Guy's Hospital, University of London; Hon. Consultant in Forensic Medicine, King's College Hospital, since 1967; *b* 11 Sept. 1919; *s* of George Arthur Mant and Elsie Muriel (*née* Slark); *m* 1947, Heather Smith, BA; two *s* one *d. Educ:* Denstone Coll., Staffs; St Mary's Hosp., Paddington. MB BS 1949, MD 1950; MRCS, LRCP 1943; FRCPath 1967; MRCP 1977; FRCP 1982. Dept Obst. and Gynæc., St Mary's Hosp., 1943; RAMC, i/c Path. Section, War Crimes Gp, 1945-48 (Major); Registrar (ex-service), Med. Unit, St Mary's Hosp., 1948-49; Research Fellow, 1949-55, Lectr, 1955-66, Dept of Forensic Med., Guy's Hosp.; Sen. Lectr in Forensic Med., KCH, 1965; Reader in Forensic Med., Guy's Hosp., 1966-74. WHO Consultant, Sri Lanka, 1982. Visiting Lectr in Med. Jurisprudence and Toxicology, St Mary's Hosp., 1955-; Niels Dungal Meml Lectr, Reykjavic, 1979; British Council Lectr, India, 1979; J. B. Firth Meml Lectr, 1981. Examiner in Forensic Medicine: NUI; 1960; St Andrews Univ., 1967; Dundee Univ., 1968; RCPath, 1971; Soc. of Apothecaries, 1971; Univ. of Riyadh, Saudi Arabia, 1976; Univ. of Garyounis-Libya, 1976; Univ. of Tripoli, 1979. A. D. Williams Distinguished Scholar Fellowship, Univ. Med. Coll. of Virginia, 1963 and 1968. President: Internat. Assoc. in Accident and Traffic Med., 1972-; British Acad. of Forensic Sci., 1975-76; Past Pres., Forensic Sci. Soc., British Assoc. in Forensic Med.; Vice-Pres., Medico-Legal Soc. Nat. correspondent for GB, Internat. Acad. of Legal and Social Med.; Corresp. Mem., Amer. Acad. of Forensic Sci.; Corresp. For. Mem., Soc. de Méd. Légale; Hon. Member: Brazilian Assoc. for Traffic Med.; Soc. de Méd. Légale, Belgium; Mem., Editorial Bd, Internat. Reference Org. in Forensic Med. (INFORM); English Editor, Zeitschrift für Rechtsmedizin; Internat. Editorial Bd, Excerpta Medica (Forensic Sci. abstracts). Fellow: Indian Acad. of Forensic Sci.; Indian Assoc. in Forensic Medicine; Swedish Soc. of Med. Scis. Hon. DMJPath Soc. of Apothecaries, 1979. *Publications:* Forensic Medicine: observation and interpretation, 1960; Modern Trends in Forensic Medicine, Series 3, 1973; contribs to med. and sci. literature. *Recreations:* fishing, orchid culture. *Address:* Department of Forensic Medicine, Guy's Hospital, SE1 9RT. *T:* 01-407 0378; 29 Ashley Drive, Walton-on-Thames, Surrey KT12 1JT. *T:* Walton-on-Thames 25005. *Club:* Athenæum.

MANT, Sir Cecil (George), Kt 1964; CBE 1955; consultant and company director; Consultant to Corporation of London; Project Co-ordinator for Barbican Arts Centre, 1972-81; *b* 24 May 1906; *o s* of late George Frederick Mant and Beatrice May Mant; *m* 1940, Hilda Florence (*née* Knowles); three *d. Educ:* Trinity County Sch.; Hornsey School of Art; Northern Polytechnic School of Architecture. ARIBA 1929, FRIBA 1944, resigned 1970. Entered HM Office of Works, 1928. Visiting Lecturer in Architecture and Building to Northern Polytechnic, 1930-39; Departmental Liaison Officer to Works and Buildings Priority Cttee, 1939-40. Ministry of Public Building and Works: Deputy Director-General of Works, 1950-60; Director-General of Works, 1960-63; Controller-Gen. of Works, 1963-67. Served as member and chairman of various cttees; to British Standards Institution and Codes of Practice; Departmental Working Parties and Investigating Boards, Civil Service Commission Selection Boards, Joint Min. of Works and P.O. Study Group on P.O. Buildings Costs and Procedure, etc. Assessor to Advisory Cttee on Building Research, 1958-67; Member, Architecture Consultative Cttee, Hammersmith College of Art and Building, 1966-75. Mem., Guild of Freemen of City of London. *Address:* 44 Hamilton Court, Maida Vale, W9 1QR. *T:* 01-286 8719. *Clubs:* City Livery, Arts.

MANTELL, Hon. Charles Barrie Knight; Hon. Mr Justice Mantell; Judge of the Supreme Court, Hong Kong, since 1982; *b* 30 Jan. 1937; *s* of Francis Christopher Knight Mantell and Elsie Mantell; *m* 1960, Anne Shirley Mantell; two *d. Educ:* Manchester Grammar Sch.; Manchester Univ. (LLM). Called to the Bar, Gray's Inn, 1960. Flying Officer, RAF, 1958-61. In practice at Bar, London and Manchester, 1961-82; a Recorder of the Crown Court, 1978-82; QC 1979. *Recreations:* golf, reading, watching cricket. *Address:* Supreme Court, Hong Kong. *Clubs:* Lansdowne; Big Four (Manchester).

MANTHORP, Rev. Brian Robert, MA; Headmaster, Worcester College for the Blind, since 1980; *b* 28 July 1934; *s* of Alan Roy Manthorp and Stella Manthorp; *m* 1955, Jennifer Mary Caradine; three *s* one *d. Educ:* Framlingham Coll.; Pembroke Coll., Oxford (MA Hons English); Westcott House, Cambridge. Instructor Lieut, RN, 1955-58. Ordained priest, Guildford, 1961. Assistant Master, Charterhouse, 1958-65; Head of English: Lawrence Coll., Pakistan, 1965-67; Aitchison Coll., Pakistan, 1968-70; Oakbank Sch., Keighley, 1970-73; Headmaster, Holy Trinity Senior Sch., Halifax, 1973-80. *Publication:* Fifty Poems for Pakistan, 1971. *Recreations:* sport, sketching. *Address:* The Headmaster's House, Worcester College for the Blind, Whittington Road, Worcester WR5 2JU. *T:* Worcester 356599; The Brew House, High Street, Chipping Campden, Glos.

MANTLE, Philip Jaques, CMG 1952; *b* 7 Aug. 1901; 2nd *s* of late Paul Mantle; *m* 1930, Gwendolen, *d* of late John Webb, CMG, CBE, MC; one *s* one *d. Educ:* Bancroft's Sch., Woodford; St John's Coll., Oxford (Scholar, Goldsmiths' exhibitioner, 1st class Mod. Hist. Finals). Entered Inland Revenue Dept, 1923 (Taxes); Secretaries' office, 1928; Asst Secretary Min. of Supply, 1940, Board of Trade, 1942; Deputy Head, Administration of Enemy Property Dept, 1949; Controller-General, 1955-57; Companies Dept, 1957-61; with

Charity Commission, 1962; retired 1966. *Address:* 27 Kensington Mansions, Trebovir Road, SW5 9TQ. *T:* 01-370 3683.

MANTON, 3rd Baron, *cr* 1922, of Compton Verney; **Joseph Rupert Eric Robert Watson;** DL; Landowner and Farmer; *b* 22 Jan. 1924; *s* of 2nd Baron Manton and Alethea (*d* 1979), 2nd *d* of late Colonel Philip Langdale, OBE; *S* father, 1968; *m* 1951, Mary Elizabeth, twin *d* of Major T. D. Hallinan, Ashbourne, Glounthaune, Co. Cork; two *s* three *d. Educ:* Eton. Joined Army, 1942; commissioned Life Guards, 1943; Captain, 1946; retired, 1947; rejoined 7th (QO) Hussars, 1951-56. DL Humberside, 1980. *Recreations:* hunting, shooting, racing. *Heir: s* Lieut the Hon. Miles Ronald Marcus Watson, Life Guards, *b* 7 May 1958. *Address:* Houghton Hall, Sancton, York. *T:* Market Weighton 3234. *Clubs:* White's, Jockey.
See also Baron Hesketh.

MANTON, Prof. Irene, BA, ScD, PhD; FRS 1961; Emeritus Professor of Botany, University of Leeds; retired 1969. *Educ:* Girton Coll., Cambridge. BA 1926, PhD 1930, ScD 1940, Cambridge. Has made studies with the light and electron microscope on the ultramicroscopic structure of plants, and studies on the cytology and evolution of ferns. Hon. Member: Danish Acad. of Sciences and Letters, 1953; Deutsche Akad. Leopoldina, 1967; Amer. Acad. of Arts and Sciences, 1969. Hon. DSc: McGill Univ., Canada; Durham Univ., 1966; Lancaster Univ., 1979; Hon. Doctorate, Oslo Univ., 1961. *Publications:* Problems of Cytology and Evolution in the Pteridophyta, 1950; papers in scientific journals. *Address:* 15 Harrowby Crescent, West Park, Leeds LS16 5HP.

MANUEL, Joseph Thomas, CBE 1970; QPM 1967; one of HM's Inspectors of Constabulary, 1963-74; *b* 10 June 1909; *s* of George and Lucy Manuel; *m* 1933, Millicent Eveline Baker; one *s. Educ:* Dorchester Boys' Sch., Dorchester, Dorset. Joined Metropolitan Police, 1929. Served in Allied Military Government, Italy (rank of Captain and Major), 1943-46. Returned Metropolitan Police and promoted: Superintendent, 1954; Chief Superintendent, 1957; Dep. Commander, 1958; Commander 1959. *Recreations:* golf, walking, motoring. *Address:* Cranbrook, Pyrford Road, West Byfleet, Weybridge, Surrey KT14 6RE. *T:* Byfleet 46360.

MANVELL, (Arnold) Roger, PhD (London), DLitt (Sussex); film historian, biographer; scriptwriter and lecturer; Director, British Film Academy, 1947-59; Consultant to the British Academy of Film and Television Arts and Editor of its Journal, 1959-76; Associate Editor, New Humanist (formerly Humanist), 1967-75; Director: Rationalist Press Association Ltd; Pemberton Publishing Co. Ltd, etc; *b* 10 Oct. 1909; *s* of Canon A. E. W. Manvell. *Educ:* Wyggeston Sch., Leicester; King's Sch., Peterborough; University College, Leicester; Univ. of London. Schoolmaster and Lecturer in adult education, 1931-37; Lecturer in Literature and Drama, Dept Extramural Studies, University of Bristol, 1937-40; Ministry of Information, specialising in film work, 1940-45; Research Officer, British Film Institute, 1945-47. Has lectured on film subjects for British Film Institute, British Council and other authorities in Great Britain, US, Canada, Far East, India, Caribbean, W Africa and most European countries; regular broadcaster, 1946-, including BBC's long-established programme The Critics. Visiting Fellow, Sussex Univ.; Bingham Prof. of Humanities, Louisville Univ., 1973; Prof. of Film, Boston Univ., 1975-. Governor, London Film School, 1966-74; Vice-Chm., Nat. Panel for Film Festivals, 1974-76; Member Cttee of Management, Society of Authors, 1954-57, 1965-68; Chairman: Society of Lecturers, 1959-61; Radiowriters' Assoc., 1962-64; Authors' Club, 1972-75. Hon. DFA New England Coll., USA, 1972; Hon. DLitt: Leicester, 1974; Louisville, 1979. Commander of the Order of Merit of the Italian Republic, 1970; Order of Merit (First Class) of German Federal Republic, 1971. *Publications:* Film, 1944, revised 1946 and 1950; A Seat at the Cinema, 1951; On the Air (a study of broadcasting in sound and vision), 1953; The Animated Film, 1954; The Film and the Public, 1955; The Dreamers (novel), 1958; The Passion (novel), 1960; The Living Screen (a study of film and TV), 1961; What is a Film?, 1965; This Age of Communication, 1967; New Cinema in Europe, 1966; The July Plot (television play), 1966; New Cinema in the USA, 1968; Ellen Terry, 1968; New Cinema in Britain, 1969; SS and Gestapo, 1969; Sarah Siddons, 1970; Shakespeare and the Film, 1971; The Conspirators: 20 July 1944, 1971; Goering, 1972; Films and the Second World War, 1974; Charles Chaplin, 1974; Love Goddesses of the Movies, 1975; The Trial of Annie Besant, 1976; Theater and Film, 1979; Ingmar Bergman, 1980; Art and Animation, 1980; (ed and contributed) Experiment in the Film, 1949; (contributed) Twenty Years of British Film, 1947; collaborated: with Rachel Low in The History of the British Film 1896-1906, 1948; with Paul Rotha in revised edn of Movie Parade, 1950; with John Huntley in The Technique of Film Music, 1957; with John Halas in The Technique of Film Animation, 1959, Design in Motion, 1962, and Art in Movement, 1970; with Heinrich Fraenkel in: Dr Goebbels, 1959, Hermann Goering, 1962, The July Plot, 1964, Heinrich Himmler, 1965, The Incomparable Crime, 1967, The Canaris Conspiracy, 1969, History of the German Cinema, 1971, Hess, 1971, Inside Adolf Hitler, 1973 (revd as Adolf Hitler, the Man and the Myth, 1977; enlarged UK edn, 1978), The Hundred Days to Hitler, 1974; Editor: Three British Screenplays, 1950; Penguin Film Review, 1946-49; The Cinema, 1950-52; The Year's Work in the Film (for British Council), 1949 and 1950; International Encyclopedia of Film, 1972; for thirty years contrib. on Cinema to the Annual Register; contributed to Encyclopædia Britannica, journals at home and overseas concerned with history and art of the film and history of the Nazi régime. *Recreation:* travel abroad. *Address:* 15 Above Town, Dartmouth, Devon.

MANWARING, Randle (Gilbert), FSS, FPMI; poet and author; retired company director; *b* 3 May 1912; *s* of late George Ernest and Lilian Manwaring; *m* 1941, Betty Violet, *d* of H. P. Rout, Norwich; three *s* one *d. Educ:* private schools. Joined Clerical, Medical and Gen. Life Assce Soc., 1929. War service, RAF, 1940-46, W/Cdr; comd RAF Regt in Burma, 1945. Clerical, Medical & Gen. Pensions Rep., 1950; joined C. E. Heath & Co. Ltd, 1956: Asst Dir, 1960, Dir, 1964, Man. Dir. 1969; Founder Dir (Man.), C. E. Heath Urquhart (Life and Pensions), 1966-71, and a Founder Dir, Excess Life Assce Co., 1967-75; Dir, Excess Insurance Group, 1975-78; Insurance Adviser, Midland Bank, 1971; first Man. Dir, Midland Bank Ins. Services, 1972-74, Vice-Chm., 1974-77, Dir, 1977-78. Chm., Life Soc., Corp. of Insce Brokers, 1965-66; Dep. Chm., Corp. of Insce Brokers, 1970-71; Pres., Soc. of Pensions Consultants, 1968-70. Chairman of Governors: Luckley-Oakfield Sch., 1972-; Northease Manor Sch., 1972-. Diocesan Reader (Chichester), 1968-; Chm., Vine Books Ltd; Dir, Crusaders Union Ltd, 1960-. MA Keele, 1982. *Publications:* The Heart of this People, 1954; A Christian Guide to Daily Work, 1963; Thornhill Guide to Insurance, 1976; *poems:* Posies Once Mine, 1951; Satires and Salvation, 1960; Under the Magnolia Tree, 1965; Slave to No Sect, 1966; Crossroads of the Year, 1975; From the Four Winds, 1976; In a Time of Unbelief, 1977; Poem Prayers for Growing People, 1980; The Swifts of Maggiore, 1981; contrib. poems and articles to learned jls in GB and Canada. *Recreations:* music, reading, following cricket. *Address:* Priory Well, Wilmington, Polegate, East Sussex BN26 5SR. *T:* Alfriston 870426. *Clubs:* Royal Air Force, MCC.

MANZIE, (Andrew) Gordon; Deputy Secretary, Department of Industry, since 1980; *b* 3 April 1930; *s* of late John Mair and Catherine Manzie; *m* 1955, Rosalind Clay; one *s* one *d. Educ:* Royal High Sch. of Edinburgh; London Sch. of Economics and Political Science (BScEcon). Joined Civil Service as Clerical Officer, Scottish Home Dept, 1947. National Service, RAF, 1949. Min. of Supply: Exec. Officer (Higher Exec. Officer, 1957). Private Sec. to Perm. Sec., Min. of Aviation, 1962; Sen. Exec. Officer, 1963; Principal, 1964; Sec. to Cttee of Inquiry into Civil Air Transport (Edwards Cttee), 1967; Asst Sec., Dept of Trade and Industry, on loan to Min. of Posts and Telecommunications, 1971; Dept of Industry, 1974; Under-Sec., Dir, Office for Scotland, Depts of Trade and Industry, 1975; Under Sec., Scottish Economic Planning Dept, 1975-79; Dir, Industrial Develt Unit, Dept of Industry, 1980-81. *Recreations:* golf, reading. *Address:* 28 Manor Links, Bishop's Stortford, Herts CM23 5RA. *Clubs:* Caledonian, Royal Commonwealth Society.

MANZINI, Raimondo; Cavaliere di Gran Croce all'Ordine della Repubblica Italiana; GCVO (Hon.) 1969; Secretary-General at Italian Foreign Ministry, since 1975; *b* 25 Nov. 1913. *Educ:* Bologna Univ.; Clark Univ., Mass; Univ. of California. Entered Diplomatic Service, 1940; Sec. to Italian Legation, Lisbon, 1941-43; Ministry of Foreign Affairs in Brindisi (1943) and Salerno (1944); Sec. to Italian Embassy, London, 1944-47; Consul General for Congo, Nigeria and Gold Coast, 1947-50; Consul General, Baden Baden, 1951-52; Head of Information Service, CED, Paris, 1952-53; Ministry of Foreign Affairs, 1953-55; Adviser to the Minister of Foreign Trade, 1955-58; Chef de Cabinet of Minister for Foreign Affairs, 1958; Diplomatic Adviser to the Prime Minister, 1958-59; Adviser to the Minister of Industry, 1959-64; Italian Ambassador to: OECD in Paris, 1965-68; UK, 1968-75. *Address:* Ministero degli Affari Esteri, Palazzo Farnesina, Rome, Italy.

MANZÙ, Giacomo; sculptor and painter; stage designer; *b* 22 Dec. 1908; *s* of Angelo and Maria Manzoni; *m* ; three *s* decd. *Educ:* Milan. Professor of Sculpture, Brera Accad., Milan, 1941-54; International Summer Acad., Salzburg, 1954-60. Sculpture Prize, Venice Biennale, 1948; Society of Portrait Sculptors' International Award (Jean Masson Davidson Medal), 1965. Works include: Cathedral main door, Salzburg, and re-designing of bronze doors of St Peter's, Rome, 1963 (commission won in open international competition); The Door of Peace and War, St Laurenz Church, Rotterdam, 1968. Exhibitions of Sculptures, Paintings and Drawings: Haus der Kunst, Munich, 1959; Tate Gall., 1960, Hanover Gall., London, 1965; Moscow, Leningrad, and Kiev, 1966; Bordeaux, 1969; Prague and Tokyo, 1973; Budapest, 1974; Rome, 1975; Münster, 1976; (retrospective exhibn) Hamilton, Ont., 1980, and in 8 other Canadian cities, 1981. Established permanent collection of his most important works at Ardea, near Rome, 1969, donated to the Republic of Italy, 1981. Hon. Member: American Academy of Arts and Letters; National Academies of Argentina and Belgium; Accademia di Belle Arti Sovietica; Acad. Européenne des Sciences, des Arts et des Lettres, Paris, 1981; For. Hon. Mem., Amer. Acad. of Arts and Sci., 1978. Hon. Dr RCA 1971. Premio Internazionale Lenin per la pace, 1966. Medaglia d'Oro Benemeriti, Scuola, Cultura, Arte (Italy), 1981. *Publication:* La Porta di S Pietro, 1965. *Relevant publications:* J. Rewald, Giacomo Manzù, 1966; B. Heynold von Graefe, The Doors of Rotterdam, 1969. *Address:* 00040 Ardea, Rome, Italy.

MAPLES, Ven. Jeffrey Stanley; Archdeacon of Swindon and Hon. Canon Diocesan, Bristol Cathedral, 1974-82; *b* 8 Aug. 1916; *o s* of Arthur Stanley and Henrietta Georgina Maples; *m* 1945, Isobel Eileen Mabel Wren; four *s* (and one *s* decd). *Educ:* Downing Coll., Cambridge; Chichester Theological Coll. Asst Curate St James, Milton, Portsmouth, 1940-46; Asst Curate, Watlington, Diocese of Oxford, 1946-48. Vicar of Swinderby, Dio. Lincoln, and Diocesan Youth Chaplain, 1948-50; Vicar of St Michael-on-the-Mount, Lincoln, and Director of Religious Education: for Lincoln Dio., 1950-56; for Salisbury Dio., 1956-63; Canon of Lincoln, 1954-56; Chancellor of Salisbury Cathedral, 1960-67; Director of the Bible Reading Fellowship, 1963-67;

Proctor in Convocation for Salisbury Diocese, 1957-70; Canon Emeritus of Salisbury Cathedral, 1967-; Vicar of St James, Milton, Portsmouth, 1967-74; Rural Dean of Portsmouth, 1968-73; Hon. Canon, Portsmouth Cathedral, 1972-74. *Address:* 88 Exeter Street, Salisbury, Wilts SP1 2SE. *T:* Salisbury 23848.

MAPLES EARLE, Ven. E. E.; *see* Earle.

MAR, Countess of (*suo jure*, 31st in line from Ruadri, 1st Earl of Mar, 1115); Premier Earldom of Scotland by descent; Lady Garioch, *c* 1320; **Margaret of Mar;** *b* 19 Sept. 1940; *er d* of 30th Earl of Mar, and Millicent Mary Salton; *S* father, 1975; recognised in surname "of Mar" by warrant of Court of Lord Lyon, 1967, when she abandoned her second forename; *m* 1st, 1959, Edwin Noel Artiss (marr. diss. 1976); one *d*; 2nd, 1976, (cousin) John Salton, recognised in surname "of Mar" by warrant of Lord Lyon, 1976 (marr. diss. 1981); 3rd, 1982, J. H. Jenkin, MA (Cantab), FRCO, LRAM. *Heir: d* Mistress of Mar, *qv. Address:* St Michael's Farm, Great Witley, Worcester WR6 6JB. *T:* Great Witley 608.

MAR, Mistress of; Lady Susan Helen of Mar; *b* 31 May 1963; *d* and *heiress* of Countess of Mar, *qv. Educ:* King Charles I School, Kidderminster; Christie College, Cheltenham.

MAR, 13th Earl of, *cr* 1565, **and KELLIE, 15th Earl of,** *cr* 1619; **John Francis Hervey Erskine;** Baron Erskine, 1429; Viscount Fentoun, 1606; Baron Dirleton, 1603; Premier Viscount of Scotland; Hereditary Keeper of Stirling Castle; Representative Peer for Scotland, 1959-63; Major Scots Guards; retired 1954; Major, Argyll and Sutherland Highlanders (TA) retired 1959; Lord Lieutenant of Clackmannan, since 1966; *b* 15 Feb. 1921; *e s* of late Lord Erskine (John Francis Ashley Erskine), GCSI, GCIE; *S* grandfather, 1955; *m* 1948, Pansy Constance (Pres., UK Cttee for UNICEF; Chm., Youth at Risk Adv. Gp; Hon. Pres., Girls Bde, Scotland; Chm. and Vice-Chm., Scottish Standing Conf., Voluntary Youth Orgns, 1967-81. Elder of Church of Scotland. JP 1971; OStJ 1977), *y d* of late General Sir Andrew Thorne, KCB; three *s* one *d. Educ:* Eton; Trinity Coll., Cambridge. 2nd Lieut, Scots Guards, 1941; served in Egypt, N. Africa, Italy and Germany with 2nd Bn Scots Guards and HQ 201 Guards' Brigade, 1942-45 (wounded, despatches). Staff Coll., Camberley, 1950; DAAG, HQ, 3rd Infantry Div., 1951-52. DL Clackmannanshire, 1954, Vice-Lieutenant, 1957, JP 1962; County Councillor for Clackmannanshire, 1955-75 (Vice-Convener, 1961-64); Chairman: Forth Conservancy Board, 1957-68; Clackmannanshire T&AFA, 1961-68. An Elder of the Church of Scotland. Member of the Queen's Body Guard for Scotland (Royal Company of Archers). KStJ 1966. *Heir: s* Lord Erskine, *qv. Address:* Claremont House, Alloa, Clackmannanshire. *T:* Alloa 212020. *Club:* New (Edinburgh).

MARA, Rt. Hon. Ratu Sir Kamisese Kapaiwai Tuimacilai, PC 1973; KBE 1969 (OBE 1961); Tui Nayau; Tui Lau; Prime Minister of Fiji, since 1970; Hereditary High Chief of the Lau Islands; *b* 13 May 1920; *s* of late Ratu Tevita Uluilakeba, Tui Nayau; *m* 1951, Adi Lady Lala Mara (Roko Tui Dreketi); three *s* five *d. Educ:* Fiji; Sacred Heart Coll., NZ; Otago Univ., NZ; Wadham Coll., Oxford (MA), Hon. Fellow, 1971; London Sch. of Economics (Dip. Econ. & Social Admin.). Administrative Officer, Colonial Service, Fiji, Oct. 1950; Fijian MLC, 1953-, and MEC, 1959-61 (elected MLC and MEC, 1959). Member for Natural Resources and Leader of Govt Business; Alliance Party, 1964-66 (Founder of Party); Chief Minister and Mem., Council of Ministers, Fiji, 1967. Hon. Dr of Laws: Univ. of Guam, 1969; Univ. of Papua New Guinea, 1982; Hon. LLD: Univ. of Otago, 1973; New Delhi, 1975; Hon. DPolSc Korea, 1978; Hon. Dr Tokai Univ., 1980; DU Univ. of South Pacific, 1980. Grand Cross, Order of Lion, Senegal, 1975; Order of Diplomatic Service Merit, Korea, 1978. *Recreations:* athletics, cricket, Rugby football, golf, fishing. *Address:* 11 Battery Road, Suva, Fiji. *T:* 311629. *Clubs:* United Oxford & Cambridge University, Achilles (London); Defence (Suva, Fiji).

MARAJ, Dr James Ajodhya; Senior Evaluation Officer, The World Bank, since 1982; Hon. Professor of Education, University of the South Pacific, since 1978 (Vice-Chancellor, 1975-82); *b* 28 Sept. 1930; *s* of Ramgoolam Maraj and Popo Maraj; *m* 1951, Etress (*née* Ouditt); two *s* two *d. Educ:* St Mary's Coll. and Govt Teachers' Coll., Trinidad; Univ. of Birmingham (BA, PhD). FRICS 1981. Teacher, Lectr, 1947-60; Sen. Lectr, Univ. of West Indies, 1965-70; Head, Inst. of Educn, UWI, 1968-70; Dir, Educn Div., Commonwealth Secretariat, 1970-72; Commonwealth Asst Sec.-Gen., 1973-75. External Examr, Educn Adviser and Consultant to WHO and to several countries; Chm. or Sec. nat. or internat. commns. Hon. DLitt Loughborough, 1980. Gold Medal of Merit, Trinidad and Tobago, 1974; Pacific Person of the Year, Fiji Times, 1978; Dist. Scholar's Award, British Council, 1979. *Publications:* miscellaneous research papers. *Recreations:* sport: cricket, squash, horse-racing; poetry, music. *Address:* The World Bank, 1818 H Street, Washington, DC 20433, USA. *Clubs:* Athenæum, Royal Commonwealth Society, Royal Over-Seas League.

'MARC'; *see* Boxer, C. M. E.

MARCEAU, Marcel; Chevalier de la Légion d'Honneur; Officier de l'Ordre National du Mérite; Commandeur des Arts et Lettres de la République Française; mime; Founder and Director, Compagnie de Mimes Marcel Marceau, since 1949; Director, International School of Mime of Paris Marcel Marceau; *b* Strasbourg, 22 March 1923; *s* of Charles and Anne Mangel; two

s two *d. Educ:* Ecole des Beaux Arts; Arts Décoratifs, Limoges; Ecole Etienne Decroux; Ecole Charles Dullin. First stage appearance, in Paris, 1946; with Barrault/Renaud Co., 1946-49; founded his company, 1949; since then has toured constantly, playing in 65 countries. Created about 100 pantomimes (most famous are The Creation of the World, The Cage, The Maskmaker, The Tree, Bip Liontamer, Bip hunts Butterfly, Bip plays David and Goliath, Bip at a Society Party, Bip in the Modern and Future Life, Bip Soldier, etc); and 26 mimodrames, and in particular the character 'Bip' (1947); *Mimodrames:* Bip et la fille des rues, 1947; Bip et L'Oiseau, 1948; Death Before Dawn, 1948; The Fair, 1949; The Flute Player, 1949; The Overcoat, 1951; Moriana and Galvan, Pierrot of Montmartre, 1952; Les Trois Perruques, 1953; Un Soir aux Funambules, 1953; La Parade en bleu et noir, 1956; le 14 juillet, 1956; Le Mont de Piéré, 1956; Le Loup de Tsu Ku Mi, 1956; Le Petit Cirque, 1958; Les Matadors, 1959; Paris qui rit, Paris qui pleure, 1959; Don Juan, 1964; Candide, 1970, with Ballet de l'Opéra de Hambourg; *films:* The Overcoat, 1951; Barbarella, 1967; Scrooge (BBC London), 1973; Shanks, US, 1973; Silent Movie, 1976. Has made frequent TV appearances and many short films for TV, incl. Pantomimes, 1954, A Public Garden, 1955, Le mime Marcel Marceau, 1965, The World of Marcel Marceau, 1966, 12 short films with Enc. Brit., NY, 1974. Member: Acad. of Arts and Letters (DDR); Akad. der schönen Künste, Munich. Emmy Awards (US), 1955, 1968. Hon. Dr, Univ. of Oregon; Dr *hc* Univ. of Princeton, 1981. Gold Medal of Czechoslovak Republic (for contribution to cultural relations). *Publications:* Les 7 Péchés Capitaux (lithographs); Les Rêveries de Bip (lithographs); La Ballade de Paris et du Monde (text, lithographs, water-colours, drawings in ink and pencil); Alphabet Book; Counting Book; L'Histoire de Bip (text and lithographs); The Third Eye (lithoprint). *Recreations:* painting, poetry, fencing. *Address:* 21 rue Jean-Mermoz, 75008 Paris, France. *T:* 225 06 05 and 256 32 76.

MARCH AND KINRARA, Earl of; Charles Henry Gordon-Lennox; DL; *b* 19 Sept. 1929; *s* and *heir* of Duke of Richmond and Gordon, *qv; m* 1951, Susan Monica, *o d* of late Colonel C. E. Grenville-Grey, CBE, Hall Barn, Blewbury, Berks; one *s* four *d. Educ:* Eton; William Temple Coll. 2nd Lieut, 60th Rifles, 1949-50. Chartered Accountant, 1956. Church Commissioner, 1963-76; Mem. Gen. Synod of Church of England, formerly Church Assembly, 1960-80 (Chm., Bd for Mission and Unity, 1967-77); Mem., Central and Exec. Cttees, World Council of Churches, 1968-75; Chairman: Christian Orgn Res. and Adv. Trust, 1965-; House of Laity, Chichester Diocesan Synod, 1976-79; Vice-Chm., Archbishop's Commn on Church and State, 1966-70; Pres., Voluntary and Christian Service, 1982-. Mem., W Midlands Regional Economic Planning Council, 1965-68; Chm., Goodwood Group of Cos, 1969-. President: Sussex Rural Community Council, 1973-; British Horse Soc., 1976-78; South of England Agricultural Soc., 1981-82; Vice-Pres., SE England Tourist Bd, 1974-; Chairman: Rugby Council of Social Service, 1961-68; Dunford Coll. (YMCA), 1969-; Hon. Treasurer, Historic Houses Assoc., 1975- (Chm., SE Region, 1975-78); Dir, Country Gentlemen's Assoc. Ltd, 1975-; Treasurer, Sussex Univ., 1979-; Chm. of Trustees, Sussex Heritage Trust, 1978-. DL W Sussex, 1975. *Heir: s* Lord Settrington, *qv. Address:* Goodwood House, Chichester, W Sussex. *T:* (office) Chichester 774107; (home) Chichester 774760.
See also Lord N. C. Gordon Lennox.

MARCH, Derek Maxwell, CBE 1982 (OBE 1973); HM Diplomatic Service; Counsellor seconded to Department of Industry, since 1982; *b* 9 Dec. 1930; *s* of Frank March and Vera (*née* Ward); *m* 1955, Sally Annetta Riggs; one *s* two *d. Educ:* Devonport High Sch.; Birkbeck Coll., London. National Service, RAF, 1949-51. Joined HM Diplomatic Service, 1949; FO, 1951; Bonn, 1955; Vice Consul, Hanover, 1957; Asst Trade Comr, Salisbury, 1959; Consul, Dakar, 1962; First Secretary: FO, 1964; Rawalpindi, 1968; Peking, 1971; FCO, 1974; Counsellor, seconded to Dept of Trade, 1975; Senior British Trade Comr, Hong Kong, 1977-82. *Recreations:* golf, cricket, Rugby Union. *Address:* Soke House, The Soke, Alresford, Hants. *T:* Alresford 2588. *Clubs:* MCC, East India, Devonshire, Sports and Public Schools; Hong Kong (Hong Kong); Alresford Golf.

MARCH, George Frederick, CMG 1946; MC 1917; *b* 6 July 1893; *o s* of late Frederick J. March, Ockbrook Grange, Derbyshire; *m* 1935, Myrtle Lloyd, Carmarthen; two *s. Educ:* Rugby Sch.; Wye Agricultural Coll. (dip. Agric. 1914). Commissioned in Sherwood Foresters, Aug. 1914; France, 1915-19 (wounded thrice); Egypt (Alexandria), 1919-21; demobilised, 1921; Inspector of Agriculture, Sudan Government, 1921; Senior Inspector of Agriculture, 1928; Asst Director, Agriculture and Forests, 1935; Dep. Director, 1942; Director, 1944-47. Chairman, Rural Water Supplies and Soil Conservation Board. Member Governor-General's Council (Sudan). Agricultural Consultant on mission to Swaziland by Colonial Development Corporation, Jan.-April, 1950; Manager and Secretary, Flishinghurst Farms Ltd, 1950-52; now farming on own (hops, fruit, etc.), in Kent. *Recreation:* fishing. *Address:* The Well House, Limes Grove Farm, Hawkhurst, Kent. *TA:* Hawkhurst. *T:* Hawkhurst 2398.

MARCH, Henry Arthur, MA (Oxon); *b* 14 March 1905; *s* of late Edward Gerald March, MD, Reading; *m* 1943, Mary (*d* 1968), *d* of late Rev. P. P. W. Gendall, Launceston; two *s* one *d. Educ:* Leighton Park Sch.; St John's Coll., Oxford. Asst Master, Merchant Taylors' Sch., 1929-39; Head of Modern Language side, 1940-54, and Housemaster, 1945-54, Charterhouse; Headmaster, Cranleigh Sch., 1954-59; Temp. Asst Master, Marlborough Coll., 1959-61; Asst Master, 1961-65. Acting Headmaster, Charterhouse, 1964. *Address:* Horsna Parc, St Tudy, Bodmin, Cornwall.

MARCH, Lionel John, ScD; FRSA; Rector and Vice-Provost, Royal College of Art, since 1981; *b* 26 Jan. 1934; *o s* of Leonard James March and Rose (*née* Edwards). *Educ:* Hove Grammar Sch. for Boys; Magdalene Coll., Cambridge (MA, ScD). FIMA, FRSA. Nat. Service: Sub-Lt, RNVR, 1953-55. Harkness Fellow, Commonwealth Fund, Harvard Univ. and MIT, 1962-64; Asst to Sir Leslie Martin, 1964-66; Lectr in Architecture, Univ. of Cambridge, 1966-69; Dir, Centre for Land Use and Built Form Studies, Univ. of Cambridge, 1969-73; Prof., Dept of Systems Design, Univ. of Waterloo, Ontario, 1974-76; Prof. of Design, Faculty of Technology, Open Univ., 1976-81. Chm., Applied Res. of Cambridge Ltd, 1969-73. Mem., Governing Body, Imperial Coll. of Science and Technology, 1981-. General Editor (with Leslie Martin), Cambridge Urban and Architectural Studies, 1970-; Editor, Environment and Planning B, Internat. Jl of Architectural and Design Science, 1974-. *Publications:* (with Philip Steadman) The Geometry of Environment, 1971; (ed with Leslie Martin) Urban Space and Structures, 1972; (ed) The Architecture of Form, 1976. *Address:* Rector's Lodge, Royal College of Art, Jay Mews, Kensington, SW7 2ES. *T:* 01-584 5020.

MARCH, Prof. Norman Henry; Coulson Professor of Theoretical Chemistry, University of Oxford, since 1977; Fellow of University College, Oxford, since 1977; *b* 9 July 1927; *s* of William and Elsie March; *m* 1949, Margaret Joan Hoyle; two *s. Educ:* King's Coll., London Univ. University of Sheffield: Lecturer in Physics, 1953-57; Reader in Theoretical Physics, 1957-61; Prof. of Physics, 1961-72; Prof. of Theoretical Solid State Physics, Imperial Coll., Univ. of London, 1973-77. Hon. DTech Chalmers, Gothenburg, 1980. *Publications:* The Many-Body Problem in Quantum Mechanics (with W. H. Young and S. Sampanthar), 1967; Liquid Metals, 1968; Theoretical Solid State Physics (with W. Jones), 1973; Self-Consistent Fields in Atoms, 1974; Orbital Theories of Molecules and Solids, 1974; Atomic Dynamics in Liquids (with M. P. Tosi), 1976; many scientific papers on quantum mechanics and statistical mechanics in Proceedings Royal Society, Phil. Magazine, etc. *Recreations:* music, chess, cricket. *Address:* Elmstead, 6 Northcroft Road, Englefield Green, Egham, Surrey. *T:* Egham 3078.

MARCH, Valerie, (Mrs Andrew March); *see* Masterson, V.

MARCHAMLEY, 3rd Baron, *cr* 1908, of Hawkstone; **John William Tattersall Whiteley;** late Lieutenant, Royal Armoured Corps; *b* 24 April 1922; *s* of 2nd Baron and Margaret Clara (*d* 1974), *d* of Thomas Scott Johnstone of Glenmark, Waipara, New Zealand; *S* father, 1949; *m* 1967, Sonia Kathleen Pedrick; one *s.* Served War of 1939-45, Captain, 19th King George V Own Lancers. *Heir: s* Hon. William Francis Whiteley, *b* 27 July 1968. *Address:* Whetcombe, North Huish, South Brent, Devon.

MARCHANT, Catherine; *see* Cookson, C.

MARCHANT, Edgar Vernon; Member, Civil Service Appeal Board; Director, Paddington Building Society; *b* 7 Dec. 1915; *s* of E. C. Marchant; *m* 1945, Joyce Allen Storey; one *s* two *d. Educ:* Marlborough Coll.; Lincoln Coll., Oxford. Engr, Bahrain Petroleum Co., 1938; various technical and scientific posts in Min. of Aircraft Production, Min. of Supply and RAE, 1940-51; Principal, Min. of Supply, 1951; Principal, BoT, 1955; Asst Sec., BoT, 1959; Asst Registrar of Restrictive Trading Agreements, 1964; Asst Sec., Dept of Economic Affairs, 1966; Nat. Board for Prices and Incomes: Asst Sec., 1967-68; Under-Sec., 1968-71; Under-Sec., DTI, later Dept of Industry, 1971-75. *Recreations:* gardening, messing about in boats. *Address:* 87 New Forest Drive, Brockenhurst, Hants SO4 7QT. *Clubs:* United Oxford & Cambridge University; Royal Southampton Yacht.

MARCHANT, Ven. George John Charles; Archdeacon of Auckland and Canon Residentiary, Durham Cathedral, since 1974; *b* 3 Jan. 1916; *s* of late T. Marchant, Little Stanmore, Mddx; *m* 1944, Eileen Lillian Kathleen, *d* of late F. J. Smith, FCIS; one *s* three *d. Educ:* St John's Coll., Durham (MA, BD); Tyndale Hall, Bristol. Deacon 1939, priest 1940, London; Curate of St Andrew's, Whitehall Park, N19, 1939-41; Licence to officiate, London dio., 1941-44 (in charge of Young Churchmen's Movement); Curate of St Andrew-the-Less, Cambridge (in charge of St Stephen's), 1944-48; Vicar of Holy Trinity, Skirbeck, Boston, 1948-54; Vicar of St Nicholas, Durham, 1954-74; Rural Dean of Durham, 1964-74; Hon. Canon of Durham Cathedral, 1972-74. Member of General Synod, 1970-80 (Proctor in Convocation for Dio. Durham). *Publications:* contribs to The Churchman. *Recreations:* record-music, bird watching. *Address:* 15 The College, Durham DH1 3EQ. *T:* Durham 47534.

MARCHANT, Sir Herbert (Stanley), KCMG 1963 (CMG 1957); OBE 1946; MA Cantab; *b* 18 May 1906; *s* of E. J. Marchant; *m* 1937, Diana Selway, *d* of C. J. Selway, CVO, CBE; one *s. Educ:* Perse Sch.; St John's Coll., Cambridge (MA 1929). Asst Master, Harrow Sch., 1928-39; Foreign Office, 1940-46; Consul, Denver, Colorado, USA, 1946-48; First Secretary, British Legation, Bucharest, 1948-49; Counsellor, British Embassy, Paris, 1950-52; Consul-General, Zagreb, 1952-54; Land Commissioner and Consul-General for North Rhine/Westphalia, 1954-55; Consul-General, Düsseldorf, 1955-57; Consul-General, San Francisco, 1957-60; Ambassador to Cuba, 1960-63; Ambassador to Tunisia, 1963-66. Asst Dir, Inst. of Race Relations, 1966-68; UK Representative, UN Cttee for Elimination of Racial Discrimination, 1969-73. Chm., British-Tunisian Soc., 1970-74. *Publications:* Scratch a Russian, 1936; His Excellency Regrets, 1980. *Recreations:* mountains, spear fishing, theatre. *Club:* Travellers'.

MARCHWOOD, 3rd Viscount *cr* 1945, of Penang and of Marchwood, Southampton; **David George Staveley Penny;** Bt 1933; Baron 1937; Président Directeur Général, Schweppes (France) Ltd; *b* 22 May 1936; *s* of 2nd Viscount Marchwood, MBE and Pamela (*d* 1979), *o d* of John Staveley Colton-Fox; *S* father, 1979; *m* 1964, Tessa Jane, *d* of W. F. Norris; three *s. Educ:* Winchester College. 2nd Lt, Royal Horse Guards (The Blues), 1955-57. Joined Schweppes Ltd, 1958; Vice-Pres. and Gen. Man., Schweppes Div. of Cadbury Schweppes Powell Montreal, Canada, 1973-75; thence to present position. *Recreations:* cricket, shooting, racing. *Heir: s* Hon. Peter George Worsley Penny, *b* 8 Oct. 1965. *Address:* Filberts, Aston Tirrold, near Didcot, Oxon. *T:* Blewbury 850386. *Clubs:* White's, MCC.

MARCUS, Frank Ulrich; playwright; Theatre Critic for The Sunday Telegraph, 1968-78; *b* Breslau, Germany, 30 June 1928; *s* of late Frederick Marcus and of Gertie Marcus; *m* 1951, Jacqueline (*née* Sylvester); one *s* two *d. Educ:* Bunce Court Sch., Kent (evac. to Shropshire during war); St Martin's Sch. of Art, London. Actor, Dir, Scenic Designer, Unity Theatre, Kensington (later Internat. Theatre Gp). *Stage plays:* Minuet for Stuffed Birds, 1950; The Man Who Bought a Battlefield, 1963; The Formation Dancers, 1964; The Killing of Sister George, 1965 (3 'Best Play of the Year' Awards: Evening Standard, Plays and Players, Variety); Cleo, 1965; Studies of the Nude, 1967; Mrs Mouse, Are You Within?, 1968; The Window, 1969; Notes on a Love Affair, 1972; Blank Pages, 1972; Carol's Christmas, 1973; Beauty and the Beast, 1975; Portrait of the Artist (mime scenario), 1977; Blind Date, 1977; The Ballad of Wilfred the Second, 1978; The Merman of Orford (mime scenario), 1978; *television plays:* A Temporary Typist, 1966; The Glove Puppet, 1968; *radio plays:* The Hospital Visitor, 1980; The Beverley Brooch, 1981; The Row over La Ronde, 1982; *translations:* Schnitzler's Reigen, 1952 (as La Ronde, TV, 1982); Liebelei (TV), 1954; Anatol, 1976; (Molnar's) The Guardsman, 1969, 1978; (Kaiser's) From Morning Till Midnight, 1979; (Hauptmann's) The Weavers, 1980. *Publications:* The Formation Dancers, 1964; The Killing of Sister George, 1965; The Window, 1968; Mrs Mouse, Are You Within?, 1969; Notes on a Love Affair, 1972; Blank Pages, 1973; Beauty and the Beast, 1977; Blind Date, 1977; contribs to: Behind the Scenes, 1972; Those Germans, 1973; On Theater, 1974 (US), etc, also to London Magazine, Plays and Players, Dramatists' Quarterly (US), New York Times, etc. *Recreation:* observing. *Address:* 42 Cumberland Mansions, Nutford Place, W1H 5ZB. *T:* 01-262 9824; c/o Margaret Ramsay Ltd, 14a Goodwin's Court, St Martin's Lane, WC2.

MARDELL, Peggy Joyce, CBE 1982; Regional Nursing Officer, North West Thames Regional Health Authority, 1974-82; *b* 8 July 1927; *d* of Alfred Edward and Edith Mary Mardell. *Educ:* George Spicer Sch., Enfield; Highlands Hosp., London (RFN); E Suffolk Hosp., Ipswich (Medallist, SRN); Queen Charlotte's Hosp. Battersea Coll. of Further Educn (Hons Dip., RNT). Queens Inst. of District Nursing, Guildford, 1951-52 (SCM); Ward Sister, Night Sister, Bethnal Green Hosp., 1953-55; Sister Tutor, Royal Surrey County Hosp., 1957-64; Asst Regional Nursing Officer, NE Metrop. Regional Hosp. Bd, 1964-70; Chief Regional Nursing Officer, NW Metrop. Regional Hosp. Bd, 1970-74. Lectr, British Red Cross, 1958-60; Examr, Gen. Nursing Council, 1962-70; Nurse Mem., Surrey AHA, 1977-82; Member: Royal Coll. of Nursing; Regional Nurse Trng Cttee, 1970-82; Assessor for Nat. Nursing Staff Cttee, 1970-82. *Recreations:* renovating old furniture, gardening, reading. *Address:* 19 East Meads, Guildford, Surrey. *T:* Guildford 75906.

MARDEN, John Louis, CBE 1976; JP; Chairman, Wheelock, Marden and Co. Ltd; Director, Hong Kong & Shanghai Banking Corporation; *b* Woodford, Essex, 12 Feb. 1919; *s* of late George Ernest Marden; *m* 1947, Anne Harris; one *s* three *d. Educ:* Gresham Sch., Norfolk; Trinity Hall, Cambridge (MA). Served War, as Captain 4th Regt RHA, in N Africa, France and Germany, 1940-46. Joined Wheelock, Marden & Co. Ltd, as trainee (secretarial and shipping, then insurance side of business), 1946; Dir of company, 1952, Chm., 1959. Chm., Hong Kong Shipowners' Assoc., 1978-. JP Hong Kong, 1964. *Recreations:* golf, water ski-ing, ski-ing. *Address:* PO Box 85, Hong Kong; c/o Wheelock Marden (UK) Ltd, 16 Finsbury Circus, EC2.

MARDER, Bernard Arthur; QC 1977; a Recorder of the Crown Court, since 1979; *b* 25 Sept. 1928; *er s* of late Samuel Marder and Marie Marder; *m* 1953, Sylvia Levy; one *s* one *d. Educ:* Bury Grammar Sch.; Manchester Univ. (LLB 1951). Called to the Bar, Gray's Inn, 1952. Asst Comr, Local Govt and Parly Boundary Commns; Chm., Panel of Inquiry into W Yorks Structure Plan, 1979. *Address:* 4/5 Gray's Inn Square, Gray's Inn, WC1R 5AU.

MARDON, Lt-Col John Kenric La Touche, DSO 1945; TD 1943; DL; MA; JP; Vice Lord-Lieutenant, Avon, 1974-80; Chairman, Mardon, Son & Hall, Ltd, Bristol, 1962-69; Director, Bristol & West Building Society; *b* 29 June 1905; *e s* of late Evelyn John Mardon, Halsway Manor, Crowcombe and late Maud Mary (*née* Rothwell); *m* 1933, Dulcie Joan, 3rd *d* of late Maj.-Gen. K. M. Body, CB, CMG, OBE; two *s* one *d. Educ:* Clifton; Christ's Coll., Cambridge. Commissioned in Royal Devon Yeomanry, 1925; Major, 1938; Lieut.-Colonel, RA, 1942; served War of 1939-45, in N.W. Europe, 1944-45 (despatches). JP Somerset, 1948; High Sheriff of Somerset, 1956-57; DL 1962. Master, Society of Merchant Venturers, Bristol, 1959-60; Governor, Clifton Coll., 1957. Pres., Bristol YMCA, 1969-79. *Recreations:* shooting, lawn tennis, squash rackets (rep. Cambridge v. Oxford, 1925). *Address:* Hemington House, Hemington, Bath BA3 5XX. *T:* Faulkland 592.

MARENGO, Kimon Evan; see Kem.

MARGADALE, 1st Baron, cr 1964; **John Granville Morrison,** TD; JP; Lord-Lieutenant of Wiltshire, 1969-81; Member Royal Company of Archers (Queen's Body Guard for Scotland); b 16 Dec. 1906; s of late Hugh Morrison; m 1928, Hon. Margaret Esther Lucie Smith (d 1980), 2nd d of 2nd Viscount Hambleden; three s one d. Educ: Eton; Magdalene Coll., Cambridge. Served 1939-45 with Royal Wilts Yeomanry; in MEF, 1939-42. MP (C) Salisbury Division of Wilts, 1942-64; Chairman, Conservative Members' (1922) Cttee, 1955-64. Yeomanry Comdt and Chm., Yeomanry Assoc., 1965-71; Hon. Col, The Royal Wiltshire Yeomanry Sqdn, 1965-71; Hon. Col, The Royal Yeomanry, 1965-71; Dep. Hon. Col, The Wessex Yeomanry, 1971-. DL 1950, JP 1936, High Sheriff, 1938, Wilts. MFH S and W Wilts Foxhounds, 1932-66. Heir: s Major Hon. James Ian Morrison, qv. Address: Fonthill House, Tisbury, Wilts. T: Tisbury 870202; Islay House, Bridgend, Argyll. Clubs: Turf, Jockey, White's.
See also Hon. C. A. Morrison, Hon. Dame M. A. Morrison, Hon. P. H. Morrison.

MARGÁIN, Hugo B.; GCVO; Ambassador of Mexico to the United States, 1965-70 and since 1977; b 13 Feb. 1913; s of Cesar R. Margáin and Maria Teresa Gleason de Margáin; m 1941, Margarita Charles de Margáin; two s three d (and one s decd). Educ: National Univ. of Mexico (UNAM); National Sch. of Jurisprudence (LLB). Prof. of Constitutional Law, 1947, of Constitutional Writs, 1951-56, and of Fiscal Law, 1952-56, Univ. of Mexico. Govt posts include: Dir-Gen., Mercantile Transactions Tax, 1951-52, and Dir-Gen., Income Tax, 1952-59, Min. for Finance. Official Mayor, Min. for Industry and Commerce, 1959-61; Dep. Minister of Finance, Sept. 1961-Dec. 1964; Sec. of Finance, Aug. 1970-May 1973; Ambassador to the UK, 1973-77. Chm., Nat. Commn on Corporate Profit-Sharing (ie labour participation), 1963-64; Govt Rep. on Bd of Nat. Inst. for Scientific Res., 1962-63 (Chm. of Bd, 1963-64). Holds hon. degrees from univs in USA. Hon. GCVO 1975. Publications: Avoidance of Double Taxation Based on the Theory of the Source of Taxable Income, 1956; Preliminary Study on Tax Codification, 1957; (with H. L. Gumpel) Taxation in Mexico, 1957; Civil Rights and the Writ of Amparo in Administrative Law, 1958; The Role of Fiscal Law in Economic Development, 1960; Profit Sharing Plan, 1964; Housing Projects for Workers (Infonavit), 1971. Recreations: riding, swimming. Address: Embassy of Mexico, 2829 16th Street, NW, Washington, DC 20009, USA.

MARGERISON, Thomas Alan; author, journalist and broadcaster on scientific subjects; Chairman, Communications Committee, UK National Commission for UNESCO; b 13 Nov. 1923; s of Ernest Alan Margerison and Isabel McKenzie; m 1950, Pamela Alice Tilbrook; two s. Educ: Huntingdon Grammar Sch.; Hymers Coll., Hull; King's Sch., Macclesfield; Sheffield University. Research Physicist, 1949; film script writer, Film Producers Guild, 1950; Scientific Editor, Butterworths sci. pubns, Ed. Research, 1951-56; Man. Editor, Heywood Pubns and National Trade Press, 1956. First Scientific Editor, The New Scientist, 1956-61; Science Corresp., Sunday Times, 1961; Dep. Editor, Sunday Times Magazine, 1962; Man. Dir, Thomson Technical Developments Ltd, 1964; Dep. Man. Dir, 1967-69, Chief Exec., 1969-71, London Weekend Television; Dir, 1966, Chm., 1971-75, Computer Technology Ltd. Worked for many years with Tonight team on BBC. Responsible for applying computers to evening newspapers in Reading and Hemel Hempstead. Publications: articles and television scripts, indifferent scientific papers; (ed) popular science books. Recreation: sailing. Address: 13 New Quebec Street, W1. T: 01-723 1634. Club: Savile.

MARGESSON, family name of Viscount Margesson.

MARGESSON, 2nd Viscount cr 1942, of Rugby; **Francis Vere Hampden Margesson;** b 17 April 1922; o s of 1st Viscount Margesson, PC, MC, and Frances H. Leggett (d 1977), New York; S father, 1965; m 1958, Helena, d of late Heikki Backstrom, Finland; one s three d. Educ: Eton; Trinity Coll., Oxford. Served War of 1939-45, as Sub-Lt, RNVR. A Director of Thames & Hudson Publications, Inc., New York, 1949-53. ADC to Governor of the Bahamas, 1956; Information Officer, British Consulate-General, NY, 1964-70. Heir: s Hon. Richard Francis David Margesson, b 25 Dec. 1960. Address: Box 245, Stone Ridge, New York, NY 12484, USA.

MARGETSON, John William Denys, CMG 1979; HM Diplomatic Service; Senior Civilian Instructor, Royal College of Defence Studies, since 1981; b 9 Oct. 1927; yr s of Very Rev. W. J. Margetson and Marion Jenoure; m 1963, Miranda, d of Sir William Menzies Coldstream, qv and Mrs Nancy Spender; one s one d. Educ: Blundell's; St John's Coll., Cambridge. Lieut, Life Guards, 1947-49. Colonial Service, District Officer, Tanganyika, 1951-60 (Private Sec. to Governor, 1956-57); entered Foreign (subseq. Diplomatic) Service, 1960; The Hague, 1962-63; speech writer to Foreign Sec., 1966-68; Head of Chancery, Saigon, 1968-70; Counsellor 1971, seconded to Cabinet Secretariat, 1971-74; Head of Chancery, UN Delegn to NATO, 1974-78; Ambassador to Vietnam, 1978-80. Recreation: music. Address: c/o Foreign and Commonwealth Office, SW1. Club: Brooks's.

MARGETSON, Major Sir Philip (Reginald), KCVO 1953 (CVO 1948); MC 1916; QPM 1956; Assistant Commissioner of Police of the Metropolis, 1946-57, retired; b 2 Jan. 1894; s of late William Parker Margetson and Ellen Maria Snell; m 1918, Diana, er d of late Sir John Edward Thornycroft, KBE;

one s (and er s killed on active service in N. Africa, 1943). Educ: Marlborough; RMC, Sandhurst. Gazetted to RSF, 1915; European War, 1914-18, served 1914-19 (MC); Adjutant 1st Bn 1923; Captain, 1923; Bt Major, 1933; Staff Captain 54th East Anglian Div. (TA) and East Anglian Area, 1928-32; retired and joined Metropolitan Police, 1933; Chief Constable No 2 District, 1936, No 1 District, Feb.-Nov. 1938, No 3 District, Nov. 1938-Feb. 1940; Dep. Asst Commissioner A Dept, New Scotland Yard, Feb.-Aug. 1940; Dep. Asst Commissioner No 1 District, Aug. 1940-June 1946; Asst Commissioner i/c D Dept, New Scotland Yard, June-Oct. 1946, transferred to A Dept, Oct. 1946. Chairman: Securicor Ltd, 1960-73 (Hon. Pres., 1973); British Security Industry Assoc., 1966-73. CStJ. Officer of the Legion of Honour; Officer of Orange Nassau (Netherlands); Commander Order of the Dannebrog (Denmark); Commander Order of St Olaf (Norway). Recreation: gardening. Address: Steyne Wood Battery, Bembridge, IoW PO35 5PG. T: Bembridge 2424. Clubs: Naval and Military, MCC; Bembridge Sailing (Bembridge).

MARGETTS, Frederick Chilton, CBE 1966 (MBE 1943); Consultant, Containerisation; b 2 Nov. 1905; m 1929, Dorothy Walls; one d. Educ: Driffield Grammar Sch.; St Martin's Grammar Sch., Scarborough. Asst Operating Supt, LNER Scotland, 1946; BR Scotland, 1949; Chief Operating Supt, BR Scotland, 1955; Chief Traffic Manager, 1958, Asst General Manager, 1959, General Manager, 1961, BR York; Member BR Cttee, 1962; Operating Mem., BR Board, 1962-67. Recreations: œnology, history of ancient gilds. Address: 9 Riseborough House, York YO3 6NQ. T: York 26207.

MARJOLIN, Robert Ernest; Commandeur de la Légion d'Honneur, 1978; Officier du Mérite Agricole, 1958; Hon. CBE 1957; economist; b 27 July 1911; s of Ernest Marjolin and Elise Vacher; m 1944, Dorothy Smith (d 1971); one s one d. Educ: Sorbonne and Law Sch., Paris; Yale Univ., New Haven, Conn. Asst to Professor Charles Rist at Institut Scientifique de Recherches Economiques et Sociales, 1934-37; Chief Asst, 1938-39. Joined General de Gaulle in London, 1941; Head of French Supply Mission in USA, 1944; Directeur des Relations Economiques Extérieures, Ministère de l'Economie Nationale, 1945; Commissaire Général Adjoint du Plan de Modernisation et d'Equipement, 1946-48; Secretary General, Organisation for European Economic Co-operation, 1948-55; Professor of Economics, University of Nancy, 1955-58; Vice-President, Commission of European Economic Community (Common Market), 1958-67; Prof. of Economics, Univ. of Paris, 1967-69. Adviser: American Express Co., 1972-; IBM, 1970-; Dir, Shell Française. Foreign Hon. Member American Academy of Arts and Sciences, 1963. Hon. LLD: Yale, 1965; Harvard, 1967; University of East Anglia, 1967. American Medal of Freedom, 1947; King's Medal, 1947; Grand-Croix de l'Ordre d'Orange-Nassau (Holland), Cavaliere di Gran Croce nell' Ordine al Merito della Repubblica (Italy). Grand-Croix du Mérite de la République Fédérale d'Allemagne, Grand-Croix de l'Ordre Royal du Phœnix (Greece), 1955, Commandeur de l'Ordre du Drapeau (Yugoslavia), 1956. Grand-Officier de l'Ordre de la Couronne (Belgique); Grand Croix de l'Ordre du Dannebrog (Denmark), 1958; Grand Croix de l'Ordre de Leopold II (Belgique), 1967. Publications: L'Evolution du Syndicalisme aux Etats-Unis, de Washington à Roosevelt, 1936; Prix, monnaie, production: Essai sur les mouvements économiques de longue durée, 1945; Europe and the United States in the World Economy, 1953; Europe in Search of its Identity, 1981. Address: 9 rue de Valois, 75001 Paris, France. T: 261.3758.

MARJORIBANKS, (Edyth) Leslia, JP; MA; Headmistress, The Henrietta Barnett School, London, since 1973; b 17 Feb. 1927; d of late Stewart Dudley Marjoribanks and Nancye (née Lee). Educ: Cheltenham Ladies' Coll.; Girton Coll., Cambridge (BA Hons Hist. 1951, MA 1955); Hughes Hall, Cambridge (Certif. Educn 1952). Talbot Heath, Bournemouth: Asst History Mistress, 1952-57; Head of History Dept, 1957-68; Headmistress, Holly Lodge High Sch., Liverpool, 1969-73. Mem. Governing Council, Examinations Cttee and Curriculum Sub-Cttee of North-West Sec. Schs Exam. Board, 1969-73. JP City of Liverpool, 1971-73, Inner London, 1976. Address: 29 Park Farm Close, N2 0PU. T: 01-883 6609.

MARJORIBANKS, Sir James Alexander Milne, KCMG 1965 (CMG 1954); Vice-President, Scottish Council (Development and Industry), since 1981; b 29 May 1911; y s of Rev. Thomas Marjoribanks, DD, and Mary Ord, d of William Logan, Madras CS; m 1936, Sonya Patricia (d 1981), d of David Stanley-Alder, Alderford Grange, Sible Hedingham, Essex, and Sylvia Marie Stanley; one d. Educ: Merchiston; Edinburgh Academy; Edinburgh Univ. (MA, 1st class hons). Entered Foreign Service, Nov. 1934; HM Embassy, Peking, 1935-38; Consulate-General, Hankow, 1938; Marseilles, 1939-40; Consul, Jacksonville, 1940-42; Vice-Consul, New York, 1942-44; Asst to UK Political Rep., Bucharest, 1944-45; Foreign Office, 1945-49; Dep. to Secretary of State for Foreign Affairs in Austrian Treaty negotiations, 1947-49; Official Secretary, UK High Commn, Canberra, 1950-52; Dep. Head of UK Delegation to High Authority of European Coal and Steel Community, 1952-55; Cabinet Office, 1955-57; HM Minister (Economic), Bonn, 1957-62; Asst Under-Secretary of State, Foreign Office, 1962-65; Ambassador and Head of UK Delegn to European Economic Community, European Atomic Energy Community and ECSC, 1965-71. Dir, The Distillers Co. Ltd, 1971-76; Governing Mem., Inveresk Research International, 1978-. Gen. Council Assessor, Edinburgh Univ. Ct, 1975-79. Chm., Scotland in Europe, 1979-. Recreations: hill walking, croquet. Address: 13 Regent Terrace, Edinburgh EH7 5BN; Lintonrig, Kirk Yetholm, Roxburghshire TD5 8PH. Club: New (Edinburgh).

MARJORIBANKS, Leslia; see Marjoribanks, E. L.

MARK, James, MBE 1943; Under-Secretary, Ministry of Overseas Development, 1965-74, retired; b 12 June 1914; s of late John Mark and Louisa Mary (née Hobson); m 1941, Mary Trewent Rowland; three s two d. Educ: William Hulme's Grammar Sch., Manchester; Trinity Coll., Cambridge; Universities of Munich and Münster. MA 1939. PhD 1939, Cambridge. Intelligence Corps, 1940-46. Principal, Control Office for Germany and Austria, 1946-48; HM Treasury, 1948-64; Asst Secretary, 1950; Economic Counsellor, Washington, 1951-53. Jt Editor, Theology, 1976-. Publications: The Question of Christian Stewardship, 1964; articles and reviews on theological and related subjects. Recreations: reading, music, gardening. Address: 6 Manorbrook, SE3. T: 01-852 9289.
See also Sir Robert Mark.

MARK, Sir Robert, GBE 1977; Kt 1973; QPM 1965; Commissioner, Metropolitan Police, 1972-77 (Deputy Commissioner, 1968-72); Director, Phoenix Assurance Co. Ltd, since 1977; Chairman, Forest Mere Ltd, since 1978; Director: Control Risks Ltd; Asset Protection International Ltd; Data Destruction Ltd; b Manchester, 13 March 1917; y s of late John Mark and Louisa Mark (née Hobson); m 1941, Kathleen Mary Leahy; one s one d. Educ: William Hulme's Grammar Sch., Manchester. Constable to Chief Superintendent, Manchester City Police, 1937-42, 1947-56; Chief Constable of Leicester, 1957-67; Assistant Commissioner, Metropolitan Police, 1967-68. Vis. Fellow, Nuffield Coll., Oxford, 1970-78 (MA Oxon 1971). Member: Standing Advisory Council of Penal System, 1966; Adv. Cttee on Police in Northern Ireland, 1969; Assessor to Lord Mountbatten during his Inquiry into Prison Security, 1966. Royal Armoured Corps, 1942-47: Lieut, Phantom (GHQ Liaison Regt), North-West Europe, 1944-45; Major, Control Commission for Germany, 1945-47. Lecture tour of N America for World Affairs Council and FCO, Oct. 1971; Edwin Stevens Lecture to the Laity, RCM, 1972; Dimbleby Meml Lecture (BBC TV), 1973. Mem. Council, AA, 1977-; Governor and Mem. Admin. Bd, Corps of Commissionaires, 1977-; Hon. Freeman, City of Westminster, 1977. Hon. LLM Leicester Univ., 1967; Hon. DLitt Loughborough, 1976; Hon. LLD: Manchester, 1978; Liverpool, 1978. KStJ 1977. Publications: Policing a Perplexed Society, 1977; In the Office of Constable, 1978. Address: Esher, Surrey KT10 8LU.
See also James Mark.

MARKALL, Most Rev. Francis, SJ; b 24 Sept. 1905; e s of late Walter James Markall and Alice Mary Gray, London. Educ: St Ignatius' College, London. Entered Society of Jesus, 1924; continued classical and philosophical studies, 1926-31; Assistant Master, Stonyhurst College, 1931-34; theological studies, 1934-38; Missionary in Rhodesia, 1939-56; Titular Archbishop of Cotieo and Coadjutor with right of succession to Archbishop of Salisbury, April 1956; Archbishop of Salisbury and Metropolitan of Province of Rhodesia, Nov. 1956; retired, 1976. Address: Hartmann House, St George's College, PO Bag 7727, Causeway, Harare, Zimbabwe. Club: Salisbury (Harare).

MARKHAM, Rt. Rev. Bernard; b 26 Feb. 1907. Educ: Bingley Grammar School; Leeds University (BA Hons History, 1928); College of the Resurrection. Deacon, 1930; Priest 1931. Curate of: Lidget Green, 1930-35; S Francis, N Kensington, 1935-37; Stoke-on-Trent, 1937-39; Vicar of Bierley, 1939-46; Rector of St Benedict, Ardwick, 1946-59; Vicar of St Margaret's, Liverpool, 1959-62; Bishop of Nassau and the Bahamas, 1962-72; Asst Bishop, Dio. of Southwell and Rector of E Bridgford, 1972-77; Asst Bishop, Dio. Southwark, 1977-80. Hon. DD Nashotah House, Wisconsin, 1979. Address: 209 London Road, Balderton, Newark, Notts NG24 3HB.

MARKHAM, Sir Charles (John), 3rd Bt, cr 1911; b 2 July 1924; s of Sir Charles Markham, 2nd Bt, and Gwladys, e d of late Hon. Rupert Beckett; S father 1952; m 1949, Valerie, o d of Lt-Col E. Barry-Johnston, Makuyu, Kenya; two s one d. Educ: Eton. Served War of 1939-45, Lieut in 11th Hussars (despatches). Vice-Chm., Nairobi Co. Council, 1953-55; MLC Kenya, 1955-60. Pres., Royal Agricultural Soc., Kenya, 1958. KStJ 1973. Heir: s Arthur David Markham [b 6 Dec. 1950; m 1977, Carolyn, yr d of Captain Mungo Park; two d]. Address: PO Box 42263, Nairobi, Kenya, East Africa. Club: Cavalry and Guards.

MARKING, Sir Henry (Ernest), KCVO 1978; CBE 1969; MC 1944; CompRAeS 1953; FCIT; Chairman, British Tourist Authority, since 1977 (Member, 1969-77); b 11 March 1920; s of late Isaac and Hilda Jane Marking. Educ: Saffron Walden Gram. Sch.; University Coll., London. Served War of 1939-45: 2nd Bn The Sherwood Foresters, 1941-45; North Africa, Italy and Middle East; Adjutant, 1944-45. Middle East Centre of Arab Studies, Jerusalem, 1945-46. Admitted solicitor, 1948. Asst Solicitor, Cripps, Harries, Hall & Co., Tunbridge Wells, 1948-49; Asst Solicitor, 1949, Sec., 1950, Chief Exec., 1964-72, Chm., 1971-72, BEA; Mem. Bd, BOAC, 1971-72; Mem., British Airways Board, 1971-80 (Man. Dir, 1972-76; Dep. Chm., 1972-77). Dir, Barclays Bank Internat. Ltd, 1977-. Chm., Carreras Rothmans Ltd, 1979-; Dir, Rothmans Internat. Ltd, 1979-. Trustee and Vice-Chm., Leonard Cheshire Foundn, 1962-. FBIM 1971. Club: Reform.

MARKOVA, Dame Alicia, DBE 1963 (CBE 1958); **(Dame Lilian Alicia Marks)**; Prima Ballerina Assoluta; Professor of Ballet and Performing Arts, College-Conservatory of Music, University of Cincinnati, since 1970; b London 1910; d of Arthur Tristman Marks and Eileen Barry. With Diaghilev's Russian Ballet Co., 1925-29; Rambert Ballet Club, 1931-33;

Vic-Wells Ballet Co., 1933-35; Markova-Dolin Ballet Co., 1935-37; Ballet Russe de Monte Carlo, 1938-41; Ballet Theatre, USA, 1941-46. Appeared with Anton Dolin, guest and concert performances, 1948-50. Co-Founder and Prima Ballerina, Festival Ballet, 1950-51; Guest Prima Ballerina: Buenos Aires, 1952; Royal Ballet, 1953 and 1957; Royal Danish Ballet, 1955; Scala, Milan, 1956; Teatro Municipal, Rio de Janeiro, 1956; Festival Ballet, 1958 and 1959; Guest appearances at Metropolitan Opera House, New York, 1952, 1953-54, 1955, 1957, 1958; Dir, Metropolitan Opera Ballet, 1963-69; produced Les Sylphides for Festival Ballet and Aust. Ballet, 1976, for Royal Ballet School and Northern Ballet Theatre, 1978, for Royal Winnipeg Ballet, Canada, 1979. Guest Professor: Royal Ballet Sch., 1973-; Paris Opera Ballet, 1975; Australian Ballet Sch., 1976. Vice-Pres., Royal Acad. of Dancing, 1958-; Governor, Royal Ballet, 1973-. Concert, television and guest appearances (general), 1952-61. BBC series, Markova's Ballet Call, 1960; Masterclass, BBC2, 1980. Queen Elizabeth II Coronation Award, Royal Acad. of Dancing, 1963. Hon. DMus: Leicester, 1966; East Anglia, 1982. Publication: Giselle and I, 1960. Address: c/o Barclays Bank Ltd, 451 Oxford Street, W1.

MARKS, family name of **Baron Marks of Broughton.**

MARKS OF BROUGHTON, 2nd Baron, cr 1961; **Michael Marks;** b 27 Aug. 1920; o s of 1st Baron and Miriam (d 1971), d of Ephraim Sieff; S father 1964; m ; one s two d. Heir: son.

MARKS, Bernard Montague; Chairman, Alfred Marks Bureau Limited, since 1946; Member of Lloyd's, since 1973; b 11 Oct. 1923; s of Alfred and Elizabeth Marks; m 1956, Norma Renton; two s. Educ: Highgate Public Sch.; Royal Coll. of Science. Chm. or Vice-Chm., Fedn of Personnel Services of GB, 1965-79. Publication: Once Upon A Typewriter, 1974. Recreations: bridge, golf, tennis, ski-ing. Address: Charters, South Ridge, St George's Hill, Weybridge, Surrey. Clubs: St George's Hill Golf, St George's Hill Tennis.

MARKS, John Emile, CBE 1970; President of DV Group Ltd since 1958; s of late Hyam and Miriam Marks; m ; two s two d. Educ: Eton College. Served War of 1939-45 (despatches 1944; 1939-45 Star, France and Germany Star, Defence and Victory Medals). Emigrated to Canada, 1951; estab. John Marks Ltd, importers and distributors of sporting goods, 1952; Pres., Douglas Engineering Co. Ltd, Toronto, 1956; estab. Canair Ltd, Windsor, England, 1962 (Chm. and majority shareholder); bought controlling interest in DV Group Ltd, 1963 (inc. Douglas Engrg, Engmark Western Ltd and EngMark Ltd). Pres., British Canadian Trade Assoc., 1966-67, 1969-70; returned to England, 1972; Pres., Canada UK Chamber of Commerce, 1975-76; Vice-Chm., Westminster Chamber of Commerce. Recreations: tennis, golf, squash. Address: 25 Montrose Court, Princes Gate, SW7 2QQ; DV Group Ltd, PO Box 5500, Don Mills, Ont, Canada. Clubs: Queen's, Royal Automobile; Toronto Cricket, Skating and Curling, Queen's (Toronto).

MARKS, Sir John (Hedley Douglas), Kt 1972; CBE 1966; FCA; Chairman: Development Finance Corporation Ltd, since inception, 1955 (Managing Director, 1955-75); Development Holdings Ltd; Garratt's Ltd; Reinsurance Co. of Australasia Ltd; Brambles Industries Ltd; Vice-Chairman, Australian Consolidated Industries Ltd; Directorships include: CHEP International Finance SA; CHEP International Investments SA; West Lakes Ltd; Borg-Warner (Aust.) Ltd; Japan Aust. Invest Co. Ltd; Alcan Australia Ltd; b 8 May 1916; s of late Frederick William Marks, CBE, and late Viva Bessie Meurant Stinson; m 1941, Judith Norma Glenwright; two d. Educ: St Peter's Prep. Sch.; Sydney Church of England Sch. Qualified as Chartered Accountant and Secretary, and commenced practice on own behalf, 1937. Served War of 1939-45: enlisted in 2nd AIF, 1939; commissioned, 1941, and rose to rank of Lt-Col. Founded Development Finance Corp. Ltd, Investment Bankers, 1955. Member: Cttee on Community Health Services (Starr Report), 1968-69; Aust. Manufacturing Council; NSW Electricity Commn, 1966-81; Chm., Cttee of Inquiry into State Taxation (NSW), 1975-76. Trustee: Shore Foundn; Nat. Parks and Wildlife Foundn, NSW, 1969-81. Mem. Council, Macquarie Univ., 1963-76; Governor, Queenwood Sch.; Chairman Emeritus: The Prince Henry Hosp.; The Prince of Wales Hosp.; Fellow, Internat. Banker Assoc. Recreations: yachting, golf, tennis. Address: 6b Raglan Street, Mosman, NSW 2088, Australia. T: 960 2221. Clubs: Australian, Royal Sydney Yacht, Elanora Country, American National, Manly Golf (all in NSW).

MARKS, Kenneth; MP (Lab) Gorton since Nov. 1967; b 15 June 1920; s of Robert P. Marks, Electrician and Edith Collins, Cotton Weaver; m 1944, Kathleen Lynch; one s one d. Educ: Peacock Street Sch., Gorton; Central High Sch., Manchester; Didsbury Coll. of Education. Worked in offices of LNER, 1936-40. Joined ranks, Grenadier Guards, 1940-42; commnd into Cheshire Regt, 1942-46 (Capt.); served in Middle East, Malta, Italy, NW Europe and Germany as Infantry Platoon and Company Comdr. Taught in Manchester schs, 1946-67; Headmaster, Clough Top Sec. Sch. for Boys, 1964-67. Parliamentary Private Secretary: to Rt Hon. Anthony Crosland, 1969-70; to Roy Hattersley, 1974-75; to Rt Hon. Harold Wilson, 1975; Opposition Whip, 1971-72; Parly Under-Sec. of State, DoE, 1975-79. Member: House of Commons Select Cttee for Educn and Science, 1968-70; Select Cttee on Expenditure, 1971-75; Exec. Cttee, CPA, 1972-75; Exec. Cttee, UK Br., IPU, 1981-. Chm., Parly Labour Party Educn Gp, 1972-75, NW Reg. Gp, 1975-; Mem., N Atlantic Assembly, 1974-75, 1979-. Vice-Pres., YHA, 1980-. Address: 1 Epping Road, Denton, Manchester M34 2GB. T: 061-336 4147.

MARKUS, Rika, (Rixi), MBE 1975 (for services to Bridge); Bridge journalist and author, since 1957; *b* 27 June 1910; *d* of Michel and Louise Scharfstein; *m* 1929, Salomon Markus (marr. diss. 1947); one *d* decd. *Educ:* Vienna and Dresden. Turned to bridge after a severe illness; arrived in London, March 1938 (3 days after Hitler occupied Austria; parents lived already in London). Bridge correspondent of The Guardian and Harpers & Queen, and formerly of the Evening Standard; writes for Express Syndication Gp. Organises annual bridge match between House of Lords and House of Commons (Challenge Cup donated by The Guardian); matches held with parliamentarians and players in other countries, *eg* France, Holland and Dubai. Acclaimed as best woman player in the world; European Bridge Champion, 1935 and 1936; World Champion, 1937; 1st Woman Grand Master, 1973; Charles Goren Award for the player of the year, 1976; 4 Olympic titles; 10 Eur. Championships; many national and internat. titles. *Publications:* Bid Boldly, Play Safe, 1965; Common-Sense Bridge, 1972; Aces and Places, 1972; Bridge around the World, 1977; Improve Your Bridge, 1977; Play Better Bridge with Rixi Markus, 1978; Table Tales by Rixi Markus, 1979. *Recreations:* music, cooking, watching all sports, theatre. *Address:* 22 Lowndes Lodge, Cadogan Place, SW1X 9RZ. *T:* 01-235 7377. *Club:* St James Bridge.

MARLAND, Michael, CBE 1977; Headmaster, North Westminster Community School, since 1980; *b* 28 Dec. 1934; *m* 1st, 1955, Eileen (*d* 1968); four *s* one *d* ; 2nd, 1971, Rose. *Educ:* Christ's Hospital Sch.; Sidney Sussex Coll., Cambridge (MA). Head of English, Abbey Wood Sch., 1961-64; Head of English and subseq. Dir of Studies, Crown Woods Sch., 1964-71; Headmaster, Woodberry Down Sch., 1971-79. Hon. Prof., Dept of Educn, Univ. of Warwick, 1980-. Member of many educn cttees, incl. Bullock Cttee, Schools Council English Cttee (Chm.), Nat. Book League Exec. *Publications:* Towards The New Fifth, 1969; The Practice of English Teaching, 1970; Peter Grimes, 1971; Head of Department, 1971; Pastoral Care, 1974; The Craft of the Classroom, 1975; Language Across the Curriculum, 1977; Education for the Inner City, 1980; Departmental Management, 1981; General Editor of: Blackie's Student Drama Series; Longman Imprint Books; The Times Authors; Heinemann Organisation in Schools Series; contrib. Times Educnl Supplement. *Recreations:* music, literature. *Address:* 22 Compton Terrace, N1 2UN. *T:* 01-226 0648; The Green Farmhouse, Cranmer Green, Walsham-le-Willows, Bury St Edmunds, Suffolk. *T:* 483.

MARLAND, Paul; MP (C) Gloucestershire West, since 1979; *b* 19 March 1940; *s* of Alexander G. Marland and Elsa May Lindsey Marland; *m* 1965, Penelope Anne Barlow; one *s* two *d*. *Educ:* Gordonstoun Sch., Elgin; Trinity Coll., Dublin (BA,BComm). Hopes Metal Windows, 1964; London Press Exchange, 1965-66; farmer, 1967-. Jt PPS to Financial Sec. to the Treasury and Economic Sec., 1981-. *Recreations:* skiing, shooting, riding, ballet. *Address:* Ford Mill Farm, Temple Guiting, Cheltenham, Glos. *T:* Guiting Power 232. *Club:* Boodle's.

MARLBOROUGH, 11th Duke of, *cr* 1702; **John George Vanderbilt Henry Spencer-Churchill;** DL; Baron Spencer, 1603; Earl of Sunderland, 1643; Baron Churchill, 1685; Earl of Marlborough, 1689; Marquis of Blandford, 1702; Prince of the Holy Roman Empire; Prince of Mindelheim in Suabia; late Captain Life Guards; *b* 13 April 1926; *s* of 10th Duke of Marlborough and Hon. Alexandra Mary Hilda Cadogan, CBE (*d* 1961), *d* of late Henry Arthur, Viscount Chelsea; *S* father, 1972; *m* 1st, 1951, Susan Mary (marr. diss., 1960; she *m* 1962, Alan Cyril Heber-Percy), *d* of Michael Hornby, *qv* ; one *s* one *d* (and one *s* decd); 2nd, 1961, Mrs Athina Livanos (marr. diss. 1971; she *d* 1974), *d* of late Stavros G. Livanos, Paris; 3rd, 1972, Rosita Douglas; one *s* one *d* (and one *s* decd). *Educ:* Eton. Lieut Life Guards, 1946; Captain, 1953; resigned commission, 1953. Chairman: Martini & Rossi 1979; London Paperweights Ltd, 1974. President: Thames and Chilterns Tourist Board, 1974-; Oxfordshire Branch, CLA, 1978-; Oxfordshire Assoc. of Boys' Clubs, 1972-; Oxford Br., SS&AFA, 1977-; Oxford United Football Club, 1964-. CC 1961-64, Oxfordshire; JP 1962; DL 1974. *Heir: s* Marquis of Blandford, *qv. Address:* Blenheim Palace, Woodstock, Oxon. *Clubs:* Portland, White's.

MARLEY, 2nd Baron *cr* 1930, of Marley in the County of Sussex; **Godfrey Pelham Leigh Aman;** *b* 6 Sept. 1913; *s* of 1st Baron Marley and Octable Turquet, Lady Marley (*d* 1969); *S* father 1952; *m* 1956, Catherine Doone Beal. *Educ:* Bedales Sch. Royal Marines, 1939-45. *Heir:* none. *Address:* 104 Ebury Mews, SW1. *T:* 01-730 4844; House of Lords, SW1.

MARLING, Sir Charles (William Somerset), 5th Bt *cr* 1882; *b* 2 June 1951; *s* of Sir John Stanley Vincent Marling, 4th Bt, OBE, and Georgina Brenda (Betty) (*d* 1961), *o d* of late Henry Edward FitzRoy Somerset, *S* father, 1977; *m* 1979, Judi P. Futrille, one *d. Address:* Woodcray Manor Farm, Wokingham, Berks RG11 3HG.

MARLOW, Antony Rivers; MP (C) Northampton North, since 1979; *b* 17 June 1940; *s* of late Major Thomas Keith Rivers Marlow, MBE, RE retd, and Beatrice Nora (*née* Hall); *m* 1962, Catherine Louise Howel (*née* Jones); three *s* two *d. Educ:* Wellington Coll.; RMA Sandhurst; St Catharine's Coll., Cambridge (2nd Cl. Hons (1) Mech. Sciences, MA). Served Army, 1958-69; retd, Captain RE; management consultant and industrial/commercial manager, 1969-79. *Recreations:* livestock farming, Rugby spectator, opera, ballet. *Address:* House of Commons, SW1A 0AA.

MARLOW, Roger Douglas Frederick, DSC 1943; JP; Deputy Director-General, Institute of Directors, 1975-77; *b* 21 Aug. 1912; *s* of Frederick George Marlow and Mabel Marlow(e), authoress; *m* 1st 1951, Mary (Bernadette Teresa) Savage, actress (*d* 1972); two *s* one *d* ; 2nd, 1977, Jean Marian White (*née* Watts); two step *d. Educ:* Christ's Hospital; London School of Economics and Political Science. BScEcon (Hons). Initial trng in merchant banking, 1934-35; Executive, Overseas Sections, London Chamber of Commerce, 1935-39. War service, 1939-46, Lt-Comdr RNVR (Commendation (Naval) 1941, DSC). Dep. Asst Sec., London Chamber of Commerce, 1946-60; concurrently, Chief Executive and Secretary: London Building Acts Cttee; Mica Trade Assoc.; Horological Trade Pool Ltd (incl. import Licence admin for BoT); British Essence Mfrs Assoc.; British Aromatic Compound Mfrs Assoc.; Asst Dir-Gen. and Educn Dir, Inst. of Dirs, 1960-75. Member: Essential Oils Adv. Cttee (Govt and Industry), 1946-51; Adv. Panel, PER, Dept of Employment, 1972-77; Co-ordinating Sec., Sino-British Trade Council, 1954-60; Mem., Negotiating Mission to USSR for Estabt of Reciprocal Trade Fairs, 1959. Mem. Council, Nat. Inst. of Industrial Psychology, 1960-74; Mem. Court and Council, Univ. of Sussex, 1970-; Governor, Christ's Hospital, 1978-. JP E Sussex, Brighton Div., 1965-. *Publications:* Selling to Finland, 1959; Trading with the Soviet Union, 1959; (with R. Earnshaw) Falcon Workshop Business Course for Sixth Formers, 1980; various articles in trade and professional jls. *Recreations:* tennis, swimming, music, painting, bridge. *Address:* 5 Surrenden Crescent, Brighton, Sussex BN1 6WE. *T:* Brighton 503072.

MARLOWE, Hugh; *see* Patterson, Harry.

MARMION, Prof. Barrie P.; Director, Division of Virology, Institute of Medical and Veterinary Science, Adelaide, S Australia, since 1978; *b* 19 May 1920; *s* of J. P. and M. H. Marmion, Alverstoke, Hants; *m* 1953, Diana Ray Newling, *d* of Dr P. Ray Newling, Adelaide, SA; one *d. Educ:* University Coll. and University Coll. Hosp., London. MD London 1947, DSc London 1963, FRCPath 1962, FRCPE 1970, FRCPA. House Surg., UCH, 1942; Bacteriologist, Public Health Laboratory Service, 1943-62; Rockefeller Trav. Fellow, at Walter and Eliza Hall Inst., Melbourne, 1951-52; Foundation Prof., Microbiology, Monash Univ., Melbourne, Australia, 1962-68; Prof. of Bacteriology, Univ. of Edinburgh, 1968-78. *Publications:* (ed) Mackie and McCartney's Medical Microbiology, 13th edn 1978; numerous papers on bacteriology and virology. *Recreations:* tennis, music. *Address:* c/o IMVS, Box 14, Rundle Street PO, Adelaide, SA 5000, Australia. *T:* 2287911; *Telex:* 82647.

MARNAN, His Honour John Fitzgerald, MBE 1944; QC 1954; a Circuit Judge, lately sitting at Central Criminal Court, 1972-80, retired; *b* 23 Jan. 1908; *s* of late T. G. Marnan, Irish Bar; *m* 1st, 1934, Morwenna (marr. diss., 1958), *d* of late Sir Keith Price; one *s* (and one *s* decd); 2nd, 1958, Mrs Diana Back (marr. diss., 1963), *o d* of late Comdr Charles Crawshay, RN (retd), and late Mrs M. L. Greville; 3rd, 1966, Joanna, *o d* of late Maj.-Gen. W. N. Herbert, CB, CMG, DSO. *Educ:* Ampleforth; Trinity Coll., Oxford. Commnd TA (Oxford Univ. OTC), 1929. Called to Bar, 1931; joined Chester and N Wales Circuit; joined Supplementary Reserve, Irish Guards, 1936; served War of 1939-45 (MBE, despatches); Western Europe with Irish Guards, and on staff of 15th (Scottish) Div.; Major (GSO2), 1944. A Metropolitan Magistrate, 1956-58, resigned. Crown Counsel in the Ministry of Legal Affairs, Kenya Government, 1958-59; Federal Justice of the Federal Supreme Court, the West Indies, 1959-62; subseq. Justice of Appeal of the British Caribbean Court of Appeal. Sat as Commissioner at Crown Courts, at Manchester, 1962-63, at Liverpool, 1963, and at Central Criminal Court, 1964-66; a Dep. Chm., Greater London Sessions, 1966-68; Chm., NE London QS, 1968-71. *Recreation:* field sports. *Address:* Cottrells, Dinton, near Salisbury, Wilts. *T:* Teffont 315. *Clubs:* Cavalry and Guards, Pratt's.

MARNHAM, Harold, MBE 1945; QC 1965; Barrister-at-Law; Leader of Parliamentary Bar, 1967-74; *b* 14 July 1911; *y s* of late Arthur Henry Marnham and late Janet Elizabeth Marnham; *m* 1947, Hilary, *y d* of late Ernest Jukes; two *s. Educ:* Stellenbosch Boys' High Sch.; Stellenbosch Univ.; Jesus Coll., Cambridge. Called to Bar, Gray's Inn, 1935; Bencher, 1969. Served War 1939-45; BEF, 1939-40; BLA, 1944-45 (despatches); 2nd Lt RA (TA); Capt. 1940; Major 1942; Lt-Col 1945. Dep. Chm., Oxfordshire QS, 1966-71. Chm., Industrial Tribunals, 1975-79. *Address:* 1 Raymond Buildings, Gray's Inn, WC1R 5BH. *T:* 01-242 2615. *Clubs:* Hawks (Cambridge); Leander (Henley-on-Thames).

MARNHAM, John Ewart, CMG 1955; MC 1944; TD 1949; HM Diplomatic Service, retired; *b* Hampstead, 24 Jan. 1916; *er s* of late Col Arthur Ewart Marnham, MC, TD, DL, JP, Foxley Grove, Holyport, Berks, and late Dorothy Clare Morgan; *m* 1944, Susan, *er d* of late Walter Foster (formerly Friedenstein), Vienna and London; two *s. Educ:* Mill Hill; Jesus Coll., Cambridge. Asst Principal, Colonial Office, 1938. Served War, 1939-45: BEF 1939-40; BLA 1944-45 (despatches); 2nd Lt RA (TA) 1938; Major, 1942; Lt-Col, Commanding 353 (London) Medium Regt RA (TA), 1954-57; Brevet Col, 1958. Principal, Colonial Office, 1946; Asst Sec. 1948; Imperial Defence Coll., 1961; Asst Under-Sec. of State: CO, 1964; Foreign Office, 1966-67; Consul-Gen., Johannesburg, 1967-70; British Govt Rep., WI Associated States, 1970-73; Ambassador to Tunisia, 1973-75. Clerk in Cttee Office, House of Commons, 1977-81. *Recreations:* reading, gardening, riding. *Address:* Glebe House, Blake's Lane, Hare Hatch, Berks RG10 9TD. *T:* Wargrave 3469. *Club:* United Oxford & Cambridge University.

MARNHAM, Sir Ralph, KCVO 1957; MChir, FRCS; Serjeant Surgeon to the Queen, 1967-71; Consulting Surgeon to: St George's Hospital; King Edward VII's Hospital for Officers; Fellow: Medical Society of London; Association of Surgeons of Great Britain and Ireland; *b* 7 June 1901; *e s* of Arthur Henry Marnham and late Janet Elizabeth Micklem; *m* 1st, 1927, Muriel, *y d* of Herbert Marnham; one *d*; 2nd, 1942, Helena Mary, *e d* of Patrick Daly; two *s*. *Educ*: Diocesan Coll., Rondebosch, South Africa; Gonville and Caius Coll., Cambridge; St George's Hospital. Allingham Scholarship Surgery; Sir Francis Laking Research Scholarship; Moynihan Fellow Assoc. of Surgeons of Great Britain and Ireland. War of 1939-45: Officer in Charge Surgical Divs of No. 62 and 6 Gen. Hospitals. Cons. Surgeon, 9th Army, East Africa and Southern Command (despatches twice). Usual House Appointments St George's Hospital; also Asst Curator of Museum, Surgical Registrar, and Resident Asst Surgeon. *Publications*: various in medical journals. *Recreation*: golf. *Address*: 74 Eyre Court, Finchley Road, NW8 9TX. *T*: 01-586 3001. *Clubs*: Buck's, Pratt's.

MAROWITZ, Charles; Artistic Director: Open Space Theatre of Los Angeles, since 1982; The Open Space Theatre, London, 1968-81; *b* 26 Jan. 1934; Austrian mother, Russian father. *Educ*: Seward Park High Sch.; University Coll. London. Dir, In-Stage Experimental Theatre, 1958; Asst Dir, Royal Shakespeare Co., 1963-65; Artistic Dir, Traverse Theatre, 1963-64. Drama Critic: Encore Magazine, 1956-63; Plays and Players, 1958-74; The Village Voice, 1955-; The NY Times, 1966-. West End Director: Loot, Criterion, 1967; The Bellow Plays, Fortune, 1966; Fortune and Men's Eyes, Comedy, 1969; productions abroad: Woyzeck, 1965, The Shrew, 1979, Nat. Theatre, Bergen; Hedda, 1978, Enemy of the People, 1979, Nat. Theatre, Oslo; Measure for Measure, Oslo New Theatre, 1981; The Father, Trondheim, 1981; Ah, Sweet Mystery of Life, Seattle, 1981. Order of the Purple Sash, 1969. *Publications*: The Method as Means, 1960; The Marowitz Hamlet, 1967; A Macbeth, 1970; Confessions of a Counterfeit Critic, 1973; Open Space Plays, 1974; Measure for Measure, 1975; The Shrew, 1975; Artaud at Rodez, 1976; Variations on The Merchant of Venice; The Act of Being, 1977; The Marowitz Shakespeare, 1978; New Theatre Voices of the 50s and 60s, 1981; Sex Wars, 1982. *Recreation*: balling. *Address*: c/o Open Space, Suite 584, 1901 Avenue of the Stars, Los Angeles, Calif 90067, USA.

MARPLES, Brian John; Emeritus Professor of Zoology, University of Otago, NZ; *b* 31 March 1907; 2nd *s* of George and Anne Marples; *m* 1931, Mary Joyce Ransford; two *s*. *Educ*: St Bees Sch.; Exeter Coll., Oxford. Lecturer in Zoology, Univ. of Manchester, 1929-35; Lecturer in Zoology, Univ. of Bristol, 1935-37; Prof. of Zoology, Univ. of Otago, NZ, 1937-67. *Publications*: Freshwater Life in New Zealand, 1962; various technical zoological and archaeological papers. *Address*: 1 Vanbrugh Close, Old Woodstock, Oxon.

MARQUAND, Prof. David (Ian); Professor of Contemporary History and Politics, Salford University, since 1978; *b* 20 Sept. 1934; *s* of Rt Hon. Hilary Marquand, PC; *m* 1959, Judith Mary (*née* Reed); one *s* one *d*. *Educ*: Emanuel Sch.; Magdalen Coll., Oxford; St Antony's Coll., Oxford (Sen. Schol.). 1st cl. hons Mod. Hist., 1957. Teaching Asst, Univ. of Calif., 1958-59; Leader Writer, The Guardian, 1959-62; Research Fellow, St Antony's Coll., Oxford, 1962-64; Lectr in Politics, Univ. of Sussex, 1964-66. Contested (Lab) Barry, 1964; MP (Lab) Ashfield, 1966-77; PPS to Minister of Overseas Develt, 1967-69; Jun. Opposition Front-Bench Spokesman on econ. affairs, 1971-72; Member: Select Cttee on Estimates, 1966-68; Select Cttee on Procedure, 1968-73; Select Cttee on Corp. Tax, 1971; British Deleg. to Council of Europe, 1970-73. Chief Advr, Secretariat-Gen., European Commission, 1977-78. Mem., Nat. Steering Cttee, SDP, 1981-; Prospective Parly Cand. (SDP) High Peak, 1982-. Thomas Jefferson Meml Lectr, Univ. of Calif at Berkeley, 1981. George Orwell Meml Prize (jtly), 1980. *Publications*: Ramsay MacDonald, 1977; Parliament for Europe, 1979; The Politics of Nostalgia, 1980; Taming Leviathan, 1980; (with David Butler) European Elections and British Politics, 1981; (ed) John Mackintosh on Politics, 1982; contrib. to: The Age of Austerity, 1964; A Radical Future, 1967; Coalitions in British Politics, 1978; Britain in Europe, 1980; The Political Economy of Tolerable Survival, 1980; The Rebirth of Britain, 1982; European Monetary Union Progress and Prospects, 1982; Social Theory and Political Practice, 1982; articles and reviews in The Guardian, The Times, The Sunday Times, New Statesman, Encounter, Commentary, etc. *Recreation*: walking. *Address*: c/o University of Salford, Salford M5 4WT.

MARQUIS, family name of **Earl of Woolton.**

MARQUIS, James Douglas, DFC 1945; Managing Director, Irvine Development Corporation, 1972-81; *b* 16 Oct. 1921; *s* of James Charles Marquis and Jessica Amy (*née* Huggett); *m* 1945, Brenda Eleanor, *d* of Robert Rayner Davey; two *s*. *Educ*: Shooters Hill Sch., Woolwich. Local Govt, 1938-41. Served War: RAF 1941-46 (RAF 1st cl. Air Navigation Warrant, 1945), Navigation Officer, 177 Sqdn, 224 Gp, and AHQ Malaya (Sqdn Ldr 1945). Local Govt, 1946-56; Harlow Develt Corp., 1957-68; Irvine Develt Corp.: Chief Finance Officer, 1968-72; Dir of Finance and Admin., 1972. Pres., Ayrshire Chamber of Industries, 1979-80. FRMetS 1945; IPFA 1950; FCIS 1953. *Publication*: An Ayrshire Sketchbook, 1979. *Recreations*: sketching and painting (five one-man exhibns, incl. one in Sweden; works in collections: Rhodesia, Japan, Sweden, Norway, Denmark, USA, Canada); angling, gardening, ornithology, golf. *Address*: 3 Knoll Park, Ayr KA7 4RH. *T*: Alloway 42212. *Club*: Royal Air Force.

MARR, Allan James, CBE 1965; Director and Chairman, EGS Co. Ltd; *b* 6 May 1907; *s* of late William Bell Marr and Hilda May Marr; *cousin* and *heir pres.* to Sir Leslie Lynn Marr, 2nd Bt, *qv*; *m* 1935, Joan de Wolf Ranken; one *s* two *d*. *Educ*: Oundle; Durham Univ. Apprenticeship, Joseph L. Thompson & Sons Ltd, 1926-31; joined Sir James Laing & Sons Ltd, 1932. Dir, Doxford and Sunderland Shipbuilding and Eng. Co. Ltd; retd from all shipbldg activities, 1973. Pres. Shipbuilding Conf., 1963-65; Fellow of North-East Coast Inst. of Engineers and Shipbuilders (Pres., 1966-68); Mem., RINA. Chm., Research Council of British Ship Research Assoc., 1965-73. *Recreations*: photography, fishing. *Address*: Dalesford, Thropton, Morpeth, Northumberland.

MARR, (Sir) Leslie Lynn, (2nd Bt, *cr* 1919, but does not use the title); MA Cambridge; painter and draughtsman; late Flight Lieutenant RAF; *b* 14 Aug. 1922; *o s* of late Col John Lynn Marr, OBE, TD, (and *g s* of 1st Bt,) and Amelia Rachel, *d* of late Robert Thompson, Overdinsdale Hall, Darlington; *S* grandfather 1932; *m* 1st, 1948, Dinora Delores Mendelson (marr. diss. 1956); one *d*; 2nd, 1962, Lynn Heneage; two *d*. *Educ*: Shrewsbury; Pembroke Coll., Cambridge. Has exhibited at Ben Uri, Drian, Woodstock, Wildenstein, Whitechapel, Campbell and Franks Galls, London; also in Norwich, Belfast, Birmingham, Newcastle upon Tyne, Bristol and Paris. *Publication*: From My Point of View, 1979. *Heir*: *cousin* Allan James Marr, *qv*. *Address*: c/o Lloyds Bank, Holt, Norfolk.

MARRACK, Rear-Adm. Philip Reginald, CB 1979; CEng, FIMechE, FIMarE; *b* 16 Nov. 1922; *s* of Captain Philip Marrack, RN and Annie Kathleen Marrack (*née* Proud); *m* 1954, Pauline Mary (*née* Haag); two *d*. *Educ*: Eltham Coll.; Plymouth Coll.; RNC Dartmouth; RN Engineering Coll., Manadon. War service at sea, HM Ships Orion and Argus, 1944-45; Advanced Engineering Course, RNC Greenwich, 1945-47; HM Submarines Templar and Token, 1947-50; served in Frigate Torquay, Aircraft Carriers Glory and Hermes, and MoD; Captain 1965; Commanded Admiralty Reactor Test Estab., Dounreay, 1967-70; CSO (Mat.) on Staff of Flag Officer Submarines, and Asst Dir (Nuclear), Dockyard Dept, 1970-74; Rear-Adm. 1974; Dir, Naval Ship Production, 1974-77; Dir, Dockyard Production and Support, 1977-81, retd. *Recreations*: fly fishing, gardening, viticulture, wine making. *Address*: c/o Barclays Bank, Princess Street, Plymouth PL1 2HA.

MARRE, Sir Alan (Samuel), KCB 1970 (CB 1955); Parliamentary Commissioner for Administration, 1971-76; ex officio Member, Council on Tribunals, 1971-76; *b* 25 Feb. 1914; *s* of late Joseph and late Rebecca Marre; *m* 1943, Romola Mary (*see* Lady Marre); one *s* one *d*. *Educ*: St Olave's and St Saviour's Grammar Sch., Southwark; Trinity Hall, Cambridge (Major open Schol.) John Stewart of Rannoch Schol. and 1st cl. hons Class. Trip. Parts I and II. Ministry of Health: Asst Principal, 1936; Principal, 1941; Asst Sec., 1946; Under-Sec., 1952-63; Under-Sec., Ministry of Labour, 1963-64; Dep. Sec.: Ministry of Health, 1964-66; Min. of Labour (later Dept of Employment and Productivity), 1966-68; Second Perm. Under-Sec. of State, Dept of Health and Social Security, 1968-71. Health Service Comr for England, Wales and Scotland, 1973-76; ex officio Mem. Commns for Local Admin, 1974-76. Chairman: Age Concern England, 1977-80; Crown Housing Assoc., 1978-; Vice-Chm., Adv. Cttee on Distinction Awards for Consultants, 1979-. *Recreations*: reading, walking, travel. *Address*: 44 The Vale, NW11 8SG. *T*: 01-458 1787. *Clubs*: Athenæum, MCC.

MARRE, Romola Mary, (Lady Marre), CBE 1979; Chairman, London Voluntary Service Council (formerly London Council of Social Service), since 1974; *b* 25 April 1920; *d* of late Aubrey John Gilling and Romola Marjorie Angier; *m* 1943, Sir Alan Samuel Marre, *qv*; one *s* one *d*. *Educ*: Chelmsford County High Sch. for Girls; Bedford Coll., Univ. of London. BA Hons Philosophy. Asst Principal (Temp.), Min. of Health, 1941-42; Sgt, subseq. Jun. Comdr, ATS Officer Selection Bd, 1942-45. Organiser, West Hampstead Citizen's Advice Bureau, 1962-65; Dep. Gen. Sec., Camden Council of Social Service, 1965-73; Adviser on Community Health Councils to DHSS, 1974-75. Member: Lord Chancellor's Adv. Cttee on Legal Aid, 1975-80; Milk Marketing Bd, 1973-; BBC and IBA Central Appeals Adv. Cttee, 1980-; Dep. Chm., Royal Jubilee Trusts, 1981-; Chairman: Volunteer Centre, 1973-78; Adv. Gp on Hospital Services for children with cancer in North Western Region, Jan-June 1979. Founder Pres., Barnet Voluntary Service Council, 1979-; Chm., Cope UK, 1981-. Trustee, City Parochial Foundn, 1975-. *Recreations*: cooking, gardening, walking, talking. *Address*: 44 The Vale, NW11 8SG. *T*: 01-458 1787.

MARRIAGE, John Goodbody, QC 1971; a Recorder of the Crown Court, since 1972; *b* 17 Aug. 1929; *s* of late Llewellyn Marriage and late Norah (*née* Goodbody); *m* 1955, Caroline June Swainson; two *s* four *d*. *Educ*: Downs Sch., Colwall; Leighton Park Sch., Reading; Trinity Hall, Cambridge (BA). Royal Marines, 1947-49. Called to Bar, Inner Temple, 1953; Bencher, 1979. Dep. Chm., W Suffolk QS, 1965-71. Dep. Chm., Horserace Betting Levy Bd, 1976-; Chm., Criminal Bar Assoc., 1979-82; Mem., Judicial Studies Bd, 1980-. *Recreation*: horses (for pleasure not profit). *Address*: South End House, Bassingbourn, Cambs. *T*: Royston 42327. *Clubs*: Norfolk (Norwich); Lough Derg Yacht.

MARRINER, Neville, CBE 1979; conductor; Founder and Director, Academy of St Martin in the Fields, since 1956; Music Director, Minnesota Orchestra, since 1979; *b* 15 April 1924; *s* of Herbert Henry Marriner and Ethel May Roberts; *m* 1955, Elizabeth Mary Sims; one *s* one *d*. *Educ*: Lincoln Sch.;

Royal College of Music (ARCM). Taught music at Eton Coll., 1948; Prof., Royal Coll. of Music, 1950. Martin String Quartet, 1949; Jacobean Ensemble, 1951; London Symphony Orchestra, 1954; Music Dir, Los Angeles Chamber Orchestra, 1968-77. Artistic Director: South Bank Summer Music, 1975-77; Meadow Brook Festival, Detroit Symphony Orchestra, 1979-83. Hon. RAM; Hon. FRCM 1983. *Address:* 67 Cornwall Gardens, SW7 4BA. *Club:* Garrick.

MARRIOTT, Hugh Leslie, CBE 1946; MD London; FRCP; Physician Emeritus, Middlesex Hospital; formerly: Consulting Physician; Lecturer in Middlesex Hospital Medical School; Hon. Consulting Physician to the Army; Examiner to the Conjoint Board of the Royal Colleges of Physicians and Surgeons and to Oxford, London and Glasgow Universities; Croonian Lecturer, Royal College of Physicians; Editor Quarterly Journal of Medicine; Member Association of Physicians of Great Britain; Fellow and ex-Member of Council Royal Society of Medicine; Fellow Royal Society of Tropical Medicine and Hygiene; *b* 6 Nov. 1900; *s* of Samuel Augustus Marriott; *m* 1930, Vida Cureton; no *c.* Served RAMC 1939-45; Brig. 1942-45; Mission to Middle East for War Office and Medical Research Council, 1941; Consulting Physician to Army and Hon. Consultant to Royal Air Force, India Command, 1942-44; Consulting Physician to Allied Land Forces and Hon. Consultant to Royal Air Force, South-East Asia Command, 1944-45; Burma campaign (CBE). *Publications:* originated (with Alan Kekwick) Continuous Drip Blood Transfusion, Lancet, 1935; various papers in medical journals and articles in medical text-books. *Address:* Shepherd's Down, Ridgeway, Friston, Eastbourne BN20 0EZ. *T:* East Dean 3123.

MARRIOTT, John Miles; County Treasurer, Greater Manchester Council, since 1978; *b* 11 Oct. 1935; *s* of Arthur James Marriott and May Lavinia (*née* Goodband); *m* 1967, Josephine Anne (*née* Shepherd). *Educ:* High Pavement Grammar Sch., Nottingham. CIPFA 1962; MBCS 1970. E Midlands Electricity Bd, Nottingham (incl. 2 yrs National Service in RAF), 1952-60; Morley Bor. Council, 1960-62; Wolverhampton County Bor. Council, 1962-67; Asst Bor. Treasurer, Torbay Co. Bor. Council, 1967-70; Dep. Bor. Treas., 1970-72, and Bor. Treas., 1972-73, Ipswich Co. Bor. Council; Dir of Finance, Bolton Metrop. Bor. Council, 1973-78. *Publications:* papers in prof. jls. *Recreations:* golf, reading, bird watching, motoring. *Address:* 12 Martinsclough, Lostock, Bolton BL6 4PF. *T:* Bolton 47444.

MARRIOTT, Sir Ralph G. C. S.; *see* Smith-Marriott.

MARRIOTT, Richard D'Arcy, CBE 1965; DFC 1944; Assistant Director of Radio (formerly of Sound Broadcasting), BBC, 1957-69; *b* 9 June 1911; *s* of late Sir Hayes Marriott, KBE, CMG, Malayan Civil Service; *m* 1951, Dawn Kingdon; two *d. Educ:* Uppingham; Corpus Christi Coll., Cambridge. Joined BBC, 1933; Foreign Liaison Officer, BBC, 1936; started BBC Monitoring Unit, at outbreak of war, 1939; served as navigator in Fighter Command, RAF, 1942-45 (DFC and Bar); attached as Wing Commander to Control Commission for Germany, in charge of German Broadcasting Service in British Zone, 1945-46. Re-joined BBC as Head of European Liaison, 1946; Head of Transcription Service, BBC, 1951-52; Head of Monitoring Service, BBC, 1952-53; Controller, BBC, Northern Ireland, 1953-56. *Address:* 6 Windmill Hill, Hampstead, NW3. *T:* 01-435 4648.

MARRIOTT, Brig. Sir Robert Ecklin, Kt 1943; VD; FInstCE; BSc; with Sir Owen Williams and Partners, on M1 Construction, 1958-68; retired, 1968; *b* 15 Oct. 1887; *m* 1920, Valerie Hoch; four *d* ; *m* 1953, Mary Bauer; no *c.* Joined Indian State Railways, 1910; Indian Sappers and Miners (East Africa), 1915-1920; Chief Engineer, 1937, Gen. Man., EI Rly, 1939; Dir Gen. Rlys Calcutta Area, 1944; Dir General Rlys, Control Commission Germany, 1945; Royal Engineers, 1945-47; Col Commandant, East Indian Rly Regt, Aux. Force, India; ADC to the Viceroy. Bursar, Administrative Staff Coll., Henley-on-Thames, 1948-50; Air Ministry Works Department, 1951-57. *Address:* Hartfield, Crick, near Rugby.

MARRIS, Adam Denzil, CMG 1944; *b* 11 June 1906; *o s* of late Sir William Marris, KCSI, KCIE; *m* 1934, B. Waterfield; one *s* two *d. Educ:* Winchester; Trinity Coll., Oxford. With Lazard Bros & Co. Ltd, 11 Old Broad Street, London, 1929-39; Ministry of Economic Warfare, London, 1939-40; First Sec., HM Embassy, Washington, 1940-41; Counsellor, War Trade Dept, British Embassy, Washington, 1941-45; Secretary-General, Emergency Economic Cttee for Europe, Aug. 1945-Feb. 1946, with temp. rank of Principal Asst Sec., Foreign Office; Deputy Leader of UK Delegn to Marshall Plan Conference, July-Sept. 1947, and to Washington Conf. of Cttee for European Economic Co-operation, Nov.-Dec. 1947. Director: Lazard Bros & Co. Ltd, 1947-73 (Man. Dir, 1947-71); Commercial Union Assce Co. Ltd 1948-78 (Vice-Chm., 1965-78); English Scottish & Australian Bank Ltd, 1951-71; Barclays Bank Ltd, 1953-77; Australia and New Zealand Banking Group Ltd, 1969-76; P&O Steam Navigation Co., 1952-72. *Address:* Hampen House, Andoversford, Glos GL54 4JJ. *T:* 279; 36 King's Court North, SW3. *T:* 01-352 8656; 01-588 2721. *Clubs:* Boodle's; Melbourne (Vic).

See also R. L. Wade-Gery.

MARRIS, Prof. Robin Lapthorn; Professor of Economics, Birkbeck College, University of London, since 1981; *b* 31 March 1924; *s* of Eric Denyer Marris, CB, and late Phyllis, *d* of T. H. F. Lapthorn, JP; *m* 1st, 1949, Marion Ellinger; 2nd, 1954, Jane Evelina Burney Ayres; one *s* two *d* ; 3rd, 1972, Anne Fairclough Mansfield; one *d. Educ:* Bedales Sch.; King's Coll., Cambridge. BA

1946, ScD 1968, Cantab. Asst Principal, HM Treasury, 1947-50; UN, Geneva, 1950-52; Fellow of King's Coll., Cambridge, 1951-76; Lectr, 1951-72, Reader, 1972-76, in Econs, Univ. of Cambridge; Prof. 1976-83 (on leave of absence, 1981-83), and Chm., 1976-79, Dept of Economics, Univ. of Maryland. Vis. Prof., Univ. California, Berkeley, 1961, and Harvard, 1967; Dir, World Economy Div., Min. of Overseas Develt, 1964-66. Mem., Vis. Cttee, Open Univ., 1982-. *Publications:* Economic Arithmetic, 1958; The Economic Theory of Managerial Capitalism, 1964; The Economics of Capital Utilisation, 1964; (with Adrian Wood) The Corporate Economy, 1971; The Corporate Society, 1974; The Theory and Future of the Corporate Economy and Society, 1979; contrib. Econ. Jl, Rev. Econ. Studies, Economica, Jl Manchester Stat. Soc., Jl Royal Stat. Soc., Amer. Econ. Rev., Qly Jl of Econs, Economie Appliquée, etc. *Recreations:* cooking, ski-ing, sailing. *Address:* Department of Economics, Birkbeck College, 7/15 Gresse Street, W1P 1PA.

See also S. N. Marris.

MARRIS, Stephen Nicholson; Economic Adviser to the Secretary-General, Organisation for Economic Co-operation and Development, since 1975; *b* 7 Jan. 1930; *s* of Eric Denyer Marris, CB, and Phyllis May Marris (*née* Lapthorn); *m* 1955, Margaret Swindells; two *s* one *d. Educ:* Bryanston School; King's College, Cambridge. MA, PhD. Parker of Waddington Research Student, Cambridge Univ., 1952-53; Nat. Inst. of Economic and Social Research, 1953-54; economist and international civil servant; with Org. for European Economic Co-operation, later Org. for Economic Co-operation and Development (OECD), 1956-; Dir, Economics Branch, 1970. Vis. Res. Prof. of Internat. Economics, Brookings Instn, Washington DC, 1969-70. Hon. Dr Stockholm Univ., 1978. *Recreation:* sailing. *Address:* 8 Sentier des Pierres Blanches, 92190 Meudon, France. *T:* (office) 524.87.70; (home) 626.34.35. *Club:* Royal Ocean Racing.

See also R. L. Marris.

MARRISON, Dr Geoffrey Edward; Director and Keeper, Department of Oriental Manuscripts and Printed Books, British Library, London, since 1974; *b* 11 Jan. 1923; *s* of John and Rose Marrison; *m* 1958, Margaret Marian Millburn; one *s* three *d. Educ:* SOAS, Univ. of London; Bishops' Coll. Cheshunt; Kirchliche Hochschule, Berlin. BA Malay 1948, PhD Linguistics 1967, London. Indian Army, 1942-46. SOAS, 1941-42 and 1946-49; ordained Priest, Singapore, 1952; in Malaya with USPG, 1952-56; Vicar of St Timothy, Crookes, Sheffield, 1958-61; Linguistics Adviser British and Foreign Bible Soc., 1962-67, incl. service in Assam, 1962-64. Asst. Keeper, British Museum, 1967-71, Dep. Keeper 1971-74. Hon. Canon of All Saints Pro-Cathedral, Shillong, 1963. FRAS. *Publications:* The Christian Approach to the Muslim, 1958; articles in Jl Malayan Branch Royal Asiatic Soc., Bible Translator. *Recreation:* ethno-linguistics of South and South East Asia. *Address:* 85 Warwick Road, Thornton Heath, Surrey CR4 7NN. *T:* 01-684 2806.

MARS-JONES, Hon. Sir William (Lloyd), Kt 1969; MBE 1945; **Hon. Mr Justice Mars-Jones;** a Judge of the High Court of Justice, Queen's Bench Division, since 1969; *b* 4 Sept. 1915; *s* of Henry and Jane Mars Jones, Llansannan, Denbighshire; *m* 1947, Sheila Mary Felicity Cobon; three *s. Educ:* Denbigh County Sch.; UCW, Aberystwyth (LLB Hons); St John's Coll., Cambridge (BA). Entrance Schol., Gray's Inn, 1936; Pres. Students' Rep. Counc. and Central Students' Rep. Counc., UCW, 1936-37; MacMahon Studentship, 1939; Barrister-at-Law, 1941, QC 1957. War of 1939-45, RNVR (MBE); Lt-Comdr RNVR 1945. Contested W Denbigh Parly Div., 1945. Joined Wales and Chester Circuit, 1947, Presiding Judge, 1971-75. Recorder of: Birkenhead, 1959-65; Swansea, 1965-68; Cardiff, 1968-69; Dep. Chm., Denbighshire Quarter Sessions, 1962-68. Bencher, Gray's Inn, 1964, Treasurer, 1982. Comr of Assize, Denbigh and Mold Summer Assize, 1965. Member: Bar Council, 1962; Home Office Inquiry into allegations against Metropolitan Police Officers, 1964; Home Secretary's Adv. Council on Penal System, 1966-68. Pres., N Wales Arts Assoc., 1976-. Hon. LLD UCW, Aberystwyth, 1973. *Publications:* contrib. Atkins' Encycl. of Court Forms and Precedents. *Recreations:* singing, acting, guitar. *Address:* 3 Gray's Inn Square, WC1. *T:* 01-405 3632. *Club:* Garrick.

MARSACK, Hon. Sir Charles (Croft), KBE 1981 (CBE 1962); **Hon. Mr Justice Marsack;** Judge, Fiji Court of Appeal, since 1957; *b* 7 May 1892; *s* of Richard Marsack and Mary Ann Marsack; *m* 1918, Ninette Padiou; two *s. Educ:* Auckland Univ., New Zealand (BA, LLB). Legal practice, New Zealand, 1914-39, except for overseas service with NZ Rifle Brigade, 1915-18; service with 2 NZEF, Middle East and Italy, 1939-45. New Zealand Stipendiary Magistrate, 1945-47; Chief Justice, Western Samoa, 1947-62; Independent Chairman, Fiji Sugar Industry, 1962-70. *Publications:* Samoan Medley, 1961, 2nd edn 1964; Teach Yourself Samoan, 1962, 3rd edn 1973. *Recreation:* gardening. *Address:* PO Box 3751, Samabula, Suva, Fiji. *T:* Suva 383150. *Club:* Returned Servicemen's (Suva).

MARSDEN, Allen Gatenby, CBE 1945; FCIT; Hon. President of International Transport-Users Commission, Paris; *b* 13 Sept. 1893; *s* of late William Allen Marsden, OBE, and Marianne Turvey; *m* 1st, 1918, Mabel Kathleen Buckley (*decd*); one *s* two *d* ; 2nd, 1933, Janet Helen Williamson (*d* 1982); one *s. Educ:* Wadham House, Hale; Bedford Grammar Sch. Joined staff of London & North-Western Railway as a probationer, 1909; served European War with commission in 8th Bn Manchester Regt, TF, 1914-16, in Egypt, Cyprus and Gallipoli, invalided home with rank of Capt.; under Dir-Gen. of Transportation, France, 1917; Transport and Storage Div., Min. of Food, 1917-18; Traffic Asst, Ministry of Transport, 1920; transport manager of Cadbury Bros Ltd, Bournville, 1921; subsequently transport Supervisor, Cadbury-Fry Joint Transport until 1940; Dir of Transport, Ministry of Food, Aug. 1940-May 1946; Transport Adviser to Bd of Unilever Ltd, 1946-58. Chm. Transport Cttee, CBI, 1946-58; Vice-Pres., Internat. Container Bureau, Paris, 1948-58; Pres., Internat. Transport Users Commn, Paris, 1948-58. *Recreations:* golf, fishing. *Address:* 64 Heathfield Road, Audlem, near Crewe, Cheshire. *T:* Audley 811555.

MARSDEN, Arthur Whitcombe, MSc, DIC, ARCS, FRIC; Education Officer/Technical Editor, Animal Production and Health Division, FAO, Rome, 1964-73; *b* Buxton, Derbyshire, 14 June 1911; *o s* of late Hubert Marsden and Margaret Augusta Bidwell; *m* 1940, Ailsa Anderson, *yr d* of late William Anderson McKellar, physician, and Jessie Reid Macfarlane, of Glasgow and Chester-le-Street, Co. Durham; one *s* two *d. Educ:* St Paul's; Imperial Coll. (Royal College of Science), London. BSc Special and ARCS, 1933; research in agricultural chemistry at Imperial Coll., 1933-36; research asst, 1936; demonstrator, 1937; asst lecturer, 1939; MSc and DIC, 1940. Temp. Instr Lieut RN, 1942; HMS Diomede, 1943; HMS King Alfred, 1944; RN Coll., Greenwich, and HMS Superb, 1945. Lecturer, Imperial Coll., London, 1946; Dept Head, Seale-Hayne Agricultural Coll., Newton Abbot, 1946-48; dir of research to grain companies in Aberdeen, 1948-49. Dir of Commonwealth Bureau of Dairy Science and Technology, Shinfield, Reading, 1950-57; Organising Secretary: 15th International Dairy Congress, London, 1957-60; 2nd World Congress of Man-made Fibres, 1960-63. Hon. Sec., Agriculture Group, Soc. of Chem. Industry, 1947-52, Chm., 1954-56; Organising Cttee of 2nd International Congress of Crop Protection, London, 1949; delegate on OEEC Technical Assistance Mission in USA and Canada, 1951; toured research centres in Pakistan, India, Australia, NZ and USA, Oct. 1954-Feb. 1955. *Publications:* papers in scientific journals. *Recreations:* gardening, music, meeting and talking to people, especially from developing countries. *Address:* 109 Willingdon Road, Eastbourne, East Sussex BN21 1TX. *T:* Eastbourne 33602.

MARSDEN, Frank; JP; *b* Everton, Liverpool, 15 Oct. 1923; *s* of Sidney Marsden and Harriet Marsden (*née* Needham); *m* 1943, Muriel Lightfoot; three *s. Educ:* Abbotsford Road Sec. Mod. Sch., Liverpool. Served War, with RAF Bomber Command, 115 Sqdn (Warrant Officer), 1941-46. Joined Lab. Party and Co-op. Movement, 1948. MP (Lab) Liverpool, Scotland, Apr. 1971-Feb. 1974. Local Councillor: Liverpool St Domingo Ward, May 1964-67; Liverpool Vauxhall Ward, 1969-71; Knowsley DC, 1976-. Chm. Liverpool Markets, 1965-67; Past Mem. Exec. Cttee: Liverpool Trades Council; Liverpool Lab. Party. JP (City of Liverpool), 1969. *Recreations:* jazz music, gardening. *Address:* 2 Thunderbolt Cottage, 6 Alder Lane, Knowsley, Prescot, Merseyside. *T:* 051-546 1959.

MARSDEN, Sir John Denton, 2nd Bt, *cr* 1924; JP; *b* 25 Aug. 1913; *s* of Sir John Marsden, 1st Bt, and Agnes Mary (*d* 1951), *d* of Thomas Robert Ronald of Little Danson, Welling, Kent; *S* father, 1944; *m* 1939, Hope, *yr d* of late G. E. Llewelyn; two *s* two *d. Educ:* Downside; St John's Coll., Cambridge (BA). Served European War of 1939-45 (prisoner); Lt RA. JP; High Sheriff of Lincs, 1955-56. *Recreations:* shooting, fishing. *Heir: s* Nigel John Denton Marsden [*b* 26 May 1940; *m* 1961, Diana Jean Dunn, *er d* of Air Marshal Sir Patrick H. Dunn, *qv* ; three *d*]. *Address:* White Abbey, Linton-in-Craven, Skipton, N Yorks.

MARSDEN, Leslie Alfred, CMG 1966; *b* 25 Sept. 1921; *s* of late William Marsden, Stanmore, Middx, and of Kitty Marsden; *m* 1947, Doris Winifred, *d* of late Walter Richard Grant and of Winifred Grant; two *d. Educ:* Kingsbury County Sch. Served War: The Queen's Own Royal West Kent Regt, 1940-42; 14th Punjab Regt, Indian Army, 1942-46; serving in India, Burma and Thailand; retd as Hon. Major. Joined Nigeria Police Force, 1946; Commissioner of Police, 1964; Asst Inspector-General, 1966-68. Associate Director, Sierra Leone Selection Trust, 1969; Security Adviser, Standard Telephones and Cables Ltd, 1970-82. Nigeria Police Medal, 1964; Queen's Police Medal, 1964; Colonial Police Medal, 1958. *Recreations:* walking, reading, public affairs. *Address:* Ashbank, 14 Orchard Rise, Groombridge, Sussex. *T:* Groombridge 486. *Club:* Royal Over-Seas League.

MARSDEN, William; HM Diplomatic Service; Counsellor, UK Representation to the European Community, since 1981; *b* 15 Sept. 1940; *s* of Christopher Marsden and Ruth (*née* Kershaw); *m* 1964, Kaja Collingham; one *s* one *d. Educ:* Winchester Coll.; Lawrenceville Sch., USA; Trinity Coll., Cambridge (MA); London Univ. (BSc Econs). FO, 1962-64; UK Delegn to NATO, 1964-66; Rome, 1966-69; seconded as Asst to Gen. Manager, Joseph Lucas Ltd, 1970; First Sec., FCO, 1971-76; First Sec. and Cultural Attaché, Moscow, 1976-79; Asst Head, European Community Dept, FCO, 1979-81. Sec., Twickenham Soc., 1979-. MBIM. *Address:* c/o Foreign and Commonwealth Office, SW1A 2AH.

MARSDEN-SMEDLEY, Susan; Chairman, Greater London Citizens' Advice Bureaux Service, since 1979; Salaried Members Officer, Royal Institute of British Architects, since 1981; *b* 6 Dec. 1931; *d* of John Marsden-Smedley and Agatha (*née* Bethell). *Educ:* Downe House Sch.; Girton Coll., Cambridge (MA). Called to the Bar, Middle Temple, 1957. Worked in consumer organisations in Britain and US, 1957-65; Senior Research Officer, Consumer Council, 1966-70; Legal Officer, Nuffield Foundation Legal Advice Research Unit, 1970-72; Exec. Dir, Legal Action Gp and Editor, LAG Bulletin, 1972-78; pt-time Course Dir, Legal Action Gp, 1978-81. Dissentient mem.,

Royal Commn on Legal Services, 1976-79. *Publication:* Justice Out of Reach, a case for Small Claims Courts, 1969. *Recreations:* tree planting and preservation, gardening, looking at modern buildings. *Address:* 15 Woodsome Road, NW5 1RX. *T:* 01-485 4938.

MARSH, family name of **Baron Marsh.**

MARSH, Baron *cr* 1981 (Life Peer), of Mannington in the County of Wiltshire; **Richard William Marsh;** PC 1966; Kt 1976; FCIT; Chairman: Newspaper Publishers' Association, since 1976; British Iron and Steel Consumers' Council, since 1977; Allied Investments Ltd, since 1977; Deputy Chairman, TV-AM, since 1980; *b* 14 March 1928; *s* of William Marsh, Belvedere, Kent; *m* 1st, 1950, Evelyn Mary (marr. diss. 1973), *d* of Frederick Andrews, Southampton; two *s* ; 2nd, 1973, Caroline Dutton (*d* 1975); 3rd, 1979, Felicity, *d* of Baron McFadzean of Kelvinside, *qv. Educ:* Jennings Sch., Swindon; Woolwich Polytechnic; Ruskin Coll., Oxford. Contested Hertford, 1951; Health Services Officer, National Union of Public Employees, 1951-59; Mem., Clerical and Administrative Whitley Council for Health Service, 1953-59; MP (Lab) Greenwich, Oct. 1959-April 1971; Promoted Offices Act 1961; Member: Select Cttee Estimates, 1961; Chm. Interdepartmental Cttee to Co-ordinate Govt Policy on Industrial Training, 1964; Parly Sec., Min. of Labour, 1964-65; Joint Parly Sec., Min. of Technology, 1965-66; Minister of Power, 1966-68; Minister of Transport, 1968-69. Chm., British Railways Bd, 1971-76; Member: NEDC, 1971-; Freight Integration Council, 1971-. Chairman: Michael Saunders Management Services, 1970-71; Allied Medical Group, 1977-81; Dep. Chm., United Medical Enterprises Ltd, 1978-81; Director: National Carbonising Co. Ltd (Chm., NCC Plant and Transport), 1970-71; Concord Rotoflex International Ltd, 1970-71; European Bd, Imperial Life of Canada, 1979-. Pres., Council ECSC, 1968. Governor: British Transport Staff Coll. (Chm.); London Business Sch. *Publication:* Off the Rails (autobiog.), 1978. *Address:* c/o 6 Bouverie Street, EC4Y 8AY. *Club:* Reform.

MARSH, Ven. Bazil Roland, BA; Archdeacon of Northampton, Non-Residentiary Canon of Peterborough, and Rector of St Peter's, Northampton, since 1964; *b* Three Hills, Alta, Canada, 11 Aug. 1921; *s* of late Ven. Wilfred Carter Marsh and late Mary Jean (*née* Stott), Devil's Lake, North Dakota, USA; *m* 1946, Audrey Joan, *d* of late Owen George Oyler, farmer, of Brookmans Park, Hatfield, and Alma Lillian Oyler; three *s* one *d. Educ:* State schs in USA and Swindon, Wilts; Leeds Univ.; Coll. of the Resurrection, Mirfield, Yorks. Curate of: St Mary the Virgin, Cheshunt, Herts, 1944-46; St John Baptist, Coventry, 1946-47; St Giles-in-Reading, Berks, 1947-51; Rector of St Peter's, Townsville, Qld, Australia, 1951-56; Vicar of St Mary the Virgin, Far Cotton, Northampton, 1956-64. *Address:* 11 The Drive, Northampton NN1 4RZ. *T:* Northampton 714015. *Club:* Royal Commonwealth Society.

MARSH, Prof. David Charles; Professor of Applied Social Science, University of Nottingham, 1954-82, now Emeritus; *b* 9 Jan. 1917; *s* of F. C. Marsh, Aberdare, Glam., S Wales; *m* 1941, Maisie Done; one *s. Educ:* University of Birmingham. Research Scholar University of Birmingham, 1938-39. Military Service, 1940-46, Royal Artillery. Lecturer, University Coll. of Swansea, 1947-49; Professor of Social Science, Victoria Univ. Coll., Wellington, NZ, 1949-54. *Publications:* National Insurance and Assistance in Great Britain, 1949; The Changing Social Structure of England and Wales, 1958, new edn 1967; The Future of the Welfare State, 1964; The Welfare State, 1970. *Recreations:* tennis, badminton. *Address:* 239 Chilwell Lane, Bramcote, Notts. *T:* 25-7567.

MARSH, George Fletcher Riley, CB 1951; *b* 16 Oct. 1895; *s* of late Richard Howard Heywood Marsh, director of Geo. Fletcher & Co. Ltd, Derby; *m* 1927, Phyllis Henderson (*d* 1973), *d* of late Frank Barton, Brasted, Kent; one *s* one *d. Educ:* Bedford Sch. Entered Civil Service (Naval Store Dept, Admiralty), 1914; Deputy Dir of Stores, 1942; Dir of Stores, 1949-55; retired, 1955. *Address:* 14 Willian Way, Letchworth, Herts.

MARSH, Gordon Victor, MA; FHA; Deputy Health Service Commissioner, since 1982; *b* 14 May 1929; *s* of late Ven. Wilfred Carter Marsh, Devil's Lake, North Dakota, USA and Rosalie (*née* Holliday); *m* Millicent, *e d* of late Christopher Thomas and Edith Rowsell; one *s* one *d. Educ:* Grammar Schs, Swindon; Keble Coll., Oxford (MA); Inst. of Health Service Administrators (FHA 1964); Sloan Business Sch., Cornell Univ., USA. NHS admin. posts, England and Wales, 1952-72; Administrator and Sec., Bd of Governors, UCH, 1972-74; Area Administrator, Lambeth, Southwark and Lewisham AHA(T), 1974-82. Vice-Chm., Assoc. of Chief Administrators of Health Authorities, 1980-82; Member: Council, National Assoc. of Health Authorities, 1979-82; Adv. Bd, Coll. of Occupational Therapists, 1974-. Chm., Trelawn Cttee of Richmond Fellowship, 1970-; Hon. Sec. to Congregational Consultation and Wandsmen, St Paul's Cathedral, 1974-. *Publications:* articles in professional jls. *Recreations:* music, gardening, home winemaking. *Address:* 43 Kendall Avenue South, Sanderstead, Surrey CR2 0QR. *T:* 01-660 2772. *Club:* Royal Society of Medicine.

MARSH, Rt. Rev. Henry Hooper, MA, DD; *b* 6 Oct. 1898; *s* of Rev. Canon Charles H. Marsh, DD; *m* Margaret D. Heakes; one *s* one *d. Educ:* University College, Toronto, BA 1921; Wycliffe College, Toronto, 1924, MA 1925; DD 1962. Deacon, 1924; Priest, 1925; Curate of St Anne, Toronto, 1924-25; Curate of St Paul, Toronto, 1925-30; Priest-in-charge of St Timothy's

Mission, City and Diocese of Toronto, 1930-36; Rector, Church of St Timothy, 1936-62; Canon of Toronto, 1956-62; Bishop of Yukon, 1962-67. Canadian Centennial Medal, 1967. *Recreation:* bird watching. *Address:* Hedgerows, RR6, Cobourg, Ont K9A 4J9, Canada.

MARSH, (Henry) John, CBE 1967; international management consultant and lecturer; director of companies; Chairman: Executive Resources International, since 1981; Indeusia Ventures Ltd; *b* 1913; *s* of late Jasper W. P. Marsh and Gladys M. Carruthers; *m* 1950, Mary Costerton; two *s* two *d. Educ:* Chefoo Sch., China; Queen Elizabeth's Grammar Sch., Wimborne. Commerce, China, 1930-32; Shanghai Volunteer Force, 1930-32; engineering apprenticeship and apprentice supervisor, Austin Motor Co., 1932-39. Served War of 1939-45, Royal Army Service Corps TA, 48th and 56th Divisions; Singapore Fortress; BEF France, 1940; Malaya, 1941-42 (despatches twice); Prisoner of War, 1942-45; released with rank of Major, 1946. Personnel Officer, BOAC, 1946-47; Dir of Personnel Advisory Services, Institute of Personnel Management, 1947-49; Dir, Industrial (Welfare) Soc., 1950-61; British Institute of Management: Dir, later Dir-Gen., 1961-73; Asst Chm. and Counsellor, 1973-75. Mem., Nat. Coal Board, 1968-74. Hon. Administrator, Duke of Edinburgh's Study Conference, 1954-56; Chm. Brit. Nat. Conference on Social Work, 1957-60; Member: Youth Service Cttee, 1958-59; BBC General Advisory Council, 1959-64; Advisory Cttee on Employment of Prisoners, 1960-63; Council for Technical Educn and Training for Overseas Countries, 1961-74; UK Advisory Council on Education for Management, 1962-66; Russell Cttee on Adult Educn, 1969-72; Court, Univ. of Cranfield, 1962-69; Court, Univ. of Surrey, 1969-; Food Manufacturing EDC, 1967-69; Adv. Council, Civil Service College, 1970-77; UK Mem., Commonwealth Team of Industrial Specialists, 1976-78. Governor, King's Coll. Hosp., 1971-74. British Information Service Lecture Tours: India and Pakistan, 1959 and 1963; Nigeria, 1964; Malaysia, 1965; Australia, 1967; Latin America, 1971, 1973; Malaysia, NZ, 1974. FIAM 1969; Hon. Fellow, Canadian Inst. of Management, 1973; CBIM (FBIM 1967); FIMC 1980. Hon. DSc Bradford, 1968. Verulam Medal, 1976. *Publications:* Ardeshir Dalal Memorial Lecture, India, 1953; The Clarke Hall Lecture, 1957; E. W. Hancock Lecture, 1960; MacLaren Memorial Lecture, 1962; People at Work; Work and Leisure Digest; Partners in Work Relations; Tullis Russell Lecture, 1967; Pursuit of God, 1968; Ethics in Business, 1970; RSA Foster Lecture, 1973; Geden Foster Lecture, 1977; Chester Lecture, 1978; Stantonbury Lecture, 1981. *Recreations:* gardening, Third World charities. *Address:* 13 Frank Dixon Way, Dulwich, SE21. *Club:* Special Forces.

MARSH, Jean Lyndsey Torren; actress; Artistic Director, Adelphi University Theatre, Long Island, New York; *b* 1 July 1934; *d* of Henry Charles and Emmeline Susannah Marsh; *m* 1955, Jon Devon Roland Pertwee (marr. diss. 1960). Began as child actress and dancer; danced in films: Tales of Hoffmann, Where's Charley?, etc. Acted in repertory companies: Huddersfield, Nottingham, etc; Broadway debut in Much Ado About Nothing, 1959; West End debut, Bird of Time, 1961. *Stage:* Habeas Corpus, The Importance of Being Earnest, Too True to be Good, Twelfth Night, Blithe Spirit, Whose Life is it Anyway?, Uncle Vanya, On the Rocks. *Television:* co-created and co-starred (Rose) in series Upstairs Downstairs; series, Nine to Five. Hon. DH Maryland Coll., NY. *Publications:* The Illuminated Language of Flowers, 1978; articles for Sunday Times and Washington Post. *Recreations:* cross-country skiing, reading, cooking, eating. *Address:* The Pheasant, Chinnor Hill, Oxfordshire OX9 4BN.

MARSH, Prof. the Rev. John, CBE 1964; MA (Edinburgh et Oxon), DPhil (Oxon); DD (Hon.) Edinburgh; Moderator, Free Church Federal Council, 1970-71; Principal, Mansfield College, Oxford, 1953-70; *b* 5 Nov. 1904; *s* of George Maurice and Florence Elizabeth Ann Marsh, East Grinstead, Sussex; *m* 1934, Gladys Walker, *y d* of George Benson and Mary Walker, Cockermouth, Cumberland; two *s* one *d. Educ:* The Skinners Company Sch., Tunbridge Wells; Yorkshire United Coll., Bradford; Edinburgh Univ.; Mansfield Coll. and St Catherine's Soc., Oxford; Marburg Univ. Lecturer, Westhill Training Coll., 1932; Minister, Congregational Church, Otley, Yorks, 1934; Tutor and Chaplain, Mansfield Coll., Oxford, 1938; Prof. of Christian Theology, The University, Nottingham, 1949-53. Gray Lectr, Duke Univ., NC; Reinecke Lectr, Prot. Episc. Semin., Alexandria, Va, 1958. Delegate: First Assembly, World Council of Churches, Amsterdam, 1948; Second Assembly, Evanston, Ill., 1954; Third Assembly, New Delhi, 1961; Fourth Assembly, Uppsala, 1968. Sec. World Conference on Faith and Order's Commn on "Intercommunion"; Chm., Section 2 of British Council of Churches Commn on Broadcasting, 1949; Mem., Working Cttee, Faith and Order Dept, World Council of Churches, 1953; Sec., European Commission on Christ and the Church, World Council of Churches, 1955; Mem. Central Religious Advisory Cttee to BBC, 1955-60; Mem. Sub-Cttee of CRAC acting as Religious Advisory Panel to ITA, 1955-65; Chm. British Council of Churches Commn of Faith and Order, 1960-62. Mem. Central Cttee, World Council of Churches, 1961-68; Chm. Division of Studies, World Council of Churches, 1961-68; Select Preacher, University of Oxford, 1962; Chm. Congregational Union of England and Wales, 1962-63; Chairman: Inter-Church Relationships Cttee, Congregational Church in England and Wales, 1964-67; Board of Faculty of Theology, Oxford Univ., 1966-68; Exec. Cttee, Congregational Church in England and Wales, 1966-72; Joint Cttee. Joint Cttee for Conversations between Congregationalists and Presbyterians, 1965-72; Lay Vice-Chm., Derwent Deanery Synod, 1979-82. Chm., Buttermere Parish Council, 1973-80. Governor, Westminster Coll., Oxford, 1967-70. *Publications:* The Living God, 1942; Congregationalism Today,

1943; (jtly) A Book of Congregational Worship, 1948; (Jt Ed.) Intercommunion, 1952; contrib. Biblical Authority Today, 1951; and Ways of Worship, 1951; The Fulness of Time, 1952; The Significance of Evanston, 1954; trans. Stauffer, Theology of the New Testament, 1955; A Year with the Bible, 1957; contributed to Essays in Christology for Karl Barth, 1957; Amos and Micah, 1959; trans. Bultmann, The History of the Synoptic Tradition, 1963; Pelican Commentary on St John's Gospel, 1968; Jesus in his Lifetime, 1981. *Recreations:* water colour painting, wood turning. *Address:* Dale House, High Lorton, Cockermouth, Cumbria CA13 9UQ. *T:* Lorton 650.

MARSH, John; *see* Marsh, H. J.

MARSH, Leonard George, MEd; Principal, Bishop Grosseteste College, since 1974; *b* 23 Oct. 1930; third *c* of late Ernest Arthur Marsh and Anne Eliza (*née* Bean); *m* 1953, Ann Margaret Gilbert; one *s* one *d. Educ:* Ashford (Kent) Grammar Sch.; Borough Road Coll., London Inst. of Educn; Leicester Univ. Teachers' Certif., Academic Dip. Lectr in Educn and Mathematics, St Paul's Coll., Cheltenham, 1959-61; Lectr, 1961-63, Sen. Lectr, 1963-65, Principal Lectr and Head of Postgraduate Primary Educn Dept, 1965-74, Goldsmiths' Coll., London; Visiting Lectr, Bank Street Coll., New York, and Virginia Commonwealth Univ.; former Consultant, OECD, Portugal; Educnl Consultant, Teacher Trng Proj., Botswana, 1981; Specialist tour to India for British Council. Mem. Gen. Adv. Council, IBA, 1977-82; Chm., Nat. Assoc. for Primary Educn, 1981-. *Publications:* Let's Explore Mathematics, Books 1-4, 1964-67; Children Explore Mathematics, 1967, 3rd edn 1969; Exploring Shapes and Numbers, 1968, 2nd edn 1970; Exploring the Metric System, 1969, 2nd edn 1969; Exploring the Metric World, 1970; Approach to Mathematics, 1970; Alongside the Child in the Primary School, 1970; Let's Discover Mathematics, Books 1-5, 1971-72; Being A Teacher, 1973; Helping your Child with Maths—a parents' guide, 1980; The Guinness Mathematics Book, 1980; The Guinness Book for Young Scientists, 1982. *Recreations:* photography, theatre going, films. *Address:* The Principal's House, Bishop Grosseteste College, Lincoln LN1 3DY. *T:* Lincoln 28241; Broomfields, The Meadow, Chislehurst, Kent BR7 6AA. *T:* 01-467 6311.

MARSH, Michael John Waller, MC 1942; TD 1954; a Recorder of the Crown Court, since 1974; *b* 12 April 1921; *s* of Arthur Percival Marsh and Gladys Adine Marsh; *m* 1948, Kathleen Harrison; one *s. Educ:* Uppingham; Pembroke Coll., Cambridge (BA). 9th Queen's Royal Lancers, 1942-46; Prince Albert's Own Leics Yeo., 1947-54, retd (Major). Admitted Solicitor, 1949. *Recreations:* shooting; playing around with small boats. *Address:* Park House, Burton Lazars, Melton Mowbray, Leics. *T:* Melton Mowbray 66730.

MARSH, Nevill Francis, CBE 1969; Director-General, St John Ambulance, 1972-76; *b* 13 Aug. 1907; *m* 1935, Betty (*née* Hide); one *s* one *d. Educ:* Oundle Sch., Northants; Clare Coll., Cambridge (MA). Traction Motor Design Staff, Metropolitan-Vickers Electrical Co. Ltd, 1930-32; Mid-Lincolnshire Electric Supply Co. Ltd: Dist Engineer, 1932-38; Engineer and Manager, 1938-48; Chief Commercial Officer, E Midlands Electricity Board, 1948-55; Dep.-Chm., N Eastern Electricity Board, 1955-57; Dep.-Chm., E Midlands Electricity Board, 1957-59; Chm., East Midlands Electricity Board, 1959-61; a Dep. Chm., Electricity Council, 1962-71; Chm., British Electrotechnical Cttee, 1970-72. Dir for Gtr London, St John Ambulance Assoc., 1971-72. Also formerly: Dir, Altrincham Electric Supply Ltd, and Public Utilities (Elec.) Ltd, and Supervising Engineer, Campbeltown & Mid-Argyll Elec. Supply Co. Ltd, and Thurso & District Elec. Supply Co. Ltd. FIEE; Pres. of Assoc. of Supervising Electrical Engineers, 1966-68. KStJ 1973. *Publications:* jt contrib. Jl Inst. Electrical Engineers, 1955. *Address:* Stocksfield, First Avenue, Frinton-on-Sea, Essex CO13 9EZ. *T:* Frinton 2995. *Club:* Royal Air Force.

MARSH, Norman Stayner, CBE 1977; QC 1967; Law Commissioner, 1965-78; Member, Royal Commission on Civil Liability and Compensation for Personal Injury, 1973-78; *b* 26 July 1913; 2nd *s* of Horace Henry and Lucy Ann Marsh, Bath, Som; *m* 1939, Christiane Christinnecke, 2nd *d* of Professor Johannes and Käthe Christinnecke, Magdeburg, Germany; two *s* two *d. Educ:* Monkton Combe Sch.; Pembroke Coll., Oxford (2nd Class Hons, Final Honour Sch. of Jurisprudence, 1935; 1st Cl. Hons BCL; Hon. Fellow, 1978). Vinerian Scholar of Oxford Univ., Harmsworth Scholar of Middle Temple, called to Bar, 1937; practice in London and on Western Circuit, 1937-39; Lieut-Col Intelligence Corps and Control Commission for Germany, 1939-46. Stowell Civil Law Fellow, University Coll., Oxford, 1946-60; University Lecturer in Law, 1947-60; Estates Bursar, University Coll., 1948-56; Secretary-General, International Commission of Jurists, The Hague, Netherlands, 1956-58. Member: Bureau of Conference of Non-Governmental Organisations with Consultative Status with the United Nations, 1957-58; Internat. Cttee of Legal Science (Unesco), 1960-63. Dir of British Institute of International and Comparative Law, 1960-65. Mem., Younger Cttee on Privacy, 1970-72. Hon. Vis. Prof. in Law, KCL, 1972-77. Vice-Chm., Age Concern, England, 1979-. General editor, International and Comparative Law Quarterly, 1961-65; Mem., Editorial Board, 1965-. *Publications:* The Rule of Law as a supra-national concept, in Oxford Essays in Jurisprudence, 1960; The Rule of Law in a Free Society, 1960; Interpretation in a National and International Context, 1974; articles on common law and comparative law in English, American, French and German law jls. *Address:* Wren House, 13 North Side, Clapham Common, SW4. *T:* 01-622 2865.

MARSH, William Thomas, OBE 1944; MA; Headmaster, St Albans School, 1931-64, retd; Commander RNVR (Sp); *b* Birmingham, 18 March 1897; *o s* of W. T. Marsh; *m* 1923, Olive Constance Nightingale; three *s. Educ:* Northampton Sch.; Queens' Coll., Cambridge (Open Classical Scholar). RNVR, 1916-19; First-class Hons Classical Tripos, 1922; VIth Form Classical Master, Brighton Coll., 1923-27; Headmaster Hertford Grammar Sch., 1927-31. Blue for Athletics and Cross Country. *Recreations:* archæology, music. *Address:* Priory Close, Bishops Cleeve, Cheltenham, Glos. *T:* Bishops Cleeve 3171.

MARSHALL, family name of Baron Marshall of Leeds.

MARSHALL OF LEEDS, Baron *cr* 1980 (Life Peer), of Shadwell in the City of Leeds; Frank Shaw Marshall, Kt 1971; Solicitor; a Vice-Chairman of the Conservative Party; Special Adviser to Government on Third London Airport Project, 1972; Chairman, The Marshall Inquiry on the Government of Greater London, 1977-78; Director: Leeds & Holbeck Building Society (President, 1967-69 and 1977-79); a Vice-President, Building Societies Association; Barr & Wallace Arnold Trust Ltd and several other companies; *b* Wakefield, 26 Sept. 1915; 4th *s* of Charles William and Edith Marshall and *g g s* of Charles Marshall (*b* Wakefield, 1827), of NY, Philadelphia, and Columbia, Miss, who fought in American Civil War; *m* 1941, Mary, *e c* of Robert and Edith Barr, Shadwell House, Leeds; two *d. Educ:* Queen Elizabeth's Sch., Wakefield; Downing Coll., Cambridge (Scholar). MA, LLB. Served 1940-46, Captain Royal Tank Regt and Staff Officer JAG's Dept, WO. Managing Trustee, Municipal Mutual Insurance Co. Ltd (Chm., 1978-). Leeds CC: Leader, and Chm. Finance Cttee, 1967-72; Alderman, 1967-73. Pres., Leeds Law Soc., 1975-76; Chairman: The London Cremation Co. Ltd; Leeds and Bradford Airport, 1968-69; Local Govt Information Office of England and Wales, 1968-73; Assoc. of Municipal Corps of England, Wales and NI, 1968-73; Jt Negotiating Cttee for Town Clerks and District Council Clerks, 1968-73; Jt Negotiating Cttee for Chief Officers of Local Authorities, 1968-73; Public Administration Adv. Bd, Sheffield Polytechnic, 1969-74; Maplin Develt Authority, 1973-74; Leeds Council of Christians and Jews, 1960-78; NE Leeds Conservative Assoc., 1962-65; City of Leeds Conservative Assoc., 1967-79; Yorks Provincial Area Nat. Union of Cons. and Unionist Assocs, 1976-78. Local Authorities Conditions of Service Adv. Bd, 1971-73; Steering Cttee on Local Authority Management Structures; Leeds Grand Theatre and Opera House Ltd, 1969-72; Yorks Reg. Cttee, RSA; Vice-Chm., Bd of Governors, Centre for Environmental Studies, 1971-80; Member: Yorks and Humberside Economic Planning Council, 1971-74; Uganda Resettlement Bd, 1972-73; Court, Leeds Univ., 1965- (Council, 1965-72 and 1975-); Court, Bradford Univ., 1967-71; Council of Management, University Coll. at Buckingham, 1975-; Court, Univ. of York, 1981-; BBC North Regional Council; Leeds Radio Council, BBC, 1969-73; Nat. Exec. Cons. and Unionist Party, 1968- (Mem., Gen. Purposes Cttee, 1969, 1976-; Mem., Party Adv. Cttee on Policy, 1977-; a Vice-Chm., Nat. Union, 1978-79); Adv. Cttee on Local Govt Audit, 1979-82; Exec. Council (British Section) of Internat. Union of Local Authorities; European Conference of Local Authorities; Council, Leeds Philosophical and Literary Soc. (Pres.); Pres., Cremation Soc. of GB; Exec. Cttee, AA. FRSA. Hon. Freedom, City of Leeds, 1976. *Publications:* The Marshall Report on Greater London, 1978; contribs to Local Govt and other jls, and press articles. *Recreations:* theatre, reading. *Address:* Holtby, North Yorks.

MARSHALL, Mrs Alan R.; *see* Marshall, V. M.

MARSHALL, Alexander Badenoch; Chairman, Bestobell plc, since 1979; Director: Commercial Union Assurance plc; TI Group plc; Maersk (UK) Ltd; The Boots Co. plc; *b* 31 Dec. 1924; *m* 1961, Mona Kurina Douglas Kirk, South Africa; two *s* one *d. Educ:* Trinity Coll., Glenalmond; Worcester Coll., Oxford (MA). Served War, Sub-Lieut RNVR, 1943-46. P&O Group of Companies: Mackinnon Mackenzie & Co., Calcutta, 1947-59; Gen. Manager, British India Steam Navigation Co., 1959-62; Managing Dir, Trident Tankers Ltd, 1962-68; Dir, 1968-72, Man. Dir, 1972-79, Peninsular and Oriental Steam Navigation Co. *Recreations:* family, gardening. *Address:* Crest House, Park View Road, Woldingham, Surrey. *T:* Woldingham 2299. *Clubs:* Oriental; Tollygunge (Calcutta).

MARSHALL, Arthur; *see* Marshall, Charles A. B.

MARSHALL, Arthur C.; *see* Calder-Marshall.

MARSHALL, Sir Arthur Gregory George, Kt 1974; OBE 1948; DL; Chairman and Joint Managing Director, Marshall of Cambridge (Engineering) Ltd, since 1942; *b* 4 Dec. 1903; *s* of David Gregory Marshall, MBE, and Maude Edmunds Wing; *m* 1931, Rosemary Wynford Dimsdale, *d* of Marcus Southwell Dimsdale; two *s* one *d. Educ:* Tonbridge Sch.; Jesus Coll., Cambridge. Engrg. MA. Joined Garage Company of Marshall (Cambridge) Ltd, 1926, which resulted in estabt of Aircraft Company, now Marshall of Cambridge (Engineering) Ltd, 1929. Chm., Aerodrome Owners Assoc., 1964-65; Member: Air Cadet Council, 1951-59 and 1965-76; Adv. Council on Technology, 1967-70. Hon. Old Cranwellian, 1979; Hon. Companion RAeS 1980. DL 1968, High Sheriff of Cambridgeshire and Isle of Ely, 1969-70. *Recreations:* Cambridge Athletics Blue, Olympic Team Reserve, 1924; flying (pilot's licence) since 1928. *Address:* Horseheath Lodge, Linton, Cambridge CB1 6PT. *T:* Cambridge 891318. *Clubs:* Royal Air Force; Hawks (Cambridge).

MARSHALL, Arthur Hedley, CBE 1956; MA; BSc (Econ); PhD; City Treasurer, Coventry, 1944-64, retired; Senior Research Fellow in Public Administration, Birmingham University, 1964-74; *b* 6 July 1904; *s* of Rev. Arthur Marshall; *m* 1933, Margaret L. Longhurst; one *s. Educ:* Wolverhampton Grammar Sch.; London Sch. of Economics. Incorporated Accountant (Hons), 1934; Fellow Institute Municipal Treasurers and Accountants and Collins gold medal, 1930 (Pres. 1953-54); DPA (London) 1932. Chm. Royal Institute of Public Administration, 1952-53; Adviser in Local Govt to Sudan Govt, 1948-49; and to Govt of British Guiana, 1955. Chm., Cttee on Highway Maintenance, 1967-70; Member: Colonial Office Local Government Advisory Panel, 1950-; Central Housing Advice Cttee, 1957-65; Cttee for Training Public Administration in Overseas Countries, 1961-62; Arts Council Drama Panel, 1965-76; Arts Council, 1973-76; Uganda Commission, 1961; Kenya Commission, 1962; Royal Commission on Local Government in England, 1966-69. Hon. LLD Nottingham, 1972. *Publications:* Local Authorities: Internal Financial Control, 1936; Consolidated Loans Funds of Local Authorities (with J. M. Drummond), 1936; Report on Local Government in the Sudan, 1949, and on British Guiana, 1955; Financial Administration in Local Government, 1960; Financial Management in Local Government, 1974; Local Authorities and the Arts, 1974; various contribs to learned jls on Local Government, Accountancy, and administration of the arts. *Recreation:* music. *Address:* 39 Armorial Road, Coventry CV3 6GH. *T:* Coventry 414652. *Club:* Reform.
See also N. H. Marshall.

MARSHALL, Arthur Stirling-Maxwell, OBE 1979; HM Diplomatic Service; Deputy High Commissioner in Southern India, since 1980; *b* 29 Jan. 1929; *s* of Victor Stirling-Maxwell Marshall and Jeannie Theodora Hunter; *m* 1955, Eleni Kapralou, Athens (*d* 1969); one *s* two *d. Educ:* Daniel Stewart's Coll., Edinburgh. Served Royal Navy, 1947-59. Foreign Office, 1959; Middle East Centre for Arab Studies, Lebanon, 1959-61; Political Officer, British Political Agency, Bahrain, 1961-64; Attaché, Athens, 1964-67; Information Officer, Rabat, Morocco, 1967-69; Commercial Secretary: Nicosia, Cyprus, 1970-75; Kuwait, 1975-79. Deputy High Commission, Madras, 1979-. *Recreations:* music, nature. *Address:* c/o Foreign and Commonwealth Office, SW1; 24 Anderson Road, Madras, 600006, India. *T:* Madras 85523. *Clubs:* Oriental; Madras (Madras).

MARSHALL, Bruce; novelist; *b* 24 June 1899; *s* of Claude Niven Marshall, Edinburgh; *m* 1928, Phyllis, *d* of late William Glen Clark, Edinburgh; one *d. Educ:* Edinburgh Acad.; Trinity Coll., Glenalmond; St Andrews and Edinburgh Univs. Served in Royal Irish Fusiliers, 1914-18 War and in Royal Army Pay Corps and Intelligence in War of 1939-45; MA Edinburgh, 1924; B Com. Edinburgh, 1925; admitted a mem. of the Soc of Accountants in Edinburgh, 1926. *Publications:* Father Malachy's Miracle, 1931; Prayer for the Living, 1934; The Uncertain Glory, 1935; Yellow Tapers for Paris, 1943; All Glorious Within, 1944; George Brown's Schooldays, 1946; The Red Danube, 1947; Every Man a Penny, 1950; The White Rabbit, 1952; The Fair Bride, 1953; Only Fade Away; Thoughts of my Cats, 1954; Girl in May, 1956; The Bank Audit, 1958; A Thread of Scarlet, 1959; The Divided Lady, 1960; A Girl from Lübeck, 1962; The Month of the Falling Leaves, 1963; Father Hilary's Holiday, 1965; The Bishop, 1970; The Black Oxen, 1972; Urban the Ninth, 1973; Operation Iscariot, 1974; Marx the First, 1975; Peter the Second, 1976; The Yellow Streak, 1977; Prayer for a Concubine, 1978. *Address:* c/o Lloyds Bank, 6 Pall Mall, SW1.

MARSHALL, (Charles) Arthur (Bertram), MBE 1944; journalist and author; *b* 10 May 1910; *s* of Charles Frederick Bertram Marshall and Dorothy (*née* Lee). *Educ:* Edinburgh House, Lee-on-Solent, Hampshire; Oundle Sch.; Christ's Coll., Cambridge (MA). Schoolmaster and Housemaster, Oundle Sch., 1931-54; Private Sec. to Lord Rothschild, 1954-58; TV Script Editor for H. M. Tennent Ltd, 1958-64. Has written for New Statesman, 1935-81; regular columnist, 1976-81; broadcaster, in variety and more serious programmes, 1934-. American Bronze Star, 1945. *Publications:* Nineteen to the Dozen, 1953; (ed) New Statesman Competitions, 1955; Salome Dear, NOT in the Fridge, 1968; Girls Will Be Girls, 1974; I SAY!, 1977; I'll Let You Know, 1981; Whimpering in the Rhododendrons, 1982. *Recreations:* reading, sitting in the sun. *Address:* Pound Cottage, Christow, Exeter, Devon EX6 7LX. *T:* Christow 52236. *Club:* Reform.

MARSHALL, David; MP (Lab) Glasgow, Shettleston, since 1979 (sponsored by TGWU); Scottish Area Secretary, Manor House Hospital; *b* May 1941; *m*; two *s* one *d. Educ:* Larbert, Denny and Falkirk High Schs; Woodside Sen. Secondary Sch., Glasgow. Joined Labour Party, 1962; former Lab. Party Organiser for Glasgow; Member: TGWU; Co-op Party; deleg., Scottish TUC. Member: Glasgow Corp., 1972-75; Strathclyde Reg. Council, 1974-79 (Chm., Manpower Cttee); Chm., Manpower Cttee, Convention of Scottish Local Authorities. Member: Police Council for UK; Nat. Jt Council for Fire Bdes; Nat. Jt Council (Scottish Councils); Nat. Jt Council, APT&C Staffs; Nat. Jt Council of Manual Workers; Local Authorities Conditions of Service Adv. Bd. *Address:* House of Commons, SW1; 30 Ardlui Street, Glasgow G32 7AY.

MARSHALL, Sir Denis Alfred, Kt 1982; solicitor; *b* 1 June 1916; *s* of Frederick Herbert Marshall and Winifred Mary Marshall; *m* 1st, 1949, Joan Edith Straker (*d* 1974); one *s* ; 2nd, 1975, Jane Lygo. *Educ:* Dulwich Coll. Served War: HAC, 1939; XX Lancs Fusiliers (Temp. Major), 1940-46. Articled to Barlow Lyde & Gilbert, Solicitors, 1932-37; admitted Solicitor,

1937; with Barlow Lyde & Gilbert, 1947-80. Mem. Council, Law Soc., 1966-, Vice-Pres., 1980-81, Pres., 1981-82. *Recreations:* sailing, gardening. *Address:* Greenways, 121 Harestone Hill, Caterham, Surrey CR3 6DL. *Clubs:* Naval and Military; Lloyds Yacht.

MARSHALL, Dr Edmund Ian; MP (Lab) Goole since May 1971; *b* 31 May 1940; *s* of Harry and Koorali Marshall; *m* 1969, Margaret Pamela, *d* of John and Maud Antill, New Southgate, N11; one *d. Educ:* Magdalen Coll., Oxford (Mackinnon Schol.). Double 1st cl. hons Maths, and Junior Mathematical Prize, Oxon, 1961; PhD Liverpool, 1965. Various univ. appts in Pure Maths, 1962-66; mathematician in industry, 1967-71. Mem., Wallasey County Borough Council, 1963-65. Contested (L) Louth Div. of Lincs, 1964 and 1966; joined Labour Party, 1967. PPS to Sec. of State for NI, 1974-76, to Home Sec., 1976-79; Chm., Trade and Industry sub-cttee of House of Commons Expenditure Cttee, 1976-79; Mem., Chairmen's Panel in House of Commons, 1981-82; Opposition Whip, 1982-. Chm., Mitcham Constituency Labour Party, 1970-71. Hon. Sec., Labour First, 1980-. Member: British Methodist Conf., 1969-72; World Methodist Conf., 1971. British Council of Churches, 1972-78. *Publications:* (jtly) Europe: What Next? (Fabian pamphlet), 1969; Parliament and the Public, 1982. *Recreations:* genealogy, music. *Address:* House of Commons, SW1A 0AA. *Club:* Reform.

MARSHALL, Frank Graham; Science and Technology Counsellor, British Embassy, Tokyo (seconded to HM Diplomatic Service), since 1980; *b* 28 March 1942; *s* of Frank and Vera Marshall; *m* 1965, Patricia Anne (*née* Bestwick); two *s* one *d. Educ:* Birmingham Univ. (BSc Physics); Nottingham Univ. (PhD Physics). Joined Royal Signals and Radar Estabt (MoD) (Physics and Electronic Device Res.), 1966; Sen. Principal Scientific Officer, 1975-80. (Jtly) IEEE Best Paper award, 1973; (jtly) Wolfe Award, 1973. *Publications:* numerous papers on electronic signal processing devices in various jls. *Recreations:* gliding, home computing, electronics. *Address:* British Embassy, 1 Ichiban Cho, Chiyoda-Ku, Tokyo 102, Japan. *T:* 265 5511.

MARSHALL, Fredda, (Mrs Herbert Marshall); see Brilliant, F.

MARSHALL, Geoffrey, MA, PhD; FBA 1971; Fellow and Tutor in Politics, The Queen's College, Oxford, since 1957; *b* 22 April 1929; *s* of Leonard William and Kate Marshall; *m* 1957, Patricia Ann Christine Woodcock; two *s. Educ:* Arnold Sch., Blackpool, Lancs; Manchester Univ. MA Manchester, MA Oxon, PhD Glasgow. Research Fellow, Nuffield Coll., 1955-57. Mem. Oxford City Council, 1965-74; Sheriff of Oxford, 1970-71. *Publications:* Parliamentary Sovereignty and the Commonwealth, 1957; Some Problems of the Constitution (with G. C. Moodie), 1959; Police and Government, 1965; Constitutional Theory, 1971. *Recreation:* middle-aged squash. *Address:* The Queen's College, Oxford. *T:* Oxford 48411.

MARSHALL, George Wicks, CMG 1974; MBE 1955; BEM 1946; *b* 6 March 1916; *e s* of G. L. Marshall, Highbury, London, N5; *m* 1946, Mary Cook Kirkland. General Post Office, 1930-48. Served War, Royal Artillery (HAA), 1940-46. Board of Trade, 1948-56; Trade Common Service, 1956-65; Asst Trade Comr, Nairobi, 1956; Trade Comr: Accra, 1958, Colombo, 1961; Principal Trade Comr, Hong Kong, 1963; Dep. Controller, BoT office for Scotland, 1965; Dep. Dir, Export Services Br., 1967; seconded to HM Diplomatic Service as Counsellor (Commercial) HM Embassy, Copenhagen, 1969-76. Asst Gen. Sec., 1976, later Gen. Sec., Assoc. of First Div. Civil Servants, until 1982. *Recreations:* theatre, television, working. *Address:* 30 Withdean Avenue, Goring by Sea, West Sussex BN12 4XD. *T:* Worthing 45158. *Clubs:* Royal Commonwealth Society; Hong Kong (Hong Kong).

MARSHALL, Prof. Herbert Percival James; film, theatre and TV producer, director, scriptwriter, author and translator; *b* London, 20 Jan. 1906; *s* of Percival Charles Marshall and Anne Marshall (*née* Organ); *m* 1935, Fredda Brilliant, *qv. Educ:* Elementary Sch., Ilford; evening classes, LCC; Higher Inst. of Cinematography, Moscow, USSR. Began as Asst Film Editor, Empire Marketing Bd Film Unit, 1929-30; Asst Dir various Moscow theatres; Drama Dir, Moscow Radio (English), 1933-35; Founder, Dir, Unity Theatre; prod. documentary films, Spanish Civil War; Principal, Unity Theatre Trng Sch.; Lectr, LCC Evening Insts, 1935-39; Founder and Artistic Dir, Neighbourhood Theatre, S Kensington; Script-writer (with Fredda Brilliant) and Associate Producer (Ealing Studios), 1939-40; apptd Dir, Old Vic (theatre bombed); toured England; Dir for Sadler's Wells Opera Co.; Lectr, RADA, 1940-41; i/c of production, Russian, Czech, Polish and Yugoslav films for Europe (8 langs); broadcasts, BBC, in Russian, 1942-45; Lectr on film art, Amer. Univ., Biarritz, 1945-46; Indep. Film Producer: prod. for J. Arthur Rank, Min. of Educn, NCB, etc; prod., scripted and dir. (with Fredda Brilliant), Tinker (Edinburgh Festival Award), 1946-50; dir. Man and Superman, Arena Theatre (Fest. of Brit.), 1951; prod. official Mahatma Gandhi Biog. Documentary, etc, India, 1951-55; Exec. Producer, TV closed circuit and films for Advision Ltd, London, 1955-56; Film Producer for Govt of India; Principal, Natya Acad. of Dramatic Art, Bombay; Producer, Natya Nat. Theatre Company, 1957-60; Dir, Centre for Soviet and E European Studies, Southern Illinois Univ., apptd Prof., Academic Affairs, 1970, Prof. Emeritus 1979. Theatre Architecture Consultant to various projects: Indian Nat. Theatres, 1955-59; Centre 42, London, 1962; Morrison Civic Arts Centre, Lambeth, 1965; Samuel Beckett Theatre, Oxford Univ., 1968-. Lecturer: RCA and NY Univ., 1965; Univ. of Illinois, and Oxford Univ., 1968; Himachal Pradesh Univ., Hong Kong Univ., La Trobe Univ., Monash Univ., Univ. of Melbourne, 1972. Distinguished Visiting Prof., Sch. of Communications, Southern Illinois

Univ., Carbondale, 1965-68. Many well-known actors and actresses have been produced or directed by him. FRSA 1967. Mather Schol. of the Year, Case Western Reserve, Ohio, 1972. *Publications:* (ed) International Library of Cinema and Theatre (20 vols), 1946-56; Mayakovsky and His Poetry, 1964 (London); Hamlet Through the Ages (jointly), 1953 (London); Ira Aldridge, The Negro Tragedian (with Mildred Stock), 1953 (London, New York); Poetry of Voznesensky (London and New York) and Yevtushenko (London and New York), 1965; Stanislavsky Method of Direction (London and New York), 1969; Anthology of Soviet Poetry, 1970; (ed) Pictorial History of the Russian Theatre, 1978; (ed and introd) Battleship Potemkin, 1979; Crippled Biographies, 1982; Collected Works of Eisenstein (London and NY): Vol. 1, Autobiography (trans.), 1982. Scores: English Text and Lyrics, Ivan the Terrible (Oratorio by S. Prokoviev and S. M. Eisenstein), 1962 (Moscow); English Texts: 13th and 14th Symphonies, and Execution of Stepan Razin, by D. Shostakovich; Mayakovsky Oratorio Pathetique, by G. Sviridov, 1974, etc. *Recreations:* reading and TV. *Address:* 1204 Chautauqua Street, Carbondale, Ill 62901, USA; Southern Illinois University, Carbondale, Ill 62901, USA.

MARSHALL, Howard Wright; Under Secretary, Department of Transport, since 1978; *b* 11 June 1923; *s* of Philip Marshall, MBE, and Mary Marshall; *m* 1st (marr. diss.); two *s* ; 2nd, 1963, Carol Yvonne (*née* Oddy); one *d. Educ:* Prudhoe West Elementary, Northumberland; Queen Elizabeth Grammar Sch., Hexham. Served War, RAF, 1941-46; POW, 1943-45. Min. of Health, Newcastle upon Tyne, 1940; Regional Offices, Ministries of Health, Local Govt and Planning, Housing and Local Govt, 1948-55; HQ, Min. of Housing and Local Govt, 1955-59; National Parks Commn, 1959-62; Min. of Housing and Local Govt, later DoE, 1962; Asst Sec., 1968; Under Sec., 1976; Regional Dir, Eastern Region, Depts of Environment and Transport, 1976-78; Chm., East Anglia Regional Economic Planning Bd, 1976-78. *Recreations:* gardening, sport. *Address:* Brackenwood, Farthing Green Lane, Stoke Poges, Bucks. *T:* Fulmer 2974. *Club:* Caterpillar.

MARSHALL, Sir Hugo Frank, KBE 1953; CMG 1950; JP; retired; *b* 1905; *s* of late Henry Mieres Marshall and Cecil Mabel Balfour; *m* 1931, Christine Phyllida, *d* of late Major R. Brinckman, OBE; two *s* one *d. Educ:* Malvern Coll.; Exeter Coll., Oxford. Colonial Service, Nigeria, 1928; Administrative Officer, Class I, 1946; Staff Grade, 1947; Administrative Sec., Nigeria, 1947-52; Lt-Governor, Western Region, Nigeria, 1952-54; Chief Sec., Federation of Nigeria, 1954-55. JP Wilts 1958. *Recreation:* ornithology. *Address:* Murrell House, Limpley Stoke, near Bath. *T:* Limpley Stoke 2162.

MARSHALL, James; MP (Lab) Leicester South, since Oct. 1974; *b* 13 March 1941; *m* 1962, Shirley, *d* of W. Ellis, Sheffield; one *s* one *d. Educ:* City Grammar Sch., Sheffield; Leeds Univ. BSc, PhD. Joined Lab Party, 1960. Mem., Leeds City Council, 1965-68; Leicester City Council: Mem., 1971-76; Chm., Finance Cttee, 1972-74; Leader, 1974. Contested (Lab): Harborough, 1970; Leicester South, Feb. 1974. An Asst Govt Whip, 1977-79. *Address:* House of Commons, SW1A 0AA; Flat 15, The Woodlands, 31 Knighton Road, Leicester. *T:* Leicester 708237.

MARSHALL, John, MA; JP; Headmaster, Robert Gordon's College, Aberdeen, 1960-77; *b* 1 July 1915; *s* of Alexander Marshall and Margaret Nimmo Carmichael; *m* 1940, May Robinson Williamson; two *d. Educ:* Airdrie Acad.; Glasgow Univ. MA (1st cl. hons Classics), 1935; Medley Memorial Prizeman, History 1934; John Clark Schol., Classics, 1935. Asst Master: Bluevale Sch., 1937-39; Coatbridge Sec. Sch., 1939-41; Principal Teacher of Classics, North Berwick High Sch., 1941-50; Rector, North Berwick High Sch., 1950-60. Mem., Adv. Coun. on Educn for Scotland, 1955-57; Trustee, Scottish Sec. Schools Travel Trust, 1960-78 (Chm., 1971-78; Sec., 1978-80); Pres., Headmasters' Assoc. of Scotland, 1962-64; Member: Gen. Teaching Coun. for Scotland, 1966-70; Exec. Cttee, UCCA, 1970-78. JP City of Aberdeen, 1967. *Publications:* numerous articles on educational subjects. *Recreations:* fishing, photography, writing, language studies. *Address:* 11 Hazledene Road, Aberdeen AB1 8LB. *T:* Aberdeen 38003. *Club:* Royal Northern and University (Aberdeen).

MARSHALL, John Alexander, CB 1982; General Secretary, Distressed Gentlefolk's Aid Association, since 1982; *b* 2 Sept. 1922; *s* of James Alexander Marshall and Mena Dorothy Marshall; *m* 1947, Pauline Mary (*née* Taylor); six *s. Educ:* LCC elem. sch.; Hackney Downs School. Paymaster General's Office, 1939; FO, 1943; HM Treasury, 1947: Principal, 1953; Asst Sec., 1963; Under-Sec., 1972; Cabinet Office, 1974-77; Northern Ireland Office, 1977-82, Dep. Sec., 1979-82. *Recreations:* literature, music. *Address:* 48 Long Lane, Ickenham, Mddx. *T:* Ruislip 72020.

MARSHALL, John Leslie; Member (C) London North, European Parliament, since 1979; *b* 19 Aug. 1940; *s* of late Prof. William Marshall and Margaret Marshall; *m* 1978, Susan Elizabeth, *d* of David Mount, Petham, Kent; two *s. Educ:* Glasgow Academy; St Andrews Univ. (MA). ACIS. Asst Lecturer in Economics, Glasgow Univ., 1962-66; Lectr in Economics, Aberdeen Univ., 1966-70; Mem., London Stock Exchange; Carr Sebag & Co., 1979-82. Contested (C): Dundee East, 1964 and 1966; Lewisham East, Feb. 1974. Member: Aberdeen Town Council, 1968-70; Ealing Borough Council, 1971- (Chm., Bd, 1978-82; Chm., Local Services Cttee, 1982-). *Publications:* articles on economics in several professional jls; pamphlets on economic questions for Aims. *Recreations:* watching cricket and Rugby; bridge, theatre. *Address:* 2

Birkdale Road, W5 1JZ. *T:* 01-991 0162. *Clubs:* Carlton; Middlesex Cricket.

MARSHALL, John Robert Neil, CMG 1977; MBE 1968; *b* 15 July 1922; *s* of William Gilchrist Marshall and Mabel Marshall. *Educ:* Wisbech Grammar Sch.; Balliol Coll., Oxford (MA). Nigerian Administrative Service, 1950-79 (Adviser, Local Govt Reforms, 1976-79); Ahmadu Bello University (Institute of Administration), Zaria, 1979-81, retired 1981. *Address:* 2 Saxon Lane, Seaford, East Sussex. *T:* Seaford 895447. *Clubs:* United Oxford & Cambridge University, Royal Commonwealth Society.

MARSHALL, Rt. Hon. Sir John (Ross), PC 1966; GBE 1974; CH 1973; BA, LLM; Prime Minister of New Zealand, Feb.-Nov. 1972; Leader of the Opposition, 1972-74; Consultant Partner, Buddle Findlay; Chairman of Directors, National Bank of New Zealand; *b* Wellington, 5 March 1912; *s* of Allan Marshall; *m* 1944, Margaret Livingston; two *s* two *d*. *Educ:* Whangarei High Sch.; Otago Boys' High Sch.; Victoria Univ. Coll. Barrister and Solicitor, 1936; served War, with 2nd NZEF, Pacific Is and Italy, 1941-46 (Inf. Major); MP (Nat.) for Mount Victoria, 1946-54, for Karori, 1954-75; Lectr in Law, Victoria Univ. Coll., 1948-51, Vis. Fellow, 1975-; Minister, Asst to Prime Minister, in charge of State Advances Corp., Public Trust Office and Census and Statistics Dept, 1949-54; Minister of Health, 1951-54, and Information and Publicity, 1951-57; Attorney-Gen. and Minister of Justice, 1954-57; Dep. Prime Minister, 1957; Dep. Leader of the Opposition, 1957-60; Minister of Customs, 1960-61; Minister of Industries and Commerce, 1960-69; Attorney-General, 1969-71; Dep. Prime Minister, and Minister of Overseas Trade, 1960-72; Minister of Labour and Immigration, 1969-72. NZ Rep. at Colombo Plan Conf., New Delhi, 1953; visited US on Foreign Leader Grant, April 1958; NZ Representative: GATT, 1961, 1963, 1966, and ECAFE, 1962, 1964, 1966, 1968, 1970; Commonwealth Prime Ministers' Conf., 1962; Commonwealth Trade Ministers' Conf., 1963, 1966; Commonwealth Parly Conf., 1965; UN 25th Annual Session, NY, 1970; ILO Conf., Geneva, 1971; EEC Negotiations, 1961-71. Mem., Adv. Council, World Peace through Law. Chairman: NZ Commn for Expo 70; Nat. Develt Council, 1969-72; Cttee of Registration of Teachers, 1976-77. Chairman: Philips Electrical Industries; Contractors Bonding Corp.; Norwich Winterthur Insurance (NZ) Ltd, 1977-82; DRG (NZ) Ltd; Director: Norwich Union Insurance Soc.; Hallenstein Bros Ltd, 1974-82. Pres., Bible Soc. in NZ, 1978-80; World Vice Pres., United Bible Socs, 1982-; Patron, World Vision in NZ. Hon. Bencher, Gray's Inn. Hon. LLD Wellington, 1975. *Publications:* The Law of Watercourses, 1957; *for children:* The Adventures of Dr Duffer, 1978; More Adventures of Dr Duffer, 1979; Dr Duffer and the Treasure Hunt, 1980; Dr Duffer and his Australian Adventures, 1981. *Recreations:* fishing, golf, breeding Connemara ponies. *Address:* 22 Fitzroy Street, Wellington, NZ. *T:* 736.631.

MARSHALL, Mark Anthony; HM Diplomatic Service; Counsellor, Consul-General and Head of Chancery, Damascus, since 1980; *b* 8 Oct. 1937; *s* of late Thomas Humphrey Marshall, CMG and of Nadine, *d* of late Mark Hambourg; *m* 1970, Penelope Lesley Seymour; two *d*. *Educ:* Westminster Sch.; Trinity Coll., Cambridge (BA). MECAS, 1958; Third Sec., Amman, 1960; FO, 1962; Commercial Officer, Dubai, 1964; FO, 1965; Aden, 1967; First Sec., 1968; Asst Dir of Treasury Centre for Admin. Studies, 1968; UK Delegn to Brussels Conf., 1970; First Sec./Head of Chancery, Rabat, 1972; First Sec., FCO, 1976; Counsellor, Tripoli, 1979-80. *Recreations:* swimming, golf, fell walking. *Address:* c/o Foreign and Commonwealth Office, King Charles Street, SW1.

MARSHALL, Martin John, CMG 1967; HM Diplomatic Service, retired; Consultant, REMAP, since 1979; *b* 21 March 1914; *s* of late Harry Edmund Marshall and late Kate Ann (*née* Bishop); *m* 1938, Olive Emily Alice, *d* of Thomas and Olive King; two *d*. *Educ:* Westminster City Sch.; London Sch. of Economics, University of London. Customs and Excise Officer, 1935-39; Technical Officer, Min. of Aircraft Prod., 1940-46; Principal, Min. of Supply, 1947-50. Called to Bar, Gray's Inn, 1947. Trade Commissioner: Montreal, 1950-52; Atlantic Provinces, 1953; Alberta, 1954-57; Principal Trade Commissioner: Montreal, 1957-60; Calcutta (for Eastern India), 1961-63; Dep. High Comr, Sydney, 1963-67; Consul-General, Cleveland, Ohio, 1968-71; Dep. High Comr, Bombay, 1971-74. Dir, Finance/Administration, Royal Assoc. for Disability and Rehabilitation, 1977-79. *Recreations:* ski-ing, golf. *Address:* 8 Sunnyside Place, SW19 4SJ. *T:* 01-946 5570. *Clubs:* Brooks's; Royal Wimbledon Golf.

MARSHALL, Michael; *see* Marshall, R. M.

MARSHALL, Rt. Rev. Michael Eric; *see* Woolwich, Bishop Suffragan of.

MARSHALL, Noël Hedley; HM Diplomatic Service; Head of North America Department, Foreign and Commonwealth Office, since 1982; *b* 26 Nov. 1934; *s* of Arthur Hedley Marshall, *qv*. *Educ:* Leighton Park Sch.; Lawrenceville Sch., NJ (E-SU Exchange Scholar, 1953-54); St John's Coll., Cambridge (BA 1957; Sir Joseph Larmor Award, 1957). Pres., Cambridge Union Soc., 1957. Entered Foreign (later Diplomatic) Service; FO, 1957-59; Third Sec., Prague, 1959-61; FO, 1961-63; Second (later First) Sec., Moscow, 1963-65; CRO, 1965-66; First Sec. (Economic): Karachi, 1966-67; Rawalpindi, 1967-70; Chargé d'affaires *ai*, Ulan Bator, 1967; FCO, 1970-74; First Sec. (later Counsellor) Press, Office of UK Permanent Rep. to European Communities,

Brussels, 1974-77; NATO Defence Coll., Rome, 1977-78; Counsellor, UK Delegn to Cttee on Disarmament, Geneva, 1978-81. *Recreations:* sailing, the theatre. *Address:* c/o Foreign and Commonwealth Office, SW1. *Clubs:* Royal Ocean Racing; Europe House.

MARSHALL, Norman Bertram, MA, ScD; FRS 1970; Professor and Head of Department of Zoology and Comparative Physiology, Queen Mary College, University of London, 1972-77, now Professor Emeritus; *b* 5 Feb. 1915; *s* of Arthur Harold and Ruby Eva Marshall; *m* 1944, Olga Stonehouse; one *s* three *d*. *Educ:* Cambridgeshire High Sch.; Downing Coll., Cambridge. Plankton Biologist, Dept of Oceanography, UC Hull, 1937-41; Army (mostly involved in operational research), 1941-44; seconded from Army for Service in Operation Tabarin to Antarctic, 1944-46; British Museum (Natural History): Marine fishes, 1947-72; Sen. Principal Scientific Officer, 1962-72. In charge of Manihine Expedns to Red Sea, 1948-50; Senior Biologist, Te Vega Expedn, 1966-67. Polar Medal (Silver), 1948; Rosenstiel Gold Medal for distinguished services to marine science; Senior Queen's Fellow in Marine Science, Aust., 1982. *Publications:* Aspects of Deep Sea Biology, 1954; The Life of Fishes, 1965; Explorations in the Life of Fishes, 1970; Ocean Life, 1971; Developments in Deep Sea Biology, 1979; various papers in learned jls. *Recreations:* music, fishing, golf. *Address:* 6 Park Lane, Saffron Walden, Essex. *T:* Saffron Walden 22528.

MARSHALL, Prof. Sir (Oshley) Roy, Kt 1974; CBE 1968; Vice-Chancellor, Hull University, since 1979, Hon. Professor since 1980; *b* 21 Oct. 1920; *s* of Fitz Roy and Corene Carmelita Marshall; *m* 1945, Eirwen Lloyd; one *s* three *d*. *Educ:* Harrison Coll., Barbados, WI; Pembroke Coll., Cambridge; University Coll., London. Barbados Scholar, 1938; BA 1945, MA 1948 Cantab; PhD London 1948. Barrister-at-Law, Inner Temple, 1947. University Coll., London: Asst Lecturer, 1946-48; Lecturer, 1948-56; Sub-Dean, Faculty of Law, 1949-56; Prof. of Law and Head of Dept of Law, Univ. of Sheffield, 1956-69, Vis. Prof. in Faculty of Law, 1969-; on secondment to University of Ife, Ibadan, Nigeria, as Prof. of Law and Dean of the Faculty of Law, 1963-65; Vice-Chancellor, Univ. of West Indies, 1969-74; Sec.-Gen., Cttee of Vice-Chancellors and Principals, 1974-79. Chairman: Commonwealth Educn Liaison Cttee, 1974-81; Cttee on Commonwealth Legal Co-operation, 1975-81; Commonwealth Standing Cttee on Student Mobility; Member: Police Complaints Bd, 1977-81; Council, RPMS, 1976-; Council, ACU, 1979-; Management Cttee, Universities Superannuation Scheme Ltd, 1980-; Vice-Chm., Governing Body of Commonwealth Inst., 1980-81; Trustee, Commonwealth Foundn, 1981. Hon. LLD: Sheffield, 1972; West Indies, 1976. *Publications:* The Assignment of Choses in Action, 1950; A Casebook on Trusts (with J. A. Nathan), 1967; Theobald on Wills, 12th edn, 1963. *Recreations:* racing and cricket. *Address:* The University of Hull, Cottingham Road, Hull HU6 7RX.

MARSHALL, Percy Edwin Alan J.; *see* Johnson-Marshall.

MARSHALL, Peter, QPM 1979; Commissioner of Police for the City of London, since 1978; *b* 21 June 1930; *s* of Christopher George Marshall and Sylvia Marshall; *m* 1954, Bridget Frances Humphreys; three *s* one *d*. *Educ:* St Clement Danes Holborn Estate Grammar Sch. Trooper, 8th Royal Tank Regt, 1948-50. Police Officer, Metropolitan Police, 1950-78. *Recreations:* riding, reading, relaxing. *Address:* 26 Old Jewry, EC2R 8DJ. *T:* 01-601 2222.

MARSHALL, Peter Harold Reginald, CMG 1974; Ambassador and UK Permanent Representative to Office of United Nations and Other International Organisations at Geneva, since 1979; *b* 30 July 1924; 3rd *s* of late R. H. Marshall; *m* 1957, Patricia Rendell Stoddart (*d* 1981); one *s* one *d*. *Educ:* Tonbridge; Corpus Christi Coll., Cambridge. RAFVR, 1943-46. Entered Foreign Service, 1949; FO, 1949-52; 2nd Sec. and Private Sec. to Ambassador, Washington, 1952-56; FO, 1956-60; on staff of Civil Service Selection Board, 1960; 1st Sec. and Head of Chancery, Baghdad, 1961, and Bangkok, 1962-64; Asst Dir of Treasury Centre for Administrative Studies, 1965-66; Counsellor, UK Mission, Geneva, 1966-69, Counsellor and Head of Chancery, Paris, 1969-71; Head of Financial Policy and Aid Dept, FCO, 1971-73; Asst Under-Sec. of State, FCO, 1973-75; UK Rep. on Econ. and Social Council of UN, 1975-79. *Recreations:* music, golf. *Address:* United Kingdom Mission, 37-39 rue de Vermont, 1202 Geneva, Switzerland. *Club:* Travellers'.

MARSHALL, Prof. Peter James, DPhil; Rhodes Professor of Imperial History, King's College, London, since 1980; *b* 28 Oct. 1933; *s* of Edward Hannaford Marshall and Madeleine (*née* Shuttleworth). *Educ:* Wellington College; Wadham Coll., Oxford (BA 1957, MA, DPhil 1962). Military service, King's African Rifles, Kenya, 1953-54. Assistant Lecturer, Lecturer, Reader, Professor, History Dept, King's Coll., London, 1959-80. Editor, Journal of Imperial and Commonwealth History, 1975-81; Associate Editor, Writings and Speeches of Edmund Burke, 1976-. *Publications:* Impeachment of Warren Hastings, 1965; Problems of Empire: Britain and India 1757-1813, 1968; (ed, with J. A. Woods) Correspondence of Edmund Burke, vol. VII, 1968; The British Discovery of Hinduism, 1972; East India Fortunes, 1976; (ed) Writings and Speeches of Edmund Burke, vol. V, 1981; (with Glyndwr Williams) The Great Map of Mankind, 1982; articles in Economic History Rev., History, Modern Asian Studies, etc. *Address:* 7 Malting Lane, Braughing, Ware, Herts SG11 2QZ. *T:* Ware 822 232.

MARSHALL, Air Cdre Philippa Frances, CB 1971; OBE 1956; Director of the Women's Royal Air Force, 1969–73; *b* 4 Nov. 1920; *d* of late Horace Plant Marshall, Stoke-on-Trent. *Educ:* St Dominic's High Sch., Stoke-on-Trent. Joined WAAF, 1941; Comd WRAF Admin. Officer, Strike Comd, 1968–69, Air Cdre 1969; ADC, 1969–73. *Recreations:* music, cookery. *Address:* 41 Moorton Avenue, Burnage, Manchester M19 2NQ. *Club:* Royal Air Force.

MARSHALL, Sir Robert (Braithwaite), KCB 1971 (CB 1968); MBE 1945; Chairman, National Water Council, since 1978; *b* 10 Jan. 1920; *s* of Alexander Halford Marshall and Edith Mary Marshall (*née* Lockyer); *m* 1945, Diana Elizabeth Westlake; one *s* three *d*. *Educ:* Sherborne Sch.; Corpus Christi Coll., Cambridge. Mod. Langs, Pt I, 1938–39; Economics Pts I and II, 1945–47. BA Cambridge. Foreign Office temp. appointment, 1939–45. Entered Home Civil Service, 1947; Ministry of Works, 1947–50; Private Sec. to Sec., Cabinet Office, 1950–53; Min. of Works, 1953–62; Min. of Aviation, 1962–66; Min. of Power, 1966–69; Min. of Technology, 1969–70; Under-Sec., 1964; Dep. Sec. 1966; Second Perm. Sec., 1970; Secretary (Industry), DTI, 1970–73; Second Permanent Sec., DoE, 1973–78. Chm., Wateraid Trust, 1981–. Mem. Council, Surrey Univ., 1975–. Coronation Medal, 1953. *Recreations:* travel, gardening, music and arts. *Address:* Brooklands, Lower Bourne, Farnham, Surrey. *T:* Frensham 2879.

MARSHALL, Robert Leckie, OBE 1945; Principal, Co-operative College, and Chief Education Officer, Co-operative Union Ltd, 1946–77; *b* 27 Aug. 1913; *s* of Robert Marshall and Mary Marshall; *m* 1944, Beryl Broad; one *s*. *Educ:* Univ. of St Andrews (MA Mediaeval and Modern History; MA 1st Cl. Hons English Lit.); Commonwealth Fellow, Yale Univ. (MA Polit. Theory and Govt). Scottish Office, 1937–39. Served War, 1939–46: RASC and AEC; finally Comdt, Army Sch. of Educn. Pres., Co-op. Congress, 1976. Missions on co-op. develt to Tanganyika, Nigeria, India, Kenya, S Yemen and Thailand. Member: Gen. Adv. Council and Complaints Rev. Bd, IBA, 1973–77; Monopolies and Mergers Commn, 1976–; Distributive Studies Bd, Business Educn Council, 1976–79; Chm., Quest House, Loughborough, 1980–; Vice-Chm., Charnwood Community Council, 1980–. Hon. MA Open Univ., 1977; Hon. DLitt Loughborough Univ. of Technol., 1977. *Publications:* contribs to educnl and co-op jls. *Recreations:* walking, reading, swimming, golf. *Address:* Holly Cottage, 15 Beacon Road, Woodhouse Eaves, Loughborough, Leics LE12 8RN. *T:* Woodhouse Eaves 890612.

MARSHALL, (Robert) Michael; MP (C) Arundel since Feb. 1974; *b* 21 June 1930; *s* of Robert Ernest and Margaret Mary Marshall, Brookside Cottages, Hathersage; *m* 1972, Caroline Victoria Oliphant, *d* of late Alexander Hutchison, Strathaivly; two step *d*. *Educ:* Bradfield Coll.; Harvard and Stanford Univs. MBA Harvard 1960. Joined United Steel Cos Ltd, 1951; Branch Man., Calcutta, 1954–58; Man. Dir, Bombay, 1960–64; Commercial Dir, Workington, 1964–66; Man. Dir, Head Wrightson Export Co. Ltd, 1967–69; Management Consultant, Urwick Orr & Partners Ltd, 1969–74. Parly Under-Sec. of State, DoI, 1979–81. Vice-Chairman: Cons. Party Parly Industry Cttee, 1976–79; All Party Parly Cttee on Management, 1974–79; Parly Information Technology Cttee, 1982–; Mem., Select Cttee on Defence, 1982–; Parly Adviser, British Aerospace and Cable and Wireless. Member: Equity; BAFTA. Hon. DL New England, 1982. FRSA. *Publications:* Top Hat and Tails: the story of Jack Buchanan, 1978; (ed) The Stanley Holloway Monologues, 1979; More Monologues and Songs, 1980; The Book of Comic and Dramatic Monologues, 1981; The Timetable of Technology, 1982. *Recreations:* writing for radio and TV, cricket commentating, golf. *Address:* Old Inn House, Slindon, Arundel, W Sussex. *Clubs:* Garrick, MCC; Lord's Taverners; Goodwood Golf.

MARSHALL, Maj.-Gen. Roger Sydenham, CB 1974; TD 1948; Director of Army Legal Services, Ministry of Defence, 1971–73, retired; *b* 15 July 1913; 2nd *s* of Robert Sydenham Cole Marshall and Enid Edith Langton Cole; *m* 1940, Beryl Marie, *d* of William Vaughan Rayner; one *d*. Solicitor, Supreme Court, 1938. Commnd N Staffs Regt, TA, 1933; mobilised TA, 1939; comd 365 Batt. 65th Searchlight Regt, RA, 1942–44; Trans. Army Legal Services, 1948; DADALS: HQ MELF, 1948–49; HQ E Africa, 1949–52; GHQ MELF, 1952–53; WO, 1953–55; ADALS: WO, 1955–56; HQ BAOR, 1956–58; WO, 1960–61; HQ E Africa Comd, 1961–62; DDALS, GHQ FARELF, 1962–63; Col Legal Staff, WO, 1964–69; Brig. Legal Staff, 1969–71; Maj.-Gen. 1971. *Recreations:* hunting; reading history. *Address:* Higher Campscott Farm, Lee, N Devon. *T:* Ilfracombe 62885.

MARSHALL, Sir Roy; *see* Marshall, Sir O. R.

MARSHALL, Maj.-Gen. Roy Stuart, CB 1970; OBE 1960; MC 1945; MM 1940; *b* 28 Oct. 1917; *s* of Andrew Adamson Marshall and Bessie Marshall, Whitley Bay, Northumberland; *m* 1946, Phyllis Mary Rawlings; two *s*. *Educ:* Whitley Bay and Monkseaton High Sch. Joined TA 88 (West Lancs) Field Regt, 1939; commd into RA, 1942; War Service in Europe and Middle East, 1939–45; Staff Coll., Camberley, 1947; GSO 2, 2 Inf. Div., 1948–50; DAA & QMG, 6 Inf. Bde, 1950–51; jssc 1952–53; AA & QMG, 1 (BR) Corps, 1958–60; CO 12th Regt RA, 1960–62; Comdr 7th Artillery Bde, 1962–64; Indian Nat. Def. Coll., 1965; Maj.-Gen. RA, BAOR, 1966–69; Dep. Master-General of the Ordnance, 1969–70, retired; Col Comdt, RA, 1972–77. Dynamics Group, British Aerospace, 1970–82. *Recreations:* fishing, golf, bridge. *Address:* Sherford Place East, Taunton. *Club:* Army and Navy.

MARSHALL, Thomas Daniel; Member, Tyne and Wear County Council, since 1974 (Chairman, 1978–79); *b* 6 Nov. 1929; *s* of James William and Leonora Mary Marshall; *m* 1953, Eileen James; one *s*. *Educ:* St George's RC Elementary Sch., Bell's Close, Newcastle upon Tyne; Ruskin Coll.; Open Univ. Post Office, then Nat. Assistance Board, 1960; DHSS, 1966. Councillor, Newburn UDC, 1967. Chairman: Microprocessor Application Research Inst. Ltd; Tyne and Wear Enterprise Trust; Director: Tyne and Wear Innovation Centre and Development Co.; Bowes Railway Co.; Trustee: MEA Trust; Industrial Monuments Trust; Building Preservation Trust Ltd. *Recreation:* reading. *Address:* 7 Hallow Drive, Throckley, Newcastle upon Tyne NE15 9AQ. *T:* Newcastle upon Tyne 670956. *Clubs:* Grange Welfare; Newburn Memorial (Newcastle).

MARSHALL, Thurgood; Associate Justice of US Supreme Court, since 1967; *b* 2 July 1908; *s* of William C. and Norma A. Marshall; *m* 1st, 1929, Vivian Burey (*d* 1955); 2nd, 1955, Cecilia A. Suyat; two *s*. *Educ:* Lincoln Univ. (AB 1930); Howard Univ. Law Sch. Admitted Maryland Bar, 1933. Special Counsel, NAACP, 1938–50 (Asst, 1936–38); Dir, NAACP Legal Defense and Educ. Fund, 1940–61. Judge, 2nd Circuit Court of Appeals, 1961–65; Solicitor-Gen. of USA, 1965–67. Holds hon. doctorates at many US Univs. Spingarn Medal, 1946.

MARSHALL, Valerie Margaret, (Mrs A. R. Marshall); Investment Executive, Scottish Development Agency, since 1980; *b* 30 March 1945; *d* of Ernest Knagg and Marion Knagg; *m* 1972, Alan Roger Marshall; two *s* one *d*. *Educ:* Brighton and Hove High Sch.; Girton Coll., Cambridge (MA); London Graduate Sch. of Business Studies (MSc). LRAM. Financial Controller, ICFC, 1969–80. Member: Scottish Cttee, Design Council, 1975–77; Monopolies and Mergers Commn, 1976–81. *Recreations:* music, ballet, collecting antiquarian books, walking, entertaining. *Address:* Kilmore, 16 Dalkeith Avenue, Dumbreck, Glasgow G41 5BJ. *T:* 041-427 0096.

MARSHALL, Sir Walter Charles, Kt 1982; CBE 1973; FRS 1971; Chairman, Central Electricity Generating Board, since 1982; *b* 5 March 1932; *s* of late Frank Marshall and Amy (*née* Pearson); *m* 1955, Ann Vivienne Sheppard; one *s* one *d*. *Educ:* Birmingham Univ. Scientific Officer, AERE, Harwell, 1954–57; Research Physicist: University of California, 1957–58; Harvard Univ., 1958–59; AERE, Harwell: Group Leader, Solid State Theory, 1959–60; Head of Theoretical Physics Div., 1960–66; Dep. Dir, 1966–68; Dir, 1968–75; Chief Scientist, Dept of Energy, 1974–77; United Kingdom Atomic Energy Authority: Dir, Research Gp, 1969–75; Mem., 1972–82; Dep. Chm., 1975–81; Chm., 1981–82. Mem., NRDC, 1969–75; Chairman: Adv. Council on R&D for Fuel and Power, 1974–77; Offshore Energy Technology Bd, 1975–77. Fellow, Royal Swedish Acad. of Engrg Scis, 1977; For. Associate, Nat. Acad. of Engineering, USA. Hon. DSc Salford, 1977. Editor, Oxford Internat. Series of Monographs on Physics, 1966–. Maxwell Medal, 1964; Glazebrook Medal, 1975. FBIM. *Publications:* Thermal Neutron Scattering, 1971; research papers on magnetism, neutron scattering and solid state theory. *Recreations:* gardening, origami. *Address:* c/o Central Electricity Generating Board, Sudbury House, 15 Newgate Street, EC1. *T:* 01-248 1202.

MARSHALL, William; Assistant Under-Secretary of State, Ministry of Defence (Navy), 1968–72, retired; *b* 30 Sept. 1912; *e s* of late Allan and Julia Marshall, Whitecraigs, Renfrewshire; *m* 1st, 1940, Jessie Gardner Miller (*d* 1962); one *s*; 2nd, 1963, Doreen Margaret Read. *Educ:* Allan Glen's Sch., Glasgow; Glasgow Univ. MA Glasgow 1932, LLB (*cum laude*) Glasgow 1935. War of 1939–45: Temp. Asst Principal, Air Ministry, 1940; Service with Royal Navy (Ord. Seaman), and Admin. Staff, Admty, 1941. Private Sec. to Permanent Sec. of Admty (Sir J. G. Lang), 1947–48; Principal Private Sec. to successive First Lords of Admty (Lord Hall, Lord Packenham and Rt Hon. J. P. L. Thomas, later Lord Cilcennin), 1951–54; Asst Sec. in Admty, 1954; on loan to HM Treasury, 1958–61; returned to Admiralty, 1961. Chm., cttee to review submarine escape trng, 1974. *Recreations:* golf, travel, gardening. *Address:* 37 West Drive, Cheam, Surrey. *T:* 01-642 3399. *Club:* Kingswood Golf (Tadworth).

MARSHALL-CORNWALL, Gen. Sir James (Handyside), KCB 1940 (CB 1936); CBE 1919; DSO 1917; MC 1916; *b* 27 May 1887; *o s* of late Jas Cornwall, Postmaster-Gen. UP, India; *m* 1921, Marjorie (*d* 1976), *d* of late W. Scott Owen, OBE, JP of Cefngwifed, Newtown, Montgomeryshire; one *d* (and one *s* killed on active service, 1944). *Educ:* Cargilfield; Rugby; RMA, Woolwich. Commissioned in Royal Artillery, 1907; served European War in France and Flanders, 1914–18, as Intelligence Officer and Gen. Staff Officer (despatches 5 times, DSO, MC, Bt Major 1916; Bt Lt-Col 1918; Legion of Honour, Belgian Ordre de la Couronne (Croix d'Officier), Belgian Croix de Guerre, American Distinguished Service Medal, Order of the Nile); served on Gen. Staff at War Office, 1918; attended Peace Conference at Paris as mem. of British Delegation, 1919 (CBE); passed Staff Coll., 1919; served in Army of the Black Sea, 1920–23; acted as British Delegate, Thracian Boundary Commission, 1924–25; served in Shanghai Defence Force, 1927; Military Attaché, Berlin, Stockholm, Oslo and Copenhagen, 1928–32; Comdr RA 51st (Highland) Div. TA, 1932–34; Chief of British Military Mission to Egyptian Army, 1937–38; Dir-Gen. Air and Coast Defence, War Office, 1938–39; Special Employment, War Office, 1939–40; III Corps, Comdr, 1940; GOC British Troops in Egypt, 1941; GOC-in-C Western Command, 1941–42 (despatches twice); retd pay, 1943; Amer. Legion of Merit (Comdr), 1946. Editor-in-Chief of Captured German Archives, attached Foreign Office, 1948–51. Pres., Royal Geographical Society, 1954–58 (Hon. Vice-Pres.; Hon.

Mem., 1975). *Publications:* Geographic Disarmament, 1935; Marshal Massena, 1965; Napoleon, 1967; Grant, 1970; Foch, 1972; Haig, 1973. *Recreation:* historical research. *Address:* Birdsall House, Malton, N Yorks YO17 9NR. *T:* North Grimston 202. *Clubs:* Brooks's, Beefsteak, Geographical.
    See also Baron Middleton.

MARSHALL EVANS, David; *see* Evans.

MARSHAM, family name of **Earl of Romney.**

MARSHAM, Thomas Nelson, CBE 1976 (OBE 1964); BSc, PhD; CEng, MIEE, MInstP, FInstF; Managing Director, Northern Division, since 1977, Member, since 1979, United Kingdom Atomic Energy Authority; part-time Director, British Nuclear Fuels Ltd, since 1979; *b* 10 Nov. 1923; *s* of late Captain Thomas Brabban Marsham, OBE, and Jane Wise Marsham (*née* Nelson); *m* 1958, Dr Sheila Margaret Griffin; two *s*. *Educ:* Merchant Taylors' Sch., Crosby; Univ. of Liverpool (BSc, PhD). Ocean Steam Ship Co., 1941–46; Oliver Lodge Fellow, Univ. of Liverpool, 1951–53; joined UKAEA, 1953; Reactor Manager, Calder Hall Nuclear Power Station, 1955–57; Dep. Gen. Man., Windscale and Calder Works, 1958–64; Dir, Technical Policy, Reactor Gp, 1964–77. Member, Adv. Council on R&D for Fuel and Power, 1974–. *Publications:* papers in scientific jls. *Recreations:* sailing, Rugby football. *Address:* Whitecroft, Broseley Avenue, Culcheth, Warrington WA3 4HL. *T:* Culcheth 2948. *Clubs:* Naval, East India, Devonshire, Sports and Public Schools.

MARSLAND, Prof. Edward Abson; Professor of Oral Pathology, since 1964 and Vice-Chancellor and Principal, since 1981, University of Birmingham; *b* Coventry, 18 May 1923; *s* of T. Marsland; *m* 1951, Jose, *d* of J. H. Evans; one *s* two *d*. *Educ:* King Edward's Sch. and Univ. of Birmingham. BDS (1st cl. hons), PhD, FDSRCS, FRCPath. House Surgeon, Gen. and Dental Hosps, Birmingham, 1946; Birmingham University: Research Fellow, 1948–50; Lectr in Dental Pathology, 1950–58; Sen. Lectr, 1958–64; Pro-Vice-Chancellor, 1977–79; Vice-Principal, 1979–81; Dir, Birmingham Dental Sch., 1969–74. Chairman: West Midlands Council for the Disabled, 1977–; Co-ord. Cttee for Welfare of Handicapped, Birmingham; Vice-Chm., Midlands Council for Preparatory Trng of Disabled, 1976–. *Publications:* An Atlas of Dental Histology, 1957; A Colour Atlas of Oral Histopathology, 1975; scientific papers in various jls. *Recreations:* gardening, music, motoring. *Address:* 9 Bryony Road, Selly Oak, Birmingham B29 4BY. *T:* 021-475 4365.

MARSON, Air Vice-Marshal John, CB 1953; CBE 1950; CEng; RAF (retired); *b* 24 Aug. 1906; *s* of late Wing Comdr T. B. Marson, MBE, and late Mrs E. G. Marson, (*née* Atkins); *m* 1935, Louise Joy Stephen Paterson; two *s*. *Educ:* Oakham Sch. RAF Coll., Cranwell, 1926. STSO, HQ, Coastal Command, 1949–50; AOC 42 Group, 1951–54; Pres., Ordnance Board, 1956–57 (Vice-Pres., 1954–56); Dir-Gen. of Technical Services, 1957–58; AOC 24 Group, 1959–61. *Recreations:* sailing, golf. *Address:* Marygold, Aldeburgh, Suffolk IP15 5HF. *Clubs:* Royal Air Force; Royal Cruising; Cruising Association; Aldeburgh Golf.

MARTELL, Edward Drewett; Chairman of The Freedom Group, since 1953; *b* 2 March 1909; *e s* of E. E. Martell and Ethel Horwood; *m* 1932, Ethel Maud Beverley; one *s*. *Educ:* St George's Sch., Harpenden. In Coal trade, 1926–28, then entered journalism. Past: News Editor, World's Press News; Gen. Manager, The Saturday Review; Managing Editor, Burke's Peerage and Burke Publishing Co.; Sports staff of The Star. Served War of 1939–45, with RAC (Capt.). On demobilisation established own bookselling and publishing company. Mem. LCC, 1946–49; contested (L) Rotherhithe, 1946, and N. Hendon, 1950; East Ham (Ind.), 1957; SE Bristol (Nat. Fellowship C), 1963; Dep. Chm., Liberal Central Assoc., 1950–51; Trustee, Winston Churchill Birthday Trust, 1954. Founded: Free Press Soc., 1955; People's League for the Defence of Freedom, 1956 (first Chm.); Anti-Socialist Front, 1958; National Fellowship (co-founder), 1962; New Daily (also Editor), 1960. *Publications:* (with R. G. Burnett) The Devil's Camera, 1932; (with R. G. Burnett) The Smith Slayer, 1940; The Menace of Nationalisation, 1952; The Menace of the Trade Unions, 1957; Need the Bell Toll?, 1958; (with Ewan Butler) Murder of the News-Chronicle and the Star, 1960; Wit and Wisdom–Old and New, 1961; A Book of Solutions, 1962. *Recreations:* lawn tennis; Sherlock Holmes and Father Brown. *Address:* BM Box 2044, WC1.

MARTELL, Vice-Adm. Sir Hugh (Colenso), KBE 1966 (CBE 1957); CB 1963; *b* 6 May 1912; *s* of late Engineer Capt. A. A. G. Martell, DSO, RN (Retd) and late Mrs S. Martell; *m*; five *s* one *d*. *Educ:* Edinburgh Academy; RNC Dartmouth. Royal Navy, 1926–67, retired; served War, 1940–45 (despatches): Gunnery Officer in HMS Berwick and HMS Illustrious. Naval Adviser to Dir Air Armament Research and Development, Min. of Supply, 1952–54; Capt. (F) 7 and in Comd HMS Bigbury Bay, 1954–55; Overall Operational Comdr, Nuclear Tests, in Monte Bello Is as Cdre, 1956; IDC, 1957; Capt., HMS Excellent, 1958; Dir of Tactical and Weapons Policy, Admiralty and Naval Mem. Defence Research Policy Staff, Min. of Defence, 1959–62; Admiral Commanding Reserves and Dir-Gen. of Naval Recruiting, 1962–65; Chief of Allied Staff, Mediterranean, Aegean and Black Sea, 1965–67. *Recreation:* sailing. *Club:* Naval.

MARTEN, Francis William, CMG 1967; MC 1943; formerly Counsellor, Foreign and Commonwealth Office; *b* 8 Nov. 1916; *er s* of late Vice-Adm. Sir Francis Arthur Marten and late Lady Marten (*née* Phyllis Raby Morgan);

m 1940, Hon. Avice Irene Vernon (*d* 1964); one *s* one *d*; 2nd, 1967, Miss Anne Tan; one *s*. *Educ:* Winchester Coll.; Christ Church, Oxford. Served HM Forces, 1939–46. Entered HM Foreign Service, 1946; served FO, 1946–48; Washington, 1948–52; FO, 1952–54; Teheran, 1954–57; NATO Defence Coll., Paris, 1957–58; Bonn, 1958–62; Leopoldville, 1962–64; Imperial Defence Coll., 1964–65; Dep. High Comr, Eastern Malaysia, 1965–67; ODM, 1967–69. *Recreation:* ski-ing. *Address:* 113 Pepys Road, SE14. *T:* 01-639 1060.

MARTEN, Rt. Hon. H. N.; *see* Marten, Rt Hon. Neil.

MARTEN, Rt. Hon. Neil; PC 1981; MP (C) Banbury Division of Oxon, since 1959; Minister of State, Foreign and Commonwealth Office, and Minister for Overseas Development, since 1979; *b* 3 Dec. 1916; 3rd *s* of F. W. Marten; *m* 1944, Joan Olive, *d* of Vice-Adm. W. J. C. Lake, CBE; one *s* two *d*. *Educ:* Rossall Sch.; Law Soc. Solicitor, 1939. Served War of 1939–45 (despatches); Army, 1940–45, Northants Yeomanry, Special Forces, French Resistance, Norwegian Resistance. Foreign Office, 1947–57, Egypt, Turkey, Germany. Croix de Guerre; Norwegian War Medal. PPS to Pres. of Board of Trade, 1960–62; Parliamentary Sec., Ministry of Aviation, 1962–64. Mem., 1922 Exec. Cttee, 1965–79; Chm., British Norwegian Parly Gp, 1964–79; Hon. Treasurer: British-Amer. Parly Gp, 1975–78; CPA, 1976–79; Vice-Pres., Disabled Drivers Assoc. Governor: Inter Amer. Develt Bank; Asian Develt Bank; Caribbean Develt Bank. Chevalier 1st Class, Order of St Olav, Norway. *Recreations:* tennis, ski-ing. *Address:* Swalcliffe House, near Banbury, Oxon. *Clubs:* Special Forces, Carlton.

MARTIN, Andrew, QC 1965; PhD (London); Professor of International and Comparative Law, University of Southampton, 1963–77; Member: Law Commission, 1965–70; Law Reform Committee, since 1970; *b* 21 April 1906; *m* 1932, Anna Szekely; one *s*. *Educ:* Lutheran Coll., Budapest; Universities of Budapest, Paris, Vienna, Berlin and London. Barrister-at-Law, Middle Temple, 1940, Bencher, 1976. *Publications:* A Commentary on the Charter of the United Nations (with Norman Bentwich), 1950; Collective Security, 1952; The Changing Charter (with J. B. S. Edwards), 1955; Restrictive Trade Practices and Monopolies, 1957; Law Reform Now (jt ed. and part-author), 1963; Legal Aspects of Disarmament, 1963; numerous papers and articles published by learned socs and jls. *Recreations:* chamber music and alpine walks. *Address:* 4 Pump Court, Temple, EC4. *T:* 01-353 9178. *Clubs:* Reform, Hurlingham.

MARTIN, Archer John Porter, CBE 1960; FRS 1950; MA, PhD; *b* 1 March 1910; *s* of Dr W. A. P. and Mrs L. K. Martin; *m* 1943, Judith Bagenal; two *s* three *d*. *Educ:* Bedford Sch.; Peterhouse, Cambridge, Hon. Fellow, 1974. Nutritional Lab., Cambridge, 1933–38; Chemist, Wool Industries Research Assoc., Leeds, 1938–46; Research Dept, Boots Pure Drug Co., Nottingham, 1946–48; staff, Medical Research Council, 1948–52; Head of Phys. Chem. Div., National Inst. of Medical Research, 1952–56; Chemical Consultant, 1956–59; Director, Abbotsbury Laboratories Ltd, 1959–70; Consultant to Wellcome Research Laboratories, 1970–73. Extraordinary Prof., Technological Univ. of Eindhoven, 1965–73; Professorial Fellow, Univ. of Sussex, 1973–78; Invited Prof. of Chemistry, Ecole Polytechnique Fédérale de Lausanne, 1980–. Berzelius Gold Medal, Swedish Medical Soc., 1951; (jointly with R. L. M. Synge) Nobel Prize for Chemistry, 1952; John Scott Award, 1958; John Price Wetherill Medal, 1959; Franklin Institute Medal, 1959; Leverhulme Medal, Royal Society, 1963; Koltoff Medal, Acad. of Pharmaceutical Science, 1969; Callendar Medal, Inst. of Measurement and Control, 1971. Hon. DSc Leeds, 1968; Hon. LLD Glasgow, 1973. *Address:* 1141 Pampigny, VD, Switzerland. *T:* (021) 77-42-76. *Club:* Chemists' (New York).

MARTIN, Bruce; *see* Martin, R. B.

MARTIN, Christopher George; Director of Personnel, British Broadcasting Corporation, since 1981; *b* 29 May 1938; *s* of George and Lizbette Martin; *m* 1st, 1960, Moira Hughes (marr. diss. 1975); one *s* one *d*; 2nd, 1981, Elizabeth Buchanan Keith. *Educ:* Beckenham Sch., Kent. FBIM. Royal Marines, 1956–62. Group Personnel Manager: Viyella Internat., 1964–70; Great Universal Stores, 1970–74; Personnel Dir, Reed Paper & Board, 1974–76; UK Personnel Dir, Air Products Ltd, 1976–78; Gp Personnel Controller, Rank Organisation Ltd, 1978–81. *Publication:* contrib. Jl of Textile Inst. *Recreations:* music, sailing. *Address:* c/o BBC, Broadcasting House, W1A 1AA. *T:* 01-580 4468.

MARTIN, Prof. David Alfred, PhD; Professor of Sociology, London School of Economics and Political Science, London University, since 1971; *b* 30 June 1929; *s* of late Frederick Martin and late Rhoda Miriam Martin; *m* 1st, 1953, Daphne Sylvia Treherne (*d* 1975); one *s*; 2nd, 1962, Bernice Thompson; two *s* one *d*. *Educ:* Richmond and East Sheen Grammar Sch.; Westminster Coll. (DipEd 1952). BSc (Ext.) 1st Cl. Hons, London Univ., 1959; PhD 1964. School teaching, 1952–59; postgrad. scholar, LSE, 1959–61; Asst Lectr, Sheffield Univ., 1961–62; Lectr, LSE, 1962–67, Reader, 1967–71; JSPS Scholar, Japan, 1978–79. Lectures: Cadbury, Birmingham Univ., 1973; Ferguson, Manchester Univ., 1977; Gore, Westminster Abbey, 1977; Firth, Nottingham Univ., 1980; Forwood, Liverpool Univ., 1982; Select Preacher, Cambridge Univ., 1979. Pres., Internat. Conf. of Sociology of Religion, 1975–83. *Publications:* Pacifism, 1965; A Sociology of English Religion, 1967; The Religious and the Secular, 1969; Tracts against the Times, 1973; A General Theory of Secularisation, 1978; Dilemmas of Contemporary Religion, 1978;

(ed) Crisis for Cranmer and King James, 1979; The Breaking of the Image, 1980; (ed jtly) Theology and Sociology, 1980; (ed jtly) No Alternative, 1981; contrib. Encounter, TLS, THES, Daedalus, TES. *Recreation:* piano accompaniment. *Address:* London School of Economics and Political Science, Houghton Street, Aldwych, WC2A 2AE. *T:* 01-405 7686; Cripplegate Cottage, 174 St John's Road, Woking, Surrey GU22 9NP. *T:* Woking 62134.

MARTIN, Prof. Derek H.; Professor of Physics, Queen Mary College, University of London, since 1967; *b* 18 May 1929; *s* of Alec Gooch Martin and Winifred Martin; *m* 1951, Joyce Sheila Leaper; one *s* one *d. Educ:* Hitchin Boys' Grammar Sch.; Eastbourne Grammar Sch.; Univ. of Nottingham. BSc; PhD. Lectr, Queen Mary Coll., London, 1954-58, 1962-63; DSIR Research Fellow, 1959-62; Reader in Experimental Physics, 1963-67; Vis. Prof., Univ. of California, Berkeley, 1965-66; Dean, Faculty of Science, Queen Mary Coll., 1968-70. Mem. Adv. Board for Mathematical and Physical Sciences, Univ. of London, 1969-73; Head of Dept of Physics, QMC, 1970-75; Member: Astronomy, Space and Radio Bd, SRC, 1975-78; Bd, Athlone Press, 1973-79; Royal Greenwich Observatory Cttee, 1977-80; Senate, Univ. of London, 1981-. Governor, Royal Grammar Sch., Colchester, 1972-. Fellow, Inst. of Physics; Member: Optical Soc. of America; Inst. of Electrical and Electronic Engrs; Internat. Astronomical Union. Editor, Advances in Physics, 1974-. *Publications:* Magnetism in Solids, 1967; Spectroscopic Techniques, 1967; numerous articles and papers in Proc. Royal Soc., Jl of Physics, etc. *Address:* Hermanus, Hillwood Grove, Brentwood, Essex. *T:* Brentwood 210546.

MARTIN, Douglas Whitwell; Chairman, Gill & Duffus Ltd, 1964-70; President, Gill & Duffus Group PLC, 1973; *b* 17 Feb. 1906; *s* of Rev. T. H. Martin, MA, and Lily Janet Vaughan Martin; *m* 1st, 1931, Jessie Milroy Lawrie (*d* 1965); three *s*; 2nd, 1967, Margaret Helen Simms, FCIS. *Educ:* Rossall Sch.; Lausanne University. Member of staff, Export Dept of Lever Brothers Ltd, 1923-27; joined Gill & Duffus Ltd, 1929. Underwriting Member of Lloyd's, 1950-69. *Recreations:* reading, theatre. *Address:* 74 Fort George, St Peter Port, Guernsey, CI. *T:* Guernsey 25381. *Club:* Boodle's.

MARTIN, Frank Vernon, RE 1961 (ARE 1955); MA; MSIA; Wood Engraver; Etcher; Book Illustrator; Head of Department of Graphic Arts, Camberwell School of Art, 1976-80, Senior Lecturer since 1965 and Teacher of Etching and Engraving since 1953; *b* 14 Jan. 1921; *er s* of late Thomas Martin; *m* 1942, Mary Irene Goodwin; three *d. Educ:* Uppingham Sch.; Hertford Coll., Oxford; St Martin's Sch. of Art. History Sch., Hertford Coll., Oxford. Served War of 1939-45, Army, 1941-46. Book illustrations for Folio Society, Hutchinson, Geoffrey Bles, Burns Oates, Vine Press and other publishers. One-man exhibitions of prints and drawings, London, 1956, 1961 and 1968; works represented in: Victoria and Albert Museum; Manchester City Art Gallery; Whitworth Art Gallery, Manchester; Fitzwilliam, Cambridge; other public collections at home and abroad. Sec., Royal Society of Painter-Etchers and Engravers, 1956-73. Hon. Academician, Accademia delle Arti del Disegno, Florence, 1962. *Publications:* articles, book reviews, etc, on Engraving and the Graphic Arts. *Recreation:* photography. *Address:* Studio L, 416 Fulham Road, SW6. *T:* 01-385 1089; 55 St Mary's Grove, W4. *T:* 01-736 8896.

MARTIN, Prof. Frederick Morris; Professor of Social Administration, University of Glasgow, since 1972; Dean of Faculty of Social Sciences, 1976-78; *b* 2 Oct. 1923; *s* of J. and M. Martin; *m* 1947, Cicely Frances Brown; one *s* two *d. Educ:* London elem. and secondary schs; Birkbeck Coll., Univ. of London. BA 1949, PhD London 1953. Asst Lectr in Social Psychology, London Sch. of Economics, 1949-52; Lectr in Social Psychology and Sociology, Birkbeck Coll., and Mem. research staff, London Sch. of Hygiene, 1952-55; Lectr, Dept of Social Med., Univ. of Edin., 1956-60, Sen. Lectr, 1960-65, Reader, 1965-67; Asst Dir of Research and Intell., GLC, 1967-69; Head of Social Research and Policy Div., 1969-71. Member: Adv. Council on Social Work, 1974-81; Personal Services Council, 1974-80; (Chm.) Cttee on Social Work Statistics, 1975-81; Data Protection Cttee, 1976-78; SSRC Sociology and Social Admin. Cttee, 1971-75; (Chm.) SSRC Panel on North Sea Oil, 1975-82; Central Council for Educn and Trng in Social Work (and Chm., Scottish Cttee), 1973-76 and 1978-. *Publications:* (with Jean Floud and A. H. Halsey) Social Class and Educational Opportunity, 1956; (with G. F. Rehin) Patterns of Performance in Community Care, 1978; (with Margaret Bone and Bernadette Spain) Plans and Provisions for the Mentally Handicapped, 1972; ed (with Kathleen Murray) Children's Hearings, 1976; ed, Social Services in Scotland, 1979; (with S. J. Fox and Kathleen Murray) Children out of Court, 1981; (with Kathleen Murray) The Scottish Juvenile Justice System, 1982; WHO Reports, PEP pamphlets, papers and reviews in social sci. and med. jls. *Recreations:* books, music. *Address:* Department of Social Administration and Social Work, 53-57 Southpark Avenue, Glasgow G12 8LF. *T:* 041-339 8855.

MARTIN, Frederick Royal, BSc, CEng, FICE, FIStructE; Under-Secretary, Department of the Environment and Director, Defence Services II, Property Services Agency, 1975-79, retired; *b* 10 Oct. 1919; *e s* of late Frederick Martin and Lois Martin (*née* Royal); *m* 1946, Elsie Winifred Parkes; one *s* three *d. Educ:* Dudley Grammar Sch.; Univ. of Birmingham (BSc (Hons)). Asst Engr, Birmingham, Tame and Rea Dist Drainage Bd, 1940; entered Air Min. Directorate-Gen. of Works, as Engrg Asst, 1941; Asst Civil Engr: Heathrow, Cardington, London, 1944-48; Civil Engr: Cambridge, Iraq, Jordan, Persian

Gulf, London, 1948-54; Sqdn Leader, RAF, 1949-52; Sen. CE, London, 1954-58; Suptg CE, London, also Chief Engr, Aden, Aden Protectorate, Persian Gulf and E Africa, 1958-62; Suptg CE, Exeter, 1962-64; Min. of Public Bdg and Works, Area Officer, Bournemouth, 1964-66; Suptg CE, Directorate of Civil Engrg Develt, 1966-70; Asst Dir, 1970-72; Dir of Directorate of Social and Research Services, Property Services Agency, 1972; Chief Engineer, Maplin Develt Authority, 1973-74. *Publications:* various papers and articles to Instn Civil Engrs, etc, on airfield pavements. *Recreations:* looking at medieval building, listening to music; taking photographs; reading; gardening. *Address:* 25 East Avenue, Bournemouth, Dorset BH3 7BS. *T:* Bournemouth 25858.

MARTIN, Geoffrey; see Martin, T. G.

MARTIN, Geoffrey Haward, DPhil; FSA, FRHistS; Keeper of Public Records, since 1982; *b* 27 Sept. 1928; *s* of late Ernest Leslie Martin and of Mary H. Martin; *m* 1953, Janet, *d* of late Douglas Hamer, MC; three *s* one *d. Educ:* Colchester Royal Grammar Sch.; Merton Coll., Oxford (MA, DPhil); Univ. of Manchester. FSA 1975; FRHistS 1958. Univ. of Leicester (formerly University Coll. of Leicester): Lectr in Econ. History, 1952-65; Reader in History, 1966-73; Prof. of History, 1973-82; Public Orator, 1971-74; Dean, Faculty of Arts, 1972-75; Pro-Vice-Chancellor, 1979-82. Vis. Prof. of Medieval History, Carleton Univ., Ottawa, 1958-59 and 1967-68; Vis. Res. Fellow, Merton Coll., Oxford, 1971. Chairman: Board of Leicester University Press, 1975-82; British Records Assoc., 1982-; Selection Cttee, Miners' Welfare National Educn Fund, 1978-. Hon. Gen. Editor, Suffolk Record Soc., 1956-. Besterman Medal, Library Assoc., 1972. *Publications:* The Town: a visual history, 1961; Royal Charters of Grantham, 1963; (with Sylvia McIntyre) Bibliography of British and Irish Municipal History, vol. 1, 1972; Ipswich Recognizance Rolls: a calendar, 1973; contrib. Archives, Cahiers Bruxellois, Jl of Soc. of Archivists, Jl of Transport History, Trans RHistS. *Recreations:* fell-walking, adjusting phrases, gardening. *Address:* 27 Woodside House, Woodside, Wimbledon, SW19 7QN. *T:* 01-946 2570. *Club:* United Oxford & Cambridge University.

MARTIN, Air Marshal Sir Harold Brownlow Morgan, KCB 1971 (CB 1968); DSO 1943 (Bar 1944); DFC 1942 (Bar 1943, 1944); AFC 1948; *b* Edgecliffe, 27 Feb. 1918; *s* of the late J. H. O. M. Martin, MD, and of Colina Elizabeth Dixon; *m* 1944, Wendy Lawrence, *d* of late Grenville Outhwaite, Melbourne; two *d. Educ:* Bloomfields; Sydney; Randwick. Served war, 1939-45, Bomber Comd; took part in raid on Möhne dam, 1943. psa 1945; won Britannia Flying Trophy, 1947; Air Attaché, British Embassy, Israel, 1952-55; jssc, 1958; idc, 1965. SASO, Near East Air Force and Jt Services Chief of Staff, 1966-67; Air Vice-Marshal 1967; AOC No 38 Gp, Air Support Command, 1967-70; Air Marshal 1970; C-in-C, RAF Germany, and Commander, NATO 2nd Tactical Air Force, 1970-73; Air Member for Personnel, MoD, 1973-74, retired. ADC to HM the Queen, 1963. Hawker Siddeley International Ltd: Advr, 1974-75, Principal, Beirut, 1975-78, Middle East Future Markets; Market Advr, Hawker Siddeley PE Ltd, 1979. Oswald Watt Memorial Medal. *Recreations:* flying, horse racing, tennis, travel. *Clubs:* Royal Air Force, Hurlingham, Chelsea Arts.

MARTIN, Lt-Gen. Henry James, CBE 1943; DFC; Chief of Defence Staff, South African Defence Force, retired; *b* 10 June 1910; *s* of Stanley Charles Martin and Susan C. Fourie; *m* 1940, Renée Viljoen; one *s* two *d. Educ:* Grey Coll. Sch., Bloemfontein; Grey Univ. Coll., Bloemfontein. Joined S African Air Force, 1936, and played important rôle in British Empire Training Scheme in South Africa; commanded No 12 Sqdn in Western Desert (DFC, Croix Militaire de première classe Belgique); commanded No 3 Wing (a unit of Desert Air Force) and campaigned from El Alamein to Tunis; returned to Union, 1943. *Recreations:* rugger (represented Orange Free State, 1931-34, Transvaal, 1935-37, South Africa, 1937), bowls. *Address:* 34 Crescent Road, Waterkloof Ridge, Pretoria, S Africa. *Club:* Harlequins Bowling.

MARTIN, Ian; General Secretary, Joint Council for the Welfare of Immigrants, since 1977 (Deputy General Secretary, 1976-77). Ford Foundn Representative's Staff, India, 1969-70, Pakistan, 1970-71, Bangladesh, 1972; Community Relations Officer, Redbridge Community Relations Council, 1973-75. *Publications:* chapter on Racial Equality, in Labour and Equality, 1980; (with Larry Grant) Immigration Law and Practice, 1981. *Address:* Joint Council for the Welfare of Immigrants, 44 Theobalds Road, WC1X 8SP. *T:* 01-405 5527/8.

MARTIN, James Arthur, CMG 1970; FASA; company director; *b* 1903; *s* of late Arthur Higgins Martin and Gertrude, *d* of George Tippins; unmarried. *Educ:* Stawell and Essendon High Schools, Victoria. FASA 1924. Joined The Myer Emporium Ltd, Melbourne, 1918; The Myer Emporium (SA) Ltd, Adelaide, 1928, Man. Dir 1936, Chm. and Man. Dir, 1956-68, retd; Dir, Myer (Melbourne) Ltd, department store, 1936-68, retd. *Recreations:* gardening, walking, motoring. *Address:* 17 Hawkers Road, Medindie, SA 5081, Australia. *T:* Adelaide 442535. *Clubs:* South Australian Cricket, South Australian Jockey (Adelaide); Tattersall's (Sydney).

MARTIN, Maj.-Gen. James Mansergh Wentworth, CB 1953; CBE 1944; late 8th King George V's Own Light Cavalry; *b* 5 Aug. 1902; *er s* of late James Wentworth Martin, Castle Jane, Glanmire, Co. Cork, Ireland, and late Mrs J. Wentworth Martin, Great Meadow, Hambledon, Surrey; *m* 1944, Mrs Jean Lindsay Barnes (*d* 1978), *d* of late Sir Henry Cowan, MP. *Educ:* Charterhouse;

Royal Military Academy, Woolwich. Joined RFA 1922; with Royal West African Frontier Force, 1925-27; Private Sec. to Governor of Assam, 1928-29; transferred to Indian Army, 1930. During War of 1939-45, Persia and Iraq, Syria, Tunisia, Sicily, Italy and Burma; Brig., Gen. Staff, 1943-44. Comd 1st Indian Armoured Bde, 1945-47; transferred to Royal Scots Greys, Jan. 1948; Chief of Staff, British Forces in Trieste, 1948-49; Comd 9th Armoured Brigade, 1949-51; Dep. Chief of Staff Allied Land Forces Central Europe, Fontainebleau, 1951-53; GOC Salisbury Plain District, 1953-56; retired Sept. 1956. Vice-Pres. Army Ski Assoc. Liveryman of the Merchant Taylors' Company. *Address:* Great Meadow, Hambledon, Godalming, Surrey. *T:* Wormley 2665. *Club:* Cavalry and Guards.

MARTIN, James Purdon, MA, MD, BCh (Belfast), FRCP; Consulting Physician to the National Hospital for Nervous Diseases, Queen Square, WC1; *b* Jordanstown, County Antrim, 1893; *s* of late Samuel Martin, Garmoyle, Bangor, Co. Down; *m* 1st, Majorie, MB, BS (*d* 1937), *d* of Richard Blandy, Madeira; two *s*; 2nd, Janet Smiles Ferguson, MA (*d* 1978). *Educ:* Royal Academical Institution and Queen's Univ., Belfast; (Medical Schs: Belfast, St Bart's, St Mary's) BA (first class hons in Mathematical subjects), 1915; Purser Studentship; MB, BCh, BAO, 1920; MRCP, 1922; FRCP 1930; Neurologist to British Post-Graduate Medical Sch., 1935-57. Examnr, London Univ. and Conjoint Bd, 1940-49. Dean: Nat. Hosp. Med. Sch., 1944-48; Inst. Neurology, 1948-49. Mem. of the Senate of Queen's Univ. (representative for Students), 1916-17. Neurologist Eastern Command, Home Forces, 1940-44. Vis. Prof. of Neurology, University of Colorado, 1959. Lumleian Lecturer, RCP, 1947; Arris and Gale Lecturer, RCS, 1963. Hon. Member: Assoc. of British Neurologists; Soc. of Brit. Neuropathologists; Neurolog. Sect., RSM; Soc. Française de Neurologie; Amer. Neurolog. Assoc.; Canadian Neurolog. Congress, etc. FRSocMed (Pres. Neurolog. Sect., 1945-46). DSc *hc* QUB, 1982. *Publications:* The Basal Ganglia and Posture, 1967; many papers on neurological subjects in Brain, The Lancet, etc. *Address:* 36 Queen Court, Queen Square, WC1. *T:* 01-278 5426.

MARTIN, Janet, (Mrs K. P. Martin); Social Services Officer, Andover area centre, since 1978; Interviewer, MRC "National" survey, since 1970; Member, Press Council, 1973-78; *b* Dorchester, Dorset, 8 Sept. 1927; *d* of James Wilkinson and Florence Steer; *m* 1951, Peter Martin (Payroll Services Manager, Southampton Health Dist); one *s* one *d. Educ:* Dorchester Grammar Sch., Dorset; Weymouth Tech. Coll.; occupational training courses. PA to Group Sec., Herrison HMC, 1949; admin./clerical work, NHS and other, 1956; social res. fieldwork, mainly NHS (Wessex mental health care evaluation team), and Social Services (Hants CC and Nat. Inst. for Social Work), 1967-76; residential social worker (children with special needs), Southampton, 1976-78. *Recreations:* local history, local pub. *Address:* Napper's Mite, Broughton, Hants. *T:* Broughton 415.

MARTIN, John Christopher; Deputy Chief Scientific Officer (Special Merit), United Kingdom Atomic Energy Authority, since 1974; *b* 21 Sept. 1926; *s* of late Percy Martin and Marjorie Etta Caselton. *Educ:* Edward Alleyn's Sch.; King's Coll., London (BSc (Hons Physics) 1946). MoS, Fort Halstead, Sept. 1947; Woolwich Arsenal, 1950; UKAEA/MoD, AWRE, Aldermaston, Nov. 1952-. USA Defense Nuclear Agency Exceptional Public Service Gold Medal, 1977. *Publications:* contribs to learned jls. *Recreations:* friends, food, snorkling, science fiction and fact (not always distinguishable). *Address:* Boundary Hall, Tadley, Basingstoke, Hants.

MARTIN, Brig. John Douglas K.; *see* King-Martin.

MARTIN, Vice-Adm. Sir John (Edward Ludgate), KCB 1972 (CB 1968); DSC 1943; FNI; retired; Lieutenant-Governor and Commander-in-Chief of Guernsey, 1974-80; *b* 10 May 1918; *s* of late Surgeon Rear-Admiral W. L. Martin, OBE, FRCS and Elsie Mary Martin (*née* Catford); *m* 1942, Rosemary Ann Deck; two *s* two *d. Educ:* RNC, Dartmouth. Sub Lt and Lt, HMS Pelican, 1938-41; 1st Lt, HMS Antelope, 1942; navigation course, 1942; Navigation Officer, 13th Minesweeping Flotilla, Mediterranean, 1943-44, including invasions N Africa, Sicily, Pantellaria, Salerno; RNAS Yeovilton, 1944; Navigation Officer: HMS Manxman and HMS Bermuda, 1944-46; HMS Nelson, 1947; HMS Victorious, 1948; Staff Coll., 1949; Navigation Officer, HMS Devonshire, 1950-51; Dirg Staff, Staff Coll., 1952-54; Jt Services Planning Staff, Far East, 1954-55; Exec. Off., HMS Superb, 1956-57; Jt Services Staff Coll., 1958; Dep. Dir Manpower Planning and Complementing Div., Admty, 1959-61; Sen. Naval Off., W Indies, 1961-62; Comdr Brit. Forces Caribbean Area, 1962-63; Capt. Britannia Royal Naval Coll., Dartmouth, 1963-66; Flag Officer, Middle East, 1966-67; Comdr, British Forces Gulf, 1967-68 (despatches); Dir-Gen., Naval Personal Services and Training, 1968-70; Dep. Supreme Allied Comdr, Atlantic, 1970-72. Comdr 1951; Captain 1957; Rear-Adm. 1966. Pres., Nautical Inst., 1975-78. *Recreations:* fishing, shooting, beagling (Jt Master Britannia Beagles, 1963-66), sailing. *Clubs:* Army and Navy; Royal Naval Sailing Association; Royal Yacht Squadron.

MARTIN, John Hanbury; *b* 4 April 1892; *s* of W. A. H. Martin, DL, JP, and Frances Hanbury-Williams; *m* 1st, 1934, Avice Blaneid (marr. diss. 1938), *d* of Herbert Trench; 2nd, 1950, Dorothy Helen, *d* of E. Lloyd-Jones, Plas Mancott, Flints. *Educ:* Wellington; Brasenose Coll., Oxford. Served War of 1914-18; Captain, Queen's Westminster Rifles, 1915-19 (wounded). Labour candidate for Great Yarmouth, 1931; MP (Lab) Central Southwark, 1939-48. Co-founder and Chm., Southwark Housing Assoc., 1930-. Mem., London

Insurance Cttee, 1936-45; Sec. Franco-British Parly Assoc., 1943-48. *Publications:* Corner of England; Peace Adventure; Portrait of a King; contrib. to New Survey of London Life and Labour; numerous articles and reviews. *Address:* c/o Barclays Bank Ltd, 68 Lombard Street, EC3. *Club:* Brooks's.

MARTIN, Sir (John) Leslie, Kt 1957; MA, PhD Manchester; MA Cantab; MA Oxon; Hon. LLD Leicester, Hull, Manchester; DUniv Essex; FRIBA; Professor of Architecture, University of Cambridge, 1956-72; Emeritus Professor, 1973; Fellow, Jesus College, Cambridge, 1956-73, Hon. Fellow 1973, Emeritus Fellow, 1976; *b* 17 Aug. 1908; *s* of late Robert Martin, FRIBA; *m*, Sadie Speight, MA, ARIBA; one *s* one *d. Educ:* Manchester Univ. Sch. of Architecture. Asst Lectr, Manchester Univ. Sch. of Architecture, 1930-34; Head of Sch. of Architecture, Hull, 1934-39; Principal Asst Architect, LMS Railway, 1939-48; Dep. Architect, LCC, 1948-53; Architect to the LCC, 1953-56. Slade Prof. of Fine Art, Oxford, 1965-66; Ferens Prof. of Fine Art, Hull, 1967-68; William Henry Bishop Vis. Prof. of Architecture, Univ. of Yale, 1973-74; Lethaby Prof., RCA, 1981. Lectures: Gropius, Harvard, 1966; Cordingley, Manchester, 1968; Kenneth Kassler, Princeton, 1974; annual, Soc. Arch. Historians, 1976; Townsend, UCL, 1976; Convocation, Leicester, 1978. Consultant to Gulbenkian Foundn, Lisbon, 1959-69. Buildings include work in Cambridge and for Univs of Cambridge, Oxford, Leicester and Hull. Mem. Council, RIBA, 1952-58 (Vice-Pres., 1955-57); Mem. Royal Fine Art Commn, 1958-72. RIBA Recognised Schs Silver Medallist, 1929; Soane Medallist, 1930; London Architecture Bronze Medallist, 1954; RIBA Distinction in Town Planning, 1956; Civic Trust Award, Oxford, 1967; Commend. Cambridge, 1972; Concrete Soc. Award, Oxford, 1972; Royal Gold Medal for Architecture, RIBA, 1973. Hon. Mem. Assoc. of Finnish Architects, Accademico corrispondente National Acad. of S Luca, Rome. Comdr, Order of Santiago da Espada, Portugal. *Publications:* Jt Editor, Circle, 1937, repr. 1971; The Flat Book, 1939 (in collab. with wife); Whitehall: a Plan for a National and Government Centre, 1965; The Framework of Planning (Inaugural Lecture) Hull, 1967; Jt Editor, Cambridge Urban and Architectural Studies, Vol. I: Urban Space and Structure, 1972; contrib. various jls; papers include: An Architect's Approach to Architecture; Education Without Walls; Education Around Architecture; Notes on a Developing Architecture. *Address:* The Barns, Church Street, Great Shelford, Cambridge. *T:* Cambridge 842399. *Club:* Athenæum.

MARTIN, Sir John (Miller), KCMG 1952; CB 1945; CVO 1943; British High Commissioner in Malta, 1965-67; *b* 15 Oct. 1904; *s* of late Rev. John Martin; *m* 1943, Rosalind Julia, 3rd *d* of late Sir David Ross, KBE; one *s. Educ:* The Edinburgh Acad.; Corpus Christi Coll., Oxford (Scholar, MA; Hon. Fellow, 1980). Entered Civil Service (Dominions Office), 1927; seconded to Malayan Civil Service, 1931-34; Sec. of Palestine Royal Commission, 1936; Private Sec. to the Prime Minister (Rt Hon. Winston Churchill), 1940-45 (Principal Private Sec. from 1941); Asst Under-Sec. of State, 1945-56, Dep. Under-Sec. of State, 1956-65, Colonial Office. KStJ 1966. *Publication:* contrib. to Action This Day-Working with Churchill, 1968. *Address:* The Barn House, Watlington, Oxford. *T:* Watlington 2487. *Club:* Athenæum.

MARTIN, Prof. John Powell; Professor of Sociology and Social Administration, University of Southampton, since 1967; *b* 22 Dec. 1925; *s* of Bernard and Grace Martin; *m* 1951, Sheila Feather (marr. diss. 1981); three *s. Educ:* Leighton Park Sch., Reading; Univ. of Reading (BA); London Sch. of Economics and Political Science (Certif. in Social Admin., PhD); Univ. of Cambridge (MA). Lectr, London Sch. of Economics, 1953-59; Asst Dir of Research, Inst. of Criminology, Univ. of Cambridge, 1960-66; Fellow, King's Coll., Cambridge, 1964-67. Hill Foundn Vis. Prof., Univ. of Minnesota, 1973; Vis. Fellow, Yale Law Sch., 1974. Mem., Jellicoe Cttee on Boards of Visitors of Penal Instns, 1974-75. *Publications:* Social Aspects of Prescribing, 1957; Offenders as Employees, 1962; The Police: a study in manpower (with Gail Wilson), 1969; The Social Consequences of Conviction (with Douglas Webster), 1971; (ed) Violence and the Family, 1978; The Future of the Prison System, 1980; articles in: Lancet, British Jl of Criminology, British Jl of Sociology, International Review of Criminal Policy, etc. *Recreations:* sailing, photography, do-it-yourself. *Address:* Department of Sociology and Social Administration, The University, Southampton SO9 5NH. *T:* Southampton 559122. *Club:* Lymington Town Sailing.

MARTIN, John Sinclair, CBE 1977; farmer; *b* 18 Sept. 1931; *s* of Joseph Martin and Claire Martin, Littleport, Ely; *m* 1960, Katharine Elisabeth Barclay, MB, BS; three *s* one *d. Educ:* The Leys Sch., Cambridge; St John's Coll., Cambridge (MA, Dip. in Agriculture). Chairman: Littleport and Downham IDB, 1971-; Eastern Regional Panel, MAFF, 1981- (Mem., 1972-78). Vice-Chm., Great Ouse Local Land Drainage Cttee, AWA, 1974-. Member: Eastern Counties Farmers' Management Cttee, 1960-72; ARC, 1968-78; Great Ouse River Authority, 1970-74; Chm., JCO Arable Crops and Forage Bd, 1973-76. Chairman: Ely Br., NFU, 1963; Cambs NFU, 1979. *Address:* Denny Abbey, Waterbeach, Cambridge CB5 9PQ. *T:* Cambridge 860282. *Club:* Farmers'.

MARTIN, John William Prior; HM Diplomatic Service; Counsellor, Kuala Lumpur, since 1982; *b* 23 July 1934; *er s* of Stanley Gordon Martin and Frances Heather (*née* Moore); *m* 1960, Jean Fleming; three *s* one *d. Educ:* CIM Sch., Chefoo and Kuling; Bristol Grammar Sch.; St John's Coll., Oxford (MA). National Service, 1953-55 (2nd Lieut Royal Signals). Joined FO, 1959; Beirut, 1960; Saigon, 1963; Language Student, Hong Kong, 1965-67; Dar es Salaam,

1968; FCO, 1971; Singapore, 1974; FCO, 1978. *Address:* c/o Foreign and Commonwealth Office, SW1A 2AH.

MARTIN, Mrs Kenneth Peter; *see* Martin, Janet.

MARTIN, Prof. Laurence Woodward; Vice-Chancellor, University of Newcastle upon Tyne, since 1978; *b* 30 July 1928; *s* of Leonard and Florence Mary Martin; *m* 1951, Betty Parnall; one *s* one *d. Educ:* St Austell Grammar Sch.; Christ's Coll., Cambridge (MA); Yale Univ. (MA, PhD). Flying Officer, RAF, 1948-50; Instr, Yale Univ., 1955-56; Asst Prof., MIT, 1956-61; Rockefeller Fellow for Advanced Study, 1958-59; Associate Prof., Sch. of Advanced Internat. Studies, The Johns Hopkins Univ., 1961-64; Wilson Prof. of Internat. Politics, Univ. of Wales, 1964-68; Prof. of War Studies, King's Coll., Univ. of London, 1968-77; Research Associate, Washington Center of Foreign Policy Research, 1964-76. Lees-Knowles Lectr, Cambridge, 1981; BBC Reith Lectr, 1981. Director: Tyne Tees Television; European-American Inst. for Security Res., 1977-. Member: SSRC, 1969-76 (Chm. Res. Grants Bd); Res. Council, Georgetown Center of Strategic Studies. Consultant, Univ. of California, Los Alamos Scientific Laboratory. *Publications:* The Anglo-American Tradition in Foreign Affairs (with Arnold Wolfers), 1956; Peace without Victory, 1958; Neutralism and Non-Alignment, 1962; The Sea in Modern Strategy, 1967; (jtly) America in World Affairs, 1970; Arms and Strategy, 1973; (jtly) Retreat from Empire?, 1973; (jtly) Strategic Thought in the Nuclear Age, 1979; The Two-Edged Sword, 1982. *Address:* University of Newcastle upon Tyne, Newcastle upon Tyne NE1 7RU.

MARTIN, Leonard Charles James; Under-Secretary, Overseas Development Administration, FCO (formerly Ministry of Overseas Development), 1968-80, retired; *b* 26 June 1920; *s* of Leonard Howard Martin and Esther Martin (*née* Avis); *m* 1945, Althea Lilian Charles; three *d. Educ:* Brighton, Hove and Sussex Grammar Sch.; London Sch. of Economics. Served RAFVR, 1941-45. Min. of Educn, and Dept of Educn and Science, 1946-64; ODM, 1965-80. UK Permanent Delegate to UNESCO, 1965-68; Mem. Exec. Bd, UNESCO, 1974-78 (Chm., 1976-78). *Address:* 87 Downside, Shoreham-by-Sea, West Sussex BN4 6HF.

MARTIN, Sir Leslie; *see* Martin, Sir J. L.

MARTIN, Sir Leslie Harold, Kt 1957; CBE 1954; FRS 1957; FAA; PhD (Cantab); DSc (Australian National University, Melbourne, Qld, NSW, Adelaide); LLD (WA); DLitt (Sydney); Dean of Military Studies, and Professor of Physics, Royal Military College, Duntroon, Canberra, 1967-70; *b* 21 Dec. 1900; *s* of Richard Martin, Melbourne; *m* 1923, Gladys Maude Elaine, *d* of H. J. Bull; one *s* (and one *s* decd). *Educ:* Melbourne High Sch.; Melbourne Univ.; Trinity Coll., Cambridge. Scholar of Exhibn of 1851, 1923; apptd to Natural Philosophy Dept of Melbourne Univ., 1927; Rockefeller Fellow, 1927; Syme Prize, 1934; Associate Professor of Natural Philosophy, University of Melbourne, 1937-45; Professor of Physics, 1945-59; Emeritus Prof., 1960. Defence Scientific Adviser to Aust. Govt, and Chm., Defence Res. and Develt Policy, 1948-67; Comr, Atomic Energy Commn of Aust, 1958-68; Chm., Aust. Univ. Commn, 1959-66. *Address:* 11 Wedge Court, Glen Waverley, Victoria 3150, Australia. *T:* 2321125.
See also R. L. Martin.

MARTIN, Leslie Vaughan; Hon. Research Fellow, Exeter University; *b* 20 March 1919; *s* of late Hubert Charles Martin and late Rose Martin (*née* Skelton); *m* 1949, Winifred Dorothy Hopkins; one *s* one *d. Educ:* Price's Sch., Fareham. FIA 1947. Served with RAMC and REME, 1940-46. Deptl Clerical Officer, Customs and Excise, 1936-38; joined Govt Actuary's Dept, 1938; Asst Actuary, 1949; Actuary, 1954; Principal Actuary, 1962; Directing Actuary (Superann. and Research), 1974-79. Mem. Council, Inst. of Actuaries, 1971-76; Vice-Chm., CS Medical Aid Assoc., 1976-79. Churchwarden, St Barnabas, Dulwich, 1965-70, 1977-79, Vice-Chm. of Parish Council, 1970-79; Treasurer: Morchard Bishop Parochial Church Council, 1980-; Cadbury Deanery Synod, 1981-. *Recreations:* crosswords, travel. *Address:* Pickwick House, Down St Mary, Crediton, Devon EX17 6EQ. *T:* Copplestone 581.

MARTIN, Michael John; MP (Lab) Springburn Division of Glasgow, since 1979; *b* 3 July 1945; *s* of Michael and Mary Martin; *m* 1965, Mary McLay; one *s* one *d. Educ:* St Patrick's Boys' Sch., Glasgow. Sheet metal worker; AUEW Shop Steward, Rolls Royce, Hillington, 1970-74; Trade Union Organiser, 1976-79; Mem., and sponsored by, Nat. Union of Sheet Metal Workers, Coppersmiths and Heating and Domestic Engineers; PPS to Rt Hon. Denis Healey, MP, 1981-. Councillor: for Fairfield Ward, Glasgow Corp., 1973-74; for Balornock Ward, Glasgow DC, 1974-79. *Recreations:* hill walking, local history. *Address:* 144 Broomfield Road, Balornock, Glasgow G21 3UE.

MARTIN, Oliver Samuel, QC 1970; **His Honour Judge Martin;** a Circuit Judge, since 1975; *b* 26 Nov. 1919; *s* of Sidney Edward Martin and Nita Martin; *m* 1954, Marion Eve; two *s. Educ:* King's College Sch., Wimbledon; London University. Served RNVR, 1939-46. Called to Bar, Gray's Inn, 1951. Dep. Chm. E Sussex QS, 1970-71; a Recorder of the Crown Court, 1972-75. *Recreations:* golf, music, reading. *Address:* 8 New Square, Lincoln's Inn, WC2. *T:* 01-242 4986.

MARTIN, Patrick William, TD; JP; MA; Headmaster of Warwick School, 1962-77; *b* 20 June 1916; *e s* of Alan Pattinson Martin, Bowness-on-Windermere, Westmorland; *m* 1939, Gwendoline Elsie Helme, MA, St Hilda's Coll., Oxford; two *d. Educ:* Windermere Grammar Sch.; Balliol Coll., Oxford. 2nd cl. hons in Modern History, Balliol Coll., 1937. Asst Master, Abingdon Sch., Berks, 1938-40. Commissioned in TA, 1938; served War of 1939-45, on active service with Royal Artillery, 1940-46; Battery Capt., 1940-42; Comdt Sch. of Artillery, S India; Staff College, Quetta; GSO 2, and 1 HQRA 14th Army in Burma (despatches); British Mil. Mission to Belgium, 1946. Schoolmaster, 1946-49; Asst Dir of Educn, Brighton, 1950-52; Headmaster: Chipping Norton Grammar Sch., 1952-57; Lincoln Sch., 1958-62. Chm., Midland Div., Headmasters' Conf., 1972-; Pres., Headmasters' Assoc., 1976. Chm., Martin Working Party, Royal Agric. Soc., 1977. CC Warwickshire, 1977- (Leader, 1981). JP Warwicks 1966, Dep. Chm., Warwick Petty Sessions. *Publications:* History of Heart of England Building Society, 1981; articles in educational and other periodicals. *Recreations:* books, music, foreign countries and people; being alone in the countryside. *Address:* 80 High Street, Kenilworth, Warwicks. *T:* Kenilworth 54140.

MARTIN, Hon. Paul Joseph James, PC (Canada) 1945; CC (Canada) 1976; QC (Canada); High Commissioner for Canada in the United Kingdom, 1974-79; *b* Ottawa, 23 June 1903; *s* of Philip Ernest Martin and Lumina Marie Chouinard; *m* 1937, Alice Eleanor Adams; one *s* one *d. Educ:* Pembroke Separate Schs; St Alexandre Coll.; St Michael's Coll.; University of Toronto (MA); Osgoode Hall Law Sch., Toronto; Harvard Univ. (LLM); Trinity Coll., Cambridge; Geneva Sch. of Internat. Studies. Wilder Fellow, 1928; Alfred Zimmern Schol., 1930; Barrister-at-Law; Partner, Martin, Laird & Cowan, Windsor, Ont, 1934-63; QC 1937. Lectr, Assumption Coll., 1931-34. Can. Govt Deleg., 19th Ass. League of Nations, Geneva, 1938; Parl. Asst to Minister of Labour, 1943; Deleg. to ILO Confs, Phila, 1944, London, 1945. Apptd Sec. of State, 1945. Deleg. to 1st, 4th, 7th, 9th, 10th General Assembly, UN (Chm. Can. Del., 9th, 18th, 19th, 20th, 21st). Deleg. 1st, 3rd, 5th sessions, Economic and Social Council, 1946-47. Minister of National Health and Welfare, Dec. 1946-June 1957; Sec. of State for External Affairs, 1963-68; Pres., N Atlantic Council, 1965-66; Govt Leader in Senate, Canada, 1968-74. First elected to Canadian House of Commons, Gen. Elec., 1935; Rep. Essex East until 1968; apptd to Senate, 1968. Chancellor, Wilfrid Laurier Univ., 1972-. Holds several hon. doctorates. Hon. Life Mem., Canadian Legion. Christian Culture Award, 1956. Freedom, City of London, 1977. Hon. LLD Cambridge, 1980. *Address:* 2021 Ontario Street, Windsor, Ontario N8Y 1N3, Canada. *Clubs:* Rideau (Ottawa); Beach Grove Golf and Country (Windsor, Ont).

MARTIN, Peter; *see* Martin, R. P.

MARTIN, Maj.-Gen. Peter Lawrence de Carteret, CBE 1968 (OBE 1964); Chairman, Lady Grover's Hospital Fund for Officers' Families, since 1975; Member: National Executive Committee, Forces Help Society, since 1975; Ex-Services Mental Welfare Society, since 1977; *b* 15 Feb. 1920; *s* of late Col Charles de Carteret Martin, MD, ChD, IMS and of Helen Margaret Hardinge Grover; *m* 1st, 1949, Elizabeth Felicia (marr. diss. 1967), *d* of late Col C. M. Keble; one *s* one *d* ; 2nd, 1973, Mrs Valerie Singer. *Educ:* Wellington Coll.; RMC Sandhurst. FBIM 1979 (MBIM 1970). Commnd Cheshire Regt, 1939; BEF (Dunkirk), 1940; Middle East, 1941; N Africa 8th Army, 1942-43 (despatches); invasion of Sicily, 1943; Normandy landings and NW Europe, 1944 (despatches); Palestine, 1945-47; GSO2 (Int.), HQ British Troops Egypt, 1947; Instructor, RMA Sandhurst, 1948-50; psc 1951; Bde Major 126 Inf. Bde (TA), 1952-53; Chief Instructor MMG Div. Support Weapons Wing, Sch. of Infantry, 1954-56; Malayan Ops, 1957-58 (despatches); DAAG GHQ FARELF, 1958-60; CO 1 Cheshire, N Ireland and BAOR, 1961-63; AA&QMG Cyprus District, 1963-65; comd 48 Gurkha Inf. Bde, Hong Kong, 1966-68; Brig. AQ HQ Army Strategic Comd, 1968-71; Dir, Personal Services (Army), 1971-74. Col 73rd (Cheshire) Regt, 1971-78; Col Comdt, Mil. Provost Staff Corps, 1972-74. Services Advr, Variety Club of GB, 1976-. *Recreations:* golf, tennis, reading and watching 1 Cheshire winning Athletics championships. *Address:* Faircrosse, Brimpton Common, Berks RG7 4RT. *T:* Tadley 5274. *Club:* Army and Navy.

MARTIN, Peter Lewis, CBE 1980; Partner, The Oscar Faber Partnership, Consulting Engineers, since 1961; *b* 22 Sept. 1918; *s* of George Lewis and Madeleine Mary Martin; *m* 1949, Elizabeth Grace, *d* of John David Melling; two *d. Educ:* Wyggeston Boys Sch., Leicester; Kibworth Beauchamp Grammar Sch.; Leicester Coll. of Art and Technology; Borough Polytechnic. CEng, FIMechE, FInstE; FCIBS; AMRAeS; MConsE. Apprenticed to engrg contractor, 1934-39. Served War, 1940-46, RAF Engrg Branch. Joined consulting engrg practice of Dr Oscar Faber, 1947. Institution of Heating and Ventilating Engineers: Pres., 1971-72; Chm. Technology Bd, 1972-75; Mem. Guide Cttee, 1953-65, Chm. 1966-74; Chm., Heating and Ventilating Res. Assoc., 1967-69; Member: Cttee for Application of Computers to the Construction Industry, 1970-72; Technical Data on Fuel Cttee, World Energy Conf., 1971-77; Council, Assoc. of Consulting Engrs, 1972-75, 1976-80, 1981; Construction and Housing Res. Adv. Council, 1975-77; Building Services Bd CNAA, 1975-80; Engrg Council, 1982-; Vice-Chm., ACE, 1982. Vis. Prof., Univ. of Strathclyde, 1974-82. Governor, Herts Coll. of Building, 1970-74. Liveryman, Worshipful Co. of Plumbers of City of London 1962, Master 1979-80. Silver Medal, 1956, Bronze Medal, 1968, Gold Medal, 1976, IHVE. *Publications:* (jtly) Heating and Air Conditioning of Buildings, by Faber and Kell, 5th edn 1971, 6th edn 1979; contribs to engrg jls and confs. *Recreation:*

avoiding gardening. *Address:* 37 The Park, St Albans, Herts AL1 4RX. *T:* St Albans 54698. *Clubs:* City Livery, Lansdowne.

MARTIN, Most Rev. Pierre, Officer, Legion of Honour, 1967; President, Episcopal Conference of The Pacific, since 1971; Former Archbishop of Noumea (1966-71); *b* 22 Feb. 1910. *Educ:* Univ. de Lyon; Lyon Séminaire and in Belgium. Priest, 1939. POW, Buchenwald and Dachau Camps, until 1945. Séminaire de Missions d'Océanie, Lyon: Professor, 1945-47; Supérieure, 1947-53; Provincial, Sté de Marie, Paris, 1953-56; Bishop of New Caledonia, 1956. Apostolic Administrator of the Diocese of Port-Vila, 1976-77. *Address:* CEPAC, PO Box 1200, Suva, Fiji.

MARTIN, Prof. Raymond Leslie, MSc, PhD, ScD, DSc; FRACI, FRSC, FAA; Vice-Chancellor, Monash University, Melbourne, since 1977; *b* 3 Feb. 1926; *s* of Sir Leslie Harold Martin, *qv* ; *m* 1954, Rena Lillian Laman; three *s* one *d*. *Educ:* Scotch Coll., Melbourne; Univ. of Melb. (BSc, MSc); Sidney Sussex Coll., Cambridge (PhD, ScD). FRACI 1956; FRSC (FRIC 1974); FAA 1971. Resident Tutor in Chemistry, Queen's Coll., Melb., 1947-49 (Fellow, 1979); Sidney Sussex Coll., Cambridge: 1851 Exhibn Overseas Scholar, 1949-51; Sen. Scholar, 1952-54; Res. Fellow, 1951-54; Sen. Lectr, Univ. of NSW, 1954-59; Section Leader, 1959-60, and Associate Res. Manager, 1960-62, ICIANZ; Prof. of Inorganic Chem., 1962-72, and Dean of Faculty of Science, 1971, Univ. of Melb.; Australian National University, Canberra: Prof. of Inorganic Chem., Inst. of Advanced Studies, 1972-77, Prof. Emeritus 1977; Dean, Res. Sch. of Chem., 1976-77; DSc. Vis. Scientist: Technische Hochschule, Stuttgart, 1953-54; Bell Telephone Labs, NJ, 1967; Vis. Prof., Columbia Univ., NY, 1972. Royal Aust. Chemical Institute: Smith Medal, 1968; Olle Prize, 1974; Inorganic Award, 1978; Fed. Pres., 1968-69. *Publications:* papers and revs on physical and inorganic chem. mainly in jls of London, Amer. and Aust. Chem. Socs. *Recreations:* golf; lawn tennis (Cambridge Univ. team *v* Oxford, Full Blue; Cambs County Colours). *Address:* Vice-Chancellor's Residence, Monash University, Clayton, Vic 3168, Australia. *Clubs:* Melbourne (Melbourne); Hawks (Cambridge).

MARTIN, Col Robert Andrew St George, OBE 1959 (MBE 1949); JP; Lord-Lieutenant and Custos Rotulorum of Leicestershire since 1965; *b* 23 April 1914; *o s* of late Major W. F. Martin, Leics Yeo., and late Violet Anne Philippa (*née* Wynter); *m* 1950, Margaret Grace (JP Leics 1967), *e d* of late J. V. Buchanan, MB, ChB; one *s*. *Educ:* Eton Coll.; RMC Sandhurst. Commissioned Oxf. and Bucks Lt Inf., 1934; ADC to Gov.-Gen. of S Africa, 1938-40; war service 4 Oxf. and Bucks, 1940-42; 2/7 R Warwick Regt, 1942-44; 5 DCLI, 1944-45 in NW Europe (despatches); DAMS, HQ ALFSEA, 1946; Mil. Asst to C of S, GHQ, SEALF, 1946-49 (MBE); Chief Instr, School of Mil. Admin., 1949-50; 1 Som. LI, 1950-52; AMS, HQ BAOR, 1952-54; 1 Oxf. and Bucks, 1954-55; Military Sec. to Gov.-Gen. of Australia, 1955-57; Comd 1 Oxf. and Bucks Lt Inf. and 1 Green Jackets, 1957-59; Bde Col Green Jackets Bde, 1959-62; Comd Recruiting and Liaison Staff, HQ Western Command, 1962-65. Pres., E Midlands TA&VRA, 1968-. JP Leics, 1965. KStJ 1966. Order of Orange Nassau, 1950. *Recreations:* hunting, shooting, cricket, gardening. *Address:* The Brand, Woodhouse Eaves, Loughborough, Leics LE12 8SS. *T:* Woodhouse Eaves 890269. *Clubs:* Army and Navy, MCC.

MARTIN, (Robert) Bruce, QC 1977; a Recorder of the Crown Court, since 1978; *b* 2 Nov. 1938; *s* of Robert Martin and Fay Martin; *m* 1967, Elizabeth Georgina (*née* Kiddie); one *s* one *d*. *Educ:* Shrewsbury Sch.; Liverpool Univ. (LLB Hons 1959). Called to the Bar, Middle Temple, 1960. Chm., The Bob Martin Co. and associated cos. *Recreations:* music, golf, fishing. *Address:* 5 Essex Court, Temple, EC4 9AH. *T:* 01-353 4365; 4 Montpelier Terrace, SW7. *T:* 01-584 0649. *Clubs:* Royal Automobile; Royal Birkdale Golf.

MARTIN, Robert George H.; *see* Holland-Martin.

MARTIN, Robin Geoffrey; *b* 9 March 1921; *s* of Cecil Martin and Isabel Katherine Martin (*née* Hickman); *m* 1946, Margery Chester Yates; two *s* one *d*. *Educ:* Cheltenham Coll.; Jesus Coll., Cambridge (MA). FIQ. Tarmac Ltd: Dir 1955; Gp Man. Dir 1963; Dep. Chm. 1967; Chm. and Chief Exec., 1971-79; Dir, Serck Ltd, 1971, Dep. Chm., 1974, Chm., 1976-81; Chm., Hewitson Holdings Ltd, 1980-; Dir, Burmah Oil Co. Ltd, 1975-; Former Dir, Ductile Steels Ltd. Mem., Midlands Adv. Bd, Legal and General Assurance Soc. Ltd, 1977; Chm., Ironbridge Gorge Develt Trust, 1976-78. Life Governor, Birmingham Univ., 1970. *Recreations:* golf, sailing, ski-ing. *Address:* The Field, The Wergs, Wolverhampton, West Midlands. *T:* Wolverhampton 751719. *Club:* East India, Devonshire, Sports and Public Schools.

MARTIN, Ronald, MBE 1945; *b* 7 Nov. 1919; *o s* of late Albert and Clara Martin; *m* 1943, Bettina, *o d* of late H. E. M. Billing; one *d*. *Educ:* St Olave's Grammar Sch. Asst Traffic Superintendent, GPO, 1939. Served War of 1939-45, Royal Signals, NW Europe. GPO: Asst Princ., 1948; Princ., 1950; Treasury, 1954; Princ. Private Sec. to PMG, 1955; Staff Controller, GPO, London, 1956; Asst Sec., 1957; Dir Establishments and Organisation, GPO, 1966; Dir Telecommunications Personnel, 1967; Dir of Marketing, Telecommunications HQ, 1968-75; Sen. Dir, Customer Services, 1975-79. *Recreations:* music, motoring, amateur mechanics. *Address:* 23 Birch Close, Send, Woking, Surrey GU23 7BZ.

MARTIN, (Roy) Peter, MBE 1970; Counsellor (Cultural), British Embassy, Tokyo, and British Council Representative, Japan, since 1979; *b* 5 Jan. 1931; *s* of Walter Martin and Annie Mabel Martin; *m* 1st, 1951, Marjorie Peacock (marr. diss. 1960); 2nd, Joan Drumwright (marr. diss. 1977); two *s* ; 3rd, 1978, Catherine Sydee. *Educ:* Highbury Grammar Sch.; Univ. of London (BA 1953, MA 1956); Univ. of Tübingen. Local Govt Officer, 1948-60; Nat. Service (RAF Educn Branch), 1949-51; schoolteacher, 1954-56; joined British Council, 1960; service in Indonesia and Hungary (Cultural Attaché). *Publications:* (with Joan Martin) Japanese Cooking, 1970; (as James Melville): The Wages of Zen, 1979; The Chrysanthemum Chain, 1980; A Sort of Samurai, 1981; The Ninth Netsuke, 1982. *Recreations:* writing, things Japanese. *Address:* c/o Foreign and Commonwealth Office, King Charles Street, SW1A 2AH. *Club:* Travellers'.

MARTIN, Rupert Claude, MA; JP; *b* 2 July 1905; *s* of late Col C. B. Martin, CMG; *m* 1931, Ellen (*d* 1966), *d* of Henry Wood, Guernsey, CI; one *s* two *d*. *Educ:* Shrewsbury Sch.; Queen's Coll., Oxford (Classical Scholar), 2nd Class in Greats, 1927; Asst Master at St Paul's Sch., 1927-37; House Master, 1930-37; Headmaster of King's Sch., Bruton, Som., 1937-46, Governor, 1949-; representative of British Council in Switzerland, 1946-48; Headmaster, St Dunstan's, Burnham-on-Sea, 1948-66. Vice-Chm., Incorporated Assoc. of Preparatory Schs, 1957. *Publications:* (Lands and Peoples Series) Switzerland; Italy; Spain; Morocco; Looking at Italy; Looking at Spain. *Recreations:* mountaineering, travel. *Address:* Quantocks, Burnham on Sea, Som. *Clubs:* MCC, I Zingari, Free Foresters, Alpine; Vincent's, Authentics (Oxford).

MARTIN, Samuel Frederick Radcliffe, CB 1979; Legal Adviser to Examiner of Statutory Rules, Northern Ireland, 1979-81; *b* 2 May 1918; 2nd *s* of late William and Margaret Martin; *m* 1947, Sarah, *y d* of late Rev. Joseph and Margaret McKane; three *s*. *Educ:* Royal Belfast Academical Instn; Queen's Univ., Belfast (LLB). Called to Bar, Gray's Inn, 1950. Examr, Estate Duty Office, NI, 1939; Professional Asst, Office of Parly Draftsmen, 1956; First Legislative Draftsman, 1973-79. Northern Ireland Editor, Current Law. *Publications:* articles in NI Legal Qly and Gazette of Incorp. Law Soc. *Recreation:* golf. *Address:* Brynburn, 114 Upper Road, Greenisland, Co. Antrim. *T:* Whiteabbey 62417.

MARTIN, Sir Sidney (Launcelot), Kt 1979; FRSC; Pro Vice-Chancellor, University of the West Indies, and Principal, Cave Hill Campus, since 1964; *b* 27 Sept. 1918; *s* of Sidney A. Martin and Miriam A. Martin (*née* McIntosh); *m* 1944, Olga Brett (*née* Dolphin); three *s*. *Educ:* Wolmers Boys' Sch., Jamaica (Jamaica schol. 1937); Royal College of Science, Imperial Coll. London, 1938-42 (BScChem, ARCS, DIC; Fellow, 1981); MSc London. FRIC 1949 (ARIC 1940). Materials Research Laboratory, Phillips Electrical Ltd, Surrey, 1942; Head. Phys. Chem. Div., 1946-49; University College of the West Indies, later University of the West Indies: Lectr, 1949-52, Sen. Lectr, 1952-63, in Phys. Chem.; Warden, Taylor Hall, 1954-64; Acting Registrar, on secondment, 1961-63; Registrar, 1963-66; Principal, Cave Hill, and Pro Vice-Chancellor on secondment, 1964-66, substantively, 1966-. Chairman: Sci. Res. Council of Jamaica, 1961-64; Barbados Nat. Council for Sci. and Technology, 1977-; Member: Bd of Management, Coll. of Arts, Sci. and Technology, Jamaica, 1958-64; Educnl Adv. Cttee, Jamaica, 1960-64; Public Services Commn of Barbados, 1964-69; Bd of Management, Codrington Coll., Barbados, 1969-. Member: Faraday Soc., London, 1943-68; Chemical Soc., London, 1942-; RSA, 1972-. Queen's Silver Jubilee Medal, 1977. *Publications:* articles in various chemical and physical jls. *Recreations:* bridge, reading. *Address:* Principal's Office, University of the West Indies, Cave Hill Campus, PO Box 64, Barbados. *T:* 51310; (home) 28 Blue Waters, Christ Church, Barbados. *T:* 70784.

MARTIN, Thomas Ballantyne; *b* 1901; *s* of late Angus Martin, FRCSE, Newcastle upon Tyne, and Robina, *d* of Thomas Pringle, Middleton Hall, Wooler, Northumberland; *m* 1953, Jean Elisabeth, *e d* of Lt-Col O. D. Bennett and Audrey, *d* of Sir Hamilton Grant, 12th Bt of Dalvey; two *d*. *Educ:* Cambridge Univ. (MA). MP (C) Blaydon Div. of Co. Durham, 1931-35. Political Correspondent of Daily Telegraph, 1937-40. RAFVR; Squadron Leader, Middle East Intelligence Centre, 1940-43; Adviser on Public Relations to UK High Comr in Australia, 1943-45; Sec. of United Europe Movement, 1947-48; Sec. to British all-party delegn to Congress of Europe at The Hague. Mem., London Stock Exchange, 1949-74, retired. *Address:* Rectory Cottage, Symonsbury, Bridport, Dorset. *T:* Bridport 22781. *Clubs:* Army and Navy, Pratt's.

MARTIN, (Thomas) Geoffrey; Head of Office, Commission of the European Communities, Northern Ireland, since 1979; *b* 26 July 1940; *s* of Thomas Martin and Saidee Adelaide (*née* Day); *m* 1968, Gay (Madeleine Annesley) Brownrigg; two *d*. *Educ:* Queen's Univ., Belfast (BSc Hons). President, National Union of Students of England, Wales and Northern Ireland, 1966-68; City of London: Banking, Shipping, 1968-73; Director, Shelter, 1973-74; Diplomatic Staff, Commonwealth Secretariat, 1974-79. *Address:* Commission of the European Communities, Windsor House, Bedford Street, Belfast BT2 7EG. *T:* Belfast 40708. *Club:* Travellers'.

MARTIN, Victor Cecil, OBE; HM Diplomatic Service, retired; *b* 12 Oct. 1915; *s* of Cecil Martin and late Isabel Katherine Martin (*née* Hickman). *Educ:* Cheltenham Coll.; Jesus Coll., Cambridge (Scholar; Classical Tripos Parts 1 and 2; MA). Asst Principal, Board of Education, 1939. Served Intelligence Corps, 1940-45; Major 1944, Persia and Iraq Force. Principal, Min. of

Education, 1946; transferred to CRO, 1948; British High Commn, New Delhi, 1951-54, 1956-60; Asst Sec., CRO, 1962; Head of West Africa Dept, 1961-64; Head of S Asia Dept, 1964-66; Head of Cultural Relations Dept, 1966-68; Dep. High Comr, Madras, 1968-71; Special Adviser to High Comr, British High Commn, New Delhi, 1972-75. *Recreations:* ornithology, travel. *Address:* 76 Swan Court, Flood Street, SW3. *Clubs:* United Oxford & Cambridge University, Royal Commonwealth Society.

MARTIN, William McChesney, Jun.; Counselor, Riggs National Bank, Washington, DC, since 1970; *b* St Louis, Mo, 17 Dec. 1906; *s* of William McChesney Martin and Rebecca (*née* Woods); *m* 1942, Cynthia Davis; one *s* two *d. Educ:* Yale Univ. (BA 1928); Benton Coll. of Law, St Louis, 1931. Graduate student (part time), Columbia Univ., 1931-37. Served in bank examination dept of Federal Reserve Bank of St Louis, 1928-29; Head of statistics dept, A. G. Edwards & Sons, St Louis, 1929-31; partner, May 1931-July 1938. Mem., New York Stock Exch., June 1931-July 1938; Gov., 1935-38; Chm. Cttee on Constitution, 1937-38; Sec. Conway Cttee to reorganize the Exchange, 1937-38; Chm. Bd and Pres. pro. tem. May-June 1938; Pres. July 1938-April 1941. Asst Exec. President's Soviet Protocol Cttee and Munitions Assignments Board, Wash., DC, 1942; appointed Mem. Export-Import Bank, Nov. 1945; Chm. and Pres., 1946-49 (as Chm. of Federal Reserve Board, serves on National Advisory Council on Internat. Monetary and Financial Problems). Asst Sec. of the Treasury, Feb. 1949-April 1951; Chm., Bd of Governors, Fed. Reserve System, 1951-70; US Exec. Dir, IBRD, 1949-52. Dir of several corporations. Trustee: Berry Schs, Atlanta, Ga; Johns Hopkins Univ., Baltimore; Nat. Geographic Soc. Holds numerous Hon. Degrees from Univs in USA and Canada. Drafted, Selective Service Act, private, US Army, 1941, Sergeant, GHQ Army War Coll., 1941; Commnd 1st Lt, Inf., Feb. 1942; Captain Aug. 1942; Major, 1943; Lt-Col 1944; Col 1945. Legion of Merit, 1945. *Recreations:* tennis, squash. *Address:* 2861 Woodland Drive, NW, Washington, DC 20008, USA; (office) 800 17th Street, NW, Washington, DC 20006, USA. *Clubs:* West Side Tennis, Yale; Metropolitan, Jefferson Island, Alibi (Washington); Chevy Chase (Md).

MARTIN-BATES, James Patrick, MA; JP; FCIS; CBIM; Director: W. S. Atkins Group Ltd; Essex Holdings, since 1981; Avery's Ltd, 1970-77; Charringtons Industrial Holdings Ltd, 1972-77; Hutchinson Ltd, 1958-78; *b* 17 April 1912; *er s* of late R. Martin-Bates, JP, Perth, Scotland; *m* 1939, Clare, *d* of late Prof. James Miller, MD, DSc; one *s* two *d. Educ:* Perth Academy; Glenalmond; Worcester Coll., Oxford. BA 1933; MA 1944. Lamson Industries, 1933-36; Dorman Long & Co. Ltd, 1936-38; PE Group, 1938-61: Man. Dir, Production Engineering Ltd, 1953-59; Vice-Chm., PE Holdings, 1959-61. Principal, Administrative Staff Coll., Henley-on-Thames, 1961-72. Chm., Management Consultants Association, 1960; Member: Council, British Institute of Management, 1961-66; UK Advisory Council on Education for Management, 1961-66; Council, Glenalmond, 1963-; Bd of Visitors, HM Borstal, Huntercombe, 1964-67; The Council for Technical Education and Training for Overseas Countries, 1962-73; Council, University Coll., Nairobi, 1965-68; Council Chartered Institute of Secretaries, 1965-74; EDC for Rubber Industry, 1965-69; Council, University Coll. at Buckingham, 1977-. UN Consultant in Iran, 1977-78. High Sheriff of Buckinghamshire, 1974; Chm., Marlow Bench, 1978-. Fellow Internat. Acad. of Management, 1964. FCIS 1961; FBIM 1960. *Publications:* various articles in Management Journals. *Recreations:* golf, fishing. *Address:* Ivy Cottage, Fingest, near Henley-on-Thames, Oxon RG9 6QD. *T:* Turville Heath 202. *Clubs:* Caledonian; Leander; Royal and Ancient (St Andrews).

MARTIN-BIRD, Col Sir Richard Dawnay, Kt 1975; CBE 1971 (OBE (mil.) 1953); TD 1950; DL; Chairman and Joint Managing Director, Yates Brothers Wine Lodges Ltd, Manchester; *b* 19 July 1910; *s* of late Richard Martin Bird and Mildred, 2nd *d* of late Peter Peel Yates; *m* 1935, Katharine Blanche, *d* of Sir Arthur Selborne Jelf, CMG; one *s* three *d* (and one *s* decd). *Educ:* Charterhouse. Served with 8th (Ardwick) Bn, The Manchester Regt (TA), 1936-53; war service 1939-45; Lt-Col comdg, 1947-53; Hon. Col, 1953-67; Hon. Col, The Manchester Regt (Ardwick and Ashton) Territorials, 1967-71; Dep. Comdr, 127 Inf. Bde (TA), 1953-57 and 1959-63; Regtl Councillor, The King's Regt, 1967-; ADC (TA) to the Queen, 1961-65; Chairman: E Lancs T&AFA, 1963-68; TA&VRA for Lancs, Cheshire and IoM, later TA&VRA for NW England and IoM, 1968-75; Vice-Chm., Council, TA&AVR Assocs, 1973-75; Mem., TAVR Adv. Cttee, 1973-75. Pres., Wine and Spirit Assoc. of GB, 1978-79. DL Lancs 1964-74, Cheshire 1974; High Sheriff Greater Manchester, 1976-82. *Address:* Stockinwood, Chelford, Cheshire SK11 9BE. *T:* Chelford 523. *Clubs:* Army and Navy; St James's (Manchester); Winckley (Preston).

MARTIN-JENKINS, Christopher Dennis Alexander; Editor, The Cricketer International, since 1981; BBC radio and television commentator on cricket; *b* 20 Jan. 1945; *s* of Dennis Frederick Martin-Jenkins, qv; *m* 1971, Judith Oswald Hayman; two *s* one *d. Educ:* Marlborough; Fitzwilliam Coll., Cambridge (BA (Modern Hist.); MA). Dep. Editor, The Cricketer, 1967-70; Sports Broadcaster, 1970-73, Cricket Correspondent, 1973-80, BBC. *Publications:* Testing Time, 1974; Assault on the Ashes, 1975; MCC in India, 1977; The Jubilee Tests and the Packer Revolution, 1977; In Defence of the Ashes, 1979; Cricket Contest, 1980; The Complete Who's Who of Test Cricketers, 1980; The Wisden Book of County Cricket, 1981; Bedside Cricket, 1981. *Recreations:* cricket, Rugby fives, tennis, golf, gardening, walking, after-dinner speaking. *Address:* Little Swains, Tismans Common, Rudgwick, West Sussex. *T:* Rudgwick 2625; (office) Redhill 72217. *Clubs:*

Eccentric, MCC; I Zingari, Free Foresters, Arabs, Marlborough Blues, Cranleigh Cricket, Albury Cricket, Rudgwick Cricket.

MARTIN-JENKINS, Dennis Frederick, TD 1945; Chairman, Ellerman Lines Ltd, 1967-81 (Managing Director, 1967-76); chairman or director of many other companies; *b* 7 Jan. 1911; 2nd *s* of late Frederick Martin-Jenkins, CA and late Martha Magdalene Martin-Jenkins (*née* Almeida); *m* 1937, Rosemary Clare Walker, MRCS, LRCP; three *s. Educ:* St Bede's Sch., Eastbourne; Marlborough College. FCIT. Served RA, 1939-45 (Lt-Col). Insce, 1930-35; joined Montgomerie & Workman Ltd, 1935; transf. City Line Ltd, 1938; transf. Hall Line Ltd, 1947 (Dir 1949); Dir, Ellerman Lines Ltd and associated cos, 1950. Chamber of Shipping of UK: Mem. 1956 (now Hon. Mem.); Vice-Pres. 1964; Pres. 1965; Chm., Deep Sea Liner Section, 1969; Chairman: Gen. Council of British Shipping for UK, 1963 (Hon. Mem.); Internat. Chamber of Shipping, 1971-77; Past Chm., London Gen. Shipowners' Soc.; formerly Member: Mersey Docks and Harbour Bd; Bd of PLA; Nat. Dock Labour Bd; Exec. Cttee, Nat. Assoc. of Port Employers; Mem., British Transport Docks Bd, 1968-81. *Recreations:* golf, gardening. *Address:* Wragmoor, Bantham, Kingsbridge, S Devon TQ7 3AJ. *T:* Thurlestone 763. *Clubs:* United Oxford & Cambridge University; Royal and Ancient Golf, Woking Golf, Royal Cinque Ports Golf, Surrey County Cricket.

See also C. D. A. Martin-Jenkins.

MARTINDALE, Air Vice-Marshal Alan Rawes; Director General of Supply (RAF), since 1982; *b* 20 Jan. 1930; *s* of late Norman Martindale and Edith (*née* Rawes); *m* 1952, Eileen Alma Wrenn; three *d. Educ:* Kendal Grammar Sch.; University Coll., Leicester (BA History, London Univ., 1950). Commissioned RAF, 1951; served, 1951-71: RAF Driffield, Oakington, Eindhoven, Stafford, Wickenby, Faldingworth and Marham; Instructor, RAF Coll., Cranwell; Staff AHQ Malta; RAF Staff Coll., Bracknell, MoD, Jt Services Staff Coll. (student and Directing Staff), and HQ Maintenance Comd; Dep. Dir of Supply Management, MoD, Harrogate, 1971-72; Comd Supply Officer, RAF Germany, 1972-74; Dir of Supply Management, MoD, Harrogate, 1974-75; RCDS, 1976; Air Cdre Supply and Movements, RAF Support Comd, 1977; Dep. Gen. Man., NAMMA, 1978-81; Dir of Supply Policy (RAF), MoD, 1981-82. *Recreations:* shooting, gardening, mountain walking, squash. *Address:* Taylors Cottage, Mountfield, Robertsbridge, East Sussex TN32 5JZ. *Club:* Royal Air Force.

MARTINEAU, Charles Herman; Chairman, Electricity Consultative Council for South of Scotland, 1972-76; *b* 3 Sept. 1908; *s* of Prof. Charles E. Martineau, Birmingham; *m* 1939, Margaret Shirley Dolphin; two *s* one *d. Educ:* King Edward's Sch., Birmingham. Jas Williamson & Son Ltd, Lancaster and Nairn-Williamson Ltd, Kirkcaldy: Man. Dir, 1952-66. Part-time Mem., S of Scotland Electricity Bd, 1971-76. Mem., Fife CC, 1967 (Vice-Convener, 1970-73); Mem., Fife Regional Council, 1978-82. *Recreations:* chess, golf. *Address:* Gladsmuir, Hepburn Gardens, St Andrews, Fife. *T:* St Andrews 73069. *Club:* Royal and Ancient (St Andrews).

See also Rt Rev. R. A. S. Martineau.

MARTINEAU, Rt. Rev. Robert Arnold Schürhoff, MA; *b* 22 Aug. 1913; *s* of late Prof. C. E. Martineau, MA, MCom, FCA, and Mrs Martineau, Birmingham; *m* 1941, Elinor Gertrude Ap-Thomas; one *s* two *d. Educ:* King Edward's Sch., Birmingham; Trinity Hall, Cambridge; Westcott House, Cambridge. Tyson Medal for Astronomy, 1935. Deacon 1938, priest 1939; Curate, Melksham, 1938-41. Chaplain: RAFVR, 1941-46; RAuxAF, 1947-52. Vicar: Ovenden, Halifax, 1946-52; Allerton, Liverpool, 1952-66; St Christopher, San Lorenzo, Calif, 1961-62. Hon. Canon of Liverpool, 1961-66; Rural Dean of Childwall, 1964-66. Proctor in Convocation, 1964-66. Bishop Suffragan of Huntingdon, 1966-72; Residentiary Canon of Ely, 1966-72; Bishop of Blackburn, 1972-81. First Jt Chm., C of E Bd of Educn and Nat. Soc. for Promoting Religious Educn, 1973-79. Chm., Central Readers Bd, C of E, 1971-76. *Publications:* The Church in Germany in Prayer (ed jtly), 1937; Rhodesian Wild Flowers, 1953; The Office and Work of a Reader, 1970; The Office and Work of a Priest, 1972; Moments that Matter, 1976; Preaching through the Christian Year; Truths that Endure, 1977; Travelling with Christ, 1981. *Recreations:* gardening, swimming. *Address:* Gwenallt, Park Street, Denbigh, Clwyd LL16 3DB.

See also C. H. Martineau.

MARTINEZ ZUVIRIA, Gen. Gustavo; historian; Argentine Ambassador to the Court of St James's, 1970-74; *b* 28 Dec. 1915; *s* of Dr Gustavo Martinez Zuviria and Matilde de Iriondo de Martinez Zuviria; *m* 1940, Maria Eugenia Ferrer Deheza; five *s* four *d* (and one *s* decd). *Educ:* Col. El Salvador, Buenos Aires; Mount St Mary's Coll. (Nr Sheffield); San Martin Mil. Academy. Promoted to 2nd Lt, 1938; Capt. 1951. He participated in attempt to overthrow the Peron regime; imprisoned, but when Peron was overthrown, he continued career in Army; among other posts he served in: Cavalry Regt No 12, 1940; Granaderos a Caballo, 1944; Cavalry Regt No 7, 1945; Military Sch.: Instr of cadets, 1944; Asst Dir and Dir of Sch., 1958. Mil. Attaché to Peru, 1955; Chief of 3rd Regt of Cavalry, 1957; Chief of Staff, Argentine Cav. Corps, 1961; Dir, in Superior War Staff Coll., 1962; Dir, Sch. of Cav. and Cav. Inspector, 1963; Comdr, 2nd Cav. Div., 1964; 2nd Comdr, 3rd Army Corps, 1965; Comdr, 1st Army Corps, 1966; Comdr, Southern Joint Forces, 1969; retd from Army and was designated Sec. of State in Intelligence (Secretario de Informaciones de Estado), in 1970. Presidente dela Comisión de Caballería, 1974-76. Member: Genealogical Studies Centre, 1962; Nat.

Sanmartinian Historical Academy, 1966; Nat. Acad. of History, 1978. Lectured in Paris and Brussels, Feb. 1978, on bicentenary of birth of Gen. San Martíin. Holds several foreign orders. *Publications:* numerous (related to professional and historical subjects); notably Los tiempos de Mariano Necochea, 1961 (2nd edn, 1969) (1st award mil. lit. and award Fundación Eguiguren); Retreta del Desierto, 1956 (14 edns); José Pidsudski; San Martin y O'Brien, 1963; Historia de Angel Pacheco, 1969. *Recreations:* riding, shooting. *Address:* Avenida del Libertador 15249, 1640 Acassuso, Buenos Aires, Argentina. *Clubs:* Naval and Military, Travellers', Hurlingham, Turf (all in London); Cowdray Park Polo (Sussex); Circulo Militar, Jockey (Buenos Aires); Club Social de Paraná (Entre Rios).

MARTINS, (Virgilio) Armando; Teacher, Institute of Oriental Studies, University of Lisbon, since 1980; *b* 1 Sept. 1914; *s* of José Júlio Martins and Elvira Janeiro; *m* 1959, Ingrid Bloser; one *s* one *d. Educ:* Coimbra and Lisbon Univs. Degree in Law. Entered Foreign Service, 1939; Attaché, Foreign Min., Lisbon, 1941; Consul: Leopoldville, 1943; Liverpool, 1947; Sydney, 1949; special mission, NZ, 1951; First Sec., Tokyo, 1952; Brussels, 1955; Substitute of Permanent Rep. to NATO, 1956; Minister, 2nd Cl., Foreign Min., Lisbon, 1959; NATO, 1961; Ambassador to: Tokyo, 1964; Rome, 1971; the Court of St James's, 1977-79. Pres. of Foundn, Internat. Univ. of Macau, 1980-. *Publications:* books on internat. law, social questions, literary criticism, history, poetry, and the theatre. *Recreations:* oriental studies reading, writing. *Address:* 40 Avenida de Portugal, 2765 Estoril, Portugal.

MARTONMERE, 1st Baron, *cr* 1964; **John Roland Robinson,** PC 1962; GBE 1973; KCMG 1966; Kt 1954; MA, LLB; Governor and C-in-C of Bermuda, 1964-72; *b* 22 Feb. 1907; *e s* of Roland Walkden Robinson, Solicitor, Blackpool; *m* 1930, Maysie, *d* of late Clarence Warren Gasque; one *d* (one *s* decd). *Educ:* Trinity Hall, Cambridge. Barrister-at-law, 1929 (Certificate of Honour and Buchanan Prize Lincoln's Inn, 1928); MP (U) Widnes Division of Lancs, 1931-35, Blackpool, 1935-45, S Blackpool, 1945-64. W/Cdr RAFVR, 1940-45. Pres. Royal Lancs Agricultural Society, 1936; Past Pres. Assoc. of Health and Pleasure Resorts; Past Pres. Residential Hotels Assoc. of Great Britain. Past Chm. Conservative Party Commonwealth Affairs Cttee; Chm. Gen. Council, Commonwealth Parliamentary Assoc., 1961-62. Past Dep. Chm. United Kingdom Branch, Commonwealth Parliamentary Association. Hon. Freeman, Town of St George and City of Hamilton (Bermuda). Officer, Legion of Merit (USA). *Heir: g s* John Stephen Robinson, *b* 10 July 1963. *Address:* Romay House, Tuckers Town, Bermuda; El Mirador, Lyford Cay, PO Box 7776, Nassau, Bahamas. *Clubs:* Carlton; Royal Lytham and St Annes Golf (St Annes); Royal Yacht Squadron (Cowes); Lyford Cay (Bahamas); Hon. Life Member: Royal Bermuda Yacht, Mid-Ocean (Bermuda).

MARTY, Cardinal François, Chevalier de la Légion d'honneur; *b* Pachins, Aveyron, 18 May 1904; *s* of François Marty, cultivateur, and Zoé (*née* Gineste). *Educ:* Collège de Graves et Villefranche-de-Rouergue; Séminaire de Rodez; Institut Catholique de Toulouse (Dr en Th.). Priest, 1930. Vicaire: Villefranche-de-Rouergue, 1932; Rodez, 1933; Parish Priest: Bournazel, 1940; Rieupeyroux, 1943; Archpriest, Millau, 1949; Vicar-General, Rodez, 1951; Bishop of Saint Flour, 1952; Coadjutor Archbishop, 1959, and Archbishop of Reims, 1960; Archbishop of Paris, 1968-81. Cardinal, 1969. Pres., Comité Episcopal of Mission de France, 1965; Mem. Bureau, then Vice-Pres., Perm. Council of French Episcopate, 1966, and Pres., French Episcopal Conf., 1969-75, responsable des Catholiques orientaux. Member: Rome Commission for Revision of Canon Law; Congregations: Divine Worship; Clergy; Eastern Church. *Address:* Monteils, 12200 Villefranche de Rouergue, France.

MARTYN, Charles Roger Nicholas; Master of the Supreme Court, since 1973; *b* 10 Dec. 1925; *s* of Rev. Charles Martyn; *m* 1960, Helen, *d* of Frank Everson; two *s* one *d. Educ:* Charterhouse, 1939-44; Merton Coll., Oxford, 1947-49. MA (Hons) Mod. Hist. Joined Regular Army, 1944; commissioned 60th Rifles (KRRC), 1945; CMF, 1946-47; special release, 1947. Articles, 1950-52, and admitted as solicitor, 1952. Sherwood & Co., Parly Agents (Partner), 1952-59; Lee, Bolton & Lee, Westminster (Partner), 1961-73. Mem. and Dep. Chm., No 14 Legal Aid Area Cttee, 1967-73; Hon. Legal Adviser to The Samaritans (Inc), 1955-73. Chm., Family Welfare Assoc., 1973-78; Member: Gtr London Citizens' Advice Bureaux Management Cttee, 1974-79; Council, St Gabriel's Coll. (Further Education), Camberwell, 1973-77 (Vice-Chm); Goldsmiths' Coll. Delegacy, 1977-. *Recreations:* walking, sailing (Vice-Cdre, Thames Barge Sailing Club, 1962-65), observing people, do-it-yourself, nigrology. *Address:* 29 St Albans Road, NW5 1RG. *T:* 01-267 1076.

MARTYN, Joan, OBE 1962; Governor Class II, HM Prison Commission; Governor, Bullwood Hall, 1962-64, retired; *b* 9 Aug. 1899; 3rd *d* of George Harold and Eve Martyn. *Educ:* Municipal Coll., Grimsby; Queenwood, Eastbourne; Bedford Physical Training Coll. (diploma). Staff of St Mary's Coll., Lancaster Gate, London, W2, 1919-36; staff of HM Borstal Institution, Aylesbury, 1937 (Governor 1946-59); Governor, HM Borstal, Cardiff, 1959-62. *Address:* 57 Bargate, Grimsby, S Humberside.

MARTYN-HEMPHILL, family name of **Baron Hemphill.**

MARWICK, Sir Brian (Allan), KBE 1963 (CBE 1954; OBE 1946); CMG 1958; *b* 18 June 1908; *s* of James Walter Marwick and Elizabeth Jane Flett; *m* 1934, Riva Lee, *d* of Major H. C. Cooper; two *d. Educ:* University of Cape

Town; CCC, Cambridge. Administrative Officer: Swaziland, 1925-36; Nigeria, 1937-40; Swaziland, 1941-46; First Asst Sec.: Swaziland, 1947-48; Basutoland, 1949-52; Dep. Resident Comr and Govt Sec., Basutoland, 1952-55; Administrative Sec. to High Comr for Basutoland, the Bechuanaland Protectorate and Swaziland, 1956; Resident Comr, Swaziland, 1957-63; HM Comr, Swaziland, 1963-64; Permanent Secretary: Min. of Works and Town Planning Dept, Nassau, Bahamas, 1965-68; Min. of Educn, Bahamas, 1968-71. *Publication:* The Swazi, 1940. *Recreation:* golf. *Address:* Sea Bank, Shore Road, Castletown, Isle of Man. *T:* Castletown 823782.

MARX, Enid Crystal Dorothy, RDI 1944; Painter and Designer; *b* London, 20 Oct. 1902; *y d* of Robert J. Marx. *Educ:* Roedean Sch.; Central Sch. of Arts and Crafts; Royal College of Art Painting Sch. Designing and printing handblock printed textiles, 1925-39. Exhibited in USA and Europe; various works purchased by Victoria and Albert Museum, Musée des Arts Décoratifs, Boston Museum, Scottish Arts Council, Sheffield Art Gall., etc. Mem. Society of Wood Engravers. Wood engraving and autolithography pattern papers, book jackets, book illustration and decorations, trademarks, etc; designed moquettes and posters for LPTB. Industrial designing for printed and woven furnishing fabrics, wallpapers, ceramics, plastics. Fellow, RCA, 1982; FRSA, FSIAD; original mem. National Register of Industrial Designers of Central Institute of Art and Design. Mem. of Bd of Trade design panel on utility furniture. Designed postage stamps: ½d-2d for first issue Elizabeth II; Christmas 1976 issue. Lectures on textiles and folk art. *Publications:* (jointly) English Popular and Traditional Art, 1947; (with Margaret Lambert), English Popular Art, 1951; articles and broadcasts on aspects of industrial design in various countries; author and illustrator of eleven books for children. *Recreations:* study of popular art in different countries; gardening. *Address:* The Studio, 39 Thornhill Road, Barnsbury Square, N1. *T:* 01-607 2286.

MARY LEO, Sister; *see* Niccol, Dame Sister Mary Leo.

MARY REGIS, Sister; *see* Morant, Dame Mary Maud.

MASCALL, Rev. Canon Eric Lionel, DD Oxon, DD Cantab, BSc London; FBA 1974; an Hon. Canon of Truro Cathedral, with duties of Canon Theologian, since 1973; Professor of Historical Theology, London University, at King's College, 1962-73, now Professor Emeritus; Dean, Faculty of Theology, London University, 1968-72; *b* 12 Dec. 1905; *s* of John R. S. Mascall and S. Lilian Mascall, *née* Grundy; unmarried. *Educ:* Latymer Upper Sch., Hammersmith; Pembroke Coll., Cambridge (Scholar); Theological Coll., Ely. BSc (London) 1926; BA (Wrangler) 1927, MA 1931, BD 1943, DD 1958 Cantab; DD Oxon, 1948. Sen. Maths Master, Bablake Sch., Coventry, 1928-31; ordained, 1932; Mem., Oratory of the Good Shepherd, 1938-; Asst Curate, St Andrew's, Stockwell Green, 1932-35; St Matthew's, Westminster, 1935-37; Sub-warden, Scholae Cancellarii, Lincoln, 1937-45; Lecturer in Theology, Christ Ch., Oxford, 1945-46; Student and Tutor of Christ Ch., Oxford, 1946-62, Emeritus Student, 1962-; University Lectr in Philosophy of Religion, 1947-62; Chaplain at Oxford to Bishop of Derby, 1947-48; Commissary to Archbishop of Cape Town, 1964-73; Examining Chaplain to: Bishop of Willesden, 1970-73; Bishop of Truro, 1973-81; Bishop of London, 1981-. Visiting Professor: Gregorian Univ., Rome, 1976; Pontifical Coll. Josephinum, Columbus, Ohio, 1977; Lectures: Bampton, Oxford, 1956; Bampton, Columbia, 1958; Boyle, 1965-66; Charles A. Hart Memorial, Cath. Univ. of America, Washington, DC, 1968; Gifford, Univ. of Edinburgh, 1970-71. FKC, 1968-. Hon. DD St Andrews, 1967. *Publications:* Death or Dogma, 1937; A Guide to Mount Carmel, 1939; Man, his Origin and Destiny, 1940; The God-Man, 1940; He Who Is, 1943 (rev. edn 1966); Christ, the Christian and the Church, 1946; Existence and Analogy, 1949; Corpus Christi, 1953 (rev. edn 1965). Christian Theology and Natural Science, 1956; Via Media, 1956; Words and Images, 1957; The Recovery of Unity, 1958; The Importance of Being Human, 1958; Pi in the High, 1959; Grace and Glory, 1961; Theology and History (Inaugural Lecture), 1962; Theology and Images, 1963; Up and Down in Adria, 1963; The Secularisation of Christianity, 1965; The Christian Universe, 1966; Theology and The Future, 1968; (jt author) Growing into Union, 1970; The Openness of Being, 1971; Nature and Supernature, 1976; Theology and the Gospel of Christ, 1977; Whatever Happened to the Human Mind, 1980; Editor: The Church of God, 1934; The Mother of God, 1949; The Angels of Light and the Powers of Darkness, 1954; The Blessed Virgin Mary, 1963; (contrib.) Man, Woman and Priesthood, 1978. *Address:* 30 Bourne Street, SW1W 8JJ. *T:* 01-730 2423. *Club:* Athenæum.

MASCHLER, Thomas Michael; Chairman of Jonathan Cape Ltd, since 1970; *b* 16 Aug. 1933; *s* of Kurt Leo Maschler and of Rita Masseron (*née* Lechner); *m* 1970, Fay Coventry; one *s* two *d. Educ:* Leighton Park School. Production Asst, Andre Deutsch, 1955; Editor, MacGibbon & Kee, 1956-58; Fiction Editor, Penguin Books, 1958-60; Jonathan Cape: Editorial Dir, 1960; Man. Dir, 1966. Exec. Producer, The French Lieutenant's Woman (film), 1981. *Publications:* (ed) Declarations, 1957; (ed) New English Dramatists Series, 1959-63. *Address:* 15 Chalcot Gardens, NW3.

MASEFIELD, John Thorold; HM Diplomatic Service; Head of Personnel Services Department, Foreign and Commonwealth Office, since 1982; *b* 1 Oct. 1939; *e s* of Dr Geoffrey Bussell Masefield, DSc and Mildred Joy Thorold Masefield (*née* Rogers); *m* 1962, Jennifer Mary, *d* of Rev. Dr H. C. Trowell, OBE and K. M. Trowell, MBE; two *s* one *d* (and one *d* decd). *Educ:* Dragon Sch., Oxford; Repton Sch.; St John's Coll., Cambridge (Scholar) (MA).

Joined CRO, 1962; Private Sec. to Permanent Under Sec., 1963–64; Second Secretary: Kuala Lumpur, 1964–65; Warsaw, 1966–67; FCO, 1967–69; First Sec., UK Delegn to Disarmament Conf., 1970–74; Dep. Head, Planning Staff, FCO, 1974–77; Far Eastern Dept, FCO, 1977–79; Counsellor, Head of Chancery and Consul Gen., Islamabad, 1979–82. *Recreations:* fruit and vegetables. *Address:* c/o Foreign and Commonwealth Office, SW1A 2AH. *Club:* Royal Commonwealth Society.

MASEFIELD, Sir Peter (Gordon), Kt 1972; MA Cantab; CEng; Hon. FRAeS; FCIT; CIMechE; Chairman, Project Management Ltd, since 1972; Joint Deputy Chairman, Caledonian Airways Group, since 1978; Director: Worldwide Estates Ltd, since 1972; Nationwide Building Society, since 1973; Worldwide Properties Ltd; Caledonian Airways, since 1975; *b* Trentham, Staffs, 19 March 1914; *e s* of late Dr W. Gordon Masefield, CBE, MRCS, and Marian A. Masefield (*née* Lloyd-Owen); *m* 1936, Patricia Doreen, 3rd *d* of late Percy H. Rooney, Wallington, Surrey; three *s* one *d*. *Educ:* Westminster Sch.; Chillon Coll., Switzerland; Jesus Coll., Cambridge (BA (Eng) 1935). On Design Staff, The Fairey Aviation Co. Ltd, 1935–37; Pilot's licence, 1937–70; joined The Aeroplane newspaper, 1937, Technical Editor, 1939–43; Air Correspondent Sunday Times, 1940–43; War Corresp. with RAF and US Army Eighth Air Force on active service, 1939–43; Editor, The Aeroplane Spotter, 1941–43; Chm. Editorial Cttee, The Inter-Services Journal on Aircraft Recognition, MAP, 1942–45; Personal Adviser to the Lord Privy Seal (Lord Beaverbrook) and Sec. of War Cabinet Cttee on Post War Civil Air Transport, 1943–45; first British Civil Air Attaché, British Embassy, Washington, DC, 1945–46 (Signator to Anglo-American Bermuda Air Agreement, 1946); Dir-Gen. of Long Term Planning and Projects, Ministry of Civil Aviation, 1946–48; Chief Executive and Mem. of Board of BEA, 1949–55; Managing Dir, Bristol Aircraft Ltd, 1956–60; Man. Dir, Beagle Aircraft Ltd, 1960–67, Chm., 1968–70; Dir, Beagle Aviation Finance Ltd, 1962–71. Chm., British Airports Authority, 1965–71. Chm., Nat. Jt Council for Civil Air Transport, 1950–51; Member: Cairns Cttee on Aircraft Accident Investigation, 1960; Min. of Aviation Advisory Cttees on Civil Aircraft Control and on Private and Club Flying and Gliding; Aeronautical Research Council, 1958–61; LTE, 1973–82 (Chm., 1980–81). Mem., Cambridge Univ. Appointments Bd, 1956–69. Director, Pressed Steel Co. Ltd, 1960–68. RAeS: Chm., Graduates and Students Sect., 1937–39; Mem. Council, 1945–65; Pres., 1959–60; British Commonwealth and Empire Lectr, 1948; RAeS/AFITA Bleriot Meml Lectr, 1966; Pres., Inst. Transport, 1955–56 (Brancker Meml Lectr, 1951, 1967); President: Inst. of Travel Managers, 1967–70; Assoc. of British Aviation Consultants; Chm., Bd of Trustees, Imperial War Museum, 1977–78; Littlewood Meml Lectr, Soc. of Automotive Engrs (USA), 1971. Mem. Council, Royal Aero Club (Chm., Aviation Cttee, 1960–65; Chm., 1968–70). Mem., HMS Belfast Trust; Chm., Bd of Governors, Reigate Grammar Sch., 1979–; Pres., IRTE, 1979–81. FRSA (Chm. Council, 1977–79; Vice-Pres., 1979–); FBIM. Hon. FAIAA; Hon. FCASI; Hon. DSc Cranfield, 1977; Hon. DTech Loughborough, 1977. Liveryman, Guild of Air Pilots and Air Navigators; Freeman, City of London. *Publications:* To Ride the Storm, 1982; articles on aviation, transport, management, and First World War. *Recreations:* reading, writing, gardening. *Address:* Rosehill, Doods Way, Reigate, Surrey RH2 0JT. *T:* Reigate 42396. *Clubs:* Athenæum, Royal Aero, Steering Wheel; National Aviation (Washington).

MASERI, Attilio, MD; FRCP; FACC; Sir John McMichael Professor of Cardiovascular Medicine, Royal Postgraduate Medical School, University of London, since 1979; *b* 12 Nov. 1935; *s* of Adriano and Antonietta Albini, Italian nobles; *m* 1960, Countess Francesca Maseri Florio di Santo Stefano; one *s*. *Educ:* Classic Lycée Cividale, Italy; Padua Univ. Med. Sch. Special beds in Cardiology, 1963, in Nuclear Medicine, 1965, Italy. Research fellow: Univ. of Pisa, 1960–65; Columbia Univ., NY, 1965–66; Johns Hopkins Univ., Baltimore, 1966–67; University of Pisa: Asst Prof., 1967–70; Prof. of Internal Medicine, 1970; Prof. of Cardiovascular Pathophysiology, 1972–79; Prof. of Medicine (Locum), 1977–79. Chevalier d'honneur et devotion, SMO Malta. *Publications:* Myocardial Blood Flow in Man, 1972; Primary and Secondary Angina, 1977; Perspectives on Coronary Care, 1979; articles in major internat. cardiological and med. jls. *Recreations:* skiing, tennis, sailing. *Address:* 51 Lennox Gardens, SW1X 0DF. *T:* 01-584 9223. *Club:* Queen's.

MASHAM OF ILTON, Baroness *cr* 1970 (Life Peer); **Susan Lilian Primrose Cunliffe-Lister (Countess of Swinton);** *b* 14 April 1935; *d* of Sir Ronald Sinclair, 8th Bt and of Reba Blair (who *m* 2nd, 1957, Lt-Col H. R. Hildreth, MBE), *d* of Anthony Inglis, MD; *m* 1959, Lord Masham (now Earl of Swinton, *qv*); one *s* one *d* (both adopted). *Educ:* Heathfield School, Ascot; London Polytechnic. Has made career in voluntary social work. Mem., Peterlee and Newton Aycliffe New Town Corp., 1974–. President: N Yorks Red Cross, 1963–; Yorks Assoc. of the Disabled, 1963–; Chm., Spinal Injuries Assoc., 1974–; Member: Yorks RHA, 1980–; Bd of Visitors, Wetherby Borstal, 1963–; Voluntere Centre, 1980–; Selection Cttee, Winston Churchill Meml Trust, 1980–; Mem. and Governor, Ditchley Foundn, 1980–. Pres., Chartered Soc. of Physiotherapists, 1975. Hon. FRCGP, 1981. Hon. MA Open Univ., 1981. *Recreations:* breeding highland ponies, swimming, table tennis, fishing. *Address:* Dykes Hill House, Masham, near Ripon, N Yorks. *T:* Ripon 89241.

See also Sir J. R. N. B. Sinclair, Bt.

MASHONALAND, Bishop of, since 1981; **Rt. Rev. Ralph Peter Hatendi;** *b* 9 April 1927; *s* of Fabian and Amelia Hatendi; *m* 1954, Jane Mary Chikumbu; two *s* three *d*. *Educ:* St Peter's Coll., Rosettenville, S Africa

(LTh). AKC. School teacher, 1952–; clergyman, 1957–; Seminary Tutor, 1968–72; Executive Secretary, 1973–75; Distribution Consultant, 1976–78; Suffragan Bishop of Mashonaland, 1979–80. *Publications:* Sex and Society, 1971; Shona Marriage and the Christian Churches, in Christianity South of the Zambezi, 1973. *Recreation:* poultry. *Address:* PO UA7, Harare, Zimbabwe. *T:* 44113. *Club:* Salisbury (Zimbabwe).

MASLIN, David Michael E.; *see* Eckersley-Maslin.

MASON, family name of **Baron Blackford.**

MASON, Ailsa Mary; *see* Garland, A. M.

MASON, Alan Kenneth; HM Diplomatic Service, retired 1979; Government Secretariat, Hong Kong, since 1979; *b* 18 May 1920; *s* of Richard Mason and Mary Mason (*née* Williams); *m* 1948 (marr. diss.); two *s*; *m* 1979, Marion Basden. *Educ:* Westcliff High School. Served with British and Indian Army, India, Burma, 1940–46. Customs and Excise, 1946–48; Min. of Works, 1949–65 (Sec., Ancient Monuments Bds, 1958–63); Diplomatic Service, 1965: Head of Chancery, Jakarta, 1967–70; Dep. Defence Sec., Hong Kong, 1972–75; Consul-General, Hanover, 1975–78. *Recreations:* archæology, bird watching, Chinese porcelain, walking, bridge. *Address:* Government Secretariat, Hong Kong. *Clubs:* Royal Commonwealth Society; Hong Kong (Hong Kong).

MASON, Hon. Sir Anthony (Frank), KBE 1972 (CBE 1969); **Hon. Mr Justice Mason;** Justice, High Court of Australia, since 1972; *b* Sydney, 21 April 1925; *s* of F. M. Mason, Sydney; *m* 1950, Patricia Mary, *d* of Dr E. N. McQueen; two *s*. *Educ:* Sydney Grammar Sch.; Univ. of Sydney. BA, LLB. RAAF Flying Officer, 1944–45. Admitted to NSW Bar, 1951; QC 1964. Commonwealth Solicitor-General, 1964–69; Judge, Court of Appeal, Supreme Court of NSW, 1969–72. Vice-Chm., UN Commn on Internat. Trade Law, 1968. Mem. Council, ANU, 1969–72; Pro-Chancellor, ANU, 1972–75; Hon. LLD ANU, 1980. *Recreations:* gardening, tennis. *Address:* Judges' Chambers, High Court of Australia, Parkes, ACT 2600, Australia.

MASON, Arthur Malcolm; Director, Reckitt & Colman Ltd, 1958–79 (Chairman, 1970–77); *b* 19 Dec. 1915; British parents; *m* 1938, Mary Hall (*d* 1981); one *s* (one *d* decd). *Educ:* Linton House, London; Blundells School. Trainee, Unilever Ltd, 1934–38; Chiswick Products Ltd: Asst Sales Man., 1938; Sales and Advertising Man., 1939; Dir, 1943; Chm., 1957; Reckitt & Colman Holdings Ltd: Assoc. Dir, 1957; Dir, 1958; Vice-Chm., 1965–70. FInstD. OStJ 1975. *Recreations:* sailing, sea fishing, gardening. *Address:* Flat 7, Pinecroft, St George's Road, Weybridge KT13 0EN. *T:* Weybridge 48690. *Clubs:* Seaview Yacht, Brading Haven Yacht.

MASON, Sir (Basil) John, Kt 1979; CB 1973; FRS 1965; DSc (London); Director-General of the Meteorological Office since 1965; Pro-Chancellor, University of Surrey, since 1979; *b* 18 Aug. 1923; *s* of late John Robert and Olive Mason, Docking, Norfolk; *m* 1948, Doreen Sheila Jones; two *s*. *Educ:* Fakenham Grammar Sch.; University Coll., Nottingham. Commissioned, Radar Branch RAF, 1944–46. BSc 1st Cl. Hons Physics (London), 1947, MSc 1948; DSc (London) 1956. Shirley Res. Fellow, Univ. of Nottingham, 1947; Asst Lectr in Meteorology, 1948, Lectr, 1949, Imperial Coll.; Warren Res. Fellow, Royal Society, 1957; Vis. Prof. of Meteorology, Univ. of Calif, 1959–60; Prof. of Cloud Physics, Imperial Coll. of Science and Technology (Univ. of London), 1961–65. Hon. Gen. Sec. British Assoc., 1965–70; President: Physics Section, British Assoc., 1965; Royal Meteorol. Soc., 1968–70; Inst. of Physics, 1976–78; a Vice-Pres., and Treasurer, Royal Soc., 1976–. UK Perm. Rep., World Meteorological Orgn, 1965– (Mem. Exec. Cttee, 1966–75 and 1977–). Chm. Council, Surrey Univ., 1970–75. Lectures: James Forrest, ICE, 1967; Kelvin, IEE, 1968; Dalton, RIC, 1968; Bakerian, Royal Soc., 1971; Hugh MacMillan, IES, 1975; Symons, Royal Meteorol. Soc., 1976; Halley, Oxford, 1977. Hon. Fellow: Imperial Coll. of Science and Technology, 1974; UMIST, 1979. Hon. DSc: Nottingham, 1966; Durham, 1970; Strathclyde, 1975; City, 1980. Hugh Robert Mill Medal, Royal Meteorol. Soc., 1959; Charles Chree Medal and Prize, Inst. Physics and Phys. Soc., 1965; Rumford Medal, Royal Soc., 1972; Glazebrook Medal, Inst. Physics, 1974; Symons Meml Gold Medal, Royal Meteorol. Soc., 1975. *Publications:* The Physics of Clouds, 1957, 2nd edn 1971; Clouds, Rain and Rain-Making, 1962, 2nd edn 1975; papers in physics and meteorological journals. *Recreations:* foreign travel, music. *Address:* 64 Christchurch Road, East Sheen, SW14 7AW. *T:* 01-876 2557.

MASON, Brewster; actor; Associate Artist, Royal Shakespeare Company, since 1965; lectures on Drama and Acting at the University of California (Irvine); *b* Kidsgrove, Staffs, 30 Aug. 1922; *s* of Jesse Mason and Constance May Kemp; *m* 1st, 1948, Lorna Whittaker (marr. diss.); one *d*; 2nd, 1966, Kate Meredith. *Educ:* privately; Royal Naval Colls; RADA (Bancroft Gold Medal); Guildhall Sch. of Music and Drama (Hons. Grad.). First appeared as a professional actor at Lyric, Hammersmith, as Flt/Sgt John Nabb in An English Summer, Sept. 1948, followed by London appearances to 1960; took over part of Gen. Allenby in Ross, Haymarket, 1960. First appearance in New York, at Henry Miller Theatre, Sept. 1962, as Sir Lewis Eliot in The Affair. Joined RSC, Aldwych, London, Feb. 1963, to play Kent in King Lear, subseq. appearing at Royal Shakespeare, Stratford, July 1963, as Earl of Warwick in trilogy The Wars of the Roses; since 1963 has appeared in repertory at Stratford and Aldwych, in productions including The Birthday Party, 1964; Hamlet, 1965; Macbeth, All's Well that Ends Well, 1967; Julius Caesar, Merry

Wives of Windsor, 1968; Major Barbara, King Henry VIII, 1970; Othello in Othello, 1972; Falstaff in Henry IV and Merry Wives of Windsor, 1975. Director, Shakespeare Festivals in New England. *Films include:* The Dam Busters, Private Potter, etc. *TV:* first appeared on television, 1953, subseq. playing leading parts, including: Abel Wharton in The Palliers, 1974; Mr Voysey in The Voysey Inheritance, 1979. FGSM 1976. *Recreations:* golf, painting. *Address:* The White House, Tredington, Shipston-on-Stour, Warwicks. *T:* Shipston-on-Stour 61280. *Clubs:* Garrick, Naval; Stage Golfing; Players (New York).

MASON, Sir Dan (Hurdis), Kt 1961; OBE 1940; ERD 1956; *b* 24 July 1911; *e s* of late Charles Mason; *m* 1933, Joyce Louise, *d* of late Horace Young Nutt, Radlett, Herts; three *s* one *d. Educ:* Blundell's; Germany. Chm., West London Hospital, 1947-48; Governor, West London Hosp. Med. Sch., 1947-62; Chm., West London Hosp. Med. Trust, 1962-; Chm., Horsham Conservative Assoc., 1951-58; Sussex Conservative Council, 1955-58; Chm., SE Area of Conservative Nat. Union, 1957-62; Chm., Nat. Union of Conservative Assocs, 1966; Mem., Nat. Exec. Cttee of Conservative Party, 1956-78; Hon. Treas., Nat. Florence Nightingale Meml Cttee, 1956-66; Dep. Pres. 1966-. Served War of 1939-45, Royal Engineers (Supplementary Reserve) (OBE). *Recreations:* gardening, do-it-yourself, crosswords. *Address:* Chatley House, Norton St Philip, Somerset BA3 6NP. *T:* Beckington 325. *Club:* Naval and Military.

MASON, Vice-Adm. Dennis Howard, CB 1967; CVO 1978; *b* 7 Feb. 1916; *s* of Wilfred Howard Mason, Broadwater, Ipswich, and Gladys (Mouse) Mason (*née* Teague), Trevenson, Cornwall; *m* 1940, Patricia D. M. (*née* Hood); three *d. Educ:* Royal Naval Coll., Dartmouth. Served War of 1939-45, Coastal Forces, Frigates and Destroyers; Comdr 1951; Captain 1956; Senior Naval Officer, Northern Ireland, 1961-63; Dir RN Tactical Sch., 1964-65; Rear-Adm. 1965; Chief of Staff to Commander, Far East Fleet, 1965-67; Vice-Adm. 1968; Comdt, Jt Services Staff Coll., 1968-70, retired 1970. ADC 1964. With Paper and Paper Products Industry Training Bd, 1971-72; Warden, St George's House, Windsor Castle, 1972-77. Mem., East Hants DC, 1979-. *Recreations:* shooting, fishing, gardening. *Address:* Church Cottage, East Meon, Hants. *T:* East Meon 466.

MASON, Vice-Adm. Sir Frank (Trowbridge), KCB 1955 (CB 1953); Hon. FIMechE; FIMarE; retired; Member of Council for Scientific and Industrial Research, 1958-63 (Vice-Chairman, 1962); *b* 25 April 1900; *s* of late F. J. Mason, MBE, JP; *m* 1924, Dora Margaret Brand; one *s* two *d. Educ:* Ipswich Sch. RNC, Keyham, 1918; RN Coll., Greenwich, 1921-22; RN Engineering Coll., Keyham, 1922-23; Fleet Gunnery Engineer Officer, Home Fleet, 1943-44; Chief Gunnery Engineer Officer and Dep. Dir of Naval Ordnance, 1947-48; idc 1949. Deputy Engineer-in-Chief of The Fleet, 1950-52; Staff of C-in-C The Nore, 1952-53; Commander, 1934; Captain, 1943; Rear-Adm., 1950; Vice-Adm., 1953; Engineer-in-Chief of the Fleet, 1953-57, retired. Parsons Memorial Lectr, 1956. Chm. Steering Cttee, Nat. Engineering Laboratory, 1958-69, Chm. Adv. Board, 1969, Chm. Adv. Cttee, 1973-75; Mem. Steering Cttee, Nat. Physical Laboratory, 1966-68; Chm., Froude Cttee, 1966. Mem. Council, Institution of Mechanical Engineers, 1953-57, and 1961 (Vice-Pres., 1962, Pres., 1964); Institute of Marine Engineers: Chm., Panel of Jt Nuclear Marine Propulsion, 1957; Mem. Council; 1958-60; Vice-Chm., 1961; Chm., 1962; Pres., 1967. Dep. Chm., Schools Science and Technology Cttee, 1968; Mem. Governing Body: National Council for Technological Awards, 1960-64; Royal Naval Sch., Haslemere, 1953; Ipswich Sch., 1961-72; Further Education Staff Coll., 1964-74; Navy League, 1967-75; Hurstpierpoint Coll., 1966-80; Brighton Polytechnic, 1969-73; Mem. Council and Exec. Cttee, City and Guilds of London Inst., 1968-77, Vice Chm., 1970-77, Hon. FCGI 1977. Chm., Standing Conf. on Schools Science and Technology, 1971-75, Vice-Pres., 1975. Founder Fellow, Fellowship of Engineering, 1976. Asst to Court, Worshipful Co. of Shipwrights. Mem. Smeatonian Soc. of Civil Engineers (Pres., 1977); Hon. MIPlantE. High Steward of Ipswich, 1967 (life appointment). *Address:* Townfield House, 114 High Street, Hurstpierpoint, Sussex. *T:* Hurstpierpoint 833375. *Club:* Naval.

See also Ven. R. J. Mason.

MASON, Sir Frederick (Cecil), KCVO 1968; CMG 1960; HM Diplomatic Service, retired; Director, New Court Natural Resources Ltd, since 1973; *b* 15 May 1913; *s* of late Ernest Mason and Sophia Charlotte Mason (*née* Dodson); *m* 1941, Karen Rørholm; two *s* one *d* (and two *d* decd). *Educ:* City of London Sch.; St Catharine's Coll., Cambridge. Vice-Consul: Antwerp, 1935-36; Paris, 1936-37; Leopoldville, 1937-39; Elisabethville, 1939-40; Consul at Thorshavn during British occupation of Faroes, 1940-42; Consul, Colon, Panama, 1943-45; First Sec., British Embassy, Santiago, Chile, 1946-48; First Sec. (Information), Oslo, 1948-50; Asst Labour Adviser, FO, 1950-53; First Sec. (Commercial), UK High Commission, Bonn, 1954-55; Counsellor (Commercial), HM Embassy, Athens, 1955-56; Counsellor (Economic), HM Embassy, Tehran, 1957-60; Head of Economic Relations Dept, Foreign Office, 1960-64; Under-Sec., Ministry of Overseas Development, 1965, and CRO, 1966; Ambassador to Chile, 1966-70; Under-Sec. of State, FCO, Oct. 1970-Apr. 1971; Ambassador and Perm. UK Rep. to UN and other Internat. Orgns, Geneva, 1971-73. British Mem., Internat. Narcotics Control Bd, Geneva, 1974-77. Chm., Anglo-Chilean Soc., 1978-82. Grand Cross, Chilean Order of Merit Bernardo O'Higgins, 1968. *Recreations:* ball games, walking, painting. *Address:* The Forge, Ropley, Hants. *T:* Ropley 2285. *Club:* Canning.

MASON, (George Frederick) Peter, QC 1963; **His Honour Judge Mason;** a Circuit Judge, since 1970; *b* 11 Dec. 1921; *s* of George Samuel and Florence May Mason, Keighley, Yorks; *m* 1st, 1950 (marr. diss. 1977); two *s* two *d* (and one *d* decd); 2nd, 1981, Sara, *er d* of Sir Robert Ricketts, Bt, *qv. Educ:* Lancaster Royal Grammar Sch.; St Catharine's Coll., Cambridge. Open Exhibnr St Catharine's Coll., 1940. Served with 78th Medium Regt RA (Duke of Lancaster's Own Yeo.) in Middle East and Italy, 1941-45, latterly as Staff Capt. RA, HQ 13 Corps. History Tripos Pt 1, 1st cl. hons with distinction, 1946; called to Bar, Lincoln's Inn, 1947; MA 1948; Cholmeley Schol., 1949. Asst Recorder of Huddersfield, 1961; Dep. Chairman: Agricultural Land Tribunal, W Yorks and Lancs, 1962; West Riding of Yorks Quarter Sessions, 1965-67; Recorder of York, 1965-67; Dep. Chm., Inner London QS, 1970; Dep. Chm., NE London QS, 1970-71; Sen. Judge, Snaresbrook Crown Ct, 1972-81. Liveryman, Wax Chandlers' Co. *Recreations:* fell walking, sailing, carpentry. *Address:* Central Criminal Court, EC4. *T:* 01-248 3277. *Clubs:* Athenæum; Hawks.

MASON, James; actor; *b* 15 May 1909; *s* of late John Mason and Mabel Gaunt; *m* 1st, 1941, Pamela Kellino (marr. diss., 1965); one *s* one *d*; 2nd, 1971, Clarissa Kaye. *Educ:* Marlborough Coll.; Peterhouse, Cambridge. Début on professional stage in The Rascal, Hippodrome, Aldershot, 1931; Old Vic, 1933-34; Gate Theatre, Dublin, 1934-35. Début in Films, Late Extra, 1935. *Films include:* I Met a Murderer; Thunder Rock; The Man in Grey; Fanny by Gaslight; A Place of One's Own; They were Sisters; The Seventh Veil; The Wicked Lady; Odd Man Out; The Upturned Glass; Caught; The Reckless Moment; Pandora and the Flying Dutchman; Rommel-Desert Fox; Five Fingers; Julius Caesar; The Man Between; A Star is Born; Bigger than Life; North by North-West; Twenty Thousand Leagues under the Sea; Journey to the Center of the Earth; Touch of Larceny; Lolita; Heroes' Island; Tiara Tahiti; The Fall of the Roman Empire; The Pumpkin Eater; Lord Jim; Les Pianos Mécaniques; The Blue Max; Georgy Girl; The Deadly Affair; Duffy; Mayerling; Age of Consent; The Seagull; Spring and Port Wine; Child's Play; Last of Sheila; The Mackintosh Man; Dr Frankenstein; Cold Sweat; 11 Harrowhouse; What are Friends For; Mandingo; Left Hand of the Law; The Deal; The Schoolteacher and the Devil; Inside Out; Autobiography of a Princess; The Voyage of the Damned; Jesus of Nazareth; The Iron Cross; Fear in the City; Heaven Can Wait; The Passage; The Boys from Brazil; The Water Babies; Murder by Decree; Sidney Sheldon's Bloodline; North Sea Hijack; The Burning Man; Evil under the Sun; The Verdict; *Stage:* The Faith Healer, NY, 1979. *Publications:* (with Pamela Kellino) The Cats in Our Lives, 1949 (US); Before I Forget (autobiog.), 1981. *Recreation:* painting. *Address:* c/o Al Parker Ltd, 50 Mount Street, W1.

MASON, James Stephen; Parliamentary Counsel, since 1980; *b* 6 Feb. 1935; *s* of Albert Wesley Mason and Mabel (*née* Topham); *m* 1961, Tania Jane Moeran; one *s* two *d. Educ:* Windsor County Grammar Sch.; Univ. of Oxford (MA, BCL). Called to the Bar, Middle Temple, 1958; in practice, 1961-67; Office of Parly Counsel, 1967-. *Recreations:* reading, walking and playing the piano. *Address:* Cannon Cottage, Well Road, Hampstead, NW3. *T:* 01-435 2917. *Club:* United Oxford & Cambridge University.

MASON, Sir John; *see* Mason, Sir B. J.

MASON, Sir John (Charles Moir), KCMG 1980 (CMG 1976); HM Diplomatic Service; High Commissioner in Australia, since 1980; *b* 13 May 1927; *o s* of late Charles Moir Mason, CBE and late Madeline Mason; *m* 1954, Margaret Newton; one *s* one *d. Educ:* Manchester Grammar Sch.; Peterhouse, Cambridge. Lieut, XX Lancs Fusiliers, 1946-48; BA 1950, MA 1955, Cantab; Captain, Royal Ulster Rifles, 1950-51 (Korea); HM Foreign Service, 1952; 3rd Sec., FO, 1952-54; 2nd Sec. and Private Sec. to Ambassador, British Embassy, Rome, 1954-56; 2nd Sec., Warsaw, 1956-59; 1st Sec., FO, 1959-61; 1st Sec. (Commercial), Damascus, 1961-65; 1st Sec. and Asst Head of Dept, FO, 1965-68; Dir of Trade Develt and Dep. Consul-Gen., NY, 1968-71; Head of European Integration Dept, FCO, 1971-72; seconded as Under-Sec., ECGD, 1972-75; Asst Under-Sec. of State (Economic), FCO, 1975-76; Ambassador to Israel, 1976-80. *Address:* c/o Foreign and Commonwealth Office, SW1. *Club:* Athenæum.

MASON, Prof. John Kenyon French, CBE 1973; Regius Professor of Forensic Medicine, University of Edinburgh, since 1973; *b* 19 Dec. 1919; *s* of late Air Cdre J.M. Mason, CBE, DSC, DFC and late Alma French; *m* 1943, Elizabeth Latham (decd); two *s. Educ:* Downside Sch.; Cambridge Univ.; St Bartholomew's Hosp. MD, FRCPath, DCP, DMJ, DTM&H. Joined RAF, 1943; Dir of RAF Dept of Aviation and Forensic Pathology, 1956; retd as Group Captain, Consultant in Pathology, 1973. Pres., British Assoc. in Forensic Medicine, 1981-83. L. G. Groves Prize for Aircraft Safety, 1957; R. F. Linton Meml Prize, 1958; James Martin Award for Flight Safety, 1972; Douglas Weightman Safety Award, 1973; Swiney Prize for Jurisprudence, 1978. *Publications:* Aviation Accident Pathology, 1962; (ed) Aerospace Pathology, 1973; Forensic Medicine for Lawyers, 1978; (ed) The Pathology of Violent Injury, 1978; papers in medical jls. *Address:* Department of Forensic Medicine, Edinburgh University Medical School, Teviot Place, Edinburgh EH8 9AG. *Club:* Royal Air Force.

MASON, Rt. Rev. Kenneth Bruce; *see* Northern Territory, Australia, Bishop of the.

MASON, Ven. Lancelot, MA; Archdeacon of Chichester, 1946-73; Canon Residentiary of Chichester Cathedral, 1949-73, now Canon Emeritus; *b* 22 July 1905; *s* of late Canon A. J. Mason, DD; unmarried. *Educ:* RN Colls Osborne and Dartmouth; Trinity Coll., Cambridge. Deacon, 1928; Priest, 1929; Rector of Plumpton, 1938; Chaplain RNVR, 1939-46 (despatches). *Address:* The Stables, Morton Hall, Retford, Notts. *T:* Retford 705477.

MASON, Monica; Senior Principal Dancer, Royal Ballet; Assistant to the Principal Choreographer, since 1980; *b* 6 Sept. 1941; *d* of Richard Mason and Mrs E. Fabian; *m* 1968, Austin Bennett. *Educ:* Johannesburg, SA; Royal Ballet Sch., London. Joined Royal Ballet in Corps de Ballet, 1958; created role of Chosen Maiden in Rite of Spring, 1962; also created roles in: Diversions, Elite Syncopations, Electra, Manon, Romeo and Juliet, Rituals, Adieu, Isadora, The Four Seasons, The Ropes of Time. *Address:* Royal Opera House, Covent Garden, WC2.

MASON, Dr Pamela Georgina Walsh, FRCPsych; Senior Principal Medical Officer (Under Secretary), Department of Health and Social Security, since 1979; *b* 11 Nov. 1925; *d* of late Captain George Mason and Marie Louise Walsh; god-daughter and ward of late Captain William Gregory, Hon. Co. of Master Mariners; *m* 1st, 1949, David Paltenghi (*d* 1961); two *s*; 2nd, 1965, Jan Darnley-Smith. *Educ:* Christ's Hosp. Sch.; Univ. of London, Royal Free Hosp. Sch. of Medicine (MRCS, LRCP, 1949; MB, BS 1950). DPM 1957; MRCPsych 1971. Various appointments at: Royal Free Hosp., 1951-53; Maudsley Hosp. and Bethlem Royal Hosp., 1954-58; Guy's Hosp., 1958-60; Home Office, 1961-71; DHSS, 1971-. Vis. Psychiatrist, Holloway Prison, 1962-67; Adviser: C of E Children's Soc., 1962-; Royal Philanthropic Soc., 1962-; WRAF Health Educn Scheme, 1962-67. Chairman: WHO Working Gp on Youth Advisory Services, 1976; WHO Meeting of Nat. Mental Health Advrs, 1979. Member: Council of Europe Select Cttee of Experts on Alcoholism, 1976-77; Cttee of Experts on Legal Problems in the Medical Field, 1979-80. FRSocMed. *Publications:* contribs to various professional jls and Govt pubns. *Recreations:* antiquities, humanities, ballet, films, tennis, seafaring and expeditions. *Address:* Millbrook Cottage, Church Square, Shepperton, Mddx. *T:* Walton-on-Thames 23278.

MASON, Peter; *see* Mason, G. F. P.

MASON, Peter Geoffrey, MBE 1946; High Master, Manchester Grammar School, 1962-78; *b* 22 Feb. 1914; *o s* of Harry Mason, Handsworth, Birmingham; *m* 1st, 1939, Mary Evelyn Davison (marr. diss.); three *d*; 2nd, 1978, Elizabeth June Bissell. *Educ:* King Edward's Sch., Birmingham; Christ's Coll., Cambridge (Scholar). Goldsmith Exhibitioner, 1935; Porson Scholar, 1936; 1st Class, Classical Tripos, Pts 1 and 2, 1935, 1936. Sixth Form Classical Master, Cheltenham Coll., 1936-40, Rugby Sch., 1946-49; Headmaster, Aldenham Sch., 1949-61. War Service, 1940-46: commissioned into Intelligence Corps, 1940; various staff appointments including HQ 21 Army Group; later attached to a dept of the Foreign Office. Member: Advisory Cttee on Education in the Colonies, 1956; ITA Educnl Adv. Council, 1964-69; Council, University of Salford; Court, Univ. of Manchester; Court of Governors, UMIST; Council, British Volunteer Programme (Chm., 1966-74); Chairman: Council of Educn for World Citizenship; Reg. Conf. on IVS. *Publications:* articles and reviews in classical and educational journals. *Recreations:* travel, fly-fishing, walking. *Address:* Leeward, Longborough, Moreton-in-Marsh, Glos GL56 0QR. *T:* Stow-on-the-Wold 30147. *Club:* Athenæum.

MASON, Philip, CIE 1946; OBE 1942; writer; *b* 19 March 1906; *s* of Dr H. A. Mason, Duffield, Derbs; *m* 1935, Eileen Mary, *d* of Courtenay Hayes, Charmouth, Dorset; two *s* two *d. Educ:* Sedbergh; Balliol. 1st Cl. Hons Philosophy, Politics and Economics, Oxford, 1927; MA 1952; DLitt 1972. ICS: Asst Magistrate United Provinces, 1928-33; Under-Sec., Government of India, War Dept, 1933-36; Dep. Commissioner Garhwal, 1936-39; Dep. Sec. Govt of India, Defence Co-ordination and War Depts, 1939-42; Sec. Chiefs of Staff Cttee, India, and Head of Conf. Secretariat, SE Asia Command, 1942-44; represented War Dept in Central Assembly, 1946; Joint Sec. to Government of India, War Dept, 1944-47; Tutor and Governor to the Princes, Hyderabad, 1947; retd from ICS, 1947. Mem. Commn of Enquiry to examine problems of Minorities in Nigeria, 1957. Dir of Studies in Race Relations, Chatham House, 1952-58; Dir, Inst. of Race Relations, 1958-69. Chairman: National Cttee for Commonwealth Immigrants, 1964-65; Exec. Cttee, UK Council for Overseas Student Affairs, 1969-75; Trustees, S African Church Develt Trust, 1976-. Hon. Fellow, Sch. of Oriental and African Studies, 1970; Hon. DSc Bristol, 1971. *Publications:* (as Philip Woodruff) Call the Next Witness, 1945; The Wild Sweet Witch, 1947; Whatever Dies, 1948; The Sword of Northumbria, 1948; The Island of Chamba, 1950; Hernshaw Castle, 1950; Colonel of Dragoons, 1951; The Founders, 1953; The Guardians, 1954; (as Philip Mason) Racial Tension, 1954; Christianity and Race, 1956; The Birth of a Dilemma, 1958; Year of Decision, 1960; (ed) Man, Race and Darwin, 1960; Common Sense about Race, 1961; Prospero's Magic, 1962; (ed) India and Ceylon: Unity and Diversity, 1967; Patterns of Dominance, 1970; Race Relations, 1970; How People Differ, 1971; A Matter of Honour, 1974; Kipling: The Glass The Shadow and The Fire, 1975; The Dove in Harness, 1976; A Shaft of Sunlight, 1978; Skinner of Skinner's Horse, 1979; The English Gentleman, 1982. *Recreation:* living in the country. *Address:* Hither Daggons, Cripplestyle, Alderholt, near Fordingbridge, Hants. *T:* Cranborne 318. *Club:* Travellers'.

MASON, Richard; author; *b* 16 May 1919. *Educ:* Bryanston School. *Publications: novels:* The Wind Cannot Read, 1947; The Shadow and the Peak, 1949; The World of Suzie Wong, 1957; The Fever Tree, 1962. *Address:* c/o A. M. Heath & Co. Ltd, 40-42 William IV Street, WC2N 4DD.

MASON, Ven. Richard John; Archdeacon of Tonbridge, since 1977; Vicar of Edenbridge, since 1973; also Priest in Charge of Crockham Hill, since 1981; *b* 26 April 1929; *s* of Vice-Adm. Sir Frank Mason, *qv. Educ:* Shrewsbury School. Newspaper journalist, 1949-55; Lincoln Theological College, 1955-58; Asst Curate, Bishop's Hatfield, Herts, 1958-64; Domestic Chaplain to Bishop of London, 1964-69; Vicar of Riverhead with Dunton Green, Kent, 1969-73. *Address:* The Vicarage, Oakdale Lane, Crockham Hill, Edenbridge, Kent TN8 6RL. *T:* Edenbridge 866515.

MASON, Robert Whyte, CMG 1956; *b* Glasgow, 1905; *s* of William Whyte Mason and Jane Miller MacKellar Watt; *m* 1952, Monica (*d* 1975), *d* of late George H. Powell, Truro. *Educ:* Glasgow Academy; Morrison's Academy, Crieff. Served War of 1939-45, in Army, 1940-45; Lt-Col Gen. Staff, Gen. Headquarters, Middle East; seconded to Ministry of Information as Dir of Policy, Middle East Services, 1943. 1st Sec., British Embassy, Baghdad, 1945; Foreign Office, 1947-48; Political Adviser in Eritrea and Somalia, 1948; 1st Sec. and Consul, British Legation, Amman, 1949; Consul-Gen., Brazzaville, 1951, Chicago, 1954-59; Dir of Research, Librarian and Keeper of the Papers at the Foreign Office, 1960-65. *Publications:* Murder to Measure, 1934; The Slaying Squad, 1934; Courage for Sale, 1939; And the Shouting Dies, 1940; Three Cheers for Treason, 1940; Cairo Communiqué, 1942; More News from the Middle East, 1943; Arab Agent, 1944; Tandra, 1945; There is a Green Hill, 1946; Tender Leaves, 1950; No Easy Way Out, 1952; (ed) Anthony Trollope's North America, 1968. *Recreations:* golf, opera; writing thrillers. *Address:* 44 Sussex Square, Brighton BN2 1GE. *T:* 685093. *Club:* Travellers'.

MASON, Prof. Sir Ronald, KCB 1980; FRS 1975; Professor of Chemistry, University of Sussex, since 1971, Pro-Vice-Chancellor, 1977; Chief Scientific Adviser, Ministry of Defence, since 1977; *b* 22 July 1930; *o s* of David John Mason and Olwen Mason (*née* James); *m* 1952, E. Pauline Pattinson; three *d* ; *m* 1979, Elizabeth Rosemary Grey-Edwards. *Educ:* Univs of Wales and London (Fellow, University College Cardiff, 1981). Research Assoc., British Empire Cancer Campaign, 1953-61; Lectr, Imperial Coll., 1961-63; Prof. of Inorganic Chemistry, Univ. of Sheffield, 1963-71. Vis. Prof., Univs in Australia, Canada, France, Israel, NZ and US, inc. A. D. Little Prof., MIT, 1970; Univ. of California, Berkeley, 1975; Ohio State Univ., 1976; North Western Univ., 1977; Prof. associc, Univ. de Strasbourg, 1976; Erskine Vis. Prof., Christchurch, NZ, 1977; Associate Prof., Texas, 1982. SRC: Mem., 1971-75; Chm. Chemistry Cttee, 1969-72; Chm. Science Bd, 1972-75; Data Cttee, 1975; Member: Chief Scientist's Requirement Bd, DTI later Dept of Industry, 1973; BBC Adv. Group, 1975-79. Adv. Bd, Res. Councils, 1977-. Corday-Morgan Medallist, 1965, and Tilden Lectr, 1970, Chemical Society; Medal and Prize for Structural Chem., Chem. Soc., 1973. Schmidt Meml Lectr, Israel, 1977. *Publications:* (ed) Advances in Radiation Biology, 1964 (3rd edn 1969); (ed) Advances in Structure Analysis by Diffraction Methods, 1968 (6th edn 1978); (ed) Physical Processes in Radiation Biology, 1964; many papers in Jl Chem. Soc., Proc. Royal Soc., etc. *Address:* Ministry of Defence, Main Building, Whitehall, SW1A 2HB; Church Farm House, Rodbourne, St Paul Malmesbury Without, Wilts. *Club:* Athenæum.

MASON, Rt. Hon. Roy, PC 1968; MP (Lab) Barnsley since March 1953; *b* 18 April 1924; *s* of Joseph and Mary Mason; *m* 1945, Marjorie *d* of Ernest Sowden; two *d. Educ:* Carlton Junior Sch.; Royston Senior Sch.; London Sch. of Economics (TUC Scholarship). Went underground at 14 years of age, 1938-53; NUM branch official, 1947-53; mem. Yorks Miners' Council, 1949. Labour party spokesman on Defence and Post Office affairs, 1960-64; Minister of State (Shipping), Bd of Trade, 1964-67; Minister of Defence (Equipment), 1967-April 1968; Postmaster-Gen., April-June 1968; Minister of Power, 1968-69; President, Bd of Trade, 1969-70; Labour party spokesman on Civil Aviation, Shipping, Tourism, Films and Trade matters, 1970-74; Secretary of State for: Defence, 1974-76; Northern Ireland, 1976-79; opposition spokesman on agriculture, fisheries and food, 1979-81. Mem., Council of Europe and WEU, 1973. Chm., Yorkshire Gp of Labour MPs, 1972-74; Chm., Miners Gp of MPs, 1974, Vice-Chm., 1980. Consultant: Amalgamated Distilled Products, 1971-74; H. P. Bulmer, 1971-74. *Recreation:* work, provided one stays on top of it. *Address:* 12 Victoria Avenue, Barnsley, S Yorks.

MASON, Stephen Finney, FRS 1982; FRSC; Professor of Chemistry, King's College, University of London, since 1970; *b* 6 July 1923; *s* of Leonard Stephen Mason and Christine Harriet Mason; *m* 1955, Joan Banus; three *s. Educ:* Wyggeston Sch., Leicester; Wadham Coll., Oxford. MA, DPhil, DSc. Demonstrator, Mus. of Hist. of Sci., Oxford Univ., 1947-53; Research Fellow in Med. Chemistry, ANU, 1953-56; Reader in Chemical Spectroscopy, Univ. of Exeter, 1956-64; Prof. of Chemistry, Univ. of East Anglia, 1964-70. *Publications:* A History of the Sciences: main currents of scientific thought, 1953; Molecular Optical Activity and the Chiral Discriminations, 1982; articles in Jl Chem. Soc., 1945-. *Recreations:* history and philosophy of science. *Address:* Department of Chemistry, King's College, Strand, WC2R 2LS. *T:* 01-836 5454.

MASON, Stewart Carlton, CBE 1968; *b* 28 Feb. 1906; *s* of Carlton Willicomb Mason and Alys Kastor; *m* 1941, Ruth Elizabeth Wise; three *s* (and one *s* decd). *Educ:* Uppingham Sch.; Worcester Coll., Oxford (Exhibr, MA).

Asst Master: Berkhamsted Sch., 1930-31; Harrow Sch., 1931-37; HM Inspector of Schools, 1937-39 and 1944-47; seconded to Admty, 1939-44; Dir of Educn for Leics, 1947-71; Curator, Inst. of Contemporary Prints, 1972-76. Mem., Nat. Adv. Council on Art Educn, 1957-71; Chairman: Nat. Council for Diplomas in Art and Design, 1970-74 (Vice-Chm., 1961-70); Art and Design Main Cttee, CNAA, 1974-75; Trustee: Tate Gallery, 1966-73; Nat. Gallery, 1971-73; Mem. Adv. Council, Victoria and Albert Museum, 1961-73; Mem., Standing Commn on Museums and Galleries, 1973-76; Chm. of Visual Arts Panel, E Mids Arts Assoc., 1971-75 and Eastern Arts Assoc., 1972-78; Chm. Management Cttee, The Minories, Colchester, 1976-80; Mem. over many years of Councils of Univs of Leicester, Nottingham, Loughborough and RCA. Hon. DSc Loughborough, 1966; Senior Fellow, RCA (Hon. ARCA 1965). *Publication:* (ed) In Our Experience, 1970. *Address:* The Orangery, Ufford Place, Woodbridge, Suffolk. *T:* Eyke 322.

MASON, Timothy Ian Godson; Director, Scottish Arts Council, since 1980; *b* 11 March 1945; *s* of Ian Godson Mason and Muriel (*née* Vaile); *m* 1975, Marilyn Ailsa Williams; one *s* one *d*. *Educ:* St Alban's Sch., Washington, DC; Bradfield Coll., Berkshire; Christ Church, Oxford (MA). Assistant Manager, Oxford Playhouse, 1966-67; Assistant to Peter Daubeny, World Theatre Season, London, 1967-69; Administrator: Ballet Rambert, 1970-75; Royal Exchange Theatre, Manchester, 1975-77; Director, Western Australian Arts Council, 1977-80. *Recreations:* the arts, family. *Address:* 37 Park Road, Trinity, Edinburgh EH6 4LA.

MASON, Walter W.; *see* Wynne Mason.

MASON, William Ernest; Deputy Secretary (Fisheries and Food), Ministry of Agriculture, Fisheries and Food, since 1982; *b* 12 Jan. 1929; *s* of Ernest George and Agnes Margaret Mason; *m* 1959, Jean (*née* Bossley); one *s* one *d*. *Educ:* Brockley Grammar Sch.; London Sch. of Economics (BScEcon). RAF, 1947-49; Min. of Food, 1949-54; MAFF, 1954; Principal 1963; Asst Sec. 1970; Under Sec., 1975; Fisheries Sec., 1980. Member: Econ. Develt Cttee for Distrib. Trades, 1975-80; Econ. Develt Cttee for Food and Drink Manufg Inds, 1976-80. *Recreations:* music, reading, gardening. *Address:* The Haven, Fairlie Gardens, SE23 3TE. *T:* 01-699 5821. *Club:* Reform.

MASSEREENE, 13th Viscount, *cr* 1660, **AND FERRARD,** 6th Viscount, *cr* 1797; **John Clotworthy Talbot Foster Whyte-Melville Skeffington;** Baron of Loughneagh, 1660; Baron Oriel, 1790; Baron Oriel (UK), 1821; DL; *b* 23 Oct. 1914; *s* of 12th Viscount (*d* 1956) and Jean Barbara (*d* 1937), *e d* of Sir John Stirling Ainsworth, MP, JP, 1st Bt, of Ardanaiseig, Argyllshire; *S* father 1956; *m* 1939, Annabelle Kathleen, *er d* of late Mr and Mrs Henry D. Lewis, Combwell Priory, Hawkhurst, Kent; one *s* one *d*. *Educ:* Eton. Lt, Black Watch SR, 1933-36, re-employed, 1939-40 (invalided); retired; served in Small Vessels Pool, Royal Navy, 1944. Mem. IPU Delegation to Spain, 1960; Whip, Conservative Peers Cttee (IUP), House of Lords, 1958-65, Jt Dep. Chm., 1965-70; introduced in House of Lords: Deer Act, 1963; Riding Establishments Act, 1964; Export of Animals for Research Bill, 1968; Riding Establishments Act, 1970; moved debates on Overseas Information Services and other matters. Pres., Monday Club, 1981-; Member: CPA delegn to Malaŵi, 1976; Select Cttee on Anglian Water Authority Bill, 1976. Posts in Cons. Constituency organisations incl. Pres., Brighton, Kemp Town Div., Vice-Pres. and former Treasurer, Ashford Div. Chm. and Dir of companies. Driver of leading British car, Le Mans Grand Prix, 1937. One of original pioneers in commercial develt of Cape Canaveral, Florida; promoted first scheduled air service Glasgow-Oban-Isle of Mull, 1968; presented operetta Countess Maritza at Palace Theatre, London. Comr, Hunterston Ore Terminal Hearing, Glasgow, 1973. Pres., of Charitable and other organisations incl.: Ponies of Britain; Kent Hotels and Restaurants Assoc. Pres., Canterbury Br., RNLI. Former Mem., Senechal Council, Canterbury Cathedral. Chief, Scottish Clans Assoc. of London, 1974-76. Chm. Kent Branch Victoria League. Treas., Kent Assoc. of Boys' Clubs. Master, Ashford Valley Foxhounds, 1953-54; Vice-Pres., Animal Welfare Year, 1976-77. Commodore, House of Lords Yacht Club. Freeman, City of London, and Mem. Worshipful Company of Shipwrights. Gold Staff Officer, Coronation, 1953. FZS. DL Co. Antrim, 1957-. Cross of Comdr, Order of Merit, SMO Malta, 1978. *Publications:* The Lords, 1973; contributes articles to newspapers, chiefly sporting and natural history. *Recreations:* all field sports; farming; forestry; racing. *Heir:* *s* Hon. John David Clotworthy Whyte-Melville Foster Skeffington [*b* 3 June 1940; *m* 1970, Ann Denise, *er d* of late Norman Rowlandson; two *s* one *d*]. *Address:* Knock, Isle of Mull, Argyll. *T:* Aros 356; (Seat) Chilham Castle, Kent. *T:* Canterbury 730319. *Clubs:* Carlton, Turf, Pratt's, Royal Yacht Squadron.

MASSEVITCH, Prof. Alla; Vice-President of the Astronomical Council of the USSR Academy of Sciences since 1952; Professor of Astrophysics, Moscow University, since 1946; Vice-President, USSR Peace Committee, 1977; *b* Tbilisi, Georgia, USSR, 9 Oct. 1918; *m* 1942; one *d*. *Educ:* Moscow Univ. Lectured at the Royal Festival Hall, London, and at the Free Trade Hall, Manchester, etc., on The Conquest of Space, 1960; she is in charge of network of stations for tracking Sputniks, in Russia. Pres. Working Group 1 (Tracking and Telemetring) of COSPAR (Internat. Cttee for Space Research) 1961-66. Pres., Commission 35 (Internal Structure of Stars) of the Internat. Astronom. Union, 1967-70; Dep. Sec. Gen., UNISPACE 82 (UN Conf. on Exploration and Peaceful Uses of Outer Space), Vienna, 1981-83. Foreign Member: Royal Astronomical Soc., 1963; Indian Nat. Acad. of Sciences, 1979; Internat. Acad. Astronautics, 1964. Vice-Pres., Inst. for Soviet-American Relations, 1967; Mem. Board, Soviet Peace Cttee, and Internat. Peace Cttee, 1965. Internat. Award for Astronautics (Prix Galabert), 1963; Govtl decorations, USSR, Sign of Honour, 1963, Red Banner, 1975; USSR State Prize, 1975. Hon. Scientist Emeritus, 1978. *Publications:* Use of Satellite Tracking Data for Geodesy (monograph), 1980; 98 scientific papers on the internal structure of the stars, stellar evolution, and optical tracking of artificial satellites, in Russian and foreign astronomical and geophysical journals. *Address:* 48 Pjatnitskaja Street, Moscow, USSR. *T:* 2315461; 1 Vostania Square 403, Moscow. *Club:* Club for Scientists (Moscow).

MASSEY, Anna (Raymond); actress; *b* 11 Aug. 1937; *d* of Raymond Massey, *qv*, and of Adrianne Allen; *m* 1958, Jeremy Huggins (marr. diss., 1963); one *s*. *Educ:* London; New York; Switzerland; Paris; Rome. *Plays:* The Reluctant Debutante, 1955; Dear Delinquent, 1957; The Elder Statesman, 1958; Double Yolk, 1959; The Last Joke, 1960; The Miracle Worker, 1961; The School for Scandal, 1962; The Doctor's Dilemma, 1963; The Right Honourable Gentleman, 1964; The Glass Menagerie, 1965; The Prime of Miss Jean Brodie, 1966; The Flip Side, 1967; First Day of a New Season, 1967; This Space is Mine, 1969; Hamlet, 1970; Spoiled, 1971; Slag, 1971; Jingo, 1975; Play, Royal Court, 1976; The Seagull, Royal Court, 1981; *at National Theatre:* Heartbreak House, 1975; Close of Play, 1979; Summer; The Importance of Being Earnest; A Kind of Alaska, and Family Voices, in Harold Pinter trio Other Places, 1982. *Films:* Gideon's Day, 1957; Peeping Tom, 1960; Bunny Lake is Missing, 1965; The Looking Glass War, 1969; David Copperfield, 1969; De Sade, 1971; Frenzy, 1972; A Doll's House, 1973; Sweet William, 1979; The Corn is Green, 1979. Numerous appearances in TV plays. *Address:* c/o Jeremy Conway Ltd, 8 Cavendish Place, W1.

See also D. R. Massey.

MASSEY, Daniel (Raymond); actor; *b* London, 10 Oct. 1933; *s* of Raymond Massey, *qv*, and of Adrianne Allen; *m* 1st, Adrienne Corri (marr. diss.); 2nd, Penelope Alice Wilton; one *d*. *Educ:* Eton; King's Coll., Cambridge. Connaught Theatre, Worthing, 1956-57. *Plays:* The Happiest Millionaire, Cambridge, 1957; Living for Pleasure, Garrick, 1958; Make Me an Offer (musical), New, 1959; The School for Scandal, Haymarket, 1962; The Three Musketeers, and A Subject of Scandal and Concern, Nottingham, 1962; She Loves Me (musical), NY, 1963; Julius Caesar, Royal Court, 1964; A Month in the Country, and Samson Agonistes, Guildford, 1965; Barefoot in the Park, Piccadilly, 1965; The Rivals, Haymarket, 1966; The Importance of Being Earnest, Haymarket, 1967; Spoiled, Glasgow, 1970; Abelard and Heloise, Wyndham's, 1970; Three Sisters, and Trelawny of The Wells, 1971; Becket, Guildford, 1972; Popkiss, Globe, 1972; Gigi, NY, 1973; Bloomsbury, Phoenix, 1974; The Gay Lord Quex, Albery, 1975; Othello, Nottingham, 1976; Rosmersholm, Haymarket, 1977; Don Juan comes back from the War, Betrayal, Nat. Theatre, 1978; The Philanderer, Nat. Theatre, 1979; Appearances, May Fair, 1980; Man and Superman, The Mayor of Zalamea, The Hypochondriac, Nat. Theatre, 1981. *Films:* include: Girls at Sea, 1957; Upstairs and Downstairs; The Entertainer; The Queen's Guard, 1960; Go to Blazes, 1962; Moll Flanders, 1966; Star, 1968; The Incredible Sarah, 1977; The Cat and the Canary, 1978; Escape to Victory, 1981. *TV:* numerous plays. *Recreations:* golf, classical music, gardening. *Address:* c/o Leading Artists Ltd, 60 St James's Street, SW1.

MASSEY, Sir Harrie Stewart Wilson, Kt 1960; PhD Cantab; LLD Melbourne; FRS 1940; Quain Professor of Physics, University College, London, 1950-75, now Emeritus; *b* 1908; *s* of Harrie and Eleanor Massey, Melbourne, Australia; *m* Jessica, *d* of Alex and Alice Mary Barton Bruce, Western Australia; one *d*. *Educ:* University High Sch., Melbourne; Melbourne Univ. (BA, MSc, Hon. LLD, Hon. DSc); Trinity Coll., Cambridge (PhD); Aitchison Travelling Scholar, Melbourne Univ., 1929-31; Research at Cavendish Laboratory, Cambridge, 1929-33; Exhibition of 1851 Senior Research Student, 1931-33; Independent Lecturer in Mathematical Physics, Queen's Univ., Belfast, 1933-38; Goldsmid Prof. of Mathematics, University of London, University Coll., 1938-50; Vice-Provost, UCL, 1969-73, Hon. Fellow, 1976. Temp. Senior Experimental Officer, Admiralty Research Laboratory, 1940; Dep. Chief Scientist, 1941-43, Chief Scientist, 1943, Mine Design Dept, Admiralty; Technical Officer, DSIR Mission to Berkeley, Calif, 1943-45. Chm., Brit. Nat. Cttee for Space Research, 1959-; Mem. Bureau of Cttee on Space Research, 1959-78; President: European Prep. Commn for Space Research, 1960-64; Council ESRO, 1964; Chm. Council for Scientific Policy, 1965-69; Member: Adv. Council, Science Museum, 1959-61; Central Advisory Council for Science and Technology, 1967-69; Royal Commn for Exhbn of 1851, 1972-; Prov. Space Science Adv. Bd for Europe, 1974-78 (Chm. Standing Cttee on Space Research, European Science Foundn); Anglo-Australian Telescope Bd, 1975-; assessor, SRC (now SERC), 1972-. Vice-President: Atomic Scientists Assoc., 1949-53 (Pres., 1953-57); Royal Astronomical Soc., 1950-53; Royal Society, 1969-78 (Council Mem., 1949-51, 1959-60; Phys. Sec. and Vice-Pres., 1969-78); Council Mem., Physical Soc., 1949- (Pres., 1954-56, Hon. Fellow, 1976). Mem., Governing Bd, Nat. Inst. for Res. in Nuclear Sci., 1957-65; Governor: Rugby Sch., 1955-59; Chelsea Polytechnic, 1956-59. Rutherford Meml Lectr, 1967. Corr. Mem., Acad. of Sci., Liège, 1974; Aust. Acad. of Scis, 1976; Mem., Amer. Philosoph. Soc., 1975; Hon. Mem., Royal Met. Soc., 1967-. Hon. DSc: QUB, 1960; Leicester, 1964; Hull, 1968; Western Ontario, 1970; Melbourne 1974; Adelaide, 1974; Heriot-Watt, 1975; Liverpool, 1975; York, 1981; Ontario, 1981; Hon. LLD: Melbourne, 1955; Glasgow, 1962. Hughes Medal, Royal Society, 1955; Royal Medal, Royal Society, 1958; Gold Medal, RAS, 1982. *Publications:* Theory of Atomic Collisions (with N. F. Mott), 1933, 3rd edn, 1965; Negative Ions,

1938, 3rd edn, 1976; Electronic and Ionic Impact Phenomena (with E. H. S. Burhop), 1952, 2nd edn 1969; Atoms and Energy, 1953; The Upper Atmosphere (with R. L. F. Boyd), 1958; Ancillary Mathematics (with H. Kestelman), 1958; New Age in Physics, 1960; Space Physics, 1964; Atomic and Molecular Collisions, 1979; various publications on atomic physics in Proc. of Royal Society and other scientific jls. *Recreations:* cricket, tennis, billiards and snooker, badminton, travel, study of other sciences. *Address:* Kalamunda, 29 Pelhams Walk, Esher, Surrey. *Clubs:* MCC; Explorers' (New York); Melbourne Cricket.

MASSEY, Raymond; Actor and Producer; *b* Toronto, Canada, 30 Aug. 1896; *s* of Chester D. Massey and Anna Vincent; *m* 1st, Margery Fremantle (marr. diss.); one *s*; 2nd, Adrianne Allen (marr. diss.); one *s* one *d*; 3rd, 1939, Dorothy (Ludington) Whitney. *Educ:* Appleby Sch., Ontario; Toronto Univ.; Balliol Coll., Oxford. Hon. DLitt Lafayette Univ. 1939; Hon. LLD Queen's Univ., Kingston, Ontario, 1949; Hon. LittD Hobart Coll., NY, 1953; Hon. Dr Fine Arts: Northwestern Univ., 1959, Ripon Coll., 1962, Wooster Coll., 1966; Hon. Dr Hum., American International Coll., 1960. Served European War, 1915-19 as Lt in Canadian Field Artillery; in France, 1916 (wounded), in USA as Instructor in Field Artillery at Yale and Princeton Univs, 1917 and in Siberia, 1918; staff of Adj.-Gen. Canadian Army, rank of Major, 1942-43; naturalized US Citizen, March 1944. First appearance on professional stage at Everyman Theatre, 1922, in In the Zone, Jonty in The Round Table, played Captain La Hire and Canon D'Estivet in Saint Joan, 1924; in 1926 with Allan Wade and George Carr, entered on management of the Everyman Theatre, producing a number of plays and taking a variety of parts; played James Bebb in At Mrs Beam's, the Khan Aghaba in The Transit of Venus, the Rev. MacMillan in An American Tragedy, Robert in Beyond the Horizon, 1926, and Reuben Manassa in the Golden Calf, 1927; Austin Lowe in The Second Man, Joe Cobb in Spread Eagle, and Lewis Dodd in The Constant Nymph, 1928; Raymond Dabney in The Man in Possession, 1930; Randall in Late Night Final, 1931; Hamlet in the Norman Bel Geddes production at Broadhurst Theatre, New York, 1931; Smith in Never Come Back, 1932; Hugh Sebastian in The Rats of Norway; Von Hagen in the Ace, 1933; David Linden in the Shining Hour: At Booth Theatre, New York, 1934, and at St James' Theatre, 1935; Ethan in Ethan Frome, at the National Theatre, New York, 1936; at Apollo Theatre 1938, presented with Henry Sherek, Idiot's Delight, playing the part of Harry Van; Abraham Lincoln in Abe Lincoln in Illinois, Plymouth Theatre, New York, 1938-39; toured the US in this play, 1939-40; in The Doctor's Dilemma, Candida, Pygmalion, Lovers and Friends, The Father, John Brown's Body, J. B.; I Never Sang for my Father, Duke of York's, 1970; Night of the Iguana, Ahmanson Theatre, LA, 1977. Productions include: The White Chateau, The Crooked Billet, Spread Eagle, The Sacred Flame, The Stag, The Silver Tassie, Symphony in Two Flats, The Man in Possession, Lean Harvest, Late Night Final, Grand Hotel, The Rats of Norway, The Shining Hour, Idiot's Delight. Films played-in include: The Scarlet Pimpernel, The Old Dark House, Things to Come, Fire Over England, Under the Red Robe, The Prisoner of Zenda, The Hurricane, The Drum, Abe Lincoln in Illinois, Santa Fé Trail, Reap the Wild Wind, Arsenic and Old Lace, Invaders (49th Parallel), Action in the North Atlantic, The Woman in the Window, God is my Co-Pilot, Hotel Berlin, A Matter of Life and Death, Possessed, Mourning Becomes Electra, Fountainhead, David and Bathsheba, Come Fill the Cup, East of Eden, The Naked and the Dead, The Queen's Guards. Co-star, as "Dr Gillespie" in Television series Dr Kildare. Author of play, The Hanging Judge, produced New Theatre, London, 1952. *Publications:* When I was Young, 1976; A Hundred Different Lives, 1979. *Recreations:* golf, carpentry. *Address:* 913 Beverly Drive, Beverly Hills, California 90210, USA. *Clubs:* Garrick, Century (New York.)
See also Anna Massey, D. R. Massey.

MASSEY, Roy Cyril; Organist and Master of the Choristers, Hereford Cathedral, since 1974; *b* 9 May 1934; *s* of late Cyril Charles Massey and of Beatrice May Massey; *m* 1975, Ruth Carol Craddock Grove. *Educ:* Univ. of Birmingham (BMus); privately with David Willcocks. FRCO (CHM); ADCM; ARCM; FRSCM (for distinguished services to church music) 1972. Organist: St Alban's, Conybere Street, Birmingham, 1953-60; St Augustine's, Edgbaston, 1960-65; Croydon Parish Church, 1965-68; Warden, RSCM, 1965-68; Conductor, Croydon Bach Soc., 1966-68; Special Comr of RSCM, 1964-; Organist to City of Birmingham Choir, 1954-; Organist and Master of Choristers, Birmingham Cath., 1968-74; Dir of Music, King Edward's Sch., Birmingham, 1968-74. Mem. Council and Examiner, RCO, 1970-; Conductor, Hereford Choral Soc., 1974-; Conductor-in-Chief, alternate years Associate Conductor, Three Choirs Festival, 1975-; Mem., RCSM Adv. Council, 1976-; Advisor on organs to dioceses of Birmingham and Hereford, 1974-. President: Birmingham Organists' Assoc., 1970-75; Cathedral Organists' Assoc., 1982. Fellow, St Michael's Coll., Tenbury, 1976. *Recreations:* motoring, old buildings, Dutch organs. *Address:* 14 College Cloisters, Hereford HR1 2NG. *T:* Hereford 272011. *Club:* Conservative (Hereford).

MASSEY, Prof. Vincent, PhD; FRS 1977; Professor of Biological Chemistry, University of Michigan, since 1963; *b* 28 Nov. 1926; *s* of Walter Massey and Mary Ann Massey; *m* 1950, Margot Eva Ruth Grünewald; one *s* two *d. Educ:* Univ. of Sydney (BSc Hons 1947); Univ. of Cambridge (PhD 1953). Scientific Officer, CSIRO, Australia, 1947-50; Ian McMaster Scholar, Cambridge, 1950-53, ICI Fellow, 1953-55; Researcher, Henry Ford Hosp., Detroit, 1955-57; Lectr, then Sen. Lectr, Univ. of Sheffield, 1957-63. Vis. Prof., Univ. of Ill, 1960; Vis. Prof., Univ. of Konstanz, Germany, 1973-74,

Permanent Guest Prof., 1975-. *Publications:* Flavins and Flavoproteins (ed jtly), 1982; over 200 articles in scholarly jls and books. *Recreations:* walking, sailing, gardening. *Address:* Department of Biological Chemistry, University of Michigan, Ann Arbor, Mich 48109, USA. *T:* (313) 7647196.

MASSEY, William Edmund Devereux, CBE 1961; retired from HM Diplomatic Service; *b* 1901; *m* 1942, Ingrid Glad-Block, Oslo; one *d.* Entered Foreign Office, 1922; served in diplomatic and consular posts in Poland, France, Japan, Brazil, Roumania, Sweden, Luxembourg, Germany; Ambassador and Consul-General to Nicaragua, 1959-61. Hon. Consul for Nicaragua in London, 1969-79. Freeman of City of London. Representative in Sweden of Order of St John of Jerusalem, 1945-47. Chm., UK Permanent Cttee on Geographical Names for Official Use, 1965-81; UK Deleg., 2nd UN Conf. on Geographical Names, 1972. FRGS. Grand Ducal Commemorative Medal, Luxembourg, 1953. *Address:* 59 Redcliffe Gardens, SW10.

MASSIGLI, René, (Hon.) GCVO 1950; (Hon.) KBE 1938; (Hon.) CH 1954; Grand Cross, Legion of Honour, 1954; *b* 22 March 1888; *s* of late Charles Massigli and late Marguerite Michel; *m* 1932, Odette Boissier; one *d. Educ:* Ecole normale supérieure. Mem. of the Ecole Française de Rome, 1910-13; Chargé de cours at the University of Lille, 1913-14; Gen. Sec. at the Conference of Ambassadors, 1920; Maître des Requêtes at the Conseil d'Etat, 1924-28; Ministre plénipotentiaire, Head of the League of Nations' Section at the Ministry of Foreign Affairs, 1928-33; Asst Dir of Political Section at the Ministry of Foreign Affairs, 1933-37, Dir, 1937-38; Ambassador to Turkey, 1939-40; escaped from France, 1943; Commissioner for Foreign Affairs, French Cttee of National Liberation, 1943-44; French Ambassador to Great Britain, Sept. 1944-Jan. 1955; Sec.-Gen. at the Quai d'Orsay, Jan. 1955-June 1956; retired 1956. French Pres., Channel Tunnel Study Gp, 1958-69. *Publications:* Quelques Maladies de l'Etat, 1958; La Turquie devant la guerre, 1964; Une Comédie des Erreurs, 1978. *Address:* 3 avenue Robert Schuman, 75007 Paris, France.

MASSINGHAM, John Dudley; HM Diplomatic Service; Governor and Commander-in-Chief, St Helena, since 1981; *b* 1 Feb. 1930; *yr s* of Percy Massingham and Amy *(née* Sanders); *m* 1952, Jean Elizabeth Beech; two *s* two *d. Educ:* Dulwich Coll.; Magdalene Coll., Cambridge (MA); Magdalen Coll., Oxford. HM Overseas Civil Service, N Nigeria, 1954-59; BBC, 1959-64; HM Diplomatic Service, 1964-: First Secretary, CRO, 1964-66; Dep. High Comr and Head of Chancery, Freetown, 1966-70; FCO, 1970-71; seconded to Pearce Commn, Jan.-May 1972; First Sec. (Information), later Aid (Kuala Lumpur), 1972-75; First Sec. and Head of Chancery, Kinshasa, 1976-77; Chief Sec., Falkland Islands Govt, 1977-79; Consul-General, Durban, June-Dec. 1979; Counsellor (Economic and Commercial), Nairobi, 1980-81. *Recreations:* bird watching, avoiding physical exercise. *Address:* Plantation House, Island of St Helena; 34 Hall Drive, Sydenham, SE26 6XB. *T:* 01-778 9340. *Club:* Royal Commonwealth Society.

MASSY, family name of **Baron Massy.**

MASSY, 9th Baron *cr* 1776 (Ire.); **Hugh Hamon John Somerset Massy;** *b* 11 June 1921; *o s* of 8th Baron and Margaret, 2nd *d* of late Richard Leonard, Meadsbrook, Ashbourne, Co. Limerick, and *widow* of Dr Moran, Tara, Co. Meath; *S* father 1958; *m* 1943, Margaret, *d* of late John Flower, Barry, Co. Meath; four *s* one *d. Educ:* Clongowes Wood Coll.; Clayesmore Sch. Served War, 1940-45, Private, RAOC. *Heir:* s Hon. David Hamon Somerset Massy, *b* 4 March 1947.

MASSY-GREENE, Sir (John) Brian, Kt 1972; Chairman, Dunlop Olympic Ltd, since 1979 (Director since 1968; Vice-Chairman, 1977-79); *b* Tenterfield, NSW, 20 April 1916; *s* of late Sir Walter Massy-Greene, KCMG, and Lula May Lomax; *m* 1942, Margaret Elizabeth Ritchie Sharp, *d* of late Dr Walter Alexander Ramsay Sharp, OBE; two *s* two *d. Educ:* Sydney C of E Grammar Sch.; Geelong Grammar Sch.; Clare Coll., Cambridge (MA). Served War 1939-45: New Guinea, AIF, as Lieut, 1942-45. Joined Metal Manufacturers Ltd, as Staff Cadet, 1939; later transferred to their wholly-owned subsid. Austral Bronze Co. Pty Ltd; Gen. Manager, 1953-62. Managing Dir, 1962-76, and Chm., 1966-77, Consolidated Gold Fields Australia Ltd; Chairman: The Bellambi Coal Co. Ltd, 1964-72; Goldsworthy Mining Ltd, 1965-76; The Mount Lyell Mining & Railway Co. Ltd, 1964-76; Lawrenson Alumasc Holdings Ltd, 1964-73 (Dir, 1962-73); Director: Associated Minerals Consolidated Ltd, 1962-76; Commonwealth Banking Corporation, 1968- (Dep. Chm., 1975-); Commonwealth Mining Investments (Australia) Ltd, 1962-72 and 1978-; Consolidated Gold Fields Ltd, London, 1963-76; Dalgety Australia Ltd, 1967-78 (Dep. Chm., 1975-78); Zip Holdings Ltd, 1964-73; Nat. Mutual Life Assoc. Ltd, 1977-. Member: Exec. Cttee, Australian Mining Industry Council, 1967-78 (Pres. 1971); Manuf. Industries Adv. Council, 1968-77; NSW Adv. Cttee, CSIRO, 1968-75. Mem., Aust. Inst. Mining and Metallurgy. FAIM. *Recreations:* farming, fishing, flying. *Address:* 1/7 Quambi Place, Edgecliff, NSW 2027, Australia. *T:* 32-2947. *Club:* Australian.

MASTEL, Royston John, CVO 1977; CBE 1969; Assistant Commissioner (Administration and Operations), Metropolitan Police, 1972-76; *b* 30 May 1917; *s* of late John Mastel and late Rose Mastel *(née* Gorton); *m* 1940, Anne Kathleen Johnson; two *s. Educ:* Tottenham Grammar School. Joined Metropolitan Police as Constable, 1937; Pilot, RAF, 1941-45; Metro. Police: Sergeant 1946; Inspector 1951; Supt 1955; Comdr, No 2 District, 1966; subseq.

Dep. Asst Comr, Head of Management Services Dept and D Dept (Personnel); Asst Comr (Personnel and Training), 1972. OStJ 1976. *Recreations:* Rugby football, boxing, riding, golf. *Address:* The Retreat, Nottage, Porthcawl.

MASTERS, Rt. Rev. Brian John; *see* Fulham, Bishop Suffragan of.

MASTERS, John, DSO 1944; OBE 1945; Author; *b* 26 Oct. 1914; *s* of late John Masters, 16th Rajputs, and Ada (*née* Coulthard); *m* Barbara Allcard; one *s* one *d* (one *d* decd). *Educ:* Wellington; RMC, Sandhurst. Commissioned 2nd Lieut, Indian Army, 1934; 2nd Bn, 4th PWO Gurkha Rifles, 1935; Adjutant, 1939; Comdt 3rd Bn, 1944; Bde Major, 114 Ind. Inf. Bde, 1942; 111 Ind. Inf. Bde, 1943; GSO1 19 Ind. Div., 1945; GSO1, MO1, GHQ (I), 1946; GSO2 Staff Coll., Camberley, 1947; retired 1948. Active service: NW Frontier, 1936–37; Iraq, Syria, Persia, 1941; Burma, 1944–45. *Publications:* Nightrunners of Bengal, 1951; The Deceivers, 1952, repr. 1966; The Lotus and the Wind, 1953; Bhowani Junction, 1954; Coromandel, 1955; Far, Far the Mountain Peak, 1957; Fandango Rock, 1959; The Venus of Konpara, 1960; To the Coral Strand, 1962; Trial at Monomoy, 1964; Fourteen Eighteen, 1965; The Breaking Strain, 1967; The Rock, 1969; The Ravi Lancers, 1972; Thunder at Sunset, 1974; The Field-Marshal's Memoirs, 1975; The Himalayan Concerto, 1976; Now, God Be Thanked, 1979; Heart of War, 1980; By the Green of the Spring, 1981; *autobiography:* Bugles and a Tiger, 1956; The Road Past Mandalay, 1961; Pilgrim Son, 1971. *Recreations:* mountains, railways. *Address:* c/o Brandt, 1501 Broadway, New York, NY 10036, USA.

MASTERSON, Valerie, (Mrs Andrew March); opera and concert singer; *d* of Edward Masterson and Rita McGrath; *m* 1965, Andrew March; one *s* one *d. Educ:* Holt Hill Convent; Royal Coll. of Music. Début, Landestheater Salzburg; appearances with: D'Oyly Carte Opera, Glyndebourne Festival Opera, ENO, Royal Opera, Covent Garden, etc; appears in principal opera houses in Paris, Aix-en-Provence, Toulouse, Munich, Geneva, Barcelona, Milan, San Francisco, Chile, etc; leading roles in: La Traviata, Le Nozze di Figaro, Manon, Faust, Alcina, Die Entführung aus dem Serail, Così fan tutte, La Bohème, Semele, The Magic Flute, Julius Caesar, Rigoletto, Romeo and Juliet, Count Ory, Mireille, Louise, Domenco, Regina. Recordings include several Gilbert and Sullivan operas, The Merry Widow, Elisabetta d'Inghilterra, Der Ring des Nibelungen, La Traviata. Broadcasts regularly on radio and TV. *Recreations:* tennis, swimming, ice skating. *Address:* c/o Music International, 13 Ardilaun Road, Highbury, N5 2QR.

MASTON, Charles James, CB 1965; CBE 1954; *b* 15 May 1912; *s* of James and Amelia Maston; *m* 1940, Eileen Sybil Stopher; no *c. Educ:* Yeadon and Guiseley Secondary Sch.; Bradford Gram. Sch.; St John's Coll., Cambridge. Asst Principal, Min. of Labour, 1934; Asst Private Sec. to Minister, 1937–39; Principal, 1939. Served HM Forces, 1942–44. Asst Sec., Min. of Labour (later Dept of Employment), 1944; Industrial Relations Dept, 1953–56; Under Secretary: Military Recruitment Dept, 1957–60; Employment Dept, 1960–64; Industrial Relations Dept, 1964–65; Safety, Health and Welfare Dept, 1965–68; Employment Services Div., 1968–72. *Recreation:* philately. *Address:* Flaska, Doggetts Wood Lane, Chalfont St Giles, Bucks. *T:* Little Chalfont 2033.

MATABELELAND, Bishop of, since 1977; **Rt. Rev. Robert William Stanley Mercer;** *b* 10 Jan. 1935; *s* of Harold Windrum Mercer and Kathleen Frampton. *Educ:* Grey School, Port Elizabeth, S Africa; St Paul's Theological Coll., Grahamstown, SA (LTh). Deacon 1959, priest 1960, Matabeleland; Asst Curate, Hillside, Bulawayo, 1959–63; Novice, CR, 1963; professed, 1965; at Mirfield, 1963–66; at St Teilo's Priory, Cardiff, 1966–68; Prior and Rector of Stellenbosch, S Africa, 1968–70; deported from SA, 1970; Chaplain, St Augustine's School, Penhalonga, Rhodesia, 1971–72; Rector of Borrowdale, Salisbury, Rhodesia, 1972–77. Sub-Prelate, Order of St John of Jerusalem, 1981. *Address:* Box 2422, Bulawayo, Zimbabwe. *T:* 61370.

MATACA, Most Rev. Petero; *see* Suva, Archbishop of, (RC).

MATCHAN, Leonard Joseph; Hon. Life President, Cope Allman International Ltd; Chairman, Guarantee Trust of Jersey Ltd, since 1978; *b* 26 March 1911; *s* of late George Matchan and Elsie Harriet Greenleaf; *m* 1933, Kathleen Artis; one *s* one *d. Educ:* Trinity, Croydon. FACCA; JDipMA; Certified Accountant. Vice President and European General Manager, Max Factor, Hollywood, 1936–49. Practice as accountant, 1950–55. President, Toilet Preparations Assoc., 1940–48. *Recreation:* work. *Address:* Island of Brecqhou, Channel Islands. *T:* Brecqhou 33 and Guernsey 25000.

MATE, Rt. Rev. Martin; *see* Newfoundland, Eastern, and Labrador, Bishop of.

MATES, Lt-Col Michael John; MP (C) Petersfield, since Oct. 1974; *b* 9 June 1934; *s* of Claude John Mates; *m* 1959, Mary Rosamund Paton (marr. diss. 1980); two *s* two *d*; *m* 1982, Rosallen, *d* of Mr and Mrs W. T. Bett. *Educ:* Salisbury Cathedral Sch.; Blundell's Sch.; King's Coll., Cambridge (choral schol.). Joined Army, 1954; 2nd Lieut, RUR, 1955; Queen's Dragoon Guards, RAC, 1961; Major, 1967; Lt-Col, 1973; resigned commn 1974. Vice-Chairman: Cons. NI Cttee, 1979–81 (Sec., 1979–); Cons. Home Affairs Cttee, 1979–; Chm., All-Party Anglo-Irish Gp, 1979–; Mem., Select Cttee on Defence, 1979–; introduced Farriers Registration Bill, 1975. Liveryman, Farriers' Co., 1975, Asst 1981. *Address:* House of Commons, SW1A 0AA.

MATHER, Carol; *see* Mather, David Carol MacDonell.

MATHER, (David) Carol (Macdonell), MC 1944; MP (C) Esher since 1970; Vice-Chamberlain of HM Household, since 1981; *b* 3 Jan. 1919; *s* of late Loris Emerson Mather, CBE; *m* 1951, Hon. Philippa Selina Bewicke-Copley, *o d* of 5th Baron Cromwell, DSO; one *s* three *d. Educ:* Harrow; Trinity Coll., Cambridge. War of 1939–45: commissioned Welsh Guards, 1940; served with Commandos, Special Air Service; Western Desert Campaigns, 1941–42; PoW, 1942; escaped, 1943; NW Europe, 1944–45; wounded, 1945; Palestine Campaign, 1946–48. Asst Mil. Attaché, British Embassy, Athens, 1953–56; GSO 1, MI Directorate, War Office, 1957–61; Mil. Sec. to GOC-in-C, Eastern Command, 1961–62; retd as Lt-Col., 1962. Conservative Research Dept, 1962–70; contested (C) Leicester (NW), 1966; Secretary, Cons. Parly Cttees: Foreign Affairs, 1972–74; Home Affairs, 1974–75; an Opposition Whip, 1975–79; a Lord Comr of HM Treasury, 1979–81. Councillor, Eton Rural Dist, 1965. FRGS. *Address:* House of Commons, SW1A 0AA. *Club:* Brooks's.
See also Sir W. L. Mather.

MATHER, Sir Kenneth, Kt 1979; CBE 1956; FRS 1949; DSc (London), 1940; Hon. Professor of Genetics, University of Birmingham, since 1971; *b* 22 June 1911; *e c* and *o s* of R. W. Mather; *m* 1937, Mona Rhodes; one *s. Educ:* Nantwich and Acton Grammar Sch.; University of Manchester (BSc 1931). Ministry of Agriculture and Fisheries Research Scholar, 1931–34; Lecturer in Galton Laboratory, University Coll., London, 1934–37; Rockefeller Research Fellow, at California Institute of Technology and Harvard University, 1937–38; Head of Genetics Dept, John Innes Horticultural Institution, 1938–48; Professor of Genetics, University of Birmingham, 1948–65; Vice-Chancellor, Univ. of Southampton, 1965–71, now Emeritus Prof. Member: Agricultural Research Council, 1949–54, 1955–60, and 1969–79; Science Research Council, 1965–69; Academic Adv. Cttee of Bath Univ. of Technology, 1967–71; DHSS Cttee on the Irradiation of Food, 1967–74; Cttee on Medical Aspects of Chemicals in Food and the Environment, 1972–74; Genetic Manipulation Adv. Gp, 1976–78; Wessex Regional Hosp. Bd, 1968–71. Hon. LLD Southampton, 1972; Hon. DSc: Bath, 1975; Manchester, 1980; Wales, 1980. *Publications:* The Measurement of Linkage in Heredity, 1938; Statistical Analysis in Biology, 1943; Biometrical Genetics, 1950, 3rd edn 1982; Human Diversity, 1964; The Elements of Biometry, 1967; Genetical Structure of Populations, 1973; (jointly): The Elements of Genetics, 1950; Genes, Plants and People, 1950; Introduction to Biometrical Genetics, 1977; many papers on Genetics, Cytology, and Statistics. *Address:* Department of Genetics, University of Birmingham, B15 2TT. *T:* 021-472 1301; The White House, 296 Bristol Road, Edgbaston, Birmingham B5 7SN. *T:* 021-472 2093. *Club:* Athenæum.

MATHER, Leonard Charles, CBE 1978; Chairman, United Dominions Trust, 1974–81; Director, Midland Bank Ltd, since 1968; a life Vice-President, Institute of Bankers, since 1970; *b* 10 Oct. 1909; *s* of Richard and Elizabeth Mather; *m* 1937, Muriel Armor Morris. *Educ:* Oldershaw Sch., Wallasey. BCom. (London). Entered Midland Bank, Dale Street, Liverpool, 1926; transf. to London, 1937; served in Gen. Managers' Dept at Head Office, 1937–45; Man., Bolton, 1945–48; Princ., Legal Dept, 1948–50; Asst Gen. Man., 1950–56; Gen. Man., Midland Bank Executor & Trustee Co. Ltd, 1956–58; Jt Gen. Man., Midland Bank Ltd, 1958–63; Asst Chief Gen. Man., 1964–66; Dep. Chief Gen. Man., 1966–68; Chief Gen. Man., 1968–72; Vice-Chm., 1972–74; Director: Midland Bank Trust Co. Ltd, 1968–74; Midland & International Banks Ltd, 1969–74; Montagu Trust, 1969–74; Chm., European Banks' International Co. SA, 1972–74 (Dir, 1970); Dep. Chm., Euro-Pacific Finance Corp. Ltd, 1970–74. FCIS; FIB (Dep. Chm., 1967–69; Pres., 1969–70); Hon. FIB 1974. Hon. DLitt Loughborough, 1978. *Publications:* The Lending Banker, 1955; Banker and Customer Relationship and the Accounts of Personal Customers, 1956; The Accounts of Limited Company Customers, 1958; Securities Acceptable to the Lending Banker, 1960. *Recreations:* golf, bridge. *Address:* Rochester House, Parkfield, Seal, Sevenoaks, Kent. *T:* Sevenoaks 61007.

MATHER, Sir William (Loris), Kt 1968; OBE 1957; MC 1945; TD and 2 clasps 1949; MA, CEng, FIMechE; Vice-Lieutenant of Cheshire, since 1975; Chairman, CompAir Ltd, since 1978 (Director, since 1973); Director: Imperial Continental Gas Association Ltd, since 1980; Manchester Ship Canal Co. Ltd, since 1970; National Westminster Bank Ltd (Chairman, Northern Board, since 1972); *b* 17 Aug. 1913; *s* of Loris Emerson Mather, CBE; *m* 1937, Eleanor, *d* of Prof. R. H. George, Providence, RI, USA; two *s* two *d. Educ:* Oundle; Trinity Coll., Cambridge (MA Engrg and Law, 1939). Commissioned Cheshire Yeomanry, 1935; served War of 1939–45: Palestine, Syria, Iraq, Iran, Western Desert, Italy, Belgium, Holland, Germany (wounded twice, MC); Instructor, Staff Coll., Camberley, and GSO1, 1944–45. Chm., Mather & Platt Ltd, 1960–78; Divisional Dir, BSC, 1968–73. Chairman: NW Regional Economic Planning Council, 1965–78; Inst. of Directors, 1979–82 (Manchester Inst. of Dirs, 1967–72); British Pump Manufrs Assoc., 1970–73; President: Manchester Chamber of Commerce, 1964–66 (Emeritus Dir, 1978); Manchester Guardian Soc. for Protection of Trade, 1971–; British Mech. Engrg Confedn, 1975–78; Civic Trust for the NW, 1979– (Chm., 1961–78); Vice Pres., Assoc. of British Chambers of Commerce, 1979–; Pres., Mech. Engrg Council, 1978–80; Member: Council of Industrial Design, 1960–71; Engineering Industries Council, 1976–80; Council, Duchy of Lancaster, 1977–. Member Court: Manchester Univ., 1956–; Salford Univ., 1968–; Royal College of Art, 1967–; Mem. Council, Manchester Business Sch., 1964–;

Governor: Manchester University Inst. of Science and Technology (Pres., 1976); Manchester Grammar Sch., 1965-80; Feoffee, Chetham's Hosp. Sch., 1961-; Chm., Manchester YMCA, 1953-. Hon. Fellow, Manchester Coll. of Art and Design, 1967; Hon. DEng Liverpool, 1980. Comdr, Cheshire Yeomanry, 1954-57; Col and Dep. Comdr, 23 Armoured Bde, TA, 1957-60; ADC to the Queen, 1961-66. CBIM; FRSA. DL City and County of Chester, 1963; High Sheriff of Cheshire, 1969-70. *Recreations:* field sports, ski-ing, swimming. *Address:* Whirley Hall, Macclesfield, Cheshire SK10 4RN. *T:* Macclesfield 22077. *Clubs:* Leander; St James's (Manchester).
See also D. C. M. Mather.

MATHER-JACKSON, Sir Anthony (Henry Mather), 6th Bt *cr* 1869; retired Mining Engineer; *b* 9 Nov. 1899; *y s* of William Birkenhead Mather Jackson (*d* 1934) (2nd *s* of 2nd Bt) and Georgiana Catherine (*d* 1932), *d* of Rev. Brabazon Hallowes, Glapwell Hall, Chesterfield; *S* brother, 1976; *m* 1923, Evelyn Mary, *d* of Sir Henry Kenyon Stephenson, 1st Bt, DSO; three *d. Educ:* Harrow. Commission, Grenadier Guards, 1918-20; coal industry, 1921-47; company director, 1947-71. *Recreations:* formerly shooting, golf, hunting, racing. *Heir:* cousin William Jackson [*b* 18 Sept. 1902; *m* 1st, 1927, Lady Ankaret Howard (*d* 1945), 2nd *d* of 10th Earl of Carlisle; one *s* one *d* ; 2nd, 1966, Ina, *d* of late James Leonard Joyce, FRCS]. *Address:* Archway House, Kirklington, Newark, Notts. *Club:* White's.
See also Viscount Cowdray.

MATHERS, Sir Robert (William), Kt 1981; Chairman and Managing Director, Mathers Enterprises Ltd (footwear retailing chain), Australia, since 1973; *b* 2 Aug. 1928; *s* of William Mathers and Olive Ida (*née* Wohlsen); *m* 1957, Betty Estelle Greasley; three *d. Educ:* Church of England Grammar Sch., E Brisbane. FAIM. General Manager/Director, Mathers Enterprises Ltd, 1963. Mem. Council: Retailers Assoc. of Qld, 1960-; Inst. of Public Affairs, 1978-; Griffith Univ., 1978-; Australian Bicentennial Authority, 1980-; Member: Inst. of Directors, 1977-; Finance Adv. Cttee for XII Commonwealth Games, 1979; Trustee, World Wildlife Fund, Australia, 1981-; Past Pres., Footwear Retailers Assoc. Fellow, Queensland Art Gallery Foundn, 1979. *Recreations:* golf, tennis, swimming. *Address:* 1 Wybelenna Street, Kenmore, Queensland 4069, Australia. *T:* (07) 378 5503. *Clubs:* Rotary, Royal Queensland Yacht Squadron, Tattersalls, Milton Tennis, Rugby Union, Indooroopilly Golf (Brisbane).

MATHESON, Sir (James Adam) Louis, KBE 1976 (MBE 1944); CMG 1972; FTS; FEng; Vice-Chancellor, Monash University, Melbourne, 1959-76; Chancellor, Papua New Guinea University of Technology, 1973-75; Chairman, Australian Science and Technology Council, 1975-76; *b* 11 Feb. 1912; *s* of William and Lily Edith Matheson; *m* 1937, Audrey Elizabeth Wood; three *s. Educ:* Bootham Sch., York; Manchester Univ. (MSc 1933). Lectr, Birmingham Univ., 1938-46 (PhD 1946); Prof. of Civil Engineering, Univ. of Melbourne, Australia, 1946-50; Beyer Prof. of Engineering, Univ. of Manchester, 1951-59. Hon. FICE (Mem. Council, 1965); FIStructE (Vice-Pres.,1967-68); Hon. FIEAust (Mem. Council, 1961-81, Vice-Pres., 1970-74, Pres., 1975-76); Fellow, Aust. Acad. of Technological Scis, 1976; Fellow, Fellowship of Engrg, 1980. Member: Mission on Technical Educn in W Indies, 1957; Royal Commn into failure of King's Bridge, 1963; Ramsay Cttee on Tertiary Educn in Victoria, 1961-63; CSIRO Adv. Council, 1962-67; Exec., Aust. Council for Educational Research, 1964-69; Interim Council, Univ. of Papua and New Guinea, 1965-68; Enquiry into Post-Secondary Educn in Victoria, 1976-78; Chairman: Council, Papua New Guinea Inst. of Technology, 1966-73; Aust. Vice-Chancellors' Cttee, 1967-68; Assoc. of Commonwealth Univs, 1967-69; Newport Power Stn Review Panel, 1977; Schools Commn Buildings Cttee, 1977-81; Victorian Planning and Finance Cttee, Commonwealth Schools Commn, 1979-; Trustee, Inst. of Applied Science (now Science Mus. of Victoria), 1963- (Pres., 1969-73). Dir, Nauru Phosphate Corp., 1977-79. Hon. DSc Hong Kong, 1969; Hon. LLD: Manchester, 1972; Monash, 1975; Melbourne, 1975. Kernot Meml Medal, 1972; Peter Nicol Russell Medal, 1976. *Publications:* Hyperstatic Structures: Vol. 1, 1959; Vol. 2, 1960; Still Learning, 1980; various articles on engineering and education. *Recreations:* music, woodcraft. *Address:* 26/166 West Toorak Road, South Yarra, Victoria 3141, Australia. *Club:* Melbourne.

MATHESON, Very Rev. James Gunn; Moderator of General Assembly of Church of Scotland, May 1975-76; Parish Minister, Portree, Isle of Skye, 1973-79; *b* 1 March 1912; *s* of Norman Matheson and Henrietta Gunn; *m* 1937, Janet Elizabeth Clarkson; three *s* one *d* (and one *d* decd). *Educ:* Inverness Royal Academy; Edinburgh Univ. (MA, BD). Free Church of Olrig, Caithness, 1936-39; Chaplain to HM Forces, 1939-45 (POW Italy, 1941-43); St Columba's Church, Blackhall, Edinburgh, 1946-51; Knox Church, Dunedin, NZ, 1951-61; Sec. of Stewardship and Budget Cttee of Church of Scotland, 1961-73. Hon. DD Edinburgh, 1975. *Publications:* Do You Believe This?, 1960; Saints and Sinners, 1975; contrib. theol jls. *Recreations:* gardening, fishing. *Address:* Husabost, Totaig, Dunvegan, Isle of Skye. *Club:* New (Edinburgh).

MATHESON, Maj.-Gen. John Mackenzie, OBE 1950; TD 1969; Postgraduate Dean, Faculty of Medicine, University of Edinburgh, 1971-80; *b* Gibraltar, 6 Aug. 1912; *s* of late John Matheson and late Nina Short, Cape Town; *m* 1942, Agnes, *d* of Henderson Purves, Dunfermline; one *d. Educ:* George Watson's Coll., Edinburgh; Edinburgh Univ. (Vans Dunlop Schol.). MB, ChB 1936; MRCP 1939; MD 1945; FRCSEd 1946; FRCS 1962; FRCP 1972. Royal Victoria Hosp. Tuberculosis Trust Research Fellow, 1936-37;

Lieut, RAMC (TA), 1936. Served War of 1939-45: Middle East, N Africa and Italy; Regular RAMC Commn, 1944 (despatches). Clinical Tutor, Surgical Professorial Unit, Edinburgh Univ., 1947-48; Med. Liaison Officer to Surgeon-Gen. US Army, Washington, DC, 1948-50; Asst Chief, Section Gen. Surgery, Walter Reed Army Hosp., Washington, DC, 1950-51; Cons. Surgeon: MELF, 1963-64; BAOR, 1967; Far East, 1967-69; Jt Prof. Mil. Surg., RAM Coll. and RCS of Eng., 1964-67; Brig. 1967; Comdt and Dir of Studies, Royal Army Med. Coll., 1969-71. QHS 1969-71. Hon. Col, 205 (Scottish) Gen. Hosp., T&AVR, 1978-80. Alexander Medal, 1961; Simpson-Smith Memorial Lectr, 1967; Gordon-Watson Lectr, RCS of Eng., 1967. Senior Fellow, Assoc. of Surgeons of GB and Ireland; President: Lothian Div., BMA, 1978-80; Scottish Br., Royal Soc. of Tropical Medicine and Hygiene, 1978-80. FRSocMed. *Publications:* (contrib.) Military Medicine, in Dictionary of Medical Ethics, 1977; papers (on gun-shot wounds, gas-gangrene and sterilisation) to medical jls. *Recreation:* travel. *Address:* 2 Orchard Brae, Edinburgh EH4 1NY.

MATHESON, Sir Louis; see Matheson, Sir J. A. L.

MATHESON OF MATHESON, Sir Torquhil (Alexander), 6th Bt *cr* 1882, of Lochalsh; Chief of Clan Matheson; one of HM Body Guard of the Honourable Corps of Gentlemen at Arms, since 1977; *b* 15 Aug. 1925; *s* of General Sir Torquhil George Matheson, 5th Bt, KCB, CMG; *S* father, 1963, *S* kinsman as Chief of Clan Matheson, 1975; *m* 1954, Serena Mary Francesca, *o d* of late Lt-Col Sir Michael Peto, 2nd Bt; two *d. Educ:* Eton. Served War of 1939-45; joined Coldstream Guards, July 1943; commnd, March 1944; 5th Bn Coldstream Guards, NW Europe, Dec. 1944-May 1945 (wounded). Served with 3rd Bn Coldstream Guards: Palestine, 1945-48 (despatches); Tripoli and Egypt, 1950-53; seconded King's African Rifles, 1961-64. Captain, 1952; Major, 1959; retd 1964. 4th Bn, Wilts Regt, TA, 1965-67; Royal Wilts Territorials (T&AVR III), 1967-69. *Heir* (to Baronetcy and Chiefship): *b* Major Fergus John Matheson, late Coldstream Guards [*b* 22 Feb. 1927; *m* 1952, Hon. Jean Elizabeth Mary Willoughby, *yr d* of 11th Baron Middleton, KG, MC, TD; one *s* two *d.* One of HM Body Guard of the Honourable Corps of Gentlemen at Arms, since 1979]. *Address:* Standerwick Court, Frome, Som. *Clubs:* Army and Navy; Leander (Henley-on-Thames).

MATHEW, John Charles, QC 1977; *b* 3 May 1927; *s* of late Sir Theobald Mathew, KBE, MC, and Lady Mathew; *m* 1952, Jennifer Jane Mathew (*née* Lagden); two *d. Educ:* Beaumont Coll. Served, Royal Navy, 1945-47. Called to Bar, Lincoln's Inn, 1949; apptd Junior Prosecuting Counsel to the Crown, 1959; First Sen. Prosecuting Counsel to the Crown, 1974-77. Elected a Bencher of Lincoln's Inn, 1970. *Recreations:* golf, backgammon, cinema. *Address:* 47 Abingdon Villas, W8. *T:* 01-937 7535. *Club:* Garrick.

MATHEW, Theobald David; Windsor Herald of Arms, since 1978; *b* 7 April 1942; *s* of Robert Mathew, Porchester Terrace, London, and West Mersea Hall, Essex, solicitor, and Joan Alison, *d* of Sir George Young, Bt, MVO, of Formosa. *Educ:* Downside; Balliol Coll., Oxford (MA). Green Staff Officer at Investiture of HRH the Prince of Wales, 1969; Rouge Dragon Pursuivant of Arms, 1970; Dep. Treasurer, Coll. of Arms, 1978-. *Recreations:* cricket and sailing. *Address:* 76 Clifton Hill, NW8. *T:* 01-624 8448; College of Arms, EC4V 4BT. *T:* 01-248 0893. *Clubs:* Athenæum, MCC; Middlesex CCC, Royal Harwich Yacht.

MATHEWS, Rev. Arthur Kenneth, OBE 1942; DSC 1944; Vicar of Thursley, 1968-76; Rural Dean of Godalming, 1969-74; *b* 11 May 1906; *s* of late Reverend Canon A. A. and Mrs Mathews; *m* 1936, Elisabeth, *d* of late E. M. Butler and Mrs Butler; no *c. Educ:* Monkton Combe Sch.; Balliol Coll., Oxford (Exhibitioner); Cuddesdon Theol. Coll. Deacon 1932, priest 1933, at Wakefield; Asst Curate of Penistone; Padre of the Tanker Fleet of the Anglo-Saxon Petroleum Co. Ltd; licensed to officiate, Diocese of Wakefield, 1935-38; Vicar of Forest Row, 1938-44; Temp. Chaplain, RNVR, 1939-44 (Chaplain HMS Norfolk, 1940-44); on staff of Christian Frontier Council, 1944-46; Vicar of Rogate and Sequestrator of Terwick, 1946-54; Rural Dean of Midhurst, 1950-54; Hon. Chaplain to Bishop of Portsmouth, 1950-55; Commissary to: Bishop of Singapore, 1949-64; Bishop of Wellington, 1962-72; Student of Central Coll. of Anglican Communion at St Augustine's Coll., Canterbury, 1954-55; Dean and Rector of St Albans, 1955-63; Rector of St Peter's, Peebles, 1963-68. Hon. Chaplain to Bishop of Norwich, 1969-71. Member: Council, Marlborough Coll., 1953-74; Governing Body, Monkton Combe Sch., 1959-77. *Recreations:* walking and gardening. *Address:* The Tallat, Westwell, near Burford, Oxon.
See also Baroness Brooke of Ystradfellte.

MATHEWS, Denis Owen, CMG 1965; OBE 1959; *b* 21 Feb. 1901; *s* of Albert Edward Mathews and Edith (*née* Benton); *m* Violet Morgan; one *s. Educ:* Latymer Sch., London; Varndean, Brighton. Served with RAF, 1918; Royal Engineers, 1940-43. Uganda Survey Dept, 1921-46; East Africa Tourist Travel Assoc., 1948-65; UN Tourist Expert, 1965; Dir of Tourism, and Information and Broadcasting, Seychelles, 1965-66; Gen. Manager, Ker, Downey & Selby Safaris, 1967-70. Hon. Pres., E African Prof. Hunters' Assoc.; Founder Mem., E African Wildlife Soc. Hon. Citizen, Dallas, Texas, USA. *Publications:* technical papers on tourism and wild-life. *Address:* Bungalow 2, Manor House, Hingham, Norfolk NR9 4HP. *T:* Attleborough 850507. *Clubs:* Kiambu (Kenya), Mount Kenya Safari (Nanyuki).

MATHEWSON, George Ross, BSc, PhD, MBA; CEng, MIEE; Chief Executive and Member, Scottish Development Agency, since 1981; *b* 14 May 1940; *s* of George Mathewson and Charlotte Gordon (*née* Ross); *m* 1966, Sheila Alexandra Graham (*née* Bennett); two *s*. *Educ:* Perth Academy; St Andrews Univ. (BSc, PhD); Canisius Coll., Buffalo, NY (MBA). Assistant Lecturer, St Andrews Univ., 1964–67; various posts in Research & Development, Avionics Engineering, Bell Aerospace, Buffalo, NY, 1967–72; joined Industrial & Commercial Finance Corp., Edinburgh, 1972; Area Manager, Aberdeen, 1974, and Asst General Manager and Director, 1979. Dir, Scottish Investment Trust Ltd; Chm., Scottish Development Finance Ltd. *Publications:* various articles on engineering/finance. *Recreations:* geriatric Rugby, golf, business. *Address:* Larach-Beg, Corsee Road, Banchory, Kincardineshire, Scotland. *T:* Banchory 3482. *Clubs:* Royal Northern (Aberdeen); Aberdeen Petroleum.

MATHIAS, Lionel Armine, CMG 1953; apple grower; *b* 23 Jan. 1907; *s* of Hugh Henry Mathias and Amy Duncan Mathias (*née* Mathias); *m* 1935, Rebecca Gordon Rogers; three *d*. *Educ:* Christs Coll., New Zealand; St Paul's Sch.; Keble Coll., Oxford. Appointed Asst District Commissioner, Uganda, 1929; Labour Commissioner, 1949–53; Member: Uganda Exec. Council, 1948, Legislative Council, 1949–53; Kampala Municipal Council, 1952–53; Uganda Students Adviser, 1953–62; Chm., Uganda Britain Soc., 1964–65. *Address:* Little Copt Farm, Shoreham, Sevenoaks, Kent. *T:* Otford 2040.

MATHIAS, Prof. Peter, MA; FBA 1977; Chichele Professor of Economic History, University of Oxford, and Fellow of All Souls College, Oxford, since 1969; *b* 10 Jan. 1928; *o c* of John Samuel and Marion Helen Mathias; *m* 1958, Elizabeth Ann, *d* of Robert Blackmore, JP, Bath; two *s* one *d*. *Educ:* Colston's Sch., Bristol; Jesus Coll., Cambridge (Schol.). 1st cl. (dist) Hist. Tripos, 1950, 1951. Research Fellow, Jesus Coll., Cambridge, 1952–55; Asst Lectr and Lectr, Faculty of History, Cambridge, 1955–68; Dir of Studies in History and Fellow, Queens' Coll., Cambridge, 1955–68; Tutor, 1957–68; Senior Proctor, Cambridge Univ., 1965–66. Vis. Professor: Univ. of Toronto, 1961; School of Economics, Delhi, 1967; Univ. of California, Berkeley, 1967; Univ. of Pa, 1972; Virginia Gildersleeve, Barnard Coll., Columbia Univ., 1972; Johns Hopkins Univ., 1979; ANU, Canberra, 1980. Chairman: Business Archives Council, 1968–72 (Vice-Chm., 1980–); Econ. and Social History Cttee, SSRC, 1975–77 (Mem., 1970–77); Acad. Adv. Council, University Coll., Buckingham, 1979–; Wellcome Trust Adv. Panel for History of Medicine, 1981–; Treasurer, Econ. Hist. Soc., 1968–; Hon. Treasurer, British Acad., 1980–; International Economic History Association: Sec., 1959–62; Pres., 1974–78; Hon. Pres., 1978–; Mem., Exec. Cttee, Internat. Inst. of Economic History Francesco Datini, Prato, 1972–; Foreign Mem., Royal Danish Acad., 1982. Curator, Bodleian Library, 1972–. FRHistS 1972 (Vice-Pres., 1976–80). Asst Editor, Econ. Hist. Rev., 1955–57. *Publications:* The Brewing Industry in England 1700–1830, 1959; English Trade Tokens, 1962; Retailing Revolution, 1967; The First Industrial Nation, 1969; (ed) Science and Society 1600–1900, 1972; The Transformation of England, 1979; General Editor: Cambridge Economic History of Europe, 1968–; Debates in Economic History, 1967–. *Recreation:* travel. *Address:* All Souls College, Oxford. *T:* Oxford 722251.

MATHIAS, Sir Richard Hughes, 2nd Bt, *cr* 1917; Member London Stock Exchange; *b* 6 April 1905; *s* of Sir Richard Mathias, 1st Bt, and Annie, *y d* of Evan Hughes, Cardiff; *S* father 1942; *m* 1st, 1937, Gladys Cecilia Turton (marr. diss., 1960), *o d* of late Edwin Hart, New Hextalls, Bletchingley, Surrey; two *d*; 2nd, 1960, Mrs Elizabeth Baird Murray (*d* 1972), *er d* of late Dr and Mrs Miles of Hendrescythan, Creigiau, Glamorgan; 3rd, 1973, Mrs Hilary Vines (*d* 1975), Malaga, Spain. *Educ:* Eton; Balliol Coll., Oxford. RAF 1940–46 (Staff appt Air Ministry, 1942–46). Mem. Council Royal Nat. Mission to Deep Sea Fishermen, 1953–54. Fellow Corp. of S Mary and S Nicolas (Woodard Schs), 1965; Mem. Council, Hurstpierpoint Coll., 1965– (Chm., 1967–74). *Address:* 8 Oakwood Court, Abbotsbury Road, W14 8JU. *T:* 01-602 2635. *Club:* Reform.

MATHIAS, Prof. William (James), DMus, FRAM; composer, conductor, pianist; Professor and Head of the Department of Music, University College of North Wales, Bangor, since 1970; *b* 1 Nov. 1934; *s* of James Hughes Mathias and Marian (*née* Evans); *m* 1959, Margaret Yvonne Collins; one *d*. *Educ:* University Coll. of Wales, Aberystwyth (Robert Bryan Schol.); Royal Academy of Music (Lyell-Taylor Schol.). DMus Wales, 1966; FRAM 1965 (LRAM 1958). Lectr in Music, UC of N Wales, Bangor, 1959–68; Sen. Lectr in Music, Univ. of Edinburgh, 1968–69. Member: Welsh Arts Council, 1974–81 (Chm., Music Cttee, 1982–); Music Adv. Cttee, British Council, 1974–; Internat. Soc. for Contemporary Music (British Section), 1976–80; BBC Central Music Adv. Cttee, 1979–; Welsh Adv. Cttee, British Council, 1979–; Council, Composers' Guild of GB, 1982–; Bd of Governors, Nat. Museum of Wales, 1973–78; Artistic Dir, N Wales Music Festival, 1972–. Arnold Bax Society Prize, 1968; John Edwards Meml Award, 1982. *Publications include:* Piano Concerto No 2, 1964; Piano Concerto No 3, 1970; Harp Concerto, 1973; Clarinet Concerto, 1976; *orchestral compositions:* Divertimento for string orch., 1961; Serenade for small orch., 1963; Prelude, Aria and Finale, 1966; Symphony No I, 1969; Festival Overture, 1973; Celtic Dances, 1974; Vistas, 1977; Laudi, 1978; Vivat Regina (for brass band), 1978; Helios, 1978; Requiescat, 1979; Dance Variations, 1979; Investiture Anniversary Fanfare, 1979; Reflections on a theme by Tomkins, 1981; *chamber compositions:* Sonata for violin and piano, 1963; Piano Sonata, 1965; Divertimento for flute, oboe and piano, 1966; String Quartet, 1970; Capriccio for flute and piano, 1971; Wind Quintet, 1976; Concertino, 1977; Zodiac Trio, 1977; Clarinet Sonatina, 1978; String Quartet No 2, 1981; *choral and vocal compositions:* Wassail Carol, 1965; Three Medieval Lyrics, 1966; St Teilo, 1970; Ave Rex, 1970; Sir Christemas, 1970; Culhwch and Olwen, 1971; A Babe is born, 1971; A Vision of Time and Eternity (for contralto and piano), 1974; Ceremony after a fire raid, 1975; This Worlde's Joie, 1975; Carmen Paschale, 1976; Elegy for a Prince (for baritone and orch.), 1976; The Fields of Praise (for tenor and piano), 1977; A Royal Garland, 1978; Nativity Carol, 1978; A May Magnificat, 1980; Shakespeare Songs, 1980; Songs of William Blake (for mezzo-soprano and orch.), 1980; Rex Gloriae (four Latin motets), 1981; Te Deum, for soli, chorus and orchestra (commnd for centenary of the Chapel at Haddo House), 1981; Lux Aeterna, for soli, chorus and orchestra (commnd for Three Choirs Fest.), 1982; *organ compositions:* Variations on a Hymn Tune, 1963; Partita, 1963; Postlude, 1964; Processional, 1965; Chorale, 1967; Toccata giocosa, 1968; Jubilate, 1975; Fantasy, 1978; Canzonetta, 1978; Antiphonies, 1982; *anthems and church music:* O Sing unto the Lord, 1965; Make a joyful noise, 1965; Festival Te Deum, 1965; Communion Service in C, 1968; Psalm 150, 1969; Lift up your heads, 1970; O Salutaris Hostia, 1972; Gloria, 1972; Magnificat and Nunc Dimittis, 1973; Alleluya Psallat, 1974; Missa Brevis, 1974; Communion Service (Series III), 1976; Arise, shine, 1978; Let the people praise thee, O God (anthem composed for the wedding of the Prince and Princess of Wales), 1981; Praise ye the Lord, 1982; All Wisdom is from the Lord, 1982; Except the Lord build the House (commnd for Harvard Univ.), 1983; *opera:* The Servants (libretto by Iris Murdoch), 1980. *Address:* Y Graigwen, Cadnant Road, Menai Bridge, Anglesey, Gwynedd LL59 5NG. *T:* Menai Bridge 712392. *Clubs:* Athenæum; Cardiff and County (Cardiff).

MATHIAS, Winifred Rachel, CBE 1974; Lord Mayor of City of Cardiff, May 1972–May 1973; Member, Local Government Boundary Commission for Wales, 1974–79; *b* 11 Feb. 1902; *d* of Charles and Selina Vodden; *m* 1923, William John Mathias (*d* 1949). *Educ:* Howard Gardens High Sch. Sec., ship-owning co., 1919–23. Member, Cardiff City Council, 1954–74; Alderman, 1967–74; formerly Mem., Estates, Public Works, Civic Buildings and Children's Cttees; Deputy Chairman: Health Cttee, 1961–64, 1967–74; Welfare Cttee, 1961–64 (Mem., 1954–70; Chm., 1967–70); Mem., Educn Cttee, 1956–74; Chairman: Social Services, 1970–74; all Primary Schs, 1965–70; Primary Schs Gp 3, 1970–74. Governor, Coll. of Food Technology and Commerce, 1957– (Dep. Chm., 1960–63, Chm., 1963–74). Life Mem., Blind Council (rep. of City Council); Mem., Management Cttee, "The Rest", Porthcawl, 1954–; Past Mem., Whitchurch Hosp. Gp; Founder Mem., Danybryn Cheshire Home, 1961–; Mem., Cardiff Council for the Elderly (Cartref Cttee). *Recreations:* reading, music, needlework, travel. *Address:* 19 Timbers Square, Cardiff CF2 3SH. *T:* Cardiff 483853. *Club:* Roath Conservative (Life Vice-Pres.) (Cardiff).

MATHIESON, William Allan Cunningham, CB 1970; CMG 1955; MBE 1945; consultant to international organisations; *b* 22 Feb. 1916; *e s* of Rev. William Miller Mathieson, BD, and Elizabeth Cunningham Mathieson (*née* Reid); *m* 1946, Elizabeth Frances, *y d* of late Henry Marvell Carr, RA; two *s*. *Educ:* High Sch. of Dundee; Edinburgh and Cambridge Univs. Joined Colonial Office, 1939; served War, 1940–45; Royal Artillery in UK, France and Germany (Major, despatches). Rejoined Colonial Office, 1945; Middle East Dept, 1945–48; Private Sec. to Minister of State, 1948–49; Asst Sec., Colonial Office, 1949; Counsellor (Colonial Affairs) UK Delegn to UN, New York, 1951–54; Head of East African Department, CO, 1955–58; Minister of Education, Labour and Lands, Kenya, 1958–60; Under-Sec., Dept of Technical Co-operation, 1963–64; Under-Sec., 1964–68, Dep. Sec., 1968–75, Min. of Overseas Development; Consultant, UN Develt Prog., 1976–81. Chm., Executive Council, Commonwealth Agricultural Bureaux, 1963; Member: Exec. Bd, Unesco, 1968–74; Bd of Trustees, Internat. Centre for Maize and Wheat Improvement (Mexico), 1976–; Council, ODI, 1977–; Council, Commonwealth Soc. for the Deaf, 1979–; Bd of Management, LSHTM, 1981–; Chm., Bd of Trustees, Internat. Service for Nat. Agr. Res., 1980. Hon. Fellow, Queen Elizabeth House, Oxford, 1973. *Recreations:* photography, travel. *Address:* 13 Sydney House, Woodstock Road, W4.

MATHIESON, William Gordon, CMG 1963; BEc; FASA; *b* 5 July 1902; *s* of James L. Mathieson; *m* 1934, Margery Macdonald; two *d* (and two *d* decd). *Educ:* Fort Street High Sch.; University of Sydney. Permanent Head, NSW State Treasury, 1959–63; Vice-Pres., Sydney Water Board, 1960–63; Mem., Sydney Harbour Transport Board, 1959–63; Chm., Companies Auditors Board, 1963–67; Auditor General of New South Wales, 1963–67. *Address:* 25 Bell Street, Gordon, NSW 2072, Australia. *T:* 498-1444.

MATILAL, Prof. Bimal Krishna, PhD; Spalding Professor of Eastern Religions and Ethics, University of Oxford, since 1976; Fellow, All Souls College, since 1976; *b* 1 June 1935; *s* of Hare Krishna Matilal and Parimal Matilal; *m* 1958, Karabi Matilal; one *s* one *d*. *Educ:* Univ. of Calcutta (BA Hons 1954, MA 1956); Harvard Univ. (AM 1963, PhD 1965). Lectr, Sanskrit Coll., Calcutta Univ., 1957–65; Asst Prof., Univ. of Toronto, 1965–67, Associate Prof., 1967–71; Associate Prof., Univ. of Pennsylvania, 1969–70; Vis. Sen. Fellow, SOAS, Univ. of London, 1971–72; Prof., Univ. of Toronto, 1971–77. Founder-Editor, Jl of Indian Philosophy, 1971–. *Publications:* The Navya-nyāya Doctrine of Negation, 1968; Epistemology, Logic and Grammar in Indian Philosophical Analysis, 1971; The Logical Illumination of Indian Mysticism, 1977; The Central Philosophy of Jainism, 1981; Logical and Ethical Issues in Indian Religions, 1982; contrib. Nyāya-Vaiśesika Literature.

Recreation: gardening. *Address:* Oriental Institute, University of Oxford, Oxford.

MATOKA, Hon. Peter Wilfred, MP; Minister of Economic and Technical Co-operation, Republic of Zambia, 1977-79; MP for Mwinilunga in Parliament of Zambia; *b* 8 April 1930; member of Lunda Royal Family; *m* 1957, Grace Joyce; two *s* one *d. Educ:* Mwinilunga Sch.; Munali Secondary Sch.; University Coll. of Fort Hare (BA Rhodes); American Univ., Washington (Dipl. Internat. Relations). Minister: of Information and Postal Services, 1964-65; of Health, 1965-66; of Works, 1967; of Power, Transport and Works, 1968; of Luapula Province, 1969; High Comr for Zambia in UK and Ambassador to the Holy See, 1970-71; Minister of Health, 1971-72; Minister of Local Govt and Housing, 1972-77. Mem. Central Cttee, United National Independence Party, 1971-. Pres., AA of Zambia, 1969-70 (Vice-Pres. 1970-71). Kt of St Gregory the Great, 1964; Kt, UAR, 1964; Kt, Ethiopia, 1965. *Recreations:* fishing, shooting, discussion, photography. *Address:* 19 Chisiza Crescent, Lusaka, Zambia. *Club:* Royal Automobile.

MATOLENGWE, Rt. Rev. Patrick Monwabisi; a Bishop Suffragan of Cape Town, since 1976; *b* 12 May 1937; *s* of David and Emma Matolengwe; *m* 1967, Crecentia Nompumelelo (*née* Nxele); three *s* two *d. Educ:* Healdtown Institution, Fort Beaufort (matric.); Lovedale Teacher Training Coll., Alice; Bishop Gray Coll., Cape Town; Federal Theol Sem., Alice (Cert. Theol.). Teaching, 1959-60; Court Interpreter, 1960-61; theological studies, 1962-65; Curacy at Herschel, Dio. Grahamstown, 1965-68; Rector of Nyanga, Dio. Cape Town, 1968-76. *Recreations:* scouting, singing, music, reading, tennis. *Address:* Bishop's House, 79 Kildare Road, Newlands, Cape Town, 7700, S Africa. *T:* Cape Town 663297.

MATTHEW, Chessor Lillie, FRIBA, FRIAS, MRTPI; JP; Principal, Duncan of Jordanstone College of Art, Dundee, 1964-78, retired; *b* 22 Jan. 1913; *s* of William Matthew and Helen Chessor Matthew (*née* Milne); *m* 1939, Margarita Ellis; one *s. Educ:* Gray's School of Art; Robert Gordon's Coll., Aberdeen. Diploma in Architecture. Lectr, Welsh Sch. of Architecture, Cardiff, 1936-40. Served RAF, 1940-46, Flt-Lt. Sen. Lectr, Welsh Sch. of Architecture, Cardiff, 1946-57; Head of Sch. of Architecture, Duncan of Jordanstone Coll. of Art, Dundee, 1958-64. *Recreations:* hill walking, foreign travel. *Address:* Craigmhor, 36 Albany Road, West Ferry, Dundee DD5 1NW. *T:* Dundee 78364.

MATTHEWMAN, Keith; QC 1979; a Recorder of the Crown Court, since 1979; *b* 8 Jan. 1936; *e s* of late Lieut Frank Matthewman and Elizabeth Matthewman; *m* 1962, Jane (*née* Maxwell); one *s. Educ:* Long Eaton Grammar Sch.; University College London (LLB). Called to the Bar, Middle Temple, 1960. Commercial Assistant, Internat. Div., Rolls-Royce Ltd, 1961-62; practice at the Bar, 1962-, Midland Circuit, later Midland and Oxford Circuit. Mem., Heanor UDC, 1960-63. *Recreations:* gardening, cine photography. *Address:* 24 The Ropewalk, Nottingham NG1 5EF. *Club:* United Services (Nottingham).

MATTHEWS, family name of Baron Matthews.

MATTHEWS, Baron *cr* 1980 (Life Peer), of Southgate in the London Borough of Enfield; **Victor Collin Matthews,** FCIOB, FRSA, CBIM; Deputy Chairman since 1973, and Group Chief Executive, since 1977, Trafalgar House plc (Group Managing Director, 1968-77); Chairman: Express Newspapers plc, since 1977 (Chief Executive, 1977-82); The Cunard Steam-Ship Co. plc, since 1971; Cunard Cruise Ships Ltd, since 1978; Cunard Line Ltd, since 1978; Trafalgar House Developments Holdings Ltd, since 1970; Trafalgar House Construction Holdings Ltd, since 1977; Fleet Publishing International Holdings Ltd, since 1978; Fleet Holdings plc, since 1982; Evening Standard Co. Ltd, since 1980; The Ritz Hotel (London) Ltd, since 1976; *b* 5 Dec. 1919; *s* of A. and J. Matthews; *m* 1942, Joyce Geraldine (*née* Pilbeam); one *s. Educ:* Highbury. Served RNVR, 1939-45. Director: Associated Container Transportation (Australia) Ltd, 1972-; Cunard Crusader World Travel Ltd, 1974-; Racecourse Holdings Trust Ltd, 1977-; Associated Communications Corp. plc, 1977-82; Goldquill Ltd, 1979-; Darchart Ltd, 1980-; Garmaine Ltd, 1980-. *Recreations:* racehorse owner, cricket, golf. *Address:* Trafalgar House plc, 1 Berkeley Street, W1X 6NN. *T:* 01-499 9020. *Clubs:* MCC, Royal Automobile.

MATTHEWS, Sir Bryan Harold Cabot, Kt 1952; CBE 1944; FRS 1940; MA, ScD; Professor of Physiology, University of Cambridge, 1952-73, Professor Emeritus, 1973; Life Fellow of King's College, 1973 (Fellow, 1929-73); *b* 14 June 1906; *s* of Harold Evan Matthews and Ruby Sarah Harrison; *m* 1926; one *s* two *d; m* 1970, Audrey, *widow* of Air Vice-Marshal W. K. Stewart. *Educ:* Clifton Coll.; King's Coll., Cambridge. BA Hons, 1st Class Part II Physiology, 1927; Beit Memorial Fellow for Med. Res., 1928-32; Corresponding Mem. Société Philomatique de Paris; British Mem. of the 1935 International High Altitude Expedition for Physiological Research; Chm. of Flying Personnel Research Cttee, RAF, 1967-78; Consultant to RAF in Applied Physiology; Head of RAF Physiological Research Unit, 1940; Head of RAF Institute of Aviation Medicine, 1944-46. Asst Dir of Physiological Research, Cambridge, 1932-48, Reader, 1948-52. Dir of Studies, King's Coll., 1932-52. Royal Soc. Leverhulme Vis. Prof. to African med. schs, 1974. Oliver-Sharpey Lecturer, RCP, 1945; Kelvin Lecturer, Instn of Electrical Engineers, 1948. Pres. Section I British Association, 1961; Vice-Pres., Royal Society, 1957 and 1958. *Publications:* Electricity in our Bodies; Essay on

Physiological Research in Cambridge University Studies, 1933; Papers on Electrical Instruments and electrical phenomena in the nervous system, etc. in the Journal of Physiology, Proceedings of the Royal Society, etc. *Recreations:* ski-ing, sailing. *Address:* King's College, Cambridge.
See also Dr P. B. C. *Matthews.*

MATTHEWS, David Napier, CBE 1976 (OBE 1945); MA, MD, MCh (Cambridge); FRCS; Hon. FDSRCS; retired; Consulting Plastic Surgeon, University College Hospital and Hospital for Sick Children; Civilian Consultant in Plastic Surgery to the Royal Navy since 1954; *b* 7 July 1911; *m* 1940, Betty Eileen Bailey Davies; two *s* one *d. Educ:* Leys Sch., Cambridge; Queens' Coll., Cambridge; Charing Cross Hosp. Qualified as doctor, 1935. Surgical Registrar, Westminster Hospital, until 1940; Surgeon Plastic Unit, East Grinstead, 1939-41; Surgical Specialist, RAFVR, 1941-46; Plastic Surgeon: UCH and Hosp. for Sick Children, 1946-76; Royal Nat. Orthopædic Hosp., 1947-54; King Edward's Hosp. for Officers, 1972-80. Adviser in Plastic Surgery, DHSS, 1962-77. Consulting Practice as Surgeon 1946-80; Hunterian Professor, RCS, 1941, 1944, 1976; President: British Assoc. of Plastic Surgeons, 1954 and 1971; Plastic Section, RSM, 1970-71; Sec., Harveian Soc. of London, 1951, Vice-Pres., 1954, Pres., 1962; Gen. Sec. Internat. Confederation for Plastic Surgery, 1959; Pres., Chelsea Clinical Soc., 1962. *Publications:* Surgery of Repair, 1943, 2nd edn, 1946; (Ed.) Recent Advances in the Surgery of Trauma, 1963; chapters in surgical books; contrib. to Lancet, BMJ and Post Graduate Jl etc. *Recreations:* golf, painting. *Address:* River Walk, Shooters Hill, Pangbourne, Reading RG8 7DU. *T:* Pangbourne 4476. *Club:* Oriental.

MATTHEWS, Prof. Denis (James), CBE 1975; Concert Pianist; (first) Professor of Music, University of Newcastle upon Tyne, since 1971; *b* Coventry, 27 Feb. 1919; *o s* of Arthur and Elsie Randall Matthews; *m* 1941, Mira Howe (marr. diss., 1960); one *s* three *d ; m* 1963, Brenda McDermott; one *s* one *d. Educ:* Warwick. Thalberg Scholar, 1935, Blumenthal Composition Scholar, 1937, at RAM; studied with Harold Craxton and William Alwyn; Worshipful Co. of Musicians' Medal, 1938; first public appearances in London at Queen's Hall and National Gallery, 1939; has broadcast frequently, made records, given talks on musical subjects; soloist at Royal Philharmonic Society's concerts, May and Nov. 1945; toured USA and visited Potsdam with Royal Air Force Orchestra, 1944-45; Vienna Bach Festival, 1950; Canada, 1951, 1957, 1963; South Africa, 1953, 1954, 1962; Poland, 1956, 1960; Egypt and Far East, 1963; World Tour, 1964; N Africa, 1966; W and E Africa, 1968; Latin America, 1968, 1970; Australia, 1977, 1979. Mem., Arts Council of GB, 1972-73. Favourite composers: Bach, Mozart, Beethoven, Wagner. Hon. DMus: St Andrews, 1973; Hull, 1978; Hon. DLitt Warwick, 1982. Cobbett Medal, Musicians' Co., 1973. *Publications:* piano pieces, works for violin, 'cello; In Pursuit of Music (autobiog.), 1966; Beethoven Piano Sonatas, 1968; Keyboard Music, 1972; Brahms's Three Phases, 1972; Brahms Piano Music, 1978; Toscanini, 1982. *Recreations:* astronomy, filing-systems, reading aloud. *Address:* Department of Music, University of Newcastle upon Tyne, NE1 7RU.

MATTHEWS, Douglas, BA; FLA; Librarian, The London Library, since 1980; *b* 23 Aug. 1927; *s* of Benjamin Matthews and Mary (*née* Pearson); *m* 1968, Sarah Maria Williams; two *d. Educ:* Acklam Hall Sch., Middlesbrough; Durham Univ. Assistant: India Office Library, 1952-62; Kungl. Biblioteket, Stockholm, 1956-57; Librarian, Home Office, 1962-64; Dep. Librarian, London Library, 1965-80. *Address:* 1 Priory Terrace, Mountfield Road, Lewes, Sussex BN7 2UT. *T:* Lewes 5635. *Club:* Garrick.

MATTHEWS, Dr Drummond Hoyle, VRD 1967; FRS 1974; Senior Research Associate, Scientific Director, British Institutions Reflection Profiling Syndicate, at the University of Cambridge, since 1982; Fellow, Wolfson College, Cambridge, since 1980; *b* 5 Feb. 1931; *s* of late Captain C. B. and late Mrs E. M. Matthews; *m* 1963, Elizabeth Rachel McMullen (marr. diss. 1980); one *s* one *d. Educ:* Bryanston Sch.; King's Coll., Cambridge. BA 1954, MA 1959, PhD 1962. FRNVR, 1949-51, retd 1967. Geologist, Falkland Islands Dependencies Survey, 1955-57; returned to Cambridge (BP student), 1958; Research Fellow, King's Coll., 1960; Sen. Asst in Research, Dept of Geophysics, 1960; Asst Dir of Research, 1966; Reader in Marine Geology, 1971. Balzan Prize (jtly), 1982. *Publications:* papers on marine geophysics in jls and books. *Recreations:* walking, sailing. *Address:* British Institutions Reflection Profiling Syndicate, Bullard Laboratories, Madingley Road, Cambridge. *Clubs:* Antarctic, Cruising Association.

MATTHEWS, Edwin James Thomas, TD 1946; Chief Taxing Master of the Supreme Court, since 1979 (Master, 1965-78); *b* 2 May 1915; *s* of Edwin Martin Matthews (killed in action, 1917); *m* 1939, Katherine Mary Hirst, BA (Oxon.), Dip. Soc. Sc. (Leeds); two *d. Educ:* Sedbergh Sch., Yorks. Admitted as Solicitor of Supreme Court, 1938; practice on own account in Middlesbrough, 1938-39. Served in Royal Artillery, 1939-46, UK, France and Belgium (Dunkirk 1940); released with rank of Major. Partner, Chadwick Son & Nicholson, Solicitors, Dewsbury, Yorks, 1946-50; Area Sec., No. 6 (W Midland) Legal Aid Area Cttee of Law Soc., 1950-56; Sec. of Law Soc. for Contentious Business (including responsibility for administration of Legal Aid and Advice Schemes), 1956-65. Toured Legal Aid Offices in USA for Ford Foundation and visited Toronto to advise Govt of Ontario, 1963. Mem., Council, British Academy of Forensic Sciences, 1965-68. Special Consultant to NBPI on Solicitors' Costs, 1967-68. Member: Lord Chancellor's Adv. Cttee on Legal Aid, 1972-77; Working Party on Legal Aid Legislation, 1974-76;

Working Party on the Criminal Trial, 1980-; Supreme Ct Procedure Cttee, 1982-. *Publications:* contrib. Halsbury's Laws of England, 1961 and Atkins Encyclopaedia of Forms and Precedents, 1962; (with Master Graham-Green) Costs in Criminal Cases and Legal Aid, 1965; (jointly) Legal Aid and Advice Under the Legal Aid and Advice Acts, 1949 to 1964, 1971; (ed jtly) Supreme Court Practice; contribs to journals. *Recreations:* trout fishing, theatre, gardening, French wines. *Address:* The Old Garden, Dunorlan Park, Tunbridge Wells, Kent. *T:* Tunbridge Wells 24027.

MATTHEWS, Prof. Ernest, DDS, PhD, MSc, ARCS, DIC, FDSRCS; Director of Prosthetics, University of Manchester, 1935-70, now Professor Emeritus; *b* 14 Dec. 1904; *s* of James Alfred Matthews, Portsmouth; *m* 1928, Doris Pipe (decd); one *d* (two *s* decd). *Educ:* Imperial Coll., London; Cambridge; Guy's Hospital, London. Demonstrator and Lecturer, Guy's Hospital Medical and Dental Schs, 1926-34; Prosthetic Dental Surgeon, Manchester Royal Infirmary, 1937; Dean and Dir, Turner Dental Sch., 1966-69; Cons. Dental Surgeon, Christie Hosp., 1945; Hon. Adviser in Dental Surgery to Manchester Regional Hospital Board, 1951. Silver Jubilee Medal, 1977. *Recreation:* gardening. *Address:* 16 The Spain, Petersfield, Hants GU32 3LA.

MATTHEWS, Ven. Frederick Albert John; Archdeacon of Plymouth, 1962-78; Archdeacon Emeritus since 1978; Vicar of Plympton St Mary, Devon, since 1961; Prebendary of Exeter Cathedral, since 1978; *b* 4 Jan. 1913; *s* of Albert and Elizabeth Anne Matthews; *m* 1941, Edna Stacey; one *d. Educ:* Devonport High Sch.; Exeter Coll., Oxford. Curate of Stoke Damerel, Plymouth, 1936-44; Vicar of Pinhoe, Devon, 1944-61; Rural Dean of Aylesbeare, 1957-61. *Recreations:* Association football (spectator), walking, photography. *Address:* St Mary's Vicarage, Plympton, Plymouth PL7 4LD. *T:* Plymouth 336157.

MATTHEWS, Prof. Geoffrey, MA, PhD; FIMA; Shell Professor of Mathematics Education, Centre for Science and Mathematics Education, Chelsea College, University of London, 1968-77, now Emeritus; *b* 1 Feb. 1917; *s* of Humphrey and Gladys Matthews; *m* 1st, 1941, Patricia Mary Jackson; one *s* one *d* ; 2nd, 1972, Julia Comber. *Educ:* Marlborough; Jesus Coll., Cambridge (MA); PhD (London). Wiltshire Regt, Intelligence Officer 43rd (Wessex) Div., 1939-45, Captain (dispatches 1945; US Bronze Star, 1945). Teacher: Haberdashers' Aske's Sch., 1945-50; St Dunstan's Coll., 1950-64, Dep. Head and head of mathematics dept; Organiser, Nuffield Mathematics Teaching Project, 1964-72; Co-director (with Julia Matthews), Schools Council Early Mathematical Experiences project, 1974-79; Co-dir (with Prof. K. W. Keohane) SSRC funded prog. Concepts in Secondary Sch. Maths and Sci., 1974-79. Presenter of BBC TV programmes in series Tuesday Term, Middle School Mathematics, and Children and Mathematics; consultant to BBC series Maths in a Box and You and Me, and to ATV series Towards Mathematics. Pres., Mathematical Assoc., 1977-78; Member: Council, Inst. of Maths and its Applications, 1978-81; Cttee, Soc. of Free Painters and Sculptors, 1978-. *Publications:* Calculus, 1964; Matrices I & II, 1964; Mathematics through School, 1972; papers in Proc. Kon. Akad. Wetensch. (Amsterdam); numerous articles in Math. Gaz., etc. *Recreations:* sculpture, travel. *Address:* 50 Sydney Road, Bexleyheath, Kent DA6 8HG. *T:* 01-303 4301.

MATTHEWS, George Lloyd; Archivist, Communist Party of Great Britain; *b* 24 Jan. 1917; *s* of James and Ethel Matthews, Sandy, Beds; *m* 1940, Elisabeth Lynette Summers; no *c. Educ:* Bedford Modern Sch.; Reading Univ. Pres., Reading Univ. Students Union, 1938-39; Vice-Pres., Nat. Union of Students, 1939-40; Vice-Pres., University Labour Fedn, 1938-39. County Chm., Nat. Union of Agricultural Workers, 1945-49; Mem. Exec. Cttee, Communist Party, 1943-79; Asst Gen. Sec., Communist Party, 1949-57; Asst Editor, 1957-59, Editor, 1959-74, Daily Worker, later Morning Star; Head of Press and Publicity Dept, Communist Party of GB, 1974-79. *Recreation:* music. *Address:* c/o Communist Party, 16 King Street, WC2E 8HY. *T:* 01-836 2151.

MATTHEWS, Gordon (Richards), CBE 1974; FCA; *m* ; one *s* one *d* (and one *d* decd). *Educ:* Repton Sch. Chartered Accountant, 1932. Contested (U) General Election, Deritend, 1945, and Yardley, 1950; MP (C) Meriden Division of Warwicks, 1959-64; PPS to the Postmaster-General, 1960-64. Hon. Treas., Deritend Unionist Assoc., 1937-45; Hon. Sec., Birmingham Unionist Association, 1948-53. Pres. City of Birmingham Friendly Soc., 1957-64; Mem. Board of Management, Linen and Woollen Drapers Institution and Cottage Homes, 1950-65 (Pres. of Appeal, 1954-55); Chm. of Exec. Cttee, Birmingham Area of YMCA, 1951-59; Mem., Nat. Council and Nat. Exec. Cttee, YMCA, 1968-71; Chm., Finance Cttee, YWCA, Birmingham Area, 1965-72. Chm., Oxfordshire Br., CPRE, 1978-81. Chm., West Midlands Cons. Council, 1970-73 (Dep. Chm., 1967-70). *Recreations:* fly-fishing and foreign travel. *Address:* Windrush Cottage, Old Minster Lovell, Oxon OX8 5RN.

MATTHEWS, Horatio Keith, CMG 1963; MBE 1946; JP; HM Diplomatic Service, 1948-74; *b* 4 April 1917; *s* of late Horatio Matthews, MD and of Ruth Matthews (née McCurry); *m* 1940, Jean Andrée Batten; two *d. Educ:* Epsom Coll.; Gonville and Caius Coll., Cambridge. Entered Indian Civil Service, 1940, and served in Madras Presidency until 1947; appointed to Foreign Service, 1948; First Sec., 1949; Lisbon, 1949; Bucharest, 1951; Foreign Office, 1953; Imperial Defence Coll., 1955; Political Office with Middle East Forces, Cyprus, 1956; Counsellor, 1958; Counsellor, UK High Commission,

Canberra, 1959; Political Adviser to GOC Berlin, 1961; Corps of Inspectors, Diplomatic Service, 1964; Minister, Moscow, 1966-67; High Commissioner in Ghana, 1968-70; UN Under-Sec.-Gen. for Admin and Management, 1971-72; Asst Under-Sec. of State, MoD (on secondment), 1973-74. Mem., Bd of Visitors, HM Prison, Albany, 1976-. JP IoW 1975. *Address:* Elm House, Bembridge, IoW. *T:* Bembridge 2327. *Club:* Travellers'.

MATTHEWS, L(eonard) Harrison, FRS 1954, MA, ScD; Scientific Director, Zoological Society of London, 1951-66; *b* 12 June 1901; *s* of Harold Evan Matthews and Ruby Sarah Matthews (née Harrison); *m* 1924, Dorothy Hélène Harris; one *s* one *d. Educ:* Bristol Grammar Sch.; King's Coll., Cambridge. BA Hons 1st Class Nat. Sci. Trip., 1922; Vintner Exhibitioner King's Coll., University Frank Smart Prize. Has carried out biological researches in Africa, S America, Arctic and Antarctic, etc. Mem. of scientific staff "Discovery" Expedition, 1924; special lectr in Zoology, Univ. of Bristol, 1935; Radio Officer, Anti-Aircraft Command, 1941; Sen. Scientific Officer, Telecommunications Research Establishment, 1942; Radar liaison duties with RAF, 1943-45; Research Fell. Univ. of Bristol, 1945. Pres. Section D, British Assoc. for the Advancement of Science, 1959; President: British Academy of Forensic Science, 1962; Ray Soc., 1965; Chm., Seals Sub-Cttee, NERC, 1967-71. Member Council: Marine Biological Assoc. of UK, 1944-51; Zoological Soc. of London, 1943-45, 1946-49, 1950-51 (Vice-Pres., 1944-45, 1947-49, 1950-51); Inst. of Biology, 1954-57; Linnean Soc., of London, 1953-57; Sec., 1947-48, Pres., 1960, Assoc. of British Zoologists; Chm., World List of Scientific Periodicals, 1959-66; Acad. Mem., Assoc. of British Sci. Writers, 1956. Has made numerous sound and TV broadcasts. *Publications:* South Georgia, the Empire's Subantarctic Outpost, 1931; Wandering Albatross, 1951; British Mammals (New Naturalist), 1952; Amphibia and Reptiles, 1952; Sea Elephant, 1952; Beasts of the Field, 1954; Animals in Colour, 1959; The Senses of Animals (with Maxwell Knight), 1963; (ed) The Whale, 1968; The Life of Mammals, Vol. I, 1969, Vol. II, 1971; Introd., Darwin's Origin of Species, 1972; Introd. and explanatory notes, Waterton's Wanderings in South America, 1973; Man and Wildlife, 1975; Penguin, 1977 (with Foreword by HRH The Duke of Edinburgh); The Life of the Whale, 1978; The Seals and the Scientists, 1979; Mammals in the British Isles, 1982; numerous scientific papers on zoological subjects in jls of learned socs, Discovery Reports, Philosophical Transactions, Encyclopædia Britannica, etc. *Address:* The Old Rectory, Stansfield, via Sudbury, Suffolk CO10 8LT. *Club:* Explorers' (New York).

MATTHEWS, Maj.-Gen. Michael; Engineer in Chief (Army), from April 1983; *b* 22 April 1930; *s* of W. Matthews and M. H. Matthews; *m* 1955, Elspeth Rosemary, *d* of late Lt-Col Sir John Maclure, 3rd Bt, OBE, and of Lady Maclure; two *s* two *d. Educ:* King's Coll., Taunton, Somerset. FBIM. rcds, psc. Commissioned, Royal Engineers, 1951; served overseas, Egypt, Cyprus, Jordan, Kenya and Aden; DAA and QMG HQ 24 Inf. Bde, Kenya, 1962-65; OC, Indep. Para Sqn RE, UK and Aden, 1965-67; GSO1 (DS) Staff College, Camberley, 1968-70; CO 35 Engr Regt, BAOR, 1970-72; Col GS Ops, Exercise Planning Staff and Trg, HQ BAOR, 1972-74; CCRE, HQ1 (BR) Corps, BAOR, 1974-76; RCDS 1977; DQMG HQ BAOR, 1978-80; Dir of Personal Services (Army), 1980-83. *Recreations:* Rugby, cricket, hockey, hang gliding. *Address:* c/o Lloyds Bank, Chagford, Newton Abbot, Devon. *Club:* Army and Navy.

MATTHEWS, Mrs Pamela Winifred, (Mrs Peter Matthews), BSc (Econ.); Principal, Westfield College (University of London), 1962-65; *b* 4 Dec. 1914; *d* of Lt-Col C. C. Saunders-O'Mahony; *m* 1938, H. P. S. Matthews (*d* 1958); one *s* one *d. Educ:* St Paul's Girls' Sch.; London Sch. of Economics. Royal Institute of International Affairs, 1938-39; Foreign Office, 1939-40; The Economist Newspaper, 1940-43; Foreign Office, 1943-45; Reuters, 1945-61; Nat. Inst. for Social Work Trg, 1961-62. Independent Mem., Advertising Standards Authority, 1964-65. Governor: Northwood Coll., Middlesex, 1962-; Cardinal Manning Boys' RC School, 1980-. *Publications:* diplomatic correspondence for Reuters. *Recreations:* travel, theatre. *Address:* 1 Edwardes Place, Kensington High Street, W8. *T:* 01-603 8458.

MATTHEWS, Paul Taunton, CBE 1975; MA, PhD; FRS 1963; Vice-Chancellor, Bath University, since 1976; *b* 19 Nov. 1919; *s* of Rev. Gordon Matthews and Janet (née Viney); *m* 1947, Margit Zohn; two *s* two *d. Educ:* Mill Hill Sch.; Clare Coll., Cambridge. Research Fellow, Inst. for Advanced Study, Princeton, USA, 1950-51; ICI Research Fellow, Cambridge, 1951-52; Lectr, Univ. of Birmingham, 1952-57; Visiting Prof., Univ. of Rochester, USA, 1957; Imperial College, London: Reader in Theoretical Physics, 1957-62; Prof. of Theoretical Physics, 1962-76; Head of Dept of Physics, 1971-76; Dean, RCS, 1972-75. Mem., SRC, 1970-74; Chm., SRC Nuclear Physics Bd, 1972-74; Mem., Scientific Policy Cttee, CERN, Geneva, 1972-78. Adams Prize, Cambridge, 1958; Rutherford Medal and Prize, IPPS, 1979. *Publications:* Quantum Mechanics, 1963 (USA); Nuclear Apple, 1971; papers on elementary particle physics in Proc. Royal Soc., Phil. Mag., Phys. Review, Nuovo Cimento, Review Mod. Phys., Annals of Physics. *Address:* Bath University, Claverton Down, Bath, Avon BA2 7AY.

MATTHEWS, Percy; *b* 24 July 1921; *s* of Samuel and Minnie Matthews; *m* 1946, Audrey Rosenthal; one *s* two *d. Educ:* Parmiters Sch., London. Hon. Fellow, St Peter's Coll., Oxford. Mem. Management Cttee, Royal Postgrad. Med. Sch., Hammersmith Hosp.; Freeman, City of London. *Recreations:* painting, golf. *Address:* 41 Avenida Del Golf, Alhoa, Marbella, Malaga, Spain.

MATTHEWS, Mrs Peter; see Matthews, Mrs Pamela W.

MATTHEWS, Sir Peter (Alec), Kt 1975; AO 1980; Chairman: Vickers Ltd, since 1980 (Managing Director, 1970-79); Pegler-Hattersley Ltd, since 1979 (Director, since 1977); Director: Lloyds Bank, since 1974 (Chairman, Central London Regional Board, 1978-); British Electric Traction Co. Ltd, since 1976; Sun Alliance and London Insurance, since 1979; Lead Industries Group, since 1980; Hamilton Oil Great Britain, since 1981; b 21 Sept. 1922; s of Major Alec Bryan Matthews and Elsie Lazarus Barlow; m 1946, Sheila Dorothy Bunting; four s one d. Educ: Shawnigan Lake Sch., Vancouver Island; Oundle Sch. Served Royal Engineers (retired as Major), 1940-46. Joined Stewarts and Lloyds Ltd, 1946; Director of Research and Technical Development, 1962; Member for R&D, BSC, 1968-70, Dep. Chm., 1973-76. Member: British Overseas Trade Bd, 1973-77; Export Guarantees Adv. Council, 1973-78; NRDC, 1974-80; Engineering Industries Council, 1976- (Chm., 1980-); Adv. Council for Applied R&D, 1976-80. Pres., Engineering Employers Fedn, 1982-83; Chm., Council, University Coll., London, 1980- (Hon. Fellow, 1982). CBIM, FRSA. Recreations: sailing, gardening. Address: Vickers House, Millbank Tower, SW1P 4RA. T: 01-828 7777.

MATTHEWS, Peter Bryan Conrad, FRS 1973; MD, DSc; Reader in Physiology since 1978 and Tutor and Student of Christ Church since 1958, University of Oxford; b 23 Dec. 1928; s of Prof. Sir Bryan Matthews, qv ; m 1956, Margaret Rosemary Blears; one s one d. Educ: Marlborough Coll.; King's Coll., Cambridge; Oxford Univ. Clinical School. Univ. Lectr in Physiology, Univ. of Oxford, 1961-77. Sir Lionel Whitby Medal, Cambridge Univ., 1959; Robert Bing Prize, Swiss Acad. of Med. Science, 1971. Publications: Mammalian Muscle Receptors and their Central Actions, 1972; papers on neurophysiology in various scientific jls. Address: University Laboratory of Physiology, Parks Road, Oxford OX1 3PT. T: Oxford 57451.

MATTHEWS, Prof. Peter Hugoe; Professor of Linguistics, University of Cambridge, since 1980; b 10 March 1934; s of John Hugo and Cecily Eileen Emsley Matthews. Educ: Montpellier Sch., Paignton; Clifton Coll.; St John's Coll., Cambridge (MA 1960). Lectr in Linguistics, UCNW, 1961-65 (on leave Indiana Univ., Bloomington, 1963-64); University of Reading: Lectr in Linguistic Science, 1965-69; Reader, 1969-75; Prof., 1975-80 (on leave as Fellow, King's Coll., Cambridge, 1970-71, and as Fellow, Netherlands Inst. of Advanced Study, Wassenaar, 1977-78). An Editor, Jl of Linguistics, 1970-79. Publications: Inflectional Morphology, 1972; Morphology, 1974; Generative Grammar and Linguistic Competence, 1979; Syntax, 1981; articles esp. in Jl of Linguistics. Recreations: cycling, bird-watching. Address: St John's College, Cambridge.

MATTHEWS, Sir Peter (Jack), Kt 1981; CVO 1978; OBE 1974; QPM 1970; DL; Chief Constable of Surrey, 1968-82; b 25 Dec. 1917; s of Thomas Francis Matthews and Agnes Jack; m 1944, Margaret, er d of Cecil Levett, London; one s. Educ: Blackridge Public Sch., West Lothian. Joined Metropolitan Police, 1937; Flt-Lt (pilot) RAF, 1942-46; Metropolitan Police, 1946-65; seconded Cyprus, 1955; Chief Supt P Div. 1963-65; Chief Constable: of East Suffolk, 1965-67; of Suffolk, 1967-68. President: British Section, Internat. Police Assoc., 1964-70 (Internat. Pres. 1966-70); Assoc. of Chief Police Officers of England, Wales and NI, 1976-77 (Chm., Sub-Cttee on Terrorism and Allied Matters, 1976-82; Rep. at Interpol, 1977-80); Chief Constables' Club, 1980-81; Vice-Chm., Home Office Standing Adv. Cttee on Police Dogs, 1982- (Chm., 1978-82; Chm., Training Sub-Cttee); led British Police Study Team to advise Singapore Police, 1982. CBIM 1978. DL Surrey, 1981. Club: Royal Air Force.

MATTHEWS, Rt. Rev. Ralph Vernon; see Waiapu, Bishop of.

MATTHEWS, Richard Bonnar, CBE 1971; QPM 1965; Chief Constable, Warwickshire, 1964-76 (Warwickshire and Coventry, 1969-74); b 18 Dec. 1915; er s of late Charles Richard Matthews, Worthing; m 1943, Joan, d of late Basil Worsley, Henstridge, Som; two d. Educ: Stowe School. Served War of 1939-45, Lieut, RNVR. Joined Metropolitan Police, 1936; Asst Chief Constable, E Sussex, 1954-56; Chief Constable of Cornwall and Isles of Scilly, 1956-64. Chm., Traffic Cttee, Assoc. of Chief Police Officers, 1973-76. Mem., Williams Cttee on Obscenity and Film Censorship, 1977-79. Recreations: ski-ing, fishing, gardening. Address: Smoke Acre, Great Bedwyn, Marlborough, Wilts SN8 3LP. T: Marlborough 870584. Club: Naval.

MATTHEWS, Prof. Richard Ellis Ford, ScD, FRS 1974, FRSNZ, FNZIC; Professor of Microbiology, Department of Cell Biology, University of Auckland, New Zealand, since 1962; b Hamilton, NZ, 20 Nov. 1921; s of Gerald Wilfrid Matthews and Ruby Miriam (née Crawford); m 1950, Lois Ann Bayley; three s one d. Educ: Mt Albert Grammar Sch.; Auckland University Coll.; Univ. of Cambridge. MSc (NZ), PhD, ScD (Cantab). Postdoctoral Research Fellow, Univ. of Wisconsin, 1949. Plant Diseases Div., DSIR, Auckland, NZ: Mycologist, 1950-53; Sen. Mycologist, 1954-55; (on leave from DSIR as a visiting worker at ARC Virus Research Unit, Molteno Inst., Cambridge, 1952-56); Sen. Principal Scientific Officer, DSIR, 1956-61; Head of Dept of Cell Biology, Univ. of Auckland, 1962-77. Pres., Internat. Cttee for Taxonomy of Viruses, 1975-81. Publications: Plant Virus Serology, 1957; Plant Virology, 1970, 2nd edn 1981; over 110 original papers in scientific jls. Recreations: gardening, sea fishing, bee keeping. Address: 3 Sadgrove Terrace, Mt Albert, Auckland 3, New Zealand. T: 866005,

Auckland; (summer residences) Rural Delivery 4, Hikurangi; 1019 Beach Road, Long Bay, Auckland.

MATTHEWS, Prof. Robert Charles Oliver, CBE 1975; FBA 1968; Master of Clare College, Cambridge, since 1975; Professor of Political Economy, Cambridge University, since 1980; b 16 June 1927; s of Oliver Harwood Matthews, WS, and Ida Finlay; m 1948, Joyce Hilda Lloyds; one d. Educ: Edinburgh Academy; Corpus Christi Coll., Oxford (Hon. Fellow, 1976). Student, Nuffield Coll., Oxford, 1947-48; Lectr, Merton Coll., Oxford, 1948-49; University Asst Lectr in Economics, Cambridge, 1949-51, and Univ. Lectr, 1951-65. Fellow of St John's Coll., Cambridge, 1950-65. Visiting Prof., University of California, Berkeley, 1961-62; Drummond Prof. of Political Economy, Oxford, and Fellow of All Souls Coll., 1965-75. Chm., SSRC, 1972-75. Managing Trustee, Nuffield Foundn, 1975-; Trustee, Urwick Orr and Partners Ltd, 1978-. Member: Council, Royal Econ. Soc., 1973-82; Exec. Cttee NIESR, 1975-; Central Adv. Council on Sci. and Tech., 1967-70; Council, British Academy, 1972-75; OECD Expert Group on Non-inflationary Growth, 1975-77. Chm., Bank of England Panel of Academic Consultants, 1977-. Pres., British Chess Problem Soc., 1971-72. Hon. DLitt Warwick, 1980. Publications: A Study in Trade Cycle History, 1954; The Trade Cycle, 1958; (with F. H. Hahn) Théorie de la Croissance Economique, 1972; (ed) Economic Growth: trends and factors, 1981; (with C. H. Feinstein and J. C. Odling-Smee) British Economic Growth 1856-1973, 1982; (ed with G. B. Stafford) The Grants Economy and Collective Consumption, 1982; articles in learned journals. (With M. Lipton and J. M. Rice) Chess Problems: Introduction to an Art, 1963. Address: The Master's Lodge, Clare College, Cambridge. Club: Reform.

MATTHEWS, Ronald Sydney, CB 1978; Deputy Secretary, Department of Health and Social Security, 1976-81; b 26 July 1922; s of George and Louisa Matthews; m 1945, Eleanor Bronwen Shaw; one s one d. Educ: Kingsbury County School. RAF, 1940-46. Clerical Officer, Min. of Health, 1939; Principal 1959; Private Sec. to Minister of Health, 1967-68; Private Sec. to Sec. of State for Social Services, 1968-69; Asst Sec. 1968; Under-Sec., DHSS, 1973-76. Recreations: walking, gardening, reading. Address: 4 Saxon Rise, Winterborne Stickland, Blandford Forum, Dorset DT11 0PQ.

MATTHEWS, Sir Russell, Kt 1982; OBE 1971; company director; retired civil engineer; b 26 July 1896; s of Robert and Grace Matthews; m 1932, Elizabeth Mary Brodie; two s two d. Educ: New Plymouth Boys' High Sch.; London Sch. of Engineering. Formed Matthews & Kirkby and ran business as Man. Dir, 1936-42, then sole Proprietor, Matthews & Co., at that time the country's leading road sealing contractor; Founder Chm., and Dir, Ivon Watkins Dows, 1944-62; Founder Director: Kaikariki Sand & Gravel Co., 1944-68; R. J. Burkitt, 1956-; Pacific Constructors, 1958-71; Russell Matthews Industries, 1959-; Taranaki Hldgs, 1959-; Fitzroy Engineering, 1960-; Maxwell Machines, 1962-71; Technic Industries, 1965-; Aid Industries, 1967-71; Technic Group, 1969-; Asheltic Construction, 1971-. Recreation: gardening. Address: Tupare, 487 Mangorei Road, New Plymouth, New Zealand. T: 86480.

MATTHEWS, Sir Stanley, Kt 1965; CBE 1957; professional footballer; b Hanley, Stoke-on-Trent, 1 Feb. 1915; s of late Jack Matthews, Seymour Street, Hanley; m 1st, 1935, Elizabeth Hall Vallance (marr. diss. 1975); one s one d ; 2nd, 1975, Gertrud (Mila) Winterova. Educ: Wellington Sch., Hanley. Played in first Football League match, 1931; first played for England, 1934, and fifty-five times subsequently; Blackpool FC, 1947-61 (FA Cup, 1953); Stoke City FC, 1961-65. Freedom of Stoke-on-Trent, 1963. Publication: The Stanley Matthews Story, 1960. Recreations: golf, tennis. Address: Idle House, Marsaxlokk, Malta. T: 71068. Club: National Sporting.

MATTHEWS, Thomas Stanley; journalist; b 16 Jan. 1901; s of late Rt Rev. Paul Matthews, sometime Bishop of New Jersey, and late Elsie Procter; m 1st, 1925, Juliana Stevens Cuyler (d 1949); four s ; 2nd, 1954, Martha Gellhorn; 3rd, 1964, Pamela, widow of Lt-Col V. Peniakoff. Educ: Park Hill, Lyndhurst, Hants; Shattuck Sch. (Minn.); St Paul's Sch. (Concord, NH); Princeton Univ.; New Coll., Oxford (MA). Doctor of Humane Letters, Kenyon Coll., Ohio; Doctor of Letters, Rollins Coll., Florida. Editorial staff: The New Republic, 1925-29; Time, 1929; Exec. Editor, Time, 1942; Managing Editor Time, 1943-50, Editor, 1950-53. Publications: To the Gallows I Must Go, 1931; The Moon's No Fool, 1934; The Sugar Pill, 1957; Name and Address, 1960; O My America!, 1962; The Worst Unsaid (verse), 1962; Why So Gloomy? (verse), 1966; Great Tom: notes towards the Definition of T. S. Eliot, 1974; Jacks or Better, 1977 (Under the Influence, UK, 1979); Journal to the End of the Day, 1979. Address: Cavendish Hall, Cavendish, Suffolk. T: Clare 296. Clubs: Athenæum, Buck's; Century Association, Coffee House (New York); Reading Room (Newport, RI).

MATTHEWS, Rt. Rev. Timothy John, CD 1963; BA, LST, STh, DCL; Chaplain Emeritus, Bishop's College School; Chaplain, Advisory Committee on Postulants for Holy Orders. Educ: Bishop's Univ., Lennoxville. Deacon 1932, priest 1933, Edmonton; Vicar of Viking, 1933-37; Incumbent of Edson, 1937-40; Rector of Coaticook, 1940-44; Lake St John, 1944-52; Rector and Archdeacon of Gaspé, 1952-57; Rector of Lennoxville, 1957-71; Archdeacon of St Francis, 1957-71; Bishop of Quebec, 1971-77. Address: 23 High Street, Lennoxville, PQ J1M 1E6, Canada. Clubs: St George's (Sherbrooke); Hole-in-One, Lennoxville Golf, Milby Golf.

MATTHEWS, Prof. Walter Bryan; Professor of Clinical Neurology, University of Oxford, since 1970; Fellow of St Edmund Hall, Oxford, since 1970; *b* 7 April 1920; *s* of Very Rev. Dr Walter Robert Matthews; *m* 1943, Margaret Forster; one *s* one *d. Educ:* Marlborough Coll.; University Coll., Oxford. MA, DM, FRCP. RAMC, 1943-46. Senior Registrar, Oxford, 1948; Chief Asst, Dept of Neurology, Manchester Royal Infirmary, 1949-52; Senior Registrar, King's College Hosp., 1952-54; Consultant Neurologist, Derbyshire Royal Infirmary, 1954-68; Consultant Neurologist, Manchester Royal Infirmary and Crumpsall Hosp., 1968-70. President: Section of Neurology, RSM, 1981; Assoc. of British Neurologists, 1982. Osler Orator, RCP, 1981. Editor-in-Chief, Jl of Neurological Scis, 1977-. *Publications:* Practical Neurology, 1963, 3rd edn 1975; (with H. G. Miller) Diseases of the Nervous System, 1972, 3rd edn 1979; (ed) Recent Advances in Clinical Neurology I, 1975; Multiple Sclerosis: the facts, 1978; (ed) Recent Advances in Clinical Neurology II, 1978; papers in Brain, Quarterly Jl of Medicine, etc. *Recreation:* walking. *Address:* Sandford House, Sandford-on-Thames, Oxford. *Club:* United Oxford & Cambridge University.

MATTHÖFER, Hans; Member of the Bundestag (Social Democrat), since 1961; *b* Bochum, 25 Sept. 1925; *m* Traute Matthöfer (*née* Mecklenburg). *Educ:* primary sch.; studied economics and social sciences in Frankfurt/Main and Madison, Wis, USA, 1948-53 (grad. Economics). Employed as manual and clerical worker, 1940-42; Reich Labour Service, 1942; conscripted into German Army, 1943 (Armoured Inf.), final rank NCO. Joined SPD (Social Democratic Party of Germany), 1950; employed in Economics Dept, Bd of Management, IG Metall (Metalworkers' Union) and specialized in problems arising in connection with automation and mechanization, 1953 (Head of Trng and Educn Dept, 1961). Member, OEEC Mission in Washington and Paris, 1957-61; Vice-Pres., Gp of Parliamentarians on Latin American Affairs (Editor of periodical Esprès Español until end of 1972); Mem., Patronage Cttee of German Section of Amnesty Internat.; Pres., Bd of Trustees, German Foundn for Developing Countries, 1971-73; Parly State Sec. in Federal Min. for Economic Co-operation, 1972; Federal Minister for Research and Technology, 1974, for Finance, 1978-82, for Posts and Telecommunications, 1982. *Publications:* Der Unterschied zwischen den Tariflöhnen und den Effektivverdiensten in der Metallindustrie der Bundesrepublik, 1956; Technological Change in the Metal Industries (in two parts), 1961-62; Der Beitrag politischer Bildung zur Emanzipation der Arbeitnehmer—Materialien zur Frage des Bildungsurlaubs, 1970; Streiks und streikähnliche Formen des Kampfes der Arbeitnehmer im Kapitalismus, 1971; Für eine menschliche Zukunft—Sozialdemokratische Forschungs—und Technologiepolitik, 1976; Humanisierung der Arbeit und Produktivität in der Industriegesellschaft, 1977, 1978, 1980; numerous articles on questions of trade union, development, research and finance policies. *Address:* Federal Ministry for Posts and Telecommunications, Bonn, West Germany.

MATTINGLY, Alan; Secretary of the Ramblers' Association, since 1974; *b* 19 May 1949; *s* of Alexander and Patricia Mattingly; *m* 1980, Wendy Mallard. *Educ:* The Latymer Sch., Edmonton; St John's Coll., Cambridge (BA). Chm., Council for Nat. Parks, 1979- (Vice-Chm., 1977-79); Vice-Pres., Countryside Holidays Assoc., 1980-. Mem., Newham Borough Council, 1980-, Chm., Labour Gp, 1982-. *Publications:* Tackle Rambling, 1981; Walking in the National Parks, 1982; contributions to: People and their Settlements, 1976; The Complete Rambler, 1978; Policies for Landscapes under Pressure, 1979; Freedom to Roam, 1980. *Recreation:* walking. *Address:* 96 Geere Road, E15 3PW.

MATTINGLY, Dr Stephen; TD 1964; FRCP; Consultant Physician, Middlesex Hospital, 1958-81; Consultant Physician, 1956-82 and Medical Director, 1972-82, Garston Manor Rehabilitation Centre; Hon. Consultant in Rheumatology and Rehabilitation to the Army, 1976-81; Member, Attendance Allowance Board, since 1978; *b* 1 March 1922; *s* of Harold Mattingly and Marion Grahame Meikleham; *m* 1945, Brenda Mary Pike; one *s. Educ:* Leighton Park Sch.; UCH (MB, BS); Dip. in Physical Med., 1953. FRCP 1970. House-surg., UCH, 1947; Regtl MO, 2/10 Gurkha Rifles, RAMC Far East, 1947-49; House-surg. and Registrar, UCH, 1950-55; Sen. Registrar, Mddx Hosp., 1955-56. Reg. Med. Consultant for London, S-Eastern, Eastern and Southern Regions, Dept of Employment, 1960-74. Lt-Col RAMC TA, 1952-67. *Publications:* (contrib.) Progress in Clinical Rheumatology, 1965; (contrib.) Textbook of Rheumatic Diseases, ed Copeman, 1969; (contrib.) Fractures and Joint Injuries, ed Watson Jones, 1976; (ed) Rehabilitation Today, 1977. *Recreation:* swimming. *Address:* Highfield House, Little Brington, Northants. *T:* East Haddon 271.

MATTURI, Sahr Thomas, CMG 1967; BSc, PhD; farmer; High Commissioner in London for Sierra Leone, 1978-80; retired from Sierra Leone Foreign Service; *b* 22 Oct. 1925; *s* of Sahr and Konneh Matturi; *m* 1956, Anna Adella Stephens; two *s* one *d. Educ:* University Coll., Ibadan; Hull Univ. School Teacher, 1944-47, 1954-55; University Lecturer, 1959-63; Principal, Njala Univ. Coll., 1963-76; Vice-Chancellor, Univ. of Sierra Leone, 1968-70; Acting Vice-Chancellor and Pro Vice-Chancellor, 1972-74, Pro Vice-Chancellor, 1966-68, 1970-72, 1973-75. Ambassador of Sierra Leone to Italy, Austria and Yugoslavia, and Perm. Rep. to UN Specialised Agencies in Rome, Geneva and Vienna, 1977-78. Chm., W African Exams Council, 1971-76. Mem., British Mycol. Soc. LLD *hc* Hull, 1981. FRSA. *Recreations:* cricket, lawn tennis, shooting. *Address:* c/o Jaiama Secondary School, Private Mail Bag, Koidu Town, Sierra Leone.

MAUCHLINE, Lord; Michael Edward Abney-Hastings; ranger with New South Wales Pastures Protection Board; *b* 22 July 1942; *s* and *heir* of Countess of Loudoun (13th in line), *qv* and *s* of Captain Walter Strickland Lord (whose marriage to the Countess of Loudoun was dissolved, 1945; his son assumed, by deed poll, 1946, the surname of Abney-Hastings in lieu of his patronymic); *m* 1969, Noelene Margaret McCormick, 2nd *d* of Mr and Mrs W. J. McCormick, Barham, NSW; one *s* three *d* (of whom one *s* one *d* are twins). *Educ:* Ampleforth. *Address:* 74 Coreen Street, Jerilderie, NSW 2716, Australia.

MAUCHLINE, Rev. Prof. John, MA, BD (Glasgow), DD (Edinburgh); Professor of Old Testament Language and Literature, University of Glasgow, 1935-72, and Principal of Trinity College, Glasgow, 1953-72; *b* 5 July 1902; *m* 1930, Helen Brisbane Paterson, MA; three *s. Educ:* Hutchesons' Grammar Sch.; Glasgow Univ. (First Class Hons in Semitic Langs); British Sch. of Archæology, American Sch. of Oriental Research, and l'Ecole St Etienne, Jerusalem. Maclean Scholar, 1926; Faulds Fellow, 1926-29; Minister of South Dalziel Church, Motherwell, 1929-34; Prof. of Old Testament Language and Literature, Trinity Coll., Glasgow, 1934. Principal Pollok Lecturer in Pine Hill Divinity Hall, Halifax, Nova Scotia, 1949. *Publications:* God's People Israel; The Balaam-Balak Songs and Saga, in W. B. Stevenson Anniversary Volume; Hosea in The Interpreter's Bible; 1st and 2nd Kings, in Peake's Commentary on The Bible (new and revised edn); Isaiah 1-39 (Torch Bible Commentary); (ed) An Introductory Hebrew Grammar, by A. B. Davidson, 26th edn, 1967; 1 and 2 Samuel (New Century Bible), 1971; articles in periodicals. *Address:* Tigh-na-Drochaidh, Benderloch, near Connel, Argyll. *T:* Ledaig 305.

MAUD; *see* Redcliffe-Maud.

MAUD, Hon. Humphrey John Hamilton, CMG 1982; HM Diplomatic Service; Ambassador to Luxembourg, since 1982; *b* 17 April 1934; *s* of Baron Redcliffe-Maud, *qv* ; *m* 1963, Maria Eugenia Gazitua; three *s. Educ:* Eton; King's Coll., Cambridge (Scholar; Classics and History); MA. Instructor in Classics, Univ. of Minnesota, 1958-59; entered Foreign Service, 1959; FO, 1960-61; Madrid, 1961-63; Havana, 1963-65; FO, 1966-67; Cabinet Office, 1968-69; Paris, 1970-74; Nuffield Coll., Oxford (Econs), 1974-75; Head of Financial Relations Dept, FCO, 1975-79; Minister, Madrid, 1979-82. *Recreations:* music ('cellist). *Address:* c/o Foreign and Commonwealth Office, SW1A 2AH; 28 Whittlesey Street, SE1. *T:* 01-928 6502. *Club:* United Oxford & Cambridge University.

MAUDE, family name of Viscount Hawarden.

MAUDE, Rt. Hon. Sir Angus (Edmund Upton), Kt 1981; TD; PC 1979; MP (C) Stratford-upon-Avon Division of Warwickshire, since Aug. 1963; author and journalist; *b* 8 Sept. 1912; *o c* of late Col Alan Hamer Maude, CMG, DSO, TD, and late Dorothy Maude (*née* Upton); *m* 1946, Barbara Elizabeth Earnshaw, *o d* of late John Earnshaw Sutcliffe, Bushey; two *s* two *d. Educ:* Rugby Sch. (Scholar); Oriel Coll., Oxford (MA). Financial journalist, 1933-39: The Times, 1933-34; Daily Mail, 1935-39. Commissioned in RASC (TA), May 1939; served in RASC 1939-45, at home and in North Africa (PoW, Jan. 1942-May 1945); Major 56th (London) Armd Divl Column RASC (TA), 1947-51. Dep. Dir of PEP, 1948-50; MP (C) Ealing (South), 1950-57, (Ind. C), 1957-58; Dir, Conservative Political Centre, 1951-55; a Dep. Chm., Cons. Party, 1975-79 (Chm. Res. Dept, 1975-79); Paymaster Gen., 1979-81. Editor of the Sydney Morning Herald, 1958-61. Contested S Dorset, by-election, Nov. 1962. *Publications:* (with Roy Lewis) The English Middle Classes, 1949; Professional People, 1952; (with Enoch Powell) Biography of a Nation, 1955; Good Learning, 1964; South Asia, 1966; The Common Problem, 1969. *Address:* South Newington House, near Banbury, Oxon. *Club:* Carlton.

MAUDE, His Honour John Cyril, QC 1942; *b* 3 April 1901; *s* of Cyril Maude and Winifred Emery; *m* 1st, 1927, Rosamond Willing Murray (from whom he obtained a divorce, 1955), *d* of late Dr T. Morris Murray, Boston, Mass, USA; one *d* ; *m* 2nd, 1955, Maureen Constance (who *m* 1st, 1930, 4th Marquess of Dufferin and Ava, killed in action, 1945; one *s* two *d* ; 2nd, 1948, Major (Harry Alexander) Desmond Buchanan, MC (from whom she obtained a divorce, 1954)), 2nd *d* of late Hon. Arthur Ernest Guinness. *Educ:* Eton; Christ Church, Oxford. Joined Gen. Staff, War Office, temporary civil asst, 1939; Intelligence Corps, actg Major, 1940; offices of War Cabinet, 1942. Barrister, Middle Temple, 1925; KC 1943; Bencher, 1951; Mem., Bar Council, 1952. Counsel to PO at Central Criminal Court, 1935-42; Jun. Counsel to Treasury at Central Criminal Court, 1942-43; Recorder of Devizes, 1939-44, of Plymouth, 1944-54; Additional Judge, Mayor's and City of London Court, 1954-65; Additional Judge, Central Criminal Court, 1965-68. MP (C) Exeter, 1945-51. Chancellor of the Diocese of Bristol, 1948-50. Dir, Old Vic Trust Ltd, 1951-54; Chairman of the British Drama League, 1952-54; Governor, Royal Victoria Hall Foundn, 1953. Chm., Family Service Units, 1954; Mem. Bd, Middlesex Hosp., 1951-62. *Address:* Great Maytham Hall, Rolvenden, Kent. *T:* Rolvenden 512.

See also Marquess of Dufferin and Ava.

MAUDE-ROXBY, John Henry; Chairman: Cameron Choat and Partners, since 1977; Maude-Roxby, Sussman Associates, since 1978; *b* 4 March 1919; *m* 1966, Katherine Jewell; one *s. Educ:* Radley Coll.; Hertford Coll., Oxford (BA). ACIS. Regular Army Officer, Royal Artillery, 1939-59; Allied

Suppliers Ltd, 1959-73; Dir, Cavenham Ltd, 1972-73; Dep. Chm. and Man. Dir, Morgan Edwards Ltd, 1973-74; Dir Gen., Inst. of Grocery Distribution, 1974-77. Regional Trading Manager, Mercia Region, Nat. Trust, 1979-. *Recreations:* shooting, golf, gardening. *Address:* Rockhill, All Stretton, Shropshire. *T:* Church Stretton 722536. *Clubs:* Army and Navy; Vincent's (Oxford).

MAUDSLAY, Major Sir (James) Rennie, GCVO 1980 (KCVO 1972; CVO 1967); KCB 1979; MBE 1945; Keeper of the Privy Purse and Treasurer to the Queen, 1971-81 (Assistant Keeper, 1958-71); Extra Equerry to the Queen, since 1973; *b* 13 Aug. 1915; *o s* of late Joseph Maudslay and of Mrs Ruth Maudslay (*née* Partridge), Pinewood Copse, Boundstone, Farnham, Surrey; *m* 1951, (Jane) Ann, *d* of A. V. McCarty, Helena, Arkansas; two *s* one *d. Educ:* Harrow Sch. 2nd Lt, KRRC, 1938; served 1938-45 (despatches five times); Hon. Major, 1945. Chm., Mid-Southern Water Co.; Dir, Lyon, Lohr & Sly Ltd; Mem. of Lloyd's. Pres., Farnham Conservative Assoc., 1954-57; Pres., Maudslay Soc., 1963-65; Hon. Mem., Jun. Instn of Engineers. Employed Lord Chamberlain's Office, 1952-53. Holds Order of: Verdienst (Germany), 1958; Taj (Iran), 1959; Dakshuna Bahu (Nepal), 1960; Legion of Honour (France), 1960; Crown of Thai (Thailand), 1960; Phœnix (Greece), 1963; Al Kawkab (Jordan), 1966; Ordine al Merito della Repubblica (Italy), 1969; Order of Kroonorde (Netherlands), 1972; Order of Merit (Germany), 1972; Order of Star (Afghanistan), 1972; Order of Dannebrog (Denmark), 1974. *Recreations:* shooting, gardening. *Address:* Mornish House, Westwood Road, Windlesham, Surrey GU20 6LP. *T:* Ascot 21699. *Clubs:* White's, MCC.

MAUGHAN, Air Vice-Marshal Charles Gilbert, CB 1976; CBE 1970; AFC; General Secretary, The Royal British Legion, since 1978; *b* 3 March 1923. *Educ:* Sir George Monoux Grammar Sch.; Harrow County Sch. Served War, Fleet Air Arm (flying Swordfishes and Seafires), 1942-46. Joined RAF, 1949, serving with Meteor, Vampire and Venom sqdns in Britain and Germany; comd No 65 (Hunter) Sqdn, Duxford, Cambridgeshire (won Daily Mail Arch-to-Arc race, 1959). Subseq. comd: No 9 (Vulcan) Sqdn; flying bases of Honington (Suffolk) and Waddington (Lincs); held a staff post at former Bomber Comd, Air Staff (Ops), Strike Command, 1968-70; Air Attaché, Bonn, 1970-73; AOA Strike Command, 1974-75; SASO RAF Strike Command, 1975-77. *Address:* The Royal British Legion, Pall Mall, SW1Y 5JY.

MAUND, Rt. Rev. John Arthur Arrowsmith, CBE 1975; MC 1946; *b* 1909; *s* of late Arthur Arrowsmith and Dorothy Jane Maund, Worcester, England; *m* 1948, Catherine Mary Maurice, Bromley, Kent; no *c. Educ:* Worcester Cathedral King's Sch.; Leeds Univ.; Mirfield Theological Coll. BA Leeds 1931; Asst Priest, All Saints and St Laurence, Evesham, Worcs, 1933-36; Asst Priest, All Saints, Blackheath, London, 1936-38; Asst Priest, Pretoria Native Mission, Pretoria, South Africa, 1938-40; CF 1940-46 (despatches, 1942); Asst Priest, Pretoria Native Mission, in charge Lady Selborne, Pretoria, 1946-50; Bishop of Lesotho, 1950-76 (diocese known as Basutoland, 1950-66). Fellow Royal Commonwealth Society. *Recreation:* horse riding. *Address:* Hengrave Hall Centre, Bury St Edmunds, Suffolk IP28 6LZ. *T:* Culford 721.

MAUNDER, Prof. Leonard, OBE 1977; BSc; PhD; ScD; FEng; FIMechE; Professor of Mechanical Engineering, since 1967 (Professor of Applied Mechanics, 1961), Dean of the Faculty of Applied Science, 1973-78, University of Newcastle upon Tyne; *b* 10 May 1927; *s* of Thomas G. and Elizabeth A. Maunder; *m* 1958, Moira Anne Hudson; one *s* one *d. Educ:* Grammar Sch., Swansea; University Coll. of Swansea (BSc); Edinburgh Univ. (PhD); Massachusetts Institute of Technology (ScD). Instructor, 1950-53, and Asst Prof., 1953-54, in Dept of Mech. Engrg, MIT; Aeronautical Research Lab., Wright Air Development Center, US Air Force, 1954-56; Lecturer in Post-Graduate Sch. of Applied Dynamics, Edinburgh Univ., 1956-61. Member: NRDC, 1976-; SRC Engrg Bd, 1976-80; Adv. Council on R&D for Fuel and Power, Dept of Energy, 1981-; British Technology Gp, 1981-; Vice-Pres., IMechE, 1976-81; Dep. Chm., Newcastle Hospitals Management Cttee, 1971-73. President: Internat. Fedn Theory of Machines and Mechanisms, 1976-79; Engrg, BAAS, 1980. *Publications:* (with R. N. Arnold) Gyrodynamics and Its Engineering Applications, 1961; numerous papers in the field of applied mechanics. *Address:* Stephenson Building, The University, Newcastle upon Tyne NE1 7RU.

MAUNDRELL, Rev. Canon Wolseley David; Rector of Rye, East Sussex, since 1982; Rural Dean of Rye, since 1978; Canon and Prebendary of Chichester Cathedral, since 1981; *b* 2 Sept. 1920; *s* of late Rev. William Herbert Maundrell, RN, and Evelyn Helen Maundrell; *m* 1950, Barbara Katharine Simmons; one *s* one *d. Educ:* Radley Coll.; New Coll., Oxford. Deacon, 1943; Priest, 1944; Curate of Haslemere, 1943; Resident Chaplain to Bishop of Chichester, 1949; Vicar of Sparsholt and Lainston, Winchester, 1950; Rector of Weeke, Winchester, 1956; Residentiary Canon of Winchester Cathedral, 1961-70 (Treasurer, 1961-70; Vice-Dean, 1966-70). Examining Chaplain to Bishop of Winchester, 1962-70; Asst Chaplain of Holy Trinity Church, Brussels, 1970-71; Vicar of Icklesham, E Sussex, 1972-82. *Address:* The Rectory, Gun Garden, Rye, East Sussex. *T:* Rye 2430.

MAURICE, Dr Rita Joy; Director of Statistics, Home Office, since 1977; *b* 10 May 1929; *d* of A. N. Maurice and F. A. Maurice (*née* Dean). *Educ:* East Grinstead County Sch.; University Coll., London. BSc (Econ) 1951; PhD 1958. Asst Lectr, subseq. Lectr in Economic Statistics, University Coll., London, 1951-58; Statistician, Min. of Health, 1959-62; Statistician, subseq.

Chief Statistician, Central Statistical Office, 1962-72; Head of Economics and Statistics Div. 6, Depts of Industry, Trade and Prices and Consumer Protection, 1972-77. *Publications:* articles in statistical jls.

MAURITIUS, Bishop of; *see under* Indian Ocean, Archbishop of the.

MAUROY, Pierre; Prime Minister of France, since 1981; Mayor of Lille, since 1973; *b* 5 July 1928; *s* of Henri Mauroy and Adrienne Mauroy (*née* Bronne); *m* 1951, Gilberte Deboudt; one *s. Educ:* Lycée de Cambrai; Ecole normale nationale d'apprentissage de Cachan. Joined Young Socialists at age of 16 (Nat. Sec., 1950-58); teacher of technical educn, Colombo, 1952; Sec.-Gen., Syndicat des collèges d'enseignement technique de la Fédération de l'Education national, 1955-59; Sec., Fedn of Socialist Parties of Nord, 1961; Mem., Political Bureau, 1963, Dep. Gen. Sec., 1966, Socialist Party; Mem. Exec. Cttee, Fédération de la gauche démocratique et socialiste, 1965-68; First Sec., Fedn of Socialist Parties of Nord and Nat. Co-ordination Sec., Socialist Party, 1971-79. Member, from Le Cateau, and Vice-Pres., Conseil Gen. du Nord, 1967-73; Town Councillor and Deputy Mayor of Lille, 1971, Vice-Pres., Town Corp., 1971-81; Deputy, Le Nord, 1973-81; Pres., Regional Council, Nord-Pas-de-Calais, 1974-81; Socialist Rep. and Vice-Pres., Political Commn, EEC, 1979-81. Political Dir, Action Socialiste Hebdo, 1979-; Pres., Fédération nationale Léo Lagrange. *Publications:* Héritiers de l'avenir, 1977; C'est ici le chemin, 1981. *Address:* Hôtel Matignon, 57 rue de Varenne, 75007 Paris, France; 38 avenue Charles-Saint-Venant, 59000 Lille, France.

MAVOR, Air Marshal Sir Leslie (Deane), KCB 1970 (CB 1964); AFC 1942; FRAeS; DL; Coordinator of Voluntary Effort in Civil Defence, since 1981; *b* 18 Jan. 1916; *s* of William David Mavor, Edinburgh; *m* 1947, June Lilian Blackburn; four *s. Educ:* Aberdeen Grammar Sch. Commissioned RAF 1937. Dir of Air Staff Briefing, Air Ministry, 1961-64; AOC, No 38 Group, 1964-66; Asst CAS (Policy), 1966-69; AOC-in-C, RAF Training Comd, 1969-72; retd Jan. 1973. Principal, Home Office Home Defence Coll., 1973-80. DL N Yorks, 1976. *Recreations:* golf, fishing, shooting, gliding. *Address:* Barlaston House, Alne, Yorks. *Clubs:* Royal Air Force, Yorkshire.

MAVOR, Michael Barclay, MA; Headmaster, Gordonstoun School, since 1979; *b* 29 Jan. 1947; *s* of William Ferrier Mavor and Sheena Watson Mavor (*née* Barclay); *m* 1970, Jane Elizabeth Sucksmith; one *s* one *d. Educ:* Loretto School; St John's Coll., Cambridge (Exhibn and Trevelyan Schol.). MA (English); CertEd. Woodrow Wilson Teaching Fellow, Northwestern Univ., Evanston, Ill, 1969-72; Asst Master, Tonbridge Sch., 1972-78; Course Tutor (Drama), Open Univ., 1977-78. *Recreations:* theatre, writing, golf, fishing, cricket. *Address:* Gordonstoun School, Elgin, Moray IV30 2RF. *T:* Hopeman 445. *Club:* Hawks (Cambridge).

MAVOR, Ronald Henry Moray, CBE 1972; author; Professor of Drama, University of Saskatchewan; *b* 13 May 1925; *s* of late Dr O. H. Mavor, CBE (James Bridie) and Rona Bremner; *m* 1959, Sigrid Bruhn; one *s* one *d* (and one *d* decd). *Educ:* Merchiston Castle Sch.; Glasgow Univ. MB, ChB 1948, MRCP(Glas) 1955. In medical practice until 1957, incl. periods in RAMC, at American Hosp., Paris, and Deeside Sanatoria. Drama Critic, The Scotsman, 1957-65; Dir, Scottish Arts Council, 1965-71. Vice-Chm., Edinburgh Festival Council, 1975-81 (Mem., 1965-81); Mem. Gen. Adv. Council, BBC, 1971-76; Mem. Drama Panel, British Council, 1973-79. Vis. Lectr on Drama, Guelph, Ontario, and Minneapolis, 1976; Vis. Prof., Univ. of Saskatchewan, 1977-78, 1979-81. *Plays:* The Keys of Paradise, 1959; Aurelie, 1960; Muir of Huntershill, 1962; The Partridge Dance, 1963; A Private Matter (originally A Life of the General), 1973; The Quartet, 1974; The Doctors, 1974; Gordon, 1978; A House on Temperance, 1980. *Publications:* Art the Hard Way, in, Scotland, 1972; A Private Matter (play), 1974. *Address:* 5 Gloucester Place, Edinburgh. *T:* 031-225 1751.

MAVROGORDATO, John George, CMG 1952; *b* 9 May 1905; 2nd *s* of late George Michel and Irene Mavrogordato. *Educ:* Charterhouse; Christ Church, Oxford (BA 1927). Called to Bar, Gray's Inn, 1932; practised as Chancery Bar, 1932-39. Asst Dir, Ministry of Aircraft Production, 1943. Advocate-Gen., Sudan Government, 1946; Legal Adviser to Governor-Gen. of the Sudan, 1953; Senior Legal Counsel, Ministry of Justice, Sudan, 1958-61; retired, 1961. MBOU. *Publications:* A Hawk for the Bush, 1960; A Falcon in the Field, 1966. *Recreations:* falconry, ornithology, wild life conservation.

MAW, (John) Nicholas; composer; *b* 5 Nov. 1935; *s* of Clarence Frederick Maw and Hilda Ellen (*née* Chambers); *m* 1960, Karen Graham; one *s* one *d. Educ:* Wennington Sch., Wetherby, Yorks; Royal Academy of Music. Studied in Paris with Nadia Boulanger and Max Deutsch, 1958-59. Fellow Commoner in Creative Arts, Trinity Coll., Cambridge, 1966-70; Midsummer Prize, Corp. of London, 1980. Compositions include: *operas:* One-Man Show, 1964; The Rising of The Moon, 1970; *for orchestra:* Sinfonia, 1966; Sonata for Strings and Two Horns, 1967; Serenade, for small orchestra, 1973, 1977; Life Studies, for 15 solo strings, 1973; Odyssey, 1974-79; Summer Dances, 1981; *for voice and orchestra:* Nocturne, 1958; Scenes and Arias, 1962; *chamber music:* String Quartet, 1965; Chamber Music for wind and piano quintet, 1962; Flute Quartet, 1981; *instrumental music:* Sonatina for flute and piano, 1957; Essay for organ, 1961; Personae for piano, nos I-III, 1973; *vocal music:* Five Epigrams for chorus, 1960; Round for chorus and piano, 1963; The Voice of Love, for mezzo soprano and piano, 1966; Six Interiors, for high voice and guitar, 1966; Five Irish Songs, for mixed chorus, 1972; Reverdie, five songs for male voices, 1975; Nonsense Rhymes, songs and rounds for children, 1975-76; La Vita Nuova, for soprano and chamber ensemble, 1979; The Ruin, 1980. *Address:* c/o Faber Music Ltd, 3 Queen Square, WC1N 3AU.

MAWBY, Colin (John Beverley); Choral Director, Radio Telefis Eireann, since 1981; *b* 9 May 1936; *e s* of Bernard Mawby and Enid Mawby (*née* Vaux); unmarried. *Educ:* St Swithun's Primary Sch., Portsmouth; Westminster Cathedral Choir Sch.; Royal Coll. of Music. Organist and Choirmaster of Our Lady's Church, Warwick St, W1, 1953; Choirmaster of Plymouth Cath., 1955; Organist and Choirmaster of St Anne's, Vauxhall, 1957; Asst Master of Music, Westminster Cath., 1959; Master of Music, 1961-75; Dir of Music, Sacred Heart, Wimbledon, 1978-81. Conductor: Westminster Chamber Choir, 1971-78; Westminster Cathedral String Orchestra, 1971-78; New Westminster Chorus, 1972-80; Horniman Singers, 1979-80; Culwick Choral Soc.; Prof. of Harmony, Trinity Coll. of Music, 1975-81. Director (Catholic) Publisher, L. J. Cary & Co., 1963; Vice-Pres., Brit. Fedn of *Pueri Cantores,* 1966; Member: Council, Latin Liturgical Assoc., 1969; Adv. Panel, Royal Sch. of Church Music, 1974; Music Sub-Cttee, Westminster Arts Council, 1974. Broadcaster and recording artist; free lance journalism. *Publications:* Church music including eight Masses, Anthems, Motets and Holy Week music. *Recreations:* politics, wine drinking. *Address:* 5 Willbrook, off Whitechurch Road, Rathfarnham, Dublin 14, Ireland. *T:* Dublin 976236.

MAWBY, Raymond Llewellyn; MP (C) Totnes Division of Devon since 1955; *b* 6 Feb. 1922; *m* 1944; one *d* (one *s* decd). *Educ:* Long Lawford Council Sch., Warwicks. One-time Pres. Rugby branch Electrical Trades Union; one-time mem. of Rugby Borough Council. Asst Postmaster-Gen., 1963-64. *Address:* 29 Applegarth Avenue, Newton Abbot, S Devon.

MAWER, Air Cdre Allen Henry, DFC 1943; *b* 16 Dec. 1921; *s* of Gordon Mawer and Emily Naomi Mawer (*née* Block); *m* 1947, Pamela Mitchell (*d* 1982), *d* of David Thomas; one *s* one *d. Educ:* Bancroft's School. Joined RAF, 1940; bomber and special duties ops, 1941-45; psc 1956; Stn Comdr, RAF Scampton, 1965-68; idc 1968; Comdt RAF Coll. of Air Warfare, 1969-71; Air Cdre Plans, HQ Strike Comd, RAF, 1971-73; Air Cdre, Malta, 1973-75, retd. Gen. Manager, Basildon Develt Corp., 1975-78; Man. Dir, Docklands Develt Organisation, 1979-80. Croix de Guerre, France, 1944. *Recreations:* painting, golf, shooting. *Address:* Richmond Cottage, Fambridge Road, Althorne, Essex CM3 6BZ. *Clubs:* Royal Air Force; Royal Burnham Yacht; Burnham Golf.

MAWER, Ronald K.; *see* Knox-Mawer.

MAWHINNEY, Brian Stanley; MP (C) Peterborough, since 1979; *b* 26 July 1940; *s* of Frederick Stanley Arnot Mawhinney and Coralie Jean Mawhinney; *m* 1965, Betty Louise Oja; two *s* one *d. Educ:* Royal Belfast Academical Instn; Queen's Univ., Belfast (BSc); Univ. of Michigan, USA (MSc); Univ. of London (PhD). Asst Prof. of Radiation Research, Univ. of Iowa, USA, 1968-70; Lectr, subsequently Sen. Lectr, Royal Free Hospital School of Medicine, 1970-. Mem., MRC, 1980-. PPS to Ministers of State in the Treasury, 1982-. Contested (C) Stockton on Tees, Oct. 1974. *Publication:* (jtly) Conflict and Christianity in Northern Ireland, 1976. *Recreations:* sport, reading. *Address:* House of Commons, SW1A 0AA.

MAWSON, David, RIBA; JP; Partner, Feilden and Mawson, Architects, Norwich, since 1957; *b* 30 May 1924; *s* of John William Mawson and Evelyn Mary Mawson (*née* Bond); *m* 1951, Margaret Kathlyn Norton; one *s* one *d. Educ:* Merchant Taylors' Sch., Sandy Lodge; Wellington Coll., NZ; Auckland Univ., NZ; Kingston-upon-Thames Coll. of Art. Royal Navy, 1945-47. Chartered Architect, 1952-. Architect, Norwich Cathedral, 1977-. Chm., Norfolk Soc. (CPRE), 1971-76, Vice Pres. 1976-; Founder and Chm., British Assoc. of Friends of Museums, 1973-; Founder Pres., World Fedn of Friends of Museums, 1975-81, Past Pres., 1981-; Mem., Cttee of Nat. Heritage, 1973-; Mem., Norfolk Assoc. of Architects, 1952- (Pres., 1979-81); Hon. Treas., Heritage Coordination Gp, 1981-. JP Norwich, 1972. FRSA 1982. *Publication:* paper on British Museum Friends Socs in Proc. of First Internat. Congress of Friends of Museums, Barcelona, 1972. *Recreations:* tennis, yachting. *Address:* Gonville Hall, Wymondham, Norfolk NR18 9JG. *T:* Wymondham 602166. *Club:* Norfolk (Norwich).

MAWSON, Stuart Radcliffe; Consultant Surgeon, Ear Nose and Throat Department, King's College Hospital, London, 1951-79, Head of Department, 1973-79; *b* 4 March 1918; *s* of late Alec Robert Mawson, Chief Officer, Parks Dept, LCC, and Ena (*née* Grossmith), *d* of George Grossmith Jr, Actor Manager; *m* 1948, June Irene, *d* of George Percival; two *s* two *d. Educ:* Canford Sch.; Trinity Coll., Cambridge; St Thomas's Hosp., London. BA Cantab 1940, MA 1976; MRCS, LRCP 1943; MB, BChir Cantab 1946; FRCS 1947; DLO 1948. House Surg., St Thomas's Hosp., 1943; RMO XIth Para. Bn, 1st Airborne Div., Arnhem, POW, 1943-44; Chief Asst, ENT Dept, St Thomas's Hosp., 1950; Consultant ENT Surgeon: King's Coll. Hosp., 1951; Belgrave Hosp. for Children, 1951; Recog. Teacher of Oto-Rhino-Laryngology, Univ. of London, 1958. Chm., KCH Med. Cttee and Dist Management Team, 1977-79. FRSocMed (Pres. Section of Otology, 1974-75); Liveryman, Apothecaries' Soc.; former Mem. Council, Brit. Assoc. of Otolaryngologists. *Publications:* Diseases of the Ear, 1963, 4th edn 1979; (jtly) Essentials of Otolaryngology, 1967; (contrib.) Scott-Brown's Diseases of the

Ear, Nose and Throat, 4th edn 1979; (contrib.) Modern Trends in Diseases of the Ear, Nose and Throat, 1972; Arnhem Doctor, 1981; numerous papers in sci. jls. *Address:* Whinbeck, Knodishall, Saxmundham, Suffolk. *Clubs:* Aldeburgh Golf, Aldeburgh Yacht.

MAXEY, Peter Malcolm, CMG 1982; HM Diplomatic Service; Ambassador to German Democratic Republic, since 1981; *b* 26 Dec. 1930; *m* 1st, 1955, Joyce Diane Marshall; two *s* two *d*; 2nd, Christine Irene Spooner. *Educ:* Bedford Sch.; Corpus Christi Coll., Cambridge. Served HM Forces, 1949-50. Entered Foreign Office, 1953; Third Sec., Moscow, 1955; Second Sec., 1956; First Sec., Helsinki, 1962; Moscow, 1965; First Sec. and Head of Chancery, Colombo, 1968; seconded to Lazard Bros, 1971; Inspector, 1972; Deputy Head UK Delegation to CSCE, Geneva, 1973; Head of UN Dept, FCO, 1974; NATO Defence Coll., Rome, 1977; Dublin, 1977; on secondment as Under Sec., Cabinet Office, 1978-81. *Address:* c/o Foreign and Commonwealth Office, SW1.

MAXTON, John Alston; MP (Lab) Glasgow, Cathcart, since 1979; *b* Oxford, 5 May 1936; *s* of John Maxton, agr. economist, and Jenny Maxton; *m* Christine Maxton; three *s. Educ:* Lord Williams' Grammar Sch., Thame; Oxford Univ. Lectr in Social Studies, Hamilton Coll. Chm., Assoc. of Lectrs in Colls of Educn, Scotland; Member: Educnl Inst. of Scotland; Socialist Educnl Assoc. Joined Lab. Party, 1970. *Recreations:* family and golf. *Address:* House of Commons, SW1.

MAXWELL, family name of **Baroness de Ros** and **Baron Farnham**.

MAXWELL, Hon. Lord; Peter Maxwell; a Senator of the College of Justice in Scotland, since 1973; *b* 21 May 1919; *s* of late Comdr and late Mrs Herries Maxwell, Munches, Dalbeattie, Kirkcudbrightshire; *m* 1941, Alison Susan Readman; one *s* two *d* (and one *s* decd). *Educ:* Wellington Coll.; Balliol Coll., Oxford; Edinburgh Univ. Served Argyll and Sutherland Highlanders, and late RA, 1939-46. Called to Scottish Bar, 1951; QC (Scotland) 1961; Sheriff-Principal of Dumfries and Galloway, 1970-73. Mem., Royal Commn on Legal Services in Scotland, 1976-80; Chm., Scottish Law Commn, 1981-. *Address:* 1c Oswald Road, Edinburgh EH9 2HE. *T:* 031-667 7444.

MAXWELL, Colonel (Arthur) Terence, TD; *b* 19 Jan. 1905; *s* of late Brig.-Gen. Sir Arthur Maxwell, KCB, CMG, DSO, and late Eva Jones; *m* 1935, Beatrice Diane, *d* of late Rt Hon. Sir J. Austen Chamberlain, KG, PC, MP, and late Ivy Muriel Dundas, GBE; two *s* one *d. Educ:* Rugby; Trinity Coll., Oxford, MA. Travelled in Africa as James Whitehead travelling student, 1926-27, and in South America; Barrister-at-Law, 1929; served 7th City of London Regt Post Office Rifles, 1923-35; Captain TA Reserve of Officers, 1935. Capt. KRRC 1940; Staff Coll., 1941; Leader Ministry of Economic Warfare Mission to the Middle East with rank of Counsellor, 1941-42; Col General Staff, AFHQ, 1943-44; Deputy Chief, Military Government Section; attached SHAEF etc. British Rep., Investments Cttee, ILO, 1937-77. A Managing Dir, Glyn, Mills & Co., bankers, until 1945; Chm., Powers-Samas Accounting Machines Ltd, 1952-70; Dep. Chm., International Computers and Tabulators Ltd, 1959-67, Chm., 1967-68; Chm., International Computers (Holdings) Ltd, 1968, Dep. Chm. 1969; Chm. Computer Leasings Ltd, 1963-69; Director: Vickers Ltd, 1934-75; Aust. and NZ Banking Group Ltd, and its predecessors, 1935-76; Steel Co. of Wales, 1948-67; English Steel Corp. Ltd, 1954-67. Vice-Chm. Cttee on Rural Bus Services (1959), Ministry of Transport; Vice-Pres. and Treas. City and Guilds of London Institute, 1959-67; Mem. Delegacy of City and Guilds Coll., Imperial Coll., University of London, 1959-64. *Recreations:* forestry, golf. *Address:* Roveries Hall, Bishop's Castle, Shropshire. *T:* Bishop's Castle 638402; Flat 7, 52 Onslow Square, SW7. *T:* 01-589 0321. *Club:* Carlton.

MAXWELL, Sir Aymer, 8th Bt of Monreith, *cr* 1681; Hon. Captain Scots Guards; *b* 7 Dec. 1911; *s* of late Lt-Col Aymer Maxwell, Royal Naval Div., Captain Grenadier Guards and Lovat Scouts, and Lady Mary Percy, 5th *d* of 7th Duke of Northumberland; *S* grandfather 1937. *Educ:* Eton; Magdalene Coll., Cambridge. BA (Hon.); JP Wigtownshire. *Heir: nephew* Michael Eustace George Maxwell, *b* 28 Aug. 1943. *Address:* Monreith, Wigtownshire. *T:* Portwilliam 248; 11 Lansdowne House, Lansdowne Road, W11 3LP. *T:* 01-727 6394. *Club:* Boodle's.

MAXWELL, David Campbell F.; *see* Finlay-Maxwell.

MAXWELL of Ardwell, Col Frederick Gordon, CBE 1967; TD; FCIT; *b* 2 May 1905; *s* of late Lt-Col Alexander Gordon Maxwell, OBE, Hon. Corps of Gentlemen-at-Arms; *m* 1st, 1935, Barbara Margaret, *d* of late Edward Williams Hedley, MBE, MD, Thursley, Surrey; two *s* one *d*; 2nd, 1965, True Hamilton Exley, *d* of Francis George Hamilton, Old Blundells Cottage, Tiverton, Devon. *Educ:* Eton. OC 2nd Bn The London Scottish, 1939-42; GSO1, 52nd (Lowland) Div., 1943-44, served in Holland and Germany (despatches); GSO1, Allied Land Forces SE Asia, 1945; OC 1st Bn The London Scottish, 1947-50. Joined London Transport, 1924; Operating Manager (Railways), London Transport, 1947-70, retired 1971. Mem., Co. of London T&AFA, 1947-68; Lt-Col RE (T&AVR, IV), 1956-70; Regimental Col, The London Scottish, 1969-73. DL, Co. of London, 1962; DL, Greater London, 1966-81. OStJ 1969. *Address:* 41 Cheyne Court, Cheyne Place, SW3 5TS. *T:* 01-352 9801. *Clubs:* Naval and Military, Highland Brigade.

MAXWELL, (Ian) Robert; MC 1945; Founder, Publisher and Chairman of Board, Pergamon Press, Oxford, London and New York; Chairman, BPCC (formerly BPC), since 1981; *b* 10 June 1923; *s* of Michael and Ann Hoch; *m* 1945, Elisabeth (*née* Meynard); three *s four d* (and one *s* decd). *Educ:* self-educated. Served War of 1939-45 (MC). In German Sect. of Foreign Office (Head of Press Sect., Berlin), 1945-47. Chm., Robert Maxwell & Co. Ltd, 1948-; Dir, Computer Technology Ltd, 1966-77; Chm. and Chief Exec., Internat. Learning Systems Corp. Ltd, 1968-69; Dir, Gauthier-Villars (Publishers), Paris, 1961-70; Co-Chm., Scottish News Enterprises Ltd, 1975. MP (Lab) Buckingham, 1964-70. Chm., Labour Nat. Fund Raising Foundn, 1960-69; Chm., Labour Working Party on Science, Govt and Industry, 1963-64; Mem., Council of Europe (Vice-Chm., Cttee on Science and Technology), 1968. Contested (Lab) Buckingham, Feb. and Oct. 1974. Treasurer, The Round House Trust Ltd (formerly Centre 42), 1965-. Chm., Oxford Utd FC, 1982-. Kennedy Fellow, Harvard Univ., 1971. Hon. Mem., Acad. of Astronautics, 1974; Mem., Club of Rome, 1979- (Exec. Dir, British Gp). Co-produced films: Mozart's Don Giovanni, Salzburg Festival, 1954; Bolshoi Ballet, 1957; Swan Lake, 1968. *Publications:* (ed) Information USSR, 1963; The Economics of Nuclear Power, 1965; Public Sector Purchasing, 1968; (jt author) Man Alive, 1968. *Recreations:* chess, mountain-climbing. *Address:* Headington Hill Hall, Oxford. *T:* 64881.

MAXWELL, Sir Nigel Mellor H.; *see* Heron-Maxwell.

MAXWELL, Patrick; Solicitor; *b* 12 March 1909; *e s* of late Alderman Patrick Maxwell, Solicitor, Londonderry; *m* 1st, 1935 (wife *d* 1962); two *d*; 2nd, 1969. *Educ:* Convent of Mercy, Artillery Street, Londonderry; Christian Brothers Sch., Brow-of-the-Hill, Londonderry; St Columb's Coll., Londonderry. Solicitor, 1932; entered Londonderry Corporation as Councillor, 1934; resigned as protest against re-distribution scheme, 1937; Leader of Anti-Partition Party in Londonderry Corporation from 1938; did not seek re-election, 1946; first Chairman of Irish Union Association, 1936; Chairman of Derry Catholic Registration Association, 1934-52. MP (Nat) Foyle Division of Londonderry City, Northern Ireland Parliament, 1937-53. Resident Magistrate, 1968-80. President: Law Society of Northern Ireland, 1967-68 (Vice-Pres., 1966-67); Londonderry Rotary Club, 1958-59; Chm. Rotary in Ireland, 1963-64; Mem., Council, International Bar Association, 1968. *Address:* 3 Talbot Park, Londonderry. *T:* Londonderry 51425.

MAXWELL, Peter; *see* Maxwell, Hon. Lord.

MAXWELL, Robert; *see* Maxwell, I. R.

MAXWELL, Sir Robert (Hugh), KBE 1961 (OBE 1942); *b* 2 Jan. 1906; *s* of William Robert and Nancy Dockett Maxwell; *m* 1935, Mary Courtney Jewell; two *s*. Comdr of Order of George I of Greece, 1961; Order of Merit of Syria. *Address:* Court Hay, Charlton Adam, Som. *Club:* Athens (Athens).

MAXWELL, Col Terence; *see* Maxwell, Col A. T.

MAXWELL, Rear-Adm. Thomas Heron, CB 1967; DSC 1942; idc, jssc, psc; Director-General of Naval Training, Ministry of Defence, 1965-67; retired, 1967; *b* 10 April 1912; *s* of late H. G. Maxwell; *m* 1947, Maeve McKinley; two *s* two *d*. *Educ:* Campbell Coll., Belfast; Royal Naval Engineering Coll. Cadet, 1930; Commander, 1946; Captain, 1956; Rear-Adm., 1965. *Recreation:* fishing. *Address:* Middle Twinhoe, Bath, Avon. *T:* Combe Down 832242.

MAXWELL, William Wayland, MA (Cantab); FEng, FIMechE; FIEE; FCIT; FIMechTE; Consultant, Mott, Hay & Anderson, since 1981; *b* 10 March 1925; *s* of Somerset Maxwell and Molly Cullen; *m* 1963, Eugenie Pamela Cavanagh, *d* of Leslie Crump and Eugenie Thurlow; no *c*. *Educ:* Bedales Sch.; Trinity Hall, Cambridge (Mech. Scis Tripos). FEng 1980. Entered London Transport, 1947; Development Engr (Victoria Line), 1963; Mechanical Engr, Development: Railways, 1964; Mechanical Engr, Running: Railways, 1969; Chief Operating Manager (Railways), 1970; Bd Mem. for Engrg, LTE, 1973; Man. Dir, Railways, LTE, 1979-80. Dir, Whelpdale, Maxwell & Codd Ltd, piano and harpsichord makers. Chm., Rly Div., IMechE, 1977-78. Pres., ITEME, 1981-. Col, Engr and Railway Staff Corps RE (TA). OStJ 1980. *Publications:* papers in Proc. IMechE and Proc. IEE. *Recreations:* reading, music, theatre and gardening. *Address:* 40 Elm Bank Gardens, Barnes, SW13 0NT. *T:* 01-876 9575. *Club:* Naval and Military.

MAXWELL-HYSLOP, Robert John, (Robin); MP (C) Tiverton Division of Devon since Aug. 1960; *b* 6 June 1931; 2nd *s* of late Capt. A. H. Maxwell-Hyslop, GC, RN, and late Mrs Maxwell-Hyslop; *m* 1968, Joanna Margaret, *er d* of Thomas McCosh; two *d*. *Educ:* Stowe; Christ Church, Oxford (MA). Joined in PPE Oxon, 1954. Joined Rolls-Royce Ltd Aero Engine Div., as graduate apprentice, Sept. 1954; served 2 years as such, then joined Export Sales Dept; PA to Sir David Huddie, Dir and GM (Sales and Service), 1958; left Rolls-Royce, 1960. Contested (C) Derby (North), 1959. Chm., Anglo-Brazilian Parly Gp; Jt Sec., Cons. Parly Aviation Cttee, 1970-81. Member: Public Expenditure Cttee (Trade and Ind. Sub-Cttee), 1971-79; Standing Orders Cttee, 1977-; Industry and Trade Select Cttee, 1979-; Procedure Cttee, 1979-. Governor, Casa do Brazil. *Recreations:* motoring, South American history. *Address:* 4 Tiverton Road, Silverton, Exeter, Devon.

MAXWELL SCOTT, Sir Michael Fergus, 13th Bt *cr* 1642; *b* 23 July 1921; *s* of Rear-Adm. Malcolm Raphael Joseph Maxwell Scott, DSO (*d* 1943), and Fearga Victoria Mary (*d* 1969) *e d* of Rt Hon. Sir Nicholas Roderick O'Conor, PC, GCB, GCMG; *S* to baronetcy of kinsman, Sir Ralph (Raphael) Stanley De Marie Haggerston, 1972; *m* 1963, Deirdre Moira, *d* of late Alexander McKechnie; two *s* one *d*. *Educ:* Ampleforth; Trinity College, Cambridge. *Publication:* Stories of Famous Scientists, 1965. *Recreations:* sailing, fishing, gardening. *Heir: s* Dominic James Maxwell Scott, *b* 22 July 1968. *Address:* 10 Evelyn Mansions, Carlisle Place, SW1. *T:* 01-828 0333. *Club:* Army and Navy.

MAY, family name of **Baron May.**

MAY, 3rd Baron, *cr* 1935, of Weybridge; **Michael St John May;** 3rd Bt, *cr* 1931; late Lieut, Royal Corps of Signals; *b* 26 Sept. 1931; *o s* of 2nd Baron May and *d* of George Ricardo Thomas; *S* father 1950; *m* 1st, 1958, Dorothea Catherine Ann (marr. diss. 1963), *d* of Charles McCarthy, Boston, USA; 2nd, 1963, Jillian Mary, *d* of Albert Edward Shipton, Beggars Barn, Shutford, Oxon; one *s* one *d*. *Educ:* Wycliffe Coll., Stonehouse, Glos; Magdalene Coll., Cambridge. 2nd Lieut, Royal Signals, 1950. *Recreations:* flying, travel. *Heir: s* Hon. Jasper Bertram St John May, *b* 24 Oct. 1965. *Address:* Gautherns Barn, Sibford Gower, Oxon.

MAY, Anthony Tristram Kenneth, QC 1979; *b* 9 Sept. 1940; *s* of Kenneth Sibley May and Joan Marguérite (*née* Oldaker); *m* 1968, Stella Gay Pattisson; one *s* two *d*. *Educ:* Bradfield Coll.; Worcester Coll., Oxford (Trevelyan Scholar 1960, Hon. Scholar 1962; MA). Inner Temple Scholar, 1965; called to the Bar, 1967. Jun. Counsel to DoE for Land Commn Act Matters, 1972. Chm., Guildford Choral Soc. *Recreations:* gardening, music, books. *Address:* 11 King's Bench Walk, Temple, EC4Y 7EQ. *T:* 01-353 9281.

MAY, Prof. Brian Albert; Head, National College of Agricultural Engineering, since 1976; Professor of Environmental Control and Processing, since 1975, and Dean, Faculty of Agricultural Engineering, Food Production and Rural Land Use, since 1977, Cranfield Institute of Technology; *b* 2 June 1936; *s* of Albert Robert and Eileen May; *m* 1961, Brenda Ann Smith; three *s*. *Educ:* Faversham Grammar Sch.; Aston Univ., Birmingham. Design Engineer, Massey Ferguson, 1958-63; National College of Agricultural Engineering: Lectr, 1963-68; Sen. Lectr, 1968-72; Principal Lectr, 1972-75; Head of Environmental Control and Processing Dept, 1972-75. *Publications:* Power on the Land, 1974; papers in agricl and engrg jls. *Recreations:* cricket, gardening, reading. *Address:* Fairfield Greenway, Campton Shefford, Beds SG17 5BN. *T:* Hitchin 813451. *Club:* Farmers'.

MAY, Charles Alan Maynard, FEng, FIEE, FBCS; Director of Research, British Telecom (formerly Post Office), since 1975; *b* 14 April 1924; *s* of Cyril P. May and late Katharine M. May; *m* 1947, Daphne, *o d* of late Bertram Carpenter; one *s* two *d*. *Educ:* The Grammar Sch., Ulverston, Cumbria; Christ's Coll., Cambridge (Mech. Sciences tripos 1944, MA). CEng, FIEE 1967; FBCS 1968. Served REME and Indian Army, 1944-47. Entered Post Office Engrg Dept, 1948; Head of Electronic Switching Gp, 1956; Staff Engr, Computer Engrg Br., 1966; Dep. Dir (Engrg), 1970. Chm., IEE Electronics Divl Bd, 1977-78; Member: Council, IEE, 1970-72 and 1976-80; BBC Engrg Adv. Cttee, 1978-; Adv. Cttee on Calibration and Measurement, 1978-; Adv. Cttee, Dept of Electronic and Electrical Engrg, Sheffield Univ., 1979-82; Communications Systems Adv. Panel, Council of Educnl Technology, 1980-; Ind. Adv. Bd, Sch. of Eng. and Applied Scis, Sussex Univ., 1981-. Graham Young Lectr, Glasgow Univ., 1979. Vis. Examr, Imperial Coll., Univ. of London, 1980-82. Governor, Suffolk Coll. of Higher and Further Educn, 1980-. *Publications:* contribs on telecommunications to learned jls. *Recreations:* gardening, camping, playing the piano. *Address:* Sherbourne, Glendene Avenue, East Horsley, Leatherhead, Surrey KT24 5AY. *T:* East Horsley 2521.

MAY, Graham; retired from Civil Service, 1981; *b* 15 Dec. 1923; *s* of Augustus May; *m* 1952, Marguerite Lucy Griffin; four *s*. *Educ:* Gravesend County Sch. for Boys; Balliol Coll., Oxford (BA). War Service, Royal Artillery, 1942-46. Asst Principal, Min. of Works, 1948, Principal 1952; seconded to Treasury, 1961-63; Asst Sec., MPBW, 1963; Under Sec., DoE, 1972-81. *Address:* 2 West Cross, Tenterden, Kent TN30 6JL.

MAY, Harry Blight, MD, FRCP, retired; Director of Clinical Laboratories, The London Hospital, 1946-74; Consultant Pathologist to Royal Navy, 1950-74; *b* 12 Nov. 1908; *s* of John and Isobel May, Plymouth, Devon; *m* 1949, Dorothy Quartermaine; no *c*. *Educ:* Devonport; St John's Coll., Cambridge (Scholar). 1st cl. Natural Science Tripos, 1929. Postgraduate study Harvard Medical Sch., 1936. Dean, Faculty of Medicine, Univ. of London, 1960-64; Dean of Med. and Dental Sch., The London Hosp. Med. Coll., 1953-68; Mem. Senate, Univ. of London; Mem. Governing Body, Royal Veterinary Coll.; Examiner, Royal College of Physicians of London and Univ. of Oxford. *Publications:* Clinical Pathology (6th edn), 1951; papers on Antibacterial Agents and other medical subjects. *Address:* 3 Littlemead, Littleworth Road, Esher, Surrey. *T:* Esher 62394.

MAY, John; Councillor, Tyne and Wear County Council, since 1974 (Vice-Chairman, 1978-79, Chairman, 1979-80); *b* 24 May 1912; *s* of William and Sara May; *m* 1939, Mary Peacock (*d* 1980); two *s*. *Educ:* Holystone Council Sch., Newcastle upon Tyne. Councillor: Seaton Valley UDC, 1949-74 (Chm.,

1963-64 and 1972-73); Northumberland CC, 1970-74; Tyne and Wear County Council: Chairman, Transport Cttee, 1980- (Vice-Chm., 1977-80). *Address:* 7 Etal Close, Shiremoor, Newcastle upon Tyne, Tyne and Wear. *T:* Whitley Bay 533204.

MAY, Rt. Hon. Sir John (Douglas), Kt 1972; PC 1982; **Rt. Hon. Lord Justice May;** a Lord Justice of Appeal, since 1982; *b* 28 June 1923; *s* of late E. A. G. May, Shanghai, and of Mrs May, Whitelands House, SW3; *m* 1958, Mary, *er d* of Sir Owen Morshead, GCVO, KCB, DSO, MC, and Paquita, *d* of J. G. Hagemeyer; two *s* one *d*. *Educ:* Clifton Coll.; Balliol Coll., Oxford. Lieut (SpSc) RNVR, 1944-46. Barrister-at-Law, Inner Temple, 1947, Master of the Bench, 1972; QC 1965; Recorder of Maidstone, 1971; Leader, SE Circuit, 1971; Presiding Judge, Midland and Oxford Circuit, 1973-77; a Judge of the High Ct, Queen's Bench Division, 1972-82; a Judge of the Employment Appeal Tribunal, 1978-82. Mem., Parole Bd, 1977-80, Vice-Chm., 1980-; Chm., Inquiry into UK Prison Services, 1978-79. *Address:* c/o Royal Courts of Justice, Strand, WC2. *Club:* Vincent's (Oxford).

MAY, John Otto, CBE 1962 (OBE 1949); HM Diplomatic Service; retired; *b* 21 April 1913; *s* of late Otto May, FRCP, MD; *m* 1939, Maureen McNally, one *d*. *Educ:* St John's Coll., Cambridge. Apptd to Dept of Overseas Trade, 1937. Private Sec. to Comptroller-General, 1939; Asst Commercial Secretary: Copenhagen, 1939; Helsinki, 1940; Ministry of Economic Warfare (Representative in Caracas), 1942-44; First Sec. (Commercial): Rome, 1945, Bucharest, 1948; Foreign Office, 1950-53; First Sec., Helsinki, 1954. Acted as Chargé d'Affaires in 1954, 1955, and 1956; Counsellor (Commercial) and Consul-General, HM Embassy, Athens, 1957-60; Consul-General: Genoa, 1960-65; Rotterdam, 1965-68; Gothenburg, 1968-72. *Recreations:* travel, photography, walking, philately. *Address:* 6 Millhedge Close, Cobham, Surrey KT11 3BE. *T:* Cobham 4645. *Club:* United Oxford & Cambridge University.

MAY, Sir Kenneth Spencer, Kt 1980; CBE 1976; Director, The News Corporation Ltd, since 1980; *b* 10 Dec. 1914; *s* of late N. May; *m* 1943, Betty C. Scott; one *s* one *d*. *Educ:* Woodville High School. Editorial staff, News, 1930; political writer, 1946-59; Asst Manager, News, Adelaide, 1959-64, Manager, 1964-69; Dir, News Ltd, 1969-; Man. Dir, News Ltd, Aust., 1977-80; Chm., Mirror Newspapers Ltd and Nationwide News Pty Ltd, 1969-80; Director: Independent Newspapers Ltd, Wellington, NZ, 1971-; Santos Ltd, 1980-. *Address:* 26 Waterfall Terrace, Burnside, SA 5066, Australia.

MAY, Paul, CBE 1970; retired 1970; *b* 12 July 1907; *s* of William Charles May and Katharine Edith May; *m* 1st, 1933, Dorothy Ida Makower (*d* 1961); two *s* one *d*; 2nd, 1969, Frances Maud Douglas (*née* Tarver); two step *s*. *Educ:* Westminster; Christ Church, Oxford (MA). United Africa Co. Ltd, 1930-32; John Lewis Partnership, 1932-40; Min. of Aircraft Production, 1940-45; John Lewis Partnership, 1945-70 (Dep. Chm., 1955-70). Mem. Exec. Cttee, Land Settlement Assoc. Ltd, 1962-71. *Recreations:* walking, reading, etc. *Address:* Chesterford, Whittingham, Northumberland. *T:* Whittingham 642.

MAY, Peter Barker Howard, CBE 1981; Lloyd's Insurance Broker since 1953; Underwriting Member of Lloyd's, 1962; Director, Willis Faber & Dumas (UK) Ltd, since 1976; *b* 31 Dec. 1929; *m* 1959, Virginia, *er d* of A. H. H. Gilligan; four *d*. *Educ:* Charterhouse; Pembroke Coll., Cambridge (MA). Cambridge cricket and football XIs v. Oxford, 1950, 1951 and 1952; Surrey County Cricket Cap, 1950; played cricket for England v. S Africa 1951, v. India 1952, v. Australia 1953, v. W Indies 1953, v. Pakistan, Australia and New Zealand 1954; captained England 41 times, incl. v. S Africa, 1955, v. Australia 1956, v. S Africa 1956-57, v. W Indies, 1957, v. New Zealand 1958, v. Australia, 1958-59, v. India, 1959, v. West Indies, 1959-60, v. Australia, 1961. Chm., England Cricket Selection Cttee, 1982-. *Publication:* Peter May's Book of Cricket, 1956. *Recreations:* golf, eventing. *Address:* Franklins, Shamley Green, Surrey. *T:* Guildford 893183. *Clubs:* MCC (Pres., 1980-81), Surrey County Cricket.

MAY, Prof. Robert McCredie, FRS 1979; Chairman, University Research Board, since 1977 and Class of 1877 Professor of Zoology, since 1975, Princeton University; *b* 8 Jan. 1936; *s* of Henry W. May and Kathleen M. May; *m* 1962, Judith (*née* Feiner); one *d*. *Educ:* Sydney Boys' High Sch.; Sydney Univ. BSc 1956, PhD (Theoretical Physics) 1959. Gordon Mackay Lectr in Applied Maths, Harvard Univ., 1959-61; Sydney Univ.: Sen. Lectr in Theoretical Physics, 1962-64; Reader, 1964-69; Personal Chair, 1969-73; Prof. of Biology, Princeton Univ., 1973-; Vis. Prof., Imperial Coll., 1975-; visiting appointments at: Harvard, 1966; California Inst. of Technology, 1967; UKAEA Culham Lab., 1971; Magdalen Coll., Oxford, 1971; Inst. for Advanced Study, Princeton, 1972; King's Coll., Cambridge, 1976. *Publications:* Stability and Complexity in Model Ecosystems, 1973, 2nd edn 1974; Theoretical Ecology: Principles and Applications, 1976, 2nd edn 1981; articles in mathematical, biol and physics jls. *Recreations:* tennis, running, bridge. *Address:* Biology Department, Princeton University, Princeton, NJ 08544, USA. *T:* (609) 452-3830. *Club:* Athenæum.

MAY, Valentine Gilbert Delabere, CBE 1969; Director, Yvonne Arnaud Theatre, Guildford, since 1975; *b* 1 July 1927; *s* of Claude Jocelyn Delabere May and Olive Gilbert; *m* 1955, Penelope Sutton; one *d*. *Educ:* Cranleigh Sch.; Peterhouse Coll., Cambridge. Trained at Old Vic Theatre Sch. Director: Ipswich Theatre, 1953-57; Nottingham Playhouse, 1957-61; Bristol Old Vic Company, 1961-75. Plays directed for Bristol Old Vic which subseq. transf.

to London incl.: War and Peace, 1962; A Severed Head, 1963 (which he also dir. as his first Broadway prodn, 1964); Love's Labour's Lost, 1964 (which also went on a British Council European tour); Portrait of a Queen, 1965; The Killing of Sister George, 1965; The Italian Girl, 1968; Mrs Mouse, Are You Within, 1968; Conduct Unbecoming, 1969; It's a Two-Foot-Six Inches Above the Ground World, 1970; Poor Horace, 1970; Trelawny, 1972, The Card, 1973. Plays directed for Arnaud Theatre transferred to London: Baggage, 1976; Banana Ridge, 1976; The Dark Horse, Comedy, 1978; House Guest, Savoy, 1981. Other prodns seen in New York incl.: Romeo and Juliet and Hamlet, (followed by a tour of USA, Berlin and Israel); Portrait of a Queen; The Killing of Sister George; Conduct Unbecoming. Hon. MA Bristol, 1975. *Recreations:* reading, architecture, music, astronomy. *Address:* Yvonne Arnaud Theatre, Millbrook, Guildford, Surrey GU1 3UX. *T:* Guildford 64571.

MAYALL, Sir (Alexander) Lees, KCVO 1972 (CVO 1965); CMG 1964; HM Diplomatic Service, retired; Ambassador to Venezuela, 1972-75; *b* 14 Sept. 1915; *s* of late Alexander Mayall, Bealings End, Woodbridge, Suffolk, and Isobel, *d* of F. J. R. Hendy; *m* 1st, 1940, Renée Eileen Burn (marr. diss., 1947); one *d*; 2nd, 1947, Hon. Mary Hermione Ormsby Gore, *e d* of 4th Baron Harlech, KG, PC, GCMG; one *s* two *d*. *Educ:* Eton; Trinity Coll., Oxford (MA). Entered HM Diplomatic Service, 1939; served with armed forces, 1940; transferred to HM Legation, Berne, 1940-44; First Secretary: HM Embassy, Cairo, 1947-49, Paris, 1952-54; Counsellor, HM Embassy: Tokyo, 1958-61; Lisbon, 1961-64; Addis Ababa, 1964-65; Vice-Marshal of the Diplomatic Corps, 1965-72. Chairman: West Wilts Conservative Assoc.; Bath Preservation Trust. *Recreations:* travelling, reading. *Address:* Sturford Mead, Warminster, Wilts. *T:* Chapmanslade 219. *Clubs:* Travellers', Pratt's, Beefsteak.

MAYBRAY-KING, family name of **Baron Maybray-King.**

MAYBRAY-KING, Baron *cr* 1971 (Life Peer), of the City of Southampton; **Horace Maybray Maybray-King,** PC 1965; DL; Deputy Speaker of the House of Lords, since 1971; *b* 25 May 1901; *s* of John William and Margaret Ann King; changed name by deed poll to Maybray-King, 1971; *m* 1st, 1924, Victoria Florence Harris (*d* 1966); one *d*; 2nd, 1967, Una Porter (*d* 1978); 3rd, 1981, Mrs Ivy Duncan Forster. *Educ:* Norton Council Sch.; Stockton Secondary Sch.; King's Coll., University of London. BA 1st Class Hons 1922, PhD 1940. Head of English Dept, Taunton's Sch., Southampton, 1930-47; Headmaster, Regent's Park Secondary Sch., 1947-50. MP (Lab): Test Div. of Southampton, 1950-55; Itchen Div. of Southampton, 1955-65 (when elected Speaker); Chairman of Ways and Means and Deputy Speaker, 1964-65; MP Itchen Division of Southampton and Speaker of the House of Commons, 1965-70. Mem., BBC Complaints Commn, 1971-74. Hon. Treasurer, Help the Aged, 1972-; Pres., Spina Bifida Assoc., 1971-. FKC; Hon. FRCP. Hon. DCL Durham, 1968; Hon. LLD: Southampton, 1967; London, 1967; Bath Univ. of Technology, 1969; Hon. DSocSci Ottawa, 1969; Hon. DLitt Loughborough Univ. of Technology, 1971. Hants County Hon. Alderman; Freeman of Southampton and Stockton-on-Tees. DL Hants, 1975. *Publications:* Selections from Macaulay, 1930; Selections from Homer, 1935; (ed) Sherlock Holmes Stories, 1950; Parliament and Freedom, 1953; State Crimes, 1967; Songs in the Night, 1968; Before Hansard, 1968; The Speaker and Parliament, 1973. *Recreations:* music and the entertainment of children. *Address:* 37 Manor Farm Road, Southampton. *T:* Southampton 555884. *Club:* Farmers'.

MAYCOCK, Sir William d'Auvergne, Kt 1978; CBE 1970 (MBE 1945); MVO 1961; MD, FRCP, FRCPath; Superintendent, Elstree Laboratories, 1949-73, and Director of Blood Products Laboratory, 1973-78, Lister Institute of Preventive Medicine; retired; *b* 7 Feb. 1911; *s* of William Perren Maycock, MIEE, and Florence Marion, *d* of Alfred Hart; *m* 1940, Muriel Mary, *d* of Duncan Macdonald, Toronto; two *s*. *Educ:* The King's School, Canterbury; McGill Univ., Montreal. MD McGill, 1935; FRCP, MRCS, FRCPath. Demonstrator in Pathology, McGill Univ., 1935; Leverhulme Scholar, RCS of Eng., 1936-39; Dept of Physiology, St Thomas's Hosp. Med. Sch., 1939. Served in RAMC, 1939-45: Temp. Col, AMS, 1945. Mem. Staff of Lister Inst., London, 1946-48; Consultant Adviser in Transfusion, Min. of Health (later Dept of Health and Social Security), 1946-78; Hon. Cons. in Transfusion and Resuscitation to War Office (later Min. of Defence), 1946-78. Oliver Memorial Award for Blood Transfusion, 1955; Karl Landsteiner Gold Medal, Netherlands Red Cross Soc., 1978; Guthrie Medal, RAMC, 1979; Pres., Brit. Soc. for Haematology, 1966-67. *Publications:* scientific and other papers. *Recreations:* various. *Address:* 59 Ivinghoe Road, Bushey, Herts. *Club:* Athenæum.

MAYER, Sir Robert, CH 1973; KCVO 1979; Kt 1939; FRCM; FTCL (Hon.); Hon. GSM; Hon. RAM; Founder: Robert Mayer Concerts for Children; Transatlantic Foundation Anglo-American Scholarships; Founder, Vice-President, since 1981, and Director, Robert Mayer Trust for Youth and Music (formerly Youth and Music Trust); Co-Chairman, until 1981); Member Council: National Music Council; English Chamber Orchestra; Wind Music Society; Anglo-Israel Association; Live Music; International Music Seminar; *b* Mannheim, 5 June 1879; *s* of Emil Mayer; *m* 1st, 1919, Dorothy Moulton Piper (*d* 1974), *d* of George Piper; two *s* one *d*; 2nd, 1980, Mrs Jacqueline Noble (*née* Norman). *Educ:* Mannheim Conservatoire. Hon. LLD Leeds, 1967; Hon. DSc City University, 1968; Hon. Dr of Music, Cleveland, O, 1970. Albert Medal, RSA, 1979. Grand Cross, Order of Merit (Germany), 1967; Ordre de la Couronne (Belgium), 1969. *Publications:* Young People in

Trouble; Crescendo; My First Hundred Years, 1979. *Recreations:* philanthropy, music. *Address:* 2 Mansfield Street, W1. *TA:* Robmayer. *T:* 01-636 1204. *Club:* Athenæum.

MAYER BROWN, Prof. Howard; see Brown, Prof. H. M.

MAYERS, Norman, CMG 1952; *b* 22 May 1895; 2nd *s* of late S. A. Mayers, Bolton, and Mary Alice, *e d* of late Charles Ditchfield. *Educ:* King's Coll., London; Caius Coll., Cambridge; abroad. Served in India, 1914-19, Middlesex and Hampshire Regts (Territorials). Entered Levant Consular Service, 1922, and served in Lebanon and Saudi Arabia; Asst Oriental Sec. at the Residency, Cairo, 1927-34; Oriental Sec., Addis Ababa, 1935-37; Consul at Alexandria, 1937; Bucharest, 1938; Shiraz and Isfahan, 1941; Mersin, 1941; served at Foreign Office, 1943-44; Chargé d'Affaires at San José, Costa Rica, 1944-45; Minister to El Salvador, 1945-48; Consul-Gen., São Paulo, 1948-51; Ambassador to Ecuador, 1951-55; retired. Consul (Hon.) Palma de Mallorca, 1957-63. *Recreations:* drawing, painting. *Address:* Calle Virgen de la Bonanova 11, Genova, Palma de Mallorca, Spain. *Clubs:* United Oxford & Cambridge University, Travellers'.

MAYFIELD, Hon. Lord; Ian MacDonald, MC 1945; QC (Scot.) 1964; a Senator of the College of Justice in Scotland, since 1981; *b* 26 May 1921; *s* of H. J. and J. M. MacDonald; *m* 1946, Elizabeth de Vessey Lawson; one *s* one *d. Educ:* Colston's Sch., Bristol; Edinburgh Univ. (MA, LLB). Served 1939-46: Royal Tank Regt (Capt.). TA Lothians and Border Horse, later Queen's Own Lowland Yeomanry, 1948-62. Called to Bar, 1952. Mem., Criminal Injuries Compensation Board, 1972-74. Sheriff Principal of Dumfries and Galloway, Feb.-Dec. 1973; Pres., Industrial Tribunals for Scotland, 1973-81. *Recreation:* sport. *Address:* 16 Mayfield Terrace, Edinburgh EH9 1SA. *T:* 031-667 5542. *Club:* Caledonian.

MAYFIELD, Ven. Christopher John; Archdeacon of Bedford, since 1979; *b* 18 Dec. 1935; *s* of Dr Roger Bolton Mayfield and Muriel Eileen Mayfield; *m* 1962, Caroline Ann Roberts; two *s* one *d. Educ:* Sedbergh School; Gonville and Caius Coll., Cambridge (MA 1961); Linacre House, Oxford (Dip. Theology). Deacon 1963, priest 1964, Birmingham; Curate of St Martin-in-the-Bull Ring, Birmingham, 1963-67; Lecturer at St Martin's, Birmingham, 1967-71; Chaplain at Children's Hospital, Birmingham, 1967-71; Vicar of Luton, 1971-80 (with East Hyde, 1971-76); RD of Luton, 1974-79. *Recreations:* marriage, evangelism, walking. *Address:* The Archdeacon's House, The Ride, Totternhoe, Dunstable, Beds LU6 1RH. *T:* Dunstable 68100.

MAYHEW, family name of **Baron Mayhew.**

MAYHEW, Baron *cr* 1981 (Life Peer), of Wimbledon in Greater London; **Christopher Paget Mayhew;** *b* 12 June 1915; *e s* of late Sir Basil Mayhew, KBE; *m* 1949, Cicely Elizabeth Ludlam; two *s* two *d. Educ:* Haileybury Coll. (Scholar); Christ Church, Oxford (Open Exhibitioner, MA). Junior George Webb-Medley Scholar (Economics), 1937; Pres., Union Soc., 1937. Gunner Surrey Yeomanry RA; BEF Sept. 1939-May 1940; served with BNAF and CMF; BLA 1944 (despatches); Major, 1944. MP (Lab) S Norfolk, 1945-50; MP (Lab) Woolwich East, later Greenwich, Woolwich East, June 1951-July 1974; PPS to Lord Pres. of the Council, 1945-46; Parly Under-Sec. of State for Foreign Affairs, 1946-50; Minister of Defence (RN), 1964, resigned 1966; MP (L) Greenwich, Woolwich East, July-Sept. 1974; contested (L): Bath, Oct. 1974 and 1979; Surrey, for European Parlt, 1979; London SW, for European Parlt, Sept. 1979; Chief Liberal Party Spokesman on Defence, 1980; Member, Standing Cttee, Liberal Party; Pres., Liberal Action Gp for Electoral Reform. Chairman: Middle East International (Publishers) Ltd; ANAF Foundn; former Chm., MIND (Nat. Assoc. for Mental Health). *Publications:* Planned Investment-The Case for a National Investment Board, 1939; Socialist Economic Policy, 1946; "Those in Favour . . ." (television play), 1951; Dear Viewer . . ., 1953; Men Seeking God, 1955; Commercial Television: What is to be done?, 1959; Coexistence Plus, 1962; Britain's Role Tomorrow, 1967; Party Games, 1969; (jtly) Europe: the case for going in, 1971; (jtly) Publish It Not . . .: the Middle East cover-up, 1975; The Disillusioned Voter's Guide to Electoral Reform, 1976. *Recreations:* music, golf. *Address:* 39 Wool Road, Wimbledon, SW20 0HN. *Clubs:* United Oxford & Cambridge University, National Liberal.

MAYHEW, Patrick Barnabas Burke, QC 1972; MP (C) Royal Tunbridge Wells, since Feb. 1974; Minister of State, Home Office, since 1981; *b* 11 Sept. 1929; *o surv. s* of A. G. H. Mayhew, MC; *m* 1963, Jean Elizabeth Gurney *d* of John Gurney; four *s. Educ:* Tonbridge; Balliol Coll., Oxford (MA). President, Oxford Union Society, 1952. Commnd 4th/7th Royal Dragoon Guards, national service and AER, captain. Called to Bar, Middle Temple, 1955, Bencher 1980. Contested (C) Camberwell and Dulwich, in Gen. Election, 1970. Parly Under Sec. of State, Dept of Employment, 1979-81. Mem. Exec., 1922 Cttee, 1976-79; Vice Chm., Cons. Home Affairs Cttee, 1976-79. *Address:* House of Commons, SW1.

MAYHEW-SANDERS, Sir John (Reynolds), Kt 1982; MA; FCA; Director since 1972, Chief Executive since 1975, and Chairman, since 1978, John Brown PLC; *b* 25 Oct. 1931; *e s* of Jack Mayhew-Sanders, FCA; *m* 1958, Sylvia Mary, *d* of George S. Colling; three *s* one *d. Educ:* Epsom Coll.; RNC, Dartmouth; Jesus Coll., Cambridge (MA Engrg). FCA 1958. RN, 1949-54. Mayhew-Sanders & Co., Chartered Accountants, 1954-58; P-E Consulting Gp

Ltd, 1958-72. Member: Management Bd, Engineering Employers' Fedn, 1977-81; BOTB, 1980-; BBC Consultative Gp on Industrial and Business Affairs, 1981-; Chm., Overseas Project Bd, 1980-; Dir, BL PLC, 1980-. *Recreations:* fishing, shooting, gardening, music. *Address:* Earlstone House, Burghclere, Hants. *T:* Burghclere 288.

MAYLAND, Rev. Canon Ralph, VRD 1962 and bar 1972; Canon and Treasurer of York Minster, since 1982; *b* 31 March 1927; *s* of James Henry and Lucy Mayland; *m* 1959, Jean Mary Goldstraw; one *d* and one adopted *d. Educ:* Cockburn High Sch., Leeds; Leeds City Training Coll.; Westminster Coll., London Univ.; Ripon Hall, Oxford. Schoolteacher, 1945-46; RN, 1946-51; perm. commn, RNR, 1952, Chaplain, 1961-82; 3rd yr student, 1951-52; schoolteacher, 1952-57; theol student, 1957-59. Curate of Lambeth, 1959-62; Priest-in-charge, St Paul's, Manton, Worksop, 1962-67; Vicar, St Margaret's, Brightside, 1968-72; Chaplain, Sheffield Industrial Mission, 1968-75; Vicar, St Mary's, Ecclesfield, 1972-82; Chaplain to Master Cutler, 1979-80. Life Mem., Royal Naval Assoc. *Recreations:* collecting Victorian children's literature, goat-keeping and rearing. *Address:* 3 Minster Court, York YO1 2JJ. *T:* York 25599.

MAYNARD, Brian Alfred, CBE 1982; FCA, CBIM; Partner, Coopers & Lybrand, Chartered Accountants, 1950-81; *b* 27 Sept. 1917; *s* of late Alfred A. Maynard and Clarissa (*née* Shawe); *m* 1946, Rosemary Graham, *y d* of late Col E. C. Boutflower; two *s. Educ:* Leighton Park Sch.; Cambridge Univ. (MA). RNVR Commission, 1939-46, served Middle East and Europe. Member: Oxford Univ. Appts Cttee, 1959-81; Cttee of Duke of Edinburgh's Award Scheme, 1961-67; Council, Industry for Management Educn, 1968-81; Cttee of Enquiry into the Financial Control of Catering in the Services, 1973; Cttee of Enquiry into Problems facing the Nat. Theatre, 1978; Council for the Securities Industry, 1978; City Panel of Takeovers and Mergers, 1978; Chm., Adv. Cttee on Local Govt Audit, 1979-82. Mem. Council, Inst. of Chartered Accountants in England and Wales, 1968-81 (Pres., 1977-78); Chairman: London Soc. of Chartered Accountants, 1966-67; Management Consultants Assoc., 1970; Pres., Inst. of Management Consultants, 1974; Vice-Pres., European Fedn of Management Consultants Assoc., 1972-75; Pres., OECD Mission to USA, on Computers, 1960. *Recreations:* golf, shooting, CPRE. *Address:* Cowage Farm, Hilmarton, Calne, Wilts SN11 8RZ. *T:* Hilmarton 222; 5 Redanchor Close, Chelsea, SW3 5DW. *T:* 01-352 6777.

MAYNARD, Edwin Francis George; Overseas Business Consultant; Member, Export Council Advisory Panel; HM Diplomatic Service, retired; Deputy High Commissioner, Calcutta, 1976-80; *b* 23 Feb. 1921; *s* of late Edwin Maynard, MD, FRCS, DPH, and late Nancy Frances Tully; *m* 1945, Patricia Baker; one *s* one *d*; *m* 1963, Anna McGettrick; two *s. Educ:* Westminster. Served with Indian Army (4/8th Punjab Regt and General Staff) (Major, GSO II), Middle East and Burma, 1939-46. BBC French Service, 1947; Foreign Office, 1949; Consul and Second Sec., Jedda, 1950; Second, later First, Sec., Benghazi, 1952; FO 1954; Bogota, 1956; Khartoum, 1959; FO, 1960; Baghdad, 1962; Founder Dir, Diplomatic Service Language Centre, 1966; Counsellor, Aden, 1967; Counsellor, New Delhi, 1968-72; Minister (Commercial), Buenos Aires, 1972-76. *Recreations:* shooting, fishing, languages, gardening. *Address:* Great Dowels, Stone Street, Stelling Minnis, Canterbury, Kent; 115 Cheyne Walk, SW10. *Club:* Brooks's.

MAYNARD, Prof. Geoffrey Walter; Director of Economics, Europe and Middle East, Chase Manhattan Bank, since 1977 (Economic consultant, 1974); Director, Chase Manhattan Ltd, since 1977; *b* 27 Oct. 1921; *s* of Walter F. Maynard and Maisie Maynard (*née* Bristow); *m* 1949, Marie Lilian Wright; two *d. Educ:* London School of Economics. BSc(Econ); PhD. Lectr and Sen. Lectr, UC of S Wales, Cardiff, 1951-62; Economic Consultant, HM Treasury 1962-64; Economic Advr, Harvard Univ. Develt Adv. Gp in Argentina, 1964-65; University of Reading: Reader, 1966-68; Prof. of Economics, 1968-76; Vis. Prof. of Economics, 1976-. Editor, Bankers' Magazine, 1968-72; Under-Sec. (Econs), HM Treasury, 1972-74 (on leave of absence); Dep. Chief Economic Advr, HM Treasury, 1976-77; occasional consultant, IBRD, Overseas Develt Administration of FCO. *Publications:* Economic Development and the Price Level, 1962; (jtly) International Monetary Reform and Latin America, 1966; (jtly) A World of Inflation, 1976; chapters in: Development Policy: theory and practice, ed G. Papanek, 1968; Commonwealth Policy in a Global Context, ed Streeten and Corbet, 1971; Economic Analysis and the Multinational Enterprise, ed J. Dunning, 1974; Special Drawing Rights and Development Aid (paper), 1972; articles in Economic Jl, Oxford Economic Papers, Jl of Development Studies, World Development, etc. *Address:* Flat 219, Queens Quay, 58 Upper Thames Street, EC4. *Club:* Reform.

MAYNARD, Joan; see Maynard, V. J.

MAYNARD, Air Chief Marshal Sir Nigel (Martin), KCB 1973 (CB 1971); CBE 1963; DFC 1942; AFC 1946; *b* 28 Aug. 1921; *s* of late Air Vice-Marshal F. H. M. Maynard, CB, AFC, and of Irene (*née* Pim); *m* 1946, Daphne, *d* of late G. R. P. Llewellyn, Baglan Hall, Abergavenny; one *s* one *d. Educ:* Aldenham; RAF Coll., Cranwell. Coastal Comd, UK, Mediterranean, W Africa, 1940-43; Flt-Lieut 1942; Sqdn-Ldr 1944; Mediterranean and Middle East, 1944; Transport Comd, 1945-49; comd 242 Sqdn on Berlin Air Lift; Air Staff, Air Min., 1949-51; Wing Comdr 1952; psa 1952; Staff Officer to Inspector Gen., 1953-54; Bomber Comd, 1954-57; jssc 1957; Gp Capt. 1957; SASO 25 Gp, 1958-59; CO, RAF Changi, 1960-62; Gp Capt. Ops, Transport

Comd, 1963-64; Air Cdre 1965; Dir of Defence Plans (Air), 1965; Dir of Defence Plans and Chm. Defence Planning Staff, 1966; idc 1967; Air Vice-Marshal, 1968; Commandant, RAF Staff College, Bracknell, 1968-70; Commander, Far East Air Force, 1970-71; Air Marshal, 1972; Dep. C-in-C, Strike Command, 1972-73; C-in-C RAF Germany, and Comdr, 2nd Allied Tactical Air Force, 1973-76; Air Chief Marshal 1976; C-in-C, RAF Strike Command, and C-in-C, UK Air Forces, 1976-77. ADC to the Queen, 1961-65. *Recreations:* tennis, squash, shooting. *Address:* Manor House, Piddington, Bicester, Oxon. *T:* Brill 238270. *Clubs:* Naval and Military, Royal Air Force; MCC.

MAYNARD, (Vera) Joan; JP; MP (Lab) Sheffield, Brightside, since Oct. 1974; *b* 1921. Mem. Labour Party Nat. Exec. Cttee, 1972-82; Sec., 1956-78, Chm., 1978-, Yorks Area, Nat. Union of Agricl and Allied Workers, sponsored as MP by the Union; Mem., Parly Select Cttee on Agriculture; Vice-Chm., Labour Party, 1980-81. Vice Pres., Rural District Councils Assoc. JP Thirsk, 1950. *Address:* House of Commons, SW1A 0AA.

MAYNARD SMITH, Prof. John, FRS 1977; Professor of Biology, University of Sussex, since 1965; *b* 6 Jan. 1920; *s* of Sidney Maynard Smith and Isobel Mary (*née* Pitman); *m* 1941; two *s* one *d. Educ:* Eton Coll.; Trinity Coll., Cambridge (BA Engrg, 1941); UCL (BSc Zool., 1951; Fellow, 1979). Aircraft stressman, 1942-47; Lectr in Zool., UCL, 1952-65; first Dean of Biol Sciences, Univ. of Sussex, 1965-72. *Publications:* The Theory of Evolution, 1958, 3rd edn 1975; Mathematical Ideas in Biology, 1968; On Evolution, 1972; Models in Ecology, 1974; The Evolution of Sex, 1978; Evolution and the Theory of Games, 1982. *Recreations:* gardening, fishing, talking. *Address:* The White House, Kingston Ridge, Lewes, East Sussex. *T:* Lewes 4659.

MAYNE, Eric; Deputy Secretary, Department of Manpower Services, Northern Ireland, since 1979; *b* 2 Sept. 1928; *s* of Robert P. Mayne and Margaret Mayne; *m* 1954, Sarah Boyd (*née* Gray); three *s* two *d. Educ:* Bangor Grammar Sch.; Univ. of Reading (BSc); Michigan State Univ. (MS). Horticultural Advisor, Min. of Agriculture, NI, 1949-56; Kellogg Foundation Fellow, 1956-57; Horticultural Advisor, HQ Min. of Agriculture, NI, 1957-64; Principal Officer, 1964-67; Gen. Manager, NI Agric. Trust, 1967-74; Sen. Asst Secretary, Dept of Agriculture, NI, 1974-79. *Recreation:* gardening. *Address:* Netherleigh, Massey Avenue, Belfast BT4 2JP.

MAYNE, John Fraser; Director General of Management Audit, Ministry of Defence, since 1981; *b* 14 Sept. 1932; *s* of late John Leonard Mayne and Martha Laura (*née* Griffiths); *m* 1958, Gillian Mary (*née* Key); one *s* one *d. Educ:* Dulwich Coll.; Worcester Coll., Oxford. National Service, Royal Tank Regt, 1951-53. Air Min., 1956-64; HM Treasury, 1964-67; MoD, 1967-70; Asst Private Sec. to Sec. of State for Defence, 1968-70; Cabinet Office and Central Policy Rev. Staff, 1970-73; MoD, 1973-78; Private Sec. to Sec. of State for Def., 1975-76; Asst Under-Sec. of State (Air Staff), 1976-78; Principal Establishments and Finance Officer, NI Office, 1979-81. FBIM 1981. *Recreations:* music, fell-walking, cooking, work. *Club:* United Oxford & Cambridge University.

MAYNE, Rev. Canon Michael Clement Otway; Vicar of Great St Mary's, Cambridge (the University Church), since 1979; *b* 10 Sept. 1929; *s* of Rev. Michael Ashton Otway Mayne and Sylvia Clementina Lumley Ellis; *m* 1965, Alison Geraldine McKie; one *s* one *d. Educ:* King's Sch., Canterbury; Corpus Christi Coll., Cambridge (MA); Cuddesdon Coll., Oxford. Curate, St John the Baptist, Harpenden, 1957-59; Domestic Chaplain to the Bishop of Southwark, 1959-65; Vicar of Norton, Letchworth, 1965-72; Head of Religious Progs, BBC Radio, 1972-79. *Recreations:* theatre, bird-watching, books. *Address:* Great St Mary's Vicarage, 39 Madingley Road, Cambridge. *T:* Cambridge 355285.

MAYNE, Richard (John); writer; Special Adviser to the Commission of the European Communities, since 1979; *b* 2 April 1926; *s* of John William Mayne and Kate Hilda (*née* Angus); *m* 1st, Margot Ellingworth Lyon; 2nd, Jocelyn Mudie Ferguson; two *d. Educ:* St Paul's Sch., London; Trinity Coll., Cambridge (1st Cl. Hons Pts I and II, Hist. Tripos; MA and PhD). War service, Royal Signals, 1944-47. Styring, Sen., and Res. Scholar, and Earl of Derby Student, Trinity Coll., Cambridge, 1947-53; Leverhulme European Scholar, Rome, and Rome Corresp., New Statesman, 1953-54; Asst Tutor, Cambridge Inst. of Educn, 1954-56; Official: ECSC, Luxembourg, 1956-58; EEC, Brussels, 1958-63; Dir of Documentation Centre, Action Cttee for United States of Europe, and Personal Asst to Jean Monnet, Paris, 1963-66; Paris Corresp., Encounter, 1966-71; Vis. Prof., Univ. of Chicago, 1971; Dir of Federal Trust for Educn and Res., 1971-73; Head of UK Offices, Commn of European Communities, 1973-79. *Publications:* The Community of Europe, 1962; The Institutions of the European Community, 1968; The Recovery of Europe, 1970 (rev. edn 1973); The Europeans, 1972; (ed) Europe Tomorrow, 1972; (ed) The New Atlantic Challenge, 1975; (trans.) The Memoirs of Jean Monnet, 1978 (Scott-Moncrieff Prize, 1979). *Recreations:* travel, sailing, fell-walking. *Address:* c/o Commission of the European Communities, 20 Kensington Palace Gardens, W8 4QQ. *T:* 01-727 8090. *Clubs:* Europe House; Les Misérables (Paris).

MAYNE, Mrs Roger; *see* Jellicoe, P. A.

MAYNE, William; writer; *b* 16 March 1928; *s* of William and Dorothy Mayne. *Educ:* Cathedral Choir Sch., Canterbury, 1937-42 (then irregularly).

Has pursued a career as novelist and has had published a large number of stories for children and young people—about 66 altogether, beginning in 1953 and going on into the foreseeable future. Lectr in Creative Writing, Deakin Univ., Geelong, Vic, Aust., academic years, 1976 and 1977; Fellow in Creative Writing, Rolle Coll., Exmouth, 1979-80. Library Assoc.'s Carnegie Medal for best children's book of the year (1956), 1957. *Address:* c/o David Higham Associates, 5-8 Lower John Street, Golden Square, W1R 4HA.

MAYNEORD, Prof. William Valentine, CBE 1957; FRS 1965; Emeritus Professor of Physics as Applied to Medicine, University of London; formerly Director of Physics Department, Institute of Cancer Research, Royal Cancer Hospital; *b* 14 Feb. 1902; *s* of late Walter Mayneord; *m* 1963, Audrey Morrell, Kingston-upon-Thames. *Educ:* Prince Henry's Grammar Sch., Evesham; Birmingham Univ. BSc 1921, MSc 1922, DSc 1933. Chairman: Hon. Adv. Scientific Cttee of Nat. Gallery, 1966-71 (Member, 1952-); Internat. Commn on Radiological Units, 1950-53; Med. Res. Coun. Cttee on Protection against Ionising Radiations, 1951-58; Member: Internat. Commn on Radiological Protection, 1950-58; UK Delegn to UN Scientific Cttee on the Effects of Atomic Radiation, 1956-57; MRC Cttee on Hazards to Man of Nuclear and Allied Radiations, 1955-60; President: British Inst. of Radiology, 1942-43; 1st Internat. Conf. on Medical Physics, 1965; Internat. Orgn for Medical Physics, 1965-69; Consultant: UKAEA, 1945-70; CEGB; WHO; Mem. Council and Scientific Cttee, Imp. Cancer Research Fund, 1965-73. A Trustee, National Gallery, 1966-71. Many awards and hon. memberships of British and foreign learned societies. Coronation Medal, 1953; Gold Medals: Royal Swedish Acad. of Science, 1965; Faculty of Radiologists (now RCR), 1966; Univ. of Arizona, 1974. Sievert Award, Internat. Radiation Protection Assoc., 1977. Hon. LLD Aberdeen, 1969; DUniv Surrey, 1978. *Publications:* Physics of X-Ray Therapy, 1929; Some Applications of Nuclear Physics to Medicine, 1950; Radiation and Health, 1964; Carcinogenesis and Radiation Risk, 1975; articles on chemical carcinogenesis, and on applications of physics to medicine and radiation hazards. *Recreation:* Italian Renaissance art and literature, particularly Dante. *Address:* 7 Downs Way Close, Tadworth, Surrey KT20 5DR. *T:* Tadworth 2297.

MAYO, 10th Earl of, *cr* 1785; **Terence Patrick Bourke;** Baron Naas, 1766; Viscount Mayo, 1781; Lieut RN (retired); Managing Director, Irish Marble Ltd, Merlin Park, Galway; *b* 26 Aug. 1929; *s* of Hon. Bryan Longley Bourke (*d* 1961) and Violet Wilmot Heathcote Bourke (*d* 1950); *S* uncle, 1962; *m* 1952, Margaret Jane Robinson Harrison; three *s. Educ:* St Aubyns, Rottingdean; RNC Dartmouth. Lieut, RN, 1952; Fleet Air Arm, 1952; Suez, 1956; Solo Aerobatic Displays, Farnborough, 1957; invalided, 1959. Mem., Gosport Borough Council, 1961-64; Pres., Gosport Chamber of Trade, 1962; Gov., Gosport Secondary Schs, 1963-64. Mem., Liberal Party, 1963-65; contested (L) Dorset South, 1964. *Recreations:* sailing, riding, shooting, fishing. *Heir: s* Lord Naas, *qv. Address:* Doon House, Maam, Co. Galway, Eire. *Clubs:* Naval; County Galway.

MAYO, Eileen; artist, author, printmaker and painter. *Educ:* Clifton High School; Slade School of Art. Exhibited Royal Academy, London Group, United Society of Artists, Festival of Britain, etc; works acquired by British Council, British Museum, Victoria and Albert Museum, Contemporary Art Society, and public galleries in UK, USA, Australia and NZ. Designer of Australian mammals series of postage stamps, 1959-62, and Barrier Reef series, 1966; four Cook Bicentenary stamps, NZ, 1969, and other NZ stamps, 1970-78. *Publications:* The Story of Living Things; Shells and How they Live; Animals on the Farm, etc. *Recreations:* printmaking, gardening.

MAYO, Rear-Adm. Robert William, CB 1965; CBE 1962; *b* 9 Feb. 1909; *s* of late Frank Mayo, Charminster; *m* 1st, 1942, Sheila (*d* 1974), *d* of late John Colvill, JP, of Campbeltown; one *s*; 2nd, 1980, Mrs Betty Washbrook. *Educ:* Weymouth Coll.; HMS Conway. Royal Naval Reserve and officer with Royal Mail Steam Packet Co., 1926-37; Master's Certificate; transferred to Royal Navy, 1937. Served War, 1939-45; Korea, 1952; Capt., 1953; Rear-Adm., 1964; retired, 1966. Hon. Sheriff Substitute of Renfrew and Argyll at Campbeltown. *Recreations:* gardening, fishing, yachting. *Address:* Bellgrove, Campbeltown, Argyll. *T:* Campbeltown 2101. *Club:* Royal Scottish Automobile.

MAYO, Simon Herbert; Hon. Mr Justice Mayo; a Judge of the High Court of Hong Kong, since 1980; *b* 15 Nov. 1937; *s* of late Herbert and Marjorie Mayo; *m* 1966, Catherine Yin Ying Young; one *s* one *d. Educ:* Harrow Sch. Admitted a solicitor, England and Wales, 1961, Hong Kong, 1963; called as barrister and solicitor, W Australia, 1967. Asst Legal Advr, GEC, 1961; Asst Solicitor, Deacons, Solicitors, Hong Kong, 1963; in private practice, WA, 1967; Asst Registrar, 1968, Registrar, 1976, Supreme Court of Hong Kong. *Recreations:* music, literature, walking. *Address:* Supreme Court, Hong Kong. *T:* 5-8914353. *Clubs:* Hong Kong, Royal Hong Kong Jockey, Hong Kong Cricket (Hong Kong).

MAYOH, Raymond Blanchflower; Under Secretary, Department of Health and Social Security, since 1979; *b* 11 Nov. 1925; *s* of Charles and Isabella Mayoh; *m* 1956, Daphne Yvonne Bayliss; one *s* one *d* (and one *s* decd). *Educ:* Colwyn Bay County Sch.; University College of North Wales. Assistant Principal, Ministry of Pensions, 1950; Principal, Ministry of Health, 1955; Assistant Secretary, 1965. *Recreations:* gardening, bird watching. *Address:* 20 Willingale Way, Thorpe Bay, Southend-on-Sea, Essex SS1 3SL. *T:* Southend 586650.

MAYS, Colin Garth; HM Diplomatic Service; Overseas Inspector, since 1981; *b* 16 June 1931; *s* of William Albert Mays and late Sophia May Mays (*née* Pattinson); *m* 1956, Margaret Patricia, *d* of Philemon Robert Lloyd; one *s*. *Educ:* Acklam Hall Sch.; St John's Coll., Oxford (Heath Harrison Scholar). Served in Army, 1949-51; entered HM Foreign (subseq. Diplomatic) Service, 1955; FO, 1955-56; Sofia, 1956-58; Baghdad, 1958-60; FO, 1960; UK Delegn to Conf. of 18 Nation Cttee on Disarmament, Geneva, 1960; Bonn, 1960-65; FO, 1965-69; Prague, 1969-72; FCO, 1972-77; Head of Information Administration Dept, 1974-77; Counsellor (Commercial), Bucharest, 1977-80; seconded to PA Management Consultants, 1980-81. Liveryman, Painter-Stainers' Co., 1981. *Recreations:* sailing, swimming, travel. *Address:* c/o Foreign and Commonwealth Office, King Charles Street, SW1A 2AH. *Club:* Travellers'.

MAZRUI, Prof. Ali A., DPhil; Professor of Political Science, since 1974, and Director of Center for Afroamerican and African Studies, since 1979, University of Michigan; *b* Kenya, 24 Feb. 1933; *s* of Al'Amin Ali Mazrui, Judge of Islamic Law, and Safia Suleiman Mazrui; *m* 1962, Molly Vickerman; three *s*. *Educ:* Univ. of Manchester (BA with distinction 1960); Columbia Univ. (MA 1961); Oxford Univ. (DPhil 1966). Makerere University, Kampala, Uganda: Lectr, 1963-65; Prof. and Head of Dept of Political Science, 1965-69; Dean, Faculty of Social Sciences, 1967-73. Vis. Prof., Univs of London, Chicago, Manchester, Harvard, Nairobi, Calif (LA), Northwestern, Singapore, Australia, Stanford, Cairo, Sussex, Colgate and Leeds, 1965-78. Pres., African Studies Assoc. of USA, 1978-79; Vice-Pres., Internat. Congress of African Studies, 1978-. BBC Reith Lectr, 1979. *Publications:* Towards a Pax Africana, 1967; Violence and Thought, 1969; The Trial of Christopher Okigbo (novel), 1971; Cultural Engineering and Nation-Building in East Africa, 1972; Soldiers and Kinsmen in Uganda, 1975; A World Federation of Cultures: an African perspective, 1976; Africa's International Relations, 1977; Political Values and the Educated Class in Africa, 1978; The African Condition (The Reith Lectures), 1980. *Address:* 1517 Wells, Ann Arbor, Mich 48104, USA. *T:* 313-668-7842.

MBEKEANI, Nyemba W.; Chief Executive, Mkulumadzi Farm Bakeries Ltd, since 1981; *b* 15 June 1929; Malawi parentage; *m* 1950, Lois Mosses (*née* Chikankheni); two *s* three *d*. *Educ:* Henry Henderson Institute, Blantyre; London Sch. of Economics (Economic and Social Administration, 1963). Local Government Officer, 1945-58; political detention in Malawi and Southern Rhodesia, 1959-60; Business Executive, 1960-61; Local Govt Officer, 1963-64; Foreign Service, 1964; High Commissioner for Malawi in London, 1964-67; Ambassador to USA and Permanent Rep. at the UN, 1967-72; Ambassador to Ethiopia, 1972-73; Gen. Manager, Malawi Housing Corp., 1973-81. Farmer, company director, tea broker. *Recreations:* football, squash and flower gardening. *Address:* PO Box 2095, Blantyre, Malawi.

M'BOW, Amadou-Mahtar; Director-General of Unesco, since Nov. 1974; *b* 20 March 1921; *s* of Fara-N'Diaye M'Bow and N'Goné Casset, Senegal; *m* 1951, Raymonde Sylvain; one *s* two *d*. *Educ:* Univ. of Paris. Teacher, Rosso Coll., Mauritania, 1951-53; Dir, Service of Fundamental and Community Educn, Senegal, 1953-57; Min. of Education and Culture, 1957-58; Teacher at Lycée Faidherbe, St-Louis, Senegal, 1958-64; Prof., Ecole Normale Supérieure, Dakar, 1964-66; Minister of Educn, 1966-68; Mem. Nat. Assembly, Senegal, 1967-70; Minister of Culture, Youth and Sports 1968-70; Asst Dir-Gen. for Educn, UNESCO, 1970-74. Mem., Acad. des Sciences d'Outre-Mer, 1977. Hon. Mem., Royal Acad. Fine Arts, San Temo, Spain, 1977. Hon. Professor: Ecole normale supérieure, Dakar; Indep. Univ. of Santo Domingo; Nat. Indep. Univ. of Mexico, 1979; Hon. Dr: Buenos Aires, 1974; Granada (Lit. and Phil.), Sherbrooke (Educn), West Indies (Laws), 1975; Open, Kliment Okhridski, Sofia, Nairobi (Lit.), 1976; Malaya (Lit.), Philippines (Laws); Venice (Geog.), Uppsala (Soc. Scis), Moscow (Soc. Scis), Paris I, 1977; Andes (Philos.), Peru (Educn Scis), Haiti, Tribhunvan Univ., Nepal (Lit.), State Univ., Mongolia, Khartoum (Law), Sri Lanka, 1978; Charles Univ., Prague (Phil.), Tashkent, Québec, 1979; Nat. Univ. of Zaïre, Madras, Belgrade, Ivory Coast, Sierra Leone, 1980; Univ. Gama Filho, Brazil, 1981; Grand Tribute, Univ. Candido Mendes, Brazil, 1981. Comdr, Nat. Order of Upper Volta; Comdr, Palmes académiques (France); Officer, Order of Merit (Senegal); Grand Croix de l'Ordre du Libérateur (Venezuela); Grand Croix de l'Ordre nat. M.A.C. y R. José Cuervo (Colombia); Grand Croix de l'Ordre de Stara Planina (Bulgaria); Grand Cross, Order of Lion of Senegal; Grand Officer: Nat. Order of Ivory Coast; Nat. Order of Guinea; Order of Merit (Indonesia); Médaille de l'Ordre Manuel José Hurtado (Panama); Etoile Kawkab (Jordan); Grand Croix, Ordre Andres Bello (Venezuela); Grand Croix, Ordre du mérite (Ecuador); Grand Croix, Ordre du Soleil (Peru); Grand Croix du Mérite de Duarte, Sanchez et Mella (Dominican Republic); Grand Cross, Order Francisco Miranda, Venezuela; Order of Merit, Syrian Arab Republic; Grand Cross, Order of Merit "Juan Montalvo", Ecuador; Grand Cross, Civil Order Alfonso X, Spain; Comdr, Nat. Order of Merit, Gabon; Order of Arab Republic of Egypt (1st class); Grand Cross, Nat. Order of Southern Cross (Brazil); Grand Officer, Nat. Order (Cameroun); Grand Officer, Nat. Order of Merit (Mauritania); Grand Medal of Order of Inconfidência, Minas Gerais (Brazil). Terre des Hommes Prize, Canada. *Publications:* numerous monographs, articles in educl jls, textbooks, etc. *Address:* 7 Place de Fontenoy, 75700 Paris, France. *T:* 577.16.10.

MEACHER, Michael Hugh; MP (Lab) Oldham (West) since 1970; *b* 4 Nov. 1939; *s* of George Hubert and Doris May Meacher; *m* 1962, Molly Christine (*née* Reid); two *s* two *d*. *Educ:* Berkhamsted Sch., Herts; New College,

Oxford. Greats, Class 1. Sec. to Danilo Dolci Trust, 1964; Research Fellow in Social Gerontology, Univ. of Essex, 1965-66; Lecturer in Social Administration: Univ. of York, 1967-69; London Sch. of Economics, 1970. Parly Under-Secretary of State: DoI, 1974-75; DHSS, 1975-76; Dept of Trade, 1976-79. Chm., Labour Co-ordinating Cttee; Member: Nat. Exec.'s Campaign for Press Freedom; Treasury Select Cttee (a Chm. of its sub-cttee). Vis. Prof., Univ. of Surrey, Dept of Sociology, 1980-. *Publications:* Taken for a Ride: Special Residential Homes for the Elderly Mentally Infirm, a study of separatism in social policy, 1972; Fabian pamphlets, The Care of the Old, 1969; Wealth: Labour's Achilles Heel, in Labour and Equality, ed P. Townsend and N. Bosanquet, 1972; Socialism with a Human Face, 1981; numerous articles. *Recreations:* music, sport, reading. *Address:* 45 Cholmeley Park, N6. *T:* 01-340 5293.

MEAD, William Howard Lloyd; *b* 14 April 1905; *yr s* of late F. J. Mead; *m* 1951, Mary Pattinson, *e d* of late L. Borthwick Greig, Kendrew, S Africa. *Educ:* Marlborough; London Univ. BSc (Econ.) Hons. Industrial and Commercial Law, 1925. Chartered Accountant, 1930; RNVR 1938. Served War of 1939-45: in HMS Orion, 1939-41; Flag Lt to Vice-Adm. at Dover, 1942-45. Lt-Comdr (Sp) RNVR, retired, 1950. Clerk to the Vintners' Co., 1947-69. Dir, Royal Insurance Gp (London Bd), 1967-69. *Address:* 20 Bowen Court, The Drive, Hove, East Sussex BN3 3JF.

MEAD, Prof. William Richard; Professor and Head of Department of Geography, University College, London, 1966-81, now Emeritus Professor; *b* 29 July 1915; *s* of William Mead and Catharine Sarah Stevens; unmarried. *Educ:* Aylesbury Gram. Sch. (Foundation Governor, 1981-); London Sch. of Economics (Hon. Fellow 1979). DSc(Econ) London, 1968. Asst Lectr and Lectr, University of Liverpool, 1947-49; Rockefeller Fellowship, held in Finland, 1949-50; Lectr, 1950, Reader, 1953, University Coll., London. Chm. Council, Sch. of Slavonic and E European Studies, 1978-80. Chm., Anglo-Finnish Soc., 1966-; President: Inst. of British Geographers, 1971; Geog. Assoc., 1981-82; Hon. Sec., Royal Geographical Society, 1967-77 (Vice Pres., 1977-81, Hon. Vice-Pres., 1981-). Hon. Member: Finnish Geog. Soc.; Fenno-Ugrian Soc.; Sydsvenska geografiska sällskapet; Det norske Videnskaps. Akademi, 1976. Gill Memorial Award, 1951, Founder's Medal, 1980, RGS. Dr hc, University of Uppsala, 1966; DPhil hc, Univ. of Helsinki, 1969. Chevalier, Swedish Order of Vasa, 1962; Comdr, Orders of: Lion of Finland, 1963 (Chevalier, 1953); White Rose of Finland, 1976; Polar Star of Sweden, 1977. *Publications:* Farming in Finland, 1953; Economic Geography of Scandinavian States and Finland, 1958; (with Helmer Smeds) Winter in Finland, 1967; Finland (Modern Nations of the World Series), 1968; (with Wendy Hall) Scandinavia, 1972; The Scandinavian Northlands, 1973; (with Stig Jaatinen) The Aland Islands, 1974; An Historical Geography of Scandinavia, 1981; other books on Norway, Canada and USA. *Recreations:* riding, music. *Address:* 6 Lower Icknield Way, Aston Clinton, near Aylesbury, Bucks.

MEADE, family name of **Earl of Clanwilliam.**

MEADE, (Charles Alan) Gerald, CMG 1951; *b* 9 Aug. 1905; *s* of Charles Austin Meade; *m* 1936, Beatrix Audibert, Paris; one *s* two *d*. *Educ:* Leighton Park Sch., Reading; St John's Coll., Oxford. Entered Consular Service, 1927; Vice-Consul: Bangkok, 1927; Saigon, 1930; Barcelona, 1932; Chargé d'Affaires, Tegucigulpa, 1935; Consul: Savannah, Ga, 1936; Jacksonville, Florida, 1937; Second Sec., 1941, First Sec., 1943, Lima; First Sec., Buenos Aires, 1946; Counsellor, Washington, 1948; Minister (Economic and Social) to UK Delegation to UN, 1952. Permanent UK Representative to Council of Europe with rank of Minister, and Consul Gen. at Strasbourg, 1955-59; British Ambassador to Ecuador, 1959-62; retired, 1963. *Address:* Casa de d'Alt, Capdepera, Mallorca, Spain. *T:* Capdepera 563295; 55 rue de la Fédération, 75015 Paris, France. *T:* 273 08 81.

MEADE, Eric Cubitt, FCA; Senior Partner, Deloitte Haskins & Sells, Chartered Accountants, since 1982; *b* 12 April 1923; *s* of William Charles Abbott Meade and Vera Alicia Maria Meade; *m* 1960, Margaret Arnott McCallum; two *s* one *d*. *Educ:* Ratcliffe College. FCA 1947. Served War, Hampshire Regt, 1942-46; N Africa, Italy, prisoner of war, 1944-45; Captain. Chartered Accountant, 1947. Mem. Council, Inst. of Chartered Accountants in England and Wales, 1969-79 (Chm., Parly and Law Cttee, 1974-76; Chm., Investigation Cttee, 1976-77); Chm., Consultative Cttee., Accountancy Bodies Ethics Cttee, 1977-. *Recreations:* tennis, gardening. *Address:* 13 St Margaret's Crescent, Putney, SW15 6HL. *T:* 01-788 1271. *Clubs:* Gresham, Hurlingham.

MEADE, Sir Geoffrey; see Meade, Sir R. G. A.

MEADE, Gerald; see Meade, C. A. G.

MEADE, James Edward, CB 1947; FBA 1951; MA Oxon, MA Cantab; Hon. Dr, Universities of Basel, Bath, Essex, Hull and Oxford; Hon. Fellow: London School of Economics; Oriel College, Oxford; Hertford College, Oxford; Christ's College, Cambridge; *b* 23 June 1907; *s* of Charles Hippisley Meade and Kathleen Cotton-Stapleton; *m* 1933, Elizabeth Margaret, *d* of Alexander Cowan Wilson; one *s* three *d*. *Educ:* Malvern Coll. (Open Schol. in Classics); Oriel Coll., Oxford (Open Schol. in Classics); Trinity Coll., Cambridge. 1st Class Hon. Mods 1928; 1st Class Philosophy, Politics, and Economics, 1930. Fellow and Lecturer in Economics, 1930-37, and Bursar, 1934-37, Hertford

Coll., Oxford; Mem. Economic Section of League of Nations, Geneva, 1938-40. Economic Asst (1940-45), and Dir (1946-47), Economic Section Cabinet Offices. Prof. of Commerce, with special reference to International Trade, London Sch. of Economics, 1947-57; Prof. of Political Economy, Cambridge, 1957-68; Nuffield Res. Fellow, 1969-74, and Fellow, Christ's Coll., Cambridge, 1957-74. Member: Coun. of Royal Economic Society, 1945-62 (Pres., 1964-66, Vice-Pres., 1966-); Council of Eugenics Soc., 1962-68 (Treasurer 1963-67). Visiting Prof., Australian National Univ., 1956. Pres. Section F, British Assoc. for the Advancement of Science, 1957; Chm. Economic Survey Mission, Mauritius, 1960. Trustee of Urwick, Orr and Partners Ltd, 1958-76. Governor: Nat. Inst. of Economic and Social Research, 1947-; LSE, 1960-74; Malvern Coll., 1972-. Chm., Cttee of Inst. for Fiscal Studies, 1975-77 (producing report on The Structure and Reform of Direct Taxation, 1978). Hon. Mem., Amer. Economic Assoc., 1962; For. Hon. Member: Soc. Royale d'Econ. Politique de Belgique, 1958; Amer. Acad. of Arts and Sciences, 1966; For. Associate, Nat. Acad. of Sciences, USA, 1981. (Jtly) Nobel Prize for Economics, 1977. *Publications:* Public Works in their International Aspect, 1933; The Rate of Interest in a Progressive State, 1933; Economic Analysis and Policy, 1936; Consumers' Credits and Unemployment, 1937; League of Nations' World Economic Surveys for 1937-38 and 1938-39; The Economic Basis of a Durable Peace, 1940; (with Richard Stone) National Income and Expenditure, 1944; Planning and the Price Mechanism, 1948; The Theory of International Economic Policy, Vol. I, 1951, Vol. II, 1955; A Geometry of International Trade, 1952; Problems of Economic Union, 1953; The Theory of Customs Unions, 1955; The Control of Inflation, 1958; A Neo-Classical Theory of Economic Growth, 1960; Three Case Studies in European Economic Union, 1962 (Joint Author); Efficiency, Equality, and the Ownership of Property, 1964; Principles of Political Economy, Vol. 1, The Stationary Economy, 1965, Vol. 2, The Growing Economy, 1968, Vol. 3, The Controlled Economy, 1972, Vol. 4, The Just Economy, 1976; The Theory of Indicative Planning, 1970; The Theory of Externalities, 1973; The Intelligent Radical's Guide to Economic Policy, 1975; Stagflation, vol. 1, Wage Fixing, 1982. *Address:* 40 High Street, Little Shelford, Cambridge CB2 5ES. *T:* Cambridge 842491. *Club:* Athenæum.
See also P. S. Dasgupta, I. W. Meade, Sir Geoffrey Wilson, Prof. R. C. Wilson, S. S. Wilson.

MEADE, Patrick John, OBE 1944; consultant in meteorology to various international organisations; Director of Services, and Deputy Director-General, Meteorological Office, 1966-73; *b* 23 Feb. 1913; *s* of late John Meade, Caterham, Surrey; *m* 1937, Winifred Jessie, *d* of Bertram Kent, Fawley, Hants; one *s* one *d* (and one *s* decd). *Educ:* Sir Joseph Williamson's Math. Sch., Rochester; Imperial Coll. of Science and Technology (Royal College of Science). ARCSc, BSc; Lubbock Mem. Prize in Maths, London Univ., 1933. Entered Met. Office, 1936; Southampton, 1937; Flt Lt RAFVR, Fr., 1939-40; Sqdn Leader, Sen. Met. Off., GHQ Home Forces, 1940-42; Wing Comdr (Gp Capt. 1944), Chief Met. Off., MAAF, 1943-45; Chief Met. Off., ACSEA, 1945-46; Head of Met. Office Trng Sch., 1948-52; London Airport, 1952-55; Research, 1955-60; idc 1958; Dep. Dir for Outstations Services, 1960-65. Hon. Sec., Royal Meteorological Society, 1956-61, Vice-Pres., 1961-63. *Publications:* papers in jls on aviation meteorology and on meteorological aspects of air pollution, atmospheric radioactivity and hydrology. *Recreations:* music, gardening. *Address:* Luccombe, Coronation Road, South Ascot, Berks. *T:* Ascot 23206.

MEADE, Sir (Richard) Geoffrey (Austin), KBE 1963; CMG 1953; CVO 1961; *b* 8 March 1902; *s* of late Austin Meade, MA; *m* 1929, Elizabeth Ord, MA Oxon, 2nd *d* of late G. J. Scott, JP; three *d. Educ:* Ecole Alsacienne, Paris; Balliol Coll., Oxford. BA 1925. Entered Consular Service, 1925; served at Tangier, 1927, Salonica, 1929, Aleppo, 1930, Athens, 1931, Salonica, 1933, Tangier, 1935, Valencia, 1939, Crete, 1940, FO, 1941, Dakar, 1943, Tetuan, 1943, Cassablanca, 1945; Istanbul, 1947; idc, 1950; Marseilles, 1951; Tangier, 1956; Düsseldorf, 1957; Milan, 1958-62. Retired, 1962. *Address:* Baker's Close, 104 Lower Radley, Abingdon, Oxon OX14 3BA. *T:* Abingdon 21327.

MEADE, Thomas Wilson, DM; FRCP, FFCM; Director, Medical Research Council Epidemiology and Medical Care Unit, Northwick Park Hospital, Harrow, since 1970; Hon. consultant in epidemiology, Northwick Park Hospital, since 1971; *b* 21 Jan. 1936; *s* of James Edward Meade, *qv; m* 1962, Helen Elizabeth Perks; one *s* two *d. Educ:* Westminster Sch.; Christ Church, Oxford; St Bartholomew's Hosp. House Officer and Registrar, St Bartholomew's Hosp. and Littlemore and Churchill Hosps, Oxford, 1961-64; Scientific Staff, MRC Social Medicine Unit, 1964-68; Sen. Lectr, Dept of Public Health, London Sch. of Hygiene and Tropical Medicine (on secondment to Schieffelin Leprosy Research Sanatorium, S India, 1969-70), 1968-70. Hon. Dir, Cardiovascular Epidemiology Res. Gp, British Heart Foundn, 1982-. Member: MRC Physiological Systems and Disorders Bd, 1974-78; MRC Health Services Res. Panel, 1981-; Sub-Cttee on Adverse Reactions of Cttee on Safety of Medicines, 1976-81; Chairman: Sub-Cttee on Screening in Medical Care of Standing Med. Adv. Cttee, DHSS, 1976-77 (Mem., 1972-77); Adv. Panel (to CSM) on Collection of data relating to Adverse Reactions to Pertussis Vaccine, 1977-81. Member, British Cardiac Soc., 1978. *Publications:* papers on haemostasis and thrombosis, medical care (mainly aspects of chronic disability), leprosy. *Recreations:* oboe, growing vegetables, fishing. *Address:* 28 Cholmeley Crescent, N6 5HA. *T:* 01-340 6260. *Club:* Leander (Henley-on-Thames).

MEADE-KING, Charles Martin, MA; Headmaster, Plymouth College, 1955-73, retired; *b* 17 Aug. 1913; *s* of late G. C. Meade-King, solicitor, Bristol; *m* 1948, Mary (*née* Frazer); one *s* one *d. Educ:* Clifton Coll.; Exeter Coll., Oxford (Stapeldon Scholar). Asst Master, King's Sch., Worcester, 1935-38; Asst Master, Mill Hill Sch., 1938-40. Intelligence Corps, 1940-45. Housemaster, Mill Hill Sch., 1945-55. *Recreations:* history, arts, games. *Address:* Whistledown, Yelverton, near Plymouth. *T:* Yelverton 852237.

MEADEN, Rt. Rev. John Alfred, DD, MA, LTh; *b* 16 Feb. 1892. *Educ:* Queen's Coll., Newfoundland; University Coll., Durham, England. LTh Durham, 1916, BA 1917, MA 1935. Deacon, 1917, Nova Scotia for Newfoundland; Priest, 1918, Newfoundland. Incumbent of White Bay, 1917-21; Rector of Burin, 1921-29; Pouch Cove, 1929-34; Sec.-treasurer of Executive Cttee of Newfoundland Diocesan Synod, 1934-47; Examining Chaplain to the Bishop of Newfoundland, 1943-47; Canon of St John Baptist's Cathedral, St John's, Newfoundland, 1938-57. Principal of Queen's Coll., St John's, 1947-57. Bishop of Newfoundland, 1956-65. Hon. DCL, Bishop's Univ., Lennoxville, 1957; Hon. DD, Trinity Coll., Toronto, 1959; Hon. LLD, Memorial Univ. of Nfld, 1961. *Address:* Saint Luke's Homes, Topsail Road, St John's, Newfoundland, Canada.

MEADOWS, Bernard William; sculptor; Professor of Sculpture, Royal College of Art, 1960-80; *b* Norwich, 19 Feb. 1915; *s* of W. A. F. and E. M. Meadows; *m* 1939, Marjorie Winifred Payne; two *d. Educ:* City of Norwich Sch. Studied at Norwich Sch. of Art, 1934-36; worked as Asst to Henry Moore, 1936-40; studied at Royal College of Art, 1938-40 and 1946-48. Served with RAF, 1941-46. Commissioned by Arts Council to produce a work for Festival of Britain, 1951. Rep. (Brit. Pavilion) in Exhib. of Recent Sculpture, Venice Biennale, 1952; in Exhib., Kassel, Germany, 1959, etc. Exhibited in International Exhibitions of Sculpture (Open Air): Battersea Park, 1951, 1960; Musée Rodin, Paris, 1956; Holland Park, 1957; in 4th International Biennial, São Paulo, Brazil, 1957; also in Exhibns (Open Air) in Belgium and Holland, 1953-. *One man exhibitions:* Gimpel Fils, London, 1957, 1959, 1963, 1965, 1967; Paul Rosenberg, New York, 1959, 1962, 1967; Taranman, London, 1979. *Works in Collections:* Tate Gallery; Victoria and Albert Museum; Arts Council; British Council; Museum of Modern Art, New York; also in public collections in N and S America, Israel, Australia, and in Europe. Mem., Royal Fine Art Commn, 1971-76. Awarded Italian State Scholarship, 1956. *Publication:* 34 etchings and box (for Molloy by Samuel Beckett), 1967. *Address:* 34 Belsize Grove, NW3. *T:* 01-722 0772.

MEADOWS, Robert; company director, motor trade; Lord Mayor of Liverpool, May 1972-May 1973; *b* 28 June 1902; *m* 1st, 1926, Ivy L. Jenkinson (*d* 1963); three *s*; 2nd, 1967, Nora E. Bullen. *Educ:* locally and Bootle Technical Coll. Engineering, 1917-21. Liverpool: City Councillor, Fairfield Ward, 1945; City Alderman, Princes Park Ward, 1961-74. *Recreations:* motor vehicle development, property improvement, landscape gardening. *Address:* 163 Prescot Road, Liverpool L7 0LD. *T:* 051-428 1032.

MEADOWS, Swithin Pinder, MD, BSc, FRCP; Consulting Physician: Westminster Hospital; National Hospital, Queen Square; Moorfields Eye Hospital; *b* 18 April 1902; *er s* of late Thomas and late Sophia Florence Meadows; *m* 1934, Doris Steward Noble; two *s* two *d. Educ:* Wigan Grammar Sch.; University of Liverpool; St Thomas' Hosp. Kanthack Medal in Pathology; Owen T. Williams Prize; House Physician and House Surgeon, Liverpool Royal Infirmary; House Physician, Royal Liverpool Children's Hospital; Medical Registrar and Tutor, St Thomas' Hosp.; RMO National Hosp., Queen Square; Medical First Asst, London Hosp.; Examiner in Neurology and Medicine, University of London; Hosp. Visitor, King Edward's Hosp. Fund for London; Mem., Assoc. of British Neurologists; Hon. Mem., Aust. Assoc. of Neurologists; Hunterian Prof., Royal College of Surgeons, 1952; Pres., Section of Neurology, Royal Society of Medicine, 1965-66; Visiting Prof., University of California, San Francisco, 1954; Doyne Meml Lectr, Oxford Ophthalmological Congress, 1969. Neurologist, British European Airways; Vice-Pres., Newspaper Press Fund. *Publications:* contributions to medical literature. *Recreations:* walking, music, country life. *Address:* 45 Lanchester Road, Highgate N6 4SX.

MEAKIN, Wilfred, CB 1982; CEng, FIMechE; Managing Director, Royal Ordnance Factories, and Deputy Chairman, Board of the Royal Ordnance Factories, since 1979; *b* 1925. *Educ:* engineering apprenticeship in industry. Served War of 1939-45, RN. Technical Asst, ROF, Maltby, 1951; posts in ROF and former Inspectorate of Armaments; Asst Dir, ROF, Blackburn, 1966-72; Dir, ROF, Birtley, 1972-75; Dir, ROF Leeds, during 1975; Dir-Gen., Ordnance Factories (Weapons and Fighting Vehicles), 1975-79. *Address:* Ministry of Defence, Royal Ordnance Factories, Northumberland House, WC2N 5BP.

MEANEY, Sir Patrick (Michael), Kt 1981; Managing Director, Thomas Tilling Ltd, since 1973; *b* 6 May 1925; *m* Mary June Kearney; one *s. Educ:* Wimbledon College. HM Forces, 1941-47. Joined Thomas Tilling Ltd, 1961. Director: Cable and Wireless plc, 1978-; Rank Organisation plc, 1979-; Midland Bank, 1979-; ICI plc, 1981-. Member Council: London Chamber of Commerce, 1977-; British North American Cttee and Res. Assoc., 1979-; CBI, 1980-; Chm., Govt Review Cttee on Harland & Wolff, 1980; Member: Adv. Bd, European Management Forum, 1979-; Cttee, Conference Bd, 1982-. CBIM 1976. Pres., Inst. of Marketing, 1981-. *Recreations:* sport, music, international business, social education. *Address:* Crewe House, Curzon Street, W1Y 8AX. *T:* 01-499 4151. *Clubs:* Harlequins, British Sportsman's.

MEATH, 14th Earl of, *cr* 1627; **Anthony Windham Normand Brabazon;** Baron Ardee, Ireland, 1616; Baron Chaworth, of Eaton Hall, Co. Hereford, UK, 1831; late Major Grenadier Guards; *b* 3 Nov. 1910; *o s* of 13th Earl of Meath, CB, CBE and Lady Aileen Wyndham-Quin (*d* 1962), *d* of 4th Earl of Dunraven; *S* father 1949; *m* 1940, Elizabeth Mary, *d* of late Capt. Geoffrey Bowlby, Royal Horse Guards, and of Hon. Mrs Geoffrey Bowlby, *qv* ; two *s* two *d. Educ:* Eton; RMC Sandhurst. Joined Grenadier Guards, 1930. ADC to Governor of Bengal, 1936; Capt., 1938; served War of 1939-45, Grenadier Guards (wounded); Major, 1941; retired, 1946. *Heir: s* Lord Ardee, *qv. Address:* Killruddery, Bray, Co. Wicklow, Ireland.

MEATH, Bishop of, (RC), since 1968; **Most Rev. John McCormack;** *b* 25 March 1921; *s* of Peter McCormack and Bridget Mulvany. *Educ:* St Finian's Coll., Mullingar; Maynooth Coll.; Lateran Univ., Rome. Priest, 1946. Ministered: Multyfarnham, 1950-52; St Loman's Hosp., 1952-58; Mullingar, 1958-68; Diocesan Sec., 1952-68. *Address:* Bishop's House, Dublin Road, Mullingar, Co. Westmeath, Ireland. *T:* Mullingar 8841.

MEATH AND KILDARE, Bishop of, since 1976; **Most Rev. Donald Arthur Richard Caird;** *b* Dublin, 11 Dec. 1925; *s* of George Robert Caird and Emily Florence Dreaper, Dublin; *m* 1963, Nancy Ballantyne, *d* of Prof. William Sharpe, MD, and Gwendolyn Hind, New York, USA; one *s* two *d. Educ:* Wesley Coll., Dublin, 1935-44; Trinity Coll., Dublin Univ., 1944-50. Sen. Exhibn, TCD, 1946; elected Schol. of the House, TCD, 1948; 1st cl. Moderatorship in Mental and Moral Science, 1949; Prizeman in Hebrew and Irish Language, 1946 and 1947; Lilian Mary Luce Memorial Prize for Philosophy, 1947; BA 1949; MA and BD 1955; HDipEd 1959. Curate Asst, St Mark's. Dundela, Belfast, 1950-53; Chaplain and Asst Master, Portora Royal Sch., Enniskillen, 1953-57; Lectr in Philosophy, University Coll. of St David's, Lampeter, 1957; Rector, Rathmichael Parish, Shankill, Co. Dublin, 1960-69; Asst Master, St Columba's Coll., Rathfarnham, Co. Dublin, 1960-67; Dept Lectr in Philosophy, Trinity Coll., Dublin, 1962-63; Lectr in the Philosophy of Religion, Divinity Hostel, Dublin, 1964-70; Dean of Ossory, 1969-70; Bishop of Limerick, Ardfert and Aghadoe, 1970-76. Fellow of St Columba's Coll., Dublin, 1971. Mem., Bord na Gaeilge, 1974. *Publication:* The Predicament of Natural Theology since the Criticism of Kant, in *Directions,* 1970 (Dublin). *Recreations:* swimming, tennis. *Address:* Ivy House, Leixlip, Co. Kildare, Ireland. *T:* Dublin 280650.

MEDAWAR, Sir Peter (Brian), OM 1981; CH 1972; Kt 1965; CBE 1958; MA, DSc (Oxford); FRS 1949; Hon. FBA 1981; President, Royal Postgraduate Medical School, since 1981; Member, Scientific Staff, Medical Research Council, since 1962; *b* 28 Feb. 1915; *s* of Nicholas Medawar and Edith Muriel Dowling; *m* 1937, Jean Shinglewood, *d* of Dr C. H. S. Taylor; two *s* two *d. Educ:* Marlborough Coll.; Magdalen Coll., Oxford. Christopher Welch Scholar and Senior Demy of Magdalen Coll., 1935; Fellow of Magdalen Coll., 1938-44, 1946-47; Fellow of St John's Coll., 1944; Mason Prof. of Zoology, Birmingham Univ., 1947-51; Jodrell Prof. of Zoology and Comparative Anatomy, University Coll., London, 1951-62; Dir, Nat. Inst. for Medical Research, Mill Hill, 1962-71, Dir Emeritus, 1975. Croonian Lectr, Royal Society, 1958; Reith Lecturer, 1959; Dunham Lectr, Harvard Med. Sch., 1959; Romanes Lectr, 1968; Prof. of Experimental Medicine, Royal Institution, 1977-. Pres., Brit. Assoc. for the Advancement of Science, 1968-69; Member: Agricultural Research Council, 1952-62; University Grants Cttee, 1955-59; Royal Commn on Med. Educn, 1965-68; Bd of Scientific Consultants, Meml Sloan-Kettering Cancer Centre; Inst. of Cellular Pathology, Brussels. Foreign Member: New York Acad. of Sciences, 1957; Amer. Acad. Arts and Sciences, 1959; Amer. Philosophical Soc., 1961; National Acad. of Sciences, 1965; Indian Acad. of Sciences, 1967. Hon. Fellow: St Catherine's Coll., 1960; Magdalen Coll., 1961; University Coll., London, 1971; London Sch. of Economics, 1975; Wolfson Coll., Oxford, 1981; American Coll. of Physicians, 1964; Royal College Physicians and Surgeons, Canada, 1966; RCS, 1967; RSE, 1965; RCPE, 1971; RCP, 1974; Prof. at Large, Cornell Univ., 1965; Royal Medal of Royal Society, 1959, Copley Medal, 1969. Nobel Prize for Medicine, 1960. Hon. ScD Cambridge; Hon. D de l'Univ.: Liège; Brussels; Hon. DSc: Aston, Birmingham, Hull, Glasgow, Brazil, Alberta, Dundee, Dalhousie, British Columbia, Chicago, Exeter, Florida, Harvard, Southampton, London. *Publications:* The Uniqueness of the Individual, 1957; The Future of Man, 1960; The Art of the Soluble, 1967; Induction and Intuition, 1969; The Hope of Progress, 1972; Life Science, 1977; Advice to a Young Scientist, 1979; Pluto's Republic, 1982. *Address:* Clinical Research Centre, Watford Road, Harrow, Mddx HA1 3UJ; 25 Downshire Hill, NW3.

See also Sir Ian McAdam.

MEDD, Patrick William, OBE 1962; QC 1973; **His Honour Judge Medd;** a Circuit Judge, since 1981; *b* 26 May 1919; *s* of E. N. Medd; *m* 1st, 1945, Jeananne Spence Powell (marr. diss.); three *d* ; 2nd, 1971, Elizabeth Spink D'Albuquerque. *Educ:* Uppingham Sch.; Selwyn Coll., Cambridge. Served in Army, 1940-46, S Staffs Regt and E African Artillery, Major. Called to Bar, Middle Temple, 1947, Bencher 1969; Mem. Gen. Council of the Bar, 1965-67. Dep. Chm., Shropshire QS, 1967-71; Jun. Counsel to Comrs of Inland Revenue, 1968-73; Recorder of Abingdon, 1964-71 (Hon. Recorder, 1972-); a Recorder of the Crown Court, 1972-81. Chm., Bd of Referees, and Finance Act 1960 Tribunal, 1978-; UK rep., panel of arbitrators, Internat. Centre for Settlement of Investment Disputes, 1979-. *Publications:* (jtly) The Rule of Law, 1955; (jtly) Murder, 1956; (jtly) A Giant's Strength, 1958; Romilly, 1968. *Recreation:* gardening. *Address:* c/o The Crown Court, Oxford.

MEDHURST, Brian; Joint Chief Investment Manager, Prudential Assurance Company Ltd, since 1981; *b* 18 March 1935; *s* of Eric Gilbert Medhurst and Bertha May (*née* Kinggett); *m* 1960, Patricia Anne Beer; two *s* one *d. Educ:* Godalming Grammar Sch.; Trinity Coll., Cambridge (MA). Fellow, Inst. of Actuaries, 1962. Joined Prudential Assurance Co. Ltd, 1958; Deputy Investment Manager, 1972; Investment Manager, 1975. Mem. Council, Inst. of Actuaries, 1982-. *Recreations:* squash, golf, piano duets, tree felling. *Address:* Longacre, Fitzroy Road, Fleet, Hants GU13 8JJ. *T:* Fleet 4159. *Clubs:* North Hants Golf; Royal Aldershot Officers'.

MEDLEY, (Charles) Robert (Owen), CBE 1982; Painter and Theatrical Designer; Chairman, Faculty of Painting, British School at Rome, 1966-77; *b* 19 Dec. 1905; *s* of late C. D. Medley, and A. G. Owen. *Educ:* Gresham's Sch., Holt. Studied art in London and Paris; Art Dir of the Group Theatre and designed the settings and costumes for plays by T. S. Eliot, W. H. Auden, Christopher Isherwood, Louis Macneice, and Verdi's Othello, Sadler's Wells Theatre, Coppelia, Sadler's Wells Theatre Ballet; exhibited in London and New York World's Fair; pictures bought by: Tate Gallery; V. & A. (collection of drawings); Walker Art Gallery, Liverpool; City Art Gallery, Birmingham, and other provincial galleries; National Gallery of Canada, Ontario; Contemporary Art Society; Arts Council for Festival of Britain, 1951. Official War Artist, 1940. Retrospective Exhibition, Whitechapel Art Gallery, 1963. Diocletian in Sebastiane (film), 1976. *Publication:* (illustr.) Milton's Samson Agonistes, 1981. *Address:* 10 Gledhow Gardens, SW5 0AY.

MEDLICOTT, Prof. William Norton, DLit, MA (London); FRHistS; Stevenson Professor of International History, University of London, 1953-67; Professor Emeritus, 1967; Senior Editor of Documents on British Foreign Policy, 1919-39, since 1965; *b* 11 May 1900; *s* of William Norton Medlicott (Editor, Church Family Newspaper, 1905-11) and Margaret Louisa McMillan; *m* 1936, Dr Dorothy Kathleen Coveney, Univ. Lectr and palaeographer (*d* 1979). *Educ:* Aske's Sch., Hatcham; University College, London; Institute of Historical Research. Gladstone Prizeman, Hester Rothschild Prizeman, UCL; Lindley Student, Univ. of London; Lecturer, University Coll., Swansea, 1926-45; Visiting Prof., Univ. of Texas, USA, 1931-32; Principal, Board of Trade, 1941-42; official historian, Ministry of Economic Warfare, 1942-58; Prof. of History, University Coll. of the South West, 1945-53; Vice-Principal, 1953. Creighton Lectr, Univ. of London, 1968. Fellow of UCL. Hon. Fellow LSE. Travel and research in US, 1946, 1952, and 1957; Hon. Sec. Historical Association, 1943-46, Pres., 1952-55; Chm. editorial board, International Affairs, 1954-62; Mem. Institute for Advanced Studies, Princeton, 1952, 1957; Chm. British Co-ordinating Cttee for Internat. Studies. Hon. DLitt Wales, 1970; Hon. LittD Leeds, 1977. *Publications:* The Congress of Berlin and After, 1938, new edn 1963; British Foreign Policy since Versailles, 1940, new edn, 1968; The Economic Blockade, vol. i, 1952, vol. ii, 1959; Bismarck, Gladstone, and the Concert of Europe, 1956; The Coming of War in 1939, 1963; Bismarck and Modern Germany, 1965; Contemporary England, 1914-1964, 1967, rev. edn 1976; Britain and Germany: The Search for Agreement, 1930-1937, 1969; (with D. K. Coveney) Bismarck and Europe, 1971; (with D. K. Coveney) The Lion's Tail, 1971; (ed) Documents on British Foreign Policy 1919-1939, 2nd series, vols x-xix, 1965-; numerous articles and reviews. *Address:* 172 Watchfield Court, Sutton Court Road, W4 4NE. *T:* 01-995 7287. *Club:* Athenæum.

MEDLYCOTT, Sir (James) Christopher, 8th Bt, *cr* 1808; *b* 17 April 1907; *e s* of Sir Hubert Mervyn Medlycott, 7th Bt, and Nellie Adah (*d* 1964), *e d* of late Hector Edmond Monro, Edmondsham, Dorset; *S* father, 1964. *Educ:* Harrow; Magdalene Coll., Cambridge. BA 1930. *Heir: nephew* Mervyn Tregonwell Medlycott, *b* 20 Feb. 1947. *Address:* The Yard House, Milborne Port, near Sherborne, Dorset. *T:* Milborne Port 250312.

MEDWAY, Lord; John Jason Gathorne-Hardy; *b* 26 Oct. 1968; *s* and *heir* of 5th Earl of Cranbrook, *qv.*

MEDWIN, Robert Joseph G.; *see* Gardner-Medwin.

MEECHIE, Brig. Helen Guild; Director, Women's Royal Army Corps, since 1982; Hon. ADC to the Queen, since 1982; *b* 19 Jan. 1938; *d* of John Strachan and Robina Guild Meechie. *Educ:* Morgan Academy, Dundee; St Andrew's University. Commissioned 1960; served in UK, Cyprus and Hong Kong, 1961-76; in UK and Germany, 1977-82. *Recreations:* golf, gardening, travel. *Address:* c/o Clydesdale Bank, 31 St James's Street, SW1A 1HW.

MEEK, Charles Innes, CMG 1961; Chief Executive, 1962-81, Chairman, 1973-81, White Fish Authority; *b* 27 June 1920; *er s* of late Dr C. K. Meek; *m* 1947, Nona Corry Hurford; two *s* one *d. Educ:* King's Sch., Canterbury; Magdalen Coll., Oxford (MA). Demyship, Magdalen Coll., Oxford, 1939. Served in Army, 1940-41; District Officer, Tanganyika, 1941; Principal Asst Sec., Tanganyika, 1958; Permanent Sec., Chief Secretary's Office, 1959; Permanent Sec. to Prime Minister, Sec. to Cabinet, 1960; Government Dir, Williamson Diamonds; Head of the Civil Service, Tanganyika, 1961-62, retd. FRSA 1969. *Publications:* occasional articles in Journal of African Administration, etc. *Recreations:* travel, Times crossword. *Address:* 30 Heriot

Row, Edinburgh EH3 6EN. *T:* 031-226 2777. *Club:* Royal Commonwealth Society.

MEEK, Prof. John Millar, CBE 1975; DEng; FInstP; FIEE; David Jardine Professor of Electrical Engineering, University of Liverpool, 1946-78; Public Orator, 1973-76, and Pro-Vice-Chancellor, 1974-77, University of Liverpool; *b* Wallasey, 21 Dec. 1912; *s* of Alexander Meek and Edith Montgomery; *m* 1942, Marjorie, *d* of Bernard Ingleby; two *d*. *Educ:* Monkton Combe Sch.; University of Liverpool. College Apprentice, Metropolitan-Vickers Electrical Co. Ltd, 1934-36; Research Engineer, Metropolitan-Vickers Electrical Co. Ltd, 1936-38, 1940-46. Commonwealth Fund Research Fellow, Physics Dept, University of California, Berkeley, 1938-40. Mem. of Council, IEE, 1945-48, 1960-63 (Vice-Pres. 1964-68, Pres., 1968-69), Faraday Medal, 1975. Mem., IBA (formerly ITA), 1969-74. Hon. DSc Salford, 1971. *Publications:* The Mechanism of the Electric Spark (with L. B. Loeb), 1941; Electrical Breakdown of Gases (with J. D. Craggs), 1953, new edn 1978; High Voltage Laboratory Technique (with J. D. Craggs), 1954; papers in various scientific journals concerning research on electrical discharges in gases. *Recreations:* golf, gardening, theatre. *Address:* 4 The Kirklands, West Kirby, Merseyside. *T:* 051-625 5850. *Club:* Royal Commonwealth Society.

MEERE, Sir Frank, (Francis Anthony), Kt 1960; CBE 1955; FAIM; Comptroller General of Customs, Canberra, 1952-60; *b* 24 July 1895; *s* of Philip Francis and Harriet Charlotte Meere of Daylesford, Vic; *m* 1st, 1920, Helena Agnes (decd), *d* of late Wm G. Doyle; two *s*; 2nd, 1970, Mary Irene Higgins. *Educ:* Christian Brothers Coll., East St Kilda, Vic. Joined Australian Commonwealth Public Service, 1913; Deputy Dir, Division of Import Procurement, Brisbane, 1942-45; Dir, Division of Import Procurement, Sydney, 1945-47; Asst Comptroller General of Customs, Canberra, 1947-52. *Recreation:* gardening. *Address:* 3 Meehan Gardens, Canberra, ACT 2603, Australia. *Club:* Commonwealth (Canberra).

MEERES, Norman Victor, CB 1963; Under-Secretary, Ministry of Defence, 1971-73, retired; *b* 1 Feb. 1913; *m* 1938, Elizabeth Powys Fowler; two *s* one *d*. *Educ:* Sloane Sch., Chelsea; Magdalene Coll., Cambridge. Asst Principal, Air Ministry, 1935; Principal, 1940, Asst Sec., 1944, Ministry of Aircraft Prod.; Asst Sec., Min. of Supply, 1946; Under Secretary: Min. of Supply, 1956; Min. of Aviation, 1959-67; seconded to Dipl. Service in Australia, with title Minister (Defence Research and Civil Aviation), 1965-68; Under-Sec., Min. of Technology, 1969-70. ARCM (piano teaching), 1974. *Recreations:* music, lawn tennis. *Address:* 89 Grove Way, Esher, Surrey. *T:* 01-398 1639.

MEESE, Edwin, III; lawyer; Counsellor to the President of the United States of America, since 1981; *b* 1931; *s* of Edwin Meese Jr and Leone Meese; *m* 1958, Ursula Herrick; one *s* one *d* (and one *s* decd). *Educ:* Oakland High Sch.; Yale Univ. (BA 1953); Univ. of Calif at Berkeley (LLB 1958). Dep Dist Attorney, Alameda County, 1958-66; Aide to Ronald Reagan, 1967-; Vice-Pres., Rohr Industries, 1975-76; Dir, Center for Criminal Justice Policy and Management, 1977-; Prof of criminal justice, Univ. of San Diego Law Sch., 1978- (on leave of absence, 1980-); Manager, Nat. Security Council, Domestic Policy and Cabinet Staffs, Washington, 1981-. Vice-Pres., First Lutheran Church, El Cajon. *Address:* White House Office, 1600 Pennsylvania Avenue, Washington, DC 20500, USA.

MEGAHY, Thomas, MBE 1979; Member (Lab) SW Yorkshire, European Parliament, since 1979; *b* 16 July 1929; *s* of Samuel and Mary Megahy; *m* 1954, Jean (*née* Renshaw); three *s*. *Educ:* Wishaw High Sch.; Ruskin Coll., Oxford, 1953-55; College of Educn (Technical), Huddersfield, 1955-56 and 1968-69; London Univ. (external student), 1959-63. BScEcon London; DipEcon and PolSci Oxon; DipFE Leeds. Left school at 14 to work on railway; National Service, RN, 1947-49; railway signalman, 1950-53. Lecturer: Rotherham Coll. of Technology, 1956-59; Huddersfield Technical Coll., 1960-65; Park Lane Coll., Leeds, 1965-79. Active member of Labour Party, and Chm., Scottish Labour League of Youth; Executive Mem., Dewsbury CLP, 1962-. Councillor, Mirfield UDC, 1963-74; Leader, Kirklees Metropolitan Borough Council, 1973-76; Opposition Leader, 1976-78. Member, Yorks and Humberside REPC, 1974-77. *Recreations:* caravanning, music. *Address:* 6 Lady Heton Grove, Mirfield, West Yorks WF14 9DY. *T:* Mirfield 492680.

MEGARRY, Rt. Hon. Sir Robert (Edgar), Kt 1967; PC 1978; FBA 1970; The Vice-Chancellor of the Supreme Court, since 1982; Vice Chancellor of the Chancery Division of the High Court of Justice, since 1976, a Judge in the Division, since 1967; *b* 1 June 1910; *e s* of late Robert Lindsay Megarry, OBE, MA, LLB, Belfast, and of late Irene, *d* of Maj.-Gen. E. G. Clark; *m* 1936, Iris, *e d* of late Elias Davies, Neath, Glam; three *d*. *Educ:* Lancing Coll.; Trinity Hall, Cambridge (Hon. Fellow, 1973). MA, LLD (Cantab); Music Critic, Varsity, 1930-32; Solicitor, 1935-41; taught for Bar and Solicitors' exams, 1935-39; Mem., Faculty of Law, Cambridge Univ., 1939-40; Certificate of Honour, and called to Bar, Lincoln's Inn, 1944, in practice, 1946-67; QC 1956-67; Bencher, Lincoln's Inn, 1962, Treasurer 1981. Principal, 1940-44, and Asst Sec., 1944-46, Min. of Supply; Book Review Editor and Asst Ed., Law Quarterly Review, 1944-67; Dir of Law Society's Refresher Courses, 1944-47; Sub-Lector, Trinity Coll., Cambridge, 1945-46; Asst Reader, 1946-51, Reader, 1951-67, Hon. Reader, 1967- in Equity in the Inns of Court (Council of Legal Educn); Member: Gen. Council of the Bar, 1948-52; Lord Chancellor's Law Reform Cttee, 1952-73; Senate of Inns of Court and Bar, 1966-70, 1980-82; Adv. Council on Public Records, 1980-;

Consultant to BBC for Law in Action series, 1953-66; Chairman: Notting Hill Housing Trust, 1967-68; Bd of Studies, and Vice-Chm., Council of Legal Educn, 1969-71; Friends of Lancing Chapel, 1969-; Incorporated Council of Law Reporting, 1972-; Comparative Law Sect., British Inst. of Internat. and Comp. Law, 1977-; President: Soc. of Public Teachers of Law, 1965-66; Lancing Club, 1974-; Selden Soc., 1976-79. Visiting Professor: New York Univ. Sch. of Law, 1960-61; Osgoode Hall Law Sch., Toronto, 1964; John F. Sounett Lectr, Fordham Univ., 1982. Hon. LLD: Hull 1963; Nottingham, 1979; Law Soc. of Upper Canada (Osgoode Hall), 1982. Hon. Life Mem., Canadian Bar Assoc., 1971. *Publications:* The Rent Acts, 1939, 10th edn 1967; A Manual of the Law of Real Property, 1946, 5th edn (ed P. V. Baker QC), 1975; Lectures on the Town and Country Planning Act, 1947, 1949; Miscellany-at-Law, 1955; (with Prof. H. W. R. Wade QC) The Law of Real Property, 1957, 4th edn 1975; Lawyer and Litigant in England (Hamlyn Lectures, 1962); Arabinesque-at-Law, 1969; Inns Ancient and Modern, 1972; A Second Miscellany-at-Law, 1973; Editor, Snell's Equity, 23rd edn 1947, 27th edn (with P. V. Baker, QC), 1973; contrib. to legal periodicals. *Recreations:* heterogeneous. *Address:* The Royal Courts of Justice, Strand, WC2A 2LL. *T:* 01-405 7641; 5 Stone Buildings, Lincoln's Inn, WC2A 3XT. *T:* 01-242 8607.

MEGAW, Arthur Hubert Stanley, CBE 1951; MA Cantab; FSA; *b* Dublin, 1910; *s* of late Arthur Stanley Megaw; *m* 1937, Elene Elektra, *d* of late Helias Mangoletsi, Koritsa, Albania; no *c*. *Educ:* Campbell Coll., Belfast; Peterhouse, Cambridge. Walston Student (University of Cambridge), 1931. Macmillan Student, British School of Archæology at Athens, 1932-33, Asst Dir, 1935-36; Dir of Antiquities, Cyprus, 1936-60; Field Dir, Byzantine Institute, Istanbul, 1961-62; Dir, British Sch. of Archæology, Athens, 1962-68. CStJ, 1967. *Publications:* (with A. J. B. Wace) Hermopolis Magna-Ashmunein, Alexandria, 1959; (with E. J. W. Hawkins) The Church of the Panagia Kanakariá in Cyprus, its Mosaics and Frescoes, 1977; various papers in archæological journals. *Recreation:* travel. *Address:* 27 Perrin's Walk, NW3; 4-6 Anapiron Polemou, Athens 140, Greece.

MEGAW, Rt. Hon. Sir John, PC 1969; Kt 1961; CBE 1956; TD 1951; a Lord Justice of Appeal, 1969-80; *b* 16 Sept. 1909; 2nd *s* of late Hon. Mr Justice Megaw, Belfast; *m* 1938, Eleanor Grace Chapman; one *s* two *d*. *Educ:* Royal Academical Institution, Belfast; St John's Coll., Cambridge Univ. (open schol. in classics; Hon. Fellow, 1967); Harvard Univ. Law Sch. (Choate Fellowship). Served War, 1939-45; Col, RA. Barrister-at-Law, Gray's Inn, 1934 (Certificate of Honour, Bar Final exam.); Bencher, 1958; Treasurer, 1976; QC 1953; QC (N Ire.) 1954; Recorder of Middlesbrough, 1957-61; Judge of the High Court of Justice, Queen's Bench Div., 1961-69; Pres., Restrictive Practices Court, 1962-68. Chm., Cttee of Inquiry into Civil Service Pay, 1981-82. Visitor, New Univ. of Ulster, 1976; Hon. LLD Queen's Univ., Belfast, 1968. Legion of Merit (US), 1946. *Address:* 14 Upper Cheyne Row, SW3.

MEGGESON, Michael; Solicitor and Notary Public; Partner, Warner, Goodman & Streat; a Recorder of the Crown Court, since 1981; *b* 6 Aug. 1930; *s* of Richard Ronald Hornsey Meggeson and Marjorie Meggeson; *m* 1975, Alison Margaret (*née* Wood). *Educ:* Sherborne; Gonville and Caius Coll., Cambridge. BA 1953; MA 1963. Nat. Service, RA, 1949-50; 5th Bn Royal Hampshire Regt, TA, 1950-63. Admitted a Solicitor, 1957; Asst Solicitor, 1957-59, Partner, 1959-, Warner & Sons, subseq. Warner Goodman & Co., and Warner, Goodman & Streat; Dep. Circuit Judge, 1978-81. Mem. Cttee, Solicitors Staff Pension Fund, 1980-; Pres., Hampshire Incorp. Law Soc., 1981-82. *Recreations:* sailing, golf, gardening, music. *Address:* Church Farm, Langrish, near Petersfield, Hants GU32 1RQ. *T:* Petersfield 4470. *Clubs:* Royal Ocean Racing; Royal Southern Yacht (Hamble); Hayling Island Golf.

MEGRAH, Maurice Henry; QC 1971; *b* 5 Feb. 1896; *e s* of Henry Barnard Megrah and Annie, *d* of H. Jepps; *m* 1917, Jessie Halstead (*d* 1977); one *d*. *Educ:* London Sch. of Economics. MCom. (London) 1931. Westminster Bank Ltd, 1914. Served European War, 1914-18, London Scottish, 1915; commissioned Royal Field Artillery, 1917. Returned Westminster Bank Ltd, 1919; Secretary, Inst. of Bankers, 1935-59, Hon. Fellow 1959. Called to Bar, Gray's Inn, 1937; Gilbart Lecturer, University of London, 1950, 1951, 1952, 1958, 1959, 1960, 1962, 1963, 1969. *Publications:* Bills of Exchange Act, 1882, 1929; The Banker's Customer, 1932; (ed) 9th edn Paget's Law of Banking, 1982; (ed) 23rd edn Byles on Bills of Exchange, 1972, 24th edn 1979; 5th edn, Gutteridge and Megrah on Law of Bankers' Commercial Credits, 1976, 6th edn 1979; contributions to Halsbury's Laws of England, and to law and banking periodicals. *Address:* 5 Paper Buildings, EC4. *T:* 01-353 8494. *Clubs:* Athenæum, Overseas Bankers'.

MEHAFFEY, Rt. Rev. James; *see* Derry and Raphoe, Bishop of.

MEHEW, Peter; Assistant Under Secretary of State (Sales Administration), Ministry of Defence, since 1981; *b* 22 Jan. 1931; *er s* of Oliver Mehew and Elsie (*née* Cox); *m* 1956, Gwyneth Sellors (*d* 1982); one *s* one *d*. *Educ:* Bishop Wordsworth's Sch.; St Catharine's Coll., Cambridge (BA 1954). Asst Principal, Admiralty, 1954, Principal 1959; Assistant Secretary: CSD, 1970-73; MoD, 1973-80; Dep. Head, UK Delegn to Negotiations on Mutual and Balanced Force Reductions, 1975-77. Fellow Commoner, CCC Cambridge, 1980. *Recreations:* badminton, tennis. *Address:* Kincraig East, 87 Hitchen

Hatch Lane, Sevenoaks, Kent. *T:* Sevenoaks 455641. *Club:* Royal Commonwealth Society.

MEHROTRA, Prof. Ram Charan, MSc, DPhil, PhD, DSc; Professor of Chemistry, and Director, Special Assistance Programme, University of Rajasthan, Jaipur, since 1979; *b* 16 Feb. 1922; *s* of late R. B. Mehrotra; *m* 1944, Suman; one *s* two *d. Educ:* Allahabad Univ. (MSc 1943, DPhil 1948); London Univ. (PhD 1952, DSc 1964). Research Chemist, Vigyan Kala Bhawan, Meerut, 1943-44; Lectr, Allahabad Univ., 1944-54; Reader, Lucknow Univ., 1954-58; Prof., 1958-62, Dean, Faculty of Science, 1959-62, Gorakhpur Univ.; Prof., 1962-74, Dean, Faculty of Science, 1962-65, Chief Rector, 1965-67, Vice-Chancellor, 1968-69 and 1972-73, Rajasthan Univ., Jaipur; Vice-Chancellor, Univ. of Delhi, 1974-79. President: Chemistry Section, Indian Sci. Congress, 1967; Indian Chemical Soc., 1976-77; Indian Science Congress, 1978-79; Vice-Pres., Indian Nat. Science Acad., 1977-78. Sir S. S. Bhatnagar award, 1965; Fedn of Indian Chambers of Commerce and Industry award, 1975; Prof. T. R. Seshadri's Birthday Commem. Medal, 1976; P. C. Ray Meml Medal, 1981. Hon. DSc Meerut, 1976. *Publications:* treatises on Metal Alkoxides and Metal β-Diketonates and Allied Derivatives, 1978; numerous research papers in nat. and internat. jls of chemistry; contribs to chemistry progress reports of Chem. Soc. London. *Recreation:* photography. *Address:* P4, University Campus, Jaipur 302004, India. *T:* (office) 60088; (home) 76275.

MEHTA, Ved Parkash; staff writer, New Yorker, since 1961; *b* Lahore, 21 March 1934; 2nd *s* of Dr Amolak Ram Mehta, retired Dep. Director General of Health Services, Govt of India, and Shanti Devi Mehta (*née* Mehra); naturalized citizen of USA, 1975. *Educ:* Arkansas Sch. for the Blind; Pomona Coll.; Balliol Coll., Oxford; Harvard Univ. BA Pomona, 1956; BA Hons Mod. Hist. Oxon, 1959; MA Harvard, 1961. Phi Beta Kappa, 1955. Hazen Fellow, 1956-59; Harvard Prize Fellow, 1959-60; Guggenheim Fellow, 1971-72, 1977-78; Ford Foundn Travel and Study Grantee, 1971-76, Public Policy Grantee, 1979-82; Vis. Schol., Case Western Reserve, 1974; Beatty Lectr, McGill Univ., 1979. Mem. Council on Foreign Relations, 1979. Hon. DLitt: Pomona, 1972; Bard College, 1982. Assoc. of Indians in America Award, 1978. *Publications:* Face to Face, 1957 (Secondary Educn Annual Book Award, 1958; BBC dramatization on Home prog., serial reading on Light prog., 1958; reissued 1967, 1978; Excerpts, 1981); Walking the Indian Streets, 1960 (rev. edn 1971); The Fly and the Fly-Bottle, 1963, 2nd edn 1983; The New Theologian, 1966; Delinquent Chacha (novel), 1967; Portrait of India, 1970; John Is Easy to Please, 1971; Daddyji, 1972; Mahatma Gandhi and his Apostles, 1977; The New India, 1978; Mamaji, 1979; Photographs of Chachaji, 1980; A Family Affair, 1982; Vedi, 1982; numerous editions and translations; articles and stories in Amer., British and Indian newspapers and magazines from 1957. Writer and commentator of TV documentary film, Chachaji: My Poor Relation, PBS, 1978, BBC, 1980 (DuPont Columbia Award for Excellence in Broadcast Journalism, 1977-78). *Recreation:* listening to Indian and Western music. *Address:* c/o The New Yorker, 25 West 43rd Street, New York, NY 10036, USA. *T:* 212-840-3800; (home) 1035 Fifth Avenue, New York, NY 10028, USA. *Club:* Century Association (NY) (Trustee, 1973-75).

MEHTA, Zubin; Director, New York Philharmonic, since 1978; Musical Adviser, Israel Philharmonic Orchestra; *b* 29 April 1936; *s* of Mehli Mehta; *m* 1st, 1958, Carmen Lasky (marr. diss. 1964); one *s* one *d*; 2nd, 1969, Nancy Kovack. *Educ:* St Xavier's Coll., Bombay; Musikakademie, Vienna. First Concert, Vienna, 1958; first prize internat. comp., Liverpool, 1958; US debut, Philadelphia Orch., 1960; debut with Israel and Vienna Philharmonic Orchs, 1961; apptd Music Director, Montreal Symphony Orch., 1961; European tour with this orch., 1962; guest conducting, major European Orchs, 1962; Music Dir, Los Angeles Philharmonic Orch., 1962-78. Opera debut, Montreal, Tosca, 1964; debut Metropolitan Opera, Aida, 1965. Australian tour, Israel Philharmonic, 1966; World tour (incl. debut in India) with Los Angeles Philharmonic, 1967; European Festivals Tour, 1971; tour with Israel Philharmonic, S and N America, 1972. Operas at Metropolitan incl.: Tosca, Turandot, Otello, Carmen, Mourning becomes Elektra (world première), Trovatore, etc. Holds hon. doctorates, and numerous awards; Padma Bhusan (India), 1967, etc. *Address:* New York Philharmonic, Avery Fisher Hall, Broadway and 65th Street, New York, NY 10023, USA. *T:* (212) 580-8700.

MEIGGS, Russell, MA; FBA 1961; *b* 1902; *s* of William Herrick Meiggs, London; *m* 1941, Pauline Gregg; two *d. Educ:* Christ's Hospital; Keble Coll., Oxford. Fellow of Keble Coll., 1930-39; Fellow and Tutor in Ancient History, Balliol Coll., Oxford, 1939-70, Hon. Fellow, 1970; Univ. Lectr in Ancient History, 1939-70; Praefectus of Holywell Manor, 1945-69. Vis. Prof., Swarthmore Coll., 1960, 1970-71, 1974, 1977-78; Kipling Fellow, Marlborough Coll., Vermont, 1967. For. Mem., Amer. Philosophical Soc., 1981. DHL Swarthmore Coll., 1971. *Publications:* Home Timber Production, 1939-1945, 1949; (ed jtly) Sources for Greek History between the Persian and Peloponnesian Wars, new edn, 1951; (ed) Bury's History of Greece, 3rd edn, 1951, 4th edn, 1975; Roman Ostia, 1960, 2nd edn, 1974; (ed with David Lewis) Selection of Greek Historical Inscriptions to the end of the 5th century BC, 1969; The Athenian Empire, 1972; Trees and Timber in the Ancient Mediterranean World, 1982. *Recreations:* gardening, America. *Address:* The Malt House, Garsington, Oxford.

MEINERTZHAGEN, Daniel; Chairman: Royal Insurance Co. Ltd, since 1974; Alexanders Discount Co., since 1981; *b* 2 March 1915; *e s* of Louis Ernest Meinertzhagen, Theberton House, Leiston, Suffolk and Gwynedd, *d* of Sir William Llewellyn, PRA; *m* 1940, Marguerite, *d* of A. E. Leonard; two *s. Educ:* Eton; New Coll., Oxford. Served War of 1939-45, RAFVR (Wing Comdr). Joined Lazard Brothers, 1936; Man. Dir 1954; Dep. Chm. 1971; Chm., 1973-80. Former Chm., Mercantile Credit Co. Ltd, Raeburn Investment Trust Ltd, and Whitehall Trust; Director: Tozer Kemsley & Millbourn (Holdings) Ltd; Brixton Estate Ltd; Former Director: S. Pearson & Son Ltd; Pearson Longman Ltd; W. T. Henley's Telegraph Works Co. Ltd; Rootes Motors Ltd; Trollope & Colls Ltd; Costain Group Ltd. *Address:* Bramshott Vale, Liphook, Hants. *T:* Liphook 723243. *Club:* White's.
See also Sir Peter Meinertzhagen.

MEINERTZHAGEN, Sir Peter, Kt 1980; CMG 1966; General Manager, Commonwealth Development Corporation, since 1973; *b* 24 March 1920; *y s* of late Louis Ernest Meinertzhagen, Theberton House, Leiston, Suffolk and Gwynnedd, *d* of Sir William Llewellyn, PRA; *m* 1949, Dido Pretty; one *s* one *d. Educ:* Eton. Served Royal Fusiliers, 1940-46 (Croix de Guerre, France, 1944). Alfred Booth & Co., 1946-57; Commonwealth Development Corporation, 1958-. Member: Council, London Chamber of Commerce, 1968-69; Council, Overseas Develt Inst., 1979-. *Address:* 59 Cleaver Square, SE11 4EA. *T:* 01-735 6263. *Club:* Muthaiga Country (Nairobi).
See also D. Meinertzhagen.

MEKIE, David Eric Cameron, OBE 1955; FRCSEd; FRSEd; FRCPEd; Conservator, Royal College of Surgeons of Edinburgh, 1955-74; *b* 8 March 1902; *s* of Dr D. C. T. Mekie and Mary Cameron; *m* 1930, Winifred Knott (*d* 1970); two *s* one *d. Educ:* George Watson's Coll., Edinburgh; University of Edinburgh. MB, ChB 1925; FRCSEd 1928; FRSEd 1962; MRCP 1962; FRCPEd, 1966. Tutor, Dept of Clinical Surgery, University of Edinburgh, 1928-33; Ernest Hart Scholar, 1931-33; Professor of Clinical Surgery and Surgery, University of Malaya, 1935-55 (now Prof. Emeritus). Dir, Postgrad. Bd for Medicine, Edinburgh, 1960-71; Postgrad. Dean of Medicine, Edinburgh Univ., 1970-71. Surgeon, Singapore General Hospital and Hon. Surgical Consultant, Far East Command. *Publications:* Handbook of Surgery, 1936; numerous surgical papers. *Recreations:* fishing, gardening. *Address:* 58 Findhorn Place, Edinburgh EH9 2NW. *T:* 031-667 6472.

MELANESIA, Archbishop of, since 1975; Most Rev. Norman Kitchener Palmer, CMG 1981; MBE 1975; Bishop of Central Melanesia; *b* 2 Oct. 1928; *s* of Philip Sydney and Annie Palmer; *m* 1960, Elizabeth Lucy Gorringe; three *s* one *d. Educ:* Kokeqolo, Pawa, Brit. Solomon Is Protectorate; Te Aute, NZ; Ardmore, NZ (Teachers' Cert.); St John's Theological Coll., NZ (LTh; ordained deacon, 1964). Appts in Brit. Solomon Is Protectorate: Deacon/Teacher, Pawa Secondary (Anglican), 1966; priest, Pawa, 1966; Priest/Headmaster: Alanguala Primary, 1967-69; St Nicholas Primary, 1970-72; Dean, St Barnabas Cathedral, 1973-75. Member, Public Service Advisory Bd, 1971-75. *Address:* Archbishop's House, PO Box 19, Honiara, Solomon Islands. *T:* 339.

MELBOURNE, Archbishop of, and Metropolitan of the Province of Victoria, since 1977; Most Rev. Robert William Dann; *b* 28 Sept. 1914; *s* of James and Ruth Dann; *m* 1949, Yvonne (*née* Newnham); one *s* two *d. Educ:* Trinity Coll., Univ. of Melbourne. BA Hons Melbourne 1946. Deacon, 1945; Priest, 1946. Dir of Youth and Religious Education, Dio. Melbourne, 1946; Incumbent: St Matthew's, Cheltenham, 1951; St George's, Malvern, 1956; St John's, Footscray, 1961; Archdeacon of Essendon, 1961; Dir of Evangelism and Extension, Dio. Melbourne, 1963; Bishop Coadjutor, Dio. Melbourne, 1969-77. *Address:* Bishopscourt, Clarendon Street, Melbourne, Victoria 3002, Australia. *Club:* Australian, Melbourne (Melbourne).

MELBOURNE, Archbishop of, (RC), since 1974; Most Rev. Thomas Francis Little, KBE 1977; DD, STD; *b* 30 Nov. 1925; *s* of Gerald Thompson Little and Kathleen McCormack. *Educ:* St Patrick's Coll., Ballarat; Corpus Christi Coll., Werribee; Pontifical Urban Coll., Rome. STD Rome, 1953. Priest 1950; Asst Priest, Carlton, 1953-55; Secretary, Apostolic Deleg. to Aust., NZ and Oceania, 1955-59; Asst Priest, St Patrick's Cathedral, Melbourne, 1959-65; Dean, 1965-70; Episcopal Vicar for Lay Apostolate, 1969; Pastor, St Ambrose, Brunswick, 1971-73; Auxiliary Bishop, Archdiocese of Melbourne, 1972; Bishop, 1973. *Address:* St Patrick's Cathedral, Melbourne, Vic. 3002, Australia. *T:* 622.2233.

MELBOURNE, Bishops Coadjutor of; *see* Grant, Rt Rev. J. A.; Penman, Rt Rev. D. J.; Shand, Rt Rev. D. H. W.

MELCHETT, 4th Baron *cr* 1928; **Peter Robert Henry Mond;** Bt 1910; *b* 24 Feb. 1948; *s* of 3rd Baron Melchett and of Sonia Elizabeth, *er d* of Lt-Col R. H. Graham; *S* father, 1973. *Educ:* Eton; Pembroke Coll., Cambridge (BA); Keele Univ. (MA). Res. Worker, LSE and Addiction Res. Unit, 1973-74. A Lord in Waiting (Govt Whip), 1974-75; Parly Under-Sec. of State, DoI, 1975-76; Minister of State, NI Office, 1976-79. Chm., working party on pop festivals, 1975-76; Chm., Community Industry, 1979-; Pres., Ramblers' Assoc., 1981-. Mem., Friends of Release. *Address:* 14 Allcroft Road, NW5 4NE.

MELCHIOR-BONNET, Christian; author; Director and founder, since 1946, Historia, Journal de la France; *b* Marseille, 10 April 1904; *s* of Daniel-Joseph Melchior-Bonnet and Geneviève (*née* de Luxer); *m* 1930, Bernardine Paul-

Dubois-Taine (*g d* of the historian Taine, herself a historian, author of several historical works, recipient of Grand Prix Gobert of Académie Française); two *s* one *d. Educ:* St Jean de Béthune, Versailles; Ecole du Louvre, Faculté de droit de Paris. Secretary to Pierre de Nolhac, de l'Académie française, historian, at Jacquemart-André museum, 1927-36; formerly, Editor-in-Chief, Petit Journal, 1936-45 and Flambeau; Dir, historical and religious series of Editions Flammarion, 1932-46; Literary Dir, Fayard editions, 1946-67; Director of the reviews: Oeuvres Libres, 1946-64; Historia, 1946-; A la Page, 1964-69; Co-dir, Jardin des Arts; Literary Adviser to Nouvelles Littéraires, 1946-70. Privy Chamberlain to Pope Paul VI. Membre du jury: Prix Historia; Prix de la Fondation de France; Prix des Ambassadeurs. Officier de la Légion d'honneur; Commandeur de l'Ordre national du Mérite; Officier des Arts et des Lettres, et décorations étrangères. Prix du Rayonnement, Académie française, 1963. *Publications:* Scènes et portraits historiques de Chateaubriand, 1928; Les Mémoires du Comte Alexandre de Tilly, ancien page de la reine Marie-Antoinette, 1929; Les Mémoires du Cardinal de Retz, 1929; Principes d'action de Salazar, 1956; Le Napoléon de Chateaubriand, 1969; et nombreuses éditions de mémoires historiques. *Address:* 17 Boulevard de Beauséjour, Paris XVIe, France.

MELDRUM, Andrew, CBE 1962 (OBE 1956); KPM; Chief Inspector of Constabulary for Scotland, 1966-69, retired; *b* 22 April 1909; *s* of late Andrew Meldrum, Burntisland, Fife; *m* 1937, Janet H., *d* of late Robert Crooks, Grangemouth; one *s* one *d. Educ:* Burntisland, Fife. Joined Stirlingshire Police, 1927; Deputy Chief Constable, Inverness Burgh, 1943, Chief Constable, 1946; Chief Constable, County of Angus, 1949; Chief Constable of Fife, 1955; Inspector of Constabulary for Scotland, 1965-66. King's Police Medal, 1952. *Recreation:* golf. *Club:* Royal Burgess Golfing Society of Edinburgh.

MELGUND, Viscount; Gilbert Timothy George Lariston Elliot-Murray-Kynynmound; *b* 1 Dec. 1953; *s* and *heir* of 6th Earl of Minto, qv. *Educ:* Eton. Lieut, Scots Guards, 1972-76. *Club:* White's.

MELHUISH, Michael Ramsay, CMG 1982; HM Diplomatic Service; Ambassador to Kuwait, since 1982; *b* 17 March 1932; *s* of late Henry Whitfield Melhuish and of Jeanette Ramsay Pender Melhuish; *m* 1961, Stella Phillips; two *s* two *d. Educ:* Royal Masonic Sch., Bushey; St John's Coll., Oxford (BA). FO, 1955; MECAS, 1956; Third Sec., Bahrain, 1957; FO, 1959; Second Sec., Singapore, 1961; First Sec. (Commercial) and Consul, Prague, 1963; First Sec. and Head of Chancery, Bahrain, 1966; DSAO (later FCO), 1968; First Sec., Washington, 1970; Counsellor, Amman, 1973; Head of N America Dept, FCO, 1976; Counsellor (Commercial), Warsaw, 1979-82. *Recreations:* tennis, golf. *Address:* c/o Foreign and Commonwealth Office, SW1A 2AH. *Club:* United Oxford & Cambridge University.

MELINSKY, Rev. Canon (Michael Arthur) Hugh; Principal, Northern Ordination Course, since 1978; *b* 25 Jan. 1924; *s* of late M. M. Melinsky and Mrs D. M. Melinsky; *m* 1949, Renate (*née* Ruhemann); three *d. Educ:* Whitgift Sch., Croydon; Christ's Coll., Cambridge (BA 1947, MA 1949); London Univ. Inst. of Education (TDip 1949); Ripon Hall, Oxford. Asst Master: Normanton Grammar Sch., 1949-52; Lancaster Royal Grammar Sch., 1952-57. Curate: Wimborne Minster, 1957-59; Wareham, 1959-61; Vicar of St Stephen's, Norwich, 1961-68; Chaplain of Norfolk and Norwich Hosp., 1961-68; Hon. Canon and Canon Missioner of Norwich, 1968-73; Chief Sec., ACCM, 1973-77. Chairman: C of E Commn on Euthanasia, 1972-75; Inst. of Religion and Medicine, 1973-77; Mem., Social Policy Cttee, C of E Bd for Social Responsibility, 1982-. *Publications:* The Modern Reader's Guide to Matthew, 1963; the Modern Reader's Guide to Luke, 1963; Healing Miracles, 1967; (ed) Religion and Medicine, 1970; (ed) Religion and Medicine 2, 1973; Patterns of Ministry, 1974; (ed) On Dying Well, 1975. *Address:* 75 Framingham Road, Brooklands, Sale, Cheshire M33 3RH. *T:* 061-962 7513.

MELLAART, James, FSA; FBA 1980; Lecturer in Anatolian Archaeology, Institute of Archaeology, University of London, since 1964; *b* 14 Nov. 1925; *s* of J. H. J. Mellaart and A. D. Van Der Beek; *m* 1954, Arlette Meryem Cenani; one *s. Educ:* University College, London. BA Hons (Ancient Hist. and Egyptology) 1951. Archaeol field surveys in Anatolia as Scholar and Fellow of British Inst. of Archaeol. at Ankara, 1951-56; excavations at Hacilar, 1957-60; Asst Dir, British Inst. of Archaeol. at Ankara, 1959-61; excavations at Çatal Hüyük, Turkey, 1961-63 and 1965; Foreign Specialist, Lectr at Istanbul Univ., 1961-63. Corresp. Mem., German Archaeol Inst., 1961. *Publications:* Earliest Civilisations of the Near East, 1965; The Chalcolithic and Early Bronze Ages in the Near East and Anatolia, 1966; Çatal Hüyük, a Neolithic Town in Anatolia, 1967; Excavations at Hacilar, 1970; The Neolithic of the Near East, 1975; The Archaeology of Ancient Turkey, 1978; chapters in Cambridge Ancient History; numerous articles in Anatolian Studies, etc. *Recreations:* geology, Turkish ceramics, clan history, Gaelic and classical music, Seljuk art. *Address:* 13 Lichen Court, 79 Queen's Drive, N4 2BH. *T:* 01-802 6984.

MELLANBY, Kenneth, CBE 1954 (OBE 1945); ScD Cantab; ecological consultant and editor; *b* 26 March 1908; *s* of late Emeritus-Professor A. L. Mellanby; *m* 1933, Helen Neilson Dow, MD (marr. diss.); one *d*; *m* 1948, Jean Copeland, MA, JP; one *s. Educ:* Barnard Castle Sch.; King's Coll., Cambridge (Exhibitioner). Research Worker, London Sch. of Hygiene and Trop. Med., 1930-36 and 1953-55; Wandsworth Fellow, 1933; Sorby Research Fellow of Royal Society of London, 1936; Hon. Lecturer,

University of Sheffield; CO (Sqdn Ldr RAFVR) Sheffield Univ. Air Sqdn. Dir Sorby Research Institute, 1941; first Principal, University Coll., Ibadan, Nigeria, 1947-53; Major, RAMC (Specialist in Biological Research), overseas service in N Africa, SE Asia, etc.; Dep. Dir, Scrub Typhus Research Laboratory, SEAC; Reader in Medical Entomology, University of London, 1945-47; Head of Dept of Entomology, Rothamsted Experimental Station, Harpenden, Herts, 1955-61; first Dir, Monks Wood Experimental Station, Huntingdon, 1961-74. Vice-Pres. and Mem. Council, Royal Entomological Soc. of London, 1953-56; Pres. Assoc. for Study of Animal Behaviour, 1957-60; Member: Inter-university Council for Higher Education Overseas, 1960-75; ARC Research Cttee on Toxic Chemicals; Council, and Chm., Tropical Group, Brit. Ecological Soc.; Nat. Exec., Cambs Br., CPRE (also Pres.); Council for Science and Technology Insts, 1976-77 (Chm.); Council for Environmental Science and Engrg, 1976- (Chm., 1981-); Pres., Sect. D (Zoology), 1972, and Sect. X (General), 1973, British Assoc.; Vice-Pres. of the Institute of Biology, 1967, Pres., 1972-73; Vice-Pres., Parly and Scientific Cttee; first Hon. Life Mem., Assoc. for Protection of Rural Australia. Hon. Professorial Fellow, University Coll. of S Wales; Hon. Prof. of Biology, Univ. of Leicester. Essex Hall Lectr, 1971. Fellow, NERC. Mem. Editorial Bd, New Naturalist series. Hon. Life Prof., Central London Polytechnic, 1980; DUniv Essex, 1980. Hon. DSc: Ibadan, 1963; Bradford, 1970; Leicester, 1972. First Charter Award, Inst. of Biology, 1981. *Publications:* Scabies, 1943, new edn 1973; Human Guinea Pigs, 1945, new edn 1973; The Birth of Nigeria's University, 1958, new edn 1975; Pesticides and Pollution, 1967; The Mole, 1971; The Biology of Pollution, 1972; Can Britain Feed Itself?, 1975; Talpa, the story of a mole, 1976; Farming and Wildlife, 1981; many scientific papers on insect physiology, ecology, medical and agricultural entomology; ed, Monographs on Biological Subjects; British Editor of Entomologia Experimentalis et Applicata; Editor, Environmental Pollution. *Recreation:* austere living. *Address:* Hill Farm, Wennington, Huntingdon. *T:* Abbots Ripton 392. *Club:* Athenæum.

MELLERS, Prof. Wilfrid Howard, OBE 1982; DMus; Composer; Professor of Music, University of York, 1964-81; *b* 26 April 1914; *s* of Percy Wilfrid Mellers and Hilda Maria (*née* Lawrence); *m* 1950, Peggy Pauline (*née* Lewis); two *d. Educ:* Leamington Coll.; Downing Coll., Cambridge. BA Cantab 1939; MA Cantab 1945; DMus Birmingham 1962. Supervisor in English and College Lecturer in Music, Downing Coll., Cambridge, 1945-48; Staff Tutor in Music, Extra Mural Dept, University of Birmingham, 1949-60; Visiting Mellon Prof. of Music, University of Pittsburgh, USA, 1960-62. *Publications:* Music and Society, 1946; Studies in Contemporary Music, 1948; François Couperin and the French Classical Tradition, 1950; Music in the Making, 1951; Man and his Music, 1957; Harmonious Meeting, 1964; Music in a New Found Land, 1964; Caliban Reborn: renewal in 20th-century music, 1967 (US), 1968 (GB); Twilight of the Gods: the Beatles in retrospect, 1973; Bach and the Dance of God, 1981; Beethoven and the Voice of God, 1982. Published Compositions include: Canticum Incarnations, 1960; Alba in 9 Metamorphoses, 1962; Rose of May, 1966; Life-Cycle, 1967; Yeibichai, 1968; Canticum Resurrectionis, 1968; Natalis Invicti Solis, 1969; The Word Unborn, 1970; The Ancient Wound, 1970; De Vegetabilis et Animalibus, 1971; Venery for Six Plus, 1971; Sun-flower = the Quaternity of William Blake, 1972-73; The Key of the Kingdom, 1976; Rosae Hermeticae, 1977; A Dream of the Green Man, 1980; Shaman Songs, 1980; The Wellspring of Loves, 1981. *Address:* 5 Wilmington House, Highbury Crescent, N5 1RU. *T:* 01-607 8889.

MELLERSH, Air Vice-Marshal Francis Richard Lee, CB 1977; DFC 1943 and Bar 1944; Air Officer Flying and Officer Training, HQ Training Command, 1974-77; *b* 30 July 1922; *s* of Air Vice-Marshal Sir Francis Mellersh, KBE, AFC; *m* 1967, Elisabeth Nathalie Komaroff; two *s* one *d. Educ:* Winchester House Sch.; Imperial Service College. Joined RAFVR, 1940; Nos 29, 600 and 96 Sqdns, 1941-45; various staff and flying appts, 1946-57; Dirg Staff, RAF Staff Coll., 1957-59; Staff of Chief of Defence Staff, 1959-61; Dep. Dir Ops (F), 1961-63; OC RAF West Raynham, 1965-67; Chief Current Plans, SHAPE, 1967-68; RCDS 1969; SASO, RAF Germany, 1970-72; ACDS (Ops), 1972-74. *Address:* Rother Lea, Lossenham Lane, Newenden, Kent. *Club:* Royal Air Force.

MELLING, Cecil Thomas, CBE 1955; MScTech, CEng, Hon. FIEE, FIMechE, Sen. FInstE, CBIM; *b* Wigan, 12 Dec. 1899; *s* of William and Emma Melling; *m* 1929, Ursula Thorburn Thorburn; two *s* one *d* (and one *s* and one *d* decd). *Educ:* Manchester Central High Sch.; College of Technology, University of Manchester. 2nd Lieut RE 1918. Metropolitan Vickers Electrical Co. Ltd, 1920-34; Yorkshire Electric Power Co., 1934-35; Edmundson's Electricity Corporation Ltd, 1935-43. Borough Electrical Engineer, Luton, 1943-48. Chm., Eastern Electricity Board, 1948-57; Member: British Electricity Authority, 1952-53 and 1957; Electricity Council, 1957-61 (a Dep. Chm., 1961-65); Clean Air Council, 1961-64; Adv. Cttee on R&D, 1961-64. Chm. Utilization Sect., Institution of Electrical Engineers, 1949-50, Vice-Pres., IEE, 1957-62, Pres., 1962-63; Chm. of Council, British Electrical Development Association, 1951-52; Founder-Chm. 1945, and Pres. 1947, Luton Electrical Soc.; Pres. Ipswich & District Electrical Assoc., 1948-57; Chm. of Council, British Electrical and Allied Industries Research Assoc., 1953-55; Pres. Assoc. of Supervising Electrical Engineers, 1952-54; Chm., British Nat. Cttee for Electro-Heat, 1958-68; Mem. Council, BIM, 1961-78; Vice-Pres. Internat. Union for Electro-Heat, 1964-68, Pres., 1968-72; Pres., Manchester Technol. Assoc., 1967; Pres., British Electrotechnical Approvals Bd, 1974- (Chm., 1964-73); Chm., Electricity Supply Industry Trg

Bd, 1965-68; Vice-Pres., Union of Internat. Engineering Organisations, 1969-75. Founder Chm., Soc. of Retired Chartered Engrs in SE Kent, 1982-. *Publications:* contribs to Proc. Engineering Instns and Confs. *Address:* Durham, The Grand, Folkestone. *Club:* Athenæum.

MELLISH, Rt. Hon. Robert Joseph, PC 1967; MP Southwark, Bermondsey (Bermondsey, Rotherhithe, 1946-50; Bermondsey, 1950-74) (Lab 1946-82, Ind. since 1982); Deputy Chairman, Docklands Urban Development Corporation, since 1981; Official, Transport and General Workers' Union; *b* 1913; *m* ; five *s.* Served War of 1939-45, Captain RE, SEAC. PPS to Minister of Pensions, 1951 (to Minister of Supply, 1950-51); Jt Parly Sec., Min. of Housing, 1964-67; Minister of Public Building and Works, 1967-69; Parly Sec. to Treasury and Govt Chief Whip, 1969-70 and 1974-76; Opposition Chief Whip, 1970-74. Chm., London Regional Lab. Party, 1956-77. *Address:* c/o House of Commons, SW1.

MELLON, James, CMG 1979; HM Diplomatic Service; High Commissioner in Ghana and Ambassador to Togo, since 1978; *b* 25 Jan. 1929; *m* 1st, 1956, Frances Murray (*d* 1976); one *s* three *d* ; 2nd, 1979, Miss Philippa Shuttleworth (*née* Hartley). *Educ:* Glasgow Univ. (MA). Dept of Agriculture for Scotland, 1953-60; Agricultural Attaché, Copenhagen and The Hague, 1960-63; FO, 1963-64; Head of Chancery, Dakar, 1964-66; UK Delegn to European Communities, 1967-72; Counsellor, 1970; Hd of Sci. and Technol. Dept, FCO, 1973-75; Commercial Counsellor, East Berlin, 1975-76; Head of Trade Relations and Export Dept, FCO, 1976-78. *Address:* c/o Foreign and Commonwealth Office, SW1. *Club:* Travellers'.

MELLON, Paul, Hon. KBE 1974; Hon. RA 1978; Trustee, National Gallery of Art, Washington, DC, since 1945 (President, 1963-79; Chairman, 1979-); *b* 11 June 1907; *s* of late Andrew William Mellon and late Nora McMullen Mellon; *m* 1st, 1935, Mary Conover (decd); one *s* one *d* ; 2nd, 1948, Rachel Lambert. *Educ:* Choate Sch., Wallingford, Conn; Yale and Cambridge Univs. Trustee: Andrew W. Mellon Foundn (successor to merged Old Dominion and Avalon Foundns), 1969-; A. W. Mellon Educational and Charitable Trust, Pittsburgh, 1930-; Trustee, Virginia Mus. of Fine Arts, Richmond, Va, 1938-68, 1969-79. Member: Amer. Philosophical Soc., Philadelphia, 1971; Grolier Soc.; Soc. of Dilettanti; Roxburghe Club. Hon. Citizen, University of Vienna, 1965. Yale Medal, 1953; Horace Marden Albright Scenic Preservation Medal, 1957; Distinguished Service to Arts Award, Nat. Inst. Arts and Letters, 1962; Benjamin Franklin Medal, Royal Society of Arts, 1965, Benjamin Franklin Fellow, 1969; Alumni Seal Prize Award, Choate Sch., 1966; Skowhegan Gertrude Vanderbilt Whitney Award, 1972. Hon. FRIBA 1978. Hon. DLitt, Oxford Univ., 1961; Hon. LLD, Carnegie Inst. of Tech., 1967; Hon. DHL, Yale, 1967. *Recreations:* fox-hunting, thoroughbred breeding and racing, sailing, swimming. *Address:* (office) 1729 H Street NW, Washington, DC 20006, USA; (home) Oak Spring, Upperville, Va 22176. *Clubs:* Buck's; Travellers (Paris); Jockey, Knickerbocker, Links, Racquet and Tennis, River, Yale (New York); Metropolitan, 1925 F Street (Washington).

MELLOR, David, OBE 1981; DesRCA; RDI 1962; FSIAD; designer, manufacturer and retailer; Chairman, Crafts Council, since 1982; *b* 5 Oct. 1930; *s* of Colin Mellor; *m* 1966, Fiona MacCarthy; one *s* one *d. Educ:* Sheffield College of Art; Royal College of Art (DesRCA and Silver Medal, 1953, Hon. Fellow 1966); British School at Rome. Set up silver-smithing workshop, Sheffield, 1954; designer and maker of silver for Worshipful Co. of Goldsmiths, Cutlers' Co., Southwell Minster, Essex Univ., Darwin Coll., Cambridge, among others, and range of silver tableware for use in British embassies; designer of fountain in bronze for Botanic Gdns, Cambridge, 1970; concurrently opened industrial design office. Consultancies, 1954-, include: Walker & Hall, Abacus Municipal, Glacier Metal, ITT, Post Office, British Rail, James Neill Tools; Cons. to DoE on design of traffic signals, 1965-70, and on design of automation half-barrier crossing, as result of Gibbens report, 1969; Chm., Design Council Cttee of Inquiry into standards of design in consumer goods in Britain, 1982-; Mem., Art and Design Working Gp, Nat. Adv. Body for Local Auth. Higher Educn, 1982-. *Work in collections:* Goldsmiths' Co., V&A, Sheffield City Mus., Mus. of Modern Art, NY. *Exhibitions:* Stedjelick Mus., Amsterdam, 1968; Nat. Mus. of Wales, 1972. Designer for retrospective exhibn A Century of British Design 1880-1980, 1979. *Awards:* Design Centre: for Pride cutlery, 1957, Pride teaset, 1959, Symbol cutlery, 1962 (all designed for Walker & Hall); for convector heater, 1959 (designed for Grahamston Ironfounders); for Embassy silver for use in Brit. embassies, 1965, also for Thrift stainless steel cutlery for use in Govt canteens, 1966 (both commnd by MPBW); Design Council: for 700 range of contract furniture, designed for Abacus Municipal, 1974; Chinese Ivory cutlery, designed and manufactured by David Mellor, 1977; RSA Presidential Award for Design Management, 1981. Opened London shop, Sloane Square, 1969; opened Sheffield factory for specialist prodn of cutlery in historic Sheffield bldg (conversion of which recd an Architectural Heritage Year Award, 1975). Hon. Fellow, Sheffield City Polytechnic, 1979; Liveryman, Goldsmiths' Co., 1980; Freeman, Cutler's Co., 1981. FSIAD 1964. *Address:* Broom Hall, Broomhall Road, Sheffield S10 2DU. *T:* Sheffield 664124.

MELLOR, David John; MP (C) Wandsworth, Putney, since 1979; Parliamentary Under-Secretary of State, Department of Energy, since 1981; *b* 12 March 1949; *s* of Mr and Mrs Douglas H. Mellor; *m* 1974, Judith Mary Hall; one *s. Educ:* Swanage Grammar Sch.; Christ's Coll., Cambridge (BA Hons 1970). FZS. Called to the Bar, Inner Temple, 1972; in practice thereafter.

Chm., Cambridge Univ. Conservative Assoc., 1970; contested West Bromwich E, Oct. 1974. PPS to Leader of Commons and Chancellor of the Duchy of Lancaster, 1981. Special Trustee, Westminster Hosp. Mem. Council, NYO. *Recreations:* classical music, reading. *Address:* House of Commons, SW1. *T:* 01-219 5481.

MELLOR, Derrick; HM Diplomatic Service; Ambassador in Asuncion, since 1979; *b* 11 Jan. 1926; *s* of William Mellor and Alice (*née* Hurst); *m* 1954, Kathleen (*née* Hodgson); two *s* one *d.* Served Army, 1945-49. Board of Trade, 1950-57; Trade Commission Service, 1958-64: served Kuala Lumpur and Sydney; HM Diplomatic Service, 1964-: served Copenhagen, Caracas and London. *Recreations:* tennis, golf, skiing. *Address:* c/o Foreign and Commonwealth Office, SW1; Frant Road, Tunbridge Wells, Kent. *Clubs:* Royal Commonwealth Society, Travellers'.

MELLOR, Hugh Wright; Secretary and Director, National Corporation for Care of Old People (now Centre for Policy on Ageing), 1973-80; *b* 11 Aug. 1920; *s* of William Algernon and Katherine Mildred Mellor; *m* 1944, Winifred Joyce Yates. *Educ:* Leys Sch., Cambridge; London Univ. (BScEcon). Friends Relief Service, 1940-45; Sec., St Albans Council of Social Service, 1945-48; Community Develt Officer, Hemel Hempstead Develt Corp., 1948-50; Asst Sec., Nat. Corp. for Care of Old People, 1951-73. Chm., Hanover Housing Assoc. *Recreations:* walking, reading, music. *Address:* Lark Rise, Risborough Road, Great Kimble, Aylesbury, Bucks HP17 0XS. *Club:* Royal Commonwealth Society.

MELLOR, Brig. James Frederick McLean, CBE 1964 (OBE 1945); Norfolk County Commandant, Army Cadet Force, 1969-72; *b* 6 June 1912; *s* of late Col A. J. Mellor, RM, Kingsland, Hereford; *m* 1942, Margaret Ashley, *d* of Major F. A. Phillips, DSO, Holmer, Hereford; one *s* one *d. Educ:* Radley Coll.; Faraday House. C. A. Parsons, 1933; Yorkshire Electric Power, 1935. Commnd in Regular Army as Ordnance Mechanical Engr, 1936; France, Belgium, Dunkirk, 1940; Burma, Malaya, HQ, SEAC, 1944-47 (despatches, 1945); Brig. A/Q Northern Comd, 1961-64; Dir of Technical Trng and Inspector of Boys' Trng (Army), MoD, 1966-69; ADC to the Queen, 1963-69. Various appts in engineering and technical educn. Chm., IMechE Eastern Branch, 1971-72. DFH, FIMechE, FIEE. *Address:* Pinewood, Saxlingham Road, Blakeney, Holt, Norfolk NR25 7PB. *T:* Cley 740990. *Clubs:* Naval and Military, Royal Automobile; Norfolk (Norwich).

MELLOR, Sir John (Serocold Paget), 2nd Bt, *cr* 1924; *b* 6 July 1893; *er s* of 1st Bt and Mabel, *d* of G. E. Serocold Pearce-Serocold, of Cherryhinton, Torquay; *S* father, 1929; *m* 1st, 1922, Rachael Margaret (who obtained a divorce, 1937), *d* of Sir Herbert F. Cook, 3rd Bt, of Doughty House, Richmond; one *s* ; 2nd, 1937, Mrs Raie Mendes (*d* 1965); 3rd, 1971, Mrs Jessica de Pass, *er d* of late Clarence de Sola, Montreal. *Educ:* Eton; New Coll., Oxford. Barrister, Inner Temple; formerly Capt. Prince Albert's Somerset LI. Served overseas 1914-18 (1914-15 Star, twice wounded, taken prisoner-of-war by Turks at Kut); rejoined Somerset LI, Sept. 1939; contested (C) Workington Division, 1929; adopted Conservative Candidate for Luton Division, 1931, but withdrew in favour of Liberal National Candidate; MP (C) Tamworth Division of Warwicks, 1935-45, Sutton Coldfield Division of Warwicks, 1945-55. Pres., Prudential Assurance Co. Ltd, 1972-77 (Dir, 1946-72; Dep. Chm., 1959-65; Chm., 1965-70); Dir, CLRP Investment Trust Ltd. *Heir: s* John Francis Mellor, *b* 9 March 1925. *Address:* Binley House, near Andover, Hants. *Club:* Carlton.

MELLOR, John Walter; a Recorder of the Crown Court, 1972-74 and since 1978; *b* 24 Sept. 1927; *s* of William Mellor and Ruth (*née* Tolson); *m* 1957, Freda Mary (*née* Appleyard); one *s* three *d. Educ:* Grammar Sch., Batley; Leeds Univ. (LLB). Called to Bar, Gray's Inn, 1953. *Recreations:* golf, sailing, visiting West Cork. *Address:* 171 Scotchman Lane, Morley, Leeds, W Yorks. *T:* Morley 4093. *Clubs:* Morley Rugby Union; Crookhaven Yacht.

MELLOR, Kenneth Wilson, QC 1975; a Recorder of the Crown Court, since 1972; *m* 1957, Sheila Gale; one *s* three *d. Educ:* King's College Cambridge (MA, LLB). RNVR (Sub Lieut). Called to the Bar, Lincoln's Inn, 1950. Dep. Chm., Hereford QS, 1969-71; Chm., Agricultural Land Tribunal (West Midlands). *Address:* 5 Fountain Court, Steelhouse Lane, Birmingham B4 6DR; 1 Paper Buildings, Temple, EC4.

MELLOWS, Prof. Anthony Roger, TD 1969; PhD, LLD; Solicitor of the Supreme Court, and Professor of the Law of Property in the University of London, since 1974; Dean of the Faculty of Laws in the University of London and at King's College, London, since 1981; *b* 30 July 1936; *s* of L. B. and M. P. Mellows; *m* 1973, Elizabeth, *d* of Ven. B. G. B. Fox, MC, TD, and of Hon. Margaret Joan Davidson, *d* of 1st Viscount Davidson, PC, GCVO, CH, CB. *Educ:* King's Coll., London. LLB (1st Cl. Hons) 1957; LLM (Mk of Distinction) 1959; PhD 1962; BD 1968; LLD 1973; Fellow 1980. Commissioned Intelligence Corps (TA), 1959, Captain 1964; served Intell. Corps (TA) and (T&AVR) and on the Staff, 1959-71; RARO, 1971-. Admitted a solicitor, 1960; private practice, 1960-; Sen. Partner, Messrs Alexanders. Chm., London Law International Ltd, 1973-. Asst Lectr in Law, King's Coll., London, 1962, Lectr, 1964, Reader, 1971; Dir of Conveyancing Studies, 1969. Mem. Council, KCL, 1972-80; Trustee, Kincardine Foundn, 1972-. AKC, London, 1957; FRSA 1969. OStJ 1981. Freeman of the City of London, 1963. *Publications:* Local Searches and Enquiries, 1964 (2nd edn 1967); Conveyancing Searches, 1964 (2nd edn 1975); Land Charges, 1966; The

Preservation and Felling of Trees, 1964; The Trustee's Handbook, 1965 (3rd edn 1975); Taxation for Executors and Trustees, 1967 (5th edn 1981); The Modern Law of Trusts (jt), 1966 (4th edn 1979); The Law of Succession, 1970 (3rd edn 1977); Taxation of Land Transactions, 1973 (3rd edn 1982). *Address:* 22 Devereux Court, Temple Bar, WC2R 3JJ. *Club:* Athenæum.

MELLY, (Alan) George (Heywood); professional blues singer; with John Chilton's Feetwarmers, since 1974; *b* 17 Aug. 1926; *s* of Francis Heywood and Edith Maud Melly; *m* 1963, Diana Campion Dawson; one *s* and one step *d*. *Educ:* Stowe School. Able Seaman, RN, 1944–47. Art Gallery Asst, London Gallery, 1948–50; sang with Mick Mulligan's Jazz Band, 1949–61. Wrote Flook strip cartoon balloons (drawn by Trog (Wally Fawkes)), 1956–71. Critic, The Observer: pop music, 1965–67; TV, 1967–71; films, 1971–73. Film scriptwriter: Smashing Time, 1968; Take a Girl Like You, 1970. Pres., British Humanist Assoc., 1972–74. Critic of the Year, IPC Nat. Press Awards, 1970. *Publications:* I Flook, 1962; Owning Up, 1965; Revolt into Style, 1970; Flook by Trog, 1970; Rum Bum and Concertina, 1977; (with Barry Fantoni) The Media Mob, 1980; Tribe of One: Great Naive and Primitive Painters of the British Isles, 1981; (with Walter Dorin) Great Lovers, 1981; Mellymobile, 1982; (ed) Edward James, Swans Reflecting Elephants: my early years, 1982. *Recreations:* trout fishing, singing and listening to blues of 1920s, collecting modern paintings. *Address:* 33 St Lawrence Terrace, W10 5SR. *Club:* Colony Room.

MELMOTH, Christopher George Frederick Frampton, CMG 1959; South Asia Department, International Bank for Reconstruction and Development, 1962–75; *b* 25 Sept. 1912; *s* of late George Melmoth and Florence Melmoth; *m* 1946, Maureen Joan (*née* Brennan); three *d*. *Educ:* Sandringham Sch., Forest Gate. Accountant Officer, Co-ordination of Supplies Fund, Malta, 1942–45; Administrative Officer, Hong Kong, 1946–55; Minister of Finance, Uganda, 1956–62. *Recreations:* tennis, golf, walking. *Address:* Hoptons Field, Kemerton, Tewkesbury, Glos.

MELONEY, Mrs W. B.; *see* Franken, Rose.

MELROSE, Prof. Denis Graham; Professor of Surgical Science, Royal Postgraduate Medical School and Consultant Clinical Physiologist to Hammersmith Hospital; *b* 20 June 1921; *s* of late Thomas Robert Gray Melrose, FRCS and of Floray Collings; *m* 1945, Ann, *d* of late Kathleen Tatham Warter; two *s*. *Educ:* Sedbergh Sch.; University Coll., Oxford; UCH London. MA, BM, BCh, MRCP, FRCS. Junior appts at Hammersmith Hosp. and Redhill County Hosp., Edgware, 1945; RNVR, 1946–48; subseq. Lectr, later Reader, Royal Postgrad. Med. Sch.; Nuffield Travelling Fellow, USA, 1956; Fulbright Fellow, 1957; Associate in Surgery, Stanford Univ. Med. Sch., 1958. *Publications:* numerous papers in learned jls and chapters in books, particularly on heart surgery, heart lung machine and med. engrg. *Recreations:* sailing, ski-ing. *Address:* 1 Lower Common South, SW15 1BP. *T:* 01-788 0116. *Club:* Royal Naval Sailing Association.

MELVILL JONES, Prof. Geoffrey, FRS 1979; FRSC 1979; FCASI; FRAeS; Hosmer Research Professor of Physiology, McGill University, Montreal, since 1978 (Associate Professor, 1961–68, Full Professor, since 1968); Director, Aviation Medical Research Unit, McGill University, since 1961; *b* 14 Jan. 1923; *s* of Sir Bennett Melvill Jones, CBE, AFC, FRS and Dorothy Laxton Jotham; *m* 1953, Jenny Marigold Burnaby; two *s* two *d*. *Educ:* King's Choir Sch.; Dauntsey's Sch.; Cambridge Univ. (BA, MA, MB, BCh). Appointments in UK, 1950–61: House Surgeon, Middlesex Hosp., 1950; Sen. Ho. Surg., Otolaryngology, Addenbrooke's Hosp., Cambridge, 1950–51; MO, RAF, 1951; Scientific MO, RAF Inst. of Aviation Medicine, Farnborough, Hants, 1951–55; Scientific Officer (external staff), Medical Research Council of Gt Britain, 1955–61. Fellow, Aerospace Medical Assoc., 1969; FCASI 1965; FRAeS 1981. *Publications:* Mammalian Vestibular Physiology, 1979 (NY); research papers in physiological jls. *Recreations:* outdoor activities, music. *Address:* Aviation Medical Research Unit, McGill University, Room 1223, McIntyre Building, 3655 Drummond Street, Montreal, Quebec H3G 1Y6, Canada. *T:* (514) 392-4217.

MELVILLE; *see* Leslie Melville, family name of Earl of Leven and Melville.

MELVILLE, 9th Viscount *cr* 1802; **Robert David Ross Dundas;** Baron Duneira 1802; *b* 28 May 1937; *s* of Hon. Robert Maldred St John Melville Dundas (2nd *s* of 7th Viscount) (killed in action, 1940), and of Margaret Connell (who *m* 2nd, 1946, Gerald Bristowe Sanderson), *d* of late Percy Cruden Ross; *S* uncle, 1971; *m* 1982, Fiona Margaret Stilgoe, *d* of late Roger and of Mrs Stilgoe, Stogumber, Som. *Educ:* Wellington College. District Councillor, Lasswade, Midlothian. Lieutenant, Ayrshire Yeomanry; Captain (Reserve), Scots Guards. *Recreations:* golf, fishing. *Heir: cousin* Hugh McKenzie Dundas [*b* 3 June 1910; *m* 1939, Catherine Sanderson, *d* of late John Wallace; one *s* one *d*]. *Address:* Esk Cottage, Melville, Lasswade, Midlothian. *T:* 031-663 8862; 3 Roland Way, Fulham, SW7. *Clubs:* Cavalry and Guards; Turf; Midlothian County.

MELVILLE, Alan; revue writer and author; *b* 9 April 1910. *Educ:* Edinburgh Academy. BBC features and drama producer and script-writer, 1936–40. Served with RAF, 1940–46. *Publications: revues:* Rise Above It (Comedy), 1940; Sky High (Phoenix), 1941; Sweet and Low, Sweeter and Lower, Sweetest and Lowest (Ambassadors), 1943–46; A La Carte (Savoy), 1948; At

the Lyric (Lyric, Hammersmith), 1953; Going to Town (St Martin's), 1954; All Square (Vaudeville), 1963; (jtly) Hulla Baloo (Criterion), 1972; Déjà Revue, 1975; *plays:* Jonathan (Aldwych), 1948; Top Secret (Winter Garden), 1949; Castle in the Air (Adelphi), 1949–50; Dear Charles (New), 1952–53; Simon and Laura, 1954; The Bargain (Ethel Barrymore Theatre, New York), 1953; Mrs Willie, 1955; Change of Tune, (Strand), 1959; Devil May Care, 1963; Fuender Bitte Melden (Stadt Theater, Baden-Baden), 1966; Demandez Vicky (Théatre des Nouveautés, Paris), 1966; Content to Whisper (adaptation from French) (Theatre Royal, York); Darling You Were Wonderful (Richmond); *musical plays:* Gay's the Word (Saville), 1951; Bet Your Life (Hippodrome), 1952; Marigold (Savoy), 1959; Congress Dances (Continental productions), 1977; Set to Music, 1979; *films:* Derby Day, 1952; Hot Ice, 1952; As Long as They're Happy, 1954; All for Mary, 1955; Simon and Laura, 1955; *novels:* Week-end at Thrackley, 1935; Death of Anton, 1936; Quick Curtain, 1937; The Vicar in Hell, 1938; Warning to Critics, 1939; *war autobiography:* First Tide, 1945; *autobiography:* Myself When Young, 1956; Merely Melville, 1970. *TV series:* A-Z, Merely Melville, Melvillainy, What's My Line?, Parade, Raise Your Glasses, Whitehall Worrier, Before the Fringe, Misleading Cases, The Very Merry Widow, The Brighton Belle; also Titipu, Iolanthe; *radio:* 1972–78: The King's Favourite, The Sun King, Mellers and Sellers, Lovely Morning this Evening, Radio Burps, The Knocker, etc. *Recreations:* tennis, swimming. *Address:* 28 Victoria Street, Brighton BN1 3FQ. *T:* Brighton 22682.

MELVILLE, Anthony Edwin; Headmaster, The Perse School, Cambridge, since 1969; *b* 28 April 1929; *yr s* of Sir Leslie Melville, *qv* ; *m* 1964, Pauline Marianne Surtees Simpson, *d* of Major A. F. Simpson, Indian Army; two *d*. *Educ:* Sydney Church of England Grammar Sch.; Univ. of Sydney (BA); King's Coll., Cambridge (MA). Sydney Univ. Medal in English, 1950; Pt II History Tripos, 1st cl. with dist., 1952; Lightfoot Schol. in Eccles. History, 1954. Asst Master, Haileybury Coll., 1953. *Recreations:* reading, gardening. *Address:* 80 Glebe Road, Cambridge. *T:* Cambridge 47964. *Club:* East India, Devonshire, Sports and Public Schools.

MELVILLE, Archibald Ralph, CB 1976; CMG 1964; agricultural consultant; Member, Commonwealth Development Corporation, 1977–81; *b* 24 May 1912; *e s* of late James Melville, MA, Edinburgh, and Mrs K. E. Melville, Lynton, Devon; *m* 1943, Theresa Kelly, SRN, SCM, QAIMNS (*d* 1976); two *d*. *Educ:* George Heriot's Sch., Edinburgh; University of Edinburgh; Royal College of Science, London; Imperial Coll. of Tropical Agriculture, Trinidad. BSc in Agriculture with Hons Zoology, Edinburgh, 1934; AICTA, Trinidad, 1936. Entomologist, Kenya Dept of Agriculture, 1936; Senior Entomologist, 1947; Chief Research Officer, 1956; Dir of Agriculture, 1960–64, Kenya Government Service; Agricultural Adviser, ODM, 1965–71; Chief Natural Resources Advr, 1971–76, under Sec., 1972–76, ODM. Pres., Tropical Agriculture Assoc. UK. Served 1939–44 with Kenya Regt and East African Army Medical Corps (Major). *Publications:* contributions to technical journals. *Recreations:* golf, gardening, natural history. *Address:* Spearpoint Cottage, Kennington, Ashford, Kent TN24 9QP. *T:* Ashford 20056. *Club:* Farmers'.

MELVILLE, Sir Eugene, KCMG 1965 (CMG 1952); HM Diplomatic Service, retired; Director-General, British Property Federation, 1974–80; *b* 15 Dec. 1911; *s* of George E. Melville; *m* 1937, Elizabeth, *d* of Chas M. Strachan, OBE; two *s* one *d*. *Educ:* Queen's Park Sch., Glasgow; St Andrews Univ. (Harkness Residential Scholar; 1st cl. Hons Classics; 1st cl. Hons Economics). Appointed to Colonial Office, 1936; Colonies Supply Mission, Washington, 1941–45; PS to Sec. of State for Colonies, 1945–46; Financial Adviser, Control Commission for Germany, 1949–52; Asst Under-Sec. of State, Colonial Office, 1952; Asst Under-Sec. of State, Foreign Office, 1961; Minister (Economic), Bonn, 1962–65; Permanent UK Delegate to EFTA and GATT, 1965; Ambassador and Permanent UK Representative to UN and other Internat. Organisations at Geneva, 1966–71; Special Advr, Channel Tunnel Studies, 1971–73. Sec-Gen., Malta Round Table Conf., 1955; Hon. Treasurer, British Sailors' Soc.; Chm., Aldeburgh Festival, Snape Maltings Foundn, 1976–81, Pres., 1981–. *Address:* Longcroft, Aldeburgh, Suffolk. *Club:* Reform.

MELVILLE, Sir Harry (Work), KCB 1958; FRS 1941; FRSC; PhD Edinburgh and Cantab; DSc Edinburgh; MSc Birmingham; Principal, Queen Mary College, University of London, 1967–76; *b* 27 April 1908; *s* of Thomas and Esther Burnett Melville; *m* 1942, Janet Marian, *d* of late Hugh Porteous and Sarah Cameron; two *d*. *Educ:* George Heriot's Sch., Edinburgh; Edinburgh Univ. (Carnegie Res. Scholar); Trinity Coll., Cambridge (1851 Exhibitioner). Fellow of Trinity College, Cambridge, 1933–44. Meldola Medal, Inst. of Chemistry, 1936; Davy Medal, Royal Society, 1955; Colwyn Medal, Instn of the Rubber Industry. Asst Dir, Colloid Science Laboratory, Cambridge, 1938–40; Prof. of Chemistry, Univ. of Aberdeen, 1940–48; Scientific Adviser to Chief Superintendent Chemical Defence, Min. of Supply, 1940–43; Superintendent, Radar Res. Station, 1943–45; Mason Prof. of Chemistry, Univ. of Birmingham, 1948–56. Chief Scientific Adviser for Civil Defence, Midlands Region, 1952–56; Bakerian Lecture, Royal Society, 1956. Member: Min. of Aviation Scientific Adv. Council, 1949–51; Adv. Council, Dept of Scientific and Industrial Res., 1946–51; Res. Council, British Electricity Authority, 1949–56; Royal Commn on Univ. Educn in Dundee, 1951–52; Res. Council, DSIR, 1961–65; Chm., Adv. Council on Research and Develt, DTI, 1970–74; Member: Nuclear Safety Adv. Cttee, DTI, 1972–; Cttee of Managers, Royal Institution, 1976–; Sec. to Cttee of the Privy Council for

Scientific and Industrial Research, 1956-65; Chm., SRC, 1965-67. Mem., London Electricity Bd, 1968-75. Mem., Parly and Scientific Cttee, 1971-75; Pres., Plastics Inst., 1970-75. Hon. LLD Aberdeen; Hon. DCL Kent; Hon. DSc: Exeter; Birmingham; Liverpool; Leeds; Heriot-Watt; Essex; Hon. DTech Bradford. *Publications*: papers in Proceedings of Royal Society, etc. *Address*: Norwood, Dodds Lane, Chalfont St Giles, Bucks. *T*: 2222. *Club*: Athenæum.

MELVILLE, Dr James, CMG 1969; Director, Waite Agricultural Research Institute, University of Adelaide, 1956-73, retired; *b* 10 July 1908; *s* of Andrew Melville, Lovells' Flat, NZ; *m* 1938, Margaret, *d* of Charles Ogilvie, Christchurch, NZ; one *s* two *d* (and one *d* decd). *Educ*: Otago, London & Yale Univs. MSc (NZ) 1930, PhD (London) 1934. Commonwealth Fund Fellow, Yale Univ., 1934-36; Asst Chemist, Wheat Research Inst., NZ, 1936-38; Dir, Plant Chemistry Laboratory, DSIR, NZ, 1939-50. War Service: S and SW Pacific Areas, 1941-45. Dir, Grasslands Div., DSIR, NZ, 1951-55. Mem., CSIRO Exec., 1958-65. Chm., Bushfire Research Cttee, 1959-77; Chm., Aust. Wool Industry Conf., 1964-66. FRACI 1958; FAIAS 1968. *Publications*: contrib. scientific jls (agricultural and chemical). *Address*: 10/47 Eve Road, Bellevue Heights, SA 5050, Australia.

MELVILLE, James; *see* Martin, R. P.

MELVILLE, Sir Leslie Galfreid, KBE 1957 (CBE 1953); Member of the Board of the Reserve Bank, 1959-63, and 1965-74; Member, Commonwealth Grants Commission, since 1979 (Chm., 1966-74); *b* 26 March 1902; *s* of Richard Ernest Melville and Lilian Evelyn Thatcher; *m* 1925, Mary Maud Scales; two *s. Educ*: Sydney Church of England Grammar Sch. Bachelor of Economics, University of Sydney, 1925; Public Actuary of South Australia, 1924-28; Prof. of Economics, University of Adelaide, 1929-31; Economic Adviser to Commonwealth Bank of Australia, 1931-49; Asst Gov. (Central Banking) Commonwealth Bank of Australia, 1949-53; Mem. of Commonwealth Bank Bd, 1951-53; Exec. Dir of International Monetary Fund and International Bank for Reconstruction and Development, 1950-53. Mem. of Cttees on Australian Finances and Unemployment, 1931 and 1932; Financial Adviser to Australian Delegates at Imperial Economic Conference, 1932; Financial Adviser to Australian Delegate at World Economic Conference, 1933; Mem. of Financial and Economic Advisory Cttee, 1939; Chm. of Australian Delegation to United Nations Monetary Conf. at Bretton Woods, 1944; Mem. of Advisory Council of Commonwealth Bank, 1945-51; Chm. UN Sub-Commn on Employment and Economic Stability, 1947-50; Member: Immigration Planning Council, 1956-61; Develt Adv. Service of Internat. Bank, 1963-65; Chm. of Tariff Bd, Australia, 1960-62; Chm., Tariff Adv. Cttee of Papua and New Guinea, 1969-71. Vice-Chancellor Australian National Univ., Canberra, ACT, 1953-60. Hon. LLD: Toronto, 1958; ANU, 1978; Hon. DSc Econ Sydney, 1980. *Address*: 71 Stonehaven Crescent, Canberra, ACT 2600, Australia. *Club*: Commonwealth.

See also A. E. Melville.

MELVILLE, Sir Ronald (Henry), KCB 1964 (CB 1952); *b* 9 March 1912; *e s* of Henry Edward Melville; *m* 1940, Enid Dorcas Margaret, *d* of late Harold G. Kenyon, Ware; two *s* one *d. Educ*: Charterhouse; Magdalene Coll., Cambridge. 1st Class Classical Tripos, Pts I and II, Charles Oldham Scholarship. Civil Servant, Air Ministry, 1934-60; Dep. Under-Sec., War Office, 1960-63; Second Permanent Under-Sec. of State, Ministry of Defence, 1963-66; Permanent Sec., Ministry of Aviation, 1966-67; Secretary (Aviation), Min. of Technology, 1967-70; Permanent Sec., Min. of Aviation Supply, 1970-71; Permanent Sec., attached Civil Service Dept, 1971-72; Director: Electronic Components Industry Fedn, 1972-81; Westland Aircraft, 1974-82. Chm., Nat. Rifle Assoc., 1972- (Captain, GB Rifle Team, touring USA and Canada, 1976, and for Kolapore match in UK, 1977); Pres., Herts Rifle Assoc., 1960-; Member Council: Herts TAA, 1960-80; ACFA, 1972-. *Recreations*: rifle shooting, painting, bird-watching, gardening. *Address*: The Old Rose and Crown, Braughing, Ware, Herts. *Club*: Brooks's.

MELVIN, Air Cdre James Douglas, CB 1956; OBE 1947; idc 1956; retired; Property Manager, Coutts & Co.; *b* 20 Feb. 1914; *s* of William Adamson Melvin, The Square, Turriff, Aberdeenshire, and Agnes Fyffe, The Hunghar, Kirriemuir; *m* 1946, Mary Wills; one *d* (one *s* decd). *Educ*: Turriff Secondary Sch. Apprentice, Halton, 1930; Cadet, Cranwell, 1933. Dep. Dir Organization, Air Ministry, 1951-53; Group Capt. Organization, MEAF, 1953-55; Dir of Organization, Air Ministry, 1957-61, retd. *Address*: Kyrenia Cottage, Old Bosham, Sussex. *Club*: Royal Air Force.

MELVIN, John Turcan, TD and star; MA Cantab; *b* 19 March 1916; *m* 1951, Elizabeth Ann Parry-Jones; one *s* three *d. Educ*: Stowe Sch.; Trinity Coll., Cambridge; Berlin Univ. (Schol.). Asst Master, Sherborne Sch., 1938. Served with Dorset Regt, 1939-46. Housemaster, Sherborne Sch., 1950; Headmaster, Kelly Coll., 1959-72; Hd of German Dept, Foster's Sch., 1972-75; Sixth Form Tutor, Sherborne Sch., 1975-82. Governor: Hall Sch., Wincanton; St Francis Sch., Hook. *Recreations*: walking, reading, tennis, dramatics. *Address*: Culverhayes Lodge, Sherborne, Dorset. *Club*: East India, Devonshire, Sports and Public Schools.

MELVYN HOWE, Prof. George; *see* Howe, Prof. G. M.

MENAUL, Air Vice-Marshal Stewart William Blacker, CB 1963; CBE 1957; DFC 1941; AFC 1942; Defence Consultant: Institute for Study of Conflict; Institute for Foreign Policy Analysis, Cambridge, Mass; *b* 17 July 1915; 2nd *s* of late Captain W. J. Menaul, MC, and Mrs M. Menaul, Co. Armagh, N Ireland; *m* 1943, Hélène Mary, *d* of late R. Taylor; one *s* one *d. Educ*: Portadown; RAF Coll., Cranwell. Bomber Command Squadrons, 1936-39; on outbreak of war serving with No 21 Sqdn until 1940; Flying Instructor, 1940-41; No 15 Sqdn, 1941-42; Air Staff No 3 Gp, Bomber Command, 1943; Pathfinder Force, 1943-45; RAF Staff Coll., 1946; Air Ministry, 1947-49; Imperial Defence Coll., 1950-51; Air Ministry, Dep. Dir of Operations, 1951-54; Comd British Atomic Trials Task Forces, Monte Bello and Maralinga (Australia), 1955-56; Commanding Officer, Bombing Sch., Lindholme, 1957-58; Air Officer Administration, Aden, 1959-60; Senior Air Staff Officer, Headquarters Bomber Command, 1961-65; Commandant, Joint Services Staff Coll., 1965-67; Dir-Gen., RUSI, 1968-76. *Publications*: Soviet War Machine, 1980; Countdown: Britain's strategic nuclear forces, 1980. *Recreations*: ornithology, painting. *Address*: The Lodge, Frensham Vale, Lower Bourne, Farnham, Surrey. *Club*: Royal Air Force.

MENDE, Dr Erich; Member of the Bundestag, German Federal Republic, since 1949; *b* 28 Oct. 1916; *m* 1948, Margot (*née* Hattje); three *s* one *d. Educ*: Humane Coll., Gross-Strehlitz; Universities of Cologne and Bonn (Dr jur). Military service in Infantry Regt 84, Gleiwitz. Served War of 1939-45, Comdr of a Regt (wounded twice, prisoner of war); Major, 1944. Co-founder of FDP (Free Democratic Party), 1945; Mem. Exec. Cttee, British Zone, FDP, 1947; Dep. Chm. FDP in North Rhine Westphalia, 1953-; Mem. 1949-, Dep. Chm. 1956-, Exec. Cttee of Federal Organisation of FDP; Mem. Exec. Cttee, German Council and Parliamentary Section of European Movement; Parliamentary Group of FDP: Whip, and Mem. Exec. Cttee, 1950-53; Dep. Chm., 1953; Chm., 1957; Chm. of FDP, 1960-68. Vice-Chancellor and Minister for All-German Affairs, Federal Republic of Germany, 1963-66. Mem., CDU Hessen, 1970. *Address*: Bundeshaus, 53 Bonn 1, Germany. *T*: 16 3255; (home) Am Stadtwald 62, 53 Bonn 2, Germany.

MENDIS, Vernon Lorraine Benjamin; Permanent Representative of the Republic of Sri Lanka to UNESCO, since 1978; *b* 5 Dec. 1925; *m* 1953, Padma Rajapathirana; one *s. Educ*: Univ. of Ceylon (BA Hons History, 1948). Post Grad. Master of Philosophy, Sch. of Oriental and African Studies, Univ. of London, 1966. High Commissioner for Sri Lanka: in Canada, 1974-75; in UK, 1975-77; Ambassador in France, 1978-80. *Publication*: The Advent of the British to Ceylon 1760-1815, Colombo 1971. *Recreations*: hiking, bird watching. *Address*: UNESCO, 7 place de Fontenoy, 75007 Paris, France. *Club*: Travellers'.

MENDL, James Henry Embleton; His Honour Judge Mendl; a Circuit Judge since 1974; *b* 23 Oct. 1927; *s* of R. W. S. Mendl, barrister and author, and Dorothy Williams Mendl (*née* Burnett), and *g s* of late Sir S. F. Mendl, KBE; *m* 1971, Helena Augusta Maria Schrama, *d* of late J. H. and H. H. Schrama-Jekat, The Netherlands. *Educ*: Harrow; University Coll., Oxford (MA). Called to Bar, Inner Temple, 1953; South Eastern Circuit. Commissioned, Worcestershire Regt, 1947; served: Egypt, with 2nd N Staffs, 1947-48; with Royal Signals (TA), 1952-54, and Queen's Royal Regt (TA) (Captain, 1955), 1954-56. Councillor, Royal Borough of Kensington and Chelsea, 1964-74 (Vice-Chm., Town Planning Cttee, 1969; Chm. (Vice-Chm. 1970), Libraries Cttee, 1971). Contested (C) Gateshead East, 1966. *Recreations*: music, skiing. *Address*: 1 Wetherby Place, SW7 4NU. *T*: 01-373 1518.

MENDOZA, June Yvonne, RP; ROI; artist; *d* of John Morton and Dot (*née* Mendoza), musicians; *m* Keith Ashley V. Mackrell; one *s* three *d. Educ*: Lauriston Girls' Sch., Melbourne; St Martin's Sch. of Art. Period of variety of illustration, design etc, also worked as actress in all media. Posting Philippines, 1960-65, Australia, 1969-73. Member: RP 1970; ROI 1968. Extensive portrait work in public and private collections, British and internat. Portraits include: Queen Elizabeth II; Duke of Edinburgh; Prince of Wales; Duke of Norfolk; Rt Rev. Lord Coggan; Margaret Thatcher; A. J. P. Taylor; Sir John Gorton; Ratu Sir Kamisese Mara; Alistair Cooke; Tom Stoppard; Dame Marie Rambert; Lord Clark; group portraits; personal series of musicians include: Dame Joan Sutherland; Yehudi Menuhin; Sir Michael Tippett; Antal Dorati; Sir Colin Davis. Occasional lectures. *Recreations*: music, theatre, travel. *Address*: 34 Inner Park Road, SW19.

MENDOZA, Maurice, CVO 1982; MSM 1946; Under Secretary, Ancient Monuments and Historic Buildings, Department of the Environment, 1978-81; *b* 1 May 1921; *e s* of Daniel and Rachel Mendoza; *m* 1949, Phyllis Kriger. *Educ*: Sir Henry Raine's Foundation. Dip. Sociology London. Clerical Officer, HM Office of Works, 1938; served Royal Signals and Cheshire Yeo., 1941-46 (Sgt); Mil. Mission to Belgium, 1944-46; Organisation Officer, Treasury, 1956-61; Principal, MPBW, 1963; Asst Sec. 1968; DoE, 1970; Under-Sec., 1973; Dir of Manpower and Management Services, DoE and later, also Dept of Transport, 1974-78. Hon. Mem., 10th Battalion Transportation Corps, US Army, 1977. *Recreations*: theatre, walking, photography. *Address*: 45 Grange Grove, Canonbury, N1 2NP. *Clubs*: Athenæum, Civil Service.

MENDOZA, Vivian P.; *see* Pereira-Mendoza.

MENDOZA-ACOSTA, Vice-Adm. Felix; Venezuelan Ambassador to the Court of St James's, since 1979; *b* 21 Feb. 1929; *s* of José Mendoza and Virginia Mendoza (*née* Acosta); *m* 1954, Patricia Hill; one *s* two *d. Educ*: Naval

Academy, Venezuela; Naval Coll., USA. Professor, Naval Academy, Venezuela, 1957-59; held high appointments at High Court of Admiralty, Min. of Defence, 1960-72; Director, Naval Academy, 1973; Chief of Operations, Headquarters, High Court of Admiralty, 1974, Commander in Chief, 1976; Chief of General Staff, 1977; Inspector General of Armed Forces, 1978; in charge, Min. of Defence, on several occasions, 1978-79. Orden: del Libertador Simón Bolívar; Francisco de Miranda; Gen. Urdaneta; Andrés Bello; Diego de Lozada; naval decorations: Spain, Italy, Colombia, Argentina, Bolivia, Peru, Venezuela; Cross, 1st Cl.: Land Forces of Venezuela, Air Force of Venezuela, Naval Merit, National Guard. *Recreations:* walking, reading, music, conversation with family. *Address:* 69 Onslow Gardens, SW7. *T:* 01-370 1008. *Clubs:* Les Ambassadeurs, Hurlingham, Annabel's, Belfry, White Elephant, Casanova; Officers' (Carácas).

MENEMENCIOGLU, Turgut; High Political Adviser, Ministry of Foreign Affairs, Ankara, since 1978; *b* Istanbul, 8 Oct. 1914; *s* of Muvatfak and Kadriye Menemencioğlu; *m* 1944, Nermin Moran; two *s. Educ:* Robert Coll., Istanbul; Geneva Univ. Joined Turkish Min. of Foreign Affairs, 1939; Permanent Delegate, European Office, UN Geneva, 1950-52; Counsellor, Turkish Embassy, Washington, 1952; Dir-Gen., Econ. Affairs, Min. of Foreign Affairs, 1952-54; Dep. Permanent Rep. to UN, 1954-60; Ambassador to Canada, 1960; Permanent Rep. to UN, 1960-62; Ambassador to USA, 1962-67; High Polit. Adviser, Mem., High Polit. Planning Bd, Min. of Foreign Affairs, 1967-68; Sec.-Gen., CENTO, 1968-72; Adviser, Min. of Foreign Affairs, 1972; Ambassador of Turkey to the Court of St James's, 1972-78. *Address:* Inünü Cad 31/12, Taksim, Istanbul, Turkey.

MENEVIA, Bishop of, (RC), since 1981; **Rt. Rev. John Aloysius Ward,** OFM Cap; *b* 24 Jan. 1929; *s* of Eugene Ward and Hannah Ward (*née* Cheetham). *Educ:* Prior Park College, Bath. Received as Capuchin Franciscan Friar, 1945; solemn profession as Friar, 1950; ordained Priest, 1953; Diocesan Travelling Mission, Menevia, 1954-60; Guardian and Parish Priest, Peckham, London, 1960-66; Provincial Definitor (Councillor), 1963-69; Minister Provincial, 1969-70; General Definitor (Councillor), 1970-80; Bishop Coadjutor of Menevia, 1980-81. *Address:* Bishop's House, Wrexham, Clwyd LL13 7EW. *T:* Wrexham 262726.

MENHENNET, Dr David; Librarian of the House of Commons, since 1976; *b* 4 Dec. 1928; *s* of William and Everill Menhennet, Redruth, Cornwall; *m* 1954, Audrey, *o d* of William and Alice Holmes, Accrington, Lancs; two *s. Educ:* Truro Sch., Cornwall; Oriel Coll., Oxford (BA 1st Cl. Hons 1952); Queen's Coll., Oxford. Open Scholarship in Mod. Langs, Oriel Coll., Oxford, 1946; Heath Harrison Trav. Scholarship, 1951; Bishop Fraser Res. Scholar, Oriel Coll., 1952-53; Laming Trav. Fellow, Queen's Coll., Oxford, 1953-54; Zaharoff Trav. Scholarship, 1953-54. MA 1956, DPhil 1960, Oxon. Library Clerk, House of Commons Library, 1954; Asst Librarian i/c Res. Div., 1964-67; Dep. Librarian, 1967-76. Member: Study of Parliament Gp, 1964-; Adv. Cttee, Bibliographic Services Divn, British Library, 1975-; Associate, Inst. of Cornish Studies, 1974-. FRSA 1966. Gen. Editor, House of Commons Library Documents series, 1972-. *Publications:* (with J. Palmer) Parliament in Perspective, 1967; The Journal of the House of Commons: a bibliographical and historical guide, 1971; (ed with D. C. L. Holland) Erskine May's Private Journal, 1857-1882, 1972; (contrib.) The House of Commons in the Twentieth Century, ed S. A. Walkland, 1979; articles in Lib. Assoc. Record, Parliamentarian, Parly Affairs, Polit. Qly, New Scientist, Contemp. Rev., Jl of Librarianship, Jl of Documentation. *Recreations:* walking, gardening, visiting old churches, music, watching sport. *Address:* (office) House of Commons Library, SW1A 0AA. *T:* 01-219 3635. *Club:* Athenæum.

MENNEER, Stephen Snow, CB 1967; retired, 1970, as Assistant Under-Secretary of State, Department of Health and Social Security; *b* 6 March 1910; *s* of Sydney Charles Menneer, LLD, and Minnie Elizabeth Menneer; *m* 1935, Margaret Longstaff Smith (*d* 1976); one *s* one *d. Educ:* Rugby Sch.; Oriel Coll., Oxford. Min. of Information, 1939; Min. of National Insurance, 1948; Under-Sec., Min. of Pensions and Nat. Insurance, then Min. of Social Security, 1961. *Address:* Cowlas, Burrington, Umberleigh, N Devon.

MENON, Prof. Mambillikalathil Govind Kumar, MSc, PhD; FRS 1970; Member, Planning Commission, Government of India and Chairman, Science Advisory Committee to the Cabinet, since 1982; *b* 28 Aug. 1928; *s* of Kizhekepat Sankara Menon and Mambillikalathil Narayaniamma; *m* 1955, Indumati Patel; one *s* one *d. Educ:* Jaswant Coll., Jodhpur; Royal Inst. of Science, Bombay (MSc); Univ. of Bristol (PhD). Royal Commn for Exhibn of 1851 Senior Award, 1953-55; Tata Inst. of Fundamental Research: Reader, 1955-58; Associate Prof., 1958-60; Prof. of Physics and Dean of Physics Faculty, 1960-64; Senior Prof. and Dep. Dir (Physics), 1964-66, Dir, 1966-75. Chm., Electronics Commn, and Sec., Dept of Electronics, Govt of India, 1971-78; Scientific Advr to Minister of Defence, Dir-Gen. of Defence Res. and Develt Orgn, and Sec. in the Ministry of Defence for Defence Res., 1974-78; Dir-Gen., Council of Scientific and Industrial Res., 1978-81; Sec. to Govt of India, Dept of Science and Technology, 1978-82; Chm., Commn for Addtnl Sources of Energy, 1981-82; Mem., UN Sec.-Gen.'s Adv. Cttee on Application of Sci. and Technol. to Develt, 1972-79 (Chm. for 2 yrs); Special Advr, Internat. Fedn of Insts for Advanced Study, Stockholm. Fellow: Indian Acad. of Sciences (Pres., 1974-76), Council Mem., 1977-; Indian Nat. Science Acad. (Pres., 1981-82); Pres., Indian Sci. Congress Assoc., 1981-82; Hon. Fellow, Nat. Acad. of Sciences, India; For. Hon. Mem., Amer. Acad. of Arts and Scis; Mem., Pontifical Acad. of Scis, Vatican; Hon. Fellow, Instn

Electronics and Telecomm. Engrs (India). Hon. DSc: Jodhpur Univ., 1970; Delhi Univ., 1973; Sardar Patel Univ., 1973; Allahabad Univ., 1977; Roorkee Univ., 1979; Banaras Hindu Univ., 1981; Jadavpur Univ., 1981; Sri Venkateswara Univ., 1982; Shanti Swarup Bhatnagar Award for Physical Sciences, Council of Scientific and Industrial Research, 1960; Khaitan Medal, RAS, 1973; Awards from Govt of India: Padma Shri, 1961; Padma Bhushan, 1968. *Publications:* about 76, on cosmic rays and elementary particle physics; about 52 major lectures, talks etc. *Recreations:* photography, bird-watching. *Address:* Yojana Bhavan, Parliament Street, New Delhi 110001, India. *T:* (office) 382148; (home) 387784. *Clubs:* National Liberal; United Services (Bombay); India International Centre (New Delhi).

MENOTTI, Gian Carlo; Composer; Founder and President, Spoleto Festival; *b* Cadegliano, Italy, 7 July 1911. *Educ:* The Curtis Institute of Music, Philadelphia, Pa. Has been resident in the United States since 1928. Teacher of Composition at Curtis Inst. of Music, 1948-55. First performances of works include: Amelia Goes to the Ball (opera), 1936; The Old Maid and the Thief (radio opera), 1939 (later staged); The Island God, 1942; Sebastian (Ballet), 1943; Piano Concerto in F, 1945; The Medium (opera), 1946 (later filmed); The Telephone (opera), 1947; Errand into the Maze (ballet), 1947; The Consul (opera), 1950 (Pulitzer Prize); Apocalypse (orchestral), 1951; Amahl and the Night Visitors (television opera), 1951; Violin Concerto in A Minor, 1952; The Saint of Bleeker Street (opera), 1954 (Pulitzer Prize); The Unicorn, The Gorgon, and the Manticore, 1956; Maria Golovin (television opera), 1958; The Last Savage (opera), 1963; The Death of the Bishop of Brindisi (oratorio), 1963; Martin's Lie (opera), 1964; Canti della Lontananza (song cycle), 1967; Help, Help, the Globolinks (opera), 1968; The Leper (drama), 1970; Triplo Concerto a Tre (symphonic piece), 1970; The Most Important Man (opera), 1971; Fantasia for 'cello and orch., 1971; Tamu-Tamu (opera), 1973; The Egg (opera), 1976; The Trial of the Gypsy (opera), 1976; Landscapes & Remembrances, for chorus and orch., 1976; Symphony no 1, 1976; Chip & his Dog (opera), 1978; Juana la Loca (opera), 1979; Song of Hope (cantata), 1980; A Bride from Pluto (opera), 1982. Wrote libretto for Vanessa (opera, by Samuel Barber), 1958. *Publications:* his major works have been published, also some minor ones; he is the author of all his libretti, most of which have been written in English. *Address:* c/o Thea Dispeker, 59 East 54th Street, New York, NY 10022, USA; Yester House, Gifford, Haddington, East Lothian EH41 4JF.

MENSFORTH, Sir Eric, Kt 1962; CBE 1945; DL; MA Cantab; FEng; FIMechE; FRAeS; Hon. FIProdE; Vice Lord-Lieutenant, South Yorkshire, 1974-81; President, Westland Aircraft Ltd, since 1979 (Director, since 1968; Chairman, 1953-68; Vice-Chairman, 1968-71); Director, John Brown & Co. Ltd, retired 1982; *b* 17 May 1906; 2nd *s* of late Sir Holberry Mensforth, KCB, CBE; *m* 1934, Betty, *d* of late Rev. Picton W. Francis; three *d. Educ:* Altrincham County High Sch.; University Coll. Sch.; King's Coll., Cambridge (Price Exhibn) (1st class mechanical sciences tripos). Engineering work at Woolwich Arsenal, Mather & Platt Ltd, Bolckow Vaughan Ltd, Kloecknerwerke A. G., Dorman Long Ltd, English Electric Ltd, Markham & Co. Ltd, T. Firth & John Brown Ltd, Rhodesian Alloys Ltd, Normalair Ltd, Chief Production Adviser to Chief Executive, Ministry of Aircraft Production, 1943-45. Master Cutler, Sheffield, 1965-66. Chairman: EDC for Electronics Industry, 1968-70; Cttee on Quality Assurance, 1968-70; Council of Engineering Instns, 1969-72; Governing Body, Sheffield Polytechnic, 1969-75; Member: British Productivity Council, 1964-69; Royal Ordnance Factories Bd, 1968-72; Council, RGS, 1968-70; Treasurer, British Assoc. for Advancement of Science, 1970-75; a Vice-Pres., Fellowship of Engineering, 1977; Pres., S Yorks Scouts' Assoc., 1969-76. Hon. Fellow, Sheffield City Polytech. Hon. DEng Sheffield, 1967; Hon. DSc Southampton, 1970. DL S (formerly WR) Yorks, 1971. *Publications:* Air Frame Production, 1947 (Instn Prize, IMechE); Future of the Aeroplane (Cantor Lectures), 1959; Production of Helicopters and Hovercraft (Lord Sempill Lecture, IProdE), 1964; Future of Rotorcraft and Hovercraft (Cierva Meml Lecture, RAeS), 1967; Extracts from the Records of the Cutlers' Company, 1972; Family Engineers, 1981. *Address:* 3 Belgrave Drive, Fulwood, Sheffield S10 3LQ. *T:* Sheffield 307737. *Clubs:* Alpine; Sheffield (Sheffield).

MENTER, Sir James (Woodham), Kt 1973; MA, PhD, ScD Cantab; FRS 1966; FInstP; Principal, Queen Mary College, London University, since 1976; *b* 22 Aug. 1921; *s* of late Horace Menter and late Jane Anne Lackenby; *m* 1947, Marjorie Jean, *d* of late Thomas Stodart Whyte-Smith, WS; two *s* one *d. Educ:* Dover Grammar Sch.; Peterhouse, Cambridge. PhD 1949, ScD 1960. Experimental Officer, Admty, 1942-45; Research, Cambridge Univ., 1946-54 (ICI Fellow, 1951-54; Sir George Beilby Mem. Award, 1954); Tube Investments Research Laboratories, Hinxton Hall, 1954-68; Dir of Research and Develt, Tube Investments Ltd, 1965-76. Director: Tube Investments Res. Labs, 1961-68; Tube Investments Ltd, 1965-; Round Oak Steelworks Ltd, 1967-76; British Petroleum Co., 1976-; Steetley Co., 1981-. Member: SRC, 1967-72; Cttee of Inquiry into Engrg Profession, 1977-79; a Vice-Pres., Royal Society, 1971-76, Treasurer, 1972-76. Fellow, Churchill Coll., Cambridge, 1966. President: Inst. of Physics, 1970-72; Metals Soc., 1976; Dep. Chm., Adv. Council Applied R&D, 1976-79. Mem. (part-time), BSC, 1976-79. Mem., Ct of Governors, City of London Polytechnic. Hon. DTech Brunel, 1974. Bessemer Medal, Iron and Steel Inst., 1973; Glazebrook Medal and Prize, Inst. of Physics, 1977. *Publications:* scientific papers in Proc. Royal Society, Advances in Physics, Jl Iron and Steel Inst., etc. *Recreation:* fishing. *Address:* 1 The Pierhead, Wapping High Street, E1. *T:* 01-488 3393.

MENTETH, Sir James (Wallace) Stuart-, 6th Bt, *cr* 1838; *b* 13 Nov. 1922; *e s* of 5th Bt and Winifred Melville (*d* 1968), *d* of Daniel Francis and *widow* of Capt. Rupert G. Raw, DSO; *S* father, 1952; *m* 1949, Dorothy Patricia, *d* of late Frank Greaves Warburton; two *s. Educ:* Fettes; St Andrews Univ.; Trinity Coll., Oxford (MA). Served War of 1939-45, with Scots Guards, 1942-44; on active service in North Africa and Italy (Anzio) (severely wounded). *Recreations:* motoring, swimming, gardening, ornithology. *Heir: s* Charles Greaves Stuart-Menteth [*b* 25 Nov. 1950; *m* 1976, Nicola St Lawrence; three *d* (one *s* decd)]. *Address:* Nutwood, Auchencairn, Castle-Douglas, Kirkcudbrightshire DG7 1QZ.

MENUHIN, Yehudi, KBE (Hon.) 1965; violinist; *b* New York, 22 April 1916; *s* of Moshe and Marutha Menuhin; *m* 1938, Nola Ruby, *d* of George Nicholas, Melbourne, Australia; one *s* one *d* ; *m* 1947, Diana Rosamond, *d* of late G. L. E. Gould and late Lady Harcourt (Evelyn Suart); two *s. Educ:* private tutors; studied music under Sigmund Anker and Louis Persinger, in San Francisco; Georges Enesco, Rumania and Paris; Adolph Busch, Switzerland. Made début with orchestra, San Francisco, aged 7, Paris, aged 10, New York, 11, Berlin, 13; since then has played with most of world's orchestras and conductors; has introduced among contemp. works Sonata for Violin alone, by Béla Bartók (composed for Mr Menuhin), as well as works by William Walton, Ben-Haim, Georges Enesco, Pizzetti, Ernest Bloch, etc. During War of 1939-45 devoted larger part of his time to concerts for US and Allied armed forces and benefit concerts for Red Cross, etc (500 concerts). Series of concerts in Moscow (by invitation), 1945; seven visits to Israel, 1950-; first tour of Japan, 1951; first tour of India (invitation of Prime Minister), 1952. Largely responsible for cultural exchange programme between US and Russia, 1955, and for bringing Indian music and musicians to West. Initiated his own annual music festival in Gstaad, Switzerland, 1957, and in Bath, 1959-68; Jt Artistic Dir, Windsor Festival, 1969-72. Founder, Live Music Now, 1977. Founded Yehudi Menuhin Sch. of Music, Stoke d'Abernon, Surrey, 1963; Founder/Pres., Internat. Menuhin Music Acad., Gstaad, 1976; President: Trinity Coll. of Music, 1971; Royal Philharmonic Orch., 1982-. Hon. Fellow, St Catharine's Coll., Cambridge, 1970; Hon. DMus: Oxford, 1962; Cambridge, 1970; Sorbonne, 1976, and 10 other degrees from Brit. Univs. Freedom of the City of Edinburgh, 1965; City of Bath, 1966. He records for several companies, both as soloist and as Conductor of Menuhin Festival Orch., with which has toured USA, Australia, NZ and Europe; appears regularly on American and British Television. Gold Medal, Royal Philharmonic Soc., 1962; Jawaharlal Nehru Award for International Understanding, 1970; Sonning Music Prize, Denmark, 1972; Handel Medal, NY; City of Jerusalem Medal; Peace Prize, Börsenverein des Deutschen Buchhandels, 1979; Albert Medal, RSA, 1981. Decorations include: Comdr, Legion of Honour, Order of Arts and Letters (France); Order of Leopold (Belgium); Ordre de la Couronne (Belgium); Kt Comdr Order of Merit (Fed. Rep. of Germany); Royal Order of the Phœnix (Greece); Comdr, Order of Orange-Nassau (Netherlands); Hon. Citizen of Switzerland, 1970. *Publications:* The Violin: six lessons by Yehudi Menuhin, 1971; Theme and Variations, 1972; Violin and Viola, 1976; Sir Edward Elgar: My Musical Grandfather (essay), 1976; (autobiography) Unfinished Journey, 1977; The Music of Man, 1980; *Relevant Publication:* Yehudi Menuhin, The Story of the Man and the Musician, by Robert Magidoff, 1956 (USA); Conversations with Menuhin, by Robin Daniels, 1979. *Films:* Stage Door Canteen; Magic Bow; The Way of Light (biog.). *Television series:* The Music of Man. *Address:* (agents) Columbia Artists Management, 165 W 57th Street, New York City, NY 10019, USA; Harold Holt, 31 Sinclair Road, W4, England. *Clubs:* Athenæum, Garrick.
See also J. C. M. Benthall.

MENZIES, John Maxwell; Chairman, John Menzies Holdings Ltd, since 1952; *b* 13 Oct. 1926; *s* of late John Francis Menzies; *m* 1953, Patricia Eleanor, *d* of late Comdr Sir Hugh Dawson, Bt, CBE; four *d. Educ:* Eton. Lieut Grenadier Guards, released 1948. Berwickshire CC, 1954-57. Director: Atlantic Assets, 1973-; Independent Investment Trust, 1973-; Ivory and Sime Ltd, 1978-; Nimslo Corp. Inc., 1980-; Nimslo European Holdings Ltd, 1980-; Rocky Mountains Oil and Gas Ltd, 1980-; Nimslo International Ltd, 1981-; Gordon & Gotch Holdings Ltd, 1981-. Trustee, Newsvendors' Benevolent Instn, 1968- (Pres., 1968-74). Mem., Royal Co. of Archers, HM's Body Guard for Scotland. *Recreations:* farming, shooting, reading, travel. *Address:* Kames, Duns, Berwickshire. *T:* Leitholm 202. *Clubs:* Turf, Boodle's; New (Edinburgh).

MENZIES, Sir Laurence James, Kt 1962; *b* 23 Dec. 1906; *yr s* of late James Menzies, Coupar Angus, Perthshire; *m* 1935, Agnes Cameron, *yr d* of late John Smart; one *s* one *d. Educ:* Wandsworth Sch. Entered Bank of England, 1925; Asst Chief Cashier, 1943; Dep. Chief Cashier, 1952; Adviser to the Governors, 1957-58, 1962-64; Sec. of the Export Credits Guarantee Dept, 1958-61. Pres., Union d'Assureurs des Crédits Internationaux (Berne Union), 1960-61. *Recreation:* golf. *Address:* Timbers, Vincent Close, Esher, Surrey. *T:* Esher 64257. *Clubs:* Overseas Bankers', MCC.

MENZIES, Dame Pattie (Maie), GBE 1954; *b* 2 March 1899; *d* of late Senator J. W. Leckie; *m* 1920, Robert Gordon Menzies (Rt Hon. Sir Robert Menzies, KT, AK, CH, QC, FRS; Prime Minister of the Commonwealth of Australia, 1939-41 and 1949-66) (*d* 1978); one *s* one *d* (and one *s* decd). *Educ:* Fintona Girls' Sch., Melbourne; Presbyterian Ladies' Coll., Melbourne. *Address:* 7 Monaro Close, Kooyong, Vic 3144, Australia. *Club:* Alexandra (Melbourne).

MENZIES, Sir Peter (Thomson), Kt 1972; Director: National Westminster Bank Ltd, 1968-82; Commercial Union Assurance Co. Ltd, 1962-82; *b* 15 April 1912; *s* of late John C. Menzies and late Helen S. Aikman; *m* 1938, Mary McPherson Alexander, *d* of late John T. Menzies and late Agnes Anderson; one *s* one *d. Educ:* Musselburgh Grammar Sch.; University of Edinburgh. MA, 1st Class Hons Math. and Natural Philosophy, 1934. Inland Revenue Dept, 1933-39; Treasurer's Dept, Imperial Chemical Industries Ltd, 1939-56 (Asst Treas. 1947, Dep. Treas. 1952); Director: Imperial Chemical Industries Ltd, 1956-72 (Dep. Chm., 1967-72); Imperial Metal Industries Ltd, 1962-72 (Chm., 1964-72). Part-time Mem., CEGB, 1960-72; Mem., Review Body on Doctors' and Dentists' Remuneration, 1971-; Chairman: Electricity Council, 1972-77; London Exec. Cttee, Scottish Council (Develt and Industry), 1977-. A Vice-Pres., Siol na Meinnrich; Pres., UNIPEDE, 1973-76; Vice-Pres. and Gen. Treas., BAAS, 1982-. FInstP; CompIEE; Fellow, Inst. Dirs. *Address:* Kit's Corner, Harmer Green, Welwyn, Herts. *T:* Welwyn 4386. *Club:* Caledonian.

MENZIES-WILSON, William Napier; Chairman, Ocean Transport & Trading Ltd, Liverpool, since 1980; *b* 4 Dec. 1926; *s* of James Robert Menzies-Wilson and Jacobine Napier Williamson-Napier; *m* 1953, Mary Elizabeth Darnell Juckes; two *s* one *d. Educ:* Winchester; New Coll., Oxford (MA); North Western Univ., Chicago. Joined Stewarts & Lloyds Ltd, 1950; Managing Director, Stewarts & Lloyds of South Africa Ltd, 1954-61, Chairman, 1961; Director, Stewarts & Lloyds Ltd, 1964; Director: Supplies & Transport, British Steel Corporation, 1967; Ocean Transport & Trading Ltd, and Chairman, Wm Cory & Son Ltd, 1973. *Recreations:* shooting, golf, gardening. *Address:* 15 Clarendon Road, W11 4JB. *T:* 01-727 1536.

MERCER, Rt. Rev. Eric Arthur John; *see* Exeter, Bishop of.

MERCER, John Charles Kenneth; a Recorder of the Crown Court, 1975-82; *b* 17 Sept. 1917; *s* of late Charles Wilfred Mercer and Cecil Maud Mercer; *m* 1944, Barbara Joan, *d* of late Arnold Sydney Whitehead, CB, CBE, and Maud Ethel Whitehead; one *s* one *d. Educ:* Ellesmere Coll.; Law Sch., Swansea University Coll. (LLB). Solicitor. War Service, 1940-45, Captain RA. Partner, Douglas-Jones & Mercer, 1946-. Mem., Royal Commn on Criminal Procedure, 1978-81; Mem., SW Wales River Authority, 1960-74. *Recreations:* fishing, shooting, golf, watching sport. *Address:* 334 Gower Road, Killay, Swansea, West Glamorgan. *T:* Swansea 202931. *Clubs:* City and County, Clyne Golf (Swansea).

MERCER, Rt. Rev. Robert William Stanley; *see* Matabeleland, Bishop of.

MERCER NAIRNE PETTY-FITZMAURICE, family name of **Marquess of Lansdowne.**

MERCHANT, Ismail; film producer, since 1960; Partner, Merchant Ivory Productions, since formation, 1961; *b* 25 Dec. 1936; *s* of Noormohamed Haji Abdul Rehman and Hazra Memon. *Educ:* St Xavier's Coll., Bombay (BA); New York Univ. (MBA). Collaborator with Ruth Prawer Jhabvala and James Ivory on most of the following: *feature films:* The Householder, 1963; Shakespeare Wallah, 1965 (won Best Actress award, Berlin Film Fest., 1965); The Guru, 1969; Bombay Talkie, 1970; Savages, 1972; The Wild Party, 1975; Roseland, 1977; The Europeans, 1979 (official Brit. entry, Cannes Film Fest.); Quartet, 1981; Heat and Dust, 1982; *shorts:* The Creation of Woman, 1960 (Academy award nomination); Helen, Queen of the Nautch Girls, 1973; (directed) Mahatma and the Mad Boy, 1973; Sweet Sounds, 1976; *television:* Adventures of a Brown Man in Search of Civilization, 1971 (BBC); Autobiography of a Princess, 1975 (TV special, NY); Hullabaloo over Georgie and Bonnie's Pictures, 1978 (feature, LWT); Jane Austen in Manhattan, 1980 (feature, LWT and Polytel). *Recreations:* squash, bicycling, cooking. *Address:* 400 East 52nd Street, New York, NY 10022, USA. *T:* 212 759 3694; 32 Motlabai Street, Bombay, India. *T:* 378-376.

MERCHANT, Rev. Prof. William Moelwyn, FRSL; writer and sculptor; *b* 5 June 1913; *s* of late William Selwyn and Elizabeth Ann Merchant, Port Talbot, Glamorgan; *m* 1938, Maria Eluned Hughes, Llanelly; one *s* one *d. Educ:* Port Talbot Grammar Sch.; (Exhibnr) University Coll., Cardiff. BA, 1st Cl. English hons 1933; 2nd Cl. 1st div. Hist., 1934; MA 1950; DLitt 1960; Hon. Fellow, University Coll., Cardiff, 1981. Hist. Master, Carmarthen Grammar Sch., 1935; English Master, Newport High Sch., 1936; English Lectr, Caerleon Trg Coll., 1937; University Coll. Cardiff: Lectr in Eng. Lang. and Lit., 1939; Sen. Lectr, 1950; Reader, 1961; Prof. of English, Univ. of Exeter, 1961-74; Vicar of Llanddewi Brefi, dio. St Davids, 1974-78; Hon. Lectr, All Saints Church, Leamington Spa, 1979. Fellow, Folger Shakespeare Library, Washington, DC, and Fulbright Fellow, 1957; Woodward Lectr, Yale Univ., 1957; Dupont Lectr, Sewanee Univ., Tenn, 1963; Willett Prof. of English and Theology, Univ. of Chicago, 1971. Founded Rougemont Press, 1970 (with Ted Hughes, Eric Cleave and Paul Merchant). Welsh Cttee of Arts Council of Gt Brit., 1960 and 1975-; Council, Llandaff Festival, 1958-61. Consultant and script-writer on film, The Bible, Rome, 1960-64. Ordained to Anglican Orders, 1940; Examining Chaplain to the Bishop of Salisbury; Canon of Salisbury Cathedral, 1967-73, Canon Emeritus, 1973 (Chancellor, 1967-71); Mem., Archbishops' Commn on Faculty Jurisdiction, 1979-. Founded Llanddewi Brefi Arts Fest., 1975. FRSL 1976; Hon. Fellow, University Coll. of Wales, Aberystwyth, 1975. Hon HLD Wittenberg Univ., Ohio, 1973. *Publications:* Wordsworth's Guide to the Lakes (illus. John

Piper), 1952 (US 1953); Reynard Library Wordsworth, 1955 (US 1955); Shakespeare and the Artist, 1959; Creed and Drama, 1965; (ed) Merchant of Venice, 1967; (ed) Marlowe's Edward the Second, 1967; Comedy, 1972; Tree of Life (libretto, music by Alun Hoddinott), 1972; Breaking the Code (poems), 1975; (ed) Essays and Studies, 1977; No Dark Glass (poems), 1979; R. S. Thomas, a critical evaluation, 1979; articles in Times Literary Supplement, Warburg Jl, Shakespeare Survey, Shakespeare Quarterly, Shakespeare Jahrbuch, Encyc. Britannica, etc. *Recreations:* theatre, typography, sculpting (one-man exhibns at Exeter, Cardiff, Swansea, Plymouth, Southampton, Aberystwyth, Glasgow, Stirling, Birmingham, 1971-). *Address:* 16 St Mary's Road, Leamington Spa, Warwicks. *T:* Leamington 314253.

MERCIECA, Most Rev. Joseph; *see* Malta, Archbishop of, (RC).

MEREDITH, John Michael; barrister-at-law; a Recorder of the Crown Court, since 1976; *b* 23 Oct. 1934; *s* of late John Stanley Meredith and of Lily Meredith; *m* 1969, Penelope Ann Sykes; one *s* two *d. Educ:* Crossley and Porter Schs, Halifax, Yorks; Leeds Univ. (LLB Hons 1956). Called to the Bar, Gray's Inn, 1958. Chm., J. T. Meredith (Carbonisers) Ltd, Sowerby Bridge, W Yorks. *Recreations:* shooting, sailing. *Address:* Cooper House, Luddenden Foot, West Yorks. *T:* Halifax 883378. *Clubs:* Pwllheli Sailing (N Wales); Queen's Sports (Halifax).

MEREDITH, Richard Alban Creed, MA; Head Master of Monkton Combe School, since 1978; *b* 1 Feb. 1935; *s* of late Canon R. Creed Meredith; *m* 1968, Hazel Eveline Mercia Parry; one *s* one *d. Educ:* Stowe Sch.; Jesus Coll., Cambridge. Asst Master (Modern Langs), 1957-70, Housemaster, 1962-70, King's Sch., Canterbury; Headmaster, Giggleswick Sch., 1970-78. *Recreations:* walking, foreign travel, music, gardening. *Address:* Head Master's House, Shaft Road, Monkton Combe School, Bath BA2 7HH. *T:* Limpley Stoke 3278.

MEREDITH DAVIES, (James) Brian; *see* Davies.

MERIFIELD, Anthony James; Under Secretary, Department of Health and Social Security, since 1978; *b* 5 March 1934; *s* of late Francis Bertram Merifield and Richardina (*née* Parker); *m* 1980, Pamela Pratt. *Educ:* Chesterfield Sch.; Shrewsbury Sch.; Wadham Coll., Oxford (BA). National Service, 1952-54, Royal Tank Regt. HM Overseas Civil Service, Kenya, 1958-65; Department of Health and Social Security: Principal, 1965-71; Asst Sec., 1971-77; Under Secretary, 1978; Director of Establishments and Personnel (HQ), 1979-. *Address:* 49 Carson Road, SE21 8HT. *T:* 01-670 1546. *Club:* Royal Commonwealth Society.

MERITT, Benjamin Dean; Visiting Scholar, University of Texas, since 1973; *b* at Durham, North Carolina, 31 March 1899; *s* of Arthur Herbert Meritt and Cornelia Frances Dean; *m* 1st, 1923, Mary Elizabeth Kirkland; two *s*; 2nd, 1964, Lucy T. Shoe. *Educ:* Hamilton Coll. (AB 1920, AM 1923, LLD 1937); American Sch. of Class. Studies at Athens. AM Princeton 1923, PhD 1924, LittD 1947; DLitt Oxford, 1936; LLD Glasgow, 1948; LHD: University of Pennsylvania, 1967; Brown Univ., 1974; Dr *hc* Sch. of Philosophy, Univ. of Athens, 1970. Instr Greek Univ. of Vermont, 1923-24; Brown Univ., 1924-25; Asst Prof. Greek, Princeton, 1925-26; Asst Dir Am. Sch. of Class. Studies at Athens, 1926-28; Associate Prof. Greek and Latin, University of Michigan, 1928-29, Prof. 1929-33; Visiting Prof. Am. Sch. Class. Studies at Athens, 1932-33; Dir Athens Coll., 1932-33; Francis White Prof. of Greek, Johns Hopkins, 1933-35; lecturer at Oxford, 1935; Annual Prof. Am. Sch. of Class. Studies at Athens, 1936, 1954-55, 1969-70; Eastman Prof., Oxford Univ., 1945-46; Sather Prof., University of California, 1959; Prof. of Greek Epigraphy, Inst. for Advanced Study, Princeton, NJ, 1935-69, Emeritus, 1969; Vis. Prof., Univ. of Texas, 1972; Member: American Philosophical Soc.; German Archae. Inst.; Fellow American Academy of Arts and Sciences; Corr. fellow British Academy; hon. councillor, Greek Archæ. Soc.; hon. mem. Michigan Acad. of Sciences, Arts and Letters, Society for the Promotion of Hellenic Studies; Assoc. Mem., Royal Flemish Acad.; Foreign Mem., Acad. of Athens; Pres. Amer. Philological Assoc., 1953. Commander: Order of the Phœnix (Greece); Order of George I (Greece). *Publications:* The Athenian Calendar in the Fifth Century, 1928; Supplementum Epigraphicum Graecum, Vol. V (with Allen B. West), 1931; Corinth, Vol. VIII, Part I-Greek Inscriptions, 1931; Athenian Financial Documents, 1932; The Athenian Assessment of 425 BC (with Allen B. West), 1934; Documents on Athenian Tribute, 1937; The Athenian Tribute Lists (with H. T. Wade-Gery and M. F. McGregor), Vol. I, 1939, Vol. II, 1949, Vol. III, 1950, Vol. IV, 1953; Epigraphica Attica, 1940; The Chronology of Hellenistic Athens (with W. K. Pritchett), 1940; The Athenian Year, 1961; (with J. S. Traill) The Athenian Councillors, 1974. *Address:* 712 W 16th Street, Austin, Texas 78701, USA.

MERLE, Robert; Croix du Combattant, 1945; Officier de l'Instruction publique, 1953; Professor of English Literature, University of Paris X, Nanterre, since 1965; Titular Professor: University of Rennes, Brittany, since 1944 (on leave, 1950-51); University of Toulouse since 1957; University of Caen-Rouen, since 1960; University of Algiers, since 1963; *b* 29 Aug. 1908; father an officer; *m* 1st; one *d*; *m* 2nd, 1949; three *s* one *d*; 3rd, 1965; one *s. Educ:* Lycée Michelet, Paris; Sorbonne, Paris. Professor, 1934. Mobilised, 1939; Liaison agent with BEF (prisoner, 1940-43). *Publications:* Oscar Wilde, 1948; Week-end à Zuydcoote, 1949 (awarded Prix Goncourt); La Mort est

mon métier, 1953; L'Ile, 1962 (awarded Prix de la Fraternité) (translated, as The Island, 1964); Un Animal doué de raison, 1967 (Campbell Award, USA) (translated, as The Day of the Dolphin, 1969); Derrière la vitre, 1970; Malevil, 1972; Les hommes protégés, 1974 (translated, as The Virility Factor, 1977); Madrapour, 1976; Fortune de France, 1978; En Nos Vertes Années, 1979; Paris Ma Bonne Ville, 1980; Le Prince que voilà, 1982; *plays:* Flamineo (inspired by Webster's White Devil), 1953; Nouveau Sisyphe; *historical essays:* Moncada, 1965; Ben Bella, 1965; translations, articles. *Recreations:* swimming, tennis, yachting. *Address:* La Malmaison, Grosrouvre, 78490 Montfort L'Amaury, France.

MERMAGEN, Air Commodore Herbert Waldemar, CB 1960; CBE 1945 (OBE 1941); AFC 1940; retired, 1960; Director, Sharps, Pixley Ltd, 1962-77; *b* 1 Feb. 1912; *s* of late L. W. R. Mermagen, Southsea; *m* 1937, Rosemary, *d* of late Maj. Mainwaring Williams, DSO and late Mrs Tristram Fox, Cheltenham; two *s. Educ:* Brighton Coll., Sussex. Joined RAF, 1930; 43(F) Sqdn, 1931-34; Instructor CFS, 1936-38; Squadron Leader, 1938; served War of 1939-45 in Fighter Command, UK, Middle East, France and Germany (SHAEF); AOC British Air Command, Berlin, 1945-46; Sen. RAF Liaison Officer, UK Services Liaison Staff, Australia, 1948-50; AOC, RAF Ceylon, 1955-57; Air Officer i/c Administration, Headquarters, RAF Transport Command, 1958-60. Air Commodore, 1955. Comdr Legion of Merit (USA), 1946; Medal for Distinguished Services (USSR), 1945; Chevalier, Légion d'Honneur (France) 1951. *Recreations:* rugby (RAF (colours), Sussex, Richmond), golf, gardening. *Address:* Allandale, Vicarage Street, Painswick, Glos. *Club:* Royal Air Force.

MERMAGEN, Patrick Hassell Frederick, TD; MA Cantab; Headmaster, Ipswich School, 1950-72; *s* of late L. H. Mermagen, MA, Taunton; *m* 1st, 1934, Neva Sonia (*d* 1953), *d* of late E. Haughton James, Forton House, Chard, Somerset; two *s* one *d* (and one *s* decd); 2nd, 1965, Inge (*née* Schütt), Hamburg; one *s* one *d. Educ:* Sherborne Sch.; Pembroke Coll., Cambridge (Open Scholar in Mathematics). Asst master, Loretto Sch., 1933-39, Radley Coll., 1939-50. Served War of 1939-45, Sept. 1940-Feb. 1946, The Royal Berkshire Regt; Staff Coll., Camberley (sc), 1944; held appointments in NW Europe and in SE Asia. *Recreations:* cricket, golf, gardening. *Address:* The Old Rectory, Otley, Ipswich IP6 9NP. *T:* Helmingham 495. *Club:* MCC.

MERRELLS, Thomas Ernest; Lord Mayor of Cardiff, May 1970-71; *b* 5 Aug. 1891; *s* of Thomas Arthur Merrells, OBE, JP, and Kate Merrells, Swansea; *m* 1922, Vera Pughe Charles; one *s* one *d. Educ:* Bishop Gore Grammar Sch., Swansea. Served European War, 1914-18, in France; commissioned in Welsh Regt; seconded to HQ Staff, Royal Engineers, 1917; War of 1939-45: Chm., S Wales Area Nat. Dock Labour Bd; Mem., Exec. Cttee, Regional Port Director of Bristol Channel. Dep. Chm., S Wales Fedn of Port Employers, 1926-47, and Chm., Jt Conciliation Cttee for S Wales Ports. Councillor, City of Cardiff, 1951-74; Alderman, 1966-74. Freeman of City of London, 1971. Chevalier, Order of Mérite Social (France), 1958. *Recreation:* golf. *Address:* 151 Cyncoed Road, Cardiff. *T:* Cardiff 753321. *Clubs:* Cardiff Athletic and Rugby; Cardiff Golf.

MERRETT, Charles Edwin, CBE 1979; Area Organiser, Union of Shop, Distributive and Allied Workers, since 1948; *b* 26 Jan. 1923; *s* of Charles and Eva Merrett; *m* 1950, Mildred Merrett; two *s. Educ:* Palfrey Junior Boys' Sch., Walsall. Bristol City Council: Councillor, 1957-, Leader, 1974-78; Lord Mayor of Bristol, 1978-79, Dep. Lord Mayor, 1979-80. Member: Policy Cttee, Assoc. of District Councils, 1974-78; Jt Consultative Cttee of Local Govt Finance, 1975-78; Chm., Adv. Council, BBC Radio Bristol, 1979-. *Recreations:* watching football; cricket, music, theatre. *Address:* 13 Gainsborough Square, Lockleaze, Bristol BS7 9XA. *T:* Bristol 515195.

MERRIMAN, Dr Basil Mandeville; FRAS, FRAI, FRGS; *b* 28 March 1911; *s* of Thomas Henry Merriman and Ida, *d* of Mandeville Blackwood Phillips; *m* 1938, Yvonne Flavelle (*d* 1974); one *s. Educ:* Colet Court Prep. Sch.; St Paul's School; St Bartholomew's Hospital Med. Coll.; MRCS, LRCP 1934. House Appointments, St Bartholomew's Hosp., 1934-36; post graduate studies, Berlin, Vienna, Prague, 1936-38; Medical Adviser, British Drug Houses, 1938; Med. Dir, Carter Foundn, 1956; Consultant, Home Office Prison Department, 1963. FRAS 1972; Fellow, Royal Soc. for Asian Affairs, 1973; FRAI 1974; FRGS 1976. *Publications:* contribs to medical and social jls on drug action and drug addiction and their relationship to crime, also various related aspects of social anthropology. *Recreation:* travel of all forms, particularly Asiatic (journeys mainly in Arab Asia, Central Asiatic region, and Japan). *Address:* 85 Holland Park, W11 3RZ. *T:* 01-727 8228.

MERRIMAN, Air Vice-Marshal Henry Alan, CBE 1973; AFC 1957, and Bar 1961; Military Deputy to Head of Defence Sales, since 1981; *b* 17 May 1929; *s* of Henry Victor Merriman and Winifred Ellen Merriman; *m* 1965, Mary Brenda Stephenson; three *d. Educ:* Hertford Grammar Sch.; RAF Coll., Cranwell. Graduate, Empire Test Pilots Sch. FRAeS 1977. Commnd, 1951; Qual. Flying Instr, 263 F Sqdn, Empire Test Pilots Sch., Fighter Test Sqdn, A&AEE, Central Fighter Estabt, and RAF Staff Coll., 1952-63; Personal Air Sec. to Minister of Defence for RAF, 1964-66; Jt Services Staff Coll., 1966; OC Fighter Test Sqdn, A&AEE, 1966-69; HQ 38 Gp, 1969-70; Stn Comdr, RAF Wittering, 1970-72; RCDS, 1973; CO Empire Test Pilots Sch., 1974-75; Comdt, A&AEE, 1975-77; Dir, Operational Requirements (1), 1977-81. Queen's Commendation for Valuable Services in the Air, 1956. *Recreations:*

sailing, gardening. *Address:* c/o Lloyds Bank Ltd, Cox's and King's Branch, 6 Pall Mall, SW1. *Clubs:* Royal Air Force; Poole Yacht.

MERRIMAN, James Henry Herbert, CB 1969; OBE 1961; MSc, MInstP, FEng, FIEE, FIEETE; Chairman, National Computing Centre, since 1977; Member for Technology, Post Office Corporation, 1969-76; *b* 1 Jan. 1915; *s* of Thomas P. Merriman, AMINA and A. Margaretta Jenkins; *m* 1942, Joan B. Frost; twin *s* one *d. Educ:* King's Coll. Sch., Wimbledon; King's Coll. University of London. BSc (Hons) 1935; MSc (Thesis) 1936. Entered GPO Engrg Dept (Research), 1936; Officer i/c Castleton Radio Stn, 1940; Asst Staff Engr, Radio Br., 1951; Imp. Def. Coll., 1954; Dep. Dir, Organisation and Methods, HM Treasury, 1956; GPO: Dep. Engr-in-Chief, 1965; Sen. Dir Engrg, 1967. Chairman: NEDO Sector Working Party on Office Machinery, 1979-; NEDO Information Technology Cttee, 1980- (Mem. NEDO Electronics EDC, 1980-); SERC/DoI/Industry Project Universe Standing Cttee, 1981-; Home Office Radio Spectrum Review Cttee, 1982-. Vis. Prof. of Electronic Science and Telecommunications, Strathclyde Univ., 1969-79. Governor, Imperial College, Univ. of London, 1971-; Chm., Inspec, 1975-79; Dir, Infoline, 1976-80; Member: Nat. Electronics Council, 1969-76; Computer Bd for Univ. and Res. Councils, 1976-81; Exec. Bd, BSI, 1981- (Chm. Council for Inf. Systems); Science Museum Adv. Council, 1976-81; Council, Spurgeon's Coll. Mem. Council, IEE, 1965-80 (Chm. Electronics Div. Bd, 1968; Vice-Pres., 1969-72, Dep. Pres., 1972; Pres., 1974-75; Hon. FIEE 1981; Faraday Lectr, 1969-70); Royal Instn Discourse, 1971. FKC 1972. Hon. DSc Strathclyde, 1974. *Publications:* contribs to scientific and professional jls on tele-communications and inf. technology subjects. *Recreations:* walking, organ playing, church work, cactus growing. *Address:* 5 Melville Avenue, Copse Hill, W Wimbledon, SW20. *T:* 01-946 9870.

MERRISON, Sir Alexander Walter, (Sir Alec Merrison), Kt 1976; FRS 1969; DL; Vice-Chancellor, University of Bristol, since 1969; *b* 20 March 1924; *s* of late Henry Walter and Violet Henrietta Merrison; *m* 1st, 1948, Beryl Glencora Le Marquand (*d* 1968); two *s*; 2nd, 1970, Maureen Michèle Barry; one *s* one *d. Educ:* Enfield Gram. Sch.; King's Coll., London. BSc (London) 1944; PhD (Liverpool) 1957. Res. in Radio Wave Propagation, as Experimental Officer, Signals Research and Development Establishment, Christchurch, 1944-46; Research in Reactor and Nuclear Physics, as Sen. Scientific Officer, AERE, Harwell, 1946-51; Research in Elementary Particle Physics, as Leverhulme Fellow and Lecturer, Liverpool Univ., 1951-57; Physicist, European Organisation for Nuclear Research (CERN) Geneva, 1957-60; Prof. of Experimental Physics, Liverpool Univ., 1960-69, and Dir, Daresbury Nuclear Physics Lab., SRC, 1962-69. Regional Dir, Lloyds Bank, 1981-. Chairman: Cttee of Inquiry into Design and Erection of Steel Box Girder Bridges, 1970-73; Cttee of Inquiry into the Regulation of the Medical Profession, 1972-75; Royal Commn on NHS, 1976-79; Adv. Bd for the Research Councils, 1979- (Mem., 1972-73); Cttee of Vice-Chancellors and Principals, 1979-81. Charles Vernon Boys Prizeman of Inst. of Physics and the Physical Soc., 1961, and Mem. Council, 1964-66; Member: Council for Scientific Policy, 1967-72; Nuclear Power Adv. Bd, 1973-76; Adv. Council for Applied R&D, 1979-; Pres. Council, CERN, 1982-. Governor, Bristol Old Vic Trust, 1969-, Chm., 1971-. Mem. Haberdashers' Co., 1982; Freeman, City of London, 1982. FRSA 1970; FKC 1973. DL Avon, 1974. Hon. LLD Bristol, 1971; Hon. DSc: Ulster, 1976; Bath, 1977; Southampton, 1980; Leeds, 1981; Liverpool 1982. *Publications:* contrib. to scientific jls on nuclear and elementary particle physics. *Address:* The University, Senate House, Bristol BS8 1TH. *T:* Bristol 24161, ext. 84. *Club:* Athenæum.

MERRITT, Prof. John Edward; Professor of Educational Studies, Open University, since 1971; *b* 13 June 1926; *s* of Leonard Merritt and Janet (*née* Hartford); *m* 1948, Denise Edmondson; two *s. Educ:* Univ. of Durham (BA); Univ. of London (DipEdPsychol). ABPsS. Sandhurst, 1945-46; Trng Officer, Border Regt, 1946-48. Educnl Psychologist, Lancs LEA, 1957-59; Sen. Educnl Psychologist, Hull LEA, 1959-63; Lectr, Inst. of Educn, Univ. of Durham, 1964-71. Pres., UK Reading Assoc., 1969-70; Chm., 5th World Congress on Reading, Vienna, 1974; Mem., Nat. Cttee of Inquiry into Reading and Use of English (Bullock Cttee), 1973-75. *Publications:* Reading and the Curriculum (ed), 1971; A Framework for Curriculum Design, 1972; (ed jtly) Reading Today and Tomorrow, 1972; (ed jtly) The Reading Curriculum, 1972; Perspectives on Reading, 1973; What Shall We Teach, 1974; numerous papers in educnl jls. *Recreations:* fell walking, climbing, theatre. *Address:* 35 Vicarage Street, Woburn Sands, Milton Keynes MK17 8RE. *T:* Milton Keynes 583546.

MERRIVALE, 3rd Baron, *cr* 1925, of Walkhampton, Co. Devon; **Jack Henry Edmond Duke;** *b* 27 Jan. 1917; *o s* of 2nd Baron Merrivale, OBE, and Odette, *d* of Edmond Roger, Paris; *S* father 1951; *m* 1st, 1939, Colette (marr. diss. 1974), *d* of John Douglas Wise, Bordeaux, France; one *s* one *d*; 2nd, 1975, Betty, *widow* of Paul Baron. *Educ:* Dulwich; Ecole des Sciences Politiques, Paris. Served War of 1939-45, RAF, 1940; Flight-Lieut, 1944 (despatches). Pres., Inst. of Traffic Administration, 1953-70; Chairman: Anglo-Malagasy Soc., 1961; British Cttee for Furthering of Relations with French-speaking Africa, 1973. Founder Mem., Club de Dakar, 1974. FRSA 1964. Chevalier, Nat. Order of Malagasy, 1968. *Recreations:* sailing, riding, photography. *Heir: s* Hon. Derek John Philip Duke, *b* 16 March 1948. *Address:* 16 Brompton Lodge, SW7 2JA. *T:* 01-581 5678.

MERSEY, 4th Viscount *cr* 1916, of Toxteth; **Richard Maurice Clive Bigham;** Baron 1910; Master of Nairne; film director; *b* 8 July 1934; *e s* of

3rd Viscount Mersey, and of 12th Lady Nairne, *qv*; *S* father, 1979; *m* 1961, Joanna, *d* of John A. R. G. Murray, *qv*; one *s. Educ:* Eton and Balliol. Irish Guards, 1952-54 (final rank Lt). FRGS. *Heir: s* hon. Edward John Hallam Bigham, *b* 23 May 1966. *Address:* 1 Rosmead Road, W11. *T:* 01-727 5057.

MERTENS DE WILMARS, Jonkheer Josse Marie Honoré Charles; Chevalier de l'Ordre de Léopold; barrister, Antwerp, since 1935; President, Court of Justice of the European Communities, since 1980 (Judge since 1967); *b* 12 June 1912; *s* of (Marie Antoine Joseph) Albert Mertens de Wilmars and Jeanne Eugénie Marie Anne Meert; *m* 1939, Elisabeth Simone M. Hubertine van Ormelingen; three *s* five *d. Educ:* Abdijschool, Zevenkerke, Bruges; Catholic Univ. of Leuven (Dr in Law, Dr in Pol. and Diplomatic Science). Assessor, Legislative Dept of Council of State, 1950-52, now Hon. Assessor; Member: Chambre des Représentants (Lower House of Belgian Parlt), 1951-62 (Mem., Parly Cttees on For. Affairs, Justice and Reform of Constitution); Belgian Council of Eur. Movement, 1950-; Flemish Bar Assoc. (also Past Pres.); Bar Council, 1964-. Professeur extraordinaire, Faculty of Law, Catholic Univ. of Louvain, 1971-. *Publications:* several works on Belgian and European Law. *Address:* 192 Jan Van Rijswijcklaan, B-2020 Antwerpen, Belgium. *T:* 0032-3-2380768; 12 rue de la Fontaine, Luxembourg.

MERTHYR, Barony of (*cr* 1911); title disclaimed by 4th Baron; *see under* Lewis, Trevor Oswin.

MERTON, Viscount; Simon John Horatio Nelson; *b* 21 Sept. 1971; *s* and heir of 9th Earl Nelson, *qv*.

MERTON, John Ralph, MBE 1942; painter; *b* 7 May 1913; *s* of late Sir Thomas Merton, KBE, FRS; *m* 1939, Viola Penelope von Bernd; two *d* (and one *d* decd). *Educ:* Eton; Balliol Coll., Oxford. Served War of 1939-45 (MBE); Air Photo reconnaissance research, Lieut-Col 1944. Works include: Mrs Daphne Wall, 1948; The Artist's daughter, Sarah, 1949; Altar piece, 1952; The Countess of Dalkeith, at Drumlanrig, 1958; A myth of Delos, 1959; Clarissa, 1960; Lady Georgina Pelham, Mrs Julian Sheffield, 1970; Sir Charles Evans, 1973; Iona Colquhoun Duchess of Argyll, 1982. Legion of Merit (USA), 1945. *Recreations:* music, making things, underwater photography. *Address:* Pound House, Oare, near Marlborough, Wilts; Fourth Floor, 50 Cadogan Square, SW1. *Club:* Garrick.
See also R. A. Morritt.

MERTON, Patrick Anthony, MD; FRS 1979; Reader in Human Physiology, Cambridge University, since 1977; Fellow of Trinity College, Cambridge, since 1962; Hon. Consultant to the National Hospital, London, since 1979; Hon. Senior Research Fellow, Royal Postgraduate Medical School, since 1981; *b* 8 Oct. 1920; *s* of Gerald Merton, MC, PhD, FRAS, and Mary Elizabeth (*née* Crowley); *m* 1951, Anna Gabriel, third *d* of Foster Garfield Howe and Annie (*née* Millhoff); one *s* three *d. Educ:* The Leys Sch.; Beaumont Coll.; Trinity Coll., Cambridge (MB 1946); St Thomas's Hosp. Med. Sch.; MD 1982. On staff of MRC's Neurol. Res. Unit, National Hosp., 1946-57; Nobel Inst. for Neurophysiology, Stockholm, 1952-54; Lectr in Physiol., Cambridge, 1957-77. *Publications:* papers on control of muscular contraction mainly in Jl of Physiol. *Address:* 12 Lansdowne Road, Cambridge CB3 0EU. *T:* Cambridge 359991.

MERTON, Air Chief Marshal Sir Walter (Hugh), GBE 1963 (OBE 1941); KCB 1959 (CB 1953); *b* 29 Aug. 1905; *s* of late G. R. Merton; *m* 1st, 1930, B. H. B. Kirby (from whom he obtained a divorce, 1932); one *s*; 2nd, 1938, Margaret Ethel Wilson, 2nd *d* of late J. C. Macro Wilson, Cossington Manor, Som. *Educ:* Eastbourne Coll.; RAF Cadet Coll., Cranwell. Commissioned, 1925; Wing Comdr, 1940; served War of 1939-45 (despatches thrice); Middle East, 1940-43: Directing Staff and Asst Comdt, RAF War Staff Coll., 1943-44; Dir of Organization, Air Ministry, 1944-45. Air Attaché, Prague, 1947-48; AOC and Head of RAF Delegation, Greece, 1949-50. AOC No. 63 (Western and Welsh) Group, 1951-52; AOC No. 22 Gp, Tech. Trg Comd, 1952-53; Chief of the Air Staff, Royal NZ Air Force, 1954-56; Air Officer in charge of Administration, Headquarters Bomber Command, RAF High Wycombe, 1956-59; Chief of Staff, Allied Air Forces, Central Europe, 1959-60; Air Mem. for Supply and Organisation, April 1960-Aug. 1963, retd; Inspector General of Civil Defence, 1964-68. Air Cdre, 1949; Air Vice-Marshal, 1953; Air Marshal, 1959; Air Chief Marshal, 1961. Air ADC to the Queen, 1962-63. Gold Cross, Royal Order of George I, with crossed swords (Greece), 1941; Order of the Phœnix, Class I (Greece), 1963. *Address:* Hart House, Martin, Fordingbridge, Hants SP6 3LF. *T:* Martin Cross 237. *Club:* Royal Air Force.

MERVYN DAVIES, David Herbert; *see* Davies, D. H. M.

MESSEL, Prof. Harry, CBE 1979; BA, BSc, PhD (NUI) 1951; Professor and Head of the School of Physics, and Director of Science Foundation for Physics, University of Sydney, Australia, since 1952; *b* 3 March 1922. *Educ:* Rivers Public High Sch., Rivers, Manitoba. Entered RMC of Canada, 1940, grad. with Governor-General's Silver Medal, 1942. Served War of 1939-45: Canadian Armed Forces, Lieut, Canada and overseas, 1942-45. Queen's Univ., Kingston, Ont., 1945-48; BA 1st Cl. Hons in Mathematics, 1948. BSc Hons in Engineering Physics, 1948; St Andrews Univ., Scotland, 1948-49; Institute for Advanced Studies, Dublin, Eire, 1949-51; Sen. Lectr in Mathematical

Physics, University of Adelaide, Australia, 1951-52. Mem., Aust. Atomic Energy Commn, 1974-81. *Publications:* Chap. 4, Progress in Cosmic Ray Physics, vol. 2, (North Holland Publishing Company), 1953; numerous papers published in: Proc. Physical Soc., London; Philosophical Magazine, London; Physical Review of America; Co-author and Editor of: A Modern Introduction to Physics (Horwitz-Grahame, Vols I, II, III, 1959, 1960, 1962); Selected Lectures in Modern Physics, 1958; Science for High School Students, 1964; Senior Science for High School Students, 1966; (jt) Electron-Photon Shower Distribution Function, 1970; editor of: From Nucleus to Universe, 1960; Space and the Atom, 1961; A Journey Through Space and the Atom, 1962; The Universe of Time and Space, 1963; Light and Life in the Universe, 1964; Time, 1965; Atoms to Andromeda, 1966; Apollo and the Universe, 1967; Man in Inner and Outer Space, 1968; Nuclear Energy Today and Tomorrow, 1969; Pioneering in Outer Space, 1970; Molecules to Man, 1971; Brain Mechanisms and the Control of Behaviour, 1972; Focus on the Stars, 1973; Solar Energy, 1974; (ed jtly and part author) Multistrand Senior Science for High School Students, 1975; (ed) Our Earth, 1975; Australian Animals and their Environment, 1977; (ed) Energy for Survival, 1979; (ed, and jt author) Tidal Rivers in Northern Australia and their Crocodile Populations (17 monographs), 1979-82; (ed) The Biological Manipulation of Life, 1981. *Recreations:* water ski-ing, hunting, fishing and photography. *Address:* University of Sydney, Sydney, NSW 2006, Australia. *T:* 692 2537, 692 3383.

MESSER, Malcolm, CBE 1949; *b* 1901; *s* of late Andrew Messer, MB, ChM; *m* 1943, Mary (*d* 1951), *er d* of G. F. Grigs; one *d*. *Educ:* Edinburgh Univ. (MA); Oxford Univ. (BA). Research Asst, Agricultural Economics Research Institute, Oxford, 1927-34; Technical Editor, Farmers' Weekly, 1934-38; Editor, Farmers' Weekly, 1938-66, retired editorship, 1 July 1966. Chm., Farm Journals Ltd, 1966-69. *Address:* 66, Tarlton, near Cirencester, Glos.

MESSERVY, Professor Albert; Professor of Veterinary Surgery, University of Bristol, 1953-73, now Emeritus Professor; *b* 8 Feb. 1908; 2nd *s* of late E. P. Messervy, Jersey; *m* May, *d* of late F. E. Luce, Jersey; two *s* one *d*. *Educ:* Victoria Coll., Jersey; Royal Veterinary Coll., London. Private practice, 1929-40; Lecturer. Dept of Veterinary Surgery, Royal Vet. Coll., 1941-45; private practice, 1945-53. Mem. of Council, RCVS, 1957-65; Pres., Royal Jersey Agric. and Hort. Soc., 1974-77. Hon. MSc, 1964. *Publications:* clinical veterinary. *Recreation:* fishing. *Address:* Ville à L'Eveque, Trinity, Jersey, Channel Islands. *T:* Jersey Central 62588.

MESSERVY, (Roney) Godfrey (Collumbell); Chairman and Chief Executive, Lucas Industries plc, since 1980 (Managing Director, 1974; Deputy Chairman, 1979); *b* 17 Nov. 1924; *s* of late Roney Forshaw Messervy and Bertha Crosby (*née* Collumbell); *m* 1952, Susan Patricia Gertrude, *d* of late Reginald Arthur Nunn, DSO, DSC, RNVR, and of Adeline Frances Nunn; one *s* two *d*. *Educ:* Oundle; Cambridge Univ. Served War, RE, 1943-47: Parachute Sqdn (Captain). CAV (then of Lucas Group): joined as trainee, 1949; Dir of Equipment Sales, 1963; Dir and Gen. Man., 1966 (also dir of various Lucas subsids at home and abroad). Director: Joseph Lucas Ltd, 1971-; Joseph Lucas (Industries) Ltd, 1972-; Costain Group plc, 1978-. Member: Council, Birmingham Chamber of Industry and Commerce, 1979- (Vice-Pres., 1980-82, Pres., 1982-); Council, SMMT, 1980- (Mem. Exec. Cttee); Engrg Industries Council, 1980-; Nat. Defence Industries Council, 1980-. Freeman, Worshipful Co. of Ironmongers, 1977, Liveryman, 1979. Hon. DSc Aston in Birmingham, 1982. *Recreations:* farming, field sports, flying, photography. *Address:* Lucas Industries Ltd, Great King Street, Birmingham B19 2XF. *T:* 021-554 5252.

MESSIAEN, Olivier; Grand Officier de la Légion d'Honneur; Grand Officier de l'Ordre national du Mérite; Commandeur des Arts et des Lettres; Member, Institut de France; composer and organist; *b* Avignon, 10 Dec. 1908; *s* of Pierre Messiaen and Cécile Sauvage; *m* 1st, Claire Delbos (*d* 1959); one *s*; 2nd, 1961, Yvonne Loriod (pianist). *Educ:* Lycée de Grenoble; Conservatoire Nat. supérieur de musique (7 1st prizes). Organist, Trinité, Paris, 1930; co-founder Jeune-France Movement, 1936. Professor: Ecole Normale and Schola Cantorum, 1936-39; of Harmony, Paris Conservatoire, 1941-47; of Analysis, Aesthetics and Rhythm, 1947-; of Composition, 1966-. Mem. Council, Order of Arts and Letters, 1975-. Member: Royal Academy; Acads of Brussels, Madrid, Stockholm. Erasmus Prize, 1971; Sibelius Prize, 1971, Van Siemens Prize, 1975, Léonie Sonning Prize, 1977. *Works for organ include:* Le Banquet Céleste, 1928; Le Diptyque, 1929; L'Ascension, 1933; La Nativité du Seigneur, 1935; Les Corps Glorieux, 1939; Messe de la Pentecôte, 1949; Livre d'Orgue, 1951; Méditations sur le Mystère de la Sainte Trinité, 1969; *other works include:* Préludes, 1929; Poèmes pour Mi, 1936; Chants de Terre et de Ciel, 1938; Quatuor pour la Fin du Temps, 1941; Visions de l'Amen, 1943; Vingt Regards sur l'Enfant Jésus, 1944; Trois Petites Liturgies de la Présence Divine, 1944; Harawi, 1945; Turangalila Symphonie, 1946-48; Cinq Rechants, 1949; Etudes de Rythme, 1949; Réveil des Oiseaux, 1953; Oiseaux exotiques, 1955; Catalogue d'Oiseaux, 1956-58; Chronochromie, 1959; Sept Haïkaï, 1963; Couleurs de la Cité Céleste, 1964; Et Exspecto Resurrectionem Mortuorum, 1965; La Transfiguration de Notre Seigneur, Jésus-Christ, 1969; Des Canyons aux Etoiles, 1970-74.

MESSITER, Air Commodore Herbert Lindsell, CB 1954; 2nd *s* of late Col Charles Bayard Messiter, DSO, OBE, Barwick Park, Yeovil, Som, and Alice Lindsell; *m* 1933, Lucy Brenda Short; one *d*. *Educ:* Bedford Sch. Served War of 1939-45 (despatches 4 times): Egypt, N Africa, Belgium, Germany.

Command Engineer Officer, Far East Air Force, 1950-52; Senior Technical Staff Officer, Bomber Command, RAF, 1952-56; Senior Technical Staff Officer, Middle East Air Force, 1956-59, retired. *Address:* c/o Lloyds Bank Ltd, 6 Pall Mall, SW1; Lion Cottage, Grateley, Hants. *Club:* Royal Air Force.

MESSMER, Pierre Auguste Joseph; Grand Officier de la Légion d'Honneur; Compagnon de la Libération; Croix de Guerre, 1939-45; Médaille de la Résistance; Député (RFR) from Moselle, since 1968; Member, European Parliament, since 1979; *b* Vincennes (Seine), 20 March 1916; *s* of Joseph Messmer, industrialist, and of Marthe (*née* Farcy); *m* 1947, Gilberte Duprez. *Educ:* Lycées Charlemagne and Louis-le Grand; Faculty of Law, Paris; Ecole Nationale de la France d'Outre-Mer. Pupil Administrator of Colonies, 1938. Served War of 1939-45: Free French Forces, 1940; African Campaigns (Bir-Hakeim), France, Germany; parachuted Tonkin; PoW of Vietminh, 1945. Sec.-Gen., Interministerial Cttee of Indochina, 1946; Dir of Cabinet of E. Bollaert (High Commissioner, Indochina), 1947-48; Administrator-in-Chief of France Overseas, 1950; Governor: of Mauritania, 1952, of Ivory Coast, 1954-56; Dir of Cabinet of G. Defferre (Minister, France Overseas), Jan.-April 1956; High Commissioner: Republic of Cameroon, 1956-58; French Equatorial Africa, 1958; French West Africa, July 1958-Dec. 1959; Minister of Armed Forces: (Cabinets: M. Debré, 5 Feb. 1958-14 April 1962; G. Pompidou, April-Nov. 1962, 6 Dec. 1962-7 Jan. 1966, 8 Jan. 1966-1 April 1967, 7 April 1967-10 July 1968; M. Couve de Murville, 12 July 1968-20 June 1969); Minister of State in charge of Depts and Territories Overseas, Feb. 1971-72; Prime Minister, 1972-74. Pres., RFR Federal Cttee, Moselle, 1969-. Mayor of Sarrebourg, 1971-. Officer, American Legion. *Recreations:* tennis, sailing. *Address:* 1 rue du Général Delanne, 92 Neuilly-sur-Seine, France.

MESTEL, Prof. Leon, PhD; FRS 1977; Professor of Astronomy, University of Sussex, since 1973; *b* 5 Aug. 1927; *s* of late Rabbi Solomon Mestel and Rachel (*née* Brodetsky); *m* 1951, Sylvia Louise Cole; two *s* two *d*. *Educ:* West Ham Secondary Sch., London; Trinity Coll., Cambridge (BA 1948, PhD 1952). ICI Res. Fellow, Dept of Maths, Univ. of Leeds, 1952-54; Commonwealth Fund Fellow, Princeton Univ. Observatory, 1954-55; University of Cambridge: Univ. Asst Lectr in Maths, 1955-58; Univ. Lectr in Maths, 1958-66; Fellow of St John's Coll., 1957-66; Vis. Mem., Inst. for Advanced Study, Princeton, 1961-62; J. F. Kennedy Fellow, Weizmann Inst. of Science, Israel, 1966-67; Prof. of Applied Maths, Manchester Univ., 1967-73. *Publications:* Magnetohydrodynamics (with N. O. Weiss), 1974 (Geneva Observatory); papers, revs and conf. reports on different branches of theoretical astrophysics. *Recreations:* reading, music. *Address:* 13 Prince Edward's Road, Lewes, E Sussex BN7 1BJ. *T:* Lewes 2731.

MESTON, family name of **Baron Meston.**

MESTON, 2nd Baron, *cr* 1919, of Agra and Dunottar; **Dougall Meston;** *b* 17 Dec. 1894; *s* of 1st Baron and Jeanie, CBE (*d* 1946), *o d* of James M'Donald; *S* father, 1943; *m* 1947, Diana Mary Came, *o d* of late Capt. O. S. Doll, 16 Upper Cheyne Row, Chelsea; two *s*. *Educ:* Charterhouse; RMA, Woolwich. Served European War, 1914-19; Capt., RA, 1917; N-W Frontier, India (Afghan War, 1919, Waziristan, 1919-20); retired, 1922; Barrister, Lincoln's Inn, 1924. Hon. Mem. Incorporated Association of Architects and Surveyors. President, British Soc. of Commerce. Contested (L) Southend Bye-Election, 1927, and General Election, 1929. *Publications:* Law of Moneylenders; Law of Nuisances; The Restrictive Trade Practices Act, 1956; The Rent Act, 1957; The Rating and Valuation Act, 1961; The Betting, Gaming and Lotteries Act, 1963; The Offices, Shops and Railway Premises Act, 1963; Weights and Measures Act, 1963; Rent Act, 1965; Leasehold Reform Act, 1967; The Gaming Act, 1968; Industrial Relations Act, 1971; Consumer Credit Act, 1974; several works on Gaming, Landlord and Tenant, War Damage, Local Government, Town and Country Planning, Highways, Trade Wastes, Public Health and Housing Acts; Jt Ed. of Mather's Sheriff and Execution Law (3rd edn). *Heir:* *s* Hon. James Meston [*b* 10 Feb. 1950; *m* 1974, Anne, *yr d* of John Carder; one *s* one *d*]. *Address:* Hurst Place, Cookham Dene, Berks; Queen Elizabeth Building, Temple, EC4. *T:* 01-353 3911. *Club:* Reform.

METCALF, Malcolm, MC 1944; DL; Chairman, Surrey County Council, 1978-81; *b* 1 Dec. 1917; *s* of Charles Almond Metcalf and Martha Fatherly Atkins Metcalf; *m* 1945, Charis Thomas; two *s*. *Educ:* Merchant Taylors' Sch., Crosby. ACIS. Army service, 1939-46. Contested (C) Barrow-in-Furness, 1959; Mem., Surrey CC, 1965- (Leader, 1973-77; Vice-Chm., 1977-78); Member: Metrop. Water Board, 1965-74 (Vice-Chm. 1971-72); Thames Conservancy, 1970-74; Thames Water Authority, 1973-78, 1981-. Mem., Assoc. of County Councils, 1975-. DL Surrey, 1979. *Address:* Linden, Clive Road, Esher, Surrey KT10 8PS. *T:* Esher 64476. *Clubs:* MCC, Burhill Golf (Walton-on-Thames).

METCALFE, Air Commodore Joan, CB 1981; RRC 1976; Director of RAF Nursing Services, and Matron in Chief, Princess Mary's Royal Air Force Nursing Service, 1978-81; *b* 8 Jan. 1923; *d* of late W. and S. H. Metcalfe. *Educ:* West Leeds High Sch. for Girls; Leeds Coll. of Commerce. St James's Hosp., Leeds, 1943-47 (SRN); St James's Hosp. and Redcourt Hostel, Leeds, 1947-48 (SCM), PMRAFNS 1948. Served in RAF Hospitals in Egypt, Iraq, Libya, Cyprus, Germany, Singapore, and UK. Sen. Matron, 1970; Principal Matron, 1973. QHNS 1978-81. OStJ 1977. *Recreations:* classical music, theatre, needlework, gardening, non-fiction literature. *Address:* 10 Amport Close,

Harestock, Winchester, Hants SO22 6LP. *T:* Winchester 880260. *Club:* Royal Air Force.

METCALFE, Stanley Gordon; Managing Director, Ranks Hovis McDougall Ltd, since 1981; *b* 20 June 1932; *s* of Stanley Hudson Metcalfe and Jane Metcalfe; *m* 1968, Sarah Harter; two *d. Educ:* Leeds Grammar Sch.; Pembroke Coll., Oxford (MA). Trainee, Ranks, Hovis McDougall, 1956-59; Director, Stokes & Dalton, Leeds, 1963-66; Managing Director, McDougalls, 1966-69; Director, Cerebos Ltd, 1969-70; Managing Director: RHM Overseas Ltd, 1970-73; RHM Cereals Ltd, 1973-79; Director, Ranks Hovis McDougall Ltd, 1979. President, Nat. Assoc. of British and Irish Millers, 1978. *Recreations:* cricket, golf, theatre. *Address:* The Oast House, Lower Froyle, Alton, Hants GU34 4LX. *T:* Bentley 22310. *Clubs:* MCC, IZ, Arabs.

METFORD, Prof. John Callan James; Professor of Spanish, 1960-81, now Emeritus Professor, Head of Department of Hispanic and Latin American Studies, 1973-81, University of Bristol; *b* 29 Jan. 1916; *s* of Oliver Metford and Florence Stowe Thomas; *m* 1944, Edith Donald; one *d. Educ:* Porth Grammar Sch.; Universities of Liverpool, Yale and California. Commonwealth Fund Fellow, 1939-41; British Council Lecturer in Brazil, 1942-44; Regional Officer, Latin American Department of the British Council, 1944-46; Lectr in Latin American Studies, Univ. of Glasgow, 1946-55; Bristol University: Head of Dept of Spanish and Portuguese, 1955-73; Prof., 1960-81; Dean of Faculty of Arts, 1973-76; Chm., Sch. of Modern Langs, 1976-79. Vis. Prof., Lehigh Univ., USA, 1968-69. Chm., Council of Westonbirt Sch.; Mem., Central Cttee of Allied Schs; Governor, Coll. of St Matthias, Bristol, 1960-79; Mem., St Matthias Trust; Professorial Mem., Council of Univ. of Bristol, 1972-74. *Publications:* British Contributions to Spanish and Spanish American Studies, 1950; San Martín the Liberator, 1950, 2nd edn 1970; Modern Latin America, 1964; The Golden Age of Spanish Drama, 1969; Falklands or Malvinas?, rev. edn of J. Goebel: The Struggle for the Falkland Islands, 1982; articles in Bulletin of Spanish Studies, Bulletin of Hispanic Studies, Liverpool Studies in Spanish, International Affairs, etc. *Recreations:* opera, iconography. *Address:* 2 Parry's Close, Bristol BS9 1AW. *T:* Bristol 682284. *Clubs:* Royal Commonwealth Society (London); Royal Commonwealth Society (Bristol).

METHUEN, family name of **Baron Methuen.**

METHUEN, 6th Baron *cr* 1838; **Anthony John Methuen,** ARICS; *b* 26 Oct. 1925; *s* of 5th Baron Methuen and Grace (*d* 1972), *d* of Sir Richard Holt, 1st Bt; *S* father, 1975. *Educ:* Winchester; Royal Agricultural Coll., Cirencester. Served Scots Guards and Royal Signals, 1943-47. Lands Officer, Air Ministry, 1951-62; QALAS 1954. *Recreation:* shooting. *Heir:* b Hon. Robert Alexander Holt Methuen [*b* 22 July 1931; *m* 1958, Mary Catharine Jane, *d* of Ven. C. G. Hooper, *qv*; two *d.] Address:* Corsham Court, Wilts. *Clubs:* Lansdowne; Royal Motor Yacht (Poole).

METZGER, Rev. Prof. Bruce Manning; George L. Collord Professor of New Testament Language and Literature, Princeton Theological Seminary, since 1964; *b* Middletown, Pa, 9 Feb. 1914; *o s* of late Maurice R. Metzger and Anna Manning Metzger; *m* 1944, Isobel Elizabeth, *e d* of Rev. John Alexander Mackay, *qv*; two *s. Educ:* Lebanon Valley Coll. (BA 1935); Princeton Theol Seminary (ThB 1938, ThM 1939); Princeton Univ. (MA 1940, PhD 1942, Classics). Ordained, United Presbyterian Church, USA, 1939; Princeton Theological Seminary: Teaching Fellow in NT Greek, 1938-40; Instr. in NT, 1940-44; Asst Prof., 1944-48; Associate Prof., 1948-54; Prof., 1954-64. Vis. Lectr, Sem. Theol. Presbyt. do Sul, Campinas, Brazil, 1952; Schol. in Residence, Tyndale Hse, Cambridge, 1969; Dist. Vis. Prof., Fuller Theol Sem., 1970; Vis. Fellow: Clare Hall, Cambridge, 1974; Wolfson Coll., Oxford, 1979; Vis. Prof., Gordon-Conwell Theol Sem., 1978; Lectr, New Coll. for Advanced Christian Studies, 1978; many lectures to other academic instns. Chairman, Amer. Cttee on Versions, Internat. Greek NT Project, 1950-; Secretary: Panel of Translators, Rev. Standard Version of Apocrypha, 1952-57; Amer. Textual Criticism Seminar, 1954-56; Member: Kurat. of Vetus Latina Inst., Beuron, 1959-; Adv. Cttee, Inst. of NT Textual Res. Münster, Germany, 1961-; Inst. for Advanced Study, Princeton, 1964 and 1974; Chairman: Cttee on Trans., Amer. Bible Soc., 1964-70; Amer. Exec. Cttee, Internat. Greek NT Project, 1970-; NT Section, Rev. Standard Version Bible Cttee, 1971-. President: Soc. of Biblical Lit., 1971; Stud. Novi Test. Soc., 1971-72; N Amer. Patristic Soc., 1972; Corresp. Fellow Brit. Acad., 1978; Hon. Fellow and Corresp. Mem., Higher Inst. of Coptic Studies, Cairo, 1955. Hon. DD: Lebanon Valley Coll., 1951 (also Dist. Alumnus award of Alumni Assoc. 1961); St Andrews, 1964; DTheol Münster, 1971; LHD Findlay Coll., 1962. *Publications:* The Saturday and Sunday Lessons from Luke in the Greek Gospel Lectionary, 1944; Lexical Aids for Students of New Testament Greek, 1946, enlarged edn 1955 (trans. Malagasy, Korean); A Guide to the Preparation of a Thesis, 1950, 2nd edn 1961; Index of Articles on the New Testament and the Early Church Published in Festschriften, 1951, Supplement 1955; Annotated Bibliography of the Textual Criticism of the New Testament, 1955; (jtly) The Text, Canon, and Principal Versions of the Bible, 1956; An Introduction to the Apocrypha, 1957; Index to Periodical Literature on the Apostle Paul, 1960, 2nd edn 1970; Lists of Words Occurring Frequently in the Coptic New Testament (Sahidic Dialect), 1961; (jtly) The Oxford Concise Concordance to the Revised Standard Version of the Holy Bible, 1962; (jtly) The Oxford Annotated Bible, 1962; Chapters in the History of New Testament Textual Criticism, 1963; The Text of the New Testament, its Transmission, Corruption, and Restoration, 1964 (trans. German, Japanese,

Chinese); The Oxford Annotated Apocrypha, 1965; The New Testament, its Background, Growth, and Content, 1965 (trans. Chinese); Index to Periodical Literature on Christ and the Gospels, 1966; Historical and Literary Studies, Pagan, Jewish, and Christian, 1968; A Textual Commentary on the Greek New Testament, 1971; The New Oxford Annotated Bible with the Apocrypha, expanded edn 1977; The Early Versions of the New Testament, their Origin, Transmission, and Limitations, 1977; New Testament Studies, Philological, Versional, and Patristic, 1980; Manuscripts of the Greek Bible, an Introduction to Greek Palaeography, 1981; (general editor) Reader's Digest Condensed Bible, 1982; ed, New Testament Tools and Studies, ten vols, 1960-80; co-ed, The Greek New Testament, 1966, 3rd edn 1975; numerous articles in learned jls and encycs. *Recreations:* reading, woodworking. *Address:* 20 Cleveland Lane, Princeton, New Jersey 08540, USA. *T:* (609) 924-4060. *Club:* Nassau (Princeton, New Jersey).

MEXBOROUGH, 8th Earl of, *cr* 1766; **John Christopher George Savile;** Baron Pollington, 1753; Viscount Pollington, 1766; *b* 16 May 1931; *s* of 7th Earl of Mexborough, and of Josephine Bertha Emily, *d* of late Captain Andrew Mansel Talbot Fletcher; *S* father, 1980; *m* 1st, 1958, Elizabeth Hariot (marr. diss. 1972), *d* of 6th Earl of Verulam; one *s* one *d*; 2nd, 1972, Mrs Catherine Joyce Vivian, *d* of J. K. Hope, *qv*; one *s* one *d. Heir: s* Viscount Pollington, *qv. Address:* Arden Hall, Hawnby, York. *T:* Bilsdale 348. *Clubs:* Turf; All England Lawn Tennis and Croquet.

MEYER, Prof. Alfred; Professor of Neuropathology in the University of London, Institute of Psychiatry, 1949-56, retired; *b* 3 Feb. 1895; *m* 1949, Nina Cohen. Assoc. Prof. of Neurology at University of Bonn, 1931; Rockefeller Research Fellow in Pathological Laboratory, Maudlsey Hosp., London, 1933; Neuropathologist in the Pathological Laboratory, Maudsley Hospital, 1943. *Publications:* (jt) Prefrontal Leucotomy and Related Operations: anatomical aspects, 1954; (jt) Neuropathology, 1958, 2nd edn 1963; Historical Aspects of Cerebral Anatomy, 1971; articles on neuroanatomical and neuropathological subjects. *Address:* 38 Wood Lane, N6 5UB.

MEYER, Sir Anthony John Charles, 3rd Bt, *cr* 1910; MP (C) West Flint since 1970; *b* 27 Oct. 1920; *s* of Sir Frank Meyer, MP, 2nd Bt, Ayot House, Ayot St Lawrence, Herts; *S* father, 1935; *m* 1941, Barbadee Violet, *o c* of late A. Charles Knight, JP, and of Mrs Charles Knight, Herne Place, Sunningdale; one *s* three *d. Educ:* Eton (Capt. of Oppidans); New Coll., Oxford. Served Scots Guards, 1941-45 (wounded); HM Treasury, 1945-46; entered HM Foreign Service, 1946; HM Embassy, Paris, 1951; 1st Sec., 1953; transferred to HM Embassy, Moscow, 1956; London, 1958. MP (C) Eton and Slough, 1964-66. Cons. Research Dept, 1968. PPS to Chief Sec., Treasury, 1970-72; PPS to Sec. of State for Employment, 1972-74. Chm., Franco-British Parly Relations Cttee, 1979-; Vice-Chm., Cons. European Affairs Cttee, 1981. Trustee of Shakespeare National Memorial Theatre. Founder and Dir of political jl, Solon, 1969. *Publication:* A European Technological Community, 1966. *Recreations:* music, travel, skiing, cooking. *Heir: s* Anthony Ashley Frank Meyer [*b* 23 Aug. 1944; *m* 1966, Susan Mathilda (marr. diss. 1980), *d* of John Freestone; one *d]. Address:* Cottage Place, Brompton Square, SW3. *T:* 01-589 7416; Rhewl House, Llanasa, Flints. *Club:* Beefsteak.

MEYER, Rt. Rev. Conrad John Eustace; see Dorchester, Bishop Suffragan of.

MEYER, Matt; Newspaperman, USA; *b* Tilden, Ala, 28 Aug. 1904; *s* of Matthew Meyer and Julia Patterson; *m* 1931, Emily Cluett Dorlon; three *d. Educ:* New York University, USA (BCS). With Scripps-Howard Newspapers, 1932: Advertising Dir, Washington Daily News, 1938-47, Pres. and Business Manager, 1947-59; Asst Gen. Business Manager, Scripps-Howard Newspapers, 1959-62; Vice Pres., Business Manager, New York World-Telegram and Sun, 1962-65, Pres., 1965-66; Dir, Scripps-Howard Investment Co.; Pres., World-Journal-Tribune Inc., 1966-68. Chm., Publishers Association, New York City, 1963-65. Chm. and Pres., Scripps Howard Foundn, 1970-. *Recreations:* golf, photography, reading. *Clubs:* Union League (New York); Bald Peak Colony (New Hampshire); Scarsdale Golf.

MEYER, Michael Leverson; free-lance writer since 1950; *b* London, 11 June 1921; 3rd and *y s* of Percy Barrington Meyer and Eleanor Rachel Meyer (*née* Benjamin); unmarried; one *d. Educ:* Wellington Coll.; Christ Church, Oxford (MA). Operational Res. Section, Bomber Comd HQ, 1942-45; Lectr in English Lit., Uppsala Univ., 1947-50. Vis. Prof. of Drama, Dartmouth Coll., USA, 1978. Mem. Editorial Adv. Bd, Good Food Guide, 1958-72. FRSL. Gold Medal, Swedish Academy, 1964. Knight Commander, Polar Star (1st class), Sweden, 1977. *Publications:* (ed, with Sidney Keyes, and contrib.) Eight Oxford Poets, 1941; (ed) Collected Poems of Sidney Keyes, 1945; (ed) The Minos of Crete, by Sidney Keyes, 1948; The End of the Corridor (novel), 1951; The Ortolan (play), 1967; Henrik Ibsen: The Making of a Dramatist, 1967; Henrik Ibsen: The Farewell to Poetry, 1971; Henrik Ibsen: The Top of a Cold Mountain, 1971 (Whitbread Biography Prize, 1971); Lunatic and Lover (play), 1981; (ed) Summer Days, 1981; *translated:* The Long Ships, by Frans G. Bengtsson, 1954; Ibsen: Brand, The Lady from the Sea, John Gabriel Borkman, When We Dead Awaken, 1960; The Master Builder, Little Eyolf, 1961; Ghosts, The Wild Duck, Hedda Gabler, 1962; Peer Gynt, An Enemy of the People, The Pillars of Society, 1963; The Pretenders, 1964; A Doll's House, 1965; Rosmersholm, 1966; Strindberg: The Father, Miss Julie, Creditors, The Stronger, Playing with Fire, Erik the Fourteenth, Storm, The Ghost Sonata, 1964; A Dream Play, 1973; To Damascus, Easter, The Dance of Death, The Virgin Bride, 1975. *Recreations:* real tennis, eating, sleeping. *Address:* 4 Montagu Square, W1H 1RA. *T:* 01–486 2573. *Clubs:* Savile, Garrick, MCC.

MEYER, Rollo John Oliver, (Jack Meyer), OBE 1967; Headmaster, St Lawrence College, Athens, since 1980; *b* 15 March 1905; *s* of Canon Rollo Meyer and Arabella Ward; *m* 1931, Joyce Symons; one *d* (and one *d* decd). *Educ:* Haileybury Coll.; Pembroke Coll., Cambridge. MA 1926. Cottonbroker, Gill & Co., Bombay, 1926–29; Private Tutor, Limbdi, Porbandar, Dhrangadhra, 1929–35; Founder, and Headmaster of Millfield School, 1935–71; founded Edgarley Hall Preparatory Sch., Glastonbury, 1945; Headmaster and President, Campion Sch., Athens, 1973–80. *Recreations:* ornithology, any game with a ball in it, chess, writing, National Hunt racing, shooting. *Address:* Little Scotland, Bleadney, Wells, Somerset BA5 1PJ. *T:* Wedmore 712399; St Lawrence College, Athens, Greece. *Clubs:* MCC, English-Speaking Union, Royal Over-Seas League.

MEYJES, Sir Richard (Anthony), Kt 1972; Chairman, Coates Brothers and Co. Ltd, since 1977 (Deputy Chairman, 1977); Director: Portals Holdings Ltd; Foseco Minsep Ltd; *b* 30 June 1918; *s* of Anthony Charles Dorian Meyjes and late Norah Isobel Meyjes; *m* 1939, Margaret Doreen Morris; three *s.* *Educ:* University College School, Hampstead. War Service, RASC, Sept. 1939-Jan. 1946 (temp. Captain). Qualified as Solicitor, June 1946; Legal Dept, Anglo-Saxon Petroleum Co., 1946-56; Manager, Thailand and Vietnam Division, Shell International Petroleum Co., 1956–58; Marketing Manager, Shell Co. of Philippines, Ltd, Manila, 1958–61; President, 1961–64; Head of Regional Marketing Div., Shell International Petroleum Co., London, 1964–66; Marketing Coordinator, 1966–70. Seconded to HM Govt (Mr Heath's Admin) as Head of Business Team, 1970–72; Dir and Group Personnel Co-ordinator, Shell International Petroleum Co. Ltd, 1972–76. Chm. Council, Univ. of Surrey, 1980-. CBIM; F.R.SA. Officer of Philippine Legion of Honour, 1964. *Recreations:* gardening, walking, golf. *Address:* Longhill House, The Sands, near Farnham, Surrey. *T:* Runfold 2601. *Clubs:* City Livery, Institute of Directors; Farnham Golf.

MEYNELL, Dame Alix (Hester Marie); (Lady Meynell), DBE 1949; *b* 2 Feb. 1903; *d* of late Surgeon Commander L. Kilroy, RN, and late Hester Kilroy; *m* 1946, Sir Francis Meynell, RDI (*d* 1975); no *c.* *Educ:* Malvern Girls' Coll.; Somerville Coll., Oxford. Joined civil service, Board of Trade, 1925. Seconded to the Monopolies and Restrictive Practices Commission as Sec., 1949–52; Under-Sec., Board of Trade, 1946–55; resigned from the Civil Service, 1955. Called to the Bar, 1956. Man. Dir, Nonesuch Press Ltd, 1976-. Member: SE Gas Board, 1963–69 (Chm. Cons. Council, 1956-63); Harlow New Town Corpn, 1956–65; Performing Right Tribunal, 1956–65; Cttees of Investigation for England, Scotland and Great Britain under Agricultural Marketing Acts, 1956–65; Monopolies Commn, 1965–68; Cosford RDC, 1970–74. *Recreations:* family bridge, entertaining my friends and being entertained. *Address:* The Grey House, Lavenham, Sudbury, Suffolk. *T:* Lavenham 247526.

MEYNELL, Benedict William; Hon. Director-General, Commission of the European Communities, since 1981; *b* 17 Feb. 1930; *s* of late Sir Francis Meynell, RDI, and of Lady (Vera) Meynell, MA; *m* 1st, 1950, Hildamarie (*née* Hendricks); two *d*; 2nd, 1967, Diana (*née* Himbury). *Educ:* Beltane Sch.; Geneva Univ. (Licencié-ès-sciences politiques); Magdalen Coll., Oxford (Doncaster schol.; MA). Asst Principal, Bd of Inland Revenue, 1954-56; Asst Principal, BoT, 1957-59; Principal, 1959-68; Principal British Trade Commissioner, Kenya, 1962-64; Board of Trade: Principal Private Sec. to Pres., 1967-68; Asst Sec., 1968-70; Commercial Counsellor, Brit. Embassy, Washington, DC, 1970-73; a Dir, EEC, responsible for relations with Far East, and for commercial safeguards and textiles negotiations, 1973-77, for relations with N America, Japan and Australasia, 1977-81. *Publications:* International Regulation of Aircraft Noise, 1971; Relations with Japan, 1982; A Survey of External Relations, 1982. *Address:* 49 rue Père Eudore Devroye, 1040 Bruxelles, Belgium. *T:* 736 4916.

MEYNELL, Laurence Walter; (Robert Eton); Author; *b* Wolverhampton, 1899; *y s* of late Herbert and Agnes Meynell; *m* 1932, Shirley Ruth (*d* 1955), *e d* of late Taylor Darbyshire; one *d*; *m* 1956, Joan Belfrage (*née* Henley). *Educ:* St Edmund's Coll., Old Hall, Ware. After serving in the Honourable Artillery Company became successively schoolmaster, estate agent and finally professional writer; Royal Air Force in War of 1939-45 (despatches). Literary Editor, Time and Tide, 1958-60, Past Pres. Johnson Soc. *Publications:* as Robert Eton: The Pattern; The Dividing Air; The Bus Leaves for the Village; Not In Our Stars; The Journey; Palace Pier; The Legacy; The Faithful Years; The Corner of Paradise Place; St Lynn's Advertiser; The Dragon at the Gate; as *Laurence Meynell:* Bluefeather; Paid in Full; The Door in the Wall; The House in the Hills; The Dandy; Third Time Unlucky; His Aunt Came Late; The Creaking Chair; The Dark Square; Strange Landing; The Evil Hour; The Bright Face of Danger; The Echo in the Cave; The Lady on Platform One; Party of Eight; The Man No One Knew; Give me the Knife; Saturday Out; Famous Cricket Grounds; Life of Sir P. Warner; Builder and Dreamer; Smoky Joe; Too Clever by Half; Smoky Joe in Trouble; Rolls, Man of Speed; Young Master Carver; Under the Hollies; Bridge Under the Water; Great Men of Staffordshire; Policeman in the Family; James Brindley; Sonia Back Stage; The Young Architect; District Nurse Carter; The Breaking Point; One Step from Murder; The Abandoned Doll; The House in Marsh Road; The Pit in the Garden; Virgin Luck; Sleep of the Unjust; Airmen on the Run; More Deadly

Than the Male; Double Fault; Die by the Book; Week-end in the Scampi Belt; Death of a Philanderer; The Curious Crime of Miss Julia Blossom; The End of the Long Hot Summer; Death by Arrangement; A Little Matter of Arson; A View from the Terrace; The Fatal Flaw; The Thirteen Trumpeters; The Woman in Number Five; The Fortunate Miss East; The Fairly Innocent Little Man; The Footpath; Don't Stop For Hooky Hefferman; Hooky and the Crock of Gold; The Lost Half Hour; Hooky Gets the Wooden Spoon; Parasol in the Park; The Secret of the Pit; as *A. Stephen Tring* (for children): The Old Gang; The Cave By the Sea; Penny Dreadful; Barry's Exciting Year; Penny Triumphant; Penny Penitent; Penny Dramatic; Penny in Italy; Penny Goodbye. *Recreations:* walking, trying to write a play. *Address:* 9 Clifton Terrace, Brighton BN1 3HA. *Club:* Authors'.

MEYNER, Robert Baumle; Lawyer since 1934; Governor, State of New Jersey, USA, 1954-62; *b* 3 July 1908; *s* of late Gustave H. Meyner and Sophia Baumle Meyner; *m* 1957, Helen Day Stevenson. *Educ:* Lafayette Coll. (AB); Columbia Univ. Law Sch. (LLB). State Senator from Warren County, 1948-52; Senate Minority (Democrat) Leader, 1950; Director: Engelhard Corp.; Phillipsburg (NJ) National Bank and Trust Co.; First National State Bancorporation, Newark (NJ); Delaware and Bound Brook Railroad; ICBO; NJ State Safety Council; NJ Historical Soc.; NJ American Revolution Bicentennial Commn. Administrator, Cigarette Advertising Code. Hon. degrees: Dr of Laws: Rutgers (The State Univ.) 1954; Lafayette Coll., 1954; Princeton Univ., 1956; Long Island Univ., 1958; Fairleigh Dickinson Univ., 1959; Syracuse Univ., 1960; Lincoln Univ., 1960; Colorado Coll., 1961. *Address:* (business) Suite 2500, Gateway 1, Newark, New Jersey 07102, USA; 16 Olden Lane, Princeton, NJ 08540, USA; 372 Lincoln Street, Phillipsburg, NJ 08865, USA. *Clubs:* River (New York); Essex, Downtown (Newark, NJ); Pomfret (Easton, Pa).

MEYRICK, Lt-Col Sir George David Eliott Tapps-Gervis-, 6th Bt, *cr* 1791; MC 1943; *b* 15 April 1915; *o s* of Major Sir George Llewelyn Tapps-Gervis-Meyrick, 5th Bt, and Marjorie (*née* Hamlin) (*d* 1972); *S* father 1960; *m* 1940, Ann, *d* of Clive Miller; one *s* one *d.* *Educ:* Eton; Trinity Coll., Cambridge (BA). 2nd Lieut, 9th Queen's Royal Lancers, 1937. Served War of 1939–45 (wounded, MC): BEF, 1940; Middle East, 1941–43; Italy, 1945; Captain, 1940 Lt-Col, 1947; retired, 1952. Dir, Southampton FC, 1953-. High Sheriff, Anglesey, 1962. *Recreations:* shooting, travel. *Heir: s* George Christopher Cadafael Tapps-Gervis-Meyrick [*b* 10 March 1941; *m* 1968, Jean Louise Montagu Douglas Scott, *d* of late Lt-Col Lord William Scott and of Lady William Scott, Beechwood, Melrose, Scotland; two *s* one *d*]. *Address:* Hinton Admiral, Christchurch, Dorset. *T:* Highcliffe 72887; Bodorgan, Anglesey, Gwynedd. *T:* Bodorgan 204. *Club:* Cavalry and Guards.

MEYRICK, Col Sir Thomas Frederick, 3rd Bt, *cr* 1880; TD; late 15th/19th Hussars; DL; JP, Pembrokeshire; *b* 28 Nov. 1899; *o s* of Brigadier-General Sir Frederick Charlton Meyrick, 2nd Bt; *S* father, 1932; *m* 1st, 1926, Ivy Frances (*d* 1947), *d* of late Lieut-Col F. C. Pilkington, DSO; three *s* three *d* ; 2nd, 1951, Gladice Joyce (*d* 1977), *d* of late Bertram W. Allen, Cilrhiw, Narberth, Pembs; one *s* ; 3rd, 1978, Suzanne (*d* 1979), *yr d* of late D. A. Evans. Capt. 15/19 Hussars, 1927; Equitation Instructor, Weedon, 1922-27, and RMC, 1930-34; retd pay, 1934; Captain 102 (Pembroke and Cardigan), Field Brigade RA (TA), 1937; Major, 1939; Hon. Col 302 Pembroke Yeo. Field Regt, RA (TA), 1955-59. Sheriff of Pembrokeshire, 1938; Master Pembrokeshire Foxhounds, 1934-35, South Pembrokeshire, 1936-39; V. W. H., Lord Bathurst's, 1939, Pembrokeshire, 1946-58; President: Royal Welsh Agricultural Soc., 1955; Hunters Improvement Soc., 1972; Chm., Pembs Branch, NFU, 1968. *Heir: s* David John Charlton Meyrick [*b* 2 Dec. 1926; *m* 1962, Penelope Anne Marsden-Smedley; three *s*]. *Address:* Gumfreston, Tenby, Dyfed SA70 8RA. *Club:* English-Speaking Union.
  See also T. O. Lewis.

MEYSEY-THOMPSON, Sir (Humphrey) Simon, 4th Bt *cr* 1874; *b* 31 March 1935; *s* of Guy Herbert Meysey-Thompson (*d* 1961), and of Miriam Beryl Meysey-Thompson; *S* kinsman, Sir Algar de Clifford Charles Meysey-Thompson, 1967. *Address:* 10 Church Street, Woodbridge, Suffolk. *T:* Woodbridge 2144.

MIALL, (Rowland) Leonard, OBE 1961; Research Historian; *b* 6 Nov. 1914; *e s* of late Rowland Miall and S. Grace Miall; *m* 1st, 1941, Lorna (*d* 1974), *o d* of late G. John Rackham; three *s* one *d* ; 2nd, 1975, Sally Bicknell, *e d* of late Gordon Leith. *Educ:* Bootham Sch., York (Scholar); Freiburg Univ.; St John's Coll., Cambridge (Sizar), MA. Pres. Cambridge Union, 1936; Ed. Cambridge Review, 1936. Lectured in US, 1937; Sec. British-American Associates, 1937-39; joined BBC; inaugurated talks broadcast to Europe, 1939; BBC German Talks and Features Editor, 1940-42. Mem. British Political Warfare Mission to US, 1942-44 (Dir of News, San Francisco, 1943; Head of New York Office, 1944); Personal Asst to Dep. Dir-Gen., Political Warfare Exec., London, 1944; attached to Psychological Warfare Division of SHAEF, Luxembourg, 1945. Rejoined BBC: Special Correspondent, Czechoslovakia, 1945; Actg Diplomatic Corresp., 1945; Chief Corresp. in US, 1945-53; Head of Television Talks, 1954; Asst Controller, Current Affairs and Talks, Television, 1961; Special Asst to Dir of Television, planning start of BBC-2, 1962; Asst Controller, Programme Services, Television, BBC, 1963-66; BBC Rep. in US, 1966-70; Controller, Overseas and Foreign Relations, BBC, 1971-74. Inaugurated BBC Lunchtime Lectures, 1962; Advisor, Cttee on Broadcasting, New Delhi, 1965; Delegate to Commonwealth Broadcasting Confs, Jamaica, 1970, Kenya, 1972, Malta, 1974. Dir, Visnews Ltd; Overseas

Dir, British Acad. of Film and Television Arts. FRSA. Cert. of Appreciation, NY City, 1970. *Publication:* Richard Dimbleby, Broadcaster, 1966. *Recreations:* gardening, doing it oneself. *Address:* Maryfield Cottage, Taplow, Maidenhead, Berks SL6 0EX. *T:* Burnham 4195. *Clubs:* Garrick; Metropolitan (Washington); Union (Cambridge).

MICHAEL, David Parry Martin, CBE 1972; MA; Headmaster, Newport High School, Gwent, 1960–76; Secretary (part-time) University College Cardiff Press Board, since 1976; *b* 21 Dec. 1910; *m* 1937, Mary Horner Hayward; one *s. Educ:* University Coll., Cardiff (Fellow, 1981). Major, RAOC, combined ops, 1941–46 (despatches). Asst Master, Bassaleg Gram. Sch., Mon., 1935–41 and 1946–50; Headmaster, Cathays High Sch. for Boys, Cardiff, 1950–60. Member: Coun., University Coll., Cardiff, 1961–; Governing Body, Church in Wales, 1963–. Gov., Nat. Library of Wales, 1967–; Mem., Broadcasting Council for Wales, 1969–73. Pres., Incorporated Assoc. of Headmasters, 1968; Mem., HMC, 1971–76; Pres., Welsh Secondary Schools Assoc., 1973. Editor, Welsh Secondary Schools' Review, 1965–76. *Publications:* The Idea of a Staff College, 1967; Guide to the Sixth Form, 1969; Arthur Machen, 1971; Town Walks, 1977; articles and reviews in educational and other jls. *Recreations:* collecting Victorian Staffordshire portrait figures; setting and solving crosswords (pseudonyn, Egma). *Address:* 28 Fields Road, Newport, Gwent. *T:* Newport (Gwent) 62747.

MICHAEL, Prof. Ian David Lewis; King Alfonso XIII Professor of Spanish Studies, University of Oxford, since 1982; Fellow, Exeter College, Oxford, since 1982; *b* 26 May 1936; *o s* of late Cyril George Michael and of Glenys Morwen (*née* Lewis). *Educ:* Neath Grammar Sch.; King's Coll., London (BA First Class Hons Spanish 1957); PhD Manchester 1967. University of Manchester: Asst Lectr in Spanish, 1957–60; Lectr in Spanish, 1960–69; Sen. Lectr in Spanish, 1969–70; University of Southampton: Prof. of Spanish and Hd of Spanish Dept, 1971–82; Dep. Dean, Faculty of Arts, 1975–77, 1980–82; Sen. Curator and Chm., Univ. Library Cttee, 1980–82. Leverhulme Faculty Fellow in European Studies (at Madrid), 1977–78. *Publications:* The Treatment of Classical Material in the Libro de Alexandre, 1970; Spanish Literature and Learning to 1474, in, Spain: a Companion to Spanish studies, 1973, 3rd edn 1977; The Poem of the Cid, 1975; Poema de Mio Cid, 1976, 2nd edn 1979; Gwyn Thomas, 1977; chapter on Poem of My Cid in New Pelican Guide to English Literature. I ii, 1983; articles in various learned jls and Festschriften. *Recreations:* horticulture; collecting Art Nouveau and Art Déco, particularly ceramics; writing pseudonymous fiction. *Address:* Exeter College, Oxford. *T:* Oxford 535152. *Clubs:* Organon; Neath Cricket (a Vice-Pres.).

MICHAEL, Ian (Lockie), CBE 1972; Deputy Director, Institute of Education, University of London, 1973–78; *b* 30 Nov. 1915; 4th *c* of late Reginald Warburton Michael and Margaret Campbell Kerr; *m* 1942, Mary Harborne Bayley, *e c* of late Rev. William Henry Bayley; one *s* one *d. Educ:* St Bees Sch.; private study. BA (London) 1938; PhD (Bristol) 1963. Schoolmaster: St Faith's Sch., Cambridge, 1935–40; Junior Sch., Leighton Park, 1941–45, Headmaster, 1946–49; Lectr in Educn, Bristol Univ., 1950–63; Prof. of Educn, Khartoum Univ., 1963–64; Vice-Chancellor, Univ. of Malaŵi, 1964–73. Leverhulme Emeritus Fellowship, 1978–79, 1979–80; Vis. Prof. of Educn, Univ. of Cape Town, 1981. Hon. DLitt Malaŵi, 1974. *Publication:* English Grammatical Categories and the Tradition to 1800, 1970. *Address:* 10A Downfield Road, Bristol BS8 2TJ.

MICHAEL, Peter Colin, CBIM; Deputy Chairman, United Engineering Industries plc, since 1981; *b* 17 June 1938; *s* of Albert and Enid Michael; *m* 1962, Margaret Baldwin; two *s. Educ:* Whitgift Sch., Croydon; Queen Mary Coll., Univ. of London (BSc Elec. Engrg). CBIM 1982. Man. Dir, Micro Consultants Ltd, 1969–82; Chm., Quantel Ltd, 1974–82. Mem., Adv. Council for Applied R&D, 1982–. Hon. FBKSTS 1981. The Guardian Young Businessman of the Year, 1982. *Recreations:* squash, tennis, opera. *Address:* 20 West Mills, Newbury, Berks RG14 5HG. *T:* Newbury 48222.

MICHAELS, Prof. Leslie, MD; FRCPath, FRCP(C); Professor of Pathology, Institute of Laryngology and Otology, since 1973 (Dean, 1976–81); *b* 24 July 1925; *s* of Henry and Minnie Michaels; *m* Edith (*née* Waldstein); two *d. Educ:* Parmiter's Sch., London; King's Coll., London; Westminster Med. Sch., London (MB, BS; MD). FRCPath 1963, FRCP(C) 1962. Asst Lectr in Pathology, Univ. of Manchester, 1955–57; Lectr in Path., St Mary's Hosp. Med. Sch., London, 1957–59; Asst Prof. of Path., Albert Einstein Coll. of Medicine, New York, 1959–61; Hosp. Pathologist, Northern Ont, Canada, 1961–70; Sen. Lectr, Inst. of Laryn. and Otol., 1970–73. *Publications:* scientific articles in jls of medicine, pathology and otolaryngology. *Recreations:* reading, music, walking. *Address:* Romany Ridge, Hillbrow Road, Bromley, Kent BR1 4JL.

MICHAELS, Michael Israel, CB 1960; *b* 22 Dec. 1908; *m* 1932, Rosina, *e d* of late Joseph Sturges; one *s* one *d. Educ:* City of London College; London Sch. of Economics (Social Science Research Fellow, 1931). Asst Sec., New Survey London Life and Labour, 1932–34. Deputy Director, Programmes and Statistics, Ministry of Supply, 1940–45. Asst Sec., Ministry of Health, 1946–54; Under-Sec., Atomic Energy Office, 1955–59; Office of the Minister for Science (Atomic Energy Division), 1959–64; Under-Sec., Min. of Technology, 1964–71, retired. British Mem., Bd of Governors, Internat. Atomic Energy Agency, 1957–71. *Recreations:* music, gardening, history.

Address: The Mill House, Kelsale, Saxmundham, Suffolk. *T:* Saxmundham 3142.

MICHALOPOULOS, André, CBE 1937 (OBE 1919); FRSA; Professor Emeritus of Classical Literatures and Civilizations, since 1964, Professor 1957–64, Fairleigh-Dickinson University; *b* 1897; *m* 1st, 1924, Aspasia Eliasco; one *s* two *d*; 2nd, 1964, Countess Eleanor von Etzdorf. *Educ:* St Paul's Sch., London; Oriel Coll., Oxford (Scholar). BA 1st Cl. Hons Litt Hum., 1920; MA 1927; Priv. Sec. to Eleutherios Venizelos, Prime Minister of Greece, 1917 and 1921–24; Mem. Greek Delegation, Lausanne Peace Conference, 1922–23; Civil Governor of Lemnos, Imbros, Tenedos, and Samothrace, 1918–19; Governor of Corfu and adjacent islands, 1924–25; left Public Service for business, 1925; Managing Dir of Athens-Piraeus Water Coy; Dir of several Banking, Industrial, and Commercial Corpns in Athens; Pres. of the Anglo-Hellenic League, Athens, 1935–45; broadcast nightly English news commentary from Athens during Greco-Italian War, 1940–41; joined Greek forces in Crete, April 1941; Gen. Sec. of Nat. Cttee of Greeks of Egypt for resistance, May 1941; followed Greek Govt to S Africa, Aug. 1941; Mem. Greek Cabinet (Minister of Information in London, Washington and Cairo), Sept. 1941–May 1943. Lectured and broadcast extensively in S Africa, Great Britain, USA, Canada, 1941–43; Minister Plenipotentiary for Greece i/c information in America, 1945–46; Special Adviser on American Affairs to Royal Greek Embassy in Washington, 1950–67; Mem., Supreme Educnl Council of Greek Orthodox Archdiocese in N and S America, 1962–70. Visiting Professor, Kansas City University, 1949. Participated as Chm. or panel-mem., in Invitation to Learning programme, Columbia Broadcasting System, 1947–65; Master of Ceremonies and political and literary commentator on weekly Hellenic Television Hour, New York, 1955–56. Broadcast to Greece on Voice of America programme, 1950–55. Participated in annual American Foreign Policy Conf., Colgate Univ., 1951–61; has lectured and broadcast in the 48 States of USA and in Canada. Archon, Order of St Andrew; Grand Protonotary of Oecumenical Patriarchate of Constantinople, 1967. Commander Order of George I (Greece) with swords, 1941; Commander Order of the Phœnix (Greece), 1936; Chevalier Legion of Honour (France), 1934; Commander Order of Orange Nassau (Netherlands), 1939. FRSA 1936; Mem. Academy of American Poets, 1956; Mem. Poetry Society of America, 1957. Fellow, Ancient Monuments Soc. (London), 1958. Hon. LittD Westminster Coll., Utah. *Publications:* Homer, an interpretative study of the Iliad and Odyssey, 1965; and Greek Fire: a collection of broadcasts, articles and addresses, 1943; two collections of Verse 1923 and 1928; contribs to Encyclopedia Americana and Funk & Wagnall's Reference Encyclopaedia; chapts and articles in Greek, English, Scottish, American, Canadian, Egyptian, French, and South African books, reviews and newspapers; weekly book reviews for King Features Syndicate (USA), 1959–75. *Address:* The Normandy, 1120 North Shore Drive, Apt 1103, St Petersburg, Florida 33701, USA. *T:* 813-823-6352.

MICHALOWSKI, Jerzy; Polish diplomat; *b* 26 May 1909; *s* of Andrzej and Maria Michalowski; *m* 1947, Mira Krystyna; two *s. Educ:* University of Warsaw. Asst In Polish Inst. of Social Affairs, 1933–36; Dir of Polish Workers Housing Organisation, 1936–39; Chief of Housing Dept of Warsaw City Council, 1945; Counsellor of Polish Embassy in London, 1945–46; Deputy Deleg. of Poland to UN, March-Nov. 1946; Ambassador of Republic of Poland to the Court of St James's 1946–53; Head of a department, Ministry of Foreign Affairs, Warsaw, 1953–54; Under Sec. of State for Educ., 1954–55; Deleg. of Poland to the Internat. Commn in Vietnam, 1955–56; Permanent Representative of Poland to UN, 1956–60; Dir-Gen., in Ministry of Foreign Affairs, Warsaw, 1960–67; Ambassador to USA, 1967–71. Pres. of ECOSOC, UN, 1962. *Publications:* Unemployment of Polish Peasants, 1934; Housing Problems in Poland (publ. by League of Nations), 1935; The Big Game for the White House, 1972. *Recreations:* tennis and winter sports. *Address:* Al. I Armii WP 16/20, Warsaw, Poland.

MICHELHAM, 2nd Baron, *cr* 1905, of Hellingly; **Herman Alfred Stern;** Bt, *cr* 1905; a Baron of Portugal; *b* 5 Sept. 1900; *e s* of 1st Baron Michelham; *S* father, 1919; *m* 1919, Berthe Isabella Susanna Flora (*d* 1961), *d* of Arthur Joseph Capel; *m* 1980, Marie-José Dupas. *Educ:* Malvern College.

MICHELIN, Reginald Townend, CMG 1957; CVO 1953; OBE 1952; General Manager: Agualta Vale Estates, Jamaica, 1958–64; Jamaica Tourist Board, 1964–73; *b* 31 Dec. 1903; *s* of V. A. Michelin, Planter, Jamaica; *m* 1940, Nina Gladys Faulkner, Iffley, Oxford; one *s* one *d. Educ:* Exeter Sch., England. Sub-Inspector, Police, Jamaica, 1924; Inspector, Police, Leeward Islands, 1928; Asst Commissioner of Police, Nigeria, 1930; Comr of Police, Barbados, 1949; Commissioner of Police, Jamaica, 1953–58, retd. *Address:* Western Mews, Winslow, Bucks.

MICHELL, Alan, CMG 1966; HM Diplomatic Service, retired; *b* 11 Nov. 1913; *s* of late Pierre William Michell and late Mary Michell; *m* 1st, 1941, Glenys Enid Davies (*d* 1965); one *s* two *d*; 2nd, 1980, Mrs Josephine Thogersen. *Educ:* Barry School; Jesus Coll., Oxford (Stanhope Univ. Prize, 1934). Served Royal Tank Regt, 1940–46. Asst Master, King's Sch., Canterbury, 1937–40; Foreign Office, 1947; Second Sec., Paris, 1952; Nicosia, 1954; Singapore, 1956; First Sec., Saigon, 1959; FO, later FCO, 1961–72. *Address:* Northwick House, Brabourne, near Ashford, Kent.

MICHELL, Francis Victor, CMG 1955; *b* 17 Jan. 1908; *s* of late Pierre William Michell and late Mary Michell; *m* 1943, Betty Enid Tempest, *d* of late William Tempest Olver, JP, Tamworth; no *c.* *Educ:* Barry Sch.; Jesus Coll., Oxford. Attaché British Embassy, Rio de Janeiro, 1943–46; First Sec., Istanbul, 1947–51; First Sec., Commissioner-General's Office, Singapore, 1951–53; Foreign Office, 1953–65. *Address:* Nettlesworth Farm, Vines Cross, Heathfield, East Sussex. *T:* Heathfield 2695. *Club:* Travellers'.

MICHELL, Keith; actor since 1948; *b* Adelaide; *s* of Joseph Michell and Alice Maud (*née* Aslat); *m* 1957, Jeannette Sterke; one *s* one *d.* *Educ:* Port Pirie High Sch.; Adelaide Teachers' Coll.; Sch. of Arts and Crafts; Adelaide Univ.; Old Vic Theatre School. Formerly taught art. *Stage:* First appearance, Playbox, Adelaide, 1947; Young Vic Theatre Co., 1950–51; first London appearance, And So To Bed, 1951; Shakespeare Mem. Theatre Co., Australian tour, 1952–53, Stratford, 1954 and 1955 (Troilus and Cressida, Romeo and Juliet, Taming of the Shrew, All's Well That Ends Well, Macbeth, Twelfth Night); Don Juan, Royal Court, 1956; Old Vic Co., 1956 (Antony and Cleopatra, Much Ado about Nothing, Comedy of Errors); Irma La Douce, Lyric, 1958, Washington, DC, 1960 and Broadway, 1960–61; The Art of Seduction, Aldwych, 1962; Chichester Festival, 1962; The Rehearsal, NY, 1963; The First Four Hundred Years, Australia and NZ, 1964; Robert and Elizabeth, Lyric, 1964; The King's Mare, 1966; Man of La Mancha, 1968–69, NY, 1970; Abelard and Heloise, 1970, Los Angeles and NY, 1971; Hamlet, Globe, 1972; Dear Love, Comedy, 1973; The Crucifer of Blood, Haymarket, 1979; On the Twentieth Century (musical), Her Majesty's, 1980; One Man Show, Perth and Pinjarra, 1981; Pete McGynty and the Dreamtime (own adap. of Peer Gynt), Melbourne Theatre Co., 1981; *Chichester Festival Theatre:* Artistic Director, 1974–77; Tonight We Improvise, Oedipus Tyrannus, 1974; Cyrano de Bergerac, Othello, 1975; (dir and designed) Twelfth Night, 1976; The Apple Cart, 1977; (dir and designed) In Order of Appearance, 1977; On the Rocks, 1982; Australian tour, 1978. *Television includes:* Henry VIII in The Six Wives of Henry VIII (series), 1972 (film, Henry VIII and His Six Wives, 1972); Keith Michell at Chichester, 1974. Many recordings. First exhibn of paintings, 1959; subseq. exhibns at John Whibley Gall., London and Wright Hepburn and Webster Gall., NY, Century Gall., Henley, Wylma Wayne Gall., London. *Publications:* ed and illus. (lithographs), Twelve Shakespeare Sonnets, 1980; illus. and recorded Captain Beaky series, 1980–. *Recreations:* painting, photography, swimming, riding. *Address:* c/o Chatto & Linnit Ltd, Globe Theatre, W1.

MICHELMORE, Clifford Arthur, CBE 1969; Television Broadcaster and Producer; Managing Director: Michelmore Enterprises Ltd, since 1969; Communications Consultants Ltd, since 1969; *b* 11 Dec. 1919; *s* of late Herbert Michelmore and Ellen Alford; *m* 1950, Jean Metcalfe (Broadcaster); one *s* one *d.* *Educ:* Cowes Senior Sch., Isle of Wight. Entered RAF, 1935; commnd 1940; left RAF 1947. Head, Outside Broadcasts and Variety, BFN, 1948; Dep. Station Dir, BFN, also returned to freelance as Commentator and Producer, 1949. Entered Television, 1950. Man. Dir, RM/EMI Visual Programmes, 1971–81. Has taken part in numerous radio and television programmes in Britain, Europe and the USA. Introduced: "Tonight" series, 1957–65; 24 Hours series, 1965–68; General Election Results programmes, 1964, 1966, 1970; So You Think ...., 1966–; Our World, 1967; With Michelmore (interviews); Talkback; Apollo Space Programmes, 1960–70; Holiday, 1969–; Chance to Meet, 1970–73; Wheelbase, 1972; Getaway, 1975; Globetrotter, 1975; Opinions Unlimited, 1977–79; Presenter, Day by Day (Southern TV), 1980; Sudden Change (HTV), 1982–. Made films: Shaping of a Writer, 1977; Hong Kong: the challenge, 1978. FRSA, 1975. Television Society Silver Medal, 1957; Guild of TV Producers Award, Personality of the Year, 1958; TV Review Critics Award, 1959; Variety Club Award, 1961. *Publications:* (ed) The Businessman's Book of Golf, 1981; contribs to Highlife, Financial Weekly; various articles on television, broadcasting and travel. *Recreations:* golf, reading and doing nothing. *Address:* White House, Reigate, Surrey; Brookfield, Bembridge, Isle of Wight. *Clubs:* Garrick, Royal Air Force.

MICHELMORE, Sir Walter Harold Strachan, Kt 1958; MBE 1945; Company Director; *b* Chudleigh, Devon, 4 April 1908; 2nd *s* of late Harold G. Michelmore; *m* 1933, Dorothy Walrond (*d* 1964), *o c* of late E. W. Bryant; one *d* ; *m* 1967, Mrs Dulcie Mary Scott, *d* of late Leonard Haughton. *Educ:* Sherborne Sch.; Balliol Coll., Oxford. Joined Bird & Co., Calcutta, 1929. Served Indian Army (Staff), 1940–46 (MBE). Managing Dir, Bird & Co. (Pvt) Ltd and F. W. Heilgers & Co. (Pvt) Ltd, Calcutta, 1948–63; Dep. Chm., 1955, Chm. 1961; retired 1963. Pres. Bengal Chamber of Commerce and Industry and Associated Chambers of Commerce of India, 1957. *Recreations:* golf, fishing, gardening. *Address:* Derriwong, 33 Derriwong Road, Round Corner, via Dural, NSW 2158, Australia. *Clubs:* Oriental, Queen's; Bengal (Calcutta); Australian (Sydney).

MICHENER, James Albert; Author; *b* New York City, 3 Feb. 1907; *s* of Edwin Michener and Mabel (*née* Haddock); *m* 1st, 1935, Patti Koon (marr. diss. 1948); 2nd, 1948, Vange Nord (marr. diss., 1955); 3rd, 1955, Mari Yoriko Sabusawa; no *c.* *Educ:* Swarthmore Coll., Pennsylvania; St Andrews Univ., Scotland; Harvard Coll., Mass. Teacher, George Sch., Pa, 1933–36; Prof., Colorado State Coll. of Educn, 1936–41; Visiting Prof., Harvard, 1940–41; Associate Editor, Macmillan Co., 1941–49. Member: Adv. Cttee on the arts, US State Dept, 1957; Adv. Cttee, US Information Agency, 1970–76; Cttee to reorganise USIS, 1976. Served with USNR on active duty in South Pacific, 1944–45. Sec., Pennsylvania Constitutional Convention, 1968. Hon. DHL, LLD, LittD, DSci and DHum, from numerous univs. US Medal of Freedom, 1977. *Publications:* Unit in the Social Studies, 1940; Tales of the South Pacific (Pulitzer prize for fiction), 1947; The Fires of Spring, 1949; Return to Paradise, 1951; The Voice of Asia, 1951; The Bridges at Toko-ri, 1953; Sayonara, 1954; Floating World, 1955; The Bridge at Andau, 1957; (with A. Grove Day) Rascals in Paradise, 1957; Selected Writings, 1957; The Hokusai Sketchbook, 1958; Japanese Prints, 1959; Hawaii, 1959; Caravans, 1964; The Source, 1965; Iberia, 1968; Presidential Lottery, 1969; The Quality of Life, 1970; Kent State, 1971; The Drifters, 1971; Centennial, 1974; Michener on Sport, 1977; Chesapeake, 1978; The Covenant, 1980; ed, Future of Social Studies for NEA, 1940. *Recreations:* photography, philately, tennis. *Address:* Pipersville, Pa 18947, USA.

MICHENER, Rt. Hon. Roland, CC, CMM, CD; Royal Victorian Chain, 1973; PC (Canada) 1962; QC (Canada); Governor-General and Commander-in-Chief of Canada, 1967–Jan. 1974; Barrister associated as Counsel with Lang, Michener, Cranston, Farquharson & Wright, Toronto, since 1974; Chairman of Council, Duke of Edinburgh's Fifth Commonwealth Study Conference, Canada 1980; Hon. Chairman of Board: Victoria Grey Trust Co., Toronto; Teck Mining Corporation Ltd; Director, Pamour Porcupine Mines Ltd; etc; *b* Lacombe, Alta, 19 April 1900; *s* of late Senator Edward Michener and Mary Edith (*née* Roland), Lincoln Co., Ontario; *m* 1927, Norah Evangeline, *d* of Robert Willis, Manitoba; two *d* (and one *d* decd). *Educ:* Universities of Alberta and Oxford. BA (Alta) 1920; Rhodes Scholar for Alta, 1919; BA 1922, BCL 1923, MA 1929, Oxon. Served with RAF, 1918. Called to Bar, Middle Temple, 1923; Barrister, Ontario, 1924; KC (Canada) 1943. Practising lawyer with Lang, Michener & Cranston, Toronto, 1924–57. Mem. Ontario Legislature for St David, Toronto, 1945–48, and Provincial Sec. for Ontario, 1946–48; elected to Canadian House of Commons, 1953; re-elected 1957 and 1958; elected Speaker, 1957 and May 1958; Canadian High Commissioner to India and Ambassador to Nepal, 1964–67. Chancellor, Queen's Univ., 1974–80. Gen. Sec. for Canada, Rhodes Scholarships, 1936–64. Mem. Bd of Governors, Toronto Stock Exchange, 1974–76. Formerly: Governor, Toronto Western Hosp.; Hon. Counsel, Chm. of Exec. Cttee (Pres., 1974–79), Canadian Inst. of Internat. Affairs; Hon. Counsel, Red Cross Ont Div.; Chm. of Exec., Canadian Assoc. for Adult Educn; Officer and Dir of various Canadian mining and financial companies. Chancellor and Principal Companion, Order of Canada, 1967–74; Chancellor and Comdr, Order of Military Merit, 1972–74. KJStJ (Prior for Canada), 1967. Hon. Fellow: Hertford Coll., Oxford, 1961; Acad. of Medicine, Toronto, 1967; Trinity Coll., Toronto, 1968; Frontier Coll., Toronto, 1972; Royal Canadian Mil. Inst., 1975; Heraldry Soc. of Canada, 1976; Hon. FRCP(C) 1968; Hon. FRAIC, 1968; Hon. FRSC, 1975. Hon. Mem., Canadian Medical Assoc., 1968; Hon. Bencher, Law Soc. of Upper Canada, 1968. Hon. LLD: Ottawa, 1948; Queen's, 1958; Laval, 1960; Alberta, 1967; St Mary's, Halifax, 1968; Toronto, 1968; RMC Canada, 1969; Mount Allison, 1969; Sackville, NB, 1969; Brock, 1969; Manitoba, 1970; McGill, 1970; York, Toronto, 1970; British Columbia, 1971; Jewish Theol Seminary of America, 1972; New Brunswick, 1972; Law Soc. of Upper Canada, 1974; Dalhousie, 1974; Hon. DCL: Bishop's, 1968; Windsor, 1969; Oxford Univ., 1970. *Address:* PO Box 10, First Canadian Place, Toronto, Ontario M5X 1A2, Canada; (home) 24 Thornwood Road, Toronto, Ontario M4W 2S1.

MICHIE, David Alan Redpath, RSA 1972 (ARSA 1964); Head, School of Drawing and Painting, Edinburgh College of Art, since 1982 (Depute Head, 1969–82); *b* 30 Nov. 1928; *s* of late James Michie and late Anne Redpath, OBE, ARA, RSA; *m* 1951, Eileen Anderson Michie; two *d.* *Educ:* Edinburgh Coll. of Art (DA). National Service, 1947–49; Edinburgh Coll. of Art, 1949–53 (studied painting); travelling scholarship, Italy, 1953–54; Lectr in Painting, Gray's Sch. of Art, Aberdeen, 1958–62; Lectr in Painting, Edinburgh Coll. of Art, 1962–, Vice-Principal, 1974–77. Vis. Prof. of Painting, Acad. of Fine Art, Belgrade, 1979. Member: Gen. Teaching Council for Scotland, 1976–80; Edinburgh Festival Soc., 1976–. Pres., Soc. of Scottish Artists, 1961–63. One Man Exhibitions: Mercury Gallery, London, 1967, 1969, 1971, 1974, 1980; Lothian Region Chambers, 1977; Scottish Gall., Edinburgh, 1980. *Recreation:* fishing. *Address:* 17 Gilmour Road, Edinburgh EH16 5NS. *T:* 031-667 2684.

MICHIE, Prof. Donald, DPhil (Oxon), DSc (Oxon); Professor of Machine Intelligence, University of Edinburgh, since 1967, and Adjunct Professor of Computer Science, University of Illinois, since 1979; *b* 11 Nov. 1923; *s* of James Kilgour Michie and Marjorie Crain Michie; *m* 1st, 1949, Zena Margaret Davies (marr. diss.); one *s* ; 2nd, 1952, Anne McLaren (marr. diss.); one *s* two *d* ; 3rd, 1971, Jean Elizabeth Crouch. *Educ:* Rugby Sch.; Balliol Coll., Oxford (Schol., MA). Sci. Fellow Zool Soc. of London, 1953; Fellow Royal Soc. Edinburgh 1969; Fellow Brit. Computer Soc. 1971. War Service in FO, Bletchley, 1942–45; Res. Associate, Univ. of London, 1952–58; Univ. of Edinburgh: Sen. Lectr, Surg. Science, 1958; Reader in Surg. Science, 1962; Dir of Expermtl Programming Unit, 1965; Chm. of Dept of Machine Intelligence and Perception, 1966; Dir, Machine Intelligence Res. Unit, 1974–. Royal Soc. Lectr in USSR, 1965; Wm Withering Lectr, Univ. of Birmingham, 1972; Vis. Lectr, USSR Acad. Sci., 1973; Geo. A. Miller Lectr, Univ. of Illinois, 1974; Herbert Spencer Lectr, Univ. of Oxford, 1976; Samuel Wilks Meml Lectr, Princeton Univ., 1978; Vis. Fellow, St Cross Coll., Oxford, 1970; Visiting Professor: Stanford Univ., 1962, 1978; Syracuse Univ., USA, 1970, 1971; Virginia Polytechnic Inst. and State Univ., 1974; Univ. of California at Santa Cruz, 1975; Dartmouth Coll., USA, 1975; Illinois Univ., 1976; Carnegie Mellon Univ., 1977; Case Western Reserve Univ., 1978; McGill Univ., 1979. Chief Editor, Machine Intelligence series, 1967–. Chm., A. M. Turing Trust, 1975–. *Publications:* (jtly) An Introduction to Molecular Biology, 1964; On Machine Intelligence, 1974; Machine Intelligence and Related Topics, 1982;

papers in tech. and sci. jls. *Recreations:* chess, travel. *Address:* 10 Bellevue Crescent, Edinburgh; 15 Canal Street, Oxford. *Club:* New (Edinburgh).

MICKLETHWAIT, Sir Robert (Gore), Kt 1964; QC 1956; Chief National Insurance Commissioner, 1966-75 (Deputy Commissioner, 1959; National Insurance Commissioner and Industrial Injuries Commissioner, 1961); *b* 7 Nov. 1902; 2nd *s* of late St J. G. Micklethwait, KC and Annie Elizabeth Micklethwait (*née* Aldrich-Blake); *m* 1936, Philippa J., 2nd *d* of late Sir Ronald Bosanquet, QC; three *s* one *d. Educ:* Clifton Coll.; Trinity Coll., Oxford (2nd Class Lit. Hum., MA). Called to Bar, Middle Temple, 1925, Bencher, 1951; Autumn Reader, 1964; Dep. Treasurer, 1970, Treasurer, 1971. Oxford Circuit; Gen. Coun. of the Bar, 1939-40 and 1952-56; Supreme Court Rule Cttee, 1952-56. Royal Observer Corps, 1938-40; Civil Asst, WO, 1940-45; Recorder of Worcester, 1946-59. Deputy Chm., Court of Quarter Sessions for County of Stafford, 1956-59. Hon. LLD Newcastle upon Tyne, 1975. Hon. Knight, Hon. Soc. of Knights of the Round Table, 1972. *Publication:* The National Insurance Commissioners (Hamlyn Lectures), 1976. *Address:* 71 Harvest Road, Englefield Green, Surrey TW20 0QR. *T:* Egham 32521.

MIDDLEDITCH, Edward, MC 1945; RA 1973 (ARA 1968); ARCA 1951; painter; Head of Fine Art Department, Norwich School of Art, since 1964; *b* 23 March 1923; *s* of Charles Henry Middleditch and Esme Buckley; *m* 1947, Jean Kathleen Whitehouse; one *d. Educ:* Mundella School, Nottingham; King Edward VI Grammar Sch., Chelmsford; Royal College of Art. Served Army, 1942-47, France, Germany, India, W Africa; commissioned Middx Regt 1944. Eleven Exhibitions, London, 1954-74; contrib. to mixed exhibitions: Paris; Rome; Venice Biennale, 1956; Six Young Painters, 1957; Pittsburgh Internat., 1958; Whitechapel, 1959; English Landscape Tradition in the 20th Century, 1969; British Painting '74, 1974; 25 Years of British Painting, 1977, etc. Gulbenkian Foundn Scholarship, 1962; Arts Council of GB Bursary, 1964; Arts Council of NI Bursary, 1968. Paintings in private and public collections, including: Tate Gall.; Arts Council; V & A Museum; Contemporary Art Soc.; Manchester City Art Gall.; Ferens Art Gall., Hull; Nat. Gall. of Victoria; Nat. Gall. of S Aust.; Nat. Gall. of Canada; Chrysler Art Museum, Mass; Toledo Museum of Art, Ohio. *Address:* School House, Edwardstone, Boxford, near Colchester, Essex CO6 5PJ. *T:* Boxford (Suffolk) 210240; c/o New Arts Centre, 41 Sloane Street, SW1.

MIDDLEMISS, Sir (John) Howard, Kt 1981; CMG 1968; Professor of Radiodiagnosis, University of Bristol, and Director of Radiology, United Bristol Hospitals, 1949-81; Dean, Faculty of Medicine, Bristol University, 1978-81; *b* 14 May 1916; *s* of Thomas Middlemiss, Monkseaton, Northumberland; *m* 1942, Isobel Mary, *d* of Ivan Pirrie, MC, MD, Maldon, Essex; one *s* two *d. Educ:* Repton; Durham Univ. MB, BS 1940; MD 1947; DMRD 1946; FFR 1948; MRCP 1964, FRCP 1972; FRCS 1976. Served with RAMC as Temp. Major and Actg Lieut-Col, 1941-46. Asst Radiologist, Royal Victoria Infirmary, Newcastle upon Tyne, 1946-48. Adviser in Radiology to Governments of: Burma, Iran, Laos, Malaysia, Nigeria, Pakistan, Philippines, South Vietnam, Tanzania, Turkey and Uganda, and to Universities of Ahmadu Bello, Ghana, Ibadan, Makerere, West Indies, for periods between 1953-80. Member: Med. Adv. Cttee, Min. of Overseas Develt; Inter-Univ. Council, 1969-81; British Deleg. to 13th Internat. Congress of Radiology, 1973 (Chm.); Accident Service Review Cttee; Jt Consultants Cttee, 1972-76; Cons. to WHO; Chm., Internat. Commn on Radiological Educn, 1978-; Past Chm., Bristol Standing Cttee on Disarmament; Examnr, FFR, UK 1958-60 and 1962-63, Aust. and NZ 1969, DM (Rad.) W Indies, 1973-81. Harkness Fellow, US, 1964. Lectures: Long Fox, Bristol, 1962; Mackenzie Davidson, BIR, 1971; Litchfield, Oxford, 1972; Skinner, FR, 1972; Lindblom, Univ. of Stockholm, 1973; Edelstein, Johannesburg, 1975; Frimann-Dahl, Univ. of Oslo, 1976; Kemp., Univ. of Oxford, 1980. Warden, Faculty of Radiologists, 1966-71, Pres. 1972-75, Pres., Royal Coll. of Radiologists, 1975-76; FRSocMed. Hon. FFR, RCSI, 1969; Hon. FACR, 1972; Mem., BIR (Past Chm. of Med. Cttee); Past Vice-Pres., Section of Radiol., RSM; Hon. Member: Soc. of Radiology, Luxembourg, 1971; W African Assoc. of Radiologists, 1971; Radiol Soc. of N America, 1976; Deutsche Röntgengesellschaft, 1977; Swedish Radiol Soc., 1978; Danish Radiol Soc., 1980; Swiss Radiol Soc., 1982; Hon. Fellow, Royal Aust. Coll. of Radiologists, 1972. *Publications:* Radiology in Surgery, 1960; Tropical Radiology, 1961; Clinical Radiology in the Tropics, 1979; numerous scientific papers in Clinical Radiology, British Jl of Radiology; contrib. Encyclopaedia Britannica. *Recreations:* international relations, arboriculture. *Address:* 48 Pembroke Road, Clifton, Bristol BS8 3DT. *T:* Bristol 738553; White Cottage, Wellington Heath, Ledbury, Herefordshire. *T:* Ledbury 2454. *Club:* English-Speaking Union.

MIDDLEMORE, Sir William Hawkslow, 2nd Bt, *cr* 1919; *b* 10 April 1908; *s* of 1st Bt and Mary, *d* of late Rev. Thomas Price, Selly Oak, Birmingham; *S* father, 1924; *m* 1934, Violet Constance (*d* 1976), *d* of Andrew Kennagh, Worcester. *Heir:* none. *Address:* St Joseph's, Shurdington Road, Cheltenham, Glos. *T:* Cheltenham 25414.

MIDDLESBROUGH, Bishop of, (RC), since 1978; **Rt. Rev. Augustine Harris;** *b* 27 Oct. 1917; *s* of Augustine Harris and Louisa Beatrice (*née* Rycroft). *Educ:* St Francis Xavier's Coll.; Upholland Coll., Lancs. Ordained, 1942; Curate at: St Oswald's, Liverpool, 1942-43; St Elizabeth's, Litherland, Lancs, 1943-52; Prison Chaplain, HM Prison, Liverpool, 1952-65; Sen. RC Priest, Prison Dept, 1957-66; English Rep. to Internat. Coun. of Sen.

Prison Chaplains (RC), 1957-66; Titular Bishop of Socia and Auxiliary Bishop of Liverpool, 1965-78. Mem. Vatican Delegn to UN Quinquennial Congress on Crime, London, 1960 and Stockholm, 1965; Liaison between English and Welsh Hierarchy (RC) and Home Office, 1966-; Episcopal Moderator to Fédération Internationale des Associations Médicales Catholiques, 1967-76; Episcopal Pres., Commn for Social Welfare (England and Wales), 1972-. Mem. Central Religious Advisory Council to BBC and IBA, 1974-78. *Publications:* articles for criminological works. *Address:* Bishop's House, 16 Cambridge Road, Middlesbrough, Cleveland TS5 5NN.

MIDDLESBROUGH, Auxiliary Bishop of, (RC); *see* O'Brien, Rt Rev. T. K.

MIDDLETON, 12th Baron *cr* 1711; **Digby Michael Godfrey John Willoughby,** MC 1945; DL; Bt 1677; *b* 1 May 1921; *er s* of 11th Baron Middleton, KG, MC, TD, and Angela Florence Alfreda (*d* 1978), *er d* of Charles Hall, Eddlethorpe Hall, Malton, Yorks; *S* father, 1970; *m* 1947, Janet, *o d* of General Sir James Marshall-Cornwall, *qv*; three *s. Educ:* Eton; Trinity Coll., Cambridge. BA 1950; MA 1958. Served War of 1935: Coldstream Guards, 1940-46; NW Europe, 1944-45 (despatches, MC, Croix de Guerre); Hon. Col, 2nd Bn Yorkshire Volunteers, TAVR, 1971-. Chm., Legal and Parly Cttee, CLA, 1973-79; Pres., CLA, 1981- (Dep. Chm., 1979-81). Land Agent, 1951-. DL 1963, JP 1958, CC 1964-74, ER of Yorks; CC N Yorks, 1974-77; Mem., Yorkshire and Humberside Economic Planning Council, 1968-79. *Heir: s* Hon. Michael Charles James Willoughby [*b* 14 July 1948; *m* 1974, Hon. Lucy Sidney, *y d* of Viscount De L'Isle, *qv*; one *s* two *d*]. *Address:* Birdsall House, Malton, N Yorks. *T:* North Grimston 202. *Club:* Boodle's.

MIDDLETON, Bishop Suffragan of, since 1982; **Rt. Rev. Donald Alexander Tytler;** *b* 2 May 1925; *s* of Alexander and Cicely Tytler; *m* 1948, Jane Evelyn Hodgson; two *d. Educ:* Eastbourne College; Christ's College, Cambridge (MA); Ridley Hall, Cambridge. Asst Curate of Yardley, Birmingham, 1949; SCM Chaplain, Univ. of Birmingham, 1952; Precentor, Birmingham Cathedral, 1955; Diocesan Director of Education, Birmingham, 1957; Vicar of St Mark, Londonderry and Rural Dean of Warley, dio. Birmingham, 1963; Canon Residentiary of Birmingham Cathedral, 1972; Archdeacon of Aston, 1977-82. *Publications:* Operation Think, 1963; (contrib.) Stirrings (essays), 1976. *Recreations:* music, gardening. *Address:* The Hollies, Manchester Road, Rochdale, Lancs OL11 3QY. *T:* Rochdale 358550.

MIDDLETON, Donald King, CBE 1981; HM Diplomatic Service, retired; British High Commissioner, Papua New Guinea, 1977-82; *b* 24 Feb. 1922; *s* of late Harold Ernest Middleton and Ellen Middleton; *m* 1945, Marion Elizabeth Ryder; one *d. Educ:* King Edward's Sch., Birmingham; Saltley Coll. Min. of Health, 1958-61; joined Commonwealth Relations Office, 1961; First Sec., British High Commn, Lagos, 1961-65; Head of Chancery, British Embassy, Saigon, 1970-72; British Dep. High Commissioner, Ibadan, 1973-75; HM Chargé d'Affaires, Phnom Penh, 1975; seconded to NI Office, Belfast, 1975-77. *Address:* 31 The Dell, St Albans. *Club:* Royal Commonwealth Society.

MIDDLETON, Drew, OBE 1947 (Hon.); Military Correspondent of The New York Times, since 1970; *b* 14 Oct. 1914; *o s* of E. T. and Jean Drew Middleton, New York; *m* 1943, Estelle Mansel-Edwards, Dinas Powis, Glamorgan; one *d. Educ:* Syracuse Univ., Syracuse, New York. Correspondent: for Associated Press in London, 1939; for Associated Press in France, Belgium, London, Iceland, with the British Army and RAF, 1939-42; for The New York Times with US and British Forces in North Africa, Sicily, Britain, Normandy, Belgium and Germany, 1942-45; Chief Correspondent in USSR, 1946-47, in Germany, 1948-53, and in London, 1953-63; Chief Correspondent in Paris, 1963-65; Chief Correspondent, UN, 1965-69; European Affairs Correspondent, 1969-70. Correspondent at four meetings of Council of Foreign Ministers, also Potsdam and Casablanca Conferences. Medal of Freedom (US). English-Speaking Union Better Understanding Award, 1955. Doctor of Letters (*hc*) Syracuse Univ., 1963. *Publications:* Our Share of Night, 1946; The Struggle for Germany, 1949; The Defence of Western Europe, 1952; The British, 1957; The Sky Suspended, 1960; The Supreme Choice: Britain and the European Community, 1963; Crisis in the West, 1965; Retreat From Victory, 1973; Where Has Last July Gone?, 1974; Can America Win the Next War?, 1975; Submarine, 1976; Duel of the Giants, 1977. *Recreations:* tennis, the theatre. *Address:* The New York Times, 229 W 43rd Street, New York, NY 10036, USA. *Clubs:* Beefsteak, Press, Garrick, Travellers' (Paris); The Brook, Century (New York).

MIDDLETON, Francis; Advocate; Sheriff of Glasgow and Strathkelvin (formerly of Lanarkshire) at Glasgow, 1956-78; Temporary Sheriff, 1979; *b* 21 Nov. 1913; Scottish; *m* 1942, Edith Muir; two *s* one *d. Educ:* Rutherglen Academy; Glasgow Univ. MA, LLB 1937. Practising as Solicitor, 1937-39; volunteered Sept. 1939; Cameronian Scottish Rifles; commissioned to 6th Battn 11th Sikh Regt, Indian Army, 1940; Captain 1940; Major 1942, injured; Interpreter 1st Class in Hindustani, 1943; posted to Judge Advocate's Branch, 1944; released Dec. 1945. Admitted Faculty of Advocates in Scotland, 1946. Sheriff Substitute of Inverness, Moray, Nairn and Ross and Cromarty, 1949-52, Fife and Kinross, 1952-56. Dir, YMCA, Glasgow. Mem., Rotary

Club. *Recreations:* reading, gardening, golf. *Address:* 23 Kirklee Road, Glasgow G12 0RQ.

MIDDLETON, Sir George (Humphrey), KCMG 1958 (CMG 1950); HM Diplomatic Service, retired; *b* 21 Jan. 1910; *e s* of George Close Middleton and Susan Sophie (*née* Harley, subsequently Elphinstone); *m* Marie Elisabeth Camille Françoise Sarthou, Bordeaux; one *s*; one step *s* one step *d. Educ:* St Lawrence Coll., Ramsgate; Magdalen Coll., Oxford. Entered Consular Service, 1933, Vice-Consul, Buenos Aires; transferred to Asuncion, 1934, with local rank of 3rd Sec. in Diplomatic Service; in charge of Legation, 1935; transferred to New York, 1936; to Lemberg (Lwow), 1939; local rank of Consul; in charge of Vice-Consulate at Cluj, 1939–40; appointed to Genoa, 1940, to Madeira, 1940, to Foreign Office, 1943; 2nd Sec. at Washington, 1944; 1st Sec. 1945; transferred to FO, 1947; Counsellor, 1949; Counsellor, British Embassy, Tehran, Jan. 1951; acted as Chargé d'Affaires, 1951 and 1952 (when diplomatic relations severed); Dep. High Comr for UK, in Delhi, 1953–56; British Ambassador at Beirut, 1956–58; Political Resident in the Persian Gulf, 1958–61; British Ambassador to: Argentina, 1961–64; United Arab Republic, 1964–66. Mem. *Ad hoc* Cttee for UN Finances, 1966. Consultant, Industrial Reorganisation Corporation, 1967–68; Director: Michael Rice Ltd; C. E. Planning Ltd; East West Group (Europe) Ltd; Liberty Life Assurance Co. Ltd; Britarge Ltd; Decor France Ltd; Johnson and Bloy Holdings; Chm., Exec. Cttee, British Road Fedn, 1972; Chief Executive, British Industry Roads Campaign, 1969–76. Chairman: Bahrain Soc.; Anglo-Peruvian Soc.; British Moroccan Soc. FRSA. Comdr, Order of Merit, Peru. *Recreations:* fishing, tennis, talking. *Address:* 53 Albert Hall Mansions, SW7 2AG. *T:* 01-589 8406. *Clubs:* Travellers', Pratt's, Royal Automobile.

MIDDLETON, Sir George (P.), KCVO 1962 (CVO 1951; MVO 1941); MB, ChB (Aberdeen); Medical Practitioner, retired 1973; Surgeon Apothecary to HM Household at Balmoral Castle, 1932–73; *b* Schoolhouse, Findhorn, Morayshire, 26 Jan. 1905; *s* of late A. Middleton, FEIS, Kincorth, Elgin; *m* 1931, Margaret Wilson (*d* 1964), and *er d* of late A. Silver; one *s* one *d. Educ:* Findhorn; Forres Academy; Aberdeen Univ. Entered the Faculty of Medicine, 1921; Graduated, 1926, Bachelor of Medicine and Bachelor of Surgery, Ogston Prize and 1st medallist in Senior Systematic Surgery, 1st Medallist in Operative Surgery, House Surgeon Ward X, and House Physician Ward 4, Aberdeen Royal Infirmary, 1926; went to practice in Sheffield, 1927; Asst to late Sir Alexander Hendry, 1928; into partnership, 1929; partnership dissolved, 1931; taken into partnership, Dr James G. Moir, 1948. *Recreations:* golf, Association football, bowling. *Address:* Highland Home, Ballater, Aberdeenshire. *TA:* Highland Home, Ballater. *T:* Ballater 55478.

MIDDLETON, Kenneth William Bruce; Sheriff of Lothian and Borders at Edinburgh and Haddington; *b* Strathpeffer, Ross-shire, 1 Oct. 1905; 2nd *s* of W. R. T. Middleton; *m* 1938, Ruth Beverly (marr. diss. 1972), *d* of W. H. Mill; one *s* one *d. Educ:* Rossall Sch.; Merton Coll., Oxford; Edinburgh Univ. BA Oxford, LLB Edinburgh; called to Scottish Bar, 1931; Vans Dunlop Scholar in International Law and Constitutional Law and History, Edinburgh Univ.; Richard Brown Research Scholar in Law, Edinburgh Univ.; served War of 1939–45 with Royal Scots and Seaforth Highlanders; attached to Military Dept, Judge Advocate-Gen.'s Office, 1941–45. Sheriff-Substitute, subseq. Sheriff: Perth and Angus at Forfar, 1946–50; Lothians and Peebles, later Lothian and Borders, at Edinburgh and Haddington, 1950–. *Publication:* Britain and Russia, 1947. *Address:* Sheriff Court House, Court Street, Haddington, East Lothian.

MIDDLETON, Lawrence John, PhD; HM Diplomatic Service; Counsellor, UK Delegation to Committee on Disarmament, Geneva, since 1982; *b* 27 March 1930; *s* of John James Middleton and Mary (*née* Horgan); *m* 1963, Sheila Elizabeth Hoey; two *s* one *d. Educ:* Finchley Catholic Grammar Sch.; King's Coll., London (BSc 1951, PhD 1954). Scientific Officer, ARC, 1954–60 and 1962–63; Cons. to FAO and to UN Cttee on Effects of Atomic Radiation, 1960–62; CENTO Inst. of Nuclear Science, 1963–65; Principal, Min. of Agriculture, 1966–68; First Sec., FO, 1968; Washington, 1969–71; Kuala Lumpur, 1971–74; Counsellor (Commercial), Belgrade, 1974–78; Dir of Research, FCO, 1978–80; Cabinet Office, 1980–82. *Publications:* articles on plant physiology and nuclear science in biology, 1954–63. *Address:* c/o Foreign and Commonwealth Office, SW1; 373A Woodstock Road, Oxford.

MIDDLETON, Lucy Annie; Vice-President, Trade Union, Labour and Co-operative Democratic History Society, since 1969; Director and Foundation Chairman of War on Want, 1958–68; *b* 9 May 1894; 2nd *d* of late Sydney J. Cox, Keynsham, Somerset; *m* 1936, James S. Middleton (*d* 1962), sometime Sec. of Labour Party. *Educ:* Elementary Sch.; Colston's Girls' High Sch., Bristol; Bristol Univ. Held teaching appts under Gloucester and Bristol Authorities until 1924 when she became Organising Sec. in the Peace Movement; political adviser to Hindu Minorities during sittings of Round Table Conferences; joined staff of Labour Party, 1934. Governor of Chelsea Polytechnic, 1936–57. Certificated Advertising Consultant. Attended Inter-Parliamentary Union Confs Brussels, Nice, Rome, Stockholm, presenting Reports on Maternity and Child Welfare, Family Allowances, and Safeguarding of Women in Employment throughout the World; formerly Mem. of House of Commons Estimates Cttee. MP (Labour) Sutton Div. of Plymouth, 1945–50 (re-elected for enlarged Div., 1950–51). Life Pres., Wimbledon Lab. Party, 1978. *Publication:* Women in the Labour Movement,

1977. *Recreations:* cooking, gardening, golf. *Address:* 7 Princes Road, Wimbledon, SW19 8RQ. *T:* 01-542 2791.

MIDDLETON, Michael Humfrey, CBE 1975; Director, Civic Trust, since 1969; *b* 1 Dec. 1917; *s* of Humfrey Middleton and Lilian Irene (*née* Tillard); *m* 1954, Julie Margaret Harrison; one *s* two *d. Educ:* King's Sch., Canterbury. Art Critic, The Spectator, 1946–56; Art Editor and Asst Editor, Picture Post, 1949–53; Exec. Editor, Lilliput, 1953–54; Editor, House and Garden, 1955–57; Sec. and Dep. Dir, Civic Trust, 1957–69; Mem. Council, Soc. of Industrial Artists and Designers, 1953–55, 1968–70; UK Sec.-Gen., European Architectural Heritage Year, 1972–75. Member: Adv. Cttee on Trunk Road Assessment, 1977–80; UK Commn for UNESCO, 1976–80. FSIA; Hon. Fellow, RIBA, 1974. Film scripts include A Future for the Past, 1972. Council of Europe Pro Merito Medal, 1976. *Publications:* Soldiers of Lead, 1948; Group Practice in Design, 1967; contributor to many conferences and jls, at home and abroad, on art, design and environmental matters. *Recreation:* looking. *Address:* 46 Holland Park Avenue, W11. *T:* 01-727 9136.

MIDDLETON, Peter Edward; Deputy Secretary, HM Treasury, since 1980; *b* 2 April 1934; *m* 1964, Valerie Ann Lindup; one *s* one *d. Educ:* Sheffield City Grammar Sch.; Sheffield Univ. (BA); Bristol Univ. Served RAPC, 1958–60. HM Treasury: Senior Information Officer, 1962; Principal, 1964; Asst Director, Centre for Administrative Studies, 1967–69; Private Sec. to Chancellor of the Exchequer, 1969–72; Treasury Press Secretary, 1972–75; Head of Monetary Policy Div., 1975; Under Secretary, 1976. Vis. Fellow, Nuffield Coll., Oxford. *Address:* HM Treasury, Parliament Street, SW1. *Club:* Reform.

MIDDLETON, Ronald George, DSC 1945; solicitor; *b* 31 July 1913; *o s* of late Sir George Middleton; *m* 1959, Sybil Summerscale (*d* 1976); no *c. Educ:* Whitgift Middle Sch.; University Coll., London. Solicitor, 1936. RNVR, 1939–47 (1st-Comdr); Radar Officer HMS Queen Elizabeth, 1944–45; Fleet Radar Officer, Indian Ocean, 1945. Partner, Coward, Chance & Co., 1949, Senior Partner, 1972–80. Director: Morgan Crucible Co. Ltd; Babcock Internat. Ltd. Part-time Mem., NBPI, 1965–68. *Recreation:* sailing. *Address:* Quin, Wineham, Henfield, W Sussex. *T:* Cowfold 236. *Clubs:* Reform, Garrick, Royal Ocean Racing.

MIDDLETON, Stanley; novelist; *b* Bulwell, Nottingham, 1 Aug. 1919; *y s* of Thomas and Elizabeth Ann Middleton; *m* 1951, Margaret Shirley, *y d* of Herbert and Winifred Vera Welch; two *d. Educ:* High Pavement Sch.; University Coll., Nottingham (later Univ. of Nottingham); Hon. MA Nottingham, 1975. Served Army (RA and AEC), 1940–46. Head of English Dept, High Pavement Coll., Nottingham, 1958–81. Judith E. Wilson Vis. Fellow, Emmanuel Coll., Cambridge, 1982–83. *Publications:* novels: A Short Answer, 1958; Harris's Requiem, 1960; A Serious Woman, 1961; The Just Exchange, 1962; Two's Company, 1963; Him They Compelled, 1964; Terms of Reference, 1966; The Golden Evening, 1968; Wages of Virtue, 1969; Apple of the Eye, 1970; Brazen Prison, 1971; Cold Gradations, 1972; A Man Made of Smoke, 1973; Holiday (jtly, Booker Prize 1974), 1974; Distractions, 1975; Still Waters, 1976; Ends and Means, 1977; Two Brothers, 1978; In A Strange Land, 1979; The Other Side, 1980; Blind Understanding, 1982. *Recreations:* music, walking, listening, argument. *Address:* 42 Caledon Road, Sherwood, Nottingham NG5 2NG. *T:* Nottingham 623085. *Club:* PEN.

MIDDLETON, Sir Stephen Hugh, 9th Bt, *cr* 1662; *b* 1909; *s* of Lt Hugh Jeffery Middleton, RN, 3rd *s* of Sir Arthur Middleton, 7th Bt; *S* uncle 1942; *m* 1962, Mary (*d* 1972), *d* of late Richard Robinson. *Educ:* Eton; Magdalene Coll., Cambridge. *Heir:* *b* Lawrence Monck Middleton, *b* 1912. *Address:* Belsay Castle, Northumberland.

MIDGLEY, Eric Atkinson, CMG 1965; MBE 1945; HM Diplomatic Service, retired; *b* 25 March 1913; *s* of Charles Ewart Midgley, Keighley, Yorks; *m* 1937, Catherine Gaminara; two *d. Educ:* Christ's Hosp.; Merton Coll., Oxford. Indian Civil Service, 1937; Trade Commissioner at Delhi, 1947; Board of Trade, 1957; Commercial Counsellor at The Hague, 1960; Minister (Economic) in India, 1963–67; Minister (Commercial), Washington, 1967–70; Ambassador to Switzerland, 1970–73. *Recreation:* sailing. *Address:* 2 Wellington Place, Captains Row, Lymington, Hants. *Club:* Royal Lymington Yacht.

MIDLETON, 11th Viscount *cr* 1717, of Midleton, Ireland; **Trevor Lowther Brodrick;** Baron Brodrick, Midleton, Ireland, 1715; Baron Brodrick, Peper Harow, 1796; *b* 7 March 1903; *s* of William John Henry Brodrick, OBE (*d* 1964) (*g s* of 7th Viscount), and Blanche Sophia Emily (*d* 1944), *e d* of F. A. Hawker; *S* to viscountcy of cousin, 2nd Earl of Midleton, MC, 1979; *m* 1940, Sheila Campbell MacLeod, *d* of Charles Campbell MacLeod. *Educ:* privately. *Recreations:* photography and gardening. *Heir:* *nephew* Alan Henry Brodrick [*b* 4 Aug. 1949; *m* 1978, Julia Helen, *d* of Michael Pitt]. *Address:* Frogmore Cottage, 105 North Road, Bourne, Lincolnshire PE10 9BU.

MIDWINTER, Eric Clare, MA, DPhil; Director, Centre for Policy on Ageing, since 1980; *b* 11 Feb. 1932; *m*; two *s* one *d. Educ:* St Catharine's Coll., Cambridge (BA Hons History); Univs of Liverpool (MA Educn) and York (DPhil). Educational posts, incl. Dir of Liverpool Educn Priority Area Project, 1955–75; Head, Public Affairs Unit, Nat. Consumer Council, 1975–80. Chairman: Council, Adv. Centre for Educn, 1976–; London Transport Users Consultative Cttee, 1977–. *Publications:* Victorian Social Reform, 1968; Law and Order in Victorian Lancashire, 1968; Social Administration in Lancashire, 1969; Nineteenth Century Education, 1970; Old Liverpool, 1971; Projections: an education priority project at work, 1972; Social Environment and the Urban School, 1972; Priority Education, 1972; Patterns of Community Education, 1973; ed, Teaching in the Urban Community School, 1973; ed, Pre-School Priorities, 1974; Education and the Community, 1975; Education for Sale, 1977; Make 'Em Laugh: famous comedians and their world, 1978; Schools and Society, 1980; W. G. Grace: his life and times, 1981; chapters in: Fit to Teach, 1971; Comparative Development in Social Welfare, 1972; Year Book of Social Policy, 1972; Cities, Communities and the Young, 1973; Equality and City Schools, 1973; Better Social Services, 1973; Education and Social Action, 1975; Action-Research in Community Development, 1975. *Recreations:* sport, comedy. *Address:* Nuffield Lodge, Regent's Park, NW1. *T:* 01-722 8871.

MIDWINTER, Stanley Walter, CB 1982; RIBA, FRTPI; Chief Planning Inspector (Director of Planning Inspectorate), Departments of the Environment and Transport, since 1978; *b* 8 Dec. 1922; *s* of late Lewis Midwinter and Beatrice (*née* Webb); *m* 1954, Audrey Mary Pepper; one *d*. *Educ:* Regent Street Polytechnic Sch.; Sch. of Architecture (DipArch, ARIBA 1948); Sch. of Planning and Res. for Regional Develt (AMTPI 1952, FRTPI 1965); Dip. in Sociol., Univ. of London, 1976. Served War, RE, 1942-46: N Africa, Italy, Greece. Planning Officer, LCC, 1949-54; Bor. Architect and Planning Officer, Larne, NI, 1955-60; joined Housing and Planning Inspectorate, 1960; Dep. Chief Inspector, 1974. Assessor at Belvoir Coalfield Inquiry, 1979. Town Planning Institute: Exam. Prize, 1952; Thomas Adams Prize, 1955; President's Prize, 1958. *Publications:* articles in TPI Jl. *Address:* Tollgate House, Houlton Street, Bristol BS2 9DJ.

MIERS, Rear-Adm. Sir Anthony (Cecil Capel), VC 1942; KBE 1959; CB 1958; DSO 1941; Royal Navy retired; joined National Car Parks as Director for Development Coordination, 1971; with London and Provincial Poster Group, since 1962, Consultant, since 1972; *b* 11 Nov. 1906; 2nd *s* of late Capt. D. N. C. C. Miers, Queen's Own Cameron Highlanders (killed in France, Sept. 1914); *m* 1945, Patricia Mary, *d* of late D. M. Millar, of the Chartered Bank of India, Australia and China; one *s* one *d*. *Educ:* Stubbington House; Edinburgh Academy; Wellington Coll. Special entry cadet RN 1924. Joined submarines, 1929; commanded HM Submarine L54, 1936-37 (Coronation medal at HM's review in 1937); HMS Iron Duke, 1937-38; naval staff course, 1938 (psc); on staff of Admiral of the Fleet Sir Charles Forbes, C-in-C Home Fleet, in HM Ships Nelson, Rodney, and Warspite (despatches), 1939-40; commanded HM Submarine Torbay, 1940-42 (DSO and Bar, VC); Staff of Fleet Adm. C. W. Nimitz, C-in-C US Pacific Fleet, 1943-44 (US Legion of Merit, degree of Officer, 1945); Comdr S/M 8th Submarine Flotilla in HMS Maidstone, 1944-45; Commanded HMS Vernon II (Ramillies and Malaya), 1946; jssc 1947; Comd HMS Blackcap (RN Air Station, Stretton), 1948-50; Comd HMS Forth and Capt. S/M, 1st Submarine Flotilla, 1950-52. Capt. of the RN Coll., Greenwich, 1952-54 (Coronation medal, 1953); Commanded HMS Theseus, 1954-55; Flag Officer, Middle East, 1956-59. With Mills and Allen Ltd, 1962-74. Obtained pilot's certificate ("A" License), 1948. Governor, Star and Garter Home, Richmond, 1970-76; Chm., RN Scholarship Fund, 1968-73. Nat. Pres., Submarine Old Comrades Assoc., 1967-81. Chm., Hudsons Offshore Ltd, 1972-73. Burgess and Freeman of Burgh of Inverness, 1955; Mem., Royal Highland Soc., 1966. Councillor, Lawn Tennis Assoc., 1954-78, Hon. Life Councillor 1979; Pres. RN Squash Rackets Assoc., 1960-70; Pres. RN Lawn Tennis Assoc., 1962-78; FInstD 1960. Freeman of the City of London, 1966; Mem., Court of Assistants, 1969, Under Warden, 1982, Worshipful Company of Tin Plate Workers; Hon. Kt, Hon. Soc. of Knights of Round Table, 1967. Silver Jubilee Medal, 1977. *Address:* 8 Highdown Road, Roehampton, SW15 5BU. *T:* 01-788 6863. *Clubs:* Army and Navy, Curzon House, Crockford's, Hurlingham, MCC, British Sportsman's; London Scottish Football; Royal Navy 1765 and 1785; Hampshire Hog Cricket; Anchorites (President 1968).

MIERS, Henry David Alastair Capel, CMG 1979; HM Diplomatic Service; Head of Middle Eastern Department, Foreign and Commonwealth Office, since 1980; *b* 10 Jan. 1937; *s* of Col R. D. M. C. Miers, DSO, QO Cameron Highlanders, and Honor (*née* Bucknill); *m* 1966, Imelda Maria Emilia, *d* of Jean-Baptiste Wouters, Huizingen, Belgium; two *s* one *d*. *Educ:* Winchester; University Coll. Oxford. Tokyo, 1963; Vientiane, 1966; Private Sec. to Minister of State, FO, 1968; Paris, 1972; Counsellor, Tehran, 1977-80. *Address:* c/o Foreign and Commonwealth Office, SW1.

MIGDALE, Hon. Lord; James Frederick Gordon Thomson, MA; DL; a Lord Commissioner of Justiciary, Scotland, and a Senator of HM College of Justice in Scotland, 1953-73; Lord Lieutenant of Sutherland, 1962-72; *b* 22 June 1897; *s* of late William Thomson, advocate, and Emmeline E. Gordon; *m* 1938, Louise Carnegie (*d* 1947), *d* of Roswell Miller and Mrs Carnegie Miller, of NY and Skibo Castle, Dornoch; one *s* four *d*. *Educ:* Edinburgh Academy and Clayesmore; Edinburgh and Glasgow Univs. Served European War, 1914-19, Royal Scots; War of 1939-45, Lt-Col Home Guard. Mem. Faculty of Advocates, 1924; Advocate-Depute, 1939-40; Standing Counsel to Board of Inland Revenue in Scotland, 1944-45; QC (Scotland) 1945; Sheriff of Ayr and Bute, 1949-52; Home Advocate Depute, 1952-53. Life Trustee, Carnegie UK Trust. DL Sutherlandshire, 1959-. *Address:* Ospisdale, Dornoch, Sutherland IV25 3RH. *Clubs:* New (Edinburgh); Hon. Company of Edinburgh Golfers.

    See also J. G. Milligan.

MIKARDO, Ian; MP (Lab) Tower Hamlets, Bethnal Green and Bow, since 1974 (Poplar, 1964-74); *b* 9 July 1908; *m* 1932, Mary Rosette; two *d*. *Educ:* Portsmouth. MP (Lab) Reading, 1945-50, South Div. of Reading, 1950-55, again Reading, 1955-Sept. 1959. Member: Nat. Exec. Cttee of Labour Party, 1950-59, and 1960-78 (Chm., 1970-71); Internat Cttee of Labour Party (Chm., 1973-78); Chm., Parly Labour Party, March-Nov. 1974; Chm., Select Cttee on Nationalized Industries, 1966-70. Pres., ASTMS, 1968-73; Vice-Pres., Socialist International, 1978-. *Publications:* Centralised Control of Industry, 1944; Frontiers in the Air, 1946; (with others) Keep Left, 1947; The Second Five Years, 1948; The Problems of Nationalisation, 1948; (joint) Keeping Left, 1950; The Labour Case, 1950; It's a Mug's Game, 1951; Socialism or Slump, 1959. *Address:* House of Commons, SW1A 0AA. *T:* 01-219 5007.

MIKES, George, LLD (Budapest); Author; *b* Siklós, Hungary, 15 Feb. 1912; *s* of Dr Alfred Mikes and Margit Gál; *m* 1st, 1941, Isobel Gerson (marr. diss.), one *s*; 2nd, 1948, Lea Hanak; one *d*. *Educ:* Cistercian Gymnasium, Pécs; Budapest Univ. Theatrical critic on Budapest newspapers, 1931-38; London correspondent of Budapest papers, 1938-41; working for Hungarian Service of BBC, 1941-51. Pres., PEN in Exile, 1972-80. Governor, London Oratory School, 1978-. *Publications:* How to be an Alien, 1946; How to Scrape Skies, 1948; Wisdom for Others, 1950; Milk and Honey, 1950; Down with Everybody!, 1951; Shakespeare and Myself, 1952; Uber Alles, 1953; Eight Humorists, 1954; Little Cabbages, 1955; Italy for Beginners, 1956; The Hungarian Revolution, 1957; East is East, 1958; A Study in Infamy, 1959; How to be Inimitable, 1960; Tango, 1961; Switzerland for Beginners, 1962, new edn 1975; Mortal Passion, 1963; Prison (ed), 1963; How to Unite Nations, 1963; Eureka!, 1965; (with the Duke of Bedford) Book of Snobs, 1965; How to be Affluent, 1966; Not by Sun Alone, 1967; Boomerang, 1968; The Prophet Motive, 1969; Humour-In Memoriam, 1970; The Land of the Rising Yen, 1970; (with Duke of Bedford) How to run a Stately Home, 1971; Any Souvenirs?, 1971; The Spy Who Died of Boredom, 1973; Charlie, 1976; How to be Decadent, 1977; Tsi-Tsa, 1978; English Humour for Beginners, 1980; How to be Seventy, 1982; The Virgin and the Bull (play), 1982. *Recreations:* tennis, cooking, and not listening to funny stories. *Address:* 1B Dorncliffe Road, SW6. *T:* 01-736 2624. *Clubs:* Garrick, Hurlingham, PEN.

MILBANK, Major Sir Mark (Vane), 4th Bt, *cr* 1882; KCVO 1962; MC 1944; Extra Equerry to the Queen since 1954; Master of HM's Household, 1954-67; *b* 11 Jan. 1907; *e s* of Sir Frederick Milbank, 3rd Bt; *S* father, 1964; *m* 1938, Hon. Verena Aileen (she *m* 1st, 1934, Charles Lambert Crawley who died 1935), *yr d* of 11th Baron Farnham, DSO; two *s*. *Educ:* Eton; RMC, Sandhurst. Coldstream Guards, 1927-36 and 1939-45; ADC to Governor of Bombay, 1933-38; Comptroller to Governor General of Canada, 1946-52; Dir, Norwich Union, London Advisory Board, 1964-74. *Heir:* *s* Anthony Frederick Milbank [*b* 16 Aug. 1939; *m* 1970, Belinda Beatrice, *yr d* of Brigadier Adrian Gore, Sellindge, Kent; two *s* one *d*]. *Address:* Gate House, Barningham, Richmond, N Yorks. *T:* Teesdale 21269.

MILBORNE-SWINNERTON-PILKINGTON, Sir T. H.; *see* Pilkington.

MILBOURN, Dr Graham Maurice; Director, National Institute of Agricultural Botany, since 1981; *b* 4 Sept. 1930; *s* of late Frank McLaren Milbourn, BSc and Winifred May Milbourn; *m* 1956, Joan Louise Lawson; three *s*. *Educ:* Reading Univ. (BSc, MSc, PhD). Asst Lectr, Reading Univ., 1953-56; Radiobiological Lab., ARC, 1956-61; Sen. Lectr, Crop Production, Wye Coll., London Univ., 1961-77; Prof. of Crop Production, Sch. of Agric., Edinburgh Univ., 1977-81. *Publications:* papers on physiology of cereals and vegetables, uptake of radio-nucleides by crops, in scientific jls. *Recreation:* sailing. *Address:* National Institute of Agricultural Botany, Huntingdon Road, Cambridge CB3 0LE. *T:* Cambridge 276381.

MILBURN, Donald B.; *see* Booker-Milburn.

MILBURN, Sir John (Nigel), 4th Bt *cr* 1905; *b* 22 April 1918; *s* of Sir Leonard John Milburn, 3rd Bt, and Joan, 2nd *d* of Henry Anson-Horton, Catton Hall, Derbs; *S* father 1957; *m* 1940, Dorothy Joan, *d* of Leslie Butcher, Dunholme, Lincoln; one *s* decd. *Educ:* Eton; Trinity Coll., Cambridge. Served War of 1939-45 with Northumberland Hussars. *Recreations:* Joint-Master West Percy Foxhounds, 1955-59, 1963-. *Heir:* nephew Anthony Rupert Milburn [*b* 17 April 1947; *m* 1977, Olivia Shirley Catlow; one *s* one *d*. *Educ:* Eton; Royal Agric. Coll., Cirencester]. *Address:* Brainshaugh, Acklington, Northumberland. *T:* Shilbottle 631. *Club:* Northern Counties (Newcastle upon Tyne).

MILBURN, Very Rev. Robert Leslie Pollington, MA; *b* 28 July 1907; *er s* of late George Leslie and Elizabeth Esther Milburn; *m* 1944, Margery Kathleen Mary, *d* of Rev. Francis Graham Harvie; one *d* (one *s* decd). *Educ:* Oundle; Sidney Sussex Coll., Cambridge; New Coll., Oxford. Asst Master, Eton Coll., 1930-32; Select Preacher, University of Oxford, 1942-44; Fellow and Chaplain of Worcester Coll., Oxford, 1934-57, Tutor, 1945-57, Estates Bursar, 1946-57 (Junior Bursar, 1936-46), Hon. Fellow, 1978. University Lectr in Church History, 1947-57; Bampton Lectr, 1952. Examining Chaplain to Bishop of St Edmundsbury and Ipswich, 1941-53, to Bishop of Southwark, 1950-57, to Bishop of Oxford, 1952-57; Dean of Worcester, 1957-68, now Emeritus; Master of the Temple, 1968-80. Mem. of Oxford City Council, 1941-47. A Trustee, Wallace Collection, 1970-76. Grand Chaplain, United Grand Lodge of England, 1969. OStJ. *Publications:* Saints and their Emblems in English Churches, 1949; Early Christian Interpretations of History, 1954; articles in Journal of Theological Studies and Church Quarterly Review. *Address:* Wallcroft, Bromyard, Herefordshire. *Club:* Athenæum.

MILCHSACK, Dame Lilo, Hon. DCMG 1972 (Hon. CMG 1968); Hon. CBE 1958; Initiator, 1949, and Hon. Chairman, since 1982, Deutsch-Englische Gesellschaft eV (Hon. Secretary, 1949-77; Chairman, 1977-82); *b* Frankfurt/Main; *d* of Prof. Dr Paul Duden and Johanna Bertha (*née* Nebe); *m* Hans Milchsack; two *d. Educ:* Univs of Frankfurt, Geneva and Amsterdam. Awarded Grosses Bundesverdienstkreuz, 1959. *Recreations:* gardening, reading. *Address:* An der Kalvey 11, D-4000 Düsseldorf 31-Wittlaer, Germany. *T:* Düsseldorf 40 13 87. *Club:* Sesame.

MILDON, Arthur Leonard, QC 1971; a Recorder, since 1972; *b* 3 June 1923; *er s* of late Rev. Dr W. H. Mildon, Barnstaple; *m* 1950, Iva, *er d* of late G. H. C. Wallis, Plymouth; one *s* one *d. Educ:* Kingswood Sch., Bath; Wadham Coll., Oxford (MA). Pres., Oxford Univ. Liberal Club, 1948. Army Service, 1942-46: Lieut, 138th (City of London) Field Regt, RA; Captain, 1st Army Group, RA. Called to Bar, Middle Temple, 1950, Bencher, 1979; Mem., Bar Council, 1973-74; Member of Western Circuit. Dep. Chm., Isle of Wight QS, 1967-71. *Recreation:* sailing. *Address:* 2 Crown Office Row, Temple, EC4. *T:* 01-583 8155. *Clubs:* Hampshire (Winchester); Royal Solent Yacht.

MILEDI, Prof. Ricardo, MD; FRS 1970; Professor of Biophysics, University College London, since 1965; *b* 15 Sept. 1927. *Educ:* Univ. of Mexico City. BSc 1948; MD 1954. Engaged in research at Nat. Inst. of Cardiology, 1953-56; Rockefeller Travelling Fellowship at ANU, 1956-58; research work in Dept of Biophysics, UCL, 1958-63, Reader, 1963-65. Royal Society Foulerton Res. Prof., 1975-. *Address:* Department of Biophysics, University College, Gower Street, WC1E 6BT. *T:* 01-387 7050; 5 Park Crescent Mews East, W1N 5HB. *T:* 01-636 3240.

MILES, family name of **Baron Miles.**

MILES, Baron *cr* 1979 (Life Peer), of Blackfriars in the City of London; **Bernard James Miles,** Kt 1969; CBE 1953; Actor; Founder, with his wife, of the Mermaid Theatre, Puddle Dock, EC4, 1959 (first opened in North London, 1950-); *b* 27 Sept. 1907; *s* of Edwin James Miles and Barbara Fletcher; *m* 1931, Josephine Wilson; one *s* two *d. Educ:* Uxbridge County Sch.; Pembroke Coll., Oxford (Hon. Fellow, 1969). Hon. DLitt, City Univ., 1974. First stage appearance as Second Messenger in Richard III, New Theatre, 1930; appeared in St Joan, His Majesty's, 1931; spent 5 years in repertory as designer, stage-manager, character-actor, etc; frequent appearances on West End Stage from 1938. Entered films, 1937, and has written for, directed, and acted in them. First went on Music-hall stage, London Palladium, etc., 1950. Mermaid Theatre seasons: Royal Exchange, 1953; Macbeth, Dido and Aeneas, As You Like It, Eastward Ho! Formed Mermaid Theatre Trust which built City of London's first theatre for 300 years, the Mermaid, Puddle Dock, EC4. Opened May 1959, with musical play Lock Up Your Daughters. *Publications:* The British Theatre, 1947; God's Brainwave, 1972; Favourite Tales from Shakespeare, 1976; (ed with J. C. Trewin) Curtain Calls, 1981. *Address:* Mermaid Theatre, Puddle Dock, Blackfriars, EC4V 3DB.

MILES, Prof. Albert Edward William, LRCP; MRCS; FDS; DSc; Professor of Dental Pathology at The London Hospital Medical College, 1950-76, retired; Hon. Curator, Odontological Collection, Royal College of Surgeons of England since 1955; *b* 15 July 1912; *m* 1939, Sylvia Stuart; one *s* decd. *Educ:* Stationers' Company Sch.; Charing Cross and Royal Dental Hosps. John Tomes Prize, RCS, 1954-56. Charles Tomes Lecturer, RCS, 1957; Evelyn Sprawson Lectr, London Hosp. Med. Coll., 1977. Hunterian Trustee, 1978-. Howard Mummery Meml Prize, 1976; Colyer Gold Medal, RCS, 1978. Exec. Editor, Archives of Oral Biology, 1969-. *Publications:* contrib. to scientific literature. *Address:* 1 Cleaver Square, Kennington, SE11. *T:* 01-735 5350. *Clubs:* Tetrapods, Zoo.

MILES, Anthony John; Chairman, since 1980 (Deputy Chairman, 1977-79), and Editorial Director, since 1975, Mirror Group Newspapers; *b* 18 July 1930; *s* of Paul and Mollie Miles; *m* 1975, Anne Hardman. *Educ:* High Wycombe Royal Grammar Sch. On staff of (successively): Middlesex Advertiser; Nottingham Guardian; Brighton Evening Argus. Daily Mirror: Feature writer, 1954-66; Asst Editor, 1967-68; Associate Editor, 1968-71; Editor, 1971-74. Dir, Reuters Ltd, 1978-. Member: Press Council, 1975-78; British Exec. Cttee, IPI, 1976-. *Address:* Mirror Group Newspapers, Holborn Circus, EC1P 1DQ. *Club:* Reform.

MILES, Sir (Arnold) Ashley, Kt 1966; CBE 1953; FRS 1961; MA, MD, FRCP, FRCPath; Professor of Experimental Pathology, University of London, 1952-71, now Emeritus Professor; Director of the Lister Institute of Preventive Medicine, London, 1952-71; Deputy Director, Department of Medical Microbiology, London Hospital Medical College, since 1976; Hon. Consultant in Microbiology, London Hospital, 1976; *b* 20 March 1904; *s* of Harry Miles, York; *m* 1930, Ellen Marguerite, *d* of Harald Dahl, Cardiff; no *c. Educ:* Bootham Sch., York; King's Coll., Cambridge, Hon. Fellow, 1971; St Bartholomew's Hosp., London. Demonstrator in Bacteriology, London Sch. of Hygiene and Tropical Medicine, 1929; Demonstrator in Pathol., University of Cambridge, 1931; Reader in Bacteriology, British Postgraduate Medical Sch., London, 1935; Prof. Bacteriology, University of London, 1937-45; Acting Dir Graham Medical Research Laboratories, University Coll.

Hosp. Medical Sch., 1943-45; London Sector Pathologist, Emergency Medical Services, 1939-44; Dir, Medical Research Council Wound Infection Unit, Birmingham Accident Hosp., 1942-46; Dep. Dir, 1947-52 and Dir of Dept of Biological Standards, 1946-52, National Institute for Medical Research, London. Biological Sec. and Vice-Pres., Royal Society, 1963-68. MRC grant holder, Clinical Res. Centre, 1971-76. Pres., Internat. Assoc. Microbiological Socs, 1974-78. Trustee, Beit Memorial Fellowships, 1970-81. For. Corresp., Acad. de Médecine de Belgique, 1972. Hon. Member: Soc. Gen. Microbiology, 1972; Amer. Soc. for Microbiol., 1974; Amer. Assoc. of Pathologists, 1977; Deutsche Gesellschaft für Hygiene und Mikrobiologie, 1978; British Acad. of Forensic Scis, 1978; Path. Soc. of GB, 1980; Fellow, World Acad. Art and Science, 1975; Hon. Fellow: Infectious Diseases Soc. of Amer., 1979; RSocMed, 1981; Hon. FInstBiol, 1975; Consejero de Honor, Consejo Superior de Investigaciones Cientiificas, Madrid, 1966. Hon. DSc, Newcastle, 1969. *Publications:* (with G. S. Wilson), Topley and Wilson's Principles of Bacteriology and Immunity, 1945, 1955, 1964, 1975; various scientific papers. *Recreations:* various. *Address:* Department of Medical Microbiology, London Hospital Medical College, Turner Street, E1 2AD. *T:* 01-377 8800, ext. 105.

MILES, Basil Raymond, CBE 1968; Puisne Judge, Kenya, 1957-67, retired; *b* 10 Oct. 1906; *s* of John Thomas Miles and Winifred Miles, Wrexham, Denbighshire; *m* 1944, Margaret Baldwin Neilson; one *s* one *d. Educ:* Harrow; Magdalen Coll., Oxford. Barrister, Inner Temple, 1931; appointed Resident Magistrate, Tanganyika, 1946; Judge of the Supreme Court, The Gambia, 1953-57. A part-time Chm. of Industrial Tribunals, 1967-74. *Recreation:* music. *Address:* Mbeya, Chesham Road, Bovingdon, Herts. *T:* 3187.

MILES, Mrs Caroline Mary; Market Development Consultant, Harwell Research Laboratory, since 1981; Member, Monopolies and Mergers Commission, since 1975; *b* 30 April 1929; *d* of Brig. A.J.R.M.Leslie, OBE. *Educ:* numerous schools; Somerville Coll., Oxford. HM Treasury, 1953-54; NIESR, 1954-56 and 1964-67; attached to UN Secretariat, NY, 1956-63. Associate Mem., Nuffield Coll., Oxford, 1972-74. Member: Textile Council, 1968-71; Inflation Accounting Cttee (Sandilands Cttee), 1974-75; NEB, 1976-79. *Recreations:* picnics, poohsticks. *Address:* c/o Messrs Coutts & Co., 162 Brompton Road, SW3 1HW.

MILES, Prof. Charles William Noel, CBE 1980; Head of Department of Land Management and Development, 1968-81, Dean of Faculty of Urban and Regional Studies, 1972-75, and Professor Emeritus 1981, University of Reading; Chairman, Agricultural Wages Board for England and Wales, 1972-81; *b* 3 Nov. 1915; 2nd *s* of late Lt-Col Sir Charles W. Miles, 5th Bt; *m* 1940, Jacqueline (Dickie) Cross; one *d* (one *s* decd). *Educ:* Stowe Sch.; Jesus Coll., Cambridge (MA). FRICS. Army Service, 1939-46; Univ. Demonstrator and Univ. Lectr, Dept of Estate Management, Cambridge, 1946-54; Chief Agent to Meyrick Estates in Hants and Anglesey, 1954-68; Agent to Bisterne Estate, 1957-68. Pres., Chartered Land Agents Soc., 1965-66; Mem., Cambs AEC, 1953-54; Mem., SE Region Adv. Cttee of Land Commn, 1967-70. Mem., Yates Cttee on Recreation Management Trng, 1977-82. Leverhulme Trust Emeritus Fellowship, 1982-84. *Publications:* Estate Finance and Business Management, 1953, 4th edn 1981; Estate Accounts, 1960; Recreational Land Management, 1977; (co-ed) Walmesley's Rural Estate Management, 6th edn, 1978. *Recreations:* walking, gardening, theatre. *Address:* Glebe Cottage, Mattingley, Basingstoke, Hants. *T:* Heckfield 357. *See also* Sir W. N. M. Miles, Bt.

MILES, Dillwyn, FRGS 1946; The Herald Bard, since 1967; Director, Dyfed Rural Council, 1975-81; Chairman, National Association of Local Councils, since 1977; *b* 25 May 1916; *s* of Joshua Miles and Anne Mariah (*née* Lewis), Newport, Pembrokeshire; *m* 1944, Joyce Eileen (*d* 1976), *d* of Lewis Craven Ord, Montreal and London; one *s* one *d. Educ:* Fishguard County Sch.; University College of Wales, Aberystwyth. Served War of 1939-45, Middle East, Army Captain. National Organiser Palestine House, London, 1945-48; Extra-mural Lectr, Univ. of Wales, 1948-51; Community Centres Officer, Wales, 1951-54; Gen. Sec., Pembrokeshire Community Council, 1954-75. Founder: Jerusalem Welsh Soc., 1940; W Wales Tourist Assoc., 1962; Assoc. of Trusts for Nature Conservation in Wales, 1973; Hon. Sec., W Wales Naturalists Trust, 1958-75 (Vice-Pres., 1975-). Grand Sword Bearer, Gorsedd of Bards of Isle of Britain, 1959-67 (Mem. Bd, 1945-). Member: Pembrokeshire CC, 1947-63; Cemaes RDC, 1947-52; Newport Parish Council, 1946-52; Haverfordwest Bor. Council, 1957-63; Pembrokeshire Coast Nat. Park Cttee, 1952-75; Exec. Cttee, Council for Protection of Rural Wales, 1946-64; Nature Conservancy's Cttee for Wales, 1966-73; Council, Soc. for Promotion of Nature Reserves, 1961-73; Countryside in 1970 Cttee for Wales, 1969-70; Sports Council for Wales, 1965-69; Mental Health Rev. Tribunal for Wales, 1959-71; Rent Trib. for Wales, 1966-; Court of Govs, Nat. Libr. for Wales, 1963-64; Court of Govs, Univ. of Wales, 1957-66; Pembroke TA Assoc., 1956-59; Council for Small Industries in Wales, 1968-72; Age Concern Wales, 1972-77; Exec. Cttee, Nat. Council for Social Service, 1978-81; Exec. Cttee, NPFA, 1977-81; Council, Royal Nat. Eisteddfod of Wales, 1967-; Prince of Wales Cttee, 1971-80 (former Chm., Dyfed Projects Gp); Welsh Environment Foundn, 1971-80; Heraldry Soc., 1974-. Former Chairman: Further Educn and Libraries and Museums Cttees, Pembs CC; Pembs Cttee, Arthritis and Rheumatism Council; Pembs Jun. Ch. of Commerce; Pembs Community Health Council; Policy and Welsh Cttees, Nat. Assoc. of Local Councils. Vice-Chm., Pembs PO Adv. Cttee, 1971-; Chm., Wales Playing Fields Assoc., 1965-81. Editor: The Pembrokeshire

Historian, 1955-81; Nature in Wales, 1970-80. Mayor of Newport, Pembs, 1950, 1966, 1967, 1979, and Sen. Alderman. Mayor and Adm. of the Port, Haverfordwest, 1961, Sheriff 1963, Burgess Warden 1974. Broadcaster, TV and radio, 1936-. *Publications:* ed, Pembrokeshire Coast National Park, 1973, 2nd impr. 1978; (jtly) Writers of the West, 1974; The Sheriffs of the Pembrokeshire, 1979; A Pembrokeshire Anthology, 1982. *Recreations:* natural history, local history, books, food and wine. *Address:* Castle Hill, Haverfordwest, Dyfed, Wales SA61 2EG. *T:* Haverfordwest 3400. *Clubs:* Savile, Wig and Pen; Pembrokeshire County (Haverfordwest).

MILES, (Frank) Stephen, CMG 1964; HM Diplomatic Service, retired; a Director of Studies, Overseas Unit, Royal Institute of Public Administration, since 1980; *b* 7 Jan. 1920; *s* of Harry and Mary Miles; *m* 1953, Margaret Joy (*née* Theaker); three *d. Educ:* John Watson's Sch., Edinburgh; Daniel Stewart's Coll., Edinburgh; St Andrews Univ. (MA); Harvard Univ. (Commonwealth Fellowship; MPA). Served with Fleet Air Arm, 1942-46 (Lt (A) RNVR). Scottish Home Dept, 1948; FCO (previously CRO), 1948-80; served in: New Zealand, 1949-52, E and W Pakistan, 1954-57; Ghana, 1959-62; Uganda, 1962-63; British Dep. High Commissioner, Tanzania, 1963-65 (Acting High Commissioner, 1963-64); Acting High Commissioner in Ghana, March-April 1966; Consul-Gen., St Louis, 1967-70; Dep. High Comr, Calcutta, 1970-74; High Comr, Zambia, 1974-78; High Comr, Bangladesh, 1978-79. Cllr, Tandridge DC, Surrey. *Recreations:* cricket, tennis, golf. *Address:* Maytrees, 71 Park Road, Limpsfield, Oxted, Surrey RH8 0AN. *T:* Oxted 3132. *Clubs:* Naval, Royal Commonwealth Society, MCC.

MILES, Geoffrey, OBE 1970; HM Diplomatic Service, retired; Consul-General, Perth, Western Australia, 1980-82; *b* 25 Oct. 1922; *s* of late Donald Frank Miles and Honorine Miles (*née* Lambert); *m* 1946, Mary Rozel Cottle; one *s* one *d. Educ:* Eltham College. Joined Home Civil Service (Min. of Shipping), 1939; War service as pilot in RAF, 1941-46 (commnd 1945); Min. of Transport, 1946-50; British Embassy, Washington 1951; Sec., Copper-Zinc-Lead Ctte, Internat. Materials Conf., Washington 1952-53; BoT, 1953-55; Asst Trade Comr, Perth, 1955-59; Second Sec., Ottawa, 1960-63; First Sec., Salisbury, 1963-66, Dublin, 1967-71; Trade Comr (later Consul) and Head of Post, Edmonton, 1971-75, Consul-Gen., 1976-78; Consul-Gen., Philadelphia, 1979-80. *Recreations:* music, golf, amateur radio. *Address:* 33 Silverdale Road, Petts Wood, Kent BR5 1NH. *Clubs:* Royal Over-Seas League; British Officers (Philadelphia).

MILES, Adm. Sir Geoffrey John Audley, KCB 1945 (CB 1942); KCSI 1947; *b* 2 May 1890; 3rd *s* of Audley Charles Miles and Eveline Cradock-Hartopp; *m* 1918, Alison Mary Cadell (*d* 1981); two *s. Educ:* Bedford; HMS Britannia. Joined the Royal Navy, served with Submarines and Destroyers during European War, 1914-18; later appointments include: Dep. Dir Staff Coll., Dir Tactical Sch.; Capt. HMS Nelson, 1939-41; Rear-Adm., 1941; Vice-Adm. 1944; Adm., 1948. Head of Mil. Mission in Moscow, 1941-43; Flag Officer Comdg Western Mediterranean, 1944-45; C-in-C, Royal Indian Navy, 1946-47. *Address:* Clunie, Rowledge, Farnham, Surrey. *Club:* Naval and Military.

MILES, Prof. Hamish Alexander Drummond; Barber Professor of Fine Arts and Director of the Barber Institute, University of Birmingham, since 1970; *b* 19 Nov. 1925; *s* of J. E. (Hamish) Miles and Sheila Barbara Robertson; *m* 1957, Jean Marie, *d* of T. R. Smits, New York; two *s* two *d. Educ:* Douai Sch.; Univ. of Edinburgh (MA); Balliol Coll., Oxford. Served War: Army, 1944-47. Asst Curator, Glasgow Art Gallery, 1953-54; Asst Lectr, then Lectr in the History of Art, Univ. of Glasgow, 1954-66; Vis. Lectr, Smith Coll., Mass, 1960-61; Prof. of the History of Art, Univ. of Leicester, 1966-70. Trustee, National Galleries of Scotland, 1967-; Convenor: Ctte for Nat. Gallery, 1980-; Ctte for Gallery of Modern Art, 1982-. *Publications:* (jtly) The Paintings of James McNeill Whistler, 2 vols, 1980; sundry articles and catalogues. *Recreations:* beekeeping and woodland management. *Address:* 37 Carpenter Road, Birmingham B15 2JJ; Burnside, Kirkmichael, Blairgowrie, Perthshire.

MILES, Prof. Herbert William, MSc (Bristol), DSc (Manchester); Adviser and Lecturer in Entomology, University of Manchester, 1927-42; Advisory Entomologist, University of Bristol (Long Ashton Research Station), 1942-46; Deputy Provincial Director (West Midland Province), National Agricultural Advisory Service, 1946-47; Prof. of Horticulture, Wye Coll., London Univ., 1947-65, now Emeritus. Hon. Consultant in Horticulture to RASE, 1948-75. President: Lincolnshire Naturalists' Union, 1938; Assoc. of Applied Biology, 1956. Officier, Ordre du Mérite Agricole, 1974. *Publications:* (with Mary Miles, MSc) Insect Pests of Glasshouse Crops, revised edn 1947; original papers on Economic Entomology in leading scientific journals; original studies on the biology of British sawflies. *Address:* 2 Wood Broughton, Grange-over-Sands, Cumbria.

MILES, John Edwin Alfred, CBE 1979 (OBE 1961; MBE 1952); HM Diplomatic Service, retired; *b* 14 Aug. 1919; *s* of late John Miles and late Rose Miles (*née* Newlyn); *m* 1952, Barbara Fergus Ferguson; two *s* one *d. Educ:* Hornsey County Sch. Apptd to Dominions Office, 1937. Served War: joined Queen's Royal West Surrey Regt, 1940; commissioned in N Staffordshire Regt, 1941; attached Royal Indian Army Service Corps, 1942 (Maj. 1943); released, Sept. 1946, and returned to Dominions Office. Served in: Wellington, NZ, 1948-51; Calcutta, 1953-56; CRO, 1957-61; Trinidad (on staff of Governor-Gen.), 1961; Jamaica (Adviser to Governor, and later First

Sec. in British High Commission), 1961-64; Wellington, NZ, 1964-68; Counsellor, 1968; Accra, Ghana, 1968-71; Dep. High Comr, Madras, India, 1971-75; High Comr to Swaziland, 1975-79. *Address:* Cartref, Ladyegate Road, Dorking, Surrey. *T:* Dorking 884346.

MILES, John Seeley, FSIAD, FSTD; typographer and partner in design group, Banks and Miles; *b* 11 Feb. 1931; *s* of Thomas William Miles and Winifred (*née* Seeley); *m* 1955, Louise Wilson; one *s* two *d. Educ:* Beckenham and Penge Grammar Sch.; Beckenham School of Art. FSIAD 1973; FSTD 1974. UN travelling schol. to Netherlands to practise typography and punch cutting under Jan van Krimpen and S. L. Hartz, 1954-55; Assistant to Hans Schmoller, *qv*, at Penguin Books, 1955-58; joined Colin Banks, *qv*, to form design partnership, Banks and Miles, 1958. Consultant to: Zoological Soc., Regent's Park and Whipsnade, 1958-82, Expanded Metal Co., 1960-, Consumers' Assoc., 1964-, British Council, 1968-, The Post Office, 1972-, E Midlands Arts Assoc., 1974-79, Curwen Press, 1970-72, Basilisk Press, 1976-79; Eschedé en Zn, Netherlands, 1980-; British Telecom, 1980-; Member, PO Design Adv. Ctte, 1972-76; American Heritage Lectr, New York, 1960; Design advisor, Agricl Inf. Workshop, Udaipur, India, 1973; held seminar, Graphic Inst., Stockholm, 1977. Chm., Wynkyn de Worde Soc., 1973-74; Governor, Central School of Arts and Crafts, 1978-. Exhibitions: London, 1971, 1978; Amsterdam and Brussels, 1977. *Publications:* articles and reviews in professional jls. *Recreations:* gardening, painting, reading aloud. *Address:* 157 Coombe Road, Croydon, Surrey CR0 5SQ. *T:* 01-688 9643. *Clubs:* Arts, Double Crown.

MILES, Dame Margaret, DBE 1970; BA; Headmistress, Mayfield School, Putney, 1952-73; *b* 11 July 1911; 2nd *d* of Rev. E. G. Miles and Annie Miles (*née* Jones). *Educ:* Ipswich High Sch., GPDST; Bedford Coll., Univ. of London. History teacher: Westcliff High Sch., 1935-39; Badminton Sch., 1939-44; Lectr, Dept of Educn, University of Bristol, 1944-46; Headmistress, Pate's Grammar Sch., Cheltenham, 1946-52. Member: Schools Broadcasting Council, 1958-68; Educ. Adv. Council, ITA, 1962-67; Nat. Adv. Council on Trng and Supply of Teachers, 1962-65; BBC Gen. Adv. Council, 1964-73; Campaign for Comprehensive Educn, 1966- (Chm., 1972; Pres., 1979-); RSA Council, 1972-77; British Assoc., 1974-79; Council, Bedford Coll., Univ. of London (Vice-Chm.); Council, Chelsea Coll., Univ. of London; Chairman: Adv. Ctte on Develt Educn, ODM, 1977-79; Central Bureau for Educl Visits and Exchanges, 1978-; Vice-Chm., Educ. Adv. Ctte, UK Nat. Commn for Unesco. Hon. DCL, Univ. of Kent at Canterbury, 1973. *Publications:* And Gladly Teach, 1965; Comprehensive Schooling, Problems and Perspectives, 1968. *Recreations:* opera, films, reading, gardening, golf, walking, travel when possible. *Address:* Tanycraig, Pennal, Machynlleth, Powys. *Clubs:* University Women's; Steering Wheel; Aberdovey Golf.

MILES, Maurice Edward; Conductor; Professor of Conducting, Royal Academy of Music; *b* 1908; *s* of T. S. Miles; *m* 1936, Eileen Spencer Wood (*d* 1977); one *s* two *d. Educ:* Wells Cathedral Gram. Sch.; Royal Academy of Music, London. Employed BBC, 1930-36; Conductor of Buxton Municipal Orchestra and of Bath Municipal Orchestra, 1936-39. Served in RAC, 1940-43. Returned to BBC, 1943; Conductor: Yorks Symphony Orchestra, 1947-54; City of Belfast Orchestra and Belfast Philharmonic Society, 1955-66; Ulster Orchestra, 1966-67. FRAM. *Publication:* Are You Beating 2 or 4?, 1977. *Recreations:* walking, reading. *Address:* 32 The Orchard, North Holmwood, Dorking, Surrey.

MILES, Maxine Frances Mary; lately Director of F. G. Miles Engineering Ltd, Riverbank Works, Old Shoreham Road, Shoreham, Sussex; *b* 22 Sept. 1901; *d* of late Sir Johnston Forbes-Robertson; *m* 1932, Frederick George Miles, FRAeS, MSAE; one *s* (and one *d* decd). *Address:* Batts, Ashurst, Steyning, W Sussex.

MILES, Oliver; see Miles, R. O.

MILES, Peter Tremayne; Keeper of the Privy Purse and Treasurer to the Queen, since 1981; *b* 26 June 1924; *er s* of late Lt-Col E. W. T. Miles, MC; *m* 1956, Philippa Helen Tremlett; two *s* one *d. Educ:* Eton Coll.; RMC, Sandhurst. First The Royal Dragoons, 1944-49; J. F. Thomasson & Co., 1949-59; Gerrard & National Discount Co. Ltd, 1959-80 (Managing Director, 1964-80). Director: P. Murray-Jones Ltd, 1966-75; Astley & Pearce Holdings Ltd, 1975-80 (Chm., 1978-80). *Address:* 15 St James's Palace, SW1A 1BG. *T:* 01-930 5642. *Clubs:* Pratt's, White's; Swinley Forest Golf.

MILES, (Richard) Oliver; HM Diplomatic Service; Head of Near East and North Africa Department, Foreign and Commonwealth Office, since 1980; *b* 6 March 1936; *s* of George Miles and Olive (*née* Clapham); *m* 1968, Julia, *d* of late Prof. J. S. Weiner; three *s* one *d. Educ:* Ampleforth Coll.; Merton Coll., Oxford (Oriental Studies). Entered Diplomatic Service, 1960; served in Abu Dhabi, Amman, Aden, Mukalla, Nicosia, Jedda; Counsellor, Athens, 1977-80. *Recreations:* bird-watching, singing. *Address:* c/o Foreign and Commonwealth Office, SW1A 2AH; Little Cowfold, Mattingley, Hants. *T:* Hook 2805. *Club:* Travellers'.

MILES, Roger Steele, PhD, DSc; Head, Department of Public Services, British Museum (Natural History), since 1975; *b* 31 Aug. 1937; *s* of John Edward Miles and Dorothy Mildred (*née* Steele); *m* 1960, Ann Blake; one *s* one *d. Educ:* Malet Lambert High Sch., Hull; King's Coll., Univ. of Durham (BSc, PhD, DSc). Sen. Res. Award, DSIR, 1962-64; Sen. Res. Fellow, Royal

Scottish Museum, 1964–66, Sen. Scientific Officer, 1966–68; Sen. Sci. Officer, BM (Nat. Hist.), 1968–71, Principal Sci. Officer, 1971–74. *Publications:* 2nd edn, Palaeozoic Fishes, 1971 (1st edn, J. A. Moy-Thomas, 1939); (ed, with P. H. Greenwood and C. Patterson) Interrelationships of Fishes, 1973; (ed, with S. M. Andrews and A. D. Walker) Problems in Vertebrate Evolution, 1977; papers and monographs on anatomy and palaeontology of fishes, articles on museums, in jls. *Recreations:* music, reading. *Address:* 1 Highfield Green, Epping, Essex CM16 5HB. *T:* Epping 74848.

MILES, Surgeon Rear-Adm. Stanley, CB 1968; FRCP, FRCS; Chairman, International Trauma Foundation, since 1978; *b* 14 Aug. 1911; *s* of late T. C. Miles, Company Dir, Sheffield; *m* 1939, Frances Mary Rose; one *s* one *d.* *Educ:* King Edward VII Sch.; University of Sheffield. MSc Sheffield, 1934; MB, ChB, 1936; DTM&HEng, 1949; MD, 1955; FRCP 1971, FRCS 1971. Joined RN Medical Service, 1936; served in China, W Africa, Pacific and Mediterranean Fleets. Medical Officer-in-Charge, RN Medical Sch. and Dir of Medical Research, 1961; Consultant in Physiology; Med. Officer-in-Charge, Royal Naval Hosp., Plymouth, 1966–69. Surg. Captain 1960; Surg. Rear-Adm. 1966. Dean, Postgraduate Med. Studies, Univ. of Manchester, 1969–76. Gilbert Blane Medal, RCS, 1957. QHP 1966–69. CStJ 1968. *Publication:* Underwater Medicine, 1962. *Recreations:* tennis, golf. *Address:* Peartree Cottage, Normansland, Salisbury, Wilts SP5 2BN. *Club:* National Liberal.

MILES, Stephen; *see* Miles, F. S.

MILES, Sir William (Napier Maurice), 6th Bt, *cr* 1859; Chartered Architect; Consultant in firm Miles Wills & Partners, Chartered Architects; *b* 19 Oct. 1913; *s* of Sir Charles William Miles, 5th Bt, OBE; *S* father, 1966; *m* 1946, Pamela, *d* of late Capt. Michael Dillon; one *s* two *d.* *Educ:* Stowe; University of Cambridge (BA). Architectural Assoc. Diploma, 1939. *Recreations:* swimming, sailing. *Heir: s* Philip John Miles, *b* 10 Aug. 1953. *Address:* Old Rectory House, Walton-in-Gordano, near Clevedon, Avon. *T:* Clevedon 873365; Flat 59, Fort Picklecombe, Maker, Torpoint, Cornwall. *Club:* Royal Western Yacht.
See also Prof. C. W. N. Miles.

MILFORD, 2nd Baron *cr* 1939; **Wogan Philipps;** Bt 1919; farmer and painter; *b* 25 Feb. 1902; *e s* of 1st Baron Milford; *S* father, 1962; *m* 1st, 1928, Rosamond Nina Lehmann, *qv* ; one *s* (and one *d* decd); 2nd, 1944, Cristina, Countess of Huntingdon (who *d* 1953); 3rd, 1954, Tamara Rust. *Educ:* Eton; Magdalen Coll., Oxford. Member of International Brigade, Spanish Civil War. Former Member of Henley on Thames RDC, Cirencester RDC; has taken active part in building up Nat. Union of Agric. Workers in Gloucestershire and served on its county cttee. Contested (Com) Cirencester and Tewkesbury, 1950. Has held one-man exhibitions of paintings in London, Milan and Cheltenham and shown in many mixed exhibns. *Heir: s* Hon. Hugo John Laurence Philipps [*b* 27 Aug. 1929; *m* 1st, 1951 (marr. diss., 1958); one *d* ; 2nd, 1959, Mary, *e d* of Baron Sherfield, *qv* ; three *s* one *d*]. *Address:* Butler's Farm, Colesbourne, Cheltenham, Glos. *T:* Coberley 260.
See also Hon. J. P. Philipps, Hon. R. H. Philipps.

MILFORD, Rev. Canon Theodore Richard; Master of the Temple, 1958–68; *b* 10 June 1895; *e s* of Robert Theodore Milford, MA, and Elspeth Barter; *m* 1st, 1932, Nancy Dickens Bourchier Hawksley; two *d* ; 2nd, 1937, Margaret Nowell Smith; two *d. Educ:* Denstone; Fonthill, East Grinstead; Clifton; Magdalen Coll., Oxford; Westcott House, Cambridge. Served European War, 1914–18, 19th Royal Fusiliers, 1914; Oxford & Bucks LI, 1915–19 (Mesopotamia, 1916–18); Magdalen Coll., Oxford, 1919–21; BA (1st Cl. Lit. Hum), 1921; Union Christian Coll., Alwaye, Travancore, 1921–23; St John's Coll., Agra, 1923–24, 1926–30, 1931–34; Sec. Student Christian Movement, 1924–26 and 1935–38; Westcott House, 1930–31; Deacon, 1931; Priest, 1934 (Lucknow); Curate All Hallows, Lombard Street, 1935–37; Vicar of St Mary the Virgin, Oxford (University Church), 1938–47; Canon and Chancellor of Lincoln, 1947–58; Canon of Norton Episcopi, Lincoln Cathedral, 1947–68, Canon Emeritus, 1968. Chm., Oxfam, 1942–47 and 1960–65. Greek Red Cross (Bronze), 1947. *Publications:* Foolishness to the Greeks, 1953; The Valley of Decision, 1961; Belated Harvest (verse), 1978. *Recreations:* music, chess. *Address:* 1 Kingsman Lane, Shaftesbury, Dorset. *T:* Shaftesbury 2843.

MILFORD HAVEN, 4th Marquess of, *cr* 1917; **George Ivar Louis Mountbatten;** Earl of Medina, 1917; Viscount Alderney, 1917; *b* 6 June 1961; *s* of 3rd Marquess of Milford Haven, OBE, DSC, and of Janet Mercedes, *d* of late Major Francis Bryce, OBE; *S* father, 1970. *Heir: b* Lord Ivar Alexander Michael Mountbatten, *b* 9 March 1963. *Address:* Flat 2, Wilton Terrace, SW1; Moyns Park, Birdbrook, Essex.

MILINGO, Most Rev. Emanuel; *see* Lusaka, Archbishop of, (RC).

MILKINA, Nina, (Mrs A. R. M. Sedgwick); Hon. RAM; concert pianist; *b* Moscow, 27 Jan. 1919; *d* of Jacques and Sophie Milkine; *m* 1943, Alastair Robert Masson Sedgwick, Dir Nielsen Sedgwick International; one *s* one *d. Educ:* privately. Musical studies with the late Leon Conus of the Moscow Conservatoire and at the Paris Conservatoire, also with Profs Harold Craxton and Tobias Matthay, London. First public appearance at age of 11 with Lamoureux Orchestra, Paris; has since been broadcasting, televising, and touring in Great Britain and abroad. Was commissioned by BBC to broadcast series of all Mozart's piano sonatas; invited to give Mozart recital for

bicentenary celebration of Mozart's birth, Edinburgh Festival; recorded for Westminster Co. of New York, and Pye Record Co., London. Widely noted for interpretation of Mozart's piano works. *Publications:* works for piano. *Recreations:* reading, chess, fly fishing. *Address:* 20 Paradise Walk, SW3; Vicarage Cottage, Rogate, Petersfield, Hants.

MILKOMANE, G. A. M.; *see* Sava, George.

MILL, Rear-Adm. Ernest, CB 1960; OBE 1944; Director General, Aircraft, Admiralty, 1959–62; *b* 12 April 1906; *s* of Charles and Rosina Jane Mill; *m* 1939, Isobel Mary Neilson (*d* 1971). *Educ:* Merchant Venturers Sch. Fleet Engr Officer on staff of C-in-C, Mediterranean, 1957; Rear-Adm., 1958. *Recreations:* sailing, fishing. *Club:* Army and Navy.

MILL, Laura Margaret Dorothea, OBE 1962; MB, ChB, Diploma Psych; Medical Commissioner, Mental Welfare Commission for Scotland, 1962–63, retired; *b* 28 Nov. 1897; *d* of Rev. William Alexander Mill, MA and Isabel Clunas. *Educ:* The Park Sch., Glasgow; Glasgow Univ. House Surg., Samaritan Hosp. for Women, and Royal Maternity Hospital, Glasgow, House Physician, Royal Hospital for Sick Children, and Senior Medical Officer Out-patient Dispensary, Glasgow; Resident Medical Officer, York General Dispensary; Asst Physician, Riccartsbar Mental Hosp., Paisley, and Murray Royal Mental Hosp., Perth; Clinical Medical Officer, Glasgow Public Health Dept. Dep. Medical Commissioner, Gen. Board of Control for Scotland, 1936; Medical Commissioner, Gen. Board of Control for Scotland (later Mental Welfare Commission), 1947, and Senior Medical Officer, Dept of Health for Scotland. *Address:* 7 Montpelier Terrace, Edinburgh EH10 4NE. *T:* 031-229 7982.

MILLAIS, Sir Ralph (Regnault), 5th Bt, *cr* 1885; *b* 4 March 1905; *s* of Sir Geoffroy William Millais, 4th Bt, and Madeleine Campbell (*d* 1963), *d* of C. H. Grace; *S* father, 1941; *m* 1st, 1939, Felicity Caroline Mary Ward Robinson (marr. diss.), *d* of late Brig.-Gen. W. W. Warner, CMG; one *s* one *d* ; 2nd, 1947, Irene Jessie (marr. diss. 1971), *er d* of E. A. Stone, FSI; 3rd, 1975, Babette Sefton-Smith, *yr d* of Maj.-Gen. H. F. Salt, CB, CMG, DSO. *Educ:* Marlborough; Trinity Coll., Cambridge. Business career. Joined RAFVR at outbreak of war, 1939, Wing Comdr. *Recreations:* fishing, travel and the restoration of famous Vintage and Historic cars. *Heir: s* Geoffroy Richard Everett Millais, *b* 27 Dec. 1941. *Address:* Gate Cottage, Winchelsea, East Sussex.

MILLAN, Rt. Hon. Bruce, PC 1975; MP (Lab) Craigton Division of Glasgow since 1959; *b* 5 Oct. 1927; *s* of David Millan; *m* 1953, Gwendoline May Fairey; one *s* one *d. Educ:* Harris Academy, Dundee. Chartered Accountant, 1950–59. Chm. Scottish Labour Youth Council, 1949–50. Contested: West Renfrewshire, 1951, Craigton Div. of Glasgow, 1955. Parly Under-Sec. of State: for Defence, (RAF), 1964–66; for Scotland, 1966–70; Minister of State, Scottish Office, 1974–76; Sec. of State for Scotland, 1976–79; opposition spokesman on Scotland, 1979–. *Address:* 10 Beech Avenue, Glasgow G41 5BY. *T:* 041-427 6483.

MILLAND, Raymond Alton, (Ray Milland); film actor and director, US; *b* Wales, 3 Jan. 1907; *s* of Alfred Milland and Elizabeth Truscott; *m* 1932, Muriel Weber; one *s* one *d. Educ:* private schs in Wales and England; Monks Preparatory Sch.; University of Wales. Served with Household Cavalry, 1926–29; became actor in 1930; went to USA, 1930, and became naturalized citizen, 1938. *Films include:* The Flying Scotsman; Payment Deferred; Bolero; Four Hours to Kill; The Glass Key; Ebb Tide; Beau Geste; The Lost Weekend; French Without Tears; So Evil My Love; Circle of Danger; A Man Alone; Lisbon; The Safecracker (also directed); Kitty; Golden Earrings; It Happens Every Spring; Alias Nick Beal; Dial M for Murder; 3 Brave Men; Man Alone; Love Story; The House in Nightmare Park; Gold; The Swiss Conspiracy; The Last Tycoon; Oliver's Story. Received Motion Picture Acad. Award for best actor, for part in The Lost Weekend. Has also appeared on stage and television. *Publication:* Wide-Eyed in Babylon (autobiog.), 1975.

MILLAR, family name of **Baron Inchyra.**

MILLAR, Betty Phyllis Joy; Regional Nursing Officer, South Western Regional Health Authority, since 1973; *b* 19 March 1929; *o d* of late Sidney Hildersly Millar and May Phyllis Halliday. *Educ:* Ursuline High Sch. for Girls; Dumbarton Academy; Glasgow Royal Infirm.; Glasgow Royal Maternity Hosp.; Royal Coll. of Nursing, London. RGN 1950; SCM 1953; NA (Hosp.) Cert. 1961. Theatre Sister, Glasgow Royal Infirm., 1953–54; Ward and Theatre Sister, Henry Brock Meml Hosp., 1954–55; Nursing Sister, Iraq Petroleum Co., 1955–57; Clinical Instructor, Exper. Scheme of Nurse Trng, Glasgow, 1957–60; Admin. Student, Royal Coll. of Nursing, 1960–61; 2nd Asst Matron, Glasgow Royal Infirm., 1961–62; Asst Nursing Officer, Wessex Regional Hosp. Bd, 1962–67; Matron, Glasgow Royal Infirm., 1967–69; Chief Regional Nursing Officer, SW Regional Hosp. Bd, 1969–73. WHO Fellowship to study nursing services in Scandinavia, 1967. Mem. Jt Bd of Clinical Nursing Studies, 1970–. *Address:* Pinedrift, 45 Stoneyfields, Easton-in-Gordano, Bristol BS20 0LL. *T:* Pill 2709.

MILLAR, Dame Elizabeth; *see* Hoyer-Millar.

MILLAR, Prof. Fergus Graham Burtholme, DPhil; FSA; FBA 1976; Professor of Ancient History, University College, University of London, since

1976; *b* 5 July 1935; *s* of late J. S. L. Millar and of Jean Burtholme (*née* Taylor); *m* 1959, Susanna Friedmann; two *s* one *d. Educ:* Edinburgh Acad.; Loretto Sch.; Trinity Coll., Oxford (1st Cl. Lit. Hum.). Fellow: All Souls Coll., Oxford, 1958-64; Queen's Coll., Oxford, 1964-76. Conington Prize, 1963. Vice-Pres., Soc. for the Promotion of Roman Studies, 1977-. FSA 1978. Corresp. Mem., German Archaeolog. Inst., 1978. Editor, Jl of Roman Studies, 1975-79. *Publications:* A Study of Cassius Dio, 1964; The Roman Empire and its Neighbours, 1967; (ed with G. Vermes) E. Schürer, history of the Jewish people in the age of Jesus Christ (175 BC-AD 135), Vol. I, 1973, Vol. II, 1979; The Emperor in the Roman World (31 BC-AD 337), 1977. *Address:* Department of History, University College, Gower Street, WC1E 6BT. *T:* 01-387 7050; 80 Harpes Road, Oxford OX2 7QL. *T:* Oxford 55782.

MILLAR, George, DSO 1944; MC; farmer and writer; *b* 19 Sept. 1910; 2nd *s* of Thomas Andrew Millar, architect, and Mary Reid Morton; *m* 1945, Isabel Beatriz, *d* of Montague Paske-Smith, CMG, CBE; no *c. Educ:* Loretto; St John's, Cambridge. Architect, 1930-32; journalist, with Daily Telegraph and Daily Express, 1934-39; Paris correspondent Daily Express, 1939; served War of 1939-45, The Rifle Bde; escaped from German POW camp to England, then served as agent in France; Chevalier de la Légion d'Honneur; Croix de Guerre avec Palmes. Tenant farmer, 400 acres, 1962; increased to 1000 acres, 1966. *Publications:* Maquis, 1945; Horned Pigeon, 1946; My Past was an Evil River, 1946; Isabel and the Sea, 1948; Through the Unicorn Gates, 1950; A White Boat from England, 1951; Siesta, 1952; Orellana, 1954; Oyster River, 1963; Horseman, 1970; The Bruneval Raid, 1974; Road to Resistance, 1979. *Recreation:* sailing. *Address:* Sydling St Nicholas, Dorset. *T:* Cerne Abbas 205. *Clubs:* Royal Cruising; Royal Yacht Squadron (Cowes).

MILLAR, Ian Alastair D.; *see* Duncan Millar.

MILLAR, John Stanley, CBE 1979; County Planning Officer, Greater Manchester Council, since 1973; *b* 1925; *s* of late Nicholas William Stanley Millar and late Elsie Baxter Millar (*née* Flinn); *m* 1961, Patricia Mary (*née* Land); one *d. Educ:* Liverpool Coll.; Univ. of Liverpool. BArch, DipCD, PPRTPI, RIBA. Planning Asst, then Sen. Asst Architect, City of Liverpool, 1948-51; Sectional Planning Officer, then Dep. Asst County Planning Officer, Lancs CC 1951-61; Chief Asst Planning Officer, then Asst City Planning Officer, City of Manchester, 1961-64; City Planning Officer, Manchester, 1964-73. *Publications:* papers in professional and technical jls. *Recreations:* walking, listening to music, travel, the sea. *Address:* 17 Pownall Road, Pownall Park, Wilmslow, Cheshire SK9 5DR. *T:* Wilmslow 523616. *Club:* National Liberal.

MILLAR, Sir Oliver Nicholas, KCVO 1973 (CVO 1963; MVO 1953); FBA 1970; Surveyor of the Queen's Pictures, since 1972; *b* 26 April 1923; *er s* of late Gerald Millar, MC and late Ruth Millar; *m* 1954, Delia Mary, 2nd *d* of late Lt-Col Cuthbert Dawnay, MC; one *s* three *d. Educ:* Rugby; Courtauld Institute of Art, University of London (Academic Diploma in History of Art). Unable, for medical reasons, to serve in War of 1939-45. Asst Surveyor of the King's Pictures, 1947-49, Dep. Surveyor 1949-72. Trustee, Nat. Portrait Gallery, 1972-. Mem., Reviewing Cttee on Export of Works of Art, 1975-. A Governor, St Mary's Sch., Calne. FSA. *Publications:* Gainsborough, 1949; William Dobson, Tate Gallery Exhibition, 1951; English Art, 1625-1714 (with Dr M. D. Whinney), 1957; Rubens's Whitehall Ceiling, 1958; Abraham van der Doort's Catalogue, 1960; Tudor, Stuart and Early Georgian Pictures in the Collection of HM the Queen, 1963; Zoffany and his Tribuna, 1967; Later Georgian Pictures in the Collection of HM the Queen, 1969; Inventories and Valuations of the King's Goods, 1972; The Age of Charles I (Tate Gallery Exhibn), 1972; The Queen's Pictures, 1977; Sir Peter Lely (Nat. Portrait Gall. Exhibn), 1978; Van Dyck in England (Nat. Portrait Gall. Exhibn), 1982; articles in the Burlington Magazine, etc; numerous catalogues, principally for The Queen's Gallery. *Recreations:* drawing, gardening, cricket, golf. *Address:* Yonder Lodge, Penn, Bucks. *T:* Penn 2124. *Club:* Brooks's.

MILLAR, Sir Ronald (Graeme), Kt 1980; playwright and screenwriter; Deputy Chairman, Theatre Royal Haymarket Ltd, since 1977; *b* 12 Nov. 1919; *s* of Ronald Hugh Millar and Dorothy Ethel Dacre Millar (*née* Hill). *Educ:* Charterhouse; King's Coll., Cambridge. Served as Sub-Lt, RNVR, 1940-43 (invalided out). Began in the Theatre as an actor. First stage appearance, London, Swinging the Gate, Ambassadors', 1940, subseq. in Mr Bolfry, The Sacred Flame, Murder on the Nile, Jenny Jones, (own play) Zero Hour, 1944. Ealing Studios, 1946-48, worked on Frieda, Train of Events, etc; screenwriter, Hollywood, 1948-54: So Evil My Love, The Miniver Story, Scaramouche, Rose-Marie, The Unknown Man, Never Let Me Go, Betrayed. Plays produced in London: Frieda, 1946; Champagne for Delilah, 1948, Waiting for Gillian, 1954; The Bride and the Bachelor, 1956; The More the Merrier, 1960; The Bride Comes Back, 1960; The Affair (from C. P. Snow novel), 1961, The New Men (from C. P. Snow), 1962; The Masters (from C. P. Snow), 1963; (book and lyrics) Robert and Elizabeth (musical), 1964; Number 10, 1967; Abelard and Heloise, 1970; The Case in Question (from C. P. Snow), 1975; A Coat of Varnish (from C. P. Snow), 1982. *Recreations:* all kinds of music, all kinds of people. *Address:* 7 Sheffield Terrace, W8. *T:* 01-727 8361. *Clubs:* Brooks's, Dramatists'.

MILLAR, Prof. William Malcolm, CBE 1971; MD; Crombie-Ross Professor of Mental Health, University of Aberdeen, 1949-77; *b* 20 April 1913; *s* of Rev. Gavin Millar, BD, Logiealmond, Perthshire, and Margaret Malcolm, Stanley, Perthshire; *m* 1941, Catherine McAuslin Rankin; two *s* four *d. Educ:*

George Heriot's Sch., Edinburgh; Edinburgh Univ. MB, ChB (Edinburgh) 1936; MD (Edinburgh) 1939; Dip. Psych. (Edinburgh) 1939; MRCPE 1958; FRCPE 1962. Asst Physician, Royal Edinburgh Hospital for Mental Disorders, 1937-39. Served 1939-46 (Lieut, Captain, Major), Specialist in Psychiatry, RAMC. Senior Lecturer, Dept of Mental Health, Aberdeen Univ., 1946-49. Dean, Faculty of Medicine to 1977. Member: MRC, 1960-64; Mental Welfare Commn for Scotland, 1964-68. FBPsS 1946. *Publications:* contributions to various learned journals. *Recreations:* golf, chess, gardening. *Address:* 2 South Avenue, Cults, Aberdeen AB2 1LP.

MILLAR-CRAIG, Hamish, CMG 1960; OBE 1958; *b* 25 Sept. 1918; *yr s* of late Captain David Millar-Craig and late Winifred Margaret Cargill; *m* 1953, Rose Ernestine Boohene. *Educ:* Shrewsbury; Keble Coll., Oxford. Served War of 1939-45, 2nd Lt Royal Scots, 1940; Colonial Civil Service, Gold Coast, 1940-57; Ghana Civil Service, 1957-62; Reader in Public Administration (UN Technical Assistance), Ghana Institute of Public Administration, 1962-65; Dir, E African Staff Coll., 1965-69; Adviser, Min. of Finance, Somalia, 1969-71; Bursar, UNITAR, 1972-77. Economic Development Institute, Washington, 1957-58. *Recreation:* philately. *Address:* c/o Lloyds Bank Ltd, Taunton, Somerset TA1 1HN.

MILLARD, Sir Guy (Elwin), KCMG 1972 (CMG 1957); CVO 1961; HM Diplomatic Service, retired; Chairman, British-Italian Society, since 1977; *b* 22 Jan. 1917; *s* of Col Baldwin Salter Millard, and Phyllis Mary Tetley; *m* 1st, 1946, Anne, *d* of late Gordon Mackenzie; one *s* one *d* ; 2nd, 1964, Mary Judy, *d* of late James Dugdale and of Pamela, Countess of Aylesford; two *s. Educ:* Charterhouse; Pembroke Coll., Cambridge. Entered Foreign Office, 1939. Served Royal Navy, 1940-41. Asst Private Sec., to Foreign Sec., 1941-45; British Embassy, Paris, 1945-49, Ankara, 1949-52; Imperial Defence Coll., 1953; Foreign Office, 1954, Counsellor, 1955; Private Sec. to Prime Minister, 1955-56; British Embassy, Tehran, 1959-62; Foreign Office, 1962-64; Minister, UK Delegation to NATO, 1964-67; Ambassador to Hungary, 1967-69; Minister, Washington, 1970-71; Ambassador to Sweden, 1971-74; Ambassador to Italy, 1974-76. Grand Officer, Order of Merit, Italy, 1981. *Address:* Fyfield Manor, Southrop, Glos. *T:* Southrop 234. *Club:* Boodle's.

MILLARD, Raymond Spencer, CMG 1967; PhD; FICE; FInstHE; consulting engineer; *b* 5 June 1920; *s* of Arthur and Ellen Millard, Ashbourne, Derbs; *m* 1st, 1945, Irene Guy (marr. diss.); one *s* one *d* ; 2nd, 1977, Sheila Taylor. *Educ:* Queen Elizabeth Grammar Sch., Ashbourne; University Coll., London (BSc (Eng)). RE and civil engineering contracting, 1941-44. Road Research Laboratory, 1944-74: Hd of Tropical Section, 1955-65; Dep. Dir, 1965-74; Partner, Peter Fraenkel & Partners, Asia, 1974-76; Highway Engrg Advisor, World Bank, 1976-82. *Publications:* scientific and technical papers on road planning and construction. *Recreations:* bonzai culture, painting, travel. *Address:* Drapers Cottage, 93 High Street, Odiham, Basingstoke, Hants RG25 1LR.

MILLEN, Brig. Anthony Tristram Patrick; Defence Advisor to British High Commissioner, Ottawa, Canada, since 1980; *b* 15 Dec. 1928; *s* of Charles Reginald Millen and Annie Mary Martin; *m* 1954, Mary Alice Featherston Johnston; two *s* two *d* (and one *s* decd). *Educ:* Mount St Mary's Coll. AMBIM. 5th Royal Inniskilling Dragoon Guards, 1948; served in Germany, Korea, Cyprus, N Ireland, Hong Kong, USA. *Publications:* articles in US military jls. *Recreation:* sailing. *Address:* British High Commission, Ottawa, Canada. *T:* 613 237 1530. *Club:* Rideau (Ottawa).

MILLER, Alan Cameron; MA; LLB; FCIT; advocate; Master at Fettes College, since 1974; Temporary Sheriff, since 1979; *b* 10 Jan. 1913; *o s* of late Arthur Miller, Edinburgh; *m* 1945, Audrey Main; one *s* one *d. Educ:* Fettes Coll.; Edinburgh Univ. MA 1934; LLB 1936; Advocate, 1938; served War of 1939-45, RN; Interim Sheriff-Substitute at Dundee, 1946; Sheriff-Substitute of Inverness, Moray, Nairn, Ross and Cromarty, at Fort William, 1946-52; Legal Adviser (Scotland): British Transport Commn, 1952-62; BR Board, 1962-73. Chm., Inst. of Transport (Scotland), 1971-72. *Recreations:* golf and music. *Address:* 42 Great King Street, Edinburgh, Scotland. *Clubs:* Arts (Edinburgh); HCEG.

MILLER, Alan John McCulloch, DSC 1941, VRD 1950; Chairman: Miller Insulation Ltd, since 1975; Low & Bonar, 1977-82; *b* 21 April 1914; *s* of late Louis M. Miller and Mary McCulloch; *m* 1940, Kirsteen Ross Orr; three *s* one *d. Educ:* Kelvinside Academy; Strathclyde Univ. CEng, MRINA, MIESS, FBIM, FRSA. Family engrg business, 1933-39. Commnd RNVR (Clyde Div.), 1938; served RN, 1939-45: Far East, Indian Ocean, S Atlantic, HMS Dorsetshire, then destroyers; in comd, HMS Fitzroy, Wolverine, Holderness, St Nazaire, Dieppe raids, Russian convoys, 1943-44; psc 1944. Rejoined family business, 1945, until sold to Bestobell Ltd, 1951; Dir, Bestobell Ltd, 1951-73, Chm. and Man. Dir, 1965-73; Chm. and Man. Dir, Wm Simons & Co. Ltd, Shipbuilders, 1956-60; Chm., Dev West Ltd, 1973-76; Chm., BNEC Southern Africa Cttee, 1970, until abolished. Member: Sports Council, 1973-80; Central Council of Physical Recreation. *Recreations:* sailing, golf, ski-ing, shooting. *Address:* Windlefield, Windlesham, Surrey GU20 6AA. *T:* Bagshot 72980. *Clubs:* Army and Navy, Royal Thames Yacht, Royal Ocean Racing, Royal Cruising; Royal and Ancient (St Andrews); Sunningdale Golf; Royal Northern Yacht.

MILLER, Alastair Cheape, MBE 1948; TD; Prison Governor, retired 1972; *b* 13 March 1912 (twin-brother); *s* of John Charles Miller, Banker, Glasgow, and Jessie Amelia Miller; *m* 1943, Elizabeth S. Hubbard (marr. diss. 1967); one *s* one *d. Educ:* Melville Coll., Edinburgh; Bedford Sch., Bedford. Territorial Army, 1930-46; War Service (Gibraltar and Italy); 5th Beds and Herts Regt, 1st Herts Regt and 4th KOYLI, 1948-51. Barclays Bank Ltd; Junior Clerk to Cashier, 1929-45. Housemaster, Approved Sch., April-Nov. 1946. Prison Service: Asst Governor, Wakefield, Dec. 1946-Jan. 1953; Governor: Dover, 1953-59; Winchester, 1959-62; Hindley Borstal, 1962-65; Parkhurst Prison, 1966-70; Pentonville, 1970-72. Associated with St Mungo Community Trust i/c Old Charing Cross Hosp. project for homeless people, 1974-75. Freeman, City of London, 1980. *Publication:* Inside Outside, 1976. *Recreations:* golf, sailing. *Address:* 3 White Hart Street, SE11. *Clubs:* Civil Service; Bantry Golf; Hampstead Golf; Seaford Golf (Seaford); Cowes Corinthian Yacht, Royal London Yacht (Cowes); Royal Solent Yacht (Yarmouth); Newport Boat (Pembroke).

MILLER, Alexander Ronald, CBE 1970; Chairman and Managing Director, Motherwell Bridge Holdings Ltd, since 1958; *b* 7 Nov. 1915; *s* of Thomas Ronald Miller and Elise Hay. *Educ:* Craigflower; Malvern Coll.; Royal Coll. of Science and Technology. Royal Engineers and Royal Bombay Sappers and Miners, 1940-46. Member: Scottish Council, CBI (formerly FBI), 1955- (Chm., 1963-65); Design Council (formerly CoID), 1965-71 (Chm. Scottish Cttee, 1965-67); Scottish Economic Planning Council, 1965-71 (Chm., Industrial Cttee, 1967-71); British Railways (Scottish) Board, 1966-70; British Rail Design Panel, 1966-; Gen. Convocation, Univ. of Strathclyde, 1967-; Steering Cttee, W Central Scotland Plan, 1970-75; Lanarkshire Area Health Bd, 1973- (Chm., 1973-77); Oil Develt Council for Scotland, 1973-78; Instn of Royal Engineers; BIM Adv. Bd for Scotland, 1974-; Coll. Council, Bell Coll. of Technology, Hamilton, 1976-; Management Cttee, Scottish Health Services Common Services Agency (Chm., 1977-); Lloyds Register of Shipping Scottish Cttee, 1977-, Gen. Cttee, 1982-; Incorporation of Hammermen, Merchants' House of Glasgow. Pres., Hamilton and Other Districts Br., Forces Help Soc. and Lord Roberts Workshops, 1979-. A Burgess of the City of Glasgow. FRSA; AIMechE; CBIM. *Address:* Lairfad, Auldhouse, by East Kilbride, Lanarks. *T:* East Kilbride 63275. *Clubs:* Directors; Royal Scottish Automobile (Glasgow), Western (Glasgow).

MILLER, Rear-Adm. Andrew John; Assistant General Secretary, Missions to Seamen, since 1981 (London and South East Regional Director, 1977-81); *b* 12 Dec. 1926; *s* of Major A. D. Miller, Baluch Regt, IA; *m* 1954, Elizabeth Rosanne Foster; one *s* two *d. Educ:* Craigflower, Fife; RNC Dartmouth. Midshipman 1944; Sub-Lt 1946; Lieut 1948; Lt-Comdr 1956; Comdr 1959; Captain 1965; Rear-Adm. 1972. Commanded ML3513, Asheldham, Grafton, Scorpion, Nubian. Dir Public Relations (Navy), 1970-71; Flag Officer Second Flotilla, 1972-73. *Recreation:* gardening. *Address:* Forge Cottage, Bosham, West Sussex. *T:* Bosham 572144. *Club:* Army and Navy.

MILLER, Arjay; Dean, and Professor of Management, Graduate School of Business, Stanford University, 1969-79, now Dean Emeritus; Vice-Chairman, Ford Motor Company, 1968-69 (President, 1963-68); *b* 4 March 1916; *s* of Rawley John Miller and Mary Gertrude Schade; *m* 1940, Frances Marion Fearing; one *s* one *d. Educ:* University of California at Los Angeles (BS with highest hons, 1937). Graduate Student and Teaching asst, University of California at Berkeley, 1938-40; Research Technician, Calif. State Planning Bd, 1941; Economist, Federal Reserve Bank of San Francisco, 1941-43. Captain, US Air Force, 1943-46. Asst Treas, Ford Motor Co., 1947-53; Controller, 1953-57; Vice-Pres. and Controller, 1957-61; Vice-Pres. of Finance, 1961-62; Vice-Pres., Staff Group, 1962-63. Member, Board of Directors: Ford Motor Co.; Levi Strauss & Co.; Transworld Corp.; Utah Internat. Inc.; The Washington Post Co.; Wells Fargo Bank; Southern Pacific Co.; Trustee: Eisenhower Exchange Fellowships; Brookings Instn, Washington; The Conference Board, 1965; Internat. Exec. Service Corps; Andrew W. Mellon Foundn; Urban Inst. Member, Board of Directors: SRI International; William and Flora Hewlett Foundn; Mem., Trilateral Commn. Hon. LLD: Univ. of California (LA), 1964; Whitman Coll., 1965; Univ. of Nebraska, 1965; Ripon Coll., 1980; Washington Univ., St Louis, 1982. *Address:* 225 Mountain Home Road, Woodside, Calif 94062, USA. *Clubs:* Bohemian, Pacific Union (San Francisco).

MILLER, Arthur; playwright; *b* 17 Oct. 1915; *s* of Isadore Miller and Augusta Barnett; *m* 1940, Mary Grace Slattery (marr. diss.); one *s* one *d* ; *m* 1956, Marilyn Monroe (marr. diss. 1961; she *d* 1962); *m* 1962, Ingeborg Morath; one *d. Educ:* University of Michigan, USA (AB). Pres. of PEN Club, 1965-69. *Publications:* Honors at Dawn, 1936; No Villains (They Too Arise), 1937; The Pussycat and the Expert Plumber who was a Man, 1941; William Ireland's Confession, 1941; The Man who had all the Luck, 1944; That They May Win, 1944; Situation Normal (reportage), 1944; Focus (novel), 1945; Grandpa and the Statue, 1945; The Story of Gus, 1947; All My Sons (play) (New York Drama Critics Award, 1948), 1947; Death of A Salesman (play) (New York Drama Critics Award, 1949, Pulitzer Prize, 1949), 1949; The Crucible (play), 1953; A View from the Bridge (play), 1955, filmed, 1962; A Memory of Two Mondays (play), 1955; Collected Plays, 1958; The Misfits (motion picture play), 1960; Jane's Blanket, 1963; After the Fall (play), 1963; Incident at Vichy (play), 1964; I Don't Need You Anymore (collected stories), 1967; The Price (play), 1968; (jt author) In Russia, 1969; Fame, and the Reason Why, 1970; The Portable Arthur Miller, 1971; The Creation of the World and Other Business (play), 1972, musical version, Up From Paradise, 1974; (with Inge Morath) In the Country, 1977; (ed Robert Martin) The Theater Essays of Arthur Miller, 1978; (with Inge Morath) Chinese

Encounters, 1979; The American Clock (play), 1980; Playing for Time (play) (Peabody Award, CBS-TV, 1981); contrib. stories and essays to Esquire, Colliers, Atlantic Monthly, etc. *Address:* c/o Kay Brown, ICM, 40 W 57th Street, New York, NY 10019, USA.

MILLER, Sir Bernard; *see* Miller, Sir O. B.

MILLER, Bruce; *see* Miller, John D. B.

MILLER, David Quentin; Metropolitan Stipendiary Magistrate, since 1982; *b* 22 Oct. 1936; *s* of Alfred Bowen Badger and Mair Angharad Evans. *Educ:* Ellesmere Coll., Shropshire; London Sch. of Econs and Pol. Science, London Univ. (LLB Hons 1956). Called to the Bar, Middle Temple, 1958; admitted Barrister and Solicitor of the Supreme Court of NZ, 1959. In practice, SE Circuit, 1960-82. *Recreations:* history, walking, gardening, art, music. *Address:* 15 Belsize Park Mews, Hampstead, NW3 5BL. *T:* 01-794 4861. *Club:* Medico-Legal.

MILLER, Desmond Campbell, QC 1961; TD; Chairman, Rossminster Group, 1973-78; *b* 17 Dec. 1914; *y s* of late Robert Miller, DD, sometime Bishop of Cashel and Waterford, and of Mary Miller, *yr d* of Dean Potter of Raphoe; *m* 1948, Ailsa, *y d* of Hon. Allan Victor Maxwell, CMG, and Margaret (*née* Lawless); two *s* one *d. Educ:* Manor Sch., Fermoy; Dean Close Sch., Cheltenham; St Columba's Coll., Rathfarnham; Pembroke Coll., Oxford. Called to Bar, Inner Temple, 1939, Gray's Inn (*ad eundem*), 1960; Master of the Bench, Inner Temple, 1968; retired from practice at the Bar, 1976. Served War of 1939-45 (despatches): Middx Yeo.; Northants Yeo.; 2nd, 6th and 11th Armoured Divs; HQ 1 Corps; HQ, ALFSEA; Staff Coll., Camberley, 1942. Lt-Col TA. Mem. General Council of the Bar, 1964-68, 1971-73 (Chm., Taxation and Retirement Benefits Cttees). *Recreations:* golf, flyfishing, reading. *Address:* Aux Cordiers, La Couperderie, St Peter Port, Guernsey, CI. *T:* Guernsey 20322. *Clubs:* Brooks's; MCC, Hurlingham; Royal Mid-Surrey Golf; Royal Guernsey Golf.

MILLER, Donald C.; *see* Crichton-Miller.

MILLER, Sir Douglas; *see* Miller, Sir I. D.

MILLER, Sir Douglas (Sinclair), KCVO 1972; CBE 1956 (OBE 1948); Development Adviser, Duke of Edinburgh's Award Scheme, since 1971; *b* 30 July 1906; British parentage; m 1933, Valerie Madeleine Carter; one *d. Educ:* Westminster Sch.; Merton Coll., Oxford. HM Overseas Colonial Service, 1930-61: Supt of Native Educn, N Rhodesia, 1930-45; Director of Education: Basutoland, 1945-48; Nyasaland, 1948-52; Uganda, 1952-58; Kenya, 1958-59; Dir of Educn and Permanent Sec., Min. of Educn, Kenya, 1959-60; Temp. Minister of Educn, Kenya, 1960-61; Sec., King George's Jubilee Trust, 1961-71. *Address:* The Lodge, 70 Grand Avenue, Worthing, Sussex. *T:* Worthing 501195. *Clubs:* Royal Commonwealth Society; Kampala (Uganda).

MILLER, Edward, FBA 1981; Master, Fitzwilliam College, Cambridge, 1971-81, Hon. Fellow, 1981; *b* Acklington, Northumberland, 16 July 1915; *e s* of Edward and Mary Lee Miller; *m* 1941, Fanny Zara Salingar; one *s. Educ:* King Edward VI's Grammar Sch., Morpeth; St John's Coll., Cambridge (Exhibnr, Schol.). BA 1937; MA 1945; Strathcona Res. Student, 1937-39, Fellow, 1939-65, and Hon. Fellow, 1974, St John's Coll., Cambridge. Nat. Service, 1940-45 in Durham Light Inf., RAC and Control Commn for Germany; Major. Dir of Studies in History, 1946-55 and Tutor, 1951-57, St John's Coll., Cambridge; Asst Lectr in History, 1946-50 and Lectr, 1950-65, University of Cambridge; Warden of Madingley Hall, Cambridge, 1961-65; Prof. of Medieval Hist., Sheffield Univ., 1965-71. FRHistS; Chm., Victoria Co. Histories Cttee of Inst. Hist. Research, 1972-79; Dep. Chm., Cttee to review Local Hist., 1978-79; Mem., St Albans Res. Cttee; Pres., Cambs Local Hist. Council; Chm., Editorial Bd, History of Parliament Trust. Hon. LittD Sheffield, 1972. *Publications:* The Abbey and Bishopric of Ely, 1951; Portrait of a College, 1961; (Jt Ed.) Cambridge Economic History of Europe, Vol. iii, 1963; Historical Studies of the English Parliament, 2 vols, 1970; (jtly) Medieval England: rural society and economic change, 1978; articles in Victoria County Histories of Cambridgeshire and York, Agrarian History of England and Wales, vol. ii, English Hist. Rev., Econ. History Rev., Trans Royal Historical Society, Past and Present, etc. *Recreations:* with advancing years watching any form of sport, especially Rugby and cricket. *Address:* 36 Almoners Avenue, Cambridge CB1 4PA. *T:* Cambridge 246794.

MILLER, Edward; Director of Education, Strathclyde, since 1974; *b* 30 March 1930; *s* of Andrew and Elizabeth Miller; *m* 1955; two *s. Educ:* Eastbank Academy; Glasgow Univ. (MA, MEd). Taught at Wishaw High Sch., 1955-57 and Whitehill Secondary Sch., 1957-59; Depute Dir of Educn, West Lothian, 1959-63; Sen. Asst Dir of Educn, Stirlingshire, 1963-66; Depute, later Sen. Depute Dir of Educn, Glasgow, 1966-74. *Recreations:* golf, reading, sailing. *Address:* 58 Heather Avenue, Bearsden, Glasgow G61 3JG.

MILLER, Lt-Gen. (retired) Sir Euan (Alfred Bews), KCB 1954 (CB 1949); KBE 1951; DSO 1945; MC 1918; Lieutenant of the Tower of London, 1957-60; *b* 5 July 1897; *s* of Dr A. E. Miller; *m* 1926, Margaret (*d* 1969) *d* of late Captain H. C. R. Brocklebank, CBE; two *d* (and one *s* decd). *Educ:* Wellington Coll.; RMC Sandhurst. 2nd Lieut, KRRC, 1915. Served European War, France and Salonika, 1915-18 (despatches, MC). Staff Coll.,

1926-27; Bt Lt-Col, 1936; served War of 1939-45, GSO1, GHQ, BEF, 1939; OC2 KRRC, 1940 (despatches, prisoner of war, DSO). Col, 1945; Brig., 1946; Dep. Mil. Sec., 1946; ADC to the King, 1946-48; Comdr Hanover Dist, 1948; Maj.-Gen., 1948; Chief of Staff, Middle East Land Forces, 1949-51; Lieut-Gen. 1951; Military Sec. to the Sec. of State for War, 1951; retired, 1955. Col Comdt, 1 KRRC, 1954-61. Chm. Kent T&AFA, 1956-61. DL Kent, 1958-81. *Address*: Farningham House Cottage, Farningham, Kent DA4 0DH. *T*: Farningham 863243. *Club*: Army and Navy.
See also J. M. Clay, E. W. F. Tomlin.

MILLER, Air Chief Marshal Frank Robert, CC (Canada) 1972; CBE 1946; CD; retired from military service, 1966; Director, United Aircraft of Canada Ltd, 1967-76; *b* Kamloops, BC, April 1908; *m* Dorothy Virginia Minor, Galveston, Texas. *Educ*: Alberta Univ. (BSc, Civil Engrg). Joined RCAF, 1931. Served War of 1939-45: commanded Air Navigation Schs at Rivers, Man., and Penfield Ridge, NB, and Gen. Reconnaisance Sch., Summerside, PEI; subseq. Dir of Trng Plans and Requirements and Dir of Trng, Air Force HQ; service overseas with Can. Bomber Gp as Station Comdr, later Base Comdr, 1944; Tiger Force, 1945 (despatches); Chief SO (later AOC), Air Material Comd, 1945; US Nat. War Coll., 1948; Air Mem. Ops and Trng, Air Force HQ, 1949; Vice Chief of Air Staff, 1951; Vice Air Deputy, SHAPE HQ, Paris, 1954; Dep. Minister, Dept of Nat. Defence, 1955; Chm., Chiefs of Staff, 1960; first Pres., NATO Mil. Cttee, 1963-64; Chief of Defence Staff, Canada, 1964-66. Air Chief Marshal, 1961. Hon. LLD Alta, 1965; Hon. DScMil, RMC Canada, 1968. *Recreations*: golf, fishing. *Address*: 1654 Brandywine Drive, Charlottesville, Va 22901, USA.

MILLER of Glenlee, Sir (Frederick William) Macdonald, 7th Bt *cr* 1788; *b* 21 March 1920; *e s* of Sir Alastair George Lionel Joseph Miller of Glenlee, 6th Bt; *S* father, 1964; *m* 1947, Marion Jane Audrey Pettit; one *s* one *d*. *Educ*: Tonbridge. Conservative Agent for: Whitehaven, 1947-50; Wembley North, 1950-52; North Norfolk, 1952-65; Lowestoft, 1965-82. County Councillor, Suffolk (Chm. Education Gen. Purposes Cttee). A Dep. Traffic Comr, Eastern Region, 1976-. *Recreation*: gardening. *Heir*: *s* Stephen William Macdonald Miller of Glenlee, FRCS [*b* 20 June 1953; *m* 1978, Mary Owens; one *s*. *Educ*: Rugby; St Bartholomew's Hosp.]. *Address*: Ivy Grange Farm, Westhall, Halesworth, Suffolk. *T*: Ilketshall 265.

MILLER, Brigadier George Patrick Rose-, DSO 1940; MC; beef farmer; inventor and export salesman; *b* 20 July 1897; 3rd *s* of late John Gardner Miller, Mayfield, Perth; *m* 1929, Millicent Rose Lang-Rose; two *s* two *d*. *Educ*: Trinity Coll., Glenalmond; RMC, Sandhurst. Gazetted to Queen's Own Cameron Highlanders, 1915; served in France and Belgium, 1916-17 (MC, immediate award); served with 1st Bn in India, Burma and Sudan; commanded 1st Bn in France 1940 (DSO); raised and commanded 227 Brigade; commanded 155 Brigade. Invented calf feeder, 1948, and new device for feeding young animals, patented 1978; having bought estate of 4,800 acres, has now produced new method of breeding out-wintered cattle with self-feed labour-saving silage in the hills of Nairnshire (losing none in the very bad winter of 1978-79). *Publications*: articles on agricultural subjects. *Address*: Barevan, Cawdor, Nairnshire. *T*: Croy 218. *Club*: Naval and Military.

MILLER, G(eorge) William; Secretary of the Treasury of the United States of America, 1979-81; private investments and business ventures; *b* Oklahoma, USA, 9 March 1925; *s* of James Dick Miller and Hazle Deane Miller (*née* Orrick); *m* 1946, Ariadna Rogojarsky. *Educ*: Borger High Sch.; Amarillo Junior Coll.; US Coast Guard Acad. (BS); School of Law, Univ. of California, Berkeley (JD). Served as US Coast Guard Officer, Pacific Area, 1945-49, stationed (one year) in China. Admitted to Bar of California, 1952, New York Bar 1953; law practice with Cravath, Swaine & Moore, NYC, 1952-56. Joined Textron Inc., Providence, RI, 1956; Vice-Pres. 1957; Treas. 1958; Pres. 1960; Chief Exec. 1968-78; also Chm., 1974-78. Chm. Bd of Governors of Federal Reserve System of US, 1978-79. Chm., The Conference Board, 1977-78; Chm., National Alliance of Business, 1978; Chm., US Industrial Payroll Savings Cttee, 1977. RI delegate to Democratic National Convention, 1968. Mem., State Bar, California. Phi Delta Phi. *Recreations*: music, golf, squash. *Address*: 1616 H Street NW, Suite 506, Washington, DC 20006, USA. *Clubs*: Chevy Chase (Maryland); The Brook (NY); Burning Tree (Bethesda, Md); Lyford Cay (Bahamas).

MILLER, Hilary Duppa, (Hal Miller); MP (C) Bromsgrove and Redditch since Feb. 1974; *b* 6 March 1929; *s* of Lt-Comdr John Bryan Peter Duppa-Miller, *qv*; *m* 1st, 1956, Fiona Margaret McDermid; two *s* two *d*; 2nd, 1976, Jacqueline Roe, *d* of T. C. W. Roe and of Lady Londesborough; one *s*. *Educ*: Eton; Merton Coll., Oxford; London Univ. MA (Oxon) 1956; BSc (Estate Management) (London), 1962. With Colonial Service, Hong Kong, 1955-68. Company Director. Contested: (C), Barrow-in-Furness, 1970; Bromsgrove by-elec. May 1971. PPS to Sec. of State for Defence, 1979-81, to Chancellor of the Duchy of Lancaster, 1981, resigned; Mem., UK delegn to Council of Europe, 1974-76. Jt Chm., All Party Motor Industry Gp, 1978. Fellow, Econ. Develt Inst. of World Bank, Washington. *Recreations*: sailing, fell walking, cricket, Rugby refereeing. *Address*: House of Commons, SW1A 0AA. *Clubs*: St Stephen's; Vincent's (Oxford); Aston Fields Royal British Legion (Bromsgrove); Eton Ramblers, Free Foresters, Blackheath Football.
See also Michael Miller.

MILLER, Sir Holmes; *see* Miller, Sir J. H.

MILLER, Mrs Horrie; *see* Durack, Dame M.

MILLER, Mrs Hugh; *see* Katzin, Olga.

MILLER, Sir (Ian) Douglas, Kt 1961; FRCS; Hon. Consulting Neurosurgeon since 1960 (Hon. Neurosurgeon, 1948), St Vincent's Hospital, Sydney, and Repatriation General Hospital; Chairman of Board, St Vincent's Hospital, 1966; Dean of Clinical School, St Vincent's Hospital, Sydney, 1931-64; *b* Melbourne, 20 July 1900; *m* 1939, Phyllis Laidley Mort; three *s* two *d*. *Educ*: Xavier Coll., Melbourne; University of Sydney. MB, ChM Sydney 1924; FRCS 1928. Hon. Asst Surgeon, St Vincent's Hosp., Sydney, 1929; Lectr in Surgical Anat., University, Sydney, 1930; Hon. Surg., Mater. Hosp. Sydney, 1934; Hon. Surg., St Vincent's Hosp., 1939; Major AIF, Surgical Specialist, 1940; Lt-Col (Surgical CO), 102 AGH, 1942; o/c Neurosurgical Centre, AIF. Chairman: Community Systems Foundn of Aust., 1965-72; Foundn of Forensic Scis, Aust. Mem. Ct of Examrs 1946, Mem. Council, 1947, RACS; President: RACS, 1957-59; Asian Australasian Soc. of Neurological Surgeons, 1964-67. Chairman: Editorial Cttee, ANZ Jl of Surgery, 1958-73; Editorial Bd, Modern Medicine in Australia. Hon. FRCSE 1980. Hon. AM 1964, Hon. LittD 1974, Singapore; Hon. MD Sydney, 1979. *Publications*: contrib. Med. Jl of Aust., 1956, 1960; Earlier Days, 1970. *Recreation*: agriculture. *Address*: 149 Macquarie Street, Sydney, NSW 2000, Australia. *T*: BU 5077, JJ 2431. *Club*: Australian (Sydney).

MILLER, Dr Jacques Francis Albert Pierre, AO 1981; FRS 1970; FAA 1970; Head of Experimental Pathology Unit, Walter and Eliza Hall Institute of Medical Research, since 1966; *b* 2 April 1931; French parents; *m* 1956, Margaret Denise Houen. *Educ*: St Aloysius' Coll., Sydney. BSc (Med.) 1953, MB, BS 1955, Sydney; PhD 1960, DSc 1965, London. Sen. Scientist, Chester Beatty Res. Inst., London, 1960-66; Reader, Exper. Pathology, Univ. of London, 1965-66. For. Mem., Académie Royale de Médicine de Belgique, 1969; For. Associate, US Nat. Acad. Scis, 1982. Langer-Teplitz Cancer Research Award (USA), 1965; Gairdner Foundn Award (Canada), 1966; Encyclopaedia Britannica (Australia) Award, 1966; Scientific Medal of Zoological Soc. of London, 1966; Burnet Medal, Austr. Acad. of Scis, 1971; Paul Ehrlich Award, Germany, 1974; Rabbi Shai Shacknai Meml Prize, Hadassah Med. Sch., Jerusalem, 1978. *Publications*: over 260 papers in scientific jls and several chapters in books, mainly dealing with thymus and immunity. *Recreations*: music, photography. *Address*: Walter and Eliza Hall Institute of Medical Research, Royal Melbourne Hospital PO, Parkville, Victoria 3050, Australia. *T*: 347-1511.

MILLER, James, RSA 1964; RSW 1934; Artist, Painter; *b* 25 Oct. 1893; *s* of William Miller and Margaret Palmer; *m* 1934, Mary MacNeill, MA (*d* 1973); no *c*. *Educ*: Woodside Sch.; Sch. of Art, Glasgow. Teaching, 1917-47. Commissioned by Artists' Adv. Coun. of Min. of Information to make drawings of buildings damaged by enemy action in Scotland, 1939-41; travelled extensively in Spain looking at buildings and making drawings; made drawings for Pilgrim Trust, 1942. Paintings have been bought by Bradford, Newport, Glasgow, Dundee, Hertford, Paisley, Nat. Gall. of S Australia, Melbourne, Aberdeen, Dumbarton, Perth and Muirhead Bequest, Edinburgh. Has held several one-man shows in Glasgow. Mem., Arts Council of GB (Scotland), 1964-65. *Recreations*: listening to gramophone records, reading. *Address*: Tigh-na-bruaich, Dunvegan, Isle of Skye. *Club*: Art (Glasgow).

MILLER, Lt-Comdr John Bryan Peter Duppa-, GC and King's Commendation 1941; *b* 22 May 1903; *er s* of Brian Stothert Miller, JP, Posbury, Devon, and Mary (*née* Sadler); *m* 1st, 1926, Barbara, *d* of Stanley Owen, 1st Viscount Buckmaster, GCVO; three *s*; 2nd, 1944, Clare, *d* of Francis Egerton Harding, JP, Old Springs, Market Drayton; 3rd, 1977, Greta, *d* of B. K. G. Landby, Royal Vasa Order, Gothenburg, Sweden. *Educ*: Rugby Sch.; Hertford Coll., Oxford. Dep. County Educn Officer, Hants, 1930-35; Asst Sec., Northants Educn Cttee, 1936-39; Torpedo and Mining Dept, Admity, 1940-45; a Dep. Dir-Gen., Trade and Econs Div., Control Commn for Germany, 1945; Inspector-Gen., Min. of Educn, Addis Ababa, 1945-47; Educn Dept, Kenya, 1947-57; Chm. of European Civil Servants' Assoc., and formation Chm. Staff Side, Central Whitley Coun. for Civil Service; Sec. to Kenya Coffee Marketing Bd, 1960-61; Sec. to Tanganyika Coffee Bd, 1961-62; Asst Sec. and Marketing Officer, Min. of Lands and Settlement, Kenya, 1963-65. *Publication*: Saints and Parachutes, 1951. *Recreations*: yachting, economics. *Address*: Box 222, Somerset West, 7130, South Africa. *Club*: Reform.
See also H. D. Miller, Michael Miller.

MILLER, Prof. J(ohn) D(onald) Bruce; Professor of International Relations, Research School of Pacific Studies, Australian National University, since 1962; *b* 30 Aug. 1922; *s* of Donald and Marion Miller, Sydney, Australia; *m* Margaret Martin (*née* MacLachlan); one *s*. *Educ*: Sydney High Sch.; University of Sydney. BEc, 1944; MEc 1951; MA Cantab 1978. Announcer and Talks Officer, Australian Broadcasting Commission, Sydney and Canberra, 1939-46; Staff Tutor, Department of Tutorial Classes, University of Sydney, 1946-54; Asst Lecturer in Political Science and International Relations, London Sch. of Economics, 1953-55; Lecturer in Politics, University Coll., Leicester, 1955-57; Prof. of Politics, University of Leicester, 1957-62; Dean of Social Sciences, 1960-62; Public Orator, 1961-62. Visiting Professor: Indian Sch. of International Studies, 1959; Columbia Univ., New York, 1962, 1966, 1981; Yale, 1977; Overseas Vis. Fellow, St John's Coll., and

Smuts Vis. Fellow, Cambridge Univ., 1977-78; Macrossan Lectr, University of Queensland, 1966. Member: Aust. Population and Immigration Council, 1975-81; Aust. Res. Grants Cttee, 1975-81. Joint Editor, Journal of Commonwealth Political Studies, 1961-62; Editor, Australian Outlook, 1963-69; Chm., Editorial Adv. Bd for Austr. documents on foreign relations, 1971-77. FASSA 1967 (Treas., 1979-). *Publications:* Australian Government and Politics, 1954, 4th edn with B. Jinks 1970; Richard Jebb and the Problem of Empire, 1956; Politicians (inaugural), 1958; The Commonwealth in the World, 1958; The Nature of Politics, 1962; The Shape of Diplomacy (inaugural), 1963; Australia and Foreign Policy (Boyer Lectures), 1963; The Disintegrating Monolith (ed with T. H. Rigby), 1965; Britain and the Old Dominions, 1966; Australia, 1966; The Politics of the Third World, 1966; (ed) India, Japan, Australia: Partners in Asia?, 1968; Survey of Commonwealth Affairs: problems of expansion and attrition 1953-1969, 1974; (ed) Australia's Economic Relations, 1975; The EEC and Australia, 1976; The World of States, 1981; Ideology and Foreign Policy, 1982. *Recreations:* books, garden, dachshund. *Address:* 16 Hutt Street, Yarralumla, ACT 2600, Australia. *T:* Canberra 813138. *Clubs:* National Press, Commonwealth (Canberra).

MILLER, Sir John Francis C.; *see* Compton Miller.

MILLER, John Harmsworth; architect in private practice; *b* 18 Aug. 1930; *s* of Charles Miller and Brenda Borrett; *m* 1957, Patricia Rhodes (marr. diss. 1975); two *d. Educ:* Charterhouse; Architectural Assoc. Sch. of Architecture (AA Dip. Hons 1957). ARIBA 1959. Private practice, Colquhoun and Miller, 1961-; works include: Forest Gate High Sch., West Ham (Newham), 1965; Chemistry Labs, Royal Holloway Coll., London Univ., 1970; Melrose Activity Centre, Milton Keynes Develt Corp. (Commendation, Steel Awards, 1975); Pillwood House, Feock, Cornwall (RIBA Regional Award, 1975). Tutor: RCA and AA, 1961-73; Cambridge Sch. of Arch., 1969-70; Prof. of Environmental Design, RCA, 1975. Vis. Critic: Cornell Univ. Sch. of Arch., Ithaca, 1966, 1968 and 1971; Princeton Univ. Sch. of Arch., NJ, 1970; Dublin Univ. Sch. of Arch., 1972-73. *Publications:* contribs to architect. jls. *Address:* 23 Regent's Park Road, NW1. *T:* 01-267 5800.

MILLER, Sir John Holmes, 11th Bt *cr* 1705, of Chichester, Sussex; *b* 1925; *er s* of 10th Bt and of Netta Mahalah Bennett; *S* father 1960; *m* 1950, Jocelyn Robson Edwards, Wairoa, NZ; two *d. Heir: b* Harry Holmes Miller [*b* 1927; *m* 1954, Gwynedd Margaret Sheriff; one *s* two *d*]. *Address:* Te Whare, Kohinui, Pahiatua, New Zealand.

MILLER, John Ireland; Vice-President, Methodist Conference of Great Britain, 1973-74; *b* 20 June 1912; *s* of John William Miller and Emma Miller (*née* Minkley); *m* 1943, Vida Bertha Bracher; one *s* one *d. Educ:* Hardye's School, Dorchester; Taunton School, Taunton. Admitted Solicitor and Member of Law Society, 1933. HM Coroner: Poole Borough, 1972-74 (Deputy Coroner, 1939-72); East Dorset, 1974-. Dir, Farney Close School Ltd. Chm., Methodist Homes for the Aged. *Address:* 25 Merriefield Drive, Broadstone, Dorset BH18 8BW. *T:* Broadstone 694057. *Club:* National Liberal.

MILLER, Air Vice-Marshal John Joseph, CB 1981; Director General, Personal Services (RAF), since 1982; Head of Administrative Branch, RAF, since 1979; *b* 27 April 1928; *s* of Frederick George Miller and Freda Ruth Miller; *m* 1950, Adele Mary Colleypriest; one *s* two *d. Educ:* Portsmouth Grammar School. Commissioned RAF, 1947; called to the Bar, Gray's Inn, 1958; CO RAF Support Unit Fontainbleau, 1965; Directing Staff, RAF Staff Coll., 1967; DGPS (RAF) Staff, MoD, 1970; Group Captain Admin., RAF Halton, 1971; Comd Accountant, HQ Strike Comd, 1973; RCDS 1975; Dir, Personnel Management (Policy and Plans) RAF, MoD, 1976; Asst Chief of Defence Staff (Personnel and Logistics), 1978-81. *Recreations:* walking, collecting (especially antiquarian books). *Address:* 3 Hemsdale, Maidenhead, Berks SL6 6SL. *T:* Maidenhead 22029. *Club:* Royal Air Force.

MILLER, Lt-Col Sir John (Mansel), KCVO 1974 (CVO 1966); DSO 1944; MC 1944; Crown Equerry since 1961; *b* 4 Feb. 1919; 3rd *s* of Brig.-Gen. Alfred Douglas Miller, CBE, DSO, DL, JP, Royal Scots Greys, and of Ella Geraldine Fletcher, Saltoun, E Lothian. *Educ:* Eton; RMA, Sandhurst. 2nd Lieut Welsh Guards, 1939; Adjt 1942-44; ADC to F-M Lord Wilson, Washington, DC, 1945-47; Regtl Adjt, 1953-56; Brigade Major 1st Guards Brigade, 1956-58; comd 1st Bn Welsh Guards, 1958-61. President: Coaching Club, 1975-82; Nat. Light Horse Breeding Soc., 1982; British Driving Soc., 1982. *Recreations:* hunting, shooting, polo, driving. *Address:* Shotover House, Wheatley, Oxon. *T:* Wheatley 2450; The Crown Equerry's House, Buckingham Palace, SW1. *T:* 01-930 4832. *Clubs:* Pratt's, White's.

MILLER, Dr Jonathan Wolfe; Director; *b* 21 July 1934; *s* of late Emanuel Miller, DPM, FRCP; *m* 1956, Helen Rachel Collet; two *s* one *d. Educ:* St Paul's Sch.; St John's Coll., Cambridge (MB, BCh 1959; Hon. Fellow 1982). Res. Fellow in Hist. of Med., UCL, 1970-73. Associate Director, Nat. Theatre, 1973-75. Mem., Arts Council, 1975-76. Vis. Prof. in Drama, Westfield Coll., London, 1977-; Fellow, UCL, 1981-. Co-author and appeared in Beyond the Fringe, 1961-64; stage directing in London and NY, 1965-67; *television:* Editor, BBC Monitor, 1965; directed films for BBC TV (incl. Alice in Wonderland), 1966; The Body in Question, BBC series, 1978; Exec. Producer, BBC Shakespeare series, 1979-81; *stage:* School for Scandal, 1968, The Seagull, 1969, The Malcontent, 1973, Nottingham Playhouse; King Lear, The Merchant of Venice, Old Vic, 1970; The Tempest, Mermaid, 1970;

Hamlet, Arts Theatre, Cambridge, 1970; Danton's Death, 1971, School for Scandal, 1972, Measure for Measure, 1974, Marriage of Figaro, 1974, The Freeway, 1974, Nat. Theatre; The Taming of the Shrew, 1972, The Seagull, 1973, Chichester; Family Romances, Greenwich, 1974; The Importance of Being Earnest, Greenwich, 1975; All's Well, Greenwich, 1975; Three Sisters, Cambridge, 1976; She Would If She Could, Greenwich, 1979; *film:* Take a Girl Like You, 1970; *operas:* Arden must die, Sadler's Wells Theatre, 1974; The Cunning Little Vixen, Glyndebourne, 1975 and 1977; English National Opera: The Marriage of Figaro, 1978; The Turn of the Screw, 1979; Arabella, 1980; Otello, 1981; Rigoletto, 1982; Kent Opera: Cosi Fan Tutte, 1975; Rigoletto, 1975; Orfeo, 1976; Eugene Onegin, 1977; La Traviata, 1979; Falstaff, 1980, 1981. Hon. DLitt Leicester, 1981. Silver Medal, Royal TV Soc., 1981. *Publications:* McLuhan, 1971; (ed) Freud: the man, his world, his influence, 1972; The Body in Question, 1978. *Recreation:* deep sleep. *Address:* 63 Gloucester Crescent, NW1. *T:* 01-485 6973.

MILLER, Maj.-Gen. Joseph Esmond, MC 1943; Medical Officer to Army Careers Information Office, Sheffield; *b* 22 Sept. 1914; *s* of Col J. F. X. Miller, OBE; *m* 1946, Kathleen Veronica Lochée-Bayne; one *s. Educ:* St George's Coll., Weybridge; London Univ. (St Bartholomew's Hosp.). MRCS, LRCP; MRCGP; MFCM; MBIM. Qualified, July 1940. Fellow RoySocMed; Member: BMA; Sheffield Medico-Chirurgical Soc. Served War of 1939-45: commissioned in RAMC, Dec. 1940 (ante-dated Sept. 1940); RAMC Depot, 1940-42; Airborne Forces, 1942-45: N Africa, Sicily, Italy, Holland, Germany. RAMC Depot, 1945-47; Staff Coll., 1948; DADMS, HQ MELF, Egypt, 1949-50; CO, 35 Field Amb., Tripoli and Egypt, 1950-54; SMO, RMA Sandhurst, 1954-57; CO, 4 Field Amb., Germany, 1957-59; CO, 10 Bde Gp Med. Co., Aden, 1959-61; ADMS, Middle East Command, Aden, 1961; Chief Instr, RAMC Depot, 1961-65; CO, BMH Hong Kong, 1965-68; ADMS, 4 Div., Germany, 1968-69; DDMS: HQ BAOR, 1969-71; HQ Scotland (Army), 1971-72; HQ UKLF, 1972-73; DMS, HQ UKLF, 1973-76. QHS 1973-76. CStJ 1975. *Recreations:* golf, gardening. *Address:* 17 Norton Green Close, Norton, Sheffield S8 8BP. *T:* Sheffield 748694. *Club:* The Club (Sheffield).

MILLER, Sir (Joseph) Holmes, Kt 1979; OBE 1958; Surveyor, New Zealand; Partner, Spencer, Holmes Miller and Jackson, Wellington, NZ; *b* Waimate, NZ, 12 Feb. 1919; *s* of Samuel Miller; *m* 1947, Marjorie, *d* of Harold Tomlinson; one *s* one *d. Educ:* Willowbridge Sch.; Waimate High Sch.; Victoria Univ., Wellington, NZ (BA). DSc 1979. Served War, 2 NZEF, 1940-44; NZ Artillery (wounded, Tunisia, 1943). Surveyor, Lands and Survey Dept, on rehabilitation farms, geodetic survey; consulting surveyor, Masterton, 1952-55; Wellington, 1959-. Fulton Medallion Exploratory Surveys, Fiordland, 1949; Expedition, Antipodes and Bounty Is, 1950; Dep. Leader, NZ Trans-Antarctic Expedn, 1955-58; Leader, NZ Expedn, Oates Land, Antarctica, 1963-64. Member: NZ Antarctic Soc. (Pres. 1960-63); NZ Inst. Surveyors, 1960-68 (Pres. 1969-71); NZ Survey Bd, 1962-71; NZ Geographic Bd, 1966-; Nature Conservation Council, 1972-. NZ Delegate to SCAR, Paris, 1964, Wyoming, 1974. *Publications:* numerous, on Antarctic and surveying literature. *Address:* 95 Amritsar Street, Khandallah, Wellington, New Zealand.

MILLER, Prof. Karl Fergus Connor; Lord Northcliffe Professor of Modern English Literature, University College London, since 1974; Editor, London Review of Books, since 1979; *b* 2 Aug. 1931; *s* of William and Marion Miller; *m* 1956, Jane Elisabeth Collet; two *s* one *d. Educ:* Royal High School, Edinburgh; Downing Coll., Cambridge. Asst Prin., HM Treasury, 1956-57; BBC TV Producer, 1957-58; Literary Editor, Spectator, 1958-61; Literary Editor, New Statesman, 1961-67; Editor, Listener, 1967-73. *Publications:* (ed) Poetry from Cambridge, 1952-54, 1955; (ed, with introd.) Writing in England Today: The Last Fifteen Years, 1968; (ed) Memoirs of a Modern Scotland, 1970; (ed) A Listener Anthology, August 1967-June 1970, 1970; (ed) A Second Listener Anthology, 1973; (ed) Henry Cockburn, Memorials of his Time, 1974; Cockburn's Millennium, 1975; (ed, with introd.) Robert Burns, 1981. *Recreation:* football. *Address:* 26 Limerston Street, SW10. *T:* 01-352 1735.

MILLER, Dr Kenneth Allan Glen, FEng; FIMechE; Director-General, Engineering Council, since 1982; *b* 27 July 1926; *s* of Dr Allan Frederick Miller and Margaret Hutchison (*née* Glen); *m* 1954, Dorothy Elaine Brown; three *s. Educ:* Upper Canada Coll., Toronto; Trinity Hall, Cambridge (BA 1946; MA 1950); PhD Wales, 1949. Res. Asst to Prof. of Physics, Aberystwyth, 1946; joined ICI, Billingham, 1949; various posts on production and design, 1949-59; seconded to BTC, 1959-60; Asst Tech. Manager, 1960, Engrg Manager, 1963, Engrg Dir, 1965, HOC Div., ICI; Engrg Advr, ICI, 1971; Managing Director: APV Co., 1974; APV Holdings, 1977-82. Member: Cttee for Industrial Technol., 1972-76; UGC, 1981-; Chm., Steering Cttee for Manufrg Adv. Service, 1977-82. Mem. Council, Fellowship of Engrg, 1982-. *Recreations:* gardening, photography. *Address:* 4 Montrose Gardens, Oxshott, Surrey KT22 0UU. *T:* Oxshott 2093. *Club:* Leander.

MILLER of Glenlee, Sir Macdonald; *see* Miller of Glenlee, Sir F. W. M.

MILLER, Prof. Marcus Hay, PhD; Professor of Economics, University of Warwick, since 1978; *b* 9 Sept. 1941; *s* of J. Irvine Miller and Rose H. (*née* Moir); *m* 1967, Margaret Ellen Hummel; two *d. Educ:* Price's Sch., Fareham, Hants; University Coll., Oxford (BA 1st Cl. PPE); Yale Univ. (Henry Fellowship, MA, PhD Econ). Lecturer, London School of Economics,

1967-76; Prof. of Economics, Univ. of Manchester, 1976-78. Economist, 1972-73, Houblon-Norman Fellow, 1981-82, Bank of England; Vis. Associate Prof. of Internat. Finance, Univ. of Chicago, 1976. Member, Academic Panel, HM Treasury, 1976- (Chm., 1979-80); Adviser, House of Commons Select Cttee on the Treasury and Civil Service, 1980-81. Mem. Management Cttee, NIESR, 1980-. Mem., Economic Policy Gp, SDP, 1981-. *Publications:* joint editor: Monetary Policy and Economic Activity in West Germany, 1977; Essays on Fiscal and Monetary Policy, 1981; papers on macro and monetary economics, incl. effects of UK entry into EEC, reform of UK monetary system, inflation, exchange rates and liquidity preference, in Amer. Economic Rev., Economica, Nat. Inst. Economic Rev., Oxford Economic Papers, Rev. of Economic Studies. *Recreations:* swimming, orienteering. *Address:* Department of Economics, University of Warwick, Coventry CV4 7AL. *T:* Coventry 24011, ext. 2484.

MILLER, Mrs Mary Elizabeth H.; *see* Hedley-Miller.

MILLER, Maurice Solomon, MB; MP (Lab) East Kilbride, since 1974 (Glasgow Kelvingrove, 1964-74); *b* 16 Aug. 1920; *s* of David Miller; *m* 1944, Renée, *d* of Joseph Modlin, Glasgow; two *s* two *d*. *Educ:* Shawlands Academy, Glasgow; Glasgow University. MB, ChB 1944. Mem. of Glasgow Corporation since 1950; Bailie of Glasgow, 1954-57; JP Glasgow, 1957. Asst Govt Whip, 1968-69. Visited Russia as mem. of medical delegation, 1955. *Publication:* Window on Russia, 1956. *Address:* House of Commons, SW1; 82 Springkell Avenue, Glasgow G41 4EH.

MILLER, Michael, RD 1966; QC 1974; Barrister since 1958; *b* 28 June 1933; 2nd *s* of John Bryan Peter Duppa-Miller, *qv*; *m* 1958, Mary Elizabeth, *e d* of Donald Spiers Monteagle Barlow, *qv*; two *s* two *d*. *Educ:* Dragon Sch., Oxford; Westminster Sch. (King's Scholar); Christ Church, Oxford (Westminster Scholar). BA Lit. Hum. 1955; MA 1958. Ord. Seaman, RNVR, 1950; Sub-Lt 1956; qual. submarines, 1956; Navigating Officer, HMS Solent, 1956; Armaments Officer: HMS Sturdy, 1956-57; HMS Tally Ho, 1957; Lt-Comdr RNR. Called to Bar, Lincoln's Inn, 1958; practice at Chancery Bar from 1958; Mem. Bar Council, 1972-74; Mem. Senate of Inns of Court and Bar, 1974-76. *Recreations:* sailing, music, chess, football. *Address:* 8 Stone Buildings, Lincoln's Inn, WC2.
See also H. D. Miller.

MILLER, Sir (Oswald) Bernard, Kt 1967; *b* 25 March 1904; *s* of late Arthur Miller and of Margaret Jane Miller; *m* 1931, Jessica Rose Marie ffoulkes; three *s*. *Educ:* Sloane Sch.; Jesus Coll., Oxford (Hon. Fellow, 1968). Stanhope Prize, 1925; BA 1927; MA 1930. Joined John Lewis Partnership, 1927; Dir, 1935; Chm., 1955-72. Chm., Retail Distributors Assoc., 1953; Member: Council of Industrial Design, 1957-66; Monopolies Commission, 1961-69; EDC for Distributive Trades, 1964-71. Chm. Southern Region, RSA, 1974-80; Mem. Council, RSA, 1977-82. Treasurer, Southampton Univ., 1974-82, Chm. Council, 1982-. Hon. LLD Southampton, 1981. *Publication:* Biography of Robert Harley, Earl of Oxford, 1927. *Recreations:* fishing, gardening, opera and theatre. *Address:* The Field House, Longstock, Stockbridge, Hants. *T:* Stockbridge 627.

MILLER, Rev. Canon Paul William; Canon Residentiary of Derby Cathedral, since 1966; Chaplain to the Queen, since 1981; *b* 8 Oct. 1918; *s* of F. W. Miller, Barnet. *Educ:* Haileybury; Birmingham Univ. (Dip. Theology). Served in ranks with Sherwood Foresters, 1939-45; POW of Japanese, 1942-45; despatches 1946. Deacon, 1949; Curate: of Staveley, Derbyshire, 1949-52; of Matlock, Derbyshire, 1952-55; Vicar of Codnor, Derbyshire, 1955-61. *Recreations:* painting, travel. *Address:* 22 Kedleston Road, Derby DE3 1GN. *T:* Derby 44773.

MILLER, Peter Francis Nigel, RIBA, FSIAD; Senior Partner, Purcell Miller Tritton and Partners, Architects, Surveyors and Design Consultants, Norwich, London, Sevenoaks, Winchester and Colchester, since 1973; *b* 8 May 1924; *s* of Francis Gerald Miller and Dorothy Emily (*née* Leftwich); *m* 1950, Sheila Gillian Branthwayt, ARCA, FSIAD, (*née* Stratton); one *s* two *d*. *Educ:* King's Sch., Canterbury; Sch. of Architecture, Coll. of Art, Canterbury. ARIBA 1952; FRIBA 1968; MSIA 1956; FSIA 1968. Served army, 1942-47, NW Europe, Austria, Italy and India; commnd Duke of Cornwall's LI, 1943. Private practice: Peter Miller and Sheila Stratton, 1954; Miller and Tritton, 1956; Purcell Miller and Tritton, 1965. Surveyor to the Fabric of Ely Cathedral, 1974-; Architect, Cathedral of St John the Baptist, Norwich, 1976-. Vice-Pres., SIAD, 1976. *Recreations:* deer stalking, shooting, wildfowling, fishing. *Address:* Thornage Hall, Holt, Norfolk NR25 7QH. *T:* Melton Constable 860305; 64 Bethel Street, Norwich NR2 1NR. *T:* Norwich 20438. *Club:* Norfolk (Norwich).

MILLER, Sir Richard Hope, Kt 1955; Chairman, North West Region, Arthritis and Rheumatism Council, since 1974; President: Knutsford Division Conservative Association, since 1975; David Lewis Epileptic Centre, since 1977; Cheshire County Lawn Tennis Association, since 1981; *b* 26 July 1904; 2nd *s* of late Hubert James Miller, The Old Court House, Knutsford, Cheshire, and of Elsa Mary Colimann; unmarried. *Educ:* Wellington Coll.; Trinity Hall, Cambridge. BA 1925; MA 1930. Served War of 1939-46: commissioned in 7th Bn (TA) The Manchester Regt; Adjutant 1941; Major 1945; served in Staff appointments (Britain, Ceylon, and Singapore), 1942-46. Hon. Sec., Greater Manchester and Area Br., Inst. of Dirs, 1966-81. *Recreations:* skiing, tennis. *Address:* 9 Carrwood, Knutsford, Cheshire WA16 8NG. *T:* Knutsford

3422; National Westminster Bank Ltd, Knutsford, Cheshire. *Club:* United Oxford & Cambridge University.

MILLER, Robert Alexander Gavin D.; *see* Douglas Miller.

MILLER, Robin Anthony; a Recorder of the Crown Court, since 1978; *b* 15 Sept. 1937; *s* of William Alexander Miller, CBE, BEM, and Winifred Miller; *m* 1962, Irene Joanna Kennedy; two *s* one *d*. *Educ:* Devonport High Sch., Plymouth; Wadham Coll., Oxford (MA). Called to the Bar, Middle Temple, 1960. *Address:* St Michael's Lodge, 192 Devonport Road, Stoke, Plymouth, Devon PL1 5RD. *T:* Plymouth 54943.

MILLER, Prof. Ronald, MA, PhD, FRSE, FRSGS; Professor of Geography, Glasgow University, 1953-76; Dean of the Faculty of Science, 1964-67; *b* 21 Aug. 1910; *o c* of late John Robert Miller and Georgina Park; *m* 1940, Constance Mary Phillips, SRN, SCM; one *s* one *d*. *Educ:* North Queensferry; Stromness Acad.; Edinburgh Univ. Silver Medal, Royal Scottish Geographical Soc.; MA 1931; Carnegie Research Fellowship at Marine Laboratory of Scottish Home Dept, Aberdeen, 1931-33; PhD 1933; Asst Lecturer Manchester Univ., 1933-36; Education Officer, Nigeria, 1936-46; Royal West African Frontier Force, 1939-44; Lecturer, Edinburgh Univ., 1947-53. Guest Lecturer: University of Montpellier, 1957; University of Oslo and Handelshøyskole Bergen, 1966; Simon Fraser Univ., 1967; Ife, 1969. Pres., RSGS, 1974-77. *Publications:* (with MacNair) Livingstone's Travels; The Travels of Mungo Park; (with Tivy) ed. The Glasgow Region, 1958; (with Watson) Ogilvie Essays, 1959; Africa, 1967; Orkney, 1976; papers in geographical journals. *Address:* Ruah, 20 South End, Stromness, Orkney. *T:* Stromness 850594.

MILLER, Ronald Kinsman; Principal Assistant Solicitor, Board of Inland Revenue, since 1981; *b* 12 Nov. 1929; *s* of William Miller and Elsie May Miller; *m* 1952, Doris Alice Dew; one *s* one *d*. *Educ:* Colchester Royal Grammar Sch. Served RN, 1948-50. Called to the Bar, Gray's Inn, 1953. Joined Inland Revenue, 1950; Asst Solicitor, 1971; Law Officers' Dept, 1977-79. *Recreations:* gardening, sailing, reading, music. *Address:* 4 Liskeard Close, Chislehurst, Kent BR7 6RT. *T:* 01-467 8041.

MILLER, Comdr Ronald S.; *see* Scott-Miller.

MILLER, Rudolph Valdemar Thor C.; *see* Castle-Miller.

MILLER, Sir Stephen (James Hamilton), KCVO 1979; MD, FRCS; Hospitaller, St John Ophthalmic Hospital, Jerusalem, since 1980; Surgeon-Oculist: to the Queen, 1974-80; to HM Household, 1965-74; Ophthalmic Surgeon: St George's Hospital, 1951-80; National Hospital, Queen Square, 1955-78; King Edward VII Hospital for Officers, since 1965; Surgeon, Moorfields Eye Hospital, 1954-80; Recognised Teacher in Ophthalmology, St George's Medical School and Institute of Ophthalmology, University of London; *b* 19 July 1915; *e s* of late Stephen Charles Miller and Isobel Hamilton; *m* 1949, Heather P. Motion; three *s*. *Educ:* Arbroath High Sch.; Aberdeen Univ. House Physician and Surgeon, Royal Infirmary, Hull, 1937-39. Surgeon Lieut-Comdr RNVR, 1939-46 (Naval Ophthalmic Specialist, RN Aux. Hosp., Kilmacolm and RN Hosp., Malta). Resident Surgical Officer, Glasgow Eye Infirmary, 1946; Registrar and Chief Clinical Asst, Moorfields Eye Hosp., 1947-50; Registrar St George's Hosp., 1949-51; Research Associate, Institute of Ophthalmology, 1949-80. Ophthalmic Surgeon, Royal Scottish Corp.; Advr in Ophthalmol., BUPA; Civilian Consultant in Ophthalmol. to RN and MoD, 1971-80. Member: Med. Commn for Accident Prevention; Transport and Road Res. Cttee. FRSocMed (Hon. Mem., Sect. of Ophthalmol.); Fellow Faculty of Ophthalmology; Editor, British Journal of Ophthalmology; Mem. Editorial Bd, Ophthalmic Literature; Ophthalmological Soc. of UK; Oxford Ophthalmological Congress (Master, 1969-70); Examiner in Ophthalmology: for Royal Colls and Brit. Orthoptic Bd; RCS and RCSE. Mem. Exec. Cttee, London Clinic; Governor, Moorfields Eye Hosp., 1961-67 and 1974-77. Trustee: Fight for Sight Charity; Frost Foundn Charity. Hon. Mem., Amer. Acad. of Ophthalmology. Freeman, City of London; Liveryman, Soc. of Apothecaries. Doyne Medal, 1972; Montgomery Medal, 1974. KStJ 1978. *Publications:* Modern Trends in Ophthalmology, 1973; Operative Surgery, 1976; Parsons Diseases of the Eye, 1977; articles in BMJ, Brit. Jl of Ophthalmology, Ophthalmic Literature. *Recreations:* golf, fishing. *Address:* 149 Harley Street, W1. *T:* 01-935 4444. *Clubs:* Garrick, Caledonian; Woking Golf.

MILLER, Terence George, TD 1960; MA Cantab; Director, Polytechnic of North London, 1971-80; *b* 16 Jan. 1918; *o s* of late George Frederick Miller, Cambridge, and late Marion Johnston, Port William, Wigtownshire; *m* 1944, Inga Catriona, 3rd *d* of Austin Priestman, MD, Folkestone, Kent; one *s* three *d*. *Educ:* Perse (foundn schol.); Jesus Coll., Cambridge (schol.). Wiltshire Prizeman, 1939. Served War of 1939-45: RA, Special Forces, Glider Pilot Regt, TA, 1947-67. Harkness Scholar, 1948; Research Fellow, Jesus Coll., 1949-54. University Demonstrator, 1948; Lectr in Geology, Univ. of Keele, 1953; Sen. Lectr, 1963. Prof. of Geography, Univ. of Reading, 1965-67; Principal, University Coll. of Rhodesia, 1967-69; Vis. Prof., Reading Univ., 1969-71. *Publications:* Geology, 1950; Geology and Scenery in Britain, 1953; scientific papers in various jls. *Recreations:* studies in military history, sailing, beachcombing, cutting and burning. *Address:* 29 Wodehouse Terrace, Falmouth, Cornwall. *T:* Falmouth 316657.

MILLER, Walter George, IPFA; FCCA; City Treasurer, Bristol, since 1980; *b* 2 March 1932; *s* of Bert and Rosina Miller; *m* 1956, Sheila Mary Daw; one *s* two *d. Educ:* Howardian High Sch., Cardiff. Cardiff, City Treasurer's Dept, Cardiff, 1948-50. Served RA, Hong Kong and Korea, 1950-52. Audit Asst, City Treasurer's Dept, Cardiff, 1952-55; Accountant, Treasurer's Dept: Nairobi, 1955-58; Cardiff, 1958-60; Caerphilly, 1960-63; Ilford, 1963-65; Redbridge, 1965; Bromley, 1965-68; Asst Borough Treasurer, Bromley, 1968-72; Bristol: Asst City Treasurer, 1972-73; Dep. City Treasurer, 1973-80. *Publications:* contrib. local government and accountancy press. *Recreations:* writing and lecturing on local government and allied topics; gardening. *Address:* 4 Nore Road, Portishead, Bristol BS20 9HN. *T:* Bristol 848559.

MILLER, William; see Miller, George William.

MILLER, Comdr William Ronald; Royal Navy (retired); Clerk to the Worshipful Company of Haberdashers since 1966; *b* 6 Dec. 1918; *s* of Col Joseph Sidney Miller, DSO and Florence Eva Drabble; *m* 1942, Betty Claelia Otto, Richmond, Natal; one *d. Educ:* Cranleigh Sch., Surrey. Entered RN, 1936. Sec. to Flag Officer (Submarines), 1955-57; Exec. Asst to Dep. Supreme Allied Comdr Atlantic (as Actg Capt.), 1958-60; Sec. to C-in-C Home Fleet (as Actg Capt.), 1960-62; Sec. to C-in-C Portsmouth (as Actg Capt.), 1963-65; retd from RN at own request, 1966. Called to Bar, Lincoln's Inn, 1958. Liveryman, 1969, Assistant *hc,* 1980, Haberdashers' Co. *Recreations:* golf, swimming, gardening. *Address:* 1 Great George Street, Godalming, Surrey. *T:* Godalming 22965.

MILLER PARKER, Agnes; see Parker, A. M.

MILLES-LADE, family name of **Earl Sondes.**

MILLETT, Peter Julian, QC 1973; *b* 23 June 1932; *s* of late Denis Millett and Adele Millett; *m* 1959, Ann Mireille, *d* of late David Harris; two *s* (and one *s* decd). *Educ:* Harrow; Trinity Hall, Cambridge (Schol.; MA). Nat. Service, RAF, 1955-57 (Flying Officer). Called to Bar, Middle Temple, 1955, *ad eundem* Lincoln's Inn, 1959 (Bencher, 1980), Singapore, 1976; Hong Kong, 1979; at Chancery Bar, 1958-. Examnr and Lectr in Practical Conveyancing, Council of Legal Educn, 1962-76. Junior Counsel to Dept of Trade and Industry in Chancery matters, 1967-73. Mem., General Council of the Bar, 1971-75. Outside Mem., Law Commn on working party on co-ownership of matrimonial home, 1972-73; Mem., Dept of Trade Insolvency Law Review Cttee, 1977-82. *Publications:* contrib. to Halsbury's Laws of England, Encycl. of Forms and Precedents; articles in legal jls. *Recreations:* philately, bridge, The Times crossword. *Address:* 18 Portman Close, W1H 9HJ. *T:* 01-935 1152; St Andrews, Kewhurst Avenue, Cooden, Sussex. *Club:* National Liberal.

MILLIGAN, James George, QC (Scot.) 1972; Advocate-Depute, since 1971; *b* 10 May 1934; *s* of Rt Hon. Lord Milligan; *m* 1961, Elizabeth Carnegie Thomson, *e d* of Hon. Lord Migdale, *qv* ; two *s* three *d. Educ:* St Mary's Sch., Melrose; Rugby Sch.; Oxford Univ. (BA); Edinburgh Univ. (LLB). Admitted to Faculty of Advocates, 1959; Standing Junior Counsel to the Scottish Home and Health Dept and Dept of Health and Social Security in Scotland. *Publication:* (contrib. small part of) Armour on Valuation for Rating, 3rd edn, 1961. *Recreations:* golf, squash. *Address:* 36 Mansionhouse Road, Edinburgh EH9 2JD. *T:* 031-667 4858. *Clubs:* New (Edinburgh); Honourable Company of Edinburgh Golfers (Muirfield).

MILLIGAN, Terence Alan, (Spike Milligan); actor; author; *b* 16 April 1918; *s* of late Captain L. A. Milligan, MSM, RA retd, and of Florence Winifred Milligan; *m* (wife *d* 1978); one *s* three *d. Educ:* Convent of Jesus and Mary, Poona; Brothers de La Salle, Rangoon; SE London Polytechnic, Lewisham. Appearances (comedy) as Spike Milligan: *stage:* The Bed-Sitting Room; Son of Oblomov; Ben Gunn, in Treasure Island, Mermaid, 1973, 1974; One man shows, 1979, 1980; writer, Ubu Roi, 1980; *radio:* Goon Show (inc. special performance, 1972, to mark 50th Anniversary of BBC); Best British Radio Features Script, 1972; *TV:* Show called Fred, ITV; World of Beachcomber, BBC; Q5, BBC; Oh in Colour, BBC; A Milligan for All Seasons, BBC, 1972-73; Marty Feldman's Comedy Machine, ITV (writing and appearing; awarded Golden Rose and special comedy award, Montreux, 1972); The Melting Pot, BBC, 1975; Q7, BBC series, 1977; Q8, 1978; Q9, 1979; TV Writer of the Year Award, 1956; *films:* The Magic Christian, 1971; The Devils, 1971; The Cherry Picker, 1972; Digby the Biggest Dog in the World, 1972; Alice's Adventures in Wonderland, 1972; The Three Musketeers, 1973; The Great McGonagall, 1975; The Last Remake of Beau Geste, 1977; The Hound of the Baskervilles, 1978; Monty Python Life of Brian, 1978; History of the World, Part 1, 1980. *Publications:* Dustbin of Milligan, 1961; Silly Verse for Kids, 1963; Puckoon, 1963; The Little Pot Boiler, 1965; A Book of Bits, 1965; Milliganimals, 1968; The Bedside Milligan, 1968; The Bed-Sitting Room (play), 1969; The Bald Twit Lion, 1970; Adolf Hitler, My Part in his Downfall, 1971 (filmed 1973; on record, 1980); Milligan's Ark, 1971; Small Dreams of a Scorpion, 1972; The Goon Show Scripts, 1972; Rommel? Gunner Who?, 1973; (for children) Badjelly the Witch, 1973; (with J. Hobbs) The Great McGonagall Scrapbook, 1975; The Milligan Book of Records, Games, Cartoons and Commercials, 1975; Dip the Puppy, 1975; Transports of Delight, 1975; William McGonagal, the truth at last, 1976; Monty, His Part in my Victory, 1976; Goblins (with Heath Robinson illus), 1978; Mussolini, His Part in my Downfall, 1978; Open Heart University, 1978; Spike Milligan's Q Annual, 1979; Get in the Q Annual, 1980; Unspun Socks from a Chicken's Laundry, 1981; Indefinite Articles and Scunthorpe, 1981; The 101

Best and Only Limericks of Spike Milligan, 1982. *Recreations:* restoration of antiques, oil painting, water colours, gardening, eating, drinking, talking, wine, jazz. *Address:* 9 Orme Court, W2. *T:* 01-727 1544.

MILLIGAN, Veronica Jean Kathleen; Senior Partner, Civlec Advisory Industrial Development Services, industrial consultants, since 1966; *b* 11 March 1926; *d* of Gilbert John O'Neill and Jennie Kathleen Robertson; *m* 1945, Francis Sutherland Milligan; one *s* (and one *s* decd). *Educ:* Pontypridd Intermediate Grammar Sch.; University Coll., Cardiff (BA Wales, DipEd); (evenings) Polytechnic of Wales (HNC Elect. and Endorsements, Dip. Management Studies). CEng, MIEE; MBIM. Sch. teacher, Glam Educn Authority, 1948-51; Grad. Trainee/Senior Elec. Engr, Electricity Supply Industry, 1952-65. Manpower Adviser/Consultant to Manpower and Productivity Services, Dept of Employment (on secondment), 1969-73. Pres., Women's Engrg Soc., 1977-79; Chm., E Wales Area, IEE, 1976-77 and Mem. Council, 1976-78. Member: Gwent AHA, 1976-; National Water Council, 1977-80; Industrial Tribunals Panel, 1977-; Commn on Energy and Environment, 1978-; Management Adv. Panel for Craftsmen, DHSS, 1979-; Nat. Staff Cttee for Works Staff, DHSS, 1981-; Rent Assessment Panel, 1981-; Monitoring Cttee, NFIS for NHS Maintenance Depts, 1982-. *Publications:* short papers in learned jls. *Recreations:* industrial careers advice to schools, industrial history, landscaping, walking. *Address:* Park Cottage, Rhiwderin, Newport, Gwent NP1 9RP. *T:* Newport 893557, Pontypridd 202451.

MILLIGAN, Wyndham Macbeth Moir, MBE 1945; TD 1947; Principal of Wolsey Hall, Oxford, 1968-80, retired; *b* 21 Dec. 1907; *s* of Dr W. Anstruther Milligan, MD, London, W1; *m* 1941, Helen Penelope Eirene Cassavetti, London, W1; three *s* two *d. Educ:* Sherborne; Caius Coll., Cambridge. Asst Master, Eton Coll., 1932-, House Master, Eton Coll., 1946; Warden, Radley Coll., 1954-68. Served 1939-45, with Scots Guards, in NW Europe (Major). Former Chm., N Berks Area Youth Cttee. Governor: St Mary's, Wantage (Chm.); Reed's Sch., Cobham; Lay Chm., Vale of White Horse Deanery Synod; Mem., Administrative Council, King George's Jubilee Trust. FRSA 1968. *Recreations:* gardening, sketching. *Address:* Church Hill House, Stalbridge, Sturminster Newton, Dorset. *T:* Stalbridge 62815.

MILLING; see Crowley-Milling.

MILLING, Geoffrey; Chairman, Bowring Steamship Company, 1965-68; Deputy Chairman, Lloyd's Register of Shipping, 1963-72; *b* 1 Sept. 1901; *s* of Henry Milling, Warrington, Lancs; *m* 1928, Dorothy Gordon Baird (*d* 1979), St John's, Newfoundland; one *s* one *d. Educ:* Radley; Merton Coll., Oxford (MA). In USA, 1923, as Sec. to Sir Wilfred Grenfell; joined Lever Brothers, England, 1924; Hudson's Bay Co., 1926 (2 years in Baffin Land, as Manager of trading post, etc.); Bowring Brothers Ltd, St John's, 1935-48, returning to parent firm, London, 1948. Chm., Royal Alfred Merchant Seamen's Soc., 1951-59; Chm., London General Shipowners' Soc., 1959-60; Mem. Port of London Authority, 1959-67. *Recreation:* golf. *Address:* Cranford, Love Lane, Bembridge, Isle of Wight. *Clubs:* Leander; Swinley Forest Golf.

MILLING, Peter Francis, MB, BChir, FRCS; formerly: Surgeon, Ear, Nose and Throat Department, University College Hospital; Surgeon in charge, Throat and Ear Department, Brompton Hospital; Consultant Ear, Nose and Throat Surgeon: Epsom District Hospital; Oxted and Limpsfield Cottage Hospital; Visiting Laryngologist Benenden Chest Hospital. *Educ:* Cambridge University. BA Hons, 1937; MRCS, LRCP, 1940; MA, MB, BChir, 1941; FRCS, 1946. Formerly Chief Assistant, Ear, Nose and Throat Department, St Thomas' Hospital; Chief Clinical Assistant and Registrar, Ear, Nose and Throat Department, Guy's Hosp.; Surgical Registrar, Ear, Nose and Throat Dept, Royal Cancer Hospital. Member British Association of Otolaryngologists. FRSocMed. *Publications:* contributions to medical textbooks and journals. *Address:* 3 Homefield Park, Ballasalla, Isle of Man. *T:* Douglas 823072.

MILLINGTON, Air Commodore Edward Geoffrey Lyall, CB 1966; CBE 1946; DFC 1943; Manager, Regional Defence Sales, SE Asia, Plessey Singapore Pte Ltd; *b* 7 Jan. 1914; *s* of late Edward Turner Millington, Ceylon CS; *m* 1st, 1939, Mary Bonynge (marr. diss. 1956), *d* of W. Heaton Smith, FRCS; 2nd, 1956, Anne Elizabeth, *d* of Robert Brennan. *Educ:* Nautical Coll., Pangbourne. Served Cameron Highlanders, Palestine, 1936 (despatches); War of 1939-45, RAF, in N Africa, Sicily, Italy (actg Gp Capt.; despatches); Air Cdre, 1960; Comdr, RAF Persian Gulf, 1964-66; Air Commander, Zambia Air Force, 1968-70; Air Defence Adviser, Singapore Air Defence Command, 1970-72. psc; idc; Order Mil. Valour (Poland). *Address:* c/o Williams & Glyn's Bank Ltd, Holt's Branch, 22 Whitehall, SW1. *Club:* Royal Air Force.

MILLINGTON, Wing Comdr Ernest Rogers, DFC 1945; Teacher in charge of Teachers' Centre, London Borough of Newham, 1967-80, retired; Founder, and Editor, Project, 1967-80; *b* 15 Feb. 1916; *s* of Edmund Rogers Millington and Emily Craggs; *m* 1st, 1937 (marr. diss. 1974); four *d* ; 2nd, 1975, Ivy Mary Robinson. *Educ:* Chigwell Sch., Essex; College of S Mark and S John, Chelsea; Birkbeck Coll., London Univ. Clerk; Accountant; Company Sec.; served War of 1939-45, soldier, gunner officer, pilot RAF, instructor and heavy bomber, CO of a Lancaster Sqdn. MP (Commonwealth) for Chelmsford, 1945-50. Re-joined Royal Air Force, 1954-57. Head of Social Educn, Shoreditch Comprehensive Sch., London, 1965-67. *Publications:*

(edited): A Study of Film, 1972; The Royal Group of Docks, 1977; A Geography of London, 1979; National Parks, 1980. *Recreations:* studying the relationship between diet and arthritis; travel writing. *Address:* 85 Upminster Road, Hornchurch, Essex. *T:* Hornchurch 43852.

MILLINGTON-DRAKE, James Mackay Henry; Managing Director, Inchcape & Co. Ltd, since 1976 (Director since 1971); Chairman, Gray Mackenzie & Co. Ltd; Director, Commonwealth Development Corporation, since 1972; *b* 10 Jan. 1928; *s* of late Sir (John Henry) Eugen Vanderstegen Millington-Drake, KCMG and Lady Effie Millington-Drake; *m* 1953, Manon Marie Redvers-Bate; two *s* two *d. Educ:* Upper Canada Coll., Toronto; RNC Dartmouth. Joined Inchcape Group, London, 1956: Sydney, 1958-65; UK 1965; now Man. Dir, Inchcape & Co. Ltd. Governor, Reed's Sch., Cobham. Chevalier, Royal Order of Swedish Sword, 1949. *Recreations:* tennis, swimming, ski-ing, water ski-ing. *Address:* Flat 2, 6 Reeves Mews, W1Y 5DG. *Clubs:* City of London, Oriental, All England Lawn Tennis and Croquet; Union (Sydney).

MILLIS, Charles Howard Goulden, DSO 1918; OBE 1946; MC; *b* 1894; *e s* of C. T. Millis; *m* 1919, Violet, *o c* of late Herbert J. Gifford; one *s* one *d. Educ:* King's Coll. Sch.; Oxford, MA. Served European War, 1914-18, Brevet Major (despatches, DSO, MC and bar, Croix de Guerre with Palm, France); served War of 1939-45 (OBE). Managing Director, Baring Brothers & Co. Ltd, 1933-55; Vice-Chm., BBC, 1937-45; Mem., Nat. Res. Develt Corp., 1955-65; Rhodes Trustee, 1948-61. *Address:* 22 Belvedere Grove, SW19 7RL.

MILLIS, Sir Leonard (William Francis), Kt 1977; CBE 1970 (OBE 1948); JP; Secretary from 1939, subsequently Director and President, 1973, British Waterworks Association; *b* 1 Aug. 1908; *o s* of William John Millis and Jessie Millis, Hackney; *m* 1932, Ethel May, *o c* of John T. W. Willmott, Enfield; two *d* (and one *d* decd). *Educ:* Grocers' Company Sch., Hackney; London Sch. of Economics (BSc Econ). Called to Bar, Inner Temple, 1936; served with Metropolitan Water Board; Asst Sec., British Waterworks Assoc. Pres., Internat. Water Supply Assoc., 1974 (Sec.-Gen., 1947-72); Chm., North Surrey Water Co., 1956-; Thames Conservator, 1959-74; Chm., Sutton District Water Co., 1971-. Member: Council, Water Companies Assoc. (Vice-Pres.); Nat. Water Council, 1973-80; Water Services Staff Commn 1973-79; Commn on High Water Charges in Wales, 1974-76. Sec., Public Works and Municipal Services Congress Council, 1965-; Vice-Pres., Freshwater Biological Assoc.; Vice-Chm. of Council, Water Research Assoc.; Master, Plumbers' Co., 1978; Mem., Water Supply Industry Trng Board, 1966-74. Hon. MIWE 1966; Hon. FIPHE 1980; FRSA. Hon. Member: Amer. Water Works Assoc., 1969; Deutsche Verein von Gas- und Wasserfachmannern, 1974. JP Mddx (Barnet Div.). *Publications:* contribs to scientific and technical papers, also other papers about water supply. *Recreations:* reading, gardening, sport. *Address:* Covenden, 17 Beech Hill, Hadley Wood, Barnet, Herts. *T:* 01-449 6164. *Club:* Lansdowne.

MILLNER, Ralph; QC 1965; Visiting Lecturer in Law, University of Leicester, since 1980; *b* 25 Jan. 1912; *o s* of Ralph Millner, Merchant, Manchester; *m* 1st, 1935, Bruna, *d* of Arturo Rosa, Este, Italy (marr. diss. 1949); one *d* decd; 2nd, 1949, Monica, *d* of Prof. P. W. Robertson, Wellington, NZ; one *s* two *d. Educ:* William Hulme's Grammar Sch., Manchester; Clare Coll., Cambridge (MA); Bedford Coll., London (BA, Italian). Called to English Bar, Inner Temple, 1934; Ghana Bar (Gold Coast), 1950; Sierra Leone Bar, 1957; Nigerian Bar and S Cameroons Bar, 1959; Guyana Bar (formerly British Guiana), 1961; has also appeared in courts of Aden and Kenya. Lectr in Italian, QUB, 1972-77. Member: Soc. for Italian Studies; Haldane Soc. *Address:* 69 Anson Road, N7.

MILLOTT, Prof. Norman; Emeritus Professor, University of London, since 1976; Director of the University Marine Biological Station, Millport, 1970-76; *b* 24 Oct. 1912; *s* of Reuben Tomlinson Millott and Mary Millott (*née* Thistlethwaite); *m* 1939, Margaret Newns; three *d. Educ:* The Brunts Sch., Mansfield, Notts; Univs of Sheffield (BSc 1935, MSc 1936, DSc 1961), Manchester, Cambridge (PhD 1944). Demonstrator in Zoology, Manchester Univ., 1935-36; Rouse Ball Student, Trinity Coll., Cambridge, 1936-38; Lectr in Zoology, Manchester Univ., 1938-40 and 1945-47. Commissioned RAFVR Technical Branch, 1940-45. Prof. of Zoology, University Coll. of the West Indies, 1948-55; Prof. of Zoology, Bedford Coll., London Univ., 1955-70. Staff Councillor, 1957-60, and Dean of Faculty of Science, Bedford Coll., 1958-60; Chm. of Board of Studies in Zoology, Univ. of London, 1961-65; Chm. Photobiology Group, UK, 1960-62; Chm. Academic Advisory Board, Kingston-upon-Thames Technical Coll., 1960-66; Vice-Pres., International Congress of Photobiology, 1964; Mem. Council, Scottish Marine Biological Assoc., 1971-76. Royal Society Vis. Prof., Univ. of Malta, 1976-77. Governor, Bedford Coll., London Univ., 1976-82. *Publications:* scientific papers chiefly on invertebrate morphology, histology, physiology, and biochemistry. *Address:* Dunmore House, Millport, Isle of Cumbrae, Scotland.

MILLS, family name of Viscount Mills.

MILLS, 2nd Viscount, *cr* 1962; **Roger Clinton Mills;** Bt 1953; Baron 1957; Company Executive since 1963; *b* 14 June 1919; *o s* of 1st Viscount Mills, PC, KBE, and Winifred Mary (*d* 1974), *d* of George Conaty, Birmingham; *S* father, 1968; *m* 1945, Joan Dorothy, *d* of James Shirreff; one *s* two *d. Educ:*

Canford Sch.; Jesus Coll., Cambridge. Served War as Major, RA, 1940-46. Administrative Officer, Colonial Service, Kenya, 1946-63. Barrister, Inner Temple, 1956. *Heir: s* Hon. Christopher Philip Roger Mills [*b* 20 May 1956; *m* 1980, Lesley, *er d* of Alan Bailey, Lichfield, Staffs]. *Address:* Whitecroft, Abbey Road, Knaresborough, N Yorks. *T:* Harrogate 866201.

MILLS, Maj.-Gen. Alan Oswald Gawler; Director-General of Artillery, Ministry of Defence (Army), 1967-69, retired; *b* 11 March 1914; *o s* of John Gawler Mills; *m* 1941, Beata Elizabeth de Courcy Morgan Richards; one *s* one *d. Educ:* Marlborough Coll.; RMA, Woolwich. Commissioned RA, 1934; Hong Kong, 1938-45; Br. Jt Services Mission, USA, 1951-53; Techn SO Grade I, Min. of Supply, 1955-57; Mil. Dir of Studies, RMCS, 1957-61; Sen. Mil. Officer, Royal Armament Research and Develt Estabt, 1961-62; BGS, WO, 1962-65; Dir, Guided Weapons Trials, Min. of Aviation, 1966. CEng, MRAeS. *Recreations:* sailing, ski-ing. *Address:* 3 Seafield Terrace, Seaview, IoW. *T:* Seaview 3166; 9 Redburn Street, Chelsea, SW3 4DA. *T:* 01-351 4272. *Clubs:* Royal London Yacht, Island Sailing (Cowes); Seaview Yacht.

MILLS, Major Anthony David; *b* 14 Dec. 1918; *y s* of late Maj.-Gen. Sir Arthur Mills, CB, DSO; *m* 1948, Anne (*née* Livingstone); two *d. Educ:* Wellington Coll.; RMC, Sandhurst. Commnd Indian Army, 1939, 9th Gurkha Rifles; served War of 1939-45, NW Frontier and Burma, regimental duty and various staff appts; seconded Indian Para. Regt, 1944; retd from Army 1948. Apptd Asst Sec., All England Lawn Tennis Club and Wimbledon Championships, 1948, Sec. Treasurer, and Sec.-Gen., 1963-79. *Recreations:* golf, dog walking, consulting Who's Who. *Address:* 29 White Hart Lane, Barnes, SW13. *Clubs:* Naval and Military, Queen's (Hon.); All England Lawn Tennis; Royal Wimbledon Golf.

MILLS, Barbara Jean Lyon; Junior Treasury Counsel, Central Criminal Court, since 1981; a Recorder of the Crown Court, since 1982; *b* 10 Aug. 1940; *d* of John and Kitty Warnock; *m* 1962, John Angus Donald Mills; four *c. Educ:* St Helen's Sch., Northwood; Lady Margaret Hall, Oxford (MA). Called to the Bar, Middle Temple, 1963. *Recreation:* my family. *Address:* 72 Albert Street, NW1 7NR. *T:* 01-387 0398.

MILLS, Prof. Bernard Yarnton, AC 1976; FRS 1963; FAA 1959; DSc Eng; Professor of Physics (Astrophysics), University of Sydney, since 1965; *b* 8 Aug. 1920; *s* of Ellice Yarnton Mills and Sylphide Mills. *Educ:* King's Sch., New South Wales; University of Sydney. BSc 1940, DSc Eng 1959 (Sydney). Joined the then Council for Scientific and Industrial Research and worked on Develt of mil. radar systems; after working for many years on radioastronomy he joined Sydney Univ. to form a radioastronomy group in Sch. of Physics, 1960; Reader in Physics, 1960-65; responsible for Mills Cross radio-telescope, near Hoskinstown, NSW. Lyle Medal of Australian Academy of Science, 1957. *Publications:* (jtly) A Textbook of Radar, 1946; many contrib. sci. jls in Australia, England and America, mainly on subject of radioastronomy. *Address:* c/o School of Physics, University of Sydney, Sydney, NSW 2006, Australia.

MILLS, (Charles) Ernest, CBE 1979; consultant; Director, United Heating Services Group, since 1978; Member, British Gas Corporation, 1973-78 (Member for Economic Planning, Gas Council, 1968-72); *b* 9 Dec. 1916; *s* of late Charles and Mary Elizabeth Mills; *m* 1943, Irene Hickman; one *s* one *d. Educ:* Barnsley and District Holgate Grammar Sch.; Manchester Coll. of Technology. Administrative Staff Coll., Henley, 1958. Inspector of Naval Ordnance, 1939-45. Engrg Asst, Rochdale Corp. Gas Dept, 1945-51; East Midlands Gas Board: Asst Divisional Engr, 1951-54; Divisional Engr, 1954-58; Asst Chief Engr and Production Controller, 1958-61; Chief Engr and Production Controller, 1961-64; Dep. Chm., E Midlands Gas Bd, 1964-66, Chm., W Midlands Gas Bd, 1966-68. Chm. and Chief Exec., Gas Gathering Pipelines (N Sea) Ltd, 1977-79. Mem., Econ. and Soc. Cttee, EEC, 1978-82. *Recreations:* travel, sports. *Address:* Long Rafters, Sheethanger Lane, Felden, Hemel Hempstead, Herts HP3 0BG. *T:* Hemel Hempstead 55220.

MILLS, Vice-Adm. Sir Charles (Piercy), KCB 1968 (CB 1964); CBE 1957; DSC 1953; *b* 4 Oct. 1914; *s* of late Capt. Thomas Piercy Mills, Woking, Surrey; *m* 1944, Anne Cumberlege; two *d. Educ:* RN College, Dartmouth. Joined Navy, 1928; Comdr 1947; Capt. 1953; Rear-Adm. 1963; Vice-Adm. 1966. Served War of 1939-45, Home Waters, Mediterranean and Far East; Korea, 1951-52; Flag Officer, Second in Command, Far East Fleet, 1966-67; C-in-C Plymouth, 1967-69; Lieut-Governor and C-in-C Guernsey, 1969-74. US Legion of Merit, 1955. KStJ 1969. *Recreations:* golf, yachting. *Address:* Park Lodge, Aldeburgh, Suffolk. *T:* Aldeburgh 2115.

MILLS, Edward (David), CBE 1959; FRIBA; Architect and Design Consultant in private practice since 1937; Senior Partner, Edward D. Mills & Partners, Architects, London, since 1956; *b* 19 March 1915; *s* of Edward Ernest Mills; *m* 1939, Elsie May Bryant; one *s* one *d. Educ:* Ensham Sch.; Polytechnic Sch. of Architecture. ARIBA 1937, FRIBA 1946. Mem. of RIBA Council, 1954-62 and 1964-69; Chm. RIBA Bd of Architectural Education, 1960-62 (Vice-Chm., 1958-60); Pres., Soc. of Architectural Illustrators, 1975-. RIBA Alfred Bossom Research Fellow, 1963; Churchill Fellow, 1969. FSIA 1975; Mem., Uganda Soc. of Architects. Chm., Faculty Architecture, British School at Rome. Architect for British Industries Pavilion, Brussels Internat. Exhibn, 1958; works include: Nat. Exhibn Centre, Birmingham, churches, schools, industrial buildings, research centres, flats and houses in Great Britain and overseas. *Publications:* The Modern Factory, 1951; The New Architecture in Great Britain, 1953; The Modern Church, 1956; Architects Details, Vols 1-6, 1952-61; Factory Building, 1967; The Changing Workplace, 1971; Planning, 1972; The National Exhibition Centre, 1976; Building Maintenance and Preservation, 1980; contribs to RIBA journal, Architectural Review, etc. *Recreations:* photography, foreign travel. *Address:* Gate House Farm, Newchapel, Lingfield, Surrey. *T:* Lingfield 832241.

MILLS, Eric Robertson, CBE 1981; Registrar of the Privy Council since 1966; *b* 27 July 1918; *s* of late Thomas Piercy Mills, Woking, Surrey; *m* 1950, Shirley Manger; two *d. Educ:* Charterhouse; Trinity Coll., Cambridge (BA). Served Royal Artillery, 1939-46; Major 1944. Called to Bar, Inner Temple, 1947; Mem. of Western Circuit. Dep. Judge Advocate, 1955; Chief Clerk, Judicial Cttee of Privy Council, 1963. *Publications:* contribs to legal text books. *Address:* Lamber Green, St Catherines Drive, Guildford, Surrey GU2 5HE. *T:* Guildford 37218.

MILLS, Prof. Eric William, CChem, FRSC; FRACI; Director, South Australian Institute of Technology, since 1978; *b* 22 April 1920; *s* of William and Lucy Margaret Mills; *m* 1945, Inge Julia Königsberger; three *d. Educ:* Liverpool Institute; Univ. of Liverpool (BSc, PhD). Chemist, British Insulated Cables, 1941-45; Research Chemist, British Oxygen Co., 1948-49; Sen. Lectr, Birmingham College of Advanced Technology, 1949-52; Head of Dept, Rutherford Coll. of Technology, 1952-57; Principal: Carlisle Technical Coll., 1959-60; Chesterfield Coll. of Technology, 1960-63; Asst Dir, SA Inst. of Technology, 1964-77. *Address:* 93 Mount Osmond Road, Mount Osmond, South Australia 5064, Australia. *T:* 79-6674.

MILLS, Ernest; *see* Mills, C. E.

MILLS, Frank, CMG 1971; HM Diplomatic Service; High Commissioner in Bangladesh, since 1981; *b* 3 Dec. 1923; *s* of Joseph Francis Mills and Louisa Mills; *m* 1953, Trilby Foster; one *s* two *d. Educ:* King Edward VI Sch., Nuneaton; Emmanuel Coll., Cambridge. RAFVR, 1942-45. CRO, 1948; served in: Pakistan, 1949-51; S Africa, 1955-58; Malaysia, 1962-63; Singapore, 1964-66; India, 1972-75; Ghana, 1975-78; Private Sec. to Sec. of State, 1960-62; RCDS, 1971; Dir of Communications, FCO, 1978-81. *Recreations:* golf, sailing. *Address:* c/o Foreign and Commonwealth Office, SW1. *Club:* Royal Commonwealth Society.

MILLS, Maj.-Gen. Giles Hallam, CB 1977; OBE 1964; Major and Resident Governor, HM Tower of London, and Keeper of the Jewel House, since 1979; *b* 1 April 1922; 2nd *s* of late Col Sir John Digby Mills, TD, Bisterne Manor, Ringwood, Hampshire, and of Lady Mills; *m* 1947, Emily Snowden Hallam, 2nd *d* of late Captain W. H. Tuck, Perrywood, Maryland, USA, and of Mrs Tuck; two *s* one *d. Educ:* Eton Coll. Served War: 2nd Lieut, KRRC, 1941; 1st Bn, KRRC, N Africa, Italy (Adjt, despatches), 1943-47. Staff Coll., 1951; Armed Forces Staff Coll. (US), 1959; Mil. Asst to CIGS, 1961-63; CO, 2 Green Jackets, KRRC, 1963-65; Admin. Staff Coll., Henley, 1965; Regtl Col, Royal Green Jackets, 1966-67; Comd, 8 Infty Bde, 1968-69; IDC 1970; Comd, British Army Staff and Mil. Attaché, Washington, 1971-73; Divl Brig., The Light Div., 1973-74; Dir of Manning (Army), 1974-77, retd. *Publications:* Annals of The King's Royal Rifle Corps, vol. VI (with Roger Nixon), 1971, vol. VII, 1979. *Recreations:* gardening, bird-watching, fishing, shooting, history. *Address:* Queen's House, HM Tower of London, EC3N 4AB. *Club:* Army and Navy.

MILLS, Herbert Horatio, MC 1944; Rector of the Edinburgh Academy, 1962-77; *b* Jan. 1917; *s* of Edward Charles and Sarah Mills. *Educ:* Marling Sch.; St Catharine's Coll., Cambridge (PhD). Commonwealth Fellow, University of Pennsylvania, USA, 1950. Asst Master, Sedbergh Sch., 1953-62. *Recreations:* mountaineering; Cambridge Rugby XV, 1947, 1948. *Clubs:* Alpine; Scottish Mountaineering; Scottish Arts (Edinburgh).

MILLS, Iain Campbell; MP (C) Meriden, since 1979; *b* 21 April 1940; *s* of John Steel Mills and Margaret Leitch; *m* 1971, Gaynor Lynne Jeffries. *Educ:* Prince Edward Sch., Salisbury, Rhodesia. Dunlop Rhodesia Ltd, 1961-64; Dunlop Ltd, UK, 1964-79 (latterly Marketing Planning Manager). PPS to Minister of State for Industry, 1981, to Sec. of State for Employment, 1982. *Address:* House of Commons, SW1A 0AA.

MILLS, Ivor; Head of Public Affairs and Deputy Director, Public Relations, British Telecommunications, since 1981 (Head of Public Affairs, Post Office, 1978-81); *b* 7 Dec. 1929; *e s* of John Mills and Matilda (*née* Breen); *m* 1956, Muriel, *o d* of Wilson and Muriel Hay; one *s* one *d. Educ:* High sch.; Stranmillis Coll.; Queen's Univ., Belfast. Radio and television journalist, and freelance writer, Ulster TV, 1959, and Southern TV, 1963; freelance writer/editor/producer/presenter, contrib. to BBC World Service and Home Radio Networks, and ITV Regions, 1964; joined ITN as Reporter, 1965; newscaster with wide experience in preparation and presentation of ITN's News Bulletins, 1967-78. Media consultant to public and private sector orgs. *Recreations:* art, music, theatre, tennis, food, wine. *Address:* British Telecommunications Headquarters, 2-12 Gresham Street, EC2V 7AG.

MILLS, Ivor Henry, FRCP; Professor of Medicine in the University of Cambridge since 1963; Fellow Churchill College, Cambridge; Hon. Consultant to United Cambridge Hospitals; *b* 13 June 1921; 3rd *s* of late J. H. W. Mills and late Priscilla Mills; *m* 1947, Sydney Elizabeth Puleston (*née*

Roberts); one *s* one *d. Educ:* Selhurst Grammar Sch., Croydon; Queen Mary Coll., London; Trinity Coll., Cambridge. BSc (London) 1942; PhD (London) 1946; BA (Cantab) 1948; MB, BChir Cantab 1951; MRCP 1953; MD Cantab 1956; MA Cantab 1963; FRCP 1964. Pres. Cambridge Univ. Medical Soc., 1947-48; Sen. Schol., Trinity Coll., Cambridge, 1948; MRC (Eli Lilly) Trav. Fellow, 1956; Vis. Scientist, Nat. Inst. of Health, 1957; Lectr in Medicine and Chem. Path., St Thomas's Hosp. Medical Sch., 1954; Reader in Medicine, St Thomas's Hosp. Medical Sch., London, 1962. Vis. Prof. in Physiology and Medicine, N Carolina Med. Sch., USA, 1972. Mem., Hunter Working Party on Medical Administrators, 1970-72. Sec., Soc. for Endocrinology, 1963-71; Mem. Council, RCP, 1971-74. Pro-Censor, RCP, 1974-75, Censor, 1975-76. Hon. FACP. *Publications:* Clinical Aspects of Adrenal Function, 1964; contrib. Lancet, Science Jl of Endocr., Clin. Science, etc. *Recreation:* gardening. *Address:* Addenbrooke's Hospital, Cambridge.

MILLS, John; *see* Mills, Laurence J.

MILLS, John F. F. P.; *see* Platts-Mills.

MILLS, Sir John (Lewis Ernest Watts), Kt 1976; CBE 1960; Actor, Producer, Director; *b* 22 Feb. 1908; *m* 1941, Mary Hayley Bell, playwright; one *s* two *d. Educ:* Norwich. 1st appearance, stage, 1929. *Plays:* Cavalcade, London Wall, Words and Music, Five O'clock Girl, Give Me a Ring, Jill Darling, Floodlight, Red Night, We at the Cross Roads, Of Mice and Men, Men in Shadow, Duet for Two Hands, etc.; Old Vic Season, 1938; Top of the Ladder; Figure of Fun, Aldwych; Ross, New York, 1961; Power of Persuasion, Garrick, 1963; Veterans, Royal Court, 1972; At the End of the Day, Savoy, 1973; The Good Companions, Her Majesty's, 1974; Separate Tables, Apollo, 1977; Goodbye, Mr Chips, Chichester Fest., 1982. *Films:* The Midshipmaid, Britannia of Billingsgate, Brown on Resolution, OHMS, Cottage To Let, The Young Mr Pitt, We Dive at Dawn, In Which We Serve, The Way to the Stars, Great Expectations, So Well Remembered, The October Man, Scott of the Antarctic, The History of Mr Polly, The Rocking Horse Winner, Morning Departure, Mr Denning Drives North, Gentle Gunman, The Long Memory, Hobson's Choice, The Colditz Story, The End of the Affair, Above Us the Waves, Town on Trial, Escapade, Its Great to be Young, The Baby and the Battleship, War and Peace, Around the World in Eighty Days, Dunkirk, Ice Cold in Alex, I Was Monty's Double, Summer of the Seventeenth Doll, Tiger Bay, Swiss Family Robinson, The Singer not the Song, Tunes of Glory, Flame in the Streets, The Valiant, Tiara Tahiti, The Chalk Garden, The Truth about Spring, King Rat, Operation X Bow, Red Waggon, Sky West and Crooked (directed), The Wrong Box, The Family Way, Chuka, Showdown, Oh What a Lovely War, The Return of the Boomerang, Ryan's Daughter (Best Supporting Actor Award, Oscar Award, 1971), Run Wild, Run Free, Emma Hamilton, Dulcima, Lamb, Young Winston, Oklahoma Crude, Trial by Combat, The Devil's Advocate, Great Expectations, The Big Sleep, Zulu Dawn, The 39 Steps, The Human Factor, Gandhi. *TV series:* The Zoo Gang, 1974; Quatermass, 1979; Tales of the Unexpected, 1979, 1980, 1981; Young at Heart, 1980, 1981, 1982. Member: SFTA (Vice-Pres.); RADA Council, 1965-; Chm., Stars Organization for Spastics, 1975-79. Patron Life Mem., Variety Club. *Publication:* Up in the Clouds, Gentlemen Please (autobiog.), 1980. *Recreations:* ski-ing, golf, painting. *Address:* c/o ICM, 388 Oxford Street, W1. *Club:* Garrick.

MILLS, John Robert, BSc, CEng, FIEE, MInstP; Under Secretary and Deputy Director (Systems) Royal Signals and Radar Establishment, Ministry of Defence, 1976-77, retired; engaged part-time by Civil Service Commission, since 1979; *b* 12 Nov. 1916; *s* of Robert Edward Mills and Constance H. Mills; *m* 1950, Pauline Phelps; two *s. Educ:* Kingston Grammar Sch., Kingston-upon-Thames; King's Coll., London (BSc 1939); MInstP; FIEE, 1971. Air Ministry Research Estab., Dundee, 1939; RAE Farnborough, 1940-42; TRE, later RRE, Malvern, 1942-60; Supt (Offensive), Airborne Radar, RRE, 1954-60; Asst Dir, Electronics R and D (Civil Aviation), Min. of Aviation, 1960-61; Head of Radio Dept, RAE Farnborough, 1961-65; Electronics Div., Min. of Technology, 1965-67; Dir, Signals R&D Establishment, MoD, 1967-76. *Publications:* (jointly) Radar article in Encyclopædia Britannica; various papers in journals. *Address:* Little Chewton, Chewton Farm Road, Highcliffe, Christchurch, Dorset.

MILLS, (John) Vivian G., DLitt; *b* 22 Sept. 1887; *s* of late Comdr J. F. Mills, ISO, RN (retd); *m* 1st, 1915, Lilian (*d* 1947), *d* of late A. Brisley; no *c*; 2nd, 1968, Marguerite Mélanie, *d* of late Jean Hoffman. *Educ:* privately; Merton Coll., Oxford; Classical Mods and Lit Hum; MA 1946; DLitt 1974. Barrister-at-law, Middle Temple, 1919; Cadet, Malayan Civil Service, 1911; qualified in Chinese, 1914; held various administrative, legal and judicial appointments, 1914-28; Solicitor-Gen., Straits Settlements, 1928-32; acting Attorney-Gen., and Mem. of the Executive and Legislative Councils, 1932; Commissioner of Currency, 1932; Puisne Judge, Straits Settlements, 1933; Judge, Johore, 1934; retired, 1940; Attached to office of Federal Attorney-Gen., Sydney, Australia, 1944-45; Additional Lecturer in Chinese Law, School of Oriental and African Studies, London, 1946-47; Pres. of Malayan Branch, Royal Asiatic Society, 1937; Joint Hon. Sec., Hakluyt Soc., 1950-53. *Publications:* Eredia's Malaca, Meridional India and Cathay, 1930; Malaya in the Wu-pei-chi Charts, 1937; (trans. and ed) Ma Huan: Ying-yai sheng-lan, The Overall Survey of the Ocean's Shores, 1970; various official publications. *Recreations:* Oriental research and watching first-class cricket. *Address:* Bellaria 62, 1814 La Tour de Peilz, Switzerland. *Club:* Athenæum.

MILLS, John William, OBE 1945; QC 1962; *b* 24 Oct. 1914; *s* of late John William Mills, OBE and Jessie Mills; *m* 1942, Phyllis Mary, *yr d* of late Arthur Gibson Pears; no *c. Educ:* Clifton; Corpus Christi Coll., Cambridge (MA). Called to Bar, Middle Temple, 1938; Bencher, 1968. Lt-Col, Royal Signals, 1944; Comdr, Royal Signals, 46 Div., 1944. Member: Bar Council, 1961-64; Clifton Coll. Council, 1967-80. *Publications:* The Building Societies Act, 1960, 1961, Wurtzbarg and Mills, Building Society Law, 1964-. *Recreations:* sailing, golf. *Address:* 38 Adam and Eve Mews, W8. *T:* 01-937 1259; 11 Old Square, Lincoln's Inn, WC2. *T:* 01-405 5243; Greenleas, Highleigh, Chichester, Sussex. *T:* Sidlesham 396.

MILLS, (Laurence) John, CBE 1978; Member, National Coal Board since 1974, a Deputy Chairman, since 1982; *b* 1 Oct. 1920; *s* of late Archibald John and Annie Ellen Mills; *m* 1944, Barbara May (*née* Warner); two *s. Educ:* Portsmouth Grammar Sch.; Birmingham Univ. BSc (Hons), FEng, Hon. FIMinE, CAMEME; CBIM. Mining Student, Houghton Main Colliery Co. Ltd, 1939; Corps of Royal Engrs, 1942-46, Major 1946; various mining appts, Nat. Coal Bd, 1949-67; Chief Mining Engr, HQ NCB, 1968; Area Dir, N Yorks Area, 1970; Area Dir, Doncaster Area, 1973. Director: Coal Develts (Queensland) Ltd; Capricorn Coal Management Pty Ltd; Coal Develts (German Creek) Pty Ltd; German Creek Pty Ltd. Member: Mining Qualifications Bd, 1975-; Safety in Mines Res. Adv. Bd, 1975-; Adv. Council on Res. Develt for Fuel and Power, 1981. Pres., IMinE, 1975. *Publications:* techn. papers in Trans IMinE. *Recreation:* coastal and inland waterway cruising. *Address:* c/o Hobart House, Grosvenor Place, SW1X 7AE.

MILLS, Lawrence William Robert; JP; Director of Trade, Hong Kong, since 1981; *b* London, 7 May 1934; *s* of William H. Mills and E. May Mills; *m* 1964, Amy Kwai Lan (*née* Poon), Shanghai and Hong Kong; two *d. Educ:* Reigate Grammar Sch., Surrey. National Service: RN, 1953; Intell. Corps, 1954. Formerly, Jun. Exec., K. F. Mayer Ltd, London. Hong Kong Govt (Mem. of HMOCS): Exec. Officer, Cl. II, 1958; Asst Trade Officer, 1960; Trade Officer, 1964; Sen. Trade Officer, 1968; Principal Trade Officer, 1969; Asst Dir of Commerce and Industry, 1971; Chief Trade Negotiator, 1974-75; Counsellor (Hong Kong Affairs), Hong Kong Office, UK Mission, Geneva, 1976-77; Director of Trade, Hong Kong, 1977; Comr of Industry, 1979-81. *Recreation:* music (classical jazz). *Address:* Trade Department, Ocean Centre, Hong Kong. *Clubs:* Hong Kong, Hong Kong Country (Hong Kong).

MILLS, Leif Anthony; General Secretary, Banking, Insurance and Finance Union (formerly National Union of Bank Employees), since 1972; Member, Monopolies and Mergers Commission, since 1982; *b* 25 March 1936; *s* of English father and Norwegian mother; *m* 1958, Gillian Margaret Smith; two *s* two *d. Educ:* Balliol Coll., Oxford. BA Hons PPE. Commnd in Royal Military Police, 1957-59. Trade Union Official, Nat. Union of Bank Employees, 1960-: Research Officer, 1960; Asst Gen. Sec., 1962; Dep. Gen. Sec., 1968. Mem. various arbitration tribunals; Member: TUC Non-Manual Workers Adv. Cttee, 1967-72; Office of Manpower Economics Adv. Cttee on Equal Pay, 1971. Member: Cttee to Review the Functioning of Financial Institutions, 1977-80; CS Pay Res. Unit Bd, 1978-81; BBC Consultative Gp on Social Effects of Television, 1978-80; Armed Forces Pay Review Body, 1980-. Contested (Lab) Salisbury, 1964, 1965 (by-elecn). Mem., Council, Industrial Soc., 1980-. *Publications:* biography (unpublished), Cook: A History of the Life and Explorations of Dr Frederick Albert Cook, SPRI ms 883, Cambridge, 1970. *Recreations:* rowing, chess, squash. *Address:* 31 Station Road, West Byfleet, Surrey. *T:* Byfleet 42829. *Clubs:* United Oxford & Cambridge University; Oxford University Boat.

MILLS, Leonard Sidney, CB 1970; Deputy Director General (2), Highways, Department of the Environment, 1970-74; *b* 20 Aug. 1914; *s* of late Albert Edward Mills; *m* 1940, Kathleen Joyce Cannicott; two *s. Educ:* Devonport High Sch.; London Sch. of Economics; Birkbeck Coll., University of London. Entered Exchequer and Audit Dept, 1933; transferred to Min. of Civil Aviation, 1946; Asst Sec., 1950; Min. of Transport: Under-Sec., 1959; Chief of Highway Administration, 1968-70. Commonwealth Fund Fellow, 1953-54. *Recreations:* walking, croquet, photography, gardening. *Address:* Pine Rise, 7A Bedlands Lane, Budleigh Salterton, Devon.

MILLS, Mary Bell McMillan, (Mrs Ian Mills); *see* MacMurray, M.B. McM.

MILLS, Neil McLay; Chairman, Sedgwick Group plc, since 1979; *b* 29 July 1923; *yr s* of late L. H. Mills and Mrs Mills; *m* 1950, Rosamund Mary Kimpton, *d* of Col and Hon. Mrs A. C. W. Kimpton; two *s* two *d. Educ:* Epsom Coll.; University Coll. London. Served War, 1939-45: commnd RN; Lieut RNVR; Coastal Forces (mentioned in despatches, 1944). Joined Bland Welch & Co. Ltd, 1948; Exec. Dir, 1955; Chm., 1965-74; Chm., Bland Payne Holdings Ltd, 1974-79. Underwriting Mem. of Lloyd's, 1955-. Director: Montagu Trust Ltd, 1966-74; Midland Bank Ltd, 1974-79. Vice-President: Insurance Inst. of London, 1971-; British Insurance Brokers Assoc., 1978- (Mem., Internat. Insurance Brokers Cttee); Mem. Cttee, Lloyd's Insurance Brokers Assoc., 1974-77. Member: (Alternate), Cttee on Invisible Exports, 1975-; Church Army Board, 1957-64 (Vice-Chm., 1959-64); Council, Oak Hill Theol Coll., 1958-62. Trustee and Governor, Lord Mayor Treloar Trust, 1975-81. *Recreation:* farming. *Address:* 15 Markham Square, SW3. *T:* 01-584 3995; The Dower House, Upton Grey, near Basingstoke, Hants. *T:* Long Sutton 435. *Clubs:* City of London, Naval and Military.

MILLS, Sir Peter (Frederick Leighton), 3rd Bt, *cr* 1921; *b* 9 July 1924; *s* of Major Sir Frederick Leighton Victor Mills, 2nd Bt, MC, RA, MICE, and Doris (*née* Armitage); *S* father 1955; *m* 1954, Pauline Mary, *d* of L. R. Allen, Calverton, Notts; one *s* one adopted *d. Educ:* Eastbourne Coll.; Cedara Coll. of Agriculture, University of Natal (BSc Agric.). Served HM Forces, 1943-47. CS, Fedn Rhodesia and Nyasaland, 1953; with Rhodesia Min. of Agric., 1964-. *Heir: s* Michael Victor Leighton Mills, *b* 30 Aug. 1957. *Address:* Henderson Research Station, P Bag 2004, Mazoe, Zimbabwe.

MILLS, Sir Peter (McLay), Kt 1982; MP (C) Devon West, since 1974 (Torrington, 1964-74); Farmer; *b* 22 Sept. 1921; *m* 1948, Joan Weatherley; one *s* one *d. Educ:* Epsom; Wye Coll. Farmer since 1943. Parly Sec., MAFF, 1972; Parly Under-Sec. of State, NI Office, 1972-74. Member: European Legislation Cttee, EEC, 1974-79; Exec. Cttee, Commonwealth Parly Assoc., 1979-; For. Affairs Select Cttee, 1980-; Chm., Cons. Agriculture Cttee, 1979-. *Recreations:* work and staying at home for a short time. *Address:* House of Commons, SW1. *T:* 01-219 4093.

MILLS, Peter William; Vice President, The Woodbridge Company Ltd, since 1980; *b* 22 July 1942; *s* of Joseph Roger Mills and Jane Eveyln (*née* Roscoe); *m* 1967, Eveline Jane (*née* Black); two *s. Educ:* Dalhousie Univ. Law Sch. (LLB); Dalhousie Univ. (BComm). Barrister and solicitor, Ont, Canada; with McInnes, Cooper and Robertson, Halifax, 1967; Solicitor, Canadian Pacific Ltd, Montreal and Toronto, 1967-71; Dir, Cammell Laird Shipbuilders Ltd, 1971-76; Mem. Org. Cttee for British Shipbuilders, 1976-77; Manager, Currie, Coopers & Lybrand Ltd, Toronto, 1977-79; Dir, Corporate Develt, FP Publications Ltd, 1979-80. *Recreations:* golf, sailing, travel, reading. *Address:* The Woodbridge Company Ltd, 65 Queen Street West, Toronto, Ont M5H 2M8, Canada; 390 Glencairn Avenue, Toronto, Ont M5N 1V1. *Clubs:* Board of Trade, York Downs Golf and Country (Toronto); Royal Liverpool Golf (Hoylake); Royal Nova Scotia Yacht Squadron.

MILLS, Air Cdre Stanley Edwin Druce, CB 1968; CBE 1959; Royal Air Force, retired; *b* 1913; *s* of Edwin J. Mills; *m* 1938, Joan Mary, *d* of Robert Ralph James; one *s* one *d. Educ:* Collegiate Sch., Bournemouth, RAF Staff Coll. Entered RAF 1939; served RAF Middle East and Italy, 1942-45; Station Comdr, RAF Innsworth, 1957-60; Comd Accountant, RAF Germany, 1960-63; Dir of Personnel (Policy) (Air), MoD, 1963-65; Dir of Personal Services (Air), MoD, 1966-68. Bursar, Roedean Sch., 1968-73. FCA. *Recreation:* travel. *Address:* Maryland, Lullington Close, Seaford, E Sussex. *Club:* Royal Air Force.

MILLS, Brig. Stephen Douglas, CBE 1943; MC; *b* 1892; *s* of late Stephen E. Mills, JP, Longmead, Havant, Hants; *m* 1923, Rosamond, *d* of late W. R. Merk, CSI, CIE, ICS; one *s* one *d. Educ:* Bradfield Coll.; RMC, Sandhurst. Late Beds and Herts Regt, European War 1914-19, in France, Belgium, and Palestine (wounded, MC); Palestine, 1936-39 (despatches); War of 1939-45 in Middle East (despatches, CBE); retired 1946. *Address:* Quidhams, Bowerchalke, near Salisbury, Wilts. *T:* Broadchalke 243.

MILLS, Stratton; *see* Mills, W. S.

MILLS, Vivian; *see* Mills, J. V. G.

MILLS, Wilbur Daigh; lawyer and politician, USA; tax consultant, Shea & Gould (Mirabelli & Gould), since 1977; *b* Kensett, Ark, 24 May 1909; *s* of Ardra Pickens Mills and Abbie Lois Daigh; *m* 1934, Clarine Billingsley; two *d. Educ:* Hendrix Coll.; Harvard Law Sch. Admitted to State Bar of Arkansas, 1933; in private legal practice, Searcy; County and Probate Judge, White County, 1934-38; Cashier, Bank of Kensett, 1934-35. Mem., US House of Representatives, 1939-76 (Chm., Ways and Means Cttee, 1958-74). Democrat. *Address:* (office) 1627 K Street NW, Washington, DC 20006, USA; Kensett, Arkansas 72082, USA.

MILLS, Maj.-Gen. William Graham Stead, CBE 1963; *b* 23 June 1917; *s* of William Stead Mills and Margaret Kennedy Mills; *m* 8 July 1941, Joyce Evelyn (*née* Ransom) (*d* 1981); three *s. Educ:* Merchiston Castle Sch., Edinburgh. Regtl duty, Royal Berks Regt, in India, 1938-43; Staff Coll., India, 1944; GSO2 and GSO1, Ops HQ 14th Army, Burma, 1944-45; WO and Washington, USA, 1946-50; Regtl duty with Parachute Regt, comdg 17th Bn, The Parachute Regt, 1958-60; GSO1, 2 Div. BAOR, 1956-58; Regtl Col The Parachute Regt, 1960-62; Comdg TA Brigade, Winchester, 1963-64; Brig. GS, HQ Middle East Comd, Aden, 1965-66; Imperial Defence Coll., Student, 1967; GOC West Midland District, 1968-70. *Recreations:* normal. *Address:* Inglenook, Field Dalling, Holt, Norfolk. *T:* Binham 388.

MILLS, (William) Stratton; Partner in Mills, Selig & Bailie, Solicitors, Belfast; Company Director; *b* 1 July 1932; *o s* of late Dr J. V. S. Mills, CBE, Resident Magistrate for City of Belfast, and Margaret Florence (*née* Byford); *m* 1959, Merriel E. R. Whitla, *o d* of Mr and Mrs R. J. Whitla, Belfast; three *s. Educ:* Campbell Coll., Belfast; Queen's Univ., Belfast (LLB). Vice-Chm., Federation of University Conservative and Unionist Assocs, 1952-53 and 1954-55; admitted a Solicitor, 1958. MP (UU) Belfast N, Oct. 1959-Dec. 1972; MP (Alliance) Belfast N, Apr. 1973-Feb. 1974; PPS to Parly Sec., Ministry of Transport, 1961-64; Member: Estimates Cttee, 1964-70; Exec. Cttee, 1922 Cttee, 1967-70, 1973; Hon. Sec. Conservative Broadcasting Cttee, 1963-70, Chm., 1970-73; Mem., Mr Speaker's Conference on Electoral Law, 1967. Mem., One Nation Gp, 1972-73. Chm., Ulster Orchestra Soc. Ltd,

1980-. *Address:* (office) 20 Callender Street, Belfast 1. *T:* Belfast 43878; (home) 17 Malone Park, Belfast 9. *T:* Belfast 665210. *Clubs:* Carlton; Ulster (Belfast).

MILLS-OWENS, Richard Hugh, CBE 1972; Puisne Judge, Hong Kong, 1967–71 (also 1961–64); Chief Justice, Fiji, 1964–67; *b* Jan. 1910; *s* of George Edward Owens and Jessie Mary Mills; *m* 1935, Elizabeth Ann Hiles (*d* 1968); two *s.* *Educ:* Rhyl Grammar Sch. Admitted Solicitor, 1932; Clifford's Inn Prizeman; Barrister-at-law, 1956, Middle Temple. Practised in Wales (including service with Carmarthenshire County Council) until 1949 when joined Colonial Legal Service as a Registrar of Titles; Principal Registrar, Kenya; Crown Counsel and Legal Draftsman, 1952; Magistrate, 1956, District Judge, 1958, Hong Kong. *Recreation:* golf. *Address:* Westwood, Hangersley, Ringwood, Hants.

MILLSON, John Albert; Assistant Under-Secretary of State, Ministry of Defence, 1972–78; *b* 4 Oct. 1918; *s* of late George Charles Millson and Annie Millson, London; *m* 1953, Megan Laura Woodiss; one *s* one *d. Educ:* St Olave's. Entered Air Min., 1936; Private Sec. to Parly Under-Sec. of State for Air, 1947–50; Principal, Air Min., 1955; Asst Sec., MoD, 1961; Asst Under-Sec. of State, 1972. Chm. of Governors, Homefield Prep. Sch., Sutton, 1975. *Recreations:* walking, listening to music. *Address:* 9 The Highway, Sutton, Surrey. *T:* 01-642 3967.

MILLWARD, William, CB 1969; CBE 1954; with Government Communications Headquarters, 1946–74, retired (Superintending Director, 1958–69); *b* 27 Jan. 1909; *s* of William John and Alice Millward; *m* 1937, Nora Florella Harper; one *s* one *d. Educ:* Solihull Sch.; St Catherine's Society, Oxford. Asst Master, Dulwich Coll., 1930–41; RAF, 1941–46. *Recreations:* music, reading, walking. *Address:* Three Poplars, Evesham Road, Cheltenham, Glos. *T:* Cheltenham 25732.

MILMAN, Sir Dermot (Lionel Kennedy), 8th Bt, *cr* 1800; *b* 24 Oct. 1912; *e s* of Brig.-Gen. Sir Lionel Charles Patrick Milman, 7th Bt, CMG, and Marjorie Aletta (*d* 1980), *d* of Col A. H. Clark-Kennedy, late Indian Civil Service; *S* father, 1962; *m* 1941, Muriel, *o d* of J. E. S. Taylor, King's Lynn; one *d. Educ:* Uppingham; Corpus Christi Coll., Cambridge. BA 1934, MA 1938. Served War of 1939–45, Royal Army Service Corps, in France, Belgium and Burma (despatches), Major. Hon. Major, RCT (formerly RARO, RASC). British Council service overseas and home, 1946–76, retired 1976. Mem., Gen. Council, Victoria League; Chairman: Assoc. for British-Arab Univ. Visits; Phyllis Konstam Meml Trust; India Arise Fund. *Heir: b* Malcolm Douglas Milman [*b* 18 May 1915; *m* 1940, Sheila Maud (marriage dissolved), *d* of Albert Maurice Dudeney; two *d*]. *Address:* 7 Old Westhall Close, Warlingham, Surrey. *T:* Upper Warlingham 4843.

MILMO, Hon. Sir Helenus Patrick Joseph, Kt 1964; DL; **Hon. Mr Justice Milmo;** Judge of High Court of Justice, Queen's Bench Division, since 1964; *b* 24 Aug. 1908; 3rd *s* of late Daniel Milmo, Furbough, Co. Galway, Eire; *m* 1st, 1933, Joan Frances (*d* 1978), *d* of late Francis Morley, London; two *s* three *d* (and one *d* decd); 2nd, 1980, Anne (Nan), widow of F. B. Brand. *Educ:* Downside; Trinity Coll., Cambridge. Barrister, Middle Temple, 1931; Bencher, 1955; QC 1961; Dep. Treasurer, 1972; Treasurer 1973. Civil Asst, General Staff, War Office, 1940–45. Dep. Chm., West Sussex QS, 1960–64. DL Sussex, 1962. *Recreations:* hunting, fishing, wine. *Address:* Church Farm, Shipley, near Horsham, W Sussex. *T:* Coolham 261. *Clubs:* Garrick, MCC.

MILNE, family name of **Baron Milne.**

MILNE, 2nd Baron, *cr* 1933, of Salonika and of Rubislaw, Co. Aberdeen; **George Douglass Milne;** *b* 10 Feb. 1909; *s* of 1st Baron Milne, GCB, GCMG, DSO, Field Marshal from 1928, and Claire Marjoribanks, MBE, DGStJ (*d* 1970), *d* of Sir John N. Maitland, 5th Bt; *S* father, 1948; *m* 1940, Cicely, 3rd *d* of late Ronald Leslie; two *s* one *d. Educ:* Winchester; New Coll., Oxford. Mem., Inst. of Chartered Accountants of Scotland. Partner, Arthur Young McClelland Moores Co., 1954–73, Dep. Chm., 1981; Dir, London & Northern Group Ltd, 1973–. Master of the Grocers' Company, 1961–62. Served War of 1939–45, Royal Artillery (TA); prisoner of war, 1941; NWEF and MEF (wounded, despatches). *Recreation:* art: has exhibited RA, ROI, RP. *Heir: s* Hon. George Alexander Milne, *b* 1 April 1941. *Address:* 33 Lonsdale Road, Barnes, SW13. *T:* 01-748 6421; (business) Essex Hall, Essex Street, WC1.

MILNE, Alasdair David Gordon; Director-General of the BBC, since 1982; *b* 8 Oct. 1930; *s* of Charles Gordon Shaw Milne and Edith Reid Clark; *m* 1954, Sheila Kirsten Graucob; two *s* one *d. Educ:* Winchester Coll.; New Coll., Oxford. Commnd into 1st Bn Gordon Highlanders, 1949. Hon. Mods Oxon 1952; BA Oxon Mod. Langs, 1954. Joined BBC, 1954; Dep. Editor, 1957–61, Editor, 1961–62, of Tonight Programme; Head of Tonight Productions, 1963–65; Partner, Jay, Baverstock, Milne & Co., 1965–67; rejoined BBC, Oct. 1967; Controller, BBC Scotland, 1968–72; Dir of Programmes, 1973–77, Man. Dir, 1977–82, BBC TV; Dep. Dir-Gen., BBC, 1980–82. *Recreations:* piping, salmon fishing, golf, tennis. *Address:* c/o BBC, Broadcasting House, W1A 1AA. *T:* 01-580 4468.

MILNE, (Alexander) Berkeley, OBE 1968; Government Communications Headquarters, since 1978; *b* 12 Feb. 1924; *s* of George and Mary Milne; *m*

1952, Patricia Mary (*née* Holderness); one *s* two *d. Educ:* Keith Grammar and Buckie High Schs, Banffshire, Scotland; Univ. of Aberdeen (MA (Hons Mental Phil.) 1943); University Coll., Oxford (BA (Hons Persian and Arabic) 1949). 3/2nd Punjab Regt, Indian Army: service in India and Java, 1943–46. Scarborough Schol., Tehran Univ., 1950–51; Lectr in Persian, Edinburgh Univ., 1951–52. Foreign Office, 1952–53; BMEO, Cyprus, 1953–54; Third, later Second Sec., Tehran, 1954–57; FO, 1958–61; Second, later First Sec., Brussels, 1961–64; FO (later FCO), 1964–65; First Sec., British Residual Mission, Salisbury, Rhodesia, 1966–67; First Sec., Jedda, Saudi Arabia, 1968–70; FCO, 1971–74; Counsellor, Tehran, 1974–77. *Recreations:* gardening, reading; playing chamber music, preferably second violin in string quartets. *Address:* 3 Paragon Terrace, Cheltenham, Glos. *T:* Cheltenham 34849.

MILNE, Alexander Taylor; Fellow of University College London; Secretary and Librarian, Institute of Historical Research, University of London, 1946–71; *b* 22 Jan. 1906; *s* of late Alexander Milne and Shanny (*née* Taylor); *m* 1960, Joyce Frederica Taylor, Dulwich. *Educ:* Christ's Coll., Finchley; University Coll., London. BA History Hons 1927; Diploma in Education, 1928; MA (London), 1930; FRHistS, 1938; Vice-Pres., Historical Assoc., 1966–75, Pres., 1970–73; Asst Officer and Librarian, Royal Historical Society, 1935–40; Hon. Librarian, 1965–70. Fellow, Huntington Library, Calif, 1975. Served War of 1939–45: Buffs and Maritime Artillery, 1940–42; Army Bureau of Current Affairs, 1942–44; Research Dept, FO, 1944–46. Director, History Today, 1962–79. *Publications:* History of Broadwindsor, Dorset, 1935; Catalogue of the Manuscripts of Jeremy Bentham in the Library of University College, London, 1937, 2nd edn 1961; Writings on British History, 1934–45: a Bibliography (8 vols), 1937–60; Centenary Guide to Pubns of Royal Historical Society, 1968; (part-author) Historical Study in the West, 1968; (ed) Librarianship and Literature, essays in honour of Jack Pafford, 1970; (ed) Correspondence of Jeremy Bentham, vols. IV and V, 1788-1797, 1981; contribs to Cambridge History of the British Empire, Encyclopædia Britannica and learned journals. *Recreation:* golf. *Address:* 9 Frank Dixon Close, Dulwich, SE21 7BD. *T:* 01-693 6942. *Clubs:* Athenæum, Dulwich (1772).

MILNE, Andrew McNicoll, MA; Headmaster, The King's School, Worcester, since 1979; *b* 9 March 1927; *s* of late John McNicoll Milne and Daviona K. Coutts; *m* 1963, Nicola Charlotte, 2nd *d* of Ian B. Anderson and Sylvia Spencer; two *d. Educ:* Bishop Wordsworth's Sch., Salisbury; Worcester Coll., Oxford (MA 1961). Oundle: apptd, 1961; Head of History Dept, 1966–70; Housemaster, 1968–75; Second Master, 1975–79. *Publications:* Metternich, 1975; contrib. to Practical Approaches to the New History. *Recreations:* music (classical and jazz), reading, writing. *Address:* 9 College Green, Worcester WR1 2LH. *T:* Worcester 24989.

MILNE, Berkeley; see Milne, A. B.

MILNE, Denys Gordon, (Tiny), CBE 1982; Director, Business in the Community; *b* 12 Jan. 1926; *s* of late Dr George Gordon Milne and of Margaret (*née* Campbell); *m* 1951, Pamela Mary Senior; two *s* one *d. Educ:* Epsom Coll.; Brasenose Coll., Oxford (MA Hons Mod. History). Pilot Officer, RAF Regt, RAFVR, 1944–47. Colonial Admin. Service, Northern Nigeria, 1951–55; British Petroleum Company, 1955–81, retired as Man. Dir and Chief Exec., BP Oil Ltd. Director: Silkolene Lubricants Ltd, 1981–; Fluor (GB) Ltd, 1981–. Member: Scottish Economic Council, 1978–81; Adv. Cttee on Energy Conservation, 1980–81. President: UK Petroleum Industry Assoc., 1980–81 (Vice-Pres., 1979–80); Inst. of Petroleum, 1978–80. *Recreations:* gardening, cruising. *Address:* Westbury, Old Lane, St Johns, Crowborough, East Sussex. *T:* Crowborough 2634. *Clubs:* Caledonian, Royal Air Force; Inanda (Johannesburg).

MILNE, Maj.-Gen. Douglas Graeme; Deputy Director General Army Medical Services, 1975–78; *b* 19 May 1919; *s* of George Milne and Mary Panton; *m* 1944, Jean Millicent Gove; one *d. Educ:* Robert Gordon's Coll.; Aberdeen Univ. MB, ChB, FFCM, DPH. Commnd into RAMC, 1943; service in W Africa, Malta, Egypt, BAOR, Singapore; Dir of Army Health and Research, 1973–75. QHS 1974–78. Col Comdt, RAMC, 1979–. *Recreations:* gardening, fishing. *Address:* 17 Stonehill Road, SW14 8RR. *T:* 01-878 2828.

MILNE, Edward James; author and lecturer; *b* 18 Oct. 1915; *s* of Edward James Milne and Isabella Stewart; *m* 1939, Emily Constable; three *d. Educ:* George Street and Kittybrewster Primary; Sunnybank Intermediate; Robert Gordon's Coll., Aberdeen (Schol.). Lecturer and Organiser, National Council of Labour Colls, 1942–47; Area Organiser, Union of Shop Distributive and Allied Workers, 1952–61. MP (Lab) Blyth, Nov. 1960-Feb. 1974, MP (Ind Lab) Blyth, Feb.-Sept. 1974; PPS to Sir Frank Soskice, Home Sec., 1964–65; Vice-Chm., Parly Labour Party, 1967–68; Secretary: Anglo-Norwegian Parly Gp, 1967–74; Anglo-Swedish Parly Gp, 1968–74; contested (Ind Lab) Blyth, 1979. Mem., (Seaton Delaval Ward), Blyth Valley DC, 1975–79. Grand Order of Star of Africa (Liberia), 1964. *Publication:* No Shining Armour, 1976. *Recreations:* walking, swimming. *Address:* 3 Scotstoun Park, South Queensferry, West Lothian EH30 9PQ.

MILNE, Ian Innes, CMG 1965; OBE 1946; a Senior Clerk, House of Commons, 1969–76; *b* 16 June 1912; *e s* of Kenneth John Milne, CBE, and Maud Innes; *m* 1939, Marie Mange; one *d. Educ:* Westminster Sch.; Christ Church, Oxford. Advertising, 1935–40; RE, 1940–46 (Lieut-Col). FO, 1946–

68; 2nd Sec., Teheran, 1948-51; 1st Sec., Berne, 1955-56; 1st Sec., Tokyo, 1960-63; retired 1968. US Leg. of Merit (Off.), 1946. *Recreations:* cricket, music, gardening. *Address:* c/o Lloyds Bank, 79 Brompton Road, SW3.

MILNE, James; General Secretary, Scottish Trades Union Congress, since 1975 (Assistant General Secretary, 1969-75); Member, General Council of Scottish TUC; Chairman, Scottish Business Education Council; patternmaker; *b* 1921. Secretary to Aberdeen Trades Council, 1948-69. Joined Young Communist League, 1939. *Address:* Scottish Trades Union Congress, 16 Woodlands Terrace, Glasgow G3 6DF. *T:* 041-332 4946.

MILNE, James L.; *see* Lees-Milne.

MILNE, Hon. Kenneth Lancelot, CBE 1971; JP; chartered accountant; MLC South Australia (Australian Democrat), since 1979; *b* 16 Aug. 1915; *s* of F. K. Milne, Adelaide; *m* 1st, 1941, Mary (*d* 1980), *d* of E. B. Hughes; two *s* one *d*; 2nd, 1982, Joan Constance Lee, *d* of Claude W. J. Lee. *Educ:* St Peter's Coll., Adelaide. Entered Public Practice as a Chartered Acct, 1946; Elected to State Council, 1951, Chm. 1958-60, Mem. Gen. Council, 1956-60. Served with RAAF, 1940-45, attaining rank of Flt Lieut. Municipality of Walkerville: Councillor, 1960; Mayor, 1961-63; Municipal Assoc. 1961 (Pres. 1964-65); Pres. SA Br Aust. Inst. of Internat. Affairs, 1958-60; Mem. Faculty of Economics, University of Adelaide, 1963-65; Agent Gen. and Trade Comr for S Aust. in UK, 1966-71. President: SA Branch, Royal Overseas League, 1975-; Royal Life Saving Soc. of SA, 1977-. Chm., State Govt Insce Commn, 1971-79; Mem., Commn on Advanced Educn, 1973-77. Freeman, City of London, 1970. JP SA, 1947. *Publications:* Ostrich Heads, 1937; Forgotten Freedom, 1952; The Accountant in Public Practice, 1959. *Recreations:* rowing, tennis, conchology. *Address:* (office) 32 Grenfell Street, Adelaide, South Australia 5000. *T:* 212 3125; (home) 50 Birch Road, Stirling, SA 5152. *T:* 339 3674. *Clubs:* Adelaide, Adelaide Rowing, Commerce (all in SA).

MILNE, Prof. Malcolm Davenport, MD, FRCP; FRS 1978; Professor of Medicine, University of London, at Westminster Medical School, 1961-80, now Emeritus; *b* 22 May 1915; *s* of Alexander Milne and Clara Lilian Milne (*née* Gee); *m* 1941, Mary Milne (*née* Thorpe); one *s* one *d*. *Educ:* Stockport Sch.; Univ. of Manchester (BSc, MD, ChB). Ho. Phys., Manchester Royal Inf., 1939-40. Served War, RAMC, 1940-46 (despatches 1942). Sen. Registrar in Med., Manchester, 1946-49; Lectr in Med.: Manchester, 1949-52; Postgrad. Med. Sch., London, 1952-61. *Publications:* numerous articles relating to renal and metabolic diseases in appropriate scientific jls. *Recreations:* horticulture, haute cuisine, mathematics. *Address:* 12 York Avenue, East Sheen, SW14 7LG. *T:* 01-876 3619. *Club:* Athenæum.

MILNE, Maurice, CB 1976; Deputy Director General of Highways, Department of the Environment, 1970-76; retired; *b* 22 July 1916; *s* of James Daniel Milne, stone mason, and Isabella Robertson Milne; *m* 1947, Margaret Elizabeth Stewart Monro; one *d* decd. *Educ:* Robert Gordon's Coll., Aberdeen; Aberdeen University. BScEng (1st cl. Hons); FEng, FICE, FIStructE, FIMunE, FIHE, FRTPI. Principal Planning Asst, Paisley Burgh Engr's Dept, 1946-47; Chief Asst, D. A. Donald & Wishart, Cons. Engrs, Glasgow, 1947-48; Sen. Engr and Chief Engr, Crawley Develt Corp., 1948-59; Engr, Weir Wood Water Board, 1953-57; County Engr and Surveyor, W Sussex CC, 1960-68; Dir, S Eastern Road Construction Unit, MoT, 1968-70. Chm., Downland Housing Soc. Ltd, 1978-. Trustee, Rees Jeffreys Road Fund, and Rees Jeffreys Vis. Lectr, Univ. of Southampton, 1976-. Hon. Sec., County Surveyors' Soc., 1963-67; Pres., Instn Highway Engineers, 1974-75; Mem. Council, ICE, 1967-71 and 1972-75; Pres., Perm. Internat. Assoc. of Road Congresses, 1977-. *Publications:* contributions to Jl Instn of Civil, Municipal and Highway Engrs. *Recreations:* gardening, camping, hill walking, photography. *Address:* Struan, Walton Lane, Bosham, Chichester, West Sussex. *T:* Bosham 573304. *Clubs:* St Stephen's, Civil Service; Bosham Sailing.

MILNE, Norman; Sheriff of North Strathclyde at Campbeltown and Oban, 1975-81, retired; *b* 31 Dec. 1915; *s* of William Milne and Jessie Ferguson; *m* 1947, Phyllis Christina Philip Rollo; no *c. Educ:* Logie Central Sch., Dundee. Solicitor, 1939. Army, 1939-46: active service in Madagascar, Sicily, Italy, and Germany (despatches). Procurator Fiscal Depute: Perth, 1946-51; Edinburgh, 1951-55; Senior Depute Fiscal, Glasgow, 1955-58; Procurator Fiscal: Banff, 1959-64; Kirkcaldy, 1964-65; Paisley, 1965-71; Edinburgh, 1971-75. *Recreation:* sailing. *Address:* The Anchorage, Machrihanish, Argyll. *Club:* Royal Scottish Motor Yacht.

MILNE, Peter Alexander, PhD, FIMechE, FIMarE, MNECInst; Board Member for Engineering, British Shipbuilders, since 1981; *b* 23 April 1935; *s* of late Alexander Ogston Milne and of Lilian Winifred Milne (*née* Murray); *m* 1961, Beatrice Taylor Reid; two *d. Educ:* Tynemouth Sch.; Harwell Reactor Sch. BSc Marine Engrg Univ. of Durham 1957; PhD Applied Sci. Univ. of Newcastle 1960. Practical experience with apprenticeship at Wallsend Slipway & Engineering and at sea with Union Castle Mail Steamship; Trainee Manager, Swan Hunter Gp, 1961; Technical Dir, Swan Hunter Shipbuilders, 1970-74; Man. Dir, 1974-77; British Shipbuilders HQ at formation of Corp., 1977; Man. Dir, Shipbuilding Ops, British Shipbuilders, 1978-80; Dir, Vosper Thornycroft, 1978-80. Bd Mem., SMTRB, 1971-75; Chm., BSI Ind. Cttee, 1972-76. Vis. Lectr in Marine Engrg, Newcastle Univ., 1970-75. *Publications:* papers related to science and

industry. *Recreations:* squash, cricket. *Address:* 104 Holywell Avenue, Whitley Bay, Tyne and Wear. *T:* Whitley Bay 522708.

MILNE HOME, Captain Archibald John Fitzwilliam, DL; RN, retired; Member of Queen's Body Guard for Scotland (Royal Company of Archers) since 1963; *b* 4 May 1909; *e s* of late Sir John Milne Home; *m* 1936, Evelyn Elizabeth, *d* of late Comdr A. T. Darley, RN; three *s* one *d. Educ:* RNC Dartmouth. Joined RN, 1923: Comdr 1946; Captain 1952; retd 1962; ADC to the Queen, 1961-62. Chm., Whitbread (Scotland), 1968-73. Chm., SE Region, Scottish Woodland Owners Assoc., 1966-78. DL Selkirkshire, 1970. Cross of Merit, SMO Malta, 1963. *Recreations:* shooting, fishing. *Address:* Horsemill House, Bemersyde, Melrose, Roxburghshire TD6 9DP.

MILNE-WATSON, Sir Michael, 3rd Bt *cr* 1937; Kt 1969; CBE 1953; MA; Director: Commercial Union Assurance Co. Ltd; *b* 16 Feb. 1910; *yr s* of Sir David Milne-Watson, 1st Bt, and Olga Cecily (*d* 1952), *d* of Rev. George Herbert; *S* brother, 1982; *m* 1940, Mary Lisette, *d* of late H. C. Bagnall, Auckland, New Zealand; one *s. Educ:* Eton; Balliol Coll., Oxford. Served War of 1939-45. RNVR, 1943-45. Joined Gas Light & Coke Co., 1933; Managing Dir, 1945; Governor, 1946-49; Chairman: North Thames Gas Board, 1949-64; Richard Thomas & Baldwins Ltd, 1964-67; The William Press Group of Companies, 1969-74; a Dep. Chm., BSC, 1967-69 (Mem. Organizing Cttee, 1966-67); Mem., Iron and Steel Adv. Cttee, 1967-69. Director: Industrial and Commercial Finance Corp. Ltd, 1963-80; Finance for Industry Ltd, 1974-80; Finance Corp. for Industry Ltd, 1974-80. President: Soc. of British Gas Industries Guild, 1970-71; Pipeline Industries Guild, 1971-72. Vice-Pres., BUPA, 1981- (Chm., 1976-81). Liveryman, Grocers' Co., 1947. Governor: Council, Reading Univ., 1971-82 (Pres., 1975-80); Nuffield Nursing Homes Trust. *Heir: s* Andrew Michael Milne-Watson [*b* 10 Nov. 1944; *m* 1970, Beverley Jane Gabrielle (marr. diss. 1981), *e d* of Philip Cotton, Majorca; one *s* one *d*]. *Address:* 39 Cadogan Place, SW1X 9RX; Oakfield, Mortimer, Berks. *T:* Burghfield Common 2200. *Clubs:* Athenæum, MCC; Leander.

MILNER, family name of Baron Milner of Leeds.

MILNER OF LEEDS, 2nd Baron, *cr* 1951; **Arthur James Michael Milner,** AE 1952; Partner, Milners, Curry & Gaskell, Solicitors, London; *b* 12 Sept. 1923; *o s* of 1st Baron Milner of Leeds, PC, MC, TD and Lois Tinsdale (*d* 1982), *d* of Thomas Brown, Leeds; *S* father, 1967; *m* 1951, Sheila Margaret, *d* of Gerald Hartley, Leeds; one *s* two *d. Educ:* Oundle; Trinity Hall, Cambridge (MA). Served: RAFVR, 1942-46, Flt Lt; 609 (W Riding) Sqn, RAuxAF, 1947-52, Flt Lt. Admitted Solicitor, 1951. Opposition Whip, House of Lords, 1971-74. Member: Clothworkers' Co.; Pilgrims; Hon. Treas, Soc. of Yorkshiremen in London, 1967-70. *Recreation:* water ski-ing. *Heir: s* Hon. Richard James Milner, *b* 16 May 1959. *Address:* 2 The Inner Court, Old Church Street, SW3 5BY. *Club:* Royal Air Force.

MILNER, Prof. Brenda (Atkinson), FRS 1979, FRSC; Professor of Psychology, Department of Neurology and Neurosurgery, McGill University, and Head of Neuropsychology Research Unit, Montreal Neurological Institute, since 1970; *b* 15 July 1918; *d* of Samuel Langford and Clarice Frances Leslie (*née* Doig). *Educ:* Univ. of Cambridge (BA, MA, ScD); McGill Univ. (PhD). Experimental Officer, Min. of Supply, 1941-44; Professeur Agrégé, Inst. de Psychologie, Univ. de Montréal, 1944-52; Res. Associate, Psychology Dept, McGill Univ., 1952-53; Lectr, 1953-60, Asst Prof., 1960-64, Associate Prof., 1964-70, Dept of Neurology and Neurosurgery, McGill Univ. Hon. LLD Queen's Univ., Kingston, Ont, 1980; Hon. DSc Manitoba, 1982. *Publications:* mainly articles in neurological and psychological jls. *Address:* Montreal Neurological Institute, 3801 University Street, Montreal, Quebec H3A 2B4, Canada. *T:* (514) 284—4518.

MILNER, George; His Honour Judge Milner; a Circuit Judge, since 1974; *b* 11 Jan. 1927; *s* of Charles and Mary Elizabeth Milner; *m* 1952, Eileen Janet Blackett; two *s. Educ:* Tadcaster Grammar Sch.; Selwyn Coll., Cambridge (MA). Instructor Lieut RN, 1947-51. Called to Bar, Lincoln's Inn, 1951; practised in Sheffield from 1951. A Recorder of the Crown Court, 1972-74. *Recreations:* gardening, music, history. *Address:* Wayside, Maunby, Thirsk, North Yorkshire. *T:* Thirsk 587279. *Club:* Durham County.

MILNER, Sir (George Edward) Mordaunt, 9th Bt *cr* 1716; *b* 7 Feb. 1911; *er s* of Brig.-Gen. G. F. Milner, CMG, DSO; *S* cousin (Sir William Frederick Victor Mordaunt Milner, 8th Bt) 1960; *m* 1st, 1935, Barbara Audrey (*d* 1951), *d* of Henry Noel Belsham, Hunstanton, Norfolk; two *s* one *d*; 2nd, 1953, Katherine Moodie Bisset, *d* of D. H. Hoey, Dunfermline. *Educ:* Oundle. Served War of 1939-45, Royal Artillery. Stipendiary Steward, Jockey Club of South Africa, 1954-59; Steward, Cape Turf Club, 1959-75; Steward, Jockey Club of SA, 1977-. Mem. Council, Thoroughbred Breeders Assoc., 1975-. *Publications:* (novels) Inspired Information, 1959; Vaulting Ambition, 1962; The Last Furlong, 1965. *Heir: s* Timothy William Lycett Milner, *b* 11 Oct. 1936. *Address:* Natte Valleij, Klapmuts, Cape, S Africa. *T:* 0251-5171. *Clubs:* Rand (Johannesburg); Jockey Club of SA.

MILNER, John Giddings; Consulting Surgeon, Moorfields Eye Hospital, since 1956; Consulting Ophthalmic Surgeon: Charing Cross Hospital since 1966; St Andrew's Hospital, Dollis Hill, since 1966; *b* 7 Dec. 1900; 2nd *s* of late T. J. Milner, Blythwood, Radlett, and late Carrie, *d* of John Carpenter; *m* 1928, Monica Thrale, *d* of late Henry Mardall, Harpenden; one *s* two *d*.

Educ: Marlborough Coll.; Trinity Coll., Cambridge; St Bartholomew's Hosp. MRCS, LRCP, 1925; MA, MB, BCh Cantab, 1929; FRCS, 1930. Ophthalmic Surgeon, Hertford County Hosp., 1929–46; Surgeon, Moorfields, Westminster and Central Eye Hosp., 1936-56; Wing Comdr RAFVR Medical Branch, 1940–45; Cons. Ophthalmic Surgeon, Hertford County Hosp., 1947; Surgeon Oculist to the late Queen Mary, 1948-53. Coronation Medal, 1953. *Publications:* Modern Treatment in General Practice (contribution), 1949; Brit. Jl Opth., 1934; Brit. Medical Jl, 1941, 1944. *Recreations:* golf, natural history. *Address:* Blythwood, Watford Road, Radlett, Herts. *T:* Radlett 5750.

MILNER, Joseph, CBE 1975; QFSM 1962; Chief Officer of the London Fire Brigade, 1970–76; *b* 5 Oct. 1922; *e s* of Joseph and Ann Milner; *m* 1943, Bella Grice (*d* 1976), *e d* of Frederick George Flinton; one *s* one *d*; *m* 1976, Anne Cunningham, *e d* of J. Cunningham. *Educ:* Ladybarn Sch., Manchester. Served King's Regt (Liverpool), 1940-46: India/Burma, 1943–46 (Wingate's Chindits). Nat. Fire Service, 1946-48; North Riding Fire Bde, 1948-50; Manchester Fire Bde, 1950-51; Hong Kong Fire Bde, 1951-60; Dep. Dir, Hong Kong Fire Services, 1961-65; Dir, Hong Kong Fire Services, and Unit Controller, Auxiliary Fire Service, 1965-70. Mem., Hong Kong Council, Order of St John, 1965-70; JP Hong Kong, 1965-70. Regional Fire Commander (designate), 1970. Mem. Bd, Fire Service College, 1970; Mem., Central Fire Brigades Adv. Council, 1970; Adviser, Nat. Jt Council for Local Authority Fire Brigades, 1970; Chm., London Fire Liaison Panel, 1970; Mem., London Local Adv. Cttee, IBA, 1974-78; Fire Adviser, Assoc. of Metrop. Authorities. Vice-President: Fire Services Nat. Benevolent Fund (Chm., 1975–77); GLC Br., Royal British Legion. Mem., Caston Parish Council, 1980–. Fellow, Instn of Fire Engineers; Associate Mem., Inst. of British Engineers. OStJ 1971. *Recreations:* walking, poetry, hacking, horse management. *Address:* Lamlow, The Street, Caston, Attleborough, Norfolk NR17 1DD. *T:* Caston 697. *Clubs:* Royal Over-Seas League; Hong Kong (Hong Kong).

MILNER, Sir Mordaunt; *see* Milner, Sir G. E. M.

MILNER, Ralph; *see* Millner, Ralph.

MILNER-BARRY, Sir (Philip) Stuart, KCVO 1975; CB 1962; OBE 1946; Ceremonial Officer, Civil Service Department (formerly Treasury), 1966-77; *b* 20 Sept. 1906; *s* of late Prof. E. L. Milner-Barry; *m* 1947, Thelma Tennant Wells; one *s* two *d. Educ:* Cheltenham Coll.; Trinity Coll., Cambridge (Major Schol.). 1st Class Hons, Classical Tripos (Pt I), Moral Science Tripos (Pt II). With L. Powell Sons & Co., Stockbrokers, 1929-38; Chess Correspondent, The Times, 1938-45; temporary civil servant, a Dept of the Foreign Office, 1940–45; Principal, HM Treasury, 1945; Asst Sec., 1947; Dir of Organisation and Methods, Treasury, 1954-58; Dir of Establishments and Organisation, Min. of Health, 1958-60; Under-Sec., Treasury, 1954-66. *Recreations:* Chess: British Boy Champion, 1923; British Championship Second, 1953; mem. British Internat. teams, 1937-61; Pres. British Chess Fedn, 1970-73; walking. *Address:* 43 Blackheath Park, SE3. *T:* 01-852 5808. *Club:* Brooks's.

MILNES COATES, Sir Anthony (Robert), 4th Bt *cr* 1911; BSc, MB BS, MRCS, MRCP; *b* 8 Dec. 1948; *s* of Sir Robert Edward James Clive Milnes Coates, 3rd Bt, DSO, and of Lady Patricia Ethel, *d* of 4th Earl of Listowel; *S* father, 1982; *m* 1978, Harriet Ann Burton; one *d. Educ:* Eton; St Thomas's Hospital, London University. BSc; MRCS 1973; MB BS 1973; MRCP (UK) 1978. *Address:* 135 Gloucester Road, SW7. *T:* 01-373 3451. *Club:* Brooks's.

MILNES WALKER, Robert; *see* Walker, R. M.

MILOSLAVSKY, Dimitry T.; *see* Tolstoy, Dimitry.

MILOSZ, Czeslaw; poet, author; Professor of Slavic Languages and Literatures, University of California, Berkeley, 1961-78, now Emeritus; *b* Lithuania, 30 June 1911; naturalised US citizen, 1970; *s* of Aleksander and Weronika Milosz. *Educ:* High Sch., Wilno; Univ. of Wilno. MJuris 1934. Programmer, Polish Nat. Radio, 1935-39; Mem., Polish diplomatic service, Washington, Paris, 1945-50. Vis. Lectr, Univ. of Calif, Berkeley, 1960-61. Guggenheim Fellow, 1976. Member: Polish Inst. Letters and Scis in America; PEN Club in Exile. Hon. LittD Michigan, 1977; Hon. doctorate, Catholic Univ. of Lublin, 1981. Prix Littéraire Européen, Les Guildes du Livre, Geneva, 1953; Neustadt Internat. Prize for Literature, Univ. of Oklahoma, 1978; citation, Univ. of Calif, Berkeley, 1978; Nobel Prize for Literature, 1980. *Publications:* Poemat o czasie zastyglym (Poem on Time Frozen), 1933; Trzy zimy (Three Winters), 1936; Ocalenie (Rescue), 1945; Zniewolony umysl (The Captive Mind), 1953; Zdobycie wladzy, 1953, trans. as The Usurpers (in US as Seizure of Power), 1955; Dolina Issy, 1955, trans. as The Issa Valley, 1981; Swiatlo dzienne (Daylight), 1955; Traktat poetycki (Poetic Treatise), 1957; Rodzinna Europa, 1958, trans. as Native Realm, 1968; Postwar Polish Poetry, 1965; Widzenia nad Zatoka San Francisco (Views from San Francisco Bay), 1969; The History of Polish Literature, 1970; Prywatne obowiazki (Private Obligations), 1972; Selected Poems, 1973, rev. edn 1981; Ziemia Ulro (The Land of Ulro), 1977; Emperor of the Earth, 1977; Bells in Winter, 1978. *Address:* Department of Slavic Languages and Literatures, 5416 Dwinelle Hall, University of California, Berkeley, Calif 94720, USA.

MILROY, Rev. Dominic Liston, OSB; MA; Headmaster, Ampleforth College, since 1980; *b* 18 April 1932; *s* of Adam Liston Milroy and Clarita Burns. *Educ:* Ampleforth Coll.; St Benet's Hall, Oxford (1st Cl. Mod. Langs, MA). Entered Ampleforth Abbey, 1950; teaching staff, Ampleforth Coll., 1957-74; Head of Mod. Langs, 1963-74; Housemaster, 1964-74; Prior of Internat. Benedictine Coll. of S Anselmo, Rome, 1974-79. *Address:* Ampleforth College, York YO6 4ER. *T:* Ampleforth 224.

MILSOM, Stroud Francis Charles, FBA 1967; Professor of Law, Cambridge University, and Fellow of St John's College, Cambridge, since 1976; *b* 2 May 1923; *yr s* of late Harry Lincoln Milsom and Isobel Vida Collins; *m* 1955, Irène, *d* of late Witold Szereszewski, Wola Krysztoporska, Poland. *Educ:* Charterhouse; Trinity Coll., Cambridge. Admiralty, 1944-45. Called to the Bar, Lincoln's Inn, 1947, Hon. Bencher, 1970; Commonwealth Fund Fellow, Univ. of Pennsylvania, 1947-48; Yorke Prize, Univ. of Cambridge, 1948; Prize Fellow, Fellow and Lectr, Trinity Coll., Cambridge, 1948-55; Fellow, Tutor and Dean, New Coll., Oxford, 1956-64; Prof. of Legal History, London Univ., 1964-76. Literary Dir, Selden Soc., 1964-80. Mem., Royal Commn on Historical Manuscripts, 1975–. Vis. Lectr, New York Univ. Law Sch., several times, 1958-70; Visiting Professor: Yale Law Sch., several times, 1968-82; Harvard Law Sch. and Dept of History, 1973; Associate Fellow, Trumbull Coll., Yale Univ., 1974–; Charles Inglis Thomson Prof., Colorado Univ. Law Sch., 1977. Maitland Meml Lectr, Cambridge, 1972; Addison Harris Meml Lectr, Indiana Univ. Law Sch., 1974; Vis. Prof. and Wilfred Fullagar Lectr, Monash Univ., 1981. Hon. LLD Glasgow, 1981. Ames Prize, Harvard, 1972; Swiney Prize, RSA/RCP, 1974. *Publications:* Novae Narrationes (introd., trans. and notes), 1963; introd. reissue Pollock and Maitland, History of English Law, 1968; Historical Foundations of the Common Law, 1969, 2nd edn 1981; The Legal Framework of English Feudalism, 1976; articles in learned jls. *Address:* St John's College, Cambridge CB2 1TP; 23 Bentley Road, Cambridge CB2 2AW. *T:* Cambridge 354100. *Club:* Athenæum.

MILSTEIN, César, PhD, FRS 1975; Scientific Staff of Medical Research Council, since 1963; Fellow, Darwin College, University of Cambridge, since 1981; *b* 8 Oct. 1927; *s* of Lázaro and Máxima Milstein; *m* 1953, Celia Prilleltensky. *Educ:* Colegio Nacional de Bahia Blanca; Univ. Nacional de Buenos Aires; Fitzwilliam Coll., Cambridge (Hon. Fellow 1982). Licenciado en Ciencias Quimicas 1952; Doctor en Quimica 1957; PhD Cantab 1960. British Council Fellow, 1958-60; Staff of Instituto Nacional de Microbiologia, Buenos Aires, 1957-63; Head of Div. de Biologia Molecular, 1961-63; Staff of MRC Laboratory of Molecular Biology, 1963–, Mem. Governing Bd, 1975-79; Head of Sub-div. of Protein Chemistry, 1969. For. Associate, Nat. Acad. of Scis, USA, 1981. Biochem. Soc. Ciba Medal, 1978; Rosenstiel Medal, 1979; Avery-Landsteiner Preis, 1979; Rosenberg Preize, 1979; Mattia Award, 1979; Gross Horwitz Prize, 1980; Koch Preis, 1980; Wolf Prize in Med., 1980; Wellcome Foundn Medal, 1980; Gimenez Diaz Medal, 1981; William Bate Hardy Prize, Camb. Philos. Soc., 1981; Gairdner Award, 1981. Silver Jubilee Medal, 1977. *Publications:* original papers and review articles on structure, evolution and genetics of immunoglobulins and phosphoenzimes. *Recreations:* open air activities, cooking. *Address:* Medical Research Council Centre, Hills Road, Cambridge. *Club:* Sefe (Cambridge).

MILSTEIN, Nathan; violinist; *b* Odessa, Russia, 31 Dec. 1904; *s* of Miron and Maria Milstein; *m* 1945, Thérèse Weldon; one *d. Educ:* with Prof. Stoliarsky, in Odessa; with Leopold Auer, at Royal Conservatory, St Petersburg; studied with Eugène Isaye, Le Zoot, Belgium. Many tours in Russia, 1920-26; left Russia, 1926; annual tours throughout Europe, also in North, Central and South America, from 1929, except for war years. Hon. Mem., Acad. of St Cecilia, Rome, 1963. Officier, Légion d'Honneur, 1967; Ehrenkreuz, Austria, 1963. *Address:* c/o Shaw Concerts Inc., 1995 Broadway, New York, NY 10023, USA; 17 Chester Square, SW1.

MILTHORPE, Prof. Frederick Leon, DSc London, MScAgr, DIC; FInstBiol; FRSA; Professor of Biology, Macquarie University, Sydney, New South Wales, since 1967; *b* 24 Sept. 1917; 2nd *s* of S. G. and Annie Milthorpe, Hillston, NSW; *m* 1941, Elma Joan, *o d* of R. K. Hobbs, Sydney; two *s. Educ:* McCaughey Memorial High Sch.; Univ. of Sydney; Imperial Coll. of Science, London. Walter and Eliza Hall Agricultural Fellow, 1940-42; Plant Pathologist, NSW Dept of Agriculture, 1942-46; Farrer Memorial Scholar, 1946-48; Leverhulme Research Fellow, 1948-49; Senior Plant Physiologist, Waite Agricultural Research Inst., University of Adelaide, 1949-54; Prof. of Agricultural Botany, University of Nottingham, 1954-67. Australian Medal of Agricultural Sciences, 1975. *Publications:* An Introduction to Crop Physiology (with J. Moorby), 1974, 2nd edn 1979; chapters, some jtly, on water relations and crop growth; various papers on plant physiology in scientific journals. *Address:* Macquarie University, North Ryde, NSW 2113, Australia.

MILVERTON, 2nd Baron *cr* 1947, of Lagos and of Clifton; **Rev. Fraser Arthur Richard Richards;** Rector of Christian Malford with Sutton Benger and Tytherton Kellaways, since 1967; *b* 21 July 1930; *s* of 1st Baron Milverton, GCMG, and Noelle Benda, *d* of Charles Basil Whitehead; *S* father, 1978; *m* 1957, Mary Dorothy, BD, *d* of Leslie Fly, ARCM, Corsham, Wilts; two *d. Educ:* De Carteret Prep. Sch., Jamaica; Ridley Coll., Ontario; Clifton Coll.; Egerton Agric. Coll., Kenya; Bishop's Coll., Cheshunt. Royal Signals, 1949-50; Kenya Police, 1952-53. Deacon 1957, priest 1958, dio. Rochester; Curate: Beckenham, 1957-59; St John Baptist, Sevenoaks, 1959-60; Great

Bookham, 1960–63; Vicar of Okewood with Forest Green, 1963–67. *Recreations:* family, reading, current affairs and history; enjoys music and walking; interested in tennis, swimming, cricket and Rugby Union. *Heir: b* Hon. Michael Hugh Richards [*b* 1 Aug. 1936; *m* 1960, Edna Leonie, *y d* of Col Leo Steveni, OBE, MC; one *s*]. *Address:* The Rectory, Christian Malford, Chippenham, Wilts. *T:* Seagry 720466.

MIMPRISS, Trevor Walter, MS; FRCS; Hon. Consultant; retired, 1970, as: Surgeon to St Thomas' Hospital; Surgeon-in-Charge, Urological Division, St Peter's Hospital, Chertsey, Surrey; *b* 12 May 1905; *s* of late S. T. Mimpriss, Bromley, Kent; *m* 1938, Eleanor Joan, *d* of Gordon Innes; two *s* one *d. Educ:* Brighton Coll.; St Thomas' Hospital, London Univ. FRCS 1932; MS London 1935. Cheselden Medal for Surgery, St Thomas' Hospital, 1932; Louis Jenner Research Scholarship, 1936–37. Hunterian Professor of Royal College of Surgeons, 1938. *Publications:* various papers in medical journals. *Recreations:* shooting, fishing, golf. *Address:* Muskoka, Kingsley Green, Haslemere, Surrey.

MIMS, Prof. Cedric Arthur, MD, FRCPath; Professor of Microbiology, Guy's Hospital Medical School, London, since 1972; *b* 9 Dec. 1924; *s* of A. H. and Irene Mims; *m* 1952, Valerie Vickery; two *s* two *d. Educ:* Mill Hill Sch.; University Coll. London (BSc (Zool)); Middlesex Hosp. Med. Sch. (MB, BS, BSc, MD). Medical Research Officer, East African Virus Research Inst., Entebbe, Uganda, 1953–56; Research Fellow and Professorial Fellow, John Curtin Sch. of Med. Research, Australian Nat. Univ., Canberra, 1957–72; Rockefeller Foundn Fellow, Children's Hosp. Med. Centre, Boston, USA, 1963–64; Visiting Fellow, Wistar Inst., Philadelphia, USA, 1969–70. *Publications:* The Biology of Animal Viruses (jtly), 1974; The Pathogenesis of Infectious Disease, 1976; numerous papers on the pathogenesis of virus infections. *Address:* Sherriff House, Highbrook Road, Ardingly, Sussex RH17 6SR. *T:* Ardingly 892243.

MINCHINTON, Prof. Walter Edward; Professor and Head of Department of Economic History, University of Exeter, since 1964; *b* 29 April 1921; *s* of late Walter Edward and Annie Border Minchinton; *m* 1945, Marjorie Sargood; two *s* two *d. Educ:* Queen Elizabeth's Hosp.; Bristol; LSE, Univ. of London. 1st cl. hons BSc (Econ). FRHistS. War Service, RAOC, REME, Royal Signals (Lieut), 1942–45. UC Swansea: Asst Lectr, 1948–50; Lectr, 1950–59; Sen. Lectr, 1959–64. Rockefeller Research Fellow, 1959–60. Vis. Prof., Fourah Bay Coll., Sierra Leone, 1965. Chairman: Confedn for Advancement of State Educn, 1964–67; Devon History Soc., 1967–; Exeter Industrial Arch. Gp, 1967–; British Agricultural History Soc., 1968–71 (Mem. Council, 1952–); Export Research Group, 1971–72; Soc. for Nautical Res., 1978– (Mem. Council, 1969–); Devon Historic Buildings Trust, 1980– (Mem. Council. 1967–). Governor, Exeter Sch. of Art. Chm., Exeter Educn Cttee, 1972. Alexander Prize, RHistS, 1953. *Publications:* The British Tinplate Industry: a history, 1957; (ed) The Trade of Bristol in the Eighteenth Century, 1957; Industrial Archaeology in Devon, 1968, 3rd edn 1976; Politics and the Port of Bristol in the Eighteenth Century, 1963; Essays in Agrarian History, 1968; Industrial South Wales 1750–1914, essays in Welsh economic history, 1969; Mercantilism, System or Expediency?, 1969; The Growth of English Overseas Trade in the Seventeenth and Eighteenth Centuries, 1969; Wage Regulation in Pre-industrial England, 1972; Devon at Work, 1974; articles in Econ. History Review, Explorations in Entrepreneurial History, Mariner's Mirror, Trans RHistS, etc. *Recreations:* walking, music, industrial archaeology. *Address:* 53 Homefield Road, Exeter EX1 2QX. *T:* Exeter 77602.

MINFORD, Prof. (Anthony) Patrick (Leslie); Edward Gonner Professor of Applied Economics, University of Liverpool, since 1976; *b* 17 May 1943; *s* of Leslie Mackay Minford and Patricia Mary (*née* Sale); *m* 1970, Rosemary Irene Allcorn; two *s. Educ:* Horris Hill; Winchester Coll. (scholar); Balliol Coll., Oxford (schol.; BA); London Sch. of Economics (grad. studies; MScEcon, PhD). Economic Asst, Min. of Overseas Development, London, 1966; Economist, Min. of Finance, Malawi, 1967–69; Economic Adviser: Director's Staff, Courtaulds Ltd, 1970-71; HM Treasury, 1971–73, and HM Treasury Delegn in Washington DC, 1973–74; Visiting Hallsworth Fellow, Manchester Univ., 1974–75; Editor, NIESR Review, 1975–76. *Publications:* Substitution Effects, Speculation and Exchange Rate Stability, 1978; articles in learned jls on monetary and international economics. *Recreations:* music, squash. *Address:* 104 Prenton Road West, Birkenhead, Merseyside L42 9PX. *T:* 051-608 9566.

MINGAY, Frederick Ray; Counsellor (Commercial), British Embassy, Washington, since 1978; *b* 7 July 1938; *s* of Cecil Stanley and Madge Elizabeth Mingay; *m* 1963, Joan Heather Roberts; three *s* one *d. Educ:* Tottenham Grammar Sch.; St Catharine's Coll., Cambridge (Exhibnr; BA); London Univ. (Postgrad. Pub. Admin.). FBIM. Nat. Service (2nd Lt RAEC) 1959–61. Administration, St Thomas' Hosp., 1961; Min. of Transport, 1962–64; BoT, 1964; Chrysler (UK) Ltd, 1968–70; Consul (Commercial), Milan, 1970–73; Asst Sec., Dept of Trade, 1973–78. *Address:* c/o Foreign and Commonwealth Office, SW1.

MINHINNICK, Sir Gordon (Edward George), KBE 1976 (OBE 1950); Cartoonist, New Zealand Herald, 1930–76, retired; *b* 13 June 1902; *s* of Captain P. C. Minhinnick, RN, and Anne Sealy; *m* 1928, Vernor Helmore; one *s* (one *d* decd). *Educ:* Kelly Coll., Tavistock, Devon. Came to NZ, 1921; studied architecture for 4 years; Cartoonist: NZ Free Lance, 1926; Sun,

Christchurch, and Sun, Auckland, 1927. *Address:* Apartment 219, Northbridge, Akarana Drive, Northcote, Auckland, New Zealand.

MINIO-PALUELLO, Lorenzo, FBA 1957; Reader in Medieval Philosophy, University of Oxford, 1956–75 (Senior Lecturer, 1948–56); Professorial Fellow of Oriel College, 1962–75, now Emeritus and (1979) Hon. Fellow; *b* 21 Sept. 1907; *s* of Michelangelo Minio and Ersilia (*née* Bisson); *m* 1938, Magda Ungar; one *s* one *d* (and one *d* decd). *Educ:* Ginnasio-Liceo Foscarini, Venice; Univ. of Padua; Sorbonne and Ecole des Hautes Etudes, Paris. Dr of Philosophy (Padua), 1929; Asst Librarian, University of Padua, 1929–32; Fellow of Warburg Inst., Univ. of London, 1947–48; DPhil Oxon, MA Oxon, 1948; Barlow Lectr, Univ. of London, 1955; Prof. straord. of medieval and humanistic philology, Univ. of Padua, for 1956–57; Hon. Dir of Aristoteles Latinus (Union Acad. Internat.), 1959–72; Mem., Inst. for Advanced Study, Princeton, 1969–70, 1974–76; Corresp. Fellow, Amer. Mediaeval Acad., 1970; Member: Amer. Philosophical Soc., 1971; Unione Accademia Nazionale (Pres., Corpus Philosophorum Medii Aevi), 1971–72; Corresp. Member: Koninklijke Academie voor Wetenschappen, Letteren en Schone Kunsten van België, 1975; Accad. Patavina di Scienze, Lettere ed Arti, 1977; Ist. Veneto di Scienze, Lettere ed Arti, 1980. Medal of the Collège de France, 1975. *Publications:* Education in Fascist Italy, 1946; editions of Aristotle's Categoriae and De interpretatione (1949, 1957), Plato's Phaedo (Medieval Latin trans., 1950), Aristotle's Categoriae, De interpretatione, Prior and Posterior Analytics, Topics (Ancient and Medieval Latin trans. and paraphrases, 1953, 1954, 1961, 1962, 1965, 1967, 1969), Pseudo-Aristotle's De Mundo (Apuleius', Rinucio's, Sadoleto's trans, 1965), Porphyry's Isagoge (Boethius' trans, 1966); 'Liber VI Principiorum' (1966); co-ed Aristoteles Latinus Codices, vol. ii, and (ed) Supplementa Altera (1955, 1961), and Poetics (Latin trans., 1953, 1968); Twelfth Century Logic, vol. i, 1956, vol. ii, 1958; Opuscula: The Latin Aristotle, 1972; articles in The Classical Quart., Jl of Hellenic Studies, Mediaeval and Renaiss. Studies, Italian Studies, Studi Danteschi, Riv. di Filos. Neoscolastica, Studi Medievali, Rev. Philos. de Louvain, Traditio, Encyclopædia Britannica, Dizion. Biograf. degli Ital., Dictionary of Scientific Biography, etc. *Address:* 22 Polstead Road, Oxford OX2 6TN. *T:* Oxford 57798.

MINION, Stephen, OBE 1954; JP; DL; *b* 2 June 1908; *s* of Stephen and Elizabeth Minion; *m* 1935, Ada, *d* of George and Jane Evans; no *c. Educ:* Liverpool Technical and Commercial Colleges. Formerly Man. Dir, The Lancashire & Cheshire Rubber Co. Ltd, retired 1980. City Councillor 1940, Alderman 1961, Lord Mayor 1969–70, Liverpool. JP Liverpool, 1954; High Sheriff Merseyside, 1976; DL Merseyside, 1976. *Recreations:* outdoor sports, reading, history, theatre and music. *Address:* Glen Cairn, 223 Booker Avenue, Liverpool L18 9TA. *T:* 051-724 2671. *Club:* Athenæum (Liverpool).

MINNITT, Robert John, CMG 1955; *b* 2 April 1913; *s* of Charles Frederick Minnitt and Winifred May Minnitt (*née* Buddle); *m* 1st, 1943, Peggy Christine Sharp (*d* 1973); one *s* two *d*; 2nd, 1975, Hon. Primrose Keighley Muncaster, widow of Claude Muncaster. *Educ:* Marlborough Coll.; Trinity Coll., Cambridge. Appointed to Colonial Administrative Service, Hong Kong, 1935; Chief Sec., Western Pacific High Commission, 1952–58, retired. Furniture designer and craftsman, 1960–66; temp. Civil Servant, CO, 1966; FCO, 1968–69. *Address:* Whitelocks, Sutton, Pulborough, W Sussex. *T:* Sutton 216.

MINOGUE, Hon. Sir John (Patrick), Kt 1976; QC; Law Reform Commissioner, Victoria, 1977–82; *b* 15 Sept. 1909; *s* of John Patrick Minogue and Emma Minogue; *m* 1938, Mary Alicia O'Farrell. *Educ:* St Kevin's Coll., Melbourne; Univ. of Melbourne (LLB). Australian Army, 1940–46; GSO1 HQ 1 Aust. Corps and HQ New Guinea Force, 1942–43 (mentioned in despatches); GSO1 Aust. Mil. Mission, Washington, 1945–46. Solicitor, Bendigo, 1937–39; called to the Bar, Melbourne, 1939; QC Victoria 1957, NSW 1958; Papua New Guinea: Judge, Supreme Court, 1962; Chief Justice, 1970–74. Vice-Pres., Aust. Section, Internat. Commn of Jurists, 1965–. Member: Council and Faculty of Law, Univ. of Papua New Guinea, 1965–74 (Pro-Chancellor, 1972–74); Law Faculty, Melbourne Univ., 1975–79; Law Faculty, Monash Univ., 1977–82. Hon. LLD Papua New Guinea, 1974. *Recreations:* reading, conversation, golf. *Address:* Marengo Vale, Seymour, Vic 3660, Australia. *T:* Seymour 922146. *Clubs:* Melbourne, Naval and Military, Royal Automobile of Victoria, Melbourne Cricket (Melbourne).

MINOGUE, Maj.-Gen. Patrick John O'Brien; computer consultant, since 1981; *b* 28 July 1922; *s* of Col M. J. Minogue, DSO, MC, late East Surrey Regt, and Mrs M. V. E. Minogue; *m* 1950, June Elizabeth (*née* Morris); one *s* two *d. Educ:* Brighton Coll.; RMCS. CBIM, FBCS, FIWSP, FIMH; jssc, psc, ato. Indian Army, 1942–46; East Surrey Regt, 1947; RAOC, 1951; served UK, BAOR, USA, Cyprus; Col, 1969; Brig., 1971; Insp. RAOC, 1971–73; Comdt, Central Ord. Depot, Bicester, 1973–75; Maj.-Gen. 1975; Comdr, Base Orgn, RAOC, 1975–78. Hon. Col, RAOC (TAVR), 1975–78; Col Comdt, RAOC, 1980–. Group Systems Controller, Lansing Bagnall Ltd, 1978–81; Chm., LT Electronics, 1979–81. *Recreations:* cricket, sailing (Cdre Wayfarer Class, UK, 1975), golf, shooting, gun-dogs, athletics. *Address:* Clare Cottage, Ellisfield, Basingstoke, Hants; Listonero, Cortijo Grande, Turre, Almeria, Spain. *Clubs:* MCC; Army Sailing Association; Milocarian Athletic; Staff College (Camberley); Basingstoke Golf; Cortijo Grande Golf.

MINTO, 6th Earl of, *cr* 1813; **Gilbert Edward George Lariston Elliot-Murray-Kynynmound,** MBE 1955; Bt 1700; Baron Minto, 1797; Viscount

Melgund, 1813; JP; late Captain Scots Guards; *b* 19 June 1928; *er s* of 5th Earl of Minto and Marion, OBE (*d* 1974), *d* of G. W. Cook, Montreal; *S* father, 1975; *m* 1st, 1952, Lady Caroline Child-Villiers (from whom he obtained a divorce, 1965), *d* of 9th Earl of Jersey; one *s* one *d* ; 2nd, 1965, Mary Elizabeth, *d* of late Peter Ballantine and of Mrs Ballantine, Gladstone, New Jersey, USA. *Educ:* Eton; RMA, Sandhurst. Served Malaya, 1949-51; ADC to C-in-C FARELF, 1951, to CIGS, 1953-55, to HE Governor and C-in-C Cyprus, 1955; transferred to RARO, 1956. Brigadier, Queen's Body Guard for Scotland (Royal Company of Archers). Regional Councillor (Hermitage Div.), Borders Region, 1974-; Chm., Scottish Council on Alcoholism, 1973-; Dep. Traffic Comr for Scotland, 1975-; Exec. Vice-Pres., S of Scotland Chamber of Commerce, 1978-. JP Roxburghshire, 1961-. *Heir: s* Viscount Melgund, *qv. Address:* Minto, Hawick, Scotland. *T:* Denholm 321. *Club:* Puffin's (Edinburgh).

MINTO, Dr Alfred, FRCPsych; Medical Director, Rampton Hospital, Retford, Notts, since 1981; *b* 23 Sept. 1928; *s* of Alfred Minto and Margaret Mavor Goudie Leask; *m* 1949, Frances Oliver Bradbrook; two *s* two *d. Educ:* Aberdeen Central Sch.; Aberdeen Univ. (MB ChB 1951); DPM RCS&P London 1961; MRCPsych 1972, FRCPsych 1974. House Physician, Huddersfield Royal Inf., 1952; Sen. House Officer/Jun. Hosp. Med. Officer, Fairmile Hosp., Wallingford, 1952-56; Sen. Registrar, St Luke's Hosp., Middlesbrough, 1956-59; Sen. Hosp. Med. Officer, 1959-63, Conslt Psychiatrist, 1963, Mapperley Hosp., Nottingham; Conslt Physchiatrist i/c, Alcoholism and Drug Addiction Service, Sheffield RHB, 1963-68; Conslt Psychiatrist, St Ann's and Mapperley Hosps, 1968-81. Clinical Teacher, Nottingham Univ. Med. Sch., 1971-; Special Lectr in Forensic Psych., Nottingham Univ., 1982-. Conslt Psychiatrist, CS Comrs, 1964-. *Publications:* Key Issues in Mental Health, 1982; papers on alcoholism, community care, toxoplasmosis. *Recreations:* books, people. *Address:* 76 Walsingham Road, Woodthorpe, Nottingham NG5 4NR. *T:* Nottingham 260221.

MINTOFF, Dominic, MP; Prime Minister of Malta, since 1971; Leader of Labour Party, since 1949; *b* 6 Aug. 1916; *s* of Lawrence Mintoff; *m* 1947, Moyra de Vere Bentinck; two *d. Educ:* Univ. of Malta (BSc; BE&A); Hertford Coll., Oxford (BA 1939; MA 1945). Practised as civil engineer in Britain, 1941-43, and as architect in Malta, 1943. Gen. Sec. Malta Labour Party, 1936-37; Rejoined Maltese Labour Party, 1944; Mem., Council of Govt and Exec. Council, 1945; MLA, 1947-; Dep. Leader, Labour Party, 1947; Dep. Prime Minister and Minister for Works and Reconstruction, 1947-49; Prime Minister and Minister of Finance, 1955-58; resigned office in 1958 to lead the Maltese Liberation Movement; Leader of Opposition, 1962-71; Minister of Foreign Affairs, 1971-81; Minister of the Interior, 1976-81. *Publications:* scientific, literary and artistic works. *Recreations:* horse-riding, swimming, water skiing, bocci. *Address:* Kastilja, Valletta, Malta; The Olives, Tarxien, Malta.

MINTON, Yvonne Fay, CBE 1980; mezzo-soprano; *er d* of R. T. Minton, Sydney; *m* 1965, William Barclay; one *s* one *d. Educ:* Sydney Conservatorium of Music. Elsa Stralia Scholar, Sydney, 1957-60; won Canberra Operatic Aria Competition, 1960; won Kathleen Ferrier Prize at s'Hertogenbosch Vocal Competition, 1961. Joined Royal Opera House as a Principal Mezzo-Soprano, 1965. Major roles include: Octavian in Der Rosenkavalier; Dorabella in Cosi Fan Tutte; Marina in Boris Godounov; Helen in King Priam; Cherubino in Marriage of Figaro; Orfeo in Gluck's Orfeo; Sextus in La clemenza di Tito; Dido in The Trojans at Carthage; Kundry in Parsifal; Charlotte in Werther; Countess Geschwitz in Lulu. Recordings include Octavian in Der Rosenkavalier, Mozart Requiem, Elgar's The Kingdom, etc. Guest Artist with Cologne Opera Company, Oct. 1969-. Hon. RAM 1975. *Recreations:* reading, gardening. *Address:* c/o Ingpen and Williams, 14 Kensington Court, W8. *T:* 01-937 5158.

MIQUEL, Raymond Clive, CBE 1981; Chairman since 1973, and Managing Director since 1968, Arthur Bell & Sons Ltd; Chairman, Canning Town Glass Ltd, since 1975; *b* 28 May 1931; *m* 1958; one *s* two *d. Educ:* Allan Glen's Sch., Glasgow; Glasgow Technical Coll. Joined Arthur Bell & Sons Ltd as Works Study Engineer, 1956; Production Controller, 1958; Production Director, 1962; Dep. Managing Director, 1965; Dep. Chairman, 1972. *Address:* Whitedene, Caledonian Crescent, Gleneagles, Perthshire, Scotland. *T:* Auchterarder 2642.

MIREPOIX, Duc de L.; *see* Lévis Mirepoix.

MIRÓ, Joan; artist; *b* Barcelona, 20 April 1893; *s* of Miguel and Dolores Miró; *m* 1929, Pilar. *Educ:* Barcelona Academy of Fine Art. Work includes paintings, ceramics, sculptures, engravings, lithographs. Guggenheim Award for ceramic mural in grounds of Unesco Building, Paris, 1958. Foundation Joan Miró, Parc Montjuic, Barcelona, opened in 1975 with exhibn of 92 paintings and sculptures dated 1917-74. *Exhibitions include:* Galérie Pierre, 1925; Goeman's Gallery, 1928; Galérie Maeght, Paris, 5 exhibns, 1948-70; Pierre Matisse Gallery, New York, 36 exhbns, 1932-80; Tate Gallery, London, 1964; Marlborough Fine Art Gallery, London, 1966; Tokyo, Kyoto, 1966; Barcelona, 1968; Fondation Maeght, St Paul de Vence, 1968, 1979; Munich, 1968; Museum of Modern Art, NY, 1974; Grand Palais, Paris, 1974; Madrid Museum of Contemp. Art, 1978; Hayward Gall., London, 1979; St Louis/Chicago, 1980; Hirshhorn Mus., Washington/Buffalo, 1980; Mexico City, 1980. Grand Cross of Isabel la Católica (Spain), 1978. *Recreation:*

walking. *Address:* Pierre Matisse Gallery, 41 East 57th Street, New York, NY 10022, USA; Galerie Maeght, 13 rue de Téhéran, Paris, 8e, France.

MIRON, Wilfrid Lyonel, CBE 1969 (OBE 1945; MBE 1944); TD 1950; JP; DL; Regional Chairman (Midlands), National Coal Board, 1967 and Regional Chairman (South Wales), 1969; National Coal Board Member (with Regional responsibilities), 1971-76; *b* 27 Jan. 1913; *s* of late Solman Miron and late Minnie Pearl Miron; *m* 1958, Doreen (*née* Hill); no *c. Educ:* Llanelli Gram. Sch. Admitted Solicitor, 1934; private practice and Legal Adviser to Shipley Collieries and associated companies. TA Commn, Sherwood Foresters, 1939; served War of 1939-45: Home Forces, 1939; France and Dunkirk, 1940; IO 139 Inf. Bde and GSO3 Aldershot Dist, 1941-42; Staff Coll., Quetta, 1942 (SC); DAAG 17 Ind. Div., 1943-44, and AA&QMG 17 Ind. Div., 1944-45, Chin Hills, Imphal, Burma (despatches, 1944). E Midlands Div. NCB: Sec. and Legal Adviser, 1946-51; Dep. Chm., 1951-60; Chm., 1960-67. Pres. and Chm., Midland Dist Miners' Fatal Accident Relief Soc.; Chairman: E Mids Regional Planning Council, 1976-79 (Mem., 1965-76); (part-time), Industrial Tribunals, 1976-; Mem. Council and Law Adv. Cttee, Nottingham Univ.; Dir, Nottingham Theatre Trust Ltd. Freeman (by redemption) City of London; Master, Pattenmakers' Company, 1979-80. Hon. Lieut-Col. JP Notts, 1964 (Chairman: Nottingham PSD, 1982-; Notts Majistrates' Cts Cttee, 1971-); DL Notts, 1970. FRSA 1965. OStJ 1961. *Publications:* Bitter Sweet Seventeen, 1946; articles and papers in mining and other jls. *Recreations:* cricket, music, reading, crosswords. *Address:* Briar Croft, School Lane, Halam, Newark, Notts. *T:* Southwell 812446. *Clubs:* Army and Navy, MCC; XL; Nottingham and Notts United Services (Nottingham).

MIRRLEES, Prof. James Alexander; Edgeworth Professor of Economics, University of Oxford, and Fellow of Nuffield College, since 1968; *b* 5 July 1936; *s* of late George B. M. Mirrlees; *m* 1961, Gillian Marjorie Hughes; two *d. Educ:* Douglas-Ewart High Sch., Newton Stewart; Edinburgh Univ.; Trinity Coll., Cambridge. MA Edinburgh Maths, 1957; BA Cantab Maths, 1959; PhD Cantab Econs, 1963. Adviser, MIT Center for Internat. Studies, New Delhi, 1962-63; Cambridge Univ. Asst Lectr in Econs and Fellow of Trinity Coll., 1963, University Lectr, 1965; Adviser to Govt of Swaziland, 1963; Res. Assoc., Pakistan Inst. of Develt Econs, Karachi, 1966-67. Vis. Prof., MIT, 1968, 1970, 1976. Mem., Treasury Cttee on Policy Optimisation, 1976-78. Econometric Society: Fellow, 1970; Vice-Pres., 1980, Pres., 1982. For. Hon. Mem., Amer. Acad. of Arts and Scis, 1981; Hon. Mem., Amer. Economic Assoc., 1982. Hon. DLitt Warwick, 1982. *Publications:* (joint author) Manual of Industrial Project Analysis in Developing Countries, 1969; (ed jtly) Models of Economic Growth, 1973; (jt author) Project Appraisal and Planning, 1974; articles in economic jls. *Recreations:* reading detective stories and other forms of mathematics, playing the piano, travelling, listening. *Address:* Nuffield College, Oxford; 11 Field House Drive, Oxford OX2 7NT. *T:* Oxford 52436.

MIRRLEES, Robin Ian Evelyn Stuart de la Lanne-; Richmond Herald of Arms, 1962-67; *b* Paris, 13 Jan. 1925; grandson of Ambassador La Lanne; godson of 11th Duke of Argyll; one *s. Educ:* Merton Coll., Oxford (MA). Several language diplomas. Served India, 1942-46; Captain RA, 1944; Gen. Staff, New Delhi, 1946; Embassy Attaché, Tokyo, 1947; Rouge Dragon Pursuivant of Arms, 1952-62 (and as such attended Coronation). Co-editor, Annuaire de France, 1966-. ADC to HM the King of Yugoslavia, 1963-70. Has raised substantial funds for humanitarian organisations; undertook restoration of Inchdrewer Castle, Scotland, and others; Laird of Island of Bernera, pop. 350. Freeman of City of London, 1960. Patrician of San Marino, 1964. Succeeded to the title of Comte de Lalanne (France), 1962 and titular Prince of Coronata. Various foreign orders of knighthood. *Recreations:* foxhunting, piloting, travelling, painting, sculpture, mystic philosophy. *Address:* 25 Holland Park Avenue, W11; 115 Rue de la Pompe, Paris 16me; Inchdrewer Castle, Banff, Scotland; Villa Lambins-Lalanne, Le Touquet, France; Schloss Ratzenegg, Carinthia, Austria. *Clubs:* Buck's; Puffin's (Edinburgh); Travellers' (Paris).

MISCAMPBELL, Norman Alexander, QC 1974; MP (C) Blackpool North since 1962; barrister; a Recorder of the Crown Court, since 1977; *b* 20 Feb. 1925; *s* of late Alexander and Eileen Miscampbell; *m* 1961, Margaret Kendall; two *s* two *d. Educ:* St Edward's Sch., Oxford; Trinity Coll., Oxford. Called to Bar, Inner Temple, 1952; N Circuit. Mem., Hoylake UDC, 1955-61. Contested (C) Newton, 1955, 1959. *Address:* House of Commons, SW1; 7 Abbey Road, West Kirby, Wirral, Merseyside.

MISCHLER, Norman Martin; Chairman: Hoechst UK Ltd, since 1975; Hoechst Ireland Ltd, since 1976; Berger Jenson & Nicholson Ltd, since 1979; *b* 9 Oct. 1920; *s* of late Martin Mischler and Martha Sarah (*née* Lambert); *m* 1949, Helen Dora Sinclair; one *s* one *d. Educ:* St Paul's Sch., London; St Catharine's Coll., Cambridge (MA). Indian Army, 1940; served in Burma Campaign (mentioned twice in despatches); released, rank of Major, 1946. Joined Burt, Boulton & Haywood, 1947, Vice-Chm. 1963; Dep. Man. Dir, Hoechst UK Ltd, 1966; Director: Berger, Jenson & Nicholson Ltd; Ringsdorff Carbon Co. Ltd; Vice-Chm., German Chamber of Industry and Commerce in London; Mem. Council, Chemical Industries Assoc. Ltd. Paviors Co.; Freeman, City of London. *Recreations:* cricket, opera, and theatre. *Address:* 12A Abbey Court, Abbey Road, NW8 0AU. *T:* 01-624 2906. *Clubs:* MCC; Hawks (Cambridge).

MISHCON, family name of **Baron Mishcon.**

MISHCON, Baron cr 1978 (Life Peer), of Lambeth in Greater London; **Victor Mishcon;** DL; Solicitor; Senior Partner, Victor Mishcon & Co.; b 14 Aug. 1915; s of Rabbi Arnold and Mrs Queenie Mishcon; m 1976, Joan Estelle Conrad; two s one d by previous marr. Educ: City of London Sch. Mem. Lambeth Borough Coun., 1945-49 (Chm. Finance Cttee, 1947-49); Mem. London CC for Brixton, 1946-65 (Chairman: Public Control Cttee, 1947-52; Gen. Purposes Cttee, 1952-54; Council, April 1954-55; Supplies Cttee, 1956-57; Fire Brigade Cttee, 1958-65); Mem. GLC for Lambeth, 1964-67 (Chm., Gen. Purposes Cttee, 1964-67). Mem., Inner London Educn Authority, 1964-67. Chm. Governors, Cormont and Loughborough Secondary Schools, 1947-60; Governor: Stockwell Manor Sch., 1960-78 (Chm. of Governors, 1960-67, 1970-78); JFS Comprehensive Sch., 1970-; Philippa Fawcett Coll. of Educn, 1970-. Member: Standing Joint Cttee, Co. of London Sessions, 1950-65 (Vice-Chm. 1959-61); Nat. Theatre Board, 1965-67, 1968- (Mem., Finance and General Purposes Cttee); South Bank Theatre Board, 1977-; London Orchestra Bd, 1966-67; Exec. Cttee, London Tourist Board, 1965-67; Government Cttee of Enquiry into London Transport, 1953-54; Departmental Cttee on Homosexual Offences and Prostitution, 1954-57; Law Sub-Cttee, House of Lords European Communities Cttee, 1978-; House of Lords Select Cttee on Procedure, 1981-. Vice-Chm., Council of Christians and Jews, 1976-77; Vice-Pres., Bd of Deputies of British Jews, 1967-73; Chm., Inst. of Jewish Studies, UCL; Hon. President, Brit. Technion Soc.; Mem. Bd of Governors, Technion, Israel; Vice-Pres. (Past Pres.) Assoc of Jewish Youth; Chm., British Council of the Shaare Zedek Hosp., Jerusalem. Contested (Lab) NW Leeds, 1950, Bath, 1951, Gravesend, 1955, 1959. DL Greater London. Comdr Royal Swedish Order of North Star, 1954; Star of Ethiopia, 1954. Address: House of Lords, SW1.

MISKIN, James William, QC 1967; **His Honour Judge Miskin;** Recorder of London, since 1975; b 11 March 1925; s of late Geoffrey Miskin and Joyce Miskin; m 1st, 1951, Mollie Joan Milne; two s two d; 2nd, 1980, Sheila Joan Collett, widow. Educ: Haileybury; Brasenose Coll., Oxford (MA). Sub-Lt, RNVR, 1943-46. Oxford, 1946-49 (Sen. Heath Harrison Exhibnr). Called to Bar, Inner Temple, 1951; Bencher, 1976; Mem. of Bar Council, 1964-67, 1970-73. Dep. Chm., Herts QS, 1968-71; a Recorder of the Crown Court, 1972-75; Leader of SE Circuit, 1974-75. City of London Magistrate, 1976. Chm., Bd of Discipline, LSE, 1972-75. Appeals Steward, British Boxing Bd of Control, 1972-75; Chm., Inner London Probation After Care Cttee, 1979-. One of HM Lieutenants, City of London, 1976-. Liveryman, Worshipful Co. of Curriers; Hon. Liveryman, Worshipful Co. of Cutlers. Recreations: golf, gardening. Clubs: Vincent's (Oxford); All England Lawn Tennis.

MISKIN, Raymond John, CEng, FIProdE, MIMechE, MRAeS, FIQA; Secretary, Institution of Production Engineers, since 1976; b 4 July 1928; s of late Sydney George Miskin and Hilda (née Holdsworth); m 1951 (marr. diss. 1981); one d (one s decd). Educ: Woking Grammar Sch.; Southall Technical Coll. The Fairey Aviation Co. Ltd: apprentice, 1945-49; devel engr, 1949-59; Dep. Chief Inspector, 1959-63; Quality Control Manager and Chief Inspector, Graviner Ltd, 1963-69; Sec., Inst. of Qual. Assurance, 1969-73; Dep. Sec., IProdE, 1973-76. Director: IPRODE Ltd, 1976-; Laleham GC Ltd, 1977-. Mem. Council and Hon. Treasurer, Inst. of Qual. Assurance, 1963-69; Member: Bd, Nat. Council for Qual. and Reliability, 1969-81 (Chm., 1975-77); Amer. Soc. for Qual. Control. Hon. FIIPE 1979. Internat. Industrial Management Award, San Fernando Valley Engineers Council, USA, 1978; Internat. Achievement Award, Los Angeles Council of Engrs, 1981. Publications: articles in technical pubns. Recreation: golf. Address: Institution of Production Engineers, 66 Little Ealing Lane, W5 4XX. Clubs: Golfers'; Burhill Golf (Surrey).

MISSELBROOK, (Bertram) Desmond, CBE 1972; FRSE 1978; Chairman, Livingston Development Corporation, 1972-78; b 28 May 1913; s of late C. J. and E. P. Misselbrook; m 1949, Anne, er d of late F. O. Goodman; two s. Educ: Chatham House, Ramsgate; Bristol Univ. Admiralty Psychologist, 1942-45. Lectr in Psychology and Dir, Unit of Applied Psychology, Edinburgh Univ., 1945-49; Senr Res. Fellow in Business Studies, 1970-71, Hon. Fellow, 1971. Personnel Adviser, 1949, Dir. 1955, Dep. Chm. 1963-70, British-American Tobacco Co. Ltd; Chm., Evershed and Vignoles Ltd, 1961-65; Chm., Mardon Packaging International Ltd, 1962-70; Dir, 1963, Dep. Chm. 1966-69, Wiggins Teape Ltd; Dir, Charterhouse Gp Ltd, 1969-72; Deputy Chairman: Standard Life Assurance Co., 1977-80 (Dir, 1970-); Anderson Mavor Ltd, 1971-74; Chairman: Anderson Strathclyde Ltd, 1974-77; Seaforth Maritime Ltd, 1977-78. Mem. Council, British Inst. of Management, 1967-72 (a Vice-Chm., 1969); Chairman: Bd of Governors, Oversea Service, 1963-70; Construction Ind. Trng Bd, 1970-73; Council, Scottish Business Sch., 1972-77; Economic Development Cttees for Building and Civil Engineering Industries, 1969-72; Member: Adv. Council on Social Work (Scotland), 1970-74; Economic Consultant, Scottish Office, 1970-72. Hon. DSc Edinburgh, 1977. Recreations: fishing, gardening, walking. Address: Cleughhead, By Annan, Dumfriesshire DG12 5LW. T: Annan 2785.

MISSEN, Leslie Robert, CMG 1956; MC 1918; Research Consultant; b 2 May 1897; e s of Robert Symonds Missen, Chesterton, Cambs; m 1932, Muriel, o d of Robert Alstead, OBE, Gathurst, Lancs, formerly MP for Altrincham; two s. Educ: Perse Sch. and Christ's Coll., Cambridge. Served European War, Capt., 7th Bn N Stafford Regt, Mesopotamia, Persia and Caucasus, 1915-19. Asst Education Officer, Leeds, 1922-26; Dep. Chief Educ. Officer,

Middlesbrough, 1926-30; Chief Educ. Officer: Wigan, 1930-36; East Suffolk County Council, 1936-62; Mem., Local Govt Commn for England, 1962-66. Educational Adviser to: Ministry of Education, 1950-57; Ministry of Agriculture, 1944-54; Colonial Sec., 1952-55; Royal Navy, 1958-64; Chairman: Working Party on Educn in Trinidad, BWI, 1954; Trustees of Homerton Coll., Cambridge, 1946-62; President: Assoc. of Education Officers, 1952; Old Persean Soc., 1953-55; Education Section of British Assoc., 1957; County Educn Officers' Soc., 1960; Chairman: Ipswich and District War Pensions Cttee, 1942-70; Suffolk War Pensions Cttee, 1971-. Publications: War History of 7th Bn N Stafford Regt, 1920; The Employment of Leisure, 1935; Anecdotes and After Dinner Stories, 1961; Quotable Anecdotes, 1966; Toptable Talk, 1968; contrib. Purnell's History of the First World War, 1971. Recreations: gardening, writing, piano. Address: 34 Saxmundham Road, Aldeburgh, Suffolk. T: Aldeburgh 3163.

MITCHELL, Adrian; writer; b 24 Oct. 1932; s of James Mitchell and Kathleen Fabian. Educ: Dauntsey's Sch.; Christ Church, Oxford. Worked as reporter on Oxford Mail, Evening Standard, 1955-63; subseq. free-lance journalist for Daily Mail, Sun, Sunday Times, New Statesman; Granada Fellow, Univ. of Lancaster, 1968-69; Fellow, Center for Humanities, Wesleyan Univ., 1972; Resident Writer, Sherman Theatre, Cardiff, 1974-75; Vis. writer, Billericay Comp. Sch., 1978-80; Judith E. Wilson Fellow, Cambridge Univ., 1980-81. Plays: Tyger, Nat. Theatre, 1971; Man Friday, 7:84 Theatre Co., 1973 (TV 1972, Screenplay 1975); Mind Your Head, Liverpool Everyman, 1973; Marat/Sade (stage adaptation), Royal Shakespeare Co.; Daft as a Brush (TV), 1975; A Seventh Man, Hampstead, 1976; White Suit Blues, Nottingham, Edinburgh and Old Vic, 1977; Houdini, Amsterdam, 1977; Glad Day (TV), 1978; Uppendown Mooney, Welfare State Theatre Co., 1978; The White Deer, 1978; Hoagy Bix and Wolfgang Beethoven Bunkhaus, 1979; In the Unlikely Event of an Emergency, 1979; Peer Gynt (adaptation), 1980; The Mayor of Zalamea (adaptation), 1981; You Must Believe All This (TV), 1981; The Tragedy of King Real, Welfare State Theatre Co., 1982. Publications: novels: If You See Me Comin', 1962; The Bodyguard, 1970; Wartime, 1973; poetry: Poems, 1964; Out Loud, 1968; Ride the Nightmare, 1971; The Apeman Cometh, 1975; For Beauty Douglas, 1981; Collected Poems 1953-1979, 1982; also plays. Address: c/o Fraser and Dunlop Scripts Ltd, 91 Regent Street, W1R 8RU.

MITCHELL, Alec Burton, CEng, MIMechE, FRINA; Director, Admiralty Marine Technology Establishment, since 1977; b 27 Aug. 1924; er s of Ronald Johnson Mitchell and Millicent Annie Mitchell; m 1952, Barbara, d of Arthur Edward and Katie Florence Jane Archer; three s. Educ: Purley County Sch.; St. John's Coll., Cambridge (MA). Mechanical Sciences Tripos, Cambridge, 1944. Aeronautical Engineer with Rolls Royce Ltd, Hucknall, 1944-46; Grad. apprentice and gas turbine design engr with English Electric Co Ltd, Rugby, 1946-48. Joined RN Scientific Service, 1948; Dep. Head of Hydrodynamic Research Div., Admty Research Lab., 1961; promoted Dep. CSO, 1966; Dep. Dir, Admty Research Laboratory, 1973, Dir, 1974-77. Publications: numerous scientific papers on hydrodynamics and under-water propulsion systems. Recreations: golf, photography, wood-work. Address: 32 Ormond Crescent, Hampton, Mddx TW12 2TH. T: 01-979 6056.

MITCHELL, Alexander Graham, CBE 1973; DFM 1945; b 2 Nov. 1923; s of Alexander Mitchell and Evelyn Mitchell (née Green); m 1954, Pamela Ann Borman; three d. Educ: Dulwich College; Downing Coll., Cambridge (Exhibnr; MA). Served RAF, 1942-45. Clerk to Governors, Dame Allan's Schs, Newcastle. Sudan Government Civil Service, 1951-55; HM Overseas Civil Service, 1955; Western Pacific High Commission: various posts in British Solomon Islands Protectorate and British Residency, New Hebrides, 1955-71; Sec., Financial Affairs, British Residency, 1968-71; Administrator, Turks and Caicos Is, 1971-73; Governor 1973-75; sabbatical, 1975-76, retired June 1977. Recreations: ancient and military history. Address: The Dene, Stocksfield, Northumberland NE43 7PB. Clubs: Royal Over-Seas League, Farmers'.

MITCHELL, Angus; see Mitchell, J. A. M.

MITCHELL, Air Cdre Sir (Arthur) Dennis, KBE 1977; CVO 1961; DFC 1944, and Bar, 1945; AFC 1943; an Extra Equerry to the Queen since 1962; b 26 May 1918; 2nd s of Col A. Mitchell, DSO, Carrickfergus, Belfast, N Ireland; m 1949, Comtesse Mireille Caroline Cornet de Ways Ruart; one s. Educ: Nautical Coll., Pangbourne; RAF Coll., Cranwell; Army Staff Coll., Camberley; RAF Flying Coll., Manby. Joined RAF, 1936. Served 1938-45, India, Burma, UK and NW Europe; RAF Delegn, Belgium, 1948-49; US Air Force, 1951-53; HQ Allied Air Forces Central Europe, NATO, Fontainebleau, 1953-56; o/c RAF Cottesmore Bomber Comd, 1959-62; Dep. Captain and Captain of the Queen's Flight, 1956-59 and 1962-64; ADC to the Queen, 1958-62. Founder: Brussels Airways; Aero Distributors SA; Aero Systems SA; Aero Consultants Ltd; Gen. Agent, Spantax SA. French Croix de Guerre, 1945. Recreation: golf. Address: 10 chemin des Chasseurs, 1328 Ohain, Belgium. T: 653.13.01; (office) 653.22.88. Clubs: Royal Air Force, Naval and Military, Anglo-Belgian.

MITCHELL, Austin Vernon, DPhil; MP (Lab) Grimsby, since April 1977; b 19 Sept. 1934; s of Richard Vernon Mitchell and Ethel Mary Mitchell; m 1st, Patricia Dorothea Jackson (marr. diss.) two d; 2nd, Linda Mary McDougall; one s one d. Educ: Woodbottom Council Sch.; Bingley Grammar Sch.; Manchester Univ. (BA, MA); Nuffield Coll., Oxford (DPhil). Lectr in

History, Univ. of Otago, Dunedin, NZ, 1959-63; Sen. Lectr in Politics, Univ. of Canterbury, Christchurch, NZ, 1963-67; Official Fellow, Nuffield Coll., Oxford, 1967-69; Journalist, Yorkshire Television, 1971; Presenter, BBC Current Affairs Gp, 1972-73; Journalist, Yorkshire TV, 1973-77. *Publications:* New Zealand Politics In Action, 1962; Government By Party, 1966; The Whigs in Opposition 1815-1830, 1969; Politics and People in New Zealand, 1970; Yorkshire Jokes, 1971; The Half-Gallon Quarter-Acre Pavlova Paradise, 1974; Can Labour Win Again, 1979. *Recreation:* worriting (*sic*). *Address:* 1 Abbey Park Road, Grimsby, South Humberside; House of Commons, SW1. *T:* 01-219 4559. *Clubs:* Willows Social (Grimsby); AEU (Saltaire, Shipley).

MITCHELL, Prof. Basil George, DD; Nolloth Professor of the Philosophy of the Christian Religion, Oxford University, and Fellow of Oriel College, since 1968; *b* 9 April 1917; *s* of George William Mitchell and Mary Mitchell (*née* Loxston); *m* 1950, Margaret Eleanor Collin; one *s* three *d*. *Educ:* King Edward VI Sch., Southampton; Queen's Coll., Oxford (Southampton Exhibitioner. 1st cl. Lit Hum 1939). Served Royal Navy, 1940-46; Lt RNVR 1942, Instructor Lt RN 1945. Lectr, Christ Church, Oxford, 1946-47; Fellow and Tutor in Philosophy, Keble Coll., Oxford, 1947-67, Emeritus Fellow, 1981; Sen. Proctor, 1956-57; Hebdomadal Council, 1959-65. Vis. Prof., Princeton Univ., 1963; Stanton Lectr in Philosophy of Religion, Cambridge Univ., 1959-62; Edward Cadbury Lectr, University of Birmingham, 1966-67; Gifford Lectr, Glasgow Univ., 1974-76. Vis. Prof., Colgate Univ., 1976. Member: C of E Working Parties on Ethical Questions, 1964-78; Doctrine Commn, 1978-. Hon. DD Glasgow, 1977; Hon. DLitHum Union Coll., Schenectady, 1979. *Publications:* (ed) Faith and Logic, 1957; Law, Morality and Religion in a Secular Society, 1967; Neutrality and Commitment, 1968; (ed) The Philosophy of Religion, 1971; The Justification of Religious Belief, 1973; Morality: Religious and Secular, 1980; articles in philosophical and theological periodicals. *Address:* Bridge House, Wootton, Woodstock, Oxford. *T:* Woodstock 811265.

MITCHELL, Bob; see Mitchell, R. C.

MITCHELL, Lt-Col Brian Granville Blayney, DSC 1940; RM (Retired); DL; *b* 14 March 1900; *er s* of William Blayney Mitchell, Drumreaske, Co. Monaghan, Eire; *m* 1937, Violet Gwyndolin, *o d* of late Major Sir Charles Price, DL, Haverfordwest, Pembs; two *d*. *Educ:* King's Sch., Bruton, Somerset. Joined Royal Marines, 2nd Lt 1917; Lt 1919; HMS Erin, 1919; Emperor of India, Mediterranean, 1921-22; Hood, Atlantic and Round the World Cruise, 1923-24; Instructor, Sigs Portsmouth, 1925-27; HMS Champion, Home, 1928; Capt. 1928; Queen Elizabeth, Mediterranean, 1929-31; St Vincent (Boys' Training Estab.), 1932-33; Hermes, China, 1934-37; Coronation Review, Spithead, 1937; Supt of Sigs, RM, 1938-40; Major 1937; Actg Lt-Col 1940; Hook of Holland, 1940; The RM Div., 1941-42; Commando Group, Chief Signal Officer, 1943-44; Actg Col 1945; CO Molcab IV, 1945; retired, 1945. DL 1956, High Sheriff, 1959, County of Pembroke. Order of Orange Nassau with Crossed Swords (Netherlands), 1940. *Address:* Manor House, Wiston, Dyfed SA62 4PN. *T:* Clarbeston 258.

MITCHELL, Charles Julian Humphrey; see Mitchell, Julian.

MITCHELL, Lt-Col Colin (Campbell); Chairman, Garrison Ltd, since 1973; *b* 17 Nov. 1925; *o s* of Colin Mitchell, MC, and Janet Bowie Gilmour; *m* 1956, Jean Hamilton Susan Phillips; two *s* one *d*. *Educ:* Whitgift Sch. Enlisted British Army, 1943; commissioned Argyll and Sutherland Highlanders, 1944, serving in Italy (wounded); Palestine, 1945-48 (wounded); Korea, 1950-51; Cyprus, 1958-59; Borneo, 1964 (brevet Lt-Col); Aden, 1967 (despatches). Qualified Camberley Staff Coll., 1955; subsequently: GSO2, 51st Highland Div. (TA); Bde Major, King's African Rifles, and GSO1 Staff of Chief of Defence Staff at MoD. Retired at own request, 1968; subseq. Special Correspondent, Vietnam; industrial management trainee. MP (C) W Aberdeenshire, 1970-Feb. 1974 (not seeking re-election); PPS to Sec. of State for Scotland, 1972-73. Hon. Pres., Scottish Military Collectors Soc.; Vice-Pres., Royal Scottish Country Dance Soc. Freedom of City of London, 1979. Liveryman, Fletchers' Co., 1980-. *Publication:* Having Been A Soldier, 1969. *Recreations:* golf, shooting, squash, poetry, antiques, travel. *Address:* 901 Nelson House, Dolphin Square, SW1V 3NJ. *T:* 01-834 3800. *Clubs:* Carlton, Garrick.

MITCHELL, David Bower; MP (C) Basingstoke since 1964; Parliamentary Under Secretary of State, Northern Ireland Office, since 1981; *b* June 1928; *er s* of James Mitchell, Naval Architect; *m* 1954, Pamela Elaine Haward; two *s* one *d*. *Educ:* Aldenham. Farming, 1945-50; businessman, wine merchant, 1951-79. An Opposition Whip, 1965-67; PPS to Sec. of State for Social Services, 1970-74; Parly Under Sec. of State, DoI, 1979-81. Chm., Cons. Smaller Business Cttee, 1974-79. *Recreations:* gardening, wine-tasting. *Address:* 46 Eaton Terrace, SW1. *T:* 01-730 4470. *Club:* Carlton.

MITCHELL, Sir Dennis; see Mitchell, Sir A. D.

MITCHELL, Sir Derek (Jack), KCB 1974 (CB 1967); CVO 1966; Senior Adviser, Lehman Brothers Kuhn Loeb International Ltd, since 1979; Director: Bowater Corporation, since 1979; Standard Chartered Bank Ltd, since 1979; Independent Director, The Observer Ltd, since 1981; *b* 5 March 1922; *s* of late Sidney Mitchell, Schoolmaster, and Gladys Mitchell; *m* 1944, Miriam, *d* of

late F. E. Jackson; one *s* two *d*. *Educ:* St Paul's Sch.; Christ Church, Oxford. Served War of 1939-45: Royal Armoured Corps and HQ London District, 1942-45. Asst Principal HM Treasury, 1947; Private Sec. to Economic Sec., 1948-49; Private Sec. to Permanent Sec. and Official Head of Civil Service (Sir Edward Bridges), 1954-56; Principal Private Sec. to: Chancellor of Exchequer (Mr Reginald Maudling), 1962-63; The Prime Minister (Mr Harold Wilson, previously Sir Alec Douglas-Home), 1964-66; Under-Sec., 1964; Dep. Under-Sec. of State, Dept of Economic Affairs, 1966-67; Dep. Sec., Min. of Agriculture, Fisheries and Food, 1967-69; Economic Minister and Head of UK Treasury and Supply Delegn, Washington, (also UK Executive Director for IMF and IBRD), 1969-72; Second Permanent Sec. (Overseas Finance), HM Treasury, 1973-77. Dir, Guinness Mahon & Co., 1977-78; Mem., PLA, 1979-82. Member: Nat. Theatre Bd, 1977-; Nat. Theatre Foundn, 1982-; Council, University Coll., London, 1978-82. Governing Trustee, Nuffield Provincial Hospitals Trust, 1978-. *Recreations:* going to opera, theatre and concerts, travel. *Address:* c/o 99 Bishopsgate, 22nd Floor, EC2M 3XD. *T:* 01-638 6911. *Club:* Garrick.

See also E. F. Jackson.

MITCHELL, Douglas Svärd; Controller of Personnel and Administrative Services, Greater London Council, 1972-78; *b* 21 Aug. 1918; *er s* of late James Livingstone Mitchell and Hilma Josefine (*née* Svärd); *m* 1943, Winifred Thornton Paterson, *d* of late William and Ellen Paterson; one *s* two *d*. *Educ:* Morgan Academy, Dundee. Royal Ordnance Factories, 1937-51; Principal, Min. of Supply, 1951-55; Dir of Personnel and Admin., in Industrial, Production and Engineering Groups, UKAEA, 1955-63; Authority Personnel Officer for UKAEA, 1963-64; Dir of Establishments, GLC, 1964-72. *Address:* The Manor House, Horncastle, Lincolnshire. *T:* Horncastle 3553.

MITCHELL, Prof. Edgar William John, CBE 1976; Dr Lee's Professor of Experimental Philosophy, Oxford University and Fellow of Wadham College, Oxford, since 1978; *b* Kingsbridge, S Devon, 25 Sept. 1925; *s* of late Edgar and Caroline Mitchell; *m* 1948; one *s*. *Educ:* Univs of Sheffield (BSc, MSc) and Bristol (PhD). FInstP. Metropolitan Vickers Research Dept, 1946-48, 1950-51; Univ. of Bristol, 1948-50; Univ. of Reading, 1951-78; Prof. of Physics, 1961-78; Dean, Faculty of Science, 1966-69; Dep. Vice-Chancellor, 1976-78. Mem., SERC (formerly SRC), 1970-74, 1982- (Mem., 1965-70, Chm., 1967-70, Physics Cttee; Chm., Neutron Beam Res. Cttee, 1966-74; Mem., Nuclear Physics Bd, 1980-); devised scheme for extensive University use of nuclear res. reactors for condensed matter res. Acting Jt Dir, 1973, Mem., 1973-, Sci. Council of Inst. Laue-Langevin, Grenoble; Member: Comité de Direction, Solid State Physics Lab., Ecole Normale and Univ. of Paris VI, 1975-79; Exec. Cttee, Univ. Council for Non-Academic Staff, 1979-; UGC Phys. Sci. Cttee, 1982-; Chairman: SE Reg. Computing Cttee, 1974-76; Science Planning Gp for Spallation Neutron Source, 1980-. *Publications:* numerous papers on solid state physics. *Recreations:* good food, opera, motoring, physics. *Address:* Clarendon Laboratory, Oxford.

MITCHELL, Mrs Eric; see Shacklock, Constance.

MITCHELL, Ewan; see Janner, Hon. G. E.

MITCHELL, Rear-Adm. Geoffrey Charles, CB 1973; retired 1975; Director, The Old Granary Art and Craft Centre, Bishop's Waltham, since 1976; *b* 21 July 1921; *s* of William C. Mitchell; *m* 1955, Jocelyn Rainger, Auckland, NZ; one *s* two *d*. *Educ:* Marlborough College. Joined RN 1940; Captain 1961; Director Officer Recruiting, 1961-63; Captain (F), 2nd Frigate Sqdn, 1963-65; Director Naval Ops and Trade, 1965-67; Comdr, NATO Standing Naval Force Atlantic, 1968-69; Director Strategic Policy, to Supreme Allied Comdr Atlantic, 1969-71; Rear Adm. 1971; Dep. Asst Chief of Staff (Ops), SHAPE, 1971-74; Chm., RNR and Naval Cadet Forces Review Bd, 1974-75. *Recreations:* golf, tennis, painting, music, languages. *Address:* Willowpool, Lockhams Road, Curdridge, Southampton. *T:* Botley 2403.

MITCHELL, Prof. George Archibald Grant, OBE 1945; TD 1950; Professor of Anatomy and Director of Anatomical Laboratories, Manchester University, 1946-74, now Professor Emeritus; late Dean of Medical School and Pro-Vice-Chancellor; *b* 11 Nov. 1906; *s* of George and Agnes Mitchell; *m* 1933, Mary Cumming; one *s* two *d*. *Educ:* Fordyce Academy; Aberdeen Central Sch.; Aberdeen Univ. MB, ChB (1st Cl. Hons); 1929; ChM 1933; MSc (Manchester); DSc (Aberdeen) 1950; FRCS 1968. Lecturer in Anatomy, 1930-33, in Surgery, 1933-34, Aberdeen Univ.; Surgical Specialist, Co. Caithness, 1934-37; Sen. Lecturer in Anatomy, Aberdeen Univ., 1937-39. Chm., Internat. Anatomical Nomenclature Commn, 1970-75. Pres., 3rd European Anatomical Congress; Pres., S Lancs and E Cheshire BMA Br. Council, 1972-73; Mem. Ct of Examnrs, RCS, 1950-68; Mem. Bd of Governors, United Manchester Hosps, 1955-74; Past President: Anatomical Soc. of GB and Ireland; Manchester Med. Soc. Served War, 1939-45: Surgical Specialist, Officer i/c No. 1 Orthopædic Centre, MEF; Officer i/c Surgical Divs, Adviser in Penicillin and Chemotherapy, 21 Army Gp. Hon. Alumnus, Univ. of Louvain, 1944; Hon. Member: Société Med. Chir. du Centre; Assoc. des Anatomistes; Amer. Assoc. Anat.; British Assoc. Clin. Anat. Chevalier First Class Order of the Dannebrog. *Publications:* The Anatomy of the Autonomic Nervous System, 1952; Basic Anatomy (with E. L. Patterson), 1954; Cardiovascular Innervation, 1956; ed Symposium, Penicillin Therapy and Control in 21 Army Group, 1945. Sections in: Penicillin (by Sir A. Fleming), 1946; Medical Disorders of the Locomotor System (by E. Fletcher), 1947; British Surgical Practice (by Sir Rock Carling and Sir J. Patterson Ross),

1951; Peripheral Vascular Disorders (by Martin, Lynn, Dible and Aird), 1956; Essentials of Neuroanatomy, 1966; Encyclopaedia Britannica, 15th edn; Editor, Nomina Anatomica, 1966. Numerous articles in Jl Anatomy, British Jl Surg., Jl Bone and Joint Surg., Brit. Jl Radiol., BMJ, Lancet, Acta Anat., Nature, Brit. Jl Urol., Edinburgh Medical Jl, Jl Hist. Med., Aberdeen Univ. Rev., Ann. Méd. Chir. du Centre, etc. *Recreations:* wood carving; studying antiques. *Address:* 16 Fellpark Road, Northern Moor, Manchester M23 0EU. *T:* 061-998 8579.

MITCHELL, George Francis, FRS 1973; MRIA; *b* 15 Oct. 1912; *s* of late David William Mitchell and late Frances Elizabeth Kirby; *m* 1940, Lucy Margaret Gwynn; two *d. Educ:* High Sch., Dublin; Trinity Coll., Dublin (MA, MSc); FTCD 1945. Joined staff of Trinity Coll., Dublin, 1934; Professor of Quaternary Studies, 1965-79. Pres., Internat. Union for Quaternary Research, 1969-73. MRIA 1939, PRIA 1976-79. HRHA 1981; Hon. Life Mem., RDS, 1981. DSc (*hc*): Queen's Univ., Belfast, 1976; NUI, 1977; fil.D(*hc*) Uppsala, 1977. *Publications:* The Irish Landscape, 1976; Treasures of Early Irish Art, 1977. *Address:* Townley Hall, Drogheda, Co. Louth, Republic of Ireland. *T:* Drogheda 8218. *Clubs:* Kildare Street and University (Dublin); Explorers' (New York).

MITCHELL, Gladys (Maude Winifred); Writer; *b* 19 April 1901; *e d* of James Mitchell and Annie Julia Maude Simmonds. *Educ:* The Green Sch., Isleworth; Goldsmiths' and University Colls, University of London. First novel published, 1929; followed by other novels, short stories, BBC short detective plays, BBC excerpts from books, BBC Talks on Home Service. Member: Ancient Monuments Soc.; Soc. of Authors; Crime Writers' Assoc.; Detection Club. *Publications:* Speedy Death, 1929; and subsequently numerous other detective novels, including Dead Men's Morris; My Father Sleeps; Rising of the Moon; Dancing Druids; Tom Brown's Body; Groaning Spinney; The Devil's Elbow; The Echoing Strangers; Merlin's Furlong; Faintley Speaking; Watson's Choice; Twelve Horses and the Hangman's Noose; The Twenty-third Man; Spotted Hemlock; The Man Who Grew Tomatoes; Say It With Flowers, 1960; The Nodding Canaries, 1961; My Bones Will Keep, 1962; Adders on the Heath, 1963; Death of a Delft Blue, 1964; Pageant of Murder, 1965; The Croaking Raven, 1966; Skeleton Island, 1967; Three Quick and Five Dead, 1968; Dance to Your Daddy, 1969; Gory Dew, 1970; Lament for Leto, 1971; A Hearse on May-Day, 1972; The Murder of Busy Lizzie, 1973; A Javelin for Jonah, 1974; Winking at the Brim, 1974; Convent on Styx, 1975; Late, Late in the Evening, 1976; Noonday and Night, 1977; Fault in the Structure, 1977; Wraiths and Changelings, 1978; Mingled with Venom, 1978; Nest of Vipers, 1979; The Mudflats of the Dead, 1979; Uncoffin'd Clay, 1980; The Whispering Knights, 1980; The Death-Cap Dancers, 1981; Lovers, Make Moan, 1981; Here Lies Gloria Mundy, 1982; Death of a Burrowing Mole, 1982; The Greenstone Griffins, 1983; *as Stephen Hockaby:* Marsh Hay, 1934; Seven Stars and Orion, 1935; Shallow Brown, 1936; Grand Master, 1939; *as Malcolm Torrie:* Heavy As Lead, 1966; Late and Cold, 1967; Your Secret Friend, 1968; Churchyard Salad, 1969; Shades of Darkness, 1970; Bismarck Herrings, 1971; *children's books:* Outlaws of the Border, The Three Fingerprints, Holiday River, 1948; Seven Stones Mystery, 1949; The Malory Secret, 1950; Pam at Storne Castle, 1951; On Your Marks, 1954; Caravan Creek, 1954; The Light-Blue Hills, 1959. *Recreations:* reading, studying architecture, writing poetry. *Address:* 1 Cecil Close, Corfe Mullen, Wimborne, Dorset.

MITCHELL, Sir Godfrey Way, Kt 1948; President, George Wimpey Ltd (Chairman, 1930-73, Executive Director, 1973-79); *b* 31 Oct. 1891; *s* of Christopher Mitchell and Margaret Mitchell (*née* Way); *m* 1929, Doreen Lilian Mitchell (*d* 1953); two *d. Educ:* Aske's Sch., Hatcham. Employed in father's business, Rowe & Mitchell, 1908, until European War, 1914-18; served in France; temp. commission RE; demobilized with rank Captain. Managing Dir of George Wimpey Ltd, 1919. Hon. Fellow, ICE, 1968; Hon. FIOB, 1971. *Address:* Copper Beech, 2 Curzon Avenue, Beaconsfield, Bucks HP9 2NN. *T:* Beaconsfield 3128.

MITCHELL, Graham Russell, CB 1957; OBE 1951; attached War Office, 1939-63, retired; *b* 4 Nov. 1905; *s* of late Capt. A. S. Mitchell; *m* 1934, Eleonora Patricia (*née* Robertson); one *s* one *d. Educ:* Winchester; Magdalen Coll., Oxford. *Recreations:* yacht racing, chess. *Address:* Barncote, Chobham, Woking, Surrey. *Clubs:* Bembridge Sailing (Bembridge, I of W); Royal Thames Yacht.

MITCHELL, Sir Hamilton, KBE 1969; Barrister and Solicitor, in private practice, New Zealand; *b* 24 Feb. 1910; *s* of Ernest Hamilton Mitchell and Catherine Mitchell; *m* 1st, 1938, Marion Frances Norman; two *s* one *d*; 2nd, 1980, Dorothy Good. *Educ:* Auckland Grammar Sch.; New Zealand Univ. (LLM). Practice on own account, 1941-. Served 2nd NZEF, 1943-46 (Captain, Egypt and Italy). President: Disabled Servicemen's Re-establishment League, 1959-63; NZ Returned Services Assoc., 1962-74; Vice-President: World Veterans' Fedn, 1964-66; British Commonwealth Ex-Services League, 1962-74; Judge, Courts Martial Appeal Court, 1962-; Dep. Chm., Winston Churchill Trust, 1966-76; Chairman: National Art Gallery Management Council, 1967-73; Canteen Fund Bd, 1967-; NZ Patriotic Fund, 1970-; Nat. War Meml Council, 1973-; War Pensions Appeal Bd, 1978-; Dep. Chm., Rehabilitation League, NZ, 1970-. Pres., Wellington Show Assoc., 1980-. *Address:* 78 Orangikaupapa Road, Wellington, New Zealand. *T:* 757224. *Clubs:* Wellington, Wellesley (Wellington); Royal New Zealand Yacht Squadron.

MITCHELL, Harold Charles, CIE 1947; Indian Police (retired); *b* 7 March 1896; *s* of late Daniel Charles Mitchell and late Helen Mitchell; *m* 1923, Edna Evadne Bion (*d* 1982); one *d. Educ:* Fairfield. RNVR, Bristol, 1912-19 (Pay Lt). Joined Indian Police, 1920; served as Dist Supt of Police, Bareilly, Benares, Cawnpore, Meerut and other UP districts; Central Intelligence Officer, UP and Ajmer, Home Dept Govt of India; Special Branch, CID, UP; Dep. Inspector-Gen. of Police, CID, UP; Personal Asst to Inspector-Gen. of Police, UP; Dep. Inspector-Gen. of Police, UP HQ and Railways. *Recreations:* golf, fishing. *Address:* Camber Cottage, Camberley, Surrey. *T:* Camberley 22675. *Clubs:* Naval; Camberley Heath.

MITCHELL, Col Sir Harold (Paton), 1st Bt, *cr* 1945; *b* 21 May 1900; *e s* of late Col. Alexander Mitchell, TD, JP, DL, of Tulliallan; *m* 1947, Mary, *d* of late William Pringle; one *d. Educ:* Eton; RMC, Sandhurst; University Coll., Oxford (MA), Hon. Fellow 1972; University of Geneva (Docteur ès Sciences Politiques). Vice-Chm. of Conservative Party, 1942-45; Contested (C) Clackmannan and East Stirlingshire in 1929; MP (C) Brentford and Chiswick Div. of Middlesex, 1931-45; Parliamentary Private Sec. to Rt Hon. John Colville, MP (Dept of Overseas Trade), 1931-35; Parliamentary Private Sec. to Rt Hon. Ralph Assheton, MP (Ministry of Labour, 1939-41, and Ministry of Supply, 1941); Mem. Departmental Cttee on Education and Training of Overseas Students, 1933-34; Mem. Selection Board for Consular Service, 1934-35; Mem. Company Law Amendment Cttee, 1943-45; Command Welfare Officer, AA Command, 1940-48, and Liaison Officer to Polish Forces (France, Belgium, Holland, 1944). Lectr, Hispanic American Studies, Stanford University 1959-65; Research Prof. of Latin American Studies, Rollins Coll. Hon. Col, 123 LAA Regt (City of London Rifles) TA, 1939-48; Hon. Col of 61st (City of Edinburgh) Signal Regt, TA, 1947-65. Chm. and Chief Exec., Luscar Ltd Group, Edmonton, Alberta; sometime Dir London and North Eastern Railway Co.; Joint Master Lauderdale Foxhounds, 1934-35; sometime Mem. Queen's Body Guard for Scotland. DL Clackmannanshire, 1943-47. Hon. LLD Alberta, Rollins and St Andrews. KStJ; Knight Commander of Polonia Restituta; Polish Cross of Valour. *Publications:* Downhill Ski-Racing, 1930; Into Peace, 1945; In My Stride, 1951; Europe in the Caribbean, 1963; Caribbean Patterns, 1967, 2nd edn 1972; The Spice of Life, 1974. *Recreation:* ski-ing, represented Gt Britain, 1929, 1931, and 1933. *Address:* Haus Gornerwald, 3920 Zermatt, Switzerland; Marshall's Island, Bermuda. *Clubs:* Alpine; Royal Bermuda Yacht.

MITCHELL, Harvey Allan; Head of Cultural and International Services, Lothian Regional Council, since 1975; *b* 23 Sept. 1932; *s* of Robert Mutter Mitchell and Margaret Massey Mitchell; *m* 1970, Karin Katharina Rapp, Tailfingen, Germany; two *s* one *d. Educ:* Edinburgh Univ. (MA Hons). Freelance Journalist, 1955-56; Press Officer, Rank Organization, 1956-58; Sen. Staff, Voice & Vision, 1958-60; Sen. Staff, Barnet & Reef (NY), 1961; Public Relations Administrator, Merck & Co., New York and Brussels, 1962-65; Asst to Vice-Pres., Massey-Ferguson (Toronto), 1965-67. Gen. Manager, New Philharmonia Orch., 1968-72; Dir of Develt, Tayside, 1972-75. Dir, Scottish Occupational Health Service, 1972-; Chm., Duntrune House Develts Ltd, 1972-. *Publications:* articles on philosophy and the arts. *Recreations:* tennis, bridge, travel. *Address:* 28A Murray Place, Edinburgh. *T:* 031-226 6108. *Club:* Scottish Arts (Edinburgh).

MITCHELL, Helen Josephine; *see* Watts, H. J.

MITCHELL, Ian Edward; Manager, CKS Products Ltd, since 1982; *b* 24 Dec. 1932; *s* of George Thomas Mitchell and Lorna May Mitchell. *Educ:* Queensland, Australia. Town Clerk's Dept, Brisbane City Council, 1953-65; Gen. Sec., British Film Producers Assoc. Ltd, 1966-81; Co. Sec. and Dir, Central Casting Ltd, 1970-81; Administrator, Fedn of Specialised Film Producers Assocs, 1970-80. Manager, Vicars Saunderson and Partners, 1981-82. *Recreations:* amateur theatricals, opera, swimming, tennis. *Address:* 80 Alexandra Road, Epsom, Surrey. *T:* Epsom 20982, (office) 01-643 0200.

MITCHELL, James; writer these many years; *b* South Shields, 12 March 1926; *s* of James Mitchell and Wilhelmina Mitchell; *m* 1968, Delia, *d* of Major and Mrs K. J. McCoy; two *s. Educ:* South Shields Grammar Sch.; St Edmund Hall, Oxford (BA 1948, MA 1950); King's Coll., Newcastle upon Tyne, Univ. of Durham (DipEd 1950). Worked in rep. theatre, 1948, then in shipyard, travel agency and Civil Service; taught for some fifteen years in almost every kind of instn from secondary modern sch. to coll. of art. Free-lance writer: novels; more than a hundred television scripts; several screenplays and a theatre play. *Publications:* Here's a Villain, 1957; A Way Back, 1959; Steady Boys, Steady, 1960; Among Arabian Sands, 1963; The Man Who Sold Death, 1964; Die Rich, Die Happy, 1965; The Money that Money can't Buy, 1967; The Innocent Bystanders, 1969; Ilion like a Mist, 1969; A Magnum for Schneider, 1969; The Winners, 1970; Russian Roulette, 1973; Death and Bright Water, 1974; Smear Job, 1975; When the Boat Comes In, 1976; The Hungry Years, 1976; Upwards and Onwards, 1977; The Evil Ones, 1982. *Recreations:* travel, military history, aristology. *Address:* 15 Zetland House, Marloes Road, W8 5LB. *Club:* Lansdowne.

MITCHELL, James; Social Security Commissioner, since 1980; *b* 11 June 1926; *s* of James Hill Mitchell and Marjorie Kate Mitchell (*née* Williams); *m* 1957, Diane Iris Mackintosh; two *d. Educ:* Merchiston Castle Sch., Edinburgh; Brasenose Coll., Oxford, 1944-45 and 1948-51 (Open Exhibnr, BCL, MA). Served RAFVR, 1945-48. Assistant Master, Edge Grove Preparatory Sch., Herts, 1952-55; called to the Bar, Middle Temple, 1954; private practice as barrister/solicitor, Gold Coast/Ghana, 1956-58; practice as barrister, London, 1958-80. Most Hon. Order of Crown of Brunei, 3rd Cl. 1959, 2nd Cl. 1972. *Recreations:* sailing, walking, railways, the Jacobites. *Address:* 6 Grosvenor Gardens, SW1W 0DH. *T:* 01-730 9236.

MITCHELL, James Alexander Hugh; publisher; Chairman, Mitchell Beazley Ltd; Founder Chairman, Mitchell Beazley Television, 1981; Senior Vice-President, Communications Division, American Express Company, since 1980; *b* 20 July 1939; *s* of William Moncur Mitchell and Christine Mary Browne; *m* 1962, Janice Page Davison; three *s. Educ:* Winchester; Trinity Coll., Cambridge (BA). Hatchards (bookseller), 1960-61; Constable & Co. (Editor), 1961-67; Editorial Director, Thomas Nelson, 1967-69; Jt Founder of Mitchell Beazley with John Beazley (*d* 1977), 1969. Chm. Bd of Trustees, RCA, 1982-. *Publications:* (ed) The God I Want, 1966; (gen. ed) The Joy of Knowledge Encyclopaedia (also called The Random House Encyclopedia, in USA, l'Univers en couleurs, in France (Larousse), etc (now 28 editions in 23 languages). *Recreations:* family, fishing, gardening, birds, dogs. *Address:* c/o Mitchell Beazley, 87-89 Shaftesbury Avenue, W1V 7AD. *T:* 01-439 7211. *Club:* Garrick.
See also Julian Mitchell.

MITCHELL, (James Lachlan) Martin, RD 1969; Sheriff of Lothian and Borders (formerly Lothians and Peebles), since 1974 (as a floating Sheriff, 1974-78, and at Edinburgh, 1978); *b* 13 June 1929; *o s* of late Dr L. M. V. Mitchell, OBE, MB, ChB and Harriet Doris Riggall. *Educ:* Cargilfield; Sedbergh; Univ. of Edinburgh. MA 1951, LLB 1953. Admitted Mem. Faculty of Advocates, 1957; Standing Junior Counsel in Scotland to Admty Bd, 1963-74. Nat. Service, RN, 1954-55; Sub-Lt (S) RNVR 1954; Perm. Reserve, 1956; Comdr RNR 1966, retd 1974. *Recreations:* fishing, photography, gramophone. *Address:* 3 Great Stuart Street, Edinburgh EH3 6AP. *T:* 031-225 3384. *Club:* New (Edinburgh).

MITCHELL, Jeremy George Swale Hamilton; Under Secretary, and Director, National Consumer Council, since 1977; *b* 25 May 1929; *s* of late George Oswald Mitchell and late Agnes Josephine Mitchell; *m* 1956, Margaret Mary Ayres; three *s* one *d. Educ:* Ampleforth; Brasenose and Nuffield Colls, Oxford (MA). Dep. Research Dir, then Dir of Information, Consumers' Assoc. (Which?), 1958-65; Asst Sec., Nat. Econ. Develt Office, 1965-66; Scientific Sec., then Sec., SSRC, 1966-74; Under Sec., and Dir of Consumer Affairs, Office of Fair Trading, 1974-77. *Publications:* (ed) SSRC Reviews of Research, series, 1968-73; (ed jtly) Social Science Research and Industry, 1971; Betting, 1972; (ed) Marketing and the Consumer Movement, 1978. *Recreation:* Swinburne. *Address:* National Consumer Council, 18 Queen Anne's Gate, SW1.

MITCHELL, Prof. Joan Eileen, (Mrs James Cattermole); Professor of Political Economy, University of Nottingham, since 1978; *b* 15 March 1920; *d* of late Albert Henry Mitchell, Paper Merchant, and Eva Mitchell; *m* 1956, James Cattermole; one *s* one *d. Educ:* Southend-on-Sea High Sch.; St Hilda's Coll., Oxford. Economist, Min. of Fuel and Power, 1942; Tutor, St Anne's Coll., Oxford, 1945; Economist, BoT, 1947; Research Officer, Labour Party, 1950; Lectr in Econs, Nottingham Univ., 1952, Reader in Econs, 1962. Mem., NBPI, 1965-68; personal economic adviser to Sec. of State for Prices and Consumer Protection, 1974-76. Member: Cttee to Review the Functioning of Financial Institutions, 1977-80 (Chm. Res. Panel); Standing Commn on Pay Comparability, 1979-81. *Publications:* Britain in Crisis 1951, 1963; Groundwork to Economic Planning, 1966; The National Board for Prices and Incomes, 1972; Price Determination and Prices Policy, 1978. *Recreations:* gardening, cooking, highbrow music. *Address:* Economics Department, University of Nottingham; 15 Ranmoor Road, Gedling, Nottingham. *Club:* National Liberal.

MITCHELL, (John) Angus (Macbeth), CB 1979; CVO 1961; MC 1946; Secretary, Scottish Education Department, since 1976; *b* 25 Aug. 1924; *s* of John Fowler Mitchell, *qv,* and Sheila Macbeth, MBE; *m* 1948, Ann Katharine Williamson; two *s* two *d. Educ:* Marlborough Coll.; Brasenose Coll., Oxford (Junior Hulme Scholar); BA Modern Hist., 1948. Served Royal Armoured Corps, 1943-46: Lieut, Inns of Court Regt, NW Europe, 1944-45; Captain East African Military Records, 1946. Entered Scottish Education Dept, 1949; Private Sec. to Sec. of State for Scotland, 1958-59; Asst Sec., Scottish Educn Dept, 1959-65; Dept of Agriculture and Fisheries for Scotland, 1965-68; Scottish Development Dept, 1968; Asst Under-Secretary of State, Scottish Office, 1968-69; Under Sec., Social Work Services Gp, Scottish Educn Dept, 1969-75; Under Sec., SHHD, 1975-76. Chairman: Scottish Marriage Guidance Council, 1965-69; Working Party on Social Work Services in NHS, 1976; Working Party on Relationships between Health Bds and Local Authorities, 1976; Consultative Cttee on the Curriculum, 1976-80. Kt, Order of Oranje-Nassau (Netherlands), 1946. *Recreations:* old Penguins; maps. *Address:* 20 Regent Terrace, Edinburgh EH7 5BS. *T:* 031-556 7671. *Clubs:* Royal Commonwealth Society; New (Edinburgh).

MITCHELL, John Fowler, CIE 1935; Indian Civil Service, retired; *b* 30 Dec. 1886; *s* of William Mitchell and Janet Woodrow; *m* 1920, Sheila Macbeth, MBE; one *s* two *d. Educ:* Allan Glen's Sch., Glasgow; Royal College of Science, S Kensington; Glasgow Univ.; Merton Coll., Oxford; London Univ. (BSc 1st cl. Hons, Exptl Physics, 1908). Entered Indian Civil Service, 1910; from 1910-19 various posts as Asst Comr Punjab, including Magistrate and Sec. Municipal Cttee, Delhi; Subdivisional Officer, Fazilka; Superintendent

Central Jail, Multan; Forest Settlement Officer, Kangra; from 1920-34 various finance and audit posts, including Under Sec. Finance, Punjab; Accountant General Madras, Central Provinces and Central Revenues; Dir of Audit Indian Railways; officiating Dep. Auditor General, India; retired 1937. Military Service, 1940-46; Allied Commission for Austria, 1946-47. *Publications:* (with Sheila Mitchell): Monumental Inscriptions in Kinross-shire, 1967; Monumental Inscriptions (pre-1855) in Clackmannanshire, 1968; similar volumes for West Lothian, 1969; Dunbartonshire, 1969; Renfrewshire, 1970; East Fife, 1971; West Fife, 1972; East Stirlingshire, 1972; West Stirlingshire, 1973; South Perthshire, 1974; North Perthshire, 1975. *Address:* 47 Connaught Mansions, Bath, Avon BA2 4BP. *T:* Bath 60107.
See also J. A. M. Mitchell.

MITCHELL, John Gall, QC (Scot.) 1970; a Social Security (formerly National Insurance) Commissioner, since 1979; *b* 5 May 1931; *s* of late Rev. William G. Mitchell, MA; *m* 1959, Anne Bertram, *d* of John Jardine; three *s* one *d. Educ:* Royal High Sch., Edinburgh; Edinburgh Univ. (MA, LLB). Advocate 1957. Standing Junior Counsel, Customs and Excise, Scotland, 1964-70; Chairman: Industrial Tribunals, Scotland, 1966-80; Legal Aid Supreme Court Cttee, Scotland, 1974-79; Pensions Appeals Tribunal, Scotland, 1974-80. Hon. Sheriff of Lanarkshire, 1970-74. *Address:* Rosemount, Park Road, Eskbank, Dalkeith, Midlothian.

MITCHELL, John Matthew, CBE 1976; PhD; Assistant Director-General, British Council, since 1981; *b* 22 March 1925; *s* of Clifford George Arthur Mitchell and Grace Maud Jamson; *m* 1952, Eva Maria von Rupprecht; three *s* one *d. Educ:* Ilford County High Sch.; Worcester Coll., Oxford; Queens' Coll., Cambridge (MA). PhD Vienna. Served War, RN, 1944-46. British Council: Lectr, Austria, 1949-52 and Egypt, 1952-56; Scotland, 1957-60; Dep. Rep., Japan, 1960-63; Reg. Dir, Zagreb, 1963-66; Reg. Rep., Dacca, 1966-69; Dep. Controller, Home Div., 1969-72; Rep., Federal Republic of Germany, 1973-77; Controller, Educn, Medicine and Sci. Div., 1977-81. Vis. Fellow, Wolfson Coll., Cambridge, 1972-73; former Lectr, univs of Vienna, Cairo and Tokyo. *Publications:* verse, short stories and trans. from German. *Recreations:* ski-ing, golf, bridge. *Address:* The Cottage, Pains Hill Corner, Pains Hill, Limpsfield, Surrey. *T:* Limpsfield Chart 3354. *Clubs:* Royal Commonwealth Society; Tandridge Golf.

MITCHELL, Prof. John Richard Anthony, FRCP; Foundation Professor of Medicine, Nottingham Medical School, since 1967; Consultant Physician, Nottingham Hospitals, since 1968; *b* 20 Oct. 1928; *s* of Richard and Elizabeth Mitchell; *m* 1954, Muriel Joyce Gibbon; two *s* two *d. Educ:* Manchester Univ. (BSc, MB ChB, MD); St Catherine's Coll., Oxford (MA, DPhil). Junior clinical posts, Manchester, 1953-54; Medical Specialist, RAMC, 1955-57; Registrar and Lectr, Regius Prof., Oxford, 1957-61; MRC Research Fellow, Oxford, 1961-63; First Asst, Oxford, 1963-68; Fellow, Linacre Coll., Oxford, 1964-68; Adviser in general medicine to DHSS, 1968-81. *Publications:* Arterial Disease, 1965; numerous papers on aspects of vascular disease. *Recreations:* music, getting on to water (sea and canal), local history, natural history, arguing. *Address:* 7 Sutton Passeys Crescent, Nottingham NG8 1BX. *T:* Nottingham 784468.

MITCHELL, John Wesley, FRS 1956; PhD, DSc; Senior Research Fellow and Emeritus Professor, University of Virginia, since 1979; *b* 3 Dec. 1913; *s* of late John Wesley Mitchell and late Lucy Ruth Mitchell; *m* 1976, Virginia Hill; one step *d* of former marriage. *Educ:* Canterbury University Coll., Christchurch, NZ; Univ. of Oxford. BSc 1934. MSc 1935, NZ; PhD 1938, DSc 1960, Oxford. Reader in Experimental Physics in the Univ. of Bristol, 1945-59; Prof. of Physics, Univ. of Virginia, 1959-63; Dir of the National Chemical Laboratory, Oct. 1963-Aug. 1964; William Barton Rogers Prof. of Physics, Univ. of Virginia, 1964-79. *Publications:* various on photographic sensitivity and on plastic deformation of crystals in scientific journals. *Recreations:* mountaineering, colour photography. *Address:* Department of Physics, University of Virginia, Charlottesville, Virginia 22901, USA. *Clubs:* Athenæum; Cosmos (Washington, DC).

MITCHELL, Joseph Rodney; Director General of Defence Accounts, Ministry of Defence, 1973, retired; *b* 11 March 1914; *s* of late Joseph William and Martha Mitchell, Sheffield; *m* 1936, Marian Richardson; two *s* three *d. Educ:* Sheffield Central Secondary School. FCCA, ACMA, ACIS. Works Recorder and Junior Costs Clerk, United Steel Cos Ltd, Sheffield, 1930-35; Senior Accounts Clerk, Cargo Fleet Iron Co. Ltd, Middlesbrough, 1936-39; Royal Ordnance Factories, 1940-55: Chief Exec. Officer, 1951-55; Min. of Supply/Aviation/Technology, 1956-71: Dir of Accounts, 1967-71; Dep. Dir Gen. of Defence Accounts, MoD, 1971-72. *Recreation:* hill-walking. *Address:* 4 Orchard Court, Hathersage Road, Grindleford, Sheffield S30 1JH.

MITCHELL, Prof. Joseph Stanley, CBE 1951; FRS 1952; Regius Professor of Physic in the University of Cambridge, 1957-75, now Emeritus; Director, Radiotherapeutic Centre, Addenbrooke's Hospital, Cambridge, 1943-76, and Professor of Radiotherapeutics, Cambridge University, 1946-57 and 1975-76; now working in Research Laboratories of the Clinical School, Radiotherapeutic Centre; Fellow, St John's College, Cambridge, since 1936; Hon. Consultant, Atomic Energy Authority; *b* 22 July 1909; *s* of late Joseph Brown Mitchell and Ethel Maud Mary Arnold, Birmingham; *m* 1934, Dr Lilian Mary Buxton, MA, MB, ChB; one *s* one *d. Educ:* Marlborough Road Council Sch., Birmingham; King Edward's High Sch., Birmingham; University of Birmingham; St John's Coll., Cambridge. Nat. Sciences Tripos

Part II, Class I, Physics, 1931; MB, BChir Cantab 1934; House Physician, Gen. Hosp., Birmingham; Beit Memorial Medical Research Fellowship; Colloid Science Laboratory, Cambridge, 1934-37; MA Cantab 1935; PhD Cantab 1937; Resident Radiological Officer, Christie Hosp., Manchester, 1937-38; Asst in Research in Radiotherapy, Dept of Medicine, University of Cambridge, 1938. Radiotherapist EMS, 1939; DMR (RCS), 1943; in charge of medical investigations, National Research Council Laboratory, Montreal, 1944-45. FFR, 1954; MRCP 1956; MD Cantab 1957; DSc (hc) Birmingham 1958; FRCP 1958. Foreign Fellow, Indian Nat. Science Acad., 1975. Linacre Lecturer, 1970. Leverhulme Emeritus Fellow, 1976-77. Pres. British Section, Anglo-German Medical Soc., 1959-68. Vice-Chm., Faith Courtauld Unit for Human Study of Cancer, King's College Hosp., London, 1977-79 (Chm., 1971-77). Hon. Mem., German Roentgen Soc., 1967; Pirogoff Medal, 1967. *Publications:* Studies in Radiotherapeutics, 1960; Cancer, if curable why not cured?, 1971; papers in scientific and medical journals on mechanism of therapeutic action of radiations, and the development of radioactive compounds. *Recreations:* walking, modern languages. *Address:* Thorndyke, Huntingdon Road, Girton, Cambridge CB3 0LG. *T:* Cambridge 276102; Research Laboratories, Radiotherapeutic Centre, Addenbrooke's Hospital, Hills Road, Cambridge CB2 2QQ. *T:* Cambridge 243619.

MITCHELL, Julian; writer; *b* 1 May 1935; *s* of late William Moncur Mitchell and of Christine Mary (*née* Browne). *Educ:* Winchester; Wadham Coll., Oxford. Mem., Literature Panel, Arts Council, 1966-69. John Llewellyn Rhys Prize, 1965; Somerset Maugham Award, 1966. *Publications:* novels: Imaginary Toys, 1961; A Disturbing Influence, 1962; As Far As You Can Go, 1963; The White Father, 1964; A Circle of Friends, 1966; The Undiscovered Country, 1968; *biography:* (with Peregrine Churchill) Jennie: Lady Randolph Churchill, 1974; *translation:* Henry IV (Pirandello), 1979 (John Florio Prize, 1980); *plays:* Half-Life, 1977; The Enemy Within, 1980; Another Country, 1981; (adapted from Ivy Compton-Burnett): A Heritage and Its History, 1965; A Family and a Fortune, 1975. Television plays include: Shadow in the Sun; A Question of Degree; Rust; Abide With Me (Internat. Critics Prize, Monte Carlo, 1977); adaptations of: Persuasion; The Alien Corn; Staying On; The Good Soldier; The Mysterious Stranger; series, Jennie, Lady Randolph Churchill, 1974. *Address:* 2 Castle Rise, Llanvaches, Newport, Gwent NP6 3BS. *T:* Newport 400848.
See also James A. H. Mitchell.

MITCHELL, Leslie Herbert, CBE 1955 (OBE 1949); *b* 28 May 1914; *s* of J. W. and A. J. Mitchell; *m* 1937, Margaret Winifred Pellow; three *s. Educ:* Christ's Hospital. Served War of 1939-45 in HM Forces in NW Europe. 2nd Sec., British Embassy, Copenhagen, 1945-50; 1st Sec., British Embassy, Washington, 1953-56; 1st Sec., Bonn, 1956-57; FO, retd 1968. Order of Dannebrog (Denmark), 1947. *Recreations:* music, railways. *Address:* 2 Lakeside Court, East Approach Drive, Cheltenham, Glos. *Club:* Reform.

MITCHELL, Martin; see Mitchell, J. L. M.

MITCHELL, Very Rev. Patrick Reynolds; Dean of Wells, since 1973; *b* 17 March 1930; *s* of late Lt-Col Percy Reynolds Mitchell, DSO; *m* 1959, Mary Evelyn (*née* Phillips); three *s* one *d. Educ:* Eton Coll.; Merton Coll., Oxford (MA Theol); Wells Theol Coll. Officer in Welsh Guards (National Service), 1948-49. Deacon, 1954; priest, 1955; Curate at St Mark's, Mansfield, 1954-57; Priest-Vicar of Wells Cathedral and Chaplain of Wells Theological Coll., 1957-60; Vicar of St James', Milton, Portsmouth, 1961-67; Vicar of Frome Selwood, Somerset, 1967-73; Director of Ordination Candidates for Bath and Wells, 1971-74. Member: Adv. Bd for Redundant Churches, 1978-; Cathedrals Adv. Commn for England, 1981-. FSA 1981. *Address:* The Dean's Lodging, 25 The Liberty, Wells, Somerset. *T:* Wells 72192.

MITCHELL, Dr Peter Dennis, FRS 1974; Director of Research, Glynn Research Institute (formerly Laboratories), since 1964; *b* 29 Sept. 1920; *s* of Christopher Gibbs Mitchell, Mitcham, Surrey; *m* 1958, Helen, *d* of Lt-Col Raymond P. T. ffrench, late Indian Army; three *s* one *d. Educ:* Queens Coll., Taunton; Jesus Coll., Cambridge; BA 1943; PhD 1950; Hon. Fellow, 1980. Dept of Biochem., Univ. of Cambridge, 1943-55, Demonstrator 1950-55; Dir of Chem. Biol. Unit, Dept of Zoology, Univ. of Edinburgh, 1955-63, Sen. Lectr 1961-62, Reader 1962-63. Sir Hans Krebs Lect. and Medal, Fed. European Biochem. Socs, 1978; Fritz Lipmann Lectr, Gesellschaft für Biol Chem., 1978; Humphry Davy Meml Lectr, RIC and Chilterns and Mddx Sect. of Chem. Soc., at Royal Instn of London, 1980; James Rennie Bequest Lectr, Univ. of Edinburgh, 1980. For. Associate, Nat. Acad. of Scis, USA, 1977. Hon. Dr rer. nat. Tech. Univ., Berlin, 1976; Hon. DSc: Exeter, 1977; Chicago, 1978; Liverpool, 1979; Bristol, 1980; Edinburgh, 1980; Hull, 1980; Hon. ScD: East Anglia, 1981; York, 1982. CIBA Medal and Prize, Biochem. Soc., for outstanding research, 1973; (jtly) Warren Trienniel Prize, Trustees of Mass Gen. Hosp., Boston, 1974; Louis and Bert Freedman Foundn Award, NY Acad. of Scis, 1974; Wilhelm Feldberg Foundn Prize, 1976; Lewis S. Rosenstiel Award, Brandeis Univ., 1977; Nobel Prize for Chemistry, 1978; Copley Medal, Royal Society, 1981; Medal of Honour, Athens Municipal Council, 1982. *Publications:* Chemiosmotic Coupling in Oxidative and Photosynthetic Phosphorylation, 1966; Chemiosmotic Coupling and Energy Transduction, 1968; papers in scientific jls. *Recreations:* enjoyment of family life, home-building and creation of wealth and amenity, restoration of buildings of architectural and historical interest, music, thinking, understanding, inventing, making, sailing. *Address:* Glynn House, Bodmin, Cornwall PL30 4AU. *T:* Cardinham 381.

MITCHELL, Richard Charles, (Bob); MP Itchen Division of Southampton, since May 1971 (Lab, 1971-81, SDP since 1981); *b* 22 Aug. 1927; *s* of Charles and Elizabeth Mitchell; *m* 1950, Doreen Lilian Gregory; one *s* one *d. Educ:* Taunton's Sch., Southampton; Godalming County Gram. Sch.; Southampton Univ. BSc(Econ) Hons 1951. Bartley County Sec. Sch.: Senior Master and Head of Maths and Science Dept, 1957-65; Dep. Headmaster, 1965-66. MP (Lab) Southampton Test, 1966-70. Mem., European Parlt, 1975-79. Member: Bureau of European Socialist Gp, 1976-79; Chairman's Panel, House of Commons, 1979-. *Recreation:* postal chess (rep. Brit. Correspondence Chess Assoc. against other countries). *Address:* 49 Devonshire Road, Polygon, Southampton. *T:* Southampton 21781.

MITCHELL, Robert; Stipendiary Magistrate, City of Glasgow, 1974-80, retired; *b* 24 June 1915; *s* of Robert Mitchell and Anne Mathie; *m* 1944, M. Dorothy Logan; two *s. Educ:* Dumbarton Acad.; Glasgow Univ. (MA, LLB 1939). LMRTPI 1962. Solicitor. Depute Town Clerk, Dumfries, 1944-53; Chief Exec., Eldoret, Kenya, 1953-55; general practice, Edinburgh, 1955-58; Town Clerk, Inverkeithing, 1958-65; Clerk to Glasgow City Courts, 1966-74. *Recreations:* walking and swimming. *Address:* 9 Dundonald Road, Glasgow G12 9LJ. *T:* 041-334 3230. *Club:* University of Glasgow College.

MITCHELL, Robert; Chairman and Managing Director, R. Mitchell (M&S) Ltd, since 1969; Councillor, Greater London Council, since 1964; *b* 14 Dec. 1913; *s* of Robert Mitchell and Lizzie Mitchell (*née* Snowdon); *m* 1946, Reinholda Thoretta L. C. Kettlitz; two *s* one step *s. Educ:* West Ham Secondary Sch.; St John's Coll., Cambridge (MA Hons NatSci). Councillor, Wanstead and Woodford Council, 1958-65, Dep. Mayor, 1960-61. Chairman: GLC, 1971-72; Fire Brigade and Ambulance Cttees, 1967-71; Nat. Jt Negotiating Cttee for Local Authority Fire Brigades, 1970-71; Covent Gdn Jt Develt Cttee, 1972-73; Professional and Gen. Services Cttee, 1977-79; Greater London Jt Supply Bd, 1977-79. Member: CBI Cttee on State Intervention in Private Industry, 1976-78; London and SE Reg. Council, 1969-79; Smaller Firms Council, 1977-79; Policy Cttee, AMA, 1978-79. Wanstead and Woodford Conservative Association: Vice-Chm., 1961-65; Chm., 1965-68; Vice-Pres., 1968-; contested (C) West Ham South, 1964 and 1966 gen. elecs. Represented: Cambridge Univ., swimming and water polo, 1932-35 (Captain, 1935); England and Gt Britain, water polo, 1934-48, incl. Olympic Games, 1936 and 1948; Gt Britain, swimming and water polo, World Univ. Games, 1933, 1935; Rest of World *v* Champions, water polo, Univ. Games, 1935; Captain, 1946-49, Pres., 1955-56, Plaistow United Swimming Club; London Rep., Cambridge Univ. Swimming Club, 1953-75. Mem. Cttee, Crystal Palace Nat. Sports Centre, 1965-. Verderer, Epping Forest, 1976-; Mem., Lea Valley Regl Park Auth., 1982-. Governor, Chigwell Sch., 1966- (Vice-Chm., 1968-). Grand Officer, Order of Orange Nassau (Holland), 1972; Order of Star (Afghanistan), 1971; Order of Rising Sun (Japan), 1971. *Recreation:* planting trees, then sitting watch them grow. *Address:* Hatchwood House, Sunset Avenue, Woodford Green, Essex. *T:* 01-504 0056; Little Brigg, Bessingham, Norfolk NR11 7JR. *Clubs:* Carlton, City Livery; Hawks (Cambridge).

MITCHELL, Maj.-Gen. Robert Imrie, OBE 1958 (MBE 1945); retired; *b* 25 Jan. 1916; *s* of James I. Mitchell; *m* 1947, Marion Lyell. *Educ:* Glasgow Academy; Glasgow Univ. BSc 1936, MB, ChB 1939. FFCM. 2/Lt 1937, Lieut 1938 (TA Gen. List); Lieut, RAMC, 1939; served war 1939-45 (despatches 1945); Captain 1940; Major 1947; Lt-Col 1958; Col 1962; Brig. 1968; DDMS, I (British) Corps, BAOR, 1968-69; Maj.-Gen. 1969; DDMS, Army Strategic Command, 1969-71; DMS, BAOR, 1971-73. QHP 1970-73. Hon. Colonel, Glasgow and Strathclyde Univs. OTC TA, 1977-82. OStJ 1966. *Recreations:* skiing, shooting, fishing, golf. *Address:* Hallam, Gargunnock, Stirlingshire FK8 3BQ. *T:* Gargunnock 600. *Clubs:* Naval and Military; Royal Scottish Automobile (Glasgow).

MITCHELL, Hon. Dame Roma (Flinders), DBE 1982 (CBE 1971); **Hon. Justice Mitchell;** Senior Puisne Judge, Supreme Court of South Australia, since 1979 (Judge of Supreme Court, since 1965); *b* 2 Oct. 1913; *d* of Harold Flinders Mitchell and Maude Imelda Victoria (*née* Wickham). *Educ:* St Aloysius Coll., Adelaide; Univ. of Adelaide (LLB 1934). Admitted as Practitioner, Supreme Court of SA, 1934; QC 1962 (first woman QC in Australia). Chairman: Parole Bd of SA, 1974-81; Criminal Law Reform Cttee of SA, 1971-81; Human Rights Commn of Australia, 1981-; State Heritage Cttee of SA, 1978-81; Dep. National Chm., Winston Churchill Meml Trust, 1975-; National Pres., Australian Assoc. of Ryder-Cheshire Foundn, 1979-. Member: Council for Order of Australia, 1980-; Bd of Governors, Adelaide Festival of Arts, 1981-. Sen. Dep. Chancellor, Univ. of Adelaide, 1972-. Boyer Lectr, ABC, 1975. *Recreations:* theatre, music, art, swimming, walking. *Address:* 256 East Terrace, Adelaide, SA 5000, Australia. *T:* 223 5373. *Clubs:* Queen Adelaide, Lyceum (Adelaide).

MITCHELL, Prof. Ross Galbraith, MD, FRCPE, DCH; Professor of Child Health, University of Dundee and Pædiatrician, Ninewells Hospital, Dundee, since 1973; Dean of the Faculty of Medicine and Dentistry, 1978-81; *b* 18 Nov. 1920; *s* of late Richard Galbraith Mitchell, OBE and Ishobel, *d* of late James Ross, Broadford, Skye; *m* 1950, June Phylis Butcher; one *s* three *d. Educ:* Kelvinside Acad.; University of Edinburgh. MB, ChB Edinburgh, 1944. Surg-Lt, RNVR, 1944-47; Jun. hosp. posts, Liverpool, London, Edinburgh, 1947-52; Rockefeller Res. Fellow, Mayo Clinic, USA, 1952-53; Lectr in Child Health, Univ. of St Andrews, 1952-55; Cons. Pædiatrician, Dundee Teaching Hosps, 1955-63; Prof. of Child Health, Univ. of Aberdeen.

Pædiatrician, Royal Aberdeen Children's and Aberdeen Maternity Hosps, 1963-72. Chairman: Scottish Adv. Council on Child Care, 1966-69; Specialist Adv. Cttee on Pædiatrics, 1975-79; Academic Bd, British Pædiatric Assoc., 1975-78; Spastics Internat. Med. Pubns, 1981-. Pres., Harveian Soc., Edinburgh, 1982-83. For. Corresp. Mem., Amer. Acad. of Cerebral Palsy and Developmental Medicine. Jt Editor, Developmental Medicine and Child Neurology, 1968-80. *Publications:* Disease in Infancy and Childhood, (7th edn) 1973; Child Life and Health (5th edn), 1970; Child Health in the Community (2nd edn), 1980; contribs to textbooks of paediatrics, medicine and obstetrics and articles in scientific and medical jls. *Recreations:* Celtic language and literature, fishing. *Address:* Department of Child Health, The University, Dundee, Tayside.

MITCHELL, Sir (Seton) Steuart (Crichton), KBE 1954 (OBE 1941); CB 1951; *b* 9 March 1902; *s* of A. Crichton Mitchell, DSc, FRSE; *m* 1929, Elizabeth (*née* Duke); no *c. Educ:* Edinburgh Acad.; RN Colls, Osborne and Dartmouth. Joined Royal Navy as Cadet, 1916; at sea in HMS Hercules, Grand Fleet, 1918, subsequently served in HM Ships Ramillies, Sportive, Tomahawk, Marlborough; qualified as Gunnery Specialist, 1927-29, subsequently Gunnery Officer of HM Ships Comus and Frobisher; Naval Ordnance Inspection Dept and Asst Supt of Design, 1931-39; War of 1939-45, Inspector of Naval Ordnance, in charge of Admiralty Ordnance contracts in Switzerland, 1939-40, in USA, 1940-44; Chief Engineer and Supt, in charge of Armament Design Establishment, Min. of Supply, 1945; Controller, Guided Weapons and Electronics, Min. of Supply, 1951-56; Controller, Royal Ordnance Factories, 1956-59; Controller, Guided Weapons and Electronics, Ministry of Aviation, 1959-62; Mem., BTC, Feb.-Nov. 1962; Vice-Chm., British Railways Bd, Nov. 1962-64; Chairman: Machine Tool Industry EDC, 1964-; Shipbuilding Industry Trng Bd, 1964-; Mem., Central Trng Council, 1965-; Adviser (part-time) to Min. of Technology, 1965-; Mem. Scottish Economic Planning Council, 1965-67; Mem. Nat. Economic Develt Council, 1967-70. Chm., Carrier Engineering Co., 1968-70; Director: Parkinson Cowan Ltd, 1964-71; Plessey Numerical Controls Ltd, 1970-73. Officer Legion of Merit (USA), 1945. *Recreations:* music, gardening, antiques. *Address:* 137 Swan Court, Chelsea Manor Street, SW3 5RY. *T:* 01-352 5571.

MITCHELL, Sir Steuart Crichton; see Mitchell, Sir S. S. C.

MITCHELL, Warren; *b* 14 Jan. 1926; *s* of Montague and Annie Misell, later Mitchell; *m* 1952, Constance Wake; three *s. Educ:* Southgate Co. Sch.; University Coll., Oxford; RADA. Demobbed RAF, 1946. First professional appearance, Finsbury Park Open Air Theatre, 1950; Theophile in Can-Can, Coliseum, 1954; Crookfinger Jake in The Threepenny Opera, Royal Court and Aldwych, 1956; Mr Godboy in Dutch Uncle, Aldwych, 1969; Satan in Council of Love, Criterion, 1970; Herbert in Jump, Queen's, 1971; Ion Will in The Great Caper, Royal Court, 1974; The Thoughts of Chairman Alf, Stratford E, 1976; Willie Loman in Death of a Salesman, Nat. Theatre, 1979; *films include :* Diamonds Before Breakfast; Assassination Bureau; Best House in London; Till Death Us Do Part; Moon Zero Two; Whatever Happened to Charlie Farthing; Jabberwocky; Stand Up Virgin Soldiers; Meetings with Remarkable Men; Norman Loves Rose; *television:* Alf Garnett in Till Death Us Do Part, BBC, 1966-78; Shylock in Merchant of Venice, BBC, 1981; Till Death, ITV, 1981; The Caretaker, BBC, 1981. TV Actor of the Year Award, Guild of Film and TV Producers, 1966; Actor of Year Award: Evening Standard, 1979; Soc. of West End Theatres, 1979; Plays and Players, 1979. *Recreations:* sailing, tennis, playing clarinet. *Address:* c/o Plunket Greene Ltd, 91 Regent Street, W1.

MITCHELL, William Eric Marcus, MC; MB; BS London; FRCS; FRCSC; MRCP; DPH; Surgeon, genito-urinary specialist, Consulting Surgeon, Royal Jubilee Hospital, Victoria, BC, retired; *b* 29 April 1897; *e s* of Dr J. F. Mitchell, formerly of Bangor, Co. Down; *m* 1922, Catherine, *d* of W. F. Hamilton, of Ashwick, NZ; one *d*; *m* 1958, Margery, *d* of D. O. Thomas, Victoria, BC. *Educ:* Campbell Coll., Belfast; St Bartholomew's Hosp., University of London. Served as a Lt with the 11th Battalion Royal Irish Rifles in France, 1916 (wounded, MC); various prizes during sch. and Univ. career; House Surg., St Bartholomew's Hosp.; Chief Asst to a Surgical Unit, St Bartholomew's Hosp.; Clinical Asst, St Peter's Hosp., London; Pres., Abernethian Soc., St Bartholomew's Hosp. War of 1939-45, Lt-Col RAMC, Officer in Charge Surgical Div. No 13 Gen. Hosp. MEF. *Publications:* Health, Wealth and Happiness, 1969; numerous papers on surgical subjects published in the Lancet, the Canadian Medical Association Journal, St Bartholomew's Hospital Journal. *Recreations:* fishing, ski-ing, mountaineering. *Address:* 2171 Granite Street, Oak Bay, Victoria, BC, Canada. *TA:* Victoria, BC. *Club:* Alpine Club of Canada.

MITCHELL, Rt. Rev. Mgr. William Joseph; Rector, Pontifical Beda College, Rome, since 1978; *b* 4 Jan. 1936; *s* of William Ernest and Catherine Mitchell. *Educ:* St Brendan's Coll., Bristol; Corpus Christi Coll., Oxford (MA); Séminaire S Sulpice, Paris; Gregorian Univ., Rome (LCL). Ordained Priest, Pro-Cathedral, Bristol, 1961; Curate, Pro-Cathedral, Bristol, 1963-64; Secretary to Bishop of Clifton, 1964-75; Parish Priest, St Bernadette, Bristol, 1975-78. Prelate of Honour, 1978. *Address:* Pontificio Collegio Beda, Viale di S Paolo 18, 00146 Rome. *T:* Rome 5561700; Loretto, 4 Stonehill, Hanham, Bristol BS15 3HL. *T:* Bristol 674306.

MITCHELL COTTS, Sir R. C.; see Cotts.

MITCHELL-THOMSON, family name of **Baron Selsdon.**

MITCHENSON, Francis Joseph Blackett, (Joe Mitchenson); Joint Founder and Director, The Raymond Mander and Joe Mitchenson Theatre Collection, since 1939 (Theatre Collection Trust, since 1977); *b* 4 Oct.; *s* of Francis William Mitchenson and Sarah Roddam. *Educ:* privately; Fay Compton Studio of Dramatic Art. First appeared on stage professionally in Libel, Playhouse, London, 1934; acted in repertory, on tour and in London, until 1948. With Raymond Mander, founded Theatre Collection, 1939; War Service with Royal Horse Artillery, invalided out, 1943; returned to stage, and collab. with Raymond Mander on many BBC progs. Collection subject of an Aquarius programme, 1971; many TV appearances on theatrical subjects; many theatrical exhbns, incl. 50 Years of British Stage Design, for British Council, USSR, 1979. Archivist to: Sadler's Wells; Old Vic. Mem., Soc. of West End Theatre Awards Panel, 1976-78. *Publications:* with Raymond Mander: Hamlet Through the Ages, 1952 (2nd rev. edn 1955); Theatrical Companion to Shaw, 1954; Theatrical Companion to Maugham, 1955; The Artist and the Theatre, 1955; Theatrical Companion to Coward, 1957; A Picture History of British Theatre, 1957; (with J. C. Trewin) The Gay Twenties, 1958; (with Philip Hope-Wallace) A Picture History of Opera, 1959; (with J. C. Trewin) The Turbulent Thirties, 1960; The Theatres of London, 1961, illus. by Timothy Birdsall (2nd rev. edn, paperback, 1963; 3rd rev. edn 1975); A Picture History of Gilbert and Sullivan, 1962; British Music Hall: A Story in Pictures, 1965 (rev. and enlarged edn 1974); Lost Theatres of London, 1968 (2nd edn, rev. and enlarged, 1976); Musical Comedy: A Story in Pictures, 1969; Revue: A Story in Pictures, 1971; Pantomime: A Story in Pictures, 1973; The Wagner Companion, 1977; Victorian and Edwardian Entertainment from Old Photographs, 1978; Introd. to Plays, by Noël Coward (4 vols), 1979; Guide to the W. Somerset Maugham Theatrical Paintings, 1980; contribs to and revs in Encyc. Britannica, Theatre Notebook, and Books and Bookmen. *Recreations:* collecting anything and everything theatrical, sun bathing. *Address:* 5 Venner Road, Sydenham, SE26 5EQ. *T:* 01-778 6730.

MITCHISON, Avrion; see Mitchison, N. A.

MITCHISON, Dr Denis Anthony; Professor of Bacteriology, Royal Postgraduate Medical School, since 1971; Director, Medical Research Council's Unit for Laboratory Studies of Tuberculosis, since 1956; *b* 6 Sept. 1919; *e s* of Baron Mitchison, CBE, QC, and of Naomi Margaret Mitchison, *qv* ; *m* 1940, Ruth Sylvia, *d* of Hubert Gill; two *s* two *d. Educ:* Abbotsholme Sch.; Trinity Coll., Cambridge; University Coll. Hosp., London (MB, ChB). House Physician Addenbrooke's Hosp., Royal Berkshire Hosp.; Asst to Pathologist, Brompton Hosp.; Prof. of Bacteriology (Infectious Diseases), RPGMS, 1968-71. FRCP; FRCPath. *Publications:* numerous papers on bacteriology and chemotherapy of tuberculosis. *Recreation:* computer programming. *Address:* 14 Marlborough Road, Richmond, Surrey. *T:* 01-940 4751.

See also J. M. Mitchison, N. A. Mitchison.

MITCHISON, Prof. John Murdoch, ScD; FRS 1978; FRSE 1966; Professor of Zoology, University of Edinburgh, since 1963; *b* 11 June 1922; *s* of Lord Mitchison, CBE, QC, and of N. Haldane (see Naomi M. Mitchison); *m* 1947, Rosalind Mary Wrong; one *s* three *d. Educ:* Winchester Coll.; Trinity Coll., Cambridge. Army Operational Research, 1941-46; Sen. and Research Scholar, Trinity Coll., Cambridge, 1946-50; Fellow, Trinity Coll., Cambridge, 1950-54; Lectr in Zoology, Edinburgh, 1953-59; Reader in Zoology, Edinburgh, 1959-62. J. W. Jenkinson Memorial Lectr, Oxford, 1971-72. Member: Edinburgh Univ. Court, 1971-74; Council, Scottish Marine Biol. Assoc., 1961-67; Exec. Cttee, Internat. Soc. for Cell Biology, 1964-72; Biol Cttee, SRC, 1972-75; Royal Commn on Environmental Pollution, 1974-79; Science Bd, SRC, 1976-79; Working Gp on Biol Manpower, DES, 1968-71; Adv. Cttee on Safety of Nuclear Installations, Health and Safety Exec., 1981-. Pres., British Soc. for Cell Biology, 1974-77. FInstBiol 1963. *Publications:* The Biology of the Cell Cycle, 1971; papers in scientific jls. *Address:* Great Yew, Ormiston, East Lothian EH35 5NJ. *T:* Pencaitland 340530.

See also D. A. Mitchison, N. A. Mitchison.

MITCHISON, Naomi Margaret, (Lady Mitchison since 1964, but she still wishes to be called Naomi Mitchison); *b* Edinburgh, 1 Nov. 1897; *d* of late John Scott Haldane, CH, FRS, and Kathleen Trotter; *m* 1916, G. R. Mitchison (*d* 1970), CBE, QC, created a Baron (Life Peer), 1964; three *s* two *d. Educ:* Dragon Sch., Oxford; home student, Oxford. Officier d'Académie Française, 1924; Argyll CC, 1945-65, on and off; Highland and Island Advisory Panel, 1947-65; Highlands and Islands Develt Consult. Council, 1966-76; Tribal Mother to Bakgatla, Botswana, 1963-. DUniv. Stirling, 1976. Hon. Fellow St Anne's Coll., Oxford, 1980. *Publications:* The Conquered, 1923; When the Bough Breaks, 1924; Cloud Cuckoo Land, 1925; The Laburnum Branch, 1926; Black Sparta, 1928; Anna Comnena, 1928; Nix-Nought-Nothing, 1928; Barbarian Stories, 1929; The Hostages, 1930; Comments on Birth Control, 1930; The Corn King and the Spring Queen, 1931; The Price of Freedom (with L. E. Gielgud), 1931; Boys and Girls and Gods, 1931; The Powers of Light, edited an Outline for Boys and Girls, 1932; The Delicate Fire, 1933; Vienna Diary, 1934; The Home, 1934; We Have Been Warned, 1935; Beyond this Limit, 1935; The Fourth Pig, 1936; Socrates (with R. H. S. Crossman), 1937; An End and a Beginning, 1937; The Moral Basis of Politics, 1938; The Kingdom of Heaven, 1939; As It was in the Beginning (with L. E. Gielgud), 1939; The Blood of the Martyrs, 1939; (ed) Re-educating Scotland, 1944; The

Bull Calves, 1947; Men and Herring (with D. Macintosh), 1949; The Big House, 1950; Spindrift (play: with D. Macintosh), Citizens' Theatre, Glasgow, 1951; Lobsters on the Agenda, 1952; Travel Light, 1952; The Swan's Road, 1954; Graeme and the Dragon, 1954; The Land the Ravens Found, 1955; To the Chapel Perilous, 1955; Little Boxes, 1956; Behold your King, 1957; The Far Harbour, 1957; Five Men and a Swan, 1958; Other People's Worlds, 1958; Judy and Lakshmi, 1959; The Rib of the Green Umbrella, 1960; The Young Alexander, 1960; Karensgaard, 1961; The Young Alfred the Great, 1962; Memoirs of a Space Woman, 1962; (ed) What the Human Race is Up To, 1962; The Fairy who Couldn't Tell a Lie, 1963; When we Become Men, 1965; Ketse and the Chief, 1965; Return to the Fairy Hill, 1966; Friends and Enemies, 1966; The Big Surprise, 1967; African Heroes, 1968; Don't Look Back, 1969; The Family at Ditlabeng, 1969; The Africans: a history, 1970; Sun and Moon, 1970; Cleopatra's People, 1972; A Danish Teapot, 1973; Sunrise Tomorrow, 1973; Small Talk: memoirs of an Edwardian childhood (autobiog.), 1973; A Life for Africa, 1973; Oil for the Highlands?, 1974; All Change Here (autobiog.), 1975; Solution Three, 1975; Snake!, 1976; The Two Magicians, 1979; The Cleansing of the Knife, 1979; You May Well Ask (autobiog.), 1979; Images of Africa, 1980; The Vegetable War, 1980; Mucking Around, 1980; What Do You Think Yourself, Scottish stories, 1982. Recreation: burning rubbish. Address: Carradale House, Carradale, Campbeltown, Scotland.

See also D. A. Mitchison, J. M. Mitchison, N. A. Mitchison.

MITCHISON, Prof. (Nicholas) Avrion, FRS 1967; Jodrell Professor of Zoology and Comparative Anatomy, University College, London, since 1970; b 5 May 1928; 3rd s of Baron Mitchison, CBE, QC, and of Naomi Margaret Mitchison, qv; m 1957, Lorna Margaret, d of Maj.-Gen. J. S. S. Martin, CSI; two s three d. Educ: Leighton Park Sch.; New Coll., Oxford (MA 1949). Fellow of Magdalen College, 1952; Commonwealth Fund Fellow, 1952-54; Lecturer, Edinburgh Univ., 1954-61; Reader, Edinburgh Univ., 1961-62; Head of Div. of Experimental Biology, Nat. Inst. for Med. Research, 1962-71. Hon. MD Edinburgh, 1977. Publications: articles in scientific journals. Address: 14 Belitha Villas, N1.

See also D. A. Mitchison, J. M. Mitchison.

MITFORD, family name of **Baron Redesdale.**

MITFORD, Jessica Lucy, (Mrs Jessica Treuhaft); author; b 11 Sept. 1917; d of 2nd Baron Redesdale; m 1st, Esmond Marcus David Romilly (d 1942); one d; 2nd, 1943, Robert Edward Treuhaft; one s. Distinguished Prof., San José State Univ., Calif, 1973-74. Publications: (as Jessica Mitford): Hons and Rebels, 1960; The American Way of Death, 1963; The Trial of Dr Spock, 1969; Kind and Usual Punishment, 1974; The American Prison Business, 1975; A Fine Old Conflict, 1977; The Making of a Muckraker, 1979. Address: 6411 Regent Street, Oakland, Calif 94618, USA.

MITFORD, Rupert Leo Scott B.; see Bruce-Mitford.

MITFORD-SLADE, Col Cecil Townley; b 19 April 1903; s of late Col William Kenyon Mitford, CMG, CVO; assumed additional name of Slade by deed poll, 1941; m 1931, Phyllis, d of late E. G. Buxton; two s one d. Educ: Eton; RMC; joined 60th Rifles, 1923; psc† 1938-39; Gen. Staff, GHQ BEF, 1940; Jt planning, WO, 1941; Gibraltar, 1942-43; comd 8th Bn KRRC, 1943-44; Burma, 1944-45; Palestine, 1946-47; 1st Bn KRRC, 1948-50; Comdt, WRAC Staff Coll., 1951; HM Bodyguard of Hon. Corps of Gentlemen-at-Arms, 1952-73. DL, Somerset, 1955-66, 1978; JP, 1953; CC, 1955; High Sheriff, 1963; Vice-Lieut, 1966-68; Lord-Lieutenant, 1968-78; Hon. County Alderman, 1978. County Comr, St John Amb. Bde, 1954-68; Chm., Taunton Race Course Co. KStJ; Order of Mercy. Recreations: shooting, fishing. Address: Montys Court, Taunton, Somerset. T: Bishop's Lydeard 432255. Club: Naval and Military.

See also P. B. Mitford-Slade.

MITFORD-SLADE, Patrick Buxton; Partner, Cazenove & Co., since 1972; Deputy Chairman, The Stock Exchange, since 1982; b 7 Sept. 1936; s of Col Cecil Townley Mitford-Slade, qv; m 1964, Anne Catharine Stanton, d of Major Arthur Holbrow Stanton, MBE; one s two d. Educ: Eton Coll.; RMA Sandhurst. Commissioned 60th Rifles, 1955, Captain; served Libya, NI, Berlin and British Guyana; Adjt, 1st Bn The Royal Green Jackets, 1962-65; Instructor, RMA Sandhurst, 1965-67. Stockbroker, Cazenove & Co., 1968-. Asst Sec., Panel on Takeovers and Mergers, 1970-72; Mem., Stock Exchange, 1972- (Mem. Council, 1976-). Recreations: shooting, fishing. Address: Damales House, Hartley Wintney, Basingstoke, Hants. Clubs: City of London, Naval and Military.

MITHEN, Dallas Alfred; Commissioner for Harvesting and Marketing, Forestry Commission, since 1977; b 5 Nov. 1923; m 1st, 1947, Peggy (née Clarke) (decd); one s one d; 2nd, 1969, Avril Teresa Dodd (née Stein). Educ: Maidstone Grammar Sch.; UC of N Wales, Bangor. BSc (Forestry). Fleet Air Arm, 1942-46. Joined Forestry Commission as District Officer, 1950; Dep. Surveyor, New Forest and Conservator SE (England), 1968-71; Senior Officer (Scotland), 1971-75; Head of Forest Management Div., Edinburgh, 1975-76. Recreations: cricket, swimming, sailing, walking. Address: Kings Knot, Bonnington Road, Peebles EH45 9HF. T: Peebles 20738.

MITMAN, Frederick S., CBE 1941; b 21 April 1900; s of late William and Elizabeth Mitman; m 1925, Helen McNary; one s one d. Educ: Lehigh Univ.,

USA (Deg. of Engineer of Mines, 1923). Dir of Light Alloys and Magnesium (Sheet and Strip) Control, Ministry of Aircraft Production, 1939-41; Co-ordinator of Aircraft Supplies for Fighter and Naval Aircraft, Ministry of Aircraft Production, 1940-41; Adviser on Light Metals Fabrication, Ministry of Aircraft Production, 1941-42. Address: 10 Campden House Close, Kensington, W8. T: 01-937 9071.

MITSAKIS, Prof. Kariofilis; Professor of Modern Greek Literature, University of Athens, since 1978; b 12 May 1932; s of Christos and Crystalli Mitsakis; m 1966, Anthoula Chalkia; two s. Educ: Univs of Thessaloniki (BA, PhD), Oxford (MA, DPhil) and Munich. Scientific Collaborator, National Research Foundn of Greece, 1959-62; Associate Prof. of Byzantine and Modern Greek Literature, Univ. of Maryland, 1966-68; Chm. of Dept of Comparative Literature, Univ. of Maryland, 1967-68; Sotheby and Bywater Prof. of Byzantine and Modern Greek Language and Literature, Univ. of Oxford, 1968-72; Prof. of Modern Greek Lit., Univ. of Thessaloniki, 1972-75; Dir, Inst. for Balkan Studies, Thessaloniki, 1972-80. Publications: Problems Concerning the Text, the Sources and the Dating of the Achilleid, 1962 (in Greek); The Greek Sonnet, 1962 (in Greek); The Language of Romanos the Melodist, 1967 (in English); The Byzantine Romance from the Cod. Vindob. theol. gr. 244, 1967 (in German); Byzantine Hymnography, 1971 (in Greek); Petrarchism in Greece, 1973 (in Greek); Introduction to Modern Greek Literature, 1973 (in Greek); Homer in Modern Greek Literature, 1976 (in Greek); George Viziynos, 1977 (in Greek); Modern Greek Prose: the generation of the '30s, 1978 (in Greek); Modern Greek Music and Poetry, 1979 (in Greek and English); contribs to Balkan Studies, Byzantinisch-Neugriechische Jahrbücher, Byzantinische Zeitschrift, Comparative Literature Studies, Diptycha, Etudes Byzantines–Byzantine Studies, Glotta, Hellenika, Jahrbuch der Oesterreichischen Byzantinischen Gesellschaft, Nea Hestia, etc. Recreations: music, travelling. Address: University of Athens, Faculty of Philosophy, 33 Hippocratous Street, Athens 144, Greece.

MITTERRAND, François Maurice Marie; Grande Croix de l'Ordre National de la Légion d'Honneur; Croix de Guerre (1939-45); President of the French Republic, since 1981; advocate; b Jarnac, Charente, 26 Oct. 1916; s of Joseph Mitterrand and Yvonne (née Lorrain); m 1944, Danielle Gouze; two s. Educ: Coll. Saint-Paul, Angoulême; Facultés de droit et des lettres, Univ. of Paris. Licencié en droit, Lic. ès lettres; Dip. d'études supérieures de droit public. Served War, 1939-40 (prisoner, escaped; Rosette de la Résistance). Missions to London and to Algiers, 1943; Sec.-Gen., Organisation for Prisoners of War, War Victims and Refugees, 1944-46. Deputy from Nièvre, 1946-58 and 1962-81; Minister for Ex-Servicemen, 1947-48; Sec. of State for Information, attached Prime Minister's Office, 1948-49; Minister for Overseas Territories, 1950-51; Chm., UDSR, 1951-52; Minister of State, Jan.-Feb. 1952 and March 1952-July 1953; Deleg. to Council of Europe, July-Sept. 1953; Minister of the Interior, June 1954-Feb. 1955; Minister of State, 1956-57; Senator, 1959-62; Candidate for Presidency of France, 1965, 1974; Pres., Fedn of Democratic and Socialist Left, 1965-68; First Sec., Socialist Party, 1971-81. Vice-Pres., Socialist International, 1972-. Pres., Conseil général de la Nièvre, 1964-. Publications: Aux frontières de l'Union française; La Chine au défi, 1961; Le Coup d'Etat permanent, 1964; Ma part de vérité, 1969; Un socialisme du possible, 1971; La rose au poing, 1973; La paille et le grain, 1975; Politique, 1977; l'Abeille et l'Architecte, 1978; Ici et Maintenant, 1980; numerous contribs to the Press. Recreation: tennis. Address: Palais de l'Elysée, 75008 Paris, France; (private) 22 rue de Bièvre, 75005 Paris, France.

MITTLER, Prof. Peter Joseph, CBE 1981; MA, PhD, MEd; FBPsS; Director, Hester Adrian Research Centre, since 1968, and Professor of Special Education, since 1973, University of Manchester; b 2 April 1930; s of Dr Gustav Mittler and Gertrude Mittler; m 1955, Helle Katscher; three s. Educ: Merchant Taylors' Sch., Crosby; Pembroke Coll., Cambridge (MA); PhD London; MEd Manchester. Clinical Psychologist, Warneford and Park Hosps, Oxford, 1954-58; Principal Psychologist, Reading Area Psychiatric Hosps, 1958-63; Lectr in Psychology, Birkbeck Coll., Univ. of London, 1963-68. Chm., Nat Develt Gp for Mentally Handicapped, 1975-80; Vice-Pres., Internat. League of Socs for Persons with Mental Handicap, 1978-. Publications: ed, Psychological Assessment of Mental and Physical Handicaps, 1970; The Study of Twins, 1971; ed, Assessment for Learning in the Mentally Handicapped, 1973; ed, Research to Practice in Mental Retardation (3 vols), 1977; People not Patients, 1979; (jtly) Teaching Language and Communication to the Mentally Handicapped, (Schools Council), 1979; (ed jtly) Advances in Mental Handicap Research, 1980; (ed) Frontiers of Knowledge in Mental Retardation (2 vols), 1981; (ed jtly) Approaches to Partnership: professionals and parents of mentally handicapped people, 1982; papers in medical and educnl jls. Recreations: music, travel. Address: 3 Dorset Avenue, Bramhall, Stockport SK7 3NU. T: 061-485 6491.

MITTON, Rev. Dr Charles Leslie, BA; MTh; PhD; Principal of Handsworth College, Birmingham, 1955-70 (Tutor, 1951-55); b 13 Feb. 1907; s of Rev. Charles W. Mitton, Bradford, Yorks; m 1937, Margaret J. Ramage; one s one d. Educ: Kingswood Sch., Bath; Manchester Univ.; Didsbury Coll., Manchester. Asst Tutor at Wesley Coll., Headingley, 1930-33; Minister in Methodist Church at: Dunbar, 1933-36; Keighley, 1936-39; Scunthorpe, 1939-45; Nottingham, 1945-51; Tutor in New Testament Studies at Handsworth Coll., Birmingham, 1951-70. Editor of Expository Times, 1965-76. Hon. DD, Aberdeen Univ., 1964. Publications: The Epistle to the Ephesians: Authorship, Origin and Purpose, 1951; Pauline Corpus of Letters,

1954; Preachers' Commentary on St Mark's Gospel, 1956; The Good News, 1961; The Epistle of James, 1966; Jesus: the fact behind the faith, 1974; The Epistle to the Ephesians: a commentary, 1976; Your Kingdom Come, 1978. *Recreations:* Rugby football, Association football, cricket, tennis. *Address:* 14 Cranbrook Road, Handsworth, Birmingham B21 8PJ. *T:* 021-554 7892.

MKONA, Callisto Matekenya, DSM (Malaŵi) 1966; High Commissioner for Malaŵi in London, since 1981; *b* 4 June 1930; *s* of late Benedicto Mkona and of Martha Matekenya Mkona; *m* 1971, Helen Victoria (*née* Sazuze); two *s* two *d. Educ:* Zomba, Malaŵi; Urbanian Univ., Rome (DCL, Dip. Soc. Scis). Secondary School teacher, 1962-64; Mission Educn Liaison Officer, 1964-67; Educn Attaché (First Sec.), Washington and London, 1967-71; Ambassador to Ethiopia, 1971-72; Minister, Washington, 1972-73; High Comr in Zambia, 1973-75; Ambassador in Bonn, 1975-78; Dep. Principal Sec., Min. of External Affairs, 1978-79; Principal Sec., Office of the President and Cabinet, 1979-81. *Recreations:* reading, walking. *Address:* Malaŵi High Commission, 33 Grosvenor Street, W1X 0DE. *T:* 01-491 4172.

MOATE, Roger Denis; MP (C) Faversham since 1970; Insurance Broker; Director, Alexander Howden Insurance Brokers Ltd; *b* 12 May 1938; *m* 1960, Hazel Joy Skinner; one *s* one *d. Educ:* Latymer Upper Sch., Hammersmith. Joined Young Conservative Movement, in Brentford and Chiswick, 1954: Vice-Chm., Greater London area Young Conservatives, 1964; contested (C) Faversham, Gen. Elec., 1966. *Recreation:* skiing. *Address:* House of Commons, SW1; 23 Ponsonby Terrace, SW1.

MOBBS, (Gerald) Nigel; Chairman and Chief Executive, Slough Estates plc, since 1976; Chairman, Charterhouse Group plc, since 1977 (Director, since 1974); Director, Barclays Bank Trust Co. Ltd, since 1973; *b* 22 Sept. 1937; *s* of Gerald Aubrey Mobbs and Elizabeth (*née* Lanchester); *m* 1961, Hon. Pamela Jane Marguerite Berry, 2nd *d* of 2nd Viscount Kemsley, *qv*; one *s* twin *d. Educ:* Marlborough Coll.; Christ Church, Oxford. Joined Slough Estates plc, 1961; Director, 1963, Man. Dir, 1971. Dir, Barclays Bank PLC, 1979-. Chairman: Slough Industrial Health Service, 1976-; Slough Social Fund, 1975-; Property Services Agency Adv. Bd, 1981-; Pres., Slough & Dist Chamber of Commerce, 1969-72; Vice-Pres., Assoc. of British Chambers of Commerce, 1976- (Chm. 1974-76); Pres., British Property Fedn, 1979-81. High Sheriff, Bucks, 1982. *Recreations:* riding, hunting, travel. *Address:* Widmer Lodge, Lacey Green, Aylesbury, Bucks HP17 0RJ. *T:* Hampden Row 265.

MOBERLY, John Campbell, CMG 1976; HM Diplomatic Service; Ambassador to Iraq, since 1982; *b* 27 May 1925; *s* of Sir Walter Moberly, GBE, KCB, DSO; *m* 1959, Patience, *d* of Major Sir Richard George Proby, 1st Bt, MC; two *s* one *d. Educ:* Winchester College; Magdalen College, Oxford. War Service in Royal Navy, 1943-47 (despatches). Entered HM Foreign (now Diplomatic) Service, 1950; Political Officer, Kuwait, 1954-56; Political Agent, Doha, 1959-62; First Secretary, Athens, 1962-66; Counsellor, Washington, 1969-73; Dir, Middle East Centre for Arab Studies, 1973-75; Ambassador, Jordan, 1975-79; Asst Under-Sec. of State, FCO, 1979-82. CStJ 1979. *Recreations:* mountain walking and climbing, skiing, swimming. *Address:* c/o Foreign and Commonwealth Office, SW1; The Cedars, Temple Sowerby, Penrith, Cumbria. *T:* Kirkby Thore 437. *Clubs:* Travellers', Royal Automobile; Leander (Henley-on-Thames).

MOBERLY, Patrick Hamilton, CMG 1978; HM Diplomatic Service; Ambassador to Israel, since 1981; *b* 2 Sept. 1928; *yr s* of G. H. Moberly; *m* 1955, Mary Penfold; two *s* one *d. Educ:* Winchester; Trinity Coll., Oxford (MA). HM Diplomatic Service, 1951-; diplomatic posts in: Baghdad, 1953; Prague, 1957; Foreign Office, 1959; Dakar, 1962; Min. of Defence, 1965; Commonwealth Office, 1967; Canada, 1969; Israel, 1970; FCO, 1974; Asst Under-Sec. of State, 1976-81. *Recreations:* sailing, opera. *Address:* c/o Foreign and Commonwealth Office, SW1A 2AH. *Club:* United Oxford & Cambridge University.

MOBERLY, Maj.-Gen. Richard James, CB 1957; OBE 1944; retired, 1960, and became Director, Communications Electronic Equipment, War Office, until 1964; *b* 2 July 1906; *o s* of late J. E. Moberly; *m* 1st, 1935, Mary Joyce Shelmerdine (*d* 1964); three *d*; 2nd, 1971, Mrs Vivien Mary Cameron (*d* 1981), *d* of Victor Bayley, CIE, CBE. *Educ:* Haileybury; Royal Military Academy, Woolwich. Commissioned Royal Signals, 1926; India, 1928-35; comd 1st Airborne Div. Signal Regt, 1942-43; CSO 1st Airborne Corps, 1943-45; Comdt Indian Signal Trng Centre, 1946-47; Dep. Comdt, Sch. of Signals, 1949-52; Dep. Dir of Signals, WO, 1952-54; CSO, Northern Army Gp, 1954-57; Signal Officer-in-Chief, War Office, 1957-60. Col Comdt, Royal Signals, 1960-66. Comr for Dorset, St John Ambulance, 1968-76. CStJ 1974. *Address:* Steeple Cottage, Westport Road, Wareham, Dorset BH20 4PR. *T:* Wareham 2697.

MOCATTA, Sir Alan Abraham, Kt 1961; OBE 1944; Judge of the High Court of Justice (Queen's Bench Division), since 1961; Member, 1961-81, President, 1970-81, Restrictive Practices Court; *b* 1907; *s* of Edward L. Mocatta and Flora Gubbay; *m* 1930, Pamela Halford, JP; four *s. Educ:* Clifton Coll.; New Coll., Oxford (exhbnr); 1st cl. History, 1928, 2nd cl. Jurisprudence, 1929; MA. Called to the Bar, Inner Temple, 1930; Bencher, 1960, Treas., 1982; Northern circuit; QC 1951. Served War of 1939-45: 2nd Lieut 12 LAA Regt, RA, TA, 1939; Bde Major, 56 AA Bde, 1940-41; GSO (2) AA HQ BTNI, 1941-42; Lt-Col GS, Army Council Secretariat, War

Office, 1942-45. Chm., Council of Jews' Coll., 1945-61; Vice-Pres., Board of Elders, Spanish and Portuguese Jews' Congregation, London, 1961-67, Pres., 1967-82; Chm. Treasury Cttee on Cheque Endorsement, 1955-56. Joint editor, 14th-18th editions of Scrutton on Charter parties; Editor, 3rd edn Rowlatt on Principal and Surety. *Address:* 18 Hanover House, NW8 7DX. *T:* 01-722 2857; 10 Breakwater Road, Bude, Cornwall. *T:* Bude 2745. *Club:* MCC.

MOERAN, Edward Warner; *b* 27 Nov. 1903; *s* of E. J. Moeran. *Educ:* Christ's Coll., Finchley; University of London. Solicitor. MP (Lab) South Beds, 1950-51. Pres., W London Law Soc., 1970-71. Chm., Solicitors' Ecology Gp, 1972-74. *Publications:* Practical Conveyancing, 1949; Invitation to Conveyancing, 1962; Practical Legal Aid, 1970; (jtly) Social Welfare Law, 1977; Legal Aid Summary, 1978; Introduction to Conveyancing, 1979. *Recreation:* carpentry. *Address:* 6 Frognal Gardens, Hampstead, NW3 6UX.

MOFFAT, Sir John Smith, Kt 1955; OBE 1944; MLC Northern Rhodesia, 1951-64; Member Federal Parliament, Salisbury, 1954-62; *b* N Rhodesia, April 1905; *s* of Rev. Malcolm Moffat; *m* 1930, Margaret Prentice; two *d. Educ:* Grey High Sch., Port Elizabeth, South Africa; Glasgow Univ. Cadet Northern Rhodesia Provincial Administration, 1927; District Officer, 1929. Served at Serenje, Fort Jameson, etc. Commissioner for National Development, 1945; retd from CS, 1951. Chm. Federal African Affairs Board, and leader Liberal Party until 1962, when disbanded. Farmer. *Address:* Kulinda, RD3, Whangarei, North Island, New Zealand.

MOFFATT, Prof. Henry Keith, PhD; Professor of Mathematical Physics, University of Cambridge, since 1980; Fellow, Trinity College, Cambridge, 1961-76, and since 1980; *b* 12 April 1935; *s* of Frederick Henry Moffatt and Emmeline Marchant Fleming; *m* 1960, Katharine Stiven; two *s* two *d. Educ:* George Watson's Coll., Edinburgh; Edinburgh Univ. (BSc); Cambridge Univ. (BA, PhD). Lecturer in Mathematics, Cambridge Univ., and Director of Studies in Mathematics, Trinity Coll., 1961-76; Tutor, 1971-75; Sen. Tutor, 1975; Professor of Applied Mathematics, Bristol Univ., 1977-80. Visiting appts, Stanford Univ. and Johns Hopkins Univ., 1965, Univ. of Paris VI, 1975-76. Co-editor, Journal of Fluid Mechanics, 1966-. *Publications:* Magnetic Field Generation in Electrically Conducting Fluids, 1978 (Russian edn 1980); papers in fluid mechanics and dynamo theory in Jl Fluid Mech. and other jls. *Recreations:* baking and brewing. *Address:* 6 Banham's Close, Cambridge. *T:* Cambridge 63338.

MOGG, Gen. Sir John, GCB 1972 (KCB 1966; CB 1964); CBE 1960; DSO 1944; Bar, 1944; Vice Lord-Lieutenant, Oxfordshire, since 1979; Deputy Supreme Allied Commander, Europe, 1973-76; *b* 17 Feb. 1913; *s* of late Capt. H. B. Mogg, MC and late Alice Mary (*née* Ballard); *m* 1939, Cecilia Margaret Molesworth; three *s. Educ:* Malvern Coll.; RMC Sandhurst. Coldstream Guards, 1933-35; RMC Sandhurst (Sword of Honour) 1935-37; commissioned Oxfordshire and Buckinghamshire Light Infantry, 1937. Served War of 1939-45 (despatches); comd 9 DLI (NW Europe), 1944-45; Instructor, Staff Coll., 1948-50; Commander 10th Parachute Bn, 1950-52; Chief Instructor, School of Infantry, Warminster, 1952-54; Instructor (GSO1), Imperial Defence Coll., 1954-56; Comdr, Commonwealth Brigade Gp, Malaya, 1958-60; Meritorious Medal (Perak, Malaya); Dir of Combat Development, War Office, 1961-62; Comdt, Royal Military Academy, Sandhurst, 1963-66; Comdr 1st (British) Corps, 1966-68; GOC-in-C Southern Comd, 1968; GOC-in-C Army Strategic Comd, 1968-70; Adjutant-Gen., MoD (Army), 1970-73. ADC Gen. to the Queen, 1971-74. Col Comdt: Army Air Corps, 1963-74; The Royal Green Jackets, 1965-73; Hon. Col, 10th Parachute Bn, TA, 1973-78. Kermit Roosevelt Lectr, 1969. President: Army Cricket Assoc.; Army Saddle Club, 1969; Army Boxing Assoc., 1970; Army Parachute Assoc., 1971; BHS, 1972; Ex Services Mental Welfare Soc.; Army Benevolent Fund, 1980- (Chm., 1976); Chairman: Army Free Fall Parachute Assoc., 1970; Army Football Assoc., 1960-63; Royal Soldiers' Daughters Sch., 1976; Operation Drake for Young Explorers, 1978-; Royal Internat. Horse Show, 1979. Pres., Council Services Kinema Corp., 1970. Dir, Lloyds Bank S Midland Regional Bd, 1976. Member Council: Wessex TA&VRA, 1976; British Atlantic Cttee, 1977. Comr, Royal Hospital Chelsea, 1976. Governor: Malvern College, 1967; Bradfield College, 1977; Chm. of Governors, Icknield Sch., 1981-. Hon. Liveryman, Fruiterers' Co. DL Oxfordshire, 1979. *Recreations:* cricket, most field sports, helicopter pilot. *Address:* Church Close, Watlington, Oxon. *Clubs:* Army and Navy, Flyfishers', MCC, Cavalry and Guards, Pitt.

MOGG, Sir William R.; *see* Rees-Mogg.

MOI, Hon. Daniel arap, EGH, EBS; President of Kenya, since 1978; Minister of Defence, since 1979; *b* Rift Valley Province, 1924. *Educ:* African Inland Mission Sch., Kabartonjo; Govt African Sch., Kapsabet. Teacher, 1946-56. MLC, 1957; Mem. for Baringo, House of Representatives, 1963-78; Minister for Educn, 1961; Minister for Local Govt, 1962-64; Minister for Home Affairs, 1964-67; Vice-Pres. of Kenya, 1967-78. Chm., Kenya African Democratic Union (KADU), 1960; Pres., Kenya African Nat. Union (KANU) for Rift Valley Province, 1966; Pres. of KANU, 1978-. Chm., Rift Valley Provincial Council. Former Member: Rift Valley Educn Bd; Kalenjin Language Cttee; Commonwealth Higher Educn Cttee; Kenya Meat Commn; Bd of Governors, African Girls' High Sch., Kikuyu. *Address:* Office of the President, PO Box 30510, Nairobi, Kenya; State House, PO Box 40530, Nairobi, Kenya.

MOIR, Alan John, CMG 1971; *b* 19 July 1903; *s* of George Allen Moir and Louise Elvina Moir (*née* Evans); *m* 1929, Eileen Walker; one *s* one *d. Educ:* Scotch Coll., Melbourne; Univ. of Melbourne. Barrister and Solicitor, Supreme Court of Victoria. Partner, Gillott Moir & Ahern, 1929–63, retd. *Recreations:* racing, bowls. *Address:* 27 Hopetoun Road, Toorak, Victoria 3142, Australia. *T:* 20-5267. *Clubs:* Athenæum (Melbourne) (ex-Pres.); Victoria Racing, Victoria Amateur Turf, Moonee Valley Racing (ex-Chm.), Melbourne Cricket.

MOIR, Sir Ernest Ian Royds, 3rd Bt, *cr* 1916; *b* 9 June 1925; *o s* of Sir Arrol Moir, 2nd Bt, and Dorothy Blanche, *d* of Admiral Sir Percy Royds, CB, CMG; *S* father, 1957; *m* 1954, Margaret Hanham Carter; three *s. Educ:* Rugby; Cambridge Univ. (BA). Served War of 1939–45 in Royal Engineers. *Heir: s* Christopher Ernest Moir, *b* 22 May 1955. *Address:* Three Gates, 174 Coombe Lane West, Kingston, Surrey. *T:* 01-942 7394. *Club:* Royal Automobile.

MOIR, (George) Guthrie, MA; with Thames Television; *b* 30 Oct. 1917; *s* of James William and May Flora Moir; *m* 1951, Sheila Maureen Ryan, SRN; one *s* two *d. Educ:* Berkhamsted; Peterhouse, Cambridge. Officer, 5th Suffolk Regt, 1940–46, POW Singapore, 1942. Chief Officer, St John Ambulance Bde Cadets, 1947–50; Dir, European Youth Campaign, 1950–52; Chm., later Pres., World Assembly of Youth, 1952–56; Education Adviser, Hollerith Tab. Machine Co., 1957; Asst Controller and Exec. Producer, Rediffusion TV, 1958–68; Controller of Educn and Religious Programmes, Thames TV, 1968–76. Serious damage under train in Sept. 1974, and in hospitals till 1976. Member: Gen. Synod (formerly House of Laity, Church Assembly), 1956–75; Bd of Church Army, 1973–; Mem. Council, Reading Univ. Mem. Cttee Athenæum, 1974–. Contested (L) Aylesbury Div., 1950. CC Bucks, 1949–75; President: Old Berkhamstedians Assoc., 1974; Ivinghoe Beacon Villages, 1973. Vice Pres., St John, Bucks. Papal Bene Merenti Medal 1970, for services to religious and educational broadcasting. OStJ. *Publications:* (ed) Why I Believe, 1964; (ed) Life's Work, 1965; (ed) Teaching and Television: ETV Explained, 1967; The Suffolk Regiment, 1969; Into Television, 1969; (ed) Beyond Hatred, 1969; contribs to Times, Times Ed. Supplement, Church Times, Contemporary Review, Frontier, etc. Many TV series, including This Week; Dialogue with Doubt; Royalist and Roundhead; Best Sellers; Treasures of the British Museum; (with Nat. Trust) A Place in the Country; A Place in History; A Place in Europe. *Recreations:* golf, poetry, churches, mountains. *Address:* The Old Rectory, Aston Clinton, Aylesbury, Bucks. *T:* Aylesbury 630393. *Club:* Nikaean.

MOIR CAREY, D. M.; *see* Carey.

MOISEIWITSCH, Prof. Benjamin Lawrence; Professor of Applied Mathematics since 1968, and Head of Department of Applied Mathematics and Theoretical Physics since 1977, Queen's University of Belfast; *b* London, 6 Dec. 1927; *s* of Jacob Moiseiwitsch and Chana Kotlerman; *m* 1953, Sheelagh M. McKeon; two *s* two *d. Educ:* Royal Liberty Sch., Romford; University Coll., London (BSc, 1949, PhD 1952). Sir George Jessel Studentship in Maths, UCL, 1949; Queen's University, Belfast: Lectr and Reader in Applied Maths, 1952–68; Dean, Faculty of Science, 1972–75. MRIA 1969. *Publications:* Variational Principles, 1966; Integral Equations, 1977; articles on theoretical atomic physics in scientific jls. *Recreations:* music, books, walking in the Mourne Mountains. *Address:* 21 Knocktern Gardens, Belfast, Northern Ireland BT4 3LZ. *T:* Belfast 658332.

MOISEIWITSCH, Tanya, (Mrs Felix Krish), CBE 1976; designer for the theatre; *b* 3 Dec. 1914; *d* of late Benno Moiseiwitsch, CBE, and 1st wife, Daisy Kennedy; *m* 1942, Felix Krish (*decd*). *Educ:* various private schs; Central School of Arts and Crafts, London; Scenic painting student at Old Vic, London. Abbey Theatre, Dublin, 1935–39; Q. Theatre, 1940; 1st West End prod. Golden Cuckoo, Duchess, 1940; Weekly Repertory, Oxford Playhouse, 1941–44. Stage designs include: Bless the Bride, Adelphi, 1947; Peter Grimes, Covent Garden, 1947; Beggar's Opera, English Opera Group, Aldeburgh Festival, 1948; Treasure Hunt, Apollo, 1949; Home at Seven, Wyndham's, 1950; The Holly and the Ivy, Lyric (Hammersmith) and Duchess, 1950; Captain Carvallo, St James's, 1950; Figure of Fun, Aldwych, 1951. Has designed for Old Vic Company since 1944; at Playhouse, Liverpool, 1944–45; at Theatre Royal, Bristol, 1945–46; productions for Old Vic Company include: (at New Theatre): Uncle Vanya, The Critic, Cyrano de Bergerac, 1945–46, The Cherry Orchard, 1948, A Month in the Country, 1949; (at Old Vic): Midsummer Night's Dream, 1951, Timon of Athens, 1952, Henry VIII, 1953; Two Gentlemen of Verona, 1957. Has designed for Royal Shakespeare Theatre, Stratford upon Avon: Henry VIII, 1950; The History Cycle (assisted by Alix Stone), 1951; Othello, 1954; Measure for Measure, 1956; Much Ado about Nothing, 1958; All's Well that Ends Well, 1959; also for 1st, and subsequent seasons, Shakespearean Festival, Stratford, Ont; for The Matchmaker, Edinburgh Festival, 1954, and New York, 1955; for Cherry Orchard, Piccolo Teatro, Milan, 1955; for Merchant of Venice, Habimah Theatre, Israel, 1959; Tyrone Guthrie Theatre, Minneapolis, USA: 1963; Hamlet, The Miser, Three Sisters; 1964: St Joan, Volpone; 1965: The Way of the World; Cherry Orchard; 1966: As You Like It; Skin of our Teeth (with Carolyn Parker); 1967: The House of Atreus; Peter Grimes (Metropolitan Opera, New York), 1967; Volpone, Nat. Theatre, 1968; Macook's Corner, Ulster Players, Belfast, 1969; Caucasian Chalk Circle, Sheffield Playhouse, 1969; Swift, Abbey Theatre, Dublin, 1969; Uncle Vanya, Minneapolis, 1969; Cymbeline, Stratford, Ont., 1970; The Barber of Seville, Brighton Festival,

1971; cons. designer, Crucible Theatre, Sheffield, 1971–73; The Misanthrope, Nat. Theatre, 1973; The Government Inspector (with J. Jensen), USA, 1973; Australian Tour for Elizabethan Theatre Trust, 1974; The Imaginary Invalid, Stratford, Ont, 1974; The Misanthrope, St James' Theater, NY, 1975; Phaedra Britannica. Nat. Theatre, 1975; The Voyage of Edgar Allan Poe (world première), Minnesota Opera Co., USA, 1976; Rigoletto, NY Met., 1977; All's Well that Ends Well, Stratford, Ont, 1977; The Double Dealer, Nat. Theatre, 1978; Œdipus the King and Œdipus at Colonus, Adelaide Fest., 1978; Red Roses for Me, Abbey Theatre, Dublin, 1980; La Traviata, Metropolitan Opera, NY, 1981. Diplôme d'Honneur, Canadian Conference of the Arts; Hon. Fellow, Ontario Coll. of Art, 1979. Hon. DLitt: Birmingham, 1964; Waterloo, Ont, 1977. *Address:* c/o National Westminster Bank, 185 Sloane Street, SW1.

MOKAMA, Hon. Moleleki Didwell, BA, LLM (Harvard), LLM (London); Barrister-at-Law; Advocate of the Supreme Court of Botswana; Attorney-General of Botswana, since 1969; Member of Parliament *ex officio* and Member of the Cabinet *ex officio*; *b* 2 Feb. 1933; *e s* of Mokama Moleleki and Baipoledi Moleleki, Maunatlala, Botswana; *m* 1962, Kgopodiso Vivien Robi; one *s. Educ:* Moeng; Fort Hare; London Univ.; Inner Temple. Crown Counsel to Botswana Govt, 1963–66; High Comr for Botswana in London, 1966–69; Botswana Ambassador Extraordinary and Plenipotentiary: to France, 1967–69; to Germany, 1967–69; to Sweden, 1968–69; to Denmark, 1968–69. Hon. Mem., American Soc. of International Law, 1965. *Recreations:* swimming, shooting, hunting, photography. *Address:* Attorney-General's Chambers, Private Bag 009, Gaborone, Botswana.

MOLAPO, Mooki Motsarapane; High Commissioner for Lesotho in the United Kingdom, 1979–82; *b* 28 April 1928; *s* of Motsarapane and Mathebe Molapo; *m* 1958, Emily Mamanasse Thamae; three *s* one *d. Educ:* Lesotho (then Basutoland) High School. Government Service, 1950–. *Recreations:* football fan, walking, movies, theatre. *Address:* c/o Ministry of External Affairs, Maseru, Lesotho.

MOLESWORTH, family name of Viscount Molesworth.

MOLESWORTH, 11th Viscount, *cr* 1716 (Ireland); **Richard Gosset Molesworth;** Baron Philipstown, 1716; secretarial work since 1959; *b* 31 Oct. 1907; *s* of 10th Viscount and Elizabeth Gladys Langworthy (*d* 1974); *S* father, 1961; *m* 1958, Anne Florence Womersley, MA; two *s. Educ:* Lancing Coll.; private tutors. Farmed for many years. Freeman, City of London, 1978. Served War, in RAF, 1941–44 (Middle East, 1941–43). *Recreations:* foreign travel, music. *Heir: s* Hon. Robert Bysse Kelham Molesworth, *b* 4 June 1959. *Address:* Garden Flat, 2 Bishopswood Road, Highgate, N6. *T:* 01-348 1366.

MOLESWORTH, Allen Henry Neville; Financial and Administrative Controller, Crown Agents for Oversea Governments and Administrations, since 1976; *b* 20 Aug. 1931; *s* of late Roger Bevil Molesworth (Colonel RA), and of Iris Alice Molesworth (*née* Kennion); *m* 1970, Gail Cheng Kwai Chan. *Educ:* Wellington Coll., Berks; Trinity Coll., Cambridge (MA). FCA, FCMA, MIMC. 2nd Lt, 4th Queen's Own Hussars, 1950. Project Accounts, John Laing & Sons (Canada) Ltd, 1954–58; Singleton Fabian & Co., Chartered Accountants, 1959–63; Consultant: Standard Telephones & Cables Ltd, 1963–67; Coopers & Lybrand Associates Ltd, 1967: India, 1970; Kuwait, 1971; France, 1972; New Hebrides, 1972; Laos, 1974; Tonga, 1975. *Recreations:* shooting, skiing, music, restoring antiques. *Address:* c/o Lloyds Bank, Cox's & King's Branch, 6 Pall Mall, SW1. *Clubs:* 1900, Coningsby.

MOLESWORTH-ST AUBYN, Sir John, 14th Bt, *cr* 1689; CBE 1968; *b* 12 Jan. 1899; *s* of Sir Hugh Molesworth-St Aubyn, 13th Bt, and Emma Sybil (*d* 1929), *d* of Admiral Charles Wake; *S* father, 1942; *m* 1926, Celia Marjorie (*d* 1965), *e d* of late Lieut-Col Valentine Vivian, CMG, DSO, MVO; one *s* two *d. Educ:* Eton; Christ Church, Oxford. Flight Lieut, RAFVR, 1941. JP Cornwall, 1942; Sheriff of Cornwall, 1948. *Heir: s* John Arscott Molesworth-St Aubyn, *qv. Address:* Pencarrow, Washaway, Bodmin, Cornwall.

See also Earl of Morley.

MOLESWORTH-ST AUBYN, Lt-Col John Arscott, MBE 1963; DL; JP; *b* 15 Dec. 1926; *s* and *heir* of Sir John Molesworth-St Aubyn, *qv*; *m* 1957, Iona Audrey Armatrude, *d* of late Adm. Sir Francis Loftus Tottenham, KCB, CBE; two *s* one *d. Educ:* Eton. 2nd Lieut KRRC 1946; Captain 1954; psc 1959; Major 1961; jssc 1964; served Malaya and Borneo, 1961–63 and 1965; Royal Green Jackets, 1966; Lt-Col 1967; retd 1969. County Comr, Scouts, Cornwall, 1969–79. Mem., Cornwall River Authority, 1969–74; Chm. Devon Exec. Cttee, 1975–77, and Mem. Nat. Exec. Cttee, 1979–, Country Landowners Assoc.; Chairman: West Local Land Drainage Cttee, SW Water Authority, 1974–; Wessex Region, Historic Houses Assoc., 1981–. Pres., Royal Cornwall Agricl Assoc., 1976; Mem. Council, Devon County Agricl Assoc., 1979–; JP Devon, 1971; DL Cornwall, 1971; High Sheriff Cornwall, 1975. *Recreations:* shooting, ornithology. *Address:* Tetcott Manor, Holsworthy, Devon. *T:* North Tamerton 220; Pencarrow, Bodmin, Cornwall. *Clubs:* Army and Navy; Cornish 1768.

MOLEYNS; *see* Eveleigh-De-Moleyns.

MOLLISON, Prof. Patrick Loudon, CBE 1979; MD; FRCP; FRCPath; FRCOG; FRS 1968; Professor of Hæmatology, St Mary's Hospital Medical School, London University, 1962-79, now Emeritus Professor; Consultant Hæmatologist, St Mary's Hospital 1960-79; Part-time Director, Medical Research Council Experimental Hæmatology Unit, 1960-79; *b* 17 March 1914; *s* of William Mayhew Mollison, Cons. Surgeon (ENT), Guy's Hospital; *m* 1st, 1940, Dr Margaret D. Peirce (marr. diss., 1964); three *s*; 2nd, 1973, Dr Jennifer Jones. *Educ:* Rugby Sch.; Clare Coll., Cambridge; St Thomas' Hosp., London. MD Cantab 1944; FRCP 1959; FRCPath 1963; FRCOG *ad eund*, 1980. House Phys., Medical Unit, St Thomas' Hosp., 1939; Medical Officer, S London Blood Supply Depot, 1939-43; RAMC, 1943-46; Dir, MRC Blood Transfusion Res. Unit, Hammersmith Hosp., 1946-60; Hon. Lectr, then Sen. Lectr, Dept of Medicine, Post-grad. Medical Sch., 1948; Cons. Hæmatologist, Hammersmith Hosp., 1947-60. Hon. FRSM 1979; Landsteiner Meml Award, USA, 1960; P. Levine Award, USA, 1973; Oehlecker Medal, Germany, 1974. *Publications:* Blood Transfusion in Clinical Medicine, 1951 (6th edn, 1979); papers on red cell survival and blood group antibodies. *Recreations:* music, gardening, golf. *Address:* 60 King Henry's Road, NW3 3RR. *T:* 01-722 1947. *Club:* Savile.

MOLLO, Joseph Molelekoa Kaibe; High Commissioner for Lesotho in the United Kingdom, since 1982; *b* 7 May 1944; *s* of Kaibe and Cyrian Mollo; *m* 1972, Makaibe; one *s* two *d*. *Educ:* Univ. of Botswana, Lesotho and Swaziland (BA Admin); Univ. of Saskatchewan (MCEd); Carleton Univ. Asst Sec., Min. of Finance, 1971; Comr of Co-operatives, 1973; Dep. Perm. Sec., Finance, 1975; High Comr, Canada, 1976; Perm. Sec., Finance, 1980. Unpublished thesis: Profit versus Co-operation: the struggle of the Western Co-operative College. *Recreations:* jogging, dancing, music, soccer. *Address:* 10 Collingham Road, SW5. *T:* 01-373 8581.

MOLLO, Victor; Bridge Correspondent, The Mail on Sunday, 1982; Bridge Editor, Pelham Books, since 1980; Bridge Cruise Director: P&O, 1973-74; Norwegian-America Line, 1975; *b* St Petersburg, 17 Sept. 1909; Russian parents; *m* 1952, Jeanne Victoria Forbes. *Educ:* privately in Paris; Cordwalles, Surrey (Prep. Sch.); Brighton Coll.; London School of Economics, London Univ. Free lance journalism, also reading French and Russian texts for publishers, 1927-40; sub editor and editor, European Services (now External) BBC, 1940 till retirement in Oct. 1969. Bridge Correspondent, The Evening Standard, 1970-75; Bridge Editor, Faber & Faber, 1966-79. *Publications:* Streamlined Bridge, 1947; Card-Play Technique (in collab. with N. Gardener), 1955; Bridge for Beginners (in collab. with N. Gardener) 1956; Bridge Psychology, 1958; Will You Be My Partner?, 1959; Bridge: Modern Bidding, 1961; Success at Bridge, 1964; Bridge in the Menagerie, 1965; Confessions of an Addict, 1966; The Bridge Immortals, 1967; Victor Mollo's Winning Double, 1968; Bridge: Case for the Defence, 1970; (with E. Jannersten) Best of Bridge, 1972; Bridge in the Fourth Dimension, 1974; Instant Bridge, 1975; (with Aksel J. Nielson) Defence at Bridge, 1976; Bridge Unlimited, 1976; Bridge Course Complete, 1977; The Finer Arts of Bridge, 1977; Masters and Monsters, 1978; Streamline Your Bidding, 1979; Streamline Your Card Play, 1981; Bridge à la Carte, 1982; also Pocket Guides: ACOL: Winning Bidding, 1969 and Winning Defence, Winning Conventions. Contributing Editor to the Official Encyclopaedia of Bridge. Regular contributor to Bridge Magazines in USA, France, Denmark, Norway and Sweden and to Bridge Magazine in Britain. *Recreations:* gastronomy, conversation, bridge. *Address:* 801 Grenville House, Dolphin Square, SW1. *Clubs:* St James's Bridge, Sesame.

MOLLOY, family name of Baron Molloy.

MOLLOY, Baron *cr* 1981 (Life Peer), of Ealing in Greater London; **William John Molloy,** FRGS; *b* 26 Oct. 1918; *m* Eva Lewis; one *d*; *m* 1980, Doris Paynes, *d* of Joseph Foxton. *Educ:* elementary sch., Swansea; University Coll., Swansea (Political Economy, extra-mural). Served Field Coy, RE, 1939-46. Member: TGWU 1936-46; Civil Service Union, 1946-52; Co-op and USDAW, 1952; Parliamentary Adviser: COHSE, 1974-; Civil Service Union, 1974-79. Editor, Civil Service Review, 1947-52; Chm., Staff-Side Whitley Council, Germany and Austria Sections, FO, 1948-52, and Staff-Side Lectr, 1946-52. Leader, Fulham Borough Council, 1959-62. MP (Lab) Ealing N, 1964-79; former Vice-Chm., Parly Labour Party Gp for Common Market and European Affairs; Parly Adviser, London Trades Council Transport Cttee, 1968-79; Mem., House of Commons Estimates Cttee, 1968-70; PPS to Minister of Posts and Telecom., 1969-70. Mem. Assemblies, Council of Europe and WEU, 1969-73; Mem., European Parlt, 1976-79. Mem., Parly and Scientific Cttee, 1982-. Chm., Parly Lab. Party Social Services Gp, 1974. Mem. Court, Reading Univ., 1968-; Mem. Exec. Council, RGS, 1976-79, 1982-. *Recreations:* horse-riding, music. *Address:* 2a Uneeda Drive, Greenford, Mddx.

MOLLOY, Michael John; Editor, Daily Mirror, since Dec. 1975; *b* 22 Dec. 1940; *s* of John George and Margaret Ellen Molloy; *m* 1964, Sandra June Foley; three *d*. *Educ:* Ealing School of Art. Sunday Pictorial, 1956; Daily Sketch, 1960; Daily Mirror, 1962-: Editor, Mirror Magazine, 1969; Asst Editor, 1970; Dep. Editor, 1975; Dir, Mirror Group Newspapers, 1976-. *Recreations:* reading, running. *Address:* Daily Mirror, 33 Holborn, EC1. *T:* 01-353 0246. *Club:* Reform.

MOLONY, Thomas Desmond, 3rd Bt. Does not use the title, and his name is not on the Official Roll of Baronets.

MOLOTOV, Vaycheslav Mikhailovich, (*pseudonym* of V. M. Skryabin); Soviet diplomat; *b* Kirov district (Vyatka), 9 March 1890; son of a ship assistant; as mem. of students' Marxist circles in Kazan, took part in first Revolution, 1905; joined Bolshevik section of Russian Social Democratic Labour Party and organised students, 1906; arrested and deported to Vologda; organised Vologda railwaymen; graduated, 1909; organised students, Petrograd; contributed to Zvezda; part-founder with Stalin and sec. of Pravda, 1911; exiled from Petrograd for political activity, 1912; continued Party work from suburbs, organising elections and work of Party deputies in Duma, 1913; reorganised Moscow Bolshevik Party; exiled to Irkutsk, Siberia, 1915; escaped, returned to Petrograd and appointed mem. of Russian Bureau of Bolshevik Central Committee, 1916; mem. of executive of Petrograd Soviet and of military revolutionary cttee, 1917; chm. of People's Economy Council, Northern Region, 1918; mem. Nijegorodsky regional executive, 1919; sec. of Donets Regional Party cttee, 1920; elected mem. and sec. of Central Cttee of Communist Party of Soviet Union and candidate mem. of Political Bureau, 1921; mem. of Political Bureau of CPSU; worked against Zinovievists, Leningrad, 1926; elected mem. of Central Executive Cttee of Russian Soviet Socialist Republic, 1927; sec., Moscow cttee of CPSU; worked against Bukharinists in Moscow, 1928; elected mem. of Presidium of Central Executive Cttee of USSR, 1929; chm. of Council, of People's Commissars of USSR, 1930-41; 1st Dep. Chm., Council of People's Commissars, 1941-46; Dep. Chm., State Defence Cttee, 1941-45; took part in Teheran, Crimean, Potsdam and San Francisco Conferences; Leader of Soviet Delegn to Paris Peace Conf., 1946, to UN Gen. Assemblies, 1945-48; People's Commissar for For. Affairs, 1930-46, For. Min., 1946-49, 1953-56; First Dep. Chm. of USSR Council of Ministers, 1953-57; Min. of State Control, 1956-57; Dep. to Supreme Soviet, 1937-57; Soviet Ambassador to Mongolia, 1957-60; Chief Permanent Representative of the Soviet Union (rank Ambassador) to the International Atomic Energy Agency, Vienna, 1960-62. Hon. Mem. USSR Acad. of Sciences, 1946. Hero of Socialist Labour (and Hammer and Sickle Medal), 1943; Order of Lenin (4 awards). *Publications:* In the Struggle for Socialism, 1934; Articles and Speeches, 1935-36, 1937; Problems of Foreign Policy, 1948. *Address:* c/o Ministry of Social Security, 14 Shabolovka, Moscow, USSR.

MOLSON, family name of Baron Molson.

MOLSON, Baron, *cr* 1961, of High Peak (Life Peer); **(Arthur) Hugh (Elsdale) Molson,** PC 1956; President, Council for Protection of Rural England, 1971-80 (Chairman, 1968-71); *b* 29 June 1903; *o surv. s* of late Major J. E. Molson, MP, Gainsborough, and Mary, *d* of late A. E. Leeson, MD; *m* 1949, Nancy, *d* of late W. H. Astington, Bramhall, Cheshire. *Educ:* Royal Naval Colleges, Osborne and Dartmouth; Lancing; New Coll., Oxford. Pres. of Oxford Union, 1925; 1st Class Hons Jurisprudence. Served 36 Searchlight Regt, 1939-41. Staff Captain 11 AA, Div., 1941-42. Barrister-at-Law, Inner Temple, 1931; Political Sec., Associated Chambers of Commerce of India, 1926-29; Contested Aberdare Div. of Merthyr Tydfil, 1929; MP (U) Doncaster, 1931-35. MP (U) The High Peak Div. of Derbyshire, 1939-61. Parly Sec., Min. of Works, 1951-53; Joint Parly Sec., Min. of Transport and Civil Aviation, Nov. 1953-Jan. 1957; Minister of Works, 1957-Oct. 1959. Mem., Monckton Commission on Rhodesia and Nyasaland, 1960; Chm., Commn of Privy Counsellors on the dispute between Buganda and Bunyoro, 1962. *Publications:* articles in various reviews on political and other subjects. *Recreation:* shooting. *Address:* Cherrytrees, Kelso, Roxburghshire. *T:* Yetholm 204. *Clubs:* Athenæum, Carlton.

MOLYNEAUX, James Henry; JP; MP (UU) South Antrim since 1970; Member (UU) South Antrim, Northern Ireland Assembly, since 1982; *b* 27 Aug. 1920; *s* of late William Molyneaux, Seacash, Killead, Co. Antrim; unmarried. *Educ:* Aldergrove Sch., Co. Antrim. RAF, 1941-46. Vice-Chm., Eastern Special Care Hosp. Man. Cttee, 1966-73; Chm. Antrim Br., NI Assoc. for Mental Health, 1967-70; Hon. Sec., S Antrim Unionist Assoc., 1964-70; Vice-Pres., Ulster Unionist Council, 1974; Leader, Ulster Unionist Party, 1979-. Leader, UU Party, House of Commons, 1974-. Dep. Grand Master of Orange Order and Hon. PGM of Canada; Sovereign Grand Master, Commonwealth Royal Black Instn, 1971. JP Antrim, 1957; CC Antrim, 1964-73. *Recreations:* gardening, music. *Address:* Aldergrove, Crumlin, Co. Antrim, N Ireland. *T:* Crumlin 52545.

MOLYNEUX, Wilfrid, FCA; *b* 26 July 1910; *s* of Charles Molyneux and Mary (*née* Vose); *m* 1937, Kathleen Eleanor Young; one *s* one *d*. *Educ:* Douai Sch. With Cooper Brothers & Co., 1934-67; Finance Mem., BSC, 1967-71. *Address:* 105 Park Road, Brentwood, Essex CM14 4TT.

MOMIGLIANO, Prof. Arnaldo Dante, Hon. KBE 1974; DLitt (Turin); FBA 1954; Professor of Ancient History in the University of London at University College, 1951-75; Alexander White Visiting Professor, University of Chicago, 1969, since 1975; *b* 5 Sept. 1908; *s* of late Riccardo Momigliano and late Ilda Levi; *m* 1932, Gemma Segre; one *d*. *Educ:* privately, and at Univs of Turin and Rome. Professore Incaricato di Storia Greca, Univ. of Rome, 1932-36; Professore Titolare di Storia Romana, 1936-38, Professore Ordinario di Storia Romana in soprannumero, 1945-64, Univ. of Turin, Id, 1964-, Scuola Normale Superiore of Pisa. Lecturer in Ancient History, 1947-49, Reader in Ancient History, 1949-51, University of Bristol; research work in Oxford, 1939-47. Sather Prof. in Classics, Univ. of California, 1961-62; J. H. Gray Lectr, Univ. of Cambridge, 1963; Wingate Lectr, Hebrew Univ. of Jerusalem, 1964; Vis. Prof. and Lauro de Bosis Lectr, Harvard Univ., 1964-65;

C. N. Jackson Lectr, Harvard Univ., 1968; Jerome Lectr, Michigan Univ., 1971-72; Vis. Schol., Harvard, 1972; Trevelyan Lectr, Cambridge Univ., 1973; Flexner Lectr, Bryn Mawr, 1974; Grinfield Lectr on the Septuagint, Oxford, 1978-82; Efroymson Lectr, Hebrew Union Coll., Cincinnati, 1978; Chr. Gauss Lectr, Princeton, 1979; Lurcy Prof., Univ. of Chicago, 1982. Socio Nazionale: Accademia dei Lincei, 1961 (corresp. mem., 1947-61); Arcadia, 1967; Accademia delle Scienze di Torino, 1968; Istituto di Studi Romani, 1970 (corresp. mem., 1954-70); Istituto Studi Etruschi, 1973. Foreign Member: Royal Dutch Academy; Amer. Philosophical Soc.; Amer. Acad. of Arts and Scis; Institut de France; Corresp. Mem., German Archæological Institute, 1935; Hon. Mem., Amer. Hist. Assoc., 1964. Pres., Soc. for Promotion of Roman Studies, 1965-68. Hon. MA Oxford; Hon. DLitt: Bristol, 1959; Edinburgh, 1964; Oxford, 1970; Cambridge, 1971; London, 1975; Chicago, 1976; Leiden, 1977; Urbino, 1978; Hon. DHL: Columbia, 1974; Brandeis, 1977; Hebrew Union Coll., 1980; Hon. DPhil: Hebrew Univ., 1974; Tel-Aviv Univ., 1981. Hon. Fellow: Warburg Inst., 1975; UCL, 1976. Premio Cantoni, Univ. of Florence, 1932; Premio Feltrinelli for historical res. (Accademia dei Lincei award), 1960; Kaplun Prize for historical res., Hebrew Univ., 1975; Gold Medal, Italian Min. of Educn, 1977; Kenyon Medal, British Acad., 1981. Co-editor of Rivista Storica Italiana, 1948-. *Publications:* La composizione della Storia di Tucidide, 1930; Prime Linee di storia della tradizione maccabaica, 1931 (2nd edn 1968); Claudius, 1934 (2nd edn 1961); Filippo il Macedone, 1934; La storiografia sull' impero romano, 1936; Contributo alla storia degli studi classici, 1955; Secondo Contributo alla storia degli studi classici, 1960; Terzo Contributo alla storia degli studi classici, 1966; Studies in Historiography, 1966; Paganism and Christianity in the Fourth Century, 1963; Quarto contributo alla storia degli studi classici, 1969; The Development of Greek Biography, 1971 (trans. Italian, Japanese); Introduzione Bibliografica alla Storia Greca fino a Socrate, 1975; Quinto Contributo alla Storia degli studi classici, 1975; Alien Wisdom, the limits of Hellenization, 1975, 2nd edn 1978 (trans. Italian, German, French); Essays on Historiography, 1977; Sesto Contributo alla Storia degli Studi Classici, 1981; La Storiografia Greca, 1982; contribs to Cambridge Ancient History, Jl of Roman Studies, History and Theory, Jl of Warburg Inst., Daedalus, Enciclopedia Italiana, Encycl. Britannica, Encycl. Judaica. *Recreation:* walking. *Address:* Department of Classics, University of Chicago, Chicago, Ill 60637, USA.

MONAGHAN, Rt. Rev. James; Titular Bishop of Cell Ausaille and Bishop Auxiliary to Archbishop of St Andrews and Edinburgh since 1970; Parish Priest of Holy Cross, Edinburgh, since 1959; *b* Bathgate, 11 July 1914; *s* of Edward and Elizabeth Monaghan. *Educ:* St Aloysius' Coll., Glasgow; Blairs Coll., Aberdeen; St Kieran's Coll., Kilkenny, Ireland. Priest, 1940; Secretary, 1953; Vicar-Gen. for Archdio. St Andrews and Edinburgh, 1958-. *Address:* 252 Ferry Road, Edinburgh EH5 3AN. *T:* 031-552 3957.

MONAHAN, James Henry Francis, CBE 1962; Director, Royal Ballet School, since Sept. 1977; *b* 16 Dec. 1912; *s* of late George John Monahan, Indian Civil Service, and Helen Monahan (*née* Kennedy); *m* 1941, Joan Barker-Mill (*née* Eaden); two *s* three *d*; *m* 1965, Merle Park, *qv* (marr. diss. 1970); one *s*; *m* 1970, Gail Thomas; one *s* one *d*. *Educ:* Stonyhurst Coll.; Christ Church, Oxford. The Manchester Guardian: critic and reporter, London office, 1937-39; film critic, 1945-63; dance critic, 1945-. Government Service and attached to BBC German Service, 1939-42; Army Service: (despatches); Special Forces and No 10 Commando, 1942-45; Captain, 1944. British Broadcasting Corporation: Asst Head, West European Services, 1946; Head, West European Services, 1946-51; Controller, European Services, 1952-70; Dir of Programmes, External Services, 1971, retired. Part-time cons., Corp. for Public Broadcasting, USA, 1973. *Publications:* Far from the Land (poems), 1944; After Battle (poems), 1947; Fonteyn, 1958; report on Deutsche Welle, West Germany, 1972; The Nature of Ballet, 1976. *Recreations:* lawn tennis, squash rackets. *Address:* 6 Elm Bank Mansions, The Terrace, Barnes, SW13. *Club:* Hurlingham.

MONCEL, Lt-Gen. Robert William, OC 1968; DSO 1944; OBE 1944; CD 1944; retired 1966; *b* 9 April 1917; *s* of René Moncel and Edith Brady; *m* 1939, Nancy Allison, *d* of Ralph P. Bell; one *d*. *Educ:* Selwyn House Sch.; Bishop's Coll. Sch. Royal Canadian Regt, 1939; Staff Coll., 1940; Bde Major 1st Armd Bde, 1941; comd 18th Manitoba Dragoons, 1942; GSO1, HQ 2 Cdn Corps, 1943; comd 4th Armd Bde, 1944; Dir Canadian Armd Corps, 1946; Nat. War Coll., 1949; Canadian Jt Staff, London, 1949-54; Comdr 3 Inf. Bde, 1957; QMG, 1960; GOC Eastern Comd, 1963; Comptroller Gen., 1964; Vice-Chief of the Defence Staff, Canada, 1965-66. Col, 8th Canadian Hussars. Chm., Fishermen's Memorial Hosp., 1980-. Croix de Guerre, France, 1944; Légion d'Honneur, France, 1944. Hon. LLD Mount Allison Univ., 1968. *Recreations:* fishing, sailing, golf. *Address:* 174 Dufferin Road, Ottawa, Ontario, Canada. *T:* 745-5061; High Head, Murder Point, Nova Scotia. *Clubs:* Royal Ottawa Golf; Royal St Lawrence Yacht; Royal Nova Scotia Yacht.

MONCK, family name of Viscount Monck.

MONCK, 7th Viscount *cr* 1801; **Charles Stanley Monck;** Baron Monck, 1797; Baron Monck (UK), 1866; *b* 2 April 1953; *s* of 6th Viscount Monck, OBE, and of Brenda Mildred, *d* of G. W. Adkins, Harpenden; *S* father, 1982. *Educ:* Eton. BTech. *Heir: b* Hon. George Stanley Monck, *b* 12 April 1957.

MONCK, Nicholas Jeremy; Under Secretary, HM Treasury, since 1977; *b* 9 March 1935; *s* of Bosworth Monck and Stella Mary (*née* Cock); *m* 1960, Elizabeth Mary Kirwan; three *s*. *Educ:* Eton; King's Coll., Cambridge; Univ. of Pennsylvania. Asst Principal, Min. of Power, 1959-62; NEDO, 1962-65; NBPI, 1965-66; Senior Economist, Min. of Agriculture, Tanzania, 1966-69; HM Treasury, 1969-; Asst Sec., 1971; Principal Private Sec. to Chancellor of the Exchequer, 1976-77. Mem., BSC, 1978-80. *Address:* 31 Lady Margaret Road, Kentish Town, NW5 2NG. *T:* 01-485 8474.

MONCKTON, family name of Viscount Galway and Viscount Monckton of Brenchley.

MONCKTON OF BRENCHLEY, 2nd Viscount *cr* 1957; **Maj.-Gen. Gilbert Walter Riversdale Monckton,** CB 1966; OBE 1956; MC 1940; DL; retired, 1967; Director: Ransome, Hoffmann Pollard Ltd; United & General Trust Ltd; Country Building Society; *b* 3 Nov. 1915; *o s* of 1st Viscount Monckton of Brenchley, PC, GCVO, KCMG, MC, QC, and Mary A. S. (*d* 1964), *d* of Sir Thomas Colyer-Fergusson, 3rd Bt; *S* father, 1965; *m* 1950, Marianna Laetitia (Dame of Honour and Devotion, SMO Malta (also Cross of Merit), OStJ, Pres., St John's Ambulance, Kent, 1975-80, High Sheriff of Kent, 1981-82), 3rd *d* of late Comdr Robert T. Bower; four *s* one *d*. *Educ:* Harrow; Trinity Coll., Cambridge. BA 1939, MA 1942. 2/Lt 5th Royal Inniskilling Dragoon Guards, SR 1938; Reg. 1939; France and Belgium, 1939-40; Staff Coll., 1941; Bde Major Armd Bde, 1942; Comd and Gen. Staff Sch., USA, 1943; Sqdn Ldr, 3rd King's Own Hussars, 1944, Italy and Syria; Sqdn Ldr, 5th Royal Inniskilling Dragoon Gds, 1945. RAF Staff Coll., 1949; GSO2, 7th Armd Div., 1949; Sqdn Ldr and 2 i/c 5th Royal Inniskilling Dragoon Gds, Korea and Egypt, 1951-52; GSO1, Mil. Ops, WO, 1954-56; Mil. Adv., Brit. Delegn, Geneva Confs on Indo-China and Korea, 1954; transf. 12th Royal Lancers and comd, 1956-58; Comdr Royal Armd Corps, 3rd Div., 1958-60; psc, idc 1961; Dep. Dir, Personnel Admin., WO, 1962; Dir of Public Relations, WO (subseq. MoD), 1963-65; Chief of Staff, HQ BAOR, 1965-67; Col 9th/12th Royal Lancers (Prince of Wales's), 1967-73; Hon. Col, Kent and Sharpshooters Yeomanry Sqdn, 1974-79. Farms 400 acres in Kent. President: Kent Assoc. of Boys' Clubs, 1965-78; Inst. of Heraldic and Genealogical Studies, 1965; Kent Archæological Soc., 1968-75; Medway Productivity Assoc., 1968-72; Kent Co. Rifle Assoc., 1970; Anglo-Belgian Union, 1973-; Chm., Thurnham Parish Council, 1968-70. DL Kent, 1970. Liveryman Broderers' Co., Master 1978; KStJ; Chm., Council of Order of St John for Kent, 1969-75; SMO Malta: Bailiff, Grand Cross of Obedience (Chancellor of the British Assoc., 1963-68, Vice-Pres., 1968-74, Pres., 1974-); Grand Cross of Merit, 1980; Comdr, Order of Crown (Belgium), 1965; Bailiff, Grand Cross of Justice, Constantinian Order of St George, 1975; Grand Officer, Order of Leopold II (Belgium), 1978. *Recreation:* archaeology. *Heir: s* Hon. Christopher Walter Monckton, *qv*. *Address:* Runhams Farm, Runham Lane, Harrietsham, Maidstone, Kent ME17 1NJ. *T:* Ulcombe 313. *Clubs:* Brooks's, Cavalry and Guards, MCC; Casino Maltese (Valetta).

MONCKTON, Hon. Christopher Walter; Leader-Writer, The Standard, since 1982; *b* 14 Feb. 1952; *s* and *heir* of Viscount Monckton of Brenchley, *qv*. *Educ:* Harrow; Churchill Coll., Cambridge; University Coll., Cardiff. BA 1973, MA 1977 (Cantab); Dip. Journalism Studies (Wales), 1974. Standing Cttee, Cambridge Union Soc., 1973; Treas., Cambridge Univ. Conservative Assoc., 1973. Reporter, Yorkshire Post, 1974-75, Leader-Writer, 1975-77; Press Officer, Conservative Central Office, 1977-78; Editor-designate, The Universe, 1978, Editor, 1979-81; Managing Editor, Telegraph Sunday Magazine, 1981-82. Freeman, City of London, and Liveryman, Worshipful Co. of Broderers, 1973-. Member: Internat. MENSA Ltd, 1975-; St John Amb. Brigade (Wetherby Div.), 1976-77; Hon. Soc. of the Middle Temple, 1979-; RC Mass Media Commn, 1979-; Secretary: Economic Acctg Study Gp, 1980-81, Forward Strategy Gp, 1981, Health Study Gp, 1981-, Employment Study Gp, 1982-, Centre for Policy Studies. Vis. Lectr in Business Studies, Columbia Univ., NY, 1980. Editor, Not the Church Times, 1982. Kt SMO, Malta, 1973; OStJ 1973. *Publication:* The Laker Story (with Ivan Fallon), 1982. *Recreations:* nil humanum a me alienum puto. *Address:* 71 Albert Road, Richmond, Surrey. *T:* 01-940 6528. *Clubs:* Brooks's, Beefsteak.

MONCKTON-ARUNDELL, family name of Viscount Galway.

MONCREIFF, family name of Baron Moncreiff.

MONCREIFF, 5th Baron *cr* 1873; **Harry Robert Wellwood Moncreiff;** Bt, Nova Scotia 1626, UK 1871; Lt-Col (Hon.) RASC, retired; *b* 4 Feb. 1915; *s* of 4th Baron; *S* father, 1942; *m* 1952, Enid Marion Watson, *o d* of Major H. W. Locke, Belmont, Dollar; one *s*. *Educ:* Fettes Coll., Edinburgh. Served War of 1939-45 (despatches). Retired, 1958. *Recreations:* Rugby football, tennis, shooting. *Heir: s* Hon. Rhoderick Harry Wellwood Moncreiff, *b* 22 March 1954. *Address:* Tulliebole Castle, Fossoway, Kinross-shire, *T:* Fossoway 236.

MONCREIFF, Rt. Rev. Francis Hamilton; *b* North Berwick, 29 Sept. 1906; *s* of late James Hamilton Moncreiff. *Educ:* Shrewsbury Sch.; St John's Coll., Cambridge; Cuddesdon Theological Coll. Ordained, 1931; Curate at St Giles, Cambridge, 1931-35, at St Augustine's, Kilburn, 1935-41; Priest-in-charge, St Salvador's, Edinburgh, 1941, Rector, 1947-51; Chaplain at HM Prison, Edinburgh, 1942-51; Canon of St Mary's Cathedral, Edinburgh, 1950; Diocesan Missioner in diocese of Edinburgh, 1951-52; Bishop of Glasgow and

Galloway, 1952-74; Primus of the Episcopal Church in Scotland, 1962-74. Went on a Mission to European parishes in Northern Rhodesia, 1948 and 1951, to Pretoria and Johannesburg, 1953. Hon. DD Glasgow, 1967. *Address:* 19 Eglinton Crescent, Edinburgh EH12 5BY. *T:* 031-337 1523.

MONCREIFFE OF THAT ILK, Sir (Rupert) Iain (Kay), 11th Bt, *cr* 1685; CVO 1980; DL; QC (Scot.) 1980; author; *b* 9 April 1919; *s* of late Lt-Comdr Gerald Moncreiffe, Royal Navy, and Hinda (*d* 1960), *d* of late Frank Meredyth, styled Count de Miremont; *S* cousin (Sir David Moncreiffe of that Ilk, Bt, 23rd Laird of Moncreiffe), 1957; *m* 1st, 1946, Countess of Erroll, 23rd in line (marr. diss. 1964; she *d* 1978); two *s* one *d*; 2nd, 1966, Hermione, *d* of late Lt-Col W. D. Faulkner, MC, Irish Guards and of the Countess of Dundee (*d* of late Lord Herbert Montagu-Douglas-Scott). *Educ:* Stowe; Heidelberg; Christ Church, Oxford (MA); Edinburgh Univ. (LLB, PhD). Capt. late Scots Guards; served 1939-46 (wounded in Italy): ADC to Gen. Sir Andrew Thorne (GOC-in-C Scottish Comd), 1944-45; Military Liaison Officer for Norway to Adm. Sir William Whitworth (C-in-C Rosyth), 1945. Private Sec. to Sir Maurice Peterson (Ambassador to USSR) and attaché at British Embassy in Moscow, 1946. Mem. Queen's Body Guard for Scotland (Royal Company of Archers), 1948-; called to Scottish Bar, 1950; Mem. of Lloyd's, 1952-. Chm., Debrett's Peerage, 1977-81. Mem Advisory Cttee Scottish Nat. Portrait Gallery, 1957-81. Pres., Assoc. of Genealogists and Record Agents, 1980-; Hon. Pres., Dozenal Soc. of GB, 1966-. Hon. Sheriff of Perth and Angus, 1958-. Albany Herald, 1961; DL Perth, 1961. FSA 1959. KStJ 1982. Cross with Swords, Grand Officer of Merit, SMO Malta, 1980; Gold Medal, Constantinian St George, 1982. *Publications:* (with D. Pottinger) Simple Heraldry, 1953; Simple Custom, 1954; Blood Royal, 1956; Map of Scotland of Old, 1960; (with David Hicks) The Highland Clans, 1967, rev. edn 1982; Royal Highness, 1982. *Recreations:* shooting and travel. *Heir: s* Earl of Erroll, *qv. Address:* Easter Moncreiffe, by Perth PH2 8QA. *T:* Bridge of Earn 2338; 7 Little Grosvenor Court, Pavilion Road, SW1. *T:* 01-235 2759. *Clubs:* Turf, White's, Pratt's, Beefsteak; Royal and Ancient Golf (St Andrews); (Founder) Puffin's, New (Edinburgh).

MONCRIEFF, William S.; *see* Scott-Moncrieff.

MONCTON, Archbishop of, (RC), since 1972; **Most Rev. Donat Chiasson;** *b* Paquetville, NB, 2 Jan. 1930; *s* of Louis Chiasson and Anna Chiasson (*née* Godin). *Educ:* St Joseph's Univ., NB; Holy Heart Seminary, Halifax, NS; Theological and Catechetical studies, Rome and Lumen Vitae, Belgium. *Address:* PO Box 248, Chartersville, Moncton, NB, Canada. *T:* 389.9531.

MOND, family name of **Baron Melchett.**

MONDALE, Walter Frederick; Vice-President of the United States of America, 1977-81; Counsel with Winston & Strawn, since 1981; Member of the Board, Control Data, since 1981; *b* Ceylon, Minnesota, 5 Jan. 1928; *s* of Rev. Theodore Sigvaard Mondale and Claribel Hope (*née* Cowan); *m* 1955, Joan Adams; two *s* one *d. Educ:* public schs, Minnesota; Macalester Coll., Univ. of Minnesota (BA *cum laude*); Univ. of Minnesota Law Sch. (LLB). Served with Army, 1951-53. Admitted to Minn. Bar, 1956; private law practice, Minneapolis, 1956-60; Attorney-Gen., Minnesota, 1960-64; Senator from Minnesota, 1964-76. Democratic Candidate for Vice-Pres., USA, 1976, 1980; Mem., Democratic Farm Labor Party. *Publication:* The Accountability of Power. *Address:* 2550 M Street NW, Washington, DC 20036, USA.

MONDAY, Horace Reginald, CBE 1967 (OBE 1958); JP; *b* 26 Nov. 1907; *s* of late James Thomas Monday, Gambia Civil Servant, and late Rachel Ruth Davis; *m* 1932, Wilhelmina Roberta Juanita, *d* of late William Robertson Job Roberts, a Gambian businessman; one *s. Educ:* Methodist Mission Schools, in Banjul, The Gambia; correspondence course with (the then) London Sch. of Accountancy. Clerk, 1925-48; Asst Acct, Treasury, 1948-52; Acct and Storekeeper, Marine Dept, 1953-54; Acct-Gen., The Gambia Govt, 1954-65; Chm., Gambia Public Service Commn, 1965-68; High Comr for The Gambia in the UK and NI, 1968-71. MP Banjul Central, 1977-82. Chairman: Management Cttee, Banjul City Council, 1971-79; Gambia Utilities Corp., 1972-76. Dir, Gambia Currency Bd, 1964-68; Governor, Gambia High Sch., 1964-68; Pres., Gambia Red Cross Soc., 1967-68. JP 1944. Comdr, National Order of Republic of Senegal, 1968. *Address:* Rachelville, 24 Clarkson Street, Banjul, The Gambia. *T:* Banjul 511.

MONEY, Ernle (David Drummond); Barrister-at-Law; *b* 17 Feb. 1931; *s* of late Lt-Col E. F. D. Money, DSO, late 4th Gurkha Rifles, and of Sidney, *o d* of D. E. Anderson, Forfar; *m* 1960, Susan Barbara, *d* of Lt-Col D. S. Lister, MC, The Buffs; two *s* two *d. Educ:* Marlborough Coll.; Oriel Coll., Oxford (open scholar). Served in Suffolk Regt, 1949-51, and 4th Bn, Suffolks Regt (TA), 1951-56; MA Hons degree (2nd cl.) in mod. hist., 1954. Tutor and lecturer, Swinton Conservative Coll., 1956. Called to Bar, Lincoln's Inn (Cholmeley Scholar), 1958. Mem., Bar Council, 1962-66. MP (C) Ipswich, 1970-Sept. 1974; Opposition Front Bench Spokesman on the Arts, 1974; Sec., Parly Cons. Arts and Amenities Cttee, 1970-73, Vice-Chm., 1974; Vice-Pres., Ipswich Cons. Assoc., 1979-. Regular columnist, East Anglian Daily Times. Governor, Woolverstone Hall Sch., 1967-70; co-opted Mem., GLC Arts Cttee, 1972-73; Mem., GLC Arts Bd, 1974-76; Mem., Cttee of Gainsborough's Birthplace, Sudbury. Fine Arts Correspondent, Contemporary Review, 1968-. Pres., Ipswich Town Football Club Supporters, 1974-; Vice-Pres., E Suffolk and Ipswich Branch, RSPCA, 1974-. *Publications:* (with Peter Johnson) The Nasmyth Family of Painters, 1970; Margaret Thatcher, First Lady of the

House, 1975; regular contrib. various periodicals and newspapers on antiques and the arts. *Recreations:* music, pictures and antiques, watching Association football. *Address:* Ipswich Chambers, 3 Princes Street, Ipswich. *T:* Ipswich 214481; High House Farm, Rendlesham, near Woodbridge, Suffolk. *T:* Eyke 335. *Clubs:* Carlton; Ipswich and Suffolk (Ipswich).

MONEY, George Gilbert; Director, Barclays Bank International Ltd, 1955-81 (Vice-Chairman, 1965-73); *b* 17 Nov. 1914; 2nd *s* of late Maj.-Gen. Sir A. W. Money, KCB, KBE, CSI and late Lady Money (*née* Drummond). *Educ:* Charterhouse Sch. Clerk, L. Behrens & Soehne, Bankers, Hamburg, 1931-32; Clerk, Barclays Bank Ltd, 1932-35, Dir 1972-73; joined Barclays Bank DCO (now Barclays Bank International Ltd), London, 1935; served in Egypt, Palestine, Cyprus, Ethiopia, Cyrenaica, E Africa, 1936-52; Local Dir, W Indies, 1952; Director: Barclays Bank of California, 1965-75; Bermuda Provident Bank Ltd, 1969; Barclays Bank of the Netherlands, Antilles NV, 1970; Republic Finance Corp. Ltd, 1972; Republic Bank Ltd, 1972; Barclays Bank of Jamaica Ltd, 1972-77; Barclays Australia Ltd, 1972-75; New Zealand United Corp., 1972-75; Chairman: Bahamas Internat. Trust Co. Ltd, 1970-72; Cayman Internat. Trust Co. Ltd, 1970-72; Mem., Caribbean Bd, Barclays Bank International Ltd. *Recreations:* tennis, water ski-ing, fishing, bridge. *Address:* 54 Lombard Street, EC3. *Clubs:* Crockfords, Royal Commonwealth Society.

MONEY, Col Reginald Angel, CBE 1943; MC 1917; ED; FRCS; FRACS; MB, ChM (Sydney); RAAMC; *b* Sydney, Australia, 3 March 1897; *s* of late Angel Money, MD, FRCP, Harley Street, W1, and of late Mrs Amy Money, 138 Ocean Street, Edgecliff, Sydney; *m* 1937, Dorothy Jean Wilkinson, Strathfield, NSW; two *d. Educ:* Sydney Grammar Sch.; Univ. of Sydney. Enlisted in AIF and was abroad with Australian Field Artillery, 1916-19 (Lt, MC); CO 2/6 Australian Gen. Hosp., AIF, 1940-44 (Col, CBE); MB, ChM from Medical Sch. of Univ. of Sydney, 1923; House Surgeon, Registrar, and Medical Supt, Royal Prince Alfred Hosp., Sydney, 1923-28, Hon. Asst Surgeon, 1928; Hon. Neuro-Surgeon, 1937-57. FRCS 1932; FRACS 1931; Tutor in Surgery, Sydney Univ., 1929-37; Lecturer in Head and Spinal Injuries, 1935-57; Mem., Bd of Directors, Royal Prince Alfred Hospital, Sydney, 1953. Hon. Consulting Neuro-Surgeon, Royal Prince Alfred Hosp., Royal North Shore Hosp., and St George Hosp., Sydney; Visiting Neuro-Surgeon, NSW Masonic Hosp., Sydney. Postgraduate Professional Tours of Great Britain, Europe, USA, Canada, USSR, Mexico, South America, Japan, S Africa, Asia, Romania, Far East, 1928-79. *Publications:* articles and case reports in med. and surgical jls, etc. *Recreations:* swimming, contract bridge, farming. *Address:* 28 Bathurst Street, Woollahra, Sydney, NSW 2025, Australia. *T:* (02) 387-2165. *Clubs:* Australian, Royal Sydney Golf, Australian Jockey (Sydney).

MONEY, Maj.-Gen. Robert Cotton, CB 1943; MC; psc; *b* 21 July 1888; *o c* of late Col R. C. Money, CMG, CBE; *m* 1st, 1917, Daphne Dorina (*d* 1968), 2nd *d* of Brig.-Gen. C. W. Gartside Spaight, Derry Castle, Killaloe, Ireland; (one *s* killed in action, 1940) one *d*; 2nd, 1978, Evelyn, 3rd *d* of late E. J. Grosstephan. *Educ:* Arnold House, Llandulas; Wellington Coll.; RMC, Sandhurst. Joined Cameronians (Scottish Rifles), 1909; served with both battalions, European War and India; commanded 1st Bn 1931-34; commanded Lucknow Bde, 1936-39; Commandant Senior Officers' Sch., 1939; comd 15th (Scottish) Div., 1940-41; District Comdr, India, 1942-44; retired pay, 1944. Ministry of Transport, 1944-52; retired, 1952. *Recreation:* gardening. *Address:* Moat House, Cholesbury, Tring, Herts.

MONEY-COUTTS, family name of **Baron Latymer.**

MONEY-COUTTS, David Burdett; Managing Director since 1970, and Chairman since 1976, Coutts & Co.; *b* 19 July 1931; *s* of Hon. Alexander B. Money-Coutts (2nd *s* of 6th Baron Latymer, TD), and Mary E., *er d* of Sir Reginald Hobhouse, 5th Bt; *m* 1958, Penelope Utten Todd; one *s* two *d. Educ:* Eton; New Coll., Oxford (MA). National Service, 1st Royal Dragoons, 1950-51; Royal Glos Hussars, TA, 1951-67. Joined Coutts & Co., 1954; Dir, 1958. Director: National Discount Co., 1964-69; Gerrard & National, 1969- (Dep. Chm. 1969-); United States & General Trust Corp., 1964-73; Charities Investment Managers (Charifund), 1964-; (Regional), SE Reg., National Westminster Bank, 1969-; National Westminster Bank, 1976-; Dun & Bradstreet, 1973-; Phoenix Assurance, 1978-. Member: Kensington and Chelsea and Westminster AHA, 1974-82 (Vice-Chm., 1978-82); Bloomsbury HA, 1982-; Health Educn Council, 1973-77. Middlesex Hospital: Governor, 1962-74 (Dep. Chm. Governors, 1973-74); Chm., Finance Cttee, 1965-74; Mem., Med. Sch. Council, 1963- (Chm., 1974-). Trustee, Multiple Sclerosis Soc., 1967-. Hon. Treas., Nat. Assoc. of Almshouses, 1960-; Hon. Sec., Old Etonian Trust, 1969-76, Chm. Council, 1976-. *Recreations:* odd jobs, living in the country. *Address:* Magpie House, Peppard Common, Henley-on-Thames, Oxon RG9 5JG. *T:* Rotherfield Greys 497. *Club:* Leander (Henley-on-Thames).

MONGER, George William; Under-Secretary, HM Treasury, since 1981; *b* 1 April 1937; *s* of George Thomas Monger and Agnes Mary (*née* Bates). *Educ:* Holloway Sch.; Jesus Coll., Cambridge (PhD 1962). Entered Home Civil Service (Admin. Class), 1961: Min. of Power, Min. of Technol., DTI, and Dept of Energy; Principal, 1965; Asst Sec., 1972; Under-Sec., Electricity Div., 1976, Coal Div., 1979, Dept of Energy. Alexander Prize, RHistS, 1962. *Publication:* The End of Isolation: British Foreign Policy, 1900-1907, 1963.

Address: Lochalsh, Christ Church Lane, Hadley Green, Barnet, Herts. *T:* 01-449 7887. *Club:* United Oxford & Cambridge University.

MONIBA, Harry Fumba, PhD; Ambassador of the Republic of Liberia to the Court of St James's, since 1981; *b* 22 Oct. 1937; *s* of Mr Moniba and Mrs Janga Sando Moniba; *m* 1969, Minita Kollie; three *s* two *d. Educ:* Cuttington Univ. Coll., Liberia (all-round student award; BSEd, *cum laude*); State University of New York, New Paltz (MSc); New York Univ., NY (post grad. studies); Michigan State Univ., USA (PhD African Hist. and Internat. Relations). Teacher and Registrar, also Vice Principal, Holy Cross Bolahun Mission Schs, 1968-70; Special Asst and Dir of Research, Min. of Educn, 1975-76; First Secretary and Consul, Liberian Embassy: Washington DC, 1976-80; Ottawa, Canada, 1978-80; Asst Minister of Foreign Affairs for European Affairs, Min. of Foreign Affairs, 1980-81. *Recreations:* reading, soccer, fishing, hunting, dancing. *Address:* Embassy of the Republic of Liberia, 21 Prince's Gate, SW7 1QB. *T:* 01-589 9405.

MONIER-WILLIAMS, Evelyn Faithfull; His Honour Judge Monier-Williams; a Circuit Judge since 1972; *b* 29 April 1920; *o s* of late R. T. Monier-Williams, OBE, Barrister-at-Law, and Mrs G. M. Monier-Williams; *m* 1948, Maria-Angela Oswald; one *s* one *d. Educ:* Charterhouse; University Coll., Oxford (MA). Admitted to Inner Temple, 1940; served Royal Artillery, 1940-46 in UK, Egypt, Libya, Tunisia, Sicily (8th Army), France, Low Countries and Germany; called to Bar, Inner Temple, 1948; South Eastern Circuit; Master of the Bench, Inner Temple, 1967; Mem. Senate of Four Inns of Court, 1969-73; Mem. Council, Selden Soc., 1970; Mem., Council of Legal Educn, 1971, Vice Chm., 1974; Mem., Adv. Cttee on Legal Educn, 1979. Livery, Glaziers Company, 1974. *Recreation:* collecting old books. *Address:* Inner Temple, EC4.

MONIZ DE ARAGÃO, José Joaquim de Lima e Silva; *b* Rio de Janeiro, Brasil, 12 May 1887; *m* 1926, Isabel Rodrigues Alves; two *s. Educ:* Faculty of Law, Rio de Janeiro. Attached to Ministry of Foreign Affairs, Rio de Janeiro, 1908; 2nd Sec., Washington, 1911; 1st Sec., Monte-Video, Madrid, Rome, 1913; Counsellor, Berlin, 1915-18; Counsellor, Brazilian Delegn Peace Conf., Versailles, 1919; Counsellor, Berlin, 1920-25; Minister, League of Nations, Geneva, 1926; Minister Delegate, Internat. Labour Office, Geneva, 1928-29; Minister, Copenhagen, Caracas, 1929-33; Under-Sec. of State for Foreign Affairs, Rio de Janeiro, 1934; Ambassador to Berlin, 1935-38; Brazilian Ambassador to Court of St James's, 1940-52. Brazilian Delegate to UNO Assembly in London, 1945; Chief Brazilian Delegate to: UNESCO Assembly, London, 1945, Paris, 1946; UNRRA Assembly, London, 1946; Internat. Cttee for Refugees in London, 1944, 1945, Paris, 1946. Mem. Royal Philatelic Society. Knight Grand Cross of the Royal Victorian Order, Gt Brit. (Hon. GCVO); Comdr Order of the British Empire (Hon. CBE). *Address:* Avenida Atlântica no 2242, 10 andar, Rio de Janeiro, Brazil. *Clubs:* Rotary, Jockey, Automovel (Rio de Janeiro).

MONK, Rear-Adm. Anthony John, CBE 1973; Director General, Brick Development Association, since 1979; *b* 14 Nov. 1923; *s* of Frank Leonard and Barbara Monk; *m* 1951, Elizabeth Ann Samson; four *s* one *d. Educ:* Whitgift Sch.; RNC Dartmouth; RNEC Keyham. MSc, BScEng, FIMarE, FRAeS, FIMechE. Cadet, 1941; served War of 1939-45, Pacific Fleet; flying trng, Long Air Engrg Course, Cranfield, 1946; RN Air Stn Ford; RNEC Manadon, 1950; Prodn Controller and Man., RN Aircraft Yard, Belfast, 1953-56; Mem. Dockyard Work Measurement Team, subseq. Engr Officer HMS Apollo, Techn. Asst to Dir-Gen. Aircraft, Sqdn Engr Officer to Flag Officer Aircraft Carriers, 1963-65; Asst Dir of Marine Engrg, 1965-68; Dir of Aircraft Engrg, 1968; Comd Engrg Officer to Flag Officer Naval Air Comd; Naval Liaison Officer for NI and Supt RN Aircraft Yard, Belfast, 1970; Port Admiral, Rosyth, 1974-76; Rear-Adm. Engineering to Flag Officer Naval Air Comd, 1976-78. Comdr 1956; Captain 1964; Rear-Adm. 1974. *Recreation:* swimming (ASA teacher). *Address:* 7 London Road, Widley, Portsmouth PO7 5AT.

MONK, Arthur James; Director, Components, Valves and Devices, Ministry of Defence, since 1981; *b* 15 Jan. 1924; *s* of late Rev. Arthur S. Monk, AKC, and late Lydia E. Monk; *m* 1953, Murial V. Peacock; one *s* two *d. Educ:* Latymer Upper School, Hammersmith; London Univ. BSc Hons Physics 1953; FIEE 1964. Served RAF, 1943-48. Services Electronic Research Labs, 1949-63; Asst Director (Co-ord. Valve Development), MoD, 1963-68; Student, Imperial Defence Coll., 1969; idc 1970; Admiralty Underwater Weapons Establishment, 1970-73; Dep. Director, Underwater Weapons Projects (S/M), MoD, 1973-76; Counsellor, Def. Equipment Staff, Washington, 1977-81. *Publications:* papers on electronics in jls of learned societies. *Recreations:* caravan touring, photography, do-it-yourself. *Address:* Empress State Building, Lillie Road, Fulham, SW6 ITR. *T:* 01-385 1244, ext. 2792.

MONK BRETTON, 3rd Baron *cr* 1884; **John Charles Dodson;** *b* 17 July 1924; *o s* of 2nd Baron and Ruth (*d* 1967), 2nd *d* of late Hon. Charles Brand; *S* father, 1933; *m* 1958, Zoë Diana Scott; two *s. Educ:* Westminster Sch.; New Coll., Oxford (MA). *Recreations:* hunting, farming. *Heir: s* Hon. Christopher Mark Dodson, *b* 2 Aug. 1958. *Address:* Shelley's Folly, Cooksbridge, near Lewes, East Sussex. *T:* Barcombe 231. *Club:* Brooks's.

MONKS, Constance Mary, OBE 1962; *b* 20 May 1911; *d* of Ellis Green and Bessie A. Green (*née* Burwell); *m* 1937, Jack Monks; one *s* (decd). *Educ:* Wheelton County Sch.; Chorley Grammar Sch.; City of Leeds Training Coll.

Apptd Asst Teacher, 1931. Started retail business as partner with husband, 1945. Councillor (C), Chorley (N Ward), 1947-67, Alderman, 1967-74; Mayor of Chorley, 1959-60; Mem. Lancs CC, 1961-64. MP (C) Chorley, Lancs, 1970-Feb. 1974. JP Chorley, 1954. *Recreations:* reading, needlework. *Address:* 17 Sandridge Avenue, Chorley, Lancs. *T:* Chorley 76744.

MONKS, John Stephen; Head of Organisation and Industrial Relations Department, Trades Union Congress, since 1977; *b* 5 Aug. 1945; *s* of Charles Edward Monks and Bessie Evelyn Monks; *m* 1970, Francine Jacqueline Schenk; two *s* one *d. Educ:* Ducie Technical High Sch., Manchester; Nottingham Univ. (BA Econ). Joined TUC, 1969. Mem. Council, ACAS, 1979-. *Recreation:* squash. *Address:* 3 Queenswood Road, Forest Hill, SE23 2QR. *T:* 01-699 4292.

MONKSWELL, Barony of (*cr* 1885); title disclaimed by 4th Baron; *see under* Collier, William Adrian Larry.

MONMOUTH, Bishop of, since 1972; **Rt. Rev. Derrick Greenslade Childs;** *b* 14 Jan. 1918; *er s* of Alfred John and Florence Theodosia Childs; *m* 1951, Elizabeth Cicely Davies; one *s* one *d. Educ:* Whitland Grammar Sch., Carmarthenshire; University Coll., Cardiff (BA Wales, 1st cl. Hons History; Fellow 1981); Sarum Theol College at Wells. Deacon 1941, priest 1942, Diocese of St David's; Asst Curate: Milford Haven, 1941-46; Laugharne with Llansadwrnen, 1946-51; Warden of Llandaff House, Penarth (Hall of Residence for students of University Coll., Cardiff), 1951-61; Gen. Sec., Provincial Council for Education of the Church in Wales, 1955-65; Director of Church in Wales Publications, 1961-65; Chancellor of Llandaff Cathedral, 1964-69; Principal of Trinity Coll. of Education, Carmarthen, 1965-72; Canon of St David's Cathedral, 1969-72. Member: Court University College, Cardiff; Council, St David's Univ. College, Lampeter; Court, Univ. of Wales; Chm., Church in Wales Provincial Council for Educn, 1972; Chm. of Council, Historical Soc. of Church in Wales, 1972; Vice-Chm., National Society, 1973; Chm. Bd, Church in Wales Publications. Sub-Prelate, Order of St John of Jerusalem, 1972. *Publications:* Editor: Cymry'r Groes, 1947-49, Province, 1949-68, and regular contributor to those quarterly magazines; contrib.: E. T. Davies, The Story of the Church in Glamorgan, 1962; Religion in Approved Schools, 1967. *Recreations:* music, walking, and watching cricket and Rugby football. *Address:* Bishopstow, Stow Hill, Newport, Gwent NPT 4EA. *T:* Newport 63510.

MONMOUTH, Dean of; *see* Jenkins, Very Rev. F. G.

MONOD, Prof. Théodore, DèsSc; Officier de la Légion d'Honneur, 1958; Professor Emeritus at National Museum of Natural History, Paris (Assistant 1922, Professor, 1942-73); *b* 9 April 1902; *s* of Rev. Wilfred Monod and Dorina Monod; *m* 1930, Olga Pickova; two *s* one *d. Educ:* Sorbonne (Paris). Docteur ès-sciences, 1926. Sec.-Gen. (later Dir) of l'Institut Français d'Afrique Noire, 1938; Prof., Univ. of Dakar, 1957-59; Doyen, Science Faculty, Dakar, 1957-58. Mem., Academy of Sciences; Member: Acad. des Sciences d'Outre-Mer; Académie de Marine; Corresp. Mem., Académie des Sciences de Lisbonne and Académie Royale des Sciences d'Outre-Mer. Dr *hc* Köln, 1965, Neuchâtel, 1968. Gold Medallist, Royal Geographical Soc., 1960; Gold Medallist, Amer. Geographical Soc., 1961; Haile Sellassie Award for African Research, 1967. Comdr, Ordre du Christ, 1953; Commandeur, Mérite Saharien, 1962; Officier de l'Ordre des Palmes Académiques, 1966, etc. *Publications:* Méharées, Explorations au vrai Sahara, 1937; L'Hippopotame et le philosophe, 1942; Bathyfolages, 1954; (ed) Pastoralism in Tropical Africa, 1976; many scientific papers in learned jls. *Address:* 14 quai d'Orléans, 75004 Paris, France. *T:* 326 79.50; Muséum national d'Histoire naturelle, 57 rue Cuvier, 75005 Paris, France. *T:* 331 40.10.

MONRO, Sir Hector (Seymour Peter), Kt 1981; JP; DL; MP (C) Dumfries since 1964; *b* 4 Oct. 1922; *s* of late Capt. Alastair Monro, Cameron Highlanders, and Mrs Monro, Craigcleuch, Langholm, Scotland; *m* 1949, Elizabeth Anne Welch, Longstone Hall, Derbs; two *s. Educ:* Canford Sch.; King's Coll., Cambridge. RAF, 1941-46, Flight Lt; RAuxAF, 1946-53 (AEM 1953). Mem. of Queen's Body Guard for Scotland, Royal Company of Archers. Dumfries CC, 1952-67 (Chm. Planning Cttee, and Police Cttee). Chm. Dumfriesshire Unionist Assoc., 1958-63; Scottish Cons. Whip, 1967-70; a Lord Comr of HM Treasury, 1970-71; Parly Under-Sec. of State, Scottish Office, 1971-74; Opposition Spokesman on: Scottish Affairs, 1974-75; Sport, 1974-79; Parly Under-Sec. of State (with special responsibility for Sport), DoE, 1979-81. Mem. Dumfries T&AFA, 1959-67; Hon. Air Cdre, No 2622 RAuxAF Regt Sqdn, 1982-. Mem., Area Executive Cttee, Nat. Farmers' Union of Scotland; JP 1963, DL 1973, Dumfries. *Recreations:* Rugby football (Mem. Scottish Rugby Union, 1958-77, Vice-Pres., 1975, Pres., 1976-77); golf, flying, vintage sports cars. *Address:* Williamwood, Kirtlebridge, Dumfriesshire. *T:* Kirtlebridge 213. *Clubs:* Royal Air Force, MCC; Royal Scottish Automobile (Glasgow).

MONRO DAVIES, William Llewellyn, QC 1974; **His Honour Judge Monro Davies;** a Circuit Judge, since 1976; *b* 12 Feb. 1927; *s* of Thomas Llewellyn Davies and Emily Constance Davies; *m* 1956, Jean, *d* of late E. G. Innes; one *s* one *d. Educ:* Christ Coll., Brecon; Trinity Coll., Oxford (MA, LitHum). Served in RNVR, 1945-48 (Sub-Lt). Called to the Bar, Inner Temple, 1954. Mem., Gen. Council of the Bar, 1971-75. A Recorder of the Crown Court, 1972-76. *Recreations:* the theatre and cinema; watching Rugby football. *Address:* Farrar's Buildings, Temple, EC4Y 7BD. *T:* 01-583 9241. *Clubs:* Garrick; Bristol Channel Yacht (Mumbles).

MONROE, Elizabeth, (Mrs Humphrey Neame), CMG 1973; MA Oxon; Fellow of St Antony's College, Oxford, 1963-73, now Emeritus Fellow; Hon. Fellow of St Anne's College; *b* 16 Jan. 1905; *d* of late Canon Horace Monroe, Vicar of Wimbledon; *m* 1938, Humphrey Neame (*d* 1968). *Educ:* Putney High Sch., GPDST; St Anne's Coll., Oxford. Secretariat of League of Nations, Geneva, 1931; staff of Royal Institute of International Affairs, 1933; Rockefeller Travelling Fellowship, held in Middle East and French N Africa, 1936-37; Min. of Information, Dir, Middle East Div., 1940; Diplomatic correspondent, The Observer, 1944. UK rep. on UN Sub-Commn for Prevention of Discrimination and Protection of Minorities, 1947-52; staff of Economist Newspaper, London, 1945-58. Leverhulme Research Fellowship, 1969. T. E. Lawrence Medal, Royal Soc. for Asian Affairs, 1980. *Publications:* (with A. H. M. Jones) A History of Abyssinia, 1935; The Mediterranean in Politics, 1938; Britain's Moment in the Middle East: 1914-1956, 1963, rev. edn 1982; The Changing Balance of Power in the Persian Gulf, 1972; Philby of Arabia, 1973; (with Robert Mabro) Oil Producers and Consumers: conflict or cooperation, 1974. *Address:* Flat 11, Ritchie Court, 380 Banbury Road, Oxford OX2 2PW. *T:* Oxford 53778.

See also J. G. Monroe.

MONROE, John George; Social Security (formerly National Insurance) Commissioner since 1973; *b* 27 July 1913; *s* of late Canon Horace G. Monroe, Vicar of Wimbledon and Sub-dean of Southwark and of Frances Alice Monroe (*née* Stokes); *m* 1943, Jane Reynolds; one *s* two *d*. *Educ:* Marlborough Coll.; Oriel Coll., Oxford. Called to Bar, Middle Temple, 1937; Master of the Bench, 1967. *Publications:* (ed, with Judge McDonnell *qv*) Kerr on Fraud and Mistake, 7th edn; The Law of Stamp Duties, 1954 (5th edn, with R. S. Nock, 1976). *Address:* Highmead, Birchwood Grove Road, Burgess Hill, West Sussex. *T:* Burgess Hill 3350.

See also Elizabeth Monroe.

MONSELL, 2nd Viscount *cr* 1935, of Evesham; **Henry Bolton Graham Eyres Monsell;** *b* 21 Nov. 1905; *s* of 1st Viscount Monsell, PC, GBE, and Caroline Mary Sybil, CBE (*d* 1959), *d* of late H. W. Eyres, Dumbleton Hall, Evesham; *S* father, 1969. *Educ:* Eton. Served N Africa and Italy, 1942-45 (despatches); Lt-Col Intelligence Corps. US Medal of Freedom with bronze palm, 1946. *Recreation:* music. *Address:* The Mill House, Dumbleton, Evesham, Worcs. *Club:* Travellers'.

See also P. M. L. Permor.

MONSON, family name of Baron Monson.

MONSON, 11th Baron *cr* 1728; **John Monson;** Bt *cr* 1611; *b* 3 May 1932; *e s* of 10th Baron and of Bettie Northrup (who *m* 1962, Capt. James Arnold Phillips), *d* of late E. Alexander Powell; *S* father, 1958; *m* 1955, Emma, *o d* of late Anthony Devas, ARA, RP; three *s*. *Educ:* Eton; Trinity Coll., Cambridge (BA). *Heir: s* Hon. Nicholas John Monson [*b* 19 Oct. 1955; *m* 1981, Hilary, *o d* of Kenneth Martin, Nairobi and Diani Beach]. *Address:* Manor House, South Carlton, near Lincoln. *T:* Scampton 263.

MONSON, Sir (William Bonnar) Leslie, KCMG 1965 (CMG 1950); CB 1964; HM Diplomatic Service, retired; *b* 28 May 1912; *o s* of late J. W. Monson and late Selina L. Monson; *m* 1948, Helen Isobel Browne. *Educ:* Edinburgh Acad.; Hertford Coll., Oxford. Entered Civil Service (Dominions Office) 1935; transferred to Colonial Office, 1939; Asst Sec., 1944; seconded as Chief Sec. to West African Council, 1947-51; Asst Under-Sec. of State, Colonial Office, 1951-64; British High Commissioner in the Republic of Zambia, 1964-66; Dep. Under-Sec. of State, Commonwealth Office, later FCO, 1967-72. Dir, Overseas Relations Branch, St John Ambulance, 1975-81. KStJ 1975. *Address:* Golf House, Goffers Road, Blackheath, SE3. *Club:* United Oxford & Cambridge University.

MONTAGU; *see* Douglas-Scott-Montagu.

MONTAGU, family name of Duke of Manchester, Earldom of Sandwich, and Baron Swaythling.

MONTAGU OF BEAULIEU, 3rd Baron *cr* 1885; **Edward John Barrington Douglas-Scott-Montagu;** *b* 20 Oct. 1926; *o s* of 2nd Baron and Pearl (who *m* 2nd, 1936, Captain Hon. Edward Pleydell-Bouverie, RN, MVO, *s* of 6th Earl of Radnor), *d* of late Major E. B. Crake, Rifle Brigade, and Mrs Barrington Crake; *S* father, 1929; *m* 1st, 1959, Elizabeth Belinda (marr. diss. 1974), *o d* of late Capt. the Hon. John de Bathe Crossley, and late Hon. Mrs Crossley; one *s* one *d*; 2nd, 1974, Fiona Herbert; one *s*. *Educ:* St Peter's Court, Broadstairs; Ridley Coll., St Catharines, Ont; Eton Coll.; New Coll., Oxford. Late Lt Grenadier Guards; released Army, 1948. Founded Montagu Motor Car Museum, 1952 and World's first Motor Cycle Museum, 1956; created Nat. Motor Museum Trust, 1970, to administer new Nat. Motor Museum at Beaulieu, opened 1972. President: Historic Houses Assoc., 1973-78; Union of European Historic Houses, 1978-81; Fédération Internationale des Voitures Anciennes; Southern Tourist Bd; Assoc. of Brit. Transport Museums; Museums Assoc., 1982-; Vice-President: Transport Trust; British Museums Assoc.; Member: Development Commn, 1980-; Council, Nat. Heritage. Founder and Editor, Veteran and Vintage Magazine, 1956-79. *Publications:* The Motoring Montagus, 1959; Lost Causes of Motoring, 1960; Jaguar, A

Biography, 1961; The Gordon Bennett Races, 1963; Rolls of Rolls-Royce, 1966; The Gilt and the Gingerbread, 1967; Lost Causes of Motoring: Europe, vol. i, 1969, vol. ii, 1971; More Equal than Others, 1970; History of the Steam Car, 1971; The Horseless Carriage, 1975; Early Days on the Road, 1976; Behind the Wheel, 1977; Royalty on the Road, 1980; Home James, 1982. *Heir: s* Hon. Ralph Douglas-Scott-Montagu, *b* 13 March 1961. *Address:* Palace House, Beaulieu, Hants. *T:* Beaulieu 612345; Flat 11, 24 Bryanston Square, W1. *T:* 01-262 2603. *Clubs:* Veteran Car, Vintage Sports-Car, Vintage Motor Cycle, Historical Commercial Vehicle (Pres.), Disabled Drivers Motor, Show Biz Car (Pres.), Steam Boat Assoc. of Gt Britain (Vice-Pres.), and many other motoring clubs.

See also Sir E. John Chichester, Bt, Viscount Garnock.

MONTAGU, (Alexander) Victor (Edward Paulet); *b* 22 May 1906; *S* father, 1962, as 10th Earl of Sandwich, but disclaimed his peerages for life, 24 July 1964; *m* 1st, 1934, Rosemary, *d* of late Major Ralph Harding Peto; two *s* four *d*; 2nd, 1962, Anne, MBE (*d* 1981), *d* of Victor, 9th Duke of Devonshire, KG, PC. *Educ:* Eton; Trinity Coll., Cambridge. MA (Nat. Sciences). Lt 5th (Hunts) Bn The Northamptonshire Regt, TA, 1926; served France, 1940, and afterwards on Gen. Staff, Home Forces. Private Sec. to Rt Hon. Stanley Baldwin, MP, 1932-34; Treasurer, Junior Imperial League, 1934-35; Chm., Tory Reform Cttee, 1943-44. MP (C) South Dorset Div. (C 1941, Ind. C 1957, C 1958-62); contested (C) Accrington Div. Lancs, Gen. Elec., 1964. Pres., Anti-Common Market League, 1962-; Chm., Conservative Trident Gp, 1973-. *Publications:* Essays in Tory Reform, 1944; The Conservative Dilemma, 1970; articles in Quarterly Review, 1946-47. *Heir: (to disclaimed peerages): s* John Edward Hollister Montagu, *qv*. *Address:* Mapperton, Beaminster, Dorset. *Clubs:* Carlton, Brooks's.

MONTAGU, Prof. Ashley; *b* 28 June 1905; *o c* of Charles and Mary Ehrenberg; *m* 1931, Helen Marjorie Peakes; one *s* two *d*. *Educ:* Central Foundation Sch., London; Univ. of London; Univ. of Florence; Columbia Univ. (PhD 1937). Research Worker, Brit. Mus. (Natural Hist.), 1926; Curator, Physical Anthropology, Wellcome Hist. Mus., London, 1929; Asst-Prof. of Anatomy, NY Univ., 1931-38; Dir, Div. of Child Growth and Develt, NY Univ., 1931-34; Assoc.-Prof. of Anat., Hahnemann Med. Coll. and Hosp., Phila, 1938-49; Prof. and Head of Dept of Anthropology, Rutgers Univ., 1949-55; Dir of Research, NJ Cttee on Growth and Develt, 1951-55. Chm., Anisfield-Wolf Award Cttee on Race Relations, 1950-. Vis. Lectr, Harvard Univ., 1945; Regent's Prof., Univ. of Calif, Santa Barbara, 1961; Lectr, Princeton Univ., 1978-83, and Dir, Inst. Natural Philosophy, 1979-. DSc, Grinnell Coll., Iowa, 1967; DLitt Ursinus Coll., Pa, 1972. *Publications:* Coming Into Being Among the Australian Aborigines, 1937, 2nd edn 1974; Man's Most Dangerous Myth: The Fallacy of Race, 1942, 5th edn 1974; Edward Tyson, MD, FRS (1650-1708): And the Rise of Human and Comparative Anatomy in England, 1943; Introduction to Physical Anthropology, 1945, 3rd edn 1960; Adolescent Sterility, 1946; On Being Human, 1950, 2nd edn 1970; Statement on Race, 1951, 3rd edn 1972; On Being Intelligent, 1951, 3rd edn 1972; Darwin, Competition, and Cooperation, 1952; The Natural Superiority of Women, 1953, 3rd edn 1974; Immortality, 1955; The Direction of Human Development, 1955, 2nd edn 1970; The Biosocial Nature of Man, 1956; Education and Human Relations, 1958; Anthropology and Human Nature, 1957; Man: His First Million Years, 1957, 2nd edn 1969; The Reproductive Development of the Female, 1957, 3rd edn 1979; The Cultured Man, 1958; Human Heredity, 1959, 2nd edn 1963; Anatomy and Physiology (with E. B. Steen), 2 vols, 1959; A Handbook of Anthropometry, 1960; Man in Process, 1961; The Humanization of Man, 1962; Prenatal Influences, 1962; Race, Science and Humanity, 1963; The Dolphin in History (with John Lilly), 1963; The Science of Man, 1964; Life Before Birth, 1964, 2nd edn 1978; The Human Revolution, 1965; The Idea of Race, 1965; Man's Evolution (with C. Loring Brace), 1965; Up the Ivy, 1966; The American Way of Life, 1967; The Anatomy of Swearing, 1967; The Prevalence of Nonsense (with E. Darling), 1967; The Human Dialogue (with Floyd Matson), 1967; Man Observed, 1968; Man: His First Two Million Years, 1969; Sex, Man and Society, 1969; The Ignorance of Certainty (with E. Darling), 1970; Textbook of Human Genetics (with M. Levitan), 1971, 2nd edn 1977; Immortality, Religion and Morals, 1971; Touching: the human significance of the skin, 1971, 2nd edn 1978; The Elephant Man, 1971, 2nd edn 1979; Man and the Computer (with S. S. Snyder), 1972; (ed) The Endangered Environment, 1973; (ed) Frontiers of Anthropology, 1974; (ed) Culture and Human Development, 1974; (ed) The Practice of Love, 1974; (ed) Race and IQ, 1975; The Nature of Human Aggression, 1976; Human Evolution (with C. L. Brace), 1977; The Human Connection (with F. Matson), 1979; Growing Young, 1981; Editor: Studies and Essays in the History of Science and Learning; The Meaning of Love, 1953; Toynbee and History, 1956; Genetic Mechanisms in Human Disease, 1961; Atlas of Human Anatomy, 1961; Culture and the Evolution of Man, 1962; International Pictorial Treasury of Knowledge, 6 vols, 1962-63; The Concept of Race, 1964; The Concept of the Primitive, 1967; Culture: Man's Adaptive Dimension, 1968; Man and Aggression, 1968; The Origin and Evolution of Man, 1973; Learning Non-Aggression, 1978; Sociobiology Examined, 1980; Science, Evolution, and Creationism, 1982. *Recreations:* book collecting, gardening. *Address:* 321 Cherry Hill Road, Princeton, NJ 08540, USA. *T:* Area Code 609 924-3756.

MONTAGU, Hon. David Charles Samuel; *b* 6 Aug. 1928; *e s* and *heir* of 3rd Baron Swaythling, *qv*, and Mary Violet, *e d* of Major Levy, DSO; *m* 1951, Christiane Françoise (Ninette), *d* of Edgar Dreyfus, Paris; one *s* one *d*

(and one *d* decd). *Educ:* Eton; Trinity Coll., Cambridge. Exec. Dir, 1954, Chm., 1970-73, Samuel Montagu & Co. Ltd; Chm. and Chief Exec., Orion Bank, 1974-79; Chairman: Ailsa Investment Trust plc, 1981; Derby Trust plc; United British Securities Trust plc; Director: Ashdown Investment Trust PLC; Drayton Japan Trust plc; Philip Hill Investment Trust PLC; Precious Metals Trust PLC; London Weekend Television; RIT and Northern plc; Rothmans International plc; Standard Telephones and Cables plc; Trades Union Unit Trust Managers Ltd. *Recreations:* shooting, racing, theatre. *Address:* 25 Kingston House South, Ennismore Gardens, SW7. *T:* 01-581 2549. *Clubs:* White's, Turf, Portland, Pratt's.

MONTAGU, Hon. Ewen Edward Samuel, CBE 1950 (OBE mil. 1944); QC 1939; The Judge Advocate of the Fleet, 1945-73; Hon. Captain RNR, 1973; *b* 29 March 1901; 2nd *s* of 2nd Baron Swaythling; *m* 1923, Iris Rachel, *d* of late Solomon J. Solomon, RA; one *s* one *d. Educ:* Westminster Sch.; Harvard Univ.; Trinity Coll., Cambridge (MA, LLB). Called to Bar, Middle Temple, 1924, Bencher, 1948, Treas., 1968; Western Circuit. Recorder of Devizes, 1944-51, of Southampton, 1951-60; Chairman of Quarter Sessions: Hampshire, 1951-60 (Dep. Chm., 1948-51, and 1960-71); Middlesex, 1956-65 (Asst Chm., 1951-54; Dep. Chm., 1954-56); Middlesex Area of Gtr London, 1965-69; Judge, 1969; Chm. Central Council of Magistrates' Courts Cttees, 1963-71 (Vice-Chm., 1954-63). Pres. United Synagogue, 1954-62; Vice-President: Anglo-Jewish Assoc.; Nat. Addiction and Research Inst., 1969; Chm. Gen. Purposes Cttee, RYA, 1960-68; RYA Award, 1972. DL County of Southampton, 1953. RNVR, 1939-45. Order of the Crown, Yugoslavia, 1943. *Publications:* The Man Who Never Was, 1953; The Archer-Shee Case, 1974; Beyond "Top Secret U", 1977. *Recreations:* sailing, fly-fishing, shooting, beagling, golf, painting, grandchildren. *Address:* 24 Montrose Court, Exhibition Road, SW7 2QQ. *T:* 01-589 9999; Warren Beach, Beaulieu, Hants. *T:* Bucklers Hard 239. *Clubs:* Royal Ocean Racing, Bar Yacht (Hon. Commodore).

See also Ivor Montagu, J. I. R. Montagu.

MONTAGU, Ivor; author; *b* 23 April 1904; 3rd *s* of 2nd Baron Swaythling; *m* 1927, Eileen, *d* of late Francis Anton Hellstern. *Educ:* Westminster Sch.; Royal Coll. of Science, London; King's Coll., Cambridge. Pres. and/or Chm., (Ping Pong Assoc., then Table Tennis Assoc., then) English Table Tennis Assoc., 1922-33, 1936-66, Life Vice-Pres., 1970-; Pres. and Chm., International Table Tennis Fedn, 1926-67, Life Founder Pres. 1967-; Chm., Film Soc., 1925-39; film critic, editor, director, writer, producer, 1925-. Mem., BAFTA; Hon. Member: Assoc. of Cine and Television Technicians, 1970; Writers Guild, 1964; Editorial Staff, Daily Worker, 1932-33 and 1937-47; Mem. Secretariat and Bureau, World Council of Peace, 1948-67, Presidential Cttee, 1969-72; Pres., Soc. for Cultural Relations with USSR, 1973-82. Order of Liberation, First Class (Bulgaria), 1952; Lenin Peace Prize, 1959; Order of Pole Star (Mongolia), 1963; Lenin Centenary Commemoration Medal, 1970; Dimitrov Anniv. Medal, 1972; Mongolian Peace Medal, 1973. *Publications:* Table Tennis Today, 1924; Table Tennis, 1936; The Traitor Class, 1940; Plot against Peace, 1952; Land of Blue Sky, 1956; Film World, 1964; Germany's New Nazis, 1967; With Eisenstein in Hollywood, 1968; The Youngest Son (Vol. I of memoirs), 1970; numerous scenarios, translations, pamphlets, articles on current affairs, contribs to Proc. Zool. Soc. London. *Recreations:* washing up, pottering about, sleeping through television. *Address:* Old Timbers, Verdure Close, Watford WD2 7NJ. *Clubs:* MCC; Hampshire County Cricket.

See also Hon. E. E. S. Montagu, Baron Swaythling.

MONTAGU, Jennifer Iris Rachel, PhD; Curator of the Photograph Collection, Warburg Institute, since 1971; *b* 20 March 1931; *d* of Hon. Ewen Edward Samuel Montagu, *qv. Educ:* Brearley Sch., New York; Benenden Sch., Kent; Lady Margaret Hall, Oxford (BA); Warburg Inst., London (PhD). Assistant Regional Director, Arts Council of Gt Britain, North West Region, 1953-54; Lecturer in the History of Art, Reading Univ., 1958-64; Asst Curator of the Photograph Collection, Warburg Inst., 1964-71. Slade Prof., Cambridge, and Fellow Jesus Coll., Cambridge, 1980-81. Member: Academic Awards Cttee, British Fedn of University Women, 1963-; Executive Cttee, National Art-Collections Fund, 1973-; Consultative Cttee, Burlington Magazine, 1975-. *Publications:* Bronzes, 1963; (with Jacques Thuillier) Catalogue of exhibn Charles Le Brun, 1963; articles in learned periodicals. *Address:* 10 Roland Way, SW7 3RE. *T:* 01-373 6691; Warburg Institute, Woburn Square, WC1H 0AB.

MONTAGU, John Edward Hollister; (Viscount Hinchingbrooke, but does not use the title); journalist; Information Officer, Christian Aid, since 1974; *b* 11 April 1943; *er s* of Victor Montagu, *qv*, and *heir* to disclaimed Earldom of Sandwich; *m* 1968, Caroline, *o d* of Canon P. E. C. Hayman, Rogate, W Sussex; two *s* one *d. Educ:* Eton; Trinity College, Cambridge. *Address:* 69 Albert Bridge Road, SW11 4QE.

MONTAGU, Montague Francis Ashley; *see* Montagu, A.

MONTAGU, Victor; *see* Montagu, A. V. E. P.

MONTAGU DOUGLAS SCOTT, family name of **Duke of Buccleuch.**

MONTAGU-POLLOCK, Sir G. S.; *see* Pollock.

MONTAGU-POLLOCK, Sir William H., KCMG 1957 (CMG 1946); *b* 12 July 1903; *s* of Sir M. F. Montagu-Pollock, 3rd Bt; *m* 1st, 1933, Frances Elizabeth Prudence (marr. diss. 1945), *d* of late Sir John Fischer Williams, CBE, KC; one *s* one *d*; 2nd, 1948, Barbara, *d* of late P. H. Jowett, CBE, FRCA, RWS; one *s. Educ:* Marlborough Coll.; Trinity Coll., Cambridge. Served in Diplomatic Service at Rome, Belgrade, Prague, Vienna, Stockholm, Brussels, and at Foreign Office; British Ambassador, Damascus, 1952-53 (Minister, 1950-52); British Ambassador: to Peru, 1953-58; to Switzerland, 1958-60; to Denmark, 1960-62. Retired from HM Foreign Service, 1962. Governor, European Cultural Foundation; Dir, European Cultural Foundn (UK Cttee); Inst. of Linguists, European Acad. GB; Vice-Pres., Soc. for Promotion of New Music. *Address:* 28 Drayton Gardens, SW10. *T:* 01-373 3685; Playa Blanca, Yaiza, Lanzarote, Canary Islands. *Club:* Athenæum.

MONTAGU-STUART-WORTLEY-MACKENZIE, family name of **Earl of Wharncliffe.**

MONTAGUE, family name of **Baron Amwell.**

MONTAGUE, Francis Arnold, CMG 1956; retired; *b* 14 June 1904; *s* of late Charles Edward Montague, OBE, author and journalist, and of Madeleine Montague (*née* Scott), Manchester; *m* 1939, Fanny Susanne, *d* of late E. S. Scorer and Mrs C. D. Scorer; one *d. Educ:* Cargilfield Sch., Edinburgh; Rugby Sch.; Balliol Coll., Oxford. Tanganyika: served in Game Preservation Dept, 1925-28; Cadet, Colonial Administrative Service, 1928; Dist Officer, 1938; Private Sec. to Governor, 1938-40; Asst Chief Sec., 1948; Administrative Sec., Sierra Leone, 1950-58; retired from Colonial Service, Jan. 1958. Deputy-Chairman: Public Service Commn, Uganda, 1958-63; Public Service Commn, Aden, 1963. Mem., Oxon CC, 1964-73, Witney (Oxon) RDC, 1966-74; W Oxon Dist. Council, 1973-76. *Recreation:* gardening. *Address:* Dolphin House, Westhall Hill, Fulbrook OX8 4BN. *T:* Burford 2147. *Club:* Lansdowne.

MONTAGUE, Leslie Clarence; Chairman, Johnson Matthey & Co. Ltd, 1966-71; *b* 28 May 1901; *s* of Albert Edward Montague and Clara Amelia Chapman; *m* 1926, Ellen Rose Margaret Keene; no *c. Educ:* Bancroft's School, Woodford. 50 years' service with Johnson Matthey & Co. Ltd; appointed Secretary, 1934, and a Director, 1946. *Recreations:* walking, gardening. *Address:* Jasmine Cottage, Piddinghoe, near Newhaven, East Sussex.

MONTAGUE, Michael Jacob, CBE 1970; Chairman: Valor Company Ltd since 1965 (Managing Director, 1963); English Tourist Board, since 1979; Member, British Tourist Authority, since 1979; *b* 10 March 1932; *s* of David Elias Montague and Eleanor Stagg. *Educ:* High Wycombe Royal Grammar Sch.; Magdalen Coll. Sch., Oxford. Founded Gatehill Beco Ltd, 1958 (sold to Valor Co., 1962). Pres., Young European Management Assoc.; Gov., Nat. Inst. of Hardware; Chairman: Asia Cttee, BNEC, 1968-71; Immigration Cttee, Kent Social Service; Hon. Treas., British Assoc. for World Government. *Address:* 17 Stratford Road, W8.

MONTAGUE BROWNE, Anthony Arthur Duncan, CBE 1965 (OBE 1955); DFC 1945; a Managing Director, Gerrard and National PLC, since 1974 (Director, since 1967); *b* 8 May 1923; *s* of late Lt-Col A. D. Montague Browne, DSO, OBE, Bivia House, Goodrich, Ross-on-Wye, and Violet Evelyn (*née* Downes); *m* 1st, 1950, Noel Evelyn Arnold-Wallinger (marr. diss. 1970); one *d*; 2nd, 1970, Shelagh Macklin (*née* Mulligan). *Educ:* Stowe; Magdalen Coll., Oxford; abroad. Pilot RAF, 1941-45. Entered Foreign (now Diplomatic) Service, 1946; Foreign Office, 1946-49; Second Sec., British Embassy, Paris, 1949-52; seconded as Private Sec. to Prime Minister, 1952-55; seconded as Private Sec. to Rt Hon. Sir Winston Churchill, 1955-65; Counsellor, Diplomatic Service, 1964; seconded to HM Household, 1965-67; Trustee and Chm. of Council, Winston Churchill Memorial Trust; Chm., Internat. Certificate of Deposit Market Assoc. *Address:* c/o R3 Section, Lloyds Bank Ltd, Cox's & King's Branch, 6 Pall Mall, SW1. *Clubs:* Boodle's, Pratt's.

MONTAGUE-JONES, Brigadier (retd) Ronald, CBE 1944 (MBE 1941); jssc; psc; *b* 10 Dec. 1909; *yr s* of late Edgar Montague Jones, until 1932 Headmaster of St Albans Sch., Herts, and of late Emmeline Mary Yates; *m* 1937, Denise Marguerite (marr. diss.), *y d* of late General Sir Hubert Gough, GCB, GCMG, KCVO; one *s*; *m* 1955, Pamela, *d* of late Lieut-Col Hastings Roy Harington, 8th Gurkha Rifles, and the Hon. Mrs Harington; one *s. Educ:* St Albans Sch., Herts; RMA, Woolwich; St John's Coll., Cambridge (BA 1933, MA 1937). 2nd Lieut RE 1930; Temp. Brig. 1943; Bt Lt-Col 1952; Brig. 1958. Egypt, 1935; Palestine, 1936-39 (despatches twice); War of 1939-45 (MBE, CBE, US Bronze Star, Africa Star, 1939-45 Star, Italy Star, Burma Star, General Service Medal with Clasps Palestine, SE Asia and Malaya). CC Dorset, for Swanage (East), 1964-74, Swanage, 1974-. *Address:* 10 Battlemead, Swanage, Dorset BH19 1PH. *T:* Swanage 3186.

MONTAGUE-SMITH, Patrick Wykeham; Editor of Debrett, 1962-80, Consulting Editor since 1980; *b* 3 Jan. 1920; *o s* of late Major Vernon Milner Montague-Smith, Richmond, Surrey, and Sybil Katherine, *d* of late William Wykeham Frederick Bourne, Kensington, and Foxbury House, Worcs; *m* 1974, Annabelle Christina Calvert, *o d* of late Noel Newton, MA and Isabella Newton, 65 Abbotsbury Close, Kensington, W14. *Educ:* Lynfield, Hunstanton and Mercers' Sch. Served RASC, 8 Corps, 1940-46; in NW Europe, 1944-46. Asst Editor of Debrett, 1946-62. Dir, Debrett's Peerage Ltd,

1976-81. A Vice-Pres., English Genealogical Congress, Cambridge, 1975. Fellow, Soc. of Genealogists, 1969; Member: Heraldry Soc.; Soc. of Descendants of Knights of the Garter (Windsor); Sublime Soc. of Beefsteaks (Hon.); Kt, Internat. Mark Twain Soc., Missouri. Freeman of the City of London. *Publications:* Royal Line of Succession, 1953; The Prince of Wales, 1958; Princess Margaret, 1961; Debrett's Correct Form, 1970, new edn 1976; Debrett's Royal Wedding: HRH Princess Anne and Captain Mark Phillips, 1973; The Royal Year, 1974, 1975, 1976; The Country Life Book of the Royal Silver Jubilee (1977), 1976; (with Charles Kidd) The Royal Betrothal, 1981; (with Hugh Montgomery-Massingberd) The Country Life Book of Royal Palaces, Castles and Homes, 1981; (with Charles Kidd) Debrett's Book of Royal Children, 1982; contribs to Encyclopædia Britannica and various journals and newspapers, principally on genealogy, heraldry, royal and historical subjects, also lectures, television and broadcasts. *Recreations:* genealogy, heraldry, British history, visiting country houses and browsing in bookshops. *Address:* Brereton, 197 Park Road, Kingston upon Thames, Surrey. *T:* 01-546 8807.

MONTAND, Simone H. C.; *see* Signoret, Simone.

MONTEAGLE OF BRANDON, 6th Baron *cr* 1839; **Gerald Spring Rice;** late Captain, Irish Guards; one of HM Body Guard, Hon. Corps of Gentlemen-at-Arms, since 1978; *b* 5 July 1926; *s* of 5th Baron and Emilie de Kosenko (*d* 1981), *d* of Mrs Edward Brooks, Philadelphia, USA; *S* father 1946; *m* 1949, Anne, *d* of late Col G. J. Brownlow, Ballywhite, Portaferry, Co. Down; one *s* three *d* (of whom two are twins). *Educ:* Harrow. Member: London Stock Exchange, 1958-76; Lloyd's, 1978-. *Heir: s* Hon. Charles James Spring Rice, *b* 24 Feb. 1953. *Address:* 242A Fulham Road, SW10. *Clubs:* Cavalry and Guards, Pratt's; Kildare Street and University (Dublin).

MONTEATH, Robert Campbell, CBE 1964; County Clerk, Treasurer and Local Taxation Officer, Kirkcudbright, 1946-72, and Clerk to the Lieutenancy, since 1966; *b* 15 June 1907; *s* of Gordon Drysdale Monteath, Dumbarton; *m* 1936, Sarah McGregor, *d* of John Fenwick, Dumbarton; two *s* one *d. Educ:* Dumbarton Academy; Glasgow Univ. Dep. County Clerk, Dunbartonshire, 1937-46; Dep. Civil Defence Controller, 1939-46; Hon. Sheriff, Kirkcudbright, 1966-. Past District Governor, Rotary Internat., District 102. *Address:* Gortonbrae, Townhead, Kirkcudbright. *T:* Townhead 251. *Clubs:* Royal Over-Seas League; Royal Scottish Automobile (Glasgow).

MONTEFIORE, Harold Henry S.; *see* Sebag-Montefiore.

MONTEFIORE, Rt. Rev. Hugh William; *see* Birmingham, Bishop of.

MONTEITH, Charles Montgomery; Senior Editorial Consultant, Faber & Faber Ltd, since 1981; Fellow of All Souls College, Oxford, since 1948; *b* 9 Feb. 1921; *s* of late James Monteith and late Marian Monteith (*née* Montgomery). *Educ:* Royal Belfast Academical Instn; Magdalen Coll., Oxford (Demy 1939, Sen. Demy 1948, MA 1948, BCL 1949). Sub-Warden, All Souls Coll., Oxford, 1967-69. Served War, Royal Inniskilling Fusiliers, India and Burma (Major), 1940-45. Called to the Bar, Gray's Inn, 1949; joined Faber & Faber, 1953, Dir, 1954, Vice-Chm., 1974-76, Chm., 1977-80. Dir, Poetry Book Soc., 1966-81; Member: Literature Panel, Arts Council of GB, 1974-78; Library Adv. Council for England, 1979-81. Hon. DLitt: NUU, Coleraine, 1980; Kent, 1982. *Address:* c/o Faber & Faber Ltd, 3 Queen Square, WC1. *T:* 01-278 6881. *Clubs:* Beefsteak, Garrick.

MONTEITH, Rt. Rev. George Rae, BA; *b* 14 Feb. 1904; *s* of John Hodge Monteith and Ellen (*née* Hall); *m* 1931, Kathleen Methven Mules; two *s* one *d. Educ:* St John's Coll., Auckland; Univ. of New Zealand. BA 1927. Deacon, 1928; priest, 1929; Curate: St Matthew's, Auckland, 1928-30; Stoke-on-Trent, 1931-33; Vicar of: Dargaville, NZ, 1934-37; Mt Eden, Auckland, NZ, 1937-49; St Mary's Cathedral Parish, Auckland, 1949-69; Dean of Auckland, 1949-69; Vicar-General, 1963-76; Asst Bishop of Auckland, NZ, 1965-76. *Address:* 7 Cathedral Place, Auckland 1, NZ. *T:* 734.449.

MONTEITH, Brig. John Cassels, CBE 1968; MC 1938; JP; Colonel, The Black Watch, 1976-81; *b* 28 Sept. 1915; *s* of Lt-Col John Cassels Monteith (killed in action 1915), Moniaive, Dumfriesshire, and of Mrs Jane Robertson Monteith (*née* Wilson), Dunning, Perthshire; *m* 1st, 1949, Winifred Elisabeth (*d* 1968), *d* of Louis Cecil Breitmeyer, Kettering; one *s* one *d*; 2nd, 1973, Pamela Joan, *d* of Col Francis E. Laughton, MC, TD. *Educ:* Stowe; Trinity Coll., Cambridge (BA). 2nd Lieut Black Watch, 1935; served War 1939-45, ME, Italy and NW Europe; CO 1st Bn Black Watch, 1957-59; Col 1961; Comdr 155 (L) Inf. Bde, TA, 1962-65; Brig. 1963; Defence and Mil. Attaché, Bonn, 1965-68; Comdr Highland Area, 1968-70; retd 1970. Chm., Highland TAVR Assoc., 1971-76. Brig., Queen's Body Guard for Scotland (Royal Company of Archers), 1972. JP Perthshire, 1972. *Recreations:* shooting, gardening. *Address:* Essendy House, Blairgowrie, Perthshire. *T:* Essendy 260. *Clubs:* Army and Navy; Royal Perth.

MONTEITH, Prof. John Lennox, FRS 1971; FRSE 1972; Professor of Environmental Physics, University of Nottingham, since 1967; *b* 3 Sept. 1929; *s* of Rev. John and Margaret Monteith; *m* 1955, Elsa Marion Wotherspoon; four *s* one *d. Educ:* George Heriot's Sch.; Univ. of Edinburgh; Imperial Coll., London. BSc, DIC, PhD. Mem. Physics Dept Staff, Rothamsted Experimental Station, 1954-67. FInstP, FIBiol. Governor, Grassland Res. Inst., 1976-. Vice

Pres., British Ecological Soc., 1977-79; Pres., Royal Meteorol Soc., 1978-80. Member: NERC, 1980-; British Nat. Cttee for the World Climate Programme, 1980-. *Publications:* Instruments for Micrometeorology (ed), 1972; Principles of Environmental Physics, 1973; (ed with L. E. Mount) Heat Loss from Animals and Man, 1974; (ed) Vegetation and the Atmosphere, 1975; (ed with C. Webb) Soil Water and Nitrogen, 1981; papers on Micrometeorology and Crop Science in: Quarterly Jl of RMetSoc.; Jl Applied Ecology, etc. *Recreations:* music, photography. *Address:* School of Agriculture, Sutton Bonington, Loughborough, Leics LE12 5RD. *T:* Kegworth 2386.

MONTEITH, Lt-Col Robert Charles Michael, OBE 1981; MC 1943; TD 1945; JP; Vice Lord-Lieutenant of Lanarkshire since 1964; Land-owner and Farmer since 1950; *b* 25 May 1914; *s* of late Major J. B. L. Monteith, CBE, and late Dorothy, *d* of Sir Charles Nicholson, 1st Bt; *m* 1950, Mira Elizabeth, *e d* of late John Fanshawe, Sidmount, Moffat; one *s. Educ:* Ampleforth Coll., York. CA (Edinburgh), 1939. Served with Lanarkshire Yeomanry, 1939-45: Paiforce, 1942-43; MEF, 1943-44; BLA, 1944-45. Contested (U) Hamilton Division of Lanarkshire, 1950 and 1951. Member: Mental Welfare Commn for Scotland, 1962-; E Kilbride Develt Corp., 1972-76. DL 1955, JP 1955, CC 1949-64, 1967-74, Lanarkshire; Chm., Lanark DC, later Clydesdale DC, 1974-. Mem. Queen's Body Guard for Scotland, Royal Company of Archers. Mem. SMO of Knights of Malta; OStJ 1973. *Recreations:* shooting, curling. *Address:* Cranley, Cleghorn, Lanark. *T:* Carstairs 330. *Clubs:* New, Puffins (Edinburgh).

MONTGOMERIE, family name of **Earl of Eglinton.**

MONTGOMERIE, Lord; **Hugh Archibald William Montgomerie;** *b* 24 July 1966; *s* and *heir* of 18th Earl of Eglinton and Winton, *qv.*

MONTGOMERY, family name of **Viscount Montgomery of Alamein.**

MONTGOMERY OF ALAMEIN, 2nd Viscount *cr* 1946, of Hindhead; **David Bernard Montgomery,** CBE 1975; Managing Director, Terimar Services (Overseas Trade Consultancy), since 1974; Director: Northern Engineering Industries, since 1981; KCA International, since 1981; *b* 18 Aug. 1928; *s* of 1st Viscount Montgomery of Alamein, KG, GCB, DSO, and Elizabeth (*d* 1937), *d* of late Robert Thompson Hobart, ICS; *S* father, 1976; *m* 1st, 1953, Mary Connell (marr. diss. 1967); one *s* one *d*; 2nd, 1970, Tessa, *d* of late Gen. Sir Frederick Browning, GCVO, KBE, CB, DSO, and of Lady Browning, DBE (*see* Dame Daphne du Maurier). *Educ:* Winchester, Trinity Coll., Cambridge (MA). Shell International, 1951-62; Yardley International (Director), 1963-74; Director of various companies, 1974-. Editorial Adviser, Vision Interamericana, 1974-. Chm., Economic Affairs Cttee, Canning House, 1973-75; Pres., British Industrial Exhibition, Sao Paulo, 1974. Councillor, Royal Borough of Kensington and Chelsea, 1974-78. Hon. Consul, Republic of El Salvador, 1973-77. Pres., Anglo-Argentine Soc., 1977-; Chairman: Hispanic and Luso Brazilian Council, 1978-80; Brazilian Chamber of Commerce in GB, 1980-82. Patron, D-Day and Normandy Fellowship, 1980-. President: Redgrave Theatre, Farnham, 1977-; Restaurateurs Assoc. of GB, 1982-. Governor, Amesbury Sch., 1976-. *Recreations:* golf, sailing. *Heir: s* Hon. Henry David Montgomery [b 2 April 1954; *m* 1980, Caroline, *e d* of Richard Odey, Hotham Hall, York]. *Address:* Isington Mill, Alton, Hants GU34 4PW. *T:* Bentley 23126. *Clubs:* Garrick; Royal Fowey Yacht.

MONTGOMERY, Sir (Basil Henry) David, 9th Bt, *cr* 1801, of Stanhope; JP; DL; landowner; Chairman, Forestry Commission, since 1979; *b* 20 March 1931; *s* of late Lt-Col H. K. Purvis-Montgomery, OBE, and of Mrs C. L. W. Purvis-Russell-Montgomery (*née* Maconochie Welwood); *S* uncle, 1964; *m* 1956, Delia, *o d* of Adm. Sir (John) Peter (Lorne) Reid, GCB, CVO; one *s* four *d* (and one *s* decd). *Educ:* Eton. National Service, Black Watch, 1949-51. Member: Nature Conservancy Council, 1973-79; Tayside Regional Authority, 1974-79. Hon. LLD Dundee, 1977. DL Kinross-shire, 1960, Vice-Lieutenant 1966-74; JP 1966; DL Perth and Kinross, 1975. *Heir: s* James David Keith Montgomery, *b* 13 June 1957. *Address:* Kinross House, Kinross. *T:* Kinross 63416.

MONTGOMERY, (Charles) John, CBE 1977; Director since 1972, and a Vice-Chairman, since 1978, Lloyds Bank Ltd; Director: Lloyds Bank International, since 1978; Yorkshire Bank, since 1980; *b* 18 Feb. 1917; *s* of late Rev. Charles James Montgomery; *m* 1950, Gwenneth Mary McKendrick; two *d. Educ:* Colwyn Bay Grammar School. Served with RN, 1940-46. Entered Lloyds Bank, 1935; Jt Gen. Man. 1968; Asst Chief Gen. Man. 1970; Dep. Chief Gen. Man. 1973; Chief Gen. Man., 1973-78. Pres., Inst. of Bankers, 1976-77, Vice-Pres., 1977. Chm., Chief Exec. Officers' Cttee, Cttee of London Clearing Bankers, 1976-78. *Recreations:* walking, photography. *Address:* High Cedar, 6 Cedar Copse, Bickley, Kent. *T:* 01-467 2410. *Clubs:* Naval, Overseas Bankers.

MONTGOMERY, David, OBE 1972; HM Diplomatic Service; British Deputy High Commissioner: to Barbados, since 1980, also (non-resident) to Antigua and Barbuda, Dominica, Grenada, St Lucia and St Vincent; concurrently, Deputy British Government Representative to the West Indies Associated States; *b* 29 July 1927; *s* of late David Montgomery and of Mary (*née* Walker Cunningham); *m* 1955, Margaret Newman; one *s* one *d*. GPO, Glasgow, 1941-45; Royal Navy, 1945-48; GPO, Glasgow, 1948-49; Foreign Office, 1949-52; Bucharest, 1952-53; FO, 1953-55; Bonn, 1955-58;

Düsseldorf, 1958-61; Rangoon, 1961-63; Ottawa, 1963-64; Regina, Saskatchewan, 1964-65; FCO, 1966-68; Bangkok, 1968-72; Zagreb, 1973-76; FCO, 1976-79. *Recreations:* golf, music (light and opera). *Address:* c/o Foreign and Commonwealth Office, SW1. *T:* 01-233 3000. *Club:* Royal Over-Seas League.

MONTGOMERY, Prof. Desmond Alan Dill, CBE 1981 (MBE 1943); MD; FRCP, FRCPI; Chairman, Northern Ireland Council for Postgraduate Medical Education, since 1979; *b* 6 June 1916; 3rd *s* of late Dr and Mrs J. Howard Montgomery, China and Belfast; *m* 1941, Dr Susan Holland, 2nd *d* of late Mr and Mrs F. J. Holland, Belfast; one *s* one *d*. *Educ:* Inchmarlo Prep. Sch.; Campbell Coll.; Queen's Univ., Belfast (3rd, 4th and final yr scholarships; MB, BCh, BAO 1st Cl. Hons 1940; MD (Gold Medal) 1946). Sinclair Medal in Surgery, Butterworth Prize in Medicine, Prize in Mental Disease, QUB. MRCP 1948, FRCP 1964; FRCPI 1975; FRCOG (*ae*) 1981. Served War, RAMC, 1941-46: Temp. Major India Comd; DADMS GHQ India, 1943-45. House Physician and Surgeon, Royal Victoria Hosp., Belfast, 1940-41, Registrar, 1946; Registrar, Royal Postgrad. Med. Sch. and Hammersmith Hosp., and National Heart Hosp., London, 1946-48; Royal Victoria Hosp., Belfast: Sen. Registrar, 1948-51; Consultant Physician, 1951-79, Hon. Consultant 1980-; Physician i/c Sir George E. Clark Metabolic Unit, 1958-79; Endocrinologist, Royal Maternity Hosp., Belfast, 1958-79; Hon. Reader in Endocrinol., Dept of Medicine, QUB, 1969-75, Hon. Prof., 1975-. Hon. Secretary: Royal Victoria Med. Staff Cttee, 1964-66 (Chm., 1975-77); Ulster Med. Soc., 1954-58 (Pres., 1975-76). Member: NI Council for Health and Personal Social Services, 1974- (Chm., Central Med. Adv. Cttee, 1974-); NI Med. Manpower Adv. Cttee, 1974, Distinction and Meritorious Awards Cttee, 1975- (Chm., 1982-83); Faculty of Medicine, QUB, 1969- (Chm., Ethical Cttee, 1975-81); Senate, QUB, 1979-; GMC, 1979-. Member: BMA; Assoc. of Physicians of GB and NI; Eur. Thyroid Assoc.; Corrigan Club (Chm., 1969); Irish Endocrine Soc. (1st Chm., Founder Mem.); Internat. Soc. for Internal Medicine; formerly Mem., Eur. Soc. for Study of Diabetes; Hon. Mem., British Dietetic Assoc. Lectured in USA, India, Greece, Australia and Nigeria; visited Russia on behalf of British Council, 1975. Pres., Belfast City Mission, 1973; Mem., Bd of Trustees, Presbyterian Church in Ireland. DSc (*hc*) NUI, 1980. Jt Editor, Ulster Med. Jl, 1974-. *Publications:* (contrib.) Whitla's Dictionary of Treatment, 1957; (contrib.) Good Health and Diabetes, 1961, 3rd edn 1976; (contrib.) R. Smith, Progress in Clinical Surgery, 1961; (with R. B. Welbourn) Clinical Endocrinology for Surgeons, 1963; (contrib.) Progress in Neurosurgery, 1964; (with R. B. Welbourn) Medical and Surgical Endocrinology, 1975; (contrib.) M. D. Vickers, Medicine for Anaesthetists, 1977; articles in med. jls on endocrinology, diabetes mellitus and related subjects. *Recreations:* travel, photography, music, gardening, philately. *Address:* 59 Church Road, Newtownbreda, Belfast BT8 4AN. *T:* Belfast 648326; 15 Carrickmore Road, Ballycastle BT54 6QS. *T:* Ballycastle 62361.

MONTGOMERY, Fergus; *see* Montgomery, (William) Fergus.

MONTGOMERY, Prof. George Lightbody, CBE 1960; TD 1942; MD, PhD, FRCPE, FRCPGlas, FRCPath, FRCSE; FRSE; Professor of Pathology, University of Edinburgh, 1954-71, now Emeritus; *b* 3 Nov. 1905; *o s* of late John Montgomery and Jeanie Lightbody; *m* 1933, Margaret Sutherland, 3rd *d* of late A. Henry Forbes, Oban; one *s* one *d*. *Educ:* Hillhead High Sch., Glasgow; Glasgow Univ. MB, ChB, 1928; Commendation and RAMC Memorial Prize; PhD (St Andrews), 1937; MD Hons and Bellahouston Gold Medal (Glasgow), 1946. House Physician, House Surgeon, Glasgow Royal Infirmary, 1928-29; Lecturer in Clinical Pathology, Univ. of St Andrews, 1931-37; Lecturer in Pathology of Disease in Infancy and Childhood, Univ. of Glasgow, 1937-48; Asst Pathologist, Glasgow Royal Infirmary, 1929-31; Asst Pathologist, Dundee Royal Infirmary, 1931-37; Pathologist, Royal Hospital for Sick Children, Glasgow, 1937-48; Professor of Pathology (St Mungo-Notman Chair), Univ. of Glasgow, 1948-54. Chm. Scottish Health Services Council, 1954-59. Hon. Member: Pathological Soc. Gt Britain and Ireland; BMA. Col (Hon.) Army Medical Service. *Publications:* numerous contribs to medical and scientific journals. *Recreation:* music. *Address:* 2 Cumin Place, Edinburgh EH9 2JX. *T:* 031-667 6792. *Club:* New (Edinburgh).

MONTGOMERY, Group Captain George Rodgers, CBE 1946; DL; RAF (Retired); Secretary, Norfolk Naturalists' Trust, 1963-75; Hon. Appeal Secretary, and Member of the Court, University of East Anglia, since Nov. 1966; *b* 31 May 1910; *s* of late John Montgomery, Belfast; *m* 1932, Margaret McHarry Heslip (*d* 1981), *d* of late William J. Heslip, Belfast; two *s*; *m* 1982, Margaret Stephanie, *widow* of Colin Vanner Hedworth Foulkes. *Educ:* Royal Academy, Belfast. Commnd in RAF, 1928; retd 1958. Served in UK and ME, 1928-38. War of 1939-45: Bomber Comd, NI, Air Min. and ME. Served UK, Japan and W Europe, 1946-58: Comdr RAF Wilmslow, 1946-47; Air Adviser to UK Polit. Rep. in Japan, and Civil Air Attaché, Tokyo, 1948-49; Chief Instr RAF Officers' Advanced Trg Sch., 1950; Comdt RAF Sch. of Admin, Bircham Newton, 1951-52; Comdr RAF Hednesford, 1953-54; DDO (Estabts) Air Min. and Comn. RAF Western European Estabts Cttee, Germany, 1955-57. On retirement, Organising Sec. Friends of Norwich Cathedral, 1959-62; Appeal Sec., Univ. of East Anglia, 1961-66; Hon. Vice-Pres., Norfolk Naturalists' Trust; Member: Great Bustard Trust Council; Broads Soc. Cttee. DL Norfolk, 1979. *Recreations:* river cruising, gardening. *Address:* 24 Cathedral Close, Norwich, Norfolk. *T:* Norwich 28024. *Club:* Royal Air Force.

MONTGOMERY, Hugh Bryan Greville; Managing Director, Andry Montgomery group of companies (organisers, managers and consultants in exhibitions), since 1952; *b* 26 March 1929; *s* of Hugh Roger Greville Montgomery, MC, and Molly Audrey Montgomery (*née* Neele). *Educ:* Repton; Lincoln Coll., Oxford (MA PPE). Founder member, Oxford Univ. Wine and Food Soc. Consultant and adviser on trade fairs and developing countries for UN. Chairman: Brit. Assoc. of Exhibn Organisers, 1970; Union des Foires Internat. Bldg Specialised Cttee, 1975-; Internat. Cttee, Amer. Nat. Assoc. of Exposition Managers, 1980-; Chm. of Trustees of ECHO (Supply of Equipment to Charity Hosps Overseas), 1978-; Vice-Chm., Bldg Conservation Trust, 1979- (Chm. Interbuild Fund, 1977). Hon. Treas., Contemporary Art Soc., 1980-; Member Executive Committee: CGLI, 1974-; Nat. Fund for Research into Crippling Diseases, 1970-. Master, Worshipful Co. of Tylers and Bricklayers, 1980-81. Silver Jubilee Medal, 1977. *Publications:* Industrial Fairs and Developing Countries (UNIDO), 1975; contrib. to Internat. Trade Forum (ITC, Geneva). *Recreations:* collecting contemparary art, theatre, wine tasting. *Address:* 11 Manchester Square, W1M 5AB. *T:* 01-486 1951. *Clubs:* United Oxford & Cambridge University, City Livery.

MONTGOMERY, John; *see* Montgomery, C. J.

MONTGOMERY, John Matthew; Clerk of the Salters' Company, since 1975; *b* 22 May 1930; *s* of Prof. George Allison Montgomery, QC, and Isabel A. (*née* Morison); *m* 1956, Gertrude Gillian Richards; two *s* one *d*. *Educ:* Rugby Sch.; Trinity Hall, Cambridge (MA). Various commercial appointments with Mobil Oil Corporation and First National City Bank, 1953-74. Chm., Surrey Trust for Nature Conservation Ltd, 1973-; Member: Exec. Cttee, Nat. Assoc. of Almshouses, 1980-; Council, Royal Soc. for Nature Conservation, 1980-; Council, London Wildlife Trust, 1981-; Conservation Cttee, Botanical Soc. of British Isles, 1982-. *Recreations:* various natural history interests. *Address:* Dunedin, Red Lane, Claygate, Esher, Surrey KT10 0ES. *T:* Esher 64780.

MONTGOMERY, Col John Rupert Patrick, OBE 1979; MC 1943; *b* 25 July 1913; *s* of George Howard and Mabella Montgomery; *m* 1st, 1940, Alice Vyvyan Patricia Mitchell (*d* 1976); one *s* two *d*; 2nd, 1981, Marguerite Beatrice Chambers (*née* Montgomery). *Educ:* Wellington Coll.; RMC, Sandhurst. Commissioned, Oxfordshire and Buckinghamshire LI, 1933; Regimental Service in India, 1935-40 and 1946-47. Served War, in Middle East, N Africa and Italy, 1942-45. Commanded 17 Bn Parachute Regt (9 DLI), 1953-56; SHAPE Mission to Portugal, 1956-59; retired, 1962. Sec., Anti-Slavery Soc., 1963-80. Silver Medal, RSA, 1973. *Address:* The Oast House, Buxted, Sussex. *Club:* Army and Navy.

MONTGOMERY of Blessingbourne, Captain Peter Stephen; Vice-Lieutenant of County Tyrone, Northern Ireland, 1971-79; *b* 13 Aug. 1909; 2nd *s* of late Maj.-Gen. Hugh Maude de Fellenberg Montgomery, CB, CMG, DL, RA, and late Mary, 2nd *d* of Edmund Langton and Mrs Massingberd, Gunby Hall, Lincs. *Educ:* Wellington Coll.; Trinity Coll., Cambridge (MA). Founder, 1927, and Conductor until 1969, of Fivemiletown Choral Soc.; employed with BBC in N Ireland and London, 1931-47; Asst Music Dir and Conductor, BBC Northern Ireland Symphony Orchestra, 1933-38. Served War of 1939-45: Captain, Royal Intelligence Corps, ADC to Viceroy of India (FM Earl Wavell), 1945-46. Mem. BBC Northern Ireland Advisory Council, 1952-71, and BBC Gen. Adv. Council, 1963-71. Hon. ADC to Governor of Northern Ireland (Lord Wakehurst), 1954-64; Member: National Trust Cttee for NI, 1955-75; Bd of Visitors, HM Prison, Belfast (Chm. 1971); Friends of National Collections of Ireland; Bd of Arts Council of NI (Pres., 1964-74). JP 1959, DL 1956, Co. Tyrone; High Sheriff of Co. Tyrone, 1964. Hon. LLD Queen's Univ. Belfast, 1976. Silver Jubilee Medal, 1977. *Address:* Blessingbourne, Fivemiletown, Co. Tyrone, Northern Ireland. *Clubs:* Oriental; Ulster (Belfast); Tyrone County (Omagh).

MONTGOMERY, (William) Fergus; MP (C) Altrincham and Sale, since Oct. 1974; *b* 25 Nov. 1927; *s* of William Montgomery and late Winifred Montgomery; *m* Joyce, *d* of George Riddle. *Educ:* Jarrow Grammar Sch.; Bede Coll., Durham. Served in Royal Navy, 1946-48; Schoolmaster, 1950-59. Nat. Vice-Chm. Young Conservative Organisation, 1954-57, National Chm., 1957-58; contested (C) Consett Division, 1955; MP (C): Newcastle upon Tyne East, 1959-64; Brierley Hill, Apr. 1967-Feb. 1974; contested Dudley W, Feb. 1974; PPS to Leader of the Opposition, 1975-76. Councillor, Hebburn UDC, 1950-58. Has lectured extensively in the USA. *Recreations:* bridge, reading. *Address:* 30 Laxford House, Cundy Street, SW1. *T:* 01-730 2341; 3 Groby Place, Altrincham, Cheshire. *T:* 061-928 1983.

MONTGOMERY CUNINGHAME, Sir John Christopher Foggo, 12th Bt *cr* 1672, of Corsehill, Ayrshire and Kirktonholm, Lanarkshire; Director: Artemis Energy Co.; Piston Powered Products and other companies; *b* 24 July 1935; 2nd *s* of Col Sir Thomas Montgomery-Cuninghame, 10th Bt, DSO (*d* 1945), and of Nancy Macaulay (his 2nd wife), *d* of late W. Stewart Foggo, Aberdeen (she *m* 2nd, 1946, Johan Frederik Christian Killander); *b* of Sir Andrew Montgomery-Cuninghame, 11th Bt; *S* brother, 1959; *m* 1964, Laura Violet, *d* of Sir Godfrey Nicholson, Bt, *qv*; three *d*. *Educ:* Fettes; Worcester Coll., Oxford (MA). 2nd Lieut, Rifle Brigade (NS), 1955-56; Lieut, London Rifle Brigade, TA, 1956-59. *Recreation:* fishing. *Heir:* none. *Address:* Lower Farm House, East Ilsley, Berks.

MONTGOMERY WATT, Prof. William; *see* Watt.

MONTMORENCY, Sir Arnold Geoffroy de; *see* de Montmorency.

MONTREAL, Archbishop of, (RC), since 1968; **Most Rev. Paul Grégoire;** *b* Verdun, 24 Oct. 1911. *Educ:* Ecole Supérieure Richard; Séminaire de Ste-Thérèse; Univ. of Montreal. Priest, 1937; became Professor, but continued his studies: PhD, STL, LèsL, MA (Hist.), dip. in pedagogy. Subseq. became Director, Séminaire de Ste-Thérèse; Prof. of Philosophy of Educn at l'Ecole Normale Secondaire and at l'Institut Pédagogique; Chaplain of the Students, Univ. of Montreal, 1950-61; consecrated Bishop, 1961, and became auxiliary to Archbishop of Montreal; Vicar-General and Dir of Office for the Clergy; Apostolic Administrator, Archdiocese of Montreal, Dec. 1967-Apr. 1968. Pres., Episcopal Commn on Ecumenism (French sector), 1965. Has presided over several Diocesan Commns (notably Commn for study of the material situation of the Clergy), 1965-68. Member: Canadian delegn to Bishop's Synod, Rome, 1971; Sacred Congregation for the Clergy, 1979. Dr *hc* : Univ. of Montreal, 1969; St Michael's Coll., Winooski, Vt, 1970. *Address:* Archbishop's House, 1071 Cathedral Street, Montreal, Quebec H3B 2V4, Canada.

MONTREAL, Bishop of, since 1975; **Rt. Rev. Reginald Hollis;** *b* 18 July 1932; *s* of Jesse Farndon Hollis and Edith Ellen Lee; *m* 1957, Marcia Henderson Crombie; two *s* one *d*. *Educ:* Selwyn Coll., Cambridge; McGill Univ., Montreal. Chaplain and Lectr, Montreal Dio. Theol Coll., 1956-60; Chaplain to Anglican Students, McGill Univ.; Asst Rector, St Matthias' Church, Westmount, PQ, 1960-63; Rector, St Barnabas' Church, Pierrefonds, PQ, 1963-70; Rector, Christ Church, Beaconsfield, PQ, 1971-74; Dir of Parish and Dio. Services, Dio. Montreal, 1974-75. Hon. DD 1975. *Address:* 3630 Mountain Street, Montreal, PQ, Canada.

MONTROSE, 7th Duke of, *cr* 1707; **James Angus Graham;** *cr* Baron Graham before 1451; Earl of Montrose, 1505; Bt (NS) 1625; Marquis of Montrose, 1645; Duke of Montrose, Marquis of Graham and Buchanan, Earl of Kincardine, Viscount Dundaff, Baron Aberuthven, Mugdock, and Fintrie, 1707; Earl and Baron Graham (Peerage of England), 1722; Hereditary Sheriff of Dunbartonshire; *b* 2 May 1907; *e s* of 6th Duke of Montrose, KT, CB, CVO, VD, and Lady Mary Douglas-Hamilton, OBE (*d* 1957), *d* of 12th Duke of Hamilton; *S* father, 1954; *m* 1st, 1930, Isobel Veronica (marr. diss. 1950), *yr d* of late Lt-Col T. B. Sellar, CMG, DSO; one *s* one *d* ; 2nd, 1952, Susan Mary Jocelyn, *widow* of Michael Raleigh Gibbs and *d* of late Dr J. M. Semple; two *s* two *d*. *Educ:* Eton; Christ Church, Oxford. Lt-Comdr RNVR. MP for Hartley-Gatooma in Federal Assembly of Federation of Rhodesia and Nyasaland, 1958-62; Minister of Agriculture, Lands, and Natural Resources, S Rhodesia, 1962-63; Minister of Agric., Rhodesia, 1964-65; (apptd in Rhodesia) Minister of External Affairs and Defence, 1966-68. *Heir:* s Marquis of Graham, *qv. Address:* Dalgoram, PO Box 1, Baynesfield, Natal, 3770, South Africa; (Seat) Auchmar, Drymen, Glasgow.

MOODY, Helen Wills; *see* Roark, H. W.

MOODY, John Percivale, OBE 1961; Counsellor to the Board, Welsh National Opera Co.; *b* 6 April 1906; *s* of Percivale Sadleir Moody; *m* 1937, Helen Pomfret Burra; one *s* decd. *Educ:* Bromsgrove; Royal Academy Schools. In publishing in the City, 1924-26; Painting; Academy Schs, 1927-28, various London Exhibitions; taught at Wimbledon Art Sch., 1928-29. Studied opera Webber Douglas Sch. Derby Day under Sir Nigel Playfair, Lyric, Hammersmith, 1931. West End plays include: The Brontës, Royalty, 1932; Hervey House, His Majesty's, 1935; After October, Criterion, 1936; played in Old Vic seasons 1934, 1937; Ascent of F6, Dog Beneath the Skin, Group Theatre, 1935; Dir Old Vic Sch., 1940-42. AFS Clerkenwell, 1940 (wounded and discharged). Producer Old Vic Co., Liverpool, 1942-44; Birmingham Repertory Theatre, 1944-45; Carl Rosa Opera Co., 1945; Sadler's Wells Opera Co., 1945-49; Drama Dir, Arts Council of Great Britain, 1949-54; Dir, Bristol Old Vic Co., 1954-59; Dir of Productions, 1960, and Jt Artistic Dir, 1970, Welsh Nat. Opera. First productions in England of Verdi's Simone Boccanegra, 1948, Nabucco, 1952, and The Battle of Legnano, 1960; Rimsky's May Night, 1960; also for Welsh Nat. Opera: Rossini's William Tell, 1961; Macbeth, 1963; Moses, 1965; Carmen, 1967; Boris Godunov, 1968; Simone Boccanegra, 1970; Rigoletto, 1972; The Pearl Fishers, 1973; What the Old Man Does is Always Right, Fishguard Festival, 1977. With wife, new translations of Carmen, Simone Boccanegra, Macbeth, La Traviata, The Pearl Fishers, Prince Igor and Fidelio. *Recreations:* swimming, gardening. *Address:* 2 Richmond Park Road, Bristol BS8 3AT. *T:* Bristol 34436.

MOODY, Leslie Howard; General Secretary, Civil Service Union, 1977-82; *b* 18 Aug. 1922; *s* of George Henry and Edith Jessie Moody; *m* 1944, Betty Doreen Walton; two *s*. *Educ:* Eltham College. Telephone Engineer, General Post Office, 1940-53. Served Royal Signals, Far East, 1944-47. Asst Sec., Civil Service Union, 1953, Dep. Gen. Sec., 1963. *Recreations:* walking, music, theatre, educating management. *Address:* 68 Shearman Road, Blackheath, SE3 9HX. *T:* 01-318 1040. *Club:* Civil Service.

MOODY, Peter Edward, CBE 1981; Joint Secretary and Group Chief Investment Manager, Prudential Corporation Ltd, 1979-80; *b* 26 Aug. 1918; *s* of late Edward Thomas Moody and Gladys (*née* Flint); *m* 1945, Peggy Elizabeth, *d* of Edward Henry Causer and Elizabeth Theodora (*née* Finke); one *s* one *d*. *Educ:* Christ's Coll., Finchley. FIA. Prudential Assurance Co. Ltd: Dep. Investment Manager, 1960; Jt Sec. and Chief Investment Manager, 1973-80. Institute of Actuaries: Hon. Sec., 1968-70; Vice-Pres., 1972-75; Pres.,

1978-80; Director: United Dominions Trust Ltd, 1972-81; Equity Capital for Industry Ltd, 1976-; Inmos International Ltd, 1981-; The Laird Gp Ltd, 1981-; British American and General Trust, 1981-; Prudential Corp. Ltd, 1981-. Part-time mem., PO Bd. *Publications:* contrib. Jl of Inst. of Actuaries. *Recreation:* golf. *Address:* 46 Brookmans Avenue, Brookmans Park, Herts AL9 7QJ.

MOODY, Theodore William, MA, PhD; Hon. DLit; Corr. FBA; Professor of Modern History, Dublin University, and Fellow of Trinity College, Dublin, 1939-77, now Fellow Emeritus; *b* 26 Nov. 1907; *o s* of William J. Moody, Belfast, and Ann I. Dippie; *m* 1935, Margaret C. P. Robertson, LLB, Bristol; one *s* four *d*. *Educ:* Royal Academical Instn, Belfast; Queen's Univ., Belfast (BA Mediæval and Modern Hist., 1930); Inst. of Historical Research, Univ. of London, 1930-32 (PhD 1934). FRHistS 1934; MRIA 1940. Queen's Univ., Belfast: Asst in History, 1932-35; Lectr in History, 1935-39. Trinity Coll., Dublin: Fellow and Prof., 1939-77; Tutor, 1939-52 (MA 1941); Sen. Tutor, 1952-58; Sen. Lectr, 1958-64; first Dean, Faculty of Arts, 1967-69. Hon. Treasurer, Social Service Co., TCD, 1942-53, Chm. 1953-. Member: Irish MSS Commn, 1943-; Adv. Cttee on Cultural Relations, Ireland, 1949-63; Govt Commn on Higher Educn in Ireland, 1960-67; Comhairle Radio Eireann (Irish Broadcasting Council), 1953-60; Irish Broadcasting Authority, 1960-72. Leverhulme Res. Fellow, 1964-66. Mem., Sch. of Historical Studies, Inst. for Advanced Study, Princeton, 1965; Mem., Acad. Council, Irish Sch. of Ecumenics, 1972- (Exec. Bd, 1978-). Jt Editor, Irish Historical Studies, 1937-77; Editor, Studies in Irish History, 1st series, 1944-56, 2nd series, 1960-75; Chm., Bd of Editors, A New History of Ireland, 1968-. Hon. DLit, Queen's Univ., Belfast, 1959; Hon. DLitt NUI, 1978. Corr. FBA, 1977. *Publications:* The Londonderry Plantation, 1609-41: the City of London and the plantation in Ulster, 1939; The Irish Parliament under Elizabeth and James I: a general survey (Proc. of RIA, vol xlv, sect C, no 6), 1939; Thomas Davis, 1814-45, 1945; (with J. C. Beckett) Queen's, Belfast, 1845-1949: the history of a university, 1959; The Ulster Question 1603-1973, 1974; Davitt and Irish Revolution, 1846-82, 1981; *Editor and contributor:* (with H. A. Cronne and D. B. Quinn) Essays in British and Irish History in honour of J. E. Todd, 1949; (with J. C. Beckett) Ulster since 1800, 1st series, 1955, 2nd series, 1957; (with F. X. Martin) The Course of Irish History, 1967; Historical Studies vi, 1968; The Fenian Movement, 1968; Irish Historiography 1936-70, 1971; (with F. X. Martin and F. J. Byrne) Early Modern Ireland, 1534-1691 (A New History of Ireland, vol. iii), 1976; Nationality and the Pursuit of National Independence, 1978; *Editor:* Ulster Plantation Papers, 1608-13 (Analecta Hibernica, no 8), 1938; An Irish Countryman in the British Navy, 1809-1815: the memoirs of Henry Walsh (The Irish Sword, iv-v, nos 16-21), 1960-62; (with J. G. Simms) The Bishopric of Derry and the Irish Society of London, 1602-70, 1968; Michael Davitt's Leaves from a Prison Diary, repr. 1972; various contribs on modern Irish history, the Irish in America, the Irish university question, and on Michael Davitt 1846-1906 (in Irish Historical Studies, Studies, History, Trans of Royal Hist. Soc., Hermathena). *Festschrift:* Ireland under the Union: essays in honour of T. W. Moody (ed F. S. Lyons and R. A. J. Hawkins), 1980. *Recreations:* listening to music, walking. *Address:* 25 Trinity College, Dublin.

MOOKERJEE, Sir Birendra Nath, Kt 1942; MA Cantab, MIE (India); Partner of Martin & Co. and Burn & Co., Managing Director, Martin Burn Ltd, Engineers, Contractors, Merchants, Shipbuilders, etc; Chairman Steel Corporation of Bengal Ltd; President Calcutta Local Board of Imperial Bank of India; Director Darjeeling Himalayan Railway Co. Ltd and many other companies; *b* 14 Feb. 1899; *s* of late Sir Rajendra Nath Mookerjee, KCIE, KCVO, MIE (India), FASB, DSc (Eng); *m* 1925, Ranu Priti Adhikari, *d* of Phani Bhusan Adhikari, late Professor Benares Hindu Univ.; one *s* two *d*. *Educ:* Bishop's Collegiate Sch., Hastings House, Calcutta; Bengal Engineering Coll.; Trinity Coll., Cambridge. Mem., Viceroy's Nat. Defence Council; Adviser, Roger Mission; Mem., Munitions Production Adv. Cttee. Fellow Calcutta Univ.; Sheriff of Calcutta 1941. *Address:* Martin Burn Ltd, Martin Burn House, 12 Mission Row, Calcutta 1, India; 7 Harington Street, Calcutta 16. *Clubs:* National Liberal; Calcutta, Calcutta Polo, Royal Calcutta Turf, Calcutta South, Cricket Club of India (Calcutta), etc.

MOOLLAN, Hon. Sir Cassam (Ismael), Kt 1982; **Hon. Mr Justice Moollan;** Chief Justice, Supreme Court of Mauritius, since 1982; *b* 26 Feb. 1927; *s* of Ismael Mahomed Moollan and Fatimah Nazroo; *m* 1954, Rassoulbibie Adam Moollan; one *s* two *d*. *Educ:* Royal Coll., Port Louis and Curepipe; London Sch. of Econs and Pol. Science (LLB 1950). Called to the Bar, Lincoln's Inn, 1951. Private practice, 1951-55; Dist Magistrate, 1955-58; Crown Counsel, 1958-64; Sen. Crown Counsel, 1964-66; Solicitor Gen., 1966-70; QC (Mauritius) 1969; Judge, Supreme Court, 1970; Sen. Judge, 1978. Editor, Mauritius Law Reports, 1982-. *Recreations:* table tennis, tennis, bridge, Indian classical and semi-classical music. *Address:* Supreme Court, Port Louis, Mauritius. *T:* 21905; 22 Hitchcock Avenue, Quatre Bornes, Mauritius. *T:* 46949. *Club:* Gymkhana (Port Louis).

MOON, Sir Edward, 5th Bt *cr* 1887; MC 1944; retired; *b* 23 Feb. 1911; *s* of Jasper Moon (*d* 1975) (*g s* of 1st Bt) and Isabel Moon (*née* Logan) (*d* 1961); *S cousin,* Sir John Arthur Moon, 4th Bt, 1979; *m* 1947, Mary, *d* of late Captain B. D. Conolly, RAMC. *Educ:* Sedbergh. Farming, Kenya, 1934-62. Served 1939-45, King's African Rifles (Major). *Recreations:* gardening, cooking, fishing and all games. *Heir:* b Roger Moon [*b* 17 Nov. 1914; *m* 1950, Meg, *d* of late Arthur Mainwaring Maxwell, DSO, MC; three *d*]. *Address:* c/o Midland Bank Ltd, Oswestry, Salop.

MOON, Sir (Edward) Penderel, Kt 1962; OBE 1941; Editor, India Office Records on the Transfer of Power, since 1972; *b* 13 Nov. 1905; *s* of Dr R. O. Moon, FRCP; *m* 1966, Pauline Marion (marr. diss.), *d* of Rev. W. E. C. Barns. *Educ:* Winchester; New Coll., Oxford (MA). Fellow of All Souls College, Oxford, 1927-35 and 1965-72. Entered ICS, 1929, resigned, 1944; Sec., Development Board and Planning Advisory Board, Govt of India; Min. of Revenue and Public Works, Bahawalpur State; Chief Comr, Himachal Pradesh; Chief Comr, Manipur; Adviser, Planning Commission. *Publications:* Strangers in India; The Future of India; Warren Hastings and British India; Divide and Quit; Gandhi and Modern India; Disbelief in God; (ed) Wavell: the Viceroy's Journal. *Recreations:* hunting, shooting and singing. *Address:* Manor Farm, Wotton Underwood, Aylesbury, Bucks.

MOON, Sir Penderel; *see* Moon, Sir E. P.

MOON, Sir Peter (James Scott), KCVO 1979; CMG 1979; HM Diplomatic Service; High Commissioner in Singapore, since 1982; *b* 1 April 1928; *m* 1955, Lucile Worms; three *d*. Home Office, 1952-54; CRO, 1954-56; Second Sec., Cape Town/Pretoria, 1956-58; Principal, CRO, 1958-60; First Sec., Colombo, 1960-63; Private Sec. to Sec. of State for Commonwealth Relations, 1963-65; First Sec., UK Mission to UN, New York, 1965-69; Counsellor, FCO, 1969-70; Private Sec. to Prime Minister, 1970-72; NATO Defence Coll., 1972; seconded to NATO Internat. Staff, Brussels, 1972-75; Counsellor, Cairo, 1975-78; Ambassador to Madagascar (non-resident), 1978-79; High Comr in Tanzania, 1978-82. *Address:* c/o Foreign and Commonwealth Office, SW1.

MOON, Sir Peter Wilfred Giles Graham-, 5th Bt, *cr* 1855; *b* 24 Oct. 1942; *s* of Sir (Arthur) Wilfred Graham-Moon, 4th Bt, and 2nd wife, Doris Patricia, *yr d* of Thomas Baron Jobson, Dublin; *S* father, 1954; *m* 1967, Sarah Gillian Chater (formerly *m* Major Antony Chater; marr. diss. 1966), *e d* of late Lt-Col Michael Lyndon Smith, MC, MB, BS, and Mrs Michael Smith; two *s*. *Recreations:* shooting, golf. *Heir: s* Rupert Francis Wilfred Graham-Moon, *b* 29 April 1968. *Address:* The Old Hundred Farm, Tormarton, Badminton, Glos GL9 1JA. *T:* Badminton 276. *Clubs:* Cricketers; Royal Cork Yacht.

MOON, Philip Burton, FRS 1947; Poynting Professor of Physics in the University of Birmingham, 1950-74, now Emeritus; Dean of the Faculty of Science and Engineering, 1969-72; *b* 17 May 1907; *o s* of late F. D. Moon; *m* 1st, 1937, Winifred F. Barber (*d* 1971); one *s* one *d*; 2nd, 1974, Lorna M. Aldridge. *Educ:* Leyton County High Sch.; Sidney Sussex Coll., Cambridge. *Publications:* Artificial Radioactivity, 1949; various papers on physics. *Address:* 42 Serpentine Road, Selly Park, Birmingham B29 7HU. *T:* 021-472 5615.

MOON, Lieut (Hon. Captain) Rupert Vance, VC 1917; *b* Bacchus Marsh, 1892; *s* of Arthur Moon, of the Nat. Bank of Australasia, Melbourne; *m* 1931, Susan Alison May, *yr d* of Robert Vincent, Prospect House, Geelong; one *s* one *d*. *Educ:* Kyneton Grammar Sch. Served European War (VC). Formerly Accountant, National Bank of Australasia Ltd, Geelong; Gen. Manager, Dennys Lascelles Ltd, retd 1960, and Dir, retd 1975. *Address:* 13 Bostock Avenue, Barwon Heads, Vic 3227, Australia. *Clubs:* Melbourne, Naval and Military, Victorian Racing, Moonee Valley Racing (Melbourne); Geelong, Geelong Racing (Geelong); Victoria Amateur Turf (Caulfield); Barwon Heads Golf.

MOONMAN, Eric; Director, Centre for Contemporary Studies, since 1979; *b* 29 April 1929; *s* of Borach and Leah Moonman; *m* 1962, Jane; two *s* one *d*. *Educ:* Rathbone Sch., Liverpool; Christ Church, Southport; Univs of Liverpool and Manchester. Dipl. in Social Science, Liverpool, 1955. Human Relations Adviser, British Inst. of Management, 1956-62; Sen. Lectr in Industrial Relations, SW Essex Technical Coll., 1962-64; Sen. Research Fellow in Management Sciences, Univ. of Manchester, 1964-66. MSc Manchester Univ., 1967. MP (Lab) Billericay, 1966-70, Basildon, Feb. 1974-1979; PPS to Minister without Portfolio and Sec. of State for Educn, 1967-68. Chairman: All-Party Parly Mental Health Cttee, 1967-70 and 1974-79; New Towns and Urban Affairs Cttee, Parly Labour Party, 1974-79; Zionist Fedn, 1975-80; Member: Stepney Council, 1961-65 (Leader, 1964-65); Tower Hamlets Council, 1964-67. Chm., Islington HA, 1981-. Mem., Council, Toynbee Hall Univ. Settlement (Chm., Finance Cttee); Governor, BFI, 1974-80. FRSA. *Publications:* The Manager and the Organization, 1961; Employee Security, 1962; European Science and Technology, 1968; Communication in an Expanding Organization, 1970; Reluctant Partnership, 1970; articles on management-trade union relations in American and British literature. *Recreations:* football, theatre, cinema. *Address:* 1 Beacon Hill, N7.

MOORBATH, Dr Stephen Erwin, FRS 1977; Reader in Geology, Oxford University, since 1978; Fellow of Linacre College, since 1970; *b* 9 May 1929; *s* of Heinz Moosbach and Else Moosbach; *m* 1962, Pauline Tessier-Varlet; one *s* one *d*. *Educ:* Lincoln Coll., Oxford Univ. (MA 1957, DPhil 1959). DSc Oxon 1969. Asst Experimental Officer, AERE, Harwell, 1948-51; Undergrad., Oxford Univ., 1951-54; Scientific Officer, AERE, Harwell, 1954-56; Research Fellow: Oxford Univ., 1956-61; MIT, 1961-62; Sen. Res. Officer, Oxford Univ., 1962-78. Wollaston Fund, Geol Soc. of London, 1968; Liverpool Geol. Medal, 1968; Murchison Medal, Geol. Soc. of London, 1978; Steno Medal, Geol. Soc. of Denmark, 1979. *Publications:* contribs to scientific jls and books. *Recreations:* music, philately, travel, linguistics.

Address: 53 Bagley Wood Road, Kennington, Oxford OX1 5LY. *T:* Oxford 739507.

MOORCRAFT, Dennis Harry; Under-Secretary, Inland Revenue, 1975-81; *b* 14 Aug. 1921; *s* of late Harry Moorcraft and Dorothy Moorcraft (*née* Simmons); *m* 1945, Ingeborg Utne, Bergen, Norway; one *s* one *d*. *Educ:* Gillingham County Grammar Sch. Tax Officer, Inland Revenue, 1938. RNVR, 1940-46. Inspector of Taxes, 1948; Sen. Inspector of Taxes, 1956; Principal Inspector of Taxes, 1963. *Recreations:* gardening, garden construction, croquet.

MOORE, family name of Earl of Drogheda.

MOORE, Viscount; Henry Dermot Ponsonby Moore; photographer; *b* 14 Jan. 1937; *o s* and *heir* of 11th Earl of Drogheda, *qv*; *m* 1st, 1968, Eliza Lloyd (marr. diss. 1972), *d* of Stacy Barcroft Lloyd, Jr, and Mrs Paul Mellon; 2nd, 1978, Alexandra, *d* of Sir Nicholas Henderson, *qv*. *Educ:* Eton; Trinity College, Cambridge. *Publications:* (with Brendan Gill) The Dream Come True, Great Houses of Los Angeles, 1980; (with George Plumptre) Royal Gardens, 1981; (with Sybilla Jane Flower) Stately Homes of Britain, 1982; (with Henry Mitchell) Washington, Houses of the Capital, 1982. *Address:* 40 Warwick Avenue, W9. *Club:* Garrick.

MOORE, Alexander Wyndham Hume S.; *see* Stewart-Moore.

MOORE, Antony Ross, CMG 1965; *b* 30 May 1918; *o s* of late Arthur Moore and late Eileen Maillet; *m* 1st, 1941, Philippa Weigall (marr. diss.); two *d*; 2nd, 1963, Georgina Mary Galbraith (*see* G. M. Moore); one *s*. *Educ:* Rugby; King's Coll., Cambridge. Served in Friends Ambulance Unit, 1939-40; HM Forces, 1940-46. Apptd Mem. Foreign (subseq. Diplomatic) Service, Nov. 1946; transf. to Rome, 1947; FO, Nov. 1949; 1st Sec., 1950; transf. to Tel Aviv, 1952; acted as Chargé d'Affaires, 1953, 1954; apptd Consul, Sept. 1953; FO, 1955; UK Perm. Delegn to UN, NY, 1957; Counsellor and transf. to IDC, 1961; FO, 1962-64; Internat. Fellow, Center for Internat. Affairs, Harvard Univ., 1964-65; Regional Information Officer, Middle East, British Embassy, Beirut, 1965-67; Head of Eastern Dept, FO, 1967; retd from HM Diplomatic Service, Dec. 1968. Dir, Iranian Selection Trust, 1969-72. *Address:* Touchbridge, Boarstall, Aylesbury, Bucks. *T:* Brill 238247.

MOORE, Bobby; *see* Moore, Robert.

MOORE, Brian; novelist; *b* 25 Aug. 1921; *s* of James Bernard Moore, FRCS, Northern Ireland, and Eileen McFadden; *m* Jean Denney. Guggenheim Fellowship (USA), 1959; Canada Council Senior Fellowship (Canada), 1960. National Institute of Arts and Letters (USA) Fiction Award 1960; Governor-Gen. of Canada's Award for Fiction, 1960, etc. *Publications: novels:* The Lonely Passion of Judith Hearne, 1955; The Feast of Lupercal, 1956; The Luck of Ginger Coffey, 1960; An Answer from Limbo, 1962; The Emperor of Ice-Cream, 1965; I am Mary Dunne, 1968; Fergus, 1970; The Revolution Script, 1972; Catholics, 1972 (W. H. Smith Literary Award, 1973); The Great Victorian Collection, 1975 (James Tait Black Meml Award, 1976); Governor Gen. of Canada's Award for Fiction, 1976); The Doctor's Wife, 1976; The Mangan Inheritance, 1979; The Temptation of Eileen Hughes, 1981; *non-fiction:* Canada (with Editors of Life), 1964. *Address:* c/o Curtis Brown Ltd, 575 Madison Avenue, New York, NY 10022, USA. *T:* Plaza 54200.

MOORE, Brian Baden; Football Commentator/Presenter: London Weekend Television, since 1968; Mid-Week Sports Special, Thames Television, since 1978; *b* 28 Feb. 1932; *m* 1955, Betty (*née* Cole); two *s*. *Educ:* Cranbrook Sch., Kent. Sports Sub-Editor, World Sports, 1954-56; journalist: Exchange Telegraph, 1956-58; The Times, 1958-61; Football Commentator/Presenter, BBC Radio, 1961-68. Presenter, Brian Moore Meets (TV documentary series), 1979-. *Publication:* The Big Matches 1970-1980, 1980. *Recreations:* being at home, animal care. *Address:* c/o London Weekend Television, South Bank Television Centre, Kent House, Upper Ground, SE1 9LT. *T:* 01-261 3434.

MOORE, Air Vice-Marshal Charles Stuart, CB 1962; OBE 1945; *b* London, 27 Feb. 1910; *s* of late E. A. Moore and late E. B. Moore (*née* Druce); *m* 1st, 1937, Anne (*d* 1957), *d* of Alfred Rogers; 2nd, 1961, Jean Mary, *d* of John Cameron Wilson; one *d*. *Educ:* Sutton Valence Sch.; RAF Coll., Cranwell. Commissioned in General Duties Branch, Dec. 1930; served in Egypt, 1932-34 and 1936-41; Sqdn Ldr 1938; Sudan, 1941-42; Wing Comdr 1940; 11 Group, 1943-44; Gp Capt. 1943; OC, OTU, 1944-45; Gp Capt. Org., HQFC, 1945-46; Staff Coll., Bracknell, 1946-47; Dep. Dir Plans, Air Ministry, London, 1947-49; Student, US National War Coll., Washington, 1949-50; Staff of USAF Air War Coll., Alabama, 1950-53; Air Commodore, 1953; AOC 66 Group, 1953-55; Dir of Intelligence, Air Ministry, London, 1955-58; AOA, NEAF, 1958-62; Actg Air Vice-Marshal, 1960; retired, 1962. Joined HM Foreign Service, Oct. 1962; posted to British Embassy, Tehran, Iran; left HM Diplomatic Service, March 1969. *Recreations:* music, photography and travelling. *Address:* Ferndene, The Avenue, Crowthorne, Berks. *T:* Crowthorne 2300. *Club:* Royal Air Force.

MOORE, David James Ladd; Under Secretary, HM Treasury, since 1982; *b* 6 June 1937; *s* of James and Eilonwy Moore; *m* 1968, Kay Harrison; two *s*. *Educ:* King Edward VI Sch., Nuneaton; Brasenose Coll., Oxford (BA). PO, 1961-67 (Asst Principal 1961, Principal 1966); Cabinet Office, 1967-69; HM

Treasury, 1969-80 (Asst Sec. 1973); Under Sec., Cabinet Office, 1980-82. *Recreations:* reading, theatre, family. *Address:* 183 Hampstead Way, NW11 7YB. *T:* 01-455 5945.

MOORE, Maj.-Gen. Denis Grattan, CB 1960; DL; retired; *b* 15 March 1909; *s* of Col F. G. Moore, CBE and Marian, *d* of Very Rev. W. H. Stone, Dean of Kilmore; *m* 1st, 1932, Alexandra, *d* of W. H. Wann; two *d* ; 2nd, 1946, Beatrice Glynn, *d* of W. S. Williamson; one adopted *d. Educ:* Wellington Coll.; Royal Military College, Sandhurst (cadet schol., 1928). Commissioned 1929, Royal Inniskilling Fusiliers; GSO1, HQ Tenth Army, 1943; Asst Dir of Artillery (Weapons), HQ Eighth Army, 1944; GSO1, War Office, 1946; GSO1 (Col) War Office, 1952-54; comd 47 Infantry Bde, TA, 1954-57; Dir of Weapons and Development, War Office, 1958-60; Dir of Equipment Policy, War Office, 1960-61; Chief, Jt Services Liaison Staff, BAOR, 1961-63. Col, The Royal Inniskilling Fusiliers, 1960-66. Chm., Ulster Timber Growers Organisation, 1965-81. High Sheriff, Co. Tyrone, 1969; DL Co. Tyrone, 1974. *Recreations:* shooting, fishing. *Address:* Pooks Hill, Alton Lane, Four Marks, Hants. *Club:* Naval and Military.

MOORE, Mrs D(oris) Langley, OBE 1971; FRSL; Founder (1955) and former Adviser, Museum of Costume, Assembly Rooms, Bath; author. Has done varied literary work in connection with films, television, and ballet, and has specialized in promoting the study of costume by means of exhibns and lectures in England and abroad. Designer of clothes for period films. *Publications: fiction:* A Winter's Passion, 1932; The Unknown Eros, 1935; They Knew Her When . . ., 1938 (subseq. re-published as A Game of Snakes and Ladders); Not at Home, 1948; All Done by Kindness, 1951; My Caravaggio Style, 1959; *non-fiction:* Anacreon: 29 Odes, 1926; The Technique of the Love Affair, 1928; Pandora's Letter Box, A Discourse on Fashionable Life, 1929; E. Nesbit, A Biography, 1933 (rev. 1966); The Vulgar Heart, An Enquiry into the Sentimental Tendencies of Public Opinion, 1945; The Woman in Fashion, 1949; The Child in Fashion, 1953; Pleasure, A Discursive Guide Book, 1953; The Late Lord Byron, 1961; Marie and the Duke of H, The Daydream Love Affair of Marie Bashkirtseff, 1966; Fashion through Fashion Plates, 1771-1970, 1971; Lord Byron: Accounts Rendered, 1974 (Rose Mary Crawshay Prize, awarded by British Academy, 1975); Ada, Countess of Lovelace, 1977; The Nieces' and Nephews' Book, 1983 (for children); (with June Langley Moore): Our Loving Duty, 1932; The Pleasure of Your Company, 1933. *Recreation:* Byron research. *Address:* 5 Prince Albert Road, NW1.

MOORE, Dudley Stuart John; actor (stage, films, TV and radio); composer (film music and incidental music for plays, etc); *b* 19 April 1935; *s* of Ada Francis and John Moore; *m* Suzy Kendall (marr. diss.); *m* Tuesday Weld (marr. diss.); one *s. Educ:* County High Sch., Dagenham, Essex; Magdalen Coll., Oxford (BA, BMus). *Stage:* Beyond the Fringe, 1960-62 (London), 1962-64 (Broadway, New York); Vic Lewis, John Dankworth Jazz Bands, 1959-60; composed incidental music, Royal Court Theatre (various plays), 1958-60. *BBC TV :* own series with Peter Cook: Not only . . . but also, 1964, 1966, 1970; in the sixties, *ITV:* Goodbye again; Royal Command Performance. Play it again Sam, Woody Allen, Globe Theatre, 1970. *BBC TV Series:* It's Lulu, not to mention Dudley Moore, 1972. Behind the Fridge, Cambridge Theatre, 1972-73; Good Evening, Broadway, New York, 1973-74; Tour of USA, 1975. Various TV and radio guest spots with Jazz piano trio. *Films* 1966-: The Wrong Box, 30 is a Dangerous Age Cynthia, Bedazzled, Monte Carlo or Bust, The Bed-sitting room, Alice in Wonderland, The Hound of the Baskervilles, Foul Play, "10", Wholly Moses, Arthur, Six Weeks, Love Sick, Romantic Comedy. *Film music* composed for: Bedazzled, 30 is a dangerous age Cynthia, The Staircase, Inadmissable Evidence, Six Weeks, and various TV films. *Publication:* Dud and Pete: The Dagenham Dialogues, 1971. *Recreations:* films, theatre, music. *Address:* c/o Louis Pitt, ICM, 8899 Beverly Boulevard, Los Angeles, Calif 90048, USA. *Club:* White Elephant.

MOORE, Rt. Rev. Edward Francis Butler, DD; *b* 1906; *s* of Rev. W. R. R. Moore; *m* 1932, Frances Olivia Scott; two *s* two *d. Educ:* Trinity Coll., Dublin (MA, PhD, DD). Deacon, 1930; Priest, 1931; Curate, Bray, 1930-32; Hon. Clerical Vicar, Christ Church Cathedral, Dublin, 1931-35; Curate, Clontarf, 1932-34; Incumbent, Castledermot with Kinneagh, 1934-40; Greystones, Diocese of Glendalough, 1940-49; Chaplain to Duke of Leinster, 1934-40; Rural Dean, Delgany 1950-59; Canon of Christ Church, Dublin, 1951-57; Archdeacon of Glendalough, 1957-59; Bishop of Kilmore and Elphin and Ardagh, 1959-81. *Recreations:* tennis, golf, fishing. *Address:* Drumlona, Sea Road, Kilcoole, Co. Wicklow, Ireland. *Club:* Royal Dublin Society (Dublin).

MOORE, Sir Edward Stanton, 2nd Bt *cr* 1923; OBE 1970; *b* 1910; *s* of Major E. C. H. Moore (killed, Vimy Ridge, 1917) and Kathleen Margaret (*d* 1970), *d* of H. S. Oliver, Sudbury, Suffolk; *S* grandfather, 1923; *m* 1946, Margaret, *er d* of T. J. Scott-Cotterell. *Educ:* Mill Hill Sch.; Cambridge. RAF 1940-46; Wing Cdr Special Duties; Managing Director, Spain and Western Mediterranean, BEA, 1965-72. Pres., British Chamber of Commerce in Spain, 1969-71; Dir, European British Chambers of Commerce, 1970-72. FCIT 1960. *Heir:* none. *Address:* Church House, Sidlesham, Sussex. *T:* Sidlesham 369. *Clubs:* Cruising Association, Royal Yachting Association, Chichester Yacht.

MOORE, the Worshipful Chancellor the Rev. E(velyn) Garth; barrister-at-law; Chancellor, Vicar-General and Official Principal of Diocese of Durham since 1954, of Diocese of Southwark since 1948 and of Diocese of Gloucester since 1957 (and Official Principal of Archdeaconries of Lewisham, Southwark, Kingston-on-Thames and Ely); Vicar, Guild Church of St Mary Abchurch, London, 1972, Priest-in-Charge since 1980; Fellow of Corpus Christi College, Cambridge, since 1947, and formerly Lecturer in Law (Director of Studies in Law, 1947-72); High Bailiff of Ely Cathedral since 1961; Member, Legal Advisory Committee (formerly Legal Board of Church of England), since 1956, Chairman since 1972; President, Churches' Fellowship for Psychical and Spiritual Studies, since 1963; *b* 6 Feb. 1906; *y s* of His Honour the late Judge (Robert Ernest) Moore and late Hilda Mary, *d* of Rev. John Davis Letts; unmarried. *Educ:* The Hall, Belsize Sch.; Durham Sch.; Trinity Coll., Cambridge (MA); Cuddesdon Theol Coll., 1962. Deacon, 1962; Priest, 1962. Called to Bar, Gray's Inn, 1928; SE Circuit. Formerly: Tutor of Gray's Inn; Lector of Trinity Coll., Cambridge; Mem. Gen. Council of Bar and of Professional Conduct Cttee. Commnd 2nd Lt RA, 1940; Major on staff of JAG; served at WO and throughout Great Britain, N Ireland, Paiforce, Middle East (for a time local Lt-Col), Greece, etc. Mem. of Church Assembly (for Dio. Ely), 1955-62; a Church Comr, 1964-77. JP and Dep. Chm. of QS, Hunts, 1948-63 and Cambs, 1959-63; Lectr in Criminal Procedure, Council of Legal Educn, 1957-68, Lectr in Evidence, 1952-68. Council, St David's Coll., Lampeter, 1949-65 and Westcott House, 1961-65; Mem. Governing Body, St Chad's Coll., Durham, 1955-78. Legal Assessor to Disciplinary Cttee, RCVS, 1963-68. Pres., Sion Coll., 1977-78. Vis. Prof., Khartoum Univ., 1961. Mere's Preacher, Cambridge Univ., 1965. *Publications:* An Introduction to English Canon Law, 1966; 8th Edn (with Suppl.) of Kenny's Cases on Criminal Law; (jt) Ecclesiastical Law, in Halsbury's Laws of England (3rd edn); Believe it or Not: Christianity and psychical research, 1977; The Church's Ministry of Healing, 1977; (ed jtly) Macmorran and Elphinstone's A Handbook for Churchwardens and Parochial Church Councillors, 1980; various contribs mainly to legal and theological jls. *Recreations:* travel, architecture, furniture, etc, psychical research. *Address:* Corpus Christi College, Cambridge. *T:* 59418; 1 Raymond Buildings, Gray's Inn, WC1. *T:* 01-242 3734; St Mary Abchurch, EC4. *T:* 01-626 0306. *Clubs:* Gresham; Pitt (Cambridge).

MOORE, Maj.-Gen. (retired) Frederick David, CB 1955; CBE 1954; *b* 27 Nov. 1902; *s* of Sir Frederick W. Moore; *m* 1932, Anna Morrell Hamilton (*d* 1974), *d* of Col T. H. M. Clarke, CMG, DSO; one *s. Educ:* Wellington Coll.; RMA Woolwich. Commnd in RFA, 1923. Served War of 1939-45: BEF 1940, 5th Regt RHA; BLA, 1944-45, CO 5th Regt RHA and CRA 53rd (W) Div.; GOC 5th AA Group, 1953-55; retd, 1956. DL Beds, 1958, Vice-Lieutenant, 1964-70. Officer Order of Crown (Belgian); Croix de Guerre (Belgian), 1940, with palm, 1945. *Recreations:* country pursuits. *Address:* Riverview, Bunclody, Co. Wexford, Ireland. *T:* Enniscorthy 77184. *Club:* Army and Navy.

MOORE, Frederick Thomas, OBE 1943; FRCS, FRCSE; Consulting Plastic Surgeon to King's College Hospital, London, since 1948; Plastic Unit East Grinstead since 1948; *b* 19 Oct. 1913; *s* of Francis Moore and Rose Perry; *m* 1957; Margrethe Johanne Holland (actress, as Greta Gynt); one *d. Educ:* St Bartholomew's Hosp. MRCS, LRCP 1936; FRCSE 1939; FRCS 1945. Served War of 1939-45 (OBE): RAF, Plastic Surgeon, 1939-48. Mem. Council, British Assoc. Plastic Surgeons, 1949. Founder Mem., British Hand Club. Legion of Honour, 1948. *Publications:* numerous on surgical problems. *Recreations:* golf, sailing, writing, research (medical). *Address:* L'Annonciade, ave L'Annonciade, Monte-Carlo. *T:* 504600. *Clubs:* Royal Thames Yacht; Monaco Yacht.

MOORE, Geoffrey Ernest, CBE 1977; FCIS, FIMI; Director, Vauxhall Motors Ltd (Chairman, 1979-81); *b* 31 Dec. 1916; *s* of late Charles Frederick Moore and Alice Isobel (*née* Large); *m* 1950, Olive Christine Moore; one *s* one *d. Educ:* Dunstable Grammar Sch. FCIS 1975; FIMI 1973. Served War, Armed Forces, 1939-45. Joined Vauxhall Motors, 1933; returned to Vauxhall Motors, Sales Dept, 1946; Asst Sales Manager, 1953; Domestic Sales Manager, 1955; Sales Dir, 1967; Dir of Govt and Public Relations, 1971; Dir of Personnel and Govt and Public Relations, 1974; Chm., Stampings Alliance Ltd (Vauxhall Subsid.), 1974-; Asst to Man. Dir, 1975. Vice-President: Inst. of Motor Industry, 1972-; Luton Indust. Coll., 1973-; Pres., SMMT, 1981-82; Member: Eastern Reg. Council, CBI, 1975-79; Council, CBI, 1981-; Exec. Council, Soc. of the Irish Motor Industry, 1981-. Trustee, National Motor Mus., Beaulieu; Governor, Luton Coll. of Higher Educn. Silver Jubilee Medal, 1977. *Recreations:* golf, gardening. *Address:* Windyacre, Gatesdene Close, Little Gaddesden, Berkhamsted, Herts HP4 1PB. *T:* Little Gaddesden 2431.

MOORE, Geoffrey Herbert; Professor of American Literature and Head of the Department of American Studies, University of Hull, 1962-82, now Professor Emeritus; *b* 10 June 1920; *e s* of late Herbert Jonathan Moore, Norwich; *m* 1947, Pamela Marguerite (marr. diss. 1962), *d* of Bertram Munn, Twickenham; one *s* one *d. Educ:* Mitcham Grammar Sch.; Emmanuel Coll., Cambridge; Univ. of Paris. 1st Cl. English Tripos, Cambridge, 1946; MA 1951. War Service (Air Ministry and RAF), 1939-43. Instr in English, Univ. of Wisconsin, 1947-49; Vis. Prof. of English, Univs of Kansas City and New Mexico, 1948, 1949; Asst Prof. of English, Tulane Univ., 1949-51; Vis. Prof. of English, Univ. of Southern California and Claremont Coll., 1950; Extra Mural Lectr, London and Cambridge Univs, 1951-52 and 1953-54; Editor and

Producer, BBC Television Talks, 1952-54; Rose Morgan Prof., Univ. of Kansas, 1954-55; Lectr in Amer. Lit., Manchester Univ., 1955-59; Vis. Lectr, Univs of Mainz, Göttingen and Frankfurt, 1959; Rockefeller Fellow, Harvard Univ., 1959-60; Sen. Lectr in Amer. Lit., Manchester Univ., 1960-62; Dean, Faculty of Arts, Univ. of Hull, 1967-69. Visiting Lecturer: Univs of Montpellier, Aix-en-Provence and Nice, 1967, 1971; Univs of Frankfurt, Heidelberg, Mainz, Saarbrücken, Tübingen, 1967, 1968; Univs of Perpignan, Turin, Florence, Pisa, Rome, New Delhi, Hyderabad, Madras, Bombay, Calcutta, 1971; Fellow, Sch. of Letters, Indiana Univ., Summer 1970; Visiting Professor: York Univ., Toronto, 1969-70; Univ. of Tunis, Spring 1970, 1971; Harvard, 1971; Univs of Düsseldorf, Heidelberg, Freiburg, Mainz, 1972; Univs of Teheran, Shiraz, Isfahan, Mashad, 1978; Research Fellow: Univ. of California at San Diego, 1974; Rockefeller Centre, Bellagio, 1979. Mem. Cttee, British Assoc. for Amer. Studies, 1957-60. Sen. Scholar Award, Amer. Coun. of Learned Socs, 1965. Ed. and Founder, The Bridge (Cambridge lit. mag.), 1946. *Publications:* Voyage to Chivalry (under pseud.), 1947; Poetry from Cambridge in Wartime, 1947; The Penguin Book of Modern American Verse, 1954; (ed) 58 Short Stories by O. Henry, 1956; Poetry Today, 1958; American Literature and the American Imagination, 1964; American Literature, 1964; The Penguin Book of American Verse, 1977; articles in TLS, Amer. Mercury, BBC Quarterly, Kenyon Review, Review of English Lit., The Year's Work in English Studies, Jl of American Studies, Studi Americani and other scholarly and literary jls. *Recreations:* swimming, walking. *Address:* The University, Hull, HU6 7RX. *T:* Hull 497611. *Club:* Savile.

MOORE, George; Chairman, Grayne Marketing Co. Ltd, since 1978; *b* 7 Oct. 1923; *s* of George Moore and Agnes Bryce Moore; *m* 1946, Marjorie Pamela Davies; three *s. Educ:* Coatbridge Secondary School; University Coll. and Royal Technical Coll., Cardiff (Jt Engineering Diploma); Hull Univ. (Post Graduate Diploma in Economics). Graduate Engineer, Electricity Authority, 1948-50; Development Engineer, Anglo-Iranian Oil Co., Abadan, 1950-52; Chief Electrical Engineer, Distillers' Solvents Div., 1952-58; Management Consultant, Urwick, Orr & Partners, 1958-64; Executive Dir, Burton Group, 1964-66; Group Managing Dir, Spear & Jackson International Ltd and Chm., USA Subsidiary, 1966-75; Dir of cos in Sweden, France, India, Australia, Canada, S Africa, 1966-75; Under Sec. and Regional Industrial Dir, NW Regional Office, DoI, 1976-78; Dir, Cordel Corporate Develt Ltd, 1978-. *Recreations:* golf, sailing. *Address:* Leasgill House, Leasgill, near Milnthorpe, Cumbria. *Club:* Reform.

MOORE, George; Member, South Yorkshire County Council (Chairman, 1978-79); *b* 29 Jan. 1913; *s* of Charles Edward Moore and Edith Alice Moore; *m* 1943, Hannah Kenworthy; two *d. Educ:* Woodhouse, Sheffield. Started work in pit at 14 yrs of age, 1927; worked in hotel business, 1930; publican in own right for several yrs, after which went into fruit and vegetable business, first as retailer and eventually as wholesaler and partner in small co. Served in RAF for short period during war. Elected to Barnsley Bor. Council, 1961: served as Vice Chm., Health and Housing Cttee, and Vice Chm., Fire and Licensing Dept; Chairman: Barnsley and Dist Refuse Disposal Cttee, 1959-64; Sanitary Cttee, Barnsley, 1963-73. Elected to County Council, 1974: first Chm., Fire Service Cttee, 1974-78. Chm., Barnsley Community Health Council, 1974-. *Recreation:* aviculture. *Address:* 34 Derwent Road, Athersley South, Barnsley, S Yorks S71 3QT. *T:* Barnsley 6644.

MOORE, His Honour George Edgar; HM First Deemster and Clerk of the Rolls, Isle of Man, 1969-74; *b* 13 July 1907; *er s* of Ramsey Bignall Moore, OBE, formerly HM Attorney-General for Isle of Man, and Agnes Cannell Moore; *m* 1937, Joan Mary Kissack; one *s* one *d. Educ:* Rydal School. Served in RAF, 1940-45 (Sqdn Ldr). Admitted to Manx Bar, 1930; Attorney-General for Isle of Man, 1957-63; HM Second Deemster, 1963-69; MLC; Chairman: IoM Criminal Injuries Compensation Tribunal, 1967-69; IoM Income Tax Appeal Comrs, 1969-74; Tynwald Common Market Select Cttee, 1970-74; Mem., Exec. Council Manx Museum and Nat. Trust, 1970-74; Chm. of Directors: Commercial Bank of Wales (IoM) Ltd, 1975-; Securicor (IoM) Ltd, 1975-; Chm., Trustees of Manx Blind Welfare Soc.; Pres., Isle of Man Badminton Assoc., 1953-72; Chm., Manx War Work Trust; Hon. County Representative of Royal Air Force Benevolent Assoc., 1948-72. *Address:* Brookdale, 8 Cronkbourne Road, Douglas, Isle of Man. *Club:* Ellan Vannin (IoM).

MOORE, George Herbert, MSc; FPS; FRSC; *b* 1 June 1903; *s* of late R. Herbert Moore and Mabel Moore, Bath; *m* 1931, Dora, *d* of Frederick and Emily Blackmore, Bath; one *d. Educ:* King Edward's Sch., Bath; Bath Coll. of Chemistry and Pharmacy. FPS 1928, FRIC 1943; MSc Bristol 1953. Merchant Venturers' Technical Coll., Bristol; Lectr in Pharmaceutical Chemistry, 1929-38; Head of Science Dept, 1938-50; Vice-Principal, Bristol Coll. of Technology, 1950-54; Principal, Bristol Coll. of Science and Technology, 1954-66; Vice-Chancellor, Bath Univ., 1966-69. Vice-Pres. Royal Inst. of Chemistry, 1955-57. Hon. LLD Bath, 1968. *Publication:* University of Bath: the formative years 1949-69, 1982. *Recreations:* music, photography. *Address:* Hilcot, Horsecombe Vale, Combe Down, Bath BA2 5QR. *T:* Bath 837417. *Club:* Bristol Savages (Bristol).

MOORE, Mrs (Georgina) Mary, MA; Principal, St Hilda's College, Oxford, since 1980; *b* 8 April 1930; *yr d* of late Prof. V. H. Galbraith, FBA, and late Georgina Rosalie Galbraith (*née* Cole-Baker); *m* 1963, Antony Ross Moore, *qv*; one *s. Educ:* The Mount Sch., York; Lady Margaret Hall, Oxford (1st Cl. Hons Modern History 1951; MA; Hon. Fellow, 1981). Joined HM Foreign

(later Diplomatic) Service, 1951; posted to Budapest, 1954; UK Permanent Delegn to United Nations, New York, 1956; FO, 1959; First Secretary, 1961; resigned on marriage. A Trustee, BM, 1982-. Under pseudonym Helena Osborne has written plays for television and radio, including: The Trial of Madame Fahmy, Granada TV, 1980; An Early Lunch, BBC Radio, 1980; An Arranged Marriage, BBC Radio, 1982. JP Bucks 1977-82. *Publications:* (also as Helena Osborne): *novels:* The Arcadian Affair, 1969; Pay-Day, 1972; White Poppy, 1977; The Joker, 1979. *Address:* St Hilda's College, Oxford. *T:* Oxford 41821; Touchbridge, Boarstall, Aylesbury, Bucks. *T:* Brill 238247. *Club:* University Women's.
See also J. H. Galbraith.

MOORE, Gerald, CBE 1954; FRCM; pianoforte accompanist; *b* Watford, Herts, 30 July 1899; *e s* of David Frank Moore, Tiverton, Devon; *m* Enid Kathleen, *d* of Montague Richard, Beckenham, Kent. *Educ:* Watford Grammar Sch.; Toronto Univ. Studied piano in Toronto; toured Canada as a boy pianist; returning to England, devoted himself to accompanying and chamber music. Associated with world's leading singers and instrumentalists. Festivals of Edinburgh, Salzburg, Holland, etc. Retired from concert platform, 1967. Ensemble Classes in USA, Tokyo, Stockholm, Helsinki, Dartington Hall, Salzburg Mozarteum, London S Bank Fest. Awarded Cobbett Gold Medal, 1951, for services to Chamber Music; Pres. Incorporated Soc. of Musicians, 1962. FRCM 1980. Hon. RAM 1962. Grand Prix du Disque: Amsterdam, 1968, 1970; Paris, 1970; Granados Medal, Barcelona, 1971; Hugo Wolf Medal, Vienna, 1973. Hon. DLitt Sussex, 1968; Hon. MusD Cambridge, 1973. *Publications:* The Unashamed Accompanist, 1943, rev. edn 1957; Careers in Music, 1950; Singer and Accompanist, 1953, repr. 1982; Am I Too Loud?, 1962; The Schubert Song Cycles, 1975; Farewell Recital, 1978; Poet's Love and other Schumann Songs, 1981; Furthermoore: interludes in an accompanist's life, 1983; arrangements of songs and folk songs. *Recreations:* reading, bridge, gardening. *Address:* Beechwood Cottage, Penn Bottom, Penn, Bucks. *T:* Penn 2507. *Clubs:* Savile, MCC.

MOORE, Gordon Charles; Chief Executive, City of Bradford Metropolitan Council, since 1974; *b* 23 July 1928; *s* of John Edward and Jessie Hamilton Moore; *m* 1956, Ursula Rawle; one *s* two *d. Educ:* Uppingham; St Catharine's Coll., Cambridge (MA, LLB). Solicitor. CBIM. Legal Asst, Cambs CC, 1955-56; Asst Solicitor: Worcester CB, 1956-58; Bath CB, 1958-60; Sen. Asst Solicitor: Bath CB, 1960-63; Croydon CB, 1963-65; Asst Town Clerk, Croydon LB, 1965; Dep. Town Clerk, Bradford CB, 1965-68, Town Clerk, 1968-73. FRSA. Silver Jubilee Medal, 1977. *Recreations:* music, railways, supporting Yorkshire County Cricket. *Address:* City Hall, Bradford, West Yorks BD1 1HY. *T:* Bradford 29577.

MOORE, Brig. Guy Newton, CBE 1941; DFC; ED; Chartered Accountant; Senior Partner, A. Capper Moore & Sons; *b* 13 Jan. 1893; *s* of A. Capper and Alice Eleanor Moore; *m* 1922, Marguerite Thompson; three *d. Educ:* Wesley Coll., Melbourne. Served with Royal Flying Corps and Royal Air Force (Capt.), 1916-18; Hon. Sqdn Leader, Citizens Air Force (Australia); Chief Paymaster, AIF. Dir of Finance Administration, Australian Commonwealth Forces, 1939-45, Brigadier. *Recreations:* golf, swimming, bowls. *Address:* 5 Brandon Road, Brighton, Vic 3186, Australia. *Clubs:* Naval and Military, Emerald Country, RACV (Melbourne); Royal Federation of Aero Clubs.

MOORE, Sir Harry, (Henry Roderick); Kt 1978; CBE 1971; Chairman, Molins Ltd, since 1978; Vice-Chairman, Philip Hill Investment Trust Ltd, since 1949; *b* 19 Aug. 1915; *er s* of late Roderick Edward Moore; *m* 1944, Beatrice Margaret, *d* of late Major J. W. Seigne; one *s* one *d. Educ:* Malvern Coll.; Pembroke Coll., Cambridge. Qualified as mem. of Institute of Chartered Accountants, 1939. Served War of 1939-45: North Africa, Italy, Europe; 2nd Lt Royal Fusiliers, 1939; Lt-Col, 1944. Director: Hill Samuel Group Ltd, 1949-80; Estates House Investment Trust Ltd, 1975-76; Chairman: Associated Engineering Ltd, 1955-75; Staveley Industries, 1970-79. Chm., Bd of Governors, The London Hospital, 1960-74; Mem. Council, British Heart Foundn; Dep. Chm., Adv. Panel on Institutional Finance in New Towns, 1970-81; Chm., North East Thames RHA, 1974-. High Sheriff of Bucks, 1966. *Address:* Bourton Grounds, near Buckingham. *T:* Buckingham 2241; 70 Chesterfield House, Chesterfield Gardens, W1Y 5TD. *T:* 01-492 0666. *Clubs:* White's, Pratt's; Leander; Rand (Johannesburg).

MOORE, Henry, OM 1963; CH 1955; FBA 1966; Hon. FRIBA; sculptor; *b* Castleford, Yorks, 30 July 1898; *s* of Raymond Spencer Moore and Mary Baker; *m* 1929, Irene Radetzky; one *d. Educ:* Castleford Grammar Sch. After serving European War, 1917-19, in Army, studied at Leeds Sch. of Art and Royal College of Art. Official War Artist, 1940-42. A Trustee: Tate Gallery, 1941-48 and 1949-56; National Gallery, 1955-63 and 1964-74; Member: Arts Council, 1963-67; Royal Fine Art Commn, 1947-71. Formed Henry Moore Foundation, 1977. *Major exhibitions of his work held:* London 1928, 1931, 1933, 1935, 1936, 1940, 1945, 1946, 1948, 1951, 1953, 1955, 1960, 1961, 1963, 1965, 1967, 1968, 1974, 1975, 1976, 1978; Leeds, 1941; New York, 1946; Chicago, 1947; San Francisco, 1947; Australia Tour, 1947; Venice Biennale, 1948 (of which he was awarded First Prize for Sculpture); Europe Tour, 1949-51; Cape Town, 1951; Scandinavian Tour, 1952-53; Rotterdam, 1953; Antwerp, 1953; São Paulo, 1953 (of which he was awarded 1st Prize in Foreign Sculpture); Germany Tour, 1953-54; USA Tour, 1955; Basle, 1955; Yugoslavia Tour, 1955; Canada, New Zealand, Australia, RSA Tour, 1955-58; Paris, 1957; Arnhem, 1957; Japan Tour, 1959; Spain and Portugal Tour, 1959; Poland Tour, 1959; Europe Tour, 1960-61; Edinburgh, 1961; USA

Tour, 1963; Latin America Tour, 1964–65; USA Tour, 1966–68; East Europe Tour, 1966; Israel Tour, 1966; Canada Tour, 1967–68; Holland and Germany Tour, 1968; Japan Tour, 1969–70; New York, 1970; Iran Tour, 1971; Munich, 1971; Paris, 1971; Florence, 1972; Luxembourg, 1973; Los Angeles, 1973; Toronto, 1974; Scandinavia Tour, 1975–76; Zurich, 1976; Paris, 1977; Madrid, 1981. *Examples of work are in:* the Tate Gallery, British Museum, the Museum of Modern Art, New York, the Allbright Knox Art Gallery, Buffalo, and other public galleries in the UK, USA, Germany, Italy, Switzerland, Holland, Sweden, Denmark, Norway, France, Australia, Brazil, Israel, South Africa and Japan. Foreign Corresp. Mem., Acad. Flamande des Sciences; For. Mem., Acad. Lettres et Beaux Arts de Belgique; For. Mem., Swedish Royal Academy of Fine Arts; For. Hon. Mem., Amer. Acad. of Arts and Sciences; Mem. de l'Institut, Acad. des Beaux-Arts, Paris, 1975; Hon. Fellow, Churchill Coll., Cambridge. Hon. Degrees: Dr of Lit: Leeds, London, Reading, Oxford, Hull, York, Durham; Dr of Arts: Yale, Harvard; Dr of Law: Cambridge, St Andrews, Sheffield, Toronto, Manchester; Dr of Letters: Sussex, Warwick, Leicester, York (Toronto), Columbia; Dr of Engineering, Berlin; Hon. Dr, RCA, 1967; Hon. Prof. Emeritus of Sculpture, Carrara Acad. of Fine Arts, 1967. Feltrinelli Foundn Internat. Sculpture Prize, 1963; Erasmus Prize, 1968; Einstein Prize, 1968. Biancoumano Prize, 1973; Goslar Prize, 1975. Order of Merit, West Germany, 1968, Grand Cross, 1980; Order of Merit, Italy, 1972; Commandeur de l'Ordre des Arts et des Lettres, Paris, 1973; Decoration of Honour for Science and Art, Austria, 1978. *Publications:* Heads, Figures and Ideas, 1958; Henry Moore on Sculpture (with Philip James), 1966; (with photographs by David Finn) Henry Moore at the British Museum, 1981; Catalogues Raisonné: Sculpture, 4 vols; Graphics, 2 vols; principal monographs by Will Grohmann, John Russell, Robert Melville, Kenneth Clark, (drawings) David Finn, John Hedgecoe, G. C. Argan, Henry Seldis. *Address:* Hoglands, Perry Green, Much Hadham, Herts. *T:* Much Hadham 2566. *Club:* Athenæum.

MOORE, Sir Henry Roderick; *see* Moore, Sir Harry.

MOORE, Rear-Adm. Humfrey John Bradley, CBE 1951; RI 1955; *b* 16 May 1898; *s* of Harry Farr Bradley and Mabel Clara Adelaide Moore; *m* 1925, Doris May Best; one *s* one *d*. *Educ:* Rugby Sch. Served European War, Grand Fleet, 1916–18. Thereafter various afloat and administrative posts, including Royal Naval Engineering Coll., Devonport staff, Admiralty (Engineer-in-Chief's and Naval Ordnance Depts) and Manager, Engineering Depts at Rosyth and Devonport and Staff of C-in-C, The Nore; retired 1952. *Recreations:* painting, music. *Address:* Prestons Cottage, Ightham, Kent. *T:* Borough Green 882668. *Club:* Arts.

MOORE, Gen. Sir (James Newton) Rodney, GCVO 1966 (KCVO 1959); KCB 1960 (CB 1955); CBE 1948; DSO 1944; PMN 1961; Chief Steward, Hampton Court Palace, since 1975; *b* 9 June 1905; *s* of late Maj.-Gen. Sir Newton Moore, KCMG, Perth, WA; *m* 1st, 1927, Olive Marion (marr. diss., 1947), *d* of late Lt-Col Sir Thomas Bilbe Robinson, GBE, KCMG; one *s* two *d*; 2nd, 1947, Patricia Margery Lillian, *d* of late James Catty, New York. *Educ:* Harrow; RMC, Sandhurst. Gazetted to Grenadier Guards, 1925, and served with Regt in England until 1933, then served in Egypt until 1936. Returned to England, 1936, and at outbreak of European War was at staff Coll., Camberley. Served War of 1939–45 (despatches, DSO): at GHQ Home Forces, 1940; Bde Major 30th Guards Bde and 6th Guards Armd Bde, 1940–42; GSO1, Guards Armd Div., 1942–44; Comd 2nd Armd Bn Gren. Guards in campaign NW Europe, 1944–45. Brig. comdg 8th Brit. Inf. Bde, Germany, Egypt and Palestine, 1945–46; Comd 1st Guards Bde, Palestine, 1946–47; Chief of Staff, HQ London Dist, 1948–50; idc 1950; Dep. Adjt Gen. HQ BAOR, 1951–53; Chief of Staff, Allied Forces, Northern Europe, 1953–55; GOC, 1st Infantry Div., MELF, 1955; GOC, 10th Armoured Div., 1955–57; Gen. Officer Commanding, London Dist; Maj.-Gen. Commanding Household Brigade, 1957–59; Chief of the Armed Forces Staff and Dir of Border Operations, Federation of Malaya, 1959–64; Defence Services Sec., Min. of Defence, 1964–66, retd. ADC Gen., 1965–66; Gentleman Usher to the Queen, 1966–75, Extra Gentleman Usher, 1975–. Col Comdt, HAC, 1966–76. Officer Order of Crown of Belgium and Belgian Croix de Guerre with Palm, 1944. Panglima Mangku Negara, 1961. *Recreations:* hunting, polo, fishing. *Address:* Hampton Court Palace, East Molesey, Surrey. *Club:* Cavalry and Guards.

MOORE, Maj.-Gen. Jeremy; *see* Moore, John J.

MOORE, Hon. Sir John (Cochrane), Kt 1976; President, Australian Conciliation and Arbitration Commission, since 1973; *b* 5 Nov. 1915; *s* of E. W. Moore and L. G. Moore; *m* 1946, Julia Fay, *d* of Brig. G. Drake-Brockman; two *s* two *d*. *Educ:* N Sydney Boys' High Sch.; Univ. of Sydney (BA, LLB). Private, AIF, 1940; R of O Hon. Captain 1945. Admitted NSW Bar, 1940; Dept of External Affairs, 1945; 2nd Sec., Aust. Mission to UN, 1946; practice, NSW Bar, 1947–59; Dep. Pres., Commonwealth Conciliation and Arbitration Commn, 1959–72, Actg Pres. 1972–73. Chm. (Pres.), Aust. Council of Nat. Trusts, 1969–82; President Nat. Trust of Aust. (NSW), 1966–69; Ind. Relations Soc. of NSW, 1972–73; Ind. Relations Soc. of Aust., 1973–74. Pres., NSW Br., Scout Assoc. of Aust., 1978–82. *Recreations:* swimming, reading. *Address:* Law Courts Building, Queen's Square, Sydney, NSW 2000, Australia. *T:* 2308506. *Club:* Athenæum (Melbourne).

MOORE, John Edward Michael; MP (C) Croydon Central since Feb. 1974; Parliamentary Under Secretary of State, Department of Energy, since 1979; *b* 26 Nov. 1937; *s* of Edward O. Moore; *m* 1962, Sheila Sarah Tillotson; two

s one *d*. *Educ:* London Sch. of Economics (BSc Econ). Nat. Service, Royal Sussex Regt, Korea, 1955–57 (commnd). Chm. Conservative Soc., LSE, 1958–59; Pres. Students' Union, LSE, 1959–60. Took part in expedn from N Greece to India overland tracing Alexander's route, 1960. In Banking and Stockbroking instns, Chicago, 1960–65; Democratic Precinct Captain, Evanston, Ill, USA, 1962; Democratic Ward Chm. Evanston, Illinois, 1964; Dir, 1968–79, Chm., 1975–79, Dean Witter Internat. Ltd. An Underwriting Mem. of Lloyds, 1978–. Conservative Councillor, London Borough of Merton, 1971–74; Chm., Stepney Green Conservative Assoc., 1968; a Vice-Chm., Conservative Party, 1975–79. Mem. Ct of Governors, LSE, 1977–. *Address:* House of Commons, SW1A 0AA.

MOORE, Captain John Evelyn, RN; Editor, Jane's Fighting Ships, since 1972; *b* Sant Ilario, Italy, 1 Nov. 1921; *s* of William John Moore and Evelyn Elizabeth (*née* Hooper); *m* 1st, 1945, Joan Pardoe; one *s* two *d*; 2nd, Barbara (*née* Kerry). *Educ:* Sherborne Sch., Dorset. Served War: entered Royal Navy, 1939; specialised in hydrographic surveying, then submarines, in 1943. Commanded HM Submarines: Totem, Alaric, Tradewind, Tactician, Telemachus. RN Staff course, 1950–51; Comdr, 1957; attached to Turkish Naval Staff, 1958–60; subseq. Plans Div., Admty; 1st Submarine Sqdn, then 7th Submarine Sqdn in comd; Captain, 1967; served as: Chief of Staff, C-in-C Naval Home Command, Defence Intell. Staff; retired list at own request, 1972. FRGS 1942. *Publications:* Jane's Major Warships, 1973; The Soviet Navy Today, 1975; Submarine Development, 1976; (jtly) Soviet War Machine, 1976; Encyclopaedia of World's Warships, 1978; World War 3, 1978; Seapower and Politics, 1979; Warships of the Royal Navy, 1979. *Recreations:* gardening, riding, swimming, archaeology. *Address:* Elmhurst, Rickney, Hailsham, Sussex BN27 1SF. *T:* Eastbourne 763294. *Clubs:* Naval, MCC, Anchorites.

MOORE, Maj.-Gen. Sir (John) Jeremy, KCB 1982 (CB 1982); OBE (mil.) 1973; MC 1952, Bar 1962; Major General Commando Forces, Royal Marines, 1979–82; Commander, Land Forces, Falkland Islands, May–July 1982; on staff of Chief of Defence Staff, since Sept. 1982; *b* 5 July 1928; *s* of Lt-Col Charles Percival Moore, MC, and Alice Hylda Mary (*née* Bibby); *m* 1966, Veryan Julia Margaret Acworth; one *s* two *d*. *Educ:* Brambletye Sch.; Cheltenham Coll. Joined RM as Probationary 2/Lt, 1947; training until 1950 (HMS Sirius, 1948); Troop subaltern, 40 Commando RM, 1950–53 (MC Malayan Emergency 1952); Housemaster, RM School of Music, 1954; ADC to MGRM Plymouth Gp, 1954–55; Instructor, NCO's Sch., RM, 1955–57; Adjt, 45 Cdo RM, 1957–59; Instr, RMA Sandhurst, 1959–62; Adjt and Company Comdr, 42 Cdo RM, 1962–63 (Bar to MC Brunei Revolt 1962); Australian Staff Coll., 1963–64; GSO2 Operations, HQ 17 Gurkha Div., 1965; Asst Sec., Chiefs of Staff Secretariat, MoD, 1966–68; HMS Bulwark, 1968–69; Officer Comdg, Officers Wing Commando Trng Centre RM, 1969–71; CO 42 Cdo RM, 1972–73 (OBE operational, NI 1973); Comdt RM School of Music (Purveyor of Music to the Royal Navy), 1973–75; RCDS 1976; Comdr 3rd Cdo Bde RM, 1977–79. *Recreations:* music (no performing ability except on a gramophone), most outdoor activities except ball games. *Address:* c/o Lloyds Bank Ltd, Cox's and King's Branch, 6 Pall Mall, SW1. *Club:* Edward Bear (RMA Sandhurst).

MOORE, John Michael, CB 1974; DSC 1944; Second Crown Estate Commissioner, since 1978; *b* 2 April 1921; *m*. *Educ:* Whitgift Middle Sch.; Selwyn Coll., Cambridge. Royal Navy, 1940–46. Royal Humane Society Bronze Medal, 1942. Ministry of Transport, 1946; Joint Principal Private Sec. to Minister (Rt Hon. Harold (later Lord) Watkinson), 1956–59; Asst Sec., 1959; Under-Sec. (Principal Estabt Officer), 1966; Under-Sec., DoE, 1970–72; Dep. Sec., CSD, 1972–78. Sec. to Jack Cttee on Rural Bus Services and Geddes Cttee on Carriers' Licensing. *Recreations:* sailing, walking hills and mountains. *Address:* High Spinney, Old Coach Road, Wrotham, Kent. *T:* Fairseat 822340. *Club:* Royal Automobile.

MOORE, John Royston, BSc, CChem, FRSC; Councillor since 1973, and Leader of the Opposition, West Yorkshire Metropolitan County Council, since 1981; Chairman: Bradford Health Authority, since 1982; Wool, Jute and Flax Industrial Training Board, since 1981; *b* 2 May 1921; *s* of late Henry Roland and Jane Elizabeth Moore; *m* 1947, Dorothy MacKay Hick, *d* of late Charles and Edith MacKay Hick; two *s*. *Educ:* Manchester Central Grammar Sch.; Univ. of Manchester (BSc Hons). War service, research and manufacture of explosives. Lecturer in schools and college, Manchester; Principal, Bradford Technical Coll., 1959–75; Sen. Vice Principal and Dir of Planning and Resources, Bradford Coll., 1975–80, retired. Leader, Baildon Urban DC, 1965–68; Councillor, West Riding CC, until 1973; Leader of West Yorkshire MCC, 1978–81. President, Baildon Conservative Assoc., 1975–; past Chm., Conservative Nat. Adv. Cttee on Educn. Hon. Mem., and Councillor, City and Guilds of London Inst., 1977–. *Recreations:* music, history, bridge. *Address:* Bicknor, 33 Station Road, Baildon, Shipley, West Yorkshire BD17 6HS. *T:* Bradford 581777.

MOORE, Prof. Leslie Rowsell, BSc, PhD, DSc, CEng, FIMinE, FGS; Consultant Geologist; Professor of Geology, University of Sheffield, 1949–77, now Emeritus Professor; *b* 23 June 1912; *m* 1946, Margaret Wilson MacRae; one *s*. *Educ:* Midsomer Norton Grammar Sch.; Bristol Univ. Univ. of Bristol, 1930–37; Lecturer and Senior Lecturer, Cardiff, 1939–46; Research Dir, Univ. of Glasgow, 1946–48; Reader in Geology, Univ. of Bristol, 1948–49. *Publications:* contributions to: Quarterly Journal Geol. Soc., London;

Geological Magazine; S Wales Inst. Engineers. *Recreations:* soccer, cricket, golf. *Address:* Moorside, The Bent, Curbar, near Sheffield S30 1YD.

MOORE, Mary; *see* Moore, G. M.

MOORE, Noel Ernest Ackroyd; Under-Secretary, Management and Personnel Office (formerly Civil Service Department), since 1975, and Principal of Civil Service College, since 1981; *b* 25 Nov. 1928; *s* of late Rowland H. Moore and Hilda Moore (*née* Ackroyd); *m* 1954, Mary Elizabeth Thorpe; two *s*. *Educ:* Penistone Grammar Sch., Yorks; Gonville and Caius Coll., Cambridge (MA; Half-Blue for chess). Asst Principal, Post Office, 1952; Asst Private Sec. to Postmaster General, 1955-56; Private Sec. to Asst PMG, 1956-57; Principal, 1957; Sec., Cttee of Inquiry on Decimal Currency, 1961-63; Treasury, 1966; Asst Sec., 1967; Sec., Decimal Currency Bd, 1966-72; Civil Service Dept, 1972. *Publication:* The Decimalisation of Britain's Currency (HMSO), 1973. *Address:* 30 Spurgate, Hutton, Brentwood, Essex CM13 2LA. *T:* Brentwood 216988.

MOORE, Prof. (Sir) Norman Winfrid (3rd Bt *cr* 1919; has established his claim but does not use the title); Senior Principal Scientific Officer, Nature Conservancy Council, since 1965 (Principal Scientific Officer, 1958-65); Visiting Professor of Environmental Studies, Wye College, University of London, since 1979; *b* 24 Feb. 1923; *s* of Sir Alan Hilary Moore, 2nd Bt; *S* father 1959; *m* 1950, Janet, *o d* of late Mrs Phyllis Singer; one *s* two *d*. *Educ:* Eton; Trinity Coll., Cambridge. Served War, 1942-45, Germany and Holland (wounded, POW). *Heir: s* Peter Alan Cutlack Moore, *b* 21 Sept. 1951. *Address:* The Farm House, Swavesey, Cambridge.

MOORE, Patrick Caldwell-, OBE 1968; free-lance author since 1968; *b* 4 March 1923; *s* of late Capt. Charles Caldwell-Moore, MC, and of Mrs Gertrude Lilian Moore. *Educ:* privately (due to illness). Served with RAF, 1940-45: Navigator, Bomber Command. Concerned in running of a school, 1945-52; free-lance author, 1952-65; Dir of Armagh Planetarium, 1965-68. TV Series, BBC, The Sky at Night, 1957-; radio broadcaster. Composed and performed in Perseus and Andromeda (opera), 1975, and Theseus, 1982. Pres., British Astronomical Assoc., 1982-. Hon. Mem., Astronomic-Geodetic Soc. of USSR, 1971. Editor, Year Book of Astronomy, 1962-. Lorimer Gold Medal, 1962; Goodacre Gold Medal, 1968; Arturo Gold Medal (Italian Astronomical Socs), 1969; Jackson-Gwilt Medal, RAS, 1977; Roberts-Klumpke Medal, Astronom. Soc. of Pacific, 1979. Hon. DSc Lancaster, 1974. *Publications:* More than 60 books, mainly astronomical, including The Amateur Astronomer, 1970; Atlas of the Universe, 1970, rev. edn 1981; Guide to the Planets, 1976; Guide to the Moon, 1976; Can You Speak Venusian?, 1977; Guide to the Stars, 1977; Guide to Mars, 1977; (jtly) Out of the Darkness: the Planet Pluto, 1980; The Unfolding Universe, 1982. *Recreations:* cricket, chess, tennis, music, xylophone playing (composer of music in record The Ever Ready Band Plays Music by Patrick Moore, 1979). *Address:* Farthings, 39 West Street, Selsey, West Sussex. *Clubs:* Lord's Taverners; Sussex County Cricket.

MOORE, Very Rev. Peter Clement; Dean of St Albans, since 1973; *b* 4 June 1924; *s* of Rev. G. G. Moore and Vera (*née* Mylrea); *m* 1965, Mary Claire, *o d* of P. A. M. Malcolm and Celia (*née* Oldham); one *s* one *d*. *Educ:* Cheltenham Coll.; Christ Church, Oxford (MA, DPhil); Cuddesdon Coll., Oxford. Minor Canon of Canterbury Cathedral and Asst Master, Cathedral Choir School, 1947-49; Curate of Bladon with Woodstock, 1949-51; Chaplain, New Coll., Oxford, 1949-51; Vicar of Alfrick with Lulsley, 1952-59; Hurd Librarian to Bishop of Worcester, 1953-62; Vicar of Pershore with Pinvin and Wick, 1959-67; Rural Dean of Pershore, 1965-67; Canon Residentiary of Ely Cathedral, 1967-73; Vice-Dean, 1971-73. Member: Archbishops' Liturgical Commission, 1968-76; General Synod, 1978-; Governing Body, SPCK. Liveryman, Worshipful Co. of Glaziers and Painters of Glass. Trustee, Historic Churches Preservation Trust. *Publications:* Tomorrow is Too Late, 1970; Man, Woman and Priesthood, 1978; Footholds in the Faith, 1980; Crown in Glory, 1982; Bishops: but what kind?, 1982. *Recreations:* gardening, music, fishing, barrel organs. *Address:* The Deanery, St Albans, Herts. *T:* St Albans 52120; Thruxton House, Thruxton, Hereford. *T:* Wormbridge 376. *Club:* United Oxford & Cambridge University.

MOORE, Prof. Peter Gerald, TD 1963; PhD; FIA; Professor of Statistics and Operational Research, since 1965, Deputy Principal, since 1972, London Business School; *b* Richmond, Surrey, 5 April 1928; *s* of Leonard Moore and late Ruby Moore; *m* 1958, Margaret Gertrude Sonja Enevoldson Thomas, Dulwich; two *s* one *d*. *Educ:* King's College Sch., Wimbledon; University Coll. London (BSc (1st Cl. Hons Statistics), PhD; Rosa Morison Meml Medal 1949). Served with 3rd Regt RHA, 1949-51, TA, 1951-65, Major 1963. Lectr, UCL, 1951-57; Commonwealth Fund Fellow, Princeton, NJ, 1953-54; Asst to Economic Adviser, NCB, 1957-59; Head of Statistical Services, Reed Paper Gp, 1959-65. Director: Shell UK, 1969-72; Copeman Paterson Ltd, 1978-; Partner, Duncan C. Fraser, 1974-77. Member: Review Body on Doctors' and Dentists' Pay, 1971-; Cttee on 1971 Census Security, 1971-73; UGC, 1979- (Vice-Chm., 1980-); Cons. to Wilson Cttee on Financial Instns, 1977-80. Member Council: Royal Statistical Soc., 1966-78 (Hon. Sec., 1968-74, Guy Medal, 1970); Inst. of Actuaries, 1966- (Vice-Pres., 1973-76); Mem., Internat. Stat. Inst., 1972-; Chm., Conf. of Univ. Management Schs, 1974-76; a Governor, London Business Sch., 1968-. J. D. Scaife Medal, Instn of Prodn Engrs, 1964. *Publications:* Principles of Statistical Techniques, 1958, 2nd edn 1969; (with D. E. Edwards) Standard Statistical Calculations, 1965; Statistics

and the Manager, 1966; Basic Operational Research, 1968, 2nd edn 1976; Risk and Business Decisions, 1972; (with H. Thomas) Anatomy of Decisions, 1976; Reason by Numbers, 1980; articles in professional jls. *Recreations:* golf, walking, travel (particularly by train). *Address:* London Business School, Sussex Place, Regent's Park, NW1 4SA. *T:* 01-262 5050. *Club:* Knole Park Golf.

MOORE, Rt. Hon. Sir Philip (Brian Cecil), KCB 1980 (CB 1973); KCVO 1976; CMG 1966; PC 1977; Private Secretary to the Queen and Keeper of the Queen's Archives, since 1977; *b* 6 April 1921; *s* of late Cecil Moore, Indian Civil Service; *m* 1945, Joan Ursula Greenop; two *d*. *Educ:* Dragon Sch.; Cheltenham Coll. (Scholar); Oxford Univ. Classical Exhibitioner, Brasenose Coll., Oxford, 1940. RAF Bomber Command, 1940-42 (prisoner of war, 1942-45). Brasenose Coll., Oxford, 1945-46 (Hon. Fellow 1981). Asst Private Sec. to First Lord of Admiralty, 1950-51; Principal Private Sec. to First Lord of Admiralty, 1957-58; Dep. UK Commissioner, Singapore, 1961-63; British Dep. High Comr in Singapore, 1963-65; Chief of Public Relations, MoD, 1965-66; Asst Private Secretary to the Queen, 1966-72, Dep. Private Secretary, 1972-77. *Recreations:* golf; Rugby football (Oxford Blue, 1945-46; International, England, 1951), hockey (Oxford Blue, 1946), cricket (Oxfordshire). *Address:* Wren House, Kensington Palace, W8. *T:* 01-937 2272. *Club:* MCC.

MOORE, Richard Valentine, GC 1940; CBE 1963; BSc (Eng); FIMechE; FIEE; retired; Managing Director (Reactor Group), UK Atomic Energy Authority, 1961-76; Member, 1971-76; *b* 14 Feb. 1916; *s* of Randall and Ellen Moore; *m* 1944, Ruby Edith Fair; three *s*. *Educ:* Strand Sch., London; London Univ. County of London Electric Supply Co., 1936-39. RNVR, 1939-46; HMS Effingham, 1939-40; HMS President, 1940-44; HMS Dido, 1942-44; British Admiralty Delegn, Washington, DC, 1944-46; Lieut-Comdr 1944. AERE Harwell, 1946-53; Dept of Atomic Energy, Risley, 1953; Design and Construction of Calder Hall, 1953-57; Chief Design Engineer, 1955; UKAEA, 1955; Dir of Reactor Design, 1958-61. Faraday Lectr, 1966. Hon. DTech Bradford, 1970. *Publications:* various papers to technical institutions. *Recreations:* golf, gardening. *Address:* Culleen House, Cann Lane, Appleton, Ches. *T:* Warrington 61023. *Club:* Naval.

MOORE, Robert, (Bobby Moore), OBE 1967; professional footballer; Manager, Oxford City Football Club, 1979-81; *b* 12 April 1941; *m* 1962, Christina Elizabeth Dean; one *s* one *d*. Captained: England Youth, at 17 years old (18 caps); England Under 23 (8 caps); made 108 appearances for England (the record number for England, and a world record until 1978), 90 as Captain (equalling Billy Wright's record). League debut for West Ham against Manchester United, Sept. 1958; England debut against Peru, 1962; played in World Cup, in Chile, 1962; Captained England for first time, against Czechoslovakia, 1963. Footballer of the Year, 1963-64; Holder of: FA Cup Winners' medal, 1964; European Cup Winners' medal, 1965; named Player of Players in World Cup (England the Winner), 1966; transferred to Fulham Football Club, 1974-77; played 1,000 matches at senior level. *Publication:* Bobby Moore (autobiog.), 1976. *Address:* 136 Greengate Street, E13. *T:* 01-472 2434.

MOORE, Robert, CBE 1973; Commissioner for Local Administration in Scotland, 1975-78; *b* 2 Nov. 1915; *m* 1940, Jean Laird Dick; two *s*. *Educ:* Dalziel High Sch., Motherwell; Glasgow Univ. (BL). Admitted solicitor, 1939. Town Clerk, Port Glasgow, 1943-48; Secretary, Eastern Regional Hosp. Bd, 1948-60; Principal Officer: Scottish Hosp. Administrative Staffs Cttee, 1960-74; Manpower Div., Scottish Health Service, 1974-75. Lectr in Administrative Law, St Andrews Univ., 1960-65; External Examr in Administrative Law, Glasgow Univ., 1967-71. Mem., Scottish Cttee, Council on Tribunals, 1964-82. *Address:* (home) 93 Greenbank Crescent, Edinburgh EH10 5TB. *T:* 031-447 5493. *Club:* New (Edinburgh).

MOORE, Gen. Sir Rodney; *see* Moore, Gen. Sir J. N. R.

MOORE, Roger; actor; *b* London, 14 Oct. 1927; *m* 1st, Doorn van Steyn (marr. diss. 1953); 2nd, 1953, Dorothy Squires (marr. diss. 1969); 3rd, Luisa Mattioli; two *s* one *d*. *Educ:* RADA. Golden Globe World Film Favourite Award, 1980. Stage début, Androcles and the Lion. *TV series include:* Ivanhoe, 1958; The Alaskans, 1960-61; Maverick, 1961; The Saint, 1962-69 (dir some episodes); The Persuaders, 1972-73; *films include:* The Last Time I Saw Paris, 1954; The Interrupted Melody, 1955; The King's Thief, 1955; Diane, 1956; The Miracle, 1959; Rachel Cade, 1961; Gold of the Seven Saints, 1961; The Rape of the Sabine Women, 1961; No Man's Land, 1961; Crossplot, 1969; The Man Who Haunted Himself, 1970; Live and Let Die, 1973; The Man With The Golden Gun, 1974; Gold, 1974; That Lucky Touch, 1975; Street People, 1975; Shout at the Devil, 1975; Sherlock Holmes in New York, 1976; The Spy Who Loved Me, 1976; The Wild Geese, 1977; Escape to Athena, 1978; Moonraker, 1978; North Sea Hijack, 1979; The Sea Wolves, 1980; Sunday Lovers, 1980; The Cannonball Run, 1980; For Your Eyes Only, 1980-81. *Publication:* James Bond Diary, 1973. *Address:* c/o London Management Ltd, 235 Regent Street, W1.

MOORE, Roy, CBE 1962; *b* 10 Jan. 1908; *s* of Harry Moore and Ellen Harriet Post; *m* 1st, 1934, Muriel Edith (*d* 1959), *d* of late C. E. E. Shill; two *s*; 2nd, 1963, Lydia Elizabeth Newell Park, *widow* of David Park, Berkeley, Calif. *Educ:* Judd Sch., Tonbridge; King's Coll., London. 2nd Cl. Hons English, 1928; AKC 1928; MA 1931; Carter Prize for English Verse. Chief English

Master, Mercers' Sch., London, 1931-40. Served War of 1939-45, Squadron Leader RAF Bomber Command, 1941-45. Head Master: Lawrence Sheriff Sch., Rugby, 1945-51; Mill Hill Sch., 1951-67. Fellow King's Coll., London, 1956. *Address:* 138 Santo Tomas Lane, Santa Barbara, Calif 93108, USA. *Club:* Athenæum.

MOORE, Thomas, OBE 1968; formerly, Chief Constable of City of Nottingham, and Deputy Chief Constable of Nottinghamshire; *b* 16 March 1903; *s* of Alfred and Fanny Moore; *m* 1932, Norah Carruthers; two *s. Educ:* The Hickling Sch., Loughborough. *Recreations:* shooting and fishing. *Address:* Lowcroft, Manvers Grove, Radcliffe-on-Trent, Notts. *T:* Radcliffe 2108.

MOORE, Thomas William, JP; Chairman (since inception) of Trojan Metals Ltd, Carseview Holdings Ltd, Dundee Timber Market Ltd, Inverlaw Property Co. Ltd; *b* 9 Aug. 1925; Scottish; *m* 1945, Mary Kathleen Thompson; four *s* two *d. Educ:* Stobswell Secondary Sch.; Leicester Coll. of Art and Technology. MBIM. Contested (Lab), Perth and East Perthshire, 1959. Lord Provost of Dundee, and Lord Lieutenant of County of City of Dundee, 1973-75; Chairman: Tay Road Bridge Jt Cttee, 1973; Tayside Steering Cttee. FInstD. *Recreations:* golf, reading. *Address:* 85 Blackness Avenue, Dundee. *Club:* Royal Automobile.

MOORE, Sir William (Roger Clotworthy), 3rd Bt *cr* 1932; TD 1962; *b* 17 May 1927; *s* of Sir William Samson Moore, 2nd Bt, and Ethel Cockburn Gordon (*d* 1973); *S* father, 1978; *m* 1954, Gillian, *d* of John Brown, Co. Antrim; one *s* one *d. Educ:* Marlborough; RMC, Sandhurst. Lieut Royal Inniskilling Fusiliers, 1945; Major North Irish Horse, 1956. High Sheriff, Co. Antrim, 1964. *Heir: s* Richard William Moore, *b* 8 May 1955. *Address:* Kenbank House, Dalry, Castle Douglas.

MOORE-BRABAZON, family name of **Baron Brabazon of Tara.**

MOORE-COULSON, Maj.-Gen. Samuel, CB 1959; ERD 1948; *b* 26 May 1908; *s* of late Samuel Coulson and Laura Elizabeth Moore, Leicestershire; *m* 1936, Joan Hardy, *d* of late J. R. H. Watkiss, London; one *s* two *d. Educ:* Wyggeston, Leicester; University Coll., Nottingham. Commnd Royal Leicestershire Regt (SRO), 1930; Asst Master, Queen Elizabeth Gram. Sch., Barnet, 1932-39; served with 2nd Bn Royal Leicestershire Regt, Palestine, 1939-40; Western Desert, 1940-41; Crete, 1941; Syria, 1941; Staff Officer, Lebanon, 1941-43; Canal Zone, 1943-44; War Office (AG1), 1945-46; transferred to RAEC, 1946; War Office (AE7/8), 1946-48; Regular Commn, 1948; SO1 Education, Far East, 1949-52; Dep. Dir of Army Education, 1952-55; Chief Education Officer, Eastern Command, 1955-57; Dir of Army Education, 1957-62; Maj.-Gen., 1957; retired, 1962. Head of Educn and Research Div., FBI, 1962-65; Asst Dir, Educn and Training, CBI, 1965-69; Chief Training and Develt Adviser, Dunlop Co. Ltd, 1969-70. Vice-Chm. Governors, Brit. Soc. for Internat. Understanding, 1964-70; Chm., Internat. Youth Science Fortnight, 1963-65, Vice-Pres., 1967-72. Hon. Fellow, Corporation of Secretaries, 1966; Mem., Adv. Cttee, Duke of Edinburgh Award, 1958-62 and 1968-70. Former Chairman: Army Rugby Referees Soc., Army Chess Soc.; MoD Foreign Language Trng Cttee; Standing Cttee on Educn of Service Children Overseas. Member: Min. of Education Cttee on R&D in Modern Languages; Co-ord. Cttee on Overseas Vol. Service; Comr Duke of York's Royal Mil. Sch.; Governor, Centre for Inf. on Language Teaching, SOAS. *Recreation:* chess. *Address:* 3 Addington Court, Keats Avenue, Milford-on-Sea, Hants SO4 0WN. *T:* Milford-on-Sea 5883.

MOOREHEAD, Alan McCrae, CBE 1968 (OBE 1946); AO 1978; *b* 22 July 1910; 2nd *s* of Richard Moorehead, Croydon, Vic., Aust.; *m* 1939, Lucy (*d* 1979), *yr d* of Dr Vincent Milner, Torquay; two *s* one *d. Educ:* Scotch Coll., Melbourne; Melbourne Univ. Editor Melbourne Univ. Magazine, 1929. Worked on various newspapers in Australia and England, mostly as war correspondent, 1930-46, when retired from active journalism to write books. *Publications:* Mediterranean Front, 1941; A Year of Battle, 1943; The End in Africa, 1943; African Trilogy, 1944; Eclipse, 1945; Montgomery, 1946; The Rage of the Vulture, 1948; The Villa Diana, 1951; The Traitors, 1952; Rum Jungle, 1953; A Summer Night, 1954; Gallipoli, 1956 (Sunday Times 1956 Book Prize and Duff Cooper Memorial Award); The Russian Revolution, 1958; No Room in the Ark, 1959; The White Nile, 1960; The Blue Nile, 1962, 2nd edn 1972; Cooper's Creek, 1963 (Royal Society of Literature Award); The Fatal Impact, 1966; Darwin and the Beagle, 1969; A Late Education: episodes in a Life, 1970. *Address:* 10 Egbert Street, NW1.

MOORER, Admiral Thomas Hinman; Defense Distinguished Service Medal, 1973; DSM 1965, 1967, 1968, 1970; Silver Star 1942; Legion of Merit, 1945; DFC 1942; Purple Heart, 1942; Presidential Unit Citation, 1942; Vice Chairman of Board, Blount Inc.; Board Member: Texaco Inc.; Fairchild Industries; *b* Mount Willing, Alabama, 9 Feb. 1912; *s* of Dr R. R. Moorer and Hulda Hill Hinson, Eufaula, Ala; *m* 1935, Carrie Ellen Foy Moorer; three *s* one *d. Educ:* Cloverdale High Sch., Montgomery, Ala; USN Acad.; Naval Aviation Trg Sch.; Naval War Coll. First ship, 1933; serving at Pearl Harbour in Fleet Air Wing, Dec. 1941; Pacific and East Indies areas, 1942; Mining Observer, C-in-C, US Fleet in UK, 1943; Strategic Bombing Survey in Japan, 1945; Naval Aide to Asst Sec. of Navy (Air), 1956; CO, USS Salisbury Sound, 1957; Special Asst to CNO, 1959; Comdr, Carrier Div. Six, 1960; Dir, Long Range Objectives Group, CNO, 1962; Comdr Seventh Fleet, 1964; C-in-C: US Pacific Fleet, 1965; Atlantic and Atlantic Fleet, and Supreme Allied

Commander, Atlantic, 1965-67; Chief of Naval Operations, 1967-70; Chm., Jt Chiefs of Staff, USA, 1970-74, retired US Navy 1974. Captain 1952; Rear-Adm. 1958; Vice-Adm. 1962; Adm. 1964. Holds seventeen foreign decorations. Hon. LLD Auburn, 1968; Hon. DH Samford, 1970. *Recreations:* golfing, fishing, hunting. *Address:* 6901 Lupine Lane, McLean, Va 22101, USA. *Clubs:* Brook (New York); International (Washington, DC); US Naval Inst. (Annapolis, Md); Army-Navy Country (Arlington, Va); Chevy Chase (Chevy Chase, Md).

MOORES, Hon. Frank Duff; MHA (Progressive C) Humber West, Newfoundland, since 1971 (MP for Bonavista-Trinity-Conception, 1968-71); Premier of the Province of Newfoundland, 1972-79; *b* 18 Feb. 1933; *s* of Silas Wilmot Moores and Dorothy Duff Moores; *m* 1973, Janis Johnson, Winnipeg; one *s* (and one *s* six *d* by a former marriage). *Educ:* United Church Academy, Carbonear; St Andrew's Coll., Aurora, Ont. Pres., Progressive Conservative Party in Canada, 1969. Is a Freemason. Hon. LLD, Meml Univ. of Newfoundland, 1975. *Recreations:* tennis, reading, fishing, hunting, golf. *Address:* Mount Scio House, St John's, Newfoundland, Canada. *Club:* Coral Beach (Bermuda).

MOORES, Sir John, Kt 1980; CBE 1972; Founder of the Littlewoods Organisation, 1924, Chairman, 1924-77 and 1980-82, Life President, 1982; *b* Eccles, Lancs, 25 Jan. 1896; *s* of John William Moores and Louisa (*née* Fethney); *m* 1923, Ruby Knowles; two *s* two *d. Educ:* Higher Elementary Sch. Founded: Littlewoods Pools, 1924; Littlewoods Mail Order Stores, 1932; Littlewoods Stores, 1936. Hon. Freeman, City of Liverpool, 1970; Hon. LLB Liverpool, 1973; first winner of Liverpool Gold Medal for Achievement, 1978. *Recreations:* painting, languages, sport, travel. *Address:* c/o The Littlewoods Organisation PLC, JM Centre, Old Hall Street, Liverpool L70 1AB. *T:* 051-235 2222.
See also Baron Grantchester, Peter Moores.

MOORES, Peter; Director: The Littlewoods Organization, since 1965 (Chairman, 1977-80); Singer & Friedlander, since 1978; *b* 9 April 1932; *s* of Sir John Moores, *qv; m* 1960, Luciana Pinto; one *s* two *d. Educ:* Eton; Christ Church, Oxford; Wiener Akademie der Musik und darstellenden Kunst. Worked in opera at Glyndebourne and Vienna State Opera; sponsor of complete recording of Wagner's Der Ring des Nibelungen in English and La Traviata by the English National Opera. Trustee, Tate Gall., 1978-; Governor of the BBC, 1981-. Hon. MA Christ Church, 1975. Gold Medal of the Italian Republic, 1974. *Recreations:* water-skiing, wind-surfing, shooting. *Address:* Parbold Hall, Parbold, near Wigan, Lancs. *Club:* Boodle's.

MOOREY, (Peter) Roger (Stuart), DPhil; FBA 1977; FSA; Keeper, Department of Antiquities, Ashmolean Museum, Oxford, since 1982; Fellow of Wolfson College, since 1976; *b* 30 May 1937; *s* of late Stuart Moorey and Freda (*née* Harris). *Educ:* Mill Hill Sch.; Corpus Christi Coll., Oxford (MA, DPhil). FSA 1967. Nat. Service, 1956-58, Intelligence Corps. Asst Keeper, 1961-73, Sen. Asst Keeper, 1973-82, Ashmolean Museum, Oxford. Editor of Levant, 1968-. *Publications:* Catalogue of the Ancient Persian Bronzes in the Ashmolean Museum, 1971; Ancient Persian Bronzes in the Adam Collection, 1974; Biblical Lands, 1975; Kish Excavations 1923-1933, 1978; Cemeteries of the First Millennium BC at Deve Hüyük, 1980; Excavation in Palestine, 1981; museum booklets and articles in learned jls. *Recreations:* travel, walking. *Address:* Ashmolean Museum, Oxford. *T:* Oxford 512651.

MOORHOUSE, (Cecil) James (Olaf); Member (C) London South, European Parliament, since 1979; Spokesman on Transport for European Democratic Group; *b* 1 Jan. 1924; *s* of late Captain Sidney James Humphrey Moorhouse and Anna Sophie Hedvig de Lövenskiold; *m* 1958, Elizabeth Clive Huxtable, Sydney, Aust.; one *s* one *d. Educ:* St Paul's School; King's Coll. and Imperial Coll., Univ. of London. BSc (Eng), DIC (Advanced Aeronautics); CEng. Designer with de Havilland Aircraft Co., 1946-48; Project Engr, BOAC, 1948-53; Technical Advr 1953-68, and Environmental Conservation Advr 1968-72, Shell International Petroleum; Environmental Advr, Shell Group of Companies in UK, 1972-73; Group Environmental Affairs Advr, Rio-Tinto Zinc Corp., 1973-80, Consultant, 1980-. Contested (C) St Pancras North, 1966 and 1970. Chm., European Parlt delegn to N Europe and Nordic Council. *Publications:* numerous articles and papers. *Recreations:* tennis, badminton, cycling, reading, travelling. *Address:* 6 St James's Square, SW1. *Clubs:* Carlton, Royal Automobile, English-Speaking Union; Croydon Conservative.

MOORHOUSE, Geoffrey; writer; *b* Bolton, Lancs, 29 Nov. 1931; *s* of Richard and Gladys Moorhouse; *m* 1st, 1956, Janet Marion Murray; two *s* one *d* (and one *d* decd); 2nd, 1974, Barbara Jane Woodward (marr. diss. 1978). *Educ:* Bury Grammar School. Royal Navy, 1950-52; editorial staff: Bolton Evening News, 1952-54; Grey River Argus (NZ), Auckland Star (NZ), Christchurch Star-Sun (NZ), 1954-56; News Chronicle, 1957; (Manchester) Guardian, 1958-70 (Chief Features Writer, 1963-70). FRGS 1972; FRSL 1982. *Publications:* The Other England, 1964; The Press, 1964; Against All Reason, 1969; Calcutta, 1971; The Missionaries, 1973; The Fearful Void, 1974; The Diplomats, 1977; The Boat and The Town, 1979; The Best-Loved Game, 1979 (Cricket Soc. Award). *Recreations:* music, cricket, hill-walking, looking at buildings. *Address:* Park House, Gayle, near Hawes, North Yorkshire. *T:* Hawes 456. *Club:* Lancashire County Cricket.

MOORHOUSE, James; *see* Moorhouse, C. J. O.

MOORMAN, Rt. Rev. John Richard Humpidge, MA, DD, Cambridge; LittD: Leeds; St Bonaventure, USA; FSA; Hon. Fellow of Emmanuel College; *b* Leeds, 4 June 1905; 2nd *s* of late Professor F. W. Moorman; *m* 1930, Mary Caroline Trevelyan (*see* M. C. Moorman). *Educ:* Gresham's School, Holt; Emmanuel College, Cambridge. Curate of Holbeck, Leeds, 1929-33; of Leighton Buzzard, 1933-35; Rector of Fallowfield, Manchester, 1935-42; Hon. and Examining Chaplain to Bishop of Manchester, 1940-44; Vicar of Lanercost, 1945-46, and Examining Chaplain to Bishop of Carlisle, 1945-59; Principal of Chichester Theological Coll. and Chancellor of Chichester Cathedral, 1946-56; Prebendary of Heathfield in Chichester Cathedral, 1956-59; Bishop of Ripon, 1959-75. Delegate-observer to 2nd Vatican Council, 1962-65. Hale Memorial Lectr, Evanston, USA, 1966. Chairman: Anglican members, Anglican-Roman Catholic Preparatory Commn, 1967-69; Advisory Council for Religious Communities, 1971-80. Member, Jt Internat. Commn of the Roman Catholic Church and the Anglican Communion, 1969-. Pres., Henry Bradshaw Soc., 1977-. *Publications:* Sources for the Life of S Francis of Assisi, 1940; Church Life in England in the Thirteenth Century, 1945; A New Fioretti, 1946; B. K. Cunningham, a Memoir, 1947; S Francis of Assisi, 1950, 2nd edn 1976; The Grey Friars in Cambridge (Birkbeck Lectures), 1952; A History of the Church in England, 1953; The Curate of Souls, 1958; The Path to Glory, 1960; Vatican Observed, 1967; A History of the Franciscan Order, 1968; The Franciscans in England, 1974; Richest of Poor Men, 1977. *Recreations:* country life, music. *Address:* 22 Springwell Road, Durham. *T:* Durham 63503.

MOORMAN, Mrs Mary Caroline; *b* 19 Feb. 1905; *d* of George Macaulay Trevelyan, OM, CBE, FRS, FBA, and Janet Penrose Ward, CH; *m* 1930, Rt Rev. J. R. H. Moorman, *qv. Educ:* Berkhamsted Sch. for Girls; Somerville Coll., Oxford. BA 1926; MA 1950. Chm., Trustees of Dove Cottage, 1974-77. Hon. Lectr, Sch. of English, Leeds Univ., 1970-, and Dept of English, Durham Univ., 1980-. Hon. LittD: Leeds, 1967; Durham, 1968. *Publications:* William III and the Defence of Holland, 1672-73, 1930; William Wordsworth, A Biography: vol. 1, The Early Years, 1957, vol. 2, The Later Years, 1965 (James Tait Black Meml Prize, 1965); (ed) Letters of William and Dorothy Wordsworth, vol. II, The Middle Years: Part 1, 1806-1811, 2nd edn (rev. and ed), 1969; vol. III, The Middle Years: Part 2, 1812-1820, 2nd edn (rev. and ed with A. G. Hill), 1970; (ed) The Journals of Dorothy Wordsworth, 1971, new edn 1976; George Macaulay Trevelyan, a Memoir, 1980. *Recreations:* country walking, bird-watching. *Address:* 22 Springwell Road, Durham DH1 4LR. *T:* Durham 63503.

MOORTHY, Arambamoorthy Thedchana; High Commissioner for Sri Lanka in London, since 1981; *b* 10 Aug. 1928; *s* of late Mr Arambamoorthy and Mrs Nesamma Arambamoorthy; *m* 1959, Suseela T. Moorthy, *d* of Justice P. Sriskandarajah; one *s* two *d. Educ:* BAEcon Hons (Sri Lanka). Called to Bar, Gray's Inn, 1965. Entered Foreign Service of Sri Lanka, 1953; Second Secretary: Indonesia, 1955-57; China, 1957-59; First Secretary: London, 1961-63; Federal Republic of Germany, 1964-66; Chargé d'Affaires, *ai,* Thailand, and Permanent Representative of Sri Lanka to Economic Commn for Asia and Far East, 1969; Chargé d'Affaires, *ai,* Iraq, 1970; Ambassador in Pakistan, 1978-Dec. 1980, and concurrently, Jan.-Dec. 1980, Ambassador to Iran with residence in Islamabad. *Address:* Sri Lanka High Commission, 13 Hyde Park Gardens, W2. *T:* 01-262 1841; (residence) 35 Avenue Road, NW8. *T:* 01-722 0617.

MOOSONEE, Bishop of, since 1980; **Rt. Rev. Caleb James Lawrence;** *b* 26 May 1941; *s* of James Otis Lawrence and Mildred Viola Burton; *m* 1966, Maureen Patricia Cuddy; one *s* two *d. Educ:* Univ. of King's College. BA (Dalhousie Univ.) 1962; BST 1964. Deacon 1963, priest 1965; Missionary at Anglican Mission, Great Whale River, Quebec, 1965-75; Rector of St Edmund's Parish, Great Whale River, 1975-79; Canon of St Jude's Cathedral, Frobisher Bay, Diocese of The Arctic, 1974; Archdeacon of Arctic Quebec, 1975-79; Bishop Coadjutor, Diocese of Moosonee, Jan.-Nov. 1980. Hon. DD, Univ. of King's Coll., Halifax, NS, 1980. *Recreations:* reading, photography. *Address:* The Diocese of Moosonee, Synod Office, Box 841, Schumacher, Ontario PON 1G0, Canada. *T:* 705-264-9759.

MOOTHAM, Sir Orby Howell, Kt 1962; *b* 17 Feb. 1901; *s* of Delmé George Mootham, ARIBA; *m* 1st, 1931, Maria Augusta Elizabeth Niemöller (*d* 1973); one *s* one *d*; 2nd, 1977, Mrs Beatrix Douglas Ward, *widow* of Basil Ward, FRIBA. *Educ:* Leinster House Sch., Putney; London Univ. MSc (Econ). Called to Bar, Inner Temple, 1926 (Yarborough-Anderson Schol., 1924; hon. Bencher, 1958). An Advocate of Rangoon High Court, 1927-40; DJAG, Army in Burma, 1940-44, thereafter service in Dept of JAG in India and as Chief Judicial Officer, Brit. Mil. Admin. (despatches). Actg Judge, Rangoon High Court, 1945-46; Judge, Allahabad High Court, 1946-55; Chief Justice, 1955-61. Chm., Allahabad Univ. Enquiry Cttee, 1953-54; Legal Adviser's Dept, CRO, 1961-63. Deputy-Chairman of QS: Essex, 1964-71; Kent, 1965-71; Surrey, 1970-71; a Recorder of the Crown Court, 1972. Chm., Med. Appeals Tribunal, 1963-73; Mem. Governing Body, Froebel Educational Inst., 1965-79. *Publications:* Burmese Buddhist Law, 1939. Articles in Brit. Year Book of Internat. Law and other legal jls. *Address:* 3 Paper Buildings, Temple, EC4Y 7EU. *T:* 01-353 1310. *Club:* Athenæum.

MORAES, Dom; Indian poet and author; *b* 1938; *s* of Frank Moraes (Editor of the Indian Express and biographer of Nehru); *m* 1970, Leela Naidu. *Educ:* Jesus Coll., Oxford. Read English, 1956-59. Took up residence in England at age of 16, after world-wide travel and a 2-yr stay in Ceylon. On loan to Govt of India from UNFPA, for a period. *Publications:* A Beginning (poems), 1957 (Hawthornden Prize, 1958); Gone Away (Travel), 1960; Poems, 1960; John Nobody (poems), 1965; The Brass Serpent (trans. from Hebrew poetry), 1964; Poems 1955-65 (collected poems), 1966; My Son's Father (autobiography), 1968; The People Time Forgot, 1972; The Tempest Within, 1972; A Matter of People, 1974; (ed) Voices for Life (essays), 1975; Mrs Gandhi, 1980; Bombay, 1980. *Recreation:* thinking. *Address:* c/o Praeger Publishers Inc., 521 Fifth Avenue, 12th floor, New York, NY 10017, USA.

MORAN, 2nd Baron *cr* 1943; **Richard John McMoran Wilson,** KCMG 1981 (CMG 1970); HM Diplomatic Service; High Commissioner in Canada, since 1981; *b* 22 Sept. 1924; *er s* of 1st Baron Moran, MC, MD, FRCP, and of Dorothy, MBE, *d* of late Samuel Felix Dufton, DSc; *S* father, 1977; *m* 1948, Shirley Rowntree Harris; two *s* one *d. Educ:* Eton; King's Coll., Cambridge. Served War of 1939-45; Ord. Seaman in HMS Belfast, 1943; Sub-Lt RNVR in Motor Torpedo Boats and HM Destroyer Oribi, 1944-45. Foreign Office, 1945; Third Sec., Ankara, 1948; Tel-Aviv, 1950; Second Sec., Rio de Janeiro, 1953; First Sec., FO, 1956; Washington, 1959; FO 1961; Counsellor, British Embassy in S Africa, 1965; Head of W African Dept, FCO, 1968-73; Ambassador to Chad, 1970-73; Ambassador to Hungary, 1973-76, to Portugal, 1976-81. Grand Cross, Order of the Infante (Portugal), 1978. *Publication:* (as John Wilson) C. B.: a life of Sir Henry Campbell-Bannerman, 1973 (Whitbread Award, 1973). *Recreations:* fishing, fly-tying, bird-watching. *Heir:* *s* Hon. James McMoran Wilson [*b* 6 Aug. 1952; *m* 1980, Hon. Jane Hepburne-Scott, *y d* of Lord Polwarth, *qv*]. *Address:* c/o Foreign and Commonwealth Office, SW1. *Clubs:* Beefsteak, Flyfishers'.

See also Baron Mountevans, Hon. G. H. Wilson.

MORAN, Rt. Rev. Monsignor John; Principal RC Chaplain and Vicar General (Army), since 1981; *b* 3 Dec. 1929; *s* of Thomas Moran and Gertrude May (*née* Sheer). *Educ:* De La Salle Coll., Sheffield; Ushaw Coll., Durham. Ordained Priest, Leeds Diocese, 1956; Curate, Dewsbury, 1956-60; Prison Chaplain, Armley, 1960-61; commissioned Army Chaplain, 1961; service in BAOR, Singapore, Malaya, Hong Kong, UK; Chaplain, RMA Sandhurst, 1968-70, Staff Chaplain, 1970-71; Senior Chaplain, HQ BAOR, 1977-79, and HQ UKLF, 1979-80. *Recreations:* music, rivers, clocks. *Address:* MoD Chaplains (A), Bagshot Park, Bagshot, Surrey GU19 5PL. *T:* Bagshot 71717.

MORAN, Prof. Patrick Alfred Pierce, FRS 1975; FAA; Visiting Fellow, Social Psychiatry Research Unit, Australian National University; Professor of Statistics, Australian National University, 1952-82; *b* 14 July 1917; *s* of late Herbert Michael Moran and of Eva Moran; *m* 1946, Jean Mavis Frame; two *s* one *d. Educ:* St Stanislaus Coll., Bathurst, NSW; Univs of Sydney (DSc) and Cambridge (ScD). Exper. Officer, Min. of Supply, 1940-42; Australian Sci. Liaison Officer, London, 1942-45; Baylis Student, Cambridge, 1945-46; Sen. Res. Officer, Oxford Inst. of Statistics, 1946-51; Lectr in Maths, Trinity Coll., Oxford, 1949-51; Univ. Lectr in Maths, Oxford, 1951. Mem. Council, Australian Acad. of Scis, 1971-74; Vice-Pres., Internat. Statistical Inst., 1971-73, 1975-77. Hon. FSS. Lyle Medal, Australian Acad. of Scis, 1963; Pitman Medal, Statistical Soc. of Aust., 1982. *Publications:* The Theory of Storage, 1960; The Random Processes of Evolutionary Theory, 1962; (with M. G. Kendall) Geometrical Probability, 1963; Introduction to the Theory of Probability, 1968. *Address:* 17 Tennyson Crescent, Forrest, Canberra, ACT 2603, Australia. *T:* Canberra 731140.

MORAN, Thomas, CBE 1946; ScD; DSc; Scientific Adviser, Home Grown Cereals Authority, 1966-69; Director of Research, Research Association of British Flour Millers, 1939-66; *b* 1899; *s* of late Thomas Moran; *m* 1st, 1924, Elizabeth Ann Flynn (*d* 1952); one *s* one *d* (and one *d* decd); 2nd, 1959, June Patricia Martin. *Educ:* St Francis Xavier's Coll., Liverpool; Liverpool Univ.; Gonville and Caius Coll., Cambridge. Sir John Willox Schol., 1920, Univ. Scholar, 1920, Liverpool Univ.; served European War, 1914-18, with Liverpool Scottish (KLR), 1917-19; with DSIR at Low Temperature Station, Cambridge, 1922-39. Mem. Advisory Scientific Cttee, Food Defence Plans Dept, 1938-39; Dir of Research and Dep. Scientific Adviser, Min. of Food, 1940-46; UK delegate, Quadripartite Food Conf., Berlin, Jan. 1946. Mem. Council, British Nutrition Foundation, 1967-70. *Publications:* Bread (with Lord Horder and Sir Charles Dodds), 1954; papers on different aspects of Food Science in scientific and medical journals, 1922-; reports on applied food research published by HM Stationery Office. *Address:* 5 Amhurst Court, Grange Road, Cambridge. *T:* Cambridge 354548.

MORANT, Dame Mary (Maud), DBE 1969, **(Sister Mary Regis)** (to be addressed as Sr Mary Regis, DBE); Headmistress, Roman Catholic Schools, 1933-70; voluntary social worker in convents at Battersea, Southwark and Woolton, 1969-81; *b* 21 Dec. 1903; *d* of Stephen Augustus and Mary Morant. *Educ:* Notre Dame High Sch. and Notre Dame Coll. of Educn, Mt Pleasant. Asst, Notre Dame Demonstration Sch., 1924; Asst, St Mary's, Battersea, 1929; Headmistress, St John's, Wigan, 1933; Headmistress, Central Sch., Embakwe Mission, S Rhodesia, 1938; Vice-Pres., Chikuni Trg. Coll., N Rhodesia, 1946; Headmistress: St Peter Claver, Kroonstad, 1948; Lowe House, St Helens, Lancs, 1956; Our Lady's, Eldon St, Liverpool, 1961; Preparatory School, Convent of Notre Dame, Birkdale, 1969-70. Pro Pontifice et Ecclesia Medal, 1969, from HH Pope Paul VI. *Recreations:* drama, music. *Address:* Convent of Notre Dame, Speke Road, Woolton, Liverpool L25 7TN.

MORAVIA, Alberto; Italian author; *b* 28 Nov. 1907; *s* of Carlo and Teresa de Marsanich; *m* 1941, Elsa Morante. Chevalier de la Légion d'Honneur (France), 1952. *Publications: novels:* Gli indifferenti, 1929 (Eng. trans.: The Time of Indifference, 1953); Le ambizioni sbagliate, 1935; La mascherata, 1941 (Eng. trans.: The Fancy Dress Party, 1948); Agostino, 1944 (Eng. trans.: Agostino, 1947); La Romana, 1947 (Eng. trans.: The Woman of Rome, 1949); La disubbidienza, 1948 (Eng. trans: Disobedience, 1950); L'amore Coniugale, 1949 (Eng. trans.: Conjugal Love, 1951); Il Conformista, 1951 (Eng. Trans.: The Conformist, 1952); La Ciociara, 1957 (Eng. trans.: Two Women, 1958); La Noia, 1961 (Viareggio Prize) (Eng. trans.: The Empty Canvas, 1961); The Fetish, 1965; L'attenzione, 1965 (Eng. trans.: The Lie, 1966); La vita interiore, 1978 (Eng. trans: Time of Desecration, 1980); *short stories:* (and selections in Eng.;) La bella vita, 1935; L'imbroglio, 1937; I sogni del pigro, 1940; L'amante infelice, 1943; L'epidemia, 1945; Racconti, 1952 (Eng. trans.: Bitter Honeymoon, and the Wayward Wife, 1959); Racconti romani, 1954 (Eng. trans.: Roman Tales, 1956); Nuovi racconti romani, 1959; L'automa, 1964; Una cosa è una cosa, 1966; Il Paradiso, 1970 (Eng. trans.: Paradise, 1971); Io e lui, 1971 (Eng. trans.: The Two of Us, 1971); Un'altra vita, 1973 (Eng. trans.: Lady Godiva and Other Stories, 1975); The Voice of the Sea, 1978; *essays:* L'uomo come fine e altri saggi, 1964 (Eng. trans.: Man as an End, 1966); Impegno Controvoglia, 1980; *plays:* Beatrice Cenci, 1955; Il mondo è quello che è, 1966; Il dio Kurt, 1967; La Vita è Gioco, 1970; *travel:* La rivoluzione culturale in Cina, 1967 (Eng. trans: The Red Book and The Great Wall, 1968); Which Tribe Do You Belong To?, 1974. *Address:* Lungotevere della Vittoria 1, Rome, Italy. *T:* 3603698.

MORAY, 20th Earl of, *cr* 1562; **Douglas John Moray Stuart;** Lord Abernethy and Strathearn, 1562; Lord Doune, 1581; Baron of St Colme, 1611; Baron Stuart (GB), 1796; *b* 13 Feb. 1928; *e s* of 19th Earl of Moray and Mabel Helen Maud Wilson (*d* 1968); *S* father, 1974; *m* 1964, Lady Malvina Murray, *er d* of 7th Earl of Mansfield and Mansfield; one *s* one *d. Educ:* Trinity Coll., Cambridge (BA), FLAS 1958. *Heir: s* Lord Doune, *qv. Address:* Doune Park, Doune, Perthshire. *T:* Doune 333; Darnaway Castle, Forres, Moray, Scotland. *Club:* New (Edinburgh).

MORAY, ROSS and CAITHNESS, Bishop of, since 1970; **Rt. Rev. George Minshull Sessford;** *b* Aintree, Lancs, 7 Nov. 1928; *o s* of Charles Walter Sessford and Eliza Annie (*née* Minshull); *m* 1952, Norah, *y d* of David Henry Hughes and Ellen (*née* Whitely); three *d. Educ:* Warbreck Primary Sch.; Oulton High and Liverpool Collegiate Sch; St Andrews Univ. (MA). Curate, St Mary's Cathedral, Glasgow, 1953; Chaplain, Glasgow Univ., 1955; Priest-in-Charge, Cumbernauld New Town, 1958; Rector, Forres, Moray, 1966. *Recreations:* Lanchester motor cars, donkey breeding, sailing. *Address:* Spynie House, 96 Fairfield Road, Inverness, Scotland IV3 5LL. *T:* Inverness 31059.

MORAY, ROSS AND CAITHNESS, Dean of; *see* Barnes, Very Rev. C. A.

MORAY, Edward Bruce D.; *see* Dawson-Moray.

MORCOM, Rev. Canon Anthony John; a Residentiary Canon of Ely Cathedral, since 1974, Vice-Dean, since 1981; *b* 24 July 1916; *s* of late Dr Alfred Farr Morcom and Sylvia Millicent Morcom (*née* Birchenough); *m* 1st, 1955, Pamela Cappel Bain (*d* 1963); 2nd, 1965, Richenda, widow of Frederick Williams. *Educ:* Repton; Clare Coll., Cambridge; Cuddesdon Coll. Curate: St Mary Magdalene, Paddington, 1939-42; St Mary the Virgin, Pimlico, 1942-47; Domestic Chaplain to the Bishop of London, 1947-55; Archdeacon of Middx, 1953-66; Vicar of St Cyprian's, Clarence Gate, 1955-66; Vicar of St Mary the Less, Cambridge, 1966-73; Rural Dean of Cambridge, 1971-73. *Recreation:* travel. *Address:* Powchers Hall, Ely, Cambs. *T:* Ely 2336. *Clubs:* United Oxford & Cambridge University, MCC.

MORCOM, John Brian; a Social Security Commissioner, since 1981; *b* 31 May 1925; *s* of Albert John Morcom and Alice Maud Morcom (*née* Jones), Carmarthen; *m* 1st, 1958, Valerie Lostie de Kerhor Rivington (*d* 1960); one *s* ; 2nd, 1965, Sheila Myfanwy Adams-Lewis; one *d. Educ:* Queen Elizabeth Grammar Sch., Carmarthen; Balliol Coll., Oxford (State schol., 1943; MA). Bevin Ballottee, Oakdale Colliery, 1944; MO, RAMC, Talgarth Mil. Mental Hosp. and BMH Suez, 1944-47. Called to the Bar, Inner Temple, 1952, Lincoln's Inn, 1955; Wales and Chester Circuit, 1954-81. *Publications:* Estate Duty Saving, 1959, 5th edn 1972; (jtly) Capital Transfer Tax, 1976, 2nd edn 1978. *Recreations:* Welsh genealogy, forestry. *Address:* Social Security Commission, 6 Grosvenor Gardens, SW1W 0DH. *Clubs:* Royal Commonwealth Society, London Welsh Association.

MORCOS-ASAAD, Prof. Fikry Naguib; Professor of Architecture, Department of Architecture and Building Science, University of Strathclyde, since 1970; *b* 27 Sept. 1930; *s* of Naguib and Marie A. Morcos-Asaad; *m* 1958, Sarah Ann (*née* Gribben); three *s. Educ:* Cairo Univ. (BArch); Georgia Inst. of Techn. (MArch); MIT (SM); IIT (PhD). RIBA; FRIAS. Lectr in Architecture, Fac. of Engrg, Cairo Univ., 1952-54 and 1958-63; Dir of Structural Studies, Sch. of Arch., Univ. of Liverpool, 1963-70; Design Critic and Vis. Prof. in Arch. Engrg, Calif State Polytechnic Univ., 1969, 1970 and 1973. Comr, Royal Fine Art Commn for Scotland; Mem. Educn Cttee, Architects Registration Council of UK; formerly Mem. Council, Glasgow Inst. of Architects; Member Council: Royal Incorp. of Architects in Scotland; Glasgow Coll. of Building and Printing. Mem., Rotary International.

Publications: Circular Forms in Architecture, 1955; High Density Concretes for Radiation Shielding, 1956; Structural Parameters in Multi-Storey Buildings under Dynamic Loading, 1956; The Egyptian Village, 1956; Architectural Construction, vol. 1 1960, vol. 2 1961; Plastic Design in Steel, 1975; Large-span Structures, 1976; Brickwork: some pertinent points, 1978; Design and Building for a Tropical Environment, 1978; various papers on structural form in architecture. *Recreations:* renovation of antique clocks, gardening, reading, travelling. *Address:* Staneacre House, Townhead Street, Hamilton ML3 7BP. *T:* Hamilton 420644, (office) 041-552 4400, ext 3000. *Club:* Hamilton Civic Society (Hamilton).

MORDAUNT, Sir Richard (Nigel Charles), 14th Bt *cr* 1611; (does not use the title at present); *b* 12 May 1940; *s* of Lt-Col Sir Nigel John Mordaunt, 13th Bt, MBE, and Anne (*d* 1980), *d* of late Arthur F. Tritton; *S* father, 1979; *m* 1964, Myriam Atchia; one *s* one *d. Educ:* Wellington. *Heir: s* Kim John Mordaunt, *b* 11 June 1966. *Address:* Elsenham Place, Bishops Stortford, Herts.

MORDECAI, Sir John Stanley, Kt 1962; CMG 1956; formerly Secretary, Development Planning, University of the West Indies; *b* 21 Oct. 1903; *s* of Segismund T. and Marie A. Mordecai; *m* 1st, 1929, Pearl K. Redmond (*d* 1947); two *s* four *d* ; 2nd, 1951, Phyllis M. Walcott; two *s. Educ:* Wolmer's Boys' High Sch., Jamaica; Syracuse Univ., New York, USA. MSc (Pub. Adm.). Entered public service as clerical asst in Treasury, Jamaica, 1920; Finance officer, 1942; asst treasurer, 1944; asst sec. in charge of local government secretariat, 1946; trade administrator and sec. trade control board, 1949; principal, seconded to Colonial Office, 1950; Executive Sec. Regional Economic Cttee of the West Indies, British Guiana and British Honduras, with headquarters in Barbados, 1952-56; Federal Sec., West Indies Federation, 1956-60 (Special work on preparatory arrangements for Federation, 1955-58); Dep. Gov.-Gen., WI Fedn, 1960-62; Gen. Manager, Jamaica Industrial Develt Corp., 1962-63. Fellow, Princeton Univ., NJ, 1964-66. Chairman: Jamaica Public Services Commn, 1962; Cttee of Inquiry into Sugar Ind., 1969. *Publication:* The West Indies, 1968. *Recreations:* horse racing, music. *Address:* 34 Mona Road, Kingston 6, Jamaica.

MORE, Sir Jasper, Kt 1979; JP, DL; *b* 31 July 1907; *s* of Thomas Jasper Mytton More and Lady Norah, *d* of 5th Marquess of Sligo; *m* 1944, Clare Mary Hope-Edwardes, Netley, Shropshire, *d* of Capt. Vincent Coldwell, 4th Indian Cavalry; no *c. Educ:* Eton (Schol.); King's Coll., Cambridge. Barrister, Lincoln's Inn, 1930, and Middle Temple, 1931; Harmsworth Law Schol., 1932; in practice, 1930-39. Served War of 1939-45: in Min. of Economic Warfare, MAP and Light Metals Control, 1939-42; commissioned as legal officer in Military Govt, 1943; with Allied Commission (Italy), 8th Army and 5th Army, 1943-45; Legal Adviser, Military Govt, Dodecanese, 1946. MP (C) Ludlow, 1960-79; An Asst Government Whip, Feb.-Oct. 1964; Asst Opposition Whip, 1964-70; Vice-Chamberlain, HM Household, 1970-71. JP Salop; 1950; DL Salop, 1955; CC Salop, 1958-70, 1973-. *Publications:* The Land of Italy, 1949; The Mediterranean, 1956; A Tale of Two Houses, 1978; The Land of Egypt, 1980; (contrib.) Shell Guide to English Villages, 1980. *Recreations:* shooting, fishing, riding, building, travel and landscape gardening. *Address:* Linley Hall, Bishop's Castle, Shropshire. *Clubs:* Travellers', Brooks's, Naval and Military, St Stephen's Constitutional.

MORE, Norman, FRICS; Managing Director, Redditch Development Corporation, since 1979; *b* 20 Dec. 1921; *s* of Herbert and Anna More; *m* 1952, Kathleen Mary Chrystal; two *s* one *d. Educ:* Royal High Sch., Edinburgh; Edinburgh Univ. FRICS 1970 (ARICS 1951). Served in Royal Engineers, Middle East, N Africa, Italy, Greece and Germany, Major, 1941-48. Surveyor, Directorate of Lands and Accommodation, Min. of Works, 1948-58; Sen. Valuer, City Assessor's Office, Glasgow Corporation, 1958-63; Valuation and Estates Officer, East Kilbride Development Corp., 1963-65; Chief Estates Officer, Redditch Develt Corp., 1965-79. Chairman, West Midlands Br., Royal Instn of Chartered Surveyors, 1974-75. *Publications:* press articles and contribs to jls. *Recreations:* music, sport. *Address:* Mead Cottage, 192 Loxley Road, Stratford-upon-Avon, Warwickshire CV37 7DU. *T:* Stratford-upon-Avon 293763. *Club:* East India, Devonshire, Sports and Public Schools.

MOREAU, Jeanne; actress; *b* 23 Jan. 1928; *d* of Anatole-Désiré Moreau and Kathleen Moreau (*née* Buckley); *m* 1949, Jean-Louis Richard (marr. diss.); one *s* ; *m* 1977, William Friedkin. *Educ:* Collège Edgar-Quinet; Conservatoire national d'art dramatique. Comédie Française, 1948-52; Théâtre National Populaire, 1953. Over 60 films including: Les amants, 1958; Les liaisons dangereuses, 1959; Le dialogue des Carmelites, 1959; Moderato cantabile, 1960; Jules et Jim, 1961; La Baie des Anges, 1962; Journal d'une femme de chambre, 1963; Viva Maria, 1965; Mademoiselle, 1965; The Sailor from Gibraltar, 1965; The Immortal Story, 1966; Great Catherine, 1967; The Bride wore Black, 1967; Monte Walsh, 1969; Chère Louise, 1971; Nathalie Granger, 1972; La Race des Seigneurs, 1974; Mr Klein, 1976; Lumière (also Dir), 1976; Le Petit Théâtre de Jean Renoir, 1976; Madame Rosa, 1978; L'Intoxe, 1980; Querelle, La Truite, 1982; Chevalier des Arts et des Lettres, 1966. *Recreation:* reading. *Address:* c/o Artmédia, 10 avenue George V, 75008 Paris, France.

MORECAMBE, Eric; *see* Bartholomew, J. E.

MORELAND, Robert John; Member (C) Staffordshire East, European Parliament, since 1979; *b* 21 Aug. 1941; *s* of Samuel John Moreland and late Norah Mary, (Molly) (*née* Haines). *Educ:* Glasgow Acad.; Dean Close Sch.,

Cheltenham; Univ. of Nottingham (BA Econs); Inst. of World Affairs, Conn, and Warwick Univ. (postgrad. work). Civil Servant, Govt of NS, Canada, 1966-67, Govt of NB, 1967-72; Sen. Economist, W Central Scotland Planning Study, 1972-74; Management Consultant, Touche Ross and Co., London, 1974-. Contested (C) Pontypool, Oct. 1974; Chm., Eur. Cttee, Bow Gp, 1977-78. *Publications:* contrib. to Crossbow. *Recreations:* tennis, skiing, watching cricket, wine and beer drinking. *Address:* 17 Barnwood Road, Gloucester GL2 0RZ. *T:* Gloucester 21867; 7 Vauxhall Walk, SE11 5JT. *T:* 01-582 2613. *Clubs:* Carlton, Royal Automobile; Conservative (Burslem); Conservative (Cannock); Conservative (Burntwood).

MORELL, Joan, (Mrs André Morell); *see* Greenwood, Joan.

MORETON, family name of **Earl of Ducie.**

MORETON, Lord; David Leslie Moreton; *b* 20 Sept. 1951; *s* and *heir* of 6th Earl of Ducie, *qv* ; *m* 1975, Helen, *er d* of M. L. Duchesne; one *s*. *Educ:* Cheltenham College; Wye Coll., London Univ. (BSc 1973). *Heir:* s Hon. James Berkeley Moreton, *b* 6 May 1981. *Address:* Talbots End Farm, Cromhall, Glos.

MORETON, Sir John (Oscar), KCMG 1978 (CMG 1966); KCVO 1976; MC 1944; HM Diplomatic Service, retired; Director, Wates Foundation, since 1978; Gentleman Usher of the Blue Rod, Order of St Michael and St George, since 1979; *b* 28 Dec. 1917; *s* of Rev. C. O. Moreton; *m* 1945, Margaret Katherine, *d* of late Sir John Fryer, KBE, FRS; three *d*. *Educ:* St Edward's Sch., Oxford; Trinity Coll., Oxford (MA). War Service with 99th (Royal Bucks Yeomanry) Field Regt RA, 1939-46: France, Belgium, 1940; India, Burma, 1942-45. Colonial Office, 1946; Private Sec. to Perm. Under-Sec. of State, 1949-50; seconded to Govt of Kenya, 1953-55; Private Sec. to Sec. of State for Colonies (Rt Hon. Alan Lennox-Boyd), 1955-59; transf. to CRO, 1960; Counsellor, British High Commn, Lagos, 1961-64; IDC 1965; Asst Under-Sec. of State, CRO, 1965-66, CO 1966-68, FCO 1968-69; Ambassador to Vietnam, 1969-71; High Comr, Malta, 1972-74; Dep. Perm. Representative, with personal rank of Ambassador, UK Mission to UN, NY, 1974-75; HM Minister, British Embassy, Washington, 1975-77. Governor, St Edward's Sch., Oxford, 1980-. Hon. DL Hanover Coll., Indiana, 1976. *Recreations:* tennis; formerly athletics (Oxford Blue and International, 880 yds, 1939). *Address:* Woodside House, Woodside Road, Cobham, Surrey. *Clubs:* Army and Navy; Union (Malta).

MOREY, Rev. Dom Adrian, MA, DPhil, LittD; FRHistS; Superior, Downside House of Studies, Cambridge; *b* 10 April 1904; *s* of late John Morey and Charlotte Helen Morey (*née* Nelson). *Educ:* Latymer Upper Sch.; Christ's Coll., Cambridge (Schol.); Univ. of Munich. 1st cl. hons Hist. Tripos Pts I and II, Cambridge. Housemaster, Downside Sch., 1934; Bursar, Downside Abbey and Sch., 1946-50; Headmaster, Oratory Sch., Reading, 1953-67; Rector, St Wulstan's, Little Malvern, Worcs, 1967-69. *Publications:* Bartholomew of Exeter, 1937; (with Prof. C. N. Brooke) Gilbert Foliot and His Letters, 1965; The Letters and Charters of Gilbert Foliot, 1967; The Catholic Subjects of Elizabeth I, 1977; David Knowles: a memoir, 1979; articles in English Hist. Review, Jl Eccles. History, Cambridge Hist. Jl. *Address:* Benet House, Mount Pleasant, Cambridge. *T:* Cambridge 354637.

MORFEE, Air Vice-Marshal Arthur Laurence, CD; CB 1946; CBE 1943; retired; *b* 27 May 1897; *s* of George Thomas Morfee; *m* Estelle Lillian, *d* of William Edward Hurd of South Carolina, USA; one *s* one *d*. *Educ:* Finchley County Sch. Canadian Army from 1915; served France and Belgium, 19th Can. Inf. (wounded); joined RAF 1918; Air Board (Civil Service), 1921-24; appointed RCAF 1924; psa Andover, Eng., 1933; Air Vice-Marshal, 1945; retd 1949. Dir of Air Cadet League; Vice-Chm., Nova Scotia Div., Corps of Commissionaires. US Legion of Merit (Comdr), 1949. *Address:* 380 St George Street, Annapolis Royal, NS, Canada.

MORGAN; *see* Elystan-Morgan.

MORGAN; *see* Vaughan-Morgan.

MORGAN, Anthony Hugh; HM Diplomatic Service; Counsellor, Vienna, since 1982; *b* 27 March 1931; *s* of late Cyril Egbert Morgan and Muriel Dorothea (*née* Nash); *m* 1957, Cicely Alice Voysey; two *s* one *d*. *Educ:* King's Norton Grammar Sch.; Birmingham Univ. (BA 1952). Served HM Forces (RAF Educn Br.), 1952-55. Joined HM Foreign (later Diplomatic) Service, 1956; Cairo, then Cyprus, 1956; Khartoum, 1957; FO, 1959; Saigon, 1962; Second Sec., 1963; UK Delegn to NATO, 1965; First Sec., 1968; FCO, 1969; First Sec. and Head of Chancery, Calcutta, 1973; FCO, 1976; Dep. Head of Inf. Policy Dept, 1977; Counsellor (Information), Brussels, 1977-79; Counsellor (Commercial), Copenhagen, 1979-82. Comdr, Order of Dannebrog, Denmark, 1979. *Recreations:* music, looking at pictures, doing-it-myself. *Address:* c/o Foreign and Commonwealth Office, SW1. *Club:* Royal Air Force.

MORGAN, Arthur William Crawford, (Tony Morgan); research consultant for overseas corporations, USA and South Africa; *b* 24 Aug. 1931; *s* of Arthur James and Violet Morgan; *m* 1955, Valerie Anne Williams; three *s*. *Educ:* Hereford High Sch.; Westcliff High Sch. Governor, BBC, 1972-77; Sailed Olympic Games, Tokyo; Silver Medal, Flying Dutchman, 1964; Jt Yachtsman of the Year, 1965; Member: British Olympic Yachting Appeal,

1970; Royal Yachting Assoc. Council, 1968-72. FRSA. *Publications:* various technical papers. *Recreations:* squash, skiing, sailing. *Address:* Chalet Bergfried, 3920 Zermatt, Switzerland. *T:* Zermatt 67.21.01.

MORGAN, Rear-Adm. Brinley John, CB 1972; Director, Administration, Social Science Research Council, 1975-80; *b* 3 April 1916; *s* of Thomas Edward Morgan and Mary Morgan (*née* Parkhouse); *m* 1945, Margaret Mary Whittles; three *s*. *Educ:* Abersychan Grammar Sch.; University Coll., Cardiff (BSc 1937). Entered Royal Navy as Instr Lt, 1939. Served War of 1939-45: Cruisers Emerald and Newcastle, 1939-41; Aircraft Carrier Formidable, 1941-43; Naval Weather Service (Admty Forecast Section), 1943-45. Staff of C-in-C Medit., 1945-48; HQ, Naval Weather Service, 1948-50; Staff of Flag Officer Trg Sqdn in HM Ships Vanguard, Indefatigable and Implacable, 1950-52; Instr Comdr, 1951; Lectr, RN Coll., Greenwich, 1952-54; Headmaster, RN Schools, Malta, 1954-59; Instr Captain, 1960; Staff of Dir, Naval Educn Service, 1959-61 and 1963-64; Sen. Officers' War Course, 1961; HMS Ganges, 1961-63; Dean, RN Engineering Coll., Manadon, 1964-69; Instr Rear-Adm., 1970; Dir, Naval Educn Service, 1970-75, retired. *Address:* 11 Selwyn House, Manor Fields, Putney Hill, SW15. *T:* 01-789 3269.

MORGAN, Rev. Chandos Clifford Hastings Mansel, CB 1973; MA; Chaplain, Dean Close School, Cheltenham, since 1976; Chaplain of the Fleet and Archdeacon of the Royal Navy, 1972-75; *b* 12 Aug. 1920; *s* of Llewelyn Morgan, Anglesey; *m* 1946, Dorothy Mary (*née* Oliver); one *s*. *Educ:* Stowe; Jesus Coll., Cambridge (MA); Ridley Hall, Cambridge. Curate of Holy Trinity, Tunbridge Wells, 1944-51; staff of Children's Special Service Mission, 1947-51; Chaplain, RN, 1951; served in HM Ships: Pembroke, 1951; Vengeance and Ceylon, 1952; Drake, 1954; Theseus, 1956; Ocean, 1957; Caledonia, 1958; Adamant, 1960; Jufair, 1961; Heron, 1963; Ark Royal, 1965; Collingwood, 1967; Royal Arthur, 1969. QHC 1972-75. *Recreations:* riding, shooting, sailing, gardening, etc. *Address:* Westwood Farmhouse, West Lydford, Somerton, Somerset. *T:* Wheathill 301.

MORGAN, Mrs Charles (L.); *see* Vaughan, Hilda.

MORGAN, Clifford Isaac, OBE 1977; Head of Outside Broadcasts Group, BBC Television, since 1975; *b* 7 April 1930; *m* 1955, Nuala Martin; one *s* one *d*. *Educ:* Tonyrefail Grammar School, South Wales. Played International Rugby Union for Wales, British Lions and Barbarians. Joined BBC, 1958, as Sports Organiser, Wales; Editor, Sportsview and Grandstand, 1961-64; Producer, This Week, 1964-66; freelance writer and broadcaster, 1966-72; Editor, Sport Radio, 1972-74; Head of Outside Broadcasts, Radio, 1974-75. Pres., London Glamorgan Soc., 1974-. *Recreation:* music. *Address:* BBC Television, W14.

MORGAN, Sir Clifford Naunton, Kt 1966; MS; FRCS; FRCOG; Hon. FRCSI; Hon. FACS; Commander of the Order of the Star of the North (Sweden); Hon. Consulting Surgeon: St Bartholomew's Hospital; St Mark's Hospital for Diseases of the Rectum and Colon; Hospital for Tropical Diseases; Surgeon, King Edward VII's Hospital for Officers; Consulting Surgeon: RAF; (Colon and Rectum) RN; *b* 20 Dec. 1901; *s* of late Thomas Naunton Morgan, Penygraig; *m* 1930, Ena Muriel Evans; two *s* one *d*. *Educ:* Royal Masonic Sch.; University Coll., Cardiff; Univ. of London (St Bartholomew's Hosp.). MB 1924; FRCS 1926. Surgeon: Metropolitan Hosp., 1930; Royal Masonic Hosp.; St Bartholomew's Hospital: Demonstrator of Anatomy, Med. Coll., 1929; Chief Asst to a Surgical Unit, 1930; Casualty Surgeon, 1936; Asst Dir of Surgery, Professorial Unit, 1937. Lectr and Examr in Surgery, Univ. of London; Examr in Surgery, Univs of Cambridge, Glasgow, and Edinburgh. Officer i/c Surgical Divs, MEF, 1941-43 (despatches); Cons. Surgeon: Persia-Iraq Force, 1943-45; E Africa Comd, 1945; Hon. Col and late Brig., AMS. Twice Pres., Section of Proctology, Royal Soc. of Medicine; Mem. Council, RCS of England, 1953-68 (Vice-Pres., 1963-65); Past Vice-Chm., Imperial Cancer Research Fund. Sims Commonwealth Travelling Prof., 1963; Bradshaw Lectr, RCS, 1964; Vicary Lectr, 1967. Fellow, Assoc. of Surgeons of Great Britain and Ireland (Pres., 1968); Hon. Fellow: Amer. Surgical Assoc.; Amer. Protologic Soc.; For. Mem., Académie de Chirurgie; Hon. Member: Pennsylvania Proctologic Soc.; Société Nationale Française de Proctologie; Sociedades Argentina, Brasileira and Chilena de Proctologia; Med. Assoc. of Thessaloniki; Burmese Med. Assoc. *Publications:* various chapters in British Surgical Practice and other surgical Text Books. Contributor St Mark's Hosp. Centenary Vol., 1935. Many articles on Surgery of the Colon and Rectum in Brit. and Amer. Jls. *Recreation:* farming. *Address:* Rolfe's Farm, Inkpen, Berks RG15 0PZ. *T:* Inkpen 259. *Club:* Royal Air Force.

MORGAN, Cyril Dion, OBE 1970; TD 1945; FCIS; Secretary, Institution of Structural Engineers, 1961-82; *b* 30 Aug. 1917; *y s* of late Robert Dymant Morgan and of Nell (*née* Barrett); *m* 1948, Anthea Grace Brown; two *d*. *Educ:* Sloane Sch., Chelsea; City of London Coll. Served War, North Africa, Italy, 1939-46. Secretary: Inst. of Road Transport Engineers, 1948-53; British Road Fedn, 1953-61. FRSA. *Publications:* articles/reports in Proc. Instn of Structural Engrs. *Recreation:* gardening. *Address:* 11 North Way, Pinner, Mddx. *T:* 01-866 0750.

MORGAN, (David) Dudley; Consultant, Theodore Goddard & Co., Solicitors, since 1980; *b* 23 Oct. 1914; *y s* of Thomas Dudley Morgan; *m* 1948, Margaret Helene, *o d* of late David MacNaughton Duncan, Loanhead, Midlothian; two *d*. *Educ:* Swansea Grammar Sch.; Jesus Coll., Cambridge

(MA, LLB). War Service with RAF in Intell. Br., UK, 1940-42 and Legal Br., India, 1942-46; Wing Comdr 1945. Admitted Solicitor, 1939, with Theodore Goddard & Co.; Partner 1948; Senior Partner, 1974-80. Director: Associated Fisheries PLC; Crown House PLC; Francis Industries PLC, and other companies. An Underwriting Member of Lloyd's. *Recreation:* gardening. *Address:* St Leonard's House, St Leonard's Road, Nazeing, Waltham Abbey, Essex EN9 2HG. *T:* Nazeing 2124. *Club:* Carlton.

MORGAN, David Gethin; County Treasurer, Avon County Council, since 1973; *b* 30 June 1929; *s* of Edgar and Ethel Morgan; *m* 1955, Marion Brook. *Educ:* Jesus Coll., Oxford (MA Hons English). IPFA, FInstAM(Dip). Graduate Accountancy Asst, Staffordshire CC, 1952-58; Computer Systems Officer, Sen. O&M Officer, Cheshire CC, 1958-62; County Management Services Officer, Durham CC, 1962-65; Leicestershire CC: Asst County Treasurer, 1965-68; Dep. County Treasurer, 1968-73. *Publication:* Vol. XV Financial Information Service (IPFA). *Recreations:* local history, church architecture. *Address:* 6 Wycliffe Road, Henleaze, Bristol, Avon BS9 4NH. *T:* Bristol 629640.

MORGAN, David Glyn; a Recorder of the Crown Court, since 1974; *b* 31 March 1933; *s* of late Dr Richard Glyn Morgan, MC, and of Nancy Morgan; *m* 1959, Ailsa Murray Strang; three *d*. *Educ:* Mill Hill Sch.; Merton Coll., Oxford (MA). Called to Bar, Middle Temple, 1958; practised Oxford Circuit, 1958-70; Wales and Chester Circuit, 1970-. 2nd Lieut, The Queen's Bays, 1955; Dep. Col, 1st The Queen's Dragoon Guards, 1976. *Recreations:* riding, fishing, Rugby football, gardening. *Address:* 2 Harcourt Buildings, Temple, EC4Y 9DB. *T:* 01-353 8549; 30 Park Place, Cardiff. *T:* Cardiff 41121. *Clubs:* Cavalry and Guards; Cardiff and County (Cardiff); Newport (Mon) Constitutional.

MORGAN, Sir David John H.; *see* Hughes-Morgan.

MORGAN, Rev. Dewi, (David Lewis); Rector, St Bride's Church, Fleet Street, EC4, since 1962; a Prebendary of St Paul's Cathedral, since 1976; *b* 5 Feb. 1916; *s* of David and Anne Morgan; *m* 1942, Doris, *d* of Samuel and Ann Povey; two *d*. *Educ:* Lewis Sch., Pengam; University Coll. Cardiff (BA); St Michael's Coll., Llandaff. Curate: St Andrew's, Cardiff, 1939-43; Aberdare, 1943-46; Aberavon, 1946-50. Soc. for the Propagation of the Gospel: Press Officer, 1950-52, Editorial and Press Sec., 1952-62; Editor, St Martin's Review, 1953-55; Associate Editor: Church Illustrated, 1955-67; Anglican World, 1960-67; Priest-in-charge, St Dunstan-in-the-West, 1978-80. Freeman of City of London, 1963. *Publications:* Expanding Frontiers, 1957; The Bishops Come to Lambeth, 1957; Lambeth Speaks, 1958; The Undying Fire, 1959; 1662 And All That, 1961; But God Comes First, 1962; Agenda for Anglicans, 1963; Seeds of Peace, 1965; Arising From the Psalms, 1965; God and Sons, 1967. Edited: They Became Anglicans, 1959; They Became Christians, 1966; The Church in Transition, 1970; The Phoenix of Fleet Street, 1973. *Recreation:* sleeping. *Address:* St Bride's Rectory, Fleet Street, EC4. *T:* 01-353 1301. *Clubs:* Athenæum; Press (Hon. Chaplain), Publicity (Hon. Chaplain).

MORGAN, Dudley; *see* Morgan, David D.

MORGAN, Prof. Edwin George, OBE 1982; Titular Professor of English, University of Glasgow, 1975-80; *b* 27 April 1920; *s* of Stanley Lawrence Morgan and Margaret McKillop Arnott. *Educ:* Rutherglen Academy; High Sch. of Glasgow; Univ. of Glasgow. MA 1st Cl. Hons, Eng. Lang. and Lit., 1947. Served War, RAMC, 1940-46. University of Glasgow: Asst, 1947, Lectr, 1950, Sen. Lectr, 1965, Reader, 1971, in English. Cholmondeley Award for Poets, 1968; Hungarian PEN Meml Medal, 1972; Scottish Arts Council Book Awards, 1968, 1973, 1975, 1977, 1978. Visual/concrete poems in many internat. exhibns, 1965-. Opera librettos (unpublished): The Charcoal-Burner, 1969; Valentine, 1976; Columba, 1976; Spell, 1979. Hon. DLitt. Loughborough, 1981. *Publications: poetry:* The Vision of Cathkin Braes, 1952; Beowulf, 1952; The Cape of Good Hope, 1955; Poems from Eugenio Montale, 1959; Sovpoems, 1961; (ed) Collins Albatross Book of Longer Poems, 1963; Starryveldt, 1965; Emergent Poems, 1967; Gnomes, 1968; The Second Life, 1968; Proverbfolder, 1969; Penguin Modern Poets 15, 1969; Twelve Songs, 1970; The Horseman's Word, 1970; (co-ed) Scottish Poetry 1-6, 1966-72; Glasgow Sonnets, 1972; Wi the Haill Voice, 1972; Instamatic Poems, 1972; The Whittrick, 1973; From Glasgow to Saturn, 1973; Fifty Renascence Love-Poems, 1975; Rites of Passage, 1976; The New Divan, 1977; Colour Poems, 1978; Platen: selected poems, 1978; Star Gate, 1979; (ed) Scottish Satirical Verse, 1980; Poems of Thirty Years, 1982; *prose:* Essays, 1974; East European Poets, 1976; Hugh MacDiarmid, 1976. *Recreations:* photography, scrapbooks, walking in cities. *Address:* 19 Whittingehame Court, Glasgow G12 0BG. *T:* 041-339 6260.

MORGAN, Edwin John; Civil Service Commissioner, since 1980; *b* 10 Jan. 1927; *s* of Thomas Grosvenor Morgan and Florence (*née* Binmore); *m* 1954, Joyce Beryl, *o d* of Reginald and Gladys Ashurst, Bebington, Wirral; two *s* one *d*. *Educ:* Dauntsey's Sch.; St Edmund Hall, Oxford (Sen. Scholar, BA 1st Cl. Hons 1951). Served Army, Intell. Corps, Palestine and Cyprus, 1944-48. Lecteur d'anglais, Ecole normale supérieure, Paris, 1952; Asst, Dept of French Studies, Glasgow Univ., 1953; Asst Principal, Air Min., 1957, Principal, 1960; MoD, 1965; Registrar, RMCS, 1968; Asst Sec., 1970; CSD, 1971; CS Commn, 1975; Under Sec., 1980. *Recreations:* reading, walking, music, swimming, domesticity. *Address:* c/o Civil Service Commission, Standard House,

Northumberland Avenue, WC2N 5AL. *T:* 01-273 4045. *Club:* Civil Service.

MORGAN, Ellis, CMG 1961; HM Diplomatic Service, retired; *b* 26 Dec. 1916; *s* of late Ben Morgan and of Mary Morgan, The Grove, Three Crosses, Gower, S Wales; *m* 1st, 1948, Molly Darby (marr. diss.); three *d*; 2nd, 1975, Mary, *d* of late Slade Baker Stallard-Penoyre; one *s* twin *d* (one decd). *Educ:* Swansea Grammar Sch. (Bishop Gore Sch.). Dep. Librarian, County Borough of Swansea, 1937-39. Commissioned Royal Artillery, 1941; served War of 1939-45, in India, Burma, Malaya, 1943-47. Entered Foreign (subseq. Diplomatic) Service, 1948; 3rd Sec., 1948-50, 2nd Sec., 1951-53, subseq. 1st Sec., British Embassy, Rangoon; 1st Sec., British Embassy, Bangkok, 1954-55; 1st Sec., Office of Commissioner-Gen., Singapore, 1957-60; Student at Imperial Defence Coll., 1961; Counsellor: UK High Commission, New Delhi, 1964; FO, later FCO, 1966-73; Political and Economic Adviser, Commercial Union Assurance, 1973-79. *Address:* Penhenllan, Cusop, Hay-on-Wye, Hereford. *T:* Hay 820826. *Club:* Farmers'.

MORGAN, Sir Ernest (Dunstan), ORSL; KBE 1971 (OBE 1951; MBE 1940); DCL; JP; *b* 17 Nov. 1896; *s* of Thomas William Morgan and Susan Barnett; *m* 1st, 1918, Elizabeth Mary Agnes Collier; one *d*; 2nd, 1972, Monica Fredericka Davies; one *s* three *d*. *Educ:* Zion Day School, Freetown; Methodist Boys' High School, Freetown. Government Dispenser, 1914-20; Druggist, 1917-. MHR Sierra Leone, 1956-61; Member: Freetown City Council, 1938-44; Fourah Bay Coll. Council, 1950-54; Chairman: Blind Welfare Soc., 1946-52; Public Service Commn, 1948-52. JP Sierra Leone, 1952. *Recreation:* tennis. *Address:* 15 Syke Street, Freetown, Sierra Leone. *T:* Freetown 23155 and 22366. *Club:* Freetown Dinner.

MORGAN, Frank Leslie, MBE 1973; Chairman, Morgan Bros (Mid Wales) Ltd, since 1959; Chairman, Development Board for Rural Wales, since 1981; *b* 7 Nov. 1926; *s* of Edward Arthur Morgan and Beatrice Morgan; *m* 1962, Victoria Stoker (*née* Jeffery); one *s* two *d*. *Educ:* Llanfair Primary Sch.; Llanfair Grammar Sch.; University College of Wales (BA Econ Hons). Post graduate trainee and parts executive in motor industry, 1950-56. Chairman and President, Montgomery Conservative Assoc., 1964-81; Member, Welsh Council, 1970-79; Dep. Chm., Mid Wales New Town Development Corp., 1973-77; Member: Development Bd for Rural Wales, 1977-81; Welsh Development Agency, 1981-; Wales Tourist Bd, 1982-; Infrastructure Cttee, BTA, 1982-; Dir, Develt Corp. for Wales, 1981-. Mem., Design Council Welsh Cttee, 1981-. *Recreations:* reading, travel, jogging, swimming, cycling. *Address:* Wentworth House, Llangyniew, Welshpool, Powys SY21 9EL. *T:* Llanfair-Caereinion 810462.

MORGAN, Col Frank Stanley, CBE 1940; ERD 1954; DL; JP; *b* 10 Jan. 1893; *s* of F. A. Morgan, Commissioner Imperial Chinese Customs; *m* 1918, Gladys Joan (*d* 1953), *d* of Lt-Col H. M. Warde, CBE, DL Kent; no *c*; *m* 1956, Minnie Helen Pine, MBE, TD, DL, Lt-Col WRAC, The Manor House, Great Barrow, Cheshire. *Educ:* Marlborough; Christ Church, Oxford. Served European War, 1914-19; public work in Wales; Territorial and Reserve Service, 1919-39; Air Formation Signals, France, North Africa, Italy, Middle East, 1939-45; DL Glamorgan, 1946; JP 1951; Hon. Col 50 and 81 AF Signal Regts, 1952-60. *Address:* Herbert's Lodge, Bishopston, Swansea. *T:* Bishopston 4222.

MORGAN, George Lewis Bush; Chief Registrar, Bank of England, since 1978; *b* 1 Sept. 1925; *s* of late William James Charles Morgan and Eva Averill Morgan (*née* Bush); *m* 1949, Mary Rose (*née* Vine); three *s*. *Educ:* Cranbrook Sch., Kent. Captain, Royal Sussex Regt, 1943-47. Entered Bank of England, 1947; Asst Chief Accountant, 1966; Asst Sec., 1969; Dep. Sec., 1973. *Recreations:* tennis, golf, gardening. *Address:* Bank of England, New Change, EC4M 9AA.

MORGAN, Geraint; *see* Morgan, W. G. O.

MORGAN, Graham, CMG 1954; FICE; Chartered Civil Engineer; *b* 12 July 1903; *m* 1931, Alice Jane Morgan; three *d*. *Educ:* King Henry VIII Grammar Sch., Abergavenny; University Coll., Cardiff. BSc Civil Engineering, Wales, 1923; Asst Engineer: Newport, Mon., 1924; Devon CC, 1924; Federated Malay States, 1926; Sen. Exec. Engineer, Malayan Public Works Service, 1941; State Engineer, Johore, 1948; Dir of Public Works, Tanganyika, 1950-Sept. 1954, retired. FICE (Mem. of Council, 1953-55). *Address:* 36 Sandfield Road, Oxford.

MORGAN, Guy, FRIBA; AIStructE; FRSA; BA; Senior Partner, in architectural practice; *b* 14 June 1902; *s* of late Francis Morgan and Miriam Hanley; *m* 1937, Violet Guy; one *d* (one *s* decd). *Educ:* Mill Hill; Cambridge; University Coll., London. Andrew Taylor Prizeman, 1923. Lecturer and Year Master, Architectural Assoc., 1931-36. In practice, 1927-; principal works include: large blocks of flats and offices in London and Provinces; aircraft factories and air bases; town planning schemes and housing in England and abroad; agricultural buildings and country houses; ecclesiastical and hospital works; film studios; racing and sports stadia. Past Joint Master, Cowdray Foxhounds. Past Master of Worshipful Company of Woolmen. *Recreations:* foxhunting, sailing, travel; music. *Address:* Lower House Farm, Fernhurst, Haslemere, Surrey. *T:* Haslemere 53022; 12A Eaton Square, SW1. *T:* 01-235 5101. *Club:* Royal Thames Yacht.

MORGAN, Gwenda, RE 1961; Wood Engraver; *b* 1 Feb. 1908; *d* of late William David Morgan, JP, and late Mary Morgan. *Educ:* Brighton and Hove High Sch. Studied Art at Goldsmiths' Coll. Sch. of Art, and at Grosvenor Sch. of Modern Art under Iain Macnab. Women's Land Army, 1939-46. Mem., Soc. of Wood Engravers. Exhibited in London, provincial and foreign exhibitions. Work represented in Victoria and Albert Museum, Brighton Art Gallery and Herefordshire Museum. *Address:* Ridge House, Petworth, West Sussex.

MORGAN, Gwyn; *see* Morgan, J. G.

MORGAN, Prof. Henry Gemmell; Professor of Pathological Biochemistry, University of Glasgow, since 1965; *b* 25 Dec. 1922; *s* of John McIntosh Morgan, MC, MD, FRCPE, and Florence Ballantyne; *m* 1949, Margaret Duncan, BSc, MB, ChB; one *d. Educ:* Dundee High Sch.; Merchiston Castle Sch., Edinburgh; Univ. of St Andrews at University Coll., Dundee. BSc 1943; MB, ChB (distinction), 1946; FRCPE 1962; FRCPGlas 1968; FR.CPath 1970; FRSE 1971. Hon. Consultant, Eastern District, Glasgow, 1966-. Chairman: Cttee on Clinical Chemistry, SHHD, 1981-; Assoc. of Clinical Biochemists, 1982-; Ext. Examnr, Clinical Biochemistry, Univ. of Dublin; Examnr in primary FRCS and MRCP, RCPGlas. Chm., Scottish Br., Nutrition Soc., 1967-68. Adviser to Greater Glasgow Health Ed, SHHD. *Publications:* chapters; papers in medical jls. *Recreations:* golf, foreign travel, history. *Address:* Royal Infirmary, Glasgow G4 0SF; Firwood House, 8 Eaglesham Road, Newton Mearns, Glasgow. *T:* 041-639 4404.

MORGAN, Hugh Travers, CMG 1966; HM Diplomatic Service, retired; Ambassador to Austria, 1976-79; *b* 3 Aug. 1919; *s* of Dr Montagu Travers Morgan, CMG, MC; *m* 1959, Alexandra Belinoff; two *s* one *d. Educ:* Winchester Coll.; Magdalene Coll., Cambridge. RAF, 1939-45, prisoner-of-war in Germany, 1941-45. Entered HM Diplomatic Service, 1945, and served: New York, 1946-48; Moscow, 1948-50; Foreign Office, 1950-53; Canadian National Defence Coll., 1953-54; Mexico City, 1954-57; Foreign Office, 1957-58; UK Delegation to Conference on Nuclear Tests, Geneva, 1958-61; Peking (Counsellor), 1961-63; Political Adviser to the British Commandant, Berlin, 1964-67; FCO, 1967-70; Ambassador, Peru, 1970-74; Asst Under-Sec. of State, FCO, 1974-75. *Address:* 42 Waldemar Avenue, SW6.

MORGAN, Janet; writer and consultant; Visiting Fellow, All Souls College, University of Oxford; Special Adviser to the Director-General, BBC, since 1983; *b* 5 Dec. 1945; *e d* of Frank Morgan and Shiela Sadler. *Educ:* Newbury Co. Girls Grammar Sch.; St Hugh's Coll., Oxford. MA, DPhil Oxon, MA Sussex. Kennedy Meml Scholar, Harvard Univ., 1968-69; Student, Nuffield Coll., Oxford, 1969-71; Res. Fellow, Wolfson Coll., Oxford and Res. Officer, Univ. of Essex, 1971-72; Res. Fellow, Nuffield Coll., Oxford, 1972-74; Lectr in Politics, Exeter Coll., Oxford, 1974-76; Dir of Studies, St Hugh's Coll., Oxford, 1975-76 and Lectr in Politics, 1976-78; Mem., Central Policy Rev. Staff, Cabinet Office, 1978-81. Dir, Satellite Television PLC. Member: Lord Chancellor's Adv. Council on Public Records; Editorial Bd, Political Quarterly. *Publications:* The House of Lords and the Labour Government 1964-70, 1975; Reinforcing Parliament, 1976; (ed) The Diaries of a Cabinet Minister 1964-70 by Richard Crossman, 3 vols 1975, 1976, 1977; (ed) Backbench Diaries 1951-63 by Richard Crossman, 1980; (ed with Richard Hoggart) The Future of Broadcasting, 1982. *Recreations:* music, sea-bathing, gardens, housekeeping, making ice cream. *Address:* Home Close, Elsfield, Oxford. *T:* Stanton St John 753.

MORGAN, John Albert Leigh, CMG 1982; HM Diplomatic Service; Ambassador to the Republic of Korea, since 1980; *b* 21 June 1929; *s* of John Edward Rowland Morgan, Bridge, Kent; *m* 1st, 1961, Hon. Fionn Frances Bride O'Neill (marr. diss. 1975), *d* of 3rd Baron O'Neill, Shane's Castle, Antrim; one *s* two *d* ; 2nd, 1976, Angela Mary Eleanor, *e d* of Patrick Warre Rathbone, Woolton, Liverpool; one *s* one *d. Educ:* London School of Economics. Served in Army, 1947-49; entered Foreign Service, 1951; FO, 1951-53; 3rd Sec. and Private Sec. to HM Ambassador, Moscow, 1953-56; 2nd Sec., Peking, 1956-58; FO, 1958-63; 1st Sec., 1960; Head of Chancery, Rio de Janeiro, 1963-64; FO, 1964-65; Chargé d'Affaires, Ulan Bator, 1965; Moscow, 1965-67; FO, 1968; Head of Far Eastern Dept, FCO, 1970-72; Head of Cultural Relations Dept, FCO, 1972-80. Served on Earl Marshal's Staff for State Funeral of Sir Winston Churchill, 1965, and for Investiture of Prince of Wales, 1969. Governor, LSE, 1971-. Fellow, Royal Asiatic Soc.; Hon. Life Member: Royal Philharmonic Orch.; GB-China Centre. *Address:* c/o Foreign and Commonwealth Office, SW1. *Club:* Travellers'.

MORGAN, John Alfred; General Manager, British Railways Pension Funds, since 1978; *b* 16 Sept. 1931; *s* of late Alfred Morgan and of Lydia Amelia Morgan; *m* 1959, Janet Mary Sclater-Jones; one *d. Educ:* Rugeley Grammar Sch.; Peterhouse, Cambridge (BA). Investment research, Cambridge, 1953-59; Investment Manager, S. G. Warburg & Co. Ltd, 1959-67; Director: Finance and Investment, Williams & Glyn's Bank Ltd, 1967-76; Glyn, Mills & Co., 1967-70; Rothschild Asset Management, 1976-77. Director: Central Trustee Savings Bank Ltd, 1982-; Zurich Life Assce Co. Ltd, 1970-. Chm., Post Office Users' Nat. Council, 1978-82. *Recreations:* music, contemporary art, fell walking. *Address:* 5 Grange Road, Highgate, N6 4AR. *Club:* Reform.

MORGAN, (John) Gwyn(fryn); Head of EEC Press and Information Office for Canada, since 1979; a Director, Development Corporation for Wales, since 1976; *b* 16 Feb. 1934; *s* of Arthur G. Morgan, coal miner, and Mary Walters;

m 1960, Joan Margaret Taylor (marr. diss. 1974); one *d* ; *m* Colette Anne Rumball; two *s* one *d. Educ:* Aberdare Boys' Grammar Sch.; UCW Aberystwyth. MA Classics 1957; Dip. Educn 1958. Senior Classics Master, The Regis Sch., Tettenhall, Staffs, 1958-60; Pres., National Union of Students, 1960-62; Sec.-Gen., Internat. Student Conf. (ISC), 1962-65; Head of Overseas Dept, British Labour Party, 1965-69; Asst Gen. Secretary, British Labour Party, 1969-72; Chef de Cabinet to Mr George Thomson, 1973-75; Head of Welsh Inf. Office, EEC, 1975-79. Mem., Hansard Commn on Electoral Reform, 1975-76. Adjunct Prof., Univ. of Guelph, 1980-. *Publications:* contribs to numerous British and foreign political jls. *Recreations:* cricket, Rugby football, crosswords, wine-tasting. *Address:* c/o EEC Press and Information Office, Suite 1110, 350 Sparks Street, Ottawa, Ont K1R 7S8, Canada. *Clubs:* Royal Commonwealth Society, Reform; Cardiff and County; Cercle Universitaire, Country (Ottawa); Mount Stephens (Montreal).

MORGAN, Kenneth, OBE 1978; Director, Press Council, since 1980; *b* 3 Nov. 1928; *s* of Albert E. and Lily M. Morgan; *m* 1950, Margaret Cynthia, *d* of Roland E. Wilson; three *d. Educ:* Stockport Grammar School. Stockport Express, 1944; Army, 1946 (served Palestine, Egypt, GHQ MELF); journalism, 1949; Central London Sec., NUJ, 1962; Nat. Organiser, NUJ, 1966; Gen. Sec., NUJ, 1970-77, Mem. of Honour, 1978. Press Council: Consultative Mem., 1970-77; Jt Sec., 1977-78; Dep. Dir and Conciliator, 1978-79. Mem. Exec. Cttee: Printing and Kindred Trades Fedn, 1970-73; Nat. Fedn of Professional Workers, 1970-77; Fedn of Broadcasting Unions, 1970-77; Confedn of Entertainment Unions, 1970-77; Bureau, Internat. Fedn of Journalists, 1970-78. Member: NEDC for Printing and Publishing Industry, 1970; Printing Industries Cttee, TUC, 1974-77; Printing and Publishing Industries Trng Bd, 1975-77; Jt Standing Cttee, Nat. Newspaper Industry, 1976-77; British Cttee, Journalists in Europe, 1977. Associate Mem. IPI, 1980; FRSA 1980. *Recreations:* theatre, military history, inland waterways. *Address:* 174 Overhill Road, Dulwich, SE22 0PS. *T:* 01-693 6585. *Club:* Press.

MORGAN, Kenneth Smith; Editor of the Official Report (Hansard), House of Commons, since 1979; *b* 6 Aug. 1925; *er s* of Edward and Florence Morgan; *m* 1952, Patricia Hunt; one *s* one *d. Educ:* Battersea and Dartford Grammar Schools. Commissioned Royal West Kent Regt, 1944; Burma, 1944-46. Weekly newspapers, 1947-51; Derby Evening Telegraph, 1951-52; Reuters Parliamentary Staff, 1952-54; joined Official Report, 1954; Dep. Asst Editor, 1972, Dep. Editor, 1978. *Recreations:* Napoleonic warfare history, model soldiers, cricket, bridge. *Address:* Official Report (Hansard), House of Commons, SW1A 0AA.

MORGAN, Leslie James Joseph; a Recorder of the Crown Court, since 1975; *b* Ballina, NSW, 2 June 1922; *er s* of late Bertram Norman Morgan and Margaret Mary Morgan, MA (née Meere); *m* 1949, Sheila Doreen Elton Williamson; one *s* one *d. Educ:* Bournemouth Sch.; University Coll., Southampton. LLB (London) 1943. Served, Home Guard, 1940, Radio Security Service, 1941-43. Solicitor (Distinction) 1944; general practice in Bournemouth, 1944-. Chairman: Southern Area Legal Aid Cttee, 1973-74; Bournemouth Exec. Council (NHS), 1962-74; Dorset Family Practitioner Cttee, 1974-77; Law Society's Standing Cttee on Criminal Law, 1979-82; Member: Council, Law Society, 1973-; Matrimonial Causes Rule Cttee, 1978-; President: Bournemouth and Dist Law Soc., 1972-73; Soc. of Family Practitioner Cttees, 1975-76. *Publications:* articles on aspects of short wave radio. *Recreations:* music, reading, wine, amateur radio (licensed as G2HNO, 1939-). *Address:* 4 Tree Tops, Martello Park, Canford Cliffs, Poole, Dorset BH13 7BA. *T:* Canford Cliffs 708405. *Club:* Reform.

MORGAN, Michael Hugh, CMG 1978; HM Diplomatic Service; Ambassador to the Philippines, since 1981; *b* 18 April 1925; *s* of late H. P. Morgan; *m* 1957, Julian Bamfield; two *s. Educ:* Shrewsbury Sch.; Downing College, Cambridge; School of Oriental and African Studies, London Univ. Army Service 1943-46. HMOCS Malaya, 1946-56. Foreign Office, 1956-57; First Secretary, Peking, 1957-60; Belgrade 1960-64; attached to Industry, 1964; First Secretary, FCO, 1964-68; Counsellor and Head of Chancery, Cape Town/Pretoria, 1968-72; Counsellor, Peking, 1972-75; Inspector, FCO, 1975-77; High Comr, Sierra Leone, 1977-81. *Address:* c/o Foreign and Commonwealth Office, SW1.

MORGAN, Rear-Adm. Sir Patrick (John), KCVO 1970; CB 1967; DSC 1942; Flag Officer, Royal Yachts, 1965-70, retired; *b* 26 Jan. 1917; *s* of late Vice-Adm. Sir Charles Morgan, KCB, DSO; *m* 1944, Mary Hermione Fraser-Tytler, *d* of late Col Neil Fraser-Tytler, DSO, Aldourie Castle, Inverness, and of Mrs C. H. Fraser-Tytler, *qv* ; three *s* one *d. Educ:* RN College, Dartmouth. Served War of 1939-45 (despatches, DSC). Naval Attaché, Ankara, 1957-59; Imperial Defence Coll. 1960; Asst Chief of Staff, Northwood, 1961-62; Commanding Officer, Commando Ship, HMS Bulwark, 1963-64. *Recreations:* sports. *Address:* Swallow Barn, Well Road, Crondall, Farnham, Surrey GU10 5PW. *T:* Aldershot 850107.

MORGAN, Peter Trevor Hopkin, QC 1972; **His Honour Judge Hopkin Morgan;** a Circuit Judge, since 1972; Liaison Judge to Gwent Magistrates, and Justice of the Peace, since 1973; a Judge of the Provincial Court of the Church in Wales, since 1980; *b* 5 Feb. 1919; *o s* of Cyril Richard Morgan and Muriel Arceta (née Hole); *m* 1942, Josephine Mouncey, *d* of Ben Travers, CBE, AFC; one *s* three *d. Educ:* Mill Hill Sch.; Magdalen Coll., Oxford (BA). Called to Bar, Middle Temple, 1949; Wales and Chester Circuit; Lectr in Law, Univ. of Wales (Cardiff and Swansea), 1950-55. Liveryman, Fishmongers'

Company. *Recreation:* inland waterways. *Address:* Itton Court, Chepstow NP6 6BW. *T:* Chepstow 3935. *Club:* Garrick.

MORGAN, Rev. Philip; General Secretary, British Council of Churches, since 1980; *b* 22 June 1930; *s* of David Lewis and Pamela Morgan; *m* 1954, Greta Mary Hanson; one *s* one *d*. *Educ:* Overdale Coll.; Selly Oaks Colls; Univ. of Birmingham (BA Hons Theology). Ordained 1952; Ministries: Aberfan, Godreaman, Griffithstown, Merthyr Tydfil and Treharris, 1952-58; Eltham, London, 1958-62; Leicester and South Wigston, 1962-67; General Secretary, Churches of Christ in Gt Britain and Ireland, 1967-80. Hon. DD Christian Theological Seminary, USA, 1980. *Recreations:* hill walking, Celtic history, steam railways. *Address:* 8 Cliveden Place, SW1. *T:* 01-730 3033.

MORGAN, Richard Martin, MA; Headmaster, Cheltenham College, since 1978; *b* 25 June 1940; *s* of His Honour Trevor Morgan, MC, QC, and late Leslie Morgan; *m* 1968, Margaret Kathryn, *d* of late Anthony Agutter and of Mrs Launcelot Fleming; three *d*. *Educ:* Sherborne Sch.; Caius Coll., Cambridge (MA, DipEd); York Univ. Assistant Master, Radley Coll., 1963; Housemaster, 1969. Member, Adv. Council, Understanding British Industry, 1977-79. *Recreations:* reading, music, games. *Address:* College House, Cheltenham, Glos GL53 7LD. *T:* Cheltenham 24841. *Clubs:* Free Foresters', Jesters'.

MORGAN, Robin Milne; Principal: Daniel Stewart's and Melville College, Edinburgh, since 1977; The Mary Erskine School, since 1979; *b* 2 Oct. 1930; *o s* of Robert Milne Morgan and Aida Forsyth Morgan; *m* 1955, Fiona Bruce MacLeod Douglas; three *s* one *d*. *Educ:* Mackie Academy, Stonehaven; Aberdeen Univ. (MA); London Univ. (BA, External). Nat. Service, 2nd Lieut The Gordon Highlanders, 1952-54; Asst Master: Arden House Prep. Sch., 1955-60; George Watson's Coll., 1960-71; Headmaster, Campbell Coll., Belfast, 1971-76. *Recreations:* music, archaeology, fishing, climbing, deer-stalking. *Address:* Daniel Stewart's and Melville College, Queensferry Road, Edinburgh EH4 3EZ.

MORGAN, Roger Hugh Vaughan Charles; Librarian, House of Lords, since 1977; *b* 8 July 1926; *s* of late Charles Langbridge Morgan, FRSL, and of Hilda Vaughan, *qv*; *m* 1st, 1951, Harriet Waterfield (marr. diss. 1965), *d* of Gordon Waterfield; one *s* one *d* (and one *s* decd); 2nd, 1965, Susan Vogel Marrian, *d* of Hugo Vogel, Milwaukee, USA; one *s*. *Educ:* Downs Sch., Colwall; Phillips Acad., Andover, USA; Eton Coll.; Brasenose Coll., Oxford. MA. Grenadier Guards, 1944-47 (Captain, 1946). House of Commons Library, 1951-63; House of Lords Library, 1963-. *Recreations:* photography, cooking. *Address:* 30 St Peter's Square, W6 9UH. *T:* 01-741 0267; Cliff Cottage, Laugharne, Dyfed. *Clubs:* Garrick, Beefsteak.
See also Marchioness of Anglesey.

MORGAN, Tom, CBE 1982; JP; Lord Provost of the City of Edinburgh and Lord Lieutenant of the City and County of Edinburgh since 1980; *b* 24 Feb. 1914; *s* of Thomas Morgan; *m* 1940, Mary Montgomery, *d* of Stephen McLauchlan; two *s*. *Educ:* Longside Public Sch., Aberdeenshire; Aberdeen Univ.; W of Scotland Coll. of Agriculture. Unigate Ltd for 36 yrs (Regional Dir for Scotland). Member, Edinburgh Corp., 1954-71 and Edinburgh DC, 1977-. Chairman: Edinburgh Festival Soc., 1980-; Edinburgh Mil. Tattoo Policy Cttee, 1980-. Curator of Patronage, Univ. of Edinburgh. Formerly: Magistrate; City Treasurer; Governor, George Heriot's Trust; Governor, Edinburgh and E of Scotland Coll. of Agric.; Dir, Edinburgh Chamber of Commerce and Manufactures; Pres., Edinburgh City Business Club; Gen. Comr of Income Tax; Chm., Edinburgh Abbeyfield Soc. *Recreations:* golf, gardening. *Address:* City Chambers, High Street, Edinburgh EH1 1PL; 400 Lanark Road, Edinburgh EH13 0LX.

MORGAN, Tony; see Morgan, A. W. C.

MORGAN, Rt. Rev. Mgr. Vaughan Frederick John, CBE 1982; Principal Roman Catholic Chaplain (Naval), and Vicar General for the Royal Navy, since 1979; *b* Upper Hutt, New Zealand, 21 March 1931; *o s* of late Godfrey Frederick Vaughan Morgan and Violet (Doreen) Vaughan Morgan. *Educ:* The Oratory Sch., S Oxon; Innsbruck Univ. Ordained, 1957; Archdiocese of St Andrews and Edinburgh, 1959-62; entered Royal Navy as Chaplain, 1962. Prelate of Honour to HH Pope John Paul II, 1979. *Publications:* contribs to journals. *Recreations:* music, swimming, painting, heraldry. *Address:* c/o Coutts & Co., Duncannon Branch, 440 Strand, WC2R 0QS. *Club:* Army and Navy.

MORGAN, Walter Thomas James, CBE 1959; FRS 1949; Director, Lister Institute of Preventive Medicine, London, 1972-75 (Deputy Director, 1952-68); *b* London, 5 Oct. 1900; *s* of Walter and Annie E. Morgan; *m* 1930, Dorothy Irene Price; one *s* two *d*. *Educ:* Univ. of London. Grocers' Company Scholar, 1925-27; Beit Memorial Med. Res. Fellow, 1927-28; First Asst and Biochemist, Lister Institute Serum Dept (Elstree), 1928-37; Rockefeller Research Fellow (Eidgenössische Tech. Hochschule, Zürich), 1937. Reader, 1938-51, Lister Inst.; Prof. of Biochemistry, Univ. of London, 1951-68, now Prof. Emeritus. PhD 1927, DSc 1937, London Univ.; DrSc (Tech.) Zürich, 1938; FRIC 1929. Hon. Secretary: Biochemical Soc., 1940-45; Biological Council, 1944-47. Chm. Bd of Studies, Biochem., Univ. of London, 1954-57; Member: Scientific Advisory Council, 1956-60; MRC, 1966-70. Mem., Lawes Agricl Trust Cttee, 1964-76. Guest Lecturer, 100th meeting of Gesellschaft Deutscher Naturforscher und Arzte, Germany, 1959; Royal Society: Croonian

Lectr, 1959; Vice-Pres., 1961-64; Royal Medal, 1968. Vis. Prof., Japan Soc. for Promotion of Science, 1979. Hon. Mem., Internat. Soc. Blood Transfusion, 1980; Hon. FRCP 1982. MD *hc* Basel, 1964; DSc *hc* Michigan, 1969. Conway Evans Prize (Royal College of Physicians, London), 1964. (Jointly) Landsteiner Memorial Award (USA), 1967. (Jointly) Paul Ehrlich and Ludwig Darmstädter Prizes (Germany), 1968. *Publications:* papers on biochemistry, immunology and pathology. *Address:* Division of Immunochemical Genetics, Medical Research Council, Clinical Research Centre, Watford Road, Harrow, Mddx HA1 3UJ. *T:* 01-864 5311; 57 Woodbury Drive, Sutton, Surrey. *T:* 01-642 2319. *Club:* Athenæum.

MORGAN, (William) Geraint (Oliver), QC 1971; MP (C) Denbigh, since Oct. 1959; a Recorder of the Crown Court, since 1972; *b* Nov. 1920; *m* 1957, J. S. M. Maxwell; two *s* two *d*. *Educ:* University Coll. of Wales, Aberystwyth; Trinity Hall, Cambridge. Served War of 1939-45 with Royal Marines; demobilised with Rank of Major, 1946. Called to the Bar, Gray's Inn, 1947; Squire Law Scholar; Holt Scholar; Northern Circuit. Contested: Merioneth, 1951; Huyton, 1955. *Address:* House of Commons, SW1.

MORGAN, Air Vice-Marshal William Gwyn, CB 1968; CBE 1960 (OBE 1945); RAF, retired 1969; *b* 13 Aug. 1914; *s* of T. S. Morgan; *m* 1962, Joan Russell. *Educ:* Pagefield Coll., Swansea. Joined Royal Air Force, 1939; Group Capt., 1958; Command Acct, HQ, FEAF, 1962; Air Commodore, 1965; DPS (2), RAF, 1965-66; AOA Technical Training Comd, 1966-68, Training Comd, 1968-69. Air Vice-Marshal, 1967; jssc; psc; FCCA; ACMA. *Recreation:* fell walking. *Address:* c/o Lloyds Bank, 6 Pall Mall, SW1. *Club:* Royal Air Force.

MORGAN, Rt. Hon. William James, PC (Northern Ireland) 1961; JP; Member (UUUC), for North Belfast, Northern Ireland Constitutional Convention, 1975-76; *b* 1914; *m* 1942; two *s* one *d*. Retired company director. MP, Oldpark Div. of Belfast, 1949-58, Clifton Div. of Belfast, 1959-69, NI Parlt; Minister: of Health and Local Government, Northern Ireland, 1961-64; of Labour and National Insurance, 1964; of Health and Social Services, 1965-69; Mem. (U), N Belfast, NI Assembly, 1973-75. *Address:* Thornleigh, 45 Tullynagardy Road, Newtownards, Co. Down. *T:* Newtownards 817906.

MORGAN, William Stanley, CMG 1965; Colonial Administrative Service, retired; *b* 29 April 1908; *s* of late J. W. Morgan; *m* 1957, Joan Ruth Dixon Williams; two *s* one *d*. *Educ:* Rendcomb Coll.; (Open Scholar in History) Queens' Coll., Cambridge (MA). Malayan Education Service, 1931-50; Colonial Administrative Service, 1950-57; Malaya, 1931-47; Sec., Commn on Univ. Educn in Malaya, 1947; Principal, Colonial Office, 1947-50; Sierra Leone, Ministerial Sec., 1950-57; Asst Adviser to Qatar Govt, 1957-60; Chm., Public and Police Service Commns, Mauritius, 1960-69. *Publication:* Story of Malaya, 1938. *Recreations:* travel and music. *Address:* Old Vicarage, Kirk Maughold, Isle of Man. *T:* Ramsey 812863.

MORGAN-GILES, Rear-Adm. Morgan Charles, DSO 1944; OBE 1943 (MBE 1942); GM 1941; *b* 19 June 1914; *e s* of late F. C. Morgan-Giles, OBE, MINA, Teignmouth, Devon; *m* 1946, Pamela (*d* 1966), *d* of late Philip Bushell, Sydney, New South Wales; two *s* four *d*; *m* 1968, Marigold, *d* of late Percy Lowe. *Educ:* Clifton Coll. Entered Royal Navy, 1932; served on China Station, and in destroyers. War Service: Atlantic convoys and Mediterranean; Tobruk garrison and Western Desert, 1941; with RAF, 1942; Sen. Naval Officer, Vis. (Dalmatia) and liaison with Commandos and Marshal Tito's Partisan Forces, 1943-44. Captain 1953; Chief of Naval Intelligence, Far East, 1955-56; Captain (D) Dartmouth Training Sqdn, 1957-58; HMS Belfast, in command, 1961-62; Rear-Adm. 1962; Adm. Pres., Royal Naval Coll., Greenwich, 1962-64; retd 1964. MP (C) Winchester, May 1964-79. Vice-Chm., Conservative Defence Cttee, 1965-75. Chm., HMS Belfast Trust, 1971-78; Mem., Management Cttee, RNLI. Mem. Ct of Assts, Shipwrights' Company. *Recreations:* sailing, country pursuits. *Address:* Upton Park, Alresford, Hants. *T:* Alresford 2443. *Clubs:* Carlton; Royal Yacht Squadron; Australian (Sydney).
See also Baron Killearn.

MORGAN HUGHES, David; see Hughes, David M.

MORGAN JONES, John; see Jones, J. M.

MORGAN-OWEN, John Gethin, MBE 1945; QC 1981; Judge Advocate General since 1979; *b* 22 Aug. 1914; *o s* of late Maj.-Gen. L. I. G. Morgan-Owen, CB, CMG, CBE, DSO, West Dene, Beech, Alton; *m* 1950, Mary, *d* of late F. J. Rimington, MBE, Master Mariner; two *s* one *d*. *Educ:* Shrewsbury; Trinity Coll., Oxford (BA). Called to Bar, Inner Temple, 1938; Wales and Chester Circuit, 1939; practised at Cardiff, 1939-52. 2nd Lieut Suppl. Reserve, S Wales Borderers, 1939; served 2nd Bn SWB, 1939-44: N Norway, 1940; NW Europe, 1944-45; DAA&QMG, 146 Inf. Bde, 1944-45; Hon. Major. Dep. Judge Advocate, 1952: Germany, 1953-56; Hong Kong, 1958-60; Cyprus, 1963-66; AJAG, 1966; DJAG, Germany, 1970-72; Vice JAG, 1972-79. *Recreations:* bad tennis, inland waterways, beagling. *Address:* Burninghams, Kingsley, Bordon, Hants GU35 9NW. *T:* Bordon 2040. *Club:* Army and Navy.

MORI, Haruki; Adviser to Japanese Foreign Office, since 1975; *b* 1911; *m* 1940, Tsutako Masaki; four *s*. *Educ:* Univ. of Tokyo. Ministry of Foreign

Affairs, served USA and Philippines, 1935–41; Head of Economic Section, Dept of Political Affairs, 1950–53; Counsellor, Italy, 1953–55, Asian Affairs Bureau, 1955–56; Private Sec. to Prime Minister, 1956–57; Dep. Dir-Gen., Economic Affairs Bureau, 1957; Dir-Gen., American Affairs Bureau, 1957–60; Minister Plenipotentiary to UK, 1960–63, to France, 1963–64; Ambassador to OECD, 1964–67; Dep. Vice-Minister for Foreign Affairs, 1967–70; Vice-Minister for Foreign Affairs, 1970–72; Japanese Ambassador to the Court of St James's, 1972–75. *Recreation:* golf. *Address:* c/o Ministry of Foreign Affairs, Tokyo, Japan.

MORIARTY, Gerald Evelyn, QC 1974; a Recorder of the Crown Court, since 1976; *b* 23 Aug. 1928; *er s* of late Lt-Col G. R. O'N. Moriarty and Eileen Moriarty (*née* Moloney); *m* 1961, Judith Mary, *er d* of Hon. William Robert Atkin; four s. *Educ:* Downside Sch.; St John's Coll., Oxford (MA). Called to the Bar, Lincoln's Inn, 1951. *Address:* 15 Campden Street, W8 7EP. *T:* 01-727 4593. *Club:* Reform.

MORIARTY, Brig. Joan Olivia Elsie, CB 1979; RRC 1977; Matron-in-Chief and Director of Army Nursing Services, 1976–80; *b* 11 May 1923; *d* of late Lt-Col Oliver Nash Moriarty, DSO, RA, and Mrs Georgina Elsie Moriarty (*née* Moore). *Educ:* Royal Sch., Bath; St Thomas' Hosp. (nursing); Queen Charlotte's Hosp. (midwifery). SRN. VAD, Somerset, 1941–42; joined QAIMNS (R), 1947; Reg. QAIMNS (later QARANC), 1948–82; appts incl.: Staff Captain, WO; Instr, Corps Trng Centre; Liaison Officer, MoD; served in UK, Gibraltar, BAOR, Singapore, Malaya, Cyprus; Matron, Mil. Hosp., Catterick, 1973–76; Comdt, QARANC Trng Centre, Aldershot, 1976. Major 1960; Lt-Col 1971; Col 1973; Brig. 1977. QHNS, 1977–80. Governor, Royal Sch., Bath, 1979–. OStJ 1977. *Recreation:* country pursuits. *Address:* 21 Pitman Court, Gloucester Road, Bath BA1 8BD. *Clubs:* VAD Ladies, Naval and Military.

MORIARTY, Michael John; Assistant Under-Secretary of State, Broadcasting Department, Home Office, since 1981; *b* 3 July 1930; *er s* of Edward William Patrick Moriarty, OBE, and May Lilian Moriarty; *m* 1960, Rachel Milward, *d* of J. S. Thompson and Isobel F. Thompson; one *s* two *d*. *Educ:* Reading Sch., Reading; St John's Coll., Oxford (Sir Thomas White schol.; MA Lit. Hum.). Entered Home Office as Asst Principal, 1954; Private Sec. to Parliamentary Under-Secretaries of State, 1957–59; Principal, 1959; Civil Service Selection Bd, 1962–63; Cabinet Office, 1965–67; Asst Sec., 1967; Private Sec. to Home Sec., 1968; Head of Crime Policy Planning Unit, 1974–75; Asst Under-Sec. of State, 1975–; seconded to NI Office, 1979–81. UK Representative, 1976–79, and Chm., 1978–79, Council of Europe Cttee on Crime Problems. *Publications:* contribs to: Proceedings, Conference on Criminal Policy, 1975; Penal Policy-Making in England, 1977. *Recreations:* music, walking, family pursuits. *Address:* 36 Willifield Way, Hampstead Garden Suburb, NW11 7XT. *T:* 01-455 8439.

MORICE, Prof. Peter Beaumont, DSc, PhD; FICE, FIStructE; Professor of Civil Engineering, University of Southampton, since 1958; *b* 15 May 1926; *o s* of Charles and Stephanie Morice; *m* 1952, Margaret Ransom; one *s* two *d*. *Educ:* Barfield Sch.; Farnham Grammar Sch.; University of Bristol; University of London. Surrey County Council, 1947–48; Research Div., Cement and Concrete Assoc., 1948–57. *Publications:* Linear Structural Analysis, 1958; Prestressed Concrete, 1958; papers on structural theory in various learned journals. *Recreations:* sailing, reading, listening to music. *Address:* 65 Shaftesbury Avenue, Highfield, Southampton. *T:* 556624.

MORINI, Erica; concert violinist; *b* Vienna, 5 Jan. 1910; *m* 1938, Felice Siracusano; no *c*. *Educ:* at age of 4 years under father, Prof. Oscar Morini, and then under Prof. Ottocar Sevcik, masterclass of Viennese Conservatory, at age of 8. Debut under Arthur Nikisch, at age of 9, in Leipzig Gewandhaus (Beethoven Festival); from there on Concert-tours to: Australia, Asia, Africa, Europe; to USA, 1920. Hon. Mem., Sigma Alpha Beta. Hon. MusD: Smith Coll., Mass, 1955; New England Conservatory of Music, Mass, 1963. *Recreations:* mountain climbing and chamber music. *Address:* 1200 Fifth Avenue, New York, NY 10029, USA.

MORISHIMA, Prof. Michio, FBA 1981; Professor of Economics, London School of Economics and Political Science, since 1970; *b* 18 July 1923; *s* of Kameji and Tatsuo Morishima; *m* 1953, Yoko; two *s* one *d*. *Educ:* Univ. of Kyoto (BAEcon). Assistant Professor: Kyoto Univ., 1950–51; Osaka Univ., 1951–63; Prof., Osaka Univ., 1963–69; Sen. Visiting Fellow, All Souls Coll, 1963–64; Visiting Prof., Stanford Univ., 1964; Temp. Prof. and Keynes Visiting Prof., Univ. of Essex, 1968–70. Associate Editor, Econometrica, 1959–69; Co-editor and Editor, Internat. Economic Review, 1960–67; Board of Editors: Economica, 1975–; Jl of Economic Lit., 1976–79; Fellow, Econometric Soc., 1958–, Vice-Pres., 1964, Pres., 1965; For. Hon. Mem., Amer. Acad. of Arts and Sciences, 1975–; For. Hon. Mem., Amer. Economic Assoc., 1976–. Order of Culture (Japan), 1976. *Publications:* Equilibrium, Stability and Growth, 1964; Theory of Economic Growth, 1969; The Working of Econometric Models, 1972; Marx's Economics, 1973; Theory of Demand: real and monetary, 1973; The Economic Theory of Modern Society, 1976; Walras' Economics, 1977; Value, Exploitation and Growth, 1978; Why Has Japan 'Succeeded'?, 1982. *Address:* Ker, Greenway, Hutton Mount, Brentwood, Essex CM13 2NP. *T:* Brentwood 219956.

MORISON, Alastair Malcolm; QC (Scotland), 1968; *b* 12 Feb. 1931; 2nd *s* of Sir Ronald Peter Morison, QC (Scotland); *m* 1st, 1957, Lindsay Balfour

Oatts (marr. diss. 1977); one *s* one *d*; 2nd, 1980, Birgitte Hendil. *Educ:* Cargilfield; Winchester Coll.; Edinburgh Univ. Admitted to Faculty of Advocates, 1956. *Recreations:* golf, fishing. *Address:* 6 Carlton Terrace, Edinburgh EH7 5DD. *T:* 031-556 6766. *Club:* New (Edinburgh).

MORISON, Air Vice-Marshal Richard Trevor, CBE 1969 (MBE 1944); RAF retired; President, Ordnance Board, 1971–72; *s* of Oscar Colin Morison and Margaret Valerie (*née* Cleaver); *m* 1964, Rosemary June Brett; one *s* one *d*. *Educ:* Perse Sch., Cambridge; De Havilland Sch. of Aeronautical Engineering. Commnd in RAF, 1940; RAF Staff Coll., 1952; Sen. Techn. Officer, RAF Gaydon, 1955–57; HQ Bomber Comd, 1958–60; STSO HQ 224 Group, Singapore, 1960–61; Dir of Techn. Services, Royal NZ Air Force, 1961–63; Comd Engrg Officer, HQ Bomber Comd, 1963–65; Air Officer i/c Engrg, HQ Flying Training Comd, 1966–68; Air Officer i/c Engrg, HQ Training Comd RAF, 1968–69; Vice-Pres. (Air) Ordnance Bd, 1969–70. *Recreation:* cabinet making. *Address:* Meadow House, Chedgrave, Loddon, Norfolk. *Club:* Royal Air Force.

MORISON, Thomas Richard Atkin, QC 1979; barrister-at-law, since 1960; *b* 15 Jan. 1939; *s* of Harold Thomas Brash Morison and Hon. Nancy Morison; *m* 1963, Judith Rachel Walton Morris; one *s* one *d*. *Educ:* Winchester Coll.; Worcester Coll., Oxford, 1959–62 (MA). Passed final Bar examinations, 1959; called to the Bar, Gray's Inn, 1960; pupil in Chambers, 1962–63; started practice, 1963. *Recreations:* camping, sailing, cooking. *Address:* 26 Sheen Common Drive, Richmond, Surrey TW10 5BN; Fountain Court, Temple, EC4. *T:* 01-353 7356.

MORITA, Akio; Chairman and Chief Executive Officer, Sony Corporation, since 1976; *b* Nagoya, Japan, 26 Jan. 1921; *m* 1950, Yoshiko Kamei; two *s* one *d*. *Educ:* Osaka Imperial Univ. (BSc Physics). Sony Corporation, Tokyo: co-founder, 1946; Man. Dir, 1947–55; Sen. Man. Dir, 1955–56; Exec. Vice-Pres., 1959–71; Pres., 1971–76; Sony Corporation of America: Pres., 1960–66, Chm., 1966–72; Chm. Finance Cttee, 1972–74; Chm. Exec. Cttee, 1974–77; Chm. Finance Cttee, 1977–. Dir, IBM World Trade Americas/Far East Corp., 1972–77; Member: Internat. Council, Morgan Guaranty Trust Co.; Bd of Dirs, Pan American World Airways Inc., 1980–. Chm., Cttee on Internat. Investment and Technol. Exchange, Keidanren (Fedn of Economic Organization), 1981–. Albert Medal, RSA, 1982. *Publications:* Gakureki Muyooron (Never Mind Education Records), 1966; Shin Jitsuryoku Shugi (A New Merit System), 1969. *Recreations:* music, golf. *Address:* Sony Corporation, 6-7-35 Kitashinagawa, Shinagawa-ku, Tokyo 141, Japan. *T:* 03-448-2600.

MORLAND, Martin Robert; HM Diplomatic Service; seconded to Hardcastle & Co. Ltd, since 1982; *b* 23 Sept. 1933; *e s* of Sir Oscar Morland, GBE, KCMG and of Alice, *d* of Rt Hon. Sir F. O. Lindley, PC, GCMG; *m* 1964, Jennifer Avril Mary Hanbury-Tracy; two *s* one *d*. *Educ:* Ampleforth; King's Coll., Cambridge (BA). Nat. Service, Grenadier Guards, 1954–56; British Embassy, Rangoon, 1957–60; News Dept, FO, 1961; UK Delegn to Common Market negotiations, Brussels, 1962–63; FO, 1963–65; UK Disarmament Delegn, Geneva, 1965–67; Private Sec. to Lord Chalfont, 1967–68; European Integration Dept, FCO, 1968–73; Counsellor, 1973–77, Rome (seconded temporarily to Cabinet Office to head EEC Referendum Information Unit, 1975); Hd of Maritime Aviation and Environment Dept, FCO, 1977–79; Counsellor and Head of Chancery, Washington, 1979–82. *Address:* c/o Foreign and Commonwealth Office, SW1. *Club:* Garrick.

MORLAND, Michael, QC 1972; a Recorder of the Crown Court, since 1972; *b* 16 July 1929; *e s* of Edward Morland, Liverpool, and Jane Morland (*née* Beckett); *m* 1961, Lillian Jensen, Copenhagen; one *s* one *d*. *Educ:* Stowe; Christ Church, Oxford (MA). 2nd Lieut, Grenadier Guards, 1948–49; served in Malaya. Called to Bar, Inner Temple, 1953, Bencher 1979; practises on Northern Circuit. Mem., Criminal Injuries Compensation Bd, 1980–. *Address:* 12 King's Bench Walk, Temple, EC4Y 7EL. *T:* 01-353 5892.

MORLEY; see Headlam-Morley.

MORLEY; see Hope-Morley, family name of Baron Hollenden.

MORLEY, 6th Earl of, *cr* 1815; **John St Aubyn Parker,** JP; Lt-Col, Royal Fusiliers; Lord-Lieutenant of Devon, since 1982; Chairman: Farm Industries Ltd, Truro, since 1970; Plymouth Sound Ltd, since 1974; Henry Norrington & Son Ltd, since 1980; Director, Lloyds Bank UK Management Ltd, since 1979; *b* 29 May 1923; *e s* of Hon. John Holford Parker (*y s* of 3rd Earl), Pound House, Yelverton, Devon; *S* uncle, 1962; *m* 1955, Johanna Katherine, *d* of Sir John Molesworth-St Aubyn, Bt, *qv* ; one *s* one *d*. *Educ:* Eton. 2nd Lt, KRRC, 1942; served NW Europe, 1944–45; Palestine and Egypt, 1945–48; transferred to Royal Fusiliers, 1947; served Korea, 1952–53; Middle East, 1953–55 and 1956; Staff Coll., Camberley, 1957; Comd, 1st Bn Royal Fusiliers, 1965–67. Dir, Lloyds Bank Ltd, 1974–78. Mem., Devon and Co. Cttee, Nat. Trust, 1969–; President: Plymouth Incorporated Chamber of Trade and Commerce, 1970–; Cornwall Fedn of Chambers of Commerce and Trader Assocs, 1972–79; West Country Tourist Bd, 1971–. Governor: Seale-Hayne Agric. Coll., 1973; Plymouth Polytechnic, 1975– (Chm., 1977–). Pres., Council of Order of St John for Devon, 1979. DL 1973, Vice Lord-Lieutenant, 1978–82, Devon. JP Plymouth, 1972. *Heir:* s Viscount Boringdon, *qv*. *Address:* Pound House, Yelverton, Devon. *T:* Yelverton 3162.

MORLEY, Cecil Denis, CBE 1967; Secretary General, The Stock Exchange, London, 1965-71; retired; *b* 20 May 1911; *s* of Cornelius Cecil Morley and Mildred Irene Hutchinson; *m* 1936, Lily Florence Younge; one *s. Educ:* Clifton; Trinity Coll., Cambridge. Solicitor. Asst Sec., Share & Loan Dept, Stock Exchange, 1936; Sec. to Coun. of Stock Exchange, 1949. Served War of 1939-45, Major RA (TA). *Recreations:* travel, gardening. *Address:* 17a Eldon Road, W8. *T:* 01-937 8383.

MORLEY, Eric Douglas; Joint Chairman and Chief Executive, Belhaven Brewery Group Ltd and many associated companies, including Miss World Ltd; orphaned age 11; *m* Julia Evelyn; four *s* one *d. Educ:* Sch at Martins in the Fields; Whitstable Grammar Sch.; Army Sch. of Educn Trng Ship Exmouth. Joined Army, band boy, Royal Fusiliers, 1934; RASC Motor Boats, 1943; demobilised 1946 (Captain). Joined Mecca, 1946 as Publicity Sales Manager; resigned as Chm. and Chief Exec., 1978. Dir, Grand Met Ltd, 1969-78; formed, and was first Chm. or Pres., main trade assocs in leisure and gaming industries; introd commercial bingo to UK, 1961; creator of Miss World contest, 1951, which has raised $20 million for charity. President: Variety Clubs Internat., world's greatest children's charity, 1977-79; Outward Bound Trust, 1980-. Chief Barker, Variety Club of GB, 1973, and Life-time Mem. of Crew. Contested (C) Southwark, Dulwich, Oct. 1974, 1979 (when reduced maj. of then Attorney Gen. from 7,500 to 122). Freeman, City of London. *Publication:* Miss World Story, 1967. *Recreations:* French horn, all forms of sport. *Address:* 21 Soho Square, W1. *Club:* MCC.

MORLEY, Sir Godfrey (William Rowland), Kt 1971; OBE 1944; TD 1946; *b* 15 June 1909; *o s* of late Arthur Morley, OBE, KC, and late Dorothy Innes Murray Forrest; *m* 1st, 1934, Phyllis Dyce (*d* 1963), *d* of late Sir Edward Duckworth, 2nd Bt; two *s* two *d* ; 2nd, 1967, Sonia Gisèle, *d* of late Thomas Ritchie; two *s. Educ:* Westminster; Christ Church, Oxford (MA). Solicitor, 1934; Partner in Allen & Overy, 1936, Senior Partner, 1960-75. Joined Territorial Army, 1937; served War of 1939-45, Rifle Bde and on Staff in Middle East and Italy (despatches); Lt-Col 1944. Law Society: Mem. Council, 1952-73; Vice-Pres., 1969-70; Pres., 1970-71. Member: Lord Chancellor's Law Reform Cttee, 1957-73; Cttee on Legal Educn of Students from Africa, 1960; Cttee of Management, Inst. of Advanced Legal Studies, 1961-77; CBI Company Affairs Cttee, 1972; Law Adv. Panel, British Council, 1974-; Council, Selden Soc., 1975- (Pres., 1979-82). Dir, Bowater Corp. Ltd, 1968-79. Trustee, Thalidomide Children's Trust, 1980-. Hon. Mem., Canadian Bar Assoc., 1970. Bronze Star Medal (US), 1945. *Address:* Hunter's Lodge, Warren Drive, Kingswood, Tadworth, Surrey KT20 6PT. *T:* Mogador 832485. *Clubs:* Athenæum, Boodle's, City of London.
See also Sir William Lindsay.

MORLEY, Herbert, CBE 1974; Chairman, Templeborough Rolling Mills Ltd, since 1977; Director, Bridon Ltd, since 1973; *b* 19 March 1919; *s* of George Edward and Beatrice Morley; *m* 1942, Gladys Hardy; one *s* one *d. Educ:* Almondbury Grammar Sch., Huddersfield; Sheffield Univ. (Assoc. Metallurgy); Univ. of Cincinnati (Post-Grad. Studies in Business Admin). Dir and Gen. Works Man., Samuel Fox & Co Ltd, 1959-65; Dir and Gen. Man., Steel Peech Tozer, 1965-68; Dir, United Steel Cos, 1966-70; British Steel Corporation: Dir, Northern Tubes Gp, 1968-70; Man. Dir, Gen. Steel Div., 1970-73; Man. Dir, Planning and Capital Develt, 1973-76. *Recreations:* music, cricket lover, weekend golfer. *Address:* Honeysuckle Cottage, Firbeck, near Worksop, Notts S81 8JY. *T:* Rotherham 815710.

MORLEY, Robert, CBE 1957; Actor-Dramatist; *b* Semley, Wilts, 26 May 1908; *s* of Major Robert Morley and Gertrude Emily Fass; *m* 1940, Joan North Buckmaster, *d* of Dame Gladys Cooper, DBE; two *s* one *d. Educ:* Wellington Coll. Originally intended for diplomatic career; studied for stage at RADA. First appearance in Treasure Island, Strand Theatre, 1929; appeared in provinces; established repertory (with Peter Bull) at Perranporth, Cornwall; parts include: Oscar Wilde in play of that name, Gate, 1936, and Fulton (first New York appearance), 1938; Alexandre Dumas in The Great Romancer, Strand, 1937; Higgins in Pygmalion, Old Vic, 1937; Sheridan Whiteside in The Man Who Came to Dinner, Savoy, 1941; Prince Regent in The First Gentleman, New, 1945, and Savoy; Arnold Holt in Edward My Son, His Majesty's and Lyric, 1947, Martin Beck Theatre, New York, 1948; toured Australia, 1949-50; The Little Hut, Lyric, 1950; Hippo Dancing, Lyric, 1954; A Likely Tale, Globe, 1956; Fanny, Drury Lane, 1957; Hook, Line and Sinker, Piccadilly, 1958; A Majority of One, Phœnix, 1960; A Time to Laugh, Piccadilly, 1962; Halfway Up The Tree, Queen's, 1968; How the Other Half Loves, Lyric, 1970; A Ghost on Tiptoe, Savoy, 1974; Banana Ridge, Savoy, 1976. Directed: The Tunnel of Love, Her Majesty's Theatre, 1957; Once More, with Feeling, New Theatre, 1959. Entered films, 1937; *films:* Marie Antoinette; Major Barbara; Young Mr Pitt; Outcast of the Islands; The African Queen; Curtain Up; Mr Gilbert and Mr Sullivan; The Final Test; Beat the Devil; The Rainbow Jacket; Beau Brummell; The Good Die Young; Quentin Durward; Loser Takes All; Law and Disorder; The Journey; The Doctor's Dilemma; Libel; The Battle of the Sexes; Oscar Wilde; Go to Blazes; The Young Ones; The Boys; The Road to Hong Kong; Nine Hours to Rama; The Old Dark House; Murder at the Gallop; Take her, She's Mine; Hot Enough for June; Sold in Egypt; Topkapi; Of Human Bondage; Those Magnificent Men in Their Flying Machines; Ghengis Khan; ABC Murders; The Loved One; Life at the Top; A Study in Terror; Way Way Out; Finders Keepers; Hotel Paradiso; Le Tendre Voyou; Hot Millions; Sinful Davey; Song of Norway; Oliver Cromwell; When Eight Bells Toll; Doctor in Trouble; Theatre of Blood; Too Many Cooks; The Human Factor. Hon. DLitt

Reading, 1980. *Publications:* Short Story, 1935; Goodness How Sad, 1937; Staff Dance, 1944; (with Noel Langley) Edward My Son, 1948; (with Ronald Gow) The Full Treatment, 1953; Hippo Dancing, 1953; (with Dundas Hamilton) Six Months Grace, 1957; (with Sewell Stokes) Responsible Gentleman (autobiography), 1966; A Musing Morley, 1974; Morley Marvels, 1976; (ed) Robert Morley's Book of Bricks, 1978; (ed) Robert Morley's Book of Worries, 1979; Morley Matters, 1980; The Best of Morley, 1981; The Second Book of Bricks, 1981. *Recreations:* conversation, horse racing. *Address:* Fairmans, Wargrave, Berks.
See also S. R. Morley.

MORLEY, Sheridan Robert; Drama Critic and Arts Editor, Punch, since 1975; London Drama Critic, International Herald Tribune, since 1979; *b* Ascot, Berks, 5 Dec. 1941; *s* of Robert Morley, *qv* and Joan Buckmaster; *m* 1965, Margaret Gudejko; one *s* two *d. Educ:* Sizewell Hall, Suffolk; Merton Coll., Oxford (MA (Hons) 1964). Newscaster, reporter and scriptwriter, ITN, 1964-67; interviewer, Late Night Line Up, BBC2, 1967-71; Presenter, Film Night, BBC2, 1972; Dep. Features Editor, The Times, 1973-75. Regular presenter: Kaleidoscope, BBC Radio 4; Meridian, BBC World Service; frequent radio and TV broadcasts on the performing arts. Mem., Drama Cttee, British Council, 1982-. *Publications:* A Talent to Amuse: the life of Noel Coward, 1969; Review Copies, 1975; Oscar Wilde, 1976; Sybil Thorndike, 1977; Marlene Dietrich, 1977; Gladys Cooper, 1979; (with Cole Lesley and Graham Payn) Noel Coward and his Friends, 1979; The Stephen Sondheim Songbook, 1979; Gertrude Lawrence, 1981; (ed, with Graham Payn) The Noel Coward Diaries, 1982; ed, series of theatre annuals and film and theatre studies, inc. Punch at the Theatre, 1980; contribs to The Times, Evening Standard, Radio Times, Playbill (NY), High Life and The Australian. *Recreations:* talking, swimming, eating, narrating Side by Side by Sondheim. *Address:* c/o Punch, 23 Tudor Street, EC4. *T:* 01-583 9199.

MORLEY, Very Rev. William Fenton, CBE 1980; Dean Emeritus of Salisbury, since 1977; *b* 5 May 1912; *s* of Arthur Fenton and Margaret Morley; *m* 1937, Marjorie Rosa, *d* of Joseph Temple Robinson, Frinton; one *s* one *d. Educ:* St David's, Lampeter; Oriel Coll., Oxford; Wycliffe Hall, Oxford; University of London. Ordained, 1935; Curate of: Ely, Cardiff, 1935-38; Porthcawl, S Wales, 1938-43; Officiating Chaplain to the Forces, 1941-43; Vicar of Penrhiwceiber, 1943-46; Rector of Haseley, Oxon, 1946-50; Director of Music and Lecturer in Hebrew at Cuddesdon Coll., Oxon, 1946-50; Examiner in Hebrew and New Testament Greek, 1947-59 and External Lecturer in Biblical and Religious Studies, 1950-61, Univ. of London; Chaplain and Lecturer of St Gabriel's Training Coll., 1956-61; Education Sec. to Overseas Council of Church Assembly, 1950-56; Warburton Lectr, Lincoln's Inn, 1963-65; Chairman: Church of England Deployment and Payment Commission, 1965-68; Church of England Pensions Bd, 1974-80; Bath and Wells Diocesan Education Council, 1978-82. Public Preacher to Diocese of Rochester, 1950-56; Canon Residentiary and Precentor of Southwark Cathedral, 1956-61; Vicar of Leeds, Rural Dean of Leeds and Hon. Canon of Ripon, 1961-71; Dean of Salisbury, 1971-77. Editor, East and West Review, 1953-64. Chaplain to HM's Household, 1965-71; Church Comr, 1968-77. *Publications:* One Church, One Faith, One Lord, 1953; The Church to Which You Belong, 1955; The Call of God, 1959; Preaching through the Christian Year: Year 4, 1974, Year 6, 1977. *Recreations:* music, writing. *Address:* 5 Cavendish Place, Bath, Avon BA1 2UB. *Club:* Royal Commonwealth Society.

MORLEY-JOHN, Michael, CBE 1979; RD 1970; Judge of the Supreme Court of Hong Kong, 1973-78; *b* 22 May 1923; *s* of late Clifford Morley-John and Norah (*née* Thompson); *m* 1951, Sheila Christine Majendie; one *s* one *d. Educ:* Wycliffe Coll.; Univ. of Bristol (LLB). Called to the Bar, Gray's Inn, 1950. Hong Kong: Crown Counsel, 1951; Dir of Public Prosecutions, 1961; Acting Solicitor Gen., 1966-67; Dist Judge, 1967; Judicial Comr, State of Brunei, 1974. Acting Comdr, RNR, 1973. *Recreations:* tennis, stamp collecting, sailing. *Address:* The Coach House, Woodland Way, Milford-on-Sea, Hants SO4 0NB. *T:* Milford-on-Sea 4824. *Clubs:* Milford and South Hants; Royal Ocean Racing; Bar Yacht; Hong Kong, Hong Kong Kennel (former Pres.) (Hong Kong).

MORLING, Col Leonard Francis, DSO 1940; OBE 1946; TD 1942; Architect; *b* 2 Nov. 1904, British; 2nd *s* of late Ernest Charles Morling and Frances Ruth Baldwin; unmarried. *Educ:* Brighton Hove and Sussex Grammar Sch. Architect, 1927-36; Mem. of firm, C. Morling Ltd, Builders and Contractors, Seaford, 1936-39; social work, in London, 1948-50, Malaya, 1950-55; Personnel and Welfare Work, London, 1956-59, Australia, 1960-63, London, 1964. Comnd, Terrtl Army, 1924; Capt. 1930; Major, 1934; Lt-Col, 1943; Col 1946; served France and Flanders (despatches, DSO); Persia, Iraq and India. *Publication:* Sussex Sappers, 1972. *Address:* c/o Lloyds Bank Ltd, Seaford, East Sussex.

MORLING, Norton Arthur; Member, Civil Aviation Authority, 1972-75; *b* 13 Feb. 1909; *o s* of Norton and Edith Morling, Hunsdon, Herts; *m* 1942, Rachel Paterson, *d* of James and Elizabeth Chapman, Johannesburg, SA; one *s* one *d. Educ:* Hertford Grammar Sch.; Cambridge Univ. (MA); Birmingham Univ. (MCom). Joined Turner & Newall Ltd as Management Trainee, 1931. War Service, N Africa and Italy, 1942-45 (despatches); Lt-Col 1944; ADS&T, AFHQ, 1944-45. Dir, and in some cases Chm., of various subsid. and associated companies, UK and overseas, 1946-64, including Turner Brothers Asbestos Co. Ltd and Ferodo Ltd; Gp Dir, 1957-67; Financial Dir, 1964-67; seconded as

Industrial Advr to Nat. Economic Develt Office, 1967-70; Mem., Air Transport Licensing Bd, 1971-72. *Recreation:* gardening. *Address:* Little Brook House, Over Wallop, Stockbridge, Hants SO20 8HT. *T:* Andover 781296.

MORNINGTON, Earl of; Arthur Gerald Wellesley; *b* 31 Jan. 1978; *s* and *heir* of Marquess of Douro, *qv.*

MORO, Peter, CBE 1977; FRIBA, FSIAD; Architect in private practice, since 1952 (partners, M. Mellis, RIBA, M. Heard, RIBA, A. Blonski, RIBA, M. Merritt, RIBA, C. Peel, RIBA); *b* 27 May 1911; *s* of Prof. Ernst Moro and Grete Hönigswald; *m* 1940, Anne Vanneck; three *d. Educ:* Stuttgart, Berlin and Zurich. Swiss Dip. Architecture, 1936; FRIBA 1948; FSIA 1957. Practice with Tecton, 1937-39; Mem. Exec. Cttee, Mars Gp, 1938; Lectr, Sch. of Arch., Regent Street Polytechnic, 1941-47; LCC Associated Architect, Royal Festival Hall, 1948-51. Architect: Fairlawn Sch., LCC, 1957; Nottingham Playhouse, 1964; alterations, Royal Opera House, Covent Garden, 1964; Birstall Sch., Leics, 1964; housing schemes, GLC and Southwark, 1967-80; theatre, Hull Univ., the Gulbenkian Centre, 1970; additions and alterations, Bristol Old Vic, 1972; theatre, New Univ. of Ulster, 1976; Plymouth Theatre Royal, 1982. Sen. Pres., Assoc. of British Theatre Technicians (Founder Mem.); Member: Council, RIBA, 1967-73; Housing the Arts Cttee, Arts Council of GB, 1975-78. Lectures in UK, Finland and Norway. Bronze Medal, RIBA, 1964; 4 Civic Trust Awards and Commendations. *Publications:* contribs to technical jls in UK, Germany, France, Italy, Portugal and Japan. *Address:* 20 Blackheath Park, SE3 9RP. *T:* 01-852 0250.

MORONY, Lt.-Gen. Sir Thomas (Lovett), KCB 1981; OBE 1969; Vice Chief of the General Staff, since 1980; *b* 23 Sept. 1926; *s* of Thomas Henry Morony, CSI, CIE, and Evelyn Myra (*née* Lovett); *m* 1961, Elizabeth, *d* of G. W. N. Clark; two *s. Educ:* Eton. Commissioned, 1947. BM, King's African Rifles, 1958-61; GSO1 (DS) at Camberley and RMCS, 1963-65; GSO1, HQ Northern Army Gp, 1966-67; commanded 22 Light Air Defence Regt, RA, 1968-69; Comdr, 1st Artillery Bde, 1970-72; Dep. Comdt, Staff Coll., Camberley, 1973-75; Director RA, 1975-78; Comdt, RMCS, 1978-80. Col Comdt, RA, 1978-. Mem. Bd of Governors, Sherborne Sch. *Recreations:* country pursuits, big game photography, music. *Address:* c/o Bank of Scotland, 8 Morningside Road, Edinburgh EH10 4DD. *Club:* Army and Navy.

MORPETH, Viscount; George William Beaumont Howard; Master of Ruthven; *b* 15 Feb. 1949; *s* and *heir* of 12th Earl of Carlisle, *qv. Educ:* Eton Coll.; Balliol Coll., Oxford. 9th/12th Royal Lancers, 1967-; Lieut 1970, Captain 1974, Major 1981. *Recreations:* reading, travel. *Address:* The Gate House, Naworth Castle, Brampton, Cumbria; 34 Epirus Road, SW6. *Clubs:* Beefsteak, Brooks's.

MORPETH, Sir Douglas (Spottiswoode), Kt 1981; TD 1959; FCA; Partner, Touche Ross & Co., Chartered Accountants, 1958; Senior Partner, Touche Ross, 1977; *b* 6 June 1924; *s* of Robert Spottiswoode Morpeth and Louise Rankine Morpeth (*née* Dobson); *m* 1951, Anne Rutherford, yr *d* of Ian C. Bell, OBE, MC, Edinburgh; two *s* two *d. Educ:* George Watson's Coll., Edinburgh; Edinburgh Univ. (BCom). Commissioned RA; served 1943-47, India, Burma, Malaya. Qualified as Mem. of Inst. of Chartered Accountants in England and Wales, 1952, Fellow, 1957 (Council of Inst., 1964, Vice-Pres., 1970, Dep. Pres., 1971, Pres., 1972). Dir, Clerical Medical and General Life Assurance Soc., 1973, Dep. Chm., 1974, Chm., 1978; Dir, Brixton Estate Ltd, 1977. Mem., Investment Grants Advisory Cttee, 1968-71; Chm., Inflation Accounting Steering Gp, 1976-80; Vice-Chm., Accounting Standards Cttee, 1970-82. Chm., Taxation Cttee, CBI, 1973-76. Honourable Artillery Company: Member, 1949-; commanded 'B' Battery, 1958-61; Lt-Col, comdg 1st Regt RHA, 1964-66; Master Gunner within the Tower of London, 1966-69. Master, Co. of Chartered Accountants in England and Wales, 1977-78. *Recreations:* golf, tennis, gardening. *Address:* Summerden House, Shamley Green, near Guildford, Surrey. *T:* Guildford 892689. *Clubs:* Athenæum, City Livery, Royal Automobile.

MORPHET, David Ian; Under-Secretary, Electricity Division, Department of Energy, since 1979; *b* 24 Jan. 1940; *s* of late A. Morphet and of Sarah Elizabeth Morphet; *m* 1968, Sarah Gillian Sedgwick; two *s* one *d. Educ:* King James's Grammar Sch., Almondbury, Yorks; St John's Coll., Cambridge. Foreign Office, 1961; Vice Consul, Taiz, 1963; Doha, 1963-64; Arabian Dept, FO, 1964-66; Asst Private Sec. to Foreign Secretary, 1966-68; First Sec., Madrid, 1969-72; Diplomatic Service Observer, CS Selection Board, 1972-74; transf. to Dept of Energy, 1974; Asst Sec., 1975; Dep. Chm., Midlands Electricity Board (on secondment), 1978-79. Dir, BICC Cables Ltd, 1981-. *Recreations:* music, theatre, reading, walking. *Address:* 11 Daisy Lane, Parsons Green, SW6 3DD. *T:* 01-736 2659.

MORPURGO, Jack Eric; Professor of American Literature, University of Leeds, since 1969; author; *b* 26 April 1918; *s* of late Mark Morpurgo, Islington; *m* 1946, Catherine Noel Kippe, *d* of late Prof. Emile Cammaerts; three *s* one *d. Educ:* Christ's Hosp.; Univ. of New Brunswick; Coll. of William and Mary, USA (BA); Durham Univ. Enlisted RA, 1939; served as regimental and staff officer in India, Middle East, Greece and Italy; GSO 2, Public Relations Directorate, War Office. Editorial Staff, Penguin Books, 1946-49; Editor Penguin Parade; General Editor, Pelican Histories, 1949-61; Asst Dir, Nuffield Foundation, 1950-54; Dir-Gen., Nat. Book League, 1955-69, Dep. Chm.,

1969-71, Vice-Pres., 1971-; Prof. of American Studies, Univ. of Geneva, 1968-70; Visiting Professor: Michigan State Univ., 1950; George Washington Univ., 1970; Vanderbilt Univ., 1981; Schol.-in-residence, Rockefeller Res. Centre, Italy, 1974; Vis. Fellow, ANU, 1975, 1977; has lectured in USA, Canada, Germany, India, Burma, etc. Dir of Unesco Seminar on Production of Reading Materials, Rangoon, 1957, Madras, 1959. Donation Governor and Almoner, Christ's Hospital; Chm. Working Pty on Medical Libraries; Dir, William and Mary Historical Project, 1970-76. Phi Beta Kappa, 1948; Hon. Fellow, Coll. of William and Mary, 1949. Hon. LitD Maine, 1961; Hon. DLitt Elmira, 1966; Hon. DHL William and Mary, 1970. *Publications:* American Excursion, 1949; Charles Lamb and Elia, 1949; The Road to Athens, 1963; Barnes Wallis, 1972; Treason at West Point, 1975; Their Majesties Royall Colledge, 1976; Allen Lane: King Penguin, 1979; Verses Humorous and Post-Humorous, 1981; contributor to: The Impact of America, 1951; joint author of: History of The United States (with Russel B. Nye), 1955; Venice (with Martin Hürlimann), 1964; edited: Leigh Hunt: Autobiography, 1949; E. J. Trelawny: Last Days of Shelley and Byron, 1952; Poems of John Keats, 1953; Rugby Football: An Anthology (with Kenneth Pelmear), 1958; Cobbett: a year's residence in USA, 1964; Cooper: The Spy, 1968. *Recreation:* watching Rugby football. *Address:* Cliff Cottage, 51 Cliff Road, Leeds LS6 2EZ; 12 Laurence Mews, W12 9AT. *Clubs:* Army and Navy, Pilgrims.

MORRAH, Ruth, (Mrs Dermot Morrah), JP; Chairman, Metropolitan Juvenile Courts, 1945-64; *b* 21 Aug. 1899; *d* of Willmott Houselander; *m* 1923, Dermot Michael Macgregor Morrah (*d* 1974); two *d. Educ:* convent schs; St Anne's Coll., Oxford. JP 1944. Pro Ecclesia et Pontifice, 1964. *Recreations:* travelling, needlework. *Address:* 3 Kennington Palace Court, Sancroft Street, SE11. *T:* 01-582 1894.

See also T. E. Utley.

MORRELL, Frances Maine; Member for Islington South and Finsbury, Greater London Council, since 1981; Deputy Leader, Inner London Education Authority, since 1981; *b* 28 Dec. 1937; *d* of Frank and Beatrice Galleway; *m* 1964, Brian Morrell; one *d. Educ:* Queen Anne Grammar Sch., York; Hull Univ. BA (Hons) English Lang. and Lit. Secondary Sch. Teacher, 1960-69; Press Officer, Fabian Soc. and NUS, 1970-72; Research into MPs' constituency role, 1973; Special Adviser to Tony Benn, as Sec. of State for Industry, then as Sec. of State for Energy, 1974-79. Chm., Islington S and Finsbury Constituency Lab Party, 1976-79. Member: Oakes Cttee, Enquiry into Payment and Collection Methods for Gas and Electricity Bills (report publ. 1976); Exec., Campaign for Labour Party Democracy, 1979-; Women's Action Cttee, 1980-. Press Advr, Nat. Children's Bureau. Contested (Lab) Chelmsford, Feb. 1974. *Publications:* (with Tony Benn and Francis Cripps) A Ten Year Industrial Strategy for Britain, 1975; (with Francis Cripps) The Case for a Planned Energy Policy, 1976; From the Electors of Bristol: the record of a year's correspondence between constituents and their Member of Parliament, 1977; (jtly) Manifesto—a radical strategy for Britain's future, 1981. *Recreations:* reading, cooking, gardening. *Address:* c/o County Hall, SE1 7PB. *T:* 01-633 5000.

MORRELL, Col (Herbert) William (James), OBE 1954; MC 1944; TD; MA Oxon; DL; JP; *b* 1 Aug. 1915; *er s* of James Herbert Morrell, MA, Headington Hill, Oxford; *m* 1947, Pamela Vivien Eleanor, *d* of Richard Stubbs, Willaston, Cheshire; one *s* two *d. Educ:* Eton; Magdalen Coll., Oxford. 2nd Lt RA, 1936; served War of 1939-45 (France, Madagascar, Burma); retired 1948. DL 1961, JP 1959, High Sheriff 1960, Oxon. *Recreations:* hunting, sailing. *Address:* Caphill, Sandford St Martin, Oxon. *T:* Great Tew 291.

MORRELL, James George; Founder Director, Henley Centre for Forecasting, since 1974; author and business forecaster; *b* 1923; *s* of Frederick Morrell and late Violet (*née* Smart); *m* 1st, 1944, Elizabeth Bristow (marr. diss. 1970); one *s* two *d* ; 2nd, 1972, Margaret Helen Nickolls. *Educ:* Christ's Hospital; Ruskin and Wadham Colls, Oxford. MA Oxon 1953. Served RAF, 1941-46. Ford Motor Co., 1955; Phillips & Drew, 1957; Charterhouse Group, 1964; founded James Morrell & Associates, 1967. Visiting Professor, Univ. of Bradford, 1970-73; Associate Fellow, Oxford Centre for Management Studies, 1981-. *Publications:* Business Forecasting for Finance and Industry, 1969; Business Decisions and the Role of Forecasting, 1972; Inflation and Business Management, 1974; 2002: Britain plus 25, 1977; The Regeneration of British Industry, 1979; Britain through the 1980s, 1980; The Future of the Dollar and the World Reserve System, 1981. *Recreations:* canals, Samuel Pepys, stock market. *Address:* 81 Speed House, Barbican, EC2Y 8AU.

MORRELL, Rt. Rev. James Herbert Lloyd; Canon and Prebend of Heathfield in Chichester Cathedral since 1959; Provost of Lancing (Southern Division Woodard Schools), 1961-82; an Assistant Bishop, Diocese of Chichester, since 1978; *b* 12 Aug. 1907; *s* of George Henry and Helen Adela Morrell. *Educ:* Dulwich Coll.; King's Coll., London; Ely Theological Coll. Deacon, 1931; Priest, 1932; Curate of St Alphage, Hendon, 1931-35; Curate of St Michael and All Angels, Brighton, 1935-39; Bishop of Chichester's Chaplain for men, 1939-41; Lecturer for The Church of England Moral Welfare Council, 1941-44; Vicar of Roffey, 1944-46; Archdeacon of Lewes, 1946-59; Bishop Suffragan of Lewes, 1959-77. Fellow of King's Coll., London, 1960. *Publications:* Four Words (broadcast talks to the Forces), 1941; The Heart of a Priest, 1958; A Priest's Notebook of Prayer, 1961; The Catholic Faith Today, 1964. *Recreations:* walking, photography. *Address:* 83 Davigdor

Road, Hove BN3 1RA. *T:* Brighton 733971. *Club:* English-Speaking Union.

MORRELL, Leslie James; JP; Hon. Secretary, James Butcher Housing Association (Northern Ireland) Ltd, since 1980 (Chairman, 1976–80); *b* 26 Dec. 1931; *s* of James Morrell; *m* 1958, Anne Wallace, BSc; two *s* one *d. Educ:* Portora Royal Sch., Enniskillen; Queen's Univ., Belfast. BAgric 1955. Mem. (U) for Londonderry, NI Assembly, 1973–75; Head of Dept of Agriculture, NI Exec., 1974; Dep. Leader, Unionist Party of NI, 1974–80. Chm., NI Fedn of Housing Assocs, 1978–. Mem., BBC Gen. Adv. Cttee, 1980–, Coleraine RDC, 1961; Londonderry CC, 1969; JP Londonderry, 1970; Coleraine District Council, 1973–77. *Address:* Dunboe House, Castlerock, Coleraine, N Ireland. *T:* Castlerock 352.

MORRELL, Col William; *see* Morrell, Col H. W. J.

MORRICE, Norman; choreographer; Director of the Royal Ballet, since 1977; *b* Mexico, of British parents. *Educ:* Rambert School of Ballet. Joined the Ballet Rambert in early 1950s as a dancer; notably danced Dr Coppélius, in Coppélia, and subseq. also choreographer; first considerable success with his ballet, Two Brothers, in America, and at first London perf., Sept. 1958; première of his 2nd ballet, Hazaña, Sadler's Wells Theatre, 1958; the New Ballet Rambert Company was formed in 1966 and he was Co-Director with Marie Rambert, to create new works by unknown and established choreographers; his ballet, Hazard, was danced at Bath Festival, 1967; he composed 10 new ballets by 1968 and had taken his place with leading choreographers; *ballets include:* 1–2–3, Them and Us and Pastorale Variée, which were staged at the Jeanetta Cochrane Theatre, 1968–69; Ladies, Ladies!, perf. by Ballet Rambert at Young Vic, 1972; Spindrift, at Round House, 1974, etc. Has danced frequently overseas. *Address:* The Royal Ballet, Royal Opera House, Covent Garden, WC2.

MORRIS; *see* Temple-Morris.

MORRIS, family name of **Barons Killanin, Morris, Morris of Grasmere** and **Morris of Kenwood.**

MORRIS, 3rd Baron *cr* 1918 **Michael David Morris;** *b* 9 Dec. 1937; *s* of 2nd Baron Morris and of Jean Beatrice (now Lady Salmon), *d* of late Lt-Col D. Maitland-Makgill-Crichton; *S* father, 1975; *m* 1st, 1959, Denise Eleanor (marr. diss. 1962), *o d* of Morley Richards; 2nd, 1962, Jennifer (marr. diss. 1969), *o d* of Squadron Leader Tristram Gilbert; two *d*; *m* 1980, Juliet, twin *d* of Anthony Buckingham; one *s* one *d. Educ:* Downside. FCA. *Heir: s* Hon. Thomas Anthony Salmon Morris, *b* 2 July 1982.

MORRIS OF GRASMERE, Baron *cr* 1967 (Life Peer), of Grasmere; **Charles Richard Morris,** KCMG 1963; Kt 1953; MA Oxon; Hon. LLD: Manchester, 1951; Aberdeen, 1963; Leeds, 1964; Malta, 1964; Hull, 1965; Hon. DLitt: Sydney, 1954; Lancaster, 1967; Hon. DTech Bradford, 1970; *b* 25 Jan. 1898; *s* of M. C. Morris, Sutton Valence, Kent; *m* 1923, Mary de Selincourt; one *s* one *d. Educ:* Tonbridge Sch.; Trinity Coll., Oxford. Lt RGA 1916–19; Fellow and Tutor of Balliol Coll., 1921–43; for one year, 1926–27 (while on leave of absence from Balliol), Prof. of Philosophy, Univ. of Michigan, USA; Senior Proctor, 1937–38; Mem. of Council of Girls Public Day Sch. Trust, 1933–38; Oxford City Councillor, 1939–41; Ministry of Supply, 1939–42; Under-Sec., Min. of Production, 1942–43; Head Master, King Edward's Sch., Birmingham, 1941–48; Chm., Cttee of Vice-Chancellors and Principals, 1952–55; Central Joint Adv. Cttee on Tutorial Classes, 1948–58; Commonwealth Univ. Interchange Cttee and Recruitment Sub-Cttee of British Council, 1951; Sch. Broadcasting Council, 1954–64; Inter-Univ. Council for Higher Education Overseas, 1957–64; Independent Chm., Jt Adv. Cttee for Wool Textile Industry, 1952; Pres., Council of Coll. of Preceptors, 1954–63. Vice-Chancellor of Leeds Univ., 1948–63; Pro-Chancellor, Univ. of Bradford, 1966–69. Member: Royal Commn on Local Govt in Greater London, 1957; Cttee of Inquiry on Australian Univs, 1957; Chairman: Adv. Bd Of Univs Quarterly, 1960; Local Govt Training Bd, 1967–75; President: Brit. Student Tuberculosis Foundn, 1960; Assoc. of Teachers in Colls and Depts of Educn, 1961–64. *Publications:* A History of Political Ideas (with Mary Morris), 1924; Locke, Berkeley, Hume, 1931; Idealistic Logic, 1933; In Defence of Democracy (with J. S. Fulton), 1936; British Democracy, 1939; various essays and papers to learned societies. *Recreation:* fell walking. *Address:* Ladywood, White Moss, Ambleside, Cumbria LA22 9SF. *T:* 286. *Club:* Athenæum.

MORRIS OF KENWOOD, 2nd Baron *cr* 1950, of Kenwood; **Philip Geoffrey Morris,** JP; Company Director; *b* 18 June 1928; *s* of 1st Baron Morris of Kenwood, and Florence (*d* 1982), *d* of Henry Isaacs, Leeds; *S* father, 1954; *m* 1958, Ruth, *o d* of late Baron Janner and of Lady Janner, *qv*; one *s* three *d. Educ:* Loughborough Coll., Leics. Served RAF, Nov. 1946–Feb. 1949; July 1951–Oct. 1955. JP Inner London, 1967. *Recreations:* tennis, golf, ski-ing. *Heir: s* Hon. Jonathan David Morris, *b* 5 Aug. 1968. *Address:* Lawn Cottage, Orchard Rise, Kingston, Surrey. *T:* 01–942 6321.

MORRIS, Air Marshal Sir Alec; *see* Morris, Air Marshal Sir Arnold A.

MORRIS, Rt. Hon. Alfred; PC 1979; MP (Lab and Co-op) Manchester (Wythenshawe) since 1964; Opposition Front Bench Spokesman on Social Services (the Disabled), 1970–74 and since 1979; *b* 23 March 1928; *s* of late

George Henry Morris and Jessie Morris (*née* Murphy); *m* 1950, Irene (*née* Jones); two *s* two *d. Educ:* elem. and evening schs, Manchester; Ruskin Coll., Oxford; St Catherine's, Univ. of Oxford (MA); Univ. of Manchester (Postgrad. certif. in Educn). Employed in office of a Manchester brewing firm from age 14 (HM Forces, 1946–48); Schoolmaster and Adult Educn Lectr, Manchester, 1954–56; Asst Sec., NW & Merseyside and N Wales Dist Jt Adv. Councils for Electricity Supply Industry, 1956–59; Asst Sec., Nat. Jt Adv. Coun. for El. Supply Ind., 1959–61; Asst Labour Relations Officer, The Electricity Coun., London, 1961–64. Nat. Chm., Labour League of Youth, 1950–52; contested Liverpool (Garston), Gen. Elec. 1951; Mem., Bureau and Chm. Control Commn, Internat. Union of Socialist Youth, 1951–54; Observer, Coun. Socialist Internat. and Coun. of Europe, 1952–53; PPS to Minister of Agric., Fisheries and Food, 1964–67, and to Lord President of the Council and Leader of House of Commons, 1968–70; Parly Under-Sec. of State, DHSS, responsible for disabled people, 1974–79. Mem. Exec. Cttee British Group, Inter-Parly Union, 1966–74, Treasurer, 1971–74; Mem., UK Parly Delegn to UN Gen. Assembly, 1966; Vice-Chm., Food and Agriculture Gp of Parly Lab. Party, 1970–71, Chm., 1971–74; Representative of Privy Council on Council of RCVS, 1969–74; promoted Chronically Sick and Disabled Persons Act, 1970, Food and Drugs (Milk) Act, 1970, Police Act, 1972, as a Private Member; Vice-Chm., Co-operative Parly Group, 1970–71, Chm., 1971–72; Vice-Chm., All-Party Parly Retail Trade Gp, 1972–74. Mem., Gen. Adv. Council, BBC, 1968–74; Patron of Disablement Income Group, 1970–74; Parly Adviser to the Police Federation, 1971–74; Mem., Exec. Cttee, Central Council for the Disabled and Nat. Fund for Research into Crippling Diseases, 1970–74. Chm., World Cttee apptd to draft "Charter for the 1980's" for disabled people worldwide, 1980–81. Field Marshal Lord Harding Award, 1971, for services to the disabled; Grimshaw Meml Award of Nat. Fedn of the Blind, 1971. *Publications:* Value Added Tax: a tax on the consumer, 1970; The Growth of Parliamentary Scrutiny by Committee, 1970; (with A. Butler) No Feet to Drag, 1972; Ed. lectures (Human Relations in Industry), 1958; Ed. Jl (Jt Consultation) publ. Nat. Jt Adv. Coun. Elec. Supply Ind., 1959–61. *Recreations:* gardening, tennis, snooker, chess. *Address:* House of Commons, SW1A 0AA.

MORRIS, Air Marshal Sir (Arnold) Alec, KBE 1982; CB 1979; Chief Engineer, RAF, since 1981; *b* 11 March 1926; *s* of late Harry Morris; *m* 1946, Moyna Patricia, *d* of late Norman Boyle; one *s* one *d* (twins). *Educ:* King Edward VI Sch., East Retford; King's Coll., Univ. of London; Univ. of Southampton. Commnd RAF, 1945; radar duties, No 90 (Signals) Gp, 1945–50; Guided Weapons Dept, RAE, 1953–56; exchange duty, HQ USAF, 1958–60; space res., Min. of Supply, 1960–63; DS, RAF Staff Coll., 1963–65; OC Eng, No 2 Flying Trng Sch., Syerston, 1966–68; Asst Dir, Guided Weapons R&D, Min. of Tech., 1968–70; OC RAF Central Servicing Develt Estabt, Swanton Morley, 1970–72; SASO, HQ No 90 (Signals) Gp, 1972–74; RCDS, 1974; Dir of Signals (Air), MoD, 1975–76; Dir Gen. Strategic Electronic Systems, MoD (PE), 1976–79; Air Officer Engineering, RAF Strike Command, 1979–81. *Recreations:* tennis, squash, gardening. *Address:* 6 Liverpool Road, Kingston-upon-Thames, Surrey KT2 7SZ. *T:* 01–549 3437. *Club:* Royal Air Force.

MORRIS, Prof. Benjamin Stephen; Professor of Education, University of Bristol, 1956–75, now Emeritus; *b* 25 May 1910; *s* of Rev. B. S. Morris, Sherborne, Dorset, and Annie McNicol Duncan, Rothesay, Bute; *m* 1938, Margaret, *d* of Mr and Mrs Lamont, Glasgow; two *s* one *d. Educ:* Rothesay Academy; Glasgow Univ. BSc 1933, MEd 1937 (Glasgow). Trained as teacher, Jordanhill Training Coll., Glasgow; teacher, primary and secondary schs, 1936–39; Lecturer: in Psychology, Logic and Ethics, Jordanhill Trng Coll., 1939–40; in Educn, Univ. of Glasgow, 1940–46. Temp. Civil Servant, Min. of Food, 1941; Army Psychologist, 1942–46; Sen. Psychologist (WOSB), 1945–46; Hon. Lt-Col 1946. Student at Inst. of Psychoanalysis, London, 1946–50; Senior staff, Tavistock Institute of Human Relations, 1946–50 (Chm. Management Cttee, 1947–49); Dir Nat. Foundation for Educl Research in England and Wales, 1950–56. Vis. Prof. of Education, Harvard Univ., 1969–70. *Publications:* Objectives and Perspectives in Education, 1972; Some Aspects of Professional Freedom of Teachers, 1977; contributed to: The Function of Teaching, 1959; How and Why Do We Learn?, 1965; Study of Education, 1966; Higher Education, Demand and Response, 1969; Towards a Policy for the Education of Teachers, 1969; Towards Community Mental Health, 1971; The Sciences, The Humanities and the Technological Threat, 1975; articles in educational and psychological jls. *Recreation:* living in the country. *Address:* 7 Howcroft, Churchdown, Gloucester GL3 2EP.

MORRIS, Prof. Brian Robert, MA, DPhil; Principal, St David's University College, Lampeter, since 1980; *b* 4 Dec. 1930; *o s* of William Robert Morris and Ellen Elizabeth Morris (*née* Shelley); *m* 1955, Sandra Mary James, JP; one *s* one *d. Educ:* Cardiff High School; Worcester Coll., Oxford (MA, DPhil). National service with Welch Regt, 1949–51. Fellow of Shakespeare Inst., Univ. of Birmingham, 1956–58; Asst Lectr 1958–60, Lectr 1960–65, Univ. of Reading; Lectr 1965–67, Sen. Lectr 1967–71, Univ. of York; Prof. of English Literature, Univ. of Sheffield, 1971–80. Gen. Editor: New Mermaid Dramatists, 1964–; New Arden Shakespeare, 1974–82. Member: Council, Yorkshire Arts Assoc., 1973–81 (Chm. Literature Panel, 1973–77); Museums and Galleries Commn (formerly Standing Commn on Museums and Galleries), 1975–; Welsh Arts Council Lit. Cttee, 1978–; Archbishops' Council on Evangelism, 1971–75; Yr Academi Gymreig, 1979–; British Library Bd, 1980–; Council, Poetry Soc., 1980–; Council, Nat. Library of Wales, 1981–. Trustee: Nat. Portrait Gall., 1977–; Nat. Heritage Meml Fund, 1980–.

Broadcaster, scriptwriter and presenter of television programmes. *Publications:* John Cleveland: a Bibliography of his Poems, 1967; (with Eleanor Withington) The Poems of John Cleveland, 1967; (ed) New Mermaid Critical Commentaries I-III, 1969-72; Mary Quant's London, 1973; (ed) Ritual Murder, 1980; *edited plays:* Ford's The Broken Heart, 1965, and 'Tis Pity She's a Whore, 1968; (with Roma Gill) Tourneur's The Atheist's Tragedy, 1976; Shakespeare's The Taming of the Shrew, 1981; *poetry:* Tide Race, 1976; Stones in the Brook, 1978; contribs to journals. *Recreations:* music, mountains, and museums. *Address:* Bryn, North Road, Lampeter, Dyfed SA48 7HZ. *T:* Lampeter 422335. *Club:* Athenæum.

MORRIS, Charles Alfred, RWS 1949 (ARWS 1943); RBA 1948; retired as Vice-Principal Brighton College of Art (1952-59); Vice-President, RWS, 1957-60; *b* 5 Sept. 1898; *s* of G. W. Morris and Susan (*née* Lee); *m* 1927, Alice Muriel Drummond, *d* of Rev. Dr W. H. Drummond; one *s* two *d. Educ:* Royal Academy Schs and Brighton Coll. of Art. Served with HAC, 1916-19. Teacher of advanced drawing and painting, Liverpool Coll. of Art, 1926; Senior Asst, County Sch. of Art, Worthing, 1931, Principal, 1942. Examples of work in following public collections: Birkenhead, Blackburn, Brighton, Eastbourne, Hove, Worthing. *Recreation:* gardening. *Address:* Hillside Cottage, Burpham, Arundel, West Sussex. *T:* Arundel 883019.

MORRIS, Rt. Hon. Charles Richard; PC 1978; MP (Lab) Openshaw Division of Manchester since Dec. 1963; *b* 14 Dec. 1926; *s* of George Henry Morris, Newton Heath, Manchester; *m* 1950, Pauline, *d* of Albert Dunn, Manchester; two *d. Educ:* Brookdale Park Sch., Manchester. Served with Royal Engineers, 1945-48. Pres., Clayton Labour Party, 1950-52. Mem. of Manchester Corporation, 1954-64: Chm. of Transport Cttee, 1959-62; Dep. Chm. of Establishment Cttee, 1963-64. Mem., Post Office Workers Union (Mem. Nat. Exec. Council, 1959-63). Contested (Lab) Cheadle Div. of Cheshire, 1959. PPS to the Postmaster-General, 1964; Govt Asst Whip, 1966-67; Vice-Chamberlain, HM Household, 1967-69; Treasurer, HM Household (Deputy Chief Whip), 1969-70; PPS to Rt Hon. H. Wilson, MP, 1970-74; Minister of State: DoE, March-Oct. 1974; CSD, 1974-79; Dep. Shadow Leader of the House, 1980. Sec., NW Gp of Labour MPs, 1979-. *Address:* 24 Buxton Road West, Disley, Stockport, Cheshire. *T:* Disley 2450.

MORRIS, Rev. Dr Colin; Head of Religious Broadcasting, BBC, since 1979 (Deputy Head, 1978-79), and Head of Religious Programmes, BBC Television, since 1978; *b* 13 Jan. 1929; *o s* of Daniel Manley Morris and Mary Alice Morris, Bolton, Lancs. *Educ:* Bolton County Grammar Sch.; Univs of Oxford and Manchester. Served RM, 1947-49. Student, Nuffield Coll., Oxford, 1953-56; Missionary, Northern Rhodesia, 1956-60; President: United Church of Central Africa, 1960-64; United Church of Zambia, 1965-68; Minister of Wesley's Chapel, London, 1969-73; Gen. Sec., Overseas Div., Methodist Church, 1973-78; Pres. of the Methodist Conference, 1976-77. Chm., Community and Race Relations Unit, BCC, 1974-76. Lectures: Willson, Univ. of Nebraska, 1968; Cousland, Univ. of Toronto, 1972; Voigt, S Illinois Conf. United Methodist Church, 1973; Hickman, Duke University, North Carolina, 1974; Palmer, Pacific NW Univ.; Select Preacher, Univ. of Cambridge, 1975, Oxford, 1976; holds several hon. degrees. Officer-Companion, Order of Freedom (Zambia), 1966. *Publications:* Black Government (with President K. D. Kaunda), 1960; Hour After Midnight, 1961; Out of Africa's Crucible, 1961; End of the Missionary, 1961; Church and Challenge in a New Africa, 1965; Humanist in Africa (with President K. D. Kaunda), 1966; Include Me Out, 1968; Unyoung, Uncoloured, Unpoor, 1969; What the Papers Didn't Say, 1971; Mankind My Church, 1971; The Hammer of the Lord, 1973; Epistles to the Apostle, 1974; The Word and the Words, 1975; Bugles in the Afternoon, 1977; Get Through Till Nightfall, 1979; (ed) Kaunda on Violence, 1980; *relevant publication:* Spark in the Stubble, by T. L. Charlton, 1969. *Recreations:* writing, walking, music. *Address:* c/o BBC TV, Wood Lane, W12 7RJ. *T:* 01-743 8000.

MORRIS, David Edward; Chief Scientist, Civil Aviation Authority, 1972-78, retired; *b* 23 July 1915; *m* 1950, Heather Anne Court; one *s* two *d. Educ:* University Coll. of North Wales, Bangor; Trinity Coll., Cambridge. Aerodynamics Dept, RAE, 1938-56; Chief Supt, A&AEE, 1956-59; Chief Supt, RAE, Bedford, 1959-61; Dir-General, Development (RAF), Min. of Aviation, 1961-65; Dir-Gen., Civil Aircraft and Gen. Services Research and Develt, 1965-69; Scientific Adviser (Civil Aviation), BoT, later DTI, 1969-72. FRAeS 1956. *Publications:* various reports and memoranda. *Recreations:* walking, bridge. *Address:* 38 Days Lane, Biddenham, Bedford. *T:* 66644.

MORRIS, David Elwyn; Registrar of the Principal Registry of the Family Division of the High Court of Justice, since 1976; *b* 22 May 1920; *s* of Rev. S. M. Morris and K. W. Morris; *m* 1st, 1947, Joyce Hellyer (*d* 1977); one *s* one *d* ; 2nd, 1978, Gwendolen Pearce, *widow* of Dr John Pearce. *Educ:* Mill Hill Sch.; Brasenose Coll., Oxford (Hulme Exhibnr; MA). With Friends' Ambulance Unit in China, 1942-44; served British Army in India, 1944-46. Called to Bar, Inner Temple, 1949; admitted Solicitor of the Supreme Court, 1955; Mem., Matrimonial Causes Rule Cttee, 1967-75. Partner, Jaques & Co. until 1975. *Publications:* China Changed My Mind, 1948; The End of Marriage, 1971; contrib. Marriage For and Against, 1972; Pilgrim through this Barren Land, 1974. *Recreation:* reading. *Address:* 8 Rodney House, Pembridge Crescent, W11 3DY. *T:* 01-727 7975.

MORRIS, Prof. David William, PhD; Principal, Welsh Agricultural College, Aberystwyth, since 1970; Professor of Agriculture, University College of Wales, Aberystwyth, since 1979; *b* 7 Dec. 1937; *s* of late David William Morris and Mary Olwen Ann Lewis; *m* 1966, Cynthia Cooper; one *s* one *d. Educ:* Ardwyn Grammar Sch.; UC of Wales (BSc Agric.); Univ. of Newcastle upon Tyne (PhD). FRAgS 1974. Develt Officer, Agric. Div., ICI, 1963-64; Asst Dir, Cockle Park Exptl Farm, Newcastle upon Tyne Univ., 1964-68; Farms Manager for Marquis of Lansdowne, Bowood, Wilts, 1968-70. Churchill Fellowship, 1973. *Publications:* Practical Milk Production, 1976, 3rd edn 1977; (with M. M. Cooper) Grass Farming, 4th edn 1977. *Recreation:* farming. *Address:* Felin Gyffin, Dolau, Bow Street, Dyfed. *T:* Aberystwyth 828574. *Club:* Farmers'.

MORRIS, Denis Edward, OBE 1958; Head, and ultimately Controller of Light Programme, BBC, 1960-67; *b* 29 June 1907; *s* of Philip and Edith Morris; *m* 1st, 1931, Angela Moore (marr. diss., 1942); one *s*; 2nd, 1943, Catharine Garrett (*née* Anderton); one *s. Educ:* Tonbridge Sch. BBC Talks Producer, 1936; BBC Midland Public Relations Officer, 1938; BBC Empire Public Relations Officer, 1939; MOI Dir, Midland Region, 1940-42; BBC Midland Regional Programme Dir, 1943-48; Head of Midland Regional Programmes, 1948-60. Leicester City Council, 1933-36; Chm., Findon Parish Council, 1971-74; Chm., Lord Mayor of Birmingham's War Relief Fund Publicity and Appeals Cttee, 1942-48; Chm., Shoreham Cons. Assoc., 1971-75, Pres., 1976-79; Member: Hosp. Management Cttee, St Francis Hosp. and Lady Chichester Hosp., 1966-71; Exec. Cttee, Nat. Cricket Assoc., 1969-74 (Chm., Public Relations Standing Cttee, 1969-72); Chm., Lord's Taverners' Council, 1963-65 (Mem., 1962-67); Public Relations Advisor to MCC and the Counties, 1967-68; Mem., Public Relations and Promotion Sub-Cttee, TCCB, 1968-75. *Publications:* Poultry-Keeping for Profit, 1949; The French Vineyards, 1958; A Guide to the Pleasures of Wine-Drinking, 1972; ABC of Wine, 1977. *Recreations:* swimming, golf, drinking wine and writing about it (for Daily Telegraph and Field). *Address:* Little Nepcote, Findon, Worthing, West Sussex BN14 0SN. *T:* Findon 3256. *Clubs:* MCC; Incogniti CC; Sussex Martlets CC; Gentlemen of Leicestershire CC; Blackheath Rugby Football; Sussex Rugby Football.

See also T. D. Morris.

MORRIS, Derek James, MA, DPhil; Economic Director, National Economic Development Office, since 1981; Fellow of Oriel College, Oxford, since 1970; *b* 23 Dec. 1945; *s* of Denis William and Olive Margaret Morris; *m* 1975, Susan Mary Whittles; one *s. Educ:* Harrow County Grammar Sch.; St Edmund Hall, Oxford; Nuffield Coll., Oxford. MA (Oxon); DPhil. Research Fellow, Centre for Business and Industrial Studies, Warwick Univ., 1969-70; Fellow and Tutor in Economics, Oriel Coll., Oxford, 1970-; Tutor and Sen. Tutor, Oxford University Business Summer Sch., 1970-78; Visiting Fellow, Oxford Centre for Management Studies, 1977-. *Publications:* (ed) The Economic System in the UK, 1977, 2nd edn 1979; (with D. Hay) Industrial Economics, Theory and Evidence, 1979; articles on import penetration, exchange rates and profitability. *Recreations:* skiing, rugby, reading history. *Club:* Reform.

MORRIS, Desmond John, DPhil; writer on animal and human behaviour; *b* 24 Jan. 1928; *s* of Capt. Harry Howe Morris and Dorothy Marjorie Fuller Morris (*née* Hunt); *m* 1952, Ramona Baulch; one *s. Educ:* Dauntsey's Sch.; Birmingham Univ. (BSc); Magdalen Coll., Oxford (DPhil). Postdoctoral research in Animal Behaviour, Dept of Zoology, Oxford Univ., 1954-56; Head of Granada TV and Film Unit at Zool. Soc. of London, 1956-59; Curator of Mammals, Zool. Soc. of London, 1959-67; Dir, Inst. of Contemp. Arts, London, 1967-68; Research Fellow, Wolfson Coll., Oxford, 1973-81. Chm. of TV programmes: Zootime (weekly), 1956-67; Life (fortnightly), 1965-68; TV series: The Human Race, 1982. *Publications:* (Jt Ed.) International Zoo Yearbook, 1959-62; The Biology of Art, 1962; The Mammals: A Guide to the Living Species, 1965; (with Ramona Morris) Men and Snakes, 1965; (with Ramona Morris) Men and Apes, 1966; (with Ramona Morris) Men and Pandas, 1966; The Naked Ape, 1967; (ed) Primate Ethology, 1967; The Human Zoo, 1969; Patterns of Reproductive Behaviour, 1970; Intimate Behaviour, 1971; Manwatching: a field guide to human behaviour, 1977; (jtly) Gestures: their origins and distribution, 1979; Animal Days (autobiog.), 1979; The Giant Panda, 1981; The Soccer Tribe, 1981; numerous papers in zoological jls. *Recreations:* painting, archæology. *Address:* c/o Jonathan Cape, 30 Bedford Square, WC1.

MORRIS, Desmond Victor; HM Diplomatic Service; Consul-General and Counsellor (Administration), Washington, since 1982; *b* 26 June 1926; *s* of late John Walter Morris and Bessie (*née* Mason); *m* 1st, 1951, Peggy Iris Mumford; two *d* ; 2nd, 1961, Patricia Irene Ward, *d* of Charles Daniel and Emma Camwell; one *d. Educ:* Portsmouth Southern Secondary Sch. for Boys; Durham Univ. Served RAF, 1945-48 (Actg Corporal). Joined HM Diplomatic Service; served at Seattle, Budapest, Saigon, Addis Ababa, Berne, Ankara and Pretoria; Dep. High Comr, Georgetown, 1973-78; Dep. Head of Accommodation and Services Dept, FCO, 1979-82. *Recreations:* gardening and the other fine arts. *Address:* c/o Foreign and Commonwealth Office, King Charles Street, SW1A 2AH.

MORRIS, Air Marshal Sir Douglas (Griffith), KCB 1962 (CB 1954); CBE 1945; DSO 1945; DFC 1941; AOC-in-C, RAF Fighter Command, 1962-66; *b* 3 Dec. 1908; *2nd s* of D. G. Morris, late of Natal, South Africa; *m* 1936, Audrey Beryl Heard; one *s* one *d. Educ:* St John's Coll., Johannesburg, South Africa. Commissioned RAF, 1930; trained as pilot, 1930-31; No. 40 (B) Sqdn,

1931–32; Fleet Air Arm, 1932–34; qualified as Flying Instructor, Central Flying Sch., 1934; on instructor duties, 1934–40; RAF Staff Coll., 1940; Air Ministry, 1940–41; on night fighting ops, 1941–42; Comdg No. 406 RCAF Sqdn, 1941–42, as Wing Comdr; Comd RAF North Weald, as Group Capt., 1942–43; on staff of Allied Exped. Air HQ, 1943–44; Comd No. 132 (F) Wing, 1944–45, in Normandy, Belgium, Holland; SASO No 84 Gp HQ, as Air Cdre, Feb.–Nov. 1945; in W Africa, Nov. 1945–46; Jt Planning staff, Min. of Defence, 1946–47; Nat. War Coll., Washington, 1947–48; on staff of Brit. Jt Services Mission, Washington, DC, 1948–50; Sector Comdr, Southern Sector, 1950–52; Sector Comdr, Metropolitan Sector, Fighter Comd, 1952–53; idc 1954; Air Vice-Marshal, 1955, and SASO, 2nd TAF; ACAS (Air Defence), Air Ministry, 1957–59; Chief of Staff, Allied Air Forces, Central Europe, 1960–62. Comdr Order of St Olav, 1945; Comdr Order of Orange-Nassau, 1947; ADC to King George VI, 1949–52; ADC to the Queen, 1952. Retired, 1966. Mem. Council, St Dunstan's, 1968–. *Recreations:* golf, ski-ing. *Address:* Friar's Côte, Northiam, Rye, East Sussex. *Club:* Royal Air Force.

MORRIS, Edward Allan, CMG 1967; OBE 1961; *b* 8 Sept. 1910; *s* of late John Morris, Twickenham; *m* 1937, Phyllis, *d* of late Francis Guise, Twickenham; one *d* (one *s* decd). *Educ:* Hampton Grammar Sch.; Univ. of London (BCom). Entered Crown Agents' Office, 1928. RAFVR, 1942–46; Sqdn Leader (King's Commendation, 1946). Crown Agents' Office: Asst Head of Dept, 1956; Head of Dept, 1958; Asst Crown Agent, 1964; Crown Agent for Oversea Governments and Administrations, 1968–70. *Recreations:* cricket, Rugby Union football, church bells and change-ringing, preserving the riverside area of Twickenham. *Address:* 56 Lebanon Park, Twickenham, Mddx. *T:* 01-892 5856. *Clubs:* Royal Air Force, MCC, Corona (Hon. Treas.); Middlesex County Cricket, Harlequin Football.

MORRIS, Air Commodore Edward James, CB 1966; CBE 1959; DSO 1942; DFC 1944; RAF, retired 1968; *b* 6 April 1915; *s* of late D. G. Morris, and late Mrs E. Morris, Bulawayo, Southern Rhodesia; *m* 1945, Alison Joan, *d* of Sir Charles Henderson, KBE; two *s*. *Educ:* Michaelhouse, Natal, S Africa. Commnd, 1937; Fighter Comd, 1938–41; Desert Air Force, 1941–45; Staff Coll., 1945–46; BAFO Germany, 1946–49; Old Sarum, 1949–52; Caledonian Sector, Fighter Command, 1952–53; RAF Flying Coll., 1953–54; Exchange Posting with USAF, Florida, 1954–56; SASO HQ 12 Group, 1956–58; OC Wattisham, 1958–59; HQ Fighter Command, 1959–60; Air Ministry, 1960–64; Chief of Staff, Headquarters Middle East Command, 1964–66; AOC Air Cadets, and Comdt Air Training Corps, 1966–68. American DFC 1945. *Recreations:* golf, fishing. *Address:* PO Box 85, Underberg, Natal 4590, South Africa.

MORRIS, Gareth; *see* Morris, J. G.

MORRIS, Gareth (Charles Walter); Principal Professor of the Flute, Royal Academy of Music, since 1945; *b* Clevedon, Som, 13 May 1920, *e s* of late Walter and Enid Morris; *m* 1954; one *d*; *m* 1975, Patricia Mary, *y d* of Neil and Sheila Murray, Romsey, Hampshire; one *s* two *d*. *Educ:* Bristol Cathedral Sch.; Royal Academy of Music, London. First studied the flute at age of twelve under Robert Murchie and later won a scholarship to RAM. Career since then has been as soloist, chamber music and symphonic player, teacher and lecturer; Principal Flautist, 1949–72, Chm., 1966–72, Philharmonia Orch. Has been mem. Arts Council Music Panel, and Warden of Incorporated Soc. of Musicians Soloists Section; Adjudicator, International Flute playing Competitions, Geneva, 1973, 1978, Munich, 1974, Leeds, 1977, 1980, Ancona, 1978, 1979. Played at Her Majesty's Coronation in Westminster Abbey in 1953. ARAM 1945; FRAM 1950; FRSA 1967 (Mem. Council, 1977-). *Recreations:* reading and collecting books; astronomy, antiquarian horology. *Address:* 4 Alwyne Place, Canonbury, N1. *T:* 01-226 4752.

MORRIS, Ivor Gray, CMG 1974; Former Chairman and Managing Director, Morris Woollen Mills (Ipswich) Pty Ltd; Chairman Queensland Export Advisory Committee; *b* 28 March 1911; *s* of John and Annie Morris, Talybont, Cards, and Ipswich, Qld; *m* 1944, Jessie Josephine Halley; two *d*. *Educ:* Scotch Coll., Melbourne; Scots Coll., Warwick, Qld; Ipswich Grammar Sch., Qld; Leeds Univ. Founded Morris Woollen Mills (Ipswich) Pty Ltd, 1934. Former Mem. Exec., Wool Textile Manufrs Assoc. of Australia; Life Mem., Nuclear Physics Foundn; Former Mem., Trade Develt Council, Canberra. Former Chm. of Trustees, Ipswich Grammar Sch.; Vice-Pres., Qld Museum Trust, 1970-; Patron, St David's Welsh Soc.; Foundn Mem. and District Governor, Ipswich Apex Club (1st Apex Club formed in Austr.), 1938. *Recreations:* music, reading. *Address:* River Road, Redbank, Queensland 4301, Australia. *T:* 88-29-35. *Clubs:* Tattersall's (Brisbane); Ipswich, Ipswich North Rotary (Ipswich, Qld).

MORRIS, James; *see* Morris, Jan.

MORRIS, James Peter; Secretary General, National Cold Storage Federation, since 1977; *b* 17 Sept. 1926; *s* of Frank Morris and Annie (*née* Collindridge); *m* 1st, Peggy Giles (marr. diss.); 2nd, Margaret Law. *Educ:* Barnsley Grammar Sch.; Manchester Univ. (BA, Teaching Dip.). Served RAF, 1945–48; Research Dept, Labour Party, 1952–59; Govt Information Services, 1960–73; Dir of Information, GLC, 1973–77. *Publication:* Road Safety: a Study of Cost Benefit in Public Service Advertising, 1972. *Recreations:* painting, brewing. *Address:* 88 Ridgmount Gardens, WC1E 7AY. *T:* 01-637 2141. *Clubs:* MCC, Reform.

MORRIS, (James) Richard (Samuel); Chairman and Managing Director, Brown and Root (UK) Ltd, since 1980; *b* 20 Nov. 1925; *o s* of James John Morris and Kathleen Mary Morris (*née* McNaughton); *m* 1958, Marion Reid Sinclair; two *s* two *d*. *Educ:* Ardingly Coll.; Birmingham Univ. BSc, 1st cl. hons Chem. Engrg; Vice-Chancellor's Prize, 1955; FEng, FIChemE. Captain Welsh Guards, 1944–48. Courtaulds Ltd, 1950–80: Man. Dir, National Plastics Ltd, 1959–64; Dep. Chm., British Cellophane Ltd, 1967–70; Chm., British Celanese Ltd, 1970–72; Chm., Northgate Gp Ltd, 1971–76; Chm., Meridian Ltd, 1972–76; Dir, 1967–78, Gp Technical Dir, 1976–78, Courtaulds Ltd; Dir, British Nuclear Fuels Ltd, 1971-. Vis. Prof. of Chem. Engrg, Univ. of Strathclyde, 1979-; Pro-Chancellor, Loughborough Univ., 1982-. Member: Nuclear Power Adv. Bd, 1973; Adv. Council for Energy Conservation, 1974–80; Adv. Bd for Res. Councils, 1981-; Dep. Chm., NEB, 1978–79; Industrial Adviser to Barclays Bank, 1980-. Mem. Council, 1974, Vice-Pres., 1976, Pres., 1977, IChemE; Vice-Pres., Soc. of Chem. Industry, 1978–81; Hon. Sec., Fellowship of Engineering, 1979–82. Hon. DSc: Leeds, 1981; Bath, 1981. *Recreations:* ski-ing, gardening, music. *Address:* Breadsall Manor, Derby DE7 6AL. *T:* Derby 831368. *Club:* Athenæum.

MORRIS, James Shepherd, ALI; ARSA; RIBA, FRIAS; Partner, Morris & Steedman, Architects and Landscape Architects; *b* 22 Aug. 1931; *s* of Thomas Shepherd Morris and Johanna Sime Malcolm; *m* 1959, Eleanor Kenner Smith; two *s* one *d*. *Educ:* Daniel Stewart's Coll.; Edinburgh Sch. of Architecture (DipArch); Univ. of Pennsylvania (MLA). *Architectural works:* Edinburgh Univ., Strathclyde Univ., Princess Margaret Rose Hosp., Countryside Commn for Scotland. Member, Arts Council of Gt Britain, 1973–80; Vice-Chm., Scottish Arts Council, 1976–80 (Chm., Art Cttee, 1976–80; Mem., Enquiry into Community Arts, 1974); Past Member: Council, RIAS and Edinburgh AA, 1969–71; Council of Cockburn Assoc., Edinburgh; Cttee of Management, Traverse Theatre, Edinburgh. Trustee, Nat. Mus. of Antiquities, 1980-. RIBA Award, 1974; Civic Trust Awards, 1962–75; British Steel Award, 1971; European Architectural Heritage Award, 1975; European Heritage Business & Industry Award, 1975. *Publications:* contribs to RIBA Jl. *Recreations:* golf, tennis, skiing, painting. *Address:* (office) 37 Young Street Lane North, Edinburgh EH2 4JE. *T:* (office) 031-226 6563. *Clubs:* New (Edinburgh); Scottish Arts (Edinburgh); Philadelphia Cricket (Philadelphia).

MORRIS, Jan, FRSL; writer; Commonwealth Fellow, USA, 1953; Editorial Staff, The Times, 1951–56; Editorial Staff, The Guardian, 1957–62. Mem., Yr Academi Gymreig. *Publications:* (as James Morris): Coast to Coast, 1956, rev. edn 1962; Sultan in Oman, 1957; The Market of Seleukia, 1957; Coronation Everest, 1958; South African Winter, 1958; The Hashemite Kings, 1959; Venice, 1960, 2nd rev. edn, 1983; The Upstairs Donkey, 1962 (for children); The World Bank, 1963; Cities, 1963; The Presence of Spain, 1964, rev. edns (as Spain), 1979, 1982; Oxford, 1965, rev. edn 1978; Pax Britannica, 1968; The Great Port, 1970; Places, 1972; Heaven's Command, 1973; Farewell the Trumpets, 1978; (as Jan Morris): Conundrum, 1974; Travels, 1976; The Oxford Book of Oxford, 1978; Destinations, 1980; My Favourite Stories of Wales, 1980; The Venetian Empire, 1980; The Small Oxford Book of Wales, 1982; A Venetian Bestiary, 1982; The Spectacle of Empire, 1982; (with Paul Wakefield) Wales, The First Place, 1982; Stones of Empire, 1983. *Address:* Trefan Morys, Llanystumdwy, Cricieth, Gwynedd, Wales. *T:* Cricieth 2222; Trefan Bach, Fforest, Y Fenni, Gwent, Wales. *T:* Crucorney 466.

MORRIS, Prof. Jeremy Noah, CBE 1972; FRCP; Professor of Community Health, University of London, at London School of Hygiene and Tropical Medicine, 1967–78; *b* 6 May 1910; *s* of Nathan and Annie Morris; *m* 1939, Galina Schuchalter; one *s* one *d*. *Educ:* Hutcheson's Grammar Sch., Glasgow; Univ. of Glasgow; University Coll. Hosp., London; London School of Hygiene and Tropical Medicine (Hon. Fellow 1979). MA, DSc, DPH. Qual., 1934; hosp. residencies, 1934–37; general practice, 1937–38; Asst MOH, Hendon and Harrow, 1939–41; Med. Spec., RAMC, 1941–46 (Lt-Col 1944–46); Rockefeller Fellow, Prev. Med., 1946–47; Dir, MRC Social Med. Unit, 1948–75; Prof., Social Med., London Hosp., 1959–67; Visiting Professor: Yale, 1957; Berkeley, 1963; Jerusalem, 1968, 1980; Adelaide, 1983. Lectures: Ernestine Henry, RCP London; Gibson, RCP Edinburgh; Fleming, RCPS Glasgow; Carey Coombs, Univ. of Bristol; Brontë Stewart, Univ. of Glasgow; St Cyres, Nat. Heart Hosp.; Alumnus, Yale; Delamar, Johns Hopkins Univ. Member: Royal Commission on Penal Reform; Cttee, Personal Social Services, Working Party Med. Admin, 1964–72; Health Educn Council, 1978–80; Nat. Adv. Cttee on Nutrition Educn, 1980-; Chm., Fitness and Health Adv. Gp, Sports Council, 1980-. Hon. Member: Amer. Epid. Soc., 1976; Soc. for Social Medicine, 1978; British Cardiac Soc., 1982. Hon. FFCM, 1977. Hon. MD Edinburgh, 1974; Hon. DSc Hull, 1982. Bisset Hawkins Medal, RCP, 1980. *Publications:* Uses of Epidemiology, 1957, 3rd edn 1975; papers on coronary disease and exercise, and on health and prevention. *Recreations:* walking, swimming, piano music. *Address:* 3 Briardale Gardens, NW3. *T:* 01-435 5024. *Club:* Royal Automobile.

MORRIS, Rt. Hon. John, PC 1970; QC 1973; MP (Lab) Aberavon Division of Glamorgan since Oct. 1959; a Recorder of the Crown Court, since 1982; *b* Nov. 1931; *s* of late D. W. Morris, Penywern, Talybont, Cardiganshire; *m* 1959, Margaret M. Morris, JP, *d* of late Edward Lewis, OBE, JP, of Llandysul; three *d*. *Educ:* Ardwyn, Aberystwyth; University Coll. of Wales, Aberystwyth; Gonville and Caius Coll., Cambridge; Academy of International Law, The Hague; Holker Senior Exhibitioner, Gray's Inn. Commissioned Royal Welch Fusiliers and Welch Regt. Called to the Bar,

Gray's Inn, 1954. Parly Sec., Min. of Power, 1964-66; Jt Parly Sec., Min. of Transport, 1966-68; Minister of Defence (Equipment), 1968-70; Sec. of State for Wales, 1974-79. Dep. Gen. Sec. and Legal Adviser, Farmers' Union of Wales, 1956-58. Member: UK Delegn Consultative Assembly Council of Europe and Western European Union, 1963-64, 1982-; N Atlantic Assembly, 1970-74. Chairman: Nat. Pneumoconiosis Jt Cttee, 1964-66; Joint Review of Finances and Management, British Railways, 1966-67; Nat. Road Safety Advisory Council, 1967; Mem. Courts of University Colls, Aberystwyth, Swansea and Cardiff. *Address:* House of Commons, SW1.

MORRIS, Maj.-Gen. John Edward Longworth, CB 1963; CBE 1956; DSO 1945; Director of Recruiting, War Office, 1960-64, retired; *b* 1 June 1909; *s* of Col A. E. Morris and M. E. Stanyon; *m* 1939, Pamela Gresley Ball; two *d. Educ:* Cheltenham Coll. Commissioned Regular Army, 1929; served War of 1939-45: India, Middle East and NW Europe, Col Comdt, RA, 1966-74. *Recreations:* sailing, model railways, electronics. *Address:* Garden House, Garden Road, Burley, Hants. *Clubs:* Royal Ocean Racing, Royal Artillery Yacht (Admiral).

MORRIS, John Evan A.; *see* Artro Morris.

MORRIS, Prof. (John) Gareth, FIBiol; Professor of Microbiology, University College of Wales, Aberystwyth, since 1971; *b* 25 Nov. 1932; *s* of Edwin Morris and Evelyn Amanda Morris (*née* Griffiths); *m* 1962, Áine Mary Kehoe; one *s* one *d. Educ:* Bridgend Grammar Sch.; Univ. of Leeds; Trinity Coll., Oxford. DPhil; FIBiol 1971. Guinness Res. Fellow, Univ. of Oxford, 1957-61; Rockefeller Fellow, Univ. of Calif at Berkeley, 1959-60; Tutor in Biochem., Balliol Coll., Oxford, 1960-61; Lectr, subseq. Sen. Lectr, Univ. of Leicester, 1961-71. Vis. Associate Prof., Purdue Univ., USA, 1965. Mem., UGC, 1981-. *Publications:* A Biologist's Physical Chemistry, 1968, 2nd edn 1974; contribs on microbial biochemistry and physiology. *Recreations:* gardening, walking. *Address:* Cilgwyn, 16 Lôn Tyllwyd, Llanfarian, Aberystwyth, Dyfed SY23 4UH. *T:* Aberystwyth 612502.

MORRIS, Dr John Humphrey Carlile, QC 1981; FBA 1966; DCL; LLD; Fellow of Magdalen College, Oxford, 1936-77, Hon. Fellow, 1977; University Reader in Conflict of Laws, 1951-77; *b* 18 Feb. 1910; *e* s of H. W. Morris, Solicitor, and J. M. Morris; *m* 1939, Mercy Jane Kinch; no *c. Educ:* Charterhouse; Christ Church, Oxford. DCL Oxford, 1949; LLD Cantab, 1979. Barrister-at-Law, 1934; Fellow and Tutor in Law, Magdalen Coll., Oxford, 1936; All Souls Lecturer in Private Internat. Law, 1939-51; Arthur Goodhart Vis. Prof. of Legal Sci., and Fellow of Gonville and Caius Coll., Cambridge, 1979-80. Hon. Bencher of Gray's Inn, 1980. Lt-Comdr RNVR, 1940-45. Visiting Prof., Harvard Law Sch., 1950-51; Assoc. Mem. Amer. Acad. of Arts and Sciences, 1960. *Publications:* Cases in Private International Law, 1939, 4th edn, 1968; (with Prof. W. Barton Leach) The Rule against Perpetuities, 1956, 2nd edn 1962; The Conflict of Laws, 1971, 2nd edn 1980; title Conflict of Laws in Halsbury's Laws of England, 4th edn, 1974; Thank You, Wodehouse, 1981; Editor, 9th, 10th and 11th edns of Theobald on Wills, 1939-54; Gen. Editor: Dicey's Conflict of Laws, 6th to 10th edns, 1949-80; Chitty on Contracts, 22nd edn, 1961. *Recreation:* yacht cruising. *Address:* Sparepenny Cottage, Front Street, Orford, Suffolk IP12 2LP. *T:* Orford 664. *Club:* Royal Cruising.

MORRIS, Rev. (John) Marcus (Harston); Editor-in-Chief, since 1964, Deputy Chairman, since 1979, The National Magazine Co. Ltd; *b* 25 April 1915; *e* s of late Rev. Canon W. E. H. Morris and Edith (*née* Nield); *m* 1941, Jessica, *d* of late John Hamlet Dunning and Alice (*née* Hunt-Jones); one *s* three *d. Educ:* Dean Close Sch., Cheltenham; Brasenose Coll., Oxford (Colquitt Exhibnr; BA Lit. Hum. 1937); Wycliffe Hall, Oxford (BA Theol. 1939, MA 1947). Deacon 1939, priest 1940. Curate: St Bartholomew's, Roby, 1939-40; Great Yarmouth, 1940-41; Chaplain, RAFVR, 1941-43; Rector of Weeley, 1943-45; Vicar of St James's, Birkdale, 1945-50; Editor, The Anvil, 1946-50; Founder and Editor, Eagle, Girl, Swift, and Robin, 1950-59; Man. Editor, Housewife, 1954-59; Editorial Dir, 1960-64, Man. Dir, 1964-82, The National Magazine Co. Ltd. Hon. Chaplain, St Bride's, Fleet Street, 1952-. *Publications:* Stories of the Old Testament, 1961; Stories of the New Testament, 1961; (ed) The Best of Eagle, 1977. *Recreation:* salmon and trout fishing. *Address:* Flat 5, 71 Portland Place, W1N 3AL. *T:* 01-637 3240; Mill House, Midford, near Bath, Avon BA2 7DE. *T:* Combe Down 833939. *Club:* Savile.

MORRIS, Keith Elliot Hedley; HM Diplomatic Service; Minister, Mexico City, since 1979; *b* 24 Oct. 1934; *m* Maria del Carmen Carratala; two *s* two *d.* Entered Foreign Office, 1959; served Dakar, Algiers, Paris, Bogota; First Sec., FCO, 1971-76; Counsellor (Commercial), Warsaw, 1976-79. *Address:* c/o Foreign and Commonwealth Office, SW1.

MORRIS, Rev. Marcus; *see* Morris, Rev. J. M. H.

MORRIS, Max; educational propagandist and reformer; pioneer of the Comprehensive School; Headmaster, Willesden High School, 1967-78, retired; *b* 15 Aug. 1913; *s* of Nathan and Annie Morris; *m* 1961, Margaret Saunders (*née* Howard), historian. *Educ:* Hutcheson's, Glasgow; Kilburn Grammar Sch., Mddx; University Coll., Univ. of London (BA 1st cl. Hons History); Inst. of Education, Univ. of London (DipEd); LSE. Began teaching, 1936, in Willesden. Served War, 1941-46, demobilised as Captain RASC. Sen. Lectr, Colls of Education, 1946-50; Dep. Head, Tottenham, 1960, after eleven years of political discrimination in Middlesex. Headmaster: Chamberlayne

Wood Secondary Sch., Willesden, 1962-67; Willesden High Sch., 1967-78. NUT: Mem. Exec., 1966-79; Pres., 1973-74; Chm. Action Cttee, 1976-79. Chairman: Mddx Regional Examining Bd, 1975-79; London Regional Examining Bd, 1979-; Vice-Chm., Centre for Information and Advice on Educnl Disadvantage, 1975-80; Member: Examinations Cttee, Schools Council; Univ. of London Entrance and Sch. Exams Council; Council, Inst. of Educn; Jt Council, GCE and CSE Boards; former Mem., Bd of NFER; alternate Mem., Schools Broadcasting Council; Finance and Priorities Cttee, Schools Council; Schoolmaster Publishing Co. (former Vice-Chm.); Burnham Cttee; Nat. Adv. Cttee on Supply and Trng of Teachers; CLEA/School Teachers Cttee. *Publications:* The People's Schools, 1939; From Cobbett to the Chartists, 1948; Your Children's Future, 1953; (with Jack Jones) An A to Z of Trade Unionism and Industrial Relations, 1982; contribs on educnl and historical subjects in newspapers, weeklies and jls. *Recreations:* baiting the Dept of Education and Science; ridiculing Trotskyists and trendies; tasting malt whiskey. *Address:* 44 Coolhurst Road, N8. *T:* 01-348 3980.

MORRIS, Michael Sachs; Director-General, British Insurance Brokers' Association, since 1980; *b* 12 June 1924; *s* of late Prof. Noah Morris, MD, DSc, and Hattie Michaelis; *m* 1952, Vera Leonie, *er d* of Paul and Lona Heller; one *s* one *d. Educ:* Glasgow Acad.; St Catharine's Coll., Cambridge. Wrangler, 1948. Scientific Officer, Admty Signals Estabt, 1943-46; Asst Principal, BoT, 1948; idc 1970; Under Secretary: Insurance Div., DoT, 1973; Shipping Policy Div., DoT, 1978. Chm., Consultative Shipping Gp, 1979-80. *Recreation:* sitting in the sun. *Address:* 53 Westbury Road, Finchley, N12 7PB. *T:* 01-445 5234. *Club:* United Oxford & Cambridge University.

MORRIS, Michael Wolfgang Laurence; MP (C) Northampton South since Feb. 1974; Proprietor, A. M. International, communication consultancy, since 1980; *b* 25 Nov. 1936; *m* 1960, Dr Ann Appleby (Dr Ann Morris, MB, BS, MRCS, MRCP); two *s* one *d. Educ:* Bedford Sch.; St Catharine's Coll., Cambridge (MA). BA Hons Econs, MIPA, MInstM. Management Trainee to Marketing Manager, UK, India and Ceylon, Reckitt & Colman Gp, 1960-63; Service Advertising Ltd, 1964-68; Marketing Exec. to Account Supervisor, Horniblow Cox-Freeman Ltd, 1968-71, Dir 1969-71; Dir, Benton & Bowles Ltd, 1971-81. Contested (C) Islington North, 1966. Islington Council: Councillor, 1968-70; Alderman, 1970-74; Chm. of Housing, 1968; Leader, 1969-71. PPS to Minister of State, NI Office, 1979-81; Mem., Public Accounts Cttee, 1979-. Chm., British Sri Lanka Cttee, 1979-; Secretary: Cons. Housing and Local Govt Cttee, 1974-76; Cons. Trade Cttee, 1974-76; Cons. Environment Cttee, 1977-79; Vice-Chm., Cons. Energy Cttee, 1981-; Sec., Parly Golf Soc. *Publications:* (jtly) Helping the Exporter, 1967; (contrib.) Marketing below the Line: Studies in Management, 1972; The Disaster of Direct Labour, 1978. *Recreations:* restoration work, clocks, squash, tennis, golf. *Address:* Caesar's Camp, Sandy, Beds. *T:* Sandy 80388. *Clubs:* Carlton, Wellington; George Row, Conservative, Whitworth, Billing Road, St George's (Northampton).

MORRIS, Nigel Godfrey, CMG 1955; MVO 1966; QPM 1954; *b* 11 Nov. 1908; 2nd *s* of late Lt-Col G. M. Morris, 2/8th Gurkha Rifles and late Mrs Morris; *m* 1941, Mrs G. E. Baughan, *widow* (*d* 1982), *e d* of late J. C. Sidebottom; one *d* and one step *d. Educ:* Wellington Coll. Asst Superintendent SS Police, 1928; Chinese language course, Amoy, China, 1929; Asst Supt of Police, Singapore CID 1931; Special Branch, 1935; Asst Supt of Police, Town Penang, 1939; interned by Japanese, 1942; repatriated to UK, 1945; Asst Dir, Malayan Security Service, 1946; Dir, Special Branch, Singapore, 1948; Dep. Commissioner, CID, Singapore, 1950, Comr, 1952; Deputy Inspector-General of Colonial Police, Colonial Office, 1957-63; Commissioner of Police, Bahamas, 1963-68, retired. Colonial Police Medal, 1949. *Recreation:* golf. *Address:* Blenheim House, Watlington, Oxon. *T:* Watlington 2228.

MORRIS, Prof. Norman Frederick, MD, FRCOG; Professor of Obstetrics and Gynæcology, University of London, Charing Cross Hospital Medical School, since 1958; Dean, Faculty of Medicine, University of London, 1971-76; Deputy Vice-Chancellor, University of London, 1976-80; *b* Luton, 26 Feb. 1920; *s* of F. W. Morris, Luton; *m* 1944, Lucia Xenia Rivlin; two *s* two *d. Educ:* Dunstable Sch., Dunstable; St Mary's Hospital Medical Sch. MRCS, LRCP 1943; MRCOG 1949; MB, BS (London) 1943; MD (London) 1949; FRCOG 1959. House appts St Mary's Hosp., Paddington and Amersham, 1944-46; Res. Obstetrician and Surg. Officer, East Ham Memorial Hosp., E6; Surg. Specialist RAF (Sqdn Ldr), 1946-48; Registrar, St Mary's Hosp., W2, and East End Maternity Hosp., E1, 1948-50; Sen. Registrar (Obst. and Gynæcol.), Hammersmith Hosp., 1950-52; First Asst, Obstetric Unit, Univ. Coll. Hosp., WC1, 1953-56; Reader, Univ. of London in Obst. and Gynæcol., Inst. of Obstetrics and Gynæcology, 1956-58. Dep. Chm., NW Thames RHA, 1974-80; Chm., NW Thames Reg. Res. Cttee, 1981-. External Examiner, Univs of Sheffield, Leeds, Dundee and Liverpool. President: Internat. Soc. of Psychosomatic Obstetrics and Gynaecology, 1972-80; Section of Obstetrics and Gynaecology, RSocMed, 1978-79. Chm., Assoc. of Profs of Obstets and Gynaecol. of UK, 1981-. Mem. Ct and Senate, Univ. of London, 1972-80; Governor: Wye Coll., 1973-80; St Paul's Sch., 1976-. Fellow, Soc. Gyn. et Obst., Italy, 1970-. Formerly Chairman: Assoc. of University Clinical Academic Staff; 3rd World Congress of Psychosomatic Medicine in Obst. and Gynæcol. (Editor, Proceedings, 1972). Editor, Midwife and Health Visitor Jl. *Publications:* The Baby Book, 1957; Non-Toxæmic Hypertension in Pregnancy (jtly), 1958; Sterilisation, 1976; articles in medical jls related to obstetric problems, 1952-. *Recreations:* travelling, collecting antiques, music.

Address: 16 Provost Road, NW3. *T:* 01-722 4244. *Clubs:* Athenæum, 1942.

MORRIS, Owen Humphrey, CB 1977; CMG 1967; Deputy Under-Secretary of State, Welsh Office, 1974-81, retired; *b* 15 June 1921; *o c* of late David Humphreys Morris, Ton Pentre, Rhondda, Glam., and Mrs Amy Ann Morris (*née* Jones); *m* 1972, Mair Annetta Evans, *d* of late Capt. Daniel Evans, DSC, Tynllys, Morfa Nefyn. *Educ:* Public Elem. Schs; King's Coll. Sch., Wimbledon (Schol.); Balliol Coll., Oxford (Schol.; MA). Served War of 1939-45: The Welch Regt and King's African Rifles, 1941-45 (Capt.). Asst Princ., Colonial Office, 1946; seconded Sierra Leone Administration, 1952-53; Asst Sec., 1955; Dept of Techn. Cooperation, 1962; Min. of Overseas Development, 1964; Min. of Housing and Local Govt, 1966; Welsh Office, 1969; Asst Under-Sec., 1970; Dep. Sec., 1974. *Address:* Taltreuddyn Fawr, Dyffryn Ardudwy, Gwynedd.

MORRIS, Peter Christopher West; a Recorder of the Crown Court, since 1980; *b* 24 Dec. 1937; *s* of C. T. R. and L. B. Morris; *m* 1959, Joy; two *s* one *d. Educ:* Seaford Coll., Christ's Coll., Cambridge, 1958-61 (MA, LLB). Hockey Blue, 1959, 1960, 1961; Hockey for Wales, 1962-65. National Service, 1956-58. Admitted Solicitor, 1965; Partner with Wild Hewitson & Shaw, 1967. *Recreations:* golf, cricket, squash, photography. *Address:* 234 Milton Road, Cambridge CB4 1LQ. *T:* Cambridge 314512. *Clubs:* Flyfishers'; Hawks (Cambridge); Royal Worlington and Newmarket Golf.

MORRIS, Prof. Peter John; Nuffield Professor of Surgery, Oxford University, since 1974; Fellow of Balliol College, since 1974; *b* 17 April 1934; *s* of Stanley Henry and Mary Lois Morris; *m* 1960, Mary Jocelyn Gorman; three *s* two *d. Educ:* Xavier Coll., Melbourne; Univ. of Melbourne (MB, BS, PhD). FRCS, FRACS, FACS. Jun. surg. appts at St Vincent's Hosp., Melbourne, Postgrad. Med. Sch., London, Southampton Gen. Hosp. and MGH Boston, 1958-64; Research Fellow, Harvard Med. Sch., 1965-66; Asst Prof. in Surgery, Med. Coll. of Virginia, 1967; 2nd Asst in Surgery, Univ. of Melbourne, 1968-69, 1st Asst 1970-71; Reader in Surgery, Univ. of Melbourne, 1972-74. WHO Consultant, 1970-; Cons. to Walter and Eliza Hall Inst. of Med. Res., 1969-74. Chm., British Transplantation Soc. Selwyn Smith Prize, Univ. of Melbourne, 1971. Hunterian Prof., RCS, 1972. Hon. Fellow, Amer. Surgical Assoc. *Publications:* Kidney Transplantation: principles and practice, 1979; Tissue Transplantation, 1982; numerous sci. articles and chapters in books concerned mainly with transplantation and surgery. *Recreations:* golf, tennis, cricket. *Address:* 19 Lucerne Road, Oxford OX2 7QB. *Clubs:* Oxford University Croquet and Lawn Tennis, Frilford Heath Golf (Oxford); Yarra Yarra Golf (Australia).

MORRIS, Rex G.; see Goring-Morris.

MORRIS, Richard; see Morris, J. R. S.

MORRIS, Sir Robert (Byng), 10th Bt *cr* 1806, of Clasemont, Glamorganshire; *b* 25 Feb. 1913; *s* of Percy Byng Morris (*d* 1957) (*g s* of 2nd Bt), and Ethel Maud (*d* 1923), *d* of William Morley Glascott, Melbourne; *S* cousin, 1982; *m* 1947, Christine Kathleen, *d* of Archibald Field, Toddington, Glos; one *s* three *d. Heir: s* Allan Lindsay Morris, *b* 27 Nov. 1961. *Address:* RR2 Norton Creek Road, St Chrysostome, Quebec, Canada.

MORRIS, Air Vice-Marshal Ronald James Arthur, CB 1974; retired; *b* 27 Nov. 1915; *s* of late Dr James Arthur Morris, Ladybank, Fife; *m* 1945, Mary Kerr Mitchell; one *s* two *d. Educ:* Madras Coll., St Andrews; St Andrews Univ. MB, ChB 1939; DPH Edinburgh, 1953; MFCM 1972. Commnd RAF, 1939; served on Fighter Comd Stns, 1940-41; India and Burma Campaign, 1941-45; HQ Techn. Trng Comd, 1946-48; SMO, HQ Air Forces Western Europe, 1948-50; Sen. Trng Officer and Comdt Med. Trng Estabt, 1950-52; Exchange Officer, Sch. of Aviation Medicine (USAF), 1955-56; Dept MA7, Air Min., 1956-60; OC RAF Chessington, 1960-61; OC RAF Hosp. Wroughton, 1961-63; PMO, Signals Comd, 1963-65; Dep. PMO, Far East Air Forces, 1965-69; PMO, Maintenance Comd, 1969-70; DDGMS (RAF), 1971-73; PMO, RAF Strike Comd, 1974-75. QHS, 1971-75. CStJ 1974. *Recreations:* golf, fishing. *Address:* 2 Cairnsden Gardens, St Andrews, Fife KY16 8SQ. *T:* St Andrews 75326.

MORRIS, Prof. Terence Patrick, JP; Professor of Social Institutions, University of London, since 1981; *b* 8 June 1931; *s* of Albert and Norah Avis Morris; *m* 1954, Pauline Jeannette Peake (*née* Morris) (marr. diss. 1973); one *d* ; *m* 1973, Penelope Jane, *y d* of Stanley and Alexandra Tomlinson. *Educ:* John Ruskin Grammar Sch., Croydon; LSE, Univ. of London (Leverhulme Schol.). BSc (Soc) 1953, PhD (Econ) 1955. Lectr in Sociology, LSE, 1955-63; Reader, 1963-69, Prof., 1969-81, Sociology (with special ref. to Criminology), London Univ. Vis. Prof. of Criminology, Univ. of California, 1964-65. Mem., Adv. Mission on Treatment of Offenders (Western Pacific, British Honduras, Bahamas), 1966. Member: Magistrates' Assoc. Treatment of Offenders Cttee (co-opted), 1969-77; Council, Inst. for Study of Drug Dependence. Man. Editor, British Jl of Sociology, 1965-74. JP Inner London, 1967. *Publications:* The Criminal Area, 1957; (with Pauline Morris) Pentonville: a sociological study of an English prison, 1963; (with L. J. Blom-Cooper) A Calendar of Murder, 1964; Deviance and Control: the secular heresy, 1976; contribs to Brit. Jl Criminology, Brit. Jl Sociology, Encycl. Britannica. *Recreations:* sailing and maintenance of small boats,

cycling, photography. *Address:* c/o London School of Economics, Houghton Street, WC2A 2AE. *Clubs:* Royal Solent Yacht; Cyclists' Touring.

MORRIS, Most Rev. Thomas; see Cashel and Emly, Archbishop of, (RC).

MORRIS, Timothy Denis, DL; Chairman, Birmingham Post & Mail Ltd, since 1982 (Director, since 1967); a Director, Press Association Ltd, since 1980; *b* 15 Feb. 1935; *s* of D. E. Morris, OBE, *qv*, and Mrs P. H. Skey; *m* 1959, Caroline Wynn; one *s* one *d. Educ:* Tonbridge Sch.; Pembroke Coll., Cambridge (MA). Managing Director, Coventry Newspapers Ltd, 1970-77; Director: British Transfer Printing Co. Ltd, 1970-; BPM Holdings Ltd, 1977-; T. Dillon & Co. Ltd, 1977-. Chairman, Birmingham Civic Soc., 1979-; Dir, Birmingham Hippodrome Theatre Trust, 1980-; President: W Midlands Newspaper Soc., 1975-76; Coventry Chamber of Commerce, 1976-77. County Comr, Warwickshire Scouts, 1974-77. DL West Midlands, 1975. *Recreations:* golf, philately. *Address:* Holly Lodge, Lodge Green Lane, Meriden, near Coventry CV7 7JZ. *T:* Coventry 22237. *Club:* Naval.

MORRIS, Walter Frederick, LLB London; ACII; MBIM; Senior Partner, Morris, Scott & Co., Solicitors, Highcliffe, Christchurch, Dorset; *b* 15 Oct. 1914; *s* of late Captain Frederick James Morris and Elsie Eleanor (*née* Williams); *m* 1945, Marjorie Vaughan, *o d* of late Thomas Vaughan Phillips and Eleanor Mirren (*née* Jones); one *s* one *d. Educ:* Cardiff High Sch.; University Coll., Cardiff (Law Prizeman), Legal practice, 1936-39; Served RA (TA), 1939-45: GHQ Home Forces (Intelligence); WO Sch. of Military Administration; Certificate of Merit, Western Comd; GSO1 (Lt-Col), HQ 21st Army Gp, BLA (later BAOR); commanded Legal Aid Organisation, which provided legal assistance to all British Army and RAF personnel in Europe; legal practice (and Hon. District Army Welfare Officer), 1945-47; entered Administrative Home Civil Service, 1947; Min. of Social Security, 1947-68 (Prin., Dep. Chief Insce Off., Asst Sec.); Admin. Staff Coll., Henley, 1953; on loan to Export Credits Guarantee Dept, 1955-57; Manchester Business Sch., 1968; trans. to HM Diplomatic Service, 1968; HM Consul-Gen., Cairo, 1968-70; ME Centre for Arab Studies, Shemlan, Lebanon, 1969; Head of Claims Dept, FCO, 1970-72; Dep. High Comr, later Consul-Gen., Lahore, 1972-73; retired from HM Diplomatic Service, 1973. Mem., Law Soc. Liveryman, City of London Solicitors' Co. *Recreations:* yachting, golf, travel. *Address:* c/o Lloyds Bank Ltd, 47 Station Road, New Milton, Hants BH25 6HU. *Clubs:* Royal Lymington Yacht; Barton-on-Sea Golf; Punjab (Lahore).

MORRIS, His Honour Sir William (Gerard), Kt 1972; a Circuit Judge and Honorary Recorder of Manchester, 1972-77; *b* 20 June 1909; *s* of Joseph Thomas and Ellen Morris; *m* 1935, Mollie Broadbent; two *s* (and one *s* decd). *Educ:* Bolton Sch.; Gonville and Caius Coll., Cambridge. Called to Bar, 1931; practised on Northern Circuit till 1961; County Court Judge, 1961-66. Served in RAFVR, 1940-45, rank Sqdn Leader. Asst Recorder of Salford, 1956-61; Recorder of Liverpool, 1966-67; Recorder of Manchester, and Judge of the Crown Court at Manchester, 1967. *Recreation:* golf. *Address:* Kingslea, Chorley New Road, Bolton, Lancs. *T:* Bolton 40900.

MORRIS, Prof. William Ian Clinch; Professor of Obstetrics and Gynaecology, University of Manchester, 1949-72, Professor Emeritus since 1972; *b* 10 May 1907; *s* of Dr J. M. Morris, Neath; *m* 1938, Mary Farquharson (*d* 1976); one *d. Educ:* Royal High Sch., Edinburgh; Edinburgh Univ. Obstetrician to Ayr County Council, 1937-46; Sen. Lectr in Obstetrics and Gynaecology, Univ. of Edinburgh, 1946-49. RAMC (TA) 1935; war service, 1939-43. *Publications:* (jointly) A Combined Text-book of Obstetrics and Gynaecology, 1950; contribs to Jl of Obstetrics and Gynaecology of British Commonwealth, Lancet, Edinburgh Med. Jl, etc. *Address:* 19 Linden Avenue, Newport-on-Tay, Fife. *T:* Newport-on-Tay 542425.

MORRIS, Rev. William James, JP; Minister of Glasgow Cathedral, since 1967; a Chaplain to the Queen in Scotland, since 1969; *b* Cardiff, 22 Aug. 1925; *o s* of William John Morris and Eliza Cecilia Cameron Johnson; *m* 1952, Jean Daveena Ogilvy Howie, MBE, *o c* of Rev. David Porter Howie and Veena Christie, Kilmarnock; one *s. Educ:* Cardiff High Sch.; Univ. of Wales; Edinburgh Univ. BA 1946, BD 1949, Wales; PhD Edinburgh, 1954. Ordained, 1951. Asst, Canongate Kirk, Edinburgh, 1949-51; Minister, Presbyterian Church of Wales, Cadoxton and Barry Is, 1951-53; Buckhaven (Fife): St David's, 1953-57; Peterhead Old Parish, 1957-67; Chaplain to the Lord High Comr to the General Assembly of the Church of Scotland, 1975-76; Chaplain: Peterhead Prison, 1963-67; Glasgow DC, 1967-; Trades House of Glasgow, 1967-; W of Scotland Engrs Assoc., 1967-; The High Sch. of Glasgow, 1974-76; Glasgow Acad., 1976-; Strathclyde Police, 1977-; Hon. Chaplain, The Royal Scottish Automobile Club; Moderator, Presbytery of Deer, 1965-66; Convener Adv. Bd, Church of Scotland, 1977-80; Vice-Chm., Bd of Nomination to Church Chairs, Church of Scotland, 1978-81. Mem. IBA, 1979- (Chm. Scottish Adv. Cttee). President: Rotary Club of Peterhead, 1965-66; Peterhead and Dist Professional and Business Club, 1967; Chairman: Iona Cath. Trust, 1976 (Trustee, 1967); Council, Soc. of Friends of Glasgow Cath., 1967; Club Service Cttee, Dist 101, RIBI, 1964-66; Prison Chaplaincies Bd (Church of Scotland Home Bd); Vice-Pres., St Andrew's Soc., Glasgow; Member: Scottish Cttee, British Sailors' Soc.; Bd of Management, W of Scotland Convalescent Home; Council of Management, Quarriers' Homes; Bd of Management, Glasgow YMCA; Gen. Convocation, Strathclyde Univ.; Scottish Council on Crime; Hon. Mem., Scottish Ambulance Assoc., 1981. JP:

Co. of Aberdeen, 1963-71; Co. of City of Glasgow, 1971. SubChapStJ 1978. Hon. LLD Strathclyde, 1974; Hon. DD Glasgow, 1979. *Recreations:* fishing, gardening. *Address:* 94 St Andrews Drive, Glasgow G41 4RX. *T:* 041-427 2757. *Clubs:* New (Edinburgh); RNVR (Scotland) (Hon.); University of Strathclyde Staff (Hon.); Rotary of Dennistoun (Hon.).

MORRIS, Wyn, FRAM; Chief Conductor and Musical Director of Symphonica of London; *b* 14 Feb. 1929; *s* of Haydn Morris and Sarah Eluned Phillips; *m* 1962, Ruth Marie McDowell; one *s* one *d. Educ:* Llanelli Grammar Sch.; Royal Academy of Music; Mozarteum, Salzburg. August Mann's Prize, 1950; Apprentice Conductor, Yorkshire Symph. Orch., 1950-51; Musical Dir, 17th Trg Regt, RA Band, 1951-53; Founder and Conductor of Welsh Symph. Orch., 1954-57; Koussevitsky Memorial Prize, Boston Symph. Orch., 1957; (on invitation George Szell) Observer, Cleveland Symph. Orch., 1957-60; Conductor: Ohio Bell Chorus, Cleveland Orpheus Choir and Cleveland Chamber Orch., 1958-60; Choir of Royal National Eisteddfod of Wales, 1960-62; London debut, Royal Festival Hall, with Royal Philharmonic Orch., 1963; Conductor: Royal Choral Society, 1968-70; Huddersfield Choral Soc., 1969-74; Ceremony for Investiture of Prince Charles as Prince of Wales, 1969; Royal Choral Soc. tour of USA, 1969. FRAM 1964. Specialises in conducting of Mahler; has recorded Des Knaben Wunderhorn (with Dame Janet Baker and Sir Geraint Evans), Das Klagende Lied, Symphonies 1, 2, 5, 8 and 10 in Deryck Cooke's final performing version. Mahler Memorial Medal (of Bruckner and Mahler Soc. of Amer.), 1968. *Recreations:* chess, Rugby football, climbing, cynghanedd and telling Welsh stories. *Address:* Symphonica Music Ltd, c/o Norton Warburg Investments, 103 Cannon Street, EC4.

MORRIS-JONES, Prof. Huw; Professor, University College of North Wales, Bangor, 1966-79; Head of Department of Social Theory and Institutions, University College, 1966-79; *b* 1 May 1912; *s* of William Oliver Jones and Margaret Jones; *m* 1942, Gwladys Evans; one *s* one *d. Educ:* Alun Grammar Sch., Mold, Flintshire; University Coll. of North Wales, Bangor; Oriel Coll., Oxford. Educn Officer, S Wales Council of Social Service, 1937-39; Tutor and Lectr, Dept of Extra-Mural Studies, Univ. of Nottingham, 1939-42; Lectr, Sen. Lectr and Prof., Bangor, 1942-79. Member: Aves Cttee of Inquiry into Voluntary Workers in Social Services, 1966-69; Welsh Hosp. Bd, 1967-70; Prince of Wales Cttee for Wales, 1967-70; Welsh Economic Council (Chm., Environmental Panel), 1967-71; Broadcasting Council for Wales, 1957-60; IBA (Chm., Welsh Adv. Cttee), 1976-82; Welsh Fourth TV Channel Auth., 1981-82. Chm., Caernarfon Borough, later Jt Caernarfon-Gwyrfai, Magistrates' Ct, 1949-; Mem. Council, Magistrates' Assoc., 1950- (Chm., Gwynedd Br., 1952-). *Publications:* Y Gelfyddyd Lenyddol yng Nghymru, 1957; contrib. Aesthetics in the Modern World (ed Osborne), 1968; Philosophy, Jl of Royal Inst. Philosophy, Monist, Efrydiau Athronyddol. *Address:* Ceredigion, Pentraeth Road, Menai Bridge, N Wales. *T:* Menai Bridge 712522. *Club:* United Oxford & Cambridge University.

MORRIS-JONES, Ifor Henry, QC 1969; His Honour Judge Morris-Jones; a Circuit Judge, since 1977; *b* 5 March 1922; *s* of late Rev. Prof. and Mrs D. Morris-Jones; *m* 1950, Anne Diana, *d* of late S. E. Ferris, OBE, Blundellsands; one *s* two *d. Educ:* Taunton Sch.; Sidney Sussex Coll., Cambridge. Called to the Bar, Lincoln's Inn, 1947. Joined Northern Circuit, 1947; Assistant Recorder, Carlisle, 1962; Dep. Chm., Cumberland Sessions, 1969; a Recorder, 1972-76. Mem., Bar Council, 1972. *Recreation:* golf. *Address:* Trewarren, Dowhills Road, Blundellsands, Liverpool L23 8SP. *T:* 051-924 4848. *Club:* Artists' (Liverpool).

MORRIS-JONES, Prof. Wyndraeth Humphreys; Professor of Commonwealth Affairs and Director, Institute of Commonwealth Studies, University of London, since 1966; *b* 1 Aug. 1918; *s* of late William James Jones, Carmarthen, and Annie Mary Jones (*née* Morris); *m* 1953, Graziella Bianca Genre; one *s* two *d. Educ:* University Coll. Sch., Hampstead; London Sch. of Economics (BSc(Econ.) First Class, 1938; Leverhulme Research Grant, 1939; Hon. Fellow, 1980); Christ's Coll., Cambridge Research Schol., 1940. Indian Army, 1941-46 (Lt-Col, Public Relations Directorate, 1944); Constitutional Adviser to Viceroy of India, 1947; Lecturer in Political Science, London Sch. of Economics, 1946-55; Prof. of Political Theory and Instns, Univ. of Durham, 1955-65. Rockefeller Travel Grants, 1954, 1960 and 1967. Vis. Prof. of Commonwealth Hist. and Instns, Indian Sch. of Internat. Studies, New Delhi, 1960; Visiting Professor: Univ. of Chicago, 1962; Univ. of California, Berkeley, 1964-65. Editor, Jl of Commonwealth and Comparative Politics (formerly Commonwealth Polit. Studies), 1964-80. *Publications:* Parliament in India, 1957; Government and Politics of India, 1964, 3rd edn, 1971; (with Biplab Dasgupta) Patterns and Trends in Indian Politics, 1976; Politics Mainly Indian, 1978; articles in Polit. Studies, Asian Survey, Modern Asian Studies, etc. *Address:* Institute of Commonwealth Studies, 27 Russell Square, WC1. *T:* 01-580 5876.

MORRIS WILLIAMS, Christine Margaret, (Mrs F. Morris Williams); *see* Puxon, C. M.

MORRISH, John Edwin, (Jack); Councillor, Deputy Leader, and Chairman, Education Committee, Northamptonshire County Council, since 1981; *b* 23 Sept. 1915; *s* of Henry Edwin Morrish and Ada Minnie (*née* Tapping); *m* 1st, 1937, Norah Lake; one *d*; 2nd, 1944, Violet Saunders (marr. diss.); one *s* one *d. Educ:* Fleet Road, Hampstead, Elem. Sch.; University Coll. Sch.; Northampton Polytechnic, London; various work-faces. Post Office Techn.

Officer, 1932-54; coalminer, 1944-45. Trade Union Official: Civil Service Union, 1954-72; Soc. of Civil and Public Servants, 1972-76 (Gen. Sec., Customs and Excise Gp). Administrator, Northants Rural Community Council, 1979. Census Officer, 1980-81. Vice-Chm., E Midlands Further Educn Council, 1982-; Member: Adv. Cttee, Supply and Educn of Teachers; Assoc. of County Councils, 1981-; Hon. Chm., Northants Child Poverty Action Gp, 1980-. *Publications:* The Future of Forestry, 1971; contrib. Trade Union jls. *Recreations:* thinking, pursuit of justice, music, walking. *Address:* The Old Coach House, Scaldwell, Northants. *T:* Northampton 880428. *Clubs:* Scaldwell; the world at large.

MORRISON, family name of **Viscount Dunrossil** and of **Barons Margadale** and **Morrison.**

MORRISON, 2nd Baron *cr* 1945, of Tottenham; **Dennis Morrison;** Manufacturing Executive with The Metal Box Co. Ltd, 1957-72, retired; *b* 21 June 1914; *e* and *o* surv. *s* of 1st Baron Morrison, PC, and Grace, *d* of late Thomas Glossop; *S* father 1953; *m* 1940, Florence Alice Helena (marr. diss. 1958), *d* of late Augustus Hennes, Tottenham; *m* 1959, Joan (marr. diss. 1975), *d* of late W. R. Meech. *Educ:* Tottenham County Sch. Employed by The Metal Box Co. Ltd on research work, 1937-51; Quality Controller, 1952-57. Lord Lieutenant's Representative for Tottenham, 1955-. FSS 1953-57. Vice-Pres., Acton Chamber of Commerce, 1972 (Mem., Exec. Cttee, 1962). Hon. President: Robert Browning Settlement, 1967-; 5th Acton Scout Group, 1969. *Recreations:* gardening, football. *Heir:* none. *Address:* 7 Ullswater Avenue, Felixstowe, Suffolk. *T:* Felixstowe 77405.

MORRISON, Maj.-Gen. (retd) Albert Edward, CB 1956; OBE 1942; *b* 17 March 1901; *s* of late Major A. Morrison; *m* 1926, Esther May Lacey. *Educ:* Dover Coll.; RMA Woolwich. Royal Artillery, 1922-26; Royal Signals, 1926-57. Retired as Chief Signal Officer, AFHQ, March 1957. Col Commandant, Royal Corps of Signals, 1959-. Legion of Merit (US), 1946; Order of Rafidain (Iraq), 1940. *Recreation:* golf. *Address:* Wesley House, 68 Fairways, Ferndown, Wimborne, Dorset BH22 8BB.

MORRISON, Alexander John Henderson; His Honour Judge Morrison; a Circuit Judge, since 1980; *b* 16 Nov. 1927; *yr s* of late Dr Alexander Morrison and Mrs A. Morrison; *m* 1978, Hon. Philippa, *y d* of 1st Baron Hives. *Educ:* Derby Sch.; Emmanuel Coll., Cambridge. MA, LLB. Called to the Bar, Gray's Inn, 1951. Mem. of Midland Circuit; Dep. Chm., Derbyshire QS, 1964-71; Regional Chm. of Industrial Tribunals, Sheffield, 1971-80; a Recorder of the Crown Court, 1971-80. Pres., Derbys Union of Golf Clubs, 1977-79. *Recreations:* golf, music. *Address:* 17 Eastwood Drive, Littleover, Derby. *T:* Derby 45376. *Club:* The Club (Sheffield).

MORRISON, Hon. Charles Andrew; MP (C) Devizes since May 1964; *b* 25 June 1932; 2nd *s* of 1st Baron Margadale, *qv*; *m* 1954, Hon. Sara Long (*see* Hon. Sara Morrison); one *s* one *d. Educ:* Eton. Nat. Service in The Life Guards, 1950-52; Royal Wilts Yeo. (TA), 1952-66. County Councillor (Wilts), 1958-65; Chairman: Wilts Educn Cttee, 1963-64; South West Regional Sports Council, 1966-68; Young Volunteer Force Foundn, 1971-74; British Trust for Conservation Volunteers, 1973-78; Member: Council, Salmon and Trout Assoc.; Game Conservancy (Vice-Chm.). A Vice-Chm., 1922 Cttee, 1974- (Mem. Exec., 1972-74). *Recreations:* gardening, shooting. *Address:* 60 Cumberland Street, SW1. *T:* 01-834 3020; Wyndham's Farm, Wedhampton, Devizes, Wilts. *T:* Chirton 690. *Clubs:* White's, Pratt's.
See also Hon. J. I. Morrison, Hon. Dame M. A. Morrison, Hon. P. H. Morrison.

MORRISON, Donald Alexander Campbell; Assistant Under-Secretary of State, Home Office, 1972-76; *b* 30 Nov. 1916; *s* of late George Alexander Morrison, sometime MP for Scottish Univs, and late Rachel Brown Morrison (*née* Campbell); *m* 1st, 1951, Elma Margaret Craig (*d* 1970); two *s* one *d*; 2nd, 1973, Jane Margaret Montgomery; one step *s. Educ:* Fettes Coll.; Christ Church, Oxford (BA). Home Office, 1939; Asst Sec., 1955. A Senior Clerk (acting), House of Commons, 1976-81. War Service, 1940-45: 79th (Scottish Horse) Medium Regt, RA, 1942-45. *Recreation:* music. *Address:* 27 High Street, Wingham, near Canterbury, Kent CT3 1AW. *T:* Wingham 774.

MORRISON, Air Vice-Marshal Ian Gordon, CB 1965; CBE 1957 (OBE 1946); RNZAF (retired); Deputy Chairman, Wm Scollay & Co., since 1980; *b* 16 March 1914; *s* of W. G. Morrison; *m* 1938, Dorothy, *d* of W. H. Franks; one *s* two *d. Educ:* Christchurch Boys' High Sch., NZ. RAF 1935; RNZAF 1939; No 75 Sqdn, UK, 1939; Comd RNZAF, Omaka, 1941; Comd RNZAF, Gisborne, 1942; SASO, Islands Gp, 1943; Comd No 3 BR Sqdn Pacific, 1944-45; jssc, UK, 1950; Comd RNZAF, Ohakea, 1952; Air Mem. for Supply, 1954; idc, 1958; AOC, RNZAF, HQ London, 1959-60; Air Mem. for Personnel, 1961-62; Chief of the Air Staff, Royal New Zealand Air Force, 1962-66. Develt Dir, A. S. Cornish Gp, 1970-80. Nat. Pres., Scout Assoc. of NZ, 1967-79. *Recreations:* golf and angling. *Address:* 2 Taungata Road, York Bay, Eastbourne, New Zealand. *T:* Wellington 683367. *Clubs:* Wellington (Pres., 1978-), Wellington Golf (both in NZ).

MORRISON, Prof. James, OBE 1963; BSc, NDA; Professor of Crop and Animal Husbandry, The Queen's University of Belfast, 1944-65, also Director, Agricultural Research Institute, Hillsborough, NI, 1934-65; retired; *b* 11 Aug. 1900; *m* 1934, Grace F. Stockdale, Clogher, Co. Tyrone; three *d. Educ:* Fordyce Academy, Banffshire, Scotland; Marischal Coll., Aberdeen

Univ. Instructor in Agriculture, Co. Tyrone and Co. Down, 1925 and 1926; Sec. and Agric. Organiser, Co. Armagh, 1927-30; Inspector, Min. of Agric. for N Ireland, 1931-33; Lectr in Crop and Animal Husbandry, QUB, 1934. *Recreation:* gardening. *Address:* Loxwood, 35 Lisburn Road, Hillsborough, Co. Down BT26 6HW. *T:* Hillsborough (Co. Down) 682208.

MORRISON, Hon. James Ian, TD, DL; director of companies; farmer; *b* 17 July 1930; *e s* and *heir* of Baron Margadale, *qv* ; *m* 1952, Clare Barclay; two *s* one *d. Educ:* Eton Coll.; Royal Agricultural Coll., Cirencester. 2nd Lieut, Life Guards, 1949-50; Major, Royal Wilts Yeo., 1960-68. Member, Queen's Body Guard for Scotland, 1960-. County Councillor, Wilts, 1955 and 1973-77, County Alderman, 1969; Chairman, W Wilts Conservative Assoc., 1967-71, Pres., 1972-; Chm., Wilts CLA, 1978-81. Chm., Tattersalls Cttee, 1969-80. DL 1977-, High Sheriff 1971, Wiltshire. *Recreations:* racing, shooting, hunting. *Address:* Hawking Down, Hindon, Salisbury, Wilts SP3 6DN; Islay House, Bridgend, Islay, Argyll PA44 7PA. *Clubs:* White's, Jockey.
See also Hon. C. A. Morrison, Hon. Dame M. A. Morrison, Hon. P. H. Morrison, Viscount Trenchard.

MORRISON, James Victor, CB 1979; TD 1950; Member, Police Authority for Northern Ireland, since 1979; *b* 13 Sept. 1917; *s* of Frederick Armand Morrison, Mountstewart, Co. Down, and Hannah Maria Snow, Kells, Co. Meath; *m* 1944, Sophie Winifred Ives; one *s* two *d. Educ:* Regent House. Entered NICS, 1937; War service, 1939-46: BEF, France; SE Asia; TA Service, 1947-57; comd 245 (Ulster) Light Air Defence Regt. NI Industrial Develt Rep., New York, 1957-60; Chief Administrative Officer, Police Authority for NI, 1970-74; Dep. Sec., NICS, seconded to NI Office, 1974-79. *Recreations:* gardening, hi-fi, reading, golf. *Address:* 49 Castlehill Road, Belfast BT4 3GP. *T:* Belfast 63344.

MORRISON, John Lamb Murray, CBE 1957; DSc; FEng; FIMechE; Formerly Professor of Mechanical Engineering, University of Bristol, Emeritus 1971; *b* 22 May 1906; *s* of late Latto A. Morrison, Biggar, Lanarkshire; *m* 1936, Olga, *d* of late M. Nierenstein, DSc; two *s. Educ:* Biggar High Sch.; Univ. of Glasgow (DSc 1939). Lecturer in Mechanical Engineering; Reader in Mechanical Engineering, Univ. of Bristol. Pres., IMechE, 1970-71. Hon. DSc Salford, 1972. *Publications:* An Introduction to the Mechanics of Machines, 1964; various papers on strength of materials and design of machines. *Recreations:* gardening, golf. *Address:* Dreva, Rayleigh Road, Bristol BS9 2AU. *T:* 681193.

MORRISON, John Sinclair; President, Wolfson College (formerly University College), Cambridge, 1966-80; *b* 15 June 1913; *s* of Sinclair Morrison (and *g s* of William Morrison, NY and Stagbury, Chipstead, Surrey) and Maria Elsie, *d* of William Lamaison, Salmons, Kenley, Surrey; *m* 1942, Elizabeth Helen, *d* of S. W. Sulman, Bexhill, Sussex; three *s* two *d. Educ:* Charterhouse; Trinity Coll., Cambridge. Fellow Trinity College, Cambridge, 1937-45; Asst Lecturer Manchester University, 1937-39; Editor of Cambridge Review, 1939-40. Ordinary Seaman (Volunteer), 1940-41. In service of British Council, Cairo, Zagazig, Baghdad, 1941-42; British Council Rep. in Palestine and Transjordan, 1942-45; Pres. Jerusalem Rotary Club, 1945; Prof. of Greek and Head of Dept of Classics and Ancient History at the Durham Colls of Univ. of Durham, 1945-50; Fellow Tutor and Senior Tutor of Trinity Coll., Cambridge, 1950-60; Vice-Master and Sen. Tutor of Churchill Coll., Cambridge, 1960-65, now Hon. Fellow. Leverhulme Fellow, 1965. Mellon Prof., 1976-77, Kenan Prof., 1981-82, Reed Coll., Oregon, USA. Mem. of Council: Hellenic Soc., 1948, 1952; Classical Assoc., 1949; Member: Sierra Leone Educn Commission, 1954; Annan Cttee on Teaching of Russian, 1961; Hale Cttee on University Teaching Methods, 1961; Schools Council, 1965-67; Jt Working Party on 6th Form Curriculum and Examinations, 1968-72; Governing Bodies Assoc., 1965; Governor: Bradfield Coll., 1963; Wellington Coll., 1963; Charterhouse Sch., 1970. Jt Editor, Classical Review, 1968-75. Trustee, National Maritime Museum, 1975-82. *Publications:* (with R. T. Williams) Greek Oared Ships, 1968; Long Ships and Round Ships, 1980. *Address:* Granhams, Granhams Road, Great Shelford, Cambridge.

MORRISON, Hon. Dame Mary Anne, DCVO 1982 (CVO 1970); Woman of the Bedchamber to the Queen since 1960; *b* 17 May 1937; *o d* of Baron Margadale, *qv. Educ:* Heathfield School. *Address:* Fonthill House, Tisbury, Wilts. *T:* Tisbury 870202; Islay House, Bridgend, Isle of Islay, Argyllshire. *T:* Bowmore 223.
See also Hon. C. A. Morrison, Hon. J. I. Morrison, Hon. P. H. Morrison.

MORRISON, Hon. Peter Hugh; MP (C) City of Chester since Feb. 1974; a Parliamentary Under-Secretary of State, Department of Employment, since 1981; *b* 2 June 1944; 3rd *s* of 1st Baron Margadale, *qv. Educ:* Eton; Keble Coll., Oxford (Hons Law). Personal Asst to Rt Hon. P. Walker, MP, 1966-67; Investment Manager, 1968-70; independent business, 1970-74. Sec., W Cons. Members' Gp, 1974-76; Jt Sec., Cons. Smaller Businesses Cttee, 1974-76. An Opposition Whip, 1976-79; a Lord Comr of HM Treasury, and Govt Pairing Whip, 1979-81. *Address:* 81 Cambridge Street, SW1V 4PS. *T:* 01-828 8228; The Stable House, Puddington, Chester. *T:* 051-336 2330; Islay House, Bridgend, Islay, Argyll. *Clubs:* White's, Pratt's.
See also Hon. C. A. Morrison, Hon. J. I. Morrison, Hon. Dame M. A. Morrison.

MORRISON, Maj.-Gen. Reginald Joseph Gordon, CB 1969; CBE 1959; MD, FRCP; Physician, The Royal Hospital, Chelsea, 1969-79; Director of Medicine, Ministry of Defence (Army), and Consulting Physician to the Army, 1965-68; *b* 29 March 1909; *s* of R. Morrison; *m* 1947, Norma Jacqueline Nicholson; two *s. Educ:* Dulwich Coll.; St Joseph's Coll., SE19; St Bartholomew's Hosp. House Phys., St Bart's Hosp., 1934; Res. MO, Hove Gen. Hosp. Commnd RAMC, 1936; served as Med. Specialist, RAMC. Adviser in Medicine, EA Command, 1947-50; OC, Med. Div., QA Mil. Hosp., 1950-56; Cons. Phys., Far East, 1956-59; Prof. of Trop. Med., Royal Army Medical College, 1959-65. QHP 1963-68. *Publications:* (with W. H. Hargreaves) The Practice of Tropical Medicine, 1965; chapter in: Exploration Medicine, 1965; Medicine in the Tropics, 1974; various articles in Lancet, BMJ, Proc. RSM, etc. *Recreations:* rose growing, golf. *Address:* Flat 2, Highclere, Old Hill, Chislehurst, Kent.

MORRISON, Hon. Sara Antoinette Sibell Frances, (Hon. Mrs Morrison); *b* 9 Aug. 1934; *d* of 2nd Viscount Long and of Laura, Duchess of Marlborough; *m* 1954, Hon. Charles Andrew Morrison, *qv* ; one *s* one *d. Educ:* in England and France. Gen. Electric Co., 1975- (Dir 1980-); Director: Abbey Nat. Building Soc., 1979-; Imperial Group Ltd, 1981-. Chairman: Nat. Council for Voluntary Orgns (formerly Nat. Council of Social Service), 1977-81; Nat. Adv. Council on Employment of Disabled People, 1981-. County Councillor, then Alderman, Wilts, 1961-71; Chairman: Wilts Assoc. of Youth Clubs, 1958-63; Wilts Community Council, 1965-70; Vice-Chairman: Nat. Assoc. Youth Clubs, 1969-71; Conservative Party Organisation, 1971-75; Member: Governing Bd, Volunteer Centre, 1972-77; Annan Cttee of Enquiry into Broadcasting, 1974-77; Nat. Consumer Council, 1975-77; Bd, Fourth Channel TV Co., 1980-. *Address:* Wyndham's Farm, Wedhampton, Devizes, Wilts. *T:* Chirton 690; 60 Cumberland Street, SW1. *T:* 01-834 3020.

MORRISON, Prof. Stuart Love; Professorial Fellow in Community Medicine, since 1976, Director, Centre for Medical Research, since 1979, University of Sussex; *b* 25 Nov. 1922; *o s* of late William James Morrison, Ironfounder, Glasgow and late Isabella Murdoch, Edinburgh; *m* 1947, Dr Audrey Butler Lornie, *yr d* of late Lt-Col W. S. Lornie, MC, TD, MRCVS, Perth; one *d. Educ:* Glasgow Acad.; Dundee High Sch.; St Andrews and London Univs. MB, ChB (St Andrews) 1951; DPH (London) 1954; MRCP Edinburgh, 1966; FRCP Edinburgh, 1968; FFCM 1975. Served in RAF, 1939-46; Hosp. and gen. practice, 1951-53; Public Health appts, 1954-56; Mem., Scientific Staff, MRC Social Medicine Research Unit, 1956-62; Vis. Fellow, Epidemiology and Statistics, Univ. of N Carolina, 1961-62; Sen. Lectr in Social Med., Univ. of Edinburgh, 1962-64, Prof. of Community Medicine, Univ. of Edinburgh, 1964-75. FSS; Mem., WHO Expert Adv. Panel on Organisation of Medical Care. *Publications:* (jtly) The Image and the Reality, 1978; contribs to med. jls on epidemiology, organisation of medical care and medical administration. *Recreation:* book collecting. *Address:* March House, Little Dene, Glynde, Lewes, Sussex BN8 6AL. *T:* Glynde 369.

MORRISON, Rear-Adm. Thomas Kenneth, CBE 1967; CBE 1962 (OBE 1941); DSC; Royal Australian Navy, retired; *b* 31 Oct. 1911; *s* of late L. N. Morrison, Sydney, Australia; *m* 1938, Dorothy C., *d* of late W. M. Hole; one *s* three *d. Educ:* Jervis Bay Sch.; Royal Australian Naval College. Served War, 1939-45: Indian Ocean, Red Sea, Pacific (despatches, OBE, DSC). Qualified (Short Staff Course) RNC, Greenwich, 1945. Dir, Training and Staff Requirements, Navy Office, Melbourne, 1946-47; Comdr, Royal Australian Naval Coll., 1948-49; Capt., HMAS Tobruk, on commissioning, 1950-51; Dir of Manning, Navy Office, 1951-52; Dep. Chief of Naval Personnel, 1952-53; Commanding: 1st Frigate Squadron, Royal Australian Navy, 1954-55; HMAS Melbourne, 1959; Royal Australian Naval Air Stn, Nowra, NSW, 1961-62; Dep. Chief of the Naval Staff, Royal Australian Navy, 1962-64; Flag Officer Commanding the Australian Fleet, 1965; Flag Officer-in-Charge, East Australia Area, 1966-68. Australian Comr-Gen. for Osaka Exposition, 1970. *Recreation:* golf. *Address:* 14 Milton Avenue, Woollahra, NSW 2025, Australia. *Club:* Royal Sydney Golf.

MORRISON-BELL, Sir William (Hollin Dayrell), 4th Bt *cr* 1905; *b* 21 June 1956; *s* of Sir Charles Reginald Francis Morrison-Bell, 3rd Bt and of Prudence Caroline, *d* of late Lt-Col W. D. Davies, 60th Rifles (she *m* 2nd, Peter Gillbanks); *S* father, 1967. *Educ:* Eton; St Edmund Hall, Oxford. *Heir:* *b* Julian Francis Tarret Morrison-Bell, *b* 14 Feb. 1959. *Address:* Highgreen, Tarset, Hexham, Northumberland. *T:* Greenhaugh 223; 38 Tournay Road, SW6. *T:* 01-381 3783.

MORRISON-LOW, Sir James; *see* Low.

MORRISON-SCOTT, Sir Terence Charles Stuart, Kt 1965; DSC 1944; DSc; FLS; Director, British Museum (Natural History), 1960-68 (Director, Science Museum, 1956-60); Member, Properties Committee, National Trust, since 1968; *b* Paris, 24 Oct. 1908; *o s* of late R. C. S. Morrison-Scott, DSO, and Douairière Jhr. R. Quarles van Ufford; *m* 1935, Rita, 4th *d* of late E. J. Layton. *Educ:* Eton; Christ Church (MA of the House, 1947), Oxford; Royal College of Science (1st Class Hons Zoology, BSc, ARCS 1935, MSc 1939); DSc London, 1952. Asst Master, Eton, 1935; Scientific Staff, Brit. Museum (Natural Hist.) in charge of Mammal Room, 1936-39, 1945-55 and part of 1956. Served War of 1939-45, with Royal Navy (DSC). Lt-Comdr RNVR. Treas., Zoological Soc. of London, 1950-76; Treas., XVth Internat. Congress of Zoology, 1958. Trustee, Imp. War Museum, 1956-60; Dir,

Arundel Castle Trustees Ltd, 1976-. Governor, Imperial Coll. of Science and Technology, 1956-76 (Fellow, 1963); Mem., Standing Commn on Museums and Galleries, 1973-76; National Trust: Chm., Nature Cons. Panel, 1970-81; Chm., Architectural Panel, 1973-82. Goodwood Flying Sch. (solo), 1975. *Publications:* Palaearctic and Indian Mammals (with J. R. E.), 1951; Southern African Mammals (with J. R. E. and R. W. H.), 1953; papers in scientific jls on taxonomy of mammals. *Address:* Upperfold House, Fernhurst, Haslemere, Surrey GU27 3JH. *Clubs:* Athenæum, Brooks's; Vincent's (Oxford); Leander.

MORRITT, (Robert) Andrew, QC 1977; *b* 5 Feb. 1938; *s* of Robert Augustus Morritt and Margaret Mary Morritt (*née* Tyldesley Jones); *m* 1962, Sarah Simonetta Merton, *d* of John Ralph Merton, *qv* ; two *s. Educ:* Eton Coll.; Magdalene Coll., Cambridge (BA 1961). 2nd Lieut Scots Guards, 1956-58. Called to the Bar, Lincoln's Inn, 1962; Mem., Gen. Council of the Bar, 1969-73. Junior Counsel: to Sec. of State for Trade in Chancery Matters, 1970-77; to Attorney-Gen. in Charity Matters, 1972-77; Attorney General to HRH The Prince of Wales, 1978-. Mem., Adv. Cttee on Legal Educn, 1972-76. *Recreations:* fishing, shooting. *Address:* 7 Stone Buildings, Lincoln's Inn, WC2A 3SZ. *T:* 01-405 3886. *Club:* Garrick.

MORROCCO, Alberto, RSA 1963 (ARSA 1952); RP 1977; RGI; Head of School of Painting, Duncan of Jordanstone College of Art, Dundee, since 1950; *b* 14 Dec. 1917; *m* 1941, Vera Cockburn Mercer; two *s* one *d. Educ:* Gray's Sch. of Art, Aberdeen. Carnegie Schol., 1937; Brough Schol., 1938. In the Army, 1940-46. Guthrie Award, 1943; San Vito Prize, Rome, 1959. Pictures in: Scottish Modern Arts Coll.; Contemporary Arts Soc.; Scottish Arts Council Coll.; Hull, Aberdeen, Glasgow, Perth and Dundee Art Galleries. Mem., Royal Fine Art Commn for Scotland, 1978-. Hon. LLD Dundee, 1980. *Recreations:* travel, swimming, eating. *Address:* Binrock, 456 Perth Road, Dundee. *T:* Dundee 69319. *Club:* Scottish Arts.

MORROGH, Henton, CBE 1969; FRS 1964; FEng 1979; Director, BCIRA (formerly British Cast Iron Research Association), since 1959; *b* 29 Sept. 1917; *s* of Clifford and Amy Morrogh; *m* 1949, Olive Joyce Ramsay; one *d.* Distinguished for his work on the microstructure and solidification of cast iron and for the development of ductile cast iron. Visiting Prof., Dept of Industrial Engineering and Management Univ. of Technology, Loughborough, 1967-72. President: Instn of Metallurgists, 1967-68; Inst. of British Foundrymen, 1972-73; Internat. Cttee of Foundry Technical Assocs, 1978. DSc (*hc*), Univ. of Birmingham, 1965; Iron and Steel Inst. Andrew Carnegie Gold Medal, 1946; E. J. Fox Medal Inst. of Brit. Foundrymen, 1951; McFadden Gold Medal, Amer. Foundrymen's Soc., 1952; Robert Hadfield Medal, Iron & Steel Inst., 1956; Gold Medal, Amer. Gray Iron Founders' Soc., 1961; Bessemer Gold Medal, Metals Soc., 1977. *Address:* BCIRA, Alvechurch, Birmingham B48 7QB. *T:* Redditch 66414; Cedarwood, Penn Lane, Tanworth-in-Arden, Warwicks. *T:* Tanworth-in-Arden 2414.

MORROW, Sir Ian (Thomas), Kt 1973; CA; FCMA, JDipMA, FBIM; CompIEE; Chairman, since 1979, and Managing Director, UKO International plc (formerly UK Optical & Industrial Holdings Ltd), and Chairman of subsidiary companies; Chairman: The Laird Group plc; Mills and Allen International plc; Harlow Meyer Savage Ltd; Mills & Allen Money Brokers Ltd; Pearl & Dean Ltd (Hong Kong); Agricultural Holdings Co. Ltd; Collett, Dickenson, Pearce International Ltd; Hugh Paul Holdings Ltd; Martin-Black Ltd; International Harvester Co. of Great Britain Ltd; Scotia DAF Trucks Ltd; Strong & Fisher (Holdings) Ltd; Deputy Chairman, Siebe Gorman Holdings Ltd; Director: Hambros Ltd; Hambros Industrial Management Ltd; Vision Screening Ltd; James North (Africa) Pty Ltd; James North (Japan) Co. Ltd; DAF Trucks (GB) Ltd; W. M. Still Service Ltd; *b* 8 June 1912; *er s* of late Thomas George Morrow and Jamesina Hunter, Pilmour Links, St Andrews; *m* 1940, Elizabeth Mary Thackray (marr. diss. 1967); one *s* one *d* ; *m* 1967, Sylvia Jane Taylor; one *d. Educ:* Dollar Academy, Dollar. Chartered Accountant 1935; FCMA 1945; Asst Accountant, Brocklehurst-Whiston Amalgamated Ltd, 1937-40; Partner, Robson, Morrow & Co., 1942-51; Financial Dir, 1951-52, Dep. Man. Dir, 1952-56, Joint Man. Dir, 1956-57, Man. Dir, 1957-58, The Brush Electrical Engineering Co. Ltd (now The Brush Group Ltd); Jt Man. Dir, H. Clarkson & Co. Ltd, 1961-72; Chairman: Associated Fire Alarms Ltd, 1965-70; Rowe Bros & Co. (Holdings) Ltd, 1960-70; Kenwood Manufacturing Co. Ltd, 1961-68; Crane Fruehauf Trailers Ltd, 1969-71; Deputy Chairman, Rolls Royce Ltd, 1970-71, Rolls Royce (1971) Ltd, 1971-73 (Man. Dir, 1971-72). Led Anglo-American Council on Productivity Team on Management Accounting to US, 1950. Council Member: British Electrical & Allied Manufacturers' Assoc., 1957-58; British Internal Combustion Engine Manufacturers' Assoc., 1957-58; Member: Grand Council, FBI, 1953-58; Council, Production Engineering Research Assoc., 1955-58; Council, Inst. of Cost and Works Accountants (now Inst. of Cost and Management Accountants), 1952-70 (Pres. 1956-67, Gold Medallist 1961); Performing Right Tribunal, 1968-74; Council, Inst. of Chartered Accountants of Scotland, 1968-72, 1979-82 (Vice-Pres. 1978-79, 1980-81, Pres., 1981-82); Inflation Accounting Steering Gp, 1976-79; Lay Member, Press Council, 1974-80; Freeman, City of London; Liveryman, Worshipful Co. of Spectaclemakers. DUniv. Stirling, 1979. *Publications:* papers and addresses on professional and management subjects. *Recreations:* reading, music, golf, ski-ing. *Address:* 23 Chester Terrace, Regent's Park, NW1 4ND. *T:* 01-486 4250. *Clubs:* National Liberal, Royal Automobile; Royal and Ancient (St Andrews).

MORROW, Martin S.; Stipendiary Magistrate, Glasgow, since 1972; *b* 16 Nov. 1923; *s* of late Thomas Morrow and Mary Lavery; *m* 1952, Nancy May, BMus, LRAM; one *s* two *d. Educ:* St Aloysius' Coll., Glasgow; Glasgow Univ. Solicitor. Private practice, 1951-56; Asst Procurator Fiscal, 1956-72. *Recreations:* music, golf, reading. *Address:* 14 Queen's Gate, Glasgow G12 9DN. *T:* 041-334 1324. *Club:* St Mungo (Glasgow).

MORSE, Sir Christopher Jeremy, KCMG 1975; Chairman, Lloyds Bank, since 1977 (Deputy Chairman, 1975-77); Deputy Chairman, Lloyds Bank International, 1975-79 and since 1980 (Chairman, 1979-80); Director: Legal & General Assurance Society Ltd; Alexanders Discount Co. Ltd; ICI plc; *b* 10 Dec. 1928; *s* of late Francis John Morse and Kinbarra (*née* Armfield-Marrow); *m* 1955, Belinda Marianne, *d* of Lt-Col R. B. Y. Mills; three *s* one *d. Educ:* Winchester; New Coll., Oxford. 1st Class Lit. Hum. 1953. 2nd Lt KRRC, 1948-49. Trained in banking at Glyn, Mills & Co., and made a director in 1964; Executive Dir, Bank of England, 1965-72; Alternate Governor for UK of IMF, 1966-72; Chm. of Deputies of Cttee of Twenty, IMF, 1972-74; Chm., Cttee of London Clearing Bankers, 1980-82 (Dep. Chm., 1978-80). Mem., NEDC, 1977-81. Governor, Henley Management Coll., 1966-; Pres., London Forex Assoc., 1978-. Freeman, City of London, 1978; Chm., City Arts Trust, 1976-79. Fellow: All Souls Coll., Oxford, 1953-68; Winchester Coll., 1966-82; Hon. Fellow, New Coll., Oxford, 1979-; Hon. DLitt City, 1977. FIDE Internat. Judge for chess compositions, 1975-; Pres., British Chess Problem Soc., 1977-79. *Recreations:* poetry, problems and puzzles, coarse gardening, golf. *Address:* 102a Drayton Gardens, SW10. *T:* 01-370 2265. *Club:* United Oxford & Cambridge University.

MORSE, David A.; partner, law firm of Surrey & Morse (Washington DC, New York City, Paris, London); *b* New York City, 31 May 1907; *m* 1937, Mildred H. Hockstader. *Educ:* Somerville Public Schs, NJ; Rutgers Coll., NJ; Harvard Law Sch. LittB (Rutgers), 1929, LLB (Harvard), 1932. Admitted to New Jersey Bar, 1932, NY Bar, Washington DC Bar; Chief Counsel Petroleum Labor Policy Bd, Dept of Interior, 1934-35. US Dept of Interior; Special Asst to US Attorney-Gen., 1934-35; Regional Attorney, National Labor Relations Bd (Second Region), 1935-38. Impartial Chm., Milk Industry Metropolitan Area of New York, 1940-42, when entered Army. Lectr on Labor Relations, Labor Law, Administrative Law, various colleges and law schools, 1938-47. Gustav Pollak Lectr on Research in Govt, Harvard Univ., 1955-56. Formerly: Perm. US Govt Mem. on Governing Body of Internat. Labor Office; US Govt Deleg. to Internat. Labor Confs; Statutory Mem. Bd of Foreign Service; Dep. Chm. Interdepartmental Cttee on Internat. Social Policy; Mem., Cttee for Conservation of Manpower in War Industry, State of NJ; served in N Africa, Sicily and Italy, 1943-44 (Chief of Labor Div., Allied Mil. Govt); arrived in England, 1944. Major, 1944; Chief of Labor Section, US Group Control Council for Germany and prepared Labor Policy and Program for Germany; also advised and assisted SHAEF in preparation of Labor Policy and Program for France, Belgium, Holland, etc; Lt-Col and Dir Labor for Mil. Govt Group, 1945; returned to US; Gen. Counsel, Nat. Labor Relations Bd, 1945-46; Asst Sec. of Labor, 1946-47; Under-Sec. of Labor, 1947-48; Actg Sec. of Labor, June-Aug. 1948; Dir-Gen., Internat. Labor Office, Geneva, 1948-70; Adviser to Administrator, UN Develt Programme. Member: Amer. Bar Assoc.; Council on Foreign Relations; World Rehabilitation Fund; NY Foundation; Albert and Mary Lasker Foundn; Nat. Council of UN Assoc. of USA; Amer. Arbitration Assoc.; US Cttee of Dag Hammarskjöld Foundn; American Legion; Impartial Chm., Coat and Suit Ind. of Metropolitan Area of NY, 1970. Hon. LLD: Rutgers, 1957; Geneva, 1962; Strasbourg, 1968; Hon. DSc, Laval, Quebec, 1969; Hon. DHL Brandeis Univ., 1971. Sidney Hillman Foundn Award, 1969; Rutgers Univ. Alumni Award, 1970; Internat. League for Rights of Man Award, 1970; Three Bronze Battle Stars; Legion of Merit; Officier de l'Etoile Equatoriale (Gabon); Ordre de la valeur (Cameroon); Order of Merit of Labour (Brazil); Grand Officer, Simon Bolivar, (Columbia), 1970; Grand Officer, Order of Merit (Italy), 1971; Grand Officer, French Legion of Honour, 1971; Orden El Sol (Peru), 1972; Grand Officer, Ordre National du Lion (Senegal), 1978. *Address:* 30 East 62nd Street, New York, NY 10021, USA. *Clubs:* Metropolitan (Washington DC); Century Association (New York).

MORSE, Sir Jeremy; see Morse, Sir C. J.

MORSON, Basil Clifford, VRD 1963; MA, DM Oxon; FRCS; FRCPath; FRCP; Consultant in Pathology to the Royal Navy, since 1975; Consultant Pathologist to St Mark's Hospital since 1956; Director of the Research Department, since 1958; Director, WHO International Reference Centre for Gastrointestinal Cancer, since 1969; *b* 13 Nov. 1921; *s* of late A. Clifford Morson, OBE, FRCS; *m* 1950, Pamela Elizabeth Gilbert; one *s* two *d. Educ:* Beaumont Coll.; Wadham Coll., Oxford; Middlesex Hosp. Medical Sch. House Surg., Middlesex Hosp., 1949; House Surg., Central Middlesex Hosp., 1950; Asst Pathologist, Bland-Sutton Institute of Pathology, Middlesex Hosp., 1950. Sub-Lt RNVR, 1943-46; Surgeon-Comdr RNR (London Div.), retd 1972. President: Sect. of Proctology, RSocMed, 1973-74; British Soc. of Gastroenterology, 1979-80; British Div., Internat. Acad. of Pathology, 1978-; Vice-Pres., RCPath, 1978. Vis. Prof. of Pathology, Univ. of Chicago, 1959; Sir Henry Wade Vis. Prof., RCSE, 1970; Vis. Prof of Pathology, Univ. of Texas System Cancer Center, 1980 (Joanne Vandenberg Hill Award); Lectures: Lettsomian, Med. Soc., 1970; Sir Arthur Hurst Meml, British Soc. of Gastroenterology, 1970; Richardson, Massachusetts Gen. Hosp., Boston, 1970. FRCS 1972; FRCP 1979 (MRCP 1973); Hon. Fellow: Amer. Soc. of Colon and Rectal Surgeons, 1974; Amer. Coll. of Gastroenterology, 1978;

French Nat. Soc. of Gastroenterology, 1982. *Publications:* section, Pathology of Alimentary Tract, in Systemic Pathology, ed G. Payling Wright and W. St C. Symmers, 1966, 2nd edn 1978; (ed) Diseases of the Colon, Rectum and Anus, 1969; Textbook of Gastrointestinal Pathology, 1972, 2nd edn 1979; numerous articles in medical journals. *Recreations:* gardening, ornithology, travel. *Address:* 52 Gordon Place, W8. *T:* 01-937 7101.

MORT, Rt. Rev. John Ernest Llewelyn, CBE 1965; Canon Residentiary and Treasurer of Leicester Cathedral, since 1970; Assistant Bishop, Diocese of Leicester, since 1972; *b* 13 April 1915; *s* of late Trevor Ll. Mort, JP, and Ethel Mary Mort; *m* 1953, Barbara Gifford. *Educ:* Malvern Coll.; St Catharine's Coll., Cambridge (BA Hist. Tripos 1938; MA 1942); Westcott House, Cambridge. Asst Curate, Dudley, 1940-44; Worcester Diocesan Youth Organiser, 1944-48; Private Chaplain to Bishop of Worcester, 1943-52; Vicar of St John in Bedwardine, Worcester, 1948-52; Bishop of N Nigeria, 1952-69. Hon. LLD Ahmadu Bello Univ., 1970. *Address:* 7 St Martin's East, Leicester LE1 5FX. *T:* Leicester 52580.

MORTIMER, Chapman; *see* Chapman-Mortimer, W. C.

MORTIMER, Clifford Hiley, DSc, DrPhil; FRS 1958; Distinguished Professor in Zoology, University of Wisconsin-Milwaukee, 1966-81, now Distinguished Professor Emeritus; *b* Whitchurch, Som, 27 Feb. 1911; *er s* of Walter Herbert and Bessie Russell; *m* 1936, Ingeborg Margarete Closs, Stuttgart, Germany; two *d. Educ:* Sibford and Sidcot Schs; Univ. of Manchester. BSc (Manchester) 1932, DSc (Manchester) 1946; Dr Phil (Berlin) 1935. Served on scientific staff of Freshwater Biological Assoc., 1935-41 and 1946-56. Seconded to Admiralty scientific service, 1941-46. Sec. and Dir, Scottish Marine Biological Assoc., 1956-66; Dir, Center for Great Lakes Studies, Univ. of Wisconsin-Milwaukee, 1966-79. *Publications:* scientific papers on lakes and the physical and chemical conditions which control life in them. *Recreations:* music, travel. *Address:* 2501 E Menlo Boulevard, Shorewood, Wisconsin 53211, USA.

MORTIMER, Gerald James, CBE 1979 (MBE (mil.) 1944); FEng, consultant mining engineer, Consolidated Gold Fields Ltd, since 1978; Board Member, Council of Engineering Institutions, since 1978 (Vice-Chairman, 1981-82, Chairman, 1982-83); Councillor, since 1973, Chairman, Finance Sub-Committee, since 1980, Surrey County Council; *b* 2 Sept. 1918; *s* of late Rev. Fernley Mortimer and Grace Mortimer (*née* Whiting); *m* 1942, Connie (*née* Dodd); two *s* two *d. Educ:* Caterham Sch.; Royal School of Mines, London Univ. (BSc (mining engrg), ARSM). Served War, Major, RE, UK and NW Europe, 1939-46. Mining official on Witwatersrand gold mines, S Africa, and in E Africa, 1946-55; Consolidated Gold Fields Ltd: Management staff, London, 1955-63; Exec. Dir, 1963-78; Dep. Chm., 1969-78; Gp Chief Exec., 1976-78; non. exec. Dir, 1978-80; Dir, other Gp cos, 1957-79; in charge Goldsworthy iron ore project, W Australia, 1964-65; Exec. Chm., Amey Roadstone Corp. Ltd, 1967-75. President: Overseas Mining Assoc., 1972-73; Instn of Mining and Metallurgy, 1977-78; Inst. of Quarrying, 1980-81; Hon. Treas., Fellowship of Engrg, 1981-. President: Old Caterhamians Assoc., 1970-71; RSM Assoc., 1976-77. Chm., E Surrey Cons. Assoc., 1980-82, Treasurer, 1982-. FRSA; CBIM; Hon. FIMM; Hon. FIQ. *Recreations:* history, politics. *Address:* 40 Harestone Valley Road, Caterham, Surrey CR3 6HD. *T:* Caterham 44853. *Club:* Carlton.

MORTIMER, James Edward; General Secretary of the Labour Party, since 1982; *b* 12 Jan. 1921; *m* ; two *s* one *d. Educ:* Junior Techn. Sch., Portsmouth; Ruskin Coll., Oxford; London Sch. of Economics. Worked in Shipbuilding and Engrg Industries as Ship Fitter Apprentice, Machinist and Planning Engr; TUC Schol., Oxford, 1945-46; TUC Economic Dept, 1946-48; full-time Trade Union Official, Draughtsmen's and Allied Technicians' Assoc., 1948-68. Dir, London Co-operative Soc., 1968-71. Mem., NBPI, 1968-71; LTE, 1971-74. Chm., ACAS (formerly Conciliation and Arbitration Service), 1974-81. Member: Wilberforce Ct of Inquiry into the power dispute, 1970; Armed Forces Pay Review Body, 1971-74; EDC for Chemical Industry, 1973-74; Chm. EDC for Mechanical and Electrical Engineering Construction, 1974-82. Vis. Fellow, Admin. Staff Coll., Henley, 1976-82; Sen. Vis. Fellow, Bradford Univ., 1977-; Vis. Prof., Imperial Coll. of Sci. and Technol., London Univ., 1981-. Hon. DLitt Bradford, 1982. *Publications:* A History of Association of Engineering and Shipbuilding Draughtsmen, 1960; (with Clive Jenkins) British Trade Unions Today, 1965; (with Clive Jenkins) The Kind of Laws the Unions Ought to Want, 1968; Industrial Relations, 1968; Trade Unions and Technological Change, 1971; History of the Boilermakers' Society, vol. 1, 1973; (with Valerie Ellis) A Professional Union: the evolution of the Institution of Professional Civil Servants, 1980. *Recreation:* camping. *Address:* 9 Blenheim Court, Stanmore Road, Richmond, Surrey. *T:* 01-940 1484.

MORTIMER, John Barry, QC 1971; a Recorder of the Crown Court, since 1972; Chancellor of Diocese of Ripon, since 1971; *b* 7 Aug. 1931; *s* of John William Mortimer and Maud (*née* Snarr) Mortimer; *m* 1958, Judith Mary (*née* Page); two *s* two *d. Educ:* St Peters' School, York, (Headmasters' Exhibitioner 1945); Emmanuel College, Cambridge; BA 1955, MA 1959. Commissioned into 4 RTR, 1951; served in Egypt, 1951-52; 45/51 RTR (TA), 1952-57. Called to the Bar, Middle Temple, 1956 (Bencher 1980); Harmsworth Law Scholar 1957; Prosecuting Counsel on NE Circuit to Post Office, 1965-69; to Inland Revenue, 1969-71. Member: Bar Council, 1970-75; Senate, 1979-. *Recreations:* reading, shooting, cricket. *Address:* 2 Park Square,

Leeds. *T:* Leeds 33277; 5 King's Bench Walk, Temple, EC4. *T:* 01-353 2882; 1A Middle Temple Lane, Temple, EC4; The Grange, Staveley, near Knaresborough. *T:* Copgrove 265. *Clubs:* Travellers'; Leeds; Durham.

MORTIMER, John (Clifford), QC 1966; barrister; playwright and author; *b* 21 April 1923; *s* of Clifford Mortimer and Kathleen May (*née* Smith); *m* 1st, 1949, Penelope Ruth Fletcher; one *s* one *d* ; 2nd, Penelope (*née* Gollop); one *d. Educ:* Harrow; Brasenose Coll., Oxford. Called to the Bar, 1948; Master of the Bench, Inner Temple, 1975. Mem. Nat. Theatre Bd, 1968-. Won the Italia Prize with short play, The Dock Brief, 1958; another short play What Shall We Tell Caroline, 1958. Full-length plays: The Wrong Side of the Park, 1960; Two Stars for Comfort, 1962; (trans.) A Flea in Her Ear, 1966; The Judge, 1967; (trans.) Cat Among the Pigeons, 1969; Come as You Are, 1970; A Voyage Round My Father, 1970 (filmed, 1982); (trans.) The Captain of Köpenick, 1971; I, Claudius (adapted from Robert Graves), 1972; Collaborators, 1973; Mr Luby's Fear of Heaven (radio), 1976; Heaven and Hell, 1976; The Bells of Hell, 1977; (trans.) The Lady from Maxim's, 1977; Film Scripts: John and Mary, 1970; Brideshead Revisited (TV), 1981. *Publications:* novels: Charade, 1947; Rumming Park, 1948; Answer Yes or No, 1950; Like Men Betrayed, 1953; Three Winters, 1956; Will Shakespeare: an entertainment, 1977; Rumpole of the Bailey, 1978 (televised; BAFTA Writer of the Year Award, 1980); The Trials of Rumpole, 1979; Rumpole's Return, 1980 (televised); Regina v Rumpole, 1981; *travel:* (in collab. with P. R. Mortimer) With Love and Lizards, 1957; *plays:* The Dock Brief and Other Plays, 1959; The Wrong Side of the Park, 1960; Lunch Hour and Other Plays, 1960; Two Stars for Comfort, 1962; (trans.) A Flea in Her Ear, 1965; A Voyage Round My Father, 1970; (trans.) The Captain of Köpenick, 1971; Five Plays, 1971; Collaborators, 1973; *autobiography:* Clinging to the Wreckage, 1982; writes TV plays; contribs to periodicals. *Recreations:* working, gardening, going to opera. *Address:* Turville Heath Cottage, Henley on Thames, Oxon. *Club:* Garrick.

MORTIMER, Penelope (Ruth), FRSL; writer; *b* 19 Sept. 1918; *d* of Rev. A. F. G. and Amy Caroline Fletcher; *m* 1st, 1937, Charles Dimont (marr. diss. 1949); four *d* ; 2nd, 1949, John Clifford Mortimer, QC (marr. diss. 1972); one *s* one *d. Educ:* Croydon High Sch.; New Sch., Streatham; Blencathra, Rhyl; Garden Sch., Lane End; St Elphin's Sch. for Daughters of Clergy; Central Educnl Bureau for Women; University Coll., London. *Publications:* Johanna (as Penelope Dimont), 1947; A Villa in Summer, 1954; The Bright Prison, 1956; (with John Mortimer) With Love and Lizards, 1957; Daddy's Gone A-Hunting, 1958; Saturday Lunch with the Brownings, 1960; The Pumpkin Eater, 1962; My Friend Says It's Bulletproof, 1967; The Home, 1971; Long Distance, 1974; About Time (autobiog), 1979 (Whitbread Prize). *Address:* The Old Post Office, Chastleton, Moreton-in-Marsh, Glos. *T:* Barton-on-the-Heath 242.

MORTIMER, Air Vice-Marshal Roger, CBE 1972; Officer Commanding RAF Institute of Pathology and Tropical Medicine and Consultant Adviser in Pathology and Tropical Medicine, 1969-76; Dean of Air Force Medicine, 1975-76; *b* 2 Nov. 1914; *s* of Henry Roger Mortimer, tea planter, Dooars, India and Lily Rose (*née* Collier); *m* 1942, Agnes Emily Balfour; two *d. Educ:* Uppingham; St Mary's Hosp. Med. School. MB, BS London, FRCPath, DCP, DTM&H. Joined RAF, 1942; Sqdn Med. Officer to Nos 23 and 85 Sqdns, 1942-44; Service Narrator and Editor to Official RAF Medical History of the War, 1944-47; specialised in Pathology and Tropical Medicine from 1947. Founder Mem. RCPath; Assoc. Editor and Council Mem., British Div. of Internat. Academy of Pathology, 1967-73; Editor, International Pathology, 1970-73; Mem. Council, Royal Soc. Trop. Med. and Hygiene, 1970-73. QHS 1973-76. *Publications:* papers on approved laboratory methods, practical disinfection, blood transfusion and infusion. *Recreations:* cars, anything mechanical, do-it-yourself, laboratory design. *Address:* The Old Forge, Askett, Aylesbury, Bucks. *T:* Princes Risborough 5566.

MORTIMER, William Charles C.; *see* Chapman-Mortimer.

MORTLOCK, Herbert Norman; Director, Materials Quality Assurance, Ministry of Defence, since 1979; *b* 1926. Superintendent, Royal Armament Research & Development Estabt, 1964-71; Asst Director, Procurement Executive, MoD, 1971-73; Deputy Director: Chemical Defence Estabt, 1973-78; Materials Quality Assurance Directorate, 1978-79. *Address:* Materials Quality Assurance Directorate, Ministry of Defence, SW1.

MORTON, 22nd Earl of, *cr* 1458 (*de facto* 21st Earl, 22nd but for the Attainder); **John Charles Sholto Douglas,** DL; Lord Aberdour, 1458; *b* 19 March 1927; *s* of Hon. Charles William Sholto Douglas (*d* 1960) (2nd *s* of 19th Earl) and of Florence, *er d* of late Major Henry Thomas Timson; *S* cousin, 1976; *m* 1949, Sheila Mary, *d* of late Rev. Canon John Stanley Gibbs, MC, Didmarton House, Badminton, Glos; two *s* one *d.* DL West Lothian, 1982. *Recreation:* polo. *Heir:* *s* Lord Aberdour, *qv. Address:* Dalmahoy, Kirknewton, Midlothian. *Clubs:* Edinburgh Polo, Dalmahoy Country.

MORTON, Alastair; *see* Morton, R. A. N.

MORTON, Alastair; *see* Morton, S. A.

MORTON, Rev. Andrew Queen; Minister of Culross Abbey since 1959; *b* 4 June 1919; *s* of Alexander Morton and Janet Queen; *m* 1948, Jean, *e d* of George Singleton and late Jean Wands; one *s* two *d. Educ:* Glasgow Univ.

MA 1942, BD 1947, BSc 1948. Minister of St Andrews, Fraserburgh, 1949–59. Dept of Computer Science, Univ. of Edinburgh, 1965–. FRSE 1973. *Publications:* The Structure of the Fourth Gospel, 1961; Authorship and Integrity in the New Testament, 1963; (with G. H. C. Macgregor) The Structure of Luke and Acts, 1965; Paul the Man and the Myth, 1965; (with S. Michaelson) The Computer in Literary Research, 1973; Literary Detection, 1979; (with S. Michaelson and N. Hamilton-Smith) Justice for Helander, 1979; (with James McLeman) The Genesis of John, 1980. *Recreations:* thinking, talking. *Address:* The Abbey Manse, Culross, Dunfermline, Fife KY12 8JD. *T:* Newmills 880231.

MORTON, Admiral Sir Anthony (Storrs), GBE 1982; KCB 1978; UK Military Representative to NATO, since 1980; *b* 6 Nov. 1923; *s* of late Dr Harold Morton. *Educ:* Loretto School. Joined RN 1941; war service in Atlantic, Mediterranean and Far East (despatches, HMS Wrangler, 1945); Commander 1956; Comd HMS Appleton and 100th MSS 1957–58; HMS Undine 1960; HMS Rocket 1960–62; Captain 1964; Captain (F) 20th Frigate Squadron, 1964–66; Chief Staff Officer, Plans and Policy, to Commander Far East Fleet, 1966–68; Senior Naval Officer, Northern Ireland, 1968–70; Senior Naval Mem., RCDS, 1971–72; ACDS (Policy), 1973–75; Flag Officer, First Flotilla, 1975–77; Vice-Chief of Defence Staff, 1977–78; Vice-Chief of Naval Staff, 1978–80. *Recreations:* fishing, sailing, shooting, watching Association football. *Address:* c/o Barclays Bank, Alresford, Hants. *Clubs:* Army and Navy, Royal Cruising; Royal Yacht Squadron; Irish Cruising.

MORTON, Rev. Arthur, CVO 1979; OBE 1961; Director, National Society for the Prevention of Cruelty to Children, 1954–79; *b* 29 June 1915; *s* of Arthur Morton and Kate Floyd Morton; *m* 1940, Medora Gertrude Harrison; two *d. Educ:* Imperial Service Coll., Windsor; Jesus Coll., Cambridge (MA); Wycliffe Hall, Oxford (GOE). Curate, St Catherine's, Neasden, NW2, 1938–41; Chaplain, Missions to Seamen, Manchester, 1941–51. Asst Dir, NSPCC, 1951–54. Member, Adv. Council in Child Care and of Central Trng Council, 1956–71; frequent broadcasts on work of NSPCC. *Publication:* (with Anne Allen) This is Your Child: the story of the NSPCC, 1961. *Recreations:* golf, fishing, reading, gardening. *Address:* 25 Cottes Way, Hill Head, Fareham, Hants PO14 3NF. *T:* Stubbington 3511. *Club:* MCC.

MORTON, Sir Brian, Kt 1973; FRICS; Chairman, Harland & Wolff, 1975–80; *b* 24 Jan. 1912; *s* of Alfred Oscar Morton and Margaret Osborne Hennessy; *m* 1937, Hilda Evelyn Elsie Hillis; one *s* (and one *s* decd). *Educ:* Campbell Coll., Belfast. Estate Agency, Brian Morton & Co., Belfast, 1936; retired, 1964. Elected Councillor (U) Cromac Ward, Belfast Corp., 1967; apptd Mem. Craigavon Development Commn, 1968; Chm., Londonderry Develt Commn, 1969–73. *Recreations:* golf, sailing, landscape painting, fishing. *Address:* Rolly Island, Comber, Co. Down, N Ireland. *T:* Killinchy 541472. *Clubs:* Royal Automobile; Royal County Down Golf (Newcastle).

MORTON, Air Commodore Crichton Charles, CBE 1945; Command Electronics Officer, HQ Bomber Command, 1962–66, retired; *b* 26 July 1912; *s* of late Charles Crichton Morton, Ramsey, IOM; *m* 1956, Diana Yvonne, *d* of late Maj.-Gen. R. C. Priest, CB, RMS and *widow* of Group Captain N. D. Gilbart-Smith, RAF; no *c. Educ:* King William's Coll., IOM; RAF Coll., Cranwell. Various flying duties, 1932–36; RAF Officers Long Signals Course, Cranwell, 1936–37; signals duties, 1937–39; radar duties at HQ Fighter Comd, No 5 Signals Wing Force, HQ 60 Signals Gp, Air HQ Iceland, HQ Air Comd SE Asia, 1939–45; Dir of Radar and Dep. Dir of Signals, Air Min., 1945–49; jssc Latimer, 1949–50; OC No 3 Radio Sch., RAF Compton Bassett, 1950–52; OC Communications Gp, Allied Air Forces Central Europe, 1952–55; Inspector of Radio Services, 1955–58; Dep. Chief Signals Office, HQ, SHAPE, 1958–60; Chm. of Brit. Jt Communications Electronics Board, Ministry of Defence, 1960–62. AMIEE 1955; AFRAeS 1965; MIERE 1965; CEng 1966. *Address:* Apartamento 102, Torre Tramontana, Apartado 50, Playa de Aro, Gerona, Spain.

MORTON, Digby; *see* Morton, H. D.

MORTON, Prof. Frank, CBE 1976 (OBE 1968); DSc 1952, PhD 1936 (Manchester); MSc Tech; MIChemE; Professor of Chemical Engineering, University of Manchester, 1956–73, now Professor Emeritus; a Pro-Vice-Chancellor, 1968–72; *b* Sheffield, 11 Aug. 1906; *s* of late Joseph Morton, Manchester; *m* 1934, Hilda May, *d* of John W. Seaston, Withington, Manchester; one *s. Educ:* Manchester Univ. Demonstrator in Chemical Technology, 1931–36; Research Chemist, Trinidad Leaseholds Ltd, 1936–40; Superintendent of Research and Development, Trinidad Leaseholds, Trinidad, 1940–45; Chief Chemist, Trinidad Leaseholds Ltd, UK, 1945–49; Prof. of Chemical Engineering, Univ. of Birmingham, 1949–56. Actg Principal, Manchester Coll. of Science and Technology, 1964–65; Dep. Principal, Univ. of Manchester Inst. of Science and Technology, 1966–71. Member: Council, Manchester Business Sch., 1964–72; Chemical and Allied Products Training Board, 1968–71; European Fedn of Chemical Engineering, 1968–72. Pres., IChemE, 1963–64. Society of Chemical Industry: Vice-Pres., 1967–; Jubilee Memorial Lectr, 1967; Medal, 1969. Hon. Fellow, UMIST, 1978. *Publications:* Report of Inquiry into the Safety of Natural Gas as a Fuel (Ministry of Technology), 1970; various papers on petroleum, organic chemistry, chemical engineering and allied subjects. *Recreation:* golf. *Address:* 47 Penrhyn Beach East, Llandudno, Gwynedd. *T:* Llandudno 48037. *Club:* Savage.

MORTON, George Martin; MP (Lab) Manchester Moss Side, since July 1978; *b* 11 Feb. 1940; *s* of Rev. Thomas Ralph Morton, DD, and Janet Maclay MacGregor Morton (*née* Baird). *Educ:* Fettes Coll., Edinburgh; Edinburgh Coll. of Art; Glasgow Univ. RIBA. Member: Manchester City Council, 1971–74; Greater Manchester Council, 1973–77. An Opposition Whip, 1979–. *Address:* 4 St Anne's Road, Manchester M21 2TG. *T:* 061-881 8195.
See also H. D. B. Morton.

MORTON, Rev. Harry Osborne; Methodist Minister, supernumerary due to ill-health; *b* 28 June 1925; *s* of John William Morton and Alice Morton (*née* Betteridge); *m* 1954, Patricia Mary McGrath; two *s* two *d* (and one *d* decd). *Educ:* The King's Sch., Pontefract, Yorks; King's Coll., Cambridge (MA Cantab); Hartley Victoria Methodist Coll., Manchester. Marconi's Wireless Telegraph Co. Ltd, 1945; Gen. Sec., Order of Christian Witness, 1947; entered Methodist Ministry, 1949; ordained Deacon, Church of South India, 1954; Presbyter, 1955; Sec. for Scholarships, World Council of Churches, Geneva, 1960; Sec. for East and Central Africa, Methodist Missionary Soc., 1963, Gen. Sec. 1972–73; Gen. Sec., BCC, 1973–80; Superintendent Minister, London Mission (East Ham) Circuit, 1980–81. Pres., Methodist Conf., 1972. Select Preacher, Cambridge Univ., 1972 and 1975. *Recreations:* fell walking, music, theatre, coarse gardening. *Address:* 34B Campbell Road, Bow, E3 4DT. *T:* 01-980 9460.

MORTON, (Henry) Digby; consultant designer (independent); *b* 27 Nov. 1906; *e s* of Digby Berkeley Morton, Dublin; *m* 1936, Phyllis May, *d* of James Harwood Panting, London. *Educ:* Dublin. Trained in Art and Architecture, Metropolitan Sch. of Art, Dublin, 1923–29. Opened Couture Establishment in London, 1930; designed WVS uniform for Lady Reading, 1939; worked in USA, 1953–57. Founder Member: Incorporated Soc. of London Fashion Designers, 1939 (Vice-Pres., 1955–56); Visual Arts Soc. of the Cayman Is, for the promotion of art in this Crown Colony. *Recreation:* painting. *Address:* PO Box 191, Grand Cayman, BW1.

MORTON, Hugh Drennan Baird, QC 1974; *b* 10 April 1930; *s* of late Rev. T. R. Morton, DD, and of J. M. M. Morton (*née* Baird); *m* 1956, Muriel Miller; three *s. Educ:* Glasgow Academy; Glasgow Univ. (BL). Admitted Faculty of Advocates, 1965. *Address:* 25 Royal Circus, Edinburgh EH3 6TL. *T:* 031-225 5139.
See also G. M. Morton.

MORTON, John Percival, CMG 1965; OBE 1946; Indian Police Medal for gallantry, 1935, Bar 1940; retired; *b* 15 May 1911; *e s* of late Henry Percy Dee Morton; *m* 1939, Leonora Margaret Sale, *d* of late Hon. Mr Justice S. L. Sale, ICS; one *d* (one *s* decd). *Educ:* Bedford Modern Sch. Indian Police, Punjab, 1930–47 (Dist Supt Police Jullundur; Central Int. Officer, Govt of India, Punjab and Delhi Provinces; seconded HQ British Troops (Egypt); Senior Supt Police, Lahore Dist.); Principal, War Office, 1947; Civil Asst, Staff of AOC RAF Iraq, 1947–49; Counsellor, Office of Comr-Gen., SE Asia, 1949–52; Dir of Int., Govt of Malaya, 1952–54; Asst Sec., War Office, 1954–59; IDC 1959; Sec. of State's Adv. Staff, Colonial Office, 1961–65; Asst Under-Sec. of State, MoD, 1968–71; retired 1971. Advisory missions for FCO to Jordan, Pakistan, Mauritius, E Caribbean and Sri Lanka, 1972–79, for MoD to N Ireland, 1973; Consultant: The De La Rue Co. Ltd, 1972–75; N. M. Rothschild & Sons Ltd, 1972–76; Panel Chm., Civil Service Commn Selection Bd, 1973–80; Chm., Aviation Industry Security Trng Steering Gp, 1978–79. *Recreations:* golf, music. *Address:* Courtlands Cottage, Green Lane, Pangbourne, Berks. *T:* Pangbourne 3908. *Clubs:* East India, Devonshire, Sports and Public Schools; Huntercombe (Oxon).

MORTON, Kenneth Valentine Freeland, CIE 1947; OBE 1971; Secretary East Anglian Regional Hospital Board, 1947–72, retired; *b* 13 May 1907; *s* of Kenneth John Morton; *m* 1936, Mary Hadwin Hargreaves; four *s* one *d. Educ:* Edinburgh Academy; University Coll., Oxford. Joined ICS, 1930; Under-Sec. (Political) Punjab Govt, 1934–36; Deputy Commissioner, 1936–39; Colonisation Officer, 1939–43; Deputy Sec., Development Dept, 1943–46; Sec. Electricity and Industries Depts, 1946–47; retired, 1947. *Address:* Temple End House, 27 Temple End, Great Wilbraham, Cambridge CBI 5JF. *T:* Cambridge 880691. *Club:* East India, Devonshire, Sports and Public Schools.

MORTON, Sir Ralph (John), Kt 1960; CMG 1954; OBE 1947; MC 1918; Judge of High Court of Southern Rhodesia, 1949–59; *b* 2 Aug. 1896; *yr s* of John Morton, Horton-under-Edge, Glos; *m* 1923, Cato Marie van den Berg; one *d. Educ:* Bishop's Stortford; Cambridge Univ. Served European War, RFA, 1915–19. Southern Rhodesia: Solicitor General, 1934; Attorney General, 1944. *Address:* 3 Dundalk Avenue, Parkview, Johannesburg, 2193, South Africa.

MORTON, (Robert) Alastair (Newton); Chief Executive, Guinness Peat Group, since 1982; Director, Massey Ferguson Ltd, Canada, since 1981; Chairman, Thames Oil & Gas plc, since 1981; *b* 11 Jan. 1938; *s* of late Harry Newton Morton and Elizabeth Martino; *m* 1964, Sara Bridget Stephens; one *s* one *d. Educ:* St John's Coll. and Witwatersrand Univ., Johannesburg (BA); Worcester Coll., Oxford (MA). Special grad. student, MIT, 1964. Anglo American Corp. of SA (mining finance), London and Central Africa, 1959–63; Internat. Finance Corp., Washington, 1964–67; Industrial Reorganisation Corp., 1967–70; Exec. Dir, 117 Group of investment trusts, 1970–72; Chm., Draymont Securities, 1972–76. Chm. or Dir, various public engineering groups, 1970-76; Man. Dir, BNOC, 1976-80. Non-Exec. Member: Royal Ordnance Factories Bd, 1974-76; British Steel Corp., 1979-82. Mem., City and East London AHA, 1974-77; Governor: London Hosp., Whitechapel, 1971-74 (Special Trustee, 1974-77); St Peter's Hosps, 1973-76. *Recreation:* sailing. *Address:* 115 Clifton Hill, NW8.

MORTON, (Stephen) Alastair, TD 1949; JP; **His Honour Judge Morton;** a Circuit Judge (formerly Deputy Chairman, Greater London Quarter Sessions), since 1971; *b* 28 July 1913; *o s* of Philip Morton, Dune Gate, Dorchester; *m* 1939, Lily Yarrow Eveline, *o d* of J. S. P. Griffith-Jones, Drews, Beaconsfield, Bucks; one *s* one *d. Educ:* private sch.; Trinity Hall, Cambridge. Commnd Dorset Heavy Bde, RA, TA, 1932; served War of 1939-45, Royal Artillery. Called to the Bar, Middle Temple, 1938; Western Circuit, 1938; Master of the Bench, 1964. Counsel to the Crown at County of London Sessions, 1954-59; Central Criminal Court: First Junior Treasury Counsel, 1959-64; Senior Treasury Counsel, 1964-71; Recorder of Devizes, 1957-71; Dep.-Chm. Quarter Sessions: Dorset, 1957-71; Norfolk, 1969-71. JP Dorset, 1957. *Recreation:* painting. *Address:* 53 Eaton Terrace, SW1. *T:* 01-730 7730; Cringles, Overy Staithe, near King's Lynn, Norfolk. *T:* Burnham Market 339. *Clubs:* White's, Pratt's.

MORTON BOYD, John; *see* Boyd, J. M.

MORTON JACK, David; barrister-at-law; a Recorder of the Crown Court, since 1979; *b* 5 Nov. 1936; *o s* of late Col W. A. Morton Jack, OBE, and late Mrs Morton Jack (*née* Happell); *m* 1972, Rosemary, *o d* of Mr and Mrs F. G. Rentoul; four *s. Educ:* Stowe (scholar); Trinity Coll., Oxford (Cholmeley Schol., MA). Called to the Bar, Lincoln's Inn, 1962. 2nd Lieut, RIF, 1955-57. *Recreations:* country pursuits, reading, music, gardening. *Address:* 1 Harcourt Buildings, Temple, EC4Y 9DA; Otter House, Oddington, Oxford OX5 2RA.

MORTON-SANER, Robert, CVO 1966; CBE 1962 (OBE 1946; MBE 1941); HM Diplomatic Service, retired; *b* 30 December 1911; *o s* of late Major A. E. Saner; *m* 1943, Katharine Mary Gordon (*d* 1981); two *d. Educ:* Westminster Sch.; Christ Church, Oxford. ICS, 1935; served in United Provinces; Under Sec., Defence Department, Government of India, 1940; Deputy Secretary and Chief Administrative Officer, General Headquarters, New Delhi, 1943-45; served with Resettlement Directorate, 1945-47. Retired from Indian Civil Service and entered Foreign (subseq. Diplomatic) Service, 1947. Served in Madras, 1947-50; Foreign Office, 1950-52; Budapest, 1953-55; NATO Defence College, 1955; Counsellor and Consul-General, Djakarta, 1955-59; Counsellor, Buenos Aires, 1960-64; Consul-General, Antwerp, 1964-70. Acted as Chargé d'Affaires, 1953, 1954, 1956, 1958, 1959, 1960. Member, Skinners' Company. Commander, Order of Leopold II (Belgium). *Recreations:* gardening, old churches. *Address:* Hethe Cottage, Hethe, Oxon. *Club:* Anglo-Belgian.

MOSDELL, Lionel Patrick; Judge of the High Court of Kenya, 1966-72, Tanganyika, 1960-64; part time Chairman: National Insurance Local Tribunal, London South Region, since 1974; Immigration Appeal Tribunal, since 1975; Pensions Appeal Tribunals, since 1976; *b* 29 Aug. 1912; *s* of late William George Mosdell and late Sarah Ellen Mosdell (*née* Gardiner); *m* 1945, Muriel Jean Sillem; one *s* one *d. Educ:* Abingdon Sch.; St Edmund Hall, Oxford (MA). Solicitor, England, 1938. Served War of 1939-45, Gunner, Sussex Yeomanry RA, 1939-41; Commnd Rifle Bde, 1941; Libyan Arab Force; Force 133; No 1 Special Force; Egypt, Cyrenaica, Eritrea, Abyssinia, Italy (Capt.). Registrar of Lands and Deeds, N Rhodesia, 1946; Resident Magistrate, 1950; Senior Resident Magistrate, 1956. Barrister, Gray's Inn, 1952. Chm., Surrey and Sussex Rent Assessment Panel, 1972-82. *Recreations:* walking, cycling. *Address:* 10 Orpen Road, Hove, East Sussex BN3 6NJ. *Clubs:* Special Forces, Royal Commonwealth Society; Mombasa (Kenya).

MOSELEY, Sir George Walker, KCB 1982 (CB 1978); Permanent Secretary, Department of the Environment, since 1981; *b* 7 Feb. 1925; *o c* of late William Moseley, MBE, and Bella Moseley; *m* 1950, Anne Mercer; one *s* one *d. Educ:* High Sch., Glasgow; St Bees Sch., Cumberland; Wadham Coll., Oxford (MA). Pilot Officer, RAF Levies, Iraq, 1943-48. Asst Principal, Min. of Town and Country Planning, 1950; Asst Private Sec. to Minister of Housing and Local Govt, 1951-52; Private Sec. to Parly Sec., 1952-54; Principal Private Sec. to Minister of Housing and Local Govt, 1963-65; Asst Sec. 1965; Under-Sec. 1970-76; Dep. Sec., DoE, 1976-78, CSD, 1978-80; Second Permanent Sec., DoE, 1980-81. *Recreations:* listening to music, gardening, sitting in front of TV set. *Address:* 1 Howard Close, Hampton, Mddx. *Club:* United Oxford & Cambridge University.

MOSELEY, (Thomas) Hywel; barrister; a Recorder of the Crown Court, since 1981; *b* 27 Sept. 1936; *s* of Rev. Luther Moseley and late Megan Eiluned Moseley; *m* 1960, Monique Germaine Thérèse Drufin; three *d. Educ:* Caterham Sch.; Queens' Coll., Cambridge (LLB, MA). Called to the Bar, Gray's Inn, 1964; in private practice, Cardiff, 1965-, and London, 1977-. Lectr in Law, 1960-65, Prof. of Law, 1970-82, UCW, Aberystwyth. *Publication:* (with B. Rudden) Outline of the Law of Mortgages, 4th edn 1967. *Recreation:* bee-keeping. *Address:* Nantceiro, Llanbadarn Fawr, Aberystwyth, Dyfed SY23 3HW. *T:* Aberystwyth 3532. *Club:* Reform.

MOSER, Sir Claus (Adolf), KCB 1973; CBE 1965; FBA 1969; Vice-Chairman, N. M. Rothschild & Sons, since 1978; Director: The Economist Newspaper, and Chairman, Economist Intelligence Unit, since 1979; Equity and Law Life Assurance Society, since 1980; International Medical Statistics, Inc., since 1982; *b* Berlin, 24 Nov. 1922; *s* of late Dr Ernest Moser and Lotte Moser; *m* 1949, Mary Oxlin; one *s* two *d. Educ:* Frensham Heights Sch.; LSE, Univ. of London. RAF, 1943-46. London Sch. of Economics: Asst Lectr in Statistics, 1946-49; Lectr, 1949-55; Reader in Social Statistics, 1955-61; Prof. of Social Statistics, 1961-70; Vis. Prof. of Social Statistics, 1970-75. Dir, Central Statistical Office and Hd of Govt Statistical Service, 1967-78. Statistical Adviser, Cttee on Higher Education, 1961-64. Vis. Fellow, Nuffield Coll., Oxford, 1972-80; Chm., Bd of Dirs, Royal Opera House, Covent Garden, 1974-; Member: Governing Body, Royal Academy of Music, 1967-79; BBC Music Adv. Cttee, 1971-. Pres., Royal Statistical Soc., 1978-80. Hon. FRAM, 1970. Hon. Fellow, LSE, 1976; Hon. DSocSci Southampton, 1975; Hon. DSc: Leeds, 1977; City, 1977; Sussex, 1980; DUniv: Surrey, 1977; Keele, 1979; York, 1980; Hon. DTech Brunel, 1981. Comdr de l'Ordre National du Mérite (France), 1976. *Publications:* Measurement of Levels of Living, 1957; Survey Methods in Social Investigation, 1958; (jtly) Social Conditions in England and Wales, 1958; (jtly) British Towns, 1961; papers in statistical jls. *Recreation:* music. *Address:* 3 Regent's Park Terrace, NW1 7EE. *T:* 01-485 1619. *Club:* Garrick.

MOSES, Sir Charles (Joseph Alfred), Kt 1961; CBE 1954; Hon. Councillor, Asian Broadcasting Union, since 1977 (Secretary-General, 1965-77); General Manager, Australian Broadcasting Commission, 1935-65; Company Director; *b* 21 Jan. 1900; *s* of Joseph Moses and Lily (*née* Henderson); *m* 1922, Kathleen, *d* of Patrick O'Sullivan, Bruree, Co. Limerick; one *s* (one *d* decd). *Educ:* Oswestry Grammar Sch.; RMC Sandhurst. Lt 2nd Border Regt, 1918-22, serving in Germany and Ireland; fruitgrower, Bendigo, Australia, 1922-24; in motor business in Melbourne, 1924-30; in radio, ABC: Announcer/Commentator, 1930-32; Talks and Sporting Editor, Sydney, 1933-34; Federal Talks Controller, 1934-35. War of 1939-45 (despatches): AIF in Malaya and Singapore, Major, 1941-42, in New Guinea, Lt-Col, 1942-43. Leader of Austr. Delegn to UNESCO Annual Gen. Conf., Paris, 1952; Chm. Commonwealth Jubilee Arts Cttee, 1951; Vice-Pres., Royal Agricultural Society of NSW, 1951-; Vice-Pres., Elizabethan Theatre Trust; Remembrance Driveway (NSW). Hon. Dir, Postgraduate Med. Foundn (NSW). Member: Internat. Broadcasting Inst., London; Council, Royal NSW Instn for Deaf and Blind Children; Vice-Chm., Asian Mass Communications and Inf. Centre, Singapore; Mem., Internat. Adv. Panel, East-West Centre, Honolulu. *Publication:* Diverse Unity: a history of the Asia-Pacific Broadcasting Union 1957-77, 1978. *Recreations:* walking, tree-felling, music. *Address:* 78 New Beach Road, Darling Point, NSW 2027, Australia. *T:* 32 4224. *Clubs:* Australian, Tattersall's, Rugby Union (Sydney).

MOSES, Eric George Rufus, CB 1973; Solicitor of Inland Revenue, 1970-79; *b* 6 April 1914; *s* of Michael and Emily Moses; *m* 1940, Pearl Lipton; one *s. Educ:* University Coll. Sch., London; Oriel Coll., Oxford. Called to Bar, Middle Temple, 1938, Hon. Bencher, 1979. Served Royal Artillery, 1940-46 (Major). Asst Solicitor, Inland Revenue, 1953-65, Principal Asst Solicitor, 1965-70. *Recreations:* walking, opera. *Address:* Broome Cottage, Castle Hill, Nether Stowey, Bridgwater, Somerset.

MOSES, Very Rev. John Henry, PhD; Rector and Provost of Chelmsford Cathedral, and Director of the Cathedral Centre for Research and Training, since 1982; *b* 12 Jan. 1938; *s* of late Henry William Moses and of Ada Elizabeth Moses; *m* 1964, Susan Elizabeth (*née* Wainwright); one *s* two *d. Educ:* Ealing Grammar School; Nottingham Univ. (Gladstone Meml Prize 1958, BA History 1959, PhD 1965); Trinity Hall and Dept of Education, Cambridge (Cert. in Education 1960); Lincoln Theological Coll. Deacon 1964, priest 1965; Asst Curate, St Andrew, Bedford, 1964-70; Priest-in-Charge, St Peter, Coventry, and Rector-designate of Coventry East Team Ministry, 1970-73; Priest-in-Charge, St Mark with St Barnabas, Coventry, 1971-73; Rector of Coventry East Team Ministry, 1973-77; Rural Dean of Coventry East, 1973-77; Examining Chaplain to Bishop of Coventry, 1972-77; Archdeacon of Southend, 1977-82. Bishop of Chelmsford's Officer for Industry and Commerce, 1978-82. *Address:* The Provost's House, 3 Harling Grove, Waterloo Lane, Chelmsford, Essex. *T:* Chelmsford 354318.

MOSLEY, family name of **Baron Ravensdale.**

MOSLEY, Nicholas; *see* Ravensdale, 3rd Baron.

MOSS, Dr Alfred Allinson; Keeper of Minerals, British Museum (Natural History), 1968-74; *b* 30 Dec. 1912; *o s* of Frank Allinson and Alice Moss; *m* 1938, Sheila Mary, *o d* of Charles H. Sendell; two *d. Educ:* Ilfracombe Grammar Sch.; University Coll., Exeter. BSc London; PhD London. Chemist: War Dept, 1936; Govt Laboratory, 1937-39; Asst Keeper, Brit. Mus., 1939-40; Chemist, Chief Chemical Inspectorate, Min. of Supply, 1940-45; Asst Keeper, Brit. Mus., 1945-49; Principal Scientific Officer: Brit. Mus., 1949-53; Brit. Mus. (Nat. Hist.), 1953-59; Dep. Keeper of Minerals, Brit. Mus. (Nat. Hist.), 1959; Keeper, 1968. Treas., Mineralogical Soc., 1966-73; FSA. *Publications:* papers on archaeological and mineralogical subjects in various jls. *Recreations:* horology, chess, photography, squash rackets. *Address:* 12 Somerfields, Lyme Regis, Dorset DT7 3EZ. *T:* Lyme Regis 3443.

MOSS, Very Rev. Basil Stanley; Provost of Birmingham Cathedral since 1973; Rector, Cathedral parish of St Philip, since 1973; *b* 7 Oct. 1918; *e s* of Canon Harry George Moss and Daisy Violet (*née* Jolly); *m* 1950, Rachel

Margaret, *d* of Dr Cyril Bailey and Gemma (*née* Creighton); three *d. Educ:* Canon Slade Grammar Sch., Bolton; The Queen's Coll., Oxford. Asst Curate, Leigh Parish Church, 1943–45; Sub-Warden, Lincoln Theological Coll., 1946–51; Sen. Tutor, St Catharine's Cumberland Lodge, Windsor Gt Pk, 1951–53; Vicar of St Nathanael with St Katharine, Bristol, 1953–60; Dir, Ordination Training, Bristol Dioc., 1956–66; Residentiary Canon of Bristol Cath., 1960–66, Hon. Canon, 1966–72; Chief Secretary, Advisory Council for the Church's Ministry, 1966–72; Chaplain to Church House, Westminster, 1966–72; Examining Chaplain to Bishop of Bristol, 1956–72. Chm., Birmingham Community Relations Council, 1973–81. *Publications:* Clergy Training Today, 1964; (ed) Crisis for Baptism, 1966; (contrib.) Living the Faith, 1980. *Recreations:* walking, music. *Address:* Cathedral Office, Colmore Row, Birmingham B3 2QB. *Club:* Birmingham Rotary.

MOSS, Charles James, CBE 1977; Director, National Institute of Agricultural Engineering, 1964–77; *b* 18 Nov. 1917; *s* of James and Elizabeth Moss; *m* 1939, Joan Bernice Smith; two *d. Educ:* Queen Mary Coll., London Univ. (BSc). CEng, FIMechE. Rotol Ltd, Gloucester, 1939–43; RAE Farnborough, 1943–45; CIBA Ltd, Cambridge, 1945–51; ICI Ltd, Billingham, 1951–58; Central Engineering Estabt, NCB, Stanhope Bretby, 1958–61; Process Develt Dept, NCB, London, 1961–63; Vis. Prof., Dept of Agric. Engrg, Univ. of Newcastle upon Tyne, 1972–75; Head of Agr. Engineering Dept, Internat. Rice Res. Inst., Philippines, 1977–80; Liaison scientist and agr. engineer, Internat. Rice Res. Inst., Cairo, 1980–81. *Publications:* papers in learned jls, confs., etc. *Recreations:* gardening, walking. *Address:* Windrush, 13 Woodlands Drive, Colsterworth, near Grantham, Lincs.

MOSS, David Francis; Assistant Chief Executive, Dockyards, Ministry of Defence, Bath, since 1981; *b* 11 July 1927; *s* of Frank William and Dorothy May Moss; *m* 1950, Beryl Eloise (*née* Horsley); one *s* one *d. Educ:* Manchester Grammar Sch.; Manchester Univ. (BSc Hons MechEng); RNC Greenwich (Naval Architecture Cert.). Devonport Dockyard, 1952; Director General Ships, Bath, 1956; HM Dockyards: Gibraltar, 1961; Devonport, 1964; Singapore, 1967; Rosyth, 1969; Chatham, 1973; Rosyth, 1975; Portsmouth, 1979. *Recreations:* hill walking, handiwork. *Address:* 16 Beaufort West, Grosvenor, Bath BA1 6QB.

MOSS, David Joseph; HM Diplomatic Service; Head of Permanent Under-Secretary's Department, Foreign and Commonwealth Office, since 1981; *b* 6 Nov. 1938; *s* of Herbert Joseph and Irene Gertrude Moss; *m* 1961, Joan Lillian Moss; one *s* one *d. Educ:* Hampton Grammar Sch. CS Commn, 1956; FO, 1957; RAF, 1957–59; FO, 1959–62; Third Sec., Bangkok, 1962–65; FO, 1966–69; First Sec., La Paz, 1969–70; FCO, 1970–73; First Sec. and Head of Chancery, The Hague, 1974–77; First Sec., FCO, 1978–79, Counsellor, 1979. *Recreations:* squash, reading, listening to music. *Address:* c/o Foreign and Commonwealth Office, SW1. *T:* 01-233 3000. *Club:* Travellers'.

MOSS, Edward Herbert St George; Under-Secretary, University Grants Committee, 1971–78; *b* 18 May 1918; *s* of late Sir George Moss, KBE, HM Consular Service in China, and late Lady (Gladys Lucy) Moss; *m* 1948, Shirley Evelyn Baskett; two *s* one *d. Educ:* Marlborough; Pembroke Coll., Cambridge. Army Service in UK and Middle East, 1940–45; entered HM Foreign (subseq. Diplomatic) Service, 1945; served in Japan, FO, Belgrade (Head of Chancery 1951–55), St Louis, Detroit, FO; transf. to Home Civil Service (MoD), 1960; Asst Sec. 1961; Dept of Educn and Science, 1969. *Recreations:* writing, gardening. *Address:* Prospect, 29 Guildown Avenue, Guildford, Surrey. *T:* Guildford 66984.

MOSS, James Richard Frederick, OBE 1955; FRINA; RCNC; Founder, and Chairman, Polynous, Cambridge, since 1978; Chief Executive, Balaena Structures (North Sea), 1974–77, retired; *b* 26 March 1916; *s* of late Lt-Cdr J. G. Moss, RN, and late Kathleen Moss (*née* Steinberg); *m* 1941, Celia Florence Lucas; three *d. Educ:* Marlborough College; Trinity Coll., Cambridge (1st Cl. Hons Mech. Sci. Tripos and Maths Pt I); RCNC, 1941; Asst Constructor, Admiralty Mission, Washington, 1941–44; Constructor Commander, Admiralty Tech. Mission, Ottawa, 1944–46; Admiralty Experimental Works, Haslar, 1946–49; Constructor Comdr to C-in-C, Far East Fleet, 1949–52; Aircraft Carrier design, Admiralty, Bath, 1952–55; Chief Constructor, HM Dockyard, Singapore, 1955–58; Chief Constructor, HM Dockyard, Devonport, 1958–62; Management Techniques, Dockyard HQ, Bath, 1962–63; Asst Director, R&D, Ship Dept, Bath, 1963–65; Supt, Naval Construction Research Estab., Dunfermline, 1965–68; Dir, Naval Ship Production, 1968–74. *Recreations:* yachting and dinghies, music. *Address:* 25 Church Street, Stapleford, Cambridge CB2 5DS. *T:* Cambridge 843108. *Clubs:* Royal Naval Sailing Association; Royal Naval.

MOSS, Jane Hope; *see* Bown, J. H.

MOSS, Sir John H. T. E.; *see* Edwards-Moss.

MOSS, John Ringer, CB 1972; Deputy Secretary, Ministry of Agriculture, Fisheries and Food, 1970–80; *b* 15 Feb. 1920; 2nd *s* of late James Moss and Louisa Moss; *m* 1946, Edith Bland Wheeler; two *s* one *d. Educ:* Manchester Gram. Sch.; Brasenose Coll., Oxford (MA). War Service, mainly India and Burma, 1940–46; Capt., RE, attached Royal Bombay Sappers and Miners. Entered Civil Service (Min. of Agric., Fisheries and Food) as Asst Princ., 1947; Princ. Private Sec. to Minister of Agric., Fisheries and Food, 1959–61; Asst Sec., 1961; Under-Sec., Gen. Agricultural Policy Gp, Min. of Agric., Fisheries

and Food, 1967–70. Mem., Economic Develt Cttee for Agriculture, 1969–70. Mem. Council, RVC, 1980–. Adviser to companies in Associated British Foods Gp, 1980–; Specialist Adviser to House of Lords' Select Cttee on European Communities, 1982–. *Recreations:* music, travel. *Address:* 16 Upper Hollis, Great Missenden, Bucks. *T:* Great Missenden 2676.

MOSS, Norman J.; *see* Jordan-Moss.

MOSS, Rosalind Louisa Beaufort, FSA; Editor of Porter-Moss Topographical Bibliography of Ancient Egyptian Hieroglyphic Texts, Reliefs, and Paintings, 1924–72, retired; *b* 21 Sept. 1890; *d* of Rev. H. W. Moss, Headmaster of Shrewsbury Sch., 1866–1908. *Educ:* Heathfield Sch., Ascot; St Anne's Coll., Oxford. Diploma in Anthropology (distinction), 1917, BSc Oxon 1922. Took up Egyptology, 1917. FSA 1949. Hon. DLitt, Oxon, 1961. Hon. Fellow, St Anne's Coll., Oxford, 1967. *Publications:* Life after Death in Oceania, 1925; Topographical Bibliography (see above); articles in Journal of Egyptian Archæology, etc. *Recreation:* travel. *Address:* 51 Yew Tree Bottom Road, Epsom, Surrey KT17 3NQ.

MOSS, Stirling, OBE 1959; FIE; Racing Motorist, 1947–62, retired; Managing Director, Stirling Moss Ltd; Director: Designs Unlimited Ltd; SM Design & Interior Decorating Co.; America St Garage Ltd; Goblin Hill Hotels Ltd; Hankoe Stove Enamelling Ltd; Templar Tillers Ltd; Motoring Editor: Harpers & Queen Magazine; Penthouse UK; *b* 17 Sept. 1929; *m* 1st, 1957, Kathleen Stuart (marr. diss. 1963), *y d* of F. Stuart Moison, Montreal, Canada; 2nd, 1964, Elaine (marr. diss. 1968), 2nd *d* of A. Barbarino, New York; one *d* ; 3rd, 1980, Susan, *y d* of Stuart Paine, London; one *s. Educ:* Haileybury and Imperial Service Coll. Brit. Nat. Champion, 1950, 1951, 1952, 1954, 1955, 1956, 1957, 1958, 1959, 1961; Tourist Trophy, 1950, 1951, 1955, 1958, 1959, 1960, 1961; Coupe des Alpes, 1952, 1953, 1954; Alpine Gold Cup (three consecutive wins), 1954. Only Englishman to win Italian Mille Miglia, 1955. Competed in 494 races, rallies, sprints, land speed records and endurance runs, and won 222 of these. Successes include Targa Florio, 1955; Brit. Grand Prix, 1955, 1957; Ital. GP, 1956, 1957, 1959; NZ GP, 1956, 1959; Monaco GP, 1956, 1960, 1961; Leguna Seca GP, 1960, 1961; US GP, 1959, 1960; Aust. GP, 1956; Bari GP, 1956; Pescara GP, 1957; Swedish GP, 1957; Dutch GP, 1958; Argentine GP, 1958; Morocco GP, 1958; Buenos Aires GP, 1958; Melbourne GP, 1958; Villareal GP, 1958; Caen GP, 1958; Portuguese GP, 1959; S African GP, 1960; Cuban GP, 1960; Austrian GP, 1960; Cape GP, 1960; Watkins Glen GP, 1960; German GP, 1961; Modena GP, 1961. Twice voted Driver of the Year, 1954 and 1961. *Publications:* Stirling Moss's Book of Motor Sport, 1955; In the Track of Speed, 1957; Stirling Moss's Second Book of Motor Sport, 1958; Le Mans, 1959; My Favourite Car Stories, 1960; A Turn at the Wheel, 1961; All But My Life, 1963; Design and Behaviour of the Racing Car, 1964; How to Watch Motor Racing, 1975; *relevant publication:* Stirling Moss, by Robert Raymond, 1953. *Recreations:* snow-ski-ing, water ski-ing, dancing, spear-fishing, model making, the theatre, and designing. *Address:* (business) Stirling Moss Ltd, 46 Shepherd Street, W1; (residence) 44 Shepherd Street, W1. *Clubs:* White Elephant; British Racing Drivers', British Automobile Racing, British Racing and Sports Car, Road Racing Drivers of America, 200 mph, Lord's Taverners, Royal Automobile; Internationale des Anciens Pilotes des Grand Prix; Chm. or Pres. of 36 motoring clubs.

MOSS, Trevor Simpson, PhD; FInstP; Editor: Journal of Infra Red Physics, since 1961; Journal of Progress in Quantum Electronics, since 1978; *b* 28 Jan. 1921; *s* of William Moss and Florence Elizabeth (*née* Simpson); *m* 1948, Audrey (*née* Nelson). *Educ:* Alleynes, Uttoxeter; Downing Coll., Cambridge. MA, PhD Cantab. Research on radar, Royal Aircraft Establishment, 1941–43; research on radar and semiconductors, Telecommunications Research Estabt, 1943–53; RAE, 1953–78; Dep. Dir, Royal Signals and Radar Estabt, 1978–81. Various hon. commissions in RAF, 1942–45. Max Born Medal, German and British Physical Societies, 1975. *Publications:* Photoconductivity, 1952; Optical Properties of Semiconductors, 1959; Semiconductor Optoelectronics, 1973; Handbook of Semiconductors, 4 vols, 1980–81. *Address:* 2 Shelsley Shelsley Meadow, Colwall, Malvern, Worcs. *T:* Colwall 40079.

MOSSBAUER, Rudolf L., PhD; Professor of Experimental Physics, Technische Universität München, since 1964; *b* Munich, 31 Jan. 1929; *m* 1957, Elisabeth Pritz; one *s* two *d. Educ:* High Sch. and Inst. of Technology, Munich (equiv. Bachelor's and Master's degrees). PhD (Munich) 1958. Research Asst Max Planck Inst., Heidelberg, 1955–57; Research Fellow: Inst. of Techn., Munich, 1958–60, and at Caltech, 1960, Sen. Research Fellow, Caltech, 1961; Prof. of Experimental Physics, Munich, 1964; Dir, Institut Max von Laue-Paul Langevin, and French-German-British High-Flux-Reactor at Grenoble, 1972–77 (on leave from Munich). Member: Bavarian Acad. of Sci.; Amer. Acad. of Sci.; Amer. Acad. of Arts and Scis; Pontifical Acad.; Acad. Leopoldina, etc. Hon. degrees Oxon, Leuwen, Madrid, Grenoble, etc. Nobel Prize for Physics, 1961, and numerous other awards. Bavarian Order of Merit, 1962. *Publications:* on gamma resonance spectroscopy and on neutrino physics. *Recreations:* photography, music, archæology. *Address:* Technische Universität München, Arcisstrasse 21, 8000 Munich 2, Federal Republic of Germany.

MOSTYN, 5th Baron, *cr* 1831; **Roger Edward Lloyd Lloyd-Mostyn,** Bt 1778; MC 1943; *b* 17 April 1920; *e s* of 4th Baron Mostyn; *S* father, 1965; *m* 1943, Yvonne Margaret Stuart (marr. diss., 1957), *y d* of A. Stuart Johnston, Henshall Hall, Congleton, Cheshire; one *s* one *d*; 2nd, 1957, Mrs Sheila Edmondson Shaw, *o c* of Major Reginald Fairweather, Stockwell Manor,

Silverton, Devon, and of Mrs Fairweather, Yew Tree Cottage, Fordcombe, Kent. *Educ:* Eton; Royal Military College, Sandhurst. 2nd Lt, 9th Queen's Royal Lancers, 1939. Served War 1939-45, France, North Africa, and Italy (wounded, despatches, MC). Temp. Major, 1946. *Heir: s* Hon. Llewellyn Roger Lloyd Lloyd-Mostyn [*b* 26 Sept. 1948; *m* 1974, Denise Suzanne, *d* of Roger Duvanel; one *d. Educ:* Eton. Called to the Bar, Middle Temple, 1973]. *Address:* Mostyn Hall, Mostyn, Clwyd, North Wales. *T:* Mostyn 222.

MOSTYN, Sir Jeremy (John Anthony), 14th Bt *cr* 1670; Senior Partner, Mostyn & Co., Estate Agents, Woodstock, and Burford, Oxford; *b* 24 Nov. 1933; *s* of Sir Basil Anthony Trevor Mostyn, 13th Bt and Anita Mary, *d* of late Lt-Col Rowland Charles Feilding, DSO; *S* father 1956; *m* 1963, Cristina, *o d* of Marchese Orengo, Turin; one *s* two *d. Educ:* Rhodesia and Downside. Contested: Ealing South (L) General Election, 1959; Cities of London and Westminster, LCC Elections, 1960. Green Staff Officer, Investiture of the Prince of Wales, 1969. FRSA; AMRSH. Kt of Honour and Devotion, SMO Malta. *Recreation:* saving and restoring old houses. *Heir: s* William Basil John Mostyn, *b* 15 Oct 1975. *Address:* The Manor House, Lower Heyford, Oxon; 29 Aynhoe Road, W14.

MOSTYN, Maj.-Gen. Joseph David Frederick, CBE 1974 (MBE 1962); GOC Berlin, and Commandant, British Sector, since 1980; *b* 28 Nov. 1928; *s* of late J. P. Mostyn, Arundel, and of Mrs J. D. S. Keenan, Farnham; *m* 1952, Diana Patricia Sheridan; four *s* two *d. Educ:* Downside; RMA Sandhurst; psc, rcds. Commnd Oxf. and Bucks LI, 1948; served BAOR, Greece, Cyprus, UK, 1948-58; Canadian Army Staff Coll., 1958; 1st Green Jackets; WO, 1959-61; Co. Comdr 1st Green Jackets, Malaya, Brunei, Borneo, 1962-63 (despatches); Instructor, Staff Coll., Camberley, 1964-67; MoD, 1967-69; CO 2 RGJ, BAOR and NI, 1969-71; Comdt Officers' Wing, Sch. of Infantry, 1972; Comdr 8 Inf. Bde, NI, 1972-74; Dep. Dir Army Training, 1974-75; RCDS 1976; BGS, HQ BAOR, 1977; Dir Personal Services (Army), 1978-80. Kt SMO Malta, 1974. *Publications:* articles in mil. and RUSI jls. *Recreations:* maintaining a home for the family; all field sports. *Address:* White Ley, Uplyme, Lyme Regis, Dorset. *T:* Lyme Regis 3159. *Club:* Army and Navy.

MOTE, Harold Trevor, DL, JP; Member for Harrow East, Greater London Council, since 1965; company director, company consultant and engineer; *b* 28 Oct. 1919; *s* of late Harold Roland Mote; *m* 1944, Amplias Pamela, *d* of late Harold Johnson, Oswestry; three *s* one *d. Educ:* Upper Latymer Sch.; St Paul's Sch.; Regent Street Polytechnic; Army Staff Coll. RE, TA, 1935; served War, Royal Signals, 1940-46 (Lt-Col); Royal Signals, TA, 1954. Councillor, Harrow, 1953-67, Alderman 1967; 1st Mayor, London Bor. of Harrow, 1965-66; Opposition Leader, Harrow Council, 1971-73, Leader, 1973-77, resigned 1978. Greater London Council, 1905-: Member, Leader's Cttee, 1977-78, 1979-81 (latterly with special responsibility for Law and Order); Dep. Leader, Planning and Communications Policy Cttee, 1977-78, 1980-81; Chm., 1978-79; Chm., London Transport Cttee, 1979-81; Opposition Spokesman on Transport, 1981-82; Member: Staff Cttee, 1981-; Planning Cttee, 1981-; Shadow Leaders Cttee, 1981-82; formerly: Chm., Scrutiny Cttee; Vice-Chm., Public Services Cttee; Member: Policy and Resources Cttee; West and North Area Planning Bds; Opposition Leader, Fire Bde Cttee; Chm., W Area Planning and Transportation Sub-Cttee; Member: Finance and Estabt Cttee; Public Services and Safety Cttee. Mem., Thames Water Authority, 1973- (Chm., Personnel Sub-Cttee, 1973-; Nat. Rep. on Personnel Matters, 1973-). JP Mddx 1965; DL Greater London 1967. *Address:* Parkville House, 8 Red Lion Parade, Pinner, Mddx. *T:* 01-868 3171; Mercury, 66 Paines Lane, Pinner, Middlesex. *T:* 01-866 8500.

MOTHERWELL, Bishop of, (RC), since 1964; **Rt. Rev. Francis Thomson**; Hon. Canon of St Andrews and Edinburgh, since 1961; *b* 15 May 1917; *s* of late Francis Thomson, MA and late Winifred Mary Clare (*née* Forsyth). *Educ:* George Watson's Coll., Edinburgh; Edinburgh Univ.; Christ's Coll., Cambridge; St Edmund's Coll., Ware; Angelicum Univ., Rome. MA Edinburgh 1938; BA Cambridge 1940; Priest, 1946; STL (Angelicum, Rome) 1949. Asst Priest: St Patrick's, Kilsyth, 1946-48; St James', St Andrews, 1949-52; St Cuthbert's, Edinburgh, 1952-53; Prof. of Dogmatic Theology, St Andrew's Coll. Drygrange, Melrose, 1953-60; Rector of St Mary's Coll., Blairs, Aberdeen, 1960-64. *Address:* 17 Viewpark Road, Motherwell ML1 3ER. *T:* Motherwell 63715.

MOTT, Gregory George Sidney, CBE 1979; Managing Director, Vickers Shipbuilding Group Ltd, since 1979; *b* 11 Feb. 1925; *s* of Sidney Cyril George Mott and Elizabeth Rolinda Mott; *m* 1949, Jean Metcalfe. *Educ:* Univ. of Melbourne (BMechE Hons). Trainee Manager, Vickers Armstrong Ltd Naval Yard, 1948-49; Supervising Engr, A. E. Turner and John Coates, London, 1950-52; Sen. Draughtsman, Melbourne Harbour Trust Comrs, 1952-56; joined Vickers Armstrong Ltd, Barrow, trng on submarine construction, 1956; seconded to Naval Section Harwell, for shielding design DS/MP1 (specialised in computer technol.), 1957-59; returned to Barrow as Project Manager, Dreadnought, 1959-61; Technical Manager, Nuclear, 1961-64; Projects Controller, 1964-67; Local Dir, Vickers Ltd Shipbuilding Gp, 1966; responsible for Special Projects Div., incl. Oceanics Dept, 1968-72; Man. Dir, Vickers Oceanics Ltd, on formation of company, 1972-75; Dir, Vickers Ltd Shipbuilding Gp, and Gen. Manager, Barrow Shipbuilding Works (retained directorship, Vickers Oceanics Ltd, resigned later), 1975-77; Dir, Vickers Shipbuilding Gp Ltd, 1977; Gen. Manager and Dir, Barrow Engrg Works, Vickers Shipbuilding Gp Ltd, 1978. *Address:* Vickers Shipbuilding and

Engineering, Barrow Shipbuilding Works, Barrow in Furness, Cumbria LA14 1AB.

MOTT, John Charles Spencer, FEng, FICE, FIStructE; Chairman: French Kier Holdings Ltd, 1974 (Director, on merger, 1973); French Kier Construction Ltd; French Kier Developments Ltd; French Kier Property Investment Ltd; Kier International Ltd; French Kier Products & Services Ltd; *b* Beckenham, Kent, 18 Dec. 1926; *m* 1953, Patricia Mary (*née* Fowler); two *s. Educ:* Balgowan Central Sch., Beckenham, Kent; Brixton Sch. of Building; Battersea Polytechnic; Rutherford Coll. of Technology, Newcastle upon Tyne. Served war, Lieut, Royal Marines, 1943-46. Indentured as Engr under agreement with L. G. Mouchel & Partners, 1949-52; joined Kier Ltd, as engr, 1952; Agent on heavy civil engrg contracts, 1952-63. Director: Kier Ltd, 1963; J. L. Kier Ltd (Holding Co.), 1968. Past Member: Council, Instn Civil Engrs; Bragg Cttee of Falsework. CBIM. *Recreations:* golf, gardening. *Address:* (home) 91 Long Road, Cambridge; (office) Tempsford Hall, Sandy, Beds SG19 2BD. *T:* Bedford 55111. *Club:* Danish.

MOTT, Sir John (Harmar), 3rd Bt, *cr* 1930; Regional Medical Officer, Department of Health and Social Security; *b* 21 July 1922; *s* of 2nd Bt and Mary Katherine (*d* 1972) *d* of late Rev. A. H. Stanton; *S* father, 1964; *m* 1950, Elizabeth (*née* Carson); one *s* two *d. Educ:* Radley Coll.; New Coll., Oxford. MA Oxford, 1948; BM, BCh, 1951. Served War of 1939-45: Pilot, Royal Air Force, 1943-46. Middlesex Hospital: House Physician, 1951; House Surgeon, 1952. Mem., RCGP. *Recreations:* sailing, photography. *Heir: s* David Hugh Mott, *b* 1 May 1952. *Address:* 64 Hodge Lane, Hartford, near Northwich, Cheshire CW8 3AG. *T:* Northwich 77021.

MOTT, Michael Duncan; a Recorder of the Crown Court, since 1980; *b* 8 Dec. 1940; *s* of Francis J. Mott and Gwendolen Mott; *m* 1970, Phyllis Ann Gavin; two *s. Educ:* Rugby Sch.; Caius Coll., Cambridge (Exhibnr, MA). Called to Bar, Inner Temple, 1963; practised Midland and Oxford Circuit, 1964-69; Resident Magistrate, Kenya, 1969-71; resumed practice, Midland and Oxford Circuit, 1972; a Deputy Circuit Judge, 1976-80. *Recreations:* fencing, tennis, travel, music. *Address:* 2 Fountain Court, Steelhouse Lane, Birmingham B4 6DR. *Clubs:* Cambridge Union Society; Union and County (Worcester).

MOTT, Sir Nevill (Francis), Kt 1962; FRS 1936; MA Cantab; Cavendish Professor of Physics, Cambridge University, 1954-71; Senior Research Fellow, Imperial College, London, 1971-73, Fellow, 1978; *b* 30 Sept. 1905; *s* of C. F. Mott, late Dir of Educn, Liverpool, and Lilian Mary Reynolds; *m* 1930, Ruth Horder; two *d. Educ:* Clifton Coll.; St John's Coll., Cambridge. Lecturer at Manchester Univ., 1929-30; Fellow and Lecturer, Gonville and Caius Coll., Cambridge, 1930-33; Melville Wills Prof. of Theoretical Physics in the Univ. of Bristol, 1933-48; Henry Overton Wills Prof. and Dir of the Henry Herbert Wills Physical Laboratories, Univ. of Bristol, 1948-54. Master of Gonville and Caius Coll., Univ. of Cambridge, 1959-66. Corr. mem., Amer. Acad. of Arts and Sciences, 1954; Pres., International Union of Physics, 1951-57; Pres., Mod. Languages Assoc., 1955; Pres., Physical Soc., 1956-58; Mem. Governing Board of Nat. Inst. for Research in Nuclear Science, 1957-60; Mem. Central Advisory Council for Education for England, 1956-59; Mem. Academic Planning Cttee and Council of University Coll. of Sussex; Chm. Ministry of Education's Standing Cttee on Supply of Teachers, 1959-62; Chairman: Nuffield Foundation's Cttee on Physics Education, 1961-73; Physics Education Cttee (Royal Society and Inst. of Physics), 1965-71. Chairman, Taylor & Francis, Scientific Publishers, 1970-75, Pres., 1976-. Foreign Associate, Nat. Acad. of Sciences of USA, 1957; Hon. Member: Akademie der Naturforscher Leopoldina, 1964; Société Française de Physique, 1970; Inst. of Metals, Japan, 1975; Royal Soc. of Spain, 1978; Hon. Fellow: St John's Coll., Cambridge, 1971; UMIST, 1975; Darwin Coll., Cambridge, 1977. Hon. DSc Louvain, Grenoble, Paris, Poitiers, Bristol, Ottawa, Liverpool, Reading, Sheffield, London, Warwick, Lancaster, Heriot-Watt, Oxon, East Anglia, Bordeaux, St Andrews, Essex, William and Mary, Stuttgart, Sussex, Marburg; Hon. Doctorate of Technology, Linköping, Sweden. Hon. FInstP 1972. Hughes Medal of Royal Society, 1941; Royal Medal, 1953; Grande Médaille de la Société Française de Métallurgie, 1970; Copley Medal, 1972; Faraday Medal, IEE, 1973; (jtly) Nobel Prize for Physics, 1977. Chevalier, Ordre Nat. du Mérite, France, 1977. *Publications:* An Outline of Wave Mechanics, 1930; The Theory of Atomic Collisions (with H. S. W. Massey), 1933; The Theory of the Properties of Metals and Alloys (with H. Jones), 1936; Electronic Processes in Ionic Crystals (with R. W. Gurney), 1940; Wave Mechanics and its Applications (with I. N. Snedden), 1948; Elements of Wave Mechanics, 1952; Atomic Structure and the Strength of Metals, 1956; Electronic Processes in Non-Crystalline Materials (with E. A. Davis), 1971, 2nd edn 1979; Elementary Quantum Mechanics, 1972; Metal-Insulator Transitions, 1974; various contribs to scientific periodicals about Atomic Physics, Metals, Semi-conductors and Photographic Emulsions and Glasses. *Recreation:* photography. *Address:* The Cavendish Laboratory, Madingley Road, Cambridge CB3 0HE; 63 Mount Pleasant, Aspley Guise, Milton Keynes MK17 8JX. *Club:* Athenæum.

MOTT, Norman Gilbert, CMG 1962; retired, 1969; *b* 7 Sept. 1910; *s* of late Albert Norman Mott and late Ada Emily Kilby; *m* 1941, Betty Mary, *d* of late Sidney Hugh Breeze; two *s. Educ:* Christ's Coll., Finchley. Served in HM Forces (Intelligence Corps), 1940-47. Joined HM Diplomatic Service, 1948; served since in Foreign Office and at Trieste. *Recreations:* gardening, photography. *Address:* 34 Ferndale Road, Chichester, West Sussex. *T:* Chichester 527960.

MOTT-RADCLYFFE, Sir Charles (Edward), Kt 1957; DL; Captain Rifle Brigade, Reserve of Officers; *b* 1911; *o s* of Lt-Col C. E. Radclyffe, DSO, Rifle Brigade (killed in action 1915), Little Park, Wickham, Hants, and Theresa Caroline, *o d* of John Stanley Mott, JP, Barningham Hall, Norfolk; *m* 1940, Diana (*d* 1955), *d* of late Lt-Col W. Gibbs, CVO, 7th Hussars; three *d* ; *m* 1956, Stella, *d* of late Lionel Harrisson, Caynham Cottage, Ludlow, Salop. *Educ:* Eton; Balliol Coll., Oxford. Hon. Attaché Diplomatic Service, Athens and Rome, 1936-38; Mem. Military Mission to Greece, 1940-41; served as Liaison Officer in Syria, 1941, and with Rifle Brigade in Middle East and Italy, 1943-44; MP (C) Windsor, 1942-70; Parliamentary Private Sec. to Sec. of State for India (Rt Hon. L. S. Amery), Dec. 1944-May 1945; Junior Lord of the Treasury, May-July 1945; Conservative Whip, Aug. 1945-Feb. 1946; Chm. Conservative Parly Foreign Affairs Cttee, 1951-59. Mem., Plowden Commn on Overseas Representational Services, 1963-64. A Governor of Gresham's Sch., Holt, 1957-; Mem., Historic Buildings Council for England, 1962-70; President: Country Landowners Assoc. (Norfolk Branch), 1972-; Norfolk CCC, 1972-74 (Chm., 1976-); Royal Norfolk Show, 1979. High Sheriff, 1974, DL 1977, of Norfolk. Comdr, Order of Phoenix (Greece). *Publication:* Foreign Body in the Eye (a memoir of the Foreign Service), 1975. *Recreations:* cricket (Captain, Lords and Commons Cricket, 1952-70), shooting. *Address:* Barningham Hall, Matlaske, Norfolk. *T:* Matlaske 250; Flat 1, 38 Cadogan Square, SW1. *T:* 01-584 5834. *Clubs:* Turf, Buck's, Pratt's, MCC.

MOTTELSON, Prof. Ben R., PhD; Danish physicist; Professor, Nordic Institute for Theoretical Atomic Physics, Copenhagen, since 1957; *b* Chicago, Ill, USA, 9 July 1926; *s* of Goodman Mottelson and Georgia Mottelson (*née* Blum); *m* 1948, Nancy Jane Reno; three *c* ; became a Danish citizen, 1971. *Educ:* High Sch., La Grange, Ill; Purdue Univ. (officers' trng, USN, V12 program; BSc 1947); Harvard Univ. (grad. studies, PhD 1950). Sheldon Trav. Fellowship from Harvard at Inst. of Theoretical Physics, Copenhagen (later, the Niels Bohr Inst.), 1950-51. His Fellowship from US Atomic Energy Commn permitted continuation of work in Copenhagen for two more years, after which he held research position in CERN (European Organization for Nuclear Research) theoretical study group, formed in Copenhagen. Visiting Prof., Univ. of Calif at Berkeley, Spring term, 1959. Nobel Prize for Physics (jtly), 1975; awarded for work on theory of Atomic Nucleus, with Dr Aage Bohr (3 papers publ. 1952-53). *Publications:* Nuclear Structure, vol. I, 1969; vol. II, 1975 (with A. Bohr); contrib. Rev. Mod. Phys (jt), etc. *Address:* Nordita, Copenhagen, Denmark.

MOTTERSHEAD, Frank William, CB 1957; Deputy Secretary, Department of Health and Social Security (formerly Ministry of Health), 1965-71; *b* 7 Sept. 1911; *o s* of late Thomas Hastings and Adeline Mottershead; unmarried. *Educ:* King Edward's Sch., Birmingham; St John's Coll., Cambridge. BA 1933, MA 1973. Entered Secretary's Dept of Admiralty, 1934; Principal Private Sec. to First Lord, 1944-46; idc 1949; Under Sec., 1950; Transferred to Ministry of Defence, 1956; Deputy Sec., 1958; Deputy Under-Sec. of State, 1964. *Address:* Old Warden, Grevel Lane, Chipping Campden, Glos. *T:* Evesham 840548. *Club:* United Oxford & Cambridge University.

MOTTERSHEAD, Peter Michael Hall, QC 1979; *b* 15 Nov. 1926; *o s* of late Harry Mottershead and Constance Helen, 7th *d* of Frederick Hall, Macclesfield; *m* All Saints Day 1952, Lorna Eden, *o d* of R. W. and Lily Evans, Manchester; one *s.* *Educ:* The King's Sch., Macclesfield; Jesus Coll., Cambridge (Exhibnr 1946, BA 1951, MA 1954). National Service, 1946-48: Border Regt and RAOC, commnd 1947. Called to the Bar, Inner Temple, 1952 (Philip Teichman Schol.; Yarborough-Anderson Schol.); in practice, 1952-; Member: General Council of the Bar and of Senate of the Inns of Court and the Bar, 1971-75. *Recreations:* water colour drawing, walking, modest climbing, compulsory gardening, avoiding people. *Address:* 11 New Square, Lincoln's Inn, WC2A 3QB. *T:* 01-405 1793; Thundridge, Ware, Herts. *Club:* Reform.

MOTTISTONE, 4th Baron, *cr* 1933, of Mottistone; **David Peter Seely;** DL; Export Secretary, Cake and Biscuit Alliance, and Cocoa, Chocolate and Confectionery Alliance, since 1981; *b* 16 Dec. 1920; 4th *s* of 1st Baron Mottistone; *S* half brother, 1966; *m* 1944, Anthea, *er d* of T. V. W. McMullan, Bangor, Co. Down, N Ireland; two *s* two *d* (and one *d* decd). *Educ:* RN Coll., Dartmouth. Convoy escorting, Atlantic and Mediterranean, 1941-44; qualified in Communications, 1944; Served in Pacific, 1945; in comd HMS Cossack, FE Flt, 1958-59; in comd HMS Ajax and 24th Escort Sqdn, FE Flt (offensive ops against Indonesian confrontation), 1963-65; Naval Advr to UK High Comr, Ottawa, 1965-66; retired at own request as a Captain, 1967. Dir of Personnel and Training, Radio Rentals Gp, 1967-69; Dir, Distributive Industry Trng Bd, 1969-75; Dir, Cake and Biscuit Alliance, 1975-81. FIERE; FIPM; FBIM. DL Isle of Wight, 1981. *Recreation:* yachting. *Heir: s* Hon. Peter John Philip Seely [*b* 29 Oct. 1949; *m* 1st, 1972, Joyce Cairns (marr. diss. 1975); one *s* ; 2nd, 1982, Linda, *d* of W. Swain, Bulphan Fen, Essex]. *Address:* The Old Parsonage, Mottistone, Isle of Wight. *Clubs:* Royal Commonwealth Society; Royal Yacht Squadron, Royal Cruising, Island Sailing, Royal Navy Sailing Association.

MOTTRAM, Maj.-Gen. John Frederick, OBE 1969; MVO 1976; Major-General Training and Reserve Forces Royal Marines, since 1980; *b* 9 June 1930; *s* of Frederick Mottram and Margaret Mottram (*née* Butcher); *m* 1956, Jennifer Thomas; one *s* one *d.* *Educ:* Enfield Central Sch.; Enfield Technical Coll. Joined RM, 1948; 42 Commando, Malaya, ME, 1951-54; Special Boat Squadron, 1955-56; HMS Loch Lomond, Persian Gulf, 1957-58; Adjutant, Commando Trng Centre, 1959-62; Student, Army Staff Coll., 1963; Staff of CGRM and RM Equerry to HRH The Duke of Edinburgh, 1964-65; Bde Major, 3 Commando Bde, Far East, 1966-68; Directing Staff, Army Staff Coll., 1969-71; CO, 40 Commando, NI and Plymouth, 1972-74 (mentioned in Despatches, 1973); Student, Naval War Coll., 1974; Jt Warfare Attaché, British Embassy, Washington DC, 1974-77; Col GS, DCGRM and RM ADC to HM The Queen, 1978-80; Maj.-Gen., 1980. *Recreation:* fishing. *Clubs:* Army and Navy, Pall Mall.

MOTYER, Rev. John Alexander; Minister of Christchurch, Westbourne, Bournemouth, since 1981; *b* 30 Aug. 1924; *s* of Robert Shankey and Elizabeth Maud Motyer; *m* 1948, Beryl Grace Mays; two *s* one *d.* *Educ:* High Sch., Dublin; Dublin Univ. (MA, BD); Wycliffe Hall, Oxford. Curate: St Philip, Penn Fields, Wolverhampton, 1947-50; Holy Trinity, Old Market, Bristol, 1950-54; Tutor, Clifton Theol Coll., Bristol, 1950-54, Vice-Principal, 1954-65; Vicar, St Luke's, Hampstead, 1965-70; Dep. Principal, Tyndale Hall, Bristol, 1970-71; Principal and Dean of College, Trinity Coll., Bristol, 1971-81. *Publications:* The Revelation of the Divine Name, 1959; After Death, 1965; The Richness of Christ (Epistle to the Philippians), 1966; The Tests of Faith (Epistle of James), 1970, 2nd edn 1975; (Old Testament Editor) New Bible Commentary Revised, 1970; The Day of the Lion (Amos), 1975; The Image of God: Law and Liberty in Biblical Ethics (Laing Lecture), 1976; contributor: New Bible Dictionary; Expositor's Bible Commentary; Law and Life (monograph); New International Dictionary of New Testament Theology. *Recreations:* reading, odd-jobbing. *Address:* Christ Church Vicarage, 43 Branksome Dene Road, Bournemouth BH4 8JW. *T:* Bournemouth 762164.

MOTZ, Prof. Hans; Professor of Engineering, University of Oxford, 1972-77, now Emeritus; Emeritus Fellow of St John's College, Oxford and St Catherine's College, Oxford; Honorary Professor, Technical University, Vienna, since 1980; Hon. Consultant, Culham Laboratory, United Kingdom Atomic Energy Authority; *b* 1 Oct. 1909; *s* of Karl and Paula Motz; *m* 1959, Lotte Norwood-Edlis; one *d.* *Educ:* Technische Hochschule, Vienna; Besançon Univ. (Schol.); Trinity Coll., Dublin (Schol.). Dipl. Ing 1932, Dr Techn. Sc. 1935, MSc TCD, MA Oxon; FInstP. Research Engr, Standard Telephones & Cables, 1939-41; Demonstrator, Dept of Engrg Science, Oxford, 1941; Lectr in Engrg Physics, Sheffield Univ., 1946-48; Research Assoc., Microwave Lab., Stanford Univ., 1949; Donald Pollock Reader in Engrg Science, Oxford, 1954; Professorial Fellow, St Catherine's Coll., Oxford, 1963. Internat. Fellow, Stanford Res. Inst., 1956; Guest Prof., Paris Univ. (Saclay), 1964; Visiting Professor: Brown Univ., 1959; Brooklyn Polytech., 1965; Innsbruck Univ., 1967; Tech. Univ., Vienna, 1979-80 (permanent Hon. Prof., 1980). Ehrenkreuz für Wissenschaft und Kunst, 1st class (Austria), 1980. *Publications:* Problems of Microwave Theory, 1951; The Physics of Laser Fusion, 1979; many papers in sci. jls. *Recreations:* ski-ing, yachting, silversmith, and enamel work. *Address:* 16 Bedford Street, Oxford. *T:* Oxford 41895.

MOULE, Rev. Prof. Charles Francis Digby, FBA 1966; Lady Margaret's Professor of Divinity in the University of Cambridge, 1951-76; Fellow of Clare College, Cambridge, since 1944; Canon Theologian (non-residentiary) of Leicester, 1955-76, Canon Emeritus, since 1976; Honorary Member of Staff, Ridley Hall, Cambridge, 1976-80; *b* 3 Dec. 1908; *s* of late Rev. Henry William Moule and Laura Clements Pope; unmarried. *Educ:* Weymouth Coll., Dorset; Emmanuel Coll., Cambridge (scholar) (Hon. Fellow 1972); Ridley Hall, Cambridge. 1st Cl. Classical Tripos Part I, 1929; BA (1st Cl. Classical Tripos Part II), 1931; Evans Prize, 1931; Jeremie Septuagint Prize, 1932; Crosse Scholarship, 1933; MA 1934. Deacon, 1933, priest, 1934; Curate, St Mark's, Cambridge, and Tutor of Ridley Hall, 1933-34; Curate, St Andrew's, Rugby, 1934-36; Vice-Principal, Ridley Hall, 1936-44, and Curate of St Mary the Great, Cambridge, 1936-40. Dean of Clare Coll., Cambridge, 1944-51; Faculty Asst Lecturer in Divinity in the Univ. of Cambridge, 1944-47; Univ. Lecturer, 1947-51. Burkitt Medal for Biblical Studies, British Acad., 1970. Hon. DD Univ. of St Andrews, 1958. *Publications:* An Idiom Book of New Testament Greek, 1953; The Meaning of Hope, 1953; The Sacrifice of Christ, 1956; Colossians and Philemon (Cambridge Greek Testament Commentary), 1957; Worship in the New Testament, 1961; The Birth of the New Testament, 1962, 3rd edn 1981; The Phenomenon of the New Testament, 1967; (co-editor) Christian History and Interpretation, 1968; The Origin of Christology, 1977 (Collins Theological Book Prize, 1977); The Holy Spirit, 1978; contrib., Encyclopædia Britannica, Interpreter's Dictionary of the Bible, Biblisch-Historisches Handwörterbuch. *Address:* 1 King's Houses, Pevensey, East Sussex.

MOULE-EVANS, David, DMus Oxon; Composer; Conductor; Professor of Harmony, Counterpoint and Composition, Royal College of Music, 1945-74; *b* 21 Nov. 1905; *s* of John Evans, MA Cantab, and Emily Blanche Evans (*née* Cookson); *m* 1935, Monica Warden Evans, *d* of Richardson Evans, ICS; no *c.* *Educ:* The Judd Sch.; Royal College of Music. Mem. of Queen's Coll., Oxford. Open Scholarship in Composition, RCM, 1925 (Senior Composition Scholar); Mendelssohn Scholarship, 1928; DMus Oxford, 1930. Carnegie

Publication Award (for Concerto for String Orchestra), 1928. Symphony in G Major awarded £1,000 Prize offered by Australian Govt, 1952. Many public and broadcast performances of orchestral and other works. *Publications: published orchestral works include:* Overture: The Spirit of London, 1947; Vienna Rhapsody, 1948; The Haunted Place (for String Orchestra), 1949; Old Tupper's Dance, 1951; chamber works: instrumental pieces and songs. *Recreations:* reading and studying subjects other than music; perambulating the countryside and looking at old churches. *Address:* Bracken, 44 Deepdene Avenue, Dorking, Surrey RH5 4AE. *T:* Dorking 880294.

MOULTON, Alexander Eric, CBE 1976; RDI; FEng; Managing Director, Moulton Developments Ltd, since 1956; *b* 9 April 1920; *s* of John Coney Moulton, DSc, The Hall, Bradford-on-Avon, and Beryl Latimer Moulton. *Educ:* Marlborough Coll.; King's Coll., Cambridge (MA). Bristol Aeroplane Co., 1939-44: Engine Research Dept; George Spencer, Moulton & Co. Ltd, 1945-56; became Techn. Dir; estab. Research Dept (originated work on rubber suspensions for vehicles, incl. own design Flexitor); formed Moulton Developments Ltd, 1956 to do develt work on own designs of rubber suspensions for BLMC incl. Hydrolastic and Hydragas (Queen's Award to Industry, 1967); formed Moulton Bicycles Ltd to produce own design Moulton Bicycle, 1962 (Design Centre Award, 1964); designer of Moulton Coach, 1968-70. RDI 1968; FRSA 1968; FEng 1980. Hon. Dr, RCA, 1967; Hon. DSc Bath, 1971. SIAD Design Medal, 1976; (jointly): James Clayton Prize, Crompton-Lanchester Medal, and Thomas Hawksley Gold Medal, IMechE, 1979. *Publications:* numerous articles and papers on engineering and education. *Recreations:* canoeing, steam boating, shooting. *Address:* The Hall, Bradford-on-Avon, Wilts. *T:* Bradford-on-Avon 2991. *Clubs:* Brooks's; Royal Southern Yacht (Hamble).

MOULTON, Maj.-Gen. James Louis, CB 1956; DSO 1944; OBE 1950; retired; *b* 3 June 1906; *s* of Capt. J. D. Moulton, RN; *m* 1937, Barbara Aline (*née* Coode); one *s* one *d. Educ:* Sutton Valence Sch. Joined Royal Marines, 1924; Pilot, Fleet Air Arm, 1930; Staff Coll., Camberley, 1938; served War of 1939-45: GSO3 GHQ, BEF, 1940; GSO1, Force 121 (Madagascar), 1942; Commanding Officer, 48 Commando, NW Europe, 1944-45 (DSO); Comd 4th Commando Bde, NW Europe, 1945; CO Commando Sch., 1947-49; Comd 3rd Commando Bde, Middle East, 1952-54; Maj.-Gen. Royal Marines, Portsmouth, 1954-57; Chief of Amphibious Warfare, 1957-61. Rep. Col Comdt RM, 1971-72. Editor, Brassey's Annual, 1969-73. *Publications:* Haste to the Battle, 1963; Defence in a Changing World, 1964; The Norwegian Campaign of 1940, 1966; British Maritime Strategy in the 1970s, 1969; The Royal Marines, 1972; Battle for Antwerp, 1978. *Address:* Fairmile, Woodham Road, Woking, Surrey GU21 4DN. *T:* Woking 5174.

MOULTON, Air Vice-Marshal Leslie Howard, CB 1971; DFC 1941; with The Plessey Co., since 1971; *b* 3 Dec. 1915; *s* of late Peter Moulton, Nantwich, Cheshire; *m* Lesley, *d* of late P. C. Clarke, Ilford; two *s* two *d. Educ:* Nantwich and Acton School. Joined RAF, 1932; served War of 1939-45. Pilot; Operations with 14 Sqdn in Africa, 1940-42; CFS, 1942-44; specialised in Signals, 1945; Staff Coll., 1950; USAF, Strategic Air Comd, 1954-56; Dep. Dir Radio, Air Min., 1958-61; Comdt RAF Cosford, 1961-63; CSO Fighter Comd, 1963-65; Min. of Technology, 1965-68. Wing Comdr 1955; Gp Captain 1959; Air Cdre 1964; Air Vice-Marshal 1969; AOC No 90 (Signals) Group, RAF, 1969-71; retired 1971. FIERE, CEng, 1959; FRSA, 1974. *Recreations:* gardening, golf, hill walking. *Address:* Hill Top, Reeth, near Richmond, N Yorks. *T:* Richmond 84320. *Club:* Royal Air Force.

MOUND, Laurence Alfred, DSc; FRES; Keeper of Entomology, British Museum (Natural History), since 1981; *b* 22 April 1934; *s* of John Henry Mound and Laura May Cape; *m* 1958, Agnes Jean Solari; one *s* two *d. Educ:* Warwick Sch.; Sir John Cass Coll., London; Imperial Coll., London (DIC); DSc London; Imperial Coll. of Tropical Agriculture, Trinidad (DipTropAgric). Nigerian Federal Dept of Agricl Research, 1959-61; Empire Cotton Growing Corp., Republic of Sudan, 1961-64; Sen. Scientific Officer, BM (NH), 1964-69; Australian CSIRO Research Award, 1967-68; PSO, 1969-75, Dep. Keeper, Dept of Entomology, BM (NH), 1975-81. Editor, Jl of Royal Entomological Soc. of London, 1973-81 (Vice-Pres., RES, 1975-76). Numerous expedns studying thrips in tropical countries. *Publications:* over 70 technical books and papers on biology of thrips and whitefly, particularly in Bull. of BM (NH), incl. Whitefly of the World (with S. H. Halsey). *Recreations:* thrips with everything. *Address:* c/o British Museum (Natural History), Cromwell Road, SW7. *T:* 01-589 6323.

MOUND, Trevor Ernest John, OBE 1977; HM Diplomatic Service; Counsellor (Economic), British Embassy Oslo, since 1981; *b* 27 July 1930; *e s* of late Harvey Mound and late Margaret Webb; *m* 1955, Patricia Kathleen de Burgh (marr. diss. 1972); two *s. Educ:* Royal Grammar Sch., Worcester; RMA Sandhurst; Univs of London and Hong Kong. 2nd Lt, Worcs Regt (Malayan Campaign), 1951-54; Parachute Regt (ME), 1954-56; Adjutant, Airborne Forces, 1956-58; GSO 3, 16 Parachute Bde (ME), 1958-60; MoD, 1965-67; retired 1967; joined HM Diplomatic Service, 1967; First Secretary and Head of Chancery: Luxembourg, 1969-71; Calcutta, 1971-73; FCO, 1973-76; Beirut, 1976-77; Counsellor (Commercial), Peking, 1978-81. *Recreation:* yoga. *Address:* c/o Foreign and Commonwealth Office, SW1A 2AH. *Club:* Bell (Peking).

MOUNSEY, John Patrick David, MA, MD, FRCP; Provost, Welsh National School of Medicine, 1969-79, retired; *b* 1 Feb. 1914; *s* of late John

Edward Mounsey and late Christine Frances Trail Robertson; *m* 1947, Vera Madeline Sara King; one *s* one *d. Educ:* Eton Coll.; King's Coll., Cambridge; King's Coll. Hosp., London. Sherbrook Res. Fellow, Cardiac Dept, London Hosp., 1951; Royal Postgraduate Medical School: Lectr, 1960; Sen. Lectr and Sub-Dean, 1962; Cons. Cardiologist, Hammersmith Hosp., 1960; Dep. Dir, British Postgrad. Med. Fedn, 1967; Member: GMC, 1970-79; GDC, 1973; Council, St David's University Coll., Lampeter, 1975-; South Glamorgan AHA (T); British Cardiac Soc.; Assoc. of Physicians; Soc. of Physicians in Wales. Corresp. Mem., Australasian Cardiac Soc.; late Asst Ed., British Heart Jl. Hon. LLD Wales, 1980. *Publications:* articles on cardiology mainly in British Heart Jl. *Recreations:* painting, gardening, music. *Address:* Esk House, Coombe Terrace, Wotton-under-Edge, Glos GL12 7NA. *T:* Wotton-under-Edge 2792. *Club:* Athenæum.

MOUNT, Air Cdre Christopher John, CBE 1956; DSO 1943; DFC 1940; retired; *b* 14 Dec. 1913; *s* of Capt. F. Mount; *m* 1947, Audrey Mabel Clarke; two *s. Educ:* Eton; Trinity Coll., Oxford. Royal Auxiliary Air Force, 1935; Royal Air Force, 1938. Consultant, C. R. Thomas & Son, Solicitors, Maidenhead (partner, 1970-79). *Address:* Garden House, Bagshot Road, Sunninghill, Ascot, Berks.

MOUNT, Ferdinand; *see* Mount, W. R. F.

MOUNT, Sir James (William Spencer), Kt 1979; CBE 1965; BEM 1946; *b* 8 Nov. 1908; *s* of Spencer William Mount and Kathleen Mount (*née* Ashenden); *m* 1931, Margaret Geikie (*d* 1973); one *s* three *d; m* 1975, Jane Mount. *Educ:* Tonbridge School. Chairman and Director, S. W. Mount & Sons Ltd, 1944-. Chairman: Horticultural Advisory Cttee, MAFF, 1963-69; National Fruit Trials Advisory Cttee, MAFF, 1973-78; Governing Body, E Malling Res. Station, 1960-80. *Recreations:* fishing, gardening. *Address:* Woolton Farm, Bekesbourne, Canterbury, Kent. *T:* Canterbury 830202. *Club:* Farmers'.

MOUNT, Sir William (Malcolm), 2nd Bt, *cr* 1921; Lieutenant-Colonel Reconnaissance Corps; *b* 28 Dec. 1904; *s* of Sir William Mount, 1st Bt, CBE, and Hilda Lucy Adelaide (*d* 1950), OBE, *y d* of late Malcolm Low of Clatto, Fife; *S* father, 1930; *m* 1929, Elizabeth Nance, *o d* of Owen John Llewellyn, Badminton Vicarage, Glos; three *d. Educ:* Eton; New Coll., Oxford. Berkshire: DL 1946; High Sheriff, 1947-48; Vice-Lieutenant, 1960-76. *Recreations:* fishing, shooting. *Heir: nephew* William Robert Ferdinand Mount, *qv. Address:* Wasing Place, Aldermaston, Berks.
See also Sir W. S. Dugdale, Bt.

MOUNT, (William Robert) Ferdinand; Head of Prime Minister's Policy Unit, since 1982; *b* 2 July 1939; *s* of late Robin and Lady Julia Mount; *heir pres.* to Sir William Mount, *qv; m* 1968, Julia Margaret, *d* of late Archibald Julian and Hon. Mrs Lucas; two *s* one *d* (and one *s* decd). *Educ:* Eton; Christ Church, Oxford. Has worked for Sunday Telegraph, Conservative Research Dept, Daily Sketch, National Review, Daily Mail; Political Columnist: The Spectator, 1977-82; The Standard, 1980-82. *Publications:* Very Like a Whale, 1967; The Theatre of Politics, 1972; The Man Who Rode Ampersand, 1975; The Clique, 1978; The Subversive Family, 1982. *Address:* 17 Ripplevale Grove, N1. *T:* 01-607 5398.

MOUNT CHARLES, Earl of; Henry Vivian Pierpoint Conyngham; *b* 23 May 1951; *s* and *heir* of 7th Marquess Conyngham, *qv; m* 1971, Juliet Ann, *yr d* of Robert Kitson; one *s* one *d. Educ:* Harrow; Harvard Univ. *Heir: s* Viscount Slane, *qv. Address:* Slane Castle, Co. Meath, Eire. *Club:* Kildare Street and University (Dublin).

MOUNT EDGCUMBE, 7th Earl of, *cr* 1789; **Edward Piers Edgcumbe;** Viscount Mount Edgcumbe and Valletort, 1781; Baron Edgcumbe of Mount Edgcumbe, Co. Cornwall (UK), 1742; *b* 13 July 1903; *s* of George Valletort Edgcumbe (*d* 1947) and Georgina Mildred (*d* 1941), *d* of T. A. Bell; *S* cousin 1965; *m* 1944, Victoria Effie Warbrick (widow) (*d* 1979), *y d* of late Robert Campbell, N Ireland and NZ. *Heir: nephew* Robert Charles Edgcumbe [*b* 1 June 1939; *m* 1960; five *d*]. *Address:* Mount Edgcumbe, Plymouth.

MOUNTAIN, Sir Denis Mortimer, 3rd Bt *cr* 1922; Chairman and Managing Director: Eagle Star Insurance Co. Ltd, since 1974; Eagle Star Holdings plc, since 1979; Chairman, Eagle Star Insurance Co. of America, since 1978; *b* 2 June 1929; *er s* of Sir Brian Edward Stanley Mountain, 2nd Bt, and of Doris Elsie, *e d* of late E. C. E. Lamb; *S* father, 1977; *m* 1958, Hélène Fleur Mary Kirwan-Taylor; two *s* one *d. Educ:* Eton. Late Lieut, Royal Horse Guards. Chairman: Australian Eagle Insurance Co. Ltd; South African Eagle Insurance Co. Ltd, and other companies both in UK and overseas; Pres., Compagnie de Bruxelles Risques Divers S.A. d'Assurances (Belgium); Director: Rank Organisation Ltd; Grovewood Securities Ltd (Dep. Chm.); Philip Hill Investment Trust plc; Bank of Nova Scotia (Toronto) and other UK and overseas companies. *Recreations:* fishing, shooting. *Heir: s* Edward Brian Stanford Mountain, *b* 19 March 1961. *Address:* Shawford Park, Shawford, near Winchester, Hants. *T:* Twyford 712289; 12 Queens Elm Square, Old Church Street, Chelsea SW3 6ED. *T:* 01-352 4331.

MOUNTBATTEN, family name of Marquess of Milford Haven.

MOUNTBATTEN OF BURMA, Countess (2nd in line) *cr* 1947; **Patricia Edwina Victoria Knatchbull;** CD; JP, DL; Viscountess Mountbatten of

Burma, 1946; Baroness Romsey, 1947; *b* 14 Feb. 1924; *er d* of Admiral of the Fleet 1st Earl Mountbatten of Burma, KG, GCB, OM, GCSI, GCIE, GCVO, DSO, PC, FRS, and Countess Mountbatten of Burma, CI, GBE, DCVO, LLD (*d* 1960) (Hon. Edwina Cynthia Annette Ashley, *e d* of 1st Baron Mount Temple, PC); *S* father, 1979; *m* 1946, Baron Brabourne, *qv* ; four *s* two *d* (and one *s* decd). *Educ:* Malta, England and New York City. Served War in WRNS, 1943-46. Colonel-in-Chief, Princess Patricia's Canadian Light Infantry, 1974. Vice-Chm. of Council, BRCS; Dep. Vice-Chm., NSPCC; Chm., Sir Ernest Cassel Educational Trust. President: WES/PNEU; SOS Children's Villages; Friends of Cassel Hosp.; Friends of William Harvey Hosp.; Kent Branches of NSPCC, Save the Children Fund and Marriage Guidance Council. Vice-President: FPA; Nat. Childbirth Trust; SSAFA; RLSS; Shaftesbury Soc. Patron, Commando Assoc.; Vice-Patron, Burma Star Assoc. Governor: Ashford School, Kent; Caldecott Community. Mem. British Legion, WI and other local orgns. JP 1971, DL 1973, Kent. DStJ 1981. *Heir: s* Lord Romsey, *qv. Address:* Newhouse, Mersham, Ashford, Kent TN25 6NQ. *T:* Ashford 23466; 39 Montpelier Walk, SW7 1JH. *T:* 01-589 8829.

MOUNTEVANS, 3rd Baron *cr* 1945, of Chelsea; **Edward Patrick Broke Evans;** Promotion Services Manager, British Tourist Authority, since 1976; *b* 1 Feb. 1943; *s* of 2nd Baron Mountevans and of Deirdre Grace, *d* of John O'Connell, Cork; *S* father, 1974; *m* 1973, Johanna Keyzer, *d* of late Antonius Franciscus Keyzer, The Hague. *Educ:* Rugby; Trinity Coll., Oxford. Reserve Army Service, 1961-66; 74 MC Regt RCT, AER; Lt 1964. Joined management of Consolidated Gold Fields Ltd, 1966; British Tourist Authority, 1972: Manager, Sweden and Finland, 1973; Head of Promotion Services, 1976. *Heir: b* Hon. Jeffrey de Corban Richard Evans [*b* 13 May 1948; *m* 1972, Juliet, *d* of Baron Moran, *qv* ; two *s*]. *Address:* 86 Portland Place, W1N 3HA.

MOUNTFIELD, Alexander Stuart; *b* 5 Dec. 1902; *s* of Robert Mountfield and Caroline (*née* Appleyard); *m* 1934, Agnes Elizabeth Gurney; two *s. Educ:* Merchant Taylors' Sch., Crosby. Entered service of Mersey Docks and Harbour Board as Apprentice, 1918; served through clerical grades and in various administrative capacities. Gen. Man. and Sec., Mersey Docks and Harbour Bd, 1957-62; retd 1962. FCIT. *Recreations:* gardening, reading. *Address:* Lanthwaite, Hightown, near Liverpool. *T:* 051-929 2115. *Club:* Athenæum (Liverpool).

See also P. Mountfield, R. Mountfield.

MOUNTFIELD, Peter; Under Secretary, HM Treasury, since 1980; *b* 2 April 1935; *s* of Alexander Stuart Mountfield, *qv* ; *m* 1958, Evelyn Margaret Smithies; three *s. Educ:* Merchant Taylors' Sch., Crosby; Trinity Coll., Cambridge (BA); Graduate Sch. of Public Admin., Harvard. RN, 1953-55. Asst Principal, HM Treasury, 1958; Principal, 1963; Asst Sec., 1970; Under Sec., Cabinet Office, 1977. *Recreations:* reading, walking, looking at buildings. *Address:* 42 Lambardes, New Ash Green, near Dartford, Kent DA3 8HX. *T:* Ash Green 873677.

See also R. Mountfield.

MOUNTFIELD, Robin; Under Secretary, Vehicle Division, Department of Industry, since 1980; *b* 16 Oct. 1939; *s* of Alexander Stuart Mountfield, *qv* ; *m* 1963, Anne Newsham; two *s* one *d. Educ:* Merchant Taylors' Sch., Crosby; Magdalen Coll., Oxford (BA). Assistant Principal, Ministry of Power, 1961, Principal, 1965; Private Sec. to Minister for Industry, 1973-74; Asst Sec., Dept of Industry, 1974: Air Division, 1974-77; seconded to Stock Exchange, 1977-78; Industrial and Commercial Policy Div., 1978-80. *Address:* 10 Oakcroft Road, SE13 7ED. *T:* 01-852 7141.

See also Peter Mountfield.

MOUNTFORT, Guy Reginald, OBE 1970; retired as Director, Ogilvy & Mather International Inc., New York (1964-66); and as Managing Director, Ogilvy and Mather Ltd, London (1964-66); *b* 4 Dec. 1905; *s* of late Arnold George Mountfort, artist, and late Alice Edith (*née* Hughes); *m* 1931, Joan Hartley (*née* Pink); two *d. Educ:* Grammar Sch. General Motors Corporation (France), 1928-38. War service, 1939-46, 12 Regt HAC and British Army Staff (Washington) Lt-Col; service in N Africa, Italy, Burma, Pacific, Germany. Procter & Gamble Inc., USA, 1946-47; Mather & Crowther Ltd, 1947, Dir, 1949; Vice-Chm., Dollar Exports Bd Advertising Cttee, 1948-49. Hon. Sec., Brit. Ornithologists' Union, 1952-62, Pres. 1970-75 (Union Medal, 1967); Leader of scientific expedns to Coto Doñana, 1952, 1955, 1956; Bulgaria, 1960; Hungary, 1961; Jordan, 1963, 1965; Pakistan, 1966, 1967. Trustee, World Wildlife Fund (Gold Medal, 1978); Scientific FZS (Stamford Raffles Award, 1969). Medal of Société d'Acclimatation, 1936. Commander, Order of the Golden Ark, Netherlands, 1980. *Publications:* A Field Guide to the Birds of Europe (co-author), 1954; The Hawfinch, 1957; Portrait of a Wilderness, 1958; Portrait of a River, 1962; Portrait of a Desert, 1965; The Vanishing Jungle, 1969; Tigers, 1973; So Small a World, 1974; Back from the Brink, 1977; Saving the Tiger, 1981; contribs to ornithological and other scientific jls; television and radio broadcasts on ornithology and exploration. *Recreations:* ornithology, gardening, photography, travel. *Address:* Hurst Oak, Sandy Lane, Lyndhurst, Hants. *T:* Lyndhurst 2462.

MOUNTGARRET, 17th Viscount (Ireland) *cr* 1550; Baron (UK) *cr* 1911; **Richard Henry Piers Butler;** *b* 8 Nov. 1936; *s* of 16th Viscount; *S* father, 1966; *heir-pres.* to earldoms of Marquess of Ormonde, *qv* ; *m* 1st, 1960, Gillian Margaret (marr. diss. 1970), *o d* of Cyril Francis Stuart Buckley, London, SW3; two *s* one *d* ; 2nd, 1970, Mrs Jennifer Susan Melville Fattorini, *yr d* of

Captain D. M. Wills, Barley Wood, Wrington, near Bristol. *Educ:* Eton; RMA, Sandhurst. Commissioned, Irish Guards, 1957; retd rank Capt., 1964. *Recreations:* shooting, stalking, cricket, golf. *Heir: s* Hon Piers James Richard Butler, *b* 15 April 1961. *Address:* Stainley House, South Stainley, Harrogate, Yorks. *T:* Harrogate 770087; 29 Trevor Place, SW7. *T:* 01-589 9846. *Clubs:* White's, Pratt's.

MOURANT, Arthur Ernest, DM, FRCP; FRS 1966; formerly Director, Serological Population Genetics Laboratory; Conseiller Scientifique Etranger, Institut d'Hématologie, Immunologie et Génétique Humaine, Toulouse, since 1974; *b* 11 April 1904; *er s* of Ernest Charles Mourant and Emily Gertrude (*née* Bray); *m* 1978, Mrs Jean E. C. Shimell. *Educ:* Victoria Coll., Jersey; Exeter Coll., Oxford; St Bartholomew's Hosp. Medical Coll. London. BA 1925, DPhil (Geol.) 1931, MA 1931, BM, BCh 1943, DM 1948, Oxford; FRCP 1960; FRCPath 1963. 1st cl. hons Chem., 1926; Sen. King Charles I Schol., Exeter Coll., Oxford, 1926; Burdett-Coutts Schol., Oxford Univ., 1926. Demonstrator in Geology, Univ. of Leeds, 1928-29; Geol Survey of Gt Brit., 1929-31; teaching posts, 1931-34; Dir, Jersey Pathological Lab., 1935-38; Med. Student, 1939-43; House med. appts, 1943-44; Med. Off., Nat. Blood Transfusion Service, 1944-45; Med. Off., Galton Lab. Serum Unit, Cambridge, 1945-46; Dir, Blood Gp Reference Lab., Min. of Health and MRC, 1946-65 (Internat. Blood Gp Reference Lab., WHO, 1952-65); Hon. Adviser, Nuffield Blood Gp Centre, 1952-65; Hon. Sen. Lectr in Haematology, St Bartholomew's Hospital Medical Coll., 1965-77. Visiting Professor: Columbia Univ., 1953; Collège de France, 1978-79. Marett Meml Lectr, Exeter Coll., Oxford, 1978. Pres., Section H (Anthropology), Brit. Assoc., 1956; Vice-Pres., Mineralogical Soc., 1971-73; Mem. Hon., Société Jersiaise (Vice-Pres., 1977-80); Corresp. Mem., Académie des Sciences, Inscriptions et Belles-Lettres, Toulouse; Honorary Member: Internat. Soc. of Blood Transfusion; British Soc. for Haematology; Peruvian Pathological Soc.; Soc. for Study of Human Biol. (Vice-Pres., 1960-63). Past or present Mem. Ed. Bd of eight British, foreign and internat. scientific jls. Oliver Meml Award, 1953; Huxley Memorial Medal, Royal Anthropological Institute, 1961; Landsteiner Meml Award, Amer. Assoc. of Blood Banks, 1973; Osler Meml Medal, Univ. of Oxford, 1980; R. H. Worth Prize, Geolog. Soc., 1982. *Publications:* The Distribution of the Human Blood Groups, 1954, (jtly) 2nd edn, 1976; (jtly) The ABO Blood Groups: Comprehensive Tables and Maps of World Distribution, 1958; (ed jtly) Man and Cattle, 1963; (jtly) Blood Groups and Diseases, 1977; (jtly) The Genetics of the Jews, 1978; numerous papers in scientific jls on blood groups and other biol subjects, geology and archæology. *Recreations:* photography, geology, archæology, travel, reading in sciences other than own, alpine gardening. *Address:* The Dower House, Maison de Haut, Longueville, St Saviour, Jersey, Channel Islands. *T:* Jersey 52280.

MOVERLEY, Rt. Rev. Gerald; *see* Hallam, Bishop of, (RC).

MOWAT, John Stuart; Sheriff of Glasgow and Strathkelvin (formerly Lanark and Glasgow), since 1974; *b* 30 Jan. 1923; *s* of George Mowat and Annie Barlow; *m* 1956, Anne Cameron Renfrew; two *s* two *d. Educ:* Glasgow High Sch.; Belmont House; Merchiston Castle Sch.; Glasgow Univ. (MA, LLB). Served RAF Transport Comd, 1941-46; Flt-Lt 1944. Journalist, 1947-52; Advocate, 1952; Sheriff-Substitute, then Sheriff, of Fife and Kinross at Dunfermline, 1960-72; Sheriff of Fife and Kinross at Cupar and Kinross, 1972-74. Contested (L) Caithness and Sutherland, 1955; Office-bearer, Scottish Liberal Party, 1954-58; Life Trustee: Carnegie Dunfermline Trust, 1967-73; Carnegie UK Trust, 1971-73. *Recreations:* golf, curling, watching football. *Address:* 31 Westbourne Gardens, Glasgow G12 9PF. *T:* 041-334 3743.

MOWBRAY (26th Baron *cr* 1283), **SEGRAVE** (27th Baron *cr* 1283), **AND STOURTON,** of Stourton, Co. Wilts (23rd Baron *cr* 1448); **Charles Edward Stourton,** CBE 1982; *b* 11 March 1923; *s* of William Marmaduke Stourton, 25th Baron Mowbray, 26th Baron Segrave and 22nd Baron Stourton, MC, and Sheila (*d* 1975), *er d* of Hon. Edward Gully, CB; *S* father, 1965; *m* 1952, Hon. Jane de Yarburgh Bateson, *o c* of 5th Baron Deramore, and of Nina Lady Deramore, OBE, *d* of Alastair Macpherson-Grant; two *s. Educ:* Ampleforth; Christ Church, Oxford. Joined Army, 1942; Commissioned Gren. Guards, 1943; served with 2nd Armd Bn Gren. Gds, as Lt, 1943-44 (wounded, France, 1944; loss of eye and invalided, 1945). Mem. of Lloyd's 1952; Mem. Securicor, 1961-64; Director: Securicor (Scotland) Ltd, 1964-70; Economic International Resources Corporation Ltd, Jersey, 1980-; GDC Ltd, Ghana, 1980-; Western Consolidated Goldfields, Ghana, 1981-. Mem., Nidderdale RDC, 1954-58. A Conservative Whip in House of Lords, 1967-70, 1974-78; a Lord in Waiting (Govt Whip), and spokesman for DoE, 1970-74; Dep. Chief Opposition Whip in House of Lords, 1978-79; a Lord in Waiting (Govt Whip), and spokesman for the arts, envt and transport, 1979-80. Chm., Govt Picture Buying Cttee, 1972-74; Trustee, College of Arms Trust, 1975-. Chancellor, Primrose League, 1974-80, 1981-. Hon. Pres., Safety Glazing Assoc., 1975-78. Bicentennial Year Award of Baronial Order of Magna Charta, USA, 1976. Kt of Hon. and Devotion, SMO Malta, 1947; Kt Gr. Cross, Mil. Order of St Lazarus, 1970. *Recreations:* reading, shooting, gardening. *Heir: s* Hon. Edward William Stephen Stourton [*b* 17 April 1953; *m* 1980, Penelope, *e d* of Dr Peter Brunet; one *d*]. *Address:* Marcus, by Forfar, Angus DD8 3QH. *T:* Finavon 219; 23 Warwick Square, SW1V 2AB. *Clubs:* Turf, White's, Pratt's, Beefsteak, Pilgrims.

See also F. P. Crowder, Hon. J. J. Stourton.

MOWBRAY, Sir John Robert, 6th Bt cr 1880; b 1 March 1932; s of Sir George Robert Mowbray, 5th Bt, KBE, and of Diana Margaret, d of Sir Robert Heywood Hughes, 12th Bt; S father, 1969; m 1957, Lavinia Mary, d of late Lt-Col Francis Edgar Hugonin, OBE, Stainton House, Stainton in Cleveland, Yorks; three d. Educ: Eton; New College, Oxford. Address: Hunts Park, Great Thurlow, Suffolk. T: Thurlow 232.

MOWBRAY, William John, QC 1974; b 3 Sept. 1928; s of James Nathan Mowbray, sugar manufr and E. Ethel Mowbray; m 1960, Shirley Mary Neilan; one s three d. Educ: Upper Canada Coll.; Mill Hill Sch.; New Coll., Oxford. BA 1952. Called to Bar, Lincoln's Inn, 1953; called to Bahamian Bar, 1971. Publications: Lewin on Trusts, 16th edn, 1964; Estate Duty on Settled Property, 1969, etc; articles in jls. Recreations: music, gardening. Address: 12 New Square, Lincoln's Inn, WC2A 3SW. T: 01-405 3808/9, 01-405 0988/9.

MOWER, Brian Leonard; Director of Information, Home Office, since 1982; b 24 Aug. 1934; s of Samuel William and Nelly Elizabeth Rachel Mower; m 1960, Margaret Ann Wildman; one s one d. Educ: Hemel Hempstead Grammar Sch. Royal Air Force, 1954-56. Executive, Service Advertising Co., 1956-66; entered Civil Service, Sen. Information Officer, HM Treasury, 1966; Principal Information Officer, Central Statistical Office, 1969; Dep. Head of Information, HM Treasury, 1978; Head of Information, Dept of Employment, 1980; Dep. Press Sec. to Prime Minister, 1982. Recreations: bridge, walking. Address: 34 Wrensfield, Hemel Hempstead, Herts HP1 1RP. T: Hemel Hempstead 52277.

MOWLEM, Rainsford, FRCS; Emeritus Cons. Plastic Surgeon, Middlesex Hospital; Surgeon i/c Department for Plastic Surgery, Middlesex Hospital, 1939-62, retired; Surgeon i/c North West Regional Centre for Plastic Surgery, Mount Vernon Hospital; Consulting Plastic Surgeon to King Edward VII Hospital, Windsor, Luton and Dunstable Hospital, Birmingham Accident Hospital; b 21 Dec. 1902; s of Arthur Manwell Mowlem, New Zealand; m 1933, Margaret West Harvey; two d. Educ: Auckland Grammar Sch.; Univ. of New Zealand. MB, ChB, NZ 1924, FRCS 1929. Asst Med. Officer i/c Plastic Surgery Unit, LCC, 1933-37; Asst Plastic Surgeon, St Andrews Hosp., Dollis Hill, 1937-39; Surgeon i/c NW Centre Plastic Surgery, Hill End Hosp., 1939-53. Hunterian Prof., RCS, 1940. President: British Assoc. of Plastic Surgeons, 1950, 1959 (Mem. Council, 1947-57; Hon. Fellow, 1975); Internat. Congress of Plastic Surgeons, 1959. Sen. Fellow, Assoc. Surgeons of GB and Ireland; Fellow: RSM; Brit. Orthopædic Assoc.; Hon. Fellow, Amer. Assoc. Plastic Surgeons. Sen. Corresp. Mem., Amer. Soc. of Plastic and Reconstructive Surgeons; Corresp. Mem., Soc. Italiana di Cirurgia Plastica; Hon. Member: Netherlands Soc. of Plastic Surgery; Soc. Française de Chirurgie Plastique et Reconstructive; Nordisk Plastikkirurgisk Forening; Soc. Espanola de Cirurgia Plástica y Reparadora; Internat. Soc. of Aesthetic Plastic Surgery; Inst. of Accident Surgery. Hon. ScD Trinity Coll., Hartford. Publications: various on subjects related to plastic surgery. Address: La Morena, Apartado 56, Mijas, Málaga, Spain.

MOWLL, Christopher Martyn; Clerk to The Clothworkers' Company of the City of London and Secretary to The Clothworkers' Foundation, since 1978; b 14 Aug. 1932; s of late Christopher Kilvinton Mowll and Doris Ellen (née Hutchinson); m 1958, Margaret Frances (née Laird); four s. Educ: Epsom Coll.; Gonville and Caius Coll., Cambridge (MA). Admitted Solicitor, 1956. Member: Council, National Library for the Blind, 1964-79; Greenwich Metropolitan Society for the Blind, 1964- (Treas., 1965-79; Vice-Chm., 1971-79; Chm., 1979-); Exec. Council, RNIB, 1982-. Address: Clothworkers' Hall, Dunster Court, Mincing Lane, EC3R 7AH. T: 01-623 7041.

MOYA, (John) Hidalgo, CBE 1966; RIBA 1956; architect; b Los Gatos, Calif, 5 May 1920; s of Hidalgo Moya; m 1947, Janiffer Innes Mary Hall; one s two d. Educ: Oundle Sch.; Royal West of England Coll. of Art; AA Sch. of Architecture; AA Dip., 1943. Partner, Powell and Moya, 1946, Powell Moya and Partners, 1976-. Major works include: Churchill Gardens Flats, Westminster, 1948-62; Houses at Chichester, 1950; Toys Hill, 1954; Mayfield Sch., Putney, 1955; Plumstead Manor Sch., Woolwich, 1970; Chichester Festival Theatre, 1962; Public Swimming Baths, Putney, 1967; British Nat. Pavilion, Expo 1970, Osaka; Dining Rooms, Bath Acad. of Art, 1970, Eton Coll., 1974; Psychiatric Hosp. extensions at Fairmile, 1957 and Borocourt, 1965; Brasenose Coll., 1961 and Corpus Christi Coll., 1969, Oxford extensions; Christ Church Coll., Oxford Picture Gall. and undergraduate rooms, 1967; St. John's Coll., 1967 and Queens' Coll., 1978, Cambridge, new buildings; Wolfson Coll., Oxford, 1974; General Hosps at Swindon, Slough, High Wycombe, Wythenshawe, Woolwich and Maidstone; new headquarters for London & Manchester Assurance Co., near Exeter, 1978; extensions for Schools for Advanced Urban Studies and of Extra Mural Studies, Univ. of Bristol, 1980; Nat. West. Bank, Shaftesbury Ave, London, 1982. Pimlico Housing Scheme, Winning Design in Open Competition, 1946; Skylon, Festival of Britain Winning Design, 1950 (Award, 1951); Mohlg Good Design in Housing Award, 1954; RIBA Bronze Medal, 1958, 1961 (Bucks, Berks, Oxon); Civic Trust Awards (Class I and II), 1961; Architectural Design Project Award, 1965; RIBA Architectural Award, (London and SE Regions), 1967; Royal Gold Medal for Architecture, RIBA, 1974. Address: Powell, Moya and Partners, Architects, 21 Upper Cheyne Row, SW3 5JW. T: 01-351 3882.

MOYERS, Bill D., BJ, BD; journalist; Senior News Analyst, CBS Evening News, since 1981; b 5 June 1934; s of John Henry Moyers and Ruby Moyers (née Johnson); m 1954, Judith Suzanne Davidson; two s one d. Educ: High Sch., Marshall, Texas; Univ. of Texas; Univ. of Edinburgh; Southwestern Theological Seminary. BJ 1956; BD 1959. Personal Asst to Senator Lyndon B. Johnson, 1959-60; Executive Asst, 1960; US Peace Corps: Associate Dir, 1961-63; Dep. Dir, 1963. Special Asst to President Johnson, 1963-66; Press Sec., 1965-67; Publisher of Newsday, Long Island, 1967-70; Exec. Ed., Bill Moyers' Jl, Public Broadcasting Service, 1971-76, 1978-81; editor and chief reporter, CBS Reports, 1976-79. Contributing Editor, Newsweek Magazine. Three Emmy Awards, inc. most outstanding broadcaster, 1974; Lowell Medal, 1975; ABA Gavel Award for distinguished service to American system of law, 1974; ABA Cert. of Merit, 1975; Peabody Award, 1977; Awards for The Fire Next Door: Monte Carlo TV Festival Grand Prize, Jurors Prize and Nymph Award, 1977; Robert F. Kennedy Journalism Grand Prize, 1978; Christopher Award, 1978; Sidney Hillman Prize for Distinguished Service, 1978, 1981; Distinguished Urban Journalism Award, Nat. Urban Coalition, 1978; George Polk Award, 1981; Columbia—Du Pont Award, 1981; Peabody Award, 1981; Emmy, 1981. Publication: Listening to America, 1971. Address: 76 Fourth Street, Garden City, Long Island, New York 11530, USA.

MOYES, Lt-Comdr Kenneth Jack, MBE (mil.) 1960; RN retd; Under-Secretary, Department of Health and Social Security, 1975-78; b 13 June 1918; s of Charles Wilfrid and Daisy Hilda Moyes; m 1943, Norma Ellen Outred Hillier; one s two d. Educ: Portsmouth Northern Grammar Sch. FCIS. Royal Navy, 1939-63. Principal, Dept of Health and Social Security, 1963; Asst Secretary, 1970. Recreations: gardening, tennis, squash, bridge. Address: Garden House, Darwin Road, Birchington, Kent CT7 9JL. T: Thanet 42015.

MOYLAN, John David FitzGerald; His Honour Judge Moylan; a Circuit Judge (formerly Judge of the County Courts), since 1967; b 8 Oct. 1915; s of late Sir John FitzGerald Moylan, CB, CBE, and late Lady Moylan (née FitzGerald); m 1946, Jean, d of late F. C. Marno-Edwards, Lavenham, Suffolk; one s two d. Educ: Charterhouse; Christ Church, Oxford. Served War of 1939-45, with Royal Marines. Inner Temple, 1946; practised on the Western Circuit. Recreations: travel and music. Address: 29 Lennox Gardens, SW1. T: 01-584 4726.

MOYLE, Rt. Hon. Roland (Dunstan); PC 1978; MP (Lab) Lewisham East, since 1974 (Lewisham North, 1966-74); b 12 March 1928; s of late Baron Moyle, CBE; m 1956, Shelagh Patricia Hogan; one s one d. Educ: Infants' and Jun. Elem. Schs, Bexleyheath, Kent; County Sch., Llanidloes, Mont.; UCW Aberystwyth (LLB); Trinity Hall, Cambridge (MA, LLB); Gray's Inn. Barrister-at-Law. Commnd in Royal Welch Fusiliers, 1949-51. Legal Dept, Wales Gas Bd, 1953-56; Industrial Relations Executive with Gas Industry, 1956-62, and Electricity Supply Industry, 1962-66. PPS to Chief Secretary to the Treasury, 1966-69, to Home Secretary, 1969-70; opposition spokesman on higher educn and science, 1972-74; Parly Sec., MAFF, 1974; Min. of State, NI Dept, 1974-76; Min. of State for the Health Service, 1976-79; opposition spokesman on health, 1979-80; deputy foreign affairs spokesman, 1980-. Mem., Select Cttee on Race Relations and Immigration, 1968-72; Vice-Chm., PLP Defence Group, 1968-72; Sec., 1971-74, Mem. Exec. Cttee, 1968-80, British Amer. Parly Gp. Recreations: gardening, motoring, swimming, reading. Address: House of Commons, SW1.

MOYNE, 2nd Baron, cr 1932, of Bury St Edmunds; **Bryan Walter Guinness**, MA; FRSL; poet, novelist and playwright; Vice-Chairman of Arthur Guinness, Son and Co., 1949-79, retired (Director, 1934-79); Trustee, Iveagh (Housing) Trust, Dublin; Barrister-at-Law; b 27 Oct. 1905; e s of 1st Baron Moyne (3rd s of 1st Earl of Iveagh) and Lady Evelyn Erskine (d 1939), 3rd d of 14th Earl of Buchan; S father 1944; m 1st, 1929, Diana Freeman-Mitford (marr. diss. 1934): two s ; 2nd, 1936, Elisabeth Nelson; three s five d (and one s decd). Educ: Eton; Christ Church, Oxford. Called to Bar, 1930. Capt., Royal Sussex Regiment, 1943; A Governor National Gallery of Ireland, 1955; Mem., Irish Acad. of Letters, 1968. Hon. FTCD 1979. Hon. LLD: TCD, 1958; NUI, 1961. Publications: (as Bryan Guinness): 23 Poems, 1931; Singing out of Tune, 1933; Landscape with Figures, 1934; Under the Eyelid, 1935; Johnny and Jemima, 1936; A Week by the Sea, 1936; Lady Crushwell's Companion, 1938; The Children in the Desert, 1947; Reflexions, 1947; The Animals' Breakfast, 1950; Story of a Nutcracker, 1953; Collected Poems, 1956; A Fugue of Cinderellas, 1956; Catriona and the Grasshopper, 1957; Priscilla and the Prawn, 1960; Leo and Rosabelle, 1961; The Giant's Eye, 1964; The Rose in the Tree, 1964; The Girl with the Flower, 1966; The Engagement, 1969; The Clock, 1973; Dairy Not Kept, 1975; Hellenic Flirtation, 1978; Potpourri from the Thirties, 1982; plays: The Fragrant Concubine, 1938; A Riverside Charade, 1954. Recreation: travelling. Heir: s Hon. Jonathan Bryan Guinness, qv. Address: Biddesden House, Andover, Hants. T: Andover 790237; Knockmaroon, Castleknock, Co. Dublin. Clubs: Athenæum, Carlton; Kildare Street and University (Dublin).
See also Hon. D. W. Guinness.

MOYNIHAN, family name of **Baron Moynihan**.

MOYNIHAN, 3rd Baron, cr 1929; **Antony Patrick Andrew Cairnes Berkeley Moynihan**; Bt 1922; b 2 Feb. 1936; s of 2nd Baron Moynihan, OBE, TD, and of Ierne Helen Candy; S father 1965; m 1st, 1955, Ann Herbert (marr. diss., 1958); 2nd, 1958, Shirin Roshan Berry (marr. diss., 1967); one *d*; 3rd, 1968, Luthgarda Maria Fernandez (marr. diss. 1979); three *d*. *Educ*: Stowe. Late 2nd Lt Coldstream Guards. *Recreation*: dog breeding. *Heir*: half-*b* Hon. Colin Berkeley Moynihan, *b* 13 Sept. 1955.

MOYNIHAN, Senator (Daniel) Patrick; US Senator from New York State, since 1977; *b* Tulsa, Oklahoma, 16 March 1927; *s* of John Henry and Margaret Ann Phipps Moynihan; *m* 1955, Elizabeth Therese Brennan; two *s* one *d*. *Educ*: City Coll., NY; Tufts Univ.; Fletcher Sch. of Law and Diplomacy. MA, PhD. Gunnery Officer, US Navy, 1944-47. Dir of Public Relations, Internat. Rescue Commn, 1954; successively Asst to Sec., Asst Sec., Acting Sec., to Governor of NY State, 1955-58; Mem., NY Tenure Commn, 1959-60; Dir, NY State Govt Res. Project, Syracuse Univ., 1959-61; Special Asst to Sec. of Labor, 1961-62; Exec. Asst to Sec., 1962-63, Asst Sec. of Labor, 1963-65; Dir, Jt Center Urban Studies, MIT and Harvard Univ., 1966-69; Prof. of Govt, 1972-77 and Senior Mem., 1966-77, Harvard (Prof. of Education and Urban Politics, 1966-73). Asst to Pres. of USA for Urban Affairs, 1969-70; Counsellor to Pres. (with Cabinet rank), 1969-70; Consultant to Pres., 1971-73; US Ambassador to India, 1973-75; US Permanent Rep. to the UN and Mem. of Cabinet, 1975-76. Democratic Candidate for the Senate, NY, 1976. Mem., US delegn 26th Gen. Assembly, UN, 1971. Fellow, Amer. Acad. Arts and Scis; Member: Amer. Philosophical Soc.; AAAS (formerly Vice-Pres.); Nat. Acad. Public Admin; President's Sci. Adv. Cttee, 1971-73. Hon. Fellow, London Sch. of Economics, 1970. Holds numerous hon. degrees. *Publications*: (co-author) Beyond the Melting Pot, 1963; (ed) The Defenses of Freedom, 1966; (ed) On Understanding Poverty, 1969; Maximum Feasible Misunderstanding, 1969; (ed) Toward a National Urban Policy, 1970; (jt ed) On Equality of Educational Opportunity, 1972; The Politics of a Guaranteed Income, 1973; Coping: On the Practice of Government, 1974; (jt ed) Ethnicity: Theory and Experience, 1975; A Dangerous Place, 1979. *Address*: Senate Office Building, Washington, DC 20510, USA. *Clubs*: Century, Harvard (NYC); Federal City (Washington).

MOYNIHAN, Martin John, CMG 1972; MC; HM Diplomatic Service, retired; *b* 17 Feb. 1916; *e s* of William John Moynihan and late Phoebe Alexander; *m* 1946, Monica Hopwood; one *s* one *d*. *Educ*: Birkenhead Sch.; Magdalen Coll., Oxford (MA). India Office, 1939. War of 1939-45: Indian Army, 1940; QVO Corps of Guides; served with Punjab Frontier Force Regt, N-W Frontier and Burma (MC); Commonwealth Service: Delhi, Madras, Bombay and London, 1946-54; Deputy High Commissioner: Peshawar, 1954-56; Lahore, 1956-58; Kuala Lumpur, 1961-63; Port of Spain, 1964-66; HM Consul-General, Philadelphia, 1966-70; Ambassador to Liberia, 1970-73; High Comr in Lesotho, 1973-76. Administering Officer, Kennedy Meml Trust, 1977-79. Member: Council, Hakluyt Soc., 1976-81; Charles Williams Soc., 1977; Pres., Lesotho Diocesan Assoc., 1976. Fellow: Internat. Scotist Congress, Padua, 1976; Internat. Arthurian Congress, Regensburg, 1979; Associate Mem. in S African Studies, Clare Hall, Cambridge, 1977-78. Hon. Knight Grand Band of Humane Order of African Redemption (Liberia), 1973. *Publications*: The Strangers, 1946; South of Fort Hertz, 1956. *Address*: The Gatehouse, 5 The Green, Wimbledon Common, SW19 5AZ. *T*: 01-946 7964. *Clubs*: Athenæum, Travellers'.

MOYNIHAN, Sir Noël (Henry), Kt 1979; MA, MB, BCh; FRCGP; family doctor; *b* 24 Dec. 1916; *o s* of Edward B. Moynihan and Ellen (*née* Shea), Cork, Ireland; *m* 1941, Margaret Mary Lovelace, JP, *d* of William John Lovelace, barrister-at-law, and Mary Lovelace, JP, Claygate, Surrey; two *s* two *d*. *Educ*: Ratcliffe; Downing Coll., Cambridge (BA English Tripos 1940, MA 1946) (represented Cambridge in athletics (mile) and cross country, v Oxford, 1939, 1940); MB 1956, BChir 1955 London; MRCS, LRCP 1954, MRCGP 1965, FRCGP 1981. Served War, RAF, Sqdn Ldr, 1940-46 (despatches twice). Medically qual., St Thomas' Hosp., 1954; Newsholme Public Health Prize, 1954; Sutton Sams Prize (Obstet. and Gynaecol.), 1954. Upjohn Travelling Fellow, RCGP, 1967; Leverhulme Travelling Res. Fellow, 1974. Co-Founder, Med. Council on Alcoholism, 1963 (Mem. Council, 1963-79; Vice-Pres., 1972-79); Mem. Bd, S London Faculty, RCGP, 1958-73; Chm., Public Relations and Fund Raising Cttee, African Med. and Res. Foundn, 1959-64; President: Harveian Soc. of London, 1967 (Mem. Council, 1963-68, 1978-79); Chelsea Clinical Soc., 1978 (Mem. Council, 1969-78); Vice-Chm., 1972-77, Chm., 1977-81, Save the Children Fund; Hon. Sec., Council, Med. Soc. of London, 1981-82. Mem. Cttee, St Francis Leper Guild, 1964-81 (Vice-Pres., 1981). Mem. Bd, Royal Med. Benevolent Fund, 1973-77. Editor, St Thomas' Hosp. Gazette, 1952-54. Mem., Inner Temple, 1948; Yeoman, Worshipful Soc. of Apothecaries, 1956; Liveryman, 1959; Freeman, City of London, 1959. CStJ 1971; Kt SMO Malta 1958 (Officer of Merit, 1964; Comdr of Merit, 1979); KSG 1966. *Publications*: The Light in the West, 1978; Rock Art of the Sahara, 1979; contribs to med. jls, 1953-78. *Recreations*: Save The Children Fund, collecting barbers' bleeding bowls, rock art of the Sahara. *Address*: 25-27 Sloane Court West, Chelsea, SW3 4TD. *T*: 01-730 1828; Herstmonceux Place, Flowers Green, East Sussex. *Clubs*: Brooks's, Carlton, MCC; Hawks (Cambridge), Achilles.

MOYNIHAN, Rodrigo, CBE 1953; RA 1954 (ARA 1944); artist; lately Professor of Painting at the Royal College of Art; *b* 17 Oct. 1910; *s* of Herbert James Moynihan and late Maria de la Puerta; *m* 1931, Elinor Bellingham Smith; one *s*; *m* 1960, Anne, *d* of Sir James Hamet Dunn, 1st Bt; one *s*. *Educ*: UCS, London, and in USA. Slade Sch., 1928-31; Mem. of London Group, 1933; one-man shows at Redfern Gall., 1940, 1958, 1961; Leicester Gallery, 1946; Hanover Gallery, 1963, 1967; Fischer Fine Art, 1973, 1982; Royal

Academy (major retrospective), 1978; New York: Egan Gallery, 1966; Tibor de Nagy, 1968; Robert Miller Gall., 1980, 1983. Vis. Prof., Slade Sch. Army Service, 1940-43; Official War Artist, 1943-44. Pictures purchased by Chantrey Bequest, Tate Gallery, Contemporary Art Soc., War Artists' Advisory Cttee, Nat. Portrait Gallery, Hirschhorn Coll., Washington. Hon. Dr RCA 1969; Fellow UCL, 1970-. Editor (jtly with wife), Art and Literature, 1963-68. *Publication*: Goya, 1951. *Address*: c/o Royal Academy, Piccadilly, W1V 0DS. *Clubs*: Buck's, Royal Automobile.

MOYOLA, Baron *cr* 1971 (Life Peer), of Castledawson; **James Dawson Chichester-Clark,** PC (Northern Ireland) 1966; DL; *b* 12 Feb. 1923; *s* of late Capt. J. L. C. Chichester-Clark, DSO and bar, DL, MP, and Mrs C. E. Brackenbury; *m* 1959, Moyra Maud Haughton (*née* Morris); two *d* one step *s*. *Educ*: Eton. Entered Army, 1942; 2nd Lieut Irish Guards, Dec. 1942; wounded, Italy, 1944; ADC to Governor-General of Canada (Field-Marshal Earl Alexander of Tunis), 1947-49; attended Staff Coll., Camberley, 1956; retired as Major, 1960. MP (U), S Derry, NI Parlt, 1960-72; Asst Whip, March 1963; Chief Whip, 1963-67; Leader of the House, 1966-67; Min. of Agriculture, 1967-69; Prime Minister, 1969-71. DL Co. Derry, 1954. *Recreations*: shooting, fishing, ski-ing. *Address*: Moyola Park, Castledawson, Co. Derry, N Ireland.
See also Sir R. Chichester-Clark.

MPUCHANE, Samuel Akuna; High Commissioner for Botswana in the United Kingdom, since 1982; *b* 15 Dec. 1943; *s* of Chiminya Thompson Mpuchane and Motshidiemang Phologolo; *m* Sisai Felicity Mokgokong; one *s* one *d*. *Educ*: Univ. of Botswana, Lesotho and Swaziland (BA Govt and Hist.); Southampton Univ. (MSc Internat. Affairs). External Affairs Officer, 1969-70; First Secretary: Botswana Mission to UN, 1970-71; Botswana Embassy, Washington, 1971-74; Under Sec., External Affairs, 1974-76; on study leave, 1976-77; Dep. Perm. Sec., Min. of Mineral Resources and Water Affairs, 1977-79; Admin. Sec., Office of Pres., 1979-80; Perm. Sec., Min. of Local Govt and Lands, 1980-81. *Recreations*: playing and watching tennis, watching soccer. *Address*: Botswana High Commission, 162 Buckingham Palace Road, SW1W 9TJ.

MTEKATEKA, Rt. Rev. Josiah; *b* 1903; *s* of Village Headman; *m* 1st, 1925, Maude Mwere Nambote (*d* 1940); one *s* four *d*; 2nd, 1944, Alice Monica Chitanda; six *s* two *d* (and five *c* decd). *Educ*: Likoma Island School; St Michael's Teachers' Training Coll., Likoma; St Andrew's Theological Coll., Likoma. Deacon, 1939; Priest, 1943. Asst Priest, Nkhotakota, Nyasaland Dio., 1943-45; Chiulu, Tanganyika, 1945-50; Priest, Mlangali, Tanganyika, Nyasaland Dio., 1950-52; Mlangali, SW Tanganyika Dio., 1952-60; rep. SW Tanganyika Dio. at UMCA Centenary Celebrations in England, 1957; Canon of SW Tanganyika Dio., 1959; Priest-in-charge, Manda, 1960-64, Njombe, 1964-65, SW Tanganyika Dio.; Archdeacon of Njombe, 1962-65; Suffragan Bishop, Nkhotakota, Dio. Malawi, 1965-71; Bishop of Lake Malawi, 1971-77. *Address*: PO Box 27, Ntchisi, Malawi.

MUDD, (William) David; MP (C) Falmouth and Camborne, since 1970; *b* 2 June 1933; *o s* of Capt. W. N. Mudd and Mrs T. E. Mudd; *m* 1965, Helyn Irvine Smith; one *s* one *d* (and one step *d*). *Educ*: Truro Cathedral Sch. Journalist, Broadcaster, TV Commentator; work on BBC and ITV (Westward Television). Became Editor of The Cornish Echo; Staff Reporter, Western Morning News and Tavistock Gazette, 1954-. Mem., Tavistock UDC, 1963-65. Secretary: Conservative West Country Cttee, 1973-76; Conservative Party Fisheries Sub-Cttee, 1974-75, 1981-; PPS, Dept of Energy, 1979-81. *Publications*: Cornishmen and True, 1971; Murder in the West Country, 1975; Facets of Crime, 1975; The Innovators, 1976; Down Along Camborne and Redruth, 1978; The Falmouth Packets, 1978; Cornish Sea Lights, 1978; Cornwall and Scilly Peculiar, 1979; About the City, 1979; Home Along Falmouth and Penryn, 1980; Around and About the Roseland, 1980; The Cruel Cornish Sea, 1981; The Cornish Edwardians, 1982. *Recreation*: jig-saw puzzles. *Address*: Peruind, Roskear, Camborne, Cornwall. *T*: Camborne 712141. *Clubs*: Athenæum; Falmouth.

MUELLER, Anne Elisabeth, CB 1980; Deputy Secretary, Department of Industry, since 1977; *b* 15 Oct. 1930; *d* of late Herbert Constantin Mueller and Phoebe Ann Beevers; *m* 1958, James Hugh Robertson (marr. diss. 1978). *Educ*: Wakefield Girls' High Sch.; Somerville Coll., Oxford. Entered Min. of Labour and Nat. Service, 1953; served with Orgn for European Econ. Co-op., 1955-56; Treasury, 1962; Dept of Economic Affairs, 1964; Min. of Technology, 1969; DTI 1970; Under-Sec., DTI, later Dept of Industry, 1972-77. *Address*: 21 Phillimore Place, W8 7BY. *T*: 01-937 9766.

MUFF, family name of **Baron Calverley.**

MUGABE, Robert Gabriel; Prime Minister of Zimbabwe since 1980; also Minister of Defence since 1980, and Minister of Public Service, since 1981; President (Co-Founder, 1963), Zimbabwe African National Union (ZANU), since 1977; *b* Kutama, 1924; *m* Sarah Mugabe. *Educ*: Kutama and Empanden Mission School; Fort Hare Univ. (BA (Educ), BSc (Econ)); London Univ. (by correspondence: BSc(Econ); BEd; LLB; LLM); Univ. of S Africa (by correspondence BAdm). Teacher, 1942-58: Kutama, Mapanzure, Shabani, Empandeni Mission, Hope Fountain Mission, Driefontein Mission, South Africa; Mbizi Govt Sch., Mambo Sch., Chalimbana Trng Coll., Zambia; St Mary's Teacher Trng Coll., Ghana. Publ. Sec. of Nat. Dem. Party, 1960-61; Publicity Sec. and acting Sec.-Gen., Zimbabwe African People's Union,

1961-62. Political detention, 1962, escaped to Tanzania, 1963; became Sec.-Gen. ZANU, Aug. 1963, but in detention in Rhodesia, 1964-74; resident in Mozambique, 1975-79. Jt Leader (with Joshua Nkomo) of the Patriotic Front, Oct. 1976. Attended Confs: Geneva Constitutional Conf. on Rhodesia, 1976; Malta Conf., 1978; London Conf., 1979. Hon. LLD Ahmadu Bello. *Address:* Office of the Prime Minister, Harare, Zimbabwe.

MUGGERIDGE, Douglas; Managing Director, External Broadcasting, BBC, since 1981; *b* 2 Dec. 1928; *s* of Col Harry Douglas Muggeridge, OBE, and late Bertha Ursula Rutland; *m* 1953, Diana Marguerite Hakim; two *d. Educ:* Shrewsbury; London Sch. of Economics. Sub-Editor and Leader-Writer, Liverpool Daily Post, 1953; joined BBC as Talks Producer, 1956; Senior Producer, 1959; Chief Publicity Officer, Overseas, 1961; Chief Asst, Publicity, 1964; Head of Overseas Talks and Features, 1965; Controller, Radio 1 and 2, 1969; Dir of Programmes, Radio, 1976; Dep. Man. Dir, BBC Radio, 1978-80. Pres., Radio Industries Club, 1977-78. *Recreations:* music, fishing, book collecting. *Address:* Castle Hill Cottage, Rotherfield, Sussex. *T:* Rotherfield 2770.

MUGGERIDGE, Malcolm; *b* 24 March 1903; *s* of late H. T. Muggeridge; *m* 1927, Katherine, *d* of G. C. Dobbs; two *s* one *d* (and one *s* decd). *Educ:* Selhurst Grammar Sch.; Selwyn Coll., Cambridge. Lecturer at Egyptian Univ., Cairo, 1927-30; Editorial Staff, Manchester Guardian, 1930-32; Manchester Guardian correspondent, Moscow, 1932-33; Asst Editor, Calcutta Statesman, 1934-35; Editorial staff, Evening Standard, 1935-36. Served in War of 1939-45, in East Africa, North Africa, Italy and France, Intelligence Corps, Major (Legion of Hon., Croix de Guerre with Palm, Médaille de la Reconnaissance Française). Daily Telegraph Washington Correspondent, 1946-47; Dep. Editor Daily Telegraph, 1950-52; Editor of Punch, Jan. 1953-Oct. 1957. Rector, Edinburgh Univ., 1967-68. *Publications:* Three Flats, produced by the Stage Society, 1931; Autumnal Face, 1931; Winter in Moscow, 1933; The Earnest Atheist, a life of Samuel Butler, 1936; In A Valley of this Restless Mind, 1938, new edn, 1978; The Thirties, 1940; edited English edn Ciano's Diary, 1947; Ciano's Papers, 1948; Affairs of the Heart, 1949; Tread Softly for you Tread on my Jokes, 1966; London à la Mode (with Paul Hogarth), 1966; Muggeridge through the Microphone (Edited by C. Ralling); Jesus Rediscovered, 1969; Something Beautiful for God, 1971; Paul: envoy extraordinary (with A. R. Vidler), 1972; Chronicles of Wasted Time (autobiog.), vol. 1, 1972, vol. 2, 1973; Malcolm's Choice, 1972; Jesus: the man who lives, 1975; A Third Testament, 1977; A Twentieth-Century Testimony, 1979; Like It Was (diaries), 1981. *Recreation:* walking. *Address:* Park Cottage, Robertsbridge, East Sussex.

MUGNOZZA, Carlo S.; *see* Scarascia-Mugnozza.

MUHAMMAD, Valiyaveettil Abdulaziz, PhD; High Commissioner for India in London, since 1980; *b* Kerala, 29 May 1923; *m* 1958, Sara Beebi; two *s* two *d. Educ:* Aligarh Muslim Univ. (MA, LLB 1st Cl. 1946); Univ. of London (PhD 1955). Called to the Bar, Inner Temple, 1953. Lawyer and Advocate Gen., Kerala State, 1965-67; Sen. Standing Counsel for State of Kerala and Union Govt in the Supreme Court, 1967-75; Mem., Rajya Sabha, 1973-77, Lok Sabha, 1977-80; Minister of State for Law, Justice, and Company Affairs, 1975-77. Sen. Adviser to Indian Delegn to UN, 1971; alternate Mem., Indian Delegn to UN Gen. Assembly, 1975; Chm., Panel on Minorities, Scheduled Castes, Scheduled Tribes and Weaker Sections, 1980. *Publications:* (ed jtly) The Indian Advocate; The Legal Framework of World Trade, 1958; Our Constitution: For Haves or Have-Nots?, 1974. *Recreations:* reading, walking, gardening. *Address:* India House, Aldwych, WC2; 9 Kensington Palace Gardens, W8.

MUIL, Maj.-Gen. David John, CB 1956; OBE 1945; *b* 18 Oct. 1898; *s* of David Muil, Kirkintilloch, Scotland; *m* 1924, Ruth, *d* of Mark Burgess, Alderley Edge, Cheshire; one *d. Educ:* Aston Grammar Sch.; Birmingham Univ. Served European War, 1917-19, with London Scottish, Royal Warwickshire Regt and RFC (France and Belgium). Joined Royal Army Dental Corps, 1923, and served with them War of 1939-45, in India and Far East; Col, 1949. Dir Army Dental Service, 1955-58. QHDS 1955. *Address:* 4 Courtslands, Court Downs Road, Beckenham, Kent. *T:* 01-650 9060.

MUIR, Air Commodore Adam, CB 1967; retired, 1977; *b* 4 Aug. 1908; *s* of George Muir and Mary Gillies Ferguson; *m* 1938, Isobel Janet Arbuckle Turnbull (*d* 1967); one *s* one *d. Educ:* Greenock Acad.; Glasgow Univ. MA 1929; BSc 1931; MB, ChB (Commend.) 1934; DTM&H (Eng) 1954; MRCPE 1955; FRCPE 1963. Joined RAF Medical Branch, 1937, retd 1967; served War of 1939-45, Iceland and Mediterranean Theatres (despatches twice); Dir of Hygiene and Research, RAF, 1959-63; PMO, RAF Germany, 1963-67; Officer i/c Reception, BMH Rinteln, 1967-70; MO, Army Careers Information Office, Glasgow, 1970-77. CStJ 1966. *Recreation:* music. *Address:* Clachan, Tighnabruaich, Argyll PA21 2DY. *T:* Tighnabruaich 378. *Club:* Royal Air Force.

MUIR, Alec Andrew, CBE 1968; QPM 1961; DL; Chief Constable of Durham Constabulary, 1967-70; *b* 21 Aug. 1909; *s* of Dr Robert Douglas Muir, MD, and Edith Muir, The Limes, New Cross, SE14; *m* 1948, Hon. Helen (who *m* 1st, 1935, Wm Farr; marr. diss., 1948), *er d* of Baron du Parcq (*d* 1949); one *s* one *d* (and one step *s* one step *d*). *Educ:* Christ's Hosp.; Wadham Coll., Oxford (MA). Receivers' Office, Metropolitan Police, 1933; Metropolitan Police Coll., 1934; Supt, 1948; Chief Constable, Durham Co.

Constabulary, 1950. DL, Co. Durham, 1964. OStJ 1957. *Recreations:* cricket, bowls, squash, sailing. *Address:* 7 Newcombe Court, 300 Woodstock Road, Oxford. *T:* Oxford 512518. *Clubs:* United Oxford & Cambridge University; County (Durham).

MUIR, (Charles) Augustus; author and journalist; Regimental Historian, The Royal Scots; *b* Carluke, Ontario, Canada, 15 Nov. 1892; *s* of late Rev. Walter Muir and Elizabeth Carlow; *m* Jean Murray Dow Walker (*d* 1972); *m* 1975, Mair Davies. *Educ:* George Heriot's Sch. and Edinburgh Univ.; contributor to various dailies, weeklies, and monthlies; Asst Editor and subsequently Editor, the World; served 1914-19 in Royal Scots, King's Own Scottish Borderers, and on Staff. *Publications:* The Third Warning; The Blue Bonnet; The Black Pavilion; The Shadow on the Left; The Silent Partner; Birds of the Night; The House of Lies; Beginning the Adventure; Scotland's Road of Romance; The Green Lantern; The Riddle of Garth; Raphael, MD; The Crimson Crescent; Satyr Mask; The Bronze Door; The Red Carnation; The Man Who Stole the Crown Jewels; Castles in the Air; The Sands of Fear; The Intimate Thoughts of John Baxter, Bookseller; Heather-Track and High Road; Joey and the Greenwings; Scottish Portrait; The Story of Jesus for Young People; The History of The Fife Coal Company; The History of the Shotts Iron Company; The History of Michael Nairn and Company; 75 Years, The History of Smith's Stamping Works (Coventry) Ltd and Smith-Clayton Forge Ltd, Lincoln; The History of Blyth, Greene, Jourdain & Co. Ltd, Merchant Bankers; Andersons of Islington, The History of C. F. Anderson & Son Ltd; The History of Churchill & Sim Ltd; The Kenyon Tradition, The History of James Kenyon & Son Ltd; The History of Baker Perkins Ltd; In Blackburne Valley, The History of Bowers Mills; The Life of the Very Rev. Dr John White, CH; Candlelight in Avalon, A Spiritual Pilgrimage; How to Choose and Enjoy Wine; The First of Foot, The History of The Royal Scots (The Royal Regiment) 1633-1961; The Vintner of Nazareth, a study of the early life of Christ; History of British Paper & Board Makers Association; (with Mair Davies) A Victorian Shipowner: A Life of Sir Charles Cayzer. Joint-Editor The George Saintsbury Memorial Volume and A Last Vintage. *Recreations:* nearly anything except golf. *Address:* Parkhill, Stansted-Mountfitchet, Essex. *T:* Bishops Stortford 812289. *Clubs:* Savage, Saintsbury; Royal Scots, Scottish Arts (Edinburgh).

MUIR, Sir David (John), Kt 1961; CMG 1959; FCIS, FASA, FAIM, AAUQ; Chairman, Queensland Cultural Centre Trust, since 1976; *b* 20 June 1916; *s* of John Arthur and Grace Elizabeth Muir, Brisbane; *m* 1942, Joan Haworth; one *s* one *d. Educ:* Kangaroo Point State Sch.; State Commercial High Sch., Brisbane. Entered Qld Public Service, 1932, as Clerk in Dept of Public Lands; transf. to Premier's Dept, 1938. Made special study of problems associated with production and marketing of sugar. Permanent Under Sec., Premier and Chief Secretary's Dept, 1948-51; also Clerk of Exec. Council of Qld and Mem. of State Stores Bd. Agent General for Qld in London and Australian Govt Rep. on Internat. Sugar Council, 1951-63 (Chm. 1958); Dir, Industrial Develt, Queensland, and Chm., Industries Assistance Bd, 1964-77; Chm., Qld Public Service Bd, 1977-79; Parly Comr for Administrative Investigations (Ombudsman), 1979-81. Pres., Chartered Institute of Secretaries, 1964. Chairman: Queensland Theatre Co. Bd, 1969-78. James N. Kirby Medal, InstProdE, Australia, 1969. JP. *Recreations:* gardening and golf. *Address:* Box 159 PO, South Brisbane, Qld 4101, Australia; 28 Buena Vista Avenue, Coorparoo, Qld 4151, Australia.

MUIR, Frank, CBE 1980; writer and broadcaster; *b* 5 Feb. 1920; *s* of Charles James Muir and Margaret Harding; *m* 1949, Polly McIrvine; one *s* one *d. Educ:* Chatham House, Ramsgate; Leyton County High Sch. Served RAF, 1940-46. Wrote radio comedy-series and compered TV progs, 1946. With Denis Norden, 1947-64; collaborated for 17 years writing comedy scripts, including: (for radio): Take it from Here, 1947-58; Bedtime with Braden, 1950-54; (for TV): And so to Bentley, 1956; Whack-O,! 1958-60; The Seven Faces of Jim, 1961, and other series with Jimmy Edwards; resident in TV and radio panel-games; collaborated in film scripts, television commercials, and revues (Prince of Wales, 1951; Adelphi, 1952); joint Advisors and Consultants to BBC Television Light Entertainment Dept, 1960-64; jointly received Screenwriters Guild Award for Best Contribution to Light Entertainment, 1961; together on panel-games My Word!, 1956-, and My Music, 1967-. Asst Head of BBC Light Entertainment Gp, 1964-67; Head of Entertainment, London Weekend Television, 1968-69, resigned 1969, and reverted to being self-unemployed; resumed TV series Call My Bluff, 1970; began radio series Frank Muir Goes Into . . ., 1971; The Frank Muir Version, 1976. Pres., Johnson Soc., Lichfield, 1975-76. Rector, Univ. of St Andrews, 1977-79. (With Simon Brett) Writers' Guild Award for Best Radio Feature Script, 1973; (with Denis Norden) Variety Club of GB Award for Best Radio Personality of 1977; Radio Personality of the Year, Radio Industries Club, 1977. Hon. LLD St Andrews, 1978; Hon. DLitt Kent, 1982. *Publications:* (with Patrick Campbell) Call My Bluff, 1972; (with Denis Norden) You Can't Have Your Kayak and Heat It, 1973; (with Denis Norden) Upon My Word!, 1974; Christmas Customs and Traditions, 1975; The Frank Muir Book: an irreverant companion to social history, 1976; What-a-Mess, 1977; (with Denis Norden) Take My Word for It, 1978; (with Simon Brett) Frank Muir Goes Into . . . , 1978; What-a-Mess the Good, 1978; (with Denis Norden) The Glums, 1979; (with Simon Brett) The Second Frank Muir Goes Into ....., 1979; Prince What-a-Mess, 1979; Super What-a-Mess, 1980; (with Simon Brett) The Third Frank Muir Goes Into . . . , 1980; (with Simon Brett) Frank Muir on Children, 1980; (with Denis Norden) Oh, My Word!, 1980; What-a-Mess and the Cat-Next-Door, 1981; (with Simon Brett) The Fourth Frank Muir Goes Into

..., 1981; (with Polly Muir) The Big Dipper, 1981; A Book at Bathtime, 1982; What-a-Mess in Spring, What-a-Mess in Summer, What-a-Mess in Autumn, What-a-Mess in Winter, 1982; (with Simon Brett) The Book of Comedy Sketches, 1982. *Recreations:* book collecting, staring silently into space. *Address:* Anners, Thorpe, Egham, Surrey TW20 8UE. *T:* Chertsey 62759. *Club:* Savile.

MUIR, (Isabella) Helen (Mary), CBE 1981; MA, DPhil, DSc; FRS 1977; Director, since 1977, and Head of Division of Biochemistry, since 1966, Kennedy Institute of Rheumatology, London; *b* 20 Aug. 1920; *d* of late G. B. F. Muir, ICS, and Gwladys Muir (*née* Stack). *Educ:* Downe House, Newbury; Somerville Coll., Oxford (Hon. Fellow, 1978). MA 1944, DPhil (Oxon) 1947, DSc (Oxon) 1973. Research Fellow, Dunn's Sch. of Pathology, Oxford, 1947-48; Scientific Staff, Nat. Inst. for Med. Research, 1948-54; Empire Rheumatism Council Fellow, St Mary's Hosp., London, 1954-58; Pearl Research Fellow, St Mary's Hosp., 1959-66. Scientific Mem. Council, Med. Research Council (first woman to serve), Oct. 1973-Sept. 1977; Member, Editorial Board: Biochemical Jl, 1964-69; Annals of the Rheumatic Diseases, 1971-. Heberden Orator, London, 1976; Bunim Lectr, New Orleans, 1978. Feldberg Foundn Award, 1977; Neil Hamilton Fairley Medal, RCP, 1981; Ciba Medal, Biochem. Soc., 1981; Steindler Award, Orthop. Soc., USA, 1982; Hon. Mem., Amer. Soc. of Biolog. Chemists, 1982. *Publications:* many scientific papers, mainly on biochem. of connective tissues in reln to arthritis and inherited diseases in Biochem. Jl, Biochim. et Biophys. Acta, Nature, etc; contribs to several specialist books. *Recreations:* gardening, music, horses and hunting, natural history and science in general. *Address:* Mathilda and Terence Kennedy Institute of Rheumatology, Bute Gardens, W6 7DW. *T:* 01-748 9966.

MUIR, Jean Elizabeth, (Mrs Harry Leuckert), RDI; Designer-Director and Co-Owner, Jean Muir Ltd, since 1967; *d* of Cyril Muir and Phyllis Coy; *m* 1955, Harry Leuckert. *Educ:* Dame Harper Sch., Bedford. Selling/sketching, Liberty & Co., 1950; Designer, Jaeger Ltd, 1956, then Jane & Jane; with Harry Leuckert as co-director, formed own company, 1966. Awards: Dress of the Year, British Fashion Writers' Gp, 1964; Ambassador Award for Achievement, 1965; Harpers Bazaar Trophy, 1965; Maison Blanche Rex Internat. Fashion Award, New Orleans, 1967, 1968 and 1974 (also Hon. Citizen of New Orleans); Churchman's Award as Fashion Designer of the Year, 1970; Neiman Marcus Award, Dallas, Texas, 1973. RDI 1972; FRSA 1973; FSIAD 1978; Hon. Dr RCA, 1981. *Address:* 22 Bruton Street, W1X 7DA. *T:* 01-499 4214.

MUIR, John Gerald Grainger, CBE 1975; DSC 1944; bee-keeper; *b* 19 Jan. 1918; *s* of George Basil Muir, ICS and Gladys Stack; *m* 1945, Lionella Maria Terni; three *d. Educ:* Rugby Sch.; Corpus Christi Coll., Oxford (MA). Bd of Educn Studentship, 1938. RN, Norway, Medit., Channel and Germany, 1939-46. British Council: Italy, 1946-49; Asst, Leeds, 1949-50; Asst Rep., Syria, 1950-55; Representative: Arab Gulf, 1955-60; Portugal, 1960-64; Iraq, 1964-67; Dep. Controller, Educn, 1968-72; Rep., Spain, 1972-76; Controller, Overseas Div. (Europe), 1976-78, retired. *Publications:* contribs to Mariner's Mirror, Bull. SOAS, and Soc. de Geographia, Lisbon. *Recreations:* music, nautical research, sailing, travel, flowers. *Address:* c/o Lloyds Bank Ltd, 6 Pall Mall, SW1Y 5NH. *Club:* Naval.

MUIR, Sir John (Harling), 3rd Bt, *cr* 1892; TD; DL; Director: James Finlay & Co. Ltd, 1946-81 (Chairman, 1961-75); Grindlay's Holdings Ltd, etc; Member, Queen's Body Guard for Scotland (The Royal Company of Archers); *b* 7 Nov. 1910; *s* of James Finlay Muir (*d* 1948), Braco Castle, Perthshire, and of Charlotte Escudier, *d* of J. Harling Turner, CBE; *S* uncle 1951; *m* 1936, Elizabeth Mary, *e d* of late Frederick James Dundas, Dale Cottage, Cawthorne, near Barnsley; five *s* two *d. Educ:* Stowe. With James Finlay & Co. Ltd, in India, 1932-40. Served War of 1939-45: joined 3rd Carabiniers, Sept. 1940, Lieut; transferred 25th Dragoons, 1941, Capt.; Major, 1942; transferred RAC Depot, Poona, i/c Sqdn, 1942; transferred to Staff, HQ 109 L of C Area, Bangalore; held various Staff appointments terminating as AA and QMG with actg rank of Lt-Col; demobilised, 1946, with rank of Major. DL, Perthshire, 1966. *Recreations:* shooting, fishing, gardening. *Heir: s* Richard James Kay Muir [*b* 25 May 1939; *m* 1965, Susan Elizabeth (marr. diss.), *d* of G. A. Gardner, Leamington Spa; two *d*; *m* 1975, Lady Linda Mary Cole, *d* of 6th Earl of Enniskillen, *qv*; two *d*]. *Address:* Bankhead, Blair Drummond, by Stirling, Perthshire. *T:* Doune 207. *Clubs:* Oriental; Tollygunge (Calcutta).

See also Sir G. J. Aird, Bt.

MUIR, Prof. Kenneth, FBA 1970; King Alfred Professor of English Literature, University of Liverpool, 1951-74, now Professor Emeritus; *b* 1907; *s* of Dr R. D. Muir; *m* 1936, Mary Ewen; one *s* one *d. Educ:* Epsom Coll.; St Edmund Hall, Oxford. Lectr in English, St John's Coll., York, 1930-37; Lectr in English Literature, Leeds Univ., 1937-51; Liverpool University: Public Orator, 1961-65; Dean of the Faculty of Arts, 1958-61. Visiting Professor: Univ. of Pittsburgh, 1962-63; Univ. of Connecticut, 1973; Univ. of Pennsylvania, 1977. Editor, Shakespeare Survey, 1965-80; Chm., Internat. Shakespeare Assoc., 1974-. Leeds City Councillor, 1945-47, 1950-51; Chm. of Leeds Fabian Soc., 1941-46; Pres., Leeds Labour Party, 1951; Birkenhead Borough Councillor, 1954-57. FRSL 1978. Docteur de l'Université: de Rouen, 1967; de Dijon, 1976. *Publications:* The Nettle and the Flower, 1933; Jonah in the Whale, 1935; (with Sean O'Loughlin) The Voyage to Illyria, 1937; English Poetry, 1938; Collected Poems of Sir Thomas Wyatt, 1949;

Arden edn Macbeth, 1951; King Lear, 1952; Elizabethan Lyrics, 1953; (ed) Wilkins' Painful Adventures of Pericles, 1953; John Milton, 1955; The Pelican Book of English Prose I, 1956; Shakespeare's Sources, 1957; (ed with F. P. Wilson) The Life and Death of Jack Straw, 1957; (ed) John Keats, 1958; Shakespeare and the Tragic Pattern, 1959; trans. Five Plays of Jean Racine, 1960; Shakespeare as Collaborator, 1960; editor Unpublished Poems by Sir Thomas Wyatt, 1961; Last Periods, 1961; (ed) U. Ellis-Fermor's Shakespeare the Dramatist, 1961; (ed) Richard II, 1963; Life and Letters of Sir Thomas Wyatt, 1963; Shakespeare: Hamlet, 1963; (ed) Shakespeare: The Comedies, 1965; Introduction to Elizabethan Literature, 1967; (ed) Othello, 1968; (ed) The Winter's Tale, 1968; (ed with Patricia Thomson) Collected Poems of Sir Thomas Wyatt, 1969; The Comedy of Manners, 1970; (ed) The Rivals, 1970; (ed) Double Falsehood, 1970; (ed with S. Schoenbaum) A New Companion to Shakespeare Studies, 1971; Shakespeare's Tragic Sequence, 1972; Shakespeare the Professional, 1973; (ed) Essays and Studies, 1974; (ed) Three Plays of Thomas Middleton, 1975; The Singularity of Shakespeare, 1977; The Sources of Shakespeare, 1977; Shakespeare's Comic Sequence, 1979; Shakespeare's Sonnets, 1979; (trans.) Four Comedies of Calderon, 1980; (ed) U. Ellis-Fermor's Shakespeare's Drama, 1980; (ed with S. Wells) Aspects of the Problem Plays, 1982; (ed with M. Allen) Shakespeare's Plays in Quarto, 1982; (ed) Troilus and Cressida, 1982. *Recreations:* acting, producing plays, local government. *Address:* 6 Chetwynd Road, Oxton, Birkenhead, Merseyside. *T:* 051-652 3301.

MUIR, Sir Laurence (Macdonald), Kt 1981; VRD 1954; company director; Chairman, Canberra Development Board, since 1979; *b* 3 March 1925; *s* of Andrew Muir and Agnes Campbell Macdonald; *m* 1948, Ruth Richardson; two *s* two *d. Educ:* Yallourn State Sch.; Scotch Coll., Melbourne; Univ. of Melbourne (LLB). Served RAN, 1942-46 (Lieut); Lt-Comdr, RANR, 1949-65. Admitted Barrister and Solicitor, Supreme Court of Victoria, 1950. Sharebroker, 1949-80; Mem., Stock Exchange of Melbourne, 1960-80; Partner, 1962-80, Sen. Partner, 1976-80, Potter Partners. Director: ANZ Banking Gp, 1980-; ACI Ltd, 1980-; Commercial Union Assce Co. of Australia, 1979-; Wormald Internat. Ltd, 1980-; Alex Harvey Industries Ltd, NZ, 1982-; Herald and Weekly Times Ltd, 1982-; ANZ Pensions Ltd, 1982-. Fellow: Securities Inst. of Australia, 1962; Australian Inst. of Dirs, 1967; FAIM 1965. Member: Parlt House Construction Authority; Council, ANU; CSIRO Vic. Adv. Cttee; Vic. Law Foundn; State Library and Nat. Mus. Bldgs Cttee (Chm.); Exec. Cttee, Vic. 150th Anniv. Celebrations (Chm., Finance and Admin Cttee); Microsurgery Foundn (Chm.); Vic. Appeals Cttee, Anti-Cancer Council (Chm.); Board, Alfred Hosp.; Business Adv. Cttee, Baker Res. Inst.; Council, Gen. Motors, Aust. *Recreations:* tennis, gardening, fishing. *Address:* 9/5 Grand View Grove, Hawthorn, Vic 3122, Australia; Meadow End, Kyla Park, Tuross Head, NSW 2537, Australia. *Clubs:* Melbourne, Melbourne Cricket, Lawn Tennis Association of Victoria (Melbourne).

MUIR BEDDALL, Hugh Richard; *see* Beddall.

MUIR MACKENZIE, Sir Alexander (Alwyne Henry Charles Brinton), 7th Bt *cr* 1805; *b* 8 Dec. 1955; *s* of Sir Robert Henry Muir Mackenzie, 6th Bt and Charmian Cecil de Vere (*d* 1962), *o d* of Col Cecil Charles Brinton; *S* father, 1970. *Educ:* Eton; Trinity Coll., Cambridge. *Address:* Sunderland Hall, near Galashiels, Selkirkshire; Park Hall, near Kidderminster, Worcestershire.

MUIR WOOD, Sir Alan (Marshall), Kt 1982; FRS 1980; FICE; Senior Partner, Sir William Halcrow & Partners, since 1979 (Partner, 1964); Director, Halcrow Fox & Associates, since 1977; *b* 8 Aug. 1921; *s* of Edward Stephen Wood and Dorothy (*née* Webb); *m* 1943, Winifred Leyton Lanagan; three *s. Educ:* Abbotsholme Sch.; Peterhouse, Cambridge Univ. (MA; Hon. Fellow 1982). FICE 1957; Fellow, Fellowship of Engrg, 1977. Engr Officer, RN, 1942-46. Asst Engr, British Rail, Southern Reg., 1946-50; Res. Asst, Docks and Inland Waterways Exec., 1950-52; Asst Engr, then Sen. Engr, Sir William Halcrow & Partners, 1952-64. Principally concerned with studies and works in fields of tunnelling, geotechnics, coastal engrg, roads and railways; major projects include: (Proj. Engr) Clyde Tunnel and Potters Bar railway tunnels; (Partner) Cargo Tunnel at Heathrow Airport, and road crossing of River Orwell; studies and works for Channel Tunnel (intermittently from 1958 to cancellation in 1975); Dir, Orange-Fish Consultants, resp. for 80 km irrigation tunnel. Mem., SERC, 1981-. Member: Adv. Council on Applied R & D, 1980-; Governing Body, Inst. of Development Studies, 1981-; Council, ITDG, 1981-. President: (first), Internat. Tunnelling Assoc., 1975-77; ICE, 1977-78. Fellow, Imperial Coll., 1981; Foreign Fellow, Royal Swedish Acad. of Engrg Sci., 1980. Hon. DSc City, 1968. Telford Medal, ICE, 1976. *Publications:* Coastal Hydraulics, 1969, 2nd edn, 1981; papers, mainly on tunnelling and coastal engrg, in Proc. ICE, and Geotechnique. *Address:* Franklands, Bere Court Road, Pangbourne, Berks. *T:* Pangbourne 2833. *Club:* Athenæum.

MUIRHEAD, Sir David (Francis), KCMG 1976 (CMG 1964); CVO 1957; HM Diplomatic Service, retired; *b* 30 Dec. 1918; *s* of late David Muirhead, Kippen, Stirlingshire; *m* 1942, Hon. Elspeth Hope-Morley, *d* of 2nd Baron Hollenden, and of Hon. Mary Gardner, *d* of 1st Baron Burghclere; two *s* one *d. Educ:* Cranbrook Sch. Commissioned Artists Rifles (Rifle Brigade), 1937; passed Officers Exam., RMC Sandhurst; apptd to Bedfs and Herts Regt, 1939; served War of 1939-45 in France, Belgium and SE Asia. Hon. Attaché, Brit. Embassy, Madrid, 1941. Passed Foreign Service Exam., 1946; appointed to Foreign Office, 1947; La Paz, 1948; Buenos Aires, 1949; Brussels, 1950; Foreign Office, 1953; Washington, 1955; Foreign Office, 1959; Head of

Personnel Dept, FO, 1960, DSAO, 1965; Under-Sec., Special Planning Duties, Foreign Office, 1966-67; HM Ambassador: Peru, 1967-70; Portugal, 1970-74; Belgium, 1974-78. Kt Grand Cross, Military Order of Christ (Portugal). *Recreation:* tennis. *Address:* 16 Pitt Street, W8. *T:* 01-937 2443. *Clubs:* Travellers', Special Forces.

MUIRSHIEL, 1st Viscount, *cr* 1964, of Kilmacolm; **John Scott Maclay,** KT 1973; CH 1962; CMG 1944; PC 1952; DL; Lord-Lieutenant of Renfrewshire, 1967-80; *b* 26 Oct. 1905; *s* of 1st Baron Maclay, PC; *m* 1930, Betty L'Estrange Astley (*d* 1974). *Educ:* Winchester; Trinity Coll., Cambridge. MP (Nat. L and C) for Montrose Burghs, 1940-50, for Renfrewshire West, 1950-64. Head of Brit. Merchant Shipping Mission, Washington, 1944; Parliamentary Sec., Min. of Production, May-July 1945; Minister of Transport and Civil Aviation, 1951-52; Minister of State for Colonial Affairs, Oct. 1956-Jan. 1957; Sec. of State for Scotland, Jan. 1957-July 1962. Pres., Assembly of WEU, 1955-56. Pres., National Liberal Council, 1957-67; Chm., Joint Exchequer Board for Northern Ireland, 1965-72. Dir, Clydesdale Bank, 1970-. DL Renfrewshire, 1981. Hon. LLD: Edinburgh, 1963; Strathclyde, 1966; Glasgow, 1970. *Heir:* none. *Address:* Knapps, Kilmacolm, Renfrewshire. *T:* Kilmacolm 2770. *Clubs:* Boodle's; Western (Glasgow); Royal Yacht Squadron.

MUKHERJEE, Pranab Kumar; Member, since 1969, and Leader, since 1980, Rajya Sabha; Finance Minister, India, since 1982; *b* 11 Dec. 1935; *s* of Kamda Kinkar Mukherjee, of an illustrious family which was involved actively in the Freedom Movement of India; *m* 1957, Suvra Mukherjee; two *s* one *d*. *Educ:* Vidyasagar Coll., Suri; Calcutta Univ. (MA (Hist. and Pol Sci.); LLB). Dep. Minister, Mins of Industrial Develt and of Shipping and Transport, 1973-74; Minister of State, Finance Min., 1974-77; Cabinet Minister i/c of Mins of Commerce, Steel and Mines, 1980-82; became youngest Minister to hold Finance Portfolio in Independent India, 1982. *Publications:* Crisis in Democracy; An Aspect of Constitutional Problems in Bengal, 1967; Mid-Term Poll, 1969. *Recreations:* music, gardening, reading. *Address:* 2 Jantar Mantar Road, New Delhi 110001, India. *T:* (home) 382875, 381328; (office) 372810.

MUKHERJEE, Tara Kumar, FLIA; Branch Manager, Save & Prosper Group, since 1978 (District Manager, 1970-78); President, Confederation of Indian Organisations (UK), since 1975; *b* 20 Dec. 1923; *s* of Sushil Chandra Mukherjee and Sova Moyee Mukherjee; *m* 1951, Betty Patricia Mukherjee; one *s* one *d*. *Educ:* Scottish Church Collegiate Sch., Calcutta, India; Calcutta Univ. (matriculated 1939). Shop Manager, Bata Shoe Co. Ltd, India, 1941-44; Buyer, Brevitt Shoes, Leicester, 1951-56; Sundries Buyer, British Shoe Corp., 1956-66; Prodn Administrator, Priestley Footwear Ltd, Great Harwood, 1966-68; Head Stores Manager, Brit. Shoe Corp., 1968-70. Pres., India Film Soc., Leicester. Chm., Leicester Community Centre Project; Member: Brit. Europ. Movement, London; Exec. Council, Leics Europ. Movement; Trustees, Haymarket Theatre, Leicester. *Recreation:* cricket (1st Cl. cricketer; played for Bihar, Ranji Trophy, 1941; 2nd XI, Leics CCC, 1949). *Address:* Tallah, 1 Park Avenue, Hutton, Brentwood, Essex CM13 2QL. *T:* Brentwood 215438. *Club:* (Gen. Sec.) Indian National (Leicester).

MULDOON, Rt. Hon. Robert David, PC 1976; CH 1977; MP Tamaki, since 1960; Prime Minister of New Zealand, and Minister of Finance, since 1975; Leader of the National Party, since 1974; *b* 25 Sept. 1921; *s* of James Henry and Mamie R. Muldoon; *m* 1951, Thea Dale Flyger; one *s* two *d*. *Educ:* Mt Albert Grammar School. FCANZ, CMANZ, FCIS, FCWA. Chartered Accountant. Pres., NZ Inst. of Cost Accountants, 1956. Parly Under-Sec. to Minister of Finance, 1963-66; Minister of Tourism, 1967; Minister of Finance, 1967-72; Dep. Prime Minister, Feb.-Nov. 1972; Dep. Leader, National Party and Dep. Leader of the Opposition, 1972-74; Leader of the Opposition, 1974-75. Chm., Bd of Governors, IMF and World Bank, 1979-80; Chm., Ministerial Council, OECD, 1982. *Publications:* The Rise and Fall of a Young Turk, 1974; Muldoon, 1977; My Way, 1981. *Recreation:* horticulture. *Address:* Vogel House, 75 Woburn Road, Lower Hutt, New Zealand. *Clubs:* Wellington, Professional (New Zealand).

MULGRAVE, Earl of; Constantine Edmund Walter Phipps; *b* 24 Feb. 1954; *s* and *heir* of 4th Marquis of Normanby, *qv*. *Educ:* Eton (Oppidan Scholar); Worcester Coll., Oxford. *Address:* Mulgrave Castle, Whitby, N Yorks.

MULHOLLAND, family name of **Baron Dunleath.**

MULHOLLAND, Hon. Mrs John, (Olivia Vernon), DCVO 1971 (CVO 1958); Woman of the Bedchamber to Queen Elizabeth The Queen Mother since 1950; Chairman, Elizabeth Garrett Anderson Hospital, 1945-72; Vice-Chairman, Royal Free Hospital Group, 1950-61; Member: North London Group Hospital Management Committee, 1961-72; King Edward's Hospital Fund Management Committee, 1961; *b* 1902; 2nd *d* of 1st Viscount Harcourt and Mary Ethel, Viscountess Harcourt, GBE, *o d* of Walter Haynes Burns, New York and North Mymms Park, Hatfield; *m* 1923, Hon. (Godfrey) John A. M. L. Mulholland (*d* 1948), *y s* of 2nd Baron Dunleath, Ballywalter Park, Co. Down, N Ireland; one *s* two *d*. *Educ:* Notting Hill High Sch.; Lady Margaret Hall, Oxford. *Address:* Weston Mark, Upton Grey, Basingstoke, Hants. *T:* Long Sutton 429.

MULHOLLAND, Major Sir Michael (Henry), 2nd Bt *cr* 1945; retired; *b* 15 Oct. 1915; *s* of Rt Hon. Sir Henry George Hill Mulholland, 1st Bt, and

Sheelah (*d* 1982), *d* of Sir Douglas Brooke, 4th Bt; *S* father, 1971; *cousin* and *heir-pres.* to 4th Baron Dunleath, *qv*; *m* 1st, 1942, Rosemary Ker (marr. diss. 1948); 2nd, 1949, Elizabeth, *d* of Laurence B. Hyde; one *s. Educ:* Eton; Pembroke College, Cambridge (BA). Regular Army Commission, 1937, Oxford and Bucks Light Infantry; retired, 1951, with rank of Major. *Heir:* *s* Brian Henry Mulholland [*b* 25 Sept. 1950; *m* 1976, Mary Joana, *y d* of Major R. J. F. Whistler; one *s* one *d*]. *Address:* Storbrooke, Massey Avenue, Belfast BT4 2JT. *T:* Belfast 63394. *Clubs:* MCC; Light Infantry (Shrewsbury).

MULKEARNS, Most Rev. Ronald Austin; see Ballarat, Bishop of, (RC).

MULKERN, John, FCIT; Managing Director and Member of Board, British Airports Authority, since 1977; *b* 15 Jan. 1931; *s* of late Thomas Mulkern and of Annie Tennant; *m* 1954, May Egerton (*née* Peters); one *s* three *d*. *Educ:* Stretford Grammar Sch. Dip. in Govt Admin. Harvard Business Sch. AMP, 1977. FCIT 1973 (Mem. Council, 1979-82). Ministries of Supply and Aviation, Civil Service, 1949-65: Exec. Officer, finally Principal, Audit, Purchasing, Finance, Personnel and Legislation branches; British Airports Authority, 1965-: Dep. Gen. Man., Heathrow Airport, 1970-73; Dir, Gatwick Airport, 1973-77. Chm., British Airports International Ltd, 1978-82; Board Mem., Airport Operators Council Internat., 1978-81; Pres., Western European Airports' Assoc., 1981-83; Chm., Co-ordinating Council, Airports Assocs, 1982. CBIM 1981. *Recreations:* family pursuits, classical recorded music, destructive gardening. *Address:* Dorwyn, 23 St Mary's Road, Leatherhead, Surrey. *T:* Leatherhead 372378. *Club:* Royal Automobile.

MULLALY, Terence Frederick Stanley; Art Critic of The Daily Telegraph since 1958; *b* 14 Nov. 1927; *s* of late Col B. R. Mullaly (4th *s* of Maj.-Gen. Sir Herbert Mullaly, KCMG, CB, CSI) and Eileen Dorothy (*née* Stanley); *m* 1949, Elizabeth Helen (*née* Burkitt). *Educ:* in India, England, Japan and Canada; Downing Coll., Cambridge (MA). Archæological studies in Tripolitania, 1948, and Sicily, 1949; has specialised in study of Italian art, particularly Venetian and Veronese painting of 16th and 17th centuries; lecturer and broadcaster. Pres. Brit. Section, Internat. Assoc. of Art Critics, 1967-73; Vice Chm., British Art Medal Soc., 1982; Mem., Adv. Cttee: Cracow Art Festival, 1974; Palermo Art Festival, 1976; Artistic Adviser, Grand Tours. FRSA 1969; FSA 1977; FRNS 1981. Commendatore, Order Al Merito, Italy, 1974 (Cavaliere Ufficiale, 1964); l'Ordre du Mérite Culturel, Poland, 1974; Order of Merit of Poland (Silver Badge), 1978; Bulgarian 1300th Anniversary Medal, 1981. *Publications:* Ruskin a Verona, 1966; catalogue of exhibition, Disegni veronesi del Cinquecento, 1971; contrib. to catalogue of exhibition Cinquant' anni di pittura veronese: 1580-1630, 1974; contrib on history of art, to Burlington Magazine, Master Drawings, Arte Illustrata, Antologia di Belle Arti, The Minneapolis Inst. of Arts Bulletin, etc. *Recreations:* collecting and travel. *Address:* 74 Greencroft Gardens, Hampstead, NW6. *T:* 01-624 8531.

MULLAN, Charles Heron, CBE 1979; VRD; DL; Resident Magistrate, 1960-82, retired; Lieutenant-Commander RNVR; retired, 1951; *b* 17 Feb. 1912; *s* of Frederick Heron Mullan, BA, DL, Solicitor, Newry, Co. Down, and Minnie Mullan, formerly of Stow Longa, Huntingdonshire; *m* 1940, Marcella Elizabeth Sharpe, *er d* of J. A. McCullagh, Ballycastle, Co. Antrim; one *s. Educ:* Castle Park, Dalkey, Co. Dublin; Rossall Sch., Fleetwood; Clare Coll., Cambridge. Hons Degree Law, Cambridge, 1934; MA 1939. Joined Ulster Div. RNVR, 1936; called up for active service with Royal Navy, Aug. 1939; served throughout the war, HMS Rodney 1939-40; destroyers and escort vessels, Channel, North Sea, North Atlantic, etc, 1940-44 (with Royal Norwegian Navy, 1941-43); King Haakon VII War Decoration. MP (UU) Co. Down, 1946-50, Westminster Parlt; contested S Down, 1945, for NI Parlt. Mem. Ulster Unionist Council, 1946-60. Solicitor 1948; JP 1960; Chm., Belfast Juvenile Courts, 1964-79. Mem., N Ireland Section of British Delegn to 3rd UN Congress on Prevention of Crime and Treatment of Offenders, Stockholm, 1965; Mem. Exec. Cttee, British Juvenile Courts Soc., 1973-79; Vice-Pres., NI Juvenile Courts Assoc., 1980-; NI Rep. to 9th Congress of Internat. Assoc. of Youth Magistrates, Oxford, 1974; Adviser, Internat. Assoc. of Youth Magistrates, 1974-. Hon. Governor, South Down Hospitals Gp, 1965-; Vice-Pres., Rossallian Club, 1974. DL Co. Down, 1974. *Recreations:* tennis, shooting, walking, boating. *Address:* Cairn Hill, Newry, Co. Down, Northern Ireland. *T:* 2003; Casanbarra, Ballycastle, Co. Antrim, Northern Ireland. *T:* 62323. *Club:* Naval.

MULLER, Franz Joseph; QC 1978; a Recorder of the Crown Court, since 1977; *b* England, 19 Nov. 1938; *s* of Wilhelm Muller and Anne Maria (*née* Ravens). *Educ:* Mount St Mary's Coll.; Univ. of Sheffield (LLB). Called to the Bar, Gray's Inn, 1961. Graduate Apprentice, United Steel Cos, 1960-61; Commercial Asst, Workington Iron and Steel Co. Ltd, 1961-63. Commenced practice at the Bar, 1964. Non-Executive Director: Richards of Sheffield (Holdings) Ltd, 1969-77; Joseph Rodgers and Son Ltd and Rodgers Wostenholm Ltd, 1975-77. *Recreations:* squash, fell walking, being in Greece, listening to music. *Address:* 13 Taptonville Road, Sheffield S10 5BQ; 11 King's Bench Walk, Temple, EC4Y 7EQ. *T:* 01-353 3337.

MULLER, Hon. Dr Hilgard; director of companies and farmer; Law Consultant with firm of Dyason, Pretoria; MP for Beaufort West, 1964-77; *b* 4 May 1914; *s* of C. J. Muller; *m* 1943, Anita Dyason; one *s. Educ:* Pretoria Univ.; Oxford Univ.; DLitt Pretoria, BLitt Oxon., LLB S Africa. Rhodes Scholar, 1937; Oxford Rugby Blue, 1938. Univ. Lecturer, Pretoria, 1941-47.

Solicitor, 1947-61; Dir of Companies and farmer. Mayor of Pretoria, 1953-55; MP for Pretoria East, 1958-61; High Commissioner for Union of South Africa in the UK, Jan.-May, 1961; South African Ambassador to the Court of St James's, 1961-63; Minister of Foreign Affairs, South Africa, 1964-77. Hon. Pres., S Africa - Republic of China (Taiwan) Chamber of Economic Co-operation, 1980. Chancellor of the Univ. of Pretoria, 1965-, formerly Pres. of Convocation. DPhil (*hc*) Pretoria; PhD (*hc*) Stellenbosch. Mem. RSA. Grand Cross, Order of Merit (Paraguay), 1966; Grand Cross, Order of Christ (Portugal), 1968; Grand Cross of Order of Infante Dom Henrique (Portugal), 1973; Grand Officer of Order of Merit of Central African Republic, 1976; Decoration for Meritorious Service (South Africa), 1976; Grand Officer's Cross of Merit, SMO Malta, 1978. *Recreations:* golf, farming, reading. *Address:* PO Box 793, Pretoria, South Africa. *Clubs:* various in South Africa.

MULLER, Mrs Robert; see Whitelaw, Billie.

MULLETT, Leslie Baden; consultant; *b* 22 Aug. 1920; *s* of Joseph and Edith Mullett; *m* 1st, 1946, Katherine Lear (marr. diss. 1968); no *c*; 2nd, 1971, Gillian Pettit. *Educ:* Gram. Sch., Hales Owen, Worcs; Birmingham Univ. BSc (Hons Physics) 1941. Telecommunications Research Estab., 1941-46; AEA, 1946-60 (Head of Accelerator Div., 1958); Asst Dir, Rutherford High Energy Lab., SRC, 1960-68; on secondment to Res. Gp, Min. of Technology, 1966-68; CSO, Min. of Transport, 1968; CSO, Res. Requirements, DoE, 1970-74; Dep. Dir, Transport and Road Res. Lab., DoE/Dept of Transport, 1974-80. *Publications:* papers in learned jls on particle accelerators. *Recreations:* fishing, caravanning. *Address:* 22 Wellington Court, Spencers Wood, Reading, Berks. *T:* (business) Crowthorne 3131.

MULLEY, Rt. Hon. Frederick William, PC 1964; MP (Lab) Park Division of Sheffield since 1950; barrister-at-law and economist; *b* 3 July 1918; *er s* of late William and M. A. Mulley, Leamington Spa; *m* 1948, Joan D., *d* of Alexander and Betty Phillips; two *d. Educ:* Bath Place Church of England Sch.; Warwick Sch. (Schol.); Christ Church, Oxford (Adult Scholar, 1945). 1st Class Hons Philosophy, Politics and Economics, 1947; Research Studentship, Nuffield Coll., Oxford, 1947; Fellowship (Economics), St Catharine's Coll., Cambridge, 1948-50. Called to Bar, Inner Temple, 1954. Son of general labourer; clerk, National Health Insurance Cttee, Warwicks; joined Labour Party and Nat. Union of Clerks, 1936. Served War of 1939-45, Worcs Regt; Lance-Sgt 1940 (prisoner of war in Germany, 1940-45, meanwhile obtaining BSc (Econ.) and becoming Chartered Sec.). Contested (Lab) Sutton Coldfield Division of Warwicks, 1945. Parliamentary delegation to Germany, 1951, and to Kenya, 1957; PPS to Minister of Works, 1951; National Exec. Cttee, Labour Party, 1957-58, 1960-64, 1965-80; Chm., Labour Party, 1974-75. Delegate to Council of Europe and WEU, 1958-61, also Vice-Pres. Economic Cttee and Vice-Pres. WEU Assembly, 1960; Pres., WEU Assembly, 1980-. Deputy Defence Sec. and Minister for the Army, 1964-65; Minister of Aviation, Dec. 1965-Jan. 1967; Jt Minister of State, FCO (formerly FO), 1967-69; Minister for Disarmament, 1967-69; Minister of Transport, 1969-70; Minister for Transport, DoE, 1974-75; Sec. of State for Educn and Science, 1975-76; Sec. of State for Defence, 1976-79. *Publications:* The Politics of Western Defence, 1962; articles on economic, defence and socialist subjects. *Address:* House of Commons, SW1A 0AA.

MULLIGAN, Andrew Armstrong; Director of Press and Information, Delegation of the Commission of the European Communities to the US, since 1975; *b* 4 Feb. 1936; *s* of Col Hugh Waddell Mulligan, CMG, MD, DSc and Rita Aimee Armstrong; *m* 1964, Pia Ursula Schioler; two *s* two *d. Educ:* Magdalene Coll., Cambridge (Geog. and Anthropol Tripos (Hons)). Personal Asst to Man. Dir, De La Rue Co., London, 1958-60; special assignment to Australia and NZ for Irish Export Bd, 1961-62; Foreign Correspondent: Daily Telegraph and London Observer in Paris, 1962-68; Independent Television News at Ten, 1968; Producer and reporter, BBC's Panorama, 1969-73; Head of General Reports Div., EEC, Brussels, 1973-74. Publisher, Europe magazine, 1975-. *Publications:* Ouvert l'Après Midi, 1963; The All Blacks, 1964. *Recreations:* rugby, tennis, skiing, sailing, landscape painting. *Address:* Suite 707, 2100 M Street, NW, Washington, DC 20037, USA. *T:* (202) 862 9532. *Clubs:* Travellers', Annabel's; Hawks (Cambridge); Anglo-American Press Association (Paris); National Press (Washington, DC).

MULLIGAN, Most Rev. Patrick; *b* 9 June 1912; *s* of James and Mary Martin. *Educ:* St Macartan's, Monaghan; Maynooth. Prof., St Macartan's, 1938; Bishop's Sec., 1943; Headmaster, Clones, 1948; Headmaster, St Michael's, Enniskillen, 1957; Parish Priest of Machaire Rois and Vicar General and Archdeacon, 1966; Bishop of Clogher, 1970-79. *Publications:* contribs to IER, JLAS, Seanchas Clochair. *Address:* 2 Clowes Road, Monaghan, Ireland.

MULLIGAN, Prof. William, FRSE; Professor of Veterinary Physiology since 1963, and Vice-Principal since 1980, University of Glasgow; *b* 18 Nov. 1921; *s* of John Mulligan and Mary Mulligan (*née* Kelly); *m* 1948, Norah Mary Cooper; one *s* two *d. Educ:* Banbridge Academy; Queen's Univ. of Belfast (BSc). PhD London. Assistant, Dept of Chemistry, QUB, 1943-45; Demonstrator/Lectr, St Bartholomew's Med. Coll., London, 1945-51; Sen. Lectr, Veterinary Biochemistry, Univ. of Glasgow, 1951-63; McMaster Fellow, McMaster Animal Health Laboratory, Sydney, Aust., 1958-60; Dean of Faculty of Veterinary Medicine, Univ. of Glasgow, 1977-80. *Publications:* (jtly) Isotopic Tracers, 1954, 2nd edn 1959; numerous contribs to scientific jls on immunology and use of radiation and radioisotopes in animal science.

Recreations: golf, tennis, gardening, pigeon racing, theatre. *Address:* Brooks House, Cardross, Dunbartonshire G82 5HD. *T:* Cardross 269. *Club:* Royal Commonwealth Society.

MULLIKEN, Prof. Robert S., PhD; Professor of Physics and Chemistry, University of Chicago; *b* Newburyport, Mass, 7 June 1896; *s* of Samuel Parsons Mulliken, Prof. of Organic Chemistry, and Katherine (*née* Mulliken); *m* 1929, Mary Helen von Noé (decd); two *d. Educ:* Massachusetts Inst. of Technology; Univ. of Chicago. BS (MIT), 1917; PhD (Chicago), 1921. Nat. Research Coun. Fellow, Univ. of Chicago, and Harvard Univ., 1921-25; Guggenheim Fellow, Europe, 1930 and 1932-33; Fulbright Scholar, Oxford Univ., 1952-53; Vis. Fellow, St John's Coll., Oxford, 1952-53. Jun. Chem. Engr, Bureau of Mines, US Dept of Interior, Washington, 1917-18; Chemical Warfare Service, US Army, 1918 (Pte First-Class); Asst in Rubber Research, New Jersey Zinc Co., Penn., 1919; Asst Prof. of Physics, Washington Sq. Coll., New York Univ., 1926-28; Univ. of Chicago: Assoc. Prof. of Physics, 1928-31; Prof. of Physics, 1931-61 and Chemistry, 1961; Ernest de Witt Burton Distinguished Service Prof., 1956-61; Distinguished Service Prof. of Physics and Chemistry, 1961-; Distinguished Research Prof. of Chemical Physics, Florida State Univ., (Jan.-March) 1965-72. Dir, Editorial Work and Information, Plutonium Project, Univ. of Chicago, 1942-45; Scientific Attaché, US Embassy, London, 1955. Baker Lectr, Cornell Univ., 1960; Silliman Lectr, Yale Univ., 1965; Visiting Professor: Bombay, 1962; Kanpur, 1962; Jan van Geuns Vis. Prof., Amsterdam Univ., 1965. Member: Amer. Acad. of Arts and Sciences; Nat. Acad. of Sciences; Amer. Philosophical Soc.; Amer. Chem. Soc.; Fellow: Amer. Physical Soc.; Amer. Acad. for Advancement of Science; Internat. Acad. of Quantum Molecular Science; Hon. Fellow: Chem. Soc. of Gt Britain; Indian Nat. Acad. of Science; Foreign Mem., Royal Soc.; Hon. Member: Soc. de Chimie Physique, Paris; Chem. Soc., Japan; Corresp. Mem., Soc. Royale des Sciences de Liège. Hon. Mem., Royal Irish Acad.; Hon. ScD: Columbia, 1939; Marquette, 1966; Cantab, 1966; Hon. PhD Stockholm, 1960. Nobel Prize for Chemistry, 1966; other medals and awards. *Publications:* (with Willis B. Person) Molecular Complexes, 1969; Selected Papers, 1975; (with Walter C. Ermler) Diatomic Molecules: results of ab initio calculations, 1977; (with Walter C. Ermler) Polyatomic Molecules: results of ab initio calculations, 1981; over 200 contributions (1919-; in recent years dealing extensively with structure and spectra of molecular complexes) to various American and foreign journals including: Jl Am. Chem. Soc.; Jl Chem. Phys; Rev. Mod. Phys; Phys Rev.; Chem. Rev.; Nature; also contributions: Proc. Nat. Acad. Sci.; Trans Faraday Soc. *Recreations:* driving a car, Oriental rugs, art. *Address:* (home) 5825 Dorchester Avenue, Chicago, Ill 60637, USA; (office) Department of Chemistry, University of Chicago, 5735 South Ellis Avenue, Chicago, Ill 60637. *Clubs:* Quadrangle (Chicago); Cosmos (Washington).

MULLIN, Chris; Editor, Tribune, since 1982; *b* 12 Dec. 1947; *s* of Leslie and Teresa Mullin. *Educ:* Univ. of Hull (LLB). Freelance journalist, travelled extensively in Indo-China and China; sub editor, BBC World Service, 1974-78. Executive Member: Campaign for Labour Party Democracy, 1975-; Labour Co-ordinating Cttee, 1978-82. Contested (Lab): Devon N, 1970; Kingston upon Thames, Feb. 1974. Editor: Arguments for Socialism, by Tony Benn, 1979; Arguments for Democracy, by Tony Benn, 1981. *Publications:* A Very British Coup (novel), 1982; pamphlets: How to Select or Reselect your MP, 1981; The Tibetans, 1981. *Address:* c/o Tribune, 308 Gray's Inn Road, WC1X 8DY. *T:* 01-278 0911.

MULLIN, Prof. John William, DSc, PhD, CChem, FRSC, CEng, FIChemE; Professor of Chemical Engineering, since 1969, Vice-Provost, since 1980, Fellow, since 1981, University College London; Dean, Faculty of Engineering, London University, since 1979; *b* Rock Ferry, Cheshire, 22 Aug. 1925; *er s* of late Frederick Mullin and Kathleen Nellie Mullin (*née* Oppy); *m* 1952, Averil Margaret Davies, Carmarthen; one *s* one *d. Educ:* Hawarden County Sch.; UCW Cardiff (Fellow, 1981); University Coll. London. 8 yrs in organic fine chemicals industry; Lectr 1956, Reader 1961, Dean, Faculty of Engrg, 1975-77, University Coll. London. Vis. Prof., Univ. New Brunswick, 1967. Chm. Bd of Staff Examrs, Chem. Eng, Univ. London, 1965-70. Hon. Librarian, IChemE, 1965-77, Mem. Council, 1973-76; Member: Cttee of Management, Inst. of Child Health, 1970-; European Space Agency Cttee, 1977-81; Founder Mem., Brit. Assoc. for Crystal Growth; Court of Governors, University Coll., Cardiff; Chm., BS and ISO Cttees on metrication, sieves, industrial screens, particle sizing, etc. Moulton Medal, IChemE, 1970. *Publications:* Crystallization, 1961, 2nd edn 1972; (ed) Industrial Crystallization, 1976; papers in Trans IChemE, Chem. Engrg Sci., Jl Crystal Growth, etc. *Address:* 4 Milton Road, Ickenham, Mddx UB10 8NQ. *Club:* Athenæum.

MULLINS, Brian Percival, PhD; Director of Research and Laboratory Services and Head of Safety in Mines Research Establishment, Health and Safety Executive, (Under-Secretary), 1975-80; *b* 5 Aug. 1920; *s* of Thomas Percival Mullins and Lillian May Mullins; *m* 1944, Margaret Fiona Howell, MA; one *s* one *d. Educ:* Shooters' Hill Sch., London; Woolwich Polytechnic Evening Inst. BSc Nat. Sciences (London), 1940; PhD Fuel Techn. (Extern. London), 1951. Clerical Officer, Air Ministry, 1937-40; Research Scientist, Engine Dept, Royal Aircraft Estabt, 1941-42; seconded to Univ. of Cambridge for high vacuum gas analysis research, 1943; fuels, combustion and aero-engine research at Power Jets (R&D) Ltd and at Nat. Gas Turbine Estabt, 1944-60; Head of Chemistry Dept, RAE, 1960-62; Head of Chemistry, Physics and Metallurgy Dept, RAE, 1962-65; idc (seconded), 1966; Head of

Structures Dept, RAE, 1967-74. Chm., Combustion Panel, AGARD-NATO, 1954-57; Sen. UK Mem., Structures and Materials Panel, AGARD-NATO, 1967-74. *Publications*: Spontaneous Ignition of Liquid Fuels, 1955; (jtly) Explosions, Detonations, Flammability and Ignition, 1959; numerous scientific research papers. *Recreation*: oriental languages. *Address*: 1 St Michael's Road, Farnborough, Hants GU14 8ND. *T*: Farnborough (Hants) 542137.

MULLINS, Rt. Rev. Daniel Joseph; Titular Bishop of Stowe, and Auxiliary Bishop in Cardiff (RC), since 1970; *b* 10 July 1929; *s* of Timothy Mullins. *Educ*: Mount Melleray; St Mary's, Aberystwyth; Oscott Coll.; UC of S Wales and Mon, Cardiff. Priest, 1953. Curate at: Barry, 1953-56; Newbridge, 1956; Bargoed, 1956-57; Maesteg, 1957-60; Asst Chaplain to UC Cardiff, 1960-64; Sec. to Archbp of Cardiff, 1964-68; Vicar General of Archdiocese of Cardiff, 1968. Pres., Catholic Record Soc.; Chairman: Dept for Catholics in Higher Educn; Oxford and Cambridge Catholic Educn Bd; Council of Bds of Religious Studies; Assoc. of Voluntary Colls. Mem. Ct, UWIST; Governor: Heythrop Coll.; Digby Stuart Coll. *Recreations*: golf, walking. *Address*: St Joseph's Presbytery, Penarth, South Glam CF6 1RL. *T*: Penarth 708247.

MULLINS, Edwin Brandt; free-lance author, journalist and film-maker; *b* 14 Sept. 1933; *s* of Claud and Gwendolen Mullins; *m* 1960, Gillian Brydone (*d* 1982); one *s* two *d*. *Educ*: Midhurst Grammar Sch.; Merton Coll., Oxford (BA Hons, MA). Co-editor, Two Cities, 1957-58; Sub-editor and Art Correspondent, Illustrated London News, 1958-62; Art Critic: Sunday Telegraph, 1962-69; Telegraph Sunday Magazine, 1965-; contributor on arts subjects, 1962-, to The Guardian, Financial Times, Director, Apollo, Art and Artists, Studio, Radio Times. Regular broadcaster on radio and television; scriptwriter and presenter of numerous BBC TV documentaries, incl. 100 Great Paintings. *Publications*: Souza, 1962; Alfred Wallis, 1967; Josef Herman, 1967; Braque, 1968; The Art of Elisabeth Frink, 1972; The Pilgrimage to Santiago, 1974; Angels on the Point of a Pin (novel), 1979; (ed) Great Paintings, 1981; Sirens (novel), 1983. *Recreations*: everything except football. *Address*: 7 Lower Common South, SW15 1BP. *T*: 01-789 2553.

MULLINS, Leonard, CMG 1976; PhD, DSc; Director of Research, Malaysian Rubber Producers' Research Association, Brickendonbury, Hertford, since 1962; *b* 21 May 1918; *s* of Robert and Eugenie Alice Mullins; *m* 1943, Freda Elaine Churchouse; two *d*. *Educ*: Eltham Coll.; University Coll., London; Inst. of Educn, London. BSc (Hons), PhD, DSc. FInstP; FPRI. Experimental Officer, Min. of Supply, 1940-44; Scientific Officer, finally Head of Physics Gp, Research Assoc. of British Rubber Manufrs, 1944-49; Malayan (previously British) Rubber Producers' Research Assoc., 1950-; Foundn Lectr, Instn of Rubber Industry, 1968. Pres., Council of Plastics and Rubber Inst., 1981- (Chm., 1976-77; Vice-Pres., 1977-81); Chm., Adv. Cttee, Nat. Coll. of Rubber Technology, 1976-; Vice-Pres., Plastics and Rubber Inst., 1977-; Member: Court, Cranfield Inst. of Technology; Adv. Bd, Inst. of Technol., Loughborough Univ.; Council, Rubber and Plastics Res. Assoc. Discovered Mullins Effect, relating to elastic behaviour of rubber. Governor of local schools. Colwyn Medal, IRI, 1966; Comdr, Malaysian Order of Chivalry, JMN, 1975. *Publications*: numerous original scientific papers in field of rubber physics. *Address*: 32 Sherrardspark Road, Welwyn Garden City, Herts AL8 7JS. *T*: Welwyn Garden 23633. *Club*: Athenæum.

MUMFORD, Sir Albert (Henry), KBE 1963 (OBE 1946); CEng, Hon. FIEE; Engineer-in-Chief, GPO, 1960-65, retd; *b* 16 April 1903; *s* of late George Mumford; *m* 1927, Eileen Berry; two *s* two *d*. *Educ*: Bancroft's Sch.; Queen Mary Coll., Univ. of London. BSc (Eng) 1st Class Hons (London) 1923. Entered GPO Engineering Dept, 1924; Staff Engineer radio branch, 1938; Imperial Defence Coll., 1948; Asst Engineer-in-Chief, 1951; Dep. Engineer-in-Chief, 1954. Treasurer, Instn of Electrical Engineers, 1969-72 (Chm. Radio Section, 1945-46; Vice-Pres. 1958-63; Pres. 1963-64; Hon. Fellow, 1980); Pres. Assoc. Supervising Electrical Engineers, 1964-66; Treas., Instn of Electrical and Electronic Incorporated Engineers, 1967- (Hon. Fellow 1978). Fellow, Queen Mary Coll., 1962; Hon. Fellow, Polytechnic of the South Bank, 1982; Hon. Mem., City and Guilds of London Inst. *Publications*: many scientific papers. *Address*: 27 Grendon Gardens, Wembley Park, Mddx. *T*: 01-904 2360.

MUMFORD, Prof. Enid; Professor of Organizational Behaviour, Manchester Business School, since 1979; *d* of Arthur McFarland and Dorothy Evans; *m* 1947, Jim Mumford; one *s* one *d*. *Educ*: Wallasey High Sch.; Liverpool Univ. (BA, MA); Manchester Univ. (PhD). CIPM. Personnel Officer, Rotol Ltd, 1946-47; Production Supervisor, J. D. Francis Ltd, 1947-48; Research Associate: Dept of Social Science, Liverpool Univ., 1948-56; Bureau of Public Health Economics, Univ. of Michigan, USA, 1956-57; Res. Lectr, Dept of Social Science, Liverpool Univ., 1957-65; Lectr, then Sen. Lectr and Reader, Manchester Business Sch., 1966-79. *Publications*: Chester Royal Infirmary 1856-1956, 1956; Living with a Computer, 1964; Computers Planning and Personnel Management, 1969; Systems Design for People, 1971; Job Satisfaction: a study of computer specialists, 1972; (with others) Coal and Conflict, 1963; (with O. Banks) The Computer and the Clerk, 1967; (with T. B. Ward) Computers: planning for people, 1968; (with E. Pettigrew) Implementing Strategic Decisions, 1975; (ed, with H. Sackman) Human Choice and Computers, 1975; (ed, with K. Legge) Designing Organizations for Efficiency and Satisfaction, 1978; (with D. Henshall) A Participative Approach to Computer Systems Design, 1978; (with M. Weir) Computer Systems in Work Design, 1979; (ed. with C. Cooper) The Quality of

Working Life, 1979; (with others) The Impact of Systems Change in Organizations, 1980; Values, Technology and Work, 1980; contribs to books and journals. *Address*: Manchester Business School, Booth Street West, Manchester M15 6PB. *T*: 061-273 8228.

MUMFORD, Lewis; writer; *b* 19 Oct. 1895; *s* of Lewis Mumford and Elvina Conradina Baron; *m* 1921, Sophia Wittenberg; (one son killed in action 1944) one *d*. *Educ*: Coll. of the City of New York, Columbia Univ. Radio operator (USN) 1918; Associate editor Fortnightly Dial, 1919; Acting Editor Sociological Review (London), 1920; Co-editor American Caravan, 1927-36. Member: National Inst. of Arts and Letters 1930-; Amer. Academy of Arts and Letters, 1956- (Pres., 1962-65); Amer. Philosophical Soc., Amer. Academy of Arts and Sciences; Bd of Higher Educn, City of New York, 1935-37; Commn on Teacher Educn, Amer. Council on Educn, 1938-44; Prof. of Humanities, Stanford Univ., 1942-44. Hon. LLD Edinburgh 1965; Hon. Dr Arch., Rome, 1967. Hon. Phi Beta Kappa, 1957; Hon. Fellow, Stanford Univ., 1941. Hon. FRIBA (Hon. ARIBA, 1942); Hon. MRTPI (Hon. Mem. TPI, 1946); Hon. Member: Amer. Inst. of Architects, 1951; Town Planning Inst. of Canada, 1960; Amer. Inst. of Planners, 1955; Colegio del Arquitectas del Peru; Prof. of City Planning, Univ. of Pennsylvania, 1951-56; Vis. Prof., MIT, 1957-60; Ford Prof., Univ. of Pennsylvania, 1959-60; Univ. of Calif., 1961; Fellow, Wesleyan Univ. Center for Advanced Studies, 1963; MIT: Vis. Lectr, 1973-74; Charles Abrams Prof., 1975. Co-chairman Wenner-Gren Foundation Conf. on Man's Use of the Earth, 1955. Made six documentary films on City for National Film Board, Canada, 1964. Hon. Fellow, Royal Inst. of Architects of Ireland. Townsend Harris Medal, 1939; Ebenezer Howard Memorial Medal, 1946; Medal of Honour, Fairmount Park Art Assoc., 1953; TPI (later RTPI) Gold Medal, 1957; RIBA Royal Gold Medal for Architecture, 1961; Presidential Medal of Freedom, 1964; Emerson-Thoreau Medal, Amer. Acad. of Arts and Sciences, 1965; Gold Medal, Belles Lettres, Nat. Inst. of Arts and Letters, 1970; Leonardo da Vinci Medal, Soc. for Hist. of Technology, 1969; Hodgkins Medal, Smithsonian Instn, 1971; Thomas Jefferson Meml Foundn Medal, 1972; Nat. Medal for Literature, 1972; Prix Mondial del Duca, 1976. Hon. KBE 1975. *Publications*: The Story of Utopias, 1922; Sticks and Stones, 1924; The Golden Day, 1926; Herman Melville, 1929; The Brown Decades, 1931; Technics and Civilization, 1934; The Culture of Cities, 1938; Whither Honolulu?, 1938; Men Must Act, 1939; Faith for Living, 1940; The South in Architecture, 1941; The Condition of Man, 1944; City Development, 1945; Values for Survival, 1946 (Programme for Survival (Eng.), 1946); Green Memories: The Story of Geddes Mumford, 1947; The Conduct of Life, 1951; Art and Technics, 1952; In the Name of Sanity, 1954; The Human Prospect, 1955; From the Ground Up, 1956; The Transformations of Man, 1956; The City in History, 1961; Highway and City, 1962; Herman Melville (rev. edn), 1963; The Myth of the Machine, 1967; The Urban Prospect, 1968; The Van Wyck Brooks-Lewis Mumford Letters, 1970; The Pentagon of Power, 1971; The Letters of Lewis Mumford and Frederic J. Osborn, 1971; Interpretations and Forecasts, 1973; Findings and Keepings: analects for an autobiography, 1975; Architecture as a Home for Man, 1975; My Works and Days: a personal chronicle, 1979. *Address*: Amenia, New York 12501, USA.

MUMFORD, Rt. Rev. Peter; *see* Truro, Bishop of.

MUMFORD, William Frederick; Assistant Under-Secretary of State (Materiel) Navy, Ministry of Defence, since 1980; *b* 23 Jan. 1930; *s* of late Frederick Charles Mumford and Hester Leonora Mumford; *m* 1958, Elizabeth Marion, *d* of Nowell Hall; three *s* one *d*. *Educ*: St Albans Sch.; Lincoln Coll., Oxford (MA PPE). Nat. Service commission, Royal Artillery, 1949-50. Appointed to Home Civil Service, 1953; Asst Principal, 1953-58, Principal, 1958-60, Air Ministry; First Secretary, UK Delegn to NATO, Paris, 1960-65; Principal, 1965-67, Asst Sec., 1967-73, Defence Secretariat, MoD; Dep. Head of UK Delegn to MBFR Exploratory Talks, Vienna, 1973; Principal Private Sec. to Secretaries of State for Defence: Rt Hon. Lord Carrington, 1973-74, Rt Hon. Ian Gilmour, MP and Rt Hon. Roy Mason, MP, 1974-75; Under-Sec., Machinery of Govt Div., CSD, 1975-76; Asst Sec.-Gen. for Defence Planning and Policy, NATO, Brussels, 1976-80. *Recreations*: antique book collecting, music, swimming. *Address*: c/o Barclays Bank Ltd, 366 Strand, WC2R 0JQ.

MUMMERY, Sir Hugh Evelyn L.; *see* Lockhart-Mummery.

MUMMERY, John Frank; Treasury Junior Counsel (Chancery), since 1981; *b* 5 Sept. 1938; *s* of Frank Stanley Mummery and Ruth Mummery (*née* Coleman), Coldred, Kent; *m* 1967, Elizabeth Anne Lamond Lackie, *d* of Dr D. G. L. Lackie and Ellen Lackie (*née* Easterbrook), Edinburgh; one *s* one *d*. *Educ*: Oakleigh House, Dover; Dover County Grammar Sch.; Pembroke Coll., Oxford, 1959-63 (MA, BCL; Winter Williams Prize in Law). National Service, The Border Regt and RAEC, 1957-59. Called to Bar, Gray's Inn (Atkin Schol.), 1964; Mem., Justice Cttee on Privacy and the Law, 1967-70; Treasury Junior Counsel in Charity Matters, 1977-81. Member, Senate of Inns of Court and Bar, 1978-81. Mem., Art Registration Cttee, 1969-. *Publication*: (co-ed) Copinger and Skone James on Copyright, 12th edn. *Recreation*: long walks with family, friends and alone. *Address*: (chambers) 5 New Square, Lincoln's Inn, WC2. *T*: 01-405 6430; (home) 5 Canonbury Grove, N1. *T*: 01-226 4140.

MUNFORD, William Arthur, MBE 1946; PhD; FLA; Librarian Emeritus, National Library for the Blind; *b* 27 April 1911; *s* of late Ernest Charles Munford and Florence Margaret Munford; *m* 1934, Hazel Despard Wilmer;

two s one d. *Educ:* Hornsey County Sch.; LSE (BScEcon, PhD). Asst, Hornsey Public Libraries, 1927-31; Chief Asst, Ilford Public Libraries, 1931-34; Borough Librarian, Dover, 1934-45 (Food Exec. Officer, 1939-45); City Librarian, Cambridge, 1945-53; Dir-Gen., Nat. Library for the Blind, 1954-82. Hon. Sec., Library Assoc., 1952-55, Hon. Fellow 1977. Trustee, Ulverscroft Foundn. *Publications:* Books for Basic Stock, 1939; Penny Rate: aspects of British public library history, 1951; William Ewart, MP, 1960; Edward Edwards, 1963; (with W. G. Fry) Louis Stanley Jast, 1966; James Duff Brown, 1968; A History of the Library Association, 1877-1977, 1976; contribs to Librarianship jls, 1933-. *Recreations:* reading, rough gardening, wood sawing, cycling, serendipity. *Address:* 11 Manor Court, Pinehurst, Grange Road, Cambridge CB3 9BE. *T:* Cambridge 62962. *Club:* National Liberal.

MUNN, James, OBE 1976; MA; Rector, Cathkin High School, Cambuslang, Glasgow, since 1970; *b* 27 July 1920; *s* of Douglas H. Munn and Margaret G. Dunn; *m* 1946, Muriel Jean Millar Moles; one *d*. *Educ:* Stirling High Sch.; Glasgow Univ. (MA (Hons)). Entered Indian Civil Service, 1941; served in Bihar, 1942-47. Taught in various schools in Glasgow, 1949-57; Principal Teacher of Modern Languages, Falkirk High Sch., 1957-62, Depute Rector, 1962-66; Rector, Rutherglen Acad., 1966-70. Member: Consultative Cttee on Curriculum, 1968-80, Chm., 1980-; University Grants Cttee, 1973-; Chm., Cttee to review structure of curriculum at SIII and SIV, 1975-77. Chevalier des Palmes Académiques, 1967. DUniv Stirling, 1978. *Recreations:* reading, bridge. *Address:* 4 Kincath Avenue, High Burnside, Glasgow G73 4RP. *T:* 041-634 4654.

MUNN, Rear-Adm. William James, CB 1962; DSO 1941; OBE 1946; *b* 15 July 1911; *s* of late Col R. G. Munn, CMG, FRGS, and late Mrs R. G. Munn; *m* 1940, Susan Astle Sperling, Teviot Bank, Hawick, Scotland; two *s*. *Educ:* Britannia Royal Naval College, Dartmouth. Cadet and Midshipman in HMS Nelson, 1929-31. Flag Lt (Battle Cruiser Sqdn during Spanish Civil War); served War of 1939-45 (despatches, DSO): First Lt Destroyer HMS Mohawk; Comd Destroyer HMS Hereward (Battle of Matapan, evacuation of Crete), 1941. POW in Italy and Germany, 1941-45. Comd HMS Venus (Mediterranean during Palestine trouble, OBE), 1945-47; Comdr 1946; psc 1949; Exec. Officer, Cruiser HMS Kenya (Far East Station, Korean War, despatches), 1949-51; Capt., 1951; Capt. of the Britannia Royal Naval College, Dartmouth, 1956-58; Capt. of HMS Gambia, Nov. 1958-Dec. 1960; Rear-Adm. 1960; Chief of Staff to the Comdr-in-Chief, Home Fleet, 1961-63, retd. *Recreation:* golf. *Address:* The Old Rectory, Langham, near Bury St Edmunds, Suffolk. *T:* Walsham-le-Willows 234. *Clubs:* Royal Worlington Golf, North Berwick Golf, Gullane Golf.

MUNRO, Alan Gordon; HM Diplomatic Service; Head of Defence Sales 1 (Middle East), Ministry of Defence, since 1981; *b* 17 Aug. 1935; *s* of late Sir Gordon Munro, KCMG, MC and Lilian Muriel Beit; *m* 1962, Rosemary Grania Bacon; twin *s* two *d*. *Educ:* Wellington Coll.; Clare Coll., Cambridge (MA). MIPM. Mil. Service, 4/7 Dragoon Guards, 1953-55; Middle East Centre for Arab Studies, 1958-60; British Embassy, Beirut, 1960-62; Kuwait, 1961; FO, 1963-65; Head of Chancery, Benghazi, 1965-66 and Tripoli, 1966-68; FO, 1968-73; Consul (Commercial), 1973-74, Consul-Gen., 1974-77, Rio de Janeiro; Head of E African Dept, FCO, 1977-78; Head of Middle East Dept, FCO, 1979; Head of Personnel Ops Dept, FCO, 1979-81. *Recreations:* historic buildings, gardening, music, history. *Address:* c/o Foreign and Commonwealth Office, SW1A 2AL; Eynham House, Chiswick Mall, W4 2PJ. *T:* 01-994 5022. *Club:* Travellers'.

MUNRO, Alison (Mrs), CBE 1964; Chairman: Chichester Health Authority, since 1982; Central Transport Consultative Committee, since 1980; *d* of late John Donald, MD; *m* 1939, Alan Lamont Munro (killed on active service, 1941); one *s*. *Educ:* Queen's Coll., Harley Street; Wynberg Girls' High Sch., South Africa; St Paul's Girls' Sch.; St Hilda's Coll., Oxford (MA). Ministry of Aircraft Production, 1942-45; Principal, Ministry of Civil Aviation, 1945; Asst Sec., 1949; Under-Sec., Ministry of Transport and Civil Aviation, 1958; Under-Sec., Ministry of Aviation, 1960; High Mistress, St Paul's Girls' Sch. Hammersmith, 1964-74. Chm., Merton, Sutton and Wandsworth AHA(T), 1974-82. Chairman: Training Council for Teachers of the Mentally Handicapped, 1966-69; Cttee of Inquiry into Children's Footwear, 1972; Member: Board, BEA, 1966-73; Board, British Library, 1973-79; BTA, 1973-81; Maternity Services Adv. Cttee, 1981-. Governor, Charing Cross Group of Hospitals, 1967-74. *Recreations:* gardening, tennis, sailing, Scottish dancing. *Address:* Harbour Way, Ellanore Lane, West Wittering, West Sussex PO20 8AN. *T:* West Wittering 3274. *Club:* University Women's.

MUNRO, Charles Rowcliffe; *b* 6 Nov. 1902; *s* of Charles John Munro, CA, Edinburgh, Hon. Sheriff Substitute, County of Selkirk, and of Edith Rowcliffe; *m* 1942, Moira Rennie Ainslie, *d* of Dr Alexander Cruickshank Ainslie; two *s*. *Educ:* Merchiston Castle Sch., Edinburgh. Hon. Treasurer W Edinburgh Unionist Assoc., 1945-61, Hon. Treas. Scottish Nat. Cttee English-Speaking Union of the Commonwealth 1952-64; Pres. Edinburgh Union of Boys' Clubs, 1957-66. *Recreation:* fishing. *Address:* 17 Succoth Place, Edinburgh EH12 6BJ. *T:* 031-337 2139.

MUNRO, Colin William Gordon R.; *see* Ross-Munro.

MUNRO, Ian Arthur Hoyle, MB, MRCP; Editor of The Lancet, since 1976; *b* 5 Nov. 1923; *o s* of Gordon Alexander and Muriel Rebecca Munro; *m* 1948, Olive Isabel, MRCS, LRCP, *o d* of Ernest and Isabella Jackson; three *s* two

d. Educ: Huddersfield Coll.; Paston Sch., North Walsham; Royal Liberty Sch., Romford; Guy's Hosp. (MB 1946). MRCP 1980. Served with RAMC, 1947-50. Joined staff of The Lancet, 1951, Dep. Editor, 1965-76. *Recreations:* cricket, crosswords. *Address:* Oakwood, Bayley's Hill, Sevenoaks, Kent TN14 6HS. *T:* Sevenoaks 454993. *Clubs:* Athenæum; Yorkshire CC.

MUNRO of Foulis-Obsdale, Sir Ian Talbot, 15th Bt *cr* 1634; *b* 28 Dec. 1929; *s* of Robert Hector Munro (*d* 1965) (*n* of 12th and 13th Bts) and Ethel Amy Edith, *d* of Harry Hudson; *S* cousin, Sir Arthur Herman Munro, 14th Bt, 1972. Heir: uncle Malcolm Munro [*b* 24 Feb. 1901; *m* 1931, Constance, *d* of William Carter; one *d* (one *s* decd)]. *Address:* 38 Clarence Gate Gardens, NW1.

MUNRO, John Bennet Lorimer, CB 1959; CMG 1953; *b* 20 May 1905; *s* of late Rev. J. L. Munro; *m* 1st, 1929, Gladys Maie Forbes Simmons (*d* 1965); three *s*; 2nd, 1965, Margaret Deacy Ozanne, Blackfort House, Foxford, County Mayo. *Educ:* Edinburgh Academy; Edinburgh University; Corpus Christi Coll., Oxford. ICS: entered, 1928; Under-Sec. Public Dept, Fort St George, 1934; HM Treasury, 1939; Min. of Supply, 1943; idc, 1949; Div. of Atomic Energy Production, 1950; Chief Administrative Officer, UK High Commission for Germany, 1951; Under-Sec.: Min. of Supply, 1953; Bd of Trade, 1955-62; Export Credits Guarantee Dept, 1962-65; Consultant, Export Council for Europe, 1966-67. *Address:* 77 Shirley Drive, Hove, Sussex BN3 6UE. *T:* Brighton 556705.

MUNRO OF FOULIS, Captain Patrick, TD 1958; DL 1949; 30th Chief of Clan Munro; landowner and farmer; Vice-Lieutenant of Ross and Cromarty, 1968-77; *b* 30 Aug. 1912; *e s* of late Col C. H. O. Gascoigne, DSO, Seaforth Highlanders, and Eva Marion, *d* of Sir Hector Munro of Foulis, 11th Bt; assumed arms and designation of Munro of Foulis on death of his grandfather; *m* 1947, Eleanor Mary, *d* of Capt. Hon. William French, French Park, Co. Roscommon, Eire; three *s* one *d*. *Educ:* Imperial Service Coll., Windsor; RMC Sandhurst. 2nd Lt Seaforth Highlanders, 1933; Capt. 1939. Served War of 1939-45, France (POW). Mem. Ross and Cromarty T&AFA, 1938. Hon. Sheriff of Ross and Cromarty, 1973. *Address:* Foulis Castle, Evanton, Ross-shire. *T:* Evanton 212. *Club:* MCC.

MUNRO, Hon. Sir Robert (Lindsay), Kt 1977; CBE 1962; President of the Senate, Fiji, since 1970; *b* NZ, 2 April 1907; *s* of Colin Robert Munro and Marie Caroline Munro; *m* 1937, Lucie Ragnhilde Mee; two *s* one *d*. *Educ:* Auckland Grammar Sch.; Auckland University Coll. (LLB). Barrister and Solicitor, 1929. Served War, 1940-46: 1st Lieut, FMF. Founder Chairman, Fiji: Town Planning Bd, 1946-53; Broadcasting Commn, 1953-61. Member: Educn Bd and Educn Adv. Council, 1943-70; Legislative Council, 1945-46; Nat. Health Adv. Cttee, 1976-. President: Law Soc., 1960-62 and 1967-69; Family Planning Assoc. of Fiji, 1963-. Internat. Planned Parenthood Federation: formerly Mem., Governing Body; Regional Vice-Pres., 1973-. Govt Representative: Bangkok reg. pre-consultation World Population Conf., ECAFE, 1974; World Pop. Conf., Bucharest, 1974; E Asian and Pacific Copyright Seminar, Sydney, 1976. Order of St Olav, Norway, 1966. Rifle shooting Blue; Captain, NZ Hockey Team, 1932. *Recreations:* literature, garden, music. *Address:* Foulis, 6 Milne Road, Suva, Fiji. *T:* 22166. *Club:* Fiji (Suva).

MUNRO, Robert Wilson, CMG 1967; HM Diplomatic Service, retired; *b* 21 Jan. 1915; *yr s* of late J. S. Munro and late Mrs E. G. Munro, Dunedin, NZ; *m* 1946, Annette Kilroy; two *s*. *Educ:* Otago Boys' High Sch., Univ. of Otago, New Zealand, MSc 1936, and Univ. of London, BSc(Econ), 1950. Research Chemist, NZ Dept of Agriculture, 1938-40. Served with 2 NZEF and UK Forces, 1941-45. Sudan Civil Service, 1945-52; HM Diplomatic Service, 1952-74: served in London, Warsaw, Paris, Baghdad and Khartoum; Inspector, Diplomatic Service, 1967-69; Dep. High Comr, Nairobi, 1969-71; RN College, Greenwich, 1971-72; Dep. High Comr, Wellington, 1972-74. Middle East Advr, NZ Meat Producers' Bd, 1978-80. Order of Nilein, 1965. *Recreations:* camping, shooting. *Address:* 7 Lynmouth Avenue, Karori, Wellington, New Zealand. *Club:* Wellington (Wellington).

MUNRO, Sir Sydney Douglas G.; *see* Gun-Munro, S. D.

MUNRO, Sir (Thomas) Torquil (Alfonso), 5th Bt, *cr* 1825; JP Angus; *b* 7 Feb. 1901; *e s* of 4th Bt and Selina Dorothea (*d* 1902), *d* of Major-General T. E. Byrne; *S* father, 1919; *m* 1st, 1925, Beatrice (who obtained a divorce, 1932), *d* of late Robert Sanderson Whitaker; one *s*; 2nd, 1934, Averil Moira Katharine (*d* 1982), *d* of Kenneth Owen Hunter; one *s* one *d*. *Educ:* Winchester. Heir: *s* Alasdair Thomas Ian Munro [*b* 6 July 1927; *m* 1954, Marguerite Lillian, *d* of late Franklin R. Loy, Dayton, Ohio, USA; one *s* one *d*]. *Address:* Lindertis, Kirriemuir, Angus. *TA:* Munro, Lindertis, Kirriemuir, Angus. *T:* Craigton 209.
See also Baron Colyton.

MUNRO, William, QC (Scotland) 1959; *b* 19 April 1900; *s* of William Munro, JP, Kilmarnock, and Janet Thomson Munro; *m* 1950, Christine Frances, *d* of W. B. Robertson, MC, DL, Colton, Dunfermline; three *d*. *Educ:* Glasgow High Sch.; Glasgow Univ. (MA, LLB). Called to Scottish Bar, 1925; called to Bar of Straits Settlements, 1927; Johore, 1927. Practised in Singapore and Malaya, 1927-57; Partner, Allen & Gledhill, Singapore. 1933-57 (Prisoner of war, Feb. 1942-Aug. 1945). Resumed practice Scottish Bar, 1958. *Recreation:* reading. *Address:* 9 The Hawthorns, Muirfield Park, Gullane

EH31 2DZ. *T:* Gullane 84 2398. *Clubs:* Caledonian; New (Edinburgh), Hon. Company of Edinburgh Golfers.

MUNRO-LUCAS-TOOTH of Teananich, Sir Hugh (Vere Huntly Duff), 1st Bt, *cr* 1920; Lieutenant-Colonel Queen's Own Cameron Highlanders; *b* 13 Jan. 1903; *er s* of Major Hugh Munro Warrand of Bught and Beatrice Maud Lucas, *e c* of late Sir Robert Lucas Lucas-Tooth, Bt, of Holme Lacy, Co. Hereford, and *co-heiress* with her sisters in the lordship of the Manor of Holme Lacy; *m* 1925, Laetitia Florence, OBE 1958 (*d* 1978), *er d* of Sir John R. Findlay, 1st Bt; one *s* two *d. Educ:* Eton; Balliol Coll., Oxford. Called to Bar, Lincoln's Inn, 1933; MP (C) Isle of Ely, 1924-29, Hendon South, 1945-70; Parliamentary Under-Sec. of State, Home Office, 1952-55. Mem., Nat. Water Council, 1973-76. Sir Robert Lucas-Tooth, 1st Bt, having died, and all his three sons having lost their lives in France during the European War, HM the King was graciously pleased to grant a re-creation of the baronetcy in favour of Sir Robert's eldest grandson, H. V. H. D. Warrand, who assumed the name and arms of Lucas-Tooth in place of Warrand by Royal Letters Patent; changed name by Deed Poll from Lucas-Tooth to Munro-Lucas-Tooth of Teananich, 1965. *Heir: s* Hugh John Lucas-Tooth [*b* 20 Aug. 1932; *m* 1955, Caroline, *e d* of 1st Baron Poole, *qv*; three *d*]. *Address:* Burgate Court, Fordingbridge, Hants. *Club:* Brooks's.
See also Sir Michael Oppenheimer.

MUNROW, Roger Davis; Principal Assistant Treasury Solicitor, since 1981; *b* 20 March 1929; *s* of William Davis Munrow, *qv*, and Constance Caroline Munrow (*née* Moorcroft); *m* 1957, Marie Jane Beresford; three *d. Educ:* Bryanston School; Oriel College, Oxford. MA; Solicitor. Entered Treasury Solicitor's Dept as Legal Assistant, 1959; Senior Legal Assistant, 1965; Assistant Treasury Solicitor, 1973. *Recreations:* swimming, cycling, tennis. *Address:* 20 Monahan Avenue, Purley, Surrey CR2 3BA. *T:* 01-660 1872.

MUNROW, William Davis, CBE 1963; Chief Inspector of Audit, Ministry of Housing and Local Government, 1965-68; *b* 28 April 1903; 2nd *s* of Alexander Gordon Davis and Charlotte Munrow; *m* 1927, Constance Caroline Moorcroft (*d* 1977); one *s. Educ:* Council Schs; Birkbeck Coll.; and London Sch. of Economics (BSc(Econ)). District Auditor for London, 1954; Dep. Chief Inspector of Audit, 1958. *Recreation:* golf. *Address:* 60 Withyham Road, Cooden, Bexhill-on-Sea, East Sussex. *T:* Cooden 2543.
See also R. D. Munrow.

MUNSTER, 6th Earl of, *cr* 1831; **Edward Charles FitzClarence;** Viscount FitzClarence, Baron Tewkesbury, 1831; *b* 3 Oct. 1899; *s* of Brig.-Gen. Charles FitzClarence, VC (*g s* of 1st Earl) (killed in action, 1914), and Violet (*d* 1941), *d* of Lord Alfred Spencer-Churchill; *S* cousin, 1975; *m* 1st, 1925, Monica Shiela Harrington (marr. diss. 1930; she *d* 1958), *d* of Lt-Col Sir Henry Mulleneux Grayson, 1st Bt, KBE; one *s* one *d* ; 2nd, 1939, Mrs Vivian Schofield, *d* of late Benjamin Schofield, JP, and step *d* of late Judge A. J. Chotzner (MP Upton Div., West Ham, 1931-34). *Educ:* Eton; RMC Sandhurst. Captain Irish Guards, retired. Served 1st Bn Irish Guards, Narvik, Norway, 1940; No 8 Commando, Western Desert, 1941. *Heir: s* Viscount FitzClarence, *qv. Address:* 98 Whitelands House, Cheltenham Terrace, SW3.

MUNTZ, (Frederick) Alan (Irving), FRAeS; Consultant; *b* 7 June 1899; *s* of Major Irving Muntz and Jessie Challoner; *m* 1st, 1923, Mary Lee (marr diss., 1934), 3rd *d* of Canon W. L. Harnett; one *s* two *d* ; 2nd, 1934, Lady Margaret Frances Anne (marr. diss., 1939), 2nd *d* of 7th Marquess of Londonderry; 3rd, 1948, Marjorie Mary Helena, 2nd *d* of Edward Strickland, Ceylon; one *d. Educ:* Winchester; Trinity Coll., Cambridge. (BA Mech. Sciences). Served in France; 2nd Lt 432nd Field Co. RE, 1918; British Petroleum Co., Ltd, 1922-26; Anglo-Iranian Oil Co., Ltd, 1926-28; with Sir Nigel Norman founded Airwork Ltd, and Heston Airport, 1928; with Talaat Harb Pasha, Banque Misr, Cairo, founded Misr Airwork SAE, 1932; with R. E. Grant Govan, Delhi, helped found Indian National Airways Ltd, 1933; founded: Alan Muntz & Co. Ltd to develop Pescara free piston engine system and other inventions, 1937; Alan Muntz Consultants, 1965, retired, 1975. *Recreations:* golf, fishing, travelling. *Address:* The Bothy, Furzedown Lane, Amport, near Andover, Hants. *T:* Weyhill 3254; rue du Baou, Callian, 83440 Fayence, Var, France. *T:* (94) 76.53.70.

MUNTZ, Thomas Godric Aylett, CMG 1951; OBE 1948; retired; *b* 31 May 1906; *s* of R. A. Muntz, Tansor Manor, Peterborough; *m* 1st, 1932, Marjorie (*d* 1968), *d* of Sir Charles Statham; two *s* ; 2nd, 1969, June Robertson (*d* 1982). *Educ:* Lancing; Pembroke Coll., Oxford. Appointed to Dept of Overseas Trade, 1929; served at office of HM Trade Commissioner, New Zealand, 1931-38; Embassy, Warsaw, 1938-39; Board of Trade, 1939-40; Montreal, 1940-42; Embassy, Rio de Janeiro, 1942-43; Lisbon, 1944-47; Ankara, 1947-50; Head of Economic Relations Dept, Foreign Office, 1950-51; Tangier, 1952-55; Antwerp, 1957-59. *Address:* Kirk's Lodge, King's Cliffe, near Peterborough.

MURCHIE, John Ivor; His Honour Judge Murchie; a Circuit Judge, since 1974; *b* 4 June 1928; *s* of Captain Peter Archibald Murchie, OBE, RD, RNR; *m* 1953, Jenifer Rosalie Luard; one *s* two *d. Educ:* Edinburgh Academy; Rossall Sch.; Exeter Coll., Oxford (MA). Called to the Bar, Middle Temple, 1953; Harmsworth Scholarship, 1956. Dep. Chm., Berkshire QS, 1969-71; a Recorder of the Crown Court, 1972-74. Chm. Council, Rossall Sch., 1979-.

Recreations: versifying and diversifying. *Address:* Brook House, Warren Row, Wargrave, Reading RG10 8QS.

MURCHISON, Very Rev. Thomas Moffat, DD; *b* 27 July 1907; *s* of Malcolm Murchison and Ann Moffat; *m* 1940, Mary Black Morton Philp; one *s* two *d. Educ:* Portree High Sch.; University and Trinity Coll., Glasgow. DD Glasgow, 1964. Minister of Glenelg, Inverness-shire, 1932-37; St Columba Copland Road Church, Glasgow, 1937-66; St Columba Summertown Church, Glasgow, 1966-72. Member: BBC National Broadcasting Council for Scotland, 1952-57; Scottish National Parks Cttee, 1946-47; Panel of Religious Advisers, ITA, 1966-70; Pres., Highland Development League; Convener, Church of Scotland Home Board, 1959-64; Convener, Church of Scotland Adv. Board, 1967-72; Moderator of Gen. Assembly of Church of Scotland, 1969-70. Internat. Pres., Celtic Congress, 1966-71. Chm. Dirs, Scottish Jl of Theology, 1970-74. Crowned Bard of the National Mod, 1958; Chief of Gaelic Society of Inverness, 1961; Bard of the Gorseth of the Bards of Cornwall, 1969. *Publications:* The Plight of the Smallholders, 1935; (Jt Editor) Alba: A Miscellany, 1948; (ed) The Golden Key, 1950; Gaelic Prose writings of Donald Lamont, 1960; Editor, The Gael, 1946-57; Editor, Gaelic Supplement, Life and Work, 1951-80; numerous English and Gaelic articles and broadcasts. *Recreations:* Gaelic literature, highland history. *Address:* Kylerhea, Isle of Skye, by Kyle, Ross-shire; 10 Mount Stuart Street, Glasgow G41 3YL. *T:* 041-632 4276.

MURDOCH, Air Marshal Sir Alister Murray, KBE 1966 (CBE 1946); CB 1960; *b* 9 Dec. 1912; *s* of Brig. T. Murdoch, DSO, Melbourne; *m* 1937, Florence Eilene, *d* of Charles Herbert Miller, Sydney; one *d. Educ:* Caulfield Grammar Sch.; RMC Duntroon, Canberra. Attached to Directorate of Operations and Intelligence, 1938-39. Served War of 1939-45 (CBE). Senior Air Staff Officer, RAAF HQ, 1944; Dir, Air Staff Plans and Policy, 1949-52; AOC RAAF Pt Cook, and Comdt RAAF Coll., Pt Cook, 1952-53; AOC Training Command, 1954-58; Dep. Chief of the Air Staff, 1958-59; RAAF Representative in London, 1959-62; AOC, HQ Operational Command, 1962-65; idc; Chief of the Air Staff, RAAF, 1965-70. *Recreations:* golf and tennis. *Address:* 11 East View Road, Church Point, NSW 2105, Australia.

MURDOCH, Dame Elisabeth (Joy), DBE 1963 (CBE 1961); *b* 1909; *d* of Rupert Greene and Marie (*née* de Lancey Forth); *m* 1928, Sir Keith (Arthur) Murdoch (*d* 1952); one *s* three *d. Educ:* Clyde Sch., Woodend, Victoria. Pres., Royal Children's Hospital, Melbourne, Victoria, Australia, 1953-65. Trustee, National Gallery, Victoria, 1968-76. Hon. LLD Melbourne, 1982. *Recreation:* gardening. *Address:* Cruden Farm, Langwarrin, Victoria 3910, Australia. *Clubs:* Alexandra, Lyceum (Melbourne).
See also K. R. Murdoch.

MURDOCH, Iris; see Murdoch, J. I.

MURDOCH, (Jean) Iris, (Mrs J. O. Bayley), CBE 1976; novelist and philosopher; Fellow of St Anne's College, Oxford, since 1948, Hon. Fellow, 1963; Lecturer at Royal College of Art, 1963-67; *b* Dublin, 15 July 1919; *d* of Wills John Hughes Murdoch and Irene Alice Richardson; *m* 1956, John Oliver Bayley, *qv. Educ:* Froebel Educational Inst., London; Badminton Sch., Bristol; Somerville Coll., Oxford (Lit. Hum. 1st Class 1942), Hon. Fellow 1977. Asst Principal, Treasury, 1942-44; Administrative Officer with UNRRA, working in London, Belgium, Austria, 1944-46; Sarah Smithson studentship in philosophy, Newnham Coll., Cambridge, 1947-48. Mem., Irish Academy, 1970; Hon. Member: Amer. Acad. of Arts and Letters, 1975; Amer. Acad. of Arts and Sciences, 1982. *Publications:* Sartre, Romantic Rationalist, 1953; Under the Net, 1954; The Flight from the Enchanter, 1955; The Sandcastle, 1957; The Bell, 1958; A Severed Head, 1961 (play, Criterion, 1963); An Unofficial Rose, 1962; The Unicorn, 1963; The Italian Girl, 1964 (play, Criterion, 1967); The Red and the Green, 1965; The Time of The Angels, 1966; The Nice and The Good, 1968; Bruno's Dream, 1969; A Fairly Honourable Defeat, 1970; The Sovereignty of Good, 1970; An Accidental Man, 1971; The Black Prince, 1973 (James Tait Black Meml Prize); The Sacred and Profane Love Machine, 1974 (Whitbread Prize); A Word Child, 1975; Henry and Cato, 1976; The Fire and the Sun, 1977; The Sea, the Sea, 1978 (Booker Prize, 1978); Nuns and Soldiers, 1980; *plays:* The Servants and the Snow (Greenwich), 1970; The Three Arrows (Arts, Cambridge), 1972; Art and Eros (Nat. Theatre), 1980; *poems:* A Year of Birds, 1978. papers in Proc. Aristotelian Soc., etc. *Recreation:* learning languages. *Address:* Cedar Lodge, Steeple Aston, Oxford OX5 3SE.

MURDOCH, (Keith) Rupert; Publisher; Group Chief Executive, News Ltd, Australia; Chairman and Chief Executive (formerly Managing Director), News International plc, UK; Chairman and President, News America Publishing Inc.; Publisher and Editor-in-Chief, New York Post; Chairman, Times Newspapers Holdings Ltd, since 1982; *b* 11 March 1931; *s* of late Sir Keith Murdoch and of Dame Elisabeth (Joy) Murdoch, *qv* ; *m* 1967, Anna Torv; two *s* two *d. Address:* New York Post, 210 South Street, New York, NY 10002, USA; 30 Bouverie Street, EC4.

MURDOCH, Richard Bernard; Actor (stage, films, broadcasting, television); *b* Keston, Kent; *s* of late Bernard Murdoch and late Amy Florence Scott, both of Tunbridge Wells; *m* 1932, Peggy Rawlings; one *s* two *d. Educ:* Charterhouse; Pembroke Coll., Cambridge. Commenced theatrical career in chorus of musical comedies, after which played dancing, light comedy and juvenile rôles in musical comedy and revue. Productions include: The Blue

Train; Oh, Kay; That's a Good Girl; The Five O'Clock Girl; C. B. Cochran's 1930 Revue; Stand Up and Sing; Ballyhoo; various Charlot revues; Over She Goes. The advent of broadcasting brought firstly several appearances as an early television star and then the famous partnership with Arthur Askey. At outbreak of War, 1939, was playing in Band Waggon at London Palladium and also making films; these include; The Terror; Over She Goes; Band Waggon; Charlie's Big-Hearted Aunt; The Ghost Train; I Thank You. In Jan. 1941 joined RAF as Pilot-Officer in Admin. and Special Duties Branch; one year at Bomber Command HQ (Intelligence Br.) and subs. Intelligence Officer at various stations all over the country; towards end of War became Sqdn Ldr under Wing-Comdr Kenneth Horne in Directorate of Administrative Plans, Air Ministry. In off-duty hours at Air Ministry during this period Much-Binding-in-the-Marsh was evolved with Kenneth Horne. Released from RAF Oct. 1945; went on tour with George Black's revue, Strike a New Note. Dame in Emile Littler's Pantomime, Little Miss Muffet, London Casino, Dec. 1949. 20 weeks in Australia for ABC recordings, 1954. Other films include: Three Men and a Girl. BBC radio series, Men from the Ministry, 1961-. Season with Shaw Festival of Canada and tour of USA, 1973. TV appearances include: Hazell; The Avengers; Owner Occupied; In the Looking Glass; This is Your Life; Rumpole of the Bailey; Doctor's Daughters; Churchill: The Wilderness Years, etc. *Recreations:* sailing, golf. *Address:* The End Cottage, Walton-on-the-Hill, Tadworth, Surrey. *Clubs:* Royal Automobile; Walton Heath Golf.

MURDOCH, Robert, (Robin Murdoch), TD 1946; MD; FRCSGlas, FRCOG; Consultant Obstetrician and Gynaecologist, Royal Maternity and Royal Samaritan Hospitals, Glasgow, 1946-76; *b* 31 July 1911; *s* of late James Bowman Young Murdoch and Christina Buntin Murdoch (*née* Wood); *m* 1941, Nora Beryl (*née* Woolley); two *s* (and one *s* decd). *Educ:* Hillhead High Sch., Glasgow; Glasgow Univ. MB ChB 1934, MD 1955; MRCOG 1940; FRCSGlas 1959; FRCOG 1961. Pres., Glasgow Univ. Union, 1933. Served War, 1939-45; Major RAMC. Examiner in Obstetrics and Gynaecology, Univs of Glasgow and Cambridge. Royal College of Gynaecologists: Examiner; Mem. Council, 1954-60, 1968-74; Jun. Vice-Pres., 1974-75; Sen. Vice-Pres., 1975-77. Pres., Scottish AAA, 1956; Mem., British Amateur Athletic Bd, 1956. *Publications:* contribs to medical jls. *Recreations:* angling, golf, gardening, athletics (rep. Scotland (British Empire Games, 1934), and GB (1931, 1933, 1934, 1935, 1938) in 220 yds). *Address:* Carrick Arden, 22 Drymen Road, Bearsden, Glasgow G61 2RD. *T:* 041-942 3677. *Clubs:* Oriental; Royal Scottish Automobile (Glasgow).

MURDOCH, Rupert; see Murdoch, K. R.

MURDOCH, William Ridley Morton, CBE 1963; DSC 1940 and Bar, 1942; VRD 1949; Sheriff of Grampian, Highland and Islands (formerly Ross and Cromarty), at Dingwall and Tain, 1971-78; *b* 17 May 1917; *s* of William Ridley Carr Murdoch and Margaret Pauline Mackinnon; *m* 1941, Sylvia Maud Pearson; one *s* one *d. Educ:* Kelvinside Academy, Glasgow; Glasgow Univ. (MA, LLB). War Service in Navy, 1939-45; Captain, RNR, 1959. Solicitor in private practice, 1947-71; Dir, Glasgow Chamber of Commerce, 1955-71; Dean, Royal Faculty of Procurators in Glasgow, 1968-71. DL, County of City of Glasgow, 1963-75. OStJ 1976. *Recreations:* sailing, gardening. *Address:* Aird House, Gairloch, Ross-shire. *T:* Badachro 243. *Clubs:* Western, Naval (Glasgow).

MURGATROYD, Prof. Walter, PhD; Professor of Thermal Power, Imperial College of Science and Technology, since 1968; Rockefeller International Fellow, Princeton University, 1979; *b* 15 Aug. 1921; *s* of Harry G. Murgatroyd and Martha W. Strachan; *m* 1952, Denise Geneviève, *d* of Robert Adolphe Schlumberger, Paris and Bénouville; one *s* one *d* (and one *s* decd). *Educ:* St Catharine's Coll., Cambridge. BA 1946, PhD 1952. Hawker Aircraft Ltd, 1942-44; Rolls Royce Ltd, 1944-46; Univ. of Cambridge (Liquid Metal and Reactor heat transfer research), 1947-54; UK Atomic Energy Authority, Harwell, 1954-56; Head of Dept of Nuclear Engineering, Queen Mary Coll., Univ. of London, 1956-67, and Dean of Engineering, 1966-67. Member: British-Greek Mixed Commn, 1963-78; British-Belgian Mixed Commn, 1964-78; British-Austrian Mixed Commn, 1965-78. Specialist Adviser to H of C Select Cttee on Energy, 1980-. *Publications:* contrib. to various scientific and technical journals. *Recreation:* music. *Address:* 3 Helme Close, SW19 7EB. *T:* 01-946 0415.

MURLESS, Sir (Charles Francis) Noel, Kt 1977; Trainer of racehorses, Newmarket, 1953-76; Owner: Woodditton Stud, Cambridgeshire; Cliff Stud, Yorkshire; *b* 1910; *m* 1940, Gwen Carlow; one *d.* Leading Trainer on the flat for ninth year at end of British flat racing season, 1973 (former years being 1948, 1957, 1959, 1960, 1961, 1967, 1968, 1970); The Queen's trainer until flat racing season of 1969. He made a new record in earnings (£256,899) for his patrons, 1967; over £2,500,000 in winning stakes; has trained the winners of 19 Classic races: Two Thousand Guineas (2); One Thousand Guineas (6); Derby (3) (Crepello, 1957; St Paddy, 1960; Royal Palace, 1967); Oaks (5); St Leger (3); other major races: King George VI and Queen Elizabeth (3); Eclipse (5); Coronation Cup (5); Champion Stakes (3). Mem., Jockey Club, 1977-. *Address:* The Bungalow, Woodditton, Newmarket, Suffolk.
See also H. R. A. Cecil.

MURLEY, John Tregarthen, DPhil; *b* 22 Aug. 1928; *s* of John Murley and Dorothea Birch; *m* 1954, Jean Patricia Harris; one *d. Educ:* University College, London (BA 1st Cl. Hons History); St Antony's Coll., Oxford (DPhil). Entered FO, 1955; Counsellor, Washington, 1976-80. *Publication:* The Origin and Outbreak of the Anglo-French War of 1793, 1959. *Recreations:* tennis, squash, piano.

MURLEY, Sir Reginald (Sydney), KBE 1979; TD 1946; FRCS; President, Royal College of Surgeons, 1977-80; *b* 2 Aug. 1916; *s* of Sydney Herbert Murley and Beatrice Maud Baylis; *m* 1947, Daphne, 2nd *d* of Ralph E. and Rowena Garrod; three *s* two *d* and one step *d. Educ:* Dulwich Coll.; Univ. of London; St Bartholomew's Hosp. (MB, BS Hons 1939, MS 1948). MRCS, LRCP 1939; FRCS 1946. Served War, RAMC 1939-45: ME, E Africa, N Africa, Sicily, Italy and NW Europe; regtl and fld ambulance MO; Surgical Specialist, No 1 and 2 Maxillo-Facial Units and Fld Surg. Units; Major. St Bartholomew's Hospital: Jun. Scholarship, 1935; Sen. Schol., and Sir William Dunn Exhibn in Anat., Univ. of London, 1936; House Surg., 1939; Anat. Demonstrator, 1946; Surg. Chief Asst, 1946-49; Cattlin Res. Fellow and Mackenzie Mackinnon Res. Fellow, RCP and RCS, 1950-51; Surgeon: St Albans Hosp., 1947; Royal Northern Hosp., London, 1953; Hon. Consultant Surgeon, St Bartholomew's Hosp., 1979. Chm., Med. Council on Alcoholism, 1980. Royal Coll. of Surgeons: formerly Tutor and Reg. Adviser; Mem. Council, 1970-82; Hunterian Orator, 1981; Bradshaw Lectr, 1981; Mem. Ct of Patrons, 1981-. Mitchiner Lectr, RAMC, 1981. FRSM; Fellow, Assoc. of Surgeons of GB and Ireland. Member: Hunterian Soc. (Pres., 1970-71; Orator, 1978); Med. Soc. of London (former Mem. Council; Pres., 1982); Harveian Soc. (former Mem. Council; Pres., 1983); Osler Club; BMA (former Councillor); Exec. Cttee, Soc. Internat. de Chirurgie, 1980-. European and internat. cardiovascular socs. Associate Mem., Brit. Assoc. of Plastic Surgs. Eponymous surg. lectures and orations; Hon. FRACS and Syme Orator, 1979; Hon. FCSSA 1979; Hon. FRCSI 1980; Hon. FDSRCS 1981; Hon. Fellow, Italian Soc. Surg., 1979. President: Alleyn Club, 1983; Fellowship for Freedom in Medicine, 1972-; Mem. Council, Freedom Assoc., 1982-. *Publications:* (contrib.) Financing Medical Care, 1962; contrib. surg. textbooks; articles in med. literature on breast, thyroid and vascular diseases; articles on med. politics and econs. *Recreations:* golf, swimming, gardening, music, reading history and economics. *Address:* (home) Cobden Hill House, Radlett, Herts. *T:* 01-779 6532; (office) 95 Harley Street, W1N 1DF. *T:* 01-935 5050. *Clubs:* Royal Automobile; Fountain and Vicarage (both St Bart's Hospital); Porter's Park Golf.

MURPHY, Rear-Adm. Anthony Albert, CBE 1976; Special Project Executive, Ministry of Defence, 1977-82; *b* 19 May 1924; *s* of Albert Edward Murphy and Jennie (*née* Giles); *m* 1954, Antonia Theresa (*née* Rayner); four *s. Educ:* Sir George Monoux Grammar Sch. National Provincial Bank, 1940-42; joined RN, 1942; commnd. 1944; Western Approaches, 1944-45; HMS Vanguard (Royal Tour of S Africa), 1945-49; HMS Bulwark (Suez); Comdr 1960; HMS Yarmouth/6th Frigate Sqdn, Kuwait, 1961-63; HMS Eagle, 1965-67; Captain 1967; Dir, Naval Guided Weapons, 1970-73; in comd HMS Collingwood, 1973-76; Rear-Adm. 1977; Vice-Pres., and Senior Naval Mem., Ordnance Board, 1977. *Recreations:* cricket, soccer (Chm. RNFA, 1973-76), country activities.

MURPHY, Mrs Brian Taunton; see Hufton, Prof. Owen.

MURPHY, Christopher Philip Yorke; MP (C) Welwyn and Hatfield, since 1979; *b* 20 April 1947; *s* of Philip John and Dorothy Betty Murphy; *m* 1969, Sandra Gillian Ashton. *Educ:* Devonport High Sch.; The Queen's Coll., Oxford (MA). London Advertising Agencies, 1968-79; Associate Dir, D'Arcy MacManus & Masius. President, Oxford Univ. Conservative Assoc., 1967; held number of Conservative Party offices, 1968-72; Parish Councillor, Windlesham, Surrey, 1972-76. Contested (C): Bethnal Green and Bow, Feb. 1974, Oct. 1974. Vice-Chairman: Urban and New Town Affairs Parly Cttee; Arts and Heritage Parly Cttee; Commonwealth Parly Sub-Cttee. Convenor, Herts MPs. *Recreations:* walking, theatre, music. *Address:* House of Commons, SW1. *Clubs:* Carlton; Hatfield Conservative; Oxford Union Society.

MURPHY, Cornelius McCaffrey, (Neil Murphy), MBE 1982; MA; Editor of Building (formerly The Builder), since 1974; Director, The Builder Ltd, since 1979; Managing Director, Building (Publishers) Ltd, since 1981; *b* 31 May 1936; 2nd *s* of Edward and Annie Murphy, Glasgow; *m* 1963, Joan Anne, *o d* of William Tytler, master carpenter, retd; two *d. Educ:* Holyrood Sch.; Univ. of Glasgow (MA 1958). *Recreations:* reading, racing. *Address:* 42 St John's Park, Blackheath, SE3 7JH. *T:* 01-853 2625. *Club:* Royal Automobile.

MURPHY, Dervla; *b* 28 Nov. 1931; *d* of Fergus Murphy and Kathleen Rochfort-Dowling; one *d. Educ:* Ursuline Convent, Waterford. American Irish Foundn Literary Award, 1975; Christopher Ewart-Biggs Meml Prize, 1978. *Publications:* Full Tilt, 1965, 5th edn 1978; Tibetan Foothold, 1966, 3rd edn 1968; The Waiting Land, 1967, 3rd edn 1969; In Ethiopia with a Mule, 1968, 2nd edn 1972; On a Shoe String to Coorg, 1976; Where the Indus is Young, 1977; A Place Apart, 1978; Wheels Within Wheels, 1979; Race to the Finish?, 1981. *Recreations:* reading, music, cycling, swimming, walking. *Address:* Lismore, Co. Waterford, Ireland.

MURPHY, Rev. Gervase; see Murphy, Rev. J. G. M. W.

MURPHY, Sheriff James Patrick; Sheriff of North Strathclyde, since 1976; *b* 24 Jan. 1932; *s* of Henry Francis Murphy and Alice (*née* Rooney); *m* 1956,

Maureen Coyne; two s one d. *Educ:* Notre Dame Convent; St Aloysius' Coll., Glasgow; Univ. of Glasgow (BL 1953). Admitted Solicitor, 1953; assumed partner, R. Maguire Cook & Co., Glasgow, 1959; founded firm of Ross Harper & Murphy, Glasgow, 1961. President: Glasgow Juridical Soc., 1962-63; Glasgow Bar Assoc., 1966-67; Mem. Council, Law Soc. of Scotland, 1974-76. Governor, St Aloysius' Coll., Glasgow, 1978-. *Recreations:* photography, canoeing, cycling, books, the history of writing. *Address:* 4 West End, Bearsden, Dunbartonshire.

MURPHY, Most Rev. John A.; *see* Cardiff, Archbishop of, (RC).

MURPHY, Rev. (John) Gervase (Maurice Walker), MA; Domestic Chaplain to the Queen, Rector of Sandringham and Leader of Sandringham Group of Parishes, since 1979; *b* 20 Aug. 1926; *s* of William Stafford and Yvonne Iris Murphy; *m* 1957, Joy Hilda Miriam Livermore; five d. *Educ:* Methodist Coll., Belfast; Trinity Coll., Dublin (BA 1952, MA 1955). Guardsman, Irish Guards, 1944-45; commissioned Royal Ulster Rifles, 1945-47. TCD, 1947-52 and Divinity Sch., TCD, 1949-52. Ordained, 1952; Curate, Shankill Parish, Lurgan, 1952-55. Royal Army Chaplains' Dept, 1955; served: Korea, 1955-57; Woolwich, 1957-59; Aden, 1959-62; Infantry Junior Leaders, Oswestry, 1962-64; Bagshot, 1964-65; Worthy Down, 1965; Commonwealth Bde Sen. Chaplain, 1965-67; Sen. Chaplain, Guards Depot, Pirbright, 1967-69; DACG, Rhine Area, 1969-72; Sen. Chaplain, RMA Sandhurst, 1972-74; Asst Chaplain General: BAOR, 1974-75; South East, 1975-77. Vicar of Ranworth and RD of Blofield, 1977-79; Chaplain for Holidaymakers on Norfolk Broads, 1977-79. *Recreations:* people and sport; Rugby football (internat. caps for Ireland, 1952, 1954, 1958; played for Barbarians 1958, British Army, 1957, 1958), cricket, swimming, etc. *Address:* Sandringham Rectory, Norfolk PE35 6EH. *T:* Dersingham 40587. *Clubs:* British Sportsman's, London Irish RFC, Public School Wanderers RFC; Leprechauns Cricket (Ireland); Mid-Ulster Cricket.

MURPHY, Sir Leslie (Frederick), Kt 1978; Chairman: Petroleum Economics Ltd, since 1980; National Enterprise Board, 1977-79 (Deputy Chairman, 1975-77); *b* 17 Nov. 1915; *s* of Frederick Charles and Lillian Annie Murphy; *m* 1940, Marjorie Iris Cowell; one s one d. *Educ:* Southall Grammar Sch.; Birkbeck Coll., Univ. of London. Principal Private Sec. to Minister of Fuel and Power, 1947-49; Asst Sec., Min. of Fuel and Power, 1949-52; Chm., Mobil Supply Co. Ltd and Mobil Shipping Co. Ltd, 1955-59; Finance Dir, Iraq Petroleum Co. Ltd, 1959-64; Dir, J. Henry Schroder Wagg & Co. Ltd, 1964-75 (Dep. Chm. 1972-73); Dep. Chm., Schroders Ltd, 1973-75, Dir, 1979-; Director: Unigate Ltd, 1968-75; Simon Engrg Ltd, 1980-; Folksam International Insurance (UK) Ltd, 1980-. Mem., NEDC, 1977-79. Mem. Royal Commn on Distribution of Income and Wealth, 1974-76; Board Mem., Church Army, 1964-; Chm., Church Army Housing Ltd, 1973-82, Pres., 1982-. *Recreations:* music, golf. *Address:* Hedgerley, Barton Common Road, Barton-on-Sea, Hants.

MURPHY, Hon. Mr Justice Lionel Keith; Justice of the High Court of Australia, since 1975; *b* 31 Aug. 1922; *s* of William and Lily Murphy; *m* 1969, Ingrid Gee; two s one d. *Educ:* Sydney Boys' High Sch.; Univ. of Sydney (BSc, LLB). Admitted to NSW Bar, 1947, to Victoria Bar, 1958; QC, NSW 1960, Vic 1961. Senator in Federal Parlt, 1962-75; Leader of Opposition in Senate, 1967-72; Leader of Govt in Senate, 1972-75; Attorney-General of Australia and Minister for Customs and Excise, 1972-75. Initiated reforms in legislative areas of human rights, family law, anti-trust, consumer protection. Mem. Executive, Australian section, Internat. Commn of Jurists; Delegate to UN Conf. on Human Rights, Teheran, 1968; represented Australia, Nuclear Tests Case, Internat. Court of Justice, 1973-74. Mem. Council, ANU, 1969-73. *Address:* c/o High Court of Australia, Parkes, ACT 2600, Australia.

MURPHY, Neil; *see* Murphy, C. McC.

MURPHY, Richard Holmes; Chairman, Industrial Tribunals, since 1972; *b* 9 July 1915; *o s* of Harold Lawson Murphy, KC, and Elsie, 4th *d* of Rt Hon. Lord Justice Holmes; *m* 1967, Irene Sybil, *e d* of Reginald and Elizabeth Swift. *Educ:* Charterhouse; Emmanuel Coll., Cambridge (MA, LLB). Called to Bar, Inner Temple, 1939. Enlisted Inns of Court Regt, 1939; Commissioned 3rd County of London Yeomanry, 1940; served Middle East and Italy, 1941-45; Judge Advocate-Gen.'s Dept, WO, 1945-46; released, rank of Major. Resident Magistrate, Tanganyika, 1948; Chief Registrar, Gold Coast Supreme Ct and Registrar of W African Ct of Appeal, 1951; Sen. Magistrate, Gold Coast, 1955; Puisne Judge, Ghana, 1957-60; Judge of High Court, Tanganyika, 1960-64; Senior Lectr in Law, Polytechnic of Central London (formerly Holborn Coll.), 1965-72. *Address:* 9 Vyvyan Terrace, Clifton, Bristol BS8 3DF. *Club:* Constitutional (Bristol).

MURPHY, Stephen Dunlop; Television Programme Officer, Independent Broadcasting Authority, since 1976; *b* Glasgow, 28 Aug. 1921; *s* of Stephen Dunlop Murphy and Jean Irwin; *m* 1944, Jean Marian Smith, Burnley; two s one d. *Educ:* Royal Grammar Sch., Newcastle upon Tyne; Manchester Grammar Sch.; Balliol Coll., Oxford (BA). Asst Master, Manchester Grammar Sch., 1943; BBC Educn Officer, 1951; BBC Producer, 1955; ITA Regional Officer North, 1961; Senior Programme Officer, ITA, 1966; Secretary, British Bd of Film Censors, 1971-75. *Address:* 204 London Road, Twickenham, Mddx. *T:* 01-892 6794.

MURPHY, Thomas A.; Director, General Motors Corporation (Chairman, 1974-80); *b* Hornell, NY, 10 Dec. 1915. *Educ:* Leo High Sch., Chicago; Univ. of Illinois. Joined General Motors Corporation, 1938; Asst Treas., 1959; Comptroller, 1967; Treas., 1968-70; Vice-Pres., 1970-72; Vice-Chm., 1972-74. *Address:* c/o General Motors Corporation, General Motors Building, Detroit, Mich 48202, USA.

MURPHY, William Parry, AB, MD; Lecturer on Medicine, Harvard Medical School, 1948-58, Lecturer Emeritus, 1958; Senior Associate in Medicine, Peter Bent Brigham Hospital, 1935-58, Senior Associate Emeritus in Medicine and Consultant in Hematology since 1958; Consultant Hematologist: Melrose Hospital, Melrose, Mass; Quincy City Hospital, Quincy, Mass; Emerson Hospital, Concord, Mass; Consultant in Internal Medicine, Delaware State Hospital, Farnhurst, Delaware; *b* 6 Feb. 1892; *s* of Thomas Francis Murphy and Rose Anna Parry; *m* 1919, Pearl Harriett Adams; one s (one d decd). *Educ:* Univ. of Oregon (AB); Harvard Med. Sch. (MD). Army, enlisted Medical Reserve, 1917-18; acted as House Officer at the Rhode Island Hosp., 1920-22; as Asst Resident Physician, 1922-23; Junior Associate in Medicine, 1923-28; Associate in Medicine, 1928-35 at Peter Bent Brigham Hospital; Asst in Medicine, 1923-28; Instructor in Medicine, 1928-35; Associate in Medicine, Harvard Medical Sch., 1935-48; has been engaged in the practice of Medicine since 1923, and carried on research at the Peter Bent Brigham Hospital in Boston; Diplomate in Internal Medicine, 1937. Mem. Bd of Dirs, Cordis Corp., 1960-70. Mem. many American and foreign medical and scientific socs; co-discoverer of the liver treatment for pernicious anemia; Cameron Prize in Medicine, Univ. of Edinburgh Medical Faculty, 1930; Bronze Medal, American Medical Association, 1934; Nobel Prize in Physiology or Medicine, 1934; Paul Harris Fellow Award, Brookline Rotary Club, 1980. Hon. Dr of Science, Gustavus Adolphus Coll., 1963; Hon. Member: Univ. of Oregon Med. Alumni Assoc., 1964; Internat. Soc. for Research on Civilisation Diseases and Vital Substances, 1969. Commander of the first rank, Order of the White Rose, Finland, 1934; gold medal, Mass Humane Soc., 1935; National Order of Merit, Carlos J. Finlay, Official, Havana, Cuba, 1952; Dist. Achievement Award, City of Boston, 1965; Internat. Bicentenial Symposium Award, Boston, 1972; Gold Badge, Mass Med. Soc. 50th Anniv., 1973. *Publications:* Anemia in Practice: Pernicious Anemia, 1939; about 75 papers published in medical journals, especially on diseases of the blood. *Recreation:* collector of rare old firearms. *Address:* 97 Sewall Avenue, Brookline, Mass 02146, USA. *Clubs:* Sigma xi (Harvard); Harvard (Boston); Rotary (Brookline, Mass).

MURPHY-O'CONNOR, Rt. Rev. Cormac; *see* Arundel and Brighton, Bishop of, (RC).

MURRAY; *see* Erskine-Murray.

MURRAY, family name of **Duke of Atholl,** of **Earl of Dunmore,** of **Earl of Mansfield and Mansfield** and of **Baron Murray of Newhaven.**

MURRAY, Rt. Hon. Lord; Ronald King Murray, PC 1974; a Senator of the College of Justice in Scotland, since 1979; *b* 15 June 1922; *s* of James King Murray, MIEE, and Muriel (*née* Aitken), Glasgow; *m* 1950, Sheila Winifred Gamlin; one s one d. *Educ:* George Watson's Coll., Edinburgh; Univ. of Edinburgh; Jesus Coll., Oxford. MA (1st cl. hons Phil) Edinburgh, 1948; LLB Edinburgh, 1952. Served HM Forces, 1941-46; commnd in REME, 1942; India and SEAC, 1943-46. Asst in Moral Philosophy, Edinburgh Univ., 1949; called to Scottish Bar, 1953; QC (Scotland) 1967; Standing Jun. Counsel to BoT (Scotland), 1961-64; Advocate-Depute, 1964-67; Senior Advocate-Depute, 1967-70. MP (Lab) Leith, Edinburgh, 1970-79; Lord Advocate, 1974-79. Assessor, Edinburgh Univ. Court, 1981. *Publications:* articles in various jls. *Recreation:* boating. *Address:* 31 Boswall Road, Edinburgh EH5 3RP. *T:* 031-552 5602. *Clubs:* Royal Forth Yacht, Forth Corinthian Yacht.

MURRAY, Bishop of The, since 1970; **Rt. Rev. Robert George Porter,** OBE 1952; *b* 7 Jan. 1924; *s* of Herbert James and Eileen Kathleen Porter; *m* 1954, Elizabeth Mary Williams; two d. *Educ:* Canterbury Boys' High School; St John's Theological Coll., Morpeth, NSW; Moore College, Sydney (ThL Hons). Served with AIF, 1942-44. Deacon 1947, priest 1948; Assistant Curate, Christ Church Cathedral, Ballarat, Victoria, 1947-49; Assistant Curate, St Paul's, Burwood, Sydney, 1949-50; Priest in charge of Isivita and Agenehambo, Diocese of New Guinea, 1950-57; Archdeacon of Ballarat, 1957-70; Assistant Bishop of Ballarat, 1967-70. *Recreations:* gardening, reading. *Address:* 48 Eleanor Terrace, Murray Bridge, SA 5253, Australia. *T:* 32 2240.

MURRAY OF NEWHAVEN, Baron *cr* 1964 (Life Peer); **Keith Anderson Hope Murray,** KCB 1963; Kt 1955; Chancellor, Southampton University, 1964-74; Visitor, Loughborough University of Technology, 1968-78; *b* 28 July 1903; 2nd surv. *s* of late Rt Hon. Lord Murray, PC, CMG, LLD. *Educ:* Edinburgh Academy; Edinburgh Univ. (BSc); Ministry of Agriculture, 1925-26; Commonwealth Fund Fellowship, 1926-29, at Cornell Univ., New York (PhD); Oriel Coll. and Agricultural Economics Research Institute, 1929-32, University of Oxford (BLitt and MA); Research Officer, 1932-39; Fellow and Bursar, Lincoln Coll., 1937-53, and Rector, 1944-53; Chm., Univ. Grants Cttee, 1953-63. Oxford City Council, 1938-40; Min. of Food, 1939-40; RAFVR 1941-42; Dir of Food and Agriculture, Middle East Supply Centre, GHQ, MEF, 1942-45; Oxfordshire Education Cttee, 1946-49; JP, City of

Oxford, 1950-53; Chm., Vice-Chancellor's Commission of Enquiry on Halls of Residence, 1947; Mem. of Commission of Enquiry into Disturbances in the Gold Coast, 1948; Development Commissioner, 1948-53; Chairman: Advisory Cttee on Colonial Colleges of Arts, Science and Technology, 1949-53, RAF Education Advisory Cttee, 1947-53; National Council of Social Service, 1947-53. Advisory Cttees on Agricultural Colls, 1954-60, Harkness Fellowship Cttee of Award, 1957-63, Cttee on Provincial Agricultural Economics Service, 1949-57, Cttee on Australian Univs, 1957; World Univ. Service, 1957-62; Dartmouth Review Cttee, 1958; Pres. Agric. Economics Soc., 1959-60; Pres. Agricultural History Soc., 1959-62; Chairman: Colonial Univ. Grants Cttee, 1964-66; London Conf. on Overseas Students, 1963-67; Academic Adv. Cttee for Stirling Univ., 1967-75. Vice-Pres., Wellington Coll., 1966-69; Governor, The Charterhouse, 1957-69. Mem. Bd, Wellcome Trustees, 1965-73; Dir, Leverhulme Trust Fund, 1965-72; Hon. Pres., Nat. Union of Students, 1967-70. Chairman: Cttee of Enquiry into Governance of London Univ., 1970-72; Royal Commn for Exhibition of 1851, 1962-71. Director: Bristol Aeroplane Co., 1963-67; Metal Box Co., 1964-68. Hon. Fellow: Downing Coll., Cambridge; Oriel Coll., Oxford; Lincoln Coll., Oxford; Birkbeck Coll., London. Hon. LLD: Western Australia and of Bristol, 1963; Cambridge, Hull, Edinburgh, Southampton, Liverpool and Leicester, 1964; Calif., 1966; London and Strathclyde, 1973; Hon. DCL Oxford, 1964; Hon. DLitt Keele, 1966; Hon. DUniv. Stirling, 1968; Hon. DU Essex, 1971; Hon. FDSRCS, 1964; Hon. FUMIST, 1965. *Address:* 224 Ashley Gardens, SW1. *T:* 01-828 4113. *Club:* United Oxford & Cambridge University.

MURRAY, Dame (Alice) Rosemary, DBE 1977; MA, DPhil; JP; DL; President, New Hall, Cambridge, 1964-81 (Tutor in Charge, 1954-64); Vice-Chancellor, Cambridge University, 1975-77 (Deputy Vice-Chancellor, 1973); *b* 28 July 1913; *2 d* of late Adm. A. J. L. Murray and Ellen Maxwell Spooner. *Educ:* Downe House, Newbury; Lady Margaret Hall, Oxford (Hon. Fellow, 1968). MA (Oxon and Cantab); BSc, DPhil (Oxon). Lecturer in chemistry: Royal Holloway Coll., 1938-41; Sheffield Univ., 1941-42. Served War of 1939-45, Experimental Officer, Admiralty Signals Establishment, 1941; WRNS, 1942-46, successively Wren, 3rd, 2nd, 1st and Chief Officer. Lectr in Chemistry, Girton Coll., Cambridge, 1946-54, Fellow, 1949, Tutor, 1951, Hon. Fellow, 1976; Demonstrator in Chemistry, Univ. of Cambridge, 1947-52. Dir, Midland Bank Ltd, 1978-; Independent Dir, The Observer, 1981-. Member: Lockwood Cttee on Higher Educn in NI, 1963-65; Wages Councils, 1968-; Council, GPDST, 1969-; Armed Forces Pay Review Body, 1971-81; Pres., Nat. Assoc. of Adult Educn, 1977-80, Vice-Pres., 1980-. Governor and Chm., Keswick Coll. of Education. Liveryman, Goldsmiths' Co., 1978-. JP City of Cambridge, 1953-; DL Cambs, 1982. Hon. Fellow, New Hall, Cambridge, 1981; Hon. DSc: New Univ. of Ulster, 1972; Leeds, 1975; Pennsylvania, 1975; Wellesley Coll., 1976; Hon. DCL Oxon, 1976; Hon. DL Univ. Southern California, 1976; Hon. LLD Sheffield, 1977. *Recreations:* foreign travel, gardening, book binding and restoring. *Address:* 9 Grange Court, Cambridge CB3 9BD. *Clubs:* University Women's, English-Speaking Union.

MURRAY, Rear-Adm. Sir Brian (Stewart), KCMG 1982; AO 1978; Governor of Victoria, since 1982; *b* 26 Dec. 1921; *s* of Alan Stewart Murray and Lily Astria (*née* Fenton); *m* 1st, 1954, Elizabeth (*d* 1962); one *s* two *d*; 2nd, 1973, Janette, *d* of Mr and Mrs J. J. Paris. *Educ:* Hampton High Sch., Vic; Royal Naval Coll., Dartmouth. Joined RAN, 1939; served War, 1939-45: cruisers and destroyers in Pacific, Indian and Atlantic Oceans, North Sea and China Sea; served Korean War, 1952-53: Sen. Air Direction Officer, HMAS Sydney (despatches); CO HMAS: Condamine, 1954-55; Queenborough, 1961-62; Parramatta, 1963; Dir of Plans, Navy Office, 1964-65; IDC, London, 1966; CO HMAS Supply, 1967; Aust. Services Attaché, Tokyo, 1968-70; served Vietnam War, 1970: CO HMAS Sydney (troop transport); Hon. ADC to the Queen, 1971-72; Dir, Jt Ops and Plans, Dept of Defence, 1971, Dir of Jt Policy, 1972-73; Naval Officer i/c, Vic, 1974-75; Dep. Chief of Naval Staff, 1975-78; retd RAN, 1978. Operator of small vineyard and winery at Murrumbateman, on southern tablelands of NSW, 1978-. *Recreations:* golf, tennis, horse racing. *Address:* Government House, Melbourne, Vic 3004, Australia. *T:* 63.9971.

MURRAY, Cecil James Boyd, MS; FRCS; Emeritus Consultant Surgeon, Middlesex Hospital, since 1975 (Surgeon, 1946-75); Surgeon, Royal Masonic Hospital, London, 1958-75; *b* 8 Jan. 1910; *s* of Richard Murray, MIEE; *m* 1940, Bona (*d* 1974), *o d* of Rev. William Askwith, MA, Ripon; two *s*. *Educ:* Warriston Sch., Moffat; King's Sch., Canterbury; Middlesex Hospital Medical Sch. MB, BS, 1935; MS 1936; MRCS, LRCP, 1933, FRCS 1936. Formerly: Surgeon, King Edward Memorial Hospital, Ealing; Lecturer in Operative Surgery, Middlesex Hospital Medical Sch. Served War of 1939-45 (despatches), temp. Lt-Col RAMC. Mem., Court of Examiners, Royal College of Surgeons of England; Fellow, Assoc. of Surgeons of Great Britain; FRSocMed. *Publications:* papers in medical journals. *Recreation:* fly-fishing. *Address:* Conifera, Comrie, Perthshire PH6 2LT. *T:* Comrie 395. *Clubs:* Flyfishers', MCC.

MURRAY, Charles Henry; Governor, Central Bank of Ireland, since 1976 (Director, 1969-76); *b* 1917; *s* of Charles and Teresa Murray; *m* 1942, Margaret Ryan; one *s* four *d*. *Educ:* Christian Brothers Sch., Synge Street, Dublin; London Univ. (BCom). Asst Secretary, Dept of Finance (Ireland), 1961, Secretary, 1969-76. Member: Council and Exec. Cttee, Economic and Social Research Inst., 1969-; Nat. Economic and Social Council, 1973-; Pres.,

Inst. of Public Admin, 1980-. Hon. LLD, NUI, 1977. *Recreations:* reading, theatre, golf. *Address:* 6 Washington Park, Dublin 14. *T:* 909007.

MURRAY, Hon. Donald Bruce; Hon. Mr Justice Murray; Judge of the High Court of Justice in Northern Ireland, since 1975; *b* 24 Jan. 1923; *y s* of late Charles Benjamin Murray and late Agnes Mary Murray, Belfast; *m* 1953, Rhoda Margaret, *o c* of late Thomas and Anna Parke, Londonderry; two *s* one *d*. *Educ:* Belfast Royal Acad.; Queen's Univ. Belfast (LLB Hons); Trinity Coll. Dublin (BA). 1st Cl., Certif. of Honour, Gray's Inn Prize, English Bar Final Exam., 1944; Called to Bar, Gray's Inn, 1945. Asst Parly Draftsman to Govt of NI, 1945-51; Asst Lectr, Faculty of Law, QUB, 1951-53. Called to NI Bar, 1953, and to Inner Bar, NI, 1964; Bencher, Inn of Court, NI, 1971; Chm., Gen. Council of Bar of NI, 1972-75. Dep. Chm., Boundary Commn for NI, 1976-. Mem. 1971, Chm. 1974, Incorporated Council of Law Reporting for NI; Dir, NI Legal Quarterly; Member: UK Delegn to Commn Consultative des Barreaux des Pays des Communautés Européennes, 1972-75; Jt Standing Cttee of Bars of UK and Bar of Ireland, 1972-75; Deptl Cttee on Registration of Title to Land in N Ireland. Chm., Deptl Cttee on Reform of Company Law in NI; Inspector apptd to report on siting of new prison in NI. Mem., Legal Adv. Cttee of Standing Cttee of General Synod of Church of Ireland. Governor, Belfast Royal Academy. *Publications:* articles in various legal periodicals. *Recreations:* playing the piano, DXing. *Address:* 40 Cadogan Park, Belfast, N Ireland.

MURRAY, Donald Frederick, CMG 1973; HM Diplomatic Service; Ambassador to Sweden, since 1980; *b* 14 June 1924; *s* of A. T. Murray and F. M. Murray (*née* Byfield); *m* 1949, Marjorie Culverwell; three *s* one *d*. *Educ:* Colfe's Grammar Sch.; King's Sch., Canterbury (King's and Entrance Schols); Worcester Coll., Oxford. Royal Marines, 1943-46 (41 (RM) Commando). Entered Foreign Office, 1948; Third Sec., Warsaw, 1948; FO 1951; Second Sec., Vienna, 1953; First Sec., Political Office, ME Forces, 1956; FO, 1957; First Sec. (Comm.), Stockholm, 1958; Head of Chancery, Saigon, 1962; FO 1964; Counsellor, 1965; Head of SE Asia Dept, 1966; Counsellor, Tehran, 1969-72; RCDS, 1973; Ambassador to Libya, 1974-76; Asst Under-Sec. of State, FCO, 1977-80. *Publication:* article in Seaford House Papers, 1973. *Recreations:* gentle sports (Oxford v Cambridge cross-country, 1942; athletics, 1943; small-bore shooting, 1947), gardening, music. *Address:* c/o Foreign and Commonwealth Office, SW1; Oxney House, Wittersham, Kent. *Club:* Buck's.

MURRAY, Sir (Francis) Ralph (Hay), KCMG 1962 (CMG 1950); CB 1957; Chairman: SAFT (UK) Ltd; CSM Parliamentary Consultants Ltd; Director, CSM European Consultants Ltd; *b* 3 March 1908; *s* of Rev. Charles Hay Murray and Mabel Umfreville; *m* 1935, Mauricette, *d* of Count Bernhard Kuenburg; three *s* one *d*. *Educ:* Brentwood Sch.; St Edmund Hall, Oxford. BBC, 1934-39; Foreign Office, 1939-45; Allied Commission for Austria, 1945-46; Special Commissioner's Staff, SE Asia, 1946-47; Foreign Office, 1947-51; Counsellor, HM Embassy, Madrid, 1951-54; Minister, HM Embassy, Cairo, 1954-56; Asst Under-Sec. of State, FO, 1957-61; Dep. Under-Sec. of State, FO, 1961-62; Ambassador to Greece, 1962-67. A Governor of the BBC, 1967-73. *Address:* 3 Whaddon Hall Mews, Whaddon, Milton Keynes. *T:* Whaddon 467. *Club:* Travellers'.

MURRAY, George Raymond B.; *see* Beasley-Murray.

MURRAY, George Sargent; Forestry Commissioner, since 1981; *b* 2 Oct. 1924; *s* of James and Helen Murray; *m* 1951, Anita Garden Fraser; two *s*. *Educ:* Buckie High School. Inland Revenue, 1941-43; Royal Navy, 1943-46; Inland Revenue, 1946-49; Dept of Agriculture and Fisheries for Scotland, 1949-67; Scottish Development Dept, 1967-71; Scottish Economic Planning Dept, Scottish Office, 1971-76; Dept of Agriculture and Fisheries for Scotland, 1976-81. *Recreations:* golf, lapidary work. *Address:* 30 Easter Currie Terrace, Currie, Midlothian EH14 5LE. *T:* 031-449 2538. *Club:* Civil Service.

MURRAY, Gen. Sir Horatius, GCB 1962 (CMG 1966; KBE 1956; DSO 1943; Colonel of The Cameronians (Scottish Rifles), 1958-64, now retired; *b* 18 April 1903; *s* of late Charles Murray; *m* 1953, Beatrice, artist, *y d* of Frederick Cuthbert. *Educ:* Peter Symonds Sch., Winchester; RMC, Sandhurst. Gazetted to Cameronians, 1923; transferred to Camerons, 1935. Served War of 1939-45, North Africa, Sicily, Italy, France (DSO, CB); GOC 6 Armoured Division, 1944-45; Dir of Personal Services, War Office, 1946-47; GOC 1st Infantry Division, 1947-50; GOC Northumbrian District, 1951-53; Commander, Commonwealth Division in Korea, 1953-54; GOC-in-C, Scottish Command and Governor of Edinburgh Castle, 1955-58; Commander-in-Chief, Allied Forces, Northern Europe, 1958-61, retired. Commander Legion of Merit (US); Knight *Clubs:* New, Puffins (Edinburgh). the Sword (Sweden). *Recreations:* golf, cricket. *Address:* 3 Duneaves, Mount Park Road, Harrow-on-the-Hill, Mddx HA1 3JS. *Club:* Royal Commonwealth Society.

MURRAY, Sir James, KCMG 1978 (CMG 1966); HM Diplomatic Service, retired; Ambassador and Permanent UK Representative to UN and other International Organisations at Geneva, 1978-79; *b* 3 Aug. 1919; *er s* of late James Hamilton Murray, King's Cross, Isle of Arran, and Hester Macneill Buie; *m* 1982, Mrs Jill Charmian Chapuisat, *d* of Maj.-Gen. Frederick William Gordon-Hall, *qv*; two step *d*. *Educ:* Bellahouston Acad.; Glasgow Univ. Royal Regt of Artillery, 1939; served India and Burma, 1943-45; Staff Coll., Quetta, 1945; Bde Major (RA) 19 Ind. Div.; GSO II (RA) ALFSEA; GSO II War Office. HM Foreign (subseq. Diplomatic) Service, 1947; Foreign

Office, 1947–49; First Sec. (Information), HM Embassy, Cairo, 1949–54; Foreign Office, 1954–56; attached National Defence Coll. of Can., 1956–57; First Sec., HM Embassy, Paris, 1957–61; HM Consul in Ruanda-Urundi, 1961–62; Special Ambassador for Independence celebrations in Ruanda, July 1962, and in Burundi, Sept. 1962; Ambassador to Rwanda and Burundi, 1962–63; Deputy Head of UK Delegation to European Communities, 1963–65; Counsellor, Djakarta, 1965–67; Head of Far Eastern Dept, FCO, 1967–70; Consul-Gen., San Francisco, 1970–73; Asst Under-Sec. of State, FCO, 1973–74; Dep. Perm. Representative to UN, 1974–78 (Ambassador, 1976). Special Envoy of 5 Western Govts for negotiations on Namibia, 1979–80; Advr, Trade Policy Res. Centre, London, 1981–. *Recreations:* horses, lawn tennis. *Address:* 220 Columbia Heights, Brooklyn Heights, New York, NY 11201, USA. *T:* (212) 852.3320. *Clubs:* Brooks's, Beefsteak; River (New York).

MURRAY, James Dalton, CMG 1957; HM Diplomatic Service, retired; *b* Edinburgh, 6 March 1911; *s* of late Dr James Murray, Edinburgh, and late Eleanor (*née* Mortimer); *m* 1st, 1949, Dora Maud (Denny) Carter (*d* 1958); one *s* two *d*; 2nd, 1959, Merriall Rose, 2nd *d* of Sir Timothy Eden, 8th Bart; two *s. Educ:* Edinburgh Acad.; Stowe; Magdalene Coll., Cambridge (Exhibitioner). Entered HM Consular Service, 1933; Vice-Consul: San Francisco, 1933, Mexico City, 1936; 2nd Sec., Embassy, Washington, 1939; 1st Sec. and Consul, La Paz, 1943; Foreign Office, 1945; Office of Comr-Gen. for SE Asia, Singapore, 1948; Counsellor, HM Foreign Service, and apptd to FO, 1950; seconded to CRO, 1952; Dep. High Comr for UK, Karachi, 1952; returned FO, 1955; Counsellor, British Embassy, Lisbon, 1959–61; Minister, 1961–63, Ambassador, 1963–65, Rumania; British High Comr, Jamaica, 1965–70, and Ambassador to Haiti (non-resident), 1966–70; retired 1970. Re-employed, 1970–76, as First Secretary and Consul (Chargé d'Affaires) resident in Port-au-Prince, Haiti. *Recreations:* golf, relaxing. *Address:* c/o Foreign and Commonwealth Office, SW1.

MURRAY, Prof. James Greig; Professor of Surgery, University of London, 1964–80, retired; Hon. Consultant Surgeon, King's College Hospital, London; *b* 1 April 1919; *s* of J. A. F. Murray and Christina (*née* Davidson); *m* 1946, Cecilia (*née* Mitchell Park); one *s* one *d. Educ:* Peterhead Acad.; Aberdeen Univ. MB, ChB 1942; FRCS Edinburgh 1950; ChM (Aberdeen) 1961; FRCS 1964. Surg.-Lt, RNVR, 1943–46. Lectr in Anatomy Dept, Univ. Coll., London, 1950–54; Clinical Research Fellow, MRC, RCS of England, 1954–56; Sen. Lectr in Surgery, Univ. of Aberdeen, 1958–59. Member: Senate of Univ. of London, 1973–77; SE Thames RHA, 1977–80. Chm., Cancer Res. Campaign Study on Breast Cancer. *Publications:* Scientific Basis of Surgery, 1965; Gastric Secretion: Mechanism and Control, 1965; After Vagotomy, 1969; articles in scientific and clinical jls on composition of vagus nerves, regeneration of nerves, physiology of gastric secretion and treatment of peptic ulceration, cancer of the breast, etc. *Recreations:* fishing, golf. *Address:* Salmon Bothy, Burghead, Moray, Scotland. *T:* Burghead 712.

MURRAY, James Patrick, CMG 1958; *b* 1906; *m* 1934, Margaret Ruth Buchanan; three *s. Educ:* St Edward's Sch., Oxford; Christ Church, Oxford. Cadet, Northern Rhodesia, 1929; District Officer, Northern Rhodesia, 1931; Provincial Commissioner, Northern Rhodesia, 1950; Senior Provincial Commissioner, Northern Rhodesia, 1955; Commissioner for Northern Rhodesia in London, 1961–64 (Country became Independent, as Zambia, 1964). Vice-Chm., Royal African Soc. *Address:* Trewen, Shaftesbury Road, Woking, Surrey. *T:* Woking 61988. *Club:* Royal Commonwealth Society.

MURRAY, John, QC (Scotland) 1974; *b* 8 July 1935; *o s* of J. H. Murray, farmer, Stranraer; *m* 1960, Bridget Jane, *d* of Sir William Godfrey, 7th Bt, and of Lady Godfrey; three *s. Educ:* Cairnryan Sch.; Park Sch., Stranraer; Stranraer High Sch.; Edinburgh Academy; Corpus Christi Coll., Oxford; Edinburgh Univ. BA Oxon 1959, LLB Edinburgh 1962. Advocate, 1962. Mem., Scottish Law Commn, 1979–. Chairman: Scottish Lawyers' European Gp, 1975–78; Agricultural Law Assoc.; Scottish Council of Law Reporting. *Publications:* contrib. Festschrift für Dr Pikalo, 1979; articles in legal and ornithological jls. *Recreations:* farming, gardening, birdwatching, opera, field sports. *Address:* 4 Moray Place, Edinburgh EH3 6DS. *T:* 031-225 1881; Fell Cottage, Craigcaffie, Stranraer. *T:* Stranraer 3356; Wood of Dervaird Farm, Glenluce. *T:* Glenluce 222. *Clubs:* New, Puffins (Edinburgh).

MURRAY, John (Arnaud Robin Grey), CBE 1975 (MBE 1945); FSA; FRSL; Senior Director of Publishing House of John Murray since 1968; *o s* of late Thomas Robinson Grey and Dorothy Evelyn Murray; *m* 1939, Diana Mary, 3rd *d* of late Col Bernard Ramsden James and Hon. Angela Kay-Shuttleworth; two *s* two *d. Educ:* Eton; Magdalen Coll., Oxford (BA Hist). Joined publishing firm of John Murray, 1930; Asst Editor, Cornhill Magazine, 1931; Asst Editor, Quarterly Review, 1933. Served with Royal Artillery and Army-Air Support, War Office, 1940–45. Relaunched Cornhill Magazine with Peter Quennell, 1945. Member: Council, Publishers' Assoc., to 1976; Council, RGS, to 1978; Pres., English Assoc., 1976. *Publication:* (editor, with Peter Quennell) Byron: A Self-Portrait, 1950. *Recreations:* Byron, archives, forestry, music. *Address:* (office) 50 Albemarle Street, W1X 4BD. *T:* 01-493 4361; (home) Cannon Lodge, 12 Cannon Place, NW3. *T:* 01-435 6537. *Clubs:* Pratt's, Beefsteak, Brooks's; Roxburghe.

See also Viscount Mersey.

MURRAY, Katherine Maud Elisabeth, MA, BLitt, FSA; Principal, Bishop Otter College, Chichester, 1948–70; *b* 3 Dec. 1909; *d* of Harold J. R. Murray

(former HMI of Schools) and Kate M. Crosthwaite. *Educ:* Colchester County High Sch.; Somerville Coll., Oxford. Tutor and Librarian, Ashburne Hall, Manchester, 1935–37; Mary Somerville Research Fellow, Somerville Coll., Oxford, 1937–38; Asst Tutor and Registrar, 1938–44, Domestic Bursar, 1942–44, and Junior Bursar, 1944–48, Girton Coll., Cambridge. Chairman of Council, Sussex Archæological Soc., 1964–77, Pres., 1977–80. Mem., Chichester District Council, 1973–, Chm. Planning Cttee, 1979–82 (Vice-Chm., 1976–79). Hon. DLitt: Sussex, 1978; Coll. of Wooster, Ohio, 1979. *Publications:* The Constitutional History of the Cinque Ports, 1935; Register of Daniel Rough, Kent Record Soc., 1945; Caught in the Web of Words: James A. H. Murray and the Oxford English Dictionary, 1977; articles in Sussex Notes and Queries, Transactions of the Royal Historical Society, Archæologia Cantiana, English Historical Review. *Recreations:* walking, archæology. *Address:* Upper Cranmore, Heyshott, Midhurst, West Sussex. *T:* Midhurst 2325.

MURRAY, Prof. Kenneth, PhD; FRS 1979; Professor of Molecular Biology, University of Edinburgh, since 1976; *b* 1930; *yr s* of Allen and Elizabeth Ann Murray; *m* 1958, Noreen Elizabeth Parker (*see* N. E. Murray). *Educ:* Birmingham. Dept of Molecular Biology, Univ. of Edinburgh: Sen. Lecturer, 1967–73; Reader, 1973–76; Prof., 1976–. Member: Biochemical Soc.; European Molecular Organisation; British Biophysical Soc. *Publications:* papers on nucleic acid biochem. and molecular genetics. *Address:* Department of Molecular Biology, University of Edinburgh, Edinburgh EH9 3JR.

MURRAY, Kenneth Alexander George, CB 1977; MA, EdB; Special Adviser to the Home Office on Police Service, Prison Service, and Fire Service selection, 1977–80; Director, Civil Service Selection Board, and Civil Service Commissioner, 1964–77; *b* 16 June 1916; *s* of late George Dickie Murray and Isabella Murray; *m* 1942, Elizabeth Ward Simpson; one *d. Educ:* Skene Street and Central Schools, Aberdeen; Aberdeen Univ. (MA English (1st Cl. Hons), EdB Psychol. (1st Cl. Hons)). RAMC and War Office Selection Bd, 1940–45, Captain. Psychological Adviser, Govt of India, 1945–47; Lectr in Psychology, Univ. of Hull, 1948–50; Principal Psychologist and Chief Psychologist, CS Selection Bd, 1951–63. Adviser to Police Service in high-grade selection, 1963–, also to Fire and Prison Services, to Church of Scotland and C of E; Adviser (earlier) to Govts of Pakistan and Western Nigeria through their Public Service Commns. *Recreations:* reading, walking, bridge, watching cricket and Rugby League. *Address:* 15 Melvinshaw, Leatherhead, Surrey KT22 8SX. *T:* Leatherhead 72995. *Clubs:* MCC, Royal Commonwealth Society.

MURRAY, Rt. Hon. Lionel, (Len Murray), PC 1976; OBE 1966; General Secretary of the Trades Union Congress, since 1973; *b* 2 Aug. 1922; *m* 1945, Heather Woolf; two *s* two *d. Educ:* Wellington (Salop) Gram. Sch.; Univ. of London, 1940–41; NCLC; New Coll., Oxford, 1945–47 (Hon. Fellow, 1975). Economic Dept, TUC, 1947, Head of Dept, 1954–69; Asst Gen. Sec., TUC, 1969–73. Member: NEDC, 1973–; Cttee to Review the Functioning of Financial Institutions, 1977–80; Bd of Trustees, Anglo-German Foundn for Study of Industrial Society, 1977–; Vice-President: ICFTU, 1973; European Trade Union Confedn, 1974. Vis. Fellow, Nuffield Coll., Oxford, 1974. Hon. Fellow, Sheffield City Polytechnic, 1979. Hon. DSc: Aston, 1977; Salford, 1978; Hon. LLD St Andrews, 1979. *Publication:* Contrib. to Economics and Technical Change. *Address:* Trades Union Congress, 23–28 Great Russell Street, WC1. *T:* 01-636 4030.

MURRAY of Blackbarony, Sir Nigel Andrew Digby, 15th Bt *cr* 1628; farmer; *b* 15 Aug. 1944; *s* of Sir Alan John Digby Murray of Blackbarony, 14th Bt, and of Mabel Elisabeth, *d* of late Arthur Bernard Schiele, Arias, Argentina; *S* father, 1978; *m* 1980, Diana Margaret, *yr d* of Robert C. Bray, Olivos, Buenos Aires; one *s. Educ:* St Paul's School, Argentina; Salesian Agricl Sch., Argentina; Royal Agricultural Coll., Cirencester. Farms dairy cattle, store cattle, crops and bees. Holds a private pilot's licence. *Heir: s* Alexander Nigel Robert Murray, *b* 1 July 1981. *Address:* Establecimiento Tinamú, CC 115, 2624 Arias, Provincia de Córdoba, Argentina. *Clubs:* Venado Tuerto Polo and Athletic; Tigre Boat.

MURRAY, Noreen Elizabeth, PhD, FRS 1982; Reader, Department of Molecular Biology, University of Edinburgh, since 1978; *b* 26 Feb. 1935; *d* of John and Lillian Grace Parker; *m* 1958, Kenneth Murray, *qv. Educ:* King's College London (BSc); Univ. of Birmingham (PhD). Research Associate: Stanford Univ., California, 1960–64; Univ. of Cambridge, 1964–67; Mem., MRC Molecular Genetics Unit, Edinburgh, 1968–74; Lectr, 1974, later Sen. Lectr, Dept of Molecular Biology, Univ. of Edinburgh; scientist in European Molecular Biol. Lab., Heidelberg, 1980–82. Member: EMBO; Genetical Soc.; Genetics Soc., USA. *Publications:* original research papers and reviews in field of genetics and molecular biology. *Recreation:* gardening. *Address:* Department of Molecular Biology, University of Edinburgh, Mayfield Road, Edinburgh. *T:* 031-667 1081.

MURRAY, Sir Patrick (Ian Keith), 12th Bt *cr* 1673; *b* 22 March 1965; *s* of Sir William Patrick Keith Murray, 11th Bt, and of Susan Elizabeth (who *m* 1976, J. C. Hudson, PhD), *d* of Stacey Jones; *S* father, 1977. *Educ:* Christ College, Brecon, Powys. *Heir: kinsman* Major Peter Keith-Murray, Canadian Forces [*b* July 1935; *m* 1960, Judith Anne, *d* of late Andrew Tinsley); one *s* one *d*]. *Address:* Old Fford Fawr, Hay-on-Wye, Powys. *T:* Hay-on-Wye 820736.

MURRAY, Peter, CMG 1959; HM Diplomatic Service, retired; *b* 18 July 1915; *m* 1960, E. M. Batchelor. *Educ:* Portsmouth Gram. Sch.; Merton Coll., Oxford. Burma Commission, 1937-49, Foreign Service, 1947; HM Ambassador to Cambodia, 1961-64; Ambassador to Ivory Coast, Upper Volta and Niger, 1970-72. *Address:* Brae Cottage, Lion Lane, Haslemere GU27 1JR. *Club:* East India.

MURRAY, Peter (John), PhD (London), FSA; Professor of the History of Art at Birkbeck College, University of London, 1967-80, now Emeritus; *b* 23 April 1920; *er s* of John Knowles Murray and Dorothy Catton; *m* 1947, Linda Bramley. *Educ:* King Edward VI Sch., Birmingham; Robert Gordon's Coll., Aberdeen; Gray's Sch. of Art, Aberdeen; Slade Sch. and Courtauld Inst., Univ. of London. Sen. Research Fellow, Warburg Inst., 1961. Trustee, British Architectural Library, 1979-. Pres., Soc. of Architectural Historians of GB, 1969-72; Chm., Walpole Soc., 1978-81. Rhind Lecturer, Edinburgh, 1967; Vis. Prof., Univ. of Victoria, BC, 1981. *Publications:* Watteau, 1948; Index of Attributions . . . before Vasari, 1959; Dictionary of Art and Artists (with Linda Murray), 1959 (4th edn 1976); History of English Architecture (with P. Kidson), 1962 (with P. Kidson and P. Thomson), 1965; The Art of the Renaissance (with L. Murray), 1963; The Architecture of the Italian Renaissance, 1963; Renaissance Architecture, 1971; The Dulwich Picture Gallery, a Catalogue, 1980; contribs to New Cambridge Mod. Hist., Encycl. Britannica, etc.; translations; articles in Warburg and Courtauld Jl, Burlington Mag., Apollo, foreign jls. *Address:* The Old Rectory, Farnborough, Banbury, Oxon.

MURRAY, Sir Ralph; *see* Murray, Sir F. R. H.

MURRAY, Rt. Hon. Ronald King; *see* Murray, Rt Hon. Lord.

MURRAY, Dr Ronald Ormiston, MBE (mil.) 1945; MD; FRCPE, DMR, FRCR; Consulting Radiologist: Royal National Orthopaedic Hospital, since 1977 (Consultant Radiologist, 1956-77); Lord Mayor Treloar's Orthopaedic Hospital, Alton, and Heatherwood Hospital, Ascot, since 1977 (Consultant Radiologist, 1951-77); *b* 14 Nov. 1912; *y s* of late John Murray and Elizabeth Ormiston Murray (*née* MacGibbon); *m* 1st, 1940, Catherine Joan Suzette Gauvain, FFCM (*d* 1980), *d* of late Sir Henry Gauvain, MD, FRCS, and Laura Louise Butler; one *s* two *d*; 2nd, 1981, Mrs Jane Mathewson. *Educ:* Glasgow Acad.; Loretto Sch.; St John's Coll., Cambridge (MA); St Thomas's Hosp. Med. Sch. Casualty Officer and Ho. Surg., St Thomas' Hosp., 1938-39; RAMC (TA), 1939-45, MO 2nd Bn The London Scottish, Hon. Lt-Col. Associate Prof., Radiology, Amer. Univ. Hosp., Beirut, 1954-56. Sen. Lectr in Orthopaedic Radiology, Inst. of Orthopaedics, London Univ., 1963-77; Robert Jones Lectr, RCS, 1973; Baker Travelling Prof. in Radiology, Australasia, 1974; Caldwell Lectr, Amer. Roentgen Ray Soc., 1975, also Corresp. Mem. of the Soc., 1973-; Skinner Lectr, RCR, 1979; other eponymous lectures. Associate Editor, Brit. Jl of Radiology, 1959-71. Founder Vice-Pres., Internat. Skeletal Soc., 1973, Pres., 1977-78. Fellow: Brit. Orthopaedic Assoc.; RSocMed (Pres., Sect. of Radiol., 1978-79); Hon. Fellow: Amer. Coll. of Radiology, 1969; Royal Australasian Coll. of Radiol., 1979; Fac. Radiol., RCSI, 1981; Hon. Member: Mexican and Peruvian Rad. Socs, 1968; Rad. Soc. of N Amer., 1975; GETROA, France, 1976. *Publications:* chapters in: Modern Trends in Diagnostic Radiology, 1970; D. Sutton's Textbook of Radiology, 1969, 2nd edn 1975; (jtly) Radiology of Skeletal Disorders: exercises in diagnosis, 1971, 2nd edn 1977; papers in med. jls, mainly concerning radiological aspects of orthopaedics. *Recreations:* golf; formerly: Rugby football (Cambridge XV 1934-35, Scotland XV 1935), swimming (Cambridge Univ. Team 1933-34, British Univs Team, Turin, 1934). *Address:* 25 Wimpole Street, W1M 7AD. *T:* 01-935 4747; Little Court, The Bury, Odiham, Hants RG25 1LY. *T:* Odiham 2982. *Clubs:* United Oxford & Cambridge University; Hawks (Cambridge); Berkshire Golf, Rye Golf.

MURRAY, Dame Rosemary; *see* Murray, Dame A. R.

MURRAY, Sir Rowland William Patrick, 14th Bt *cr* 1630; General Manager, Miles Motor Inn, Augusta, Georgia; *b* 26 Oct. 1910; *s* of late Rowland William Murray, 2nd *s* of 12th Bt, and Gertrude Frances McCabe; *S* uncle 1958; *m* ; four *s* two *d*. Served in US Army during War of 1939-45. Captain. *Heir: s* Rowland William Murray, *b* 22 Sept. 1947.

MURRIE, Sir William (Stuart), GCB 1964 (CB 1946); KBE 1952; Permanent Under-Secretary of State for Scotland, 1959-64, retired; *b* Dundee, 19 Dec. 1903; *s* of Thomas Murrie and Catherine Burgh; *m* 1932, Eleanore Boswell (*d* 1966). *Educ:* S America; Harris Acad., Dundee; Edinburgh Univ.; Balliol Coll., Oxford. Entered Scottish Office, 1927; transferred to Dept of Health for Scotland, 1935; Under-Sec., Offices of War Cabinet, 1944; Deputy Sec. (Civil), Cabinet Office, 1947; Deputy Under-Sec. of State, Home Office, 1948-52; Sec. to the Scottish Education Dept, 1952-57; Sec., Scottish Home Dept, 1957-59. Chm., Board of Trustees for Nat. Galls of Scotland, 1972-75; Member: Council on Tribunals, 1965-77; Adv. Cttee on Rhodesian Travel Restrictions, 1968-79 (Chm., 1979). General Council Assessor, Edinburgh Univ. Court, 1967-75. Hon. LLD, Dundee Univ., 1968. *Address:* 7 Cumin Place, Edinburgh EH9 2JX. *T:* 031-667 2612.

MURSELL, Sir Peter, Kt 1969; MBE 1941; Vice-Lord-Lieutenant, West Sussex, since 1974; *b* 20 Jan. 1913; *m* 1938, Cicely, *d* of late Mr and Mrs M. F. North; two *s* two *d*. *Educ:* Bedales Sch.; Downing Coll. Cambridge. Fruit growing, 1934. War Service: Air Transport Auxiliary, 1940-44, Sen. Comdr. West Sussex County Council: Mem., 1947-74; Chm., 1962-67 and 1969-74. Member: Cttee on Management in Local Govt, 1965-66; Royal Commn on Local Govt in England, 1966-69; Water Space Amenity Commn, 1973-76; Inland Waterways Amenity Adv. Council, 1974-77. DL West Sussex, 1962. *Recreations:* sailing, mountain walking, skiing, squash, canal cruising. *Address:* Dounhurst Farm, Wisborough Green, Billingshurst, West Sussex. *T:* Kirdford 501. *Club:* Farmers'.

MURTAGH, Miss Marion; Chairman: Stats (MR) Ltd; Midas Research Ltd; CSB Data Processing Ltd. *Educ:* Waverley Gram. Sch., Birmingham. Qualified as: Certified Accountant, 1947; Chartered Secretary, 1948. Proprietor, The Calculating Bureau, 1938-51, Joint Owner, 1951-61. Member: Anglo-Thai Soc.; West Midlands Bridge Club (Pres.). *Recreation:* bridge. *Address:* 116 Chessetts Wood Road, Lapworth, Solihull, West Midlands B94 6EL. *T:* Lapworth 2089.

MURTON, family name of **Baron Murton of Lindisfarne.**

MURTON OF LINDISFARNE, Baron *cr* 1979 (Life Peer), of Hexham in the County of Northumberland; **(Henry) Oscar Murton,** PC 1976; OBE 1946; TD 1947 (Clasp 1951); JP; a Deputy Chairman of Committees, House of Lords, since 1981; *b* 8 May 1914; *o s* of late H. E. C. Murton, and of E. M. Murton (*née* Renton), Hexham, Northumberland; *m* 1939, Constance Frances (*d* 1977), *e d* of late F. O'L. Connell; one *s* one *d* ; 2nd, 1979, Pauline Teresa (Freeman, City of London, 1980; Chevalier, Nat. Order of Merit, France, 1976), *y d* of late Thomas Keenan. *Educ:* Uppingham Sch. Commissioned, TA, 1934; Staff Coll., Camberley, 1939; tsc; active service, Royal Northumberland Fusiliers, 1939-46; GSO1, HQ Salisbury Plain Dist, 1942-44; GSO1, SD1, War Office, 1944-46. Managing Dir, Henry A. Murton Ltd, Departmental Stores, Newcastle-upon-Tyne and Sunderland, 1949-57. Dep. Sec. Northern Div. Nat. Coal Board, 1947-49. MP (C) Poole, 1964-79; Sec., Cons. Parly Cttee for Housing, Local Government and Land, 1964-67; Vice-Chm., 1967-70; Chm., Cons. Parly Cttee for Public Building and Works, 1970; introduced Highways (Amendment) Act, 1965; PPS to Minister of Local Government and Development, 1970-71; an Asst Govt Whip, 1971-72; a Lord Comr, HM Treasury, 1972-73; Second Dep. Chm., 1973-74, First Dep. Chm., 1974-76, Dep. Speaker and Chm. of Ways and Means, House of Commons, 1976-79. Member: Exec. Cttee, Inter-Parliamentary Union British Group, 1970-71; Panel of Chairmen of Standing Cttees, 1970-71; a former Vice-Pres., Assoc. of Municipal Corporations; Mem. Herrison (Dorchester) Hosp. Group Management Cttee, 1963-74. Governor, Canford Sch., 1972-76. Freeman, City of London, 1977; Freeman, Wax Chandlers' Co., 1978; Liveryman, 1979, Mem. Ct of Assistants, 1981-, Clockmakers' Co.; Pres., League of Friends of Poole Gen. Hosp., 1978-. JP, Poole, 1963. *Recreations:* sailing, painting. *Address:* 49 Carlisle Mansions, Carlisle Place, SW1P 1HY. *T:* 01-834 8226; Flat 5 Seaview Court, North Road, Parkstone, Poole, Dorset BH14 0LX. *T:* Parkstone 730243.

MUSCHAMP, Rt. Rev. Cecil Emerson Barron, AM 1982; MA, ThL; *b* Wing, Bucks, England, 16 June 1902; *s* of late Canon E. G. Muschamp, Launceston, Tasmania; *m* 1931, Margaret Warren Crane; two *s* two *d*. *Educ:* Church Grammar Sch., Launceston, Tasmania; Univ. of Tasmania; Univ. of Oxford; St Stephen's House, Oxford. BA Univ. of Tasmania, 1924, Oxon (Hon. Sch. of Theology), 1927; ThL Australian Coll. of Theology, 1925; MA Oxon, 1934. Schoolmaster, 1920-25, Hutchins Sch., Hobart, and St Peter's Coll., Adelaide. Deacon, 1927; Priest, 1928. Curate of St Luke, Bournemouth, 1927-30; in charge of St Albans and St Aidan's, Aldershot, 1930-32; Curate, Withycombe Raleigh (in charge of All Saints, Exmouth), 1932-37; Vicar of St Michael and All Angels, City and Diocese of Christchurch, NZ, 1937-50; Asst Bishop of Perth, 1950-55; Bishop of Kalgoorlie, 1950-67; Dean of Brisbane, 1967-72, Dean Emeritus, 1981-. Retired 1972. Served War of 1939-45: Chaplain in Royal New Zealand Air Force, 1942-45; Sen. Chaplain, 1944, S Pacific Comd. Pres., WCC in WA, 1953-55; Councillor, Royal Flying Doctor Service, Kalgoorlie Base, 1955-67. *Publications:* Table Manners, 1945; Sin and its Remedy, 1961; The Church of England and Roman Catholicism, 1962. *Recreations:* golf, gardening. *Address:* 9 Samson Street, Mosman Park, WA 6012, Australia. *Club:* Rotary (Mosman Park) (Paul Harris Fellow of Rotary, 1982).

MUSCROFT, Harold Colin; a Recorder of the Crown Court, 1972-82; *b* Leeds, 12 June 1924; *s* of Harold and Meta Catrina Muscroft; *m* 1958; three *d*. *Educ:* Dept of Navigation, Southampton Univ.; home; Exeter Coll., Oxford (MA). Volunteer, Royal Corps of Signals, 1942; commnd RA, 1943; served in India, Burma (wounded), Malay and Java; demobilised 1947 (Captain). Oxford, 1947-51. Called to Bar, Inner Temple, 1953; practised NE Circuit. Huddersfield Town Councillor, 1958-59. *Recreation:* writing. *Address:* 11 Chelmsford Road, Harrogate, North Yorks. *T:* Harrogate 503344.

MUSGRAVE, Sir Christopher (Patrick Charles), 15th Bt *cr* 1611; *b* 14 April 1949; *s* of Sir Charles Musgrave, 14th Bt and of Olive Louise Avril, *o d* of Patrick Cringle, Norfolk; *S* father, 1970; *m* 1978, Megan, *d* of Walter Inman, Hull; one *d*. *Recreations:* sailing, tennis, table-tennis, painting. *Heir: b* Nigel Chardin Musgrave, *b* 8 Dec. 1951. *Address:* c/o Williams & Glyn's Bank, Silver Street, Hull.

MUSGRAVE, Sir Cyril; *see* Musgrave, Sir F. C.

MUSGRAVE, Dennis Charles, FICE; Director, British Water Industries Group, since 1981; *b* 10 Feb. 1921; *s* of Frederick Charles Musgrave and Jane Elizabeth (*née* Gulliver); *m* 1942, Marjorie Cynthia (*née* Chaston); one *s*. *Educ:* privately. MIStructE, FIWES. Engineering Assistant: Howard Humphreys and Sons, Consulting Engrs; Coode and Partners, Cons. Engrs, 1938-45; Asst Port Engr, Lagos, Nigeria, 1945-47; Engrg Asst, Borough of Willesden, 1947-49; Agent, Ruddock and Meighan, Civil Engrg Contractors, 1949-56; Associate Partner, Sandford, Fawcett and Partners, Cons. Engrs, in Canada, 1956-63, in Westminster, 1963-66. Engineering Inspector, Min. of Housing and Local Govt, 1966, Sen. Inspector, 1971; Asst Dir, DoE, 1974; Chief Water Engr, DoE, 1977-82. *Publications:* various technical papers. *Recreations:* music, literature. *Address:* 5 Old Forge Close, Stanmore, Mddx HA7 3EB. *T:* 01-954 2971.

MUSGRAVE, Sir (Frank) Cyril, KCB 1955 (CB 1946); retired; *b* 21 June 1900; *s* of late Frank Musgrave; *m* 1st, Elsie Mary, *d* of late Christopher Williams; one *s* one *d*; 2nd, Jean Elsie, *d* of late John Soulsby; two *s*. *Educ:* St George's Coll., London. Entered Civil Service, 1919; served Inland Revenue, 1920-37; Air Ministry, 1937-40; Ministry of Aircraft Production, 1940-46; Min. of Supply, 1946-59, Permanent Sec., 1956-59. Chm., Iron and Steel Bd, 1959-67; Mem. (part time), BSC, 1967-70; Dir various companies, 1960-76. *Recreations:* music, gardening. *Address:* Black Horse Cottage, Towersey, Thame, Oxon OX9 3QR. *T:* Thame 3269.

MUSGRAVE, Sir Richard James, 7th Bt, *cr* 1782; *b* 10 Feb. 1922; *s* of Sir Christopher Norman Musgrave, 6th Bt, OBE, and Kathleen (*d* 1967), 3rd *d* of late Robert Chapman, Co. Tyrone; *S* father 1956; *m* 1958, Maria, *d* of late Col M. Cambanis, and Mrs Cambanis, Athens, Greece; two *s* four *d*. *Educ:* Stowe. Capt., The Poona Horse (17th Queen Victoria's Own Cavalry), 1940-45. *Recreation:* shooting. *Heir: s* Christopher John Shane Musgrave, *b* 23 Oct. 1959. *Address:* Riverstown, Tara, Co. Meath. *T:* Drogheda 25121; Komitu, Syros, Greece. *Club:* Kildare Street and University (Dublin).

MUSGRAVE, Thea; composer; *b* 1928; *d* of James P. Musgrave and Joan Musgrave (*née* Hacking); *m* 1971, Peter, *s* of Irving Mark, NY. *Educ:* Moreton Hall, Oswestry; Edinburgh Univ.; Paris Conservatoire; privately with Nadia Boulanger. *Works include:* Cantata for a summer's day, 1954; The Abbot of Drimock (Chamber opera), 1955; Triptych for Tenor and orch., 1959; Colloquy for violin and piano, 1960; The Phoenix and the Turtle for chorus and orch., 1962; The Five Ages of Man for chorus and orch., 1963; The Decision (opera), 1964-65; Nocturnes and arias for orch., 1966; Chamber Concerto No. 2, in homage to Charles Ives, 1966; Chamber Concerto No 3 (Octet), 1966; Concerto for orchestra, 1967; Music for Horn and Piano, 1967; Clarinet Concerto, 1968; Beauty and the Beast (ballet), 1968; Night Music, 1969; Memento Vitae, a concerto in homage to Beethoven, 1970; Horn concerto, 1971; From One to Another, 1972; Viola Concerto, 1973; The Voice of Ariadne (opera), 1972-73; Rorate Coeli, for chorus, 1974; Space Play, 1974; Orfeo I and Orfeo II, 1975; Mary, Queen of Scots (opera), 1976-77; Christmas Carol (opera), 1979. Performances and broadcasts: UK, France, Germany, Switzerland, Scandinavia, USA, USSR, etc., Edinburgh, Cheltenham, Aldeburgh, Zagreb, Venice and Warsaw Festivals. Hon. MusDoc, CNAA. *Address:* c/o Novello & Co. Ltd, Borough Green, Kent.

MUSGRAVE, Prof. William Kenneth Rodgerson, PhD, DSc (Birmingham); Professor of Organic Chemistry, 1960-81, now Emeritus, and Head of Department of Chemistry, 1968-71, 1974-77, 1980-81, University of Durham; *b* 16 Sept. 1918; *s* of late Charles Musgrave and late Sarah Alice Musgrave; *m* 1944, Joyce Cadman; two *s*. *Educ:* Stanley Grammar Sch., Co. Durham; Univ. of Birmingham. British-Canadian Atomic Energy Project, 1944-45; Univ. of Durham: Lecturer in Chemistry, 1945-56; Senior Lecturer, 1956-60; Personal Readership in Organic Chem., 1960; Second Pro-Vice-Chancellor, 1970-73; Pro-Vice-Chancellor and Sub-Warden, 1973-78; Acting Vice-Chancellor, 1979. *Publications:* (joint) Advances in Fluorine Chemistry, Vol. I, edited by Stacey, Tatlow and Sharpe, 1960; Rodd's Chemistry of Carbon Compounds, vols Ia and IIIa, edited by Coffey; scientific papers in chemical journals. *Recreations:* gardening, rough shooting. *Address:* The Orchard, Potter's Bank, Durham City. *T:* Durham 43196.

MUSGROVE, Prof. Frank, DLitt; Sarah Fielden Professor of Education, University of Manchester, 1970-82, now Emeritus; Dean of the Faculty of Education, 1976-78; *b* 16 Dec. 1922; *e s* of late Thomas and Fanny Musgrove, New Brinsley, Nottingham; *m* 1944, Dorothy Ellen (*née* Nicholls); one *d*. *Educ:* Henry Mellish Grammar Sch., Nottingham; Magdalen Coll., Oxford; Univ. of Nottingham. BA Oxon, PhD Nottingham, MEd Manchester. Served War, RAFVR, Navigator, Bomber Command (commnd), Ops 149 Sqdn, 1941-45 (tour of bombing missions completed 1944). Educational appts in England and in the Colonial Educn Service, E Africa, 1947-57; Lectureships in Univs of Leicester and Leeds, 1957-65; Vis. Prof. of Educn, Univ. of British Columbia, 1965; Prof. of Research in Educn, Univ. of Bradford, 1965-70; Vis. Prof. of Sociology, Univ. of California (Davis), 1969; The Chancellor's Lectr, Univ. of Wellington, NZ, 1970; Raymond Priestley Lectr, Univ. of Birmingham, 1975. Co-editor, Research in Education, 1971-76. FRSA 1971. DLitt Open, 1982. *Publications:* The Migratory Elite, 1963; Youth and the Social Order, 1964; The Family, Education and Society, 1966; Society and the Teacher's Role (with P. H. Taylor), 1969; Patterns of Power and Authority in English Education, 1971; Ecstasy and Holiness: counter culture and the open society, 1974; Margins of the Mind, 1977; School and the Social Order, 1979; Education and Anthropology, 1982; research papers in: Africa;

Sociological Review; Brit. Jl of Sociology; Brit. Jl of Educational Psychology; Economic History Review; Brit. Jl of Social and Clinical Psychology, etc. *Recreations:* fell walking, fly fishing. *Address:* Fin Cop, Moody Sty Lane, Grassington, N Yorks BD23 5LX. *T:* Grassington 752744. *Club:* Linton and Grassington Angling.

MUSGROVE, Prof. John, RIBA; Haden Pilkington Professor of Environmental Design and Engineering, University of London at University College, since 1978; Head of the Bartlett School of Architecture and Planning, University College London, since 1980; *b* 20 June 1920; *s* of James Musgrove and Betsy (*née* Jones); *m* 1941, Gladys Mary Webb; three *s*. *Educ:* Univ. of Durham (King's Coll.). (BArch, 1st Cl. Hons). Asst to late Baron Holford, RA, 1952-53; Research Architect, Nuffield Foundn, 1953-60; Sen. Lectr and Reader in Architecture, University Coll. London, 1960-70, Prof., 1970-78. Hon. Fellow, Inst. of Architects, Sri Lanka, 1972. *Publications:* (jtly) The Function and Design of Hospitals, 1955; (jtly) The Design of Research Laboratories, 1960; numerous articles and papers in Architects' Jl, RIBA Jl, and reviews. *Recreations:* painting in oils, gardening. *Address:* Netherby, Green End Road, Boxmoor, Hemel Hempstead, Herts HP1 1QW.

MUSHIN, Prof. William W(oolf), CBE 1971; MA Oxon, 1946; MB, BS (Hons) London, 1933; FRCS 1966; FFARCS 1948; Professor and Director of Anaesthetics, Welsh National School of Medicine, University of Wales, 1947-75, now Emeritus; *b* London, Sept. 1910; *y s* of Moses Mushin and Jesse (*née* Kalmenson); *m* 1939, Betty Hannah Goldberg; one *s* three *d*. *Educ:* Davenant Sch.; London Hosp. Med. Sch. Buxton Prize in Anatomy, Anderson Prize in Clinical Medicine). Various resident hosp. posts; formerly: Anaesthetist, Royal Dental Hosp.; first Asst, Nuffield Dept of Anaesthetists, Univ. of Oxford. Lectures: Clover, RCS, 1955; Kellogg, George Washington Univ., 1950; Guedel, Univ. of Calif, 1957; John Snow, 1964; Baxter Travenol, Internat. Anaesth. Research Soc., 1970; Macgregor, Univ. of Birmingham, 1972; Rovenstine, Amer. Soc. of Anesthesiol., 1973; Crawford Long, Emory Univ., USA, 1981. Visiting Professor or Consultant to univs, academic and other bodies in USA, Argentine, Uruguay, Brazil, Denmark, NZ, Australia, India, Germany, Ghana, Kenya, S Africa, and Holland. Examiner: Univ. of Oxford for MD and PhD; FFARCS, 1953-73; FRCSI, 1962-67. Welsh Regional Hospital Board: Cons. Adviser in Anaesthetics, 1948-74; Mem., 1961-74. Member: Central Health Services Council, 1962-72; Safety of Drugs Cttee, Dept of Health and Social Security, 1964-76; Medicines Commn, 1976-; Assoc. of Anaesthetists, 1936- (Mem. Council, 1946-59 and 1961-73; Vice-Pres., 1953-56); Anaesthetists Group Cttee, BMA, 1950-69; Bd of Governors, United Cardiff Hosps, 1956-65; Court, Univ. of Wales, 1957-58; Commonwealth Scholarships Commn, 1969-78. Welsh National School of Medicine: Mem. Senate, 1947-75; Mem. Council, 1957-58; Vice-Provost, 1958-60; Royal College of Surgeons: Mem. Bd, Faculty of Anaesthetists, 1954-71; Mem. Council, 1961-64; Dean, Faculty of Anaesthetists, 1961-64. Mem. Bd of Management and Consulting Editor, British Jl of Anaesthesia, 1947-75. Hon. Mem., various societies of anaesthetists. Hon. FFARACS 1959; Hon. FFA(SA) 1962; Hon. FFARCSI 1962; Hon. DSc Wales, 1982. John Snow Silver Medal, 1974. *Publications:* Anaesthesia for the Poor Risk, 1948; (with Sir R. Macintosh) Local Analgesia: Brachial Plexus, 1954, 4th edn 1967; Physics for the Anaesthetist, 1946, 3rd edn 1964; Automatic Ventilation of Lungs, 1959, 3rd edn 1980; (ed) Thoracic Anaesthesia, 1963. Numerous papers on anaesthesia and allied subjects in British and foreign jls. *Address:* 30 Bettws-y-Coed Road, Cardiff CF2 6PL. *T:* Cardiff 751002. *Club:* United Oxford & Cambridge University.

MUSKER, Sir John, Kt 1952; Banker; Director, Cater, Ryder & Co., Ltd, Bankers, 1960-79 (Chairman, 1960-71); Chairman, Cater, Brightwen & Co. Ltd, Bankers, since 1938; *b* 25 Jan. 1906; *o s* of late Capt. Harold Musker, JP, Snarehill Hall, Thetford, Norfolk; *m* 1st, 1932, Elizabeth (decd), *d* of Captain Loeffler, 51 Grosvenor Square, W1; two *d*; 2nd, 1955, Mrs Rosemary Pugh (*d* 1980), *d* of late Maj.-Gen. Merton Beckwith-Smith; 3rd 1982, Hon. Audrey Elizabeth Paget, *d* of 1st Baron Queenborough, GBE. *Educ:* privately; St John's Coll., Cambridge (BA). Mem. LCC for City of London, 1944-49. Lt, RNVR, 1940. Hon. Treas., London Municipal Soc., 1936-46. *Address:* Shadwell Park, Thetford, Norfolk. *T:* Thetford 3257; 71 Cadogan Gardens, SW3. *Club:* White's.

MUSKERRY, 8th Baron (Ireland), *cr* 1781; Hastings Fitzmaurice Tilson Deane; 13th Bt (Ireland), *cr* 1710; Radiologist to Regional Health Authority, Limerick, 1961-77; *b* 12 March 1907; 3rd and *o surv. s* of 7th Baron Muskerry and Mabel Kathleen Vivienne (*d* 1954), *d* of Charles Henry Robinson, MD, FRCSI; *S* father, 1966; *m* 1944, Betty Fairbridge, *e d* of George Wilfred Reckless Palmer, South Africa; one *s* one *d*. *Educ:* Sandford Park Sch., Dublin; Trinity Coll., Dublin; MA, MB, BCh, BAO; DMR London. Served War of 1939-45, S African Army (Western Desert; seconded RAMC, Italy, Greece). Specialised in Radiology, London Univ., 1946-48; Consultant Radiologist to Transvaal Administration, 1949-57. *Heir: s* Hon. Robert Fitzmaurice Deane, BA, BAI [*b* 26 March 1948; *m* 1975, Rita Brink, Pietermaritzburg. *Educ:* Sandford Park Sch., Dublin; Trinity Coll. Dublin]. *Address:* Springfield Castle, Drumcollogher, Co. Limerick. *T:* Drumcollogher 5.

MUSKETT, Prof. Arthur Edmund, OBE 1957; DSc London, ARCS, MRIA; FIBiol; Professor of Plant Pathology and Head of Department of Mycology and Plant Pathology, The Queen's University, Belfast, 1945-65; Professor Emeritus, since 1966; Head of Plant Pathology Division, Ministry of Agriculture, N Ireland, 1938-65; *b* 15 April 1900; *s* of late Arthur Muskett,

Wood Farm, Ashwellthorpe, Norwich, Norfolk; *m* 1926, Hilda Elizabeth, *d* of late Henry Smith, Manor Farm, Fundenhall, Norwich; three *s* one *d. Educ:* City of Norwich Sch., Norwich; Imperial Coll. of Science, London. BSc, ARCS (Botany); MSc (London) 1931; MRIA 1933; DSc (London) 1938. RAF Flight Cadet A, 1918-19. Asst in Plant Pathology, Min. of Agr., NI and QUB, 1923-26, Junior Lectr QUB 1926; Dep. Head Plant Pathology Div., Min. of Agric. NI and Lectr QUB, 1931; Dean of Faculty of Agriculture, Queen's Univ., Belfast, 1950-57. Pres. British Mycological Soc., 1948; Vice-Pres., Assoc. Applied Biologists, 1954-55. Chairman: Central Gardens Assoc. for Northern Ireland; Ulster Countryside Cttee, 1965-72; N Ireland Amenity Council; Ulster Tree Cttee. *Publications:* Diseases of the Flax Plant, 1947; A. A. McGuckian: A Memorial Volume, 1956; Autonomous Dispersal: Plant Pathology (An Advanced Treatise), Vol. III, 1960; Mycology and Plant Pathology in Ireland, 1976; Catalogue of Irish Fungi, I Gasteromycetes, 1978, II Hymenomycetes, 1980, III Teliomycetes, 1980; Ulster Garden Handbook (annually); numerous papers in Annals of Applied Biology, Annals of Botany, Trans Brit. Mycological Soc., etc. *Recreations:* horticulture; extra work. *Address:* The Cottage, 29 Ballynahinch Road, Carryduff, Belfast. *T:* Carryduff 812350.

MUSKIE, Edmund Sixtus; Secretary of State, USA, 1980-81; lawyer and politician; *b* Rumford, Maine, 28 March 1914; *s* of Stephen Muskie and Josephine Czarnecki; *m* 1948, Jane Frances Gray; two *s* three *d. Educ:* Bates Coll., Maine (AB); Cornell Law Sch., Ithaca, New York (LLB). Served War, Lt USNR, 1942-45. Admitted to Bar: Massachusetts, 1939; Maine, 1940, and practised at Waterville, Maine, 1940 and 1945-55; Federal District Court, 1941. Mem., Maine House of Reps, 1947-51; Democratic Floor Leader, 1949-51; Dist. Dir for Maine, Office of Price Stabilisation, 1951-52; City Solicitor, Waterville, Maine, 1954-55; Governor of State of Maine, 1955-59; US Senator from Maine, 1959-80; Senate Assistant Majority Whip, 1966-80; Chm., Senate Budget Cttee, 1974-80. Cand. for Vice-Presidency of US, 1968. Mem., Senate Foreign Relations Cttee, 1970-74, 1979-80; Former Chm., and Mem. *ex officio*, Democratic Senatorial Campaign Cttee; Chairman, Senate Sub-Cttees on: Environmental Pollution, Senate Environment and Public Wks Cttee; Intergovtl Relations, Senate Governmental Affairs Cttee, 1959-78; Former Member: Special Cttee on Aging; Exec. Cttee, Nat. Governors' Conf.; Chm., Roosevelt Campobello Internat. Park Commn. Mem, Amer. Acad. of Arts and Sciences. Has numerous hon. doctorates. Phi Beta Kappa; Phi Alpha Delta. Presidential Medal of Freedom, 1981; Notre Dame Laetare Medal, 1981; Distinguished Service Award, Former Members of Congress Assoc., 1981. *Publication:* Journeys, 1972. *Address:* Chadbourne, Parke, Whiteside & Wolff, 1101 Vermont Ave, NW, Washington, DC 20005, USA.

MUSSEN, Surgeon Rear-Adm. Robert Walsh, CB 1954; CBE 1949; MD; FRCP; retired; *b* 13 May 1900; *s* of Hugh Harper Mussen, JP, Belfast, late Crown Solicitor, N Ireland; *m* 1932, Mary Katherine Anne, *d* of late Surgeon Rear-Adm. H. E. R. Stephens; one *s* two *d* (and one *s* decd). *Educ:* Campbell Coll., Belfast; Queen's Univ., Belfast; Charing Cross Hosp., London. Entered Royal Navy, 1922. Served in ships and Naval hosps at home and abroad; specialized in Clin. Pathology and Internal Medicine. MD (Belfast); MRCP 1935; FRCP 1949. Sqdn MO, 1st Battle Sqdn, 1938; Brit. Naval Med. Liaison Officer with US Navy, 1943-45; Surgeon Capt., 1944; MO i/c and Dir Med. Studies, RN Medical Sch., 1945-48. Surgeon Rear-Adm., 1952; QHP 1952-55; Medical Officer in Charge, RN Hosp., Chatham, and Command MO on staff of Comdr-in-Chief, the Nore, 1952-55; Min. of Health, 1955-65. Chm., Chailey RDC, 1972-74. Comdr Order of St John, 1954. *Publications:* various papers on medical subjects and on naval medical history. *Recreations:* walking, reading and writing. *Address:* Cleves, 40 Lewes Road, Ditchling, Sussex BN6 8TU. *T:* Hassocks 2920.

MUSSON, Maj.-Gen. Alfred Henry, CB 1958; CBE 1956; pac; late RA; President, Ordnance Board, 1957-58, retired (Vice-President, 1955-57); *b* 14 Aug. 1900; *s* of Dr A. W. Musson, Clitheroe, Lancs; *m* 1932, Joan Wright Taylor; three *s. Educ:* Tonbridge Sch.; RMA Woolwich. Served War of 1939-45. *Address:* Lyndon, The Ridgeway, Tonbridge, Kent. *T:* Tonbridge 364978.

MUSSON, Gen. Sir Geoffrey (Randolph Dixon), GCB 1970 (KCB 1965; CB 1959); CBE 1945; DSO 1944; BA; *b* 9 June 1910; *s* of late Robert Dixon Musson, Yockleton, Shrewsbury; *m* 1939, Hon. Elspeth L. Bailey, *d* of late Hon. Herbert Crawshay Bailey; one *s* one *d. Educ:* Shrewsbury; Trinity Hall, Cambridge. 2nd Lt KSLI, 1930. Served War of 1939-45, North Africa and Italy; Comdr 2nd Bn DCLI, 1943-44; Comdr 36th Infantry Bde, 1944-46. Comdr Commonwealth Forces in Korea, 1954-55; Comdr Sch. of Infantry, 1956-58, Comdr 7th Armoured Div., BAOR, 1958; Maj.-Gen. 1958; Comdr of the 5th Div., 1958-59. Chief of Staff, GHQ, Near East Land Forces, 1959-62; Vice-Adjutant-Gen., War Office, subseq. Min. of Defence, 1963-64; GOC-in-C, N Command, 1964-67; Adjutant-General, 1967-70, retired. Colonel: King's Shropshire Light Infantry, 1963-68; The Light Infantry, 1968-72. A Vice-Chm., Nat. Savings Cttee, 1970-78; Chairman: HM Forces Savings Cttee, 1970-78; Regular Forces Employment Assoc., 1978-80; Vice-Pres., Royal Patriotic Fund Corporation, 1974-; Pres., Victory Services Club, 1970-80. *Address:* Barn Cottage, Hurstbourne Tarrant, Andover, Hants SP11 0BD. *T:* Hurstbourne Tarrant 354. *Club:* Army and Navy.

MUSSON, John Nicholas Whitaker; Warden, Trinity College, Glenalmond, since 1972; *b* 2 Oct. 1927; *s* of late Dr J. P. T. Musson, OBE and Gwendoline

Musson (*née* Whitaker); *m* 1953, Ann Priest; one *s* three *d. Educ:* Clifton; Brasenose Coll., Oxford (MA). Served with Welsh Guards and Lancs Fusiliers, 1945-48 (commnd); BA Hons Mod. Hist., Oxford, 1951; HM Colonial Admin. Service, 1951-59; District and Provincial Administration, N Nigeria; Lectr, Inst. of Administration, N Nigeria; Staff Dept, British Petroleum, London, 1959-60; Asst Master and Housemaster, Canford Sch., 1961-72. *Recreations:* hill walking, history, fine arts. *Address:* Trinity College, Glenalmond, Perthshire. *T:* Glenalmond 205. *Club:* East India, Devonshire, Sports and Public Schools.

MUSSON, Samuel Dixon, CB 1963; MBE 1943; Chief Registrar of Friendly Societies and Industrial Assurance Commissioner, 1963-72; *b* 1 April 1908; *e s* of late R. Dixon Musson, Yockleton, Salop; *m* 1949, Joan I. S., 2nd *d* of late Col D. Davies-Evans, DSO, Penylan, Carmarthenshire. *Educ:* Shrewsbury Sch.; Trinity Hall, Cambridge. Called to Bar (Inner Temple), 1930; practised as Barrister, 1930-46; commnd, Pilot Officer, RAFVR, 1941; served Egypt, N Africa, Italy, 1942-45 (despatches). Ministry of Health: Senior Legal Asst, 1946; Asst Solicitor, 1952; Principal Asst Solicitor, 1957. Vice-Pres., Building Socs Assoc., 1972-77; Mem., Trustee Savings Bank Inspection Cttee. *Recreations:* golf, country pursuits. *Address:* Prospect Hill Farm, Headley, Bordon, Hants. *T:* Headley Down 713183. *Club:* Savile.

MUSTAFA, Nasr El-Din; Medal of Merit, First Class, 1972; Order of the Dedicated Son of Sudan, 1978; Order of the Two Niles, First Class, 1979; Ambassador of the Democratic Republic of Sudan to the Court of St James's, since 1982; *b* 10 Oct. 1930; *m* 1962, Raga Yousif Sukkar; three *s* three *d. Educ:* University Coll. Khartoum. BSc(Eng), London; FICE. Sudan Railways (Civil Engrg), 1956-68; Messrs Goode & Partners, Consulting Engrs, UK, 1958-60; Sudanese Estate Bank, 1968-69; Sudanese People's Armed Forces, 1969-74; Chm., Sea Ports Corp., 1974-76; Minister of State for Planning, 1976-77; Minister of Nat. Planning, 1977-81 (and as such Governor for Sudan in IBRD, Arab Fund for Socio-Econ. Develt, IDB, ADB/F, NAO, EDF); Dep. Pres., Ministerial Cttee for Economic Sector, 1979-81. Mem., Sudan Railway Bd of Dirs, 1973-76; Chm., Bd of Dirs, Khartoum Polytechnic, 1976-79. *Recreations:* reading, swimming. *Address:* Sudan Embassy, 3 Cleveland Row, St James's, SW1. *Club:* Royal Automobile.

MUSTILL, Hon. Sir Michael (John), Kt 1978; **Hon. Mr Justice Mustill;** Judge of the High Court of Justice, Queen's Bench Division, since 1978; Presiding Judge, North Eastern Circuit, since 1981; *b* 10 May 1931; *o s* of Clement William and late Marion Mustill; *m* 1960, Beryl Reid Davies. *Educ:* Oundle Sch.; St John's Coll., Cambridge. Royal Artillery, 1949-51 (commissioned, 1950). Called to Bar, Gray's Inn, 1955, Bencher, 1976. QC 1968. Dep. Chm., Hants QS, 1971; a Recorder of the Crown Court, 1972-78. Chm., Civil Service Appeal Tribunal, 1971-78. *Publications:* The Law and Practice of Commercial Arbitration in England (with S. C. Boyd, QC), 1982; Joint Editor: Scrutton on Charterparties and Bills of Lading; Arnould on Marine Insurance; articles in legal periodicals. *Recreations:* visiting France, reading, music, active sports. *Address:* 8 Prior Bolton Street, N1.

MUSTON, Rt. Rev. Gerald Bruce; *see* Australia, North-West, Bishop of.

MUTI, Riccardo; Principal Conductor and Music Director, Philadelphia Orchestra, since 1980; Conductor Laureate, Philharmonia Orchestra, since 1982; *b* 28 July 1941; *m* 1969, Cristina Mazzavillani; two *s* one *d. Educ:* Diploma in pianoforte, Conservatorio di Napoli; Diploma in conducting and composition, Milan. Principal Conductor, 1973-82, Music Dir, 1979-82, New Philharmonia, later Philharmonia Orchestra; Principal Conductor, Orchestra Maggio Musicale Fiorentino, 1969-81; Principal Guest Conductor, Philadelphia Orchestra, 1977-80. Concert tours in USA: with Boston, Chicago, and Philadelphia orchestras; concerts at Salzburg, Edinburgh, Lucerne, Flanders and Vienna Festivals; concerts with Berlin Philharmonic, Vienna Philharmonic, Concertgebouw Amsterdam; opera in Florence, Salzburg, Vienna, Munich, Covent Garden, Milan. Recording prizes from France, Germany, Italy and Japan. Accademico: dell'Accademia di Santa Cecilia, Rome; dell'Accademia Luigi Cherubini, Florence. Verdienstkreuz, 1st class (Germany), 1976. *Address:* Via Corti alle Mura 25, Ravenna, Italy.

MWANZA, Dr Jacob Mumbi; Vice-Chancellor, University of Zambia, since 1976; *b* 2 Feb. 1937; *m* 1964, Elizabeth Maria; three *d. Educ:* Univ. of Munster, W Germany (MA Econ. 1968); Cornell Univ., USA (PhD 1973). Lectr, then Sen. Lectr, 1968-74, Head of Econs Dept, 1973-74, Univ. of Zambia. Man. Dir, Zambia Energy Corp., 1974-76. Mem., UN Cttee for Develt Planning; Vice-Chm., Senate, UN Inst. for Namibia, 1980-; Pres., Council for Develt of Economic and Social Research in Africa, 1982-. Mem. Council, Univ. of Dar es Salaam. *Publications:* Orienting Economics Teaching to Development Needs, in The Teaching of Economics in African Universities, 1973; The Operation of Public Enterprises in Zambia, 1978; contrib. Developing Economies. *Recreations:* fishing, tennis. *Address:* (home) Hawndsworth Park, Lumubashi Road 1-5, Lusaka, Zambia; (office) Box 302811, Lusaka, Zambia. *Clubs:* Flying, Economics (Lusaka).

MWENDWA, Maluki Kitili; Chief Justice of Kenya, 1968-71; Chairman: United Nations Association, Kenya; Chania Enterprises Ltd; ExpoAfrica Ltd; Fad Investments Ltd; Export Promotion Services; Inter Continental Holdings Ltd; Kenya Advertising Corporation Ltd; Kenya Allied Travel Enterprises Ltd; Kenya Pisci-Culture Ltd; Mugie Ltd; Pasha Club Ltd; Qwicklear (EA) Ltd; Ranching and Agricultural Consultants Ltd; Research, Editorial and

Design Services Ltd; Wendo Ltd; Consultant General, Private Sector; *b* 24 Dec. 1929; *s* of Senior Chief M. Kitavi Mwendwa and Mrs Kathuka Mwendwa; *m* 1964, Winifred Nyiva Mangole (Hon. Mrs Winifred Mwendwa, MP Kitui West; one of first four Kenya women MPs, Oct. 1974); one *s* three *d. Educ:* Alliance High Sch., Kenya; Makerere University Coll.; London Univ.; Exeter Univ.; St Catherine's Coll., Oxford. DipEd 1950; LLB 1955 (Sir Archibald Bodkin Prize for Criminal Law, 1953); DPA 1956; BA 1959, MA 1963. President: Cosmos Soc., 1959; Jowett Soc., 1959; St Catherine's Debating Soc., 1959, Oxford. Called to the Bar, Lincoln's Inn, 1961. Lectr Kagumo Teacher Training Coll., 1951. Asst Sec., Min. of Commerce and Industry, 1962, Min. of Works and Communications, 1962; Sen. Asst Sec., Min. of Tourism, Forests and Wild Life, 1962-63; Perm. Sec., Min. of Social Services, 1963, and Min. of Home Affairs, 1963-64; Solicitor Gen., 1964-68 (acting Attorney Gen., 1967). Leader, Kenya Delegn: Commonwealth and Empire Law Conf., Sydney, 1965; World Peace through Law Conf., Washington, 1965; Conf. on Intellectual Property, Stockholm, 1967 (Vice-Pres. of Conf.); UN Special Cttee on Friendly Relations, Geneva, 1967; Conf. on Law of Treaties, Vienna, 1968; Kenya Rep. on 6th Cttee, 21st Session, and on 2nd and 6th Cttees (Vice-Chm. of 6th Cttee), 22nd Session, UN Gen. Assembly; Ambassador to 22nd Session, UN Gen. Assembly, 1967 (Vice-Chm., Kenya Delegn to April/May 1967 Special Session); Mem., UN Internat. Trade Law Commn, 1967-74; Mem., Executive Council: African Inst. of Internat. Law, Lagos; Kenya Farmers' Assoc.; Donovan Maule Theatre, Nairobi; Agricultural Soc. of Kenya, Nairobi, 1970-73 (Life Governor, 1978); African Automobile Assoc., Nairobi. Chm., Bd of Governors: Ngara Sch., 1965-73; Parklands Sch., 1967-73; Kitui Sch., 1972-74. *Publication:* Constitutional Contrasts in the East African Territories, 1965. *Recreations:* hunting, swimming, cycling, walking. *Address:* c/o Gigi House, Gigiri Road, PO Box 40198, Nairobi, Kenya. *T:* Nairobi 23450. *Clubs:* Pasha (Nairobi), Mount Kenya Safari (Nanyuki).

MYDDELTON, Lt-Col Ririd, MVO 1945; JP; Extra Equerry to The Queen since 1952; Vice-Lieutenant of Denbighshire, 1968-74; *b* 25 Feb. 1902; *s* of late Col Robert Edward Myddelton, TD, DL, JP, Chirk Castle, and late Lady Violet, *d* of 1st Marquess of Abergavenny; *m* 1931, Margaret Elizabeth Mercer Nairne (now Lady Margaret Elizabeth Myddelton; granted rank as *d* of a Marquess, 1946), *d* of late Lord Charles Mercer Nairne; two *s* one *d. Educ:* Eton; RMC Sandhurst. 2nd Lt Coldstream Guards, 1923; Adjutant, 3rd Bn, 1928-31; Staff Capt., London District, 1934-37; seconded as Dep. Master of the household to King George VI, 1937-39; DAAG London District, 1939-40; Staff Coll., Camberley, War Course, 1942; Commanded: 1st (Armd) Bn, Coldstream Guards, 1942-44 (Normandy); retired, 1946. JP 1948, DL 1949, High Sheriff, 1951-52, Denbigh. KStJ 1961. *Recreations:* hunting, fishing. *Address:* Chirk Castle, North Wales. *T:* Chirk 772460. *Club:* Turf.
See also Captain A. S. Aird.

MYER, Sidney Baillieu; Chairman, Myer Emporium Ltd, since 1978 (Director, since 1955); *b* 11 Jan. 1926; *s* of late Sidney Myer and Dame (Margery) Merlyn Baillieu Myer, DBE; *m* 1955, Sarah J., *d* of late S. Hordern; two *s* one *d. Educ:* Geelong Grammar Sch.; Pembroke Coll., Cambridge (MA). Sub-Lieut, RANVR, 1944-46. Joined Myer Emporium, 1953; Vice-Pres., Myer Foundn, 1959-. Director: Elders IXL Ltd, 1972-; Cadbury Schweppes Aust. Ltd, 1976-82; Nat. Mutual Life Assoc. of Australasia, 1978-; Commonwealth Banking Corp., 1979-. Part-time Mem. Executive, CSIRO, 1981-. Pres., French Chamber of Commerce (Vic), 1962-64; Rep. Chm., Aust.-Japan Foundn, 1976-81; Member: Consultative Cttee on Relations with Japan, 1978-81; Aust.-China Council, 1979-81. Councillor: Aust. Conservation Foundn, 1964-73; Vic. Coll. of Arts, 1973-78; Vice-Pres., Nat. Gall. Soc. of Vic., 1964-68; Trustee, Nat. Gall. of Vic., 1973- (Vice-Pres., 1977-); Chm., Commonwealth Research Centres of Excellence Cttee, 1981-82. *Address:* 250 Elizabeth Street, Melbourne, Victoria 3000, Australia.

MYERS, Dr David Milton, CMG 1974; Vice-Chancellor, La Trobe University, Melbourne, 1965-76; *b* 5 June 1911; *s* of W. H. Myers, Sydney; *m* 1937, Beverley A. H., *d* of Dr T. D. Delprat; three *s. Educ:* Univs of Sydney and Oxford. BSc, BE, DScEng; FIE Aust., FIEE, FInstP. 1st Chief of Div. of Electrotechnology, CSIR, 1939-49; P. N. Russell Prof. of Elec. Engrg, Univ. of Sydney, 1949-59; Dean, Faculty of Applied Science, and Prof. of Elec. Engrg, Univ. of British Columbia, 1960-65. Mem. Adv. Council, CSIRO, 1949-55; Mem. Nat. Res. Council of Canada, 1965; Chairman: Cttee on Overseas Professional Qualifications, 1969-; Inquiry into Unemployment Benefits, for Aust. Govt, 1977; Cttee of Inquiry into fluoridation of Victorian water supplies, 1979-80; Consultative Council on Victorian Mental Health Act, 1981. Pres., Aust. Inst. of Engineers, 1958. Kernot Meml Medal, 1974; P. N. Russell Meml Medal, 1977. *Publications:* various research papers in sci. jls. *Recreations:* golf, tennis, music. *Address:* 76 Glenard Drive, Heidelberg, Vic. 3084, Australia. *T:* 459 9629. *Clubs:* Melbourne (Melbourne); Green Acres Golf.

MYERS, Brig. (Retired) Edmund Charles Wolf, CBE 1944; DSO 1943; BA Cantab; MICE; *b* 12 Oct. 1906; *er s* of late Dr C. S. Myers, CBE, FRS; *m* 1943, Louisa, *er d* of late Aldred Bickham Sweet-Escott; one *d. Educ:* Haileybury; Royal Military Academy, Woolwich; Caius Coll., Cambridge. Commissioned into Royal Engineers, 1926. Served Palestine, 1936 (despatches); War of 1939-45; Comdr, British Mil. Mission to Greek Resistance Forces, 1942-43; Middle East, including Balkans, until 1944 (African Star, Italy Star, DSO, CBE); North-West Europe, 1944-45 (France and Germany Star, Dutch Bronze Lion, Norwegian Liberty Medal); Far East,

1945; Korea, 1951-52 (despatches, American Legion of Merit). Chief Engineer, British Troops in Egypt, 1955-56; Dep. Dir, Personnel Administration in the War Office, 1956-59; retired 1959. Chief Civil Engineer Cleveland Bridge & Engineering Co. Ltd, 1959-64. Construction Manager, Power Gas Corp. Ltd, Davy-Ashmore Group, 1964-67. Regional Sec., British Field Sports Soc., 1968-71. *Publication:* Greek Entanglement, 1955. *Recreations:* horse training and riding, sailing, flying (1st Sec. RE Flying Club, 1934-35), fishing. *Address:* Wheatsheaf House, Broadwell, Moreton-in-Marsh, Glos GL56 0TY. *T:* Stow-on-the-Wold 30183. *Clubs:* Army and Navy, Special Forces.

MYERS, Geoffrey, CEng; FCIT; Member, British Railways Board, since 1980; *b* 12 July 1930; *s* of Ernest and Annie Myers; *m* 1959, Patricia Mary (*née* Hall); two *s. Educ:* Belle Vue Grammar Sch.; Bradford Technical Coll. (BScEng London). CEng, MICE 1963; FCIT 1973. RE, 1955-57. British Rail: civil engrg positions, 1957-64; Planning Officer, N Eastern Reg., 1964-66; Divl Movements Manager, Leeds Div., 1966-68; Dir of Studies, British Transport Staff Coll., 1968-70; Divl Man., Sheffield, 1970-76; Dep. Gen. Man., Eastern Reg., 1976-77, Gen. Man., 1977-78; Dir of Strategic Develt, 1978-80. OStJ 1979. *Recreations:* golf, walking. *Address:* The Spinney, Lands Lane, Knaresborough, N Yorks. *T:* Harrogate 863719.

MYERS, Geoffrey Morris Price; Under-Secretary, Agricultural Research Council, since 1973; *b* 8 May 1927; *o s* of late Sam Price Myers, Liverpool and Deptford, and M. E. (Nancy) Price Myers, London. *Educ:* Reigate Grammar Sch.; King's Coll., London. BSc 1st cl. hons Botany 1947, MSc Plant Physiology 1950. Captain, RAEC, 1947-49; Asst Principal, Home Civil Service, 1950; UKAEA, 1959-67, Private Sec. to Chm.; Nat. Econ. Develt Office, 1967-69; Agric. Research Council, 1970; Asst Sec., Plants and Soils Research, 1970-73. *Address:* 160 Great Portland Street, W1N 6DT. *Club:* Athenæum.

MYERS, Gordon Elliot, CMG 1979; Under-Secretary, Food Policy Group, Ministry of Agriculture, Fisheries and Food, since 1980; *b* 4 July 1929; *s* of William Lionel Myers and Yvonne (*née* Arthur); *m* 1963, Wendy Jane Lambert; two *s* one *d. Educ:* Kilburn Grammar Sch.; University Coll., Oxford (BA 1st Cl. Hons Modern History). Asst Principal, MAFF, 1951; Principal, 1958; Asst Sec., 1966; Head successively of Land Drainage Div., Sugar and Tropical Foods Div., and EEC Div., 1966-74; Under-Sec., MAFF, 1975; Minister (Agriculture), Office of UK Perm. Rep. to EEC, 1975-79. *Address:* Woodlands, Nugents Park, Hatch End, Mddx. *Club:* United Oxford & Cambridge University.

MYERS, Harry Eric, QC 1967 (Gibraltar 1977); *b* 10 Jan. 1914; *s* of Harry Moss Myers and Alice Muriel Serjeant; *m* 1951, Lorna Babette Kitson (*née* Blackburn); no *c. Educ:* Bedford Sch. Admitted Solicitor of Supreme Court, 1936; called to Bar, Middle Temple, 1945. Prosecuting Counsel to Bd of Inland Revenue on SE Circuit, 1965. *Address:* 3 Hare Court, Temple, EC4. *T:* 01-353 7741.

MYERS, Sir Kenneth (Ben), Kt 1977; MBE 1944; FCA; Director, South British Insurance Co. Ltd, 1934-82 (Chairman, 1945-78); *b* 5 March 1907; *s* of Hon. Sir Arthur Myers and Lady (Vera) Myers (*née* Levy); *m* 1933, Margaret Blair Pirie; one *s* two *d. Educ:* Marlborough Coll.; Gonville and Caius Coll., Cambridge (BA 1928). FCA 1933. Returned to NZ, 1933; served War with 2nd NZEF, ME and Italy, 1940-45. Dir, cos in NZ and Australia. *Recreations:* looking after my business connections and my family. *Address:* 21 Upland Road, Auckland 5, New Zealand. *T:* Auckland 545499. *Clubs:* Boodle's; Northern (Auckland).

MYERS, Mark, QC 1977; a Recorder of the Crown Court, since 1979; *b* 22 July 1930; *s* of late Lewis Myers and Hannah Myers; *m* 1964, Katherine Ellen Desormeaux Waldram; one *s* one *d. Educ:* King's Sch., Ely; Trinity Coll., Cambridge (Exhibnr; MA). Called to the Bar, Gray's Inn, 1954. Sublector in Law, Trinity Coll., Cambridge, 1954-61; Part-time Lectr in Law, Southampton Univ., 1959-61. Mem., Consumers Cttee for England and Wales, and Consumers Cttee for GB, 1974-. *Publications:* articles in legal jls. *Recreations:* music and country life. *Address:* 73 Cholmeley Crescent, Highgate, N6 5EX. *T:* 01-340 7623; 11 King's Bench Walk, Temple, EC4Y 7EQ. *T:* 01-353 9281.

MYERS, Philip Alan, OBE 1977; QPM 1972; one of Her Majesty's Inspectors of Constabulary, since 1982; *b* 7 Feb. 1931; *s* of John and Catherine Myers; *m* 1951, Hazel Gittings; two *s. Educ:* Grove Park, Wrexham. RAF, 1949-50. Shropshire Constabulary, 1950-67; West Mercia Police, 1967-68; Dep. Chief Constable, Gwynedd Constabulary, 1968-70; Chief Constable, North Wales Police, 1970-81. OStJ 1972. *Address:* 5 Woodlands Road West, Colwyn Bay, Clwyd.

MYERS, Sir Rupert (Horace), KBE 1981 (CBE 1976); FTS 1979; Professor Emeritus; Chairman: New South Wales State Pollution Control Commission, since 1971; Coastal Council of New South Wales, since 1982; *b* 21 Feb. 1921; *s* of Horace Alexander Myers and Dorothy (*née* Harris); *m* 1944, Io Edwina King; one *s* three *d. Educ:* Melbourne High Sch.; Univ. of Melbourne. BSc 1942; MSc 1943; PhD 1947; CEng, FIM, FRACI; FAIM; MAusIMM. Commonwealth Res. Fellow, Univ. of Melbourne, 1942-47; Principal Res. Officer, CSIRO, AERE Harwell, 1947-52; Univ. of New South Wales: Dean, Faculty of Applied Science, 1956-61; Pro-Vice-Chancellor, 1961-69;

Foundation Professor of Metallurgy, Vice-Chancellor and Principal, 1969-81. Chairman: Aust. Vice-Chancellors' Cttee, 1977-79; Cttee of Inquiry into Technol Change in Australia, 1979-80; Director: CSR Ltd, 1982-; Energy Resources of Australia Ltd, 1982-; Member: Nat. Energy Adv. Cttee, 1980-82; Australian Manufacturing Council, 1980-. Mem., Sydney Opera House Trust, 1976-. Hon. LLD Strathclyde, 1973; Hon. DSc Wollongong, 1976; Hon. DEng Newcastle, 1981; Hon. DLitt NSW, 1981. *Publications:* Technological Change in Australia, 1980; numerous on metallurgy and atomic energy (also patents). *Recreations:* tennis, music, working with silver. *Address:* 135 Neerim Road, Castlecove, NSW 2069, Australia.

MYERSON, Arthur Levey, QC 1974; **His Honour Judge Myerson;** a Circuit Judge, since 1978; *b* 25 July 1928; *o s* of Bernard and Eda Myerson; *m* 1960, Elaine Shirley Harris; two *s. Educ:* Blackpool Grammar Sch.; Queens' Coll., Cambridge. BA 1950, LLB 1951. Called to the Bar, 1952. A Recorder of the Crown Court, 1972-78. RAF, 1946-48. *Recreations:* reading, sailing, golf. *Address:* 25 Sandmoor Drive, Leeds LS17 2RE. *T:* Leeds 684169. *Clubs:* Royal Commonwealth Society; Moor Allerton Golf (Leeds), Leeds Sailing.

MYERSON, Aubrey Selwyn, QC 1967; a Recorder of the Crown Court, since 1972; *b* Johannesburg, S Africa, 10 Dec. 1926; *o s* of late Michael Colman Myerson, MRCSI, LRCPI, and late Lee Myerson; *m* 1955, Helen Margaret, *d* of late Hedley Lavis, Adelaide, S Austr.; one *s* one *d. Educ:* Cardiff High Sch.; University Coll., Cardiff (Fellow, 1981). Called to Bar, Lincoln's Inn, 1950, Bencher, 1975. Leader, Wales and Chester Circuit, 1981-. *Recreations:* competing aggressively at all pursuits, including squash, fencing, tennis, gardening. *Address:* 8 Sloane Court East, Chelsea, SW3. *T:* 01-730 4707; Laurustina Cottage, Inkpen, Berks. *T:* Inkpen 468; 1 Dr Johnson's Buildings, Temple, EC4. *T:* 01-353 9328. *Club:* Bristol Channel Yacht.

MYINT, Prof. Hla; Professor of Economics, London School of Economics, since 1966; *b* Bassein, Burma, 20 March 1920; *m* 1944, Joan (*née* Morris); no *c. Educ:* Rangoon Univ.; London Sch. of Economics. Prof. of Econs, Rangoon Univ., and Econ. Adviser to Govt of Burma, 1946-49; Univ. Lectr in Econs of Underdeveloped Countries, Oxford Univ., 1950-65; Rector of Rangoon Univ., 1958-61. Vis. Prof., Univs of Yale, Cornell and Wisconsin; has served on UN Expert Cttees; Hon. DLitt, Rangoon, 1961. Order of Sithu (Burma), 1961. *Publications:* Theories of Welfare Economics, 1948; The Economics of the Developing Countries, 1964; Economic Theory and the Underdeveloped Countries, 1971; Southeast Asia's Economy: development policies in the 1970s, 1972; many papers in learned jls. *Recreations:* walking, garden watching. *Address:* 12 Willow Drive, Barnet, Herts. *T:* 01-449 3028.

MYLAND, Howard David; Deputy Secretary, Exchequer and Audit Department, since 1979; *b* 23 June 1929; *s* of John Tarrant and Frances Grace Myland; *m* 1951, Barbara Pearl Mills; two *s* one *d. Educ:* Fairfields Sch; Queen Mary's Sch., Basingstoke. Served Intelligence Corps, 1948-50. Entered Exchequer and Audit Dept, 1948; Dep. Dir of Audit, 1972; Dir of Audit, 1977. Member: Basingstoke Round Table, 1962-70; Basingstoke Ex-Tablers, 1970-. *Recreations:* travel, caravanning, contract bridge. *Address:* 20 Wallis Road, Basingstoke, Hants RG21 3DN. *T:* Basingstoke 64347.

MYLES, David Fairlie; MP (C) Banff, since 1979; tenant hill farmer; *b* 30 May 1925; *s* of Robert C. Myles and Mary Anne S. (*née* Fairlie); *m* 1951, Janet I. (*née* Gall); two *s* two *d. Educ:* Edzell Primary Sch.; Brechin High Sch. National Farmers Union of Scotland: Mem. Council, 1970-79; Convenor of Organisation and Publicity Cttee, 1976-79. Director, Kincardineshire Auction Mart Ltd, 1963-. Sec., Cons. backbench Cttees on European Affairs and on Agriculture, Fisheries and Food (Jt Sec.); Mem., Select Cttees on Agriculture and on European Legislation. *Recreations:* curling, Scottish fiddle music. *Address:* Dalbog, Edzell, Brechin, Angus DD9 7UU. *Clubs:* Farmers'; Brechin Rotary.

MYLLENT, Peter; *see* Hamylton Jones, K.

MYNETT, George Kenneth, QC 1960; JP; **His Honour Judge Mynett;** a Circuit Judge, Oxford Crown Court, since 1972; *b* 16 Nov. 1913; *s* of E. Mynett, Wellington, Salop; *m* 1940, Margaret Verna Bass-Hammonds; two *s. Educ:* Adams Grammar Sch., Newport, Salop; London Univ. Admitted solicitor of Supreme Court, 1937; LLB Hons (London) 1938. Served War of 1939-45, RAF, 1940-46; Dep. Judge Advocate Staff, Dept of JAG, 1945, 1946. Barrister, Middle Temple, 1942, 1st Cl. Hons, Certificate of Honour; after demobilisation practised on Oxford Circuit. Master of the Bench, Middle Temple, 1967. Recorder of Stoke-on-Trent, 1961-71, Honorary Recorder 1972-; JP Stoke-on-Trent, 1961; JP Oxon, 1969-71; Dep. Chm., Oxfordshire QS, 1969-71; Comr of Assize: SE Circuit, 1970; Oxford Circuit, 1971. UK Representative, Conferences of Judges of Supreme Administrative Courts of EEC Countries in Berlin, Rome, The Hague, Luxembourg etc. Member: Council for the Training of Magistrates, 1967; Gen. Council of the Bar, 1968; Court of Governors, Univ. of Keele, 1961-. *Recreations:* landscape painting, golf, travel. *Address:* Tanglewood House, Boar's Hill, Oxford. *T:* Oxford 730439; 12 King's Bench Walk, Temple, EC4. *T:* 01-353 7008.

MYNORS, Sir Humphrey (Charles Baskerville), 1st Bt, *cr* 1964; *b* 28 July 1903; 2nd *s* of Rev. A. B. Mynors, Rector of Langley Burrell, Wilts; *m* 1939, Lydia Marian, *d* of late Sir Ellis Minns, LittD, FSA, FBA; one *s* four *d. Educ:*

Marlborough; Corpus Christi Coll., Cambridge. Fellow of Corpus Christi Coll., Cambridge, 1926-33; Hon. Fellow, 1953. Entered the service of the Bank of England, 1933; a Dir, 1949-54; Dep. Governor, 1954-64. Chm., Panel on Take-overs and Mergers, 1968-69; Dep. Chm., 1969-70. Hon. DCL Durham. *Heir: s* Richard Baskerville Mynors [*b* 5 May 1947; *m* 1970, Fiona Bridget, *d* of Rt Rev. G. E. Reindorp, *qv*; two *d*]. *Address:* Treago, St Weonards, Hereford. *T:* St Weonards 208.

MYNORS, Sir Roger (Aubrey Baskerville), Kt 1963; FBA 1944; *b* 28 July 1903; *s* of Rev. A. B. Mynors, Rector of Langley Burrell, Wilts; *m* 1945, Lavinia Sybil, *d* of late Very Rev. C. A. Alington, DD. *Educ:* Eton; Balliol College, Oxford. Fellow and Classical Tutor of Balliol, 1926-44 (Hon. Fellow 1963); Kennedy Prof. of Latin in the Univ. of Cambridge and Fellow of Pembroke Coll., 1944-53 (Hon. Fellow, 1965); Corpus Christi Prof. of Latin Language and Literature, Oxford, 1953-70 (Hon. Fellow, Corpus Christi Coll., 1970). Vis. Lectr, Harvard, 1938. Temp. Principal, HM Treasury, 1940. Longman Vis. Fellow, Leeds Univ., 1974. Pres., Classical Assoc., 1966. Hon. DLitt: Edinburgh; Durham; Hon. LittD: Cambridge; Sheffield; Hon. LLD Toronto. Hon. Fellow, Warburg Inst.; Hon. Member: Amer. Acad. of Arts and Sciences; Istituto di Studi Romani. *Publications:* Cassiodori Senatoris Institutiones, 1937; Durham Cathedral MSS before 1200, 1939; Catulli Carmina, 1958; Catalogue of Balliol MSS, 1963; Plinii Epistulae, 1963; Panegyrici Latini, 1964; Vergilii Opera, 1969. *Address:* Treago, St Weonards, Hereford HR2 8QB. *T:* St Weonards 208.

MYRDAL, Alva; former Swedish Cabinet Minister, diplomatist, sociologist and author; Ambassador at large since 1961; Member of Swedish Parliament, 1962-70; Minister without Portfolio (in charge of disarmament and Church affairs) in Swedish Government, 1967-73; *b* 31 Jan. 1902; *d* of Albert and Lova Reimer; *m* 1924, Dr Gunnar Myrdal, *qv* ; one *s* two *d. Educ:* Stockholm Univ. (AB); Uppsala Univ. (AM); USA; Geneva. Founder 1936, and Dir, 1936-48, Training Coll. for Pre-Sch. Teachers, Stockholm; Principal Dir, UN Dept of Social Affairs, 1949-50; Dir, Unesco Dept of Social Sciences, 1951-55; Minister to India, Burma, Ceylon and Nepal, 1955-56, Ambassador, 1956-61. Delegate to: ILO Conf., Paris, 1945, Geneva, 1947; Unesco Conf., Paris, 1946, New Delhi, 1956; UN General Assemblies, 1962, 1963, 1965-73. Chief Swedish Delegate to UN Disarmament Cttee, Geneva, 1962-73. Fellow, Center for Study of Democratic Instns, Santa Barbara, Calif., 1974. Vis. Professor: MIT 1974, 1975; Wellesley Coll., 1976; Texas Univ., 1978. Chairman: Internat. Inst. for Peace Research, Stockholm, 1965-66; UN Expert Group on South Africa, 1964; Swedish Govt Cttees: on relations between State and Church, 1968-72; on Research on the Future, 1971-72; UN Expert Gp on Disarmament and Development, 1972. World Council on Pre-School Educn, 1947-49. Board Member: Internat. Fedn of Univ. Women; Swedish Organisation for Cultural Relief in Europe; Swedish Fedn of Business and Professional Women (Chm. 1935-38, 1940-42). Hon. LLD: Mount Holyoke Coll., USA, 1950; Edinburgh Univ., 1964; Dr Humane Letters, Columbia Univ., 1965; Temple Univ., 1968; Hon. PhD, Leeds Univ., England, 1956; Hon. DD: Gustavus Adolphus, Miami, 1971; Brandeis, 1974; Gothenburg, 1975; East Anglia, 1976; Helsinki, 1981. West German Peace Prize (with G. Myrdal), 1970; Wateler Peace Prize, Hague Acad., 1973; Royal Inst. of Technology award, Stockholm, 1975; Albert Einstein Peace Award, 1980; People's Peace Prize, Oslo, 1982; (jtly) Nobel Peace Prize, 1982. *Publications:* (with G. Myrdal) Crisis in the Population Problem, 1934; City Children, 1935; Nation and Family, 1941; Postwar Planning, 1944; Are We Too Many?, 1950; (with V. Klein) Women's Two Roles, 1956; Towards Equality, 1970; Game of Disarmament, 1976, etc.; numerous contribs to newspapers, periodicals, books and reports. *Recreations:* travel, theatre, cooking, reading. *Address:* Vaesterlaanggatan 31, 11129 Stockholm, Sweden.

MYRDAL, Prof. (Karl) Gunnar; Swedish economist; *b* 6 Dec. 1898; *s* of Carl Adolf Pettersson and Anna Sofia Carlsdotter; *m* 1924, Alva Reimer (*see* Alva Myrdal); one *s* two *d. Educ:* Stockholm Univ. Studied in Germany and Britain, 1925-29; Rockefeller Fellow, US, 1929-30; Assoc. Prof., Post-Grad. Inst. of Internat. Studies, Geneva; Lars Hierta Prof. of Polit. Econ. and Public Finance, Stockholm Univ., 1933; Mem. Swedish Senate (Social Democrat), 1934; directed study of Amer. Negro problem for Carnegie Corp., NY, 1938; returned to Sweden, 1942, re-elected to Senate, Mem. Bd of Bank of Sweden, Chm. Post-War Planning Commn; Minister of Commerce, 1945-47; Exec. Sec., UN Econ. Commn for Europe, 1947-57; directed study of econ. trends and policies in S Asian countries for Twentieth Century Fund, 1957-67; Prof. of Internat. Econs, Stockholm Univ., 1961; founded Inst. for Internat. Econ. Studies, Stockholm Univ., 1961; past Chm., Bd of Stockholm Internat. Peace Research Inst. (Mem. Bd); Vis. Res. Fellow, Center for Study of Democratic Instns, Santa Barbara, 1973-74; Distinguished Vis. Prof., New York City Univ., 1974-75; Regents' Prof., Univ. of California, Irvine, Spring 1977; Dist. Vis. Prof., Univ. of Madison, Autumn 1977; Jt Slick Prof. of Peace, L. B. Johnson Sch. of Public Affairs, Univ. of Texas, 1978. Member: British Acad.; Amer. Acad. of Arts and Scis; Royal Swedish Acad. of Scis; Hungarian Acad. of Scis; Fellow, Econometric Soc.; Hon. Mem., Amer. Econ. Assoc. Holds numerous hon. degrees and has received many awards, incl. Nitti Prize, 1976 and Nobel Prize for Economics (jtly), 1974. *Publications:* numerous sci. works, incl: The Cost of Living in Sweden 1830-1930, 1933; Monetary Equilibrium, 1939; An American Dilemma: The Negro Problem and Modern Democracy, 1944; The Political Element in the Development of Economic Theory, 1953; An International Economy: Problems and Prospects, 1956; Econimic Theory and Underdeveloped Regions, 1957; Value in Social Theory, 1958; Beyond the Welfare State: Economic Planning and its

International Implications, 1960; Challenge to Affluence, 1963; Asian Drama: An Inquiry into the Poverty of Nations, 1968; Objectivity in Social Research, 1969; The Challenge of World Poverty: A World Anti-Poverty Program in Outline, 1970; Against the Stream: Critical Essays on Economics, 1973. *Address:* Västerlânggatan 31, 111 29 Stockholm, Sweden. *T:* (08) 21-36-41.

MYRES, John Nowell Linton, CBE 1972; LLD, DLitt, DLit, MA; FBA 1966; FSA; President, Society of Antiquaries, 1970-75 (Vice-President, 1959-63; Director, 1966-70), now Hon. Vice-President; Bodley's Librarian, University of Oxford, 1947-65; Hon. Student of Christ Church, 1971 (Student 1928-70), and Fellow of Winchester College, 1951-77; *b* 27 Dec. 1902; *yr s* of late Emeritus Prof. Sir John Linton Myres, OBE; *m* 1929, Joan Mary Lovell, *o d* of late G. L. Stevens, Jersey; two *s. Educ:* Winchester Coll. (Scholar); New Coll., Oxford (Scholar), Hon. Fellow, 1973. 1st Class Lit Hum., 1924; 1st Class Modern History, 1926; BA 1924; MA 1928; Lecturer, 1926, Student and Tutor, 1928-48, Librarian, 1938-48, of Christ Church; Univ. Lectr in Early English History, 1935-47; served in Min. of Food, 1940-45 (Head of Fruit and Veg. Products Div., 1943-45); mem. of Council of St Hilda's Coll., Oxford, 1937-52; Pres. Oxford Architectural and Historical Soc., 1946-49. Mem. Institute for Advanced Study, Princeton, 1956; Pres. Council for British Archæology, 1959-61; Member: Ancient Monuments Board (England), 1959-76; Royal Commn on Historical Monuments (England), 1969-74; Chm. Standing Conference of National and Univ. Libraries, 1959-61. Pres: Library Assoc., 1963; Soc. for Medieval Archæology, 1963-66. Lectures: Ford's, in English History, 1958-59; O'Donnell, Edinburgh Univ., 1961; Oxford 1966-67; Rhind, Edinburgh, 1964-65; Raleigh, British Acad., 1970. Hon. Mem., Deutsches Archäologisches Institut. Hon. LLD Toronto, 1954; Hon. DLitt Reading, 1964; Hon DLit Belfast, 1965. Has supervised excavations at Caerleon Amphitheatre, 1926, St Catharine's Hill, Winchester, 1925-28, Colchester, 1930, Butley Priory, 1931-33, Aldborough, 1934-35 and elsewhere. Gold Medal, Soc. of Antiquaries, 1976. Hon. Foreign Corresp. Mem. Grolier Club, New York. *Publications:* part-author: St Catharine's Hill, Winchester, 1930; Roman Britain and the English Settlements, 1936; Anglo-Saxon Pottery and the Settlement of England, 1969; A Corpus of Anglo-Saxon Pottery, 1977; articles and reviews in learned periodicals. *Recreations:* growing of vegetables and fruit; bibliophily, study of antiquities. *Address:* Manor House, Kennington, Oxford. *T:* Oxford 735353.

N

NAAS, Lord; Charles Diarmuidh John Bourke; *b* 11 June 1953; *e s* and *heir* of 10th Earl of Mayo, *qv*; *m* 1975, Marie Antoinette Cronnelly; one *d. Educ:* St Aubyn's, Rottingdean; Portora Royal Sch., Enniskillen; QUB; Bolton Street Coll. of Technology, Dublin. *Address:* Doon House, Maam, Co. Galway, Eire.

NABARRO, Prof. Frank Reginald Nunes, MBE 1946; FRS 1971; Professor of Physics, University of the Witwatersrand, since 1953; *b* 7 March 1916; *s* of late Stanley Nunes Nabarro and Leah Nabarro; *m* 1948, Margaret Constance, *d* of late James Dalziel, ARAM; three *s* two *d. Educ:* Nottingham High Sch.; New Coll., Oxford (MA, BSc). DSc Birmingham. Sen. Exper. Officer, Min. of Supply, 1941-45; Royal Soc. Warren Research Fellow, Univ. of Bristol, 1945-49; Lectr in Metallurgy, Univ. of Birmingham, 1949-53; University of Witwatersrand: Prof. and Head of Dept of Physics, 1953-77, City of Johannesburg Prof. of Physics, 1970-77; Dean, Faculty of Science, 1968-70; Representative of Senate on Council, 1967-77; Deputy Vice-Chancellor, 1978-80. Vis. Prof., Nat. Research Council, Ottawa, 1956; Vice-Pres., S African Inst. of Physics, 1956-57; Republic Steel Vis. Prof., Dept of Metallurgy, Case Inst. of Techn., Cleveland, Ohio, 1964-65; Overseas Fellow of Churchill Coll., Cambridge, 1966-67; Gauss Prof., Akademie der Wissenschaften, Göttingen, 1970; Professeur-associé, Univ. Paris-Sud, 1971, Montpellier II, 1973; Vis. Prof. Dept of Material Science, Univ. of Calif., Berkeley, 1977; Vis. Fellow, Robinson Coll., Cambridge, 1981. Hon. FRSSAf 1973. Beilby Memorial Award, 1950; South Africa Medal, 1972. *Publications:* Theory of Crystal Dislocations, 1967; scientific papers, mainly on solid state physics. *Recreation:* gardening. *Address:* 32 Cookham Road, Auckland Park, Johannesburg, South Africa. *T:* (011) 726-7745.

NABARRO, Dr John David Nunes, FRCP; Consultant Physician, The Middlesex Hospital, London, 1954-81, now Emeritus Consultant Physician; Hon. Research Associate, Departments of Medicine and Biochemistry, Middlesex Hospital Medical School, since 1981; Director, Cobbold Laboratories, Middlesex Hospital Medical School, 1970-81; Hon. Consultant Physician, Royal Prince Alfred Hospital, Sidney, since 1959; *b* 21 Dec. 1915; *s* of David Nunes Nabarro and Florence Nora Nabarro (*née* Webster); *m* 1948, Joan Margaret Cockrell; two *s* two *d. Educ:* Oundle Sch.; University Coll., London (Howard Cluff Meml Prize 1935; Fellow, UCL, 1963); University Coll. Hosp. Med. Sch. (Magrath Schol., Atkinson Morley Schol., Atchison Schol., 1938). MD London. Medical Specialist, OC Med. Div., RAMC, 1939-45: served in Iraq; 8th Army, Italy (Salerno Anzio); Middle East (despatches). UCH: House Phys., 1939; Med. Registrar, 1945-47; Res. Asst

Phys., 1948-49; First Asst, Med. Unit, UCH Med. Sch., 1950-54; WHO Travelling Fellowship, 1952. Hon. Cons. Endocrinologist to Army, 1965-81. Examiner in Medicine, Univs of Cambridge, London and Sheffield. Chm., Jt Consultants Cttee, 1979-. Mem., Assoc. of Physicians of GB and Ire., 1952; Pres., Sect. of Endocrinology, RSM, 1968-70; Chm., Med. and Sci. Sects, Brit. Diabetic Assoc., 1975-77, Mem. Council, 1981-; RCP: Mem. Council, 1954-55; Oliver Sharpey Lectr, 1960; Joseph Senior White Fellow, 1960; Examiner for MRCP, 1964-; Procensor, 1973; Censor, 1974; Croonian Lectr, 1976; Sen. Censor and First Vice-Pres., 1977. William McIlwrath Guest Prof., Royal Prince Alfred Hosp., Sidney, 1959; John Mathison Shaw Lectr, RCPE, 1963; Guest Visitor, St Vincent's Hosp., Sidney, 1963; Guest Lectr, Postgrad. Cttee, Christchurch Hosps, NZ, 1973; Banting Meml Lectr, Brit. Diabetic Assoc., 1978. *Publications:* Biochemical Investigations in Diagnosis and Treatment, 1954, 3rd edn, 1962; papers on endocrinology and diabetes in med. jls. *Recreation:* gardening. *Address:* 33 Woodside Avenue, N12. *T:* 01-445 7925; 121 Harley Street, W1. *T:* 01-935 7200.

NADER, Ralph; author, lecturer, lawyer; *b* Winsted, Conn, USA, 27 Feb. 1934; *s* of Nadra Nader and Rose (*née* Bouziane). *Educ:* Gilbert Sch., Winsted; Woodrow Wilson Sch. of Public and Internat. Affairs, Princeton Univ. (AB *magna cum laude*); Law Sch. of Harvard Univ. (LLB). Admitted to Bar of Connecticut, 1958; to Bar of Massachusetts, 1959, and US Supreme Court; US Army, 1959; Law practice in Hartford, Conn, 1959-. Member: Amer. Bar Assoc.; AAAS; Phi Beta Kappa. Lectr in History and Govt, Univ. of Hartford, 1961-63; Lectr, Princeton Univ., 1967-68. Has pursued, actively, better consumer protection; improving the lot of the American Indian, etc; lobbyed in Washington for safer gas pipe-lines and nuclear reactors, also played a very important role in work for the passing of: National Traffic and Motor Vehicle Safety Act, 1966; Wholesome Meat Act, 1967. Niemen Fellows Award, 1965-66; named one of the Ten Outstanding Young Men of the Year by US Junior Chamber of Commerce, 1967. *Publications:* Unsafe at Any Speed: The Designed-in Dangers of the American Automobile, 1965; (ed) The Consumer and Corporate Accountability, 1974; (ed jtly) Taming the Giant Corporation, 1976; contrib. articles to New Republic, etc. *Address:* (home) 53 Hillside Avenue, Winsted, Conn 06098, USA.

NADESAN, Pararajasingam, CMG 1955; OBE 1954; Governor, Rotary International, District 321; Member, Legislative Council, Rotary International; Director: Cargills (Ceylon) Ltd; Associated Hotels Co. Ltd; Past Chairman, Low Country Products Association; *b* 20 Dec. 1917; *s* of Sir Sangarapillai Pararajasingam, *qv*; *m* 1st, 1941, Gauri Nair (decd); one *s* one *d*; 2nd, 1953, Kamala Nair; three *d. Educ:* Royal College, and Ceylon Univ. Coll.; Univ. of London (BA Hons). Tutor, Ceylon Univ. Coll., 1940; entered Ceylon Civil Service, 1941; held various appts in sphere of provincial administration, 1941-47; Asst Permanent Sec., Min. of Transport and Works, 1948-53; Dir of Civil Aviation in addition to duties as Asst Sec. Min. of Transport and Works, 1954-56; Sec. to the Prime Minister and Information Officer, Ceylon, 1954-56; Member: Ceylon Delegation to the Bandung Conf.; Commonwealth Prime Minister's Conf.; ICAO Gen. Assembly; ILO Cttee on Plantations. FCIT. Officer Order of Merit (Italy), 1954; Knight Comdr Order of the Crown, Thailand, 1955; Comdr Order of Orange Nassau, Netherlands, 1955; Defence Medal, 1947; Coronation Medal, 1953; Ceylon Armed Services Inauguration Medal, 1956. *Recreations:* golf, tennis, gardening, collecting antiques. *Address:* Six 28th Lane A, Inner Flower Road, Colombo 3, Sri Lanka. *T:* 28202 (Residence), 25919 (Office). *Clubs:* Colombo, Orient, Rotary (Colombo); Gymkhana.

NAGDA, Kanti; Manager, Community Centre; *b* 1 May 1946; *s* of Vershi Bhoja Nagda and Zaviben Nagda; *m* 1972, Bhagwati Desai; two *s. Educ:* City High Sch., Kampala, Uganda; Coll. of Further Educn, Chippenham, Wilts; E African Univ., Uganda. Sec.-Gen., Confedn of Indian Organisations (UK), 1975-. Exec. Cttee Member: Harrow Community Relations Council, 1974-76; Gujarati Literary Acad. (GB), 1976-82. Mem., European Movement. President: Uganda Art Circle, 1968-71; Anglo Indian Circle, 1973-82; Indian Cricket Club, Harrow, 1976-80. Representative: Harrow Youth Council; Brent Youth Council; Harrow Arts Council. Hon. Editorial Consultant, International Asian Guide & Who's Who, 1975-; Asst Editor, Oswal News, 1977-. *Publications:* Muratiyo Ke Nokar (Gujarati novel), Kenya 1967; stories and articles in newspapers and jls. *Recreations:* cricket, photography. *Address:* 11 North Avenue, Harrow, Mddx HA2 7AE. *T:* 01-427 0696. *Club:* Indian National.

NAGEON de LESTANG, Sir (Marie Charles Emmanuel) Clement, Kt 1960; *b* 20 Oct. 1910; *e s* of late M. F. C. Nageon de Lestang, Solicitor and Simone Savy; *m* 1933, Danielle Sauvage; one *s* three *d* (and one *s* decd). *Educ:* St Louis' Coll., Seychelles; King's Coll., London. LLB (Hons) London, 1931. Called to the Bar, Middle Temple, 1931. Private practice, Seychelles, 1932-35; Legal Adviser and Crown Prosecutor to Govt of Seychelles, 1936-39; Actg Chief Justice, Seychelles, 1939-44; Resident Magistrate, Kenya, 1944-47; Puisne Judge, Kenya, 1947-56; Federal Justice, Federal Supreme Court of Nigeria, 1956-58; Chief Justice of the High Court of Lagos, 1958-64, and of the Southern Cameroons, 1958-60; Justice of Appeal, Court of Appeal for Eastern Africa, 1964, Vice-Pres., 1966-69. *Recreations:* yachting, fishing. *Address:* Pennies, Court Drive, Shillingford, Oxon.

NAGY, János L.; *see* Lörincz-Nagy, J.

NAIPAUL, Vidiadhar Surajprasad; author; *b* 17 Aug. 1932; *m* 1955, Patricia Ann Hale. *Educ:* Queen's Royal Coll., Trinidad; University Coll., Oxford. *Publications:* The Mystic Masseur, 1957 (John Llewelyn Rhys Memorial Prize, 1958); The Suffrage of Elvira, 1958; Miguel Street, 1959 (Somerset Maugham Award, 1961); A House for Mr Biswas, 1961; The Middle Passage, 1962; Mr Stone and the Knights Companion, 1963 (Hawthornden Prize, 1964); An Area of Darkness, 1964; The Mimic Men, 1967 (W. H. Smith Award, 1968); A Flag on the Island, 1967; The Loss of El Dorado, 1969; In a Free State, 1971 (Booker Prize, 1971); The Overcrowded Barracoon, and other articles, 1972; Guerrillas, 1975; India: a wounded civilization, 1977; A Bend in the River, 1979; The Return of Eva Perón, 1980; Among the Believers, 1981. *Address:* c/o André Deutsch Ltd, 105 Great Russell Street, WC1.

NAIRN, Sir George; *see* Nairn, Sir M. G.

NAIRN, Air Vice-Marshal Kenneth Gordon, CB 1945; chartered accountant; *b* 9 Nov. 1898; *m* 1920, Mary Fleming Martin; two s one d. *Educ:* George Watson's Coll., Edinburgh; Univ. of Manitoba. Lived in Edinburgh till 1911; proceeded to Canada; service in Strathcona Horse and transferred to RFC 1916-19; Pilot, rank Lt; moved to Vancouver from Winnipeg, 1921; retired. Hon. Wing Commander of 111 Aux. Squadron RCAF 1933; Active Service, 1939-45; on Air Council as Air Mem. Accounts and Finance till Oct. 1944, then Special Adviser to Minister for Air on Finance. Hon. ADC for Province of BC to the Governor-General, Viscount Alexander, 1947. Norwegian Cross of Liberation, 1948. *Recreations:* golf, fishing, yachting. *Address:* 1611 Drummond Drive, Vancouver, BC. *T:* 224-1500. *Clubs:* Royal Air Force; Vancouver, Royal Vancouver Yacht (Vancouver).

NAIRN, Margaret, RGN, SCM; Chief Area Nursing Officer, Greater Glasgow Health Board, since 1974; *b* 20 July 1924; *d* of James R. Nairn and Anne G. Nairn. *Educ:* Aberdeen Academy. Nurse Training: general: Aberdeen Royal Infirmary, to 1945 (RGN); midwifery: Aberdeen Maternity Hosp., until 1948 (State Certified Midwife); Health Visitors: Aberdeen Coll. for Health Visitors, until 1952 (Health Visitors Cert.); administrative: Royal Coll. of Nursing, London, to 1959 (Nursing Admin. Cert.); 6 months study in USA as British Commonwealth and Empire Nurses Scholar, 1956. Ward Sister and Night Supt, Aberdeen Maternity Hosp., 1945-52; Director of Nursing Services in Aberdeen and Glasgow, 1952-74. *Publications:* articles in medical and nursing press: A Study of 283 Families with Rent Arrears; Liaison Services between Hospital and Community Nursing Services; Health Visitors in General Practice. *Recreations:* reading, gardening, swimming. *Address:* Flat 18, 20 Kensington Road, Glasgow G12 9UX. *T:* 041-339 1150.

NAIRN, Sir (Michael) George, 3rd Bt, *cr* 1904; TD 1948; *b* 30 Jan. 1911; *s* of Sir Michael Nairn, 2nd Bt, and Mildred Margaret, *e* d of G. W. Neish; *S* father 1952; *m* 1936, Helen Louise, *yr* d of late Major E. J. W. Bruce, Melbourne, Aust., and late Mrs L. Warre Graham-Clarke; two s. *Educ:* Trinity Coll., Glenalmond. Chairman: Kirkcaldy and Dist Trustee Savings Bank, 1952-71; Michael Nairn & Greenwich Ltd, 1958-62; Nairn Williamson (Holdings) Ltd, 1962-70. Served War of 1939-45, with The Black Watch (wounded); Major, 1939. Mem. of the Queen's Body Guard for Scotland (Royal Company of Archers). *Heir:* s Michael Nairn [*b* 1 July 1938; *m* 1972, Diana (d 1982), *er* d of Leonard Blight; two s one d]. *Address:* Pitcarmick, Bridge of Cally, Blairgowrie, Perthshire PH10 9NW. *T:* Strath Ardle 214. *Club:* Caledonian.
See also Sir W. G. N. Walker.

NAIRN, Sir Robert Arnold S.; *see* Spencer-Nairn.

NAIRNE, Lady (12th in line, of the Lordship *cr* 1681); **Katherine Evelyn Constance Bigham;** *b* 22 June 1912; *d* of 6th Marquess of Lansdowne and Elizabeth (she *m* 2nd, Lord Colum Crichton-Stuart, who *d* 1957; she *d* 1964); *S* to brother's Lordship of Nairne, 1944; *m* 1933, Hon. Edward Bigham (later 3rd Viscount Mersey, who *d* 1979); three s. *Heir:* s Viscount Mersey, *qv. Address:* Bignor Park, Pulborough, W Sussex. *T:* Sutton (Sussex) 214.

NAIRNE, Rt. Hon. Sir Patrick (Dalmahoy), GCB 1981 (KCB 1975; CB 1971); MC 1943; PC 1982; Master, St Catherine's College, Oxford, since 1981; *b* 15 Aug. 1921; *s* of late Lt-Col C. S. and Mrs E. D. Nairne; *m* 1948, Penelope Chauncy Bridges, *d* of Lt-Col R. F. and Mrs L. C. Bridges; three *s* three d. *Educ:* Radley Coll.; University Coll., Oxford (Exhibr; Hon. Fellow, 1981). Seaforth Highlanders, 1941-45 (Capt.). 1st cl. hons Mod. Hist. (Oxon), 1947. Entered Civil Service and joined Admty, Dec. 1947; Private Sec. to First Lord of Admty, 1958-60; Asst Sec., 1960; Private Sec. to Sec. of State for Defence, 1965-67; Assistant Under-Sec. of State (Logistics), MoD, 1967-70; Dep. Under-Sec. of State, MoD, 1970-73; Second Perm. Sec., Cabinet Office, 1973-75; Perm. Sec., DHSS, 1975-81. Chm., Soc. of Italic Handwriting, 1981-; Trustee: Nat. Maritime Museum, 1981-; Rowntree Meml Trust; Member: W Midlands Bd, Central TV; VSO Council; Council, RCA; President: Radleian Soc., 1980-; Seamen's Hosp. Soc. FRSA 1978. Hon. LLD Leicester, 1980. *Recreations:* watercolour painting, calligraphy. *Address:* Master's Lodgings, St Catherine's College, Oxford. *Club:* United Oxford & Cambridge University.

NAIROBI, Archbishop of, (RC), since 1971; **HE Cardinal Maurice Otunga;** *b* Jan. 1923. Priest, 1950; Titular Bishop of Tacape, 1957; Bishop of Kisii, 1960; Titular Archbishop of Bomarzo, 1969; Cardinal 1973. *Address:* Archbishop's House, PO Box 14231, Nairobi, Kenya.

NAISBY, John Vickers, MC 1918; TD 1935; QC 1947; *b* 1894; *m* 1954, Dorothy Helen (d 1977), d of late J. H. Fellows. *Educ:* Rossall; Emmanuel Coll., Cambridge. Called to Bar, Inner Temple, 1922. Lt-Col and Brevet Col.

NALDER, Hon. Sir Crawford David, Kt 1974; farmer; active in voluntary and charitable organisations; *b* Katanning, WA, 14 Feb. 1910; *s* of H. A. Nalder, Wagin; *m* 1st, 1934, Olive May (d 1973), d of S. Irvin; one s two d; 2nd, 1974, Brenda Wade. *Educ:* State Sch., Wagin; Wesley Coll., Perth, WA. Sheep, wheat and pig farmer, 1934-; Country rep. for Perth butchers. Entered parliament, 1947; MLA (CP) for Katanning, Parliament of Western Australia, 1950-73 (for Wagin, 1947-50); Dep. Leader, Country Party, 1956; Minister: for War Service Land Settlement, 1959-66; for Agriculture, 1959-71; for Electricity, 1962-71; Leader, Parly Country Party, 1962-73. Chm., Girls College Council. Knighted for services to the state and in local govt. *Recreations:* tennis, gardening. *Address:* 7 Morriett Street, Attadale, WA 6156, Australia.

NALL, Sir Michael (Joseph), 2nd Bt *cr* 1954; DL; *b* 6 Oct. 1921; *er* s of Colonel Sir Joseph Nall, 1st Bt; *S* father, 1958; *m* 1951, Angela Loveday Hanbury, *e* d of Air Chief Marshal Sir Alec Coryton, KCB, KBE, MVO, DFC; two s. *Educ:* Wellington College, Berks. Joined Royal Navy, 1939. Served War of 1939-45 (at sea); psc (MM) 1944; Lt-Comdr, 1950-61, retired. General Manager, Guide Dogs for the Blind Association, 1961-64. Pres., Nottingham Chamber of Commerce and Industry, 1972-74. DL Notts, 1970-; High Sheriff, Notts, 1971. Chm., Notts Scout Assoc., 1968- (Silver Acorn, 1979). *Recreations:* field sports, flying. *Heir:* s Captain Edward William Joseph Nall, 13th/18th Royal Hussars (QMO), *b* 24 Oct. 1952. *Address:* Hoveringham Hall, Nottingham NG14 7JR. *T:* Lowdham 3634.

NALL-CAIN, family name of **Baron Brocket.**

NANCE, Francis James, LLM; **His Honour Judge Nance;** a Circuit Judge (formerly a Judge of County Courts and Commissioner, Liverpool and Manchester Crown Courts), since 1966; *b* 5 Sept. 1915; *s* of late Herbert James Nance, South Africa, and of Margaret Ann Nance, New Brighton; *m* 1943, Margaret Gertrude Roe (d 1978); two s. *Educ:* St Francis Xavier's College, Liverpool; University of Liverpool (LLM 1938). Called to the Bar, Gray's Inn, 1936. Served War of 1939-45, Royal Corps of Signals (Captain): Normandy invasion, NW Europe (despatches). Practised on Northern Circuit, 1936-66. Deputy Chairman, Lancashire QS, 1963-71. *Recreation:* chess. *Address:* c/o St George's Hall, Liverpool, Merseyside. *Club:* Athenæum (Liverpool).

NANDY, Dipak; Deputy Chief Executive, Equal Opportunities Commission, since 1976; *b* 21 May 1936; *s* of B. C. Nandy and Leela Nandy; *m* 1st, 1964, Margaret Gracie; 2nd, 1972, Hon. Luise Byers; two d. *Educ:* St Xavier's Coll., Calcutta; Univ. of Leeds BA 1st Cl. Hons English Literature, 1960; C.E. Vaughan Research Fellowship, 1960-62. Lectr, English Literature, Univ. of Leicester, 1962-66; Lectr and Fellow of Rutherford College, Univ. of Kent at Canterbury, 1966-68; founder-Director, The Runnymede Trust, 1968-73; Vis. Fellow, Adlai Stevenson Inst. of International Affairs, Chicago, 1970-73; Research Fellow, Social and Community Planning Research, 1973-75. Mem., Cttee of Inquiry into Future of Broadcasting, 1974-77. *Publications:* numerous essays in books, periodicals and newspapers on literature, political thought, race relations, urban problems, and equality for women. *Recreations:* collecting records, opera, mathematics. *Address:* c/o Equal Opportunities Commission, Overseas House, Quay Street, Manchester M3 3HN. *T:* 061-833 9244. *Club:* Film Exchange (Manchester).

NANKIVELL, Owen; Group Chief Economist, Lucas Industries, since 1979; *b* 6 April 1927; *s* of John Hamilton Nankivell and Sarah Ann Mares; *m* 1956, Mary Burman Earnshaw; one s two d. *Educ:* Torquay Grammar Sch.; Univ. of Manchester. BA (Econ) 1951, MA (Econ) 1963. FRSS. Admty, 1951-52; Colonial Office, 1952-55; Central Statistical Office, 1955-65; DEA, 1965-69; HM Treasury, 1969-72; Asst Dir, Central Statistical Office, 1972-79. *Publication:* All Good Gifts, 1978. *Recreations:* Christian, tennis, choral music, singing. *Address:* 12 Whittington Road, Worcester. *T:* Worcester 352948.

NAPIER, family name of **Lord Napier and Ettrick** and **Baron Napier of Magdala.**

NAPIER, 14th Lord, *cr* 1627 (Scotland), **AND ETTRICK,** 5th Baron, *cr* 1872 (UK); **Francis Nigel Napier,** MVO 1980; DL; a Bt of Nova Scotia, 1666, 11th Bt of Thirlestane; Major, Scots Guards (Reserve of Officers); Private Secretary, Comptroller and Equerry to HRH the Princess Margaret, Countess of Snowdon, since 1973; *b* 5 Dec. 1930; *e* s of 13th Baron Napier and 4th Ettrick, TD, and Muir, *e* d of Sir Percy Newson, Bt; *S* father 1954; *m* 1958, Delia Mary, *yr* d of A. D. B. Pearson; two s two d. *Educ:* Eton; RMA, Sandhurst. Commissioned, 1950; served Malaya, 1950-51; Adjt 1st Bn Scots Guards, 1955-57. Equerry to His late Royal Highness The Duke of Gloucester, 1958-60, retd, 1960. Deputy Ceremonial and Protocol Secretary, CRO, 1962-66; Purple Staff Officer at State Funeral of Sir Winston Churchill, 1966. A Cons. Whip, House of Lords, 1970-71; handed over

Instruments of Independence to Tuvalu (formerly Ellice Is), 1978. Mem. Royal Co. of Archers (Queen's Body Guard for Scotland), 1953-. Pres., St John Ambulance Assoc. and Brigade for County of London, 1975-. DL Selkirkshire, 1974, Ettrick and Lauderdale, 1975-. Freeman, City of London; Liveryman, Worshipful Company of Grocers. OStJ 1982. *Heir: s* Master of Napier, *qv. Address:* Forest Lodge, The Great Park, Windsor SL4 2BU. *T:* Windsor 61262; Apartment 2, St James's Palace, SW1A 1BA. *T:* 01-930 0242; (seat) Thirlestane, Ettrick, Selkirkshire. *Clubs:* White's, Pratt's.

NAPIER OF MAGDALA, 5th Baron (UK), *cr* 1868; **Robert John Napier,** OBE 1944; MICE; late Royal Engineers; Brigadier, Chief Engineer, HQ, Scottish Command, retd; *b* 16 June 1904; *o s* of 4th Baron and Florence Martha (*d* 1946), *d* of Gen. John Maxwell Perceval, CB; *S* father, 1948; *m* 1939, Elizabeth Marian, *y d* of E. H. Hunt, FRCS; three *s* two *d. Educ:* Wellington. Served Waziristan, 1936-37 (despatches); War of 1939-45, Sicily (OBE). *Heir: s* Hon. Robert Alan Napier [*b* 6 Sept. 1940; *m* 1964, Frances Clare, *er d* of A. F. Skinner, Monks Close, Woolpit, Suffolk; one *s* one *d*]. *Address:* 8 Mortonhall Road, Edinburgh EH9 2HW.

NAPIER, Master of; Hon. Francis David Charles Napier; *b* 3 Nov. 1962; *s* and *heir* of 14th Lord Napier (and 5th Baron Ettrick), *qv. Educ:* Stanbridge Earls School. *Address:* Forest Lodge, The Great Park, Windsor.

NAPIER, Barbara Langmuir, OBE 1975; Senior Tutor to Women Students in the University of Glasgow, 1964-74; Member, the Industrial Arbitration Board (formerly Industrial Court), 1963-76; *b* 21 Feb. 1914; *y c* of late James Langmuir Napier, Consultant Engineer, and late Siblie Agnes Mowat. *Educ:* Hillhead High Sch., Glasgow; Univ. of Glasgow (MA); Glasgow and West of Scotland Coll. of Domestic Science. Org. Sec. Redlands Hosp., Glasgow, 1937-41; Univ. of Glasgow: Warden, Queen Margaret Hall, 1941-44; Gen. Adv. to Women Students, 1942-64; Appts Officer (Women), 1942-65. Founder Mem. Assoc. of Principals, Wardens and Advisers to Univ. Women Students, 1942, Hon. Mem., 1977- (Pres. 1965-68); Local Rep. and later Mem. Coun., Women's Migration and Overseas Appts Soc., 1946-64; Winifred Cullis Lecture Fellowship (midwest USA) of Brit. Amer. Associates, 1950. Founder Dir, West of Scotland Sch. Co. Ltd, 1976-77. Member, Tribunal under National Insurance Acts, 1954-60; President, Standing Conference of Women's Organisations (Glasgow), 1955-57; Member: Scottish Committee, ITA, 1957-64; Executive Cttee, Nat. Advisory Centre on Careers for Women, (formerly Women's Employment Fedn), 1963-68, 1972-77; Indep. Member: Flax and Hemp Wages Council (GB), 1962-70 (Dep. Chm. 1964-70); Hat, Cap and Millinery Wages Council (GB), 1963-70; Laundry Wages Council (GB), 1968-70. Governor: Westbourne Sch., Glasgow, 1951-77 (Chm., 1969-77; Hon. Governor, 1981); Notre Dame Coll. of Educn, Glasgow, 1959-64. JP Glasgow 1955-75, Stirling 1975-80. *Publications:* (with S. Nisbet) Promise and Progress, 1970; contrib. The College Courant, etc. *Recreations:* reading, travel, gardening, painting, being with cats. *Address:* 67 Brisbane Street, Largs, Ayrshire KA30 8QP. *T:* Largs 675495. *Club:* College (Glasgow).

NAPIER, Sir Joseph William Lennox, 4th Bt, *cr* 1867; OBE 1944; *b* 1 Aug. 1895; *s* of 3rd Bt and Mabel Edith Geraldine (*d* 1955), *d* of late Rev. Charles Thornton Forster; *S* father (killed in action, Gallipoli), 1915; *m* 1931, Muriel Isabel, *yr d* of late Maj. Siward Surtees, DL, JP, Redworth Hall, Co Durham; two *s. Educ:* Rugby; Jesus College, Cambridge. Served European War, 1914-18, in South Wales Borderers, Gallipoli and Mesopotamia (wounded three times; POW, Turkey). Joined 57 Home Counties Bde RFA (TF), 1920; re-employed 1939, Lt-Col (AQMG (Movt)) HQ Staff, Eastern Command and Italy (OBE mil.). Mem., Lloyds, 1921-73. Former Dir of public companies and Mem., Council of Inst. of Directors. Gold Staff Officer, Coronations 1937 and 1953. *Recreations:* painting, fishing. *Heir: s* Robert Surtees Napier [*b* 5 March 1932; *m* 1971, Jennifer Beryl, *d* of late H. Warwick Daw; one *s*]. *Address:* 17 Cheyne Gardens, Chelsea, SW3. *Club:* Alpine.
See also Brigadier V. J. L. Napier.

NAPIER, Maj.-Gen. Lennox Alexander Hawkins, OBE 1970; MC 1957; General Officer Commanding Wales, since 1980; *b* 28 June 1928; *s* of Major Charles McNaughton Napier and D. C. Napier; *m* 1959, Jennifer Dawn Wilson; one *s* two *d. Educ:* Radley; RMA Sandhurst. Joined Army, 1946; commnd into South Wales Borderers, 1948; commanded 1st Bn S Wales Borderers and 1st Bn Royal Regt of Wales, 1967-70; Instructor, JSSC, 1970-72; served Min. of Defence, 1972-74; Brigade Commander, Berlin Infantry Bde, 1974-76; Prince of Wales's Division: Divisional Brigadier, 1976-80; Col Commandant, 1980. *Recreations:* shooting, riding. *Address:* c/o Barclays Bank, 17/18 Agincourt Square, Monmouth, Gwent. *Club:* Lansdowne.

NAPIER, Oliver John; Member (Alliance) Belfast East, Northern Ireland Assembly, since 1982; Councillor for East Belfast, Belfast City Council, since 1977; *b* 11 July 1935; *e s* of James J. and Sheila Napier; *m* 1962, Brigid (*née* Barnes); three *s* five *d* (and one *s* decd). *Educ:* Ballycruttle Public Elem. Sch., Downpatrick; St Malachy's Coll., Belfast; Queen's Univ., Belfast (LLB). Qual. Solicitor, NI, 1959; Lectr and Mem. Bd of Examrs, Incorp. Law Soc. of NI, 1965-71. Mem. Exec., Ulster Liberal Party, 1962-69; Founder Mem., New Ulster Movt, 1969; Founder Mem., Alliance Party, 1970, Leader 1973-. Mem. (Alliance), E Belfast, NI Assembly, 1973-75; Minister of Legal Affairs, NI Executive, Jan.-May 1974; Mem. (Alliance), N Ireland Constitutional Convention for E Belfast, 1975-76. Contested (Alliance), E Belfast, 1979.

Recreations: many and varied. *Address:* 83 Victoria Road, Holywood, Co. Down.

NAPIER, Brigadier Vivian John Lennox, MC 1918; late S Wales Borderers; Vice-Lieutenant, Brecknock, 1964-74; *b* 13 July 1898; 3rd *s* of Sir William Lennox Napier, 3rd Bt; *m* 1958, Marion Avis, OBE, *d* of late Sir John and Lady Lloyd. *Educ:* Uppingham; RMC. Served European War, 1914-18: France and Belgium (wounded, MC); served War of 1939-45: HQ Cairo Bde and 1 Bn Welch Regt, North Africa (despatches, prisoner). Brig. Comdg Mombasa Area, 1948-49; Dep. Comdr S-W District, UK, 1949-51; retd, 1952. Commissioner, St John Ambulance, Breconshire, 1957-62. DL Brecknock, 1958. Order of Leopold (Belgium), 1925; OStJ 1959. *Recreation:* fishing. *Address:* Ty Nant, Groesffordd, Brecon, Powys.
See also Sir Joseph Napier, Bt.

NAPIER, Sir William Archibald, 13th Bt, of Merchiston, *cr* 1627; *b* 19 July 1915; *s* of Sir Robert Archibald Napier, 12th Bt and Violet Payn; *S* father 1965; *m* 1942, Kathleen Mabel, *d* of late Reginald Greaves, Tafelberg, CP; one *s. Educ:* Cheam School; Stowe. Captain S African Engineers, Middle East, 1939-45. Mechanical Engineer. AM Inst. of (SA) Mech. Engineers; AM Inst. of Cert. Engineers (Works); Fellow, Inst. of Matériel Handling. *Recreations:* shooting, golf, squash. *Heir: s* John Archibald Lennox Napier [*b* 6 Dec. 1946; *m* 1969, Erica, *d* of late Kurt Kingsfield; one *s* one *d*]. *Address:* Merchiston Croft, PO Box 65177, Benmore, Transvaal, 2010, S Africa. *T:* 7832651. *Clubs:* Carlton; Rand, Johannesburg Country, Wanderers' (Johannesburg).

NAPLEY, Sir David, Kt 1977; Solicitor; Senior Partner in Kingsley, Napley & Co.; President of the Law Society, 1976-77 (Vice-President, 1975-76); *b* 25 July 1915; *s* of late Joseph and Raie Napley; *m* 1940, Leah Rose, *d* of Thomas Reginald Saturley; two *d. Educ:* Burlington College. Solicitor, 1937. Served with Queen's Royal (W Surrey) Regt, 1940; commnd 1942; Indian Army, 1942; Captain 1942; invalided 1945. Contested (C): Rowley Regis and Tipton, 1951; Gloucester, 1955. Pres., London (Criminal Courts) Solicitors Assoc., 1960-63; Chm. Exec. Council, British Academy of Forensic Sciences, 1960-74 (Pres. 1967; Director, 1974-); Mem. Council, Law Soc., 1962-; Mem. Judicial Exchange with USA, 1963-64; Chm., Law Soc's Standing Cttee on Criminal Law, 1963-76; Pres., City of Westminster Law Soc., 1967-68; Mem. Editorial Bd, Criminal Law Review, 1967-; Chairman: Contentious Business, Law Soc., 1972-75; Legal Aid Cttee, 1976-79; Exam. Bd, Incorp. Soc. of Valuers and Auctioneers, 1981-; Mem. Home Office Law Revision Cttee, 1971-. Mem. Council, Imperial Soc. of Kts Bachelor, 1981-. Chm., Mario & Franco Restaurants Ltd, 1968-74. Trustee, W Ham Boys' Club, 1979-, Pres., 1981-. *Publications:* Law on the Remuneration of Auctioneers and Estate Agents, 1947; (ed) Bateman's Law of Auctions, 1954; The Law of Auctioneers and Estate Agents Commission, 1957; Crime and Criminal Procedure, 1963; Guide to Law and Practice under the Criminal Justice Act, 1967; The Technique of Persuasion, 1970, 2nd edn 1975; a section, Halsbury's Laws of England; contrib. legal and forensic scientific jls, press, legal discussions on radio and TV. *Recreations:* painting, reading, writing, music, eating. *Address:* 107-115 Long Acre, WC2E 9PT. *T:* 01-240 2411. *Club:* Garrick.

NAPOLITAN, Leonard, CB 1970; Director of Economics and Statistics, Ministry of Agriculture, Fisheries and Food, 1965-77; *b* 9 April 1919; *s* of late Domenic and Rose G. Napolitan; *m* 1945, Dorothy Laycock; two *d. Educ:* Univ. of London (BSc Econ. 1944); LSE (MSc Econ. 1946). Asst Agric. Economist, Univ. of Bristol, 1947-48; joined Min. of Agric. and Fisheries as Agric. Economist, 1948. Pres., Agric. Econs Soc., 1974-75. *Address:* High Lee, Sandford Avenue, Church Stretton, Shropshire SY6 7AE.

NAPPER, John (Pelham); painter; *b* 17 Sept. 1916; *e s* of late John Mortimer Napper and late Dorothy Charlotte (*née* Hill); *m* 1st, 1935, Hedvig Sophie Armour; 2nd, 1945, Pauline Davidson. *Educ:* Frensham Heights, Surrey and privately; Dundee Sch. of Art; Royal Acad. Schs of Art. Served War of 1939-45: commnd RA, 1941; Ceylon, 1942, War Artist to Ceylon comd, 1943-44; seconded to RNVR, 1944, E Africa, 1944; demobilised, 1945. One-man exhibitions: Leicester Galleries, London, 1949, 1961, 1962; The Adams Gallery, London, 1957 and 1959; The Walker Art Gallery, Liverpool, 1959; La Maison de la Pensée Française, Paris, 1960; Galerie Lahumière, Paris, 1963; Galleries Hervé and Lahumière, Paris, 1965; Larcada Gallery, New York, 1968, 1970, 1972, 1975, 1977; Browse and Darby Gall., 1978, 1980; represented in many public and private collections. Vis. Prof. of Fine Arts, Southern Illinois Univ., USA, 1968-69. Awarded prize at International Exhibition of Fine Arts, Moscow, 1957; Awarded International Assoc. of Art Critics Prize, 1961. *Address:* Steadvallets Farm, Bromfield, Ludlow, Salop. *T:* Bromfield 247.

NARAIN, Sase, OR 1976; CMG 1969; JP (Guyana); solicitor; Speaker of the National Assembly, Guyana, since 1971; Chairman, Berger Paints (Guyana) Ltd; *b* 27 Jan. 1925; *s* of Oudit and Sookdai Naraine; *m* 1952, Shamshun Narain (*née* Rayman); four *s. Educ:* Modern Educational Inst.; Gibson and Weldon Law Tutors. Solicitor, admitted in England and Guyana, 1957. Town Councillor, City of Georgetown, 1962-70; Member: History and Arts Council, 1969-; Republic Cttee of Guyana, 1969; Pres., Guyana Sanatan Dharma Maha Sabha, 1963-. Comr for Oaths to Affidavits, 1961; Notary Public, 1968. Dep. Chm., Public Service Commn, Guyana, 1966-71; Mem., Police Service Commn, 1961-71. Mem., Nat. Awards Cttee of Guyana. JP 1962. *Recreations:* golf, cricket, swimming. *Address:* 217 South Street,

Lacytown, Georgetown, Demerara, Guyana. *T:* 66611. *Clubs:* Georgetown, Georgetown Cricket, Everest Cricket (Guyana).

NARAIN, Sir Sathi, KBE 1980 (MBE 1971); Managing Director, Narain Construction Co. Ltd, since 1945; *b* 26 Sept. 1919; *s* of Suramma and Appalsamy Narain; *m* 1969, Hannah Shakuntla (*née* Pratap); three *s*. *Educ:* Suva, Fiji. Government apprentice carpenter, 1933-44; Man. Dir, Narain Construction Co. Ltd, 1945-, and of subsidiary companies (hotels, land development, road development, shipping), 1950-; Director: Burns Philps South Sea Co. Ltd; Queensland Insurance Co. Ltd. Suva City Councillor, 1956-59; Member of Parliament, 1963-67. *Recreations:* golf, bowling. *Address:* (business) Narain Construction Co. Ltd, Box 412, Suva, Fiji. *T:* 23873; (residence) 20 Narain Place, Tamavua, Suva, Fiji. *T:* 381027. *Clubs:* Defence, Royal Yacht, Fiji (Suva, Fiji); Tattersall (Sydney, Aust.).

NARASIMHAN, Chakravarthi Vijayaraghava; Senior Fellow, UN Institute for Training and Research, since 1978; *b* 21 May 1915; *s* of Chakravarthi V. and Janaki Vijayaraghavachari; *m* 1938, Janaki, *d* of Dr M. T. Chari; two *d*. *Educ:* University of Madras (BA); Oxford (MA). Indian Civil Service, 1936; Dep. Sec., Development Dept, Government of Madras, 1945-48; Min. of Agriculture, Govt of India, 1950-53; Joint Sec., Economic Affairs Dept, Ministry of Finance, 1953-56; Executive Sec., UN Economic Commission for Asia and Far East, 1956-59; Under-Sec. for Special Political Affairs, UN, 1959-62; Chef de Cabinet of the Sec.-Gen., UN, 1961-73; Under-Sec., 1962-67, Under-Sec.-Gen. 1967-69, for Gen. Assembly Affairs, UN; Dep. Administrator, UN Develt Prog., 1969-72; Under-Sec.-Gen. for Inter-Agency Affairs and Co-ordination, UN, 1973-78; Organizing Exec. Sec., Cotton Develt Internat., UN Develt Programme, 1979-81. Hon. Doctor of Laws, Williams Coll. Williamstown, Mass, 1960; Hon. Dr of Humane Letters, Colgate Univ., 1966. *Recreations:* Sanskrit literature, South Indian classical music, tennis. *Address:* 210 East 47th Street, New York, NY 10017, USA. *T:* (212) 355-2092.

NARAYAN, R. K.; Author; *b* Madras, India, 1906. *Educ:* Maharaja's College, Mysore, India. Padma Bushan award for distinguished services to literature. Hon. LittD Leeds, 1967. *Publications: novels:* Swami and Friends, 1935; The Bachelor of Arts, 1937; The Dark Room, 1939; The English Teacher, 1945; Mr Sampath, 1947; The Financial Expert, 1952; Waiting for the Mahatma, 1955; The Guide, 1958; The Man-Eater of Malgudi, 1961; Gods, Demons and Others, 1964; The Sweet Vendor, 1967; The Painter of Signs, 1977; (ed) The Ramayana, 1973; (ed) The Mahabharata, 1978; *autobiography* My Days, 1975; *short stories:* An Astrologer's Day; The Lawley Road; A Horse and Two Goats, 1970, etc; *essays:* Next Sunday, 1955 (India); My Dateless Diary, 1960 (India). *Address:* c/o Anthony Sheil Associates, 2/3 Maxwell Street, WC1B 3AR; Yadavagiri, Mysore 2, India.

NARAYAN, Rudy; barrister-at-law; *b* Guyana, 11 May 1938; *s* of Sase Narayan and Taijbertie (*née* Sawh); *m* 1969, Dr Naseem Akbar; two *d*. *Educ:* Lincoln's Inn. Came to UK, 1953; Served HM Forces, BAOR and HQ MELF, 1958-65. Lincoln's Inn: Founder/1st Pres., Students Union, 1966; Chm. of Debates, and Captain of Cricket, 1967; called to the Bar, 1968. Joined Labour Party, 1970; nominated Parly B List by Streatham Lab. Party, 1974; Mem., Lab. Parly Assoc. Councillor, Lambeth, 1974-76; Vice-Chm., Lambeth Council for Community Relations. Founder Chairman: Lambeth's 1st Community Advice Centre; Lambeth Law Centre; founded Community Law Centres in Birmingham, Manchester, Leeds and Leicester; Founder/Sec., Soc. of Immigrant Lawyers; Sec., Soc. of Black Lawyers; Delegate to Select Cttee on Race Relations, Royal Commn on Legal Services, and Royal Commn on Criminal Procedure. Member: Soc. of Lab. Lawyers; NCCL; Fabian Soc.; Legal Action Gp; Justice. Formerly: Chm. Management Cttee, BBC's Black Londoners; Mem., Race Relations Bd. Legal Officer: London W Indian Standing Conf. (PRO 1980); Mutual Protection Assoc., Birmingham. Legal Adviser: Black People's Inf. Centre, Notting Hill; Notting Hill Carnival Cttee; Melting Pot Youth Foundn, Brixton; Consortium of Ethnic Minorities in Lambeth; West Indian World newspaper (also contributing journalist); Legal Correspondent, Caribbean Times; Fraternal Delegate to: Standing Conf. of Pakistani Orgns, 1980-; Indian Workers Assoc. (GB), 1980-; Chm., Black Rights (UK), 1982-. *Publications:* Black Community on Trial, 1976; Black England, 1977; The Criminal Trial, 1978; contrib. newspapers. *Recreations:* cricket, debating, theatre, ballet, opera. *Address:* 23 Woodbourne Avenue, SW16. *T:* 01-769 0345. *Club:* Albany (Birmingham).

NARJES, Karl-Heinz; Member, Commission of the European Communities, since 1981; *b* 30 Jan. 1924; *s* of Heinrich Narjes; *m* 1951, Eva-Maria Rahe; one *s* one *d*. *Educ:* Hamburg Univ. Entered Foreign Service, 1953; Chef du Cabinet, Pres. of EEC, 1963; Dir-Gen., Press and Inf. Directorate, EEC, 1968-69; Minister of Econs and of Transport, Schleswig-Holstein, 1969-73. Mem., Bundestag, 1972-; Mem., For. Affairs Cttee, 1976-80; Pres., Econ. Affairs Cttee, 1972-76, 1980-. *Address:* 200 rue de la Loi, 1049 Brussels, Belgium.

NASH, (Denis Frederic) Ellison, OBE 1982; FRCS; Consulting Surgeon: St Bartholomew's Hospital; Chailey Heritage Hospital; *b* 10 Feb. 1913; *m* 1938, Joan Mary Andrew; two *s* two *d*. *Educ:* Dulwich College; St Bartholomew's Medical College. MRCS, LRCP, 1935; FRCS 1938. Served war of 1939-45, RAFVR, Wing-Comdr (Air Efficiency Award, 1943). Hunterian Professor, 1949 and 1956. Arris and Gale Lecturer, 1950. Consultant Surgeon: St Bartholomew's Hosp., 1947-78; Chailey Heritage Hosp., 1952-78; Dean, St

Bartholomew's Hospital Medical College, 1957-62; Special Trustee, St Bartholomew's Hosp., 1974-78; Regional Postgraduate Dean, and Asst Dir, British Postgraduate Medical Fedn, Univ. of London, 1948-74. Special interest in the education and care of the physically handicapped; Hon. Med. Adviser: Shaftesbury Soc.; John Groom's Assoc. for Disabled. Senior Member, British Assoc. of Urological Surgeons. Senior Fellow, British Orthopædic Assoc.; Fellow, Assoc. of Surgeons of GB. Hon. Fellow, Med. Artists Assoc. Chm., Dulwich Coll. Preparatory Sch. Trust. *Publications:* The Principles and Practice of Surgery for Nurses and Allied Professions, 1955, 7th revised edn, 1980; scientific papers in medical journals particularly concerned with surgery of childhood. *Recreations:* photography, fuchsias. *Address:* 28 Hawthorne Road, Bickley, Bromley, Kent BR1 2HH. *T:* 01-467 1142. *Club:* City of London Guild of Freemen.

NASH, John Edward; Director, S. G. Warburg & Co. Ltd, since 1977; Chairman, S. G. Warburg Bank AG, Zürich, since 1980 (Director, since 1977; Deputy Chairman, 1977-80); Director: Reckitt & Colman plc, 1966-73 and since 1977; Ailsa Investment Trust plc, since 1981; Chairman: Mercury Money Market Trust Ltd, since 1979; Mercury Far Eastern Trust Ltd, since 1980; *b* 25 June 1925; *s* of Joseph and Madeleine Nash; *m* 1947, Ralda Everard Herring; two *s* two *d*. *Educ:* Univ. of Sydney (BEc); Balliol Coll., Oxford (BPhil). Teaching Fellow in Economics, Sydney Univ., 1947. Exec. Dir, Samuel Montagu & Co. Ltd, 1956; also Director, 1960-73: British Australian Investment Trust; Montagu Trust Ltd; Midland Montagu Industrial Finance Ltd; Capel Court Corp. (in Melb.); resigned all directorships on appt to Brussels, 1973; Dir of Monetary Affairs, EEC, 1973-77. Dir, Oxford Univ. Business Summer Sch., 1965; Research Fellow, Nuffield Coll., Oxford (part-time), 1966-69. Hon. Treasurer, PEP, 1964-73. *Recreations:* golf, skiing, horse-racing, music. *Address:* Chalet Gstelli, 3781 Gsteig bei Gstaad, Switzerland. *T:* (030) 51162. *Clubs:* Turf, Buck's, MCC, University (Sydney).

NASH, Thomas Arthur Manly, CMG 1959; OBE 1944; Dr (Science); retired; *b* 18 June 1905; *s* of late Col L. T. Nash, CMG, RAMC; *m* 1930, Marjorie Wenda Wayte; (one *s* decd). *Educ:* Wellington Coll.; Royal Coll. of Science. Entomologist, Dept Tsetse Research and Reclamation, Tanganyika Territory, 1927; Entomologist, Sleeping Sickness Service, Med. Dept, Nigeria, 1933. Doctorate of Science, 1933. In charge Anchau Rural Development Scheme, 1937-44; seconded as Chief Entomologist, W African Institute for Trypanosomiasis Research, 1948; Deputy Director, WAITR, 1953; Director, 1954-59; Dir, Tsetse Research Lab., Univ. of Bristol, Veterinary Field Station, Langford, 1962-71. *Publications:* Tsetse Flies in British West Africa, 1948; Africa's Bane, The Tsetse Fly, 1969; numerous scientific publications on tsetse and trypanosomiasis. *Recreation:* fishing. *Address:* Spring Head Farm, Upper Langford, near Bristol. *T:* Churchill 852321.

NASH, Ven. Trevor Gifford; Archdeacon of Basingstoke, since 1982; *b* 3 May 1930; *s* of Frederick Walter Gifford Nash and Elsie Violet Louise Nash; *m* 1957, Wanda Elizabeth (*née* Freeston); four *d*. *Educ:* Haileybury College, Hertford; Clare Coll., Cambridge (MA); Cuddesdon Coll., Oxford. Curate: Cheshunt, 1955-57; Kingston-upon-Thames, 1957-61; Priest-in-Charge, Stevenage, 1961-63; Vicar, Leagrave, Luton, 1963-67; Senior Chaplain, St George's Hosp., London, 1967-73; Rector, St Lawrence with St Swithun, Winchester, 1973-82; Priest-in-Charge, Holy Trinity, Winchester, 1977-82; RD of Winchester, 1978-82; Bishop's Adviser for Ministry of Healing, 1973-; Hon. Canon of Winchester, 1980-. RAChD (TA), 1956-67. *Recreations:* clay modelling, music, walking. *Address:* Rivendell, 3 Crossborough Hill, Basingstoke, Hants RG21 2AG. *T:* Basingstoke 28572.

NASHDOM, Abbot of; *see* Weston, Rt Rev. Dom D. W. V.

NASIR, Rt. Rev. Eric Samuel; *b* 7 Dec. 1916. *Educ:* St Stephen's College, Delhi (MA); St Xavier's College, Calcutta (BT); Westcott House, Cambridge; Bishop's College, Calcutta. Warden, St Paul's Hostel, Delhi, 1942-45, 1951-52, 1956-62; Principal, Delhi United Christian School, 1956-62. Vicar: St Andrew's Church, Rewari, 1942-47; St Mary's Church, Ajmer, 1947-49; St James' Church, Delhi, 1949-51; St Thomas' Church, New Delhi, 1953-56; Holy Trinity Church, Delhi, 1952. Chaplain, St Stephen's College, Delhi, 1945-47. Bishop of Delhi, 1970-81; Moderator, Church of N India, 1971-81. Member, Central Committee, World Council of Churches, 1968-81. *Address:* c/o Bishop's House, 1 Church Lane, New Delhi 1. *T:* 387471.

NASMITH; *see* Dunbar-Nasmith.

NATAL, Bishop of, since 1982; **Rt. Rev. Michael Nuttall;** *b* 3 April 1934; *s* of Neville and Lucy Nuttall; *m* 1959, Dorris Marion Meyer; two *s* one *d*. *Educ:* Maritzburg Coll. (matric. 1951); Univ. of Natal (BA 1955); Rhodes Univ. (BA Hons in History 1956). MA (Cantab), MA, DipEd (Oxon), BD Hons (London). Teacher at Westville High Sch., Natal, 1958; Lectr in History, Rhodes Univ., 1959-62; Theological Student, St Paul's Coll., Grahamstown, 1963-64; ordained deacon, 1964, priest 1965; Assistant Priest, Cathedral of St Michael and St George, Grahamstown, 1965-68; Lectr in Ecclesiastical History, Rhodes Univ., 1969-74; Dean of Grahamstown, 1975; Bishop of Pretoria, 1975-81. *Publications:* a chapter on Raymond Raynes in Better Than They Knew, Volume 2 (ed R. M. de Villiers); articles in Dictionary of S African Biography. *Recreations:* walking, tennis, trout fishing. *Address:* Bishop's House, 5 Chaceley Place, Morningside, Durban 4001, South Africa.

NATALI, Lorenzo; politician and lawyer, Italy; a Vice-President, Commission of the European Communities, since 1977; *b* 2 Oct. 1922. *Educ:* Collegio d'Abruzzo dei Padri Gesuiti; Univ. of Florence. MP (Christian Democrat); Under-Secretary of State: for the Press and Information, 1955-57; Min. of Finance, 1957-59; Treasury, 1960-64; Minister: for Merchant Marine, 1966-68; of Public Works, 1968; of Tourism and Entertainments, 1968-69; of Agriculture, 1970-73. *Recreations:* sport, scholasticism. *Address:* 200 rue de la Loi, 1040 Brussels, Belgium; (home) Via Nibby 18, Rome, Italy.

NATHAN, family name of **Baron Nathan.**

NATHAN, 2nd Baron, *cr* 1940; **Roger Carol Michael Nathan;** *b* 5 Dec. 1922; *s* of 1st Baron Nathan, PC, TD, and Eleanor Joan Clara (*d* 1972), *d* of C. Stettauer; *S* father, 1963; *m* 1950, Philippa Gertrude, *d* of Major J. B. Solomon, MC; one *s* two *d. Educ:* Stowe Sch.; New Coll., Oxford (MA). Served War of 1939-45: Capt., 17/21 Lancers (despatches, wounded twice). Admitted Solicitor (Hons), 1950. Associate Member: Bar Assoc. of City of New York; NY County Lawyers' Assoc.; FSA; FRSA; FRGS. Pres., Jewish Welfare Board, 1967-71; Chm., Central British Fund for Jewish Relief and Rehabilitation, 1971-77; Chm. Exec. Cttee, British Empire Cancer Campaign, 1970-75, Hon. Treasurer, 1979-; a Vice-Pres., The Jewish Museum; Chm., Working Party on Energy and the Environment (reported 1974); Vice Chm., Cttee on Charity Law and Practice (reported 1976); Mem., Royal Commn on Environmental Pollution, 1979-. Chm., RSA, 1975-77, Vice-Pres., 1977-. Chm., City Festival of Flowers, 1964; Master, Worshipful Company of Gardeners, 1963-64. *Heir: s* Hon. Rupert Harry Bernard Nathan, *b* 26 May 1957. *Address:* 20 Copthall Avenue, EC2. *T:* 01-628 9611. *TA:* Client, London; Collyers Farm, Lickfold, Petworth, West Sussex. *T:* Lodsworth 284. *TA:* Ronath, Lodsworth. *Clubs:* Athenæum, Cavalry and Guards.

See also Hon. Lady Waley-Cohen.

NATHAN, Sir Maurice (Arnold), KBE 1963 (CBE 1957); *b* Kew, Vic, 17 July 1914; *s* of late Harold B. Nathan, Melbourne; *m* 1942, Margaret Frances, *d* of David McKay; one *s. Educ:* Geelong C of E Gram. Sch. Served War of 1939-45, Capt. AIF. Formerly Chm. and Man. Dir, Patersons (Australia) Ltd and associated cos; Pres., Victorian Industries Confederation, Furnishers Soc. of Victoria and Aust. Retail Furnishers Assoc., 1951-53; Mem. Melbourne City Council, 1952-72; Lord Mayor of Melbourne, 1961-63; Founder and Chm., Victoria Promotion Cttee; Chm., Olympic Park Cttee of Management; Founder and Chairman, Australian World Exposition Project; Pres., Victorian Football League, 1971-77. *Recreations:* gardening, racing, squash, football, tennis, golf. *Address:* c/o Suite 600, 55 Exhibition Street, Melbourne, Vic 3000, Australia. *T:* 63.9384; 25 St Georges Road, Toorak, Vic 3142. *T:* 2412282. *Clubs:* Victoria Amateur Turf, Victoria Racing, Moonee Valley Racing, Melbourne Cricket, Lawn Tennis Assoc. of Vic, Metropolitan Golf.

NATHANS, Prof. Daniel; Professor of Molecular Biology and Genetics, The Johns Hopkins University School of Medicine; *b* 30 Oct. 1928; *s* of Samuel Nathans and Sarah Nathans (*née* Levitan); *m* 1956, Joanne Gomberg; three *s. Educ:* Univ. of Delaware, Newark, Del (BS Chemistry); Washington Univ., St Louis, Mo (MD). Intern, 1954-55, and resident, 1957-59, in Medicine, Columbia-Presbyterian Medical Center, NYC; Clinical Associate, Nat. Cancer Inst., Bethesda, Md, 1955-57; Guest Investigator, Rockefeller Inst., NYC, 1959-62; Prof. of Microbiology, 1962 and Faculty Mem., Johns Hopkins Univ. Sch. of Medicine, Baltimore, Md, 1962-. Nobel Prize in Physiology or Medicine, 1978. *Address:* 2227 Crest Road, Baltimore, Md 21209, USA.

NATWAR-SINGH, Kanwar; Secretary, Ministry of External Affairs, India, since 1982; *b* 16 May 1931; *s* of Govind Singh and Prayag Kaur; *m* 1967, Princess Heminder Kumari, *e d* of Maharaja of Patiala; one *s* one *d. Educ:* St Stephen's Coll., Delhi Univ.; Corpus Christi Coll., Cambridge; Peking Univ. 1st cl. hons History Delhi. Joined Indian Foreign Service, 1953; 3rd Sec., Peking, 1956-58; Adviser, Indian Delegn to UN, NY, 1961-66; Rapporteur, UN Cttee on Decolonisation, 1962-66; Rapporteur, UN Trusteeship Council, 1965; Alt. Deleg. of India to UN Session for 1962; Rep. of India on Exec. Bd of UNICEF, NY, 1962-65; Dep. Sec. to Prime Minister of India, 1966-67; Dir, Prime Minister's Secretariat, New Delhi, 1967-70; Jt Sec. to Prime Minister, 1970-71; Ambassador to Poland, 1971-73; Dep. High Comr in London, 1973-77; High Comr for India in Zambia and Botswana, 1977-80; Ambassador to Pakistan, 1980-82. Attended Commonwealth Heads of Govt Meetings: Jamaica, 1975; Lusaka, 1979; Mem., Commonwealth Cyprus Cttee, 1977; Mem., Indian Deleg. to Zimbabwe Indep. Celebrations, 1980. Hon. Res. Fellow, UCL. *Publications:* E. M. Forster: A Tribute, 1964; The Legacy of Nehru, 1965; Tales from Modern India, 1966; Stories from India, 1971; Maharaja Suraj Mal, 1707-1763, 1981; book reviews for Financial Times. *Recreations:* tennis, reading, writing, good conversations followed by periods of uninterrupted silence. *Address:* Ministry of External Affairs, New Delhi 110011, India. *Clubs:* Garrick, Royal Over-Seas League (Life Mem.); India International Centre (Life Mem.), Gymkhana (Life Mem.) (Delhi).

NAUNTON MORGAN, Sir Clifford; *see* Morgan, Sir C. N.

NAYLOR, Arthur Holden, MSc; FICE; FIMechE; Emeritus Professor; *b* 1897; *er s* of Rev. John and Eunice Naylor; *m* 1925, Edith Riley; one *s* one *d.* RE, 1916-19 and 1940-43; Aeroplane Research under DSIR 1919; engaged on construction of Johore Causeway and Prai Power Station, Malaya,

1921-24; Sir Lawrence Guillemard Service Reservoir, Penang, 1925-29; Severn Barrage Investigation, 1930-31; Lochaber Water Power Scheme, 1931-34; Kenya and Uganda Hydro-Electric Investigations, 1934-35; Research Officer, Institution of Civil Engineers, 1935-38; Professor of Civil Engineering, Queen's University, Belfast, 1938-63; Professor of Civil Engineering, Ahmadu Bello University, Nigeria, 1963-66; Visiting Lecturer, 1966-67, Senior Research Fellow, School of Engineering, 1967-70, University College of Swansea. *Publication:* Siphon Spillways, 1935. *Address:* 2 Hael Lane, Southgate, near Swansea, West Glamorgan.

NAYLOR, Rev. Canon Charles Basil; Chancellor and Canon Residentiary of Liverpool Cathedral, 1956-81; Canon Emeritus, Diocese of Liverpool, since 1981; *b* 29 Oct. 1911; *s* of Charles Henry Naylor and Eva Garforth Naylor. *Educ:* Rugby School; Keble College, Oxford. BA 2nd class Lit. Hum., 1934; MA 1939. Deacon, 1939, priest, 1940, Liverpool; Asst Master, Llandovery Coll., 1935-39; Asst Master, Chaplain and Housemaster, Liverpool College, 1939-43; Chaplain RNVR, 1943-46, East Indies Station and Fleet. Curate, St Peter le Bailey Oxford, 1946-56; Chaplain of St Peter's Coll., 1946-56, Dean, 1946-52, Fellow, 1950-56; Tutor in Theology, 1952-56. Examining Chaplain: to Bishop of Blackburn, 1951-; and to Bishop of Liverpool, 1954-; Senior Proctor of Univ. of Oxford, 1952-53. Exchanged duties with Dean of Christchurch, New Zealand, Dec. 1960-April 1961. Dir of Ordination Candidates and Dir of Post-Ordination Training, Liverpool dio., 1956-72; Dir of In-service Trng, Liverpool dio., 1973-81. Librarian, Radcliffe Library, Liverpool Cathedral, 1958-81. Mem., Liturgical Commn, 1962-66. Trustee, St Peter's Coll., Oxford, 1971-. *Publications:* Why Prayer Book Revision at all, 1964; contrib. Theological Collections: The Eucharist Then and Now, 1968; Ground for Hope, 1968; contrib. Arias of J. S. Bach, 1977; (ed) Front Line Praying, 1981. *Recreations:* music, walking. *Address:* 50 Park Road, Rugby, Warwickshire CV21 2QH. *Clubs:* National Liberal; Athenæum (Liverpool).

NAYLOR, Prof. Ernest, PhD, DSc; FIBiol; Lloyd Roberts Professor of Zoology, University College of North Wales, Bangor, since 1982; *b* 19 May 1931; *s* of Joseph and Evelyn Naylor; *m* 1956, Carol Gillian Bruce; two *d. Educ:* Univ. of Sheffield (BSc); Univ. of Liverpool (PhD, DSc). FIBiol 1972. Successively Asst Lectr, Lectr, Sen. Lectr and Reader in Zoology, University Coll. of Swansea, Wales, 1956-71; Prof. of Marine Biology, Univ. of Liverpool, 1971-82. Vis. Professor: Duke Univ., USA, 1969, 1970; Univ. of Otago, NZ, 1982. *Publications:* British Marine Isopods, 1972; (co-ed with R. G. Hartnoll) Cyclic Phenomena in Marine Plants and Animals, 1979; over 70 papers in learned jls. *Recreations:* gardening, theatre. *Address:* School of Animal Biology, University College of North Wales, Bangor, Gwynedd LL57 2DG. *T:* Bangor 51151.

NAYLOR, (Gordon) Keith, TD 1973; a Recorder of the Crown Court, since 1980; *b* 26 Feb. 1933; *yr s* of late Henry and Elizabeth Naylor, Hoylake; *m* 1962, Anthea Laverock, *d* of late G. E. Shaw and Mrs Elizabeth Douglas; two *s. Educ:* Wallasey Grammar Sch.; Univ. of Liverpool (Grotius Prize, 1953; LLB 1955). Called to the Bar, Gray's Inn, 1957; in practice on Northern Circuit, 1957-. National Service, Cheshire Regt, 1955-57 (commnd, 1956); served TA, 4th and 4th/7th Bns Cheshire Regt, 1957-70; Lt-Col, comd Liverpool Univ. OTC, 1975-78 (Jubilee Medal); TA Col, HQ NW Dist, 1979-80. *Publications:* book revs and articles in legal pubns. *Address:* 1 Exchange Flags, Liverpool L2 3XN. *T:* 051-236 7747; Hantsport, Lightfoot Lane, Gayton, Wirral, Merseyside L60 2TP. *T:* 051-342 6739. *Clubs:* Athenæum (Liverpool); Border and County (Carlisle).

NAYLOR, Prof. Malcolm Neville, RD 1967; BSc, BDS, PhD; FDSRCS; Professor of Preventive Dentistry, University of London, since 1970; Head of Department of Periodontology and Preventive Dentistry, Guy's Hospital, since 1980; *b* 30 Jan. 1926; *er s* of late Roland B. Naylor, MBE and Mabel L. (*née* Neville), Walsall, Staffs; *m* 1956, Doreen Mary, *d* of late H. E. Jackson, CBE; one *s. Educ:* Queen Mary's Grammar Sch., Walsall; Univ. of Glasgow; Univ. of Birmingham (BSc 1951, BDS 1955; Nuffield Scholar, 1949-51); Univ. of London (PhD 1963). FDSRCS 1958. Hosp. appts, Birmingham and Dundee, 1955-59; Guy's Hosp. Dental School: Res. Fellow, 1959-62; Sen. Lectr in Preventive Dentistry, 1962-66; Reader in Preventive Dentistry, 1966-70; Hon. Consultant Dental Surgeon, Guy's Hosp., 1966-. William Waldorf Astor Fellow, USA, 1963. Hon. Treasurer, British Div., IADR. Served RNVR and RNR, retiring as Surg. Captain (D), 1943-76; Hon. Dental Surgeon to the Queen, 1976; Hon. Col, Univ. of London OTC, 1978-; Sec., COMEC, 1978-; Chairman: Mil. Educn Cttee, Univ. of London, 1979-; Sea Cadet Assoc., Sports Council, 1976-. Governor: Roehampton Inst. for Higher Educn, 1978-; Whitelands Coll., 1975-; Bacons Sch., Bermondsey, 1979- (Vice Chm., 1981-). Lay Reader, C of E, 1974-. *Publications:* papers and articles in prof. and scientific jls. *Recreations:* sailing, music, restoring church organs. *Address:* Carrick Lodge, Roehampton, SW15 5BN. *T:* 01-788 5045. *Clubs:* Royal Society of Medicine; Royal Solent Yacht, Yarmouth Sailing.

NAYLOR, Maurice; *see* Naylor, W. M.

NAYLOR, Peter Brian; Controller, European Division, British Council, since 1978; *b* 10 July 1933; *s* of Eric Sydney Naylor and Phyllis Marian Jolly; *m* 1958, Barbara Pearson; three *s* one *d. Educ:* Grange High Sch., Bradford; Selwyn Coll., Cambridge (Open Exhibnr; BA 1957). Wool Top Salesman, Hirsch, Son & Rhodes, Bradford, 1957; British Council: Asst Rep., Bangkok,

1959; Courses Dept and E Europe Dept, London, 1962; Asst Rep., Warsaw, 1967; Reg. Rep., Dacca, E Pakistan, 1969; Actg Rep., Athens, 1971; Rep., Argentina, 1972, Brazil, 1975. *Recreations:* painting, music, books, games. *Address:* Cheston, London Road, Great Chesterford, near Saffron Walden, Essex CB10 1NY. *T:* Saffron Walden 30408.

NAYLOR, (William) Maurice, CBE 1973; FHA; JP; Director, National Association of Health Authorities, since 1981; *b* 1920; *s* of late Thomas Naylor; *m* 1948, Maureen Ann, *d* of John Walsh; one *s* two *d. Educ:* St Joseph's Coll., Market Drayton; Manchester Univ. (BA Admin). FHA 1956. Asst Sec., Manchester Regional Hosp. Bd, 1955-57; Dep. Sec., Sheffield Regional Hosp. Bd, 1957-63, Sec., 1963-73; Regional Administrator, Trent RHA, 1973-81. Pres., IHSA, 1975-76. Hon. MBA Sheffield, 1982. *Address:* 9 Derriman Close, Sheffield S11 9LB.

NAYLOR-LEYLAND, Sir Vivyan (Edward), 3rd Bt, *cr* 1895; *b* 5 March 1924; *e s* of Sir Edward Naylor-Leyland, 2nd Bt, and Marguerite Helene (*d* 1945), 2nd *d* of late Baron de Belabre; *S* father 1952; *m* 1st, 1952, Elizabeth Anne (marr. diss. 1960), *yr d* of 2nd Viscount FitzAlan of Derwent, OBE; one *s*; 2nd, 1967, Starr Anker-Simmons (marr. diss. 1975); one *d*; 3rd, 1980, Jameina F. Reid, *d* of James Freeman Reid, High Park, Co. Offaly, Eire. *Educ:* Eton; Christ Church, Oxford; Royal Agricultural Coll., Cirencester. Grenadier Guards, 1942-47. *Heir: s* Philip Vyvyan Naylor-Leyland [*b* 9 August 1953; *m* 1980, Lady Isabella Lambton, *d* of Antony Lambton, *qv*; one *s*]. *Address:* 6 Harbour Mews, Nassau, Bahamas. *T:* Nassau 77523. *Club:* White's (overseas mem.).

NEAGLE, Dame Anna, (Dame Marjorie Wilcox), DBE 1969 (CBE 1952); Hon. Vice-President, FANY Corps, 1972 (Hon. Ensign 1950); actress, producer; Member: Executive Council, King George VI Memorial Foundation; Council Edith Cavell Homes of Rest for Nurses; Council, King George's Pension Fund for Actors and Actresses; Vice-President, Forces Help Society; *b* Forest Gate, Essex; *d* of late Captain Herbert William Robertson, RNR, and Florence Neagle Robertson; *m* 1943, Herbert Wilcox, CBE (*d* 1977). *Educ:* High School, St Albans, Herts; Wordsworth's Physical Training College. Theatre Royal, Drury Lane, Charlot and Cochran revues, London and New York, 1926-30; Stand up and Sing, with Jack Buchanan, 1931; Open Air Theatre—Rosalind and Olivia, 1934; Peter Pan, 1937; Jane Austen's Emma, 1944-45; *later plays include:* The Glorious Days, Palace Theatre, 1952-53; The More the Merrier, Strand, 1960; Person Unknown, 1964; Charlie Girl, Adelphi, 1965-71, Aust. and NZ presentation 1971-72; No, No, Nanette, Drury Lane, 1973; The Dame of Sark, Duke of York's and O'Keefe Centre, Toronto, 1975; The First Mrs Fraser; Maggie, Shaftesbury, 1977; Most Gracious Lady, 1978; Relative Values, 1978 (Vienna); Nat. tour, My Fair Lady, 1979, Adelphi, 1980, Canada tour, 1980, 1981, 1982. Has appeared in plays on television. *Films:* Good Night, Vienna, 1931; Bitter Sweet, 1933; Nell Gwyn, 1934; Peg of Old Drury, 1935; Victoria The Great, 1937; Sixty Glorious Years, 1938; Hollywood: Edith Cavell, 1939; Irene, No, No, Nanette, Sunny, 1939-40; England: They Flew Alone, 1941; Yellow Canary, 1943; I Live in Grosvenor Square, 1944; Piccadilly Incident, 1946; The Courtneys of Curzon Street, 1947; Spring in Park Lane, Elizabeth of Ladymead, 1948; Maytime in Mayfair, 1949; Odette, 1950; The Lady With The Lamp, 1951; Derby Day, 1951; Lilacs in the Spring, 1954; King's Rhapsody, 1955; My Teenage Daughter, 1956; No Time for Tears, 1957; The Man Who Wouldn't Talk, 1957; The Lady is a Square, 1958. *Produced:* These Dangerous Years, 1957; Wonderful Things, 1958; Heart of a Man, 1959. Has received numerous awards both international and national. *Publication:* There's Always Tomorrow (autobiog.), 1974, rev. edn 1979. *Recreations:* walking, travel, reading. *Address:* 117b Hamilton Terrace, NW8. *Club:* FANY Regimental.

NEAL, Prof. Bernard George, MA, PhD, ScD; Professor of Civil Engineering, Imperial College of Science and Technology, since 1981; *b* 29 March 1922; *s* of late Horace Bernard Neal, Wembley, and Hilda Annie Webb; *m* 1948, Elizabeth Ann, *d* of late William George Toller, Woodbridge, and Bertha Catharine Toller; one *s* one *d. Educ:* Merchant Taylors'; Trinity College, Cambridge (Schol.). MA Cantab, 1947; PhD Cantab 1948; ScD Cantab 1965; FInstCE 1960; FIStructE 1966; FEng 1980. Temp. Experimental Officer, Admiralty, 1942-45; Research Student, Univ. of Cambridge, 1945-48; Research Associate, Brown University, USA, 1948-49; Demonstrator, 1949-51, Lecturer, 1951-54, Univ. of Cambridge; Research Fellow, 1947-50, Staff Fellow, 1950-54, Trinity Hall, Cambridge; Prof. of Civil Engineering, University Coll. of Swansea, 1954-61; Imperial College, London: Prof. of Applied Science (with special reference to Engineering), 1961-72; Prof. of Engineering Structures, 1972-81; Head of Civil Engrg Dept, 1976-82; Pro-Rector, 1972-74. Dean of City and Guilds Coll., 1964-67; Visiting Prof., Brown Univ., USA, 1959-60. Underwriting Mem. of Lloyd's, 1977. Telford Premium, 1951, Manby Premium, 1952, Instn Civil Engineers. *Publications:* The Plastic Methods of Structural Analysis, 1956; Structural Theorems and their Applications, 1964; technical papers on theory of structures, strength of materials. *Recreations:* lawn tennis, croquet. *Address:* Imperial College of Science and Technology, South Kensington, SW7. *T:* 01-589 5111.

NEAL, Sir Eric (James), Kt 1982; CEng, FInstE; Director and Chief Executive, Boral Ltd, since 1973; *b* 3 June 1924; *s* of James and May Neal; *m* 1950, Thelma Joan, *d* of R. E. Bowden; two *s. Educ:* Adelaide Univ.; South Australian Sch. of Mines and Industries. CEng, MIGasE; FInstE. Works Engr,

Broken Hill Gas Co., NSW, 1950, Manager 1956; Manager, Ballarat Gas Co., Vic, 1959; Asst Gen. Man., Boral Gas Ltd, 1963, Chief Gen. Man., Sydney, 1970; Chief Gen. Man. and Dir, Boral Gp, 1972. Director: Wormald Internat. Ltd, 1977-; Oil Co. of Australia NL, 1982-; Australian Inst. of Petroleum, 1977-. Mem., Defence Review Cttee, 1981- (apptd by Prime Minister of Australia to review Australia's Higher Defence Orgn). *Recreations:* horse racing, motor boating. *Address:* 93 Pentecost Avenue, St Ives, NSW 2075, Australia. *T:* 02/44 2122. *Clubs:* Union, Australasian Pioneers, American National (Sydney); Queensland Turf (Brisbane).

NEAL, Frederick Albert, FIL; Assistant Secretary, Department of Trade, since 1980; *b* 22 Dec. 1932; *s* of Frederick William George Neal and Frances Elizabeth (*née* Duke); *m* 1958, Gloria Maria Moirano. *Educ:* Royal Grammar Sch., High Wycombe; Birkbeck Coll., London (BA). FIL 1965. Min. of Supply, 1953; Asst Defence Supply Attaché, Bonn, 1958-64; Principal, Min. of Technology (subseq. DTI), 1967; Asst Sec., DTI, 1974; Counsellor (Economic and Commercial), Ottawa, 1975-80. *Recreations:* golf, bridge, music. *Address:* 70 Greenway, Totteridge, N20. *Clubs:* Naval and Military, Royal Over-Seas League; South Herts Golf.

NEAL, Harry Morton; Managing Director, Harry Neal Ltd, since 1963; *b* 21 Nov. 1931; *s* of Godfrey French Neal and late Janet Bryce Morton; *m* 1954, Cecilia Elizabeth Crawford, *d* of late Col M. Crawford, DSO; one *s* three *d. Educ:* Uppingham Sch.; London Univ. (BSc(Eng)); City and Guilds Coll. (ACGI). Flying Officer, RAF, 1953. Chm., Connaught Hotel Ltd, 1980-; Dir, Savoy Hotel Ltd, 1982-. Member of Lloyd's. Chm., City and Guilds of London Inst., 1979-; Mem., Technician Educn Council, 1982-. Liveryman, Carpenters' Co., 1955-. FCIOB, FRSA. Chevalier de Tastevin, 1981. *Recreations:* gardening, shooting. *Address:* Great Sarratt Hall, Sarratt, near Rickmansworth, Herts. *T:* Kings Langley 64321.

NEAL, Sir Leonard (Francis), Kt 1974; CBE 1971; FCIT; Industrial Relations Consultant to number of industrial and commercial companies; *b* 27 Aug. 1913; *s* of Arthur Henry Neal and Mary Neal; *m* 1939, Mary Lilian Puttock; one *s* one *d. Educ:* London School of Economics; Trinity College, Cambridge (MA). Labour Manager, Esso, 1956; Employee Relations Manager, Fawley Refinery, 1961; Labour Relations Adviser, Esso Europe Inc. Mem., British Railways Board, 1967-71; Chm., Commn on Industrial Relations, 1971-74. Prof. (part-time) of Industrial Relations, UMIST, 1970-76; Chairman: MAT Transport International Gp Ltd, 1974-; Employment Conditions Abroad Ltd; Dir (non-exec.), Pilkington Bros, 1976-; Dir (non-exec.), Rosgill Holdings Ltd, 1980-. *Publication:* (with A. Robertson) The Managers Guide to Industrial Relations. *Recreations:* reading, gardening, motoring. *Address:* Brightling, Sussex. *Club:* Institute of Directors.

NEAL, Michael David; Headmaster, Cranborne Chase School, since 1969; *b* 27 Jan. 1927; *s* of David Neal, FCA; *m* 1952, Barbara Lisette, *d* of late Harold Carter, MA; two *s* two *d. Educ:* Winchester; University Coll., Oxford (BA). Rifle Bde, 1945-48 (Captain); Asst Master, RNC Dartmouth, 1952-54; Eton Coll., 1954-69 (Housemaster, 1963-69). Mem., Eton UDC, 1960-63. *Address:* Wardour Castle, Tisbury, Salisbury, Wilts. *T:* Tisbury 870464.

NEALE, Sir Alan (Derrett), KCB 1972 (CB 1968); MBE 1945; Member, since 1981, and a Deputy Chairman, since 1982, Monopolies and Mergers Commission; Director, Borthwicks, since 1979; *b* 24 Oct. 1918; *o* s of late W. A. Neale; *m* 1956, Joan, *o d* of late Harry Frost, Wisbech; one *s. Educ:* Highgate School; St John's College, Oxford. War Service, Intelligence Corps, 1940-45. Board of Trade, 1946-68; Second Sec., 1967; Dep. Sec., Treasury, 1968-71, Second Permanent Sec., 1971-72; Perm. Sec., MAFF, 1973-78. Commonwealth Fund Fellowship, USA, 1952-53; Fellow of Center for Internat. Affairs, Harvard Univ., 1960-61. *Publications:* The Anti-Trust Laws of the USA, 1960; The Flow of Resources from Rich to Poor, 1961. *Recreations:* music, bridge. *Address:* 95 Swains Lane, N6 6PJ. *T:* 01-340 5236. *Club:* Reform.

NEALE, Gerrard Anthony; MP (C) North Cornwall, since 1979; *b* 25 June 1941; *s* of Charles Woodhouse Neale and Phyllis Muriel Neale; *m* 1965, Deirdre Elizabeth McCann; one *s* two *d. Educ:* Bedford Sch. Articled to solicitors, Bedford, 1961; admitted 1966; established Gerrard Neale Fennemore & Co., Solicitors, Milton Keynes, 1966. Founder Dir, Woburn Chemicals Ltd, 1968; Dir, Telephone Rentals, 1979.- Councillor, Borough of Milton Keynes, 1973-79; Mayor, 1976-77. Founder Patron, Milton Keynes City Forum, 1977-; Chm., Milton Keynes Area Crime Prevention Panel, 1978. Chm., Buckingham Constituency Cons. Assoc., 1974-76. Contested (C) N Cornwall, Oct. 1974; PPS to Minister for Consumer Affairs, 1981-82, to Minister of State for Trade, 1981-. Mem. Court, Cranfield Inst. of Technology. *Recreations:* sailing, tennis. *Address:* The Manor, Woughton on the Green, Milton Keynes. *T:* Milton Keynes 679532.

NEALE, Rt. Rev. John Robert Geoffrey; *see* Ramsbury, Bishop Suffragan of.

NEALE, Kenneth James, OBE 1959; FSA; author and lecturer; Assistant Under Secretary of State, Home Office, 1976-82; *b* 9 June 1922; *s* of late James Edward and Elsie Neale; *m* 1943, Dorothy Willett; three *s* one *d. Educ:* Hackney Downs (Grocers') Sch., London. Entered Civil Service as Clerical Officer, Tithe Redemption Commn, 1939. Lieut, RNVR, 1941-46. Exec. Officer, Min. of Nat. Insce, 1947-51; Asst Princ., 1951-55, Principal, 1955-64,

Colonial Office; Sec. for Interior and Local Govt, Cyprus, 1957; Dep. Admin Sec., Cyprus, 1958–59; Central African Office, 1962–64; Asst Sec., Commonwealth Office, Diplomatic Service, 1964–67; Home Office: Asst Sec., 1967–70; Dir, Industries and Supply, 1970–75; Controller, Planning and Devel, 1976–80; Dir, Regimes and Services, 1980–82. Member: Prisons Bd, 1967–69, 1976–82; European Cttee on Crime Problems, 1976–; Chairman: Council of Europe Select Cttee on Standard Minimum Rules for Treatment of Prisoners, 1978–80; Council of Europe Cttee for Co-operation in Prison Affairs, 1981–. *Publications:* Discovering Essex in London, 1970; Victorian Horsham, 1975; Work in Penal Institutions, 1976; Essex in History, 1977; Her Majesty's Commissioners, 1978; various articles and papers on local history and natural history. *Recreations:* reading, local history, natural history. *Address:* The Forge Cottage, West Chiltington, West Sussex. *T:* West Chiltington 3410.

NEALE, Michael Cooper, CEng, FIMechE, FRAeS; Director General Engines (Procurement Executive), Ministry of Defence, since 1980; *b* 2 Dec. 1929; *s* of Frank and Edith Kathleen Neale; *m* 1956, Thelma Weare; one *s* two *d*. *Educ:* West Bridgford Grammar Sch., Nottingham; Queen Mary Coll., Univ. of London (BScEng, MScEng). Postgraduate research on fuel injection in diesel engines, 1951–53; Engr Officer, Royal Air Force, 1953–56; joined Civil Service, 1956; Aeroplane and Armament Experimental Estabt, Boscombe Down, 1956–58; joined Nat. Gas Turbine Estabt, Pyestock, 1958; Asst Director of Engine Develt, MoD Headquarters, 1971; Dep. Director (R&D), Nat. Gas Turbine Estabt, 1973–80. *Publications:* papers in Aeronautical Research Council reports and memoranda series and elsewhere in the technical press, mainly concerning engines. *Recreations:* old railways, cricket. *Address:* 108 Wargrave Road, Twyford, Reading, Berks RG10 9PJ. *T:* Twyford 341759.

NEALON, Dr Catherina Theresa, (Rina), CBE 1979; JP; Chairman, Lothian Health Board, 1973–81; *d* of John and Margaret O'Reilly, Glasgow; *m* 1940, James Patrick Nealon; one *s*. *Educ:* Convent of Mercy, Garnethill, Glasgow. Mem., Edinburgh Town Council for Pilton Ward, 1949–74; served as Magistrate, 1954–57; Licensing Court, 1954–57; Judge of Police, 1957–62; Chm., Health Cttee, 1972–73. Member: Educn Cttee, Civil Defence Commn, 1949–73; Royal Infirmary and Associated Hosp's Bd of Management, 1952–56; NHS Exec. Council for City of Edinburgh, 1953–74 (Vice-Chm., May 1966–74); Exec. Cttee of Scottish Assoc. of Exec. Councils, 1967–74 (Vice-Pres., 1971, Pres., 1972); SE Regional Hosp. Bd, Scotland, 1966–74 (Chm., 1969–74); Med. Educn Cttee, 1969–74 (Chm., 1972–74); Scottish Health Service Planning Council, 1974–81; Common Services Agency, Management Cttee, and Convenor, Estabt and Accommodation Sub-Cttee, Scottish Health Service, 1974–77; Univ. Liaison Cttee, 1974– (Chm., 1978–81); Edinburgh and SE District Cttee, Scottish Gas Consultative Council, 1967–74 (Chm., 1970–74; Mem. Council, 1969–74); Clean Air Council for Scotland, 1966–75; Nat. Soc. for Clean Air, Scottish Div., 1963– (Vice-Pres., 1970–72, Pres., 1972–74); A&C Whitley Council, 1973–81 (Vice-Chm., 1975–81); Nat. Negotiating Cttee; Ambulance Officers' Negotiating Cttee (Management Side Chm., 1979–81); Gen. Whitley Council (Mem., Gen. Purposes Cttee and Jt Negotiating Cttee, 1980–); Nat. Appeals Panel; Chm., Scottish Hosp. Supplies Steering Cttee, 1972–74. Former Member: Edin. and Lothian Probation Cttee; Animal Disease Res. Assoc.; Marriage Guidance Council; Nat. Assoc. for Maternal and Child Welfare; Nat. Council on recruitment of Nurses and Midwives; Scottish Assoc. for Mental Health; Assoc. of Sea and Airport Authorities; Edin. and Lothians Tourist Assoc.; Youth Employment Cttee; Extra-Mural Cttee, Edin. Univ., 1960–65; Mem. Bd of Governors: Napier Coll. of Science and Technology, 1964–73 (Vice-Chm., 1971–73); Telford Coll. for Further Education, 1969–72; Moray House Coll. of Educn; Wellington Farm Approved Sch.; Dr Guthrie's Girls' Sch. JP Edinburgh, 1957; Mem. Justices Cttee, 1975; Justice on District Court, 1975; Mem. Extra-Parliamentary Panel, 1976. Attended 25th Anniv. Meeting, President's Cttee on Employment of Handicapped, Washington, 1972. Travelled to many countries with Internat. Hosp. Fedn study tours. Member, Church of Scotland. Dr *hc* Edinburgh, 1977. *Recreations:* dancing, dressmaking. *Address:* 34 Learmonth Crescent, Edinburgh EH4 1DE.

NEAME, Captain Douglas Mortimer Lewes, DSO 1940, Bar 1942; RN retired; *b* Oct. 1901; *s* of late Douglas John Neame; *m* 1937, Elizabeth Ogilvy Carnegy; one *s* two *d*. *Educ:* RN Colleges, Osborne and Dartmouth. Served European War, 1917–19; Fleet Air Arm, 1927–31; Commander, 1936; Capt. 1940. Commanded HM Ships Carlisle and Vengeance in War of 1939–45; Commodore 2nd Class, 1947–50; retd 1950. Member of Olympic Team, Amsterdam, 1928, British Empire Games, Canada, 1930. Vice-Patron AAA; Vice-Pres. LAC. *Recreation:* gardening. *Address:* de Vaux Lodge, Salisbury, Wilts. *Clubs:* Naval; Milocarian, London Athletic.

NEAME, Mrs Humphrey; see Monroe, E.

NEAME, Ronald; film producer and director; *b* 23 Apr. 1911; *s* of Elwin Neame and Ivy Close; *m* 1933, Beryl Yolanda Heanly; one *s*. *Educ:* University College School; Hurstpierpoint College. Entered film industry, 1928; became Chief Cameraman, 1934. In charge of production on: In Which We Serve, This Happy Breed, Blithe Spirit, Brief Encounter, 1942–45; produced: Great Expectations, Oliver Twist, The Magic Box; directed: Take My Life, The Card, 1945–51; The Million Pound Note, 1953; The Man Who Never Was, 1954; Windom's Way, 1957; The Horse's Mouth, 1958; Tunes of Glory, 1960; I Could Go On Singing, 1962; The Chalk Garden, 1963; Mr Moses, 1964;

Gambit, 1966; The Prime of Miss Jean Brodie, 1968; Scrooge, 1970; The Poseidon Adventure, 1972; Odessa File, 1973; Meteor, 1978; Hopscotch, 1979; First Monday in October, 1980. *Address:* c/o Hutton Management Ltd, 194 Old Brompton Road, SW5 0AS. *Club:* Savile.

NEARY, Martin Gerard James; Organist and Master of Music, Winchester Cathedral, since 1972; Organ Recitalist and Conductor; Founder and Conductor, Martin Neary Singers, since 1972; Conductor, Waynflete Singers, since 1972; *b* 28 March 1940; *s* of Leonard Walter Neary and Jeanne Marguerite (*née* Thébault); *m* 1967, Penelope Jane, *d* of Sir Brian Warren, *qv*, and Dame A. J. M. T. Barnes, *qv*; one *s* two *d*. *Educ:* HM Chapels Royal, St James's Palace; City of London Sch.; Gonville and Caius Coll., Cambridge (Organ Schol., MA). FRCO. St Margaret's, Westminster: Asst Organist, 1963–65; Organist and Master of Music, 1965–71; Prof. of Organ, Trinity Coll., London, 1963–72. Organ Advr to dio. of Winchester, 1975–. Conductor, Twickenham Musical Soc., 1966–72; Founder and Conductor, St Margaret's Westminster Singers, 1967–71; Dir, Southern Cathedrals Festival, 1972, 1975, 1978, 1981, 1982. Mem. Council, RCO, 1982–. Many organ recitals and broadcasts in UK, incl. Royal Festival Hall and music festivals; has conducted many premières of music by British composers incl. John Taverner's Ultimos Ritos, 1979, Jonathan Harvey's Hymn, 1979, and Passion and Resurrection, 1981; with Martin Neary Singers perf. madrigals and graces at 10 Downing Street, 1970–74. Toured US and Canada, 1963, 1968, 1971, 1973, 1975, 1977, 1979; BBC Promenade Concerts, 1979, 1982; Conductor with: ECO, 1978, 1980, 1981; LSO, 1979, 1980, 1981; Bournemouth SO and Sinfonietta, 1975–; many European tours and recordings. Hon. FTCL, 1969. Hon. Citizen of Texas, 1971. Prizewinner, St Alban's Internat. Organ Festival, 1963; Conducting Scholarship, Berkshire Music Center, USA, 1963; Diploma, J. S. Bach Competn, Leipzig, 1968; UK/USA Bicentennial Fellow, 1979–80. *Publications:* edns of early organ music; contribs to organ jls. *Recreation:* watching cricket. *Address:* 10 The Close, Winchester, Hants. *T:* Winchester 4392.

NEAVE, Sir Arundell Thomas Clifton, 6th Bt, *cr* 1795; JP; late Major Welsh Guards; *b* 31 May 1916; *e s* of Col Sir Thomas Lewis Hughes Neave, 5th Bt, and Dorina (*d* 1955) (author of 26 years on the Bosphorus, Remembering Kut, 1937, Romance of the Bosphorus, 1950), *d* of late George H. Clifton; *S* father, 1940; *m* 1946, Richenda, *o c* of Sir Robert J. Paul, 5th Bt; two *s* two *d*. *Educ:* Eton. Served in 1939–45 war, Welsh Guards (Major); Dunkirk, 1940, retired 1947. JP for Anglesey, 1950. *Heir: s* Paul Arundell Neave [*b* 13 December 1948; *m* 1976, Coralie Jane Louise, *e d* of Sir Robert Kinahan, *qv*; one *s*. *Address:* Greatham Moor, Liss, Hants. *Clubs:* Carlton, Pratt's.
See also Sir Richard Williams-Bulkeley.

NEAVE, Julius Arthur Sheffield, CBE 1978 (MBE (mil.) 1948); JP; General Manager, since 1966, Director since 1977, Mercantile & General Reinsurance Co. Ltd (Managing Director, 1980–82); Director, Prudential Corporation plc, since 1982; *b* 19 July 1919; *s* of Col Richard Neave and Helen Mary Elizabeth (*née* Miller); *m* 1951, Joseph Margery, *d* of Col P. M. Acton-Adams, DSO, Clarence Reserve, Marlborough, NZ; three *d*. *Educ:* Sherborne School. Joined Mercantile & General Reinsurance Co. Ltd, 1938. Served War, 1939–46: called as Territorial, commnd 13th/18th Royal Hussars, Adjt 3 years, final rank Major (despatches 1945). Returned to Mercantile & General, 1946; Asst Gen. Manager, 1964. (First) Chairman, Reinsurance Offices Assoc., 1969–74, Hon. Pres., 1974–; Chm., Reinsurance Panel, British Insce Assoc., 1971–; representative, Gt Britain: Cttee, annual internat. meeting of reinsurers, Monte Carlo, 1969–; Vice-Pres., Assoc. Internat. pour l'Etude de l'Assurance, Geneva, 1976–. Dir and Governor, Internat. Insce Seminars, 1977– (Founder's Gold Medal, 1977); Pres., Insce Inst. of London, 1976–77; Mem. Council, Chartered Insce Inst., 1975–; Mem. Court, Insurers' Co., 1979–. Hon. Fellow, RSA, 1975. JP (Brentwood) Essex, 1975. *Recreations:* shooting, fishing, golf, tennis. *Address:* Mill Green Park, Ingatestone, Essex CM4 0JB. *T:* Ingatestone 3036. *Club:* Cavalry and Guards.

NEAVE AIREY, family name of **Baroness Airey of Abingdon.**

NEEDHAM, family name of **Earl of Kilmorey.**

NEEDHAM, Dorothy Mary Moyle, ScD Cantab; FRS 1948; Research Worker, Biochemical Laboratory, Cambridge, 1920–63; Foundation Fellow, Lucy Cavendish Collegiate Society, University of Cambridge, 1965, Emeritus Fellow, 1966; *b* London, 22 Sept. 1896; *d* of John Moyle and Ellen Daves; *m* 1924, Joseph Needham, *qv*; no *c*. *Educ:* Claremont Coll., Stockport; Girton Coll., Cambridge (Hon. Fellow, 1976). Research for DSIR, 1920–24; Gamble Prize, 1924; Beit Meml Research Fellow, 1925–28. Specialised in biochemistry of muscle, carbohydrate metabolism and phosphorylations; carried out research and teaching at Cambridge and in laboratories in USA, France, Germany, Belgium, etc., 1928–40; Research Worker for Ministry of Supply (Chemical Defence), 1940–43; Chemical Adviser and Acting Director, Sino-British Science Cooperation Office, Chungking, China, 1944–45; Research Worker for MRC 1946–52; Research grant from Broodbank Fund, Univ. of Cambridge, 1952–55; Research Worker for ARC, 1955–62; Foulerton Gift Donation, Royal Society, 1961–62; Leverhulme Award, 1963. Hon. Fellow, Gonville and Caius Coll., Cambridge, 1979. *Publications:* Biochemistry of Muscle, 1932; Science Outpost (ed jtly), 1948; Machina Carnis: the biochemistry of muscle contraction in its historical development, 1971; Source-Book in the History of Biochemistry 1740 to 1940, 1983; numerous original papers in biochemical journals and Proc. Royal Soc. *Address:* 42 Grange Road, Cambridge CB3 9DG. *T:* Cambridge 352183.

NEEDHAM, Prof. John, MA (Sheffield); FRIBA, DipArch (Leeds); Professor of Architecture, The University, Sheffield, 1957-72, now Professor Emeritus; *b* 2 April 1909; British; *s* of P. Needham; *m* 1934, Bessie Grange; three *d. Educ:* Belle Vue Grammar School, Bradford; Leeds School of Architecture. Diploma in Architecture, Leeds, 1931; ARIBA 1931, FRIBA 1948; RIBA; Alfred Bossom Silver Medal, 1937; Alfred Bossom Gold Medal, 1938; Soane Medal, 1938; Athens Bursar, 1949. Head, Dundee School of Architecture, 1938-57. 1st Premium in Open Architectural Competition for new County Buildings, Cupar, Fife, 1947. Mem. Amenity Cttee set up by Sec. of State for Scotland under Hydro Electric (Scotland) Development Acts, 1956-81. Hon. Editor, Quarterly Jl of Royal Incorporation of Architects in Scotland, 1946-50. *Address:* 16 Ferndene Court, Moor Road South, Gosforth, Newcastle upon Tyne NE3 1NN.

NEEDHAM, Commissioner John Edward Dunmore; National Commander of The Salvation Army in the USA, since 1982; *b* 13 July 1917; *s* of Major Walter Needham and Major Miriam Needham; *m* 1935, Florence E. M. Jolly; three *s* one *d. Educ:* Alabama, USA. Member: Nat. Assoc. of Social Workers; Acad. of Certified Social Workers. Salvation Army Officer, 1939-, serving in pastoral work, youth work, training work, public relations, senior administrative positions; has had charge of Salvation Army operations in the Caribbean, 1974-77, and in central USA, 1977-80; British Comr, 1980-81. *Address:* The Salvation Army National Headquarters, 799 Bloomfield Avenue, Verona, NJ 07044, USA. *Club:* Rotary.

NEEDHAM, Joseph, MA, PhD, ScD (Cantab); FRS 1941; FBA 1971; Director, East Asian History of Science Library, Cambridge, since 1976; Master of Gonville and Caius College, 1966-76; Hon. Counsellor, UNESCO; *b* 1900; *s* of late Joseph Needham, MD, of Harley Street and Clapham Park, and Alicia A. Needham; *m* 1924, Dorothy Mary (*see* D. M. M. Needham), *d* of John Moyle, Babbacombe, Devon. *Educ:* Oundle School. Fellow Gonville and Caius Coll., 1924-66 (Librarian, 1959-60, Pres., 1959-66); Univ. Demonstrator in Biochem., 1928-33; Sir William Dunn Reader in Biochemistry, 1933-66, now Emeritus; Vis. Prof. of Biochem. at Stanford Univ., California, USA, 1929; Hitchcock Prof., Univ. of California, 1950; Visiting Professor: Univ. of Lyon, 1951; Univ. of Kyoto, 1971; Collège de France, Paris, 1973; Univ. of British Columbia, Vancouver, 1975; Hon. Prof., Inst. of History of Science, Acad. Sinica, Peking, 1980-. Lectures: Terry and Carmalt, Yale Univ.; Goldwin-Smith, Cornell Univ.; Mead-Swing, Oberlin College, Ohio, USA, 1935; Oliver Sharpey, RCP, 1935-36; Herbert Spencer, Oxford, 1936-37; for Polskie Towarzystwo Biologicznej in the Universities of Warsaw, Lwów, Kraków and Wilno, 1937; Comte Memorial, London, 1940; Conway Memorial, London, 1947; Boyle, Oxford, 1948; Noguchi, Johns Hopkins Univ., 1950; Hobhouse, London Univ., 1950; Dickinson, Newcomen Soc., 1956; Colombo, Singapore, Peking and Barua Universities, 1958; Wilkins, Royal Society, 1958; Wilde, Manchester, 1959; Earl Grey, Newcastle upon Tyne, 1960-61; Henry Myers, Royal Anthropological Institute, 1964; Harveian, London, 1970; Rapkine, Paris, 1971; Bernal, London, 1971; Ballard Matthews, Bangor, 1971; Fremantle, Oxford, 1971; Irvine, St Andrews, 1973; Dressler, Leeds, 1973; Carr-Saunders, London, Gerald Walters, Bath, First John Caius, Padua, 1974; Bowra, Oxford, 1975; Danz, Seattle, 1977; Harris, Northwestern, 1978; First Wickramasinghe, Colombo, 1978; Ch'ien Mu and Huang Chan, Hong Kong, 1979; Creighton, London, 1979; Radhakrishnan, Oxford, 1980. Head of the British Scientific Mission in China and Counsellor, British Embassy, Chungking, and Adviser to the Chinese National Resources Commission, Chinese Army Medical Administration and Chinese Air Force Research Bureau, 1942-46; Director of the Dept of Natural Sciences, UNESCO, 1946-48. Chm. Ceylon Government University Policy Commission, 1958. Pres., Internat. Union of Hist. of Science, 1972-75. Foreign Member: Nat. Acad. of Science, USA; Amer. Acad. Arts and Sciences; National Academy of China (Academia Sinica); Mem. Internat. Academies of Hist. of Science and of Med.; Hon. Member Yale Chapter of Sigma Xi. Hon. Prof., Academia Sinica Hist. of Sci. Inst., Peking, 1980. Hon. Fellow, UMIST. Hon. DSc Brussels and Norwich; Hon. LLD Toronto and Salford; Hon. LittD Cambridge, Hongkong, Newcastle upon Tyne, Hull, Chicago and Wilmington, NC; DUniv Surrey; Hon. PhD Uppsala. Sir William Jones Medallist, Asiatic Society of Bengal, 1963; George Sarton Medallist, Soc. for History of Science, 1968; Leonardo da Vinci Medallist, Soc. for History of Technology, 1968; Dexter Award for History of Chemistry, 1979. Order of the Brilliant Star (China). *Publications:* Science, Religion and Reality (ed), 1925; Man a Machine, 1927; The Sceptical Biologist, 1929; Chemical Embryology (3 vols), 1931; The Great Amphibium, 1932; A History of Embryology, 1934; Order and Life, 1935; Christianity and the Social Revolution (ed), 1935; Adventures before Birth (tr.), 1936; Perspectives in Biochemistry (Hopkins Presentation Volume; ed), 1937; Background to Modern Science (ed), 1938; Biochemistry and Morphogenesis, 1942; The Teacher of Nations, addresses and essays in commemoration of John Amos Comenius (ed), 1942; Time, the Refreshing River, 1943; History is on Our Side, 1945; Chinese Science, 1946; Science Outpost, 1948; Hopkins and Biochemistry (ed), 1949; Science and Civilisation in China (7 vols, 20 parts), 1954-: vol. I, Introductory Orientations, 1954; vol. II, History of Scientific Thought, 1956; vol III, Mathematics and the Sciences of the Heavens and the Earth, 1959; vol. IV, Physics and Physical Technology, part 1, Physics, 1962, part 2, Mechanical Engineering, 1965, part 3, Civil Engineering and Nautics, 1971; vol. V, Chemistry and Chemical Technology, part 2, Spagyrical

Discovery and Invention, 1974, part 3, History of Alchemy, 1976, part 4, Apparatus, Theory and Comparative Macrobiotics, 1980, part 5, Physiological Alchemy, 1982; The Development of Iron and Steel Technology in China, 1958; Heavenly Clockwork, 1960; Within the Four Seas, 1970; The Grand Titration, 1970; Clerks and Craftsmen in China and the West, 1970; (ed) The Chemistry of Life, 1970; Moulds of Understanding, 1976; Celestial Lancets, a history and rationale of Acupuncture and Moxa, 1980. Chart to illustrate the History of Physiology and Biochemistry, 1926; original papers in scientific, philosophical and sinological journals. *Address:* 42 Grange Road, Cambridge; East Asian History of Science Library, Brooklands Avenue at Clarendon Road, Cambridge. *T:* Cambridge 311545. *Club:* United Oxford & Cambridge University.

NEEDHAM, N. J. T. M.; *see* Needham, Joseph.

NEEDHAM, Richard Francis; (6th Earl of Kilmorey, but does not use the title); MP (C) Chippenham, since 1979; *b* 29 Jan. 1942; *e s* of 5th Earl of Kilmorey (*d* 1977), and of Helen Bridget (who *m* 2nd, 1978, Harold William Elliott, *qv*), *y d* of Sir Lionel Faudel-Phillips, 3rd and last Bt; *m* 1965, Sigrid Juliane Thiessen-Gairdner, *o d* of late Ernst Thiessen and of Mrs John Gairdner, Hamburg; two *s* one *d. Educ:* Eton College. Chairman, R. G. M. Print Holdings Ltd. CC Somerset, 1967-74. Contested (C): Pontefract and Castleford, Feb. 1974; Gravesend, Oct. 1974; Personal Asst to Rt Hon. James Prior, MP, Shadow Minister of Employment, 1974-79. Cons. Vice-Chm., Employment Cttee, 1981-; Mem., Public Accts Cttee. *Heir: s* Viscount Newry and Morne, *qv. Address:* House of Commons, SW1.

NEEDHAM, Prof. Roger Michael; Professor of Computer Systems, since 1981, Head of Computer Laboratory, since 1980, and Fellow of Wolfson College, since 1967, University of Cambridge; *b* 9 Feb. 1935; *s* of Leonard William Needham and Phyllis Mary Needham; *m* 1958, Karen Ida Boalth Spärck Jones. *Educ:* Cambridge Univ. (MA, PhD). FBCS. Cambridge University: Sen. Asst in Research, Computer Lab., 1963-64; Asst Dir of Research, 1964-73; Reader in Computer Systems, 1973-81. Member: Chesterton RDC, 1971-74; South Cambs DC, 1974-; Chm., Barton and Dist Labour Party, 1973-. Mem., assorted bds and cttees of Govt organizations. *Publications:* (with M. V. Wilkes) The Cambridge CAP Computer and its operating system, 1979; contribs to publications on computer operating systems, communications, security and protection. *Recreations:* sailing, politics. *Address:* 7 Brook Lane, Coton, Cambridge CB3 7PY. *T:* Madingley 210366; (work) Cambridge 352435. *Clubs:* Naval; Royal Harwich Yacht.

NÉEL, Prof. Louis Eugène Félix, Grand Croix de la Légion d'Honneur; Croix de Guerre avec Palme; Président d'Honneur, Institut National Polytechnique de Grenoble; *b* Lyon, 22 Nov. 1904; *m* 1931, Hélène Hourticq; one *s* two *d. Educ:* Ecole Normale Supérieure. Agrégé de l'Université; DèsS. Prof. of Science, Strasbourg, 1937-45. Dir, Centre d'Études Nucléaires, Grenoble, 1956-71, and Delegate of High Comr for Atomic Energy at the centre, 1971-76; rep. France at Scientific Council, NATO; Pres., Conseil Sup. Sûreté Nucléaire. Mem., Acad. of Science, Paris, 1953; For. Member: Acad. of Science, USSR, 1959, Rumania, 1965, Poland, 1975; Royal Netherlands Acad., 1959; Deutsche Akademie der Naturforscher Leopoldina, 1964; Royal Society, 1966; Amer. Acad. of Arts and Sciences, 1966; Pres., Internat. Union of Pure and Applied Physics, 1963-66. Gold Medal, CNRS, 1965; Nobel Prize for Physics, 1970. Hon. Dr: Graz, 1948; Nottingham, 1951; Oxford, 1958; Louvain, 1965; Newcastle, 1965; Coïmbra, 1966; Sherbrooke, 1967; Madrid, 1978. *Publications:* numerous on magnetism. *Address:* 15 rue Marcel-Allégot, 92190 Meudon-Bellevue, France. *T:* (1) 534 3651.

NEELY, Air Vice-Marshal John Conrad, CB 1957; CBE 1952; DM; FRCS; retired; Senior Consultant, 1955, and Consultant in Ophthalmology, RAF Central Medical Establishment, 1950-59; *b* 29 Mar. 1901; *s* of late William Neely; *m* 1st, 1938, Marjorie Monica (*d* 1964), *d* of Dr Ernest Bramley, Eastbourne; 2nd, 1966, Roma, *widow* of Group Capt. Neil McKechnie, GC. *Educ:* Stonyhurst; Oxford Univ.; Guy's Hosp. MRCS, LRCP, 1927; MA, BM, BCh, 1928, DO (Oxon) 1935, DM 1945, Oxford; DOMS London, 1933. Joined RAF 1928; served War of 1939-45; Middle East (despatches); RAF Hosp., Halton. KHS 1951. Wing Comdr, 1940; Air Cdre, 1950; Air Vice-Marshal, 1955; retired, 1959. FRCS 1958. CStJ 1955. *Address:* 27 Vicarage Drive, Eastbourne, East Sussex.

NEGUS, Arthur George, OBE 1982; Partner, Messrs Bruton, Knowles & Co., Gloucester, since 1972; *b* 29 March 1903; *s* of Arthur George Negus and Amy Julia Worsley; *m* 1926, Irene Amy Hollett; two *d. Educ:* Reading Sch. Dealer in Antiques, 1920-40; Police War Reserve, 1941-45; joined Messrs Bruton, Knowles & Co., Fine Art Auctioneers, as Appraiser, 1944. BBC Television, 1966-, and BBC Radio, 1968-. Freeman of the City of London, 1976; Liveryman, Plaisterers' Co., 1977. *Publication:* Going for a Song: English Furniture, 1969, 5th edn 1977. *Recreations:* watching sport, philately. *Address:* 31 Queens Court, Cheltenham, Glos GL50 2LU. *T:* Cheltenham 45696. *Club:* Lord's Taverners.

NEGUS, Richard; Senior Partner, Negus & Negus, since 1967; Consultant Designer to British Airways, since 1973; *b* 29 August 1927; *s* of Bertie and Kate Negus; *m* 1949, Pamela Wheatcroft-Hancock; two *s* one *d. Educ:* Battersea Grammar Sch.; Camberwell Sch. of Arts and Crafts. PPSIAD, FSTD. Staff designer, Festival of Britain, 1948-51; Partner, Negus & Sharland, 1951-67; Lecturer, Central Sch. of Art, 1951-53. Consultant to: Cotton Board

Design Centre, 1960-67; BNEC, 1969-75; Pakistan Airlines, 1975-; Rank Organisation, 1979-; City of Westminster, 1973-75; National Exhibition Centre, 1974-77; Lloyds Bank, 1972-75; Godfrey Davis, 1971-; John Laing, 1970-73; Andry Montgomery, 1967-; Celltech, 1980-; Vickers Ltd, 1980-; SDP, 1981-. Member: Design Council Poster Awards Cttee, 1970-72; PO Stamps Adv. Cttee, 1977-; (CNAA, 1980-;) Design Council, 1981-; Art and Design Cttee, Technician Educn Council, 1981-. Advisor, Norwich Sch. of Art, 1969-71; Assessor, Birmingham and Bradford Colls of Art, 1969-73; Governor: Camberwell Sch. of Art, 1964-78; Chelsea Sch. of Art, 1977-; Mem. Court, RCA, 1979-. Pres., SIAD, 1977-79, Vice Pres. 1966-68. *Publications:* Designing for Export Printing, 1972; contribs to: Design Mag., The Designer, Graphis, Gebrauchgraphick, Architectural Review. *Address:* Myddelton Cottage, Canonbury Park South, N1. *T:* 01-226 2381. *Club:* Reform.

NEHRU, Braj Kumar; Governor of Jammu and Kashmir, since 1981; *b* Allahabad, 4 Sept. 1909; *s* of Brijlal and Rameshawri Nehru; *m* 1935, Magdalena Friedmann; three *s. Educ:* Allahabad Univ.; LSE (Fellow); Balliol Coll., Oxford. BSc; BSc(Econ.). Called to Bar, Inner Temple. Joined ICS, 1934; Asst Comr, 1934-39; Under-Sec., Dept of Education, Health and Lands, 1939; Mem., Indian Legislative Assembly, 1939; Officer on special duty, Reserve Bank of India, and Under-Sec., Finance Dept, 1940; Jt Sec., 1947; Exec. Dir, IBRD (World Bank), and Minister, Indian Embassy, Washington, 1949-54 and 1958-62; Sec., Dept of Econ. Affairs, 1957-58; Comr-Gen. for Econ. Affairs, Min. of Finance, 1958-61; Ambassador to USA, 1961-68; Governor: Assam and Nagaland, 1968-73; Meghalaya, Manipur and Tripura, 1972-73; High Comr in London, 1973-77. Rep. of India: Reparations Conf. 1945; Commonwealth Finance Ministers Confs, UN Gen. Assembly, 1949-52, and 1960; FAO Confs, 1949-50; Sterling Balance Confs, 1947-49; Bandung Conf., 1955; deputed to enquire into Australian Fed. Finance, 1946; Mem., UN Adv. Cttee on Admin and Budgetry Questions, 1951-53; Advr to Sudan Govt, 1955; Mem., UN Investments Cttee, 1962- (Chm., 1977-). Hon. LLD Mo Valley Coll.; Hon. LittD Jacksonville. *Publications:* Australian Federal Finance, 1947; Speaking of India, 1966. *Recreations:* bridge, reading, conversation. *Address:* Raj Bhavan, Srinagar 190001, India. *Club:* Gymkhana (Delhi).

NEIDPATH, Lord; Hon. James Donald Charteris, Lord Douglas of Neidpath; *b* 22 June 1948; *s* and *heir* of 12th Earl of Wemyss and March, *qv. Educ:* Eton; University College, Oxford (BA 1969, MA 1974); St Antony's Coll., Oxford (DPhil 1975); Royal Agricultural Coll., Cirencester (Diploma, 1978); ARICS 1982. Page of Honour to HM Queen Elizabeth the Queen Mother, 1962-64. *Publication:* The Singapore Naval Base and the Defence of Britain's Eastern Empire 1919-42, 1981. *Address:* Stanway, Cheltenham, Glos. *Clubs:* Brooks's, Pratt's, Ognisko Polskie; Puffin's (Edinburgh).

NEIGHBOUR, Oliver Wray, FBA 1982; Music Librarian, Reference Division of the British Library, since 1976; *b* 1 April 1923; *s* of Sydney William Neighbour, OBE, TD, and Gwenydd Joyce (*née* Prentis). *Educ:* Eastbourne Coll.; Birkbeck Coll., London (BA 1950). Entered Dept of Printed Books, BM, 1946; Asst Keeper in Music Room, 1951; Dep. Keeper, 1976. *Publications:* (with Alan Tyson) English Music Publishers' Plate Numbers, 1965; The Consort and Keyboard Music of William Byrd, 1978; (ed) Music and Bibliography: essays in honour of Alec Hyatt King, 1980; article on Schoenberg in New Grove Dictionary of Music and Musicians, 1980; editor of first publications of works by Schumann, Schoenberg and Byrd. *Recreations:* walking, ornithology. *Address:* 12 Treborough House, 1 Nottingham Place, W1M 3FP. *T:* 01-935 1772.

NEIL, Prof. Eric; John Astor Professor of Physiology in the University of London, at the Middlesex Hospital Medical School, since 1956; *b* 15 Feb. 1918; *s* of George Neil, MC, and Florence Neil; *m* 1946, Anne Baron, *d* of late T. J. M. B. Parker and of Evelyn Maud Parker; two *d. Educ:* Heath Grammar School; University of Leeds. BSc Hons (Physiology) (Leeds), 1939; MB, ChB, 1942; MD (Dist.), 1944 and DSc, 1953 (Leeds); FRCP 1978. Demonstrator and Lecturer in Physiology, Univ. of Leeds, 1942-50; Sen. Lecturer and later Reader in Physiology, Middx Hosp. Med. School., 1950-56. Hon. Treas., Physiological Soc.; Chm., European Editorial Bd of Physiological Reviews, 1960-67; Mem., Brit. Nat. Cttee of Physiological Sciences, 1960-; Pres., Internat. Union of Physiological Sciences, 1974-77, 1977- (Treasurer, 1968-74). Hon. For. Mem., Royal Acad. of Medicine, Belgium, 1978. Examiner in Physiology, Univs of London, Oxford, Cambridge, Birmingham, Trinity Coll., Dublin. Hon. MD Ghent, 1977. Queen's Silver Jubilee Medal, 1977. *Publications:* (with Prof. C. Heymans) Reflexogenic Areas in the Cardiovascular System, 1958; (with Prof. C. A. Keele) Samson Wright's Applied Physiology, 10th edn 1961, 12th edn 1971; (with Prof. B. Folkow) Circulation, 1971; The Mammalian Circulation, 1974, 2nd edn, 1978; The Life and Work of William Harvey, 1975; papers on physiological topics in British and foreign med. scientific jls. *Recreations:* pianoforte, golf. *Address:* 53 Talbot Road, Highgate, N6. *T:* 01-340 0543.

NEIL, Matthew, CBE 1976; Secretary and Chief Executive, Glasgow Chamber of Commerce, since 1954; *b* 19 Dec. 1917; *s* of John Neil and Jean Wallace. *Educ:* John Neilson High Sch., Paisley; Glasgow Univ. (MA, LLB). Served War, 1939-46: Far East, ME, Mediterranean and Western Europe; RHA, RA and Air Observation Post; RAuxAF, 1950-57. Admitted solicitor, 1947. Mem., British Overseas Trade Adv. Council, 1975-. *Recreations:* skiing, golf,

music. *Address:* 39 Arkleston Road, Paisley PA1 3TH. *T:* 041-889 4975. *Clubs:* East India, Devonshire, Sports and Public Schools; Erskine Golf, Lamlash Golf, Prestwick Golf.

NEIL, Thomas, CMG 1962; TD 1951; Director, Thomson Foundation, 1963-79; *b* 23 December 1913; *s* of late W. R. Neil; *m* 1939, Phyllis Selina Gertrude Sargeant; one *d. Educ:* King's College, University of Durham (now University of Newcastle upon Tyne) (BSc, NDA). Lectr in Agriculture, Devon County Council, 1936-39; Chief Technical Officer, 1946. Colonial Service: District Officer, Kenya, 1947; Assistant Chief Secretary, 1957; Permanent Secretary, 1957; Permanent Secretary, Ministry of State, Kenya, 1959-63. Director, Kenya Famine Relief, 1961-63. Directed Africanisation of CS. Served War of 1939-45 with Devonshire Regiment (TA), Lieutenant-Colonel, in UK, E Africa, Middle East. *Recreation:* country life. *Address:* Summerhill, Bourne End, Bucks. *T:* Bourne End 20403.

NEILD, Prof. Robert Ralph; Professor of Economics, University of Cambridge, since 1971; Fellow of Trinity College, Cambridge; *b* 10 Sept. 1924; *o s* of Ralph and Josephine Neild, Letchmore Heath, Hertfordshire; *m* 1960, Elizabeth Walton Griffiths; one *s* four *d* (incl. twin *d*). *Educ:* Charterhouse; Trinity Coll., Cambridge. Royal Air Force, 1943-44; Operational Research, 1944-45. Secretariat of United Nations Economic Commission for Europe, Geneva, 1947-51; Economic Section, Cabinet Office and Treasury, 1951-56; Lecturer in Economics, and Fellow, Trinity College, Cambridge, 1956-58; National Institute of Economic and Social Research: at first as Editor of its Quarterly Economic Review; then as Deputy Director of the Institute, 1958-64; MIT Center for International Studies, India Project, New Delhi, 1962-63; Economic Adviser to HM Treasury, 1964-67; Dir, Stockholm Internat. Peace Research Inst., 1967-71. Mem., Fulton Cttee on Reform of CS, 1966-68; Vice-Chm., I. F. S. Armstrong Cttee on Budgetary Reform in UK, 1979-80. Director: Nat. Mutual Life Assce Soc., 1959-64; Investing in Success Equities Ltd, 1961-64, 1972-. *Publications:* Pricing and Employment in the Trade Cycle, 1964; (with T. S. Ward) The Measurement and Reform of Budgetary Policy, 1978; How to Make Up Your Mind about the Bomb, 1981; various articles. *Address:* 5 Cranmer Road, Cambridge. *T:* Cambridge 56902.

NEILL, Hon. Sir Brian (Thomas), Kt 1978; **Hon. Mr Justice Neill;** a Judge of the High Court, Queen's Bench Division, since 1978; *b* 2 Aug. 1923; *s* of late Sir Thomas Neill and of Lady (Annie) Neill (*née* Bishop); *m* 1956, Sally Margaret, *d* of late Sydney Eric Backus and late Marguerite Backus; three *s. Educ:* Highgate Sch.; Corpus Christi Coll., Oxford. Rifle Brigade, 1942-46 (Capt.). MA Oxford. Called to the Bar, Inner Temple, 1949, Bencher, 1976. QC 1968; a Recorder of the Crown Court, 1972-78. Mem., Departmental Cttee to examine operation of Section 2 of Official Secrets Act, 1971; Chm., Adv. Cttee on Rhodesia Travel Restrictions, 1973-78. Mem., Ct of Assts, 1972-, Master, 1980-81, Turners' Co. Governor, Highgate Sch., 1969. *Address:* c/o Royal Courts of Justice, Strand, WC2. *Clubs:* MCC, Hurlingham.
See also F. P. Neill.

NEILL, Prof. Derrick James, DFC 1943; Professor of Prosthetic Dentistry, University of London, since 1969; Sub-Dean of Dental Studies, Guy's Hospital Dental School, 1969-76; Consultant Dental Surgeon, Guy's Hospital, since 1960; *b* 14 March 1922; *s* of Jameson Leonard Neill, MBE, and Lynn Moyle; *m* 1st, 1952, Iris Jordan (*d* 1970); one *s* one *d*; 2nd, 1971, Catherine Mary Daughtry. *Educ:* East Sheen County Grammar Sch.; Guy's Hosp. Dental Sch., Univ. of London. LDSRCS 1952; FDSRCS 1955; MDS London, 1966. Served RAFVR, 1941-46, 150 Sqdn, Bomber Comd (Sqdn Ldr). Dept of Dental Prosthetics, Guy's Hosp. Dental School: Lectr, 1954; Sen. Lectr, 1959; Univ. Reader in Dental Prosthetics, 1967. Examr, Univs of London, Liverpool and Manchester. Council Member, Odontological Section, Royal Soc. of Medicine, 1966-73; Past Pres., British Soc. for Study of Prosthetic Dentistry. Mem. Council of Governors: Guy's Hosp. Med. Sch., 1980-82; United Med. Schs of Guy's and St Thomas's Hosps, 1982-. *Publications:* (jtly) Complete Dentures, 1968; Partial Denture Construction, 1976; numerous papers in dental jls. *Recreations:* golf, music. *Address:* Hurst, Clenches Farm Road, Kippington, Sevenoaks, Kent. *T:* Sevenoaks 452374. *Club:* Royal Automobile.

NEILL, Francis Patrick, QC 1966; Warden of All Souls College, Oxford, since 1977; a Judge of the Courts of Appeal of Jersey and Guernsey, since 1977; Chairman, Press Council, since 1978; first Chairman, Council for Securities Industry, since 1978; *b* 8 Aug. 1926; *s* of late Sir Thomas Neill, JP, and of Lady (Annie Strachan) Neill (*née* Bishop); *m* 1954, Caroline Susan, *d* of late Sir Piers Debenham, 2nd Bt, and Lady (Angela) Debenham; four *s* two *d. Educ:* Highgate Sch.; Magdalen College, Oxford. Gibbs Law Scholar, 1949; Eldon Law Scholar, 1950. BA 1950; BCL 1951; MA 1972. Served Rifle Brigade, 1944-47 (Captain); GSO III (Training), British Troops Egypt, 1947. Fellow of All Souls, 1950-77, Sub-Warden 1972-74; Lectr in Air Law, LSE, 1955-58. Called to the Bar, Gray's Inn, 1951; Bencher, 1971; Member, Bar Council, 1967-71, Vice-Chm., 1973-74, Chm., 1974-75; Chm., Senate of the Inns of Court and the Bar, 1974-75; a Recorder of the Crown Court, 1975-78. Chm., Justice—All Souls Cttee for Rev. of Admin. Law, 1978-. Hon. LLD Hull. *Recreations:* music and forestry. *Address:* All Souls College, Oxford OX1 4AL. *T:* Oxford 722251. *Clubs:* Athenæum, Garrick, Beefsteak.
See also Hon. Sir Brian Neill.

NEILL, Major Rt. Hon. Sir Ivan, Kt 1973; PC (N Ireland) 1950; DL; b Belfast 1 July 1906; m 1928, Margaret Helena Allen. Educ: Ravenscroft Nat. Sch., Belfast; Shaftesbury House Tutorial Coll., Belfast; Queen's Univ., Belfast (BSc Econ). FRGS. Served War of 1939-45: RE in UK and FE, 1939-46; Major. MP Ballynafeigh Div. of Belfast, Parlt of Northern Ireland, 1949-73; Government of Northern Ireland: Minister of Labour and National Insurance, 1950-62; Minister of Home Affairs, Aug.-Oct. 1952; Minister of Education, 1962-64; Minister of Finance, 1964-65; Leader of House of Commons, Oct. 1964; resigned from Govt, April 1965; Minister of Develt, Dec. 1968-March 1969; Speaker of House of Commons, 1969-73. Represented N Ireland at Internat. Labour Confs, 1950-61. Councillor and Alderman in Belfast Corp., 1946-50 (specialised in educn, housing and youth welfare). DL Belfast, 1966. Address: Greenlaw, Ballywilliam, Donaghadee, Co. Down, Northern Ireland.

NEILL, Very Rev. Ivan Delacherois, CB 1963; OBE 1958; Provost of Sheffield and Vicar of the Cathedral Church of St Peter and St Paul, 1966-74, now Emeritus; Chaplain to the Queen, 1962-66; b 10 July 1912; s of Rev. Robert Richard Neill and Bessie Montrose (née Purdon); m 1938, Enid Eyre Godson (née Bartholomew); one s one d. Educ: St Dunstan's College; Jesus College, Cambridge (MA); London College of Divinity. Curate: St Mary, West Kensington, 1936-38; Christ Church, Crouch End, 1938-39. CF 4th Cl., Chatham; served BEF and UK with 3rd Div., Orkneys, Sandhurst, 1941-43; Sen. Chaplain, N Aldershot, 1943; 43rd (Wessex) Div., 1943-45 (despatches); DACG, 1st British Corps, 1945-46; Sen. Chaplain, Guards Depot, Caterham, 1947-50; DACG, N Canal, Egypt, 1950-53; Catterick, 1953; Warden, Royal Army Chaplains Dept Trg Centre Depot, 1954-57; Sen. Chaplain, SHAPE 1957-58; Asst Chaplain-Gen., Middle East Land Forces, 1958-60; QHC 1960; Chaplain General to HM Forces, 1960-66. Chairman of Governors, Monkton Combe Sch., Bath, 1969-81; Pres. of Foundn, St Paul's and St Mary's C of E Coll. of Educn, Cheltenham, 1978-. Knight Officer, Order of Orange Nassau (with Swords) 1946. Address: Rodborough Crest, Rodborough Common, Stroud, Glos GL5 5BT. T: Amberley 3224; Churchtown, Broadway, Co. Wexford, Republic of Ireland. T: Wexford 31221. Club: National.

NEILL, James Hugh, CBE 1969; TD 1950; DL; Chairman, James Neill Holdings Ltd, since 1963; Member, Eastern Regional Board, National Westminster Bank Ltd, since 1969; b 29 March 1921; o s of Col Sir Frederick Neill, CBE, DSO, TD, DL, JP, and Lady (Winifred Margaret) Neill (née Colver); m 1943, Jane Margaret Shuttleworth; two d; m 1982, Anne O'Leary. Educ: Rugby School. War service with RE and Royal Bombay Sappers and Miners, UK, Norway, India, Burma and Germany, 1939-46 (despatches, Burma, 1945). Mem., British Overseas Trade Bd, 1973-78; Pres., European Tool Cttee, 1972-76; Mem., Trent Regional Health Authority, 1974-80; Chm. Exec. Cttee, Sheffield Council for Voluntary Service, 1953-; Mem. Council, CBI, 1965-; Chm., E and W Ridings Regional Council, FBI, 1962-64; Pres., Nat. Fedn of Engrs Tool Manufrs, 1963-65; Pres., Fedn of British Hand Tool Manufrs, 1960-61; Vice-Pres., Inst. of Export. FBIM. Master Cutler of Hallamshire, 1958; High Sheriff of Hallamshire, 1971; DL South Yorkshire, 1974. Recreations: golf, horse trials, racing, shooting. Address: Barn Cottage, Lindrick Common, near Worksop S81 8BA. T: Dinnington 562806. Clubs: East India; Sheffield (Sheffield); Lindrick (Worksop); Royal and Ancient (St Andrews).

NEILL, Patrick; see Neill, F. P.

NEILL, Rt. Rev. Stephen Charles, FBA 1969; an Assistant Bishop, Diocese of Oxford, since 1979; b 31 Dec. 1900; s of Rev. Charles Neill, MB, and of Margaret, d of late James Monro, CB. Educ: Dean Close School; Trinity College, Cambridge (MA 1926, DD 1980). Fellow of Trinity College, Cambridge, 1924-28; Missionary in dioceses of Tinnevelly and Travancore, 1924-30; Warden, Bishop's Theological College, Tirumaraiyur, Nazareth, S India, 1930-38; Bishop of Tinnevelly, 1939-45; Chaplain of Trinity Coll., Cambridge; Univ. Lecturer in Divinity, 1945-47; Co-Director Study Dept of World Council of Churches, 1947-48; Asst Bishop to Archbishop of Canterbury, 1947-50; Associate Gen. Sec. of World Council of Churches, 1948-51; General Editor, World Christian Books, 1952-62, Director, 1962-70: Prof. of Missions and Ecumenical Theology, Univ. of Hamburg, 1962-67; Prof. of Philosophy and Religious Studies, Nairobi Univ., 1969-73. Lectures: Hulsean, Cambridge, 1946-47; Birkbeck, Trinity Coll., Cambridge, 1949-50; Godfrey Day in Missions, TCD, 1950; Earle, Pacific School of Religions, Berkeley, California, 1950; Cody Meml, Toronto, 1956; Carnahan, Faculty of Theology, Buenos Aires, 1958; Duff in Missions, Edinburgh and Glasgow, 1958-59; Moorhouse, Melbourne, 1960; Firth, Nottingham, 1962; Bampton, Oxford, 1964; Ziskind, Dartmouth Coll., NH, 1966; Westcott-Teape, Delhi and Madras, 1972; Livingstone Meml, Blantyre, Malawi, 1973. Visiting Professor: of Missions, Hamburg Univ., 1956-57, 1961; of Theol., Colgate-Rochester Divinity Sch., 1961-62; of Theol., Wycliffe Coll., Toronto, 1962; Drew Univ., NJ, 1967; of Religion, Univ. Coll., Nairobi, 1968; of Science of Religion, Durban-Westville Univ., SA, 1975; of World Christianity, Union Theol. Seminary, NY, 1979. Hon. DD: Trinity Coll., Toronto, 1950; Culver-Stockton, 1953; Glasgow, 1961; Acadia, 1976; Hon. ThD: Hamburg, 1957; Uppsala, 1965; Hon. LittD St Paul's Univ., Tokyo, 1960. Publications: Out of Bondage, 1928; Builders of the Indian Church, 1933; Beliefs, 1940; Foundation Beliefs, 1942; The Challenge of Jesus Christ, 1944; Christ, His Church and His World, 1948; The Cross over Asia, 1948; On the Ministry, 1952; The Christian Society, 1952; Christian Partnership, 1952; Towards

Church Union, 1937-1952, 1952; Under Three Flags, 1954; The Christian's God, 1954; Christian Faith To-day, 1955; The Christian Character, 1955; Who is Jesus Christ?, 1956; The Unfinished Task, 1957; Anglicanism, 1958; A Genuinely Human Existence, 1959; Creative Tension, 1959; Christian Holiness, 1960; Men of Unity, 1960; Christian Faith and other Faiths, 1961; The Eternal Dimension, 1963; The Interpretation of the New Testament, 1964; A History of Christian Missions, 1964; Colonialism and Christian Missions, 1966; The Church and Christian Union, 1968; Christianity in India and Pakistan, 1970; Bible Words and Christian Meanings, 1970; What do we know of Jesus?, 1970; Bhakti Hindu and Christian, 1974; Salvation Tomorrow, 1976; Jesus Through Many Eyes, 1976. (Editor) Twentieth Century Christianity, 1961; (ed jtly) A History of the Ecumenical Movement, 1517-1948, 1951-54; (ed jtly) The Layman in Christian History, 1963; (ed jtly) The Concise Dictionary of the Christian World Mission, 1970; contrib. to: Encyclopædia Britannica; Chambers's Encyclopædia; Die Religion in Geschichte und Gegenwart; Evangelisches Kirchenlexikon; Weltkirchenlexicon. Address: Wycliffe Hall, Oxford.

NEILSON, Ian (Godfrey), DFC 1944; TD 1951; b 4 Dec. 1918; er s of James Wilson Neilson, solicitor, Glasgow; m 1945, D. Alison St Clair Aytoun, Ashintully; one s one d. Educ: Glasgow Acad.; Glasgow Univ. (BL). Legal Trng, Glasgow, 1935-39; Territorial Army, 1938; War Service, 1939-45: Field Artillery; Air Observation Post, 1941; RA Staff, 1944; Lt-Col comdg War Crimes Investigation Unit, Germany, 1945-46; formed and commanded No 666 (Scottish) Sqdn, RAuxAF, 1948-53. Enrolled Solicitor, 1946. Royal Institution of Chartered Surveyors: Scottish Sec., Edinburgh, 1946-53; Asst Sec., London, 1953-61; Under-Sec., 1961-65; Brigade Sec., The Boys' Brigade, 1966-74 (officer, 5th Mid-Surrey Co., 1972-78); Clerk to Governors of the Cripplegate Foundn, Cripplegate Educnl Foundn, Trustees of St Giles and St Luke's Jt Parochial Charities, and Governors of the Cripplegate Schs Foundn, 1974-81. Hon. Treasurer, Thames Youth Venture Adv. Council (City Parochial Foundn), 1968-76. Vice-Chm., British Council of Churches Youth Dept, 1971-74; Trustee: St George's Chapel, London Airport, 1978-; Douglas Haig Meml Homes, 1979-; Mem., Nat. Council for Voluntary Youth Services, 1966-74; Pres., London Br., Glasgow Academical Club, 1977-79; Chm. of Governors, Lucas-Tooth Leadership Training Fund for Boys, 1976-; Governor, Kingsway-Princeton Coll. of Further Educn, 1977-. Elder, United Reformed Church, St Andrew's, Cheam, 1972-; Lay Mem., Provincial Ministerial Cttee, URC, 1974-; Dir and Asst Sec., URC Trust, 1982-. FBIM 1980: Hon. Sec., City of London Branch, 1976-79, Chm., 1979-81, Vice Pres. and Mem. Council, 1981-; Chm., Inner London Branches Area Cttee, 1981-. Sen. Instr, Royal Yachting Assoc., 1977-; Vice-Pres., Air Observation Post Officers Assoc., 1978-; Chm., Epsom Choral Soc., 1977-81. Freeman, Guild of Air Pilots and Air Navigators, 1976-78, Liveryman, 1978; Freeman, City of London, 1975; Chm., Queenhithe Ward Club, 1977-78. Recreations: golf, music, gardening, sailing. Address: 103 Longdown Lane South, Epsom Downs, Epsom, Surrey KT17 4JJ. T: Epsom 20670. Clubs: Athenæum; St Mawes Sailing.

NEILSON, Nigel Fraser, MC 1943; Chairman and Managing Director, Neilson McCarthy, since 1962; b 12 Dec. 1919; s of Lt-Col W. Neilson, DSO, 4th Hussars and Maud Alice Francis Anson; m 1949, Pamela Catherine Georgina Sheppard; one s one d. Educ: Hereworth Sch.; Christ's Coll., New Zealand; RADA. Inns of Court Regt; commnd Staffs Yeomanry, 1939; seconded Cavalry Regt, Transjordanian Frontier Force; served Syrian Campaign; returned Staffs Yeo., Seventh Armoured Div., GSO 111 Ops; served desert and Italy; Staff Coll., 1944; served in Germany, Holland and France; C of S, Bergen area, Norway; served with SAS and French SAS. On demobilisation worked in theatre, cabaret, films, London, USA and NZ; joined J. Walter Thompson, 1951; became personal rep. to Aristotle Onassis, 1955, later consultant to his daughter, Christina; founded Neilson McCarthy Internat. Public Relations Consultants in UK, USA, Australia, NZ and SE Asia, 1962. Past Pres., NZ Soc., 1978-79. Chevalier de la Légion d'Honneur 1946, Croix de Guerre avec Palme 1946. Recreations: riding, shooting, music, theatre. Address: Woolfield Farm, Froxfield, Hants; 24 Bruton Place, W1. T: 01-493 8606. Club: Buck's.

NEILSON, Richard Alvin, MVO 1968; HM Diplomatic Service; Deputy Governor and Political Adviser, Gibraltar, since 1981; b 9 July 1937; s of Robert and Ethel Neilson; m 1961; Olive Tyler; one s. Educ: Burnley Grammar Sch.; Leeds Univ. (BA Hons 1958, MA 1960). Fulbright Fellow, Univ. of Wisconsin, 1959-60; Asst Lectr, Univ. of Edinburgh, 1960-61; joined FO, 1961; Third (later Second) Sec., Kinshasa, 1963-65; Treasury Centre for Admin. Studies, 1965; Second (later First) Sec. (Information), Santiago, 1966-69; First Sec., Canberra, 1969-73; FCO, 1973-77; Counsellor, seconded to NI Office as Head of Political Affairs Div., 1977-79; Dep. High Comr, Lusaka, 1979-80, Acting High Comr, Nov. 1979-June 1980. Publications: contribs to geomorphological literature. Recreations: tennis, golf, chess, sailing. Address: c/o Foreign and Commonwealth Office, SW1A 2AH; Maynes Hill Farm, Hoggeston, Buckingham, Bucks. T: Winslow 2308. Clubs: Royal Commonwealth Society; Royal Gibraltar Yacht.

NEILSON, Hon. William Arthur, AC 1978; Agent-General for Tasmania, in London, 1978-81; b 27 Aug. 1925; s of late Arthur R. Neilson; m 1948, Jill, d of A. H. Benjamin; one s three d. Educ: Ogilvie Commercial High Sch., Hobart. When first elected to Tasmanian Parlt in 1946, aged 21, youngest MP in British Commonwealth and youngest member ever elected to any Australian parlt. Re-elected, 1948, 1950, 1955, 1956, 1959, 1964, 1969 and

1972, resigned 1977. Labor Party Whip, Dec. 1946–Feb. 1955; Minister for Tourists and Immigration and Forests, Oct. 1956–Aug. 1958; Attorney-Gen. and Minister for Educn, Aug.–Oct 1958; Minister for Educn, until April 1959, then Treasurer and Minister for Educn, April–May 1959; Minister for Educn, 1959–69 and May 1972–March 1974; Attorney-Gen., also Dep. Premier, Minister for Environment and Minister administering Police Dept and Licensing Act, April 1974–March 1975; Premier and Treasurer, 1975–77. *Recreations:* reading, writing, chess, Australian Rules football, amateur theatre. *Address:* 61 Red Chapel Hill, Sandy Bay, Hobart, Tasmania 7005, Australia.

NELDER, John Ashworth, DSc; FRS 1981; Head of Statistics Department, Rothamsted Experimental Station, since 1968; Visiting Professor, Imperial College of Science and Technology, since 1971; *b* 8 Oct. 1924; *s* of Reginald Charles and Edith May Ashworth Nelder; *m* 1955, Mary Hawkes; one *s* one *d*. *Educ:* Blundell's Sch., Tiverton; Cambridge Univ. (MA); DSc Birmingham. Head, Statistics Section, National Vegetable Research Station, 1950–68. Hon. DSc Paul Sabatier, Toulouse, 1981. *Publications:* Computers in Biology, 1974; responsible for statistical programs (computer) Genstat and GLIM; numerous papers in statistical and biological jls. *Recreations:* piano-playing, music, natural history. *Address:* Cumberland Cottage, 33 Crown Street, Redbourn, St Albans, Herts AL3 7JX. *T:* Redbourn 2907.

NELIGAN, Desmond West Edmund, OBE 1961; National Insurance Commissioner, 1961–76, retired; *b* 20 June 1906; *s* of late Rt Rev. M. R. Neligan, DD (one time Bishop of Auckland, NZ), and Mary, *d* of Edmund Macrory, QC; *m* 1st, 1936, Penelope Ann, *d* of Henry Mason (marr. diss., 1946); two *s*; 2nd, 1947, Margaret Elizabeth, *d* of late Captain Snook, RN; one step *d*. *Educ:* Bradfield Coll.; Jesus Coll., Cambridge. BA Cantab, 1929; Barrister, Middle Temple, 1940. Practising Barrister until 1961. Appointed Umpire under National Service Acts, Nov. 1955. Dep. Comr for National Insurance, 1955–61. Served War of 1939–45, in 2 NZ Division, in Greece, Crete and Western Desert. *Publications:* (ed) 6th, 7th and 8th Editions Dumsday's Parish Councils Handbook; (with Sir A. Safford, QC) Town and Country Planning Act, 1944, and *ibid*, 1947; Social Security Case Law: digest of Commissioners' decisions, 1979. *Recreations:* formerly: hockey, cricket (Mem. MCC), tennis and hunting. *Address:* Frobishers, Danhill Cross Roads, West Chiltington, Pulborough, West Sussex. *T:* Coolham 434.

NELSON, family name of **Earl Nelson** and **Baron Nelson of Stafford.**

NELSON, 9th Earl *cr* 1805, of Trafalgar and of Merton; **Peter John Horatio Nelson;** Baron Nelson of the Nile and of Hilborough, Norfolk, 1801; Viscount Merton, 1805; Detective Sergeant, Hertfordshire Police Force; *b* 9 Oct. 1941; *s* of Captain Hon. John Marie Joseph Horatio Nelson (*d* 1970) (*y s* of 5th Earl) and of Kathleen Mary, *d* of William Burr, Torquay; *S* uncle, 1981; *m* 1969, Maureen Diana, *d* of Edward Patrick Quinn, Kilkenny; one *s* one *d. Heir:* *s* Viscount Merton, *qv. Address:* c/o Hertfordshire Police Headquarters, Stanborough Road, Welwyn Garden City, Herts AL8 6XF.

NELSON OF STAFFORD, 2nd Baron, *cr* 1960; **Henry George Nelson,** Bt 1955; MA, FEng, FICE, Hon. FIMechE, FIEE, FRAeS; Director: The General Electric Company plc (Chairman, 1968–83); Bank of England; International Nickel Company of Canada; Royal Worcester Ltd (Chairman); *b* Manchester, 2 Jan. 1917; *s* of 1st Baron Nelson of Stafford and late Florence Mabel, *o d* of late Henry Howe, JP; *S* father, 1962; *m* 1940, Pamela Roy Bird, *yr d* of late Ernest Roy Bird, formerly MP for Skipton, Yorks; two *s* two *d. Educ:* Oundle; King's Coll., Cambridge. Exhibnr 1935; Mechanical Sciences Tripos, 1937. Practical experience in England, France and Switzerland, 1937–39. Joined the English Electric Co. Ltd, 1939; Supt, Preston Works, 1939–40; Asst Works Man., Preston, 1940–41; Dep. Works Man., Preston, 1941–42; Man. Dir, D. Napier & Son Ltd, 1942–49; Exec. Dir, The Marconi Co. Ltd, 1946–58; Dep. Man. Dir, 1949–56, Man. Dir, 1956–62, Chm. and Chief Exec., 1962–68, The English Electric Co. Ltd. Dep. Chm., British Aircraft Corp., 1960–77; Director: ICL, 1968–74; Nat. Bank of Australasia Ltd (London Bd of Advice), 1950–81. Outside Lectr, Univ. of Cambridge (Mech. Sciences Tripos course on Industrial Management), 1947–49. Chancellor of Aston Univ., 1966–79. Member: Govt. Adv. Council on Scientific Policy, 1955–58; Adv. Council on Middle East Trade, 1958–63 (Industrial Leader and Vice-Chm., 1959–63); Civil Service Commn (Part time Mem. Final Selection and Interview Bds), 1956–61; Engrg Adv. Council, 1958–61; Council, Inst. Electrical Engineers, 1959–76 (Vice-Pres. 1957–62 and 1965–70, Pres., 1970–71); Middle East Assoc. (Vice-Pres., 1962–); Gen. Bd of NPL, 1959–66; Council, SBAC, 1943–64 (Pres. 1961–62); Council Foundn on Automation and Employment Ltd, 1963–68; Council, BEAMA, 1964– (Pres., 1966); Adv. Council, Min. of Technology, 1964–70; Engineering Industries Council, 1975–. World Power Conference: Mem., British Nat. Cttee, 1954–71, Chm., 1971–74. Mem., Nat. Def. Industries Council, 1969–77 (Chm., 1971–77); President: Locomotive and Allied Manufacturers Assoc., 1964–66; British Electrical Power Convention, 1965–67; Orgalime (Organisme de Liaison des Industries Métalliques Européennes), 1968–70; Sino-British Trade Council, 1973–. Liveryman: Worshipful Co. of Coachmakers and Coach Harness Makers of London, 1944; Worshipful Co. of Goldsmiths, 1961. Lord High Steward of Borough of Stafford, 1966–71. Hon. DSc: Aston, 1966; Keele, 1967; Cranfield, 1972; Hon. LLD Strathclyde, 1971; Fellow, Imp. Coll. of Science and Technology, 1969. Benjamin Franklin Medal, RSA, 1959. *Recreations:* shooting, tennis, ski-ing. *Heir:* *s* Hon. Henry Roy George Nelson [*b* 26 Oct. 1943; *m* 1968, Dorothy, *yr d* of Leslie Caley, Tibthorpe Manor,

Driffield, Yorks; one *s* one *d*]. *Address:* 8 Carlton Lodge, 37 Lowndes Street, SW1X 9HX. *T:* 01-235 6551. *Clubs:* Carlton, Hurlingham.

NELSON, NZ, Bishop of, since 1965; **Rt. Rev. Peter (Eves) Sutton;** *b* Wellington, NZ, 7 June 1923; *m* 1956, Pamela Cherrington, *e d* of R. A. Dalley, Patin House, Kidderminster; one *s* one *d. Educ:* Wellesley Coll.; Nelson Coll.; University of New Zealand. BA 1945; MA 1947; LTh 1948. Deacon, 1947; Priest, 1948 (Wellington); Curate of Wanganui, New Zealand, 1947–50; St John the Evangelist, Bethnal Green, 1950–51; Bishops Hatfield, Diocese of St Albans (England), 1951–52; Vicar of St Cuthberts, Berhampore (NZ), 1952–58; Whangarei, Diocese of Auckland, New Zealand, 1958–64; Archdeacon of Waimate, 1962–64; Dean of Dunedin and Vicar of St Paul's Cathedral, Dunedin, 1964–65. *Publication:* Freedom for Convictions, 1971. *Recreations:* golf (Canterbury Univ. Blue), tennis. *Address:* Bishopdale, Nelson, New Zealand.

NELSON, Anthony; *see* Nelson, R. A.

NELSON, Bertram, CBE 1956; FCA; *b* 1905; *s* of W. E. Nelson, Liverpool; *m* 1954, Eleanor Kinsey; one *s* one *d. Educ:* The Leys School, Cambridge. Hon. Sec. Merseyside Civic Soc. 1938-53. Chm. Liverpool Chamber of Commerce, 1951–53, Treas., 1953–60; a Vice-Pres. of Assoc. of British Chambers of Commerce, 1956. Pres. Soc. of Incorporated Accountants, 1954–56; Mem. Council of Inst. of Chartered Accountants, 1957–75 (Chairman of Education Committee, 1961–66). Chm., Liverpool Daily Post and Echo Gp, 1972–76. BBC North Regional Council, 1947-57. Mem. Board of Trade Consultative Cttee on Companies, 1954–73, and of Bd of Trade Treas. Cttee on Export Credit Guarantees Dept., 1958; Part-time Mem., Merseyside and N Wales Electricity Bd 1967–76. Treas. of Liverpool Univ., 1948–57, Vice-Pres., 1957–63, Pres. and Pro-Chancellor, 1963–67, Senior Pro-Chancellor, 1967–73; Chm., Univ. Develt Cttee, 1961–68; Governor: The Leys Sch., Cambridge (Vice-Chm., 1970); Staff Coll. for Further Education; Mem. Mersey Docks and Harbour Bd, 1951–65; Chm. Liverpool Youth Welfare Advisory Cttee, 1952–65; Dir, the Playhouse, Liverpool, 1949–63; Chm. of Appeals Cttee on Gradings and Salaries in Colls of Advanced Technology, 1964–65. Trustee, Civic Trust for NW. JP Liverpool, 1944. Hon. LLD Liverpool, 1972. *Publication:* Tables of Procedure, 1933. *Address:* Maylands, Gayton Lane, Heswall, Wirral, Merseyside. *Clubs:* Reform, Athenæum (Pres. 1962); University Staff House (Liverpool).

NELSON, Campbell Louis; Chairman, 1971–80, and Managing Director, 1960–80, Ultramar Co. Ltd (Director, since 1947; Executive Director, 1947–80); *b* 14 Dec. 1910; *s* of George Francis Nelson and Kate Nelson (*née* Wilson); *m* 1939, Pauline Frances Blundell (*d* 1978); one *s* one *d. Educ:* Seaford Coll.; King's Coll., London Univ. FCA. Partner of Limebeer & Co., Chartered Accountants, 1933–41. Served War, KRRC (Motor Bns), 1941–44. Sen. Partner, Limebeer & Co., 1944–74 (retd); Exec. Dir, 1948–, Chm., 1957–, British-Borneo Petroleum Syndicate Ltd; Dir, 1970–81, Chm., 1976–81, Gellatly Hankey & Co. Ltd (retd); Chm., 1975–, Scottish Offshore Investors Ltd; Dir, Harrisons (Clyde) Ltd, 1981–. Councillor: Maritime Trust, 1979–; Indonesia Assoc., 1980–; Patron, St James and St Vedast Schools, 1980–. *Recreations:* golf, bridge. *Address:* 2 Chelsea House, 26 Lowndes Street, SW1X 9JD. *T:* 01-235 8260; Queenshill, Sunningdale, Berks. *T:* Ascot 20088. *Clubs:* City of London; Royal and Ancient Golf (St Andrews), Royal Wimbledon Golf, Sunningdale Golf.

NELSON, Air Cdre Eric Douglas Mackinlay, CB 1952; DL; retired, Sept. 1963; *b* 2 Jan. 1912; *e s* of late Rear-Adm. R. D. Nelson, CBE, and the late Ethel Nelson (*née* MacKinlay); *m* 1939, Margaret Yvonne Taylor; one *s* one *d. Educ:* Dover Coll.; RAF Coll., Cranwell. Commissioned RAF, 1932; served War of 1939–45 (despatches); CO 103 (HB) Sqdn Elsham Wolds, 1943–44; Group Capt., 1944; ADC to the Queen, 1953–57; Air Commodore 1956; Commandant, RAF, Halton, 1956–58; Commandant, Royal Air Force Staff College, Andover, 1958–60; AOA Transport Command, 1960–61; Air Officer Commanding and Commandant, Royal Air Force College, Cranwell, 1961–63. DL Lincs, 1966, Hon. Clerk to Lieutenancy, 1973–. *Recreations:* sailing, beagling. *Address:* (permanent) Jasmine Cottage, Carlton-le-Moorland, Lincoln. *T:* Bassingham 309. *Club:* Royal Air Force.

NELSON, Maj.-Gen. Sir (Eustace) John (Blois), KCVO 1966 (MVO 1953); CB 1965; DSO 1944; OBE 1948; MC 1943; *b* 15 June 1912; *s* of late Roland Hugh Nelson and late Hylda Letitia Blois; *m* 1936, the Lady Jane FitzRoy (granted rank and precedence of *d* of a duke, 1931), *er d* of (William Henry Alfred FitzRoy) Viscount Ipswich; two *d. Educ:* Eton; Trinity College, Cambridge. BA (Hons) History. Commissioned Grenadier Guards, Sept. 1933; served 1939–45 with 3rd and 5th Bns, Belgium, N Africa, Italy (wounded three times, despatches); comd 3rd Bn Grenadier Guards, 1944–45, Italy. Contested (C) Whitechapel, 1945. Comd 1st Guards Parachute Bn, 1946–48, Palestine; comd 1st Bn Gren. Gds, 1950–52, Tripoli, N Africa. Planning Staff Standing Group, Washington, DC, 1954–56, Imperial Defence College, 1958; comd 4th Guards Bde, 1959–61, Germany; GOC London District, and Maj.-Gen. comdg Household Brigade 1962–65; GOC Berlin (British Sector), 1966–68. Chm., Internat. Students' House; Vice-Pres., Nat. Playing Fields Assoc. (Gen. Sec. 1969–72). Silver Star (USA), 1944. *Recreations:* the countryside, sailing. *Address:* Tigh Bhaan, Appin, Argyll. *T:* Appin 252.

NELSON, Geoffrey Sheard, CBE 1970; Director, Leased Hotels Ltd; *b* 1 Jan. 1909; *s* of late William Nelson and Sarah Nelson (*née* Sheard); *m* 1932, Gladys, *d* of late C. W. Brown; two *d. Educ:* Leeds Central High Sch. Chartered Accountant (Incorporated Accountant, 1931). Min. of Supply (Costing Br.), 1942-45. Subseq. with Finance Corp. for Industry Ltd., Gen. Manager, 1948-73. FCA, ACMA. *Recreations:* golf, photography, travel. *Address:* 4 Norman Way, Southgate, N14 6NA. *T:* 01-886 0442.

NELSON, Air Marshal Sir Richard; *see* Nelson, Air Marshal Sir S. R. C.

NELSON, (Richard) Anthony; MP (C) Chichester, since Oct. 1974; *b* 11 June 1948; *o s* of Gp Captain R. G. Nelson, BSc, CEng, FRAeS, MICE, and Mrs J. M. Nelson; *m* 1974, Caroline Victoria Butler; one *s* one *d. Educ:* Harrow Sch.; Christ's Coll., Cambridge (MA (Hons) Economics and Law). State Scholarship to Harrow, 1961; Head of School, 1966; Rothschild Scholar, 1966. N. M. Rothschild & Sons Ltd, 1969-73. Founder Mem., Nat. Victims Assoc., 1972; Member: Bow Gp Council, 1973; Howard League Council, 1977-. Contested (C) E Leeds, Feb. 1974. Mem., Select Cttee on Science and Technology, 1975-79; PPS to Minister for Housing and Construction, 1979-. FRSA 1979. *Recreations:* music, rugby. *Address:* The Old Vicarage, Easebourne, Midhurst, West Sussex.

NELSON, St Elmo Dudley, CMG 1964; Permanent Secretary, Military Governor's Office, Kano, 1968-76; Acting Secretary to Military Government, and Head of Kano State Civil Service, 1970, 1973 and 1975; *b* 18 March 1919; *s* of Dudley Nelson and Dorothy Maida (*née* Browne), Highton, Victoria, Australia; *m* 1958, Lynette Margaret, *o d* of late Phillip Anthony Browne, Yarram and Frankston, Victoria, Australia. *Educ:* privately; Geelong School; Oxford University; Sorbonne. Served War of 1939-45 (despatches): 2/7 Australian Infantry Bn (Major); campaigns N Africa, Greece, Crete, New Guinea; Instructor Staff Coll., Cabalah, 1944. Joined HM Colonial Administrative Service. Nigeria: Cadet 1947; Administrative Officer (Class II), 1957; Resident, Plateau Province, 1961; Resident and Provincial Sec., Kabba Province, 1962; Provincial Sec., Kano Province, 1963-67, Sokoto, 1967-68. Chm., Cttee which divided assets of Northern Region between the six Northern States, 1967. Election supervisor, Rhodesian independence elecns, 1980. Gen. Tax Comr, S Wilts, 1980-. *Recreations:* fishing, polo, squash. *Address:* Burcombe Manor, Burcombe, near Salisbury, Wilts SP2 0EJ. *Club:* MCC.

NELSON, Air Marshal Sir (Sidney) Richard (Carlyle), KCB 1963 (CB 1962); OBE 1949; Director-General, Royal Air Force Medical Services, 1962-67; Director of Research and Medical Services, Aspro-Nicholas Ltd, 1967-72; *b* Ponoka, Alberta, Canada, 14 Nov. 1907; *s* of M. O. Nelson, BA; *m* 1939, Christina Elizabeth Powell; two *s. Educ:* University of Alberta (MD). Commissioned in RAF, 1935; served: England 1935-36; Egypt and Western Desert, 1936-42; Fighter Command, 1943; UK Delegation (Canada), 1943-44; British Jt Services Mission (Washington), 1945-48; RAF Staff Coll., 1949; Air Ministry, 1949-52; Comd RAF Hosp., Nocton Hall, 1953-55; SMO British Forces, Arabian Peninsula, 1956-57; PMO Technical Training Comd, 1957-59; Bomber Comd, 1959-62, QHP 1961-67. *Recreations:* fishing, golf. *Address:* Caffyn's Copse, Shappen Hill Lane, Burley, Hants. *T:* Burley 3308. *Clubs:* Royal Air Force; Royal Lymington Yacht.

NELSON, Sir William Vernon Hope, 3rd Bt, *cr* 1912; OBE 1952; Major (retired) late 8th Hussars; *b* 25 May 1914; *s* of late William Hope Nelson (2nd *s* of 1st Bt); *S* uncle, Sir James Hope Nelson, 2nd Bt, 1960; *m* 1945, Elizabeth Ann Bevil, *er d* of Viscount Falkland, *qv*; three *s* three *d. Educ:* Beaumont; Royal Military College, Sandhurst. Commissioned 2nd Lt, 8th Hussars, 1934. Served in Palestine, 1936-39 (despatches, medal with clasp). Served War of 1939-45; served Korea, 1950-51 (OBE). *Heir: s* Jamie Charles Vernon Hope Nelson, *b* 23 Oct. 1949. *Address:* c/o Hoare & Co., 16 Waterloo Place, SW1.

NEMETZ, Hon. Nathaniel Theodore; Hon. Chief Justice Nemetz; Canada Medal 1967; Chief Justice of British Columbia and Administrator of the Province of British Columbia, since 1979; *b* 8 Sept. 1913; *s* of Samuel and Rebecca (*née* Birch); *m* 1935, Bel Newman; one *s. Educ:* Univ. of British Columbia (BA (1st Cl. Hons)). Called to the Bar, 1938; QC (Canada) 1951. Justice, Supreme Court of BC, 1963-67; Justice, Court of Appeal of BC, 1968-73; Chief Justice, Supreme Court of BC, 1973-78. Special counsel to: City of Vancouver, City of New Westminster and Municipality of Burnaby; Electrical Assoc.; BC Hosp. Assoc.; Public Utilities Commn of BC; Royal Commission on: Expropriation, 1961; Fishing, 1964; Election Regulations, 1965; Forest Industry, 1966. Chm., Educational Delegn to People's Republic of China, 1974; Advisor to Canadian Govt Delegn, ILO, Geneva, 1973. University of British Columbia: Chm., Bd of Governors, 1965-68; Chancellor, 1972-75; Pres., Alumni Assoc., 1957; Mem., Bd of Governors, Canadian Inst. for Advanced Legal Studies, Cambridge, England. Hon. Fellow, Hebrew Univ., Jerusalem, 1976. Hon. LLD: Notre Dame (Nelson), 1972; Simon Fraser, 1975; British Columbia, 1975; Victoria, 1976. Silver Jubilee Medal, 1977. *Publications:* Swedish Labour Law and Practice, 1967; Judicial Administration and Judicial Independence, 1976. *Recreations:* swimming, billiards. *Address:* 5688 Newton Wynd, Vancouver, BC V6T 1H5, Canada. *T:* (604) 224-5383; (office) (604) 668-2710. *Clubs:* Vancouver, University, Faculty of University of British Columbia (all Vancouver).

NEMON, Oscar; Sculptor; *b* 13 March 1906; *s* of Mavro and Eugenia Nemon, Yugoslavia; *m* 1939, Patricia Villiers-Stuart; one *s* two *d. Educ:* Osijek; Brussels; Paris. Exhibitions held in principal capitals of Europe. Examples of his work are in: House of Commons; Windsor Castle; The Guildhall, London; The Union, Oxford. His sitters include: HM The Queen, HM the Queen Mother, Rt Hon. Sir Winston Churchill, Rt Hon. Harold Macmillan, Lord Beaverbrook, Sigmund Freud, Sir Max Beerbohm, Lord Montgomery, President Eisenhower; other work: Lord Portal, 1975. Hon. DLitt St Andrews, 1978. *Recreation:* searching for lost opportunities. *Address:* Pleasant Land, Boars Hill, Oxford. *T:* Oxford 735583.
See also Sir George Young, Bt.

NEPEAN, Lt-Col Sir Evan Yorke, 6th Bt, *cr* 1802; late Royal Signals; *b* 23 Nov. 1909; *s* of Sir Charles Evan Molyneux Yorke Nepean, 5th Bt, and Mary Winifred, *o d* of Rev. William John Swayne, formerly Vicar of Heytesbury, Wilts, and Custos of St John's Hospital, Heytesbury; *S* father 1953; *m* 1940, (Georgiana) Cicely, *o d* of late Major Noel Edward Grey Willoughby, Middlesex Regiment, of Chancel End House, Heytesbury, Wilts; three *d. Educ:* Winchester; Downing College, Cambridge. BA 1931, MA 1946. North West Frontier of India (Mohmand), 1935. Served War of 1939-45: GSO3, War Office, 1939-40; with Royal Signals (Lt-Col 1943), UK, and Middle East, Major 1946; on Staff Southern Command, 1947; GSO1 Royal Signals, Ministry of Defence, 1950-53; Lt-Col 1952; Cmdg 11 Air Formation Signal Regt, BAOR, 1955-56, retired. Civil Servant, 1957-59; CSO's branch at HQ Southern Command (Retired Officers' Staff appt), 1959-73. MIEE. *Recreations:* sailing, amateur radio. *Heir:* none. *Address:* Goldens, Teffont, Salisbury, Wilts. *T:* Teffont 275. *Club:* Royal Lymington Yacht.

NERINA, Nadia; (*née* Nadine Judd**);** Prima Ballerina; Ballerina with Royal Ballet, 1951-69; *b* Cape Town, Oct. 1927; *m* 1955, Charles Gordon. Joined Sadler's Wells Sch., 1946; after two months joined Sadler's Wells Theatre Ballet; transferred Sadler's Wells Ballet, Royal Opera House (now Royal Ballet), as soloist, 1967. *Rôles:* Princess Aurora in The Sleeping Beauty; Ondine; Odette-Odile in Swan Lake; Swanhilda in Coppelia; Sylvia; Giselle; Cinderella; Firebird; Can Can Dancer in La Boutique Fantasque; Ballerina in Petrushka; Colombine in Carnaval; Mazurka, Little Waltz, Prelude, in Les Sylphides; Mam'zelle Angot; Ballet Imperial; Scènes de Ballet; Flower Festival of Genzano; Les Rendezvous; Polka in Façade; The Girl in Spectre de la Rose; Casse Noisette; Laurentia; Khadra; Vagabonds; The Bride in A Wedding Bouquet; *creations:* Circus Dancer in Mardi Gras; Fairy Spring in Cinderella; Queen of the Earth in Homage to the Queen; Faded Beauty in Noctambules; Variation on a Theme; Birthday Offering; Lise in La Fille Mal Gardée; Electra; The Girl in Home; Clorinda in Tancredi. Appeared with Royal Ballet: Europe; South Africa; USA; Canada; USSR; Bulgaria; Romania. Recital Tours with Alexis Rassine: South Africa, 1952-55; England, 1956-57; concert performances, Royal Albert Hall and Royal Festival Hall, 1958-60. *Guest appearances include:* Turkish Nat. Ballet, 1957; Bolshoi Ballet, Kirov Ballet, 1960; Munich Ballet, 1963; Nat. Finnish Ballet, Royal Danish Ballet, 1964; Stuttgart Ballet, 1965; Ballet Theatre, Opera House Chicago, 1967; Royal Command Variety Performances, 1963-66. Mounted, dir. and prod three Charity Gala performances, London Palladium, 1969, 1971, 1972. Many TV appearances, UK and USA. Hon. Consultant on Ballet, Ohio Univ., 1967-69. British Jury Member, 3rd Internat. Ballet Competition, Moscow, 1977. Fellow, 1959, Patron, 1964, Cecchetti Soc. Mem. Council, RSPCA, 1969-74. *Publications:* contrib: La Fille Mal Gardée, 1960; Ballet and Modern Dance, 1974; *relevant publication:* Ballerina, ed Clement Crisp, 1975. *Address:* c/o Royal Opera House, Covent Garden, WC2.

NESS, Air Marshal Sir Charles, KCB 1980 (CB 1978); CBE 1967 (OBE 1959); Air Member for Personnel, since 1980; *s* of late Charles W. Ness and Jessica Ness; *m* 1951, Audrey, *d* of late Roy and Phyllis Parker; one *s. Educ:* George Heriot's Sch.; Edinburgh Univ. CBIM, MIPM. Joined RAF, 1943; flying and staff appts in Bomber Comd and with USAF, 1943-62; Commander, British Skybolt Trials Force, Florida, 1962-63; Station Commander, Royal Air Force, Steamer Point, Aden, 1965-67; Air Comdr, Gibraltar, 1971-73; Director of Organisation and Administrative Plans (RAF), MoD, 1974-75; Comdr, Southern Maritime Air Region, 1975-76; Dir Gen., Personnel Management (RAF), 1976-80. Pres., Aries Assoc., 1976-. *Address:* Perseverance Cottage, Wentworth, near Ely, Cambs. *T:* Ely 778968. *Club:* Royal Air Force.

NETHERTHORPE, 2nd Baron *cr* 1959, of Anston, W Riding; **James Andrew Turner,** FCA; Deputy Chairman, Dalgety Ltd, since 1978 (Chief Executive, 1978-81); *b* 23 July 1936; *s* of 1st Baron Netherthorpe, and of Margaret Lucy, *d* of James Arthur Mattock; *S* father, 1980; *m* 1960, Belinda Nicholson; two *s* two *d. Educ:* Rugby Sch.; Pembroke Coll., Cambridge. Peat, Marwick, Mitchell & Co., Chartered Accountants, 1958-61; joined Lazard Brothers & Co. Ltd, 1961; seconded to Australian United Corp. Ltd, 1966-67; apptd Head of Lazards' Corporate Finance Dept, 1969; Dir, Lazards, 1971-; Dalgety Ltd: Director; Vice-Chm. and Exec. Dir, 1972-75; Man. Dir, 1975-78; also Director: Dalgety UK Ltd; Dalgety Australia Ltd; Dalgety New Zealand Ltd; Babcock International Ltd, 1971-82. Mem., Council of British Australia Soc. Chairman of Tree Foundation. *Heir: s* Hon. James Frederick Turner, *b* 7 Jan. 1964. *Address:* Boothby Hall, Boothby Pagnell, Grantham, Lincs NG33 4DQ. *T:* Ingoldsby 374.

NEUBERGER, Albert, CBE 1964; PhD (London), MD (Würzburg); FRCP; FRS 1951; FRSC; Professor of Chemical Pathology, St Mary's Hospital,

University of London, 1955-73, now Emeritus Professor; Physician-in-Chief (*Pro Tem.*), at Peter Bent Brigham Hospital, Boston, and Visiting Lecturer on Biological Chemistry, Harvard Univ., 1964; *b* 15 April 1908; *s* of late Max Neuberger and Bertha Neuberger; *m* 1943, Lilian Ida, *d* of late Edmond Dreyfus and Marguerite Dreyfus, London; four *s* one *d*. *Educ:* Gymnasium, Würzburg; Univs of Würzburg and London. Beit Memorial Research Fellow, 1936-40; Research at the Biochemistry Department, Cambridge, 1939-42; Mem. of Scientific Staff, Medical Research Council, 1943; Adviser to GHQ, Delhi (Medical Directorate), 1945; Head of Biochemistry Dept, Nat. Inst. for Medical Research, 1950-55; Principal of the Wright Fleming Institute of Microbiology, 1958-62. Visiting Lectr on Medicine, Harvard Univ. 1960. Mem. of Editorial Bd Biochemical Jl, 1947-55, Chm., 1952-55; Associate Man. Editor, Biochimica et Biophysica Acta, 1968-. Member: MRC, 1962-66; Council of Scientific Policy, 1968-69; ARC, 1969-79; Indep. Cttee on Smoking and Health, 1973-; Chm., Jt ARC/MRC Cttee on Food and Nutrition Res., 1971-73; Chairman: Governing Body, Lister Inst., 1971- (Mem., 1968-); Advisory Board, Beit Memorial Fellowships, 1967-73; Biochemical Soc., 1967-69 (Hon. Mem., Biochemical Soc., 1973); Dep. Chm., Bd of Governors, Hebrew Univ., Jerusalem. Pres., Assoc. of Clinical Biochemists, 1972-73; Hon. Pres., British Nutrition Foundn, 1982-. For. Hon. Mem., Amer. Acad. Arts and Sciences, 1972. FRCPath 1964; FRCP 1966. William Julius Mickle Fellowship of Univ. of London, 1946-47; Heberden Medal, 1959; Frederick Gowland Hopkins Medal, 1960; Kaplun Prize, 1973. Hon. LLD, Aberdeen, 1967; Hon. PhD, Jerusalem, 1968; Hon. DSc Hull, 1981. *Publications:* papers in Biochemical Jl, Proceedings of Royal Society and other learned journals. *Address:* 37 Eton Court, Eton Avenue, NW3 3HJ. *T:* 01-586 5470; Lister Institute of Preventive Medicine, Charing Cross Hospital Medical School, The Reynolds Building, St Dunstan's Road, W6 8RP. *Club:* Athenæum.

NEUBERT, Michael Jon; MP (C) Havering, Romford, since Feb. 1974; Parliamentary Private Secretary to Ministers of State, Northern Ireland Office, since 1981, and to Secretary of State for Trade, since 1982; *b* 3 Sept. 1933; *s* of Frederick Henry and Mathilda Marie Louise Neubert; *m* 1959, Sally Felicity Bilger; one *s*. *Educ:* Queen Elizabeth's Sch., Barnet; Bromley Grammar Sch.; Royal Coll. of Music; Downing Coll., Cambridge. MA (Cantab) Modern and Medieval Langs. Travel and industrial consultant. Councillor, Borough of Bromley, 1960-63; London Borough of Bromley: Councillor, 1964-68; Alderman, 1968-74; Leader of the Council, 1967-70; Mayor, 1972-73. Prospective Parly Candidate (C), N Hammersmith, 1965; contested (C): N Hammersmith, Gen. Elec., 1966; Romford (Prosp. Cand., 1969), Gen. Elec., 1970; PPS to Minister for Social Security and for the Disabled, 1980, to Minister of State for Employment, 1981-82. Chm., Bromley Conservative Assoc., 1968-69. *Publication:* Running Your Own Society, 1967. *Recreations:* music, literature, cinema, theatre, the countryside. *Address:* 12 Greatwood, Chislehurst, Kent BR7 5HU. *T:* 01-467 0040. *Club:* Romford Conservative and Constitutional.

NEUMANN, Prof. Bernhard Hermann, FACE 1970; FAA 1964; FRS 1959; Honorary Research Fellow, CSIRO Division of Mathematics and Statistics, since 1978; *b* Berlin-Charlottenburg, 15 Oct. 1909; *s* of late Richard Neumann and late Else (*née* Aronstein); *m* 1st, 1938, Hanna Neumann (*née* von Caemmerer) (*d* 1971), DPhil, DSc, FAA, formerly Prof. and Head of Dept of Pure Mathematics, Sch. of Gen. Studies, ANU; three *s* two *d*; 2nd, 1973, Dorothea Neumann (*née* Zeim). *Educ:* Herderschule, Berlin; Univs of Freiburg, Berlin, Cambridge. Dr phil Berlin, 1932; PhD Cambridge 1935; DSc Manchester 1954. Asst Lectr, University Coll, Cardiff, 1937-40. Army Service, 1940-45. Lectr, University Coll., Hull, 1946-48; Lectr, Senior Lectr, Reader, Univ. of Manchester, 1948-61; Prof. and Hd of Dept of Maths, Inst. of Advanced Studies, ANU, Canberra, 1962-74, Emeritus Prof., 1975-; Sen. Res. Fellow, CSIRO Div. of Maths and Stats, 1975-77. Visiting Lecturer: Australian Univs, 1959; Univ. of Cambridge, 1970; Monash Univ., 1980; Visiting Professor: Tata Inst. of Fundamental Research, Bombay, 1959; New York Univ., 1961-62; Univ. of Wisconsin, 1966-67; Vanderbilt Univ., 1969-70; G. A. Miller Vis. Prof., Univ. of Illinois at Urbana-Champaign, 1975; Univ. of Manitoba, 1979; Vis. Fellow, Fitzwilliam Coll., Cambridge, 1970. Wiskundig Genootschap te Amsterdam Prize, 1949; Adams Prize, Univ. of Cambridge, 1952-53. Chm., Aust. Subcommn, Internat. Commn Math. Instruct., 1967-75; Mem.-at-large, Internat. Commn Math. Instruct., 1975-, Mem. Exec. Cttee, 1979-82; Mem., Programme Adv. Cttee, Congress Math. Educn, Karlsruhe, 1976, Berkeley, Calif., 1980, Adelaide, Australia, 1984. Member Council: London Math. Society, 1954-61 (Vice-Pres., 1957-59); Aust. Math. Society, 1963-79 (Vice-Pres., 1963-64, 1966-68, 1971-73, Pres., 1964-66; Hon. Mem. 1981-); Aust. Acad. of Science, 1968-71 (a Vice-Pres., 1969-71). Mem. Aust. Nat. Cttee for Mathematics, 1963-75 (Chm., 1966-75); (Foundation) Pres., Aust. Assoc. Math. Teachers, 1966-68, Vice-Pres., 1968-69, Hon. Mem., 1975-; (Foundn) Pres., Canberra Math. Assoc., 1963-65, Vice-Pres., 1965-66, Hon. Mem., 1975-; Hon. Mem., NZ Math. Soc., 1975-; Mem., Acad. Adv. Council, RAN Coll., 1978-. Hon. DSc: Univ. of Newcastle, NSW, 1974; Monash Univ., 1982; Non-res. Fellow (Tutor), Bruce Hall, ANU, 1963-; Hon. Fellow, Dept of Maths, Inst. of Advanced Studies, ANU, 1975-. Pres., Amateur Sinfonia of Canberra Inc., 1978-80, Vice-Pres., 1980-81. Hon. Editor, Proc. London Math. Soc., 1959-61; Assoc. Editor, Pacific Jl Math., 1964-; (Foundation) Editor, Bulletin of Aust. Math. Soc., 1969-79, Hon. Editor, 1979-; Member Editorial Board: Communications in Algebra, 1973-; Houston Math. Jl, 1974-; Indian Jl Math. Educn, 1974-; Mem., Adv. Bd, Zentralblatt Didaktik Math. 1970-; Founder Editor and Publisher, IMU Canberra Circular, 1972-; Mem. and Regional Chm., IMU Exchange Commn, 1975-78. *Publications:* Appendix to German and Hungarian translations of A. G. Kuroš: Teoriya Grupp, 1953, 1955: Topics in the Theory of Infinite Groups, Bombay, 1961; Special Topics in Algebra, Vol. I: Universal Algebra, Vol. II: Order Techniques, New York, 1962; papers, mainly on theory of groups, in various mathematical journals. *Recreations:* chess, cycling, music. *Address:* 20 Talbot Street, Forrest, ACT 2603, Australia. *T:* (062) Canberra 733447.

NEVE, David Lewis; President, Immigration Appeal Tribunal, since 1978; *b* 7 Oct. 1920; *s* of Eric Read Neve, QC, and Nellie Victorine Neve (*née* Uridge); *m* 1948, Betsy Davida Bannerman; one *s* (decd). *Educ:* Repton; Emmanuel Coll., Cambridge (BA). Served war, Royal Artillery, 1940-46. Called to Bar, Middle Temple, 1947; Resident Magistrate, Uganda, 1952-59; Sen. Resident Magistrate, Uganda, 1959-62; Acting Judge, Uganda, 1962. Immigration Appeals Adjudicator, 1970; Vice-Pres., Immigration Appeals Tribunal, 1976. *Recreations:* sailing, music, reading. *Address:* Deans, Lewes Road, Ditchling, Hassocks, East Sussex.

NEVILE, Henry Nicholas; Lord-Lieutenant of Lincolnshire, since 1976; *b* 1920; *s* of Charles Joseph Nevile, Wellingore, Lincoln; *m* 1944, Jean Rosita Mary, *d* of Cyril James Wenceslas Torr; two *s* three *d*. *Educ:* Ampleforth; Trinity Coll., Cambridge. Served war, Scots Guards, in France and Germany, 1940-46. JP 1950, DL 1962, Lincs; High Sheriff of Lincolnshire, 1963. *Address:* Aubourn Hall, Lincoln. *T:* Bassingham 224.

NEVILL, family name of **Marquess of Abergavenny.**

NEVILL, Air Vice-Marshal Sir Arthur de Terrotte, KBE 1950 (CBE 1941); CB 1946; CEng; FRAeS; Director of Civil Aviation, New Zealand, 1956-65, retired; Royal New Zealand Air Force; *b* 29 April 1899; *s* of late H. G. Nevill; *m* 1927, Mary Seton, *d* of E. T. Norris; two *d*. *Educ:* Auckland Grammar School; Royal Military College, Duntroon. BSc 1921; MSc 1952. Chief of Air Staff, NZ, 1946-51; Member Air Licensing Authority, 1952; Deputy Director of Civil Aviation, New Zealand, 1952-56, Director, 1956-65. President NZ Div., RAeS, 1949-52. Member: NZ Univ. Grants Cttee, 1955-68 (Dep.-Chm., 1961-68); Research and Scholarships Cttee, UGC, 1968-79; US Educational Foundation in NZ, 1958-70; NZ Architects Educn and Registration Board, 1964-79; engaged in research administration, UGC, until resignation in 1979. President: Air Force Association, 1967-72; Air Cadet League, 1972-76. Hon. D Waikato Univ., 1969. Legion of Merit (USA). *Address:* 27 Colway Street, Ngaio, Wellington 4, New Zealand. *Club:* United Services (Wellington).

NEVILL, Bernard Richard, FSIAD; designer; *b* 24 Sept. 1934; *s* of R. Nevill. *Educ:* privately; St Martin's Sch. of Art; Royal Coll. of Art. FSIA 1970. Designed exhibn, Opera and Ballet, for Cotton Bd, Manchester, 1950; lectured in art, fashion, history of costume, textile design and fashion drawing, Shoreditch Coll., 1954-56 (resp. for first dress show staged at GLC Chm.'s annual reception, County Hall); Lectr, St Martin's Sch. of Art and RCA, 1959-74 (liaised between Fashion and Textile Schs, devising projs and themes for finale to RCA annual diploma show); lectured in theatre design and book illustration, Central Sch. of Art and Design, 1957-60; freelance illustrator, Good Housekeeping, Woman's Jl, Vogue, Harper's Bazaar, incl. covers for Queen and Sketch, 1956-60; freelance journalist, Vogue, Sketch and textile and fashion periodicals, 1956-66; Art Critic, Vogue, 1965-66; Designer (later Design Dir), Liberty Prints, 1961: for next decade, produced collections which became fashion landmarks and re-estabd Liberty's as major source of fashion textiles worldwide; collections designed: Islamic, 1963 (anticipated Eastern revival in fashion); Jazz, 1964 (first re-appraisal of Art Deco); Tango, 1966; Renaissance, 1967; Chameleon, 1969 (co-ordinated prints); Designer and Design Dir, Ten Cate, Holland, 1969-71; Design Consultant in dress fabrics to Cantoni (founders of cotton industry in Italy), 1971-: printed velvets and cottons have placed Cantoni in fore-front of internat. ready-to-wear; designed printed sheet collection for Cantoni Casa, 1977. Designed: two collections for Internat. Wool Secretariat, 1975-77; English Country House Collection for Sekers Internat., 1981-82 (collection used when redesigned Long Gall., Lutyen's British Embassy, Washington). Designed costumes: films: Genevieve, 1953; Next To No Time, 1955; The Admirable Crichton, 1957; musical: Marigold, 1958; opera: Cosi fan tutte (Glyndebourne), 1962. Mem., Adv. Panel, National Dip. of Design, 1964-66; Governor, Croydon Coll. of Art, 1966-67. FRSA 1967, resigned 1977. Illustrated articles on his work have appeared in the Press. *Recreations:* looking at large well-built walls and buildings; passionate conservationist and environmentalist, collector, bibliophil; tree-worship, chamber music. *Address:* West House, 35 Glebe Place, SW3; Fonthill Abbey, Fonthill Gifford, near Salisbury, Wilts.

NEVILL, Maj.-Gen. Cosmo Alexander Richard, CB 1958; CBE 1954; DSO 1944; War Office, 1958-60; Colonel, Royal Fusiliers, 1959-63, retired; *b* 14 July 1907; *s* of late Maj. Cosmo Charles Richard Nevill, DSO, OBE, Eccleston, Leamington Spa; *m* 1934, Grania, *d* of late Maj. G. V. Goodliffe, MC, Birdstown, co. Donegal; one *s* one *d*. *Educ:* Harrow; Royal Military College. Commissioned as Second Lieutenant, Royal Fusiliers, 1927; served War of 1939-45 (DSO, OBE): on staff, India; commanded 2nd battalion Devonshire Regiment, Normandy; Lieutenant-Colonel, 1944. A General Staff Officer, Military Staff Committee, United Nations, New York, 1946-48; commanded 1st battalion Royal Fusiliers, 1950-51; temporary Brigadier, 1951; a Brigade Commander, 1951-54; Commandant School of Infantry, 1954-56; Major-General 1957; GOC 2nd Infantry Division, 1956-58. CC West Suffolk,

1962. Lay Canon, St Edmundsbury Cathedral, 1979-. *Address:* Holt, Edwardstone, Boxford, Suffolk CO6 5PJ. *T:* Boxford 210428. *Club:* Army and Navy.

NEVILLE, family name of **Baron Braybrooke.**

NEVILLE, Prof. Adam Matthew, MC 1944; TD 1963; Principal and Vice-Chancellor, University of Dundee, since 1978; *b* 5 Feb. 1923; *m* 1952, Mary Hallam Cousins; one *s* one *d.* BSc 1st cl. Hons, MSc, PhD, DSc (Eng) London; DSc Leeds; FIStructE, FAmSCE, MSocCE (France), FCIArb; formerly FICE, resigned. Lectr, Southampton Univ., 1950-51; Engr, Min. of Works, NZ, 1951-54; Lectr, Manchester Univ., 1955-60; Prof. of Civil Engrg, Nigerian Coll. of Technology, 1960-62; Dean of Engrg, Calgary Univ., 1963-67, also Dean of Graduate Studies, 1965-66; Vis. Prof., Swiss Federal Inst. of Technology, 1967-68; Prof. and Head of Dept of Civil Engineering, Univ. of Leeds, 1968-78. Consultant on concrete and structural design and failures. Former Chm., Permanent Concrete Commn, RILEM (Internat. Union of Testing and Res. Labs for Materials and Structures); Dir, Petroleum Recovery Res. Inst.; Advr to Canadian Govt on management of concrete research. Member Council: Concrete Soc., 1968-77, Pres., 1974-75; IStructE, 1976-79; Faculty of Building, 1976-80; Open University, 1979-; Europe Standing Conference on Univ. Problems, 1980- (Vice-Pres., 1983-); Member: Bd, Architectural Educn, ARC, 1980-; Exec. Cttee, IUPC, 1979-. Mem. Editorial Boards of various technical jls. Fellow, Amer. Concrete Inst., 1973; Hon. Fellow, Inst. of Concrete Technologists, 1976; For. Mem., Académie Royale des Sciences d'Outre-Mer, Belgium, 1974. IStructE Research Award, 1960; Reinforced Concrete Assoc. Medal, 1961; Senior Research Fellowship, Nat. Research Council of Canada, 1967. Stanton Walker Award (US) 1968; Medal of Univ. of Liège (Belgium), 1970; Arthur R. Anderson Award, Amer. Concrete Inst., 1972. *Publications:* Properties of Concrete, 1963, 3 edns, trans. into 8 languages; (with J. B. Kennedy) Basic Statistical Methods, 1964, 2 edns; Creep of Concrete: plain, reinforced and prestressed, 1970; (with A. Ghali) Structural Analysis: a unified classical and matrix approach, 1971, 2 edns, trans. into Chinese; Hardened Concrete: physical and mechanical aspects, 1971; High Alumina Cement Concrete, 1975; numerous research papers on concrete and concrete structures. *Recreations:* ski-ing, travel. *Address:* The University, Dundee. *Club:* Athenæum.

NEVILLE, (Eric) Graham; His Honour Judge Neville; a Circuit Judge, since 1980; *b* 12 Nov. 1933; *s* of late Frederick Thomas Neville and Doris Winifred (*née* Toye); *m* 1966, Jacqueline Catherine, *d* of late Major Francis Whalley and Alexandrina Whalley (*née* MacLeod). *Educ:* Kelly Coll.; Sidney Sussex Coll., Cambridge. Served Royal Air Force, General Duties. Called to Bar, Middle Temple, 1958. A Recorder of the Crown Court, 1975-80. *Recreations:* sailing, fishing. *Address:* Trillow House, Nadderwater, Exeter EX4 2LD. *T:* Exeter 54403. *Clubs:* Royal Western Yacht (Plymouth); Royal Fowey Yacht.

NEVILLE, John, OBE 1965; actor, stage and film; Hon. Professor in Drama, Nottingham University, since 1967; Artistic Director, Neptune Theatre, Halifax, Nova Scotia, 1978-May 1983; *b* Willesden, 2 May 1925; *s* of Reginald Daniel Neville and Mabel Lillian (*née* Fry); *m* 1949, Caroline Hooper; three *s* three *d. Educ:* Willesden and Chiswick County Schools; Royal Academy of Dramatic Art. Worked as a stores clerk before studying at RADA. First appearance on stage, walking-on part in Richard II; subseq. parts at Open Air Theatre, in repertory at Lowestoft, and with Birmingham Repertory Co.; Bristol Old Vic Co., 1950-53; Old Vic Co., London, 1953-61; Nottingham Playhouse, 1961-63; Theatre Director, Nottingham Playhouse, 1963-68; Dir, Park Theatre Co., Fortune, 1969; Theatre Director: Citadel Theatre, Edmonton, Canada, 1973-78; Neptune Theatre, Halifax, NS, 1978. Parts with Old Vic include: Ferdinand in The Tempest, Macduff, Richard II, Orlando in As You Like It, Henry Percy in Henry IV, Part I, Mark Antony; during Old Vic tour of Europe, 1958, Hamlet, Sir Andrew Aguecheek. Played lead in Irma La Douce, Lyric, 1959-60; produced Henry V, Old Vic, 1960; The Lady From the Sea, Queen's, 1961; The School for Scandal, Haymarket, 1962; Alfie, Mermaid and Duchess, 1963. Acted in: The Chichester Festival Theatre, 1962; Beware of the Dog, St Martin's, 1967; Iago in Othello, Nottingham Playhouse, 1967; Mr and Mrs, Palace, 1968; The Apple Cart, Mermaid, 1970; The Beggar's Opera, The Doctor's Dilemma, Chichester, 1972; Sherlock Holmes, NY, 1975; Happy Days, Nat. Theatre, 1977. Tour W Africa (Jt Dir and acting), 1963. *Films:* Oscar Wilde; Topaze; Billy Budd; A Study in Terror. Has appeared on television, incl. The First Churchills, series for BBC 2. Hon. Dr Dramatic Arts Lethbridge Univ., 1979; Hon. DFA Nova Scotia Coll. of Art and Design, 1981. *Address:* 6370 Pepperell Street, Halifax, NS, Canada; c/o Larry Dalzell Associates, 3 Goodwin's Court, St Martin's Lane, WC2.

NEVILLE, Sir Richard (Lionel John Baines), 3rd Bt *cr* 1927; *b* 15 July 1921; *s* of Sir Reginald James Neville Neville, 1st Bt (*d* 1950), and Violet Sophia Mary (*d* 1972), *widow* of Captain Richard Jocelyn Hunter, Rifle Bde and *d* of Lt-Col Cuthbert Johnson Baines, Gloucester Regt, The Lawn, Shirehampton, Glos; *S* half-brother, 1982; unmarried. *Educ:* Eton; Trinity Coll., Cambridge (BA 1941, MA 1948). Served War of 1939-45 as Captain, Oxford and Bucks Light Infantry; seconded Royal West African Frontier Force (1st Gold Coast Regt), Burma Campaign, 1944-45. Journalist and Director of English Broadcasts of Radio-Television Française (RTF), Indochina, 1953-55; Dir of Foreign Broadcasts, RTF (English, Spanish and Portuguese), French Equatorial Africa (Congo), 1956-57; Algeria, 1957-60.

Master, Worshipful Co. of Bowyers, 1972-74. *Recreations:* history, genealogy, heraldry and supporting lost causes. *Heir:* none. *Address:* Sloley Hall, Norwich NR12 8HA. *T:* Swanton Abbott 236.

NEVILLE, Maj.-Gen. Sir Robert Arthur Ross, KCMG 1952; CBE 1948; late RM; *b* 17 Dec. 1896; *s* of late Col William Neville, DSO, Cheshire Regt; *m* 1943, Doris Marie (*d* 1977), *y d* of late Capt. Philip Collen, 14th Sikh Regiment; one *s* one *d. Educ:* Cheltenham College. Joined Royal Marines, 1914, served European War, 1914-18, Grand Fleet and France (despatches); Lt-Col, 1940; served War of 1939-45, Admlty, as Asst Dir of Naval Intelligence, Combined Ops, and in Mediterranean; Colonel, 1945; ADC to the King, 1946-48; Maj.-Gen., 1948. Governor and C-in-C, Bahamas, 1950-Dec. 1953. Dir, Epsylon Industries Ltd, 1954-61; Chm., Vectron Electronics, 1961-66. *Address:* 10 Chiltley Lane, Liphook, Hants GU30 7HJ. *T:* Liphook 722454. *Club:* White's.

NEVILLE, Royce Robert; Agent-General for Tasmania, in London, 1971-78; Governing Director, Neville Constructions Pty Ltd, Burnie; *b* 5 Oct. 1914; *s* of R. P. Neville, Launceston, Tasmania; *m* 1941, Joan, *d* of G. A. Scott; two *s* two *d. Educ:* Launceston Technical Coll. Served War, Sqdn Ldr (OC Flying, Chief Flying Instr, Gen Reconnaissance Sqdn), RAAF, 1941-45. OC Air Trg Corps, Burnie, 1947. Past President: Air Force Assoc., 1947; Tas. Apex, 1948; Tas. Master Builders' Assoc., 1965-67; Master Builders' Fedn of Aust., 1965-66; Comr of Oaths for Tasmania, 1971; Mem., Australia Soc., London; Life Mem., Tasmanian Master Builders' Assoc. FInstD, FRAIB, AFAIM, Fellow, Inst. of Dirs, Aust., 1971; MIEx 1973; FFB 1976; FIArb 1977. Freeman, City of London, 1975; Freeman, Guild of Air Pilots and Air Navigators, 1976. JP 1974. *Recreations:* boating, fishing, water skiing, painting, tennis. *Address:* 29 Seaview Avenue, Burnie, Tasmania 7320, Australia. *Clubs:* Wig and Pen; Naval, Military and Air Force (Hobart).

NEVILLE-JONES, (Lilian) Pauline; Chef de Cabinet to Christopher Tugendhat, European Commissioner for Budget, Financial Control, Financial Institutions, Personnel and Administration, since 1979; *b* 2 Nov. 1939; *d* of Roland Neville-Jones and Cecilia Emily Millicent Rath. *Educ:* Leeds Girls' High Sch.; Lady Margaret Hall, Oxford (BA Hons Mod. History). Harkness Fellow of Commonwealth Fund, USA, 1961-63; joined FO, 1963; Third Sec., Salisbury, Rhodesia, 1964-65; Third, later Second Sec., Singapore, 1965-68; FCO, 1968-71; First Sec., Washington, 1971-75; FCO, 1975-77. *Recreations:* antiques, cooking, gardening. *Address:* 3 Donne Place, SW3. *T:* 01-581 3274; 1 Square Marguerite, 1040 Brussels, Belgium. *T:* Brussels 735-9660.

NEVIN, Thomas Richard, TD 1949 (and Bar); JP; LLB; **His Honour Judge Nevin;** a Circuit Judge and Crown Court Liaison Judge (formerly Judge of County Courts), since 1967; a Dep. High Court Judge, since 1974; *b* 9 Dec. 1916; *e s* of late Thomas Nevin, JP, and Phyllis (*née* Strickland), Ebchester Hall and Mirfield; *m* 1955, Brenda Micaela (marr. diss. 1979), *e d* of Dr B. C. Andrade-Thompson, MC, Scarborough; one *s* (and one *s* decd). *Educ:* Bilton Grange; Shrewsbury School; Leeds University. LLB 1939. 2nd Lt, W Yorks Regt (Leeds Rifles) TA, 1935. Served London Bombardment, India and Burma, 1939-46; Indian Artillery, Lt-Col 1944 (despatches), SEAC; DJAG, XII Army, 1945. Major, TARO, 1951. WR Special Constab., 1938-66. Articled Clerk to Sir A. M. Ramsden, CB, Solicitor, 1935. Called to Bar, Inner Temple, 1948; practised 19 years on NE Circuit; Law Lectr, Leeds Coll. of Commerce, 1949-51; Asst Recorder of Leeds, 1961-64; Recorder of Doncaster, 1964-67; Dep. Chm., Quarter Sessions: W Riding, 1965-71; E Riding, 1968-71, Yorkshire; Chm., Northern Agricultural Land Tribunal, 1963-67 (Dep. Chm. 1961-63); a special Divorce Comr, 1967-72; Mem., County Court Rule Cttee, 1974-80; Chm., Lord Chancellor's Adv. Cttee on JP's, Hull, 1968-74; Founder Chm., Leeds Family Mediation Service, 1979-. Director, Bowishott Estates Ltd; Member: Leeds Gp Hospital Management Cttee, 1965-67; Thoresby Soc.; Yorks Archæological Soc.; President, Yorks Numismatic Soc., 1968; Life Member: Guild of Freemen of London; British Numismatic Soc.; Vice-Pres. Leeds Univ. Law Graduates; Mem., Leeds Univ. Adv. Cttee on Law. FRNS; FRSA; FRGS; FCIArb. Freeman of City of London. JP West Yorks 1965-. *Publications:* Hon. Editor, Yorkshire Numismatic Soc.; and various articles. *Recreations:* coinage, our past, gardening, and rest therefrom. *Address:* The Court House, 1 Oxford Row, Leeds; 11 King's Bench Walk, Temple, EC4.

NEW WESTMINSTER, Archbishop of, since 1981; **Most Rev. Douglas Walter Hambidge,** DD; Metropolitan of the Ecclesiastical Province of British Columbia, since 1981; *b* London, England, 6 March 1927; *s* of Douglas Hambidge and Florence (*née* Driscoll); *m* 1956, Denise Colvill Lown; two *s* one *d. Educ:* London Univ.; London Coll. of Divinity. BD, ALCD; DD, Anglican Theol. Coll. of BC, 1970. Asst Curate, St Mark's, Dalston, 1953-56; Rector: All Saints, Cassiar, BC, 1956-58; St James, Smithers, BC, 1958-64; Vicar, St Martin, Fort St John, BC, 1964-69; Canon, St Andrew's Cathedral, Caledonia, 1965-69; Bishop of Caledonia, 1969-80; Bishop of New Westminster, 1980. *Address:* 101-325 Howe Street, Vancouver, BC V6C 1Z7, Canada.

NEW ZEALAND, Primate and Archbishop of, since 1980; **Most Rev. Paul Alfred Reeves;** Bishop of Auckland, 1979; *b* 6 Dec. 1932; 2nd *s* of D'Arcy Lionel and Hilda Mary Reeves; *m* 1959, Beverley Gwendolen Watkins; three *d. Educ:* Wellington Coll., New Zealand; Victoria Univ. of Wellington (MA); St John's Theol. Coll., Auckland (LTh); St Peter's Coll., Univ. of Oxford (MA; Hon. Fellow, 1980). Deacon, 1958; Priest, 1960;

Curate, Tokoroa, NZ, 1958-59; Curate: St Mary the Virgin, Oxford, 1959-61; Kirkley St Peter, Lowestoft, 1961-63; Vicar, St Paul, Okato, NZ, 1964-66; Lectr in Church History, St John's Coll., Auckland, NZ, 1966-69; Dir of Christian Educn, Dio. Auckland, 1969-71; Bishop of Waiapu, 1971-79. Chm., Environmental Council, 1974-76. *Publications:* Life is Liturgy, 1966; contrib. NZ Theological Review. *Recreations:* jogging, sailing, swimming. *Address:* Bishop's House, 2 Arney Crescent, Remuera, Auckland 5, NZ. *T:* 543473.

NEWALL, family name of **Baron Newall.**

NEWALL, 2nd Baron, *cr* 1946; **Francis Storer Eaton Newall;** company director and Chairman of several companies; *b* 23 June 1930; *o s* of 1st Baron (Marshal of the RAF Lord) Newall, GCB, OM, GCMG, CBE, AM; *S* father, 1963; *m* 1956, Pamela Elizabeth, *e d* of E. H. L. Rowcliffe, Pinkney Park, Malmesbury, Wilts; two *s* one *d. Educ:* Eton College; RMA Sandhurst. Commissioned 11th Hussars (Prince Albert's Own), 1950; served in: Germany, 1950-53; Malaya, 1953-55; on staff of GHQ FarELF, Singapore, 1955-56; Adjt Royal Gloucestershire Hussars, 1956-58; retired 1961. Introduced Farriers Registration Bill and Betting Gaming and Lotteries Amendment Act (Greyhound Racing) in House of Lords and saw into law. Cons. Whip and front bench spokesman, 1976-79; Founder Mem., House of Lords all party Defence Study Group; official visits to NATO, SHAPE, Norway, Morocco, Bonn, Cyprus, BAOR, Qatar, Oman, Bahrain. Mem., Select Cttee on Laboratory Animals Protection Bill. Hon. Pres., Corp. of Mortgage Brokers and Life Assurance Consultants. Mem., Merchant Taylors' Co. *Recreations:* shooting, travel, meeting people. *Heir: s* Hon. Richard Hugh Eaton Newall, *b* 19 Feb. 1961. *Address:* 18 Lennox Gardens, SW1X 0DG; Wotton Underwood, near Aylesbury, Bucks. *Club:* Cavalry and Guards.

NEWARK, Archdeacon of; *see* Leaning, Ven. D.

NEWBIGGING, David Kennedy, OBE 1982; Chairman and Senior Managing Director, Jardine Matheson & Co. Ltd, Hong Kong, since 1975; Chairman: Hongkong Land Co. Ltd, since 1975; Jardine Fleming & Co. Ltd, since 1975; Hongkong Electric Holdings Ltd, since 1982; Director, Hongkong & Shanghai Banking Corporation Ltd, since 1975; *b* 19 Jan. 1934; *s* of late David Locke Newbigging, CBE, MC, and Lucy Margaret; *m* 1968, Carolyn Susan (*née* Band); one *s* two *d. Educ:* in Canada; Oundle Sch., Northants. Joined Jardine, Matheson & Co. Ltd, 1954; Man. Dir, 1970; Chm., Hongkong & Kowloon Wharf & Godown Co. Ltd, 1970-80. Mem., Internat. Council, Morgan Guaranty Trust Co. of NY, 1977-. Member (unofficial): Hong Kong Exec. Council, 1980-; Hong Kong Legislative Council, 1978-. Chairman: Hong Kong Tourist Assoc., 1977-; Hong Kong Gen. Chamber of Commerce, 1980-; Steward, Royal Hong Kong Jockey Club, 1975-. JP (unofficial) Hong Kong, 1971. *Recreations:* most outdoor sports; Chinese art. *Address:* Bangour, 35 Mount Kellett Road, The Peak, Hong Kong. *T:* 5-96334. *Clubs:* Hurlingham, Turf; Hongkong (Hong Kong).

NEWBIGIN, Rt. Rev. (James Edward) Lesslie, CBE 1974; DD; Minister, United Reformed Church, Winson Green, since 1980; *b* 8 Dec. 1909; *s* of Edward Richmond Newbigin, Shipowner, Newcastle, and Annie Ellen Newbigin (*née* Affleck); *m* 1936, Helen Stewart, *d* of Rev. Robert Henderson; one *s* three *d. Educ:* Leighton Park Sch.; Queens' Coll., Cambridge; Westminster Coll., Cambridge. Intercollegiate Secretary, Student Christian Movement, Glasgow, 1931-33. Ordained by Presbytery of Edinburgh and appointed to Madras Mission of Church of Scotland, 1936; served as missionary in Chingleput and Kancheepuram, 1936-46; Bishop in Madura and Ramnad, Church of South India, 1947. Chairman, Advisory Cttee on Main Theme for Second Assembly, World Council of Churches, 1954; Vice-Chairman, Commission on Faith and Order, 1956; Chairman, International Missionary Council, 1958. Resigned from See of Madura, 1959. General Secretary, International Missionary Council, 1959; Associate General Secretary, World Council of Churches, 1959-65; Bishop in Madras, 1965-74; Lectr in Theology, Selly Oak Colls, Birmingham, 1974-79. Moderator, Gen. Assembly of URC, 1978. Hon. DD: Chicago Theological Seminary, 1954; St Andrews Univ., 1958; Hamburg, 1960; Basel, 1965; Hull, 1975; Newcastle, 1981. *Publications:* Christian Freedom in the Modern World, 1937; The Reunion of the Church, 1948; South India Diary, 1951; The Household of God, 1953; Sin and Salvation, 1956; A Faith for This One World?, 1962; Honest Religion for Secular Man, 1966; The Finality of Christ, 1969; The Good Shepherd, 1977; The Open Secret, 1978; The Light has come, 1982. *Recreations:* music, walking. *Address:* 15 Fox Hill, Birmingham B29 4AG.

NEWBOLD, Sir Charles Demorée, KBE 1970; Kt 1966; CMG 1957; QC (Jamaica) 1947; President, Court of Appeal for East Africa, 1966-70; *b* 11 June 1909; *s* of late Charles Etches and Laura May Newbold; *m* 1936, Ruth, *d* of Arthur L. Vaughan; two *d. Educ:* The Lodge Sch., Barbados; Keble Coll., Oxford (BA). Called to Bar, Gray's Inn, 1931. Private practice at the Bar, Trinidad, 1931-35; joined Colonial Legal Service, 1936, as Principal Officer, Supreme Court Registry, Trinidad; Magistrate, Trinidad, 1937; Legal Draftsman, Jamaica, 1941; Solicitor-General Jamaica, 1943; Member of Commission of Enquiry into Land Taxation, Jamaica, 1942-43; represented Jamaica at Quarantine Conf. in Trinidad, 1943; at US Bases Conf. in Trinidad, 1944; at Washington, USA, for labour contracts, 1945; Actg Attorney-Gen., 1946; Legal Secretary, East Africa High Commn, 1948-61. Mem. of East Africa Central Legislative Assembly, 1948-61 (Chm. of Committee of Supply, 1948-61); Commissioner for Revision of High Commn Laws, 1951; Vice-

Chm. Governing Council of Royal Technical Coll., 1954-59; Justice of Appeal, Court of Appeal for Eastern Africa, 1961-65; Vice-Pres., 1965-66. Star of Africa (Liberia). *Publications:* Joint Editor of Trinidad Law Reports, 1928-33; Editor of East African Tax Cases Reports, 1948-61. *Recreations:* cricket, tennis, croquet, reading. *Address:* Low Water, Harbour Way, Bosham, W Sussex.

NEWBOROUGH, 7th Baron, *cr* 1776; **Robert Charles Michael Vaughan Wynn,** Bt 1742; DSC 1942; *b* 24 April 1917; *er s* of 6th Baron Newborough, OBE, JP, DL, and Ruby Irene (*d* 1960), 3rd *d* of Edmund Wigley Severne, of Thenford, Northamptonshire and Wallop, Shropshire; *S* father, 1965; *m* 1st, 1945, Rosamund Lavington Barbour (marr. diss. 1971); one *s* two *d* ; 2nd, 1971, Jennifer, *y d* of late Captain C. C. A. Allen, RN, and Lady Morgan. *Educ:* Oundle. Served as 2nd Lt, SR, 1935-39, with 9th Lancers, 5th Inniskilling Dragoon Guards, then as Lt with 16th/5th Lancers after 6 months attachment with Royal Dragoon Guards; invalided out of Army, 1940. Took command of vessel attached to Fleet Air Arm, 1940, as civilian, and took part in Dunkirk evacuation; then joined RNVR as Sub Lieut; later had command of MTB 74 and took part in St Nazaire raid, 1942 (wounded, despatches, DSC, POW, escaped from Colditz 1944). High Sheriff of Merionethshire, 1963. *Recreation:* yachting. *Heir: s* Hon. Robert Vaughan Wynn, *b* 11 Aug. 1949. *Address:* Rhug, Corwen, Clwyd, North Wales. *T:* Corwen 2510. *Clubs:* Goat, Naval and Military.

NEWBURGH, 11th Earl of, *cr* 1660; **Don Giulio Cesare Taddeo Cosimo Maria Rospigliosi;** Viscount Kynnaird, Baron Levingston, 1660; 10th Prince Rospigliosi (Holy Roman Empire), 10th Duke of Zagarolo, 13th Prince of Castiglione, Marquis of Giuliana, Count of Chiusa, Baron of La Miraglia and Valcorrente, Lord of Aidione, Burgio, Contessa and Trappeto, and Conscript Roman Noble, Patrician of Venice, Genoa and Pistoia; *b* 26 Oct. 1907; *s* of Prince Giambattista Rospigliosi (*d* 1956) and Ethel (*d* 1924), *d* of Isaac Bronson; *S* cousin, 1977; *m* 1940, Donna Giulia, *d* of Don Guido Carlo dei Duchi Visconti di Mondrone, Count of Lonate Pozzolo; two *s. Educ:* Corpus Christi College, Cambridge (Engineering Tripos, MA). *Heir: s* Viscount Kynnaird, *qv. Address:* Via Corridoni 3, 20. 122 Milan, Italy.

NEWBY, (George) Eric, MC 1945; FRSL 1972; FRGS 1975; writer; *b* 6 Dec. 1919; *s* of George Arthur Newby and Hilda Pomeroy, London; *m* 1946, Wanda, *d* of Viktor Skof and Gisella Urdih, Trieste; one *s* one *d. Educ:* St Paul's School. With Dorland Advertising, London, 1936-38; apprentice and ord. seaman, 4-masted Finnish barque, Moshulu, 1938-39; served War of 1939-45, The Black Watch and Special Boat Section, POW 1942-45; Women's Fashion Business, 1946-56 (with Worth Paquin, 1955-56); explored in Nuristan and made unsuccessful attempt to climb Mir Samir, Afghan Hindu Kush, 1956; with Secker & Warburg, 1956-59; with John Lewis Partnership (Central Buyer, Model Dresses), 1959-63; descended Ganges with wife, 1963. Travel Editor, The Observer, and Gen. Editor, Time Off Books, 1964-73. Mem., Assoc. of Cape Horners. *Publications:* The Last Grain Race, 1956; A Short Walk in the Hindu Kush, 1958; Something Wholesale, 1962; Slowly Down the Ganges, 1966; Time Off in Southern Italy, 1966; Grain Race: Pictures of Life Before the Mast in a Windjammer, 1968; (jointly) The Wonders of Britain, 1968; (jointly) The Wonders of Ireland, 1969; Love and War in the Apennines, 1971; (jointly) The World of Evelyn Waugh, 1973; Ganga (with photographs by Raghubir Singh), 1973; World Atlas of Exploration, 1975; Great Ascents, 1977; The Big Red Train Ride, 1978; A Traveller's Life, 1982. *Recreations:* walking, running, cycling, gardening. *Address:* West Bucknowle House, Bucknowle, Wareham, Dorset BH20 5PQ. *T:* Corfe Castle 480374. *Club:* Garrick.

NEWBY, (Percy) Howard, CBE 1972; novelist; Chairman, English Stage Company, since 1978; *b* 25 June 1918; *o s* of Percy Newby and Isabel Clutsam Newby (*née* Bryant); *m* 1945, Joan Thompson; two *d. Educ:* Hanley Castle Grammar Sch., Worcester; St Paul's Coll., Cheltenham. Served War of 1939-45, RAMC, 1939-43; BEF, France, 1939-40; MEF, 1941-42; seconded as Lecturer in English Literature, Fouad 1st University, Cairo, 1942-46. Joined BBC, 1949; Controller: Third Programme, 1958-69; Radio Three, 1969-71; Dir of Programmes, Radio, 1971-75; Man. Dir, BBC Radio, 1975-78. Atlantic Award, 1946; Somerset Maugham Prize, 1948; Yorkshire Post Fiction Award, 1968; Booker Prize, 1969 (first recipient). *Publications:* A Journey to the Interior, 1945; Agents and Witnesses, 1947; The Spirit of Jem, 1947; Mariner Dances, 1948; The Snow Pasture, 1949; The Loot Runners, 1949; Maria Edgeworth, 1950; The Young May Moon, 1950; The Novel, 1945-50, 1951; A Season in England, 1951; A Step to Silence, 1952; The Retreat, 1953; The Picnic at Sakkara, 1955; Revolution and Roses, 1957; Ten Miles from Anywhere, 1958; A Guest and his Going, 1959; The Barbary Light, 1962; One of the Founders, 1965; Something to Answer For, 1968; A Lot to Ask, 1973; Kith, 1977; (with F. Maroon) The Egypt Story, 1979; Warrior Pharaohs, 1980; Feelings Have Changed, 1981. *Address:* Garsington House, Garsington, Oxford OX9 9AB. *T:* Garsington 420.

NEWCASTLE, 9th Duke of, *cr* 1756; **Henry Edward Hugh Pelham-Clinton-Hope,** OBE 1945; Earl of Lincoln, 1572; Wing Comdr, retd; *b* 8 April 1907; *o s* of 8th Duke and Olive Muriel (*d* 1912), *d* of George Horatio Thompson, banker, Melbourne, formerly wife of Richard Owen; *S* father 1941; *m* 1st, 1931, Jean (from whom he obtained a divorce 1940), *d* of D. Banks, Park Avenue, New York; 2nd, 1946, Lady Mary Diana Montagu-Stuart-Wortley (marr. diss., 1959), 2nd *d* of 3rd Earl of Wharncliffe; two *d* ; 3rd, 1959, Mrs Sally Ann Wemyss Hope (Jamal), *d* of Brig. John Henry

Anstice, DSO. *Educ:* Eton; Cambridge. Sqdn Ldr Comdg No 616 Sqdn, 1938-39; served War of 1939-45 in RAF at home and overseas. *Heir:* cousin Edward Charles Pelham-Clinton, *b* 18 Aug. 1920. *Address:* 5 Quay Hill, Lymington, Hants SO4 9AB.

NEWCASTLE, Bishop of, since 1981; **Rt. Rev. Andrew Alexander Kenny Graham;** *b* 7 Aug. 1929; *o s* of late Andrew Harrison and Magdalene Graham; unmarried. *Educ:* Tonbridge Sch.; St John's Coll., Oxford; Ely Theological College. Curate of Hove Parish Church, 1955-58; Chaplain and Lectr in Theology, Worcester Coll., Oxford, 1958-70; Fellow and Tutor, 1960-70, Hon. Fellow, 1981; Warden of Lincoln Theological Coll., 1970-77; Canon and Prebendary of Lincoln Cathedral, 1970-77. Examining Chaplain to: Bishop of Carlisle, 1967-77; Bishop of Bradford, 1972-77; Bishop of Lincoln, 1973-77; Bishop Suffragan of Bedford, 1977-81. *Recreation:* hill walking. *Address:* Bishop's House, 29 Moor Road South, Newcastle upon Tyne NE3 1PA. *T:* Gosforth 852220. *Club:* United Oxford & Cambridge University.

NEWCASTLE, Provost of; *see* Spafford, Very Rev. C. G. H.

NEWCASTLE, NSW, Bishop of, since 1978; **Rt. Rev. Alfred Charles Holland;** *b* 23 Feb. 1927; *s* of Alfred Charles Holland and Maud Allison; *m* 1954, Joyce Marion Embling; three *s* one *d. Educ:* Raine's Sch., London; Univ. of Durham (BA 1950, DipTh 1952). RNVR, 1945-47; Univ. of Durham, 1948-52; Assistant Priest, West Hackney, London, 1952-54; Rector of Scarborough, WA, 1955-70; Asst Bishop, Dio. Perth, WA, 1970-77. Life Mem., Stirling Rugby Football Club, 1969; Mem., Newcastle RUFC. *Publication:* Luke Through Lent, 1980. *Recreations:* reading, painting. *Address:* Bishopscourt, Newcastle, NSW 2300, Australia. *T:* 21311, (home) 26 2767. *Club:* Australian (Sydney); Newcastle (NSW).

NEWDEGATE, Francis Humphrey Maurice F.; *see* FitzRoy Newdegate.

NEWE, Rt. Hon. Gerard Benedict, PC (N Ireland) 1971; CBE 1977 (OBE 1961); Chairman, Personal Social Services Advisory Committee for Northern Ireland, 1974-81; *b* 5 Feb. 1907; *s* of Patrick Newe and Catherine Newe (*née* McCanny); unmarried. *Educ:* St Malachy's Coll., Belfast; Belcamp Coll., Dublin. Editor, The Ulster Farmer, 1931-67. Area Admin. Officer, Min. of Health and Local Govt, NI, 1941-48; Regional Officer and Dir, NI Council of Social Service, 1948-72. First Roman Catholic Minister of State, Govt of NI, 1971-72. Last Minister to be appointed to HM Privy Council in Northern Ireland. Chief Welfare Officer, Civil Defence, Belfast, 1951-68; Member: BBC's NI Agr. Adv. Cttee, 1954-58; BBC's NI Appeals Adv. Cttee, 1956-59; ITA NI Cttee, 1960-66; Nat. Trust Cttee for NI, 1962-71; NI Indust. Trng Council, 1964-73 (Chm., Res. Cttee); NI Cttee, Nuffield Provincial Hosps Trust, 1954-63; First Bd of Governors, Rupert Stanley Coll. of Further Educn, Belfast, 1964-72; NI Legal Aid Adv. Cttee, 1967-75; NI Adv. Cttee, Council for Trng in Social Work, 1966-70; N Area Health and Social Services Bd, 1973-77 (Chm., Personal Social Services Cttee); Founder Member: Ulster Folklife Soc. (Vice-Pres.); PACE (and co-Patron); NIACRO (a Vice-Pres.); The Assissi Fellowship (Chm.). Council of Europe Fellow, 1970. Hon. MA The Queen's Univ. of Belfast, 1967; Hon. DLitt New Univ. of Ulster, Coleraine, 1971. *Publications:* The Catholic in the Community, 1958, 2nd edn 1965; The Story of the Northern Ireland Council of Social Service, 1963; contribs to Tablet, The Furrow, Christus Rex, Aquarius. *Recreations:* reading, trying to be lazy. *Address:* Prospect House, 28 Coast Road, Cushendall, Ballymena, Co. Antrim BT44 0RY. *T:* Cushendall 219.

NEWELL, Philip Staniforth, CB 1961; *b* 1903; *m* 1927, Sylvia May Webb (*d* 1982); two *s* one *d. Educ:* Uppingham; Emmanuel College, Cambridge (Scholar). First Class Part I, Mathematical Tripos, First Class Mechanical Sciences Tripos; Assistant Master at Uppingham; Chief Mathematical Master, Repton; Headmaster of Gresham's School, Holt, 1935-44; Admiralty, 1944-64; Imperial Defence College, 1955; Under-Secretary, 1956; Principal Finance Officer, 1961-65. Director, Greenwich Hosp., 1964-69; a Maths Master, Pierrepont Sch., Surrey, 1969-72. *Address:* Dawson's, Tilford, Surrey. *T:* Frensham 2787. *Club:* Athenæum.

NEWELL, Rt. Rev. Phillip Keith; *see* Tasmania, Bishop of.

NEWENS, (Arthur) Stanley; MP (Lab and Co-op) Harlow, since 1974; *b* 4 Feb. 1930; *s* of Arthur Ernest and Celia Jennie Newens, Bethnal Green; *m* 1st, 1954, Ann (*d* 1962), *d* of J. B. Sherratt, Stoke-on-Trent; two *d* ; 2nd, 1966, Sandra Christina, *d* of J. A. Frith, Chingford; two *d. Educ:* Buckhurst Hill County High Sch.; University Coll., London (BA Hons History); Westminster Training Coll. (Post-Graduate Certificate of Education). Coal face worker in N Staffs mines, 1952-55. Secondary Sch. Teacher, 1956-65, 1970-74. MP (Lab) Epping, 1964-70 (NUT sponsored). Chm., Eastern Area Gp of Lab. MPs, 1974-; Vice-Chairman: E Reg. Council, Lab. Party; Party Foreign Affairs Gp, 1976-77; Labour Action for Peace. Active Member: Labour Party, holding numerous offices, 1949-; NUM, 1952-55; NUT, 1956-. Chm., Liberation (Movement for Colonial Freedom), 1967-. Dir, London Co-operative Soc., 1971-77 (Pres., 1977-81); Member: Central Exec., Co-op. Union, 1974-80; Tribune Gp of MP's (Vice-Chm., 1981-82). *Publications:* numerous pamphlets and articles, incl. The Case Against NATO, 1972; Nicolae Ceausescu, 1972; Third World: change or chaos, 1977. *Recreations:* local historical research, family, reading. *Address:* The Leys, 18 Park Hill, Harlow, Essex. *T:* Harlow 20108.

NEWEY, John Henry Richard, QC 1970; **His Honour Judge Newey;** a Circuit Judge appointed to perform Official Referee duties in London, since 1980; Commissary General of the City and the Diocese of Canterbury, since 1971; *b* 20 Oct. 1923; *s* of Lt-Col T. H. Newey, ED and Mrs I. K. M. Newey (*née* Webb); *m* 1953, Mollie Patricia (*née* Chalk), JP; three *s* two *d. Educ:* Dudley Grammar Sch.; Ellesmere Coll.; Queens' Coll., Cambridge (MA, LLB (1st class); Foundn Scholar). Served Central India Horse, Indian Army, 1942-47 in India, Middle East, Italy and Greece, Captain (US Bronze Star, 1944). Called to Bar, Middle Temple, 1948, Bencher 1977. Prosecuting Counsel to Post Office, South Eastern Circuit, 1963-64; Standing Counsel to Post Office at Common Law, 1964-70; Personal Injuries Junior to Treasury, 1968-70; Dep. Chm., Kent County QS, 1970-71; a Recorder of the Crown Court, 1972-80. Legal Assessor, GMC and GDC, 1973-80; an Advr to the Home Sec., 1978-80; Parly Boundary Comm', 1980-. Chm., Cheshire Structure Plan Exam., 1977; Inspector: Calder Valley Motorway Inquiry, 1978; Gatwick Air Port Inquiry, 1980. Legal Mem., Rhodesian Travel Facilities Cttee, 1978-80. Lectr, (part-time), Coll. of Estate Mgt, Univ. of London, 1951-59. Contested (C and L) Cannock Div. of Staffs, 1955. Alternate Chm., Burnham and other Teachers' Remuneration Cttees, 1969-80. Chairman: Sevenoaks Preservation Soc., 1962-65; Sevenoaks Div. Conservative Assoc., 1965-68. *Recreations:* history, excursions. *Address:* St David's, 68 The Drive, Sevenoaks, Kent TN13 3AF. *T:* Sevenoaks 54597.

NEWFOUNDLAND, CENTRAL, Bishop of, since 1976; **Rt. Rev. Mark Genge;** *b* 18 March 1927; *s* of Lambert and Lily Genge; *m* 1959, Maxine Clara (*née* Major); five *d. Educ:* Queen's Coll. and Memorial Univ., Newfoundland; Univ. of Durham (MA); BD Gen. Synod of Canada. Deacon, Corner Brook, Newfoundland, 1951; priest, Stephenville, 1952; Durham, 1953-55; Vice-Principal, Queen's Coll., St John's, Newfoundland, 1955-57; Curate, St Mary's Church, St John's, 1957-59; Rector: Foxtrap, 1959-64; Mary's Harbour, 1964-65; Burgeo, 1965-69; Curate, Marbleton, PQ, 1969-71; Rector, South River, Port-de-Grave, 1971-73; District Sec., Canadian Bible Soc., 1973-76. *Recreations:* badminton, swimming. *Address:* (home) 35 Airport Boulevard, Gander, Newfoundland A1V 1K7, Canada; (office) 34 Fraser Road, Gander, Newfoundland A1V 2E8.

NEWFOUNDLAND, EASTERN, AND LABRADOR, Bishop of, since 1980; **Rt. Rev. Martin Mate;** *b* 12 Nov. 1929; *s* of John Mate and Hilda Mate (*née* Toope); *m* 1962, Florence Hooper, Registered Nurse; two *s* three *d. Educ:* Meml Univ. of Newfoundland and Queen's Coll., St John's, Newfoundland (LTh); Bishop's Univ., Lennoxville, PQ. BA (1st Cl. Hons), MA. Deacon 1952, priest 1953; Curate, Cathedral of St John the Baptist, St John's, Newfoundland, 1952-53; Deacon-in-charge and Rector, Parish of Pushthrough, 1953-58; Incumbent, Mission of St Anthony, 1958-64; Rural Dean, St Barbe, 1958-64; Rector of Cookshire, Quebec, 1964-67; Rector of Catalina, Newfoundland, 1967-72; RD of Bonavista Bay, 1970-72; Rector of Pouch Cove/Torbay, 1972-76; Treasurer, Diocesan Synod of E Newfoundland and Labrador, 1976-80. *Publication:* Pentateuchal Criticism, 1967. *Recreations:* carpentry, hunting, fishing, camping. *Address:* 19 King's Bridge Road, St John's, Newfoundland A1C 3K4, Canada.

NEWFOUNDLAND, WESTERN, Bishop of, since 1978; **Rt. Rev. Sidney Stewart Payne;** *b* 6 June 1932; *s* of Albert and Hilda Payne; *m* 1960, Selma Carlson Penney, St Anthony, Newfoundland; two *s* two *d. Educ:* Elementary and High School, Fogo, Newfoundland; Memorial Univ. of Newfoundland (BA); Queen's Coll., Newfoundland (LTh); BD(General Synod). Incumbent of Mission of Happy Valley, 1957-65; Rector, Parish of Bay Roberts, 1965-70; Rector, Parish of St Anthony, 1970-78. DD *hc* Univ. of King's Coll., Halifax, NS, 1981. *Address:* 13 Cobb Lane, Corner Brook, Newfoundland A2H 2V3, Canada. *T:* 709-639-9987.

NEWHOUSE, Ven. Robert John Darrell; Archdeacon of Totnes and Canon Residentiary of Exeter Cathedral, 1966-76, now Archdeacon Emeritus and Canon Emeritus; Treasurer of Exeter Cathedral, 1970-76; *b* 11 May 1911; *s* of Rev. R. L. C. Newhouse; *m* 1938, Winifred (*née* Elton); two *s. Educ:* St Edward's Sch.; Worcester Coll., Oxford; Cuddesdon College. Ordained, 1936. Curate of: St John's, Peterborough, 1936-40; St Giles, Cambridge, 1940-46; Chaplain, RNVR, 1941-46; Rector of Ashwater, Devon, 1946-56; Rural Dean of Holsworthy, 1954-56; Vicar of Littleham-cum-Exmouth, 1956-66; Rural Dean of Aylesbeare, 1965-66. *Recreation:* gardening. *Address:* Pound Cottage, Northlew, Okehampton, Devon. *T:* Beaworthy 532.

NEWING, Rt. Rev. Kenneth Albert; *see* Plymouth, Bishop Suffragan of.

NEWINGTON, Michael John, CMG 1982; HM Diplomatic Service; Consul-General, Düsseldorf, since 1981; *b* 10 July 1932; *er s* of J. T. Newington, Spalding, Lincs; *m* 1956, Nina Gordon-Jones; one *s* one *d. Educ:* Stamford Sch.; St John's Coll., Oxford. MA. RAF, 1951-52, Pilot Officer. Joined Foreign Office, 1955; Economic Survey Section, Hong Kong, 1957-58; resigned 1958. ICI, 1959-60. Rejoined FO, 1960; Second, later First Sec. (Economic), Bonn, 1961-65; First Sec., Lagos, 1965-68; Asst Head of Science and Technology Dept, FCO, 1968-72; Counsellor (Scientific), Bonn, 1972-75; Counsellor and Consul-Gen., Tel Aviv, 1975-78; Head of Republic of Ireland Dept, FCO, 1978-81. *Recreations:* skiing, golf, gardening. *Address:* c/o Foreign and Commonwealth Office, SW1.

NEWIS, Kenneth, CB 1967; CVO 1970 (MVO 1958); *b* 9 Nov. 1916; *o s* of late H. T. and G. Newis, Manchester; *m* 1943, Kathleen, *o d* of late John

Barrow, Davenport, Cheshire; two d. *Educ:* Manchester Grammar Sch.; St John's Coll., Cambridge (Scholar). BA 1938, MA 1942. Entered HM Office of Works, 1938; Private Sec. to Minister of Works (Rt Hon. C. W. Key), 1948-49; Asst Sec., 1949; Under-Sec., 1959; Dir of Management Services, MPBW, 1969-70; Under-Sec., Scottish Develt Dept, 1970-73, Sec., 1973-76. Chairman: Queen's Hall (Edinburgh) Ltd; Budget Cttee, Methodist Church of GB, 1979-; Edinvar Housing Assoc.; MHA Housing Assoc. Member: Historic Buildings Council for Scotland, 1978-; Cockburn Conservation Trust; Council, Scottish Fedn of Housing Assocs; Bd, Methodist Homes for the Aged; Scottish Baroque Ensemble Ltd; Bd, RSAMD. Conservator of Wimbledon and Putney Commons, 1963-70. Governor: Farrington's School, 1964-70; Richmond College, 1964-70. *Recreation:* music. *Address:* 11 Abbotsford Park, Edinburgh EH10 5DZ. *Club:* New (Edinburgh).

NEWLAND, Prof. David Edward, ScD, FEng, FIMechE; Professor of Engineering (1875), University of Cambridge, since 1976; Fellow, Selwyn College, Cambridge, since 1976; consulting engineer (part-time), since 1963; *b* 8 May 1936; *s* of late Robert W. Newland and of Marion A. Newland (*née* Dearman); *m* 1959, Patricia Frances Mayne; two *s. Educ:* Alleyne's Sch., Stevenage; Selwyn Coll., Cambridge (Lyttleton Scholar, 1956; Mech. Sciences Tripos: Rex Moir Prize, 1956, Ricardo Prize, 1957; MA); Massachusetts Inst. of Technol. (ScD thesis on nonlinear vibrations, 1963). English Electric Co., 1957-61; Instr and Asst Prof. of Mech. Engrg, MIT, 1961-64; Lectr and Sen. Lectr, Imperial Coll. of Science and Technol., 1964-67; Prof. of Mech. Eng., Sheffield Univ., 1967-76. Past or present mem., cttees of IMechE, Dept of Industry, BSI, SERC and Design Council; technical witness, Flixborough Inquiry, 1974-75, and other legal cases; Governor, St Paul's Schs, 1978-; Churchwarden, St Mary Magdalene, Ickleton, 1979-. *Publications:* An Introduction to Random Vibrations and Spectral Analysis, 1975; technical papers, mostly in British and Amer. engrg jls. *Recreations:* golf, cycling, engineering memorabilia. *Address:* c/o University Engineering Department, Trumpington Street, Cambridge CB2 1PZ. *T:* Cambridge 366466.

NEWLEY, Edward Frank, CBE 1960; consultant; *b* 9 June 1913; *s* of Frederick Percy Newley; *m* 1946, Sybil Madge Alvis; two *s* one d. *Educ:* King's Coll., London. 1st class hons BSc; MSc. GPO Engrg Dept, Radio Research Br, 1937-44; GPO Factories Dept, 1944-49; Royal Naval Scientific Service, 1949-55; joined UKAEA, 1955; Dep. Dir, AWRE, 1959; Dir, Atomic Weapons Establishment, Aldermaston, 1965-76. *Publications:* sundry scientific and technical papers. *Address:* Reades, Heads Hill, Newbury, Berks. *T:* Headley 371.

NEWLEY, (George) Anthony; actor since 1946; author, composer; *b* 24 Sept. 1931; *m* 1956, Ann Lynn; *m* 1963, Joan Collins; one *s* one d ; *m* Dareth Rich; one *s* one d. *Educ:* Mandeville Street Sch., Clapton, E5. Appeared on West End stage in: Cranks, 1955; Stop the World, I Want to Get Off (co-author and co-composer, with Leslie Bricusse), 1961-62; subseq. starred in New York production, 1962-63; The Good Old Bad Old Days (co-author and co-composer with Leslie Bricusse), 1972; The Roar of the Greasepaint-the Smell of the Crowd (co-author and composer, with Leslie Bricusse, star and director), New York, 1965. Has acted in over 40 films in last 17 years. *Films include:* Adventures of Dusty Bates; Oliver Twist; Up To His Neck; Cockleshell Heroes; High Flight; Idle on Parade; Jazz Boat; The Small World of Sammy Lee; Dr Doolittle; Sweet November; (wrote, produced and acted) Can Heironymus Merkin ever forget Mercy Humppe and find True Happiness?; (directed) Summertree, 1970; (score) Willy Wonka and the Chocolate Factory (Academy Award nomination, 1972); Quilp, 1974; It Seemed Like a Good Idea at the Time, 1974. *TV appearances include:* Anthony Newley Shows; The Strange World of Gurney Slade, 1960-61; Johnny Darling Show, 1962; Lucy in London, 1966; appears on TV and stars in leading night clubs and theatres in US. He is also a successful recording star. *Recreations:* photography, painting, fishing. *Address:* c/o Katz-Gallin, 9255 Sunset Boulevard, Los Angeles, Calif 90069, USA.

NEWMAN, Dr Barry Hilton; Director, Propellants, Explosives and Rocket Motor Establishment, since 1980; Head of Rocket Motor Executive, Ministry of Defence, since 1980; *b* 16 Sept. 1926; *s* of Charles Ernest Newman and Kathleen (*née* Hilton); *m* 1950, Dorothy Ashworth Truesdale; one *s* one d. *Educ:* Bishop Vesey's Grammar Sch., Sutton Coldfield; Univ. of Birmingham (BSc (Hons) 1947, PhD 1950). Joined Scientific Civil Service, 1950; Explosives R&D Estabt, 1950-63; Defence Research Staff, Washington, 1963-66; Supt Explosives Br., Royal Armament R&D Estabt, 1966-71; Asst Dir, Directorate General Weapons (Army), 1971-72; Dir, Research Armaments, 1972-74; RCDS 1975; Head of Terminal Effects Dept, RARDE, 1976-77; Dep. Dir, RARDE, 1977-80. *Publications:* official reports. *Recreations:* cricket, bridge, reading, music. *Address:* Chevy Chase, St Mary's Drive, Riverhead, Sevenoaks, Kent TN13 2AR. *T:* Sevenoaks 454809.

NEWMAN, Charles, CBE 1965; MD (Cantab); FRCP; retired; Emeritus Dean, Postgraduate Medical School (now Royal Postgraduate Medical School); Harveian Librarian, 1962-79, Royal College of Physicians; *b* 16 March 1900; *s* of Charles Arnold Newman and Kate Beck; *m* 1st, 1932, Phyllis (d 1965), d of I. Bloomfield; 2nd, 1971, Anne (d 1982), d of F. W. Stallard. *Educ:* Shrewsbury Sch.; Magdalene Coll., Cambridge (Scholar); King's College Hospital (Scholar; Fellow of Med. School, 1980). Murchison Scholar RCP, 1926; FRCP 1932; Volunteer Asst to Prof. Aschoff, Univ. of Freiburg i B. 1930; Hon. Treas., RSocMed, 1946-50; Fellow Medical Society of London (Orator, 1961); Hon. Member Assoc. of Physicians, 1965. Hon.

Secretary, 1942-47. Hon. Treasurer, 1948-58; Mem., British Gastro-enterological Soc. (Pres., 1964); Governor, St Clement Dane's Sch., 1955-76, Vice-Chm., 1958-76; Mem. Cttee of Management of Conjoint Board in England, 1958-68 (Chm., 1965-68). Goulstonian Lectr, 1933; FitzPatrick Lectr, 1954, 1955 and 1968; Linacre Fellow, 1966; Harveian Orator, 1973; Assistant Registrar, RCP, 1933-38; Sub-Editor, EMS, Official Medical History of the War, 1942-47; late Physician, Medical Tutor and Vice-Dean, King's College Hospital and Asst Physician, Belgrave Hospital for Children. *Publications:* Medical Emergencies, 1932, 3rd edn 1946, repr. 1948; Evolution of Medical Education in the Nineteenth Century, 1957; articles in medical text-books and encyclopædias; papers on diseases of the liver and gall-bladder, medical history and education. *Address:* Basset, South Road, Oundle, Peterborough, Northants. *T:* Oundle 3310. *Club:* Athenæum.

NEWMAN, Cyril Wilfred Francis, QC 1982; a Recorder of the Crown Court, since 1982; *b* 2 July 1937; *s* of Wilfred James Newman and Cecilia Beatrice Lily Newman; *m* 1966, Winifred de Kok; two *s* one d. *Educ:* Sacred Heart Coll., Droitwich; Lewes County Grammar Sch. for Boys; Merton Coll., Oxford (BA 1959, MA 1964). Blackstone Entrance Scholar, Blackstone Pupillage Prize, and Harmsworth Major Scholar, Middle Temple, 1958-60; called to the Bar, Middle Temple, 1960. Asst Comr, Boundary Commn for England, 1976. President: Oxford Univ. Law Soc., 1959; Oxford Univ. Middle Temple Soc., 1959. Hon. Treasurer, Bar Yacht Club, 1973-. *Recreations:* sailing, ski-ing, beagling, squash, swimming, opera, church music. *Address:* 3 Gray's Inn Place, Gray's Inn, WC1R 5EA. *T:* 01-831 8441; Redriff, 11 Cedar Road, Farnborough, Hants GU14 7AU. *T:* Farnborough 546063. *Clubs:* Royal Officers (Aldershot); Bar Yacht.

NEWMAN, Sir Geoffrey (Robert), 6th Bt, *cr* 1836; *b* 2 June 1947; *s* of Sir Ralph Alured Newman, 5th Bt, and of Hon. Ann Rosemary Hope, *d* of late Hon. Claude Hope-Morley; *S* father, 1968; *m* 1980, Mary, *y d* of Colonel Martin St John Valentine Gibbs, *qv*. *Educ:* Heatherdown, Ascot; Kelly Coll., Tavistock. 1st Bn, Grenadier Guards, 1967-70. FRGS. *Recreations:* sub-aqua, sailing, all sports. *Heir: b* Richard Claude Newman, *b* 2 May 1951. *Address:* Blackpool House, Dartmouth, Devon.

NEWMAN, George Michael, QC 1981; *b* 4 July 1941; *s* of Wilfred James Newman and Cecilia Beatrice Lily Newman; *m* 1966, Hilary Alice Gibbs (*née* Chandler); two *s* one d. *Educ:* Lewes County Grammar Sch.; St Catharine's Coll., Cambridge (BA Hons Law). Called to the Bar, Middle Temple, 1965. *Recreations:* tennis, skiing, alpine walking, the countryside. *Address:* 1 Crown Office Row, Temple, EC4Y 7HH. *T:* 01-353 9292.

NEWMAN, Sir Gerard (Robert Henry Sigismund), 3rd Bt, *cr* 1912; farmer, since 1969; *b* 19 July 1927; *s* of Sir Cecil Gustavus Jacques Newman, 2nd Bt, and Joan Florence Mary, CBE (*d* 1969), *e d* of late Rev. Canon Hon. Robert Grimston; *S* father, 1955; *m* 1960, Caroline Philippa, *d* of late Brig. Alfred Geoffrey Neville, CBE, MC; three *s* one d. *Educ:* Eton; Jesus Coll., Oxford (BA 1951). Dir, APL Engineering Ltd, 1951-53; Asst to Man. Dir, Enfield Rolling Mills Ltd, 1953-56; Director: Enfield Zinc Products Ltd, 1953-56; The Rom River Co. Ltd, 1954-72 (Chm., 1955); Galloway (Mechanical Services) Ltd, Dundee, 1973- (Chm., 1980); Chairman: Seven Seas Engineering Ltd, Glasgow, 1975-78; Woodcote Grove Estate Ltd, 1975-. Dep. Traffic Comr for the Metropolitan Area, 1972-. Governor, Wellesley House & St Peter's Court Schs Trust, 1963-; Pres., Friends of Royston and District Hosp., 1975-; Trustee, Cambridge Symphony Orchestra Trust, 1979-. High Sheriff, Herts, 1981-82. *Recreations:* travel and pursuits of the countryside. *Heir: s* Francis Hugh Cecil Newman, *b* 12 June 1963. *Address:* Burloes, Royston, Herts. *T:* Royston 42150; 27 Bloomfield Terrace, SW1. *T:* 01-730 7540. *Club:* Boodle's.

NEWMAN, Graham Reginald, FICS; Chairman: Tatham Bromage (Holdings) Ltd and group of companies, since 1953; Baltic Exchange, 1977-79; *b* 26 July 1924; *s* of late A. H. G. Newman and Ethel (*née* Wadey); *m* 1950, Joycelyn Helen Newman, MB, ChB, DPH (*née* Sandison). *Educ:* Canford Sch.; Hertford Coll., Oxford. War service, Royal Signals, India and Far East, 1941-46, retd Captain. Director, Tatham Bromage & Co. Ltd, 1945. Elected to Baltic Exchange, 1947; Dir, 1967; Chm., 1977-79. *Recreations:* golf, sailing. *Address:* 46 St Mary Axe, EC3A 8EY. *Clubs:* RAC, Highgate Golf; Bosham Sailing; Vancouver (Canada).

NEWMAN, Sir Jack, Kt 1977; CBE 1963; FCIT 1955; JP; Founder, 1938, President, 1981, TNL Group Ltd, Nelson, New Zealand; *b* 3 July, 1902; *s* of Thomas Newman and Christina Thomson; *m* 1926, Myrtle O. A. Thomas; four d. *Educ:* Nelson Coll. for Boys, NZ. Joined Newman Bros Ltd (family business), 1922; Manager, 1927; Managing Director, 1935. Director: L & M Oil (NZ) Ltd; Moller Holdings Ltd. Past President and Life Member: NZ Cricket Council; NZ Travel Assoc.; NZ Passenger Transport Fedn; former Dir, Pacific Area Travel Assoc. Represented: NZ, 1931-33; Nelson, Canterbury and Wellington, at cricket; Nelson, at Rugby football, golf, and lawn bowls. JP Nelson, 1950. *Recreations:* lawn bowls, golf. *Address:* (home) 36 Brougham Street, Nelson, New Zealand; (office) TNL Group Ltd, PO Box 48, Nelson, NZ. *Clubs:* MCC; Wellesley (Wellington); Nelson (Nelson).

NEWMAN, Karl Max, CB 1979; Second Counsel to the Chairman of Committees and Legal Adviser to the European Communities Committee, House of Lords, since 1982; *b* 26 March 1919; *s* of Karl Neumann, DrJur, and Licie Neumann; *m* 1952, Annette, *d* of late Ronald Cross Sheen; one *s* one *d. Educ:* Ottershaw Coll., Surrey; Christ Church, Oxford (MA). Bacon Scholar of Gray's Inn, 1939. Served War in Army, 1940–42. Called to Bar, Gray's Inn, 1946; joined Lord Chancellor's Office, 1949; Asst Solicitor, 1962; Under-Sec., 1972–82; part-time Legal Adviser to European Unit of Cabinet Office, 1972–82; Head of Delegn negotiating UK accession to EEC Convention on Jurisdiction and Judgments, 1972–78. Member: UK delegns to Internat. Diplomatic Confs on Nuclear Liability, 1962–63; expert Cttees of Council of Europe, 1961–68; 10th and 11th Session of Hague Conf. on Private Internat. Law, 1964–68. Mem., EEC expert cttees, 1972–82. *Publications:* Das Englisch-Amerikanische Beweisrecht, 1949 (Heidelberg); contribs to legal publications on internat. jurisdiction and recognition of judgments. *Recreations:* philately, looking at paintings. *Address:* 17 Marryat Road, Wimbledon, SW19 5BB. *Club:* United Oxford & Cambridge University.

NEWMAN, Sir Kenneth (Leslie), Kt 1978; QPM 1982; Commissioner of the Metropolitan Police, since 1982; *s* of John William Newman and Florence Newman; *m* 1949, Eileen Lilian. *Educ:* London Univ. (LLB Hons). Served War, RAF, 1942–46. Palestine Police, 1946–48; Metropolitan Police, 1948–73; Comdr, New Scotland Yard, 1972; Royal Ulster Constab., 1973–79; Sen. Dep. Chief Constable, 1973; Chief Constable, 1976–79; Comdt, Police Staff Coll., and HM Inspector of Constabulary, 1980–82. CBIM (FBIM 1977). OStJ 1978. *Recreations:* squash, walking. *Address:* c/o Metropolitan Police, New Scotland Yard, Broadway, SW1H 0BG.

NEWMAN, Maxwell Herman Alexander, MA, FRS 1939; Professor Emeritus, University of Manchester; *b* 7 Feb. 1897; *m* 1st, 1934, Lyn (*d* 1973), *d* of Rev. J. A. Irvine; two *s*; 2nd, 1973, Margaret, *widow* of Prof. L. S. Penrose, FRS. *Educ:* City of London School; St John's College, Cambridge; Vienna Univ., 1922–23. MA 1924; Fellow of St John's College, Cambridge, 1923–45 (Hon. Fellow, 1973); Rockefeller Research Fellow at Princeton, 1928–29; University Lecturer in Mathematics, Cambridge University, 1927–45; Fielden Professor of Mathematics, Manchester Univ., 1945–64; Visiting Professor in Australian National Univ., 1964–65 and 1967; in Univ. of Wisconsin and Rice Univ., 1965–66. Royal Soc. Council, 1946–47; Pres., London Mathematical Soc., 1950–51; Pres. Mathematical Assoc., 1959. Hon. DSc Hull, 1968. Sylvester Medal of Royal Society, 1959; De Morgan Medal, 1962. *Publications:* Topology of Plane Sets of Points, 1939, 2nd edn 1951; papers on mathematics in various journals. *Address:* Cross Farm, Comberton, Cambridge.

NEWMAN, Nanette, (Mrs Bryan Forbes); *b* 29 May 1939; *d* of Sidney and Ruby Newman; *m* 1958, Bryan Forbes, *qv* ; two *d. Educ:* Sternhold Coll., London; Italia Conti Stage Sch.; RADA. Appeared as a child in various films for Children's Film Foundn; other film appearances include: The L-Shaped Room, 1962; The Wrong Arm of the Law, 1962; Seance on a Wet Afternoon, 1963; The Wrong Box, 1965; The Whisperers, 1966; Deadfall, 1967; The Madwoman of Chaillot, 1968; The Raging Moon, 1971 (Variety Club Best Film Actress Award); The Stepford Wives, 1974; International Velvet, 1978 (Evening News Best Film Actress Award); *television:* Call My Bluff, What's My Line, The Fun Food Factory (own series), London Scene, Stay with me till Morning (Yorkshire), Jessie (title role, BBC TV), Let There Be Love (Thames series). *Publications:* God Bless Love, 1972 (repr. 16 times); Lots of Love, 1973 (repr. 7 times); Vote for Love, 1976 (repr. 4 times); All Our Love, 1978; Fun Food Factory, 1976 (repr. twice); Fun Food Feast, 1978; The Root Children, 1978; The Pig Who Never Was, 1979; Amy Rainbow, 1980; The Facts of Love, 1980; That Dog, 1980; Reflections, 1981; The Dog Lovers Coffee Table Book, 1982. *Recreations:* needlepoint, working for children's charities. *Address:* c/o The Bookshop, Virginia Water, Surrey. *T:* Wentworth 2463.

NEWMAN, Philip Harker, CBE 1976; DSO 1940; MC; FRCS; FCS(SA); Hon. Consulting Orthopædic Surgeon, Middlesex Hospital, Royal National Orthopædic Hospital, King Edward VII's Hospital for Officers, W1; *b* 22 June 1911; *s* of John Harker Newman, Mannofield, Ingatestone, Essex; *m* 1943, Elizabeth Anne, *er d* of Rev. G. H. Basset, Turners, Belchamp St Paul, Suffolk; two *s* one *d. Educ:* Cranleigh; Middlesex Hospital Medical School (Senior Broderip Scholar and 2nd Year Exhibitioner), MRCS, LRCP, 1934; FRCS, 1938; Hunterian Prof., RCS, 1954; late Lt-Col RAMC; Served War of 1939–45 (DSO, MC); FRSM (formerly Pres., Section of Orthopaedics); Fellow Brit. Orthopædic Assoc. (Pres., 1975–76); Chm., British Editorial Soc. of Bone and Joint Surgery, 1973–75; Chm., Medical Br., St John, 1976–82; Member British Medical Association. Corresp. Member: Amer. Orthopaedic Assoc.; S African Orthopaedic Assoc. *Publications:* The Prisoner of War Mentality, 1944; Early Treatment of Wounds of the Knee Joint, 1945; Sacroiliac Arthrodesis, 1946; The Etiology of Spondylolisthesis, 1962; The Spine, the Wood and the Trees, 1968; Spinal Fusion, Operative Surgery, 1969; Orthopædic Surgery, Medical Encyclopædia, 1956. *Recreations:* sailing, golf. *Address:* 72A Saxmundham Road, Aldeburgh, Suffolk. *T:* Aldeburgh 3373. *Club:* Army and Navy.

NEWMAN, Ronald William; HM Diplomatic Service, retired; *b* 6 April 1921; *s* of William James Newman and Louisa Ellen Taylor; *m* 1943, Victoria Brady; three *d. Educ:* Wandsworth Sch. Served War, RAF, 1940–46. Min. of Agriculture and Fisheries, later MAFF, 1946–58; Statistical Org. Adviser to Central Bureau of Statistics, Jerusalem, 1958; O&M Adviser to Basutoland, Bechuanaland and Swaziland, 1959–61; MAFF, 1962–65; CRO, 1965–67; First Secretary: (Econs), Accra, 1967; (Capital Aid), Nairobi, 1968–72; (Econs), Islamabad, 1973–75; Counsellor, Khartoum, 1975–76; Consul General,

Casablanca, 1977. *Recreations:* squash, swimming, diving, flying. *Address:* Dene Bank, Cranley Close, Guildford, Surrey GU1 2JN. *T:* Guildford 76728.

NEWMAN, Sydney Cecil, OC 1981; film and television producer and executive; President, Sydney Newman Enterprises Inc.; Chief Creative Consultant, Canadian Film Development Corporation; *b* Toronto, 1 April 1917; *m* 1944, Margaret Elizabeth (*d* 1981), *d* of Rev. Duncan McRae, DD; three *d. Educ:* Ogden Public School and Central Technical School, Toronto. Painter, stage, industrial and interior designer; still and cinema photographer, 1935–41. Joined National Film Board of Canada under John Grierson as splicer-boy, 1941. Editor and Director of Armed Forces training films and war information shorts, 1942. Producer of Canada Carries On, 1945. Exec. Producer in charge of all films for cinemas, including short films, newsreels, films for children and travel, 1947–52. Over 300 documentaries, including: Suffer Little Children (UN), It's Fun to Sing (Venice Award), Ski Skill, After Prison What? (Canada Award). For Canadian Govt to NBC in New York to report on American television techniques, 1949–50. Joined Canadian Broadcasting Corporation as Television Director of Features and Outside Broadcasts, 1953. Supervisor of Drama and Producer of General Motors Theatre, On Camera, Ford Theatre, Graphic, 1954. Produced first plays by Arthur Hailey, inc. Flight Into Danger, Course for Collision. Ohio State Award for Religious Drama; Liberty Award, Best Drama Series. Supervisor of Drama and Producer Armchair Theatre, ABC Television, England, 1958–62 (devised, The Avengers, 1961); Head of Drama Group, TV, BBC, 1963–67 (devised, Adam Adamant Lives!, 1966); Producer, Associated British Productions Ltd, Elstree, 1968–69; Special Advisor to Chm. and Dir, Broadcast Programmes Branch, Canadian Radio and Television Commn, 1970; Canadian Govt Film Comr and Chm., Nat. Film Bd of Canada, 1970–75; Special Advisor on Film to Sec. of State for Canada, 1975–77. Producer: Stephen D, 1963; The Rise and Fall of the City of Mahagonny, 1965; The Tea Party, 1965. Commissioned and prod. first on-air plays of Alun Owen, Harold Pinter, Angus Wilson, Robert Muller, Peter Luke; also plays by Clive Exton, David Perry and Hugh Leonard. Trustee, Nat. Arts Center, Ottawa, 1970–75; Director: Canadian Film Develt Corp., Montreal, 1970–75; Canadian Broadcasting Corp., 1972–75. Governor, Canadian Conf. of the Arts; Mem., New Western Film and TV Foundn. FRSA 1970; Fellow Soc. of Film and Television Arts. Desmond Davis Award, 1967, Soc. of Film and Television Arts; President's Award, 1969, and Zeta Award, 1970, Writers Guild of Great Britain; Canadian Picture Pioneers Special Award, 1973; Special Recognition Award, SMPTE, 1975. Kt of Mark Twain, USA. *Address:* 3 Nesbitt Drive, Toronto, Ontario M4W 2G2, Canada.

NEWNHAM, Captain Ian Frederick Montague, CBE 1955; RN Retired; *b* 20 Feb. 1911; *s* of late John Montague Newnham, OBE, DL, JP, and Hilda Newnham; *m* 1947, Marjorie Warden; no *c. Educ:* RN College, Dartmouth. Served War of 1939–45 (despatches). Captain, 1952; retd 1961. Lent to Indian Navy as Chief of Material, 1952–55; Chief of Staff to Admiral, British Joint Service Mission, and Naval Attaché, Washington, 1959–61. Gen. Manager, Precision Engineering Div., Short Brothers and Harland, Belfast, 1961–68. *Recreations:* golf, fishing. *Address:* Elsted Green, near Midhurst, West Sussex.

NEWNS, Sir (Alfred) Foley (Francis Polden), KCMG 1963 (CMG 1957); CVO 1961; MA Cantab; *b* 30 Jan. 1909; *s* of late Rev. Alfred Newns, AKC; *m* 1936, Jean, *d* of late A. H. Bateman, MB, BS; one *s* one *d. Educ:* Christ's Hospital; St Catharine's College, Cambridge. Colonial Administrative Service, Nigeria, 1932; served E Reg. and Colony; Enugu Secretariat, 1947; Lagos Secretariat, 1949; attached Cabinet Office, London, 1951; Resident, 1951; Secretary to Council of Ministers, 1951; Secretary to Governor-General and the Council of Ministers, Federation of Nigeria, 1955–59; Dep. Governor, Sierra Leone, 1960–61; Acting Gov. during 1960; Adviser to the Government of Sierra Leone after Independence, 1961–63; Sec. to Cabinet, Govt of the Bahamas, 1963–71. FRSA 1969. *Publications:* various papers on Cabinet procedure and government machinery, circulated in Commonwealth. *Recreations:* astronomy, natural history, gardening. *Address:* Cedar House, Caxton Lane, Foxton, Cambridge CB2 6SR. *T:* Cambridge 870629.
See also J. Ounsted.

NEWNS, George Henry, MD, FRCP; Physician, The Hospital for Sick Children, Great Ormond Street, WC1, 1946–73, Hon. Consulting Physician since 1974; Dean, Institute of Child Health, University of London, 1949–73, Emeritus Dean, 1974; Chairman, Leukaemia Research Fund, since 1963; *b* 27 July 1908; *s* of late George Newns, Dartford, Kent; *m* 1936, Deirdre, *d* of late Lawrence Kenny, Clonmel, Tipperary, Eire; one *s* one *d. Educ:* Whitgift School; King's Coll., and King's Coll. Hosp., London. MB, BS (London) 1931; MRCP 1932; MD (London), 1933; FRCP 1951. Registrar: Roy. Northern Hosp., 1933–34; to Children's Dept, King's Coll. Hosp., 1934–35; Med. Registrar and Pathologist, Hosp. for Sick Children, Gt Ormond St, 1935–38; Physician: Bolingbroke Hosp., London, 1938–45; Queen Elizabeth Hosp. for Children, 1939–46; Pædiatrician to Barnet Gen. Hosp., 1946–67; Civilian Pædiatric Consultant to Admiralty, 1962–74; Hon. Consultant in Pædiatrics to Army, 1966–74. Mem., British Pædiatric Assoc., 1945–; Pres., Pædiatric Section, RSM, 1966–67. *Publications:* contributor to Medical Annual, 1953–61; (with Dr Donald Paterson) Modern Methods of Feeding in Infancy and Childhood, 10th edn, 1955; contrib. to Pædiatric Urology (ed D. I. Williams), 1968; Urology in Childhood, 1974; numerous contributions to med. journals. *Recreations:* reading and looking at paintings. *Address:* 12

Milborne Grove, SW10 9SN. *T:* 01-373 2011; 34 Great Ormond Street, WC1N 3JH. *T:* 01-405 1306.

NEWPORT, Viscount; Alexander Michael Orlando Bridgeman; *b* 6 Sept. 1980; *s* and *heir* of 7th Earl of Bradford, *qv.*

NEWRY AND MORNE, Viscount; Robert Francis John Needham; *b* 30 May 1966; *s* and *heir* to Earl of Kilmorey (*see* R. F. Needham).

NEWSAM, Peter Anthony; Chairman, Commission for Racial Equality, since 1982; *b* 2 Nov. 1928; *s* of late W. O. Newsam and of Mrs D. E. Newsam; *m* 1953, Elizabeth Joy Greg; four *s* one *d. Educ:* Clifton Coll.; Queen's Coll., Oxford (MA, DipEd). Asst Principal, BoT, 1952-55; teacher, 1956-63; Asst Educn Officer, N Riding of Yorks, 1963-66; Asst Dir of Educn, Cumberland, 1966-70; Dep. Educn Officer: W Riding of Yorks, 1970-72; ILEA, 1972-76; Educn Officer, ILEA, 1977-82. Vis. Fellow, Nuffield Coll., Oxford, 1982-83. *Address:* 48 Dartmouth Row, Greenwich, SE10.
See also R. W. Newsam.

NEWSAM, Richard William, CVO 1961; HM Diplomatic Service, retired; *b* 23 June 1918; *s* of late W. O. Newsam, ICS; *m* 1952, Joan Rostgard; one *s. Educ:* St Paul's; Trinity Coll., Oxford. Commnd RASC; served War of 1939-45: with East African Forces, Kenya, Abyssinia, Ceylon and Burma. Temporary Administrative Assistant, Colonial Office, 1946; Assistant Principal, Colonial Office, 1947; Principal, 1948; Nigeria secondment, 1952-53; joined Commonwealth Relations Office, 1957; served in: Ceylon, 1958; Pakistan, 1960; Dept of Technical Co-operation, 1963; Ministry of Overseas Development, 1964; Deputy High Commissioner, Dar es Salaam, 1965; Accra, 1967-69. *Recreations:* golf, sailing. *Club:* Dulwich and Sydenham Hill Golf.

NEWSOM, George Harold, QC 1956; Chancellor: Diocese of St Albans, since 1958; Diocese of London, since 1971; Diocese of Bath and Wells, since 1971; *b* 29 Dec. 1909; *e s* of late Rev. G. E. Newsom, Master of Selwyn Coll., Cambridge; *m* 1939, Margaret Amy, *d* of L. A. Allen, OBE; two *s* one *d. Educ:* Marlborough; Merton College, Oxford. 2nd Class Lit Hum, 1931; 1st Class Jurisprudence, 1932; Harmsworth Senior Scholar; Merton College, 1932; Cholmeley Student, 1933, called to Bar, 1934, Lincoln's Inn; Bencher, 1962; Treasurer, 1980; practised at Chancery Bar, 1934-79. Min. of Economic Warfare, 1939-40; Trading with the Enemy Dept, Treasury and Bd of Trade, 1940-45; Junior Counsel to Charity Comrs, 1947-56; Conveyancing Counsel to PO, 1947-56; Dep. Chm., Wilts QS, 1964-71; a Recorder of the Crown Court, 1972-74. Member Gen. Council of the Bar, 1952-56. Vis. Prof. in Law, Auckland Univ., NZ, 1971. *Publications:* Restrictive Covenants affecting freehold land, 1st edn (with late C. H. S. Preston), 1940, 7th edn 1982; Limitation of Actions, 1st edn (with late C. H. S. Preston), 1939, 2nd edn 1943, 3rd edn (with L. Abel-Smith), 1953; The Discharge and Modification of Restrictive Covenants, 1957; (with J. G. Sherratt) Water Pollution, 1972. *Recreations:* wine, walking. *Address:* The Old Vicarage, Bishop's Cannings, Devizes, Wilts. *T:* Cannings 660. *Club:* Athenæum.

NEWSOME, David Hay, MA; LittD Cantab 1976; FRSL 1981; Master of Wellington College, since 1980; *b* 15 June 1929; *s* of Captain C. T. Newsome, OBE; *m* 1955, Joan Florence, *d* of Lt-Col L. H. Trist, DSO, MC; four *d. Educ:* Rossall Sch., Fleetwood; Emmanuel Coll., Cambridge (Scholar). First Cl. in Hist. Tripos Parts I and II, 1952, 1953. Asst Master, Wellington Coll., 1954-59 (Head of History Dept, 1956-59); Fellow of Emmanuel Coll., Cambridge, 1959-70; Asst Lectr in Ecclesiastical History, Univ. of Cambridge, 1961-66; Univ. Lectr, 1966-70; Sen. Tutor, Emmanuel Coll., Cambridge, 1965-70; Headmaster of Christ's Hospital, 1970-79. Lectures: Gore Memorial, Westminster Abbey, 1965; Bishop Westcott Memorial, Cambridge, 1968; Birkbeck, Univ. of Cambridge, 1972. Council of: Ardingly Coll., 1965-69; Eastbourne Coll., 1966-70; Epsom Coll., 1966-70. FRHistS, 1970. *Publications:* A History of Wellington College, 1859-1959, 1959; Godliness and Good Learning, Four Studies in a Victorian Ideal, 1961; The Parting of Friends, a study of the Wilberforces and Henry Manning, 1966; Bishop Westcott and the Platonic Tradition, 1969; Two Classes of Men: Platonism and English Romantic Thought, 1974; On the Edge of Paradise: A. C. Benson the Diarist, 1980 (Whitbread Book of the Year Award); (ed) Edwardian Excursions, 1981; articles in Jl of Theological Studies, Jl of Ecclesiastical History, Theology, History Today, Historical Jl. *Recreations:* music, fell-walking. *Address:* Wellington College, Crowthorne, Berks RG11 7PU. *T:* Crowthorne 2261; The Retreat, Thornthwaite, Keswick, Cumbria. *T:* Braithwaite 372. *Clubs:* Athenæum, MCC.

NEWSOME, William Antony; Director-General, Association of British Chambers of Commerce, since 1974; *b* 8 Nov. 1919; *s* of William F. Newsome and Elizabeth (*née* Thompson); *m* 1951, Estella Ann (*née* Cope); one *s. Educ:* King Henry VIII Sch., Coventry; Bedford Modern Sch. Student Engineer, W. H. Allen, Sons & Co. Ltd, Bedford, 1937-40. Served War, Royal Engineers: N Africa, Sicily, Italy campaigns, 1940-47. Engrg Dept, Crown Agents for Oversea Governments and Administrations, 1949-61; Principal: Home Office, 1961-64; Min. of Technology, 1964-70; Dept of Trade and Industry, 1970-71; Asst Sec., Dept of Trade, 1971-74. Member: SITPRO, 1972-; Production Statistics Adv. Cttee, 1975-; Home Office Standing Cttee on Crime Prevention, 1978-. *Recreations:* photography, swimming, lawn tennis. *Address:* Bourdon Lacey, Old Woking Road, Woking, Surrey GU22 8HR. *T:* Woking 62237.

NEWSON-SMITH, Sir John (Kenneth), 2nd Bt *cr* 1944; DL; Member of HM Commission of Lieutenancy for City of London, since 1947; Deputy Chairman, London United Investments Ltd, since 1971 (Chairman, 1968-71); *b* 9 Jan. 1911; *s* of Sir Frank Newson-Smith, 1st Bt and Dorothy (*d* 1955), *d* of late Sir Henry Tozer; *S* father, 1971; *m* 1st, 1945, Vera Margaret Allt (marr. diss. 1971); one *s* two *d* ; 2nd, 1972, Anne, *d* of late Harold Burns. *Educ:* Dover Coll.; Jesus Coll., Cambridge (MA). Joined Newson-Smith & Co, 1933, Partner 1938. Served War, Royal Navy, 1939-40; RNVR 1940. Rejoined Newson-Smith & Co, 1946 (which subseq. became Fielding Newson-Smith & Co.). Master of Turners Co., 1969-70; Liveryman: Merchant Taylors' Co.; Spectaclemakers' Co. Court of Common Council, 1945-78; Deputy, Ward of Bassishaw, 1961-76. DL City of London, 1947. *Recreations:* travelling, gardening. *Heir: s* Peter Frank Graham Newson-Smith [*b* 8 May 1947; *m* 1974, Mrs Mary-Ann Owens, *o d* of Cyril C. Collins; one *s* one *d*]. *Address:* Orchard Cottage, Babcary, Somerton, Somerset. *T:* Charlton Mackrell 3547. *Clubs:* City Livery, Naval.

NEWTH, Prof. David Richmond; Regius Professor of Zoology, University of Glasgow, 1965-81; *b* 10 Oct. 1921; *s* of Herbert Greenway Newth and Annie Munroe (*née* Fraser); *m* 1946, Jean Winifred (*née* Haddon); two *s* one *d. Educ:* King Edward VI High Sch., Birmingham. Entered University Coll., London, 1938; graduated in Zoology, 1942. Served War of 1939-45, REME, commnd 1943. Asst Lectr in Zoology at University Coll., London, 1947; Lectr, 1949; Prof. of Biology as Applied to Medicine in the Univ. of London, at the Middlesex Hospital Medical Sch., 1960-65. Mem., Nature Conservancy Council, 1978-81. President: Scottish Marine Biol. Assoc., 1973-79; British Soc. for Developmental Biology, 1979-. FRSE 1966. Editor, Journal of Embryology and Experimental Morphology, 1960-69. *Publications:* Animal Growth and Development, 1970; original articles in scientific journals, translations, and contrib. (popular) scientific works. *Recreation:* resting. *Address:* Monevechadan, Lochgoilhead, Cairndow, Argyll PA24 8AN. *T:* Lochgoilhead 287.

NEWTON, 4th Baron, *cr* 1892; **Peter Richard Legh;** *b* 6 April 1915; *er s* of 3rd Baron Newton, TD, DL, JP, and Hon. Helen Meysey-Thompson (*d* 1958); *S* father 1960; *m* 1948, Priscilla, *yr d* of late Capt. John Egerton-Warburton and *widow* of William Matthew Palmer, Visc. Wolmer; two *s. Educ:* Eton; Christ Church, Oxford (MA). 2nd Lt, Grenadier Guards (SR), 1937; Captain, 1941; Major, 1945. JP 1951; CC Hampshire, 1949-52 and 1954-55. Chairman East Hampshire Young Conservatives, 1949-50. MP (C) Petersfield Division of Hants, Oct. 1951-June 1960; PPS to Fin. Sec. to Treasury, 1952-53; Asst Govt Whip, 1953-55; a Lord Comr of Treasury, 1955-57; Vice-Chamberlain of the Household, 1957-59; Treasurer of the Household, 1959-60; Capt. Yeomen of the Guard and Govt Asst Chief Whip, 1960-62; (Joint) Parly Sec., Min. of Health, 1962-64; Min. of State for Education and Science, April-Oct. 1964. *Recreations:* photography, clock repairing, making gadgets. *Heir: s* Hon. Richard Thomas Legh [*b* 11 Jan. 1950; *m* 1978, Rosemary Whitfoot Clarke, *yr d* of Herbert Clarke, Eastbourne; one *s*]. *Address:* Vernon Hill House, Bishop's Waltham, Hampshire. *T:* Bishop's Waltham 2301. *Clubs:* Carlton, St Stephen's Constitutional, Pratt's; Hampshire (Winchester).
See also Major Hon. Sir F. M. Legh, Earl of Selborne.

NEWTON, Antony Harold, OBE 1972; MP (C) Braintree since Feb. 1974; Parliamentary Under Secretary of State for Social Security, since 1982; economist; *b* Aug. 1937; *m* ; two *c. Educ:* Friends' Sch., Saffron Walden; Trinity Coll., Oxford. Hons PPE. President: OU Conservative Assoc., 1958; Oxford Union, 1959. Formerly Sec. and Research Sec., Bow Group. Head of Conservative Research Dept's Economic Section, 1965-70; Asst Dir, Conservative Research Dept, 1970-74. Chm. Coningsby Club, 1965-66. Contested (C) Sheffield, Brightside, 1970. An Asst Govt Whip, 1979-81; a Lord Comr of HM Treasury, 1981-82. Vice-Chm., Fedn of Univ. Conservative and Unionist Assocs. Governor: City Literary Inst.; Felstead Sch. Interested in taxation and social services. *Address:* House of Commons, SW1A 0AA.

NEWTON, Clive Trevor; Director of Consumer Affairs, Office of Fair Trading, since 1980; *b* 26 Aug. 1931; *s* of Frederick Norman and Phyllis Laura Newton; *m* 1961, Elizabeth Waugh Plowman; one *s* one *d. Educ:* Hove Grammar School for Boys. LLB London; called to Bar, Middle Temple, 1969; certified accountant. Examiner, Insolvency Service, Board of Trade, 1952; Sen. Examiner, 1963, Asst Official Receiver, 1967; Principal, Marine Div., BoT, 1969; Sen. Principal, Marine Div., Dept of Trade, 1973; Asst Director of Consumer Credit, Office of Fair Trading, 1974; Asst Sec., Regional Development Grants Div., Dept of Industry, 1978. *Recreations:* golf, watching cricket and football. *Address:* 115 Hangleton Way, Hove, Sussex BN3 8AF. *T:* Brighton 416048. *Clubs:* Sussex County Cricket; East Brighton Golf; West Hove Golf.

NEWTON, Douglas Anthony, CB 1976; Senior Registrar, Principal Registry, Family Division of High Court, 1972-75, retired; *b* 21 Dec. 1915; *s* of John and Janet May Newton; *m* 1946, Barbara Sutherland; one *s* one *d. Educ:* Westminster Sch. Joined Civil Service, 1934. Served War, British and Indian Armies, 1940-46. Apptd Registrar, 1959; Sen. Registrar, 1972. *Recreations:* beer, boats, building.

NEWTON, Sir Gordon; *see* Newton, Sir L. G.

NEWTON, Sir (Harry) Michael (Rex), 3rd Bt, cr 1900; Director Thos Parsons & Sons Ltd; b 7 Feb. 1923; 2nd and e surv. s of Sir Harry K. Newton, 2nd Bt, OBE, DL, and Myrtle Irene (d 1977), e d of W. W. Grantham, Balneath Manor, Lewes; S father, 1951; m 1958, Pauline Jane, o d of late R. J. F. Howgill, CBE; one s; three adopted d. Educ: Eastbourne College. Served War of 1939-45, with KRRC, in 8th Army and Middle East, 1941-46 (wounded). Master, Girdlers' Company, 1975-76; Freeman of City of London. Recreations: shooting, sailing (winner of 1953 Fastnet Race), ski-ing, fencing. Heir: s George Peter Howgill Newton, b 26 March 1962. Address: Weycroft Hall, near Axminster, Devon. T: 3169. Club: Royal Ocean Racing.

NEWTON, Sir Hubert, Kt 1968; Chairman, Britannia Building Society, since 1976; b 2 Sept. 1904; s of Joe Newton and Gertrude Eliza Newton; m 1931, Elsie (née Wilson); one d. Educ: Burnley Gram. School. Burnley Building Soc., 1918-23; Mortgage Dept Controller, Northampton Town Building Soc., 1923-26; Controller of Investment Dept, Leeds Perm. Building Soc., 1926-30; Asst Sec., Bristol & West Building Soc., 1930-33; Leek and Moorlands Building Soc.: Sec., 1933-40; Gen. Man., 1940-63; Chm. and Man. Dir, 1963-66, when Leek and Moorlands amalgamated with Westbourne Park Building Soc. to form Leek and Westbourne Building Soc.; Man. Dir, 1966-69, Chm., 1966-74, Leek and Westbourne Building Soc.; on further amalgamation, Jt Dep. Chm., Leek Westbourne and Eastern Counties Building Soc. (name changed to Britannia Building Soc., 1975), 1974-76. Local Dir, N Staffs, Royal Insce Co. Ltd. Former Member Council: Building Socs Assoc. of Gt Britain (Chm., 1952-54); and Mem., Exec. Cttee. Internat. Union of Building Socs and Savings Assocs (Dep. Pres., Washington Congress, 1962; Pres., London Congress, 1965); Vice-President: Chartered Building Socs Inst., 1962; Building Socs Assoc. of Jamaica Ltd, 1967; President: Midland Assoc. of Building Socs, 1979; N Staffs Chamber of Commerce, 1964-65. Former Mem., Skelmersdale Develt Corp. Past Mem., Central Housing Adv. Cttee; Mem. Council, Nat. House-Building Council (Vice-Pres.); Founder Pres., Rotary Club, Leek, 1937; Liveryman, Gold and Silver Wyre Drawers' Company. Hon. MA Keele, 1971. Coronation Medal, 1953. Publications: contribs to Building Socs Gazette. Recreations: golf, travel. Address: Birchall, Leek, Staffs ST13 5RA. T: Leek 382397. Club: English-Speaking Union.

NEWTON, Rev. Dr John Anthony; Superintendent Minister of the London Mission (West London) Circuit of the Methodist Church, since 1978; b 28 Sept. 1930; s of late Charles Victor Newton and of Kathleen Marchant; m 1963, Rachel, d of late Rev. Maurice H. Giddings and of Hilda Giddings, Louth, Lincs; four s. Educ: Grammar School, Boston, Lincs; University Coll., Hull; London Univ.; Wesley House, Cambridge. BA, PhD (Lond), MA (Cantab). Jun. Research Fellow, Inst. of Historical Research, London Univ., 1953-55; Housemaster and actg Chaplain, Kent Coll., Canterbury, 1955-56; trained for Methodist Ministry, Wesley House, 1956-58; Asst Tutor, Richmond Coll., Surrey, 1958-61, having been ordained, 1960; Circuit Minister at Louth, Lincs, 1961-64, and Stockton-on-Tees, 1964-65; Tutor at Didsbury Coll. (from 1967, Wesley Coll.), Bristol, 1965-72; taught Church History, St Paul's United Theolog. Coll., Limuru, Kenya, and Univ. of Nairobi, 1972-73; Principal of Wesley Coll., Bristol, 1973-78. President of the Methodist Conference, 1981-82. Governor, Kingswood Sch., Bath, 1973-; Chm. of Governors, Westminster Coll., Oxford, 1979-; Trustee, Wesley House, Cambridge, 1979-. Hon. DLitt Hull, 1982. Publications: Methodism and the Puritans, 1964; Susanna Wesley and the Puritan Tradition in Methodism, 1968; The Palestine Problem, 1972; Search for a Saint: Edward King, 1977; The Fruit of the Spirit in the Lives of Great Christians, 1979. Recreations: music, gardening, tennis, fretwork. Address: 36 Priory Avenue, Bedford Park, Chiswick, W4 1TY. T: 01-994 5147.

NEWTON, John Mordaunt, CB 1964; retired from Post Office Central HQ, 1973; b 24 April 1913; o s of late Wallis and Mabel Newton; m 1939, Pamela Frances, e d of late Sir E. John Maude, KCB, KBE; five d. Educ: Manchester Gram. Sch.; CCC, Cambridge (Scholar). BA 1st Cl. History Tripos, 1935. Assistant Principal, Post Office, 1936; Principal: Ministry of Home Security, 1941; Home Office, 1943; Treasury, 1945-47; Post Office 1947-73: Assistant Secretary, 1949; Under Secretary, 1957; Director of Personnel, GPO, 1957-67; Dir, Management Develt, 1967-73. Mem., London Diocesan Synod, 1979-82. Hon. Secretary, Abbeyfield Chiswick Soc., 1965-77. Recreations: reading, bookbinding, historic buildings. Address: Thames Bank, Chiswick Mall, W4 2PR. T: 01-994 1803.

NEWTON, Sir Kenneth (Garnar), 3rd Bt cr 1924; OBE 1970 (MBE 1944); TD; Managing Director, since 1972, Garnar Booth Ltd; b 4 June 1918; s of Sir Edgar Henry Newton, 2nd Bt, and Gladys Maud (d 1966), d of late Sir James Garnar; S father, 1971; m 1st, 1944, Margaret Isabel (d 1979), d of Rev. Dr George Blair, Dundee; two s; 2nd, 1980, Mrs Pamela S. Wilson. Educ: Wellington College, Berks. Served War of 1939-45 (MBE); Lt-Col, RASC (TA). General Commissioner for Income Tax, 1961-. Pres., Internat. Council of Tanners, 1972-78; Past President, British Leather Federation (1968-69); Liveryman and Member of Court of Assistants, Leathersellers' Company (Master, 1977-78) and Feltmakers' Company (Renter Warden, 1981-82). Heir: s John Garnar Newton [b 10 July 1945; m 1972, Jacynth A. K. Miller; three s]. Address: Wildways, High Broom Lane, Crowborough, Sussex TN6 3SP. T: Crowborough 61089.

NEWTON, Sir (Leslie) Gordon, Kt 1966; Editor of The Financial Times, 1950-72, Director 1967-72; Director, Mills & Allen (International) Ltd,

1974-81; b 1907; s of John and Edith Newton; m 1935, Peggy Ellen Warren; one s. Educ: Blundell's School; Sidney Sussex College, Cambridge. Chm., LBC, 1974-77; Dir, Trust Houses Forte Ltd, 1973-80. Hannen Swaffer Award for Journalist of the Year, 1966; Granada Television special award, 1970. Address: Little Basing, Vicarage Walk, Bray-on-Thames, Berks.

NEWTON, Margaret; General Secretary, Friends of the Elderly, since 1981; b 20 Dec. 1927; 2nd d of F. L. Newton, KStJ, MB, ChB, and Mrs A. C. Newton, MBE, BA. Educ: Sherborne School for Girls; St Andrews Univ.; Oxford University. MA Hons St Andrews, 1950; Educn Dip. Oxon 1951. Asst Mistress, King Edward VI Grammar School, Handsworth, Birmingham, 1951-54; Classics Mistress, Queen Margaret's Sch., York, 1954-60 (House Mistress, 1957); House Mistress, Malvern Girls' College, 1960-64 (Head of Classics Dept, 1962); Headmistress, Westonbirt Sch., 1965-80. Address: The Comedy, Sherborne Street, Lechlade, Glos.

NEWTON, Sir Michael; see Newton, Sir H. M. R.

NEWTON, Robert, CMG 1953; retired as Colonial Secretary, Mauritius, 1961; b Newcastle upon Tyne, 12 Oct. 1908; m 1933, Muriel Winifred, d of late Mr and Mrs R. P. Chinneck; one s two d. Educ: Aysgarth School; Malvern College; Pembroke College, Cambridge. Joined Colonial Administrative Service as Administrative Officer (Cadet), Nigeria, 1931; served there as an Assistant District Officer until 1937; served Palestine until 1946; IDC 1947; seconded for duty in Colonial Office, 1948; Financial Secretary, Jamaica, 1949. Member, British Ornithologists Union. PhD (Exon) 1966. FRSA 1972. Publications: Tarnished Brocade, 1937; Swords of Bronze, 1939; Victorian Exeter, 1968; The Northumberland Landscape, 1972. Recreations: ornithology, walking. Address: 14 Howell Road, Exeter, Devon. Club: United Oxford & Cambridge University.

NEWTON-CLARE, Herbert Mitchell, (Bill), CBE 1976; MC 1943; Chairman and Managing Director, NCAS Ltd, since 1978; b 5 May 1922; s of Herbert John and Eileen Margaret Newton-Clare; m 1970, Maureen Mary Thorp; three d. Educ: Cheltenham Coll. TA, Middlesex Regt, 1938; served War of 1939-45: mobilised, 1939; commnd, Wiltshire Regt, 1941; wounded, Normandy, 1944; demobilised, 1945 (Major). Joined Bowyers (Wiltshire) Ltd, as trainee, 1945; Factory Manager, 1955, Gen. Manager, 1957, Man. Dir, 1960, Chm., 1966; following take-over by Unigate of Scot Bowyers (formerly Bowyers (Wiltshire) Ltd), became Director of Unigate, 1973, Vice-Chm., 1974-76; Dir, FMC Ltd, and ancillary cos, 1976-77. Director: Aidaco (Finance) Ltd, 1980-; Hilliers Bacon Curing Co. Ltd, 1980-. Chm., Meat Manufrs Assoc.; Member: Exec. and Council, Food Manufrs Fedn; Food and Drink Industries Fedn; Exec. Centre de Liaison des Industries Transformatrice de Viandes de la Commune Européenne. Recreations: golf, tennis, swimming, fishing. Address: Hurtmore Holt, Shackleford, near Godalming, Surrey GU8 6AY. T: Godalming 7116; 28 Chesham Place, SW1X 8HG. T: 01-235 4172. Club: Sunningdale Golf.

NEWTON DUNN, William Francis; Member (C) Lincolnshire, European Parliament, since 1979; b 3 Oct. 1941; s of Lt-Col Owen Newton Dunn, OBE, and Barbara (née Brooke); m 1970, Anna Terez Arki; one s one d. Educ: Marlborough Coll. (scholar); Gonville and Caius Coll., Cambridge (MA); INSEAD Business Sch., Fontainebleau (MBA). With Fisons Ltd (Fertilizer Division), 1974-79: General Manager of subsid. shipping company, 1974-77; Purchasing Controller for raw materials, 1977-79. Contested (C): general elections: Carmarthen, Feb. 1974; Cardiff West, Oct. 1974. Recreation: spending time with his children. Address: c/o 6 Upgate, Louth, Lincs LN11 9ET. T: Louth 603713.

NGAIZA, Christopher Pastor; Special Personal Assistant to the President of Tanzania and Commissioner for Kagera River Basin Organisation, since 1977; b 29 March 1930; parents decd; m 1952, Thereza; three s two d (and one s decd). Educ: Makerere University Coll.; Loughborough Co-operative College. Local Courts Magistrate, 1952-53; Secretary/Manager, Bahaya Co-operative Consumer Stores, 1955-57; Loughborough Co-operative Coll., 1957-59; Auctioneer and Representative of Bukoba Native Co-operative Union, Mombasa, 1959-61; Foreign Service, 1961-; Counsellor, Mission to UN, 1961-62; Counsellor, Tanganyika High Commn, London, 1962-63; High Commissioner for United Republic of Tanganyika and Zanzibar in London, 1964-65; Tanzanian Ambassador: to Netherlands, 1965-67, to Arab Republic of Egypt, 1972-77; Mem., E African Common Market Tribunal, 1968-69; Tanzania's first High Comr to Zambia, 1969-72. Recreations: music, tennis. Address: State House, PO Box 9120, Dar es Salaam, Tanzania.

NGATA, Sir Henare Kohere, KBE 1982 (OBE); chartered accountant, Gregory Chambers, Gisborne, New Zealand; b Waiomatatini, 19 Dec. 1917; s of Sir Apirana Ngata and Arihia, d of Tuta Tamati; m 1940, Rora Lorna, d of Maihi Rangipo Mete Kingi; one s. Educ: Waiomatatini Sch.; Te Aute Coll., Victoria Univ. of Wellington, BA, BCom; FCA (NZ Soc. of Accountants). Served 28th Maori Bn, 1939-45: POW, Greece; Germany, 1941-45. Chm., Mangatu 1, 3 & 4 Blocks Incorp., 1959-; Director: Fieldair Ltd, 1960-79; Gisborne Sheepfarmers Mercantile Co. Ltd; Gisborne Sheepfarmers Freezing Co. Ltd. Member: Gisborne Reg. Commn, NZ Historic Places Trust, 1962-70; NZ Maori Council, 1962-; C of E Provincial Commn on Maori Schs, 1964-; Gisborne/East Coast Regional Develt Council, 1973-78; Finance Cttee, Bishopric of Aotearoa. Nat. Pres., 28th Maori Bn Assoc., 1964-66. Vice-Pres., NZ Nat. Party, 1967-69. Hon. LLD,

Victoria Univ. of Wellington, 1979. *Address:* Grant Road, Gisborne, New Zealand; Gregory Chambers, Derby Street, Gisborne, New Zealand.

NG'ETHE NJOROGE; businessman; High Commissioner for Kenya in London, 1970–78; *m* 1972, Dr Njeri Ng'ethe Njoroge; one *s. Educ:* Kenya and Uganda (Cambridge Sch. Cert., 1949); United States: Central State Coll., Wilberforce, Ohio (BSc (Gen. Sci.) 1955); Univ. of Dayton, Dayton, Ohio (Sociology, 1955–56); Boston Univ. (MSc (Pol. Sci. and Journalism) 1962). Began as journalist, Patriot Ledger, Quincy, Mass; subseq., Kenya Govt: Asst Sec. (Admin), in Min. of Lands and Settlement, and Min. of Works, 1963–64; Min. of Foreign Affairs, 1964; Head of Africa Div., 1964–67; Counsellor, Kenya Embassy, Bonn, 1968–70. Delegate: Commonwealth Conf., 1965, 1966, 1971; Organization of African Unity Confs, 1964–67; UN Gen. Assembly, 1964, 1965, 1966. *Recreations:* music (collector of jazz and classical records), photography (colour slides); reading; interest in current public and international issues. *Address:* PO Box 30384, Nairobi, Kenya.

NGONDA, Putteho Muketoi; Zambian Ambassador to USA, Peru, Brazil and Venezuela, since 1977; *b* 16 Aug. 1936; *m* 1965, Lungowe Mulala; three *s. Educ:* Mongu and Munali Secondary Schs, Zambia; UC of Rhodesia and Nyasaland, Salisbury. BScEcon (Hons). District Officer, 1963–64; 2nd Sec., Zambia Perm. Mission to UN, 1964–65; 1st Sec., Zambian Embassy, Washington, 1967–68; Asst Sec. (Political), Min. of Foreign Affairs, 1968–70; Under-Sec., Min. of Foreign Affairs, 1970–72; Ambassador to Ethiopia, 1972–74; High Comr to UK, 1974–75; Perm. Sec., Ministry of Foreign Affairs, 1975–77. *Recreation:* mainly tennis. *Address:* Embassy of the Republic of Zambia, 2419 Massachusetts Avenue, NW, Washington, DC 20008, USA.

NIALL, Sir Horace Lionel Richard, Kt 1974; CBE 1957 (MBE 1943); Civil Servant (retd); *b* 14 Oct. 1904; *s* of late Alfred George Niall and Jane Phyllis Niall; *m* 1965, Una Lesley Niall (*née* de Salis); one *d. Educ:* Mudgee High Sch., NSW; Sydney Univ., NSW. Served War of 1939–45: with AIF, four yrs in New Guinea, rank Major, No NGX 373, all campaigns in New Guinea. NSW Public Service (Water Conservation Commn), 1923–27. Public Service of Papua, New Guinea, 1927–64: joined as a Cadet and retd as Dist Comr; rep. PNG at South Pacific Commn, 1954, and UN Trusteeship Council, 1957; Mem. for Morobe in first House of Assembly and Speaker First House, 1964. *Recreations:* golf, surfing. *Address:* 9 Commodore, 50 Palm Beach Road, Palm Beach, NSW 2108, Australia. *T:* 919 5462. *Clubs:* Palm Beach Golf, RSL Palm Beach (NSW).

NIARCHOS, Stavros Spyros; Grand Cross of Order of the Phœnix (Greece), 1957; Commander of Order of George I of Greece, 1954; Commander of Order of St George and St Constantine (Greece), 1964; Head of Niarchos Group of Shipping Companies which controls over 5.75 million tons of shipping (operational and building); *b* 3 July 1909; *s* of late Spyros Niarchos and of Eugenie Niarchos; *m* 1st, 1939, Melpomene Capparis (marr. diss., 1947); no *c*; 2nd, 1947, Eugenie Livanos (*d* 1970); three *s* one *d*; 3rd, 1965, Charlotte Ford (marr. diss., 1967); one *d*; 4th, 1971, Mrs Athina Livanos (*d* 1974). *Educ:* Univ. of Athens (Dr of Laws). On leaving Univ. joined family grain and shipping business; started independent shipping concern, 1939. Joined Royal Hellenic Navy Volunteer Reserve, 1941; served on destroyer engaged in North Atlantic convoy work (despatches). Demobilised, 1945, with rank of Lieut-Comdr. Returned to Shipping business. Pioneered super-tankers. *Recreations:* yachting, ski-ing. *Address:* c/o Niarchos (London) Ltd, 41/43 Park Street, W1. *T:* 01–629 8400. *Clubs:* Athenian, Royal Yacht Club of Greece (both in Athens).

NIBLETT, Prof. William Roy, CBE 1970; BA, MLitt; Professor of Higher Education, University of London, 1967–73, Professor Emeritus, 1973; *b* 25 July 1906; *m* 1938, Sheila Margaret, OBE 1975, *d* of A. C. Taylor, Peterborough; one *s* one *d. Educ:* Cotham Sch., Bristol; University of Bristol (1st cl. hons English); St Edmund Hall, Oxford. Lectr in Educn, King's Coll., Newcastle, 1934–45 (Registrar of Univ. Durham, 1940–44); Prof. of Educn, University Coll., Hull, 1945–47; Prof. of Education, and Dir, Inst. of Education, Univ. of Leeds, 1947–59. Dean, Univ. of London Inst. of Education, 1960–68; Mem., UGC, 1949–59; Hibbert Lectr, 1965; Kellogg International Fellow, 1954; sometime Visiting Professor, Universities of California, Melbourne, Otago and Univs of Japan. Chairman: UGC Sub-Cttee on Halls of Residence, 1956 (Report 1957); Educn Dept, BCC, 1965–71; Higher Educn Policy Gp, 1969–72; Pres., European Assoc. for Res. in Higher Educn, 1972. Vice-President: World Univ. Service (UK), 1963–; Soc. for Res. in Higher Educn, 1978–; Gloucestershire Historic Churches Preservation Trust, 1981–. Member: Nat. Advisory Coun. on Trng and Supply of Teachers, 1950–61; Adv. Council on Army Educn, 1961–70; Council, Royal Holloway College, 1963–76; Council, Cheltenham Ladies' College, 1967–79; Trustee: Lucy Cavendish Coll., Cambridge; St Luke's Coll. Foundn, Exeter; Westhill Coll., Birmingham; Higher Educn Foundn (Chm. of Trustees, 1980–81). Chm., Editorial Bd, Studies in Higher Education, 1975–82. FRSA. *Publications:* Education and the Modern Mind, 1954; Christian Education in a Secular Society, 1960; (ed) Moral Education in a Changing Society, 1963; (ed) Higher Education: Demand and Response, 1969; (ed with R. F. Butts) World Year Book of Education, 1972–73; Universities Between Two Worlds, 1974; (with D. Humphreys and J. Fairhurst) The University Connection, 1975; (ed) The Sciences, The Humanities and the Technological Threat, 1975; (contrib.) International Encyclopedia of Higher Education, 1977; (contrib.) The Study of Education, 1980. *Address:* Pinfarthings, Amberley, Stroud, Glos GL5 5JJ. *Club:* Athenæum.

NIBLOCK, Henry, (Pat), OBE 1972; HM Diplomatic Service, retired; HM Consul-General, Strasbourg, 1968–72; *b* 25 Nov. 1911; *s* of Joseph and Isabella Niblock, Belfast; *m* 1940, Barbara Mary Davies, *d* of late Captain R. W. Davies, Air Ministry; two *s.* Vice-Consul: Bremen, 1947–50; Bordeaux, 1951; Second Sec. (Commercial), Copenhagen, 1951–53; Consul, Frankfurt-on-Main, 1954–57; First Sec. and Consul, Monrovia, 1957–58; Consul, Houston, 1959–62; Chargé d'Affaires, Port-au-Prince, 1962–63; First Sec. and Consul, Brussels, 1964; Consul (Commercial), Cape Town, 1964–67. *Recreations:* walking, photography. *Address:* 10 Clifton House, 2 Park Avenue, Eastbourne, East Sussex BN22 9QN. *T:* Eastbourne 55695. *Club:* Civil Service.

NICCOL, Dame Sister Mary Leo, (Kathleen Agnes Niccol), DBE 1973 (MBE 1963), of Auckland, New Zealand; Member of the Sisters of Mercy, Auckland. Specialised in vocal training. Entered Order of Sisters of Mercy, 1923. Has been a singing teacher for over 40 years; pupils who have gained international success include Dame Kiri Te Kanawa, DBE, now living in London, Heather Begg, Mina Foley and Malvina Major. Biography in preparation. *Address:* St Mary's Convent, PO Box 47025, Ponsonby, Auckland 1, New Zealand.

NICHOL, Duncan Kirkbride; Regional Administrator, Mersey Regional Health Authority, since 1981; *b* 30 May 1941; *s* of James and Mabel Nichol; *m* 1972, Elizabeth Wilkinson; one *s* one *d. Educ:* Bradford Grammar Sch.; St Andrews Univ. (MA Hons). AHA 1967. Asst Gp Sec. and Hosp. Sec. to Manchester Royal Infirmary, 1969–73; Dep. Gp Sec. and Actg Gp Sec., Univ. Hosp. Management Cttee of S Manchester, 1973–74; Dist Administrator, Manchester S Dist, 1974–77; Area Administrator, Salford AHA(T), 1977–81. *Recreations:* caravanning, golf, squash. *Address:* 1 Pipers Close, Heswall, Wirral, Merseyside L60 9LJ. *T:* 051-342 2699.

NICHOL, Mrs Muriel Edith; JP; *e d* of late R. C. Wallhead, MP Merthyr Tydfil, 1922–34; *m* James Nichol, MA; one *s.* Counsellor, Welwyn Garden City UDC, 1937–45 (Chm. 1943–44); formerly Dep. Chm., Welwyn Magistrates' Court. MP (Lab) North Bradford, 1945–50; Mem. Parly Delegation to India, Jan.–Feb. 1946; Mem. "Curtis" Cttee (Home Office) on Care of Children, 1945–46. JP Herts, 1944. *Recreations:* local government, social welfare, education.

NICHOLAS, Sir Alfred James, Kt 1967; CBE 1960 (OBE 1954); Chairman: Aberdare Holdings Ltd, 1963–70; South Wales Switchgear Ltd, 1965–70; Glyn John Transport Ltd; *b* 1900; *s* of George and Harriet Nicholas; *m* 1927, Ethel (*d* 1978), *d* of Thomas Platt; one *s. Educ:* Bishop's Castle Sch.; Wellington Sch., Salop; Manchester Coll. of Technology. With Metropolitan Vickers Ltd, and Ferguson-Pailin Ltd until 1941. Formerly Chm. and Man. Director: Aberdare Cables Ltd; Aberdare Engineering Ltd; Erskine Heap & Co. Ltd; South Wales Group (Pty) Ltd South Africa; South Wales Electric (Pvt) Ltd Rhodesia; South Wales Electric Australia (Pty) Ltd; South Wales Electric Zambia Ltd. Founder Mem. and former Chm., Develt Corp. for Wales, President, 1971–; founder Mem. and former Pres., Industrial Assoc. of Wales and Monmouthshire; a Vice-Chm., Welsh Economic Council, 1966–68; Vice-Pres., Welsh Council, 1968–71; Past President: Electrical Res. Assoc.; Cardiff Chamber of Commerce and Industry. Member: Court of Governors, University Coll., Cardiff; Court of Governors, UWIST; Governor, Christ Coll., Brecon, 1965–81. Assoc. Mem. Manchester Coll. of Technology; FIEE; MIEEE (USA); CEng; FBIM. Freeman of the City of London; Liveryman, Worshipful Co. of Tin Plate Workers. Hon. LLD Wales. CStJ (Pres., East Mon area). *Recreations:* photography, gardening. *Address:* Bovil House, Machen, Gwent NP1 8SN.

NICHOLAS, (Angela) Jane (Udale); Dance Director, Arts Council of Great Britain, since 1979; *b* 14 June 1929; *d* of Bernard Alexander Royle Shore, *qv*; *m* 1964, William Alan Nicholas. *Educ:* Norland Place Sch.; Rambert Sch. of Ballet; Arts Educnl Trust; Sadler's Wells Ballet Sch. Founder Mem., Sadler's Wells Theatre Ballet, 1946–50; Mem., Sadler's Wells Ballet at Royal Opera House, 1950–52; freelance dancer, singer, actress, 1952–60; British Council Drama Officer, 1961–70; Arts Council of Great Britain: Dance Officer, 1970–75; Asst Dance Dir, 1975–79. *Recreations:* pruning, weeding, collecting cracked porcelain. *Address:* 21 Stamford Brook Road, W6 0XJ. *T:* 01-741 3035.

NICHOLAS, Barry; see Nicholas, J. K. B. M.

NICHOLAS, David, CBE 1982; Editor and Chief Executive, Independent Television News, since 1977; *b* 25 Jan. 1930; *s* of late Daniel and Bernice Nicholas; *m* 1952, Juliet, *d* of late William and Gladys Davies; one *s* one *d. Educ:* Neath Grammar School; University Coll. of Wales, Aberystwyth. BA (Hons) English. National Service, 1951–53. Journalist with Yorkshire Post, Daily Telegraph, Observer; joined ITN, 1960; Deputy Editor, 1963–77. Produced ITN General Election Results, Apollo coverage, and ITN special programmes, 1963–77. Fellow, Royal Television Soc., 1980. Producers' Guild Award 1967, on return of Sir Francis Chichester. *Recreations:* walking, sailing. *Address:* 103 Kidbrooke Grove, Blackheath, SE3. *T:* 01-858 2654. *Club:* Reform.

NICHOLAS, Sir Harry; see Nicholas, Sir Herbert Richard.

NICHOLAS, Prof. Herbert George, FBA 1969; Rhodes Professor of American History and Institutions, Oxford University, 1969-78; Fellow of New College, Oxford, 1951-78, Emeritus 1978-80, Honorary Fellow since 1980; *b* 8 June 1911; *s* of late Rev. W. D. Nicholas. *Educ:* Mill Hill Sch.; New Coll., Oxford (1st cl. Lit. Hum., 1934). Commonwealth Fund Fellow in Modern History, Yale, 1935-37; MA Oxon, 1938; Exeter College, Oxford: Lectr, 1938, Fellow, 1946-51; Amer. Div., Min. of Information, and HM Embassy, Washington, 1941-46; Faculty Fellow, Nuffield Coll., Oxford, 1948-57; Nuffield Reader in the Comparative Study of Institutions at Oxford Univ., 1956-69. Chm., British Assoc. for American Studies, 1960-62; Vice-Pres., British Academy, 1975-76. Vis. Prof., Brookings Instn, Washington, 1960; Albert Shaw Lectr in Diplomatic History, Johns Hopkins, 1961; Vis. Fellow, Inst. of Advanced Studies, Princeton, 1964; Vis. Faculty Fellow, Inst. of Politics, Harvard, 1968. Hon. DCL Pittsburgh, 1968. *Publications:* The American Union, 1948; The British General Election of 1950, 1951; To the Hustings, 1956; The United Nations as a Political Institution, 1959, 5th edn 1975; (ed) Tocqueville's De la Démocratie en Amérique, 1961; Britain and the United States, 1963; The American Past and The American Present, 1971; The United States and Britain, 1975; The Nature of American Politics, 1980; (ed) Washington Despatches, 1941-45, 1981; articles. *Recreations:* gardening, listening to music. *Address:* 3 William Orchard Close, Old Headington, Oxford. *T:* Oxford 63165. *Clubs:* Athenæum; Lotos (New York).

NICHOLAS, Sir Herbert Richard, (Sir Harry Nicholas), Kt 1970; OBE 1949; General Secretary of the Labour Party, 1968-72; *b* 13 March 1905; *s* of Richard Henry and Rosina Nicholas; *m* 1932, Rosina Grace Brown. *Educ:* Elementary sch., Avonmouth, Bristol; Evening Classes; Correspondence Courses. Clerk, Port of Bristol Authority, 1919-36. Transport and Gen. Workers Union: District Officer, Gloucester, 1936-38; Regional Officer, Bristol, 1938-40; National Officer, London: Commercial Road Transport Group, 1940-42; Chemical Section, 1942-44; Metal and Engineering Group, 1944-56; Asst Gen. Sec., 1956-68 (Acting Gen. Sec., Oct. 1964-July 66). Mem., TUC General Council, 1964-67. Mem., Labour Party Nat. Exec. Cttee, 1956-64, 1967-; Treasurer, Labour Party, 1960-64. *Publications:* occasional articles in press on Industrial Relations subjects. *Recreations:* Rugby football, fishing, reading, gardening. *Address:* 33 Madeira Road, Streatham, SW16. *T:* 01-769 7989.

NICHOLAS, Jane; *see* Nicholas, A. J. U.

NICHOLAS, (John Keiran) Barry (Moylan); Principal of Brasenose College, Oxford, since 1978 (Fellow, 1947-78); *b* 6 July 1919; *s* of Archibald John Nicholas and Rose (*née* Moylan); *m* 1948, Hildegart, *d* of Prof. Hans Cloos, Bonn; one *s* one *d*. *Educ:* Downside; Brasenose Coll., Oxford (Scholar). 1st cl. Class. Mods, 1939 and Jurisprudence, 1946. Royal Signals, 1939-45: Middle East, 1941-45; Major, 1943. Called to Bar, Inner Temple, 1950. Tutor, 1947-71 and Vice-Principal, 1960-63, Brasenose Coll.; All Souls Reader in Roman Law, Oxford Univ., 1949-71; Prof. of Comparative Law, Oxford, 1971-78. Vis. Prof.: Tulane Univ., 1960; Univ. of Rome Inst. of Comparative Law, 1964; Fordham Univ., 1968. *Publications:* Introduction to Roman Law, 1962; Jolowicz's Historical Introduction to Roman Law, 3rd edn, 1972; French Law of Contract, 1982. *Address:* Brasenose College, Oxford. *T:* Oxford 48641.

NICHOLAS, Sir John (William), KCVO 1981; CMG 1979; HM Diplomatic Service; High Commissioner to Sri Lanka, and Ambassador to the Republic of Maldives, since 1979; *b* 13 Dec. 1924; *m* 1947, Rita (*née* Jones); two *s*. *Educ:* Birmingham Univ. Served 7th Rajput Regt, Indian Army, 1944-47; joined Home Civil Service, 1949; War Office, 1949-57; transf. to CRO 1957; First Sec., Brit. High Commn, Kuala Lumpur, 1957-61; Economic Div., CRO, 1961-63; Dep. High Comr in Malawi, 1964-66; Diplomatic Service Inspector, 1967-69; Dep. High Comr and Counsellor (Commercial), Ceylon, 1970-71; Dir, Establishments and Finance Div., Commonwealth Secretariat, 1971-73; Hd of Pacific Dependent Territories Dept, FCO, 1973-74; Dep. High Comr, Calcutta, 1974-76; Consul Gen., Melbourne, 1976-79. *Address:* c/o Foreign and Commonwealth Office, SW1. *Clubs:* Royal Over-Seas League, Travellers'.

NICHOLAS, William Ford, OBE 1954; Director, London Chamber of Commerce and Industry, since 1974; *b* 17 March 1923; *s* of William and Emma Nicholas; *m* 1954, Isobel Sybil Kennedy; two *s*. *Educ:* Stockport Grammar School. Called to Bar, Middle Temple, 1965. Joined S Rhodesia Civil Service, 1947; Private Sec. to Prime Minister, S Rhodesia, 1950; Private Sec. to Prime Minister, Fedn of Rhodesia and Nyasaland, 1953; Counsellor, High Comr's Office, London, 1960; retd 1963. Dir, UK Cttee, Fedn of Commonwealth Chambers of Commerce, 1964; Dep. Dir, London Chamber of Commerce, 1966. *Address:* 2 Lime Close, Frant, Tunbridge Wells, Kent. *T:* Frant 428. *Club:* Gresham.

NICHOLETTS, Air Marshal Sir Gilbert (Edward), KBE 1956; CB 1949; AFC 1931 and Bar, 1933; retired; *b* 9 Nov. 1902; *s* of Edward Cornewall Nicholetts and Ellen Fanny Hollond; *m* 1956, Nora Beswick, *d* of Francis John Butt, MB, Chester. *Educ:* RN Colleges, Osborne and Dartmouth. Cranwell Cadet Coll., 1921-22; Calshot, Lee-on-Solent, 1922-24; HMS Eagle (Med. Fleet), 1924-26; Far East Flight and 205 Sqdn, 1927-30; 209 Sqdn, 1931-32; long distance flight (World Record, 5309 miles non-stop), 1933; Air Staff, 23 Group HQ, 1934; Staff Coll., 1935; Air Staff, AHQ Iraq, 1936-38; Air Ministry organization, 1938-39; War of 1939-45, OC 228 Sqdn, 1939-41;

Haifa, Shallufa, 1941; POW Far East, 1942-45; AOC Central Photographic Establishment, 1946-48; Dir of Organization, Air Ministry, 1948-51; SASO Coastal Command, 1951; AOC No 21 Group, Flying Training Command, 1953; AOC-in-C Flying Training Command, Sept.-Dec. 1955; AOC Malta, and Dep. C-in-C (Air), Allied Forces, Mediterranean, Jan. 1956-Dec. 1957; Inspector-Gen., Royal Air Force, Jan. 1958-June, 1959; retired, 1959. *Address:* Stoborough Croft, Wareham, Dorset. *T:* Wareham 2992. *Club:* Royal Air Force.

NICHOLL, Anthony John David; a Recorder of the Crown Court, since 1978; barrister-at-law; *b* 3 May 1935; *s* of late Brig. and Mrs D. W. D. Nicholl; *m* 1961, Hermione Mary Landon; one *s* two *d*. *Educ:* Eton; Pembroke Coll., Oxford. Called to Bar, Lincoln's Inn, 1958. Practising in Birmingham, 1961-. *Recreations:* history, gardening and other rural pursuits. *Address:* 2 Fountain Court, Steelhouse Lane, Birmingham B4 6DR. *T:* 021-236 3882.

NICHOLLS; *see* Harmar-Nicholls.

NICHOLLS, Brian; Director: John Brown Engineering Ltd, since 1979; John Brown Engineering Gas Turbines Ltd, since 1979; *b* 1928; *s* of Ralph and Kathleen Nicholls; *m* 1961, Mary Elizabeth Harley; one *s* two *d*. *Educ:* Haberdashers' Aske's Sch., Hampstead; London Univ. (BSc Econ); Harvard Business Sch. George Wimpey & Co., 1951-55; Constructors John Brown Ltd, 1955-75; Director: CJB Projects Ltd, 1972-75; CJB Pipelines Ltd, 1974-75; Industrial Adviser, Dept of Trade, 1975-78; Dep. Chm., CJB Mohandessi Iran Ltd, 1974-75. Member: Council, British Rly Industry Export Gp, 1976-78; Overseas Projects Bd, 1976-78; BOTB, 1978. Member: Council, British Chemical Engineering Contractors Assoc., 1973-75; Trade and Industry Cttee, British Algerian Soc., 1974-75. *Recreations:* writing, walking, music. *Address:* Croy, Shandon, by Helensburgh, Dunbartonshire. *T:* Rhu 388. *Club:* Royal Northern and Clyde Yacht (Rhu).

NICHOLLS, Clive Victor, QC 1982; *b* 29 Aug. 1932; twin *s* of Alfred Charles Victor Nicholls and Lilian Mary (*née* May); *m* 1960, Alison Virginia, *d* of late Arthur and Dorothy Oliver; three *s* three *d*. *Educ:* Brighton Coll.; Trinity Coll., Dublin (MA, LLB); Sidney Sussex Coll., Cambridge (BA ad eund, LLB). Called to the Bar, Gray's Inn, 1957. *Recreations:* farming, sailing, fishing. *Address:* Queen Elizabeth Building, Temple, EC4 9BS. *T:* 01-583 9744.
See also C. A. A. Nicholls.

NICHOLLS, Colin Alfred Arthur, QC 1981; *b* 29 Aug. 1932; twin *s* of Alfred Charles Victor Nicholls and Lilian Mary (*née* May); *m* 1976, Clarissa Allison Spenlove, *d* of late Clive and of Theo Dixon; two *s*. *Educ:* Brighton Coll.; Trinity Coll., Dublin. MA, LlB. Called to the Bar, Gray's Inn, 1957 (Albion Richardson Schol.). Auditor, 1956, and Hon. Mem., 1958-, TCD Historical Soc. *Recreations:* painting (exhib. RHA), English domestic architecture, farming, sailing. *Address:* Queen Elizabeth Building, Temple, EC4Y 9BS. *T:* 01-583 9744.
See also C. V. Nicholls.

NICHOLLS, David Alan; Assistant Secretary General for Defence Planning and Policy, NATO, since 1980; *s* of Thomas Edward and Beatrice Winifred Nicholls; *m* 1955, Margaret (*née* Lewis); two *d*. *Educ:* Cheshunt Grammar School; St John's Coll., Cambridge (Schol., Wright's Prizeman 1952, 1953; BA Hons 1954). Served RAF (Flying Officer), 1950-51. Admiralty, 1954-64; Asst Principal, 1954; Private Sec. to Parliamentary Sec., 1958-59; Principal, 1959; MoD, 1964-75; Private Sec. to Minister of Defence for Admin, 1968-69; Asst Sec., 1969; Cabinet Office, 1975-77; Asst Under-Sec. of State, MoD, 1977-80. *Recreations:* sketching, printmaking. *Address:* c/o Midland Bank, Church Stretton, Shropshire.

NICHOLLS, Donald James, QC 1974; *b* 25 Jan. 1933; *yr s* of William Greenhow Nicholls and late Eleanor Jane (*née* Looney); *m* 1960, Jennifer Mary, *yr d* of late W. E. C. Thomas, MB, BCh, MRCOG, JP; two *s* one *d*. *Educ:* Birkenhead Sch.; Liverpool Univ.; Trinity Hall, Cambridge (Foundn Schol.). LLB 1st cl. hons Liverpool, BA 1st cl. hons with dist., Pt II Law Tripos Cantab, LLB 1st cl. hons with dist. Cantab. Certif. of Honour, Bar Final, 1958; called to Bar, Middle Temple, 1958, Bencher, 1981; in practice, Chancery Bar, 1958-. Mem., Senate of Inns of Court and the Bar, 1974-76. *Recreations:* gardening, history, music. *Address:* Little Blakeney, Leigh Hill Road, Cobham, Surrey. *T:* Cobham 4740. *Club:* Athenæum.

NICHOLLS, Pastor Sir Douglas (Ralph), KCVO 1977; Kt 1972; OBE 1968; Governor of South Australia, 1976-77; *b* Cummeragunja, NSW, 9 Dec. 1906; *s* of H. Nicholls, Cummeragunja; *m* 1942, Gladys, *d* of M. Bux; one *s* one *d*. *Educ:* at Cummeragunja. Formerly one of the best-known aborigines of Australia in the field of athletics and football; Pastor, Churches of Christ Aborigines' Mission, Fitzroy, Victoria; Dir, Aborigines Advancement League, 1969-76. KStJ 1977. *Publications:* contribs AAL quarterly magazines. *Recreations:* formerly running (won Nyah Gift and Warracknabeal Gift, 4th Melbourne Thousand, 1929); football (rep. Vic. in interstate matches). *Address:* 688 Canterbury Road, Vermont, Vic 3133, Australia.

NICHOLLS, Rear-Adm. Francis Brian Price B.; *see* Brayne-Nicholls.

NICHOLLS, Air Marshal Sir John (Moreton), KCB 1978; CBE 1970; DFC 1953; AFC 1965; Director in Charge, British Aircraft Co. (British Aerospace),

Saudi Arabia, 1980-82; *b* 5 July 1926; *s* of Alfred Nicholls and Elsie (*née* French); *m* 1st, 1945, Enid Jean Marjorie Rose (*d* 1975); two *d*; 2nd, 1977, Shelagh Joyce Hall (*née* Strong). *Educ:* Liverpool Collegiate; St Edmund Hall, Oxford. RAF Coll., 1945-46; No 28 Sqdn, 1947-49; No 257 Sqdn, 1949-52; 335th Ftr Sqdn USAF, Korea, 1952; CFE, 1953-56 and 1962-64; 435th and 83rd Ftr Sqdns USAF, 1956-58; attached British Aircraft Co., Lightning Project, 1959-61; psa 1961; jssc 1964; MoD, 1964-67; comd RAF Leuchars, 1967-70; idc 1970; SASO 11 Gp, 1971; Principal Staff Officer to CDS, 1971-73; SASO, Strike Comd, 1973-75; ACAS (Op. Requirements), 1976-77; Air Mem. for Supply and Orgn, 1977-79; Vice-Chief of the Air Staff, 1979-80. CBIM. DFC (USA) and Air Medal (USA), 1953. *Address:* 17 The High Street, Morton, Lincs. *Club:* Royal Air Force.

NICHOLLS, Nigel Hamilton, CBE 1982; Assistant Secretary, Ministry of Defence, since 1974; *b* 19 Feb. 1938; *s* of late Bernard Cecil Hamilton Nicholls and Enid Kathleen Nicholls (*née* Gwynne); *m* 1967, Isobel Judith, *d* of Rev. Canon Maurice Dean; two *s. Educ:* King's School, Canterbury; St John's College, Oxford (Exhibr). BA 1962; MA 1966. Asst Principal, Admiralty, 1962, MoD, 1964; Asst Private Sec. to Minister of Defence for RN, 1965-66; Principal, 1966; Directing Staff, RCDS, 1971-73; Asst Private Sec. to Sec. of State for Defence, 1973-74; Defence Counsellor, UK Delegation to MBFR Talks, Vienna, 1977-80. *Recreations:* choral singing, genealogy. *Address:* Trystings, Red Lane, Claygate, Esher, Surrey KT10 0ES. *T:* Esher 66086.

NICHOLLS, Philip, CB 1976; *b* 30 Aug. 1914; *yr s* of late W. H. Nicholls, Radlett; *m* 1955, Sue, *yr d* of late W. E. Shipton; two *s. Educ:* Malvern; Pembroke Coll., Cambridge. Asst Master, Malvern, 1936; Sen. Classical Master, 1939; resigned, 1947. Served in Army, 1940-46: 8th Bn, The Worcestershire Regt; HQ, East Africa Command; Allied Commn for Austria. Foreign Office (German Section), 1947; HM Treasury, 1949; a Forestry Commissioner (Finance and Administration), 1970-75, retired. Mem. Council, Malvern Coll. (Vice-Chm., 1963). *Address:* Barnards Green House, Barnards Green, Malvern, Worcs. *T:* Malvern 4446.

NICHOLLS, Robert Michael; Regional Administrator, South Western Regional Health Authority, since 1981; *b* 28 July 1939; *s* of late Herbert Edgar Nicholls and of Bennetta L'Estrange (*née* Burges); *m* 1961, Dr Deirín Deirdre (*née* O'Sullivan); four *s. Educ:* Hampton Sch.; University Coll. of Wales (BA 1961); Univ. of Manchester (DSA 1962). AHA 1963. Asst Sec., Torbay Hosp., 1964; House Governor, St Stephen's Hosp., Chelsea, 1966; Asst Clerk to the Governors, St Thomas' Hosp., 1968; Dep. Gp Sec., Southampton Univ. Hosp. Management Cttee, 1972; Dist Administrator, Southampton and SW Hampshire Health Dist, 1974; Area Administrator, Newcastle upon Tyne AHA(T), 1977. National Council, Inst. of Health Service Administrators: Mem., 1976-; Hon. Treasurer, 1980-81; Vice Chm., 1981-82; Chm., 1982-83. Mem., Education Cttee, King Edward's Hosp. Fund for London, 1975-81. *Publications:* (contrib.) Resources in Medicine, 1970; contrib. Hosp. and Health Services Rev., Health and Soc. Services Jl and The Health Services. *Recreations:* bird-watching, jazz, opera, sport. *Address:* 47 Woodhill Road, Portishead, Bristol BS20 9EY. *T:* Bristol 848215.

NICHOLLS, Rt. Rev. Vernon Sampson; *see* Sodor and Man, Bishop of.

NICHOLS, Beverley; author and composer; *b* 9 Sept. 1898; *y s* of late John Nichols, Solicitor, of Bristol; unmarried. *Educ:* Marlborough Coll.; Balliol Coll., Oxford (Pres. of the Union, Editor of the Isis, Founder and Editor of the Oxford Outlook). *Publications:* Prelude (a public school novel), 1920; Patchwork, 1921; Self, 1922; Twenty-Five (an autobiography), 1926; Crazy Pavements, 1927; Are They the Same at Home?, 1927; The Star Spangled Manner, 1928; Women and Children Last, 1931; Evensong, 1932; Down the Garden Path, 1932; For Adults Only, 1932; Failures, 1933; Cry Havoc, 1933; A Thatched Roof, 1933; A Village in a Valley, 1934; The Fool Hath Said, 1936; No Place Like Home, 1936; News of England, 1938; Revue, 1939; Green Grows the City, 1939; Men do not Weep, 1941; Verdict on India, 1944; The Tree that Sat Down, 1945; The Stream that Stood Still, 1948; All I Could Never Be, 1949; Uncle Samson, 1950; The Mountain of Magic, 1950; Merry Hall, 1951; A Pilgrim's Progress, 1952; Laughter on the Stairs, 1953; No Man's Street, 1954; The Moonflower, 1955; Death to Slow Music, 1956; Sunlight on the Lawn, 1956; The Rich Die Hard, 1957; The Sweet and Twenties, 1958; Murder by Request, 1960; Beverley Nichols' Cats ABC, 1960; Beverley Nichols' Cats XYZ, 1961; Garden Open Today, 1963; Forty Favourite Flowers, 1964; Powers That Be, 1966; A Case of Human Bondage, 1966; The Art of Flower Arrangement, 1967; Garden Open Tomorrow, 1968; The Sun in My Eyes, 1969; The Wickedest Witch in the World, 1971; Father Figure (autobiog.), 1972; Down the Kitchen Sink, 1974; The Unforgiving Minute (autobiog.), 1978; *poems:* Songs at Twilight, 1982; *plays:* (Musical and otherwise): The Stag, 1929; Cochran's 1930 Revue, 1930; Avalanche, 1931; Evensong, 1932; When The Crash Comes, 1933; Dr Mesmer, 1934; Floodlight, 1937; Song on the Wind (Operette), 1948; Shadow of the Vine, 1949; Lady's Guide, 1950. *Address:* Sudbrook Cottage, Ham Common, Surrey. *Club:* Garrick.

NICHOLS, Clement Roy, CMG 1970; OBE 1956; Chairman, Alpha Spinning Mills Pty Ltd and associated companies; *b* 4 Jan. 1909; *s* of C. J. Nichols, Melbourne; *m* 1933, Margareta, *d* of A. C. Pearse, Melbourne; one *s* one *d. Educ:* Scotch Coll., Melbourne. ATI. Lifetime in wool worsted manufacturing. Past Pres., Wool Textile Mfrs of Australia; Vice-Pres., Internat. Wool Textile Organisation, 1970-75; President: Victorian Chamber

of Mfrs, 1970-72, 1977-78; Associated Chambers of Mfrs of Australia, 1971-74. Mem., World Scouts' Cttee, 1959-65, 1967-73; Chm., Asia Pacific Region, 1962-64; Chief Comr, Scout Assoc., 1963-66; Chief Comr, Victorian Br., 1952-58; Nat. Chm., 1973-79. *Address:* 82 Studley Park Road, Kew, Victoria 3101, Australia. *Clubs:* Australian (Melbourne); Rotary (Heidelberg).

NICHOLS, Sir Edward (Henry), Kt 1972; TD; Town Clerk of City of London, 1954-74; *b* 27 Sept. 1911; *o s* of Henry James and Agnes Annie Nichols, Notts; *m* 1941, Gwendoline Hetty, *d* of late Robert Elgar, Leeds; one *s. Educ:* Queen Elizabeth's Gram. Sch., Mansfield; Selwyn Coll., Cambridge (BA, LLB). Articled Town Clerk, Mansfield, 1933; Asst Solicitor, Derby, 1936-40. Served War of 1939-45, Hon. Lt-Col RA. Dep. Town Clerk, Derby, 1940-48, Leicester, 1948-49; Town Clerk and Clerk of the Peace, Derby, 1949-53. Hon. DLitt City Univ., 1974. Chevalier, Order of N Star of Sweden; holds other foreign orders. *Address:* Hillrise, Park Close, Esher KT10 8LG. *T:* Esher 65102. *Club:* City Livery.

NICHOLS, John; *see* Nichols, K. J. H.

NICHOLS, John Winfrith de Lisle, BSc (Eng); CEng; FIEE; Director: National Maritime Institute, 1976-79; Computer Aided Design Centre, Cambridge, 1977-79; *b* 7 June 1919; *er s* of late John F. Nichols, MC, PhD, FRHistS, FSA, Godalming; *m* 1942, Catherine, *er d* of Capt. A. V. Grantham, RNR, Essex; two *s* two *d. Educ:* Sir Walter St John's Sch., Battersea; London Univ. Royal Navy, 1940-46; GPO, Dollis Hill, 1946-47; RN Scientific Service, 1947-55; Chief Research Officer, Corp. of Trinity House, 1955-59; UKAEA, 1959-65; Min. of Technology, later DTI and Dept of Industry, 1965-; Under-Sec., and Chm., Requirement Bd for Computers, Systems and Electronics, 1972-74; Under Sec., Research Contractors Div., DoI, 1974-76. *Recreations:* gardening, sailing, caravanning. *Address:* West House, Leybourne, Wormley, Godalming, Surrey. *T:* Wormley 3252.

NICHOLS, (Kenneth) John (Heastey); Metropolitan Stipendiary Magistrate, since 1972; *b* 6 Sept. 1923; *s* of Sidney Kenneth Nichols, MC and Dorothy Jennie Heastey Richardson; *m* 1st, 1946, Audrey Heather Powell; one *d* ; 2nd, 1966, Pamela Marjorie Long, *qv. Educ:* Westminster School. Served War of 1939-45: 60th Rifles, 1941-43; Parachute Regt, NW Europe, SE Asia Comd, 1943-46 (Captain). Admitted Solicitor, 1949; Partner, Speechly, Mumford & Soames (Craig), 1949-69. Mem. Council of Law Soc., 1959-68. *Recreations:* cricket, music, walking. *Address:* Flat 1, 36 Buckingham Gate, SW1; Dolphin House, Porthgwarra, St Levan, Cornwall. *Club:* MCC.

NICHOLS, Pamela Marjorie, (Mrs John Nichols); *see* Long, P. M.

NICHOLS, Peter, OBE 1982; Rome Correspondent of The Times, since 1957; *b* 15 Feb. 1928; *s* of Walter and Beatrice Nichols; *m* 1974, Paola Rosi; one *s* (and four *c* by a previous marriage). *Educ:* Portsmouth Grammar Sch.; Oxford Univ. BA (Mod. Hist.). Correspondent, The Times, London, Berlin, Bonn, Rome, 1954-. Peripheral activities include BBC TV documentaries, radio and television programmes for Italian broadcasting corporation. Internat. prize for journalism, Città di Roma, 1973. *Publications:* Piedmont and the English, 1967; Politics of the Vatican, 1968; Italia, Italia, 1973 (Book of the Year Prize, 1976, for Italian edn); Italian Decision, 1977; Ruffo in Calabria, 1977; The Pope's Divisions, The Roman Catholic Church Today, 1981; contrib. Foreign Affairs, etc. *Recreation:* relaxing. *Address:* 20 Piazza della Torretta, Rome, Italy. *T:* Rome 6788406.

NICHOLS, Peter Richard; playwright since 1959; *b* 31 July 1927; *s* of late Richard George Nichols and Violet Annie Poole; *m* 1960, Thelma Reed; one *s* two *d* (and one *d* decd). *Educ:* Bristol Grammar Sch.; Bristol Old Vic Sch.; Trent Park Trng College. Actor, mostly in repertory, 1950-55; worked as teacher in primary and secondary schs, 1958-60. Mem., Arts Council Drama Panel, 1973-75. Playwright in residence, Guthrie Theatre, Minneapolis, 1976. *TV plays:* Walk on the Grass, 1959; Promenade, 1960; Ben Spray, 1961; The Reception, 1961; The Big Boys, 1961; Continuity Man, 1963; Ben Again, 1963; The Heart of the Country, 1963; The Hooded Terror, 1963; The Brick Umbrella, 1964; When the Wind Blows, 1964 (later adapted for radio); Daddy Kiss It Better, 1968; The Gorge, 1968; Hearts and Flowers, 1971; The Common, 1973; The Atkinsons (in 6 parts), 1978; *films:* Catch Us If You Can, 1965; Georgy Girl, 1967; Joe Egg, 1971; The National Health, 1973; *stage plays:* A Day in The Death of Joe Egg, 1967 (Evening Standard Award, Best Play); The National Health, 1969 (Evening Standard Award, Best Play); Forget-me-not Lane, 1971; Chez Nous, 1973; The Freeway, 1974; Privates on Parade, 1977 (Evening Standard Best Comedy, Soc. of West End Theatres Best Comedy and Ivor Novello Best Musical Awards); Born in the Gardens, 1979; Passion Play, 1980 (Standard Best Play award, 1981); *musicals:* A Better Mousetrap, 1981; Poppy, 1982. *Publications:* some TV plays in anthologies; all above stage plays published. *Recreations:* listening to jazz, looking at cities. *Address:* Margaret Ramsay Ltd, 14 Goodwin's Court, WC2. *T:* 01-240 0691.

NICHOLS, William Henry, CB 1974; *b* 25 March 1913; *s* of William and Clara Nichols. *Educ:* Owens School. Entered Inland Revenue, 1930; Exchequer and Audit Dept, 1935, Secretary, 1973-75, retired. *Address:* 17 Park House, Winchmore Hill Road, N21 1QL. *T:* 01-886 4321; 11 Old Street, Haughley, Stowmarket, Suffolk IP14 3NT.

NICHOLS, William Reginald, CBE 1975; TD; MA; Clerk of the Worshipful Company of Salters, 1946-75, Master, 1978-79; *b* 23 July 1912; *s* of late Reginald H. Nichols, JP, FSA, Barrister-at-Law; *m* 1946, Imogen, *d* of late Rev. Percy Dearmer, DD, Canon of Westminster, and late Nancy (who *m* 1946, Sir John Sykes, KCB; he died, 1952); one *s* one *d*. *Educ:* Harrow; Gonville and Caius Coll., Cambridge (Sayer Classical Scholar). MA 1938. Called to the Bar, Gray's Inn, 1937. Served War of 1939-45 with Hertfordshire Regt (despatches) and on staff 21st Army Group. Former Jt Hon. Sec., CGLI; Governor of Christ's Hospital; former Governor of Grey Coat Hospital Foundation. *Address:* The Farriers Cottage, St Nicholas-at-Wade, Birchington, Kent.

NICHOLSON, Air Commodore Angus Archibald Norman, CBE 1961; AE 1945; Deputy Secretary-General, International Shipping Secretariat, 1971-80; *b* 8 March 1919; *s* of Major Norman Nicholson and Alice Frances Nicholson (*née* Salvidge), Hoylake, Cheshire; *m* 1943, Joan Mary, *d* of Ernest Beaumont, MRCVS, DVSM; one *s* one *d*. *Educ:* Eton; King's Coll., Cambridge. Cambridge Univ. Air Sqn, 1938-39; commissioned, 1939. Served War 1939-45: flying duties in Bomber Command and Middle East. Air Cdre, 1966; Dir of Defence Plans (Air), Min. of Defence, 1966-67; Defence Adviser to British High Comr in Canada and Head of British Defence Liaison Staff, 1968-70; retired from RAF, 1970. MBIM 1967, FBIM 1980. *Recreations:* sailing, ski-ing, golf, fishing. *Address:* 12 Captain's Row, Lymington, Hants. *Clubs:* Army and Navy; Leander (Henley); Royal Lymington Yacht.

NICHOLSON, Anthony Thomas Cuthbertson; a Recorder of the Crown Court, since 1980; *b* 17 May 1929; *s* of Thomas and Emma Cuthbertson Nicholson, Stratford, E; *m* 1955, Sheila Rose, *er d* of Albert and Rose Pigram, Laindon, Essex; two *s* one *d*. *Educ:* St Bonaventure's Grammar Sch., Forest Gate, E7. Journalist, 1944-62. Served Army, 1947-49, RAF, 1950-53. Called to the Bar, Gray's Inn, 1962. *Publications:* (play) Van Call, 1954; Esprit de Law, 1973. *Recreation:* wildfowling. *Address:* The Old Vicarage, Southminster, Essex CM0 7ES; 3 Hare Court, Temple, EC4.

NICHOLSON, Charles Gordon Brown; Member, Scottish Law Commission, since 1982; *b* 11 Sept. 1935; *s* of William Addison Nicholson, former Director, Scottish Tourist Board, and late Jean Brown; *m* 1963, Hazel Mary Nixon; two *s*. *Educ:* George Watson's Coll., Edinburgh; Edinburgh Univ. MA Hons (English Lit.) 1956, LLB 1958. 2nd Lieut Queen's Own Cameron Highlanders, 1958-60. Admitted Faculty of Advocates, Edinburgh, 1961; in practice at Bar; Standing Junior Counsel, Registrar of Restrictive Trading Agreements, 1968; Advocate-Depute, 1968-70; Sheriff of: South Strathclyde, Dumfries and Galloway, 1970-76; Lothian and Borders, 1976-82. Vice-Pres., Sheriffs' Assoc., 1979-82 (Sec., 1975-79). Member: Scottish Council on Crime, 1972-75; Dunpark Cttee on Reparation by Offenders, 1974-77; May Cttee of Inquiry into UK Prison Service, 1978-79; Chairman: Scottish Assoc. for Study of Delinquency, 1974-79; Edinburgh CAB, 1979-82. *Publication:* The Law and Practice of Sentencing in Scotland, 1981. *Recreations:* music, philately. *Address:* 23 Lennox Street, Edinburgh EH4 1PY. *T:* 031-332 5861. *Club:* New (Edinburgh).

NICHOLSON, Hon. Sir David (Eric), Kt 1972; company director; Speaker of the Legislative Assembly of Queensland, 1960-72 (record term); MLA (CP) for Murrumba, 1950-72; *b* 26 May 1904; *s* of J. A. Nicholson; *m* 1934, Cecile F., *d* of M. E. Smith; two *s* two *d*. *Recreations:* bowls, swimming, gardening. *Address:* 8/178 Bowen Terrace, New Farm, Qld 4005, Australia. *Clubs:* Redcliffe Trotting (Life Mem.), Redcliffe Agricl, Horticultural and Industrial Soc. (Life Mem.); Returned Servicemen's (Caboolture); New Farm Bowls.

NICHOLSON, Douglas; *see* Nicholson, F. D.

NICHOLSON, (Edward) Max, CB 1948; CVO 1971; Chairman, Land Use Consultants, since 1966; *b* 1904; *m* 1st, 1932, Eleanor Mary Crawford (marr. diss., 1964); two *s*; 2nd, Marie Antoinette Mauerhofer; one *s*. *Educ:* Sedbergh; Hertford Coll., Oxford. Head of Allocation of Tonnage Division, Ministry of War Transport, 1942-45; Secretary of Office of The Lord President of the Council, 1945-52. Member Advisory Council on Scientific Policy, 1948-64; Dir-Gen., Nature Conservancy, 1952-66; Convener, Conservation Section, Internat. Biological Programme, 1963-74; Secretary, Duke of Edinburgh's Study Conference on the Countryside in 1970, 1963; Albright Lecturer, Univ. of California, 1964; a Dir and Managing Editor, Environmental Data Services Ltd, 1978-80. Pres., RSPB, 1980-; Vice-President: RSA, 1978-82; PSI (formerly PEP); Wildfowl Trust; Trustee: Fair Isle Bird Observatory; Simon Population Trust; Member: Council, Internat. Inst. of Environment and Devel; Bd and Editorial Cttee, Birds of the Western Palearctic, 1965-. Chairman: Environmental Cttee, London Celebrations for the Queen's Silver Jubilee, 1976-77; London Looks Forward Conf., 1977; Ecological Parks Trust, 1977-; UK Standing Cttee for World Conservation Strategy Prog., 1981-; Common Ground Internat., 1981-. Hon. Member: IUCN; World Wildlife Fund; RTPI. Scientific FZS; Corr. Fellow, American Ornithologists' Union. Hon. Fellow RIBA; Hon. LLD Aberdeen, 1964; Hon. Dr, RCA, 1970. John C. Phillips Medallist International Union for Conservation of Nature and Natural Resources, 1963; Europa Preis für Landespflege, 1972. Comdr, Order of Golden Ark, Netherlands, 1973. *Publications:* Birds in England, 1926; How Birds Live, 1927; Birds and Men, 1951; Britain's Nature Reserves, 1958; The System, 1967; The Environmental Revolution, 1970 (Premio Europeo Cortina-Ulisse, 1971); The Big Change, 1973; and other books, scientific papers and articles. *Address:* 13 Upper Cheyne Row, SW3 5JW. *Club:* Athenæum.

NICHOLSON, Edward Rupert, FCA; Partner, Peat Marwick Mitchell & Co. (UK), 1949-77; *b* 17 Sept. 1909; *s* of late Alfred Edward Nicholson and late Elise (*née* Dobson); *m* 1935, Mary Elley; one *s* one *d*. *Educ:* Whitgift Sch., Croydon. Articled to father, 1928-33; joined Peat Marwick Mitchell & Co., 1933. Apptd by BoT, jointly, Inspector of Majestic Insurance Co. Ltd and two others, 1961; apptd Liquidator, Davies Investments Ltd, 1967; apptd Receiver, Rolls-Royce Ltd, 1971; Receiver, Northern Developments (Holdings), 1975. Chm., Techn. Adv. Cttee, Inst. Chartered Accountants, 1969-70; Liquidator, Court Line Ltd, 1974; Mem., Post Office Review Cttee, 1976; Governor, Whitgift Foundn, 1976, Chm., 1978. *Publications:* articles in learned jls. *Address:* Grey Wings, The Warren, Ashtead, Surrey. *T:* Ashtead 72655. *Club:* Caledonian.

NICHOLSON, Rev. Prof. Ernest Wilson, DD; Oriel Professor of the Interpretation of Holy Scripture and Fellow of Oriel College, Oxford University, since 1979; *b* 26 Sept. 1938; *s* of Ernest Tedford Nicholson and Veronica Muriel Nicholson; *m* 1962, Hazel (*née* Jackson); one *s* three *d*. *Educ:* Portadown Coll.; Trinity Coll., Dublin (Scholar, BA 1960, MA 1964); Glasgow Univ. (PhD 1964). MA (by incorporation) 1967, BD 1971, DD 1978, Cambridge; DD Oxford (by incorporation) 1979. Lectr in Hebrew and Semitic Languages, TCD, 1962-67; Univ. Lectr in Divinity, Cambridge Univ., 1967-79; Fellow: University Coll. (now Wolfson Coll.), Cambridge, 1967-69; Pembroke Coll., Cambridge, 1969-79; Chaplain, Pembroke Coll., Cambridge, 1969-73, Dean, 1973-79. *Publications:* Deuteronomy and Tradition, 1967; Preaching to the Exiles, 1971; Exodus and Sinai in History and Tradition, 1973; (with J. Baker) The Commentary of Rabbi David Kimḥi on Psalms 120-150, 1973; Commentary on Jeremiah 1-25, 1973; Commentary on Jeremiah 26-52, 1975; articles in biblical and Semitic jls. *Recreation:* music. *Address:* Oriel College, Oxford OX1 4EW.

NICHOLSON, (Frank) Douglas, TD; MA Cantab; JP; DL; President, Vaux Breweries Ltd and subsidiary cos (Chairman, 1953-76; Joint Managing Director, 1937-52; Director 1928-77); Vice-President, The Brewers' Society (Chairman 1970-71); *b* 30 July 1905; *o s* of late Sir Frank Nicholson, CBE; *m* 1937, Pauline, *y d* of late Sir Thomas Lawson Tancred, 9th Bt, Borobridge; five *s*. *Educ:* Harrow; Clare Coll., Cambridge. Scottish Horse (TA), 1928; served in Scottish Horse and RA, War of 1939-45, in charge of British and American Supply Mission to Saudi Arabia, 1944. Contested (C) Spennymoor, at 1945 Election. Chm., Durham Police Authority, 1955-64. Pres. and Treasurer, Durham Co. Assoc. of Boys' Clubs, 1952-78. High Sheriff Durham County, 1948-49; DL 1948; JP 1949. British Team Winner, World Driving Championship, Munster, W Germany, 1972. *Recreations:* farming, etc. *Address:* Southill Hall, near Chester-le-Street, Co. Durham DH3 4EQ. *T:* Chester-le-Street 882286.

NICHOLSON, Sir Godfrey, 1st Bt, *cr* 1958; Distiller; *b* 9 Dec. 1901; *s* of late Richard Francis Nicholson of Woodcott, Hants, and late Helen Violet Portal; *m* 1936, Lady Katharine Constance Lindsay (*d* 1972), 5th *d* of 27th Earl of Crawford; four *d*. *Educ:* Winchester; Christ Church, Oxford. MP (Nat. C) Morpeth, 1931-35; Royal Fusiliers, 1939-42; MP (C) Farnham Division of Surrey, 1937-66; retired. Chairman, Estimates Cttee, 1961-64. Pres., British Assoc. of Parascending Clubs, 1973-. Chm., Friends of Friendless Churches. FSA. *Address:* Bussock Hill House, Newbury, Berks. *T:* Chieveley 260. *Clubs:* Athenæum, Pratt's.

See also R. N. Luce, Sir J. C. F. Montgomery Cuninghame.

NICHOLSON, Dr Howard, FRCP; Physician, University College Hospital, since 1948; Physician, Brompton Hospital, 1952-77, retired; Fellow of University College, London, since 1959; *b* 1 Feb. 1912; *s* of Frederick and Sara Nicholson; *m* 1941, Winifrid Madeline Piercy. *Educ:* University Coll., London, and University Coll. Hospital. MB, BS, London, 1935; MD London 1938; MRCP 1938, FRCP 1949. House appointments and Registrarship, UCH, 1935-38; House Physician at Brompton Hosp., 1938. Served War, 1940-45, RAMC; Physician to Chest Surgical Team and Officer i/c Medical Div. (Lt-Col). Registrar, Brompton Hosp., and Chief Asst, Inst. of Diseases of Chest, 1945-48. Goulstonian Lecturer, RCP, 1950. *Publications:* sections on Diseases of Chest in The Practice of Medicine (ed J. S. Richardson), 1961, and in Progress in Clinical Medicine, 1961; articles in Thorax, Lancet, etc. *Recreations:* reading, going to the opera. *Address:* Chelwood, Laughton, Lewes, E Sussex BN8 6BE.

NICHOLSON, Sir John (Charles), 3rd Bt, *cr* 1859; TD 1954; FRCS 1934; BM, BCh; Consulting Surgeon; Senior Surgeon, Bethnal Green, St Leonard's and St Matthew's Hospitals, London, retired 1969; *b* 10 Jan. 1904; *s* of Sir Charles Nicholson, 2nd Bt, and Evelyn Louise (*d* 1927), *d* of Rev. H. Oliver; *S* father, 1949; *m* 1928, Caroline Elizabeth (*d* 1981), *d* of late Rt Rev. John Frederick McNeice, Bishop of Down; no *c*. *Educ:* Brighton Coll.; New Coll., Oxford; St Bartholomew's Hospital. Major, RAMC, TA (commissioned 1932); Temp. Lieut-Colonel, RAMC, 1942; Hon. Lieut-Colonel 1945. Late Surgical Registrar, Royal National Orthopædic Hospital, etc.; Clinical Fellow in Surgery, Harvard Univ., 1947-48. Qualified 1929; BM, BCh, Oxford, 1929. *Publications:* various on professional subjects in British Medical Journal and other periodicals. *Recreation:* yachting. *Heir:* none. *Address:* Thames Cottage, Thames Street, Sunbury-on-Thames. *T:* Sunbury 82148.

NICHOLSON, (John) Leonard; Senior Fellow, Policy Studies Institute, since 1977; b 18 Feb. 1916; er s of late Percy Merwyn Nicholson and late Jane Winifred Nicholson (née Morris). Educ: Stowe; Institute of Actuaries; London School of Economics. MSc(Econ). Mem., Oxford University Inst. of Statistics, 1940-47; Statistician with Ministry of Home Security, 1943-44; Statistician, 1947-52, Chief Statistician, 1952-68, Central Statistical Office; Chief Economic Advr to DHSS, 1968-76. Simon Research Fellow, Manchester Univ., 1962-63; Assoc. Prof. of Quantitative Econs, Brunel Univ., 1972-74. Publications: The Beveridge Plan for Social Security (jtly), 1943; Variations in Working Class Family Expenditure, 1949; The Interim Index of Industrial Production, 1949; Redistribution of Income in the United Kingdom, 1965; The Changing Impact of Taxes and Benefits on Personal Incomes, 1981; contrib. D. Wedderburn, Poverty, Inequality and Class Structure, 1974; contrib. A. B. Atkinson, The Personal Distribution of Incomes, 1976; contrib. V. Halberstadt and A. J. Culyer, Public Economics and Human Resources, 1977; contrib. DHSS Social Security Research, 1977; contrib. DHSS Definition and Measurement of Poverty, 1979; various papers concerned with national income, family expenditure, economic welfare and statistics in academic journals. Recreations: listening to music, looking at paintings, real and lawn tennis, skiing. Address: 53 Frognal, NW3 6YA.

NICHOLSON, Rev. John Malcolm; b 26 May 1908; 2nd s of John and Madeleine Nicholson; m 1939, Dorothy Lisle Preston; one s two d. Educ: Whitgift Sch.; King's Coll., Cambridge; Cuddesdon Theological Coll. Asst Curate, St John's, Newcastle upon Tyne, 1932-36; Vicar, St Mary's, Monkseaton, 1936-38; Vicar, Sugley, 1938-46; Vicar, St George's, Cullercoats, 1946-55; Archdeacon of Doncaster, 1955-59; Vicar of High Melton, 1955-59; Headmaster, The King's School, Tynemouth, 1959-70. Examining Chaplain: to Bishop of Newcastle, 1944-55; to Bishop of Sheffield, 1955-59; Select Preacher, Cambridge Univ., 1959. Address: 12 Carrsfield, Corbridge NE45 5LJ.

NICHOLSON, Sir John (Norris), 2nd Bt, cr 1912; KBE 1971; CIE 1946; JP; Lord-Lieutenant, since 1980, and Keeper of the Rolls, since 1974, of the Isle of Wight; b 19 Feb. 1911; o c of late Captain George Crosfield Norris Nicholson, RFC, and Hon. Evelyn Izme Murray, y d of 10th Baron and 1st Viscount Elibank (she m 2nd 1st Baron Mottistone, PC); S grandfather, 1918; m 1938, Vittoria Vivien, y d of late Percy Trewhella, Villa Sant' Andrea, Taormina; two s two d. Educ: Winchester Coll., Trinity Coll., Cambridge. Captain 4th Cheshires (TA), 1939-41. BEF Flanders 1940 (despatches). Min. of War Transport, India and SE Asia, 1942-46. Chairman: Ocean Steam Ship Co. Ltd, 1957-71; Liverpool Port Employers Assoc., 1957-61; Martins Bank Ltd, 1962-64 (Dep. Chm., 1959-62); Management Cttee, HMS Conway, 1958-65; British Liner Cttee, 1963-67; Cttee, European Nat. Shipowners Assoc., 1965-69; Mem., Shipping Advisory Panel, 1962-64; Pres., Chamber of Shipping of the UK, 1970-71; Mem., Economic and Social Cttee, EEC, 1973-74. Director: Barclays Bank Ltd, 1969-81; Royal Insurance Co. Ltd, 1955-81. Pres., E Wessex TA&VRA, 1982-. Governor, IoW Technical Coll. Vice Lord-Lieutenant, IoW, 1974-80. Silver Jubilee Medal, 1977. Heir: s Charles Christian Nicholson [b 15 Dec. 1941; m 1975, Martie, widow of Niall Anstruther-Gough-Calthorpe and d of Stuart Don]. Address: Mottistone Manor, Isle of Wight. T: Brighstone 740322. Clubs: Brooks's; Royal Yacht Squadron (Commodore).

NICHOLSON, Hon. John Paton; Hon. Chief Justice Nicholson; Chief Justice, Supreme Court of Prince Edward Island, Canada, since 1977; b 16 Nov. 1922; s of Robert H. Nicholson and Beatrice Paton; m 1950, Grace Diamond; one s two d. Educ: Prince of Wales Coll., Charlottetown, PEI; Dalhousie Univ., Halifax, NS (LLB). Called to Bar of PEI, 1948; private law practice, 1948-70; QC 1966; apptd Judge, Supreme Court, PEI, 1970. Recreations: sailing, sport fishing. Address: Law Courts Building, Charlottetown, PEI C1A 7K4, Canada. T: (area code) 902-892-9131. Clubs: Canadian, United Services Officers' (Hon.) (PEI).

NICHOLSON, Leonard; see Nicholson, J. L.

NICHOLSON, Lewis Frederick, CB 1963; b 1 May 1918; s of Harold and May Nicholson; m 1947, Diana Rosalind Fear; one s two d. Educ: Taunton Sch.; King's Coll., Cambridge. Research Laboratories of GEC, 1939; Royal Aircraft Establishment, 1939-59; Head of Aerodynamics Dept, RAE, 1953-59; Imperial Defence Coll., 1956; Director-General of Scientific Research (Air), Ministry of Aviation, 1959-63; Dep. Director (Air) Royal Aircraft Establishment, 1963-66; Chief Scientist, RAF, 1966-69; Vice Controller Aircraft, MoD (PE), 1969-78, retired. Publications: (Joint) Compressible Airflow-Tables; Compressible Airflow-Graphs; papers on aerodynamic subjects. Address: Ravenswood, Charles Hill, Tilford, Farnham, Surrey. T: Elstead 702376.

NICHOLSON, Max; see Nicholson, E. M.

NICHOLSON, Michael Constantine; a Recorder of the Crown Court, since 1980; b 3 Feb. 1932; m 1960, Kathleen Mary Strong; two d. Educ: Wycliffe Coll., Stonehouse; University Coll. of Wales, Aberystwyth (LLB). Called to the Bar, Gray's Inn, 1957; Crown Counsel, Nyasaland, 1960-63; Wales and Chester circuit, 1963-. Recreations: cinema, theatre. Address: (home) 11 The Rise, Cardiff. T: Cardiff 756212; (chambers) 33 Park Place, Cardiff. T: Cardiff 33313. Club: Cardiff Golf.

NICHOLSON, Norman Cornthwaite, OBE 1981; poet and critic; b Millom, Cumberland, 8 Jan. 1914; s of Joseph and Edith Nicholson; m 1956, Yvonne Edith Gardner. Educ: local schools. Literary criticism in weekly press. FRSL 1945; Hon. Fellow, Manchester Polytechnic, 1979. MA (Hon.): Manchester Univ., 1959; Open Univ., 1975; Hon. DLitt Liverpool, 1980. Cholmondley Award for Poetry, 1967; Soc. of Authors Travelling Award, 1972; Queen's Medal for Poetry, 1977. Publications: poetry: Five Rivers, 1944 (Heinemann Prize, 1945); Rock Face, 1948; The Pot Geranium, 1954; Selected Poems, 1966; A Local Habitation, 1973; Sea to the West, 1981; Selected Poems 1940-1982, 1982; verse drama: The Old Man of the Mountains (produced Mercury Theatre), 1946; A Match for the Devil, 1955; Birth by Drowning, 1960; criticism: Man and Literature, 1943; William Cowper, 1951; topography: Cumberland and Westmorland, 1949; The Lakers, 1955; Provincial Pleasures, 1959; Portrait of the Lakes, 1963; Greater Lakeland, 1969; autobiography: Wednesday Early Closing, 1975; anthology: The Pelican Anthology of Modern Religious Verse, 1943; A Choice of Cowper's Verse, 1975; The Lake District, 1977. Address: 14 St George's Terrace, Millom, Cumbria. T: Millom 2024.

NICHOLSON, Robert; publisher, designer, artist, writer; b Sydney, Australia, 8 April 1920; m 1951, Kate Poulter, ARCA (marr. diss. 1976); one s one d. Educ: Troy Town Elementary Sch., Rochester; Rochester Tech. Sch.; Medway Sch. of Art. Served 1939-45, RAMC (mainly pathology in Middle East). Responsible with brother for major design projects during post-war design boom, 1945-55: Festival of Britain in Edinburgh, 1951; British Council exhibn in Zürich; Jamestown centenary exhibn, British Heritage; extensive redecoration of public rooms, Caledonian Hotel, Edinburgh; wallpapers, furniture and industrial design; original Design Centre in the Haymarket, 1956. Founded and ran small advertising agency, 1963-66: main client, Palladio wallpapers (WPM). Writer and publisher of guide books, 1966-, including: Nicholson's London Guide; Street Finder; Guide to Great Britain. Benjamin Franklin medal, 1960. First one man exhibn of paintings, Patrick Seale Gallery, Knightsbridge, 1976, with sporadic exhibitions each year in provinces. Recreations: collecting, travelling to hot places—preferably volcanic; loves Spain, his own cooking and travelling by foot in out of way places. Lives in Brighton, Sussex.

NICHOLSON, Robin Buchanan, PhD; FRS 1978; FEng; Chief Scientist, Central Policy Review Staff, since 1981; b 12 Aug. 1934; s of Carroll and Nancy Nicholson; m 1958, Elizabeth Mary, d of late Sir Sydney Caffyn; one s two d. Educ: Oundle Sch.; St Catharine's Coll., Cambridge. BA 1956, PhD 1959, MA 1960. FIM; MInstP; FEng 1980. University of Cambridge: Demonstrator in Metallurgy, 1960; Lectr in Metallurgy, 1964; Fellow of Christ's Coll., 1962-66; Prof. of Metallurgy, Univ. of Manchester, 1966. Inco Europe Ltd: Dir of Research Lab., 1972; Dir, 1975; Man. Dir, 1976-81. Mem., SERC (formerly SRC), 1978-. Rosenhain Medallist, Inst. of Metals, 1971; Platinum Medal, Metals Soc., 1982. Publications: Precipitation Hardening (with A. Kelly), 1962; (jtly) Electron Microscopy of Thin Crystals, 1965; (ed and contrib. with A. Kelly) Strengthening Methods in Crystals, 1971; numerous papers to learned jls. Recreations: family life, gardening, music. Address: Whittington House, 8 Fisherwick Road, Whittington, near Lichfield, Staffs WS14 9LH. T: Whittington 432081. Club: MCC.

NICHOLSON, Rupert; see Nicholson, E. R.

NICHOLSON, William Ewart, CBE 1941; BA, FRAI; b 29 Dec. 1890; s of Robert Francis Nicholson, Leeds; m 1920, Alice Elgie, d of W. E. Cork; one d. Educ: Leeds Grammar Sch.; Jesus Coll., Oxford. Education Dept, N Nigeria, 1914; Lieut, Nigeria Regt, 1917; Principal, Katsina Coll., 1934; Director of Education, Sierra Leone, 1935-45; Member Fourah Bay College Commission, 1938; Member of Exec. Council, JP, Sierra Leone; Educational Adviser to Government of The Gambia, 1944-45; Secretary Commission of Enquiry into the system of Education of the Jewish Community in Palestine, 1945-46; Director of Training, Ministry of Food, 1946-48. Hon. Keeper of Ethnography, Leeds City Museum, 1959-74. Address: 2 Washington Road, PO Box 153, Chinhoyi, Zimbabwe.

NICKELL, Prof. Stephen John; Professor of Economics, London University at the London School of Economics and Political Science, since 1979; b 25 April 1944; s of John Edward Hilary Nickell and Phyllis Nickell; m 1976, Susan Elizabeth (née Pegden); one d. Educ: Merchant Taylors' Sch.; Pembroke Coll., Cambridge (BA); LSE (MSc). Maths teacher, Hendon County Sch., 1965-68; Lectr, LSE, 1970-77, Reader, 1977-79. Publications: The Investment Decisions of Firms, 1978; articles in learned jls. Recreations: jogging, cricket, cooking. Address: 92 Woodland Gardens, N10 3UB.

NICKERSON, Albert Lindsay; retired as Chairman and Chief Executive Officer, Mobil Oil Corporation; b 17 Jan. 1911; s of Albert Lindsay Nickerson and Christine (née Atkinson); m 1936, Elizabeth Perkins; one s three d. Educ: Noble and Greenough Sch., Mass; Harvard. Joined Socony-Vacuum Oil Co. Inc. as Service Stn Attendant, 1933; Dist. Man., 1940; Div. Manager, 1941; Asst General Manager, Eastern Marketing Div., 1944; Director, 1946; name of company changed to Socony Mobil Oil Co. Inc., 1955; President, 1955-61; Chairman Exec. Cttee and Chief Exec. Officer, 1958-69; Chm. Bd, 1961-69; name of company changed to Mobil Oil Corporation, 1966. Chairman, Vacuum Oil Co. Ltd, London (later Mobil Oil Co. Ltd), 1946. Director, Placement Bureau War Manpower Commission, Washington, 1943. Chm., Federal Reserve Bank of NY, and Federal Reserve Agent, 1969-71; Mem.,

The Business Council (Chm. 1967-69). Director: American Management Assoc., NY, 1948-51, 1953-56, 1958-61; Federal Reserve Board of NY, 1964-67; Metrop. Life Insurance Co., 1965-81; Mobil Oil Corp., 1946-75; Raytheon Co.; State Street Investment Corp.; Federal Street Fund Inc.; Harvard Management Co.; Transportation Assoc. of America, 1969; Partner, State Street Exchange Fund; Trustee: International House, NY City, 1952-62; Cttee for Economic Development, NY, 1961-65; Brigham and Women's Hosp., Boston; Rockefeller Univ.; Boston Symphony Orch.; American Museum of Natural History, 1958-62, 1964-69; Mem. of Corp., Woods Hole Oceanographic Instn, Mass; former Director and Treas., American Petroleum Institute; former Member: Council on Foreign Relations; National Petroleum Council; Harvard Corp., 1965; Fellow, Harvard Univ., 1965-75; Overseer Harvard Univ., 1959-65. Hon. LLD: Hofstra Univ., 1964; Harvard Univ., 1976. Comdr, Order of Vasa (Sweden), 1963; Grand Cross of the Republic (Italy), 1968. *Recreations:* golfing, fishing, sailing, camping. *Address:* (office) Room 3540, 150 East 42nd Street, New York, NY 10017, USA. *T:* 212 883-5225; (home) Lexington Road, Lincoln, Mass 01773, USA. *T:* (617) 259-9664. *Clubs:* Thames Rowing; Harvard Varsity, Cambridge Boat (Cambridge, Mass); Country (Brookline, Mass); Harvard (NY City); Harvard (Boston); 25 Year Club of Petroleum Industry.

NICKLAUS, Jack William; golfer; *b* 21 Jan. 1940; *s* of Louis Charles Nicklaus and Helen (*née* Schoener); *m* 1960, Barbara Jean Bash; four *s* one *d. Educ:* Upper Arlington High Sch.; Ohio State Univ. Won US Amateur golf championship, 1959, 1961; became professional golfer, 1961; designs golf courses in USA, Europe, and Far East; Pres., Golden Bear Inc. *Major wins include:* US Open, 1962, 1967, 1972, 1980; US Masters, 1963, 1965, 1966, 1972, 1975; US Professional Golfers' Assoc., 1963, 1971, 1973, 1974, 1975, 1980; Colonial National Invitation Tournament, 1982; British Open, 1966, 1970, 1978, and many other championships in USA, Europe, Australia and Far East. *Publications:* My 55 Ways to Lower Your Golf Score, 1962; Take a Tip from Me, 1964; The Greatest Game of All, 1969; Golf My Way, 1974; The Best Way to Better Your Golf, vols 1-3, 1974; Total Golf Techniques, 1977; On and Off the Fairway, 1979. *Address:* (office) 1208 US Highway, Suite 1, North Palm Beach, Florida 33408, USA.

NICKOLS, Herbert Arthur; Headmaster, Westonbirt School, Tetbury, Gloucestershire, since 1981; *b* 17 Jan. 1926; *s* of Herbert and Henrietta Elizabeth Nickols; *m* 1953, Joyce Peake; two *s* one *d. Educ:* Imperial Coll., Univ. of London (BSc). ACGI. Res. Demonstrator, Imperial Coll., 1947-49; Housemaster, Sen. Science Master and later Dep. Headmaster, St Edmund's Sch., Canterbury, Kent, 1949-81. *Recreations:* music, travel, cricket. *Address:* Rose Cottage, Westonbirt, Tetbury, Glos. *T:* Westonbirt 306; 146 New Dover Road, Canterbury, Kent. *T:* Canterbury 52605.

NICKSON, David Wigley, CBE 1981; DL; CBIM; Chairman, Countryside Commission for Scotland, since 1983; *b* 27 Nov. 1929; *s* of Geoffrey Wigley Nickson and Janet Mary Nickson; *m* 1952, Helen Louise Cockcraft; three *d. Educ:* Eton; RMA, Sandhurst. Commnd Coldstream Guards, 1949-54. Joined Wm Collins, 1954; Dir, 1961; Jt Man. Dir, 1967; Vice Chm., 1976-; Gp Man. Dir, 1979-82. Director: Scottish United Investors plc, 1970-; General Accident Fire and Life Assurance Corp. plc, 1971-; Clydesdale Bank plc, 1981-; Scottish & Newcastle Breweries plc, 1981- (Dep. Chm., 1982-); Radio Clyde Ltd, 1982-. Member: Scottish Indust. Develt Adv. Bd, 1975-80; Scottish Econ. Council, 1980-; Scottish Cttee, Design Council, 1978-81. Chm., CBI in Scotland, 1979-81; CBIM 1980. Mem. Management Cttee, Atlantic Salmon Trust. Mem., Queen's Body Guard for Scotland, Royal Co. of Archers. DL Stirling and Falkirk, 1982. *Recreations:* fishing, bird watching, the countryside. *Address:* Renagour, Aberfoyle, Stirling FK8 3TF. *T:* Aberfoyle 275. *Clubs:* Boodle's; Western (Glasgow).

NICKSON, Francis; Chief Executive and Town Clerk, London Borough of Camden, since 1977; *b* 9 Sept. 1929; *s* of Francis and Kathleen Nickson; *m* 1957, Helena (*née* Towers). *Educ:* Preston Catholic College; Liverpool Univ. (LLB). LMRTPI. Admitted Solicitor (Hons), 1953; Asst Solicitor, Newcastle-under-Lyme, 1953-56; Senior Asst Solicitor, Wood Green, 1956-60; Assistant Town Clerk, Enfield, 1960-71; Deputy Town Clerk, Camden, 1971-77. Hon. Clerk, Housing and Works Cttee, London Boroughs Assoc. FRSA. *Recreations:* listening to music, country walking. *Address:* 14 Waggon Road, Hadley Wood, Barnet, Herts EN4 0HL. *T:* 01-449 9390.

NICOL, Angus Sebastian Torquil Eyers; barrister; a Recorder of the Crown Court, since 1982; *b* 11 April 1933; *s* of Henry James Nicol and Phyllis Mary Eyers; *m* 1968, Eleanor Denise Brodrick; two *d. Educ:* Dartmouth. Served RN, 1947-56. Called to the Bar, Middle Temple, 1963. *Recreations:* music, Gaelic language and literature, shooting, fishing, sailing, gastronomy. *Address:* 32 Elm Park Road, SW3. *T:* 01-352 4702; 5 Paper Buildings, Temple, EC4Y 7HB. *T:* 01-353 8494. *Club:* Wig and Pen.

NICOL, Claude Scott, CBE 1977; TD; Hon. Physician, Genitourinary Medicine Department, St Thomas' Hospital, London; Hon. Consultant to the Army; late Adviser in Genitourinary Medicine to Department of Health and Social Security; *b* 1914; *s* of late Dr C. G. Nicol, barrister-at-law (Lincoln's Inn); *m* 1939, Janet Wickham Bosworth Smith; one *s* two *d. Educ:* Harrow Sch.; St Mary's Hospital; St John's Coll., Oxford. MRCS, LRCP, 1936; MB, BS, 1938; MD 1946; MRCP, 1946; FRCP, 1962. Formerly: Physician in charge of Venereal Diseases Dept, St Bartholomew's Hosp., London; Physician, Whitechapel Clinic, London Hospital; Fellow in Medicine, Johns Hopkins Hospital, Baltimore; House Physician, St Mary's Hosp., London. Former Asst Dist Surgeon, St John Amb. Assoc. and Brigade. Ex-Pres., Medical Soc. for Study of Venereal Diseases; FRSM. QHP 1967-69. *Publications:* contributions to medical textbooks and journals. *Recreations:* squash racquets, tennis. *Address:* 40 Ferncroft Avenue, NW3 7PE. *T:* 01-435 1310; The Albert Embankment Consulting Rooms, 199 Westminster Bridge Road, SE1 7EH. *T:* 01-928 5485.

NICOL, Davidson Sylvester Hector Willoughby, CMG 1964; MA, MD, PhD (Cantab); FRCPath; Under-Secretary-General of the United Nations and Executive Director, United Nations Institute for Training and Research (UNITAR), since 1972; Hon. Consultant Pathologist, Sierra Leone Government; *b* 14 Sept. 1924, of African parentage; *m* 1950, Marjorie Esme Johnston, MB, ChB; three *s* two *d. Educ:* Schools in Nigeria and Sierra Leone; Cambridge and London Univs. Science Master, Prince of Wales Sch., Sierra Leone, 1941-43. Cambridge: Foundation Schol., Prizeman, 1943-47, Fellow and Supervisor in Nat. Sciences and Med., 1957-59, Christ's Coll. (Hon. Fellow, 1972); BA 1946; 1st Cl. Hons (Nat. Sciences), 1947; Beit Meml Fellow for Medical Research, 1954; Benn Levy Univ. Studentship, Cambridge, 1956; Univ. Schol., House Physician (Medical Unit and Clinical Pathology), Receiving Room Officer, and Research Asst (Physiology), London Hosp., 1947-52; Univ. Lectr, Medical School, Ibadan, Nigeria, 1952-54; Visiting Lecturer: Univs of Toronto, California (Berkeley), Mayo Clinic, 1958; Aggrey-Fraser-Guggisberg Meml Lectr, Univ. of Ghana, 1963; Danforth Fellowship Lectr in African Affairs, Assoc. of Amer. Colls, USA, 1968-71. Sen. Pathologist, Sierra Leone, 1958-60; Principal, Fourah Bay Coll., Sierra Leone, 1960-68, and first Vice-Chancellor, Univ. of Sierra Leone, 1966-68; Perm. Rep. and Ambassador for Sierra Leone to UN, 1969-71 (Security Council, 1970-71, Pres. Sept. 1970; Chm., Cttee of 24 (Decolonisation); Mem., Economic and Social Council, 1969-70); High Comr for Sierra Leone in London, and Ambassador to Norway, Sweden and Denmark, 1971-72. Margaret Wrong Prize and Medal for Literature in Africa, 1952; Chm., Sierra Leone Nat. Library Bd, 1959-65; Member: Governing Body, Kumasi Univ., Ghana; Public Service Commn, Sierra Leone, 1960-68; W African Council for Medical Research, 1959-62; Exec. Council, Assoc. of Univs of British Commonwealth, 1960 and 1966; Commn for proposed Univ. of Ghana, 1960; Chm., Univ. of E Africa Visiting Cttee, 1962; Chm., UN Mission to Angola, July 1976. Director: Central Bank of Sierra Leone; Consolidated African Selection Trust Ltd (London); Davesme Corp. President: W African Science Assoc., 1964-66; Sierra Leone Red Cross Soc., 1962-66; Chm., W African Exams Council, 1964-69; Conference Delegate to: WHO Assembly, 1960; UNESCO Higher Educn Conf., Tananarive, 1963; Commonwealth Prime Ministers' Conf., London, 1965 and 1969, Singapore 1971. Hon. Fellow: Ghana Acad. of Scis. Hon. LLD: Leeds; Barat, Ill; Univ. of West Indies (St Augustine), 1981; Tuskegee, Ala, 1981; Hon. DSc: Newcastle upon Tyne; Kalamazoo, Mich; Hon. DLitt Davis and Elkins Coll., W Va. Independence Medal, Sierra Leone, 1961. Grand Commander: Order of Rokel, Sierra Leone, 1974; Star of Africa, Liberia, 1974. *Publications:* Africa, A Subjective View, 1964; contribs to: Malnutrition in African Mothers and Children, 1954; HRH the Duke of Edinburgh's Study Conference, Vol. 2, 1958; The Mechanism of Action of Insulin, 1960; The Structure of Human Insulin, 1960; Africanus Horton and Black Nationalism (1867), 1969; New and Modern Rôles for Commonwealth and Empire, 1976; The United Nations and Decision Making: the role of women, 1978; Nigeria and the Future of Africa, 1980; (ed) Paths to Peace, 1981; (ed) Essays on the UN Security Council and its Presidency, 1981; (ed) Regionalism and the New International Economic Order, 1981; The United Nations Security Council: towards greater effectiveness, 1981; also to Jl Trop. Med., Biochem. Jl, Nature, Jl of Royal African Soc., Times, Guardian, New Statesman, Encounter, West Africa, etc. *Recreation:* creative writing. *Address:* UNITAR, 801 United Nations Plaza, New York, NY 10017, USA. *T:* 754-1234, ext. 8621. *Clubs:* United Oxford & Cambridge University, Royal Commonwealth Society; Senior Dinner (Freetown).

NICOL, Prof. Donald MacGillivray, FBA 1981; Koraës Professor of Modern Greek and Byzantine History, Language and Literature, University of London, King's College, since 1970; Fellow and Vice Principal, King's College, since 1980 (Assistant Principal, 1977-80); *b* 4 Feb. 1923; *s* of late Rev. George Manson Nicol and Mary Patterson (*née* MacGillivray); *m* 1950, Joan Mary Campbell, *d* of Sir Walter Campbell, KCIE; three *s. Educ:* King Edward VII Sch., Sheffield; St Paul's Sch., London; Pembroke Coll., Cambridge (MA, PhD). Friends' Ambulance Unit, 1942-46; Scholar at British Sch. of Archæology, Athens, 1949-50; Lectr in Classics, University Coll., Dublin, 1952-64; Vis. Fellow, Dumbarton Oaks, Washington, DC, 1964-65; Vis. Prof. of Byzantine History, Indiana Univ., 1965-66; Sen. Lectr and Reader in Byzantine History, Univ. of Edinburgh, 1966-70. Birkbeck Lectr, Cambridge, 1976-77. Pres., Ecclesiastical Hist. Soc., 1975-76. MRIA 1960; FRHistS 1971. Editor, Byzantine and Modern Greek Studies, 1973-. *Publications:* The Despotate of Epiros, 1957; Meteora, the Rock Monasteries of Thessaly, 1963, rev. edn, 1975; The Byzantine Family of Kantakouzenos (Cantacuzenus) ca 1100-1460: a genealogical and prosopographical study, 1968; The Last Centuries of Byzantium, 1261-1453, 1972; Byzantium: Its Ecclesiastical History and Relations with the Western World, 1972; Church and Society in the Last Centuries of Byzantium, 1979; The End of the Byzantine Empire, 1979; articles in Byzantine, classical and historical jls. *Recreation:* bookbinding. *Address:* 19 Highshore Road, SE15 5AA. *T:* 01-732 6164. *Club:* Athenæum.

NICOL, Dr Joseph Arthur Colin, FRS 1967; Professor of Zoology, University of Texas Institute of Marine Science, 1967-80, now Professor Emeritus; *b* 5 Dec. 1915; *s* of George Nicol and Noele Petrie; *m* 1941, Helen Wilhelmina Cameron; one *d*. *Educ:* Universities of McGill, Western Ontario and Oxford. BSc (hons Zool.) 1938, McGill; MA 1940, Western Ontario; DPhil 1947, DSc 1961, Oxford. Canadian Army, RCCS, 1941-45. Asst Professor in Zoology, University of British Columbia, 1947-49; Experimental Zoologist, Marine Biological Assoc., UK, 1949 (research on marine animals, comparative physiology, luminescence, vision, at Plymouth Laboratory, 1949-66). Guggenheim Fellow, Scripps Inst. Oceanography, 1953-54. Vis. Prof., Univ. of Texas, 1966-67. *Publications:* Biology of Marine Animals, 1960; papers on comparative physiology and anatomy in Jl Marine Biol. Assoc. UK, Proc. Royal Soc, Jl Exp. Biol., Biol. Review, etc. *Recreation:* English literature. *Address:* Ribby, Lerryn, Lostwithiel, Cornwall PL22 0PG. *T:* Bodmin 872319.

NICOL, Prof. Thomas, MD, DSc (Glasgow and London); FRCS; FRCSE; FRSE; FKC; Emeritus Professor of Anatomy, University of London; Professor of Anatomy and Head of Anatomical Department, King's College, University of London, 1936-67 (Senior Professor in all Faculties, since Oct. 1966); Director of Department of Clinical Anatomy, Institute of Laryngology and Otology; Member: New York Academy of Sciences; Anatomical Society of Great Britain and Ireland; American Assoc. of Anatomists; International Reticulo-Endothelial Society; Society of Endocrinology; Fellow, Medical Society of London; Hon. Member, Mark Twain Society, in succession to Sir Alexander Fleming; *b* 4 Aug. 1900; *s* of Wm. Nicol and Mary Wilson Gilmour; *m* 1927, Evelyn Bertha (*d* 1966), *d* of Thomas Keeling, MICE, Engineer-in-Chief late Glasgow and South Western Railway; one *s* one *d*. *Educ:* University of Glasgow. Honours and Bellahouston Gold Medal for MD Thesis, University of Glasgow, 1935; Struthers Gold Medal and Prize, University of Glasgow, 1935. Sen. House Surgeon to Sir William Macewen, FRS (the discoverer of asepsis), Western Infirmary, Glasgow, 1921; Demonstrator of Anatomy, 1922-27, Senior Lecturer in Anatomy, 1927-35, University of Glasgow. Pioneer of experimental stimulation of phagocytes as suggested by Bernard Shaw in The Doctor's Dilemma; succeeded in doing this with oestrogen in late twenties; later discovered that body defence is under hormone control and that 17 β-oestradiol is the principal stimulant in both sexes. Lately: Dean of Faculty of Medicine, King's Coll., Univ. of London; Chm., Board of Studies in Human Anatomy and Morphology, Univ. of London; Examiner, Univs of London, Birmingham, Durham, Glasgow, and St Andrews, RCS England, Edinburgh and Ireland, and RCP; John Hunter Lectr in Applied Anatomy, St George's Hosp. Med. Sch.; Malcolm McHardy Lectr, Royal Eye Hosp. Lord of the Manor of Heveningham, Suffolk. *Publications:* research articles on raising body defence against infection and cancer, in British Jl of Surgery, Jl of Obstetrics and Gynaec. of British Empire, Jl of Anatomy, Trans. and Proc. Royal Society of Edinburgh, BMJ, Nature, Jl of Endocrinology, Jl of Reticuloendothelial Soc. *Recreations:* music, golf, swimming. *Address:* 18 Penn House, Moor Park, Northwood, Mddx. *T:* Northwood 25081.

NICOL, William Allardyce, CA, FCIS; President, Midland Assurance Ltd, since 1975 (Chairman, 1964-75); Director, Eagle Star Insurance Co. Ltd (Isle of Man), since 1975; Deputy Chairman, Eagle Star (International Life), since 1982; Chairman, Isle of Man Assurance Group, since 1976; *s* of William Nicol and Mary Wilson Gilmour; *m* 1st, 1933, Elizabeth (*d* 1967), *d* of James Miller; one *s* one *d*; 2nd, 1970, Sally Philippa, *d* of Robert Patrick Vernon Brettell; one *s* one *d*. *Educ:* Glasgow University. Guest, Keen & Nettlefolds: Asst to Man. Dir, 1939-48; Group Sec., 1948-60; Dir, 1958-77; full-time Exec. Admin. Dir, 1960-68; Dep. Chm., Eagle Star Insurance Co. Ltd, 1968-75; Director: Powell Duffryn Ltd, 1968-75; Barclays Bank Ltd (Birmingham Bd), 1961-75; Stait Carding Gp Ltd (Chm., 1973-75); Chm., John Stait Gp, 1972-75. Chm., Assoc. Scottish Chartered Accountants in Midlands, 1953-68; Mem. Grand Council, CBI, 1965-67. *Recreations:* golf, fishing, music. *Address:* Longmead, Ballakillowey, Colby, Isle of Man. *T:* Port Erin 832005.

NICOLL, Douglas Robertson, CB 1980; retired; *b* 12 May 1920; *s* of James George Nicoll and Mabel Nicoll (*née* Styles); *m* 1949, Winifred Campion; two *s*. *Educ:* Merchant Taylors' School; St John's College, Oxford (MA 1946). FCO (GCHQ), 1946-80; Joint Services' Staff College, 1953; Under Secretary, 1977-80. *Address:* c/o National Westminster Bank, 31 The Promenade, Cheltenham, Glos GL50 1LH.

NICOLL, Prof. Ronald Ewart, MSc, FRTPI, FRICS; Professor of Urban and Regional Planning, University of Strathclyde, 1966-80; Partner, PEIDA, since 1980; *b* 8 May 1921; *s* of William Ewart Nicoll and Edith May Choat; *m* 1943, Isabel Christina McNab; one *s* one *d*. *Educ:* Southend Municipal Coll.; Hammersmith Sch. of Architecture and Building; Royal College of Science and Technology, Glasgow. Served War, Royal Navy, 1939-46. Planning Asst, 1949-53: Southend CB; Derbyshire CC; Northamptonshire CC. Dep. Dir of Planning, Glasgow City, 1953-64; Chief Planning Officer, Scottish Development Dept, 1964-66. Consultant to UN and WHO. Member: Scottish Social Advisory Council, 1970; Scottish Council on Crime, 1971; Scottish Council (Develt and Industry), 1971; Glasgow Chamber of Commerce, 1971; Royal Commn on Environmental Pollution, 1973-79. RICS Gold Medal, 1975. FRSA. *Publications:* Oceanspan, 1970; Energy and the Environment, 1975; contribs to: The Future of Development Plans, 1965 (HMSO); How Do You Want to Live?, 1972 (HMSO); A Future for Scotland, 1973. *Recreations:*

travel, photography, hill walking. *Address:* 78 Victoria Park Drive North, Glasgow G14 9PJ. *T:* 041-959 7854. *Clubs:* Royal Commonwealth Society; Carrick (Glasgow).

NICOLL, William, CMG 1974; a Director General, Secretariat of the Council of Ministers of the European Communities, since 1982; *b* 28 June 1927; *s* of Ralph Nicoll and Christina Mowbray Nicoll (*née* Melville); *m* 1954, Helen Morison Martin; two *d*. *Educ:* Morgan Acad., Dundee; St Andrews Univ. Entered BoT, 1949; British Trade Comr, India, 1955-59; Private Sec. to Pres. of BoT, 1964-67; Commercial Inspector, FCO, 1967-69; DTI, 1969-72; Office of UK Perm. Rep. to European Communities, 1972-75; Under Sec., Dept of Prices and Consumer Protection, 1975-77; Dep. UK Rep. to EEC, 1977-82. *Address:* Council of the European Communities, 107 Rue de la Loi, 1048 Brussels, Belgium.

NICOLSON, family name of **Baron Carnock.**

NICOLSON, Sir David (Lancaster), Kt 1975; Chairman: BTR PLC, since 1969 (Deputy Chairman, 1965-69); Rothmans International, since 1975; Oppenheimer International Ltd, since 1980; Selincourt Plc, since 1982; Co-Chairman, European Channel Tunnel Group, since 1980; Member (C) London Central, European Parliament, since 1979; Industrial Advisor, European Democratic Group, since 1980; *b* 20 Sept. 1922; *s* of Charles Tupper Nicolson, consulting engineer, and Margaret Lancaster Nicolson; *m* 1945, Joan Eileen, *d* of Major W. H. Griffiths, RA; one *s* two *d*. *Educ:* Haileybury; Imperial Coll., London Univ., Hon. Fellow 1971. BSc, FCGI, FEng, FIMechE, FIProdE; FIAM; FBIM; FRSA. Constructor Lt, Royal Corps Naval Constructors, 1942-45; served N Atlantic and Normandy, 1944 (despatches). Management Consultant, Production-Engineering Ltd, 1946-50; Production Manager, Bucyrus Erie Co., Milwaukee, 1951-52; Manager, later Dir, Production-Engineering Ltd, 1953-62; Chairman: P-E Consulting Gp, 1963-68; Associated British Maltsters Ltd, 1965-71; Howden Gp Ltd, 1971-72; Chm., British Airways Board, 1971-75. Director: Bank of Montreal; Todd Shipyards Corp.; Drayton Consolidated Trust Ltd; CIBA-Geigy (UK); Confederation Life Insce Co. Mem. Council: CBI, 1972- (Chm., Environment Cttee, 1976-79); Inst. of Directors, 1971-76; Brit. Inst. of Management, 1964-69; Inst. of Production Engrs 1966-68; City and Guilds of London Inst. 1968-76; Member: SRC, 1970-71; SRC Engineering Bd, 1969-71; Chm. Management Consultants Assoc., 1964; Mem. Brit. Shipbuilding Mission to India, 1957; Chm., BNEC Cttee for Canada, 1970-71. Founder Chm., Amer. European Community Assoc., 1981; Pres., European Acad., 1981. Mem. Council, Oxford Centre for Management Studies, 1982-; Governor: Imperial Coll., London Univ., 1966-77; Cranleigh Sch., 1979-. *Publications:* contribs to technical jls; lectures and broadcasts on management subjects in UK, USA, Australia, etc. *Recreation:* sailing. *Address:* Howicks, Dunsfold, Surrey. *T:* Dunsfold 296. *Clubs:* Carlton; Royal Thames Yacht.

NICOLSON, Malise Allen, MC 1945; Director, Booker McConnell plc, since 1968; *b* 31 Oct. 1921; *e s* of late Sir Kenneth Nicolson, MC; *m* 1946, Vivien Bridget, *y d* of late Arthur Hilton Ridley, CBE; one *s* two *d*. *Educ:* Eton. Served War, Probyn's Horse, 1940-45 (MC; Burma); served 1st Royal Dragoons, 1946-47. Gladstone, Lyall Ltd, Calcutta, 1948-55; joined Booker McConnell, 1956; Chairman: Booker Line, 1968- (Dir, 1957-); Coe Metcalf Shipping, 1977-; Govt 'A' Dir, Mersey Docks and Harbour Co., 1974-80. Chairman: Liverpool Steam Ship Owners, 1971-72; Employers Assoc., Port of Liverpool, 1972-74; Vice-Chm., British Shipping Fedn, 1968-71; Pres., Gen. Council of British Shipping, 1982-83. *Recreation:* country sports. *Address:* Frog Hall, Tilston, Malpas, Cheshire SY14 7HB. *T:* Tilston 320. *Club:* Cavalry and Guards.

NICOLSON, Nigel, MBE 1945; FSA; FRSL; author; Director of Weidenfeld and Nicolson Ltd since 1947; *b* 19 Jan. 1917; 2nd *s* of late Hon. Sir Harold Nicolson, KCVO, CMG and Hon. V. Sackville-West, CH; *heir-pres.* to 4th Baron Carnock, *qv* ; *m* 1953, Philippa Janet (marr. diss. 1970), *d* of Sir Gervais Tennyson d'Eyncourt, 2nd Bt; one *s* two *d*. *Educ:* Eton Coll.; Balliol Coll., Oxford. Capt. Grenadier Guards. Served War of 1939-45 in Tunisian and Italian Campaigns (MBE). Contested (C) NW Leicester, 1950, and Falmouth and Camborne, 1951; MP (C) Bournemouth East and Christchurch, Feb. 1952-Sept. 1959. Chm. Exec. Cttee, UNA, 1961-66. *Publications:* The Grenadier Guards, 1939-45, 1949 (official history); People and Parliament, 1958; Lord of the Isles, 1960; Great Houses of Britain, 1965; (editor) Harold Nicolson: Diaries and Letters, 1930-39, 1966; 1939-45, 1967; 1945-62, 1968; Great Houses, 1968; Alex (FM Alexander of Tunis), 1973; Portrait of a Marriage, 1973; (ed) Letters of Virginia Woolf, 1975-80 (6 vols); The Himalayas, 1975; Mary Curzon, 1977 (Whitbread Award). *Recreation:* archæology. *Address:* Sissinghurst Castle, Kent. *T:* Cranbrook 712850. *Club:* Beefsteak.

NIDDITCH, Prof. Peter Harold; Professor and Head of Department of Philosophy, University of Sheffield, since 1969; *b* 15 Sept. 1928; *o s* of Lazarus Nidditch and Matilda Nidditch (*née* Freeman); *m* 1951, Bridget Veronica McDonnell; no *c*. *Educ:* Clifton Coll.; Birkbeck Coll., Univ. of London (BA (External) 1949, MA 1951, PhD 1953, DLit 1980). Asst, Birkbeck Coll., 1953-54; Asst Lectr, Queen's Univ., Belfast, 1954-56; Lectr, Univ. of Liverpool, 1956-59; Univ. of Bristol, 1959-63; Univ. of Sussex: Sen. Lectr, 1963-64; Reader in Phil. and History of Science, and Chm. of Logic, History, and Policy of Science Div., Sch. of Math. and Phys. Scis, 1964-70; Editor, official pubns of Univ. of Sussex, 1965-69. Univ. of Sheffield: Dean, Faculty of Arts, 1977-79; Chm., Library Cttee, 1979-82; Chm., Academic Staffing Cttee, 1980-. Gen. Editor, Clarendon Edn of Works of John Locke (30 vols), in progress. *Publications:* Introductory Formal Logic of Mathematics, 1957; Elementary Logic of Science and Mathematics, 1960; Propositional Calculus, 1962; Russian Reader in Pure and Applied Mathematics, 1962; The Development of Mathematical Logic (in C. K. Ogden's Basic English), 1962 (Spanish edn 1978); (ed) Philosophy of Science, 1968 (Spanish edn 1978); The Intellectual Virtues, 1970; A Bibliographical and Text-Historical Study of the Early Printings of Locke's Some Thoughts concerning Education, 1972; critical edn, Locke's Essay concerning Human Understanding, 1975, revd edn 1979; (ed) Hume's Enquiries, 1975; An Apparatus of Variant Readings for Hume's Treatise of Human Nature, 1976; critical edn, Hume's Treatise of Human Nature, 1978; Preface to the Grammar of Postulates (Proc. Aristotelian Soc. supp. vol.), 1979; The Earliest Extant Autograph Version (Draft A) of Locke's Essay, transcribed with critical apparatus, 1980; Index to J. L. Austin, How To Do Things With Words, 1980; (ed) Draft B of Locke's Essay, 1982; chapters in several other books; contribs to learned jls. *Address:* Sparlands, Grindleford, Derbyshire S30 1HQ. *T:* Hope Valley 30670.

NIELD, Sir Basil Edward, Kt 1957; CBE 1956 (MBE 1945); DL; Judge of High Court of Justice, Queen's Bench Division, 1960-78; *b* 7 May 1903; *yr s* of late Charles Edwin Nield, JP, and Mrs F. E. L. Nield, MBE, LLA, Upton-by-Chester. *Educ:* Harrow Sch.; Magdalen Coll., Oxford (MA). Officers Emergency Reserve, 1938; served War of 1939-45: commnd Captain, 1940; 1941; GHQ MEF (Major), HQs E Africa Force, Abyssinia, Palestine and Syria; Pres., Palestine Military Courts in Jerusalem; 1942; HQs Eritrea and 8th Army; 1943: HQ Persia and Iraq; Asst Dep. Judge Advocate-Gen., ME (Lt-Col; despatches); Home Estab.; 1944: 21 Army Gp; HQ Lines of Communication, BLA, Normandy; HQ 2nd Army, France, Belgium, Holland and Germany (MBE); Home Estab., 1945; RARO until 1948. Called to Bar, Inner Temple, 1925, Reader, 1976, Treasurer, 1977; Northern Circuit, Chambers in Liverpool; KC 1945; Recorder of Salford, 1948-56; Recorder and first permanent Judge of Crown Court at Manchester, 1956-60. MP (C) City of Chester, 1940-56; sponsored as Private Member's Bill the Adoption of Children Act, 1949; Hon. Parly Chm., Dock and Harbour Authorities Assoc., 1944-50; Mem., Special Cttee under Reorganisation Areas Measure for Province of York, 1944. Mem., Gen. Council of Bar, 1951; Master of Bench of Inner Temple, 1952-. Member: Magistrates' Rules Cttee, 1952-56; Legal Bd, Church Assembly, 1952-56; Home Secretary's Adv. Cttee on Treatment of Offenders, 1957. Chancellor, Diocese of Liverpool, 1948-56. Vice-President: Nat. Chamber of Trade, 1948-56; Graduate Teachers Assoc., 1950-56; Corp. of Secretaries, 1950; Assoc. of Managers of Approved Schools, 1956; Cheshire Soc. in London; Spastics Soc., Manchester. Chm., Chester Conservative Assoc., 1930-40. Member: Court, Liverpool Univ., 1948-56; Adv. Council, E-SU, 1951; Oxford Soc.; Imperial Soc. of Knights Bachelor; Life Mem., Royal Soc. of St George. Governor, Harrow Sch., 1961-71. FAMS. JP Co. Lancaster, 1956; DL County Palatine of Chester, 1962-. Freeman, City of London, 1963. *Publication:* Farewell to the Assizes, 1972. *Address:* 7 King's Bench Walk, Temple, EC4. *T:* 01-353 3868. *Clubs:* Carlton, Garrick, Royal Automobile; City, Grosvenor (Chester).

NIELD, Sir William (Alan), GCMG 1972; KCB 1968 (CB 1966); Deputy Chairman, Rolls Royce (1971) Ltd, 1973-76; *b* 21 Sept. 1913; *s* of William Herbert Nield, Stockport, Cheshire, and Ada Nield; *m* 1937, Gwyneth Marion Davies; two *s* two *d. Educ:* Stockport Gram. Sch.; St Edmund Hall, Oxford. Research and Policy Dept of Labour Party, 1937-39; K-H News Letter Service, 1939. Served Royal Air Force and Royal Canadian Air Force, 1939-46 (despatches, 1944); demobilised as Wing Comdr, 1946. Min. of Food, 1946-47; HM Treasury, 1947-49; Min. of Food and Min. of Agric., Fisheries and Food, 1949-64 (Under-Sec., 1959-64); Dept of Economic Affairs: Under-Sec., 1964-65; Dep. Under-Sec. of State, 1965-66; a Dep. Sec., Cabinet Office, 1966-68; Permanent Under-Sec. of State, DEA, 1968-69; Permanent Secretary: Cabinet Office, 1969-72; NI Office, 1972-73. *Address:* South Nevay, Stubbs Wood, Chesham Bois, Bucks. *T:* Amersham 3869. *Club:* Farmers'.

NIEMEYER, Oscar; architect; *b* Rio de Janeiro, 15 Dec. 1907; *s* of Oscar Niemeyer Soares; *m* Anita Niemeyer; one *d. Educ:* Escola Nacional de Beles Artes, Univ. of Brazil. Joined office of Lúcio Costa, 1935; worked on Min. of Education and Health Building, Rio de Janeiro, Brazilian Pavilion, NY World Fair, etc., 1936-41. Major projects include: Pamphulha, Belo Horizonte, 1941-43; also Quintandinha, Petrópolis; Exhibition Hall, São Paulo, 1953; Brasilia (Dir of Architecture), 1957-. Brazilian Rep., UN Bd of Design Consultants, 1947. Lenin Peace Prize, 1963; Prix Internat. de l'Architecture Aujourd'hui, 1966. *Address:* 3940 avenida Atlàntica, Rio de Janeiro, Brazil.

NIEMÖLLER, Rev. Dr (Friedrich Gustav Emil) Martin; a President of the World Council of Churches, 1961-68; Church President of Evangelical Church in Hesse and Nassau, Germany, 1947-64, retired; *b* Lippstadt, Westphalia, 14 Jan. 1892; *s* of Pastor Heinrich Niemoeller; *m* 1st, 1919, Else (*née* Bremer) (*d* 1961); three *s* two *d* (and one *s* one *d* decd); 2nd, 1971, Sibylle (*née* von Sell). *Educ:* Gymnasium, Elberfeld. Midshipman in German Navy, 1910; retd 1919, as Kapitänleutnant; studied Theology, Münster, Westfalen; Pastor, 1924; Pastor of Berlin-Dahlem, 1931; creator of Pastors' Union and Confessing Church; prisoner in concentration camps at Sachsenhausen and Dachau, 1937-45; Pres. Office of Foreign Affairs of Evangelical Church in Germany, 1945-56. Holds Hon. DD of Univ. of Göttingen (Germany), and several foreign hon. doctorates. *Publications:* Vom U-Boot zu Kanzel

(Berlin), 1934; . . . Dass wir an Ihm bleiben: Sechzehn Dahlemer Predigten (Berlin), 1935; Alles und in allem Christus; Fünfzehn Dahlemer Predigten (Berlin), 1935; Fran U-Bat till Predikstol (trans.) (Stockholm), 1936; Dennoch getrost: Die letzten 28 Predigten (Switzerland), 1939; Ach Gott vom Himmel sieh darein: Sechs Predigten (Munich), 1946; . . . Zu verkündigen ein Gnädiges: Jahr des Herrn: Sechs Dachauer Predigten (1944-45), (Munich), 1946; Herr ist Jesus Christus: Die letzten 28 Predigten (Gütersloh), 1946; Herr, wohin sollen wir gehen? Ausgewählte Predigten (Munich), 1956; some hundred articles about theological, cultural and political themes. *Address:* Brentanostrasse 3, Wiesbaden, Germany.

NIGERIA, Archbishop of, since 1979; **Most Rev. Timothy Olufosoye,** OON 1964; Bishop of Ibadan; *b* 31 March 1918; *s* of Chief D. K. Olufosoye and Felecia O. Olufosoye; *m* 1947; one *s* three *d. Educ:* St Andrew's Coll., Oyo, Nigeria; Vancouver School of Theology, Univ. of BC (STh). Headmaster, 1942-44; deacon 1946, priest 1947; appointments in Ondo, Lagos, and overseas in St Helens, Lancs, Sheffield Cathedral, Yorks, and Christ Church Cathedral, Vancouver, BC; Canon, 1955; Provost, St Stephen's Cathedral, Ondo, 1959; Vicar-Gen., 1963; Bishop of Gambia and Rio Pongas, 1965-70. Member: World Council of Churches; Gen. and Exec. Cttee, All Africa Conf. of Churches. Hon. DD, St Paul's Univ., Tokyo, 1958. Knight Comdr, Humane Order of African Redemption, Republic of Liberia. *Publications:* Egbogi fun Ibanuje, 1967; editor of The Beacon, Ibadan Ecclesia Anglicana, The Rubric. *Recreation:* poultry farming. *Address:* Bishopscourt, Arigidi Street, Bodija Estate, PO Box 3075, Ibadan, Nigeria. *T:* 411331 Ibadan. *Club:* Ibadan Dining.

NIGHTINGALE, Sir Charles (Manners Gamaliel), 17th Bt *cr* 1628; Higher Executive Officer, Department of Health and Social Security, since 1977; *b* 21 Feb. 1947; *s* of Sir Charles Athelstan Nightingale, 16th Bt, and of Evelyn Nadine Frances, *d* of late Charles Arthur Diggens; *S* father, 1977. *Educ:* St Paul's School. Entered DHSS as Executive Officer, 1969; Higher Executive Officer, 1977. *Heir: cousin* Edward Lacy George Nightingale, *b* 11 May 1938. *Address:* 14 Frensham Court, 27 Highbury New Park, N5 2ES.

NIGHTINGALE, Edward Humphrey, CMG 1955; Farmer in Kenya since 1954; *b* 19 Aug. 1904; *s* of Rev. Edward Charles Nightingale and Ada Mary Nightingale; *m* 1944, Evelyn Mary Ray; three *s* one *d. Educ:* Rugby Sch.; Emmanuel Coll., Cambridge. Joined Sudan Political Service, 1926; Dep. Civil Sec., Sudan Government, 1951-52; Gov., Equatoria Province, Sudan, 1952-54. Order of the Nile, 4th Class, 1940. *Recreations:* polo, ski-ing, photography. *Address:* Nunjoro Farm, PO Box 100, Naivasha, Kenya. *T:* Naivasha 53Y1. *Clubs:* Rift Valley Sports (Nakuru); Muthaiga Country (Nairobi).

NIGHTINGALE, Sir John (Cyprian), Kt 1975; CBE 1970; BEM 1941; QPM 1965; DL; Chief Constable, Essex, 1962-69 and 1974-78, retired (Essex and Southend-on-Sea Joint Constabulary, 1969-74); *b* 16 Sept. 1913; *s* of Herbert Paul Nightingale, Sydenham, London; *m* 1947, Patricia Mary, *d* of Norman Maclaren, Glasgow University. *Educ:* Cardinal Vaughan Sch., Kensington; University Coll., London. Joined Metropolitan Police, 1935; Asst Chief Constable, Essex, 1958. Chm., Police Council, 1976-; Mem., Parole Bd, 1978-. Served with RNVR, 1943-45. DL Essex 1975. *Publications:* various police. *Address:* Great Whitman's Farm, Purleigh, Essex.

NIGHTINGALE of Cromarty, Michael David, OBE 1960; BSc; BLitt; FSA; Baron of Cromarty; Chairman, The Anglo-Indonesian Corporation Ltd; Esquire Bedell, University of London, since 1953; *b* 6 Dec. 1927; *s* of late Victor Russell John Nightingale, Wormshill, Kent; *m* 1956, Hilary Marion Olwen, *d* of late John Eric Jones, Swansea; two *s* three *d. Educ:* Winchester; Wye Coll.; Magdalen Coll., Oxford. Organised Exhibition from Kent Village Churches, Canterbury, 1951; Asst to Investment Manager, Anglo-Iranian Oil Co., 1951-53; Asst to Principal, Univ. of London, 1953-54; Investment Adviser, Univ. of London, 1954-66; Dir, Charterhouse Japhet Ltd, 1965-70. Secretary: Museums Assoc. (and Editor of Museums Jl), 1954-60; Museum Cttee, Carnegie UK Trust, 1954-60; Member: Advisory Council on Export of Works of Art, 1954-60; British Cttee of International Council of Museums, 1956-60; Canterbury Diocesan Advisory Cttee, 1964-79; Exec. Cttee, SE Arts Assoc., 1974-77; Area Archaeol. Adv. Cttee for SE England, 1975-79. Mem., Gen. Synod of C of E, 1979-. Mem., Kent CC, 1973-77; Chm., Planning Cttee, Maidstone Borough Council, 1973-77, Leader, 1976-77. Vice-Pres., Swale & North Downs Soc.; Chm., Churches Cttee, and Vice-Pres., Kent Archaeological Soc. Dep. Steward, Royal Manor of Wye, 1954-. *Publications:* articles on agrarian and museum subjects. *Address:* Wormshill Court, Sittingbourne, Kent. *T:* Wormshill 235; Perceval House, 21 Dartmouth Row, Greenwich, SE10. *T:* 01-692 6033; Cromarty House, Ross and Cromarty. *T:* Cromarty 265. *Club:* Athenæum.

NIKLASSON, Frau Bertil; see Nilsson, Birgit.

NIKLAUS, Prof. Robert, BA, PhD London; LèsL Lille; DrUniv Rennes *hc* 1963; Hon. DLitt Exon 1981; Officier de l'Ordre National du Mérite, 1972; Professor of French, 1956-75, now Emeritus, also Head of Department of French and Spanish, 1958-64, French and Italian, 1964-75, University of Exeter; *b* 18 July 1910; *s* of late Jean Rodolphe and Elizabeth Niklaus; *m* 1st, 1935, Thelma (*née* Jones) (*d* 1970); two *s* one *d*; 2nd, 1973, Kathleen (*née* Folta). *Educ:* Lycée Français de Londres; University Coll., London; Univ. of Lille. Sen. Tutor, Toynbee Hall, London, 1931-32; Asst and Asst Lecturer at University Coll., 1932-38; Asst Lecturer, Lecturer, Univ. of Manchester,

1938-52; Prof. of French, UC of the SW, 1952-56. Dean of the Faculty of Arts, Exeter, 1959-62; Dep. Vice-Chancellor, 1965-67. Visiting Professor: Univ. of Calif., Berkeley, 1963-64; Univ. of British Columbia, 1975-76; Hd of Dept of Langs, Univ. of Nigeria, Nsukka, 1977-78. Pres., Assoc. of Univ. Teachers, 1954-55, Mem. Executive Cttee, 1948-62; Pres. Internat. Assoc. of Univ. Profs and Lecturers, 1960-64 (Vice-Pres., 1958-60, 1964-66); Member: Cttee of Modern Humanities Research Association, 1956-71; Cttee, Soc. for French Studies, 1965-72 (Vice-Pres., 1967-68 and 1970-71, Pres. 1968-70); Pres., British Soc. for XVIIIth Century Studies, 1970-72; Treasurer, Internat. Soc. for Eighteenth-century Studies, 1969-79; Post-graduate Awards Cttee of Min. of Education, 1956-61; Management Cttee, British Inst., Paris, 1965-67. Gen. Editor, Textes Français Classiques et Modernes, Univ. of London Press. *Publications:* Jean Moréas, Poète Lyrique, 1936; The Nineteenth Century (Post-Romantic) and After (in The Year's Work in Modern Language Studies, VII-XIII), 1937-52; Diderot and Drama, 1942; Beaumarchais, Le Barbier de Séville, 1968; A Literary History of France, the Eighteenth Century, 1970; critical editions of: J.-J. Rousseau, Les Rêveries du Promeneur Solitaire, 1942; Denis Diderot, Pensées Philosophiques, 1950; Denis Diderot, Lettre sur les Aveugles, 1951; Marivaux, Arlequin poli par l'Amour, 1959 (in collab. with Thelma Niklaus); Sedaine, La Gageure imprévue, 1970; (contrib.) Diderot: Œuvres Complètes, vol. II, 1975, vol. IV, 1979; articles in Encyclopaediæ and learned journals; textbooks for schools and universities. *Recreations:* aviculture, the theatre, the cinema. *Address:* 17 Elm Grove Road, Topsham, Exeter, Devon. *T:* Topsham 3627.

NIKOLAYEVA-TERESHKOVA, Valentina Vladimirovna; Hero of the Soviet Union; Order of Lenin; Gold Star Medal; Order of October Revolution; Joliot-Curie Peace Medal; Soviet cosmonaut; *b* Maslennikovo, 6 March 1937; *d* of late Vladimir and of Elena Fyodorovna Tereshkova; *m* 1963, Andrian Nikolayev; one *d*. Formerly textile worker, Krasny Perekop mill, Yaroslavl; served on cttees; Sec. of local branch, Young Communist league, 1960; Member: CPSU, 1962-; Central Cttee, CPSU, 1971; Deputy, 1966, Mem. of Presidium, 1970, Supreme Soviet of Russia; Pres., Soviet Women's Cttee, 1968. Joined Yaroslavl Air Sports Club, 1959, and started parachute jumping; joined Cosmonaut Training Unit, 1962; became first woman in the world to enter space when she made 48 orbital flights of the earth in spaceship Vostok VI, 16-19 June 1963. Nile Collar (Egypt), 1971; holds honours and citations from other countries. *Address:* Soviet Women's Committee, 6 Nemirovich-Danchenko Street, 103009 Moscow, USSR.

NILSSON, Birgit, (Fru Bertil Niklasson); Swedish operatic soprano; *b* Karup, Kristianstadslaen, 1922. *Educ:* Stockholm Royal Academy of Music. Debut as singer, 1946; with Stockholm Opera, 1947-51. Has sung at Glyndebourne, 1951; Bayreuth, 1953, 1954, 1957-70; Munich, 1954-58; Hollywood Bowl, Buenos Aires, Florence, 1956; La Scala, Milan, 1958-; Covent Garden, 1957, 1960, 1962, 1963, 1973 and 1977; Edinburgh, 1959; Metropolitan, New York, 1959-; Moscow, 1964; also in most leading opera houses and festivals of the world. Particularly well-known for her Wagnerian rôles. Austrian Kammersängerin, 1968; Bavarian Kammersängerin, 1970. Swedish Royal Acad. of Music's Medal for Promotion of Art of Music, 1968. Comdr of the Vasa Order, Sweden, 1968.

NIMMO, Hon. Sir John (Angus), Kt 1972; CBE 1970; Justice of the Federal Court of Australia, 1977-80; Justice of Australian Industrial Court, 1969-80; *b* 15 Jan. 1909; *s* of John James Nimmo and Grace Nimmo (*née* Mann); *m* 1935, Teanie Rose Galloway; two *s*. *Educ:* Univ. of Melbourne. Admitted to practise at Victorian Bar, 1933. QC 1957. Mem., Commonwealth Taxation Bd of Review No 2, 1947-54; Actg Supreme Court Justice, Victoria, 1963; Dep. Pres., Commonwealth Conciliation and Arbitration Commn, 1964-69; Chm., Health Insce Cttee of Enquiry, 1968-69. Dep. Pres., Trade Practices Tribunal, 1966-73, also a Justice of Supreme Courts of ACT and NT, 1966-74; on secondment as Chief Justice of Fiji, 1972-74. Royal Comr into future of Norfolk Is, 1975-76; Chm., Commonwealth Legal Aid Commn, 1978-79; Mem., Cttee on Overseas Professional Qualifications, 1978. OStJ 1945. *Recreations:* reading, bowls, walking. *Address:* 2/28 Clarkestown Avenue, Mount Eliza, Victoria 3930. *T:* 787-7420. *Clubs:* Australian (Melbourne); Melbourne Cricket.

NIMMO SMITH, William Austin, QC (Scot.) 1982; *b* 6 Nov. 1942; *s* of Dr Robert Herman Nimmo Smith and Mrs Ann Nimmo Smith; *m* 1968, Jennifer Main; one *s* one *d*. *Educ:* Eton Coll. (King's Scholar, 1956); Balliol Coll., Oxford (BA 1965); Edinburgh Univ. (LLB 1967). Admitted to Faculty of Advocates, 1969. *Recreations:* hill-walking, music. *Address:* 29 Northumberland Street, Edinburgh EH3 6LR. *T:* 031-556 1625. *Club:* New (Edinburgh).

NIND, Philip Frederick, OBE 1979; TD 1946; Director, Foundation for Management Education, since 1968; Secretary, Council of Industry for Management Education, since 1969; *b* 2 Jan. 1918; *s* of W. W. Nind, CIE; *m* 1944, Fay Allardice Crofton (*née* Errington); two *d*. *Educ:* Blundell's Sch.; Balliol Coll., Oxford (MA). War service, 1939-46, incl. Special Ops in Greece and Albania (despatches), 1943-44, Mil. Govt Berlin, 1945-46 (Major). Shell Gp of Cos in Venezuela, Cyprus, Lebanon, Jordan and London, 1939-68. Educn and Trng Cttee, CBI (formerly FBI), 1961-68; OECD Working Gp on Management Educn, 1966-69; Nat. Adv. Council on Educn for Industry and Commerce, 1967-70; UGC Management Studies Cttee, 1968-; NEDO Management Educn Trng and Develt Cttee, 1968-; Chm., NEDO Management Teacher Panel, 1969-72; Member: Council for Techn. Educn and

Trng for Overseas Countries, 1970-75; CNAA Management Studies Bd, 1971-; Vice-Pres., European Foundn for Management Develt, 1978-. Member: Oxford Univ. Appts Cttee, 1967-; Exec. Cttee, Royal Academy of Dancing, 1970-; Governor: Univ. of Keele, 1961-; Bedford Coll., London Univ., 1967-. Chevalier, Order of Cedars of Lebanon, 1959; Grand Cross, Orders of St Mark and Holy Sepulchre, 1959. *Publications:* (jtly) Management Education and Training Needs of Industry, 1963; Fourth Stockton Lecture, 1973; articles in various jls. *Address:* Foundation for Management Education, Management House, Parker Street, WC2B 5PT. *T:* 01-405 3456. *Clubs:* Travellers', Special Forces.

NINEHAM, Rev. Prof. Dennis Eric, DD (Oxon); BD (Cantab); Hon. DD (Birmingham); Hon. DD (BDS Yale); Professor of Theology and Head of Theology Department, Bristol University, since 1980; Honorary Canon of Bristol Cathedral, since 1980; *b* 27 Sept. 1921; *o c* of Stanley Martin and Bessie Edith Nineham, Shirley, Southampton; *m* 1946, Ruth Corfield, *d* of Rev. A. P. Miller; two *s* two *d*. *Educ:* King Edward VI Sch., Southampton; Queen's Coll., Oxford. Asst Chaplain of Queen's Coll., 1944; Chaplain, 1945; Fellow and Praelector, 1946; Tutor, 1949; Prof. of Biblical and Historical Theology, Univ. of London (King's Coll.), 1954-58; Prof. of Divinity, Univ. of London, 1958-64; Regius Prof. of Divinity, Cambridge Univ., and Fellow, Emmanuel Coll., 1964-69; Warden of Keble Coll., Oxford, 1969-79, Hon. Fellow, 1980. FKC 1963. Examining Chaplain: to Archbishop of York and to Bishop of Ripon; to Bishop of Sheffield, 1947-54; to Bishop of Norwich, 1964-73; to Bishop of Bristol, 1981-. Select Preacher to Univ. of Oxford, 1954-56, 1971, and to Univ. of Cambridge, 1959; Proctor in Convocation of Canterbury: for London Univ., 1955-64; for Cambridge Univ., 1965-69. Mem. General Synod of Church of England for Oxford Univ., 1970-76; Mem., C of E Doctrine Commn, 1968-76. Roian Fleck Resident-in-Religion, Bryn Mawr Coll., Pa, 1974. Governor of Haileybury, 1966-. *Publications:* The Study of Divinity, 1960; A New Way of Looking at the Gospels, 1962; Commentary on St Mark's Gospel, 1963; The Use and Abuse of the Bible, 1976; Explorations in Theology, no 1, 1977; (Editor) Studies in the Gospels: Essays in Honour of R. H. Lightfoot, 1955; The Church's Use of the Bible, 1963; The New English Bible Reviewed, 1965; contrib. to: Studies in Ephesians (editor F. L. Cross), 1956; On the Authority of the Bible, 1960; Religious Education, 1944-1984, 1966; Theologians of Our Time, 1966; Christian History and Interpretation, 1967; Christ for us To-day, 1968; Christian Believing, 1976; The Myth of God Incarnate, 1977; Imagination and the Future, 1980. *Recreation:* reading. *Address:* Department of Theology, Bristol University, Royal Fort House, Tyndall Avenue, Bristol BS8 1UJ. *T:* Bristol 24161; 52 Granby Hill, Bristol BS8 4LS. *T:* Bristol 23565.

NINIS, Ven. Richard Betts; Archdeacon of Lichfield (formerly Stafford) and Treasurer of Lichfield Cathedral, since 1974; *b* 25 Oct. 1931; *s* of late George Woodward Ninis and of Mary Gertrude Ninis; *m* 1967, Penelope Jane Harwood; two *s* one *d*. *Educ:* Lincoln Coll., Oxford (MA); Bishop's Hostel, Lincoln (GOE). Curate, All Saints, Poplar, 1955-62; Vicar of: St Martins, Hereford, 1962-71; Bullinghope and Dewsall with Callow, 1966-71. Diocesan Missioner for Hereford, 1971-74. *Recreations:* gardening, viticulture, travel. *Address:* 24 The Close, Lichfield, Staffs. *T:* Lichfield 23535.

NIRENBERG, Dr Marshall Warren; Research Biochemist; Chief, Laboratory of Biochemical Genetics, National Heart, Lung and Blood Institute, National Institutes of Health, Bethesda, Md, since 1966; *b* New York, 10 April 1927; *m* 1961, Perola Zaltzman; no *c*. *Educ:* Univs of Florida (BS, MS) and Michigan (PhD). Univ. of Florida: Teaching Asst, Zoology Dept, 1945-50; Res. Associate, Nutrition Lab., 1950-52; Univ. of Michigan: Teaching and Res. Fellow, Biol Chemistry Dept, 1952-57; Nat. Insts of Health, Bethesda: Postdoctoral Fellow of Amer. Cancer Soc., Nat. Inst. Arthritis and Metabolic Diseases, 1957-59, and of Public Health Service, Section of Metabolic Enzymes, 1959-60; Research Biochemist, Section of Metabolic Enzymes, 1960-62 and Section of Biochem. Genetics, 1962-66. Member: Amer. Soc. Biol Chemists; Amer. Chem. Soc.; Amer. Acad. Arts and Sciences; Biophys. Soc.; Nat. Acad. Sciences; Washington Acad. Sciences; Sigma Xi; Soc. for Study of Development and Growth; (Hon.) Harvey Soc.; Leopoldina Deutsche Akademie der Naturforscher; Neurosciences Research Program, MIT; NY Acad. Sciences; Pontifical Acad. Science, 1974. Robbins Lectr, Pomona Coll., 1967; Remsden Mem. Lectr, Johns Hopkins Univ., 1967. Numerous awards and prizes, including Nobel Prize in Medicine or Physiology (jtly), 1968. Hon. Dr Science: Michigan, Yale, and Chicago, 1965; Windsor, 1966; Harvard Med. Sch., 1968; Hon. PhD, Weitzmann Inst. of Science, Israel, 1978. *Publications:* numerous contribs to learned jls and chapters in symposia. *Address:* Laboratory of Biochemical Genetics, National Heart, Lung and Blood Institute, Bethesda, Md 20014, USA; 7001 Orkney Parkway, Bethesda, Maryland, USA.

NISBET, Prof. Hugh Barr; Professor of Modern Languages, University of Cambridge, since 1982; Professorial Fellow, Sidney Sussex College, since 1982; *b* 24 Aug. 1940; *s* of Thomas Nisbet and Lucy Mary Hainsworth; *m* 1962, Monika Luise Ingeborg Uecker; two *s*. *Educ:* Dollar Acad.; Univ. of Edinburgh. MA, PhD 1965. University of Bristol: Asst Lectr in German, 1965-67; Lectr, 1967-72; Reader, 1972-73; Prof. of German Lang. and Lit., Univ. of St Andrews, 1974-81. Mem., Gen. Teaching Council for Scotland, 1978-81. Governor, Dollar Acad., 1978-. Mem. Cttee, MHRA, 1972-; Jt Editor, MHRA texts and dissertations, 1978-; Germanic Editor, 1973-80, Gen. Editor, 1981-, Modern Language Rev. *Publications:* Herder and the Philosophy and History of Science, 1970; (ed with Hans Reiss) Goethe's Die

Wahlverwandtschaften, 1971; Goethe and the Scientific Tradition, 1972; *translations:* Kant, Political Writings, 1970, 2nd edn 1977; Hegel, Lectures on the Philosophy of World History, 1975, 2nd edn 1980; articles and reviews on German literature and thought. *Recreations:* music, art history, cycling. *Address:* Sidney Sussex College, Cambridge CB2 3HU. *T:* Cambridge 61501.

NISBET, Prof. John Donald, OBE 1981; MA, BEd, PhD; FEIS; FRSA; Professor of Education, Aberdeen University, since 1963; *b* 17 Oct. 1922; *s* of James Love Nisbet and Isabella Donald; *m* 1952, Brenda Sugden; one *s* one *d. Educ:* Dunfermline High Sch.; Edinburgh Univ. (MA, BEd); PhD (Aberdeen); Teacher's Certif. (London). FEIS 1975; FRSA 1982. Royal Air Force, 1943-46. Teacher, Fife, 1946-48; Lectr, Aberdeen Univ., 1949-63. Editor: British Jl of Educnl Psychology, 1967-74; Studies in Higher Education, 1979-; Chairman: Educnl Research Bd, SSRC, 1972-75; Cttee on Primary Educn, 1974-80; Scottish Council for Research in Educn, 1975-78; Pres., British Educnl Research Assoc., 1975. *Publications:* Family Environment, 1953; Age of Transfer to Secondary Education, 1966; Transition to Secondary Education, 1969; Scottish Education Looks Ahead, 1969; Educational Research Methods, 1970; Educational Research in Action, 1972; Impact of Research, 1980; Towards Community Education, 1980; papers in jls on educnl psychology and curriculum develt. *Recreations:* golf, orienteering. *Address:* 5 The Chanonry, Aberdeen AB2 1RP. *T:* Aberdeen 44375.
See also S. D. Nisbet.

NISBET, Prof. Robin George Murdoch, FBA 1967; Corpus Christi Professor of Latin, Oxford, since 1970; *b* 21 May 1925; *s* of R. G. Nisbet, Univ. Lecturer, and A. T. Husband; *m* 1969, Anne, *d* of Dr J. A. Wood. *Educ:* Glasgow Academy; Glasgow Univ.; Balliol Coll., Oxford (Snell Exhibitioner). Fellow and Tutor in Classics, Corpus Christi College, Oxford, 1952-70. *Publications:* Commentary on Cicero, in *Pisonem,* 1961; (with M. Hubbard) on Horace, *Odes I,* 1970; *Odes II,* 1978; articles and reviews on Latin subjects. *Recreation:* 20th century history. *Address:* 80 Abingdon Road, Cumnor, Oxford. *T:* Oxford 862482.

NISBET, Prof. Stanley Donald; Professor of Education, University of Glasgow, 1951-78; *b* 26 July 1912; *s* of Dr J. L. and Isabella Nisbet; *m* 1942, Helen Alison Smith; one *s* one *d. Educ:* Dunfermline High Sch., Edinburgh Univ. MA (1st Cl. Hons Classics), 1934; Diploma in Education, 1935; BEd (with distinction in Education and Psychology), 1940. Taught in Moray House Demonstration Sch., Edinburgh, 1935-39. Served War in RAF, 1940-46; research officer at Air Ministry, 1944-46. Lecturer in Education, Univ. of Manchester, Feb.-Sept. 1946; Prof. of Education, Queen's Univ. of Belfast, 1946-51. FRSE 1955; FEIS 1976. *Publications:* Purpose in the Curriculum, 1957; (with B. L. Napier) Promise and Progress, 1970; articles in psychological and educational journals. *Recreations:* walking, sailing. *Address:* 6 Victoria Park Corner, Glasgow G14 9NZ.
See also J. D. Nisbet.

NISBET-SMITH, Dugal; Senior Executive, headquarters of HH the Aga Khan, Aiglemont, France, since 1981; *b* 6 March 1935; *s* of David and Margaret Homeward Nisbet-Smith; *m* 1959, Dr Ann Patricia Taylor; one *s* two *d. Educ:* Southland Boys' High Sch., Invercargill, NZ. Journalist on Southland Daily News, NZ, 1952-56; Features writer and reporter, Beaverbrook Newspapers, London, 1956-60; variously Asst Editor, Gen. Manager and Man. Dir, Barbados Advocate Co., Barbados, WI, Gen. Manager, Sierra Leone Daily Mail Ltd, W Africa, Dep. Gen. Manager, Trinidad Mirror Co., 1960-66; Sen. Industrial Relations Manager, Mirror Gp Newspapers, London, 1966-68; Develt Manager, 1969-71, Production Dir, 1971-73, Man. Dir, 1974-78, Scottish Daily Record and Sunday Mail Ltd, Glasgow; joined Bd, Mirror Gp Newspapers, 1976; Dir/General Manager, 1978-80, Man. Dir, 1980-81, Times Newspapers Ltd. *Recreations:* travel, sculpture, painting. *Address:* 19 Highgate Close, Hampstead Lane, N6. *T:* 01-340 9457. *Clubs:* Royal Automobile; Nairobi.

NISSAN, Prof. Alfred Heskel, PhD, DSc (Chem. Eng, Birmingham), MIChemE, MAIChE, MACS; Member Sigma XI; Consultant to WESTVACO (formerly West Virginia Pulp and Paper), New York (Vice-President, 1967-79, and Corporate Director of Research, 1962-79); Professor, College of Environmental Science and Forestry, Syracuse, New York, since 1979; *b* 14 Feb. 1914; *s* of Heskel and Farha Nissan, Baghdad, Iraq; *m* 1940, Zena Gladys Phyllis, *o d* of late Phillip and Lillian Frances Pursehouse-Ahmed, Birmingham; one *d. Educ:* The American Sch. for Boys, Baghdad, Iraq; Univ. of Birmingham. Instn of Petroleum Scholarship, 1936; first cl. Hons BSc 1937; Sir John Cadman Medal, 1937; Instn of Petroleum Medal and Prize and Burgess Prize, 1937; Research Fellow, 1937, Lectr, 1940, Univ. of Birmingham; Head of Central Research Laboratories, Bowater Paper Corporation Ltd, 1947; Technical Director in charge of Research, Bowaters Development and Research Ltd, 1950; Research Prof. of Wool Textile Engineering, the Univ. of Leeds, 1953; Prof. of Chemical Engineering, Rensselaer Polytechnic Inst., Troy, NY, USA, 1957. Hon. Vis. Prof., Uppsala Univ., 1974. Schwarz Memorial Lectr, Amer. Soc. of Mech. Engrs, 1967. Member: Adv. Council for Advancement of Industrial R&D, State of NY, 1965-; Board of Directors: Technical Assoc. of Pulp & Paper Industry, 1968-71 (R&D Div. Award, 1976); Industrial Res. Inst., 1973-77. Alexander Mitscheslich Medal, Zellchening, W Germany, 1980; Gold Medal, Technical Assoc. of Pulp and Paper Industry, 1982. *Publications:* (ed) Textile

Engineering Processes, 1959; (ed) Future Technical Needs and Trends in the Paper Industry, 1973; Lectures on Fiber Science in Paper, 1977; papers on physical chemistry and chemical engineering problems of petroleum, paper and textile technology in scientific jls. *Address:* 6A Dickel Road, Scarsdale, NY 10583, USA.

NISSEN, George Maitland; Partner, Pember & Boyle, Stockbrokers, since 1956; *b* 29 March 1930; *s* of Col Peter Norman Nissen, DSO, and Lauretta Maitland; *m* 1956, Jane Edmunds, *d* of late S. Curtis Bird, New York; two *s* two *d. Educ:* Eton; Trinity Coll., Cambridge (MA). National Service, KRRC, 1949-50, 2/Lieut. Dep. Chm., Stock Exchange, 1978-81 (Mem. Council, 1973-); Mem., Inflation Accounting Steering Gp, 1976-80. Governor: Reed's Sch., Cobham; St Paul's Girls' Prep. Sch., Hammersmith. *Recreations:* railways, music. *Address:* Swan House, Chiswick Mall, W4 2PS. *T:* 01-994 8203.

NISSEN, Karl Iversen, MD, FRCS; retired Surgeon, Royal National Orthopædic Hospital, W1, 1946-71; Orthopædic Surgeon: Harrow Hospital 1946-71; Peace Memorial Hospital, Watford, 1948-71; *b* 4 April 1906; *s* of Christian and Caroline Nissen; *m* 1935, Margaret Mary Honor Schofield (*d* 1981); one *s* one *d. Educ:* Otago Boys' High Sch., Dunedin, NZ; Univ. of Otago, NZ. BSc (NZ) 1927; MB, ChB (NZ) 1932; MD (NZ) 1936; FRCS 1936. Served as Orthopædic Specialist, RNVR, 1943-46. Corresp. mem. Belgian, French, Swiss, German, Scandinavian, Norwegian, Finnish Socs of Orthopædics. *Recreation:* gardening. *Address:* Prospect House, The Avenue, Sherborne, Dorset. *T:* Sherborne 3539. *Club:* Naval.

NIVEN, Sir (Cecil) Rex, Kt 1960; CMG 1953; MC 1918; *b* 20 Nov. 1898; *o s* of late Rev. Dr G. C. and Jeanne Niven, Torquay, Devon; *m* 1st, 1925, Dorothy Marshall (*d* 1977), *e d* of late D. M. Mason, formerly MP (Coventry and E Edinburgh); one *d* (and one *d* decd); 2nd, 1980, Mrs Pamela Beerbohm, *d* of late G. C. Leach, ICS, Sibton Ct, Lyminge, Kent, and Mrs Leach, and widow of Dr O. H. B. Beerbohm. *Educ:* Blundell's Sch., Tiverton; Balliol Coll. Oxford (MA Hons). Served RFA 1917-19, France and Italy. Colonial Service Nigeria, 1921-54; served Secretariats and Provinces; PRO, Nigeria, 1943-45; Senior Resident, 1947; twice admin. Northern Govt; Mem. N House of Assembly, 1947-59 (Pres. 1952-58; Speaker, 1958-59); Mem., N Executive Council, 1951-54; Comr for Special Duties in N Nigeria, 1959-62; Dep. Sec., Southwark Dio. Bd of Finance, 1962-68. Life Mem., BRCS; Member: Council, RSA, 1963-69; Council, N Euboea Foundation; Council, Imp. Soc. of Knights Bachelor, 1969-; Gen. Synod of C of E, 1975-80; St Charles's (formerly Paddington) Group Hosp. Management Cttee, 1963-72. FRGS. *Publications:* A Short History of Nigeria, 1937, 10th edn 1966; Nigeria's Story, 1939; Nigeria: the Outline of a Colony, 1946; How Nigeria is Governed, 1950; West Africa, 1958; Short History of the Yoruba Peoples, 1958; You and Your Government, 1958; Nine Great Africans, 1964; Nigeria (in Benn's Nations of the Modern World), 1967; The War of Nigerian Unity, 1970; (collab.) My Life, by late Sardauna of Sokoto, 1962; A Nigerian Kaleidoscope, 1982. *Recreations:* walking, architecture, philately. *Address:* West Hill House, Finglesham, Deal, Kent. *T:* Sandwich 611317. *Club:* Royal Over-Seas League.

NIVEN, David; see Niven, J. D. G.

NIVEN, Ian; see Niven, J. R.

NIVEN, (James) David (Graham); Actor-producer (international); author; *b* 1 March 1910; *s* of late William Graham Niven and late Lady Comyn-Platt, Carswell Manor, Abingdon, Berks; *m* 1st, Primula (*d* 1946), *d* of Hon. William and Lady Kathleen Rollo; two *s*; 2nd, Hjördis Tersmeden, Stockholm; two *d. Educ:* Stowe; RMC Sandhurst. Commissioned HLI, 1929, Malta and Home Service; resigned commission, 1932; roamed Canada, USA, West Indies and Cuba till 1935. Journalist; Whisky Salesman; indoor pony-racing promoter; delivery of laundry; etc. Arrived California; became "extra" in films in Hollywood, 1935 ("English Type No 2008"); played bits and small parts; first starring rôle, Bachelor Mother, 1938, with Ginger Rogers. Returned to England at outbreak of War of 1939-45; rejoined Army; commissioned Rifle Brigade, later to Phantom Reconnaissance Regt; served Normandy, Belgium, Holland, Germany (usual campaign decorations, American Legion of Merit). Important films: Wuthering Heights, Dawn Patrol, Raffles, The First of the Few, The Way Ahead, A Matter of Life and Death, The Bishop's Wife, Bonnie Prince Charlie, The Elusive Pimpernel, Enchantment, Soldiers Three, Happy Go Lovely, The Moon is Blue, The Love Lottery, Happy Ever After, Carrington VC, Around the World in 80 Days, The Birds and the Bees, Silken Affair, The Little Hut, Oh, Men, Oh, Women, Bonjour Tristesse, My Man Godfrey, Separate Tables, Ask Any Girl, Please don't eat the Daisies, The Guns of Navarone, The Best of Enemies, Guns of Darkness, 55 Days at Peking, The Pink Panther, The King of the Mountain, Bedtime Story, Lady L., Where the Spies Are, Eye of the Devil, Casino Royale, Extraordinary Seaman, Prudence and the Pill, The Impossible Years, Before Winter Comes, The Brain, The Statue; King, Queen, Knave; Vampira, Paper Tiger, No Deposit No Return, Murder by Death, Candleshoe, Death on the Nile, Escape to Athena, A Man Called Intrepid, A Nightingale Sang in Berkeley Square, Rough Cut, Sea Wolves, Ménage à Trois, Trail of the Pink Panther, Curse of the Pink Panther. Formed Four Star Television, 1952, which has since produced over 2000 films for TV. Winner Academy Award, 1959; New York Critics' Award, 1960. *Publications:* Round the Rugged Rocks, 1951; The Moon's a Balloon (autobiog.), 1971; Bring on the Empty

Horses, 1975; Go Slowly, Come Back Quickly, 1981. *Recreations:* ski-ing, skin diving, oil painting. *Address:* c/o Coutts & Co., 440 Strand, WC2. *Club:* White's.

NIVEN, John Robertson, (Ian Niven); Under-Secretary, Department of the Environment, formerly Ministry of Housing and Local Government, 1974-79; *b* 11 May 1919; *s* of Robert Niven and Amelia Mary Hill; *m* 1946, Jane Bicknell; three *s. Educ:* Glasgow Academy; Jesus Coll., Oxford. Entered Min. of Town and Country Planning, 1946; Sec., Royal Commn on Local Govt in Greater London, 1957-60. *Address:* White Gates, Parham, Woodbridge, Suffolk.

NIVEN, Margaret Graeme, ROI 1936; Landscape and Portrait Painter; *b* Marlow, 1906; *yr d* of William Niven, FSA, ARE, JP, Marlow Place, Marlow, Bucks, and Eliza Mary Niven. *Educ:* Prior's Field, Godalming. Studied at Winchester Sch. of Art, Heatherley Sch. of Fine Art, and under Bernard Adams, RP, ROI; Mem. of National Soc. Painters, Sculptors, and Engravers, 1932. Exhibitor at Royal Academy and Royal Soc. of Portrait Painters. Works purchased by Bradford Art Gallery, The Ministry of Works, Homerton Coll., Cambridge, and Bedford Coll., London. Served with WRNS, 1940-45. *Address:* Broomhill, Sandhills, Wormley, near Godalming, Surrey.

NIVEN, Sir Rex; *see* Niven, Sir C. R.

NIVEN, Col Thomas Murray, CB 1964; TD 1941; FICE (retired); FIMechE (retired); *b* 20 Aug. 1900; *s* of Thomas Ogilvie Niven, Civil Engineer, Glasgow. *Educ:* Glasgow Academy; Glasgow Univ. Served War of 1939-45 with Royal Signals: comdg 52 (Lowland) Div. Signals, 1938-40; comdg Royal Signals Mobilisation Centre, 1941-43; Dep. Chief Signal Officer, Northern Command, 1944. Comdg 6 Glasgow Home Guard Bn, 1952-56; Hon. Col 52 (Lowland) Signal Regt (TA), 1950-66; Chm., Glasgow T & AFA, 1959-62. Formerly Dir of Mechans Ltd, Engineers, Scotstoun Iron Works, Glasgow. DL Glasgow, 1949-75. *Recreation:* walking. *Address:* c/o Barclays Bank, High Street, Guernsey. *Clubs:* Naval and Military; Royal Channel Islands Yacht (Guernsey).

NIVISON, family name of **Baron Glendyne.**

NIXON, Edwin Ronald, CBE 1974; Chairman and Chief Executive since 1979, and Managing Director since 1965, IBM United Kingdom Ltd; Managing Director since 1965: IBM United Kingdom Holdings Ltd; IBM United Kingdom Rentals Ltd; Chairman of IBM United Kingdom Laboratories Ltd, since 1965; Director, IBM Information Services Ltd, since 1967; *b* 21 June 1925; *s* of William Archdale Nixon and Ethel (*née* Corrigan); *m* 1952, Joan Lilian (*née* Hill); one *s* one *d. Educ:* Alderman Newton's Sch., Leicester; Selwyn Coll., Cambridge; MA. Dexion Ltd, 1950-55; IBM United Kingdom Ltd, 1955-; Director: National Westminster Bank PLC, 1975-; Royal Insurance PLC, 1980-. Mem. Council: Foundn for Automation and Employment, 1967-77; Electronic Engineering Assoc., 1965-76; CBI, 1971- (Chm. Standing Cttee on Marketing and Consumer Affairs to 1978; Mem., Cttee on Industrial Policy, 1978-); Foundn for Management Educn, 1973-; Member: British Cttee of Awards for Harkness Fellowships, 1976-82; Adv. Council, Business Graduates Assoc., 1976-; Board of Governors, United World Coll. of Atlantic, 1977-; Council: Manchester Business Sch., 1974- (Chm., 1979-); Westfield Coll., London, 1969- (Vice Chm., 1980-); William Temple Coll., Manchester, 1972-80; Oxford Centre for Management Studies, 1973-. Pres., Nat. Assoc. for Gifted Children, 1980-; Hon. Vice Pres., Inst. of Marketing, 1980-. Trustee: Royal Opera House, Covent Garden, 1980-; Monteverdi Choir and Orch., 1980-. *Recreations:* music, tennis, golf, sailing, ski-ing. *Address:* Starkes Heath, Rogate, Petersfield, Hants. *T:* Rogate 504. *Clubs:* Athenæum, Reform.

NIXON, Rear-Adm. Harry Desmond, CB 1973; MVO 1958; DL; *b* 6 May 1920; *s* of Harry Earle Nixon and Ethel Maude Nixon; *m* 1946, Elizabeth June Witherington; one *s* two *d. Educ:* Brigg. CEng, FIMechE. Joined RN as Cadet, 1938; RNEC, 1939-42; HMS: Suffolk, 1942; Indomitable, 1943-45; HM Dockyard, Malta, 1954-55; HM Yacht Britannia, 1956-58; Ship Dept, Admty, Bath, 1958-60; RNEC, 1960-62; Naval District Engr Overseer Midlands, 1962-64; CO, HMS Sultan, 1964-66; idc 1967; Dir of Fleet Maintenance, 1968-71. Comdr 1953; Captain 1962; Rear-Adm. 1971; Vice-Pres. (Naval), 1971-73, Pres., 1973-74, Ordnance Board. Mem., Public Inquiries Panel for Dept of Transport, 1974-82. Chm., 1974-77, Vice-Chm., 1977-79, Wilts Assocs of Boys' Clubs and Youth Clubs. DL Wilts 1978. *Address:* Ashley Cottage, Ashley, Box, Corsham, Wilts SN14 9AJ. *Club:* Army and Navy.

NIXON, Howard Millar, FSA; Librarian, Westminster Abbey, since 1974; *b* 3 Sept. 1909; *s* of Rev. Leigh H. Nixon, MVO, and Harrie (*née* Millar); *m* 1951, Enid Dorothy Bromley; three *s. Educ:* Marlborough; Keble Coll., Oxford. BA 1931; MA 1974. Served in Army, 1939-46 (Major, RA). Asst Cataloguer, Dept of Printed Books, British Museum, 1936; Asst Keeper, 1946, Dep. Keeper, 1959-74. Lectr in Bibliography, Sch. of Library Studies, University Coll., London, 1959-76; Sandars Reader in Bibliography, Univ. of Cambridge, 1967-68; Lyell Lecturer in Bibliography, Oxford, 1978-79. Pres., Bibliographical Soc., 1972-74. Editor, British Library Jl, 1974-77. Chm., Panel for allocation of Printed Books received in lieu of Death Duties, 1976-. Hon. Fellow: Keble Coll., Oxford; Pierpont Morgan Library, NY. Gold

Medal, Bibliographical Soc., 1978. Officier, Ordre de la Couronne (Belgium), 1979. *Publications:* Twelve Books in Fine Bindings, 1953; Broxbourne Library, 1956; Bookbindings from the Library of Jean Grolier, 1965; Sixteenth-century Gold-tooled Bookbindings in the Pierpont Morgan Library, 1971; English Restoration Bookbindings, 1974; Five Centuries of English Bookbinding, 1978; British Bookbindings presented by Kenneth H. Oldaker to the Chapter Library of Westminster Abbey, 1982; articles in The Library, Book Collector, etc. *Recreation:* golf. *Address:* 4A Little Cloister, Westminster Abbey, SW1P 3PL. *T:* 01-222 6428. *Club:* Grolier (New York).

NIXON, Rev. Sir Kenneth Michael John Basil, SJ; 4th Bt *cr* 1906; Teaching Member of the Jesuit Community at St George's College, Harare, since 1954; *b* 22 Feb. 1919; *s* of Sir Christopher William Nixon, 2nd Bt, DSO, and Louise (*d* 1949), *d* of Robert Clery, JP, The Glebe, Athlacca, Limerick; *S* brother, 1978. *Educ:* Beaumont College; Heythrop College, Oxon. Catholic priest and member of the Society of Jesus; ordained, 1952. *Recreation:* cricket. *Heir: b* Major Cecil Dominic Henry Joseph Nixon, MC [*b* 5 Feb. 1920; *m* 1953, Brenda, *d* of late Samuel Lycett Lewis and *widow* of Major M. F. McWhor; three *s* one *d*]. *Address:* St George's College, PB7727, Causeway, Zimbabwe. *T:* Harare 24650.

NIXON, Richard M.; President of the United States of America, 1969-74, resigned 10 Aug. 1974; *b* 9 Jan. 1913; *s* of Francis A. and Hannah Milhous Nixon; *m* 1940, Patricia Ryan; two *d. Educ:* Whittier Coll., Whittier, California (AB); Duke University Law Sch., Durham, North Carolina (LLB). Lawyer, Whittier, California, 1937-42; Office of Price Administration, 1942; Active duty, US Navy, 1942-46. Member 80th, 81st Congresses, 1947-50; US Senator from California, 1950-53. Vice-President of the USA, 1953-61; Republican candidate for the Presidency of the USA, 1960. Lawyer, Los Angeles, 1961-63, NY, 1963-68. Republican Candidate for Governor of California, 1962. Member: Board of Trustees, Whittier Coll., 1939-68; Society of Friends; Order of Coif. *Publications:* Six Crises, 1962; Memoirs, 1978; The Real War, 1980; Leaders, 1982. *Address:* 26 Federal Plaza, New York, NY 10278, USA.

NOAD, Sir Kenneth (Beeson), Kt 1970; Consulting Physician since 1931; Patron, Australian Postgraduate Federation in Medicine; *b* 25 March 1900; *s* of James Beeson and Mary Jane Noad; *m* 1935, Eileen Mary Ryan; no *c. Educ:* Maitland, NSW; Sydney University. MB, ChM 1924, MD 1953, Sydney; MRCP 1929; FRCP 1948; Foundn FRACP 1938 (PRACP 1962-64). Hon FACP 1964; Hon. FRCPE 1968. Served War of 1939-45, Palestine, Egypt, Greece, Crete, New Guinea; Lt-Col Comdr Medical Div. of an Australian General Hospital. Hon. DLitt and Hon. AM Singapore. *Publications:* papers in Brain, Med. Jl of Australia. *Recreations:* golf, gardening. *Address:* 22 Billyard Avenue, Elizabeth Bay, NSW 2011, Australia. *Clubs:* Australian (Sydney); Royal Sydney Golf.

NOAKES, Col Geoffrey William, OBE 1958; TD 1948; JP; DL; Past Managing Director, William Timpson Ltd, Footwear Retailers; Member, Industrial Tribunal, Manchester; *b* Manor House, Basingstoke, Hants, 19 Nov. 1913; *s* of Charles William Noakes; *m* 1936, Annie, *d* of Albert Hough, Peel Green; two *s* two *d. Educ:* Wyggeston Sch. Commissioned RA, 1936. Served War: in France, 1940; Burma, 1940-46 (despatches); Staff Coll., Quetta, 1944; AQMG, Fourteenth Army, 1944-45. In command 252 Field Regt RA, 1951-57; DCRA, 42 Div., 1957-62. Past Pres., Multiple Shoe Retailers' Assoc.; Past Pres. and Chm., Footwear Distributors' Fedn; Past Leader and Sec., Employer's side, Boot and Shoe Repairing Wages Council; Past Pres., Nat. Assoc. of Shoe Repair Factories. Past Chm., Publicity and Recruiting Cttee, and Vice-Chm., NW of England and IOM TAVR Assoc.; Pres., Burma Star Assoc., Altrincham; Past Mem., Bd of Examiners, Sch. of Business Studies, Manchester Polytechnic; Mem. Exec. Cttee, Manchester and Dist Boys' Clubs; Governor, Manchester Univ.; formerly Rep. Col Comdt, RA Uniformed Staff; Vice-Pres., Cholmondeley Cons. Assoc.; Chm., Border Castles Driving Club. JP Manchester, 1963; DL Lancs 1974. FBIM, FIWM, MIPM, ABSI. *Recreations:* hunting, shooting, fishing (Pres. Altrincham Angling Club), golf. *Address:* The Mill House, Bickley, near Malpas, Cheshire SY14 8EG. *T:* Hampton Heath 309. *Club:* Army and Navy.

See also P. R. Noakes.

NOAKES, Rt. Rev. George; *see* St Davids, Bishop of.

NOAKES, Michael, PPROI, RP; portrait and landscape painter; *b* 28 Oct. 1933; *s* of late Basil and of Mary Noakes; *m* 1960, Vivien Noakes (*née* Langley), writer; two *s* one *d. Educ:* Downside; Royal Academy Schs, London. Nat. Dipl. in Design, 1954; Certificate of Royal Academy Schools, 1960. Commnd: National Service, 1954-56. Has broadcast and appeared on TV on art subjects in UK and USA; Art Correspondent, BBC TV programme Town and Around, 1964-68; subject (with Eric Morley) of BBC film, Portrait, 1977, 1978. Member Council: ROI, 1964-78 (Vice-Pres. 1968-72; Pres., 1972-78; Hon. Mem. Council, 1978-); RP, 1969-71, 1972-74, 1978-80; NS, 1962-76 (Hon. Mem., 1976-); Chm., Contemp. Portrait Soc., 1971; Dir, Fedn of British Artists, 1981- (Governor, 1972-). *Exhibited:* Royal Acad.; Royal Inst. Oil Painters; Royal Soc. Portrait Painters; Contemp. Portrait Soc.; Nat. Society; Young Contemporaries, Grosvenor Galleries, Upper Grosvenor Galls, Woodstock Galls, Royal Glasgow Inst. of Fine Arts, Nat. Portrait Gall.; Roy. Soc. of British Artists; Grafton Gall.; New Grafton Galls; Art Exhibitions Bureau, touring widely in Britain, USA and Canada. Judge, Miss

World Contest, 1976. Platinum disc, 1977 (record sleeve design Portrait of Sinatra). *Portraits include:* The Queen (unveiled Silver Jubilee year, for Manchester; Queen's Lancs Regt); Queen Elizabeth The Queen Mother (as Chancellor, Univ. of London; as Patron, RADAR); Lord Aberconway; Lord Amory; Princess Anne (for Saddlers' Co.; Royal Signals); Princess Ashraf; Lord Benson; Lord Barnetson; Lord Boothby; Lady Boothby; Lord Bowden; Lord Boyd; FM Lord Carver; Lord Chuter-Ede; Lord Denning; Paul Dirac; Abbot of Downside; Lord Elwyn-Jones; Archbishop Lord Fisher; Lord Fulton; Sir Alec Guinness; Sir H. John Habakkuk; Gen. Sir John Hackett; Gilbert Harding; Robert Hardy; Sir Alan Hodgkin; Lord Iveagh; Sir Douglas Logan; Lord Selwyn-Lloyd; Cliff Michelmore; Eric Morley; Robert Morley; Malcolm Muggeridge; Sir Gerald Nabarro; Sir David Napley; Valerie Profumo; J. B. Priestley; Sir Ralph Richardson; Edmund de Rothschild; Archbishop Runcie; Dame Margaret Rutherford; Very Rev. M. Sullivan; Lord Todd; Sir Anthony Tuke; Dennis Wheatley; Sir Mortimer Wheeler; Lord Wolfenden; Sir Donald Wolfit; *major group portraits:* Royal Family, with Lord and Lady Mayoress, for Guildhall; Members and Officers, Metropolitan Water Board (47 figures); Lords of Appeal in Ordinary (for Middle Temple); Queen Elizabeth the Queen Mother opening Overlord Embroidery to public view, with Princess Alice, Lord Mountbatten, Duke of Norfolk, etc. *Represented in collections:* The Prince of Wales; British Mus.; Nat. Portrait Gall. (Hugill Fund Purchase, RA, 1972); numerous Oxford and Cambridge colleges; County Hall, Westminster; various livery companies and Inns of Court; House of Commons; Bradford Art Gall.; Univs of London, Nottingham, East Anglia; City Univ.; Frank Sinatra. *Publications:* A Professional Approach to Oil Painting, 1968; contributions to various art journals. *Recreation:* idling. *Address:* 146 Hamilton Terrace, St John's Wood, NW8 9UX. *T:* 01-328 6754.

NOAKES, Philip Reuben, OBE 1962; HM Diplomatic Service, retired; *b* 12 Aug. 1915; *y s* of late Charles William and Elizabeth Farey Noakes; *m* 1940, Moragh Jean Dickson; two *s. Educ:* Wyggeston Grammar Sch.; Wycliffe Coll.; Queens' Coll., Cambridge (Open Schol.). Mod. Langs Tripos Part I, Hist. Tripos Part II; BA 1937; MA 1945; Pres., Cambridge Union Soc., 1937. Served War, 1940-46; Capt.-Adjt 2nd Fife and Forfar Yeomanry, RAC (despatches). Public Relations Officer, Royal Over-Seas League, 1947-48; Sen. Information Officer, Colonial Office, 1948; Prin. Information Officer, CO, 1953; Information Adviser to Governor of Malta, 1960-61; Chief Information Officer, CO, 1963-66; Commonwealth Office, 1967; Counsellor (Information), Ottawa, 1967-72; Consul-Gen., Seattle, 1973-75. *Recreations:* bird-watching, fishing, ski-ing. *Address:* Eaton Hey, The Drive, Eaton Park, Cobham, Surrey. *Club:* Royal Over-Seas League.
See also G. W. Noakes.

NOAKES, His Honour Sidney Henry; a Circuit Judge (formerly County Court Judge), 1968-77; *b* 6 Jan. 1905; *s* of Thomas Frederick Noakes (Civil Servant) and Ada Noakes. *Educ:* Merchant Taylors' Sch.; St John's Coll., Oxford (MA). Called to Bar, Lincoln's Inn, 1928; SE Circuit; Bencher, 1963. War Service, Lt-Col., Intelligence Corps, England and NW Europe. Deputy Chairman: Surrey QS, 1963; Herts QS, 1964; Recorder of Margate, 1965-68. *Publication:* Fire Insurance, 1947. *Recreations:* regretfully now only walking and gardening. *Address:* 14 Meadway Crescent, Hove, E Sussex BN3 7NL. *T:* Brighton 736143.

NOBAY, Prof. (Avelino) Robert, PhD; Brunner Professor of Economic Science, University of Liverpool, since 1980; *b* 11 July 1942; *s* of Theodore Anastasio Nobay and Anna Gracia D'Silva; *m* 1965, Susan Clare Saunders; two *s. Educ:* Univ. of Leicester (BA); Univ. of Chicago (PhD Southampton. Jun. Economist, Electricity Council, London, 1964-66; Res. Officer, NIESR, 1966-70; Sen. Lectr, Univ. of Southampton, 1970-80. Vis. Associate Prof., Univ. of Chicago, 1977-79. *Publications:* (with H. G. Johnson) The Current Inflation; (with H. G. Johnson) Issues in Monetary Economics. *Recreations:* sailing, golf, music. *Address:* Springfield, 28 Knowsley Road, Cressington Park, Liverpool L19 0PG. *T:* 051-427 2093.

NOBES, (Charles) Patrick; Headmaster, Weymouth Grammar School, since 1981; *b* 17 March 1933; *o c* of Alderman Alfred Robert Nobes, OBE, JP, and Marguerite Violet Vivian (*née* Fathers), Gosport, Hants; *m* 1958, Patricia Jean (*née* Brand); three *s. Educ:* Price's Sch., Fareham, Hants; University Coll., Oxford. MA. With The Times, reporting and editorial, 1956-57; Head of English Dept, King Edward VI Grammar Sch., Bury St Edmunds, 1959-64; Head of English and General Studies and Sixth Form Master, Ashlyns Comprehensive Sch., Berkhamsted, 1964-69; Headmaster: The Ward Freman Sch., Buntingford, Herts, 1969-74; Bedales Sch., 1974-81. Chm., HMC Co-ed Schs Gp, 1976-80; Chm., Soc. of Headmasters of Independent Schs, 1978-80. General Editor and adapter, Bulls-Eye Books (series for adults and young adults with reading difficulties), 1972-. *Recreations:* cricket and hockey, King Arthur, Hampshire, music, First World War. *Address:* Weymouth Grammar School, Chickerell Road, Weymouth, Dorset DT4 9SY; 54 Coombe Valley Road, Preston, Weymouth, Dorset DT3 6NL. *Club:* Athenæum.

NOBLE, family name of **Baron Glenkinglas.**

NOBLE, Comdr Rt. Hon. Sir Allan (Herbert Percy), PC 1956; KCMG 1959; DSO 1943; DSC 1941; DL; a Member of Lloyd's; *b* 2 May 1908; *s* of late Admiral Sir Percy Noble, GBE, KCB, CVO, and Diamantina Campbell; *m* 1938, Barbara Janet Margaret, *o d* of late Brigadier Kenneth Gabbett. *Educ:* Radley College. Entered Royal Navy, 1927; ADC to Viceroy of India (Lord

Linlithgow), 1936-38; commanded HM Destroyers Newport, Fernie and Quentin, 1940-42; Commander, 1943. Attended Quebec and Yalta Conferences. Served War of 1939-45 (despatches, DSC, DSO); retired list, 1945. MP (C) for Chelsea, 1945-59, retired; Government Observer, Bikini Atomic Bomb Tests, 1946; PPS to Mr Anthony Eden, 1947-51; Parly and Financial Sec., Admiralty, 1951-55; Parly Under-Sec. of State for Commonwealth Relations, 1955-56; Minister of State for Foreign Affairs, 1956-59; Leader, UK Delegation: to UN Gen. Assembly, 1957-58; to UN Disarmament Sub-Cttee, 1957; Special Ambassador, Ivory Coast Independence, 1961; Mem., Adv. Cttee on Service Parly candidates, 1963-74. Dir and Chm., Tollemache & Cobbold Breweries Ltd, 1960-73; Dir, Colonial Mutual Life Assurance Soc. Ltd (UK Br.), 1960-76. Member Cttee of Management, Inst. of Cancer Research, Royal Cancer Hosp., 1959-67. President: Chelsea Cons. Assoc., 1962-66; Cambridgeshire Cons. Assoc., 1967-72; a Mem. of Radley Coll. Council, 1947-63; Chm., National Trainers' Assoc., 1963-66. Hon. Freeman: Chelsea, 1963; Royal Borough of Kensington and Chelsea, 1965. DL Suffolk, 1973. Inter Services Athletics (Hurdles), 1931. *Address:* Troston Cottage, Bury St Edmunds, Suffolk IP31 1EX. *T:* Honington 250. *Club:* White's.

NOBLE, Sir Andrew Napier, 2nd Bt, *cr* 1923; KCMG 1954 (CMG 1947); *b* 16 Sept. 1904; *s* of Sir John Henry Brunel Noble, 1st Bt, and Amie (*d* 1973), *d* of S. A. Walker Waters; *S* father, 1938; *m* 1934, Sigrid, 2nd *d* of M. Michelet, of Royal Norwegian Diplomatic Service; two *s* one *d. Educ:* Eton; Balliol Coll., Oxford. Counsellor of the British Embassy, Buenos Aires, 1945-47; Assistant Under-Secretary of State, Foreign Office, 1949; HM Minister at Helsinki, 1951-54; HM Ambassador: Warsaw, 1954-56; Mexico, 1956-60; Netherlands, 1960-64, retired. *Publications:* (jt author) Centenary History, OURFC, 1969; History of the Nobles of Ardmore and of Ardknglas, 1971. *Heir: s* Ian Andrew Noble, *b* 1935. *Address:* 11 Cedar House, Marloes Road, W8 5LA. *T:* 01-937 7952. *Club:* Boodle's.
See also Baron Glenkinglas.

NOBLE, Barrie Paul; HM Diplomatic Service; Counsellor, United Kingdom Mission to United Nations, Geneva, since 1980; *b* 17 Oct. 1938; *s* of late Major F. A. Noble and Mrs Henrietta Noble; *m* 1965, Alexandra Helene Giddings; one *s. Educ:* Hele's, Exeter; New Coll., Oxford (BA Jurisprudence); Univ. of Dakar. RAF, 1957-59. Joined HM Diplomatic Service, 1962; Third, later Second Sec., (Leopoldville) Kinshasa, 1965-67; Second Sec. (Commercial), Kaduna, 1967-69; FCO, 1969-72; First Sec., 1972-75 and Head of Chancery, 1975, Warsaw; FCO, 1976-80. *Publication:* Droit Coutumier, Annales Africaines, 1965. *Recreations:* grass cutting, bridge, skiing. *Address:* UK Mission to United Nations, 37-39 Rue de Vermont, 1211 Geneva 20, Switzerland; 147 Cambridge Street, SW1; South Leigh Manor, near Witney, Oxon. *Club:* Royal Air Force.

NOBLE, Dr Denis, FRS 1979; Fellow and Tutor in Physiology, Balliol College, Oxford and University Lecturer, since 1963; *b* 16 Nov. 1936; *s* of George and Ethel Noble; *m* 1965, Susan Jennifer Barfield; one *s* one *d. Educ:* Emanuel Sch., London; University Coll. London (BSc, MA, PhD). Asst Lectr, UCL, 1961-63; Vis. Prof., Alberta, 1969-70. Editor, Progress in Biophysics, 1967-. Praefectus of Holywell Manor (Balliol/St Anne's Graduate Centre), 1971-. Hon. Sec., Physiol Soc., 1974-80. Darwin Lectr, British Assoc., 1966; Nahum Lectr, Yale, 1977. Scientific Medal, Zoolog. Soc., 1970. *Publications:* Initiation of the Heartbeat, 1975, 2nd edn, 1979; Electric Current Flow in Excitable Cells, 1975; papers mostly in Jl of Physiology. *Recreations:* Indian and French cooking, Occitan. *Address:* Holywell Manor, Manor Road, Oxford OX1 3UH. *T:* Oxford 48738.

NOBLE, Sir Fraser; *see* Noble, Sir T. A. F.

NOBLE, Kenneth Albert, CBE 1975; Member, Price Commission, 1973-77 (Deputy Chairman, 1973-76); Director, 1954-73, Vice-Chairman, 1966-73, Co-operative Wholesale Society Ltd; Director of associated organisations and subsidiaries. Member: CoID, 1957-65; Post Office Users Nat. Council, 1965-73; Monopolies Commn, 1969-73; London VAT Tribunals Panel, 1977-. Served War, 1940-46 (despatches); Major RASC. *Publication:* (jtly) Financial Management Handbook, 1977, new edn 1980. *Address:* Flat 1, York Mansions, Kings Parade, Holland-on-Sea, near Clacton-on-Sea, Essex CO15 5JP.

NOBLE, Major Sir Marc (Brunel), 5th Bt, *cr* 1902; *b* 8 Jan. 1927; *er s* of Sir Humphrey Brunel Noble, 4th Bt, MBE, MC, and Celia (*d* 1982), *d* of late Captain Stewart Weigall, RN; *S* father, 1968; *m* 1956, Jennifer Lorna, *yr d* of late John Mein-Austin, Flint Hill, West Haddon, Northants; two *s* one *d* (and one *d* decd). *Educ:* Eton. Commissioned into King's Dragoon Guards as 2nd Lieut, 1947; on amalgamation, transferred Royal Dragoons, 1958. Training Major and Adjutant, Kent and County of London Yeomanry (Sharpshooters), 1963-64; retired 1966. Commonwealth Comr, 1972, Chm., Cttee of Council, 1979-80, Scout Assoc. *Heir: er s* David Brunel Noble, *b* 25 Dec. 1961. *Address:* Deerleap House, Knockholt, Sevenoaks, Kent TN14 7NP. *T:* Knockholt 33222. *Club:* Cavalry and Guards.

NOBLE, Michael Alfred, (Mike); *b* 10 March 1935; *s* of Alfred and Olive Noble; *m* 1956, Brenda Kathleen Peak; one *s* two *d. Educ:* Hull Grammar Sch.; Sheffield Univ. (BA); Hull Univ. (DipEd). Secondary Sch. Teacher, Hull, 1959-63; WEA Tutor in Industrial Relations, 1963-73; Consultant in Industrial Relations and Trng, 1973-74. MP (Lab) Rossendale, Oct. 1974-1979; PPS to Sec. for Prices and Consumer Protection, 1976-79. *Recreations:*

golf, fishing, reading. *Address:* 10 Kingsway, Hapton, Burnley, Lancs. *T:* Padiham 74416. *Club:* Workingmen's (Ramsbottom).

NOBLE, Sir Peter (Scott), Kt 1967; Principal of King's College, University of London, 1952-July 1968; *b* 17 Oct. 1899; *s* of Andrew Noble and Margaret Trail; *m* 1928, Mary Stephen; two *s* one *d. Educ:* Aberdeen Univ.; St John's Coll., Cambridge. First Bursar at Aberdeen Univ., 1916, MA, with 1st Class Honours in Classics 1921, Simpson Prize and Robbie Gold Medal in Greek, Seafield Medal and Dr Black prize in Latin, Jenkyns Prize in Comparative Philology, Liddell Prize in Greek Verse, Fullerton Scholarship in Classics, 1921, Croom Robertson Fellow (1923-26); Scholar of St John's Coll., Cambridge; 1st class Classical Tripos Part I (1922) Part II (1923), 1st Class Oriental Langs Tripos Part I (1924) Part II (1925), Bendall Sanskrit Exhibition (1924), (1925), Hutchison Student (1925); Lecturer in Latin at Liverpool Univ., 1926-30; Professor of Latin Language and Literature in the University of Leeds, 1930-37; Fellow of St John's Coll., Cambridge, 1928-31; Regius Professor of Humanity, University of Aberdeen, 1938-52; Member of University Grants Cttee, 1943-53; Vice-Chancellor, University of London, 1961-64; Member of General Dental Council, 1955; Member of Educational Trust, English-Speaking Union, 1958; Governor of St Thomas' Hospital, 1960. Hon. LLD Aberdeen, 1955. *Publications:* Joint editor of Kharosthi Inscriptions Vol. III; reviews, etc, classical journals. *Address:* 17 Glenorchy Terrace, Edinburgh EH9 2DG.

NOBLE, Robert More Hilary; a Recorder of the Crown Court since 1972; Chairman: National Health Service Tribunal for England and Wales, since 1970; West Sussex Supplementary Benefits Appeal Tribunal, since 1970; Industrial Tribunals, since 1975 (part-time); *b* 23 Aug. 1909; *s* of late Mr Justice Noble, KCSG, Colonial Legal Service, and of late Mrs Robert Noble; *m* 1936, Faith (*née* Varley); two *s* three *d* (and one *d* decd). *Educ:* Beaumont Coll.; Balliol Coll. (BA Hons). Admitted Solicitor, 1934. Served War, 1939-45: Commissioned RAFVR, Air Force Dept of Judge Advocate General's Office, France and Middle East, also Accidents Investigation Br., 1940-41, ranks Sqdn Ldr, Actg Wing Comdr. Partner: Underwood & Co., 1946-59, Vernor Miles & Noble, 1959-70 (both of London). Trustee of a number of Charitable Trusts (concerned with educn and the disabled); Chm., Possum Controls Ltd. *Address:* 14 East Street, Lewes, Sussex BN7 2LJ. *Club:* Oriental.

NOBLE, Sir (Thomas Alexander) Fraser, Kt 1971; MBE 1947; Principal and Vice-Chancellor, University of Aberdeen, 1976-81; *b* 29 April 1918; *s* of late Simon Noble, Grantown-on-Spey and Jeanie Graham, Largs, Ayrshire; *m* 1945, Barbara A. M. Sinclair, Nairn; one *s* one *d. Educ:* Nairn Acad; Univ. of Aberdeen. After military service with Black Watch (RHR), entered Indian Civil Service, 1940. Served in NW Frontier Province, 1941-47, successively as Asst Comr, Hazara; Asst Polit. Agent, N Waziristan; Controller of Rationing, Peshawar; Under-Sec., Food Dept and Develt Dept; Sec., Home Dept; Joint Dep. Comr, Peshawar; Civil Aide to Referendum Comr. Lectr in Political Economy, Univ. of Aberdeen, 1948-57; Sec. and Treas., Carnegie Trust for Univs of Scotland, 1957-62; Vice-Chancellor, Leicester Univ., 1962-76. Mem. and Vice-Chm., Bd of Management, Aberdeen Mental Hosp. Group, 1953-57. Sec., Scottish Economic Soc., 1954-58; Vice-Pres., 1962-. Chm., Scottish Standing Conf. of Voluntary Youth Organisations, 1958-62; Vice-Chm., Standing Consultative Council on Youth Service in Scotland, 1959-62. Mem., Departmental Cttee on Probation Service, 1959-62; Chairman: Probation Advisory and Training Board, 1962-65; Television Research Cttee, 1963-69; Advisory Council on Probation and After-Care, 1965-70; Univs Council for Adult Education, 1965-69; Min. of Defence Cttee for Univ. Assistance to Adult Educn in HM Forces, 1965-70; Advisory Board, Overseas Students' Special Fund, 1967-71, Fees Awards Scheme, 1968-75; Cttee of Vice-Chancellors and Principals of Univs of UK, 1970-72; British Council Cttee on Exchanges between UK and USSR, 1973-78; Scottish Council for Community Educn, 1979-80. Member: Academic Advisory Cttee, Univs of St Andrews and Dundee, 1964-66; E Midlands Economic Planning Council, 1965-68; Council, Assoc. Commonwealth Univs, 1970-79; Exec. Cttee, Inter-Univ. Council for Higher Educn Overseas, 1972-79; Exec. Cttee, British Council, 1973-79; British Council Cttee for Commonwealth Univ. Interchange, 1973-79; US-UK Educnl Commn, 1973-76. Hon. LLD: Aberdeen, 1968; Leicester, 1976; Glasgow, 1981; Washington Coll., 1981. *Publications:* articles in economic journals and on education. *Recreation:* golf. *Address:* Hedgerley, Victoria Street, Nairn. *Clubs:* Athenæum; Royal Northern and University (Aberdeen); Royal Aberdeen Golf, Nairn Golf.

NOCK, Rt. Rev. Frank Foley; *see* Algoma, Bishop of.

NOCK, Sir Norman (Lindfield), Kt 1939; Director, Nock & Kirby Holdings Ltd, Sydney (Chairman, 1926-79); *s* of Thomas Nock, Stanhope Road, Killara, Sydney; *m* 1927, Ethel Evelina Bradford; one *s. Educ:* Sydney Church of England Grammar Sch. Alderman for Gipps Ward, City of Sydney, 1933-41; Lord Mayor of Sydney, 1938-39; Chairman, Federal Australian Comforts Fund, 1939-43; Chairman, Australian Comforts Fund, NSW Division, 1939-45; President of the National Roads and Motorists Association, 1954-69; Chairman Royal North Shore Hospital of Sydney, 1940-69; Member National Health and Medical Research Council, 1946-69. JP for New South Wales. *Recreations:* golf, sailing and motoring. *Address:* Box 4250, GPO Sydney, NSW 2001, Australia. *Club:* Royal Sydney Golf (Sydney).

NOCKOLDS, Stephen Robert, FRS 1959; PhD; Reader in Geochemistry in the University of Cambridge, 1957-72, now Emeritus Reader; *b* 10 May 1909; *s* of Dr Stephen and Hilda May Nockolds; *m* 1st, 1932, Hilda Jackson (*d* 1976); 2nd, 1978, Patricia, *d* of late Flying Officer F. Horsley; one step *s* two step *d. Educ:* Felsted; University of Manchester (BSc); University of Cambridge (PhD). Fellow of Trinity Coll. and formerly Lectr in Petrology, Univ. of Cambridge. Murchison Medal, Geol Soc., 1972. Hon. Fellow, Geol. Soc. of India. *Publications:* (jtly) Petrology for Students, 1978; various papers in mineralogical and geological journals. *Recreation:* gardening. *Address:* Elm Lodge, Station Road, Keyingham, North Humberside HU12 9TB.

NODDER, Timothy Edward, CB 1982; Deputy Secretary, Department of Health and Social Security, since 1978; *b* 18 June 1930; *s* of Edward Nodder. *Educ:* St Paul's Sch.; Christ's Coll., Cambridge. Under-Sec., DHSS, 1972. *Recreation:* natural history. *Address:* 10 Frognal Lane, NW3.

NOEL, family name of **Earl of Gainsborough.**

NOËL, Sir Claude; *see* Noël, Sir M. E. C.

NOEL, Rear-Adm. Gambier John Byng, CB 1969; retired; *b* 16 July 1914; *s* of late G. B. E. Noel; *m* 1936, Miss Joan Stevens; four *d. Educ:* Royal Naval Coll., Dartmouth. Joined Royal Navy, 1931; Served in War of 1939-45, HMS Aurora and HMS Norfolk (despatches twice). Captain 1959; Imperial Defence Coll., 1962; Staff of Commander Far East Fleet, 1964-67; Rear-Admiral 1967; Chief Staff Officer (Technical) to C-in-C, Western Fleet, 1967-69. *Recreations:* gardening, golf. *Address:* Woodpeckers, Church Lane, Haslemere, Surrey. *T:* Haslemere 3824. *Club:* Anglo-Belgian.

NOEL, Major Geoffrey Lindsay James; Metropolitan Stipendiary Magistrate, since 1975; Deputy Circuit Judge, since 1980; *b* 19 April 1923; *s* of Major James Noel and Maud Noel; *m* 1st, 1947; two *d* ; 2nd, 1966, Eileen Pickering (*née* Cooper); two step *s. Educ:* Crewkerne Sch., Somerset. Enlisted Royal Regt of Artillery, 1941; commnd, 1942; attached 9th Para Bn, 6 Airborne Div., 1944, Captain; regular commnn, 1946; Major 1957; retd 1960. Called to Bar, Middle Temple, 1962; practised London and SE circuit. Chm., Juvenile Courts, 1977-79. *Recreation:* gardening. *Address:* Patchings, Henfield, Sussex. *T:* Henfield 492098.

NOEL, Hon. Gerard Eyre Wriothesley; author, publisher and journalist; Editor, Catholic Herald, 1971-76 and since 1982; *b* 20 Nov. 1926; *s* of 4th Earl of Gainsborough, OBE, TD, and Alice (*née* Eyre); *m* 1958, Adele Julie Patricia, *d* of Major V. N. B. Were; two *s* one *d. Educ:* Georgetown, USA; Exeter Coll., Oxford (MA, Modern History). Called to Bar, Inner Temple, 1952. Dir, Herder Book Co., 1959-66; Chm., Sands & Co. (Publishers) Ltd, 1967-; Dir, Search Press Ltd, 1972-. Literary Editor, Catholic Times, 1958-61; Catholic Herald: Asst Editor, 1968; Editorial Dir, 1976-81. Mem. Exec. Cttee, 1974-, Hon. Treasurer, 1979-81, Council of Christians and Jews. Contested (L) Argyll, 1959. Liveryman, Co. of Stationers and Newspapermakers. Freeman, City of London. *Publications:* Paul VI, 1963; Harold Wilson, 1964; Goldwater, 1964; The New Britain, 1966; The Path from Rome, 1968; Princess Alice: Queen Victoria's Forgotten Daughter, 1974; contrib. The Prime Ministers, 1974; The Great Lock-Out of 1926, 1976; The Anatomy of the Roman Catholic Church, 1980; Ena, Spain's English Queen, 1983; *translations:* The Way to Unity after the Council, 1967; The Holy See and the War in Europe (Official Documents), 1968; articles in: Church Times, Catholic Times, Jewish Chronicle, Baptist Times, Catholic Herald, Universe. *Recreations:* walking, travel, exploring London. *Address:* 105 Cadogan Gardens, SW3. *T:* 01-730 8734; Westington Mill, Chipping Campden, Glos. *T:* Evesham 840240. *Clubs:* Beefsteak, Garrick.

NOËL, Sir (Martial Ernest) Claude, Kt 1976; CMG 1973; Director and Chairman of sugar and other companies; *b* 1 Feb. 1912; *m* 1937, Hélène Fromet de Rosnay; three *s* three *d. Educ:* College du St Esprit, Mauritius. Maths teacher, 1930; joined sugar industry, 1931; Manager sugar estate, 1939-. Chairman: Central Cttee of Estate Managers on several occasions; Mauritius Sugar Producers; Mauritius Employers Fedn, 1962-63. Membre d'Honneur, Mauritius Chamber of Agriculture, 1980 (Chm., 1971-72, Pres., 1974-). Citoyen d'Honneur Escalier Village. *Address:* Floréal, Mauritius. *T:* Curepipe 2235. *Clubs:* Dodo, Mauritius Turf (Mauritius).

NOEL-BAKER, Hon. Francis Edward; Director: North Euboean Enterprises Ltd, since 1973; Fini Fisheries, Cyprus, since 1976; *b* 7 Jan. 1920; *o s* of late Baron Noel-Baker, PC, and late Irene, *o d* of Frank Noel, British landowner, of Achmetaga, Greece; *m* 1957, Barbara Christina, *yr d* of late Joseph Sonander, Sweden; four *s* one *d. Educ:* Westminster Sch.; King's Coll., Cambridge (Exhibitioner). Founder and Chm., CU Lab. Club, 1939; left Cambridge to join Army, summer 1940, as Trooper, Royal Tank Regt; Commissioned in Intelligence Corps and served in UK, Force 133, Middle East (despatches); returned to fight Brentford and Chiswick Div.; MP (Lab) Brentford and Chiswick Div. of Mddx, 1945-50; Editor, United Nations World/World Horizon, 1945-47, Go! magazine, 1947-48; PPS Admiralty, 1949-50; BBC European Service, 1950-54; MP (Lab) Swindon, 1955-69, resigned from Labour Party, 1969; Sec., 1955-64, Chm., 1964-68, UN Parly Cttee; Vice-Chm., Lab. Cttee for Europe, 1976-78; Member: SDP 1981-; NUJ, 1946-81. Chm., Advertising Inquiry Council, 1951-68. Chm., North Euboean Foundation Ltd; Hon. Pres., Union of Forest Owners of Greece, 1968-. Member: Parochial Church Council, St Martin in the Fields, 1960-68;

Freedom from Hunger Campaign UK Cttee Exec. Cttee, 1961; Ecology Party, 1978–; Soil Assoc., 1979–. Governor, Campion Sch., Athens, 1973–78. *Publications:* Greece, the Whole Story, 1946; Spanish Summary, 1948; The Spy Web, 1954; Land and People of Greece, 1957; Nansen, 1958; Looking at Greece, 1967. *Recreation:* gardening. *Address:* Sisini 13, Athens 612, Greece. *Telex:* 214716; Achmetaga Estate, Prokopion, Euboea, Greece. *T:* 0227 41204; (office) 10 Drayton Gardens, SW10. *T:* 01-373 6345. *London Telex:* 917506. *Clubs:* Special Forces; Athens.

NOEL-BUXTON, family name of **Baron Noel-Buxton.**

NOEL-BUXTON, 3rd Baron *cr* 1930; **Martin Connal Noel-Buxton;** Partner, Speechly Bircham, Solicitors; *b* 8 Dec. 1940; *s* of 2nd Baron Noel-Buxton and Helen Nancy (*d* 1949), *yr d* of late Col K. H. M. Connal, CB, OBE, TD; *S* father, 1980; *m* 1st, 1964, Miranda Mary (marr. diss. 1968), *er d* of H. A. Chisenhale-Marsh; 2nd, 1972, Sarah Margaret Surridge (marr. diss. 1982), *o d* of N. C. W. Barrett, TD; one *s* one *d. Educ:* Bryanston School; Balliol College, Oxford (MA). Admitted a Solicitor, 1966. *Heir: s* Hon. Charles Connal Noel-Buxton, *b* 17 April 1975. *Address:* Speechly Bircham, Bouverie House, 154 Fleet Street, EC4A 2HX. *T:* 01-353 3290.

NOEL-PATON, family name of **Baron Ferrier.**

NOGUEIRA, Albano Pires Fernandes; Ambassador of Portugal; *b* 8 Nov. 1911; *m* 1937, Alda Maria Marques Xavier da Cunha. *Educ:* Univ. of Coimbra. 3rd Sec., Washington, 1944; 2nd Sec., Pretoria, 1945; 1st Sec., Pretoria, 1948; Head of Mission, Pretoria, 1950; Counsellor, London, 1953; Consul-Gen., Bombay, 1955; Consul-Gen., NY, 1955; Asst Perm. Rep. UN, NY, 1955; Asst Dir-Gen., Econ. Affairs, Lisbon, 1959; Dir Gen., Econ. Affairs, Lisbon, 1961; Ambassador to: European Communities, Brussels, 1964; NATO, 1970; Court of St James's, 1974–76; Sec.-Gen., Ministry for Foreign Affairs, 1977. Vis. Prof., Univ. of Minho, Braga, 1979, 1980. Grand Cross: Merito Civil (Spain), 1961; Order of Infante Don Henrique (Portugal), 1963; Isabel la Católica (Spain), 1977; Merit (Germany), 1977; St Olav (Norway), 1978; Christ (Portugal), 1981; the Flag with golden palm (Yugoslavia), 1978; Grand Officer: Cruzeiro do Sul (Brazil), 1959; White Elephant (Thailand), 1960. *Publications:* Imagens em espelho Côncavo (essays); Portugal na Arte Japonesa (essay); Uma Agulha no Céu (novel); contrib. leading Portuguese papers and reviews. *Recreations:* reading, writing. *Address:* 18 Avenue Gaspar Corte-Real, 18, Apt 4D, 2750 Cascais, Portugal. *T:* 2868264; 5 Rua Alberto de Oliveira, 5-3, 3000 Coimbra, Portugal. *T:* 75035. *Clubs:* Grémio Literário, Automóvel de Portugal (Lisbon).

NOLAN, Brig. Eileen Joan, CB 1976; Director, Women's Royal Army Corps, 1973–77; *b* 19 June 1920; *d* of late James John and Ethel Mary Nolan. *Educ:* King's Norton Grammar Sch. for Girls. Joined ATS, Nov. 1942; commissioned, 1945. Lt-Col, 1967; Col, 1970; Brig., 1973. Hon. ADC to the Queen, 1973–77; Chm., NATO Senior Women Officers' Cttee, 1975–77; Dep. Controller Comdt, WRAC, 1977–. *Address:* 34 The Brambles, Lower Wokingham Road, Crowthorne, Berks. *T:* Crowthorne 6584.

NOLAN, Michael Patrick, QC 1968; QC (NI) 1974; a Recorder of the Crown Court, since 1975; *b* 10 Sept. 1928; *yr s* of James Thomas Nolan and Jane (*née* Walsh); *m* 1953, Margaret, *yr d* of Alfred Noyes, CBE, and Mary (*née* Mayne); one *s* four *d. Educ:* Ampleforth; Wadham Coll., Oxford. Served RA, 1947–49; TA, 1949–55. Called to Bar, Middle Temple, 1953; Bencher, 1975. Member: Bar Council, 1973–74; Senate of Inns of Court and Bar, 1974–81 (Treasurer, 1977–79); called to Bar, NI, 1974. Mem., Sandilands Cttee on Inflation Accounting, 1973–75. Mem. Governing Body, Convent of the Sacred Heart, Woldingham, 1973–; Governor, Combe Bank Sch., 1974–. *Recreations:* fishing, shooting. *Address:* Tanners, Brasted, Westerham, Kent. *T:* Westerham 63758. *Club:* MCC.

NOLAN, Sir Sidney (Robert), Kt 1981; CBE 1963; artist; *b* Melbourne, 22 April 1917; *s* of late Sidney Henry Nolan; *m* 1939, Elizabeth Patterson (marr. diss. 1942); *m* 1948, Cynthia Hansen (*d* 1974). *Educ:* State and technical schools, Melbourne; National Art Gallery Sch., Victoria. Italian Government Scholar, 1956; Commonwealth Fund Fellow, to USA, 1958; Fellow: ANU, 1965 (Hon. LLD, 1968); York Univ., 1971; Bavarian Academy, 1971. Hon. DLit London, 1971. Exhibited: Paris, 1948, 1961; New Delhi, 1953; Pittsburgh International, 1953, 1954, 1955, 1964, 1967, 1970; Venice Biennale, 1954; Rome, 1954; Pacific Loan Exhibition, 1956; Brussels International Exhibition, 1958; Documenta II, Kassel, 1959; Retrospective, Art Gallery of New South Wales, Sydney, 1967; Retrospective, Darmstadt, 1971; Ashmolean Museum, Oxford, 1971; Retrospective, Royal Dublin Soc., 1973. Exhibits Tate Gallery, Marlborough New London Gallery, Marlborough Gallery, New York. Ballet Designs for Icare, Sydney, 1941; Orphée (Cocteau), Sydney, 1948; The Guide, Oxford, 1961; Rite of Spring, Covent Garden, 1962; The Display, Adelaide Festival, 1964; opera designs for Samson et Delilah, Covent Garden, 1981. Works in Tate Gallery, Museum of Modern Art, New York, Australian national galleries, Contemporary Art Society and Arts Council of Great Britain, etc. *Publication:* Paradise Garden (poems, drawings and paintings), 1972; *Illustrated:* Near the Ocean, by Robert Lowell, 1966; The Voyage, by Baudelaire, trans. Lowell, 1968; Children's Crusade, by Benjamin Britten, 1973; *Relevant publications:* Kenneth Clark, Colin MacInnes, Bryan Robertson: Nolan, 1961; Robert Melville: Ned Kelly, 1964; Elwyn Lynn: Sydney Nolan: Myth and Imagery, 1967; Melville and Lynn: The Darkening Ecliptic: Ern Malley Poems, Sidney Nolan Paintings, 1974; Cynthia Nolan:

Open Negative, 1967; Sight of China, 1969; Paradise, and yet, 1971. *Address:* c/o Marlborough Fine Art Ltd, 6 Albemarle Street, W1. *Club:* Athenæum.

NONWEILER, Prof. Terence Reginald Forbes, BSc; PhD; CEng; FRAeS; FIMA; Professor of Mathematics, Victoria University of Wellington, since 1975; *b* 8 Feb. 1925; *s* of Ernest James Nonweiler and Lilian Violet Amalie Nonweiler (*née* Holfert); *m* 1949, Patricia Hilda Frances (*née* Neame); four *s* two *d. Educ:* Bethany Sch., Goudhurst, Kent; University of Manchester, BSc 1944, PhD 1960. Scientific Officer, Royal Aircraft Establishment, Farnborough, Hants, 1944–50; Scientific Officer, Scientific Advisor's Dept, Air Ministry, 1950–51; Senior Lecturer in Aerodynamics, College of Aeronautics, Cranfield, Beds, 1951–57; Senior Lecturer in Aeronautical Engineering, The Queen's Univ. of Belfast, 1957–61; Mechan Prof. of Aeronautics and Fluid Mechanics, Glasgow Univ., 1961–75. Consultant: to Admiralty, 1951; to Ministry of Aviation, 1959; to Ministry of Agriculture, 1966; to Wellington City Corp., 1977. Member, International Academy of Astronautics. *Publications:* Jets and Rockets, 1959; numerous technical papers on aeronautics, space flight, and submarine motion. *Recreations:* acting and stage production. *Address:* Victoria University, Private Bag, Wellington, New Zealand.

NORBURY, 6th Earl of, *cr* 1827; **Noel Terence Graham-Toler;** Baron Norwood, 1797; Baron Norbury, 1800; Viscount Glandine, 1827; *b* 1 Jan. 1939; *s* of 5th Earl and Margaret Greenhalgh; *S* father 1955; *m* 1965, Anne Mathew; one *s* one *d. Heir: s* Viscount Glandine, *qv. Address:* Stock Exchange, EC2.

NORBURY, Brian Martin; Assistant Under Secretary of State (Ordnance), Ministry of Defence, since 1981; *b* 2 March 1938; *s* of Robert Sidney Norbury and Doris Lilian (*née* Broughton). *Educ:* Churcher's Coll., Petersfield; King's Coll., London (BA; AKC 1959). National Service, RAEC, 1959–61. Asst Principal, WO, 1961; Private Sec. to Under Sec. of State for War, 1962; Asst Private Sec. to Dep. Sec. of State for Defence, 1964; Principal, MoD, 1965, Cabinet Office, 1969; Private Sec. to Sec. of the Cabinet, 1970–73; Asst Sec., MoD, 1973; Private Sec. to Sec. of State for Def., 1979–81; Under Sec., 1981. *Address:* c/o Ministry of Defence, Main Building, Whitehall, SW1. *Club:* Reform.

NORCROSS, Lawrence John Charles; Headmaster, Highbury Grove School, since 1975; *b* 14 April 1927; *s* of Frederick Marshall Norcross and Florence Kate (*née* Hedges); *m* 1958, Margaret Wallace; three *s* one *d. Educ:* Ruskin Coll., Oxford; Univ. of Leeds (BA Hons English). Training Ship, Arethusa, 1941–42; RN, 1942–49 (E Indies Fleet, 1944–45); clerical asst, 1949–52; Asst Teacher: Singlegate Sch., 1957–61; Abbey Wood Sch., 1961–63; Housemaster, Battersea County Sch., 1963–74; Dep. Headmaster, Highbury Grove Sch., 1974–75. Member: Secondary Heads' Assoc.; NAS/UWT; Exec. Cttee, Nat. Council for Educnl Standards; Educn Study Gp, Centre for Policy Studies; Univ. Entrance and Schs Examinations Council, Univ. of London; Steering Cttee, Campaign for a Gen. Teaching Council. Founder and Hon. Sec., John Ireland Soc.; former Chm., Contemp. Concerts Co-ordination. Occasional broadcasts and television appearances. *Publications:* occasional articles. *Recreations:* talking to friends, playing bridge badly, watching cricket, listening to music. *Address:* 17 Devereux Road, SW11 6JR. *T:* 01-228 8478. *Club:* Surrey County Cricket.

NORDEN, Denis, CBE 1980; scriptwriter and broadcaster; *b* 6 Feb. 1922; *s* of George Norden and Jenny Lubell; *m* 1943, Avril Rosen; one *s* one *d. Educ:* Craven Park Sch., London; City of London Sch. Theatre Manager, 1939–42; served RAF, 1942–45; staff-writer in Variety Agency, 1945–47. With Frank Muir, 1947–64: collaborated for 17 years writing comedy scripts, including: (for radio): Take it from Here, 1947–58; Bedtime with Braden, 1950–54; (for TV): Whack-O!, 1958–60; The Seven Faces of Jim, 1961, and other series with Jimmy Edwards; resident in TV and radio panel-games; collaborated in film scripts, television commercials, and revues; joint Advisors and Consultants to BBC Television Light Entertainment Dept, 1960–64; jointly received Screenwriters Guild Award for Best Contribution to Light Entertainment, 1961; together on panel-games My Word!, 1956–, and My Music, 1967–. Since 1964, solo writer for television and films; Chm., Looks Familiar (Thames TV), 1973–; It'll Be Alright on the Night (LWT), 1977, 1979, 1980. Film Credits include: The Bliss of Mrs Blossom; Buona Sera, Mrs Campbell; The Best House in London; Every Home Should Have One; Twelve Plus One; The Statue; The Water Babies. Variety Club of GB Award for Best Radio Personality (with Frank Muir), 1978; Male TV Personality of the Year, 1980. *Publications:* (with Frank Muir): You Can't Have Your Kayak and Heat It, 1973; Upon My Word!, 1974; Take My Word for It, 1978; The Glums, 1979; Oh, My Word!, 1980. *Recreations:* reading, loitering. *Address:* 8/20 Short's Gardens, WC2H 9AU. *Club:* Saturday Morning Odeon.

NORDMEYER, Hon. Sir Arnold (Henry), KCMG 1975 (CMG 1970); JP; Leader of the Opposition (Labour), New Zealand, 1963–65; *b* Dunedin, New Zealand, 7 Feb. 1901; *s* of Arnold and Martha Nordmeyer; *m* 1931, Frances Maria Kernahan; one *s* one *d. Educ:* Waitaki Boys' High Sch.; Otago Univ. (BA, DipSocSci.). Presbyterian Minister for 10 years. Entered New Zealand Parliament, 1935; MP for Oamaru, 1935–49, for Brooklyn, 1951–54, for Island Bay, 1954–69; Minister of: Health, 1941–47; Industries and Commerce, 1947–49; Finance, 1957–60. JP 1970. Hon. LLD Otago, 1970. *Recreations:* shooting, fishing. *Address:* 53 Milne Terrace, Wellington, New Zealand.

NORFOLK, 17th Duke of, *cr* 1483; **Miles Francis Stapleton Fitzalan-Howard**, CB 1966; CBE 1960; MC 1944; DL; Earl of Arundel, 1139; Baron Beaumont, 1309; Baron Maltravers, 1330, Earl of Surrey, 1483; Baron FitzAlan, Clun, and Oswaldestre, 1627; Earl of Norfolk, 1644; Baron Howard of Glossop, 1869; Earl Marshal and Hereditary Marshal and Chief Butler of England; Premier Duke and Earl; a Director of Robert Fleming Holdings Ltd, since 1969; *b* 21 July 1915; *s* of 3rd Baron Howard of Glossop, MBE, and Baroness Beaumont (11th in line), OBE; *S* to barony of mother, 1971, and of father, 1972, and to dukedom of cousin, 1975; *m* 1949, Anne Mary Teresa, *e d* of late Wing Commander Gerald Joseph Constable Maxwell, MC, DFC, AFC; two *s* three *d*. *Educ:* Ampleforth Coll.; Christ Church, Oxford (MA). 2nd Lieut, Grenadier Guards, 1937. Served War of 1939-45, France, North Africa, Sicily, Italy (despatches, MC), NW Europe. Appointed Head of British Military Mission to Russian Forces in Germany, 1957; Commanded 70 Bde KAR, 1961-63; GOC, 1 Div., 1963-65 (Maj.-Gen.); Dir, Management and Support Intelligence, MoD, 1965-66; Director, Service Intelligence, MoD, 1966-67; retd 1967. Chm., Arundel Castle Trustees, Ltd. DL West Sussex, 1977. Knight of the Sovereign Order of Malta. *Heir:* s Earl of Arundel and Surrey, *qv*. *Address:* Arundel Castle, Sussex BN18 9AB. *T:* Arundel 882173; Carlton Towers, Goole, North Humberside DN14 9LZ. *T:* Goole 860 243; Bacres House, Hambleden, Henley-on-Thames, Oxfordshire RG9 6RY. *T:* Hambleden 350. *Club:* Pratt's.

See also Lord Michael Fitzalan-Howard.

NORFOLK, Lavinia Duchess of; Lavinia Mary Fitzalan-Howard, CBE 1971; Lord-Lieutenant of West Sussex, since 1975; *b* 22 March 1916; *d* of 3rd Baron Belper and of Eva, Countess of Rosebery, DBE; *m* 1937, 16th Duke of Norfolk, KG, PC, GCVO, GBE, TD (*d* 1975); four *d*. *Educ:* Abbotshill, Hemel Hempstead, Herts. President: Riding for the Disabled Assoc., 1970-; Nat. Canine Defence League, 1969-; Pony Riding for the Disabled Trust, Chigwell, 1964-; BHS, 1980-82. Vice-President: ASBAH, 1970-; Spastic Soc., 1969-; NSPCC, 1967-. Chairman, King Edward VII Hosp., Midhurst, 1975-. Steward, Goodwood, 1976-78. BRCS Certificate of Honour and Badge, Class 1, 1969. Silver Jubilee Medal, 1977. *Address:* Arundel Park, Sussex. *T:* Arundel 882041.

See also Earl of Ancram, Lady Herries.

NORFOLK, Archdeacon of; *see* Dawson, Ven. Peter.

NORFOLK, Ven. Edward Matheson; Archdeacon of St Albans, since 1982; *b* 29 Sept. 1921; *s* of Edward and Chrissie Mary Wilson Norfolk; *m* 1947, Mary Louisa Oates; one *s* one *d* (and one *s* decd). *Educ:* Latymer Upper School; Leeds Univ. (BA); College of the Resurrection, Mirfield. Deacon, 1946; priest, 1947; Assistant Curate: Greenford, 1946-47; King Charles the Martyr, South Mymms, 1947-50; Bushey, 1950-53; Vicar: Waltham Cross, 1953-59; Welwyn Garden City, 1959-69; Rector, Great Berkhamsted, 1969-81; Vicar, King's Langley, 1981-82. Hon. Canon of St Albans, 1972-82. *Recreations:* walking, bird-watching. *Address:* 6 Sopwell Lane, St Albans, Herts AL1 1RR. *T:* St Albans 59773.

NORFOLK, Leslie William, CBE 1973 (OBE 1944); TD 1946; CEng; engineering consultant; *b* 8 April 1911; *e s* of late Robert and Edith Norfolk, Nottingham; *m* 1944, A. I. E. W. (Nancy) Watson (then WRNS), *d* of late Sir Hugh Watson, IFS (retd); two *s* one *d*. *Educ:* Southwell Minster Grammar Sch., Notts; University Coll., Nottingham. Assistant and later Partner, E. G. Phillips, Son & Norfolk, consulting engineers, Nottingham, 1932-39. Served with RE, France, Gibraltar, Home Forces, 1939-45, Lt-Col. Engineer, Dyestuffs Div., ICI Ltd, 1945-53; Resident Engineer, ICI of Canada, Kingston, Ont., 1953-55; Asst Chief Engr, Metals Div., ICI Ltd, 1955-57; Engineering Manager, Severnside Works, ICI Ltd, 1957-59; Engineering Director, Industrias Quimicas Argentinas Duperial SAIC, Buenos Aires, 1959-65; Director, Heavy Organic Chemicals Div., ICI Ltd, 1965-68; retired from ICI, 1968; Chief Exec., Royal Dockyards, MoD, 1969-72. *Recreations:* home workshop, industrial archaeology. *Address:* Beechwoods, Beechwood Road, Combe Down, Bath, Avon. *T:* Combe Down 832104. *Club:* Bath & County (Bath).

NORGARD, John Davey, AO 1982; Chairman, Australian Broadcasting Commission, 1976-81; retired as Executive General Manager, Operations, BHP Co. Ltd, and as Chairman, Associated Tin Smelters, 1970; *b* 3 Feb. 1914; *s* of John Henry and Ida Elizabeth Norgard; *m* 1943, Irena Mary Doffkont; one *s* three *d*. *Educ:* Adelaide Univ. (BE); SA Sch. of Mines. Part-time Chm., Metric Conversion Bd, Australia, 1970-81; Chairman: Commonwealth Employment Service Review, 1976-77; Pipeline Authority, 1976-81; Mem., Nat. Energy Adv. Cttee, 1977-80. Dep. Chancellor, La Trobe Univ., 1972-75. Chm., Grad. Careers Council of Australia, 1979-. FSASM. *Recreation:* golf. *Address:* 29 Montalto Avenue, Toorak, Victoria 3142, Australia. *T:* (03) 244937. *Clubs:* Australian, Royal Melbourne Golf, Sciences (all Melbourne); Newcastle (NSW).

NORLAND, Otto Realf; Director, Hambros Bank Ltd, since 1964; Chairman, Alcoa of Great Britain Ltd, since 1978; *b* 24 Feb. 1930; *s* of Realph I. O. Norland and Aasta S. Sæther; *m* 1955, Gerd Ellen Andenæs; one *s* two *d*. *Educ:* Norwegian University College of Economics and Business Administration, Bergen. FIB. Hambros Bank Ltd, 1953-; Manager, 1963. Director: Alcoa of Great Britain Ltd, 1968; Norsk Alcoa A/S, 1978-. Pres., Aluminium Fedn, 1982. *Recreations:* tennis, skiing, books (polar explorations). *Address:* 41

Bishopsgate, EC2. *T:* 01-588 2851. *Clubs:* Den Norske; Norske Selskab (Oslo).

NORMAN, Baroness (Priscilla), CBE 1963; JP; *b* 1899; *o d* of late Major Robert Reyntiens and late Lady Alice Bertie; *m* 1st, 1921, Alexander Koch de Gooreynd (marr. diss. 1929); two *s*; 2nd, 1933, 1st Baron Norman, PC, DSO (*d* 1950). Member: London County Council, 1925-33; Chelsea Borough Council, 1928-31; Bethlem Royal and the Maudsley Hospital Board, 1951-75; South-East Metropolitan Regional Board, 1951-74; Hon. Pres., World Fedn for Mental Health, 1972. Vice-Chm., Women's Voluntary Services for Civil Defence, 1938-41; Vice-Pres., Royal College of Nursing. JP 1944. *Address:* Aubrey Lodge, Aubrey Road, W8 7JJ.

See also S. P. E. C. W. Towneley, P. G. Worsthorne.

NORMAN, (Alexander) Vesey (Bethune); Master of the Armouries, HM Tower of London, since 1977; *b* 10 Feb. 1930; *s* of Lt-Col A. M. B. Norman and Sheila M. Maxwell; *m* 1954, Catherine Margaret Barne; one *s*. *Educ:* Alford Sch.; Trinity Coll., Glenalmond; London Univ. (BA Gen.). FSA; FSAScot; FMA. Asst Curator, Scottish United Services Museum, Edinburgh Castle, 1957; Hon. Curator of Arms and Armour, Abbotsford, 1957; Asst to Dir, Wallace Collection, 1963; Inspector of Armouries, 1977. Liveryman, Gunmakers' Co., 1981-. *Publications:* Arms & Armour, 1964 (also foreign edns); (with Don Pottinger) Warrior to Soldier, 449-1660, 1966 (USA edn as A History of War and Weapons, 449-1660, reprinted as English Weapons and Warfare, 449-1660, 1979); Small Swords and Military Swords, 1967; The Medieval Soldier, 1971 (also USA); Arms and Armour in the Royal Scottish Museum, 1972; A Catalogue of Ceramics, Wallace Collection, Pt I, 1976; The Rapier and Small-Sword, 1460-1820, 1980; articles in learned jls. *Recreation:* study of arms and armour. *Address:* The Armouries, HM Tower of London, EC3N 4AB.

NORMAN, Archibald Percy, MBE 1945; FRCP; MD; Physician, Hospital for Sick Children, 1950-77, now Hon. Physician; Paediatrician, Queen Charlotte's Maternity Hospital, 1951-77, now Hon. Paediatrician; *b* 19 July 1912; *s* of Dr George Percy Norman and Mary Margaret MacCallum; *m* 1950, Aleida Elisabeth M. M. R. Bisschop; five *s*. *Educ:* Charterhouse; Emmanuel Coll., Cambridge. Served War of 1939-45, in Army, 1940-45. Chm., Med. and Res. Cttee, Cystic Fibrosis Res. Trust, 1976-. *Publications:* (ed) Congenital Abnormalities, 1962, 2nd edn 1971; (ed) Moncrieff's Nursing and Diseases of Sick Children, 1966; contributions to medical journals. *Address:* White Lodge, Heather Close, Kingswood, Surrey. *T:* Mogador 832626.

NORMAN, Sir Arthur (Gordon), KBE 1969 (CBE 1966); DFC 1943; and Bar 1944; Chairman, The De La Rue Company, since 1964 (Chief Executive, 1972-77); *b* N Petherton, Som, 18 Feb. 1917; *m* 1944, Margaret Doreen Harrington; three *s* two *d*. *Educ:* Blundell's Sch. Joined Thomas De La Rue & Co., 1934. RAF 1939-45 (DFC and Bar); Wing-Comdr, 1943. Rejoined Thomas De La Rue & Co., 1946; Director, 1951; Managing Director, 1953. Director: Sun Life Assurance Society; SKF (UK) Ltd, 1970-; Thomas Tilling Ltd, 1979-; Whitbread & Co. Ltd, 1979-. Pres., CBI, 1968-70. Trustee: Royal Air Force Museum; World Wildlife Fund Internat.; Chm., World Wildlife Fund, UK, 1977-; Mem., Nature Conservancy Council. *Recreations:* tennis, golf, country life. *Address:* De La Rue House, 3/5 Burlington Gardens, W1A 1DL. *T:* 01-734 8020.

NORMAN, Barry (Leslie); author, journalist and broadcaster; *b* 21 Aug. 1933; *s* of Leslie and Elizabeth Norman; *m* 1957, Diana, *o d* of late A. H. and C. A. Narracott; two *d*. *Educ:* Highgate Sch. Entertainments Editor, Daily Mail, 1969-71, then made redundant; Writer and Presenter of Film, 1973-81, BBC1; Presenter of: Today, Radio 4, 1974-76; Going Places, Radio 4, 1977-81; Breakaway, Radio 4, 1979-80; Omnibus, BBC1, 1982; Writer and Presenter of: The Hollywood Greats, BBC1, 1977-79; The British Greats, 1980. Weekly columnist, The Guardian, 1971-80. *Publications:* The Matter of Mandrake, 1967; The Hounds of Sparta, 1968; Tales of the Redundance Kid, 1975; End Product, 1975; A Series of Defeats, 1977; To Nick a Good Body, 1978; The Hollywood Greats, 1979; The Movie Greats, 1981; Have a Nice Day, 1981. *Recreation:* playing village cricket. *Address:* c/o Curtis Brown Ltd, 1 Craven Hill, W2 3EP.

NORMAN, Sir Edward (James), Kt 1958; Chief Inspector of Taxes, 1956-64, retired; *b* Bridport, Dorset, 8 Jan. 1900; *s* of Edward Robert Norman; *m* 1923, Lilian May Sly (*d* 1974); three *d*. *Educ:* Weymouth Grammar Sch. Entered Inland Revenue Department, 1917; Assistant Inspector of Taxes, 1920; Principal Inspector, Somerset House, 1947; Assistant Secretary, Board of Inland Revenue, 1948; Dep. Chief Inspector of Taxes, 1950-55. Member, and later Dep. Chm., Housing Corporation, 1964-69. Financial Advr, 1964-72, Indep. Chm., Building & Civil Engineering Holidays Scheme Management Ltd, 1972-78, Benefits Scheme Trustee Ltd, 1975-78. *Address:* Bourn Cottage, Westhumble, Dorking, Surrey.

NORMAN, Rt. Rev. Edward Kinsella; *see* Wellington, Bishop of.

NORMAN, Rev. Dr Edward Robert; Dean of Peterhouse, Cambridge, since 1971; Lecturer in History, University of Cambridge, since 1965; *b* 22 Nov. 1938; *o s* of Ernest Edward Norman and Yvonne Louise Norman. *Educ:* Chatham House Sch.; Monoux Sch.; Selwyn Coll., Cambridge (MA, PhD, DD). FRHlstS. Deacon, 1965; Priest, 1971. Asst Master, Beaconsfield Sec. Mod. Sch., Walthamstow, 1957-58; Fellow of Selwyn Coll., Cambridge,

1962-64; Fellow of Jesus Coll., Cambridge, 1964-71; Wilkinson Prof. of Church History, Wycliffe Coll., Univ. of Toronto, 1981-82. NATO Res. Fellow, 1966-68. Asst Chaplain, Addenbrooke's Hosp., Cambridge, 1971-78. Reith Lectr, 1978; Prideaux Lectr, 1980. *Publications:* The Catholic Church and Ireland, 1965; The Conscience of the State in North America, 1968; Anti-Catholicism in Victorian England, 1968; The Early Development of Irish Society, 1969; A History of Modern Ireland, 1971; Church and Society in Modern England, 1976; Christianity and the World Order, 1979; Christianity in the Southern Hemisphere, 1981. *Recreation:* watching television. *Address:* Peterhouse, Cambridge. *T:* Cambridge 50256. *Club:* Athenæum.

NORMAN, Vice-Adm. Sir Geoffrey; *see* Norman, Vice-Adm. Sir H. G.

NORMAN, Geoffrey; JP; Secretary, The Magistrates' Association, since 1977; *b* 25 March 1935; *s* of late William Frederick Trafalgar Norman and of Vera May Norman (*née* Goodfellow); *m* 1958, Dorothy Frances King (*d* 1978); two *s* two *d. Educ:* Harrow County Sch.; Brasenose Coll., Oxford (MA). Admitted Solicitor, 1959. Deputy Clerk to the Justices, Uxbridge, 1961-66; Clerk to the Justices, N Hertfordshire and Stevenage, 1966-77. JP Inner London, 1982. Freeman, City of London, 1982. *Publications:* articles on magistrates' courts and related subjects. *Recreations:* painting, badminton. *Address:* 7 Dale Close, Hitchin, Herts SG4 9AS. *T:* Hitchin 50783.

NORMAN, George Alfred B.; *see* Bathurst Norman.

NORMAN, Vice-Admiral Sir (Horace) Geoffrey, KCVO 1963; CB 1949; CBE 1943; *b* 25 May 1896; *m* 1924, Noreen Frances, *o d* of late Brig.-General S. Geoghegan; one *s* one *d. Educ:* Trent Coll.; RN Coll., Keyham. HMS Queen Elizabeth and destroyers, 1914-18; Long Gunnery Course, 1921; passed RN Staff Coll., 1929; Commander, 1932; Captain, 1938; idc 1939; Rear-Admiral, 1947; Chief of Staff to C-in-C, Mediterranean Station, 1948-50; Admiralty, 1950; Vice-Admiral (retired), 1951. Sec., Nat. Playing Fields Assoc., 1953-63. *Recreations:* fishing and outdoor sports. *Address:* Chantry Cottage, Wickham, Hants. *T:* Wickham 832248.

NORMAN, Jessye; soprano, concert and opera singer; *b* Augusta, Ga, USA, 15 Sept. 1945; *d* of Silas Norman and Janie King. *Educ:* Howard Univ., Washington, DC (BM *cum laude*). Peabody Conservatory, 1967; Univ. of Michigan, 1967-68 (MMus). Operatic début, Deutsche Oper, Berlin, 1969; La Scala, Milan, 1972; Royal Opera House, Covent Garden, 1972; American début, Hollywood Bowl, 1972; Lincoln Centre, NYC, 1973-. First Covent Garden recital, 1980. Tours include North and South America, Europe, Middle East, Australia, Israel. Many international festivals, including Aix-en-Provence, Aldeburgh, Berlin, Edinburgh, Flanders, Helsinki, Lucerne, Salzburg. Hon. DMus Harvard, 1982. Musician of the Year, Musical America, 1982; prizes include: Grand Prix du Disque (Acad. du Disque Français), 1973, 1976, 1977, 1981; Deutsche Schallplattenpreis, 1975, 1981. *Address:* c/o Ingpen and Williams, 14 Kensington Court, W8 5DN.

NORMAN, Sir Mark (Annesley), 3rd Bt, *cr* 1915; Chairman, IU Europe Ltd; Director, Gotaas-Larsen Shipping Corporation, and other companies; *b* 8 Feb. 1927; *s* of Sir Nigel Norman, 2nd Bt, CBE, and Patricia Moyra (who *m* 2nd, 1944, Sir Robert Perkins, *qv*), *e d* of late Lieut-Colonel J. H. A. Annesley, CMG, DSO; *S* father, 1943; *m* Joanna Camilla, *d* of late Lt-Col I. J. Kilgour, Bampton, Oxon; two *s* one *d. Educ:* Winchester Coll. Coldstream Guards, 1945-47; Flying Officer, 601 (County of London) Sqdn, RAuxAF, 1953-56. *Recreations:* gardening, field sports, the building of follies. *Heir: s* Nigel James Norman, Major 13th/18th Royal Hussars (Queen Mary's Own), *b* 5 Feb. 1956. *Address:* Wilcote Manor, Charlbury, Oxon. *T:* Ramsden 357. *Clubs:* White's, Travellers', Pratt's, MCC; St Moritz Tobogganing.
See also N. D. Norman, W. R. Norman.

NORMAN, Mark Richard, CBE 1977 (OBE 1945); Managing Director of Lazard Brothers & Co. Ltd, 1960-75; Chairman, Gallaher Ltd, 1963-75; Director of other public companies, 1947-75; Deputy Chairman, National Trust, 1977-80 (Chairman, Finance Committee, 1969-80); *b* 3 April 1910; *s* of late Ronald C. Norman; *m* 1933, Helen, *d* of late Thomas Pinckney Bryan, Richmond, Virginia; two *s* three *d. Educ:* Eton; Magdalen Coll., Oxford. With Gallaher Ltd, 1930-32; Lazard Brothers & Co. Ltd, 1932-39. Served War of 1939-45: Hertfordshire Yeomanry; wounded Greece, 1941; an Asst Military Secretary, War Cabinet Offices, 1942-45 (Lieut-Colonel). Partner Edward de Stein & Co., 1946-60. *Address:* Garden House, Moor Place, Much Hadham, Herts. *T:* Much Hadham 2703. *Club:* Brooks's.

NORMAN, Nigel Desmond, CBE 1970; CEng; FRAeS; Managing Director, NDN Aircraft Ltd, Isle of Wight, and NDN Aeroculture Ltd, since 1979; *b* 13 Aug. 1929; 2nd *s* of Sir Nigel Norman, 2nd Bt (*d* 1943), CBE, and Patricia Moyra (who *m* 2nd, 1944, Sir Robert Perkins, *qv*); *m* 1st, Anne Fogg-Elliott; two *s*; 2nd, 1965, Mrs. Boel Elizabeth Holmsen; two *s* two *d. Educ:* Eton; De Havilland Aeronautical Technical Sch. (1946-49). RAF GD Pilot, thereafter 601 Sqdn, RAuxAF Fighter Sqdn, until disbandment, 1948-57. Export Asst at SBAC, 1951-53; Founder of Britten-Norman Ltd with F. R. J. Britten, 1954, Jt Man. Dir, 1954-71. Non-Exec. Director: Bridport Aviation Products Ltd, 1980-; Bridport-Gundry plc, 1981-. *Recreations:* aviation, sailing, shooting. *Address:* NDN Aircraft Ltd, Isle of Wight Airport, Sandown, IoW. *T:* Sandown 406421; Portland House, High Street, Bembridge, IoW. *T:* Bembridge 3574. *Clubs:* Royal Air Force, Royal Yacht Squadron.
See also Sir Mark Norman, Bt, W. R. Norman.

NORMAN, Prof. Richard Oswald Chandler, DSc; FRS 1977; CChem, FRSC; Professor of Chemistry, University of York, since 1965; *b* 27 April 1932; *s* of Oswald George Norman and Violet Maud Chandler. *Educ:* St Paul's Sch.; Balliol Coll., Oxford (MA, DSc). CChem; FRIC 1963. Jun. Res. Fellow, Merton Coll., Oxford, 1956-58, Fellow and Tutor, 1958-65; Univ. Lectr in Chemistry, Oxford, 1958-65. Pres., RIC, 1978-80; Dir, Salters' Inst. of Indust. Chemistry, 1975-. *Publications:* Principles of Organic Synthesis, 1968; (with D. J. Waddington) Modern Organic Chemistry, 1972; papers in Jl Chem. Soc. *Recreations:* cricket, music, gardening. *Address:* 129 The Mount, York YO2 2DA. *T:* York 53900. *Club:* Athenæum.

NORMAN, Sir Robert (Wentworth), Kt 1970; JP; Director, Bank of New South Wales, since 1970 (Chief General Manager, 1964-77); *b* 10 April 1912; *s* of William Henry Norman and Minnie Esther Brown; *m* 1942, Grace Hebden, *d* of Sidney Percy Hebden; one *s* one *d. Educ:* Sydney Grammar Sch. Served Army 1940-46: Captain, AIF. Joined Bank of New South Wales, 1928; Manager, Head Office, 1961; Dep. Gen. Manager, 1962. Director: Australian Guarantee Corp. Ltd; Australian Gas Light Co. Ltd; Reckitt & Colman Australia Ltd; Ciba-Geigy Australia Ltd; Chrysler Australia Ltd; Partnership Pacific Ltd. Councillor: Science Foundn for Physics within Univ. of Sydney; Inst. of Public Affairs; Senator and Life Mem., Junior Chamber Internat. FAIM (Vice-Pres.). JP NSW, 1956. *Recreations:* bowls, reading. *Address:* 432 Edgecliff Road, Edgecliff, NSW 2027, Australia. *T:* 32 1900. *Clubs:* Union, Tattersalls, Royal Sydney Golf, Australian Jockey (Sydney).

NORMAN, Vesey; *see* Norman, A. V. B.

NORMAN, Willoughby Rollo; Hon. President, The Boots Co. Ltd, since 1972 (Chairman, 1961-72); Deputy Chairman, English China Clays Ltd; 2nd *s* of Major Rt Hon. Sir Henry Norman, 1st Bt; *m* 1st, 1934, Hon. Barbara Jacqueline Boot, *er d* of 2nd and last Baron Trent, KBE; one *s* two *d*; 2nd, 1973, Caroline Haskard, *d* of William Greville and Lady Diana Worthington. *Educ:* Eton; Magdalen Coll., Oxford. Served War of 1939-45, Major, Grenadier Guards. Director: National Westminster Bank (Chm. Eastern Region), 1963-79; Sheepbridge Engineering Ltd, 1979; Guardian Royal Exchange Assurance, until 1979. Under-writing member of Lloyd's. Vice-Chairman Boots Pure Drug Co. Ltd, 1954-61. High Sheriff of Leicestershire, 1960. *Recreations:* shooting, farming, gardening. *Address:* Hurst Mill, Petersfield, Hants; 28 Ranelagh House, Elystan Place, SW3. *T:* 01-584 9410. *Clubs:* White's, Pratt's.
See also Sir Mark Norman, Bt, N. D. Norman.

NORMAN-WALKER, Sir Hugh (Selby), KCMG 1966 (CMG 1964); OBE 1961; *b* 17 Dec. 1916; *s* of late Colonel J. N. Norman-Walker, CIE; *m* 1948, Janet Baldock; no *c. Educ:* Sherborne; Corpus Christi Coll., Cambridge. MA. Indian Civil Service, 1938-48; Colonial Administrative Service, 1949; Development Secretary, Nyasaland, 1954; Secretary to the Treasury, Nyasaland, 1960-64; Malawi, 1964-65; HM Commissioner, Bechuanaland, 1965-66; Governor and C-in-C, Seychelles, and Comr, British Indian Ocean Territory, 1967-69; Colonial Sec., Hong Kong, 1969-74. KStJ 1967. *Recreations:* sailing, shooting, bridge. *Address:* Houndwood, Farley, Wilts SP5 1AN. *Clubs:* East India, Devonshire, Sports and Public Schools, etc.

NORMANBY, 4th Marquis of, *cr* 1838; **Oswald Constantine John Phipps,** CBE 1974 (MBE (mil.) 1943); Baron Mulgrave (Ireland), 1767; Baron Mulgrave (Great Britain), 1794; Earl of Mulgrave and Viscount Normanby, 1812; Lord-Lieutenant of North Yorkshire, since 1974 (of North Riding of Yorkshire, 1965-74); *b* 29 July 1912; *o s* of Rev. the 3rd Marquess and Gertrude Stansfeld, OBE, DGStJ (*d* 1948), *d* of Johnston J. Foster of Moor Park, Ludlow; *S* father, 1932; *m* 1951, Hon. Grania Maeve Rosaura Guinness, *d* of 1st Baron Moyne; two *s* five *d. Educ:* Eton; Christ Church, Oxford. Served War of 1939-45, The Green Howards (wounded, prisoner, repatriated). PPS to Sec. of State for Dominion Affairs, 1944-45, to Lord President of the Council, 1945; a Lord-in-Waiting to the King, 1945. High Steward of York Minster, 1980-. Mem., Council of St John for N Yorks (formerly NR of Yorks), 1948- (Chm., 1948-77; Pres., 1977-); Chairman: KCH, 1948-74; Nat. Art-Collections Fund, 1981-; Pres., Nat. Library for the Blind, 1977-; Vice-Pres., St Dunstans; Member: Cttee of Management, RNLI; Gen. Council, King Edward's Hosp. Fund; Chapter-Gen., OStJ. Hon. Col Comdt, The Green Howards, 1970-82; Dep. Hon. Col, 2nd Bn Yorks Volunteers, 1971-72; President: TA&VRA for N of England, 1971-74 (Vice-Pres., 1968-71); TA&VRA N Yorks and Humberside, 1980-. KStJ. Hon. DCL Durham Univ. *Heir: s* Earl of Mulgrave, *qv. Address:* Mulgrave Castle, Whitby; Argyll House, 211 King's Road, SW3. *T:* 01-352 5154. *Club:* Yorkshire (York).

NORMANTON, 6th Earl of, *cr* 1806; **Shaun James Christian Welbore Ellis Agar;** Baron Mendip, 1794; Baron Somerton, 1795; Viscount Somerton, 1800; Baron Somerton (UK), 1873; Royal Horse Guards, 1965; Blues and Royals, 1969; left Army, 1972, Captain; *b* 21 Aug. 1945; *er s* of 5th Earl of Normanton; *S* father, 1967; *m* 1970, Victoria Susan *d* of J. H. C. Beard, Turmer House, Somerley, Ringwood, Hants; one *s* two *d. Educ:* Eton. *Recreations:* shooting, motor racing. *Heir: s* Viscount Somerton, *qv. Address:* Somerley, Ringwood, Hants. *T:* Ringwood 3253. *Clubs:* White's; Royal Yacht Squadron.

NORMANTON, Tom, TD; BA (Com); MP (C) Cheadle since 1970; Member (C) European Parliament, since 1973, elected for Cheshire East, 1979; chairman of a group of companies; *b* 12 March 1917; *m* 1942, Annabel Bettine (*née* Yates); two *s* one *d. Educ:* Manchester Grammar Sch.; Manchester Univ. (BA (Com); Chm., Cons. Assoc., 1937-38; Vice-Pres. Students' Union, 1938). Joined family group of textile cos, 1938. Served War of 1939-45: Army (commnd TA 1937) Europe and N Africa; GS appts, GHQ BEF, HQ First and Eighth Armies; HQ 21 Army Gp (wounded, Calais, 1940; despatches, 1944); demob., rank Major, 1946. Chm., Rochdale YC, 1948; Mem. Rochdale CB Council, 1950-53; contested (C) Rochdale, 1959 and 1964. Hon. Sec., Cons. Backbencher Industry Cttee, 1972-74; Mem., Expenditure Cttee, 1972-73; opposition front bench spokesman on energy, 1975-79; European Parliament: Member: Cttee on Energy and Research, 1973-79 (Vice-Chm., 1976-79 and (as elected Member), 1979-); Cttee on Economic and Monetary Affairs, 1973-79; Jt Africa, Caribbean, Pacific States Standing Conf., 1975-79; spokesman on Competition Policy, 1975; Deleg. to US Congress, 1975-78; Mem. European Cons. Gp, resp. Indust. Policy; special interests energy and defence. Manager, Lancashire Fusiliers Compassionate Fund, 1964-; Trustee, Cotton Industry War Memorial Fund, 1965; apptd Employer panel, NBPI, 1966-68; Member: Council, British Employers Confedn, 1959-64; Council, CBI, 1964-76 (Mem. Europe Cttee, 1964, and Econ. Policy Cttee, 1964-70), 1979- (co-opted); Stockport Chamber of Commerce, 1970-; Central Training Council, 1968-74; Exec., UK Automation Council, 1966- (Vice-Chm., 1970-73); Cotton and Allied Textiles Ind. Trng Bd, 1966-70; Exec. Council, British Textile Confederation, 1972-76; Vice-Chm. Manchester Br. of Inst. of Dirs, 1969-71; Chm., European Textile Industries Cttee; President: British Textile Employers Assoc., 1970-71; Internat. Fedn of Cotton & Allied Textiles Industries, 1976- (Vice-Pres., 1972-76, Pres., 1976-78). Director: Industrial Training Services Ltd, 1972-; N Reg. Bd, Commercial Union Assurance Ltd, 1974-; Manchester Chamber of Commerce, 1970-. Consultant, Midland Bank Gp, EEC, Brussels, 1979-. Speaks French and German. AMBIM. *Recreations:* sailing, walking, gardening. *Address:* Bollin Court, Macclesfield Road, Wilmslow, Cheshire. *T:* Wilmslow 524930. *Clubs:* Beefsteak, House of Commons Yacht (Hon. Treasurer, 1972-74, Commodore, 1976); St James's (Manchester).

NORREYS, Lord; Henry Mark Willoughby Bertie; *b* 6 June 1958; *s* and *heir* of the Earl of Lindsey (14th) and Abingdon (9th), *qv. Educ:* Eton; Univ. of Edinburgh. *Address:* Gilmilnscroft, Sorn, Mauchline, Ayrshire KA5 6ND. *Clubs:* Brooks's; Puffin's (Edinburgh).

NORRIE, family name of **Baron Norrie.**

NORRIE, 2nd Baron, *cr* 1957; **George Willoughby Moke Norrie;** Director, Fairfield Nurseries (Hermitage) Ltd; *b* 27 April 1936; *s* of 1st Baron Norrie, GCMG, GCVO, CB, DSO, MC, and Jocelyn Helen (*d* 1938), *d* of late R. H. Gosling; *S* father, 1977; *m* 1964, Celia Marguerite, *d* of John Pelham Mann, MC; one *s* two *d. Educ:* Eton College; RMA Sandhurst. Commissioned 11th Hussars, 1956; ADC to C-in-C Middle East Comd, 1960-61; GSO 3 (Int.) 4th Guards Brigade, 1967-69; retired, 1970. Pres. Royal British Legion (Newbury Branch). *Recreations:* skiing, tennis. *Heir:* *s* Hon. Mark Willoughby John Norrie, *b* 31 March 1972. *Address:* Henwick Old Farm, Newbury, Berks RG16 9EP. *T:* Thatcham 62808. *Clubs:* Cavalry and Guards, MCC.

NORRIE, Marian Farrow; a Recorder of the Crown Court, since 1979; *b* 25 April 1940; *d* of Arthur and Edith Jackson; *m* 1964; two *d. Educ:* Manchester High Sch. for Girls; Nottingham Univ. (LLB). Admitted Solicitor of Supreme Court, 1965. Sen. Partner, Norrie, Bowler & Wrigley, Solicitors, Sheffield, 1968-. *Recreations:* reading, skiing. *Address:* 16 Ivy Park Court, Sheffield S10 3LA. *T:* Sheffield 301794.

NORRINGTON, Roger Arthur Carver, OBE 1980; Musical Director: London Classical Players, since 1978; London Baroque Players, since 1975; Schütz Choir of London, since 1962; Principal Conductor, Kent Opera, since 1966; *b* 16 March 1934; *s* of late Sir Arthur Norrington and Edith Joyce, *d* of William Moberly Carver; *m* 1964, Susan Elizabeth McLean May (marr. diss. 1982); one *s* one *d. Educ:* Dragon Sch., Oxford; Westminster; Clare Coll., Cambridge (BA); Royal Coll. of Music. Freelance singer, 1962-72. Guest conducts many British and European orchestras, appears at Proms, City of London, Bath, Aldeburgh, Edinburgh and Harrogate festivals; broadcasts regularly at home and abroad. Debuts: British, 1962; BBC Radio, 1964; TV 1967; Germany, Austria, Denmark, Finland, 1966; Portugal, 1970; Italy, 1971; France and Belgium, 1972; USA, 1974; Holland, 1975; Switzerland, 1976. Many gramophone recordings. Cavaliere, Order al Merito della Repubblica Italiana, 1981. *Publications:* occasional articles in various musical journals. *Recreations:* reading, walking, sailing. *Address:* 17 Lancaster Grove, NW3. *T:* 01-794 1640.

NORRIS, Dame Ada (May), DBE 1976 (OBE 1954); CMG 1969; *b* 28 July 1901; *d* of Allan Herbert Bickford and Alice Hannah (*née* Baggs); *m* 1929, Hon. Sir John Gerald Norris, *qv*; two *d. Educ:* Melbourne High Sch.; Melbourne Univ. (MA, DipEd). Teacher, 1925-29. Vice-Chm., Victorian Council on the Ageing, 1951-80; Member-at-Large, Aust. Council on the Ageing; Vice-Pres., Victorian Soc. for Crippled Children and Adults, 1951-; President: Australian Adv. Council for the Physically Handicapped, 1955-57; Children's Book Council of Victoria, 1954-60, of Aust., 1960; Member: Commonwealth Immigration Adv. Council, 1950-71 (Dep. Chm., 1968-71);

Exec. Cttee, Internat. Council of Women, 1950-79; Life-Vice-Pres., Nat. Council of Women of Australia (Pres., 1967-70); Chairman: Nat. Cttee for Internat. Women's Year, 1974-76; UNAA Nat. Cttee for Status of Women and Decade for Women, 1976-; Mem. Exec. Cttee, Melbourne Internat. Centenary Exhbn 1980, 1979-. Australian Rep., UN Commn on Status of Women, 1961-63. Chm., Appeal Cttee, Hall of Residence for Women Students, Univ. of Papua New Guinea, 1969-73. Hon. LLD Melbourne, 1980. UN Peace Medal, 1975. *Publications:* The Society: history of the Victorian Society for Crippled Children and Adults, 1974; Champions of the Impossible, 1978; papers on status of women and social welfare matters. *Recreations:* gardening, travel. *Address:* 10 Winifred Crescent, Toorak, Vic 3142, Australia. *T:* Melbourne (03) 2415166. *Club:* Lyceum.

NORRIS, Sir Alfred (Henry), KBE 1961 (OBE 1950; MBE 1938); *b* 27 April 1894; *s* of late Alfred James Norris, Hornchurch, Essex, and Charlotte Norris; *m* 1925, Betty K. R. Davidson (decd); *m* 1936, Winifred Gladys, *d* of late Archibald Henry Butler; three *s. Educ:* Cranbrook Sch., Kent. Served War of 1914-18, King's Own Royal (Lancaster) Regt. Retired Company Director and Chartered Accountant; formerly of Brazil. *Recreations:* social work, gardening. *Address:* 11 Abbey Close, Elmbridge, Elmbridge Road, Cranleigh, Surrey. *Clubs:* Canning; Royal British (Lisbon).

NORRIS, Vice-Adm. Sir Charles (Fred Wivell), KBE 1956; CB 1952; DSO 1944; *b* 16 Dec. 1900; *m* 1924, Violet Cremer; one *s. Educ:* RNC Osborne and Dartmouth. Comdr, 1934; RN Staff Course, 1935; commanded HMS Aberdeen, 1936-39; Captain, 1941; commanded HMS Bellona, 1943-45; commanded HMS Dryad (Navigation and Direction School), 1945-46; Imperial Defence Coll., 1947; Captain of the Fleet, Home Fleet, 1948-50; Rear-Admiral, 1950; Director of Naval Training, and Deputy Chief of Naval Personnel, 1950-52; Vice-Admiral, 1953; Flag Officer (Flotilla), Mediterranean, 1953-54. Commander-in-Chief, East Indies Station, 1954-56, retired, 1956. Director of the British Productivity Council, 1957-65. *Address:* Clouds, 56 Shepherd's Way, Liphook, Hants GU30 7HH. *T:* Liphook 722456.

NORRIS, Air Chief Marshal Sir Christopher Neil F.; *see* Foxley-Norris.

NORRIS, Rt. Rev. Mgr David Joseph; Prelate of Honour to the Pope; General Secretary to RC Bishops' Conference of England and Wales, since 1967; *b* 17 Aug. 1922; *s* of David William and Anne Norris. *Educ:* Salesian Coll., Battersea; St Edmund's Coll., Ware; Christ's Coll., Cambridge (MA). Priest, 1947; teaching at St Edmund's Coll., Ware, 1948-53; Cambridge, 1953-56; Private Secretary to Cardinal Godfrey, 1956-64; National Chaplain to Catholic Overseas Students, 1964-65; Private Secretary to Cardinal Heenan, 1965-72; Vicar General of Westminster Diocese, 1972-. *Recreations:* reading, music, sport. *Address:* Archbishop's House, Westminster, SW1P 1QJ. *T:* 01-834 4717.

NORRIS, Sir Eric (George), KCMG 1969 (CMG 1963); HM Diplomatic Service, retired; Deputy Chairman, Inchcape & Co., since 1981 (Director, since 1977); Director: London Sumatra Plantations Ltd; Gray Mackenzie Ltd; *b* 14 March 1918; *s* of late H. F. Norris, Bengeo, Hertford; *m* 1941, Pamela Crane; three *d. Educ:* Hertford Grammar Sch.; St Catharine's Coll., Cambridge. Served Royal Corps of Signals, 1940-46 (Major). Entered Dominions Office, 1946. Served in British Embassy, Dublin, 1948-50; UK High Commission in Pakistan, 1952-55; UK High Commission in Delhi, 1956-57; Dep. High Commissioner for the UK, Bombay, 1957-60; IDC 1961; British Dep. High Comr, Calcutta, 1962-65; Commonwealth Office, 1966-68; High Comr, Kenya, 1968-72; Dep. Under Sec. of State, FCO, 1972-73; High Comr, Malaysia, 1974-77. Chm., Zebra Trust, 1977-. PMN (Malaysia), 1974. *Address:* Homestead, Great Amwell, Herts. *T:* Ware 870739. *Clubs:* East India, Royal Commonwealth Society (Chm. 1980-).

NORRIS, Maj.-Gen. Sir (Frank) Kingsley, KBE 1957 (CBE 1943); CB 1953; DSO; ED; MD; Hon. Consultant Pædiatrician, Alfred Hospital, Melbourne, since 1948; *b* 25 June 1893; *s* of Dr W. Perrin Norris; *m* 1920, Dorothy Leonard Stevenson; two *d. Educ:* Melbourne Church of England Grammar Sch.; Trinity Coll., Melbourne Univ. Served War of 1914-18, Australian Imperial Forces, ME; CO 1 CCS, AIF, 1939; ADMS 7 Australian Div. AIF, 1940-43; DDMS 1 Australian Corps AIF, 1943; Service in Middle East, Libya, 1940; Palestine 1941; Syria, 1941; Java, 1942; New Guinea, 1942-44; Korea, 1951-53. DGMS Commonwealth Military Forces, 1948-55; President: Royal Empire Soc., Vic. Br., 1948-54; BMA, Vic. Br., 1947; Good Neighbour Council, Vic., 1958-63; Alcoholic Foundn of Vic., 1961-68. Comr St John's Ambulance Bde, 1956, Chief Comr, 1963-; Chief Comr, Priory of St John Ambulance in Australia. Medical Adviser, Civil Defence, Australia, 1956-61. KStJ 1961 (CStJ 1959). KHP 1948; QPH 1953-55. *Publications:* The Syrian Campaign, 1944; The New Guinea Campaign, 1946; Major-General Sir Neville Howse, VC, 1965; No Memory for Pain (autobiography), 1970; various papers to medical journals. *Recreations:* bridge, chess, golf, model-ship building, cooking. *Address:* 69 Broadway, Camberwell, Victoria 3124, Australia. *Clubs:* MCC; Beefsteak, Melbourne, Naval and Military (Melbourne).

NORRIS, Gilbert Frank; Chief Road Engineer, Scottish Development Department, 1969-76; *b* 29 May 1916; *s* of Ernest Frank Norris and Ada Norris; *m* 1941, Joan Margaret Catherine Thompson; one *s. Educ:* Bemrose

Sch., Derby; UC Nottingham. FICE. Served with Notts, Bucks and Lindsey County Councils, 1934–39; Royal Engineers, 1939–46; Min. of Transport: Highways Engr in Nottingham, Edinburgh and Leeds, 1946–63; Asst Chief Engr, 1963–67; Dep. Chief Engr, 1967; Dir, NE Road Construction Unit, 1967–69. *Recreations:* motoring, photography. *Address:* Woodhead Lea, Lamlash, Isle of Arran KA27 8JU. *T:* Lamlash 323.

NORRIS, Col Graham Alexander, OBE (mil.) 1945; JP; company director and management consultant, since 1972; Vice Lord-Lieutenant of County of Greater Manchester, since 1975; *b* 14 April 1913; *er s* of late John O. H. Norris and Beatrice H. Norris (*née* Vlies), Manchester; *m* 1st, 1938, Frances Cicely, *d* of late Walter Gorton, Minchinhampton, Glos; one *d*; 2nd, 1955, Muriel, *d* of late John Corris, Manchester. *Educ:* William Hulme's Grammar Sch.; Coll. of Technology, Manchester; Regent St Polytechnic, London; Merchant Venturers Techn. Coll., Bristol. CEng, FIMechE, FIMI. Trng as automobile engr, Rolls Royce Ltd, Bristol Motor Co. Ltd; Joseph Cockshoot & Co. Ltd: Auto Engr, Works Man., 1937, Works Dir 1946, Jt. Man. Dir 1964, Chm. and Man. Dir, 1968; Dir, Lex Garages Ltd, 1968–70; Dir, Red Garages (N Wales) Ltd, 1973–. War service, RAOC and REME, UK, ME and Italy, 1940–46 (Lt-Col); Comdr REME 32 (W) Corps Tps (TA), 1947–51; Hon. Col, 1957–61. Mem., NEDC for Motor Vehicle Distrib. and Repair, 1966–; Pres., Motor Agents Assoc., 1967–68; Vice-Pres., Inst. of Motor Industry, 1973; Mem., Industrial Tribunal Panel, 1976. Pres., Manchester and Dist Fedn of Boys' Clubs, 1968–74; Vice-Pres., NABC, 1972–; Chm. Council and Mem. Court, UMIST; Mem. Court, Univ. of Manchester. Master, Worshipful Co. of Coachmakers and Coach Harness Makers, 1961–62; Freeman, City of London, 1938. JP, Lancashire 1963; DL Co. Palatine of Lancaster, 1962. *Recreations:* gardening, walking, social service activities. *Address:* Beech Rigg, Birthwaite Road, Windermere, Cumbria LA23 1DW. *Club:* East India, Devonshire, Sports and Public Schools.

NORRIS, Herbert Walter; Regional Director, South East Region, National Westminster Bank Ltd, 1969–73; Deputy Chief General Manager, 1962–65, Director, 1965–68, Westminster Bank Ltd; *b* 9 Dec. 1904; *s* of Walter Norris, Farnworth, Widnes, Lancs; *m* 1935, Laura Phyllis Tardif, *d* of A. Tardif, St Martin's, Guernsey; no *c*. *Educ:* Liverpool Collegiate School. Joined Westminster Bank, Liverpool Office, 1921; Joint General Manager, Westminster Bank Ltd, 1949. FIB (Mem. Council, Inst. of Bankers, 1952–65; Dep. Chairman, 1959–61). Master of Coopers' Company, 1973–74. *Recreations:* reading, music. *Address:* 53 Chancellor House, Tunbridge Wells, Kent.

NORRIS, Hon. Sir John (Gerald), Kt 1982; ED 1945; Judge of the Supreme Court of Victoria, 1972–75, retired; *b* 12 June 1903; *s* of John Alexander Norris, CMG and Mary Ellen (*née* Heffernan); *m* 1929, Ada May Bickford (*see* Dame Ada Norris); two *d*. *Educ:* Camberwell State Sch.; Melbourne High Sch.; Univ. of Melbourne (LLM; (jtly) Supreme Court Prize, 1924). Called to the Victorian Bar, 1925; KC 1950. Served War, 1939–45: Australia and New Guinea; Lt-Col. Actg County Court Judge, 1950; County Court Judge, 1955–72; Actg Supreme Court Judge for periods during 1968–72. Royal Comr on admin of law relating to prostitution in WA, 1975–76; Chm., Victorian Govt Cttee to consider recommendations of Bd of Inquiry into allegations against Victorian Police, 1976–78; reviewed law relating to coroners for Victorian Govt, 1979–80; conducted inquiry into concentration of ownership and control of press in Vic, 1980–81. Univ. of Melbourne: Lectr in Commercial Law, 1932–52; Mem., Standing Cttee of Convocation, 1952–62; Warden of Convocation, 1962–65; Mem. Council, 1965–81. Pres., Baden Powell Scout Guild of Australia, 1979–81. Hon. Col, 4th/19th Prince of Wales's Light Horse, 1964–72; Patron, Vic Br., Royal Aust. Armoured Corps Assoc., 1975–. Hon. LLD Melb., 1980. *Publications:* The Financial Emergency Acts, 1932; articles in legal jls. *Recreations:* gardening, walking, reading. *Address:* 10 Winifred Crescent, Toorak, Vic 3142, Australia. *T:* 241 5166. *Clubs:* Australian, Royal Automobile of Victoria (Melbourne); Toorak Services.

NORRIS, John Robert, PhD; Director, Group Research, Cadbury Schweppes Ltd, since 1979; *b* 4 March 1932; *s* of Albert Norris and Winifred May Perry; *m* 1956, Barbara Jean Pinder; two *s* one *d* (and one *s* decd). *Educ:* Depts of Bacteriology and Agriculture, Univ. of Leeds (BSc 1st Cl. Hons 1954, PhD 1957). Lectr in Bacteriology, Univ. of Glasgow, 1957–63; Microbiologist, Shell Research Ltd, 1963–73 (Dir, Borden Microbiol Lab., 1970–73); Dir, Agr. Res. Council's Meat Res. Inst., 1973–79. Editor, Methods in Microbiology, 1969–. *Publications:* papers in microbiol jls. *Recreations:* walking, wood carving, Yoga. *Address:* 32 Redland Grove, Bristol BS6 6PR. *T:* Bristol 47175. *Club:* Farmers'.

NORRIS, Maj.-Gen. Sir Kingsley; *see* Norris, Maj.-Gen. Sir F. K.

NORSTAD, Gen. Lauris, DSM (US) with Oak Leaf Cluster and Silver Star; Legion of Merit (US) with Cluster; Air Medal; United States Air Forces, retired; Hon. Chairman (formerly Chairman and Chief Executive Officer, 1967–72), Owens-Corning Fiberglas Corporation (President, Owens-Corning Fiberglas International, January–December 1963); *b* Minneapolis, USA, 24 March 1907; *s* of Martin Norstad; *m* 1935, Isabelle Helen Jenkins; one *d*. *Educ:* US Military Academy (BS). 2nd Lieut, Cavalry, 1930; graduated, Air Corps Sch., 1931. Served in various branches of Air Force; duty at GHQ Air Force, Langley Field, Va., 1940; Assistant Chief of Staff for Operations, 12th Air Force, 1942, served with 12th Air Force, England and Algiers; Director of

Operations, Allied Air Forces, Mediterranean, Dec. 1943; Chief of Staff, 20th Air Force, Washington, 1944; Asst Chief of Staff for Plans, Army Air Force HQ, 1945; Director of Plans and Operations Div., War Dept, Washington, 1946; Dep. Chief of Staff for Operations, USAF, 1947; Acting Vice Chief of Staff, Air Force, May 1950; C-in-C US Air Forces in Europe and C-in-C Allied Air Forces Central Europe, 1951; Deputy (Air) to Supreme Allied Commander, Europe, 1953; C-in-C, US European Comd, 1956–62, and Supreme Allied Commander, Europe, 1956–62; retired, 1963. Has several hon. degrees. Hon. CBE (GB). Holds other foreign orders. *Address:* (business) 717 Fifth Avenue, New York, NY 10022, USA.

NORTH, family name of **Earl of Guilford.**

NORTH, Lord; Piers Edward Brownlow North; *b* 9 March 1971; *s* and *heir* of Earl of Guilford, *qv.*

NORTH, John Joseph; Chief Agricultural Officer, Agricultural Development Advisory Service, Ministry of Agriculture, Fisheries and Food, since 1979; *b* 7 Nov. 1926; *s* of Frederick James North and Annie Elizabeth North (*née* Matthews); *m* 1958, Sheila Barbara Mercer; two *s*. *Educ:* Rendcomb College; Univ. of Reading (BSc, DipAgric); Univ. of California (MS). Agricultural Adviser, Nat. Agricultural Advisory Service, 1951; Kellogg Fellowship, USA, 1954–55; Regional Agricultural Officer, Cambridge, 1972; Senior Agricultural Officer, 1976. *Recreations:* golf, gardening. *Address:* 28 Hauxton Road, Little Shelford, Cambridge. *T:* Shelford 3369.

NORTH, Sir Jonathan; *see* North, Sir W. J. F.

NORTH, Dr Peter Machin, DCL; a Law Commissioner, since 1976; Fellow of Keble College, Oxford, since 1965; *b* Nottingham, 30 Aug. 1936; *o s* of late Geoffrey Machin North and Freda Brunt (*née* Smith); *m* 1960, Stephanie Mary, *e d* of T. L. Chadwick; two *s* one *d*. *Educ:* Oakham Sch.; Keble Coll., Oxford (BA 1959, BCL 1960, MA 1963, DCL 1976). National Service, Royal Leics Regt, 2nd Lieut, 1955–56. Teaching Associate, Northwestern Univ. Sch. of Law, Chicago, 1960–61; Lecturer: University Coll. of Wales, Aberystwyth, 1961–63; Univ. of Nottingham, 1963–65; Tutor in Law, Keble Coll., Oxford, 1965–76. Vis. Professor: Univ. of Auckland, 1969; Univ. of BC, 1975–76. Dir of Studies, Hague Acad. of Internat. Law, 1970; Mem., Lord Chancellor's Adv. Cttee on Legal Educn, 1973–75. *Publications:* Occupiers' Liability, 1971; The Modern Law of Animals, 1972; Private International Law of Matrimonial Causes, 1977; (ed jtly) Chitty on Contracts, 24th edn 1977, 25th edn 1982; Cheshire and North's Private International Law, 10th edn 1979; Contract Conflicts, 1982; articles and notes in legal jls. *Recreations:* children, gardening, cricket (both playing and sleeping through). *Address:* 10 Coln St Aldwyns, Cirencester, Glos. *T:* Oxford 862001; Law Commission, Conquest House, 37–38 John Street, Theobald's Road, WC1N 2BQ. *T:* 01-242 0861.

NORTH, Roger, JP; a Recorder of the Crown Court, 1971–73; Chairman West Norfolk Valuation Panel, since 1949; *b* 10 Dec. 1901; *s* of F. K. North, Rougham Hall, King's Lynn, and Grace, *d* of Gen. Sir Percy Feilding; *m* 1934, Pamela Susan, *d* of Rev. H. W. L. O'Rorke, North Litchfield, Hants; one *s* three *d*. *Educ:* Eton; Trinity Coll., Cambridge. Called to the Bar, 1925. Began farming at Rougham, Norfolk, 1932. Dep. Chm., Norfolk QS, 1962–71 (apptd by Royal Warrant); Chm., King's Lynn QS, 1942–71. Late Chm. Tractor Users' Assoc. and Oxford Farming Conf. Cttee; Council Mem. Instn of Agricultural Engineers, 1954–58; Chm., Norfolk Br., Mathematical Assoc. JP Norfolk, 1941. *Publication:* The Art of Algebra, 1965. *Recreations:* veteran motor cars and mathematics. *Address:* Rougham Hall, Rougham, King's Lynn, Norfolk. *T:* Weasenham St Peter 230. *Clubs:* Royal Institution; Norfolk.

NORTH, Sir Thomas (Lindsay), Kt 1982; FAIM, FAInstD, FRMIA; Chairman, G. J. Coles & Coy Limited, Melbourne, since 1979; *b* 11 Dec. 1919; *s* of John North and Jane (*née* Irwin); *m* 1944, Kathleen Jefferis; two *d*. *Educ:* Rutherglen, Vic. FAIM 1972; FAInstD 1979. Joined G. J. Coles & Co. Ltd, 1938; Gen. Man., 1966; Dep. Man. Dir, 1969; Man. Dir, 1975–79; Chm., various G. J. Coles subsid. cos. Dep. Chm., K. Mart (Australia) Ltd, 1975–; Director: Viscount Holdings Ltd, 1981–; Advance Australia, 1982–; Life Be In It, 1982–. *Recreations:* horse racing, swimming. *Address:* 31 Power Street, Toorak, Vic 3142, Australia. *T:* 03.203161. *Clubs:* Athenæum (Melbourne); Australian, Australian Armoured Corps (Sydney); Victorian Amateur Turf (Mem. Cttee), Victorian Racing Club, Moonee Valley Race; Melbourne Cricket, Sydney Cricket.

NORTH, Sir (William) Jonathan (Frederick), 2nd Bt, *cr* 1920; *b* 6 Feb. 1931; *s* of Muriel Norton (2nd *d* of 1st Bt) and Hon. John Montagu William North (who *m* 2nd, 1939, Marion Dyer Chase, Boston, Mass); *g s* of Sir William Hicking, 1st Bt; *S* grandfather, 1947 (under special remainder); *m* 1956, Sara Virginia, *d* of Air Chief Marshal Sir Donald Hardman, GBE, KCB, DFC; one *s* two *d*. *Educ:* Marlborough Coll. *Heir:* *s* Jeremy William Francis North, *b* 5 May 1960. *Address:* Frogmore, Weston-under-Penyard, Herefordshire.

NORTHAMPTON, 7th Marquess of, *cr* 1812; **Spencer Douglas David Compton;** DL; Earl of Northampton, 1618; Earl Compton, Baron Wilmington, 1812; *b* 2 April 1946; *s* of 6th Marquess of Northampton, DSO, and of Virginia, *d* of Lt-Col David Heaton, DSO; *S* father, 1978; *m* 1st, 1967, Henriette Luisa Maria (marr. diss. 1973), *o d* of late Baron Bentinck; one *s* one *d*; 2nd, 1974, Annette Marie (marr. diss. 1977), *er d* of C. A. R. Smallwood; 3rd, 1977, Hon. Mrs Rosemary Dawson-Damer; one *d*. *Educ:* Eton. DL Northants 1979. *Heir: s* Earl Compton, *qv*. *Address:* Compton Wynyates, Tysoe, Warwick. *T:* Tysoe 629. *Club:* Turf.

NORTHAMPTON, Bishop of, (RC), since 1982; **Rt. Rev. Francis Gerard Thomas;** Prelate of Honour, 1969; *b* 29 May 1930; *s* of Edward James and Elizabeth May Thomas. *Educ:* St Dominic's Primary School, Stone, Staffs; Cotton College, Staffs; Oscott College, Sutton Coldfield. Priest, 1955; Curate at St Peter's, Leamington Spa, 1955–56; further study in theology, Gregorian Univ., Rome, 1956–59; Lectr in Theology, Oscott Coll., 1959; Rector of the College, 1968–79; Chapter Canon and Vicar General, Archdiocese of Birmingham, 1979–82; Parish Priest of Holy Trinity, Newcastle-under-Lyme, 1979–82. Assistant Editor of Liturgy and Music. *Address:* Bishop's House, Marriott Street, Northampton NN2 6AW. *T:* Northampton 715635.

NORTHAMPTON, Archdeacon of; *see* Marsh, Ven. Bazil Roland.

NORTHBOURNE, 5th Baron *cr* 1884; **Christopher George Walter James;** Bt 1791; FRICS; agricultural consultant; company director; *b* 18 Feb. 1926; *s* of 4th Baron Northbourne and Katherine Louise (*d* 1980), *d* of late George A. Nickerson, Boston, Mass; *S* father, 1982; *m* 1959, Marie Sygne, *e d* of Henri Claudel, Chatou-sur-Seine, and *g d* of late Paul Claudel; three *s* one *d*. *Educ:* Eton; Magdalen Coll., Oxford (MA). *Heir: s* Hon. Charles Walter Henri James, *b* 14 June 1960. *Address:* 11 Eaton Place, SW1. *T:* 01-235 6790; Coldharbour, Northbourne, Deal, Kent. *T:* Sandwich 611277. *Clubs:* Brooks's, Farmers'.

NORTHBROOK, 5th Baron, *cr* 1866; **Francis John Baring,** Bt 1793; DL; Chairman, Winchester District Health Authority, since 1981; *b* 31 May 1915; *s* of 4th Baron Northbrook and Evelyn Gladys Isabel (*d* 1919), *d* of J. G. Charles; *S* father 1947; *m* 1951, Rowena Margaret, 2nd *d* of late Brig-General Sir William Manning, and of Lady Manning, Hampton Court Palace; one *s* three *d*. *Educ:* Winchester; Trinity Coll., Oxford. Chm., Hants AHA, 1978–81. JP 1955, DL 1972, Hants. *Heir: s* Hon. Francis Thomas Baring, *b* 21 Feb. 1954. *Address:* East Stratton House, East Stratton, Winchester, Hants.

NORTHCHURCH, Baroness (Life Peer); *see under* Davidson, Dowager Viscountess.

NORTHCOTE, family name of **Earl of Iddesleigh.**

NORTHCOTE, Prof. Donald Henry, FRS 1968; Master of Sidney Sussex College, Cambridge, since 1976; Professor of Plant Biochemistry, University of Cambridge, since 1970 (Reader, 1965–72); *b* 27 Dec. 1921; *m* Eva Marjorie Mayo; two *d*. *Educ:* Sir George Monoux Grammar Sch., London; London Univ.; Cambridge Univ. Fellow, St John's College, Cambridge, 1960–76. Hon. Fellow, Downing Coll., Cambridge, 1976. Mem. Governing Council, John Innes Inst., 1980–. *Publication:* Differentiation in Higher Plants, 1974, 2nd edn 1980. *Recreations:* sitting and chatting; strolling about. *Address:* The Master's Lodge, Sidney Sussex College, Cambridge. *T:* Cambridge 355860. *Club:* United Oxford & Cambridge University.

NORTHCOTE, Peter Colston; His Honour Judge Northcote; a Circuit Judge since 1973; *b* 23 Oct. 1920; *s* of late William George Northcote and late Edith Mary Northcote; *m* 1947, Patricia Bickley; two *s*. *Educ:* Ellesmere Coll.; Bristol Univ. Called to Bar, Inner Temple, 1948. Chm., Nat. Insce Tribunal; Chm., W Midland Rent Tribunal; Dep. Chm., Agric. Land Tribunal. Commnd KSLI, 1940; served 7th Rajput Regt, Far East (Major). *Recreations:* music, travel, ski-ing. *Address:* Wroxeter Grange, Wroxeter, Shrewsbury, Salop. *T:* Cross Houses 279. *Clubs:* Army and Navy; Union and County (Worcester).

NORTHCOTE-GREEN, Roger James, MC 1944; TD 1950; JP; Headmaster, Worksop College, Notts, 1952–70; *b* 25 July 1912; *s* of Rev. Edward Joseph Northcote-Green and Mary Louisa Catt; *m* 1947, Joan, *d* of Ernest Greswell and Grace Lillian (*née* Egerton); three *s* one *d*. *Educ:* St Edward's Sch. and The Queen's Coll., Oxford (MA). Served with Oxford and Bucks Light Infantry, 1939–44, in India and Burma; Staff Coll., Quetta, 1944–45; Bde Major, 53rd Ind. Inf. Bde, Malaya, 1945. Assistant Master, St Edward's Sch., 1936–39, 1946–52; Housemaster, 1947. Representative OURFC on RU Cttee, 1946–52. S Western Sec., Independent Schs Careers Orgn, 1970–77. JP Nottinghamshire, 1964. *Recreations:* shooting, fishing. *Address:* Manor Cottage, Woolston, Williton, Som. *T:* Williton 32445. *Clubs:* East India, Devonshire, Sports and Public Schools, MCC; Vincent's (Oxford).

NORTHCOTT, Rev. Cecil; *see* Northcott, Rev. (William) C.

NORTHCOTT, Prof. Douglas Geoffrey, FRS 1961; MA, PhD, Cambridge; Town Trust Professor of Mathematics, University of Sheffield, 1952–82; *b* London, 1916; *m* 1949, Rose Hilda Austin, Twickenham, Middlesex; two *d*. *Educ:* Christ's Hospital; St John's Coll., Cambridge. *Publications:* Ideal Theory, 1953; An Introduction to Homological Algebra, 1960; Lessons on Rings, Modules and Multiplicities, 1968; A First Course of Homological Algebra, 1973; Finite Free Resolutions, 1976; Affine Sets and Affine Groups, 1980. *Address:* 25 Parkhead Road, Ecclesall, Sheffield S11 9RA.

NORTHCOTT, Rev. (William) Cecil, MA; PhD; Religious Affairs Adviser and Churches Correspondent, Daily Telegraph, 1967–79; Editorial Secretary United Society for Christian Literature and Editor, Lutterworth Press, 1952–72; Editor-at-large, Christian Century of USA, 1945–70; *b* Buckfast, Devon, 5 April 1902; *s* of William Ashplant Northcott and Mary Nance; *m* 1930, Jessie Morton, MA, 2nd *d* of J. L. Morton, MD, Hampstead and Colyford, Devon; one *s* one *d*. *Educ:* Hele's Sch., Exeter; Fitzwilliam Coll. and Cheshunt Coll., Cambridge. 2nd Class Hons Historical and Theological Triposes; BA 1927; MA 1930; PhD London Univ. (School of Oriental and African Studies), 1961. Three years social work East End of London; Member Cambridge delegation to League of Nations, Geneva, 1926; Joint Proprietor and Editor The Granta, 1927–28; Asst Minister Ormskirk Street Congregational Church, St Helens, 1929–32; Minister Duckworth Street Congregational Church, Darwen, Lancs, 1932–35; Home Secretary and Literary Superintendent London Missionary Society, 1935–50; General Secretary and Editor United Council for Missionary Education (Edinburgh House Press), 1950–52; Chairman London Missionary Society, 1954–55; Delegate World Conferences, Amsterdam, 1948, Willingen, 1952, Evanston, 1954, New Delhi, 1961, Uppsala, 1968, Nairobi, 1975. Member, World Council of Churches Information Cttee, 1954–61; Member, British Council of Churches Christian Aid Cttee, 1946–64. Select Preacher, Cambridge, 1958; Danforth Foundation Lecturer, USA, 1961; Visiting Lecturer, Garrett Theological Seminary, USA, 1965, 1967, 1969, 1971. British Information Services, USA, 1944; editor, Congregational Monthly, 1953–58. Leverhulme Research Award, 1958. *Publications:* Time to Spare (Collab. BBC Talks), 1935; Southward Ho!, 1936; Guinea Gold, 1937; Who Claims the World?, 1938; John Williams Sails On, 1939; Change Here for Britain, 1942; Glorious Company, 1945; Whose Dominion?, 1946; Religious Liberty, 1948; Venturers of Faith, 1950; Voice Out of Africa, 1952; Robert Moffat: Pioneer in Africa, 1961; Christianity in Africa, 1963; David Livingstone: his triumph, decline and fall, 1973; Slavery's Martyr, 1976; ed Encyclopedia of the Bible for Children, 1964; People of the Bible, 1967. *Recreation:* old books. *Address:* 34 Millington Road, Cambridge. *T:* Cambridge 62905. *Club:* Royal Commonwealth Society.

NORTHEDGE, Prof. Frederick Samuel; Professor of International Relations, London School of Economics and Political Science, University of London, since 1968; *b* 16 Oct. 1918; *s* of William and Alice Northedge; *m* 1939, Betty Cynthia Earnshaw; two *s* one *d*. *Educ:* Bemrose Sch., Derby; Merton Coll., Oxford; Univ. of Nottingham; LSE. BSc (Econ) 1st class, PhD, DSc (Econ), London. London School of Economics: Asst Lectr in Internat. Relations, 1949–52; Lectr, 1952–60; Reader, 1960–68; Convener, Dept of Internat. Relations, 1969–72, 1975–78 and 1981–. Vis. Prof., Makerere Univ., Uganda, 1965. *Publications:* British Foreign Policy: the process of readjustment, 1945–1961, 1962; The Troubled Giant: Britain among the Great Powers, 1916–1939, 1966; (ed) The Foreign Policies of the Powers, 1968, 2nd edn, 1974; (jtly) A Hundred Years of International Relations, 1971; (jtly) International Disputes: the Political Aspects, 1971; Order and the Nature of International Relations, 1971; Freedom and Necessity in British Foreign Policy, 1972; East-West Relations: Détente and After, 1973; Descent from Power: British foreign policy, 1945–1973, 1974; (ed) The Use of Force in International Relations, 1974; The International Political System, 1976; Britain and Soviet Communism, 1982; articles and reviews in acad. jls on politics and internat. affairs. *Recreations:* talking, music, drinking wine. *Address:* 21 Marlborough Road, Chiswick, W4. *T:* 01-995 3171.

NORTHERN TERRITORY, AUSTRALIA, Bishop of the, since 1968; **Rt. Rev. Kenneth Bruce Mason;** *b* 4 Sept. 1928; *s* of Eric Leslie Mason and Gertrude Irene (*née* Pearce); unmarried. *Educ:* Bathurst High Sch.; Sydney Teachers' Coll.; St John's Theological Coll., Morpeth; Univ. of Queensland. Deacon, 1953; Priest, 1954. Primary Teacher, 1948–51; St John's Theological Coll., Morpeth, 1952–53 (ThL); Member, Brotherhood of the Good Shepherd, 1954; Parish of: Gilgandra, NSW, 1954–58; Darwin, NT, 1959–61; Alice Springs, NT, 1962; University of Queensland, 1963–64 (BA, Dip Div); resigned from Brotherhood, 1965; Trinity Coll., Melbourne Univ.: Asst Chaplain, 1965; Dean, 1966–67. Member, Oratory of the Good Shepherd, 1962; Superior, 1981–. *Recreations:* listening to music, railways. *Address:* The Lodge, PO Box 2267, Darwin, NT 5794, Australia.

NORTHESK, 13th Earl of, *cr* 1647; **Robert Andrew Carnegie;** Lord Rosehill and Inglismaldie, 1639; Landowner, Farmer; *b* 24 June 1926; *yr s* of 12th Earl of Northesk and Dorothy Mary (*d* 1967), *er d* of late Col Sir William Robert Campion, KCMG, DSO; *S* father, 1975; *m* 1949, Jean Margaret, *yr d* of Captain (John) Duncan George MacRae, Ballimore, Otter Ferry, Argyll; one *s* two *d* (and one *s* decd). *Educ:* Pangbourne RNR Coll.; Tabor Naval Acad., USA. Served with Royal Navy, 1942–45. Mem., Council, Fédération Internationale des Assocs d'éleveurs de la race bovine Charolaise. Chm. Bd, Chandler, Hargreaves Whittal IoM Ltd, 1980–; Member: Bd of Dirs, IoM Bank, 1980–; IoM Br., CPA; Bd of Governors, Buchan Sch., IoM. *Heir: s* Lord Rosehill, *qv*. *Address:* Springwaters, Ballamodha, Isle of Man.

See also Baron Fisher.

NORTHFIELD, Baron *cr* 1975 (Life Peer), of Telford, Salop; **(William) Donald Chapman;** Visiting Fellow, Centre for Contemporary European Studies, University of Sussex, since 1973; Chairman, Telford Development Corporation, since 1975; *b* 25 Nov. 1923; *s* of Wm H. and Norah F. E. Chapman, Barnsley. *Educ:* Barnsley Grammar Sch.; Emmanuel Coll.,

Cambridge, MA (1st Cl. Hons) Economics, also degree in Agriculture; Senior Scholar of Emmanuel Coll. Research in Agric. Economics, Cambridge, 1943-46; Cambridge City Councillor, 1945-47; Sec., Trades Council and Labour Party, 1945-57; MP (Lab) Birmingham (Northfield), 1951-70. Research Sec. of the Fabian Soc., 1948-49, Gen. Sec., 1949-53. Gwilym Gibbon Fellow, Nuffield Coll., Oxford, 1971-73. Special Adviser to EEC Commn, 1978-; Chairman: Develt Commn, 1974-80; Inquiry into recent trends in acquisition and occupancy of agric. land, 1977-79. *Publications:* The European Parliament: the years ahead, 1973; The Road to European Union, 1975; articles and Fabian pamphlets. *Recreation:* travel. *Address:* Priorslee Hall, Telford TF2 9NT. *T:* Telford 613131. *Club:* Reform.

NORTHOLT, Archdeacon of; *see* Butler, Ven. T. F.

NORTHROP, Filmer S(tuart) C(uckow), PhD, LittD, LLD; Sterling Professor of Philosophy and Law Emeritus, the Law School and the School of Graduate Studies, Yale University, USA, since 1962; *b* 27 Nov. 1893; *s* of Marshall Ellsworth Northrop and Ruth Cuckow; *m* 1st, 1919, Christine Johnston; two *s*; 2nd, 1969, Marjorie Carey. *Educ:* Beloit Coll. (BA 1915, LittD 1946); Yale (MA 1919); Harvard (MA 1922, PhD 1924); Imperial Coll. of Science and Technology, London; Trinity Coll., Cambridge. Instr. at Yale, 1923-26; Asst Prof., Yale, 1926-29; Associate Prof., Yale, 1929-32, Prof., 1932-47; Master of Silliman Coll., 1940-47; Sterling Prof. of Philosophy and Law, Yale, 1947-62; Visiting Prof., summer session, Univ. of Iowa, 1926; Univ. of Michigan, 1932; Univ. of Virginia, 1931-32; Visiting Prof. and Mem. of East-West Conf. on Philosophy at Univ. of Hawaii, 1939; Prof. Extraordinario, La Universidad Nacional Autonoma de Mexico, 1949; Fellow: American Acad. of Arts and Sciences, 1951; American Acad. of Political and Social Science, 1957; Pres., American Philosophical Assoc. (Eastern Div.), 1952. Hon. Founder: Macy Foundn Conferences, 1944-53; Amer. Soc. of Cybernetics, 1964; Mem., SEATO Round Table, Bangkok, 1958. Hon. LLD: Univ. of Hawaii, 1949, Rollins Coll., 1955; Hon. LittD: Beloit Coll., 1946; Pratt Inst., 1961. Order of the Aztec Eagle (Mexican), 1946, *Publications:* Science and First Principles, 1931; The Meeting of East and West, 1946; The Logic of the Sciences and the Humanities, 1947; The Taming of the Nations, A Study of the Cultural Bases of International Policy, 1952 (Wilkie Memorial Building Award, 1953); European Union and United States Foreign Policy, 1954; The Complexity of Legal and Ethical Experience, 1959; Philosophical Anthropology and Practical Politics, 1960; Man, Nature and God, 1962; Co-Editor, Cross-cultural Understanding: Epistemology in Anthropology, 1964; Chapter 5 in Contemporary American Philosophy, second series, 1970; (with J. Sinões da Fonseca) Interpersonal Relations in Neuropsychological and Legal Science, 1975; ed, Ideological Differences and World Order, 1949; Prolegomena to a Philosophia Naturales, 1982. *Recreations:* travel, baseball. *Address:* Red Jacket Inn, North Conway, NH, USA. *Clubs:* Century (New York); Beaumont, Berzilius, Elizabethan, Graduates, Mory's (New Haven); American Academy of Arts and Sciences (Philosophy Section) (Boston).

NORTHROP, John Howard; Member Rockefeller University (formerly Institute), 1924, Emeritus 1962; Visiting Professor of Bacteriology, University of California, 1949, Emeritus, 1959; Professor Biophysics, 1958, Emeritus 1959; Research Biophysicist, Donner Laboratory, 1958; *b* Yonkers, NY, 5 July 1891; *s* of Dr John I. Northrop, of Department of Zoology, Columbia Univ., and Alice Rich Northrop, of Dept of Botany, Hunter Coll., NY City; *m* 1917, Louise Walker, NY City; one *s* one d. *Educ:* Columbia Univ. BS 1912; AM 1913; PhD 1915; W. B. Cutting Travelling Fellow, Columbia Univ. (year in Jacques Loeb's laboratory at Rockefeller Inst.), 1915; on staff of Rockefeller Inst. 1916; Member, 1924; Stevens prize, Coll. of Physicians and Surgeons, Columbia Univ., 1931; Captain, Chemical Warfare Service, 1917-18; discovered and worked on fermentation process for manufacturing acetone; ScD Harvard 1936, Columbia 1937, Yale 1937, Princeton 1940, Rutgers 1941; LLD, University of California, 1939; Chandler Medal, Columbia Univ., 1937; DeLamar Lectr, Sch. of Hygiene and Public Health, Johns Hopkins, 1937; Jesup Lectr, Columbia Univ., 1938; Hitchcock Lectr, Univ. of California, 1939; Thayer Lectr, Johns Hopkins, 1940; Daniel Giraud Elliot Medal for 1939 of National Acad. of Science, 1944; Consultant, OSRD, 1941-45. Shared Nobel Prize in Chemistry, 1946. Certificate of Merit, USA, 1948. Alex. Hamilton Medal, Columbia Univ., 1961. Member: Sons of the American Revolution; Delta Kappa Epsilon fraternity, Sigma Xi, Phi Lambda Upsilon; American Society of Biological Chemists; National Acad. of Sciences, Halle Akademie der Naturforscher; Société Philomathique (Paris); American Philosophical Society; Society of General Physiologists; Chemical Society (Hon. Fellow); Fellow World Academy; Benjamin Franklin Fellow, RSA. *Publications:* Crystalline Enzymes, 1939; numerous papers on physical chemistry of proteins, agglutination of bacteria, kinetics of enzyme reactions, and isolation and chemical nature of enzymes; editorial board of Journal of General Physiology, Experimental Biology Monographs; Contrib. Editor, Funk & Wagnell's Encyclopedia. *Recreations:* field shooting, salmon fishing. *Address:* PO Box 1387, Wickenburg, Arizona 85358, USA. *Club:* Century Association (New York).

NORTHUMBERLAND, 10th Duke of, *cr* 1766; **Hugh Algernon Percy,** KG 1959; GCVO 1981; TD 1961; PC 1973; JP; FRS 1970; Earl of Northumberland, Baron Warkworth, 1749; Earl Percy, 1776; Earl of Beverly, 1790; Lord Lovaine, Baron of Alnwick, 1784; Bt, *cr* 1660; Baron Percy (by writ), 1722; Lord Steward of HM Household, since 1973; Lord-Lieutenant and Custos Rotulorum of Northumberland since 1956; Chancellor of University of Newcastle since 1964; *b* 6 April 1914; 2nd *s* of 8th Duke of Northumberland, KG, CBE, MVO (d 1930), and Lady Helen Gordon-Lennox (Helen, Dowager Duchess of Northumberland, who *d* 1965), *y d* of 7th Duke of Richmond and Gordon; *S* brother (killed in action), 1940; *m* 1946, Lady Elizabeth Diana Montagu-Douglas-Scott, *er d* of 8th Duke of Buccleuch and Queensberry, KT, PC, GCVO; three *s* three d. *Educ:* Eton; Oxford. Lieut, Northumberland Hussars, 1936; RA, 1940; Captain, 1941; Captain, Northumberland Hussars, 1947; TARO, 1949-64; Chm., T&AFA, 1950-56; Pres., Northumberland T&AFA, 1956-68; Pres., TA&VR Assoc. for North of England, 1968-71; Hon. Colonel: 7th Bn, Royal Northumberland Fusiliers, 1948-70; The Northumbrian Volunteers, 1971-75; 6th (V) Bn, Royal Regt of Fusiliers, T&AVR, 1975-. A Lord in Waiting, May-July 1945. Mem., Northumberland CC, 1944-55, Alderman, 1955-67. President: Northern Area, British Legion; Northumberland Boy Scouts' Assoc., 1946-; Northumb. Assoc. of Boys' Clubs, 1942-; British Horse Soc., 1950; North of England Shipowners' Assoc., 1952-78; Hunters Improvement and Light Horse Breeding Soc., 1954; Royal Agricultural Soc. of England, 1956, 1962; BSJA 1959; The Wildfowl Trust, 1968-72. Chairman: Departmental Cttee on Slaughter of Horses, 1952; Court of Durham Univ., 1956-64; Border Forest Park Cttee, 1956-68; ARC, 1958-68; Departmental Cttee for Recruitment of Veterinary Surgeons, 1964; Cttee of Enquiry on Foot-and-Mouth Disease, 1968-69; MRC, 1969-77; Agricultural EDC, 1971-78. Member: Agricultural Improvement Council, 1953-62; National Forestry Cttee for England and Wales, 1954-60; Hill Farming Advisory Cttee for England and Wales, 1946-60; County Agricultural Exec. Cttee, 1948-59; Royal Commn on Historical Manuscripts, 1973-. Chm. Council, RASE, 1971-74. Hon. Treasurer, RNLI; Associate, RCVS, 1967. Master of Percy Foxhounds, 1940-. KStJ 1957. Hon. DCL Durham, 1958. *Heir: s* Earl Percy, qv. *Address:* Alnwick Castle, Northumberland NE66 1NQ. *T:* Alnwick 2456; Syon House, Brentford. *T:* Isleworth 2353; Clive Lodge, Albury Park, Guildford. *T:* Shere 2695. *Clubs:* Boodle's, Northern Counties, Turf.
See also Duke of Hamilton and Brandon, Sir Aymer Maxwell, Bt, Lord Richard Percy, Duke of Sutherland.

NORTHUMBERLAND, Archdeacon of; *see* Thomas, Ven. W. J.

NORTON; *see* Hill-Norton, family name of Baron Hill-Norton.

NORTON, family name of **Barons Grantley** and **Rathcreedan.**

NORTON, 7th Baron, *cr* 1878; **John Arden Adderley,** OBE 1964; *b* 24 Nov. 1915; *s* of 6th Baron Norton; *S* father, 1961; *m* 1946, Betty Margaret, *o d* of late James McKee Hannah; two *s*. *Educ:* Radley; Magdalen Coll., Oxford (BA). Oxford University Greenland Expedition, 1938; Assistant Master, Oundle School, 1938-39. Served War, 1940-45 (despatches); RE (N Africa, Europe). Major, 1944. Asst Secretary, Country Landowners Assoc., 1947-59. *Recreations:* mountaineering, shooting, heraldry and genealogy. *Heir: s* Hon. James Nigel Arden Adderley [*b* 2 June 1947; *m* 1971, Jacqueline Julie Willett, *e d* of Guy W. Willett, Woking, Surrey; one d]. *Address:* Fillongley Hall, Coventry, West Midlands. *T:* Fillongley 303.

NORTON, Sir Clifford John, KCMG 1946 (CMG 1933); CVO 1937; *b* 17 July 1891; *o surv. s* of late Rev. George Norton and Clara, *d* of late John Dewey; *m* 1927, Noel Evelyn (d 1972), *d* of late Sir Walter Charleton Hughes, CIE, MInstCE; no *c. Educ:* Rugby Sch.; Queen's Coll., Oxford, MA 1915. Suffolk Regt, 1914, Gallipoli, Palestine; Captain, General Staff EEF, 1917; Political Officer, Damascus, Deraa, Haifa, 1919-20; entered Diplomatic Service, 1921; Private Secretary to the Permanent Under-Secretary of State for Foreign Affairs, 1930-37; First Secretary, 1933; Counsellor British Embassy, Warsaw, 1937-39; Foreign Office, 1939-42; Minister, Berne, 1942-46; HM Ambassador in Athens, 1946-51; retired, 1951; Hon. Citizen of Athens, 1951. UK Delegate (alternate) to United Nations Assembly, 1952 and 1953. Past President, Anglo-Swiss Society. Hon. Fellow, Queen's Coll., Oxford, 1963. *Address:* 21a Carlyle Square, SW3.

NORTON, Maj.-Gen. Cyril Henry, CB 1952; CBE 1945; DSO 1943; Colonel Commandant RA, 1958-63; *b* 4 Nov. 1898; *s* of late F. H. Norton, Tilehurst, Caterham, Surrey; *m* 1934, Ethel, *d* of Kapten R. E. G. Lindberg, Stockholm, Sweden; one *s* one d. *Educ:* Rugby Sch.; RMA, Woolwich. 2nd Lieut, RFA, 1916; Captain, 1929; Major, 1938; Lieut-Colonel, 1945; Colonel, 1946. Brig., 1950; Maj.-Gen., 1951; GOC 5th Anti-Aircraft Group, 1950-53; retired Nov. 1953. Served European War, 1914-19 (Salonika); Palestine, 1937-39 (despatches); War of 1939-45: in Middle East, Sicily and NW Europe. *Address:* Dunn House, Long Melford, Sudbury, Suffolk. *Club:* Army and Navy.
See also Viscount Colville of Culross.

NORTON, Donald; Regional Administrator, Oxford Regional Health Authority, 1973-80, retired; *b* 2 May 1920; *s* of Thomas Henry Norton and Dora May Norton (née Prentice); *m* 1945, Miriam Joyce, *d* of Herbert and Florence Mann; two *s* one d. *Educ:* Nether Edge Grammar Sch., Sheffield; Univs of Sheffield and London. LLB, DPA; FHA. Senior Administrator Sheffield Regional Hosp. Bd, 1948-51; Sec. Supt, Jessop Hosp. for Women and Charles Clifford Dental Hosp., Sheffield, 1951-57; Dep. Sec., Archway Gp of Hosps, London, 1957-60; Gp Sec., Dudley Road Gp of Hosps, Birmingham 1960-70; Sec., Oxford Regional Hosp. Bd, 1970-73. *Recreations:* marriage, golf, gardening. *Address:* The Squirrels, 14 Pullens

Field, Headington, Oxford OX3 0BU. *T:* Oxford 67291. *Clubs:* Victory; Management (Oxford); Frilford Heath.

NORTON, Captain Gerard Ross, VC 1944; MM; 1/4th Hampshire Regiment; *b* S Africa, 7 Sept. 1915; *m* 1942, Lilia Morris, East London, S Africa; one *d. Educ:* Selborne Coll., East London, S Africa. Bank clerk. *Recreations:* Rugger-provincial, tennis, cricket. *Address:* Minnehaha, PO Raffingora, Zimbabwe.

NORTON-GRIFFITHS, Sir Peter, 2nd Bt, *cr* 1922; Barrister-at-Law, Inner Temple, 1931; *b* 3 May 1905; *e s* of late Sir John Norton-Griffiths, 1st Bt, KCB, DSO; *S* father, 1930; *m* 1935, Kathryn (*d* 1980), *e d* of late George F. Schrafft, Boston, Massachusetts, USA; two *s* one *d. Educ:* Eton; Magdalen Coll., Oxford. Asst to President, Shell Union Oil Corporation, NY, 1936-39; enlisted Intelligence Corps, 1940; Asst Military Attaché, British Embassy, Madrid (GSO2) 1941-42; Instructor School of Military Intelligence, GSO3, 1943-44; GSO3, Intelligence Staff, SHAEF, 1944-45. Asst to General Manager, Deutsche Shell AG, 1948-50; General Manager, Shell Co. of Portugal Ltd, 1950-53; Managing Director, Belgian Shell Co., SA, 1953-60; retired from business. Officier de l'Ordre de la Couronne (Belgium); Officier de l'Ordre de la Couronne de Chêne (Luxembourg). *Recreations:* music, sight-seeing. *Heir: s* John Norton-Griffiths [*b* 4 Oct. 1938; *m* 1964, Marilyn Margaret, *er d* of Norman Grimley]. *Address:* Apartado 4, Santo António (Oeiras), 2780 Oeiras, Portugal. *Clubs:* Boodle's; Eça de Queiroz (Lisbon). *See also* Rt Hon. J. J. Thorpe.

NORWICH, 2nd Viscount, *cr* 1952, of Aldwick; **John Julius Cooper,** FRSL; writer and broadcaster; *b* 15 Sept. 1929; *s* of 1st Viscount Norwich, PC, GCMG, DSO, and of Lady Diana Cooper, *qv, d* of 8th Duke of Rutland; *S* father, 1954; *m* 1952, Anne (Frances May), *e d* of late Hon. Sir Bede Clifford, GCMG, CB, MVO; one *s* one *d. Educ:* Upper Canada Coll., Toronto, Canada; Eton; University of Strasbourg; New Coll., Oxford. Served 1947-49 as Writer, Royal Navy. Entered Foreign Office, 1952; Third Secretary, British Embassy, Belgrade, 1955-57; Second Secretary, British Embassy, Beirut, 1957-60; worked in Foreign Office (First Secretary from 1961) and in British Delegation to Disarmament Conference, Geneva, from 1960 until resignation from Foreign Service 1964. Chairman: Venice in Peril Fund; British Theatre Museum, 1966-71; Member: Exec. Cttee, National Trust, 1969- (Properties Cttee, 1970-); Franco-British Council, 1972-79; English Nat. Opera Cttee, 1977-81; Trustee, Civic Trust, 1976-. Makes historical documentary films for BBC TV. Chm., Serenissima Travel Ltd. Commendatore, Ordine al Merito della Repubblica Italiana. *Publications:* Mount Athos (with Reresby Sitwell), 1966; The Normans in the South (as The Other Conquest, US), 1967; Sahara, 1968; The Kingdom in The Sun, 1970; Gen. Editor, Great Architecture of the World, 1975; A History of Venice, vol. I, The Rise to Empire, 1977, vol. II, The Greatness and the Fall, 1981; Christmas Crackers, 1980. *Recreation:* sight-seeing. *Heir: s* Hon. Jason Charles Duff Bede Cooper, *b* 27 Oct. 1959. *Address:* 24 Blomfield Road, W9. *T:* 01-286 5050. *Clubs:* Beefsteak, Garrick.

NORWICH, Diana, Viscountess; *see* Cooper, Lady Diana.

NORWICH, Bishop of, since 1971; **Rt Rev. Maurice Arthur Ponsonby Wood,** DSC 1944; MA; RNR; *b* 26 Aug. 1916; *o s* of late Arthur Sheppard Wood and of Jane Elspeth Dalzell Wood (*née* Piper); *m* 1st, 1947, Marjorie (*née* Pennell) (*d* 1954); two *s* one *d* ; 2nd, 1955, M. Margaret (*née* Sandford); two *s* one *d. Educ:* Monkton Combe Sch.; Queens' Coll., Cambridge (MA); Ridley Hall, Cambridge. Curate, St Paul's, Portman Square, 1940-43. Royal Naval Chaplain, 1943-47 (still a Chap. to Commando Assoc.); attached RM Commandos, 1944-46; Chaplain, RNR, 1971. Rector, St Ebbe's, Oxford, 1947-52; Vicar and RD of Islington, and Pres. Islington Clerical Conf., 1952-61; Principal, Oak Hill Theological Coll., Southgate, N14, 1961-71; Prebendary of St Paul's Cathedral, 1969-71. Proctor in Convocation of Canterbury and Mem. House of Clergy and Gen. Synod of Church of England (formerly Church Assembly), 1954-; Member: various standing cttees on Liturgical Reform; Archbishops' Council on Evangelism; Church Comrs' Houses Cttee. Chairman: Theological Colls Principals' Conf., 1970-71; Norfolk Water Safety Assoc.; Anglican Council of Boys' Brigade. Governor: Monkton Combe Sch., Bath; Gresham's Sch., Holt. Abbot of St Benet's; Visitor, Langley Sch., Norfolk. Took his seat in House of Lords, 1975. *Publications:* Like a Mighty Army, 1956; Comfort in Sorrow, 1957; Your Suffering, 1959; Christian Stability, 1968; To Everyman's Door, 1968; Into the Way of Peace, 1982. *Recreations:* hockey, tennis, swimming, painting; supporting Norwich City FC. *Address:* The Bishop's House, Norwich NR3 1SB. *T:* Norwich 29001. *Club:* Royal Commonwealth Society.

NORWICH, Archdeacon of; *see* Handley, Ven. A. M.

NORWOOD, Suzanne Freda, (Mrs John Lexden Stewart); Her Honour Judge Norwood; a Circuit Judge, since 1973; *b* 24 March 1926; *d* of late Frederic Francis Norwood and of Marianne Freda Norwood (*née* Thomas); *m* 1954, John Lexden Stewart (*d* 1972); one *s. Educ:* Lowther Coll., Bodelwyddan; St Andrews Univ. MA English, MA Hons History. Called to Bar, Gray's Inn, 1951; practised at Bar, SE Circuit. Mem., Parole Bd, 1976-78. Mem., Greenwich and Bexley AHA, 1979-82. *Recreations:* walking, housekeeping, opera. *Address:* 69 Lee Road, SE3. *T:* 01-852 1954.

NORWOOD, Sir Walter (Neville), Kt 1971; President, New Zealand Motor Corporation; *b* 14 July 1907; *s* of late Sir Charles Norwood; *m* 1935, Rana Muriel, *d* of David Redpath; two *s* one *d. Educ:* Wellington and Wanganui. Trustee: Nuffield Trust for Crippled Children; Laura Fergusson Trust for Disabled Persons; C. J. B. Norwood Crippled Children's Trust; Norwood Cricket Trust. Past President: Wellington Rotary Club; Wellington Racing Club. *Recreations:* racing, farming, sailing. *Address:* Hillcrest, 24 Mataroa Avenue, Wellington, New Zealand. *Clubs:* Wellesley, Wellington (Wellington, NZ).

NOSSAL, Sir Gustav (Joseph Victor), Kt 1977; CBE 1970; FRS 1982; FAA; Director, The Walter and Eliza Hall Institute of Medical Research, Melbourne, since 1965; Professor of Medical Biology, University of Melbourne, since 1965; *b* 4 June 1931; *m* 1955, Lyn B. Dunnicliff; two *s* two *d. Educ:* Sydney Univ. (MB, BS, BScMed); Melbourne Univ. (PhD 1960). FAA 1967; FRACP 1967; Hon. FRCPA 1971; FACMA 1971; FRCP 1980. Jun., then Sen. Resident Officer, Royal Prince Alfred Hosp., Sydney, 1955-56; Res. Fellow, Walter and Eliza Hall Inst. of Med. Res., 1957-59; Asst Prof., Dept of Genetics, Stanford Univ. Sch. of Medicine, Calif, 1959-61; Dep. Dir, Walter and Eliza Hall Inst. of Med. Res., 1961-65. Special Consultant, Tropical Disease Res. Prog., WHO, 1976. Mem., Aust. Science and Technol. Council, 1975-. Hon. Mem., Amer. (1975), French (1979), Indian (1976), Soc. of Immunology; Foreign Hon. Mem., Amer. Acad. of Arts and Scis, 1974. For. Associate, US Nat. Acad. of Scis, 1979; Fellow, New York Acad. of Scis, 1977; Foreign Fellow, Indian Nat. Sci. Acad., 1980. Hon. MD Johannes Gutenberg Univ., Mainz, 1981. Emil von Behring Prize, Philipps Univ., Marburg, Germany, 1971; Rabbi Shai Shacknai Memorial Prize, Univ. of Jerusalem, 1973; Ciba Foundn Gold Medal, 1978; Burnet Medal, Aust. Acad. of Sci., 1979. *Publications:* Antibodies & Immunity, 1968 (rev. edn 1977); Antigens Lymphoid Cells & The Immune Response, 1971; Medical Science & Human Goals, 1975; Nature's Defences (Boyer Lectures), 1978. *Recreations:* golf, literature. *Address:* 46 Fellows Street, Kew, Vic 3101, Australia. *T:* 861 8256. *Clubs:* Melbourne (Melbourne); Rosebud Country.

NOSSITER, Bernard Daniel; United Nations Bureau Chief, New York Times, since 1979; *b* 10 April 1926; *s* of Murry and Rose (Weingarten) Nossiter; *m* 1950, Jacqueline Robinson; four *s. Educ:* Dartmouth Coll., Hanover, NH (BA); Harvard Univ., Cambridge, Mass. (MA Econ). Washington Post: Nat. Econs Corresp., 1955-62; European Econs Corresp., 1964-67; S Asia Corresp., 1967-68; Nat. Bureau Reporter, 1968-71; London Corresp., 1971-79. Nieman Fellow, Harvard, 1962-63. *Publications:* The Mythmakers, 1964; Soft State, 1970; Britain: a future that works, 1978; contribs to Amer. Econ. Rev., Harvard Business Rev., Annals Amer. Acad. Pol. Sci. *Address:* c/o New York Times, 229 West 43rd Street, New York, NY 10036, USA. *T:* 556-1234.

NOSWORTHY, Harold George, CMG 1965; *b* 15 March 1908; *m* 1941, Marjorie Anjelique; two *d. Educ:* Kingston Technical High Sch.; private tuition. Entered Jamaica Civil Service, 1929; 2nd class Clerk, 1938; Examiner of Accounts, 1943; Asst Commissioner, Income Tax, 1947; Asst Trade Administrator, 1950; Trade Administrator and Chairman Trade Control Board, 1953; Principal Asst Secretary, Ministry of Finance, 1955; Auditor-General, 1957-66; Dir, Internal Audit Service, UN, 1966-68. Queen's Coronation Medal, 1953; Jamaica Independence Medal, 1962. *Recreations:* reading, billiards, bridge, swimming. *Address:* 18 Hyperion Avenue, PO Box 127, Kingston 6, Jamaica. *T:* 9279889. *Club:* Kingston Cricket (Jamaica).

NOTT, Charles Robert Harley, CMG 1959; OBE 1952; retired, New Zealand; *b* 24 Oct. 1904; *e s* of late John Harley Nott, JP, Leominster, Herefordshire and late Mrs Nott, formerly of Bodenham Hall, Herefordshire; *m* 1935, Marion (*née* Macfarlane), Auckland, NZ; one *s* one *d. Educ:* Marlborough; Christ's Coll., Cambridge (MA). Colonial Administrative Service: Fiji, 1926; Administrative Officer (Grade II), 1938, (Grade I), 1945. Member of the Legislative Council, Fiji, 1950; HBM's Agent and Consul, Tonga, 1954-57; Sec. for Fijian Affairs, 1957-59; MLC, MEC, retired, 1960. *Recreation:* trout fishing. *Address:* Matakana, PO Box 106, Havelock North, New Zealand.

NOTT, Rt. Hon. John William Frederic; PC 1979; MP (C) St Ives Division of Cornwall since 1966; Secretary of State for Defence, since 1981; *b* 1 Feb. 1932; *s* of Richard William Kandahar Nott, Bideford, Devon, and late Phyllis (*née* Francis); *m* 1959, Miloska Sekol, Maribor, Yugoslavia; two *s* one *d. Educ:* King's Mead, Seaford; Bradfield Coll.; Trinity Coll., Cambridge. Lieut, 2nd Gurkha Rifles (regular officer), Malayan emergency, 1952-56; Trinity Coll., Cambridge, 1957-59 (BA Hons Law and Econs); Pres., Cambridge Union, 1959; called to the Bar, Inner Temple, 1959; Gen. Manager, S. G. Warburg & Co. Ltd, Merchant Bankers, 1960-66; Sec., Cons. Parly Finance Cttee, 1969-70; Minister of State, HM Treasury, 1972-74; Cons. front bench spokesman on: Treasury and Economic Affairs, 1975-76; Trade, 1976-79; Sec. of State for Trade, 1979-81. *Address:* House of Commons, SW1. *T:* 01-219 4157.

NOTT, Kathleen Cecilia, FRSL; author, broadcaster, lecturer and journalist; *d* of Philip and Ellen Nott; *m* Christopher Bailey (marr. diss.). *Educ:* Mary Datchelor Sch., London; Somerville Coll., Oxford (BA Hons, PPE); King's Coll., London. FRSL 1977. President: Progressive League, 1959-61; English PEN, 1974-75. Editor, Internat. PEN Bulletin of Selected Books, 1960-. *Publications: poetry:* Landscapes and Departures, 1947; Poems from the North,

1956; Creatures and Emblems, 1960; Elegies and Other Poems, 1980; *novels:* Mile End, 1938; The Dry Deluge, 1947; Private Fires, 1960; An Elderly Retired Man, 1963; *criticism and philosophy:* The Emperor's Clothes, 1954; A Soul in the Quad, 1969; Philosophy and Human Nature, 1970; The Good Want Power, 1977; *general:* A Clean Well-lighted Place, 1961 (Sweden); contribs to collections of essays, and to periodicals. *Recreations:* playing the piano, gardening. *Address:* 5 Limpsfield Avenue, Thornton Heath, Surrey CR4 6BG. *T:* 01-684 2889. *Clubs:* University Womens', PEN, Society of Authors.

NOTT, Very Rev. Michael John, BD; FKC; Provost of Portsmouth, 1972-82; Hon. Officiating Chaplain, Royal Navy, 1978-82; *b* 9 Nov. 1916; *s* of Frank and Ann Nott; *m* 1942, Elisabeth Margaret Edwards; one *s* one *d. Educ:* St Paul's; King's Coll., London, FKC 1972; Lincoln Theological Coll. Curate of: Abington, Northampton, 1939-45; St Mary, Reading, 1945-46; Vicar of St Andrew, Kettering, 1946-54; Rural Dean of Kettering, 1952-54; Warden and Chaplain, Heritage Craft Sch. and Hospital, Chailey; Vicar of Seaford, 1957-64; Rural Dean of Seaford, 1961-64; Senior Chaplain to Archbishop of Canterbury, 1964-65; Archdeacon of Maidstone, 1965-67; Archdeacon of Canterbury, 1967-72; Canon Residentiary of Canterbury Cathedral, 1965-72. *Recreations:* reading, walking, travel. *Address:* 9 Clarence Parade, Southsea, Hants. *Club:* Royal Naval (Portsmouth).

NOTT, Rt. Rev. Peter John; *see* Taunton, Bishop Suffragan of.

NOTTAGE, Raymond Frederick Tritton, CMG 1964; Chairman: Gilmartin Investment Management Ltd; Growth Investments Ltd; Director-General, Royal Institute of Public Administration, 1949-78; *b* 1 Aug. 1916; *s* of Frederick and Frances Nottage; *m* 1941, Joyce Evelyn, *d* of Sidney and Edith Philpot; three *d. Educ:* Hackney Downs Secondary Sch. Civil servant, Post Office Headquarters, 1936-49; Editor of Civil Service Opinion, and Member Exec. Cttee, Soc. of Civil Servants, 1944-49; Mem. Hornsey Borough Council, 1945-47; Mem. Cttee on Training in Public Admin. for Overseas Countries, 1961-63; Vice-Pres. Internat. Inst. of Admin. Sciences, 1962-68; Mem. Governing Body, Inst. of Development Studies, Univ. of Sussex, 1966-76; travelled abroad as Consultant and Lectr. Treasurer, Arkwright Arts Trust, Hampstead. *Publications:* Sources of Local Revenue (with S. H. H. Hildersley), 1968; Financing Public Sector Pensions, 1975; articles in Public Administration and similar jls. *Recreations:* enjoying music, taking exercise. *Address:* 36e Arkwright Road, NW3. *T:* 01-794 7129.

NOTTINGHAM, Bishop of, (RC), since 1974; **Rt. Rev. James Joseph McGuinness;** *b* 2 Oct. 1925; *s* of Michael and Margaret McGuinness. *Educ:* St Columb's College, Derry; St Patrick's College, Carlow; Oscott College, Birmingham. Ordained, 1950; Curate of St Mary's, Derby, 1950-53; Secretary to Bishop Ellis, 1953-56; Parish Priest, Corpus Christi Parish, Clifton, Nottingham, 1956-72; Vicar General of Nottingham Diocese, 1969; Coadjutor Bishop of Nottingham and Titular Bishop of St Germans, 1972-74. *Recreations:* gardening, golf. *Address:* Bishop's House, 27 Cavendish Road East, The Park, Nottingham NG7 1BB.

NOTTINGHAM, Archdeacon of; *see* Williamson, Ven. R. K.

NOURSE, Hon. Sir Martin (Charles), Kt 1980; **Hon. Mr Justice Nourse;** a Judge of the High Court of Justice, Chancery Division, since 1980; *b* 3 April 1932; *yr s* of late Henry Edward Nourse, MD, MRCP, of Cambridge, and Ethel Millicent, *d* of Rt Hon. Sir Charles Henry Sargant, Lord Justice of Appeal; *m* 1972, Lavinia, *yr d* of Comdr D. W. Malim, *qv* ; one *s* one *d. Educ:* Winchester; Corpus Christi Coll., Cambridge. National Service as 2nd Lieut, Rifle Bde, 1951-52; Lieut, London Rifle Bde Rangers (TA), 1952-55. Called to Bar, Lincoln's Inn, 1956; Bencher, 1978; Mem., General Council of the Bar, 1964-68; a Junior Counsel to BoT in Chancery matters, 1967-70; QC 1970; Attorney Gen., Duchy of Lancaster, 1976-80; a Judge of the Courts of Appeal of Jersey and Guernsey, 1977-80. *Address:* North End House, Grantchester, Cambridge CB3 9NQ; 214 Old Brompton Road, SW5; Royal Courts of Justice, Strand, WC2. *Club:* Cambridge County (Cambridge).
See also Sir Edmund Sargant.

NOVA SCOTIA, Bishop of, since 1980; **Rt. Rev. Leonard Fraser Hatfield;** *b* 1 Oct. 1919; *s* of Otto Albert Hatfield and Ada Hatfield (*née* Tower). *Educ:* Port Greville and Amherst High School; King's and Dalhousie Univ., Halifax (BA 1940, MA 1943, Sociology). Deacon 1942, priest 1943; Priest Assistant, All Saints Cathedral, Halifax, NS, 1942-46; Rector of Antigonish, NS, 1946-51; Asst Sec., Council for Social Service of Anglican Church of Canada, 1951-54; Gen. Sec., 1955-61; Rector: Christ Church, Dartmouth, NS, 1961-71; St John's, Truro, NS, 1971-76. Canon of All Saints Cathedral, Halifax, 1969; Bishop Suffragan, Dio. NS, 1976. Member: Dio. Council, NS Synod; Corpn of Anglican Dio. Centre; Dean and Chapter, All Saints Cathedral; Bd of Governors, King's Coll. Has served: Program Cttee and Unit of Public Social Responsibility; Gen. Synod; Council of Churches on Justice and Corrections; Anglican Cons. Council, and various cttees of WCC; Organizing Sec., Primate's World Relief and Develt Fund; founding mem., Vanier Inst. of the Family, Ottawa; convened Primate's Task Force on Ordination of Women to the Priesthood; rep. Anglican Church of Canada at Internat. Bishops' Seminar, Anglican Centre in Rome, 1980. Hon. DD, Univ. of King's Coll., Halifax, NS, 1956. *Publication:* He Cares, 1958. *Recreations:* fishing, gardening, travelling, and playing bridge. *Address:* 5732 College Street, Halifax, Nova Scotia B3H 1X3. *T:* 423-8301.

NOVE, Prof. Alexander, FRSE 1982; FBA 1978; Professor of Economics, University of Glasgow, 1963-82, now Emeritus; Hon. Senior Research Fellow, Glasgow University, since 1982; *b* Leningrad, 24 Nov. 1915; *s* of Jacob Novakovsky; *m* 1951, Irene MacPherson; three *s. Educ:* King Alfred Sch., London; London Sch. of Economics (Hon. Fellow, 1982). BSc (Econ) 1936. Army, 1939-46. Civil Service (mainly BoT), 1947-58; Reader in Russian Social and Economic Studies, Univ. of London, 1958-63. Hon. Dr.agr Giessen, 1977. *Publications:* The Soviet Economy, 1961 (3rd edn 1969); (with J. A. Newth) The Soviet Middle East, 1965; Was Stalin Really Necessary?, 1965; Economic History of the USSR, 1969; (ed, with D. M. Nuti) Socialist Economics, 1972; Efficiency Criteria for Nationalised Industries, 1973; Stalinism and After, 1976; The Soviet Economic System, 1977; Political Economy and Soviet Socialism, 1979. *Recreations:* walking in Scottish hills, travel, music, theatre, exotic dishes. *Address:* 55 Hamilton Drive, Glasgow G12 8DP. *T:* 041-339 1053. *Club:* Royal Commonwealth Society.

NOWAR, Maj.-Gen. Ma'an Abu, Jordanian Star 1st Class; Minister of Tourism and Antiquities, and of Culture and Youth, Hashemite Kingdom of Jordan; *b* 26 July 1928; *m* Vivian Ann Richards; two *s* seven *d* ; *m* 1976, Susan Ann Coombs, Bath, Som; one *d. Educ:* London Univ. (Dip. World Affairs, 1963). Joined Jordanian Armed Forces, 1943; comd Regt, 1956; comd Bde, 1957; Counsellor, Jordan Embassy, London, 1963; Dir of Civil Defence, 1964; Dir of Public Security, 1967; Asst Chief of Staff, Jordan Armed Forces, 1969; Minister of Culture and Information, 1972-73; Ambassador of Jordan to the Court of St James's, 1973-76; Mayor of Amman, 1976-80; Minister of Public Works, 1980. *Publications:* The Battle of Karameh, 1968; For Jerusalem, 1969; 40 Armoured Brigade, 1970; The State in War and Peace, 1971; History of the Jordan Army, 1972. *Recreation:* swimming. *Address:* Ministry of Tourism and Antiquities, Amman, Jordan.

NOWELL-SMITH, Prof. Patrick Horace, AM (Harvard); MA (Oxon); Professor of Philosophy, York University, Toronto, since 1969; *b* 17 Aug. 1914; *s* of Nowell Charles Smith; *m* 1st, 1946, Perilla Thyme (marr. diss. 1968), *d* of Sir Richard Vynne Southwell; three *s* one *d* ; 2nd, 1968, Felicity Margret, *d* of Dr Richard Leonard Ward; two *d. Educ:* Winchester Coll.; New College, Oxford. Commonwealth Fellow, Harvard Univ., 1937-39. Served War of 1939-45, in Army, 1939-45. Fellow and Lecturer, Trinity Coll., Oxford, 1946-57, Estates Bursar, 1951-57. Professor of Philosophy: University of Leicester, 1957-64; University of Kent, 1964-69. *Publications:* Ethics, 1954; articles in Mind, Proc. Aristotelian Soc., Theoria, etc. *Address:* Department of Philosophy, York University, Downsview, Ont, Canada.
See also S. H. Nowell-Smith, Sir S. S. T. Young.

NOWELL-SMITH, Simon Harcourt, FSA; *b* 5 Jan. 1909; *s* of late Nowell Charles Smith, sometime Headmaster of Sherborne; *m* 1938, Marion Sinclair (*d* 1977), *d* of late W. S. Crichton, Liverpool; two *s* one *d. Educ:* Sherborne; New Coll., Oxford (MA). Editorial Staff of The Times, 1932-44; Assistant Editor, Times Literary Supplement, 1937-39; attached to Intelligence Division, Naval Staff, 1940-45; Secretary and Librarian, The London Library, 1950-56; Secretary, Hospital Library Services Survey, 1958-59; President, Bibliographical Society, 1962-64; Lyell Reader in Bibliography, Oxford Univ., 1965-66. Pres., Oxford Bibliographical Soc., 1972-76. Trustee, Dove Cottage Trust, 1974-. OStJ. *Publications:* Mark Rutherford, a bibliography, 1930; The Legend of the Master (Henry James), 1947; The House of Cassell, 1958; (ed) Edwardian England, 1964; Letters to Macmillan, 1967; International Copyright Law and the Publisher, 1968; Postscript to Autobiography of William Plomer, 1975. *Address:* 7 Beaumont Road, Headington, Oxford OX3 8JN. *Clubs:* Athenæum, Roxburghe.
See also Prof. P. H. Nowell-Smith.

NSEKELA, Amon James; Chairman and Managing Director, National Bank of Commerce, 1967-74 and since 1981; *b* 4 Jan. 1930; *s* of Ngonile Reuben Nsekela and Anyambilile Nsekela (*née* Kalinga); *m* 1957, Christina Matilda Nsekela; two *s. Educ:* Rungwe Dist Sch.; Malangali Secondary Sch.; Tabora Govt Sen. Sec. Sch.; Makerere UC (DipEd); Univ. of Pacific (Scholar, MA). Entered Civil Service as DO, Moshi, 1960; Perm. Sec., Min. of External Affairs and Defence, 1963; Perm. Sec. to Min. of Commerce, 1964; Prin. Sec. to Treasury, 1966-67. MP 1973-75, and Mem. E African Legis. Assembly, 1967-70. High Comr, UK, 1974-81, and Ambassador Extraordinary and Plenipotentiary to Ireland, 1979-81. Chm. or Dir of many cos and corporations, 1967-, incl.: Chm., Nat. Insurance Corp. of Tanzania, 1967-72; Director: Nat. Develt Corp. (past Chm. when Tanganyika Develt Corp.); Bd of Internal Trade; E African Airways Corp. Mem./Sec., Presidential Commn on Estabt of Democratic One-Party State in Tanzania. Chm. Council, Inst. of Finance Management, 1971-; Chm. Council, Univ. of Dar es Salaam; Past Pres., Economic Assoc. of Tanzania. *Publications:* Minara ya Historia ya Tanganyika: Tanganyika hadi Tanzania, 1965, new edns 1966 and 1971; Demokrasi Tanzania, 1973; (with A. L. Nhonoli) The Development of Health Services in Mainland Tanzania: Tumetoka Mbali, 1973; Socialism and Social Accountability in a Developing Nation, 1977; Towards Rational Alternatives, 1982; A Time to Act, 1982; contribs to Jl of Administration Overseas (ODM), African Review, Development Dialogue. *Address:* Box 1863, Dar-es-Salaam, Tanzania.

NTIWANE, Nkomeni Douglas; Group Personnel, Training and Localisation Officer, Swaki Group of Companies, since 1980; *b* 16 Feb. 1933; *s* of Isaiah Myotha and Jane Dlamini; *m* 1960, Sophia Pulane Kali; three *s. Educ:* DOT Coll., Middelburg, Transvaal, SA; Columbia Univ. (1967-68; Carnegie

Fellow in Dipl.). Teacher, East Transvaal, 1955-61; Headmaster (Swaziland): Mponono Sch., 1961-62; Mbekelweni Sch., 1962-63; Mhlume Central Sch., 1964-66; Lozitha Central Sch., Jan.-Sept. 1967. High Commissioner in London, 1968-71; Ambassador: Federal Republic of Germany, March 1969; Republic of France, April 1969. Permanent Secretary: Dept of Foreign Affairs, Swaziland, 1971-72; Ministry of Health, 1972-77; Ministry of Commerce, Industry, Mines and Tourism, 1977-80; retired from Civil Service, 1980. Swaziland Independence Medal, 1968; Meritorious Service Medal, Royal Swaziland Umbutfo Defence Force, 1978. *Publication:* Asive Ngwane (siSwati poetry). *Address:* E Mangweni, PO Box 41, Malkerns, Swaziland.

NUGEE, Edward George, TD 1964; QC 1977; *b* 9 Aug. 1928; *o s* of late Brig. George Travers Nugee, CBE, DSO, MC, RA, and of Violet Mary (*née* Richards, now Brooks); *m* 1955, Rachel Elizabeth Makower (*see* R. E. Nugee); four *s. Educ:* Brambletye; Radley Coll. (Open Scholar.) Worcester Coll., Oxford (Open Exhibnr; Law Mods, Distinction, 1950; 1st Cl. Hons Jurisprudence, 1952; Eldon Law Scholar, 1953; MA 1956). National Service, RA, 1947-49 (Office of COS, GHQ, FARELF); service with 100 Army Photographic Interpretation Unit, TA, 1950-64 (retd Captain, Intell. Corps, 1964). Read as pupil with Lord Justice Templeman and Lord Brightman; called to the Bar, Inner Temple, 1955, Bencher 1976; *ad eundem* Lincoln's Inn, 1968. Jun. Counsel to Land Commn (Chancery and Conveyancing), 1967-71; Counsel for litigation under Commons Registration Act, 1965, 1968-77; Conveyancing Counsel to Treasury, WO, MAFF, Forestry Commn, MoD (Admiralty), and DoE, 1972-77; Conveyancing Counsel of Court, 1976-77. Poor Man's Lawyer, Lewisham CAB, 1954-72. Member: CAB Adv. Cttee, Family Welfare Assoc., 1969-72; Management Cttee, Greater London Citizens Advice Bureaux Service Ltd, 1972-74; Man. Cttee, Forest Hill Advice Centre, 1972-76; Bar Council, 1962-66 (Mem., External Relations Cttee, 1966-71); Council of Legal Educn, 1967- (Vice-Chm. 1976-, and Chm. of Bd of Studies, 1976-); Adv. Cttee on Legal Educn, 1971-; Common Professional Exam. Bd, 1976- (Chm., 1981-); Lord Chancellor's Law Reform Cttee, 1973-; various working parties and consultative groups of Law Commn, 1966-; Inst. of Conveyancers, 1971-. Chm. Governors, Brambletye Sch., 1972-77; Mem. Council, Radley Coll., 1975-. *Publications:* (jtly) Nathan on the Charities Act 1960, 1962; (ed jtly) Halsbury's Laws of England, titles Landlord and Tenant (3rd edn 1958), Real Property (3rd edn 1960, 4th edn 1982); contribs to legal jls. *Recreations:* travel, cooking, the family. *Address:* 3 New Square, Lincoln's Inn, WC2A 3RS. *T:* 01-405 5296; 10 Heath Hurst Road, Hampstead, NW3 2RX. *T:* 01-435 9204.

NUGEE, Rachel Elizabeth, JP, MA; *b* 15 Aug. 1926; *d* of John Moritz Makower and Adelaide Gertrude Leonaura Makower (*née* Franklin); *m* 1955, Edward George Nugee, *qv*; four *s. Educ:* Roedean Sch., Brighton; Lady Margaret Hall, Oxford; MA (EngLang and Lit); Reading Univ. (Dip. Soc. Studies). Joined Mothers' Union, 1956; Vice-Chm., Central Publications Cttee, 1971-74; Diocesan Pres., London Dio., 1974-77; Central Pres., 1977-83. JP Inner London, Dec. 1971-. Member: Royal Free Hosp. (Hampstead Gen. Hosp.) House Cttee and Patients' Services Cttee, 1961-72. *Publications:* several religious articles and booklets for children. *Recreations:* active support of Church and family life; reading, especially history, visiting friends. *Address:* 10 Heath Hurst Road, Hampstead, NW3 2RX. *T:* 01-435 9204.

NUGENT, family name of **Earl of Westmeath** and **Baron Nugent of Guildford.**

NUGENT OF GUILDFORD, Baron, *cr* 1966 (Life Peer), of Dunsfold; **George Richard Hodges Nugent;** Bt 1960; PC 1962; *b* 6 June 1907; *s* of late Colonel George H. Nugent, RA; *m* 1937, Ruth, *d* of late Hugh G. Stafford, Tilford, Surrey. *Educ:* Imperial Service Coll., Windsor; RMA, Woolwich. Commissioned RA, 1926-29. MP (C) Guildford Division of Surrey, 1950-66. Parliamentary Secretary: Ministry of Agriculture, Fisheries and Food, 1951-57; Min. of Transport, 1957-Oct. 1959. A Dep. Speaker, House of Lords. JP Surrey; CC and sometime Alderman, Surrey, 1944-51. Member: Exec. Council, NFU, 1945-51; Agricl Improvement Council, 1947-51; Chairman: Thames Conservancy Board, 1960-74; Nat. Water Council, 1973-78; House of Commons Select Cttee for Nationalised Industries, 1961-64; Agricultural Market Development Cttee, 1962-68; Animal Virus Research Institute, 1964-77; Standing Conf. on London and SE Regional Planning, 1962-; Defence Lands Cttee, 1971-73; Vice-Chairman: Nat. Fedn of Young Farmers, 1948-51; Wye Agricl Coll., 1946-51; Harper Adams Agricl Coll., 1947-51; President, Assoc. of River Authorities, 1965-74; Mem., Guildford Diocesan Synod, 1970-. Pres., RoSPA, 1980-82. FRSA 1962. Hon. FIPHE. DUniv Surrey, 1968. *Address:* Blacknest Cottage, Dunsfold, Surrey. *Club:* Royal Automobile (Vice-Pres., 1974).

NUGENT, David James Douglas, (Prince HSH, title of Austrian Empire, *cr* 1816; also 7th Baron Nugent, Austrian title *cr* 1859, confirmed by Royal Warrant of Edward VII, 1908); *b* 24 Nov. 1917; 2nd *s* of Albert Beauchamp Cecil Nugent (HSH Prince Nugent, and 5th Baron) and Frances Every Douglas, niece of 3rd Baron Blythswood, KCB, CVO; *S* brother, 1944; *m* 1968, Mary Louise (*d* 1975), *d* of William Henry Wroth, Bigbury Court, Devonshire; *m* 1979, Evelyn Diana, *er d* of late Lt-Col Francis Noel, OBE, and *widow* of Sir Hector Lethbridge, 6th Bt. *Educ:* Lancing Coll. *Recreation:* historical research. *Address:* Alford House, Castle Cary, Somerset.

NUGENT, Sir Hugh Charles, 6th Bt, *cr* 1795; Count of the Holy Roman Empire; *b* 26 May 1904; *s* of late Charles Hugh Nugent, *o s* of 5th Bt and

Anna Maria (she *m* 2nd, Edwin John King, Danemore Park, Speldhurst, Kent), *d* of Edwin Adams; *S* grandfather, 1927; *m* 1931, Margaret Mary Lavallin, *er d* of late Rev. H. L. Puxley, The White House, Chaddleworth, Newbury, Berks; two *s. Educ:* Stonyhurst Coll. Knight of Malta. *Heir: s* John Edwin Lavallin Nugent [*b* 16 March 1933; *m* 1959, Penelope Ann, *d* of late Brig. R. N. Hanbury, of Braughing, Hertfordshire; one *s* one *d. Educ:* Eton]. *Address:* Ballinlough Castle, Clonmellon, Co. Westmeath, Ireland. *T:* Trim 33135.

NUGENT, Sir Peter Walter James, 5th Bt, *cr* 1831; *b* 26 Jan. 1920; *s* of Sir Walter Richard Nugent, 4th Bt and of Aileen Gladys, *y d* of late Middleton Moore O'Malley, JP, Ross, Westport, Co. Mayo; *S* father, 1955; *m* 1947, Anne Judith, *o d* of Major Robert Smyth, Gaybrook, Mullingar, Co. Westmeath; two *s* two *d. Educ:* Downside. Served War of 1939-45; 2nd Lieut, Hampshire Regt, 1941; Major, 1945. *Heir: s* Walter Richard Middleton Nugent, *b* 15 Nov. 1947.

NUGENT, Sir Robin (George Colborne), 5th Bt *cr* 1806; *b* 11 July 1925; *s* of Sir Guy Nugent, 4th Bt and of Maisie, Lady Nugent, *d* of J. A. Bigsby; *S* father, 1970; *m* 1st, 1947, Ursula Mary (marr. diss. 1967), *d* of late Lt-Gen. Sir Herbert Fothergill Cooke, KCB, KBE, CSI, DSO; two *s* one *d* ; 2nd, 1967, Victoria Anna Irmgard, *d* of late Dr Peter Cartellieri. *Educ:* Eton; RWA School of Architecture. Lt Grenadier Guards, 1943-48; served Italy, 1944-45. ARIBA 1959. *Recreations:* golf, skiing, travel. *Heir: s* Christopher George Ridley Nugent, *b* 5 Oct. 1949. *Address:* Bannerdown House, Batheaston, Bath, Avon. *T:* Bath 858481. *Club:* Cavalry and Guards.

NUNAN, Manus, QC (Nigeria) 1962; a Recorder of the Crown Court, since 1978; *b* 26 March 1926; *s* of Manus Timothy Nunan, Dist Justice, and Nan (*née* FitzGerald); *m* 1960, Anne Monique Fradin; one *s* one *d. Educ:* St Mary's Coll., Dublin; Trinity Coll., Dublin (BA, LLB). Called to the Irish Bar, King's Inns, 1950; called to the English Bar, Gray's Inn, 1956. Asst d'Anglais, Lycée Masséna, Nice, 1949-50; practised at Irish Bar, 1950-53; Crown Counsel, Nigeria, 1953-62; Solicitor-Gen., Northern Nigeria, 1962-64; Minister of Govt, Northern Nigeria, 1962; in practice at English Bar, 1965-. *Address:* 2B Mosslea Park, Liverpool L18 8DS. *T:* 051-724 5373. *Clubs:* Racquet (Liverpool); Kildare Street and University (Dublin).

NUNBURNHOLME, 4th Baron *cr* 1906; **Ben Charles Wilson;** Major, Royal Horse Guards, retired; *b* 16 July 1928; *s* of 3rd Baron Nunburnholme, and Lady Mary Thynne, *y d* of 5th Marquess of Bath, KG, PC, CB; *S* father, 1974; *m* 1958, Ines Dolores Jeanne, *d* of Gerard Walravens, Brussels; four *d* (including twin *d*). *Educ:* Eton. *Heir: b* Hon. Charles Thomas Wilson [*b* 27 May 1935; *m* 1969, Linda Kay, *d* of Cyril James Stephens; one *s* one *d*]. *Address:* Shillinglee Park, Chiddingfold, Surrey. *T:* Northchapel 461.

NUNN, Janet; see Suzman, J.

NUNN, Jean Josephine, CB 1971; CBE 1966; Deputy Secretary, Cabinet Office, 1966-70; *b* 21 July 1916; *d* of late Major John Henry Nunn, RHA, and Mrs Doris Josephine Nunn (*née* Gregory); unmarried. *Educ:* The Royal School for Daughters of Officers of the Army, Bath; Girton Coll., Cambridge, Hon. Fellow 1971. Entered Home Office, 1938; Secretary, Royal Commission on the Press, 1947-49; Private Secretary to the Secretary of State, 1949-51; Assistant Secretary, 1952; Assistant Under-Secretary of State, 1961-63; Under-Secretary, Cabinet Office, 1963-66. *Recreations:* gardening, bird-watching, reading. *Address:* Garden Cottage, School Lane, Washington, Pulborough, West Sussex. *T:* Ashington 892280. *Club:* Royal Commonwealth Society.

NUNN, John Francis, PhD; MD; FFARCS; Head of Division of Anaesthesia, Medical Research Council Clinical Research Centre, since 1968; *b* 7 Nov. 1925; *s* of late Francis Nunn, Colwyn Bay; *m* 1949, Sheila, *d* of late E. C. Doubleday; one *s* two *d. Educ:* Wrekin Coll.; Birmingham Univ. MO, Birmingham Univ. Spitzbergen Expedition, 1948; Colonial Med. Service, Malaya, 1949-53; University Research Fellow, Birmingham, 1955-56; Leverhulme Research Fellow, RCS, 1957-64; Part-time Lectr, Postgrad. Med. Sch., Univ. of London, 1959-64; Consultant Anæsth., Hammersmith Hosp., 1959-64; Prof. of Anaesthesia, Univ. of Leeds, 1964-68. Member: Council, RCS, 1977-82 (Mem. Board, Faculty of Anaesthetists, Vice-Dean, 1977-79, Dean, 1979-82); Council, Assoc. of Anaesthetists, 1973-76; Hunterian Professor, RCS, 1960; Visiting Professor to various American Universities, 1960-; British Council Lecturer: Switzerland, 1962; USSR, 1963; Czechoslovakia, 1969; China, 1974. Joseph Clover Lectr, RCS, 1968. Mem., Egypt Exploration Soc. *Publications:* Applied Respiratory Physiology, 1969, 2nd edn 1977; Jt Editor, General Anaesthesia, 3rd edn, 1971, 4th edn 1980; several chapters in medical text-books, and publications in Journal Appl. Physiol., Lancet, Nature, British Journal Anæsth., etc. *Recreations:* archaeology, model engineering, ski-ing. *Address:* MRC Clinical Research Centre, Northwick Park, Harrow, Middx; 3 Russell Road, Moor Park, Northwood, Mddx. *T:* Northwood 26363.

NUNN, Rear-Adm. John Richard Danford, CB 1980; Editor, The Naval Review, since 1980; Bursar and Official Fellow, Exeter College, Oxford, since 1981; *b* 12 April 1925; *s* of Surg. Captain Gerald Nunn and Edith Florence (*née* Brown); *m* 1951, Katharine Mary (*née* Paris); three *d. Educ:* Epsom Coll. CEng, FIMechE; MPhil Cantab. Entered RN, 1943; RN Engrg Coll., Keyham, 1943-47; HMS Devonshire, Second Cruiser Sqdn, 1945; HMS

Vengeance, 1947; Advanced Engineering Course, RNC Greenwich, 1949-51. HMS Amethyst, Korea, 1952-53; HMS Tiger, 1957-59; Commander, 1960; HMS Glamorgan, 1967-68; Captain, 1969; Sea Dart and Seaslug Chief Engineer, 1970-72; Cabinet Office, 1973-74; Staff of SACLANT, 1975-77; Rear-Adm., 1978; Port Adm., Rosyth, 1977-80. Fellow Commoner, Downing Coll., Cambridge, 1980-. *Recreations:* sailing, tennis, gliding, travel. *Address:* Warner's Cottage, Corhampton, Hants SO3 1LL; 2 Sadler Walk, St Ebbes, Oxford. *Clubs:* Naval; Automobile Association; Royal Naval Sailing Association (Portsmouth).

NUNN, Trevor Robert, CBE 1978; Chief Executive and Joint Artistic Director, Royal Shakespeare Company, since 1978 (Artistic Director, 1968-78); *b* 14 Jan. 1940; *s of* Robert Alexander Nunn and Dorothy May (*née* Piper); *m* 1969, Janet Suzman, *qv*; one *s*. *Educ:* Northgate Grammar Sch., Ipswich; Downing Coll., Cambridge (BA). Producer, Belgrade Theatre, Coventry; subseq. Associate Dir, Royal Shakespeare Company. Hon. MA: Newcastle upon Tyne, 1982; Warwick. *Address:* c/o Barbican Centre, Silk Street, EC2.

NUNNELEY, John Hewlett, FCIT; Managing Director, British Transport Advertising Ltd, since 1969; *b* Sydney, NSW, 26 Nov. 1922; *o s of* late Wilfrid Alexander Nunneley and Audrey Mary (*née* Tebbitt); *m* 1945, Lucia, *e d of* Enrico Ceruti, Milan, Italy; one *s* one *d*. *Educ:* Lawrence Sheriff Sch., Rugby. Served War of 1939-45: Somerset LI, seconded KAR; Abyssinia, Brit. Somaliland, 1942; Burma campaign, 1944 (wounded, despatches); Captain and Adjt. Various management posts in aircraft, shipping, printing and publishing industries, 1946-55. Exec., Beaverbrook Newspapers, 1955-62; joined BTC, 1962: Chief Publicity Officer, 1962-63; Chief Development Officer (Passenger) BR Bd, 1963-64; Chief Passenger Manager, 1964-69; Pres. and Chm., BR-Internat. Inc., New York, USA, 1966-69. Principal Advertising Consultant, Hong Kong Govt, 1981-. Member: Passenger Co-ordination Cttee for London, 1964-69; Outdoor Advertising Council, 1969-. Vice-Pres., European Fedn of Outdoor Advertising (FEPE), 1978-. Introduced BR Corporate Identity, 1964 and Inter-City concept, 1965. FRSA. *Publications:* numerous articles on transport and advertising subjects. *Recreations:* walking, gliding. *Address:* 6 Ashfield Close, Petersham, Surrey.

NUREYEV, Rudolf Hametovich; ballet dancer and choreographer; *b* Ufa, E Siberia, 1939, of a farming family. Joined Kirov Ballet School and at age 17 appeared with the Company in 1959; when on tour, in Paris, sought political asylum, May 1961. Joined Le Grand Ballet du Marquis de Cuevas Company and has made frequent appearances abroad; London debut at Royal Academy of Dancing Gala Matinée, organised by Dame Margot Fonteyn, Dec. 1961; debut at Covent Garden in Giselle with Margot Fonteyn, Feb. 1962; Choreographic productions include: La Bayadère, Raymonda, Swan Lake, Tancredi, Sleeping Beauty, Nutcracker, Don Quixote, Romeo and Juliet, Manfred; guest artist in England and America in wide variety of rôles. Has danced in many countries of the world. Gold Star, Paris, 1963. *Films:* Romeo and Juliet, 1965; I am a Dancer, 1972; Don Quixote, 1974; Valentino, 1977. *Publication:* Nureyev, 1962. *Recreations:* listening to and playing music. *Address:* c/o S. A. Gorlinsky Ltd, 35 Dover Street, W1X 4NJ.

NURJADIN, Air Chief Marshal Roesmin; Minister of Transport, Communications and Tourism, Indonesia, since 1978; *b* 31 May 1930; *m* 1962, Surjati Subali; two *s* one *d*. *Educ:* Indonesian Air Force Academy; Techn. Coll., Univ. Gadjahmada. Student Army, 1945-50. Comdr 3rd Fighter Sqdn, 1953; RAF CFS, England, 1954; Law Sch., 1956; Instructor, Jet Sqdn, 1957-59; Junior Staff Sch., 1959; Defence Services Staff Coll., Wellington, India, 1960-61; Dir Operation AF HQ, 1961-62; Dep. Comdr Operational Comd, Chief of Staff Air Defence Comd, 1962-64; Air Attaché: Bangkok, 1964-65; Moscow, 1965-66; Minister/C-in-C/Chief of Staff, Indonesian Air Force, 1966-70; Ambassador to the UK, 1970-74, to the USA, 1974-78. *Recreations:* golf, swimming. *Address:* Ministry of Transport, Communications and Tourism, Merdeka Barat 8, Jakarta, Indonesia. *Clubs:* Highgate Golf; Djakarta Golf.

NURSAW, James; Legal Adviser to the Home Office and the Northern Ireland Office, since 1983; *b* 18 Oct. 1932; *s of* William George Nursaw, *qv*; *m* 1959, Eira, *yr d of* late E. W. Caryl-Thomas, MD, BSc, Barrister-at-law; two *d*. *Educ:* Bancroft's School; Christ's Coll., Cambridge (Schol.; MA, LLB). Called to Bar, Middle Temple, 1955 (Blackstone Entrance Schol. and Prize, Harmsworth Schol.). Senior Research Officer, Cambridge Univ. Dept of Criminal Science, 1958. Joined Legal Adviser's Branch, Home Office, 1959; Principal Asst Legal Advr, HO and NI Office, 1977-80; Legal Secretary, Law Officers' Dept, 1980-83. Liveryman, Loriners' Co. *Address:* Legal Adviser's Office, Home Office, 50 Queen Anne's Gate, SW1H 9AT. *Club:* United Oxford & Cambridge University.

NURSAW, William George; investment consultant since 1961; financial writer and company director; *b* 5 Sept. 1903; *s of* George Edward Nursaw and Amy Elizabeth (*née* Davis); *m* 1931, Lilian May (*née* Howell); one *s* two *d*. *Educ:* Rushmore Road LCC Primary Sch.; Holloway Grammar Sch. (Schol.). Insurance, 1920-61: Trustee Man., Atlas Assce Co.; subseq. Dir Throgmorton Management (Man. Dir, 1962-71) and Hogg Robinson Gardner Mountain Pensions Management (Chm., 1963-71); Hon. Financial Adviser, RAF Escapers Soc., 1964-, and National Birthday Trust, 1947- (and Hon. Treas.); Co-founder and Dep. Chm., Covenanters Educational Trust and Perry Foundn, 1945-; Freeman, City of London; Assistant, Loriners' Co.;

Deacon, Chingford Congregational Church, 1944-62; Youth Leader, 1942-67; Chm., Chingford and Waltham Forest Playing Fields Assoc., 1959-79; Exec., Greater London Playing Fields. Civil Defence (Post Warden), 1938-65. FSS; ACII; FCIS (Mem. Council, 1962-70, Chm., London, 1968-69); FCIArb (Mem. Council, 1968-74); Associate, Soc. of Investment Analysts. *Publications:* Investment in Trust: problems and policies, 1961; Art and Practice of Investment, 1962, 4th edn 1974; Purposeful Investment, 1965; Principles of Pension Fund Investment, 1966, 2nd edn 1976; Investment for All, 1972; articles for national press on investment and insurance, incl. over 200 articles for The Guardian, Observer, etc. *Recreations:* rose-growing, cricket (Pres. and Captain, Chingford Park CC), writing, portrait painting, playing-fields movement, 1934- (Duke of Edinburgh award). *Address:* 603 Mountjoy House, Barbican, EC2Y 8BP. *T:* 01-628 7638; 6 Carlton Road East, Westgate, Kent. *T:* Thanet 32105. *Clubs:* City Livery, MCC, Pen International.

See also James Nursaw.

NURSTEN, Prof. Harry Erwin, PhD, DSc; FRSC, FIFST; Professor and Head of Department of Food Science, Reading University, since 1976; *s of* Sergius Nursten and Helene Nursten; *m* 1950, Jean Patricia Frobisher. *Educ:* Ilkley Grammar Sch.; Leeds Univ. (BSc 1st Cl. Hons Colour Chemistry, 1947; PhD 1949; DSc 1973). FRIC 1957; FIFST 1972. Bradford Dyers Assoc. Res. Fellow, Dept of Colour Chem. and Dyeing, Leeds Univ., 1949-52; Lectr in Textile Chem. and Dyeing, Nottingham and Dist Tech. Coll., 1952-54; Lectr 1955-65, Sen. Lectr 1965-70, and Reader 1970-76, Procter Dept of Food and Leather Science, Leeds Univ. Res. Associate, Dept of Nutrition, Food Science and Technol., MIT, 1961-62; Vis. Prof., Dept of Food Science and Technol., Univ. of Calif, Davis, 1966. Pres., Soc. of Leather Technologists and Chemists, 1974-76. Bill Littlejohn Memorial Medallion Lectr, Brit. Soc. of Flavourists, 1974. *Publications:* (ed jtly) Progress in Flavour Research, 1979; papers in Jl Sci. Food Agric., Jl Soc. Leather Technol. Chem., and Jl Chem. Soc. *Address:* Department of Food Science, University of Reading, London Road, Reading, Berks RG1 5AQ. *T:* Reading 875234.

NUTMAN, Dr Phillip Sadler, FRS 1968; Head of Department of Soil Microbiology, Rothamsted Experimental Station, Harpenden, 1957-79; *b* 10 Oct. 1914; *s of* John William Nutman and Elizabeth Hester Nutman (*née* Hughes); *m* 1940, Mary Meta Stanbury; two *s* one *d*. *Educ:* Teignmouth Grammar Sch.; Imperial Coll., London Univ. Research Asst, Rothamsted Experimental Station, 1940; Senior Research Fellow, Canberra, Australia, 1953-56; Rothamsted, 1956-79; Hannaford Res. Fellow, Waite Inst., Adelaide, 1980. Huxley Medal, 1959. *Publications:* research papers in plant physiological, genetical and microbiological journals. *Recreations:* music, woodworking. *Address:* Great Hackworthy Cottage, Tedburn St Mary, Exeter EX6 6DW. *T:* Tedburn St Mary 364.

NUTTALL, Rev. Derek; Director, Cruse, the National Organisation for the Widowed and their Children, since 1978 (National Organiser, 1974-78); *b* 23 Sept. 1937; *s of* Charles William Nuttall and Doris Nuttall; *m* 1965, Margaret Hathaway Brown; two *s* one *d*. *Educ:* Ironville Sch.; Somercotes Sch.; Overdale Coll., Selly Oak (Diploma). Semi-skilled worker in industry, 1953-60; office clerk, 1960-61; college, 1961-65; ministry in Falkirk, 1965-67; ordained, 1967; ministry and community work in Aberfan, 1967-74: Gen. Sec., Community Assoc.; mem., church and community cttees. Member: Exec., Internat. Fedn of Widow/Widower Orgns, 1980-; Internat. Workgroup on Death and Dying, 1980-. *Publications:* articles and papers on bereavement and on needs of widows, widowers and bereaved children. *Recreations:* music, reading, sport (mainly spectating), supporting the children's activities. *Address:* Cruse House, 126 Sheen Road, Richmond, Surrey TW9 1UR. *T:* 01-940 4818; 51 Spinney Hill, Addlestone, Surrey. *T:* Weybridge 46897. *Club:* Royal Society of Medicine.

NUTTALL, Dr Geoffrey Fillingham; Ecclesiastical historian, retired; Visiting Professor, King's College, London, 1977-80; *b* Colwyn Bay, Wales, 8 Nov. 1911; *s of* Harold Nuttall and Muriel Fillingham (*née* Hodgson); *m* 1944, Mary (*née* Preston) (*d* 1982), widow of George Philip Powley. *Educ:* Bootham Sch., York; Balliol Coll., Oxford (MA 1936); Mansfield Coll., Oxford (BD 1938, DD 1945). Ordained Congregational Minister, 1938: Warminster, Wilts, 1938-43; Fellow, Woodbrooke, Selly Oak Colls, Birmingham, 1943-45; Lectr in Church Hist., New Coll. (Sch. of Divinity), London Univ., 1945-77; Chm., Bd of Studies in Theol., Univ. of London, 1957-59; Dean, Faculty of Theol., 1960-64; FKC 1977. University Preacher: Leeds, 1950; Cambridge, 1958; London, 1968; Oxford, 1972, 1980. Lectures: Friends of Dr Williams's Library, 1951; Drew, New Coll., London, 1956; Hibbert, 1962; W. M. Llewelyn, Memorial Coll., Swansea, 1966; Charles Gore, Westminster Abbey, 1968; Owen Evans, Aberystwyth, 1968; F. D. Maurice, King's Coll., London, 1970; R. T. Jenkins, Bangor, 1976; Ethel M. Wood, London, 1978; Dr Williams Meml, Swansea, 1978. External Examiner: Belfast, Birmingham, Cambridge, Canterbury, Durham, Edinburgh, Leeds, McMaster, Manchester, Nottingham, Oxford, Wales. President: Friends' Hist. Soc., 1953; Congregational Hist. Soc., 1965-72; London Soc. for Study of Religion, 1966; Eccles. History Soc., 1972; United Reformed Church History Soc., 1972-77. Trustee, Dr Daniel Williams's Charity. A Vice-Pres., Hon. Soc. of Cymmrodorion, 1978-. Mem., Adv. Editorial Bd, Jl of Eccles. History, 1950-. For. Hon. Mem., Kerkhistorisch Gezelschap, 1981. Hon. DD Wales, 1969. *Publications:* (ed) Letters of John Pinney 1679-1699, 1939; The Holy Spirit in Puritan Faith and Experience, 1946 (2nd edn 1947); The Holy Spirit and Ourselves, 1947 (2nd edn 1966);

Studies in Christian Enthusiasm illustrated from Early Quakerism, 1948; (ed) Philip Doddridge 1702-1751: his contribution to English religion, 1951; Richard Baxter and Philip Doddridge: a study in a tradition, 1951; The Reality of Heaven, 1951; James Nayler: a fresh approach, 1954; (contrib.) Studies in Christian Social Commitment, 1954; Visible Saints: the Congregational Way 1640-1660, 1957; The Welsh Saints 1640-1660: Walter Cradock, Vavasor Powell, Morgan Llwyd, 1957; Christian Pacifism in History, 1958 (2nd edn 1971); (ed with Owen Chadwick) From Uniformity to Unity 1662-1962, 1962; Better Than Life: the lovingkindness of God, 1962; (contrib.) Man's Faith and Freedom: the theological influence of Jacobus Arminius, 1962; (contrib.) The Beginnings of Nonconformity, 1964; (contrib.) Choose your Weapons, 1964; Richard Baxter (Leaders of Religion), 1965; Howel Harris 1714-1773: the last enthusiast, 1965; The Puritan Spirit: essays and addresses, 1967; Congregationalists and Creeds, 1967; (contrib.) A Declaration of Faith (Congregational Church in England and Wales), 1967; The Significance of Trevecca College 1768-91, 1969; The Faith of Dante Alighieri, 1969; Christianity and Violence, 1972; (contrib.) Violence and Oppression: a Quaker Response, 1973; (contrib.) Christian Spirituality: essays in honour of Gordon Rupp, 1975; (contrib.) Der Pietismus in Gestalten und Wirkungen: Martin Schmidt zum 65 Geburtstag, 1975; New College, London and its Library, 1977; The Moment of Recognition: Luke as story-teller, 1978; contrib. Studies in Church History: Vol. VII, 1971; Vol. X, 1973; (contrib.) Pietismus und Réveil, 1978; (ed) Calendar of the Correspondence of Philip Doddridge, DD 1702-1751, 1979; (contrib.) Reformation Principle and Practice: essays in honour of A. G. Dickens, 1980; (contrib.) Philip Doddridge, Nonconformity and Northampton, 1981; contrib. Dict. of Nat. Biog., Encyc. Brit., Dict. d'Histoire et de Géog. Eccés., Evang. Kirchenlexikon; articles and revs in Jl Eccles. History and Jl Theol Studies; *Festschrift:* Reformation, Conformity and Dissent: essays in honour of Geoffrey Nuttall, 1977. *Recreations:* walking, motoring (as passenger), languages. *Address:* 35 Queen Mother Court, 151 Selly Wood Road, Birmingham B30 1TH. *T:* 021-472 2320. *Club:* Penn.

NUTTALL, Rt. Rev. Michael; *see* Natal, Bishop of.

NUTTALL, Sir Nicholas Keith Lillington, 3rd Bt, *cr* 1922; *b* 21 Sept. 1933; *s* of Lieut-Colonel Sir E. Keith Nuttall, 2nd Bt, RE (who died on active service, Aug. 1941), and Gytha Primrose Harrison (*d* 1967), *e d* of Sidney H. Burgess, of Heathfield, Bowdon, Cheshire; *S* father, 1941; *m* 1st, 1960, Rosemary Caroline (marr. diss. 1971), *e d* of Christopher York, *qv*; one *s* one *d*; 2nd, 1971, Julia Jill Beresford (marr. diss. 1975), *d* of Thomas Williamson; 3rd, 1975, Miranda, *d* of Richard St John Quarry and of Lady Mancroft; three *d*. *Educ:* Eton; Royal Military Academy, Sandhurst. Commissioned Royal Horse Guards, 1953; Captain, 1959; Major 1966; retd 1968. *Heir: s* Harry Nuttall, *b* 2 Jan. 1963. *Address:* Lyford Cay, PO Box N7776, Nassau, Bahamas. *Club:* White's.

NUTTER, Most Rev. Harold Lee; *see* Fredericton, Archbishop of.

NUTTGENS, Patrick John; Director, Leeds Polytechnic, since 1969; *b* 2 March 1930; 2nd *s* of Joseph Edward Nuttgens, stained glass artist, and Kathleen Mary Nuttgens (*née* Clarke); *m* 1954, Bridget Ann Badenoch; five *s* three *d*. *Educ:* Ratcliffe Coll., Leicester; Univ. of Edinburgh; Edinburgh Coll. of Art. MA, PhD, DA(Edin), ARIBA. Lectr, Dept of Architecture, Univ. of Edinburgh, 1956-61; Dir, Inst. of Advanced Architectural Studies, Univ. of York, 1962-68; Prof. of Architecture, Univ. of York, 1968-69; Hoffman Wood Prof. of Architecture, Univ. of Leeds, 1968-70. Member: Royal Commn on Ancient and Historical Monuments of Scotland, 1967-76; Ancient Monuments Bd, 1975-78; Chairman: BBC North Region Adv. Council, 1970-75; BBC Continuing Educn Adv. Council, 1977-. *Publications:* Reginald Fairlie, a Scottish Architect, 1959; York, City Building Series, 1971; The Landscape of Ideas, 1972; (contrib.) Spirit of the Age, 1975; York: the continuing city, 1976; Leeds, Old and New, 1976; Leeds, 1979; Yorkshire section, Shell Book of English Villages, 1980; Pocket Guide to Architecture, 1980; (Gen. Editor) World's Great Architecture, 1980; (contrib.) Study Service, 1982; regular contributor to jls on architecture, planning, education and environmental studies. *Recreations:* drawing, painting. *Address:* Churchwood, Beckett Park, Leeds LS6 3QS. *Club:* Savile.

NUTTING, Rt. Hon. Sir (Harold) Anthony, 3rd Bt *cr* 1902; PC 1954; *b* 11 Jan. 1920; 3rd and *y s* of Sir Harold Stansmore Nutting, 2nd Bt, and Enid Hester Nina (*d* 1961), *d* of F. B. Homan-Mulock; *S* father, 1972; *m* 1st, 1941, Gillian Leonora (marr. diss., 1959), *d* of Edward J. Strutt, Hatfield Peverel, Essex; two *s* one *d*; 2nd, 1961, Anne Gunning, *d* of Arnold Parker, Cuckfield, Sussex. *Educ:* Eton; Trinity College, Cambridge. Leics. Yeo., 1939; invalided, 1940. In HM Foreign Service, 1940-45; MP (C) Melton Division of Leics, 1945-56, resigned. Chairman: Young Conservative and Unionist Movement, 1946; National Union of Conservative and Unionist Associations, 1950; Conservative National Executive Cttee, 1951. Parliamentary Under-Secretary of State for Foreign Affairs, 1951-54; Minister of State for Foreign Affairs, 1954-56, resigned. Leader, UK Delegn to UN General Assembly and to UN Disarmament Commn, 1954-56. *Publications:* I Saw for Myself, 1958; Disarmament, 1959; Europe Will Not Wait, 1960; Lawrence of Arabia, 1961; The Arabs, 1964; Gordon, Martyr and Misfit, 1966; No End of a Lesson, 1967; Scramble for Africa: the Great Trek to The Boer War, 1970; Nasser, 1972. *Recreation:* fishing. *Heir: s* John Grenfell Nutting [*b* 28 Aug. 1942; *m* 1973, Diane Countess Beatty; one *s* one *d*]. *Address:* Achentoul, Kinbrace, Sutherland.

NUTTING, Prof. Jack, MA, ScD, PhD; FEng, FIM; Professor of Metallurgy, Houldsworth School of Applied Science, University of Leeds, since 1960; *b* 8 June 1924; *o s* of Edgar and Ethel Nutting, Mirfield, Yorks; *m* 1950, Thelma Kippax, *y d* of Tom and Florence Kippax, Morecambe, Lancs; one *s* two *d*. *Educ:* Mirfield Grammar School, Yorks; Univ. of Leeds. BSc Leeds, 1945; PhD Leeds, 1948; MA Cantab, 1952; ScD Cantab, 1967. Research at Cavendish Laboratory, Cambridge, 1948-49; University Demonstrator, 1949-54, University Lecturer, 1954-60, Department of Metallurgy, Cambridge University. Past Pres., Metals Soc.; Past Pres., Instn of Metallurgists. Awarded Beilby medal and prize, 1961; Hadfield medal and prize, 1964. Hon. DSc: Acad. of Mining and Metallurgy, Cracow, 1969; Moratuwa Univ., Sri Lanka, 1981. *Publications:* numerous papers in Jls of Iron and Steel Inst., Inst. of Metals and Metals Soc. *Recreations:* foreign travel, mountain walking. *Address:* St Mary's, 57 Weetwood Lane, Headingley, Leeds LS16 5NP. *T:* Leeds 751400.

NYAKYI, Anthony Balthazar; High Commissioner for Tanzania in London, since 1981; *b* 8 June 1936; *m* 1969, Margaret Nyakyi; two *s* two *d*. *Educ:* Makerere Coll., Univ. of E Africa (BA Gen.). Admin. Office, Prime Minister's Office and Min. of Educn, 1962-63; Head of Political Div., Foreign Service Office, 1963-68; Ambassador: to the Netherlands, 1968-70; to Fed. Republic of Germany, 1970-72; Principal Sec., Foreign Affairs, 1972-78; Principal Sec., Defence, 1978-80; High Comr to Zimbabwe, 1980-81. *Address:* Tanzania High Commission, 43 Hertford Street, W1Y 7TF. *T:* 01-499 8951.

NYE, Prof. John Frederick, FRS 1976; Professor of Physics, University of Bristol, since 1969; *b* 26 Feb. 1923; *s* of Haydn Percival Nye and Jessie Mary, *d* of Anderson Hague, painter; *m* 1953, Georgiana Wiebenson; one *s* two *d*. *Educ:* Stowe; King's Coll., Cambridge (Maj. Schol.; MA, PhD 1948). Research, Cavendish Laboratory, Cambridge, 1944-49; Univ. Demonstrator in Mineralogy and Petrology, Cambridge, 1949-51; Bell Telephone Laboratories, NJ, USA, 1952-53; Lectr, 1953, Reader, 1965, Univ. of Bristol; Visiting Professor: in Glaciology, California Inst. of Technol., 1959; of Applied Sciences, Yale Univ., 1964; of Geophysics, Univ. of Washington, 1973. President: Internat. Glaciological Soc., 1966-69; Internat. Commn of Snow and Ice, 1971-75. For. Mem., Royal Swedish Acad. of Scis, 1977. Kirk Bryan Award, Geol. Soc. of Amer., 1961; Seligman Crystal, Internat. Glaciol Soc., 1969; Antarctic Service Medal, USA, 1974. *Publications:* Physical Properties of Crystals, 1957, rev. edn 1972; papers on physics of crystals, glaciology, and applications of catastrophe theory in scientific jls. *Address:* 45 Canynge Road, Bristol BS8 3LH. *T:* Bristol 733769.

See also P. H. Nye.

NYE, Ven. Nathaniel Kemp; retired; *b* 4 Nov. 1914; *s* of Charles Frederick and Evelyn Nye; *m* 1941, Rosa Jackson; two *s* one *d*. *Educ:* Merchant Taylors' Sch.; King's College London (AKC 1935); Cuddesdon College, Oxford. Ordained 1937 to St Peter's, St Helier Estate, Morden, Surrey; Chaplain RAF, 1940-46 (POW 1941-43; escaped from Italy at liberation); Rector, Holy Trinity, Clapham, 1946-54; Vicar, St Peter's, St Helier Estate, 1954-60; Vicar, All Saints, Maidstone (Parish Church), Canon, and Rural Dean, 1960-66; Tait Missioner, Canterbury Diocese, 1966-72; Archdeacon of Maidstone, 1972-79. Hon. Canon of Canterbury, 1960; Canon Emeritus, 1979; Archdeacon Emeritus, dio. Canterbury, 1982. *Recreations:* woodcraft, sailing, travel; family life! *Address:* Lees Cottage, Boughton Lees, Ashford, Kent. *T:* Ashford 26175.

NYE, Peter Hague; Reader in Soil Science, University of Oxford, since 1961; Fellow of St Cross College, since 1966; *b* 16 Sept. 1921; *s* of Haydn Percival Nye and Jessie Mary (*née* Hague); *m* 1953, Phyllis Mary Quenault; one *s* two *d*. *Educ:* Charterhouse; Balliol Coll., Oxford (MA, BSc (Domus Exhibnr)); Christ's Coll., Cambridge. Agricl Chemist, Gold Coast, 1947-50; Lectr in Soil Science, University Coll. of Ibadan, Nigeria, 1950-52; Sen. Lectr in Soil Science, Univ. of Ghana, 1952-60; Res. Officer, Internat. Atomic Energy Agency, Vienna, 1960-61; Vis. Professor, Cornell Univ., 1974, 1981; Commonwealth Vis. Prof., Univ. of Western Aust., 1979. Pres., British Soc. Soil Science, 1968-69; Mem. Council, Internat. Soc. Soil Science, 1968-74. Governor, Nat. Vegetable Res. Station, 1972-. *Publications:* The Soil under Shifting Cultivation, 1961; Solute Movement in the Soil-Root System, 1977; articles, mainly in Jl of Soil Science, Plant and Soil, Jl of Agricl Science. *Recreations:* gardening; formerly cricket, tennis, squash. *Address:* Hewl Barn, Common Road, Beckley, Oxon.

See also J. F. Nye.

NYE, Robert; writer; *b* 15 March 1939; *s* of Oswald William Nye and Frances Dorothy Weller; *m* 1st, 1959, Judith Pratt (marr. diss. 1967); three *s*; 2nd, 1968, Aileen Campbell; one *d*. *Educ:* Southend High School, Essex. Freelance writer, 1961-. FRSL 1977. *Publications: poetry:* Juvenilia 1, 1961; Juvenilia 2, 1963 (Eric Gregory Award, 1963); Darker Ends, 1969; Divisions on a Ground, 1976; *fiction:* Doubtfire, 1967; Tales I Told My Mother, 1969; Falstaff, 1976 (The Guardian Fiction Prize, 1976; Hawthornden Prize, 1977); Merlin, 1978; Faust, 1980; The Voyage of Destiny, 1982; *plays:* (with Bill Watson) Sawney Bean, 1970; The Seven Deadly Sins: A Mask, 1974; Penthesilea, Fugue and Sisters, 1976; *children's fiction:* Taliesin, 1966; March Has Horse's Ears, 1966; Wishing Gold, 1970; Poor Pumpkin, 1971; Out of the World and Back Again, 1977; Once Upon Three Times, 1978; The Bird of the Golden Land, 1980; Harry Pay the Pirate, 1981; *translation:* Beowulf, 1968; *editions:* A Choice of Sir Walter Ralegh's Verse, 1972; William Barnes:

Selected Poems, 1973; A Choice of Swinburne's Verse, 1973; The English Sermon 1750-1850, 1976; The Faber Book of Sonnets, 1976; contribs to British and American periodicals. *Recreation:* gambling. *Address:* The Anchorage, Summer Cove, Kinsale, County Cork, Ireland.

NYERERE, Julius Kambarage; President, United Republic of Tanzania (formerly Tanganyika and Zanzibar), since 1964; President, Tanganyika African National Union, since 1954; Chairman, Chama cha Mapinduzi (The Revolutionary Party) (born of merger between mainland's TANU and Zanzibar Afro-Shiraz Party), since 1977; Chancellor, University of Dar es Salaam, since 1970; *b* 1922; *m* 1953, Maria Magige; five *s* two d. *Educ:* Tabora Secondary School; Makerere University College; Edinburgh University (MA). Began as Teacher; became President African Association, Dar es Salaam, 1953; formed Tanganyika African National Union, left teaching and campaigned for Nationalist Movement, 1954; addressed Trusteeship Council, 1955, and Cttee of UN Gen. Assembly, 1956. MLC Tanganyika, July-Dec. 1957, resigned in protest; elected Mem. for E Prov. in first elections, 1958, for Dar es Salaam, 1960; Chief Minister, 1960; Prime Minister of Tanganyika, 1961-62; President, Tanganyika Republic, 1962-64. First Chancellor, Univ. of East Africa, 1963-70. Holds hon. degrees. *Publications:* Freedom and Unity-Uhuru Na Umoja, 1966; Freedom and Socialism-Uhuru na Ujamaa, 1969; Essays on Socialism, 1969; Freedom and Development, 1973; Swahili trans of Julius Caesar and The Merchant of Venice, 1969. *Address:* State House, Dar es Salaam, United Republic of Tanzania.

O

OAKELEY, Sir (Edward) Atholl, 7th Bt *cr* 1790; author; *b* 31 May 1900; *s* of late Major E. F. Oakeley, South Lancashire Regiment, and late Everilde A. Oakeley, *d* of Henry Beaumont; *S* cousin (Sir Charles Richard Andrew Oakeley, 6th Bt), 1959; *m* 1st, 1922, Ethyl Felice O'Coffey (marr. diss.); 2nd, (Patricia) Mabel Mary (*née* Birtchnell) (marr. diss.); one *s*; 3rd, Doreen (*née* Wells) (marr. diss.); 4th, 1960, Shirley Church; one d. *Educ:* Clifton and Sandhurst. Lieutenant, Oxfordshire and Buckinghamshire Light Infantry, 1919-23; then Chief Contact to late Sir Charles Higham in Advertising; Captain, Amateur International Wrestling Team, 1928-29; Heavyweight Wrestling Champion of Europe, 1932; Heavyweight Wrestling Champion of Gt Britain, 1930-35; Manager to World Heavyweight Wrestling Champion, Jack Sherry, 1935-39; Promoter of Championship Wrestling, Harringay Arena, 1949-54. *Publications:* The Facts on which R. D. Blackmore based Lorna Doone, 1969; Blue Blood on the Mat, 1971. *Recreations:* cricket; hunting; athletics; sailing; wrestling; boxing; weight-lifting. *Heir:* s John Digby Atholl Oakeley [*b* 27 Nov. 1932; *m* 1958, Maureen, *d* of John and Helen Cox, Hamble, Hants; one *s* one d]. *Address:* Nomad, Lynton, Devon.
See also M. Oakeley.

OAKELEY, Mary, MA Oxon; Headmistress, St Felix School, Southwold, 1958-April 1978; *b* 2 April 1913; *d* of Maj. Edward Francis Oakeley, S Lancs Regt, and Everilde Anne (*née* Beaumont). *Educ:* St John's Bexhill-on-Sea; St Hilda's Coll., Oxford. MA Hons History. Asst Mistress: St James's, West Malvern, 1935-38; St George's, Ascot, 1938-39; Headmistress, Craighead Diocesan Sch., Timaru, NZ, 1940-55; Head of American Section, La Châtelainie, St Blaise, Switzerland, 1956-58. *Recreations:* ski-ing, gardening, embroidery. *Address:* Cherwell Lodge, Eynsham, Oxon. *T:* Oxford 880759. *Club:* Royal Over-Seas League.
See also Sir Atholl Oakeley, Bt.

OAKES, Sir Christopher, 3rd Bt, *cr* 1939; *b* 10 July 1949; *s* of Sir Sydney Oakes, 2nd Bt, and Greta (*d* 1977), *yr* d of Gunnar Victor Hartmann, Copenhagen, Denmark; *S* father, 1966; *m* 1978, Julie Dawn, *d* of Donovan Franklin Cowan, Regina, Canada; one d. *Educ:* Bredon, Tewkesbury; Georgia Mil. Acad., USA. *Heir:* uncle Harry Philip Oakes [*b* 30 Aug. 1932; *m* 1958, Christiane, *o d* of Rudolf Botsch, Hamburg; three *s* one d]. *Address:* PO Box 1002, Nassau, Bahamas.

OAKES, Rt. Hon. Gordon James; PC 1979; MP (Lab) Widnes, since Sept. 1971; *b* 22 June 1931; *o s* of late James Oakes and Florence (*née* Hewitt), Widnes, Lancs; *m* 1952, Esther O'Neill, *e d* of late Councillor Joseph O'Neill; three *s*. *Educ:* Wade Deacon Gram. Sch., Widnes; Univ. of Liverpool. BA (Hon.) English, 1952; Admitted Solicitor, 1956. Entered Widnes Borough Council, 1952 (Mayor, 1964-65). Chm. Widnes Constituency Labour Party, 1953-58; contested (Lab): Bebington, 1959; Moss Side (Manchester) by-election, 1961; MP (Lab) Bolton West, 1964-70; PPS, Home Office, 1966-67, DES, 1967-70; Front Bench Opposition spokesman on local govt and the environment, 1970-74; Parly Under-Secretary of State: DoE, 1974-76; Dept of Energy, 1976; Minister of State, DES, 1976-79; Front Bench Opposition spokesman on Environment, 1979-. British Deleg., NATO Parliamentarians, 1967-70; Member: Select Cttee on Race Relations, 1969-70; Executive, NW Region of Labour Party, 1971-73; Exec. Cttee, Commonwealth Parly Assoc., 1979-; Chm., All Party Energy Efficiency Gp, 1980-. Vice-President: Rural District Councils Assoc., 1972-74; County Councils Assoc., 1982-; Inst. of Public Health Inspectors, 1973-; Jt Chm., Nat. Waste Management Adv.

Council, 1974-76. *Publications:* The Management of Higher Education in the Maintained Sector, 1978; various articles. *Recreations:* conversation, motoring with the family, caravanning, maps. *Address:* Upton Bridle Path, Widnes, Cheshire.

OAKES, Joseph Stewart; a Recorder of the Crown Court, since 1975; barrister-at-law; *b* 7 Jan. 1919; *s* of Laban Oakes and Mary Jane Oakes; *m* 1950, Irene May Peasnall. *Educ:* Royal Masonic Sch., Bushey; Stretford Grammar Sch.; Manchester Univ., 1937-40 (BA Hons). Royal Signals, 1940-48, Captain. Called to Bar, Inner Temple, 1948; practised on Northern Circuit, 1948-. *Recreations:* horticulture, photography, music. *Address:* 38 Langley Road, Sale, Greater Manchester M33 5AY. *T:* 061-962 2068; 28 St John Street, Manchester M3 4DJ. *T:* 061-834 8418.

OAKESHOTT, Michael Joseph, FBA 1966; MA; Professor Emeritus, University of London, 1969; *b* 11 Dec. 1901; *s* of Joseph Francis Oakeshott and Frances Maude Hellicar. *Educ:* St George's School, Harpenden; Gonville and Caius College, Cambridge. Fellow: Gonville and Caius College, 1925-; Nuffield College, Oxford, 1949-50; University Prof. of Political Science at LSE, Univ. of London, 1951-69. Served in British Army, 1940-45. Muirhead Lecturer, Univ. of Birmingham, 1953. *Publications:* Experience and its Modes, 1933: A Guide to the Classics (with G. T. Griffith), 1936, 1947; Social and Political Doctrines of Contemporary Europe, 1939; Hobbes's Leviathan, 1946; The Voice of Poetry in the Conversation of Mankind, 1959; Rationalism in Politics and other Essays, 1962; Hobbes on Civil Association, 1975; On Human Conduct, 1975; On History, 1982. *Address:* Victoria Cottage, Acton, Swanage, Dorset.

OAKESHOTT, Sir Walter (Fraser), Kt 1980; MA; FBA 1971; FSA; Hon. LLD (St Andrews); Rector of Lincoln College, Oxford, 1953-72, Hon. Fellow, 1972; *b* 11 Nov. 1903; *s* of Walter Field Oakeshott, MD, and Kathleen Fraser; *m* 1928, Noël Rose (*d* 1976), *d* of R. O. Moon, MD, FRCP; twin *s* two d. *Educ:* Tonbridge; Balliol Coll., Oxford. Class. Mods 1924; Lit. Hum. 1926; Hon. Fellow, 1974. Assistant Master, Bec School, SW17, 1926-27; Assistant Master Merchant Taylors', 1927-30; Kent Education Office, 1930-31; Assistant Master Winchester College, 1931-38; released for 15 months (1936-37) for membership of Pilgrim Trust Unemployment Enquiry; High Master of St Paul's School, 1939-46; Headmaster of Winchester College, 1946-54. Vice-Chancellor, Oxford University, 1962-64; Pro-Vice-Chancellor, 1964-66. President, Bibliographical Society, 1966-68. Trustee, Pilgrim Trust, 1949-76. Rhind Lecturer, Edinburgh Univ., 1956. Master, Skinners' Co., 1960-61. *Publications:* Men Without Work (joint), 1938; The Artists of the Winchester Bible, 1945; The Mosaics of Rome, Fourth to Fourteenth Centuries, 1967; Sigena Wall Paintings, 1972; The Two Winchester Bibles, 1981; various semi-popular books on literature and medieval art. *Recreations:* pictures, books. *Address:* The Old School House, Eynsham, Oxford. *Club:* Roxburghe.

OAKHAM, Archdeacon of; see Fernyhough, Ven. B.

OAKLEY, Brian Wynne, CBE 1981; Secretary, Science and Engineering Research Council (formerly Science Research Council), since 1978; *b* 10 Oct. 1927; *s* of Bernard and Edna Oakley; *m* 1953, Marian Elizabeth (*née* Woolley); one *s* three d. *Educ:* Exeter Coll., Oxford. MA. FInstP, FBCS. Telecommunication Res. Establishment, 1950; Head, Industrial Applications Unit, RRE, 1966-69; Head, Computer Systems Branch, Min. of Technology, 1969-72; Head, Res. Requirements Div., DTI, 1972-78. *Recreations:* theatre, sailing. *Address:* 120 Reigate Road, Ewell, Epsom, Surrey KT17 3BX. *T:* 01-393 4096.

OAKLEY, John Davidson, CBE 1981; DFC 1944; Chairman, Grosvenor Development Capital, since 1981; Deputy Chairman, Robert Jenkins Ltd, since 1978; Director: Beau Brummel Ltd, since 1972; Ionian Securities Ltd, since 1978; Gardners Transformers Ltd, since 1982; Member, British Overseas Trade Advisory Council, since 1977; *b* 15 June 1921; *s* of Richard Oakley and Nancy Davidson; *m* 1943, Georgina Mary Hare; two *s*. *Educ:* Green Lane Sch. Joined Briggs Motor Bodies Ltd, 1937. Served War in RAF, 1941-46: commissioned 1942; Flt Lt 1943; actg Sqdn Ldr 1944; apptd to Air Min. Directorate Staff, 1945. Engrg Buyer, Briggs Motor Bodies Ltd, 1946-53; Dep. Purchase Manager, Body Div., Ford Motor Co. Ltd, 1953-56; Production Dir/General Manager, Standard Triumph (Liverpool) Ltd, until 1962; Managing Director: Copeland & Jenkins Ltd, 1963-71; R. Woolf & Co. Ltd, 1964-67; Gp Man. Dir, L. Sterne & Co., 1967-69; Chairman: General Electric & Mechanical Systems Ltd, 1970-73; Berwick Timpo Ltd, 1970-82; Edgar Allen Balfour Ltd, 1974-79; Australian British Trade Assoc., 1977-81; BOTB Adv. Gp Australia and NZ, 1977-81; Director: Blairs Ltd, 1976-82; Eagle & Globe Steel Ltd, NSW, 1978-79; Nexos Office Systems Ltd, 1981-82; Isis Industrial Services plc, 1982. Dir, Oxford Univ. Business Summer Sch. for 1978; Mem., Steering Cttee, Oxford Univ. Business Summer Sch., 1981-. Cons. Mem., Essex CC, 1982-. Member: Glovers' Co.; Cutlers' Co. in Hallamshire; Inst. of British Carriage & Automobile Manufacturers. CBIM; FIPS. FRSA. *Recreations:* golf, tennis, walking, bridge. *Address:* Lower Meadows, White Roding, Essex CM6 1RG. *T:* White Roding 386. *Clubs:* Reform, Royal Air Force; Bishop's Stortford Golf (Bishop's Stortford, Herts).

OAKLEY, Wilfrid George, MD, FRCP; Hon. Consulting Physician, King's College Hospital, since 1971; Vice President, British Diabetic Association, since 1971; *b* 23 Aug. 1905; *s* of late Rev. Canon G. D. Oakley and Mrs Oakley; *m* 1931, Hermione Violet Wingate-Saul; one *s*. *Educ*: Durham School; Gonville and Caius College, Cambridge; St Bartholomew's Hospital. Tancred studentship in Physic, Gonville and Caius Coll., 1923; Bentley Prize and Baly Research Schol., St Bart's Hosp., 1933. Formerly Physician i/c Diabetic Dept, King's College Hosp., 1957-70. Examr, Cambridge and Glasgow Univs. MD (Hon. Mention) Cantab 1934; FRCP 1942. FRSocMed; Pres., Med. Soc., London, 1962; Mem. Assoc. of Physicians of Great Britain; Vice-Pres., British Diabetic Assoc., 1971. *Publications*: (jtly) Clinical Diabetes and its Biochemical Basis, 1968; Diabetes and its Management, 1973, 3rd edn 1978; scientific articles and chapters in various text-books on diabetes. *Address*: 149 Harley Street, W1. *T*: 01-935 4444.

OAKSEY, 2nd Baron *cr* 1947 (properly **TREVETHIN,** 4th Baron *cr* 1921, **AND OAKSEY); John Geoffrey Tristram Lawrence;** JP; Racing Correspondent to Daily Telegraph since 1957, to Horse and Hound since 1959 and to Sunday Telegraph since 1960; racing commentator for ITV, since 1970; Director, HTV, since 1980; *b* 21 March 1929; *o s* of 1st Baron Oaksey and 3rd Baron Trevethin and of Marjorie, *d* of late Commander Charles N. Robinson, RN; *S* father, 1971; *m* 1959, Victoria Mary, *d* of late Major John Dennistoun, MBE; one *s* one *d*. *Educ*: Horris Hill; Eton; New College, Oxford (BA); Yale Law School. JP Malmesbury, 1978. *Publications*: History of Steeplechasing (jointly), 1967; The Story of Mill Reef, 1974. *Recreations*: hunting, skiing, tennis, riding. *Heir*: *s* Hon. Patrick John Tristram Lawrence, *b* 29 June 1960. *Address*: Hill Farm, Oaksey, Malmesbury, Wilts. *T*: Crudwell 303. *Club*: Brooks's.

See also H. S. L. Dundas.

OAKSHOTT, Hon. Sir Anthony (Hendrie), 2nd Bt *cr* 1959; *b* 10 Oct. 1929; *s* of Baron Oakshott, MBE (Life Peer), and of Joan, *d* of Marsden Withington; *S* to baronetcy of father, 1975; *m* 1965, Mrs Valerie de Pret-Roose, *d* of Jack Vlasto. *Educ*: Rugby. *Heir*: *b* Hon. Michael Arthur John Oakshott [*b* 12 April 1932; *m* 1957, Christina Rose Methuen, *d* of late Thomas Banks; three *s*]. *Address*: 42 Eaton Square, SW1. *T*: 01-235 2107. *Club*: White's.

OATES, Prof. (Edward Ernest) David (Michael), FSA; FBA 1974; Professor of Western Asiatic Archaeology, University of London, since 1969; *b* 25 Feb. 1927; *s* of Thomas Oates and Dora B. Strike; *m* 1956, Joan Louise Lines; one *s* two *d*. *Educ*: Callington County Sch.; Oundle Sch.; Trinity Coll., Cambridge (BA, MA). Fellow of Trinity Coll., Cambridge, 1951-65; Director, British School of Archaeology in Iraq, 1965-69. FSA 1954. *Publications*: Studies in the Ancient History of N Iraq, 1968; (with J. Oates) The Rise of Civilisation, 1976; contribs to The Dark Ages, ed D. Talbot Rice, 1965; papers of the British School in Rome, Iraq, etc. *Recreations*: history, carpentry. *Address*: 86 High Street, Barton, Cambridge CB3 7BG. *T*: Comberton 2273.

OATES, John Claud Trewinard, FBA 1976; Emeritus Reader in Historical Bibliography, University of Cambridge; Emeritus Fellow of Darwin College, Cambridge; *b* 24 June 1912; *s* of Claud Albert Oates and Clarissa Alberta Wakeham; *m* 1960, Helen Cooke (*née* Lister). *Educ*: Crypt Sch., Gloucester; Trinity Coll., Cambridge (Scholar; 1st Cl. Class. Tripos Pt I 1933, Pt II 1935; BA 1935, MA 1938). Sch. of Tank Technol., Mil. Coll. of Science, 1941-46. Univ. of Cambridge: Walston Student, 1935; Asst Under-Librarian, 1936, Under-Librarian, 1949, Dep. Librarian, 1975, Acting Librarian, 1979-80, Univ. Library; Sandars Reader in Bibliography, 1952, 1965. Pres., Bibliograph. Soc., 1970-72; Pres., Cambridge Bibliograph. Soc., 1978-81; Trustee, Laurence Sterne Trust, 1968-. Editor, The Library (Trans Bibliograph. Soc.), 1953-60. *Publications*: A Catalogue of the Fifteenth-Century Printed Books in the University Library, Cambridge, 1954; (contrib.) The English Library before 1700 (ed F. Wormald and C. E. Wright), 1958; Shandyism and Sentiment 1760-1800 (bicentenary lecture), 1968; contrib. bibliograph. jls. *Recreation*: walking the dog. *Address*: 144 Thornton Road, Cambridge. *T*: Cambridge 276653.

OATES, Sir Thomas, Kt 1972; CMG 1962; OBE 1958 (MBE 1946); Governor and Commander-in-Chief of St Helena, 1971-76; *b* 5 November 1917; *er s* of late Thomas Oates, Wadebridge, Cornwall; unmarried. *Educ*: Callington Grammar School, Cornwall; Trinity College, Cambridge (MA). Mathematical Tripos (Wrangler). Admiralty Scientific Staff, 1940-46; HMS Vernon, Minesweeping Section, 1940-42; British Admiralty Delegn, Washington, DC, 1942-46; Temp. Lieut, RNVR. Colonial Administrative Service, Nigeria, 1948-55; seconded to HM Treasury, 1953-55; Adviser to UK Delegn to UN Gen. Assembly, 1954. Financial Sec. to Govt of: British Honduras, 1955-59, Aden, 1959-63; Dep. High Comr, Aden, 1963-67; Permanent Sec., Gibraltar, 1968-69; Dep. Governor, Gibraltar, 1969-71. *Recreations*: photography, walking. *Address*: Tristan, Trevone, Padstow, Cornwall. *Clubs*: East India, Devonshire, Sports and Public Schools, Royal Commonwealth Society.

OATLEY, Sir Charles (William), Kt 1974; OBE 1956; MA; FRS 1969, FEng, FIEE, FIEEE; Professor of Electrical Engineering, University of Cambridge, 1960-71, now Emeritus; Fellow of Trinity College, Cambridge, since 1945; *b* 14 Feb. 1904; *s* of William Oatley and Ada May Dorrington; *m* 1930, (Dorothy) Enid West; two *s*. *Educ*: Bedford Modern Sch.; St John's Coll., Cambridge. Demonstrator, later lecturer, Dept of Physics, KCL, 1927-39. Min. of Supply, Radar Research and Development Establishment, 1939-45. Actg Superintendent in charge of scientific work, 1944-45. Lecturer,

later Reader, Dept of Engineering, Cambridge Univ., 1945-60. Director, English Electric Valve Company, 1966. Member: Council, Inst. of Electrical Engineers, 1954-56, 1961-64 (Chm. of Radio Section, 1954-55); Council, Royal Society, 1970-72. FEng 1976. Hon. Fellow, Royal Microscopical Soc., 1970; FKC 1976; Foreign Associate, Nat. Acad. of Engineering, USA, 1979. Hon. DSc: Heriot-Watt, 1974; Bath, 1977. Achievement Award, Worshipful Co. of Scientific Instrument Makers, 1966; Duddell Medal, Inst. of Physics and Physical Soc., 1969; Royal Medal, Royal Soc., 1969; Faraday Medal, IEE, 1970; Mullard Award, Royal Soc., 1973; James Alfred Ewing Medal, ICE, 1981. *Publications*: Wireless Receivers, 1932; The Scanning Electron Microscope, 1972; Electric and Magnetic Fields, 1976; papers in scientific and technical journals. *Recreation*: gardening. *Address*: 16 Porson Road, Cambridge. *T*: Cambridge 56194. *Club*: Athenæum.

See also M. C. Oatley.

OATLEY, Michael Charles, OBE 1975; HM Diplomatic Service; Counsellor, Harare (formerly Salisbury), since 1981; *b* 18 Oct. 1935; *s* of Sir Charles Oatley, *qv* and Lady Oatley (*née* Enid West); *m* 1965, Pippa Howden; two *s* one *d*. *Educ*: The Leys Sch.; Trinity Coll., Cambridge. FO, 1959-61; seconded to CO, Nairobi and Kampala, 1961-62; FO, 1962-63; Lome, 1963-65; FO, 1965-66; Kampala, 1966-68; Accra, 1968-69; FCO, 1969-73; seconded to NI Office, Belfast, 1973-75; Hong Kong, 1975-77; FCO, 1977-81. *Address*: c/o Foreign and Commonwealth Office, SW1. *Club*: Athenæum.

OBASANJO, Gen. Olusegun; Nigerian Head of State, Head of the Federal Military Government and Commander-in-Chief of the Armed Forces, Nigeria, 1976-79; Member, Advisory Council of State, since 1979; farmer; *b* Abeokuta, Ogun State, Nigeria, 5 March 1937; *m*; two *s* three *d*. *Educ*: Abeokuta Baptist High Sch.; Mons Officers' Cadet Sch., England. Entered Nigerian Army, 1958; commission, 1959; served in Zaire (then, the Congo), 1960. Comdr, Engrg Corps, 1963; Comdr of 2nd (Rear) Div. at Ibadan; GOC 3rd Inf. Div., 1969; Comdr, 3rd Marine Commando Div.; took surrender of forces of Biafra, in Nigerian Civil War, 1969-70; Comdr Engrg Corps, 1970-75. Political post as Federal Comr for Works and Housing, Jan.-July 1975. Chief of Staff, Supreme HQ, July 1975-Feb. 1976. Mem., Internat. Indep. Commn on Disarmament and Security. Part-time Associate, Univ. of Ibadan. *Publication*: My Command (autobiog.), 1980. *Recreations*: squash, table tennis, billiards, snooker. *Address*: PO Box 2286, Abeokuta, Nigeria.

O'BEIRNE, Cornelius Banahan, CBE 1964; QC; Assistant Director (Commonwealth), British Institute of International and Comparative Law, since 1978; *b* 9 September 1915; *e s* of late Captain C. B. O'Beirne, OBE; *m* 1949, Ivanka, *d* of Miloc Tupanjanin, Belgrade; one *s* one *d*. *Educ*: Stonyhurst Coll. Solicitor (Eng.), 1940. Served War, 1940-46; Maj. RA, Eur., Mid. E; Polit. Adviser's Office, Brit. Emb., Athens, 1945-46. Colonial Office, 1947-48. Called to Bar, Lincoln's Inn, 1952. Crown Counsel: Nigeria, 1949-53; High Commn Territories, SA, 1953-59; Solicitor-Gen., 1959; Attorney-General, High Commission Territories, South Africa, 1961-64; Counsellor (Legal), British Embassy, SA, 1964-65; Senior Legal Asst, Lord Chancellor's Office, 1966-71 (seconded as Attorney-Gen., Gibraltar, 1966-70); Council on Tribunals, 1971-78. QC: Basutoland, Bechuanaland and Swaziland, 1962; Gibraltar, 1967. Member: RIIA; Justice; Plowden Soc.; Commonwealth Parly Assoc. *Publications*: Laws of Gibraltar, rev. edn 1968; contribs to jls. *Recreations*: reading, photography. *Address*: Nanhoran Cottage, Claremont Lane, Esher, Surrey.

O'BEIRNE RANELAGH, John, (John Ranelagh), PhD; Commissioning Editor and Secretary to the Board, Channel Four Television Company, since 1981; *b* 3 Nov. 1947; *o s* of James O'Beirne Ranelagh and Elaine Lambert O'Beirne Ranelagh; *m* 1974, Elizabeth Grenville, *y d* of Sir William Hawthorne, *qv*. *Educ*: St Christopher's Sch.; Cambridgeshire Coll. of Arts and Technology; Christ Church, Oxford (MA); Eliot Coll., Univ. of Kent (PhD). Chase Manhattan Bank, 1970; Campaign Dir, Outset Housing Assoc., 1971; Univ. of Kent Studentship, 1972-74; BBC TV, 1974; Conservative Res. Dept, 1975-79; Associate Producer, Ireland: a television history, BBC TV, 1979-81. Mem., Political Cttee, UNA, 1978-. Governor, Daneford Sch., 1977-81. *Publications*: Science, Education and Industry, 1978; (with Richard Luce) Human Rights and Foreign Policy, 1978; Ireland: an illustrated history, 1981; A Short History of Ireland, 1983. *Recreations*: old Bentley motor cars, quarter horses, Ireland. *Address*: The Garner Cottages, Mill Way, Grantchester, Cambridge. *Club*: Travellers'.

OBOLENSKY, Prof. Dimitri, MA, PhD, DLitt; FBA 1974; FSA; FRHistS; Professor of Russian and Balkan History in the University of Oxford since 1961, and Student of Christ Church since 1950; *b* Petrograd, 1 April 1918; *s* of late Prince Dimitri Obolensky and late Countess Mary Shuvalov; *m* 1947, Elisabeth Lopukhin. *Educ*: Lycée Pasteur, Paris; Trinity College, Cambridge. Cambridge: 1st Class Modern and Medieval Langs Tripos Parts I and II; Amy Mary Preston Read and Allen Schol.; Fellow of Trinity Coll., 1942-48; Faculty Asst Lecturer, 1944; Lecturer, Trinity Coll., 1945; Univ. Lecturer in Slavonic Studies, 1946. Reader in Russian and Balkan Medieval History in Univ. of Oxford, 1949-61; Vis. Schol., Dumbarton Oaks Center for Byzantine Studies, Harvard Univ., 1952, 1964, 1977, Vis. Fellow, 1981-82; Vis. Prof. of Russian History, Yale Univ., 1957; Birkbeck Lecturer in Ecclesiastical History, Trinity Coll., Cambridge, 1961; Raleigh Lectr, British Acad., 1981; Gen. Sec. Thirteenth Internat. Congress of Byzantine Studies, Oxford, 1966; Vis. Prof. of European History, Univ. of California, Berkeley, 1973; Davis Prof. in Slavic Studies, Wellesley Coll., Mass, 1982. British

Co-Chairman: Anglo-Bulgarian Conf. of Historians, 1973; Anglo-Romanian Conf. of Historians, 1975. Corresp. Mem., Acad. of Athens. Hon. Dr Univ. Paris, Sorbonne, 1980. *Publications:* The Bogomils, A Study in Balkan Neo-Manichaeism, 1948; (ed) The Penguin Book of Russian Verse, 1962; (jointly) The Christian Centuries, vol. 2: The Middle Ages, 1969; Byzantium and the Slavs, 1971; The Byzantine Commonwealth, 1971; (ed jtly) Companion to Russian Studies, 3 vols, 1976-80; The Byzantine Inheritance of Eastern Europe, 1982. *Recreations:* lawn tennis, motoring. *Address:* Christ Church, Oxford. *T:* 47224. *Club:* Athenæum.

OBOTE, Dr (Apollo) Milton; President of Uganda and Minister of Foreign Affairs, since 1980; Leader, Uganda People's Congress Party; *b* 1924; *m* ; three *s.* Migrated to Kenya and worked as labourer, clerk and salesman, 1950-55; Founder Mem., Kenya Africa Union. Mem., Uganda Nat. Congress, 1952-60; Mem., Uganda Legislative Council, 1957-71; Founder and Mem., Uganda People's Congress, 1960-71; Leader of the Opposition, 1961-62; Prime Minister, 1962-66; Minister of Defence and Foreign Affairs, 1963-65; President of Uganda, 1966-71 (deposed by military coup); in exile in Tanzania, 1971-80; returned to Uganda, 1980. *Address:* Office of the President, Kampala, Uganda.

Ó BRIAIN, Hon. Barra, MSM; President of the Circuit Court and, *ex officio,* Judge of High Court in Ireland 1959-73 (seconded as President of the High Court of Justice, Cyprus, 1960-62); *b* 19 September 1901; *s* of Dr Christopher Michael and Mary Theresa Ó Briain, Merrion Square, Dublin; *m* 1928, Anna Flood, Terenure, Dublin (*d* 1968); three *s* eight *d. Educ:* Belvedere College; University Coll., Dublin; Paris University. Served in IRA in Irish War of Independence, 1920-21; National Army, 1922-27; Mil. Sec. to Chief of Staff, 1926-27. Called to Irish Bar, 1926; Hon. Bencher, King's Inns, 1974. Sen. Counsel, 1940; Circuit Judge, 1943 (S Western Circuit). Mem., Cttee of Inquiry into operation of Courts in Ireland, 1962; Chm., Cttee to recommend safeguards for persons in police custody, 1977. *Publication:* The Irish Constitution, 1927. *Recreations:* fishing, gardening, walking. *Address:* Dún Ard, Islington Avenue, Sandycove, Co. Dublin.

O'BRIEN, family name of **Barons Inchiquin** and **O'Brien of Lothbury.**

O'BRIEN OF LOTHBURY, Baron *cr* 1973 (Life Peer), of the City of London; **Leslie Kenneth O'Brien,** PC 1970; GBE 1967; President, British Bankers' Association, 1973-80; *b* 8 Feb. 1908; *e s* of late Charles John Grimes O'Brien; *m* Isabelle Gertrude Pickett; one *s. Educ:* Wandsworth School. Entered Bank of England, 1927; Deputy Chief Cashier, 1951; Chief Cashier, 1955; Executive Director, 1962-64; Deputy Governor, 1964-66; Governor, 1966-73; Director: Commonwealth Develt Finance Co. Ltd, 1962-64; The Prudential Assurance Co. Ltd, 1973-80; The Prudential Corp. Ltd, 1979-; The Rank Organisation, 1974-78; Bank for International Settlements, 1966-73, 1974- (Vice-Chm., 1979-); Saudi Internat. Bank, 1975-; Vice-Chm., Banque Belge, 1981-; Mem., Adv. Bd, Unilever Ltd, 1973-78; Consultant to J. P. Morgan & Co., 1973-79; Chm., Internat. Council of Morgan Guaranty Trust Co., NY, 1974-78; Mem. Internat. Adv. Council, Morgan Grenfell & Co. Ltd, 1974-. Chm., Cttee of Inquiry into export of animals for slaughter, 1973. Member: Finance and Appeal Cttee, RCS, 1973-; Council, RCM, 1973-; Bd of National Theatre, 1973-78; Council, Marie Curie Meml Foundn, 1963-78; Investment Adv. Cttee, Mercers' Co., 1973-; City of London Savings Cttee, 1966-78. A Trustee of Glyndebourne Arts Trust, 1974-78; Hon. Treasurer and Mem. Exec. Cttee, Royal Opera House Develt Appeal, 1977-. Pres., United Banks' Lawn Tennis Assoc., 1958-81; Vice-Pres., Squash Rackets Assoc., 1972-78. One of HM Lieutenants for City of London, 1966-73; Freeman, City of London in Co. of Mercers; Hon. Liveryman, Leathersellers Co. Hon. DSc City Univ., 1969; Hon. LLD Univ. of Wales, 1973. FRCM 1979. Hon. Fellow, Inst. of Bankers. Cavaliere di Gran Croce al Merito della Repubblica Italiana, 1975; Grand Officier, Ordre de la Couronne (Belgium), 1976. *Address:* 23 Burghley House, Somerset Road, SW19 5JB. *T:* 01-946 7749. *Clubs:* Athenæum, Boodle's, Grillions, MCC, All England Lawn Tennis.

O'BRIEN, Brian Murrough Fergus; Special Commissioner of Income Tax since 1981; *b* 18 July 1931; *s* of Charles Murrough O'Brien, MB, BCh and Elizabeth Joyce O'Brien (*née* Peacocke). *Educ:* Bedford Sch.; University Coll., Oxford (BA 1954, MA 1959). Nat. Service, Royal Inniskilling Fusiliers, 1949-50. Called to the Bar, Lincoln's Inn, 1955; Office of Solicitor of Inland Revenue, 1956-70; Asst Solicitor, Law Commn, 1970-80; Secretary, Law Commn, 1980-81. Mem., Senate of Inns of Court and Bar Council, 1977-80; Hon. Gen. Sec., 1962-67 and Chm., 1974-76, CS Legal Soc.; Chm., Assoc. of First Div. Civil Servants, 1979-81. Mem., London Diocesan (1974-), and London Area (1980-) Synods; Lay Chm., Westminster (St Margaret's) Deanery Synod, 1978-; Chm., Trustees, St Mary's, Bourne St, 1968-. *Recreations:* music, travel, light-hearted bridge. *Address:* 20 Manchester Street, W1. *T:* 01-935 4285. *Clubs:* Reform; Kildare Street and University (Dublin).

O'BRIEN, Charles Michael, MA; FIA, FSS, FPMI; Manager and Actuary, Royal National Pension Fund for Nurses, since 1955; *b* 17 Jan. 1919; *s* of late Richard Alfred O'Brien, CBE, MD, and Nora McKay; *m* 1950, Joy, *d* of late Rupert Henry Prebble and Phyllis Mary Langdon; two *s. Educ:* Westminster Sch.; Christ Church, Oxford (MA). Commissioned, Royal Artillery, 1940 (despatches, 1945). Asst Actuary, Equitable Life Assce Soc., 1950; Royal National Pension Fund for Nurses: Asst Manager, 1953; Manager and Actuary, 1955. Institute of Actuaries: Fellow, 1949; Hon. Sec., 1961-62; Vice-Pres.,

1965-68; Pres., 1976-78. Mem., Governing Body, Westminster Sch. *Recreations:* lawn tennis, training gundogs. *Address:* Furzedown, Grubb Street, Limpsfield, Surrey RH8 0SH. *T:* Limpsfield Chart 2197.

O'BRIEN, Conor Cruise; Consultant Editor, The Observer, since 1981 (Editor-in-Chief, 1978-81); Pro-Chancellor, University of Dublin, since 1973; *b* 3 November 1917; *s* of Francis Cruise O'Brien and Katherine Sheehy; *m* 1st, 1939, Christine Foster (marr. diss. 1962); one *s* two *d* ; 2nd, 1962, Máire Mac Entee; one adopted *s* one adopted *d. Educ:* Sandford Park School, Dublin; Trinity College, Dublin (BA, PhD). Entered Department of External Affairs of Ireland, 1944; Counsellor, Paris, 1955-56; Head of UN section and Member of Irish Delegation to UN, 1956-60; Asst Sec., Dept of External Affairs, 1960; Rep. of Sec.-Gen. of UN in Katanga, May-Dec. 1961; resigned from UN and Irish service, Dec. 1961. Vice-Chancellor, Univ. of Ghana, 1962-65; Albert Schweitzer Prof. of Humanities, New York Univ., 1965-69. TD (Lab) Dublin North-East, 1969-77; Minister for Posts and Telegraphs, 1973-77. Mem. Senate, Republic of Ireland, 1977-79. Vis. Fellow, Nuffield Coll., Oxford, 1973-75; Fellow, St Catherine's Coll., Oxford, 1978-81. Mem., Royal Irish Acad. Hon. DLitt: Bradford, 1971; Ghana, 1974; Edinburgh, 1976; Nice, 1978; Coleraine, 1981. Valiant for Truth Media Award, 1979. *Publications:* Maria Cross (under pseud. Donat O'Donnell), 1952 (reprinted under own name, 1963); Parnell and his Party, 1957; (ed) The Shaping of Modern Ireland, 1959; To Katanga and Back, 1962; Conflicting Concepts of the UN, 1964; Writers and Politics, 1965; The United Nations: Sacred Drama, 1967 (with drawings by Felix Topolski); Murderous Angels, 1968; (ed) Power and Consciousness, 1969; Conor Cruise O'Brien Introduces Ireland, 1969; (ed) Edmund Burke, Reflections on the Revolution in France, 1969; Camus, 1969; A Concise History of Ireland, 1972; (with Máire Cruise O'Brien) The Suspecting Glance, 1972; States of Ireland, 1972; Herod, 1978; Neighbours: the Ewart-Biggs memorial lectures 1978-79, 1980. *Recreation:* travelling. *Address:* Whitewater, Howth Summit, Dublin, Ireland. *T:* Dublin 322474. *Club:* Athenæum.

O'BRIEN, Sir David (Edmond), 6th Bt *cr* 1849; *b* 19 Feb. 1902; *s* of Edmond Lyons O'Brien (*y b* of 3rd Bt) and Audrey Townshend, *d* of late David Crawford, New York; *S* brother, 1969; *m* 1927, Mary Alice (*d* 1974), *y d* of Sir Henry Foley Grey, 7th Bt; one *s* one *d* (and one *s* decd). *Educ:* Oratory School. *Recreations:* fishing, gardening. *Heir: g s* Timothy John O'Brien, *b* 6 July 1958. *Club:* Kildare Street and University (Dublin).

O'BRIEN, Dermod Patrick; a Recorder of the Crown Court, since 1978; *b* 23 Nov. 1939; *s* of Lieut D. D. O'Brien, RN, and Mrs O'Brien (*née* O'Connor); *m* 1974, Zoë Susan Norris; two *s. Educ:* Ampleforth Coll., York; St Catherine's Coll., Oxford. BA (Jurisprudence); MA. Called to Bar, Inner Temple, 1962; joined Western Circuit, 1963. *Recreations:* fishing, shooting, skiing. *Address:* 55 Doneraile Street, SW6 6EW. *T:* 01-736 6413; (chambers) 2 Temple Gardens, Temple, EC4Y 9AY. *T:* 01-583 6041.

O'BRIEN, Edna; writer; *b* 15 Dec. 1936; marr. diss.; two *s. Educ:* Irish convents; Pharmaceutical Coll. of Ireland. Yorkshire Post Novel Award, 1971. *Publications:* The Country Girls, 1960; The Lonely Girl, 1962; Girls in Their Married Bliss, 1963; August is a Wicked Month, 1964; Casualties of Peace, 1966; The Love Object, 1968; A Pagan Place, 1970; (play) A Pagan Place, 1971; Night, 1972; (short stories) A Scandalous Woman, 1974; Mother Ireland, 1976; Johnnie I hardly knew you, 1977; Mrs Reinhardt and other stories, 1978; Virginia (play), 1979; The Dazzle, 1981; Returning, 1982; A Christmas Treat, 1982. *Recreations:* reading, writing, remembering. *Address:* c/o Douglas Rae Ltd, 28 Charing Cross Road, WC2H 0DB.

O'BRIEN, Frederick William Fitzgerald, QC (Scotland) 1960; Sheriff Principal of Lothian and Borders, since 1978; Sheriff of Chancery in Scotland, since 1978; *b* 19 July 1917; *s* of Dr Charles Henry Fitzgerald O'Brien and Helen Jane; *m* 1950, Audrey Muriel Owen; two *s* one *d. Educ:* Royal High Sch.; Univ. of Edinburgh; MA 1938; LLB 1940. Admitted Faculty of Advocates, 1947. Comr, Mental Welfare Commission of Scotland, 1962-65; Home Advocate Depute, 1964-65; Sheriff-Principal of Caithness, Sutherland, Orkney and Shetland, 1964-75; Interim Sheriff-Principal of Aberdeen, Kincardine and Banff, 1969-71; Sheriff Principal of N Strathclyde, 1975-78; Interim Sheriff Principal of Strathclyde, 1981; Member: Scottish Medical Practices Cttee, 1973-76; Scottish Records Adv. Council, 1974-; Convener of Sheriffs Principal, 1972-; Chm., Sheriff Court Rules Council, 1975-81. Convener, Gen. Council Business Cttee, Edinburgh Univ., 1980-. Hon. Pres., Royal High Sch. Former Pupils Club, 1982 (Pres. 1975-76). Mem., Inst. of Advanced Motorists. *Recreations:* golf, music. *Address:* 22 Arboretum Road, Edinburgh EH3 5PN. *T:* 031-552 1923. *Clubs:* New (Edinburgh); Bruntsfield Golf, Scottish Arts.

O'BRIEN, Rt. Rev. James Joseph; Auxiliary Bishop of Westminster (Bishop in Hertfordshire) (RC), and Titular Bishop of Manaccenser, since 1977; *s* of John and Mary Elizabeth O'Brien. *Educ:* St Ignatius College, Stamford Hill; St Edmund's Coll., Ware. Priest, 1954; Assistant, St Lawrence's, Feltham, 1954-62; Catholic Missionary Society, 1962-68; Director of Catholic Enquiry Centre, 1967-68; Rector of Allen Hall, 1968-77. Prelate of Honour, 1969. *Address:* The Farm Cottage, All Saints Pastoral Centre, London Colney, St Albans, Herts AL2 1AQ. *T:* Bowmansgreen 24664.

O'BRIEN, Prof. John W., PhD, DCL, LLD; Rector and Vice-Chancellor, Concordia University (incorporating Loyola College and Sir George

Williams University, Montreal), since 1969; Professor of Economics, since 1965; *b* 4 Aug. 1931; *s* of Wilfred Edmond O'Brien and Audrey Swain; *m* 1956, Joyce Helen Bennett; two *d. Educ:* McGill Univ., Montreal, Que. BA 1953, MA 1955, PhD 1962. Sir George Williams Univ.: Lectr in Economics, 1954; Asst Prof. of Economics, 1957; Associate Prof. of Economics and Asst Dean, 1961; Dean, Faculty of Arts, 1963; Vice-Principal (Academic), 1968-69. Hon. DCL Bishop's Univ., 1976; Hon. LLD McGill Univ., 1976. *Publication:* Canadian Money and Banking, 1964 (2nd edn, with G. Lermer, 1969). *Address:* Concordia University, 1455 de Maisonneuve Boulevard West, Montreal, Que H3G 1M8, Canada. *T:* 879-2862.

O'BRIEN, Rt. Rev. Kevin; *see* O'Brien, Rt Rev. T. K.

O'BRIEN, (Michael) Vincent; trainer of horses for flat and National Hunt racing, England and Ireland; *b* 9 April 1917; *s* of Daniel P. O'Brien and Kathleen (*née* Toomey); *m* 1951, Jacqueline (*née* Wittenoom), Perth, Australia; two *s* three *d. Educ:* Mungret Coll., Ireland. Started training in Co. Cork, 1944; moved to Co. Tipperary, 1951. Won all principal English and Irish steeple-chases, incl. 3 consecutive Grand Nationals, Gold Cups and Champion Hurdles. From 1959 has concentrated on flat racing and has trained winners of 14 English classics, incl. 6 Derbys; trainer of Nijinsky, first triple crown winner since 1935; also 3 Irish Derbys, 3 Prix de l'Arc de Triomphe and Washington International. *Recreations:* fishing, golf. *Address:* Ballydoyle House, Cashel, Co. Tipperary, Ireland. *T:* 062-61222; Telex 28214.

O'BRIEN, Owen; Joint General Secretary, Society of Graphical and Allied Trades 1982, (SOGAT 82), since amalgamation of Unions in 1982; *b* Stepney, 22 June 1920; *m* ; two *s* two *d. Educ:* Tower Hill Sch., E1. Entered printing industry, 1934. Served War: Merchant Navy, 1939-41; RAF, 1941-46. Elected: Asst Sec., London Machine Br. of NATSOPA, Dec. 1951; (unopposed) Sec. of Br., Nov. 1952; Sec. of Union's London Jt Branches, 1952-63; Nat. Asst Sec., 1964-75; Gen. Sec., 1975-82. Past Mem., local Labour Party and London Labour party; Mem., Stepney Borough Council, 1947-50; Chm., Printing and Publishing Industry Training Board, 1977- (Mem. Exec. Cttee and Chm., Levy and Grant Cttee from Bd's constitution, 1968-77); Mem. Council, Industrial Soc. Governor, London Coll. of Printing, 1964- (Chm., Governors, 1969, 1977). *Recreations:* walking, reading, swimming. *Address:* SOGAT House, 274/288 London Road, Hadleigh, Essex SS7 2DE. *T:* Southend-on-Sea 553131.

O'BRIEN, Raymond Francis; DL; Chief Executive, Merseyside Metropolitan County Council, since 1978; *b* 13 Feb. 1936; *s* of Ignatius and Anne O'Brien; *m* 1959, Mary Agnes (Wendy) Alcock; two *s* two *d. Educ:* St Mary's Coll., Great Crosby, Liverpool; St Edmund Hall, Oxford. BA Hons 1959, MA 1962; IPFA. Accountant, Cheshire CC, 1959-65; Head of Data Processing, Staffs CC, 1965-67; Asst County Treas., Notts CC, 1967-70; Dep. Clerk, Notts CC, 1970-73; Clerk of CC and Chief Executive, Notts, 1973-77. Director: Merseyside Economic Development Co. Ltd, 1981-; Merseyside Cablevision Ltd. DL Merseyside, 1980. *Recreations:* cricket, rugby, gardening, music, reading. *Address:* Loch Sloigh, 16 Sea Road, Wallasey, Merseyside. *T:* (business) 051-227 5234; (home) 051-639 9175.

O'BRIEN, Sir Richard, Kt 1980; DSO 1944, MC 1942 (Bar 1944); Chairman, Manpower Services Commission, 1976-82; *b* 15 Feb. 1920; *s* of late Dr Charles O'Brien and of Marjorie Maude O'Brien; *m* 1951, Elizabeth M. D. Craig; two *s* three *d. Educ:* Oundle Sch.; Clare Coll., Cambridge (MA). Served, 1940-45, with Sherwood Foresters and Leicesters, N Africa, ME, Italy and Greece; Personal Asst to C-in-C, 21st Army Gp, 1945-46. Develt Officer, Nat. Assoc. of Boys' Clubs, 1946-48; Richard Sutcliffe Ltd, Wakefield (latterly Prodn Dir), 1948-58; Dir and Gen. Man., Head Wrightson Mineral Engrg Ltd, 1958-61; Dir, Industrial Relns, British Motor Corp., 1961-66; Industrial Adviser (Manpower), DEA, 1966-68; Delta Metal Co. Ltd (subseq. Dir of Manpower, and Dir 1972-76), 1968-76. Chairman: CBI Employment Policy Cttee, 1971-76; Crown Appointments Commn, 1979; Engineering Industry Trng Bd, 1982-; Pres., British Inst. of Industrial Therapy, 1982-; Mem., NEDC, 1977-82. Member Council: Industrial Soc., 1962-; Univ. of Birmingham, 1969-; Policy Studies Inst., 1978-; Mem. Ct of Governors, ASC, 1977-. Hon. DSc Aston, 1979; Hon. LLD: Bath, 1981; Liverpool, 1981; Birmingham, 1982; Hon. Fellow Sheffield City Polytech., 1980. JP Wakefield, 1955-61. *Publications:* contrib. Conflict at Work (BBC pubn), 1971; articles in various jls. *Recreation:* reading. *Address:* 24 Argyll Road, W8. *T:* 01-937 8944.

O'BRIEN, Robert Stephen; *b* 14 Aug. 1936; *s* of Robert Henry and Clare Winifred O'Brien; *m* 1958, Zoë T. O'Brien; two *s* two *d. Educ:* Sherborne Sch., Dorset. Joined Charles Fulton & Co. Ltd, 1956; Dir, 1964; Chm., 1970-82. Chairman: Foreign Exchange and Currency Deposit Brokers Assoc., 1968-72; Fullemploy Ltd, 1973-; Dir, Kirkland-Whittaker Gp Ltd, 1981-82. Ordained Deacon, 1971; Hon. Curate, St Lawrence Jewry, 1973-; Chm., Christian Action, 1976-. *Recreations:* family life, rough gardening, tennis. *Address:* Bedford Farm House, Thursley, Godalming, Surrey. *T:* Wormley 2340. *Club:* Island Cruising (Salcombe, Devon).

O'BRIEN, Terence John, CMG 1971; MC 1945; HM Diplomatic Service, retired; *b* 13 Oct. 1921; *s* of Joseph O'Brien; *m* 1950, Phyllis Mitchell (*d* 1952); *m* 1953, Rita Emily Drake Reynolds; one *s* two *d. Educ:* Gresham's Sch., Holt; Merton Coll., Oxford. Ayrshire Yeo., 1942-45. Dominions Office, 1947; CRO, 1947-49; British High Comr's Office, Ceylon, 1950-52; Princ.,

Treasury, 1953-56; 1st Sec. (Financial), Canberra, 1956-58; Planning Officer, CRO, 1958-60; 1st Sec., Kuala Lumpur, 1960-62; Sec. to Inter-Governmental Cttee, Jesselton, 1962-63; Head of Chancery, New Delhi, 1963-66; Imp. Def. Coll., 1967; Counsellor, FCO (formerly FO), 1968-70; Ambassador: Nepal, 1970-74; Burma, 1974-78; Indonesia, 1978-81. *Address:* Beaufort House, Woodcutts, Dorset. *Club:* Royal Commonwealth Society.

O'BRIEN, Rt. Rev. (Thomas) Kevin; Auxiliary Bishop of Middlesbrough, (RC), and Titular Bishop of Ard Carna, since 1981; *b* Cork City, Republic of Ireland, 18 Feb. 1923; *s* of Jack and Mary O'Brien. *Educ:* Christian Brothers Coll., Cork. Ordained, All Hallows College, Dublin, 1948; Curate at Batley, Yorks, 1948-51, and St Anne's Cathedral, Leeds, 1951-56; Catholic Missionary Society, 1956-71, Superior 1960-71; Vicar General, Diocese of Leeds, 1971-81; Parish Priest: St Patrick's, Huddersfield, 1971-79; St Francis, Bradford, 1979-81. *Address:* St Charles Rectory, Jarratt Street, Hull HU1 3HB.

O'BRIEN, Timothy Brian; designer; *b* 8 March 1929; *s* of Brian Palliser Tiegue O'Brien and Elinor Laura (*née* Mackenzie). *Educ:* Wellington Coll.; Corpus Christi, Cambridge (MA); Yale Univ. Design Dept, BBC TV, 1954; Designer, Associated Rediffusion, 1955-56; Head of Design, ABC Television, 1956-66 (The Flying Dutchman, 1958); partnership in stage design with Tazeena Firth estabd 1961; output incl.: The Bartered Bride, The Girl of the Golden West, 1962; West End prodns of new plays, 1963-64; London scene of Shakespeare Exhibn, 1964; Tango, Days in the Trees, Staircase, RSC, and Trafalgar at Madame Tussaud's, 1966; All's Well that Ends Well, As You Like It, Romeo and Juliet, RSC, 1967; The Merry Wives of Windsor, Troilus and Cressida (also Nat. Theatre, 1976), The Latent Heterosexual, RSC, 1968; Pericles (also Comédie Française, 1974), Women Beware Women, Bartholomew Fair, RSC, 1969; 1970: Measure for Measure, RSC; Madame Tussaud's in Amsterdam; The Knot Garden, Royal Opera; 1971: Enemies, Man of Mode, RSC; 1972: La Cenerentola, Oslo; Lower Depths, The Island of the Mighty, RSC; As You Like It, OCSC; 1973: Richard II, Love's Labour's Lost, RSC; 1974: Next of Kin, NT; Summerfolk, RSC; The Bassarids, ENO; 1975: John Gabriel Borkman, NT; Peter Grimes, Royal Opera (later in Göteborg, Paris); The Marrying of Ann Leete, RSC; 1976: Wozzeck, Adelaide Fest.; The Zykovs, RSC; The Force of Habit, NT; 1977: Tales from the Vienna Woods, Bedroom Farce, NT; Falstaff, Berlin Opera; 1978: The Cunning Little Vixen, Göteborg; Evita, London (later in Australia, Austria, USA); A Midsummer Night's Dream, Sydney Opera House; 1979: The Rake's Progress, Royal Opera; 1981: Lulu, Covent Garden; 1982: La Ronde, RSC. (Jtly) Gold Medal for Set Design, Prague Quadriennale, 1975. *Recreation:* sailing. *Address:* 33 Lansdowne Gardens, SW8 2EQ. *T:* 01-622 5384.

O'BRIEN, Turlough Aubrey, CBE 1959; Public Relations Consultant, since 1972; *b* 30 Sept. 1907; *er s* of late Lieut-Colonel A. J. O'Brien, CIE, CBE; *m* 1945, Phyllis Mary, twin *d* of late E. G. Tew; two *s* one *d. Educ:* Charterhouse; Christ Church, Oxford. Assistant to Director of Public Relations, Board of Trade, 1946-49; Public Relations Officer: Home Office, 1949-53; Post Office, 1953-64; Chief Public Relations Officer, 1964-66; Director, Public Relations, 1966-68; Public Relations Manager, Bank of London and South America, 1968-72. President, Institute of Public Relations, 1965. *Recreation:* fishing. *Address:* Claremount, 11 Kiln Gardens, Hartley Wintney, Basingstoke, Hants RG27 8RG. *Club:* United Oxford & Cambridge University.

O'BRIEN, Vincent; *see* O'Brien, M. V.

O'BRIEN, Adm. Sir William (Donough), KCB 1969 (CB 1966); DSC 1942; Commander-in-Chief, Western Fleet, Feb. 1970-Sept. 71, retd Nov. 1971; Rear-Admiral of the United Kingdom, since 1979; *b* 13 Nov. 1916; *s* of late Major W. D. O'Brien, Connaught Rangers and I. R. Caroe (*née* Parnis); *m* 1943, Rita Micallef, Sliema, Malta; one *s* two *d. Educ:* Royal Naval Coll., Dartmouth. Served War of 1939-45: HM Ships Garland, Wolsey, Witherington, Offa, 1939-42; Cottesmore i/c, 1943-44; Arakan Coast, 1945. HMS Venus i/c, 1948-49; Commander 1949; HMS Ceylon, 1952; Admiralty, 1953-55; Captain, 1955; Captain (D) 8th DS in HMS Cheviot, 1958-59; HMS Hermes i/c, 1961-64; Rear-Admiral 1964; Naval Secretary, 1964-66; Flag Officer, Aircraft Carriers, 1966-67; Comdr, Far East Fleet, 1967-69; Admiral 1969. Chairman: Kennet and Avon Canal Trust, 1974; King George's Fund for Sailors, 1974. Pres., Assoc. of RN Officers, 1973. *Address:* Drew's Mill, Potterne Road, Devizes, Wilts. *T:* Devizes 3243. *Club:* Army and Navy.

OCHOA, Dr Severo; Distinguished Member, Roche Institute of Molecular Biology, New Jersey, since 1974; *b* Luarca, Spain, 24 Sept. 1905; *s* of Severo Ochoa and Carmen (*née* Albornoz); *m* 1931, Carmen G. Coblan. *Educ:* Malaga Coll.; University of Madrid. AB, Malaga, 1921; MD, Madrid, 1929. Lecturer in Physiology, University of Madrid Medical School, 1931-35; Head of Physiology Div., Institute for Medical Research, 1935-36; Guest Research Asst, Kaiser Wilhelm Inst., Heidelberg, 1936-37; Marine Biological Lab., Plymouth, July-Dec. 1937; Demonstrator and Nuffield Research Assistant in Biochemistry, University of Oxford Medical School, 1938-41; Instructor and Research Assoc. in Pharmacology, Washington Univ. School of Medicine, St Louis, 1941-42; New York University School of Medicine: Research Assoc. in Medicine, 1942-45; Asst Professor of Biochemistry, 1945-46; Professor of Pharmacology, and Chairman of Dept of Pharmacology, 1946-54; Prof. of Biochemistry, and Chm. of Dept of Biochemistry, 1954-74. Carlos Jimenez Diaz lectr, Madrid Univ., 1969. Pres., Internat. Union of Biochemistry,

1961-67. Member: US National Academy of Sciences; American Academy of Arts and Sciences; American Philosophical Society; Deutsche Akademie der Naturforscher (Leopoldina), etc. Nobel Prize (joint) in Physiology and Medicine, 1959. Hon. degrees from universities and colleges in Argentina, Brazil, Chile, England, Italy, Peru, Philippines, Scotland, Spain and USA. Foreign Member: Royal Society, 1965; USSR Academy of Science, 1966; Polish Acad. of Science; Acad. of Science, DDR, 1977; Acad. of Med. Scis, Argentina, 1977; Chilean Acad. of Scis, 1977; Indian Nat. Sci. Acad., 1977. Hon. Mem., Royal Acad. Med., Sevilla, 1971. Gold Medal, Madrid Univ., 1969; Quevedo Gold Medal, Madrid, 1969; Albert Gallatin Medal, NY Univ., 1970. Order of Rising Sun, 2nd class, 1967. *Publications:* papers on biochemistry and molecular biology. *Recreations:* colour photography and swimming. *Address:* 530 East 72nd Street, New York, NY 10021, USA. *T:* 879-1480.

O'COLLINS, Most Rev. Sir James (Patrick), KBE 1980; DD 1930; *b* Melbourne, Australia, 31 March 1892. *Educ:* St Columba's, Springwood; St Patrick's, Sydney; Urban Coll., Rome. Ordained Priest, Rome, 1922 for the Diocese of Melbourne; R.C Bishop of Geraldton, 1930-41; Bishop of Ballarat, 1942-71. Nominated Asst Bishop at the Papal Throne, 1955. *Address:* 1444 Sturt Street, Ballarat, Victoria 3350, Australia.

O'CONNELL, Sir Bernard Thomas, Kt 1972; Deputy Chairman, New Zealand Breweries Ltd, since 1970; *b* 31 Dec. 1909; *s* of Bernard O'Connell and Mary Walker, Yorkshire, England; *m* 1939, Margaret Mary Collins; three *s*. *Educ:* Christian Brothers Schools in Australia and New Zealand. New Zealand Breweries Ltd, Wellington, New Zealand: Sec. 1939; Gen. Manager, 1946; Man. Dir, 1958; Dep. Chm., 1970. FCA. *Recreations:* golf, racing. *Address:* 7 Wai-te-ata Road, Wellington, New Zealand. *T:* Wellington 726-704. *Clubs:* Wellesley, Wellington Golf, Wellington Racing (all in Wellington, NZ).

O'CONNELL, John Eugene Anthony, MS (London), FRCS; Consulting Neurological Surgeon, St Bartholomew's Hospital; *b* 16 Sept. 1906; *s* of Thomas Henry and Catherine Mary O'Connell; *m* Marjorie Hutchinson Cook. *Educ:* Clongowes Wood and Wimbledon Colleges; St Bartholomew's Hospital. Held posts of House Surgeon, Senior Demonstrator of Anatomy, and Surgical Chief Assistant, St Bartholomew's Hospital, 1931-39; Studied at Universities of Michigan and Chicago on Rockefeller Foundation Travelling Fellowship, 1935-36; Surgeon in charge of an EMS Neurosurgical Unit, 1941-46; Surgeon i/c Dept of Neurol Surgery, St Bartholomew's Hosp., 1946-71; Hunterian Professor, Royal College of Surgeons, 1943 and 1950. Emeritus Mem., Soc. of Brit. Neurol Surgeons (ex-Pres.); FRSM (ex-Vice-Pres.); Hon. Member: Neurosurgical Soc. Australasia; Deutsche Gesellschaft für Neurochirurgie; Corresp. Mem., Amer. Assoc. Neurol Surgeons. *Publications:* papers in neurological, surgical and other journals and books. *Recreations:* fly-fishing, bird watching. *Address:* Fishing Cottage, Itchen Abbas, Winchester, Hants. *T:* Itchen Abbas 227. *Club:* Athenæum.

O'CONNELL, Sir Morgan (Donal Conail), 6th Bt, *cr* 1869; *b* 29 Jan. 1923; *o s* of Captain Sir Maurice James Arthur O'Connell, 5th Bt, KM, MC, and Margaret Mary, *d* of late Matthew J. Purcell, Burton Park, Buttevant; *S* father, 1949; *m* 1953, Elizabeth, *o d* of late Major and Mrs John MacCarthy O'Leary, Lavenders, West Malling, Kent; two *s* four *d*. *Educ:* The Abbey School, Fort Augustus, Scotland. Served War of 1939-45, in Royal Corps of Signals, 1943-46; BLA, 1944-46. *Recreations:* fishing and shooting. *Heir:* *s* Maurice James Donagh MacCarthy O'Connell, *b* 10 June 1958. *Address:* Lakeview, Killarney, Co. Kerry. *T:* 31845.

O'CONNOR, Surgeon Rear-Adm. Anthony, MVO 1967; Director, Red Cross Blood Transfusion Service, Western Australia, since 1981 (Deputy Director, 1975-81); *b* 8 Nov. 1917; *s* of Armel John O'Connor and Lucy Violet O'Connor (*née* Bullock-Webster); *m* 1946, Catherine Jane (*née* Hayes); three *d*. *Educ:* Kings Coll., Strand, London; Westminster Hosp. Med. Sch. MRCS, LRCP, MB, BS, FFARCS, MFCM. Qualified Medical Practitioner, 1941; joined Royal Navy (RNVR), 1942; Permanent Commn, 1945; Dep. Medical Director General (Naval), 1969; MO i/c, Inst. of Naval Med. and Dean of Naval Med., 1972-75. QHP 1970-75. *Recreations:* gardening, photography. *Address:* c/o Lloyds Bank Ltd, Ludlow, Shropshire.

O'CONNOR, Cormac Murphy; *see* Murphy-O'Connor.

O'CONNOR, Professor Daniel John; Professor of Philosophy, University of Exeter, 1957-79, now Emeritus; *b* 2 April 1914; *m* 1948, Kathleen Kemsley; no *c*. *Educ:* Birkbeck Coll., University of London. Entered Civil Service, 1933; Commonwealth Fund Fellow in Philosophy, University of Chicago, 1946-47; Professor of Philosophy, University of Natal, SA, 1949-51; Professor of Philosophy, University of the Witwatersrand, Johannesburg, 1951-52; Lecturer in Philosophy, Univ. Coll. of North Staffordshire, 1952-54; Professor of Philosophy, University of Liverpool, 1954-57. Visiting Professor, University of Pennsylvania, 1961-62. *Publications:* John Locke, 1952; Introduction to Symbolic Logic (with A. H. Basson), 1953; Introduction to the Philosophy of Education, 1957; A Critical History of Western Philosophy (ed), 1964; Aquinas and Natural Law, 1968; Free Will, 1971; (ed jtly) New Essays in the Philosophy of Education, 1973; The Correspondence Theory of Truth, 1975; various papers in philosophical journals. *Address:* c/o

Department of Philosophy, University of Exeter, Queen's Building, The Queen's Drive, Exeter EX4 4QH.

O'CONNOR, Lt-Gen. Sir Denis (Stuart Scott), KBE 1963 (CBE 1949; OBE 1946); CB 1959; DL; *b* Simla, 2 July 1907; *s* of Lieut-Colonel Malcolm Scott O'Connor and Edith Annie (*née* Rees); *m* 1936, Martha Neill Algie (*née* Johnston), Donaghadee, Co. Down; two *s* one *d*. *Educ:* Glengorse, Eastbourne; Harrow School; RMA Woolwich. Commnd 2nd Lieut, Royal Artillery, 1927; India, 1929-35; France, 1939, Captain; Student Staff Coll., 1940; Major Instructor, Staff Coll., 1941, Lieut-Colonel GSO 1, 11th Armoured Division, 1942-44; N.W. Europe, CO Artillery Regt, 1944 (despatches); Colonel, 14th Army, 1945; Brigadier, Director of Plans, Supreme Allied Commander, South East Asia, 1945-46; Middle East, BGS, 1946-49; Student, IDC 1950; School of Artillery, 1951-52; CRA, 11th Armoured Division, BAOR, 1953-54; Director of Plans, War Office, 1955-56; Maj.-General, Commander, 6th Armoured Division, BAOR, 1957-58; Chief Army Instructor, Imperial Defence Coll., London, 1958-60; GOC, Aldershot District, 1960-62; Vice Chief of Defence Staff, Ministry of Defence, 1962-64; Commander British Forces, Hong Kong, 1964-66, retired. Colonel Commandant, RA, 1963-72. Member of Administrative Board of Governors, Corps of Commissionaires, 1964-75, Life Governor, 1975. HQ Staff, Army Benevolent Fund, 1967-75. DL Surrey, 1968. *Recreations:* shooting, fishing, golf. *Address:* Springfield Lodge, Camberley, Surrey.

O'CONNOR, Sir Kenneth Kennedy, KBE 1961; Kt 1952; MC 1918; QC (Kenya) 1950; *b* 21 Dec. 1896; *s* of Rev. William O'Connor and Emma Louisa O'Connor; *m* 1928, Margaret Helen (*née* Wise); two *s*. *Educ:* Abbey Sch., Beckenham; St Columba's Coll., near Dublin. Indian Army, 14th (KGO) Sikhs, 1915-18 (despatches, MC). Pol. Dept, Mesopotamia, 1919. Foreign and Pol. Dept, Government of India, 1920-22; resigned, 1922. Called to Bar, Gray's Inn, 1924; practised at Bar, London and Singapore, 1924-41. President, Straits Settlements Assoc., 1938, 1939, 1940. Colonial Legal Service, 1943; Acting Attorney-General, Nyasaland, 1944; Colonel, 1945; Attorney-General, Malaya, 1946-48; Attorney-General, Kenya, 1948-51; Chief Justice, Jamaica, 1951-54; Chief Justice of Kenya, 1954; President, Court of Appeal for Eastern Africa, 1957-62, retired. *Publications:* Index Guide to the Law of Property Act, 1925, 1926. Editor Straits Settlements Law Reports. Contributions to legal journals. *Recreations:* cricket, lawn tennis, golf. *Address:* 7 Westfield Close, Wimborne, Dorset. *Club:* Royal Over-Seas League.

O'CONNOR, Rt. Rev. Kevin, JCL; Titular Bishop of Glastonbury and an Auxiliary Bishop of Liverpool, (RC), since 1979; *b* 20 May 1929. *Educ:* St Francis Xavier, Liverpool; Junior and Senior Seminaries, Upholland; Gregorian Univ., Rome. Priest, 1954; Member, Archdiocesan Marriage Tribunal; Parish Priest, St Anne's and Chancellor of Archdiocese of Liverpool, 1977. *Address:* 12 Richmond Close, Eccleston, St Helens WA10 5JE.

O'CONNOR, Air Vice-Marshal Patrick Joseph, CB 1976; OBE 1943; MD; FRCPE, FRCPsych; Civil Consultant in Neuropsychiatry, Royal Air Force, since 1978; Consultant in Neurology and Psychiatry to Civil Aviation Authority, British Airways and British Caledonian Airways, since 1978; *b* 21 Aug. 1914; *s* of Charles O'Connor, Straffan, Co. Kildare, Eire, farmer; *m* 1946, Elsie, *o d* of David Craven, Leeds, Yorks; one *s* two *d* (and one *d* decd). *Educ:* Roscrea Coll.; University of Dublin. MB, BCh 1938. Joined RAF, 1940; Air Cdre 1966; Air Vice-Marshal 1971; Consultant Adviser in Neurology and Psychiatry to RAF, 1964-78; Senior Consultant to RAF at Central Medical Establishment, 1975-78, retired. MD 1950; MRCPE 1950; DPM 1953; FRCPE 1960; MRCP 1960; FRCPsych 1970. QHP 1967-78. Member: Med. Council on Migraine Trust; Med. Council on Alcoholism; The EEG Soc.; Assoc. of British Neurologists; Internat. Acad. of Aviation and Space Med., 1977; Internat. League against Epilepsy; Flying Personnel Res. Cttee. Fellow, Aerospace Med. Assoc; FRSM. *Publications:* contrib.: Journal Neurology, Psychiatry and Neurosurgery; British Journal Psychiatry; BMJ. *Recreations:* gardening, shooting. *Address:* 108 Harley Street, WI. *T:* 01-935 8033; St Benedicts, Bacombe Lane, Wendover, Bucks. *T:* Aylesbury 623329. *Club:* Royal Air Force.

O'CONNOR, Rt. Hon. Sir Patrick McCarthy, Kt 1966; PC 1980; **Rt. Hon. Lord Justice O'Connor;** a Lord Justice of Appeal, since 1980; *b* 28 Dec. 1914; *s* of late William Patrick O'Connor; *m* 1938, Mary Garland, *d* of William Martin Griffin, KC, of Vancouver, BC; two *s* two *d*. *Educ:* Downside; Merton Coll., Oxford. Called to the Bar, Inner Temple, 1940; Master of the Bench, 1966. Junior Counsel to the Post Office, 1954-60; QC 1960; Recorder: of King's Lynn, 1959-61; of Southend, 1961-66; a Judge of the High Ct of Justice, QBD, 1966-80; Dep. Chairman, IoW QS, 1957-71. Vice-Chm., Parole Bd, 1974-75. A Governor of Guy's Hospital, 1956-60. *Recreation:* golf. *Address:* Royal Courts of Justice, Strand, WC2; 1 Old Mill House, West Mills, Newbury, Berks. *T:* Newbury 43283. *Club:* Huntercombe.

O'CONNOR, Rory; Hon. Mr Justice O'Connor; Judge of the High Court of Hong Kong, since 1977; *b* Co. Down, 26 Nov. 1925; *s* of late James O'Connor and Mary Savage; *m* 1963, Elizabeth, *d* of late Frederick Dew; one *s* two *d*. *Educ:* Blackrock Coll., Dublin; Univ. Coll., Dublin (BCom). Called to Irish Bar, King's Inns, 1949. Resident Magistrate, Kenya, 1956-62; Hong Kong: Magistrate, 1962-70; District Judge, 1970-75. *Address:* Courts of Justice, Hong Kong. *Clubs:* Royal Hong Kong Jockey, United Services Recreation, Ladies Recreation (Hong Kong).

O'CONNOR HOWE, Mrs Josephine Mary; HM Diplomatic Service, retired; *b* 25 March 1924; *d* of late Gerald Frank Claridge and late Dulcie Agnes Claridge (*née* Waldegrave); *m* 1947, John O'Connor Howe (decd); one *d. Educ:* Wychwood Sch., Oxford; Triangle Coll. (course in journalism). Inter-Allied Information Cttee, later, United Nations Information Office, 1942-45; Foreign Office: The Hague, 1945-46; Internat. News Service and freelance, 1946-50; FO, 1952; Counsellor, FCO, 1974-1979. Magazine Administrator, Reader's Digest, 1979-. *Recreations:* theatre, gardening, grandchildren. *Address:* Dering Cottage, Little Chart, Ashford, Kent TN27 0PT. *T:* Pluckley 328. *Club:* Royal Commonwealth Society.

ODDIE, Christopher Ripley; His Honour Judge Oddie; a Circuit Judge, since 1974; *b* Derby, 24 Feb. 1929; *o s* of Dr and Mrs J. R. Oddie, Uttoxeter, Staffs; *m* 1957, Margaret Anne, *d* of Mr and Mrs J. W. Timmis; one *s* three *d. Educ:* Giggleswick Sch.; Oriel Coll., Oxford (MA). Called to Bar, Middle Temple, 1954, Oxford Circuit. Contested (L) Ludlow, Gen. Election, 1970. A Recorder of the Crown Court, 1972-74. Mem., County Court Rule Cttee, 1981-. Mem. Council, St Mary's Hosp. Med. Sch., 1980-. *Recreations:* reading, gossip, opera, fishing. *Address:* 89 The Vineyard, Richmond, Surrey. *T:* 01-940 4135; Woodside Cottage, Clun, Craven Arms, Salop.

ODDIE, Prof. Guy Barrie; Robert Adam Professor of Architecture, 1968-82, Head of Department of Architecture, 1968-80, University of Edinburgh; *b* 1 Jan. 1922; *o s* of Edward Oddie and Eleanor Pinkney; *m* 1952, Mabel Mary Smith; no *c. Educ:* Hookergate Grammar Sch.; Univ. of Newcastle upon Tyne. BArch, DipTP, RIBA, FRIAS. Demonstrator, Univ. of Newcastle upon Tyne, 1944; Sen. Lectr, Birmingham Sch. of Architecture, 1950-52; Research Architect, Building Res. Stn, 1947-50; Develt Gp, Min. of Educn, 1952-58; Staff architect, UGC, 1958-63; Consultant to OECD, 1963-66; Dir, Laboratories Investigation Unit, DES, 1966-68. Sen. Advr to OECD Prog. on Educnl Bldg, 1972-; Mem., Bldg Res. Estabt Scottish Adv. Cttee. *Publications:* School Building Resources and their Effective Use, 1966; Development and Economy in Educational Building, 1968; Industrialised Building for Schools, 1975; contrib. Architects Jl, Architectural Rev., RIBA Jl. *Recreations:* dry-fly fishing, gardening. *Address:* The Causeway, Edinburgh EH15 3QA. *T:* 031-661 5492.

ODDY, Revel; Keeper, Department of Art and Archaeology, Royal Scottish Museum, Edinburgh, since 1974; *b* 11 April 1922; *s* of Sidney Oddy and Muriel Barnfather; *m* 1949, Ariadne Margaret, *d* of late Sir Andrew Gourlay Clow, KCSI, CIE; two *s* two *d. Educ:* Worksop Coll.; Pembroke Coll., Cambridge (MA). Served War, Loyal Regt and King's African Rifles, 1941-46. Mod. langs master, Dr Challoner's Grammar Sch., Amersham, 1949; Res. Asst, V&A Mus., London, 1950-55; Asst Keeper, Royal Scottish Mus., Edinburgh, 1955-74. *Recreations:* mild gardening, reading. *Address:* 44 Findhorn Place, Edinburgh EH9 2NT. *T:* 031-667 5815. *Clubs:* Civil Service; University of Edinburgh Staff (Edinburgh).

O'DEA, Sir Patrick Jerad, KCVO 1974; retired public servant, New Zealand; public affairs consultant; Extra Gentleman Usher to the Queen, since 1981; *b* 18 April 1918; 2nd *s* of late Patrick O'Dea; *m* 1945, Jean Mary, *d* of Hugh Mulholland; one *s* three *d. Educ:* St Paul's Coll. and Univ. of Otago, Dunedin, NZ; Victoria Univ., Wellington, NZ. Joined NZ Public Service, 1936; served in Agriculture Dept, 1936-47. Served War in Royal New Zealand Artillery of 2 NZEF, 1941-45. With Industries and Commerce Dept, 1947-49; subseq. served with Dept of Internal Affairs in various posts interrupted by 2 years' full-time study at Victoria Univ. of Wellington (DPA). Group Exec. Officer, Local Govt, 1959-64; Dep. Sec., 1964-67; Sec. for Internal Affairs, NZ, 1967-78; formerly Sec. for: Local Govt; Civil Defence; Sec. of Recreation and Sport; Clerk of the Writs; NZ Sec. to the Queen, 1969-78, reapptd 1981, for visit of Queen and Duke of Edinburgh to NZ. Dep. Chm., Accumulas Fund Ltd. Member: Nat. Parks Authority; NZ Ballet and Opera Trust Bd; Chm., NZ Ballet Sch. Bd; Nat. Co-ordinator, Duke of Edinburgh's Award Scheme in NZ; Chm., Adv. Cttee of YMCA for RYDUM (Re-directing Youth Using Mini-cycles) Youth Scheme; Dep. Chm., NZ Racing Authority. *Publications:* several papers on local govt in New Zealand. *Recreations:* gardening, golf, bowls. *Address:* 1 Tensing Place, Khandallah, Wellington, New Zealand. *T:* Wellington 792-424. *Clubs:* Shandon Golf (Petone, NZ); Khandallah Bowling (Khandallah, NZ).

ODELL, John William, (Jack), OBE 1969; Joint Vice-Chairman, Lesney Products & Co. Ltd, Diecasting Engineers, London E9, 1981-82 (Joint Managing Director, 1947-73; Deputy Chairman, 1973-81).

ODELL, Prof. Noel Ewart; geological research worker, since retirement from last professorship in 1962; *b* 25 Dec. 1890; *s* of Rev. R. W. Odell and M. M. Odell (*née* Ewart); *m* 1917, Gwladys Jones; one *s. Educ:* Brighton College; Imperial Coll. of Science and Technology (ARSM); Clare Coll., Cambridge (PhD). MIMM, FGS, FRSE, FRGS. Served RE: 1915-19 (wounded three times); 1940-42, British and Indian Armies (Major, Bengal Sappers and Miners). Staff Lectr, Council for Adult Educn in Forces, 1942-47. Geologist, Anglo Persian Oil Co. Ltd, 1922-25; cons. geologist and mining engineer, Canada, 1927-30; Univ. Lectr in Geology and Tutor, Harvard Univ., 1928-30; Research Student and Univ. Lectr, Cambridge, 1931-40 (Fellow Commoner and Supervisor of Studies, Clare Coll.); Leverhulme Fellowships, 1934 and 1938; Lectr, McGill Univ. and Vis. Prof., Univ. of BC, Canada, 1948-49; Prof. of Geology and Head of Dept, Univ. of Otago, NZ, 1950-56, Peshawar Univ., Pakistan, 1960-62. British Council Lectr, Scandinavian univs 1946, 1959, Swiss

Univ. 1947. Foreign expeditions: Mt Everest 1924 (geologist, to 27,500 ft without oxygen, search for Mallory and Irvine) (private audience of HM King George V at Buckingham Palace, Nov. 1924); Mt Everest 1938, to 25,000 ft; Norway 1929 and British Columbia 1930, geological research; mountaineering and exploration in Canadian Rockies, 1927-47; Nanda Devi, 26,640 ft, first ascent with H. W. Tilman, 1936 (for 14 years highest peak climbed to summit); geol exploration in N Labrador, 1931; NE Greenland, 1933; Lloyd George Mts, Rockies, 1947; St Elias Mts, Yukon, Alaska, 1949 and 1977. *Publications:* Chapters in: Norton: The Fight for Everest, 1925; Tilman: Everest, 1938; contribs to journals, scientific *et al. Recreations:* fell-walking, watching Rugby football, listening to music. *Address:* Clare College, Cambridge CB2 1TL; 5 Dean Court, Cambridge. *T:* Cambridge 47701. *Clubs:* (Hon. Mem.) Alpine, Himalayan, and many foreign alpine and mountaineering clubs in Canada, NZ, SA, USA, Switzerland, Norway, Japan, inc. Arctic (former Pres.), and Arctic Inst. of N America.

ODELL, Prof. Peter Randon; Director, Centre for International Energy Studies, Erasmus University, Rotterdam, since 1981; *b* 1 July 1930; *s* of late Frank James Odell and late Grace Edna Odell; *m* 1957, Jean Mary McKintosh; two *s* two *d. Educ:* County Grammar Sch., Coalville; Univ. of Birmingham (BA, PhD); Fletcher Sch. of Law and Diplomacy, Cambridge, Mass. (AM). RAF 1954-57. Economist, Shell International Petroleum Co., 1958-61; Lectr, LSE, 1961-65; Sen. Lectr, LSE, 1965-68; Prof. of Economic Geography, Erasmus Univ., 1968-81. Stamp Meml Lectr, London Univ., 1975. Adviser, Dept of Energy, 1977-78. *Publications:* An Economic Geography of Oil, 1963; Natural Gas in Western Europe, 1969; Oil and World Power, 1970, 7th edn 1983; (with D. A. Preston) Economics and Societies in Latin America, 1973, 2nd edn 1978; Energy: Needs and Resources, 1974, 2nd edn 1977; (with K. E. Rosing) The North Sea Oil Province, 1975; The West European Energy Economy: the case for self-sufficiency, 1976; (with K. E. Rosing) The Optimal Development of the North Sea Oilfields, 1976; (with L. Vallenilla) The Pressures of Oil: a strategy for economic revival, 1978; British Oil Policy: a Radical Alternative, 1980; (with K. E. Rosing) The Future of Oil, 1980-2080, 1980, 2nd edn 1982. *Address:* Postbus 4002, 3006 AA Rotterdam, The Netherlands. *T:* Rotterdam 525341.

ODEY, George William, CBE 1945; DL; Honorary President, Barrow, Hepburn Group Ltd, since 1974 (Chairman, 1937-74); *b* 21 April 1900; *s* of late George William Odey; *m* 1st, 1926, Dorothy Christian (*d* 1975), *d* of late James Moir; one *s*; 2nd, 1976, Mrs Doris Harrison-Broadley (*d* 1981); 3rd, 1981, Denise, *widow* of Sir Richard Barwick, 3rd Bt. *Educ:* Faversham Grammar Sch.; University College, London. President Union Society, UCL, 1921-22. University of London Union Society, 1922. Fellow, UCL 1953; Assistant Secretary, University of London Appointments Board, 1922-25. Joined firm of Barrow, Hepburn & Gale, Ltd, 1925; Board of Barrow, Hepburn & Gale, Ltd, 1929, Managing Director, 1933. Representative Ministry of Supply in Washington for negotiations in connection with joint purchase of hides between UK and USA, 1941; Member joint UK and USA Mission on Hides and Leather to S. America, 1943; Chairman: Board of Governors, National Leathersellers Coll., 1951-77; United Tanners' Federation, 1951. MP (C) Howdenshire Division of E Yorks, Nov. 1947-Feb. 1950, Beverley Division of the East Riding of Yorkshire, 1950-55; CC East Riding, Yorkshire, 1964-74. Leathersellers' Company Livery, 1939. Hon. Air Commodore (RAuxAF), retired. Commodore House of Commons Yacht Club, 1954. President: International Tanners' Council, 1954-67; British Leather Manufacturers Research Assoc., 1964; British Leather Federation, 1965; Federation of Gelatine and Glue Manufacturers, 1955-57; British Gelatine and Glue Research Assoc., 1950-. Member: Western Hemisphere Export Council, 1960-64; Cttee for Exports to the US, 1964; Member of Lloyd's. Hon. Freeman of Beverley, 1977. DL Humberside, 1977. *Recreations:* farming, yachting, tennis. *Address:* Keldgate Manor, Beverley, North Humberside. *T:* Beverley 882418. *Clubs:* Carlton, Royal Automobile; Royal Yorkshire Yacht; Lloyds Yacht; Scarborough Yacht; House of Commons Yacht.

ODGERS, Graeme David William; Group Finance Director, Tarmac, since 1979; *b* 10 March 1934; *s* of William Arthur Odgers and Elizabeth Minty (*née* Rennie); *m* 1957, Diana Patricia Berge; one *s* three *d. Educ:* St John's Coll., Johannesburg; Gonville and Caius Coll., Cambridge (Mech. Scis Tripos); Harvard Business Sch. (MBA, Baker Scholar). Investment Officer, Internat. Finance Corp., Washington DC, 1959-62; Management Consultant, Urwick Orr and Partners Ltd, 1962-64; Investment Executive, Hambros Bank Ltd, 1964-65; Director: Keith Shipton and Co. Ltd, 1965-72; C. T. Bowring (Insurance) Holdings Ltd, 1972-74; Chm., Odgers and Co. Ltd (Management Consultants), 1970-74; Dir, Industrial Develt Unit, DoI, 1974-77; Assoc. Dir (Finance), General Electric Co., 1977-78. *Recreations:* tennis, swimming. *Address:* The Old Rectory, Eaton Constantine, Shrewsbury, Shropshire. *T:* Cressage 295. *Club:* Lansdowne.

ODGERS, James Rowland, CB 1980; CBE 1968; *b* 9 Aug. 1914; *s* of Matthew John Odgers and Lilian Odgers; *m* 1939, Helen Jean Horner; two *s* one *d. Educ:* South Australian public schools. Parliamentary officer, 1937-79; Clerk of the Australian Senate, 1965-79; retired 1979. *Publication:* Australian Senate Practice, 1954, 5th edn 1976. *Recreations:* bowls, writing. *Address:* 30 Barnett Close, Swinger Hill, Canberra, ACT 2606, Australia. *T:* 864224.

ODGERS, Paul Randell, CB 1970; MBE 1945; TD 1949; Deputy Secretary, Department of Education and Science, 1971-75; *b* 30 July 1915; *e s* of late

Dr P. N. B. Odgers and Mrs M. A. Odgers (*née* Higgins); *m* 1944, Diana, *d* of late R. E. F. Fawkes, CBE; one *s* one *d. Educ:* Rugby; New Coll., Oxford. Entered CS, Board of Education, 1937. Army Service, 1939-45 (despatches three times). Asst Secretary: Min. of Educn, 1948; Cabinet Office, 1956; Under-Secretary: Min. of Educn, 1958; Office of First Secretary of State, 1967; Office of Lord President of the Council, 1968; Office of Sec. of State for Social Services, 1968; Cabinet Office, 1970. Vice-Pres., Soc. for Promotion of Roman Studies; Mem. Council, GPDST. *Address:* Stone Walls, Aston Road, Haddenham, Bucks. *T:* Haddenham 291830. *Club:* United Oxford & Cambridge University.

ODLING, Thomas George, CB 1974; *b* 18 Sept. 1911; *yr s* of late Major W. A. Odling, Paxford, Glos and late Mary Bennett Odling (*née* Case); *m* 1st, Camilla Haldane Paterson (marr. diss.); two *s* ; 2nd, Hilary Katharine, *d* of late W. J. Palgrave-Ker, Lilliput, Dorset. *Educ:* Temple Grove; Rugby Sch.; New Coll., Oxford (MA). House of Commons: Asst Clerk, 1935; Clerk of Private Bills, Examr of Petitions for Private Bills and Taxing Officer, 1961-73; Clerk of Select Cttee on Parly Comr for Admin, 1969-73; Clerk of Committees, 1974-76, retired 1976. Temp. attached to Consultative Assembly of Council of Europe during 1949 and later sessions. *Recreations:* music, gardening. *Address:* Paxford, Campden, Glos. *Clubs:* Athenæum, MCC.
See also Maj.-Gen. W. Odling.

ODLING, Maj.-Gen. William, CB 1963; OBE 1951; MC; DL; President, English-Speaking Union (Eastern Counties); Chairman, Roman River (Colchester) Conservation Zone; Vice Chairman: Friends of Essex Churches; Fingringhoe Parish Council, School and Hall; Treasurer/Secretary, Fingringhoe Ancient Charities; *b* 8 June 1909; *s* of late Major and Mrs W. A. Odling, Paxford, Campden, Glos; *m* 1939, Margaret Marshall (*née* Gardner); one *s* two *d. Educ:* Temple Grove; Wellington Coll.; RMA, Woolwich. Subaltern RHA and RA, chiefly in India until 1938; Captain, 1938; Major, 1946; Lieut-Colonel, 1951; Colonel, 1953; Brigadier 1957; Maj.-General, 1961; Adjutant, TA, 1939; CRA, Madagascar Force, 1942 (MC); GSO 1, RA, COSSAC, Planning Staff for Operation Overlord, 1943; N.W. Europe Campaign (despatches), 1944; GSO 1, War Office, 1945; GSO 1, Training, GHQMELF, 1948; AQMG, MELF, 1950; AAG Colonel, War Office, 1953; CRA E Anglian Div., 1957; Brig. AQ, HQ E Comd, 1959; Maj.-Gen. i/c Admin, GHQ FELF, 1961-62; COS GHQ FELF 1962-64. DL Essex, 1975. *Recreations:* sailing (Vice Pres., Atalanta (Yacht) Owners Assoc.), print collecting, gardening, brick building, economising. *Address:* Gun House, Fingringhoe, Colchester CO5 7AL. *T:* Peldon 320. *Club:* Army and Navy.
See also T. G. Odling.

ODLUM, Dr Doris Maude; Hon. Consultant, since 1955, formerly Senior Physician for Psychological Medicine, Elizabeth Garrett Anderson (Royal Free) Hospital, London; Consultant Emeritus, Marylebone Hospital for Psychiatry and Child Guidance, London; Consultant Emeritus, Bournemouth and East Dorset Hospital Group; Fellow, British Medical Association, 1959; *b* 26 June 1890; *d* of Walter Edward and Maude Gough Odlum. *Educ:* Talbot Heath, Bournemouth; St Hilda's Coll., Oxford (Hon. Fellow 1981); St Mary's Hospital and London School of Medicine for Women. MA Oxon; BA London; MRCS; LRCP, Foundn Fellow, Royal Coll. Psychiatrists, 1971; DPM; DipEd. Hon. Consultant Phys., Lady Chichester Hospital for Nervous Diseases, Hove, 1928-48; Hon. Phys. for Psychiatry, Royal Victoria and W. Hants Hospital, Bournemouth, 1928-48; President, British Med. Women's Federation, 1950-53; President, European League for Mental Hygiene, 1953-56; Vice-President, International Med. Women's Assoc., 1950-54; Vice-President, National Assoc. for Mental Health, 1946-; Member Exec. World Federation for Mental Health, 1948-51; Hon. Cons. Psychiatrist to the Samaritans Inc., 1961-, Life Pres., 1973-. Corresponding Member Swiss Psychiatric Assoc., 1946-; Member Home Office Cttee on Adoption, 1954. *Publications:* You and Your Children, 1948; Psychology, the Nurse and the Patient (3rd edn 1959, US edn 1960); Journey Through Adolescence, 1957 (2nd edn, 1965, 3rd edn 1977); The Mind of Your Child, 1959; L'Età Difficile, 1962 (2nd edn 1968); Puber Puberteit, 1965; The Male Predicament, 1975; Understanding Your Child, 1976; Adolescence, 1978; articles in British Medical Journal, Lancet, Practitioner, etc. *Recreations:* painting, golf, swimming, travel. *Address:* (Residence) 11 Golden Gates, Ferry Way, Sandbanks, Poole, Dorset BH13 7QH. *T:* Canford Cliffs 707915. *Club:* Naval and Military.

O'DONNELL, Dr Michael; author and journalist; *b* 20 Oct. 1928; *o s* of late James Michael O'Donnell and Nora (*née* O'Sullivan); *m* 1953, Catherine Dorrington Ward; one *s* two *d. Educ:* Stonyhurst; Trinity Hall, Cambridge (Lane Harrington Schol.); St Thomas's Hosp. Med. Sch., London (MB, BChir). Editor, Cambridge Writing, 1948; Scriptwriter, BBC Radio, 1949-52. General Medical Practitioner, 1954-64. Editor, World Medicine, 1966-82. Member: General Medical Council, 1971-; Longman Editorial Adv. Bd, 1978-. Inaugural lecture, Green Coll., Oxford, 1981. Scientific Adviser: O Lucky Man (film), 1972; Inside Medicine (BBC TV), 1974; Don't Ask Me (Yorkshire TV), 1977; Don't Just Sit There (Yorkshire TV), 1979-80; Where There's Life (Yorkshire TV), 1981-82. *Television plays:* Suggestion of Sabotage, 1963; Dangerous Reunion, 1964; Resolution, 1964; *television documentaries:* You'll Never Believe It, 1962; Cross Your Heart and Hope to Live, 1975; The Presidential Race, 1976; From Europe to the Coast, 1976; Chasing the Dragon, 1979; Second Opinion, 1980; Judgement on Las Vegas, 1981; Is Your Brain Really Necessary, 1982; contributor to Stop the Week

(BBC Radio), 1976-. Medical Journalists Assoc. Award, 1971 and 1982; British Science Writers' Award, 1979. *Publications:* Cambridge Anthology, 1952; The Europe We Want, 1971; My Medical School, 1978; The Devil's Prison, 1982; contrib. Punch, New Scientist, Vogue, The Times, Sunday Times, Daily Telegraph, Daily Mail. *Recreations:* golf, listening to music, loitering (with and without intent). *Address:* Cedar Tree House, Weybridge Park, Weybridge, Surrey KT13 8SJ. *T:* Weybridge 46095. *Club:* Garrick.

O'DONNELL, Peadar; Member Irish Academy of Letters. *Educ:* St Patrick's, Dublin. *Publications:* Storm; Islanders, 1925; Adrigoole, 1928; The Knife, 1930; The Gates Flew Open; On The Edge of the Stream, 1934; Salud; An Irishman in Spain, 1937; The Big Windows, 1955; Proud Island, 1976. *Address:* c/o O'Brien Press, 11 Clare Street, Dublin 2, Ireland.

O'DONNELL, Rt. Hon. Turlough; PC 1979; **Rt. Hon. Lord Justice O'Donnell;** Lord Justice of Appeal, Supreme Court of Northern Ireland, since 1979; *b* 5 Aug. 1924; *e s* of Charles and Eileen O'Donnell; *m* 1954, Eileen McKinley; two *s* two *d. Educ:* Abbey Grammar Sch., Newry; Queen's Univ., Belfast (LLB). Called to Bar of Northern Ireland, 1947; called to Inner Bar, 1964; Puisne Judge, NI, 1971-79. Chairman: NI Bar Council, 1970-71, Council of Legal Educn, NI, 1980-. *Recreations:* golf, folk music. *Address:* 155 Glen Road, Belfast 11. *T:* 613965; Royal Courts of Justice (Ulster), Belfast BT1 3JF.

O'DONOGHUE, Michael; His Honour Judge O'Donoghue; a Circuit Judge, since 1982; *b* 10 June 1929; *s* of late Dr James O'Donoghue, MB, ChB and Vera O'Donoghue. *Educ:* Rhyl County School; Univ. of Liverpool. LLB (Hons) 1950. Called to the Bar, Gray's Inn, 1951; National Service as Flying Officer, RAF, 1951-53; practised at the Chancery Bar, 1954-82; Lectr in Law (part time), Univ. of Liverpool, 1966-82. *Recreations:* music, sailing, photography. *Address:* 21 Princes Park Mansions, Liverpool L8 3SA; Helen View, 29 Rhes Segontiwm, Caernarfon, Gwynedd LL55 2PH. *Clubs:* Athenæum (Liverpool); Royal Welsh Yacht (Caernarfon) (Commodore, 1980-82).

O'DONOGHUE, Philip Nicholas, FIBiol; General Secretary, Institute of Biology, since 1982; *b* 9 Oct. 1929; *s* of Terence Frederick O'Donoghue and Ellen Mary (*née* Haynes); *m* 1955, Veronica Florence Campbell; two *d. Educ:* East Barnet Grammar Sch.; Univ. of Nottingham (BSc; MSc 1959). FIBiol 1975. Experimental Officer, ARC's Field Stn, Compton, 1952-55 and Inst. of Animal Physiology, Babraham, 1955-61; Scientific Officer, National Inst. for Res. in Dairying, Shinfield, 1962-66; Lectr in Exptl Vet. Science and later Sen. Lectr in Lab. Animal Science, Royal Postgrad. Med. Sch., Univ. of London, 1966-82. Vice-Pres., Inst. of Animal Technicians, 1969-; Hon. Sec., Inst. of Biology, 1972-76; Member: TEC, 1973-79 (Chm., Life Sciences Cttee, 1973-80). Editor, Laboratory Animals, 1967-82. *Publications:* editor of books and author of articles chiefly on the law relating to and the effective use and proper care of laboratory animals. *Recreations:* music, local history, talking. *Address:* 21 Holyrood Road, New Barnet, Herts EN5 1DQ. *T:* 01-449 3692. *Club:* Royal Society of Medicine.

O'DONOVAN, Rev. Canon Oliver Michael Timothy, DPhil; Regius Professor of Moral and Pastoral Theology, University of Oxford, since 1982; Canon of Christ Church, Oxford, since 1982; *b* 28 June 1945; *s* of Michael and Joan M. O'Donovan; *m* 1978, Joan Elizabeth Lockwood; one *s. Educ:* University Coll. Sch., Hampstead; Balliol Coll., Oxford (MA, DPhil); Wycliffe Hall, Oxford; Princeton Univ. Ordained deacon 1972, priest 1973, dio. of Oxford. Tutor, Wycliffe Hall, Oxford, 1972-77; Prof. of Systematic Theology, Wycliffe Coll., Toronto, 1977-82. *Publications:* The Problem of Self-Love in Saint Augustine, 1980; contrib. Jl of Theol Studies and Jl of Religious Ethics. *Address:* Christ Church, Oxford OX1 1DP.

OESTREICHER, Rev. Canon Paul; Assistant General Secretary and Secretary of the Division of International Affairs, British Council of Churches, and Public Preacher in the Diocese of Southwark, since 1981; Hon. Canon of Southwark Cathedral, since 1978; journalist; *b* Germany, 29 Sept. 1931; *s* of Paul Oestreicher and Emma (*née* Schnaus); *m* 1958, Lore Feind; two *s* two *d. Educ:* King's High Sch., Dunedin; Otago and Victoria Univs, NZ; Bonn Univ. (Humboldt Res. Fellow); Lincoln Theol College. BA Mod. Langs Otago 1953; MA Hons Polit. Sci. Victoria 1955. Ordained 1959. Fled to NZ with refugee parents, 1939; returned to Europe, 1955. Fraternal worker with German Lutheran Church at Rüsselsheim, trng in problems of industrial soc. (Opel, Gen. Motors), 1958-59; Curate, Dalston, E London, 1959-61; Producer, Relig. Dept, BBC Radio, 1961-64; Assoc. Sec., Dept of Internat. Affairs, Brit. Council of Churches with special resp. for East-West Relations, 1964-69; Vicar, Church of the Ascension, Blackheath, 1968-81; Dir of (Lay) Trng, Dio. Southwark, 1969-72. Hon. Chaplain to Bp of Southwark, 1975-. Mem. Gen. Synod of C of E, 1970-; Member: Brit. Council of Churches working parties on Southern Africa and Eastern Europe; Anglican Pacifist Fellowship (sometime exec. mem.), 1960-; Exec. Mem., Christian Concern for Southern Africa, 1978-. Chm., British Section, Amnesty International, 1974-79. Mem. Council, Keston Coll. (Centre for the Study of Religion and Communism), 1976-. Vice-Chm., Campaign for Nuclear Disarmament, 1980-81. Editor, Critic (Otago Univ. newspaper), 1952-53; subseq. free-lance journalist and broadcaster. *Publications:* (ed English edn) Helmut Gollwitzer, The Demands of Freedom, 1965; (trans.) H. J. Schultz, Conversion to the World, 1967; (ed, with J. Klugmann) What Kind of Revolution: A Christian-Communist Dialogue, 1968; (ed) The Christian Marxist Dialogue, 1969.

Address: 50 Handen Road, SE12. *T:* 01-852 5766; (office) 2 Eaton Gate, SW1. *T:* 01-730 9611.

O'FAOLAIN, Sean; writer. *Publications:* Midsummer Night Madness, 1932; A Nest of Simple Folk, 1933; Constance Markievicz: a biography, 1934; Bird Alone, 1936; A Purse of Coppers, 1937; King of the Beggars: a biography, 1938; She Had to Do Something (play), 1938; An Irish Journey, 1940; Come Back to Erin, 1940; The Great O'Neill: a biography, 1942; Teresa, 1946; The Short Story, 1948; Summer in Italy, 1949; Newman's Way, 1952; South to Sicily, 1953; The Vanishing Hero, 1956; The Stories of Sean O'Faolain, 1958; I Remember! I Remember!, 1962; Vive Moi!, 1965; The Heat of the Sun, 1966; The Talking Trees, 1970; Foreign Affairs and Other Stories, 1976; Selected Stories of Sean O'Faolain, 1978; And Again?, 1979; The Collected Stories, 1980. *Address:* 17 Rosmeen Park, Dunlaoire, Dublin.

O'FERRALL, Ven. Basil Arthur, CB 1979; MA; Chaplain to the Queen, since 1980; Vicar of Ranworth with Panxworth and Woodbastwick (Norwich) and Bishop's Chaplain for the Broads, since 1980; *b* 25 Aug. 1924; *s* of Basil James and Mabel Violet O'Ferrall, Dublin; *m* 1952, Joyce Forbes (*née* Taylor); one *s* two *d. Educ:* St Patrick's Cathedral Gram. Sch., Dublin; Trinity Coll., Dublin (BA 1948, MA 1966). Curate Assistant, St Patrick's, Coleraine, 1948; Chaplain RN, 1951; served: HMS Victory, 1951; Ganges, 1952; Gambia, 1952-54; Curlew, 1955; Daedalus, 1956; Amphibious Warfare Sqdn, 1956-58; HMS Adamant, 1958-60; 40 Commando, RM, 1960-62; RN Hosp., Bighi, 1962; HMS Victorious, 1963-64; Condor, 1964-66; Maidstone, 1966-68; St Vincent, 1968; Commando Training Centre, RM, 1969-71; HM Naval Base, Portsmouth, 1971-74; CTC, RM, 1975; Chaplain of the Fleet and Archdeacon of the Royal Navy, 1975-80. Hon. Canon of Gibraltar, 1977-80. QHC 1975-80. *Recreations:* sailing, ornithology. *Address:* Ranworth Vicarage, Norwich NR13 6HT.

OFFALY, Earl of; Thomas FitzGerald; *b* 12 Jan. 1974; *s* of Marquess of Kildare, *qv.*

OFFICER, Maj.-Gen. William James, CB 1962; CBE 1959 (OBE 1945); MB, ChB; late RAMC; *b* 24 August 1903; *s* of John Liddell Officer, OBE, WS, Edinburgh; *m* 1934, Doris, *d* of William Charles Mattinson, Keswick, Cumberland; three *d. Educ:* Edinburgh Acad.; Durham School; Edinburgh University. MB, ChB, Edin., 1927. Joined RAMC, 1929; Major, 1939; Commanding Officer British Military Hosp., Deolali, and Officer-in-Charge RAMC Records, India and Burma, 1939-41; Served War of 1939-45 (despatches twice); in Burma, 1941-45; ADMS, 17th Indian Division and 2nd British Division; DDMS, Chindits Special Force and 33rd Indian Corps. Lt-Col, 1946; Asst Commandant, RAMC Depot and Training Establishment; Commanding Officer, British Military Hospital, Fayid (T/Col), 1949; Col 1951; ADMS, Hannover Dist, 1952; ADMS, N Midland Dist, 1954; DDMS (Actg Brig.), 2 (Br) Corps (Suez), 1956; Brig., 1957; Dir of Medical Services (temp. Maj.-Gen.), Middle East Land Forces, 1957-60; Maj.-Gen., 1960; Dir of Medical Services, Far East Land Forces, 1960-63; QHS 1961-63, retired 1963. *Address:* c/o Williams & Glyn's Bank Ltd, Kirkland House, SW1. *Club:* Naval and Military.

OFFICER BROWN, Sir (Charles) James; *see* Brown, Sir C. J. O.

OFFLER, Prof. Hilary Seton, MA; FBA 1974; Professor of Medieval History in the University of Durham, 1956-78, now Professor Emeritus; *b* 3 Feb. 1913; *s* of Horace Offler and late Jenny Whebby; *m* 1951, Betty Elfreda, *d* of late Archibald Jackson, Sawbridgeworth; two *s. Educ:* Hereford High School; Emmanuel College, Cambridge. 1st Cl. Historical Tripos Pt I, 1932, Part II, 1933, Theological Tripos Pt II, 1934; Lightfoot Schol., Cambridge, 1934; Research Fellow, Emmanuel Coll., 1936-40. Served with RA in N Africa, Sicily and NW Europe, 1940-46. Lecturer, Univ. of Bristol, 1946; Reader in Medieval History, Univ. of Durham, 1947. Pres., Surtees Society, 1980- (Sec., 1950-66). *Publications:* edited: Ockham, Opera politica, vol. i (jtly) 1940, ed. altera 1974; vol. ii (jtly) 1963; vol. iii 1956; (with E. Bonjour and G. R. Potter) A Short History of Switzerland, 1952; Medieval Historians of Durham, 1958; Durham Episcopal Charters 1071-1152, 1968; articles in English and foreign hist. jls. *Address:* 28 Old Elvet, Durham. *T:* Durham 46219.

OFFORD, Albert Cyril, DSc London; PhD Cantab; FRS 1952; FRSE; Emeritus Professor of Mathematics, University of London; Professor, 1966-73, Hon. Fellow, 1978, London School of Economics and Political Science; *b* 9 June 1906; *s* of Albert Edwin and Hester Louise Offord; *m* 1945, Marguerite Yvonne Pickard; one *d. Educ:* Hackney Downs School, London; University Coll. London (Fellow, 1969); St John's Coll., Cambridge. Fellow of St John's Coll., Cambridge, 1937-40; Lectr, UC N Wales, Bangor, 1940-41; Lectr, King's Coll., Newcastle upon Tyne, 1941-45; Professor: King's College, Newcastle upon Tyne, 1945-48; Birkbeck Coll., Univ. of London, 1948-66. *Publications:* papers in various mathematical journals. *Recreation:* early, especially Renaissance, music. *Address:* West Cottage, 24A Norham Gardens, Oxford OX2 6QD. *T:* Oxford 513703.

O'FIAICH, His Eminence Cardinal Tomás Séamus; *see* Armagh, Archbishop of, (RC).

O'FLAHERTY, Dr Coleman Anthony; Principal, Tasmanian College of Advanced Education, Australia, since 1978; *b* 8 Feb. 1933; *s* of Michael and Agnes O'Flaherty; *m* 1957, Nuala Rose Silke. *Educ:* Nat. Univ. of Ireland (BE); Iowa State Univ. (MS, PhD). FIMunE; FIEI; FIHE; FCIT. Engineer: Galway Co. Council, Ireland, 1954-55; Canadian Pacific Railway Co., Montreal, 1955-56; M. W. Kellogg Co., USA, 1956-57; Asst Prof., Iowa State Univ., 1957-62; Leeds University: Lectr, 1962-66; Prof. of Transport Engineering, Inst. for Transport Studies and Dept of Civil Engineering, 1966-74; First Asst Comr (Engineering), Nat. Capital Develt Commn, Canberra, 1974-78. Vis. Prof., Univ. of Melbourne, 1973. *Publications:* Highways, 1967, 2nd edn 1974; (jtly) Passenger Conveyors, 1972; (jtly) Introduction to Hovercraft and Hoverports, 1975; contribs to professional jls. *Recreations:* walking, squash. *Address:* Tasmanian College of Advanced Education, PO Box 1214, Launceston, Tasmania 7250, Australia. *T:* (003) 260531. *Club:* Launceston.

O'FLAHERTY, Liam; novelist; *b* Aran Islands, Co. Galway. *Educ:* Rockwell College; Blackrock College; University College, Dublin. Hon. DLitt Nat. Univ. of Ireland, 1974. Allied Irish Bank-Irish Academy of Letters Literary Award, 1979. *Publications:* Thy Neighbour's Wife, a novel; The Black Soul, a novel; Spring Sowing, short stories; The Informer, a novel; The Tent, and other stories, 1926; Mr Gilhooley, 1926; The Life of Tim Healy, 1927; The Assassin, 1928; Return of the Brute, 1929; The Mountain Tavern, and other stories, 1929; A Tourist's Guide to Ireland, 1929; The House of Gold, 1929; Two Years, 1930; I went to Russia, 1931; The Puritan, 1932; Skerrett, 1932, repr. 1977; The Martyr, 1933; Shame the Devil, 1934; Hollywood Cemetery, 1935; Famine, 1937; Short Stories of Liam O'Flaherty, 1937; Land, 1946; Two Lovely Beasts, short stories, 1948; Insurrection, 1950; The Short Stories of Liam O'Flaherty, 1956; The Pedlar's Revenge and other stories, 1976; The Wilderness, 1978. *Address:* c/o A. D. Peters, 10 Buckingham Street, Adelphi, WC2.

O'FLYNN, Brigadier (Retd) Dennis John Edwin, CBE 1960 (MBE 1937); DSO 1945; Army Officer retired; *b* 2 Aug. 1907; *s* of late Patrick Horace George O'Flynn and of Katie Alice (*née* Pye); *m* 1936, Winifred Madge Cairn Hogbin; (one *s* and one *d* decd). *Educ:* St Paul's School; RMC Sandhurst. Commissioned 2nd Lieut, Royal Tank Corps, 1928; served in Trans-Jordan Frontier Force, 1932-36; commanded: Westminster Dragoons (2nd Co. Lond. Yeo.), 1947-48; 3rd Royal Tank Regiment, 1948-50. Brigade Commander, 1953-60; retired 1960. Area Comr, St John Ambulance Brigade, 1966-69. OStJ 1967. *Recreations:* golf, gardening, photography. *Address:* High Copse, Pinemount Road, Camberley, Surrey. *T:* Camberley 63736. *Club:* Army and Navy.

of MAR, family name of **Countess of Mar.**

OGDEN, (Edward) Michael, QC 1968; Barrister since 1950; a Recorder (formerly Recorder of Hastings), since 1971; *b* 9 Apr. 1926; *er s* of late Edward Cannon Ogden and Daisy (*née* Paris); *m* 1951, Joan Kathleen, *er d* of late Pius Charles Brodrick and Kathleen (*née* Moran); two *s* two *d. Educ:* Downside Sch.; Jesus Coll., Cambridge (MA). Served in RAC (Royal Glos Hussars and 16th/5th Lancers), 1944-47 (Capt.); Inns of Court Regt (TA) 1950-56. Jesus Coll., Cambridge, 1948-49; called to Bar, Lincoln's Inn, 1950; Bencher, 1977. Mem. Bar Council, 1960-64, 1966-70, 1971-78 (responsible for fee negotiations, 1968-72, Treas., 1972-74, Chm., Internat. Relns Cttee, 1974-75); Mem. Senate of the Inns of Court, 1966-70, 1972-78. Leader, SE Circuit, 1975-78. Member: Council of Union Internationale des Avocats, 1962-; Council of Legal Educn, 1969-74; Chm., Criminal Injuries Compensation Bd, 1975- (Mem., 1968-); Mem., Lord Chancellor's Adv. Cttee on Legal Education, 1972-74. Dir, Internat. Assoc. of Crime Victim Compensation Bds, 1978-. Assessor for Home Sec. of compensation for persons wrongly convicted, 1978-. *Address:* 2 Crown Office Row, Temple, EC4Y 7HJ. *T:* 01-353 9337.

OGDEN, Eric; MP West Derby Division of Liverpool since 1964 (Lab 1964-81, SDP since 1981); *b* 23 Aug. 1923; *s* of Robert and Jane Lillian Ogden, Rhodes, Co. Lancaster; *m*; one *s*; *m* Marjorie (*née* Smith); two *s* two step *d. Educ:* Queen Elizabeth's Grammar School, Middleton, Lancs; Leigh Tech. Coll.; Wigan Mining and Tech. Coll. Merchant Service, 1942-46. Textiles, 1946-52; NCB, 1952-64. Mem., Nat. Union of Mineworkers. Councillor, Borough of Middleton, 1958-65. NUM sponsored candidate, West Derby, Liverpool, 1962. Hon. Vice-Pres., Socialist Medical Assoc.; Jt Hon. Chm., Parly Channel Tunnel Gp; Mem., PO Stamps Adv. Cttee. *Recreations:* painting, gardening, motoring. *Address:* House of Commons, SW1. *T:* 01-219 5201.

OGDEN, Frank Collinge, CBE 1956; FRGS; *b* 30 Mar. 1907; *s* of Paul and Nora Ogden; *m* 1944, Margaret, *o d* of Fred and Elizabeth Greenwood; one *s* two *d* (and one *d* decd). *Educ:* Manchester Grammar School; King's College, Cambridge. Entered Levant Consular Service, 1930; served in Cairo, Alexandria, Bagdad and Damascus; served War, 1941-42; Min. of Information, 1942; Tabriz, 1942; 1st Sec., Bogotá, 1944, Chargé d'Affaires, 1945; Consul, Shiraz, 1947; transferred to Seattle, 1949; Consul-General, Seattle, 1952; Basra, 1953; Gothenburg, 1955; Couns., Brit. Emb. in Libya, 1958; Chargé d'Affaires, 1958, 1959; Counsellor and Consul-General, Brit. Emb., Buenos Aires, 1960-65; retired. *Recreations:* swimming, motoring. *Address:* Yellow Sands, Thorney Drive, Selsey, Chichester, West Sussex. *Club:* Royal Automobile.

OGDEN, Sir George (Chester), Kt 1973; CBE 1966; DL; Chief Executive, Greater Manchester Metropolitan County Council, 1973-76; *b* 7 June 1913; *s* of late Harry and Florence A. Ogden, Burnley, Lancs; *m* 1942, Nina Marion (*née* Lewis); one *s* two *d*. *Educ*: Burnley Gram. Sch.; Giggleswick Sch.; Corpus Christi Coll., Oxford (MA). Asst Solicitor, Middlesbrough Corp., 1940. Served in Royal Marines, Middle East, Sicily and NW Europe, 1941-45 (Major). Dep. Town Clerk: Middlesbrough, 1947-53; Leicester, 1953-54; Town Clerk, Leicester, 1955-66; Town Clerk, Manchester, 1966-73. Dep. Chm., Police Complaints Bd, 1977-. DL Greater Manchester (formerly Co. Palatine of Lancaster), 1971. FBIM, Hon. LLD Manchester, 1976. *Recreations*: golf, fell walking. *Address*: Wood Lea, Twemlow, Holmes Chapel, Crewe. *T*: Holmes Chapel 33362. *Club*: National Liberal.

OGDEN, Michael; *see* Ogden, E. M.

OGDON, John (Andrew Howard); Pianist, Composer; *b* Mansfield Woodhouse, Notts, 27 Jan. 1937; *m* 1960, Brenda Mary Lucas; one *s* one *d*. *Educ*: Manchester Gram. Sch.; Royal Manchester Coll. of Music. Concert Appearances include: Michelangeli Festival, Brescia, 1966; Festivals of Spoleto, Edinburgh, Prague Spring, Zagreb Biennale, Cheltenham. Founded Cardiff Festival (with Alun Hoddinott), 1967, Jt Artistic Dir. Two-piano recitals with Brenda Lucas; concert appearances, USA, USSR, Australia, Far East, European capitals. Prof. in Music Dept, Univ. of Indiana, Bloomington, 1977-80. Awards: Liverpool, 1959; Liszt Prize, 1961; Tschaikovsky Prize (*ex aequo* with Vladimir Ashkenazy), Moscow, 1962; Harriet Cohen International Award. *Compositions*: large and small, mainly for piano. *Recreation*: history of literature, especially P. G. Wodehouse. *Address*: c/o Basil Douglas Ltd, 8 St George's Terrace, Regent's Park Road, NW1 8XJ.

OGILVIE, Sir Alec (Drummond), Kt 1965; Chairman, Powell Duffryn Ltd, 1969-78 (Deputy Chairman, 1967-69); *b* 17 May 1913; *s* of late Sir George Drummond Ogilvie, KCIE, CSI; *m* 1945, Lesley Constance, *d* of E. B. Woollan; two *s*. *Educ*: Cheltenham College. Served War of 1939-45; 2/2nd Gurkha Rifles (Indian Army), 1940-45; Captain 1941; PoW, Singapore, 1942-45. Joined Andrew Yule & Co. Ltd, Calcutta, 1935, Man. Dir, 1956, and Chm., 1962-65. Director: Westinghouse Brake & Signal Co. Ltd, 1966-79; Lindustries Ltd, 1973-79; J. Lyons & Co. Ltd, 1977-78. Pres., Bengal Chamber of Commerce and Industry, 1964-65; Pres., Associated Chambers of Commerce and Industry of India, 1964-65. Member: Council, King Edward VII Hosp. for Officers, 1967- (Vice-Pres., 1979-); Council, Cheltenham Coll., 1973-. *Recreations*: golf, walking. *Address*: Townlands, High Street, Lindfield, West Sussex RH16 2HT. *T*: Lindfield 3953. *Clubs*: Oriental, MCC; Bengal (Calcutta).

OGILVIE, Lady, (Mary Helen); Principal of St Anne's College, Oxford, 1953-66; *b* 22 March 1900; *e d* of late Rev. Professor A. B. Macaulay, DD, of Glasgow; *m* 1922, (Sir) Frederick Wolff Ogilvie, LLD (*d* 1949), Principal of Jesus College, Oxford, 1945-49; one *s* (and two *s* decd). *Educ*: St George's, Edinburgh; Somerville College, Oxford (Hon. Fellow, 1978). BA Hon. Sch. of Mod. Hist., Oxford, 1922, MA 1937. Member: Royal Commission on Population, 1944-49; Archbp's Commn on Church and State, 1967-70. Tutor of Women Students, University of Leeds, 1949-53. Member of Arts Council of Great Britain, 1953-58; on Governing Board of Cheltenham Ladies' College, 1951-75; Governing Board of Clifton College, 1960-72. Hon. LLD: Wilson College, Pa, 1956, QUB 1960; Leeds Univ., 1962; Trent Univ., Ont, 1972; Hon. DCL Stirling, 1973. Hon. Fellow: St Anne's College, Oxford, 1966; Lucy Cavendish Collegiate Soc., 1971. *Recreation*: travel. *Address*: Flat 5, Fairlawn, First Turn, Wolvercote, Oxford. *T*: 58137. *Club*: University Women's.

OGILVIE-GRANT, family name of Earl of Seafield.

OGILVY, family name of Earl of Airlie.

OGILVY, Lord; David John Ogilvy; *b* 9 March 1958; *s* and *heir* of 13th Earl of Airlie, *qv*; *m* 1981, Hon. Geraldine Harmsworth, *d* of Viscount Rothermere, *qv*. *Educ*: Eton and Oxford (MA). *Address*: 13 St Leonards Terrace, Chelsea, SW3. *T*: 01-730 8741.

OGILVY, Hon. Angus James Bruce; company director; *b* 14 Sept. 1928; *s* of 12th (*de facto* 9th) Earl of Airlie, KT, GCVO, MC; *m* 1963, HRH Princess Alexandra of Kent; one *s* one *d*. *Educ*: Eton Coll.; Trinity Coll., Oxford. Scots Guards, 1946-48; Mem., HM Body Guard for Scotland (The Royal Company of Archers), 1958-. Patron: Scottish Wildlife Trust, 1969-; Nat. Assoc. of Ladies' Circles, 1973-82; British Rheumatism and Arthritis Soc., 1977- (Pres., 1963-76); President: Imperial Cancer Research Fund, 1964-; National Association of Youth Clubs, 1971-; Vice-Pres., The Friends of the Elderly and Gentlefolk's Help, 1963-; Vice-Patron, Toc H, 1963-; Trustee: Leeds Castle Foundn, 1975-; Petroleum Press Foundn, 1979-. Director: London Trust Co. Ltd; MEPC Ltd; Rank Organisation Ltd; Sotheby & Co. and other cos. *Recreations*: architecture, music. *Address*: Thatched House Lodge, Richmond Park, Surrey. *T*: 01-546 8833. *Club*: White's.
See also under Royal Family.

OGILVY, Sir David (John Wilfrid), 13th Bt, *cr* 1626; DL; farmer and landowner; *b* 3 February 1914; *e s* of Gilbert Francis Molyneux Ogilvy (*d* 1953) (4th *s* of 10th Bt) and Marjory Katharine, *d* of late M. B. Clive, Whitfield, Herefordshire; *S* uncle, Sir Herbert Kinnaird Ogilvy, 12th Bt,

1956; *m* 1966, Penelope Mary Ursula, *d* of Arthur Lafone Frank Hills, White Court, Kent; one *s*. *Educ*: Eton; Trinity College, Oxford. Served in the RNVR in War of 1939-45. JP 1957, DL 1971, East Lothian. *Heir: s* Francis Gilbert Arthur Ogilvy, *b* 22 April 1969. *Address*: Winton Cottage, Pencaitland, East Lothian EH34 5AT. *T*: Pencaitland 340222. *Club*: New (Edinburgh).

OGILVY, David Mackenzie, CBE 1967; Chairman, Ogilvy and Mather, International, 1965-75; *b* 23 June 1911; *s* of Francis John Longley Ogilvy and Dorothy Fairfield. *Educ*: Fettes College, Edinburgh; Christ Church, Oxford (Scholar). British Security Coordination, 1942; Second Secretary, British Embassy, Washington, 1944. Mem. of Honor, World Wildlife Fund. Dr of letters (*hc*), Adelphi Univ., USA, 1977. *Publications*: Confessions of an Advertising Man, 1964; Blood, Brains and Beer (autobiog.), 1978. *Recreation*: gardening. *Address*: Château de Touffou, 86300 Bonnes, France. *Club*: Brook (NY).

OGILVY-WEDDERBURN, Sir Andrew John Alexander, 13th and 7th Bt *cr* 1704 and 1803; Captain, The Black Watch (Royal Highland Regiment); *b* 4 Aug. 1952; *s* of Sir (John) Peter Ogilvy-Wedderburn, 12th and 6th Bt, and of Elizabeth Katharine, *e d* of late John A. Cox, Drumkilbo; *S* father, 1977. *Educ*: Gordonstoun. *Heir: cousin* Caryl Eustace Wedderburn Ogilvy, ARIBA [*b* 10 Dec. 1925; *m* 1953, Katharine Mary, *o d* of William Steele; one *s* two *d*]. *Address*: Silvie, Alyth, Perthshire.

OGLE-SKAN, Peter Henry, CVO 1972; TD 1948; Director, Scottish Services, Department of the Environment, 1970-75; *b* 4 July 1915; 2nd *s* of Dr H. W. Ogle-Skan, Hendon; *m* 1941, Pamela Moira Heslop; one *s* one *d*. *Educ*: Merchant Taylors' Sch., London. Clerk with Arbuthnot-Latham & Co. Ltd, London, 1933-39. Commnd into Royal Engineers (TA), 1936; War Service, 1939-46; England, 1939-42; India, 1942-45. Min. of Works: Temp. Principal, 1946; Principal, 1948; Asst Sec., 1955; Under-Sec., Scottish HQ, MPBW, 1966-70. *Recreations*: golf, walking, photography. *Address*: 44 Ravelston Garden, Edinburgh EH4 3LF. *T*: 031-337 6834.

OGLESBY, Peter Rogerson, CB 1982; Deputy Secretary, Department of Health and Social Security, 1979-82; *b* 15 July 1922; *s* of late Leonard William Oglesby and late Jessie Oglesby (*née* Rogerson); *m* 1947, Doreen Hilda Hudson; three *d*. *Educ*: Woodhouse Grove Sch., Apperley Bridge. Clerical Officer, Admlty, 1939-47; Exec. Officer, Min. of Nat. Ins., 1947-56; Higher Exec. Officer, MPNI, 1956-62, Principal 1962-64; Principal Private Secretary: to Chancellor of Duchy of Lancaster, 1964-66; to Minister without Portfolio, 1966; to First Sec. of State, 1966-68; to Lord President, 1968; Asst Sec., Cabinet Office, 1968-70, Asst Sec., DHSS, 1970-73; Sec., Occupational Pensions Bd, 1973-74; Under Sec., DHSS, 1974-79. *Address*: 41 Draycot Road, Wanstead, E11 2NX. *T*: 01-989 5526.

OGMORE, 2nd Baron *cr* 1950, of Bridgend; **Gwilym Rees Rees-Williams**; *b* 5 May 1931; *er s* of 1st Baron Ogmore, PC, TD, and of Constance, *er d* of W. R. Wills; *S* father, 1976; *m* 1967, Gillian Mavis, *d* of M. K. Slack; two *d*. *Educ*: Mill Hill School; St Luke's Coll., Exeter. *Heir: b* Hon. Morgan Rees-Williams [*b* 19 Dec. 1937; *m* 1964, Patricia (marr. diss. 1970), *o d* of C. Paris Jones; *m* 1972, Roberta (marr. diss. 1976), *d* of Captain Alec Cunningham-Reid, DFC]. *Address*: 4 Foster Road, Chiswick, W4 4NY. *Club*: London Welsh Rugby Football.

OGNALL, Harry Henry, QC 1973; a Recorder of the Crown Court since 1972; *b* 9 Jan. 1934; *s* of Leo and Cecilia Ognall; *m* 1st, 1962, Jean Mary Stalker; two *s* one *d*; 2nd, 1977, Elizabeth Young. *Educ*: Leeds Grammar Sch.; Lincoln Coll., Oxford (MA (Hons)); Univ. of Virginia, USA (LLM). Called to Bar (Gray's Inn), 1958. Joined NE Circuit. *Recreations*: photography, music, travel. *Address*: 4 Brick Court, Temple, EC4; 2 Park Square, Leeds LS1 2NE; Netherfield House, Menston, Ilkley, W Yorks.

O'GORMAN, Rev. Brian Stapleton; President of the Methodist Conference, 1969-70; *b* 4 March 1910; *s* of William Thomas and Annie Maria O'Gorman; *m* 1939, Margaret, *d* of William and Margaret Huggon, Carlisle; two *d*. *Educ*: Bowdon College, Cheshire; Handsworth Theological College, Birmingham. Porlock, 1931-32; Handsworth College, 1932-35; Manchester Mission, 1935-40; Islington Mission, London, 1940-43; Longton Mission, Stoke on Trent, 1943-50; Sheffield Mission, 1950-57; Chm., Wolverhampton and Shrewsbury Dist of Methodist Church, 1957-75. *Address*: 9 Trysull Gardens, Wolverhampton WV3 7LD. *T*: Wolverhampton 762167.

O'GRADY, Prof. Francis William, TD 1970; MD; FRCP, FRCPath; Foundation Professor of Microbiology, University of Nottingham, since 1974; Hon. Consultant Microbiologist: Public Health Laboratory Service and Nottinghamshire District Health Authority, since 1974; to the Army, since 1982; *b* 7 Nov. 1925; *s* of Francis Joseph O'Grady and Lilian Maud Hitchcock; *m* 1951, Madeleine Marie-Thérèse Becquart; three *d*. *Educ*: Middlesex Hosp. Med. Sch., London (BSc 1st Cl. Hons; MB, BS Hons; MSc; MD). FRCP 1976; FRCPath 1972. House Physician, Mddx and North Mddx Hosps, 1951; Asst Pathologist, Bland-Sutton Inst. of Pathol., Mddx Hosp., 1952-53, 1956-58 and 1961-62; Pathologist, RAMC, 1954-55, AER, 1956-72; Asst Prof. of Environmental Medicine, Johns Hopkins Univ., Baltimore, 1959-60; Reader, 1962-66, and Prof. of Bacteriology, 1967-74, Univ. of London; Bacteriologist, St Bartholomew's Hosp., 1962-74. Mem., MRC, 1980-; Chm., MRC Physiol Systems and Disorders Bd, 1980- (Mem., 1977-80; Mem., Grants Cttee,

1975-76); Chm., MRC Cttee on Hosp. Infection, 1977-80 (Mem., 1967-77). Member: Antibiotics Panel, Cttee on Med. Aspects of Food Policy, 1968-72; Sub-Cttee on Toxicity, Clin. Trials and Therapeutic Efficacy, 1971-75, and Sub-Cttee on Biol Substances, 1971-81, Cttee on Safety of Medicines; Jt Sub-Cttee on Antimicrobial Substances, Cttee on Safety of Medicines and Vet. Products Cttee, 1973-80; Cttee on Rev. of Medicines, 1975-; Public Health Lab. Service Bd, 1980-. William N. Creasy Vis. Prof. of Clin. Pharmacology, Duke Univ., NC, 1979. Erasmus Wilson Demonstrator, RCS, 1967; Foundn Lectr, Univ. of Hong Kong, 1974; Sydney Watson Smith Lectr, RCPE, 1975; Jacobson Vis. Lectr, Univ. of Newcastle upon Tyne, 1979; Berk Lectr, British Assoc. of Urol Surgeons, 1980. Pres. Council, British Jl of Exper. Pathol., 1980- (Mem., 1968-80); Mem. Editorial Boards: Jl of Med. Microbiol., 1970-75; Pathologie Biologie, 1973-78; British Jl of Clin. Pharmacol., 1974-; Drugs, 1976-; Gut, 1977-; Jl of Infection, 1978-; Revs of Infectious Diseases, 1979-. *Publications:* Airborne Infection: transmission and control, 1968; Antibiotic and Chemotherapy, 1968, 5th edn 1981; (ed) Urinary Tract Infection, 1968; (ed) Microbial Perturbation of Host Defences, 1981; papers on clin. and exper. infections and on antimicrobial chemotherapy. *Recreations:* admiring other people's furniture, houses and gardens; occasionally restoring my own. *Address:* Department of Microbiology, University Hospital, Queen's Medical Centre, Nottingham NG7 2UH. *T:* Nottingham 700111, ext. 3523.

OGSTON, Alexander George, MA, DSc; FRS 1955; President of Trinity College, Oxford, 1970-78, Hon. Fellow 1978; Fellow, 1937, and Bedford Lecturer, 1950, Balliol College; *b* 30 January 1911; *s* of late Walter Henry Ogston and late Josephine Elizabeth Ogston (*née* Carter); *m* 1934, Elizabeth Wicksteed; one *s* three *d. Educ:* Eton College (King's Scholar); Balliol College, Oxford. DPhil 1936, MA 1937, DSc 1970. Demonstrator, Balliol College, 1933; Freedom Research Fellow, London Hospital, 1935; Departmental Demonstrator (Biochemistry), 1938; University Demonstrator, 1944. Oxford; Reader in Biochemistry, University of Oxford, 1955-59; Prof. of Physical Biochemistry, John Curtin School of Medical Research, ANU, 1959-70, Prof. Emeritus, 1970. Vis. Fellow, Inst. for Cancer Research, Philadelphia, Nov. 1978-Jan. 1979 and March-June 1981; Silver Jubilee Vis. Fellow, University House, ANU, March-Aug. 1979. Chairman, Editorial Bd, Biochemical Journal, 1955-59 (Member of Board, 1951-55). Chm., Central Council, Selly Oak Colleges, Birmingham, 1980- (Vice-Chm., 1976-80). Fellow, Australian Acad. of Science, 1962; Hon. Fellow: Balliol Coll., Oxford, 1969; Univ. of York, 1980; Hon. Mem. American Soc. of Biological Chemists, 1965; Hon. DMed Uppsala, 1977. *Publications:* scientific papers on physical chemistry and biochemistry. *Address:* 6 Dewsbury Terrace, York YO1 1HA.

OGSTON, Prof. Derek, MD, PhD, DSc; FRCP; FRSE 1982; Regius Professor of Physiology, University of Aberdeen, since 1977; *b* 31 May 1932; *s* of Frederick John Ogston and Ellen Mary Ogston; *m* 1963, Cecilia Marie Clark; one *s* two *d. Educ:* King's Coll. Sch., Wimbledon; Univ. of Aberdeen (MA, MD, PhD, DSc). FRCP Edin 1973; FRCP 1977. Univ. of Aberdeen: Res. Fellow, 1959-62; Lectr in Medicine, 1962-69; Sen. Lectr in Med., 1969-75; Reader in Med., 1975-76. MRC Trav. Fellow, 1967-68. *Publications:* scientific papers on haemostasis. *Recreation:* home maintenance. *Address:* 64 Rubislaw Den South, Aberdeen AB2 6AX. *T:* Aberdeen 36587.

O'HAGAN, 4th Baron, *cr* 1870; **Charles Towneley Strachey;** Member (C) Devon, European Parliament, since 1979; *b* 6 Sept. 1945; *s* of Hon. Thomas Anthony Edward Towneley Strachey (*d* 1965; having assumed by deed poll, 1938, the additional Christian name of Towneley, and his mother's maiden name of Strachey, in lieu of his patronymic) and of Lady Mary (who *m* 1981, St John Gore), *d* of 3rd Earl of Selborne, PC, CH; *S* grandfather, 1961; *m* 1967, Princess Tamara Imeretinsky; one *d. Educ:* Eton; (Exhibitioner) New College, Oxford. Page to HM the Queen, 1959-62. Independent Member, European Parliament, 1973-75; Junior Opposition Whip, House of Lords, 1977-79. *Heir: b* Hon. Richard Towneley Strachey, *b* 29 Dec. 1950. *Address:* Sutton Court, Stowey, Pensford, Bristol, Avon. *T:* Chew Magna 2933. *Clubs:* Beefsteak, Pratt's.

O'HAGAN, Desmond, CMG 1957; *b* 4 Mar. 1909; *s* of Captain Claud O'Hagan, Nyeri, Kenya and Eva O'Hagan (*née* Napier Magill); *m* 1942, Pamela, *d* of Major A. H. Symes-Thompson, DSO, Kiambu, Kenya; one *s* two *d. Educ:* Wellington Coll.; Clare Coll., Cambridge. Entered Colonial Administrative Service, Kenya, 1931. Called to Bar, Inner Temple, 1935. Private Secretary to British Resident, Zanzibar, 1937; served with E African Forces in N Province, Kenya, 1940-42; Native Courts Adviser, 1948-51; Provincial Commissioner, Coast Province, Kenya, 1952-59; Chairman, Transport Licensing Authority, Tanganyika, 1959-63. *Recreations:* bridge, golf. *Address:* Kianjibbi, Kiambu, Kenya. *Clubs:* East India, Devonshire, Sports and Public Schools; Muthaiga (Nairobi).

O'HALLORAN, Sir Charles (Ernest), Kt 1982; Convener, Strathclyde Regional Council, 1978-82; *b* 26 May 1924; *s* of Charles and Lily O'Halloran; *m* 1943, Annie Rowan; one *s* two *d. Educ:* Conway St Central Sch., Birkenhead. Telegraphist, RN, 1942-46. Elected Ayr Town Council, 1953; Provost of Ayr, 1964-67; Freeman of Ayr Burgh, 1975. Parly Cand. (Lab) Ayr Burghs, 1966. Dir, Radio Clyde, 1980-; Mem., BRB(Scot.), 1981-. *Recreations:* politics, golf, soccer spectating. *Address:* 1 Park Terrace, Ayr. *T:*

Ayr 266234. *Clubs:* Royal Scottish Automobile (Glasgow); Labour, Ex-Servicemen's (Ayr).

O'HALLORAN, Michael Joseph; MP Islington North since Oct. 1969 (Lab, 1969-81, SDP since 1981); *b* 20 Aug. 1929; British; *m* 1956, Stella Beatrice McDonald; three *d* (one *s* decd). *Educ:* Clohanes National School, Eire; self-educated. Railway worker, 1948-63; building works manager, 1963-69. Mem., NI Civil Rights Assoc. *Recreations:* boxing, football. *Address:* 40 Tytherton Road, N19. *Clubs:* Finsbury Park Railwaymen's, Irish Centre, Irish, Challoner, St Joseph's, St Gabriel's.

O'HARA, Bill; National Governor of the BBC for Northern Ireland, 1973-78; *b* 26 Feb. 1929; *s* of William P. O'Hara and Susanna Agnes O'Hara (*née* Gill); *m* 1953, Anne Marie Finn; two *s* two *d. Address:* Ashvale, 14 Raglan Road, Bangor, Co. Down, N Ireland. *T:* Bangor 60869. *Clubs:* Royal Ulster Yacht, Royal Belfast Golf, Sunnyland Beagles.

O'HARA, Rear-Adm. Derek; Director, Post Design (Ships), Ministry of Defence, 1980-83, retired; *b* 5 March 1927; *s* of William and Hilda O'Hara; *m* 1953, Irene Margaret (*née* Pirie); one *s* one *d. Educ:* Tadcaster Grammar Sch., W Hartlepool; RNEC Keyham and Manadon; RNC Greenwich. FIMechE. Entered RN, 1944; served in HM Ships Berwick, Indomitable, Liverpool, Newcastle, Ocean and Cardigan Bay; various MoD appointments, 1958-67; HMS Bulwark, 1967-69; Gibraltar Dockyard, 1969-72; Dir, Naval Officer Appointments (E), 1976-78; Rear-Adm. 1978; Chief Staff Officer (E), Fleet, 1978-80. ADC to HM the Queen, 1978. *Recreations:* cabinet making, gardening, British Sailors Society (Bath Chm.). *Address:* c/o Barclays Bank, Milsom Street, Bath.

O'HARA, Air Vice-Marshal Derek Ive, CB 1981; CBIM; Director General of Supply, Royal Air Force, 1979-82; *b* 14 Feb. 1928; *s* of late William Edward O'Hara and Daisy Bathurst O'Hara (*née* Ive); *m* 1953, Angela Elizabeth (*née* Marchand); two *s* one *d. Educ:* Ardingly Coll., Sussex; RAF Coll., Cranwell. Commnd RAF Coll., 1950; RAF Horsham St Faith and Tuddenham, 1950-54; Egypt, 1954-56; HQ Bomber Comd, 1956-59; Instructor, RAF Coll., 1959-61; RAF Staff Coll., Andover, 1961; Jt Planning HQ ME, Aden, 1962-64; OC Supply, RAF Finningley, 1964; Manchester Univ., 1965; OC Supply, 14 MU RAF Carlisle, 1966-68; Directing Staff, RAF Staff Coll., Andover, 1968-70; Comd of RAF Stafford, 1970-72; Dep. Dir, Supply Management, MoD Harrogate, 1972; RCDS, 1973; Air Commodore Supply and Movements, HQ Strike Comd, 1974-75; Dir, Engrg and Supply Policy, 1975-79. *Recreations:* sailing, fishing, gardening. *Address:* Dillows, Fox Hill Close, Haywards Heath, Sussex RH16 4RA. *Club:* Royal Air Force.

O'HARA, Frank, MA, CEng, FRAeS; Senior Research Fellow, Glasgow University, since 1978; *b* 1 Oct. 1917; *s* of Francis O'Hara and Lily May O'Hara (*née* Slaven); *m* 1943, Mhuire Wheldon Hattle; one *s* three *d. Educ:* Alloa Academy; Edinburgh Univ.; Christ's Coll., Cambridge. MA Hons Maths and Nat. Phil., Edinburgh, 1938; BA Hons Maths 1940, MA Cantab 1944. Marine Aircraft Experimental Estab., 1940; Airborne Forces Exper. Estab., 1942; Aircraft and Armament Exper. Estab., 1950; RAE Bedford, 1954; Head, 3' Supersonic Tunnel, 1956; Head, Aero Flight, 1959; Chief Supt and Head Flight Group, 1966. Dir-Gen. Civil Aircraft, MoD, 1970-73; Dir-Gen. Equipment, MoD (PE), 1973-77. FRAES 1966. Alston Medal for Flight Testing, 1970; Busk Prize, 1965. *Publications:* papers in Reports and Memoranda of ARC, and various jls. *Recreations:* literature and the arts, gardening. *Address:* 11 Glasgow Street, Helensburgh, Dunbartonshire. *T:* Helensburgh 3412.

O'HARA, Prof. Michael John, PhD; FRS 1981; FRSE 1969; Professor of Geology and Head of Geology Department, University College of Wales, Aberystwyth, since 1978; *b* 22 Feb. 1933; *s* of Michael Patrick O'Hara, OBE, and Winifred Dorothy O'Hara; *m* 1st, 1962, Janet Tibbits; one *s* two *d*; 2nd, 1977, Susan Howells; one *s. Educ:* Dulwich Coll. Prep. Sch.; Cranleigh; Peterhouse, Cambridge (MA, PhD). Asst, Lectr, Reader and Prof. (1971), Edinburgh Univ., 1958-78; Principal Investigator, NASA Lunar Science Prog., 1968-75. Associate Mem., Geol Soc. of France. *Publications:* numerous in learned jls. *Recreation:* mountaineering. *Address:* Geology Department, University College of Wales, Aberystwyth, Dyfed SY23 3DB. *T:* Aberystwyth 3111.

O'HIGGINS, Hon. Thomas Francis, SC (Ireland) 1954; Chief Justice of Ireland, since 1974; *b* 23 July 1916; *e s* of Dr Thomas F. O'Higgins and Agnes McCarthy; *m* 1948, Therese Keane; five *s* two *d. Educ:* St Mary's Coll., Rathmines, Clongowes Wood Coll.; University Coll., Dublin (BA, BL); King's Inns, Dublin. Called to Irish Bar, 1938; Bencher of King's Inns, 1967; Judge of High Court, 1973. Elected to Dail Eireann, 1948; Minister for Health, 1954; contested Presidency, 1966 and 1973. *Recreations:* fishing, golf. *Address:* Jerpoint, Elton Park, Sandycove, Co. Dublin. *T:* 803605. *Clubs:* Stephen's Green, Miltown Golf.

OHLSON, Sir Eric James, 2nd Bt, *cr* 1920; *b* 16 March 1911; *s* of Sir Erik Ohlson, 1st Bt, and Jennie (*d* 1952), *d* of J. Blakeley; *S* father 1934; *m* 1935, Marjorie Joan, *d* of late C. H. Roosmale-Cocq, Dorking, Surrey; two *s* one *d. Heir: s* Brian Eric Christopher Ohlson, *b* 27 July 1936.

OISTRAKH, Igor Davidovich; Soviet Violinist; *b* Odessa, 1931; *s* of late David Oistrakh. *Educ:* Music Sch. and State Conservatoire, Moscow. Many foreign tours (USSR, Europe, South America, Japan); many gramophone records; many concerts with father. 1st prize, Violin Competition, Budapest, 1952, Wieniawki Competition, Poznan, 1952; Honoured Artist of RSFSR. *Address:* State Conservatoire, 13 Ulitsa Herzen, Moscow, USSR.

O'KEEFE, John Harold; Production Director, Central London, Thames Television, since 1981; *b* 25 Dec. 1938; *s* of Terence Harold O'Keefe and Christian Frances (*née* Foot); *m* 1959, Valerie Anne Atkins; two *s* two *d. Educ:* Acton County Grammar School. Dir, Newspaper Publishers Assoc., 1974; Hd of Industrial Relations, Thames TV, 1974–81. *Address:* 189 Kingshall Road, Beckenham, Kent. *T:* 01-778 8010.

O'KEEFFE, Georgia; artist; *b* Sun Prairie, Wisconsin, USA, 15 Nov. 1887; *d* of Francis O'Keeffe and Ida Totto; *m* 1924, Alfred Stieglitz. *Educ:* Sacred Heart Acad., Madison, Wis; Chatham (Va) Episcopal Inst.; Art Inst., Chicago; Art Students' League, NY; Univ. of Va; Columbia Univ. Head of Art Dept, West Texas State Normal Coll., Canyon, 1916–18. Painting, only, 1918–; annual one-man shows, 1923–46, in Stieglitz galls. Retrospective exhibitions: Brooklyn Museum, 1927; Art Inst. of Chicago, 1943; Museum of Modern Art (New York), 1946; Worcester Art Museum, USA, 1960; Whitney Mus. of Mod. Art, 1970; Art Inst. of Chicago, 1971; San Francisco Mus. of Art, 1971. Paintings in permanent collections of many museums and galleries in USA. Member National Institute of Arts and Letters; Benjamin Franklin Fellow, Royal Soc. for Encouragement of Arts, Manufactures and Commerce, 1969. Holds many hon. degrees. Creative Arts Award, Brandeis Univ., 1963; Wisconsin Governor's Award, 1966; Gold Medal, Nat. Inst. of Arts and Letters, 1970; M. Carey Thomas Award, Bryn Mawr Coll., 1971; Nat. Assoc. of Schs of Art award, 1971; Skowhegan Sch. of Painting and Sculpture award, 1973. Film, Georgia O'Keeffe (Public Broadcasting Service, dir. P. M. Adato), 1977. Presidential Medal of Freedom, 1976. *Publications:* Georgia O'Keeffe (portfolio of 12 reproductions with text), 1937; Georgia O'Keeffe Drawings, 1968; Georgia O'Keeffe (autobiog.), 1976. *Address:* Abiquiu, Rio Arriba County, New Mexico 87510, USA.

O'KEEFFE, Peter Laurence, CVO 1974; HM Diplomatic Service; Ambassador to Senegal, since 1982; concurrently Ambassador (non-resident) to Guinea, Guinea-Bissau, Mali, Mauritania and Cape Verde, since 1982; *b* 9 July 1931; *s* of Richard O'Keeffe and Alice (*née* Chase); *m* 1954, Suzanne Marie Jousse; three *d. Educ:* St Francis Xavier's Coll., Liverpool; University Coll., Oxford (schol). HM Customs and Excise, 1953–62; 2nd, later 1st Sec. (Economic), Bangkok, 1962–65; FO, 1965–68; 1st Sec. and Head of Chancery, Athens, 1968–72; Commercial Counsellor, Jakarta, 1972–75; Head of Hong Kong and Indian Ocean Dept, FCO, 1975–76; Dir-Gen., British Information Services, and Dep. Consul General (Information), New York, 1976–78; Counsellor, Nicosia, 1978–81; Research Associate, Inst. for the Study of Diplomacy, Georgetown Univ., Washington, DC, 1981–82. *Publication:* (as Laurence Halley) Simultaneous Equations (novel), 1975. *Recreations:* photography, music. *Address:* c/o Foreign and Commonwealth Office, SW1.

O'KELLY, Surgeon Rear-Adm. Francis Joseph, OBE 1965; Royal Navy, retired 1980; Occupational Health Consultant, Medical and Health Department, Government of Hong Kong, since 1980; *b* 24 Dec. 1921; *s* of Francis John O'Kelly and Elizabeth Mary O'Kelly (*née* Rogan); *m* 1954, Winifred Mary Teresa Henry; one *s* three *d. Educ:* St Patrick's Coll., Cavan; University Coll., Dublin. MB, BCh 1945; FFCM, FFOM (RCPI), MFOM (RCPE) 1980; DPH, DIH. Hosp. appts in Dublin, 1946–48; joined RN 1948; served with RM Commandos, Middle and Far East, 1948–52; HM Ships Unicorn, St Bride's Bay and Centaur, RNB Chatham and RN Air Station, Brawdy, 1952–63; Naval MOH appts, Far East Fleet, Scotland and NI Comd, Portsmouth and Chatham Comd, 1963–72; Dep. Dir, Health and Research, 1972–74; MO i/c RN Hosp. Gibraltar, 1974–77; Surgeon Rear-Adm. (Ships and Establishments), 1977–78; Surg. Rear-Adm. (Naval Hosps), 1978–80; QHP 1977–80. Adviser in Preventive and Industrial Medicine to Med. Dir Gen. (Naval), 1972–77, in Community Medicine, 1977–80. Fellow, RSM; Member: Soc. of Community Medicine; Soc. of Occupational Medicine. *Publications:* articles in Annals of Occupational Hygiene. *Recreations:* reading and travel. *Address:* Breffni, 38 Seamead, Stubbington, Fareham, Hants PO14 2NG; Flat 15B, Manhattan Tower, 63 Repulse Bay Road, Hong Kong.

O'KENNEDY, Michael E.; TD (Fianna Fáil) Tipperary North, 1969–80 and since 1982; *b* Nenagh, Co. Tipperary, 21 Feb. 1936; *s* of Eamonn and Helena O'Kennedy; *m* 1965, Breda, *d* of late Andrew Heavey and of Mary Heavey; one *s* two *d. Educ:* St Flannan's College, Ennis, Co. Clare; Univ. Coll., Dublin. MA 1957. Called to Irish Bar, 1961; Senior Counsel 1973. Elected to Seanad Eireann, 1965; Mem., Oireachtas Select Constitutional Cttee, 1966. Parly Sec. to Minister for Educn, 1970–72; Minister without Portfolio, Dec. 1972–Jan. 1973; Minister for Transport and Power, Jan.–March 1973; Opposition spokesman on Foreign Affairs, 1973–77; Minister for Foreign Affairs, 1977–79; Minister for Finance, 1979–81. Mem., Commn of the European Communities, 1981–82. Member: All-Party Cttee on Irish Relns, 1973–77; Dáil and Seanad Jt Cttee on Secondary Legislation of the European Communities, 1973–77; Chm., Inter-Party Cttee on Implications of Irish Unity, 1972-73. Pres., Council of Ministers of the European Communities, July-Dec. 1979. *Address:* Gortlandroe, Nenagh, Co. Tipperary, Ireland.

OKEOVER, Sir Peter Ralph Leopold W.; *see* Walker-Okeover.

OKOGIE, Most Rev. Anthony Olubunmi; *see* Lagos, Archbishop of, (RC).

OLAGBEGI II, The Olowo of Owo, (Sir Olateru), Kt 1960; Oba Alaiyeluwa, Olagbegi II, Olowo of Owo, since 1941; Minister of State, Western Region (now Western Provinces) of Nigeria, 1952; President of the House of Chiefs, Western Region (now Western Provinces), 1965; *b* 1910; *s* of Oba Alaiyeluwa, Olagbegi I, Olowo of Owo; married; many *s* and *d* (some decd). *Educ:* Owo Government School. A Teacher in 1934; Treasury Clerk in Owo Native Administration, 1935-41. Queen's Medal, 1957. *Recreations:* lawn tennis, squash racquets. *Address:* PO Box 1, Afin Oba Olowo, Owo, Western Provinces of Nigeria. *T:* Owo 1.

OLANG', Most Rev. Festo Habakkuk; *b* 11 Nov. 1914; *m* 1937, Eseri D. Olang'; four *s* eight *d. Educ:* Alliance High School. Teacher, 1936-43; ordained 1945; consecrated Assistant Bishop of Mombasa in Namirembe Cathedral, by Archbishop of Canterbury, 1955; Bishop of Maseno, 1961; Bishop of Nairobi, 1970; Archbishop of Kenya, 1970-79. Hon. DD Univ. of the South Sewanee, USA. *Address:* PO Box 1, Maseno, Kenya.

OLDENBOURG-IDALIE, Zoë; Chevalier, Légion d'Honneur; Officier du Mérite des Arts et des Lettres; writer (as Zoë Oldenbourg); *b* 31 March 1916; *d* of Sergius Oldenbourg, writer and historicist, and of Ada (*née* Starynkevitch); *m* 1948, Heinric Idalie; one *s* one *d. Educ:* Lycée Molière and Sorbonne, Paris. Prix Fémina, 1953. *Publications:* Argile et cendres, 1946 (The World is Not Enough, 1949); La Pierre angulaire, 1953 (The Cornerstone, 1954); Réveillés de la Vie, 1956 (The Awakened, trans. E. Hyams, 1957); Les Irréductibles, 1958 (The Chains of Love, 1959); Bûcher de Montségur, 1959 (Massacre at Montségur, 1962); Les Brûlés, 1961 (Destiny of Fire, trans. P. Green, 1961); Les Cités charnelles, 1961 (Cities of the Flesh, 1963); Les Croisades: un essai historique, 1963 (The Crusades, trans. Anne Carter, 1966); Catherine de Russie, 1965 (Catherine the Great, 1965); Saint Bernard, 1969; La Joie des pauvres, 1970 (The Heirs of the Kingdom, trans. Anne Carter, 1972); L'Epopée des cathédrales, 1973; Que vous a donc fait Israël?, 1974; Visages d'un autoportrait (autobiog.), 1977; La Joie-Souffrance, 1980; Le Procès du Rêve, 1982. *Recreation:* painting. *Address:* c/o Victor Gollancz Ltd, 14 Henrietta Street, WC2; 4 rue de Montmorency, 92100 Boulogne, France.

OLDFIELD, John Richard Anthony; *b* July 1900; *s* of late Major H. E. Oldfield; *m* 1953, Jonnet Elizabeth, *d* of late Maj. H. M. Richards, DL, JP. *Educ:* Eton; Trinity College, Cambridge; Served in: Coldstream Guards, 1918-20; RN, 1939-45. MP (Lab) South-East Essex, 1929-31; Parliamentary Private Secretary to Sec. of State for Air, 1929-30. Mem. LCC, 1931-58 (Vice-Chairman, 1953). CC (C) Kent, 1965. *Address:* Doddington Place, near Sittingbourne, Kent.

OLDFIELD, Michael Gordon, (Mike); musician and composer; *b* 15 May 1953; *s* of Dr Raymond Henry Oldfield and Maureen Bernadine Liston; one *s* one *d* by Sally A. Cooper. *Educ:* St Edward's, Reading; Presentation Coll., Reading. Records include: Tubular Bells, 1973 (over 10 million copies sold to date); Hergest Ridge; Ommadawn; Incantations; Platinum; QE2, 1980; Five Miles Out, 1982. Extensive world wide concert tours, 1979–. Mem., Assoc. of Professional Composers. Freeman, City of London, 1982. Hon. Pict. *Recreations:* helicopter pilot, squash. *Address:* Little Halings, Tilehouse Lane, Denham, Bucks. *Club:* Jacobs Larder (Ealing).

OLDFIELD-DAVIES, Alun Bennett, CBE 1955; MA; Controller, Wales, British Broadcasting Corporation, 1945-67; *b* 1905; *s* of Rev. J. Oldfield-Davies, Wallasey, Cheshire; *m* 1931, Lilian M. Lewis, BA. *Educ:* Porth County Sch., Rhondda; University College, Aberystwyth. Schoolmaster and Lecturer to University Extension Classes in Ammanford, Carmarthenshire, and Cardiff, 1926-37. British Broadcasting Corporation: Schools Asst, 1937-40; Welsh Executive, 1940-44; Overseas Services Establishment Officer, 1944-45. Mem., Court, Univ. of Wales; Vice-Pres., University Coll., Cardiff; President: Nat. Museum of Wales, 1972-77; Welsh Council for Education in World Citizenship. Formerly Warden, University of Wales Guild of Graduates. Hon. LLD, Univ. of Wales, 1967. *Address:* Ty Gwyn, Llantrisant Road, Llandaff, Cardiff. *T:* 565920.

OLDHAM, Rev. Canon Arthur Charles Godolphin; *b* 5 Apr. 1905; *s* of late Sidney Godolphin and Lilian Emma Oldham; *m* 1934, Ursula Finch Wigham Richardson, *d* of late George and Isabel Richardson, Newcastle upon Tyne; one *s* two *d. Educ:* King's College School; King's College, London. Business, music and journalism to 1930. Ordained, to Witley, Surrey, 1933; Vicar of Brockham Green, 1936; Rector of Merrow, 1943; Rural Dean of Guildford, 1949; Vicar of Godalming, 1950; Rural Dean of Godalming, 1957; Director of Ordination Training, and Bishop's Examining Chaplain, 1958; Hon. Canon of Guildford, 1959; Canon Residentiary of Guildford Cathedral, 1961-71, retired. *Recreations:* music, sketching. *Address:* Dora Cottage, Beech Hill, Hambledon, Surrey. *T:* Wormley 2087.

OLDMAN, Col Sir Hugh (Richard Deare), KBE 1974 (OBE 1960); MC 1942; retired; *b* 24 June 1914; *s* of late Maj.-Gen. R. D. F. Oldman, CB, CMG, DSO, and Mrs Helen Marie Oldman (*née* Pigot); *m* 1947, Agnes Fielding Murray Oldman (*née* Bayles) (*d* 1978); *m* 1979, Susan V. Oldman (*née*

Vance). *Educ:* Wellington Coll.; RMC Sandhurst. CO 8th Bn Durham LI, 1944–45; psc 1945; Chief Instructor, Quetta Staff Coll.; comd Bn, Aden Protectorate Levies, 1957–60; comd Sultan's Armed Forces, Oman, 1961–64; Staff, HQ Allied Forces Southern Europe (NATO), 1965–67; retd from Army, 1967; subseq. Sec. for Defence, Sultanate of Oman. Croix de Guerre (Palme), 1944; Order of Merit 1st cl., Oman, 1972. *Recreations:* polo, yachting, golf. *Address:* PO Box 73, White Marsh, Va 23183, USA. *Clubs:* Royal Lymington Yacht; Liphook Golf; Muthaiga Country, Muthaiga Golf, Mount Kenya Safari (Kenya).

OLDROYD, Prof. James Gardner, MA, PhD, ScD (Cantab); Professor of Applied Mathematics since 1965 and Head of Department of Applied Mathematics and Theoretical Physics since 1973, University of Liverpool; *b* 25 April 1921; *o s* of late H. and R. Oldroyd; *m* 1946, Marged Katryn, *e d* of late Rev. J. D. Evans; three *s. Educ:* Bradford Grammar Sch.; Trinity Coll., Cambridge (Schol.). Min. of Supply (PDE), 1942–45; Fundamental Research Lab., Courtaulds Ltd, Maidenhead, 1945–53; Fellow, Trinity Coll., Cambridge, 1947–51; Prof. of Applied Maths, UC Swansea, Univ. of Wales, 1953–65; Dean, Faculty of Science, UC Swansea, 1957–59. Pres., Brit. Soc. of Rheology, 1955–57 (Gold Medal 1980). Adams Prize, Cambridge Univ., 1963–64. *Publications:* papers on mathematical theory of deformation and flow in Proc. Royal Soc., Proc. Cambridge Phil. Soc., etc. *Address:* Department of Applied Mathematics and Theoretical Physics, University of Liverpool, Liverpool L69 3BX. *T:* 051-709 6022; Ardenmohr, Graham Road, West Kirby, Wirral, Merseyside L48 5DN. *T:* 051-632 2684.

O'LEARY, Michael; barrister; TD for Dublin Central, since 1965; Tánaiste (Deputy Prime Minister) and Minister for Industry and Energy, 1981–82; *b* 8 May 1936; *s* of John O'Leary and Margaret McCarthy; unmarried. *Educ:* Presentation Coll., Cork; University Coll., Cork; Columbia Univ., NY; King's Inns, Dublin. Educn Officer, Irish TUC, 1962–65. Minister for Labour, 1973–77; Dep. Leader, 1977–81, Leader, 1981–, Labour Party. President, ILO, 1976. Mem. for Ireland, European Parlt, 1979–81. *Recreations:* reading, walking. *Address:* Leinster House, Kildare Street, Dublin 2, Ireland. *T:* Dublin 789911.

O'LEARY, Patrick; *see* Guerisse, A. M. E.

O'LEARY, Peter Leslie; Under-Secretary, Inland Revenue, since 1978; *b* 12 June 1929; *s* of Archibald and Edna O'Leary; *m* 1960, Margaret Elizabeth Debney; four *d. Educ:* Portsmouth Southern Grammar Sch.; University Coll., London (BA). Joined Inland Revenue as Inspector, 1952; Sen. Principal Inspector, 1974. *Recreations:* horology, gardening, wine-making. *Address:* Windy Ridge, 38 Seven Ash Green, Chelmsford CM1 5SE. *T:* Chelmsford 50072.

O'LEARY, Terence Daniel, CMG 1982; MA; HM Diplomatic Service; High Commissioner in Sierra Leone, since 1981; *b* 18 Aug. 1928; 2nd *s* of late Daniel O'Leary; *m* 1960, Janet Douglas Berney, *d* of Dr H. B. Berney, Masterton, NZ; twin *s* one *d. Educ:* Dulwich; St John's Coll., Cambridge. BA 1950. Army, commnd Queen's Royal Regt, 1946–48. Commerce, 1951–53; Asst Principal, CRO, 1953; 2nd Sec., British High Commn, Wellington, 1956–58; Principal, PSO's Dept, CRO, 1958; 1st Sec., New Delhi, 1960–63; 1st Sec., Dar es Salaam, 1963–64; CRO, 1964–65; 1st Sec. and Defence Sec., Canberra, 1965–68; Actg Head, S Asia Dept, FCO, 1969; Asst Sec., Cabinet Office, 1970–72; Counsellor, Pretoria/Cape Town, 1972–74; Dep. High Comr, Wellington, 1974–78; Senior Civil Mem., Directing Staff, Nat. Defence Coll., 1978–81. *Recreations:* cutting grass, tennis, reading. *Address:* c/o Foreign and Commonwealth Office, SW1; The Old Rectory, Petworth, W Sussex. *T:* Petworth 43335. *Club:* Travellers'.

OLINS, Wally, MA Oxon; FSIAD; Chairman, Wolff Olins Ltd, since 1979; *b* 19 Dec. 1930; *s* of Alfred Olins and Rachel (*née* Muscovitch); *m* 1957, Maria Renate Olga Laura Steinert; two *s* one *d. Educ:* Highgate Sch.; St Peter's Coll., Oxford (Hons History, MA). National Service, Army, in Germany, 1950–51. S. H. Benson Ltd, London, 1954–57; Benson, India, 1957–62; Caps Design Group, London, 1962–65; Wolff Olins, London, 1965–. Vice-Pres., SIAD. *Publications:* The Corporate Personality, 1978; various articles in Design and Management publications. *Recreations:* theatre, reading, old cars. *Address:* 15 South Grove, N6 6BJ. *T:* 01-340 5184; (office) 22 Dukes Road, WC1H 9AB. *T:* 01-387 0891.

OLIPHANT, Air Vice-Marshal David Nigel Kington B.; *see* Blair-Oliphant.

OLIPHANT, Sir Mark, (Marcus Laurence Elwin), AC 1977; KBE 1959; FRS 1937; FAA 1954; Governor of South Australia, 1971–76; *b* Adelaide, 8 Oct. 1901; *e s* of H. G. Oliphant; *m* 1925, Rosa Wilbraham, Adelaide, S Australia; one *s* one *d. Educ:* Unley and Adelaide High Schools; University of Adelaide; Trinity Coll., Cambridge (1851 Exhibitioner, Overseas 1927, Senior 1929; PhD 1929). Messel Research Fellow of Royal Society, 1931; Fellow and Lecturer St John's Coll., 1934. Hon. Fellow, 1952; Assistant Director of Research, Cavendish Laboratory, Cambridge, 1935, Poynting Professor of Physics, University of Birmingham, 1937–50; Dir, Research Sch. of Physical Sciences, ANU, Canberra, 1950–63; Prof. of Physics of Ionised Gases, Inst. of Advanced Studies, ANU, 1964–67, now Professor Emeritus. Pres., Aust. Acad. of Sciences, 1954–57. Hon. DSc (Toronto, Belfast, Melbourne, Birmingham, New South Wales, ANU, Adelaide, Flinders); Hon.

LLD (St Andrews). KStJ 1972. *Publications:* Rutherford: recollections of the Cambridge days, 1972; various papers on electricity in gases, surface properties and nuclear physics. *Address:* 37 Colvin Street, Hughes, ACT 2605, Australia. *Club:* Athenæum.

OLIVER, Benjamin Rhys; a Recorder of the Crown Court, since 1972; *b* 8 June 1928; *m* 1955; one *s* one *d. Educ:* Llandovery and Aberystwyth. Called to the Bar, Inner Temple, 1954. *Recreation:* golf. *Address:* 86 St Helen's Road, Swansea, West Glamorgan SA4 1AQ. *T:* Swansea 52988.

OLIVER, Dennis Stanley, CBE 1981; PhD, FEng, FIM, FInstP; Director, Pilkington Brothers plc, since 1977; *b* 19 Sept. 1926; *s* of late James Thomas Oliver and Lilian Mabel Oliver (*née* Bunn); *m* 1952, Enid Jessie Newcombe. *Educ:* Deacon's School, Peterborough; Birmingham Univ. BSc, PhD. Research Fellowship, Univ. of Bristol, 1949–52; Senior Scientific Officer, UKAEA, Culcheth, 1952–55; Head of Metallurgy Div., UKAEA, Dounreay, 1955–63; Chief R & D Officer, Richard Thomas & Baldwin Ltd, 1963–68; Group R & D Dir, Pilkington Brothers plc, 1968–77. Member: Nat. Enterprise Bd, 1981–; NRDC, 1981–; Court and Council, Cranfield Inst. of Technology, 1976–; Dir, Anglo-American Venture Fund Ltd, 1980–; Chm., Industrial Experience Projects Ltd, 1981–; Pres., European Industrial Res. Management Assoc., 1977–81; Patron, Science and Technology Educn on Merseyside, 1982– (Pres., 1978–81); Governor: Liverpool Inst. of Higher Educn, 1979–; Christ's and Notre Dame Coll., Liverpool, 1979–; Royal Nat. Coll. for the Blind, 1981–; Dir, L'Ecole Supérieure du Verre, Belgium, 1971–; Governor, Community of St Helens Trust Ltd, 1978–; Freeman of City of London; Liveryman of Spectaclemakers Co. FBIM. KSG 1980. *Publications:* The Use of Glass in Engineering, 1975; Glass for Construction Purposes, 1977; various publications on technical subjects and technology transfer. *Recreations:* music, gardening, travel. *Address:* Spinningdale, 3 Preston Road, Southport, Merseyside PR9 9EG.

OLIVER, Sir (Frederick) Ernest, Kt 1962; CBE 1955; TD 1942; DL; Chairman, George Oliver (Footwear) Ltd, 1950–73; *b* 31 Oct. 1900; *s* of late Colonel Sir Frederick Oliver and late Lady Oliver, CBE; *m* 1928, Mary Margaret (*d* 1978), *d* of late H. Simpson; two *d* (one *s* decd). *Educ:* Rugby School. Member Leicester City Council, 1933-73, Lord Mayor, 1950. Officer, Territorial Army, 1922-48. Served UK and Burma, 1939-45. President: Multiple Shoe Retailers' Assoc., 1964–65; Leicester YMCA, 1955–76; Leicester Conservative Assoc., 1952–66. Leicester: DL 1950; Hon. Freeman, 1971. *Address:* 6 Westminster Road, Leicester. *T:* 705310. *Club:* Leicestershire (Leicester).

OLIVER, George Harold, QC 1949; *b* 24 Nov. 1888; *m* 1910, Christina Bennett; one *s*. Barrister, Middle Temple, 1927. MP (Lab) Ilkeston Division of Derbys, 1922-31 and 1935-64; Parliamentary Under-Secretary of State, Home Office, 1945–47. *Address:* c/o 79 Bedford Road, Little Houghton, Northampton.

OLIVER, Brig. James Alexander, CB 1957; CBE 1945; DSO 1942 (and Bar to DSO 1943); TD; DL; Vice-Lieutenant, County of Angus, 1967–81; *b* 19 March 1906; *s* of Adam Oliver, Arbroath, Angus; *m* 1932, Margaret Whytock Scott; no *c. Educ:* Trinity Coll., Glenalmond. 2nd Lieut, Black Watch (TA), 1926; commanded: 7th Black Watch, 1942; 152 Infantry Bde (Highland Div.), 1943; 154 Infantry Bde (Highland Div.), 1944; served War of 1939-45 in N Africa, Sicily and NW Europe (despatches). ADC to the Queen, 1953–63; Hon. Colonel, 6/7th Black Watch, 1960–67; Hon. Colonel, 51st Highland Volunteers, 1967–70. Member, Angus and Dundee T&AFA, 1938-59 (Chairman, 1954-59). Chm., 1972-73, Vice-Pres., 1973, The Earl Haig Fund, Scotland. Hon. LLD Dundee, 1967. DL Angus, 1948. *Address:* West Newton, Arbroath, Angus, Scotland. *T:* Arbroath 72579. *Club:* Naval and Military.

OLIVER, Dr John Andrew, CB 1968; *b* 25 Oct. 1913; *s* of Robert John Oliver, Limavady, Co. Londonderry and Martha Sherrard, Magilligan, Co. Londonderry; *m* 1943, Stella Ritson; five *s. Educ:* Royal Belfast Academical Institution; Queen's Univ., Belfast; Bonn Univ.; Königsberg Univ.; Zimmern School of International Studies, Geneva; Imperial Defence Coll., London. BA 1936; DrPhil, 1951; IDC, 1954. Ministry of Development, NI: Second Sec., 1964–71; Permanent Sec., 1971–74; Permanent Sec., Housing, Local Govt and Planning, NI, 1974–75; Chief Adviser, NI Constitutional Convention, 1975-76. Hon. Sec., Assoc. of Governing Bodies of Voluntary Grammar Schs in NI, 1964–77; Chm., Bd of Governors, Royal Belfast Academical Instn, 1970–77. UK Election Supervisor, Que Que, Rhodesia, 1980. Chm. Management Review, Royal Victoria Hosp. Gp, Belfast, 1981–82. Chm., S Lakeland Council for Voluntary Action, 1980; Vice-Chm., Voluntary Action Cumbria, 1980–. Hon. MRTPI, 1964; Hon. Member, Assoc. for Housing and Town Planning, W Germany, 1966. Rhodesia Medal, 1980; Zimbabwe Independence Medal, 1980. *Publications:* Ulster Today and Tomorrow, 1978; Working at Stormont, 1978. *Recreations:* walking, maps, languages. *Address:* Laundry Cottage, Hale, Milnthorpe, Cumbria LA7 7BL. *T:* Milnthorpe 2698. *Club:* Royal Over-Seas League.

OLIVER, John Laurence; Journalist; *b* 14 Sept. 1910; *s* of late Harold and Teresa Oliver; *m* 1936, Renée Mary Webb; two *s. Educ:* Haberdashers' Aske's Hampstead School. Publicity Manager, The Book Society, 1934; Art Editor, The Bystander, 1935-39. War of 1939-45: served in the Field Security Corps; commissioned 1941, The Suffolk Regt (transferred The Cambridgeshire Regt). Joined staff of The Sphere, 1946; Art Editor, 1947; Assistant Editor,

1956; Editor, 1960-64; Editor, The Tatler, 1961-65. *Publications:* Saint John's Wood Church (with Rev. Peter Bradshaw), 1955; occasional short stories and articles. *Recreations:* reading, theatre going, watching cricket. *Address:* 10 Wellington Place, NW8 9JA. *T:* 01-286 5891. *Clubs:* Garrick, MCC.

OLIVER, Group Captain John Oliver William, CB 1950; DSO 1940; DFC 1940; RAF retired; *b* 1911; *e s* of William Oliver; *m* 1935 (marr. diss., 1951); one *s* two *d*; *m* 1962, Anne Fraser Porteous; one *s* two *d* (of whom *s* and *yr d* are twins). *Educ:* Christ's Hospital; Cranwell. Commissioned from Cranwell, GD Pilot Branch p., 1931; served 43 (F) Squadron and 55 (B) Squadron, Iraq; qualified CFS. Served War of 1939-45 (despatches thrice); commanded 85 (F) Squadron, 1940; Fighter Command and Tactical Air Force; Wing Commander, 1940; Group Captain, 1942. Assistant Commandant, RAF Coll., Cranwell, 1948-50; ACOS Ops, Allied Forces Northern Europe, 1958-60; retired, 1961. Personnel Officer, ENV (Engineering) Ltd, 1961; Staff Institute Personnel Management, 1962; Personnel Manager, Humber Ltd, 1963; Manager, Training and Administrative Service, Rootes, Coventry, 1965; Senior Training Officer, Engineering Industry Training Board, 1968; Personnel and Trng Manager, Thorn Gp, 1970-76, retired. *Address:* 9 Magdala Road, Hayling Island, Hants PO11 0BH. *Clubs:* Seacourt Tennis; Hayling Island Sailing.

OLIVER, Leslie Claremont, FRCS; FACS; Consulting Neurosurgeon: Charing Cross Hospital; Westminster Hospital; West London Hospital; Royal Northern Hospital; Founder, Neurosurgical Centre, Oldchurch Hospital, Romford. *Educ:* Latymer Sch.; Guy's Hospital. LRCP, MRCS, 1933; MB, BS, London, 1953; FRCS England, 1935; FACS 1957. Formerly: 1st Assistant and Registrar, Dept of Neurosurgery, London Hospital; Resident Asst Surgeon, W London Hospital; Surgical Registrar and Teacher in Surgery, Bristol General Hospital. Member Society British Neurological Surgeons; Corr. Member Soc. de Neurochirurgie de Langue Française. Formerly Chm. Court of Examiners, RCS. *Publications:* Essentials of Neurosurgery, 1952; Parkinson's Disease and its Surgical Treatment, 1953; (ed and contrib.) Basic Surgery, 1958; Parkinson's Disease, 1967; Removable Intracranial Tumours, 1969; Le Français Pratique. *Recreation:* travel. *Address:* 94 Harley Street, W1. *T:* 01-935 5896. *Clubs:* Royal Society of Medicine, Hurlingham.

OLIVER, Martin Hugh, PhD, CEng; Director General, Research Electronics, Procurement Executive, Ministry of Defence, 1972-76; *b* 9 July 1916; *s* of late Thomas Frederick Oliver and late Jessie Oliver (née Gibson), Peterborough; *m* 1963, Barbara Rivcah, *d* of late Richard Burgis Blakeley, Worcester; one *d*. *Educ:* King's Sch., Peterborough; Imperial Coll. (City and Guilds Coll.), Univ. of London. BSc (Eng) 1937, PhD (Eng) 1939; ACGI, DIC, MIEE. Metropolitan Vickers Electrical Co. Ltd, Manchester, 1938-41; National Physical Laboratory, Teddington, 1941-43; RRE, Malvern, 1943-65; Head of Radio Dept, RAE, Farnborough, 1965-68; Dir, Services Electronics Res. Lab., MoD, 1968-72.

OLIVER, Prof. Michael Francis, MD, FRCP, FRCPEd, FFCM; Duke of Edinburgh Professor of Cardiology, University of Edinburgh, since 1979; *b* 3 July 1925; *s* of late Captain Wilfrid Francis Lenn Oliver, MC (DLI), and Cecilia Beatrice Oliver (née Daniel); *m* 1948, Margaret Yool Abbey (separated); two *s* one *d* (and one *s* decd). *Educ:* Marlborough Coll.; Univ. of Edinburgh. MB, ChB 1947, MD (Gold Medal) 1957. Consultant Physician, Royal Infirmary and Sen. Lectr in Medicine, Univ. of Edinburgh, 1961; Reader in Medicine, 1973 and Personal Prof. of Cardiology, 1977, Univ. of Edinburgh. Mem., Cardiovascular Panel, Govt Cttee on Medical Aspects of Food Policy, 1971-74, 1982-; UK Rep. Mem., Adv. Panel for Cardiovascular Disease, WHO, 1972-79; Chm., BBC-Medical Adv. Gp in Scotland, 1975-81; Mem. Scientific Bd, Internat. Soc. of Cardiology, 1968-78 (Chm., Council on Atherosclerosis and Ischaemic Heart Disease, 1968-75); Chairman: Brit. Atherosclerosis Gp, 1970-75; Science Cttee, Fondation Cardiologique Princess Lilian, Belgium, 1976-; Convener, Cardiology Cttee, Scottish Royal Colls, 1978-81; Council Mem., Brit. Heart Foundn, 1976-. Pres., British Cardiac Soc., 1981-. Hon. Fellow, Amer. Coll. of Cardiology, 1973. Hon. MD *hc* Karolinska Inst., Stockholm, 1980. Purkinje Medal, 1981. *Publications:* Acute Myocardial Infarction, 1966; Intensive Coronary Care, 1970, 2nd edn 1974; Effect of Acute Ischaemia on Myocardial Function, 1972; Modern Trends in Cardiology, 1975; High-Density Lipoproteins and Atherosclerosis, 1978; Coronary Heart Disease in Young Women, 1978; contribs to sci. and med. jls on causes of coronary heart disease, biochemistry of fats, myocardial metabolism, mechanisms of sudden death, clinical trials of drugs, and population studies of vascular diseases. *Recreations:* work, questioning, talking. *Address:* Barley Mill House, West Saltoun, East Lothian EH34 5EP. *T:* Pencaitland 340433; 28 Chalcot Road, NW1. *T:* 01-722 4460. *Clubs:* Athenæum; New (Edinburgh).

OLIVER, Rt. Hon. Sir Peter (Raymond), Kt 1974; PC 1980; **Rt. Hon. Lord Justice Oliver;** a Lord Justice of Appeal, since 1980; *b* 7 March 1921; *s* of David Thomas Oliver, Fellow of Trinity Hall, Cambridge, and Alice Maud Oliver; *m* 1945, Mary Chichester Rideal, *d* of Sir Eric Keightley Rideal, MBE, FRS; one *s* one *d*. *Educ:* The Leys, Cambridge; Trinity Hall, Cambridge (Hon. Fellow, 1980). Military Service, 1941-45, 12th Bn RTR (despatches). Called to Bar, Lincoln's Inn, 1948, Bencher 1973; QC 1965; Judge of the High Ct of Justice, Chancery Div., 1974-80; Mem., Restrictive Practices Court, 1976-80; Chm., Review Body on Chancery Div. of High Court, 1979-81. *Recreations:* gardening, music. *Address:* 24 Westbourne Park Road, W2. *T:* 01-229 1058.

OLIVER, Peter Richard, CMG 1965; HM Diplomatic Service, retired; Ambassador to Uruguay, 1972-77; *b* 3 June 1917; *yr s* of William Henry Oliver and Muriel Daisy Elisabeth Oliver (née Widdicombe); *m* 1940, Freda Evelyn Gwyther; two *s* two *d*. *Educ:* Felsted Sch.; Hanover; Berlin; Trinity Hall, Cambridge. Indian Civil Service, 1939-47; served in Punjab and Bahawalpur State. Transferred to HM Foreign (subsequently Diplomatic) Service, 1947; served in Karachi, 1947-49; Foreign Office, 1949-52; The Hague, 1952-56; Havana, 1956-59; Foreign Office, 1959-61; Djakarta, 1961-64; Bonn, 1965-69; Dep. High Comr, Lahore, 1969-72. *Recreations:* gardening, Bumboclasm. *Address:* Bridge Cottage, Little Petherick, Wadebridge, Cornwall PL27 7QT. *T:* Rumford 358. *Clubs:* Royal Commonwealth Society; Hawks (Cambridge); Union (Cambridge).

OLIVER, Prof. Emeritus Richard Alexander Cavaye; Professor of Education and Director of the Department of Education in the University of Manchester, 1938-70; Dean of Faculty of Education, 1938-48, 1962-65; Dean of Faculty of Music, 1952-62, 1966-70; *b* 9 Jan. 1904; *s* of Charles Oliver and Elizabeth Smith; *m* 1929, Annabella Margaret White, MA Edin, MA Oxon; one *s* one *d*. *Educ:* George Heriot's Sch.; University of Edinburgh; Stanford Univ., California, USA. Held Commonwealth Fund Fellowship at Stanford Univ., 1927-29; research educational psychologist in Kenya, 1929-32; Asst Master Abbotsholme Sch. and on staff of Edinburgh Education Cttee, 1933-34; University Extension Lecturer, 1933-34; Asst Director of Education, Wilts Education Cttee, 1934-36; Dep. Secretary, Devon Education Cttee, 1936-38. Director, University of Manchester School of Education, 1947-51; Pro Vice-Chancellor, 1953-57 and 1960-61; Presenter of Hon. Graduands, 1959-64, 1966. Member National Advisory Council on Training and Supply of Teachers, 1949-59; Chairman, Northern Universities Joint Matriculation Board, 1952-55; Member Secondary School Examinations Council, 1958-64. FBPsS. Hon. Research Fellow, Princeton Univ., 1961. Hon. LLD Manchester, 1981. *Publications:* General Intelligence Test for Africans, 1932; (with others) The Educational Guidance of the School Child, 1936; Research in Education, 1946; The Content of Sixth Form General Studies, 1974; Joint Matriculation Board Occasional Publications; contrib. to Africa, British Journal of Psychology, Yearbook of Education, Universities Quarterly, Research in Education, etc. *Recreation:* gardening. *Address:* Waingap, Crook, Kendal, Cumbria LA8 9HT. *T:* Staveley 821277.

See also H. A. Hetherington.

OLIVER, Prof. Roland Anthony, MA, PhD (Cantab); Professor of the History of Africa, London University, since 1963; *b* Srinagar, Kashmir, 30 March 1923; *s* of late Major D. G. Oliver and of Lorimer Janet (née Donaldson); *m* 1947, Caroline Florence, *d* of late Judge John Linehan, KC; one *d*. *Educ:* Stowe; King's Coll., Cambridge. Attached to Foreign Office, 1942-45; R. J. Smith Research Studentship, King's Coll., Cambridge, 1946-48; Lecturer, School of Oriental and African Studies, 1948-58; Reader in African History, University of London, 1958-63; Françqui Prof., University of Brussels, 1961; Visiting Professor: Northwestern Univ., Illinois, 1962; Harvard Univ., 1967; travelled in Africa, 1949-50 and 1957-58; org. international Conferences on African History and Archæology, 1953-61; Haile Sellassie Prize Trust Award, 1966. President: African Studies Assoc., 1967-68; British Inst. in Eastern Africa, 1981-. Member: Perm. Bureau, Internat. Congress of Africanists, 1973-78; Council, Royal African Society; Chm., Minority Rights Group. Corresp. Member, Académie Royale des Sciences d'Outremer, Brussels. *Publications:* The Missionary Factor in East Africa, 1952; Sir Harry Johnston and the Scramble for Africa, 1957; (ed) The Dawn of African History, 1961; A Short History of Africa (with J. D. Fage), 1962; A History of East Africa (ed with Gervase Mathew), 1963; Africa since 1800 (with A. E. Atmore), 1967; (ed) The Middle Age of African History, 1967; Ed. (with J. D. Fage) The Journal of African History, 1960-73; (with B. M. Fagan) Africa in the Iron Age, 1975; (with A. E. Atmore) The African Middle Ages, 1981; Gen. Editor (with J. D. Fage), Cambridge History of Africa, 8 vols, 1975-. *Address:* 7 Cranfield House, Southampton Row, WC1. *T:* 01-636 5343; Frilsham Woodhouse, Newbury, Berks. *T:* Hermitage 201407.

OLIVER, Dr Ronald Martin, RD 1973; Senior Principal Medical Officer (Under Secretary), Department of Health and Social Security, since 1979; *b* 28 May 1929; *s* of late Cuthbert Hanson Oliver and Cecilia Oliver; *m* 1957, Susanna Treves Blackwell; three *s* one *d*. *Educ:* King's Coll. Sch., Wimbledon; King's Coll., London; St George's Hosp. Med. Sch. (MB, BS 1952). MRCS, LRCP 1952; DCH 1954; DPH 1960; DIH 1961; MD London 1965; MFOM 1978. Served RNR: Surg. Lieut, 1953-55; Surg. Lt-Comdr, retd 1974. St George's Hosp., London: House Surgeon and Physician, 1952-53; Resident Clin. Pathologist, 1955-56; trainee asst, gen. practice, 1956-57; Asst County MO, Surrey CC, 1957-59; MO, London Transport Exec., 1959-62; MO, later SMO, Treasury Med. Service (later CS Med. Adv. Service), 1962-74; seconded Diplomatic Service as Physician, British Embassy, Moscow, 1964-66; SMO, DHSS, 1974-79. *Publications:* papers in med. jls on epidemiology of heart disease, public health, toxicology, and health service admin. *Recreations:* golf, sailing, gardening, bad bridge. *Address:* The Cottage, The Street, Effingham, Surrey KT24 5LQ. *T:* Bookham 52887. *Club:* Effingham Golf.

OLIVER, Stephen John Lindsay, QC 1980; barrister-at-law; *b* 14 Nov. 1938; *s* of Philip Daniel Oliver and Audrey Mary Oliver; *m* 1967, Anne Dawn Harrison Taylor; one *s* two *d*. *Educ:* Rugby Sch.; Oriel Coll., Oxford (MA Jurisprudence). National Service, RN, 1957-59: served submarines; Temp. Sub-Lieut. Called to the Bar, Middle Temple, 1963. Asst Boundary Comr,

Parly Boundary Commn, 1977. *Recreations:* music, sailing. *Address:* 4 Pump Court, Temple, EC4Y 7AN. *T:* 01-583 9770; 14 Eliot Place, Blackheath, SE3 0QL. *T:* 01-852 2727.

OLIVIER, family name of **Baron Olivier.**

OLIVIER, Baron *cr* 1970 (Life Peer), of Brighton; **Laurence Kerr Olivier,** OM 1981; Kt 1947; Actor; Director, 1962-73, Associate Director, 1973-74, National Theatre; Member, South Bank Theatre Board, since 1967 (South Bank Theatre and Opera House Board, 1962-67); *b* 22 May 1907; *s* of late Rev. G. K. Olivier and Agnes Louise Crookenden; *m* 1st, 1930, Jill Esmond (marr. diss., 1940); one *s*; 2nd, 1940, Vivien Leigh (marr. diss., 1961; she *d* 1967); 3rd, 1961, Joan Plowright, *qv*; one *s* two *d*. *Educ:* St Edward's Sch., Oxford. MA Hon. Tufts, Mass, 1946; Hon. DLitt: Oxon, 1957; Manchester, 1968; Sussex, 1978; Hon. LLD Edinburgh 1964; Hon. DLitt London, 1968. Sonning Prize, Denmark, 1966; Gold Medallion, Swedish Acad. of Literature, 1968; Special Award for directorship of Nat. Theatre, Evening Standard, 1973; Albert Medal, RSA, 1976; Hon. Oscar, 1979, for lifetime's contrib. to films. Commander, Order Dannebrog, 1949; Officier Legion d'Honneur, 1953; Grande Ufficiale dell' Ordino al Merito della Repubblica (Italian), 1953; Order of Yugoslav Flag with Golden Wreath, 1971. First appeared in 1922 at Shakespeare Festival, Stratford-on-Avon special boys' performance, as Katherine in Taming of the Shrew; played in Byron, King Henry IV, toured in sketch Unfailing Instinct, with Ruby Miller, Season with Lena Ashwell, King Henry VIII, 1924-25; played with Birmingham Repertory Company till 1928; Stanhope in Journey's End, for Stage Society; Beau Geste; Circle of Chalk, Paris Bound, The Stranger Within; went to America, 1929; returned 1930 and played in The Last Enemy, After All and in Private Lives; New York, 1931, played Private Lives, 1933; Rats of Norway, London; Green Bay Tree, New York; returned London, 1934, Biography, Queen of Scots, Theatre Royal; Ringmaster under his own management, Golden Arrow, Romeo and Juliet, 1935; Bees on the Boat Deck and Hamlet at Old Vic, 1936; Sir Toby Belch in Twelfth Night, and Henry V, Hamlet at Kronborg, Elsinore, Denmark, 1937; Macbeth, 1937; Iago in Othello, King of Nowhere, and Coriolanus, 1938; No Time for Comedy, New York, 1939; under his own management produced and played Romeo and Juliet with Vivien Leigh. Lieut (A) RNVR until released from Fleet Air Arm, 1944, to co-direct The Old Vic Theatre Company with Joan Burrell and Ralph Richardson, at New Theatre; played in Old Vic, 1944-45 Season; Peer Gynt, Arms and the Man, Richard III, Uncle Vanya; toured Continent in May 1945 with Peer Gynt, Arms and the Man, Richard III; Old Vic Season, 1945-46; Henry IV, Parts I and II, Oedipus, The Critic, Uncle Vanya, Arms and the Man; six weeks' season in New York with Henry IV, Parts I and II, Oedipus, The Critic and Uncle Vanya; Old Vic, 1946-47 Season, produced and played King Lear. Made a tour of Australia and New Zealand, 1948, with Old Vic Company, in Richard III, School for Scandal, Skin of our Teeth, Old Vic, 1949 Season, Richard III, The School for Scandal, Antigone. Directed A Street Car Named Desire, Aldwych, 1949; St James's, 1950-51; produced and acted in Venus Observed, under own management, produced Captain Carvallo, 1950, Antony in Antony and Cleopatra, Caesar in Caeser and Cleopatra, 1951; also in US, 1951-52; The Sleeping Prince, Phoenix, 1953; Stratford Season, 1955; Macbeth, Malvolio in Twelfth Night, Titus in Titus Andronicus; Archie Rice in The Entertainer, Royal Court Theatre, 1957; presented The Summer of the Seventeenth Doll, 1957; toured Europe in Titus Andronicus, 1957; Titus in Titus Andronicus, Stoll, 1957; Archie Rice in The Entertainer (revival), Palace Theatre, 1957, and New York, 1958; Coriolanus in Coriolanus, Stratford, 1959; directed The Tumbler, New York; Berenger in Rhinoceros, Royal Court Theatre and Strand Theatre, 1960; Becket in Becket, New York, 1960; Henry II in Becket, US Tour and New York, 1961; Fred Midway in Semi-Detached, Saville Theatre, 1962. Apptd Dir of National Theatre (first, as Old Vic): 1963: (produced) Hamlet; 1963-64; acted in Uncle Vanya and in The Recruiting Officer, 1964; acted in Othello and in The Master Builder, 1964-65. Chichester Festival: first Director, also acted, 1962 (Uncle Vanya; The Broken Heart; also Director, The Chances), 1963 (Uncle Vanya, also Director); National Theatre (produced) The Crucible; in Love for Love, Moscow and London, 1965; Othello, Moscow and London, 1965; Othello, Love for Love, (dir.) Juno and the Paycock, 1966; Edgar in The Dance of Death, Othello, Love for Love (dir.) Three Sisters, National Theatre, 1967; A Flea in Her Ear, 1968; Home and Beauty, Three Sisters (directed and played Chebutikin), 1968-69; Shylock in Merchant of Venice, 1970, Long Day's Journey into Night, 1971, 1972; Saturday, Sunday, Monday, 1973; The Party, 1974; (dir.) Eden End, 1974; *films:* Potiphar's Wife, The Yellow Passport, Perfect Understanding, No Funny Business, Moscow Nights, Fire Over England, As You Like It, The First and the Last, Divorce of Lady X, Wuthering Heights, Rebecca, Pride and Prejudice, Lady Hamilton, 49th Parallel, Demi-Paradise; produced, directed, played Henry V; produced, directed, played Hamlet (International Grand Prix, 1948, Oscar award, 1949); Carrie (Hollywood), 1950; Macheath in film The Beggar's Opera, 1953; produced, directed, played Richard III (British Film Academy's Award), 1956; produced, directed and played in The Prince and the Showgirl, 1957; General Burgoyne in The Devil's Disciple, 1959; The Entertainer; Spartacus; Term of Trial; Bunny Lake is Missing; Othello; Khartoum; The Power and The Glory, 1961, (TV) USA; Dance of Death; Shoes of the Fisherman; Oh! What a Lovely War; Battle of Britain; David Copperfield; directed and played Chebutikin in Three Sisters; Nicholas and Alexandra; Lady Caroline Lamb; Sleuth (NY Film Critics Award, Best Actor, 1972); Seven-per-cent Solution; Marathon Man (Variety Club of GB Award, 1977); A Bridge Too Far; The Betsy; Boys from Brazil; A Little Romance; Dracula; Clash of the Titans; Inchon; The Jazz Singer; *television:* John Gabriel Borkmann, 1959; Long Day's Journey Into Night, 1972 (Emmy Award, 1973); The Merchant of Venice, 1973; Love Among The Ruins, USA, 1974 (Emmy Award, 1975); Jesus of Nazareth, 1976; The Collection, 1976; Cat on a Hot Tin Roof, 1976; Hindle Wakes, 1976; Come Back Little Sheba, Daphne Laureola, Saturday Sunday Monday, 1977; Brideshead Revisited, 1981; A Voyage Round My Father, 1982. Narrated World at War (TV), 1963. *Recreations:* tennis, swimming, motoring, flying, gardening. *Address:* 33-34 Chancery Lane, WC2A 1EW. *Clubs:* Garrick, Green Room, MCC.

OLIVIER, Henry, CMG 1954; MScEng, PhD London, DEng; FICE, FASCE, Beit Fellow; specialist consulting engineer in water resources engineering, Henry Olivier & Associates, since 1973; *b* 25 Jan. 1914; *s* of J. Olivier, Umtali, S Rhodesia; *m* 1st, 1940, Lorna Renée Collier; one *d* (one *s* decd); 2nd, 1979, Johanna Cecilia van der Merwe. *Educ:* Umtali High Sch.; Cape Town Univ. (BSc 1936; MSc 1947); University College, London (PhD 1953); DEng Witwatersrand, 1967. Beit Engineering Schol., 1932-38; Beit Fellow for two Rhodesias, 1939. Engineering post-grad. training with F. E. Kanthack & Partners, Consulting Engineers, Johannesburg, 1937; Sir Alex. Gibb & Partners, Cons. Engineers, London: training 1938, Asst Engineer, 1939. Experience covers design and construction of steam-electric power-stations, hydro-electric, floating harbour, irrigation, and water resources development schemes in UK, Africa, Middle East, and USA; Chief Engineer in charge civil engineering contracts, Owen Falls Hydro-Electric Scheme, Uganda, 1950-54; Partner in firm of Sir Alexander Gibb and Partners (Africa), 1954-55; Resident Director and Chief Engineer (Rhodesia), in firm of Gibb, Coyne & Sogei (Kariba), 1955-60; Consultant (mainly in connection with Indus Basin Project in Pakistan) to Sir Alexander Gibb and Partners, London, 1960-69 (Sen. Consultant, 1967); Partner, Gibb Hawkins and Partners, Johannesburg, 1963-69, associated with design and construction of Hendrik Verwoerd and P. K. le Roux dams on Orange River, RSA; Chm. LTA Ltd and LTA Engineering Ltd, 1969-73. Mem., Exec. Cttee, SA Nat. Cttee on Large Dams, 1972-81; Pres., SA Inst. of Civil Engineers, 1979. FRSA. Hon. DSc: Cape, 1968; Rhodesia, 1977. *Publications:* Irrigation and Climate, 1960; Irrigation and Water Resources Engineering, 1972; Damit, 1975; Great Dams in Southern Africa, 1977; Papers to Institution Civil Engineering Journal; Int. Commn on Irrigation and Drainage; Water for Peace Conference, Washington, DC. *Recreation:* tennis. *Address:* Henry Olivier and Associates, PO Box 6844, Johannesburg, South Africa. *Clubs:* Salisbury (Zimbabwe); Country (Johannesburg).

OLIVIER, Lady, (Joan); *see* Plowright, Joan.

OLLERENSHAW, Dame Kathleen (Mary), DBE 1971; MA, DPhil; FIMA, FCP; Member, Manchester City Council, 1956-80, Leader of Conservative Opposition, 1977-79; Alderman, 1970-74, Hon. Alderman since 1980; Lord Mayor, 1975-76, Deputy Lord Mayor, 1976-77; Chairman of Court, Royal Northern College of Music, Manchester, since 1968 (Companion, 1978); *b* 1 Oct. 1912; *d* of late Charles Timpson, JP, and late Mary Elizabeth Timpson (*née* Stops); *m* 1939, Robert Ollerenshaw; one *s* (one *d* decd). *Educ:* Ladybarn House Sch., Manchester; St Leonards Sch., St Andrews; (open schol. in maths) Somerville Coll., Oxford (Hon. Fellow, 1978). BA (Hons) 1934, MA 1943, DPhil 1945; Foundation Fellow, Institute of Mathematics and its Applications (FIMA), 1964 (Mem. Council, 1973-75, Vice-Pres., 1976-77, Pres., 1978-79). Research Assistant, Shirley Institute, Didsbury, 1937-40. Chairman: Educn Cttee, Assoc. of Municipal Corporations, 1968-71; Assoc. of Governing Bodies of Girls' Public Schs, 1963-69; Manchester Educn Cttee, 1967-70 (Co-opted Mem., 1954-56); Manchester Coll. of Commerce, 1964-69; Council, Science and Technology Insts, 1980-81; Member: Central Adv. Council on Educn in England, 1960-63; CNAA, 1964-74; SSRC, 1971-75; Tech. Educn Council, 1973-75; (Vice-Pres.,) British Assoc. for Commercial and Industrial Educn (Mem. Delegn to USSR, 1963); Exec., Assoc. of Educn Cttees, 1967-71; Nat. Adv. Council on Educn for Industry and Commerce, 1963-70; Gen. Adv. Council of BBC, 1966-72; Schools Council, 1968-71; Management Panel, Burnham Cttee, 1968-71; Nat. Foundn of Educnl Res., 1968-71; Layfield Cttee of Inquiry into Local Govt Finance, 1974-76; Council of Univ. of Salford, 1967-; Court, Univ. of Manchester, 1964-; Manchester Polytechnic, 1968-(Chm., 1969-72; Dep.-Chm., 1972-75; Hon. Fellow, 1979); Court, UMIST, 1971- (Vice-Pres., 1976-); Council, Lancaster Univ., 1975- (Dep. Pro-Chancellor, 1978); Council, CGLI, 1972- (Hon. Fellow, 1978; Vice-Pres., 1979); Sen. Res. Fellow (part-time), 1972-75, Hon. Res. Fellow, 1975-77, Lancaster Univ.; Rep. Governor: Union of Lancashire and Cheshire Institutes, 1967-73; Manchester and Dist Adv. Council for Further Educn, 1967-71; Associated Local Educn Authorities of Lancashire, 1967-70; NW Reg. Council for Further Educn, 1959-63, 1967-71; Univ. of Manchester Sch. of Educn Delegacy for the Trng of Teachers, 1967-70; Royal Coll. of Advanced Technol., Salford, 1959-67; Governor: St Leonards Sch., St Andrews, 1950-72 (Pres., 1980-); Manchester High Sch. for Girls, 1959-69; Ladies Coll., Cheltenham, 1966-68; Chethams Hosp. Sch., Manchester, 1967-77; Further Educn Staff Coll., Blagdon, 1960-74; Mem., Manchester Statistical Soc., 1950- (Mem. Council, 1977-; Vice-Pres., 1977, Pres., 1981-); Hon. Member: Manchester Technology Assoc., 1976- (Pres., 1982); Manchester Literary and Philosophical Soc., 1981-; Hon. Col, Manchester and Salford Univs OTC, 1977-81. Dir, Manchester Independent Radio, Ltd, 1972-83. Winifred Cullis Lecture Fellow to USA, 1965; Fourth Cockroft Lecture, UMIST and Manchester Tech. Assoc., 1977. CStJ 1978 (Chm. Council for Greater Manchester, 1974-; Mem., Chapter Gen., 1974-). Hon. LLD CNAA, 1975; Hon. DSc Salford, 1975; Hon LLD Manchester, 1976. Mancunian of the

Year, Jnr Chamber of Commerce, 1977. *Publications:* Education of Girls, 1958; Education for Girls, 1961; The Girls' Schools, 1967; Returning to Teaching, 1974; The Lord Mayor's Party, 1976; First Citizen, 1977; Mathematical Games and Modelling; papers in mathematical journals on Geometry of Numbers, 1945-54, 1977-; articles on education and local govt in national and educational press. *Address:* 2 Pine Road, Didsbury, Manchester M20 0UY. *T:* 061-445 2948. *Club:* English-Speaking Union.

OLLIS, Prof. William David, BSc, PhD; FRS 1972; Professor of Organic Chemistry, since 1963, Head of Department of Chemistry, since 1973, University of Sheffield; *b* 22 Dec. 1924; *s* of Albert George and Beatrice Charlotte Ollis; *m* 1951, Sonia Dorothy Mary Weekes; two *d. Educ:* Cotham Grammar Sch., Bristol; University of Bristol. Assistant Lecturer in Organic Chemistry, University of Bristol, 1946-49, Lecturer, 1949-62, Reader, 1962-63. Visiting Research Fellow, Harvard, 1952-53; Visiting Professor: University of California, Los Angeles, 1962; University of Texas, 1966; Nat. Science Foundn Sen. Fellowship, 1970-71; Hon. Prof., Universidade Federal Rural do Rio de Janeiro, Brasil, 1969. Robert Gnehm Lecture, 1965; Chemical Soc. Tilden Lectr, 1969. *Publications:* Recent Developments in the Chemistry of Natural Phenolic Compounds, 1961; scientific papers mainly in Journal of Chemical Society. *Address:* Department of Chemistry, University of Sheffield, Sheffield S3 7HF. *Club:* Athenæum.

O'LOGHLEN, Sir Colman (Michael), 6th Bt, *cr* 1838; *b* 6 April 1916; *s* of Henry Ross O'Loghlen (*d* 1944; 6th *s* of 3rd Bt) and of Doris Irene, *d* of late Major Percival Horne, RA; *S* uncle 1951; *m* 1939, Margaret, *d* of Francis O'Halloran, Melbourne, Victoria; six *s* two *d. Educ:* Xavier Coll., Melbourne; Melbourne Univ. (LLB). Formerly Captain AIF. Sometime Magistrate and Judge of Supreme Court, PNG. *Heir: s* Michael O'Loghlen, *b* 21 May 1945. *Address:* 98 Williamsons Road, Doncaster, Victoria 3108, Australia.

OLUFOSOYE, Most Rev. Timothy; *see* Nigeria, Archbishop of.

OLUWASANMI, Hezekiah Adedunmola, MA, PhD Harvard; Vice-Chancellor, University of Ife, Nigeria, 1966-75; *b* 12 Nov. 1919; *s* of late John Oluwasanmi and Jane Ola Oluwasanmi; *m* 1959, Edwina Marie Clarke (decd); one *s* two *d. Educ:* Morehouse Coll. (BA); Harvard University. Secondary School Teacher, 1940-41; Meteorological Observer, 1941-44; Clerk, Shell Oil Co., 1944-47; Student, 1948-55; Lectr, Sen. Lectr, and Prof. of Agricultural Economics, Univ. of Ibadan, 1955-66, Dean, Faculty of Agriculture, 1963-66. Member: W Nigeria Economic Planning Cttee, 1961-62; W Nigeria Economic Adv. Cttee, 1966-71. Chairman: Cttee of Vice-Chancellors of Nigerian Univs, 1970-72; Univ. of Zambia Grants Cttee; Member: Council, Univ. of Ghana; Assoc. of Commonwealth Univs; Bd of Governors, Internat. Develt Res. Centre, Ottawa; Bd of Trustees, Internat. Inst. of Tropical Agriculture, 1970-72. Member: Nigerian Econ. Soc.; Agricultural Soc., Nigeria; Internat. Assoc. Agricultural Economists. Hon DSc, Univ. of Nigeria, Nsukka, 1971; Hon. LLD: Univ. of Wisconsin, 1974; Univ. of Ife, Nigeria, 1980; Hon. LHD, Morehouse Coll., Georgia, USA, 1974. *Publications:* Agriculture and Nigerian Economic Development, 1966; (jt author) Uboma, a socio-economic and nutritional survey of a rural community in Eastern Nigeria, 1966; various reports, contribs to symposia and papers in learned jls. *Recreations:* reading, walking, listening to music. *Address:* 19 Osuntokun Avenue, Bodija, UIPO Box 4162, Ibadan, Oyo State, Nigeria.

OLVER, Sir Stephen (John Linley), KBE 1975 (MBE 1947); CMG 1965; HM Diplomatic Service, retired; *b* 16 June 1916; *s* of late Rev. S. E. L. Olver and Mrs Madeleine Olver (*née* Stratton); *m* 1953, Maria Morena, Gubbio, Italy; one *s. Educ:* Stowe. Indian Police, 1935-44; Indian Political Service, Delhi, Quetta, Sikkim and Bahrain, 1944-47; Pakistan Foreign Service, Aug.-Oct. 1947; Foreign Service, Karachi, 1947-50; Foreign Office, 1950-53; Berlin, 1953-56; Bangkok, 1956-58; Foreign Office, 1958-61; Washington, 1961-64; Foreign Office, 1964-66; The Hague, 1967-69; High Comr, Freetown, 1969-72; High Comr, Nicosia, 1973-75. *Recreations:* golf, photography, painting. *Address:* 7 Seymour Square, Brighton, Sussex. *Club:* MCC.

OLYOTT, Ven. Leonard Eric; Archdeacon of Taunton and Prebendary of Milverton, since 1977; *b* 11 Jan. 1926; *s* of Thomas Olyott and Maude Ann Olyott (*née* Purser); *m* 1951, Yvonne Winifred Kate Keele; two *s* one *d. Educ:* Colchester Royal Grammar School; London Univ. (BA 1950); Westcott House, Cambridge. Served RNVR, 1944-47; commissioned, 1945. Asst Curate, St George, Camberwell, 1952-55; Priest-in-Charge, St Michael and All Angels, Birchwood, Hatfield, Herts, 1955-60; Vicar of Chipperfield, Herts, 1960-68; Vicar of Crewkerne, 1968-71; Rector of Crewkerne with Wayford, 1971-77; Rural Dean of Crewkerne, 1972-77; Prebendary of Timberscombe, 1976. *Recreations:* sailing, gardening, elkhounds, music. *Address:* Summerhayes, Higher Street, Curry Mallet, Taunton, Somerset. *T:* Hatch Beauchamp 480758.

O'MALLEY, Stephen Keppel; a Recorder of the Crown Court, Western Circuit, since 1978; *b* 21 July 1940; *s* of late D. K. C. O'Malley and of Mrs R. O'Malley; *m* 1963, Frances Mary, *e d* of James Stewart Ryan, *qv*; four *s* two *d. Educ:* Ampleforth Coll.; Wadham Coll., Oxford (MA). Called to Bar, Inner Temple, 1962; Mem. Bar Council, 1968-72; Co-Founder, Bar European Gp, 1977. *Publication:* Legal London, a Pictorial History, 1971.

Address: 24 Montague Road, Richmond, Surrey TW10 6QW. *T:* 01-940 2727.

OMAN, Julia Trevelyan, (Lady Strong), RDI 1977; designer; Director, Oman Productions Ltd; *b* 11 July 1930; *d* of late Charles Chichele Oman and Joan Trevelyan; *m* 1971, Sir Roy Colin Strong, *qv. Educ:* Royal College of Art, London. Royal Scholar, 1953 and Silver Medal, 1955, RCA. Designer: BBC Television, 1955-67; Alice in Wonderland, BBC TV Film, 1966; Brief Lives, London and New York, 1967; Country Dance, London and Edinburgh, 1967; Art Director (England), The Charge of the Light Brigade, 1967; Art Director, Laughter in the Dark, 1968; Designer: 40 Years On, 1968; (Production designer) Julius Caesar, 1969; The Merchant of Venice, National Theatre, 1970; Eugene Onegin, Covent Garden, 1971; The Straw Dogs (film), 1971; Othello, Stratford, 1971; Samuel Pepys Exhibn, Nat. Portrait Gall., 1971; Getting On, Queen's, 1971; Othello, RSC, Aldwych, 1972; Un Ballo in Maschera, Hamburgische Staatsoper, 1973; La Bohème, Covent Garden, 1974; The Importance of Being Earnest, Burgtheater, Vienna, 1976; Die Fledermaus, Covent Garden, 1977; Mme Tussaud's hist. tableaux, 1979; Danish TV, 1979; Hay Fever and The Wild Duck, Lyric, Hammersmith, 1980; The Shoemakers' Holiday, Nat. Theatre, 1981; The Bear's Quest for Ragged Staff, Warwick, 1981; Die Csardasfürstin, Kassel, 1982; *ballet:* Enigma Variations, 1968; A Month in the Country, 1976; Sospiri, 1980; Swan Lake, 1981. Des RCA (1st class), 1955; FSIAD. Designer of the Year Award for Alice in Wonderland, 1967. *Publications:* Street Children (photographs by Julia Trevelyan Oman; text by B. S. Johnson), 1964; (with Roy Strong) Elizabeth R, 1971; (with Roy Strong) Mary Queen of Scots, 1972; introd. The Merchant of Venice, Folio Soc. edn, 1975; (with Roy Strong) The English Year, 1982; contrib. Architectural Review (photographs), Vogue (text and photographs). *Address:* c/o Curtis Brown, 1 Craven Hill, W2 3EP. *T:* 01-262 1011.

OMOLODUN, John Olatunji, (Chief), The Ottun-Balogun of Awe (Oyo State, Nigeria); Director, Department of Asian and Pacific Affairs, Ministry of External Affairs, Lagos; *b* 24 June 1935; *s* of late Chief Omolodun and Mrs Emmanuel Owolabi Omolodun; *S* father, 1965; *m* 1959, Risikatu Fowoshere; two *s* three *d. Educ:* King's Coll., Lagos; Univ. of London (LLB); Council of Legal Educn. Called to the Bar, Lincoln's Inn, 1959. Barrister and Solicitor, Supreme Court of Nigeria, 1960-65; Chm., Tax Appeal Bd, W Reg. Nigeria, 1963-65; Director: Nat. Bank of Nigeria, 1964-65; Wrought Iron Co. of Nigeria, 1964-65; Councillor, Oyo Div. Council, 1964-65; Agent-General for Western Reg. of Nigeria, UK, 1965-66; Actg High Commissioner of Nigeria: Pakistan, 1966-67; Sierra Leone, 1967-70; Chargé d'Affaires, Ivory Coast, 1971-73; Dep. Dir of African Affairs Dept, Min. of Ext. Affairs, Lagos, 1973-75; Actg High Comr, UK, 1976-77; High Comr, India, with concurrent accreditation to Sri Lanka, Burma, Thailand and Bangladesh, 1977. Order of Grand Star of Africa, Liberia, 1971. Sec.-Gen., UN Assoc. of Nigeria, 1960-63; Vice-Pres., World Fedn of UN Assocs, 1963-64. *Publications:* Economic Prospects in Sub-Saharan Africa, 1978; Nigeria, Africa and the World, 1981; pamphlet on overseas students in UK, and paper on International Court of Justice. *Recreations:* cricket, golf, cycling, table tennis. *Heir: s* Folarin Owolabi Omolodun, *b* 13 March 1968. *Address:* PO Box 3159, General Post Office, Marina, Lagos, Nigeria. *Clubs:* Royal Over-Seas League (Hon. Mem); Yoruba Tennis, Island (Lagos).

O'MORCHOE, David Nial Creagh, CB 1979; MBE 1967; (The O'Morchoe); Chief of O'Morchoe of Oulartleigh and Monamolin; *b* 17 May 1928; *s* of Nial Creagh O'Morchoe and Jessie Elizabeth, *d* of late Charles Jasper Joly, FRS, FRIS, MRIA, Astronomer Royal of Ireland; *S* father as Chief of the Name (O'Morchoe), 1970; *m* 1954, Margaret Jane, 3rd *d* of George Francis Brewitt, Cork; two *s* one *d. Educ:* St Columba's Coll., Dublin; RMA Sandhurst. Commissioned Royal Irish Fusiliers, 1948; served in Egypt, Jordan, Gibraltar, Germany, Kenya, Cyprus, Oman; psc 1958, jssc 1966; CO 1st Bn RIrF, later 3rd Bn Royal Irish Rangers, 1967-68; Directing Staff, Staff Coll., Camberley, 1969-71; RCDS 1972; Brigade Comdr, 1973-75; Brig. GS, BAOR, 1975-76; Maj.-Gen. 1977; Comdr, Sultan of Oman's Land Forces, 1977-79, retired. Dep. Col, 1971-76, Col 1977-79, The Royal Irish Rangers. *Recreations:* sailing and most sports. *Heir: s* Dermot Arthur O'Morchoe, *b* 11 Aug. 1956. *Address:* c/o Ulster Bank, Patrick Street, Cork. *Clubs:* Rotary, Irish Cruising.

O'NEIL, Most Rev. Alexander Henry, MA, DD; *m* 1931, Marguerite (*née* Roe); one *s. Educ:* Univ. of W Ontario; BA 1928, BD 1936, MA 1943; Huron Coll., London, Ont; LTh 1929. Deacon, 1929; Priest, 1930; Principal, Huron Coll., London, Ont, 1941-52; Gen. Sec., British and Foreign Bible Soc. in Canada, 1952-57; Bishop of Fredericton, 1957-63; Archbishop of Fredericton and Metropolitan of the Province of Canada, 1963-71. Hon. DD: Univ. of W Ontario, 1945; Wycliffe Coll., Toronto, 1954; King's Coll., Halifax, 1958; Hon. LLD: W Ontario, 1962; St Thomas Univ., Fredericton, 1970; Hon. DCL Bishop's Univ., Lennoxville, 1964. *Address:* Apt 807 Grosvenor Gates, 1 Grosvenor Street, London N6A 1Y2, Ont, Canada.

O'NEIL, Hon. Sir Desmond (Henry), Kt 1980; Chairman: Western Australia Lotteries Commission, since 1981; Western Australia Greyhound Racing Association, since 1981; *b* 27 Sept. 1920; *s* of late Henry McLelland O'Neil and Lilian Francis O'Neil; *m* 1944, Nancy Jean Culver; two *d. Educ:* Aquinas Coll., Perth; Claremont Teachers Coll., WA. Served War, Australian Army, 1939-46: Captain, Aust. Corps of Signals. Educn Dept, WA, 1939-58; Mem., Legislative Assembly, WA, 1959-80; Govt Whip, 1962-65; Minister for

Housing and Labour, 1965-71; Dep. Leader of Opposition, 1972-73; Minister for: Works and Housing, 1974-75; Works, Housing and the North-West, 1975-77; Dep. Premier, Chief Sec., Minister for Police and Traffic, Minister for Regional Admin and the NW, Western Australia, 1977-80. Col Comdt. Royal Aust. Corps of Signals 5 Mil. Dist, 1980–. *Recreations:* power boating, fishing. *Address:* 42 Godwin Avenue, South Como, WA 6152, Australia. *T:* 450-4682. *Clubs:* South of Perth Yacht (Vice-Patron); Mt Pleasant Bowling (Patron).

O'NEILL, family name of **Barons O'Neill, O'Neill of the Maine,** and **Rathcavan.**

O'NEILL, 4th Baron *cr* 1868; **Raymond Arthur Clanaboy O'Neill,** TD 1970; DL; *b* 1 Sept. 1933; *s* of 3rd Baron and Anne Geraldine (she *m* 2nd, 1945, 2nd Viscount Rothermere, and 3rd, 1952, late Ian Fleming, and *d* 1981), *e d* of Hon. Guy Charteris; *S* father, 1944; *m* 1963, Georgina Mary, *er d* of Lord George Montagu Douglas Scott; three *s. Educ:* Eton; Royal Agricultural Coll. 2nd Lieut, 11th Hussars, Prince Albert's Own; Major, North Irish Horse, AVR; Lt-Col, RARO. Chm., Ulster Countryside Cttee, 1971-75. Trustee, Ulster Folk and Transport Mus., 1969–; Member: NI Tourist Bd, 1973-80 (Chm., 1975-80); NI Nat. Trust Cttee, 1980– (Chm., 1981–); Pres., NI Assoc. of Youth Clubs, 1965–. DL Co. Antrim. *Recreations:* vintage motoring, railways, gardening. *Heir: s* Hon. Shane Sebastian Clanaboy O'Neill, *b* 25 July 1965. *Address:* Shane's Castle, Antrim, Ireland. *T:* Antrim 63264. *Clubs:* Turf, Ulster.
See also J. A. L. Morgan.

O'NEILL OF THE MAINE, Baron *cr* 1970 (Life Peer), of Ahoghill, Co. Antrim; **Terence Marne O'Neill,** PC (N Ireland) 1956; DL; *b* 10 Sept. 1914; *s* of Capt. Hon. Arthur O'Neill, MP (killed in action, 1914; *s* of 2nd Baron O'Neill, Shane's Castle, Antrim) and of late Lady Annabel Crewe-Milnes, *e d* of 1st and last Marquis of Crewe, KG; *m* 1944, Katherine Jean, *y d* of late W. I. Whitaker, Pylewell Park, Lymington, Hants; one *s* one *d. Educ:* Eton. Served, 1939-45, Irish Guards. MP (Unionist) Bannside, Parlt of N Ireland, 1946-70; Parl. Sec., Min. of Health, 1948; Deputy Speaker and Chairman of Ways and Means, 1953; Joint Parl. Sec., Home Affairs and Health, 1955; Minister: Home Affairs, 1956; Finance, 1956; Prime Minister of N Ireland, 1963-69. Mem., Hansard Soc. Commn on Electoral Reform, 1975-76. Director: S. G. Warburg & Co.; International Holdings Ltd; Phoenix Assurance, 1969–. Trustee, Winston Churchill Meml Trust. DL Co. Antrim, 1948; High Sheriff County Antrim, 1953. Hon. LLD, Queen's Univ., Belfast, 1967. *Publications:* Ulster at the Crossroads, 1969; The Autobiography of Terence O'Neill, 1972. *Address:* Lisle Court, Lymington, Hants. *Clubs:* Brooks's; Ulster (Belfast).

O'NEILL, Alan Albert; Clerk to the Drapers' Company, 1973-80, Member, Court of Assistants, since 1981; *b* 11 Jan. 1916; *o s* of late Albert George O'Neill; *m* 1939, Betty Dolbey; one *s. Educ:* Sir George Monoux Grammar Sch., Walthamstow. Joined staff Drapers' Co., 1933, Dep. Clerk 1967. Clerk to Governors, Bancroft's School, 1951-73, Governor, 1980–; Governor, Queen Mary Coll., 1973-80. Served War of 1939-45, Royal Navy: Telegraphist, RNV(W)R, 1939; DEMS Gunnery Officer, SS Aquitania and SS Nieuw Amsterdam; Lt-Comdr, RNVR, 1943; DEMS Staff Officer, Aberdeen and NE Coast Scotland, 1945. *Recreations:* tennis, gardening. *Address:* Wickenden Farm, Plaxtol, Sevenoaks, Kent. *T:* Plaxtol 810334.

O'NEILL, Hon. Sir Con (Douglas Walter), GCMG 1972 (KCMG 1962; CMG 1953); Director, Unigate Ltd, since 1974; *b* 3 June 1912; 2nd *s* of 1st Baron Rathcavan, *qv*; *m* 1st, 1940, Rosemary (marriage dissolved 1954), *d* of late H. Pritchard, MD; one *s* one *d*; 2nd, 1964, Baroness Mady Marschall von Bieberstein (*d* 1960), *d* of late Baron von Holzing-Berstett; 3rd, 1961, Mrs Anne-Marie Lindberg, Helsinki. *Educ:* Eton College; Balliol Coll., Oxford (History Scholar). BA 1934 (1st Class, English), MA 1937; Fellow, All Souls College, Oxford, 1935-46; called to Bar, Inner Temple, 1936; entered Diplomatic Service, 1936; Third Secretary, Berlin, 1938; resigned from Service, 1939. Served War of 1939-45 in Army (Intelligence Corps), 1940-Nov. 1943; temp. employed in Foreign Office, 1943-46; Leader-writer on staff of Times, 1946-47; returned to Foreign Office, 1947; re-established in Foreign Service, 1948; served in Frankfurt and Bonn, 1948-53; Counsellor, HM Foreign Service, 1951; Imperial Defence College, 1953; Head of News Department, Foreign Office, 1954-55; Chargé d'Affaires, Peking, 1955-57; Asst Under-Sec., FO, 1957-60; Ambassador to Finland, 1961-63; Ambassador to the European Communities in Brussels, 1963-65; Dep. Under-Sec. of State, FO, 1965-68; Dir, Hill, Samuel & Co. Ltd, 1968-69; Dep. Under-Sec. of State, FCO, and Leader at official level of British delegn to negotiate entry to EEC, 1969-72; Chm., Intervention Bd for Agricl Produce, 1972-74. Dir, Britain in Europe Campaign, 1974-75. *Publication:* Our European Future, 1972 (Stamp Meml Lecture). *Recreations:* shooting, fishing. *Address:* 37 Flood Street, SW3.

O'NEILL, Martin (John); MP (Lab) Stirlingshire, East and Clackmannan, since 1979; *b* 6 Jan. 1945; *s* of John and Minnie O'Neill; *m* 1973, Elaine Marjorie Samuel; two *s. Educ:* Trinity Academy, Edinburgh; Heriot Watt Univ. (BA Econ.); Moray House Coll. of Education, Edinburgh. Insurance Clerk, Scottish Widows Fund, 1963-67; Asst Examiner, Estate Duty Office of Scotland, 1971-73; Teacher of Modern Studies, Boroughmuir High School, Edinburgh, 1974-77; Social Science Tutor, Craigmount High School, Edinburgh, 1977-79; Open Univ., 1976-79. Member: Select Cttee, Scottish

Affairs, 1979–; GMWU; MATSA; EIS. *Recreations:* watching football, playing squash, reading, listening to jazz, the cinema. *Address:* House of Commons, SW1. *T:* 01-219 4548.

O'NEILL, Most Rev. Michael Cornelius, OBE 1945; MM 1918; *b* 15 Feb. 1898; Irish Canadian. *Educ:* St Michael's College, University of Toronto; St Augustine's Seminary, Toronto. Overseas Service, Signaller, CFA, European War, 1916-19. St Joseph's Seminary, Edmonton; Professor, 1928-39; Rector, 1930-39. Overseas Service, Canadian Chaplain Services, War of 1939-45; Principal Chaplain (Army) Overseas, (RC), 1941-45; Principal Chaplain (Army), (RC), 1945-46. Archbishop of Regina, 1948-73. Hon. Chaplain, Saskatchewan Comd, Royal Canadian Legion, 1973. Nat. Lutheran Merit Award, 1974. Hon. LLD: Toronto, 1952; Univ. of Saskatchewan (Regina Campus), 1974; Hon. DD Univ. of St Michael's Coll., Toronto, 1977. *Address:* 67 Hudson Drive, Regina, Sask, Canada. *Club:* East India, Devonshire, Sports and Public Schools.

O'NEILL, Prof. Patrick Geoffrey, BA, PhD; Professor of Japanese, University of London, since 1968; *b* 9 Aug. 1924; *m* 1951, Diana Howard; one *d. Educ:* Rutlish Sch., Merton; Sch. of Oriental and African Studies, Univ. of London. Lectr in Japanese, Sch. of Oriental and African Studies, Univ. of London, 1949. *Publications:* A Guide to Nō, 1954; Early Nō Drama, 1958; (with S. Yanada) Introduction to Written Japanese, 1963; A Programmed Course on Respect Language in Modern Japanese, 1966; Japanese Kana Workbook 1967; A Programmed Introduction to Literary-style Japanese, 1968; Japanese Names, 1972; Essential Kanji, 1973; (ed) Tradition and Modern Japan, 1982. *Address:* School of Oriental and African Studies, University of London, WC1E 7HP.

O'NEILL, Rt. Hon. Phelim Robert Hugh, PC (N Ireland) 1969; Major, late RA; *b* 2 Nov. 1909; *s* and *heir* of 1st Baron Rathcavan, *qv* ; *m* 1st, 1934, Clare Désirée (from whom he obtained a divorce, 1944), *d* of late Detmar Blow; one *s* one *d*; 2nd, 1953, Mrs B. D. Edwards-Moss, *d* of late Major Hon. Richard Coke; three *d* (and one *d* decd). *Educ:* Eton. MP (UU) for North Antrim (UK Parliament), 1952-59; MP (U) North Antrim, Parliament of N Ireland, 1959-72; Minister, N Ireland: Education, 1969; Agriculture, 1969-71.

O'NEILL, Robert James, CMG 1978; HM Diplomatic Service; Under Secretary, Cabinet Office, since 1981; *b* 17 June 1932; *m* 1958, Helen Juniper; one *s* two *d. Educ:* King Edward VI Sch., Chelmsford; Trinity Coll., Cambridge (Schol.). 1st cl. English Tripos Pts I and II. Entered HM Foreign (now Diplomatic) Service, 1955; FO, 1955-57; British Embassy, Ankara, 1957-60; Dakar, 1961-63; FO, 1963-68, Private Sec. to Chancellor of Duchy of Lancaster, 1966, and to Minister of State for Foreign Affairs, 1967-68; British Embassy, Bonn, 1968-72; Counsellor Diplomatic Service, 1972; seconded to Cabinet Office as Asst Sec., 1972-75; FCO, 1975-78; Dep. Governor, Gibraltar, 1978-81. *Recreation:* hill-walking. *Address:* 11 Castle Close, Parkside, SW19 5NH. *T:* 01-947 2748. *Club:* Travellers'.

O'NEILL, Thomas P(hilip), Jr; Speaker, House of Representatives, USA, since Nov. 1976; *b* Cambridge, Mass, 9 Dec. 1912; *s* of Thomas P. O'Neill and Rose Anne (*née* Tolan); *m* 1941, Mildred Anne Miller; three *s* two *d. Educ:* St John's High Sch.; Boston Coll., Mass. Grad. 1936. In business, insurance, in Cambridge, Mass. Mem., State Legislature, Mass, 1936-52: Minority Leader, 1947 and 1948; Speaker of the House, 1948-52. Member, Camb. Sch. Cttee, 1946, 1949. Member of Congresses: 83rd-87th, 11th Dist, Mass; 88th-96th, 8th Dist, Mass. Democrat: Majority Whip, 1971-73; Majority Leader, 1973-77. *Address:* Room H204, US Capitol, Washington, DC 20515, USA.

ONIANS, Richard Broxton, MA (Liverpool), PhD (Cantab); Hildred Carlile Professor of Latin in University of London, 1936-66; now Emeritus; *b* 11 January 1899; *s* of late Richard Henry Onians, Liverpool; *m* 1937, Rosalind, *d* of late Lt-Col Ernest Browning Lathbury, OBE, MD, RAMC, Chipperfield, Herts; two *s* four *d. Educ:* Liverpool Inst.; Liverpool Univ. (1st Class Hons Classics); Trinity Coll. Cambridge (Senior Scholarship Examination, Open Research Studentship, Hooper English Oration Prize); Craven Grant for archæological research in Greece, and Hare Prize (Univ. of Cambridge). Member Council Assoc. of Univ. Teachers, 1945-53; Exec. Cttee 1946-51; Chm. London Consultative Cttee (AUT), 1946-48; Chm., Nat. Campaign Cttee for Expansion of Higher Educ., 1947-Feb. 1948 and June 1948-53; Chm. Joint Standing Cttee and Conf. on Library Cooperation, 1948-60; Mem. Exec. Cttee and Finance Committee of National Central Library, 1947-53. Formerly 4th South Lancs and RAF (1917-18); Lecturer in Latin, Univ. of Liverpool, 1925-33; Professor of Classics, Univ. of Wales (Swansea), 1933-35. *Publications:* The Origins of European Thought about the Body, the Mind, the Soul, the World, Time, and Fate: new interpretations of Greek, Roman, and kindred evidence, also of some basic Jewish and Christian beliefs, 1951, enlarged edn 1954; articles and reviews in Classical Journals. *Recreation:* walking. *Address:* Stokesay, 21 Luard Road, Cambridge. *T:* Cambridge 244250.

ONION, Francis Leo, CMG 1968; JP; Director, NZ Co-operative Dairy Co. Ltd (Chairman, 1961-69); Chairman, NZ Dairy Board, 1968-76 (Deputy Chairman, 1964-68); *b* 10 July 1903; *s* of Edwin Joseph Onion, Blenheim, NZ; *m* 1931, *d* of D. Ross, Otorohanga, NZ; two *s* one *d. Educ:* Hamilton High School. Farmer and Company Director; Chairman: Waipa County Council,

NZ, 1947-61; New Zealand Counties Ward, 1947-61; Central Waikato Electric Power Board, 1947-61; Maramurua Coalfields Ltd, 1961-69; Auckland Farm Products Ltd, 1967-; New Zealand Dairy Exporter Newspaper, 1963-; Mem. Bd, NZ Meat Producers, 1969-75. JP Hamilton, 1961. Coronation Medal, 1953. *Recreations:* shooting and bowls. *Address:* Te-Kowhai, RD8, Frankton, New Zealand. *T:* HOT 832 NZ. *Club:* National (Hamilton, NZ).

O'NIONS, Prof. Robert Keith, PhD; Royal Society Research Professor, Cambridge University, since 1979; Official Fellow, Clare Hall, Cambridge, since 1980; *b* 26 Sept. 1944; *s of* William Henry O'Nions and Eva O'Nions; *m* 1967, Rita Margaret Bill; three *d. Educ:* Univ. of Nottingham (BSc 1966); Univ. of Alberta (PhD 1969). Post-doctoral Fellow, Oslo Univ., 1970; Demonstr in Petrology, Oxford Univ., 1971-72, Lectr in Geochem., 1972-75; Associate Prof., then Prof., Columbia Univ., NY, 1975-79. Mem., Norwegian Acad. of Sciences, 1980. Macelwane Award, Amer. Geophys. Union, 1979. *Publications:* contrib. to jls related to earth and planetary sciences. *Address:* Department of Earth Sciences, Cambridge University, Cambridge. *T:* Cambridge 355463.

ONSLOW, family name of **Earl of Onslow.**

ONSLOW, 7th Earl of, *cr* 1801; **Michael William Coplestone Dillon Onslow,** Bt 1660; Baron Onslow, 1716; Baron Cranley, 1776; Viscount Cranley, 1801; *b* 28 Feb. 1938; *s of* 6th Earl of Onslow, KBE, MC, TD, and of Hon. Pamela Louisa Eleanor Dillon, *o d* of 19th Viscount Dillon, CMG, DSO; *S* father, 1971; *m* 1964, Robin Lindsay, *o d* of Major Robert Lee Bullard III, US Army, and of Lady Aberconway; one *s* two *d. Educ:* Eton; Sorbonne. Life Guards, 1956-60, served Arabian Peninsula. Farmer. Governor: University Coll. at Buckingham; Royal Grammar Sch., Guildford. High Steward of Guildford. *Heir:* s Viscount Cranley, *qv. Address:* Temple Court, Clandon Park, Guildford, Surrey. *Clubs:* White's, Beefsteak.
See also A. A. Waugh.

ONSLOW, Cranley Gordon Douglas; MP (C) Woking since 1964; Minister of State, Foreign and Commonwealth Office, since 1982; *b* 8 June 1926; *s of* late F. R. D. Onslow and Mrs M. Onslow, Effingham House, Bexhill; *m* 1955, Lady June Hay, *yr d* of 13th Earl of Kinnoull; one *s* three *d. Educ:* Harrow; Oriel Coll., Oxford; Geneva Univ. Served in RAC, Lieut 7th QO Hussars, 1944-48, and 3rd/4th Co. of London Yeo. (Sharpshooters) (TA) as Captain, 1948-52. Joined HM Foreign Service, 1951; Third Sec. Br. Embassy, Rangoon, 1953-55; Consul at Maymyo, N Burma, 1955-56; resigned, 1960. Served on Dartford RDC, 1960-62, and Kent CC, 1961-64. Parly Under-Sec. of State, Aerospace and Shipping, DTI, 1972-74; an Opposition spokesman on health and social security, 1974-75, on defence, 1975-76. Chairman: Select Cttee on Defence, 1981-82; Cons. Aviation Cttee, 1970-72, 1979-82. Mem. Exec., 1922 Cttee, 1968-72, 1981-82. Mem., UK deleg to Council of Europe and WEU, 1977-81. Council Member: Nat. Rifle Assoc.; Salmon & Trout Assoc.; Anglers' Co-operative Assoc. Mem. Council, St John's Sch., Leatherhead. *Publication:* Asian Economic Development (ed), 1965. *Recreations:* fishing, shooting, watching cricket. *Address:* Highbuilding, Fernhurst, W Sussex. *Club:* English-Speaking Union.

ONSLOW, Maj.-Gen. Sir Denzil M.; *see* Macarthur-Onslow.

ONSLOW, Sir John (Roger Wilmot), 8th Bt, *cr* 1797; Captain, Royal Yacht of Saudi Arabia; *b* 21 July 1932; *o s of* Sir Richard Wilmot Onslow, 7th Bt, TD, and Constance (*d* 1960), *o d of* Albert Parker; *S* father, 1963; *m* 1955, Catherine Zoia (marr. diss. 1973), *d of* Henry Atherton Greenway, The Manor, Compton Abdale, near Cheltenham, Gloucestershire; one *s* one *d* ; *m* 1976, Susan Fay, *d of* E. M. Hughes, Frankston, Vic, Australia. *Educ:* Cheltenham College. *Heir:* s Richard Paul Atherton Onslow, *b* 16 Sept. 1958. *Address:* c/o Barclays Bank Ltd, Fowey, Cornwall.

ONSLOW, William George, CB 1970; Chairman Yorkshire and Humberside Economic Planning Board, 1965-71; *b* 12 June 1908; *s of* Albert Edward and Ann Onslow; *m* Joyce Elizabeth Robson; two *s* one *d. Educ:* Medway Technical College; London University. Board of Trade: Patent Examiner, 1930-39; Principal, 1942-46; Assistant Secretary, 1946-65; Under Secretary, Department of Economic Affairs, 1965, Min. of Housing and Local Govt, 1969, DoE, 1970-71. *Recreation:* golf. *Address:* 9 Elmete Avenue, Leeds, West Yorkshire. *T:* Leeds 659706.

ONTARIO, Metropolitan of; *see* Toronto, Archbishop of.

ONTARIO, Bishop of, since 1981; **Rt. Rev. Allan Alexander Read;** *b* 19 Sept. 1923; *s of* Alex P. Read and Lillice M. Matthews; *m* 1949, Mary Beverly Roberts; two *s* two *d. Educ:* Trinity Coll., Univ. of Toronto (BA, LTh). Incumbent, Mono East and Mono West, 1947-54; Rector, Trinity Church, Barrie, 1954-71; Canon of St James Cathedral, Toronto, 1957; Archdeacon of Simcoe, 1961-72; Bishop Suffragan of Toronto, 1972-81. Hon. DD: Trinity Coll., Toronto, 1972; Wycliffe Coll., Toronto, 1972; Hon. STD Thornloe Coll., Sudbury. Citizen of the Year, Barrie, 1969; Honorary Reeve, Black Creek, Toronto, 1980. *Publication:* Shepherds in Green Pastures, 1952. *Recreation:* organ music. *Address:* 90 Johnston Street, Kingston, Ont. K7L 1X7, Canada. *Club:* Albany (Toronto).

OPHER, William David, CBE 1963; CEng, FIMechE; Joint Managing Director, Vickers Limited, 1967-68, retired; Pro-Chancellor, Lancaster University, 1978-80; *b* 30 May 1903; *s of* William Thomas Opher, London, and Margaret Mary Carson, Belfast; *m* 1930, Marie Dorothy, 3rd *d of* William Fane; one *s. Educ:* Borough Polytechnic, London. Apprenticed Arnold Goodwin & Son, Bankside; joined Vickers, 1928; Director: Vickers Ltd, Shipbuilding Group, 1955; Vickers Ltd, 1959; Rolls-Royce & Associates Ltd, 1959; Vickers & Bookers Ltd, 1959; British Hovercraft Corporation, 1966; Chairman Vickers, Ltd, Engineering Group, 1962-67. Mem. Council, Lancaster Univ., 1968; Governor, Polytechnic of the South Bank (formerly Borough Polytechnic), 1969-73. Freeman, City of London, 1949. Hon. LLD Lancaster, 1980. Serving Brother, Order of St John, 1962, Officer Brother, 1973. *Recreations:* golfing, fishing, shooting. *Address:* 1 Dunkeld, The Esplanade, Grange-over-Sands, Cumbria LA11 7HH. *T:* (home) Grange-over-Sands 3151. *Club:* Bexleyheath Golf.

OPIE, Evelyn Arnold; Matron, King's College Hospital, SE5, 1947-60; *b* 21 Aug. 1905; *d of* George and Annie Opie. *Educ:* Wentworth School for Girls, Bournemouth. Westminster Sick Children's Hosp., 1924-26 (sick children's trng); Guy's Hosp., SE1, 1926-29; SRN Oct. 1929. Midwifery Trng SCM, 1930, Sister, 1930-32, Guy's Hosp.; private nursing, Bournemouth, 1932-33; Sister (Radium Dept and Children's Ward), 1933-39, Administrative Sister, Asst Matron, Dep. Matron, 1939-47, Guy's Hosp. Diploma in Nursing of London Univ., 1935. *Recreations:* music, gardening. *Address:* 29 Muir House, Beaulieu Road, Dibden Purlieu, Southampton SO4 5NY. *T:* Hythe 842232.

OPIE, Iona Margaret Balfour; folklorist; *b* 13 Oct. 1923; *d of* late Sir Robert Archibald, CMG, DSO, MD, and of Olive Cant; *m* 1943, Peter Mason Opie (*d* 1982); two *s* one *d. Educ:* Sandecotes Sch., Parkstone. Served 1941-43, WAAF meteorological section. Hon. Mem., Folklore Soc., 1974. Coote-Lake Medal (jtly with husband), 1960. Hon. MA Oxon, 1962. *Publications:* (all with Peter Opie): I Saw Esau, 1947; The Oxford Dictionary of Nursery Rhymes, 1951; The Oxford Nursery Rhyme Book, 1955; Christmas Party Games, 1957; The Lore and Language of Schoolchildren, 1959; Puffin Book of Nursery Rhymes, 1963 (European Prize City of Caorle); Children's Games in Street and Playground, 1969 (Chicago Folklore Prize); The Oxford Book of Children's Verse, 1973; Three Centuries of Nursery Rhymes and Poetry for Children (exhibition catalogue), 1973, enl. edn-1977; The Classic Fairy Tales, 1974; A Nursery Companion, 1980. *Recreations:* reading, walking. *Address:* Westerfield House,West Liss, Hants.

OPIE, Redvers, CMG 1944; MA (Oxon and Harvard); PhD (Harvard); Director: Business International (New York), since 1954; Fomentadora Rural SA (Mexico); Mexico-US Chamber of Commerce, since 1979; Chairman: Amparo Servicios Turisticos SA, since 1979; Ecanal SA de CV, publisher of reports on Mexico, since 1978; *b* 20 January 1900; *s of* late James Reid and Bessie Hockaday Opie; naturalised US citizen, 1948, Mexican citizen, 1978; *m* 1st, 1929, Catharine Crombie Taussig (marr. diss., 1948), Cambridge, Mass; one *s* one *d* ; 2nd, 1971, Blanca Bolaños Aceves, México, DF. *Educ:* Rutherford Coll.; Univ. of Durham. Lectr in Economics, Univ. of Durham, 1919-23, Wellesley Coll. (USA), 1923-24, Harvard Univ. 1924-30; Fellow of Magdalen College, Oxford, 1931-45, Home Bursar, 1935-40 (on leave of absence for National Service from Sept. 1939); University Lecturer in Economic Science, 1936-39; Counsellor and Economic Adviser to British Embassy, Washington, DC (resigned 1946). Adviser, UK Delegation, International Food Conference, 1943; UK Delegate, International Monetary and Financial Conference, 1944; Member US Govt Mission, on Private Foreign Investment, to Turkey, 1953; Senior Staff Mem., Brookings Institution, Washington, DC, 1947-53. Economic Counsellor, Amer. Chamber of Commerce, Mexico City, 1966-78. President, American Ligurian Company Inc., New York, 1947-54. Gen. Editor, Oxford Economic Papers, 1938-39. *Publications:* (joint) Major Problems of US Foreign Policy, annually, 1947-52; Anglo-American Economic Relations, 1950; Current Issues in Foreign Economic Assistance, 1951; The Search For Peace Settlements, 1951; American Foreign Assistance, 1953; Selected papers on the Mexican and International Economies, 1966-68, 1968. *Recreations:* tennis and music. *Address:* Rio Lerma 156, 06500 Mexico, DF. *T:* 5145373. *Clubs:* Harvard (New York); Metropolitan (Washington, DC); Churubusco, University (Mexico).

OPIE, Roger Gilbert, CBE 1976; Fellow and Lecturer in Economics, New College, Oxford, since 1961; *b* Adelaide, SA, 23 Feb. 1927; *o s of* late Frank Gilbert Opie and late Fanny Irene Grace Opie (*née* Tregoning); *m* 1955, Norma Mary, *o d of* late Norman and Mary Canter; two *s* one *d. Educ:* Prince Alfred Coll. and Adelaide Univ., SA; Christ Church and Nuffield Coll., Oxford. BA 1st Cl. Hons 1948, MA Adelaide 1950; SA Rhodes Schol., 1951; Boulter Exhibnr, 1952; George Webb Medley Jun. Schol., 1952, Sen. Schol., 1953; PPE 1st Cl. 1953; Nuffield Coll. Studentship, 1954; BPhil 1954. Tutor and Lectr, Adelaide Univ., 1949-51; Asst Lectr and Lectr, LSE, 1954-61; Econ. Adviser, Econ. Section, HM Treasury, 1958-60; Asst Dir, HM Treasury Centre for Administrative Studies, 1964; Asst Dir, Planning Div., Dept of Economic Affairs, 1964-66; Economic Adviser to Chm., NBPI, 1967-70; Special Univ. Lectr in Econs, Oxford, 1970-75; Tutor and Sen. Tutor, Oxford Univ. Business Summer Sch., 1974-79. Vis. Prof., Brunel Univ., 1975-77. Member: Monopolies and Mergers Commn, 1968-81; Price Commn, 1977-80. Mem., ILO Mission to Ethiopia, 1982. City Councillor, Oxford, 1972-74; Oxford Dist Councillor, 1973-76. Economic Correspondent, New Statesman,

1967-71, 1974-76; Editor: The Bankers' Magazine, 1960-64; International Currency Review, 1970-71. Governor: Bryanston Sch.; Harpur Trust Schs, Bedford. FRSA 1980. *Publications:* co-author of a number of works in applied economics. *Recreations:* sailing, photography, domestic pyromania. *Address:* 8 New College Lane, Oxford OX1 3BL. *T:* Oxford 41769. *Club:* Lilliput Sailing (Dorset).

OPPENHEIM, Tan Sri Sir Alexander, Kt 1961; OBE 1955; FRSE; MA, DSc (Oxon); PhD (Chicago); Visiting Professor, University of Benin, Nigeria, 1973-77; Vice-Chancellor, University of Malaya, 1957-65 (Acting Vice-Chancellor, 1955); *b* 4 Feb. 1903; *o s* of late Rev. H. J. and Mrs F. Oppenheim; *m* 1930, Beatrice Templer (marr. diss. 1977), *y d* of Dr Otis B. Nesbit, Indiana, USA; one *d*; and two *s*. *Educ:* Manchester Grammar Sch.; Balliol Coll., Oxford (Scholar). Sen. Mathematical Schol., Oxf., 1926; Commonwealth Fund Fell., Chicago, 1927-30; Lectr, Edinburgh, 1930-31; Prof. of Mathematics, 1931-42, 1945-49; Dep. Principal, 1947, 1949, Raffles Coll., Singapore; Prof. of Mathematics, 1949-57; Dean, Faculty of Arts, 1949, 1951, 1953. Hon. degrees: DSc (Hong Kong) 1961; LLD: (Singapore) 1962; (Leeds) 1966; DLitt (Malaya) 1965. L/Bdr, SRA(V), POW (Singapore, Siam), 1942-45; Dean POW University, 1942; Pres. Malayan Mathematical Soc., 1951-55, 1957. Pres. Singapore Chess Club, 1956-60; Pres., Amer. Univs. Club, 1956. Chm. Bd of Management, Tropical Fish Culture Research Institute (Malacca), 1962; Member: Unesco-International Assoc. of Universities Study of Higher Education in Development of Countries of SE Asia, 1962; Academic Adv. Cttee, Univ. of Cape Coast, 1972. Visiting Professor: Univ. of Reading, in Dept of Mathematics, 1965-68; Univ. of Ghana, 1968-73. Alumni Medal, Univ. of Chicago Alumni Assoc., 1977. Panglima Mangku Negara (Fedn of Malaya), 1962; FWA, 1963. *Publications:* papers on mathematics in various periodicals. *Recreations:* chess, bridge, walking, swimming. *Address:* Matson House, Remenham, Henley-on-Thames RG9 3HB. *T:* Henley-on-Thames 2049. *Clubs:* Royal Over-Seas League; Selangor (Kuala Lumpur).

OPPENHEIM, Sir Duncan (Morris), Kt 1960; Adviser to British-American Tobacco Co. Ltd, 1972-74 (Chairman 1953-66, President, 1966-72); Chairman, Tobacco Securities Trust Co. Ltd, 1969-74; Deputy Chairman, Commonwealth Development Finance Co., 1968-74; *b* 6 Aug. 1904; *s* of Watkin Oppenheim, BA; TD; and Helen, 3rd *d* of Dr Duncan McKechnie; *m* 1st, 1932, Joyce Mary (*d* 1933), *d* of Stanley Mitcheson; no *c* ; 2nd, 1936, Susan May (*d* 1964), *e d* of Brig.-Gen. E. B. Macnaghten, CMG, DSO; one *s* one *d*. *Educ:* Repton Sch. Admitted Solicitor of the Supreme Court, 1929; Messrs Linklaters & Paines, London, Assistant Solicitor, 1929-34; joined British-American Tobacco Ltd group as a Solicitor, 1934; Director: British-American Tobacco Co. Ltd, 1943; Lloyds Bank Ltd, 1956-75; Equity and Law Life Assurance Society, 1966-80. Chairman: Council, Royal College of Art, 1956-72; Council of Industrial Design, 1960-72 (Mem. 1959); British Nat. Cttee of Internat. Chamber of Commerce, 1963-74; Overseas Investment Cttee CBI, 1964-74; RIIA (Chatham House), 1966-71; Member: Adv. Council, V&A Mus., 1967-80 (Chm. V&A Associates, 1976-79); Crafts Council (formerly Crafts Adv. Cttee), 1972- (acting Chm., 1977; Dep. Chm., 1978); Governing Body of Repton School, 1959-79; Chm. Court of Governors, Admin. Staff Coll., 1963-71. Hon. Dr and Senior Fellow, Royal College of Art; Hon. FSIA, 1972. Bicentenary Medal, RSA, 1969. *Recreations:* painting, sailing. *Address:* 43 Edwardes Square, Kensington, W8. *T:* 01-603 7431. *Clubs:* Athenæum; Royal Yacht Squadron.

OPPENHEIM, Rt. Hon. Mrs Henry M.; *see* Oppenheim, Rt Hon. Sally.

OPPENHEIM, Rt. Hon. Sally; PC 1979; MP (C) Gloucester since 1970; *b* 26 July 1930; *d* of Mark and Jeanette Viner; *m* 1949, Henry M. Oppenheim (*d* 1980); one *s* two *d*. *Educ:* Sheffield High Sch.; Lowther Coll., N Wales. Formerly: Exec. Dir, Industrial & Investment Services Ltd; Social Worker, School Care Dept, ILEA. Trustee, Clergy Rest House Trust. Vice Chm., 1971-73, Chm., 1973-74, Cons. Party Parly Prices and Consumer Protection Cttee; Opposition Spokesman on Prices and Consumer Protection, 1974-79; Mem. Shadow Cabinet, 1975-79; Min. of State (Consumer Affairs), Dept of Trade, 1979-82. Nat. Vice-Pres., Nat. Union of Townswomen's Guilds; Pres., Glos Dist Br., BRCS; *Recreations:* tennis, bridge. *Address:* 1 Ardmore Close, Tuffley, Gloucester; House of Commons, SW1. *Clubs:* (Pres.) Conservative (Gloucester).

OPPENHEIMER, Harry Frederick; Chairman: Anglo-American Corporation of SA Ltd, 1957-82 (Director, 1934-82); De Beers Consolidated Mines, Ltd; Director, Metals and Resources Corporation Ltd, and other companies in Anglo American and De Beers Groups; *b* Kimberley, S Africa, 28 Oct. 1908; *s* of late Sir Ernest Oppenheimer, DCL; LLD; *m* 1943, Bridget, *d* of late Foster McCall; one *s* one *d*. *Educ:* Charterhouse; Christ Church, Oxford (MA; Hon. Student). MP (SA) Kimberley City, 1948-58. Served 4th SA Armoured Car Regt 1940-45. Chancellor, Univ. of Cape Town; Hon. DEcon, Univ. of Natal; Hon. DLaws, Univs of Leeds, Rhodes and Witwatersrand. Instn MM Gold Medal, 1965. *Recreations:* horse breeding and racing. *Address:* Brenthurst, Parktown, Johannesburg, South Africa. *Clubs:* Brooks's; Rand, Inanda (Johannesburg); Kimberley (SA); Salisbury (Rhodesia).

OPPENHEIMER, Sir Michael (Bernard Grenville), 3rd Bt, *cr* 1921; BLitt, MA; *b* 27 May 1924; *s* of Sir Michael Oppenheimer, 2nd Bt, and Caroline Magdalen (who *m* 2nd, 1935, late Sir Ernest Oppenheimer), *d* of Sir Robert

G. Harvey, 2nd Bt; *S* father, 1933; *m* 1947, Laetitia Helen, BPhil, MA, *er d* of Sir Hugh Munro-Lucas-Tooth of Teananich, *qv* ; three *d*. *Educ:* Charterhouse; Christ Church, Oxford. Served with South African Artillery, 1942-45. Lecturer in Politics: Lincoln Coll., Oxford, 1955-68; Magdalen Coll., Oxford, 1966-68. *Heir:* none. *Address:* L'Aiguillon, Rue des Cotils, Grouville, Jersey. *Clubs:* Victoria (Jersey); Kimberley (Kimberley).

OPPENHEIMER, Peter Morris; Student of Christ Church, Oxford, and University Lecturer in Economics, since 1967; *b* 16 April 1938; *s* of Friedrich Rudolf and Charlotte Oppenheimer; *m* 1964, Catherine, *er d* of Dr Eliot Slater, *qv*, and Dr Lydia Pasternak; two *s* one *d*. *Educ:* Haberdashers' Aske's Sch.; The Queen's Coll., Oxford (BA 1961). National Service, RN, 1956-58. Bank for International Settlements, Basle, 1961-64; Research Fellow, Nuffield Coll., Oxford, 1964-67; Vis. Prof., London Graduate Sch. of Business Studies, 1976-77. Director: Investing in Success Equities Ltd, 1975-; Target Hldgs, 1982-; J. Rothschild Investment Management, 1982-. Mem., Royal Commn on Legal Services, 1976-79. Mem. Council, Trade Policy Research Centre, 1976-, and co-Editor, The World Economy, 1977-. Presenter: BBC radio File on 4, 1977-80; BBC TV Outlook, 1982. *Publications:* (ed) Issues in International Economics, 1980; contribs to symposia, conference procs, prof. jls, bank reviews, etc. *Recreations:* music, opera, amateur dramatics, skiing. *Address:* 8 Lathbury Road, Oxford OX2 7AU. *T:* Oxford 58226.

OPPENHEIMER, Sir Philip (Jack), Kt 1970; Chairman, The Diamond Trading Co. (Pty) Ltd; *b* 29 Oct. 1911; *s* of Otto and Beatrice Oppenheimer; *m* 1935, Pamela Fenn Stirling; one *s* one *d*. *Educ:* Harrow; Jesus Coll., Cambridge. Director: De Beers Consolidated Mines Ltd; Anglo American Corp. of SA Ltd. Bronze Cross of Holland, 1943; Commandeur, Ordre de Léopold, 1977. *Recreations:* golf, horse-racing and breeding. *Address:* 39 Egerton Terrace, SW3 2BU. *Clubs:* Jockey, Portland, White's.

OPPENHEIMER, Raymond Harry, CBE 1959; *b* 13 Nov. 1905; *s* of Louis Oppenheimer and Charlotte Emily Pollak. *Educ:* Harrow; Christ Church, Oxford. Served in RAFVR, 1940-45 (Fighter Controller). *Recreations:* golf, dog breeding (bull terriers). *Address:* White Waltham Place, Berkshire. *T:* Maidenhead 27103. *Clubs:* Royal and Ancient; Royal Lytham, etc.

OPPERMAN, Hon. Sir Hubert (Ferdinand), Kt 1968; OBE 1952; Australian High Commissioner in Malta, 1967-72; *b* 29 May 1904; Australian; *m* 1928, Mavys Paterson Craig; one *s* (one *d* decd). *Educ:* Armadale, Vic.; Bailieston, Vic. Served RAAF 1940-45; commissioned 1942. Commonwealth Public Service: PMG's Dept, 1918-20; Navigation Dept, Trade and Customs, 1920-22. Cyclist: Australian Road Champion, 1924, 1926, 1927, 1929; Winner French Bol d'Or, 1928, and Paris-Brest-Paris, 1931; holder, numerous world's track and road unpaced and motor paced cycling records. Director, Allied Bruce Small Pty Ltd, 1936-60. MHR for Corio, Vic., 1949-67; Convenor: Commonwealth Jubilee Sporting Sub-Cttee, 1951; Mem. Australian Delegn to CPA Conf., Nairobi, 1954; Chief Govt Whip, 1955-60; Minister for Shipping and Transport, 1960-63; Minister for Immigration, 1963-66. Nat. Patron, Aust. Sportsmen's Assoc., 1980-. KStJ (Bailiff Prior, Victoria, 1980-). Medals of City of Paris, 1971, Brest, 1971, Verona, 1972; Médaille Mérite, French Cycling Fedn, 1978. *Publication:* Pedals, Politics and People (autobiog.), 1977. *Recreations:* cycling, swimming. *Address:* c/o Bruce Small Enterprises, 12 Marine Parade, St Kilda, Vic 3182, Australia. *T:* 534-6288. *Clubs:* USI, Air Force (Victoria).

ORAM, family name of **Baron Oram.**

ORAM, Baron *cr* 1975 (Life Peer), of Brighton, E Sussex; **Albert Edward Oram;** *b* 13 Aug. 1913; *s* of Henry and Ada Edith Oram; *m* Frances Joan, *d* of Charles and Dorothy Barber, Lewes; two *s*. *Educ:* Burgess Hill Element. Sch.; Brighton Grammar Sch.; University of London (London School of Economics and Institute of Education). Formerly a teacher. Served War 1942-45; Royal Artillery, Normandy and Belgium. Research Officer, Co-operative Party, 1946-55. MP (Lab and Co-op) East Ham South, 1955-Feb. 1974; Parly Secretary, ODM, 1964-69; a Lord in Waiting (Govt Whip), 1976-78. Chm., Co-op. Devel. Agency, 1978-81. Co-ordinator, Develt Programmes, Internat. Co-operative Alliance, 1971-73; Develt Administrator, Intermediate Technol. Develt Gp. Mem., Commonwealth Develt Corp., 1975-76. *Recreations:* country walking, cricket, chess. *Address:* 19 Ridgeside Avenue, Patcham, Brighton BN1 8WD. *T:* Brighton 505333. *Club:* MCC.

ORAM, Rt. Rev. Kenneth Cyril; *see* Grahamstown, Bishop of.

ORAM, Samuel, MD (London); FRCP; Consultant Cardiologist and Emeritus Lecturer; former Senior Physician, and Director, Cardiac Department, King's College Hospital; Censor, Royal College of Physicians; Medical Adviser: Rio Tinto Zinc Corporation Ltd; Sun Life Assurance Co. of Canada; *b* 11 July 1913; *s* of Samuel Henry Nathan Oram, London; *m* 1940, Ivy, *d* of Raffaele Amato; two *d*. *Educ:* King's College, London; King's College Hospital, London. Senior Scholar, KCH, London; Sambrooke Medical Registrar, KCH. Served War of 1939-45, as Lt-Col, RAMC. Examiner in Medicine for RCP and Univs of Cambridge and London; Examiner: in Pharmacology and Materia Medica, The Conjoint Bd; in Medicine, The Worshipful Soc. of Apothecaries. Member: Assoc. of Physicians; Br. Cardiac Society; American Heart Assoc.; Canada Club; Corresp. Member Australasian Cardiac Soc. *Publications:* Clinical Heart

Disease (textbook), 1971, 2nd edn 1981; various cardiological and medical articles in Quart. Jl Med., British Heart Jl, BMJ, Brit. Encyclopaedia of Medical Practice, The Practitioner, etc. *Recreation:* golf (execrable). *Address:* 73 Harley Street, W1. *T:* 01-935 9942. *Club:* Athenæum.

ORANMORE and BROWNE, 4th Baron (Ireland), *cr* 1836; Baron Mereworth of Mereworth Castle (UK), *cr* 1926; **Dominick Geoffrey Edward Browne;** *b* 21 Oct. 1901; *e s* of 3rd Baron and Lady Olwen Verena Ponsonby (*d* 1927), *e d* of 8th Earl of Bessborough; *S* father, 1927; *m* 1st, 1925, Mildred Helen (who obtained a divorce, 1936; she *d* 1980), *e d* of Hon. Thomas Egerton; two *s* one *d* (and two *d* decd); 2nd, 1936, Oonagh (marr. diss., 1950), *d* of late Hon. Ernest Guinness; one *s* (and two *s* decd); 3rd, 1951, Sally Gray, 5b Mount Street, London, W. *Educ:* Eton; Christ Church, Oxford. *Heir: s* Hon. Dominick Geoffrey Thomas Browne [*b* 1 July 1929; *m* 1957, Sara Margaret (marr. diss. 1974), *d* of late Dr Herbert Wright, 59 Merrion Square, Dublin, and late Mrs C. A. West, Cross-in-Hand, Sussex]. *Address:* 52 Eaton Place, SW1. *Club:* Kildare Street (Dublin).
See also Hon. *M. A. R. Cayzer.*

ORCHARD, Edward Eric, CBE 1966 (OBE 1959); *b* 12 Nov. 1920. *Educ:* King's Sch., Grantham; Jesus Coll., Oxford (MA). War Service, 1941-46; FO, and HM Embassy, Moscow, 1948-51; Lectr in Russian, Oxford, 1951-52; HM Embassy Moscow and FCO, 1953-76 (Dir of Res., 1970-76). *Publications:* various articles. *Recreations:* swimming, gardening, youth and social welfare. *Address:* Sturt Meadow House, Haslemere, Surrey. *T:* Haslemere 3034. *Club:* Athenæum.

ORCHARD, Peter Francis, CBE 1982; Chief Executive, The De La Rue Co. plc, since 1977, Director, since 1963; *b* 25 March 1927; *s* of Edward Henslowe Orchard and Agnes Marjory Willett; *m* 1955, Helen Sheridan; two *s* two *d*. *Educ:* Downside Sch., Bath; Magdalene Coll., Cambridge (MA). CBIM. Service, KRRC, 1944-48. Joined Thomas De La Rue & Co. Ltd, 1950; Managing Director: Thomas De La Rue (Brazil), 1959-61; Thomas De La Rue International, 1962-70. Dir, Delta Group plc, 1981-. Mem., Court of Assistants, Drapers' Co., 1974-, Master 1982. *Recreations:* gardening, swimming, building, cricket. *Address:* Willow Cottage, Little Hallingbury, Bishop's Stortford, Herts CM22 7PX. *T:* Bishop's Stortford 54101. *Clubs:* Travellers', MCC.

ORCHARD-LISLE, Aubrey Edwin, CBE 1973; Consultant Partner, Healey & Baker, Surveyors, London, Amsterdam, Paris, New York and Brussels (Senior Partner until 1973); *b* 12 March 1908; *s* of late Edwin Orchard-Lisle and late Lucy Ellen Lock; *m* 1934, Phyllis Muriel Viall (*d* 1981); one *s* one *d*. *Educ:* West Buckland Sch., N Devon; Coll. of Estate Management. FRICS. Joined Healey & Baker, 1926. Governor, Guy's Hosp. 1953-74; Vice-Chm. of Bd, 1963-74; Governor, Guy's Hosp. Med. Sch.; Chm., Special Trustees, Guy's Hosp., 1974-; Mem., Lambeth, Southwark, Lewisham, AHA (Teaching) 1974-79; Property Consultant, NCB Superannuation Schemes, 1953-; Mem. Bd, Gen. Practice Finance Corp., 1966-80; Chm., Adv. Panel for Institutional Finance in New Towns, 1969-80; part-time Mem., Nat. Bus Co., 1971-77 (Member: Nat. Bus Co. Property Cttee, 1971-; Investment Adv. Panel, Nat. Bus Co. Pension Schemes (Best (Estates) Ltd), 1974-). *Recreations:* gardening and gardens, travel. *Address:* 30 Mount Row, Grosvenor Square, W1Y 5DA. *T:* 01-499 6470; White Walls, Quarry Wood Road, Marlow, Bucks. *T:* Marlow 2573. *Clubs:* St Stephen's Constitutional, Naval and Military, Buck's, MCC.

ORD, Andrew James B.; *see* Blackett-Ord.

ORDE, Alan C. C.; *see* Campbell Orde.

ORDE, Denis Alan; His Honour Judge Orde; a Circuit Judge, since 1979; *b* 28 Aug. 1932; *s* of John Orde, CBE, Littlehoughton Hall, Northumberland, and late Charlotte Lilian Orde, County Alderman; *m* 1961, Jennifer Jane, *d* of Dr John Longworth, Masham, Yorks; two *d*. *Educ:* Oxford Univ. (MA). Served Army, 1950-52, 2nd Lieut 1951; TA, 1952-64 (RA). Pres., Oxford Univ. Conserv. Assoc., 1954; Mem. Cttee, Oxford Union, 1954-55; Vice-Chm., Fedn of Univ. Conserv. Assocs., 1955. Called to Bar, Inner Temple, 1956; Pupil Studentship, 1956; Profumo Prize, 1959. North-Eastern Circuit, 1958; Northern Area Legal Aid Cttee, 1969-. Asst Recorder: Kingston upon Hull, 1970; Sheffield, 1970-71; a Recorder of the Crown Court, 1972-79. Contested (C): Consett, Gen. Elec. 1959, Newcastle upon Tyne West, Gen. Elec. 1966, Sunderland South, Gen. Elec. 1970. *Recreations:* listening to music; cricket, golf, painting. *Address:* Chollerton Grange, Chollerton, near Hexham, Northumberland NE46 4TF; 11 King's Bench Walk, Temple, EC4. *Clubs:* Carlton, Coningsby, United and Cecil.

ORDE, Sir John (Alexander) Campbell-, 6th Bt *cr* 1790, of Morpeth; *b* 11 May 1943; *s* of Sir Simon Arthur Campbell-Orde, 5th Bt, TD, and of Eleanor, *e d* of Col Humphrey Watts, OBE, TD, Haslington Hall, Cheshire; *S* father, 1969; *m* 1973, Lacy Ralls, *d* of Grady Gallant, Nashville, USA; one *s* three *d*. *Educ:* Gordonstoun. *Heir: s* John Simon Arthur Campbell-Orde, *b* 15 Aug. 1981. *Address:* 228 West Hillwood Drive, Nashville, Tennessee, USA. *Clubs:* Caledonian, Lansdowne.

ORDE-POWLETT, family name of **Baron Bolton.**

O'REILLY, Anthony John Francis, (Tony O'Reilly); President and Chief Executive Officer, H. J. Heinz Co. Inc., since 1979; *b* Dublin, 7 May 1936; *o c* of J. P. O'Reilly, former Inspector-General of Customs; *m* 1962, Susan, *d* of Keith Cameron, Australia; three *s* three *d* (of whom two *s* one *d* are triplets). *Educ:* Belvedere Coll., Dublin; University Coll., Dublin (BCL 1958); Bradford Univ. (PhD 1980). Admitted Solicitor, 1958. Industrial Consultant, Weston Evans UK, 1958-60; PA to Chm., Suttons Ltd, Cork, 1960-62; Chief Exec. Officer, Irish Dairy Bd, 1962-66; Man. Dir, Irish Sugar Bd, 1966-69; Man. Dir, Erin Foods Ltd, 1966-69; Jt Man. Dir, Heinz-Erin, 1967-70; Man. Dir, H. J. Heinz Co. Ltd, UK, 1969-71; Sen. Vice-Pres., N America and Pacific, H. J. Heinz Co., 1971-72; Exec. Vice-Pres. and Chief Op. Off., 1972-73, Pres. and Chief Operating Officer, 1973-79, H. J. Heinz Co. Lectr in Business Management, UC Cork, 1960-62. Director: Robt McCowen & Sons Ltd, 1961-62; Agricl Credit Corp. Ltd, 1965-66; Nitrigin Eireann Teoranta, 1965-66; Allied Irish Investment Bank Ltd, 1968-71; Thyssen-Bornemisza Co., 1970-72; Ulster Bank Ltd, 1973; Independent Newspapers (Vice Chm., 1973-80; Chm., 1980-); Nat. Mine Service Co., 1973-76; Mobil, 1979-; Bankers Trust Co., 1980-; Allegheny Internat. Inc., 1982-; Chm., Fitzwilliam Securities Ltd, 1971-77; Fitzwilton Ltd, 1978- (Dep. Chm., 1972-78). Member: Incorp. Law Soc.; Council, Irish Management Inst.; Hon. LLD: Wheeling Coll., 1974; Rollins Coll., 1978; Trinity Coll., 1978. *Publications:* Prospect, 1962; Developing Creative Management, 1970; The Conservative Consumer, 1971; Food for Thought, 1972. *Recreations:* Rugby (played for Ireland 29 times), tennis. *Address:* 835 Fox Chapel Road, Pittsburgh, Pa 15238, USA; Castlemartin, Kilcullen, Co. Kildare, Ireland. *Clubs:* Annabels; Stephen's Green (Dublin); Union League (New York); Duquesne, Allegheny, Fox Chapel, Pittsburgh Golf (Pittsburgh); Rolling Rock (Ligonier); Lyford Cay (Bahamas).

O'REILLY, Francis Joseph; Director, Irish Distillers Group Ltd (Chairman, 1966-83); Chairman, Ulster Bank Ltd, since 1982 (Deputy Chairman, 1974-82); Director, National Westminster Bank, since 1982; *b* 15 Nov. 1922; *s* of Lt-Col Charles J. O'Reilly, DSO, MC, MB, KSG and Dorothy Mary Martin; *m* 1950, Teresa Mary, *e d* of Captain John Williams, MC; three *s* seven *d*. *Educ:* St Gerard's Sch., Bray; Ampleforth Coll., York; Trinity Coll., Dublin (BA, BAI). Served HM Forces, RE, 1943-46. John Power & Son, 1946-66 (Chm., 1955-66); Chm., Player & Wills (Ire.) Ltd, 1964-81; Dir, Ulster Bank Ltd, 1961-. Pres., Equestrian Fedn of Ireland, 1963-79; Chm., Royal Dublin Soc., 1980- (Mem. Cttees, 1959-80). LLD *hc* Univ. of Dublin, 1978. *Recreations:* fox-hunting, racing, gardening. *Address:* Rathmore, Naas, Co. Kildare, Ireland. *T:* Naas 97416. *Clubs:* Kildare Street and University (Dublin); Irish Turf (The Curragh, Co. Kildare).

O'REILLY, William John, CB 1981; OBE 1971; Commissioner of Taxation, Australian Taxation Office, since 1976; *b* 15 June 1919; *s* of William O'Reilly and Ruby (*née* McCrudden). *Educ:* Nudgee Coll., Brisbane, Qld; Univ. of Queensland (Associate in Accountancy). Served RAAF, 1942-44. Joined Australian Public Service, 1946; Australian Taxation Office: Brisbane, 1946-55; Melbourne, 1955-61; Canberra, 1961-; Asst Comr of Taxation, 1963; First Asst Comr of Taxation, 1964; Second Comr of Taxation (Statutory Office), 1967. *Recreations:* reading, walking. *Address:* Canberra Rex Hotel, Northbourne Avenue, Braddon, ACT 2601, Australia. *T:* 47-4670. *Clubs:* Commonwealth, Canberra (Canberra).

ORESCANIN, Bogdan; Ambassador of Yugoslavia to the Court of St James's, 1973-76; *b* 27 Oct. 1916; *m* 1947, Sonja Dapcevic; no *c*. *Educ:* Faculty of Law, Zagreb; Higher Mil. Academy. Organised uprising in Croatia; i/c various mil. and polit. duties in Nat. Liberation Struggle, War of 1939-45; Asst, then DCGS and Asst Defence Sec. of State, Yugoslav People's Army (Col General); formerly Mem. Fed. Parlt, Mem. Council of Fedn, Chm. Parly Cttee for Nat. Defence, Mem. For. Affairs Cttee of Fed. Parlt and Mem. Exec. Bd, Yugoslav Gp of IPU; Mil. Attaché in Gt Britain, 1952-54; Yugoslav Ambassador, People's Republics of China, Korea and Vietnam, 1970-73. Holds various Yugoslav and foreign decorations. *Publications:* articles on military-political theory; (study) Military Aspects of the Struggle for World's Peace, National Independence and Socialism. *Address:* Federal Secretariat for Foreign Affairs, Kneza Milosa 24, 11000 Belgrade, Yugoslavia.

ORGAN, (Harold) Bryan; painter; *b* Leicester, 31 Aug. 1935; *o c* of late Harold Victor Organ and Helen Dorothy Organ; *m* (marr. diss. 1981); *m* 1982, Sandra Mary Mills. *Educ:* Wyggeston Sch., Leicester; Coll. of Art, Loughborough; Royal Academy Schs, London. Lectr in Drawing and Painting, Loughborough Coll. of Art, 1959-65. One-man exhibns: Leicester Museum and Art Gallery, 1959; Redfern Gallery, 1967, 1969, 1971, 1973, 1975, 1978, 1980; Leicester 1973, 1976; New York, 1976, 1977; Turin, 1981. Represented: Kunsthalle, Darmstadt, 1968; Mostra Mercatao d'Arte Contemporanea, Florence, 1969; 3rd Internat. Exhibn of Drawing, Germany, 1970; Sao Paolo Museum of Art, Brazil; Baukunst Gallery, Cologne, 1977. Works in public and private collections in England, USA, Germany, France, Canada, Italy. Portraits include: Malcolm Muggeridge, 1966; Sir Michael Tippett, 1966; David Hicks, 1968; Mary Quant, 1969; Nadia Nerina, 1969; Princess Margaret, 1970; Dr Roy Strong, 1971; Elton John, 1973; Lester Piggott, 1973; Lord Ashby, 1975; Sir Rex Richards, 1977; Harold Macmillan, 1980; Prince of Wales, 1981; Lady Diana Spencer, 1981; Lord Denning, 1982; Jim Callaghan, 1982. Hon. MA Loughborough, 1974. *Address:* c/o Redfern Gallery, 20 Cork Street, W1. *T:* 01-734 1732.

ORGANE, Sir Geoffrey (Stephen William), Kt 1968; MD, FFARCS; FRCS; Emeritus Professor of Anæsthetics, University of London, Westminster Medical School; formerly: Civilian Consultant in Anæsthetics to Royal Navy; Consultant Adviser in Anæsthetics, Ministry of Health; *b* Madras, 25 Dec. 1908; *er s* of Rev. William Edward Hartland Organe, K-i-H, and Alice (*née* Williams); *m* 1935, Margaret Mary Bailey, *e d* of Rev. David Bailey Davies, MC; one *s* two *d*. *Educ*: Taunton Sch.; Christ's Coll., Cambridge; Westminster Med. Sch. MRCS, LRCP, 1933; DA, RCP&S, 1937; MA, MD Cantab 1941; FFARCS 1948; FRCS 1965. Various resident appointments and first Anæsthetic Registrar (1938-39), Westminster Hospital; two years in general practice. Hon. Secretary, Medical Research Council's Anæsthetics Sub-Committee of Committee on Traumatic Shock, 1941-47; formerly Hon. Sec. Anæsthetics Cttee, Cttee on Analgesia in Midwifery; Vice-Pres., BMA Sect. Anæsthetics, Harrogate, 1949, Toronto, 1955; Pres., World Fedn of Socs. of Anæsthesiologists, 1964-68 (Sec.-Treas., 1955-64); Mem. Coun., RCS, 1958-61, Joseph Clover Lectr, Fac. of Anæsthetics; Royal Society of Medicine: Mem. Council; Hon. Sec. 1953-58; Hon. Fellow, 1974; Pres. Sect. of Anæsthetics, 1949-50 (Hon. Mem.); Assoc. of Anæsthetists of Gt Brit. and Ire.: Hon. Sec. 1949-53; Vice-Pres. 1953-54; Mem. Council, 1957-59; Pres. 1954-57; Hon. Mem., 1974; John Snow Silver Medal, 1972; Mem. Cttee of Anæsthetists' Group of BMA (Chm. 1955-58); Pres. SW Metropolitan Soc. of Anæsthetists, 1957-59; Dean, Faculty of Anæsthetists, 1958-61; Examr in Anæsthetics, Conjoint Bd; Examiner for FFARCS. Visited Italy, Turkey, Greece, Syria, Lebanon for Brit. Council; Denmark, Norway for WHO; also Portugal, France, Switzerland, Spain, Belgium, Netherlands, Germany, Finland, USA, Canada, Argentina, Australia, Venezuela, Mexico, Uganda, Peru, Japan, Hong Kong, Philippines, Brazil, Ceylon, Egypt, India, Iran, Israel, Malaysia, Uruguay, Austria, Sweden, Poland, USSR, Bulgaria, Czechoslovakia, Malta. Hon. or Corr. Mem., Danish, Argentine, Australian, Austrian, Brazilian, Canadian, Greek, Portuguese, French, German, Italian, Philippine, Spanish, Venezuelan Societies of Anæsthetists; Hon. FFARACS 1957; Hon. FFARCS 1975. *Publications*: various articles and chapters in medical journals and textbooks. *Recreations*: travel, gardening, photography, competitive sports; (formerly Pres., Vice-Pres., Hon. Treas., Capt. 1933) United Hospitals Athletic Club. *Address*: 38 Newlands Park, Seaton, Devon EX12 2SF. *T*: Seaton 20266.

ORGEL, Leslie Eleazer, DPhil Oxon, MA; FRS 1962; Senior Fellow, Salk Institute, La Jolla, California, USA, and Adjunct Professor, University of California, San Diego, Calif, since 1964; *b* 12 Jan. 1927; *s* of Simon Orgel; *m* 1950, Hassia Alice Levinson; two *s* one *d*. *Educ*: Dame Alice Owen's Sch., London. Reader, University Chemical Laboratory, Cambridge, 1963-64, and Fellow of Peterhouse, 1957-64. *Publication*: An Introduction to Transition-Metal Chemistry, Ligand-Field Theory, 1960; The Origins of Life: molecules and natural selection, 1973. *Address*: Salk Institute, PO Box 85800, San Diego, Calif 92138, USA.

ORIGO, Marchesa Iris, DBE 1977; FRSL; author; *b* Birdlip, Glos, 15 August 1902; *o d* of W. Bayard Cutting, Westbrook, Long Island, USA, and Lady Sybil Cuffe; *m* 1924, Marchese Antonio Origo (*d* 1976); two *d*. *Educ*: privately, mostly in Florence. Holds honorary doctorates from Smith College and Wheaton College, USA; Isabella d'Este medal for essays and historical studies, Mantua, Italy, 1966. *Publications*: Leopardi, a biography, 1935 (revised 1953); Allegra, 1935; Tribune of Rome, 1938; War in Val d'Orcia, 1947; Giovanna and Jane, 1948; The Last Attachment, 1949; The Merchant of Prato, 1957; A Measure of Love, 1957; The World of San Bernardino, 1963; Images and Shadows, Part of a Life, 1970; The Vagabond Path: an anthology, 1972; Bearing Witness, 1983. *Recreations*: travel, gardening. *Address*: La Foce, Chianciano Terme, 53042 Siena, Italy. *T*: Rome 6541324.

ORKNEY, 8th Earl of, *cr* 1696; Cecil O'Bryen Fitz-Maurice; Viscount of Kirkwall and Baron of Dechmont, 1696; *b* 3 July 1919; *s* of Douglas Frederick Harold FitzMaurice (*d* 1937; *g g s* of 5th Earl) and Dorothy Janette (who *m* 2nd, 1939, Commander E. T. Wiggins, DSC, RN), *d* of late Capt. Robert Dickie, RN; *S* kinsman 1951; *m* 1953, Rose Katharine Durk, *yr d* of late J. W. D. Silley, Brixham. Joined RASC, 1939; served in North Africa, Italy, France and Germany, 1939-46, and in Korea, 1950-51. *Heir*: kinsman Oliver Peter St John [*b* 27 Feb. 1938; *m* 1963, Mary Juliet, *d* of W. G. Scott-Brown, *qv*; one *s* four *d*]. *Address*: Summerlanes, Princes Road, Ferndown, Dorset.

ORLEBAR, Michael Keith Orlebar S.; *see* Simpson-Orlebar.

ORMANDY, Eugene, KBE (Hon.) 1976; MusD; Conductor and Music Director of Philadelphia Orchestra, 1936-80, now Conductor Laureate; *b* 18 Nov. 1899; Hungarian; *s* of Benjamin and Rosalie Ormandy; *m* 1st, 1922, Steffy Goldner (marr. diss. 1947; decd), harpist, NY Philharmonic Orchestra; no *c* ; 2nd, 1950, Margaret Frances Hitsch. *Educ*: Royal State Acad. of Music, BA 1914; state diploma for art of violin playing, 1916, and as prof., 1917; Grad. Gymnasium; student Univ. of Budapest, 1917-20. Hon. MusD: Hamline Univ., St Paul, 1934; Univ. of Pennsylvania, 1937; Philadelphia Academy of Music, 1939; Curtis Inst. of Music, 1946; Temple Univ., 1949; Univ. of Michigan, 1952; Lehigh Univ., 1953; Villanova Univ., 1968; Rensselaer Polytechnic Inst., 1968; Peabody Inst., 1968; Univ. of Illinois, 1969; Doctor of Letters: Clark Univ., 1956, Miami Univ., 1959, Rutgers Univ., 1960, Long Island Univ., 1965; Lafayette Coll., 1966; Jefferson Medical Coll., 1973; Moravian Coll., 1976; holds many other hon. degrees. Toured Hungary as child prodigy; Head of master classes, State Conservatorium of Music,

Budapest, at age of 20; arrived in United States, 1921, naturalised 1927; substituted for Toscanini as Conductor Philadelphia Orchestra; Conductor Minneapolis Symphony Orch., 1931-36; toured Australia, 1944, S America, 1946, Europe, 1950, 1951, 1952, 1953, 1954, 1955, 1957, 1958, 1975, Japan, 1967, 1972, 1978. Appeared Edinburgh Festival, 1955, 1957. Caballero, Order of Merit of Juan Pablo Duarte, Dominican Republic, 1945; Commandeur, French Legion of Honour, 1958; Knight, Order of Dannebrog, 1st cl., 1952; Knight 1st cl., Order of the White Rose, Finland, 1955; Comdr. Order of Lion of Finland, 1966; Honor Cross for Arts and Sciences, Austria, 1967; Golden Medallion, Vienna Philharmonic Orch., 1967; Freedom Medal, USA, 1970; Commendatore, Italy, 1972; Gold Baton Award, Amer. Symph. Orch. League, 1979. *Address*: 1420 Locust Street, Philadelphia, Pa 19102, USA.

ORMATHWAITE, 6th Baron, *cr* 1868; John Arthur Charles Walsh, Bt 1804; Farming since 1950; *b* 25 December 1912; *s* of 5th Baron Ormathwaite and Lady Margaret Jane Douglas-Home (*d* 1955), 3rd *d* of 12th Earl of Home; *S* father, 1944; unmarried. *Educ*: Eton College; Trinity College, Cambridge. *Heir*: none. *Address*: Pen-y-Bont Hall, Llandrindod Wells, Powys. *T*: Pen-y-Bont 228.

ORME, Ion G.; *see* Garnett-Orme.

ORME, John Samuel, CB 1963; OBE (mil.) 1945; *b* 7 May 1916; *m* 1940, Jean Harris; three *s* one *d*. *Educ*: The High School, Newcastle under Lyme; St John's College, Oxford; Ecole des Sciences Politiques, Paris. BA 1937, 1st Cl. Hons, Sch. of Mod. Hist.; MA 1957. Air Ministry, 1938; served RAF, 1941-45; Wing Comdr, 1944 (despatches, OBE); Air Ministry, 1945; Internat. Staff of NATO, Paris, 1954-57; Assistant Under Secretary of State, Air Ministry, 1957-58, and again 1960-64; Under-Secretary; Cabinet Office, 1958-60; Min. of Transport, 1964-66; Assistant Under-Secretary of State: Welsh Office, 1966-70; DHSS, 1970-75. LSE, 1976-77. Cleveland, USA, Foundation Fellow, 1977. *Address*: Third House, Manor Crescent, Seer Green, Bucks HP9 2QX. *T*: Beaconsfield 5920. *Club*: Reform.

ORME, Rt. Hon. Stanley, PC 1974; MP (Lab) Salford West since 1964; *b* 5 April 1923; *s* of Sherwood Orme, Sale, Cheshire; *m* 1951, Irene Mary, *d* of Vernon Fletcher Harris, Worsley, Lancashire. *Educ*: elementary and technical schools; National Council of Labour Colleges and Workers' Educational Association classes. Warrant Officer, Air-Bomber Navigator, Royal Air Force Bomber Command, 1942-47. Joined the Labour party, 1944; contested (Lab) Stockport South, 1959. Minister of State: NI Office, 1974-76; DHSS, 1976; Minister of State for Social Security, 1976-77, Minister for Social Security, and Mem. Cabinet, 1977-79; Opposition Spokesman on Health and Social Services, June-Nov. 1979, on Industry, Nov. 1979-. Member of Sale Borough Council, 1958-65; Member: AEU; District Committee, Manchester; shop steward. *Address*: House of Commons, SW1; 47 Hope Road, Sale, Cheshire. *Clubs*: ASE (Altrincham); Ashfield Labour (Salford).

ORMEROD, Major Sir (Cyril) Berkeley, KBE 1960 (CBE 1954, OBE 1946); Director, Public Relations, British Information Services, New York, 1945-62 (Financial Adviser, British Press Service, 1940-45); formerly Chairman, Director and Trustee of public companies and trusts, now retired; *b* London, 3 Oct. 1897; *s* of late Ernest Berkeley Ormerod, Ashton-under-Lyne, Lancs, and late Alice Heys; *m* 1962, Beatrice (*d* 1981), widow of Frederick Sigrist, Nassau, Bahamas. *Educ*: Colet Court; St Paul's Sch.; Royal Military Academy. Royal Regt of Artillery, 1916-26; European War, active service in France and Belgium, 1917-18. London Stock Exchange (Foster and Braithwaite), 1929-39. Regular contributor to Financial Times, Investor's Chronicle, Barron's (New York), 1934-39. Member UK Delegation, UN organizational Conference, San Francisco, 1945; Public Relations Adviser to Secretary of State (late Ernest Bevin), Foreign Ministers' Conference, New York, 1946. Specially attached to the Ambassador's Staff as Press Adviser to the Royal Party during American visit of the Queen and the Duke of Edinburgh, Oct. 1957; Press Advisor to the Governor of the Bahamas during Nassau talks between Prime Minister Macmillan and late President Kennedy, Dec. 1962. Member of The Pilgrims; RIIA (Chatham House); FIPR; Hon. Life Mem., Assoc. of Radio and TV News Analysts, USA. *Publication*: Dow Theory Applied to the London Stock Exchange, 1937. *Recreations*: cricket (Oxfordshire, The Army, RA, MCC, I Zingari, Free Foresters, etc), golf (won Army Championship, 1924), bridge. *Address*: PO Box N 969, Nassau, Bahamas. *Clubs*: Cavalry and Guards, Boodle's, MCC; Royal and Ancient (St Andrews); Berkshire Golf; Knickerbocker, Lotos, Dutch Treat (New York); Travellers' (Paris); Lyford Cay (Nassau).

ORMESSON, Comte Jean d'; Chevalier des Palmes académiques 1962; Commandeur des Arts et Lettres 1973; Chevalier de la Légion d'honneur 1973; Officier de l'Ordre national du Mérite, 1978; Membre Académie française 1973; Secretary-General, International Council for Philosophy and Humanistic Studies (UNESCO), since 1971 (Deputy, 1950-71); writer and journalist; *b* 16 June 1925; 2nd *s* of Marquis d'Ormesson, French diplomat and Ambassador; *m* 1962, Françoise Béghin; one *d*. *Educ*: Ecole Normale Supérieure. MA (History), Agrégé de philosophie. Mem. French delegns to various internat. confs, 1945-48; Mem. staff of various Govt Ministers, 1958-66; Mem. Council ORTF, 1960-62; Mem. Control Cttee of Cinema, 1962-69; Mem. TV Programmes Cttee, ORTF, 1973-74. Dep. Editor, Diogenes, 1952-72, Mem. Managing Cttee, 1972; Dir, 1974-77, Editor-in-Chief, 1975-77, Le Figaro. *Publications*: L'Amour est un plaisir, 1956; Du côté de chez Jean, 1959; Un amour pour rien, 1960; Au revoir et merci, 1966; Les Illusions de la mer, 1968; La Gloire de l'Empire, 1971 (Grand Prix du Roman de l'Académie française), Amer. edn (The Glory of the Empire), 1975, Eng. edn 1976; Au Plaisir de Dieu, 1974, Amer. edn (Àt God's Pleasure), 1977, Eng. edn 1978; Le Vagabond qui passe sous une ombrelle trouée, 1978; Dieu, savie, son œuvre, 1981; articles and essays, columns in Le Figaro, Le Monde, Le Point, La Revue des Deux Mondes, La Nouvelle Revue Française. *Recreation:* ski-navigation. *Address:* CIPSH-UNESCO, 1 rue Miollis, 75732 Paris Cedex 15, France. *T:* 577-16-10; (home) 10 avenue du Parc Saint-James, 92200 Neuilly-sur-Seine, France.

ORMOND, Sir John (Davies Wilder), Kt 1964; BEM 1940; JP; Chairman: Shipping Corporation of New Zealand Ltd, since 1973; Container Terminals Ltd, since 1975; Exports and Shipping Council, since 1964; *b* 8 Sept. 1905; *s* of J. D. Ormond and Gladys Wilder; *m* 1939, Judith Wall; four *s* one *d.* *Educ:* Christ's Coll., Christchurch, New Zealand. Chairman, Waipukurau Farmers Union, 1929; President, Waipukurau Jockey Club, 1950; Member, New Zealand Meat Producers Board, 1934-72, Chm., 1951-72. Active Service Overseas (Middle East), 1940. JP, NZ, 1945. DSc (*hc*), 1972. *Recreations:* tennis, polo, Rugby Union football. *Address:* Wallingford, Waipukurau, New Zealand. *T:* Waipukurau 542M. *Club:* Hawke's Bay (New Zealand).

ORMONDE, 7th Marquess of, *cr* 1825; **James Hubert Theobald Charles Butler,** MBE 1921; Earl of Ormonde, 1328; Viscount Thurles, 1525; Earl of Ossory, 1527; Baron Ormonde (UK), 1821; 31st Hereditary Chief Butler of Ireland; retired; *b* 19 April 1899; *s* of Lord Theobald Butler (4th *s* of 2nd Marquess) and Annabella Brydon (*d* 1943), *o d* of Rev. Cosmo Reid Gordon, DD; *S* cousin, 1971; *m* 1st, 1935, Nan Gilpin (*d* 1973); two *d* ; 2nd, 1976, Elizabeth Liles (*d* 1980). *Educ:* Haileybury College; RMC Sandhurst. Commissioned Dec. 1917, King's Royal Rifle Corps; resigned commission, May 1926 (Lieut). Various business connections in USA. *Heir:* (to earldoms of Ormonde and Ossory) Viscount Mountgarret, *qv. Address:* 10 N Washington, Apt 120, Hinsdale, Ill 60521, USA. *Club:* Naval and Military.

ORMROD, Rt. Hon. Sir Roger (Fray Greenwood), PC 1974; Kt 1961; a Lord Justice of Appeal, 1974-82; *b* 20 Oct. 1911; *s* of late Oliver Fray Ormrod and Edith Muriel (*née* Pim); *m* 1938, Anne, *d* of Charles Lush; no *c. Educ:* Shrewsbury Sch.; The Queen's Coll., Oxford. BA Oxon (Jurisprudence) 1935. Called to Bar, Inner Temple, 1936; QC 1958; Judge of High Court of Justice, Family Division (formerly Probate, Divorce and Admiralty Division), 1961-74. Hon. Fellow, Queen's Coll., Oxford, 1966. BM, BCh Oxon, 1941; FRCP 1969. House Physician, Radcliffe Infirmary, Oxford, 1941-42. Served in RAMC, 1942-45, with rank of Major. DADMS 8 Corps. Lecturer in Forensic Medicine, Oxford Medical Sch., 1950-59. Hon. Prof. of Legal Ethics, Univ. of Birmingham, 1973-74. Chairman: The London Marriage Guidance Council; Lord Chancellor's Cttee on Legal Education, 1968; Notting Hill Housing Trust, 1968-. Pres., British Acad. of Forensic Science, 1970-71; Chm., Cttee of Management, Institute of Psychiatry. Visitor, Royal Postgrad. Med. Sch., 1975-; Chm., British Med. Postgrad. Fedn. Hon. Fellow, Manchester Polytechnic, 1972; Hon. FRCPsych 1975; Hon. LLD Leicester, 1978. *Publications:* ed, (with E. H. Pearce) Dunstan's Law of Hire-Purchase, 1938; (with Harris Walker) National Health Service Act 1946, 1949. *Address:* 4 Aubrey Road, W8. *T:* 01-727 7876. *Club:* Garrick.

ORMSBY GORE, family name of **Baron Harlech.**

OROWAN, Egon, DrIng; FRS 1947; Professor of Mechanical Engineering, Massachusetts Institute of Technology, Cambridge, Massachusetts, USA, 1950-67, now Emeritus; Senior Lecturer, MIT, 1967-73; *b* Budapest, 2 Aug. 1902; *s* of Berthold Orowan and Josephine Ságvári; *m* 1941, Yolande Schonfeld; one *d. Educ:* University of Vienna; Technical Univ., Berlin-Charlottenburg. Demonstrator Technical Univ., Berlin-Charlottenburg, 1928; i/c Krypton Works, United Incandescent Lamp and Electrical Co. Ltd, Ujpest, Hungary, 1936; Research in Physics of Metals, Physics Dept, University of Birmingham, 1937, and Cavendish Laboratory, Cambridge, 1939; Reader in the Physics of Metals, University of Cambridge. Alcoa Vis. Prof., Univ. of Pittsburgh, 1972-73. Mem., Nat. Acad. of Sciences; Corresp. Mem., Akademie der Wissenschaften, Göttingen. Thomas Hawksley Gold Medal, MechE, 1944; Bingham Medal, Society of Rheology, 1959; Carl Friedrich Gauss Medal, Braunschweigische Wissenschaftliche Gesellschaft, 1968; Vincent Bendix Gold Medal, Amer. Soc. of Engrg Educn, 1971; Paul Bergsøe Medal, Dansk Metallurgisk Selskab, 1973. DrIng (*hc*) Technische Universität, Berlin, 1965. *Publications:* Papers in scientific and engineering journals. *Address:* 44 Payson Terrace, Belmont, Mass 02178, USA.

ORR, Rt. Hon. Sir Alan (Stewart), PC 1971; Kt 1965; OBE 1944; A Lord Justice of Appeal, 1971-80; *b* 21 Feb. 1911; *s* of late William Orr and Doris Kemsley, Great Wakering, Essex; *m* 1933, Mariana Frances Lilian, *d* of late Captain J. C. Lang, KOSB; four *s. Educ:* Fettes; Edinburgh Univ. (1st Class Hons Classics); Balliol Coll., Oxford (1st Class Hons Jurisprudence). Barrister Middle Temple, 1936 (Cert. Hon.); Master of the Bench, 1965; Barstow Law Scholar; Harmsworth Scholar. RAF, 1940-45 (despatches, OBE), Wing Comdr. Lectr in Law (pt-time), UCL, 1948-50. Member of General Council of the Bar, 1953-57; Junior Counsel (Common Law) to Commissioners of Inland Revenue, 1957-63; QC 1963; Recorder of: New Windsor, 1958-65; Oxford, Jan.-Aug. 1965; Dep. Chairman, Oxford Quarter Sessions, 1964-71; Judge of High Court of Justice, Probate, Divorce and Admiralty Division,

1965-71; Presiding Judge, North-Eastern Circuit, 1970-71. Mem., Chancellor's Law Reform Cttee, 1966-80 (Chm., 1973-80). Chm., Court of Governors, Mill Hill Sch., 1976-79. *Recreation:* golf. *Address:* Highfield, Harmer Green, Welwyn, Herts. *T:* Welwyn 4250. *Club:* United Oxford & Cambridge University.

ORR, Sir David (Alexander), Kt 1977; MC and bar 1945; LLB; Executive Chairman, Inchcape PLC, since 1983; Director, Shell Transport & Trading Co., since 1982; Chairman, Armed Forces Pay Review Board, since 1982; *b* 10 May 1922; *s* of late Canon Adrian William Fielder Orr and Grace (*née* Robinson); *m* 1949, Phoebe Rosaleen Davis; three *d. Educ:* High Sch., Dublin; Trinity Coll., Dublin (Hon. LLD 1978). Served Royal Engineers attached QVO Madras Sappers and Miners, 1941-46. With various Unilever companies, 1948-82; Hindustan Lever, 1955-60; Mem. Overseas Cttee, Unilever, 1960-63; Lever Bros Co., New York, 1963, Pres. 1965-67; Dir, 1967-82, Vice-Chm. 1970-74, Chm., 1974-82, Unilever Ltd; Vice-Chm., Unilever NV, 1974-82. Dir, RTZ, 1981-. Chm., Leverhulme Trust. Pres., Liverpool Sch. of Tropical Medicine, 1981-. Mem. Council, Chatham House; Governor, LSE, 1980-. FRSA. Hon. LLD TCD, 1978. Comdr, Order of Oranje Nassau, 1979. *Recreations:* golf, Rugby, travel. *Address:* 81 Lyall Mews West, SW1; Oakhill, Enton Green, Godalming, Surrey. *T:* Godalming 7032. *Club:* Sunningdale Golf.

ORR, James Bernard Vivian, CVO 1968 (MVO 1962); Secretary, Medical Commission on Accident Prevention, since 1970; *b* 19 Nov. 1917; *s* of Dr Vivian Bernard Orr and Gladys Constance Orr (*née* Power); unmarried. *Educ:* Harrow; Gordonstoun; RMC, Sandhurst. British South Africa Police, Southern Rhodesia, 1939-46. Attached occupied Enemy Territory Administration in Ethiopia and Eritrea Police Forces, 1941-49; Kenya Police, 1954-57. Private Secretary to HRH The Duke of Edinburgh, 1957-70, an Extra Equerry, 1970-. *Recreations:* horse racing, watching cricket. *Address:* 10 Mulberry Trees, Shepperton, Mddx. *T:* Walton-on-Thames 45274.

ORR, Dr James Henry; Consultant in forensic psychiatry, since 1982; *b* 2 Feb. 1927; *s* of Hubert Orr and Ethel Maggs; *m* 1950, Valerie Elizabeth Yates; two *s* one *d. Educ:* Bristol Grammar Sch.; Bristol Univ. (MB, ChB 1955). DPM; FRCPsych. Enlisted, 1944; commnd RE, 1947; demobilised, 1949. Hosp. appts, 1955-56; gen. practice, 1956-58; Medical Officer, HM Prison: Leeds, 1958; Winchester, 1962; Lincoln, 1966; SMO, Leeds, 1967; Asst Dir, Prison Med. Services, 1973; Dir, Prison Med. Services, and Mem., Prisons Bd, 1976-82. *Recreation:* gardening. *Address:* Stanley Royd Hospital, Wakefield, W Yorks. *T:* Wakefield 375217.

ORR, Jean Fergus Henderson; Director, Office of Manpower Economics, 1973-80; *b* 3 April 1920; *yr d* of late Peter Orr, OBE and Janet Muir Orr (*née* Henderson). *Educ:* privately; University Coll., London (BA). Min. of Aircraft Prodn, temp. Asst Principal, 1942; Min. of Supply: Asst Principal, 1946; Principal, 1949; HM Treasury, 1954: Principal, Official Side Sec. to Civil Service Nat. Whitley Council negotiations on Report of Royal Commn on Civil Service, 1953-55; Asst Sec. 1961; on loan to Office of Manpower Econs as Sec. to Top Salaries Review Body, 1971. *Recreations:* music, travel, natural history. *Address:* 27 Primrose Hill Road, NW3 3DG. *T:* 01-722 2933. *Club:* United Oxford & Cambridge University.

ORR, Sir John Henry, Kt 1979; OBE 1972; QPM 1977; Chief Constable, Lothian and Borders Police, since 1975; *b* 13 June 1918; *m* 1942, Isobel Margaret Campbell; one *s* one *d. Educ:* George Heriot's Sch., Edinburgh. Edinburgh City Police, 1937; served in RAF 1943-45 (Flying Officer; Defence and War Medals); Chief Constable: of Dundee, 1960; of Lothians and Peebles, 1968. Hon. Sec., Assoc. of Chief Police Officers (Scotland), 1974. FBIM 1978. Coronation Medal, 1953; Police Long Service and Good Conduct Medal, 1959; Jubilee Medal, 1977; OStJ, 1975. Comdr, Polar Star, class III, Sweden, 1975; Legion of Honour, France, 1976. *Recreations:* Rugby (capped for Scotland; Past Pres., Scottish Rugby Union); golf. *Address:* 12 Lanark Road West, Currie, Midlothian EH14 5ET.

ORR, Prof. John Washington; Professor of Pathology and Director of Cancer Research, University of Birmingham, and Hon. Pathologist, United Birmingham Hospitals, 1948-66; Professor Emeritus, 1967; *b* 5 Aug. 1901; *er s* of Frederick William and Elizabeth Orr, Belfast; *m* 1932, Nora Margaret (*d* 1965), 2nd *d* of David James and Margaret Carmichael; one *s* one *d. Educ:* Royal Academical Institution, Belfast; Queen's University of Belfast. MB, BCh, BAO, Belfast, 1923; BSc (1st class Hons) Belfast, 1924, DPH 1924; MD (Gold Medal) Belfast, 1926; MRCP London, 1940; MD Birmingham, 1948; FRCP London, 1950. Hon. MD Perugia, 1961. Riddell Demonstrator of Pathology, Belfast, 1924; Musgrave student in Pathology, Belfast, 1925; First Assistant Pathologist and Asst Curator of the Museum, St Mary's Hospital, W2, 1926; Lecturer in Exp. Pathology and Asst Director of Cancer Research, University of Leeds, 1932; Reader in Exp. Pathology, 1937; President of Leeds Pathological Club, 1946-47. Senior Research Pathologist, Detroit Institute of Cancer Research, 1966-67; Research Pathologist, Royal Victoria Hosp., Bournemouth, 1967-69. Served War of 1939-45 as Pathologist in EMS and Battalion MO, Home Guard. *Publications:* articles on medical subjects in Journal of Pathology and Bacteriology, British Journal of Exp. Pathology, British Journal of Cancer, Lancet, American Journal of Cancer, etc, especially papers on experimental cancer research. *Address:* c/o Lloyds Bank, 359 Bristol Road, Birmingham B5 7SS.

ORR, Captain Lawrence Percy Story; Director, Associated Leisure Ltd, since 1972; *b* 16 Sept. 1918; *s* of late Very Rev. W. R. M. Orr, MA, LLD, sometime Dean of Dromore; *m* 1939, Jean Mary (separated 1952; marr. diss. 1976), *d* of F. C. Hughes; four *s* (one *d* decd). *Educ:* Campbell Coll., Belfast; Trinity Coll., Dublin. Served with East Lancashire Regt, Royal Armoured Corps, and Life Guards, 1939–46. MP (UU) South Down, 1950–Sept. 1974. Mem. Exec., British Chamber of Commerce, 1951–56. Dir, Pye (Scottish) Telecommunications, 1952–62. Vice-Chairman, Conservative Broadcasting Cttee, 1959–62; Leader, Ulster Unionist Parly Party, 1964–74; Vice-Pres., Ulster Unionist Council. Imperial Grand Master, Orange Order, 1964–73. *Recreations:* fishing, painting, chess. *Address:* Flat 72, River Court, Upper Ground, SE1 9OT.

ORR, Prof. Robin, (Robert Kemsley Orr), CBE 1972; MA, MusD (Cantab); FRCM; Hon. RAM; Hon. DMus, Hon. LLD; Composer; Professor of Music, Cambridge University, and Fellow of St John's College, 1965–76, now Professor Emeritus; *b* Brechin, Scotland, 2 June 1909; *s* of Robert Workman Orr and Florence Mary Kemsley; *m* 1st, 1937, Margaret (marr. diss. 1979), *er d* of A. C. Mace; one *s* two *d*; 2nd, 1979, Doris Winny-Meyer, *d* of Leo Meyer-Bechtler, Zürich. *Educ:* Loretto Sch.; Royal Coll. of Music; Pembroke Coll., Cambridge (Organ Scholar); Accademia Musicale Chigiana, Siena. Studied privately with Casella and Nadia Boulanger. Dir of Music, Sidcot Sch., Somerset, 1933–36; Asst Lecturer in Music, Univ. of Leeds, 1936–38. Served War of 1939–45, RAFVR, Photographic Intelligence (Flight Lieut). Organist and Dir of Studies in Music, St John's Coll., 1938–51, and Fellow, 1948–56, Univ. Lecturer in Music, 1947–56, Cambridge; Prof. of Theory and Composition, RCM, 1950–56; Gardiner Prof. of Music, Univ. of Glasgow, 1956–65. Mem., Carl Rosa Trust, 1953–; Chm., Scottish Opera, 1962–76; Director: Arts Theatre, Cambridge, 1970–75; Welsh Nat. Opera, 1977–. Compositions include: Sonatina for violin and piano, 1941; Three Chinese Songs, 1943; Sonata for viola and piano, 1947; Winter's Tale (Incidental Music), BBC, 1947; Overture, The Prospect of Whitby, 1948; Oedipus at Colonus (Cambridge Univ. Greek Play), 1950; Four Romantic Songs (for Peter Pears), 1950; Festival Te Deum, 1950; Three Pastorals for soprano, flute, viola and piano, 1951; Deirdre of the Sorrows (Incidental Music), BBC, 1951; Italian Overture, 1952; Te Deum and Jubilate in C, 1953; Motet, I was glad, 1955; Spring Cantata, 1955; Sonata for violin and clavier, 1956; Rhapsody for string orchestra; Antigone (Bradfield College Greek Play), 1961; Symphony in one movement, 1963; Full Circle (Opera), 1967; From the Book of Philip Sparrow, 1969; Journeys and Places (mezzo-sop. and strings), 1971; Symphony No 2, 1971; Hermiston (Opera), 1975; Symphony No 3, 1978; Versus from Ogden Nash for medium voice and strings, 1978; Songs of Zion (choir), 1978; ed, The Kelvin Series of Scots Songs. Hon DMus Glasgow, 1972; Hon. LLD Dundee, 1976. *Recreations:* gardening, mountain walks. *Address:* 16 Cranmer Road, Cambridge CB3 9BL. *T:* Cambridge 352858; Chesa Maya, Rüefaweg 4, 7250 Klosters, Switzerland. *T:* 083 43467.

ORR-EWING, family name of **Baron Orr-Ewing.**

ORR-EWING, Baron *cr* 1971 (Life Peer), of Little Berkhamsted; **(Charles) Ian Orr-Ewing,** OBE 1945; 1st Bt *cr* 1963; Consultant and Director various companies; Chairman, Metrication Board, 1972–77; *b* 10 Feb. 1912; *s* of Archibald Ian Orr Ewing and Gertrude (*née* Runge); *m* 1939, Joan McMinnies; four *s*. *Educ:* Harrow; Trinity Coll., Oxford. MA (Physics). Graduate apprentice, EMI, Hayes, 1934–37; BBC Television Service, 1938–39, 1946–49. Served RAFVR, 1939–46, N Africa, Italy, France and Germany, Wing Comdr, 1941; Chief Radar Officer, Air Staff, SHAEF, 1945 (despatches twice); BBC Television Outside Broadcasts Manager, 1946–48. MP (C) North Hendon, 1950–70; Joint Secretary, Parliamentary Scientific Cttee, 1950; Vice-Chm., Civil Air Cttee, 1955–57; Vice-Pres., Parliamentary and Scientific Cttee, 1965–68; Vice-Chm., 1922 Cttee, 1966–70 (Secretary, 1956); Vice-Chairman, Defence Cttee, 1966–70. PPS to Sir Walter Monckton, Minister of Labour and National Service, Nov. 1951–1955; Parliamentary Under-Secretary of State for Air, Air Ministry, 1957–59; Parliamentary and Financial Secretary to Admiralty, 1959; Civil Lord of the Admiralty, 1959–63. Dep. Chm., Assoc. of Cons. Peers, 1980–. Mem., Royal Commn on Standards of Conduct in Public Life, 1975–76. Pres. and Chm. of Council, Electronic Engineering Assoc., 1969–70. Pres., Nat. Ski Fedn of GB, 1972–76. FIEE. *Recreations:* tennis, light-hearted cricket and ski-ing. *Heir* (to baronetcy only): *s* (Alistair) Simon Orr-Ewing [*b* 10 June 1940; *m* 1968, Victoria, *e d* of late Keith Cameron, Fifield House, Milton-under-Wychwood, Oxon; two *s* one *d*]. *Address:* The Old Manor, Little Berkhamsted, near Hertford, Herts. *Clubs:* Boodle's, MCC; Vincent's (Oxford).

ORR-EWING, Hamish; Chairman, Rank Xerox Ltd, since 1980; Director, Tricentrol Ltd, since 1975; Chairman, European Government Business Relations Council, since 1980; *b* 17 Aug. 1924; *o s* of Hugh Eric Douglas Orr-Ewing and Esme Victoria (*née* Stewart), Strathgarry, Killiecrankie, Perthshire; *m* 1st, 1947, Morar Margaret Kennedy; one *s* (one *d* decd); 2nd, 1954, Ann Mary Teresa Terry. *Educ:* Heatherdown, Ascot; Eton. Served War, Captain Black Watch. Salesman, EMI, 1950; Ford Motor Co., 1954; Ford Light Car Planning Manager, 1959–63; Leyland Motor Corp. Ltd, 1963–65; joined Rank Xerox, 1965; apptd to Bd as Dir of Product Planning, 1968; Dir of Personnel, 1970; Man. Dir, Rank Xerox (UK) Ltd, 1971; Reg. Dir for Rank Xerox Ops in UK, France, Holland, Sweden and Belgium, 1977. Chm., Jobs in the 80s; Mem., Overseas Cttee, CBI. *Recreations:* anything mechanical,

country life, the Roman Empire. *Address:* 51 Clifton Hill, NW8 0OE. *T:* 01-624 5702; Fox Mill, Purton, Wilts SN5 9EF. *T:* Swindon 770496.

ORR EWING, Major Sir Ronald Archibald, 5th Bt, *cr* 1886; Major (retired) Scots Guards; *b* 14 May 1912; *e s* of Sir Norman Orr Ewing, 4th Bt, CB, DSO, and Lady Orr Ewing (*née* Robarts), Tile House, Buckingham; *S* father, 1960; *m* 1938, Marion Hester, *yr d* of late Colonel Sir Donald Walter Cameron of Lochiel, KT, CMG, and of Lady Hermione Cameron of Lochiel, *d* of 5th Duke of Montrose, KT; two *s* two *d*. *Educ:* Eton; RMC, Sandhurst. Scots Guards, 1932–53, Major. Served War of 1939–45, Middle East (POW 1942). JP Perthshire, 1956; DL Perthshire, 1963. Grand Master Mason of Scotland, 1965–69. *Recreation:* shooting. *Heir: s* Archibald Donald Orr Ewing [*b* 20 Dec. 1938; *m* 1st, 1965, Venetia Elizabeth (marr. diss. 1972), *y d* of Major and Mrs Richard Turner, Co. Dublin; 2nd, 1972, Nicola Jean-Anne, *d* of Reginald Baron Black, Co. Cork; one *s*]. *Address:* Cardross, Port of Menteith, Stirling. *T:* Port of Menteith 220. *Clubs:* Army and Navy; New (Edinburgh).

ORSON, Rasin Ward, FSS; Comp IEE; Member, The Electricity Council, since 1976; Director, Chloride Silent Power Ltd, since 1974; *b* 16 April 1927; *s* of Rasin Nelson Orson and Blanche Hyre; *m* 1st, 1950, Marie Goodenough; two *s* ; 2nd, 1979, Lesley Jean Vallance. *Educ:* Stratford Grammar Sch.; London School of Economics (BScEcon 1948). Asst Statistician, Min. of Civil Aviation, 1948, Statistician, 1953; Electricity Council: Head of Economics and Forecasting Branch, 1963; Dep. Commercial Adviser, 1968; Commercial Adviser, 1972. *Recreations:* music, pottering. *Address:* 128 De Beauvoir Road, N1. *T:* 01-254 7784.

ORTIZ DE ROZAS, Carlos; Head of Argentine Special Mission to the Holy See, since 1982; *b* 26 April 1926; *m* 1952, María del Carmen Sarobe. *Educ:* School of Diplomacy, Min. of Foreign Affairs, Buenos Aires (grad. 1949). Lawyer, Faculty of Law, Univ. of Buenos Aires, 1950. Entered Argentine Foreign Service, 1948; served Bulgaria, Greece, UAR and UK (Minister); Ambassador to Austria, 1967–70; Permanent Rep. to UN, 1970–77; Pres. UN Security Council, 1971–72; Chairman: First (Polit. and Security) Cttee of 29th Gen. Assembly, 1974; Preparatory Cttee of Special Session on Disarmament, 1977–78; Cttee on Disarmament, Geneva, 1979; Mem. Adv. Bd on Disarmament Studies, New York, 1978–81; Ambassador to UK, 1980–82. Universidad del Salvador, Buenos Aires: Prof. of History and Constitutional Law, 1958, Prof. of Political Science, 1958–, Faculty of Law; Prof. of Internat. Relations, School of Political Sciences, 1962–, and at School of Diplomacy, 1962–. Holds many foreign decorations. *Address:* Via Archimede 44, Rome, Italy. *Clubs:* Jockey, Circolo de Armas (Buenos Aires); Circolo della Càccia (Rome); Metropolitan Doubles (New York).

ORTOLI, François-Xavier; a Vice-President, with responsibility for economic and financial affairs, Commission of the European Communities, since 1977 (President, 1973–76); *b* 16 Feb. 1925. *Educ:* Hanoi Faculty of Law; Ecole Nationale d'Administration. Inspector of Finances, 1948–51; Tech. Adv., Office of Minister of Econ. Affairs and Information, 1951–53; Asst Dir to Sec. of State for Econ. Affairs and Sec.-Gen., Franco-Italian Cttee of EEC, 1955; Head, Commercial Politics Service of Sec. of State for Econ. Affairs, 1957; Dir-Gen., Internal Market Div., EEC, 1958; Sec.-Gen., Inter-Ministerial Cttee for Questions of European Econ. Co-operation, Paris, 1961–; Dir of Cabinet to Prime Minister, 1962–66; Comr-Gen. of the Plan, 1966–67; Minister: of Works, 1967–68; of Educn, 1968; of Finance, 1968–69; of Industrial and Scientific Develt, 1969–72. Hon. DCL Oxon, 1975; Hon Dr Sch. of Political Scis, Athens, 1975. Officier de la Légion d'Honneur; Médaille Militaire; Croix de Guerre, 1945; Médaille de la Résistance. *Address:* 18 rue de Bourgogne, 75007 Paris, France.

OSBORN, Sir Danvers (Lionel Rouse), 8th Bt, *cr* 1662; *b* 31 Jan. 1916; *s* of Sir Algernon K. B. Osborn, 7th Bt, JP and Beatrice Elliot Kennard, *d* of William Bunce Greenfield, JP, DL; *S* father, 1948; *m* 1943, Constance Violette, JP, SSStJ, *d* of late Major Leonard Frank Rooke, KOSB; one *s* one *d* (one *s* and one *d* decd). *Educ:* Eton; Magdalene Coll., Cambridge. Employed as Civil Assistant in Intelligence Dept of War Office, 1940–45. Joined Spicers Ltd, 1955. Director of two Picture Galleries. *Recreations:* golf, tennis, bridge. *Heir: s* Richard Henry Danvers Osborn, *b* 12 Aug. 1958. *Address:* The Dower House, Moor Park, Farnham, Surrey. *Club:* MCC.

OSBORN, John Holbrook; MP (C) (NL and U, 1959–64), Hallam Division of Sheffield, since 1959; *b* 14 Dec. 1922; *s* of Samuel Eric Osborn and Aileen Decima, *d* of Colonel Sir Arthur Holbrook, KBE, MP; *m* 1st, 1952, Molly Suzanne (*née* Marten) (marr. diss.); two *d* ; 2nd, 1976, Joan Mary MacDermot (*née* Wilkinson). *Educ:* Rugby; Trinity Hall, Cambridge. MA Cantab; Part 2 Tripos in Metallurgy; Diploma in Foundry Technology, National Foundry Coll., 1949. Served in Royal Corps of Signals, West Africa, 1943–47 (Captain); served in RA (TA) Sheffield, 1948–55, Major. Director of Samuel Osborn & Co. Ltd, and associated companies, 1951–79. Chairman, Hillsborough Divisional Young Conservative and Liberal Association, 1949–53. PPS to the Secretary of State for Commonwealth Relations and for the Colonies, 1963–64. Chm., Cons. Parly Transport Cttee, 1970–74, Vice-Chm., Energy Cttee, 1979–81; Vice Chm., Parly and Scientific Cttee (Officer), 1959); Mem., Educn, Science and Arts Select Cttee, 1979–. Mem., UK Delegn to Council of Europe and WEU, 1972–75, 1980–; Vice Chm., Science and Technol. Cttee, Council of Europe, 1981–; Mem., European Parlt, 1975–79; an Hon. Sec., 1922 Cttee, 1968–; Mem. Exec., British Br., IPU, 1968–75,

1979-. Freeman (Searcher), Co. of Cutlers in Hallamshire, 1950-. Fellow, Institute of British Foundrymen, 1948-72 (Member Council, Sheffield Branch, 1954-64); Fellow, Institute of Directors; Member Council: Sheffield Chamber of Commerce, 1956-; Assocs British Chambers of Commerce Council, 1960-62 (Hon. Secretary, 1962-64); British Iron and Steel Res. Association, 1965-68; CBI and Yorks and WR Br., CBI, 1968-79; Member: Metals Soc.; Council, Industrial Soc. (Life Mem.); Court and Cttee of Sheffield Univ., 1951-. Travels widely in business and politics. *Recreations:* golf, tennis, photography, gardening, skiing. *Address:* Folds Head Close, Calver, Sheffield S30 1XJ. *T:* Hope Valley 30253; Flat 13, 102 Rochester Row, SW1. *T:* 01-219 4108. *Clubs:* Carlton; Sheffield.

OSBORN, Margaret, MA; High Mistress of St Paul's Girls' School, Hammersmith, 1948-63, retired; *b* 23 April 1906; *d* of Rev. G. S. Osborn, late Rector of Milton, Cambridge. *Educ:* St Leonard's Sch., St Andrews, Fife; St Hugh's Coll., Oxford. Graduated 1929; MA Hons Lit Hum Oxon. Pelham Student at British School at Rome, 1931; Headmistress of St George's School for Girls, Edinburgh, 1943-48. *Publication:* A Latin Epithet, article in Mnemosyne (Leyden Journal), 1932. *Recreations:* music and reading. *Address:* Woodstock House, Woodstock, Oxford OX7 1UG.

OSBORNE, Sir Basil, Kt 1967; CBE 1962; Lord Mayor of Hobart, Tasmania, 1959-70, Alderman, 1952-76; Chairman, Metropolitan Transport Trust, 1971-78; business administrator; *b* 19 April 1907; *s* of late Alderman W. W. Osborne, MBE; *m* 1934, Esma, *d* of late T. Green; one *s*. *Educ:* Metropolitan Business Coll. Dir, Australian Brain Foundn (formerly Aust. Neurol Foundn), 1970-. Chairman: Board of Management, Royal Hobart Hospital, 1968-81 (Vice-Chairman, 1952-68); St John's Ambulance Assoc., 1960-76. Australian Pres., Royal Life Saving Soc., 1979- (Life Governor, Commonwealth Council); Hon. Life Member: Hobart Orpheus Club, 1977; Hospital Public Relns Officers' Assoc. of Australia, 1977. Hon. Fellow: Australian Marketing Inst., 1967; Inst. of Ambulance Officers (Aust.), 1975. OStJ 1972. *Recreations:* music, sport. *Address:* 6 Myella Drive, Chigwell, Tasmania 7011, Australia. *Club:* Royal Autocar (Tasmania).

OSBORNE, Charles (Thomas); author; Literature Director, Arts Council of Great Britain, since 1971; *b* 24 Nov. 1927; *s* of Vincent Lloyd Osborne and Elsa Louise Osborne; *m* 1970, Marie Korbelárová (marr. diss. 1975). *Educ:* Brisbane State High Sch. Studied piano and voice, Brisbane and Melbourne; acted in and directed plays, 1944-53; wrote poetry and criticism, published in Aust. and NZ magazines; co-owner, Ballad Bookshop, Brisbane, 1947-51; actor, London, provincial rep. and on tour, also TV and film, 1953-57; Asst Editor, London Magazine, 1958-66; Asst Lit. Dir, Arts Council of GB, 1966-71. Broadcaster, musical and literary progs, BBC, 1957-; Dir, Poetry International, 1967-; Sec., Poetry Book Soc., 1971-. Mem. Editorial Board: Opera, 1970-; Annual Register, 1971-. *Publications:* (ed) Australian Stories of Today, 1961; (ed) Opera 66, 1966; (with Brigid Brophy and Michael Levey) Fifty Works of English Literature We Could Do Without, 1967 (USA 1968); Kafka, 1967; Swansong (poems), 1968; The Complete Operas of Verdi, 1969 (USA 1970; Italian trans. 1975); Ned Kelly, 1970; (ed) Australia, New Zealand and the South Pacific, 1970; (ed) Letters of Giuseppe Verdi, 1971 (USA 1972); (ed) The Bram Stoker Bedside Companion, 1973 (USA 1974); (ed) Stories and Essays by Richard Wagner, 1973 (USA 1974); The Concert Song Companion, 1974; Masterpieces of Nolan, 1976; Masterpieces of Drysdale, 1976; Masterpieces of Dobell, 1976; Wagner and his World, 1977 (USA 1977); Verdi, 1977; (ed) Dictionary of Composers, 1977; The Complete Operas of Mozart, 1978 (USA 1978); (ed) Masterworks of Opera: Rigoletto, 1979; The Opera House Album, 1979; W. H. Auden: the Life of a Poet, 1980 (USA 1979); (ed with Kenneth Thomson) Klemperer Stories, 1980 (trans. German 1981); The Complete Operas of Puccini, 1981 (USA 1981); The Life and Crimes of Agatha Christie, 1982 (USA 1982); The World Theatre of Wagner, 1982 (USA 1982); poems in: The Oxford Book of Australian Verse, 1956; Australian Poetry, 1951-52, etc; The Queensland Centenary Anthology, 1959; Australian Writing Today, 1968; various ils; contrib.: TLS, Observer, Sunday Times, Times, Guardian, New Statesman, Spectator, London Mag., Encounter, Opera, Chambers Encyc. Yearbook, and Enciclopedia dello spettacolo; also cassettes. *Recreations:* travel, reading, theatre and opera-going, watching old movies on TV, visiting Austrian baroque churches, writing. *Address:* 26 Evelyn Mansions, Carlisle Place, SW1P 1NH.

OSBORNE, Maj.-Gen. the Rev. Coles Alexander, CIE 1945; Indian Army, retired; *b* 29 July 1896; *s* of late W. E. Osborne, formerly of Dover, Kent; *m* 1930, Joyce, *o d* of late R. H. Meares of Forbes and Sydney, NSW, Australia; two *d*. *Educ:* Dover County Sch. European War, 1914-18 served with HAC, Royal West Kent Regt, and RFC (wounded); transferred to 15th Sikhs, 1918; served in Afghan War 1919 and in NW Frontier Operations 1920-22 and 1939; Palestine 1938; Middle East 1940. Tactics Instructor at Royal Military Coll., Duntroon, Australia, 1928-30; Bt Major 1933; General Staff (Operations), War Office, 1934-38; Bt Lieut-Col 1936; Comd 1 Bombay Grenadiers, 1940; Deputy Director Military Training, India, 1940; Colonel, 1940; Commandant, Staff Coll., Quetta, 1941-42; Brigadier, 1941; Director Military Operations, GHQ, India and Burma, 1942-43; Temp. Maj.-Gen. 1942; Comd Kohat District, 1943-45; retired 1946. Student at Moore Theological Coll., Sydney, 1947; ordained, 1947. Asst Minister St Andrew's Cathedral, Sydney, Australia, 1947-53; Hon. Asst Minister, St Mark's Church, Darling Point, 1953-66; Personal Chaplain to Anglican Archbishop of Sydney, 1959-66. Director, Television Corp., 1956-75. Fellow of St Paul's Coll., Sydney Univ., 1953-69. Chairman, Freedom from Hunger Campaign, NSW, 1970-72. *Address:* 126 Hopetown Avenue, Vaucluse, NSW 2030, Australia. *T:* 337-2969. *Club:* Australian (Sydney).

OSBORNE, Helena; see Moore, G. M.

OSBORNE, Prof. John; (First) Professor of Dental Prosthetics, University of Birmingham, 1948-73; *b* 6 April 1911; *s* of John W. and Gertrude Osborne; *m* 1937, Virginia Preston, *d* of W. H. Fruish; one *s* one *d*. *Educ:* Bishop Vesey Grammar Sch.; Birmingham Univ. LDS Birmingham, 1933; PhD Sheffield, 1945; MDS 1948; FDS, RCS, 1948; FFD, RCSI, 1964; House Surgeon and junior staff appointments at Birmingham Dental Hospital, 1933-37; also private practice during same period; Lectr in Dental Prosthetics, Univ. of Sheffield, 1937, Univ. of Birmingham, 1946; Dir of Dental Studies, Univ. of Birmingham, 1965-69 (Dep. Dir, 1953-65). Visiting Professor: NW University, Chicago, 1956-57; Univ. of Adelaide, 1971; Univ. of Malaya, 1973-74. Guest lecturer, Australian Dental Assoc., 1962. External Examiner to Universities of Malaya, Liverpool, Durham, London, Manchester, Glasgow, Dundee, Bristol, Edinburgh, Sheffield, Belfast, Lagos, Singapore, and to RCS and RCSI. President: British Dental Students Assoc., 1956-58; Central Counties Branch, British Dental Assoc., 1958-59, Hospitals Group, 1968-69. Queen's Silver Jubilee Medal, 1977; Tomes Medal, British Dental Assoc., 1981. *Publications:* Dental Mechanics for Students, 1939, 6th edn 1970; Acrylic Resins in Dentistry, 1942, 3rd edn 1948; Partial Dentures (with Dr G. A. Lammie), 1954, 4th edn, 1974; Dental Technology and Materials (with H. J. Wilson and M. Mansfield), 1978; scientific papers in leading dental journals. *Recreations:* philately, gardening. *Address:* Vesey Cottage, Warlands Lane, Shalfleet, Isle of Wight. *T:* Calbourne 384. *Clubs:* Island Sailing (Cowes); Royal Solent Yacht.

OSBORNE, John (James); dramatist and actor; Director of Woodfall Films; *b* 12 Dec. 1929; *s* of Thomas Godfrey Osborne and Nellie Beatrice Grove; *m* 1st, 1951, Pamela Elizabeth Lane (marr. diss. 1957); 2nd, 1957, Mary Ure (marr. diss. 1963, she *d* 1975); 3rd, 1963, Penelope Gilliatt, *qv* (marr. diss. 1968); one *d*; 4th, 1968, Jill Bennett, *qv* (marr. diss. 1977); 5th, 1978, Helen Dawson. *Educ:* Belmont Coll., Devon. First stage appearance at Lyceum, Sheffield, in No Room at the Inn, 1948; toured and in seasons at: Ilfracombe, Bridgwater, Camberwell, Kidderminster, Derby, etc; English Stage Company season at Royal Court: appeared in Death of Satan, Cards of Identity, Good Woman of Setzuan, The Making of Moo, A Cuckoo in the Nest; Directed Meals on Wheels, 1965; appeared in: The Parachute (BBC TV), 1967; First Night of Pygmalion (TV), 1969; First Love (film, as Maidanov), 1970; Get Carter (film), 1971; Lady Charlotte (TV), 1977; Tomorrow Never Comes (film), 1978. First play produced, 1949, at Theatre Royal, Huddersfield; other plays include: Personal Enemy, Opera House, Harrogate, 1955; The Blood of the Bambergs, 1962; Under Plain Cover, 1962; The Right Prospectus (TV), 1969. *Plays filmed:* Look Back in Anger, 1958; The Entertainer, 1959, 1975; Inadmissible Evidence, 1965; Luther, 1971. *Film:* Tom Jones, 1964 (Oscar for best screenplay). Hon. Dr RCA, 1970. *Publications:* Look Back in Anger (play), 1957 (produced 1956); The Entertainer (play), 1957 (also produced); Epitaph for George Dillon (with A. Creighton), 1958 (produced 1957); The World of Paul Slickey (comedy of manners with music), 1959 (produced 1959); Luther (play), 1960 (produced 1961, New York, 1964); A Subject of Scandal and Concern (TV play), 1960; Plays for England, 1963; Inadmissible Evidence (play), 1964 (produced 1965); A Patriot for Me (play), 1964 (produced 1965); A Bond Honoured, 1966 (produced 1966); The Hotel in Amsterdam, 1967 (produced 1968); Time Present, 1967 (produced 1968); Hedda Gabler (adaptation), 1970 (produced 1972); The Right Prospectus and Very Like a Whale (TV plays), 1971; West of Suez, 1971 (produced 1971); The Gift of Friendship (TV play), 1971; A Sense of Detachment, 1972 (produced 1972); A Place Calling Itself Rome, 1972; The Picture of Dorian Gray (play), 1973; The Gift of Friendship (TV play), 1974; Jill and Jack (TV play), 1974; The End of Me Old Cigar (play), 1975; Watch it come down (play), 1975; You're Not Watching Me, Mummy and Try a Little Tenderness (TV plays), 1978; A Better Class of Person (autobiog.), 1981; contrib. to Declaration (a symposium), 1957; various newspapers, journals. *Address:* c/o Fraser and Dunlop, 91 Regent Street, W1. *Clubs:* Garrick; Portscatho Social.

OSBORNE, Kenneth Hilton, QC (Scot.) 1976; *b* 9 July 1937; *s* of Kenneth Osborne and Evelyn Alice (*née* Hilton); *m* 1964, Clare Ann Louise Lewis; one *s* one *d*. *Educ:* Larchfield Sch., Helensburgh; Merchiston Castle Sch., Edinburgh; Edinburgh Univ. (MA, LLB). Admitted to Faculty of Advocates in Scotland, 1962; Standing Junior Counsel to Min. of Defence (Navy) in Scotland, 1974-76; Advocate-Depute, 1982-. Chm., Disciplinary Cttee, Potato Marketing Bd, 1975-. *Recreations:* skiing, fishing, gardening, music, cooking. *Address:* 11 Ann Street, Edinburgh EH4 1PL. *T:* 031-332 1455; Primrose Cottage, Bridgend of Lintrathen, by Kirriemuir, Angus DD8 5JH. *T:* Lintrathen 316. *Club:* New (Edinburgh).

OSBORNE, Surgeon Rear-Admiral (D) Leslie Bartlet, CB 1956; *b* 16 Sept. 1900; *s* of late Rev. Joseph Osborne, MA, and of Miriam Duke James; *m* 1929; two *s* one *d*; *m* 1955, Joan Mary Williams (*née* Parnell). *Educ:* Caterham Sch.; Guy's Hospital. LDS, RCS England 1923; FDS, RCS (Edinburgh) 1955. Dental House Surgeon, Guy's Hospital, 1923. Entered Royal Navy, Surgeon Lieutenant (D), 1923; Surgeon Commander (D), 1936; Surgeon Captain (D), 1948; Surgeon Rear-Admiral (D), 1954; Deputy Director-General for Dental Services in the Royal Navy, 1954-57, retired. Served War of 1939-45. KHDS 1951; QHDS 1953-58. *Recreations:* Rugby

Football (rep. RN, Sussex and Devonport Services; Hon. Manager British Isles Rugby Union Team to New Zealand and Australia, 1950; Chairman Rugby Football Union Selection Cttee, 1949-51; President, Rugby Football Union, 1956); gardening. *Address:* 4 Westbourne Court, Cooden Drive, Cooden Beach, Bexhill-on-Sea, East Sussex TN39 3AA. *T:* Cooden 4431.

OSBORNE, Sir Peter (George), 17th Bt, *cr* 1629; *b* 29 June 1943; *s* of Lt-Col Sir George Osborne, 16th Bt, MC, and Mary (Grace), *d* of C. Horn; *S* father, 1960; *m* 1968, Felicity, *d* of Grantley Loxton-Peacock; three *s. Educ:* Wellington Coll., Berks; Christ Church Coll., Oxford. *Heir: s* Gideon Oliver Osborne, *b* 23 May 1971. *Address:* 36 Porchester Terrace, W2. *T:* 01-402 3903.

O'SHEA, Alexander Paterson, CMG 1962; North American Director, New Zealand Meat Producers' Board, USA, 1964-68, retired, 1968; *b* 29 Dec. 1902; *s* of John O'Shea; *m* 1935; one *d. Educ:* Otago Boys' High Sch.; Victoria University College (now Victoria Univ. of Wellington). (BCom). Farming, 1919-27. Wellington City Corporation, 1928-35; Secretary, Farmers' Union, 1935-46 (later Federated Farmers of NZ Inc.); General Secretary, Federated Farmers of New Zealand Inc., Wellington, NZ, 1946-64. Fellow (Chartered Accountant) New Zealand Society of Accountants. *Publication:* The Public Be Damned, 1946. *Recreation:* onlooker, Rugby football. *Address:* Herbert Gardens, The Terrace, Wellington 1, New Zealand. *Clubs:* Civil Service, Wellesley (Wellington, NZ).

O'SHEA, David Michael; Solicitor to the Metropolitan Police, since 1982; *b* 27 Jan. 1927; *s* of late Francis Edward O'Shea and Helen O'Shea; *m* 1953, Sheila Winifred; two *s. Educ:* St Ignatius Coll., London; King's Coll., London Univ. (LLB). Served RN, 1946-48. Articled H.C.L. Hanne & Co., London, 1949-52; admitted solicitor, 1952; in practice with H. C. L. Hanne & Co., 1952-56; joined Solicitor's Dept, Metropolitan Police Office, 1956; Dep. Solicitor, 1976-82. *Recreation:* travel. *Address:* New Scotland Yard, SW1. *T:* 01-230 7353. *Club:* Sutton and Epsom Rugby Football.

OSIFELO, Sir Frederick (Aubarua), Kt 1977; MBE 1972; Speaker of Legislative Assembly, Solomon Islands, 1974-78; Chairman: Public Service Commission, since 1975; Police and Prison Service Commission, since 1977; Member, Judicial and Legal Service Commission, since 1977; *b* 15 Oct. 1928; *s* of late Paul Iromea and Joy Ngangale Iromea; *m* 1949, Margaret Tanai; three *s* three *d. Educ:* Torquay Technical Coll., England (Dip. Public Admin). Office cleaner, 1945; clerk, 1950; 1st Cl. Magistrate, 1967; Admin. Officer, Cl. B, 1967; Admin. Officer, Cl. A, 1972; District Comr, Eastern Solomons, 1972; Sen. Sec., 1973; Comr of Lands, 1974. Chairman: Cttee of Prerogative of Mercy, 1979; ad hoc cttee on Solomon Islands Honours and Awards, 1979. Pres., Amateur Sports Assoc., 1975–. Lay Canon, 1977. *Address:* PO Box 548, Honiara, Solomon Islands. *T:* 01-125.

OSMAN, Sir (Abdool) Raman (Mahomed), GCMG 1973; CBE 1963; Governor-General of Mauritius, 1972-77; *b* 29 Aug. 1902, of Mauritian parents; unmarried. *Educ:* Royal College, Mauritius; Inns of Court, London. District Magistrate, Mauritius, 1930-38; Additional Substitute Procureur and Advocate General, 1938-50; Actg Procureur and Advocate-General, 1950-51; Actg Chief Justice, Apr.-Nov. 1958; Puisne Judge, Supreme Court of Mauritius, 1950-59, Sen. Puisne Judge, 1959-60, retired. Hon. DCL Mauritius, 1975. *Address:* Le Goulet Terrace, Tombeau Bay, Mauritius. *Club:* Port Louis Gymkhana.

OSMAN, Louis, BA (Arch.); FRIBA; architect, artist, medalist, goldsmith; *b* 30 January 1914; *s* of Charles Osman, Exeter; *m* 1940, Dilys Roberts, *d* of Richard Roberts, Rotherfield, Sussex; one *d. Educ:* Hele's School, Exeter; London University. Open exhibn at Bartlett School of Architecture, University Coll. London, 1931, and at Slade School; Donaldson Medallist of RIBA, 1935. With British Museum and British School of Archæology Expeditions to Syria, 1936, 1937; designed private and public buildings, 1937-39. Served War of 1939-45, Major in Intelligence Corps: Combined Ops HQ and Special Air Service as specialist in Air Photography, Beach Reconnaissance Cttee, prior to invasion of Europe. Resumed practice in London, 1945, designed buildings, furniture, tapestries, glass, etc; work in Westminster Abbey, Lincoln, Ely and Exeter Cathedrals; Staunton Harold for National Trust; Bridge, Cavendish Square, with Jacob Epstein; Newnham Coll., Cambridge; factory buildings for Cambridge Instrument Co., aluminium Big Top for Billy Smart's Circus, two villages on Dartmoor, etc; consultant architect to British Aluminium Co.; executed commissions as goldsmith and jeweller, 1956–; commissioned by De Beers for 1st Internat. Jewellery Exhibn, 1961; designed and made Prince of Wales' crown for investiture, 1969; British Bicentennial Gift to America housing Magna Carta, 1976; Verulam Medal for Metals Soc., 1975; EAHY Medal, 1975; Olympic Medal, 1976; work in precious metals exhibited GB, Denmark, Holland, Germany, American, S Africa, Australia, Japan, etc; one-man retrospective exhibn, Goldsmiths' Hall, 1971. Mem. Exec. Cttee: The Georgian Group, 1952-56; City Music Soc., 1960-70. *Publications:* reviews and contributions to learned jls. *Recreations:* music, riding. *Address:* Byford Court, Hereford HR4 7LD. *T:* Bridge Sollars 248.

OSMAN, Dr Mohammed Kheir; Ambassador of Sudan to the Court of St James's, 1975-76; Consultant to UNESCO, since 1976; *b* 1928; *s* of Osman Khalifa Taha and Khadija el Sharif; *m* 1953, Sara Ahmed. *Educ:* Khartoum Univ. (BA); London Univ. (PGCE; AcDip; MA); Univ. of California (PhD).

Director: Educational Research, 1970-71; Productivity Centre, Khartoum, 1972; Minister of Education, 1972-75; Member: Sudan Nat. Assembly, 1972-75; Sudan Socialist Union Central Cttee, 1972–. Constitution Award, 1973; Two-Niles Decoration for Public Service, 1979. *Address:* UNESCO Project, PO Box 4085, Ruwi, Muscat, Sultanate of Oman. *Club:* Athenæum.

OSMAN, Sir Raman; *see* Osman, Sir A. R. M.

OSMOND, Sir Douglas, Kt 1971; CBE 1968 (OBE 1958); QPM 1962; DL; Chief Constable, Shropshire, 1946-62, Hampshire, 1962-77. *Educ:* University Coll., London. Metropolitan Police Coll., Metropolitan Police, RN, Control Commn for Germany (Public Safety Branch; Dep. Asst Inspector Gen.), 1935-46. Pres., Assoc. of Chief Police Officers of England and Wales, 1967-69; Chm., Police Council for UK, 1972, 1974; Provincial Police Representative, Interpol, 1968-70; Member: Inter-Deptl Cttee on Death Certification and Coroners, 1964-71; Bd of Governors, Police Coll., 1968-72 (Adv. Cttee, 1959-77); Royal Commn on Criminal Procedure, 1978-81. DL Hants, 1981. OStJ 1971. *Address:* Woodbine Cottage, Ovington, Alresford, Hants SO24 0RF.

OSMOND, Mervyn Victor, OBE 1978; Secretary, Council for the Protection of Rural England, 1966-77 (Assistant Secretary, 1946; Deputy Secretary 1963); *b* 2 July 1912; *s* of Albion Victor Osmond and Florence Isabel (*née* Edwards), Bristol; *m* 1940, Aimée Margaret Moir; one *d. Educ:* Clifton Coll. (Schol.); Exeter Coll., Oxford (Schol.). 1st cl. Hon. Class. Mods.; 2nd cl. Lit. Hum.; 2nd cl. Jurisprudence; Poland Prizeman (Criminal Law), 1937; called to Bar (Inner Temple), 1938; MA 1939. Practising Barrister, Western Circuit, 1938-40. Joined Gloucestershire Regt, TA, 1931; served war of 1939-45; Royal Fusiliers; DAAG (Major) 352 L of C Sub-Area and 303 L of C Area (Calcutta). *Recreations:* reading, enjoying rural England. *Address:* 39 Stonehill Road, East Sheen, SW14 8RR. *T:* 01-876 7138.

OSMOND, Michael William Massy, CB 1977; Solicitor to the Department of Health and Social Security, and to the Office of Population Censuses and Surveys, and the General Register Office, 1974-78; *b* 1918; *s* of late Brig. W. R. F. Osmond, CBE, and Mrs C. R. E. Osmond; *m* 1943, Jill Ramsden; one *s* one *d. Educ:* Winchester; Christ Church, Oxford. 2nd Lieut Coldstream Guards, 1939-40. Called to Bar, Inner Temple, 1941; Asst Principal, Min. of Production, 1941-43; Housemaster, HM Borstal Instn, Usk, 1943-45; Legal Asst, Min. of Nat. Insce, 1946; Sen. Legal Asst, 1948; Asst Solicitor, Min. of Pensions and Nat. Insce, 1958; Principal Asst Solicitor, DHSS, 1969. *Recreations:* music, fishing. *Address:* Waylands, Long Newnton, near Tetbury, Glos. *T:* Tetbury 53308. *Club:* United Oxford & Cambridge University.

OSMOND, Sir (Stanley) Paul, Kt 1980; CB 1966; *b* 13 May 1917; *o s* of late Stanley C. and Susan Osmond; *m* 1942, Olivia Sybil, JP, *yr d* of late Ernest E. Wells, JP, Kegworth, Leicestershire; two *s. Educ:* Bristol Grammar School; Jesus College, Oxford. 2nd Cl. Final Hons School of Modern History, Oxford, 1939. Served War of 1939-45, in Army (Gloucestershire Regiment and staff), 1940-46. Home Civil Service, 1939-75: Ministry of Education, 1946-48; Private Secretary to Prime Minister, 1948-51; Admiralty, 1951, Asst Secretary, 1954; Under-Secretary, 1959; HM Treasury, 1962, Third Secretary, 1965; Deputy Secretary: Civil Service Dept, 1968-70; Office of the Lord Chancellor, 1970-72; DHSS, 1972-75. Sec. to the Church Commissioners, 1975-80. Mem., Lord Chancellor's Cttee on Public Records, 1978-80. Royal Institution: a Manager, 1966-69, 1970-73; Hon. Treas. and Vice-Pres., 1981–. Chm., Nat. Marriage Guidance Council, 1982–. Mem., Clergy Orphan Corp., 1980–. Governor, Bristol Grammar Sch., 1972–; Chm., Lingfield Hosp. Sch., 1981–. CBIM 1978. *Recreations:* theatre, unavoidable gardening. *Address:* 20 Beckenham Grove, Bromley, Kent BR2 0JU. *T:* 01-460 2026. *Club:* Athenæum.

OSMOND, Thomas Edward, BA (hons), MB Cantab; MRCS, LRCP; late Hon. Consulting Venereologist to the British Army; *b* Thorpe-le-Soken, 7 Oct. 1884; *s* of Edward Osmond, JP; *m* 1920, Daisy Stewart Mathews (*d* 1963); one *s* one *d. Educ:* King's Sch., Rochester; Emmanuel Coll., Cambridge; St Bart.'s Hospital. MB Cantab 1912; joined RAMC; service in India and Mesopotamia, 1914-18 (despatches); transferred to RARO 1920 and appointed Pathologist VD Dept St Thomas' Hospital; recalled to Army 1 Sept. 1939; served in France; late Brig. RAMC; adviser in venereology to the Army, 1939, Consultant 1943-45; late MO i/c Male VD Dept and Marlborough Path. Lab. Royal Free Hospital, London; late Pres. Med. Society for the Study of Venereal Diseases; Fellow Med. Society of London; President Middlesex Partial County Committee and Ashford (Middlesex) Branch British Legion. *Publications:* Article, Venereal Disease, Encyclopædia Britannica, Book of the Year, 1939; Aids to the diagnosis and treatment of Venereal Diseases, 1946; articles, Venereal Disease and Social Implications of Venereal Disease, Chambers's Encyclopædia, 1947; Venereal Disease in Peace and War, British Journal of Venereal Diseases, 1949; contributions to British Medical Journal, The Practitioner, etc. *Recreations:* gardening, bridge. *Address:* Lavender Cottage, Passage Hill, Mylor Bridge, near Falmouth, Cornwall.

OSMOND-CLARKE, Sir Henry, KCVO 1969; CBE 1947; FRCS; Consulting Orthopædic Surgeon: London Hospital, E1 (Orthopædic Surgeon, 1946-70); Robert Jones and Agnes Hunt Orthopædic Hospital, Oswestry (Senior Visiting Surgeon, 1930-70); Hon. Civilian Consultant in

Orthopædics, RAF, since 1946; Orthopædic Surgeon to Queen, 1965-73; e s of W. J. Clarke, Brookeborough, Co. Fermanagh, NI; m Freda, e d of Richard Hutchinson, Bury, Lancs; two d. Educ: Clones High School; Trinity College, Dublin University; Vienna, Bologna, New York, Boston, London. BA 1925; MB, BCh (stip. cond.) 1926; FRCSIre 1930; FRCS 1932; Surgical Travelling Prize, TCD 1930. Consultant Orthopædic Surgeon, Oldchurch, Black Notley, Tilbury and East Grinstead Hosps; Orthopædic Surgeon, King Edward VII Hosp. for Officers, London; Cons. King Edward VII Convalescent Home for Officers, Osborne; Hunterian Prof. RCS, 1936. Service Cons. in Orthop. Surg., Air Cdre, RAF, 1941-46; Mayo Clinic Foundation Lecturer, 1948; Orthop. Mem. WHO Mission to Israel, 1951, to India, 1953, to Persia, 1957. Past President, British Orthop. Assoc. (former Editorial Sec. and Acting Sec.); FRSocMed and several Brit. Med. Socs. Formerly: Clinical Tutor in Orthop. Surg., Manchester Roy. Infirmary and Lecturer in Surg. Pathology (Orthop.), Univ. of Manchester; Orthop. Surg., Crumpsall Hosp., Manchester, and Biddulph Grange Orthop. Hosp., Stoke-on-Trent; Sen. Ho. Surg. and Orthop. Ho. Surg. Ancoats Hosp., Manchester, and Royal Nat. Orthop. Hospital, London. Mem. Council, RCS, 1959-75, Vice-Pres. 1970-72. Chm. Accident Services Review Cttee of Great Britain and Ireland, 1960. Hon. Mem. American Orthop. Assoc.; American Acad. of Orthopædic Surgery; Australian, New Zealand and Canadian Orthopædic Assocs; Corresp. Mem., French Orthopædic Society and Surg. Soc. of Lyon; Mem. International Soc. of Orthopædics and Traumatology. Publications: papers on surgical and orthopædic subjects in leading surgical text-books and med. jls, including Half a Century of Orthopædic Progress in Great Britain, 1951. Recreations: travel, reading, fishing. Address: 46 Harley House, Marylebone Road, NW1 5HJ. T: 01-486 9975. Club: Royal Air Force.

OSOLA, (Victor) John, (Väinö Juhani), CBE 1980; FEng, FIMechE; Group Chief Executive, Redman Heenan International plc, since 1979; b 24 Jan. 1926; s of Väinö Kaarlo Osola and Violet Agenoria (née Jones); m 1948, Brenda Lilian Davison; two s one d. Educ: Hymers Coll., Hull; Sunderland Technical Coll., Univ. of Durham (BSc). FEng 1979; FIMechE 1966; Mem., ASME; MInstE. Technical Commn, RE, 1945-48. Gas Turbine Res. Engr, C. A. Parsons & Co. Ltd, 1951-52; Sen. Proj. Design Engr, Procter & Gamble Ltd, 1952-57; Chief Engr, Lankro Chemicals Ltd, 1957-65; Technical Director: Fibreglass Ltd, 1965-72; Triplex Safety Glass Co. Ltd, 1972-79; Chm., Fibreglass Pilkington Ltd, Bombay, 1967-72; Director: Triplex Ireland Ltd, 1976-79; Triclover Safety Glass Co. Ltd, 1976-79; Mem., Pilkington Brothers European Safety Glass Bd, 1977-79. Pres., IMechE, 1982-; Ind. Mem., Mech. Engrg and Machine Tool Requirements Bd, Dept of Industry, 1974-77, Chm. 1977-79; Member: Court of Cranfield Inst. of Technol., 1979-; Policy Bd, Cranfield Product Engrg Centre, 1980-. Associate, St George's House, Windsor, 1980-; Governor, Malvern Coll., 1981-. FRSA 1976. MacRobert Award, 1978. Publications: papers in specialised engrg jls. Recreations: offshore sailing (BoT yachtmaster), music, theatre. Address: Whiddon End, Yarhampton Cross, near Stourport-on-Severn, Worcs DY13 0UY. T: Great Witley 293. Clubs: Army and Navy, St Stephen's Constitutional; Royal Dee Yacht (Cheshire); Royal Irish Yacht (Dublin); North West Venturers Yacht (Beaumaris).

OSTLERE, Dr Gordon; see Gordon, Richard.

O'SULLEVAN, Peter John, OBE 1977; Daily Express Racing Correspondent, since 1950, and BBC Television Commentator; b 3 March 1918; o s of late Col John Joseph O'Sullevan, DSO, formerly Resident Magistrate, Killarney, and Vera, o d of Sir John Henry, DL, JP; m 1951, Patricia, o d of Frank Duckworth, Winnipeg, Manitoba, Canada. Educ: Hawtreys; Charterhouse; Collège Alpin, Switzerland. Specialised in ill-health in early life and not accepted for fighting forces in 1939-45 war, during which attached to Chelsea Rescue Services. Subsequently worked for John Lane, the Bodley Head, on editorial work and MSS reading. Joined Press Assoc. as Racing Correspondent, 1945, until appointed Daily Express, 1950, in similar capacity. Race-broadcasting 1946- (incl. Australia, S Africa, Italy, France, USA); in 1953 became first regular BBC TV and horse-racing commentator to operate without a race-reader; commentated: first television Grand National, 1960; world's first televised electronic horse race from Atlas computer at Univ. of London, transmitted by BBC TV Grandstand, 1967; first horse race transmitted "live" via satellite, from NY, to invited audience in London, 1980. (With late Clive Graham) Derby Award for Racing Journalist of the Year, 1971; Racehorse Owner of the Year Award, Horserace Writers' Assoc., 1974; Timeform Racing Personality, 1974; Clive Graham Meml Award for services to racing, Press Club, 1978; Evening News Sports Commentator of the Year, 1978. Recreations: racehorse owning, in minor way (happiest broadcasting experience commentating success of own horses, Be Friendly, 1966-67, and Attivo, 1974); travel, reading, art, food and wine. Address: 37 Cranmer Court, SW3 3HW. T: 01-584 2781.

O'SULLIVAN, (Carrol Austin) John (Naish), CB 1973; LLB (London); Public Trustee, 1971-75; b 24 Jan. 1915; s of late Dr Carrol Naish O'Sullivan and late Stephanie O'Sullivan (née Manning); m 1939, Lillian Mary, y d of Walter Frank Yate Molineux, Ulverston; one s one d. Educ: Mayfield College. Admitted Solicitor, 1936. Served War of 1939-45, Gordon Highlanders and HQ Special Force SEAC (Captain). Joined Public Trustee Office, 1945; Chief Administrative Officer, 1963-66; Asst Public Trustee, 1966-71. Pres., Holborn Law Soc., 1965-66. Chm. of Governors of St Thomas More High Sch. for Boys, Westcliff-on-Sea, 1964-66. Publications: articles in legal jls; short stories. Recreations: golf, gadgets, and the hobby of the

moment. Address: 3 The Leeway, Hopping Jack's Lane, Danbury, Chelmsford CM3 4PS. T: Danbury 3829.

O'SULLIVAN, Rt. Rev. Mgr. James, CBE 1973 (MBE 1963); Officiating Chaplain (RC), RAMC Depot and Training Centre, since 1973; b 2 Aug. 1917; s of Richard O'Sullivan and Ellen (née Ahern). Educ: St Finnbar's Coll., Cork; All Hallows Coll., Dublin. Ordained, 1941; joined Royal Army Chaplain's Dept, 1942; 49 Infantry Div., Normandy, 1944; Senior RC Chaplain, Malaya, 1952-54 (despatches 1953); Chaplain Irish Guards, 1954-56; Senior RC Chaplain, Berlin, 1956-59; Staff Chaplain (RC), War Office, 1959-64; Senior RC Chaplain, BAOR, 1965-69; Principal RC Chaplain (Army), 1969-73. Recreation: golf. Address: Osgil, Vicarage Lane, Ropley, Alresford, Hants.

O'SULLIVAN, John; see O'Sullivan, C. A. J. N.

OSWALD, Maj.-Gen. Marshall St John, CB 1965; CBE 1961; DSO 1945; MC 1943; retired as Director of Management and Support Intelligence, Ministry of Defence, 1966; b 13 Sept. 1911; s of William Whitehead Oswald and Katharine Ray Oswald; m 1st, 1938, Mary Georgina Baker (d 1970); one s two d; 2nd, 1974, Mrs Barbara Rickards. Educ: Rugby Sch.; RMA, Woolwich. Commissioned RA, 1931; served in RHA and Field Artillery, UK and India, 1931-39. Served War of 1939-45 (despatches, MC, DSO): Battery Comdr 4 RHA and Staff Officer in Egypt and Western Desert, 1939-42; GSO1, Tactical HQ, 8th Army, 1942-43; 2nd in Comd Field Regt, Italy, 1943-44; CO South Notts Hussars, Western Europe, 1944-45; Col on staff of HQ 21 Army Group, 1945. Mil. Govt Comdr (Col) of Cologne Area, 1946-47; Staff Officer, War Office (Lt-Col) 1948-49; Instructor (Col) Staff Coll., Camberley 1950-52; CO 19 Field Regt, Germany/Korea, 1953-55; GHQ, MELF (Col), 1955-56 (despatches 1957); IDC 1958; CCRA and Chief of Staff (Brig.) 1st Corps in Germany, 1959-62; DMI, War Office, 1962-64, Min. of Defence (Army), 1964-65. Recreations: fishing, shooting, ski-ing. Address: Eastfield House, Longparish, near Andover, Hants. T: Longparish 228. Club: Army and Navy.

OSWALD, Dr Neville Christopher, TD 1946; MD Cantab 1946, FRCP 1947; retired 1975; formerly: Consultant Physician: St Bartholomew's Hospital; Brompton Hospital; King Edward VII's Hospital for Officers, London; King Edward VII's Hospital, Midhurst; b 1 Aug. 1910; s of late Col Christopher Percy Oswald, CMG; m 1st, 1941, Patricia Rosemary Joyce Cooke (d 1947); one s one d; 2nd, 1948, Marjorie Mary Sinclair; one d. Educ: Clifton Coll.; Queens' Coll., Cambridge. Research Fellow, USA, 1938-39. Royal Army Medical Corps, 1939-45. Hon. Physician to the Queen, 1956-58; Hon. Consultant in Diseases of the Chest to the Army, 1972-75. Hon. Col, 17th (London) General Hospital RAMC (TA), 1960-70, 217 (Eastern) General Hospital RAMC (V), 1967-70. President: British Tuberculosis Assoc., 1965-67; Thoracic Soc., 1974. DL Greater London, 1973-78. RCP: Mitchell Lectr; Tudor Edwards Lectr. Publications: Recent Trends in Chronic Bronchitis, 1958; Diseases of the Respiratory System, 1962; many articles upon respiratory diseases. Recreations: travel, golf. Address: 2 The Old Rectory, Thurlestone, South Devon. T: Thurlestone 555.

OSWALD, Thomas; b 1 May 1904; s of John Oswald and Agnes Love, Leith; m 1933, Colina MacAskill, d of Archibald MacAlpine and Margaret MacAskill, Ballachulish, Argyllshire; three s one d. Educ: Yardheads and Bonnington Elementary Schools. Shipyard worker, transport worker. Official of Transport and General Workers' Union; Scottish Regional Trade Group Secretary, 1941-69. Contested (Lab) West Aberdeenshire, 1950. MP (Lab) Edinburgh Central, 1951-Feb. 1974; PPS to Secretary of State for Scotland, 1967-70. Sec. Treasurer, Scottish Parly Lab. Group, 1953-64; Sec., Members' Parly Cttee, 1956-66. Dir, St Andrew Animal Fund; Mem. Cttee, Scottish Soc. for Prevention of Vivisection; Nat. Pres., Scottish Old Age Pensions Assoc. Recreations: student economic and industrial history; swimming, camping, etc. Address: 28 Seaview Crescent, Joppa, Edinburgh EH15 2LU. T: 031-669 5569.

O'TOOLE, Peter; actor; b 1932; s of Patrick Joseph O'Toole; m Sian Phillips qv (marr. diss.); two d. Educ: Royal Academy of Dramatic Art. With Bristol Old Vic Company, 1955-58; first appearance on London stage as Peter Shirley in Major Barbara, Old Vic, 1956. Associate Dir, Old Vic Co., 1980. Plays include: Oh, My Papa!, Garrick, 1957; The Long and the Short and the Tall, Royal Court and New, 1959; season with Shakespeare Memorial Theatre Company, Stratford-on-Avon, 1960; Baal, Phœnix, 1963; Hamlet, National Theatre, 1963; Ride a Cock Horse, Piccadilly, 1965; Juno and the Paycock, Man and Superman, Pictures in the Hallway, Gaiety, Dublin, 1966; Waiting for Godot, Happy Days (dir.), Abbey, Dublin, 1969; Uncle Vanya, Plunder, The Apple Cart, Judgement, Bristol Old Vic, 1973; Uncle Vanya, Present Laughter, Chicago, 1978; Macbeth, Old Vic, 1980. Films include: Kidnapped, 1959; The Day They Robbed the Bank of England, 1959; The Savage Innocents, 1960; Lawrence of Arabia, 1962; Becket, 1963; Lord Jim, 1964; What's New, Pussycat, 1965; How to Steal a Million, 1966; The Bible . . . in the Beginning, 1966; The Night of the Generals, 1967; Great Catherine, 1968; The Lion in Winter, 1968; Goodbye Mr Chips, 1969; Brotherly Love, 1970; Murphy's War, 1971; Under Milk Wood, 1971; The Ruling Class, 1972; Man of La Mancha, 1972; Rosebud, 1975; Man Friday, 1975; Foxtrot, 1975; The Stunt Man, 1977; Coup d'Etat, 1977; Zulu Dawn, 1978; Power Play, 1978; The Antagonists, 1981; My Favorite Year, 1981; television: Rogue Male, BBC, 1976; Strumpet City, RTE, 1979; Masada, ABC, 1981; Svengali,

CBS, 1982. *Address:* c/o Veerline Ltd, 54 Baker Street, W1M 1DJ. *T:* 01-486 5888. *Club:* Garrick.

OTTAWA, Archbishop of, (RC), since 1967; **Most Rev. Joseph Aurèle Plourde;** *b* 12 Jan. 1915; *s* of Antoine Plourde and Suzanne Albert. *Educ:* Bathurst Coll.; Bourget Coll.; Rigaud; Major Seminary of Halifax; Inst. Catholique, Paris, Gregorian Univ., Rome. Auxiliary Bishop of Alexandria, Ont., 1964. Hon. DEducn, Moncton Univ., 1969. *Address:* Archbishop's Residence, 145 Saint Patrick Street, Ottawa, Ont K1N 5K1, Canada. *T:* 237-4540.

OTTAWA, Bishop of, since 1981; **Rt. Rev. Edwin Keith Lackey.** *Educ:* Bishop's Univ., Lennoxville (BA 1953). Deacon 1953, priest 1954, Ottawa; Curate of Cornwall, 1953-55; Incumbent of Russell, 1955-60, Vankleek Hill, 1960-63; Rector of St Michael and All Angels, Ottawa, 1963-72; Director of Programme, dio. Ottawa, 1972-78; Hon. Canon, 1972-78; Archdeacon of the Diocese, 1978-81. *Address:* Bishop's Office, 71 Bronson Avenue, Ottawa, Ontario K1R 6G6, Canada.

OTTER, Rt. Rev. Anthony, MA; an Assistant Bishop, Diocese of Lincoln, since 1965; *b* 8 Sept. 1896; *s* of Robert Charles and Marianne Eva Otter; *m* 1929, Dorothy Margaret Ramsbotham (*d* 1979); no *c. Educ:* Repton; Trinity College, Cambridge. Served European War, 1914-18, in RNVR, 1914-19. BA (2nd cl. History Tripos), 1920; MA 1925. Cambridge Mission to Delhi, 1921-24; Westcott House, Cambridge, 1924-25; Deacon, 1925; Priest, 1926; Curate of Holy Trinity, St Marylebone, 1925-31; London Secretary of SCM, 1926-31; Vicar of Lowdham with Gunthorpe, Dio. of Southwell, 1931-49; Chaplain of Lowdham Grange Borstal Institution, 1931-45; Ed. of Southwell Diocesan Magazine, 1941-46; Hon. Canon of Southwell Cathedral, 1942-49; Rural Dean of Gedling, 1946-49; Bishop Suffragan of Grantham, 1949-65; Dean of Stamford, 1949-71. *Publications:* William Temple and the Universal Church, 1949; Beginning with Atoms, 1971, rev. edn, From Atoms to Infinity, 1977. *Recreations:* country, birds; maintenance of domestic machinery. *Address:* The Old Rectory, Belton, Grantham, Lincs. *T:* Grantham 2061.

OTTER, Air Vice-Marshal Victor Charles, CBE 1967 (OBE 1945); Air Officer Engineering, Air Support Command Royal Air Force, 1966-69, retired; *b* 9 February 1914; *s* of Robert and Ada Annie Otter; *m* 1943, Iris Louise Dykes; no *c. Educ:* Weymouth Gram. School. RAF Aircraft Apprentice, 1929-32; flying duties, 1935-37; commissioned Engr. Br., 1940; SO (Techn) Controller Research and Development (MAP), 1942-47; Asst Air Attaché, Budapest, 1947-48; Officer Comdg Central Servicing Develt Establt, 1953-55; Chief Engrg Officer, Bomber Comd, 1956-59; OC No 32 Maintenance Unit, 1959-61; STSO Flying Trng Comd, 1961-63; Project Dir, P1154/P1127, 1963-66. CEng, FRAeS, psc. *Address:* Harpenden, 21 Keats Avenue, Littleover, Derby DE3 7EE. *T:* Derby 512048. *Club:* Royal Air Force.

OTTEWILL, Prof. Ronald Harry, PhD; FRS 1982; FRSC; Professor of Colloid Science, University of Bristol, since 1970; *b* 8 Feb. 1927; *m* Ingrid Geraldine Roe; one *s* one *d. Educ:* Southall Grammar Sch.; Queen Mary Coll., London (BSc 1948; PhD 1951); Fitzwilliam Coll., Cambridge (MA 1955; PhD 1956). Sen. Asst in Res., 1955-58, Asst Dir of Res., 1958-63, Dept of Colloid Sci., Cambridge Univ.; Bristol University: Lectr, 1964-66; Reader, 1966-70; Head of Dept of Physical Chem., 1973. Mem., Faraday Soc. *Publications:* contribs to learned jls. *Address:* School of Chemistry, The University, Bristol BS8 1TS.

OTTLEY, Agnes May; retired as Principal, S Katharine's College, Tottenham, N17, Dec. 1959; *b* 29 June 1899; *d* of late Rev. Canon Robert Lawrence Ottley, Professor of Moral and Pastoral Theology, Oxford. *Educ:* privately; Society of Oxford Home Students. Final Honours School of Modern History, Oxford, 1921; MA Oxon; Assistant Mistress at S Felix School, Southwold, 1925; Lecturer in History, Avery Hill Training College, 1927. *Address:* 104 Lyndhurst Road, Hove, East Sussex BN3 6FD. *T:* Brighton 733958.

OTTON, Sir Geoffrey (John), KCB 1981 (CB 1978); Second Permanent Secretary, Department of Health and Social Security, since 1979; *b* 10 June 1927; *s* of late John Alfred Otton and Constance Alma Otton; *m* 1952, Hazel Lomas (*née* White); one *s* one *d. Educ:* Christ's Hosp.; St John's Coll., Cambridge (MA). Home Office: Asst Principal, 1950; Principal, 1954-64 (seconded to Cabinet Office, 1959-61); Principal Private Sec. to Home Sec., 1963-65; Asst Sec., 1964-70; Asst Under-Sec. of State, Home Office Children's Dept, 1970; transf. with that Dept to DHSS, 1971, Under-Sec., DHSS, 1971-75, Dep. Sec., 1975-79. Chief Advr to Supplementary Benefits Commn, 1976-79. *Recreation:* music. *Address:* 72 Cumberland Road, Bromley, Kent. *T:* 01-460 9610.

OTTON, Philip Howard, QC 1975; a Recorder of the Crown Court, since 1972; Barrister-at-Law; *b* 28 May 1933; *o s* of H. A. Otton, Kenilworth; *m* 1965, Helen Margaret, *d* of late P. W. Bates, Stourbridge; two *s* one *d. Educ:* Bablake School, Coventry; Birmingham Univ. LLB 1954. Called to the Bar, Gray's Inn, 1955. Dep. Chm., Beds QS, 1970-72; Junior Counsel to the Treasury (Personal Injuries), 1970-75. Governor, Nat. Heart and Chest Hosps, 1979-. *Address:* 2 Crown Office Row, Temple, EC4Y 7HJ. *T:* 01-353 9337; 6 Parkmead, SW15 5BS. *T:* 01-789 6262. *Clubs:* Garrick, Roehampton.

OTUNGA, HE Cardinal Maurice; *see* Nairobi, Archbishop of, (RC).

OULTON, Antony Derek Maxwell, CB 1979; MA, PhD; Permanent Secretary, Lord Chancellor's Office, and Clerk of the Crown in Chancery, since 1982; barrister-at-law; *b* 14 Oct. 1927; *y s* of late Charles Cameron Courtenay Oulton and Elizabeth, *d* of T. H. Maxwell, KC; *m* 1955, Margaret Geraldine, *d* of late Lt-Col G. S. Oxley, MC, 60th Rifles; one *s* three *d. Educ:* St Edward's Sch., Oxford; King's Coll., Cambridge (scholar; BA (1st Cl.), MA; PhD 1974). Called to Bar, Gray's Inn, 1952; in private practice, Kenya, 1952-60; Private Sec. to Lord Chancellor, 1961-65; Sec., Royal Commn on Assizes and Quarter Sessions, 1966-69. Dep. Sec., 1976-82, and Dep. Clerk of the Crown in Chancery, 1977-82, Lord Chancellor's Office. *Publication:* (jtly) Legal Aid and Advice, 1971. *Address:* 35 St John's Wood Terrace, NW8 6JL. *T:* 01-586 1555.

OULTON, Air Vice-Marshal Wilfrid Ewart, CB 1958; CBE 1953; DSO 1943; DFC 1943; CEng; FRIN; FIERE; Chairman: Medsales Ltd; Medfurn Ltd; *b* 27 July 1911; *s* of Llewellyn Oulton, Monks Coppenhall, Cheshire; *m* 1935, Sarah, *d* of Rev. E. Davies, Pitsea, Essex; three *s. Educ:* University Coll., Cardiff; Cranwell. Commissioned, 1931; Director, Joint Anti-Submarine School, 1946-48; Joint Services Staff College, 1948-50; Air Attaché, Buenos Aires, Montevideo, Asuncion, 1950-53; idc 1954; Director of Operations, Air Ministry, 1954-56; commanded Joint Task Force "Grapple" for first British megaton weapon tests in the Pacific, 1956-58; Senior Air Staff Officer, RAF Coastal Command, HQ, 1958-60; retd. *Recreations:* music, squash, golf, travel. *Address:* Farthings, Hollywood Lane, Lymington, Hants. *T:* Lymington 73498. *Clubs:* Royal Air Force; Royal Lymington Yacht.

OUNSTED, John, MA Cantab; HM Inspector of Schools, 1971-81; *b* London, 24 May 1919; *e s* of late Rev. Laurence J. Ounsted, Dorchester Abbey, Oxon (ordained 1965; formerly with Sun Life Assurance); *m* 1940, Irene, 3rd *d* of late Rev. Alfred Newns; one *s* four *d. Educ:* Winchester (Scholar); Trinity College, Cambridge (Major Scholar). Math. Tripos Part I, 1st Class; Moral Science Tripos Part II, 1st Class; Senior Scholarship, Trinity College. Assistant Master, King Edward's School, Birmingham, 1940-48; Headmaster, Leighton Park School, 1948-70. First layman ever to be Select Preacher, Oxford Univ., 1964. Page Scholarship to visit USA, 1965. Liveryman, Worshipful Company of Mercers. *Publications:* verses from various languages in the 2 vols of Translation, 1945 and 1947; contributions to Watsonia, The Proceedings of the Botanical Society of the British Isles, and various other educational and botanical periodicals. *Recreations:* botany, camping, being overtaken when motoring. *Address:* Dumney Lane Cottage, Great Leighs, Chelmsford, Essex. *T:* Great Leighs 445.

See also Sir A. Foley Newns.

OUTERBRIDGE, Col Hon. Sir Leonard Cecil, Kt 1946; CC (Canada) 1967; CBE 1926; DSO 1919; CD 1954; Director, Harvey & Co., Ltd, and other Cos, St John's, Newfoundland; *b* 1888; *s* of late Sir Joseph Outerbridge; *m* 1915, Dorothy Winifred (*d* 1972), *d* of late John Alexander Strathy, Barrie, Ontario. *Educ:* Marlborough; Toronto Univ. (BA, LLB; Hon. LLD, 1950); Hon. LLD: Laval Univ., 1952; Memorial Univ. of Newfoundland, 1961. Solicitor and Barrister, Ontario, 1914; President, Newfoundland Board of Trade, 1923-24; Chairman, Newfoundland Committee arranging Exhibits at British Empire Exhibition (1924 and 1925) (CBE); served European War, 1914-19 (despatches twice, DSO). Hon. Private Sec. to the Governor of Newfoundland, 1931-44; Director of Civil Defence, 1942-45; Lieutenant-Governor of Newfoundland, 1949-57. Hon. Col, Royal Newfoundland Regt, 1950-75. KStJ 1951. *Address:* Littlefield, 3 Pringle Place, St John's, Newfoundland.

OUTERIÑO, Felix C.; *see* Candela Outeriño.

OUTRAM, Sir Alan James, 5th Bt, *cr* 1858; MA; Housemaster, Harrow School; *b* 15 May 1937; *s* of late James Ian Outram and Evelyn Mary Littlehales; *S* great-uncle, 1945; *m* 1976, Victoria Jean, *d* of George Dickson Paton, Bexhill-on-Sea; one *s* one *d. Educ:* Spyway, Langton Matravers, Swanage; Marlborough College, Wilts; St Edmund Hall, Oxford. Lt-Col TAVR. *Recreations:* golf, tennis, bridge. *Heir: s* Douglas Benjamin James Outram, *b* 15 March 1979. *Address:* Druries, Harrow-on-the-Hill, Middlesex.

OVENDEN, John Frederick; *b* 17 Aug. 1942; *s* of late Richard Ovenden and Margaret Louise Ovenden (*née* Lucas); *m* 1963, Maureen (*née* White); one *d. Educ:* Salmestone County Primary Sch., Margate; Chatham House Grammar Sch., Ramsgate. Asst Exec. Engr, Post Office, 1961-74. MP (Lab) Gravesend, Feb. 1974-1979. *Recreation:* football (as a spectator). *Clubs:* Gillingham Labour (Gillingham); Gravesend Trades Hall (Gravesend).

OVENS, Maj.-Gen. Patrick John, OBE 1968; MC 1951; Commandant, Joint Warfare Establishment, 1976-79; retired; *b* 4 Nov. 1922; *s* of late Edward Alec Ovens and late Mary Linsell Ovens, Cirencester; *m* 1952, Margaret Mary White; one *s* two *d. Educ:* King's Sch., Bruton. Commnd into Royal Marines, 1941; HMS Illustrious, 1942-43; 46 Commando, 1945; HQ 3rd Commando Bde, 1946-48; 41 Indep. Commando, Korea, 1950-52; HQ Portsmouth Gp, 1952-55; psa 1955-56; Staff of CGRM, 1959-61; Amphibious Warfare Sqdn, 1961-62; 41 Commando, 1963-65, COS 1965-67; C-in-C Fleet Staff, 1968-69; Comdr 3 Commando Bde, 1970-72; RCDS 1973; COS to Comdt Gen., RM, MoD, 1974-76. *Recreations:* sailing, music, gardening. *Address:* Virginia House, Netherhampton, Salisbury, Wilts SP2 8PU. *T:* Salisbury 743113.

OVERALL, Sir John (Wallace), Kt 1968; CBE 1962; MC and Bar; Director: CSR Ltd, since 1973; Land Lease Corporation Ltd, since 1973; Alliance Holdings Ltd, since 1975; General Property Trust, since 1976; b 15 July 1913; s of late W. Overall, Sydney; m 1943, Margaret J., d of C. W. Goodman; four s. Educ: Sydney Techn. College. AIF, 1940-45: CO, 1 Aust. Para. Bn (Lt-Col). Chief Architect, S Australian Housing Trust, 1946-48; private practice, Architect and Town Planner, 1949-52; Dir of Architecture, Commonwealth Dept of Works, 1952-57; Comr, Nat. Capital Develt Commn, 1958-72; Chm., Nat. Capital Planning Cttee, 1958-72; Comr, Cities Commn (Chm., Adv. Cttee), 1972-73; Mem., Parliament House Construction Authority (Commonwealth Govt of Australia), 1979-; Chm. Assessors, Parlt House Design Competition, 1979-80. Chm. of Olympic Fine Arts Architecture and Sculpture Exhibn, Melb., 1956. Life Fellow, RAIA; FAPI, FRTPI; Pres., Austr. Inst. of Urban Studies, 1970-71. Past Pres., Canberra Legacy Club. Sydney Luker Meml Medal, 1970; Sir James Barrett Medal, 1970. *Publication:* Observations on Redevelopment Western Side of Sydney Cove, 1967; sundry papers to professional jls. *Recreations:* golf, tennis. *Address:* 10 Wallaroy Road, Double Bay, NSW 2028, Australia. *T:* 367719. *Clubs:* Australian (Sydney); Royal Sydney Golf.

OVEREND, Prof. William George; Professor of Chemistry in the University of London, since 1957; Master, Birkbeck College, since 1979 (Vice-Master, 1974-79); b 16 Nov. 1921; e s of Harold George Overend, Shrewsbury, Shropshire; m 1949, Gina Olava, y d of late Horace Bertie Cadman, Birmingham; two s one d. Educ: Priory School, Shrewsbury; Univ. of Birmingham. BSc (Hons) 1943, PhD 1946, DSc 1954, Birmingham; CChem; FRSC (FRIC 1955). Asst Lecturer, Univ. Coll., Nottingham, 1946-47; Research Chemist with Dunlop Rubber Co. Ltd and subsequently British Rubber Producers' Assoc., 1947-49; Hon. Research Fellow, 1947-49, Lecturer in Chemistry, 1949-55, Univ. of Birmingham; Vis. Associate Prof., Pennsylvania State Univ., 1951-52; Reader in Organic Chemistry, Univ. of London, 1955-57; Hd of Dept of Chem., Birkbeck Coll., London, 1957-79. Univ. of London: Mem., Academic Council, 1963-67 and 1976-79; Mem., Collegiate Council, 1979-; Mem., University Entrance and Schools Examination Council, 1966-67; Chm., Bd of Studies in Chemistry, 1974-76; Mem., Senate, 1976-; Mem., Finance and General Purposes Cttee, 1976-; Mem., Jt Cttee of Court and Senate for collective planning, 1976-79; Dean, Faculty of Science, 1978-79; Chm., Acad. Adv. Bd in Sci., 1978-79; Mem., Extra-Mural Council, 1979-; Mem. Council, Inst. of Educn to 1979; Mem. Chem. Bd, CNAA, 1981-. Royal Institute of Chemistry: Examiner, 1958-62; Assessor, 1959-72; Mem., Institutions and Examinations Cttee, 1969-75 (Chm., 1976-); Mem. Council, 1977-80; Mem. Qual and Admissions Cttee, 1977-80; Mem. Qual. and Exam. Bd, RSC, 1980-; Chemical Society: Mem. Council, 1967-70, 1972-77; Mem. Publications Bd, 1967-78; Hon. Sec. and Hon. Treasurer, Perkin Div., 1972-75; Vice-Pres., 1975-77; Mem., Interdivisional Council, 1972-75; Mem., Educn and Trng Bd, 1972-78; Soc. of Chemical Industry: Mem., Council, 1955-65, Mem., Finance Committee, 1956-65, Mem., Publications Cttee, 1955-65 (Hon. Sec. for publications and Chairman of Publications Committee, 1958-65); Brit. Nat. Cttee for Chemistry, 1961-66, 1973-78; Brit. Nat. Cttee for Biochemistry, 1975-81; Chemical Council, 1960-63 and 1964-69 (Vice-Chm. 1964-69); European Cttee for Carbohydrate Chemists, 1970- (Chm.); Hon. Sec., Internat. Cttee for Carbohydrate Chemistry, 1972-75 (Pres., 1978-80); Mem., Jt IUPAC-IUB Commn on Carbohydrate Nomenclature, 1971-. Jubilee Memorial Lecturer, Society of Chemical Industry, 1959-60; Lampitt Medallist, Society of Chemical Industry, 1965; Member: Pharmacopœia Commission, 1963-81; Home Office Poisons Board. Governor: Polytechnic of the South Bank, 1970- (Chm., 1980-); Thomas Huxley Coll., 1971-77. Mem., Cttee of Management, Inst. of Archaeology, 1980-. *Publications:* The Use of Tracer Elements in Biology, 1951; papers in Nature, and Jl of Chemical Soc. *Recreation:* gardening. *Address:* Master's Office, Birkbeck College, Malet Street, WC1E 7HX. *T:* 01-580 6622; The Retreat, Nightingales Lane, Chalfont St Giles, Bucks HP8 4SR. *Club:* Athenæum.

OVERTON, Hugh Thomas Arnold, CMG 1975; HM Diplomatic Service; Consul-General, New York, and Director-General, British Trade Development in the USA, since 1980; b 2 April 1923; e s of late Sir Arnold Overton, KCB, KCMG, MC; m 1948, Claire-Marie Binet; one s two d. Educ: Dragon Sch., Oxford; Winchester; Clare Coll., Cambridge. Royal Signals, 1942-45. HM Diplomatic Service, 1947-; served: Budapest; UK Delegn to UN, New York; Cairo; Beirut; Disarmament Delegn, Geneva; Warsaw; Bonn; Canadian Nat. Defence Coll.; Head of N America Dept, FCO, 1971-74; Consul-Gen., Düsseldorf, 1974-75; Minister (Econ.), Bonn, 1975-80. *Recreations:* reading, walking, sailing, fishing. *Address:* c/o Barclays Bank, 276 Kensington High Street, W8. *Clubs:* Travellers', Royal Commonwealth Society, Royal Automobile.

OWEN, (Alfred) David; Chairman since 1975, and Managing Director since 1969, Rubery Owen Holdings Ltd; b 26 Sept. 1936; m 1966, Ethne (née Sowman); two s one d. Educ: Brocksford Hall; Oundle; Emmanuel Coll., Cambridge Univ. (MA). Joined Rubery Owen Gp, 1960; Gen. Man., Rubery Owen Motor Div., 1962-67; Dep. Man. Dir, Rubery Owen & Co. Ltd, 1967; Acting Chm., Rubery Owen Holdings Ltd, 1969. Trustee, Community Projects Foundn, 1978-; Member: Council, Univ. of Aston, 1981-; Bd, British Library, 1982-; Bd, Nat. Exhibn Centre, 1982-. *Recreations:* hockey, squash, photography, music, industrial archaeology, local history, collecting books. *Address:* Mill Dam House, Mill Lane, Aldridge, Walsall, West Midlands. *T:* 021-353 1221. *Club:* National.

OWEN, Alun, MC 1945; retired; Under-Secretary, Land Use Planning Group, Welsh Office, 1975-79; b 14 March 1919; s of late Evan Thomas Owen and of Gwladys (née David); m 1946, Rhona Evelyn Griffiths; one s four d. Educ: West Monmouth Grammar Sch.; Bridgend Grammar Sch.; LSE (BScEcon). Mil. Service, 1939-46: Ches. Regt, 1940-46 (Captain) (despatches, Normandy, 1944); Civil Service, Cadet Officer, Min. of Labour NW Region, 1946-48; Asst Principal, Min. of Fuel and Power, 1948-50; Customs and Excise, 1950-59, Principal 1951; Welsh Office, Min. of Housing and Local Govt, 1959-62; Admin. Mem., Welsh Bd of Health, 1962-69; Welsh Office: Asst Sec., hosp., health and social work services, 1969-72; Estabt Officer, 1972-73; Under-Sec., Health Services, 1974-75. Mem., Panel examining structure plans of Clwyd, Powis and Dyfed. *Address:* 78 Stanwell Road, Penarth, South Glamorgan. *T:* Penarth 709276.

OWEN, Alun (Davies); writer since 1957; b 24 Nov. 1925; s of Sidney Owen and Ruth (née Davies); m 1942, (Theodora) Mary O'Keeffe; two s. Educ: Cardigan County School, Wales; Oulton High School, Liverpool. Worked as Stage Manager, Director and Actor, in theatre, TV and films, 1942-59. Awards: Screenwriters and Producers Script of the Year, 1960; Screenwriters Guild, 1961; Daily Mirror, 1961; Golden Star, 1967. Acted in: stage: Birmingham Rep., 1943-44; Humoresque, 1948; Snow White and the Seven Dwarfs, 1951; Old Vic season, 1953; Tamburlaine the Great, As You Like It, King Lear, Twelfth Night, The Merchant of Venice, Macbeth, The Wandering Jew, The Taming of the Shrew, 1957; Royal Court Season, 1957; Man with a Guitar, The Waiting of Lester Abbs, The Samson Riddle, 1972; The Ladies, 1977; films: Every Day Except Christmas, 1957; I'm All Right Jack, 1959; The Servant, 1963. Author of productions: stage: The Rough and Ready Lot, 1959 (Radio 1958), publ. 1960; Progress to the Park, 1959 (Radio 1958), publ. 1962; The Rose Affair, 1966 (TV 1961), publ. 1962; A Little Winter Love, 1963, publ. 1964; Maggie May, 1964; The Game, 1965; The Goose, 1967; Shelter, 1971 (TV 1967), publ. 1968; There'll Be Some Changes Made, 1969; Norma, We Who Are About To (later title Mixed Doubles), 1969, publ. 1970; The Male of the Species, 1974 (TV 1969), publ. 1972; screen: The Criminal, 1960; A Hard Day's Night, 1964; Caribbean Idyll, 1970; radio: Two Sons, 1957; It Looks Like Rain, 1959; television: No Trams to Lime Street, 1959, After the Funeral, 1960, Lena, Oh My Lena, 1960, publ. as Three TV Plays, 1961; The Ruffians, 1960; The Ways of Love, 1961; Dare to be a Daniel, 1962, publ. in Eight Plays, Book 1, 1965; The Hard Knock, You Can't Wind 'em All, 1962; The Strain, Let's Imagine Series, The Stag, A Local Boy, 1963; The Other Fella, The Making of Jericho, 1966; The Wake, 1967, publ. in A Collection of Modern Short Plays, 1972; George's Room, 1967, publ. 1968; The Winner, The Loser, The Fantasist, Stella, Thief, 1967; Charlie, Gareth, Tennyson, Ah There You Are, Alexander, Minding the Shop, Time for the Funny Walk, 1968; Doreen, 1969, publ. in The Best Short Plays, 1971; The Ladies, Joan, Spare Time, Park People, You'll Be the Death of Me, Male of the Species, 1969; Hilda, And a Willow Tree, Just the Job, Female of the Species, Joy, 1970; Ruth, Funny, Pal, Giants and Ogres, The Piano Player, 1971; The Web, 1972; Ronnie Barker Show (3 scripts), Buttons, Flight, 1973; Lucky, Norma, 1974; Left, 1975; Forget Me Not (6 plays), 1976; For Old Times Sake, 1978; Passing Through, publ. 1979; The Runner, 1980; Sealink, 1980; Lancaster Gate End, 1982; Cafe Society, 1982; Kish-Kisch, 1982; Colleagues, 1982. *Recreations:* languages and history. *Address:* c/o Felix de Wolfe & Associates, 1 Robert Street, Adelphi, WC2N 6BH.

OWEN, Aron, PhD; His Honour Judge Owen; a Circuit Judge, since 1980; b 16 Feb. 1919; m 1946, Rose (née Fishman), JP; one s two d. Educ: Tredegar County Grammar Sch.; Univ. of Wales (BA Hons, PhD). Called to the Bar, Inner Temple, 1948. *Recreations:* travel, gardening. *Address:* 44 Brampton Grove, Hendon, NW4 4AQ. *T:* 01-202 8151.

OWEN, David; see Owen, A. D.

OWEN, Rt. Hon. David Anthony Llewellyn, PC 1976; MP Plymouth, Devonport, since 1974 (Plymouth, Sutton, 1966-74) (Lab, 1966-81, SDP since 1981); Deputy Leader, Social Democratic Party, since 1982; b Plympton, South Devon, 2 July 1938; s of Dr John William Morris Owen and Mary Llewellyn; m 1968, Deborah Schabert; two s one d. Educ: Bradfield College; Sidney Sussex College, Cambridge (Hon. Fellow, 1977); St Thomas' Hospital. BA 1959; MB, BChir 1962; MA 1963. St Thomas' Hospital: house appts, 1962-64; Neurological and Psychiatric Registrar, 1964-66; Research Fellow, Medical Unit, 1966-68. Contested (Lab) Torrington, 1964. PPS to Minister of Defence, Administration, 1967; Parly Under-Sec. of State for Defence, for RN, 1968-70; Opposition Defence Spokesman, 1970-72, resigned over EEC, 1972; Parly Under-Sec. of State, DHSS, 1974; Minister of State: DHSS, 1974-76; FCO, 1976-77; Sec. of State for Foreign and Commonwealth Affairs, 1977-79; opposition spokesman on energy, 1979-80. Sponsored 1973 Children's Bill; ministerially responsible for 1975 Children's Act. Co-founder, SDP, 1981; Chm., Parly Cttee, SDP, 1981-82. Chm., Decision Technology Internat., 1970-72. Mem., Independent Commn on Disarmament and Security Issues, 1980-82. Governor of Charing Cross Hospital, 1966-68; Patron, Disablement Income Group, 1968-. Chairman of SW Regional Sports Council, 1967-71. *Publications:* (ed) A Unified Health Service, 1968; The Politics of Defence, 1972; In Sickness and in Health, 1976; Human Rights, 1978; Face the Future, 1981; contrib. to Social Services for All, 1968; articles in Lancet, Neurology, and Clinical Science. *Recreation:* sailing. *Address:* 78 Narrow Street, Limehouse, E14. *T:* 01-987 5441; Castlehayes, Plympton, Plymouth, Devon. *T:* Plymouth 336130; House of Commons, SW1. *T:* 01-219 4203.

OWEN, Dr David Elystan, CBE 1972; Director, Manchester Museum, 1957-76; *b* 27 Feb. 1912; *s* of Dr John Griffith Owen, Kingston-on-Thames, and Mrs Gertrude Owen (*née* Heaton); *m* 1936, Pearl Jennings, Leicester; one *s* one *d. Educ:* The Leys Sch., Cambridge; King's Coll., London Univ. 1st cl. hons BSc 1933, PhD 1935. Keeper, Dept of Geology, Liverpool Museum, 1935-47; War Service, 1939-45 in Artillery (Major, RA); Dir, Leeds City Museums, 1947-57. Treas. 1956-61, Pres. 1968-69, Museums Assoc. *Publications:* The Story of Mersey and Deeside Rocks, 1939; A History of Kirkstall Abbey, 1955; Water Highways, 1967; Water Rallies, 1969; Water Byways, 1973; Canals to Manchester, 1977; Cheshire Waterways, 1979; The Manchester Ship Canal, 1982; numerous palaeontological papers in Palaeontology, Geological Jl, etc. *Recreation:* cruising the British canal and river system. *Address:* 9 Carleton Road, Higher Poynton, Cheshire. *T:* Poynton 872924.

OWEN, Maj.-Gen. David Lanyon Ll.; *see* Lloyd Owen.

OWEN, Sir Dudley H. C.; *see* Cunliffe-Owen.

OWEN, Rt. Rev. Edwin, MA; *b* 3 Nov. 1910; *s* of late William Rowland Owen; *m* 1940, Margaret Mary Williams, BA; one *s* one *d. Educ:* Royal School, Armagh; Trinity College, Dublin (MA). Deacon 1934, priest 1935, Dublin; Curate of Glenageary, 1934-36; Christ Church, Leeson Park, Dublin, 1936-38; Minor Canon of St Patrick's Cathedral, Dublin, 1935-36; Chancellor, 1936-38; Succentor, 1938-42; Incumbent of Birr with Eglish, 1942-57; Canon, Killaloe Cathedral, 1954-57; Rector of Killaloe and Dean of Killaloe Cathedral, 1957-72; Diocesan Secretary of Killaloe and Kilfenora, 1957-72; Bishop of Killaloe, Kilfenora, Clonfert and Kilmacduagh, 1972-76, when diocese amalgamated with Limerick, Ardfert and Aghadoe, and Emly; Bishop of Limerick and Killaloe, 1976-81. *Recreation:* classical music. *Address:* 5 Frankfort Avenue, Rathgar, Dublin 6. *Club:* Friendly Brothers (Dublin).

OWEN, Eric Hamilton; retired; *b* 4 Aug. 1903; *s* of Harold Edwin Owen and Hilda Guernsey; *m* 1937, Margaret Jeannie Slipper. Served Artists' Rifles, 1921-39; RASC, 8th Army, 1940-45; 21st SAS Regt (Artists), 1946-48 (despatches). Formerly: Chm., Charterhouse Investment Trust; Dep. Chm., Charterhouse Gp Ltd and Grindlays Bank Ltd. Dir, Gabbitas-Thring Educational Trust Ltd. Member Board of Trade Mission to Ghana, 1959. CBIM. *Recreations:* photography, travel. *Address:* 11 Broom Hall, Oxshott, Surrey. *Club:* Army and Navy.

OWEN, Dr Gareth, DSc; MRIA; FIBiol; Principal, University College of Wales, Aberystwyth, since 1979; *b* 4 Oct. 1922; *s* of J. R. and B. M. Owen; *m* 1953, Beti Jones; one *s* two *d. Educ:* Pontypridd Boys' Grammar Sch.; University Coll., Cardiff (BSc 1950; Fellow, 1982). DSc Glasgow, 1959. FIBiol 1964. Served War, RAF Pilot, 1942-47. Lectr in Zoology, Univ. of Glasgow, 1950-64; Prof. of Zool., 1964-79, and Pro-Vice-Chancellor, 1974-79, Queen's Univ. of Belfast, MRIA 1976. *Publications:* contrib. Trans Royal Soc., Proc. Malacol. Soc. London, Jl Mar. Biol. Soc., and Qly Jl Micro. Sci. *Recreation:* photography. *Address:* Plas Penglais, Aberystwyth, Dyfed SY23 3DF. *T:* Aberystwyth 3583. *Club:* Royal Commonwealth Society.

OWEN, Gerald Victor, QC 1969; a Recorder of the Crown Court, since 1979; *b* London, 29 Nov. 1922; *m* 1946, Phyllis (*née* Ladsky); one *s* one *d. Educ:* Kilburn Grammar Sch.; St Catharine's Coll., Cambridge. Exhibr, St Catharine's Coll., Cambridge, 1940; Drapers' Company Science Schol., Queen Mary Coll., London, 1940. 1st cl. Maths Tripos I, 1941; Senior Optimes Tripos II, 1942; BA 1943, MA 1946, Cantab; Royal Statistical Soc. Certif., 1947; LLB London (Hons) 1949. Research Ballistics, Min. of Supply, 1942-45; Statistical Officer, LCC, 1945-49. Called to Bar, Gray's Inn, 1949; *ad eundem* Inner Temple, 1969. A Dep. Circuit Judge, 1971. Member, Cttees of Justice on: Legal Aid in Criminal Cases; Complaints against Lawyers, 1970; False Witness, the problem of perjury, 1973. *Address:* Wellington House, Eton Road, NW3; 3 Paper Buildings, Temple, EC4. *T:* 01-353 1182. *Club:* Maccabaeans.

OWEN, Maj.-Gen. Harry, CB 1972; Chairman, Medical Appeal Tribunal, since 1972; *b* 17 July 1911; *m* 1952, Maureen (*née* Summers); one *s* one *d. Educ:* University Coll., Bangor. BA Hons Philosophy, 1934. Solicitor of Supreme Court, 1939. Commissioned in Queen's Own Cameron Highlanders, 1940-43; joined Mil. Dept of Office of Judge Advocate General, 1943: served in: W Africa, 1945-46; Middle East, 1947-50; Austria, 1952-53; Dep. Dir of Army Legal Services: Far East, 1960-62; HQ, BAOR, 1962-67; Brig. Legal Staff, 1968-69; Maj.-Gen. 1969; Dir, Army Legal Services, 1969-71, retd. *Recreations:* philosophy, history of art, walking, gardening. *Address:* Clavering, 40 North Park, Gerrards Cross, Bucks. *T:* Gerrards Cross 86777.

OWEN, Sir Hugh (Bernard Pilkington), 5th Bt *cr* 1813; *b* 28 March 1915; *s* of Sir John Arthur Owen, 4th Bt and of Lucy Fletcher, *e d* of F. W. Pilkington; *S* father, 1973. *Educ:* Chillon Coll., Switzerland. *Heir: b* John William Owen [*b* 7 June 1917; *m* 1963, Gwenllian Mary, *er d* of late E. B. Phillips]. *Address:* 63 Dudsbury Road, Ferndown, Dorset.

OWEN, Idris Wyn; a director of a company in the construction industry; *b* 1912; *m. Educ:* Stockport Sch. and Coll. of Technology; Manchester Sch. of Commerce. Contested (C): Manchester Exchange, 1951; Stalybridge and Hyde, 1955; Stockport North 1966; MP (C) Stockport North, 1970-Feb. 1974;

contested (C) Stockport North, Oct. 1974. Member, Stockport Borough Council, 1946; Mayor, 1962-63. Vice-Pres., Nat. Fedn of Building Trades Employers, 1965. FIOB. *Address:* Gawsworth Old Rectory, Cheshire.

OWEN, John Arthur Dalziel, QC 1970; a Recorder of the Crown Court, since 1972; Dean of the Arches Court of Canterbury and Auditor of the Chancery Court of York, since 1980; *b* 22 Nov. 1925; *s* of late R. J. Owen and Mrs O. B. Owen; *m* 1952, Valerie, *d* of W. Ethell; one *s* one *d. Educ:* Solihull Sch.; Brasenose Coll., Oxford. MA, BCL 1949. Commnd 2nd King Edward VII's Own Goorkha Rifles, 1944. Called to Bar, Gray's Inn, 1951, Bencher, 1980. Dep. Chm., Warwickshire QS, 1967-71. Mem. Senate of the Inns of Court and the Bar, 1977-80. Dep. Leader, Midland and Oxford Circuit, 1980-. Mem., General Synod of Church of England, Dio. Coventry, 1970-80; Chancellor, Dio. Derby, 1973-80, Dio. Coventry, 1976-80, Dio. Southwell, 1979-80. *Address:* Lansdowne House, Shipston-on-Stour, Warwicks. *T:* Shipston-on-Stour 61521; 1 Verulam Buildings, Gray's Inn, WC1R 5LQ. *Club:* Garrick.

OWEN, Prof. John Benjamin Brynmor, DSc (Oxon), MSc (Wales); CEng; John William Hughes Professor of Civil Engineering, University of Liverpool, 1950-77, now Emeritus Professor; *b* 2 Sept. 1910; *s* of David Owen (Degwyl) and Mary Alice Owen; *m* 1938, Beatrice Pearn (*née* Clark); two *d. Educ:* Universities of Oxford and Wales. Drapers Company Scholar, Page Prize and Medal, University College, Cardiff, 1928-31 (Fellow, 1981); Meyricke Scholar, Jesus Coll., Oxford, 1931-32; British Cotton Industry Research Association, 1933-35; Messrs A. V. Roe, Manchester, 1935-36; Royal Aircraft Establishment, Farnborough, 1936-48; Naval Construction Research Establishment, 1948-50. *Publications:* Light Structures, 1965; many contributions to learned journals on design of structures, on helicopters and on investigation of aircraft accidents. *Address:* Department of Civil Engineering, The University of Liverpool, PO Box 147, Brownlow Street, Liverpool L69 3BX. *T:* 051-709 6022.

OWEN, John Gethin M.; *see* Morgan-Owen.

OWEN, Maj.-Gen. John Ivor Headon, OBE 1963; Chef de Cabinet to Thomson McLintock & Co, Chartered Accountants, since 1974 (the British Member of KMG, Klynveld Main Goerdeler, since 1979); *b* 22 Oct. 1922; *s* of Major William H. Owen; *m* 1948, Margaret Jean Hayes; three *d. Educ:* St Edmund's Sch., Canterbury. FBIM; psm, jssc, idc. Joined Royal Marines (as Marine), 1942; temp. 2nd Lieut RM, 1942; 44 Commando RM, Far East, 1942-46; demobilised 1946 (Captain RM); Constable, Metropolitan Police, 1946-47; rejoined Royal Marines as Lieut, 1947; regimental service, 1948-55; Staff Coll., Camberley, 1956; Bde Major, HQ 3 Cdo Bde, 1959-62; Naval Plans, Admty/MoD, 1962-64; 42 Cdo RM, 1964-66; Instructor, Jt Services Staff Coll., 1966-67; CO 45 Cdo RM, 1967-68 (despatches); Col GS, Staff of CGRM, 1969-70; Royal Coll. of Defence Studies, 1971-72; Maj.-Gen, Commando Forces RM, Plymouth, 1972-73; Col Comdt, RM, 1983-. Lt-Col 1966; Col 1970; Maj.-Gen. 1972. Treas., Clergy Orphan Corp.; Mem., Ct of Assistants, Sons of the Clergy. *Publications:* Brassey's Infantry Weapons of the World, 1975, 2nd edn 1979; Brassey's NATO Infantry Weapons, 1979; Brassey's Warsaw Pact Infantry Weapons, 1979; contrib. Seaford House Papers, 1971; articles in Contemporary Review and the press. *Recreations:* woodworking, gardening. *Address:* c/o Midland Bank Ltd, 89 Queen Victoria Street, EC4V 4AQ. *Club:* Army and Navy.

OWEN, John Simpson, OBE 1956; conservationist; *b* 1912; *s* of late Archdeacon Walter Edwin Owen and late Lucy Olive (*née* Walton); *m* 1946, May Patricia, *d* of late Francis Gilbert Burns and late May (*née* Malone); three *d. Educ:* Christ's Hospital; Brasenose Coll., Oxford. Sudan Political Service, 1936-55; Director of National Parks, Tanzania, 1960-70, Asst to Director, 1971; Consultant on National Parks in Eastern and Central Africa, 1972-74; Woodrow Wilson Internat. Centre for Scholars, Washington, DC, 1973; Council of the Fauna Preservation Soc., 1975-80. Hon. DSc (Oxon) 1971; World Wildlife Fund Gold Medal, 1971. *Publications:* papers and articles on National Parks and African Zoology. *Address:* 5 Calverley Park Crescent, Tunbridge Wells TN1 2NB. *T:* Tunbridge Wells 29485.

OWEN, Prof. John V.; *see* Vallance-Owen.

OWEN, Joslyn Grey, CBE 1979; Chief Education Officer, Devon, since 1972; *b* 23 Aug. 1928; *s* of W. R. Owen, (Bodwyn), and Nell Evans Owen; *m* 1961, Mary Patricia Brooks; three *s. Educ:* Cardiff High Sch.; Worcester Coll., Oxford (MA). Asst Master, Chigwell Sch., and King's Sch., Canterbury, 1952-58; Asst Educn Officer, Croydon, 1959-62, and Somerset, 1962-66; Jt Sec., Schs Council, 1966-68; Dep. Chief Educn Officer, Devon, 1968-72. Adviser, ACC and Council of Local Educn Authorities, 1977-. Pres., BAAS Educn Section, 1978-79; Chairman: IBA Educnl Adv. Council, 1982- (Vice-Chm., 1980-82); County Educn Officers' Soc., 1980-81; Member: Assessment of Perf. Unit Consultative Cttee, 1974-80; NFER Management Cttee, 1973-; Council of Educnl Technol., 1972-; Gulbenkian Working Party, Arts in the Curriculum, 1978-81; Macfarlane Working Party, 16-19 Educn, 1979-80; Educnl Research Board of SSRC, 1976-82; Nat. Adv. Bd for Local Auth. Higher Educn; Nat. Joint Council, Further Education, 1980-; Cttee for Academic Policy, CNAA, 1981-. Mem. Council, Univ. of Exeter, 1976-. FRSA 1977; Hon. FCP 1979; Hon. Fellow Plymouth Polytechnic, 1981. *Publications:* The Management of Curriculum Development, 1973; chapters in edited works, papers and contribs to learned jls. *Address:* 4 The Quadrant, Exeter, Devon EX2 4LE. *T:* Exeter 74326.

OWEN, Prof. Paul Robert, CBE 1974; FRS 1971; Zaharoff Professor of Aviation, London University, at Imperial College of Science and Technology, since 1963; *b* 24 Jan. 1920; *s* of Joseph and Deborah Owen; *m* 1958, Margaret Ann, *d* of Herbert and Dr Lily Baron; two *s* two *d. Educ:* Queen Mary Coll., London Univ. BSc (London) 1940, MSc (Manchester), FEng, FRAeS, FRMetS. Aerodynamics Dept, RAE, Farnborough, 1941-53; Reader and Director of Fluid Motion Laboratory, Manchester Univ., 1953-56; Professor of the Mechanics of Fluids and Director of the Laboratory, Manchester Univ., 1956-62. Member: ARC, 1964-67, 1969-80 (Chm., 1971-79); Safety in Mines Research Adv. Bd, 1956-73; Environmental Design Res. Cttee, DoE (Chm., 1973-); British Nat. Cttee for Theoretical and Applied Mechanics, 1971-78 (Chm., 1973-78); Construction and Housing Res. Adv. Council, 1976-80; Anglo-French Mixed Commn on Cultural Exchange, 1976-. Fellow, Queen Mary Coll., 1967. Founder Fellow, Fellowship of Engineering, 1976. Hon. Dr Aix-Marseille, 1976. *Publications:* papers on Aerodynamics in R & M series of Aeronautical Research Council, Journal of Fluid Mechanics, etc. *Recreations:* music, theatre. *Address:* 1 Horbury Crescent, W11. *T:* 01-229 5111.

OWEN, Peter Francis; Under Secretary, Departments of the Environment and Transport (Regional Director of Northern and Yorkshire and Humberside Regions), since 1980; *b* 4 Sept. 1940; *s* of Arthur Owen and Violet (*née* Morris); *m* 1963, Ann Preece; one *s* one *d. Educ:* The Liverpool Inst.; Liverpool Univ. (BA French). Joined MPBW, 1964; Cabinet Office, 1971-72; Private Sec. to successive Ministers of Housing and Construction, 1972-74; Asst Sec., Housing Policy Review, 1975-77, Local Govt Finance, 1977-80. *Recreations:* reading, gardening, French language and literature. *Address:* Oakmead, The Avenue, Hampton, Mddx TW12 3RS. *T:* 01-979 3586; 10 Hampden Street, York YO1 1EA. *T:* York 38251.

OWEN, Peter Granville, CMG 1965; QPM 1964; CPM 1960; Deputy Director, Fund Raising, Save the Children Fund, since 1978; *b* 28 Oct. 1918; *s* of Walter Lincoln Owen, Highgate, and Ethel Belton, London, N6; *m* 1943, Mercia Louvaine Palmer; one *s* one *d. Educ:* Grove House Sch., Highgate; City of Norwich Sch. Great Yarmouth Borough Police, 1938-42; RAF, F/O, 1942-46; Public Prosecutor, Somalia Gendarmerie, 1946; Resident Magistrate, Mogadishu, Somalia, 1948; District Commissioner: Somalia, 1949-50; Eritrea, 1950; Tanganyika Police: Cadet, Asst Superintendent and Dep. Superintendent of Police, 1950; Somaliland Police: Superintendent and Senior Superintendent of Police, 1956; Commissioner of Police: Gibraltar, 1960; British Guiana, 1962; Aden, 1965; UN Police Adviser, Govt of Somali Republic, 1968. Adjudication Officer, Cadastral Surveys, British Virgin Is, 1971, Cayman Is, 1973, Blantyre, Malawi, 1976. OStJ 1960. *Recreations:* cricket, swimming, walking. *Address:* 7 Thakeham Close, Lawrie Park Gardens, SE26 6HN. *Clubs:* Royal Commonwealth Society, MCC.

OWEN, Philip Loscombe Wintringham, TD 1950; QC 1963; JP; a Recorder of the Crown Court, since 1972; *b* 10 Jan. 1920; *er s* of Rt Hon. Sir Wintringham Stable, MC, and late Lucie Haden (*née* Freeman); assumed surname of Owen in lieu of Stable by deed poll, 1942; *m* 1949, Elizabeth Jane, *d* of late Lewis Trelawny Widdicombe, Effingham, Surrey; three *s* two *d. Educ:* Winchester; Christ Church, Oxford (MA). Served War of 1939-45, Royal Welch Fusiliers: W Africa, India, Ceylon, Burma, 1939-47; Major TARO. Received into Roman Catholic Church, 1943. Called to Bar, Middle Temple, 1949; Bencher, 1969; Mem., Gen. Council of the Bar of England and Wales, 1971-77; a Deputy Chairman of Quarter Sessions: Montgomeryshire, 1959-71; Cheshire, 1961-71; Recorder of Merthyr Tydfil, 1971; Leader, Wales and Chester Circuit, 1975-77. Chm., Adv. Bd constituted under Misuse of Drugs Act, 1974-. Legal Assessor to: Gen. Med. Council, 1970-; Gen. Dental Council, 1970-; RICS, 1970-. Contested (C) Montgomeryshire, 1945. JP Montgomeryshire, 1959; JP Cheshire, 1961. Vice-Pres., Montgomeryshire Cons. and Unionist Assoc.; Pres., Montgomeryshire Soc., 1974-75. Dir, Swansea City AFC Ltd. *Recreations:* shooting, fishing, forestry, music, Association football. *Address:* 1 Brick Court, Temple, EC4Y 9BY. *T:* 01-583 0777; Plas Llwyn Owen, Llanbrynmair, Powys SY19 7BE. *T:* Llanbrynmair 229. *Clubs:* Carlton, Pratt's; Cardiff and County; Welshpool and District Conservative; Bristol Channel Yacht (Mumbles).

See also R. O. C. Stable.

OWEN, Rear-Adm. Richard Arthur James, CB 1963; *b* 26 Aug. 1910; *s* of late Captain Leonard E. Owen, OBE, JP; *m* 1941, Jean Sophia (*née* Bluett); one *s* two *d. Educ:* Sevenoaks Sch. Joined RN, 1927; Commander (S) 1945; Captain, 1954; Rear-Admiral, 1961; Director-General, Personal Services, Admiralty, 1962-64; retired. *Address:* High Bank, Martin, near Fordingbridge, Hants. *T:* Martin Cross 295.

OWEN, Robert Davies, CBE 1962; FRCS; FRCSE; Senior Ear and Throat Surgeon, Cardiff Royal Infirmary, 1928-64, retired; Lecturer in Oto-Laryngology, Welsh National School of Medicine, 1929-64, retired; *b* 8 May 1898; 2nd *s* of late Capt. Griffith Owen and late Mrs Jane Owen; *m* 1928, Janet Miles, Llantrisant; two *d. Educ:* Towyn Grammar Sch. Cadet, Harrison Line, Liverpool, 1916-18; University College, Cardiff, 1918-21; Guy's Hospital, London, 1921-27. BSc (Wales) 1921. MRCS, LRCP 1923; FRCS 1930; FRCSEd 1926. *Publications:* contrib. BMJ, Lancet, Proc. Royal Society

of Medicine. *Recreations:* shooting, fishing. *Address:* 1 The Mount, Cardiff Road, Llandaff, Cardiff. *T:* Cardiff 568739. *Club:* Cardiff and County.

OWEN, Robert Penrhyn; Director and Secretary, The Water Companies' Association; *b* 17 Dec. 1918; *s* of late Captain Richard Owen; *m* 1949, Suzanne, *d* of late L. H. West; one *s* one *d. Educ:* Friar's School. War service in Royal Welch Fusiliers, 1939-46, in Madagascar, India, The Arakan and North and Central Burma. Admitted Solicitor, 1947. Asst Solicitor: Berks CC, 1948-50; Leics CC, 1950-54; Chief Asst Solicitor, Lancs CC, 1954-60; 2nd Dep. Clerk and 2nd Dep. Clerk of the Peace, Lancs CC, 1960-63; Gen. Manager, Telford Develt Corp. (New Town), 1963-69; Sec., Chief Exec. Officer and Solicitor, Thames Conservancy, 1969-74. *Recreations:* all sport, reading. *Address:* Pilgrims Wood, Fawley Green, Henley-on-Thames, Oxon. *T:* Henley-on-Thames 2994. *Clubs:* St Stephen's Constitutional, MCC.

OWEN, Sir Ronald (Hugh), Kt 1980; Director: Prudential Assurance Co. Ltd, 1974-80 (Chairman, 1975-80); Prudential Corporation Ltd, since 1978 (Chairman, 1978-80); *b* 2 June 1910; *er s* of late Owen Hugh Owen and late Jane Tegwedd Owen; *m* 1939, Claire May Tully; one *s. Educ:* King's College Sch., Wimbledon. FIA 1936. Served War of 1939-45: 52 Field Regt, RA (Major); Bde Major RA, 8 Ind. Division, Middle East and Italy. Joined Prudential, 1929: India, 1936-39; Dep. General Manager, 1959-67; Chief General Manager, 1968-73. Dep. Chm., British Insurance Assoc., 1971-72. Member, Governing Body and Chairman of Finance Cttee, King's College Sch., Wimbledon. *Recreation:* golf. *Address:* 110 Rivermead Court, Hurlingham, SW6. *T:* 01-736 4842. *Clubs:* MCC, Hurlingham; Royal Wimbledon Golf.

OWEN, Rowland Hubert, CMG 1948; Deputy Controller, HM Stationery Office, 1959-64, retired; *b* 3 June 1903; *s* of William R. and Jessie M. Owen, Armagh, NI; *m* 1st, 1930, Kathleen Margaret Evaline Scott (*d* 1965); no *c*; 2nd, 1966, Shelagh Myrle Nicholson. *Educ:* Royal Sch., Armagh; Trinity Coll., Dublin (BA, LLB). Entered Dept of Overseas Trade, 1926; Private Secretary to Comptroller-General, 1930; Secretary Gorell Cttee on Art and Industry, 1931; idc, 1934; Commercial Secretary, Residency, Cairo, 1935; Ministry of Economic Warfare, 1939; Rep. of Ministry in Middle East, 1942; Director of Combined (Anglo-American) Economic Warfare Agencies, AFHQ, Mediterranean, 1943; transferred to Board of Trade and appointed Senior UK Trade Commissioner in India, Burma and Ceylon, 1944; Economic Adviser to UK High Commissioner in India, 1946; Adviser to UK Delegation at International Trade Conf., Geneva, 1947. Comptroller-General, Export Credits Guarantee Dept, 1953-58; Member Managing Cttee, Union d'Assureurs des Crédits Internationaux, 1954-58. Staff, NPFA, 1964-68. Vice-Chm., Haslemere Br., British Heart Foundn Appeal. Vice-President, Tilford Bach Society, 1962-69; Organist: St Mary's, Bramshott, 1964-70; St John the Evangelist, Farncombe, 1970-75; St Luke's, Grayshott, 1975-; Pres., Surrey Organists' Assoc., 1976, Secretary, 1977-. US Medal of Freedom. *Publications:* Economic Surveys of India, 1949 and 1952; Insurance Aspects of Children's Playground Management, 1966; Children's Recreation: Statutes and Constitutions, 1967. *Recreations:* music, theatre, gardening. *Address:* Oak Tree Cottage, Holdfast Lane, Haslemere, Surrey.

OWEN, Samuel Griffith, CBE 1977; MD, FRCP; Second Secretary, Medical Research Council, 1968-82, retired; *b* 3 Sept. 1925; *e s* of late Rev. Evan Lewis Owen and of Marjorie Lawton; *m* 1954, Ruth, *e d* of Merle N. Tate, Philadelphia, Pa, USA; two *s* two *d. Educ:* Dame Allen's Sch.; Durham Univ. MB, BS Dunelm 1948; MRCP 1951; MD Dunelm 1954; FRCP 1965; clinical and research appts at Royal Victoria Infirmary, Newcastle upon Tyne, 1948-49 and 1950-53; RAMC, SMO, HM Troopships, 1949-50; Med. Registrar, Nat. Heart Hosp., 1953-54; Instr in Pharmacology, Univ. of Pennsylvania Sch. of Med., 1954-56; Reader in Med., Univ. of Newcastle upon Tyne, 1964-68 (First Asst, 1956, Lectr, 1960, Sen. Lectr, 1961); Hon. Cons. Physician, Royal Victoria Infirmary, Newcastle upon Tyne, 1960-68; Clin. Sub-Dean of Med. Sch., Univ. of Newcastle upon Tyne, 1966-68 (Academic Sub-Dean, 1964-66); Examr in Med., Univ. of Liverpool, 1966-68; Examr in Membership, RCP, 1967-68 and Mem., Research Cttee, RCP, 1968-76; Member: Brit. Cardiac Soc., 1962-82; Assoc. of Physicians of GB, 1965-82; European Molec. Biol. Conf., 1971-82; European Molec. Biol. Lab., 1974-82; Exec. Council, European Science Foundn, 1974-78; Comité de la Recherche Médicale et de la Santé Publique, EEC, 1977-82; Scientific Coordinating Cttee, Arthritis and Rheumatism Council, 1978-82; NW Thames RHA, 1978-82. Consultant to WHO, SE Asia, 1966 and 1967-68; Commonwealth Fund Fellow, Univ. of Illinois, 1966; Fellow, Hunterian Soc., 1978. Chm., Feldberg Foundn, 1974-78; Governor, Queen Charlotte's Hosp. for Women, 1979-82. Liveryman, Soc. of Apothecaries, 1976-. *Publications:* Essentials of Cardiology, 1961 (2nd edn 1968); Electrocardiography, 1966 (2nd edn 1973); contribs to med. jls on heart disease, cerebral circulation, thyroid disease, med. research, etc. *Recreations:* chess, gastronomy. *Address:* 60 Bath Road, Chiswick, W4. *T:* 01-995 3228. *Club:* Royal Society of Medicine.

OWEN, Thomas Joseph, DL; Town Clerk, Nottingham, 1951-66; *b* 3 Nov. 1903; *s* of late Richard Owen, Sarn, Caernarvonshire; *m* 1935, Marjorie Ethel Tilbury. Articled to late Sir Hugh Vincent, 1921-26; admitted a Solicitor, 1926; Asst Solicitor with Town Clerk, Stoke-on-Trent, 1926-27; Asst Solicitor, Leeds, 1927-30; Asst Solicitor, Brighton, 1930-36; Deputy Town Clerk, Nottingham, 1936-50. President: Nottinghamshire Law Society, 1957-58; Commn of Income Tax for Nottingham Dist. Trustee: Nottingham

Roosevelt Travelling Scholarship Fund; Holbrook Trust (Painting and Sculpture). DL Notts, 1966. *Recreations:* watching Rugby football and cricket; travel abroad, reading. *Address:* Woodlands, Sherwood, Nottingham. *T:* Nottingham 61767. *Club:* United Services (Nottingham).

OWEN, Trevor Bryan, CBIM, CIPM; Managing Director, Remploy Ltd, since 1978; *b* 3 April 1928; *s* of Leonard Owen, CIE and Dilys (*née* Davies Bryan); *m* 1955, (Jennifer) Gaie (*née* Houston); one *s* one *d. Educ:* Rugby Sch.; Trinity Coll., Oxford (Scholar; MA). CBIM 1981; CIPM 1982. Sch. Student, British Sch. of Archaeology, Athens, 1953-54; ICI, 1955-78: wide range of jobs culminating in, successively: Chm., J. P. MacDougall Ltd; Dir, Paints, Agricl and Plastics Divs; Co. Personnel Manager. Member: Higher Educn Review Gp, Govt of NI, 1979-81; CNAA, 1973-79; Continuing Educn Adv. Council, BBC, 1977-; Bd of Governors, National Inst. of Social Work, 1982- (Mem., Working Party on Role and Tasks of Social Workers, 1981-82); Council, CBI, 1982-; Council, Industrial Soc., 1967-; Council, Inst. of Manpower Studies, 1975-. *Publications:* Business School Programmes—the requirements of British manufacturing industry (with D. Casey and N. Huskisson), 1971; Making Organisations Work, 1978; The Manager and Industrial Relations, 1979; articles in jls. *Address:* 9 Rochester Terrace, NW1 9JN.

OWEN, Prof. Walter Shepherd, PhD, DEng; Professor of Materials Science and Engineering, Massachusetts Institute of Technology, since 1973; *b* 13 March 1920; *s* of Walter Lloyd and Dorothea Elizabeth Owen; *m* ; one *d. Educ:* Alsop High Sch.; University of Liverpool. Metallurgist, D. Napier and Sons and English Electric Co., 1940-46; Asst Lecturer and Lecturer in Metallurgy, 1946-54, Commonwealth Fund Fellow, Metallurgy Dept, Massachusetts Inst. of Technology, USA, 1951-52, on research staff, 1954-57; Henry Bell Wortley Professor of Metallurgy, University of Liverpool, 1957-66; Thomas R. Briggs Prof. of Engineering and Dir of Materials Science and Engineering, Cornell Univ., 1966-70; Dean of Technological Inst., Northwestern Univ., 1970-71; Vice Pres. for Science and Research, Northwestern Univ., 1971-73. Mem., Nat. Acad. of Engineering, USA, 1977. *Publications:* papers in British and American journals on aspects of physical metallurgy. *Address:* Massachusetts Institute of Technology, 77 Massachusetts Avenue, Room 13-5082, Cambridge, Mass 02139, USA.

OWEN-JONES, John Eryl, CBE 1969; JP; DL; Clerk of Caernarvonshire County Council, 1956-74, and Clerk of Lieutenancy; *b* 19 Jan. 1912; *s* of late John Owen-Jones, Rhydwenfa, Old Colwyn; *m* 1944, Mabel Clara, *d* of Grant McIlvride, Ajmer, Rajputana; one *s* one *d. Educ:* Portmadoc Grammar Sch.; University Coll. of Wales, Aberystwyth; Gonville and Caius Coll., Cambridge. LLB Wales 1933; MA Cantab 1939. Admitted Solicitor, 1938; Asst Solicitor, Chester Corp., 1939. Sqdn Ldr, RAFVR, 1945; Legal Staff Officer, Judge Advocate General's Dept, Mediterranean. Dep. Clerk, Caernarvonshire CC, 1946; Clerk of the Peace, Caernarvonshire, 1956-71; formerly: Sec., N Wales Combined Probation and After-Care Cttee; Dep. Clerk, Snowdonia Jt Adv. Cttee; Dep. Clerk, Gwynedd Police Authority, 1967. Member: Central Council, Magistrates' Cts Cttees, 1980-; Bd, Civic Trust for Wales, 1982-. Hon. Sec., Caernarvonshire Historical Soc. Mem., Gorsedd of Royal National Eisteddfod of Wales. DL Caernarvonshire, 1971; JP 1974, DL 1974, Gwynedd. *Recreations:* music, gardening, photography. *Address:* Rhiw Dafnau, Caernarvon, Gwynedd. *T:* Caernarvon 3370. *Club:* National Liberal.

OWENS, Ernest Stanley, CBE 1979 (OBE 1971); FCA; chartered accountant and company director, since 1947; Chairman, Enterprise Australia, since 1976; Director, Bank of New South Wales, since 1978; *b* 22 Sept. 1916; *s* of Rev. William James Owens, MA Oxon, and Juanita (*née* Stanley); *m* 1943, Margaret Clara Brown, Killara; one *s* one *d. Educ:* The King's Sch., Parramatta, NSW. Accountants' Clerk, 1935-39; war service, Trooper to Lt-Col 1946 (despatches); own practice as chartered accountant, 1956-69; Chairman: Monier Group Ltd, 1967; Hill Samuel Aust. Ltd, 1969; Simon Engrg (Aust.) Pty Ltd, 1971; Coates Brothers Aust. Pty Ltd, 1977; Internat. Computers Aust. Pty Ltd, 1979; AUSSAT Pty Ltd, 1981; Director: Standard Telephones & Cables Pty Ltd, 1964; Byrne & Davidson Industries Ltd, 1975; Renison Goldfields Consolidated Ltd, 1977; Bank of New South Wales, 1978; Australian National Industries Ltd, 1982. Dir, Royal Prince Alfred Hosp., 1975-. Governor, Thalidomide Foundn Ltd. Freeman of City of London. *Publication:* Annual Reports of Companies (with R. K. Yorston), 1958. *Recreations:* surfing, bowls. *Address:* 11/576 Pacific Highway, Killara, NSW 2071, Australia. *T:* 498.8990; 50 Bridge Street, Sydney, NSW 2000, Australia. *Clubs:* Australian, American National (Sydney); Elanora Country, Killara Golf.

OWENS, Frank Arthur Robert, CBE 1971; Editor, Birmingham Evening Mail, 1956-74; Director, Birmingham Post & Mail Ltd, 1964-75; *b* 31 Dec. 1912; *s* of Arthur Oakes Owens; *m* 1st, 1936, Ruby Lilian Long; two *s* ; 2nd, Olwen Evans, BSc; one *s* one *d. Educ:* Hereford Cathedral School. Served with RAF, 1940-46 (despatches). Vice-Pres., Newspapers Mutual Insurance Soc.; Member: Deptl Cttee on Official Secrets Act 1911; Defence, Press and Broadcasting Cttee, 1964-75; West Midlands Econ. Planning Council, 1975-77; Press Council, 1976-79. Pres., Guild of British Newspaper Editors, 1974-75. Hon. Mem., Mark Twain Soc. *Address:* Fox Hill, 30 Linden Road, Bournville, Birmingham B30 1JU. *T:* 021-472 1509.

OWENS, Richard Hugh M.; *see* Mills-Owens.

OWER, Dr David Cheyne, TD 1975; Senior Principal Medical Officer, Department of Health and Social Security, since 1976; *b* 29 July 1931; *s* of Ernest Ower and Helen Edith Cheyne (*née* Irvine); *m* 1954, June Harris; two *s* two *d. Educ:* King's Coll. Sch., Wimbledon; King's Coll., London; King's Coll. Hosp. Med. Sch. (MB, BS 1954). DObstRCOG 1959; MFCM 1976. Jun. hosp. appts, King's Coll. Hosp. and Kingston Hosp., 1955; RAF Med. Br., 1956-58; gen. practice, 1959-64; DHSS (formerly Min. of Health) Med. Staff, 1965-. T&AVR, and RAMC(V), 1962-; Lt-Col RAMC(V); CO 221 (Surrey) Field Amb., 1973-75. *Recreations:* music, bridge, thinking about playing golf. *Address:* Merlewood, 94 Coombe Lane West, Kingston-upon-Thames, Surrey. *T:* 01-942 8552.

OWO, The Olowo of; *see* Olagbegi II.

OXBURGH, Prof. Ernest Ronald, PhD; FRS 1978; Professor of Mineralogy and Petrology, University of Cambridge, since 1978; Head of Department of Earth Sciences, since 1980; President, Queens' College, Cambridge, since 1982; Fellow of Trinity Hall, Cambridge, 1978; *b* 2 Nov. 1934; *m* Ursula Mary Brown; one *s* two *d. Educ:* Liverpool Inst.; Univ. of Oxford (BA 1957, MA 1960); Univ. of Princeton (PhD 1960). Departmental Demonstrator, 1960-61, Lectr in Geology, 1962-78, Fellow of St Edmund Hall, 1964-78, Univ. of Oxford, Emeritus Fellow, 1978. Vis. Professor: California Inst. of Technology, 1967-68; Stanford and Cornell Univs, 1973-74. FGS; Member: Geol Socs of Switzerland and USA; Amer. Geophys. Union. Hon. Mem., Geologists' Assoc.; Foreign Corresp., Geologische Bundesanstalt, Austria and of Geological Soc. of Vienna. Bigsby Medal, 1979. *Publications:* The Geology of the Eastern Alps, 1968; (ed and contrib.) Structural, Metamorphic and Geochronological Studies in the Eastern Alps, 1971; contribs to Nature, Jl Geophys Res. *Recreations:* mountaineering, reading, theatre. *Address:* Department of Earth Sciences, Downing Street, Cambridge CB2 3EQ. *T:* Cambridge 355463.

OXBURY, Harold Frederick, CMG 1961; Deputy Director-General, British Council, 1962-66 (Assistant Director-General, 1959); *b* 11 Nov. 1903; *s* of Fredric Thomas Oxbury; *m* 1st, 1928, Violet Bennets (*d* 1954); one *s* one *d* ; 2nd, 1954, Helen Shipley (*d* 1975), *d* of Amos Perry, FLS, VMH. *Educ:* Norwich Sch.; Trinity Coll., Cambridge (Senior Scholar). Entered Indian Civil Service, 1928; Chief Collector of Customs, Burma, 1940; Government of Burma Representative, Burma Office, 1942-44; Dep. Controller Finance (Colonel), Military Administration, Burma, 1945; Finance Secretary, Government of Burma, 1946; British Council: Director, Colonies Dept, 1947; Controller Finance, 1956. *Publications:* contribs to biographical works. *Recreations:* gardening, writing, painting. *Address:* Huntersmoon, Horton-cum-Studley, Oxon. *Club:* East India and Sports.

OXFORD, Bishop of, since 1978; **Rt. Rev. Patrick Campbell Rodger;** *b* 28 Nov. 1920; *s* of Patrick Wylie and Edith Ann Rodger; *m* 1952, Margaret Menzies Menzies, MBE; one *s* (and one *s* decd). *Educ:* Cargilfield; Rugby; Christ Church, Oxford; Theological College, Westcott House, Cambridge; Deacon, 1949; Priest, 1950. Asst Curate, St John's Church, Edinburgh, 1949-51, and Chaplain to Anglican Students in Edinburgh, 1951-54. Study Secretary, SCM of Gt Brit. and Ire., 1955-58; Rector, St Fillan's, Kilmacolm, with St Mary's Bridge of Weir, 1958-61; Exec. Sec. for Faith and Order, World Council of Churches, 1961-66; Vice-Provost, St Mary's Cathedral, Edinburgh, 1966-67; Provost, 1967-70; Bishop of Manchester, 1970-78. Chm., Churches' Unity Commn, 1974-78; Pres., Conf. of European Churches, 1974-. *Publications:* The Fourth World Conference on Faith and Order, Montreal (ed), 1964. *Recreations:* music and walking. *Address:* Bishop's House, 27 Linton Road, Oxford OX2 6UL. *Club:* Royal Commonwealth Society.

OXFORD, Archdeacon of; *see* Weston, Ven. F. V.

OXFORD AND ASQUITH, 2nd Earl of, *cr* 1925; **Julian Edward George Asquith,** KCMG 1964 (CMG 1961); Viscount Asquith, *cr* 1925; Governor and Commander-in-Chief, Seychelles, 1962-67; Commissioner, British Indian Ocean Territory, 1965-67; *b* 22 April 1916; *o s* of late Raymond Asquith and Katharine Frances (*d* 1976), *d* of late Sir John Horner, KCVO; *S* grandfather, 1928; *m* 1947, Anne Mary Celestine, CStJ, *d* of late Sir Michael Palairet, KCMG; two *s* three *d. Educ:* Ampleforth; Balliol Coll., Oxford (Scholar). 1st Class Lit. Hum., 1938. Lieut, RE, 1941; Assistant District Commissioner, Palestine, 1942-48; Dep. Chief Secretary, British Administration, Tripolitania, 1949; Director of the Interior, Government of Tripolitania, 1951; Adviser to Prime Minister of Libya, 1952; Administrative Secretary, Zanzibar, 1955; Administrator of St Lucia, WI, 1958. KStJ. *Heir:* *s* Viscount Asquith, *qv. Address:* The Manor House, Mells, Frome, Somerset. *T:* Mells 812324. *See also Baron Hylton.*

OXFORD, Kenneth Gordon, CBE 1981; QPM 1976; Chief Constable, Merseyside Police, since 1976; *b* Lambeth, 25 June 1924; *s* of Ernest George Oxford and late Gladys Violet (*née* Seaman); *m* 1954, Muriel (*née* Panton). *Educ:* Caldecot Sch., Lambeth. RAF, 1942-47. Metropolitan Police, 1947-69, with final rank Det. Ch. Supt, following Intermed. Comd Course, 1966, Sen. Staff Course, 1968, The Police Coll., Bramshill; Asst Chief Constable (Crime), Northumberland Constabulary, 1969; Northumbria Police, 1974; Dep. Chief Constable, Merseyside Police, 1974-75. Member: Forensic Science Soc., 1970; Medico-Legal Soc., 1975; Chairman: Crime Cttee, Assoc. of Chief Police Officers of Eng., Wales and NI, 1977-; Jt Standing Cttee on Police Use of Firearms, 1979-; President: NW Police Benevolent Fund, 1978-; Assoc. of

Chief Police Officers of England, Wales and NI, 1982-83. Chm., Merseyside Br., BIM, 1978-81 (Vice-Chm., 1975-78); CBIM 1980. Merseyside County Dir, St John's Ambulance Assoc., 1976-. OStJ 1977. *Publications:* contrib. articles and papers to prof. papers on crime and kindred matters. *Recreations:* shooting, cricket, music, books, roses. *Address:* Chief Constable's Office, PO Box 59, Liverpool L69 1JD. *T:* 051-709 6010. *Clubs:* Royal Commonwealth Society; Surrey CCC; Liverpool Cricket.

OXFUIRD, 12th Viscount of, *cr* 1651; **(John) Donald (Alexander Arthur) Makgill;** Bt 1627; Lord Macgill of Cousland 1651; late Lt Coldstream Guards; RARO; *b* 31 Dec. 1899; *e s* of Sir George Makgill, 11th Bt (*de jure* 11th Viscount) and Frances Elizabeth (*d* 1947), *e d* of Alexander Innes Grant, of Merchiston, Otago, NZ; *S* father, 1926; claim to Viscountcy admitted by Committee for Privileges, House of Lords, 1977; *m* 1927, Esther Lilian (marr. diss. 1943), *y d* of late Sir Robert Bromley, 6th Bt; one *d*; *m* 1955, Mrs Maureen Gillington, *y d* of late Lt-Col A. T. S. Magan, CMG. *Educ:* Eton; RMC. *Recreation:* fishing. *Heir: nephew* George Hubbard Makgill [*b* 7 Jan. 1934; *m* 1967, Alison Campbell (marr. diss. 1977), *d* of late Neils Max Jensen, Randers, Denmark; three *s* (inc. twin *s*); *m* 1980, Valerie Steward, *d* of Major Steward, late 9th Lancers]. *Address:* The Flat, Blairquhan, Maybole, Ayrshire. *T:* Straiton 278. *Clubs:* Royal Over-Seas League; New (Edinburgh).

OXLADE, Zena Elsie, SRN, RNT; Regional Nursing Officer, East Anglian Regional Health Authority, since 1981; Chairman, General Nursing Council for England and Wales, since 1977; *b* 26 April 1929; *d* of James and Beatrice May Oxlade. *Educ:* Latymer Grammar Sch., N9. SRN 1950; RNT (London Univ.). Ward Sister, 1952; Theatre Sister, 1953; Night Sister, 1954; Sister Tutor, 1956; Principal Tutor, 1963; Principal Nursing Officer, 1969; Chief Nursing Officer, 1973; District Nursing Officer, 1974; Area Nursing Officer, Suffolk AHA, 1978-81. Member, General Nursing Council, 1975. *Publication:* Ear, Nose and Throat Nursing, 1972. *Recreations:* motoring, reading, handicrafts. *Address:* (home) 29 Ballater Close, Ipswich, Suffolk IP1 6LL. *T:* Ipswich 43354; (office) East Anglian Regional Health Authority, Union Lane, Chesterton, Cambridge CB4 1RF. *T:* Cambridge 61212.

OXLEY, Humphrey Leslie Malcolm, CMG 1966; OBE 1956; HM Diplomatic Service, retired; *b* 9 Oct. 1909; *s* of W. H. F. Oxley, MRCS, LRCP, FRCOG, and Lily Malcolm; *m* 1945, Frances Olga, *d* of George Bowden, San Jose, Costa Rica; twin *s*. *Educ:* Epsom Coll. Admitted Solicitor, 1933; Junior Legal Assistant, India Office, 1933; Commissioner for Oaths, 1934; Assistant Solicitor, 1944; Commonwealth Relations Office, 1947; Assistant Legal Adviser, 1961; Legal Counsellor, Commonwealth Office, 1965-67; HM Diplomatic Service, 1967; Dep. Legal Adviser, FCO, 1967-69. Legal Consultant to HM Comr, Magistrate, various legal appts, Anguilla, 1971-72. *Recreations:* sailing, gardening. *Address:* Sandpipers, Crooked Lane, Birdham, Chichester, West Sussex. *Club:* Civil Service.

OXLEY, James Keith R.; *see* Rice-Oxley.

OXMANTOWN, Lord; Laurence Patrick Parsons; *b* 31 March 1969; *s* and heir of Earl of Rosse, *qv*.

OZAWA, Seiji; Japanese conductor; Music Director, Boston Symphony Orchestra, since 1973; *b* Shenyang, China, 1 Sept. 1935; 3rd *s* of Kaisaku and Sakura Ozawa; *m* 1st, Kyoko Edo; 2nd, Vera Ilyan; one *s* one *d*. *Educ:* Toho School of Music, Tokyo; studied with Hideo Saito, Eugène Bigot, Herbert von Karajan, Leonard Bernstein. Won Besançon Internat. Comp., 1959, Koussevitzky Meml Scholarship, 1960. Asst Conductor, NY Philharmonic Orch., 1961-62 and 1964-65; music dir, Ravinia Fest., Chicago, 1964-69; conductor, Toronto Symph. Orch., 1965-69; music dir, San Francisco Symph. Orch., 1970-76, music advisor, 1976-77. Tours with Boston Symphony Orchestra: Europe, 1976; Japan, 1978; China (musical and cultural exchange), 1979; European music festivals, 1979; 14 USA cities (orchestra's hundredth birthday), 1982; Japan, France, Germany, Austria and England, 1982. Guest conductor with major orchestras in Canada, Europe, Far East and USA; many recordings (awards). *Address:* c/o Ronald A. Wilford, Columbia Artists Management Inc. Conductors Division, 165 West 57th Street, New York, USA; c/o Harold Holt Ltd, 31 Sinclair Road, W14.

P

PÄCHT, Otto Ernst, MA, DPhil; FBA 1956; Professor in the History of Art, and Director of the Kunsthistorisches Institut, Vienna University, 1963-72, now Professor Emeritus; *b* Vienna, 7 Sept. 1902; *s* of David and Josephine Pächt; *m* 1940, Jeanne Michalopulo (*d* 1971); one *s*. *Educ:* Vienna and Berlin Universities. Lecturer in History of Art: Heidelberg Univ., 1933; Oriel Coll., Oxford, 1945. Senior Lecturer in Medieval Art, 1952, Reader, 1962, Oxford Univ. Lyell Reader, Oxford, 1971. Membre de la Société Archéologique française. Wirkl. Mitgl. Oesterr. Akad. d. Wissenschaft, 1972. Hon. DLitt Oxon, 1971. *Publications:* Oesterreichische Tafelmalerei der Gotik, 1929; Master of Mary of Burgundy, 1948; The St Albans Psalter, 1960; The Rise of Pictorial Narrative in Twelfth-century England, 1962; Vita Sancti

Simperti, 1964; (ed with J. J. G. Alexander) Illuminated Manuscripts in the Bodleian Library, 1973; (ed with D. Thoss) Illuminated Manuscripts in the Austrian National Library, French School, 1974-77; (ed with U. Jenni) Illuminated Manuscripts in the Austrian National Library, Dutch School, 1975; Methodisches zur kunsthistorischen Praxis, 1977; contribs to Kritische Berichte, Kunstwissenschaftliche Forschungen, Burlington Magazine, Journal of the Warburg Institute, Revue des Arts, Jahrbuch der Kunsthistorischen Sammlungen Wien, Pantheon, Revue de l'Art, Gazette des Beaux-Arts. *Address:* Pötzleinsdorferstreasse 66, 1180 Vienna, Austria.

PACK, Prof. Donald Cecil, CBE 1978 (OBE 1969); MA, DSc, FIMA, FRSE, FEIS; Professor of Mathematics, University of Strathclyde, Glasgow, since 1953, Vice-Principal, 1968-72; *b* 14 March 1920; *s* of late John Cecil and late Minnie Pack, Higham Ferrers; *m* 1947, Constance Mary Gillam; two *s* one *d*. *Educ:* Wellingborough School; New Coll., Oxford. Lecturer in Mathematics, University College, Dundee, University of St Andrews, 1947-52; Visiting Research Associate, University of Maryland, 1951-52; Lecturer in Mathematics, University of Manchester, 1952-53. Guest Prof., Technische Hochschule Darmstadt, 1981. Member: Dunbartonshire Educn Cttee, 1960-66; Gen. Teaching Council for Scotland, 1966-73; Chairman: Scottish Certificate of Educn Examn Bd, 1969-77; Cttee of Inquiry into Truancy and Indiscipline in Schools in Scotland, 1974-77; Member: various Govt Scientific Cttees, 1952-; British Nat. Cttee for Theoretical and Applied Mechanics, 1973-78; Council, Gesellschaft für Angewandte Mathematik und Mechanik, 1977-83; Scottish Arts Council, 1980-; Founder Chm., NYO of Scotland, 1978-; Mem., European Music Year Cttee (Chm., Scottish Sub-Cttee); Hon. Treasurer, IMA, 1964-72; Governor, Hamilton Coll. of Education, 1977-81. *Publications:* papers on fluid dynamics. *Recreations:* music, gardening, golf. *Address:* 18 Buchanan Drive, Bearsden, Glasgow. *T:* 041-942 5764.

PACKARD, Lt-Gen. Sir (Charles) Douglas, KBE 1957 (CBE 1945; OBE 1942); CB 1949; DSO 1943; retired as GOC-in-C Northern Ireland Command, 1958-61; *b* 17 May 1903; *s* of late Capt. C. T. Packard, MC, Copdock, near Ipswich; *m* 1937, Marion Lochhead (*d* 1981); one *s* two *d*; *m* 1982, Mrs Patricia Miles Sharp. *Educ:* Winchester; Royal Military Academy, Woolwich. 2nd Lieut, RA, 1923; served War of 1939-45, in Middle East and Italy (despatches, OBE, DSO, CBE); Dep.-Chief of Staff, 15th Army Group, 1944-45; Temp. Maj.-Gen. and Chief of Staff, Allied Commission for Austria (British Element), 1945-46; Director of Military Intelligence, WO, 1948-49; Commander British Military Mission in Greece, 1949-51; Chief of Staff, GHQ, MELF, 1951-53; Vice-Quarter-Master-General War Office, 1953-56; Military Adviser to the West African Governments, 1956-58. Lt-Gen. 1957. Col Comdt, RA, 1957-62. Officer Legion of Merit (USA). *Recreation:* sailing. *Address:* Park Side, Lower Road, Ufford, Woodbridge, Suffolk IP13 6DL. *T:* Eyke 418.

PACKARD, Vance (Oakley); Author; *b* 22 May 1914; *s* of Philip and Mabel Packard; *m* 1938, Mamie Virginia Mathews; two *s* one *d*. *Educ:* Pennsylvania State Univ.; Columbia Univ. Reporter, The Boston Record, 1938; Feature Editor, The Associated Press, 1939-42; Editor and Staff Writer, The American Magazine, 1942-56; Staff writer, Colliers, 1956; Distinguished Alumni Award, Pennsylvania State University, 1961; Outstanding Alumni Award, Columbia University Graduate School of Journalism, 1963. LittD Monmouth Coll., 1974. *Publications:* (books on social criticism): The Hidden Persuaders, 1957; The Status Seekers, 1959; The Waste Makers, 1960; The Pyramid Climbers, 1962; The Naked Society, 1964; The Sexual Wilderness, 1968; A Nation of Strangers, 1972; The People Shapers, 1977; numerous articles for The Atlantic Monthly. *Recreations:* reading, boating. *Address:* Mill Road, New Canaan, Conn 06840, USA. *T:* WO 6-1707.

PACKER, Kerry Francis Bullmore; Chairman and Managing Director: Consolidated Press Holdings Ltd, since 1974; Publishing and Broadcasting Ltd, since 1974; Chairman: Australian Consolidated Press Ltd, since 1974; Conpress Printing Ltd, since 1974; Director, General Television Corporation Ltd, since 1974; *b* 17 Dec. 1937; *s* of late Sir Douglas Frank Hewson Packer, KBE, and Lady (Gretel Joyce) Packer (*née* Bullmore); *m* 1963, Roslyn Redman Weedon; one *s* one *d*. *Educ:* Cranbrook Sch., Sydney, NSW; Geelong C of E Grammar Sch., Vic. Trainee Exec., Aust. Consolidated Press and Conpress Printing, 1955. *Recreations:* golf, tennis, shooting, cricket. *Address:* 54 Park Street, Sydney, NSW 2000, Australia. *T:* (02) 268-0666. *Clubs:* Athenæum (Melbourne); Royal Sydney Golf, Australian Golf, Elanora Country, Tattersall's (NSW).

PADLEY, Walter Ernest; Member National Executive Committee of Labour Party, 1956-79 (Chairman, Labour Party, 1965-66; Chairman, Overseas Cttee, 1963-71); *b* 24 July 1916; *s* of Ernest and Mildred Padley; *m* 1942, Sylvia Elsie Wilson; one *s* one *d*. *Educ:* Chipping Norton Grammar Sch.; Ruskin Coll., Oxford. Active in distributive workers' trade union, 1933-; President, Union of Shop, Distributive and Allied Workers, 1948-64. Member of National Council of Independent Labour Party, 1940-46. MP (Lab) Ogmore, Mid-Glam, 1950-79; Minister of State for Foreign Affairs, 1964-67. *Publications:* The Economic Problem of the Peace, 1944; Am I My Brother's Keeper?, 1945; Britain: Pawn or Power?, 1947; USSR: Empire or Free Union?, 1948. *Address:* 73 Priory Gardens, Highgate, N6. *T:* 01-340 2969.

PADMORE, Sir Thomas, GCB 1965 (KCB 1953; CB 1947); MA; FCIT; *b* 23 April 1909; *e s* of Thomas William Padmore, Sheffield; *m* 1st, 1934, Alice (*d* 1963), *d* of Robert Alcock, Ormskirk; two *d* (one *s* decd); 2nd, 1964,

Rosalind Culhane, qv. Educ: Central Sch., Sheffield; Queens' Coll., Cambridge (Foundation Scholar; Hon. Fellow, 1961). Secretaries' Office, Board of Inland Revenue, 1931-34; transferred to Treasury, 1934; Principal Private Secretary to Chancellor of Exchequer, 1943-45; Second Secretary, 1952-62; Permanent Sec., Min. of Transport, 1962-68. Dir, Laird Gp Ltd, 1970-79; Dep. Chm., Metropolitan Cammell Ltd, 1969-80. Chairman: Rehearsal Orchestra, 1961-71; Handel Opera Soc., 1963-. Hon. Treas., Inst. of Cancer Res., 1973-81. Address: 39 Cholmeley Crescent, Highgate, N6. T: 01-340 6587. Club: Reform.

PADMORE, Lady (Thomas); see Culhane, Rosalind.

PAFFARD, Rear-Admiral (retired) Ronald Wilson, CB 1960; CBE 1943; b Ludlow, 14 Feb. 1904; 4th s of Murray Paffard and Fanny (née Wilson); m 1933, Nancy Brenda Malim; one s one d. Educ: Maidstone Grammar Sch. Paymaster Cadetship in RN, 1922; Paymaster Commander, 1940; Captain (S), 1951; Rear-Admiral, 1957. Secretary to Adm. of the Fleet Lord Tovey in all his Flag appointments, including those throughout the War of 1939-45; Supply Officer of HMS Vengeance, 1946-48; Portsmouth Division, Reserve Fleet, 1948-50; HMS Eagle, 1950-51; Asst Director-General, Supply and Secretarial Branch, 1952-54; Commanding Officer, HMS Ceres, 1954-56; Chief Staff Officer (Administration) on staff of Commander-in-Chief, Portsmouth, 1957-60, retired. Recreations: painting, golf. Address: 2 Little Green Orchard, Alverstoke, Hants PO12 2EY.

PAFFORD, John Henry Pyle, MA, DLit (London); FSA; FLA; Goldsmiths' Librarian of the University of London, 1945-67; b 6 March 1900; s of John Pafford and Bessie (née Pyle); m 1941, Elizabeth Ford, d of R. Charles Ford and Margaret Harvey; one d (and one d decd). Educ: Trowbridge High Sch.; University Coll., London (Fellow, 1956). Library Asst, University College, London, 1923-25; Librarian, and Tutor, Selly Oak Colleges, 1925-31; Sub-Librarian, National Central Library, 1931-45; Lecturer at University of London School of Librarianship, 1937-61. Editor, Year's Work in Librarianship, 1935-38 (jointly), and 1939-46; Library Adviser, Inter-Univ. Council for Higher Education Overseas, 1960-68. Publications: Bale's King Johan, 1931, and The Sodder'd Citizen, 1936 (Malone Society); Library Co-operation in Europe, 1935; Accounts of Parliamentary Garrisons of Great Chalfield and Malmesbury, 1645-46, 1940; Books and Army Education, 1946; W. P. Ker, A Bibliography, 1950; The Winter's Tale (Arden Shakespeare), 1963; Watts's Divine Songs for Children, 1971; L. Bryskett's Literary Works, 1972; (with E. R. Pafford) Employer and Employed, 1974. Address: Hillside, Allington Park, Bridport, Dorset DT6 5DD. T: Bridport 22829.

PAGAN, Brig. Sir John (Ernest), Kt 1971; CMG 1969; MBE (Mil.) 1944; ED; Chairman: P. Rowe Holdings Pty Ltd, since 1958; Associated National Insurance Co. Ltd, since 1973; Medical Journal Pty Ltd; Deputy Chairman: NSW Permanent Building Society Ltd; Mercantile Mutual Holdings Ltd (Group); Director, Angus & Coote (Holdings) Ltd; b 13 May 1914; s of late D. C. Pagan, Hay, NSW; m 1948, Marjorie Hoskins, d of late Sir Cecil Hoskins; one s two d. Educ: St Peter's Coll., Adelaide. Served RAA, AIF, Middle East, Papua/New Guinea, 1939-45, 2/1st AA Regt; 2/4th LAA Regt 9 Div. Finschhafen 1943; Citizen Military Forces, E Command; Lt-Col 1948, Brig. 1958; Hon. Col, Corps of School Cadets, 1970-72; Representative Col Comdt in Australia, Royal Regt of Australian Artillery, 1974-78. Hon. ADC to Governor of NSW, 1950-55; Member: Nat. Council, Scout Assoc. of Austr., 1975-; NSW Council, Girl Guides Assoc.; Board, NSW Soc. for Crippled Children, 1967-; Council, Big Brother Movement, 1947 (Chm., 1965, Pres., 1981); Mem. Board, Church of England Retirement Villages, 1961-; Vice-Pres., Neurological Foundn; Federal Vice-Pres., Aust. Brain Foundn, 1977-; Dir, James McGrath Foundn (Odessey Drug Prevention and Cure); Hon. Treas., Australiana Fund, NSW, 1978-; Federal Dep. Chm, Cttee for Employer Support for Reserve Forces of Aust.; Mem. Nat. Cttee, Sir Robert Menzies Meml Trust, 1978-; Trustee, World Wildlife Fund, 1978-. Mem., Commonwealth Immigration Adv. Council, 1959-70. Mem. Exec. Council, Nat. Parks and Wildlife Foundn, 1970-. Governor, Frensham Sch., 1968-70; Councillor, Nat. Heart Foundn, 1969-; Chm., Red Shield Appeal, 1975; Trustee, Salvation Army Darwin Relief Fund, 1974-78; Member: Bd, Royal Prince Alfred Hospital, 1974-; NSW Exec., Inst. of Public Affairs, 1975-. Liberal Party of Australia: State Pres., NSW, 1963-66; Federal Pres., 1966-70; Agent-General for NSW in London, 1970-72. Freeman, City of London, 1973. CStJ 1972. Address: 2 Lincoln Place, Edgecliff, NSW 2027, Australia; Kennerton Green, Mittagong, NSW 2575, Australia. Clubs: White's, MCC (London); Imperial Service, Union, Royal Sydney Golf (Sydney); Melbourne (Melbourne).

PAGE, family name of **Baron Whaddon.**

PAGE, Sir Alexander Warren, (Sir Alex Page), Kt 1977; MBE 1943; Chairman: Paine & Co. Ltd, since 1981; G. T. Pension Services Ltd, since 1981; b 1 July 1914; s of Sydney E. Page and Phyllis (née Spencer); m 1st, 1940, Anne Lewis Hickman (marr. diss.); two s one d ; 2nd, 1981, Mrs Anne Mary Wharton. Educ: Tonbridge; Clare Coll., Cambridge (MA). Served REME, with Guards Armoured Div., 1940-45, Lt-Col REME. Joined The Metal Box Co. Ltd, 1936; joined board as Sales Dir, 1957; Man. Dir 1966; Dep. Chm. 1969; Chief Exec., 1970-77; Chm., 1970-79. Director: J. Lyons & Co Ltd Feb.–Oct. 1978; C. Shippam Ltd, 1979-; Chm., Electrolux, 1978-82. Mem., IBA (formerly ITA), 1970-76; Mem., Food Science and Technology Bd, 1973-. Pres., BFMIRA, 1980. FIMechE; CBIM. Governor, Colfe's Grammar

---

Sch., Lewisham, 1977-. Recreations: golf, tennis. Address: 2 Montagu Square, W1. T: 01-935 9894; Merton Place, Dunsfold, Godalming, Surrey. T: Dunsfold 211.

PAGE, Ven. Alfred Charles; Archdeacon of Leeds, 1969-81, now Archdeacon Emeritus; b 24 Dec. 1912; s of late Henry Page, Homersfield, Suffolk; m 1944, Margaret Stevenson, d of late Surtees Foster Dodd, Sunderland, Co. Durham. Educ: Bungay Grammar Sch.; Corpus Christi Coll., Cambridge (MA); Wycliffe Hall, Oxford. Curate: Wortley-de-Leeds, 1936; Leeds Parish Church, 1940 (Sen. Curate and Priest-in-charge of S Mary, Quarry Hill, 1941); Vicar: St Mark, Woodhouse, Leeds, 1944; Rothwell, Yorks, 1955. Rural Dean of Whitkirk, 1961-69; Surrogate, 1963; Hon. Canon of Ripon, 1966; Vicar of Arthington, 1969-73. Recreation: photography. Address: 602 King Lane, Alwoodley Park, Leeds LS17 7AN. T: Leeds 696458.

PAGE, Col Alfred John, CB 1964; TD 1945; DL; Chairman, TA&VR Association for Greater London, 1968-71 (Chairman, County of London T&AFA, 1957-68); b 3 January 1912; s of Harry Gould Page, Surbiton, Surrey; m 1941, Sheila Margaret Aileen (marr. diss. 1966), d of Charles Skinner Wilson, Ugley, Essex; one s two d ; m 1969, Margaret Mary Juliet Driver, widow of Harold Driver. Educ: Westminster School. 2nd Lt 19th London Regt (TA), 1931. Served 1939-45 with RA in AA Comd. Brevet Colonel 1952; ADC (TA) to the Queen, 1961-69; Hon. Col, Greater London Regt RA (Territorials), 1967-71; Dep. Hon. Col, 6th Bn, Queen's Regt, T&AVR, 1971-72. Master, Worshipful Co. of Pattenmakers, 1973-74. DL Co. of London, 1951; DL Greater London, 1965. Address: 66 Iverna Court, W8. T: 01-937 2590. Club: Army and Navy.

PAGE, Annette, (Mrs Ronald Hynd); Ballerina of the Royal Ballet, 1959-67, retired; b 18 Dec. 1932; d of James Lees and Margaret Page; m 1957, Ronald Hynd, qv ; one d. Educ: Royal Ballet School. Audition and award of scholarship to Roy. Ballet Sch., 1944. Entry into touring company of Royal Ballet (then Sadler's Wells Theatre Ballet), 1950; promotion to major Royal Ballet Co. (Sadler's Wells Ballet), 1955. Mem., Arts Council of GB, 1976-79. Roles include: The Firebird, Dec. 1958; Princess Aurora, May 1959; Odette-Odile, June 1959; Giselle, March 1960; Lise in La Fille Mal Gardée, 1963; Romeo and Juliet, 1965; Cinderella, 1966. Recreations: music, books.

PAGE, Anthony (Frederick Montague); b India, 21 Sept. 1935; s of Frederick Charles Graham Page and Pearl Valerie Montague Hall. Educ: Oakley Hall, Cirencester; Winchester Coll. (Schol.); Magdalen Coll., Oxford (Schol., BA); Neighborhood Playhouse Sch. of the Theater, NY. Asst, Royal Court Theatre, 1958: co-directed Live Like Pigs, directed The Room; Artistic Dir, Dundee Repertory Theatre, 1962; The Caretaker, Oxford and Salisbury; Women Beware Women, and Nil Carborundum, Royal Shakespeare Co., 1963; BBC Directors' Course, then several episodes of Z-Cars, Horror of Darkness and 1st TV prodn Stephen D; Jt Artistic Dir, Royal Court, 1964-65; directed Inadmissible Evidence (later Broadway and film), A Patriot for Me, 1st revival of Waiting for Godot, Cuckoo in the Nest; Diary of a Madman, Duchess, 1966; Artistic Dir, two seasons at Royal Court: Uncle Vanya, 1970; Alpha Beta (also film); Hedda Gabler; Krapp's Last Tape; Not I; Cromwell; other plays transf. from Royal Court to West End: Time Present; Hotel in Amsterdam; revival, Look Back in Anger; West of Suez; directed Hamlet, Nottingham, 1970; Rules of the Game, National Theatre; King Lear, Amer. Shakespeare Fest., 1975; television: The Parachute; Emlyn; Hotel in Amsterdam; Speaking of Murder; You're Free; Pueblo (nominated for Emmy award); The Changeling; Headmaster; Missiles of October (nominated for Emmy award); Scott Fitzgerald in Hollywood; Adam's Chronicle; Sheppey; FDR's Last Year (USA); Bill; Patricia Neal Story; films: I Never Promised You a Rose Garden; Absolution; The Lady Vanishes. Directors' and Producers' Award for TV Dir of Year, 1966. Recreations: movies, reading, riding, travelling. Address: 68 Ladbroke Grove, W11.

PAGE, (Arthur) John; MP (C) Harrow West since March 1960; b 16 Sept. 1919; s of Sir Arthur Page, QC (late Chief Justice of Burma), and Lady Page, KiH; m 1950, Anne, d of Charles Micklem, DSO, JP, DL, Longcross House, Surrey; four s. Educ: Harrow, Magdalene College, Cambridge. Joined RA as Gunner, 1939, commissioned, 1940; served War of 1939-45, Western Desert (wounded), France, Germany; demobilised as Major, comdg 258 Battery Norfolk Yeomanry, 1945; various positions in industry and commerce, 1946-63. Chm. Bethnal Green and E London Housing Assoc., 1957-70; contested (C) Eton and Slough, Gen. Election, 1959. PPS to Parly Under-Sec. of State, Home Office, 1961-63; Conservative Parly Labour Affairs Cttee: Sec., 1960-61, 1964-, Vice-Chm., 1964-69, Chm., 1970-74; Sec., Conservative Broadcasting Cttee, 1974-76. Pres., Cons. Trade Unionists Nat. Adv. Council, 1967-69; Member: Parly Select Cttee on Race Relations and Immigration, 1970-71; British Delegn to Council of Europe and WEU, 1972- (Chm. Budget Cttee, 1973-74, Social and Health Cttee, 1975-78). Mem. Exec., IPU, British Gp, 1970 (Treasurer, 1974-77; Vice-Chm., 1977-79; Chm., 1979-82); Pres., Independent Schools Assoc., 1971-78; Chm., Council for Indep. Educn, 1974-80. Recreations: painting and politics. Address: Hitcham Lodge, Taplow, Bucks. T: Burnham 5056. Clubs: Brooks's, MCC.

PAGE, Bertram Samuel; University Librarian and Keeper of the Brotherton Collection, University of Leeds, 1947-69, Emeritus Librarian, since 1969; b 1 Sept. 1904; s of Samuel and Catherine Page; m 1933, Olga Ethel, d of E. W. Mason. Educ: King Charles I School Kidderminster; University of

Birmingham. BA 1924, MA 1926. Asst Librarian (later Sub-Librarian), Univ. of Birmingham, 1931–36; Librarian, King's College, Newcastle upon Tyne, 1936–47. Pres. Library Assoc., 1960 (Hon. Fellow, 1961); Chairman: Standing Conf. of Nat. and Univ. Libraries, 1961–63; Exec. Cttee, Nat. Central Library, 1962–72 (Trustee, 1963–75); Librarianship Bd, Council for Nat. Academic Awards, 1966–71. Mem. Court of Univ. of Birmingham, 1954–69. Hon. DUniv. York, 1968. Publications: contrib. to Stephen MacKenna's trans. of Plotinus, vol. 5, 1930 (revised whole trans. for 2nd, 3rd, 4th edns, 1958, 1962, 1969); A Manual of University and College Library Practice (jt ed.), 1940; articles and reviews in classical and library jls. Address: 24 St Anne's Road, Headington, Oxford. T: Oxford 65981.

PAGE, Bruce; journalist; b 1 Dec. 1936; s of Roger and Beatrice Page; m 1st, 1964, Anne Gillison (marr. diss. 1969); 2nd, 1969, Anne Louise Darnborough; one s one d. Educ: Melbourne High Sch.; Melbourne Univ. The Herald, Melbourne, 1956–60; Evening Standard, 1960–62; Daily Herald, 1962–64; Sunday Times, 1964–76; Daily Express, 1977; Editor, The New Statesman, 1978–82. Publications: (jtly) Philby, 1968, 3rd edn 1977; (jtly) An American Melodrama, 1969; (jtly) Do You Sincerely Want to be Rich?, 1971; (jtly) Destination Disaster (a title imposed, while he was not looking, by a New York publisher), 1976; contrib. Ulster, 1972; The Yom Kippur War, 1974; The British Press, 1978. Recreations: sailing, reading. Address: 35 Duncan Terrace, N1 8AL. T: 01-359 1000.

PAGE, Maj.-Gen. Charles Edward, CB 1974; MBE 1944; Independent Telecommunications Consultant; b 23 Aug. 1920; s of late Sir (Charles) Max Page, KBE, CB, DSO, FRCS and Lady (Helen) Page; m 1948, Elizabeth Marion, d of late Sir William Smith Crawford, KBE; two s one d. Educ: Marlborough Coll.; Trinity Coll., Cambridge. BSc (Eng) London 1949; CEng, FIEE 1968. Commissioned 2nd Lieut Royal Signals from TA, 1941; regimental appts Guards Armd Divisional Signals, 1941–45; CO 19 Indian Div. Signals, 1945–46; GSO1 Air Formation Signals Far East, 1946–47; Student RMCS, 1947–49; psc 1951; GSO2 British Middle East Office, 1952–55; GSO2 Staff Coll., 1955–58; Sqdn Comdr 30 Signal Regt, 1959; GSO1 Combat Develt Directorate, WO, 1960–63; CO 1st Div. Signal Regt, 1963–65; Student NATO Defence Coll., 1965–66; CCR Signals 1 (BR) Corps, 1966–68; Sec., NATO Mil. Cttee, Brussels, 1968–70; DCD(A) MoD, 1971–74; retired 1974. Col Comdt, Royal Corps of Signals, 1974–80. Hon. Col, Women's Transport Service (FANY), 1976. Recreations: shooting, golf, fishing, photography. Address: 6 Cheyne Gardens, SW3 5QU. T: 01-352 5674. Clubs: Naval and Military; Royal and Ancient (St Andrews).

PAGE, Cyril Leslie, OBE 1965; Controller, Personnel, Television, BBC Television Service, 1971–76, retired; b 20 Oct. 1916; s of Cyril Herbert Page and Rosamund Clara Page; m 1939, Barbara Mary Rowland; one s one d. Educ: Sherborne Sch. Royal Air Force, 1936–46 (Wing Comdr). British Broadcasting Corporation, 1946–: Asst, Appts Dept, 1947; Asst Admin. Officer, Overseas Services, 1949; Asst Head of TV Admin., 1951; Estabt Officer, TV, 1958; Head of TV Estabt Dept, 1961; Asst Controller, TV Admin., 1964. Member: Council, Royal Postgrad. Med. Sch., 1975; Cttee of Management, Inst. of Obstetrics and Gynaecology, 1973; Industrial Tribunals in England and Wales, 1978; Special Trustee, Hammersmith Hosp., 1974; Governor, Queen Charlotte's Hosp. for Women, 1978. Recreations: reading, gardening. Address: 95 Fountain Gardens, Windsor, Berks SL4 3SU.

PAGE, Rt. Rev. Dennis Fountain; see Lancaster, Bishop Suffragan of.

PAGE, Brig. (Edwin) Kenneth, CBE 1951 (OBE 1946); DSO 1945; MC 1918; b 23 Jan. 1898; s of G. E. Page, Baldock, Herts; m 1921, Kate Mildred (d 1975), d of G. H. Arthur, Yorkshire, Barbados, BWI; two s. Educ: Haileybury College; RMA, Woolwich. 2nd Lt, RFA, 1916; BEF, France, 1916–18. Adjt TA, 1924–27; Staff College, Camberley, 1928–29; Staff Captain, India, 1931–35; GSO2, War Office, 1936–39; Lt-Col, 1939; served War of 1939–45: BEF, France, 1940; Col, 1945; Brig., 1946; Dep. Director, WO, 1946–48; Commander, Caribbean Area, 1948–51; employed War Office, 1951; retired pay, 1952. CC 1961–74, CA 1968–74, Dorset. Address: 12 De Maulley Road, Canford Cliffs, Poole, Dorset. T: Canford Cliffs 707181. Club: Army and Navy.

See also Prof. J. K. Page.

PAGE, Ewan Stafford, PhD, MA, BSc; Vice-Chancellor, University of Reading, since 1979; b 17 Aug. 1928; s of late Joseph William Page and Lucy Quayle (née Stafford); m 1955, Sheila Margaret Smith; three s one d. Educ: Wyggeston Grammar Sch., Leicester; Christ Coll., Cambridge (MA, PhD, Raleigh Prize 1952); Univ. of London (BSc). Instr, RAF Techn. Coll., 1949–51; Lectr in Statistics, Durham Colls, 1954–57; Director: Durham Univ. Computing Lab., 1957–63; Newcastle Univ. Computing Lab., 1963–78; Visiting Prof., Univ. of N Carolina, Chapel Hill, USA, 1962–63; University of Newcastle upon Tyne: Prof. of Computing and Data Processing, 1965–78; Pro-Vice Chancellor, 1972–78 (Actg Vice-Chancellor, 1976–77). Mem. Bd, Aycliffe and Peterlee Develt Corp., 1969–78. Hon. Fellow, Amer. Statistical Assoc., 1974; Hon. FBCS, 1976; Hon. Fellow, Newcastle upon Tyne Polytechnic, 1979. Publications: (jtly) Information Representation and Manipulation in a Computer, 1973, 2nd edn 1978; (jtly) Introduction to Computational Combinatorics, 1978; papers in statistical and computing jls. Recreations: golf, music, reading, vegetable gardening, country wine and beer making. Address: University of Reading, Whiteknights, Reading, Berks RG6 2AH. T: Reading 875123.

PAGE, Sir Frederick (William), Kt 1979; CBE 1961; FRS 1978; FEng, Hon. FRAeS; Member of the Board, British Aerospace PLC; Chairman and Chief Executive, Aircraft Group of British Aerospace PLC, 1977–82; b 20 Feb. 1917; s of Richard Page and Ellen Potter; m 1940, Kathleen Edith de Courcy; three s one d. Educ: Rutlish Sch., Merton; St Catharine's Coll., Cambridge (MA). Hawker Aircraft Co., 1938; English Electric, 1945; Chief Engr, 1950, and Dir and Chief Exec. (Aircraft), English Electric Aviation, 1959; Managing Dir, Mil. Aircraft Div. of BAC, 1965–72, Chm., 1967; apptd Managing Dir (Aircraft), BAC, and Chm., Commercial Aircraft Div., 1972. Jt Chm. of SEPECAT, the Anglo-French co. formed for management of Jaguar programme, 1966–73; apptd to Bd of Panavia Aircraft GmbH, 1969, Chm. 1977; apptd Chm. BAC Ltd (a co. of Brit. Aerospace), 1977. Mem. Council, Soc. of Brit. Aerospace Cos Ltd; apptd to Bd of BAC (Operating) Ltd, 1963; Dir, BAC (USA) Inc., 1975–77. FRAeS, 1951–80, Hon. FRAeS, 1980 (Gold Medal, 1974); Fellow, Fellowship of Engrg, 1977. Hon. Fellow, UMIST, 1970. Hon. DSc Cranfield, 1979. British Gold Medal for Aeronautics, 1962. Recreation: gardening. Address: Renvyle, 60 Waverley Lane, Farnham, Surrey GU9 8BN. T: Farnham 714999. Club: United Oxford & Cambridge University.

PAGE, Sir Harry (Robertson), Kt 1968; Chairman: National Transport Tokens Ltd; Butler, Laing Cruickshank Ltd; b 14 Apr. 1911; s of late Henry Page and Dora (née Robertson); m 1937, Elsie Dixon; two s. Educ: Manchester Grammar Sch.; Manchester University. BA (Admin) 1932; MA (Admin) 1934. IPFA 1938 (Pres. 1968). Appointed City Treasurer's Dept, Manchester, 1927, Dep. Treasurer, 1952; Treasurer, 1957–71. Consultant, Butler Till Ltd, 1971–81. Sen. Hon. Financial Adviser to Assoc. of Municipal Corps, 1962–71; Chm., Chancellor's Cttee to review Nat. Savings, 1971–73. Hon. Fellow, Manchester Polytechnic, 1970. Hon. Simon Res. Fellow, Manchester Univ., 1974–. Freeman, City of London, 1976. Haldane Medal (RIPA), 1933. Publications: Co-ordination and Planning in the Local Authority, 1936; Councillor's Handbook, 1945; Local Government up-to-date, 1946; contrib. to symposium of papers given to British Assoc., Leeds, 1968; contribs to Local Govt Finance, Bank Reviews, financial jls, etc. Recreation: collecting Victorian and other nineteenth century ephemera; heraldry. Address: 205 Old Hall Lane, Fallowfield, Manchester M14 6HJ. T: 061-224 2891.

PAGE, John; see Page, A. J.

PAGE, John Brangwyn; Chairman, Agricultural Mortgage Corporation, since 1982; Director: Standard Chartered Bank, since 1982; Nationwide Building Society, since 1982; b 23 Aug. 1923; s of late Sidney John Page, CB, MC; m 1948, Gloria Vail; one s one d. Educ: Highgate Sch. (Foundation Schol.); King's Coll., Cambridge (BA). RAF, 1942–46; Cambridge, 1946–48; Bank of England, 1948; seconded to IMF, 1953; Chief Cashier, 1970–80; Exec. Dir, 1980–82. FIB; CBIM; FRSA. Recreations: gardening, music, travel. Address: Agricultural Mortgage Corp., Bucklersbury House, Queen Victoria Street, EC4.

PAGE, Maj.-Gen. John Humphrey, CB 1977; OBE 1967; MC 1952; Director of the London Law Trust, since 1979; a non-executive Director, RBM (Holdings), since 1980; b 5 March 1923; s of late Captain W. J. Page, JP, Devizes and late Alice Mary Page (née Richards); m 1956, Angela Mary Bunting; three s one d. Educ: Stonyhurst. Commnd into RE, 1942; served in NW Europe, India, Korea, Middle East and UK, 1942–60; Instr, Staff Coll., Camberley, 1960–62; comd 32 Armd Engr Regt, 1964–67; idc 1968; CCRE 1st Br. Corps, 1969–70; Asst Comdt, RMA Sandhurst, 1971–74; Dir of Personal Services (Army), MoD, 1974–78, retd. Col Comdt, RE, 1980–. Mem. Council, Officers' Pension Soc. Address: Vanner's Farm House, Stour Provost, Gillingham, Dorset.

PAGE, Sir John (Joseph Joffre), Kt 1979; OBE 1959; Chairman: Mersey Docks and Harbour Co., since 1980; North Western Regional Health Authority, since 1982; b 7 Jan. 1915; 2nd s of late William Joseph and Frances Page; m 1939, Cynthia Maynard, d of late L. M. Swan, CBE; two s. Educ: Emanuel School. FCIT. RAF, 1933–38 and 1939–46 (despatches, 1943); Group Captain. Iraq Petroleum Group of Cos, 1938–39 and 1946–70; served in Palestine, Jordan, Lebanon, Syria, Iraq, Qatar, Bahrain and Abu Dhabi; Head Office, London, 1958–61; Gen. Man., 1955–58; Chief Representative, 1961–70; Chm., 1972–77, and Chief Exec., 1975–77, Mersey Docks and Harbour Co. Dep. Chm., British Ports Assoc., 1974–77; Chm., Nat. Ports Council, 1977–80. Chm., Chester DHA, 1981–82. Recreations: photography, fishing, music. Address: Springhill, Hill Road, Helsby, Cheshire WA6 9AG. T: Helsby 2994. Clubs: Oriental, Royal Air Force, MCC.

PAGE, Prof. John Kenneth; Professor of Building Science, University of Sheffield, since 1960; b 3 Nov. 1924; s of Brig. E. K. Page, qv; m 1954, Anita Bell Lovell; two s two d. Educ: Haileybury College; Pembroke College, Cambridge. Served War of 1939–45, Royal Artillery, 1943–47. Asst Industrial Officer, Council of Industrial Design, 1950–51; taught Westminster School, 1952–53; Sen. Scientific Officer, Tropical Liaison Section, Building Research Station, 1953–56; Chief Research Officer, Nuffield Div. for Architectural Studies, 1956–57; Lecturer, Dept. of Building Science, Univ. of Liverpool, 1957–60. Former Chm., Environmental Gp, and Mem., Econ. Planning Council, Yorks and Humberside Region, 1965–78. Former Chm., UK Section, Internat. Solar Energy Soc. Mem., UN Technical Panel on Solar Energy for New and Renewable Sources of Energy. Publications: 200 papers on Energy policy, Environmental Design and Planning, Building Climatology and Solar Energy. *Address:* c/o Department of Building Science, University of Sheffield, Western Bank, Sheffield S10 2TN. *T:* Sheffield 78555.

PAGE, Kenneth; *see* Page, Edwin Kenneth.

PAGE, Norman John, OBE 1981; MC 1945; FCCA; Secretary-General, Institute of Actuaries, since 1977; *b* 11 June 1920; *s* of John Francis Page and Ellen Catherine (*née* Fox); *m* 1949, Valerie Gascoine; two *d. Educ:* Harrow County Grammar Sch. for Boys. Fellow: Inst. of Chartered Secs and Administrators, 1955; Royal Statistical Soc., 1965; Assoc. of Certified Accountants, 1970. Served War, RAF, 1941-46: commnd RAF regt; active service in UK, NW Europe, India, Singapore and Sumatra; Flt Lieut. Prudential Assurance Co. Ltd, 1937-41, and 1946-52; Asst Sec., Inst. of Actuaries, 1952-62, Sec. 1962-77. Mem., Chartered Secretaries and Administrators' Co., 1980. *Recreations:* gardening, travel. *Address:* Trehaven, 17 Grange Road, Bushey, Watford, Herts WD2 2LQ. *T:* Watford 34177. *Clubs:* Reform, Royal Air Force.

PAGE, Richard Lewis; MP (C) Hertfordshire South West, since Dec. 1979; Director of family company, since 1964; *b* 22 Feb. 1941; *s* of Victor Charles and Kathleen Page; *m* 1964, Madeleine Ann Brown; one *s* one *d. Educ:* Hurstpierpoint Coll.; Luton Technical Coll. Apprenticeship, Vauxhall Motors, 1959-64; HNC Mech Engineering. Young Conservatives, 1964-66; Councillor, Banstead UDC, 1968-71; contested (C) Workington, Feb. and Oct. 1974; MP (C) Workington, Nov. 1976-1979; PPS to Sec. of State for Trade, 1981-82. *Recreation:* most sport. *Address:* House of Commons, SW1A 0AA.

PAGE, Russell, OBE 1951; garden designer; *b* 1 Nov. 1906. *Educ:* Charterhouse; Slade Sch.; University College London. Resident in France, 1945-62. Battersea Festival Gardens, 1951; designed gardens in UK, Belgium, Egypt, France, Germany, Italy, Portugal, Spain, Switzerland, W Indies and USA. French Academy of Architecture Medal, 1977. *Publication:* The Education of a Gardener, 1962.

PAGE, Simon Richard; Registrar, Guildford, Epsom and Reigate County Courts, and District Registrar, High Court of Justice, since 1980; a Recorder of the Crown Court, since 1980; *b* 7 March 1934; *s* of Eric Rowland Page and Vera (*née* Fenton); *m* 1963, Elizabeth Esther Broom (marr. diss. 1977); three *s* one *d. Educ:* Lancing; LSE (LLB External, 1956). Admitted solicitor (hons), 1957. National Service, Second Lieut RA, 1957-59. Private practice as solicitor, 1959-75; Pres., West Surrey Law Soc., 1972-73; Registrar, Croydon County Court, 1975-80; Junior Vice-Pres., Assoc. of County Court and District Registrars, 1982. *Recreations:* squash racquets, cricket, bridge. *Address:* Rosedene, Peaslake, Guildford, Surrey GU5 9RJ.

PAGE WOOD, Sir Anthony John, 8th Bt, *cr* 1837; *b* 6 Feb. 1951; *s* of Sir David (John Hatherley) Page Wood, 7th Bt and Evelyn Hazel Rosemary, *d* of late Captain George Ernest Bellville; *S* father 1955. *Heir:* uncle, Matthew Page Wood [*b* 13 Aug. 1924; *m* 1947; two *d*]. *Address:* 22 Godfrey Street, SW3 3TA.

PAGET, family name of **Marquess of Anglesey** and **Baron Paget of Northampton.**

PAGET OF NORTHAMPTON, Baron *cr* 1974 (Life Peer), of Lubenham, Leics; **Reginald Thomas Paget,** QC 1947; *b* 2 Sept. 1908; *m* 1931. *Educ:* Eton; Trinity College, Cambridge. Barrister, 1934. Lt RNVR, 1940-43 (invalided). Contested Northampton, 1935; MP (Lab) Northampton, 1945-Feb. 1974. Hon. Sec., UK Council of European Movement, 1954. Master, Pytchley Hounds, 1958-71. *Publications:* Manstein-Campaigns and Trial, 1951; (with late S. S. Silverman, MP) Hanged—and Innocent?, 1958; The Human Journey, 1979. *Address:* 9 Grosvenor Cottages, SW1. *T:* 01-730 4034.

PAGET, Sir John (Starr), 3rd Bt *cr* 1886; CEng, FIMechE; Chairman, Thermal Syndicate Ltd, Wallsend, 1973-80, now Chairman Emeritus (Director since 1939); Proprietor, Sir John Paget Woodworker and Proprietor and Senior Partner, Haygrass Cider Orchards; *b* 24 Nov. 1914; *s* of Sir Richard Paget, 2nd Bt and Lady Muriel Paget, CBE; *S* father 1955; *m* 1944, Nancy Mary Parish, JP, *d* of late Lieutenant-Colonel Francis Parish, DSO, MC; two *s* five *d. Educ:* Oundle; Chateau D'Oex; Trinity College, Cambridge (MA). Joined English Electric Co. Ltd, 1936; Asst Works Supt, English Electric, Preston, 1941; Joined D. Napier & Son Ltd, 1943; Assistant Manager, D. Napier & Son Ltd, Liverpool, 1945; Manager, D. Napier & Son Ltd, London Group, 1946; Works Director, Napier Aero Engines, 1961-62 (Dir and Gen. Man. D. Napier & Son Ltd, 1959-61). Director: Glacier Metal Group, 1963-65; Hilger & Watts, 1965-68; Rank Precision Industries Ltd, 1968-70. Hon. DTech Brunel, 1956. Silver Medal, Instn of Production Engineers, 1950. *Recreation:* cooking. *Heir:* *s* Richard Herbert Paget, *b* 17 February 1957. *Address:* Haygrass House, Taunton, Somerset. *T:* Taunton 81779; 20 Marloes Road, W8. *T:* 01-373 9760. *Clubs:* Athenæum; Northern Counties (Newcastle upon Tyne).

PAGET, Lt-Col Sir Julian (Tolver), 4th Bt *cr* 1871; Gentleman Usher to the Queen, since 1971; author; Public Relations Officer, Strutt and Parker, 1968-81; *b* 11 July 1921; *s* of General Sir Bernard Paget, GCB, DSO, MC

(*d* 1961) (*g s* of 1st Bt), and of Winifred, *d* of Sir John Paget, 2nd Bt; *S* uncle, Sir James Francis Paget, 3rd Bt, 1972; *m* 1954, Diana Frances, *d* of late F. S. H. Farmer; one *s* one *d. Educ:* Radley College; Christ Church, Oxford (MA). Joined Coldstream Guards, 1940; served North West Europe, 1944-45; retired as Lt-Col, 1968. *Publications:* Counter-Insurgency Campaigning, 1967; Last Post: Aden, 1964-67, 1969; The Story of the Guards, 1976; The Pageantry of Britain, 1979. *Recreations:* fishing, shooting, travel, writing. *Heir:* *s* Henry James Paget, *b* 2 Feb. 1959. *Address:* 4 Trevor Street, SW7. *T:* 01-584 3524. *Clubs:* Cavalry and Guards, Pratt's, Flyfishers'.

PAGET, Paul Edward, CVO 1971; FSA, FRIBA; Chairman, Norwich Diocesan Advisory Committee, 1973-76; Master, Art Workers Guild, 1971; Member: Redundant Churches Fund, 1969-76; Crafts Advisory Committee, 1971-75; Surveyor to the Fabric of St Paul's Cathedral, 1963-69; Senior Partner in Firm of Seely & Paget, Chartered Architects, 1963-69 (from death of late Lord Mottistone, OBE, FSA, FRIBA, in Jan. 1963); Architect to St George's Chapel, Windsor, and Portsmouth Cathedral, 1950-69; *b* 24 Jan. 1901; 2nd and *o surv s* of Bishop Henry Luke Paget and Elma Katie (*née* Hoare); *m* 1971, Verily, *d* of late Rev. F. R. C. Bruce, DD, and widow of Captain Donald Anderson. *Educ:* Winchester; Trinity Coll., Cambridge. Asst Private Sec. to 1st Viscount Templewood, PC, GCSI, GBE, CMG, 1924-26. Flight Lieutenant, RAuxAF, 1939-44. Asst Director, Emergency Works, 1941-44; Common Councilman, Corporation of London, 1949-55. CStJ 1962. *Principal Works:* Restorations: Eltham Palace; Lambeth Palace; Upper Sch., Eton Coll.; London Charterhouse, Deanery and Little Cloister, Westminster Abbey; Churches: Lee-on-Solent, Six Mile Bottom, All Hallows-by-the-Tower, City Temple, Stevenage New Town; Colleges of Education: Oxford, Norwich, Bristol, Culham. *Address:* Templewood, Northrepps, near Cromer, Norfolk. *T:* Overstrand 243. *Club:* Norfolk (Norwich).

PAIBA, Denis Anthony; a Recorder of the Crown Court, since 1980; *b* 10 Dec. 1926; *e s* of late Geoffrey Paiba and Geraldine Paiba; *m* 1955, Lesley Patricia Dresden; two *s. Educ:* University Coll. Sch. (Junior); Magdalen Coll. Sch., Oxford; Jesus Coll., Cambridge. 44 Royal Marine Commando, 1945-47. Financial Times, 1954-55. Called to the Bar, Gray's Inn, 1955. *Recreations:* theatre, music, gardening, archery, watching rugby and cricket, wining and dining. *Address:* Roehampton, SW15; 3 Temple Gardens, Temple, EC4Y 5BG. *T:* 01-353 3102.

PAICE, Karlo Bruce; Assistant Under-Secretary of State, Home Office, 1955-66; *b* 18 August 1906; *s* of H. B. Paice, Horsham, Sussex; *m* 1st, 1935, Islay (*d* 1965), *d* of late Paymaster Comdr Duncan Cook; four *s* ; 2nd, 1966, Mrs Gwen Morris (*née* Kenyon). *Educ:* Collyer's School, Horsham; Jesus Coll., Cambridge (MA). Second Clerk, Metropolitan Police Courts, 1928; Assistant Principal, Home Office, 1929; Asst Sec. to the Poisons Bd, 1933-35; Private Sec. to successive Parliamentary Under-Secretaries of State for Home Affairs, 1935-39. Principal, 1936; Assistant Secretary, 1941, serving in London Civil Defence Region, Fire Service Department, and Aliens Department. Secretary to the Prison Commission and a Prison Commissioner, 1949-55. *Recreations:* walking, history, music. *Address:* Flat 5, Windsor Lodge, Third Avenue, Hove, East Sussex. *T:* Brighton 733194. *Clubs:* Athenæum; Hove.

PAIGE, Prof. Edward George Sydney, PhD; Professor of Engineering (Electrical), University of Oxford, since 1977; *b* 18 July 1930; *s* of Sydney and Maude Paige; *m* 1953, Helen Gill; two *s* two *d. Educ:* Reading University (BSc, PhD). FInstP; FIEE. Junior Research Fellow to DCSO, Royal Radar Establishment, Malvern, 1955-77. *Address:* Department of Engineering Science, University of Oxford, Parks Road, Oxford. *T:* Oxford 59988.

PAIGE, Rear-Adm. Richard Collings, CB 1967; *b* 4 October 1911; *s* of Herbert Collings Paige and Harriet Pering Paige; *m* 1937, Sheila Brambles Ward, *d* of late Dr Ernest Ward, Paignton; two *s. Educ:* Blundell's School, Tiverton; RNE College, Keyham. Joined Navy, 1929. Served in HMS Neptune, Curaçao, Maori, King George V, Superb, Eagle (despatches twice); Captain, 1957; Commanding Officer, RNE College, 1960-62; Commodore Supt, HM Naval Base, Singapore, 1963-65; Admiral Supt HM Dockyard, Portsmouth, 1966-68. Rear-Adm. 1965. *Address:* Court, Churchstow, Kingsbridge, Devon TQ7 3QW.

PAIGE, Victor Grellier, CBE 1978; Chairman, Port of London Authority, since 1980; Deputy Chairman, National Freight Consortium, since 1982; *b* 5 June 1925; *s* of Victor Paige and Alice (*née* Grellier); *m* 1948, Kathleen Winifred, 3rd *d* of Arthur and Daisy Harris; one *s* one *d. Educ:* East Ham Grammar Sch.; Univ. of Nottingham. CIPM, FCIT, CBIM. Roosevelt Mem. Schol. 1954. Dep. Personnel Manager, Boots Pure Drug Co. Ltd, 1957-67; Controller of Personnel Services, CWS Ltd, 1967-70; Dir of Manpower and Organisation,1970-74, Exec. Vice-Chm. (Admin), 1974-77, Nat. Freight Corp.; Dep. Chm., Nat. Freight Corp., later Nat. Freight Co., 1977-82. Mem., Manpower Services Commn, 1974-80. Member: Notts Educn Cttee, 1957-63; Secondary Schs Examn Council, 1960-63; UK Adv. Council for Educn in Management, 1962-65; Careers Adv. Bd, Univ. of Nottingham, 1975-81; Chairman: Regional Adv. Council for Further Educn, E Mids, 1967; Exec. Council, British Assoc. for Commercial and Industrial Educn, 1974 (Vice-Pres. 1980); Member Council: Chartered Inst. of Transport, 1976-79; CBI; Chm., Educn and Trng Cttee, CBI; Vice-Pres., London Fedn of Boys' Clubs. Freeman, Co. of Watermen and Lightermen of the River Thames. *Publications:* contrib. techn. press on management. *Recreations:* reading, sport generally, athletics in particular (Pres. Notts Athletic Club, 1962-67). *Address:* Queen's Wood, Frithsden, Berkhamsted, Herts. *T:* Berkhamsted 5030.

PAIN, Barry Newton, CBE 1979; QPM 1976; Commandant, Police Staff College, Bramshill, and HM Inspector of Constabulary, since 1982; *b* 25 Feb. 1931; *s* of Godfrey William Pain and Annie Newton; *m* 1952, Marguerite Agnes King; one *s* one *d. Educ:* Waverley Grammar Sch., Birmingham. Clerk to Prosecuting Solicitor, Birmingham, 1947-51; 2nd Lieut (Actg Captain) RASC, Kenya, 1949-51. Birmingham City Police, 1951-68; Staff Officer to HM Inspector of Constabulary, Birmingham, 1966-68; Asst Chief Constable, Staffordshire and Stoke-on-Trent Constabulary, 1968-74; JSSC 1970. Adviser to Turkish Govt on Reorganization of Police, 1972. Pres., Assoc. of Chief Police Officers, 1981-82. *Recreations:* golf, shooting, boating. *Address:* Police Staff College, Bramshill House, near Hartley Wintney, Hants.

PAIN, Lt-Gen. Sir (Horace) Rollo (Squarey), KCB 1975 (CB 1974); MC 1945; farmer; late 4th/7th Royal Dragoon Guards; Head of British Defence Staff, Washington, 1975-78, retired; *b* 11 May 1921; *s* of late Horace Davy Pain, Levenside, Haverthwaite, Ulverston, and late Audrey Pain (*née* Hampson); *m* 1950, Denys Sophia (*née* Chaine-Nickson); one *s* two *d.* Commissioned into Reconnaissance Corps during War of 1939-45: served NW Europe (MC). After War, served for two years in E Africa and Brit. Somaliland before joining 4th/7th Royal Dragoon Gds in Palestine, 1947; attended Staff Coll., Camberley, 1951; subseq. served in Mil. Ops Directorate, in War Office; served with his Regt in BAOR, 1955-56; Mem. Directing Staff, Staff Coll., Camberley, 1957; GSO1, Brit. Army Staff, Washington, DC, 1960; commanded his Regt in BAOR, 1962; commanded one of the three divs, Staff Coll., Camberley, 1964; commanded 5 Inf. Bde in Borneo, 1965; IDC, 1968; ADC to the Queen, 1969; BGS, HQ, BAOR, 1969-70; GOC 2nd Div., 1970-72; Dir of Army Training, MoD, 1972-75; Col Comdt, Mil. Provost Staff Corps, 1974-; Col. 4th/7th Royal Dragoon Guards, 1979-. *Recreation:* hunting. *Address:* Eddlethorpe Hall, Malton, North Yorkshire. *T:* Burythorpe 218. *Club:* Cavalry and Guards.

PAIN, Hon. Sir Peter (Richard), Kt 1975; **Hon. Mr Justice Pain;** a Judge of the High Court of Justice, Queen's Bench Division, since 1975; *b* 6 Sept. 1913; *s* of Arthur Richard Pain and Elizabeth Irene Pain (*née* Benn); *m* 1941, Barbara Florence Maude Riggs; two *s. Educ:* Westminster; Christ Church, Oxford. Called to the Bar, Lincoln's Inn, 1936, Bencher 1972. QC 1965. Chairman: Race Relations Board Conciliation Cttee for Greater London, 1968-; South Metropolitan Conciliation Cttee, 1971-73; Mem., Parole Bd, 1978-. Pres., Holiday Fellowship, 1977. *Publications:* Manual of Fire Service Law, 1951; The Law Relating to the Motor Trade (with K. C. Johnson-Davies), 1955. *Recreations:* forestry, cricket, mountain walking. *Address:* Loen, St Catherine's Road, Frimley, Surrey. *T:* Deepcut 5639.

PAIN, Sir Rollo; *see* Pain, Sir H. R. S.

PAINE, George, CB 1974; DFC 1944; *b* 14 Apr. 1918; 3rd *s* of late Jack Paine and Helen Margaret (*née* Hadow), East Sutton; *m* 1969, Hilary (*née* Garrod), widow of Dr A. C. Frazer. *Educ:* Bradfield Coll.; Peterhouse, Cambridge. External Ballistics Dept, Ordnance Bd, 1941; RAF, 1942-46; Min. of Agriculture, 1948; Inland Revenue, 1949; Central Statistical Office, 1954; Board of Trade, 1957; Dir of Statistics and Intelligence, Bd of Inland Revenue, 1957-72; Dir, OPCS and Registrar Gen. for Eng. and Wales, 1972-78. Hon. Treasurer, Royal Statistical Soc., 1974-78. *Recreations:* fruit growing, beekeeping. *Address:* Springfield House, Broad Town, near Swindon, Wilts SN4 7RU. *T:* Broad Hinton 377.

PAINE, Peter Stanley, CBE 1981; DFC 1944; Managing Director, Tyne Tees Television Ltd, since 1974; *b* 19 June 1921; *s* of Arthur Bertram Paine and Dorothy Helen Paine; *m* 1942, Sheila Mary, *d* of Frederick Wigglesworth, MA; two *s* two *d. Educ:* King's Sch., Canterbury. Served 1940-46, 2 Gp RAF (Flt-Lt). Worked in Punch Publishing Office, 1945-47; Sales Promotion Man., Newnes Pearson, 1948-52, Odhams Press, then Sales Dir and Dir of Tyne Tees Television, 1958-67; Sales Dir and Dir of Yorkshire Television, 1967; Director: Independent Television News Ltd, 1982-; Independent Television Publications Ltd, 1977-; Broadcasters Audience Res. Bd, 1980-; Mem. Council, Independent Television Companies Assoc., 1974- (4 yrs Chm. Marketing Cttee). *Recreations:* golf, fishing, theatre, music, reading. *Address:* Briarfield, Ashwood Road, Woking, Surrey. *T:* Woking 73183. *Clubs:* Thirty; West Hill Golf.

PAINE, Dr Thomas Otten; Thomas Paine Associates, Los Angeles, since 1982; *b* 9 Nov. 1921; *s* of George Thomas Paine, Cdre, USN retd and Ada Louise Otten; *m* 1946, Barbara Helen Taunton Pearse; two *s* two *d. Educ:* Maury High, Norfolk, Va; Brown Univ.; Stanford Univ. Served War of 1939-45 (US Navy Commendation Ribbon 1944; Submarine Combat Award with two stars, 1944-45). Research Associate: Stanford Univ., 1947-49; General Electric Res. Lab., Schenectady, 1949-50; Manager, TEMPO, GE Center for Advanced Studies, Santa Barbara, 1963-67; Dep. Administrator, US Nat. Aeronautics and Space Admin., Washington, 1968; Administrator 1968-70; Group Executive, GE, Power Generation Group, 1970-73; Sen. Vice-Pres., GE, 1974-76; Pres. and Chief Operating Officer, Northrop Corp., 1976-82. Member, Board of Directors: Eastern Air Lines, 1981-; Quotron Systems, Inc., 1982-; RCA, 1982-; NBC, 1982-; Dir, Arthur D. Little Inc., 1982-; Chm., Pacific Forum, 1980-. MInstMet; Member: Newcomen Soc.; Nat. Acad. of Engineering; Acad. of Sciences, NY; Sigma Xi; Trustee: Occidental Coll.;

Brown Univ.; Asian Inst. Tech.; Harvey Mudd Coll. Outstanding Contribution to Industrial Science Award, AAS, 1956; NASA DSM, 1970; Washington Award, Western Soc. of Engrs, 1972; John Fritz Medal, United Engrg Soc., 1976; Faraday Medal, IEE, 1976. Hon. Dr of Science: Brown, 1969; Clarkson Coll. of Tech., 1969; Nebraska Wesleyan, 1970; New Brunswick, 1970; Oklahoma City, 1970; Hon. Dr Engrg: Worcester Polytechnic Inst., 1970; Cheng Kung Univ., 1978. Grand Ufficiale della Ordine Al Merito della Repubblica Italiana, 1972. *Publications:* various technical papers and patents. *Recreations:* sailing, beachcombing, skin diving, photography, book collecting, oil painting. *Address:* (office) Thomas Paine Associates, 10880 Wilshire Blvd, Suite 1109, Los Angeles, Calif 90024, USA; (home) 765 Bonhill Road, Los Angeles, Calif 90049. *Clubs:* Sky, Lotos, Explorers (New York); Army and Navy, Space, Cosmos (Washington); California, Regency (Los Angeles).

PAINTAL, Prof. Autar Singh, MD, PhD, DSc; FRS 1981; FRSE; Professor of Physiology and Director, Vallabhbhai Patel Chest Institute, Delhi University, since 1964 (Assistant Director, 1954-56); *b* 24 Sept. 1925; *s* of Dr Man Singh and Rajwans Kaur; *m* 1949; one *s* two *d. Educ:* SSBS Khalsa High Sch., Lahore; Forman Christian Coll., Lahore; Lucknow Univ. (MB, BS, MD); Edinburgh Univ. (PhD, DSc). Lectr in Physiol., King George's Med. Coll., Lucknow Univ., 1949; Rockefeller Fellow, 1950; Lectr in Physiol., Edinburgh Univ., 1951; Control Officer, Technical Develt Estabt Labs, Min. of Defence, Kanpur, 1952-54; Prof. of Physiology, All-India Inst. of Med. Sciences, New Delhi, 1958-64; Dean, Faculty of Med. Sciences, Delhi Univ., 1966-77. Associate Prof., Albert Einstein Coll. of Medicine, New York, 1956; Vis. Associate Prof. of Physiol., Univ. of Utah, 1957; Commonwealth Vis. Prof., St Bartholomew's Hosp. Med. Sch., London, 1966. FRSE 1966; Fellow: Indian Acad. of Med. Sciences, 1966; Indian National Science Acad., 1971 (Vice Pres., 1981-); Member: Physiol Soc., UK, 1953; Ergonomics Res. Soc., UK, 1954. B. C. Roy Orator, New Delhi, 1973. Basanti Devi Amir Chand Prize, 1967; Silver Jubilee Res. Award, 1978. *Publications:* (ed) Morphology and Mechanisms of Chemoreceptors, 1976; (ed) Respiratory Adaptations, Capillary Exchange and Reflex Mechanisms, 1977; papers in Jl of Physiol. and in other physiol jls. *Recreations:* swimming, rowing, bird watching. *Address:* Vallabhbhai Patel Chest Institute, Delhi University, PO Box 2101, Delhi 110007, India. *T:* Delhi 223846. *Club:* Roshanara (Delhi).

PAINTER, George Duncan, OBE 1974; Biographer and Incunabulist; Assistant Keeper in charge of fifteenth-century printed books, British Museum, 1954-74; *b* Birmingham, 5 June 1914; *s* of George Charles Painter and Minnie Rosendale (*née* Taylor); *m* 1942, Isabel Joan, *d* of Samuel Morley Britton, Bristol; two *d. Educ:* King Edward's Sch., Birmingham; Trinity Coll., Cambridge (Schol.). Bell Exhibr; John Stewart of Rannoch Schol.; Porson Schol.; Waddington Schol.; 1st cl. hons Class. Tripos pts I and II; Craven Student; 2nd Chancellor's Class. Medallist, 1936; MA Cantab 1945. Asst Lectr in Latin, Univ. of Liverpool, 1937; joined staff of Dept of Printed Books, BM, 1938. FRSL 1965. Hon. DLitt Edinburgh, 1979. *Publications:* André Gide, A Critical Biography, 1951, rev. edn 1968; The Road to Sinodun, Poems, 1951; André Gide, Marshlands and Prometheus Misbound (trans.), 1953; Marcel Proust, Letters to his Mother (trans.), 1956; Marcel Proust, A Biography, vol. 1, 1959, vol. 2, 1965 (Duff Cooper Memorial Prize); The Vinland Map and the Tartar Relation (with R. A. Skelton and T. E. Marston), 1965; André Maurois, The Chelsea Way (trans.), 1966; William Caxton, a Quincentenary Biography, 1976; Chateaubriand, A Biography, vol. 1, The Longed-for Tempests, 1977 (James Tait Black Meml Prize); articles on fifteenth-century printing in The Library, Book Collector, Gutenberg-Jahrbuch. *Recreations:* family life, walking, gardening, music. *Address:* 10 Mansfield Road, Hove, East Sussex. *T:* Brighton 416008.

PAINTER, Terence James; Under-Secretary, Board of Inland Revenue, since 1975; *b* 28 Nov. 1935; *s* of late Edward Lawrence Painter and Ethel Violet (*née* Butler); *m* 1959, Margaret Janet Blackburn; two *s* two *d. Educ:* City of Norwich Sch.; Downing Coll., Cambridge (BA (History)). Entered Inland Revenue as Asst Principal, 1959; Principal, 1962; seconded to Civil Service Selection Bd, 1967-68; Asst Sec., 1969; seconded to HM Treasury, 1973-75. *Recreations:* music, books. *Address:* 9 Grant Gardens, Harpenden, Herts AL5 4QD. *T:* Harpenden 60269.

PAISH, Frank Walter, MC 1918; MA; Professor Emeritus, University of London; *b* 15 January 1898; *e s* of late Sir George Paish; *m* 1927, Beatrice Marie, *d* of late G. C. Eckhard; two *s* one *d. Educ:* Winchester College; Trinity College, Cambridge. Served European War (RFA), 1916-19. Employed by Standard Bank of South Africa, Ltd, in London and South Africa, 1921-32. Lecturer, London School of Economics, 1932-38; Reader, 1938-49; Professor of Economics (with special reference to Business Finance), 1949-65; Hon. Fellow, 1970. Secretary, London and Cambridge Economic Service, 1932-41 and 1945-49; Editor, 1947-49. Deputy-Director of Programmes, Ministry of Aircraft Production, 1941-45. Consultant on Economic Affairs, Lloyds Bank Ltd, 1965-70. *Publications:* (with G. L. Schwartz) Insurance Funds and their Investment, 1934; The Post-War Financial Problem and Other Essays, 1950; Business Finance, 1953; Studies in an Inflationary Economy, 1962; Long-term and Short-term Interest Rates in the United Kingdom, 1966; (ed) Benham's Economics, 8th edn, 1967, (with A. J. Culyer) 9th edn, 1973; How the Economy Works and Other Essays, 1970; The Rise and Fall of Incomes Policy, 1969; articles in The Economic Journal, Economica, London and Cambridge Bulletin, etc. *Address:* The Old Rectory Cottage, Kentchurch, Hereford.

PAISLEY, Bishop of, (RC), since 1968; **Rt. Rev. Stephen McGill;** *b* Glasgow, 4 Jan. 1912; *s* of Peter McGill and Charlotte Connolly. *Educ:* St Aloysius', Glasgow; Blairs College, Aberdeen; Coutances, France; Institut Catholique, Paris. Ordained Priest of St Sulpice, 1936. STL Paris. St Mary's College, Blairs, Aberdeen: Spiritual Director, 1940-51; Rector, 1951-60. Bishop of Argyll and the Isles, 1960-68. *Address:* Bishop's House, Porterfield Road, Kilmacolm, Renfrewshire.

PAISLEY, Rev. Ian Richard Kyle; MP (Democratic Unionist) North Antrim, since 1974 (ProtU 1970-74); Member (DemU) Northern Ireland, European Parliament, since 1979; Member (DemU) North Antrim, Northern Ireland Assembly, since 1982; Minister, Martyrs Memorial Free Presbyterian Church, Belfast, since 1946; *b* 6 April 1926; 2nd *s* of late Rev. J. Kyle Paisley and Mrs Isabella Paisley; *m* 1956, Eileen Emily Cassells; two *s* three *d* (incl. twin *s*). *Educ:* Ballymena Model Sch.; Ballymena Techn. High Sch.; S Wales Bible Coll.; Reformed Presbyterian Theol. Coll., Belfast. Ordained, 1946. Moderator, Free Presbyterian Church of Ulster, 1951. Commenced publishing The Protestant Telegraph, 1966. Contested (Prot U) Bannside, NI Parlt, 1969; MP (Prot U), Bannside, Co. Antrim, NI Parlt, 1970-72; Leader of Opposition, 1972; Chm., Public Accounts Cttee, 1972. Co-Founder, Democratic Unionist Party, NI, 1972. Mem. (Democratic Unionist), N Antrim, NI Assembly, 1973-75. Mem. (UUUC), N Antrim, NI Constitutional Convention, 1975-76. Hon. DD Bob Jones Univ., SC. FRGS. Mem., Internat. Cultural Soc., Korea, 1977. *Publications:* History of the 1859 Revival, 1959; Christian Foundations, 1960; Ravenhill Pulpit, Vol. 1, 1966, Vol. 2, 1967; Exposition of the Epistle to the Romans, 1968; Billy Graham and the Church of Rome, 1970; The Massacre of St Bartholomew, 1972; America's Debt to Ulster, 1976; (jtly) Ulster—the facts, 1981; No Pope Here, 1982. *Address:* House of Commons, SW1; The Parsonage, 17 Cyprus Avenue, Belfast BT5 5NT.

PAISLEY, John Lawrence, CB 1970; MBE 1946; Consultant with L. G. Mouchel & Partners, Consulting Engineers, 1971-82, retired; *b* Manchester, 4 Sept. 1909; *e s* of J. R. and Mrs E. W. Paisley; *m* 1937, Angela Dorothy Catliff; three *d. Educ:* King George V Sch., Southport; Univ. of Liverpool. BEng 1930, MEng 1935. Asst Engineer: Siemens Bros & Co. Ltd, North Delta Transmission Lines, Egypt, 1930-34; Howard Humphreys & Sons, Cons. Engrs, Tunnels and Viaduct on A55, in N Wales, 1934-35; W Sussex CC, 1935-37; Asst Engr in Scotland, Min. of Transport, 1937-39. War Service with Royal Engineers, 1939-46: took part in Dunkirk evacuation and finally as Major, RE (now Hon. Major), commanded 804 Road Construction Co. in UK, France and Germany (MBE). Ministry of Transport: Engr in Scotland, 1946-52; Senr Engr in HQ, London, 1952-60; Divl Rd Engr, NW Div. at Manchester, 1960-64; Dep. Chief Engr, HQ, London, 1964-66; Chief Highway Engr, Min. of Transport, 1966-70. Hon. Vice-Pres., Permanent Internat. Assoc. of Road Congresses. FICE; FInstHE. *Publications:* contribs Proc. Instn of Civil Engrs, Proc. Instn of Highway Engrs. *Recreation:* fell walking. *Address:* Weybrook, Warren Road, Guildford, Surrey. *T:* Guildford 62798. *Clubs:* Civil Service, Victory; Rucksack (Manchester).

PAISLEY, Robert, OBE 1977; Manager, Liverpool Football Club, 1974-May 1983; *b* 23 Jan. 1919; *s* of Samuel and Emily Paisley; *m* 1946, Jessie Chandler; two *s* one *d. Educ:* Eppleton Sen. Mixed Sch., Tyne and Wear. Apprentice bricklayer, 1934; also Hetton Juniors Amateur FC, 1934-37; Bishop Auckland Amateur FC, 1937-39; signed as professional for Liverpool FC, 1939; Army Service, RA, 1939-46; Liverpool FC: 2nd Team Trainer, 1954-59; 1st Team Trainer, 1959-70; Asst Manager, 1970-74. Successes since becoming manager: UEFA Cup, 1976; League Championship, 1976, 1977, 1979, 1980, 1982; European Cup, 1977, 1978, 1981; League Cup (now known as Milk Cup), 1981-82. *Publication:* Bob Paisley's Liverpool Scrap Book, 1979. *Recreations:* all types of sport. *Address:* 29 Bower Road, Woolton, Liverpool L25 4RG.

PAKENHAM, family name of **Earl of Longford.**

PAKENHAM, Elizabeth; *see* Longford, Countess of.

PAKENHAM, Henry Desmond Verner, CBE 1964; HM Diplomatic Service, retired; *b* 5 Nov. 1911; *s* of Hamilton Richard Pakenham and Emilie Willis Stringer; *m* 1st, 1946, Crystal Elizabeth Brooksbank (marr. diss., 1960); one *s* one *d* (and one *s* decd); 2nd, 1963, Venetia Maude; one *s* one *d. Educ:* Monkton Combe; St John Baptist College, Oxford. Taught modern languages at Sevenoaks School, 1933-40. Served in HM Forces, 1940-45. Entered Foreign Service, 1946; served in Madrid, Djakarta, Havana, Singapore, Tel Aviv, Buenos Aires and Sydney; retired 1971. Chm., Suffolk Preservation Soc., 1979-82. Asst Editor, Satow's Guide to Diplomatic Practice, 5th edn, 1979. *Recreations:* music and wild life. *Address:* Rose Farm, Brettenham, Suffolk.

PAKENHAM, Thomas (Frank Dermot); writer; *b* 14 Aug. 1933; *e s* of 7th Earl of Longford, *qv* and of Countess of Longford, *qv* ; (does not use courtesy title); *m* 1964, Valerie, *d* of Major R. G. McNair Scott; two *s* two *d. Educ:* Dragon School, Oxford; Belvedere Coll., Dublin; Ampleforth Coll., York; Magdalen Coll., Oxford (BA Greats 1955). Travelled, Near East and Ethiopia, 1955-56 (discovered unrecorded medieval Ethiopian church at Bethlehem, Begemdir, 1956). Free-lance writing, 1956-58. Editorial staff: Times Educational Supplement, 1958-60; Sunday Telegraph, 1961; The Observer, 1961-64. Founder Mem. 1958, and Member Cttee 1958-64, Victorian Soc.; Founder Mem., and Mem. Cttee 1968-72, Historic Irish Tourist Houses and

Gardens Assoc. (HITHA); Treas., British-Irish Assoc., 1972-; Sec. (co-founder), Christopher Ewart-Biggs Memorial Trust, 1976-. Research Fellow, St Antony's Coll., Oxford, 1979-81. *Publications:* The Mountains of Rasselas: An Ethiopian Adventure, 1959; The Year of Liberty: The Story of the Great Irish Rebellion of 1798, 1969; The Boer War, 1979 (Cheltenham Prize, 1980). *Recreation:* water. *Address:* 111 Elgin Crescent, W11. *T:* 01-727 7624; Tullynally, Castlepollard, Westmeath, Ireland. *T:* Mullingar 61159. *Clubs:* Beefsteak, Brooks's; Stephen's Green (Dublin).

PAKENHAM-WALSH, John; Principal Assistant Legal Adviser to the Home Office, since 1980; *b* 7 Aug. 1928; *s* of late Rev. W. P. Pakenham-Walsh, formerly ICS, and Guendolen (*née* Elliott); *m* 1951, Deryn, *er d* of Group Captain R. E. G. Fulljames, MC, and Mrs Muriel Fulljames; one *s* four *d. Educ:* Bradfield Coll.; University Coll., Oxford (MA). Called to the Bar, Lincoln's Inn, 1951. Crown Counsel, Hong Kong, 1953-57; Parly Counsel, Fedn of Nigeria, 1958-61; joined Legal Adviser's Br., Home Office, 1961; seconded to Law Officers Dept, 1971-73; Asst Legal Adviser, Home Office, 1973-80. *Address:* Home Office, Queen Anne's Gate, SW1H 9AT. *Clubs:* United Oxford & Cambridge University; Liphook Golf (Hants).

PAKES, Ernest John, CBE 1954; Under-writing Member of Lloyd's, since 1956; *b* 28 Jan. 1899; *s* of Ernest William Pakes; *m* 1928, Emilie Pickering (*d* 1981); one *s. Educ:* Hampton Gram. Sch. Served with London Scottish Regt, 1917-19; Ceylon Defence Force, 1940-44; Min. of War Transport, Karachi, 1945-46. Employed in shipping industry, P&O Group, 1916-62 including: Mackinnon Mackenzie & Co., India, Ceylon etc., 1921-54 (Chm., 1951-54); British India Steam Navigation Co. Ltd, 1954-62 (Chm., 1960-62); Director: Allahabad Bank, India, 1947-54 (Chm., 1951-54); Chartered Bank, London, 1958-62. Chm., Karachi Chamber of Commerce, 1946-47; Pres., Bengal Chamber of Commerce and Assocd Chambers of Commerce of India, 1953-54. Liveryman, Worshipful Co. of Shipwrights. *Recreation:* golf. *Address:* Staneway, Tyrrells Wood, Leatherhead, Surrey. *T:* Leatherhead 73243. *Club:* Walton Heath.

PAKINGTON, family name of **Baron Hampton.**

PAL, Dr Benjamin Peary, Padma Shri 1958; Padma Bhushan 1968; FRS 1972; Chairman, National Committee on Environmental Planning and Coordination, 1977-81; *b* 26 May 1906; *s* of Dr R. R. Pal; unmarried. *Educ:* Rangoon Univ.; Downing Coll., Cambridge University. MSc hons, PhD Cantab. 2nd Economic Botanist, Imperial Agric. Research Inst., 1933; Imperial Economic Botanist, 1937; Dir, Indian Agric. Res. Inst., 1950; Dir-Gen., Indian Council of Agric. Research, 1965-72, Scientist Emeritus 1972. Hon. DSc: Punjab Agric. Univ.; Sardar Patel Univ.; UP Agric. Univ.; Haryana Agric. Univ.; Orissa Agric. Univ.; Foreign Mem., All Union Lenin Acad. of Agric. Sciences; Hon. Member: Japan Acad.; Acad. d'Agriculture de France; Fellow: Linnean Soc. of London; Indian Nat. Science Acad. (Pres., 1975-76). *Publications:* Beautiful Climbers of India, 1960; Wheat, 1966; Charophyta, The Rose in India, 1966; Flowering Shrubs, 1967; All About Roses, 1973; Bougainvilleas, 1974. *Recreations:* rose gardening, painting. *Address:* P11, Hauz Khas Enclave, New Delhi 110016, India. *T:* 660245.

PALADE, Prof. George Emil; scientist, USA; Professor of Cell Biology, Yale University, since 1973; *b* Iassy, Roumania, 19 Nov. 1912; *s* of Emil Palade and Constanta Cantemir; *m* 1st, 1941, Irina Malaxa (decd); one *s* one *d* ; 2nd, 1970, Dr Marilyn Farquhar. *Educ:* Liceul Al. Hasdeu, Buzau, Roumania; Med. Sch., Univ. of Bucharest (MD). Arrived in US, 1946; naturalized US citizen, 1952. Instructor, Asst Prof., then Lectr in Anatomy, Sch. of Med., Univ. of Bucharest, 1940-45; Visiting Investigator, Rockefeller Inst. for Med. Research, 1946-48; continuing as an Assistant (later the Inst. became Rockefeller Univ., NYC); promoted to Associate, 1951, and Associate Mem., 1953; Prof. of Cell Biology, Rockefeller Univ. and Full Member of Rockefeller Inst., 1956. Fellow, Amer. Acad. of Arts and Sciences; Member: Nat. Acad. of Sciences; Amer. Soc. Cell Biology; Amer. Assoc. for the Advancement of Science. Awards include: Albert Lasker Basic Research, 1966; Gairdner Award, 1967; Hurwitz Prize, 1970; Nobel Prize for Medicine, 1974. *Publications:* Editor: Jl of Cell Biology (co-founder); Jl of Membrane Biology; numerous contribs med. and sci. jls. *Address:* Section of Cell Biology, Yale University School of Medicine, 333 Cedar Street, New Haven, Conn. 06510, USA. *T:* (203) 436-2376.

PALAMOUNTAIN, Edgar William Irwin; Chairman of Council, University College Buckingham, since 1979; *m* 1948, Eleanor, *d* of Maj.-Gen. Sir Richard Lewis, KCMG, CB, CBE; one *s* two *d. Educ:* Charterhouse; St John's Coll., Oxford (MA). Served War, Army, 1941-47 (mentioned in despatches): RHA and staff; Captain 1943, Major 1945, Actg Lt-Col 1946; Allied Commn for Austria, 1945-47. Anglo-Iranian Oil Co., London and Tehran, 1948-51; Tootal Ltd, 1952-56 (Personal Asst to Chm.; Prodn Manager); M & G Group, 1957-79: Exec. Dir, 1962; Man. Dir, 1968; Chm., 1977. Chairman: Unit Trust Assoc., 1977-79; Institutional Shareholders Cttee, 1978-79; Wider Share Ownership Council, 1967-. Trustee: Nat. Assoc. of Almshouses, 1963-80; Esmée Fairbairn Charitable Trust, 1966-80 (Dir, 1980-); Thames Help Trust, 1980-; Social Affairs Unit, 1982-. Patron, Inst. of Economic Affairs, 1972-; Governor, NIESR, 1981-; Mem. Bd, Adam Smith Inst., 1982-. Mem. Cttee, London Voluntary Service Council, 1969-. *Publication:* Taurus Pursuant: a history of the Eleventh Armoured Division, 1945. *Recreations:* lawn tennis, golf, stalking. *Address:* Duns Tew Manor,

Oxford; 35 Chelsea Towers, SW3. *Clubs:* Boodle's, City of London, MCC.

PALETHORPE-TODD, Richard Andrew; *see* Todd, Richard.

PALETTE, John; Director of Personnel, British Rail, since 1982; *b* 19 May 1928; *s* of Arthur and Beatrice Palette; *m* 1950, Pamela Mabel Palmer; three *s. Educ:* Alexandra Sch., Hampstead. MCIT. Gen. Railway Admin, 1942-69; Divl Manager, Bristol, 1969-72; Asst Gen. Manager, Western Region, 1972-74; Divl Manager, Manchester, 1974-76; Gen. Manager, Scottish Region, 1976-77, Southern Region, 1977-82, British Railways. Chm., British Transport Ship Management (Scotland) Ltd, 1976-. *Recreations:* walking, reading, gardening, watching sport. *Address:* 90 Wargrave Road, Twyford, Reading, Berks. *T:* Twyford (Berks) 340965.

PALING, Helen Elizabeth, (Mrs W. J. S. Kershaw); a Recorder of the Crown Court, since 1972; *b* 25 April 1933; *o d* of A. Dale Paling and Mabel Eleanor Thomas; *m* 1961, William John Stanley Kershaw, PhD; one *s* three *d. Educ:* Prince Henry's Grammar Sch., Otley; London Sch. of Economics. LLB London 1954. Called to Bar, Lincoln's Inn, 1955. *Address:* 46 Grainger Street, Newcastle upon Tyne. *T:* Newcastle upon Tyne 21980, 22392.

PALING, William Thomas; *b* 28 Oct. 1892; *s* of George Thomas Paling, Sutton-in-Ashfield, Notts; *m* 1919, Gladys Nellie, MBE, *d* of William Frith, James Street, Nuncar Gate, Nottinghamshire; one *s* one *d.* MP (Lab) Dewsbury, 1945-59, retired. *Address:* 3 Lancaster Close, Tickhill, near Doncaster, South Yorks. *T:* Doncaster 742875.

PALLEY, Prof. Claire Dorothea Taylor; Professor of Law, University of Kent at Canterbury, since 1973; *b* 17 Feb. 1931; *d* of Arthur Aubrey Swait, Johannesburg; *m* 1952, Ahrn Palley; five *s. Educ:* Durham Girls' Coll.; Univs of Cape Town and London. BA 1950, LLB 1952, Cape Town; PhD London 1965. Called to Bar, Middle Temple; Advocate, S Africa and Rhodesia. Lecturer: Cape Town Univ., 1953-55; UC Rhodesia and Nyasaland, 1960-65; QUB, 1966-67; Reader, QUB, 1967-70, Prof. of Public Law, 1970-73, and Dean of Faculty of Law, 1971-73; Master of Darwin Coll., UKC, 1974-82. Chm., SE Area Cttee, Nat. Assoc. of Citizens' Advice Bureaux, 1974-79; Mem. Council, Minority Rights Group, 1975-; Constitutional Adviser to: African Nat. Council at Const. Talks on Rhodesia, 1976; Govt of Republic of Cyprus, 1980-. Mem., Commonwealth Scholarships Commn, 1980-82. Governor: Polytechnic of the South Bank, 1975-81; King's Sch., Canterbury, 1977-. *Publications:* The Constitutional History and Law of Southern Rhodesia, 1966; contrib. learned jls. *Address:* Darwin College, University of Kent at Canterbury, Canterbury, Kent CT2 7NY.

PALLISER, Sir (Arthur) Michael, GCMG 1977 (KCMG 1973; CMG 1966); HM Diplomatic Service, retired; Permanent Under-Secretary of State, Foreign and Commonwealth Office, and Head of the Diplomatic Service, 1975-82; *b* 9 Apr. 1922; *s* of late Admiral Sir Arthur Palliser, KCB, DSC, and of Lady Palliser (*née* Margaret Eva King-Salter); *m* 1948, Marie Marguerite, *d* of late Paul-Henri Spaak; three *s. Educ:* Wellington Coll.; Merton Coll., Oxford. Served with Coldstream Guards, 1942-47; Capt. 1944. Entered HM Diplomatic Service, 1947; SE Asia Dept, Foreign Office, 1947-49; Athens, 1949-51; Second Sec., 1950; Foreign Office: German Finance Dept, 1951-52; Central Dept, 1952-54; Private Sec. to Perm. Under-Sec., 1954-56; First Sec., 1955; Paris, 1956-60; Head of Chancery, Dakar, 1960-62 (Chargé d'Affaires in 1960, 1961 and 1962); Counsellor, and seconded to Imperial Defence College, 1963; Head of Planning Staff, Foreign Office, 1964; a Private Sec. to PM, 1966; Minister, Paris, 1969; Ambassador and Head of UK Deleg. to European Communities, Brussels, 1971; Ambassador and UK Permanent Representative to European Communities, 1973-75. Chevalier, Order of Orange Nassau, 1944; Chevalier, Légion d'Honneur, 1957. *Club:* Buck's.

PALLOT, Arthur Keith, CB 1981; CMG 1966; Secretary and Director-General, Commonwealth War Graves Commission, 1975-82 (Director of Finance and Establishments, 1956-75); *b* 25 Sept. 1918; *s* of Harold Pallot, La Tourelle, Jersey; *m* 1945, Marjorie, *d* of J. T. Smith, Rugby; two *d. Educ:* Newton College. Royal Navy, 1936; retired as Lt-Comdr, 1947. Commonwealth War Graves Commission, 1947. Awarded the Queen's Commendation for brave conduct, 1958. *Recreations:* walking, squash, cricket. *Address:* Northways, Stubbles Lane, Cookham Dean, Berks. *T:* Marlow 6529.

PALMAR, Derek James, FCA; Chairman and Chief Executive, Bass, since 1976 (Director, 1970-76); Chairman: Rush & Tompkins Group, since 1974; Yorkshire Television, since 1982; *b* 25 July 1919; *o s* of late Lt-Col F. J. Palmar; *m* 1946, Edith Brewster; one *s* one *d. Educ:* Dover College. Served RA and Staff, 1941-46; psc; Lt-Col 1945; Peat, Marwick, Mitchell & Co., 1937-57; Director: Hill Samuel Group, 1957-70; Howard Machinery, 1967-; Grindlays Bank Ltd, 1973-; Grindlays Holdings, 1979-; Drayton Consolidated Trust, 1982-. Adviser, Dept of Economic Affairs, 1965-67. Mem., British Railways Bd, 1969-72; Chm., BR Southern Regional Adv. Bd, 1972-79. Vice-Pres., Brewers' Soc., 1982- (Chm., 1980-82, Vice-Chm., 1978-80). Trustee: Civic Trust; World Wildlife Fund UK. Mem. Ct, Brewers' Co; Freeman, City of London. CBIM. FRSA. *Recreations:* shooting, gardening. *Address:* 30 Portland Place, W1N 3DF. *T:* 01-637 5499. *Club:* Boodle's.

PALMER, family name of **Earl of Selborne, Baron Palmer** and **Baroness Lucas of Crudwell.**

PALMER; *see* Prior-Palmer.

PALMER, 3rd Baron, *cr* 1933, of Reading; **Raymond Cecil Palmer,** OBE 1968; Bt *cr* 1916; former Director, Associated Biscuit Manufacturers Ltd, retired 1980; Chairman: Huntley & Palmers Ltd, 1969-80; Huntley Boorne & Stevens Ltd, Reading, 1956-80 (Deputy Chairman, 1948); *b* 24 June 1916; *er s* of 2nd Baron Palmer and Marguerite (*d* 1959), *d* of William McKinley Osborne, USA, Consul-General to Great Britain; *S* father 1950; *m* 1941, Victoria Ellen, *o c* of late Captain J. A. R. Weston-Stevens, Maidenhead; two *d* (and one *d* decd). *Educ:* Harrow; University Coll., Oxford. Joined Huntley & Palmers Ltd, 1938, Dep. Chm., 1966-69, Man. Dir, 1967-69. Served War of 1939-45 in Grenadier Guards as Lieut, in UK and North Africa, 1940-43 (invalided). Mem., Southern Electricity Bd, 1965-77. Pres., Berks CCC. *Recreations:* cricket, rackets, music and gardening; shooting. *Heir:* b Col Hon. Gordon William Nottage Palmer, *qv. Address:* Farley Hill House, Farley Hill, Reading, Berkshire. *T:* Eversley 732260. *Club:* Cavalry and Guards.

See also Lord Wodehouse.

PALMER, Andrew Eustace, CVO 1981; HM Diplomatic Service; Counsellor, Head of Chancery and Consul-General, Oslo, since 1979; *b* 30 Sept. 1937; *s* of Lt-Col Rodney Howell Palmer, MC, and Mrs Frances Pauline Ainsworth (*née* Gordon-Duff); *m* 1962, Davina, *d* of Sir Roderick Barclay, *qv* ; two *s* one *d. Educ:* Winchester Coll.; Pembroke Coll., Cambridge (MA). Second Lieut. Rifle Bde, 1956-58. Joined HM Foreign (later Diplomatic) Service, 1961; American Dept, FO, 1962-63; Third, later Second, Secretary (Commercial), La Paz, 1963-65; Second Sec., Ottawa, 1965-67; Treasury Centre for Administrative Studies, 1967-68; Central Dept, FO, later Southern European Dept, FCO, 1968-72; First Sec. (Information), Paris, 1972-76; Asst Head of Defence Dept, FCO, 1976-77; RCDS 1978. *Recreations:* fishing, tennis, ski-ing, following most other sports. *Address:* c/o Foreign and Commonwealth Office, SW1; Town Farm Cottage, Little Missenden, Amersham, Bucks. *T:* Great Missenden 2785; 46 Pont Street, SW1. *T:* 01-584 4931. *Clubs:* Brooks's, MCC.

PALMER, Anthony Wheeler, QC 1979; a Recorder of the Crown Court, since 1980; *b* 30 Dec. 1936; *s* of late Philip Palmer and of Doris Palmer; *m* Jacqueline, *d* of Reginald Fortnum, Taunton; one *s* two *d. Educ:* Wrekin Coll., Salop. Called to the Bar, Gray's Inn, 1962. *Address:* 17 Warwick Avenue, Coventry CV5 6DJ. *T:* Coventry 75340.

PALMER, Arnold Daniel; professional golfer since 1954; golf course designer; *b* 10 ept. 1929; *s* of Milfred J. and Doris Palmer; *m* 1954, Winifred Walzer; two *d. Educ:* Wake Forest Univ. Winner of numerous tournament titles, including: British Open Championship, 1961, 1962; US Open Championship, 1960; Masters Championship, 1958, 1960, 1962, 1964; Spanish Open Championship, 1975; Professional Golfers' Assoc. Championship, 1975; Canadian PGA, 1980; USA Seniors' Championship, 1981. Hon. Dr of Laws: Wake Forest; Nat. Coll. of Educn; Hon. Dr Hum: Thiel Coll.; Florida Southern College. *Publications:* (all jointly) Arnold Palmer Golf Book, 1961; Portrait of a Professional Golfer, 1964; My Game and Yours, 1965; Situation Golf, 1970; Go for Broke, 1973; Arnold Palmer's Best 54 Golf Holes, 1977. *Recreations:* aviation (speed record for flying round world in twin-engine jet, 1976), bridge, tennis, hunting, fishing. *Address:* PO Box 52, Youngstown, Pa 15696, USA. *T:* (412) 537-7751. *Clubs:* (Owner and Pres.) Latrobe Country; (Pres. and Part-Owner) Bay Hill (Orlando, Fla); (Tournament Professional) Laurel Valley Golf; numerous other country, city, golf.

PALMER, Arthur Montague Frank, CEng, FIEE, FInstF; MP (Lab and Co-op) Bristol North East, since 1974 (Bristol Central, 1964-74); *b* 4 Aug. 1912; *s* of late Frank Palmer, Northam, Devon; *m* 1939, Dr Marion Ethel Frances Woollaston, medical consultant; two *d. Educ:* Ashford Gram. Sch.; Brunel Technical College (now Brunel Univ.). Is a Chartered Engineer and a Chartered Fuel Technologist. Studied electrical supply engineering, 1932-35, in London; Member technical staff of London Power Co., 1936-45; former Staff Mem., Electrical Power Engineers Assoc. Member Brentford and Chiswick Town Council, 1937-45. MP (Lab) for Wimbledon, 1945-50; MP (Lab and Co-op) for Cleveland Div. of Yorks, Oct. 1952-Sept. 1959; Front bench Opposition spokesman on fuel and power, 1957-59; Chairman: Parly and Scientific Cttee, 1965-68; House of Commons Select Cttee on Science and Technology, 1966-70, 1974-79; Co-operative party Parly Gp, 1970-; Vice-Chm., Select Cttee on Energy, 1979-. *Publications:* The Future of Electricity Supply, 1943; Modern Norway, 1950; Law and the Power Engineer, 1959; articles on political, industrial, and economic subjects. *Recreations:* walking, motoring, gardening, reading novels, history and politics. *Address:* 14 Lavington Court, Putney, SW15. *T:* 01-789 1967; Hill Cottage, Charlcutt, near Calne, Wilts. *T:* Kellaways 653. *Club:* Athenæum.

PALMER, Bernard Harold Michael, MA; Editor of the Church Times since 1968; *b* 8 Sept. 1929; *e s* of late Christopher Harold Palmer; *m* 1954, Jane Margaret, *d* of late E. L. Skinner; one *s* one *d. Educ:* St Edmund's School, Hindhead; Eton (King's Scholar); King's College, Cambridge. BA 1952; MA 1956. Member of editorial staff, Church Times, 1952-; Managing Director, 1957-; Editor-in-Chief, 1960-68; Chm., 1962-. *Recreations:* cycling, penmanship. *Address:* 143 Bradbourne Vale Road, Sevenoaks, Kent. *T:* Sevenoaks 53327. *Club:* Royal Commonwealth Society.

PALMER, Brian Desmond; Under Secretary, Northern Ireland Office, since 1981; *b* 1 May 1939; *m* 1964, Hilary Eileen Latimer; one *s* one *d. Educ:* Royal Belfast Academical Instn; Queen's Univ. of Belfast (LLB 1962). Northern Ireland Civil Service, 1957-: Estate Duty Office, 1957-62; Min. of Home Affairs, 1962-65; Dept of the Environment, 1965-77; Head of Central Secretariat, 1977-81. *Recreation:* golf. *Address:* Northern Ireland Office, Dundonald House, Belfast BT4 3SU. *T:* Belfast 63255.

PALMER, Charles Alan Salier, CBE 1969; DSO 1945; Chairman, Associated Biscuit Manufacturers Ltd, 1969-72 (Vice-Chm., 1963); *b* 23 Oct. 1913; *s* of late Brig. Eric Palmer, Shinfield Grange, near Reading; *m* 1939, Auriol Mary, *d* of late Brig.-Gen. Cyril R. Harbord, CB, CMG, DSO. *Educ:* Harrow; Exeter Coll., Oxford. Joined Huntley & Palmer's, 1934 (Bd, 1938; Dep.-Chm. 1955; Chm., Huntley & Palmer's, 1963). Served War of 1939-45: with Berks Yeo., Adjt, 1939-41; GSO3, HQ 61 Div., 1941-42; GSO2, HQ III Corps, 1942-43; Lt-Col; commanded SOE mission, Albania, 1943-45 (despatches). Pres., Reading Conservative Assoc., 1946-; Chm., Cake & Biscuit Alliance, 1967-70; Mem. Council, CBI 1967-70; Mem. British Productivity Council, 1970-73. *Recreations:* shooting, fishing, tropical agriculture. *Address:* Forest Edge, Farley Hill, Reading, Berks. *T:* Arborfield Cross 760223.

PALMER, Sir (Charles) Mark, 5th Bt, *cr* 1886; *b* 21 Nov. 1941; *s* of Sir Anthony Frederick Mark Palmer, 4th Bt, and of Henriette (*see* Lady Abel Smith); *S* father 1941; *m* 1976, Hon. Catherine Elizabeth Tennant, *y d* of Baron Glenconner, *qv*; one *s* one *d. Heir: s* Arthur Palmer, *b* 9 March 1981. *Address:* Mill Hill Farm, Sherborne, Northleach, Glos. *T:* Windrush 395.

PALMER, Maj.-Gen. Charles Patrick Ralph, CBE 1982 (OBE 1974); General Officer Commanding North East District, since 1982; Commander 2nd Infantry Division, since 1983; *b* 29 April 1933; *s* of late Charles Dudley Palmer and Catherine Anne (*née* Hughes-Buller); *m* 1st, 1960, Sonia Hardy Wigglesworth (*d* 1965); one *s*; 2nd, 1966, Joanna Grace Baines; two *d. Educ:* Marlborough Coll. psc 1963. Commnd Argyll and Sutherland Highlanders, 1953; served British Guiana, Berlin, Suez Operation and Cyprus; Instructor, RMA Sandhurst, 1961-62; BM 153(H) Inf. Bde, 1964-65; 1 Argyll and Sutherland Highlanders, Borneo, Singapore and Aden, 1965-68; MA to Dep. CDS (Intell.), MoD, 1968-70; Instructor, Staff Coll., 1970-72; reformed and commanded 1st Bn Argyll and Sutherland Highlanders, 1972-74; Chief of Staff to Comdr British Forces Hong Kong, 1974-76; RCDS, 1977; Comd 7th Armoured Bde, 1977-78; Dep. Comd 1 Armoured Div., 1978-80; Comd British Mil. Adv. and Training Team, Zimbabwe, 1980-82. Col of the Argyll and Sutherland Highlanders, 1982-. *Recreations:* travel, books, outdoor interests. *Address:* c/o Royal Bank of Scotland, Comrie, Perthshire PH6 2DW. *Club:* Army and Navy.

PALMER, David Vereker; Chief Executive since 1978 and Chairman since 1982, Willis Faber plc; *b* 9 Dec. 1926; *s* of late Brig. Julian W. Palmer and Lena Elizabeth (*née* Vereker); *m* 1950, Mildred Elaine O'Neal Palmer; three *d. Educ:* Stowe. ACII 1950. Commnd The Life Guards, 1944; served as regular officer in Europe and ME, 1944-49; joined Edward Lumley & Sons, 1949; Manager, New York office, 1953-59; joined Willis, Faber & Dumas Ltd, 1959; Dir, 1961; Partner, 1965; Dep. Chm., 1972. Master, Worshipful Co. of Insurers, 1982. *Recreations:* farming, hunting. *Address:* 8 Egerton Terrace, SW3 2BT. *T:* 01-584 3869; Burrow Farm, Hambleden, near Henley-on-Thames, Oxon RG9 6LT. *T:* Hambleden 256. *Clubs:* City of London; Swinley Forest Golf.

PALMER, Ven. Derek George; Archdeacon of Rochester and Canon Residentiary of Rochester Cathedral, since 1977; *b* 24 Jan. 1928; *s* of George Palmer, MBE and Edna Palmer; *m* 1952, June Cecilie Goddard; two *s* two *d. Educ:* Clifton Coll.; Selwyn Coll., Cambridge (MA); Wells Theological Coll. Deacon 1952, priest 1953; Priest in Charge, Good Shepherd, Bristol, 1954-58; first Vicar of Hartcliffe, 1958-68; Vicar of Christ Church, Swindon, 1968-77. Mem., General Synod, 1971-81. Canon of Bristol Cathedral, 1975-. *Publications:* All Things New, 1963; Quest, 1971. *Recreation:* canals. *Address:* The Archdeaconry, The Precinct, Rochester, Kent ME1 1SX. *T:* Medway 42527.

PALMER, Edward Hurry, CB 1972; retired Civil Servant; *b* 23 Sept. 1912; *s* of late Harold G. Palmer and late Ada S. Palmer; *m* 1940, Phyllis Eagle; no *c. Educ:* Haileybury. Dep. Chief Surveyor of Lands, Admty, 1942; Chief Surveyor of Lands, Admty, 1950; Chief Surveyor of Defence Lands, MoD, 1964; Comptroller of Defence Lands and Claims, MoD, 1968-72; Property Services Agency, DoE: Dir, Defence Lands Services, 1972-73; Dir, Estate Surveying Services, 1973-74. *Recreations:* gardening, walking. *Address:* 49 Paines Lane, Pinner, Middlesex. *T:* 01-866 5961.

PALMER, Felicity Joan; soprano/mezzo-soprano; *b* 6 April 1944. *Educ:* Erith Grammar Sch.; Guildhall Sch. of Music and Drama. AGSM (Teacher/Performer), FGSM. Kathleen Ferrier Meml Prize, 1970; major appearances at concerts in Britain, America, Belgium, France, Germany, Italy and Spain; operatic début, Marriage of Figaro, Houston, USA, Oct. 1973; The Magic Flute, London, 1975; Don Giovanni, London, 1976; Alcina, Bern, 1977; Julius Caesar, Frankfurt, 1978; Idomeneo, Zürich, 1980; Tristan und Isolde, ENO, 1981; recitals in Amsterdam, Paris, Vienna, 1976-77; concert tours with BBC SO, Europe, 1973 and 1977-, Australasia, Far East and Eastern Europe, 1977-; ABC tour of Australia, 1978. Recordings include: Poèmes pour Mi,

with Pierre Boulez; Holst Choral Symphony, with Sir Adrian Boult; recitals, with John Constable, of songs by Poulenc, Ravel and Fauré, and of Victorian ballads. *Address:* 7 Bayham Road, W4 1BJ.

PALMER, Rev. Francis Harvey; Diocesan Missioner, Diocese of Lichfield, since 1980; *b* 13 Jan. 1930; *s* of Harry Hereward North Palmer and Ada Wilhelmina Annie Utting; *m* 1955, Mary Susan Lockhart; three *d. Educ:* Nottingham High Sch.; Jesus Coll., Cambridge (Exhibr); Wycliffe Hall, Oxford. MA. Deacon, 1955; Priest, 1956. Asst Curate: Knotty Ash, Liverpool, 1955-57; St Mary, Southgate, Crawley, 1958-60; Chaplain, Fitzwilliam House, Cambridge, 1960-64; Vicar of Holy Trinity, Cambridge and Chaplain to Cambridge Pastorate, 1964-71; Principal, Ridley Hall, Cambridge, 1971-72; Rector of Worplesdon, Surrey, 1972-80; Diocesan Ecumenical Officer, Guildford, 1974-80. *Publication:* (contrib.) New Bible Dictionary, 1959. *Recreation:* stamp collecting. *Address:* 14 Gorway Gardens, Walsall WS1 3BJ.

PALMER, Prof. Frank Robert, FBA 1975; Professor and Head of Department of Linguistic Science, University of Reading, since 1965; *b* 9 April 1922; *s* of George Samuel Palmer and Gertrude Lilian (*née* Newman); *m* 1948, Jean Elisabeth Moore; three *s* two *d. Educ:* Bristol Grammar Sch.; New Coll., Oxford (Ella Stephens Schol., State Schol.) 1942-43 and 1945-48; Merton Coll., Oxford (Harmsworth Sen. Schol.) 1948-49. MA Oxon 1948; Craven Fellow, 1948. Served war, E Africa, 1943-45. Lectr in Linguistics, Sch. of Oriental and African Studies, Univ. of London, 1950-60 (study leave in Ethiopia, 1952-53); Prof. of Linguistics, University Coll. of N Wales, Bangor, 1960-65; Dean of Faculty of Letters and Social Sciences, Univ. of Reading, 1969-72; Linguistic Soc. of America Prof., Buffalo, 1971. Professional visits to Canada, USA, Mexico, Venezuela, Peru, Chile, Argentine, Uruguay, Brazil, India, China, Indonesia, Morocco, Tunisia, Uganda, Kuwait and most countries of Europe. *Publications:* The Morphology of the Tigre Noun, 1962; A Linguistic Study of the English Verb, 1965; (ed) Selected Papers of J. R. Firth, 1968; (ed) Prosodic Analysis, 1970; Grammar, 1971; The English Verb, 1974; Semantics, 1976, 2nd edn 1981; Modality and the English Modals, 1979; articles and reviews on Ethiopian langs, English and linguistic theory, in learned jls. *Recreations:* gardening, crosswords. *Address:* Whitethorns, Roundabout Lane, Winnersh, Wokingham, Berks RG11 5AD. *T:* Wokingham 786214.

PALMER, Sir Geoffrey (Christopher John), 12th Bt, *cr* 1660; *b* 30 June 1936; *er s* of Lieutenant-Colonel Sir Geoffrey Frederick Neill Palmer, 11th Bt, and Cicely Katherine (who *m* 1952, Robert W. B. Newton), *o d* of late Arthur Radmall, Clifton, nr Watford; *S* father 1951; *m* 1957, Clarissa Mary, *er d* of Stephen Villiers-Smith, Knockholt, Kent; four *d. Educ:* Eton. *Recreations:* squash, racquets, cricket, shooting. *Heir: b* Jeremy Charles Palmer [*b* 16 May 1939; *m* 1968, Antonia, *d* of late Ashley Dutton; two *s*]. *Address:* Carlton Curlieu Hall, Leicestershire. *T:* Great Glen 2656. *Clubs:* Boodle's; MCC, I Zingari, Free Foresters, Eton Ramblers, Butterflies, Gentlemen of Leicestershire, Lincolnshire Gentlemen's Cricket, Derbyshire Friars, Oakham Cricket, XL, Frogs, Pedagogues, Market Harborough CC, Stoneygate, Old Etonian Golfing Society, Langtons CC.

PALMER, Gerald Eustace Howell, Hon. DLitt Reading, 1957; farmer, forester and iconographer; *b* 9 June 1904; *s* of late Eustace Exall Palmer, Chairman of Huntley and Palmers Ltd, and Madeline Mary Howell. *Educ:* Winchester; New College, Oxford (Scholar). MP (Nat. C) for Winchester Division of Hampshire, 1935-45. Served RA, Capt (despatches). President of the Council, Univ. of Reading, 1966-69; A Verderer of the New Forest, 1957-66; Chm., Forestry Commission Regional Adv. Cttee for South-East England, 1954-63; A Forestry Commissioner, 1963-65; Chm., Forestry Commn Nat. Cttee for England, 1964-65. Hon. Fellow, Soc. of Foresters of GB. *Publications:* following translations (in collab. with E. Kadloubovsky): Writings from the Philokalia, 1951; Unseen Warfare, 1952; The Meaning of Icons, by Lossky and Ouspensky, 1952; Early Fathers, from the Philokalia, 1954; (with Philip Shevrard and Father Kallistos Ware) The Philokalia, vol. I, 1979, vol. II, 1981. *Address:* Bussock Mayne, Newbury, Berks. *T:* Chieveley 265. *Club:* Brooks's.

PALMER, Col Hon. Gordon William Nottage, OBE 1957 (MBE 1944); TD 1950; Chairman, Huntley & Palmer Foods plc (formerly Associated Biscuit Manufacturers), since 1978; Chairman and Managing Director, Associated Biscuits Ltd; Managing Director, Huntley & Palmers Ltd, 1959-65; Lord-Lieutenant, Berkshire, since 1978; *b* 18 July 1918; *yr s* of 2nd Baron Palmer and Marguerite Osborne, USA; *heir-pres.* to 3rd Baron Palmer, *qv*; *m* 1950, Lorna Eveline Hope, *d* of Major C. W. H. Bailie; two *s. Educ:* Eton Coll.; Christ Church, Oxford. Served War of 1939-45, with Berks Yeo., 1939-41; staff Capt. RA, HQ 61 Div., 1941; DAQMG, Malta, 1942; GSO2, Ops, GHQ Middle East, 1943-44; GSO2, HQ 5 Div., 1944-45; Lt-Col, Instructor Staff College, Camberley, 1945; Comd Berkshire Yeo., TA, 1954-56. Hon. Col Berkshire and Westminster Dragoons, 1966-67; Hon. Col, Royal Yeomanry, 1972-75. Dir, Huntley, Boorne & Stevens Ltd, 1948-69; Chm. Cake and Biscuit Alliance, 1957-59. Dir, Marlands Brewery (Abingdon). Mem., British National Export Council, 1966-69. Dir, S Midlands Regional Bd, Lloyds Bank Ltd. Pres., Council, Reading Univ., 1973-75 (Mem. 1954-, Treas., 1955-59, Vice-Pres., 1966-73; Hon. LLD, 1975); Chm. Council, Royal Coll. of Music, 1973-; FRCM 1965; Mem. Council, Bradfield College; DL Berks, 1960; JP 1956; High Sheriff, 1965; Vice Lord-Lieutenant, 1976; Chairman, Berkshire T&AFA, 1961-68. KStJ.

Recreation: gardening. *Address:* Harris House, Mortimer, Berkshire. *T:* Mortimer 332317; Edrom Newton, Duns, Berwickshire. *T:* Chirnside 292. *Club:* Cavalry and Guards.

PALMER, John; Under Secretary, Department of Transport, since 1976; *b* 13 Nov. 1928; 2nd *s* of William Nathaniel Palmer and Grace Dorothy May Palmer (*née* Procter); *m* 1958, Lyliane Marthe Jeanjean, *o d* of René Jeanjean and Jeanne Jeanjean (*née* Larrouy); two *d. Educ:* Heath Grammar Sch., Halifax; The Queen's Coll., Oxford (Lit. Hum.) (MA). Entered Min. of Housing and Local Govt, 1952; Cabinet Office, 1963-65; Asst Sec., 1965; Under Sec., DoE, 1971. *Address:* 2 The Hermitage, Richmond, Surrey; 64 Escou, France. *Club:* United Oxford & Cambridge University.

PALMER, Sir John (Chance), Kt 1979; solicitor; Partner, Ashford Sparkes and Harward, Tiverton, Exeter and Crediton; *b* 21 March 1920; *s* of Ernest Clephan Palmer and Claudine Pattie Sapey; *m* 1945, Mary Winifred Ellyatt; four *s. Educ:* St Paul's Sch.; St Edmund Hall, Oxford (MA). Served War, RNVR, Atlantic and Mediterranean, 1939-46. Admitted a Solicitor, 1948; Elected Council of Law Society, 1963, President, 1978-79; Mem., Criminal Injuries Compensation Board, 1981-. Governor, Coll. of Law, 1965; Pres., Devon and Exeter Law Society, 1972; Pres., S Western Law Societies, 1973; Chm., Governors of Blundells Sch.; Chm. Trustees, London Sailing Project. Member: Exeter HA; Council, Exeter Univ. Hon. Member: Amer. Bar Assoc.; Canadian Bar Assoc. Hon. LLD Exeter, 1980. *Recreations:* gardening, sailing. *Address:* Hensleigh, Tiverton, Devon EX16 5NJ. *T:* Tiverton 252959. *Clubs:* Naval, RNSA; Royal Yacht Squadron; Teign Corinthian Yacht (Teignmouth).

PALMER, Sir John (Edward Somerset), 8th Bt, *cr* 1791; Consultant; Director, Atkins Land and Water Management, since 1979; *b* 27 Oct. 1926; *e s* of Sir John A. Palmer, 7th Bt; *S* father, 1963; *m* 1956, Dione Catharine Skinner; one *s* one *d. Educ:* Canford School; Cambridge Univ. (MA); Durham Univ. (MSc). Colonial Service, Northern Nigeria, 1952-61. Senior Executive, R. A. Lister & Co. Ltd, Dursley, Glos, 1962-63; Min. Overseas Develt, 1964-68. Mem. Amer. Soc. of Agric. Engrs; MIAgrE. *Heir: s* Robert John Hudson Palmer, *b* 20 Dec. 1960. *Address:* Gayton House, Gayton, Northampton NN7 3EZ. *T:* Northampton 858336; 14 Hale Street, Cambridge. *T:* Cambridge 521929. *Clubs:* Institute of Directors; Rock Sailing.

PALMER, Maj.-Gen. (Joseph) Michael; Defence Services Secretary, since 1982; *b* 17 Oct. 1928; *s* of late Lt-Col William Robert Palmer, DSO, and late Joan Audrey Palmer (*née* Smith); *m* 1953, Jillean Monica Sherston; two *s* one *d. Educ:* Wellington College. Commissioned 14th/20th King's Hussars, 1948; Adjutant 14th/20th King's Hussars, 1953-55; Adjutant Duke of Lancaster's Own Yeomanry, 1956-59; psc 1960; jssc 1965; CO 14th/20th King's Hussars, 1969-72; Comdr RAC 1st (BR) Corps, 1974-76; Asst Chief of Staff, Allied Forces Central Europe, 1976-78; Director, Royal Armoured Corps, 1978-81. Col, 14th/20th King's Hussars, 1981-. Liveryman, Salters' Co., 1965. MBIM. *Recreations:* riding, shooting, music, reading. *Club:* Cavalry and Guards.

PALMER, Leonard Robert; Professor of Comparative Philology, University of Oxford, and Fellow of Worcester College, 1952-71, Emeritus Professor, 1971, Emeritus Fellow, 1972; *b* 5 June 1906; *m* ; one *d. Educ:* High School, Canton, Cardiff; University College of South Wales and Monmouthshire; Trinity College, Cambridge; University of Vienna. BA Wales 1927; PhD Vienna 1931; PhD Cambridge 1936; MA Oxford 1952. Fellow of Univ. of Wales, 1930-31; Assistant Lecturer in Classics, 1931-35, Lecturer in Classics, 1935-41, Victoria University of Manchester; temp. Civil Servant in Foreign Office, 1941-45; Professor of Greek and Head of Dept of Classics at King's Coll., London, 1945-52. Hon. Secretary Philological Society, 1947-51, President, 1957-61. Corresponding Member Deutsches Archäologisches Institut, 1958. Dr. Phil *hc* Innsbruck, 1981. *Publications:* Translation of E. Zeller: Outlines of the History of Greek Philosophy, 14th edn, 1931; Introduction to Modern Linguistics, 1936; A Grammar of the Post-Ptolemaic Papyri, Vol. 1 (Publications of the Philological Society), 1945; The Latin Language, 1954 (as Introduccion al Latin, rev. Spanish edn, 1974; as La Lingua Latina, Italian edn, 1977); Mycenaeans and Minoans, 1961, 2nd edn 1965 (trans. as De Aegeische Wereld, 1963, Knossos och Mykene, 1963, Minoici e Micenei, 1970); The Language of Homer (in A Companion to Homer), 1962; The Interpretation of Mycenaean Greek Texts, 1963, rev. edn 1969; The Find Places of the Knossos Tablets, 1963; A New Guide to the Palace of Knossos, 1969; The Penultimate Palace at Knossos, 1969; Descriptive and Comparative Linguistics: a critical introduction, 1972 (Spanish edn, Introduccion critica a la linguistica descriptiva y comparada, 1975, rev. Italian edn, Linguistica descrittiva e comparativa, 1979, rev. Japanese edn 1979); The Greek Language, 1981; various articles in English and foreign learned journals. *Festschrift:* Studies in Greek, Italic, and Indo-European Linguistics, offered to Leonard R. Palmer on the occasion of his seventieth birthday, ed Anna M. Davies and W. Meid, 1976. *Address:* Church Hill, Pitney, Langport TA10 9PE.

PALMER, Leslie Robert, CBE 1964; Director-General, Defence Accounts, Ministry of Defence, 1969-72; *b* 21 Aug. 1910; *s* of Robert Palmer; *m* 1937, Mary Crick; two *s* one *d. Educ:* Battersea Grammar School; London University. Entered Admiralty Service, 1929; Assistant Dir of Victualling, 1941; Dep. Dir of Victualling, 1954; Dir of Victualling, Admiralty, 1959-61; Principal Dir of Accounts, Admiralty, 1961-64; Principal Dir of Accounts

(Navy) MoD, 1964-68. Hon. Treasurer and Chm., Finance and Admin Dept, United Reformed Church, 1973-79; Hon. Treasurer, BCC, 1980-82. *Recreation:* music. *Address:* 3 Trossachs Drive, Bath BA2 6RP. *T:* Bath 61981.

PALMER, Sir Mark; *see* Palmer, Sir C. M.

PALMER, Maj.-Gen. Michael; *see* Palmer, Maj.-Gen. J. M.

PALMER, Monroe Edward, OBE 1982; FCA; Joint Treasurer, Liberal Party, since 1977; Partner, Palmer Marshall, Chartered Accountants, London; *b* 30 Nov. 1938; *s* of William and Sybil Polikoff; *m* 1962, Susette Sandra (*née* Cardash); two *s. Educ:* Orange Hill Grammar Sch. FCA 1963. Chm., Hendon Citizens Advice Bureau, 1981-; Treasurer: Disablement Assoc., London Borough of Barnet, 1971-; Liberal Parly Party, 1978-. Prospective Parly Cand. (L) Hendon South; contested seat, 1979. *Recreation:* politics. *Address:* 31 The Vale, NW11 8SE. *T:* 01-455 5140. *Club:* National Liberal.

PALMER, Most Rev. Norman Kitchener; *see* Melanesia, Archbishop of.

PALMER, Maj.-Gen. (Retd) Philip Francis, CB 1957; OBE 1945; Major-General late Royal Army Medical Corps; *b* 8 Aug. 1903. MB, BCh, BAO, Dublin, 1926; DPH 1936. Served North West Frontier of India, 1930-31 (medal and clasp). Adjutant Territorial Army, 1932-36. War of 1939-45 (OBE). Director of Medical Services, Middle East Land Forces, Dec. 1955; QHS, 1956-60, retired. Col Comdt, RAMC, 1963-67. *Address:* c/o Williams & Glyn's Bank Ltd, Whitehall, SW1.

PALMER, Robert Henry Stephen; His Honour Judge Palmer; a Circuit Judge, since 1978; *b* 13 Nov. 1927; *s* of Henry Alleyn Palmer and Maud (*née* Obbard); *m* 1955, Geraldine Elizabeth Anne Evens; one *s* two *d. Educ:* Charterhouse; University Coll., Oxford. Called to the Bar, 1950. Dep. Chm., Berks QS, 1970. A Recorder of the Crown Court, 1972-78. *Publications:* Harris's Criminal Law, 1960; Guide to Divorce, 1965. *Recreation:* self-sufficiency. *Address:* 44 Staveley Road, Chiswick, W4 3ES. *T:* 01-994 3394.

PALMER, Sidney John, CB 1972; OBE 1953; Deputy Director General, Ships, and Head of Royal Corps of Naval Constructors, 1968-73; *b* 28 Nov. 1913; *m* 1941, Mavis Beatrice Blennerhassett Hallett; four *s. Educ:* RNC Greenwich. WhSch 1937. Admty Experiment Works, Haslar, 1938; Portsmouth Dockyard, 1942; Chief Constructor, Sydney, 1945; Constructor Comdr, Hong Kong, 1946; Chief Constructor Aircraft Carriers, 1948; Prof. of Naval Architecture, RNC Greenwich, 1952; Asst Dir Dreadnought Project, 1959; Dep. Dir Polaris Programme, 1963; Dir Naval Ship Production, 1966; Dep. Dir General Ships, 1968. Mem. Council, RINA, 1960; Liveryman, Shipwrights' Co., 1968; Hon. Research Fellow, UCL, 1968. Mem., Cttee of Management, RNLI, 1974-78. *Recreations:* tennis, golf, bridge. *Address:* Bloomfield Avenue, Bath, Avon. *T:* Bath 312592.

PALMER, William John, CBE 1973; Judge of Her Majesty's Chief Court for the Persian Gulf, 1967-72; Member, Court of Appeal for Anguilla, 1973-81; *b* 25 April 1909; *o s* of late William Palmer and late Mary Louisa Palmer (*née* Dibb), Suffolk House, Cheltenham; *m* 1st, 1935, Zenaida Nicolaevna (*d* 1944), *d* of late Nicolai Maropoulo, Yalta, Russia; 2nd, 1949, Vanda Ianthe Millicent, *d* of late William Matthew Cowton, Kelvin Grove, Queensland; one *s* two *d. Educ:* Pate's Grammar School, Cheltenham; Christ's College, Cambridge (Lady Margaret Scholar). Barrister, Gray's Inn. Joined Indian Civil Service, 1932; Deputy Commissioner, Jalpaiguri, 1943, Chief Presidency Magistrate, Calcutta, 1945; retired from ICS, 1949. Joined Colonial Legal Service as Magistrate, Nigeria, 1950; Chief Registrar, High Court, Eastern Region, 1956; Judge, 1958; Acting Chief Justice of Eastern Nigeria, Oct.-Dec. 1963 and Aug.-Nov. 1965. Judge of HM's Court for Bahrain and Assistant Judge of the Chief Court for the Persian Gulf, 1965-67. A part-time Chm. of Industrial Tribunals, 1975-78. *Recreations:* swimming, travel, history. *Address:* Guys Farm, Icomb, Glos GL54 1JD. *T:* Stow-on-the-Wold 30219. *Clubs:* East India, Devonshire, Sports and Public Schools; Union (Sydney, NSW).

PALMES, Peter Manfred Jerome; Principal Assistant Director, Public Prosecutions Department, 1979-81; *b* 28 Feb. 1920; *s* of Manfred Palmes and Gwendoline Robb; *m* 1st, 1945, Sylvia Theodor (decd); 2nd, 1969, Brenda Laban; one step *d. Educ:* Charterhouse; Worcester Coll., Oxford. Served War of 1939-45: Oxford and Bucks LI and 1/8th Gurkha Rifles, 1940-45. Called to Bar, Inner Temple, 1948. Public Prosecutions Dept: Legal Assistant, 1948; Sen. Legal Asst, 1958; Asst Solicitor, 1969; Asst Director, 1977. Jubilee Medal, 1977. *Address:* 4/12 Queen Anne's Gate, SW1. *T:* 01-213 3440.

PALUELLO, L. M.; *see* Minio-Paluello.

PANAYIDES, Tasos Christou; High Commissioner of Cyprus in the UK and Malta, and Ambassador to Sweden, Norway, Denmark, and Iceland since 1979; *b* 9 April 1934; *s* of Christos Panayides and Efrosini Panayides; *m* 1969, Pandora Constantinides; two *s* one *d. Educ:* Paphos Gymnasium; Teachers' Training Coll.; Univ. of London (Diploma in Education); Univ. of Indiana, USA (MA Political Science, Diploma in Public Administration). Teacher, 1954-59; First sec. to Pres., 1960-68; Director President's Office, 1969; Ambassador of Cyprus to Federal Republic of Germany, Switzerland, Austria, and Atomic Energy organisation, Vienna, 1969-78. 1st Cl., Grand Order and Grand Cross with Star and Sash, Federal Republic of Germany; Grand Cross in Gold with Star and Sash, Austria. *Publications:* articles in newspapers and magazines. *Recreations:* swimming, reading books. *Address:* 5 Cheyne Walk, SW3. *T:* 01-351 3989.

PANCKRIDGE, Surg. Vice-Adm. Sir (William) Robert (Silvester), KBE 1962; CB 1960; Medical Director-General of the Navy, 1960-63, retired; *b* 11 Sept. 1901; *s* of W. P. Panckridge, OBE, MB, MRCS, LRCP, and Mrs Panckridge; *m* 1932, Edith Muriel, *d* of Sir John and Lady Crosbie, St John, Newfoundland; one *d. Educ:* Tonbridge School; Middlesex Hospital. FRSM 1955; QHP 1958. PMO, RN Coll., Dartmouth, 1948; Medical Officer-in-Charge; RN Hosp., Hong Kong, 1952; RN Hosp., Chatham, 1958; Surgeon Captain, 1952; Surgeon Rear-Admiral, 1958; Surgeon Vice-Admiral, 1960. QHP, 1958-63. CStJ 1959. *Recreations:* shooting, fishing, gardening. *Address:* Waterfall Lodge, Oughterard, Co. Galway. *T:* Galway 82168.

PANDIT, Vijaya Lakshmi, (Mrs Ranjit S. Pandit); Padma Vibhusan, India, 1962; *b* 18 August 1900; *d* of Motilal Nehru and Sarup Rani Nehru; *m* 1921, Ranjit S. Pandit; three *d. Educ:* privately. Member Municipal Board, Allahabad, and Chm. Education Cttee, 1935; MLA, UP, and Minister of Local Govt and Health in Congress Cabinet of UP, 1937-39, and 1946-47. Leader India delegation to UN General Assembly, 1946, 1947, 1948; Ambassador to Moscow, 1947-49; Ambassador of India to the USA and Mexico, 1949-51; Member of Indian Parliament, 1952-54; High Commissioner for India in London, and Indian Ambassador to Ireland, 1954-61, concurrently Indian Ambassador to Spain, 1958-61; Governor of Maharashtra, 1962-64; MP, Phulpur, UP, 1964-69. Imprisoned three times for participation in national movement, 1932, 1941, 1942. President of the United Nations Assembly, 1953-54, Mem. Indian Delegn to UN, 1963. Trustee, Mountbatten Meml Trust, 1980-. Hon. DCL, Oxford, 1964, and numerous other Hon. degrees from Universities and Colleges. *Publications:* The Evolution of India (Whidden Lectures), 1958; The Scope of Happiness: a personal memoir, 1979. *Address:* 181B Rajpur Road, Dehra Dun, Uttar Pradesh, India.

PANET, Brig. Henri de Lotbinière, CBE 1943 (OBE 1941); *b* 21 Apr. 1896; *s* of late Brig.-Gen. A. E. Panet, CB, CMG, DSO; *m* 1931, Truda Buchanan Hope; one *d. Educ:* Loyola Coll., Montreal; Royal Military Coll., Canada. Served European War, 1915-18. Royal Engineers, France and Salonica (wounded, despatches); Indian State Railways, 1920-34; served Egypt and Palestine, 1935-36 (despatches); Hong Kong, 1938-41 (OBE); Iraq and Persia, 1941-43 (CBE); BLA, 1944-45 (despatches); Director of Fortifications and Works, War Office, 1947-49; retired, 1949. *Recreation:* fishing. *Address:* 161 Wilton Road, Salisbury, Wilts. *T:* Salisbury 3615.

PANKHURST, Air Vice-Marshal (Retd) Leonard Thomas, CB 1955; CBE 1944; *b* 26 August 1902; *s* of late Thomas William Pankhurst, Teddington, Middlesex; *m* 1939, Ruth, *d* of late Alexander Phillips, Cromer, Norfolk; one *s* two *d. Educ:* Hampton Grammar School. Joined Royal Air Force, 1925; Group Captain, 1942; Air Commodore, 1947; Actg Air Vice-Marshal, 1954. Served War of 1939-45 (despatches, CB); Directorate of War Organisation, Air Ministry, 1938-41; Coastal Command, 1941-42; Mediterranean Air Forces, 1942-45. Air Officer Commanding 44 Group Transport Command, 1945-46; Asst Comdt RAF Staff Coll., 1946; idc, 1947; Dir Staff Trg, Air Ministry, 1948-50; Air Officer Commanding RAF E Africa, 1950-52; Dir of Postings, Air Ministry, 1953-54; Director-General of Personnel (I), Air Ministry, 1954-57. *Address:* Earl's Eye House, 8 Sandy Lane, Chester CH3 5UL. *T:* Chester 20993.

PANNETT, Juliet Kathleen, (Mrs M. R. D. Pannett), PS; FRSA; Portrait Painter; Free Lance Artist to The Times, Daily Telegraph, Radio Times, etc; Special Artist to Illustrated London News, 1958-65; *b* Hove; 2nd *d* of Charles Somers and May Brice; *m* 1938, Major M. R. D. Pannett (*d* 1980), late the Devonshire Regt; one *s* one *d. Educ:* Wistons Sch., Brighton; Brighton College of Art. *Exhibitions:* Royal Festival Hall, 1957, 1958; Qantas Gallery, 1959; New York, 1960; Cleveland, Ohio, 1960; Cooling Gallery, 1961; Coventry Cathedral Festival, 1962; Gloucester Three Choirs Festival, 1962; Brighton Corporation Gallery, Rottingdean, 1967; Arun Art Centre, 1967, 1969, 1972; Fine Art Gall., 1969; Mignon Gall., Bath, 1970. *Exhibitor:* Royal Academy; Royal Society of Portrait Painters; Royal Inst. of Painters in Watercolours, etc. Official Artist on Qantas Inaugural Jet Flight, London to Sydney, 1959, London to Hong Kong, 1964; Air Canada Inaugural Flight, London to Vancouver, 1968. Freeman: City of London; Painter Stainers' Company. *Work in Permanent Collections:* portraits in: National Portrait Gall., Brighton Art Gall.; Hove Art Gall.; Worthing Art Gall.; Cambridge Colleges; Maudsley Hospital; Army Phys. Training Sch., Aldershot; Painter Stainers' Hall, London; Edinburgh Univ.; Portraits, many for official bodies, include: HRH Prince Andrew, HRH Prince Edward, for HM The Queen; HRH Princess Marina, Duchess of Kent, 1968; Lord Annan; Field-Marshal Sir Claude Auchinleck; Lord Ashby; Sir Alfred Ayer; Lord Baden-Powell; Lady Baden-Powell; Group Captain Sir Douglas Bader; Sir Adrian Boult; Lord George-Brown; Sir Arthur Bryant; Lord Butler; Lord Caldecote; Lord David Cecil; Group Captain Leonard Cheshire; Canon Collins; Dame Margery Corbett Ashby; Lord Denning; Sir Theodore Fox; Lord Fulton; Lt-Gen. Sir John Glubb; Lord Goodman; Rear-Adm. Sir Alexander Gordon Lennox; Lord Hailsham; Field Marshal Lord Harding; Rt Hon. Edward Heath; Ivon Hitchens; Lt-Gen. Sir Brian Horrocks; Bishop Huddleston; Gen. Sir Charles Jones; Sir John Kendrew; Sir Bernard Lovell; Lord McLeod; Sir William

McTaggart; Bishop Marshall; Dr Quett Masire, President of Botswana; Lord Montagu; Lady Montagu; Patrick Moore; Sir Nevill Mott; Lord Mountbatten of Burma; Sir David Napley; Lavinia Duchess of Norfolk; Sir Leon Radzinowicz; Dame Marie Rambert; Bishop Roberts; Lord Salmon; Dame Evelyn Sharp; Lord Shawcross; Gilbert Spencer; Canon Stancliffe; Rt Hon. Margaret Thatcher; Rt Hon. George Thomas; Lord Todd; Prof. Hugh Trevor-Roper; Sir Barnes Wallis; Lord Widgery; Rt Hon. Sir Harold Wilson; R. E. S. Wyatt; Lord Wemyss; Lady Wemyss; Prof. Yigael Yadin. Commemorative Stained Glass Window, Garrison church, Münster, 1967. *Publications:* Illustr. articles in The Artist; Leisure Painter; Illustr. for article in The Lancet; cover portraits: Gerald Pawle's The War and Colonel Warden; Law Guardian; Guardian Gazette; frontispieces, etc. *Recreations:* watercolour landscape, travel, music. *Address:* Pound House, Angmering Village, Sussex BN16 4AL. *T:* Rustington 4446. *Club:* Press.

PANT, Apasaheb Balasaheb; Padma Shri 1954; retired 1975; *b* 11 Sept. 1912; *s* of Pratinidhis of Aundh; *m* 1942, Nalini Pant, MB, BS, FRCS; two *s* one *d. Educ:* Univ. of Bombay (BA); Univ. of Oxford (MA). Barrister-at-Law, Lincoln's Inn. Educn Minister, Aundh State; Prime Minister, 1944-48 (when State was merged into Bombay State). Member, AICC, 1948; an alternate Deleg., of India, at UN, 1951 and 1952; Comr for Govt of India in Brit. E Africa, 1948-54; apptd Consul-Gen. for Belgian Congo and Ruanda-Urundi, Nov. 1950, and Comr for Central Africa and Nyasaland, Dec. 1950; Officer on Special Duty, Min. of Ext. Affairs, 1954-55; Polit. Officer in Sikkim and Bhutan with control over Indian Missions in Tibet, 1955-61; Ambassador of India: to Indonesia, Oct. 1961-June 1964; to Norway, 1964-66; to UAR, 1966-69; High Comr in London, 1969-72; Ambassador to Italy, 1972-75. Vis. Fellow, The Indian Institute of Advanced Studies. *Publications:* Tensions and Tolerance, 1965; Aggression and Violence: Gandhian experiments to fight them, 1968; Yoga, 1968 (Arabic edn); Surya Namaskar, 1969 (Italian edn); Mahatma Gandhi; A Moment in Time, 1973; Mandala, An Awakening, 1976; Progress, Power, Peace and India, 1978; Survival of the Individual, 1981. *Recreations:* photography, yoga, tennis, ski-ing, gliding. *Address:* Pant Niwas, Bhandarkar Road, Deccan Gymkhana, Poona 4, India. *T:* 58615.

PANTCHEFF, Theodore Xenophon Henry, CMG 1977; HM Diplomatic Service, retired; *b* 29 Dec. 1920; *s* of Sophocles Xenophon Pantcheff and Ella Jessie, *d* of Dr S. H. Ramsbotham, Leeds; *m* 1954, Patricia Mary Tully; two *s. Educ:* Merchant Taylors' Sch.; Gonville and Caius Coll., Cambridge (MA). HM Forces, 1941-47; Control Commn for Germany, 1948-51; joined Foreign Office, 1951; Vice-Consul, Munich, 1954-56: 1st Sec., Lagos, 1958-60; 1st Sec., Leopoldville, 1961-63; seconded MoD, 1969-71; Counsellor, FCO, 1971-77. Jurat of the Court of Alderney, 1979. *Publication:* Alderney: fortress island, 1981. *Recreations:* reading and conversation. *Address:* Butes Cottage, Alderney. *Clubs:* Carlton; Alderney Society (Alderney).

PANTER-DOWNES, Mollie Patricia, (Mrs Clare Robinson); London Correspondent, The New Yorker, since 1939; *b* 25 Aug. 1906; *o c* of late Major Edward Panter-Downes, Royal Irish Regt; *m* 1927, Clare, 3rd *s* of late Aubrey Robinson; two *d. Educ:* mostly private. Wrote novel, The Shoreless Sea, at age of 16 (published John Murray, 1924); wrote in various English and American publications. *Publications:* Letter from England, 1940; Watling Green (children's book), 1943; One Fine Day, 1947; Ooty Preserved, 1967; At the Pines, 1971; London War Notes, 1972; contributed to The New Yorker Book of War Pieces, 1947. *Address:* Roppelegh's, near Haslemere, Surrey. See also *J. M. F. Baer.*

PANTIN, Most Rev. Anthony; *see* Port of Spain, Archbishop of.

PANTON, Air Cdre Alastair Dyson, CB 1969; OBE 1950; DFC 1939; Provost Marshal and Director of RAF Security, 1968-71; retired; *b* 2 Nov. 1916; third *s* of William Dickson Panton, Aberdeen, and Mary Ethel Langley, Bedford; *m* 1939, Eileen Isabel Lumley, Bedford; three *s* (and one *s* decd). *Educ:* Bedford School; RAF Coll., Cranwell. Pilot Officer, No 53 Sqdn RAF, 1937; POW 1940-45; OC, Nos 58 and 540 Sqdns, 1946-47; Air Staff, Hong Kong, 1948-50; Wing Comdr Flying, RAF Coningsby, 1951-53; Staff Coll., 1953-54; Air Ministry, 1954-57; Station Comdr, RAF Cranwell, 1957-60, RAF Bircham Newton, 1961-62, RAF Tern Hill, 1963-64; HQ Far East Air Force, 1965-67. *Recreations:* gardening, poetry, Tchaikovsky. *Address:* Penrhyn Castle, Bangor, Gwynedd. *T:* Bangor 53084.

PANTON, Dr Francis Harry, MBE 1948; Director, Royal Armament Research and Development Establishment, Ministry of Defence, since 1980; *b* 25 May 1923; 3rd *s* of George Emerson Panton and Annie Panton; *m* 1952, Audrey Mary (*née* Lane); two *s. Educ:* City Sch., Lincoln; University College and Univ. of Nottingham. PhD Nottingham 1952. Served War of 1939-45: commissioned, Bomb Disposal, Royal Eng., 1943-47. Pres., Univ. of Nottingham Union, 1950-51; Vice-Pres., Nat. Union of Students, 1952-54; Technical Officer, ICI, Billingham, 1952-53; Permanent Under-Secretary's Dept, FO, 1953-55; Office of Political Adviser, Berlin, 1955-57; Dep. Head, Technical Research Unit, MoD, 1957-58; Attaché, British Embassy, Washington, DC, 1958-59; Technical Adviser, UK Delegn to Conf. on Discontinuance of Nuclear Tests, Geneva, 1959-61; Permanent Under-Secretary's Dept, FO, 1961-63; Counsellor (Defence), British Embassy, Washington, DC, 1963-66; Head of Defence Science 6, MoD, 1966-68; Asst Chief Scientific Adviser (Nuclear), MoD, 1969-76; Dir Gen., Estabs, Resources and Programmes (B), MoD, April-Sept. 1976; Dir, Propellants, Explosives and Rocket Motor Estabt, and Head, Rocket Motor Exec., MoD,

1976-80. FRIC 1961; FRSA 1973. *Recreations:* bridge, reading local history. *Address:* 1 St Peter's Lane, Canterbury, Kent. *T:* Canterbury 52902. *Club:* Reform.

PANTRIDGE, Prof. (James) Frank, CBE 1978; MC 1942; MD, FRCP, FACC; Director, Regional Medical Cardiology Centre, Northern Ireland, since 1977; *b* 3 Oct. 1916. *Educ:* Queen's Univ., Belfast (MD). FRCP 1957; FACC 1967. Res. Fellow, Univ. of Mich, 1948-49; Physician i/c Cardiac Dept, Royal Victoria Hosp., Belfast, 1954; Hon. Prof. of Cardiol., QUB. Canadian Heart Foundn Orator; St Cyres Orator, National Heart Hosp., London. Chm., Cardiac Soc., 1978. Hon. FRCPI. DUniv Open, 1981; Hon. DSc NUU, 1981. *Publications:* The Acute Coronary Attack, 1975; articles in Brit. Heart Jl, Circulation, Amer. Heart Jl, Lancet, and BMJ. *Recreation:* fishing. *Address:* Hillsborough, Co. Down, N Ireland. *T:* Hillsborough 682911. *Club:* Athenæum.

PANUFNIK, Andrzej; composer and conductor; *b* 24 Sept. 1914; 2nd *s* of Tomasz Panufnik and Mathilda Thonnes Panufnik; *m* 1963, Camilla Ruth Jessel, FRPS, *yr d* of Commander R. F. Jessel, DSO, OBE, DSC, RN (retired); one *s* one *d. Educ:* Warsaw State Conservatoire; Vienna State Acad. for Music (under Professor Felix von Weingartner). Diploma with distinction, Warsaw Conservatoire, 1936. Conductor of the Cracow Philharmonic, 1945-46; Director and Conductor of the Warsaw Philharmonic Orchestra, 1946-47. Conducting leading European orchestras such as L'Orchestre National, Paris, Berliner Philharmonisches Orchester, L'Orchestre de la Suisse Romande, Geneva, and all principal British orchestras, 1947-. Polish decorations: Standard of Labor 1st class (1949), twice State Laureate (1951, 1952). Left Poland and settled in England, 1954; naturalized British subject, 1961. Vice-Chairman of International Music Council of UNESCO, Paris, 1950-53; Musical Director and Conductor, City of Birmingham Symphony Orchestra, 1957-59. Hon. Member of International Mark Twain Society (USA), 1954; Knight of Mark Twain, 1966. The Sibelius Centenary Medal, 1965. *Ballets:* Elegy, NY, 1967; Cain and Abel, Berlin, 1968; Miss Julie, Stuttgart, 1970; Homage to Chopin (SW Royal Ballet), 1980; Adieu (Royal Ballet), 1980; Polonia (SW Royal Ballet), 1980. *Publications:* Piano Trio, 1934; Five Polish Peasant Songs, 1940; Tragic Overture, 1942; Twelve Miniature Studies for piano, 1947; Nocturne for orchestra, 1947; Lullaby for 29 stringed instruments and 2 harps, 1947; Sinfonia Rustica, 1948; Hommage à Chopin-Five vocalises for soprano and piano, 1949; Old Polish Suite for strings, 1950; Concerto in modo antico, 1951; Heroic Overture, 1952; Rhapsody for orchestra, 1956; Sinfonia Elegiaca, 1957; Polonia-Suite for Orchestra, 1959; Piano Concerto, 1961; Autumn Music, 1962; Landscape, 1962; Two Lyric Pieces, 1963; Sinfonia Sacra, 1963 (first prize, Prix de Composition Musicale Prince Rainier III de Monaco, 1963); Song to the Virgin Mary, 1964; Katyn Epitaph, 1966; Jagiellonian Triptych, 1966; Reflections for piano, 1967; The Universal Prayer, 1969; Thames Pageant, 1969; Violin Concerto, 1971; Triangles, 1972; Winter Solstice, 1972; Sinfonia Concertante, 1973; Sinfonia di Sfere, 1974; String Quartet No 1, 1976, No 2, 1980; Dreamscape, 1976; Sinfonia Mistica, 1977; Metasinfonia, 1978; Concerto Festivo, 1979; Concertino, 1980; Sinfonia Votiva, 1982. *Address:* Riverside House, Twickenham, Middlesex. *Club:* Garrick.

See also O. R. Jessel, T. F. H. Jessel.

PAO, Sir Yue-Kong, Kt 1978; CBE 1976; JP; LLD; Chairman, World-Wide Shipping Group, since 1974; *b* Chekiang, China, 10 Nov. 1918; *s* of Sui-Loong Pao and of late Chung Sau-Gin Pao; *m* 1940, Sue-Ing Haung; four *d. Educ:* Shanghai, China. Banking career in China until went to Hong Kong, 1949; engaged in import and export trade; shipowner, 1955-. Founder, World-Wide Sea Trng Sch. Chairman: World Finance Internat. Ltd; IBJ Finance (HK) Ltd; World International (Holdings) Ltd; Vice-Chm., Hongkong & Shanghai Banking Corp.; Director: Hang Seng Bank Ltd; Mass Transit Railway Corp.; Hong Kong Electric Gp; South China Morning Post; Cathay Pacific Airways Ltd; Inchcape Far East Ltd; Harbour Centre Development Ltd. Adviser, Indust. Bank of Japan. Chairman: Hong Kong and Kowloon Wharf and Godown Co. Ltd; E Asia Cttee, Lloyd's Register of Shipping; Internat. Assoc. of Independent Tanker Owners; Hon. Chm., Hong Kong Cttee, Nippon Kaiji Kyokai of Japan. Member: Internat. Gen. Cttee, Bureau Veritas of France; Asia/Pacific Adv. Council, Amer. Telephone & Telegraph Internat.; Internat. Adv. Cttee, Chase Manhattan Bank of New York; (Life), Court of Univ. of Hong Kong; Rockefeller Univ. Council, New York; Hon. Mem., INTERTANKO. Hon. Vice-Pres., Maritime Trust. Overseas Hon. Trustee, Westminster Abbey Trust. Trustee, Hong Kong Arts Centre. Hon. LLD: Univ. of Hong Kong, 1975; Chinese Univ. of Hong Kong, 1977. JP Hong Kong, 1971. Comdr, National Order of Cruzeiro do Sul, Brazil, 1977. *Recreations:* swimming, golf. *Address:* World-Wide Shipping Agency Ltd, 15-17th floor, World Shipping Centre, Harbour City, 7 Canton Road, Kowloon, Hong Kong. *T:* 3-7327333. *Clubs:* Royal Automobile; Woking Golf (Surrey); Royal and Ancient Golf (St Andrews, Fife); Sunningdale Golf (Berks).

PAOLOZZI, Eduardo Luigi, CBE 1968; RA 1979 (ARA 1972); Sculptor; Tutor in Ceramics, Royal College of Art, since 1968; Professor of Sculpture at Akademie der Bildenden Künste, Munich, since 1981; *b* 7 March 1924; *s* of Rudolpho Antonio Paolozzi and Carmella (*née* Rossi), both Italian; *m* 1951, Freda Elliott; three *d. Educ:* Edinburgh School of Art; Slade Sch. Worked in Paris, 1947-50; Instructor, Central School of Arts and Crafts, London, 1950-55; Lecturer, St Martin's School of rt, 1955-56; Prof. of Ceramics at Fachhochschule, Cologne, 1977-81. Hon. Dr RCA, 1979; Hon.

DLitt Glasgow, 1980. British Critics Prize, 1953; David E. Bright Foundn Award, 1960; Watson F. Blaire Prize, 1961; Purchase Prize, Internat. Sculpture Exhibn at Solomon R. Guggenheim Mus., 1967; First Prize for Sculpture, Carnegie Internat. Exhibn, 1967; Sculpture Prize, European Patent Office, Munich, 1978; First Prize, Rhinegarten Cologne comp., 1981. *One-man exhibitions:* first in London, Mayor Gallery, 1947; first in New York, Betty Parsons Gallery, 1960, also 1962; Tate Gallery, 1971; V&A Mus., 1973, 1977 (print retrospective); Nationalgal., W Berlin, 1975; Fruit Market Gall., Edinburgh, 1976; Marlborough Fine Art Gallery, 1976; Anthony d'Offay Gall., 1977; Kassel, Germany, 1978; Glasgow League of Artists, 1979; Edinburgh Univ., 1979; Cologne, Germany, 1979; Museum for Künste und Gewerbe, Hamburg, 1982. Work in permanent collections: Tate Gallery; Contemporary Art Society; Museum of Modern Art, New York, etc. Work exhibited in: British Pavilion, Venice Biennale, 1952; Documenta 2, Kassel, 1959; New Images of Man, New York, 1959; British Pavilion, 30th Venice Biennale; International Exhibition of Sculpture, Boymans Museum, Rotterdam; Open Air Sculpture, Battersea Park, London; Critics Choice, Tooths Gallery, London; City Art Gallery, Manchester, Oct. 1960; British Sculpture in the Sixties, Tate Gallery, March 1965; Chelsea School of Art, 1965; Hanover Gallery, 1967; Tate Gall., 1971. *Recreation:* music. *Address:* 107 Dovehouse Street, SW3; Landermere, Thorpe-le-Soken, Essex. *T:* Thorpe-le-Soken 210. *Club:* Athenæum.

PAPADOPOULOS, Achilles Symeon, CMG 1980; MVO 1972; MBE 1954; HM Diplomatic Service; High Commissioner in the Bahamas, since 1981; *b* 16 Aug. 1923; *s* of late Symeon Papadópoulos and of Polyxene Papadopoulos; *m* 1954, Joyce Martin (*née* Stark); one *s* two *d. Educ:* The English School, Nicosia, Cyprus. British Mil. Admin, Eritrea, 1943; HMOCS: Cyprus, 1953; Dar es Salaam, 1959; Malta, 1961; HM Diplomatic Service: Malta, 1965; Nairobi, 1965; FCO, 1968; Colombo, 1971; Washington, 1974; Havana, 1974; Ambassador to El Salvador, 1977-79, to Mozambique, 1979-80; attached UK Mission to UN, Sept.-Dec. 1980. *Recreations:* golf, bridge. *Address:* c/o Foreign and Commonwealth Office, SW1A 2AH; 5 Lansdowne Close, Wimbledon, SW20 8AS. *Club:* Royal Commonwealth Society.

PAPE, Hon. Sir George (Augustus), Kt 1968; Judge of Supreme Court of Victoria, 1975, retired; *b* 29 Jan. 1903; *s* of George Frederick Pape and Minnie Maud Pape (*née* Bryan); *m* 1952, Mabel, *d* of Alfred Lloyd; no *c. Educ:* All Saints Grammar Sch., St Kilda; University of Melbourne (LLB). QC 1955. RAAF, 1940-46. *Recreation:* golf. *Address:* 146 Kooyong Road, Toorak, Victoria 3142, Australia. *T:* 20-6158. *Club:* Australian (Melbourne).

PAPE, Jonathan Hector Carruthers, OBE 1980; FCIT; International Port/Dock Labour Consultant; Chief General Manager, National Dock Labour Board, 1975-82 (General Manager and Secretary, 1970-75); *b* 8 March 1918; *er s* of Jonathan Pape, MA and Florence Muriel Myrtle; *m* 1944, Mary Sullins (*née* Jeffries); one *s. Educ:* Merchant Taylors' Sch., Crosby. Mercantile Marine, 1934-46; Master Mariner (FG), 1944 (Liverpool Qualif.). Manager, Master Stevedoring Co., Liverpool, 1947-51; National Dock Labour Board: Dep. Port Manager, London, 1952-57; Asst Gen. Manager, Bd HQ, 1957-69; Dep. Gen. Manager and Secretary, Bd HQ, 1969. Mem., Honourable Co. of Master Mariners, 1965. Freeman, City of London. *Recreations:* swimming, gardening, and riding at anchor in what spare time is left. *Address:* 4 Knole Way, Sevenoaks, Kent. *T:* Sevenoaks 452820. *Club:* Wig and Pen.

PAPUA NEW GUINEA, Archbishop of, 1977-May 1983; **Most Rev. Geoffrey David Hand,** CBE 1975; Bishop of Port Moresby, 1977-83; *b* 11 May 1918; *s* of Rev. W. T. Hand. *Educ:* Oriel College, Oxford; Cuddesdon Theological Coll., BA 1941, MA 1946. Deacon, 1942; Priest, 1943. Curate of Heckmondwike, 1942-46; Missioner, Diocese of New Guinea, 1946-50; Priest in charge: Sefoa, 1947-48; Sangara, 1948-50; Archdeacon, North New Guinea, 1950-65; Bishop Coadjutor of New Guinea, 1950-63; Bishop of New Guinea (later Papua New Guinea), 1963-77. *Address:* PO Box 806, Port Moresby, Papua New Guinea.

PAQUET, Dr Jean-Guy, FRSC; Rector, Université Laval, Québec, Canada, since 1977; *b* Montmagny, Qué, 5 Jan. 1938; *s* of Laurent W. Paquet and Louisianne Coulombe. *Educ:* Université Laval (BSc Engrg Physics, 1959; DSc Elec. Engrg, 1963); Ecole Nat. Sup. de l'Aéronautique, Paris (MSc Aeronautics, 1960). FRSC 1978; FAAAS 1981. Université Laval: Asst Prof. of Elec. Engrg, 1962; Associate Prof., 1967; Head, Elec. Engrg Dept, 1967-69; Vice-Dean (Research), Faculty of Science, 1969-72; Prof. of Elec. Engrg, 1971; Vice-Rector (Academic), 1972-77. Fellowships: French Govt, 1959; NATO, 1962; Nat. Science Foundn, 1964; Québec Govt, 1965. Def. Res. Bd of Canada Grant, 1965-76. National Research Council of Canada: Fellowship, 1961; Grant, 1964-77; Mem., Associate Cttee on Automatic Control, 1964-70; Special Asst to Vice-Pres. (Scientific), 1971-72. Pres., Conf. of Rectors and Principals of Univs of Prov. of Québec, 1979-81. Member: Council, Univs of Prov. of Qué, 1973-77; Bd, Assoc. of Scientific, Engrg and Technol Community of Canada, 1970-77 (Pres., 1975-76); Bd, French Canadian Assoc. for Advancement of Science, 1969-71; Canadian Assoc. of Univ. Res. Administrators; Special Task Force on Res. and Develt, Science Council of Canada, 1976; Order of Engrs, Qué; Amer. Soc. for Engrg Educn; New York Acad. of Science, 1980-; Amer. Management Assoc., 1980-; Soc. for Res. Administrators. Member Board: Hockey Canada, 1980-; Interamerican Univs Assoc., 1980-; Assoc. des universités partiellement ou entièrement de langue française, 1981-; Assoc. of Commonwealth Univs, 1981-; Inst. of Canadian

Bankers, 1980-. DSc *hc* McGill Univ., 1982. *Publications:* (with P. A. Roy) Rapport d'études bibliographiques: l'automation dans la production et la distribution de l'énergie électrique, 1968; (with J. F. Le Maître) Méthodes pratiques d'étude des oscillations non-linéaires: application aux systèmes par plus-ou-moins, 1970; more than fifty pubns in scientific jls, on control systems engrg; articles on research, develt and scientific policy. *Recreations:* jogging, travels, golf. *Address:* Université Laval, Québec G1K 7P4, Canada. *Clubs:* Cercle universitaire de Québec, Club de Golf Cap-Rouge (Qué).

PARARAJASINGAM, Sir Sangarapillai, Kt 1955; Senator, Ceylon, 1954-59; Chairman, Board of Directors, Colonial Motors Ltd, 1961-74; former Member, Board of Trustees, Ceylon Social Service League; *b* 25 June 1896; *s* of late W. Sangarapillai, social worker and philanthropist; *m* 1916, Padmavati, *d* of Sir Ponnambalam Arunachalam; one *s* one *d. Educ:* St Thomas' Coll., Mt Lavinia. Past President, Board of Directors, Manipay Hindu Coll., Manager, 1929-61; Past President Ceylon Poultry Club; Member National Savings Cttee; Past Chairman, Board Governors, Ceylon Inst. of Scientific and Industrial Research. Formerly Chairman: Board of Directors, Agricultural and Industrial Credit Corporation of Ceylon; Education Cttee, Ceylon Social Service League; Low Country Products Assoc., 1943-44 and 1944-45; Ceylon Coconut Board; Coconut Commn; Past Member: Textile Tribunal; Land Advisory Cttee; Ceylon Tea Propaganda Board; Coconut Research Scheme; Radio Advisory Board; Excise Advisory Cttee; Central Board of Agriculture; Income Tax Board of Review; Rice Advisory Board; Services Standing Wages Board; Board for Approval of Credit Agencies; Commn on Broadcasting; Past President Vivekananda Society; Rotary Club of Colombo; Governor, Rotary Internat. District 320, 1951-52; formerly Trustee and Hon. Treasurer, Ceylon Society of Arts; formerly Manager, all Schools managed by Ceylon Social Service League. JP Ceylon 1923. Travelled widely in the UK, Europe, USA, India, Far East. Coronation Medals, 1937 and 1953. *Recreations:* gardening, agriculture and farming. *Address:* No 50, Pathmalaya, Flower Road, Colombo 7, Sri Lanka. *T:* 23159.
See also P. Nadesan.

PARAYRE, Jean-Paul Christophe; Officier, l'Ordre National du Mérite, 1978; Chairman and Chief Executive Officer, Peugeot SA, since 1977; *b* 5 July 1937; *s* of Louis Parayre and Jehanne Malarde; *m* 1962, Marie-Françoise Chaufour; two *s* two *d. Educ:* Lycées de Casablanca et Versailles; Ecole Polytechnique, Paris; Ecole Nationale des Ponts et Chaussées. Engr, Dept of Highways, 1963-67; Technical Adviser: Min. of Social Affairs, 1967; Min. of Economy and Finance, 1968; Min. of Industry and Res., 1969; Dir of Mech. Industries, Min. of Industry and Res., 1970-74; Chief Adviser to Chm. and Gen. Management, Banque Vernes et Commerciale de Paris, 1974; Chief Attaché to Gen. Management of Peugeot SA, 1974; Manager of Automobile Planning, Peugeot, 1975; Manager, Atuomobile Div., Peugeot-Citroen, 1976; Mem. Exec. Cttee, PSA Peugeot-Citroen, 1977. Mem., Board of Directors: Dumez, 1974-; Crédit National, 1978-; Gefco, 1980-. *Recreation:* tennis. *Address:* 3 Rond-Point Saint-James, 92200 Neuilly-sur-Seine, France. *Club:* Polo de Paris.

PARBO, Sir Arvi (Hillar), Kt 1978; Chairman and Managing Director, Western Mining Corporation Ltd, since 1974; Chairman: Alcoa of Australia Ltd, since 1978; BH South Ltd, since 1980; *b* 10 Feb. 1926; *s* of Aado and Hilda Parbo; *m* 1953, Saima Soots; two *s* one *d. Educ:* Clausthal Mining Acad., Germany; Univ. of Adelaide (BE). Western Mining Corporation: Underground Surveyor, 1956; Techn. Asst to Managing Dir, 1960; Dep. Gen. Supt, WA, 1964; Gen. Manager, 1968; Dep. Managing Dir, 1971; Managing Director, 1971. Dir, Aluminium Co. of America, 1980-. Comdr, Order of Merit, Germany, 1979. *Recreations:* reading, carpentry. *Address:* Western Mining Corporation Ltd, 360 Collins Street, Melbourne, Vic. 3000, Australia; GPO Box 860K, Melbourne, Vic. 3001. *T:* 602 0300. *Clubs:* Melbourne, Australian (both Melbourne); Weld (Perth); Commonwealth (Canberra); Hannans (Kalgoorlie).

PARBURY, George Mark, CB 1980; Chief Registrar of the High Court of Justice in Bankruptcy, 1975-80; *b* 27 April 1908; *s* of late Norman Cecil Parbury and Ellen Parbury; *m* 1942, Roma Constance, *d* of late James Robert Raw, JP, New Zealand, and Clare Raw. *Educ:* Geelong, Australia; Jesus Coll., Cambridge. Called to Bar, Lincoln's Inn, 1934. Practised at Chancery Bar, 1934-39. Served War of 1939-45, 1940-45, Temp. Lt-Col, 1944; AAG, AG3e War Office, Mil. Govt 21 Army Group. Again practised at Chancery Bar, 1946-65; Mem. Bar Council, 1961-62. Registrar, High Court of Justice in Bankruptcy, 1965-75. *Recreations:* walking on the Downs; gardening. *Address:* 5 Bolsover Court, Bolsover Road, Eastbourne, East Sussex. *T:* Eastbourne 639343. *Club:* Army and Navy.

PARDOE, Geoffrey Keith Charles, CEng, FRAeS; Chairman and Managing Director, General Technology Systems Ltd, since 1973; Managing Director, General Technology Systems (Netherlands) BV, Den Haag, since 1982; President, General Technology Systems SA, Belgium, since 1979; *b* 2 Nov. 1928; *s* of James Charles Pardoe and Ada Violet Pardoe; *m* 1953, Dorothy Patricia Gutteridge; one *s* one *d. Educ:* Wanstead County High Sch., London; London Univ. (BScEng Hons); Loughborough Coll. (DLC Hons Aeronautics). CEng, FRAeS 1968. Sen. Aerodynamicist, Armstrong Whitworth Ltd, 1949-51; Chief Aerodynamicist, Guided Weapons, De Havilland Props Ltd, 1951-56, Proj. Manager, Blue Streak, 1956-60; Chief Engr, Weapons and Space, De Havilland Aircraft, 1960-63; Chief Proj. Engr, Space Div., Hawker Siddeley Dynamics Ltd, 1963-69, Sales Exec., 1969-73;

Exec. Dir, British Space Develt Co. Ltd, 1960-74. Chm., Procogen Computer Systems Ltd, 1981-; Director: Philip A. Lapp Ltd, Canada, 1973-; Eurosat SA, Switzerland, 1971-; Eurotech Develts Ltd, 1981-. Vice President: Eurospace (Paris), 1961-73; RAeS, 1981-; Dep. Chm., Watt Cttee on Energy, 1981-. MInstD. *Publications:* The Challenge of Space, 1964; Integration of Payload and Stages of Space Carrier Vehicles, 1964; Project Apollo: The way to the Moon, 1969, 2nd edn 1970; The Future of Space Technology, 1982; over 50 main pubns in learned society pubns and jls; about 100 articles. *Recreations:* skiing, flying, badminton, photography, wind-surfing. *Address:* 23 Stewart Road, Harpenden, Herts AL5 4QE. *T:* Harpenden 4719. *Clubs:* Royal Air Force, Ski of GB.

PARDOE, John George Magrath, CBE 1975; FRAeS; Director-General, Airworthiness, Civil Aviation Authority, 1972-79. *Educ:* Coll. of Aeronautical Engineering. Entered design work in Aircraft Industry, 1935; joined Accidents Inspection Br. of Air Ministry, 1942; joined Staff, Air Registration Bd, 1945; Chief Technical Officer, 1969. Médaille de l'aéronautique, 1980.

PARDOE, John Wentworth; Managing Director, Sight and Sound Education Ltd; Senior Research Fellow of Policy Studies Institute; *b* 27 July 1934; *s* of Cuthbert B. Pardoe and Marjorie E. W. (*née* Taylor); *m* 1958, Joyce R. Peerman; two *s* one *d. Educ:* Sherborne; Corpus Christi Coll., Cambridge (MA). Television Audience Measurement Ltd, 1958-60; Osborne Peacock Co. Ltd, 1960-61; Liberal News, 1961-66. MP (L) Cornwall N, 1966-79; Treasurer of the Liberal Party, 1968-69. Presenter, Look Here, LWT, 1979-81. Consultant to Nat. Assoc. of Schoolmasters, 1967-73. Director: William Schlackman Ltd, 1968-71; Gerald Metals; Mem. London Metal Exchange. *Recreations:* cricket, walking, singing. *Address:* 18 New End Square, NW3.

PARE, Rev. Philip Norris; *b* 13 May 1910; *s* of Frederick William and Florence May Pare; *m* 1943, Nancy Eileen, *d* of late Canon C. Patteson; two *s* two *d. Educ:* Nottingham High Sch.; King's Coll., Cambridge; Cuddesdon Theological Coll. Curate, All Saints, W Dulwich, 1934-37; Chaplain and Vice-Principal, Bishops Coll., Cheshunt, 1937-39; Curate, St Mary the Less, Cambridge, 1939-40. Chaplain RNVR, 1940-46. Vicar of Cheshunt, Herts, 1946-57; Rural Dean of Ware, 1949-56; Examining Chaplain to Bishop of St Albans, 1952-56; Missioner Canon Stipendiary, Diocese of Wakefield, 1957-62; Diocesan Adviser for Christian Stewardship, 1959-68; Provost, and Vicar of Cathedral Church of All Saints, Wakefield, 1962-71; Vicar of Cholsey, dio. Oxford, 1973-82. A Church Commissioner, 1968-71; Member Board of Ecclesiastical Insurance Office, 1966-; Provost of Woodard Schools (Northern Div.), 1977-. *Publications:* (with Donald Harris) Eric Milner-White, A Memoir, 1965; Re-Thinking Our Worship, 1967; articles in Theology, The Reader, etc. *Recreations:* modern stained glass and architecture; railways, motor cars; church music. *Address:* 73 Oaklands Drive, Ledbury, Herefordshire HR8 2EX.

PARES, Peter; *b* 6 Sept. 1908; 2nd *s* of late Sir Bernard Pares, KBE, DCL, and late Margaret Pares (*née* Dixon); unmarried. *Educ:* Lancing Coll.; Jesus Coll., Cambridge (Scholar). Entered Consular Service, 1930; served in Philadelphia, 1930; Havana, 1932; Consul, Liberec and Bratislava, Czechslovakia, 1936-39; Budapest, 1939; Cluj, Rumania, 1940; New York, 1941; Washington, as First Secretary, 1944; Control Commission for Germany, 1946; Foreign Office, 1949; Casablanca, 1952; Strasbourg, 1956; Deputy Consul-General, Frankfurt, 1957; Consul-General, Asmara, Eritrea, 1957-59; Head of Education and Cultural Relations Dept, CRO, 1960-63. *Address:* 17 Beechwood Crescent, Eastbourne, East Sussex.

PARFITT, Rt. Rev. Thomas Richards; Assistant Bishop, diocese of Derby since 1962; *b* 24 May 1911; *s* of Charles Henry John and Maud Sarah Parfitt. *Educ:* S John Baptist Coll., Oxford. BA Oxon 1933 (2nd class Lit. Hum., 1933; 2nd class Theology, 1934); MA 1936. Cuddesdon Coll., 1934-35. Deacon, 1935; Priest, 1936; Asst Curate of New Mills, 1935-39; Curate of Rugby (in charge of Holy Trinity), 1939-43; Chaplain RNVR, 1943-46; Vicar of S Andrew, Derby, 1946-52; Rural Dean of Derby, 1951-52; Bishop in Madagascar, 1952-61; Rector of Matlock with Tansley, 1962-80. *Address:* St Paul's Vicarage, Old Chester Road, Derby DE1 3SA.

PARGETER, Edith; *b* 28 Sept. 1913; 3rd *c* of Edmund Valentine Pargeter and Edith Hordley; unmarried. *Educ:* Dawley C of E Elementary Sch.; County High School for Girls, Coalbrookdale. Worked as a chemist's assistant, and at twenty succeeded in finding a publisher for first-and unsuccessful-book. WRNS Aug. 1940, teleprinter operator (BEM 1944); dispersed from the Service, Aug. 1945. FIIAL 1962. Gold Medal and Ribbon, Czechoslovak Society for International Relations, 1968. *Publications:* Hortensius, Friend of Nero, Iron Bound, 1936; The City Lies Foursquare, 1939; Ordinary People, 1941; She Goes to War, 1942; The Eighth Champion of Christendom, 1945; Reluctant Odyssey, 1946; Warfare Accomplished, 1947; By Firelight, 1948; The Fair Young Phoenix, 1948; The Coast of Bohemia, 1949; Lost Children, 1950; Fallen Into the Pit, 1951; Holiday with Violence, 1952; This Rough Magic, 1953; Most Loving Mere Folly, 1953; The Soldier at the Door, 1954; A Means of Grace, 1956; Tales of the Little Quarter (trans. from the Czech of Jan Neruda), 1957; Don Juan (trans. from the Czech of Josef Toman), 1958; Assize of the Dying, 1958; The Heaven Tree, 1960; The Green Branch 1962; The Scarlet Seed, 1963; The Terezín Requiem (trans. from the Czech of Josef Bor), 1963; The Lily Hand and other stories, 1965;

Close Watch on the Trains (trans from the Czech of Bohumil Hrabal), 1968; Report on my Husband (trans. from the Czech of Josefa Slánská), 1969; A Bloody Field by Shrewsbury, 1972; Sunrise in the West, 1974; The Dragon at Noonday, 1975; The Hounds of Sunset, 1976; Afterglow and Nightfall, 1977; The Marriage of Meggotta, 1979; as *Ellis Peters:* 22 crime and mystery novels including: Monk's-hood, 1980 (Silver Dagger, Crime Writers Assoc.); Saint Peter's Fair, 1981; The Leper of Saint Giles, 1981; The Virgin in the Ice, 1982. *Recreations:* collecting gramophone records, particularly of voice; reading anything and everything; theatre. *Address:* Parkville, Park Lane, Madeley, Telford, Salop. *T:* Telford 585178.

PARGITER, Maj.-Gen. Robert Beverley, CB 1942; CBE 1945; *b* 11 July 1889; *s* of late F. E. Pargiter, ICS; *m* 1st, 1917, Muriel Huxley (*d* 1971); one *s* two *d* ; 2nd, 1973, Elaine Ilma, *widow* of Colin C. Gulliland. *Educ:* Rugby; RMA, Woolwich. Commissioned RA 1909; served with RA, European War, 1914-18, on NWF, India, France, and Belgium (severely wounded, despatches); Military Mission to Baltic States, 1919-21 (Brevet of Major); psc Camberley, 1924; Instructor Staff Coll., Quetta, 1930-33; idc 1934; GSO 1 Operations, WO, 1936-38; War Service, 1939-45; Commander 1st AA Brigade; 4th, 7th and 5th AA Divisions; 3rd AA Group; Maj.-Gen. Anti-Aircraft, Allied Force HQ, N. Africa and Central Mediterranean Forces (despatches, CBE, Commander of Legion of Merit); retired, 1945; Commissioner, British Red Cross and St John's War Organisation, Middle East, 1945, Malaya, 1946. Colonel Comdt RA, 1951-54. *Publication:* (with late Colonel H. Eady) The Army and Sea Power, 1927. *Recreations:* fishing, gardening, braille. *Address:* The Dye House, Biddenden, Kent.

PARHAM, Adm. Sir Frederick Robertson, GBE 1959 (CBE 1949); KCB 1955 (CB 1951); DSO 1944; *b* 9 Jan. 1901; *s* of late Frederick James Parham, Bath, and late Jessie Esther Brooks Parham (*née* Robertson), Cheltenham; *m* 1st, 1926, Kathleen Dobrée, (*d* 1973), *d* of Eugene Edward Carey, Guernsey; one *s* ; 2nd, 1978, Mrs Joan Saunders (*née* Charig). *Educ:* RN Colleges, Osborne and Dartmouth. Joined HMS Malaya as Midshipman, 1917; specialised in gunnery, 1925; Commander, 1934. Commanded HMS Shikari, 1937, HMS Gurkha, 1938-40. Captain, 1939. Commanded HMS Belfast, 1942-44 (despatches), HMS Vanguard, 1947-49; Dep. Chief, Naval Personnel, 1949-51; Rear-Admiral, 1949; Vice-Admiral, 1952; Flag Officer (Flotillas) and 2nd in command, Mediterranean, 1951-52; a Lord Commissioner of the Admiralty, Fourth Sea Lord and Chief of Supplies and Transport, 1954-55; Commander-in-Chief, The Nore, 1955-58; retired list, 1959. Member British Waterways Board, Jan. 1963-1967, Vice-Chairman (part-time) Aug. 1963-1967. Naval ADC to the King, 1949. Grand Cross of Military Order of Avis (Portugal), 1955; Order of Al Rafidain (Class II, Mil., conferred by the King of Iraq), 1956; Ordine al merito della Repubblica, Grande Ufficiale (Italy) 1958. *Address:* The Coach House, Church Road, West Lavington, Midhurst, West Sussex GU29 0EH. *T:* Midhurst 3183.

PARIKIAN, Manoug; violinist; Professor of Violin, Royal Academy of Music, since 1959; *b* Mersin, Turkey, 15 Sept. 1920, of Armenian parentage; *s* of late Stepan Parikian and Vanouhi (*née* Bedelian); *m* 1957, Diana Margaret (*née* Carbutt); two *s. Educ:* Trinity College of Music, London (Fellow). Leader: Liverpool Philharmonic Orchestra, 1947-48; Philharmonia Orchestra, London, 1949, until resignation, 1957; has appeared in all European countries as solo violinist. Introduced Shostakovitch Violin Concerto to Scandinavia (Stockholm), 1956; first public performance of works by Iain Hamilton, Rawsthorne, Musgrave, Alexander Goehr, Elizabeth Maconchy, Gordon Crosse and Hugh Wood. Toured: USSR, April-May 1961, and Nov. 1965; Latin America, July-Aug. 1974. Member Jury, Tchaikovsky violin competition, Moscow, 1970. Dir, Yorkshire Sinfonia, 1976-78; Musical Dir, Manchester Camerata, 1980-; Artistic Dir, Giggleswick Summer Music Fest., 1981. Formed trio with Amaryllis Fleming ('cello) and Bernard Roberts (piano), 1977. Sir Robert Mayer Vis. Lectr, Leeds Univ., 1974-75. Hon. RAM, 1963. *Recreations:* collecting early printed books in Armenian; backgammon. *Address:* The Old Rectory, Waterstock, Oxford. *T:* Ickford 603.

PARIS, Archbishop of; *see* Lustiger, Most Rev. Mgr J.-M.

PARIS, Sir Edward (Talbot), Kt 1954; CB 1947; DSc (London), FInstP; *b* 23 Jan. 1889; *s* of late Edward and Eliza Paris; *m* 1925, Eveline Amy (*d* 1968), *d* of late J. W. Shortt, MD; three *d. Educ:* Dean Close Sch., Cheltenham; Imperial College of Science; University College, London. Fellow University College, London, 1921; served European War, 1914-18, RA, 1915-18; seconded to Ministry of Munitions, 1918; Signals Experimental Establishment, War Dept, 1919; Experimental Officer in Air Defence Experimental Establishment, 1923; Dep. Director of Scientific Research, WO, 1938; transferred Ministry of Supply, 1939; Controller of Physical Research, 1941; Controller of Physical Research and Signals Development, 1942; Principal Director of Scientific Research (Defence), Ministry of Supply, 1946; Chief Scientific Adviser, Home Office, 1948-54. US Medal of Freedom with Bronze Palm, 1947. *Publications:* various papers in scientific journals. *Address:* Apartado 57, San Vicente de la Barquera, Santander, Spain.

PARIS, John; Director, National Army Museum, 1967-69; *b* Hove, 2 May 1912; *s* of Herbert Henry Paris, Comptroller of Telegraphs and Postmaster, Durban, during Boer War; *m* 1940, Beryl Maria Thomson; no *c. Educ:* Brighton Coll.; Brighton College of Art; Worcester Coll., Oxford. BA (English) 1936; MA 1938; BLitt 1938. Commissioned into RA, 1940; SO

Fixed Defences Scottish Command, 1942; Major. Dep. Director, Walker Art Gallery, Liverpool, 1938-49; Director, National Gallery of S Africa, Cape Town, 1949-62. Hon. Life Vice-President, Friends of Italy; Past President, S African Museums Assoc.; Kolbe Memorial Lecturer, University of Cape Town, 1961. Has made broadcasts. *Publications:* English Water-Colour Painters, 1945; William Gilpin and the Cult of the Picturesque; introductions, catalogues and articles in learned journals; occasional poems, etc. *Address:* 5 Brook House, Ardingly, Sussex. *T:* Ardingly 892274.

PARISH, Sir David (Elmer) W.; *see* Woodbine Parish.

PARK, Andrew Edward Wilson, QC 1978; *b* 27 Jan. 1939; *s* of late Dennis Edward Park and of Margaret Alison Park; *m* 1962, Ann Margaret Woodhead; two *s* one *d* (and one *s* decd). *Educ:* Leeds Grammar Sch.; University Coll., Oxford. Winter Williams Law Schol., 1959; BA (Jurisp.) 1960, MA 1964. Various academic posts in UK and abroad, 1960-68. Called to the Bar, Lincoln's Inn, 1964; practice at Revenue Bar, 1965-; Chm., Taxation and Retirement Benefits Cttee of the Bar Council, 1978-82; Treasurer, Senate of the Inns of Court and Bar, 1982-. *Publications:* The Sources of Nigerian Law, 1963; various articles, notes and reviews in legal periodicals, mainly concerning taxation. *Recreations:* squash, hill walking, Rugby League cup finals. *Address:* Blandford Cottage, Weston Green Road, Thames Ditton, Surrey KT7 0HX. *T:* 01-398 5349.

PARK, Daphne Margaret Sybil Désirée, CMG 1971; OBE 1960; HM Diplomatic Service, retired; Principal of Somerville College, Oxford, since 1980; *b* England, 1 Sept. 1921; British parents; unmarried. *Educ:* Rosa Bassett Sch.; Somerville Coll., Oxford. WTS (FANY), 1943-47 (Allied Commn for Austria, 1946-48). FO, 1948; UK Delegn to NATO, 1952; 2nd Sec., Moscow, 1954; FO, 1956; Consul and 1st Sec., Leopoldville, 1959; FO, 1961; Lusaka, 1964; FO, 1967; Consul-Gen., Hanoi, 1969-70; Hon. Res. Fellow, Univ. of Kent, 1971-72, on sabbatical leave from FCO; Chargé d'Affaires *a i*, Ulan Bator, Apr.-June 1972; FCO, 1973-79. Member: British Library Bd; RIIA; Royal Asiatic Soc. Governor, BBC, 1982-. *Recreations:* good talk, politics, and difficult places. *Address:* Somerville College, Oxford OX2 6HD. *Clubs:* United Oxford & Cambridge University, Naval and Military, Royal Commonwealth Society, Special Forces.

PARK, George Maclean, JP; MP (Lab) Coventry North East since Feb. 1974; *b* 27 Sept. 1914; *s* of James McKenzie Park and Mary Gorman Park; *m* 1941, Joyce, *d* of Robert Holt Stead and Gertrude Stead; one *d. Educ:* Onslow Drive Sch., Glasgow; Coventry Techn. College. Sen. AEU Shop Steward, Chrysler UK Ltd, Ryton, 1958-73. Coventry City Councillor, 1961-74; Coventry District Councillor, 1973-74; Leader of Council Labour Gp, 1967-74; W Mids Metropolitan CC, 1973-77; Chm. Coventry and District Disablement Adv. Cttee, 1960-74; Leader, Coventry City and District Councils, 1972-74; Chm. Policy Adv. Cttee, 1972-74. PPS to Dr J. Gilbert, Minister for Transport, 1975-76; PPS to Sec. of State for Industry, 1976-79. Chm., W Midland Group Labour MPs. Chm. Belgrade Theatre Trust, 1972-74. JP Coventry, 1961. AEU Award of Merit, 1967. *Recreations:* reading, walking. *Address:* 170 Binley Road, Coventry CV3 1HG. *T:* Coventry 458589.

PARK, Hon. Sir Hugh (Eames), Kt 1965; Hon. Mr Justice Park; Judge of the High Court of Justice, Queen's Bench Division, since 1973 (Family Division, 1965-73); *b* 24 April 1910; *er s* of late William Robert and late Helen Beatrice Park; *m* 1938, Beryl Josephine, *d* of late Joseph and Margery Coombe; three *d. Educ:* Blundell's; Sidney Sussex Coll., Cambridge (Hon. Fellow, 1968). Called to the Bar, Middle Temple, 1936; QC 1960; Bencher, 1965. Member Western Circuit. Served War, 1940-45; Sqdn Leader, 1945. Recorder of Penzance, 1959-60; of Exeter, 1960-64; of Southampton, 1964-65. Member, Court of Exeter Univ., 1961; Member, Board of Governors, Blundell's Sch., 1961. Commn of Assize, North East Circuit, 1963; Judge of the Courts of Appeal, Channel Islands, 1964-65; Chairman, County of Devon Quarter Sessions, 1964-71; Deputy Chairman, Cornwall County Quarter Sessions, 1959-71; Presiding Judge, Western Circuit, 1970-75. *Recreation:* fishing. *Address:* Royal Courts of Justice, Strand, WC2; 34 Ordnance Hill St John's Wood, NW8. *T:* 01-586 0417; Gorran Haven, Cornwall. *T:* Mevagissey 2333.

PARK, Ian Grahame; Managing Director, Northcliffe Newspapers Group Ltd, since 1982; *b* 15 May 1935; *s* of William Park and Christina (*née* Scott); *m* 1965, Anne Turner; one *s. Educ:* Lancaster Royal Grammar Sch.; Queens' Coll., Cambridge. 1st Bn Manchester Regt, Berlin (Nat. Service Commn), 1954-56. Trainee Journalist, Press and Journal, Aberdeen, 1959; Asst Lit. Editor, Sunday Times, 1960-63; various management posts, Thomson Newspapers, 1963-65; Liverpool Daily Post and Echo, 1965-, Man. Dir and Editor in Chief, 1972-82. Mem. Council, Newspaper Soc., 1967- (Pres., 1980-81); Dir, Press Assoc., 1973- (Chm., 1978-79 and 1979-80); Dir, Reuters, 1978-82. Dir, Radio City (Sound of Merseyside Ltd), 1973-82; Dir, Liverpool Playhouse, 1973-80; Trustee, Blue Coat Soc. of Arts, Liverpool, 1973-82. *Recreations:* reading, theatre, visiting galleries. *Address:* 6 Cheyne Row, SW3. *Clubs:* Reform; Press (Pittsburgh).

PARK, (Ian) Michael (Scott), CBE 1982; Partner, Paull & Williamsons, Advocates, Aberdeen, since 1964; *b* 7 April 1938; *m* 1964, Elizabeth Mary Lamberton Struthers; two *s. Educ:* Aberdeen Grammar Sch.; Aberdeen Univ. (MA, LLB). Admitted Mem. Soc. of Advocates, Aberdeen, 1962. Law Society of Scotland: Mem. Council, 1974-; Vice-Pres., 1979-80; Pres., 1980-81. Chm.,

Aberdeen Citizens Advice Bureau, 1976-. Frequent broadcaster on legal topics. *Recreations:* golf, gardening. *Address:* Beechwood, 46 Rubislaw Den South, Aberdeen AB2 6AX. *T:* Aberdeen 33799. *Club:* New (Edinburgh).

PARK, Dame Kiri; *see* Te Kanawa, Dame K.

PARK, Merle Florence, (Mrs Sidney Bloch), CBE 1974; Principal, Royal Ballet; founded Ballet School, St Peter's Square, W6, 1977; *b* Salisbury, S Rhodesia, 8 Oct. 1937; *d* of P. J. Park, Eastlea, Salisbury, S Rhodesia, C Africa; *m* 1st, 1965, James Monahan, *qv* (marr. diss. 1970); one *s*; 2nd, 1971, Sidney Bloch. *Educ:* Elmhurst Ballet Sch. Joined Sadler's Wells Ballet, 1955; first rôle, a Mouse (Sleeping Beauty prologue); first solo, Milkmaid (Façcce); principal soloist, 1959. First danced: Blue Bird (Act III, Sleeping Beauty), 1956; Swanhilda (Coppelia), Mamzelle Angot (Mamzelle Angot), 1958; Lise (Fille Mal Gardée), 1960; Cinderella, 1962; Juliet (Romeo and Juliet), 1965; Giselle, Celestial (Shadow Play), 1967; Clara (Nutcracker), Aurora (Sleeping Beauty), 1968; Odette (Swan Lake), 1971; A Walk to Paradise Garden, 1972; Firebird, Odette/Odile (Swan Lake), Dances at a Gathering, 1973; Manon, Emilia (The Moor's Pavane), Aureole, Terpsichore (Apollo), Elite Syncopations, 1974; Lulu, 1976; Kate (The Taming of the Shrew), La Bayadère, Tuesday's Child (Jazz Calendar), Triad, Symphonic Variations, Waltzes of Spring (in Royal Opera Fledermaus), Le Papillon, 1977; Countess Larisch (Mayerling), 1978; La Fin du Jour, 1979; Mary Vetsera (Mayerling), Natalia (A Month in the Country), Adieu, 1980; Chloë (Daphnis and Chloë), Isadora, 1981. *Recreations:* teaching at her own ballet school. *Address:* Chiswick Mall, W4.

PARK, Michael; *see* Park, I. M. S.

PARK, Trevor; Lecturer in Industrial Relations, Department of Adult Education and Extramural Studies, University of Leeds, since 1972; *b* 12 Dec. 1927; *s* of late Stephen Clifford Park and Annie Park (*née* Jackson); *m* 1953, Barbara Black; no *c. Educ:* Bury Grammar Sch.; Manchester Univ. (MA). History Master, Bacup and Rawtenstall Grammar Sch., 1949-56; WEA, Tutor and Organiser (NW District), 1956-60; Lecturer, Extramural Dept, Univ. of Sheffield (politics and internat. relations), 1960-64; WEA Tutor and Organiser, Manchester, 1970-72. Parliamentary Labour Candidate: Altrincham and Sale, General Election, 1955; Darwen, General Election, 1959; MP (Lab) South East Derbyshire, 1964-70. Mem. (Lab) Leeds CC, 1979- (Chm., Mun. Services Cttee, 1980-). Member: TGWU; Select Cttees on Nationalised Industries, 1966-68, and on Education and Science, 1968-70; Yorkshire and Humberside Economic Planning Council, 1977-79. Chm. ATAE, 1972-75. *Recreation:* walking. *Address:* Department of Adult Education and Extramural Studies, The University, Leeds LS2 9JT.

PARKE, Prof. Dennis Vernon William, PhD, DSc; CChem, FRSC, FIBiol, FRCPath; (first) Professor and Head of Department of Biochemistry, University of Surrey, since 1967; *b* London, 15 Nov. 1922; *e s* of William Parke and Florence Parke; *m* 1943, Doreen Joan Dunn; two *s* one *d. Educ:* West Ham Municipal Secondary Sch. (Gurney Scholar); Chelsea and University Colls, Univ. of London 1940-48; St. Mary's Hosp. Med. Sch., London (PhD DSc). War Service, RA RAMC, 1942-47. Head, Dept of Microbiol Chem., Glaxo Labs Ltd, 1948-49; St. Mary's Hosp. Med. Sch., Univ. of London: Res. Asst to Prof. R. T. Williams, FRS, 1949-52; Lectr in Biochem., 1952-58, Sen. Lectr, 1958-62; Reader in Biochem., 1962-67; Dean, Faculty of Biol and Chem. Sciences, Univ. of Surrey, 1971-75. Sometime Examnr, Univs of Dublin (Trinity), Edinburgh, Glasgow, Liverpool, London, Newcastle upon Tyne, Reading, Strathclyde, Wales, Auckland, Ibadan, Nairobi, Singapore, Sydney and Wellington. Sigma Xi Lectr, Univ. of Calif (Davis), 1978. Member: Cttee on Safety of Drugs, 1968-70; Cttee on Safety of Medicines, 1970-; Cttee on Med. Aspects of Chemicals in Food and Environment, DHSS, 1972-; Food Additives and Contaminants Cttee, MAFF, 1972-80; WHO Expert Panel on Food Additives, 1975-; WHO Sci. Gp on Toxicity Evaluation of Chemicals, 1975; WHO Cons. in Indust. Toxicol., Poland, 1974; Sci. Dir, NATO Workshop on Ecotoxicology, July-Aug. 1977. Mem., Internat. Acad. of Environmental Safety. Editor, Xenobiotica, 1970-. *Publications:* The Biochemistry of Foreign Compounds, 1968; (ed) Enzyme Induction, 1975; chapters in books and res. papers in Biochem. Jl and Biochem. Pharmacol. *Recreations:* landscape gardening, music. *Address:* Trevelen, Poyle Road, Guildford, Surrey. *T:* Guildford 73667. *Club:* Athenæum.

PARKE, Herbert William, MA (Oxon); LittD (Dublin); Fellow Emeritus of Trinity College, Dublin, since 1973, Fellow, 1929-73; Professor of Ancient History, 1934-73, Vice-Provost, 1952-73, Librarian 1949-65, Curator, 1965-73; *b* Moneymore, Co. Londonderry, 7 Sept. 1903; *o s* of William and Bertha Blair Parke; *m* 1930, Nancy Bankart (*d* 1980), *y d* of Arthur R. Gurney, Cracoe, Yorks; one *d. Educ:* Coleraine Academical Institution; Bradford Grammar Sch.; Wadham Coll., Oxford (Scholar). 1st Class Hon. Mods, 1924; 1st Class Lit. Hum. 1926; A. M. P. Read Scholar, 1927; Craven Fellow, 1928; Cromer Essay Prize, 1928; Member of Royal Irish Academy, 1933; L. C. Purser Lect. in Archæology, 1934; Temp. Principal, Board of Trade, 1942-44; FRNS, 1947. Member Institute for Advanced Study, Princeton, USA, 1960; Vis. Schol., Arts Faculty, Southampton Univ., 1979. Hon. Fellow Durham Univ.; Hon. DLit QUB, 1974; Hon. LittD NUU, 1978. *Publications:* Greek Mercenary Soldiers, 1933; Delphic Oracle, 1939 (2nd edition with Professor D. E. W. Wormell, 1956); Oracles of Zeus, 1967; Greek Oracles, 1967; Festivals of the Athenians, 1977; contrib. to Journal of Hellenic Studies, Hermathena, etc, articles on Greek History and Mythology in Chambers's

Encyclopædia, Encyclopædia Britannica, and Oxford Classical Dictionary. *Address:* 275 West Dyke Road, Redcar, Cleveland TS10 4JU.

PARKER, Dr Mary, FRS 1972; Senior Phycologist, Marine Biological Association, Plymouth, 1947-73, retired; *b* 23 March 1908. *Educ:* Notre Dame Convent, Everton Valley; Univ. of Liverpool. DSc, PhD; FLS, FIBiol. Isaac Roberts Research Schol. in Biology, 1929; Phycologist, Marine Biological Stn, Port Erin, IoM, 1930-40; research on algae for Develt Commn and Min. of Supply, 1941-46. Corresp. Mem., Royal Botanical Soc. of Netherlands, 1970; Mem., Norwegian Acad. of Science and Letters, 1971. *Publications:* (with M. Knight) Manx Algae, 1931; papers in Jl of Marine Biol Assoc., Plymouth, etc. *Address:* 6 Alfred Street, Plymouth PL1 2RP. *T:* Plymouth 668609.

PARKER, family name of **Earls of Macclesfield** and **Morley.**

PARKER, Viscount; Richard Timothy George Parker; *b* 31 May 1943; *s* and *heir* of 8th Earl of Macclesfield, *qv*; *m* 1967, Tatiana Cleone, *d* of Major Craig Wheaton-Smith; three *d* (including twins). *Educ:* Stowe; Worcester Coll., Oxford. *Address:* Portobello Farm, Shirburn, Watlington, Oxon.

PARKER, A(gnes) Miller, RE; Artist and Wood-engraver; *b* Irvine, Ayrshire, 25 March 1895; *d* of William McCall and Agnes Mitchell Parker; *m* 1918, William McCance, Artist (marr. diss. 1963, and she legally assumed maiden name); no *c. Educ:* Glasgow School of Art (Diploma, Haldane Scholar). Instructress, Glasgow School of Art, 1918-20; Art Mistress, Maltmans Green School, Gerrards Cross, 1920-28; Art Mistress, Clapham High School and Training Coll., 1928-30; Walter Brewster Prize, 1st International Exhibition of Engraving and Lithography, Chicago, 1929; Wood-engraver to Gregynog Press, Newtown, Montgomeryshire, 1930-33. *Publications:* Chief Illustrated Editions; Esopes Fables by Caxton, 1931; Daisy Matthews and three other tales by Rhys Davies, 1932; XXI Welsh Gypsy Folk-Tales, collected by John Sampson, 1933; The House with the Apricot by H. E. Bates, 1933; Forest Giant-translated from the French by J. H. Ross (Colonel T. E. Lawrence), 1935; Through the Woods by H. E. Bates, 1936; Down the River by H. E. Bates, 1937; Gray's Elegy written in a Country Church-yard (Limited Editions Club of NY), 1938; Richard II-Shakespeare (Limited Editions Club of NY), 1940; A Shropshire Lad by A. E. Housman, 1940; The Return of the Native by Thomas Hardy (Limited Editions Club of NY), 1942; Essays in Russet by Herbert Furst, 1944; Spring of the Year by Richard Jefferies, 1946; The Life of the Fields, 1947, Field and Hedgerow, 1948, The Open Air, 1948, The Old House at Coate, 1948, by Richard Jefferies; Animals Under the Rainbow by Aloysius Roche, 1952; The Faerie Queene by Edmund Spenser, vols I and II, 1953; Lucifer by J. C. Powys, 1956; Tess of the D'Urbervilles, 1956, and Far From the Madding Crowd, 1958, by Thomas Hardy (New York); The Tragedies of Shakespeare (New York), 1959; The Mayor of Casterbridge by Thomas Hardy (Limited Editions Club of NY), 1964; Poems of Shakespeare (Limited Editions Club of NY), 1967; Jude the Obscure by Thomas Hardy (Limited Editions Club of NY), 1969. *Recreations:* fishing and cats.

PARKER, Sir Alan; *see* Parker, Sir W. A.

PARKER, Alan William; film director and writer; *b* 14 Feb. 1944; *s* of William and Elsie Parker; *m* 1966, Annie Inglis; three *s* one *d. Educ:* Owen's Sch., Islington. Advertising Copywriter, 1965-67; Television Commercials Director, 1968-78. Wrote screenplay, Melody, 1969; wrote and directed: No Hard Feelings, 1972; Our Cissy, 1973; Footsteps, 1973; Bugsy Malone, 1975; directed: The Evacuees, 1974; Midnight Express, 1977; Fame, 1979; Shoot the Moon, 1981; The Wall, 1982. *Publications: novels:* Bugsy Malone, 1976; Puddles in the Lane, 1977. *Address:* Pinewood Studios, Iver Heath, Bucks SL0 09H. *T:* Iver 655052.

PARKER, Prof. Alexander Augustine, MA, LittD; Professor of Spanish Literature, University of Texas at Austin, 1970-78, now Emeritus; *b* Montevideo, 1908; *er s* of Arthur Parker and Laura Bustamante; *m* 1941, Frances Ludwig; two *s* two *d. Educ:* Hawkesyard School (later Blackfriars School, Laxton); Gonville and Caius Coll., Cambridge (Exhibn. and scholar). First Class Mod. and Medieval Langs Tripos, Part I 1928, Part II 1930; Gibson Schol., 1931. Fellow of Gonville and Caius Coll., 1933-39. Lecturer and Head of Dept of Spanish, University of Aberdeen, 1939-49; Reader in Spanish, University of Aberdeen, 1949-53; Cervantes Professor of Spanish, University of London (King's Coll.), 1953-63; Prof. of Hispanic Studies, Univ. of Edinburgh, 1963-69. Seconded to University College of the West Indies as Prof. of Modern Languages, 1960-61; Andrew Mellon Visiting Prof., University of Pittsburgh, 1964, 1968, 1969-70. Pres., MHRA, 1982. Hon. Councillor of Consejo Superior de Investigaciones Científicas, 1953. Corr. Member Royal Acad. of Letters of Seville, 1958; Corr. Member Hispanic Society of America, 1960, Member, 1976; Corr. Member Spanish Academy, 1964. Hon. DLitt: Durham, 1975; St Andrews, 1978; Hon. LittD Liverpool, 1978. Commander of the Order of Isabel la Católica, 1956. *Publications:* The Allegorical Drama of Calderón, An Introduction to the Autos Sacramentales, 1943; No hay más Fortuna que Dios, by Calderón, ed. with Introd. and notes, 1949; Literature and the Delinquent: the Picaresque Novel in Spain and Europe (1599-1753), 1967; Luis de Góngora, Fable of Polyphemus and Galatea: a study of a baroque poem, 1977; papers and articles in The Mod. Lang. Review, Bulletin of Spanish Studies, Revista de Filología Española, etc.

Recreations: opera, horticulture and lepidoptera. *Address:* 9 West Castle Road, Edinburgh EH10 5AT. *T:* 031-229 1632.

PARKER, Cameron Holdsworth; Chairman and Chief Executive, Scott Lithgow Ltd, Port Glasgow, since 1980; *b* 14 April 1932; *s* of George Cameron Parker and Mary Stevenson Parker; *m* 1957, Elizabeth Margaret Thomson; three *s. Educ:* Morrison's Acad., Crieff; Glasgow Univ. (BSc Hons). John G. Kincaid & Co. Ltd, Greenock: Asst Manager, 1958; Asst Gen. Man., 1961; Dir, 1963; Man. Dir, 1967; Chm., 1976. Bd Mem., British Shipbuilders, 1981-. *Recreation:* golf. *Address:* Heath House, Rowantreehill Road, Kilmacolm, Renfrewshire PA13 4PE. *T:* Kilmacolm 3197. *Club:* Caledonian.

PARKER, Christopher William Oxley, MA; JP; DL; *b* 28 May 1920; *s* of late Lieut-Col John Oxley Parker, TD, and Mary Monica (*née* Hills); *m* 1947, Jocelyn Frances Adeline, *d* of late Colonel C. G. Arkwright, Southern Rhodesia; one *s* two *d. Educ:* Eton; Trinity Coll., Oxford. Local Director, Barclays Bank, Chelmsford Local Board; Director: Strutt and Parker (Farms) Ltd; Lord Rayleighs Farms Inc. Served War of 1939-45, with 147th Field Regt (Essex Yeomanry) Royal Artillery, 1939-42. JP Essex, 1952; High Sheriff of Essex, 1961; DL Essex 1972. *Recreations:* shooting, tennis, golf, estate management. *Address:* Faulkbourne Hall, Witham, Essex. *T:* Witham 513385. *Clubs:* Boodle's, MCC.

PARKER, Clifford Frederick, MA, LLB Cantab; JP; Bracton Professor of Law at the University of Exeter since 1957 (Deputy Vice-Chancellor, 1963-65, Public Orator, 1977-81); *b* 6 March 1920; *yr s* of late Frederick James Parker and Bertha Isabella (*née* Kemp), Cardiff; *m* 1945, Christine Alice (*née* Knowles); two *d. Educ:* Cardiff High Sch.; Gonville and Caius Coll., Cambridge. Royal Air Force, 1940-43. Solicitor of Supreme Court, 1947. Lecturer in Common Law, University of Birmingham, 1951-57; Senior Tutor and Asst Director of Legal Studies, Faculty of Law, University of Birmingham, 1956-57. Pres., Soc. of Public Teachers of Law, 1974-75. Chm., Exeter Area, Supplementary Benefit Appeal Tribunal, 1978-. JP Devon, 1969. *Publications:* contrib. to legal periodicals. *Recreation:* touring. *Address:* Lynwood, Exton, Exeter EX3 0PR. *T:* Topsham 4051.

PARKER, Sir Douglas D.; *see* Dodds-Parker.

PARKER, Rear-Adm. Douglas Granger, CB 1971; DSO 1945; DSC 1945; AFC 1952; Assistant Chief of Naval Staff (Operations and Air), 1969-71, retired; *b* 21 Nov. 1919; *s* of R. K. Parker; *m* 1953, Margaret Susan, *d* of late Col W. Cooper; one *s* one *d. Educ:* W Hartlepool Technical Coll. Joined Royal Navy, 1940; Command Fleet Air Arm Fighter Squadrons, 1948-51; Commanded: HMS Cavendish, 1961-62; RN Air Station, Lossiemouth, 1965-67; HMS Hermes, 1967-69. Captain 1959; Rear-Adm. 1969. *Address:* High Meadow, Walhampton, Lymington, Hants. *T:* Lymington 3259. *Club:* Royal Lymington Yacht.

PARKER, Sir Douglas William Leigh, Kt 1966; OBE 1954; retired as Director of Orthopædic Services, Tasmanian Government Health Dept, 1966. *Educ:* University of Sydney; University of Liverpool. MB, ChM (Sydney), 1923; FRCSEd 1925; MChOrth (Liverpool), 1930; FRACS, 1935. War of 1939-45: Surgeon, 2/9 AGH, 1940-42, 111 AGH, 1942-46. Senior Orthopædic Surgeon, Royal Hobart Hospital. Comr St John Ambulance Bde, Tasmania. Member Legacy, Hobart. OStJ. *Address:* 30 Fisher Avenue, Lower Sandy Bay, Hobart, Tasmania, Australia. *Clubs:* Tasmanian, Naval and Military and Air Force (Hobart).

PARKER, Geoffrey, CB 1966; Under-Secretary, Department of Industry, formerly Department of Trade and Industry, 1970-76; *b* 17 Jan. 1917; *m* 1942, Janet Crawford Chidley; two *s* one *d. Educ:* Hulme Grammar Sch., Oldham; New Coll., Oxford; Queen's Coll., Oxford; Universities of Berlin and Berne, MA, DPhil (Oxon). Entered Board of Trade as temp. Assistant Principal, May 1940; established as Principal, 1946. Counsellor (Commercial), HM Embassy, Washington, DC, 1952-55; Under-Sec., 1961; Principal Establishment and Organisation Officer, 1965-70. *Recreations:* reading, languages. *Address:* 5 Hove Court, Raymond Road, Wimbledon SW19 4AG. *T:* 01-946 9300.

PARKER, Geoffrey John; Managing Director: Atlantic Steam Navigation Co. Ltd, since 1974; Felixstowe Dock & Railway Co., since 1976; Member, National Bus Co. Ltd, since 1980; *b* 20 March 1937; *s* of Stanley John Parker and Alice Ellen Parker; *m* 1957, Hazel Mary Miall; two *s* two *d. Educ:* County Grammar Sch., Hendon. Commercial Dir, Townsend Car Ferries Ltd, 1972-74. *Recreation:* golf. *Address:* 101 Valley Road, Ipswich, Suffolk IP1 4NF. *T:* Ipswich 216003. *Clubs:* Ipswich Golf (Purdis Heath, Ipswich); Felixstowe Master Mariners.

PARKER, Herbert John Harvey; *see* Parker, John.

PARKER, Hugh; Senior Director, McKinsey & Co. Inc.; *b* 12 June 1919; *s* of Ross Parker and Ruth Baker Parker; *m* 1957, Elsa del Carmen Mijares Osorio; one *s* one *d. Educ:* Tabor Academy; Trinity Hall, Cambridge; Massachusetts Inst. of Technology. North Carolina Shipbuilding Co., 1941-43; General Electric Co., 1945-46; Ludlow Manufacturing Co., 1947-50; McKinsey & Co. Inc., 1951-. Pres., American Chamber of Commerce (UK), 1976-79; Mem., Council of Management, Oxford Centre for Management Studies. Pres., MIT Alumni Club of GB. Mem. and Governor, Ditchley Foundn. *Publications:* Letters to a New Chairman, 1979; articles on

management. *Recreations:* reading, sculling, cooking. *Address:* 9 Cheyne Walk, SW3. *T:* 01-352 9592. *Clubs:* American, The Pilgrims, United Oxford & Cambridge University; Leander (Henley-on-Thames); Racquet and Tennis (New York); Eastern Yacht (Mass.)

PARKER, James Roland Walter, CMG 1978; OBE 1968; HM Diplomatic Service, retired; Governor and Commander-in-Chief, Falkland Islands and Dependencies, and High Commissioner, British Antarctic Territory, 1976-80; *b* 20 Dec. 1919; *s* of late Alexander Roland Parker, ISM; *m* 1941, Deirdre Mary Ward. Served War of 1939-45: 1st London Scottish, 1940-41. Ministry of Labour, 1938-57; Labour Attaché, Tel Aviv, 1957-60; Labour Adviser: Accra, 1960-62; Lagos, 1962-64; seconded to Foreign Office, 1965-66; Dep. High Comr, Enugu, 1966-67; Commonwealth Office (later FCO), 1968-70; Head of Chancery, Suva, Fiji, 1970-71; High Comr in The Gambia, 1972-75; Consul-Gen., Durban, 1976. *Address:* 1 St Edmund's Court, NW8 7QL; Crockers Hill, Yarlington, Somerset BA9 8DJ. *Clubs:* Travellers', MCC.

PARKER, John, CBE 1965; MP (Lab) Dagenham, since 1945; President, Fabian Society, since 1980 (Vice-President, 1972-80); *b* 15 July 1906; *s* of H. A. M. Parker, schoolmaster; *m* 1943, Zena Mimardiere; one *s. Educ:* Marlborough; St John's College, Oxford. Chm., Oxford Univ. Labour Club, 1928; Asst to Director, Social Survey of Merseyside (Liverpool Univ.), 1929-32; Gen. Sec., New Fabian Res. Bureau, 1933-39; Fabian Society: Gen. Sec., 1939-45; Vice-Chm., 1946-50; Chm., 1950-53. Contested (Lab) Holland with Boston, 1931; MP (Lab) Romford, Essex, 1935-45; PPS to Miss Ellen Wilkinson, Min. of Home Security, 1940-42; Parly Under-Sec. of State, Dominions Office, 1945-46; Member: Speaker's Conferences, 1944, 1965-67, 1973-74; Procedure Cttee, 1966-73; Parly Delegation to USSR, 1945; National Executive Labour Party, 1943-44; Executive London Labour Party, 1942-47; Select Cttee Parliamentary Disqualifications, 1956; Parly Delegations to Italy, 1957, Ethiopia, 1964, Forestry Delegation, Yugoslavia, 1971; Leader, Delegation to Windward Islands, 1965; Chm., British-Yugoslav Parly Gp, 1960-; Father of the House of Commons, 1979-; Chairman: History of Parlt Trust, 1979-; H of C Pensions Fund, 1969-. Hon. Sec., Webb Trustees; Governor, LSE, 1949-81; Member: Court, Essex Univ., 1968-; Exec. Cttee, Nat. Trust, 1969-81; Historic Buildings Council, 1974-; Inland Waterways Amenity Council, 1968-. Mem., TGWU. Yugoslav Red Star, 1975. *Publications:* The Independent Worker and Small Family Business, 1931; Public Enterprise (Forestry Commission), 1937; Democratic Sweden (Political Parties); Modern Turkey, 1940; 42 Days in the Soviet Union, 1946; Labour Marches On, 1947; Newfoundland, 1950; (ed) Modern Yugoslav Novels (English edn), 1958-64; (comp. and ed) biographies, inc. Harold Wilson and Willy Brandt, 1964; Father of the House: 50 Years in Politics, 1982. *Recreations:* architecture and gardening. *Address:* 4 Essex Court, Temple, EC4. *T:* 01-353 8521.

PARKER, John; *see* Parker, T. J.

PARKER, Sir John; *see* Parker, Sir W. J.

PARKER, Sir John (Edward), Kt 1975; BCEng; Hon. FIEAust; retired; *b* 28 Sept. 1904; *s* of late Matthew Parker and Edith Florence Parker; *m* 1932, Winifred Mary Becher; two *s* one *d. Educ:* Wesley Coll., Melbourne, Vic.; Queen's Coll., Melbourne Univ. (BCE). Served War: RAE, AIF, in SW Pacific Area, rank Major, 1942-45. Dep. Dir of Works, Public Works Dept, Perth, WA, 1953-62; Dir of Engineering, PWD, Perth, WA, 1962-69. Chm., State Electricity Commn of WA, 1969-74. *Recreations:* golf, fishing, gardening. *Address:* 11 Hopetoun Street, South Perth, WA 6151, Australia. *T:* Perth 67 1272. *Clubs:* Weld (Perth, WA); Royal Perth Golf.

PARKER, Comdr (John) Michael (Avison), CVO 1957 (MVO 1953); RN (retired); Chairman, Mann's Transport; Director, Leo Burnett-Australia; *b* 23 June 1920; *s* of late Capt. C. A. Parker, CBE, Royal Australian Navy, Melbourne; *m* 1st, 1943, Eileen Margaret Anne (*née* Allan) (marr. diss. 1958); one *s* one *d* ; 2nd, 1962, Carol (marr. diss.; she *d* 1977), *d* of Ivo Thomson, 2nd Bt, and Mrs Brian Whitmee; one *s* one *d* ; 3rd, 1976, Mrs Jean Ramsay. *Educ:* Xavier College, Melbourne, Australia. Royal Navy, 1938-47. Equerry-in-Waiting to Princess Elizabeth and the Duke of Edinburgh, 1947-52; Private Sec. to Duke of Edinburgh, 1947-57. Member: Nat. Cttee, Aust.-Britain Soc. (Vice-Pres.); Council for Res. and Rehabilitation of Retarded Children; Trustee: Australian Ballet Trust; Victorian Conservation Trust. Chm., Plain English Speaking Award, Aust. *Recreations:* reading, tennis and sailing. *Address:* Santosa, 33 Albany Road, Toorak, Vic 3142, Australia.

PARKER, Jonathan Frederic, QC 1979; barrister; *b* 8 Dec. 1937; *s* of Sir (Walter) Edmund Parker, CBE and of Elizabeth Mary Butterfield; *m* 1967, Maria-Belen Burns; three *s* one *d. Educ:* Winchester College; Magdalene College, Cambridge (MA). Called to Bar, Inner Temple, 1962; joined Chambers of Mr John Mills, QC; practising member of the Bar, 1962-. *Recreations:* golf, gardening. *Address:* The Grange, Radwinter, Saffron Walden, Essex. *T:* Radwinter 375; 11 Old Square, Lincoln's Inn, WC2A 3TS. *T:* 01-405 5243. *Club:* Garrick.

PARKER, Sir Karl (Theodore), Kt 1960; CBE 1954; MA, PhD; FBA 1950; Hon. DLitt Oxon, 1972; Hon. Antiquary to the Royal Academy, 1963; Hon. Fellow, Oriel College, Oxford; Trustee, National Gallery, 1962-69; Keeper of the Ashmolean Museum, Oxford, 1945-62 (retired); Keeper of the Department of Fine Art, Ashmolean Museum, and of the Hope Collection of

Engraved Portraits, 1934-62; *b* 1895; *s* of late R. W. Parker, FRCS, and Marie Luling; *m* Audrey (*d* 1976), *d* of late Henry Ashworth James, of Hurstmonceux Place; two *d. Educ:* Bedford; Paris; Zürich. Studied art at most continental centres and at the British Museum; edited Old Master Drawings, a Quarterly Magazine for Students and Collectors, since its inception, 1926; late Asst Keeper, Dept of Prints and Drawings, British Museum. *Publications:* North Italian Drawings of the Quattrocento; Drawings of the Early German Schools; Alsatian Drawings of the XV and XVI Centuries; Drawings of Antoine Watteau; Catalogue of Drawings in the Ashmolean Museum, Vol. I, 1938, Vol. II, 1956; Catalogue of Holbein's Drawings at Windsor Castle, 1945; The Drawings of Antonio Canaletto at Windsor Castle, 1948; Antoine Watteau: Catalogue Complet de son œuvre Dessiné, Vol. I (with J. Mathey), 1957, Vol. II, 1958; and articles, mostly on Old Master drawings, in various English and continental periodicals. *Address:* 4 Saffrons Court, Compton Place Road, Eastbourne.

PARKER, Keith John; Editor, Express and Star, Wolverhampton, since 1977; *b* 30 Dec. 1940; *s* of Sydney John Parker and Phyllis Mary Parker; *m* 1962, Marilyn Ann Edwards; one *s.* Various editorial appointments; Editor, Shropshire Star, 1972-77. *Recreations:* reading, travel. *Address:* 20 Corfton Drive, Tettenhall, Wolverhampton, West Midlands WV6 8NR. *T:* Wolverhampton 758595.

PARKER, Kenneth Alfred Lamport; CB 1959; Receiver for the Metropolitan Police District, 1967-74; *b* 1 April 1912; *e s* of A. E. A. and Ada Mary Parker; *m* 1938, Freda Silcock (OBE 1975); one *s* one *d. Educ:* Tottenham Grammar Sch.; St John's College, Cambridge. Home Office, 1934; London Civil Defence Region, 1938-45; (Assistant Secretary, 1942, Deputy Chief Administrative Officer, 1943); Assistant Under-Secretary of State, Home Office, 1955-67 (Head of Police Dept, 1961-66). Imperial Defence College, 1947. *Publications:* articles on police matters. *Address:* 18 Lichfield Road, Kew, Surrey. *T:* 01-940 4595. *Club:* United Oxford & Cambridge University.

PARKER, Margaret Annette McCrie Johnston, (Margaret Johnston); actress; *d* of James and Emily Dalrymple Johnston; *m* 1946, Albert E. W. Parker (*d* 1974). *Educ:* North Sydney and Neutral Bay High School; Sydney University, Australia. Student, RADA; studied with Dr Stefan Hock; in repertory and acted as understudies. *Plays:* Murder without Crime, 1943; Fifth Column, 1944; Last of Summer, 1944; Time of Your Life, 1946; Shouting Dies, 1946; Barretts of Wimpole Street, 1947; Always Afternoon, 1949; Summer and Smoke, 1950; Second Threshold, 1951; The Dark is Light Enough, 1954; Sugar in the Morning, 1959; The Ring of Truth, 1959; Masterpiece, 1961. Stratford Memorial Theatre, 1956 season: Othello, The Merchant of Venice, Measure for Measure; Chichester Festival Theatre, 1966 Season: Lady Macbeth. *Films:* Rake's Progress, 1945; Man About the House, 1946; Portrait of Clare, 1949; Magic Box, 1951; Knave of Hearts, 1953; Touch and Go, 1955; Nose on her Face; Life at the Top, 1965; Psychopath; Sebastian. Television plays. *Address:* 50 Mount St, W1. *T:* 01-499 4232.

PARKER, Dame Marjorie Alice Collett, DBE 1977; welfare worker, Tasmania; Deputy-Chairman, Australian National Council of Women, 1960-64 (Life Member, since 1974); *b* Ballarat; *d* of W. Shoppee, Ballarat, Vic; *m* 1926, Max Parker; one *s. Educ:* Ballarat State Sch. Announcer and Dir Women's Interests, Radio Launceston, 1941-69; Public Relations Adviser for Girl Guide Assoc., 1954-68; Pres. and Org., Red Cross Meals on Wheels, Launceston, Tas., 1961-71; State Exec. and Public Relations Officer, Good Neighbour Council, Tas., 1964-70; N Regional Pres., Aust. Red Cross Soc., Tas. Div., 1965-68; Pres., Victoria League, Launceston, 1966-69; Exec. Mem., Soc. for Care of Crippled Children (Life Mem. 1973). Past Pres., N Tas. Branch, Royal Commonwealth Soc. Vice-Pres., United Nations Assoc., Launceston, 1964-68. *Recreation:* gardening. *Address:* Apsley, 5 Croydon Grove, Cypress Street, Launceston, Tasmania 7250, Australia. *Clubs:* Soroptomist (Pres. 1951), Royal Commonwealth Soc. (Launceston, Tas).

PARKER, Comdr Michael; *see* Parker, Comdr (J.) M. (A.).

PARKER, Michael Clynes, QC 1973; **His Honour Judge Parker;** a Circuit Judge, since 1978; *b* 2 Nov. 1924; *s* of Herbert Parker and Elsie Vera Parker (sometime Pres., NUT); *m* 1950, Molly Leila Franklin; one *s* two *d. Educ:* City of London Sch.; Pembroke Coll., Cambridge (BA, LLB). Sec., Cambridge Union, 1943. Flt-Sgt/Air Gunner, RAF, 1943-47. Called to Bar, Gray's Inn, 1949; practised in London and SE Circuit. A Recorder of the Crown Court, 1972-78. Contested (Lab) S Kensington, 1951. *Recreations:* theatre, watching cricket. *Address:* 17 Courtnell Street, W2. *Club:* United Oxford & Cambridge University.

PARKER, Michael St J.; *see* St John Parker.

PARKER, Sir Peter, Kt 1978; MVO 1957; Chairman, British Rail Board, since 1976; *b* 30 Aug. 1924; *s* of late Tom and Dorothy S. Parker; *m* 1951, Gillian Rowe-Dutton, *d* of late Sir Ernest Rowe-Dutton, KCMG, CB, and of Lady Rowe-Dutton; three *s* one *d. Educ:* Bedford Sch.; London Univ.; Lincoln Coll., Oxford (Hon. Fellow, 1980). Major, Intelligence Corps, 1943-47. Commonwealth Fund Fellowship to Cornell and Harvard, 1950-51. Contested (Lab) Bedford, 1951. Phillips Electrical, 1951-53; Head of Overseas Dept, Industrial Soc. 1953-54; Sec., Duke of Edinburgh's Study Conf. on Human Problems of Industry, 1954-56; joined Booker McConnell Ltd, 1956;

Chairman: Bookers Engineering & Industrial Holdings Ltd, 1966-70; Associated British Maltsters Ltd, 1971-73; Curtis Brown Ltd, 1971-76; Victoria Deep Water Terminal Ltd, 1971-76; Dawnay Day Group, 1971-76; Director: Booker Bros McConnell & Co. Ltd, 1960-70; Renold Group Ltd; Rockware Group Ltd, 1976- (Chm., 1971-76; Dep. Chm., 1981-); H. Clarkson & Co. (Holdings) Ltd, 1976- (Chm., 1975-76); Chm.-designate, Nat. Ports Authority, 1970; Chm., Clothing EDC, 1971-78; Member: BSC, 1967-70; British Tourist Authy Bd, 1969-75; British Airways Bd, 1971-81; Ct of London Univ. (Dep. Chm. 1970-); Political and Econ. Plannning Exec. (Vice-Chm., 1969-70; Hon. Treasurer, 1973-78); Council, BIM (Vice-Chm.); Foundn on Automation & Human Develt, 1971-; Engineering Industries Council, 1975-76; NEDC, 1980-; Founder Mem., Council of Foundn for Management Educn; Chairman: Westfield College, 1969-76 (Hon. Fellow, 1979); Adv. Council, Business Graduates Assoc. Vis. Fellow, Nuffield Coll., Oxford, 1980 (Hon. Fellow, 1980). Hon. LLD: London, 1981; Manchester Polytechnic, 1981. *Recreations:* Rugby (played for Bedford and E Mids); swimming, browsing. *Address:* British Railways Board, Rail House, Euston Square, NW1 2DZ. *Club:* Savile.

PARKER, Rev. Reginald Boden; *b* Wallasey, Cheshire, 4 June 1901; *s* of Joseph William and Ada Parker. *Educ:* Wallasey Grammar School; St Catherine's College, Oxford University; Ripon Hall, Oxford. BSc (London), 1923; MA (Oxon), 1938. Assistant Master, Ashton Gram. Sch., Lancs 1925-30; Asst Master, Newton Gram. Sch., Lancs 1930-32; Curate, Childwall, Liverpool, 1935-37; Curate, St Margaret's, Westminster, 1937-39; Asst Master and Chaplain, Oundle School, 1940-48; Headmaster, Igbobi College, Lagos, 1948-58; Bishop's Chaplain in Liverpool University, 1958-61; Residentiary Canon, Liverpool Cathedral, 1958-61; Precentor, Liverpool Cathedral, 1959-61; Asst Master, Wellington Coll., 1961-64; Rector of Bentham, dio. of Bradford, 1964-72. Hon. Lecturer in Hellenistic Greek, Liverpool University, 1959; Select Preacher, Oxford University, 1960. Member of Headmasters' Conference, 1950. *Publications:* (with J. P. Hodges): The Master and the Disciple, 1938 (SPCK); The King and the Kingdom, 1939 (SPCK); The Holy Spirit and The Kingdom, 1941 (SPCK). *Address:* 3 Yew Tree Cottages, Sheepscombe, Stroud, Glos GL6 7RB. *T:* Painswick 812650.

PARKER, Sir Richard (William) Hyde, 12th Bt, *cr* 1681; *b* 5 April 1937; *o s* of Sir William Stephen Hyde Parker, 11th Bt, and Ulla Ditlef, *o d* of C. Ditlef Nielsen, Dr of Philosophy, Copenhagen; *S* father 1951; *m* 1972, Jean, *d* of late Sir Lindores Leslie, 9th Bt; three *d* (incl. twins). *Educ:* Millfield, Street, Somerset; Royal Agricultural College, Cirencester. *Heir: cousin* Laurence Edmond Hyde Parker [*b* 24 Feb. 1912; *m* 1953, Margarethe Van Thörne; two *s* one *d*]. *Address:* Melford Hall, Long Melford, Suffolk.

PARKER, Rear-Adm. Robert William, CBE 1954; JP; *b* 1902; *s* of Colonel W. F. Parker, Delamore, Cornwood, Devon; *m* 1935, Noemi Vyvian, *d* of C. V. Espeut; no *c. Educ:* Royal Naval Colleges Osborne and Dartmouth. Midshipman, 1918; served in Grand Fleet; specialised Engineering, 1922-24; served as Engineer Officer: HMS Rodney, 1942-44; HMS Indomitable (British Pacific Fleet), 1944-46; comd HMS Caledonia, RN Apprentices Training Establishment, Rosyth, 1949-52; Rear-Adm. (E), 1952, on staff of C-in-C, Plymouth; Deputy Engineer-in-Chief of the Fleet, 1953-55; retired 1955. JP Somerset, 1961. *Recreation:* model engineering. *Address:* The Hermitage, Freshford, near Bath, Avon. *T:* Limpley Stoke 3220.

PARKER, Hon. Sir Roger (Jocelyn), Kt 1977; **Hon. Mr Justice Parker;** a Judge of the High Court, Queen's Bench Division, since 1977; Judge of the Courts of Appeal, Jersey and Guernsey, since 1974; *b* 25 Feb. 1923; *s* of Captain Hon. T. T. Parker, DSC, RN (Retired) and Marie Louise Leonie (née Kleinwort); *m* 1948, Ann Elizabeth Frederika (née White); one *s* three *d. Educ:* Eton; King's Coll., Cambridge. Served Rifle Bde, 1941-46. Called to Bar, Lincoln's Inn, 1948, QC 1961; Bencher, 1969. Member, Bar Council, 1968-69, Vice-Chm., 1970-72, Chm., 1972-73. Vice-Pres., Senate of Four Inns of Court, 1972-73. Dep. Chm., Herts QS, 1969-71. Conducted Windscale Nuclear Fuel Reprocessing Inquiry, 1977. Chm., Court of Inquiry into Flixborough Explosion, 1974. *Address:* The Old Rectory, Widford, near Ware, Herts. *T:* Much Hadham 2593. *Clubs:* Lansdowne; Leander.

PARKER, Ronald William, CBE 1959; JP; *b* 21 Aug. 1909; *s* of late Ernest Edward Parker, MBE, Accountant of Court, and Margaret Parker (née Henderson); *m* 1937, Phyllis Mary (née Sherren); two *s. Educ:* Royal High School, Edinburgh. Chartered Accountant, 1933. Secretary, later Dir, Weston Group of Companies, 1935; Asst Dir of Finance, Ministry of Fuel and Power, 1942; Partner, J. Aikman, Smith & Wells, CA, 1946. National Coal Board: Finance Dir, Scottish Division, 1947; Dep. Chm., North Western Division, 1954; Chm., Scottish Division, 1955-67; Regional Chm., Scottish Region, 1967-68; Chm., Scottish Gas Region (formerly Scottish Gas Bd), 1968-74. JP City and County of Edinburgh, 1972. *Recreations:* golf, gardening, fishing. *Address:* Claremont, 3 South Lauder Road, Edinburgh EH9 2LL. *T:* 031-667 7666. *Clubs:* Caledonian; New (Edinburgh).

PARKER, (Thomas) John; Board Member for Shipbuilding, since 1978 and Deputy Chief Executive, since 1980, British Shipbuilders; Corporation Managing Director with responsibility for Technology; Chairman, British Shipbuilders Training, Education and Safety Co., since 1981; *b* 8 April 1942; *s* of Robert Parker and Margaret Elizabeth Parker (née Bell); *m* 1967, Emma Elizabeth (née Blair); one *s* one *d. Educ:* Belfast Coll. of Technology. CEng; FRINA; FIMarE; MNECInst. Harland & Wolff Ltd, Belfast: Student

Apprentice Naval Architect, 1958-63; Ship Design Staff, 1963-69 (Nat. Physical Lab. (Ship Hydrodynamics), on secondment, 1964); Numerical Applications Manager, 1969-72; Gen. Manager, Sales and Projects, 1972-74; Man. Dir, Austin-Pickersgill Ltd, Sunderland, 1974-78. Member: Council, RINA, 1979-; Bd of Governors, Sunderland Polytechnic, 1976-81; Internat. Cttee, Bureau Veritas, Paris, 1979-. *Publications:* papers to Trans IES, RINA. *Recreations:* reading, motoring in the countryside, music, family pursuits, ships. *Address:* White Gables, 24 West Meadows Road, Cleadon Village, Sunderland. *T:* Boldon 363386.

PARKER, Rev. Thomas Maynard, DD; Fellow and Praelector in Theology and Modern History, University College, Oxford, 1952-73; now Emeritus Fellow; *b* 7 March 1906; *s* of late Thomas Maynard and Emily Mary Parker; unmarried. *Educ:* King Edward VI School, Stratford-upon-Avon; Exeter College, Oxford, (Scholar). 1st Class Hon. School of Modern History, 1927; BA 1927; 1st Cl. Hon. Sch. of Theology, 1929; Liddon Student, 1928-30; MA 1931; BD, DD 1956. St Stephen's House, Oxford, 1927-29. Liveryman of Butchers' Company, 1927 (Mem. Ct of Assistants, 1955-57, 1963-65; Warden, 1957-61; Providitor, 1960-61; Renter Asst, 1961-62; Master, 1962-63; Past Master, 1963-); Freeman of City of London, 1927. Deacon, 1930; Priest, 1931; Librarian and Tutor, Chichester Theological College, 1930-32; Curate of St Mary's, Somers Town, London, NW1, 1932-35; Librarian of Pusey House, Oxford, 1935-52; Custodian of the Pusey Memorial Library, 1946-52; University of Oxford: Mem., Faculty of Modern History, 1935-81, Faculty of Theology, 1935-73; Univ. Lectr in Theology, 1950-73; Bampton Lecturer, 1950; Acting Chaplain and Lecturer in Medieval History and Political Science, Pembroke College, 1951-52; Assistant Chaplain, Exeter College, 1946-52; Chaplain, University Coll., 1952-70; Lecturer in Theology, Pembroke Coll., 1952-61; Chairman: Faculty of Theology, 1963-65; Board of Faculty of Theology, 1964-65; Examiner in: Honour School of Theology, 1963-65; Honour School of Mod. Hist., 1953-55. Select Preacher: Cambridge Univ., 1955; Oxford Univ., 1960-61. Examining Chaplain to Bishop of Bradford, 1943-55; Birkbeck Lecturer, Trinity College, Cambridge, 1956-57. External Examr, QUB, 1964-66; External Examr in Church History for BD, St David's Coll., Lampeter, 1968-70; Examr for BPhil in European History, Oxford Univ., 1972-74. Member Central Advisory Council for Training of Ministry, 1948-55; Member Faith and Order Department of Brit. Council of Churches, 1949-55. FRHistS, 1956 (Mem. Council 1964-68); FSA, 1962. *Publications:* The Re-Creation of Man, 1940; The English Reformation to 1558, 1950 (2nd edn 1966); Christianity and the State in the Light of History (Bampton Lectures), 1955. Contributor to: Union of Christendom, 1938; The Apostolic Ministry, 1946; Ideas and Beliefs of the Victorians (Broadcast Talks), 1949, new edn 1966; Augustinus Magister, 1955; Oxford Dictionary of the Christian Church, 1957, 2nd edn, 1974; Miscellanea Historiæ Ecclesiasticæ, Congrès de Oxford, 1960; Studies in Church History, vol. I, 1964; Trends in Mediæval Political Thought, 1965; Essays in Modern English Church History in Memory of Norman Sykes, 1966; Anglican Initiatives in Christian Unity, 1967; The Rediscovery of Newman, 1967; The New Cambridge Modern History, Vol. III, 1968; Encyclopædia Britannica, Chambers's Encycl., Journal Theol. Studies, English Historical Review, Journal of Eccles. Hist., Speculum, Medium Aevum, Church Quarterly Review, Time and Tide, Oxford Magazine, Proc. of British Academy. *Recreation:* study of railways. *Address:* 36 Chalfont Road, Oxford OX2 6TH. *T:* Oxford 58494. *Club:* Athenæum.

PARKER, Vice-Adm. Sir (Wilfred) John, KBE 1969 (OBE 1953); CB 1965; DSC 1943; *b* 12 Oct. 1915; *s* of Henry Edmond Parker and Ida Mary (*née* Cole); *m* 1943, Marjorie Stuart Jones, Halifax, NS, Canada; two *d*. *Educ:* RN College, Dartmouth. Joined Royal Navy, 1929; War Service in N Atlantic, N Russia, Mediterranean, Pacific, Korea; sunk in HMS Edinburgh and HMS Trinidad; mined in HMS Sheffield; torpedoed in HMS Newfoundland; DSC (twice mentioned in despatches) 1943; Imperial Defence College, 1957; Commodore West Indies, 1958-60; Captain RNC Dartmouth, 1961-63; an Asst Chief of Defence Staff, Min. of Defence, 1963-66; Flag Officer, Medway, and Adm. Supt HM Dockyard, Chatham, 1966-69, retd 1969. *Recreations:* tennis, ski-ing, sailing. *Address:* Flint Cottage, Harting, Petersfield, Hants. *Club:* Royal Navy.

PARKER, Sir (William) Alan, 4th Bt *cr* 1844; *b* 20 March 1916; *er s* of Sir William Lorenzo Parker, 3rd Bt, OBE, and late Lady Parker; *S* father, 1971; *m* 1946, Sheelagh Mary, *o d* of late Dr Sinclair Stevenson; one *s* one *d*. *Educ:* Eton; New College, Oxford. Served War of 1939-45, RE (Captain); Middle East, 1941-45. *Heir: s* William Peter Brian Parker, FCA [*b* 30 Nov. 1950; *m* 1976, Patricia Ann, *d* of R. Filtness; one *s* one *d*]. *Address:* Apricot Hall, Sutton-cum-Beckingham, Lincoln LN5 0RE. *T:* Fenton Claypole 322.

PARKER BOWLES, Dame Ann, DCVO 1977; CBE 1972; Chief Commissioner, Girl Guides, 1966-75; *b* 14 July 1918; *d* of Sir Humphrey de Trafford, 4th Bt, MC; *m* 1939, Derek Henry Parker Bowles (*d* 1977); three *s* one *d*. County Comr, Girl Guides (Berkshire), 1959-64; Dep. Chief Comr, Girl Guides, 1962-66. *Recreation:* horse racing. *Address:* Forty Hill, Highclere, Newbury, Berkshire. *T:* Highclere 253735.

PARKES, Sir Alan (Sterling), Kt 1968; CBE 1956; FRS 1933; MA, PhD, DSc, ScD; Fellow of Christ's College, Cambridge, 1961-69, Hon. Fellow 1970; Fellow of University College, London; Chairman, Galton Foundation, since 1969; *b* 1900; *y s* of E. T. Parkes, Purley; *m* 1933, Ruth, *d* of Edward Deanesly, FRCS, Cheltenham; one *s* two *d*. *Educ:* Willaston School; Christ's College, Cambridge; BA Cantab, 1921, ScD 1931; PhD Manchester, 1923; Sharpey Scholar, University College, London, 1923-24; Beit Memorial Research Fellow, 1924-30; MA Cantab 1925; Schäfer Prize in Physiology, 1926; DSc London 1927; Julius Mickle Fellowship, University of London, 1929; Hon. Lecturer, University College, London, 1929-31; Member of the Staff of the National Institute for Medical Research, London, 1932-61; Mary Marshall Prof. of the Physiology of Reproduction, Univ. of Cambridge, 1961-67, Professor Emeritus 1968. Consultant, Cayman Turtle Farm Ltd, Grand Cayman, BWI, 1973-80. Foulerton Student of the Royal Society, 1930-34. Mem., Biol. and Med. Cttee, Royal Commn on Population, 1944-46. Lectures: Sidney Ringer, University College Hospital, 1934; Ingleby, Univ. of Birmingham, 1940; Galton, Eugenics Society, 1950; Addison, Guy's Hospital, 1957; Darwin, Inst. of Biology; Robert J. Terry, Washington Univ., Sch. of Medicine, 1963; Ayerst, Amer. Fertility Soc., 1965; Dale, Soc. for Endocrinology, 1965; Dick, Univ. of Edinburgh, 1969; Cosgrave, Amer. Coll. of Obstetricians and Gynaecologists, 1970; Tracy and Ruth Storer, Univ. of Calif, Davis, 1973. President: Section of Endocrinology, Roy. Soc. Med., 1949-50, Section of Comparative Medicine, 1962-63; Section D Brit. Assoc. for the Advancement of Science, 1958; Eugenics Soc., 1968-70; Inst. of Biology, 1959-60; Assoc. of Scientific Workers, 1960-62. Chairman: Soc. for Endocrinology, 1944-51; Soc. for Study of Fertility, 1950-52, 1963-66; Nuffield Unit of Tropical Animal Ecology, 1966-69; Breeding Policy Cttee, Zool Soc. of London, 1960-67; Scientific Adv. Cttee, Brit. Egg Mkting Bd, 1961-70. Mem. Adv. Cttee on Med. Research of the WHO, 1968-71. Executive Editor, Jl Biosocial Science, 1969-; Sec., Jls of Reproduction & Fertility Ltd, 1960-76. Consultant, IPPF, 1969-79. Cameron Prize, 1962; Sir Henry Dale Medal, Soc. for Endocrinology, 1965; John Scott Award (jtly with Dr A. U. Smith and Dr C. Polge), City of Philadelphia, 1969; Marshall Medal, Soc. Stud. Fert., 1970; Oliver Bird Medal, FPA, 1970. *Publications:* The Internal Secretions of the Ovary, 1929; Sex, Science and Society, 1966; Patterns of Sexuality and Reproduction, 1976; papers on the Physiology of Reproduction, on Endocrinology and on the behaviour of living cells at low temperatures in Jl of Physiology, Proc. Royal Society, and other scientific jls. Ed. Marshall's Physiology of Reproduction, 3rd edn, 1952, consultant 4th edn (in preparation). *Address:* 1 The Bramleys, Shepreth, Royston, Hertfordshire SG8 6PY.

PARKES, Sir Basil (Arthur), Kt 1971; OBE 1966; *b* 20 Feb. 1907; *s* of late Sir Fred Parkes, Boston, Lincs, and Blackpool, Lancs, and late Gertrude Mary Parkes (*née* Bailey); *m* 1933, May Lewis McNeill; two *s* one *d*. *Educ:* Boston Grammar Sch., Lincs. Joined family trawler owning Co., 1924 (Dir, 1928; Man. Dir, 1946). Pres., North British Maritime Gp Ltd (formerly United Towing Ltd), 1960-. Hon. Brother, Hull Trinity House. Mem., Worshipful Co. of Fishmongers; Mem., Worshipful Co. of Poulters; Officier de l'ordre du Mérite National Français, 1973. *Recreations:* golf, shooting. *Address:* Loghan-y-Yuiy, The Garey, Lezayre, near Ramsey, Isle of Man. *T:* Ramsey 814614. *Clubs:* City Livery, Constitutional.

PARKES, Dr Edward Walter; Chairman, University Grants Committee, 1978-Sept. 1983; Vice-Chancellor, University of Leeds, from Oct. 1983; *b* 19 May 1926; *o s* of Walter Frederick Parkes; *m* 1950, Margaret Parr (*see* Margaret Parkes); one *s* one *d*. *Educ:* King Edward's, Birmingham; St John's College, Cambridge; Scholar; 1st cl. hons Mech. Sci. Tripos, 1945; MA, PhD, ScD; FIMechE, FEng. At RAE and in the aircraft industry, 1945-48; research student and subsequently Univ. Lecturer, Cambridge, 1948-59; Fellow and Tutor of Gonville and Caius College; Vis. Prof., Stanford Univ., 1959-60; Head of the Department of Engineering, Univ. of Leicester, 1960-65; Prof. of Mechanics, Cambridge, and Professorial Fellow, Gonville and Caius Coll., 1965-74 (Mem. Gen. Bd, Dep. head of Dept of Engineering); Vice-Chancellor, City Univ., 1974-78. Member: Brynmor Jones Cttee, 1964-65; Adv. Bd for Res. Councils, 1974-; University and Polytechnic Grants Cttee for Hong Kong, 1974-. *Publications:* Braced Frameworks, 1965, 2nd edn 1974; papers on elasticity, dynamic plasticity or thermal effects on structures in Proc. and Phil. Trans. Royal Society and other jls. *Address:* (to Sept. 1983) University Grants Committee, 14 Park Crescent, W1N 4DH; (from Oct. 1983) University of Leeds, Leeds LS2 9JT. *Club:* Athenæum.

PARKES, Geoffrey, CMG 1947; FTI 1942; Deputy Chairman, National Westminster Bank Ltd, North Region, 1969-72; *b* 24 April 1902; *er s* of late Harry Clement Parkes, JP, and late Edith Newton; *m* 1st, 1925, Marjorie Syddall (*d* 1976); no *c*; 2nd, 1979, Bertha Livesley. *Educ:* Clifton College; L'Institut Technique, Roubaix. Director: Small & Parkes Ltd, 1927-64; Geigy (UK) Ltd, 1943-66; Director of Narrow Fabrics, Ministry of Supply, and Hon. Adviser to Board of Trade, 1939-44; Director-General Textiles & Light Industries Branch, CCG, 1944-46; Dep. Chief (Exec.) Trade and Industry Div., CCG, 1946. Director: District Bank Ltd, 1949-69; National Provincial Bank Ltd, 1963-69. Mem. Court, Manchester Univ., 1949-69. MA (*hc*) Manchester Univ., 1966. FRSA 1952. JP Manchester, 1949-65. *Recreation:* gardening. *Address:* Berth-y-Coed, Walshaw Avenue, Colwyn Bay, North Wales. *T:* Colwyn Bay 30377.

PARKES, Margaret, (Mrs E. W. Parkes), JP; Member, Press Council, since 1978; *b* 26 Sept. 1925; *d* of John and Dorothy Parr; *m* 1950, Edward Walter Parkes, *qv*; one *s* one *d*. *Educ:* Perse School for Girls, Cambridge; Leicester Univ. (MEd). Homerton Coll., Cambridge, 1965-74. Chairman: London and Southwark Diocesan Cttee for Personal Relationships, 1976-81; London Diocesan Bd of Educn, 1976-80; London Diocesan Family Educn Cttee, 1981-; Colleges Adv. Cttee, Gen. Synod Bd of Educn, 1982-; Radio London

Adv. Council, 1979-. Chm. of Governors, Whitelands Coll., London, 1981-. JP Inner London 1977. *Address:* 89 Defoe House, Barbican, EC2Y 8DN.

PARKES, Norman James, CBE 1976 (OBE 1960); Clerk of the Australian House of Representatives, 1971-76, retired; *b* 29 July 1912; *s* of Ernest William Parkes; *m* 1937, Maida Cleave, *d* of James Nicholas Silk; two *s. Educ:* Victorian State Schools. AASA. Parliamentary officer, 1934: with Reporting Staff, 1934-37; with House of Representatives, 1937-76. *Recreation:* bowls. *Address:* 3/3 Nuyts Street, Red Hill, Canberra, ACT 2603, Australia. *T:* Canberra 957320. *Clubs:* Canberra Bowling, National Press (Canberra).

PARKHOUSE, Prof. James, MD, FFARCS; Professor of Postgraduate Medical Education, University of Newcastle upon Tyne, and Postgraduate Dean and Director, Northern Postgraduate Institute for Medicine and Dentistry, since 1980; *b* 30 March 1927; *s* of Charles Frederick Parkhouse and Mary Alice Sumner; *m* 1952, Hilda Florence Rimmer; three *s* two *d. Educ:* Merchant Taylors' Sch., Great Crosby; Liverpool Univ. (MD 1955). MB ChB, 1950; MA Oxon 1960; MSc Manchester 1974. DA; FFARCS 1952. Anaesthetist, RAF Med. Br., 1953-55. Sen. Resident Anaesth., Mayo Clinic, 1957-58; First Asst, Nuffield Dept of Anaesths, Oxford, and Hon. Cons. Anaesth., United Oxford Hosps, 1958-66; Prof. and Head of Dept of Anaesths, Univ. of Manitoba, and Chief Anaesth., Winnipeg Gen. Hosp., 1967-68; Postgrad. Dean, Faculty of Med., Sheffield Univ., and Hon. Cons. Anaesth., United Sheffield Hosps, 1969-70; Prof. of Anaesths, Manchester Univ., and Hon. Cons. Anaesth., Manchester and Salford AHAs (Teaching), 1970-80. Consultant, postgrad. med. trng, WHO, 1969-; Specialist Adviser, H of C Social Services Cttee, 1980-. Member: Sheffield Reg. Hosp. Bd, 1969-70; Bd, Faculty of Anaesthetists, 1971-82; Neurosciences Bd, MRC, 1977-80; GMC, 1979-; Nat. Trng Council, NHS, 1981-; North Tyneside HA, 1982-. *Publications:* a New Look at Anaesthetics, 1965; Medical Manpower in Britain, 1979; contrib. to The Lancet, BMJ and specialist jls. *Recreations:* music, golf. *Address:* 69B Monkseaton Drive, Whitley Bay, Tyne and Wear. *Clubs:* Royal Air Force; Royal Birkdale Golf.

PARKHOUSE, Peter; Under Secretary, Ministry of Agriculture, Fisheries and Food; *b* 22 July 1927; *s* of late William Richard Parkhouse, MBE, and late Alice Vera Parkhouse (*née* Clarke); *m* 1950, Mary Alison Holland; one *s* one *d. Educ:* Blundell's Sch.; Peterhouse, Cambridge; Cologne Univ. BA 1947, MA 1950. Instr Lieut, RN, 1947-50; Asst Master, Uppingham Sch., 1951-52; Asst Principal, Min. of Food, 1952; transf. to MAFF, 1955; served in private office of successive Ministers and Parly Secs, 1954-58; Principal 1958; Principal Private Sec. to Minister, 1966-67; Asst Sec. 1967; Under-Sec. 1973; Dir in Directorate-Gen. for Agriculture, Commn of European Communities, 1973-79; Under Sec., 1979-. Mem., EDC for Agriculture, 1982-. *Recreations:* music, fishing. *Address:* Stafford House, The Chipping, Tetbury, Glos GL8 8ET. *T:* Tetbury 52540. *Club:* United Oxford & Cambridge University.

PARKHURST, Raymond Thurston, BSc(Agr), MSc, PhD; Director of South Central Poultry Research Laboratory, State University, Mississippi, 1960-68, retired; *b* Everett, Massachusetts, USA, 24 April 1898; *o s* of Fred Lincoln and Celeste Elizabeth Parkhurst; *m* 1922, Norma F. Langroise; one *s* one *d. Educ:* Fitchburg (Massachusetts) High School; Universities of Massachusetts, Idaho and Edinburgh. Extension Poultryman, Iowa State College, 1919-21; Professor of Poultry Husbandry, Experiment Station Poultry Husbandman, and Head, Dept of Poultry Husbandry, University of Idaho, 1921-27; Director, Brit. Nat. Institute of Poultry Husbandry, 1927-32; Head, Department Agricultural Research, National Oil Products Co., 1932-38; Head, Dept of Poultry Husbandry, University of Massachusetts, Amherst, 1938-44; Director, Nutrition and Research, Flory Milling Co., Bangor, Pa, 1944-49; Director of Nutrition and Research, Lindsey-Robinson and Company, Roanoke, Va, USA, 1949-60; Member: Amer. Poultry Science Assoc.; Amer. Assoc. of Retired Persons; Nat. Assoc. of Retired Persons, etc.; First President of British Poultry Education Association. *Publications:* Vitamin E in relation to Poultry; The Comparative Value of various Protein Feeds for Laying Hens; Factors Affecting Egg Size; Mixed Protein Foods for Layers; Ricketts and Perosis in Growing Chickens; Rexing the Rabbit; Corn Distillers By-Products in Poultry Rations; Calcium and Manganese in Poultry Nutrition; Crabmeal and Fishmeal in Poultry Nutrition; Commercial Broiler Raising; Gumboro Disease, etc. *Recreations:* roses, camellias, stamps, coins. *Address:* 700 Sassafras Drive, Starkville, Miss 39759, USA. *Club:* Kiwanis International.

PARKIN, John Mackintosh; Administrator, Royal Courts of Justice, since 1982; *b* 18 June 1920; *s* of Thomas and Emily Cecilia Parkin; *m* Biancamaria Giuganino, Rome; two *d. Educ:* Nottingham High Sch.; Emmanuel Coll., Cambridge (Sen. Schol.; MA). Royal Artillery, 1939-46 (Captain). Asst Principal, WO, 1949; Registrar, RMCS, 1957-60; Principal Private Sec. to Sec. of State for War, 1960-62; Asst Sec. 1962; Sen. Fellow, Harvard Univ., 1966-67; Comd Sec., BAOR, 1967-70; Asst Under-Sec. of State, MoD, 1974-80. Mem., Royal Patriotic Fund Corpn, 1977-80. *Recreation:* history of architecture and art. *Address:* 35 Little Bornes, Dulwich, SE21 8SD. *T:* 01-670 5564.

PARKINSON, Rt. Hon. Cecil Edward, PC 1981; MP (C) Hertfordshire South, since 1974 (Enfield West, Nov. 1970-1974); Paymaster General and Chairman of the Conservative Party, since 1981; Chancellor of the Duchy of Lancaster, since 1982; *b* 1 Sept. 1931; *s* of Sidney Parkinson, Carnforth, Lancs; *m* 1957, Ann Mary, *d* of F. A. Jarvis, Harpenden, Herts; three *d. Educ:* Royal

Lancaster Grammar Sch., Lancaster; Emmanuel Coll., Cambridge. BA 1955, MA 1961. Joined Metal Box Company as a Management Trainee; joined West, Wake, Price, Chartered Accountants, 1956; qualified 1959; Partner, 1961-71; founded Parkinson Hart Securities Ltd, 1967; Director of several cos, 1965-79. Constituency Chm., Hemel Hempstead Conservative Assoc.; Chm., Herts 100 Club, 1968-69; contested (C) Northampton, 1970. PPS to Minister for Aerospace and Shipping, DTI, 1972-74; an Asst Govt Whip, 1974; an Opposition Whip, 1974-76; Opposition Spokesman on trade, 1976-79; Minister for Trade, Dept of Trade, 1979-81. Sec., Cons. Parly Finance Cttee, 1971-72; Chm., Anglo-Swiss Parly Gp. *Recreations:* reading, golf, skiing; ran for combined Oxford and Cambridge team against Amer. Univs, 1954 and 1955; ran for Cambridge against Oxford, 1954 and 1955. *Address:* The Old Vicarage, Northaw, Potters Bar, Herts. *Clubs:* Reform; Hawks (Cambridge).

PARKINSON, Cyril Northcote, MA, PhD, FRHistS; author, historian and journalist; Seigneur of Anneville, Mauxmarquis and Beavoir; Professor Emeritus, Troy State University, Alabama, since 1970; *b* 30 July 1909; *yr s* of late W. Edward Parkinson, ARCA and late Rose Emily Mary Curnow; *m* 1st, 1943, Ethelwyn Edith Graves (marr. diss.); one *s* one *d* ; 2nd, 1952, Elizabeth Ann Fry; two *s* one *d. Educ:* St Peter's School, York; Emmanuel College, Cambridge; King's College, London. Fellow of Emmanuel Coll., Cambridge, 1935; Sen. History Master, Blundell's Sch., Tiverton, 1938; Master, RNC, Dartmouth, 1939. Commissioned as Captain, Queen's Roy. Regt, 1940; Instructor in 166 OCTU; attached RAF, 1942-43; Major, 1943; trans. as GSO2 to War Office (General Staff), 1944; demobilised, 1945; Lectr in History, Univ. of Liverpool, 1946; Raffles Professor of History, University of Malaya, Singapore, 1950-58. Visiting Professor: Univ. of Harvard, 1958; Univs of Illinois and California, 1959-60. Mem. French Académie de Marine and US Naval Inst.; Mem. Archives Commission of Govt of India. Hon. LLD Maryland, 1974; Hon. DLitt Troy State, 1976. *Plays:* Helier Bonamy, Guernsey, 1967; The Royalist, Guernsey, 1969. *Publications:* many books including: Edward Pellew Viscount Exmouth, 1934; Trade in the Eastern Seas, 1937; (ed.) The Trade Winds, 1948; The Rise of the Port of Liverpool, 1952; War in the Eastern Seas, 1954; Britain in the Far East, 1955; Parkinson's Law, the Pursuit of Progress, 1958; The Evolution of Political Thought, 1958; British Intervention in Malaya, 1867-1877, 1960; The Law and the Profits, 1960; In-laws and Outlaws, 1962; East and West, 1963; Ponies Plot, 1965; A Law unto Themselves, 1966; Left Luggage, 1967; Mrs Parkinson's Law, 1968; The Law of Delay, 1970; The Life and Times of Horatio Hornblower, 1970; Big Business, 1974; Gunpowder, Treason and Plot, 1977; Britannia Rules, 1977; The Rise of Big Business, 1977; Jeeves: a Gentleman's Personal Gentleman, 1979; (with H. Le Compte) The Law of Longer Life, 1980; *novels:* Devil to Pay, 1973; The Fireship, 1975; Touch and Go, 1977; Dead Reckoning, 1978; So Near So Far, 1981; The Guernseyman, 1982; contribs to Encyclopædia Britannica, Economist, Guardian, New York Times, Fortune, Saturday Evening Post, Punch and Foreign Policy. *Recreations:* painting, travel, sailing. *Address:* Anneville Manor, Rue Anneville, Vale, Guernsey, CI. *Club:* Royal Channel Islands Yacht.

PARKINSON, Dr David Hardress; science writer and consultant; formerly Director General, Establishments Resources and Programmes, A, Ministry of Defence (1973-77); *b* Liverpool, 9 March 1918; *s* of E. R. H. Parkinson; *m* 1st, 1944, Muriel Gwendoline Patricia (*d* 1971), *d* of Captain P. W. Newenham; two *s* ; 2nd, 1974, Daphne Margaret Scott-Gall (marr. diss. 1978). *Educ:* Gravesend County Grammar Sch.; Wadham Coll., Oxford (MA, DPhil). FInstP. Royal Artillery, 1939-45 (Major); Oxford Univ., 1937-39 and 1945-49; Civil Service: TRE, Malvern, 1949; Supt Low Temp. and Magnetics Div., RRE, Malvern, 1956-63; Head Physics Gp, RRE, 1963-68; Head Physics and Electronics Dept, RRE and Dep. Dir, 1968-72. Hon. Prof. Physics, Birmingham Univ., 1966-73. Chm. Midland Br., Inst. Physics, 1968-70; Vice-Pres. (Exhibns), Inst. Physics, 1973-78. *Publications:* (with B. Mulhall) Generation High Magnetic Fields, 1967; many scientific papers and articles. *Recreations:* antiques, silversmithing. *Address:* South Bank, 47 Abbey Road, Great Malvern, Worcs WR14 3HH. *T:* Malvern 5423. *Club:* Royal Commonwealth Society.

PARKINSON, Desmond Frederick, CMG 1975; HM Diplomatic Service, retired; *b* 26 Oct. 1920; *m* 1977, Patricia Jean Campbell Taylor; two *s* two *d* of former *m*. HM Forces, 1939-49; served FO, 1949-51; Rangoon, 1951-53; Jakarta, 1954-55; FO, 1955-57; Rabat, 1957-60; Lagos, 1960-61; FO, 1961-63; Singapore, 1963-65; Delhi, 1965-67; FCO, 1967-78. *Address:* Woodrow, Silchester, near Reading. *T:* Reading 700257. *Clubs:* MCC; Huntercombe Golf.

PARKINSON, Desmond John, OBE 1950; Under-Secretary, Agricultural Research Council, 1971-73; *b* 8 March 1913; *s* of late Frederick A. Parkinson, Rio de Janeiro; *m* 1st, 1940, Leonor Hughes (marr. diss. 1954); 2nd, 1955, Lorna Mary Britton (*née* Wood); no *c. Educ:* Hereford Cathedral Sch.; St John's Coll., Cambridge; Brasenose Coll., Oxford. BA Cantab 1935; Colonial Admin. Service, 1936-60 (Gold Coast, Colonial Office, British Guiana, Nigeria); UK MAFF, 1960-63; ARC, 1963-73. *Recreation:* gardening. *Address:* Bourton Orchard, Penselwood, Wincanton, Somerset. *T:* Bourton (Dorset) 840423. *Club:* United Oxford & Cambridge University.

PARKINSON, Ewart West, BSc, DPA, CEng, FICE, PPRTPI, FIMunE; OStJ; Director of Environment and Planning, County of South Glamorgan, since 1973; *b* 9 July 1926; *s* of Thomas Edward Parkinson and Esther Lilian

West; *m* 1948, Patricia Joan Wood; two *s* one *d. Educ:* Wyggeston Sch., Leicester; Coll. of Technology, Leicester (BSc, DPA). Miller Prize (bridge design), Instn CE, 1953. After working with Leicester, Wakefield, Bristol and Dover Councils, he became Dep. Borough Engr, Chelmsford, 1957-60; Dep. City Surveyor Plymouth, 1960-64; City Planning Officer, Cardiff, 1964-73. Mem. Council, RTPI, 1971- (Vice-Pres., 1973-75, Pres., 1975-76, Chm. Internat. Affairs Bd, 1975-80); Member: Sports Council for Wales, 1966-78 (Chm., Facilities Cttee); Internat. Soc. of City and Regional Planners, 1972; Govt Deleg. to UN Conf. on Human Settlements, 1976; Watt Cttee for Energy, 1977- (Chm., Working Gp on Energy and Envt, 1980-); UK mem., Internat. Wkg Party on Urban Land Policy, Internat. Fedn for Housing and Planning, 1979-; Chm., Internat. Wkg Party on Energy and the Environment, Internat. Fedn for Housing and Planning; led Study Tours to Soviet Union, 1977, India and Bangladesh, 1979, China, 1980, Kenya, Zimbabwe and Tanzania, 1981; study visit, People's Republic of China at invitation of State Admin of Urban Construction, 1982. Chm., STAR Community Trust Ltd, 1979-; Vice-Pres., Wales Council for the Disabled. Diamond Jubilee Silver Medal, Nat. Housing and Town Planning Council, 1978. OStJ 1980 (S Glamorgan Council, 1975-). *Publications:* The Land Question, 1974; And Who is my Neighbour?, 1976; articles in prof. jls on land policy, energy and the environment, and public participation. *Recreations:* working, watching football, being with family, talking with friends. *Address:* County of South Glamorgan Headquarters, Newport Road, Cardiff. *T:* Cardiff 499022; 42 South Rise, Llanishen, Cardiff. *T:* Cardiff 756 394.

PARKINSON, Graham Edward; Metropolitan Stipendiary Magistrate, since 1982; *b* 13 Oct. 1937; *s* of Norman Edward Parkinson and Phyllis (*née* Jaquiss); *m* 1963, Dinah Mary Pyper; one *s* one *d. Educ:* Loughborough Grammar Sch. Admitted Solicitor of the Supreme Court, 1961. Articled to J. Tempest Bouskell, Leicester, 1955-60; Asst Solicitor: Slaughter & May, 1961-63; Amery Parkes & Co., 1963-67; Partner, Darlington and Parkinson, Ealing, 1967-82. Pres., Central and S Mddx Law Soc., 1978-79; Vice Chm. Exec. Cttee, Soc. of Conservative Lawyers, 1978-82; Mem. Cttee, London Criminal Courts Solicitors Assoc., 1978-80. *Recreations:* going to the opera, reading, piano playing, listening to music. *Address:* Highbury Corner Magistrates' Court, 51 Holloway Road, N7 8JA. *Club:* Carlton.

PARKINSON, Dr James Christopher, MBE 1963; TD 1962; Deputy Director, Brighton Polytechnic, since 1970; *b* 15 Aug. 1920; *s* of late Charles Myers Parkinson, Pharmacist, Blackburn, Lancs.; *m* 1950, Gwyneth Margot, *d* of late Rev. John Raymond Harrison, Macclesfield, Ches.; three *s. Educ:* Queen Elizabeth's Gram. Sch., Blackburn; Univ. Coll., Nottingham. BPharm, PhD (London), FRSC, FPS. Served in Mediterranean area, Parachute Regt, 1943-46; Parachute Regt TA: 16 AB Div. and 44 Parachute Bde, 1949-63 (Major). Lectr, Sch. of Pharmacy, Univ. of London, 1948-54; Head of Sch. of Pharmacy, Brighton Coll. of Technology, 1954-64; Dep. Sec., Pharmaceutical Soc. of Gt Britain, 1964-67; Principal, Brighton Coll. of Technology, 1967-70. Mem. various pharmaceutical cttees of British Pharmacopœia, British Pharmaceutical Codex and British Veterinary Codex, 1956-64; Examr, Pharmaceutical Soc. of Gt Britain, 1954-64; Mem. Bds of Studies in Pharmacy and Librarianship, CNAA, 1965-75. Member, Gen. Synod of Church of England, 1970-. *Publications:* research papers on applied microbiology in Jl Appl. Bact. and Jl Pharm. (London) and on pharmaceutical education in Pharm. Jl. *Recreation:* do-it-yourself. *Address:* 92 Wickham Hill, Hurstpierpoint, West Sussex BN6 9NR. *T:* Hurstpierpoint 833369.

PARKINSON, Michael; interviewer, television presenter, writer; *b* 28 March 1935; *m* Mary Heneghan; three *s. Educ:* Barnsley Grammar School. Journalist on local paper; The Guardian; Daily Express; columnist on Sunday Times; radio work; has written for Punch, The Listener, New Statesman; Producer and interviewer: Granada's Scene; Granada in the North; World in Action; What the Papers Say; reporter on 24 Hours (BBC); Exec. producer and presenter, London Weekend Television, 1968; Presenter: Cinema, 1969-70; Tea Break, Where in the World, 1971; host of own chat show, Parkinson, 1972-. Founder-Director, Pavilion Books, 1980-. *Publications:* Football Daft, 1968; Cricket Mad, 1969; Sporting Fever, 1974; (with Willis Hall) Football Classified, 1974; George Best: An Intimate Biography, 1975; (with Willis Hall) A-Z of Soccer, 1975; Bats in the Pavilion, 1977; The Woofits, 1980. *Address:* c/o Michael Parkinson Enterprises Ltd, 58 Queen Anne Street, W1M 0DX.

PARKINSON, Sir Nicholas (Fancourt), Kt 1980; Australian Ambassador to the United States, since 1979; *b* 5 Dec. 1925; *s* of late Rev. C. T. Parkinson, MA Oxon, and Dorothy Fancourt (*née* Mitchell); *m* 1952, Roslyn Sheena Campbell; two *d. Educ:* King's Sch., Parramatta, NSW; Univ. of Sydney (BA). Entered Aust. Foreign Service, 1951; Third Sec., Cairo, 1953-56; First Sec., Hong Kong, 1958-61; Counsellor, Moscow, Wellington, Kuala Lumpur, 1963-67; Chm., Jt Intell. Cttee, Dept of Defence, Canberra, 1967-70; High Comr, Singapore, 1970-74; Dep. Sec., Dept of For. Affairs, Canberra, 1974-76; Ambassador to the US, 1976-77; Sec., Dept of For. Affairs, Canberra, 1977-79. *Recreations:* tennis, bridge. *Address:* 3120 Cleveland Avenue NW, Washington, DC 20008, USA. *T:* Washington 7973235. *Club:* Commonwealth (Canberra).

PARKINSON, Norman, CBE 1981; photographer; *b* 21 April 1913; *m* 1945, Wenda (*née* Rogerson); one *s. Educ:* Westminster School. Always a photographer of people old and young, horses, birds, still-life, active life, fashion, reportage and travel. Has recently photographed, together and separately, all members of the Royal Family (in particular 21st Birthday and Engagement pictures of HRH The Princess Anne, and official 80th Birthday photographs of Queen Elizabeth, the Queen Mother, incl. the stamp issued to mark the occasion). Retrospective Exhibn, Fifty Years of Portraits and Fashion, National Portrait Gall., 1981. *Publications:* Life, Look Magazines, (USA); continually contributing to all the Vogues; his photographs have appeared in almost all the world's periodicals; Sisters Under the Skin (photographs, with text by leading authors), 1978; Photographs by Norman Parkinson, 1981. *Recreations:* pig farming (manufactures the famous Porkinson banger in Tobago); sun worshipping, bird watching, breeding Creole racehorses. *Address:* Tobago, West Indies. *T:* none fortunately. *Clubs:* Annabel's; Union (Trinidad); Turf (Tobago).

PARKINSON, Ronald Dennis; Assistant Keeper in charge of Education, Victoria and Albert Museum, since 1978; *b* 27 April 1945; *s* of Albert Edward Parkinson and Jennie Caroline Clara Meager. *Educ:* St Dunstan's Coll.; Clare Coll., Cambridge (MA). Res. Assistant: Paul Mellon Foundn for British Art, 1971-72; V&A Mus., 1972-74; Asst Keeper, Tate Gall., 1974-78. *Publications:* articles in Apollo, Burlington Mag., Cambridge Res., Connoisseur, Country Life, Times Higher Educn Sup. *Recreations:* reading, shopping. *Address:* Victoria and Albert Museum, South Kensington, SW7 2RL. *T:* 01-589 6371. *Club:* Algonquin.

PARKINSON, Thomas Harry, CBE 1972; DL; Town Clerk, 1960-72, Clerk of the Peace, 1970-72, Birmingham; *b* Bilston, 25 June 1907; *y s* of G. R. J. Parkinson; *m* 1936, Joan Catherine, *d* of C. J. Douglas-Osborn; two *s* one *d. Educ:* Bromsgrove; Birmingham University. LLB Hons 1929. Admitted Solicitor, 1930. RAF, 1939-45. Asst Solicitor, Birmingham Corp., 1936-49; Dep. Town Clerk, Birmingham, 1949-60. Pres., Birmingham Law Soc., 1969-70. Sec., W Midlands Passenger Transport Authority, 1969-72; Member: Water Services Staff Adv. Commn, 1973-78; W Midlands Rent Assessment Panel, 1972-78; Sec., Nat Exhibn Centre Ltd, 1972-78; Hon. Member: Birmingham Assoc. of Mech. Engrs; Inst. of Housing. DL Warwickshire, 1970. Hon. DSc Aston, 1972. *Recreations:* walking, sailing, gardening. *Address:* Stuart House, Middlefield Lane, Hagley, Worcs. *T:* Hagley 882422.

PARKS, Sir Alan (Guyatt), Kt 1977; MD; FRCP, FRCPE, FRCS; Consultant Surgeon to the London Hospital and St Mark's Hospital, since 1959; *b* 19 Dec. 1920; *s* of Harry Parks and Grace Parks; *m* 1956, Caroline Jean Cranston; three *s* one *d. Educ:* Epsom Coll.; Brasenose Coll., Oxford (Exhibnr; MA, MCh); Johns Hopkins Univ. Med. Sch. (Rockefeller Student; MD); Guy's Hosp. Med. Sch. FRCS 1948; FRCP 1976; FRCPE 1981. Captain, RAMC, 1950-52. Med. Internship, Johns Hopkins Hosp., 1945-46; house appts, Guy's Hosp., 1946, registrar appts, 1952-59. Hon. Consultant in Colon and Rectal Surgery to the Army, 1974-. Hunterian Prof., RCS, 1965. Pres., Sect. Proctol., RSocMed. 1974-75, Chm., Jt Consultants Cttee, 1974-79. Mem. Council, RCS, 1971- (Pres., 1980-); Chm., Conference of Medical Royal Colls, 1982; Lectures: Howard M. Frykman Meml, Minnesota, 1978; Fleming, RCPGlas, 1979; Sir Arthur Hurst, British Soc. of Gastroenterology, 1980; William Mitchell Banks Meml, Univ. of Liverpool, 1982. Pres., Assoc. Européenne et Méditerranéenne de Colo-Proctologie, 1979-81. Hon. FRCSEd 1981; Hon. FRCSGlas 1981; Hon. Fellow: Amer. Soc. of Colon and Rectal Surgeons, 1975-; Amer. Coll. of Surgeons, 1981; RACS, 1982; Royal Coll. of Physicians and Surgeons of Canada, 1982; Corresp. Mem., Deutsche Gesell. für Chirurgie, 1980. Ernst Jung Prize for Medicine, 1980; Cecil Joll Prize, RCS, 1981; Nessim Habif Prize, Univ. of Geneva, 1981. *Publications:* articles on various aspects of intestinal surgery in med. jls. *Recreations:* natural history; formerly Rugby and athletics for Oxford University. *Address:* 33 Alwyne Road, N1 2HW. *T:* 01-226 8045. *Club:* Athenæum.

PARKYN, Brian (Stewart); General Manager, Training Services, British Caledonian Airways Ltd, since 1981; Director: Scott Bader Ltd, since 1953; Hunting Industrial Plastics Ltd, since 1979; *b* 28 April 1923; *o s* of Leslie and Gwen Parkyn, Whetstone, N20; *m* 1951, Janet Anne, *o d* of Charles and Jessie Stormer, Eastbourne; one *s* one *d. Educ:* King Edward VI Sch., Chelmsford; technical colleges. Principal, Glacier Inst. of Management (Associated Engineering Ltd), 1976-80. British Plastics Federation: Chm., Reinforced Plastics Gp, 1961-63; Mem. Council, 1959-75. Vice Pres., Rubber and Plastics Inst., 1972-75. Has travelled widely and lectured in N and S America, Africa, Australasia, India, Japan, USSR and China, etc.; Plastics Lectr, Worshipful Co. of Horners, 1967. Contested (Lab) Bedford, 1964; MP (Lab) Bedford, 1966-70; Mem., Select Cttee on Science and Technology, 1967-70; Chm., Sub-Cttee on Carbon Fibres, 1969; contested (Lab) Bedford, Oct. 1974. Member: Council, Cranfield Inst. of Technology, 1971-; Council, RSA, 1976- (Hon. Treas., 1977-82). FPRI. *Publications:* Democracy, Accountability and Participation in Industry, 1979; various papers and books on polyester resins and reinforced plastics. *Recreations:* writing, industrial democracy. *Address:* 9 Clarendon Square, Leamington Spa, Warwicks. *T:* Leamington 30066.

PARMOOR, 4th Baron *cr* 1914; **Milo Cripps;** *b* 18 June 1929; *s* of 3rd Baron Parmoor, DSO, TD, DL, and of Violet Mary Geraldine, *d* of Sir William Nelson, 1st Bt; *S* father, 1977. *Educ:* Ampleforth; Corpus Christi College, Oxford. *Heir: cousin* (Matthew) Anthony Leonard Cripps, *qv. Address:* Manor House, Sutton Veny, Wilts.

PARNELL, family name of **Baron Congleton.**

PARNIS, Alexander Edward Libor, CBE 1973; *b* 25 Aug. 1911; *s* of Alexander T. J. Parnis and Hetty Parnis (*née* Dams). *Educ:* Malvern Coll.; London Univ. BSc(Econ); MA (Cantab). Entered HM Consular Service, 1933: Acting British Vice-Consul, Paris, 1933-34; transferred to HM Treasury, 1937; Finance Officer, Friends' Ambulance Unit, 1941-45; returned to HM Treasury, 1945. Sec., Gowers Cttee on Houses of Outstanding Historic or Architectural Interest, 1950; Sec., Waverley Cttee on Export of Works of Art, etc, 1952; Treasurer, Univ. of Cambridge, 1953-62; Fellow, King's Coll., Cambridge, 1959-62; Asst Sec., Univ. Grants Cttee, 1962-72. Sec., Church's Main Cttee, 1973-81. *Recreations:* music, travel, cycling, walking. *Address:* 26 Ardilaun Road, N5 2QR. *T:* 01-226 2688. *Clubs:* Reform; The Casino (1852) (Malta).

PARR, Martin Willoughby, CBE 1944 (OBE 1929); Foundation Committee, Gordon Boys' School, Woking; *b* 22 Nov. 1892; *s* of Rev. Willoughby Chase Parr and Laura, *d* of Colonel Francklyn, Speen Hill Lodge, Newbury; unmarried. *Educ:* Winchester (Scholar); BNC Oxford (Scholar). Commissioned HLI (SR), 1914; served France 1914-15, Palestine 1917-18, France 1918 (wounded); Sudan Political Service, 1919; Private Secretary to Governor-General, 1927-33; Deputy Civil Secretary, 1933-34; Governor Upper Nile, 1934-36; Governor Equatoria, 1936-42; retired, 1942. Member: NABC Council, 1944; Vice-President: B&FBS, CMS and NABC; Alderman, LCC, 1954-61. *Recreations:* rifle-shooting; played Rugby football for Oxford 1913-14, half-blue rifle shooting, 1913-14. Shot for Sudan and for England in Elcho Shield at Bisley on several occasions. *Address:* Delves House, 31 Queen's Gate Terrace, SW7. *T:* 01-584 8639, 01-584 1334. *Clubs:* Royal Commonwealth Society; Vincent's (Oxford).

PARR, Stanley, CBE 1975; QPM 1968: Chief Constable of Lancashire, 1972-78; *b* 14 July 1917; *s* of Thomas Walmsley and Ada Parr; *m* 1943, Charlotte Lilian Wilson, St Helens; three *s. Educ:* St Helens, Lancashire. Joined Lancashire Constabulary, 1937. Served War: commissioned RNVR, 1942-46. Dep. Chief Constable, Blackpool, 1958; Chief Constable, Blackpool, 1962; Dep. Chief Constable, Lancashire, 1967. DL Lancs, 1976-78. OStJ 1970. *Address:* 2 Holly Road, Blackpool FY1 2SF.

PARRINDER, Prof. (Edward) Geoffrey (Simons); Professor of Comparative Study of Religions, University of London, at King's College, 1970-77, Professor Emeritus, 1977; *b* 30 April 1910; *s* of William Patrick and Florence Mary Parrinder; *m* 1936, Esther Mary Burt; two *s* one *d. Educ:* private sch.; Richmond Coll., London Univ.; Faculté libre de théologie protestante, Montpellier. MA, PhD, DD London. Minister of Methodist Church, Dahomey and Ivory Coast, 1933; ordained 1936; Principal, Séminaire Protestant, Dahomey, 1936-40, 1945-46; Methodist Church: Redruth, 1940; Dahomey, 1943; Guernsey, 1946; Lectr in Religious Studies, 1949, Sen. Lectr, 1950-58, UC Ibadan; Reader in Comparative Study of Religions, Univ. of London, 1958-70; Dean, Faculty of Theology, KCL, 1972-74. Mem. Editorial Bd of Religious Studies and Jl of Religion in Africa. Hon. Sec., Internat. Assoc. for History of Religions, British Br., 1960-72, Pres., 1972-77. Pres., London Soc. for Study of Religion, 1980-; Co-Pres., London Soc. of Jews and Christians, 1981-. Lectures: Charles Strong (Australian Church), 1964; Wilde, in Natural and Comparative Religion, Oxford Univ., 1966-69; Teape, Delhi, Madras, 1973. Vis. Prof., Internat. Christian Univ., Tokyo, 1977-78; Vis. Lectr, Surrey Univ., 1978-82. FKC 1972; Hon. DLitt Lancaster, 1975. *Publications:* West African Religion, 1949; Bible and Polygamy, 1950; West African Psychology, 1951; Religion in an African City, 1953; African Traditional Religion, 1954; Story of Ketu, 1956; Introduction to Asian Religions, 1957; Witchcraft, 1958; (ed) African Ideas of God, 1961; Worship in the World's Religions, 1961; Comparative Religion, 1962; Upanishads, Gita and Bible, 1962; What World Religions Teach, 1963; The Christian Debate, 1964; The World's Living Religions, 1965; A Book of World Religions, 1965; Jesus in the Qur'an, 1965; African Mythology, 1967; Religion in Africa, 1969 repr. as Africa's Three Religions, 1976; Avatar and Incarnation, 1970; Dictionary of Non-Christian Religions, 1971; (ed) Man and his Gods, 1971; The Indestructible Soul, 1973; Themes for Living, 1973; The Bhagavad Gita, a Verse Translation, 1974; Something after Death?, 1974; The Wisdom of the Forest, 1975; Mysticism in the World's Religions, 1976; The Wisdom of the Early Buddhists, 1977; Sex in the World's Religions, 1980; articles and reviews in Times Lit. and Educnl Supplements, and jls of theology, African and Asian religions and Annual Register, 1958-. *Recreations:* travel, gardening, literature. *Address:* 31 Charterhouse Road, Orpington, Kent. *T:* Orpington 23887.
See also D. M. Boston.

PARRIS, Matthew Francis; MP (C) West Derbyshire, since 1979; *b* 7 Aug. 1949; *s* of Leslie Francis Parris and Theresa Eunice Parris (*née* Littler). *Educ:* Waterford School, Swaziland; Clare Coll., Cambridge (BA Hons); Yale Univ., USA (Paul Mellon Fellowship). Foreign Office, 1974-76; Conservative Research Dept, 1976-79. *Recreation:* distance running. *Address:* 41 Bramfield Road, SW11.

PARRISH, Alfred Sherwen; Chief Constable, Derbyshire, since 1981; *b* 21 Feb. 1931; *s* of Claude Tunstall Parrish and Georgena Parrish (*née* Sherwen); *m* 1953, Amy Johnston; one *s* one *d. Educ:* Whitehaven (West Cumberland) Grammar School. FBIM. Joined Cumberland and Westmorland Constabulary, 1953; Police Constable, Traffic, CID; Det/Sgt 1964; transf. to E Riding of Yorkshire, Det/Inspector 1966; Head of CID, 1967; York and NE Yorks Police, 1968, Supt; West Mercia Police, 1973, Chief Supt; Director,

Police Staff Coll., Bramshill, Hants, 1976; Asst Chief Constable (Operations), N Yorkshire Police, 1976-79; Dep. Chief Constable, Derbyshire, 1979. *Recreations:* music, photography, golf. *Address:* Police Headquarters, Butterley Hall, Ripley, Derbyshire DE5 3RS. *T:* Ripley 43551. *Club:* Special Forces.

PARROTT, Sir Cecil (Cuthbert), KCMG 1964 (CMG 1953); OBE 1947; MA; FRSL 1979; Hon. FIL; Professor Emeritus in Central and South-Eastern European Studies, University of Lancaster; Founder, and Hon. Pres., Comenius Centre, University of Lancaster (Director, 1968-76); *b* 29 Jan. 1909; *s* of Engineer Captain Jasper W. A. Parrott, RN, and Grace Edith West; *m* 1935, Ellen Julie, *d* of Hermann and Marie Matzow, Trondhjem, Norway; three *s. Educ:* Berkhamsted Sch.; Peterhouse, Cambridge. Asst Master at Christ's Hospital and at Edinburgh Acad., 1931-34. Tutor to King Peter of Yugoslavia, at Belgrade, 1934-39; HM Legation, Oslo, 1939-40; Stockholm, 1940-45; HM Embassy, Prague, 1945-48; Foreign Office, 1948-50; Head of UN Political Dept, 1950-52; Principal Political Adviser to UK Delegation to the United Nations, 1951-52; Counsellor, HM Embassy, Brussels, 1952-54; HM Minister, Moscow, 1954-57; Director of Research, Librarian and Keeper of the Papers, at the Foreign Office, 1957-60; Ambassador to Czechoslovakia, 1960-66; Univ. of Lancaster: Prof. of Russian and Soviet Studies, 1966-71; Prof. of Central and SE Europ. Studies, 1971-76. *Publications:* The Good Soldier Svejk (first complete English trans.), 1973; The Tightrope (memoirs), 1975; The Serpent and The Nightingale (memoirs), 1977; The Bad Bohemian Hašek, 1977; trans. The Red Commissar and Other Tales, short stories of J. Hašek, 1981; Hašek, a study of Svejk and the short stories, 1982; various articles and broadcast talks on Slavonic history, music, art and literature. *Recreations:* music, theatre, literature, languages. *Address:* c/o University of Lancaster, Bailrigg, Lancaster LA1 4YN.

PARRY, family name of **Baron Parry.**

PARRY, Baron *cr* 1975 (Life Peer), of Neyland, Dyfed; **Gordon Samuel David Parry;** Chairman, Wales Tourist Board, since 1978; *b* 30 Nov. 1925; *s* of Thomas Lewis Parry and Anne Parry (*née* Evans); *m* 1948, Glenys Parry (*née* Incledon); one *d. Educ:* Neyland Board Sch.; Pembroke County Intermediate Sch.; Trinity Coll., Carmarthen; Univ. of Liverpool (Dipl. Advanced Educn). Teacher: Coronation Sch., Pembroke Dock, 1945-46; Llanstadwell Voluntary Primary Sch., Neyland, 1946-47; Barn St Voluntary Sch., Haverfordwest, 1947; County Primary Sch., Neyland, 1947-52; Librarian, Housemaster, County Sec. Sch., Haverfordwest, 1952-62 and 1963-68; Inst. of Educn, Univ. of Liverpool, 1962-63; Warden, Pembs Teachers' Centre, 1969-78. Former member: Welsh Develt Authority; Gen. Adv. Council, IBA; Welsh Arts Council; Schs Council Cttee for Wales; Member: Fac. of Educn, Univ. Coll. of Wales Aberystwyth; Council, Open Univ. (Chm., Adv. Cttee on Studies in Educn); British Tourist Authority, 1978-; President: Pembs Br., Multiple Sclerosis Soc.; Pembs Spastics Soc.; Spastics Soc., Wales; Commonwealth Games Appeal Cttee for Wales, 1979; Keep Wales Tidy Cttee, 1979-; Vice President: Nat. Chamber of Trade, 1980; Internat. Year of Disabled People in Wales, 1979; Nat. Soc. for Mentally Handicapped Children, S Wales Region; Soc. of Handicapped Drivers in Wales; Welsh Nat. Council of YMCAs. Contested (Lab) Monmouth 1959, Pembroke 1970, and Feb. and Oct. 1974. Writer, broadcaster, and TV panel Chm. Fellow, Tourism Soc. *Recreations:* travel; watching Welsh Rugby XV win the Grand Slam; reading. *Address:* Marlborough House, 164 Marlborough Road, Roath, Cardiff. *T:* Cardiff 491139.

PARRY, Emyr Owen; solicitor; a Recorder of the Crown Court, since 1979; *b* 26 May 1933; *s* of Ebenezer Owen Parry and Ellen Parry; *m* 1959, Enid Griffiths; one *s* one *d. Educ:* Caernarfon Grammar Sch.; University Coll. of Wales, Aberystwyth (LLB Hons Wales, 1954). Admitted solicitor, 1957. Estabd own practice in Llangefni, Anglesey, 1958; formed partnership (Emyr Parry & Davies) with Mrs Elinor C. Davies, 1964; Dep. Circuit Judge, 1975. Chm., National Insurance Appeals Tribunal, Holyhead Area, 1969-; Solicitor Mem., Lord Chancellor's County Court Rule Cttee, 1975-80. *Recreations:* cricket, music. *Address:* Bryn Meillion, Rhosmeirch, Llangefni, Anglesey, Gwynedd. *T:* Llangefni 722469. *Clubs:* Llangefni Cricket (Chm., Life Mem.); Anglesey County Cricket (Vice Pres.).

PARRY, Sir Ernest J.; *see* Jones-Parry.

PARRY, Sir Hugh (Nigel), Kt 1963; CBE 1954; *b* 26 Aug. 1911; *s* of Charles Frank Parry and Lilian Maud Parry (*née* Powell); *m* 1945, Ann Maureen Forshaw; two *d. Educ:* Cheltenham Coll.; Balliol Coll., Oxford. Entered Colonial Administrative Service, 1939. Chief Secretary, Central African Council, Salisbury, S Rhodesia, 1951-53; Secretary, Office of Prime Minister and External Affairs, Federal Government of Rhodesia and Nyasaland, 1953-63; Ministry of Overseas Development, 1965; Acting Head, Middle East Develt Div., 1969-71, retd 1971. *Recreations:* sailing, motoring. *Address:* c/o Grindlays Bank, 13 St James's Square, SW1.

PARRY, Mrs Margaret Joan; Headmistress of Heathfield School, Ascot, 1973-82; *b* 27 Nov. 1919; *d* of W. J. Tamplin, Llantrisant, Glamorgan; *m* 1946, Raymond Howard Parry; two *s* one *d. Educ:* Howell's Sch., Llandaff, Cardiff; Univ. of Wales. Hons English Cl I. Married to a schoolmaster at Eton; taught and coached interesting people from time to time; Examiner for: Civil Service, LCC, Schools Examination Boards. Mem. Council, Univ. Coll. at

Buckingham, 1975-. *Recreations:* books, music, tapestry. *Address:* 5 Gulliver's, Eton College, Windsor, Berks. *T:* Windsor 60902.

PARRY, Robert; MP (Lab) Liverpool, Scotland Exchange, since 1974 (Liverpool Exchange, 1970-74); *b* 8 Jan. 1933; *s* of Robert and Sarah Parry (*née* Joyce); *m* 1956, Marie (*née* Hesdon). *Educ:* Bishop Goss RC School, Liverpool. Became a building trade worker. Full-time organizer for National Union of Public Employees, 1960-67; now Member of Transport and General Workers' Union. Member of Co-operative Party. Member, Liverpool City Council, 1963-74, Labour Group Whip, 1967-70. Chm., Merseyside Gp of Labour MPs, 1976-. Patron: UNA Hong Kong, 1977-; Rotunda Boxing Club, 1975-; KIND (Kids in Need and Distress); President: Liverpool and Dist Sunday Football League (largest in Europe), 1973-; Assoc. for Democracy in Hong Kong, 1980-. Special interests: human rights, civil liberties, foreign affairs, particularly Central and SE Asia, overseas aid and the third world. *Address:* House of Commons, SW1A 0AA. *Club:* Scotland Exchange Labour.

PARRY, Robert Hughes; *see* Hughes Parry, R.

PARRY, Sir Thomas, Kt 1978; MA, DLitt (Wales); FBA 1959; President, National Library of Wales, 1969-77; Principal of the University College of Wales, Aberystwyth, 1958-69; *b* 14 Aug. 1904; *e s* of Richard and Jane Parry, Carmel, Caernarvonshire; *m* 1936, Enid, *o d* of Picton Davies, Cardiff. *Educ:* Pen-y-groes Grammar Sch.; University College of North Wales, Bangor. Assistant Lecturer in Welsh and Latin, University College, Cardiff, 1926-29; Lecturer in Welsh, University College, Bangor, 1929-47; Prof. of Welsh, 1947-53; Librarian of National Library of Wales, Aberystwyth, 1953-58; Vice-Chancellor, University of Wales, 1961-63, 1967-69; Chairman, UGC Cttee on Libraries, 1963-67. Pres., Hon. Soc. of Cymmrodorion, 1978-82 (Cymmrodorion Medal, 1976). Hon. Professorial Fellow, University Coll. of Wales, 1971-80. Hon. DLitt Celt. NUI; Hon. LLD Wales. *Publications:* Peniarth 49, 1929; Theater du Mond, 1930; Awdl "Mam", 1932; Saint Greal, 1933; Baledi'r Ddeunawfed Ganrif, 1935; Mynegai i Weithiau Ifor Williams, 1939; Hanes Llenyddiaeth Gymraeg, 1945; Llenyddiaeth Gymraeg, 1900-45, 1945; Hanes ein Llên, 1946; Lladd wrth yr Allor (translation of T. S. Eliot's Murder in the Cathedral), 1949; Gwaith Dafydd ap Gwilym, 1952; Llywelyn Fawr (a play), 1954; (ed) Oxford Book of Welsh Verse, 1962; (ed jtly) Llyfryddiaeth Llenyddiaeth Gymraeg, 1976; articles in Bulletin of Board of Celtic Studies, Trans. Hon. Society of Cymmrodorion, Y Traethodydd, Yr Athro, Yorkshire Celtic Studies. *Address:* Gwyndy, 2 Victoria Avenue, Bangor, Gwynedd LL57 2EP. *T:* Bangor 4460.

PARRY BROWN, Arthur Ivor; *see* Brown, A. I. P.

PARRY-EVANS, Air Vice-Marshal David, CBE 1978; Commandant, RAF Staff College, since 1981; *b* 19 July 1935; *s* of late Group Captain John Parry-Evans, MRCS, LRCP, DLO, and of Dorothy Parry-Evans; *m* 1960, Ann, 2nd *d* of late Charles Reynolds and of Gertrude Reynolds; two *s. Educ:* Berkhamsted School. Joined RAF, 1956; served FEAF, Coastal Command, United States Navy, RN Staff Coll., 1958-70; Headquarters Strike Command, 1970-74; OC 214 Sqn, 1974-75; OC RAF Marham, 1975-77; MoD, 1977-81: Director of Defence Policy, 1979-81. *Recreation:* Rugby (Chairman, RAFRU, 1978-). *Address:* 47 Pound Lane, Marlow, Buckinghamshire SL7 2AZ. *T:* Marlow 3405. *Club:* Royal Air Force.

PARRY EVANS, Mary Alethea, (Lady Hallinan); a Recorder of the Crown Court, since 1978; *b* 31 Oct. 1929; *o c* of Dr Evan Parry Evans, MD, JP, and Dr Lilian Evans; *m* 1955, Sir Adrian Lincoln Hallinan, *qv* ; two *s* two *d. Educ:* Malvern Girls' Coll.; Somerville Coll., Oxford (BCL, MA). Called to Bar, Inner Temple, 1953; Wales and Chester Circuit. Member: Cardiff City Council, 1961-70; S Glamorgan CC, 1972-; S Glamorgan Health Authority, 1977-. Lady Mayoress of Cardiff, 1969-70. *Address:* (home) 63 Cathedral Road, Cardiff. *T:* Cardiff 20511; (chambers) 33 Park Place, Cardiff. *T:* Cardiff 33313.

PARS, Dr Leopold Alexander, MA, ScD Cantab; Fellow, formerly President, of Jesus College, Cambridge; *b* 2 Jan. 1896; *o s* of late Albertus Maclean Pars and Emma Laura Pars (*née* Unwin). *Educ:* Latymer Upper School; Jesus Coll., Cambridge. Smith's Prizeman, 1921; Fellow of Jesus Coll., 1921-. University Lectr in Mathematics, Cambridge, 1926-61. Visiting Professor: Univ. of California, Berkeley, 1949; Florida Atlantic Univ., 1964; Univ. of Sydney, 1965. *Publications:* Introduction to Dynamics, 1953; Calculus of Variations, 1962; A Treatise on Analytical Dynamics, 1965. Papers on Mathematics in scientific jls. *Recreations:* rock climbing, travel, theatre. *Address:* Jesus College, Cambridge. *T:* Cambridge 68611. *Clubs:* Athenæum, United Oxford & Cambridge University.

PARSHALL, Horace Field, TD 1947; Receiver-General, Venerable Order of St John of Jerusalem, 1968-72 (Chancellor, 1961-66); *b* 16 June 1903; *o s* of late Horace Field Parshall, DSc, and Annie Matilda Rogers; *m* 1st, 1929, Hon. Ursula Mary Bathurst (marr. diss. 1942, she *d* 1976), *o d* of 1st Viscount Bledisloe; one *s* decd; 2nd, 1953, Margaret Savage, MB, BS, DPH (*d* 1961), *d* of late Captain Philip Alcock, DL, JP, Wilton Castle, Enniscorthy, and Overton Lodge, Ludlow; one *s* two *d* ; 3rd, 1965, Lady (Phyllis Gabrielle) Gore, *o d* of M. von den Porten, New York. *Educ:* Eton Coll.; New Coll., Oxford (MA). Barrister-at-Law, Inner Temple. Served War of 1939-45, with Oxford and Bucks Light Inf.; Hon. Major, TARO. Dep. Commissioner-in-

Chief, St John Ambulance Brigade, 1950; Director-General, St John Ambulance Assoc., 1951-60; Vice-Chancellor, Order of St John, 1960. Member Court of Assistants, Merchant Taylors' Company (Master, 1958-59); Director, Pyrene Co. Ltd, 1947-68 (Dep.-Chairman, 1962-68). GCStJ 1960. *Recreations:* reading and travel. *Address:* Flat 2, 55 Onslow Square, SW7. *T:* 01-589 3371. *Club:* Garrick.

PARSLOE, Charles Guy, MA; Secretary, Institute of Welding, 1943-67, Hon. Fellow, 1968; Vice-President, International Institute of Welding, 1966-69 (Secretary-General, 1948-66); *b* London, 5 Nov. 1900; *o* surv. *s* of Henry Edward Parsloe; *m* 1929, Mary Zirphie Munro, *e d* of J. G. Faiers, Putney; one *s* one *d. Educ:* Stationers' Company's School and University College, London. First Class hons. History, 1921; Franks student in Archæology, 1922; Secretary and Librarian, Institute of Historical Research, 1927-43; Assistant in History, University Coll., 1925-27. Secretary OEEC Welding Mission to USA, 1953; organised Commonwealth Welding Conferences, 1957, 1965; President, Junior Institution of Engineers, 1967. Hon. Freeman, Founders' Company, 1964. Pres., John Evelyn Soc. for Wimbledon, 1975-81. Wheatley Medal, Library Association, 1965; Edstrom Medal, Internat. Inst. of Welding, 1971. *Publications:* The English Country Town, 1932; The Minute Book of the Corporation of Bedford, 1647-64, 1949; some 400 bibliographies in the Cambridge Bibliography of English Literature, 1940; Wimbledon Village Club and Lecture Hall, 1858-1958, 1958; Wardens' Accounts of the Worshipful Company of Founders of the City of London, 1497-1681, 1964; (jtly) A Present from Seaview, 1979; papers on historical and bibliographical subjects. *Recreation:* historical research. *Address:* 1 Leopold Avenue, SW19 7ET. *T:* 01-946 0764. *Club:* Athenæum.
See also Phyllida Parsloe.

PARSLOE, Prof. Phyllida; Professor of Social Work, Bristol University, since 1978; *b* 25 Dec. 1930; *d* of C. G. Parsloe, *qv. Educ:* Bristol Univ. (BA, PhD); London Univ. (Cert. in Mental Health). Probation Officer, Devon CC, 1954-59; Psychiatric Social Worker, St George's Hospital, 1959-65; Lectr, London Sch. of Economics, 1965-70; Associate Prof., Sch. of Law, Indiana Univ., 1970-73; Prof. of Social Work, Univ. of Aberdeen, 1973-78. *Publications:* The Work of the Probation and After Care Officer, 1967; Juvenile Justice in Britain and America, 1978; (with Prof. O. Stevenson) Social Service Teams: the practitioner's view, 1978; Social Service Area Teams, 1981; contribs to: British Jl of Social Work, Community Care, Social Work Today, British Jl Criminology. *Recreations:* hill walking, crafts, gardening, squash. *Address:* 15 Elliston Road, Bristol BS6 6QG. *Club:* University Women's.

PARSONS, family name of **Earl of Rosse.**

PARSONS, Adrian; *see* Parsons, C. A. H.

PARSONS, Sir Anthony (Derrick), GCMG 1982 (KCMG 1975; CMG 1969); MVO 1965; MC 1945; HM Diplomatic Service, retired; United Kingdom Permanent Representative to the United Nations, 1979-82; *b* 9 Sept. 1922; *s* of late Col H. A. J. Parsons, MC; *m* 1948, Sheila Emily Baird; two *s* two *d. Educ:* King's Sch., Canterbury; Balliol Coll., Oxford. HM Forces, 1940-54; Asst Mil. Attaché, Baghdad, 1952-54; Foreign Office, 1954-55; HM Embassy: Ankara, 1955-59; Amman, 1959-60; Cairo, 1960-61; FO, 1961-64; HM Embassy, Khartoum, 1964-65; Political Agent, Bahrain, 1965-69; Counsellor, UK Mission to UN, NY, 1969-71; Under-Sec., FCO, 1971-74; Ambassador to Iran, 1974-79; FCO, 1979. Order of the Two Niles (Sudan), 1965. *Recreations:* modern poetry, tennis. *Address:* 53 Peckarmans Wood, SE26 6RZ. *Clubs:* MCC, English-Speaking Union.

PARSONS, (Charles) Adrian (Haythorne); Charity Commissioner since 1974; *b* 15 June 1929; *s* of Dr R. A. Parsons and Mrs W. S. Parsons (*née* Haythorne); *m* 1951, Hilary Sharpe; one *d. Educ:* Bembridge Sch.; Wadham Coll., Oxford. Called to Bar, Gray's Inn, 1964. Coutts & Co., Bankers, 1952-64; joined Charity Commn, 1964; Dep. Comr, 1972. *Address:* c/o Charity Commission, 14 Ryder Street, St James's, SW1Y 6AH. *Club:* United Oxford & Cambridge University.
See also Sir R. E. C. F. Parsons.

PARSONS, Geoffrey Penwill, OBE 1977; concert accompanist; *b* 15 June 1929; *s* of Francis Hedley Parsons and Edith Vera Buckland. *Educ:* Canterbury High Sch., Sydney; State Conservatorium of Music (with Winifred Burston), Sydney. Winner ABC Concerto Competition, 1947; first tour of Australia, 1948; arrived England, 1950; has accompanied many of world's greatest singers and instrumentalists, incl. Elisabeth Schwarzkopf, Victoria de los Angeles, Nathan Milstein, Paul Tortelier, Janet Baker, in 40 countries of world on all six continents. Master Classes, South Bank Summer Festival, 1977 and 1978. Harriet Cohen Internat. Music Award, 1968. Hon. RAM, 1975. *Address:* 176 Iverson Road, NW6 2HL. *T:* 01-624 0957.

PARSONS, Mrs J. D.; *see* Beer, Patricia.

PARSONS, Sir (John) Michael, Kt 1970; Deputy Chairman and Chief Executive, 1979-81, Senior Managing Director, 1976-81, Director, 1971-81, Inchcape & Co. Ltd; Deputy Chairman and Director, Inchcape Insurance Holdings Ltd, 1979; Chairman and Director, Paxall Investments Ltd, 1982; Director, Commonwealth Development Finance Co. Ltd, since 1973; *b* 29 Oct. 1915; *s* of late Rt Rev. Richard Godfrey Parsons, DD, Bishop of Hereford; *m* 1st, 1946, Hilda Mary Frewen (marr. diss. 1964); one *s* two *d* ;

2nd, 1964, Caroline Inagh Margaret Frewen. *Educ:* Rossall Sch.; University Coll., Oxford. Barry & Co., Calcutta, 1937. Served in Royal Garhwal Rifles (Indian Army), 1939-45: Bde Major, 1942; POW, Singapore, 1942. Macneill & Barry Ltd, Calcutta, 1946-70; Chm. & Managing Dir., 1964-70; Chm., Macdonald Hamilton & Co. Pty Ltd, 1970-72; Chm. and Dir, Assam Investments, 1976-81. Vice-Chm., Indian Jute Mills Assoc., 1960-61; President: Bengal Chamber of Commerce, 1968-69; Associated Chambers of Commerce of India, 1969; Chm., UK Cttee, Fedn of Commonwealth Chambers of Commerce, 1974; Mem., Advisory Council on Trade, Bd of Trade, India, 1968-69. Chm. Council, Royal Commonwealth Soc., 1976-80, Vice Pres., 1980-; Pres., India, Pakistan and Bangladesh Assoc., 1973-78, Vice Pres., 1978. Mem., Internat. Bd, United World Colls, 1981-. *Recreation:* golf. *Address:* Tall Trees, Warren Hill Lane, Aldeburgh, Suffolk IP15 5QB. *T:* Aldeburgh 2917. *Clubs:* Oriental; Bengal, Tollygunge (Calcutta); Union (Sydney).

PARSONS, Kenneth Charles, CMG 1970; OBE 1962; HM Diplomatic Service, retired; Counsellor, Foreign and Commonwealth Office, 1972-80; *b* 9 Jan. 1921; *m* 1st, 1949, Monica (*née* Howell) (decd); two *d* ; 2nd, 1977, Mary Woolhouse. *Educ:* Haverfordwest Grammar Sch.; Exeter Coll., Oxford. Served War of 1939-45: with Oxfordshire and Buckinghamshire LI, 1941-46. 1st Class Hons, Mod. Langs (at Oxford), 1948. Joined Diplomatic Service, 1949; served FO, Moscow, Tokyo, Rangoon and Athens, 1951-72; FCO, 1972-77; Counsellor, with British Forces, Hong Kong, 1977-79. *Recreations:* rowing, swimming, walking. *Address:* Grove End, Lower Park Road, Chipstead, Surrey. *T:* Downland 53907. *Club:* Carlton.

PARSONS, Sir Michael; *see* Parsons, Sir J. M.

PARSONS, Peter John, FBA 1977; Lecturer in Papyrology, University of Oxford, since 1965; Student of Christ Church, Oxford, since 1964; *b* 24 Sept. 1936; *s* of Robert John Parsons and Ethel Ada (*née* Frary). *Educ:* Raynes Park County Grammar Sch.; Christ Church, Oxford (MA 1961). Oxford University: Craven Scholar, 1955; 1st Cl. Hons Mods and de Paravicini Scholar, 1956; Chancellor's Prize for Latin Verse and Gaisford Prize for Greek Verse, 1st Cl. Lit. Hum., Derby Scholar, Dixon and Sen. Scholar of Christ Church, 1958; Passmore Edwards Scholar, 1959; Lectr in Documentary Papyrology, 1960-65; J. H. Gray Lectr, Univ. of Cambridge, 1982. *Publications:* (jtly) The Oxyrhynchus Papyri XXXI, 1966, XXXIII and XXXIV, 1968; The Oxyrhynchus Papyri XLII, 1974; (with H. Lloyd-Jones) Supplementum Hellenisticum, 1982; articles in learned jls. *Recreations:* music, cinema, cooking and eating. *Address:* Christ Church, Oxford OX1 1DP. *T:* Oxford 43979.

PARSONS, Sir Richard (Edmund Clement Fownes), KCMG 1982 (CMG 1977); HM Diplomatic Service; Ambassador to Spain, since 1980; *b* 14 March 1928; *s* of Dr R. A. Parsons; *m* 1960, Jenifer Jane Mathews (*d* 1981); three *s. Educ:* Bembridge Sch.; Brasenose Coll., Oxford. Served in Army, 1949-51; joined HM Foreign (subseq. Diplomatic) Service, 1951; FO, 1951-53; 3rd Sec., Washington, 1953-56; 2nd Sec., Vientiane, 1956-58; FO, 1958-60; 1st Sec., Buenos Aires, 1960-63; FO, 1963-65; 1st Sec., Ankara, 1965-67; FO, 1967-69; Counsellor, Lagos, 1969-72; Head of Personnel Ops Dept, FCO, 1972-76; Ambassador to Hungary, 1976-79. *Recreations:* reading, writing, music, travel. *Address:* c/o Foreign and Commonwealth Office, King Charles Street, SW1. *Club:* Travellers'.

See also C. A. H. Parsons.

PARSONS, Roger, PhD, DSc; FRS 1980; FRSC; Director, Laboratoire d'Electrochimie Interfaciale, Centre National de la Recherche Scientifique, Meudon, France, since 1977; *b* 31 Oct. 1926; *s* of Robert Harry Ashby Parsons and Ethel Fenton; *m* 1953, Ruby Millicent Turner; three *s* one *d. Educ:* King Alfred Sch., Hampstead; Strathcona High Sch., Edmonton, Alta; Imperial Coll. of Science and Technol., (BSc, PhD). DSc Bristol 1962; ARCS 1946; FRIC 1962. Asst Lectr, Imp. Coll. of Science and Technol., 1948-50; Deedes Fellow, Dundee Univ., 1950-54; Lectr, then Reader in Electrochem., Bristol Univ., 1954-79. Unesco Specialist, Buenos Aires, 1961; Vis. Prof., Calif Inst. of Technol., 1966-67. Hon. Fellow, Polish Chem. Soc., 1981. Palladium Medal, US Electrochem. Soc., 1979. Editor, Jl of Electroanal. Chem., 1962-. *Publications:* Electrochemical Data, 1956; *circa* 130 papers in scientific jls. *Recreations:* listening to music, going to the opera. *Address:* 3 Petite Place, 78000 Versailles, France. *T:* 951 44 85.

PARSONS, Thomas Alan, LLB; Principal Assistant Solicitor, Department of Health and Social Security, since 1977; *b* 25 Nov. 1924; *s* of late Arthur and Laura Parsons; *m* 1st, 1947, Valerie Vambeck; one *s* ; 2nd, 1957, Muriel Lewis; two *s. Educ:* Clifton Coll.; Bristol Univ. (LLB). Called to the Bar, Middle Temple, 1950. Served, Royal Marines, 1943-46. Legal Asst, Min. of Nat. Insurance, 1950; Sen. Legal Asst, Min. of Pensions and Nat. Insurance, 1955; Asst Solicitor, DHSS, 1968. *Recreations:* walking, listening to music. *Address:* 18 St James' Mansions, West End Lane, NW6 2AA. *T:* 01-624 6974. *Club:* University Women's (Dining Mem.).

PARSONS-SMITH, Basil Gerald, OBE 1945; MA, MD, FRCP; Hon. Consulting Neurologist, Charing Cross Hospital; Hon. Consulting Physician, St Mary's Hospital Group; Teacher in Medicine, London University; *b* 19 Nov. 1911; *s* of late Dr Basil Parsons-Smith, FRCP, and Marguerite, *d* of Sir David Burnett, 1st Bt; *m* 1939, Aurea Mary, *d* of late William Stewart Johnston, Sunningdale; two *s* one *d. Educ:* Harrow; Trinity Coll., Cambridge.

St George's Hospital; Entrance Exhib., 1933; Brackenbury Prize in Medicine, 1936; House Surgeon, House Physician, Med. Registrar. Physician: Western Ophthalmic Hospital (St Mary's), 1938-60; Electro Encephalograph Dept, Middlesex Hospital Medical Sch., 1950-55; Dept of Neurology, West London and Charing Cross Hosps, 1950-77; Graylingwell Hosp., Chichester, 1950; West End Hosp. for Neurology, 1951-72; Neurologist, Florence Nightingale Hosp., 1955. MRCP 1939. Served War of 1939-45, as Blood Transfusion Officer, Chelsea EMS, then as medical specialist i/c medical divisions in RAF Hospitals in ME; Sqdn Leader RAFVR (despatches, OBE). MD (Cantab) 1949, Prox. Acc. Raymond Horton-Smith Prize; FRCP 1955. Examiner, RCP. FRSocMed. Member: Med. Appeals Trib., 1966-83; Association of British Neurologists; Ophthalmic Society of UK. Liveryman, Society of Apothecaries. Appeared in Hospital 1922, BBC TV, 1972. *Publications:* Electro Encephalographic Studies, 1949; 56 contribs to medical, neurological and ophthalmic jls mostly on the immediate treatment of acute stroke of the brain and eye. *Recreation:* managing riding school. *Address:* Roughets House, Bletchingley, Surrey RH1 4QX. *T:* Caterham 43929. *Clubs:* Army and Navy; Pitt (Cambridge).

PART, Sir Antony (Alexander), GCB 1974 (KCB 1966; CB 1959); MBE 1943; Chairman, Orion Insurance Company; Director: Life Association of Scotland; Lucas Industries; Metal Box; Savoy Hotel Group; *b* 28 June 1916; *s* of late Alexander Francis Part and late Una Margaret Reynolds (*née* Snowdon); *m* 1940, Isabella Bennett; no *c. Educ:* Wellesley House, Broadstairs; Harrow; Trinity Coll., Cambridge. First Class Hons Modern and Mediæval Langs Tripos. Entered Board of Education, 1937; Asst Private Secretary to successive Ministers of Supply, 1939-40. Served War of 1939-45 (despatches); Army Service, 1940-44; Lt-Col GS(1), 21st Army Group, 1944. Principal Private Secretary to successive Ministers of Education, 1945-46; Home Civil Service Commonwealth Fund Fellow to USA, 1950-51; Under-Secretary, Ministry of Education, 1954-60; Deputy Secretary: Ministry of Education, 1960-63; MPBW, 1963-65; Permanent Secretary: MPBW, 1965-68; BoT, 1968-70; DTI, 1970-74; DoI, 1974-76. Director: Debenhams, 1976-80; EMI, 1976-80. Chairman: Cttee on N Sea Oil Taxation, 1981; Adv. Panel on tech. transmission standards for UK services of direct broadcasting by satellite, 1982; Mem. Council, Regular Forces Employment Assoc., 1982-; Governor, Administrative Staff Coll., 1968-; Vice-Chm. of Governors, LSE, 1979- (Governor, 1968-). Hon. DTech Brunel, 1966; Hon. DSc: Aston, 1974; Cranfield, 1976. CBIM. *Recreation:* travel. *Address:* Flat 5, 71 Elm Park Gardens, SW10. *T:* 01-352 2950. *Clubs:* MCC, United Oxford & Cambridge University.

PARTON, Prof. John Edwin; Professor of Electrical Engineering, University of Nottingham, 1954-78, now Emeritus; *b* Kingswinford, Staffordshire, 26 Dec. 1912; *s* of Edwin and Elizabeth Parton; *m* 1940, Gertrude Brown; one *s* one *d. Educ:* Huntington Church of England Sch.; Cannock Chase Mining Coll.; University of Birmingham. BSc (1st Class Hons), 1936, PhD, 1938, Birmingham; DSc Glasgow, 1971. Training: Littleton Collieries, 1934; Electrical Construction Co., 1935; Asst Engineer, PO Engineering Dept, Dollis Hill Research Station, 1938-39; Part-time Lecturer: Cannock Chase Mining Coll., 1931-38; Northampton Polytechnic, 1938-39. Served RNVR Electrical Branch, Sub-Lt, 1939, to Lt-Comdr, 1943-45. Sen. Sci. Officer, British Iron and Steel Research Assoc., 1946; Lecturer, 1946-54, Senior Lecturer, 1954, University of Glasgow. Sen. Vis. Scientist, Nat. Sci. Foundn at Univ. of Tennessee, 1965-66; Vis. Prof., Univ. of W Indies, Trinidad, 1979, 1980. Chairman, East Midland Centre Institution of Electrical Engineers, 1961-62. FIEE 1966; Sen. Mem. IEEE 1966; FIMechE 1967. *Publications:* Applied Electromagnetics (jtly), 1975; papers in Proc. IEE, Trans. IEEE, Trans. IES, Instrument Practice, International Journal of Electrical Engineering Education, etc. *Recreations:* golf, gardening, bowls. *Address:* 6 Coopers Green, Wollaton, Nottingham NG8 2RP. *T:* Nottingham 286942.

PARTRIDGE, Bernard B.; *see* Brook-Partridge.

PARTRIDGE, Derek William; HM Diplomatic Service; Counsellor and Head of Migration and Visa Department, Foreign and Commonwealth Office, since 1981; *b* 15 May 1931; *o s* of Ernest and Ethel Elizabeth Partridge (*née* Buckingham), Wembley. *Educ:* Preston Manor County Grammar Sch., Wembley. Entered Foreign Service (later Diplomatic Service), 1949. Royal Air Force, 1949-51. Served: Foreign Office, 1951-54; Oslo, 1954-56; Jedda, 1956; Khartoum, 1957-60; Sofia, 1960-62; Bangkok, 1962; Manila, 1962-65; Djakarta, 1965-67; FCO, 1967-70; Diplomatic Service Inspectorate, 1970-72; British Consul-General, Brisbane, 1972-74; First Sec. (Economic and Commercial), Colombo, 1974-77; FCO, 1977-. *Address:* 54 Chester Court, Albany Street, NW1.

PARTRIDGE, Harry Cowderoy; Member of Civil Aviation Authority since 1974, Controller Finance and Administration since 1975; *b* 29 Aug. 1925; *y s* of late Harry Ewart Partridge and Edith Cowderoy; *m* 1st, 1950, Margaret Neill Cadzow (*d* 1967), *o d* of Charles J. M. Cadzow, OBE; two *s* one *d* ; 2nd, 1973, Jeanne Margaret Henderson; one *s. Educ:* George Watson's Coll., Edinburgh; Edinburgh Univ. CA. Air-gunner, RAF, 1943-47. Company Accountant, McGrouther Ltd, 1955-59; Plant Controller, IBM UK Ltd, 1959-63; Sec., George Kent Ltd, 1963, Financial Dir 1965-71; Controller of Finance and Planning, CAA, 1972. *Recreations:* house and garden. *Address:* Rushey Ford House, Box End, Kempston, Beds. *T:* Bedford 851594. *Club:* Savile.

PARTRIDGE, Ian (Harold); concert singer (tenor); *b* 12 June 1938; *s* of Harold Partridge and Ena Stinson; *m* 1959, Ann Glover; two *s. Educ:* New Coll., Oxford (chorister); Clifton Coll. (music scholar); Royal Coll. of Music; Guildhall Sch. of Music (LGSM, singing and teaching). Began as piano accompanist, although sang tenor in Westminster Cath. Choir, 1958-62; full-time concert singer, 1963-; performs in England and all over the world, both in recitals (with sister Jennifer) and in concerts; has worked with many leading conductors, incl. Stokowski, Boult, Giulini, Boulez and Colin Davis. Opera debut at Covent Garden as Iopas in Berlioz, Les Troyens, 1969. Title role, Britten's St Nicolas, Thames Television (Prix Italia, 1977). Many records and radio broadcasts. Governor, Clifton Coll., 1981-. *Recreations:* bridge, horse racing (strictly watching), cricket. *Address:* 127 Pepys Road, SW20 8NP. *T:* 01-946 7140.

PARTRIDGE, John Albert, CBE 1981; ARA; FRIBA; architect in private practice; a Senior and Founder Partner, Howell, Killick, Partridge & Amis (HKPA), since 1959; *b* 26 Aug. 1924; *s* of George and Gladys Partridge; *m* 1953, Doris (*née* Foreman); one *s* one *d. Educ:* Shooter's Hill Grammar Sch., Woolwich; Polytechnic School of Architecture, Regent Street. FRIBA 1966 (ARIBA 1951); ARA 1980. London County Council Housing Architects Dept, 1951-59. The work of HKPA includes universities, colleges, public buildings and housing; principal commissions include: Wolfson, Rayne and Gatehouse building, St Anne's Coll., Oxford; New Hall and Common Room building, St Antony's Coll., Oxford; Wells Hall, Reading Univ.; Middlesex Polytechnic College of Art, Cat Hill; Medway Magistrates Court; The Albany, Deptford; Hall of Justice, Trinidad and Tobago. Vice-Pres., RIBA, 1977-79, Hon. Librarian, 1977-81. External Examiner in Architecture: Bath Univ., 1975-78; Thames Polytechnic, 1978-; Cambridge Univ., 1979-81; Manchester Univ., 1982-. Governor, Building Centre Trust, 1982-. *Publications:* articles in technical press. *Recreations:* looking at buildings, travel, sketching and taking photographs. *Address:* Cudham Court, Cudham, near Sevenoaks, Kent TN14 7QF. *T:* Biggin Hill 71294.

PARTRIDGE, Michael John Anthony; Deputy Secretary, Department of Health and Social Security, since 1981; *b* 29 Sept. 1935; *s* of late Dr John Henry Partridge, DSc, PhD, and of Ethel Green; *m* 1968, Joan Elizabeth Hughes; two *s* one *d. Educ:* Merchant Taylors'; St John's Coll., Oxford. BA (1st Cl. Hons. Mods and Lit Hum) 1960, MA 1963. Entered Home Civil Service (Min. of Pensions and Nat. Insce), 1960; Private Sec. to Permanent Sec., 1962-64; Principal, 1964-71 (MPNI, Min. of Social Security and DHSS); Asst Sec., 1971-76, Under Sec., 1976-81. *Recreations:* Do-it-Yourself, Greece, reading, skiing. *Address:* 27 High View, Pinner, HA5 3NZ. *T:* 01-868 0657. *Club:* United Oxford & Cambridge University.

PARTRIDGE, Prof. (Stanley) Miles, FRS 1970; Professor of Biochemistry, University of Bristol, since 1976; *b* Whangarei, NZ, 2 Aug. 1913; *s* of Ernest Joseph Partridge and Eve Partridge (later Eve McCarthy) (*d* 1977); *m* 1940, Ruth Dowling; four *d. Educ:* Harrow County Sch.; Battersea Coll. of Technology. PhD Chemistry 1937; MA 1946, ScD 1964, Cantab. Beit Memorial Fellow, Lister Inst. of Preventive Medicine, 1940; Techn. Adviser, Govt of India, 1944; returned to Low Temperature Stn, Cambridge, 1946; Principal Scientific Officer 1952; Dep. Chief Scientific Officer, ARC, 1964; Head of Dept of Biochem. and Physiol., ARC Meat Research Inst., 1968-78. Member: Biochemical Soc. Cttee, 1957-61; Nuffield Foundn Rheumatism Cttee, 1965-77. Fourth Tanner Lectr and Award, Inst. of Food Technologists, Chicago, 1964. *Publications:* scientific papers, mainly in Biochemical Jl. *Recreation:* gardening. *Address:* Millstream House, St Andrew's Road, Cheddar, Somerset. *T:* Cheddar 742130.

PARTRIDGE, Rt. Rev. William Arthur; Assistant Bishop of Hereford, 1963-75; Prebendary Emeritus, Hereford Cathedral, since 1977; *b* 12 Feb. 1912; *s* of Alfred and Sarah Partridge; *m* 1945, Annie Eliza Joan Strangwood; one *s. Educ:* Alcester Grammar Sch.; Birmingham Univ.; Scholæ Cancellarii, Lincoln. Curate of Lye, Worcs, 1935; SPG Studentship at Birmingham Univ. Education Dept, 1938-39; Educational Missionary, Dio. Madras, 1939-43; Chaplain, RAFVR, 1943-46; Lecturer Meston Training Coll., Madras, 1947-51; Metropolitan's Commissary and Vicar-General in Nandyal, 1951; Asst Bishop of Calcutta (Bishop in Nandyal), 1953-63; Vicar of Ludford, 1963-69. *Publication:* The Way in India, 1962. *Recreation:* the organ. *Address:* Meadow Cottage, 50 The Crescent, Colwall, Malvern, Worcs WR13 6QN. *T:* Colwall 40050.

PASCO, Richard Edward, CBE 1977; actor; Associate Artist, Royal Shakespeare Company; *b* 18 July 1926; *s* of Cecil George Pasco and Phyllis Irene Pasco; *m* 1st, Greta (*née* Watson) (marr. diss.); one *s*; 2nd, 1967, Barbara (*née* Leigh-Hunt). *Educ:* Colet Court; King's Coll. Sch., Wimbledon. Served HM Forces, 1944-48. 1st stage appearance, She Stoops to Conquer, 1943; 1st London appearance, Zero Hour, Lyric, 1944; 1st New York appearance, The Entertainer, 1958. London appearances include: leading roles, English Stage Co., Royal Court, 1957; The Entertainer, Palace, 1957; The Lady from the Sea, Queen's, 1961; Teresa of Avila, Vaudeville, 1961; Look Homeward, Angel, Phoenix, 1962; The New Men, Strand, 1962; The Private Ear and the Public Eye, Globe, 1963; Bristol Old Vic: Henry V (title role), Berowne in Love's Labour's Lost, 1964; Peer Gynt (title role), Angelo in Measure for Measure, Hamlet (title role), 1966 (and world tour); Ivanov, Phoenix, 1965; The Italian Girl, Wyndham's, 1968. Joined RSC, 1969; leading roles include: Becket, Murder in the Cathedral, Aldwych, 1972; (alternated with Ian Richardson) Richard and Bolingbroke in Richard II, Stratford-on-Avon,

1973, and Stratford and Aldwych, 1974; tour of Amer. univs; Jack Tanner in Man and Superman, Malvern Festival, tour and Savoy, 1977; Timon in Timon of Athens, Clarence in Richard III, Arkady Schatslivtses in The Forest, Stratford, 1980-81; La Ronde, Aldwych, 1982. Many foreign tours; accompanied HRH Princess Grace of Monaco at Edinburgh, Stratford and Aldburgh Festivals and on tour of USA, 1977-78; Aldeburgh Festival, E. M. Forster, 1979; film, radio and television appearances including Henry Irving, Ghosts, As You Like It, A Watcher in the Woods, and Julius Caesar, BBC TV, Wagner and Disraeli; records of poems and plays. *Recreations:* music, gardening, the protection of rural England. *Address:* c/o MLR Ltd, 194 Old Brompton Road, SW5. *Club:* Garrick.

PASCO, Rowanne; Editor, The Universe, since 1981 (Deputy Editor, 1979-81); *b* 7 Oct. 1938; *d* of John and Ann Pasco. *Educ:* Dominican Convent, Chingford; Ursuline Convent, Ilford; Open Univ. (BA). Reporter, 1956-57, Editor, 1957-58, Chingford Express; Publicity Officer, NFU, 1958-59; Account Exec., Leslie Frewin PR, 1959-60; Travel Rep., Horizon Holidays, 1960-64; Publicity Asst, Paramount Pictures Corp., Hollywood, 1964-66; Publicity Officer, Religious Progs, Radio and TV, BBC, 1966-71; Reporter, BBC Radio London, 1971-72; TV Editor, Ariel, BBC Staff Newspaper, 1972-74; Radio 4 Reporter, 1974-76; Researcher, Religious Progs, BBC TV, 1976-77; Producer and Presenter, Religious Progs, BBC Radio, 1977-78. *Recreations:* taking the Daily Service on BBC Radio 4, gardening, Italian, creative cooking, rock and roll. *Address:* (office) 33/39 Bowling Green Lane, EC1R 0AB. *T:* 01-278 7321.

PASCOE, Alan Peter, MBE 1975; Director, MSW Promotions Ltd, since 1976; *b* 11 Oct. 1947; *s* of Ernest George Frank Pascoe and Joan Rosina Pascoe; *m* 1970, Della Patricia (*née* James); one *d. Educ:* Portsmouth Southern Grammar Sch.; Borough Road Coll. (Cert. in Educn); London Univ. (Hons degree in Educn). Master, Dulwich Coll., 1971-74; Lectr in Physical Educn, Borough Road Coll., Isleworth, 1974-80. Member: Sports Council, 1974-80; Minister for Sport's Working Party on Centres of Sporting Excellence; BBC Adv. Council, 1975-79. European Indoor Champion, 50m Hurdles, 1969; Europ. Games Silver Medallist, 110m Hurdles, 1971; Silver Medal, Olympic Games, Munich, 4×400m Relay, 1972; Europa Gold Cup Medallist, 400m Hurdles, 1973; Commonwealth Games Gold Medal, 400m Hurdles, and Silver Medal, 4×400m Relay, 1974; Europ. Champion and Gold Medallist in both 400m Hurdles and 4×400m Relay, 1974; Europa Cup Gold Medallist, 400m Hurdles, 1975; Olympic Finalist (injured), Montreal, 1976; Europe's Rep., World Cup Event, 1977. *Publication:* An Autobiography, 1979. *Recreation:* gardening. *Address:* c/o MSW Promotions Ltd, 27 Catherine Street, WC2B 5JG. *T:* 01-240 1951. *Clubs:* Sportsman, Eccentric.

PASCOE, Dr Michael William; Head of Science, Camberwell School of Arts and Crafts; *b* 16 June 1930; *s* of Canon W. J. T. Pascoe and Mrs D. Pascoe; *m* 1st, 1956, Janet Clark (marr. diss. 1977); three *d*; 2nd, 1977, Brenda Hale Reed; one *d. Educ:* St John's, Leatherhead; Selwyn Coll., Cambridge (BA, PhD). MInstP. Res. Student (Tribology), Cambridge, 1951-55; Physicist: Mount Vernon Hosp., Northwood, 1956-57; British Nylon Spinners Ltd, 1957-60; Chemist/Physicist, ICI Paints Div., 1960-67; Lectr (Polymer Science), Brunel Univ., 1967-77; Principal Scientific Officer, 1976-79, Keeper of Conservation and Technical Services, 1979-81, British Museum. Tutor and Counsellor, Open Univ., 1971-76. Consultant to: Royal Acad. of Arts; Mary Rose Trust; Council for the Care of Churches. FRSA. *Publications:* contrib. to books on polymer tribol. and technol.; articles in scientific, engrg and conservation jls on tribol., materials technol. and on conservation methods. *Recreations:* painting and drawing *inter alia. Address:* Camberwell School of Arts and Crafts, Peckham Road, SE5. *T:* 01-703 0987.

PASCOE, Nigel Spencer Knight; a Recorder of the Crown Court, since 1979; *b* 18 Aug. 1940; *er s* of late Ernest Sydney Pascoe and of Cynthia Pascoe; *m* 1964, Elizabeth Anne Walter; two *s* four *d. Educ:* Epsom Coll. Called to the Bar, Inner Temple, 1966. County Councillor for Lyndhurst, Hants, 1979-. Founder, 1976, and Editor, All England Qly Law Cassettes. *Publications:* articles in legal jls. *Recreations:* theatre, cricket, writing. *Address:* 3 Pump Court, Temple, EC4 7AJ. *T:* 01-353 0711. *Clubs:* Garrick; Hampshire (Winchester).

PASCOE, Maj.-Gen. Robert Alan, MBE 1968; Chief of Staff, Headquarters, United Kingdom Land Forces, since 1983; *b* 21 Feb. 1932; *er s* of C. Pascoe; *m* 1955, Pauline (*née* Myers); one *s* three *d. Educ:* Tavistock Grammar Sch.; RMA, Sandhurst. rcds, psc. Commissioned Oxford and Bucks LI, 1952; served with 1 Oxf. Bucks, 1 DLI and 4 Oxf. Bucks (TA), 1953-57; Middle East Centre for Arab Studies, Lebanon, 1958-59; 1st Cl. Interpretership (Arabic); GSO2 Land Forces Persian Gulf, 1960-62; sc Camberley, 1963; Co. Comd 2RGJ, UK and Malaysia, 1964-66 (despatches (Borneo) 1966); GSO2 HQ 2 Div. BAOR, 1967-68; Co. Comd 1RGJ, UK and UNFICYP, 1968-69; Second in Comd 2RGJ, BAOR, 1969; MA to QMG, 1970-71; Comd 1RGJ, 1971-74, BAOR and NI (despatches (NI) 1974); Col General Staff HQ UKLF, 1974-76; Comd 5 Field Force BAOR, 1976-79; rcds 1979; Asst Chief of Gen. Staff (Operational Requirements), MoD, 1980-82. Governor, Royal Sch. for Daughters of Officers of the Army, 1981-. *Recreations:* gardening, tennis, windsurfing, ski-ing. *Address:* c/o Lloyds Bank Ltd, Cox's & King's Branch, 6 Pall Mall, SW1.

PASHLEY, Prof. Donald William, FRS 1968; Professor of Materials and Head of Department of Metallurgy and Materials Science, Imperial College of Science and Technology, since 1979; *b* 21 Apr. 1927; *s* of late Harold William Pashley and Louise Pashley (*née* Clarke); *m* 1954, Glenys Margaret Ball; one *s* one *d*. *Educ:* Henry Thornton Sch., London; Imperial Coll., London (BSc). 1st cl. hons Physics, 1947; PhD 1950. Research Fellow, Imp. Coll., 1950-55; TI Res. Labs., Hinxton Hall: Res. Scientist, 1956-61; Gp Leader and Div. Head, 1962-67; Asst Dir, 1967-68; Dir, 1968-79 (also Dir of Research, TI Ltd, 1976-79). Mem. Council, Royal Soc., 1982-. Rosenhain Medal, Inst. of Metals, 1968. *Publications:* (jtly) Electron Microscopy of Thin Crystals, 1965; numerous papers on electron microscopy and diffraction, thin films and epitaxy in Phil. Mag., Proc. Roy. Soc., etc. *Address:* 32 Beeches Close, Saffron Walden, Essex CB11 4BT. *T:* Saffron Walden 23509; Department of Metallurgy and Materials Science, Imperial College, SW7 2AZ.

PASLEY, Sir (John) Malcolm (Sabine), 5th Bt *cr* 1794; Fellow and Tutor, Magdalen College, Oxford, since 1958; *b* 5 April 1926; *s* of Sir Rodney Marshall Sabine Pasley, 4th Bt, and of Aldyth Werge Hamber; *S* father, 1982; *m* 1965, Virginia Killigrew Wait; two *s*. *Educ:* Sherborne Sch.; Trinity Coll., Oxford (MA). War service, Royal Navy, 1944-46. Laming Travelling Fellow, Queen's Coll., Oxford, 1949-50; Lectr in German, Brasenose and Magdalen Colls, 1950-58; Vice-Pres., Magdalen Coll., 1979-80. *Publications:* (co-author) Kafka-Symposion, 1965; (ed) Germany: A Companion to German Studies, 1972, 2nd edn 1982; (trans.) Kafka Shorter Works, vol. 1, 1973; (ed) Nietzsche: Imagery and Thought, 1978; (ed) Franz Kafka, Das Schloss, 1982. *Heir: s* Robert Killigrew Sabine Pasley, *b* 23 Oct. 1965. *Address:* 25 Lathbury Road, Oxford.

PASMORE, (Edwin John) Victor, CH 1981; CBE 1959; MA; Artist; *b* Chelsham, Surrey, 3 Dec. 1908; *s* of late E. S. Pasmore, MD; *m* 1940, Wendy Blood; one *s* one *d*. *Educ:* Harrow; attended evening classes, LCC Central School of Arts & Crafts. Local government service, LCC County Hall, 1927-37; joined the London Artists' Assoc., 1932-34, and the London Group, 1932-52. Associated with the formation of the Euston Road School, 1937-39, and the first post-war exhibitions of abstract art, 1948-53; joined the Penwith Society, St Ives, 1951-53. Visiting teacher, LCC Camberwell School of Art, 1945-49; Central School of Arts and Crafts, 1949-53. Master of Painting, Durham University, 1954-61; consultant urban and architectural designer, South West Area, Peterlee New Town, 1955-77. *Retrospective exhibitions:* Venice Biennale, 1960; Musée des Arts Décoratifs, Paris, 1961; Stedelijk Museum, Amsterdam, 1961; Palais des Beaux Arts, Brussels, 1961; Louisiana Museum, Copenhagen, 1962; Kestner-Gesellschaft, Hanover, 1962; Kunsthalle, Berne, 1963; Tate Gallery, 1965; São Paolo Biennale, 1965; Cartwright Hall, Bradford, 1980; RA, London, 1980; Marlborough Galleries, London, Rome, NY and Zurich. *Retrospective graphic exhibitions:* Marlborough Gallery, Tate Gallery, Galleria 2RC, Rome, Milan, Lubjlana, Messina, Oslo. Carnegie Prize for painting, Pittsburgh International, 1964. Grand Prix d'Honneur, International Graphics Biennale, Lubjlana, 1977. Works represented in: Tate Gallery and other public collections in Gt Britain, Canada, Australia, Holland, Italy, Austria, Switzerland and the USA. Trustee, Tate Gall., 1963-66. *Publication:* Monograph and Catalogue Raisonnée, 1980. *Address:* Dar Gamri, Gudja, Malta; 12 St Germans Place, Blackheath, SE3. *Club:* Arts.

PASQUILL, Frank, DSc; FRS 1977; retired from Meteorological Office, 1974; *b* 8 Sept. 1914; *s* of late Joseph Pasquill and Elizabeth Pasquill (*née* Rudd), both of Atherton, Lancs; *m* 1937, Margaret Alice Turnbull, West Rainton, Co. Durham; two *d*. *Educ:* Henry Smith Sch., Hartlepool; Durham Univ. BSc (1st Cl. Hons Physics) 1935, MSc, 1949, DSc 1950. Meteorological Office, 1937-74, with posts at Chem. Defence Res. Estabt, Porton, 1937-46 (incl. overseas service in Australia); Sch. of Agric., Cambridge Univ., 1946-49; Atomic Energy Res. Estabt, Harwell, 1949-54; Chem. Defence Res. Estabt, Porton, 1954-61; Meteorological Office HQ Bracknell, 1961-74 (finally Dep. Chief Scientific Officer, and Head of Boundary Layer Research Br.). Visiting Prof., Pennsylvania State Univ., Autumn, 1974, N Carolina State Univ., Spring, 1975; Visiting Scientist, Penn. State Univ., 1975, Winter, 1976, Winter, 1977, Savannah River Lab., S Carolina, Winter, 1976. Royal Meteorological Society: Editor, 1961-64; Pres., 1970-72; Hon. FRMetS 1978; Chm., Aero Res. Council's Gust Res. Cttee, 1963-68; Chm., CEGB's Adv. Panel on Environmental Res., 1962-80. *Publications:* Atmospheric Diffusion, 1962, 2nd edn 1974; papers on atmospheric turbulence and diffusion in various jls. *Address:* Woodwell, 37 Arbor Lane, Winnersh, Wokingham, Berks RG11 5JE.

PASTERFIELD, Rt. Rev. Philip John; *see* Crediton, Bishop Suffragan of.

PASTON-BEDINGFELD, Sir Edmund George Felix, 9th Bt, *cr* 1661; Major late Welsh Guards; Managing Director, Handley Walker (Europe) Ltd, 1969-80; *b* 2 June 1915; *s* of 8th Bt and Sybil, *e d* of late H. Lyne Stephens of Grove House, Roehampton; *S* father, 1941; *m* 1st, 1942, Joan Lynette (*née* Rees) (*d* 1965); one *s* one *d*; 2nd, 1957, Agnes Kathleen (*d* 1974), *d* of late Miklos Gluck, Budapest; 3rd, 1975, Mrs Peggy Hannaford-Hill, Fort Victoria, Rhodesia. *Educ:* Oratory School; New College, Oxford. Under-Sec., Head of Agricultural Div., RICS, 1966-69. *Heir: s* Henry Edgar Paston-Bedingfeld [*b* 7 Dec. 1943; *m* 1968, Mary, *er d* of Brigadier R. D. Ambrose, CIE, OBE, MC; two *s* two *d*]. *Address:* Arundell House, Brettenham, Ipswich. *T:* Rattlesden 607.

PASTON BROWN, Dame Beryl, DBE 1967; *b* 7 March 1909; *d* of Paston Charles Brown and Florence May (*née* Henson). *Educ:* Streatham Hill High School; Newnham Coll., Cambridge (MA); London Day Training College. Lecturer: Portsmouth Training Coll., 1933-37; Goldsmiths' Coll., Univ. of London, 1937-44 and 1946-51. Temp. Asst Lecturer, Newnham Coll., 1944-46. Principal of City of Leicester Training Coll., 1952-61; Principal, Homerton College, Cambridge, 1961-71. Chairman, Assoc. of Teachers in Colleges and Depts of Educn, 1965-66. *Address:* 21 Keere Street, Lewes, East Sussex. *T:* Lewes 3608.

PATCH, Air Chief Marshal Sir Hubert (Leonard), KCB 1957 (CB 1952); CBE 1942; *b* 16 Dec. 1904; *s* of late Captain Leonard W. Patch, RN (retd), St Margarets-on-Thames; *m* 1960, Claude Renée, *d* of Major Jean-Marie Botéculet (Légion d'Honneur, Croix de Guerre, Médaille Militaire, MC (British), killed in action in Morocco, 1925). *Educ:* Stonyhurst; RAF Coll., Cranwell, Lincs. Joined RAF, 1925; Acting Group Captain, 1942; Group Captain, 1946; Air Cdre, 1947; Air Vice-Marshal, 1951. Served 1939-44 (despatches, CBE). Senior Air Staff Officer, HQ Far East Air Force, 1952-53; AOC No 11 Gp, Fighter Comd, Nov. 1953-Jan. 1956; Air Officer Commanding-in-Chief (Temp.), Fighter Command, Jan.-Aug. 1956; Commander-in-Chief, Middle East Air Force, 1956-58; Air Member for Personnel April-Sept. 1959; Commander-in-Chief, British Forces, Arabian Peninsula, October 1959-May 1960; Acting Air Marshal, 1956; Air Marshal, 1957; Air Chief Marshal, 1959. Retired from Royal Air Force, 1961. Representative of British Aircraft Corporation to the NATO countries, 1961-63. *Address:* Loma de Rio Verde, Marbella, Spain; c/o Barclays Bank, Colchester, Essex. *Club:* Royal Air Force.

PATEL, Ambalal Bhailalbhai, CMG 1949; *b* 1 May 1898; *e s* of late Bhailalbhai Dharamdas Patel, Changa, Gujarat; *m* Gangalaxmi Patel (decd); three *s* one *d* (and one *s* decd). *Educ:* Petlad High School; Baroda Coll. (BA); Bombay University (LLB). Barrister-at-Law, Lincoln's Inn, 1923. Advocate, Supreme Court of Kenya, 1924; as Kenya Indian Deleg. gave evidence before Joint Parl. Committee on Closer Union, London, 1931. Pres. E African Indian National Congress, 1938-42, and 1945-46; Pres. Kenya Indian Conf., 1942; Mem. standing and exec. Cttees of EAIN Congress, 1924-56; Chm. Indian Elected Members Organization, 1941-48; Hon. Sec. Coast Elected Members Organization, 1949-56; Mem. Makerere Coll. Assembly, 1938-48. Chm. Central Indian Advisory Man-Power Cttee and Indian E Dist Man-Power Cttee during War of 1939-45. Chm. Indian and Arab Land Settlement Bd, 1946-54; attended African Conf. in London, 1948; Mem. E African Central Legislative Assembly, 1948-52; Minister without Portfolio, Govt of Kenya, 1954-56, retired. MLC 1938-56, MEC Kenya, 1941-56. Mem. Royal Technical College Council, Nairobi, and Makerere University Coll. Council, 1954-56. Gen. Sec. and Treasurer, World Union, 1964-; Member: Emergency Council for World Govt, World Union Movement (Hesbjerg, Denmark), 1974-; World Federal Authority Cttee (Geneva), 1975-81; Co-pres., World Constitution and Parliament Assoc., 1977; First signatory, Constitution for Fedn of Earth, 1977. Pres. or trustee various political, social and cultural institutions at different times. Coronation Medal, 1953. *Publication:* Toward a New World Order, 1974. *Address:* c/o Sri Aurobindo Ashram, Pondicherry (via Madras), India.

PATEL, Praful Raojibhai Chaturbhai; Company Director; Investment Adviser in UK, since 1962; Hon. Secretary, All-Party Parliamentary Committee on UK Citizenship, since 1968; *b* Jinja, Uganda, 7 March 1939; *s* of Raojibhai Chaturbhai Patel, Sojitra, Gujarat, India, and Maniben Jivabhai Lalaji Patel, Dharmaj, Gujarat; unmarried. *Educ:* Government Sec. Sch., Jinja, Uganda; London Inst. of World Affairs, attached to University Coll., London (Extra Mural Dept). Sec., Uganda Students Union, 1956-58; Deleg. to Internat. Youth Assembly, New Delhi, 1958; awarded two travel bursaries for visits to E, Central and S Africa, and Middle East, to study and lecture on politics and economics; arrived in Britain as student, then commenced commercial activities, 1962; increasingly involved in industrial, cultural and educational projects affecting immigrants in Britain. Spokesman for Asians in UK following restriction of immigration resulting from Commonwealth Immigrants Act 1968; Council Mem., UK Immigrants Advisory Service, 1970-; Mem., Uganda Resettlement Bd, 1972-74; Hon. Sec., Uganda Evacuees Resettlement Advisory Trust, 1974-; Pres., Nava Kala India Socio-Cultural Centre, London, 1962-75; Chm. Bd of Trustees, Swaminarayan Hindu Mission, UK, 1970-76; Jt Convener, Asian Action Cttee, 1976; Convener, Manava Trust, 1979-. *Publications:* articles in newspapers and journals regarding immigration and race relations. *Recreations:* cricket; campaigning and lobbying; current affairs; and inter-faith co-operation. *Address:* 60 Bedford Court Mansions, Bedford Avenue, Bedford Square, WC1B 3AD. *T:* 01-580 0897. *Club:* Royal Commonwealth Society.

PATEMAN, Jack Edward, CBE 1970; Chairman, GEC Computers Ltd, since 1978 (Director, since 1971); Managing Director, Marconi Avionics Ltd, since 1971; Director: Canadian Marconi Co., since 1971; Elliott Bros (London) Ltd, since 1979; Marconi Avionics Projects Ltd, since 1980; Marconi Electronic Devices Ltd, since 1980; GEC Information Systems Ltd, since 1982; *b* 29 Nov. 1921; *s* of William Edward Pateman and Lucy Varley (*née* Jetten); *m* 1949, Cicely Hope Turner; one *s* one *d*. *Educ:* Gt Yarmouth Grammar Sch. Served War of 1939-45, RAF, 1940-46. Research Engineer: Belling & Lee, 1946-48; Elliott Bros (London) Ltd, 1948-51. Formed Aviation Div. of EBL at Borehamwood, 1951-62; Dep. Chm. and Jt Man. Dir, Elliott Flight

Automation Ltd, 1962-71. British Gold Medal, RAeS, 1981. *Recreation:* sailing. *Address:* Spindles, Ivy Hatch, Sevenoaks, Kent. *T:* Plaxtol 810364.

PATEMAN, Prof. John Arthur Joseph, FRS 1978; FRSE 1974; Professor of Genetics, Australian National University, since 1979; *b* 18 May 1926; *s* of John and Isobel May Pateman; *m* 1952, Mary Phelps; one *s* two *d*. *Educ:* Clacton County High Sch., Essex; University Coll., Leicester. BSc, PhD (Lond); MA(Cantab). Lectr, Univ. of Sheffield, 1954-58; Sen. Lectr, Univ. of Melbourne, Australia, 1958-60; Lectr, Univ. of Cambridge, 1960-67; Prof., Flinders Univ., S Australia, 1967-70; Prof. of Genetics, Univ. of Glasgow, 1970-79. Fellow, Churchill Coll., Cambridge, 1961-67. *Publications:* scientific papers in genetical, biochemical and microbiological jls. *Recreations:* reading, music, walking. *Address:* 46 Amaroo Street, Reid, ACT 2601, Australia. *T:* 48-8327.

PATER, John Edward, CB 1953; Under Secretary, Ministry of Health and Department of Health and Social Security, 1947-73 (retired); *b* 15 March 1911; *s* of Edward Rhodes and Lilian Pater; *m* 1938, Margaret Anderson, *yr d* of M. C. Furtado; two *s* one *d*. *Educ:* King Edward VI School, Retford; Queens' College, Cambridge. Foundation Scholar, Queens' College; BA 1933, MA 1935, PhD 1982. Assistant Principal, Ministry of Health, 1933; Principal, 1938; Assistant Secretary, 1943; Principal Assistant Secretary, 1945; Director of Establishments and Organisation, 1960-65. Treasurer: Methodist Church Dept of Connexional Funds and Finance Bd, 1959-73; Div. of Finance, 1973-; Central Finance Bd, 1968-74. Governor, Kingswood Sch. *Publication:* The Making of the National Health Service, 1981. *Recreations:* reading, archæology, walking (preferably on hills). *Address:* 1B Croham Mount, South Croydon CR2 0BR. *T:* 01-651 1601.

See also R. A. Furtado.

PATERSON, Arthur Spencer, MA (Oxon); MD; FRCPE, MRCP; FRCPsych; Consultant Psychiatrist; Physician in Charge, Department of Psychiatry, and Director Psychiatric Laboratory, West London Hospital, 1946-66; *b* 22 Feb. 1900; 4th *s* of late Professor W. P. Paterson, Edinburgh Univ., and late Jane Sanderson; *m* 1933, Antoinette, *d* of late Chas Baxter, WS; two *s*. *Educ:* Edinburgh Academy; Fettes (Scholar); 2nd Lt RHA 1919. Oriel, Oxford (Hon. Mods and Lit. Hum.; BA 1923); Edinburgh Univ. (MB, ChB 1928). Ho. Phys to Prof. of Medicine, Roy. Infirmary, Edinburgh, 1928-29; Asst Phys., Glasgow Royal Mental Hospital, 1929-30; Rockefeller Fellow, 1930-31; Pinsent-Darwin Research Student in Mental Pathology, Cambridge University, 1931-33; held research posts at: Johns Hopkins Univ., Baltimore, Md, USA, Research Inst. of Psychiatry, Munich; Maudsley Hosp., London. Asst Phys., Cassel Hosp., Penshurst, 1933-36; First Asst, Dept of Psychiatry, Middlesex Hosp., 1936-45, Psychiatrist, Sector V. EMS Metrop. Area, 1939-45. Honeyman-Gillespie Lectr, Edin. Univ., 1948. Membre d'honneur Soc. Méd. Ment. Belge, 1969; Membre Etranger, Soc. Méd.-Psychol., Paris, 1969; Corr. Member: American Psychiat. Association; American Pavlovian Soc. Hon. Secretary, Internat. Soc. for Experimental and Clin. Hypnosis, 1968-73. Hermann Goldman Lectr, NY Coll., Med., 1964. Foundation FRCPsych, 1971; FRSM (Pres. Sect., Hypnosis, 1981); FBPsS. *Publications:* Electrical and Drug Treatments in Psychiatry, 1963; Control of the Autonomic Nervous Functions by Conditioning and Hypnosis, in Hypnosis and Behaviour Therapy, ed E. Dengrove, 1975; numerous articles on psychiatric and allied subjects in British and foreign scientific periodicals. *Recreations:* travel, golf, chess. *Address:* 5 Cranley Mews, SW7 3BX. *T:* 01-373 0773. *Club:* Athenæum.

PATERSON, Dame Betty (Fraser Ross), DBE 1981 (CBE 1973); JP; DL; Chairman: NW Thames Regional Health Authority, since 1973; National Staff Advisory Committee for England and Wales (Nurses and Midwives), since 1975; *b* 14 March 1916; *d* of Robert Ross Russell and Elsie Marian Russell (*née* Fraser); *m* 1940, Ian Douglas Paterson; one *s* one *d*. *Educ:* Harrogate Coll.; Western Infirmary, Glasgow. Mem. Chartered Soc. of Physiotherapy (MCSP). County Comr, Herts Girl Guides, 1950-57. Member: Herts CC, 1952-74 (Alderman 1959-74; Chm., 1969-73); NE Metropolitan Regional Hosp. Bd, 1960-74; Governing Body, Royal Hosp. of St Bartholomew, 1960-74; Commn for the New Towns, England and Wales, 1961-75 (Dep. Chm., 1971-75); Governing Body, Bishop's Stortford Coll., 1967-81; Central Health Services Council, 1969-74; Gen. Council, King Edward's Hosp. Fund for London, 1975- (Management Cttee, 1975-80); Pres., Herts Assoc. of Local Councils, 1980. JP Herts, 1950 (Chm. Bishop's Stortford Bench, 1978-); DL Herts, 1980. *Recreations:* music, cooking, foreign travel. *Address:* Twyford Bury, Bishop's Stortford, Herts. *T:* Bishop's Stortford 53184.

PATERSON, Sir Dennis (Craig), Kt 1976; FRCS, FRACS; Director and Chief Orthopaedic Surgeon, Adelaide Children's Hospital, since 1970; Consultant Orthopaedic Surgeon: Royal Adelaide Hospital, since 1964; Queen Victoria Hospital, since 1968; *b* 14 Oct. 1930; *s* of Gilbert Charles Paterson and Thelma Drysdale Paterson; *m* 1955, Mary, *d* of Frederick Mansell Hardy; one *s* three *d*. *Educ:* Collegiate Sch. of St Peter; Univ. of Adelaide (MB, BS 1953). FRCS 1958, FRACS 1961. Res. Med. Officer: Royal Adelaide Hosp., 1954; Adelaide Children's Hosp., 1956; Registrar, Robert Jones & Agnes Hunt Orthop. Hosp., Oswestry, Shropshire, 1958-60; Sen. Registrar, Royal Adelaide Hosp., 1960-62; Cons. Orthop. Surg., Repatriation Gen. Hosp., Adelaide, 1962-70; Adelaide Children's Hospital: Asst Hon. Orthop. Surg., 1964-66; Sen. Hon. Orthop. Surg., 1966-70; Mem. Bd of Management, 1976-; Chm., Med. Adv. Cttee, 1976-; Chm., Med. Staff Cttee,

1976-. Amer./British/Canadian Trav. Prof., 1966. Royal Australasian Coll. of Surgeons: Mem., Bd of Orthop. Surg., 1974-82 (Chm., 1977-82); Mem., Court of Examnrs, 1974-; Mem., SA Cttee, 1974-78; Fellow: British Orthopaedic Assoc.; RSocMed; Member: Aust. Orthopaedic Assoc. (Censor-in-Chief, 1976-80; Dir, Continuing Educn, 1982-); AMA; Internat. Scoliosis Res. Soc.; Scientific Internat. Soc. of Traumatol. and Orthopaedics (Aust. Nat. Delegate, 1975-). Pres., Crippled Children's Assoc. of South Australia Inc., 1970- (Mem. Council, 1966-70). Life Mem., S Aust. Cricket Assoc. Queen's Jubilee Medal, 1977. *Publications:* over 60 articles in Jl of Bone and Joint Surg., Clin. Orthopaedics and Related Res., Aust. and NZ Jl of Surg., Med. Jl of Aust., Western Pacific Jl of Orthop. Surg. *Recreations:* golf, gardening. *Address:* 31 Myall Avenue, Kensington Gardens, SA 5068, Australia. *T:* 08 3323364. *Clubs:* Adelaide, Royal Adelaide Golf, Kooyonga Golf (Adelaide).

PATERSON, Francis, (Frank), FCIT; General Manager, Eastern Region, British Rail, York, since 1978; Member, British Railways (Eastern) Board, since 1978; *b* 5 April 1930; *s* of Francis William Paterson and Cecilia Eliza Reid Brownie; *m* 1950, Grace Robertson; two *s* two *d*. *Educ:* Robert Gordon's Coll., Aberdeen. Joined LNER as Junior Clerk, 1946; clerical and supervisory positions in NE Scotland; management training, Scotland, 1956-59; various man-management, operating and marketing posts, Scotland, Lincs and Yorks, 1960-66; Operating Supt, Glasgow North, 1967-68; Sales Manager, Edinburgh, 1968; Asst Divl Manager, S Wales, 1968-70; Dir, United Welsh Transport, 1968-70; Harbour Comr, Newport Harbour, 1968-70; Divl Manager, Central Div., Southern Region, 1970-75; Director: Southdown Motor Services Ltd, 1970-73; Brighton, Hove & District Omnibus Co., 1970-73; Dep. Gen. Man., Southern Region, 1975-77; Chief Freight Manager, British Railways Bd, 1977-78. Member: CBI Southern Regional Council, 1975-77; CBI Transport Policy Cttee, 1977-78; Nat. Railway Museum Cttee, 1978-; Council, CIT, 1979-. FCIT 1978. Mem. Court, Univ. of York, 1981-. Officer Brother of St John. *Publications:* papers to transport societies. *Recreations:* transport, travel, hill walking, country pursuits, Scottish culture, enjoying grandchildren. *Address:* Alligin, 97 Main Street, Askham Bryan, York YO2 3QS. *T:* York 708478; British Rail Headquarters, York YO1 1HT. *T:* York 53022.

PATERSON, Frank David; His Honour Judge Paterson; a Circuit Judge (formerly County Court Judge), since 1968; *b* 10 July 1918; *yr s* of late David Paterson and Dora Paterson, Liverpool; *m* 1953, Barbara Mary, 2nd *d* of late Oswald Ward Gillow and Alice Gillow, Formby; one *s* two *d*. *Educ:* Calderstones Preparatory Sch. and Quarry Bank High Sch., Liverpool; Univ. of Liverpool (LLB). Called to Bar, Gray's Inn, 1941; Warden, Unity Boys' Club, Liverpool, 1941; Asst Warden, Florence Inst. for Boys, Liverpool, 1943. Practised on Northern Circuit. Chairman: Min. of Pensions and Nat. Insce Tribunal, Liverpool, 1957; Mental Health Review Tribunal for SW Lancashire and Cheshire, 1963. Asst Dep. Coroner, City of Liverpool, 1960. *Address:* Vailima, 2 West Lane, Formby, Liverpool L37 7BA. *T:* Formby 74345. *Club:* Athenæum (Liverpool).

PATERSON, Sir George (Mutlow), Kt 1959; OBE 1946; QC (Sierra Leone) 1950; Chairman, Industrial Tribunals, 1965-79; *b* 3 Dec. 1906; *e s* of late Dr G. W. Paterson; *m* 1935, Audrey Anita, *d* of late Major C. C. B. Morris, CBE, MC; one *s* two *d*. *Educ:* Grenada Boys' School; St John's College, Cambridge. Appointed to Nigerian Administrative Service, 1929. Called to the Bar, Inner Temple, 1933. Magistrate, Nigeria, 1936; Crown Counsel, Tanganyika, 1938. War of 1939-45: served with the King's African Rifles, 1939 (wounded 1940); Occupied Enemy Territories Admin., 1941; Lieutenant-Colonel 1945. Solicitor-General, Tanganyika, 1946; Attorney-General, Sierra Leone, 1949, Ghana, 1954-57; Chief Justice of Northern Rhodesia, 1957-61, retired 1961; appointed to hold an inquiry into proposed amendments to the Potato Marketing Scheme, 1962; appointed legal chairman (part-time), Pensions Appeal Tribunals, 1962; appointed chairman Industrial Tribunals, South Western Region, 1965. *Recreations:* shooting, gardening, genealogy. *Address:* Buckshaw House, Sherborne, Dorset DT9 5LD. *T:* Bishop's Caundle 318.

See also T. P. P. Clifford.

PATERSON, Sqdn-Ldr Ian Veitch, CBE 1969; DL; JP; Deputy Chairman, Local Government Boundary Commission for Scotland, 1974-80; *b* 17 Aug. 1911; *s* of Andrew Wilson Paterson; *m* 1940, Anne Weir, *d* of Thomas Brown; two *s* one *d*. *Educ:* Lanark Grammar School; Glasgow University. Served RAF, 1940-45. Entered local govt service, Lanark, 1928; Principal Legal Asst, Aberdeen CC; Lanarkshire: Dep. County Clerk, 1949; County Clerk, 1956, resigned 1974. Chm., Working Party who produced The New Scottish Local Authorities Organisation and Management structures, 1973. DL Lanarkshire (Strathclyde), 1963; JP Hamilton (formerly Lanarkshire). *Address:* 35 Stewarton Drive, Cambuslang, Glasgow.

PATERSON, (James Edmund) Neil, MA; Author; *b* 31 Dec. 1915; *s* of late James Donaldson Paterson, MA, BL; *m* 1939, Rosabelle, MA, 3rd *d* of late David MacKenzie, MC, MA; two *s* one *d*. *Educ:* Banff Academy; Edinburgh Univ. Served in minesweepers, War of 1939-45, Lieut RNVR, 1940-46. Director: Grampian Television; Scottish Film Production Trust; Consultant, Films of Scotland (Mem., 1954-76; Dir, 1976-78); Member: Scottish Arts Council, 1967-76 (Vice-Chm., 1974-76); Arts Council of Great Britain, 1974-76; Governor: Nat. Film Sch., 1970-80; Pitlochry Festival Theatre, 1966-76; British Film Institute, 1958-60; Atlantic Award in Literature, 1946; Award of American Academy of Motion Picture Arts and Sciences, 1960.

Publications: The China Run, 1948; Behold Thy Daughter, 1950; And Delilah, 1951; Man on the Tight Rope, 1953; The Kidnappers, 1957; film stories and screen plays. *Recreations:* golf, fishing. *Address:* St Ronans, Crieff, Perthshire. *T:* 2615.

PATERSON, James Rupert; HM Diplomatic Service; Ambassador to the Mongolian People's Republic, since 1982; *b* 7 Aug. 1932; *s* of late Major Robert Paterson, MC, Seaforth Highlanders and of Mrs Josephine Paterson; *m* 1956, Kay Dineen; two *s* two d. *Educ:* Nautical Coll., Pangbourne; RMA, Sandhurst. Commnd RA, 1953 (Tombs Meml Prize); Staff Coll., Camberley, 1963; retd from Army with rank of Major, 1970; joined FCO, 1970; First Sec., Pakistan, 1972; Dep. High Comr, Trinidad and Tobago, 1975. *Recreations:* entertaining, letter-writing, ballet, golf. *Address:* c/o Foreign and Commonwealth Office, King Charles Street, SW1A 2AH; c/o Barclays Bank, Carshalton Beeches, Surrey SM5 3LA. *Club:* Royal Commonwealth Society.

PATERSON, James Veitch; Sheriff of the Lothian and Borders (formerly Roxburgh, Berwick and Selkirk) at Jedburgh, Selkirk and Duns, since 1963; *b* 16 April 1928; *s* of John Robert Paterson, ophthalmic surgeon, and Jeanie Gouinlock; *m* 1956, Ailie, *o d* of Lt-Comdr Sir (George) Ian Clark Hutchison, *qv* ; one *s* one d. *Educ:* Peebles High School; Edinburgh Academy; Lincoln College, Oxford; Edinburgh University. Admitted to Faculty of Advocates, 1953. *Recreations:* fishing, shooting, gardening. *Address:* Sunnyside, Melrose, Roxburghshire. *T:* Melrose 2502. *Club:* New (Edinburgh).

PATERSON, John Allan; Agent-General in London and Deputy Minister Abroad for Province of New Brunswick, 1968–75; *b* Montreal, 20 May 1909; *s* of William A. and M. Ethel Paterson; *m* 1935, Elizabeth Stewart Messenger; four s. *Educ:* Westmount, Quebec; Mount Allison Univ. (BSc 1932); Queen's Univ. Prudential Insurance Co. of America, 1934–46; RCAF 1941–45 (Sqdn Ldr); New Brunswick Dept of Industry, 1946–68 (Deputy Minister, 1956); Provincial Co-ordinator of Civil Defence, 1950–55; Bd of Comrs, Oromocto, 1956–63; Chm., Provincial Govts of Canada Trade and Industry Council, 1956–57, 1961–62, 1964–65 and 1966–67. Mem. Bd of Regents, Mount Allison Univ., 1959–63; Pres. Oromocto Develt Corp., 1963–68. *Publication:* (co-author) The New Brunswick Economy, Past Present and Future, 1955. *Recreations:* golf, motoring, fishing. *Address:* The Coach House, Back Lane, Great Malvern, Worcs.

PATERSON, Sir John (Valentine) J.; *see* Jardine Paterson.

PATERSON, Neil; *see* Paterson, James Edmund N.

PATERSON, Noel Kennedy, CIE 1947; OBE 1943; lately United Kingdom Trade Commissioner, Dublin; *b* 25 Dec. 1905; *s* of Rev. David Paterson, BD, Edinburgh; *m* 1934, Margaret Winifred Schreiber; two *s* two d. *Educ:* George Heriot's School, Edinburgh; Edinburgh University; St John's College, Cambridge. Entered Indian Civil Service, 1929; Asst Comr, 1929–34; Under Sec. to Govt of Central Provinces, 1934–36; Deputy Comr, 1936–37 and 1939–45; Under Sec. to Govt of India, 1937–38; Chief Comr, Andaman and Nicobar Islands, 1945–47. *Recreation:* travel. *Address:* Chestnut Cottage, Gabriels Farm, Park Lane, Twyford, Hants. *T:* Twyford 713116.

PATERSON, Robert Lancelot, OBE 1980; MC 1945; ERD 1957; part-time Adjudicator, Home Office Immigration Appeals, since 1970; Director, Merseyside Chamber of Commerce and Industry, 1967–81; *b* 16 May 1918; *e s* of Lancelot Wilson and Sarah Annie Paterson; *m* 1940, Charlotte Orpha, d of James and Elizabeth Nicholas; three s. *Educ:* Monmouth Sch.; University Coll. of Wales, Aberystwyth (BA); London School of Economics. Commissioned into Border Regt, SR, Dec. 1937; served War of 1939–45, 4th Bn, Border Regt, France, ME, Syria, Tobruk, Burma and India (Chindits, 1943–44); Asst Chief Instr 164 (Inf.), OCTU, 1946. Entered Colonial Admin. Service, Tanganyika, 1947; Dist Officer, 1947–60; Principal Asst Sec., Min. of Home Affairs, 1960–62; prematurely retired on attainment of Independence by Tanganyika. Dep. Sec., Liverpool Chamber of Commerce, 1963–67; Member, Nat. Council, Assoc. of Brit. Chambers of Commerce, 1969–81; Pres., Brit. Chambers of Commerce Executives, 1977–79; Governor, Liverpool Coll. of Commerce, 1967–71; Member: Liverpool Univ. Appts Bd, 1968–72; Council of Industrial Advisers, NW Reg. Management Centre, 1973–76. *Recreations:* archaeology, gardening. *Address:* c/o Standard Chartered Bank Ltd, 73 King William Street, EC4N 7AB. *Club:* Athenæum (Liverpool).

PATEY, Very Rev. Edward Henry; Dean of Liverpool, 1964–82, now Dean Emeritus; *b* 12 Aug. 1915; *s* of Walter Patey, MD, and Dorothy Patey; *m* 1942, Margaret Ruth Olivia Abbott; one *s* three d. *Educ:* Marlborough College; Hertford College, Oxford; Westcott House, Cambridge. Assistant Curate, St Mary-at-the-Walls, Colchester, 1939; MA (Oxon) 1941; Assistant Curate Bishopwearmouth Parish Church, Sunderland, 1942; Youth Chaplain to the Bishop of Durham, 1946; Vicar of Oldland, with Longwell Green, Bristol, 1950; Secretary, Youth Department, The British Council of Churches, 1952; Assistant Gen. Secretary, The British Council of Churches, 1955; Canon Residentiary of Coventry Cathedral, 1958. Hon. LLD Liverpool, 1980. *Publications:* Religion in the Club, 1956; Boys and Girls Growing Up, 1957; Worship in the Club, 1961; A Doctor's Life of Jesus, 1962; Young People Now, 1964; Enquire Within, 1966; Look out for the Church, 1969; Burning Questions, 1971; Don't Just Sit There, 1974; Christian Lifestyle, 1975; All in

Good Faith, 1978; Open the Doors, 1978; Open the Book, 1981. *Recreations:* reading, listening to music. *Address:* 139 High Street, Malmesbury, Wilts.

PATON; *see* Noel-Paton, family name of **Baron Ferrier.**

PATON, Major Adrian Gerard Nigel H.; *see* Hadden-Paton.

PATON, Alan (Stewart); writer; was National President of the South African Liberal Party until it was made an illegal organisation in 1968; living at Botha's Hill, Natal; *b* Pietermaritzburg, 11 Jan. 1903; *s* of James Paton; *m* 1st, 1928, Doris Olive (d 1967), d of George Francis; two *s* ; 2nd, 1969, Anne Hopkins. *Educ:* Natal Univ. (BSc, BEd). Formerly Principal Diepkloof Reformatory, 1935–48. Chubb Fellow, Yale Univ., 1973. Hon. LHD, Yale, 1954; Hon. DLitt: Kenyon Coll., 1962; Univ. of Natal, 1968; Trent Univ., 1971; Harvard, 1971; Rhodes, 1972; Williamette Univ., 1974; Michigan, 1977; Hon DD Edinburgh, 1971; Hon. LLB, Univ. of Witwatersrand, 1975. Freedom House Award (USA), 1960. *Publications:* Cry, the Beloved Country, 1948; Too Late the Phalarope, 1953; Land and People of South Africa, 1955; South Africa in Transition (with Dan Weiner), 1956; Debbie Go Home (short stories), 1961; Hofmeyr (biography), 1965; Instrument of Thy Peace, 1968; The Long View, 1969; Kontakion For You Departed, 1969; Apartheid and the Archbishop, 1973; Knocking on the Door, 1975; Towards the Mountain (autobiog.), 1981; Ah, But Your Land is Beautiful, 1981. *Address:* PO Box 278, Hillcrest, Natal, South Africa.

PATON, Col Alexander, DSO 1937; MC; RA, retired; *b* 13 Jan. 1897; *s* of Alexander Paton, Glasgow; *m* 1923, Sybil, *er d* of late Sir Grimwood Mears, KCIE; two s. *Educ:* Marlborough Coll.; RMA, Woolwich. Commissioned, 1915; served European War, France, 1916–19; Staff Captain, 1918; 15th Corps (despatches twice, MC and bar, General Service and Victory Medals); India, 1919–25; Staff Captain RA, Afghan War, 1919 (1908, General Service Medal, India, and clasp, 1919); Staff Officer RA, Simla, 1921–22; Chitral, NWF India, 1922–24; Home Service, 1925–36; Terr. Adjt. 13th (Highland) Brigade, TA, Argyllshire, 1926–30; Company Officer at Royal Military Academy, Woolwich, 1932–34; Adjutant, 3rd Medium Brigade RA, Shoeburyness, 1934–36; India, NWF, 1937 (wounded, despatches, DSO, Medal and clasp); Burma, 1938–40; Comd 21 Mtn Regt NWF, 1940; Comdt MATC Ambala, Punjab, 1941–42; Comdt FATC Muttra, UP, 1942–44; Col 1943–44; Recruiting Staff, Rawalpindi, Punjab, 1944–45. Defence Medal, 1939–45, and War Medal (1939–45). Retd pay, 1947. *Recreation:* philately. *Address:* Willow Cottage, 33 Crofton Lane, Hillhead, Fareham, Hants. *T:* Stubbington 2116.

PATON, Sir Angus; *see* Paton, Sir T. A. L.

PATON, Rev. Canon David Macdonald; Chaplain to the Queen, since 1972; Rector of St Mary de Crypt and St John the Baptist, Gloucester, 1970–81; Vicar of Christ Church, Gloucester, 1979–81; Hon. Canon of Canterbury Cathedral, 1966–80 (now Canon Emeritus); *b* 9 Sept. 1913; *e s* of late Rev. William Paton, DD and Grace Mackenzie Paton (née Macdonald); *m* 1946, Alison Georgina Stewart; three s. *Educ:* Repton; Brasenose Coll., Oxford. BA 1936, MA 1939. SCM Sec., Birmingham, 1936–39; Deacon 1939, Priest 1941; Missionary in China, 1940–44 and 1947–50; Chaplain and Librarian, Westcott House, Cambridge, 1945–46; Vicar of Yardley Wood, Birmingham, 1952–56; Editor, SCM Press, 1956–59; Sec., Council for Ecumenical Co-operation of Church Assembly, 1959–63; Sec., Missionary and Ecumenical Council of Church Assembly, 1964–69; Chairman: Churches' China Study Project, 1972–79; Gloucester Civic Trust, 1972–77. Hon. Fellow, Selly Oak Colls, 1981. *Publications:* Christian Missions and the Judgment of God, 1953; (with John T. Martin) Paragraphs for Sundays and Holy Days, 1957; (ed) Essays in Anglican Self-Criticism, 1958; (ed) The Ministry of the Spirit, 1960; Anglicans and Unity, 1962; (ed) Reform of the Ministry, 1968; (ed) Breaking Barriers (Report of WCC 5th Assembly, Nairobi, 1975), 1976. *Address:* 37A Cromwell Street, Gloucester GL1 1RE. *T:* Gloucester 422051.
See also Bishop of Birmingham, Ven. M. J. M. Paton, Prof. Sir W. D. M. Paton.

PATON, Douglas Shaw F.; *see* Forrester-Paton.

PATON, George Campbell Henderson, QC (Scotland) 1967; LLD Edin 1969; Reader in Scots Law, Edinburgh University, 1967–75; *b* 6 Aug. 1905; *s* of George Grieve Paton, MA, LLB, Solicitor, Glasgow and Mary Campbell Sclanders; *m* 1950, Eva French, d of David French Cranston, Edinburgh; two d. *Educ:* Glasgow Academy; Glasgow University. MA 1927; LLB (Distinction) 1930. Solicitor 1931; Advocate 1951. Served Admiralty, 1942–46. Faulds Fellow in Law, Glasgow Univ., 1931–34; Asst to Professor of Law, Glasgow, 1934–46. Lectr in History of Scots Law, Glasgow, 1951–59; Senior Lectr, Dept of Scots Law, Edinburgh, 1959–67. Literary Dir, Stair Soc., 1954–60. *Publications:* Ed., Baron Hume's Lectures (Stair Soc.), 1939–57; Ed. and Contrib., Introductory History of Scots Law (Stair Soc.), 1958; Asst Ed., A Source Book and History of Administrative Law in Scotland, 1956; (with J. G. S. Cameron) Law of Landlord and Tenant in Scotland, 1967; articles in various legal periodicals. *Recreations:* golf, tennis, walking. *Address:* 163 Colinton Road, Edinburgh EH14 1BE. *T:* 031-443 1660.

PATON, Sir George Whitecross, Kt 1957; Vice-Chancellor, University of Melbourne, 1951–68; *b* 16 August 1902; *s* of Rev. Frank H. L. Paton; *m* 1931, Alice Watson, CBE; one *s* three d. *Educ:* Scotch Coll., Melbourne; University of Melbourne; Magdalen College, University of Oxford. MA (Melb.), 1926; BA (Oxon), 1928; BCL (Oxon), 1929. Barrister-at-Law, Gray's Inn, 1929. Asst Lecturer, LSE, 1930; Professor of Jurisprudence, Univ. of Melbourne, 1931-51; Dean of Faculty of Law, 1946-51. Chairman Royal Commission on Television (Australia, 1953-54). LLD (Hon.): Glasgow, 1953; Sydney, 1955; Queensland, 1960; Tasmania, 1963; London, 1963; Monash, 1968; Melbourne, 1971; DCL (Hon.), Western Ontario, 1958. *Publications:* A Text Book of Jurisprudence, 1946, 4th edn 1972; Bailment in the Common Law, 1952; (with Barry and Sawer), Criminal Law in Australia, 1948. *Recreations:* tennis, walking, gardening. *Address:* Dunraven Avenue, Toorak, Victoria 3142, Australia. *T:* 240 1034. *Club:* Melbourne (Victoria, Aust.).

PATON, His Honour Harold William, DSC 1943; Judge of County Courts, Circuit No 54 (Bristol, etc) 1950-71; Chairman, Somerset Quarter Sessions, 1965-71; *b* 6 Oct. 1900; *s* of late Clifford James Paton; *m* 1947, Joan Orby, *d* of late Lt-Col Cecil Gascoigne, DSO, Seaforth Hldrs; one *d. Educ:* Winchester College; Christ Church, Oxford. Called to the Bar (Inner Temple), 1923 and practised at Common Law Bar. Served War of 1939-45 in RNVR (Coastal Forces); Lt-Comdr, 1944. *Recreations:* fishing, gardening. *Address:* Ardullie Farmhouse, Dingwall, Rossshire.

PATON, Sir Leonard (Cecil), Kt 1946; CBE 1944; MC 1915; MA; Director, Harrisons & Crosfield Ltd (Chairman, 1957-62); *b* 7 May 1892; 4th *s* of John Paton, Dunfermline, Fife, Headmaster; *m* 1917, Muriel, *yr d* of William Searles, Maidstone; one *s* one *d. Educ:* George Watson's Coll.; Edinburgh University (MA, 1st Class Hons Classics, 1914); Christ Church, Oxford (Exhibitioner). European War, 1914-18, Captain Cameronians (MC, despatches). *Recreations:* fishing, golf. *Address:* 52 Wilbury Road, Hove, Sussex.

PATON, Ven. Michael John Macdonald; Archdeacon of Sheffield, since 1978; *b* 25 Nov. 1922; *s* of late Rev. William Paton, DD, and Grace Mackenzie Paton (*née* Macdonald); *m* 1952, Isobel Margaret Hogarth; one *s* four *d. Educ:* Repton School; Magdalen Coll., Oxford (MA). Indian Army, 1942-46; HM Foreign Service, 1948-52; Lincoln Theological Coll., 1952-54; Deacon 1954, priest 1955; Curate, All Saints', Gosforth, Newcastle upon Tyne, 1954-57; Vicar, St Chad's, Sheffield, 1957-67; Chaplain, United Sheffield Hosps, 1967-70; Vicar, St Mark's, Broomhill, Sheffield, 1970-78. *Publications:* contrib. to: Essays in Anglican Self-criticism, 1958; Religion and Medicine, 1976. *Recreations:* hill walking, music. *Address:* 62 Kingfield Road, Sheffield S11 9AU. *T:* Sheffield 57782.
   See also Bishop of Birmingham, Rev. Canon D. M. Paton, Prof. Sir W. D. M. Paton.

PATON, Sir Stuart (Henry), KCVO 1965; CBE 1945; Captain RN, retired; *b* 9 July 1900; *s* of William Henry Paton and Winifred Powell, Norwood; *m* 1925, Dorothy Morgan, Shrewsbury; two *s* two *d. Educ:* Hillside, Godalming; RN Colleges, Osborne and Dartmouth. Served European War: Midshipman, HMS Marlborough, Grand Fleet, 1916; Sub-Lt, HMS Orcadia, English Channel, 1918. Specialised as Torpedo Officer; posts Lieut to Commander: Mediterranean and Home Fleets, Admiralty Plans Division, and New Zealand. War of 1939-45: HMS Vernon, Captain, 1940; Admiralty, Joint Intelligence Staff, 1941; Comd HMS Curacoa, E. Coast Convoys, 1942; Comd HMS Nigeria, Home Fleet and Eastern Fleet, 1942-44 (despatches Malta Convoy); Admiralty and served as a Dep.-Director, Admin. Planning, 1945-46; student, IDC, 1947; Comd HMS Newcastle, Mediterranean Fleet, 1948-49; Appointed ADC to King George VI, 1949; retired, 1950; General Secretary to King George's Fund for Sailors, 1950-65. *Recreations:* gardening, photography. *Address:* West Stroud, Grayswood, Haslemere, Surrey. *T:* Haslemere 3973.
   See also J. E. C. Kennon.

PATON, Sir (Thomas) Angus (Lyall), Kt 1973; CMG 1960; FRS 1969; FEng; Senior Consultant, Sir Alexander Gibb & Partners, since 1977 (Senior Partner, 1955-77); *b* 10 May 1905; *s* of Thomas Lyall Paton and Janet (*née* Gibb); *m* 1932, Eleanor Joan Delmé-Murray (*d* 1964); two *s* two *d. Educ:* Cheltenham Coll.; University College, London. Fellow of University College. Joined Sir Alexander Gibb & Partners as pupil, 1925; after experience in UK, Canada, Burma and Turkey on harbour works, hydro-electric projects and industrial development schemes, was taken into partnership, 1938. Responsible for design and supervision of construction of many large industrial factories and for major hydro-electric and irrigation projects, including Owen Falls and Kariba Schemes, and for overall supervision of Indus Basin Project in W. Pakistan; also for economic surveys in Middle East and Africa on behalf of Dominion and Foreign Governments. Member UK Trade Mission to: Arab States, 1953; Egypt, Sudan and Ethiopia, 1955. Mem. NERC, 1969-72. Pres. ICE, 1970-71; Chm., Council of Engineering Instns, 1973; Past Chairman Assoc. of Consulting Engineers. FICE (Hon. FICE, 1975); FIStructE, Fellow Amer. Soc. of Civil Engineers, Past Pres., British Section, Soc. of Civil Engineers (France); a Vice-Pres., Royal Soc., 1977-78; For. Associate, Nat. Acad. of Engineering, USA, 1979. Founder Fellow, Fellowship of Engineering, 1976; FRSA. Fellow, Imperial Coll., London, 1978. Hon. DSc: London, 1977; Bristol, 1981. *Publications:* Power from Water, 1960; technical articles on engineering subjects. *Address:* L'Epervier, Route Orange, St Brelade, Jersey. *T:* 45619. *Club:* Athenæum.

PATON, Prof. Sir William (Drummond Macdonald), Kt 1979; CBE 1968; MA, DM; FRS 1956; FRCP 1969; JP; Professor of Pharmacology in the

University of Oxford, and Fellow of Balliol College, since Oct. 1959; *b* 5 May 1917; 3rd *s* of late Rev. William Paton, DD, and Grace Mackenzie Paton; *m* 1942, Phoebe Margaret, *d* of Thomas Rooke and Elizabeth Frances (*née* Pearce); no *c. Educ:* Winchester House Sch., Brackley; Repton Sch.; New Coll., Oxford (Scholar; Hon. Fellow, 1980); University College Hospital Medical Sch. BA (Oxon) Natural Sciences, Physiology, 1st class hons, 1938; Scholarships: Theodore Williams (Physiology), 1938; Christopher Welch, 1939; Jesse Theresa Rowden, 1939; Demonstrator in Physiology, Oxford, 1938-39; Goldsmid Exhibition, UCH Medical Sch., 1939; Ed. UCH Magazine, 1941; Fellowes Gold Medal in Clinical Med., 1941; BM, BCh Oxon, 1942; House physician, UCH Med. Unit, 1942. Pathologist King Edward VII Sanatorium, 1943-44; Member scientific staff, National Institute for Medical Research, 1944-52; MA 1948. Reader in Pharmacology, University College and UCH Med. Sch., 1952-54; DM 1953; Professor of Pharmacology, RCS, 1954-59. Delegate, Clarendon Press, 1967-72; Rhodes Trustee, 1968- (Chm., 1978-82). Chm., Cttee for Suppression of Doping, 1970-71; Member: Pharmacological Soc. (Chm. Edtl Bd, 1969-74, Hon. Mem., 1981); Physiological Soc. (Hon. Sec. 1951-57); British Toxicological Soc., 1980- (Chm., 1982-83); Med. Research Soc.; MRC, 1963-67; Council, Royal Society, 1967-69; British Nat. Cttee for History of Science, 1972- (Chm., 1980-); Council, Inst. Study of Drug Dependence, 1969-75; Central Adv. Council for Science and Technology, 1970; DHSS Independent Cttee on Smoking, 1978-; Adv. Cttee on Animal Experiments, 1980-. Pres., Inst. of Animal Technicians, 1969-75, Vice-Pres., 1976-; Chm., Research Defence Soc., 1972-78 (Paget Lectr, 1978); Wellcome Trustee, 1978-. Consultant, RN (Diving), 1978-82. Hon. Member: Soc. Franc. d'Allergie; Australian Acad. Forensic Sci.; Corresp. Mem., German Pharmacological Soc.; Hon. Lectr, St Mary's Hosp. Med. Sch., 1950; Visiting Lecturer, Swedish Univs, 1953; Brussels, 1956. Robert Campbell Oration, 1957; Lectures: Clover, 1958; Bertram Louis Abrahams, RCP, 1962; Ivison Macadam, RCSE, 1973; Osler, RCP, 1978; Cass, Dundee, 1981; Scheuler, Tulane, 1981; Hope Winch, Sunderland, 1982. Editor with R. V. Jones, Notes and Records of Royal Soc., 1971-. FRSA 1973; Hon FFARCS 1975; Hon FRSM 1982. JP St Albans, 1956. Bengue Meml Prize, 1952; Cameron Prize, 1956; Gairdner Foundn Award, 1959; Gold Medal, Soc. of Apothecaries, 1976. *Publications:* (with J. P. Payne) Pharmacological Principles and Practice, 1968; papers on diving, caisson disease, histamine, synaptic transmission, drug action and drug dependence in physiological and pharmacological journals. *Recreations:* music, old books. *Address:* 13 Staverton Road, Oxford. *Club:* Athenæum.
   See also Bishop of Birmingham, Rev. Canon D. M. Paton, Ven. M. J. M. Paton, Dr J. F. Stokes.

PATRICK, Graham McIntosh, CMG 1968; CVO 1981; DSC 1943; Under Secretary, Department of the Environment, 1971-81, retired; *b* 17 Oct. 1921; *m* 1945, Barbara Worboys; two *s. Educ:* Dundee High Sch.; St Andrews Univ. RNVR (Air Branch), 1940-46. Entered Ministry of Works, 1946; Regional Director: Middle East Region, 1965-67; South West Region, DoE, 1971-75; Chm., South West Economic Planning Bd, 1971-75; Dir, Scottish Services, PSA, 1975-81. *Address:* 1 Saxon Way, Wedmore, Somerset. *Clubs:* Naval; New (Edinburgh).

PATRICK, (James) McIntosh, ROI 1949; ARE; RSA 1957 (ARSA, 1949); Painter and Etcher; *b* 1907; *s* of Andrew G. Patrick and Helen Anderson; *m* 1933, Janet, *d* of W. Arnot Watterston; one *s* one *d. Educ:* Morgan Academy, Dundee; Glasgow School of Art. Awarded Guthrie Award RSA, 1935; Painting Winter in Angus purchased under the terms of the Chantrey Bequest, 1935; paintings purchased for Scottish Nat. Gall. of Modern Art; National Gallery, Millbank; National Gallery of South Africa, Cape Town; National Gallery of South Australia; Scottish Contemp. Art Assoc.; and Municipal collections Manchester, Aberdeen, Hull, Dundee, Liverpool, Glasgow, Greenock, Perth, Southport, Newport (Mon.), Arbroath, also for Lady Leverhulme Art Gallery, etc.; etchings in British Museum and other print collections. Served War of 1939-46, North Africa and Italy; Captain (General List). Hon. LLD Dundee, 1973. *Recreations:* gardening, music. *Address:* c/o Fine Art Society, New Bond Street, W1; The Shrubbery, Magdalen Yard Road, Dundee. *T:* Dundee 68561. *Club:* Scottish Arts (Edinburgh).

PATRICK, Brig. John, MC; *b* 10 June 1898; *s* of Lt-Col John Patrick, DL, and Florence Annie Rutherfoord; *m* (dissolved); two *s. Educ:* Harrow-on-the-Hill; RMA, Woolwich. 2nd Lieut, RFA, 1916; Chestnut Troop, RHA, 1919-28; Captain, 15/19th The King's Royal Hussars, 1928-38; psc 1934; retired, 1938; Lt-Col RA (SR), 1939; Brigadier, 1940-45; MP for Mid Antrim in Northern Ireland House of Commons, 1938-45. *Address:* Slemish, Preston, Hitchin, Herts. *T:* 2776.

PATRICK, John Bowman; Sheriff of North Strathclyde (formerly Renfrew and Argyll) at Greenock, since Oct. 1968; *b* 29 Feb. 1916; *s* of late John Bowman Patrick, Boot and Shoe maker, Greenock, and late Barbara Patrick (*née* James); *m* 1945, Sheina Struthers McCrea; one *d. Educ:* Greenock Academy; Edinburgh Univ.; Glasgow Univ. MA Edinburgh, 1937. Served War in Royal Navy, Dec. 1940-Dec. 1945; conscripted as Ordinary Seaman, finally Lieut RNVR. LLB Glasgow 1946. Admitted as a Solicitor in Scotland, June 1947; admitted to Faculty of Advocates, July 1956. Sheriff of Inverness, Moray, Nairn, Ross and Cromarty at Fort William and Portree (Skye), 1961-68. *Address:* 77 Union Street, Greenock, Renfrewshire. *T:* 20712.

PATRICK, Margaret Kathleen, OBE 1976; District/Superintendent Physiotherapist, Central Health District, Birmingham Area Health Authority

(Teaching) (formerly United Birmingham Hospitals Hospital Management Committee), since 1951; *b* 5 June 1923; *d* of late Roy and Rose Patrick. *Educ:* Godolphin and Latymer Sch., London; Guy's Hosp. Sch. of Physiotherapy. BA, Open Univ., 1980. MCSP. Chm. Physio. Adv. Cttee. and Mem. Health Care Planning for Elderly, Birmingham AHA (T). Member: Exec., Whitley Council PTA, 1960-75 (Chm., PTA Cttee C, 1960-75); Tunbridge Cttee on Rehab. Services, 1971-72; Hosp. Adv. Service on Geriatrics, 1972; DHSS Working Party on Stat. Data in Physio., 1969-76; Council, Chartered Soc. of Physio., 1953-75 (Exec. Mem., 1960-75; Vice Chm., 1971-75); Birmingham AHA (Teaching), 1979-. Assoc. of Supt Chartered Physiotherapists: Chm., 1964-75; Pres., 1971-72. *Publications:* Ultrasound Therapy: a textbook for physiotherapists, 1965; (contrib.) Physiotherapy in some Surgical Conditions, ed Joan Cash, 1977, 2nd edn 1979; contrib. Physiotherapy, and articles on ultrasound therapy, geriatric care, and paediatrics. *Recreation:* gardening. *Address:* 7 Hawthorn Coppice, Hagley, West Midlands DY9 0PE.

PATTEN, Brian; poet; *b* 7 Feb. 1946. *Publications: poetry:* Penguin Modern Poets, 1967; Little Johnny's Confession, 1967; Notes to the Hurrying Man, 1969; The Irrelevant Song, 1971; The Unreliable Nightingale, 1973; Vanishing Trick, 1976; The Shabby Angel, 1978; Telepoems and Grave Gossip, 1979; Love Poems, 1981; Clare's Countryside: a book on John Clare, 1982; *for younger readers:* The Elephant and the Flower, 1969; Jumping Mouse, 1971; *novels:* Mr Moon's Last Case, 1975 (Mystery Writers of Amer. Award, 1976); Emma's Doll, 1976; The Sly Cormorant and the Fish: adaptations of The Aesop Fables, 1977; Gangsters, Ghosts and Dragonflies, 1981; *play:* The Pig And The Junkle, 1975; *records:* Brian Patten Reading His Own Poetry, 1969; British Poets Of Our Time, 1974; Vanishing Trick, 1976; The Sly Cormorant, 1977. *Address:* c/o Allen and Unwin Ltd, Publishers, 40 Museum Street, WC1.

PATTEN, Christopher Francis; MP (C) Bath, since 1979; *b* 12 May 1944; *s* of late Francis Joseph Patten and Joan McCarthy; *m* 1971, Mary Lavender St Leger Thornton; three *d. Educ:* St Benedict's School, Ealing; Balliol College, Oxford. Conservative Research Dept, 1966-70; Cabinet Office, 1970-72; Home Office, 1972; Personal Asst to Chairman of Conservative Party, 1972-74; Director, Conservative Research Dept, 1974-79; PPS to Chancellor of Duchy of Lancaster and Leader of House of Commons, 1979-81, to Secretary of State for Social Services, 1981. Vice Chm., Cons. Parly Finance Cttee; Member: Select Cttee on Defence; Select Cttee on Procedure. *Recreations:* reading, gardening, travelling in France. *Address:* 47 Morpeth Mansions, Morpeth Terrace, SW1. *T:* 01-828 3082; Cromwell's Rest, 207 Conkwell, near Winsley, Wilts. *T:* Limpley Stoke 3378. *Clubs:* Brooks's, Beefsteak.

PATTEN, John Haggitt Charles; MP (C) City of Oxford, since 1979; Parliamentary Under Secretary of State, Northern Ireland Office, since 1981; Fellow of Hertford College, Oxford, since 1972; *b* 17 July 1945; *s* of Jack Patten and late Maria Olga (*née* Sikora); *m* 1978, Louise Alexandra Virginia, 2nd *d* of John Rowe, Norfolk, and Claire Rowe, London. *Educ:* Wimbledon Coll.; Sidney Sussex Coll., Cambridge (PhD 1972). University Lectr, Univ. of Oxford, 1969-79. Oxford City Councillor, 1973-76. PPS to Mr Leon Brittan and Mr Tim Raison, Ministers of State at the Home Office, 1980-81. Editor: Journal of Historical Geography, 1975-80; (jt), Mainstream Book Club, 1978-. Mem. Council, Univ. of Reading. *Publications:* The Conservative Opportunity (with Lord Blake), 1976; English Towns, 1500-1700, 1978; Pre-Industrial England, 1979; articles on economic, regional and envl matters. *Recreation:* talking to my wife. *Address:* House of Commons, SW1; Hertford College, Oxford. *Clubs:* Beefsteak; Clarendon (Oxford).

PATTEN, Prof. Thomas Diery, CBE 1981; PhD; CEng, FIMechE; FRSE; Professor and Head of Department of Mechanical Engineering, Heriot-Watt University, 1967-82; *b* 1 Jan. 1926; *s* of late William Patten and of Isabella (*née* Hall); *m* 1950, Jacqueline McLachlan (*née* Wright); one *s* two *d. Educ:* Leith Acad.; Edinburgh Univ. (BSc, PhD). CEng, FIMechE 1965; FRSE 1967. Captain REME, 1946-48: served Palestine and Greece. Barry Ostlere & Shepherd Ltd, Kirkcaldy, 1949; Asst Lectr, Lectr and Sen. Lectr, Dept of Engrg, Univ. of Edinburgh, 1950-67; Dir, Inst. of Offshore Engineering, Heriot-Watt Univ., 1972-79; Vice-Principal, Heriot-Watt Univ., 1978-80, Acting Principal, 1980-81. Vis. Res. Fellow, McGill Univ., Canada, 1958. Researches in heat transfer, 1950-; British and foreign patents for heat exchange and fluid separation devices. Man. Dir, Compact Heat Exchange Ltd, 1970-; Director: Scottish Elect. Trng Scheme Ltd, 1977-82; Pict Petroleum PLC, 1981-. Member: Council, IMechE, 1971-73 and 1975-; Oil Develt Council for Scotland, 1973-78; Offshore Technol. Bd, Dept of Energy, 1975-82; SRC Marine Technol. Task Force, 1975-76; Brit. Nat. Cttee for Oceanic Res., 1978-82; Design Council (Scottish Cttee), 1979-82; Council, RSE, 1969-79 (Vice-Pres. RSE, 1976-79). *Publications:* technical and scientific papers in field of heat transfer in Proc. IMechE, and Internat. Heat Transfer Conf. Proc.; also papers on offshore engineering. *Recreations:* squash, gardening, music. *Address:* 15 Frogston Road West, Edinburgh EH10 7AB. *T:* 031-445 1464. *Club:* Caledonian.

PATTERSON, Arthur, CMG 1951; Assistant Secretary, Department of Health and Social Security, 1968-71; *b* 24 June 1906; 2nd *s* of late Alexander Patterson; *m* 1942, Mary Ann Stocks, *er d* of late J. L. Stocks; two *s* one *d. Educ:* Methodist Coll., Belfast; Queen's Univ., Belfast; St John's Coll., Cambridge. Entered Ministry of Labour, 1929; Assistant Secretary, 1941; transferred to Ministry of National Insurance, 1945; lent to Cyprus, 1953;

Malta, 1956; Jamaica, 1963; Kuwait, 1971. *Address:* 42 Campden Hill Square, W8. *T:* 01-229 3894.

PATTERSON, Maj.-Gen. Arthur Gordon, CB 1969; DSO 1964; OBE 1961; MC 1945; Director of Army Training, 1969-72; retired; *b* 24 July 1917; *s* of late Arthur Abbey Patterson, Indian Civil Service; *m* 1949, Jean Mary Grant; two *s* one *d. Educ:* Tonbridge Sch.; RMC Sandhurst. Commnd, 1938; India and Burma, 1939-45; Staff Coll., Camberley, 1949; jssc 1955; CO 2nd 6th Queen Elizabeth's Own Gurkha Rifles, 1959-61; Comdr 99 Gurkha Inf. Brigade, 1962-64; idc 1965; GOC 17 Div. and Maj.-Gen., Bde of Gurkhas, 1965-69. Col, 6th Queen's Own Gurkha Rifles, 1969-73. *Address:* Burnt House, Benenden, Cranbrook, Kent. *Club:* Naval and Military.

PATTERSON, Rt. Rev. Cecil John, CMG 1958; CBE 1954; DD (Lambeth), 1963; DD (University of Nigeria, Nsukka), 1963; Commander of the Federal Republic (CFR) (Nigeria), 1965; *b* 9 Jan. 1908. *Educ:* St Paul's School; St Catharine's Coll., Cambridge; Bishop's Coll., Cheshunt. London Curacy, 1931-34; Missionary in S Nigeria, 1934-41; Asst Bishop on the Niger, 1942-45; Bishop on the Niger, 1945-69; Archbishop of West Africa, 1961-69; Representative for the Archbishops of Canterbury and York for Community Relations, 1970-72; Hon. Asst Bishop, Diocese of London, 1970-76. Hon. Fellow, St Catharine's Coll., Cambridge, 1963. *Address:* 6 High Park Road, Kew, Surrey. *T:* 01-876 1697.

PATTERSON, Mrs (Constance) Marie, CBE 1978 (OBE 1973); National Officer, Transport and General Workers' Union, since 1976 (National Woman Officer, 1963-76); Member of General Council of TUC since 1963 (Chairman, 1974-75 and 1977); *b* 1 April 1934; *d* of Dr Richard Swanton Abraham; *m* 1960, Thomas Michael Valentine Patterson (marr. diss. 1976). *Educ:* Pendleton High Sch.; Bedford Coll., Univ. of London (BA). Joined Staff of TGWU, 1957; serves on various negotiating cttees; Member: Exec., Confedn of Shipbuilding and Engrg Unions, 1966- (Pres., 1977-78); Hotel and Catering Trng Bd, 1966-; Equal Opportunities Commn, 1975-; Central Arbitration Commn, 1976-. Dir of Remploy, 1966-. Lay Mem., Press Council, 1964-70. Hon. DSc Salford, 1975. *Recreations:* cooking, sight-seeing. *Address:* 15 Mackeson Road, NW3. *T:* 01-485 1327; Transport House, Smith Square, SW1. *T:* 01-828 7788.

PATTERSON, Eric, MBE 1970; HM Diplomatic Service; Consul-General, Auckland, New Zealand, since 1982; *b* 2 May 1930; *s* of Harold and Elizabeth Patterson; *m* 1953, Doris (*née* Mason); two *s. Educ:* Hookergate Grammar Sch., Co. Durham. Served Royal Signals, 1948-50. County Public Assistance Dept, Durham, 1947; City Architect's Dept, Newcastle upon Tyne, 1948; County Court (Lord Chancellor's Dept), Newcastle upon Tyne, 1950-52; Board of Trade: London, 1952-54; Newcastle upon Tyne, 1954-60; Manchester, 1960-62; Asst Trade Comr, Halifax, NS, 1962-67; Second Sec. (Commercial), Khartoum, 1967-70; First Sec. (Commercial), The Hague, 1970-74; FCO, 1974-76; First Sec. (Commercial), Warsaw, 1976-80; FCO, 1980-82. *Recreations:* golf, sailing, photography, fly-fishing. *Address:* c/o Foreign and Commonwealth Office, SW1; 19 Glen Atkinson Street, Auckland 5, New Zealand. *T:* 583 557. *Clubs:* Civil Service; Royal Over-Seas League, Northern, Auckland, Remuera Golf (Auckland).

PATTERSON, Geoffrey Crosbie, OBE 1975; Partner, Scott-Moncrieff, Thomson & Shiells, Chartered Accountants, 1936-79 (Senior Partner, 1966-79); *b* 24 Sept. 1912; *s* of late John George and late Elizabeth Louise Patterson; *m* 1939, Fay Mary, *d* of late James Wilson, solicitor; two *s. Educ:* Edinburgh Academy. Served War of 1939-45, Major, RA (Despatches). Qualified as Chartered Accountant, 1935; Chm., Anderson Brown Ltd, steel stock holders, Edinburgh, retd 1981; Chm., William Muir (Bond 9) Ltd, whisky bottlers and blenders, Edinburgh, 1979-82. Pres., Inst. of Chartered Accountants of Scotland, 1971-72. Hon. Nat. Treasurer, The Royal British Legion, Scotland, 1958-77; Sec. and Treasurer, Scottish National War Memorial, retd 1979. *Recreations:* shooting, golf. *Address:* Bankhead, Humbie, East Lothian EH36 5PD. *Club:* New (Edinburgh).

PATTERSON, George Benjamin; Member (C) Kent West, European Parliament, since 1979; *b* 21 April 1939; *s* of late Eric James Patterson and of Ethel Patterson; *m* 1970, Felicity Barbara Anne Raybould; one *s* one *d. Educ:* Westminster Sch.; Trinity Coll., Cambridge (MA). Lecturer, Swinton Conservative Coll., 1961-65; Editor (at Conservative Political Centre), CPC Monthly Report, 1965-74; Dep. Head, London Office of European Parlt, 1974-79. *Publications:* The Character of Conservatism, 1973; Direct Elections to the European Parliament, 1974. *Recreations:* squash, reading science fiction. *Address:* Birchenholt, Wellingtonia Avenue, Crowthorne, Berkshire RG11 6AF. *T:* 01-839 1340. *Clubs:* Europe House (National Liberal); International Chateau St Anne (Brussels).

PATTERSON, Harry; novelist; *b* 27 July 1929; *s* of Henry Patterson and Rita Higgins Bell; *m* 1958, Amy Margaret Hewitt; one *s* three *d. Educ:* Roundhay Sch., Leeds; Beckett Park Coll. for Teachers; London Sch. of Economics as external student (BSc(Hons) Sociology). FRSA. NCO, The Blues, 1947-50. 1950-58: tried everything from being a clerk to a circus tent-hand; 1958-72: variously a schoolmaster, Lectr in Liberal Studies, Leeds Polytechnic, Sen. Lectr in Education, James Graham Coll. and Tutor in Sch. Practice, Leeds Univ.; since age of 41, engaged in full-time writing career. Dual citizenship, British/Irish. *Publications include:* (as Jack Higgins) The Eagle has Landed, 1975 (filmed 1976); Storm Warning, 1976; Day of Judgement, 1978; Solo,

1980; Luciano's Luck, 1981; Touch the Devil, 1982; (as Harry Patterson) The Valhalla Exchange, 1978; To Catch a King, 1979; and many others under pseudonyms (Martin Fallon, Hugh Marlowe, Henry Patterson); some books trans. into 42 languages. *Recreations:* tennis, old movies. *Address:* c/o Higham Associates Ltd, 5/8 Lower John Street, Golden Square, W1R 4HA. *T:* 01-437 7888.

PATTERSON, Hugh Foggan, MA; Secretary, King's College London, since 1977; *b* 8 Nov. 1924; *s* of late Sir John Robert Patterson, KBE, CMG, and late Esther Margaret Patterson; *m* 1956, Joan Philippa Abdy Collins; one *s* two *d. Educ:* Royal Grammar Sch., Newcastle upon Tyne; King's Coll., Cambridge (MA). Served War, Royal Artillery, 1943-47. HM Oversea Civil Service, Nigeria, 1950-61; Universities of: Birmingham, 1962-63; Warwick, 1964-69; London, 1969- (Clerk of the Senate, 1976-77). *Recreations:* music, golf, badminton. *Address:* Lower Beechcroft, Chesham Road, Berkhamsted HP4 3AB. *T:* Berkhamsted 4353.

PATTERSON, John Allan; Deputy Director (Under Secretary), Department for National Savings, since 1981; *b* 10 Oct. 1931; *s* of William Gilchrist Patterson and May (*née* Eggie); *m* 1956, Anne Marie Lasson; one *s* two *d. Educ:* Epsom Coll.; Clare Coll., Cambridge (Major Scholar in Classics, Stewart of Rannoch Scholar; BA 1954). HM Diplomatic Service, 1954-65: served in Bangkok, 1957-61 and in Rome, 1961-64 (Private Sec. to the Ambassador); HM Treasury, 1965-81 (on loan to Cabinet Office, 1974-78). *Recreations:* church and garden. *Address:* 5 Nelson Gardens, Guildford, Surrey GU1 2NZ. *T:* Guildford 64369.

PATTERSON, Mrs Marie; *see* Patterson, Mrs C. M.

PATTERSON, Dr Mark Lister; Consultant Haematologist to the National Heart and Chest Hospitals, since 1967; *b* 2 March 1934; *s* of Alfred Patterson and Frederica Georgina Mary Lister Nicholson; *m* 1958, Jane Teresa Scott Stokes; one *s* two *d. Educ:* privately; St Bartholomew's Hosp. Med. Coll., Univ. of London (MB 1959). MRCP. Jun. hosp. appts at St Bartholomew's Hosp., Royal Postgrad. Med. Sch., and MRC Exptl Haematol. Unit. Mem., GLC, 1970-73 and 1977-; Parly Candidate (C) Ealing N, 1974. *Recreations:* medicine, politics. *Address:* Woolverton Manor, Shorwell, Newport, Isle of Wight. *T:* Brighstone 740609; 32 Christchurch Hill, NW3 1JL. *T:* 01-435 7233. *Club:* Carlton.

PATTERSON, Ven. William James; Archdeacon of Wisbech, since 1979; Vicar of Wisbech St Mary, since 1980; *b* 25 Sept. 1930; *s* of William Moscrop and Alice Patterson; *m* 1955, Elisabeth Roederer; one *s* two *d. Educ:* Haileybury; Balliol College, Oxon. MA. Asst Curate of St John Baptist, Newcastle upon Tyne, 1955-58; Priest-in-Charge, Rio Claro with Mayaro, Dio. Trinidad, 1958-65; Rector of Esher, 1965-72; RD of Emly, 1968-72; Rector of Little Downham, 1972-80; Priest-in-Charge of Coveney, 1978-80. *Recreation:* canalling. *Address:* The Vicarage, Church Road, Wisbech St Mary, Wisbech, Cambs PE13 4RN. *T:* Wisbech St Mary 596.

PATTIE, Geoffrey Edwin; MP (C) Chertsey and Walton since Feb. 1974; Parliamentary Under Secretary of State for Defence Procurement, since 1981; *b* 17 Jan. 1936; *s* of late Alfred Edwin Pattie and Ada Olive (*née* Carr); *m* 1960, Tuěma Caroline (*née* Eyre-Maunsell); one *s* one *d. Educ:* Durham Sch.; St Catharine's Coll., Cambridge (MA). BA Cantab 1959. Called to Bar, Gray's Inn, 1964. Served: Queen Victoria's Rifles (TA), 1959-61; (on amalgamation) Queen's Royal Rifles (TA), now 4th Royal Green Jackets, 1961-65; Captain, 1964. Mem. GLC, Lambeth, 1967-70; Chm. ILEA Finance Cttee, 1968-70. Chm. of Governors, London Coll. of Printing, 1968-69. Contested (C) Barking, 1966 and 1970. Sec., Cons. Parly Aviation Cttee, 1974-75, 1975-76, Vice Chm., 1976-77, 1977-78; Jt Sec., Cons. Parly Defence Cttee, 1975-76, 1976-77, 1977-78, Vice Chm., 1978-79; Mem., Cttee of Public Accounts, 1976-79; Vice-Chm., All Party Cttee on Mental Health, 1977-79. Parly Under Sec. of State for Defence for the RAF, 1979-81. Mem. General Synod of Church of England, 1970-75. *Publications:* Towards a New Defence Policy, 1976; (with James Bellini) A New World Role for the Medium Power: the British Opportunity, 1977. *Recreations:* travel, opera, cricket. *Address:* c/o House of Commons, SW1A 0AA. *Club:* Royal Green Jacket.

PATTINSON, Hon. Sir Baden, KBE 1962; LLB; Member, legal firm Pattinson, McLaughlin & Reid Smith; *b* 22 Dec. 1899; *m* 1926, Florence, *d* of T. A. Doman. Mayor of Maitland, 1928-30, and 1933; Mayor of Glenelg, 1944-47; MHA, South Australia: for Yorke Peninsula, 1930-38; for Glenelg, 1947-65; Minister of Education, SA, 1953-65. *Recreations:* horse riding, reading. *Address:* 12 Maturin Road, Glenelg, Adelaide, SA 5045, Australia.

PATTINSON, John Mellor, CBE 1943; MA; *b* 1899; *s* of late J. P. Pattinson, JP, Mobberley, Cheshire; *m* 1927, Wilhelmina, *d* of late W. J. Newth, Cheltenham; two *s. Educ:* Rugby Sch.; RMA; Cambridge Univ. RFA with BEF, 1918-19. Anglo-Iranian Oil Co., South Iran, 1922-45, General Manager, 1937-45. Director until 1969, British Petroleum Co. of Canada Ltd; Triad Oil Co. Ltd; BP Germany AG; Dep. Chm. 1960-65, and Man. Dir 1952-65, British Petroleum Co. Ltd; Chartered Bank, 1965-73. *Recreations:* gardening, travel. *Address:* Oakhurst, West Byfleet, Surrey. *Club:* East India, Devonshire, Sports and Public Schools.

PATTINSON, Peter L. F.; *see* Foden-Pattinson, P. L.

PATTINSON, William Derek; Secretary-General, General Synod of Church of England, since 1972; *b* 31 March 1930; *s* of late Thomas William Pattinson and of Mrs Elizabeth Pattinson. *Educ:* Whitehaven Grammar Sch.; Queen's Coll., Oxford (Stanhope Historical Essay Prize, 1951). BA 1952; MA 1956. Entered Home Civil Service, 1952; Inland Revenue Dept, 1952-62 and 1965-68; HM Treasury, 1962-65 and 1968-70; Assoc. Sec., General Synod, 1970-72. Chm., William Temple Assoc., 1966-70; Member: Archbishops' Commn on Church and State, 1966-70; British Council of Churches; London Diocesan Synod. Mem., Governing Body: SPCK; Sir John Cass Foundn; Greycoat Foundn; Vice-Chm., Grosvenor Chapel Cttee, 1973-81; Chm. of Governors, Liddon House, 1972-. Mem., Parish Clerks' Co. Freeman, City of London. *Address:* 4 Tufton Street, SW1P 3QY. *T:* 01-222 6307. *Club:* Athenæum.

PATTISON, Prof. Bruce; Professor of Education, University of London Institute of Education, 1948-76, now Emeritus; *b* 13 Nov. 1908; *s* of Matthew and Catherine Pattison; *m* 1937, Dorothy Graham (*d* 1979). *Educ:* Gateshead Grammar Sch.; King's Coll., Newcastle upon Tyne; Fitzwilliam House, Cambridge. Henry Mellish Sch., Nottingham, 1933-35; Hymers Coll., Hull, 1935-36; Lecturer in English, University College, London, 1936-48 (Reader, 1948). Board of Trade, 1941-43; Ministry of Supply, 1943-45. *Publication:* Music and Poetry of the English Renaissance, 1948, 2nd edn 1970. *Address:* Coombe Bank, 6 Church Road, Kenley, Surrey CR2 5DU. *T:* 01-660 2991. *Clubs:* Athenæum, National Liberal.

PATTISON, David Arnold, PhD; Chief Executive, Scottish Tourist Board, since 1981; *b* 9 Feb. 1941; *s* of David Pattison and Christina Russell Bone; *m* 1967, Anne Ross Wilson; two *s* one *d. Educ:* Glasgow Univ. (BSc 1st Cl. Hons, PhD). Planning Assistant, Dunbarton County Council, 1966-67; Lecturer, Strathclyde Univ., 1967-70; Head of Tourism Division, Highlands and Islands Development Board, 1970-81. *Publications:* Tourism Development Plans for: Argyll Bute, Ayrshire, Burgh of Ayr, Ulster. *Recreations:* reading, watching soccer and Rugby, golf, gardening. *Address:* 7 Cramond Glebe Gardens, Cramond, Edinburgh EH4 6NZ.

PATTULLO, (David) Bruce; Treasurer and General Manager, Bank of Scotland, since 1979 (Deputy Treasurer and General Manager, 1978); *b* 2 Jan. 1938; *s* of Colin Arthur Pattullo and Elizabeth Mary Bruce; *m* 1962, Fiona Jane Nicholson; three *s* one *d. Educ:* Rugby Sch.; Hertford Coll., Oxford (MA). FIB (Scot.). Commnd Royal Scots and seconded to Queen's Own Nigeria Regt. Gen. Man., Bank of Scotland Finance Co. Ltd, 1975-; Dir and Chief Exec., British Linen Bank Ltd, 1977. Director: Bank of Scotland; British Linen Bank Ltd; Melville Street Investments (Edinburgh) Ltd. Chm., Cttee, Scottish Clearing Bankers; Mem., Council, Inst. of Bankers in Scotland. First Prizeman (Bilsland Prize), Inst. of Bankers in Scotland, 1964. *Recreation:* tennis. *Address:* 6 Cammo Road, Edinburgh EH4 8EB. *T:* 031-339 6012. *Clubs:* Caledonian; New (Edinburgh).

PAUK, György; violinist; Professor at Guildhall School of Music and Drama; *b* 26 Oct. 1936; *s* of Imre and Magda Pauk; *m* 1959, Susanne Mautner; one *s* one *d. Educ:* Franz Liszt Acad. of Music, Budapest. Toured E Europe while still a student; won three internat. violin competitions, Genoa 1956, Munich 1957, Paris 1959; soon after leaving Hungary, settled in London, 1961, and became a British citizen. London début, 1961; seasonal appearances there and in the provinces, with orchestra, in recital and chamber music; also plays at Bath, Cheltenham and Edinburgh Fests and London Promenade Concerts; performs in major European music venues, with Stockholm Philharmonic, Vienna Symphony, Berlin RIAS and others; US début, under Sir George Solti, with Chicago Symph. Orch., 1970, followed by further visits to USA and Canada to appear with major orchs; holds master classes, in Colo; plays regularly in Hungary following return in 1973; overseas tours to Australia, NZ, S America, S Africa, Middle and Far East; many performances for BBC, incl. Berg and Bartók concertos, with Boulez. As conductor/soloist, has worked with the English, Scottish and Franz Liszt chamber orchs and London Mozart Players; guest dir, Acad. of St Martin-in-the-Fields. Has made many recordings. With Peter Frankl and Ralph Kirshbaum, formed chamber music trio, 1973; performances at major fests; public concerts in Gt Britain have incl. complete Brahms and Beethoven Cycles; the trio has also made many broadcasts for the BBC; first perf. of Penderecki's Violin Concerto, Japan, 1979, UK, 1980; first perf. of Tippett's Triple Concerto, London, 1980. Hon. Mem., Guildhall Sch. of Music, 1980. *Address:* c/o Ingpen & Williams, Management, 14 Kensington Court, W8 5DN. *T:* 01-937 5158.

PAUL, Geoffrey David; Editor, Jewish Chronicle, since 1977; *b* 26 March 1929; *s* of Reuben Goldstein and Anne Goldstein; *m* 1st, 1952, Joy Stirling (marr. diss. 1972); one *d*; 2nd, 1974, Rachel Mann; one *s. Educ:* Liverpool, Kendal, Dublin. Weekly newspaper and news agency reporter, 1947-57; asst editor, Jewish Observer and Middle East Review, 1957-62; Jewish Chronicle, 1962-: successively sub-editor, foreign editor, Israel corresp., deputy editor. *Publication:* Living in Jerusalem, 1981. *Address:* 25 Furnival Street, EC4A 1JT. *T:* 01-405 9252. *Club:* Press.

PAUL, Rt. Rev. Geoffrey John; *see* Bradford, Bishop of.

PAUL, Air Cdre Gerard John Christopher, CB 1956; DFC 1944; MA; CEng; FRAeS; *b* 31 Oct. 1907; *s* of E. W. Paul, FRCS; *m* 1937, Rosemary (*d* 1975), *d* of Rear-Admiral H. G. E. Lane, CB; two *s* one *d. Educ:* Cheltenham Coll.; St John's Coll., Cambridge. Entered Royal Air Force,

1929; Fleet Air Arm, 1931-36; served War of 1939-45 in England and N.W. Europe; Commandant, Central Flying School, 1954-56; retired, 1958. Secretary-General of the Air League, 1958-71. Life Vice-Pres., RAF Gliding and Soaring Assoc.; Pres., Popular Flying Assoc., 1969-78; Chm., Hampshire Gundog Soc. Croix de Guerre avec Palme (Belgium), 1944; Military Cross (Czechoslovakia), 1945. *Recreations:* dogs, garden. *Address:* Wearne House, Old Alresford, Hants. *Club:* Royal Air Force.

PAUL, Hugh Glencairn B.; *see* Balfour-Paul.

PAUL, Sir John (Warburton), GCMG 1965 (KCMG 1962); OBE 1959; MC 1940; Director, Overseas Relations, St John Ambulance, since 1981; *b* 29 March 1916; 2nd *s* of Walter George Paul and Phoebe (*née* Bull), Weymouth; *m* 1946, Kathleen Audrey, CStJ 1962, *d* of Dr A. D. Weeden, Weymouth; three *d. Educ:* Weymouth Coll., Dorset; Selwyn Coll., Cambridge (MA). Secretary, Maddermarket Theatre, Norwich, 1936. Commissioned Royal Tank Regt (Suppl. Res.), 1937; regular commission, RTR, 1938; BEF 1940 (despatches, prisoner-of-war); ADC and Private Secretary to Governor of Sierra Leone, 1945 (seconded). Called to the Bar, Inner Temple, 1947. Colonial Administrative Service, Sierra Leone, 1947; District Commissioner, 1952; Permanent Secretary, 1956; Provincial Commissioner, 1959; Secretary to the Cabinet, 1960; Governor and C-in-C, The Gambia, 1962-65; Governor-General of The Gambia, 1965-66; Governor and C-in-C: British Honduras, 1966-72; The Bahamas, 1972-73; Governor-General, The Bahamas, July-Oct. 1973; Lt Governor, Isle of Man, 1974-80. Member Board, West African Airways Corporation, 1954-56. Chm., St Christopher Motorists' Security Assoc., and associated cos, 1980-. A Patron, Pain Relief Foundn, 1980-. Mem., Bd of Governors, Pangbourne Coll., 1981-. KStJ 1962. *Recreation:* painting. *Address:* Sherrens Mead, Sherfield-on-Loddon, Hampshire. *T:* Turgis Green 331. *Clubs:* Athenæum, MCC.

PAUL, Leslie (Allen); MA, DLitt, FRSL; author; Writer-in-Residence, St Paul and St Mary College, Cheltenham, since 1981; *b* Dublin, 1905. *Educ:* at a London Central School. Entered Fleet Street at age of 17; founded The Woodcraft Folk, a youth organisation, when 20; first Book (poems) when 21. Headed a delegation, on co-operation, to USSR, 1931; Editor, Plan, 1934-39; worked on Continent (refugees and underground movement); Tutor, WEA and LCC, 1933-40; called up, infantry, 1941; Middle East (AEC); Staff Tutor, Mount Carmel Coll. (MEF). Atlantic Award in Literature, 1946. Asst Director of Studies, Ashridge College of Citizenship, 1947-48; Director of Studies, at Brasted Place, Brasted, 1953-57. Leverhulme Research Fellow, 1957-59. Member Departmental Cttee on the Youth Service, 1958-60; Research Fellow, King George's Jubilee Trust and Industrial Welfare Society, 1960-61; Research Director, Central Advisory Council for the Ministry, for Church Assembly Enquiry into Deployment and Payment of the Clergy, 1962-64. Resident Fellow, Kenyon Coll. Ohio, 1964; Selwyn Lectr, St John's Coll., NZ, 1969; Lectr in Ethics and Social Studies, Queen's Coll., Birmingham, 1965-70; Scholar-in-Residence, Eastern Baptist Coll., Pa, USA, 1970. Mem., Gen. Synod of Church of England, 1970-75; Vice-Pres., Philosophical Soc., 1973-; Chm., Diocesan Council of Social Action (Hereford), 1972-78. Hale Meml Lectr, and Hon. DCL, Seabury-Western, USA, 1970. *Publications:* (chief books, 1944-): Annihilation of Man, 1944; The Living Hedge, 1946; The Meaning of Human Existence, 1949; Angry Young Man, 1951; The English Philosophers, 1953; Sir Thomas More, 1953; The Boy Down Kitchener Street, 1957; Nature into History, 1957; Persons and Perception, 1961; Son of Man, 1961; The Transition from School to Work, 1962; Traveller on Sacred Ground, 1963; The Deployment and Payment of the Clergy, 1964; Alternatives to Christian Belief, 1967; The Death and Resurrection of the Church, 1968; Coming to Terms with Sex, 1969; Eros Rediscovered, 1970; Journey to Connemara and other poems, 1972; A Church by Daylight, 1973; The Waters and the Wild, 1975; First Love, 1977; The Bulgarian Horse, 1979; The Springs of Good and Evil, 1979; Early Days of the Woodcraft Folk, 1980. *Recreations:* bird-watching, photography, making lawns. *Address:* 73 Shurdington Road, Cheltenham, Glos GL53 0JQ. *T:* Cheltenham 511762. *Club:* Royal Commonwealth Society.

PAUL, Noël Strange, CBE 1978; Member, Steering Committee on the Mass Media, Council of Europe, since 1976; Governor, English-Speaking Union, since 1980; *b* 1914; *y s* of late S. Evan Paul, SSC, and Susan, *d* of Dr Henry Habgood; *m* 1950, Mary, *yr d* of Philip J. Bone, FRSA, MRST, Luton. *Educ:* Kingston Grammar School. Journalist, Press Assoc., 1932; served War of 1939-45, Iran and Italy, Major seconded RAF (despatches). Home Counties Newspapers, 1949; Liverpool Daily Post, 1958; Press Council: Asst Sec., 1964; Sec., 1968-76; Dir, 1976-79. *Recreations:* sailing, photography. *Address:* The Lodge, St Catherine's, Strachur, Argyllshire PA25 8AZ. *T:* St Catherine's 208; Camus Lusta, Loch Bay, Waternish, Isle of Skye. *Clubs:* Athenæum, English-Speaking Union.

PAULET, family name of **Marquess of Winchester.**

PAULING, Linus (Carl); Research Professor, Linus Pauling Institute of Science and Medicine, since 1974; *b* 28 Feb. 1901; *s* of Herman William Pauling and Lucy Isabelle Darling; *m* 1923, Ava Helen Miller (*d* 1981); three *s* one *d. Educ:* Oregon State Coll.; California Institute of Technology. BS Oregon State Coll., 1922; PhD California Inst. of Technology, 1925; Hon. DSc: Oregon State Coll., 1933; Univ. of Chicago, 1941; Princeton Univ., 1946; Yale, 1947; Cambridge, 1947; London, 1947; Oxford, 1948; Brooklyn Polytechnic Inst., 1955; Humboldt Univ. (Berlin), 1959; Melbourne, 1964;

York (Toronto), 1966; LLD Reed Coll., 1959; LHD Tampa, 1949; Dr *hc*: Paris, 1948; Toulouse, 1949; Liège, 1955; Montpellier, 1958; Warsaw, 1969; Lyon, 1970; UJD, NB, 1950; DFA, Chouinard Art Inst., 1958. Asst in Chemistry and in Mechanics and Materials, Oregon State Coll., 1919-22; Graduate Asst, California Inst. Technology, 1922-23; Teaching Fellow, 1923-25; Research Associate, 1925-26; Nat. Res. Fellow in Chemistry, 1925-26; Fellow of John Simon Guggenheim Meml Foundn, 1926-27 (Univs of Munich, Zürich, Copenhagen); Asst Prof., California Inst. of Technology, 1927-29; Associate Prof., 1929-31; Prof. of Chemistry, 1931-63; Dir of Gates and Crellin Labs of Chemistry, and Chm., Div. of Chemistry and Chemical Engrg, 1936-58; Prof. of Chemistry, Stanford Univ., 1969-74. George Fisher Baker Lectr in Chemistry, Cornell Univ., Sept. 1937-Feb. 1938; George Eastman Prof., Oxford Univ., Jan.-June 1948, etc. Amer. Chem. Soc. Award in Pure Chemistry, 1931; William H. Nichols Medal, 1941; J. Willard Gibbs Medal, 1946; Theodore William Richards Medal, 1947; Davy Medal of Royal Society, 1947; Presidential Medal for Merit, 1948; Gilbert Newton Lewis Medal, 1951; Thomas Addis Medal, 1955; Amedeo Avogadro Medal, 1956; Pierre Fermat Medal, Paul Sabatier Medal, 1957; International Grotius Medal, 1957; Nobel Prize for Chemistry, 1954; Nobel Peace Prize for 1962, 1963; Linus Pauling Medal, 1966; Internat. Lenin Peace Prize, 1971; 1st Martin Luther King Jr Medical Award, 1972; Nat. Medal of Science, 1975; Lomonosov Gold Medal, Soviet Acad. of Scis, 1978. Member: Nat. Acad. of Sciences; Amer. Phil. Soc.; Amer. Acad. of Arts and Sciences, etc.; Hon. Fellow: Chemical Society (London), Royal Institution, etc.; For. Member: Royal Society, Akademia Nauk, USSR, etc.; Associé étranger, Acad. des Sciences, 1966. War of 1939-45, Official Investigator for projects of National Defense Research Cttee on Medical Research, and Office of Scientific Research and Development. Grand Officer, Order of Merit, Italian Republic. *Publications:* The Structure of Line Spectra (with S. Goudsmit), 1930; Introduction to Quantum Mechanics (with E. B. Wilson, Jun), 1935; The Nature of the Chemical Bond, 1939 (3rd ed., 1960); General Chemistry, 1947 (2nd ed., 1953); College Chemistry, 1950 (3rd ed., 1964); No More War!, 1958 (revised edn, 1962); The Architecture of Molecules (with Roger Hayward), 1964; The Chemical Bond, 1967; Vitamin C and the Common Cold, 1971; (with Peter Pauling) Chemistry, 1975; Vitamin C, the Common Cold and the Flu, 1976; (with Ewan Cameron) Cancer and Vitamin C, 1979; also numerous scientific articles in the fields of chemistry, physics, and biology including the structure of crystals, quantum mechanics, nature of the chemical bond, structure of gas molecules, structure of antibodies and nature of serological reactions, etc. *Address:* Linus Pauling Institute of Science and Medicine, 440 Page Mill Road, Palo Alto, California 94306, USA.

PAULL, Sir Gilbert (James), Kt 1957; Judge of High Court of Justice, Queen's Bench Division, 1957-71; *b* 18 April 1896; *s* of Alan Paull, FSI, JP; *m* 1922, Maud Winifred (*d* 1978), *d* of Charles Harris, Streatham; one *s* one *d. Educ:* St Paul's Sch.; Trinity Coll., Cambridge. Called to Bar, Inner Temple, 1920; QC, 1939; Bencher of Inner Temple 1946, Reader 1969, Treasurer 1970; Member of the Council of Legal Education, 1947-65; Recorder of Leicester, 1944-57.

PAULSON, Godfrey Martin Ellis, CB 1966; CMG 1959; OBE (mil.) 1945; HM Diplomatic Service, retired 1970; *b* 6 July 1908; *s* of late Lt-Col P. Z. Paulson, OBE, Manchester Regt and Royal Signals, and late Mrs M. G. Paulson, *d* of late Dr W. H. Ellis, Shipley Hall, Bradford, Yorkshire; *m* 1936, Patricia Emma, *d* of late Sir Hugh Murray, KCIE, CBE, and late Lady Murray, Englefield Green House, Surrey; one *s* one *d. Educ:* Westminster and Peterhouse, Cambridge. BA (Hons), 1930, MA 1940. Colonial Service; Assistant District Commissioner, Gold Coast Colony, 1930-32. Admitted Solicitor, 1936; practised in City of London until outbreak of war, 1939. Served 1939-45, Manchester Regt and on General Staff in Africa, UK, and North West Europe, including Military Mission to Free French; Lt-Col, 1945 (OBE 1945). Control Commn for Germany, 1945, for Austria, 1947-48. Joined Foreign Service, 1948, and served in Venice, Stockholm, Far East (Singapore), Beirut, Rome, Nice and Foreign Office. Member: British Sect., Franco-British Council, 1978-; Exec. Cttee, Franco-British Soc., 1972-. Officer, Order of St Charles, Monaco, 1981. *Address:* Eastley House, Brightwalton, near Newbury, Berks. *T:* Chaddleworth 226. *Clubs:* United Oxford & Cambridge University, Garrick, Special Forces, MCC.

PAULUSZ, Jan Gilbert; a Recorder of the Crown Court, since 1980; *b* 18 Nov. 1929; *s* of Jan Hendrik Olivier Paulusz and Edith (*née* Gilbert); *m* 1973, Luigia Maria Attanasio. *Educ:* The Leys Sch., Cambridge. Called to the Bar, Lincoln's Inn, 1957; South Eastern Circuit, 1959-. *Recreations:* mountain walking, photography. *Address:* 50 Royston Gardens, Redbridge, Ilford, Essex IG1 3SY. *Club:* Lansdowne.

PAUNCEFORT-DUNCOMBE, Sir Philip; *see* Duncombe.

PAVITT, Laurence Anstice; MP (Lab and Co-op) Brent South, since 1974 (Willesden West, Oct. 1959-1974); *b* 1 Feb. 1914; *s* of George Anstice Pavitt and May (*née* Brooshooft); *m* 1937, Rosina (*née* Walton); one *s* one *d. Educ:* Elementary and Central Sch., West Ham. National Organising Secretary, British Fedn of Young Co-operators, 1942-46; Gen. Secretary, Anglo Chinese Development Soc., 1946-52; Regional Education Officer, Co-operative Union, 1947-52; UN Technical Assistance Programme, Asian Co-operative Field Mission, 1952-55; National Organiser, Medical Practitioners' Union, 1956-59. PPS to: Secretary for Education and Science, 1964-65; Secretary of State for Foreign Affairs, 1965-66; Secretary of State for Economic Affairs,

1966-67; an Asst Govt Whip, 1974-76. Vice-Chairman: Parly Labour Party's Health Gp, 1977-80 (Chm., 1964-77); British China All Party Gp, 1978- (Chm., 1974-78); Chm., All Party Gp on Action on Smoking and Health, 1974-78; Member: Select Cttee on Overseas Aid, 1969-71; Exec. Cttee, Inter-Parly Union, 1967-81; Exec. Cttee, Commonwealth Parly Assoc.; UK Delegn to Council of Europe, 1980-; UK Delegn to WEU, 1980; Nat. Exec., Cooperative Party (Chm. Parly Gp), 1980. Vice-Pres., Brit. Assoc. for the Hard of Hearing; Member: Hearing Aid Council, 1968-74; MRC, 1969-72. *Recreations:* reading, walking. *Address:* House of Commons, SW1. *T:* 01-219 5225.

PAWSEY, James Francis; MP (C) Rugby, since 1979; *b* 21 Aug. 1933; *s* of William Pawsey and Mary Mumford; *m* 1956, Cynthia Margaret Francis; six *s* (including twins twice). *Educ:* St Osburg's School, Coventry; Coventry Tech. School; Coventry Tech. Coll. Chairman and Chief Exec., Autobar Machine Division; Director: Autobar Ltd; Autobar Group Industries Ltd; Autobar Contract Maintenance Ltd; Vend Finance Ltd; Autobar Pension Trustees Ltd; Corinium Ltd. PPS, DES, 1982-; Member: H of C Cons. European Reform Gp; H of C Cons. Middle East Council; Sec., British Solidarity with Poland Campaign. Member: Rugby RDC, 1965-73; Rugby Borough Council, 1973-75; Warwickshire CC, 1974-79; former Chm. and Pres., Warwickshire Assoc. of Parish Councils. Mem., Inst. of Dirs. *Address:* Shilton House, Shilton, Coventry, Warwickshire. *T:* Coventry 612922; (office) Autobar House, 61 Somers Road, Rugby. *T:* Rugby 71414.

PAWSON, Albert Guy, CMG 1935; Secretary General, International Rubber Study Group, 1948-60 (Secretary, 1944-48); *b* 30 May 1888; *s* of Albert Henry and Alice Sarah Pawson; *m* 1917, Helen Humphrey Lawson (*d* 1980); two *s*. *Educ:* Winchester College; Christ Church, Oxford. 2nd Class Honours School of History; joined Sudan Political Service, 1911; Governor, White Nile Province, 1927-31; Governor, Upper Nile Province, 1931-34; Sec., Internat. Rubber Regulation Cttee, 1934-42; Colonial Office, 1942-44. *Recreations:* fishing, cricket, tennis, Oxford Cricket Blue, 1908, 1909, 1910 and 1911, Captain 1910. *Address:* c/o P. H. C. Pawson, MBE, Lower Grenofen, Tavistock, Devon PL19 9ES.

PAXTON, John; author, also writing as Jack Cherrill; Editor, The Statesman's Year-Book, since 1969; *b* 23 Aug. 1923; *m* 1950, Joan Thorne; one *s* one *d*. Head of Economics department, Millfield, 1952-63. Asst Editor, 1964-68, and Dep. Editor, 1968, of The Statesman's Year-Book. *Publications:* (with A. E. Walsh) Trade in the Common Market Countries, 1965; (with A. E. Walsh) The Structure and Development of the Common Market, 1968; (with A. E. Walsh) Trade and Industrial Resources of the Common Market and Efta Countries, 1970; (with John Wroughton) Smuggling, 1971; (with A. E. Walsh) Into Europe, 1972; (ed) Everyman's Dictionary of Abbreviations, 1974; World Legislatures, 1974; (with C. Cook) European Political Facts 1918-1973, 1975; The Statesman's Year-Book World Gazetteer, 1975 (2nd edn, 1979); (with A. E. Walsh) Competition Policy: European and International Trends and Practices, 1975; The Developing Common Market, 1976; (with C. Cook) European Political Facts 1848-1918, 1977; A Dictionary of the European Economic Community, 1977, 2nd edn, A Dictionary of the European Communities, 1982 (commended, McColvin Medal Cttee); (with C. Cook) Commonwealth Political Facts, 1979; (with S. Fairfield) Calendar of Creative Man, 1980; (with C. Cook) European Political Facts 1789-1848, 1981; Companion to Russian History, 1983; contrib. to Keesing's Contemporary Archives, TLS. *Address:* Moss Cottage, Hardway, Bruton, Somerset BA10 0LN. *T:* Bruton 3423. *Clubs:* National, Royal Over-Seas League, PEN.

PAXTON, Peter James, FCIS; FCCA; FIB; Chief Executive Officer, Cambridge and District Co-operative Society Ltd, since 1972; Chairman: Co-operative Wholesale Society Ltd, since 1980; Co-operative Bank Ltd, since 1980; *b* 27 April 1923; *m* 1947, Betty Jane Madden; one *s* one *d*. *Educ:* Lawrence Sherriff Sch., Rugby. Served RAF, 1941-46. Accountant, Rugby Co-operative Society Ltd, 1949-55; Chief Accountant, Cambridge and District Co-operative Society Ltd, 1955. *Recreation:* sailing. *Address:* 11 Grange Gardens, Grange Road, Cambridge CB3 9AT. *T:* Cambridge 311442.

PAYNE, Alan Jeffrey; HM Diplomatic Service; Consul-General, Lyons, since 1982; *b* 11 May 1933; *s* of Sydney Ellis Payne and Lydia Payne; *m* 1959, Letitia Freeman; three *s*. *Educ:* Enfield Grammar Sch.; Queens' Coll., Cambridge (Exhibnr). RN, 1955-57. EMI, London, later Paris, 1957-62; Secretariat, NATO, Paris, 1962-64; joined Diplomatic Service, 1965; Commonwealth Relations Office (later FCO), 1965-67; British High Commn, Kuala Lumpur, 1967-70; FCO, 1970-72; British Embassy, Budapest, 1972-75; Counsellor, Mexico City, 1975-79; FCO, 1979-82. *Recreations:* music, theatre. *Address:* c/o Foreign and Commonwealth Office, King Charles Street, SW1A 2AH. *Club:* Royal Commonwealth Society.

PAYNE, Anson; *see* Payne, J. A.

PAYNE, Maj.-Gen. George Lefevre, CB 1966; CBE 1963; Director of Ordnance Services, Ministry of Defence, 1964-68; retired, 1968; *b* 23 June 1911; *s* of Dr E. L. Payne, MRCS, LRCP, Brunswick House, Kew, Surrey; *m* 1938, Betty Maud (*d* 1982), *d* of Surgeon Captain H. A. Kellond-Knight, RN, Eastbourne, Sussex; three *s*. *Educ:* The King's Sch., Canterbury; Roy. Mil. Coll., Sandhurst. Royal Leicestershire Regiment: England, Northern

Ireland, 1931-33; India, 1933-37; Royal Army Ordnance Corps: England, 1938-39; France, 1939-40; England, 1941-. Deputy Director Ordnance Services: HQ, BAOR, 1952-54; War Office, 1955-57; Commandant, Central Ordnance Depot, Chilwell, 1957-59; Deputy Director Ordnance Services, War Office, 1959-63; Commander, Stores Organization, RAOC, 1963-64; Col Comdt, RAOC, 1968-72. *Recreations:* shooting, gardening. *Address:* 17 Highridge Court, Downs Avenue, Epsom, Surrey. *Club:* Royal Commonwealth Society.

PAYNE, Maj.-Gen. Henry Salusbury Legh D.; *see* Dalzell-Payne.

PAYNE, Ian; a Recorder of the Crown Court, since 1972; *b* 15 July 1926; *s* of late Douglas Harold Payne and of Gertrude (*née* Buchanan); *m* 1st, 1951, Babette (marr. diss. 1975), *d* of late Comte Clarence de Chalus; four *s* two *d*; 2nd, 1977, Colette Eugénie, *d* of late Marinus Jacobus van der Eb, Rotterdam. *Educ:* Wellington Coll. Commnd 60th Rifles, 1944-48. Called to the Bar, Lincoln's Inn, 1953, Hong Kong, 1981; Dep. Recorder of Derby, 1969-72. *Address:* 2 Crown Office Row, Temple, EC4; 603 Hang Chong Building, 5 Queen's Road C, Hong Kong. *T:* 5-212616. *Clubs:* Garrick; Refreshers Cricket.

PAYNE, Prof. Jack Marsh; Director, ARC Institute for Research on Animal Diseases, since 1973; *b* 9 March 1929; *m* 1952, Sylvia Bryant; two *s* two *d*. *Educ:* Royal Veterinary Coll., London; University Coll. Hosp. Med. Sch., London. PhD, BSc; MRCVS; FIBiol. Res. Fellowship under Sir Roy Cameron, FRS, 1952-57; apptd, 1957, to staff of IRAD, Compton, Newbury, Berks, where principal res. has involved investigation of metabolic disorders of dairy cattle; esp. interest has centred around the concept of prodn disease and the develt of the Compton Metabolic Profile Test; Head of Dept of Functional Pathology, IRAD, 1961-73. Member: British Veterinary Assoc.; Assoc. of Veterinary Teachers and Res. Workers; Pathological Soc. Chm., VETEC (round table of experts on vet. science in EEC), 1976. Veterinary Advr, British Council, 1977. FRSA. G. Norman Hall Gold Medal, 1972; RASE: Res. Gold Medal, 1972; Bledisloe Trophy and Medal, 1981. *Publications:* Metabolic Disorders in Farm Animals, 1977; numerous references in sci. jls, esp. on subject of metabolic disorders. *Recreations:* fell walking, music (especially collecting rare operas), painting. *Address:* ARC Institute for Research on Animal Diseases, Compton, Newbury, Berks RG16 0NN. *T:* Compton 411. *Club:* Veterinary Research.

PAYNE, Rev. James Richmond, MBE 1982; ThL; JP; General Secretary, Bible Society in Australia, since 1968; Chairman, United Bible Societies World Executive Committee, since 1976; *b* 1 June 1921; *s* of late R. A. Payne, Sydney, New South Wales; *m* 1943, Joan, *d* of late C. S. Elliott; three *s*. *Educ:* Drummoyne High School; Metropolitan Business College, Moore Theological College, Sydney. Served War of 1939-45: AIF, 1941-44. Catechist, St Michael's, Surry Hills, NSW, 1944-47; Curate, St Andrew's, Lismore, NSW, 1947-50; Rector, St Mark's, Nimbin, NSW, 1950-52; Chaplain, RAAF, Malta and Amberley, Qld, 1952-57; Rector, St Stephen's, Coorparoo, Qld, 1957-62; Dean of Perth, Western Australia, 1962-68. JP, Queensland, 1960; JP, ACT, 1969. *Publication:* Around the World in Seventy Days, 1965. *Recreations:* sport, walking, reading, family. *Address:* PO Box 507, Canberra City, ACT 2601, Australia. *T:* 485188. *Clubs:* Weld (Perth); Commonwealth (Canberra).

PAYNE, Jane Marian, (Mrs A. E. Payne); *see* Manning, J. M.

PAYNE, (John) Anson, OBE 1945; Chairman, FMC, 1974-75 (Executive Vice-Chairman, 1972-74); formerly Director: FMC (Meat); C. & T. Harris (Calne); Marsh and Baxter, and other cos; *b* 19 May 1917; *yr s* of late Major R. L. Payne, DSO and of Mrs L. M. Payne (*née* Duncan); *m* 1949, Deirdre Kelly; one *s* one *d*. *Educ:* St Lawrence Coll., Ramsgate; Trinity Hall, Cambridge (MA). Entered Civil Service as Assistant Principal, 1939. Served War of 1939-45 (despatches twice, OBE): RAFVR, 1940-45; Wing Commander, 1943. Principal Private Secretary to Minister of Agriculture and Fisheries, 1947-51; Asst Secretary, 1951; seconded to Treasury, 1953-54; Under-Secretary, Min. of Agriculture, 1960-68. *Address:* Sandpit Cottage, 4 High Street, Ditchling, Sussex BN6 8TA. *T:* Hassocks 2310.

PAYNE, Keith, VC 1969; *b* 30 Aug. 1933; *s* of Henry Thomas Payne and Remilda Payne (*née* Hussey); *m* 1954, Florence Catherine Payne (*née* Plaw); five *s*. *Educ:* State School, Ingham, North Queensland. Soldier, Department of Army, Aug. 1951-75; 1 RAR, Korea, 1952-53; 3 RAR, Malaya, 1963-65; Aust. Army Trng Team, Vietnam, 1969 (Warrant Officer); WO Instructor: RMC, Duntroon, ACT, 1970-72; 42 Bn, Royal Qld Regt, Mackay, 1973-75; Captain, Oman Army, 1975-76. Member: VC and GC Assoc.; Returned Services League; Korea and South East Asia Forces Assoc. Freeman City of Brisbane and of Shire of Hinchinbrook. Vietnamese Cross of Gallantry, with bronze star, 1969; US Meritorious Unit Citation; Vietnamese Unit Citation Cross of Gallantry with Palm. *Recreations:* football, fishing, hunting. *Address:* 11 Canberra Street, North Mackay, Qld 4740, Australia. *T:* (079) 578497.

PAYNE, Leonard Sidney; Director, J. Sainsbury Ltd, since 1974; *b* 16 Dec. 1925; *s* of Leonard Sydney Payne and Lillian May Leggatt; *m* 1944, Marjorie Vincent; two *s*. *Educ:* Woodhouse Grammar School. FCCA, FBIM, FCIT, FCIT, MBCS, MIRTE. Asst Accountant, Peek Frean & Co. Ltd, 1949-52; Chief Accountant, Administrator of various factory units, head office appts, Philips Electrical Industries, 1952-62; Dep. Gp Comptroller, Morgan Crucible

Co. Ltd, 1962-64; British Road Services Ltd: Finance Dir, 1964-67; Asst Man. Dir, 1967-69; Man. Dir, 1969-71; Dir of Techn. Services and Develt, Nat. Freight Corp., 1971-74, Vice-Chm. Executive 1974; Pres., Freight Transport Assoc., 1980-82. Chm., CBI Transport Policy Cttee, 1980-. *Recreations:* gardening, swimming, squash, chess. *Address:* Wisley, Gills Hill Lane, Radlett, Herts.

PAYNE, Norman John, CBE 1976 (OBE 1956; MBE (mil.) 1944); Chairman, British Airports Authority, since 1977 (Chief Executive, 1972-77); *b* 9 Oct. 1921; *s* of late F. Payne, Folkestone; *m* 1946, Pamela Vivien Wallis; four *s* one *d*. *Educ:* Lower Sch. of John Lyon, Harrow; City and Guilds Coll., London. BSc Eng Hons; FCGI, FICE, MIHE, FCIT, MSocCE (France); Mem. Architectural Assoc. Royal Engrs (Captain), 1939-45 (despatches twice); Imperial Coll. of Science and Technology London (Civil), 1946-49; Sir Frederick Snow & Partners, 1949, Partner 1955; British Airports Authority: Dir of Engrg, 1965; Dir of Planning, 1969, and Mem. Bd 1971. Pres., West European Airports Assoc., 1975-77; Chm., Airports Assoc. Co-ordinating Council, 1976. Chm., British Sect., Centre for European Public Enterprise, 1979-82. Chm., NICG, 1982-83. FBIM 1975. *Publications:* various papers on airports and air transport. *Recreations:* gardening, photography. *Address:* British Airports Authority, Head Office, Gatwick Airport, Gatwick, W Sussex RH6 0HZ. *T:* Gatwick 595200. *Clubs:* Reform, RAC.

PAYNE, Peter Charles John, PhD; MScAgrEng; agricultural consultant and farmer, since 1975; *b* 8 Feb. 1928; *s* of late C. J. Payne, China Clay Merchant, and Mrs F. M. Payne; *m* 1961, Margaret Grover; two *s* one *d*. *Educ:* Plymouth Coll.; Teignmouth Grammar School; Reading University. BSc Reading 1948; Min. of Agriculture Scholar, Durham Univ., MSc (Agr. Eng.) 1950; Scientific Officer, Nat. Institute of Agricultural Engineering, 1950-55; PhD Reading 1954; Lecturer in Farm Mechanisation, Wye College, London Univ., 1955-60; Lecturer in Agricultural Engineering, Durham Univ., 1960-61; Principal, Nat. Coll. of Agricultural Engineering, Silsoe, 1962-75; Visiting Professor: Univ. of Reading, 1969-75; Cranfield Inst. of Technology, 1975-80. Chm., Agricl Panel, Intermed. Technol. Develt Gp, 1979-; Mem., British Inst. of Agricl Consultants, 1978. Vice-Pres., Section III, Commn Internationale du Génie Rural, 1969. FIAgrE 1968; FRAgSs 1971; CEng 1980. *Publications:* various papers in agricultural and engineering journals. *Recreation:* sailing. *Address:* Garlidna Farm, Porkellis, Helston TR13 0JX. *T:* Constantine 40301. *Club:* Farmers'.

PAYNE, Sir Robert (Frederick), Kt 1970; President, The Law Society, 1969-70; Principal in Payne & Payne, Solicitors, Hull; *b* 22 Jan. 1908; *s* of late Frederick Charles Payne and of Edith Constance Payne (*née* Carlton); *m* 1st, 1937, Alice Marguerite, *d* of William Sydney Cussons, one *s* one *d* ; 2nd, 1951, Maureen Ruth, *d* of William Charles Walsh; one *s*. *Educ:* Hymers Coll., Hull. Solicitor, 1931. Served in RAF (Fighter Command), 1940-44, Sqdn Ldr, 2nd TAF. Chm., Cttee of Inquiry into Whittingham Hosp., 1971-72; Mem., Home Office Cttee on Liquor Licensing, 1971-72. Pres., Hull Incorporated Law Soc., 1954-55. Founder Mem., British Acad. of Forensic Sciences, 1959. Sheriff of Kingston-upon-Hull, 1957. Hon. Fellow, Victoria Coll. of Music, 1978. *Recreations:* golf, music. *Address:* High Woodgates, North Ferriby, North Humberside. *T:* Hull 631533. *Clubs:* East India, Devonshire, Sports and Public Schools; Royal Yorkshire Yacht (Life Member).

PAYNE, Rt. Rev. Sidney Stewart; *see* Newfoundland, Western, Bishop of.

PAYNE, (Trevor) Ian; *see* Payne, I.

PAYNE-BUTLER, George William; County Treasurer, Surrey County Council, 1973-79 (Assistant, 1962; Deputy, 1970); *b* 7 Oct. 1919; *s* of late George and Letitia Rachel Payne; *m* 1947, Joyce Louise Cockburn; one *s* two *d*. *Educ:* Woking Sch. for Boys. Joined Surrey CC, 1937. Served War, RAF, 1940-45. Chartered Municipal Treasurer, 1950 (CIPFA). *Recreations:* gardening, handicraft work in wood, reading. *Address:* Janston, Hillier Road, Guildford, Surrey GU1 2JQ. *T:* Guildford 65337.

PAYNE-GALLWEY, Sir Philip (Frankland), 6th Bt, *cr* 1812; *b* 15 March 1935; *s* of late Lt-Col Lowry Philip Payne-Gallwey, OBE, MC and of Janet, *d* of late Albert Philip Payne-Gallwey; *S* cousin, 1964. *Educ:* Eton; Royal Military Academy, Sandhurst. Lieut, 11th Hussars, 1957. *Recreations:* hunting, shooting, golf. *Heir:* none. *Address:* The Little House, Boxford, Newbury, Berks. *T:* Boxford 315. *Club:* Cavalry and Guards.

PAYNTER, Dr John Frederick; Professor of Music Education, University of York, since 1982; *b* 17 July 1931; *s* of late Frederick Albert Paynter and late Rose Alice Paynter; *m* 1956, Elizabeth Hill; one *d*. *Educ:* Emanuel Sch., London; Trinity Coll. of Music, London (GTCL 1952). DPhil York, 1971. Teaching appts, primary and secondary schs, 1954-62; Lectr in Music, City of Liverpool C. F. Mott Coll. of Educn, 1962-65; Principal Lectr (Head of Dept of Music), Bishop Otter Coll., Chichester, 1965-69; Lectr, Dept of Music, Univ. of York, 1969, Sen. Lectr, 1974-82. Composer and writer on music-educn. Dir, Schs Council Proj., Music in the Secondary School Curriculum, 1973-82. Gen. Editor, series, Resources of Music. *Publications:* Sound and Silence (with Peter Aston), 1970; Hear and Now, 1972; (with Elizabeth Paynter) The Dance and the Drum, 1974; All Kinds of Music, vols 1-3, 1976, vol. 4, 1979; Sound Tracks, 1978; Music in the Secondary School Curriculum: trends and developments in class music teaching, 1982; articles and revs in

Music in Educn, Music Teacher, Times Educnl Sup., Music Now (Aust. Contemp. Music Qtly), Music Educn Rev., Canadian Music Educator, Kreativ Musik Undervining, Muzikale vorming, Proposte di musica creativa nella scuola, Investigating Music (Australian Broadcasting Commn); scripts and commentaries for schs broadcasts and TV; *musical compositions:* choral and instrumental works including: Landscapes, 1972; The Windhover, 1972; May Magnificat, 1973; God's Grandeur, 1975; Sacraments of Summer, 1975; Galaxies for Orchestra, 1977; The Voyage of Brendan, 1978; The Visionary Hermit, 1979; The Inviolable Voice, 1980; String Quartet, 1981; Cantata for the Waking of Lazarus, 1981; The Laughing Stone, 1982; solo vocal and instrumental works and music-theatre works for children. *Recreations:* walking, wine-making. *Address:* Westfield House, Newton on Derwent, York YO4 5DA.

PAYNTER, Air Cdre Noel Stephen, CB 1946; DL; retired; *b* 26 Dec. 1898; *s* of late Canon F. S. Paynter, sometime Rector of Springfield, Essex; *m* 1925, Barbara Grace Haagensen; one *s* one *d*. *Educ:* Haileybury; RMC, Sandhurst. Flying Brevet, 1917; France and Russia, 1918-19 (St Anne 3rd Class); North-West Frontier, 1919-21; North-West Frontier, 1925-30; Malta, 1934; Directorate of Intelligence, Air Ministry, 1936-39; Chief Intelligence Officer, Middle East, 1939-42 (despatches); Chief Intelligence Officer, Bomber Command, 1942-45 (CB); Directorate of Intelligence, Air Ministry, 1946. Chm. Buckinghamshire Playing Fields Assoc., 1958-65; Chm. Bucks Army Cadet Force (TA), 1962-65. High Sheriff, Bucks, 1965. DL Buckinghamshire, 1963. *Address:* Lawn House, Edgcott, near Aylesbury, Bucks. *T:* Grendon Underwood 238.

PAYNTER, (Thomas) William; Secretary, National Union of Mineworkers, 1959-68; Member, Arbitration Panel for the Advisory Arbitration and Conciliation Service (formerly the TUC-CBI Conciliation Panel), since 1972; *b* 6 Dec. 1903; *s* of a Miner; *m* 1st, 1937; two *s* (twins); 2nd, 1943; five *s* (one set of twins). *Educ:* Whitchurch (Cardiff) and Porth Elementary Schools. Left school at age of 13 to work on a farm, 1917; commenced work in Rhondda Pits; elected Checkweigher at Cymmer Colliery, Porth, 1929; removed by Court injunction, 1931. Took part in hunger marches, 1931, 1932, 1936. Elected to Executive Committee, South Wales Miners' Federation for Rhondda, 1936; joined International Brigade, 1937; Miners' agent for Rhymney Area, 1939; President South Wales Miners, 1951. Mem., Commn on Industrial Relations, 1969-70. Chm., London Region, Nat. Fedn of Pension Assocs; Sec., London Jt Council for Senior Citizens. *Publications:* British Trade Unions and the Problem of Change, 1970; My Generation (autobiog.), 1972. *Recreations:* reading and gardening. *Address:* 32 Glengall Road, Edgware, Mddx.

PAYTON, Stanley Walden, CMG 1965; Chief of Overseas Department, Bank of England, 1975-80, retired; *b* 29 May 1921; *s* of late Archibald Walden Payton and late Ethel May Payton (*née* Kirtland); *m* 1941, Joan (*née* Starmer); one *s* one *d*. *Educ:* Monoux School. Fleet Air Arm, 1940-46; Entered Bank of England, 1946; UK Alternate on Managing Board of European Payments Union, Paris, 1957-59; First Governor of Bank of Jamaica, 1960-64.

PAYTON, Rev. Wilfred Ernest Granville, CB 1965; Vicar of Abingdon, 1969-79; Rural Dean of Abingdon, 1976-79; *b* 27 Dec. 1913; *s* of Wilfred Richard Daniel Payton and Alice Payton (*née* Lewin); *m* 1946, Nita Mary Barber; one *s* one *d*. *Educ:* Nottingham High School; Emmanuel College, Cambridge (MA); Ridley Hall, Cambridge. Ordained, 1938; Chaplain, RAF, 1941; Asst Chaplain-in-Chief, 1959; Chaplain-in-Chief, 1965-69; Archdeacon, Prebendary and Canon of St Botolph, Lincoln Cathedral, 1965-69. Hon. Chaplain to the Queen, 1965-69. *Recreations:* cricket (Cambridge Univ. 1937), hockey (Notts 1938-39), tennis. *Address:* Westwood, Nailsworth, Gloucester. *Clubs:* MCC; Hawks (Cambridge).

PAZ, Octavio; Mexican author; poet; Director, Revista Vuelta; *b* Mexico City, 31 March 1914; *s* of Octavio Paz and Josefina Lozano; *m* Marie José Tramini; one *d*. *Educ:* National Univ. of Mexico. Founded and directed Mexican literary reviews: Barandal, 1931; Taller, 1939; El Hijo Pródigo, 1943. Guggenheim Fellowship, USA, 1944. Former Sec., Mexican Embassy, Paris; Chargé d'Affaires *ad interim*, Japan, 1951; posted to Secretariat for External Affairs; Ambassador to India, 1962-68, resigned. Simon Bolivar Prof. of Latin-American Studies, Cambridge, 1970; Fellow of Churchill Coll., Cambridge, 1970-71; Charles Eliot Norton Prof. of Poetry, Harvard Univ., 1971-72. Formerly Editor, Plural. Prizes include: Internat. Poetry Grand Prix, 1963; Ollin Yoliztli, Mexico, 1980; Cervantes, Spain, 1982; Neustadt Internat. Prize for Literature, US, 1982. *Publications: poetry:* Luna Silvestre, 1933; Raiz del Hombre, 1937; Entre la Piedra y la Flor, 1941; A la Orilla del Mundo, 1942; Libertad bajo palabra, 1949; Aguila o Sol?, 1951; Semillas para un Himno, 1956; Piedra de Sol, 1957 (trans. as Sun Stone, 1960); La Estación Violenta, 1958; Libertad bajo palabra (poetical works 1935-58), 1960; Salamandra, 1962; Blanco, 1967; Topoemas, 1967; Discos Visuales, 1968; Ladera Este, 1969; Renga, 1971; Vuelta, 1976; in English: Selected Poems (1935-57), 1963; Configurations (1958-69), 1971; *prose:* El Laberinto de la soledad, 1951 (trans. as Labyrinth of Solitude, 1960); El Arco y la Lira, 1956 (trans. as The Bow and The Lyre, 1974); Las Peras del Olmo, 1957; Cuadrivio, 1965; Puertas al campo, 1966; Corriente Alterna, 1967 (trans. as Alternating Current, 1972); Claude Levi-Strauss o el Nuevo Féstin de Esopo, 1967 (trans. as On Levi-Strauss, 1970); Marcel Duchamp o El Castillo de la Pureza, 1967 (trans. as Marcel Duchamp or the Castle of Purity, 1970); Conjunciones y

Disyunciones (essay), 1969 (trans. as Conjunctions and Disjunctions, 1974); Postdata, 1970 (trans. as The Other Mexico, 1972); El Mono Gramático, 1971; Los Hijos del Limo, 1974 (trans. as Children of the Mire, 1974); El Signo y el Garabato, 1975; Marcel Duchamp: Apariencia Desnuda, 1978 (trans. as Marce Duchamp: Appearance Stripped Bare, 1979). *Address:* c/o Revista Vuelta, Leonardo da Vinci 17, México 19 DF, México.

PEACH, Captain Charles Lindsay K.; *see* Keighly-Peach.

PEACH, Denis Alan; Chief Charity Commissioner, since 1982; *b* 10 Jan. 1928; *s* of late Richard Peach and Alice Ellen Peach; *m* 1957, Audrey Hazel Chamberlain. *Educ:* Selhurst Grammar Sch., Croydon. Home Office, 1946-82; Asst Principal, 1951; Private Sec. to Perm. Under Sec of State, 1956; Principal, 1957; Sec. to Anglo-Egyptian Resettlement Bd, 1957-58; Prison Commn, 1958-62; Asst Sec., 1967; Asst Under Sec. of State, 1974-82 (Prin. Finance Officer, 1974-80). *Recreations:* painting, gardening. *Address:* 36 The Vale, Coulsdon, Surrey CR3 2AW. *T:* 01-660 6752. *Club:* Reform.

PEACOCK, Prof. Alan Turner, DSC 1945; MA; FBA 1979; Principal, University College at Buckingham, since 1980; *b* 26 June 1922; *s* of late Professor A. D. Peacock, FRSE and of Clara Mary (*née* Turner); *m* 1944, Margaret Martha Astell Burt; two *s* one *d. Educ:* Dundee High School; University of St Andrews (1939-42, 1945-47). Royal Navy, 1942-45 (Lieut RNVR). Lecturer in Economics: Univ. of St Andrews, 1947-48; London Sch. of Economics, 1948-51 (Hon. Fellow, 1980); Reader in Public Finance, Univ. of London, 1951-56; Prof. of Economic Science, Univ. of Edinburgh, 1957-62; Prof. of Economics, Univ. of York, 1962-78; Prof. of Economics, and Principal-designate, University Coll. at Buckingham, 1978-80. Seconded from Univ. of York as Chief Economic Adviser, Depts of Industry and Trade, 1973-76. Visiting Prof. of Economics, Johns Hopkins Univ., 1958. Member: Commission of Enquiry into land and population problems of Fiji, 1959; Adv. Council, Inst. Economic Affairs, 1959-; Departmental Committee on Electricity in Scotland, 1961; Council, REconS, 1961-78; Cttee of Enquiry on impact of rates, 1964; Commn on the Constitution, 1970-73; SSRC, 1972-73; Pres., Internat. Inst. of Public Finance, 1966-69; Chairman: Arts Council Enquiry on Orchestral Resources, 1969-70; Council, London Philharmonic Orch., 1975-79. Non-exec. Dir, Economist Intelligence Unit Ltd, 1977-. Hon. DUniv Stirling, 1974. *Publications:* Economics of National Insurance, 1952; (ed) Income Redistribution and Social Policy 1954; National Income and Social Accounting (with H. C. Edey), 1954, 3rd imp. 1967; The National Income of Tanganyika (1952-54) (with D. G. M. Dosser), 1958; The Growth of Public Expenditure in the UK, 1890-1955 (with J. Wiseman), 1961; Economic Theory of Fiscal Policy (with G. K. Shaw), 1971, 2nd edn, 1976; The Composer in the Market Place (with R. Weir), 1975; Welfare Economics: a liberal re-interpretation (with C. K. Rowley), 1975; Economic Analysis of Government, 1979; (ed and contrib.) Structural Economic Policies in West Germany and the UK, 1980; (ed jtly) Political Economy of Taxation, 1981; articles on applied economics in Economic Jl, Economica and other journals. *Recreation:* music. *Address:* University College at Buckingham, Buckingham MK18 1EG. *T:* Buckingham 4161. *Clubs:* Caledonian, Naval.

PEACOCK, Hon. Andrew Sharp; MP (L) Kooyong, since 1966; Minister for Industry and Commerce, Australia, since 1982; *b* 13 Feb. 1939; *s* of late A. S. Peacock and Iris Peacock. *Educ:* Scotch Coll., Melbourne, Vic; Melbourne Univ. (LLB). Former Partner, Rigby & Fielding, Solicitors; Chm., Peacock and Smith Pty Ltd, 1962-69. CMF Reserve (Captain), 1966. Pres., Victorian Liberal Party, 1965-66; Minister for Army and Minister assisting Prime Minister, 1969-71; Minister for Army and Minister asstg Treasurer, 1971-72; Minister for External Territories, Feb.-Dec. 1972; Mem., Opposition Exec., 1973-75; Oppos. Shadow Minister for For. Affairs, 1973-75; Minister for Foreign Affairs, 1975-80, for Industrial Relns, 1980-81. *Recreations:* horse racing, surfing, Australian Rules football. *Address:* 400 Flinders Street, Melbourne, Vic 3000, Australia. *T:* 622521. *Clubs:* Melbourne, Melbourne Cricket (Melbourne).

PEACOCK, Sir Geoffrey (Arden), Kt 1981; CVO 1977; MA; Remembrancer, City of London, 1968-81; *b* 7 Feb. 1920; *s* of Warren Turner Peacock and Elsie (*née* Naylor); *m* 1949, Mary Gillian Drew, *d* of Dr Harold Drew Lander, Rock, Cornwall; two *d. Educ:* Wellington Coll.; Jesus Coll., Cambridge. Served in War, 1939-46; RA and Roy. Lincs. Regt; Lt-Col 1945; Pres. of War Crimes Court, Singapore. Called to the Bar, Inner Temple. Legal Asst, Treasury Solicitor's Dept, 1949; Princ., HM Treasury, 1954; Sen. Legal Asst, Treasury Solicitor's Dept, 1958. Hon. Steward, Westminster Abbey, 1981-. Member: Court of Assistants, Worshipful Co. of Pewterers; Co. of Watermen and Lightermen (Jun. Warden, 1982). Chm., Brighton and Storrington Beagles, 1970-73. Various foreign decorations. *Recreations:* beagling, sailing, rowing. *Address:* Cowfold Lodge, Cowfold, West Sussex. *T:* Cowfold 237. *Clubs:* Cruising Association, London Rowing, City Livery, Leander.

PEACOCK, (Ian) Michael; Managing Director, Video Arts Television Ltd, since 1978; Chairman, Monitor Enterprises Ltd, since 1970; Director: Video Arts Ltd; Greater Manchester Independent Radio Ltd; *b* 14 Sept. 1929; *e s* of Norman Henry and Sara Barbara Peacock; *m* 1956, Daphne Lee; two *s* one *d. Educ:* Kimball Union Academy, USA; Welwyn Garden City Grammar School; London School of Economics (BSc Econ.). BBC Television: Producer, 1952-56; Producer Panorama, 1956-58; Asst Head of Television Outside Broadcasts, 1958-59; Editor, Panorama, 1959-61; Editor, BBC Television News, 1961-63; Chief of Programmes, BBC-2, 1963-65; Controller, BBC-1, BBC Television Service, 1965-67; Managing Dir, London Weekend Television Ltd, 1967-69; Man. Dir, Warner Bros TV Ltd, 1972-74; Exec. Vice-Pres., Warner Bros Television Inc., 1974-76. Pres., Video Arts Inc., 1976-78. First Chm., Ind. Programme Producers' Assoc., 1981-. Mem., Ct of Governors, LSE, 1982-. *Recreations:* theatre, cinema, concerts, gardening, sailing. *Address:* 21 Woodlands Road, Barnes, SW13. *T:* 01-876 2025. *Club:* Savile.

PEACOCK, Prof. Joseph Henry, MD, FRCS; Professor of Surgical Science, University of Bristol, since 1969; *b* 22 Oct. 1918; *s* of Harry James Peacock and Florence Peacock; *m* 1950, Gillian Frances Pinckney; one *s* one *d. Educ:* Bristol Grammar Sch.; Univ. of Birmingham (MB, ChB 1941, ChM 1957, MD 1963). MRCS, LRCP 1941, FRCS 1949. House appts, 1942; served RAMC, 1942-47: surgical and orthopaedic specialist, England and Far East; Hon. Major; Demonstr in Anat., Univ. of Birmingham, 1947; Surg. Registrar, 1948-51, and Sen. Surg. Registrar, 1952-53, United Bristol Hosp.; Rockefeller Fellow, Ann Arbor, 1951; Lectr in Surgery, 1953, and Reader in Surg., 1965, Univ. of Bristol; Consultant Surgeon: United Bristol Hosp., 1955; SW Reg. Hosp. Bd, 1960. Member: GMC, 1975-; SW RHA, 1975- (Chm., Res. Cttee, 1981-); Vascular Surgical Soc. of GB (also Pres.); Founder Member: Surgical Res. Soc.; European Soc. of Surg. Res.; Fellow, Assoc. of Surgeons of GB. Royal Coll. of Surgeons of England: Jacksonian Prize, 1954 and 1967; Hunterian Prof., 1956; Arris and Gale Lectr, 1960; Examr, LDS, 1958-63, and primary FRCS, 1965-71; Mem., Ct of Examrs, 1976-82 (Chm., 1982). Examr in Surg., Univs of Bristol, Birmingham, London, Wales and Ghana. *Publications:* Raynaud's Disease: British surgical practice, 1960; scientific pubns on vascular surgery and liver transplantation. *Recreations:* short wave radio, gardening. *Address:* The Old Manor, Ubley, near Bristol BS18 6PJ. *T:* Blagdon 62733. *Club:* Army and Navy.

PEACOCK, Michael; *see* Peacock, I. M.

PEACOCK, Ronald, MA, LittD (Leeds), MA (Manchester), DrPhil (Marburg); Professor of German, Bedford College, University of London, 1962-75, now Emeritus Professor; Fellow of Bedford College, 1980; President, Modern Humanities Research Association, 1983; *b* 22 Nov. 1907; *s* of Arthur Lorenzo and Elizabeth Peacock; *m* 1933, Ilse Gertrud Eva, *d* of Geheimer Oberregierungsrat Paul Freiwald; no *c. Educ:* Leeds Modern Sch.; Universities of Leeds, Berlin, Innsbruck, Marburg. Assistant Lecturer in German, University of Leeds, 1931-38; Lecturer, 1938-39; Professor, 1939-45; Henry Simon Professor of German Language and Literature, University of Manchester, 1945-62; Dean of the Faculty of Arts, 1954-56; Pro-Vice-Chancellor, 1958-62; Visiting Professor of German Literature, Cornell Univ. (USA), 1949; Visiting Professor of German Literature and Comparative Literature, University of Heidelberg, 1960-61; Professor of Modern German Literature, University of Freiburg, 1965, 1967-68. Hon. LittD Manchester, 1977. *Publications:* The Great War in German Lyrical Poetry, 1934; Das Leitmotiv bei Thomas Mann, 1934; Hölderlin, 1938; The Poet in the Theatre, 1946 (reprinted with additional essays, 1960); The Art of Drama, 1957; Goethe's Major Plays, 1959; Criticism and Personal Taste, 1972; various articles on literature contributed to reviews and periodicals. *Recreations:* music, theatre, travel. *Address:* Greenshade, Woodhill Avenue, Gerrards Cross, Bucks.

PEACOCK, Dr William James, BSc, PhD; FRS 1982; FAA; Chief, Division of Plant Industry, Commonwealth Scientific and Industrial Research Organization, since 1978; *b* 14 Dec. 1937; *m* 1961, Margaret Woodward; one *s two d. Educ:* Katoomba High Sch.; Univ. of Sydney (BSc, PhD). FAA 1976. CSIRO Postdoctoral Fellow, 1963 and Vis. Associate Prof. of Biology, 1964-65, Univ. of Oregon; Res. Consultant, Oak Ridge National Lab., USA, 1965; res. staff, Div. of Plant Industry, CSIRO, 1965-. Adjunct Prof. of Biology, Univ. of Calif, San Diego, 1969; Vis. Professor: of Biochem., Stanford Univ., 1970; of Molecular Biol., Univ. of Calif, LA, 1977. Edgeworth David Medal, Royal Soc. of NSW, 1967; Lemberg Medal, Aust. Biochem. Soc., 1978. *Publications:* editor of 4 books on genetics and molecular biology; approx. 100 papers. *Recreations:* squash, sailing, bush-walking. *Address:* 16 Brassey Street, Deakin, ACT 2600, Australia. *T:* (home) (062) 814485, (office) (062) 465250.

PEACOCKE, Rev. Dr Arthur Robert, DSc, ScD, BD; Dean and Fellow, Clare College, Cambridge, since 1973; *b* 29 Nov. 1924; *s* of Arthur Charles Peacocke and Rose Elizabeth (*née* Lilly); *m* 1948, Rosemary Winifred Mann; one *s* one *d. Educ:* Watford Grammar Sch.; Exeter Coll., Oxford (Scholar; BA Chem., BSc 1946; MA, DPhil 1948). DSc Oxon, 1962; ScD Cantab (incorp.), 1973; DD Oxon, 1982. DipTh 1960, BD 1971, Birmingham. Asst Lectr, Lectr and Sen. Lectr in Biophys. Chemistry, Univ. of Birmingham, 1948-59; Lectr in Biochem., Oxford Univ., and Fellow and Tutor in Chem., subseq. in Biochem., St Peter's Coll., 1959-73; Lectr in Chem., Mansfield Coll., Oxford, 1964-73. Rockefeller Fellow, Univ. of Calif at Berkeley, and Univ. of Wis, 1951-52; Vis. Fellow, Weizmann Inst., Israel, 1956; Bishop Williams Meml Lectr, Rikkyo (St Paul's) Univ., Japan, 1981; Shann Lectr, Univ. of Hong Kong, 1982-83. Lay Reader, Oxford Dio., 1960-71; ordained, 1971; Mem., Archbps' Commn on Christian Doctrine, 1969-76 (Mem. sub-gp on Man and Nature, 1972-74); Chm., Science and Religion Forum, 1972-78, Vice-Pres., 1981-; Select Preacher, Oxford Univ., 1973; Hulsean Preacher, Cambridge Univ., 1976; Bampton Lectr, Oxford Univ., 1978; Judge, Templeton Foundn Prize, 1979-. Meetings Sec., Sec. and Chm., Brit. Biophys.

Soc., 1965-69. Mem. Editorial Bd, Biochem. Jl, and Biopolymers, 1966-71, Zygon, 1973-. Editor, Monographs in Physical Biochemistry (OUP), 1967-. Lecomte du Noüy Prize, 1973. *Publications:* Molecular Basis of Heredity (with J. B. Drysdale), 1965 (repr. 1967); Science and the Christian Experiment, 1971; (with M. P. Tombs) Osmotic Pressure of Biological Macromolecules, 1974; (with J. Dominian) From Cosmos to Love, 1977; Creation and the World of Science, 1979; (ed) The Sciences and Theology in the Twentieth Century, 1982; articles and papers in scientific and theol jls, and symposia vols. *Recreations:* piano, music, mountain walking, churches. *Address:* Clare College, Cambridge. *T:* Cambridge 358681; 70 Gough Way, Cambridge.

PEACOCKE, Rt. Rev. Cuthbert Irvine, TD; MA; *b* 26 April 1903; *er s of* late Rt Rev. Joseph Irvine Peacocke, DD; *m* 1931, Helen Louise Gaussen; one *s* one *d. Educ:* St Columba's Coll., Dublin; Trinity Coll., Dublin; Curate, Seapatrick Parish, 1926-30; Head of Southern Mission, 1930-33; Rector, Derriaghy, 1933-35; Rector, St Mark's, Dundela, 1935-56; CF, 1939-45; Archdeacon of Down, 1950-56; Dean of St Anne's Cathedral, Belfast, 1956-69; Bishop of Derry and Raphoe, 1970-75. *Publication:* The Young Parson, 1936. *Recreations:* games, garden and reading. *Address:* Culmore House West, Culmore Point, Londonderry.

PEAKE, family name of **Viscount Ingleby.**

PEAKE, Air Cdre (retired) Dame Felicity (Hyde), (Lady Peake), DBE 1949 (MBE 1941); AE; JP; *b* 1 May 1913; *d* of late Colonel Humphrey Watts, OBE, TD, and Mrs Simon Orde; *m* 1st, 1935, John Charles Mackenzie Hanbury (killed on active service, 1939); no *c* ; 2nd, 1952, Sir Harald Peake, AE (*d* 1978); one *s. Educ:* St Winifreds, Eastbourne; Les Grands Huguenots, Vaucresson, Seine et Oise, France. Joined ATS Company of the RAF, April 1939; commissioned in the WAAF, Aug. 1939; served at home and in the Middle East; Director, Women's Auxiliary Air Force, 1946-49; Director Women's Royal Air Force, from its inception, 1949, until her retirement, 1950. Member Advisory Cttee, Recruitment for the Forces, 1958. Trustee, Imperial War Museum, 1963-; Governor, London House, 1958-76, 1978-; Mem. Council, RAF Benevolent Fund (a Vice-Pres., 1978-); Mem. Council, Union Jack Club, 1950-78. Hon. ADC to King George VI, 1949-50. *Address:* 2 Shepherd's Close, Shepherd's Place, Upper Brook Street, W1. *T:* 01-629 1264; Court Farm, Tackley, Oxford OX5 3AQ. *T:* Tackley 221.

PEAKE, Sir Francis, Kt 1951; *b* 31 Jan. 1889; *s* of late John Henry Hill Peake, Chingford, Essex; *m* 1914, Winifred Marie, *d* of late Thomas McKinnon Clark, Wood Green; two *d. Educ:* Tottenham Grammar Sch. Entered Civil Service, 1907. Called to Bar, Lincoln's Inn, 1915. Controller of Death Duties, Aug. 1948-31 July 1951. *Address:* 5 Churchfield House, Guessens Road, Welwyn Garden City, Herts. *T:* Welwyn Garden 20456.

PEAKER, Prof. Malcolm, PhD; FZS, FIBiol; Director, Hannah Research Institute, Ayr, since 1981; Hannah Professor of Dairy Science, University of Glasgow, since 1981; *b* 21 Aug. 1943; *s* of Ronald Smith Peaker and Marian (*née* Tomasin); *m* 1965, Stephanie Jane Large; three *s. Educ:* Henry Mellish Grammar Sch., Nottingham; Univ. of Sheffield (BSc Zoology); Univ. of Hong Kong (SRC NATO Scholar; PhD). FZS 1969; FIBiol 1979. Inst. of Animal Physiology, ARC, 1968-78; Head, Dept of Physiol., Hannah Res. Inst., 1978-81. Mem. Editorial Board: Jl of Dairy Science, 1975-78; Internat. Zoo Yearbook, 1978-82; Jl of Endocrinology, 1981-; Editor: British Jl of Herpetology, 1977-81; Internat. Circle of Dairy Research Leaders, 1982-. *Publications:* Salt Glands in Birds and Reptiles, 1975; (ed) Avian Physiology, 1975; (ed) Comparative Aspects of Lactation, 1977; papers in physiol, endocrinol, zool, biochem., vet. and agricl science jls. *Recreations:* vertebrate zoology, natural history, gardening, grumbling about bureaucrats. *Address:* 13 Upper Crofts, Alloway, Ayr KA7 4QX. *T:* Alloway 43999. *Club:* Farmers'.

PEARCE, family name of **Baron Pearce.**

PEARCE, Baron (Life Peer) *cr* 1962, of Sweethaws; **Edward Holroyd Pearce,** PC 1957; Kt 1948; RBA 1940; Chairman of the Press Council, 1969-74; Chairman, Appeals Committee, Take-over Panel, 1969-76; *b* 9 Feb. 1901; *s* of late John W. E. Pearce and Irene, *d* of Holroyd Chaplin; *m* 1927, Erica, *d* of late Bertram Priestman, RA; two *s. Educ:* Charterhouse; Corpus Christi Coll., Oxford. Hon. Fellow, Corpus Christi Coll., 1950. Called to Bar, 1925; QC 1945; Bencher, Hon. Society of Lincoln's Inn, 1948; Treasurer, 1966. Deputy Chairman, East Sussex Quarter Sessions, 1947-48; Judge of High Court of Justice, Probate, Divorce and Admiralty Division, 1948-54, Queen's Bench Division, 1954-57; a Lord Justice of Appeal, 1957-62; a Lord of Appeal in Ordinary, 1962-69. Chairman, Cttee on Shipbuilding Costs, 1947-49; Mem., Royal Commission on Marriage and Divorce, 1951; Chairman: Commn to test Rhodesian approval of proposed British-Rhodesian settlements, 1971-72; Cttee on the organisation of Bar and Inns of Court, 1971-73; Indep. Chm., Press discussions on Charter of Press Freedom, 1976-77. Mem., Governing Body, Charterhouse Sch., 1943-64; Governor: Tonbridge Sch., 1945-78; Sutton's Hospital in Charterhouse; Fedn of British Artists, 1970-73. Prof. of Law, Royal Acad. of Arts, 1971-. Past Master and past Member of Court of Company of Skinners; President, Artists League of GB, 1950-74; Trustee, Chantrey Bequest; Hon. FRBS. One-man show of landscapes at The Mall Galleries, 1971 and (with wife) 1973, 1976; also in provinces; one-man show of Alpine landscapes at Chur, Switzerland, 1977.

Recreations: painting and pictures. *Address:* House of Lords, SW1; Sweethaws, Crowborough. *T:* 61520. *Club:* Athenæum. *See also* Hon. J. E. H. Pearce, Hon. R. B. H. Pearce.

PEARCE, Andrew; Member (C) Cheshire West, European Parliament, since 1979; *b* 1 Dec. 1937; *s* of late Henry Pearce, Liverpool cotton broker, and of Evelyn Pearce; *m* 1966, Myra Whelan; three *s* one *d. Educ:* Rydal School, Colwyn Bay; University of Durham. BA. Formerly in construction industry; in Customs Dept, EEC, Brussels, 1974-79. Contested (C) Islington North, 1969 and 1970; Founder and Vice-Pres., British Cons. Assoc. in Belgium; Vice-Pres., Consultative Assembly of Lomé Convention. Governor, Archway Comprehensive School, 1967-70. *Address:* (office) 30 Grange Road, West Kirby, Wirral, Merseyside. *T:* 051-625 1896.

PEARCE, (Ann) Philippa, (Mrs M. J. G. Christie); freelance writer of children's fiction, since 1967; *d* of Ernest Alexander Pearce and Gertrude Alice (*née* Ramsden); *m* 1963, Martin James Graham Christie (decd); one *d. Educ:* Perse Girls' Sch., Cambridge; Girton Coll., Cambridge (MA Hons English Pt I, History Pt II). Temp. civil servant, 1942-45; Producer/Scriptwriter, Sch. Broadcasting, BBC Radio, 1945-58; Editor, Educn Dept, Clarendon Press, 1958-60; Children's Editor, André Deutsch Ltd, 1960-67. Also lectures. *Publications:* Minnow on the Say, 1955 (3rd edn 1974); Tom's Midnight Garden, 1958 (3rd edn 1976; Carnegie Medal, 1959); Mrs Cockle's Cat, 1961 (2nd edn 1974); A Dog So Small, 1962 (2nd edn 1964); (with Sir Harold Scott) From Inside Scotland Yard, 1963; The Strange Sunflower, 1966; (with Sir Brian Fairfax-Lucy) The Children of the House, 1968 (2nd edn 1970); The Elm Street Lot, 1969 (enlarged edn, 1979); The Squirrel Wife, 1971; What the Neighbours Did and other stories, 1972 (2nd edn 1974); (ed) Stories from Hans Christian Andersen, 1972; Beauty and the Beast (re-telling), 1972; The Shadow Cage and other stories of the supernatural, 1977; The Battle of Bubble and Squeak, 1978 (Whitbread Award, 1978); Wings of Courage (trans. and adapted from George Sand's story), 1982; reviews in TLS and Guardian. *Address:* c/o Kestrel Books, 17 Grosvenor Gardens, SW1W 0BD.

PEARCE, Sir Austin (William), Kt 1980; CBE 1974; PhD; Chairman, British Aerospace, since 1980; *b* 1 Sept. 1921; *s* of William Thomas and Florence Annie Pearce; *m* 1st, 1947, Maglona Winifred Twinn (*d* 1975); three *d* ; 2nd, 1979, Dr F. Patricia Grice (*née* Forsythe). *Educ:* Devonport High Sch. for Boys; Univ. of Birmingham. BSc (Hons) 1943, PhD 1945; Cadman Medallist. Joined Agwi Petroleum Corp., 1945 (later Esso Petroleum Co., Ltd): Asst Refinery Manager, 1954-56; Gen. Manager Refining, 1956-62; Dir, 1963; Man. Dir, 1968-71; Chm., 1972-80; Director: Esso Europe Inc., 1972-80; Esso Africa Inc., 1972-80; Pres., Esso Holding Co. UK Inc., 1971-80; Chairman: Esso Pension Trust Ltd, 1972-80; Irish Refining Co. Ltd, 1965-71; Director: Williams & Glyns Bank Ltd, 1974- (a Dep. Chm., 1980-); Royal Bank of Scotland Gp (formerly Nat. & Commercial Banking Gp), 1978-. Part-time Mem., NRDC, 1973-76; Member: Adv. Council for Energy Conservation, 1974-79; Energy Commn, 1977-79; British Aerospace, 1977- (Mem., Organising Cttee, 1976); Standing Commn on Energy and the Environment, 1978-81; Chm., UK Petroleum Industry Adv. Cttee, 1977-80; Pres., UK Petroleum Industry Assoc. Ltd, 1979-80; Chm., Industrial Policy Cttee, CBI, 1982-. President: Inst. of Petroleum, 1968-70; The Pipeline Industries Guild, 1973-75; Oil Industries Club, 1975-77; Pres., SBAC, 1982- (Vice-Pres., 1981-82). Mem., Bd of Governors, English-Speaking Union, 1974-80; Mem. Council, Surrey Univ., 1981-; Vice-Pres., RoSPA. Hon. DSc Southampton, 1978. *Recreations:* golf, woodwork. *Address:* British Aerospace, Brooklands Road, Weybridge, Surrey KT13 0SJ. *T:* Weybridge 45522. *Clubs:* Athenæum, Royal Wimbledon Golf.

PEARCE, Clifford James, CB 1974; Under Secretary (Local Government), Department of the Environment (formerly Ministry of Housing and Local Government), 1968-76; *b* 14 Aug. 1916; *s* of late Samuel Lightfoot Pearce and Maude Evelyn Neville; *m* 1944, Elaine Hilda (*née* Baggley); one *s* one *d. Educ:* Strand Sch.; King's Coll., London; London Sch. of Economics. Entered Inland Revenue, 1935; served in RN, 1941-46 (Lieut, RNVR); entered Min. of Health, 1946; Asst Sec., Min. of Housing and Local Govt, 1957; Under Sec. 1968. Hon. Res. Fellow, Birmingham Univ., 1976-78. *Publication:* The Machinery of Change in Local Government 1888-1974, 1980. *Recreation:* bookbinding. *Address:* Elm Cottage, The Street, Boxgrove, Chichester.

PEARCE, Sir Eric (Herbert), Kt 1979; OBE 1970; Director of Community Affairs, General Television Corporation, Channel Nine, Melbourne, Australia, since 1979; *b* 5 March 1905; *s* of Herbert Clement Pearce and Louise Mary Pearce; *m* 1956, Betty Constance Ham; one *d. Educ:* Raynes Sch., Hants. Served War, FO RAAF, 1942-44. Studio Manager/Chief Announcer, Radio Stn 3DB, Melbourne, 1944-50; Gen. Man., Radio Stns 5KA-AO-RM, SA, 1950-55; Dir of Progs, major broadcasting network, Australia, 1955-56; Chief Announcer/Sen. Newsreader, General TV, Channel Nine, 1957-79. *Recreations:* walking, swimming, golf. *Address:* 48 Lansell Road, Toorak, Vic 3142, Australia. *Clubs:* Athenæum, Toorak Services (Melbourne).

PEARCE, Most Rev. George; former Archbishop of Suva; *b* 9 Jan. 1921; *s* of George H. Pearce and Marie Louise Duval. *Educ:* Marist Coll. and Seminary, Framingham Center, Mass, USA. Entered Seminary, 1940; Priest, 1947; taught in secondary sch. in New England, USA, 1948-49; assigned as missionary to Samoa, 1949; consecrated Vicar Apostolic of Samoa, 1956; first Bishop of Apia, 1966; Archbishop of Suva, 1967-76, retired 1976. *Address:*

Bethany House of Intercession, Jackson Avenue, Hastings-on-Hudson, NY 10706, USA. *T:* (914) 478-0010.

PEARCE, Howard Spencer; Director for Wales, Property Services Agency, Department of Environment, since 1977; *b* 23 Sept. 1924; *s* of Ivor Stanley Pearce and Evelyn Pearce; *m* 1951, Enid Norma Richards; one *s. Educ:* Barry County Sch.; College of Estate Management. ARICS. Armed Services, Major RE, 1943-47. Ministry of Works: Cardiff, 1953-61; Salisbury Plain, 1961-64; Ministry of Public Building and Works: Sen. Quantity Surveyor: Hong Kong, 1964-67; Abingdon, 1967-70; Area Officer, Abingdon, 1970-72; Regional Works Officer, SW Region, Bristol, PSA, Dept of Environment, 1972-77. *Recreations:* music, playing golf and watching Rugby football. *Address:* 2 Longhouse Close, Lisvane, Cardiff CF4 5XR. *T:* Cardiff 762029. *Club:* Civil Service.

PEARCE, Hon. James Edward Holroyd, QC 1979; *b* 18 March 1934; *s* of Lord Pearce, *qv,* and Erica, *d* of late Bertram Priestman, RA; *m* 1969, Julia, *yr d* of late C. D. Hill; two *s* two *d. Educ:* Charterhouse; Corpus Christi Coll., Oxford (1st Cl. Hons Jurisprudence, MA). Military service, RE, 2nd Lieut, 1953-54. Teaching Associate, Northwestern Univ. Law Sch., Chicago, 1959; called to Bar: Middle Temple, 1960, NI, 1974. Hon. Legal Adviser to National Skating Assoc., 1970-. Mem. Council, Artists' General Benevolent Instn, 1978-. Second Warden, Skinners' Company, 1982. *Address:* Turf Lodge, Sheep Plain, Crowborough, Sussex TN6 3ST. *T:* Crowborough 5505. *Club:* Athenæum.

See also Hon. R. B. H. Pearce.

PEARCE, John Brian; Under-Secretary, HM Treasury, since 1981 (Civil Service Department, 1976-81); *b* 25 Sept. 1935; *s* of late George Frederic Pearce and Constance Josephine Pearce; *m* 1960, Michelle Etcheverry; four *s. Educ:* Queen Elizabeth Grammar Sch., Wakefield; Brasenose Coll., Oxford (BA). Asst Principal: Min. of Power, 1959; Colonial Office, 1960; Private Sec. to Parly Under-Sec. of State, 1963; Principal: Colonial Office, 1964; Dept of Economic Affairs, 1967; Principal Private Sec. to Sec. of State for Economic Affairs, 1968-69; Asst Sec., Civil Service Dept, 1969. *Recreations:* comparative theology, music, architecture. *Address:* 124 Court Lane, SE21 7EA.

PEARCE, John Dalziel Wyndham, MA, MD, FRCP, FRCPEd, FRCPsych, DPM, FBPsS; Consulting Psychiatrist: St Mary's Hospital; Queen Elizabeth Hospital for Children; *b* 21 Feb. 1904; *s* of John Alfred Wyndham Pearce and Mary Logan Dalziel; *m* 1929, Grace Fowler (marr. diss., 1964), no *c; m* 1964, Ellinor Elizabeth Nancy Draper. *Educ:* George Watson's Coll.; Edinburgh Univ. Formerly: Physician-in-charge, Depts of Psychiatry, St Mary's Hosp. and Queen Elizabeth Hosp. for Children; Cons. Psychiatrist, Royal Masonic Hosp.; Hon. physician, Tavistock Clinic and West End Hospital for Nervous Diseases; Medical co-director Portman Clinic, Institute for Study and Treatment of Delinquency (ISTD); medico-psychologist, LCC remand homes; Mem. Academic Boards, Inst. of Child Health, and St Mary's Hosp. Med. Sch. (Univ. of London); Examiner in Medicine: RCP; Univ. of London; Royal Coll. of Psychiatrists; Chm., Adv. Cttee on delinquent and maladjusted children, Internat. Union for Child Welfare; Mem., Army Psychiatry Adv. Cttee; Lt-Col, RAMC; adviser in psychiatry, Allied Force HQ, CMF (despatches). Member: Council, National Assoc. for Mental Health; Home Sec's Adv. Council on Treatment of Offenders. *Publications:* Juvenile Delinquency, 1952; technical papers in scientific journals. *Recreations:* golf, fishing, painting. *Address:* Stamford House, 4 Hampstead Square, NW3 1AB. *Club:* Caledonian.

PEARCE, John Trevor Archdall, CMG 1964; *b* 7 May 1916; *s* of late Rev. W. T. L. A. Pearce, Seven Hills, NSW, Australia, and late N. B. Pearce, Prahran, Victoria, Australia; *m* 1948, Isabel Bundey Rankine, Hindmarsh Island, S Australia; no *c. Educ:* The King's Sch., Parramatta, Australia; Keble Coll., Oxford, Eng. MA. District Officer, Tanganyika, 1939. War Service: Kenya, Abyssinia, Ceylon, India, Burma, 1940-46, Major RE. Tanganyika: District Commissioner, 1950; Provincial Commissioner, 1959; Permanent Secretary (Admin), Office of the Vice-President, 1961; Chairman, Public Service Commn, Basutoland, 1963, Swaziland, 1965; Registrar, Papua and New Guinea Univ. of Technology, 1969-73. *Recreations:* golf, piano music, solitude, travel in remote places. *Address:* Clippings, Ferguson Avenue, Buderim, Qld 4556, Australia.

PEARCE, Kenneth Leslie; retired as Chairman, East Midlands Gas Region (formerly East Midlands Gas Board), 1968-74; *b* 2 May 1910; *s* of late George Benjamin Pearce and Eliza Jane Pearce; *m* 1940, Evlyn Sarah Preedy (*d* 1957); two *s. Educ:* Dudley Grammar Sch.; Birmingham Central Techn. Coll. Engr and Man., Bilston Gas Light & Coke Co., 1939-48; Engr and Man., City of Leicester Gas Dept, 1948-49; East Midlands Gas Board: Divisional Gen. Man., Leicester and Northants, 1949-50; Divisional Gen. Man., Notts and Derby, 1950-62; Chief Distribution Engr, 1962-67; Dep. Chairman, 1968-74. *Recreations:* fishing, gardening. *Address:* 48 Wergs Road, Tettenhall, Wolverhampton, West Midlands WV6 8TD. *T:* Wolverhampton 751105.

PEARCE, Maj.-Gen. Leslie Arthur, CB 1973; CBE 1971 (OBE 1964; MBE 1956); Chief of General Staff, NZ Army, 1971-73, retd; *b* 22 Jan. 1918; British parents; *m* 1944, Fay Mattocks, Auckland, NZ; two *s* one *d. Educ:* in New Zealand. Joined Army, 1937; served War: Greece, Western Desert, Italy, 1939-45. Staff Coll., Camberley, 1948. Directing Staff, Australia Staff Coll., 1958-59; Commandant, Army Schools, NZ, 1960; Comdg Officer, 1 NZ

Regt, in NZ and Malaysia, 1961-64; Dep. QMG, NZ Army, 1964-65; Dir of Staff Duties, NZ Army, 1966; IDC, 1967; QMG, 1968-69; Dep. Chief of Defence Staff, 1970. Chm., Vocational Training Council, 1975-81. *Recreations:* golf, fishing, gardening; Provincial and Services Rugby representative, in youth. *Address:* 13 Stapleford Crescent, Browns Bay, Auckland, New Zealand.

PEARCE, Neville John Lewis; Chief Executive, Avon County Council, since 1982; *b* 27 Feb. 1933; *s* of John and Ethel Pearce; *m* 1958, Eileen Frances Potter; two *d. Educ:* Queen Elizabeth's Hosp., Bristol; Silcoates Sch., Wakefield; Univ. of Leeds (LLB Hons 1953, LLM 1954). Asst Solicitor: Wakefield CBC, 1957-59; Darlington CBC, 1959-61; Chief Asst Solicitor, Grimsby CBC, 1961-63, Dep. Town Clerk, 1963-65; Dep. Town Clerk, Blackpool CBC, 1965-66; Town Clerk, Bath CBC, 1967-73; Dir of Admin and County Solicitor, Avon CC, 1973-82. *Recreations:* home, family, Anglican and ecumenical church affairs. *Address:* Penshurst, Weston Lane, Bath BA1 4AB. *T:* (home) Bath 26925, (office) Bristol 290777.

PEARCE, Philippa; *see* Pearce, A. P.

PEARCE, Hon. Richard Bruce Holroyd, QC 1969; a Recorder of the Crown Court, since 1972; *b* 12 May 1930; *s* of Lord Pearce, *qv,* and Erica, *d* of late Bertram Priestman, RA; *m* 1958, Dornie Smith-Pert; one *s* one *d. Educ:* Charterhouse; Corpus Christi Coll., Oxford (MA). Served HM Forces, 1949-56: RE and E African Engrs, 1949-50; 119 Field Engr Regt RE, TA, 1950-56. Called to Bar, Lincoln's Inn, 1955, Bencher, 1977; *ad eund.* Mem., Middle Temple, 1958. A Legal Assessor to GMC, 1974-, GDC, 1974-, GNC, 1975-. Master, Skinner's Co., 1976-77. Governor, Tonbridge School. *Address:* Sweethaws, Crowborough, East Sussex. *T:* Crowborough 3888. *Club:* Beefsteak.

See also Hon. J. E. H. Pearce.

PEARCE-HIGGINS, Rev. Canon John Denis; Hon. Chaplain to the Forces; Residentiary Canon and Vice-Provost of Southwark, 1963-71, now Emeritus; *b* 1 June 1905; 2nd *s* of late Prof. Alexander Pearce Higgins and Mina MacLennan; *m* 1938, Margaret Edna, 2nd *d* of Harry and Marguerite Hodge, Kettering; two *s* three *d. Educ:* St Faith's Sch., Cambridge; Rugby Sch. (scholar); Gonville and Caius Coll., Cambridge (schol. and prizeman). Charles Winter Warr Research Schol. in Ancient Philosophy, 1928; 1st class hons Parts I and II Class. Tripos; Research at Vienna Univ., 1928-29; Ripon Hall Theological Coll., 1934-37. Priest, 1937; Curate: St Agnes, Cotteridge; Priory Church, Malvern, 1940. Chaplain in RAChD, Oct. 1940-Nov. 1945 (invalided; Overseas, Africa Star, Italy, Defence and Victory medals). Vicar of Hanley Castle, Worcs, 1945-53; OCF; Chaplain and Sen. Divinity Lecturer, City of Worcester Training Coll., 1946-53; Vicar of Putney, St Mary with St John and All Saints, Surrogate, 1953-63. Chairman, Modern Churchmen's Union, 1958-68. Vice-Chairman, Churches' Fellowship for Psychical and Spiritual Studies, 1961-. Member Society for Psychical Research. *Publications:* Resurrection, 1959; (ed) Life, Death and Psychical Research, 1973; articles in: Modern Churchman, Journal of SPR. *Recreations:* music, painting, swimming. *Address:* 13 Abbotstone Road, Putney, SW15 1QR. *T:* 01-788 4573.

PEARD, Rear-Admiral Sir Kenyon (Harry Terrell), KBE 1958 (CBE 1951); retired; *b* 1902; *s* of Henry T. Peard; *m* 1935, Mercy Leila Bone; one *s* one *d. Educ:* RN Colleges, Osborne and Dartmouth. Went to sea, 1919; Torpedo Specialist, 1929; transferred to Electrical Branch, 1946, Director, Naval Electrical Dept, Admiralty, 1955-58; retired 1958. *Address:* Finstead, Shorefield Crescent, Milford-on-Sea, Hants.

PEARKES, Maj.-Gen. Hon. George Randolph, VC 1918; CC (Canada) 1967; PC (Canada) 1957; CB 1943; DSO 1919; MC; Legion of Merit (US); Lieutenant-Governor, British Columbia, 1960-68, retired; *b* Watford, Herts, 26 Feb. 1888; *m* Constance Blytha, *o d* of W. F. U. Copeman, Sidney, BC; one *s. Educ:* Berkhamsted Sch. Went to Canada; farmed for three years; joined Royal N-W Mounted Police, 1909; enlisted in Canadian Expeditionary Force, 1914; arrived in France, Sept. 1915; Bombing Sgt, Dec. 1915; Lieut on the field, March 1916; Battalion Bombing Officer; Brigade Bombing Officer; Captain, Oct. 1916; Major, Nov. 1917; took command of Battalion, Dec. 1917 (VC, MC, despatches, wounded several times); passed Staff Coll., Camberley, 1919; served on the General Staff of Permanent Force of Canada as GSO at Calgary, Winnipeg, Esquimalt and Kingston; DMT and SD; at Imperial Defence Coll., 1937; DOC, MD 13, Calgary, 1938-40; GOC First Canadian Division, 1940; GOC-in-C Pacific Command, Canada, 1942-45; retired April, 1945. Minister of National Defence, 1957-60. Hon. LLD, University of British Columbia. *Address:* 1268 Tattersall Drive, Victoria, BC V8P 1Z3, Canada. *Club:* Union (Victoria).

PEARL, Valerie Louise, DPhil; President, New Hall, Cambridge, since 1981; *b* 31 Dec. 1926; *d* of Cyril R. Bence, *qv,* and late Florence Bence; *m* 1949, Morris Leonard Pearl; one *d. Educ:* King Edward VI High Sch., Birmingham; St Anne's Coll., Oxford (Exhibnr). BA Hons Mod. History; MA, DPhil (Oxon). Allen Research Studentship, St Hugh's Coll., Oxford, 1951; Eileen Power Studentship, 1952; Sen. Research Studentship, Westfield Coll., London, 1962; Leverhulme Research Award, 1962; Graham Res. Fellow and Lectr in History, Somerville Coll., Oxford, 1965; Reader in History of London, 1968, Prof. of History of London, 1976-81, University College London. Convenor of confs to found The London Journal, Chm. of Editorial

Bd, Editor-in-Chief, 1973-77; McBride Vis. Prof., Cities Program, Bryn Mawr Coll., Pennsylvania, 1974; Woodward Lectr, Yale Univ., New Haven, 1974; Lectr, Indian Council for Soc. Sci., Calcutta, Research on Indian Cities, New Delhi, 1977; John Stow Commem. Lectr, London, 1979; James Ford Special Lectr, Oxford, 1980; Sir Lionel Denny Lectr, London, 1981. Literary Dir, Royal Historical Soc., 1975-77 (Mem. Studies in History Bd, 1976); Mem., Greater London Archaeological Adv. Cttee, 1975; Pres., London and Mddx Archaeol. Soc., 1980-; Governor, Museum of London, 1978; Mem. Cttee of Management, Inst. of Hist. Research, 1978. FSA 1976. *Publications:* London and the Outbreak of the Puritan Revolution, 1625-43, 1961; (ed jtly) History and Imagination: essays for Hugh Trevor-Roper, 1981; contribs to: Nuove Questione (ed L. Bulferetti), 1965; Studies in London History (ed W. Kellaway, A. Hollaender), 1969; The Interregnum (ed G. Aylmer), 1972; Puritans and Revolutionaries (ed K. Thomas, D. Pennington), 1978; also to learned jls and other works, including Trans Royal Hist. Soc., Eng. Historical Review, History of English Speaking Peoples, Past and Present, Archives, Economic Hist. Review, History, Jl of Eccles. History, Times Literary Supplement, London Review of Books, Listener, BBC. *Recreations:* walking and swimming. *Address:* New Hall, Cambridge. *T:* Cambridge 51721.

PEARLMAN, Valerie Anne; a Recorder of the Crown Court, since 1982; *b* 6 Aug. 1936; *d* of Sidney and Marjorie Pearlman; *m* 1972; one *s* one *d. Educ:* Wycombe Abbey Sch. Called to the Bar, Lincoln's Inn, 1958. *Recreations:* gardening, painting, reading. *Address:* Lamb Building, Temple, EC4Y 7AS. *T:* 01-353 0774. *Club:* English-Speaking Union.

PEARMAN, Sir James (Eugene), Kt 1973; CBE 1960; Senior Partner, Conyers, Dill & Pearman; *b* 24 Nov. 1904; *o s* of Eugene Charles Pearman and Kate Trott; *m* 1st, 1929, Prudence Tucker Appleby (*d* 1976); two *s*; 2nd, 1977, Mrs Antoinette Trott, *d* of Dr and Mrs James Aiguier, Philadelphia, Pa. *Educ:* Saltus Grammar Sch., Bermuda; Bromsgrove Sch., Worcs; Merton Coll., Oxford; Middle Temple. Law partnership with N. B. Dill, 1927-29; law partnership with Sir Reginald Conyers and N. B. Dill, 1929 and still continuing as firm of Conyers, Dill & Pearman. Member Colonial Parlt, Bermuda, 1943-72; MEC, 1955-63 and 1968-72; MLC, 1972-. Hon. Consul for Bolivia. *Recreations:* deep-sea fishing, bridge. *Address:* Tideway, Point Shares, Pembroke, Bermuda. *T:* 21125. *Clubs:* Carlton; Anglers' (New York); Rod and Reel (Miami); Royal Bermuda Yacht.

PEARS, David Francis, FBA 1970; Student of Christ Church, Oxford, since 1960; Reader in Philosophy, Oxford University, since 1972; *b* 8 Aug. 1921; *s* of Robert and late Gladys Pears; *m* 1963, Anne Drew; one *s* one *d. Educ:* Westminster Sch.; Balliol Coll., Oxford. Research Lecturer, Christ Church, 1948-50; Univ. Lectr, Oxford, 1950-72; Fellow and Tutor, Corpus Christi Coll., 1950-60. Visiting Professor: Harvard, 1959; Univ. of Calif, Berkeley, 1964; Rockefeller Univ., 1967; Hill Prof., Univ. of Minnesota, 1970; Humanities Council Res. Fellow, Princeton, 1966. Mem., l'Inst. Internat. de Philosophie, 1978-. Governor, Westminster Sch., 1976; Delegate of Oxford Univ. Press, 1976. *Publications:* (trans. with B. McGuinness), Wittgenstein, Tractatus Logico-Philosophicus, 1961, repr. 1975; Bertrand Russell and the British Tradition in Philosophy, 1967, 2nd edn 1972; Ludwig Wittgenstein, 1971; What is Knowledge?, 1971; (ed) Russell's Logical Atomism, 1973; Some Questions in the Philosophy of Mind, 1975. *Address:* 31 Northmoor Road, Oxford. *T:* Oxford 54767.

PEARS, Sir Peter, Kt 1978; CBE 1957; Tenor; *b* 22 June 1910; *s* of Arthur and Jessie Pears. *Educ:* Lancing; Oxford; Royal College of Music. BBC Singers, 1934-37; New English Singers, 1936-38; began American and European tours with Benjamin Britten, 1939, with Julian Bream, 1956, with Osian Ellis, 1972. Sadler's Wells Opera, 1943-46; Peter Grimes in Peter Grimes 1945 and 1960; English Opera Gp. 1947; Covent Garden Opera, 1948; Aschenbach in Death in Venice, NY Met., 1974; Vere in Billy Budd, NY Met., 1978; Co-Founder of Aldeburgh Festival, 1948; Founder and Dir of Singing, Britten-Pears Sch. of Advanced Musical Studies, 1972-. Pres., Incorporated Soc. of Musicians, 1970. First performed many new works by Britten, Tippett, Berkeley, etc. Cramb Lectr, Univ. of Glasgow, 1961. FRCM; Hon. RAM; Hon. Fellow, Keble Coll., Oxford, 1978; DUniv York, 1969; Hon. DLitt Sussex, 1971; Hon. MusD Cantab, 1972; Hon. DMus Evansville (Indiana), 1976; Hon. DMus Edinburgh, 1976; Hon. DMus East Anglia, 1980; Hon. DMus Oxon, 1981; DUniv Essex, 1981. Musician of the Year, ISM, 1978; Queen's Jubilee Medal, 1977; Royal Opera House Long Service Medal, 1979. *Publications:* (with Benjamin Britten) Purcell Edition; occasional articles. *Address:* The Red House, Aldeburgh, Suffolk IP15 5PZ.

PEARSE, Prof. Anthony Guy Everson, MA, MD (Cantab); FRCP, FRCPath; DCP (London); Professor of Histochemistry, University of London, Royal Postgraduate Medical School, 1965-81, now Emeritus; *b* 9 Aug. 1916; *o s* of Captain R. G. Pearse, DSO, MC, Modbury, Devon, and Constance Evelyn Steels, Pocklington, Yorks; *m* 1947, Elizabeth Himmelhoch, MB, BS (Sydney), DCP (London); one *s* three *d. Educ:* Sherborne Sch.; Trinity Coll., Cambridge. Kitchener Scholar, Raymond Horton-Smith prizeman, 1949-50. Posts, St Bart's Hospital, 1940-41; Surg.-Lt, RNVR, 1941-45. Registrar, Edgware General Hospital, 1946; Asst Lecturer in Pathol., PG Med. School, London, 1947-51, Lecturer, 1951-57; Cons. Pathol., Hammersmith Hospital, 1951; Fulbright Fellow and Visiting Prof. of Path., University of Alabama, 1953-54; Guest Instructor in Histochemistry, University of Kansas, 1957, 1958; Vanderbilt Univ., 1967; Reader in Histochemistry, University of London, 1957-65; Middleton Goldsmith Lectr,

NY Path. Soc., 1976. Member: Path. Society (GB), 1949; Biochem. Society (GB), 1957; European Gastro Club, 1969; Hon. Member or Member various foreign societies incl. Deutsche Akademie der Naturforscher Leopoldina, 1973 and Amer. Assoc. Endocrine Surgeons, 1981; Corresp. Mem., Deutsche Gesellschaft für Endokrinologie, 1978; Hon. Fellow, Royal Microscop. Society, 1964 (Vice-Pres., 1970-72; Pres., 1972-74). Hon. Mem., Mark Twain Soc., 1977. Hon. MD: Basel, 1960; Krakow, 1978. John Hunter Medal and Triennial Prize, RCS, 1976-78; Ernest Jung Prize for Medicine, 1979; Fred W. Stewart Medal and Prize, Sloan-Kettering Cancer Center, NY, 1979. Member Editorial Board: Histochemie, 1958-73; Jl Histochem. Cytochem., 1959-68; Enzymol. biol. clin., 1961-67; Brain Research, 1968-76; Cardiovascular Research, 1968-75; Virchow's Archiv 'B', 1968-; Histochemical Jl, 1968-; Jl of Royal Microscopical Soc., 1967-69; Jl Microscopy, 1969-; Jl of Neuro-visceral Relations, 1969-73; Jl of Molecular and Cellular Cardiology, 1970-; Histochem. Jl, 1970-; Scand. Jl Gastroenterol., 1971-; Jl Neural Transmission, 1973-76; Jl of Pathology, 1973-; Histochemistry, 1974-; Mikroscopie, 1977-; Editor, Medical Biology, 1974-. *Publications:* Histochemistry Theoretical and Applied, 2nd edn, 1960, 3rd edn, vol. I, 1968, vol. II, 1972, 4th edn vol. I, 1980; numerous papers on theoretical and applied histochemistry, esp. endocrinology (Diffuse Neuroendocrine System). *Recreations:* horticulture (plant hybridization, Liliaceae, Asclepiadaceae); ship modelling, foreign touring (motoring, camping). *Address:* The Fortress, Letchmore Heath, Hertfordshire WD2 8EE. *T:* Radlett 6466. *Club:* Naval.

PEARSE, Rear-Adm. John Roger Southey G.; *see* Gerard-Pearse.

PEARSON, family name of Viscount Cowdray.

PEARSON, Brig. Alastair Stevenson, CB 1958; DSO; OBE 1953; MC; TD; Farmer; Lord Lieutenant of Dunbartonshire, since 1979; Keeper of Dumbarton Castle, since 1981; *b* 1 June 1915; *m* 1944, Mrs Joan Morgan Weld-Smith; three *d. Educ:* Kelvinside Acad.; Sedbergh. Co. Director, 1936-39; served War of 1939-45 (MC, DSO, and three Bars); embodied 6th Bn Highland LI, TA, 1939; transferred to Parachute Regt, 1941; Lt-Col 1942; CO 1st and 8th Para Bns, 1942-45, CO 15th (Scottish) Bn The Parachute Regt (TA), 1947-53; Dep. Comd 46 Parachute Bde (TA), 1953-59. Comd Scotland Army Cadet Force, Brigadier, 1967-81. ADC to the Queen, 1956-61. Hon. Colonel: 15th (Scottish) Bn The Parachute Regt (TA), 1963-77; Renfrew and Bute Bn ACF, 1981-. DL Glasgow, 1951, Dunbartonshire, 1975. KStJ 1980. *Address:* Tullochan, Gartocharn, By Alexandria, Dunbartonshire. *T:* Gartocharn 205.

PEARSON, Bertram Lamb, CB 1947; DSO 1917; MC; *b* 1893; *y s* of late William Pearson of Wakefield, Yorkshire, and late Mary Ann Pearson; *m* 1920, Gladys Mary (*d* 1980), *er d* of John Stewart of Yapham Hall, Pocklington, East Yorkshire. *Educ:* Bedford Grammar Sch.; Wakefield Grammar Sch.; The Queen's Coll., Oxford; 1st Hastings Exhibitioner and Honorary Scholar; 1st Class Honour (Classical) Moderations, 1913; 1st Class Literæ Humaniores, 1919. Served European War, 1914-19, as Captain, The Green Howards (wounded twice, despatches, MC, DSO); tutor, The Queen's Coll., Oxford, 1919-20; Private Sec. to Permanent Sec., Bd of Educn, 1924-28; Principal Private Sec. to President, Board of Educn, 1937; Accountant-General to Min. of Educn, 1944-55; Under-Secretary, 1946-55. Member Council: Central Council of Physical Recreation, 1956-; Girls' Public Day School Trust, 1958-69. *Recreations:* cricket, bowls, reading. *Address:* 15 Queen's Court, Queen's Road, Cheltenham, Glos GL50 2LU.

PEARSON, David Morris, OBE 1969 (MBE 1945); HM Diplomatic Service, retired; Ambassador to the Republic of Honduras, 1972-75; *b* 21 July 1915; *s* of late Isaac Bedlington Pearson and late Margaret Elizabeth Williams; *m* 1945, Camille Henriette Etey; no *c. Educ:* Kelvinside Academy, Glasgow; Sedbergh Sch.; Glasgow University. HM Forces, 1939-46 (Intell. Corps, then SOE in France, leading Pedagogue Mission). Personnel Manager, Gold Coast Main Reef Ltd, 1946-50; Sierra Leone Administrative Service, 1950-59; seconded to Foreign Service, in Consulate-General, Dakar, Senegal, 1954-59; entered Foreign Service, 1959; FO, 1960-62; Head of Chancery, Brazzaville, 1962-65; Rio de Janeiro, 1965-67; Kinshasa, 1967-69; Consul-Gen., Casablanca, 1969-72. French Croix de Guerre (with star), 1945. *Recreations:* music, reading, foreign travel. *Address:* 32 Les Trompettes Hautes, Montesquieu, 66740 St Génis-des-Fontaines, Pyrénées-Orientales, France. *Club:* Atalanta (Glasgow).

PEARSON, Sir Denning; *see* Pearson, Sir J. D.

PEARSON, Derek Leslie, CB 1978; Deputy Secretary, Overseas Development Administration (formerly Ministry of Overseas Development), 1977-81; *b* 19 Dec. 1921; *s* of late George Frederick Pearson and Edith Maud Pearson (*née* Dent); *m* 1956, Diana Mary, *d* of late Sir Ralph Freeman; no *c. Educ:* William Ellis Sch.; London Sch. of Economics. BSc (Econ). Observer, FAA, 1941-45. Colonial Office: Asst Principal, 1947; Principal, 1949; seconded to Kenya, 1954-56; Principal Private Sec. to Sec. of State for Colonies, 1959-61; Dept of Technical Cooperation, 1961; Asst Sec., 1962; ODM, 1964; Under Secretary: CSD, 1970-72; Min. of Overseas Develt, 1972-75; Dep. Sec., Cabinet Office, 1975-77. *Address:* Hadlow, Hazelwood Lane, Chipstead, Surrey. *Clubs:* Naval, Civil Service.

PEARSON, Sir Francis Fenwick, 1st Bt, *cr* 1964; MBE 1945; JP; DL; Chairman, Central Lancashire New Town Development Corporation, since 1971; *b* 13 June 1911; *s* of Frank Pearson, solicitor, Kirby Lonsdale, and Susan Mary Pearson; *m* 1938, Katharine Mary Fraser; one *s* one *d*. *Educ*: Uppingham; Trinity Hall, Cambridge. 1st Gurkha Rifles, 1932; ADC to Viceroy of India, 1934–36; Indian Political Service, 1936; Under-Secretary, Political Dept, 1942–45; Chief Minister, Manipur State, 1945–47; retired, 1947. MP (C) Clitheroe, Oct. 1959–1970; Assistant Whip (unpaid), 1960–62; a Lord Commissioner of the Treasury, 1962–63; PPS to Prime Minister, Nov. 1963–Oct. 1964. JP Lancs, 1952; DL Co. Palatine of Lancaster, 1971. *Recreation:* fishing. *Heir: s* Francis Nicholas Fraser Pearson [*b* 28 Aug. 1943; *m* 1978, Henrietta, *d* of Comdr Henry Pasley-Tyler]. *Address:* Beech Cottage, Borwick, Carnforth. *T:* Carnforth 4191. *Club:* Carlton.

PEARSON, Dr Graham Scott; Deputy Director, Royal Armament Research and Development Establishment, Ministry of Defence, since 1980; *b* 20 July 1935; *s* of Ernest Reginald Pearson and Alice (*née* Maclachlan); *m* 1960, Susan Elizabeth Meriton Benn; two *s*. *Educ*: Woodhouse Grove Sch., Bradford; St Salvator's Coll., Univ. of St Andrews (BSc 1st Cl. Hons Chemistry, 1957; PhD 1960). Postdoctoral Fellow, Univ. of Rochester, NY, USA, 1960–62; joined Scientific Civil Service, 1962; Rocket Propulsion Estab., 1962–69; Def. Res. and Develt Staff, Washington, DC, 1969–72; PSO to Dir Gen. Res. Weapons, 1972–73; Asst Dir, Naval Ordnance Services/Scientific, 1973–76; Technical Adviser/Explosives, Materials and Safety (Polaris), 1976–79; Principal Supt, Propellants Explosives and Rocket Motor Estab., Westcott, 1979–80. *Publications:* contrib. to: Advances in Photochemistry, vol. 3, 1964; Advances in Inorganic and Radio Chemistry, vol. 8, 1966; Oxidation and Combustion Reviews, vol. 3, 1968 and vol. 4, 1969; articles on combustion in scientific jls; official reports. *Recreations:* long distance walking, reading, gardening, photography, bridge. *Address:* Fort Halstead, Sevenoaks, Kent TN14 7PB. *T:* Knockholt 32222.

PEARSON, Air Commodore Herbert Macdonald, CBE 1944; RAF retired; *b* Buenos Aires, Argentina, 17 Nov. 1908; *s* of John Charles Pearson; *m* 1939, Jane Leslie; one *s* two *d*. *Educ*: Cheltenham Coll.; Cranwell. Left Cranwell, 1928; Malta, 1929–31; Central Flying Sch., 1932; Instructor, Cranwell, 1933–34; attached to Peruvian Government, 1935–36; Asst Air Attaché in Spain, 1936–38; comd No. 54 Sqdn, 1938–39. War of 1939–45, in Fighter Command; then France, Belgium and Germany; Air Attaché, Lima, Peru, 1946; Deputy Director Air Foreign Liaison, Air Ministry, 1949; Commanding Royal Air Force, Kai Tak, Hong Kong, 1951–53; Assistant Chief of Staff Intelligence, Headquarters of Allied Air Forces, Central Europe, 1953–55. Air Commodore, 1953; retired, 1955. *Address:* Mapleridge Barn, Horton, S Glos. *Club:* Naval and Military.

PEARSON, Sir (James) Denning, Kt 1963; JP; Chairman and Chief Executive, Rolls-Royce Ltd, 1969–70; Chairman, Gamma Associates, 1972–80; *b* 8 Aug. 1908; *s* of James Pearson and Elizabeth Henderson; *m* 1932, Eluned Henry; two *d*. *Educ*: Canton Secondary Sch., Cardiff; Cardiff Technical Coll. Senior Wh. Scholarship; BSc Eng. Joined Rolls-Royce Ltd, 1932; Technical Production Engineer, Glasgow Factory, 1941; Chief Quality and Service Engineer (resident in Canada for one year), 1941–45; Gen. Man. Sales and Service, 1946–49; Director, 1949; Director and Gen. Man., Aero Engine Division, 1950; Managing Director (Aero Engine Div.), 1954–65; Chief Exec. and Dep. Chm., 1957–68. President, SBAC, 1963; Member: NEDC, 1964–67; Fellowship of Engrg. CEng; FRAeS, 1957–64, Hon. FRAeS, 1964; Hon. FIMechE; FBIM; DrIngEh Brunswick Univ., 1962. Member: Council, Manchester Business Sch.; Governing Body, London Graduate Sch. of Business Studies, 1968–70; Governing Body, Admin. Staff Coll., Henley, 1968–73; Council, Voluntary Service Overseas. Fellow, Imperial Coll. of Science and Technology, 1968–; Hon. Fellow, Manchester Univ. Inst. of Science and Technology, 1969; Hon. DSc Nottingham, 1966; Wales, 1968; Cranfield Inst. of Technology, 1970; Hon. DTech: Loughborough, 1968; CNAA, 1969. Gold Medal, Royal Aero Club, 1969; Benjamin Franklin Medal, RSA, 1970. FRSA, 1970. *Recreations:* reading, golf, tennis, sailing. *Address:* Green Acres, Holbrook, Derbyshire. *T:* Derby 881137.

PEARSON, Prof. James Douglas; Emeritus Professor of Bibliography, with reference to Asia and Africa, School of Oriental and African Studies, University of London (Professor, 1972–79); *b* 17 Dec. 1911; *m* 1st, Rose Betty Burden (marr. diss.); one *s*; 2nd, Hilda M. Wilkinson; three *s*. *Educ*: Cambridge Univ. (MA). Asst Under-librarian, Cambridge Univ. Library, 1939–50; Librarian, Sch. of Oriental and African Studies, Univ. of London, 1950–72. Hon. FLA, 1976. *Publications:* Index Islamicus, 1958–; Oriental and Asian Bibliography, 1966; Oriental Manuscripts in Europe and North America, 1971; (ed jtly) Arab Islamic Bibliography, 1977; (ed) South Asia Bibliography, 1978. *Recreations:* natural history, walking. *Address:* 79 Highsett, Hills Road, Cambridge CB2 1NZ.

PEARSON, Sir (James) Reginald, Kt 1959; OBE 1950; retired in Nov. 1962 as Deputy Chairman (1958) and Executive Assistant to Managing Director (1953), Vauxhall Motors Ltd, Luton, Beds; *b* 17 Nov. 1897; *s* of George Henry Pearson and Annie Pearson (*née* Stringer); *m* 1925, Nellie Rose Vittery (*d* 1977); one *d*. *Educ*: Dudley, Worcestershire. Apprenticed at Bullers Ltd, Tipton; National Projectile Factory, Dudley; Vauxhall Motors Ltd (1919); Craftsman, Journeyman, Foreman, Area Manager, Production Manager, Factory Manager, Director (1946). Chairman, Dawley Development

Corporation, 1962–68 (now Telford). Vice-President, Royal Society for the Prevention of Accidents. High Sheriff of Bedfordshire, 1964; DL Beds, 1968–78. FIMechE; MIProdE. *Recreations:* golf, gardening; interested in all forms of sport; Hon. Life President, Vauxhall Motors Recreation Club. *Address:* 45 Bloomfield Road, Harpenden, Herts. *T:* Harpenden 3052.

PEARSON, Captain John William, CBE 1981; Regional Administrator, Mersey Regional Health Authority, 1977–81; *b* 19 Sept. 1920; *s* of Walter and Margaret Jane Pearson; *m* 1945, Audrey Ethel Whitehead; two *s*. *Educ*: Holloway Sch. FCIS, FHA, FCCA, IPFA. Served War, RA (Field), 1939–46. Hospital Service, LCC, 1947–48; NW Metropolitan Regional Hosp. Bd, 1948–49; Northern Gp, HMC, Finance Officer, 1949–62; Treasurer: St Thomas' Bd of Governors, 1962–73; Mersey Regional Health Authority, 1973–77. Pres., Assoc. of Health Service Treasurers, 1970–71. *Recreations:* tennis, golf, gardening, snooker. *Address:* 20 Weare Gifford, Shoeburyness, Essex SS3 8AB. *T:* Southend 585039.

PEARSON, Sir Neville, 2nd Bt *cr* 1916; *b* 13 Feb. 1898; *s* of 1st Bt, and Ethel Lady Pearson, DBE; *S* father, 1921; *m* 1st, 1922, Mary Angela (marr. diss. 1928, she *m* 1928, C. Willoughby Hordern and *d* 1937), 2nd *d* of 1st Baron Melchett; one *d* (one *s* decd); 2nd, 1928, Gladys Cooper (later Dame Gladys Cooper, DBE) (*d* 1971), (marr. diss. 1937; she *m* 1937, Philip Merivale); one *d*; 3rd, 1943, Mrs Anne Davis Elebash (*d* 1981), New York. *Educ*: Eton. RFA, European War, 1917–18; subsequently entered firm of C. Arthur Pearson, Ltd, publishers; retired from all directorships, 1968. President, St Dunstan's, 1947–77; President, Fresh Air Fund. AA Artillery, War of 1939–45. *Heir:* none. *Address:* c/o Wyndham L. Gary, 37 Highland Avenue, Fair Haven, NJ 07701, USA.
See also Baron Glenkinglas, T. S. R. Hardy.

PEARSON, Norman Charles, OBE 1944; TD 1944; Lay Member, Restrictive Practices Court, since 1968; Deputy Chairman, Cincinnati Milacron Ltd, since 1972; *b* 12 Aug. 1909; *s* of late Max Pearson and Kate Pearson; *m* 1951, Olive May, *d* of late Kenneth Harper and Ruth Harper, Granston Manor, Co. Leix; one *s* one *d*. *Educ*: Harrow Sch. (Scholar). Gonville and Caius Coll., Cambridge (Sayer Scholar). Commnd Royal Signals (TA), 1932; Middx Yeomanry; served War of 1939–45, N Africa (despatches, OBE), Italy, Greece; Lt-Col, comd 6th Armd Div. Signals, 1942; 10 Corps Signals, 1944; Mil. Comd Athens Signals; 4th Div. Signals, 1945; subseq. re-formed 56 Div. Signals Regt (TA). Boots Pure Drug Co. Ltd, 1931–37; Borax (Holdings) Ltd, 1937–69; Director, 1951; Dir, UK Provident Instn, 1965–80. Mem., Air Transport Licensing Bd, 1971–72. *Recreation:* gardening. *Address:* 19 Cornwall Gardens, SW7 4AW. *T:* 01-937 8477; Copt Heath, Cold Ash, Newbury, Berks. *Club:* Carlton.

PEARSON, Mrs R. O'Neill; see Robins, Mrs Denise.

PEARSON, Sir Reginald; see Pearson, Sir J. R.

PEARSON, Maj.-Gen. Ronald Matthew, MBE 1959; QHDS 1978; Director Army Dental Service, since 1982; *b* 25 Feb. 1925; *s* of Dr John Pearson and Sheila Pearson (*née* Brown); *m* 1956, Florence Eileen Jack; two *d*. *Educ*: Clifton Hall Sch., Ratho, Midlothian; Glasgow Acad.; Glasgow Univ./Glasgow Dental Hosp. LDS RFPS(Glas) 1948; FBIM 1979. Civilian Dental Practice, 1948–49. Commnd RADC, 1949; served: RWAFF, 1950–53; UK, 1953–57; BAOR, 1957–60; UK, 1961–67; CO No 1 Dental Gp, BAOR, 1967–70; CO Army Dental Centres, Cyprus, 1970–73; CO No 8 Dental Gp, UK, 1973–75; CO No 4 Dental Gp, UK, 1975–76; Dep. Dir Dental Service, UKLF, 1976–78; Dep. Dir Dental Service, BAOR, 1978–82. *Recreations:* trout fishing, photography, gardening, caravanning. *Address:* c/o Williams & Glyn's Bank Ltd, Holts Branch, Victoria Road, Farnborough, Hants.

PEARSON, Rt. Rev. Thomas Bernard; Titular Bishop of Sinda, since 1949; Bishop Auxiliary in the Diocese of Lancaster, 1952–62, and since 1965; Episcopal Vicar for Cumbria (formerly Cumberland, Westmorland and Furness), since 1967; *b* Preston, Lancs, 18 January 1907; *s* of Joseph Pearson and Alice (*née* Cartmell). *Educ*: Upholland College; Ven. English College, Rome. Pontifical Gregorian University, Rome; PhD 1930; Bachelor of Canon Law, Licent. Sacred Theology, 1933. Priest, 1933; Assistant Priest, 1934–44; Parish Priest, St Cuthbert's, Blackpool, 1944–67. Mem., Order of Discalced Carmelites, 1974. *Recreation:* mountaineering. *Address:* Howard Lodge, 90 Warwick Road, Carlisle CA1 1JU. *T:* Carlisle 24952. *Clubs:* Alpine, Fell and Rock, English Lake District; Achille Ratti Climbing (Founder President).

PEARSON, Gen. Sir Thomas (Cecil Hook), KCB 1967 (CB 1964); CBE 1959 (OBE 1953); DSO 1940, and Bar, 1943; retired 1974; *b* 1 July 1914; *s* of late Vice-Admiral J. L. Pearson, CMG; *m* 1947, Aud, *d* of late Alf Skjelkvale, Oslo; two *s*. *Educ*: Charterhouse; Sandhurst. 2nd Lieutenant Rifle Bde, 1934. Served War of 1939–45, M East and Europe; CO 2nd Bn The Rifle Bde, 1942; Dep. Comdr 2nd Independent Parachute Bde Gp 1944; Dep. Comdr 1st Air-landing Bde 1945; GSO1 1st Airborne Div. 1945; CO 1st Bn The Parachute Regt 1946; CO 7th Bn The Parachute Regt 1947; GSO1 (Land Air Warfare), WO, 1948; JSSC, GSO1, HQ Malaya, 1950; GSO1 (Plans), FARELF, 1951; Directing Staff, JSSC, 1953; Comdr 45 Parachute Bde TA 1955; Nat. Defence Coll., Canada, 1956; Comdr 16 Indep. Parachute Bde 1957; Chief of Staff to Dir of Ops Cyprus, 1960; Head of Brit. Mil. Mission to Soviet Zone of Germany, 1960; Major-General Commanding 1st Division, BAOR, 1961–63; Chief of Staff, Northern Army Group, 1963–67; Comdr,

FARELF, 1967–68; Military Sec., MoD, 1968–72; C-in-C, Allied Forces, Northern Europe, 1972–74; psc 1942; jssc 1950; ndc Canada 1957. ADC Gen. to the Queen, 1974. Col Comdt, the Royal Green Jackets, 1973–77. Fisheries Mem., Welsh Water Auth., 1980–. Haakon VII Liberty Cross, 1948; Medal of Honour, Norwegian Defence Assoc., 1973. *Recreations:* field sports, yachting. *Address:* Streete House, Weston under Penyard, Ross on Wye, Herefordshire HR9 7NY. *Clubs:* Naval and Military; Island Sailing, Kongelig Norsk Seilforenning.

PEARSON, William Thomas Shipston; retired from Civil Service, 1980; *b* 21 Aug. 1917; *s* of William Pearson and Alice (*née* Shipston); *m* 1948, Pauline Daphne Scott (*née* Wilkinson); one *s* two *d. Educ:* High Pavement Sch., Nottingham; University Coll., Nottingham (BSc). MRAeS, CEng. Appts at RAE, 1939–45; Hon. Commn, Flying Officer, RAFVR, 1944; Blind Landing Experimental Unit, Martlesham Heath, 1945–47; RAF Transport Comd Develt Unit, 1947–50; TRE, 1950–52; seconded to Australian Scientific Service, Long Range Weapons Estab., 1952–56; RAE, Farnborough, 1956–62; Asst Dir, Air Armaments, Min. of Aviation, 1962–65; Div. Head, Weapons Dept, RAE (concerned with various projs), 1965–76; seconded to FCO, as Counsellor (Defence Res.), British High Commn, Canberra, and Head of British Defence Res. and Supply Staffs, Australia, 1977–79. *Publications:* official reports. *Recreation:* photography. *Address:* Cooinda, Pine Avenue, Camberley, Surrey GU15 2LY.

PEART, family name of **Baron Peart.**

PEART, Baron *cr* 1976 (Life Peer), of Workington; **(Thomas) Frederick Peart,** PC 1964; Leader of the Opposition in the House of Lords, since 1979; *b* 30 Apr. 1914; *m* 1945, Sarah Elizabeth Lewis; one *s. Educ:* Crook Council; Wolsingham Grammar; Henry Smith Secondary, Hartlepool; Bede Coll., Durham Univ. (BSc); Inner Temple, Inns of Court. Pres. Durham University Union Soc. Councillor Easington RDC, 1937–40. Became a Schoolmaster. Served War of 1939–45, commissioned Royal Artillery, served in North Africa and Italy. MP (Lab) Workington Div. of Cumberland, 1945–76; PPS to Minister of Agriculture, 1945–51; Minister of Agriculture, Fisheries and Food, 1964–68 and 1974–76; Leader of the House of Commons, 1968–70; Lord Privy Seal, April–Oct. 1968; Lord President of the Council, Oct. 1968–1970; Opposition Spokesman; House of Commons Matters, 1970–71; Agriculture, 1971–72; Defence, 1972–74; Lord Privy Seal and Leader of the House of Lords, 1976–79; British Delegate to Council of Europe, 1952–55 (Rep. Agriculture Cttee and Cttee for Culture and Science (Vice-Pres.)). Privy Council Rep. on Council of RCVS, Dir, FMC, 1971–74. Chairman: Adv. Council for Applied R&D, 1976–80; Retail Consortium, 1979–81. Hon. DSc Cranfield, 1977. *Address:* House of Lords, SW1.

PEART, Brian; Under-Secretary, Ministry of Agriculture, Fisheries and Food, since 1976; *b* 17 Aug. 1925; *s* of late Joseph Garfield Peart and Frances Hannah Peart (*née* English); *m* 1952, Dorothy (*née* Thompson); one *s* one *d. Educ:* Wolsingham Grammar Sch.; Durham Univ. (BA). Served War, RAF, 1943–47. Agricultural Economist, Edinburgh Sch. of Agric., 1950–57; Sen. Agricultural Economist, 1957–64; Regional Farm Management Adviser, MAFF, West Midlands Region, 1964–67; Chief Farm Management Adviser, MAFF, 1967–71; Regional Manager, MAFF, Yorks/Lancs Region, 1971–74; Head of Intelligence and Trng Div., 1974–76; Chief Administrator, ADAS, 1976–80. *Recreations:* golf, bridge, The Times crossword. *Address:* 18 Derwent Close, Claygate, Surrey KT10 0RF. *Clubs:* Farmers', Civil Service.

PEART, Prof. William Stanley, MD; FRS 1969; Professor of Medicine, University of London, at St Mary's Hospital Medical School since 1956; *b* 31 March 1922; *s* of J. G. and M. Peart; *m* 1947, Peggy Parkes; one *s* one *d. Educ:* King's College School, Wimbledon; Medical School, St Mary's Hospital. MB, BS (Hons), FRCP, 1959; MD (London), 1949. Lecturer in Medicine, St Mary's Hospital, 1950–56. Chm., Beit Fellowship Cttee. Trustee, Wellcome Trust, 1975–. Goulstonian Lectr, 1959, Croonian Lectr, 1979, RCP. Stouffer Prize, 1968. *Publications:* chapters in: Cecil-Loeb, Textbook of Medicine; Renal Disease; Biochemical Disorders in Human Disease; articles in Biochemical Journal, Journal of Physiology, Lancet. *Recreations:* reading, tennis. *Address:* 17 Highgate Close, N6 4SD; Medical Unit, St Mary's Hospital, Praed Street, W2 1NY. *T:* 01-262 1280.

PEASE, family name of **Barons Daryngton, Gainford,** and **Wardington.**

PEASE, Sir (Alfred) Vincent, 4th Bt *cr* 1882; *b* 2 April 1926; *s* of Sir Alfred (Edward) Pease, 2nd Bt (*d* 1939), and of his 3rd wife, Emily Elizabeth (Dowager Lady Pease, JP) (*d* 1979); *S* half-brother, 1963; unmarried. *Educ:* Bootham School, York. *Heir: b* Joseph Gurney Pease [*b* 16 Nov. 1927; *m* 1953, Shelagh Munro, *d* of C. G. Bulman; one *s* one *d*]. *Address:* The Woolpack Inn, Boot, Eskdale, Cumbria CA19 1TH. *T:* Eskdale 230.

PEASE, Dr Rendel Sebastian, FRS 1977; Programme Director for Fusion, UKAEA, since 1981; *b* 1922; *s* of Michael Stewart Pease and Helen Bowen (*née* Wedgwood); *m* 1952, Susan Spickernell; two *s* three *d. Educ:* Bedales Sch.; Trinity Coll., Cambridge (MA, ScD). Scientific Officer, Min. of Aircraft Prodn at ORS Unit, HQ, RAF Bomber Comd, 1942–46; research at AERE, Harwell, 1947–61; Div. Head, Culham Lab. for Plasma Physics and Nuclear Fusion, UKAEA, 1961–67; Vis. Scientist, Princeton Univ., 1964–65;

Asst Dir, UKAEA Research Gp, 1967; Dir, Culham Lab., UKAEA, 1968–81. Chairman: Adam Hilger Ltd, 1976–77; Plasma Physics Commn, Internat. Union of Pure and Applied Physics, 1975–78; Internat. Fusion Res. Council, Internat. Atomic Energy Agency, 1976–. Member: Fabian Soc.; Inst. of Physics (Vice-Pres., 1973–77; Pres., 1978–80); Amer. Inst. of Physics; IEE. DUniv Surrey, 1973; Hon. DSc Aston, 1981. *Publications:* articles in physics jls. *Recreation:* music. *Address:* The Poplars, West Ilsley, Newbury, Berks RG16 0AW.

PEASE, Sir Richard (Thorn), 3rd Bt *cr* 1920; Director, Barclays Bank, since 1965; Deputy Chairman, Yorkshire Bank, since 1981 (Director, since 1977); *b* 20 May 1922; *s* of Sir Richard Arthur Pease, 2nd Bt, and Jeannette Thorn (*d* 1957), *d* of late Gustav Edward Kissel, New York; *S* father, 1969; *m* 1956, Anne, *d* of late Lt-Col Reginald Francis Heyworth; one *s* two *d. Educ:* Eton. Served with 60th Rifles, Middle East, Italy and Greece, 1941–46 (Captain). Director: Owners of the Middlesbrough Estate Ltd, 1954–; Bank of Scotland, 1977–; Vice-Chairman: Barclays Bank Ltd, 1970–82; Barclays Bank UK Management, 1971–82. *Heir: s* Richard Peter Pease, *b* 4 Sept. 1958. *Address:* Hindley House, Stocksfield-on-Tyne, Northumberland.

PEASE, Robert John Claude; HM Diplomatic Service, retired; Counsellor (Administration) and Consul-General, British Embassy, Moscow, 1977–80; *b* 24 April 1922; *s* of Frederick Robert Hellier Pease and Eileen Violet Pease (*née* Beer); *m* 1945, Claire Margaretta Whall; one *s* two *d. Educ:* Cattedown Road Sch., Plymouth; Sutton High Sch., Plymouth. Served War of 1939–45; Telegraphist, RN, 1942; commnd Sub Lt RNVR, 1944. Clerk, Lord Chancellor's Dept, Plymouth County Court, 1939, Truro County Court, 1946; Foreign Office, 1948; Moscow, 1952; HM Consul, Sarajevo, 1954; 2nd Sec., Bangkok, 1958; HM Consul, Gdynia, 1959, Düsseldorf, 1961; 1st Sec., Pretoria, 1964, Bombay, 1966; FCO, 1969; Dep. High Commissioner, Mauritius, 1973. *Recreations:* golf, opera. *Address:* 5 Springfield Road, Camberley, Surrey.

PEASE, Sir Vincent; *see* Pease, Sir A. V.

PEAT, William Wood Watson, CBE 1972; JP; farmer; Director of F. M. C. Ltd; broadcaster; *b* 14 Dec. 1922; *o s* of William Peat and Margaret Hillhouse; *m* 1955, Jean Frew Paton McHarrie; two *s* one *d. Educ:* Denny Public School. Served with Royal Signals, Europe and India, 1941–46; Lieut 1944. Member: Nat. Council, Scottish Assoc. of Young Farmers' Clubs, 1949 (Chm., 1953–54; Vice-Pres., 1975; Pres., 1979); Stirling CC, 1959–70 (Vice-Convenor, 1967–70); Council, NFU Scotland, 1959–78 (Pres., 1966–67); Scottish River Purification Adv. Cttee, 1960–79; Bd of Management, Royal Scottish Nat. Hosp., 1962–72; Council, Hannah Research Inst., 1963–82; Council, Scottish Agricultural Organisation Soc. Ltd, 1963 (Pres., 1974–77); Bd of Management, British Farm Produce Council, 1964 (Vice-Chm., 1980); Agric. Marketing Develt Exec. Cttee, 1966; Central Council for Agric. and Horticultural Co-operation, 1967; Bd of Management, Oatridge Agric. Coll., 1967–75; Gen. Comr of Income Tax, 1962; Governor, West of Scotland Agric. Coll., 1964– (Vice Chm., 1975); Dir, Agri-Finance (Scotland) Ltd, 1968–79; Chm., BBC Scottish Agric. Adv. Cttee, 1971–75; Chm., Scottish Adv. Cttee, Assoc. of Agriculture, 1974–79, Vice Pres., 1979–; Dir, Fedn of Agricultural Co-operatives (UK) Ltd, 1974–77; Mem., British Agricl Council, 1974–. JP Stirlingshire, 1963. *Recreations:* amateur radio, flying. *Address:* Carbro, 61 Stirling Road, Larbert, Stirlingshire FK5 4SG. *T:* Larbert 562420. *Clubs:* Farmers'; Stirling and County (Stirling); Turnhouse Flying (Edinburgh).

PECHELL, Sir Ronald (Horace), 9th Bt *cr* 1797; *b* 4 June 1918; *o s* of Major Hugh Charles Pechell (and *g g s* of Commander Charles Pechell, *b* of 5th Bt), and Caroline Charlotte, *d* of G. A. Strickland; *S* kinsman, Sir Paul Pechell, 8th Bt, 1972; *m* 1949, Dora Constance, *d* of late John Crampthorne. *Educ:* St Paul's Sch.; HMS Worcester. Naval Cadet, Royal Air Force (Marine Craft Section) and Civil Aviation. Served War of 1939–45; Air-Sea Rescue five medals. Royal Humane Society Medal, 1950. *Recreations:* sailing and overseas travel. *Heir:* none. *Address:* c/o Child & Co., 1 Fleet Street, EC4.

PECK, Antony Dilwyn, CB 1965; MBE 1945; Deputy Secretary, Department of Trade and Industry, 1970–73; retired; *b* 10 April 1914; *s* of late Sir James Peck, CB, and late Lady Peck; *m* 1st, 1939, Joan de Burgh Whyte (*d* 1955); one *s* one *d* ; 2nd, 1956, Sylvia Glenister; one *s* two *d. Educ:* Eton; Trinity College, Oxford. Fellow of Trinity College, 1938–46. Served War of 1939–45, Army, 1940–46 (Major). Joined Treasury as Principal, 1946; Asst Secretary, 1950; Under-Secretary, 1959; Dep. Under-Sec. of State, MoD, 1963–68; Second Sec., BoT, 1968–70. *Recreations:* tennis, bridge. *Address:* Holly Tree House, Compton, Chichester, W Sussex PO18 9HD. *Club:* Hurlingham.

PECK, David (Edward); His Honour Judge Peck; a Circuit Judge (formerly Judge of County Courts), since Oct. 1969; *b* 6 April 1917; *m* 1st, 1950, Rosina Seton Glover Marshall (marr. diss.); one *s* three *d* ; 2nd, 1973, Frances Deborah Redford (*née* Mackenzie); one *s. Educ:* Charterhouse School; Balliol College, Oxford. Served Army (Cheshire Regiment), 1939–46. Called to Bar, Middle Temple, 1949. Mem., County Court Rule Cttee, 1978– (Chm., 1981–); Jt Editor, County Court Practice, 1982–. *Address:* 8 New Square, Lincoln's Inn, WC2A 3QP.

PECK, Sir Edward (Heywood), GCMG 1974 (KCMG 1966; CMG 1957); HM Diplomatic Service, retired; British Permanent Representative to North

Atlantic Council, 1970-75; *b* 5 Oct. 1915; *s* of Lt-Col Edward Surman Peck, IMS, and Doris Louise Heywood; *m* 1948, Alison Mary MacInnes; one *s* two *d*. *Educ:* Clifton College; The Queen's College, Oxford. 1st Cl. Hons (Mod. Langs), 1937; Laming Travelling Fellow, 1937-38. Entered Consular Service, 1938; served in Barcelona, 1938-39; Foreign Office, 1939-40; Sofia, 1940; Ankara, 1940-44; Adana, 1944; Iskenderun, 1945; Salonica, 1945-47; with UK Deleg. to UN Special Commn on the Balkans, 1947; Foreign Office, 1947-50; seconded to UK High Commissioner's Office, Delhi, 1950-52; Counsellor, Foreign Office, 1952-55; Dep. Comdt, Brit. Sector, Berlin, 1955-58; on staff of UK Commissioner-General for S-E Asia, 1959-60; Assistant Under-Secretary of State, Foreign Office, 1961-66; British High Commissioner in Kenya, 1966-68; Dep. Under-Secretary of State, FCO, 1968-70. Hon. Vis. Fellow in Defence Studies, Aberdeen Univ., 1976-. *Publication:* North-East Scotland (Bartholomew's Guides Series), 1981. *Recreations:* mountaineering, ski-ing, reading: history and guide books. *Address:* Easter Torrans, Tomintoul, Banffshire. *Club:* Alpine.

PECK, Gregory; film actor, US, since 1943; *b* 5 April 1916; *s* of Gregory P. Peck and Bernice Ayres; *m* 1st, 1942, Greta Konen Rice (marr. diss. 1954); two *s* (and one *s* decd); 2nd, 1955, Veronique Passani; one *s* one *d*. *Educ:* Calif Public Schools; Univ. of Calif (BA). Broadway stage, 1941-43. *Films:* Days of Glory, 1943; Keys of the Kingdom, Valley of Decision, 1944; Spellbound, 1945; Duel in the Sun, The Yearling, 1946; The Macomber Affair, Gentlemen's Agreement, 1947; The Paradine Case, 1948; Yellow Sky, The Great Sinner, Twelve O'Clock High, 1949; The Gun Fighter, 1950; Only the Valiant, Captain Horatio Hornblower, David and Bathsheba, 1951; The World in his Arms, 1952; The Snows of Kilimanjaro, 1952; Roman Holiday, 1953; The Million Pound Note, 1953; Night People, 1954; The Purple Plain, 1954; The Man in the Grey Flannel Suit, 1956; Moby Dick, 1956; Designing Woman, 1957; The Bravados, 1958; The Big Country (co-producer), 1958; Pork Chop Hill, 1959; On the Beach, 1959; Guns of Navarone, 1960; Cape Fear, 1961; To Kill a Mocking Bird, 1962; Captain Newman, MD, 1963; Behold a Pale Horse, 1964; Mirage, 1965; Arabesque, 1965; Mackenna's Gold, 1967; The Chairman, 1968; The Stalking Moon, 1968; Marooned, 1970; I Walk the Line, 1971; Shoot Out, 1971; The Trial of the Catonsville Nine, 1972; Billy Two-Hats, 1974; The Boys From Brazil, 1978; The Sea Wolves, 1980; *produced:* The Dove, 1974; The Omen, 1976; MacArthur, 1977. Nat. Chm., Amer. Cancer Soc., 1966. Mem., Nat. Council on Arts, 1965-67, 1968-; Pres., Acad. Motion Pictures and Sciences, 1967-70; Chm., Board of Trustees, Amer. Film Inst., 1967-69. Medal of Freedom Award, 1969; Jean Hersholt Humanitarian Award, Acad. of Motion Picture Arts and Sciences, 1968. *Recreations:* riding, swimming, bicycling, gardening. *Address:* PO Box 24817 Los Angeles, Calif 90077, USA. *Club:* Players (New York).

PECK, Sir John (Howard), KCMG 1971 (CMG 1956); HM Diplomatic Service, retired; *b* Kuala Lumpur, 16 Feb. 1913; *o s* of late Howard and Dorothea Peck; *m* 1939, Mariska Caroline (*d* 1979), *e d* of Josef Somló; two *s*. *Educ:* Wellington College; CCC, Oxford. Assistant Private Secretary to First Lord of Admiralty, 1937-39; to Minister for Coordination of Defence, 1939-40; to the Prime Minister, 1940-46; transferred to Foreign Service, 1946; served in United Nations Dept, 1946-47; in The Hague, 1947-50; Counsellor and Head of Information Research Dept, 1951-54; Counsellor (Defence Liaison) and Head of Political Division, British Middle East Office, 1954-56; Director-General of British Information Services, New York, 1956-59; UK Permanent Representative to the Council of Europe, and Consul-General, Strasbourg, 1959-62; Ambassador to Senegal, 1962-66, and Mauritania, 1962-65; Asst Under-Sec. of State, FO, then FCO, 1966-70; Ambassador to the Republic of Ireland, 1970-73. *Publications:* Dublin from Downing Street (memoirs), 1978; various essays and light verse. *Recreations:* photography, gardening. *Address:* 4 Eglinton Park, Dun Laoghaire, Co. Dublin. *T:* Dublin 806315. *Club:* Stephen's Green (Dublin).

PECK, Stanley Edwards, CBE 1974; BEM 1954; QPM 1964; DL; HM Inspector of Constabulary, 1964-78; *b* 1916; *er s* of late Harold Edwards Peck, Edgbaston and Shanghai; *m* 1939, Yvonne Sydney Edwards, *er d* of late John Edwards Jessop, LDS; two *s* two *d*. *Educ:* Solihull School; Birmingham University. Served with RAF, 1941-45 (Flt-Lt). Joined Metropolitan Police, 1935; Chief Inspector and Supt, New Scotland Yard, 1950-54; Asst Chief Constable, Staffs, 1954-61; Chief Constable, Staffs, 1961-64. DL Staffs, 1962. Pres., Royal Life Saving Soc., UK, 1969-74 (Chm., East Midlands Region, RLSS, 1968-80). OStJ. *Recreations:* golf and dog walking. *Address:* Lodge Gardens, Walnut Grove, Radcliffe-on-Trent, Nottinghamshire. *Club:* Royal Air Force.

PECKFORD, Hon. (Alfred) Brian; MHA (Progressive C), Green Bay, Newfoundland, since 1972; Premier of the Province of Newfoundland and Labrador, since 1979; *b* Whitbourne, Newfoundland, 27 Aug. 1942; *s* of Ewart Peckford and Allison (*née* Young), St John's; *m* 1969, Marina, *d* of Raymond Dicks and Hope (*née* Adams), Halls Bay; two *d*. *Educ:* Lewisporte High Sch.; Memorial Univ. of Newfoundland (BAEd). Schoolmaster, 1962-63 and 1966-72. MHA Green Bay, 1972-; Special Asst to Premier, 1973; Minister: of Dept of Municipal Affairs and Housing, 1974; of Mines and Energy, 1976, also of Rural Development, 1978. Leader of Progressive Cons. Party, Newfoundland and Labrador, 1979-. *Recreations:* reading, sport, swimming. *Address:* Premier's Office, 8th Floor, Confederation Building, St John's, Newfoundland A1C 5T7, Canada.

PECKHAM, Arthur John; UK Permanent Representative, Food and Agriculture Organisation, Rome, 1977-80; *b* 22 Sept. 1920; *s* of Richard William Peckham and Agnes Mercy (*née* Parker); *m* 1949, Margaret Enid Quirk; two *s* one *d*. *Educ:* The Judd Sch., Tonbridge. RAF (Pilot), 1942-46, 59 Sqdn Coastal Command. Cadet, Min. of Labour and Nat. Service, 1948; Colonial Office: Asst Principal, 1950; Private Sec. to Perm. Under-Sec., 1952; Principal, 1954; Counsellor (Technical Assistance), Lagos, 1964; Asst Sec., Min. of Overseas Develt, 1966; Minister, FAO, Rome, 1977. *Recreations:* gardening, hill walking. *Address:* 7 Yardley Park Road, Tonbridge, Kent. *T:* Tonbridge 353735.

PEDDER, Vice-Adm. Sir Arthur (Reid), KBE 1959; CB 1956; retired as Commander, Allied Naval Forces, Northern Europe (1957-59); *b* 6 July 1904; *s* of late Sir John Pedder, KBE, CB; *m* 1934, Dulcie, *d* of O. L. Bickford; two *s*. *Educ:* Osborne and Dartmouth. Served in various ships, 1921-; qualified as Naval Observer, 1930; promoted Commander and appointed Admiralty, 1937-40; Executive Officer, HMS Mauritius, 1940-42; Admiralty Asst, Dir of Plans (Air), 1942-45; Capt. 1944; comd HM Ships Khedive and Phoebe, 1945-47; idc 1948; Admiralty (Dep. Dir of Plans), 1949-50; Fourth Naval Member of Australian Commonwealth Naval Board, 1950-52; Rear-Adm. 1953; Asst Chief of Naval Staff (Warfare), Admiralty, 1953-54; Flag Officer, Aircraft Carriers, December 1954-May 1956; Vice-Adm. 1956. *Recreation:* everything outdoors. *Address:* Langhurst Barn Cottage, Hascombe, Godalming, Surrey. *T:* Hascombe 294. *Club:* Athenæum.

PEDDER, Air Marshal Sir Ian Maurice, KCB 1982; OBE 1963; DFC 1949; Controller, National Air Traffic Services, since 1981 (Deputy Controller, 1977-81); Board Member, Civil Aviation Authority, since 1981; *b* 2 May 1926; *s* of Maurice and Elsie Pedder; *m* 1949, Jean Mary (*née* Kellett); one *s* two *d*. *Educ:* Royal Grammar Sch., High Wycombe; Queen's Coll., Oxford. Service in Nos 28, 60, 81, 213 Sqdns, CFS, and with Burma Air Force, 1946-59; Staff Coll., Andover, and MoD, 1959-62; Far East, 1962-64; Staff appts, 1965-70; RCDS, 1971; Comdg RAF Chivenor, 1972-74; NATS, 1974-. *Publications:* contribs to Service jls, UK and US. *Recreations:* study of Victorian times, photography, riding (a bicycle). *Address:* Pilton, Barnstaple, North Devon. *Club:* Royal Air Force.

PEDDIE, Maj.-Gen. Graham, CB 1959; DSO 1945; MBE 1941; *b* 15 Oct. 1905; *s* of late Graham Peddie and of Mrs Peddie; *m* 1937, Dorothy Mary Humfress (decd); one *s* one *d*; *m* 1959, Alexandra Mavrojani. *Educ:* Sherborne School, Royal Military Academy, Woolwich. Commissioned into RA, 1926; served in UK, 1926-30, in Egypt and Sudan, 1930-36; Instructor, RMA, Woolwich, 1937-39. War of 1939-45, in UK and NW Europe; 1st AA Group (Dep. Comd), 1948-50; idc, 1950-51. BAOR 1953-56; Director of Manpower Planning, War Office, 1957-60; retired, 1960. *Address:* Sundridge, Stratton, Cirencester, Glos GL7 2LJ.

PEDDIE, Robert Allan; Chairman, South Eastern Electricity Board, since 1977; *b* 27 Oct. 1921; *s* of Robert Allan Peddie and Elizabeth Elsie (*née* Sharp); *m* 1946, Ilene Ivy Sillcock; one *d*. *Educ:* Nottingham Univ. (BSc Eng). Electricity Dept, Hull Corp., 1946; joined nationalised electricity supply industry, 1948, and held various appts; Supt, Bradwell Nuclear Power Stn, 1958; Asst Reg. Dir, NW Region, 1962; Dep. Reg. Dir, Mids Region, 1967; Dir-Gen., SE Region, 1970; Mem. CEGB, 1972-77; part-time Mem., UKAEA, 1972-77. *Recreations:* swimming, golf, walking. *Address:* Torness, The Mount Drive, Reigate, Surrey. *T:* Reigate 44996.

PEDDIE, Ronald, CBE 1971; JP; *b* 24 May 1905; *s* of Rev. James Peddie, BA and Elsie Mary, *d* of John Edward Corby; *m* 1931, Vera (*d* 1981), *d* of W. G. Nicklin, Guildford; three *s* one *d*. *Educ:* Glasgow Academy; Leys Sch., Cambridge; St John's Coll., Cambridge (MA). CA 1930; Jt Dipl. Management Accounting, 1967. McClelland Ker & Co., CA, Glasgow, 1926-31; Accountant and Asst Sec., C. & J. Clark Ltd, Street, Som, 1931-43; The United Steel Cos Ltd, 1943-67 (Sec. from 1946, later Dir Finance and Admin); British Steel Corp.: Dir, Finance and Admin, Midland Group, 1967-69; Man. Dir, Administration, 1969-71; retd. Dir, Iron Trades Employers' Insurance Assoc. Ltd, 1970-75. Sec., Trevelyan Scholarships, 1958-81; Governor, Ashorne Hill Management Coll., 1967-71. Past Mem., Cambridge and Leeds Univs Appt Bds. JP Sheffield, 1964. *Publications:* The United Steel Companies, 1918-1968: a History, 1968; The Trevelyan Scholarships, 1975; articles in Accountants Magazine and Accountancy. *Recreations:* gardening, reading, all games (now as a spectator). *Address:* Little Glebe, 15 Lime Close, West Clandon, Surrey. *T:* Guildford 222513.

PEDLER, Sir Frederick (Johnson), Kt 1969; *b* 10 July 1908; *s* of Charles Henry Pedler and Lucy Marian (*née* Johnson); *m* 1935, Esther Ruth Carling; two *s* one *d*. *Educ:* Watford Grammar School; Caius College, Cambridge (MA). Colonial Office, 1930; seconded to Tanganyika, 1934; Secretary to Commission on Higher Educn in E Africa and Sudan, 1937; Sec. to Lord Privy Seal, 1938; Sec. to Lord Hailey in Africa, 1939, Congo, 1940; Chief Brit. Econ. Representative, Dakar, 1942; Finance Dept, Colonial Office, 1944. Joined United Africa Co., 1947, Director, 1951, Deputy Chairman, 1965-68. Director: Unilever Ltd and NV, 1956-68; William Baird Ltd, 1969-75. Chm., Council for Technical Educn and Training for Overseas Countries, 1962-73. Chm., E Africa and Mauritius Assoc., 1966-68; Mem., Inter-University Council, 1967-73. Treas., SOAS, Univ. of London, 1969-81. Hon. Fellow, 1976. *Publications:* West Africa, 1951 (2nd edn 1959); Economic Geography of W Africa, 1955; The Lion and the Unicorn in Africa, 1974; Main Currents of West African History 1940-78, 1979. *Recreations:* languages, history. *Address:* 36 Russell Road, Moor Park, Northwood, Mddx.

PEDLEY, Alan Sydney, DFC 1946; Lord Mayor of Leeds, 1975-1976; District Insurance Manager, 1974-82; *b* 16 Aug. 1917; *s* of Herbert Leonard Pedley and Edith Mary (*née* Skipsey); *m* 1st, 1949, Evelyn Anderson (*née* Scott) (*d* 1977); 2nd, 1981, Shirley Elizabeth, widow of Reg Howard. *Educ:* Leeds Modern Sch. Entered Insurance, 1934; retd (Commercial Union), 1971; joined Barclays Insurance Services Co. Ltd, 1971. Member: Leeds City Council, 1951-81; W Yorkshire Metropolitan CC, 1973-81; Dep. Lord Mayor, 1971-72. FCII 1949. *Recreations:* cricket, Association football, Rugby League, music, theatre, the Arts. *Address:* Sandylands, 44 Lidgett Lane, Leeds LS8 1PQ. *T:* Leeds 661666. *Clubs:* Leeds, Leeds Taverners.

PEDLEY, Prof. Robin; Professor Emeritus, University of Southampton, since 1979; *b* 11 Aug. 1914; *s* of Edward and Martha Jane Pedley; *m* 1951, Jeanne Lesley Hitching, BA; one *s* one *d. Educ:* Richmond Sch., Yorks; Durham Univ. (MA, PhD, Teaching Dip.; Gibson Prize in Archaeology, Gladstone Meml Prize in Mod. Hist.). Research Fellow, Durham Univ., 1936-38; Teacher, Friends' Sch., Great Ayton, 1938-42, and Crossley and Porter Schs, Halifax, 1943-46. Lecturer: Coll. of St Mark and St John, Chelsea, 1946-47; Leicester Univ. Dept of Educn, 1947-63. Dir, Exeter Univ. Inst. of Educn, 1963-71; University of Southampton: Head of Sch. of Educn and Dean, Faculty of Educn, 1971-75; Head, Dept of Educn, 1976-79. *Publications:* Comprehensive Schools Today, 1955; Comprehensive Education: a new approach, 1956; The Comprehensive School, 1963, 3rd edn 1978; The Comprehensive School (with J. Orring, publ. in Hebrew, Jerusalem), 1966; Towards the Comprehensive University, 1977; many articles various educational jls. *Recreations:* sport, reading. *Address:* Annerley, Waters Green, Brockenhurst, Hants, SO4 7RG. *T:* Brockenhurst 3001.

PEEBLES, Prof. Phillip James Edwin, FRS 1982; Professor of Physics, Princeton University, since 1965; *b* Winnipeg, 25 April 1935; *s* of Andrew Charles Peebles and Ada Marian (*née* Green); *m* 1958, Jean Alison; three *d. Educ:* Univ. of Manitoba (BSc 1958); Princeton Univ. (Ma 1959; PhD 1962). Member: Amer. Phys. Soc.; Amer. Astron. Soc.; AAAS; Amer. Acad. of Arts and Scis; Internat. Astron. Union. *Publications:* Physical Cosmology, 1971; The Large Scale Structure of the Universe, 1979; (ed jtly) Objects of High Redshift, 1980. *Address:* 24 Markham Road, Princeton, NJ 08540, USA; Joseph Henry Laboratories, Physics Department, Princeton University, Princeton, NJ 08544, USA.

PEECH, Alan James; *b* 24 August 1905; *s* of late Albert Orlando Peech; *m* 1948, Betty Leese; no *c. Educ:* Wellington College; Magdalen College, Oxford (BA). Former Governor, Wellington College, retd 1975. Independent Chm., Cement Makers' Fedn, 1970-76; former Dep. Chm., Steetley Co. Ltd, retd 1976; Pres., British Iron and Steel Fedn, Jan.-June 1967; Jt Man. Dir, United Steel Cos Ltd, 1962-67, Chm., 1962-71; a Dep. Chm., BSC, 1967-70; Man. Dir, Midland Gp BSC, 1967-70. Hon. LLD Sheffield, 1966. *Recreations:* fishing and shooting. *Address:* High House, Blyth, Worksop, Notts. *T:* Blyth 255. *Club:* MCC.

PEECH, Neil Malcolm; President for life, The Steetley Co. Ltd, since 1976 (Managing Director, 1935-68, Chairman, 1935-76); *b* 27 Jan. 1908; *s* of Albert Orlando Peech; *m* 1932, Margaret Josephine, *d* of late R. C. Smallwood, CBE, Worplesdon, Surrey; one *s* one *d. Educ:* Wellington College; Magdalen College, Oxford. Developed the production of magnesia from seawater and dolomite, 1939. Consul for Sweden, 1974-76 (Vice Consul, 1949-74). Underwriting member of Lloyd's, 1950-69; Director, Sheepbridge Engineering Ltd, 1949-79, and Albright & Wilson Ltd, 1958-79. Chairman, Ministry of Power Solid Smokeless Fuel Committee, 1959. High Sheriff of Yorkshire, 1959. Chevalier, Order of Vasa, Sweden, 1963. *Recreations:* fishing and shooting. *Address:* Park House, Firbeck, Worksop. *T:* Worksop 730338. *Club:* MCC.

PEEK, Sir Francis (Henry Grenville), 4th Bt, *cr* 1874; *b* 16 Sept. 1915; *o s* of 3rd Bt and Edwine Warner (*d* 1959), *d* of late W. H. Thornburgh, St Louis, USA; *S* father, 1927; *m* 1st, 1942, Ann (marr. diss., 1949), *d* of late Captain Gordon Duff and widow of Sir Charles Mappin, Bt (she *m* 1951, Sir William Rootes, later 1st Baron Rootes); 2nd, Marilyn (marr. diss., 1967; she *m* 1967, Peter Quennell), *d* of Dr Norman Kerr, London and Bahamas; one *s* decd; 3rd, Mrs Caroline Kirkwood, *d* of Sir Robert Kirkwood, qv. *Educ:* Eton; Trinity College, Cambridge. ADC to Governor of Bahamas, 1938-39; served Irish Guards, 1939-46. *Heir: cousin* William Grenville Peek [*b* 15 Dec. 1919; *m* 1950, Lucy Jane, *d* of late Major Edward Dorrien-Smith, DSO; one *s* three *d*]. *Address:* 60 Grosvenor Close, Nassau, Bahamas. *Club:* White's.

PEEK, Vice-Adm. Sir Richard (Innes), KBE 1972 (OBE 1944); CB 1971; DSC 1945; pastoralist; *b* 30 July 1914; 2nd *s* of late James Norman and Kate Doughty Peek; *m* 1943, Margaret Seinor (*née* Kendall) (*d* 1946); one *s* ; *m* 1952, Mary Catherine Tilley (*née* Stops); two *d. Educ:* Royal Australian Naval College. Joined RAN, 1928; served War of 1939-45 in HMS Revenge, HMAS Cerberus, Hobart, Australia, Navy Office; Korean War Service in HMAS Tobruk, 1951; Flag Officer Comdg HMA Fleet, 1967-68; Chief of Naval Staff, Australia, 1970-73. Legion of Merit (US), 1951. *Recreations:* gardening, golf. *Address:* Rothlyn, RMB, Monaro Highway, via Cooma, NSW 2630, Australia. *Clubs:* Imperial Service (Sydney); Royal Commonwealth Society (Canberra).

PEEL, family name of **Earl Peel.**

PEEL, 3rd Earl *cr* 1929; **William James Robert Peel;** Bt 1800; Viscount Peel, 1895; Viscount Clanfield, 1929; *b* 3 Oct. 1947; *s* of 2nd Earl Peel and Kathleen (*d* 1972), *d* of Michael McGrath; *S* father, 1969; *m* 1973, Veronica Naomi Livingston, *d* of Alastair Timpson; one *s* one *d. Educ:* Ampleforth; University of Tours; Cirencester Agric. Coll. *Heir: s* Viscount Clanfield, qv. *Address:* Gunnerside Lodge, Richmond, North Yorks. *Club:* Turf.

PEEL, Lady; (Beatrice); see Lillie, Beatrice.

PEEL, Prof. Edwin Arthur, DLit; Professor of Education, University of Birmingham, 1950-78, and Chairman of School of Education, 1965-70; *b* 11 March 1911; *s* of late Arthur Peel and Mary Ann Miller; *m* 1939, Nora Kathleen Yeadon; two *s* two *d. Educ:* Prince Henry's Grammar School, Otley, Yorks; Leeds University; London University. Teaching in various London Schools, 1933-38; LCC School of Building, 1938-41; MA London, 1938; Ministry of Supply, 1941-45; PhD London 1945; Part-time Lecturer London Univ. Institute of Education, 1945; Lecturer in Education, King's College, Newcastle, 1946; Reader in Psychology, Durham University, 1946-48; Professor of Educational Psychology, University of Durham, 1948-50. President British Psychological Society 1961-62. DLit, London, 1961. *Publications:* The Psychological Basis of Education, 1956; The Pupil's Thinking, 1960; The Nature of Adolescent Judgment, 1971; various in leading British and foreign journals of psychology; Editor and contrib., Educational Review. *Recreation:* painting. *Address:* 47 Innage Road, Birmingham B31 2DY. *T:* 021-475 2820.

PEEL, Jack Armitage, CBE 1972; DL; industrial relations consultant; *b* 8 Jan. 1921; *s* of Martha and George Henry Peel; *m* 1950, Dorothy Mabel Dobson; one *s* one *d. Educ:* elem. and modern sch.; Ruskin Coll., Oxford (Schol., Social Sci.), 1948-49. Railwayman, 1936-47. National Union of Dyers, Bleachers and Textile Workers: full-time Officer, 1950; Asst Gen.-Sec., 1957-66, Gen. Sec., 1966-73; Mem. Gen. Council of TUC, 1966-72; Dir, Industrial Relations, in the Social Affairs Directorate, EEC, 1973-79, Chief Adviser, 1979-81. Part-time Director: British Wool Marketing Board, 1968-73; NCB, 1969-73. Served on several courts of inquiry, incl. Rochdale Cttee of Inquiry into Merchant Navy. Hon. MA Bradford, 1979. DL West Yorks, 1971; JP Bradford, 1960-72. *Publication:* The Real Power Game, 1979. *Recreations:* cricket, painting, guitar music, swimming. *Address:* Timberleigh, 39 Old Newbridge Hill, Bath, Avon. *T:* Bath 23959.

PEEL, Sir John; see Peel, Sir W. J.

PEEL, John; see Ravenscroft, J. R. P.

PEEL, Sir John (Harold), KCVO 1960; FRCP 1971; FRCS 1933; FRCOG 1944; Surgeon-Gynæcologist to the Queen, 1961-73; Consulting Obstetric and Gynæcological Surgeon, King's College Hospital, since 1969; Emeritus Consulting Gynæcologist, Princess Beatrice Hospital, since 1965; *b* 10 December 1904; *s* of Rev. J. E. Peel; *m* 1947, Freda Margaret Mellish; one *d. Educ:* Manchester Grammar Sch.; Queen's Coll., Oxford. MA, BM, BCh Oxon 1932. King's College Hospital Med. Sch., qualified 1930; Obstetric and Gynæcological Surgeon: King's Coll. Hosp., 1936-69; Princess Beatrice Hosp., 1937; Queen Victoria Hosp., East Grinstead, 1941-69; Surgeon EMS, 1939-45. Director of Clinical Studies, King's College Hospital Medical School, 1948-67. Mem., Economic and Social Cttee, EEC, 1973-78. Litchfield Lecturer, Oxford University, 1961 and 1969; Sir Kadar Nath Das Lecturer, Bengal O and G Soc., 1962; Sir A. Mudaliar Lecturer, Madras Univ., 1962; Vis. Prof., Cape Town Univ., 1963; Travelling Prof., S African Council, RCOG, 1968. Past Examiner, Universities of Oxford, Cambridge, London, Liverpool, Bristol, Glasgow, Newcastle, Nat. Univ. of Ireland, Birmingham, Dundee, Sheffield, Conjoint Board, RCOG and CMB. Nuffield visitor to Colonies, 1950 and 1953. President, RCOG, 1966-69 (Hon. Treasurer, 1959-66, Councillor, 1955-); President: Internat. Fedn of Obstetrics and Gynæcology, 1970-73; Chelsea Clinical Society, 1960; BMA 1970 (Chm., Bd of Science and Educn, 1972-76); Family Planning Assoc., 1971-74; Chm., DHSS Cttees of Enquiry: Domiciliary Midwifery and Bed Needs, 1971; The Use of Fetus and Fetal Material for Research, 1972. Hon. Fellow: American Association of Obstetricians and Gynæcologists, 1962 (Joseph Price Oration, 1961); Edinburgh Obstetrical Soc., 1971; RSM, 1973; Hon. Member: Canadian Assoc. of O and G, 1955; Italian Assoc of O and G, 1960; Hon. Treas., GMC, 1972-75; Hon. FRCS (Canada), 1967; Hon. FCOG (SA), 1968; Hon. MMSA 1970; Hon. FACS 1970; Hon. FACOG 1971; Hon. Fellow, American Gynæcological Soc., 1974. Hon. DSc Birmingham, 1972; Hon. DM Southampton, 1974; Hon. DCh Newcastle, 1980. *Publications:* Textbook of Gynæcology, 1943; Lives of the Fellows of Royal College of Obstetricians and Gynaecologists 1929-69, 1976; numerous contributions to Medical Journals. *Recreations:* fishing, golf. *Address:* Gean Trees, 78 Countess Road, Amesbury, Wilts SP4 7AT. *Club:* Naval & Military.

PEEL, Jonathan Sidney, MC 1957; JP; Vice Lord-Lieutenant of Norfolk, since 1981; Director, Norwich Union Insurance Group, since 1973; *b* 21 June 1937; *s* of Major D. A. Peel (killed in action 1944) and Hon. Mrs David Peel (*née* Vanneck); *m* 1965, Jean Fulton Barnett, *d* of Air Chief Marshal Sir Denis Barnett, qv; one *s* four *d. Educ:* Norwich Sch.; Eton; St John's Coll., Cambridge (BA Land Economy; MA 1970). Commnd, Rifle Bde, Royal Green Jackets, 1956; served Malaya, 1956-57; UN forces, Congo (Zaire),

1960-61; Cyprus, 1962-63; resigned, 1966. Chairman: Norfolk Naturalists Trust, 1980-; Nat. Trust Cttee for East Anglia, 1982-. Mem., Norfolk CC, 1973-. JP North Walsham, 1973. *Publication:* (with M. J. Sayer) Towards a Rural Policy for Norfolk, 1973. *Recreations:* farming, music. *Address:* Barton Hall, Barton Turf, Norwich NR12 8AU. *T:* Smallburgh 250, and 298. *Clubs:* Boodles; Norfolk (Norwich).

PEEL, Prof. Ronald Francis Edward Waite, MBE 1945; MA (Cambridge) 1937; Professor of Geography, University of Bristol, 1957-77, now Emeritus; Dean of Science, 1968-70; *b* 22 Aug. 1912; *s* of late Albert Edward Peel, Bridgnorth, Shropshire, and Matilda Mary Peel (*née* Anderson), Helensburgh, Dunbartonshire; *m* 1938, Mary Annette Preston, MA Cantab, *o d* of H. Preston, Northampton; one *d. Educ:* Northampton Gram. Sch.; St Catharine's Coll., Cambridge (scholar). Lecturer in Geography, King's College, University of Durham, 1935-39; accompanied Brig. R. A. Bagnold, OBE, FRS, on exploring expedition in Libyan Desert, 1938. Served War of 1939-45, with RE; France, 1939-40; UK (staff appts), 1940-44; N Africa and Italy, 1944-45; UK, 1945. King's College, Newcastle, 1945-46; Department of Geography, Cambridge University, 1946, Lecturer in Geography, 1949; Prof. of Geography, University of Leeds, 1951-57, Head of Dept, 1953-57. Fellow of St Catharine's Coll., Cambridge, 1949. Cuthbert Peake Award of RGS, 1950; Livingstone Gold Medal, RSGS, 1979. Expeditions to Ruwenzori Mountains, 1952; W and C Sahara, 1961. President: Inst. British Geographers, 1965; Section E, British Assoc., 1967; Colston Research Soc., Bristol, 1973-76. FRGS, FRMetSoc. Editor, Geographical Jl, 1978-80. *Publications:* Physical Geography, 1951; (ed) Processes in Physical and Human Geography, 1975; (ed) Remote Sensing of Terrestrial Environment, 1976; articles on geographical subjects to technical jls, British and foreign. *Recreation:* travel. *Address:* 18 Porson Road, Cambridge. *Club:* Hawks (Cambridge).

PEEL, Sir (William) John, Kt 1973; *b* 16 June 1912; *s* of late Sir William Peel, KCMG, KBE, and Violet Mary Drake, *er d* of late W. D. Laing; *m* 1936, Rosemary Mia Minka, *er d* of Robert Readhead; one *s* three *d. Educ:* Wellington College; Queens' College, Cambridge. Colonial Administrative Service, 1933-51; on active service, 1941-45; British Resident, Brunei, 1946-48; Res. Comr, Gilbert and Ellice Is Colony, 1949-51. Personal Asst to Man. Dirs of Rugby Portland Cement Co. Ltd, 1952-54. Contested (C) Meriden Division of Warwickshire, 1955; MP (C) Leicester SE, 1957-Feb. 1974; Parliamentary Private Secretary to: Economic Secretary to the Treasury, 1958-59; Minister of State, Board of Trade, 1959-60; Asst Govt Whip (unpaid), 1960-61; a Lord Comr of the Treasury, Nov. 1961-Oct. 1964. Parly Delegate to: Assemblies of Council of Europe, 1961-74; WEU 1961-74 (Vice-Pres., 1967, Pres. 1972, Chm., Defence and Armaments Cttee, 1970-72, WEU); N Atlantic Assembly, 1959-74 (Leader, 1970-74; Pres., N Atlantic Assembly, Nov. 1972); Mem., British Delegn to European Parlt, Strasbourg, 1973-74; Hon. Dir, Cons. Party Internat. Office, 1975-76. Member Council: Victoria League for Commonwealth Friendship, 1974 (Dep. Chm., 1976-81; Chm., 1982-); Royal Over-Seas League, 1980-; British Atlantic Cttee; Chairman: Hospitality and Branches Cttee of Victoria League, 1974-78, Hospitality Cttee, 1978-81; Overseas Students Adv. Cttee, 1980-81; Jt Standing Cttee of Victoria League and Royal Commonwealth Soc., 1975-; Westminster for Europe Branch, European Movement. Mem. Ct of Assistants, Framework Knitters' Co. (Under Warden 1982). Dato Seri Laila Jasa Brunei 1969; Dato Setia Negara Brunei 1971. *Recreations:* varied. *Address:* 51 Cambridge Street, SW1. *T:* 01-834 8762. *Clubs:* Carlton; Hawks (Cambridge).

PEELER, Joseph; Under Secretary, Departments of the Environment and Transport, since 1978; Regional Director for the South-East, since 1979; *b* 22 April 1930; *s* of late Edward Francis Peeler and Marjorie Cynthia Peeler; *m* 1958, Diana Helen (*née* Wynne); three *s* one *d. Educ:* King Edward VI Grammar Sch., Stratford-on-Avon; Wimbledon Coll.; Jesus Coll., Oxford (Scholar, 1948; BA 1st Cl. Hons Modern History, 1951; MA 1955). RAF, 1951-53. Entered Civil Service (Min. of Transport and Civil Aviation), 1953; Private Sec. to Parly Sec., 1956-58; Principal, 1958; seconded to Home Office, 1964-66; Asst Sec., 1966. *Recreations:* reading, walking, family pastimes. *Address:* Farthings, The Folly, Lightwater, Surrey. *T:* Bagshot 72228.

PEERS, Most Rev. Michael Geoffrey; *see* Qu'Appelle, Archbishop of.

PEET, Ronald Hugh, CBE 1974; Group Chief Executive, Legal and General Group Plc, since 1980; Director and Chief Executive since 1972 and Chairman since 1980, Legal and General Assurance Society Ltd; *b* 12 July 1925; *s* of Henry Leonard and Stella Peet; *m* 1st, 1949, Winifred Joy Adamson (*d* 1979); two *s* two *d*; 2nd, 1981, Lynette Judy Burgess Kinsella. *Educ:* Doncaster Grammar Sch.; Queen's Coll., Oxford (MA). Served in HM Forces, Captain RA, 1944-47. Joined Legal and General Assurance Soc. Ltd, 1952; emigrated to Australia, 1955; Sec., Legal and General's Australian Branch, 1955-59; Asst Life Manager, 1959-65; Manager and Actuary for Australia, 1965-69; returned to UK as General Manager (Ops), 1969. Chm., Aviation & General Insurance Co. Ltd, 1978-80. Director: City Arts Trust Ltd, 1976- (Chm., 1980-); Royal Philharmonic Orchestra Ltd, 1977-; English National Opera, 1978-. Chm., British Insurance Assoc., 1978-79. FIA. *Recreations:* music, opera. *Address:* 36 Shawfield Street, SW3. *Club:* Hurlingham.

PEGG, Michael Anstice, PhD; University Librarian and Director, John Rylands University Library, University of Manchester, since April 1981; *b* 3 Sept. 1931; *s* of Benjamin and Rose Pegg; *m* 1955, Jean Williams; three *s.*

Educ: Burton-on-Trent Grammar Sch.; Univ. of Southampton. BA (London), PhD (Southampton). Captain, Royal Army Education Corps, Educn Officer, SHAPE, Paris, 1958-61; Asst Keeper, Nat. Library of Scotland, Edinburgh, 1961-67; Sec. and Establt Officer, Nat. Library of Scotland, Edinburgh, 1967-76; Librarian, Univ. of Birmingham, 1976-80. Member: British Library Bd, 1981-; Standing Conference of Nat. and Univ. Libraries' Council, 1981-. *Publications:* Les Divers Rapports d'Eustorg de Beaulieu (édn critique), 1964 (Geneva); Catalogue of German Reformation Pamphlets in Libraries of Great Britain and Ireland, 1973 (Baden Baden); Catalogue of Sixteenth-century German Pamphlets in Collections in France and England, 1977 (Baden Baden); Catalogue of Reformation Pamphlets in Swiss Libraries, 1982; occasional papers to learned jls. *Recreations:* cricket, tennis, squash, railway modelling. *Address:* John Rylands University Library, University of Manchester, Oxford Road, Manchester M13 9PP.

PEGGIE, Robert Galloway Emslie; Chief Executive, Lothian Regional Council, since 1974; *b* 5 Jan. 1929; *s* of John and Euphemia Peggie; *m* 1955, Christine Jeanette Simpson; one *s* one *d. Educ:* Lasswade High Sch. Certified accountant; Accountancy apprenticeship, 1946-52; Accountant in industry, 1952-57; Public Service, Edinburgh City, 1957-74. *Recreation:* golf. *Address:* 54 Liberton Drive, Edinburgh EH16 6NW. *T:* 031-664 1631.

PEGLER, Alfred Ernest, OBE 1978; DL; Councillor: Crawley Borough Council, since 1956; West Sussex County Council, since 1959; *b* 18 Jan. 1924; *s* of Frank Walter James Pegler and Violet Maud Pegler; *m* 1944, E. E. McDonald; one *s* one *d. Educ:* Cork Street Sch., Peckham; Oliver Goldsmith Sch., Peckham. Engrg apprentice, 1938-42; served War, RAF Air Crew, 1942-46; toolmaker, 1946-62. Chm., Crawley Council, 1959 and 1966; Chm. Housing Cttee, 1971-77. Leader, Labour Gp, W Sussex CC, 1977-. Mem., Crawley Cttee, New Towns Commn, 1962- (Chm., 1974-). Mayor, Crawley Borough Council, 1982-83. Mem., Sussex Police Authority, 1973-77. Parly Candidate (Labour): Horsham, 1959 and 1964; Gloucester, Feb. 1974. DL Sussex, 1982. *Recreations:* gardening, politics. *Address:* 7 Priors Walk, Three Bridges, Crawley, West Sussex RH10 1NX. *T:* Crawley 27330.

PEGLER, James Basil Holmes, TD; BA; FIA, FSS, FIS, FIMA; Professor of Actuarial Science, City University, 1976-79, Visiting Professor since 1979; Director, Clerical, Medical and General Life Assurance Society (General Manager and Actuary, 1950-69, Managing Director, 1970-75); *b* 6 Aug. 1912; *s* of late Harold Holmes Pegler and late Dorothy Cecil (*née* Francis); *m* 1937, Enid Margaret Dell; one *s* three *d. Educ:* Charterhouse; Open Univ. Joined Clerical, Medical and Gen. Life Assce Soc., 1931. War service, Queen's Royal Regt and RA, 1939-45 (Major). Inst. of Actuaries: Fellow, 1939; Hon. Sec., 1955-57; Pres., 1968-70. Chm., Life Offices' Assoc., 1959-61; Chm., Life Gp of Comité Européen des Assurances, 1964-70. *Publications:* contribs to Jl Inst. Actuaries. *Recreations:* mathematics, music, languages, squash rackets. *Address:* Dormers, Deepdene Wood, Dorking, Surrey RH5 4BQ. *T:* Dorking 885955. *Club:* Army and Navy.

PEIERLS, Sir Rudolf (Ernst), Kt 1968; CBE 1946; FRS 1945; MA Cantab; DSc Manchester, DPhil Leipzig; Wykeham Professor of Physics, Oxford University, and Fellow, New College, Oxford, 1963-74, now Emeritus Fellow (Hon. Fellow 1980); Professor of Physics (part-time), University of Washington, Seattle, 1974-77; *b* Berlin, 5 June 1907; *s* of H. Peierls; *m* 1931, Eugenia, *d* of late N. Kannegiesser; one *s* three *d. Educ:* Humboldt School, Oberschöneweide, Berlin; Universities of Berlin, Munich, Leipzig. Assistant, Federal Institute of Technology, Zürich, 1929-32; Rockefeller Fellow, 1932-33; Honorary Research Fellow, Manchester University, 1933-35; Assistant-in-Research, Royal Society Mond Laboratory, 1935-37; Professor of Mathematical Physics (formerly Applied Mathematics), University of Birmingham, 1937-63; worked on Atomic Energy Project in Birmingham, 1940-43, in USA, 1943-46. Royal Medal of Royal Society, 1959; Lorentz Medal of Royal Netherlands Academy of Sciences, 1962; Max Planck Medal, Association of German Physical Societies, 1963; Guthrie Medal, IPPS, 1968; first British recipient of Enrico Fermi Award, US Dept of Energy, 1980. FInstP 1973. Hon. DSc: Liverpool, 1960; Birmingham, 1967; Edinburgh, 1969; Sussex, 1978; Chicago, 1981. Foreign Hon. Member, American Academy of Arts and Sciences, 1962; Hon. Associate, College of Advanced Technology, Birmingham, 1963; Foreign Associate, Nat. Acad. of Sciences, USA, 1970; Hon. Mem., French Phys. Soc., 1979; For. Mem., Royal Danish Acad., 1980; Mem., Leopoldina Acad., E Germany, 1981. *Publications:* Quantum Theory of Solids, 1955; The Laws of Nature, 1955; Surprises in Theoretical Physics, 1979; papers on Quantum Theory. *Address:* 2B Northmoor Road, Oxford OX2 6UP; Nuclear Physics Laboratory, Keble Road, Oxford. *Club:* Athenæum.

PEILE, Vice-Admiral Sir Lancelot Arthur Babington, KBE 1960; CB 1957; DSO 1941; MVO 1947; DL; retired; *b* 22 Jan. 1905; *s* of late Basil Wilson Peile and Katharine Rosamond (*née* Taylor); *m* 1928, Gertrude Margaret (*née* Tolcher); two *s. Educ:* RN Colleges, Osborne and Dartmouth. Commander (E) 1939; Captain (E), 1947; Rear-Admiral, 1955; Vice-Admiral, 1958. Asst Engineer-in-Chief, 1948; Command of RN Engineering College, 1951; idc 1954. Asst Director of Dockyards, 1955-57; Admiral Superintendent, Devonport Dockyard, 1957-60; retired, 1960. DL Devon, 1969. *Address:* Strawberry How, Thurlestone, Kingsbridge, Devon. *T:* Thurlestone 209.

PEIRIS, Dr Mahapitage Velin Peter, OBE 1956; *b* 28 July 1898; *s* of M. A. Peiris and H. D. Selestina, Panadura, Ceylon; *m* 1945, Edith Doreen Idona

Carey, Negombo, Ceylon; three *s* one *d. Educ:* St John's Coll., Panadura; St Joseph's Coll., Colombo; Ceylon Medical Coll., Colombo. LMS Ceylon, 1926; MB, BS London, 1936; FRCS 1930; FICS 1957; FACS 1959. Served in Ceylon Army Med. Corps, 1930-45: Surg. to Mil. Hosps, Ceylon, 1940-45. Vis. Surgeon: Gen. Hosp., 1936-60; Children's Hosp., Colombo, 1951-60; Surg. to Orthop. Clinic, 1950-60; Cons. Orthop. Surg., Gen. Hosp., Colombo; Medico-Legal Adviser to Crown; Prof. of Surgery, Univ. of Ceylon, 1952-60. Senator, Ceylon Parlt, 1954-68: Minister of Health, 1960; Leader of Senate, and Minister of Commerce and Trade, 1965-68. Ambassador of Ceylon to USSR, 1968-69; High Comr for Ceylon in the UK, 1969-70. Mem. Coun., Univ. of Ceylon, 1960; President: Ceylon Med. Assoc., 1954; University Teachers' Assoc.; UNA of Ceylon, 1966-68. *Publications:* contribs to Indian and Ceylon medical jls. *Recreations:* swimming, photography. *Address:* 19 Beverley Court, Wellesley Road, W4 4LQ.

PEIRSE, Sir Henry G. de la P. B.; *see* Beresford-Peirse.

PEIRSE, Air Vice-Marshal Richard Charles Fairfax; Air Officer Commanding and Commandant, Royal Air Force College, Cranwell, since 1982; *b* 16 March 1931; *s* of late Air Chief Marshal Sir Richard Peirse, KCB, DSO, AFC and late Lady Peirse; *m* 1st, 1955, Karalie Grace Cox (marr. diss. 1963); two *d*; 2nd, 1963, Deirdre Mary O'Donovan (*d* 1976); one *s*; 3rd, 1977, Anna Jill Margaret Long (*née* Latey). *Educ:* Bradfield Coll.; RAF Coll., Cranwell. Commnd 1952; 2nd TAF No 266 Sqdn and HQ 2 Gp, 1952; Flying Instructor, Cranwell, 1956; Air Staff No 23 Gp, 1960; Staff Coll., 1962; Flt Comdr No 39 Sqdn and OC Ops Wg, Luqa, Malta, 1965; Air Sec.'s Dept, 1965; jssc 1968; OC No 51 Sqdn, 1968; Dep. Captain, The Queen's Flight, 1969; RCDS 1972; OC RAF Waddington, 1973; Dep. Dir, Op Requirements, 1976; Dir of Personnel (Air), 1977; Dir of Op requirements, 1980. *Recreations:* squash, theatre, archaeology. *Address:* 10 Pembroke Road, W8. *T:* 01-602 5888. *Club:* Royal Air Force.

PELHAM, family name of **Earls of Chichester** and **Yarborough.**

PELHAM, Sir (George) Clinton, KBE 1957; CMG 1949; FRGS; HM Ambassador to Czechoslovakia, 1955-57, retired; *b* 20 May 1898; *s* of George Pelham; *m* 1930, Jeanie Adelina Morton; two *d. Educ:* privately. Served European War, 1915-18. Foreign Office, 1920; China Consular Service, 1923; HM Trade Commissioner and Commercial Secretary for South China, 1933; Acting Consul-General, Madagascar, 1943; First Secretary (Commercial), Bagdad, 1945; Counsellor (Commercial), Bagdad, 1946; Counsellor (Commercial), Madrid, 1948-51; HM Ambassador to Saudi Arabia, 1951-55. County Councillor, West Sussex, 1963-70. *Recreations:* music, painting, travel. *Address:* Belcroute, Boughton Hall Avenue, Send, Surrey GU23 7DF. *Club:* Carlton.

PELHAM BURN, Angus Maitland; farmer; Vice-Lord-Lieutenant for Kincardineshire, since 1978; Director, Bank of Scotland, since 1977 (Director, since 1973, Chairman, since 1977, Aberdeen Local Board); Director: Aberdeen and Northern Marts Ltd, since 1970 (Chairman); Aberdeen Meat Marketing Co. Ltd, since 1973 (Chairman); Pelett Administration Ltd, since 1973 (Chairman); MacRobert Farms (Douneside) Ltd, since 1970 (Chairman); Jessfield Ltd, since 1970; Scottish Provident Institution, since 1975; Prime Space Design (Scotland) Ltd, since 1981; Member Accounts Commission, since 1980; *b* 13 Dec. 1931; *s* of late Brig. Gen. H. Pelham Burn, CMG, DSO, and K. Pelham Burn; *m* 1959, Anne R. Pelham Burn (*née* Forbes-Leith); four *d. Educ:* Harrow; N of Scotland Coll. of Agriculture. Hudson's Bay Co., 1951-58. Member: Kincardine CC, 1967-75 (Vice Convener, 1973-75); Grampian Regional Council, 1974-. Member, Queen's Body Guard for Scotland (Royal Co. of Archers), 1968-. Liveryman, Farmers' Co. DL Kincardineshire 1978. OStJ 1978. *Recreations:* fishing, vegetable gardening, photography, stalking. *Address:* Knappach, Banchory, Kincardineshire AB3 3JS. *T:* Crathes 555. *Clubs:* Caledonian; New (Edinburgh); Royal Northern (Aberdeen).

PELHAM-CLINTON-HOPE, family name of **Duke of Newcastle.**

PELIZA, Major Robert John, ED 1955; Leader of the Opposition, Gibraltar, 1972; Chief Minister, 1969-72; *b* 16 Nov. 1920; *s* of late Robert Peliza; *m* 1950, Irma Risso; three *s* four *d. Educ:* Christian Brothers' Coll., Gibraltar. Served in Gibraltar Defence Force (now Gibraltar Regt), 1939-61. Company Director, 1962-. Founder Mem., Integration with Britain Party (first leader), 1967; apptd Chief Minister, following Gen. Elections, 1969. *Recreations:* walking, painting, reading, rowing. *Address:* Buena Vista Cottage, Buena Vista Road, Gibraltar. *Club:* Royal Gibraltar Yacht.

PELLEREAU, Maj.-Gen. Peter John Mitchell, MA, CEng, FIMechE, FBIM; Secretary, Association of Consulting Engineers, since 1977; *b* Quetta, British India, 24 April 1921; *s* of late Col J. C. E. Pellereau, OBE and of Mrs A. N. V. Pellereau (*née* Betham), Penshurst; *m* 1949, Rosemary, *e d* of late S. R. Garnar; two *s. Educ:* Wellington Coll.; Trinity Coll., Cambridge. BA 1942, MA 1957. Commnd into Royal Engrs, 1942; War Service in NW Europe, 1942-45; OC 26 Armd Engr Sqdn, RE, 1946; ptsc, psc, 1950-51; Sec., Defence Research Policy Cttee, 1960; Asst Mil. Sec., WO, 1961; CO 131 Parachute Engr Regt RE TA, 1963; Mil. Dir of Studies, RMCS, 1965; Asst Dir RE Equipment Develt, 1967; Sen. Mil. Officer, Royal Armament R&D Estabt, 1970; Vice-Pres., 1973-75, Pres., 1975-76, Ordnance Board; retired 1976. Hon. Col, RE (Vol.) (Explosive Ordnance Disposal), 1980-.

Liveryman, Worshipful Co. of Plumbers, 1977. Mem., Smeatonian Soc. of Civil Enginters, 1981-. *Recreations:* lawn tennis, hockey (as umpire; Vice-Pres., Surrey Hockey Umpires' Assoc.; Pres., Oxted Hockey Club). *Address:* Woodmans Folly, Crockham Hill, Edenbridge, Kent. *T:* Crockham Hill 309.

PELLEW, family name of **Viscount Exmouth.**

PELLING, Anthony Adair; Deputy Director, Business in the Community, since 1981 (on loan from Department of the Environment); *b* 3 May 1934; *s* of Brian and Alice Pelling; *m* 1958, Margaret Lightfoot; one *s* one *d. Educ:* Purley Grammar Sch.; London Sch. of Economics. BSc (Econ); MIPM. National Coal Board, 1957-67; entered MPBW as Principal, 1967; Asst Sec., 1970, Under Sec., 1981, DoE. *Address:* Bishops Fold, Sprucedale Gardens, Shirley Hills, Croydon. *T:* 01-654 6349. *Club:* Reform.

PELLING, Henry Mathison; Fellow of St John's College, Cambridge, 1966-80 and since 1980; *b* 27 Aug. 1920; *s* of late D. L. Pelling, Prenton, Cheshire, and late Mrs M. M. Pelling; unmarried. *Educ:* Birkenhead School; St John's Coll., Cambridge. Class. Tripos Part I, 1941; History Tripos Part II, 1947 (MA 1945; PhD 1950; LittD 1975). Army service, 1941-45; Commnd RE, 1942; served NW Europe campaign, 1944-45. Fellow, Queen's Coll., Oxford, 1949-65; Tutor, 1950-65; Dean, 1963-64; Supernumerary Fellow, 1980; Asst Dir of Research (History), Cambridge, 1966-76; Reader in Recent British History, Cambridge, 1976-80. Smith-Mundt Schol., University of Wisconsin, USA, 1953-54. *Publications:* Origins of the Labour Party, 1954; Challenge of Socialism, 1954; America and the British Left, 1956; British Communist Party, 1958; (with Frank Bealey) Labour and Politics, 1958; American Labor, 1960; Modern Britain, 1885-1955, 1960; Short History of the Labour Party, 1961, 7th edn 1982; History of British Trade Unionism, 1963, 3rd edn 1976; Social Geography of British Elections, 1967; Popular Politics and Society in Late Victorian Britain, 1968, 2nd edn 1979; Britain and the Second World War, 1970; Winston Churchill, 1974; articles and reviews in learned journals. *Recreations:* theatre, films. *Address:* St John's College, Cambridge CB2 1TP. *T:* Cambridge 61621. *Clubs:* National Liberal, Royal Commonwealth Society.

PELLOE, Rev. Canon John Parker; a Chaplain to the Queen, 1964-75; Hon. Canon of Ely Cathedral, 1952-53, and 1965-79; now Canon Emeritus; *b* 31 May 1905; *e s* of late Rev. E. P. Pelloe; *m* 1945, Kathleen, *d* of late Arthur Bland. *Educ:* Charterhouse; Queen's Coll., Oxford (MA); Cuddesdon Theological Coll. In business, 1922-32. Ordained 1936; Curate: St Columba, Sunderland, 1936-39; St Cuthbert, Kensington, 1939-42; Domestic Chaplain to Bishop of Ely, 1942-46; Vicar of Wisbech, 1946-60 (Rural Dean, 1946-53); Vicar of Stuntney, 1960-68; Archdeacon of Wisbech, 1953-64. *Recreation:* walking. *Address:* 14 Lynn Road, Ely, Cambs. *T:* Ely 2232.

PELLY, Cornelius James, CMG 1952; OBE 1944; *b* 8 April 1908; *e s* of Hyacinth Albert and Charity Mary Pelly, Benmore, Rushbrooke, Co. Cork, Eire; *m* 1949, Una O'Shea, *y d* of Patrick Seaborn O'Shea, Lismore, Co. Waterford; one *s* one *d. Educ:* Clongowes Wood Coll., Co. Kildare; Trinity Coll., Dublin. Entered Indian Civil Service by competitive examination, 1930; appointed to Punjab, 1931; Under-Secretary Punjab Government, 1935-36; transferred to Indian Political Service, 1936; Colonization Officer, Bahawalpur State, 1936-39; Political Agent and HM's Consul, Muscat, 1941-44; Consul, Bushire, 1946-47; Political Agent, Bahrain, 1947-51; Political Agent, Kuwait, 1951-55; Acting Political Resident, Persian Gulf, 1950 and 1952; Secretary for Financial Affairs, Sultanate of Muscat and Oman, 1968-70. *Address:* 12 Stokewater House, Beaminster, Dorset DT8 3LW.

PELLY, Major Sir John (Alwyne), 6th Bt *cr* 1840; JP, DL; landowner and farmer; *b* 11 Sept. 1918; *s* of Sir (Harold) Alwyne Pelly, 5th Bt, MC, and Caroline (*d* 1976), *d* of late Richard Heywood Heywood-Jones; *S* father, 1981; *m* 1950, Elsie May, (Hazel), *d* of late L. Thomas Dechow, Rhodesia; one *d. Educ:* Canford; RMC Sandhurst; Royal Agricultural Coll. Commissioned Coldstream Guards, 1938; served War of 1939-45: Malaya, 1948-50; retired (Major), 1950. Rhodesia, 1950-61; Royal Agric. Coll., 1962-63 (Certificate of Merit). JP 1966, High Sheriff 1970-71, DL 1972, Hants. *Recreations:* ski-ing, shooting. *Heir:* *b* Richard Heywood Pelly [*b* 25 April 1920; *m* 1948, Mary Elizabeth, *d* of late John Luscombe; one *s* one *d*]. *Address:* Preshaw House, Upham, Hants SO3 1HP. *T:* Bishop's Waltham 2531. *Club:* Royal Over-Seas League.

PEMBERTON; *see* Leigh-Pemberton.

PEMBERTON, Sir Francis (Wingate William), Kt 1976; CBE 1970; DL; FRICS; *b* 1 Oct. 1916; *s* of late Dr William Warburton Wingate (assumed Arms of Pemberton, by Royal Licence, 1921) and Viola Patience Campbell Pemberton; *m* 1941, Diana Patricia, *e d* of Reginald Salisbury Woods, *qv*, and late Irene Woods, CBE, TD; two *s. Educ:* Eton; Trinity Coll., Cambridge (MA). Senior Partner, Bidwells, Chartered Surveyors. Director: Agricultural Mortgage Corp. Ltd, 1969-; Barclays Bank UK Ltd, 1977-81. Hon. Dir, Royal Show, 1963-68; Royal Agricultural Society of England: Mem. Council, 1951- (Pres., 1974-75, Dep. Pres., 1975-76); Chm. Exec. Bd, 1969-71; Trustee, 1969-. Trustee, Robinson Coll., Cambridge, 1973-. Member: Water Resources Board, 1964-74; Winston Churchill Meml Trust, 1965-80; Economic Planning Council for East Anglia, 1965-74; National Water Council, 1974-81. High Sheriff, Cambridgeshire and Isle of Ely, 1965-66; DL

Cambs, 1979. *Address:* Trumpington Hall, Cambridge. *T:* Cambridge 841941. *Club:* Farmers'.

PEMBERTON, Prof. John, MD London; FRCP, FFCM; DPH Leeds; Academic Co-ordinator, Northern Consortium, Trent Regional Health Authority, since 1977; *b* 18 Nov. 1912; British; *m* 1937, Winifred Ethel Gray; three *s. Educ:* Christ's Hospital; University College and UCH, London. House Physician and House Surgeon, University College Hospital, 1936-37; Rowett Research Institute under the late Lord Boyd Orr, 1937-39; Rockefeller Travelling Fellow in Medicine, Harvard, Mass., USA, 1954-55; Director of MRC Group for research on Respiratory Disease and Air Pollution, and Reader in Social Medicine, University of Sheffield, 1955-58; Prof. of Social and Preventive Medicine, The Queen's Univ., Belfast, 1958-76. Mem., Health Educn Council, DHSS, 1973-76. Milroy Lectr, RCP, 1976. *Publications:* (with W. Hobson) The Health of the Elderly at Home, 1954; (ed) Recent Studies in Epidemiology, 1958; (ed) Epidemiology: Reports on Research and Teaching, 1963; Will Pickles of Wensleydale, 1970; articles in Lancet, BMJ, etc. *Recreations:* visual arts and fishing. *Address:* Iona, Cannon Fields, Hathersage, Sheffield S30 1AG.

PEMBROKE, 17th Earl of, *cr* 1551, **AND MONTGOMERY,** 14th Earl of, *cr* 1605; **Henry George Charles Alexander Herbert;** Baron Herbert of Caerdiff, 1551; Baron Herbert of Shurland, 1605; Baron Herbert of Lea (UK), 1861; Hereditary Grand Visitor of Jesus College, Oxford; *b* 19 May 1939; *s* of 16th Earl of Pembroke and Montgomery, CVO, and of Mary Countess of Pembroke, *qv* ; *S* father, 1969; *m* 1966, Claire Rose (marr. diss. 1981), *o d* of Douglas Pelly, Swaynes Hall, Widdington, Essex; one *s* three *d. Educ:* Eton Coll.; Oxford Univ. Royal Horse Guards, 1958-60 (National Service); Oxford University, 1960-63. *Recreations:* photography, gardening, horse racing. *Heir: s* Lord Herbert, *qv. Address:* Wilton House, Salisbury, Wilts. *T:* Salisbury 743211.

PEMBROKE, Mary Countess of; Mary Dorothea Herbert, CVO 1947; DL; Extra Lady-in-Waiting to Princess Marina, Duchess of Kent, 1950-68 (Lady-in-Waiting, 1934-50); *o d* of 1st Marquess of Linlithgow; *m* 1936, Lord Herbert (later 16th Earl of Pembroke and Montgomery, who *d* 1969); one *s* one *d.* DL Wilts, 1980. *Address:* The Old Rectory, Wilton, near Salisbury, Wilts. *T:* Salisbury 743157.

PENDER, 3rd Baron, *cr* 1937; **John Willoughby Denison-Pender;** Joint Chairman, Bremar Trust Ltd, since 1977; *b* 6 May 1933; *s* of 2nd Baron and Camilla Eardley, *o d* of late Willoughby Arthur Pemberton; *S* father, 1965; *m* 1962, Julia, *yr d* of Richard Nevill Cannon; one *s* two *d. Educ:* Eton. Formerly Lieut, 10th Royal Hussars and Captain, City of London Yeomanry (TA). *Heir: s* Hon. Henry John Richard Denison-Pender, *b* 19 March 1968. *Address:* North Court, Tilmanstone, Kent. *Clubs:* White's, Pratt's.

PENDERECKI, Krzysztof; Rector, State Academy of Music, Kraków, since 1972; Professor of Composition, School of Music, Yale University, New Haven, Conn, since 1973; *b* Debica, Poland, 23 Nov. 1933; *s* of Tadeusz Penderecki and Zofia Penderecki; *m* 1965, Elzbieta Solecka; one *s* one *d. Educ:* State Acad. of Music, Kraków, Poland (Graduate 1958). Compositions include: Threnody to the Victims of Hiroshima, 1959-61 (52 strings); Passion According to St Luke, 1965-66 (oratorio); Utrenja, 1969-71 (oratorio); Devils of Loudun, 1969 (opera); First Symphony, 1972; Magnificat, 1974 (oratorio); Awakening of Jacob, 1974 (orchestra); violin concerto, 1976; Paradise Lost, 1977-78 (rappresentazione for Chicago Lyric Opera; Milton libretto; Christopher Fry). Hon. Dr Univ. of Rochester, NY; Hon. Member: Kungl. Musikaliska Akademien, Sweden; Akademie der Künste, Germany; Royal Academy of Music, England; Accademia Nazionale di Santa Cecilia, Italy. Preis Nordrhein-Westfalen, 1966; Prix Italia, 1967/68. *Publications:* all works published. *Recreation:* collecting old furniture, clocks and paintings. *Address:* Cisowa 22, 30229 Kraków, Poland. *T:* 25760; 324 Livingston Street, New Haven, Conn 06511, USA. *T:* 203-789 0354.

PENDRED, Air Marshal Sir Lawrence Fleming, KBE 1954 (MBE 1933); CB 1947; DFC; DL; *b* 5 May 1899; *s* of Dr B. F. and Eleanor Pendred; *m* 1923, Nina Chour; two *s. Educ:* Epsom Coll. Served European War, 1914-18, with RNAS and RAF in France, 1918; Permanent Commission RAF, 1920; served in Egypt and Turkey (208 Squadron), 1920-23; Flying Instructor, including 4 years at Central Flying School, 1924-30; Staff Officer Intelligence, Transjordan and Palestine, 1930-34; psa Andover, 1935; Sqdn Leader, 1935; Chief Flying Instructor, Montrose, 1936-37; Air Ministry, 1937-40; Wing Comdr, 1938; Bomber Station Commander, 1940-41, Group Captain; Chief Intelligence Officer, Bomber Command, 1942; Director of Intelligence, Air Ministry, 1943; Air Commodore, Chief Intelligence Officer, AEAF, 1944; Asst Comdt RAF, Staff Coll., 1944-45; AOC 227 Group, India, 1945; Director of Intelligence to Supreme Commander, South East Asia, 1946; acting Air Vice-Marshal, Dec. 1945; Air Vice-Marshal, 1948; Assistant Chief of Air Staff (Intelligence), 1947-49; Commandant, School of Land-Air Warfare, 1950-52; Air Officer Commanding-in-Chief, Flying Training Command, 1952-55; retired, 1955. Regional Director Civil Defence (Midland), 1955-63. DL Warwickshire, 1959. Grand Officer Polonia Restituta; Commander, Legion of Merit. *Address:* 13 Lansdowne Circus, Leamington Spa, Warwicks. *T:* Leamington Spa 23559.

PENDRY, Thomas; MP (Lab) Stalybridge and Hyde since 1970; *b* 10 June 1934; *m* 1966, Moira Anne Smith; one *s* one *d. Educ:* St Augustine's,

Ramsgate; Oxford Univ. RAF, 1955-57. Full time official, Nat. Union of Public Employees, 1960-70; Mem., Paddington Borough Council, 1962-65; Chm., Derby Labour Party, 1966. An Opposition Whip, 1971-74; a Lord Comr of the Treasury and Govt Whip, 1974, resigned 1977; Parly Under-Sec. of State, NI Office, 1978-79; Opposition Spokesman on NI, 1979-, on overseas development, 1981-, on regional affairs and devolution, 1982-. Member: Speaker's Conf., 1973; UK delegn to WEU and Council of Europe, 1973-75; Industrial Law Soc. Mem., Nat. Adv. Cttee, Duke of Edinburgh's Award Scheme. Pres., Stalybridge Public Band. *Recreations:* sport; football, cricket, boxing (sometime Middleweight Champion, Hong Kong; boxed for Oxford Univ.). *Address:* Chapel House, Gorsey Brow, Broadbottom, Cheshire. *Clubs:* Reform; Manchester Press; Stalybridge and Hyde Labour.

PENFOLD, Maj.-Gen. Robert Bernard, CB 1969; MVO 1957; *b* 19 Dec. 1916; *s* of late Bernard Hugh Penfold, Selsey, and late Ethel Ives Arnold; *m* 1940, Ursula, *d* of late Lt-Col E. H. Gray; two *d. Educ:* Wellington; RMC, Sandhurst. 2nd Lieut, Royal Leics Regt, 1936; commnd into 11th Sikh Regt, Indian Army, 1937; served in NWFP and during War of 1939-45 in Middle East, Central Mediterranean Forces; Instructor, Staff Coll., Quetta, 1946-47; transf. to British Army, RA, 1947; RN Staff Coll., 1953; Secretary, British Joint Services Mission, Washington, 1957-59; comdg 6 King's African Rifles, Tanganyika, 1959-61; Comdr 127 Inf. Bde (TA), 1962-64; Security Ops Adviser to High Commissioner, Aden, 1964-65; Imperial Defence Coll., 1966; Chief of Defence Staff, Kenya, 1966-69; GOC South East District, 1969-72. Gen. Manager, Royal Hong Kong Jockey Club, 1972-80. Chm., Horseracing Adv. Council, 1980-. *Recreations:* shooting, golf, gardening. *Address:* Park House, Amport, Andover, Hants. *Club:* Army and Navy.

PENGELLY, Richard Anthony; Under Secretary, Welsh Office, since 1977; *b* 18 Aug. 1925; *s* of Richard Francis Pengelly and Ivy Mildred Pengelly; *m* 1st, 1952, Phyllis Mary Rippon; one *s* ; 2nd, 1972, Margaret Ruth Crossley; two *s* one *d. Educ:* Plymouth Coll.; School of Oriental and African Studies; London Sch. of Economics and Political Science (BScEcon). Served War: Monmouthshire Regt and Intell. Corps, 1943-47. Joined Min. of Supply as Asst Principal, 1950, Principal, 1954; NATO Defence Coll., 1960-61; Asst Sec., Min. of Aviation, 1964; RCDS 1971; Min. of Defence, 1972. *Recreations:* skiing, golf. *Address:* Byways, Wern Goch Road, Cyncoed, Cardiff, S Wales CF2 6SD. *T:* Cardiff 764418.

PENGELLY, William Lister; Master of Supreme Court of Judicature, Chancery Division, 1950-64; *b* 21 Dec. 1892; *s* of Frederick Charles Goldsworthy Pengelly; *m* 1919; two *d. Educ:* Varndean, Brighton; Culham Coll., Culham, Oxfordshire. Lady Aubrey Fletcher Exhib. for violin, Brighton School of Music, 1908. Solicitor, 1921; Senior Partner in Pengelly & Co., 8 New Court, Lincoln's Inn, WC2, solicitors, until 1950. Served European War, 1914-18; 2nd Lieut, 2/5 Devon Regt, 1914; Lieut, 1915; in Egypt, 1915-16; in Mesopotamia, 1916 and 1917 with 4th Devon Regt (wounded); Asst Adjutant with 4th (R) Devon Regt, 1918-19; Captain, 1919. War of 1939-45, Major and Supervising Military Liaison Officer (Z Sector), Home Guard. Chairman of The Comedy Club, 1932-59; Captain London Solicitors Golfing Society, 1950-51; Founder Royal Courts of Justice Music Club, 1953. Member Worshipful Company of Musicians; Freeman of the City of London. *Recreations:* music, bridge, croquet. *Address:* 11 West Hill Court, Budleigh Salterton, Devon. *Club:* Budleigh Salterton Bridge and Croquet.

PENHALIGON, David Charles; MP (L) Truro since Oct. 1974; *b* 6 June 1944; *s* of late Robert Charles Penhaligon and of Sadie Jewell; *m* 1968, Annette Lidgey; one *s* one *d. Educ:* Truro Sch.; Cornwall Techn. College. CEng, MIMechE. R&D Engr, Holman Bros, Camborne, 1962-74. Liberal Party Spokesman on Industry and Energy. *Address:* 54 Daniell Road, Truro, Cornwall. *T:* Truro 70977. *Club:* National Liberal.

PENLEY, William Henry, CB 1967; CBE 1961; PhD; FEng; Engineering Director, Marconi Underwater Systems Ltd, since 1982; *b* 22 March 1917; *s* of late William Edward Penley and late Clara (née Dodgson), Wallasey, Cheshire; *m* 1st, 1943, Raymonde Evelyn (*d* 1975), *d* of late Frederick Richard Gough, Swanage, Dorset; two *s* one *d* ; 2nd, 1977, Marion Claytor, *d* of late Joseph Enoch Airey, Swanage, Dorset. *Educ:* Wallasey Grammar Sch.; Liverpool Univ.; BEng, 1937; PhD, 1940. FIEE (MIEE 1964); FRAeS 1967; FRSA 1975; FEng 1978. Head of Guided Weapons Department, Royal Radar Establishment, 1953-61; Director, Royal Radar Establishment, 1961-62; Director-General of Electronics Research and Development, Ministry of Aviation, 1962-64; Deputy Controller of Electronics, Ministry of Aviation, then Ministry of Technology, 1964-67; Dir, Royal Armament R&D Establishment, 1967-70; Chief Scientist (Army), 1970-75, Dep. Controller, Establishments and Res. B, 1971-75, MoD; Controller, R&D Establishments, and Research, MoD, and Professional Head of Science Gp of the Civil Service, 1976-77; Chm., Appleton Lab. Establishment Cttee, 1977-79; Dep. Dir, Under Water Weapons, Marconi Space and Defence Systems Ltd, Stanmore, 1979-82. Silver Jubilee Medal, 1977. *Address:* 28 Walrond Road, Swanage, Dorset BH19 1PD. *T:* Swanage 5042.

PENLINGTON, Ross Grange, OBE (mil.) 1980; AE 1972 (Clasp 1979); **Hon. Mr Justice Penlington;** a Judge of the High Court of Hong Kong, since 1980; *b* 3 March 1931; *s* of Cedric Grange Penlington and Elsie May Penlington; *m* 1956, Valerie Ann Wacher; two *d. Educ:* Christ Coll., NZ; Univ. of Canterbury, NZ. LLB 1954. Barrister and Solicitor, Christchurch, NZ, 1954-59; Legal Officer, Magistrate and Attorney Gen., Western Samoa,

1959-64; Hong Kong: Crown Counsel, 1965-75; Dir of Public Prosecutions, 1976-77; District Court Judge, 1977-80. Commnd Hong Kong RAuxAF, 1964; Pilot's Brevet, 1965; CO (Wing Comdr), 1975-. *Recreations:* flying, golf, tennis, fishing, racing. *Address:* 19 Peak Mansions, Hong Kong. *T:* 5-97106. *Clubs:* Royal Air Force; Hong Kong, Royal Hong Kong Jockey (Hong Kong); Canterbury (NZ).

PENMAN, Rt. Rev. David John; a Bishop Coadjutor, Diocese of Melbourne, since 1982; *b* 8 Aug. 1936; *s* of John James and Irene May Penman; *m* 1962, Jean Frances (*née* Newson); one *s* three *d*. *Educ:* Keith St School, Wanganui, NZ; Intermediate School, Wanganui and Hutt Valley High Sch., NZ; Teachers' Coll., Wellington; Univ. of New Zealand (BA 1962) Christchurch Theol Coll. (LTh 1964); Univ. of Karachi, Pakistan (MA 1970, PhD 1977, Sociology and Islam). Teacher in Hutt Valley and Palmerston North, NZ, 1957-59; Asst Curate, Christ Church Anglican Church, Wanganui, 1961-64; Missionary work with NZ Church Missionary Soc. in W Asia and Middle East, 1965-76; Principal, St Andrew's Hall, CMS Federal Training Coll., Melbourne, Aust., 1976-79; Vicar of All Saints' Anglican Church, Palmerston North, NZ, 1979-82. *Recreations:* sport, music, stamp collecting and reading. *Address:* 66 Baroda Street, Ascot Vale, Victoria 3032, Australia. *T:* 370. 4147.

PENMAN, Gerard Giles, MA, MD (Cantab), FRCS; Hon. Consulting Ophthalmic Surgeon, St Thomas' Hospital; Hon. Consulting Surgeon, Moorfields Eye Hospital; Consulting Ophthalmic Surgeon, Royal Hospital for Incurables, Putney; Fellow, Royal Society of Medicine and Hunterian Society; Member Ophthalmological Society of the UK and Oxford Ophthalmological Congress; *b* Port Elizabeth, 7 March 1899; *s* of late J. C. Penman and Grace Penman, Salisbury, Rhodesia, and Sherborne, Dorset; *m* 1928, Janet (*d* 1979), *d* of late Dr J. Walter Carr, CBE; three *s*. *Educ:* Sherborne Sch.; Pembroke Coll., Cambridge; St Thomas' Hospital. Royal Field Artillery, 1917-19; Ophthalmic Surgeon, Royal Northern Hospital, 1926-31; Ophthalmic Surgeon, Hospital for Sick Children, Great Ormond Street, 1931-36; Examiner in Ophthalmology, RCP, 1962-65. Vice-President: Dorset County Assoc. for the Blind; Sherborne Historical Soc. *Publications:* The Projection of the Retina in the Lateral Geniculate Body (with W. E. le Gros Clark) (Proceedings of the Royal Society, 1934); The Position occupied by the Peripheral Retinal Fibres at the Nerve Head (with E. Wolff) (Internat. Ophthalmological Congress, 1950), etc. *Recreations:* archaeology, philately. *Address:* c/o National Westminster Bank, 50 Cheap Street, Sherborne, Dorset DT9 3BH.

PENMAN, Dr Howard Latimer, OBE 1962; FRS 1962; Head of Physics Department, Rothamsted Experimental Station, 1955-74. Doctorate, Durham Univ., 1937. Has made physical studies of agricultural and botanical problems, particularly on transpiration and the irrigation of crops. Hon. FRMetS, 1978. *Publications:* Humidity (Monographs for Students, Inst. of Physics), 1955; Vegetation and Hydrology (Comm. Agric. Bur.), 1963. *Recreations:* music, golf. *Address:* 11A Kirkwick Avenue, Harpenden, Herts AL5 2QU. *T:* Harpenden 3366.

PENMAN, Ian Dalgleish; Under-Secretary (Housing), Scottish Development Department, since 1978; *b* 1 Aug. 1931; *s* of John B. Penman and Dorothy Dalgleish; *m* 1963, Elisabeth Stewart Strachan; three *s*. *Educ:* Glasgow Univ. (MA Classics); Balliol Coll., Oxford (MA Lit. Hum.; Snell Exhibnr and Ferguson Scholar). National Service, RAF, 1955-57 (Educn Br.). Asst Principal, HM Treasury, 1957-58; Scottish Office, 1958-: Private Sec. to Parly Under-Sec. of State, 1960-62; Principal, Scottish Develt Dept, 1962-69; Asst Sec., Estab. Div., 1970-72; Asst Sec., Scottish Home and Health Dept, 1972-78. *Recreations:* learning about Galloway, swimming. *Address:* 4 Wardie Avenue, Edinburgh EH5 2AB. *T:* 031-552 2180.

PENMAN, John, FRCP; Consulting Neurologist to The Royal Marsden Hospital; Clinical Assistant to the Neurosurgical Department, Atkinson Morley's Hospital; *b* 10 Feb. 1913; *er s* of late William Penman, FIA; *m* 1st, 1938, Joan, *d* of late Claude Johnson (marr. diss. 1975); one *s* two *d*; 2nd, 1975, Elisabeth Quin. *Educ:* Tonbridge Sch.; University College, Oxford (Senior Classical Scholar); Queen Mary Coll., E1; The London Hospital. MB, BS (London) 1944; MRCP 1948, FRCP 1969. Neurologist to The Royal Marsden Hospital, 1954-77. Member of Association of British Neurologists. *Publications:* The Epodes of Horace: a new English version, 1980; contributions to medical journals, mainly on tic douloureux and brain tumours; section on trigeminal injection, in Operative Surgery, 1957; chapters in Handbook of Clinical Neurology, 1968. *Recreations:* poetry; etymology; looking at Norman cathedrals. *Address:* Atkinson Morley's Hospital, Copse Hill, Wimbledon, SW20; Forest View, Forest Lane, Upper Chute, Andover, Hants. *Club:* Royal Automobile.

PENN, Lt-Col Sir Eric, GCVO 1981 (KCVO 1972; CVO 1965); OBE 1960; MC 1944; Extra Equerry to The Queen since 1963; *b* 9 Feb. 1916; *o s* of Capt. Eric F. Penn (killed in action 1915), Grenadier Guards, and late Gladys Ebden; *m* 1947, Prudence Stewart-Wilson, *d* of late Aubyn Wilson and late Murie Stewart-Stevens, Balnakeilly, Pitlochry, Perthshire; two *s* one *d*. *Educ:* Eton; Magdalene Coll., Cambridge. Grenadier Guards, 1938-60. Assistant Comptroller, Lord Chamberlain's Office, 1960-64, Comptroller, 1964-81. *Address:* Sternfield House, Saxmundham, Suffolk. *T:* Saxmundham 2456. *Clubs:* White's, Pratt's.

PENNANT; *see* Douglas-Pennant.

PENNANT, David Edward Thornton; His Honour Judge Pennant; a Circuit Judge (formerly County Court Judge), since 1961; *b* 2 Aug. 1912; *s* of David Falconer Pennant, DL, JP, Barrister-at-law, late of Nantlys, St Asaph, N. Wales, and late Lilla Agnes Pennant; *m* 1938, Alice Catherine Stainer; three *s* one *d*. *Educ:* Charterhouse; Trinity Coll., Cambridge. Called to Bar, Inner Temple, 1935. Served, 1939-45, with Royal Signals (TA); OC, Signals Officers' Training Sch., Mhow, India, 1944-45. Chancellor, Dio. Monmouth, 1949-77. Governing, and Representative Bodies, Church in Wales, 1946-. Chm., Radnorshire QS, 1962-64; Deputy Chairman: Brecknockshire QS, 1956-64; Flintshire QS, 1962-71; Dorset QS, 1971. Joint Chairman, Medical Appeals Tribunal for Wales, 1957-61; Mem., County Court Rule Cttee, 1970-78. *Recreation:* gardening. *Address:* Parkbury, Balcombe Road, Branksome Park, Poole, Dorset. *T:* Bournemouth 765614.

PENNELL, Rev. Canon (James Henry) Leslie, TD and Bar, 1949; Rector of Foxearth and Pentlow (Diocese of Chelmsford), 1965-72, and of Borley and Lyston (Diocese of Chelmsford), 1969-72; Hon. Canon, Inverness Cathedral, since 1965 (Provost, 1949-65); *b* 9 Feb. 1906; *s* of late J. H. L. Pennell and late Elizabeth Esmé Gordon Steel; *m* 1939, Ursula Mary, *d* of Rev. A. E. Gledhill; twin *s* and *d*. *Educ:* Edinburgh Academy; Edinburgh University (BL); Edinburgh Theological College. Precentor, Inverness Cathedral, 1929-32; Rector, St Mary's, Dunblane, and Offic. Chaplain to Queen Victoria School, 1932-49; Officiating Chaplain, Cameron Barracks, 1949-64. TA, 1934; BEF, 1940; SCF, 1943; DACG, 34th Ind. Corps, 1945; SCF Corps Troops, Scottish Comd, 1946-50. *Recreations:* reading and travel. *Address:* The Croft, Hundon, Clare, Suffolk. *T:* Hundon 221.

PENNEY, family name of **Baron Penney.**

PENNEY, Baron, *cr* 1967, of East Hendred (Life Peer); **William George Penney,** OM 1969; KBE 1952 (OBE 1946); MA; PhD; DSc; FRS 1946; Rector of the Imperial College of Science and Technology, 1967-73; *b* 24 June 1909; *s* of W. A. Penney, Sheerness, Kent; *m* 1st, 1935, Adele Minnie Elms (decd); two *s*; 2nd, 1945, Eleanor Joan Quennell. *Educ:* Tech. School, Sheerness; Royal College of Science, London Univ. (BSc, PhD). Commonwealth Fund Fellowship. University of Wisconsin (MA), 1931-33; Senior Student of 1851 Exhibition, Trinity Coll., Cambridge, 1933-36; PhD (Cambridge), DSc (London), 1935; Stokes Student of Pembroke Coll., 1936; Assistant Professor of Mathematics at Imperial College of Science, London, 1936-45; on loan for scientific work to Ministry of Home Security and Admiralty, 1940-44; Principal Scientific Officer, DSIR, at Los Alamos Laboratory, New Mexico, 1944-45; Chief Superintendent, Armament Research, Ministry of Supply, 1946-52; Director Atomic Weapons Research Establishment, Aldermaston, 1953-59; Member for Weapons R&D, UKAEA, 1954-59; Member for Research, UKAEA, 1959-61; Dep. Chm., 1961-64; Chm., 1964-67. Director: Tube Investments, 1968-79; Standard Telephones and Cables, 1971-. Treasurer, Royal Society, 1956-60 (Vice-President, 1957-60); Fellow, Imperial Coll.; Fellow, Winchester Coll., 1959; Supernumerary Fellow, St Catherine's Coll., Oxford, 1960; Hon. Fellow: Manchester College of Science and Technology, 1962; Trinity Coll., Cambridge, 1969; Pembroke Coll., Cambridge, 1970; Hon FRSE, 1970; For. Assoc., National Academy of Sciences, USA, 1962. Hon. DSc: Durham, 1957; Oxford, 1959; Bath University of Technology, 1966; Hon. LLD Melbourne, 1956. Rumford Medal, Royal Society, 1966; Glazebrook Medal and Prize, 1969; Kelvin Gold Medal, 1971. *Publications:* articles in scientific journals on theory of molecular structure. *Recreations:* golf, cricket. *Address:* Cat Street, East Hendred, Wantage, Oxford OX12 8JT. *Club:* Athenæum.

PENNEY, Most Rev. Alphonsus Liguori; *see* St John's (Newfoundland), Archbishop of, (RC).

PENNEY, Jennifer Beverly; Senior Principal, Royal Ballet; *b* 5 April 1946; *d* of Beverley Guy Penney and Gwen Penney. *Educ:* in Canada (grades 1-12). Entered Royal Ballet Sch., 1962; joined Royal Ballet, 1963; became soloist during 1967, principal dancer during 1970, and senior principal dancer during 1974. Evening Standard Award, 1981. *Recreation:* painting (water-colours). *Address:* 31 Ennismore Avenue, W4. *T:* 01-995 0933.

PENNEY, Reginald John; Assistant Under-Secretary of State, Ministry of Defence, 1964-73, retired; *b* 22 May 1919; *s* of Herbert Penney and Charlotte Penney (*née* Affleck); *m* 1941, Eileen Gardiner; one *s* two *d*. *Educ:* Westminster School. War Service, Royal West Kent Regt, 1939-46. Civil Servant, Air Ministry, until 1964, including service with Far East Air Force, Singapore, 1960-63. Chm., Sherborne Soc., CPRE, 1976. *Recreation:* golf. *Address:* Rumbow Cottage, Acreman Street, Sherborne, Dorset.

PENNINGTON, Prof. Robert Roland; Professor of Commercial Law, Birmingham University, since 1968, and Dean of Faculty of Law, since 1979; *b* 22 April 1927; *s* of R. A. Pennington; *m* 1965, Patricia Irene; one *d*. *Educ:* Birmingham Univ. (LLB, LLD). Solicitor. Reader, Law Soc.'s Sch. of Law, 1951-62; Mem. Bd of Management, Coll. of Law, 1962; Sen. Lectr in Commercial Law, Birmingham Univ., 1962-68. Govt Adviser on Company Legislation, Trinidad, 1967 and Seychelles, 1970; UN Adviser on Commercial Law, 1970-; Special Legal Adviser to EEC, 1972-79. Editor, European Commercial Law Library, 1974-. *Publications:* Company Law, 1959, 4th edn 1979; Companies in the Common Market, 1962, 2nd edn 1970; The Investor and the Law, 1967; Stannary Law: A History of the Mining Law of Cornwall and Devon, 1973; Commercial Banking Law, 1978; Gesellschaftsrecht des Vereinigten Königreichs, 1981 (in Jura Europae: Gesellschaftsrecht). *Recreations:* travel, walking, history, archaeology. *Address:* Gryphon House, Langley Road, Claverdon, Warwicks.

PENNINGTON-RAMSDEN, Major Sir (Geoffrey) William, 7th Bt, *cr* 1689; Major, Life Guards, retired; *b* 28 Aug. 1904; *yr* (but *o* surv.) *s* of Sir John Frecheville Ramsden, 6th Bt and Joan (*d* 1974), *d* of late G. F. Buxton, CB, Hoveton Hall; *S* father 1958; assumed by deed poll, 1925, surname of Pennington in lieu of Ramsden; resumed surname of Ramsden after that of Pennington by deed poll, 1958; *m* 1927, Veronica Prudence Betty, *o d* of F. W. Morley, formerly of Biddestone Manor, Chippenham, Wilts; three *d*. *Educ:* Ludgrove; Eton; Jesus Coll., Cambridge (BA). Joined 11th Hussars, 1925; transferred Life Guards, 1927-38; served War of 1939-45; seconded to Provost Branch; APM 9th Armd Div. and APM 14th Army; Major, 1942. High Sheriff, Cumberland, 1962-63. *Heir: kinsman* Caryl Oliver Imbert Ramsden, *qv*. *Address:* Versions Farm, Brackley, Northants. *T:* Brackley 702412; Ardverikie, Newtonmore, Scotland; (seat) Muncaster Castle, Ravenglass, Cumbria. *T:* Ravenglass 203. *Club:* Lansdowne.
See also P. A. N. P. Laing.

PENNISON, Clifford Francis, CBE 1977; *b* 28 June 1913; *s* of Henry and Alice Pennison; *m* 1940, Joan Margaret Hopkins; three *d*. *Educ:* Taunton Sch.; Bristol Univ. (BA, 1st Cl. Hons, Hist.). Barrister-at-Law, Inner Temple, 1951. Appointed senior management trainee, Unilever Ltd, 1938. Field Security Officer, Army, 1940-46 (Captain). Principal, Home Civil Service, 1946; Assistant Secretary, and Director of Organisation and Methods, Ministry of Food, 1949; Ministry of Agriculture: Director of Statistics Div., 1953; Director of Public Relations Div., 1958; Director of External Relations Div., 1961; FAO: Permanent UK representative, 1963-66; Director, Economic Analysis Div., 1966-67; Asst Dir-Gen., Admin and Finance, 1967-74; Consultant, EEC/FAO relations, 1974-76; retired 1976. *Recreations:* travel, reading, foreign languages, tennis. *Address:* 54 Clarendon Road, Sheffield S10 3TR. *Club:* Beaulieu Tennis.

PENNOCK, family name of **Baron Pennock.**

PENNOCK, Baron *cr* 1982 (Life Peer), of Norton in the County of Cleveland; **Raymond William Pennock;** Kt 1978; Chairman, BICC plc, since 1980; *b* 16 June 1920; *s* of Frederick Henry Pennock and Harriet Anne Pennock (*née* Mathieson); *m* 1944, Lorna Pearse; one *s* two *d*. *Educ:* Coatham Sch.; Merton Coll., Oxford (Hon. Fellow, 1979). MA; 2nd cl. hons History, Dipl. Educn. Royal Artillery (Captain), 1941-46 (despatches 1945). Joined ICI Ltd, 1947; Personnel Management and Commercial duties, 1947-61; Commercial Dir, Billingham Div., 1961-64; Dep. Chm., Billingham Div., 1964-68; Chm., Agric. (formerly Billingham) Div. 1968-72; Director, ICI Ltd, 1972, Dep. Chm., 1975-80. Dep. Pres., CBI, 1979-80, Pres., 1980-82 (Chm., Economic Situation Cttee, 1977-80); Pres., CIA, 1978-79; Mem., Plessey Bd, 1979-. Mem., NEDC, 1979-82. Governor, Durham Sch.; Mem. Nat. Council, Oxford Soc. *Recreations:* tennis, music, ballet, travel. *Address:* c/o BICC plc, 21 Bloomsbury Street, WC1B 3QN. *Clubs:* Queen's, Royal Tennis Court.

PENNY, family name of **Viscount Marchwood.**

PENNY, (Francis) David, CBE 1982; FRSE; Chairman: Control Systems Ltd; Automatic Revenue Controls Ltd; Deputy Chairman, Y-ARD Ltd; Managing Director, Yarrow Public Limited Company; *b* 20 May 1918; *s* of late David Penny and Esther Colley; *m* 1949, Betty E. Smith, *d* of late Oswald C. Smith. *Educ:* Bromsgrove County High School; University Coll., London (BSc), Fellow 1973. Engineering Apprenticeship, Cadbury Bros Ltd, 1934-39; Armament Design Establishment, Ministry of Supply, 1939-53; Chief Development Engineer, Fuel Research Station, 1954-58; Dep. Dir, Nat. Engineering Laboratory, 1959-66, Dir, 1967-69. FEng 1980; FIMarE; FIMechE; Member Council, IMechE, 1964- (a Vice-Pres., 1977-81, Pres., 1981-82); Chm., Quality Assurance Council, BSI, 1982-. *Publications:* various technical papers. *Recreations:* gardening, cricket, walking. *Address:* Forefaulds, East Kilbride, Glasgow. *T:* East Kilbride 20102.

PENNY, Joseph Noel Bailey, QC 1971; *b* 25 Dec. 1916; *s* of Joseph A. Penny, JP and Isabella Downie, JP; *m* 1st, 1947, Celia (*d* 1969), *d* of Mr and Mrs R. H. Roberts; three *s* one *d* ; 2nd, 1972, Sara Margaret, *d* of Sir Arnold France, *qv* ; one *d*. *Educ:* Worksop College; Christ Church, Oxford; MA (Oxon). Major, Royal Signals, 1939-46 (despatches). Called to Bar, Gray's Inn, 1948. A Social Security (formerly Nat. Ins.) Comr, 1977-. *Recreations:* wine and song, travel and amateur dramatics. *Address:* Fair Orchard, Lingfield, Surrey. *T:* Lingfield 832191.
See also N. B. Penny.

PENNY, Nicholas Beaver, MA, PhD; Senior Research Fellow in the History of Western Art, King's College, Cambridge, since 1982; *b* 21 Dec. 1949; *s* of Joseph Noel Bailey Penny, *qv* ; *m* 1971, Anne Philomel Udy; two *d*. *Educ:* Shrewsbury Sch.; St Catharine's Coll., Cambridge (BA, MA); Courtauld Inst., Univ. of London (MA, PhD). Leverhulme Fellow in the History of Western Art, Clare Hall, Cambridge, 1973-75; Lectr, History of Art Dept, Univ. of Manchester, 1975-82; Slade Prof. of Fine Art, Univ. of Oxford, 1980-81. *Publications:* Church Monuments in Romantic England, 1977; Piranesi, 1978;

(with Francis Haskell) Taste and the Antique, 1981; Mourning, 1981; (ed jtly) The Arrogant Connoisseur, 1982; articles in Apollo, Burlington Magazine, Connoisseur, Jl of Warburg and Courtauld Insts, Past and Present, and elsewhere. *Address:* 71 Montague Road, Cambridge CB4 1BU.

PENNYBACKER, Joseph Buford, CBE 1967; Director, Department of Neurological Surgery, Radcliffe Infirmary, Oxford, 1954-71; *b* 23 Aug. 1907; *s* of Claude Martin Pennybacker and Katherine Miller Mershon; *m* 1941, Winifrid Dean (*d* 1980); one *s*. *Educ:* Universities of Tennessee and Edinburgh. BA (Tennessee) 1926; MB, ChB (Edinburgh) 1930; FRCS 1935; MA (Oxon) 1938; MD (Edinburgh) 1941. Resident appointments: Royal Infirmary, Edinburgh; Grimsby District Hospital; National Hospital, Queen Square; First Asst, Neurosurgical Dept, London Hospital; First Asst to Nuffield Prof. of Surgery, University of Oxford. Cross of Royal Order of George I, Greece, 1966. *Publications:* papers in neurological and surgical journals. *Recreations:* history, horticulture. *Address:* Creagandarraich, Tighnabruaich, Argyll. *T:* Tighnabruaich 260. *Club:* Athenæum.

PENRHYN, 6th Baron *cr* 1866; **Malcolm Frank Douglas-Pennant,** DSO 1945; MBE 1943; *b* 11 July 1908; 2nd *s* of 5th Baron Penrhyn and Alice Nellie (*d* 1965), *o d* of Sir William Charles Cooper, 3rd Bt; *S* father 1967; *m* 1954, Elisabeth Rosemary, *d* of late Brig. Sir Percy Laurie, KCVO, CBE, DSO, JP; two *d*. *Educ:* Eton; RMC, Sandhurst. Colonel (retd), KRRC. *Heir: b* Hon. Nigel Douglas-Pennant [*b* 22 Dec. 1909; *m* 1st, 1935, Margaret Dorothy (*d* 1938), *d* of T. G. Kirkham; one *s* ; 2nd, 1940, Eleanor Stewart, *d* of late Very Rev. H. N. Craig; one *s* one *d*]. *Address:* Littleton Manor, Winchester, Hants. *T:* Winchester 880205. *Clubs:* Naval and Military, MCC, Flyfishers.

PENRICE, Geoffrey, CB 1978; Director of Statistics, and Deputy Secretary, Department of Employment, 1978-81; *b* Wakefield, 28 Feb. 1923; *s* of Harry and Jessie Penrice; *m* 1947, Janet Gillies Allardice; three *s*. *Educ:* Thornes House Grammar Sch.; London Sch. of Economics. Control Commn for Germany, 1947; Asst Lectr in Statistics, LSE, 1952; Statistician, Inland Revenue, 1956; Statistician and Chief Statistician, Central Statistical Office, 1964; Chief Statistician, Min. of Housing and Local Govt, 1968; Under-Sec., BoT, Min. of Technology, DTI, 1968-73; Principal Dir of Stats, DoE, later DoE and Dept of Transport, 1973-78. Statistical Adviser to Cttee on Working of Monetary System, 1957-59. *Publications:* articles on wages, earnings, financial statistics and housing statistics. *Address:* 10 Dartmouth Park Avenue, NW5. *T:* 01-267 2175. *Club:* Reform.

PENRITH, Bishop Suffragan of, since 1979; **Rt. Rev. George Lanyon Hacker;** *b* 27 Dec. 1928; *s* of Edward Sidney Hacker and Carla Lanyon; *m* 1969, June Margaret Erica Smart; one *s* one *d*. *Educ:* Kelly College, Tavistock; Exeter College, Oxford (BA 1952, MA 1956); Cuddesdon College, Oxford. Deacon 1954, priest 1955, Bristol; Curate of St Mary Redcliffe, Bristol, 1954-59; Chaplain, King's College London at St Boniface Coll., Warminster, 1959-64; Perpetual Curate, Church of the Good Shepherd, Bishopwearmouth, 1964-71; Rector of Tilehurst, Reading, 1971-79. *Recreations:* photography, boating. *Address:* Great Salkeld Rectory, Penrith, Cumbria CA11 9NA. *T:* Lazonby 273.

PENROSE, Prof. Edith Tilton; Professor, since 1977, Associate Dean for Research and Development, since 1982, Institut Européen d'Administration des Affaires, Fontainebleau; Professor of Economics (with reference to Asia), School of Oriental and African Studies, University of London, 1964-78; *b* 29 Nov. 1914; *d* of George Albert Tilton and Hazel Sparling Tilton; *m* 1st, 1934, David Burton Denhardt (*d* 1938); 2nd, 1944, Ernest F. Penrose; three *s* (and one *s* decd). *Educ:* Univ. of California, Berkeley (AB); Johns Hopkins Univ. (MA, PhD). Research Assoc., ILO, Geneva and Montreal, 1939-41; Special Asst, US Ambassador, London, 1941-46; US Delegn to UN, IV, 1946-47; research at Johns Hopkins Univ., 1948-50; Lectr and Res. Assoc., Johns Hopkins Univ., 1950-60; Vis. Fellow, Australian Nat. Univ., 1955-56; Assoc. Prof. of Econs, Univ. Baghdad, 1957-59; Reader in Econs, Univ. of London (LSE and SOAS), 1960-64; Actg Head, Dept of Econs and Polit. Studies, 1961-64; Head, Dept of Econs, SOAS, 1964-69; Visiting Professor: Univ. Dar Es Salaam, 1971-72; Univ. of Toronto, 1977. Member: Sainsbury Cttee of Enquiry into Relationship of Pharmaceutical Industry with Nat. Health Service, 1965-67; SSRC, 1974-76 (Econ. Cttee, 1970-76, Chm., 1974-76); Medicines Commn, 1975-78; Dir, Commonwealth Develt Corp., 1975-78; Mem. Council, Royal Economic Soc., 1975-; Governor, NIESR, 1974-. *Publications:* Food Control in Great Britain, 1940; Economics of the International Patent System, 1951 (trans. Japanese, Spanish); The Theory of the Growth of the Firm, 1959 (trans. Japanese, French, Spanish, Italian); The Large International Firm in Developing Countries: The International Petroleum Industry, 1968 (trans. Japanese); The Growth of Firms, Middle East Oil and Other Essays, 1971; contrib. Amer. Econ. Rev., Bus. Hist. Rev., Econ. Jl, Economica, Jl Dev. Studies, Jl Econ. History, Yearbook of World Affairs, Etudes Internationales, Mondes en Développement. *Recreations:* travel, theatre, gardening. *Address:* 48 rue St Merry, 77300 Fontainebleau, France. *T:* 422.69.88.

PENROSE, George William, QC 1978; *b* 2 June 1938; *s* of late George W. Penrose and Janet L. Penrose; *m* 1964, Wendy Margaret Cooper; one *s* two *d*. *Educ:* Glasgow Univ. (MA, LLB). CA. Advocate, 1964. *Recreation:* walking. *Address:* 5 Cobden Road, Edinburgh EH9 2BJ. *T:* 031-667 1819.

PENROSE, Maj.-Gen. (retd) John Hubert, OBE 1956; MC 1944; *b* 24 Oct. 1916; *e s* of late Brig. John Penrose, MC and late Mrs M. C. Penrose (*née* Hendrick-Aylmer); *m* 1941, Pamela Elizabeth, *d* of late H. P. Lloyd, Neath, Glam.; four *d. Educ:* Winchester Coll.; RMA Woolwich, 2nd Lieut, RA, 1936; war service in European Theatre, BEF, 1939-40, and BLA, 1944; subseq. service in India, Germany, Malaya and UK; idc 1964; Defence Adviser to British High Comr, New Delhi, 1968-71; retired 1972. *Address:* West Hoe House, Bishop's Waltham, Southampton SO3 1DT. *T:* Bishop's Waltham 2363.

PENROSE, Prof. Roger, FRS 1972; Rouse Ball Professor of Mathematics, University of Oxford, since 1973; *b* Colchester, Essex, 8 Aug. 1931; *s* of Lionel Sharples Penrose, FRS; *m* 1959, Joan Isabel Wedge; three *s. Educ:* University Coll. Sch.; University Coll., Univ. of London (BSc spec. 1st cl. Mathematics), Fellow 1975; St John's Coll., Cambridge (PhD). NRDC (temp. post, Feb.-Aug. 1956); Asst Lectr (Pure Mathematics), Bedford Coll., London, 1956-57; Research Fellow, St John's Coll., Cambridge, 1957-60; NATO Research Fellow, Princeton Univ. and Syracuse Univ., 1959-61; Research Associate King's Coll., London, 1961-63; Visiting Associate Prof., Univ. of Texas, Austin, Texas, 1963-64; Reader, 1964-66, Prof. of Applied Mathematics, 1966-73, Birkbeck Coll., London. Visiting Prof., Yeshiva, Princeton, Cornell, 1966-67 and 1969. Adams Prize (Cambridge Univ.), 1966-67; Dannie Heineman Prize (Amer. Phys. Soc. and Amer. Inst. Physics), 1971; Eddington Medal, RAS, 1975. Member: London Mathematical Soc.; Cambridge Philosophical Soc.; American Mathematical Soc. *Publications:* Techniques of Differential Topology in Relativity, 1973; many articles in scientific jls. *Recreations:* reading science fiction, 3 dimensional puzzles, making things with or for his three young sons. *Address:* 25 Aylmer Drive, Stanmore, Mddx HA7 3EJ. *T:* 01-954 3173; Mathematical Institute, 24-29 St Giles, Oxford OX1 3LB. *T:* Oxford 54295.

PENROSE, Sir Roland (Algernon), Kt 1966; CBE 1961; Chairman, Institute of Contemporary Arts, 1947-69, President, 1969-78 and since 1980; *b* 14 Oct. 1900; *s* of James Doyle Penrose and Hon. Elizabeth Josephine Peckover; *m* 1st, 1925, Valentine Andrée Boué; 2nd, 1947, Lee Miller (*d* 1977); one *s. Educ:* Leighton Park School, Reading; Queens' College, Cambridge. BA Cantab 1922; lived in France, studied and painted, 1922-34; returned to London, organised Internat. Surrealist Exhibition, 1936; painted and exhibited in London and Paris with Surrealist Group, 1936-39. Served War, 1940-45, WO Lecturer to Home Guard, 1940-42; commissioned Army, Gen. List, Capt. 1943-45. Founder, Inst. of Contemporary Arts; Fine Arts Officer, British Council, Paris, 1956-59; Member Fine Arts Panel: Brit. Council, 1955-79; Arts Coun., 1959-67; Trustee, Tate Gall., 1959-66; organised Exhibitions at Tate Gallery for Arts Council: Picasso, 1960; Max Ernst, 1961; Miró, 1964; Picasso (sculpture), 1967. *Publications:* The Road is Wider than Long, 1939, rev. edn 1980; In the Service of the People, 1945; Picasso his Life and Work, 1958, 3rd rev. edn 1980; Portrait of Picasso, 1958, 2nd rev. edn 1980; Miró, 1970; (ed with John Golding) Picasso 1881-1973, 1973; Man Ray, 1975; Tàpies, 1978; Scrapbook 1900-1981, 1981. *Recreation:* gardening. *Address:* Farley Farm, Chiddingly, nr Lewes, E Sussex. *T:* Chiddingly 308. *Club:* Garrick.

PENRUDDOCK, Sir Clement (Frederick), Kt 1973; CBE 1954; Consultant with Lawrance, Messer & Co., Solicitors (Senior Partner, 1947-81); *b* 30 Jan. 1905; *s* of Rev. Frederick Fitzpatrick Penruddock and Edith Florence Smith; *m* 1945, Philippa Mary Tolhurst; one *s* three *d. Educ:* Marlborough Coll.; Keble Coll., Oxford. BA 1927. Admitted Solicitor, 1931. Sec., Chequers Trust, 1941-72. Chairman: Atlanta Baltimore & Chicago Investment Trust Ltd; Channel Islands & Internat. Investment Trust Ltd; Paten & Co. (Peterborough) Ltd; West Coast and Texas Regional Investment Trust Ltd; Director: Save & Prosper Group Ltd, 1947-80; The Steetley Co. Ltd, 1951-75; Ocean Wilsons (Holdings) Ltd; Lancashire & London Investment Trust Ltd. *Recreations:* golf, ski-ing. *Address:* Venars, Nutfield, Redhill, Surrey. *T:* Nutfield Ridge 2218, (office) 01-606 7691. *Clubs:* City, United Oxford & Cambridge University.

PENTLAND, 2nd Baron, *cr* 1909, of Lyth, Caithness; **Henry John Sinclair,** BA; Member American IEE, MICE, MIEE; Director: American British Electric Corporation (New York); Hunting Surveys Inc. (New York); *b* 1907; *o s* of 1st Baron and Lady Marjorie Gordon, DBE, JP (*d* 1970), *o d* of 1st Marquis of Aberdeen and *sister* of 2nd Marquis; *S* father, 1925; *m* 1941, Lucy Elisabeth, 3rd *d* of late Sir Henry Babington Smith, GBE, KCB, CH; one *d. Educ:* Cargilfield; Wellington; Trinity College, Cambridge; President, Cambridge Union Society, 1929; Asst Secretary Ministry of Production, and CPRB, Washington, 1944-45. *Address:* 131 East 66th Street, New York, NY 10021, USA.

PENTNEY, Richard George; employed by Kent Social Services Committee, since 1981; *b* 17 Aug. 1922; *s* of late Rev. A. F. Pentney, MC; *m* 1953, Elisabeth, *d* of Sir Eric Berthoud, *qv* ; four *d. Educ:* Kingswood School, Bath; St John's Coll., Cambridge. Mem., Univ. Cricket and Hockey XIs. RNVR (Lieut), 1942-46. Asst Master, Sedbergh School, 1947-58; Headmaster, St Andrew's Coll., Minaki, Tanzania, 1958-64; Asst Master, Oundle School, 1964-65; Headmaster, King's Coll., Taunton, 1965-69; Sec. for Appeals, St Christopher's Fellowship, 1969-70; Commoner Fellow, St John's Coll., Cambridge, 1970; Dir, Attlee House, Toynbee Hall, 1970-73. *Recreations:* walking, water-colour painting. *Address:* Rectory Cottage, Frant, Tunbridge Wells, Kent. *T:* Frant 659; Loughanacreen, Lauragh, Co. Kerry, Eire.

PENTREATH, Rev. Canon Arthur Godolphin Guy Carleton, MA (Cambridge); Hon. Secretary, Hellenic Travellers' Club; Residentiary Canon, Rochester Cathedral, 1959-65, Emeritus, 1965; Headmaster of Cheltenham College, 1952-59, retired; *b* 30 March 1902; *s* of late Reverend Dr A. G. Pentreath, Royal Army Chaplains' Department, and Helen Guy Carleton, County Cork; *m* 1927, Margaret Lesley Cadman (*d* 1980); two *s* one *d. Educ:* Haileybury College; Magdalene College, Cambridge. (Classical Scholar), 1st class Hon. with distinction in Classical Archæology, Class. Tripos Part II. Westcott House, Cambridge, 1925-26. Master at Oundle School, 1927; Deacon, 1928; Priest, 1929; Chaplain and Master at Michaelhouse School, Natal, 1928-30; Master of the King's Scholars, Westminster School, 1930-34; Headmaster St Peter's College, Adelaide, S Australia, 1934-43; Headmaster of Wrekin College, 1944-51. *Publication:* Hellenic Traveller, 1964. *Recreation:* sailing. *Address:* Wooden Walls, Dock Lane, Beaulieu, Hants. *T:* Beaulieu 612348.

PENZIAS, Dr Arno Allan; Vice-President, Research, Bell Laboratories, since 1981; *b* 26 April 1933; *s* of Karl and Justine Penzias; *m* 1954, Anne Barras Penzias; one *s* two *d. Educ:* City Coll. of New York (BS Physics, 1954); Columbia Univ. (MA Physics, 1958; PhD Physics, 1962). Bell Laboratories: Mem., Technical Staff, 1961-72; Head, Radio Physics Res., 1972-76; Dir, Radio Res. Lab., 1976-79; Exec. Dir, Research, Communications Sciences, 1979-81. Lectr, Princeton Univ., 1967-72; Res. Associate, Harvard Univ., 1968-80; Adjunct Prof., State Univ. of NY, Stony Brook, 1974-; Trustee, Trenton State Coll., 1977-79. MNAS; Wissenschaftliche Fachbeirat, Max-Planck Inst., Bonn, 1978-; hon. degrees: Paris Observatory, 1976; Wilkes Coll., City Coll. of NY, Yeshiva Univ., and Rutgers Univ., 1979. Henry Draper Medal, National Acad. of Sciences, 1977; Herschel Medal, RAS, 1977; (jtly) Nobel Prize for Physics, 1978. Mem. Editorial Bd, Annual Revs of Astronomy and Astrophysics, 1974-78; Associate Editor, Astrophysical Jl Letters, 1977-. *Publications:* 80 published articles, principally in Astrophysical Jl. *Address:* Bell Laboratories, 600 Mountain Avenue, Murray Hill, NJ 07974, USA. *T:* (201) 582-3361.

PEPLOE, Denis (Frederic Neil), RSA 1966 (ARSA 1956); former Teacher of drawing and painting at Edinburgh College of Art; *b* 25 March 1914; *s* of late Samuel John Peploe, RSA, and late Margaret Peploe (*née* Mackay); *m* 1957, Elizabeth Marion (*née* Barr); one *s* one *d. Educ:* Edinburgh Academy. Studied at Edinburgh College of Art and Académie André Lhote, 1931-37. Served War of 1939-45: Royal Artillery and Intelligence Corps. Appointed Lecturer at Edinburgh College of Art, 1954. *Recreations:* hill-walking, mycology. *Address:* 18 Mayfield Gardens, Edinburgh EH9 2BZ. *T:* 031-667 6164.

PEPPARD, Nadine Sheila, CBE 1970; Adviser on Race Relations, Home Office, since 1972; *b* 16 Jan. 1922; *d* of late Joseph Anthony Peppard and May Peppard (*née* Barber). *Educ:* Macclesfield High Sch.; Manchester Univ. (BA, Teacher's Dip.). French Mistress, Maldon Grammar Sch., 1943-46; Spanish Editor, George G. Harrap & Co. Ltd, 1946-55; Trg Dept, Marks and Spencer, 1955-57; Dep. Gen-Sec., London Council of Social Service, 1957-64; Nat. Advisory Officer for Commonwealth Immigrants, 1964-65; Gen. Sec., Nat. Cttee for Commonwealth Immigrants, 1965-68; Chief Officer, Community Relations Commn, 1968-72. *Publications:* (trans.) Primitive India, 1954; (trans.) Toledo, 1955. *Recreations:* cookery, gardening. *Address:* 17 Kentmere Close, Hatherley, Cheltenham, Glos. *T:* Cheltenham 42583.

PEPPER, Claude Denson; Member of United States House of Representatives, former United States Senator (Democrat); *b* Dudleyville, Alabama, USA, 8 Sept. 1900; *s* of Joseph Wheeler Pepper and Lena (*née* Talbot); *m* 1936, Irene Mildred Webster (*d* 1979), St Petersburg, Fla; no *c. Educ:* University of Alabama (AB); Harvard Law School (JD, Phi Beta Kappa). Served with Armed Forces, 1918. Instr in Law, Univ. of Arkansas, 1924-25. Admitted to Alabama Bar, 1924; Florida Bar, 1925; practised law at Perry, Fla, 1925-30; House Mem. Fla State Legislature, 1929; practised law, Tallahassee, Fla, 1930-37; Mem. State Bd of: Public Welfare, 1931-32; Law Examiners, 1933-34; US Senator from Fla, 1936-51; Mem., various cttees; Chm., Middle East Sub-Cttee of Senate Foreign Relations Cttee (12 yrs) etc.; Chm. Fla Delegation to Dem. Nat. Convention, 1940-44; subseq. alternate Delegate, 1948, 1952, 1956, 1960, 1964, Delegate, 1968. Elected to: 88th Congress, 1962; 89th Congress, 1964; 90th Congress, 1966 (without opposition); 91st Congress, 1968; 92nd Congress, 1970; 93rd Congress, 1972; 94th Congress, 1974; 95th Congress, 1976; 96th Congress, 1978; 97th Congress, 1980; Member: (88th Congress) House Cttee on Banking and Currency, and sub cttees on Domestic Finance, Internat. Trade, and Internat. Finance; (89th, 90th, 91st, 92nd, 93rd, 94th, 95th, 96th and 97th Congress) House Rules Cttee; Chm. (91st and 92nd Congress) House Select Cttee on Crime, Cttee on Internal Security; Chm. (95th, 96th and 97th Congress) House Select Cttee on Aging and Sub-Cttee on Health and Long Term Care. Member: Board of Directors, Washington Federal Savings & Loan Assoc.; American Bar Assoc.; International Bar Association, etc. Mary and Albert Lasker Public Service Award, 1967; various other awards. Holds hon. degrees. Member, American Legion; Baptist; Mason; Shriner; Elk; Moose, Kiwanian. *Publications:* contributor to periodicals. *Recreations:* hunting, golf, swimming. *Address:* (home) 2121 North Bayshore Drive, Miami, Florida 33137, USA; 4201 Cathedral Avenue, NW, Washington, DC 20016, USA; (offices) 2239 Rayburn House Office Building, Washington, DC 20515. *Clubs:* Harvard, Jefferson Island, Army-Navy, Columbia Country, Burning

Tree, etc (Washington); Miami, Bankers (Miami); various country (Florida).

PEPPER, Kenneth Bruce, CB 1965; Commissioner of HM Customs and Excise, 1957-73; *b* 11 March 1913; *s* of late E. E. Pepper; *m* 1945, Irene Evelyn Watts; two *s. Educ:* County High Sch., Ilford; London Sch. of Economics. Joined HM Customs and Excise, 1932; Asst Sec., 1949; Commissioner, 1957. Lieutenant, Intelligence Corps, 1944. *Address:* Fairfield, Cae Mair, Beaumaris, Gwynedd.

PEPPERCORN, Trevor Edward, BA Oxon; *b* 4 June 1904; *s* of late William and Kate Peppercorn; *m* 1st, 1935, Sheila (*d* 1972), *d* of F. W. Ayre, St John's Newfoundland; one *s* ; 2nd, 1977, Mary Gertrude (*née* Cumming), *widow* of L. G. Williamson. *Educ:* Beaumont College; Balliol College, Oxford. Dunlop Rubber Co. Ltd, 1928; Dunlop Rubber Co. (India) Ltd, 1929; Dunlop South Africa Ltd, 1940 (Managing Director, 1943-52); Director, Dunlop Rubber Co. Ltd, 1957-76; Dir, Triplex Holdings, 1966-77 (Chm., 1966-75); Chairman: Weldall Engineering Ltd, 1971-77; Fibreglass-Pilkington Ltd, Bombay, 1972-77. Chm., Overseas Develt Inst., 1967-72. *Recreations:* gardening, shooting. *Address:* The Grange, Yattendon, Newbury, Berks.

PEPPIATT, Sir Kenneth Oswald, KBE 1941; MC; *b* 25 March 1893; *s* of late W. R. Peppiatt; *m* 1929, Pamela, *d* of late Captain E. W. Carter, MC; two *s* one *d. Educ:* Bancrofts. Entered service of Bank of England, 1911; Principal of Discount Office, 1928-34; Chief Cashier, 1934-49; Exec. Dir, 1949-57. Dir, Coutts and Co., 1958-69. Fellow, Inst. of Bankers. Hon. Treasurer, Army Benevolent Fund, 1949-64. Served European War 1914-18, retd rank Major (despatches, MC and Bar, twice wounded). *Recreations:* racing, fishing. *Address:* 7 Harvey Orchard, Beaconsfield, Bucks. *T:* Beaconsfield 3158.

PEPPITT, John Raymond, QC 1976; Barrister-at-law; a Recorder of the Crown Court, since 1976; *b* 22 Sept. 1931; *s* of late Reginald Peppitt and Phyllis Claire Peppitt; *m* 1960, Judith Penelope James; three *s. Educ:* St Paul's Sch.; Jesus Coll., Cambridge (BA Classical Tripos). Called to the Bar, Gray's Inn, 1958. *Recreations:* collecting water-colours, shooting. *Address:* Chegworth Manor Farm, Chegworth, near Harrietsham, Kent ME17 1DD.

PEPYS, family name of **Earl of Cottenham.**

PEPYS, Lady (Mary) Rachel, DCVO 1968 (CVO 1954); Lady-in-Waiting to Princess Marina, Duchess of Kent, 1943-68; *b* 27 June 1905; *e d* of 15th Duke of Norfolk, KG, PC, CVO (*d* 1917); *m* 1st, 1939, as Lady Rachel Fitz-Alan Howard, Lieutenant-Colonel Colin Keppel Davidson, CIE, OBE, RA (killed in action, 1943), *s* of Col Leslie Davidson, CB, RHA, and Lady Theodora, *d* of 7th Earl of Albemarle; one *s* one *d* ; 2nd, 1961, Brigadier Anthony Hilton Pepys, DSO (*d* 1967). *Address:* Highfield House, Crossbush, Arundel, W Sussex. *T:* Arundel 883158.

PERCEVAL, family name of **Earl of Egmont.**

PERCEVAL, Viscount; Thomas Frederick Gerald Perceval; *b* 17 Aug. 1934; *e s* of 11th Earl of Egmont, *qv.*

PERCEVAL, Michael; HM Diplomatic Service; Counsellor (Political and Economic) and Consul-General, Brasilia, since 1982; *b* 27 April 1936; *o s* of Hugh Perceval and late Guida Brind; *m* 1968, Alessandra Grandis; one *s* one *d. Educ:* Downside Sch.; Christ Church, Oxford (Schol.; 2nd Cl. Hons English Lit.). Served Royal Air Force, Nicosia, 1956-60; film production asst, Athens, 1960; freelance correspondent, Madrid, 1961-69. Joined FCO, 1970; First Sec. (Press), UK Rep. to EC, Brussels, 1972-74; First Sec. and subseq. Head of Chancery, British High Commission, Nicosia, 1974-78; Asst Head of Mexico and Caribbean Dept, FCO, 1978-79; Counsellor, Havana, 1980-82. *Publication:* The Spaniards, 1969, 2nd edn 1972. *Recreations:* music, walking, the Mediterranean. *Address:* c/o Foreign and Commonwealth Office, King Charles Street, Whitehall, SW1. *Club:* Royal Commonwealth Society.

PERCEVAL, Robert Westby, TD 1968; Clerk Assistant, House of Lords, 1964-74; retired; *b* 28 Aug. 1914; *m* 1948, Hon. J. I. L. Littleton, *er d* of 5th Baron Hatherton; two *s* two *d. Educ:* Ampleforth; Balliol College, Oxford. Joined Parliament Office, House of Lords, 1938. Royal Artillery, 1939-44; General Staff, War Office, 1944-45. *Address:* Pillaton Hall, Penkridge, Staffs ST19 5RZ. *Clubs:* Beefsteak, Turf.

PERCIVAL, Allen Dain, CBE 1975; Executive Chairman, Stainer & Bell Publishers, since 1978; Gresham Professor of Music, The City University, since 1980; *b* 23 April 1925; *s* of Charles and Gertrude Percival, Bradford; *m* 1952, Rachel Hay. *Educ:* Bradford Grammar Sch.; Magdalene Coll., Cambridge. MusB Cantab 1948. Served War of 1939-45, RNVR. Music Officer of British Council in France, 1948-50; Music Master, Haileybury and Imp. Service Coll., 1950-51; Dir of Music, Homerton Coll., Cambridge, 1951-62; Conductor, Cambridge Univ. Musical Soc., 1954-58; Dir of Music Studies, GSM, 1962-65, Principal, GSMD, 1965-78. Also professional continuo playing, broadcasting and conducting. FRCM; FGSM. Hon. RAM 1966; Hon. FTCL 1967. Hon. DMus City, 1978; Fellow, Hong Kong Conservatory of Music, 1980. *Publications:* The Orchestra, 1956; The Teach Yourself History of Music, 1961; Music at the Court of Elizabeth I, 1975; Galliard Book of Carols,

1980; English Love Songs, 1980; contribs to musical and educnl jls. *Recreation:* travel. *Address:* 7 Park Parade, Cambridge. *T:* 353953.

PERCIVAL, Sir Anthony (Edward), Kt 1966; CB 1954; Chairman: Gordon & Gotch Holdings Ltd, 1971-81; Brameast Gotch, since 1972; Director: Simon Engineering Ltd, since 1971; Bank of Adelaide, since 1971; Switzerland (General) Insurance Co., since 1971; *b* 23 Sept. 1910; *m* 1935, Doris Cuff; one *d. Educ:* Manchester Gram. Sch.; Cambridge. Entered Board of Trade, 1933; Assistant Secretary, 1942; Commercial Counsellor, Washington, on secondment, 1946-49; Under-Secretary, Board of Trade, 1949-58; Sec., Export Credits Guarantee Dept, 1962-71. Dir, Trade Indemnity Co., 1973-81. President: Berne Union of Export Credit Insurance Organisations, 1966-68; Export Credit Gp, OECD, Paris, 1967-70. *Address:* 16 Hayes Way, Beckenham, Kent. *T:* 01-650 2648.

PERCIVAL, Edgar Wikner, CEng, FRAeS, FIMechE, FIMarE, MSAE, MIAeE, AFIAeS, FRSA; engaged on Research and Design for national purposes; Founder, Chairman, Managing Director and Chief Designer, Percival Aircraft Ltd, Aircraft Manufacturers; Director: Valbank Ltd; Percival Power Units Ltd; *b* Albury, New South Wales; *s* of late William and Hilda Percival, Clarendon Park, Richmond, NSW; unmarried. *Educ:* Sydney Tech. Coll.; Sydney Univ. Served 7th Australian Light Horse, 60 Sqdn RFC and founder member 111 Sqdn RFC, RAF, 1914-18; RAFO, 1929-39; RAFVR, 1939-45; Air Ministry approved test pilot on flying boats, seaplanes and land planes; is the first to have produced low-wing cantilever monoplanes in British Commonwealth; winner of numerous Air races and trophies, both national and international; won Melbourne Herald Air Race, Melbourne-Geelong-Melbourne, 1923; has flown fastest time in King's Cup Air Races for 5 years; holds record for fastest time ever flown in King's Cup; designed, built and flew man-carrying gliders, Richmond, Aust., 1910-11; designed and built: King's Cup Air Race winners for the 3 consecutive years prior to world war II, and winners for 3 years since War; Saro-Percival Mail Plane, 1930; Percival Gull, 1931-32; Percival Mew Gull (first civil aircraft in British Commonwealth to have a speed of over 200 m.p.h.), 1933; Vega Gull, Q6 and Proctor; first aeroplane in British Empire to carry 1000 pounds load for 1000 miles range; a group of lakes discovered in Australia in 1934 was named Percival Lakes in his honour; first person to have flown to Africa and back in a day (1935); winner of Johnstone Memorial Trophy and of Oswald Watt Memorial Gold Medal; three times winner of International Speed Trophy. By enactment in 1948 of US Senate Bill specifically for him, he became a permanent resident of US; this was in recognition of his valuable research work in US on high-altitude flying; he is allowed the exceptional privilege of unlimited periods of stay, at his option, outside US. Founder Mem., Guild of Air Pilots and Air Navigators; Mem., Institute of Directors. Mem., Lloyd's of London, 1944-. *Recreations:* flying, horse riding and hunting, swimming, squash, shooting, ski-ing. *Address:* 72 Chesterfield House, Chesterfield Gardens, Curzon Street, W1. *T:* 01-499 2895. *Clubs:* Royal Air Force, Royal Automobile, Naval and Military.

PERCIVAL, George Hector, MD, PhD, FRCPE, DPH; Professor Emeritus of Dermatology, University of Edinburgh (Grant Professor, 1946); *b* 1901; *s* of late E. J. Percival, Kirkcaldy; *m* 1937, Kathleen, *d* of late John Dawson, MD, Buckhaven; one *s* one *d. Educ:* George Watson's Coll., Edinburgh; Univs of Edinburgh and Paris. Physician to the Skin Dept, Edinburgh Royal Infirmary, 1936. *Publications:* An Introduction to Dermatology; The Histopathology of the Skin; scientific articles in British Med. Journ., Lancet, etc., Encyclopædia of Med., System of Bacteriology (Med. Res. Council). *Recreations:* golf, fishing. *Address:* Woodcroft, Barnton Avenue, Edinburgh EH4 6JJ. *T:* 031-336 2438.

PERCIVAL, Sir Ian, Kt 1979; QC 1963; MP (C) Southport since 1959; Solicitor-General, since 1979; *b* 11 May 1921; *s* of Eldon and Chrystine Percival; *m* 1942, Madeline Buckingham Cooke; one *s* one *d. Educ:* Latymer Upper School; St Catharine's College, Cambridge (MA). Served HM Forces, 1940-46: 2nd Bn the Buffs, N Africa and Burma; Major. Called to the Bar, Inner Temple, 1948, Bencher, 1970. Recorder of Deal, later of the Crown Court, 1971-. Sec., Cons. Parly Legal Cttee, 1964-68, Vice-Chm. 1968-70, Chm. 1970-74. Fellow, Inst. of Taxation (Chm., Parly Cttee, 1965-71); Mem., Royal Economic Soc. *Recreations:* golf and tennis. *Address:* 9 King's Bench Walk, Temple, EC4. *T:* 01-583 2939. *Clubs:* Carlton, Beefsteak; Rye Golf.

PERCIVAL, Prof. Ian Colin, PhD; Professor of Applied Mathematics, Queen Mary College, University of London, since 1974; *b* 27 July 1931; *m* 1955, Jill Cuff (*née* Herbert); two *s* one *d. Educ:* Ealing County Grammar Sch.; UCL (BSc, PhD). Lectr in Physics, UCL, 1957-61; Reader in Applied Maths, QMC, 1961-67; Prof. of Theoret. Physics, Univ. of Stirling, 1967-74. *Publications:* papers in learned jls on scattering theory, atomic and molecular theory, statistical mechanics and classical dynamics. *Address:* Queen Mary College, Mile End Road, E1 4NS. *T:* 01-980 4811.

PERCIVAL, Robert Clarendon, FRCS, FRCOG; Consulting Obstetric Surgeon, The London Hospital; *b* 16 Sept. 1908; British; *m* 1st, 1944, Beryl Mary Ind (*d* 1967); one *d* ; 2nd, 1972, Beatrice Myfanwy Evans, FFARCS. *Educ:* Barker College, NSW; Sydney University; The London Hospital, Qualified, 1933. Resident appointments: Poplar Hospital; Hosp. for Sick Children, Gt Ormond St; The London Hosp.; Southend Gen. Hosp. Obstetric and Gynæcological 1st Asst, The London Hosp., 1937. Surgeon-Lt-Comdr,

RNVR, 1941-45 (Surgical Specialist); Obstetric Surgeon, The London Hospital, 1947-73, Director, Obstetric Unit, 1968-73. Chm., Obst. Adv. Cttee, NE Region Met. Hosp. Bd, 1967-73; President: Section of Obst. and Gyn., R.SocMed., 1973-74; The London Hosp. Clubs' Union, 1965 (Treasurer, 1955-73); United Hosps RFC, 1969-72; London Hosp. Cricket Club, 1946-72. *Publications:* (jtly) Ten Teachers' Midwifery, 1958, new edition as Ten Teachers' Obstetrics, 1972; (jtly) Ten Teachers' Diseases of Women, 1965, new edition as Ten Teachers' Gynaecology, 1971; (jtly) British Obstetric Practice, 1963; (ed) Holland and Brews Obstetrics, 1969, 14th edn 1979; contribs to Lancet, British Jl of Obst. and Gynaecol. *Recreations:* fishing, tennis, golf, ski-ing. *Address:* Coker Wood Cottage, Pendomer, near Yeovil, Somerset BA22 9PD. *T:* Corscombe 328. *Club:* MCC.

PERCIVAL, Sir (Walter) Ian; see Percival, Sir Ian.

PERCIVAL-PRESCOTT, Westby William, FIIC; Keeper and Head of Picture Department, National Maritime Museum, since 1977; practising conservator and painter; *b* 22 Jan. 1923; *s* of William Percival-Prescott and Edith Percival; *m* 1948, Silvia Haswell Miller; one *s*. *Educ:* Edinburgh Coll. of Art (DA Hons). FIIC 1957. Andrew Grant Scholar, National Gall., 1945; restoration of Rubens Whitehall ceiling, 1947-51; Restorer i/c House of Lords frescos, 1953; worked in National Gall. Conservation Dept, 1954-56; directed restoration of Painted Hall, Greenwich, 1957-60; National Maritime Museum: estabd Picture Conservation Dept, 1961; organised first internat. conf. on Comparative Lining Techniques, 1973 (Ottawa, 1974); produced and designed historical exhibitions: Idea and Illusion, 1960; Four Steps to Longitude, 1963; The Siege of Malta, 1970; Captain Cook and Mr Hodges, 1979; The Art of the Van de Veldes, 1982. Vis. Sen. Lectr, Dept of Fine Art, Univ. of Leeds, 1980. Internat. Council of Museums: Co-ordinator, Conservation Cttee, 1975-; Mem., Directory Bd, Conservation Cttee, 1981-. *Publications:* The Coronation Chair, 1957; The Lining Cycle, 1974, Swedish edn 1975; Handbook of Lining Terms, 1974; Thornhill at Greenwich, 1978; Micro X-Ray Techniques, 1978; Techniques of Suction Lining, 1981; The Art of the Van de Veldes, 1982; technical papers. *Recreations:* listening to music, travel. *Address:* 34 Compayne Gardens, NW6 3DP. *T:* 01-624 4577. *Club:* Chelsea Arts.

PERCY, family name of **Duke of Northumberland.**

PERCY, Earl; Henry Alan Walter Richard Percy; *b* 1 July 1953; *s* and *heir* of 10th Duke of Northumberland, *qv. Educ:* Eton; Christ Church, Oxford. *Address:* Alnwick Castle, Northumberland; Syon House, Brentford, Mddx.

PERCY, Lord Richard Charles; Lecturer, Department of Zoology, in the University of Newcastle upon Tyne; *b* 11 February 1921; *s* of 8th Duke of Northumberland and Lady Helen Gordon-Lennox (who *d* 1965, as Dowager Duchess of Northumberland, GCVO, CBE); *m* 1st, 1966, Sarah Jane Elizabeth Norton (*d* 1978), *o d* of Mr and Mrs Petre Norton, La Charca, Coin, Malaga, Spain; two *s*; 2nd, 1979, Hon. Mrs Clayre Ridley, 2nd *d* of 4th Baron Stratheden and Campbell, CBE. *Educ:* Eton; Christ Church, Oxford; Durham University. BSc. Lieut-Colonel Comdg Northumberland Hussars, TA, 1959-61; late Capt. Gren. Guards. Served War, 1941-45. DL Northumberland, 1968. *Address:* Department of Zoology, The University, Newcastle upon Tyne NE1 7RU; Lesbury House, Alnwick, Northumberland NE66 3PT. *T:* Alnmouth 830330; 58 Woodsford Square, W14 8DS; 212 Lambeth Road, SE1. *T:* 01-928 3441. *Clubs:* Turf; Northern Counties (Newcastle upon Tyne).

PERCY, Rodney Algernon; His Honour Judge Percy; a Circuit Judge, since 1979; *b* 15 May 1924; 3rd *s* of late Hugh James Percy, Solicitor, Alnwick; *m* 1948, Mary Allen, *d* of late J. E. Benbow, Aberystwyth; one *s* three *d. Educ:* Uppingham; Brasenose Coll., Oxford (MA). Lieut, Royal Corps of Signals, 1942-46, served in Burma, India, Malaya, Java. Called to Bar, Middle Temple, 1950. Dep. Coroner, N Northumberland, 1957; Asst Recorder, Sheffield QS, 1964; Dep. Chm., Co. Durham QS, 1966-71; a Recorder of the Crown Court, 1972-79. *Publications:* (ed) Charlesworth on Negligence, 4th edn 1962, 5th edn 1971 and 6th edn 1977. *Recreations:* golf, gardening, hill walking, King Charles spaniels, beach-combing. *Address:* Brookside, Lesbury, Alnwick, Northumberland NE66 3AT. *T:* Alnmouth 326.

PERDUE, Rt. Rev. Richard Gordon; *b* 13 Feb. 1910; *s* of Richard Perdue; *m* 1943, Evelyn Ruth Curry, BA; two *d. Educ:* Trinity Coll., Dublin. BA 1931; MA and BD 1938. Deacon 1933, priest 1934, Dublin. Curate of Drumcondra with N Strand, 1933-36; Rathmines, 1936-40; Incumbent of Castledermot with Kinneagh, 1940-43; Roscrea, Diocese of Killaloe, 1943-54; Archdeacon of Killaloe and Kilfenora, 1951-54; Examining Chaplain to Bishop of Killaloe, 1951-54; Bishop of Killaloe, Kilfenora, Clonfert and Kilmacduagh, 1953-57; Bishop of Cork, Cloyne and Ross, 1957-78. *Address:* Shalom, Clonleigh, Kinsale, Co. Cork.

PEREIRA, Arthur Leonard, FRCS; Consulting Ear, Nose and Throat Surgeon to St George's Hospital, London; *b* 10 March 1906; British; *m* 1973, Mrs Jane Wilson (*née* Lapworth). *Educ:* Merchant Taylors' School. MRCS, LRCP 1929; MB, BS London 1931; FRCS 1936. Otologist to: the Metropolitan Hospital, E8, 1941-47; St George's Hospital, 1946-71. *Address:* Dormers, The Drive, Old Bosham, Sussex. *T:* Bosham 572086. *Club:* Bosham Sailing.

PEREIRA, Sir Charles; see Pereira, Sir H. C.

PEREIRA, Helio Gelli, DrMed; FRS 1973; FIBiol 1975; Head of Department of Epidemiology and of World Reference Centre for Foot-and-Mouth Disease, Animal Virus Research Institute, 1973-79; Consultant, Centre of Comparative Virology, Fundação Oswaldo Cruz, Rio de Janeiro, since 1979; *b* 23 Sept. 1918; *s* of Raul Pereira and Maria G. Pereira; *m* 1946, Marguerite McDonald Scott (*see* Marguerite Pereira); one *s* one *d* (and one *d* decd). *Educ:* Faculdade Fluminense de Medicina, also Instituto Oswaldo Cruz, Rio de Janeiro, Brazil. British Council Scholarship, Dept of Bacteriology, Manchester Univ. and Div. of Bacteriology and Virus Research, Nat. Inst. for Med. Research, London, 1945-47; Rickettsia Laboratory, Instituto Oswaldo Cruz, 1948-51; Asst to Prof. of Microbiology, Faculdade Fluminense de Medicina, 1943-45 and 1948-51. Nat. Inst. for Med. Research, Mill Hill, London: Mem. Scientific Staff, 1951-73; Head of Div. of Virology, 1964-73; Dir, World Influenza Centre, 1961-70. *Publication:* (with C. H. Andrewes) Viruses of Vertebrates (3rd edn), 1972, 4th edn (with C. H. Andrewes and P. Wildy) 1978. *Recreations:* skiing, music. *Address:* 3 Ducks Walk, Twickenham, Mddx TW1 2DD. *T:* 01-892 4511; Fundação Oswaldo Cruz, Caixa Postal 926, 21040 Rio de Janeiro, Brazil.

PEREIRA, Sir (Herbert) Charles, Kt 1977; DSc; FRS 1969; Consultant, tropical agriculture research; *b* 12 May 1913; *s* of H. J. Pereira and Maud Edith (*née* Machin), both of London; *m* 1941, Irene Beatrice, *d* of David Sloan, Belfast; three *s* one *d. Educ:* Prince Albert Coll., Saskatchewan; St Albans Sch.; London Univ. Attached Rothamsted Expl Stn for PhD (London) 1941. Royal Engineers, 1941-46 (despatches). Colonial Agric. Service, Coffee Research Stn, Kenya, 1946-52; Colonial Research Service, established Physics Div. at East African Agriculture and Forestry Research Org., Kenya, 1952-61; DSc London 1961; Dir, ARC of Rhodesia and Nyasaland, 1961-63; Dir, ARC of Central Africa (Rhodesia, Zambia and Malawi), 1963-67; Chm., ARC of Malawi, 1967-74; Dir, East Malling Research Station, 1969-72; Chief Scientist, MAFF, 1972-77. Member: Natural Environment Res. Council, 1971-77; ARC, 1972-77; ABRC, 1973-77; Chm., Sci. Panel, Commonwealth Develt Corp., 1978-. FInstBiol; FRASE 1977; CompICE, 1971; Hon. DSc Cranfield, 1977. Haile Selassie Prize for Research in Africa, 1966. *Publications:* (jtly) Hydrological Effects of Land Use Changes in East Africa, 1962; Land Use and Water Resources, 1973; papers in research jls; Founding Editor, Rhodesian Jl Agric. Research. *Recreations:* swimming, sailing. *Address:* Peartrees, Teston, Maidstone, Kent ME18 5AD. *T:* Maidstone 813333. *Clubs:* Athenæum; Salisbury (Zimbabwe).

PEREIRA, Marguerite Scott, MD; Director, Virus Reference Laboratory, Public Health Laboratory Service, London, since 1970; *b* 29 July 1921; *d* of Dr William McDonald Scott and Alice Clotilde Mollard Scott; *m* 1946, Dr Helio Gelli Pereira, *qv*; one *s* one *d* (and one *d* decd). *Educ:* James Allens Girls' Sch., Dulwich; Univ. of Aberdeen (MB, ChB, MD). Bacteriologist, Univ. of Manchester, 1944-46; Clinical Pathologist, Rio de Janeiro, 1947-49; Dir, Public Health Laboratory, Salisbury, 1954-57; Sen. Bacteriologist, Virus Reference Lab., and Dir, WHO Nat. Influenza Centre for England and Wales, 1957-69; Co-Dir, WHO Collaborating Centre for Reference and Research on Influenza, 1975-. *Publications:* mostly on medical virology and epidemiology, espec. influenza and respiratory disease. *Recreation:* reading. *Address:* 3 Ducks Walk, Twickenham, Mddx. *T:* 01-892 4511.

PEREIRA-MENDOZA, Vivian, MScTech, CEng, FIEE; Director, Polytechnic of the South Bank, 1970-80; *b* 8 April 1917; *o s* of Rev. Joseph Pereira-Mendoza, Manchester; *m* 1942, Marjorie, *y d* of Edward Lichtenstein; two *d. Educ:* Manchester Central High Sch.; Univ. of Manchester. Asst Lectr, Univ. of Manchester, 1939. Served War, 1940-45, in Royal Corps of Signals; Major, and GSO II (War Office). Sen. Lectr, Woolwich Polytechnic, 1948; Head of Dept: of Electrical Engrg, NW Kent Coll. of Technology, 1954; of Electrical Engrg and Physics, Borough Polytechnic, 1957; Vice-Principal, Borough Polytechnic, 1964; Principal, Borough Polytechnic, and Dir of Nat. Coll. of Heating, Ventilating, and Refrigeration and Fan Engrg, 1966-70. Has been member of numerous professional and acad. cttees and bds concerned with educn and trng, esp. in electrical engrg; Member: Council for Educn and Trng of Health Visitors, 1971-77; Council, Chelsea Coll., Univ. of London, 1972-. *Address:* 183 Salmon Street, Kingsbury, NW9. *T:* 01-205 0200.

PÉREZ DE CUÉLLAR, Javier; Secretary-General, United Nations, since 1982; *b* 19 Jan. 1920; *m* ; two *c. Educ:* Law Faculty, Catholic Univ., Lima, Perú. Joined Peruvian Foreign Ministry, 1940; Diplomatic Service, 1944; Sec., Peruvian Embassies in France, UK, Bolivia and Brazil and Counsellor, Embassy, Brazil, 1944-60; Dir, Legal and Personnel Dept, Ministry of External Relations, Perú, Dir of Administration, Dir, Protocol and Dir, Political Affairs, 1961-63; Peruvian Ambassador to Switzerland and Perm. Under-Sec. and Sec.-Gen. of Foreign Office, 1964-66; Ambassador of Perú to USSR and to Poland, 1969-71; Perm. Rep. of Perú to UN, 1971-75; Special Rep. of Sec.-Gen. in Cyprus, 1975-77; Ambassador of Perú to Venezuela, 1978; UN Under-Sec.-Gen. for Special Political Affairs, 1979-81. Former Prof. of Diplomatic Law, Academia Diplomática del Perú; Prof. of Internat. Relations, Academia de Guerra Aérea del Perú. Mem., Peruvian Delegn to First Session of General Assembly, UN, 1946. *Publication:* Manual de Derecho Diplomático, 1964. *Address:* United Nations, New York, NY 10017, USA. *T:* (212) 754-5012. *Clubs:* Nacional, Ecuestre Huachipa, Villa, Jockey (Lima, Perú).

PÉREZ ESQUIVEL, Adolfo; sculptor; General Co-ordinator, Servicio de Paz y Justicia en América Latina, since 1974; *b* 26 Nov. 1931; *m* 1956, Amanda

Pérez; three s. *Educ:* Nat. Sch. of Fine Arts, Buenos Aires. Prof. of Art, Manuel Belgrano Nat. Sch. of Fine Arts, Buenos Aires, 1956-71; Prof., Faculty of Architecture and Urban Studies, Univ. Nacional de la Plata. Work in permanent collections: Buenos Aires Mus. of Modern Art; Mus. of Fine Arts, Córdoba; Fine Arts Mus., Rosario. Joined group dedicated to principles of militant non-violence, and engaged in projects to promote self-sufficiency in urban areas, 1971; founded Paz y Justicia magazine, 1973. Co-founder, Ecumenical Movement for Human Rights, Argentina; Pres., Permanent Assembly for Human Rights. Premio la Nación de Escultura; Pope John XXIII prize, Pax Christi Orgn, 1977; Nobel Peace Prize, 1980. *Address:* Servicio de Paz y Justicia, Calle México 479, Buenos Aires, Argentina.

PERINAT, Marqués de, Luis Guillermo; Spanish Ambassador to the Soviet Union, since 1981; *b* 27 Oct. 1923; *s* of Luis Perinat and Ana Maria, Marquesa de Campo Real; *m* 1955, Blanca Escriva de Romani, Marquesa de Alginet; two *s* one *d. Educ:* Univs of Salamanca and Valladolid. Barrister-at-law. Sec., Spanish Embassy, Cairo, 1949-51; Dep. Consul-Gen., New York, 1954-56; Counsellor, Spanish Embassy, Paris, 1962-65; Permanent Sec., Spanish-American Jt Defence Cttee, 1965-70; Dir-Gen., N American and Far Eastern Affairs, Min. of Foreign Affairs, Madrid, 1973-76; Spanish Ambassador to the Court of St James's, 1976-81. Grand Cross, Order of Civil Merit (Spain); Kt Comdr, Order of Isabel La Católica (Spain); Kt Comdr, Order of Merito Aeronautico (Spain); also holds foreign decorations. *Heir: s* Guillermo Perinat y Escriva de Romani. *Address:* Calle del Prado 26, Madrid, Spain. *Clubs:* White's, Travellers'; Puerto de Hierro, Nuevo (Madrid).

PERKINS, Bernard James; Chairman, Harlow Development Corporation, 1972-79; *b* 25 Jan. 1928; *y s* of George and Rebecca Perkins; *m* 1956, Patricia (née Payne); three *d. Educ:* Strand School. Member: Lambeth Council, 1962-71 (Leader, 1968-71); Community Relations Commn, 1970-72; SE Econ. Planning Council, 1971-79; Alderman, GLC, 1971-73; Chm., GLC Housing Cttee, 1972-73. *Recreation:* social service. *Address:* 25 Croxted Road, West Dulwich, SE21 8SZ. *T:* 01-670 9056. *Club:* Effra (Norwood).

PERKINS, Surg. Vice-Adm. Sir Derek Duncombe S.; *see* Steele-Perkins.

PERKINS, Dexter; Professor Emeritus, University of Rochester, USA, also of Cornell University; President, Salzburg Seminar in American Studies, 1950-62; Prof. of History from 1922 and Chairman, Department of History, 1925-54, University of Rochester; John L. Senior Prof. of American Civilization, Cornell University, 1954-59; City Historian of City of Rochester, 1936-48; *b* 20 June 1889; *s* of Herbert William Perkins and Cora Farmer, Boston, Mass; *m* 1918, Wilma Lois Lord, Rochester, NY; two *s. Educ:* Boston Latin School and Sanford School, Redding Ridge, Conn; Harvard University (AB 1909, PhD 1914). Instructor in history, Univ. of Cincinnati, 1914-15; instructor and asst prof. history, Univ. of Rochester, 1915-22; lecturer on Commonwealth Fund at University College, London, 1937; secretary of American Historical Assoc., 1928-39. Served as 1st lieut, later captain, in USA, 1918; attached to historical section, GHQ, Chaumont, France, Oct. 1918-Feb. 1919; work connected with the Peace Conf., Feb.-June 1919; gave Albert Shaw Lectures on Diplomatic History at Johns Hopkins Univ., 1932 and 1937; Professor of American History and Institutions, Cambridge Univ., 1945-46, MA Camb., 1946. Official historian for Overseas Branch of Office of War Information for San Francisco Conf. Lectures, Nat. War College, US, 1946-; Lectures, British Universities and RIIA, 1948 and 1952; Visiting Professor, University of Uppsala 1949; Chm. Council, Harvard Foundation for Advanced Study and Research, Harvard Univ., 1951-56. LLD, Union Coll., 1951, LittD, Harvard, 1953. Moderator of Unitarian Churches of US and Canada, 1952-54; Pres., Amer. Hist. Assoc., 1955-56. Pres., Salzburg Seminar in Amer. Studies, 1950-62. Member of Phi Beta Kappa. *Publications:* John Quincy Adams as Secretary of State; The Monroe Doctrine, 1823-26, 1927; The Monroe Doctrine, 1826-67, 1933; The Monroe Doctrine, 1867-1907, 1938; Hands Off! A History of the Monroe Doctrine, 1823-1940, 1941; America and Two Wars, 1944; The United States and the Caribbean, 1947; The Evolution of American Foreign Policy, 1948; The American Approach to Foreign Policy, 1952; The History of The Monroe Doctrine (revised edn, 1955); Charles Evans-Hughes and American Democratic Statesmanship, 1956; Short Biography of Charles Evans Hughes; The New Age of Franklin Roosevelt, 1957; The American Way, 1957; The American Quest for Peace, 1960; The United States and Latin America, 1960; The United States of America: A History (with G. G. Van Deusen), 1962; The American Democracy: its rise to power, 1964; The Yield of the Years, 1969. *Recreations:* bridge and Russian Bank. *Address:* The Brightonian, 1919 Elmwood Avenue, Rochester, NY 14620, USA.

PERKINS, Prof. Donald Hill, FRS 1966; Professor of Elementary Particle Physics, Oxford University, since October 1965; *b* 15 Oct. 1925; *s* of George W. and Gertrude Perkins; *m* 1955, Dorothy Mary (née Maloney); two *d. Educ:* Malet Lambert High School, Hull. BSc London 1945; PhD London 1948; 1851 Senior Scholar, 1948-51. G. A. Wills Research Associate in Physics, Univ. of Bristol, 1951-55; Lawrence Radiation Lab., Univ. of California, 1955-56; Lectr in Physics, 1956-60, Reader in Physics, 1960-65, Univ. of Bristol. Guthrie Medal, Inst. of Physics, 1979. *Publications:* The Study of Elementary Particles by the Photographic Method (with C. F. Powell and P. H. Fowler), 1959; Introduction to High Energy Physics, 1972; about 50 papers and review articles in Nature, Physical Review, Philosophical Magazine,

Physics Letters, Proc. Royal Soc., Nuovo Cimento, etc. *Recreations:* squash, tennis. *Address:* c/o Dept of Nuclear Physics, Keble Road, Oxford.

PERKINS, Dudley; *see* Perkins, G. D. G.

PERKINS, Francis Layton, CBE 1977; DSC 1940; Chairman, Insurance Brokers' Registration Council, since 1977; Solicitor since 1937; *b* 7 Feb. 1912; *s* of Montague Thornton and Madge Perkins; *m* 1st, 1941, Josephine Brice Miller (marr. diss. 1971); one *s* two *d* ; 2nd, 1971, Jill Patricia Greenish. *Educ:* Charterhouse. Served War of 1939-45, Comdr RNVR, in command of minesweepers. Partner in Clifford Turner & Co., 1946; Dir, Hogg Robinson & Capel-Cure Ltd, 1962; Chairman: Hogg Robinson and Gardner Mountain Ltd, 1967-74; Hogg Robinson Group Ltd (formerly Staplegreen Insurance Holdings Ltd), 1971-77; Dir, Transport Holding Co., 1971-73. Master of Skinners' Company, 1966; Dep. Pres., 1971, Pres., 1972-77, Corp. of Insurance Brokers; Chairman: UK Insurance Brokers European Cttee, 1973-80; British Insurance Brokers' Assoc., 1976-80; Common Mkt Cttee, Bureau International des Producteurs d'Assurances et de Réassurances, 1977-79; Dep. Chm., Cttee of Management, Inst. of Laryngology and Otology, 1976-78 (Mem., 1974-78); Mem. Council, Industrial Soc., 1976- (Treasurer, 1976-). Governor and Chm. of Cttee, Tonbridge Sch.; Governor: Sutton's Hospital in Charterhouse, 1974-; Royal National Throat, Nose and Ear Hospital, 1974-80; Chairman: Fund Raising Cttee, St Bartholomew's Hosp., 1980; City of London and Thames Estuary Panel, Duke of Edinburgh's 1974 Commonwealth Conf.; Trustee, Barts Res. Develt Trust. *Recreations:* tennis, golf, fishing. *Address:* Flat 9, 34 Sloane Court West, SW3. *T:* 01-730 9775; Seawinds, Sandwich Bay, Kent. *T:* Sandwich 612832. *Clubs:* Boodle's, MCC, All England Lawn Tennis.

PERKINS, (George) Dudley (Gwynne), MA; Director-General of the Port of London Authority, 1964-71; *b* 19 March 1911; *s* of Gwynne Oliver Perkins and Sarah Perkins; *m* 1st, 1939, Enid Prys-Jones (*d* 1943); one *d* ; 2nd, 1946, Pamela Marigo Blake (*d* 1980); one *d. Educ:* Clifton College (Scholar); King's College, Cambridge (Choral Scholar; 1st cl. hons Eng. Lit.). Solicitor, 1937; Asst Legal Adviser, BBC, 1945-48; Asst Legal Adviser, National Coal Board, 1948-51; Chief Solicitor, PLA, 1955-62; Jt Dep. General Manager, PLA, 1962-64. Member: Council of Law Society, 1954-62; Central Transport Consultative Cttee, 1962-69; SE Economic Planning Council, 1966-71; Performing Right Tribunal, 1974-. Governor, Clifton Coll., 1969-. FCIT; FBIM. Regular broadcaster on Can I Help You and other broadcasts on law and current affairs, 1950-62. *Publications:* Can I Help You, 1959; Family Lawyer, 1962. *Recreations:* music, walking. *Address:* 63 Netherhall Gardens, Hampstead, NW3 5RE. *T:* 01-435 0609. *Clubs:* Garrick, MCC.

PERKINS, Air Vice-Marshal Irwyn Morse, MBE 1957; Principal Medical Officer, Royal Air Force Support Command, 1977-80, retired; Medical Officer, Royal Military College of Science; *b* 15 Dec. 1920; *s* of William Lewis Perkins and Gwenllian Perkins, Ystalyfera, Swansea; *m* 1948, Royce Villiers Thompson, *d* of William Stanley Thompson and Zöe Thompson, The Mountain, Tangier; one *s* one *d. Educ:* Pontardawe, Swansea; St Mary's Hospital, Paddington, W2. MRCS, LRCP 1945; MFCM 1973. Commnd RAF, 1946; SMO: RAF Gibraltar, 1946-49; several flying stations in UK; RAF Laarbruch, Germany, 1958-61; RAF Khormaksar, Aden, 1964-66; DPMO, Bomber and Strike Commands, 1966-69; CO RAF Hospital, Ely, Cambs, 1969-72; PMO RAF Germany, 1972-75; CO PMRAF Hospital, Halton, 1975-77. Hon. Surgeon to HM the Queen, 1975-80. *Recreations:* sporting shooting, bodging. *Address:* 5 Redlands Close, Highworth, Swindon, Wilts SN6 7SN. *T:* Highworth 765097. *Club:* Royal Air Force.

PERKINS, James Alfred, MA, PhD; Chairman and Chief Executive Officer, International Council for Educational Development, since 1970; *b* 11 Oct. 1911; *s* of H. Norman Perkins and Emily (née Taylor); *m* 1st, 1938, Jean Bredin (*d* 1970); two *s* three *d* ; 2nd, 1971, Ruth B. Aall; one step *s* three step *d. Educ:* Swarthmore Coll., Pa (AB); Princeton Univ., NJ (MA, PhD). Instructor Polit. Sci., Princeton Univ., 1937-39; Asst Prof. and Asst Dir, Sch. of Public and Internat. Affairs, Princeton, 1939-41; Dir, Pulp and Paper Div., Office of Price Admin., 1941-43; Asst to Administrator, For. Econ. Admin., 1943-45; Vice-Pres. Swarthmore Coll., 1945-50; Exec. Associate, Carnegie Corp. of NY, 1950-51; Dep. Chm. (on leave) Res. and Develt Bd, Dept of Defense, 1951-52; Vice-Pres., Carnegie Corp. of NY, 1951-63; Pres., Cornell Univ., 1963-69. Carnegie Foundn for the Advancement of Teaching: Sec. 1954-55; Vice-Pres., 1955-63. Chm., Pres. Johnson's Gen. Adv. Cttee on Foreign Assistance Prog., 1965-68; Trustee: Rand Corp., 1961-71; United Negro Coll. Fund (Chm. of Bd), 1965-69; Educl Testing Service, 1964-68; Dir Emeritus, Council on Foreign Relations; Mem. Gen. Adv. Cttee of US Arms Control and Disarmament Agency, 1963-; Chm. NY Regents Adv. Cttee on Educational Leadership, 1963-67. Member: Bd of Directors, Chase Manhattan Bank, 1967-75; Stevenson Memorial Fund, 1966-; Trustee, Aspen Inst., 1973-; Director: Overseas Develt Council, 1969-; Center for Inter-Amer. Relations, 1969-; Inst. of Internat. Educn, 1981-. Chm., President Carter's Commn on Foreign Language and Internat. Studies, 1978-79. Mem. Society of Friends, Swarthmore, Pa. Hon. LLD and Hon. LHD various colls and univs. *Publications:* The University in Transition, 1966; Higher Education: from Autonomy to Systems, 1972; The University as an Organization, 1973; contrib. to: Public Admin. Review, Amer. Polit. Sci. Review, Educational Record, etc. *Address:* (home) 94 North Road, Princeton, NJ 08540, USA; (office) 680 Fifth Avenue, New York City, NY 10019, USA. *Clubs:* Century Association, Coffee House, University (NYC).

PERKINS, Maj.-Gen. Kenneth, CB 1977; MBE 1955; DFC 1953; with British Aerospace Dynamics Group, since 1982; *b* 15 Aug. 1926; *s* of George Samuel Perkins and Arabella Sarah Perkins (*née* Wise); *m* 1949, Anne Theresa Barry; three *d. Educ:* Lewes County Sch. for Boys; New Coll., Oxford. Enlisted 1944; commnd RA 1946; various appts in Middle and Far East, BAOR and UK until 1965, incl. Korean War, Malayan Emergency, and Staff Coll. Quetta 1958; Instructor, Staff Coll. Camberley, 1965-66; CO 1st Regt Royal Horse Artillery, 1967-69; GSO 1 Singapore, 1970; Comdr 24 Bde, 1971-72; RCDS 1973; Central Staff, MoD, 1974; Maj.-Gen., 1975; Comdr, Sultan's Armed Forces, Oman, 1975-77 (successfully concluded Dohfar War); Asst Chief of Defence Staff (Ops), 1977-80; Dir, Military Assistance Office, MoD, 1980-82. Col Comdt, RA, 1980-. Selangor Distinguished Conduct Medal (Malaya), 1955; Hashemite Order of Independence, first class, 1975; Order of Oman, 1977. *Publications:* articles in various Service jls. *Recreations:* painting, physical exercise. *Address:* c/o National Westminster Bank Ltd, Seaford, Sussex. *Club:* Army and Navy.

PERKINS, Air Vice-Marshal Maxwell Edmund Massy, CB 1962; CBE 1957; Director of Engineering, Aviation Division, Smiths Industries Ltd, retired; *b* Portsmouth, Hants, 22 Aug. 1907; *s* of late Donald Maxwell Perkins; *m* 1st, 1934, Helena Joan Penelope (*d* 1973), *d* of Herbert John Newberry, Hitchin; one *s* two *d*; 2nd, 1974, Sylvia Mary, *widow* of Willson Gatward, Hitchin, Herts. *Educ:* Portsmouth College; London University (BA). Entered RAF, 1929; 13 Sqdn, 1930-32; India, 1934-38. Served War of 1939-45, Bomber Command and Burma; America, 1952-54; STSO Fighter Command, 1954-56; Commandant, St Athan, 1956-58; Senior Technical Staff Officer, Bomber Command, 1958-61; Dir-Gen. of Engineering, Air Min., 1961-64, retired. Air Cdre, 1957; Air Vice-Marshal, 1961. CEng 1966, FIMechE (MIMechE 1957); FRAeS 1960. Co. Councillor, Herts, 1977-81. *Recreations:* sailing, golf. *Address:* Little Court, London Road, Hitchin, Herts. *Clubs:* Royal Air Force; Letchworth Golf.

PERKINS, Sir Robert Dempster, Kt 1954; *b* 1903; *s* of late W. Frank Perkins; *m* 1944, Lady Norman, *widow* of Sir Nigel Norman, 2nd Bt. *Educ:* Eton; Trinity Coll., Cambridge, MA. Mechanical Engineer. MP (C) Stroud (by-election May), 1931-45; MP (C) Stroud and Thornbury Division of Gloucestershire, 1950-55; Parliamentary Secretary, Ministry of Civil Aviation, 1945. *Recreations:* aviation and fishing. *Address:* The Manor House, Downton, Wilts.

PERKINS, Sir Walter Robert Dempster; *see* Perkins, Sir R. D.

PERKS, John Clifford, MC 1944; TD; **His Honour Judge Perks;** a Circuit Judge (formerly County Court Judge), since 1970; *b* 20 March 1915; *s* of John Hyde Haslewood Perks and Frances Mary Perks; *m* 1940, Ruth Dyke Perks (*née* Appleby); two *s* (one *s* two *d* decd). *Educ:* Blundell's; Balliol Coll., Oxford. Called to Bar, Inner Temple, 1938; joined Western Circuit; Chancellor, diocese of Bristol, 1950-71; Dep. Chm., Devon QS, 1965-71. *Recreation:* castles. *Address:* 32 Melbury Close, Chislehurst, Kent.

PERLMAN, Itzhak; violinist; *b* Tel Aviv, 31 Aug. 1945; *s* of Chaim and Shoshana Perlman; *m* 1967, Toby Lynn Friedlander; two *s* two *d*. Studied at Tel Aviv Acad. of Music with Ryvka Goldgart, and at Juilliard Sch., NY, under Dorothy Delay and Ivan Galamian. First solo recital at age of 10 in Israel; New York début, 1958. Leventritt Meml Award, NY, 1964. Has toured extensively in USA and played with all major American symphony orchestras; recital tours of Canada, South America, Europe, Israel, Far East and Australia; recorded many standard works for violin. *Recreations:* cooking Chinese style and watching basketball. *Address:* c/o Sheldon Gold, ICM Artists Ltd, 40 West 57th Street, New York, NY 10019, USA.

PEROWNE, Rear-Adm. Benjamin Cubitt, CB 1978; General Secretary, Royal United Kingdom Beneficent Association, since 1978; *b* 18 Feb. 1921; *s* of late Bernard Cubitt Perowne and of Gertrude Dorothy Perowne; *m* 1946, Phyllis Marjorie, *d* of late Cdre R. D. Peel, RNR, Southampton; two *s* one *d. Educ:* Culford Sch. Joined RN, 1939; Sec. to Adm. Sir Deric Holland-Martin, GCB, DSO, DSC, 1955-64; Acting Captain, 1957-64, Captain 1966; Staff, Chief of Personnel and Logistics, 1967-70; (Cdre, 1969-70); comd, HMS Cochrane, 1971-73; Dir of Defence Policy, 1973-75 (Cdre); Dir, Management and Support Intelligence, 1976-78, also Chief Naval Supply and Secretariat Officer, 1977-78. *Recreations:* shooting, gardening. *Address:* c/o Barclays Bank, Haslemere, Surrey. *Club:* Army and Navy.

PEROWNE, Dame Freya; *see* Stark, Dame Freya.

PEROWNE, Stewart Henry, OBE 1944; FSA; Orientalist and Historian; Colonial Administrative Service (retired); *b* 17 June 1901; 3rd *s* of late Arthur William Thomson Perowne, DD, Bishop of Worcester, and late Helena Frances Oldnall-Russell; *m* 1947, Freya Madeline Stark (*see* Dame Freya Stark). *Educ:* Haileybury Coll. (champion sprinter); Corpus Christi Coll., Cambridge (Hon. Fellow, 1981); Harvard Univ., USA. BA 1923, MA 1931, Cambridge. Joined Palestine Government Education Service, 1927; Administrative Service, 1930 (Press Officer 1931); Asst District Commissioner, Galilee, 1934; Asst Secretary Malta, 1934 (pioneered Pasteurization); Political Officer, Aden Prot., 1937; recovered inscriptions and sculpture from Imadia and Beihan; Arabic Programme Organiser, BBC, 1938 (pioneered programme, English by Radio); Information Officer, Aden, 1939; Public Relations Attaché, British Embassy, Baghdad, 1941; Oriental

Counsellor, 1944; Colonial Secretary, Barbados, 1947-51; seconded as Principal Adviser (Interior), Cyrenaica, 1950-51; retired 1951. Discovered ancient city of Aziris, 1951. Adviser, UK delegation to UN Assembly, Paris, Nov. 1951. Helped design stamps for Malta, 1936, Aden, 1938, Barbados, 1949, Libya, 1951; currency notes for W. Indies Federation, 1949, and Libya, 1951; Assistant to the Bishop in Jerusalem for Refugee work, 1952; designer and supervisor of Refugee model villages. FSA 1957. KStJ 1954. Coronation Medal, 1937; Iraq Coronation Medal, 1953; Metropolitan Police Mounted Officers certificate. Member, C. of E. Foreign Relations Council. *Publications:* The One Remains, 1954; Herod the Great, 1956; The Later Herods, 1958; Hadrian, 1960; Cæsars and Saints, 1962; The Pilgrim's Companion in Jerusalem and Bethlehem, 1964; The Pilgrim's Companion in Roman Rome, 1964; The Pilgrim's Companion in Athens, 1964; Jerusalem, 1965; The End of the Roman World, 1966; The Death of the Roman Republic: from 146 BC to the birth of the Roman Empire, 1969; Roman Mythology, 1969; (contrib.) Ancient Cities of the Middle East, 1970; The Siege within the Walls: Malta 1940-43, 1970; Rome, 1971; The Journeys of St Paul, 1973; The Caesars' Wives, 1974; The Archaeology of Greece and the Aegean, 1974; Holy Places of Christendom, 1976; articles in Encyclopædia Britannica, The Times, History Today, etc. *Recreations:* horses, the arts, archæology. *Address:* 44 Arminger Road, W12 7BB. *T:* 01-743 8363. *Clubs:* Travellers'; Casino (1852) Malta; Savannah (Bridgetown); Phoenix-SK (Harvard).

PERRETT, Desmond Seymour; QC 1980; a Recorder of the Crown Court, since 1978; *b* 22 April 1937; *s* of His Honour Judge Perrett, *qv*; *m* 1961, Pauline Merriel, *yr d* of late Paul Robert Buchan May, ICS, and of Esme May; one *s* one *d. Educ:* Westminster Sch. National Service, RN, 1955-57: midshipman RNVR, 1955; active service, Suez, 1956, and Cyprus, 1957; Sub-Lieut RNVR, 1958. Called to the Bar, Gray's Inn, 1962; Oxford Circuit, 1963-72; Midland and Oxford Circuit, 1972-. *Recreations:* cricket, fishing, cooking. *Address:* The Old Tap House, Upper Wootton, Basingstoke, Hants. *T:* Basingstoke 850027; 2 Crown Office Row, Temple, EC4Y 7HJ. *T:* 01-353 9337. *Club:* MCC.

PERRETT, His Honour John, JP; a Circuit Judge (formerly a Judge of County Courts), 1969-81; *b* 22 Oct. 1906; *er s* of late Joseph and Alice Perrett, Birmingham; *m* 1933, Elizabeth Mary, *y d* of late William Seymour, Nenagh, Co. Tipperary; two *s* two *d. Educ:* St Anne's RC and Stratford Road Schools, Birmingham; King's Coll., Strand, WC2. Entered office of Philip Baker & Co., Solicitors, Birmingham, 1922; joined late Alfred W. Fryzer, Solicitor, Arundel St, WC2, 1925; joined Herbert Baron & Co., Solicitors, Queen Victoria St, EC4, 1934. Served War of 1939-45: RAPC, 1939-45; RASC, 1945. Called to Bar, Gray's Inn, 1946; practised in London and on Midland Circuit; Dep. Chm., Warwicks QS, 1970-71; JP Warwicks, 1970. *Address:* 9 The Close, Lichfield, Staffs. *T:* Lichfield 52320.

See also D. S. Perrett, G. H. Rooke.

PERRIN, John Henry; *b* 14 Jan. 1916; *s* of Walter William Perrin, Faringdon and Sonning, Berks, and Amelia (*née* Honey), Oxford; *m* 1940, Doris Winifred Barrington-Brider; two *s. Educ:* Minchenden Sch.; London Univ. HM Customs and Excise; Royal Navy, 1939-46; Min. of Agriculture, 1948-76: Principal Private Sec. to Minister (Lord Amory), 1955-57; Regional Controller, Eastern Region, 1957-68; Under Sec., 1968-76. Dir-Gen., British Agricl Export Council, 1976-77. Inspector, Public Inquiries, Depts of the Environment and Transport, 1978-. *Recreations:* painting, Chinese porcelain, soccer, sailing. *Clubs:* Naval, Civil Service, Royal Yachting.

PERRIN, Sir Michael (Willcox), Kt 1967; CBE 1952 (OBE 1946); FRSC; Chairman, The Wellcome Foundation Ltd, 1953-70; Director: Inveresk Research International, 1961-74 (Chairman, 1971-73); Radiochemical Centre Ltd, 1971-75; *b* 13 Sept. 1905; *s* of late Bishop W. W. Perrin; *m* 1934, Nancy May, *d* of late Bishop C. E. Curzon; one *s* one *d. Educ:* Winchester; New Coll., Oxford (BA, BSc). Post-graduate research, Toronto Univ. (MA), 1928-29; Amsterdam Univ., 1929-33; ICI (Alkali) Research Dept, Northwich, 1933-38; Asst Director, Tube Alloys (Atomic Energy), DSIR, 1941-46; Dep. Controller, Atomic Energy (Technical Policy), Ministry of Supply, 1946-51; Research Adviser, ICI, 1951-52. Chm. (Treasurer) Bd of Governors, St Bartholomew's Hosp. and Pres., Med. Coll. of St Bartholomew's Hosp., 1960-69; Member: Council, Royal Veterinary Coll., London Univ., 1967-76 (Chm. 1967-72); Council, Sch. of Pharmacy, London Univ., 1963-76; Central Adv. Council for Science and Technology, 1969-70; Governing Body, British Postgrad. Med. Fedn, 1970-77 (Chm., 1972-77). Trustee, British Museum (Natural History), 1974-. Chm. Council, Roedean Sch., 1974-79. Hon. DSc Univ. of British Columbia, 1969. *Publications:* papers in scientific and technical journals. *Address:* 14 Christchurch Hill, Hampstead, NW3 1LB. *T:* 01-794 3064. *Club:* Athenæum.

PERRING, John Raymond, TD 1965; Chairman, Perring Furnishings Ltd, since 1981; *b* 7 July 1931; *e s* and *heir* of Sir Ralph Perring, Bt, *qv*; *m* 1961, Ella Christine, *e d* of late A. G. Pelham and Mrs Ann Pelham; two *s* two *d. Educ:* Stowe School. Nat. Service, then TA, RA, 1949-60; Royal Fusiliers (City of London), 1960-65. Joined family furnishing business, 1951, Dir 1957, Jt Man. Dir 1964, Vice-Chm., 1972. One of HM Lieutenants of City of London, 1963-; Mem. Ct of Assistants, Merchant Taylors' Co., 1980-; Master, Furniture Makers' Co., 1978; Nat. Pres., Nat. Assoc. of Retail Furnishers, 1971-73; Chm., Retail Alliance, 1973-75; Mem. Council, Retail Consortium, 1972-80; Mem. EDC (Distributive Trades), 1974-78. FRSA. *Recreations:*

sailing, ski-ing, swimming, gardening. *Address:* 21 Somerset Road, Wimbledon, SW19. *T:* 01-946 8971. *Clubs:* City Livery, Royal Automobile; Royal Wimbledon Golf; Bembridge Sailing.

PERRING, Sir Ralph (Edgar), 1st Bt *cr* 1963; Kt 1960; Chairman, Perring Furnishings Ltd; *b* 23 March 1905; *yr s* of late Colonel Sir John Perring, DL, JP; *m* 1928, Ethel Mary, OStJ, *o d* of late Henry T. Johnson, Putney; two *s* (and one *s* decd). *Educ:* University College Sch., London. Lieut, RA (TA) 1938–40, invalided. Member Court of Common Council (Ward of Cripplegate), 1948–51; Alderman of City of London (Langbourn Ward), 1951–75, one of HM Lieutenants of the City of London, and Sheriff, 1958–59. Lord Mayor of London, 1962–63. Chairman, Spitalfields Market Cttee, 1951–52; JP County of London, 1943–; Member: LCC for Cities of London and Westminster, 1952–55; County of London Licensing Planning Cttee; New Guildford Cathedral Council; Consumer Advisory Council, BSI, 1955–59; Bd of Governors, E-SU, 1976–. Governor: St Bartholomew's Hospital, 1964–69; Imperial College of Science and Technology, 1964–67; Christ's Hospital; Vice-Chairman, BNEC Cttee for Exports to Canada, 1964–67, Chairman, 1968–70; Dir, Confederation Life Insurance Co. of Canada, 1969–81. Vice-President, Royal Bridewell Hospital (King Edward's Sch., Witley, 1964–75); Trustee, Morden Coll., Blackheath, 1970–, Chm. 1979–. Master Worshipful Company of Tin Plate Workers, 1944–45; Master, Worshipful Company of Painters-Stainers, 1977–78; Mem. Court, Farmers' Co.; President Langbourn Ward Club, 1951–75. FRSA 1975. KStJ. Grand Cross of Merit (Republic of Germany), 1959; Order of Homayoun (Iran), 1959; Grand Officer, Order of Leopold (Belgium), 1963; Knight Commander, Royal Order of George I (Greece), 1963; Commander la Valeur Camerounaise, 1963. *Heir: s* John Raymond Perring, *qv. Address:* 15 Burghley House, Somerset Road, Wimbledon, SW19. *T:* 01-946 3433. *Clubs:* Constitutional, Royal Automobile, City Livery (President, 1951–52).

PERRINS, Wesley, MBE 1952; an official of Municipal and General Workers' Union, Birmingham District Secretary; Member, Worcestershire County Council until 1974 (formerly Alderman); formerly Member, West Midlands Economic Planning Council; *b* 21 Sept. 1905; *s* of Councillor Amos Perrins, Stourbridge; *m* 1932, Mary, *d* of Charles Evans; one *s* one *d. Educ:* Wollescote Council Sch.; Upper Standard Sch., Lye. MP (Lab) Yardley Division of Birmingham, 1945–50. Member of: Lye & Wollescote UDC, 1928–31; Stourbridge Borough Council, 1931–46, 1971. Mem., Court of Governors, Birmingham Univ. *Address:* Cromlech Cottage, 19 Walker Avenue, Wollescote, Stourbridge, West Midlands. *T:* Stourbridge 4640.

PERRIS, Sir David (Arthur), Kt 1977; MBE 1970; JP; Secretary, Trades Union Congress West Midlands Regional Council, since 1974; Secretary, Birmingham Trades Council, since 1966; Chairman, National Health Service National Training Council, since 1975; Director, Central Independent Television Ltd, since 1982 (Vice-Chairman, West Midlands Board); *b* 25 May 1929; *s* of Arthur Perris; *m* 1955, Constance Parkes, BPharm, FPS; one *s* one *d. Educ:* Sparkhill Commercial Sch., Birmingham. Film distribution industry, 1944–61; Reed Paper Group, 1961–65; Vice-Chm., ATV Midlands Ltd, 1980–81. Chairman: Birmingham Regional Hosp. Bd, 1970–74; West Midlands RHA, 1974–82; Mem. Bd of Governors: United Birmingham Hosps, 1965–74; Birmingham Coll. of Commerce, 1966–70; Mem., Birmingham Children's Hosp. House Cttee, 1958–71 (Chm. 1967–71); Vice-Chm., Birmingham Hosp. Saturday Fund, 1975–; Mem., W Mids Econ. Planning Council, 1968–70; Life Governor, Univ. of Birmingham, 1972; Mem. Convocation, Univ. of Aston in Birmingham, 1975–; Sec., Polytechnic Bursaries Cttee, 1966–; Mem., Midlands Postal Bd, 1974–; Chm. Magistrates' Assoc., Birmingham Br., 1975–. Hon. LLD Birmingham, 1981. JP Birmingham, 1961. *Recreations:* cinema, reading. *Address:* 24 Mayfield Road, Moseley, Birmingham B13 9HJ. *T:* 021-449 3652.

PERROTT, Sir Donald (Cyril Vincent), KBE 1949; *b* 12 April 1902; *s* of late Frederick John Perrott and of Alice Perrott, Southampton; *m* 1st, 1925, Marjorie May (*d* 1969), *d* of late William Holway, Taunton; one *s*; 2nd, 1969, Mrs L. L. Byre. *Educ:* Taunton's' Sch., Southampton; University College, Southampton. Inland Revenue Dept, 1920; Ministry of Aircraft Production, 1941; Ministry of Supply, 1942; Dep. Secretary Ministry of Food, 1947–49; Deputy Chairman, Overseas Food Corporation, 1949–51; Chairman: Queensland British Food Corporation, 1950–53; British Ministry of Supply, European Purchasing Commission, 1951–52; Interdepartmental Cttee, Woolwich Arsenal, 1953; Secretary, Department of Atomic Energy, 1954 and Member for Finance and Administration of Atomic Energy Authority, 1954–60; Member, Governing Board of National Institute for Research in Nuclear Science, 1957–60. *Recreations:* golf and bridge. *Address:* 5 Plane Tree House, Duchess of Bedford's Walk, W8 7QT.

PERROW, (Joseph) Howard; Chairman, Co-operative Union Ltd, since 1975; Chief Executive Officer and Secretary, Greater Lancastria Co-operative Society Ltd, since 1976; *b* 18 Nov. 1923; *s* of Joseph and Mary Elizabeth Perrow; *m* 1947, Lorraine Strick; two *s. Educ:* St Just, Penzance, Cornwall; Co-operative Coll., Stanford Hall, Leics (CSD). Joined Penzance Co-operative Soc., 1940. Served RAF, 1943–47. Various managerial positions in Co-operative Movement: in W Cornwall, with CRS N Devon, Carmarthen Soc., Silverdale (Staffs) and Burslem Socs; Mem., Co-operative Union Central Exec., 1966–, Vice-Chm., 1973–75; Vice-Chm., NW Sectional Bd, 1970–75; Director: CWS, 1970–; Nat. Co-operative Chemists, 1973–; Greater Manchester Independent Radio, 1973–; Mem., Central Cttee, Internat. Co-

operative Alliance, 1975–; Mem. Council (rep. Co-operative Union), Retail Consortium, 1976–. President, Co-operative Congress, 1979. *Recreations:* football, cricket. *Address:* Ravenscourt, The Clough, Chorley New Road, Bolton, Lancs BL1 5BB. *T:* Bolton 44017.

PERRY, family name of **Baron Perry of Walton.**

PERRY OF WALTON, Baron *cr* 1979 (Life Peer), of Walton, Bucks; **Walter Laing Macdonald Perry,** Kt 1974; OBE 1957; FRSE; Vice-Chancellor, The Open University, 1969–80, Fellow, since 1981; *b* 16 June 1921; *s* of Fletcher S. Perry and Flora M. Macdonald; *m* 1st, 1946, Anne Elizabeth Grant (marr. diss. 1971); three *s*; 2nd, 1971, Catherine Hilda Crawley; two *s* one *d. Educ:* Ayr Acad.; Dundee High Sch. MB, ChB 1943, MD 1948, DSc 1958 (University of St Andrews); MRCP (Edinburgh), 1963; FRCPE 1967; FRCP 1978; Fellow, UCL, 1981–. Medical Officer, Colonial Medical Service (Nigeria), 1944–46; Medical Officer, RAF, 1946–47; Member of Staff, Medical Research Council, 1947–52; Director, Department of Biological Standards, National Institute for Medical Research, 1952–58. Prof. of Pharmacology, University of Edinburgh, 1958–68, Vice-Principal, 1967–68. Member, British Pharmacopœia Commission, 1952–68; Secretary, British Pharmacological Society, 1957–61. Chairman: Community Radio Milton Keynes, 1979; Living Tapes Ltd, 1980; Research Defence Soc., 1979; Delegacy of Goldsmiths' Coll., 1981. Vice-Chm., SDP peers in House of Lords, 1981–. Hon. DSc Bradford, 1974; Hon. LLD Dundee, 1975; Hon. DHL: Maryland, 1978; State Univ. of NY, 1982; Hon. Dr Athabasca, 1979; DUniv: Stirling, 1980; Open, 1981; Hon. DLitt Deakin Univ., Australia, 1981. *Publications:* Open University, 1976; papers in Journal of Physiology, British Journal of Pharmacology and Chemo-therapy, etc. *Recreations:* making music and playing games. *Address:* The Open University, Sherwood House, Sherwood Drive, Bletchley, Milton Keynes. *Clubs:* Savage; Scottish Arts.

PERRY, Hon. Sir (Alan) Clifford, Kt 1976; Senior Puisne Judge, Supreme Court of New Zealand, 1976–79 (Judge, 1962); *b* 10 July 1907; *s* of George Perry and Agnes Mary Jenkins; *m* 1943, Barbara Jean Head; two *s* one *d. Educ:* Hornby Primary Sch.; Christ's Coll., Christchurch; Canterbury University Coll., Univ. of NZ (LLM, 2nd Cl. Hons). Admitted barrister and solicitor, 1928; Partner, Wilding & Acland (legal firm), 1935–62; part-time Lectr in Commercial Law, Canterbury University Coll., 1939–47. Chairman Court of Enquiry: into fire on M. V. Holmburn, 1959; into loss of M. V. Holmglen, 1960. Pres., Canterbury Dist Law Soc., 1950; Chm., Council of Legal Educn, 1975–79 (Mem., 1954–62 and 1964–79); Mem., Disciplin. Cttee, NZ Law Soc., 1952–62. Silver Jubilee Medal, 1977. Royal Danish Consul for S Island, NZ, 1948–62. Chevalier, Royal Order of Dannebrog, 1955. *Recreations:* reading, cottage in Arthur's Pass National Park. *Address:* 54 Mountain Road, Epsom, Auckland 3, New Zealand. *T:* 601-035. *Clubs:* Northern (Auckland); Canterbury (Christchurch).

PERRY, Alan Joseph; Assistant Secretary, HM Treasury, since 1980; *b* 17 Jan. 1930; *s* of late Joseph and Elsie Perry; *m* 1961, Vivien Anne Ball; two *s. Educ:* John Bright Grammar Sch., Llandudno; Dartford Grammar Sch. Served RE, 1948–50. HM Treasury, 1951–68 and 1970–78; CSD, 1968–70; Principal 1968, Asst Sec. 1976; Counsellor (Economic), Washington, 1978–80. *Address:* c/o HM Treasury, Parliament Street, SW1.

See also P. G. Perry.

PERRY, Charles Bruce; Professor of Medicine, University of Bristol, 1935–69, Emeritus since 1969; *b* 1903; *s* of Charles E. and Sarah Duthie Perry; *m* 1929, Mildred Bernice Harvey; three *d. Educ:* Bristol Grammar Sch.; University of Bristol, MB, ChB 1926; FRCP, 1936; MD Bristol, 1928; Physician, Bristol Royal Hospital for Sick Children and Women, 1928; Physician, Winford Orthopædic Hospital, 1930; Buckston Browne Prize, Harveian Society of London, 1929; Markham Skeritt Memorial Prize, 1931; Asst Physician, Bristol General Hospital, 1933. Lectures: Long Fox Memorial, 1943; Bradshaw, RCP, 1944; Lumleian, RCP, 1969; Carey Coombs, Univ. of Bristol, 1969; Cyril Fernando Meml, Ceylon, 1971. Pro-Vice-Chancellor, University of Bristol, 1958–61; President Assoc. of Physicians of Great Britain and Ireland, 1961–62; Chairman, British Cardiac Society, 1961–62; Censor, RCP, 1962–64; Medical Mem., Pensions Appeals Tribunals, 1969–79. *Publications:* Bacterial Endocarditis, 1936; The Bristol Royal Infirmary 1904–1974, 1981; various papers in the Medical Press dealing with research in Diseases of the Heart. *Address:* Beechfield, 54 Grove Road, Coombe Dingle, Bristol BS9 2RR. *T:* Bristol 682713.

PERRY, Hon. Sir Clifford; see Perry, Hon. Sir A. C.

PERRY, David Howard; Chief of Defence Procurement, Ministry of Defence, from June 1983; *b* 13 April 1931; *s* of Howard Dace Perry and Annie Evelyn Perry; *m* 1961, Rosemary Grigg; one *s* two *d. Educ:* Berkhamsted Sch.; Pembroke Coll., Cambridge (MA). CEng, MRAeS. Joined Aero Dept, RAE, 1954; Aero Flt Div., 1954–66; Aero Projs Div., 1966–71; Head of Dynamics Div., 1971–73; RCDS, 1974; Head of Systems Assessment Dept, RAE, 1975–77; Ministry of Defence (Procurement Executive): Dir-Gen. Future Projects, 1978–80; Dir-Gen. Aircraft 1, 1980–81; Dep. Controller of Aircraft, 1981–82, Controller 1982. *Recreations:* gardening, walking, painting. *Address:* 23 Rectory Road, Farnborough, Hants. *T:* Farnborough 541117.

PERRY, Sir David Norman; see Perry, Sir Norman.

PERRY, Ernest George; b 25 April 1908; British; m 1950, Edna Joyce Perks-Mankelow; one s. Educ: LCC secondary school. Textiles, 1923-33; Insurance, 1933-64. Member Battersea Borough Council, 1934-65 (Mayor of Battersea, 1955-56); Alderman, London Borough of Wandsworth, 1964-72. MP (Lab) Battersea S, 1964-74, Wandsworth, Battersea S, 1974-79; Asst Govt Whip, 1968-69; Lord Commissioner, HM Treasury, 1969-70; an Opposition Whip, 1970-74; an Asst Govt Whip, 1974-75. Served with Royal Artillery, 1939-46: Indian Army and Indian Artillery (Troop Sgt); Far East, 1942-45. Recreations: local government, sport, reading. Address: 30 Old Park Avenue, Balham, SW12.

PERRY, Frances Mary, (Mrs Roy Hay), MBE 1962; VMH 1971; horticulturist; b 19 Feb. 1907; d of Richard and Isabella Everett; m 1st, 1930, Gerald Amos Perry (d 1964); one s (and one s decd); 2nd, 1977, Robert Edwin Hay, qv. Educ: Enfield County Sch.; Swanley Horticultural Coll. (later Wye Coll.). Diploma in Horticulture. Organiser for Agricl and Horticultural Educn, Mddx CC, 1943; Principal, Norwood Hall Inst. and Coll. of Horticulture, 1953-67. Veitch Meml Medal in Gold, RHS, 1964; Sara Francis Chapman Medal, Garden Club of America, 1973. Publications: Water Gardening, 1938; The Herbaceous Border, 1949; The Garden Pool, 1954; The Woman Gardener, 1955; (as Charles Hewitt) Flower Arrangement, 1955; Guide to Border Plants, 1957; Making Things Grow, 1960; Shrubs & Trees for the Smaller Garden, 1961; Penguin Water Gardens, 1962; Colour in the Garden, 1964; Book of Flowering Bulbs, Corms & Tubers, 1966; Flowers of the World, 1972; Gardening in Colour, 1972; Plants & Flowers, 1974; Good Gardeners Guide, 1976; Beautiful Leaved Plants, 1979; Water Garden, 1981; (with Roy Hay) Tropical and Subtropical Plants, 1982. Recreations: flower stamps, photography. Address: Bulls Cross Cottage, Enfield, Mddx EN2 9HE.

PERRY, George Henry; b 24 Aug. 1920; s of Arthur and Elizabeth Perry; m 1944, Ida Garner; two d. Educ: elementary sch. and technical college. Engineering Apprentice, 1934-41. Naval Artificer, 1941-46 (Atlantic and Italy Stars; 1939-45 Star). Railway Fitter, 1946-66. Derby Town Councillor, 1955-66. Chairman: Derby Water Cttee, 1957-61; S Derbys Water Board, 1961-66; Derby Labour Party, 1961-62; Secretary, Derby Trades Council, 1961-66. Contested (Lab) Harborough, 1964; MP (Lab) Nottingham South, 1966-70. Recreation: walking. Address: 123 Hawthorn Street, Derby. T: Derby 44687.

PERRY, Ven. John Neville; Rector of Orlestone with Ruckinge and Warehorne, since 1982; b 29 March 1920; s of Robert and Enid Perry; m 1946, Rita Dyson Rooke; four s four d. Educ: The Crypt Gram. Sch., Gloucester; Univ. of Leeds (BA 1941), College of the Resurrection, Mirfield. Asst Curate, All Saints', Poplar, 1943-50; Vicar, St Peter De Beauvoir Town, Hackney, 1950-63; Vicar, St Dunstan with St Catherine, Feltham, Mddx, 1963-75; Rural Dean of Hounslow, 1967-75; Archdeacon of Middlesex, 1975-82. Mem. Latey Cttee on the Age of Majority, 1966-67. Recreations: D-I-Y handyman. Address: The Rectory, Ham Street, Ashford, Kent TN26 2NU.

PERRY, Kenneth Murray Allan, MA, MD (Cantab); FRCP; Consulting Physician to: The London Hospital (Physician, 1946-72); the Royal Masonic Hospital (Physician, 1949-72); Medical Advisor to Central Advisory Council for Training for the Ministry of the Church of England, 1958-70; b 1 Feb. 1909; s of Major H. Perry, Ware, Herts; m 1938, Winifred, d of F. P. Grassi; no c. Educ: Christ's Hospital; Queens' Coll., Cambridge. Kitchener Scholar, 1927; Price University Entrance Scholarship, 1930; Medical Registrar, London Hospital, 1935-38; Dorothy Temple Cross Fellowship, Mass. General Hospital, Boston, 1938-39; Research Fellow, Harvard, 1939. Member of Scientific Staff, Medical Research Council, 1942-46. Ernestine Henry Lecturer, Royal College of Physicians, 1955. Visiting Physician, Papworth Village Settlement, 1946-72; Consulting Physician, Brentwood District and Warley Hospitals, 1947-72. Examiner in Medicine, Universities of Cambridge, London, Liverpool and Hong Kong; Royal College of Physicians, London; Society of Apothecaries of London. UK representative, International Society of Internal Medicine, 1969-72. Member: Assoc. of Physicians of Great Britain and Ireland, 1946-72; Thoracic Society, 1946-72. Miembro Correspondiente Extranjeo de Academia Nacional de Medicina de Buenos Aires. Publications: (with Sir Geoffrey Marshall) Diseases of the Chest, 1952; Pulmonary Œdema, in British Encyclopædia of Medical Practice, 1948; Industrial Medicine in Chambers's Encyclopædia, 1948; (with Sir Thomas Holmes Sellors) Chest Diseases, 1963. Recreations: travel, photography. Address: One Tower House, Old Portsmouth PO1 2JR. T: Portsmouth 21446. Clubs: Royal Over-Seas League, Royal Automobile; Royal Naval and Royal Albert Yacht (Portsmouth).

PERRY, Ven. Michael Charles, MA; Archdeacon of Durham and Canon Residentiary of Durham Cathedral since 1970; b 5 June 1933; o s of late Charlie Perry; b 1963, Margaret, o d of late John Middleton Adshead; two s one d. Educ: Ashby-de-la-Zouch Boys' Grammar Sch.; Trinity Coll., Cambridge (Sen. Schol.); Westcott House, Cambridge. Asst Curate of Berkswich, Stafford, 1958-60; Chaplain, Ripon Hall, Oxford, 1961-63; Chief Asst for Home Publishing, SPCK, 1963-70; Examining Chaplain to Bishop of Lichfield, 1965-74; Sec., Archbishops' Commn on Christian Doctrine, 1967-70. Diocesan Chm., 1970-81, Mem. Council, 1975-81, USPG; Mem., 1981-, Vice-Chm., 1982-, Hosp. Chaplaincies Council, Gen. Synod. Mem., Durham HA, 1982-. Trustee, 1970-, Chm., 1982-, Lord Crewe's Charity. Lectures: Selwyn, NZ, 1976; Marshall Meml, Melbourne, 1976; Beard Meml,

London, 1977. Editor, Church Quarterly, 1968-71; Editor, Christian Parapsychologist, 1977-. Publications: The Easter Enigma, 1959; The Pattern of Matins and Evensong, 1961; (co-author) The Churchman's Companion, 1963; Meet the Prayer Book, 1963; (contrib.) The Miracles and the Resurrection, 1964; (ed) Crisis for Confirmation, 1967; (co-author) Declaring The Faith: The Printed Word, 1969; Sharing in One Bread, 1973; The Resurrection of Man, 1975; The Paradox of Worship, 1977; A Handbook of Parish Worship, 1977; (contrib.) Yes to Women Priests, 1978; (co-author) A Handbook of Parish Finance, 1981. Address: 7 The College, Durham DH1 3EQ. T: Durham 61891. Club: Royal Commonwealth.

PERRY, Sir Norman, Kt 1977; MBE; Consultant: Whakatohea Maori Trust Board; Coast Resource Developments. Knighthood awarded for services to the community and the Maori people, New Zealand. Address: Waiotahi, Opotiki, New Zealand. T: Opotiki 1961; PO Box 162, Opotiki, New Zealand.

PERRY, Mrs Pauline; Chief Inspector, HM Inspectorate of Schools, since 1981; b 15 Oct. 1931; d of John George Embleton Welch and Elizabeth Welch; m 1952, George Walter Perry; three s one d. Educ: Girton Coll., Cambridge (MA). Teaching in English Secondary Sch., Canadian and American High Schs, 1953-54 and 1959-61; High School Evaluator, New England, USA, 1959-61; Research Fellow, Univ. of Manitoba, 1956-57; Lecturer in Philosophy (part-time): Univ. of Manitoba, 1957-59; Univ. of Massachusetts at Salem, 1960-62; Lectr in Education (part-time), Univ. of Exeter, 1962-66; Tutor for In-Service Trng, Berks, 1966-70; Part-time Lectr in Educn, Dept of Educational Studies, Oxford Univ., 1966-70; HM Inspector of Schools, 1970-; Staff Inspector, 1975. Publications: Case Studies in Teaching, 1969; Case Studies in Adolescence, 1970; Your Guide to the Opposite Sex, 1970; articles in various educnl jls; freelance journalism for radio and TV. Recreations: music, walking, cooking. Address: 9 Ditchley Road, Charlbury, Oxford. T: Charlbury 810044. Club: National Liberal.

PERRY, Peter George, JP; Under Secretary, Department of Health and Social Security, since 1975; b 15 Dec. 1923; s of late Joseph and Elsie Perry; m 1957, Marjorie Margaret Stevens; no c. Educ: Dartford Grammar Sch.; London Univ. (LLB). Normandy with Northants Yeomanry, 1944. Joined Min. of Health, 1947; Private Sec. to Minister of State, 1968-70; Asst Sec., 1971. JP City of London, 1974; Freeman, City of London, 1975. Recreations: sailing, squash, opera, wine. Address: 50 Great Brownings, College Road, Dulwich, SE21. T: 01-670 3387. Club: Little Ship.

See also A. J. Perry.

PERRY, Lt-Col Robert Stanley Grosvenor, DSO 1943; DL; b 1909; s of late Robert Grosvenor Perry, CBE, Barton House, Moreton-in-Marsh, Glos; m 1937, Margaret Louisa Elphinstone, o c of Horace Czarnikow; one s. Educ: Harrow; RMC, Sandhurst. 2nd Lieut, 9th Lancers, 1929, Major, 1941; Adjutant, Cheshire Yeomanry, 1938-40; Commanding: 2nd Lothians and Border Yeomanry, 1943; 9th Lancers, 1944-45; served War of 1939-45, Palestine, Western Desert, N Africa, Italy (despatches, wounded twice); Commandant, RACOCTU, 1945-48. One of HM Bodyguard of Hon. Corps of Gentlemen at Arms, 1959-79. High Sheriff of Dorset, 1961. DL Dorset, 1962. Member British Olympic Yachting Team, Helsinki, 1952, Melbourne (Silver Medal), 1956; Winner: Cup of Italy with Vision (5.5 Metre), 1956; One Ton Cup with Royal Thames (6 Metre), 1958. Recreations: yacht racing, foxhunting, National Hunt racing. Address: Crendle Court, Purse Caundle, Sherborne, Dorset. T: Milborne Port 250364. Clubs: Cavalry and Guards, Royal Yacht Squadron.

PERRY, Prof. Samuel Victor, BSc (Liverpool), PhD, ScD (Cantab); FRS 1974; Professor of Biochemistry, since 1959 and Head of Department of Biochemistry, since 1968, University of Birmingham; b 16 July 1918; s of late Samuel and Margaret Perry; m 1948, Maureen Tregent Shaw; one s two d. Educ: King George V Sch., Southport; Liverpool Univ.; Trinity Coll., Cambridge. Served in War of 1939-45, home and N. Africa; Royal Artillery, 1940-46, Captain; POW 1942-45. Research Fellow, Trinity Coll., Cambridge, 1947-51; Commonwealth Fund Fellow, University of Rochester, USA, 1948-49; University Lecturer, Dept of Biochemistry, Cambridge, 1950-59. Member: Standing Cttee for Research on Animals, ARC, 1965-72; Biol Scis and Enzyme Cttees, SERC, 1968-71; Medical Res. Cttee, Muscular Dystrophy Gp of GB, 1970-; Systems Bd, MRC, 1974-77; Research Funds Cttee, British Heart Foundn, 1974-; British Nat. Cttee for Biochemistry, 1978- (Chm., 1982-); Chairman: Cttee of Biochemical Soc., 1980-; Adv. Bd, Meat Res. Inst., 1981-. Hon. Mem., Amer. Soc. of Biol Chemists, 1978; Corresponding Mem., Société Royale des Sciences, Liège, 1978; Mem., Accad. Virgiliana, Mantova, 1979. CIBA Medal, Biochemical Soc., 1977. Publications: scientific papers in Biochemical Journal, Nature, Biochemica Biophysica Acta, etc. Recreations: gardening, building stone walls, Rugby football (Cambridge, 1946, 1947, England, 1947, 1948). Address: 64 Meadow Hill Road, King's Norton, Birmingham B38 8DA. T: 021-458 1511.

PERRY, William Arthur; Counsellor (Defence Supply), British Embassy, Bonn, since 1980; b 5 Aug. 1937; s of Arthur Perry and Elizabeth Grace (née Geller); m 1962, Anne Rosemary Dight; two d. Educ: St Dunstan's Coll. Min. of Aviation, 1960-61; Second Sec. (Defence Supply), Bonn, 1964-66; Principal: Min. of Technology, 1969; MoD, 1970-74; First Sec., UK Delegn to NATO, 1974-77; Asst Sec., MoD, 1977-80. Recreations: philately, music. Address: c/o Foreign and Commonwealth Office, SW1A 2AH.

PERRY-KEENE, Air Vice-Marshal Allan Lancelot Addison, CB 1947; OBE 1940; RAF (retired); *b* 10 Nov. 1898; *s* of late L. H. A. and M. Perry-Keene; *m* 1923, K. L., *d* of late C. A. S. Silberrad, ICS; two *d*. *Educ:* Wolverley; King Edward's, Birmingham. Served European War, 1914-18; joined RFC, 1917; France, 1918-19; transferred RAF, 1918; Iraq, 1927-29; India, 1935-41; Burma and India, 1942; Director of Ground Training and Training Plans, Air Ministry, 1943-45; AOC 227 Group, India, and 3 (Indian) Group, 1946; Air Officer i/c Administration, Air HQ, India, 1946; Air Commander, Royal Pakistan Air Force, 1947-49. *Address:* Wayfarers Cottage, St Mary Bourne, Andover, Hants SP11 6AR. *T:* St Mary Bourne 210.

PERRYMAN, Francis Douglas; Board Member for Finance, British Telecommunications, since 1981; *b* 23 April 1930; *s* of Frank Smyth Perryman and Caroline Mary Anderson; *m* 1955, Margaret Mary Lamb; two *d*. *Educ:* West Hartlepool Grammar School; Durham Univ. BCom (Hons); FCA. Articled Clerk, 1951-55; Nat. Service, commnd RAPC, 1955-57; National Coal Board: Area Chief Accountant, Fife and Scottish South Areas, 1963-72; Finance Dir, Opencast Exec., 1972; Dir Gen. of Finance, 1978-81; Board Mem. for Finance, PO, 1981. FRSA. *Recreations:* golf, Rugby football, music, Francophile. *Address:* Long Mynd, 69 Copperkins Lane, Amersham, Bucks. *T:* Amersham 21611.

PERSSON, Rt. Rev. William Michael Dermot; *see* Doncaster, Bishop Suffragan of.

PERTH, 17th Earl of, *cr* 1605; **John David Drummond,** PC 1957; Baron Drummond of Cargill, 1488; Baron Maderty, 1609; Baron Drummond, 1686; Lord Drummond of Gilston, 1685; Lord Drummond of Rickertoun and Castlemaine, 1686; Viscount Strathallan, 1686; Hereditary Thane of Lennox, and Hereditary Steward of Menteith and Strathearn; Representative Peer for Scotland, 1952-63; First Crown Estate Commissioner, 1962-77; Chairman, Ditchley Foundation, 1963-66; *b* 13 May 1907; *o s* of 16th Earl of Perth, PC, GCMG, CB, and Hon. Angela Constable-Maxwell (*d* 1965), *y d* of 11th Baron Herries; *S* father 1951; *m* 1934, Nancy Seymour, *d* of Reginald Fincke, New York City; two *s*. *Educ:* Downside; Cambridge Univ. Lieut, Intelligence Corps, 1940; seconded to War Cabinet Offices, 1942-43, Ministry of Production, 1944-45; Minister of State for Colonial Affairs, 1957-62 (resigned). Chm., Reviewing Cttee on Export of Works of Art, 1972-76. Member: Court of St Andrews Univ., 1967-; Adv. Council, V&A Museum, 1971-72; Trustee, Nat. Library of Scotland, 1968-. Hon. FRIBA 1978. *Heir: s* Viscount Strathallan, *qv*. *Address:* 14 Hyde Park Gardens Mews, W2. *T:* 01-262 4667; Stobhall, by Perth.

PERTH, Provost of (St Ninian's Cathedral); *see* Forbes, Very Rev. G. J. T.

PERTH (Australia), Archbishop of, and Metropolitan of Western Australia, since 1981; **Most Rev. Peter Frederick Carnley;** *b* 17 Oct. 1937; *s* of Frederick Carnley and Gweyennetth Lilian Carnley (*née* Read); *m* 1966, Carol Ann Dunstan; one *s* one *d*. *Educ:* St John's Coll., Morpeth, NSW (ThL 1st Cl., ACT, 1962); Univ. of Melbourne (BA, 1st Cl. Hons, 1966); Univ. of Cambridge (PhD 1969). Deacon 1962, priest 1964, Bath; Licence to Officiate, dio. Melbourne, 1963-65; Asst Curate of Parkes, 1966; Licence to Officiate, dio. Ely, 1966-69; Chaplain, Mitchell Coll. of Advanced Education, Bath, 1970-72; Research Fellow, St John's Coll., Cambridge, 1971-72; Warden, St John's College, St Lucia, Queensland, 1972-81; Residentiary Canon, St John's Cathedral, Brisbane, 1975-81; Examining Chaplain to Archbishop of Brisbane, 1975-81. ChStJ 1982. *Publication:* The Poverty of Historical Scepticism, in Christ, Faith and History (ed S. W. Sykes and J. P. Clayton), 1972. *Recreations:* sailing, gardening, bush walking. *Address:* Bishop's House, 90 Mounts Bay Road, Perth, WA. *T:* 322 1777. *Clubs:* Western Australian (Perth); Royal Perth Yacht; St John's (Brisbane).

PERTH (Australia), Archbishop of, (RC), since 1968; **Most Rev. Launcelot John Goody,** KBE 1977; PhD, DD; *b* 5 June 1908; *s* of late Ernest John Goody and of Agnes Goody. *Educ:* Christian Brothers' College, Perth, WA; Urban University, Rome. PhD 1927, DD 1931. Ordained priest at Rome, 1930; Asst Parish Priest, Perth Cathedral, 1932-35, Kalgoorlie, 1935-37; Parish Priest, Toodyay, 1937; Director of Seminary, Guilford, 1940-47; Domestic Prelate to the Pope, 1947; Parish Priest, Bedford Park, 1947-51; Auxiliary Bishop of Perth, 1951; first RC Bishop of Bunbury, 1954-68. *Address:* St Mary's Cathedral, Perth, WA 6000, Australia. *T:* 259177.

PERTH (Australia), Assistant Bishops of; *see* Challen, Rt Rev. M. B.; Kyme, Rt Rev. B. R.

PERU, Bishop of, since 1978; **Rt. Rev. David Richard John Evans;** with delegated jurisdiction of Bolivia, since 1980; *b* 5 June 1938; *s* of William Henry Reginald Evans and Beatrix Catherine Mottram; *m* 1964, Dorothy Evelyn Parsons; one *s* two *d*. *Educ:* Caius College, Cambridge. Hons degree in Mod. Langs and Theology, 1963, MA 1966. Curate, Christ Church, Cockfosters, 1965-68; Missionary Pastor and Gen. Sec., Argentine Inter-Varsity Christian Fellowship, in Buenos Aires, Argentina, 1969-77; Chaplain, Good Shepherd Church, Lima, Peru, 1977-82. *Publication:* En Diálogo con Dios, 1976. *Recreations:* squash and philately. *Address:* Apartado 5152, Lima 18, Peru, S America. *T:* 45-2121.

PERUTZ, Max Ferdinand, CH 1975; CBE 1963; FRS 1954; PhD; Member, scientific staff, Medical Research Council Laboratory of Molecular Biology, 1979- (Chairman, 1962-79); *b* 19 May 1914; *s* of Hugo and Adèle Perutz; *m* 1942, Gisela Peiser; one *s* one *d*. *Educ:* Theresianum, Vienna; Univ. of Vienna; Univ. of Cambridge (PhD 1940). Hon. Fellow, Peterhouse, Cambridge, 1962. Dir, MRC Unit for Molecular Biology, 1947-62; Chm., European Molecular Biology Orgn, 1963-69. Reader, Davy Faraday Res. Lab., 1954-68, and Fullerian Prof. of Physiology, 1973-79, Royal Instn. Hon. FRSE, 1976; Hon. Member American Academy of Arts and Sciences, 1963; Corresp. Member, Austrian Acad. of Sciences, 1963; Mem., Akademie Leopoldina, Halle, 1964; Foreign Member: American Philosophical Society, 1968; Royal Netherlands Acad., 1972; French Acad. of Sciences, 1976; For. Associate, Nat. Acad. of Sciences, USA, 1970; Mem., Pontifical Acad. of Sciences, Rome, 1981. Nobel Prize for Chemistry (jointly), 1962; Royal Medal, 1971, Copley Medal, 1979, Royal Soc. Hon. degrees: in philosophy: Vienna, 1965; Salzburg, 1972; in science: Edinburgh, 1965; East Anglia, 1967; Cambridge, 1981. *Publications:* Proteins and Nucleic Acids, Structure and Function, 1962; Atlas of Haemoglobin and Myoglobin, 1981; Ging's auch ohne Forschung, 1982. *Address:* 42 Sedley Taylor Road, Cambridge; Laboratory of Molecular Biology, Hills Road, Cambridge.

PERY, family name of **Earl of Limerick.**

PESKETT, Stanley Victor, MA; Principal, Royal Belfast Academical Institution, 1959-78; *b* 9 May 1918; *o s* of late Sydney Timber and late Mary Havard Peskett; *m* 1948, Prudence Eileen, OBE 1974, *o d* of late C. R. A. Goatly, Calcutta; two *s* one *d* (and one *d* decd). *Educ:* Whitgift Sch.; St Edmund Hall, Oxford. Served War, 1939-46 (despatches) in Royal Marines, Norway, Shetland, Normandy, India and Java; Lt-Col, 1944; two Admiralty awards for inventions. Senior English Master, 1946-59, Housemaster 1954-59, The Leys School. Mem. Cttee, Headmasters' Conf., 1976; Mem. Council, Headmasters' Assoc., and Pres., Ulster Headmasters' Assoc., 1973-75; Chm., Northern Ireland Cttee, Voluntary Service Overseas, 1969-78; Founder Pres., Irish Schools Swimming Assoc., 1968-69 (Chm., Ulster Branch, 1968-78); Chm., NI Branch, School Library Assoc., 1964-73; Governor, Belfast Sch. of Music, 1974-77; Mem. Adv. Council, UDR, 1975-78. *Publications:* The Metfield Clock, 1980; articles in educational jls. *Address:* Huntsman and Hounds Cottage, Metfield, Harleston, Norfolk IP20 0LB. *T:* Fressingfield 425.

PESTELL; *see* Wells-Pestell.

PESTELL, Catherine Eva; HM Diplomatic Service; Diplomatic Service Inspector, since 1980; *b* 24 Sept. 1933; *d* of Edmund Ernest Pestell and Isabella Cummine Sangster. *Educ:* Leeds Girls' High Sch.; St Hilda's Coll., Oxford (MA). FO, 1956; Third Sec., The Hague, 1958; Second Sec., Bangkok, 1961; FO, 1964; First Sec., UK Delegn to OECD, Paris, 1969; FCO, 1971; St Antony's Coll., Oxford, 1974; Counsellor, East Berlin, 1975-78; Cabinet Office, 1978-80. *Address:* c/o Foreign and Commonwealth Office, SW1A 2AH.
See also J. E. Pestell.

PESTELL, John Edmund; Under Secretary, HM Treasury, since 1981 (Civil Service Department, 1976-81); *b* 8 Dec. 1930; *s* of late Edmund Pestell and of Isabella (*née* Sangster); *m* 1958, Muriel Ada (*née* Whitby); three *s*. *Educ:* Roundhay Sch.; New Coll., Oxford (MA). National Service (Intell. Corps), 1949-50. Jt Intell. Bureau, 1953-57; Asst Principal, WO, 1957-60; Private Sec. to Parly Under Sec. of State for War, 1958-60; Principal, WO and MoD, 1960-70; Admin. Staff Coll., Henley, 1963; Private Sec. to Minister of Defence (Equipment), 1969-70; Asst Sec., MoD, 1970-72; Press Sec. (Co-ordination), Prime Minister's Office, 1972-74; Asst Sec., CSD, 1974-76. Governor, Cranleigh Sch. *Address:* New House, Bridge Road, Cranleigh, Surrey. *T:* Cranleigh 3489.
See also C. E. Pestell.

PESTELL, Sir John Richard, KCVO 1969; an Adjudicator, Immigration Appeals, Harmondsworth, since 1970; *b* 21 Nov. 1916; *s* of late Lt-Comdr Frank Lionel Pestell, RN, and Winifred Alice Pestell; *m* 1951, Betty Pestell (*née* Parish); three *d*. *Educ:* Portsmouth Northern Secondary Sch. Joined British South Africa Police, Southern Rhodesia, 1939; retired, 1965, with rank of Asst Commissioner. Served, 1944-47, Gen. List, MELF, in Cyrenaica Defence Force. Secretary/Controller to Governor of S Rhodesia, Rt Hon. Sir H. V. Gibbs, 1965-69. *Recreations:* walking, golf. *Address:* Monks Walk, Ferry Lane, Medmenham, Marlow, Bucks.

PETCH, Barry Irvine, FCA; Controller, IBM Europe, since 1981; *b* 12 Oct. 1933; *s* of Charles Reginald Petch and Anne (*née* Fryer); *m* 1966, Anne Elisabeth (*née* Johannessen); two *s* one *d*. *Educ:* Doncaster Grammar Sch. FCA 1967. IBM United Kingdom Ltd, 1959-80. Part-time Mem., Price Commn, 1973-77. *Recreations:* tennis, sailing. *Address:* Chemin de la Mare Close, 78240 Chambourcy, France. *Club:* Reform.

PETCH, Prof. Norman James, FRS 1974; FEng; Professor of Metallurgy, University of Strathclyde, 1973-82; *b* 13 Feb. 1917; 3rd *s* of George and Jane Petch, Bearsden, Dunbartonshire; *m* 1949, Eileen Allen (*d* 1975); two *d*; *m* 1976, Marjorie Jackson. *Educ:* Queen Mary Coll., London; Sheffield Univ. Research at Cavendish Lab., Cambridge, 1939-42; Royal Aircraft Establishment, 1942-46; Cavendish Laboratory, 1946-48; British Iron and

Steel Research Assoc., Sheffield, 1948-49; Reader in Metallurgy, Leeds Univ., 1949-56; First Professor of Metallurgy, Leeds Univ., 1956-59; Cochrane Prof. of Metallurgy, 1959-73, a Pro-Vice-Chancellor, 1968-71, Univ. of Newcastle upon Tyne. Mem. Council, Royal Soc., 1979-81. *Address:* Abbotsford, 17 Printer's Row, Balfron, Stirlingshire. *T:* Balfron 40249.

PETERBOROUGH, Bishop of, since 1972; **Rt. Rev. Douglas Russell Feaver;** *b* 22 May 1914; *s* of late Ernest Henry Feaver, Bristol; *m* 1939, Katharine, *d* of late Rev. W. T. Stubbs; one *s* two *d. Educ:* Bristol Grammar School; Keble College, Oxford (Scholar; 1st cl. Hons. Mod. History, 1935; 1st cl. Hons. Theology, 1937; Liddon Student, 1935-37; MA); Wells Theological College. Deacon 1938, priest 1939, St Albans; Curate, St Albans Abbey, 1938-42. Chaplain, RAFVR, 1942-46. Canon and Sub-Dean of St Albans, 1946-58; Chaplain to St Albans School, 1946-58; Proctor in Convocation, 1951-58; Examining Chaplain to Bp of St Albans, 1948-58, to Bp of Portsmouth, 1960-72; Vicar of St Mary's, Nottingham and Rural Dean of Nottingham, 1958-72; Hon. Canon of Southwell, 1958-72; Treasurer, 1959-69; Proctor in Convocation for Southwell, 1970-72. Chairman of Trent House Boys' Probation Hostel, 1967-72; Governor of Nottingham Bluecoat School, 1958-72. *Publications:* reviews and articles in Church Times. *Address:* The Palace, Peterborough. *T:* Peterborough 62492.

PETERBOROUGH, Dean of; *see* Wise, Very Rev. R. G.

PETERKEN, Laurence Edwin; Controller, Operational Services, Greater London Council, since 1977; *b* 2 Oct. 1931; *s* of Edwin James Peterken and Constance Fanny (*née* Giffin); *m* 1st, 1955, Hanne Birgithe Von Der Recke (decd); one *s* one *d;* 2nd, 1970, Margaret Raynal Blair; one *s* one *d. Educ:* Harrow Sch. (Scholar); Peterhouse, Cambridge (Scholar); MA. Pilot Officer, RAF Regt, Adjt No 20 LAA Sqdn, 1950-52. Service Div. Manager, Hotpoint Ltd, 1961-63, Commercial Dir, 1963-66; Man. Dir, British Domestic Appliances Ltd, 1966-68; Dir, British Printing Corporation Ltd, 1969-73; Debenhams Ltd: Man. Dir, Fashion Multiple Div., 1974-76; Management Auditor, 1976-77. *Recreations:* opera, painting, squash. *Address:* Blair House, Three Gates Lane, Haslemere, Surrey. *T:* Haslemere 51777. *Club:* Athenæum.

PETERKIEWICZ, Prof. Jerzy; novelist and poet; Professor of Polish Language and Literature, University of London, 1972-79; *b* 29 Sept. 1916; *s* of late Jan Pietrkiewicz and Antonina (*née* Politowska). *Educ:* Dlugosz Sch., Wloclawek; Univ. of Warsaw; Univ. of St Andrews (MA 1944); King's Coll., London (PhD 1947). Freelance writer until 1950; Reader (previously Lectr) in Polish Language and Literature, Sch. of Slavonic and East European Studies, Univ. of London, 1952-72, Head of Dept of E European Lang. and Lit., 1972-77. *Publications:* Prowincja, 1936; Wiersze i poematy, 1938; Pogrzeb Europy, 1946; The Knotted Cord, 1953; Loot and Loyalty, 1955; Polish Prose and Verse, 1956; Antologia liryki angielskiej, 1958; Future to Let, 1958; Isolation, 1959; (with Burns Singer) Five Centuries of Polish Poetry, 1960 (enlarged edn 1970); The Quick and the Dead, 1961; That Angel Burning at my Left Side, 1963; Poematy londynskie, 1965; Inner Circle, 1966; Green Flows the Bile, 1969; The Other Side of Silence (The Poet at the Limits of Language), 1970; The Third Adam, 1975; (ed and trans.) Easter Vigil and other Poems, by Karol Wojtyla (Pope John Paul II), 1979; Kula magiczna (Poems 1934-52), 1980; (ed and trans.) Collected Poems, by Karol Wojtyla (Pope John Paul II), 1982; essays, poems and articles in various periodicals. *Recreation:* travels, outward and inward. *Address:* 7 Lyndhurst Terrace, NW3.

PETERKIN, Sir Neville (Allan Mercer), Kt 1981; **Hon. Chief Justice Peterkin;** Chief Justice, West Indies Associated States, since 1980; *b* 27 Oct. 1915; *s* of Joseph Allan Peterkin and Evelyn Peterkin; *m* 1942, Beryl Thompson; two *s* one *d. Educ:* Wellington Sch., Somerset, England. Called to Bar, Middle Temple, 1939. Registrar, St Lucia, 1943; Magistrate, Trinidad and Tobago, 1944; Resident Magistrate, Jamaica, 1954; High Court Judge: Trinidad, 1957; Associated States, 1967; Justice of Appeal, Associated States, 1975. *Recreations:* golf, bridge. *Address:* 16 Becune Point, Cap Estate, St Lucia, West Indies. *T:* 8447.

PETERS, Prof. David Keith, FRCP; Professor of Medicine, and Director of the Department of Medicine, Royal Postgraduate Medical School, Hammersmith Hospital, London, since 1977; *b* 26 July 1938; *s* of Herbert Lionel and Olive Peters; *m* 1st, 1961, Jean Mair Garfield (marr. diss. 1978); one *s* one *d;* 2nd, 1979, Pamela Wilson Ewan; one *s. Educ:* Welsh National Sch. of Medicine. MB, BCh, 1961; MRCP 1964; FRCP 1975. Junior posts in United Cardiff Hosps, 1961-65; Med. Research Council, Clinical Res. Fellowship, 1965-68; Lectr in Med., Welsh Nat. Sch. of Med., 1968-69; Royal Postgraduate Medical School: Lectr, 1969, Sen. Lectr, 1974, Reader in Med., 1975; Consultant Physician, Hammersmith Hosp., 1969-. *Publications:* in various jls on immunology of renal disease. *Recreations:* tennis, chess. *Address:* 53 Loftus Road, W12 7EH. *T:* 01-743 6298. *Club:* Hurlingham.

PETERS, Ellis; *see* Pargeter, E.

PETERS, John; Assistant Under Secretary (Air Staff), Ministry of Defence, since 1979; *b* 5 Dec. 1929; *s* of Dr G. F. Peters and Mrs C. P. Peters; *m* 1955, Jane Catherine Mary Sheldon; one *s* two *d. Educ:* Downside Sch. (Scholar); Balliol Coll., Oxford (Exhibnr, MA). HM Forces, commissioned RAEC, 1948-49. Pres., Oxford Union Soc., 1953. Entered Administrative Class,

Home Civil Service, Admiralty, 1953; PS to Civil Lord, 1956-59; Principal, 1959; PS to Navy Minister, 1964-67; PS to Minister of Defence (Equipment), 1967-68; Asst Sec., 1968; Dir of Naval Sales, 1968-72; Cabinet Office, 1974-75; Defence Counsellor, UK Delegn to NATO, Brussels, 1975-78. *Address:* 60 Scotts Lane, Bromley, Kent. *T:* 01-650 0063. *Club:* United Oxford & Cambridge University.

PETERS, Kenneth Jamieson, CBE 1979; JP; DL; FSAScot; Director: Thomson North Sea Ltd, since 1981; Thomson Scottish Petroleum Ltd, since 1981; Aberdeen Journals Ltd, since 1960 (Managing Director, 1960-80; Chairman, 1980-81); Member, Scottish Region Board, British Rail, since 1982; *b* 17 Jan. 1923; *s* of William Jamieson Peters and Edna Rosa Peters (*née* Hayman); *m* 1951, Arunda Merle Jane Jones. *Educ:* Aberdeen Grammar Sch.; Aberdeen Univ. Served War of 1939-45: last rank Captain/Adjutant, 2nd Bn King's Own Scottish Borderers. Editorial staff, Daily Record and Evening News Ltd, 1947-51; Asst Editor: Evening Express, Aberdeen, 1951-52; Manchester Evening Chronicle, 1952-53; Editor: Evening Express, Aberdeen, 1953-56; The Press and Journal, Aberdeen, 1956-60; Pres., Scottish Daily Newspaper Soc., 1964-66 and 1974-76; Mem., Press Council, 1974-77; Director: Highland Printers Ltd (Inverness), 1968-; Aberdeen Assoc. of Social Service, 1973-78; Thomson Regional Newspapers, 1974-80; Pres., Publicity Club of Aberdeen, 1972-; Member: Scottish Adv. Cttee of British Council, 1967-; Cttee, Films of Scotland, 1970-; Chm., NE Cttee, Scottish Council for Develt and Industry, 1982-; etc. FSAScot 1980; FBIM 1980. JP City of Aberdeen, 1961; DL Aberdeen, 1978. *Publications:* The Northern Lights, 1978; (ed) Great North Memories, vol. 1, 1978, vol. 2, 1981. *Recreations:* cricket, Rugby football, walking. *Address:* 47 Abergeldie Road, Aberdeen AB1 6ED. *T:* Aberdeen 27647. *Club:* Royal Northern and University (Aberdeen).

PETERS, Mary Elizabeth, MBE 1973; self employed; Managing Director, Mary Peters Sports Ltd, since 1977; *b* 6 July 1939; *d* of Arthur Henry Peters and Hilda Mary Peters. *Educ:* Portadown Coll., Co. Armagh; Belfast Coll. of Domestic Science (DipDomSc). Represented Great Britain: Olympic Games: 4th place, Pentathlon, 1964; 1st, Pentathlon (world record), 1972; Commonwealth Games: 2nd, Shot, 1966; 1st, Shot, 1st Pentathlon, 1970; 1st, Pentathlon, 1974. Member: Sports Council, 1974- (Vice-Chm., 1977-81). Director: Barwell Sports Management Ltd, 1974-; Churchill Foundn Fellowship Scholarship, Calif, 1972. Asst Sec., Multiple Sclerosis Soc., 1974-78; Pres., Old-Age Pensioners' Coal and Grocery Fund. Hon. Senior Athletic Coach, 1975-; BAAB Pentathlon Coach, 1976; Team Manager: GB women's athletic team, European Cup, 1979; GB women's athletic team, Moscow, 1980. Vice-President: NIWAAA; Riding for the Disabled; Trustee, Ulster Sports Trust, 1972. Awards: BBC Sports personality, 1972; Athletic Writers', 1972; Sports Writers', 1972; Elizabeth Arden Visible Difference, 1976; Athletics, Dublin (Texaco), 1970 and 1972. Hon. DSc, New Univ. of Ulster, 1974. *Publication:* Mary P., an autobiography, 1974. *Recreations:* squash, swimming, parachuting. *Address:* Willowtree Cottage, River Road, Dunmurry, Belfast, N Ireland.

PETERS, Prof. Raymond Harry; Professor of Polymer and Fibre Science, University of Manchester, since 1955; *b* 19 Feb. 1918. *Educ:* County High Sch., Ilford; King's Coll., London Univ.; Manchester Univ. BSc (London) 1939, PhD (London), 1942, in Chemistry; BSc (Manchester), 1949, BSc (London), 1949, in Mathematics; DSc (London), 1968. Scientist at ICI Ltd, 1941-46 and 1949-55. President, Society of Dyers and Colourists, 1967-68. *Publications:* Textile Chemistry: Vol. I, The Chemistry of Fibres, 1963; Vol. II, Impurities of Fibres: Purification of Fibres, 1967; Vol. III, Physical Chemistry of Dyeing, 1975; contributions to Journals of Chemical Society, Society of Dyers and Colourists, Textile Institute, British Journal of Applied Physics, etc. *Recreation:* gardening. *Address:* University of Manchester Institute of Science and Technology, Manchester M60 1QD. *T:* 061-236 3311.

PETERS, Prof. Richard Stanley, BA (Oxon), BA (London), PhD (London); Professor of the Philosophy of Education, University of London Institute of Education, since 1962; Dean, Faculty of Education, London University, 1971-74; *b* 31 Oct. 1919; *s* of late Charles Robert and Mabel Georgina Peters; *m* 1943, Margaret Lee Duncan; one *s* two *d. Educ:* Clifton Coll., Bristol; Queen's Coll., Oxford; Birkbeck Coll., University of London. War service with Friends' Ambulance Unit and Friends' Relief Service in E. London, 1940-44. Classics Master, Sidcot School, Somerset, 1944-46; Birkbeck Coll., University of London: Studentship and part-time Lecturer in Philos. and Psychol., 1946-49; full-time Lecturer in Philos. and Psychol., 1949-58; Reader in Philosophy, 1958-62. Visiting Prof. of Education: Grad. School of Education, Harvard Univ., 1961; Univ. of Auckland, 1975; Visiting Fellow, Australian National Univ., 1969. Part-time lectureships, Bedford Coll., LSE; Tutor for University of London Tutorial Classes Cttee and Extension Cttee. Member, American National Academy of Education, 1966. *Publications:* (revised) Brett's History of Psychology, 1953; Hobbes, 1956; The Concept of Motivation, 1958; (with S. I. Benn) Social Principles and the Democratic State, 1959; Authority, Responsibility and Education, 1960; Ethics and Education, 1966; (ed) The Concept of Education, 1967; (ed) Perspectives on Plowden, 1969; (with P. H. Hirst) The Logic of Education, 1970; (ed with M. Cranston) Hobbes and Rousseau, 1971; (ed with R. F. Dearden and P. H. Hirst) Education and the Development of Reason, 1972; Reason and Compassion (Lindsay Meml Lectures), 1973; (ed) The Philosophy of Education, 1973; Psychology and Ethical Development, 1974; (ed) Nature and Conduct, 1975; (ed) The Role of the Head, 1976; Education and the

Education of Teachers, 1977; (ed) John Dewey Reconsidered, 1977; Essays on Educators, 1981; Moral Development and Moral Education, 1981. *Address:* 16 Shepherd's Hill, N6.

PETERS, Theophilus, CMG 1967; HM Diplomatic Service, retired; Director, Theophilus Knapman & Co., since 1979; *b* 7 Aug. 1921; *er s* of late Mark Peters and Dorothy Knapman; *m* 1953, Lucy Bailey Summers, *d* of late Lionel Morgan Summers, Winter Park, Fla; two *s* three *d. Educ:* Exeter Sch., Exeter; St John's Coll., Cambridge (MA). Served War of 1939-45: 2nd Lieut, Intelligence Corps, 1942; Captain, 8 Corps HQ, 1944; Normandy, 1944; Holland, 1944-45 (despatches); Germany; Major. Entered HM Foreign (subseq. Diplomatic) Service; Vice-Consul/2nd Secretary, Peking, 1948; FO, 1951-52; Tripoli and Benghazi (Libya), 1953; FO, 1956; Dep. Secretary-General, Cento, 1960; Head of Chancery, Manila, 1962; Counsellor (Commercial), Peking, 1965; Dir, Diplomatic Service Language Centre, 1968-71, and Head of Training Dept, FCO, 1969-71; Counsellor and Consul-Gen., Buenos Aires, 1971-73; Consul-Gen., Antwerp, 1973-78. *Address:* c/o National Westminster Bank Ltd, Stamford, Lincs.

PETERS, Prof. Wallace, MD, DSc; FRCP; Professor of Medical Protozoology, London School of Hygiene and Tropical Medicine, University of London, since 1979; Joint Director, Malaria Reference Laboratory, Public Health Laboratory Service, since 1979; *b* 1 April 1924; *s* of Henry and Fanny Peters; *m* 1954, Ruth (*née* Scheidegger). *Educ:* Haberdashers' Aske's Sch.; St Bartholomew's Hosp., London. MB BS, 1947; MRCS, DTM&H. Served in RAMC, 1947-49; practised tropical medicine in West and East Africa, 1950-52; Staff Mem., WHO, Liberia and Nepal, 1952-55; Asst Dir (Malariology), Health Dept, Territory of Papua and New Guinea, 1956-61; Research Associate, CIBA, Basle, Switzerland, 1961-66; Walter Myers Prof. of Parasitology, Univ. of Liverpool, 1966-79. Dean, Liverpool Sch. of Tropical Medicine, 1975-78. Vice-Pres. and Pres., Brit. Soc. Parasit., 1972-76; Pres., Brit. Sect., Soc. Protozool., 1972-75; Member: Editorial Bd, Ann. trop. Med. Parasit., 1966-79; Expert Adv. Panel, WHO, 1967-; Trop. Med. Research Bd, MRC, 1973-77; Sec., European Fedn Parasit., 1979- (Vice-Pres., 1975-79). *Publications:* A Provisional Checklist of Butterflies of the Ethiopian Region, 1952; Chemotherapy and Drug Resistance in Malaria, 1970; (with H. M. Gilles) A Colour Atlas of Parasitology and Tropical Medicine, 1976; (with R. Killick-Kendrick) Rodent Malaria, 1978; numerous papers in jls, on trop. med. and parasitology. *Recreation:* photography. *Address:* London School of Hygiene and Tropical Medicine, Keppel Street, WC1E 7HT. *T:* 01-636 8636.

PETERS, William, CMG 1981; MVO 1961; MBE 1959; HM Diplomatic Service; High Commissioner in Malaŵi, since 1980; *b* 28 Sept. 1923; *o s* of John William Peters and Louise (*née* Woodhouse), Morpeth, Northumberland; *m* 1944, Catherine B. Bailey; no *c. Educ:* King Edward VI Grammar Sch., Morpeth; Balliol Coll., Oxford. MA Lit. Hum. 1948. War Service, Queen's Royal Rifles, KOSB, and 9th Gurkha Rifles, 1942-46. Joined HMOCS as Asst District Comr, Gold Coast, 1950; served in Cape Coast, Bawku and Tamale; Dep. Sec., Regional Comr, Northern Region, 1958-59; joined CRO as Asst Prin., 1959; Prin., 1959; 1st Sec., Dacca, 1960-63; 1st Sec., Cyprus, 1963-67; Head of Zambia and Malawi Dept, CRO, 1967-68; Head of Central African Dept, FCO, 1968-69; Dir, Internat. Affairs Div., Commonwealth Secretariat, 1969-71; Counsellor and Head of Chancery, Canberra, 1971-73; Dep. High Comr, Bombay, 1974-77; Ambassador to Uruguay, 1977-80. *Publications:* contribs to Jl of African Administration, Illustrated Weekly of India; Noticias (Uruguay); Diplomatic Service: Formation and Operation. *Recreations:* music, gardening, carpentry. *Address:* c/o Foreign and Commonwealth Office, SW1A 2AH. *Clubs:* United Oxford & Cambridge University, Royal Commonwealth Society; Society of Malaŵi; Royal African Society.

PETERSEN, Sir Jeffrey (Charles), KCMG 1978 (CMG 1968); HM Diplomatic Service, retired; Chairman: British Materials Handling Board; Banco de Valladolid; *b* 20 July 1920; *s* of Charles Petersen and Ruby Petersen (*née* Waple); *m* 1962, Karin Kristina Hayward; two *s* four *d. Educ:* Westcliff High Sch.; London School of Economics. Served RN (Lieut, RNVR), 1939-46. Joined Foreign Office, 1948; 2nd Secretary, Madrid, 1948; 3rd Secretary, Ankara, 1951-52; 1st Secretary, Brussels, 1953-56; NATO Defence College, 1956-57; FO, 1957-62; 1st Secretary, Djakarta, 1962-64; Counsellor, Athens, 1964-68; Minister (Commercial), Rio de Janeiro, 1968-71; Ambassador to: Republic of Korea, 1971-74; Romania, 1975-77; Sweden, 1977-80. Vice-Pres., Swedish Chamber of Commerce for UK; Chm., Anglo-Korean Soc. *Recreations:* painting, entomology, sailing. *Address:* 32 Longmoore Street, SW1. *T:* 01-834 8262; Crofts Wood, Petham, Kent.

PETERSHAM, Viscount; Charles Henry Leicester Stanhope; *b* 20 July 1945; *s* and *heir* of 11th Earl of Harrington, qv; *m* 1966, Virginia Alleyne Freeman Jackson, Mallow; one *s* one *d. Educ:* Eton. *Heir:* s Hon. William Henry Leicester Stanhope, *b* 14 Oct. 1967. *Address:* c/o Greenmount, Patrickswell, Co. Limerick, Ireland.

PETERSON, Alexander Duncan Campbell, OBE 1946; Vice-President, International Council of United World Colleges, since 1980; *b* 13 Sept. 1908; 2nd *s* of late J. C. K. Peterson, CIE; *m* 1946, Corinna May, *d* of late Sir Arthur Cochrane, KCVO; two *s* one *d. Educ:* Radley; Balliol Coll., Oxford. Assistant master, Shrewsbury Sch., 1932-40; commissioned in MOI (SP), 1940; Deputy Director of Psychological Warfare, SEAC, 1944-46; Headmaster, Adams'

Grammar Sch., 1946-52; Director-General of Information Services, Federation of Malaya, 1952-54; Headmaster, Dover College, 1954-57; Director: Dept of Educn, Oxford Univ., 1958-73; Internat. Baccalaureate Office, 1968-77. Contested (L) Oxford City, 1966. Chm., Army Educn Adv. Bd, 1959-66. Chairman: Farmington Trust, 1963-71; Internat. Council of United World Colls, 1978-80. *Publications:* The Far East, 1948; 100 Years of Education, 1952; Educating our Rulers, 1957; The Techniques of Teaching (ed), 1965; The Future of Education, 1968; International Baccalaureate, 1972; The Future of the Sixth Form, 1973. *Address:* 107A Hamilton Terrace, NW8. *T:* 01-286 3995. *Clubs:* Travellers', Special Forces.

PETERSON, Sir Arthur (William), KCB 1973 (CB 1963); MVO 1953; Chairman: Family Service Units, since 1978; British Refugees Council, since 1981; *b* 22 May 1916; *s* of J. C. K. Peterson and F. Campbell; *m* 1940, Mary Isabel Maples; one *s* two *d. Educ:* Shrewsbury; Merton College, Oxford. Asst Principal, Home Office, 1938; Principal Private Secretary to Home Secretary, 1946-49; Secretary, Royal Commission on Betting and Lotteries, 1949-51; Asst Secretary, Home Office, 1951-56; Personal Assistant to Lord Privy Seal, 1957; Dep. Chm., Prison Commission, 1957-60, Chm., 1960-63; Asst Under-Sec. of State, Prison Dept, Home Office, 1963-64; Dep. Sec., DEA, 1964-68; Dir-Gen. and Clerk to GLC, 1968-72; Permanent Under-Sec. of State, Home Office, 1972-77; Chairman: Mersey Docks & Harbour Co., 1977-80; Nat. Ports Council, 1980-81. Mem., Royal Commn on Criminal Procedure, 1978-80. Chm., Jt Cttee on Refugees from Vietnam, 1979-82. Hon. Fellow, Inst. of Local Government Studies, Birmingham Univ. *Address:* 7 Lincoln House, Basil Street, SW3. *T:* 01-589 2237. *Club:* Travellers'.

PETERSON, Colin Vyvyan, CVO 1982; Under Secretary, Management and Personnel Office, since 1982; *b* 24 Oct. 1932; *s* of late Sir Maurice Drummond Peterson, GCMG; *m* 1966, Pamela Rosemary Barry; two *s* two *d. Educ:* Winchester Coll.; Magdalen Coll., Oxford. Joined HM Treasury, 1959; Sec. for Appointments to PM and Ecclesiastical Sec. to the Lord Chancellor, 1974-82. *Recreation:* fishing. *Address:* 87 Christchurch Road, Winchester, Hants. *T:* Winchester 3784. *Club:* Brooks's.

PETERSON, Oscar Emmanuel, OC 1973; concert jazz pianist; *b* 15 Aug. 1925; *s* of Daniel Peterson and Kathleen Peterson; *m* 1947, Lillian Alice Ann; two *s* three *d. Educ:* (academic) Montreal High Sch.; (music) private tutors. 1st prize, amateur show, 1940; Carnegie Hall debut, 1950; 1950-: numerous jazz awards; TV shows; composer and arranger; yearly concert tours in N America, Europe, GB and Japan; has performed also in S America, Mexico, WI, Australia, NZ and Russia. Hon. LLD: Carleton Univ., 1973; Queen's Univ., Kingston, 1976. Civic Award of Merit, Toronto, 1972; Diplôme d'Honneur, Canadian Conf. of the Arts, 1974. *Publications:* Oscar Peterson New Piano Solos, 1965; Jazz Exercises and Pieces, 1965. *Recreations:* audio, photography, ham radio, sports. *Address:* 2421 Hammond Road, Mississauga, Ont, Canada. *T:* 416/255 5651.

PETHERBRIDGE, Edward; actor and director; Member, Royal Shakespeare Company, since 1978; *b* 3 Aug. 1936; *s* of William and Hannah Petherbridge; *m* 1st, 1957, Louise Harris (marr. diss. 1980); one *s* ; 2nd, 1981, Emily Richard, actress. *Educ:* Grange Grammar Sch., Bradford; Northern Theatre Sch. Early experience in repertory and on tour; London début, Dumain in Love's Labours Lost and Demetrius in A Midsummer Night's Dream, Regent's Park Open Air Theatre, 1962; All in Good Time, Mermaid, and Phoenix, 1963; with Nat. Theatre Co. at Old Vic, 1964-70, chief appearances in: Trelawny of the Wells, Rosencrantz and Guildenstern are Dead, A Flea in her Ear, Love for Love, Volpone, The Advertisement, The Way of the World, The White Devil; Alceste in The Misanthrope, Nottingham, Lulu, Royal Court, and Apollo, 1970; John Bull's Other Island, Mermaid, Swansong, opening of Crucible, Sheffield, 1971; Founder Mem., Actors' Co., 1972; chief appearances at Edinburgh Fests, NY, and on tour, 1972-75: 'Tis Pity she's a Whore, Rooling the Roost, The Way of the World, Tartuffe, King Lear; also devised, dir. and appeared in Knots (from R. D. Laing's book), The Beanstalk, a wordless pantomime, and dir. The Bacchae; RSC tour of Australia and NZ, 1976; dir. Uncle Vanya, Cambridge Theatre Co., 1977; Chasuble in The Importance of Being Earnest, and dir., devised and appeared in Do You Love Me (from R. D. Laing's book), Actors' Co. tour and Round House, 1977; Crucifer of Blood, Haymarket, 1979; Royal Shakespeare Company: tour, 1978, Twelfth Night; Three Sisters, 1979; Suicide, Newman Noggs in Nicholas Nickleby (Best Supporting Actor, London Drama Critics' Award, 1981), No Limits to Love, 1980. Numerous television appearances include: Vershinin in Three Sisters (from RSC prod.); Lytton Strachey in No Need to Lie. Member: Theatre Performers Working Group, Arts Council, 1978-; Specialist Allocations Bd, Arts Council, 1980-. *Recreations:* listening to music, photography, theatre history. *Address:* c/o John French, 26 Binney Street, W1. *T:* 01-629 4159.

PETHERICK, Maurice, MA; *b* 5 Oct. 1894; *s* of George Tallack and Edith Petherick. *Educ:* St Peter's Court, Broadstairs; Marlborough College; Trinity College, Cambridge. 2nd Lieutenant Royal 1st Devon Yeomanry 1914; invalided out, 1915; served in Foreign Office, 1916-17; recommissioned Royal Scots Greys, 1917; served in France, 1918; recommissioned General List Army, Oct. 1939, Captain, Temp. Major. Contested (C) Penryn and Falmouth Division, 1929 and 1945; MP (C) Penryn and Falmouth, 1931-45; Financial Secretary, War Office, May-July, 1945; High Sheriff of Cornwall, 1957. Director, Prudential Assurance Co. Ltd, 1953-71. *Publications:* Captain Culverin, 1932; Victoire, 1943; Restoration Rogues, 1950. *Recreations:*

racing, gardening. *Address:* Porthpean House, St Austell, Cornwall. *Club:* United Oxford & Cambridge University.

PETHICK, Brig. Geoffrey Loveston, CBE 1960; DSO 1944; *b* 25 Nov. 1907; *s* of late Captain E. E. Pethick, RN and May (*née* Brook); *m* 1st, 1939, Nancy Veronica Ferrand (*d* 1980); one *d*; 2nd, 1981, Mrs Paula Usborne. *Educ:* Newton College. Commissioned, Royal Artillery, 1927; RHA 1934; served War of 1939–45; CO, Field Regt, 1942; Far East, 1945. Comdr 3 Army Group, RA, 1951. Chief Instructor, idc, 1950. Commander, RA 3 Div. 1953; War Office, 1957; retired, 1960. Dir, British Paper Makers' Association, 1960–74. *Recreations:* golf, gardens. *Address:* Little Croft, Fireball Hill, Sunningdale, Ascot, Berks. *T:* Ascot 22018.

PETHYBRIDGE, Frank, CBE 1977; Regional Administrator, North Western Regional Health Authority, 1973–82, retired; *b* 19 Jan. 1924; *s* of Frank and Margaret Pethybridge; *m* 1947, Jean Ewing; one *s* one *d*. *Educ:* William Hulme's Grammar Sch., Manchester; Univ. of Manchester (BA Admin). FHA, FRSH. Served with RAF, 1942–47 (Flt-Lt). Town Clerk's Dept, Manchester CBC, 1940–42 and 1947–62; Manchester Regional Hosp. Bd, 1962–73. *Recreations:* woodwork, walking, swimming. *Address:* 12 The Leylands, West Beach, Lytham St Annes FY8 5QS. *T:* Lytham 739854.

PETIT, Sir Dinshaw Manockjee, 3rd Bt, *cr* 1890; *b* 24 June 1901; *s* of Sir Dinshaw Manockjee Petit, 2nd Bt, and Dinbai, *d* of Sir J. Jeejeebhoy, 3rd Bt; *S* father, 1933; *m* 1928, Sylla (*d* 1963), *d* of late R. D. Tata; one *s* one *d*. *Educ:* St Xavier's, Bombay; Trinity Hall, Cambridge. Called to Bar, Inner Temple, 1925. President: SPCA, Bombay; Petit Boys Sch., Poona; Petit Girls' Sch., Pali Hill, Bombay; Petit Sanatorium, Cumballa Hill, Bombay; Trustee: V.J.T. Technical Inst., Bombay; Parsee Gen. Hosp., Bombay. Pres., Northbrook Soc., London; Life Gov., Royal Hosp. for Incurables; Hon. Life Mem., RSPCA. Vice-Pres., British Assoc. of Riviera. Citizen of Honour of France. *Heir: s* Nasserwanjee Dinshaw Petit [*b* 13 Aug. 1934; *m* 1964, Nirmala Nanavatty; two *s*]. *Address:* Petit Hall, 66 Nepean Sea Road, Bombay, India; Savaric, 06 Eze-Village, France; 8 Mount Row, W1.

PETIT, Roland; Chevalier de la Légion d'honneur; Chevalier des Arts et des Lettres; French choreographer and dancer; Artistic Director and Choreographer, Ballets de Marseille; *b* Villemomble, 13 Jan. 1924; *m* 1954, Renée Jeanmaire; one *s*. *Educ:* Ecole de Ballet de l'Opéra de Paris, studying under Ricaux and Lifar. Premier danseur, l'Opéra de Paris, 1940–44; founded Les Vendredis de la Danse, 1944, Les Ballets des Champs-Elysées, 1945, Les Ballets de Paris de Roland Petit, 1948. Choreographic works include: Les Forains, Le Jeune Homme et la Mort, Les Demoiselles de la nuit, Carmen, Deuil en 24 heures, Le Loup, L'éloge de la Folie, Les Chants de Maldoror, Notre Dame de Paris, Paradise Lost, Les Intermittences du coeur, La Symphonie fantastique, La Dame de Pique, Die Fledermaus, etc; choreographer and dancer: La Belle au Bois Dormant; Cyrano de Bergerac. Appeared in films Hans Christian Andersen; Un, Deux, Trois, Quartre (arr. ballets, for film, and danced in 3); 4 ballets, Black Tights. *Address:* Ballets de Marseille, place Auguste-Carli, 13001 Marseille, France.

PETO, Sir Henry (George Morton), 4th Bt *cr* 1855; consultant and company director; *b* 29 April 1920; *s* of Comdr Sir Henry Francis Morton Peto, 3rd Bt, RN, and Edith (*d* 1945), *d* of late George Berners Ruck Keene; *S* father, 1978; *m* 1947, Frances Jacqueline, JP, *d* of late Ralph Haldane Evers; two *s*. *Educ:* Sherborne; Corpus Christi College, Cambridge. Served War with Royal Artillery, 1939–46. Manufacturing industry, 1946–80. *Recreations:* tennis, fishing, gardening. *Heir: s* Francis Michael Morton Peto [*b* 11 Jan. 1949; *m* 1974, Felicity Margaret, *d* of Lt-Col John Alan Burns; two *s*]. *Address:* Stream House, Selborne, Alton, Hants. *T:* Selborne 246.

PETO, Sir Michael (Henry Basil), 4th Bt *cr* 1927; *b* 6 April 1938; *s* of Brig. Sir Christopher Henry Maxwell Peto, 3rd Bt, DSO, and of Barbara, *yr d* of Edwyn Thomas Close; *S* father, 1980; *m* 1st, 1963, Sarah Susan (marr. diss. 1970), *y d* of Major Sir Dennis Stucley, Bt, *qv* ; two *s* two *d* ; 2nd, 1971, Lucinda Mary, *yr d* of Major Sir Charles Douglas Blackett, 9th Bt; two *s*. *Educ:* Eton; Christ Church, Oxford (MA). Called to the Bar, Inner Temple, 1960. Mem., Stock Exchange, 1965–. *Heir: s* Henry Christopher Morton Bampfylde Peto, *b* 8 April 1967. *Address:* Lower Church Cottage, Cliddesden, near Basingstoke, Hants. *Club:* Turf.

PETRE, family name of Baron Petre.

PETRE, 17th Baron, *cr* 1603; **Joseph William Lionel Petre;** Captain Essex Regiment; *b* 5 June 1914; *s* of 16th Baron and Catherine (who *m* 2nd, 1921, Sir Frederic Carne Rasch, 2nd Bt, TD, *d* 1963) *d* of late Hon. John and late Lady Margaret Boscawen, Tregye, Falmouth, Cornwall; *S* father, 1915; *m* 1941, Marguerite, *d* of late Ion Wentworth Hamilton, Westwood, Nettlebed, Oxfordshire; one *s*. *Heir: s* Hon. John Patrick Lionel Petre [*b* 4 Aug. 1942; *m* 1965, Marcia Gwendolyn, *o d* of Alfred Plumpton; two *s* one *d*]. *Address:* Ingatestone Hall, Essex.

PETRE, Francis Herbert Loraine; His Honour Judge Petre; a Circuit Judge, since 1972; *b* 9 March 1927; *s* of late Maj.-Gen. R. L. Petre, CB, DSO, MC and Mrs Katherine Sophia Petre; *m* 1958, Mary Jane, *d* of Everard White, Masterton, NZ; three *s* one *d*. *Educ:* Downside; Clare Coll., Cambridge. Called to Bar, Lincoln's Inn, 1952; Dep. Chm., E Suffolk QS, 1970; Dep.

Chm., Agricultural Lands Tribunal (Eastern Area), 1972; a Recorder, 1972.

PETRIE, Cecilia, (Lady Petrie); *d* of late F. J. G. Mason, Kensington; *m* 1926, Sir Charles Petrie, 3rd Bt, CBE, FRHistS (*d* 1977); one *s*. Mem. Kensington Borough Council (Queen's Gate Ward), 1946–62; Alderman, 1965–71; Freeman, 1971; Mayor of the Royal Borough of Kensington, 1954–56. Member: (C) LCC, for S Kensington, 1949–65; Fulham & Kensington Hospital Management Committee, 1948–59 (Chairman, 1955–59); Chelsea and Kensington Hospital Management Cttee, 1959–72; Board of Governors, Charing Cross Hospital, 1959–68; Member Board of Governors of Hospital for Diseases of the Chest, 1951–73; Mem. Central Health Services Council, 1955–61; Dep.-Chm. of the London County Council, 1958–59; UK Delegate to United Nations Assembly, 14th Session, 1959; Member: SW Metropolitan Regional Hospital Board, 1959–65; London Exec. Council, Nat. Health Service, 1965–74; Family Practitioner Service, 1974–78; Whitley Council Committee C, 1949–71. *Recreation:* reading detective stories. *Address:* 31 Queen's Gate Terrace, SW7 5PP. *T:* 01-581 0112.

See also P. C. Petrie.

PETRIE, Sir (Charles) Richard (Borthwick), 4th Bt *cr* 1918; TD; MA (Oxon); Director, Richard Petrie Ltd Audio-Visual Programme Production; *b* 19 Oct. 1921; *s* of Sir Charles Alexander Petrie, 3rd Bt, CBE, and Ursula Gabrielle Borthwick (*d* 1962), *d* of late Judge Harold Chaloner Dowdall, QC; *S* father, 1977; *m* 1962, Jessie Ariana Borthwick, *d* of late Comdr Patrick Straton Campbell, RN. *Educ:* Radley College; Heidelberg Univ.; New Coll., Oxford. Served REME, 1942–47 and again (TA), 1949–67, Lt-Col; Commander REME, 43rd (Wessex) Inf. Div., TA, 1962–65. Member of Exec. Cttee, Assoc. of Professional Recording Studios, 1968–75. *Publications:* Ghana: Portrait of a West African State, 1974; (contrib.) Sound Recording Practice, 1976. *Recreations:* music, shrub gardening. *Address:* 3 Northmoor Road, Oxford. *T:* Oxford 56081.

PETRIE, Edward James, CMG 1955; *b* 1907; retired from HM Treasury, Nairobi. Assistant Revenue Officer, Kenya, 1933; Assistant Treasurer, 1934; Senior Accountant, 1943; Assistant Financial Secretary, 1946; Financial Secretary, Barbados, 1948; Accountant-General, Kenya, 1951; Sec. to Treasury, Kenya, 1953–56; retd 1956. *Address:* 19 Stirling Road, Edinburgh EH5 3JA.

PETRIE, Joan Caroline, (Mrs M. E. Bathurst); HM Diplomatic Service, retired 1972; *b* 2 Nov. 1920; *d* of late James Alexander Petrie, Barrister-at-law, and Adrienne Johanna (*née* van den Bergh); *m* 1968, Maurice Edward Bathurst, *qv* ; one step *s*. *Educ:* Wycombe Abbey Sch.; Newnham Coll., Cambridge (Mary Ewart Schol.). 1st cl. Med. and Mod. Langs Tripos, 1942, MA 1964. Entered HM Foreign Service, 1947: FO, 1947–48; 2nd Sec., The Hague, 1948–50; FO, 1950–54; 1st Sec., 1953; Bonn, 1954–58; FO (later FCO), 1958–71; Counsellor 1969; Head of European Communities Information Unit, FCO, 1969–71. Mem., UK Delegn to Colombo Plan Consultative Cttee, Jogjakarta, 1959. Adviser, British Group, Inter-Parly Union, 1962–68. Officer, Order of Leopold (Belgium), 1966. *Recreations:* music, genealogy. *Address:* Airlie, The Highlands, East Horsley, Surrey. *T:* East Horsley 3269. *Club:* United Oxford & Cambridge University.

PETRIE, Peter Charles, CMG 1980; HM Diplomatic Service; Minister, Paris, since 1979; *b* 7 March 1932; *s* of Sir Charles Petrie, 3rd Bt, CBE, FRHistS and of Lady (Cecilia) Petrie, *qv* ; *b* and *heir presumptive* to Sir Richard Petrie, *qv* ; *m* 1958, Countess Lydwine Maria Fortunata v. Oberndorff, *d* of Count v. Oberndorff, The Hague and Paris; two *s* one *d*. *Educ:* Westminster; Christ Church, Oxford. BA Lit. Hum., MA. 2nd Lieut Grenadier Guards, 1954–56. Entered HM Foreign Service, 1956; served in UK Delegn to NATO, Paris 1958–61; UK High Commn, New Delhi (seconded CRO), 1961–64; Chargé d'Affaires, Katmandu, 1963; Cabinet Office, 1965–67; UK Mission to UN, NY, 1969–73; Counsellor (Head of Chancery), Bonn, 1973–76; Head of European Integration Dept (Internal), FCO, 1976–79. *Recreations:* shooting, tennis. *Address:* 16A Cambridge Street, SW1V 4QH; 40 rue Lauriston, 75116 Paris, France. *Clubs:* Brooks's; Jockey (Paris).

PETRIE, Sir Richard; see Petrie, Sir C. R. B.

PETTIFER, Julian; freelance writer and broadcaster; *b* 21 July 1935; *s* of Stephen Henry Pettifer and Diana Mary (*née* Burton); unmarried. *Educ:* Marlborough; St John's Coll., Cambridge. Television reporter, writer and presenter: Southern TV, 1958–62; Tonight, BBC, 1962–64; 24 Hours, BBC, 1964–69; Panorama, BBC, 1969–75. Numerous television documentaries, including: Vietnam, War without End, 1970; The World About Us, 1976; The Spirit of '76, 1976; Diamonds in the Sky, 1979; Nature Watch, 1981–82. Reporter of the Year Award, Guild of Television Directors and Producers, 1968. *Publications:* (jtly) Diamonds in the Sky: a social history of air travel, 1979; (jtly) Nature Watch, 1981. *Recreations:* travel, sport, cinema. *Address:* c/o Curtis Brown, 1 Craven Hill, W2 3EP. *T:* 01-262 1011. *Club:* Queen's.

PETTINGELL, Sir William (Walter), Kt 1972; CBE 1965 (OBE 1959); Deputy Chairman, The Australian Gas Light Co. (General Manager, 1952–74); *b* Corrimal, NSW, 4 Sept. 1914; *s* of H. G. W. Pettingell, Cootamundra, NSW; *m* 1942, Thora M., *d* of J. Stokes; one *s* two *d*. *Educ:* Wollongong High Sch.; Univ. of Sydney. BSc (Sydney) 1st cl. hons, 1934. The Australian

Gas Light Co.: Research Chemist, 1936; Production Engr, 1948; Works Manager, 1950; Asst Gen. Manager (Technical), 1951; Gen. Manager, 1952-74; Dir, 1974-. Chairman: Hanimex Corp., 1978-; Leighton Holdings Ltd; Prudential Cornhill Insurance; Blackwood Hodge Ltd. Deputy Chairman: Australian Consolidated Industries; Foreign Investment Review Bd; Director: Howard Smith Ltd; Coal and Allied Industries Ltd. FAIM, FIAM, FInstF, MInstGasE. *Recreation:* yachting (sails a 35 foot ocean racer and has taken part in annual Sydney to Hobart and other ocean yacht races). *Address:* 54 Linden Way, Castlecrag, NSW 2068, Australia. *T:* 95 1976. *Clubs:* Union, American, Royal Prince Alfred Yacht, Royal Sydney Yacht Squadron, Elanora Golf (all in NSW).

PETTIT, Sir Daniel (Eric Arthur), Kt 1974; Chairman, Post Office Staff Superannuation Fund, since 1979; Member (Part-time), National Ports Council, 1971-80; *b* Liverpool, 19 Feb. 1915; *s* of Thomas Edgar Pettit and Pauline Elizabeth Pettit (*née* Kerr); *m* 1940, Winifred, *d* of William and Sarah Bibby; two *s. Educ:* Quarry Bank High Sch., Liverpool; Fitzwilliam Coll., Cambridge (MA). School Master, 1938-40 and 1946-47; War Service, Africa, India, Burma, 1940-46 (Major, RA); Unilever: Management, 1948-57; Associated Company Dir and Chm., 1958-70. Chm., Nat. Freight Corp., 1971-78 (part-time Mem. Bd, 1968-70); Member: Freight Integration Council, 1971-78; Bd, Foundn of Management Educn, 1973-; Waste Management Adv. Council, 1971-78; Chm., EDC for Distributive Trades, 1974-78; Director: Lloyds Bank Ltd, 1977-78 (Chm., Birmingham & W Midlands Bd, 1978-); Lloyds Bank (UK) Ltd, 1979-; Bransford Farmers Ltd; Chm., Incpen, 1979-; Mem. Council, British Road Fedn Ltd. Hon. Col, 162 Regt RCT (V), 1978-80. Freeman, City of London; Liveryman, Worshipful Co. of Carmen. FBIM; FCIT (Pres. 1971-72); FRSA; MIPM. *Publications:* various papers on transport and management matters. *Recreations:* cricket, Association football (Olympic Games, 1936; Corinthian FC, 1935-); fly-fishing. *Address:* Bransford Court Farm, Worcester. *Clubs:* Farmers', MCC; Hawks (Cambridge).

PETTY, Hon. Sir Horace (Rostill), Kt 1964; BCom, FASA; Agent-General for State of Victoria, in London, 1964-69; *b* 29 March 1904; *m* 1st, 1930 (marr. diss.); two *s* two *d* ; 2nd, 1959, Beryl Anne Hoelter. *Educ:* South Yarra School; University High School; Melbourne University. Accountant and auditor (managerial appts in retail business field, etc.) from mid-twenties to 1939. Australian Army, 1940-44; Infty, Aust. Armd Div. and AHQ in North, rank Major. Mem. Municipal Council, City of Prahran, 1949-64 (Mayor, 1951-52). MLA for Toorak (Liberal) in Victorian Parl., 1952-64. (Victorian Govt) Minister of: Housing, July 1955-July 1961; Immigration, July 1956-Dec. 1961; Public Works, Victorian State Government, July 1961-Apr. 1964. Mem., RSSAILA. *Recreations:* golf, racing, motoring. *Address:* 593 Toorak Road, Toorak, Victoria 3142, Australia. *Clubs:* Naval and Military (Melbourne), Melbourne Cricket, Victoria Racing, RAC of Victoria.

PETTY, William Henry, CBE 1981; County Education Officer, Kent, since 1973; *b* 7 Sept. 1921; *s* of Henry and Eveline Ann Petty, Bradford; *m* 1948, Margaret Elaine, *o d* of Edward and Lorna Bastow, Baildon, Yorks; one *s* two *d. Educ:* Bradford Grammar Sch.; Peterhouse, Cambridge; London Univ. MA 1950, BSc 1953. Served RA, India and Burma, 1941-45. Admin, teaching and lectrg in London, Doncaster and N R Yorks, 1946-57; Sen. Asst Educn Officer, W R Yorks CC 1957-64; Dep. County Educn Officer, Kent CC, 1964-73. Member: Council and Court, Univ. of Kent at Canterbury, 1974-; Local Govt Trng Bd, Careers Service Trng Cttee, 1975-; Careers Service Adv. Council, 1976-; Trng and Further Educn Cons. Gp, 1977-; Vital Skills Task Gp, 1977-78; Manpower Services Commn, SE Counties Area Bd, 1978-; Bd of Dirs, Industrial Trng Service, 1978-; Exec. Mem. and Sec. for SE Reg., Soc. of Educn Officers, 1978-; Pres., Soc. of Educn Officers, 1980-81; Chairman: Assoc. of Educn Officers, 1979-80 (Vice-Chm., 1978-79); JNC for Chief Officers, Officers' side, 1981-; C of E Bd of Educn, Schs Cttee, 1981-; County Educn Officers' Soc., 1982-. Prizewinner: Cheltenham Fest. of Lit., 1968; Camden Fest. of Music and Arts, 1969. Greenwood Prize, 1978; Lake Aske Meml Award, 1980. *Publications:* No Bold Comfort, 1957; Conquest, 1967; (jtly) Educational Administration, 1980; contrib. educnl and lit. jls and anthologies. *Recreations:* literature, travel. *Address:* Godfrey House, Hollingbourne, Maidstone, Kent ME17 1TX. *T:* Hollingbourne 346. *Club:* United Oxford & Cambridge University.

PETTY-FITZMAURICE; *see* Mercer Nairne Petty-Fitzmaurice, family name of Marquess of Lansdowne.

PEVSNER, Sir Nikolaus (Bernhard Leon), Kt 1969; CBE 1953; FBA 1965; MA Cantab; MA Oxon; PhD; FSA; Hon. FRIBA; Hon. ARCA; Hon. FNZIA; Hon. Academician, Accademia di Belle Arti, Venice; Hon. Fellow, Royal Scottish Academy; Hon. Member, American Academy of Arts and Sciences; Hon. Fellow, Akademie der Wissenschaften Göttingen; Emeritus Professor of History of Art, Birkbeck College, University of London; *b* 30 Jan. 1902; *s* of late Hugo Pevsner; *m* 1923, Karola Kurlbaum (*d* 1963); two *s* one *d. Educ:* St Thomas's Sch., Leipzig; Univs of Leipzig, Munich, Berlin and Frankfort. PhD History of Art and Architecture, 1924; Asst Keeper, Dresden Gallery, 1924-28; Lectr, History of Art and Architecture, Goettingen Univ., 1929-33; Slade Prof. of Fine Art, Univ. of Cambridge, 1949-55; Fellow, St John's Coll., Cambridge, 1950-55, Hon. Fellow, 1967-; Slade Prof. of Fine Art, Univ. of Oxford, 1968-69. Former Chm., Victorian Soc. (to 1976); Member: Historic Buildings Council, 1966-79; Council, Wm Morris Soc.; (formerly) Adv. Bd for Redundant Churches (to 1977). Reith Lectr,

BBC, 1955. Royal Gold Medal for Architecture (RIBA), 1967; Albert Medal, RSA, 1976; other medals: Howland, Yale, 1963; Hitchcock, London, 1966; Thomas Jefferson, Univ. of Virginia, 1975; German Prize, Nat. Cttee for Monumental Preservation, 1982. Hon. Doctorates: Leicester, York, Leeds, Oxford, Cambridge, E Anglia, Zagreb, Keele, Open Univ., Heriot-Watt Univ., Edinburgh, Univ. of Pennsylvania; Hon. DLitt Cantab. 1979. Grand Cross of Merit, Fed. Rep. of Germany. *Publications:* The Baroque Architecture of Leipzig, 1928; Italian Painting from the end of the Renaissance to the end of the Rococo (a vol. of the Handbuch der Kunstwissenschaft), 1927-30; Pioneers of the Modern Movement, from William Morris to Walter Gropius, 1936 (revised edn: Pioneers of Modern Design, Museum of Modern Art, New York, 1949; new edn 1972; also foreign edns); An Enquiry into Industrial Art in England, 1937; German Baroque Sculpture (with S. Sitwell and A. Ayscough), 1938; Academies of Art, Past and Present, 1940; An Outline of European Architecture, Pelican Books, 1942, most recent edn, 1973 (also edns in numerous foreign langs); High Victorian Design, 1951; The Buildings of England (46 vols), 1951-74; The Planning of the Elizabethan Country House, 1961; The Englishness of English Art, 1956; Sir Christopher Wren (in Italian), 1958; Sources of Modern Art, 1962 (re-issued as The Sources of Modern Architecture and Design, 1968); Dictionary of Architecture (with John Fleming and Hugh Honour), 1966; Studies in Art, Architecture and Design (2 vols), 1968; (with J. M. Richards) The Anti-Rationalists, 1973; Some Architectural Writers of the Nineteenth Century, 1973; A History of Building Types, 1976 (Wolfson Literary Award). *Address:* 2 Wildwood Terrace, North End, NW3.

PEYREFITTE, (Pierre-) Roger; French author; *b* 17 Aug. 1907; *o s* of Jean Peyrefitte, landowner, and Eugénie Jamme; unmarried. *Educ:* Collège St Benoit, Ardouane, Hérault (Lazarist); Collège du Caousou, Toulouse, Hte. Garonne (Jesuit); Lycée de Foix, Ariège; Université de Toulouse; Ecole libre des Sciences Politiques, Paris. Bachelier de l'enseignement secondaire; Diplôme d'études supérieures de langue et de littérature française; Diplômé de l'Ecole libre des Sciences Politiques (major de la section diplomatique). Concours diplomatique, 1931; attaché to Ministry of Foreign Affairs, 1931-33; Secretary, French Embassy, Athens, 1933-38; attached to Ministry of Foreign Affairs, 1938-40 and 1943-45. *Publications:* Les Amitiés Particulières, novel, 1944 (Prix Théophraste Renaudot, 1945); Mademoiselle de Murville, novel, 1947; Le Prince des neiges, play, 1947; L'Oracle, novel, 1948; Les Amours Singulières, 1949; La Mort d'une mère, 1950; Les Ambassades, novel, 1951; Du Vésuve à l'Etna, 1952; La Fin des Ambassades, novel, 1953; Les Clés de saint Pierre, novel, 1955; Jeunes Proies, 1956; Chevaliers de Malte, 1957; L'Exilé de Capri, novel, 1959; Le Spectateur Nocturne, play, 1960; Les Ambassades, play (adaptation of A. P. Antoine), 1961; Les Fils de la Lumière, 1962; La Nature du Prince, 1963; Les Juifs, 1965; Notre Amour, 1967; Les Américains, novel, 1968; Des Français, novel, 1970; La Coloquinte, novel, 1971; Manouche, 1972; Un Musée de l'Amour, 1972; La Muse garçonnière, 1973; Catalogue de la collection de monnais grecques et romains de l'auteur, 1974; Tableaux de chasse, ou la vie extraordinaire de Fernand Legros, 1976; Propos secrets, 1977; La Jeunesse d'Alexandre, 1977; L'Enfant de coeur, 1978; Roy, novel, 1979; Les Conquêtes d'Alexandre, 1980; Propos secrets 2, 1980; Alexandre le Grand, 1981; L'Illustre écrivain, novel, 1982. *Recreations:* travel, walks, collecting antiques. *Address:* 9 Avenue du Maréchal Maunoury, 75016 Paris, France.

PEYTON, Rt. Hon. John Wynne William, PC 1970; MP (C) Yeovil Division of Somerset since 1951; *b* 13 Feb. 1919; *s* of late Ivor Eliot Peyton and Dorothy Helen Peyton; *m* 1947, Diana Clinch (marr. diss., 1966); one *s* one *d* (and one *s* decd); *m* 1966, Mrs Mary Cobbold. *Educ:* Eton; Trinity College, Oxford. Commissioned 15/19 Hussars, 1939; Prisoner of War, Germany, 1940-45. Called to the Bar, Inner Temple, 1945. Parly Secretary, Ministry of Power, 1962-64; Minister of Transport, June-Oct. 1970; Minister for Transport Industries, DoE, 1970-74. Chm., Texas Instruments Ltd, 1974-. *Address:* The Old Malt House, Hinton St George, Somerset. *T:* Crewkerne 73618; 6 Temple West Mews, West Square, SE11. *T:* 01-582 3611. *Club:* Boodle's.

PEYTON, Kathleen Wendy; writer (as K. M. Peyton); *b* 2 Aug. 1929; *d* of William Joseph Herald and Ivy Kathleen Herald; *m* 1950, Michael Peyton; two *d. Educ:* Wimbledon High Sch.; Manchester Sch. of Art (ATD). Taught art at Northampton High Sch., 1953-55; started writing seriously after birth of first child, although had already had 4 books published. *Publications:* as *Kathleen Herald:* Sabre, the Horse from the Sea, 1947, USA 1963; The Mandrake, 1949; Crab the Roan, 1953; as *K. M. Peyton:* North to Adventure, 1959, USA 1965; Stormcock Meets Trouble, 1961; The Hard Way Home, 1962; Windfall, 1963, USA (as Sea Fever), 1963; Brownsea Silver, 1964; The Maplin Bird, 1964, USA 1965 (New York Herald Tribune Award, 1965); The Plan for Birdsmarsh, 1965, USA 1966; Thunder in the Sky, 1966, USA 1967; Flambards Trilogy (Guardian Award, 1970): Flambards, 1967, USA 1968; The Edge of the Cloud, 1969, USA 1969 (Carnegie Medal, 1969); Flambards in Summer, 1969, USA 1970; Fly-by-Night, 1968, USA 1969; Pennington's Seventeenth Summer, 1970, USA (as Pennington's Last Term), 1971; The Beethoven Medal, 1971, USA 1972; The Pattern of Roses, 1972, USA 1973; Pennington's Heir, 1973, USA 1974; The Team, 1975; The Right-Hand Man, 1977; Prove Yourself a Hero, 1977, USA 1978; A Midsummer Night's Death, 1978, USA 1979; Marion's Angels, 1979, USA 1979; Flambards Divided, 1981; Dear Fred, 1981. *Recreations:* riding, walking, gardening. *Address:* Rookery Cottage, North Fambridge, Chelmsford, Essex CM3 6LP.

PEYTON, Sidney Augustus, PhD; Librarian of Sheffield University, 1941-56; *b* 1891; *e s* of late Sidney Peyton, Newbury; *m* Muriel Kathleen Pearse (*d* 1980). *Educ:* University Coll., Reading. Lectr, University Coll., Reading, 1919; Univ. Librarian, Reading, 1922-41. Hon. LittD Sheffield. *Publications:* Oxfordshire Peculiars (Oxford Record Society); Kesteven Quarter Sessions Minutes (Lincoln Record Society); Kettering Vestry Minutes (Northamptonshire Record Society); Northamptonshire QS Records, Introduction; various historical papers. *Recreation:* music. *Address:* 14 Brincliffe Court, Nether Edge Road, Sheffield S7 1RX. *T:* Sheffield 52767.

PHALP, Geoffrey Anderson, CBE 1968; TD; Secretary, King Edward's Hospital Fund for London, 1968-80; *b* 8 July 1915; *s* of late Charles Anderson Phalp and late Sara Gertrude Phalp (*née* Wilkie); *m* 1946, Jeanne Margaret, OBE, JP, *d* of late Emeritus Prof. G. R. Goldsborough, CBE, FRS; one *s* one *d. Educ:* Durham Sch.; Univ. of Durham (BCom). Served with RA (despatches), 1939-46. Asst Registrar, Med. Sch., King's Coll., Newcastle upon Tyne, 1946-49; Dep. House Governor and Sec., United Newcastle upon Tyne Hosps, 1949-51; Sec. and Principal Admin. Officer, United Birmingham Hosps, 1951-68. *Recreations:* fly fishing, gardening, music. *Address:* 86 Marryat Road, Wimbledon, SW19. *T:* 01-946 5132. *Club:* Savile.

PHAROAH, Prof. Peter Oswald Derrick, MD, FFCM; Professor of Community Health, University of Liverpool, since 1979; *b* 19 May 1934; *s* of Oswald Higgins Pharoah and Phyllis Christine Gahan; *m* 1960, Margaret Rose McMinn; three *s* one *d. Educ:* Lawrence Memorial Royal Military School, Lovedale, India; Palmers School, Grays, Essex; St Mary's Hospital Medical School. MD, MSc. Graduated, 1958; Med. House Officer and Med. Registrar appointments at various London Hosps, 1958-63; MO and Research MO, Dept of Public Health, Papua New Guinea, 1963-74; Sen. Lectr in Community Health, London School of Hygiene and Tropical Medicine, 1974-79. *Publication:* Endemic Cretinism, 1971. *Recreations:* squash, walking, philately. *Address:* 11 Fawley Road, Liverpool L18 9TE. *T:* 051-724 4896.

PHELAN, Andrew James; His Honour Judge Phelan; a Circuit Judge, since 1974; *b* 25 July 1923; *e s* of Cornelius Phelan, Clonmel, Eire; *m* 1950, Joan Robertson McLagan; one *s* two *d. Educ:* Clongoweswood, Co. Kildare; National Univ. of Ireland (MA); Trinity Coll., Cambridge. Called to: Irish Bar, King's Inn, 1945; English Bar, Gray's Inn, 1949. Jun. Fellow, Univ. of Bristol, 1948-50; in practice at English Bar, 1950-74. *Publication:* The Law for Small Boats, 2nd edn, 1970. *Recreations:* sailing, mountain walking. *Address:* 17 Hartington Road, Chiswick, W4 1PD. *T:* 01-994 6109. *Club:* Bar Yacht.

PHELPS, Anthony John, CB 1976; Deputy Chairman, Board of Customs and Excise, 1973-82; *b* 14 Oct. 1922; *s* of John Francis and Dorothy Phelps, Oxford; *m* 1st, 1949, Sheila Nan Rait (*d* 1967), *d* of late Colin Benton Rait, Edinburgh; one *s* two *d* ; 2nd, 1971, Janet M. T., *d* of late Charles R. Dawson, Edinburgh. *Educ:* City of Oxford High Sch.; University Coll., Oxford. HM Treasury, 1946; Jun. Private Sec. to Chancellor of the Exchequer, 1949-50; Principal, 1950; Treasury Rep. in Far East, 1953-55; Private Sec. to the Prime Minister, 1958-61; Asst Sec., 1961; Under-Sec., 1968. Freeman, City of Oxford, 1971. *Recreations:* music, watching sport. *Address:* 1 Woodsyre, Sydenham Hill, SE26 6SS. *T:* 01-670 0735. *Clubs:* City Livery, MCC.

PHELPS, Charles Frederick, DPhil; Principal, Chelsea College, London, since 1981; *b* 18 Jan. 1934; *s* of Seth Phelps and Rigmor Kaae; *m* 1960, Joanna Lingeman; one *s* one *d. Educ:* Bromsgrove Sch.; Oxford Univ. (MA, DPhil). Lecturer, Univ. of Bristol: in Chemical Physiology, 1960-63; in Biochemistry, 1963-70; Reader in Biochemistry, Univ. of Bristol, 1970-74; Prof. of Biochemistry, Univ. of Lancaster, 1974-80. Visiting Fellow, Univ. of Rome, 1968-69. Consultant, World Bank Educational Mission to China, 1980 and to Korea, 1982. Mem. Cttee, Biochemical Soc., 1980-; Member: British Biophysical Soc., 1974-; Research Cttee of Arthritis and Rheumatism Council, 1974-78; Editorial Board, Biochim. Biophys. Acta, 1976-80. *Publications:* numerous papers in medical and science jls. *Recreations:* enjoying things Italian, 17th Century science, Brahms. *Address:* 28 Limerston Street, SW10 0HH. *T:* 01-352 3258. *Club:* Athenæum.

PHELPS, Howard Thomas Henry Middleton; Operations Director since 1979 and Board Member since 1973, British Airways Board; *b* 20 Oct. 1926; *s* of Ernest Henry Phelps, Gloucester, and Harriet (*née* Middleton); *m* 1949, Audrey (*née* Ellis); one *d. Educ:* Crypt Grammar Sch., Gloucester; Hatfield Coll.; Durham Univ. BA Hons Politics and Econs 1951. National Coal Board, Lancs, Durham and London, 1951-72, finally Dep. Dir-Gen. of Industrial Relations; Personnel Dir, BOAC, 1972; Gp Personnel Dir, BAB, 1972. FIPM; FCIT; CBIM. Chm., Alice Ruston Housing Assoc. Chm., Durham Univ. Soc.; Pres., Hatfield Assoc. *Recreations:* gardening, musical appreciation. *Address:* Littlecroft, Heathside Road, Woking, Surrey. *T:* Woking 62027. *Clubs:* Reform, Royal Automobile.

PHELPS, Maj.-Gen. Leonard Thomas Herbert, CB 1973; OBE 1963; CBIM 1979; Managing Director, The Warrior Group, 1975-78; *b* 9 Sept. 1917; *s* of Abijah Phelps; *m* 1945, Jean Irene, *d* of R. Price Dixon; one *s* one *d*. FBIM 1973. Served War, Hong Kong, 1940-41; India/Burma, 1941-47. Student, Staff Coll., Quetta, 1946; DAQMG, HQ Land Forces Hong Kong, 1951-53; Second in Command, 4th Trng Bn, RAOC, 1955-57; War Office:

DAAG, 1957-59; ADOS, 1961-63; AA & QMG Singapore Mil. Forces, 1963; Chief of Staff, 4th Malaysian Inf. Bde, 1964; ADOS, WO, 1965-67; Chief Inspector, Land Service Ammunition, 1967-70; Comdr, Base Organisation, RAOC, 1970; Dir, Ordnance Services, MoD (Army), 1971-73; retired 1973; Col Comdt, RAOC, 1976-78. *Recreations:* shooting, golf. *Address:* South Port Cottage, Sutton Courtenay, Oxon.

PHELPS, Maurice Arthur; Board Member for Personnel and Industrial Relations, British Shipbuilders, since 1980; *b* 17 May 1935; *s* of H. T. Phelps; *m* 1960, Elizabeth Anne Hurley; two *s* one *d. Educ:* Wandsworth School; Corpus Christi College, Oxford Univ. BA Hons Modern History. Shell Chemical Co. Ltd, 1959-68; Group Personnel Planning Adviser, Pilkington Bros Ltd, 1968-70; Group Personnel Dir, Unicorn Industries Ltd, 1970-72; Dir of Labour and Staff Relations, W Midland Passenger Transport Exec., 1973-77; Dir of Personnel, Heavy Vehicle Div., Leyland Vehicles Ltd, 1977-80. *Address:* 5 Dunelm Court, South Street, Durham. *T:* Durham 46881.

PHELPS, Richard Wintour; General Manager, Central Lancashire New Town Development Corporation, since 1971; *b* 26 July 1925; *s* of Rev. H. Phelps; *m* 1955, Pamela Marie Lawson; two *d. Educ:* Kingswood Sch.; Merton Coll., Oxford (MA). 14th Punjab Regt, IA, 1944-46. Colonial Admin. Service, Northern Region and Fed. Govt. of Nigeria, 1948-57 and 1959-61; Prin., HM Treasury, 1957-59 and 1961-65; Sen. Administrator, Hants CC, 1965-67; Gen. Manager, Skelmersdale New Town Develt Corp., 1967-71. Winston Churchill Trust Travelling Fellowship, 1971. *Recreations:* reading, travel, music. *Address:* Fell Foot House, Newby Bridge, Ulverston, Cumbria LA12 8NL. *T:* Newby Bridge 31274. *Club:* Royal Commonwealth Society.

PHELPS BROWN, Sir Ernest Henry; see Brown, Sir E. H. P.

PHEMISTER, James, MA, DSc, FRSE, FGS; FMSA; *b* 3 April 1893; 2nd *s* of John Clark Phemister and Elizabeth G. Crawford; *m* 1921, Margaret Clark, MA; two *s* one *d. Educ:* Govan High Sch.; Glasgow Univ. Served European War, RE and RGA; disabled 1917, and placed on retired list, 1918; teacher of Mathematics and Science, 1918-21; appointed Geological Survey, 1921; Petrographer, 1935-45; Curator, Museum of Practical Geology, 1945-46; Asst Dir Specialist Services, 1946-53; Pres. Mineralogical Soc., 1951-54; Pres. Glasgow Geol. Soc., 1961-64. Editor, Mineralogical Abstracts, 1959-66. *Publications:* papers on Petrological and Geophysical subjects. *Recreation:* swimming. *Address:* 39A Fountainhall Road, Edinburgh EH9 2LN. *T:* 031-667 4700.

PHEMISTER, Prof. Thomas Crawford, MSc (Chicago), PhD (Cantab), DSc (Glasgow); FRSE, FGS; Dr de l'Univ. de Rennes (hon. causa); Professor and Head of Department of Geology and Mineralogy, Aberdeen University, 1937-72, now Professor emeritus; *b* 25 May 1902; 4th *s* of John Clark Phemister and Elizabeth G. Crawford; *m* 1926, Mary Wood Reid, MA; three *d. Educ:* Allan Glen's School and University of Glasgow; St John's College, Cambridge; Chicago University. Assoc. Prof. of Geology and Mineralogy, Univ. of British Columbia, 1926-33; Field Officer, Geological Survey of Canada, 1928-30; University Demonstrator in Mineralogy and Petrology, Cambridge Univ., 1933-37. Served in Royal Engineers, War of 1939-45. Dean of Faculty of Science, 1945-48, Vice-Principal, 1963-66, Aberdeen University. Chm., Macaulay Inst. for Soil Research, 1958-. Chm., Robert Gordon's Colleges, 1971-82. *Publications:* papers on mineralogical and petrological subjects. *Address:* Department of Geology and Mineralogy, University of Aberdeen, Aberdeen AB9 1AS. *T:* Aberdeen 36489.

PHILBIN, Most Rev. William J.; see Down and Connor, Bishop of, (RC).

PHILIP, John Robert, DSc; FRS 1974; FAA 1967; Chief, Division of Environmental Mechanics, Commonwealth Scientific and Industrial Research Organization, Australia, 1971-80 and since 1983; *b* 18 Jan. 1927; *e s* of Percival Norman Philip and late Ruth (*née* Osborne), formerly of Ballarat and Maldon, Vic., Australia; *m* 1949, Frances Julia, *o d* of E. Hilton Long; two *s* one *d. Educ:* Scotch Coll., Melbourne; Univ. of Melbourne (Queen's Coll.). BCE 1946, DSc 1960. Research Asst, Melb. Univ., 1947; Engr, Qld Irrig. Commn, 1948-51; Research Staff, CSIRO, 1951-; Sen. Princ. Res. Scientist, 1961-63; Chief Res. Scientist and Asst Chief, Div. of Plant Industry, 1963-71; Associate Mem., CSIRO Exec., 1978; Dir, Inst. of Physical Scis, 1980-83. Visiting Scientist, Cambridge Univ., 1954-55; Res. Fellow, Calif. Inst. Techn., 1957-58; Vis. Prof., Univ. of Illinois, 1958 and 1961; Nuffield Foundn Fellow, Cambridge Univ., 1961-62; Res. Fellow, Harvard Univ., 1966-67; Vis. Prof., Univ. of Florida, 1969; Vinton-Hayes Fellow, Harvard Univ., 1972; Vis. Res. Fellow, Cornell Univ., 1979. Horton Award, 1957, Horton Medal, 1982, Amer. Geophys. Union; David Rivett Medal, 1966; Thomas Ranken Lyle Medal, 1981. Mem. Council, Australian Acad. of Sci., 1972-78 (Biol. Sec., 1974-78); ANZAAS: Pres. Section 1 (Physics), 1970; Pres. Sect. 8 (Maths), 1971. FRMetS; Fellow, Amer. Geophys. Union, 1981. *Publications:* papers in scientific jls on soil and porous medium physics, fluid mechanics, hydrology, micrometeorology, mathematical and physical aspects of physiology and ecology. *Recreations:* reading, writing, architecture. *Address:* CSIRO Division of Environmental Mechanics, PO Box 821, Canberra City, ACT 2601, Australia. *T:* (062) 46-5645; 42 Vasey Crescent, Campbell, ACT 2601. *T:* (062) 47-8958.

PHILIP, Sir William (Shearer), Kt 1975; CMG 1961; MC 1918; President of Board of Management, Alfred Hospital, Melbourne, since 1948 (Member Board of Management, since 1935, Hon. Treasurer, 1939-48); Company Director; b Williamstown, Victoria, 18 Aug. 1891; s of Capt. William Philip, Aberdeen and Williamstown; m 1920, Irene Laura (d 1960), d of William Cross; two s two d. Educ: Scotch College, Melbourne. Flack and Flack and Price Waterhouse & Co., Chartered Accountants, 1909-56, Partner, 1925-56. Member Charities Board of Victoria, 1942-48, Chairman, 1946-47. Business Adviser, AAMC, 1940-45. Recreations: golf and fishing. Address: Glenshee, No 1 Macquarie Road, Toorak, Victoria 3142, Australia. T: 20.3973. Clubs: Melbourne, Australian and Royal Melbourne Golf (Melbourne).

PHILIPPE, André J., Hon. GCVO 1972; Luxembourg Ambassador to France, since 1978; b Luxembourg City, 28 June 1926. Dr-en-Droit. Barrister-at-Law, Luxembourg, 1951-52. Joined Luxembourg Diplomatic Service, 1952; Dep. to Dir of Polit. Affairs, Min. of Foreign Affairs, 1952-54; Dep. Perm. Rep. to NATO, 1954-61 and to OECD, 1959-61; Dir of Protocol and Legal Adviser, Min. of For. Affairs, 1961-68; Ambassador and Perm. Rep. to UN and Consul-Gen., New York, 1968-72 (Vice-Pres., 24th Session of Gen. Assembly of UN, 1969); Ambassador to UK, Perm. Rep. to Council of WEU, and concurrently Ambassador to Ireland and Iceland, 1972-78. Commander, Order of Adolphe Nassau and Order of Oaken Crown (Luxembourg); Commander, Légion d'Honneur (France). Address: Luxembourg Embassy, 33 avenue Rapp, 75007 Paris, France. T: 555.13.37.

PHILIPPS, family name of Viscount St Davids and Baron Milford.

PHILIPPS, Hon. Hanning; see Philipps, Hon. R. H.

PHILIPPS, Hon. James Perrott, TD; b 25 Nov. 1905; 3rd s of 1st Baron and b of 2nd Baron Milford, qv; m 1930, Hon. Elizabeth Joan, d of 1st Baron Kindersley; one s two d. Educ: Eton; Christ Church, Oxford. Chm., Dalham Farms Ltd. Mem., Jockey Club. Served War of 1939-45; Leicestershire Yeomanry and Shropshire Yeomanry (despatches). Major TA Reserve. High Sheriff of Suffolk, 1955-56. Recreations: breeding, racing. Address: Dalham Hall, Newmarket, Suffolk. T: Ousden 242. Club: Jockey.
See also Hon. R. H. Philipps.

PHILIPPS, Lady Marion (Violet), FRAgS; JP; farmer, since 1946; b 1 Feb. 1908; d of 12th Earl of Stair, KT, DSO; m 1930, Hon. Hanning Philipps, qv; one s one d. Educ: privately. FRAgS 1973. War Service: original Mem., WVS HQ Staff, i/c Canteen and Catering Information Services, 1938-41; Min. of Agriculture, 1942-45. Mem., Narberth Rural Dist Council, 1970-73. Chm., Picton Land & Investment Pty Ltd, WA. Trustee, Picton Castle Trust (Graham Sutherland Gallery), 1976-. Founder Mem., British Polled Hereford Soc., 1950- (also first Pres.); Member: Welsh Council, Historic Houses Assoc., 1975; Gardens Cttee, National Council of Historic Houses Assoc., 1975; Royal Welsh Agricultural Soc., 1978-. JP Dyfed (formerly Pembrokeshire), 1965. CStJ; Order of Mercy, 1926. Recreation: gardening. Address: Picton Castle, The Rhos, Haverfordwest, Dyfed. T: Rhos 201.

PHILIPPS, Hon. (Richard) Hanning, MBE 1945; JP; Hon. Major Welsh Guards; Lord-Lieutenant of Dyfed, 1974-79 (HM Lieutenant of Pembrokeshire, 1958-74); b 14 Feb. 1904; 2nd s of 1st Baron and b of 2nd Baron Milford, qv; m 1930, Lady Marion Violet Dalrymple (see Lady Marion Philipps); one s one d. Educ: Eton. Contested (Nat) Brecon and Radnor, 1939. Served War of 1939-45, NW Europe, 1944-45 (MBE). Vice-Lieutenant of Pembrokeshire, 1957. Hon. Colonel Pembroke Yeomanry, 1959. Chairman: Milford Haven Conservancy Bd, 1963-75; Northern Securities Trust Ltd, 1950-80; Hon. Pres. (former Chm.) Schweppes Ltd; Dir, Picton Land and Investment Pty Ltd, W Australia; Trustee, Picton Castle Trust, Graham and Kathleen Sutherland Foundn. Pres., Order of St John, Pembrokeshire, 1958-. CStJ. Recreations: painting, forestry, gardening. Address: Picton Castle, Haverfordwest, Pembrokeshire SA62 4AS. T: Rhos 201. Club: Boodle's.
See also Hon. J. P. Philipps.

PHILIPS, Prof. Sir Cyril (Henry), Kt 1974; Professor of Oriental History, University of London, 1946-80; Director, School of Oriental and African Studies, London, 1957-76; Vice-Chancellor, University of London, 1972-76 (Deputy Vice-Chancellor, 1969-70); b Worcester, 27 Dec. 1912; s of William Henry Philips; m 1st, 1939, Dorcas (d 1974), d of John Rose, Wallasey; one d (one s decd); 2nd, 1975, Joan Rosemary, d of William George Marshall. Educ: Rock Ferry High School; Univs of Liverpool (MA) and London (PhD). Bishop Chavasse Prizeman; Gladstone Memorial Fellow. Frewen Lord Prizeman (Royal Empire Soc.); Alexander Prizeman (Royal Hist. Soc.); Sir Percy Sykes Meml Medal; Asst Lectr, Sch. of Oriental Studies, 1936. Served in Suffolk Infantry, Army Education Corps, 1940-43; Commandant, Army School of Education, 1943. HM Treasury, Dept of Training, 1943-46. Colonial Office Mission on Community Development, Africa, 1947. Lectures: Montague Burton, Univ. of Leeds, 1966; Creighton, Univ. of London, 1972; James Smart, on Police, 1979; Home Office Bicentenary, 1982. Chairman: UGC Cttee on Oriental, African and Slavonic Studies, 1965-70; UGC Cttee on Latin American Studies, 1966-70; India Cttee of Inter-University Council and British Council, 1972-; Royal Commn on Criminal Procedure, 1978-80; Police Complaints Bd, 1980-; Inst. of Archaeology, 1979-, Inst. of Latin American Studies, 1978- (Univ. of London); Member: Social Development Cttee, Colonial Office, 1947-55; Colonial Office Research Council, 1955-57; University Grants Cttee, 1960-69; Commonwealth Education Commn, 1961-

70; Postgraduate Awards Cttee (Min. of Education), 1962-64; Modern Languages Cttee (Min. of Education), 1964-67; Inter-Univ. Council, 1967-; Court, London Univ., 1970-; Governor: Chinese Univ. of Hong Kong, 1965-; Mill Hill Sch., 1980- (Chm., 1982); Governor and Trustee, Richmond Coll., 1979-. Pres., Royal Asiatic Soc., 1979-82. Hon. DLitt Warwick, 1967; Hon. LLD Hong Kong, 1971. Publications: The East India Company, 1940 (2nd edn 1961); India, 1949; Handbook of Oriental History, 1951 (2nd edn 1962); Correspondence of David Scott, 1951; Historians of India, Pakistan and Ceylon, 1961; The Evolution of India and Pakistan, 1962; Politics and Society in India, 1963; Fort William-India House Correspondence, 1964; History of the School of Oriental and African Studies, 1917-67, 1967; The Partition of India, 1970; The Correspondence of Lord William Bentinck, Governor General of India 1828-35, 1977. Address: School of Oriental and African Studies, Malet Street, WC1E 7HP. T: 01-637 2388. Club: Athenæum.

PHILIPSON, Garry, DFC 1944; Managing Director (formerly General Manager), Aycliffe and Peterlee Development Corporations, since 1974; b 27 Nov. 1921; s of George and Marian Philipson; m 1949, June Mary Miller Somerville; one d. Educ: Stockton Grammar Sch.; Durham Univ. (BA (Hons)). Jubilee Prize, 1947. Local Govt, 1937-40. Served War, RAFVR (2 Gp Bomber Comd), 1940-46. Colonial Service and Overseas Civil Service, 1949-60. Various Dist and Secretariat posts, incl. Clerk, Exec. Council and Cabinet Sec., Sierra Leone; Principal, Scottish Develt Dept, 1961-66; Under Sec., RICS, 1966-67; Dir, Smith and Ritchie Ltd, 1967-70; Sec., New Towns Assoc., 1970-74. Publications: Press articles and contribs to various jls. Recreations: country pursuits, history, archaeology. Address: Tunstall Grange, Tunstall, Richmond, North Yorks. T: Richmond 833327. Club: Royal Air Force.

PHILIPSON, Oliphant James; b 9 Sept. 1905; 2nd s of late Hylton Philipson; m 1946, Helen Mabel (d 1976), d of David Fell. Educ: Eton. Served War of 1939-45, RNVR. Address: Manor House, Everton, near Lymington, Hampshire SO4 0HE. Clubs: Carlton; Royal Yacht Squadron.

PHILIPSON, Sir Robert James, (Sir Robin Philipson), Kt 1976; RA 1980 (ARA 1973); PRSA 1973 (RSA 1962; ARSA 1952); RSW 1954; Head of the School of Drawing and Painting, The College of Art, Edinburgh, 1960-82; President, Royal Scottish Academy, since 1973 (Secretary, 1969-73); b 17 Dec. 1916; s of James Philipson; m 1949, Brenda Mark; m 1962, Thora Clyne (marr. diss. 1975); m 1976, Diana Mary Pollock. Educ: Whitehaven Secondary School; Dumfries Academy; Edinburgh College of Art, 1936-40. Served War of 1939-45: King's Own Scottish Borderers, 1942-46, in India and Burma; attached to RIASC. Member of teaching staff, Edinburgh College of Art, 1947. Exhibits with Browse & Darby Ltd and Scottish Gallery, Edinburgh. Mem., Royal Fine Art Commn for Scotland, 1965-80. Hon. RA 1973; Hon. Mem., RHA 1979; Hon. Mem., RCA 1980. Commandeur de l'Ordre National du Mérite de la République française, 1976. FRSA 1965; FRSE 1977. DUniv Stirling 1976; Hon. LLD Aberdeen 1977. Address: 23 Crawford Road, Edinburgh EH16 5PQ. T: 031-667 2373. Club: Scottish Arts (Edinburgh).

PHILIPSON-STOW, Sir Christopher, 5th Bt cr 1907; DFC 1944; retired; b 13 Sept. 1920; s of Henry Matthew Philipson-Stow (d 1953) (3rd s of 1st Bt) and Elizabeth Willes (d 1979), d of Sir Thomas Willes Chitty, 1st Bt; S cousin, 1982; m 1952, Elizabeth Nairn, d of late James Dixon Trees and widow of Major F. G. McLaren, 48th Highlanders of Canada; two s. Educ: Winchester. Heir: er s Robert Matthew Philipson-Stow, b 29 Aug. 1953. Address: RR2, Port Carling, Ontario P0B 1J0. T: 705-765-3000.

PHILLIMORE, family name of Baron Phillimore.

PHILLIMORE, 3rd Baron, cr 1918, of Shiplake in County of Oxford; **Robert Godfrey Phillimore**, Bt, cr 1881; b 24 Sept. 1939; s of Capt. Hon. Anthony Francis Phillimore, 9th Queen's Royal Lancers (e s of 2nd Baron) and Anne, 2nd d of Maj.-Gen. Sir Cecil Pereira, KCB; S grandfather, 1947. Heir: u Major Hon. Claud Stephen Phillimore [b 15 Jan. 1911; m 1944, Anne Elizabeth, e d of Maj. Arthur Algernon Dorrien-Smith, DSO; one s one d]. Address: Coppid Hall, Henley-on-Thames, Oxon.

PHILLIMORE, John Gore, CMG 1946; DL; a Managing Director of Baring Brothers & Co. Ltd, 1949-72; Director, Tribune Investment Trust Ltd; b 16 April 1908; 2nd s of late Adm. Sir Richard and Lady Phillimore, Shedfield, Hants; m 1951, Jill, d of late Captain Mason Scott, Royal Navy retd, Buckland Manor, Broadway, Worcs, and of Hon. Mrs Scott; two s two d. Educ: Winchester College; Christ Church, Oxford. Partner of Roberts, Meynell & Co., Buenos Aires, 1936-48; Representative of HM Treasury and Bank of England in South America, 1940-45. Prime Warden, Fishmongers' Co., 1974-75. High Sheriff of Kent, 1975, DL Kent, 1979. Condor de los Andes (Bolivia), 1940; Commander, Orden de Mayo (Argentina), 1961. Address: The Postern, Tonbridge, Kent. T: 352178. Clubs: White's, Beefsteak, Overseas Bankers.

PHILLIPS, family name of Baroness Phillips.

PHILLIPS, Baroness cr 1964 (Life Peer); **Norah Phillips**, JP; Lord-Lieutenant of Greater London, since 1978; Director, Association for the Prevention of Theft in Shops; President (and former General Secretary), National Association of Women's Clubs; President: Institute of Shops, Health and

Safety Acts Administration; Association for Research into Restricted Growth; Keep Fit Association; Age Concern Greater London; Territorial Auxiliary & Volunteer Reserve Association for Greater London; Greater London Playing Fields Association; Industrial Catering Association; International Professional Security Association; London Marriage Guidance Council; Small Electrical Appliance Marketing Association; Vice-President: National Association of Local Councils; Pre-Retirement Association; National Chamber of Trade; Greater London Home Safety; Fair Play for Children; Chairman, Beatrice Webb House Trust; *d* of William and Catherine Lusher; *m* 1930, Morgan Phillips (*d* 1963); one *s* one *d* (*see* G. P. Dunwoody). *Educ:* Marist Convent; Hampton Training College. A Baroness in Waiting (Govt Whip), 1965–70. *Address:* 115 Rannoch Road, W6. *T:* 01-839 6614.

PHILLIPS, Adrian Alexander Christian; Director, The Countryside Commission, since 1981; *b* 11 Jan. 1940; *s* of Eric Lawrance Phillips, *qv* ; *m* 1963, Cassandra Frances Ela's Hubback; two *s. Educ:* The Hall, Hampstead; Westminster Sch.; Christ Church, Oxford (1st Cl. Hons MA Geography). MRTPI. Planning Services, Min. of Housing and Local Govt, 1962–68; Sen. Research Officer and Asst Director, Countryside Commission, 1968–74; Special Asst, Executive Director, United Nations Environment Programme (UNEP), Nairobi, Kenya, 1974–75; Head, Programme Coordination Unit, UNEP, Nairobi, 1975–78; Director of Programmes, Internat. Union for Conservation of Nature and Natural Resources, Switzerland, 1978–81. *Publications:* articles on countryside planning and conservation in professional jls. *Recreations:* walking, skiing, squash, stroking the cat. *Address:* c/o Countryside Commission, John Dower House, Crescent Place, Cheltenham, Glos GL50 3RA. *T:* Cheltenham 21381.

PHILLIPS, Alan; *see* Phillips, D. A.

PHILLIPS, Arthur, OBE 1957; MA, PhD; JP; Barrister at Law (Middle Temple and Western Circuit); Chancellor, Diocese of Winchester; Professor Emeritus, University of Southampton; *b* 29 May 1907; *e s* of Albert William Phillips and Agnes Phillips (*née* Edwards); *m* 1934, Kathleen Hudson; two *s* two *d. Educ:* Highgate School; Trinity College, Oxford. In chambers in Temple, 1929; joined Colonial Service, 1931, and served in Kenya: Dist Officer, 1931; Actg Resident Magistrate, 1933–35; Crown Counsel, 1936; Actg Solicitor-Gen., 1940 and 1946; Judicial Adviser, 1945; Mem. of Kenya Leg. Council, 1940. Served in Kenya Regt, Somaliland and Abyssinia, 1940–42; Chm. War Claims Commn, Br. Somaliland, 1942; retd from Colonial Service on medical grounds and practised at Bar, England, 1947–49. Reader in Law, LSE, Univ. of London, 1949–56; Prof. of English Law, Univ. of Southampton, 1956–67; Dean of Faculty of Law, 1956–62; Deputy Vice-Chancellor, 1961–63. Dep. Chm., Hants QS, 1960–71; a Recorder of the Crown Court, 1972–79. Director of Survey of African Marriage and Family Life, 1948–52. Chairman Milk and Dairies Tribunal, South-Eastern Region, 1961–79; Pres., Southern Rent Assessment Panel, 1965–72. JP Hants; Chairman Winchester County Magistrates' Court, 1956–61. Member, Church Assembly, 1965–70. Lay Reader, Diocese of Winchester, Counsellor to the Dean and Chapter of Winchester. *Publications:* Report on Native Tribunals (Kenya), 1945; (ed. and part-author) Survey of African Marriage and Family Life, 1953; (jt) Marriage Laws in Africa, 1971; principal contribr on Ecclesiastical Law, Halsbury's Laws of England, 1975. *Address:* Church Cottage, Compton, near Winchester, Hants. *T:* Twyford 713295. *Club:* Royal Commonwealth Society.

PHILLIPS, Prof. Calbert Inglis, FRCS, FRCSE; Professor of Ophthalmology, University of Edinburgh and Ophthalmic Surgeon, Royal Infirmary, Edinburgh, since 1972; *b* 20 March 1925; *o s* of Rev. David Horner Phillips and Margaret Calbert Phillips; *m* 1962, Christina Anne Fulton, MB, FRCSE; one *s. Educ:* Glasgow High Sch.; Robert Gordon's Coll., Aberdeen; Aberdeen Univ. MB, ChB Aberdeen 1946; DPH Edinburgh 1950; FRCS 1955; MD Aberdeen 1957; PhD Bristol 1961; MSc Manchester 1969; FRCSE 1973. Lieut and Captain, RAMC, 1947–49. House Surgeon: Aberdeen Royal Infirmary, 1946–47 (House Phys., 1951); Aberdeen Maternity Hosp., 1949; Glasgow Eye Infirmary, 1950–51; Asst Anatomy Dept, Glasgow Univ., 1951–52; Resident Registrar, Moorfields Eye Hosp., 1953–54; Sen. Registrar, St Thomas' Hosp. and Moorfields Eye Hosp., and Res. Asst, Inst. of Ophthalmology, 1954–58; Consultant Surg., Bristol Eye Hosp., 1958–63; Alexander Piggott Wernher Trav. Fellow, Dept of Ophthal., Harvard Univ., 1960–61; Consultant Ophthalmic Surg., St George's Hosp., 1963–65; Prof. of Ophthal., Manchester Univ., and Hon. Consultant Ophthalmic Surg. to United Manchester Hosps, 1965–72. Hon. FBOA 1975. *Publications:* (ed jtly) Clinical Practice and Economics, 1977; papers in Brit. and Amer. Jls of Ophthal., Nature, Brain, BMJ, etc, mainly on intra-ocular pressure and glaucoma, retinal detachments, ocular surgery and hereditary diseases. *Address:* Princess Alexandra Eye Pavilion, Chalmers Street, Edinburgh EH3 9HA. *T:* 031-229 2477.

PHILLIPS, Prof. Charles Garrett, FRS 1963; DM; FRCP; Dr Lee's Professor of Anatomy, University of Oxford, since 1975; Fellow of Hertford College; *b* 13 October 1916; *s* of Dr George Ramsey Phillips and Flora (*née* Green); *m* 1942, Cynthia Mary, *d* of late L. R. Broster, OBE, FRCS; two *d. Educ:* Bradfield; Magdalen College, Oxford; St Bartholomew's Hospital. Captain, RAMC, 1943–46. Reader in Neurophysiology, 1962–66, Prof., 1966–75, Oxford Univ.; Fellow, Trinity Coll., 1946–75, Emeritus Fellow, 1975. Mem., MRC, 1980–. Hon. Sec., Physiological Society, 1960–66; President: Sect. of Neurology, RSocMed, 1978–79; Assoc. of British Neurologists, 1980–81.

Hon. Member: Canadian Neurol Soc.; Belgian Soc. of Electromyography and Clin. Neurophysiology. Editor, Brain, 1975–81. Hon. DSc Monash, 1971. Lectures: Ferrier, 1968; Hughlings Jackson (and Medal), 1973; Victor Horsley Meml, 1981. Feldberg Prize, 1970. *Publications:* Papers on neurophysiology in Jl of Physiology, etc. *Address:* Department of Human Anatomy, Oxford. *T:* 58686. *Club:* United Oxford & Cambridge University.

PHILLIPS, (David) Alan; Stipendiary Magistrate for Mid-Glamorgan, since 1975; a Recorder of the Crown Court, since 1974; *b* 21 July 1926; *s* of Stephen Thomas Phillips and Elizabeth Mary Phillips; *m* 1960, Jean Louise (*née* Godsell); two *s. Educ:* Llanelli Grammar Sch.; University Coll., Oxford (MA). Left school, 1944. Served War, Army, 1944; commnd, 1946, RWF; Captain (GS), 1947; demobilised, 1948. Oxford, 1948–51. Lectr, 1952–59. Called to Bar, Gray's Inn, 1960. *Recreations:* music, chess, swimming. *Address:* The Magistrates' Court, Union Street, Pontypridd, Mid-Glamorgan.

PHILLIPS, Prof. Sir David (Chilton), Kt 1979; FRS 1967; BSc, PhD (Wales); FInstP; Professor of Molecular Biophysics and Fellow of Corpus Christi College, Oxford, since Oct. 1966; *b* 7 March 1924; *o s* of late Charles Harry Phillips and Edith Harriet Phillips (*née* Finney), Ellesmere, Shropshire; *m* 1960, Diana Kathleen (*née* Hutchinson); one *d. Educ:* Ellesmere C. of E. Schools; Oswestry Boys' High Sch.; UCW, Cardiff. Radar Officer, RNVR, 1944–47. UCW, 1942–44 and 1947–51. Post-doctoral Fellow, National Research Council of Canada, 1951–53; Research Officer, National Research Laboratories, Ottawa, 1953–55; Research Worker, Davy Faraday Research Lab., Royal Institution, London, 1955–66; Mem., MRC, 1974–78; Royal Soc. Assessor, 1978–. UK Co-ordinator, Internat. Science Hall, Brussels Exhibition, 1958; Member, European Molecular Biology Organization (EMBO), 1964, Mem. Council, 1972–78; Royal Society: Vice-Pres., 1972–73, 1976–; Biological Sec., 1976–; Fullerian (Vis.) Prof. of Physiology, Royal Institution, 1979–, Christmas lectures, 1980. For. Hon. Member, Amer. Academy of Arts and Sciences, 1968; Hon. Mem., Amer. Society of Biological Chemists, 1969 (Lecturer, 1965); Almroth Wright Memorial Lecturer, 1966; Plenary Lectures, Internat. Biochem. Congress, Tokyo, 1967, Hamburg, 1976, Internat. Crystallography Congress, Kyoto, 1972; Hassel Lecture, Oslo, 1968; Krebs Lecture and Medal, FEBS, 1971; Feldberg Prize, 1968; CIBA Medal, Biochem. Soc., 1971; Royal Medal, Royal Society, 1975; (jtly) Prix Charles Léopold Mayer, French Académie des Sciences, 1979. Hon. DSc: Leicester, 1974; Univ. of Wales, 1975; Chicago, 1978; Exeter, 1982; Warwick, 1982. Member, Ed. Board, Journal of Molecular Biology, 1966–76. *Publications:* papers in Acta Cryst. and other journals. *Address:* Molecular Biophysics Laboratory, Zoology Department, South Parks Road, Oxford OX1 3PS. *T:* Oxford 50454; 3 Fairlawn End, Upper Wolvercote, Oxford OX2 8AR. *T:* Oxford 55828; Corpus Christi College, Oxford.

PHILLIPS, Prof. Dewi Zephaniah; Professor of Philosophy, University College, Swansea, since 1971; *b* 24 Nov. 1934; *s* of David Oakley Phillips and Alice Frances Phillips; *m* 1959, Margaret Monica Hanford; three *s. Educ:* Swansea Grammar Sch.; UC Swansea (MA); St Catherine's Society, Oxford (BLitt). Asst Lectr, Queen's Coll., Dundee, Univ. of St Andrews, 1961–62; Lectr: at Queen's Coll., Dundee, 1962–63; UC Bangor, 1963–65; UC Swansea, 1965–67; Sen. Lectr, UC Swansea, 1967–71. Hintz Meml Lectr, Univ. of Arizona, Tucson, 1975; Vis. Prof. and McMartin Lectr, Univ. of Carleton, 1976; Agnes Cuming Visitor, Univ. Coll. Dublin, 1982. *Publications:* The Concept of Prayer, 1965; (ed) Religion and Understanding, 1967; (ed) Saith Ysgrif Ar Grefydd, 1967; (with H. O. Mounce) Moral Practices, 1970; Death and Immortality, 1970; Faith and Philosophical Enquiry, 1970; (with Ilham Dilman) Sense and Delusion, 1971; Athronyddu Am Grefydd, 1974; Religion Without Explanation, 1976; (ed) John Anderson: Education and Inquiry, 1980; Through A Darkening Glass: Philosophy, Literature and Cultural Change, 1981; Dramau Gwenlyn Parry, 1981; General Editor: Studies in Ethics and the Philosophy of Religion, 1968–74; Values and Philosophical Enquiry, 1976–; papers in philosophical jls. *Recreations:* lawn tennis and supporting Swansea City AFC. *Address:* 45 Queen's Road, Sketty, Swansea. *T:* Swansea 203935.

PHILLIPS, Douglas Herbert Charles; HM Diplomatic Service, retired; Deputy High Commissioner, Sri Lanka, and Counsellor, Maldives, 1978–81; *b* 4 Nov. 1924; *s* of late Herbert Henry Phillips and Aida Phillips (*née* Gervasi); *m* 1st, 1950, Olwen Laverick (*d* 1971); one *d* ; 2nd, 1972, Noreen Evelyn Mendelsohn; one step *s* one step *d. Educ:* Vaughan Sch., Kensington. RN, 1943–46; Min. of Civil Aviation, 1947; joined Commonwealth Service, 1948; served in Pakistan (Karachi and Peshawar), 1950–53; Second Sec., Calcutta, 1954–57; First Sec., Bombay, 1959–62; CRO, 1962–64; Diplomatic Service Admin., 1965–67; First Sec. (Commercial), Melbourne, 1967–72; FCO, 1972–75; First Sec. (Commercial), Singapore, 1975–78. *Address:* 7 Talbots Drive, Maidenhead, Berks. *T:* Maidenhead 35240. *Clubs:* Royal Colombo Golf; Warren (Singapore); Gymkhana (Bombay).

PHILLIPS, Edwin William, MBE 1946; Director, Lazard Bros & Co. Ltd, since 1960; Chairman, Friends Provident Life Office, since 1968; Director, Higgs and Hill (Deputy Chairman, 1974; Chairman, 1975–83); *b* 29 Jan. 1918; *s* of C. E. Phillips, Chiswick; *m* 1951, P. M. Matusch; two *s. Educ:* Latymer Upper Sch. Joined Edward de Stein & Co., Merchant Bankers, 1934. Army, 1939–46; Major, Sherwood Rangers Yeomanry. Rejoined Edward de Stein & Co., 1946, Partner, 1954; merged into Lazard Bros & Co. Ltd, 1960. Director: British Rail Property Bd, 1970; Phoenix Assurance, 1975; Woolwich Equitable Building Soc., 1977. *Recreation:* cricket. *Address:* Latymer House,

Pennymead Rise, East Horsley, Surrey. *T*: East Horsley 4810. *Club*: MCC.

PHILLIPS, Eric Lawrance, CMG 1963; retired; *b* 23 July 1909; *s* of L. Stanley Phillips, London, NW1; *m* 1938, Phyllis Bray, Artist; two *s* one step *d*. *Educ*: Haileybury Coll.; Balliol Coll., Oxford (Scholar, BA). With Erlangers Ltd, 1932-39. Served War of 1939-45, Captain, RA. Principal, Bd of Trade, 1945, Monopolies Commn, 1949; Asst Secretary, Monopolies Commn, 1951, Bd of Trade, 1952; Under-Sec., Bd of Trade, 1964-69; Sec., Monopolies Commn, 1969-74; consultant to Monopolies and Mergers Commn, 1974-75. Hon. Chm., Abbeyfield West London Soc., 1981-. *Recreations*: looking at pictures, places and buildings. *Address*: 46 Platts Lane, NW3. *T*: 01-435 7873. *Club*: Royal Automobile.
See also A. A. C. Phillips.

PHILLIPS, Sir Fred (Albert), Kt 1967; CVO 1966; Governor of St Kitts/Nevis/Anguilla, 1967-69; Special Representative, Cable and Wireless (West Indies); *b* 14 May 1918; *s* of Wilbert A. Phillips, Brighton, St Vincent. *Educ*: London Univ. (LLB); Toronto Univ.; McGill Univ. (MCL); Hague Acad. of International Law. Called to the Bar, Middle Temple. Legal Clerk to Attorney-General of St Vincent, 1942-45; Principal Officer, Secretariat, 1945-47; Windward Island: Chief Clerk, Governor's Office, 1948-49; District Officer/Magistrate of District III, 1949-53; Magistrate, Grenada, and Comr of Carriacou, 1953-56; Asst Administrator and MEC, Grenada, 1957-58 (Officer Administrating the Govt, April 1958); Senior Asst Sec., Secretariat, Fedn of W Indies (dealing with constitutional development), 1958-60; Permanent Sec. (Sec. to Cabinet), 1960-62 (when Fedn dissolved); actg Administrator of Montserrat, 1961-62; Sen. Lectr, Univ. of W Indies and Sen. Resident Tutor, Dept of Extra-mural Studies, Barbados, 1962-63; Registrar, Coll. of Arts and Science, Univ. of W Indies, 1963-64; Sen. Res. Fellow, Faculty of Law and Centre for Developing Area Studies, McGill Univ., 1964-65; Guggenheim Fellow, 1965; Administrator of St Kitts, 1966-67. Has attended numerous conferences as a Legal or Constitutional Adviser. KStJ 1968. *Publications*: Freedom in the Caribbean: a study in constitutional change, 1977; The Evolving Legal Profession in the Commonwealth, 1978; papers in various jls. *Recreations*: reading, bridge. *Address*: Chambers, Kingstown, St Vincent, West Indies; PO Box 206, Bridgetown, Barbados.

PHILLIPS, (Gerald) Hayden; Assistant Under-Secretary of State, Home Office, since 1981; *b* 9 Feb. 1943; *s* of Gerald Phillips and Dorothy Phillips; *m* 1st, 1967, Dr Ann Watkins (marr. diss.); one *s* one *d*; 2nd, 1980, Hon. Laura Grenfell; one *d*. *Educ*: Cambridgeshire High Sch.; Clare Coll., Cambridge (MA); Yale Univ., USA (MA). Home Office: Asst Principal, 1967; Economic Adviser, 1970-72; Principal, 1972-74; Asst Sec., and Principal Private Sec. to Sec. of State for Home Dept, 1974-76; Dep. Chef de Cabinet to Pres., Commn of European Communities, 1977-79; Asst Sec., Home Office, 1979-81. *Address*: c/o Home Office, 50 Queen Anne's Gate, SW1. *Club*: Brooks's.

PHILLIPS, Rev. Gordon Lewis; Gresham Professor of Divinity, 1971-73; Chaplain to the English-Speaking Church in Luxembourg, 1972-74; *b* 27 June 1911; *s* of Herbert Lewis and Margaret Gertrude Phillips. *Educ*: Cathedral Sch., Llandaff; Dean Close Sch., Cheltenham; Brasenose Coll., Oxford (scholar; exhibitioner; BA 1st cl. Lit. Hum., 1933; 3rd cl. Theology, 1935; MA 1937); Kelham Theological Coll. Deacon 1937; Priest 1938; Curate, St Julian, Newport, Mon, 1937-40; Rector: Northolt, Mddx, 1940-55; Bloomsbury, Diocese of London, 1956-68; Anglican Chaplain, London Univ., 1955-68; Examg Chaplain to Bishop of St Albans, 1957; Prebendary of Hoxton in St Paul's Cathedral, 1966-68; Proctor, Convocation of London, 1960-65; Dean of Llandaff, 1968-71. Mem., Standing Cttee on Anglican and Roman Catholic Relations; Select Preacher: Univ. of Oxford, 1942, 1964; Univ. of Cambridge, 1963. Hon. Fellow, University Coll., Cardiff, 1970. *Publications*: Seeing and Believing, 1953; Flame in the Mind, 1957; contrib. to Studies in the Fourth Gospel, 1957. *Address*: Tŷ Cornel, Cilycwm, Llandovery, Dyfed.

PHILLIPS, Hayden; *see* Phillips, G. H.

PHILLIPS, Sir Henry (Ellis Isidore), Kt 1964; CMG 1960; MBE 1946; Director of Companies; *b* 30 Aug. 1914; *s* of late Harry J. Phillips, MBE; *m* 1st, 1941, Vivien Hyamson (marr. diss., 1965); two *s* one *d*; 2nd, 1966, Philippa Cohen. *Educ*: Haberdashers' Sch., Hampstead; University College, London. BA (London) 1936; MA 1939. Inst. of Historical Research, 1936-39. FRHistS. Commissioned in Beds and Herts Regt, 1939; served War of 1939-45, with 5th Bn, becoming Adjutant; POW, Singapore, 1942. Joined Colonial Administrative Service and appointed to Nyasaland, 1946 (until retirement in 1965); Development Secretary, 1952; seconded to Federal Treasury of Rhodesia and Nyasaland, 1953-57; Dep. Sec., 1956; Financial Sec., Nyasaland Govt, 1957-64, and Minister of Finance, 1961-64. Man. Dir, Standard Bank Finance and Development Corp., 1966-72. Mem., Civil Aviation Authority, 1975-80. Hon. Treasurer, Stonham Meml Trust, 1977-. Active in the Housing Association movement. *Address*: 34 Ross Court, Putney Hill, SW15. *T*: 01-789 1404. *Clubs*: MCC, Royal Commonwealth Society.

PHILLIPS, Herbert Moore, CMG 1949; MA; *b* 7 Feb. 1908; *s* of Herbert Phillips and Beatrice Moore; *m* 1934, Martha Löffler (marr. diss.); one *d*; *m* 1952, Doris Rushbrooke. *Educ*: St Olave's; Wadham Coll., Oxford (MA (Hons) Oxon 1931). Entered Min. of Labour, 1934; Asst Sec., Manpower Dept, 1942-45, Overseas Dept 1946; FO, 1946-49, as Counsellor for Econ. and

Soc. Affairs in UK Delegn at seat of UN, Alternate UK Delegate to ECOSOC and Delegate to ECLA; Consultant, ECLA, 1950-51; UNESCO, 1952-68, as Head of Div. of Applied Social Sciences and Dir Analysis Office. Consultant, 1968-: OECD; UNESCO, UN, UNICEF, World Bank; Leader of World Bank Missions to Ethiopia, Taiwan and Turkey for preparation of educn loans; Mem., UN Family Planning Mission to Iran. *Publications*: Literacy and Development, 1970; Basic Education, a World Challenge, 1975; Educational Cooperation between Developed and Developing Countries, 1976. *Address*: 9 rue de Mézières, 75006 Paris, France.

PHILLIPS, Sir Horace, KCMG 1973 (CMG 1963); HM Diplomatic Service, retired; Resident Representative, Taylor Woodrow International Ltd, in Iran, 1978-79, in Hong Kong, since 1979; *b* 31 May 1917; *s* of Samuel Phillips; *m* 1944, Idina Doreen Morgan; one *s* one *d*. *Educ*: Hillhead High Sch., Glasgow. Joined Board of Inland Revenue, 1935. Served War of 1939-45, Dorsetshire and 1st Punjab Regts, 1940-47. Transf. to FO, Oct. 1947; Acting Vice-Consul, Shiraz, Nov. 1947; Vice-Consul, Bushire, 1948 (Acting Consul, 1948); 1st Secretary and Consul, 1949; Kabul, Oct. 1949; Foreign Office, 1951; 1st Secretary, and Consul, Jedda, 1953; Counsellor, 1956; seconded to Colonial Office, Dec. 1956, as Protectorate Secretary, Aden, until Aug. 1960; Counsellor, British Embassy, Tehran, Oct. 1960; Deputy Political Resident in the Persian Gulf, at Bahrain, 1964-66; Ambassador to Indonesia, 1966-68; High Comr in Tanzania, 1968-72; Ambassador to Turkey, 1973-77. Hon. LLD Glasgow, 1977. Order of the Taj (Iran), 1961. *Recreations*: swimming, languages, long-distance car driving especially in the Middle East. *Address*: 34a Sheridan Road, Merton Park, SW19 3HP. *T*: 01-542 3836, 1780. *Clubs*: Travellers', Royal Commonwealth Society; Hong Kong (Hong Kong).

PHILLIPS, Ian, FCA; Member, London Transport Executive, since 1980; *b* 16 July 1938; *s* of Wilfrid and Dorothy Phillips; *m* 1961, Fay Rosemary Stoner; two *s*. *Educ*: Whitgift Sch., South Croydon. Articled clerk, Hatfield Dixon Roberts Wright & Co., Accountants, 1955-61; Senior Asst, Robert J. Ward & Co., Accountants, 1961-65; Management Services Dept, John Lewis' Partnership, 1965-69; London Transport Executive: Director of Corporate Planning, 1969-75; Chief Business Planning Officer, 1975-78; Group Planning Director, 1978-80; Mem. Board, 1980-. *Recreations*: playing golf, watching any sport, the country, spending time with my family. *Address*: 74 Barnfield Wood Road, Beckenham, Kent BR3 2SU. *T*: 01-650 5756; Bakers Cottage, Church Road, Quenington, near Cirencester, Glos.

PHILLIPS, Ivan L.; *see* Lloyd Phillips.

PHILLIPS, Jeremy Patrick Manfred, QC 1980; *b* 27 Feb. 1941; *s* of late Manfred Henry Phillips, CA, and late Irene Margaret (née Symondson); *m* 1968, Virginia Gwendoline (née Dwyer) (marr. diss. 1974); two *s*; *m* 1976, Judith Gaskell (née Hetherington); one *s* two *d*. *Educ*: St Edmund's Sch., Hindhead, Surrey; Charterhouse. Apprentice Accountant, Thomson McLintock & Co., 1957-61; worked in commerce and for BBC, etc, while studying for Bar, 1961-64; called to Bar, Gray's Inn, 1964; in practice, 1964-. Owner of Kentwell Hall, Long Melford, Suffolk, 1971-; originator and organizer of Kentwell's Historical Re-Creations, 1978, 1979, 1980, 1981, 1982. *Publications*: contrib. Cooper's Students' Manual of Auditing, 1970, 2nd edn 1979; contrib. Cooper's Manual of Auditing, 2nd edn 1981; various pamphlets, papers, guides, etc, on Kentwell Hall. *Recreations*: Kentwell Hall, historic buildings, Tudor history and domestic life. *Address*: Kentwell Hall, Long Melford, Suffolk.

PHILLIPS, John Fleetwood Stewart, CMG 1965; HM Diplomatic Service, retired; *b* 16 Dec. 1917; *e s* of late Major Herbert Stewart Phillips, 27th Light Cavalry, and Violet Gordon, *d* of late Sir Alexander Pinhey, KCSI; *m* 1948, Mary Gordon Shaw, MB, BS; two *s* two *d*. *Educ*: Brighton; Worcester Coll., Oxford (Open Exhibition in Classics, MA). Represented Univ. and County intermittently at Rugby football, 1938-39. Served with 1st Bn, Argyll and Sutherland Highlanders in N Africa and Crete (wounded and captured, 1941). Appointed to Sudan Political Service, 1945; served in Kordofan and Blue Nile Provinces. HM Diplomatic Service, 1955; served in Foreign Office; Oriental Secretary in Libya, 1957; Consul-General at Muscat, 1960-63; Counsellor, British Embassy, Amman, 1963-66; Imperial Defence Coll., 1967; Dep. High Comr, Cyprus, 1968; Ambassador to Southern Yemen, 1969-70, to Jordan, 1970-72, to Sudan, 1973-77. *Recreations*: gardening and feuding. *Address*: Southwood, Gordon Road, Horsham, Sussex. *T*: Horsham 2894. *Club*: Travellers'.

PHILLIPS, John Francis, CBE 1977 (OBE 1957); QC 1981; arbitrator; Chairman, Provident Association for Medical Care (Private Patients Plan), since 1977 (Vice-Chairman, 1972-77; Director, since 1958); *b* 1911; *e s* of late F. W. Phillips and late Margaret (née Gillan); *m* 1937, Olive M. Royer; one *s* two *d*. *Educ*: Cardinal Vaughan Sch.; London Univ.; Trinity Hall, Cambridge. LLB (Hons) London; LLB (1st Cl. Hons), LLM Cantab. Barrister-at-law, Gray's Inn, 1944. Civil Servant (Lord Chancellor's Dept, Royal Courts of Justice), 1933-44; Parly Sec. and Asst Gen. Sec., Nat. Farmers' Union of England and Wales, 1945-57; Institute of Chartered Secretaries and Administrators: Sec. and Chief Exec., 1957-76; Mem. Council, 1976-81; Pres., 1977. Member: Council, Chartered Inst. of Arbitrators, 1969- (Vice-Pres., 1974-76; Pres., 1976-77); Gen. Cttee, Bar Assoc. for Commerce, Finance and Industry, 1967- (Vice-Chm., 1976-78 and 1980-81; Chm., 1978-80; Vice-Pres., 1982); Senate of the Inns of Court and the Bar; Bar Council; Cttees of Senate and Council, 1978-; Council for Accreditation of Correspondence Colls,

1969-80 (Hon. Treas., 1969-74; Chm., 1975-80); British Egg Marketing Bd, 1969-71; Departmental Cttee of Enquiry into Fowl Pest, 1971; Vice-Chm. and Mem., Business Educn Council, 1974-80; Chairman: Jt Cttee for Awards in Business Studies and Public Admin., 1968-75 (Mem. Jt Cttee for Awards, 1960-75); Associated Examining Bd, GCE, 1976- (Mem., 1958-; Vice-Chm., 1973-76); Houghton Poultry Res. Station, 1976-82 (Governor, 1973-82); Dep. Chm., Eggs Authority, 1971-80. Governor: Christ's Hospital, 1957-; Crossways Trust, 1959-71 (Financial Advisor, 1966-71); Nuffield Nursing Homes Trust, 1975-81 (Vice-Pres., 1981-); Mem. Council and Exec. Cttee, Animal Health Trust, 1976-; Deleg. to Internat. Labour Conf., 1950-56. FCIS 1958; FCIArb (FIArb 1966); CBIM (Council of Inst., 1969-74). Master, Co. of Chartered Secretaries and Administrators, 1978; Founder Master, Worshipful Co. of Arbitrators, 1980-82; Master, Co. of Scriveners, 1982-83. *Publications:* The Agriculture Act, 1947, 1948; Heywood and Massey's Lunacy Practice, 1939; many articles on aspects of law relating to land and agriculture. *Recreation:* travel. *Address:* 17 Ossulton Way, Hampstead Garden Suburb, N2 0DT. *T:* 01-455 8460; (office) Private Patients Plan, Tavistock House, Tavistock Square, WC1H 9LJ; (chambers) 1 Verulam Buildings, Gray's Inn, WC1. *Clubs:* Athenæum, United Oxford & Cambridge University, City Livery.

PHILLIPS, Sir John (Grant), KBE 1972 (CBE 1968); Governor and Chairman of Board, Reserve Bank of Australia, 1968-75; *b* 13 March 1911; *s* of Oswald and Ethel Phillips, Sydney; *m* 1935, Mary W. Debenham; two *s* two *d. Educ:* C of E Grammar Sch., Sydney; University of Sydney (BEc). Research Officer, NSW Retail Traders' Assoc., 1932-35; Econ. Asst, Royal Commn Monetary and Banking Systems, 1936-37; Econ. Dept, Commonwealth Bank of Australia, 1937-51; Investment Adviser, Commonwealth Bank, 1954-60; Dep. Governor and Dep. Chairman of Board, Reserve Bank of Australia, 1960-68. Leader, Australian Delegation to 6th Conf. GATT, Geneva, 1951; Member: Council, Macquarie Univ., 1967-79; Bd, Howard Florey Inst. of Experimental Physiology and Medicine, 1971-; Adv. Cttee, The Australian Birthright Movement, Sydney Br., 1971-; Dir, Lend Lease Corp. Ltd, 1976-81. Chm., Aust. Stats Adv. Council, 1976-81. *Recreations:* lawn bowls, contract bridge. *Address:* 2/25 Marshall Street, Manly, NSW 2095, Australia.

PHILLIPS, Prof. John Guest, PhD, DSc; FRS 1981; Wolfson Professor and Senior Science and Engineering Research Council (formerly Science Research Council) Fellow since 1979, and Dean of the Faculty of Science, 1978-80, University of Hull; Director, Wolfson Institute, since 1979; Secretary, Zoological Society of London, since 1982 (Member, Council, since 1979); *b* 13 June 1933; *s* of Owen Gwynne Phillips and Dorothy Constance Phillips; *m* 1961, Jacqueline Ann Myles-White; two *s. Educ:* Llanelli Grammar Sch. (County Major Scholar); Univ. of Liverpool (State Scholar, Univ. Studentship; ARC Studentship). BSc 1954, PhD 1957, Liverpool; DSc Hong Kong 1967; FIBiol; FRSocMed. Vis. Scientist: Collège de France, 1955; CIBA Ag, Basel, 1956; Commonwealth Fund Fellow, Yale Univ., 1957-59; Fellow, Davenport Coll., Yale Univ., 1957-59; Lectr in Zoology, Univ. of Sheffield, 1959-62; Vis. Asst Prof., Univ. of BC, 1959; Milton Res. Assoc., Harvard Univ., 1960; Prof. of Zoology, Univ. of Hong Kong, 1962-67; Dir, Nuffield Unit, Univ. of Hong Kong, 1963-67; Dean of Faculty of Science, Hong Kong, 1965-66, acting Vice-Chancellor, 1966; Vis. Scientist, US Navy Namru 2, Manilla, 1963; Prof. and Head of Dept of Zoology, Univ. of Hull, 1967-79; Public Orator, Univ. of Hull, 1970, 1972, 1976, 1979-81; Dir, Wolfson Lab. for Res. in Gerontology, 1975-79. Vis. Prof. of Biology, Univ. of California, 1975; Vis. Prof. in Pharmacology and Therapeutics, Univ. of Texas, 1979. Member: Commonwealth Scholarships Commn, 1968-; Council, Marine Biological Assoc. of UK, 1969-71; Biology Cttee, SRC, 1975-78; Cttee of Soc. for Endocrinology, 1971-74, 1975-; Treasurer, Soc. for Endocrinology, 1975-81, Chm., 1981-; Chm., British Endocrine Socs, 1982-. Chm., Hull DHA, 1981-; Member: Council of Management, Jl of Endocrinology, 1971-; Humberside AHA, 1974-81 (Vice-Chm., 1979-81); Humberside Area Nurse Educn Adv. Cttee (Chm., 1976-); Internat. Cttee for Comparative Endocrinology, 1974-; Humber Adv. Gp, 1975-80; Internat. Cttee for Endocrinology, 1976-; Commonwealth Human Ecology Council, 1976-80; Exec. Cttee, British Soc. for Res. in Ageing, 1976- (Treas., 1980-); Pres. Yorkshire Br., Inst. Biol., 1969-72. Fellow, Acad. of Zoology of India, 1966-. Governor: Endsleigh Coll. of Educn, Hull, 1967-77; St Anne's Special Sch., Hull, 1975- (Vice-Chm., 1978-); Bridgeview Special Sch., 1977-. Assessor: Univ. of Malaya, 1979-; Univ. of Singapore, 1981-. Mem., Academic Adv. Council, University Coll. of Buckingham, 1978-. Annual Lecture, Biological Council, 1982. Zoological Soc. of London Scientific Medal, 1970; Medal of Soc. for Endocrinology, 1971. *Publications:* Hormones and the Environment, 1971; Environmental Physiology, 1975; numerous papers in zoological, endocrinological and physiological jls. *Recreations:* gardening, music, travel. *Address:* Tremayne Lodge, Brough, N Humberside. *T:* Brough 668574. *Club:* Royal Commonwealth Society.

PHILLIPS, Rt. Rev. John Henry Lawrence; *b* 2 Feb. 1910; *s* of Rev. H. L. Phillips, Wimborne, Dorset; *m* 1936, Morna, *d* of E. H. W. Winfield-King, OBE; one *s* three *d. Educ:* Weymouth Coll., Trinity Hall, Cambridge, BA 1932; MA 1937; Ridley Hall, Cambridge, 1932-34. Deacon, 1934; priest, 1935. Curate of Christ Church, Harrogate, 1934-35; Curate of Methley, 1935-38; Rector of Farnley, Leeds, 1938-45; Surrogate, 1939-45; Chaplain RNVR, 1942-45; Director of Service Ordination Candidates, 1945-47; General Secretary Central Advisory Council of Training for the Ministry, 1947-49; Vicar of Radcliffe-on-Trent and of Shelford, 1949-57; Archdeacon of

Nottingham, 1949-60; Rector of Clifton with Glapton, 1958-60; Bishop of Portsmouth, 1960-75; Priest-in-charge, West with East Lulworth, 1975-78. Chaplain to the Queen, 1959-60. Provincial Grand Master, Masonic Order, Hampshire and Isle of Wight, 1975-79. *Recreations:* cricket, golf, Rugby football, etc. *Address:* Highlands, Harkstead, Ipswich. *T:* Holbrook 328261. *Club:* Naval.

PHILLIPS, Sir Leslie (Walter), Kt 1962; CBE 1947; Chairman, Baltic Exchange, 1963-65 (Vice-Chairman 1961-63); *b* 12 Aug. 1894; 2nd *s* of late Charles Phillips; *m* 1915, Mary (*d* 1971), *d* of late John Corby; one *s*; *m* 1972, Patricia, *d* of late Claude Palmer. Chm., T. A. Jones Co. Ltd, Grain Brokers, 1943-70. President National Federation of Corn Trade Associations, 1949-52; President, London Corn Trade Assoc., 1959-60; Vice-Chairman, Sugar Board, 1966-68. Director of Freight, Ministry of Food, 1941-45; Controller of Freight and Warehousing, 1946-47. *Address:* 18 The Village, Meads, Eastbourne, E Sussex. *T:* Eastbourne 37624.

PHILLIPS, Air Cdre Manfred Norman; retired, RAF Medical Branch; Consultant Radiologist, RAF Hospital, Ely, 1968-77; *b* 6 Nov. 1912; *s* of Lewis and Norah Phillips, Portsmouth; *m* 1942, Dorothy Ellen (*née* Green); two *s. Educ:* Liverpool Coll.; Liverpool Univ. Med. Sch.; Middlesex Hospital. MB, ChB 1936; DMRD 1954. *Publications:* articles in Brit. Jl Clinical Practice and Brit. Jl Radiology. *Recreations:* gardening, golf, walking. *Address:* Quaney, 83C Cambridge Road, Ely, Cambs. *T:* Ely 3539.

PHILLIPS, Captain Mark Anthony Peter, CVO 1974; ADC(P); student, Royal Agricultural College, Cirencester, 1978; *b* 22 Sept. 1948; *s* of P. W. G. Phillips, MC, and Anne Patricia (*née* Tiarks); *m* 1973, HRH The Princess Anne; one *s* one *d. Educ:* Marlborough Coll.; RMA Sandhurst. Joined 1st The Queen's Dragoon Guards, July 1969; Regimental duty, 1969-74; Company Instructor, RMA Sandhurst, 1974-77; Army Trng Directorate, MoD, 1977-78, retired. Personal ADC to HM the Queen, 1974-. In Three Day Equestrian Event, GB winning teams: Team Championships: World, 1970; European, 1971; Olympic Gold Medallists (Team), Olympic Games, Munich, 1972; Mem., Equestrian Team (Reserve), Olympic Games, Mexico, 1968 and Montreal, 1976. Winner, Badminton Three Day Event, 1971, 1972, 1974, 1981. Liveryman: Farriers' Co.; Farmers' Co; Saddlers' Co.; Freeman: Loriners Co.; City of London. *Recreations:* riding, Rugby football, athletics. *Address:* Buckingham Palace, SW1. *Club:* (Hon. Mem.) Buck's.
See also under Royal Family.

PHILLIPS, Max; Assistant Under Secretary of State, Ministry of Defence, since 1977; *b* 31 March 1924; *m* 1953, Patricia Moore; two *s* two *d. Educ:* Colston's Sch., Bristol; Christ's Hospital; Magdalene Coll., Cambridge (Schol.; 1st cl. Hist. Tripos, pts I and II; MA). Served War, RA, 1943-46. Appointed to Home Civil Service, 1949; Colonial Office, 1949-59; Sec., Nigeria Fiscal Commn, 1957-58; UKAEA, 1959-73; Procurement Exec., MoD, 1973-74; HM Treasury, 1974-77. Governor and Almoner, Christ's Hospital. *Recreations:* modern myths, exploring the imagination and the countryside. *Address:* 2 Wilderness Farmhouse, Onslow Village, Guildford, Surrey GU2 5QP. *T:* Guildford 61308.

PHILLIPS, Prof. Neville Crompton, CMG 1973; Vice-Chancellor and Rector, University of Canterbury, Christchurch, New Zealand 1966-77; retired; *b* 7 March 1916; 2nd *s* of Samuel and Clara Phillips, Christchurch, NZ; *m* 1940, Pauline Beatrice, 3rd *d* of Selby and Dorothy Palmer, Te Aratipi, Havelock North, NZ; one *s* two *d. Educ:* Dannevirke High Sch.; Palmerston North Boys' High Sch.; Canterbury University College; Merton Coll., Oxford. BA (NZ) 1936; MA 1938; Hon. LittD (Cantuar) 1977; NZ University Post-Grad. Schol. in Arts, Arnold Atkinson Prizeman, 1938; Journalist, Sun and Press, Christchurch, 1932-38; read PPE at Oxford, 1938-39; RA (Gunner, subseq. Major), 1939-46; service in Tunisia and Italy (despatches). Lecturer in History and Political Science, Canterbury University College, 1946-47; Senior Lecturer, 1948; Prof. of History and Political Science, 1949-62; Prof. of History, 1962-66; Emeritus Prof., 1966; Chairman: Canterbury Centennial Provincial Historical Cttee, 1948-66; Management Cttee, Canterbury Archaeological Trust, 1980-; 1st Pres., Canterbury Historical Assoc., 1953; Editorial Adviser, NZ War Histories, 1957-67; US Dept of State Leader Grantee, 1966; Member: Council, Canterbury Manufacturers' Assoc., 1967-77; Christchurch Teachers' Coll. Council, 1968-76; NZ Vice-Chancellors' Cttee, 1966-77 (Chm., 1973-74); Council, Assoc. of Commonwealth Univs, 1973-74; NZ Council Educational Research, 1973-77. *Publications:* Italy, vol. 1 (The Sangro to Cassino), 1957 (New Zealand War Histories); Yorkshire and English National Politics, 1783-84, 1961; The Role of the University in Professional Education, 1970; (ed) A History of the University of Canterbury, 1873-1973, 1973; articles, mainly on eighteenth-century English politics, in English and NZ jls. *Recreations:* reading history, watching cricket, things Italian. *Address:* Tyle House, Hackington Road, Tyler Hill, Canterbury, Kent CT2 9NF. *T:* Blean 708. *Club:* University (Christchurch).

PHILLIPS, Nicholas Addison, QC 1978; a Recorder of the Crown Court, since 1982; *b* 21 Jan. 1938; *m* 1972, Christylle Marie-Thérèse Rouffiac (*née* Doreau); two *d*, and one step *s* one step *d. Educ:* Bryanston Sch.; King's Coll., Cambridge (MA). Nat. Service with RN; commnd RNVR, 1956-58. Called to Bar, Middle Temple (Harmsworth Schol.), 1962. In practice at Bar, 1962-. Jun. Counsel to Minister of Defence and to Treasury in Admiralty matters, 1973-78. Mem., Panel of Wreck Comrs, 1979. Governor, Bryanston Sch.,

1975- (Chm. of Governors, 1981-). *Recreations:* sea and mountains. *Address:* 28 Chalcot Square, NW1. *T:* 01-586 2813.

PHILLIPS, Prof. Owen Hood, DCL, MA, Oxon; MA, LLB, Dublin; LLM Birmingham; QC 1970; JP; *b* 30 Sept. 1907; *yr s* of late Surgeon-Captain J. E. Hood Phillips, RN, Portsmouth; *m* 1949, Lucy Mary Carden, 3rd *d* of late Arnold Philip, and formerly Lecturer in Physical Educn, Univ. of Birmingham. *Educ:* Weymouth Coll.; Merton Coll., Oxford. Asst Lecturer in Laws, King's Coll., London, 1931-35; Lectr in General Jurisprudence, Univ. of Dublin (Trinity Coll.), 1935-37; Reader in English Law, Univ. of London, 1937-46; Vice-Dean of Faculty of Laws, King's Coll., London, 1937-40; University of Birmingham: Barber Prof. of Jurisprudence, 1946-74; Dean, Faculty of Law, and Dir Legal Studies, 1949-68, Public Orator, 1950-62, Vice-Principal and Pro-Vice-Chancellor, 1971-74. Vis. Prof. in English Law, University Coll. at Buckingham, 1974-78, Mem., Acad. Adv. Council, 1978-. Min. of Labour and National Service, 1940; Min. of Aircraft Production, 1940-45; adviser to Singapore Constitutional Commn, 1953-54; delegate to Malta Round Table Conf., 1955, to Malta Constitutional Conf., 1958. Governor King Edward VI Schs, Birmingham, 1951-76 (Bailiff, 1958-59); President: Soc. of Public Teachers of Law, 1963-64; British and Irish Assoc. of Law Librarians, 1972-76; Hon. Mem., Midland and Oxford Circuit Bar Mess. *Publications:* Principles of English Law and the Constitution, 1939; A First Book of English Law, 1948, 7th edn (with A. H. Hudson), 1977; Consitutional and Administrative Law, 1952, 6th edn (with P. Jackson), 1978; Leading Cases in Constitutional and Administrative Law, 1952, 5th edn 1979; Reform of the Constitution, 1970; Shakespeare and the Lawyers, 1972; contributions to various legal periodicals. *Address:* 24 Heaton Drive, Edgbaston, Birmingham B15 3LW. *T:* 021-454 2042; Easter Cottage, Clee St Margaret, Shropshire SY7 9DT.

PHILLIPS, Prof. Owen Martin, FRS 1968; Decker Professor of Science and Engineering, Johns Hopkins University, since 1975; *b* 30 Dec. 1930; *s* of Richard Keith Phillips and Madeline Lofts; *m* 1953, Merle Winifred Simons; two *s* two *d*. *Educ:* University of Sydney; Trinity Coll., Cambridge Univ. ICI Fellow, Cambridge, 1955-57; Fellow, St John's Coll., Cambridge, 1957-60; Asst Prof., 1957-60, Assoc. Prof., 1960-63, Johns Hopkins Univ.; Asst Director of Research, Cambridge, 1961-64; Prof. of Geophysical Mechanics, Johns Hopkins Univ., 1963-68, of Geophysics, 1968-75. Assoc. Editor Jl of Fluid Mechanics, 1964-; Mem. Council, Nat. Center of Atmospheric Research, Boulder, Colorado, 1964-68; US Nat. Cttee Global Atmospheric Research Project, 1968. Mem.-at-large, Amer. Meteorol. Soc. Publications Commn, 1971-75; Pres., Maryland Acad. of Scis, 1979-. Sec., Bd of Trustees, Chesapeake Res. Consortium, 1973-74 (Trustee, 1972-75). Adams Prize, Univ. of Cambridge, 1965; Sverdrup Gold Medal, Amer. Metereol. Soc., 1975. *Publications:* The Dynamics of the Upper Ocean, 1966, 3rd edn 1976, Russian edn 1968; The Heart of the Earth, 1968, Italian edns 1970, 1975; The Last Chance Energy Book, 1979; various scientific papers in Jl Fluid Mechanics, Proc. Cambridge Philos. Soc., Jl Marine Research, Proc. Royal Society, Deep Sea Research, Journal Geophys. Research. *Address:* 23 Merrymount Road, Baltimore, Maryland 21210, USA. *T:* 433-7195. *Clubs:* Johns Hopkins (Baltimore), Hamilton Street (Baltimore); Quissett Yacht (Mass).

PHILLIPS, Reginald Arthur, CMG 1965; OBE 1951; Deputy Director-General, British Council, 1966-73, retired; *b* 31 Jan. 1913; *y s* of late James and Catherine Ann Phillips, Tredegar, Mon; *m* 1939, Doris Tate, *d* of William and Angelina Tate, São Paulo, Brazil; one *s* two *d*. *Educ:* Tredegar Grammar Sch.; Balliol Coll., Oxford (MA). Asst Master, St Paul's School, Brazil, 1936; Lecturer, Anglo-Brazilian Cultural Society, 1937-39. War of 1939-45: Intelligence Corps (Major), 1940-46. British Council: Latin America Dept, 1947; Home Div., 1948-54; Colonies Dept, 1954-57; Controller, Commonwealth Div., 1957-59; Controller, Finance Div., 1959-62; Assistant Director-General, 1962-66. *Recreations:* golf, walking, television, gardening. *Address:* 76 Chiltley Way, Liphook, Hants. *T:* Liphook 722610. *Club:* Athenæum.

PHILLIPS, Surgeon Rear-Adm. Rex Philip, CB 1972; OBE 1963; Medical Officer-in-Charge, Royal Naval Hospital, Plymouth, 1969-72, retired; *b* 17 May 1913; 2nd *s* of William John Phillips, late Consultant Anaesthetist at Royal Victoria Infirmary, Newcastle upon Tyne, and Nora Graham Phillips; *m* 1939, Gill Foley; two *s*. *Educ:* Epsom Coll.; Coll. of Med., Newcastle upon Tyne, Univ. of Durham (now Univ. of Newcastle upon Tyne). Qual. MB, BS 1937; Ho. Surg., Ingham Infirmary, S Shields, 1938. Joined RN, 1939; served War of 1939-45: HMS Rochester, 1939-41; Royal Marines, 1941-43; HMS Simba, 1943-45. HMS Excellent, 1945-47; qual. Dip. in Ophthalmology (London), 1948; HMS Implacable, Fleet MO, 1949-51; Specialist in Ophthalmology: HMS Ganges, 1951-53; Central Air Med. Bd, 1953-55; RN Hosp., Malta (Senior), 1955-57; Admty Adv. in Ophth. to Med. Dir-Gen., 1957-65; Surg. Captain 1963; SMO, RN Hosp., Malta, 1965-68; Staff MO to Flag Officer Submarines, 1968-69. QHS 1969-72. CStJ 1970. *Recreations:* golf, bridge. *Address:* Langstone House, Langstone Village, Havant, Hants. *T:* Havant 484668. *Club:* Royal Western Yacht (Plymouth).

PHILLIPS, Robin; actor and director; *b* 28 Feb. 1942; *s* of James William Phillips and Ellen Anne (*née* Barfoot). *Educ:* Midhurst Grammar School, Sussex. Trained as director, actor and designer, Bristol Old Vic Co.; first appearance, Bristol, as Mr Puff in The Critic, 1959; Associate Dir, Bristol Old Vic, 1960-61; played at Lyric, Hammersmith, 1961, Chichester Fest., 1962, and with Oxford Playhouse Co., 1964. Asst Dir, Timon of Athens and Hamlet, Royal Shakespeare Co., Stratford upon Avon, 1965; Dir or Associate Dir, Hampstead, Exeter, (Thorndike) Leatherhead, 1966-69; Artistic Dir, Stratford Festival, Canada, 1974-80; *London prodns include:* Tiny Alice, RSC, Aldwych, 1970; Abelard and Heloise, Wyndhams and Broadway; The Two Gentlemen of Verona, Stratford and Aldwych, 1970; Miss Julie, for RSC (also directed film); Virginia, Haymarket, 1981; *Chichester:* Caesar and Cleopatra and Dear Antoine, 1971; played Dubedat in The Doctor's Dilemma and directed The Lady's Not for Burning and The Beggar's Opera, 1972; The Jeweller's Shop, 1982; *Greenwich:* formed Company Theatre and apptd Artistic Dir, 1973: plays directed include: The Three Sisters, Rosmerholm, Zorba; *Stratford Festival prodns incl.:* 1975: The Two Gentlemen of Verona and The Comedy of Errors (both also Nat. tour), Measure for Measure, Trumpets and Drums and The Importance of Being Earnest; 1976-78: Hamlet, The Tempest, Antony and Cleopatra, A Midsummer Night's Dream, The Way of the World, Richard III, The Guardsman, As You Like It, Macbeth, The Winter's Tale, Uncle Vanya, The Devils, Private Lives, Hay Fever, Judgement; 1979: Love's Labours Lost, The Importance of Being Earnest, King Lear; 1980: Virginia, Long Day's Journey into Night; Farther West, Theatre Calgary, 1982. Directorate, NY, 1978. *Films:* as actor: Decline and Fall, David Copperfield (title part), Tales from the Crypt. *TV:* Wilfred Desert in The Forsyte Saga, Constantin in The Seagull. *Address:* PO Box 51, Stratford, Ontario N5A 6S8, Canada.

PHILLIPS, Sir Robin Francis, 3rd Bt, *cr* 1912; *b* 29 July 1940; *s* of Sir Lionel Francis Phillips, 2nd Bt, and Camilla Mary, *er d* of late Hugh Parker, 22 Chapel Street, Belgrave Square, SW1; *S* father, 1944. *Educ:* Aiglon Coll., Switzerland. *Heir:* none. *Address:* 12 Manson Mews, Queen's Gate, SW7.

PHILLIPS, Siân; actress; *d* of D. Phillips and Sally Phillips; *m* 1st, 1960, Peter O'Toole, *qv* (marr. diss. 1979); two *d*; 2nd, 1979, Robin Sachs. *Educ:* Pontardawe Grammar Sch.; Univ. of Wales (Cardiff Coll.) (BA Hons English); RADA (Maggie Albanesi Scholarship, 1956; Bancroft Gold Medal, 1958). BBC Radio Wales, mid 1940s-, and BBC TV Wales, early 1950s-; Newsreader and Announcer, and Mem. Rep. Co., BBC, 1953-55; toured for Welsh Arts Council with National Theatre Co., 1953-55; Arts Council Bursary to study drama outside Wales, 1955. London productions: Hedda Gabler, 1959; Ondine, and the Duchess of Malfi, 1960-61 (1st RSC season at Aldwych); The Lizard on the Rock, 1961; Gentle Jack, Maxibules, and The Night of the Iguana, 1964; Ride a Cock Horse, 1965; Man and Superman, and Man of Destiny, 1966; The Burglar, 1967; Epitaph for George Dillon, 1972; A Nightingale in Bloomsbury Square, 1973; The Gay Lord Quex, 1975; Spinechiller, 1978; You Never Can Tell, Lyric, Hammersmith, 1979; Pal Joey, Half Moon, 1980 and Albery, 1981; Dear Liar, Mermaid, 1982. TV drama series include: Shoulder to Shoulder, 1974; How Green was my Valley, 1975; I, Claudius, 1976; Boudicca, and Off to Philadelphia in the Morning, 1977; The Oresteia of Aeschylus, 1978; Crime and Punishment, 1979; Sean O'Casey (RTE), 1980; Winston Churchill, The Wilderness Years, 1981. Films include: Becket, 1963; Goodbye Mr Chips, and Laughter in the Dark, 1968; Murphy's War, 1970; Under Milk Wood, 1971; The Clash of the Titans, 1979. Critics Circle Award, New York Critics Award, and Famous 7 Critics Award, for Goodbye Mr Chips, 1969; BAFTA Award for How Green was my Valley and I, Claudius, 1978; Royal Television Soc. Award for I, Claudius (Best Performer), 1978. Mem., Gorsedd of Bards, 1960 (for services to drama in Wales). *Publications:* gen. journalism, specifically for Radio Times. *Recreation:* gardening. *Address:* c/o Saraband Ltd, 348A Upper Street, Islington, N1 0PD.

PHILLIPS, Sydney William Charles, CB 1955; Second Civil Service Commissioner, 1968-70, a part-time Commissioner, 1970-72; *b* 1 Dec. 1908; *s* of late Frederick Charles and Elizabeth Phillips; *m* 1932, Phyllis, *d* of James Spence; two *s*. *Educ:* Bridport Grammar Sch.; University College, London. Administrative Asst, University College, Hull, 1932-37; Asst Registrar, Liverpool Univ., 1937-45; seconded to Min. of Works, 1941-43; Min. of Town and Country Planning, 1943-51 (Principal Private Sec. to Minister, 1943-44); Asst Sec., 1944; Under-Sec., Min. of Housing and Local Govt, 1952-68, Dir of Establishments, 1963-68. Fellow, UCL, 1969. *Recreations:* walking and gardening. *Address:* Innisfree, Higher Drive, Purley, Surrey. *T:* 01-660 8617. *Club:* Royal Commonwealth Society.

PHILLIPS GRIFFITHS, Allen; *see* Griffiths.

PHILLIS, Robert Weston; Managing Director, Central Independent Television plc, since 1981; *b* 3 Dec. 1945; *s* of Francis William Phillis and Gertrude Grace Phillis; *m* 1966, Jean (*née* Derham); three *s*. *Educ:* John Ruskin Grammar Sch.; Nottingham Univ. (BA Industrial Econs 1968). Apprentice, printing industry, 1961-65; Thomson Regional Newspapers Ltd, 1968-69; British Printing Corp. Ltd, 1969-71; Lectr in Industrial Relations, Edinburgh Univ. and Scottish Business Sch., 1971-75; Vis. Fellow, Univ. of Nairobi, 1974; Personnel Dir, later Man. Dir, Sun Printers Ltd, 1976-79; Man. Dir, Independent Television Publications Ltd, 1979-82. Director: Ind. Television Publications Ltd, 1979-; ITN Ltd, 1982-; Periodical Publishers Assoc., 1979-82; Ind. Television Cos Assoc., 1982-. *Recreations:* family, sport, art, theatre, gardening. *Address:* Central Independent Television plc, Central House, Broad Street, Birmingham B1 2JP. *T:* 021-643 9898.

PHILLPOTTS, Christopher Louis George, CMG 1957; HM Diplomatic Service, retired; Adviser to Employment Conditions Abroad Ltd, 1972-82; *b*

23 April 1915; *s* of Admiral Edward Montgomery Phillpotts, CB, and Violet Selina (*née* Cockburn); *m* 1942, Vivien Chanter-Bowden; one *s* one *d. Educ:* Royal Naval Coll., Dartmouth. Served in Royal Navy, 1932-43 (despatches twice). Joined Foreign Office, Nov. 1943. Appointed Vice-Consul, Malmö, March 1945; transferred Foreign Office, July 1945; Copenhagen, 3rd Secretary, 1947; 2nd Secretary, 1949; Foreign Office, 1951; Athens, 1st Secretary, 1953; Counsellor HM Embassy, Paris, 1957. Transferred Foreign Office, April 1962; Counsellor, Washington, 1964-66; Foreign and Commonwealth Office, 1966-70. *Recreation:* theatre. *Address:* 27 Merrick Square, SE1. *T:* 01-407 5995. *Clubs:* White's, Pratt's, Army and Navy.

PHILLPOTTS, (Mary) Adelaide Eden, (Mrs Nicholas Ross); writer; *b* Ealing, Middlesex; *d* of late Eden Phillpotts; *m* 1951, Nicholas Ross. *Publications: novels:* The Friend, 1923; Lodgers in London, 1926; Tomek, the Sculptor, 1927; A Marriage, 1928; The Atoning Years, 1929; Yellow Sands, 1930; The Youth of Jacob Ackner, 1931; The Founder of Shandon, 1932; The Growing World, 1934; Onward Journey, 1936; Broken Allegiance, 1937; What's Happened to Rankin?, 1938; The Gallant Heart, 1939; The Round of Life, 1940; Laugh with Me, 1941; Our Little Town, 1942; From Jane to John, 1943; The Adventurers, 1944; The Lodestar, 1946; The Fosterling, 1949; Stubborn Earth, 1951; *plays:* Arachne, 1920; Savitri the Faithful, 1923; Camillus and the Schoolmaster, 1923; Akhnaton, 1926; (with Eden Phillpotts) Yellow Sands, 1926; Laugh With Me, 1938; *poetry:* Illyrion, and other Poems, 1916; A Song of Man, 1959; *travel:* Panorama of the World, 1969; *miscellaneous:* Man, a Fable, 1922; (selected with Nicholas Ross) Letters to Nicholas Ross from J. C. Powys (ed A. Uphill), 1971; A Wild Flower Wreath, 1975; Reverie: An Autobiography, 1981. *Address:* Cobblestones, Kilkhampton, Bude, Cornwall.

PHILO, Gordon Charles George, CMG 1970; MC 1944; HM Diplomatic Service, retired; *b* 8 Jan. 1920; *s* of Charles Gilbert Philo and Nellie Philo (*née* Pinnock); *m* 1952, Mavis (Vicky) Ella, *d* of John Ford Galsworthy and Sybel Victoria Galsworthy (*née* Strachan). *Educ:* Haberdashers' Aske's Hampstead Sch.; Wadham Coll., Oxford. Methuen Scholar in Modern History, Wadham Coll., 1938. Served War, HM Forces, 1940-46: Royal West African Frontier Force, 1942-43; Airborne Forces, Normandy and Europe, 1944-45; India 1945-46. Alexander Korda Scholar, The Sorbonne, 1948-49; Lectr in Modern History, Wadham Coll., 1949-50; Foundn Mem., St Antony's Coll., Oxford, 1950-51. Foreign Office, 1951; Russian course, Christ's Coll., Cambridge, 1952-53; Istanbul, Third Sec., 1954-57; Ankara, Second Sec., 1957-58; FO, 1958-63; Kuala Lumpur, First Sec., 1963-67; FO, 1968; Consul-Gen., Hanoi, 1968-69; FCO, 1969-78. Kesatria Mangku Negara (Hon.), Order of Malaysia, 1968. *Recreations:* travel, writing. *Club:* Athenæum.

PHILPOT, Oliver Lawrence Spurling, MC 1944; DFC 1941; Managing Director, Remploy Ltd, 1974-78; *b* Vancouver, BC, Canada, 6 March 1913; *s* of Lawrence Benjamin Philpot, London, and Catherine Barbara (*née* Spurling), Bedford; *m* 1st, 1938 (marr. diss. 1951); one *s* two *d*; 2nd, 1954, Rosl Widhalm, BA Hons History, PhD (Lond.), Vienna; one *s* one *d. Educ:* Queen Mary Sch., N Vancouver; Aymestrey Court, Worcester; Radley Coll.; Worcester Coll., Oxford (BA Hons PPE; MA). RAFVR: Pilot, 42 Torpedo/Bomber Sqdn, RAF Coastal Comd, 1940; shot down off Norway, 1941; 5 prison camps, Germany and Poland; escaped to Sweden and Scotland, as 3rd man in Wooden Horse, from Stalag Luft III at Sagan, Silesia, 1943; Sen. Scientific Officer, Air Min., 1944 (wrote 33 RAF Stations Manpower Survey, 1944). Management Trainee, Unilever Ltd, 1934; Asst (commercial) Sec., Unilever Home Margarine Exec., 1936; Exec., Maypole Dairy Ltd, 1946; Chm., Trufood Ltd, 1948; Office Manager, Unilever House, EC4, 1950; Gen. Manager (admin.), T. Walls & Sons Ltd, 1951; Coast-to-Coast Lecture Tour in N America on own book, Stolen Journey, with Peat Agency, Canadian Clubs and USAAF, 1952; Dir, Arthur Woollacott & Rappings Ltd, 1953; Chm. and Man. Dir, Spirella Co. of Great Britain Ltd, 1956; Man. Dir, Venesta (later Aluminium) Foils Ltd, 1959; Exec., Union International Ltd, 1962 (also Dep. Chm. and Chief Exec., Fropax Eskimo Frood Ltd, 1965-67), i/c Lonsdale & Thompson Ltd, John Layton Ltd, Merseyside Food Products Ltd, Union Distribution Co. Ltd, Weddel Pharmaceuticals Ltd, John Gardner (Printers) Ltd, and Union Internat. Res. Centre. Chairman: Royal Air Forces Escaping Soc., and RAFES Charitable Fund, 2 terms, 1963-69. Overseas Administrator, Help the Aged, 1979-82; Mem., Nat. Adv. Council on Employment of Disabled People, 1978; Chm., London NW Area Cttee for Employment of Disabled People, 1981-; Mem., Gen. Adv. Council, IBA, 1982-. Fights local environmental battles. *Publication:* Stolen Journey, 1950 (5th edn 1951,repr. 1970; Swedish, Norwegian and Amer. edns, 1951-52; paperback 1954, repr. 4 times, 1962-66). *Recreations:* the river; talking and walking; idling; listening to sermons; reading Financial Times and obituaries in Lancet; films; following the political scene. *Address:* 30 Abingdon Villas, Kensington, W8 6BX. *T:* 01-937 6013. *Clubs:* London Rowing, Ends of the Earth, Society of Authors, United Oxford & Cambridge University, Institute of Directors, Goldfish, RAF Escaping Society; Worcester College Society (London and Oxford).

PHILPOTT, Air Vice-Marshal Peter Theodore, CB 1966; CBE 1954 (OBE 1945); Director of Service Intelligence, Ministry of Defence, 1968-70, retired; *b* 20 March 1915; *s* of late Rev. and Mrs R. G. K. F. Philpott, Worcester; *m* 1942, Marie, *d* of Charles Griffin, Malvern; two *d. Educ:* Malvern Coll.; RAF Coll., Cranwell, 1933; No. 31 Sqn, India, 1936-41; Staff Coll., Quetta, 1941; Directorate of Op. Trg., Air Ministry, 1942-44; OC, RAF, Horsham St Faith, 1945-46; JSSC, 1947; HQ, Fighter Command, 1948-51; OC, RAF

Deversoir, 1952-54; DD Policy, Air Ministry, 1954-56; IDC Student, 1957; Director of Policy and Plans, Air Ministry, 1958-61; Senior RAF Directing Staff, Imperial Defence Coll., 1961-63; AOC No. 23 Group, Flying Training Comd, 1963-65; Head of British Defence Liaison Staff, Canberra, 1965-68. *Address:* c/o Lloyds Bank Ltd (Cox's and King's Branch), 6 Pall Mall, SW1. *Club:* Royal Air Force.

PHILPS, Dr Frank Richard, MBE 1946; retired; Consultant in Exfoliative Cytology, University College Hospital, WC1, 1960-73; Director, Joint Royal Free and University College Hospitals, Department of Cytology, 1972-73; *b* 9 March 1914; *s* of Francis John Philps and Matilda Ann Philps (*née* Healey); *m* 1941, Emma L. F. M. Schmidt; two *s* one *d. Educ:* Christ's Hospital, Horsham, Sussex. MRCS, LRCP, 1939; MB, BS, 1939; DPH 1947; MD London, 1952; FRCPath, 1966; Fellow, International Academy of Cytology, 1967. RAF Medical Service, 1940-46. Junior Hospital Appointments, UCH, 1950-54; Consultant Pathologist, Eastbourne, 1954-64; Research Asst, UCH, 1955-60. Hon. Cons. in Cytology, Royal Free Hosp., 1972-73. Producer, with wife, Wild Life Series of Educational Nature Films and films on pottery making, for Educational Foundation for Visual Aids; made BBC films, The Magic of a Dartmoor Stream, 1977, The Magic of a Dartmoor Wood, 1979. Exhibitor in the annual exhibition of the Royal Inst. of Painters in Watercolours, 1980, 1981 and 1982. BBC Nature Film Prize, 1963; Council for Nature Film Prize, 1966. *Publications:* A Short Manual of Respiratory Cytology, 1964; Watching Wild Life, 1968, 2nd edn 1978. Papers on Cytology to several medical journals, 1954-67. *Recreations:* living in the country; watching wild animals and filming them, painting. *Address:* Woodlands, Sydenham Wood, Lewdown, Okehampton EX20 4PP. *T:* Chillaton 347.

PHIPPS, family name of **Marquess of Normanby.**

PHIPPS, Colin Barry, PhD; Deputy Chairman and Chief Executive, Clyde Petroleum Ltd, since 1979; *b* 23 July 1934; *s* of Edgar Reeves Phipps and Winifred Elsie Phipps (*née* Carroll); *m* 1956, Marion May Phipps (*née* Lawrey); two *s* two *d. Educ:* Townfield Elem. Sch., Hayes, Mddx; Acton County; Swansea Grammar; University Coll. London; Birmingham Univ. BSc, 1st cl. Hons Geol. London 1955; PhD, Geol. Birm. 1957. Royal Dutch/Shell Geologist: Holland, Venezuela, USA, 1957-64; Consultant Petroleum Geologist, 1964-79. Contested (Lab), Walthamstow East, 1969; MP (Lab) Dudley W, Feb. 1974-1979. FGS 1956, FInstPet 1972; Mem. Instn of Geologists, 1978. *Publications:* contrib.: Qly Jl Geol. Soc., Geol. Mag., Geol. Jl, etc. *Recreations:* swimming, reading, collecting English water colours. *Address:* Mathon Court, Mathon, Malvern WR13 5NZ. *T:* Malvern 5606; 38 Cheyne Walk, SW3. *T:* 01-352 5381. *Club:* Reform.

PHIPPS, John Constantine; Metropolitan Magistrate, 1959-75; *b* 19 Jan. 1910; *er s* of Sir Edmund Phipps, CB, and Margaret Percy, *d* of late Dame Jessie Phipps, DBE; *m* 1st, 1945, Priscilla Russell Cooke (*d* 1947); 2nd, 1949, Sheila (formerly Dilke; *née* Seeds) (from whom he obtained a divorce 1965); two *d*; 3rd, 1965, Hermione Deedes. *Educ:* Winchester Coll.; Trinity Coll., Oxford. Called to Bar, Middle Temple, 1933. RE (TA) 1938; War Office, 1940; Intelligence Corps, Captain, 1941, Major, 1943; Personal Asst to Lord Justice Lawrence (later 1st Baron Oaksey), President of International Military Tribunal, Nuremburg, 1945-46. County of London Sessions: Prosecuting Counsel to Post Office, 1951-53, Junior Counsel to the Crown in Appeals, 1953-59, Prosecuting Counsel to the Crown, 1958-59; Recorder of Gravesend, 1957-59. *Address:* St Giles, Burwash, Etchingham, East Sussex TN19 7HT. *T:* Burwash 882031. *Club:* Army and Navy.

PHIPPS, Air Vice-Marshal Leslie William, AFC 1959; Senior Directing Staff, Royal College of Defence Studies, since 1983; *b* 17 April 1930; *s* of late Frank Walter Phipps and Beatrice Kate (*née* Bearman); unmarried. *Educ:* SS Philip and James Sch., Oxford. Commnd RAF, 1950; served, 1951-69: Fighter Sqdns; Stn Comdr, RAF Aqaba, Jordan; OC No 19 (F) Sqdn; Central Fighter Estab.; RN Staff Coll.; HQ 1 (British) Corps; Stn Comdr, RAF Labuan, Borneo; OC No 29 (F) Sqdn; Jt Services Staff Coll.; Dir, RAF Staff Coll., 1970-72; Comdr, Sultan of Oman's Air Force, 1973-74; RCDS, 1975; Comdr, UK Team to Kingdom of Saudi Arabia, 1976-78; Dir of Air Def. and Overseas Ops, 1978-79; Dir Gen., Personnel Management (RAF), 1980-82. *Recreations:* sailing, squash, music. *Address:* c/o Lloyds Bank, Cox's and King's Branch, 6 Pall Mall, SW1Y 5NH. *Clubs:* Royal Air Force; Royal Air Force Yacht (Hamble).

PHIPPS, Vice-Adm. Sir Peter, KBE 1964 (CBE 1962); DSC 1941 (Bar 1943); VRD 1945; retired, 1965; *b* 7 June 1909; *m* 1937, Jean Hutton; two *s* one *d. Educ:* Sumner Primary School; Christchurch Boys' High School. Joined staff of National Bank of NZ Ltd, 1927. Joined RNZNVR as Ord. Seaman, 1928; Sub-Lieut, 1930; Lieut, 1933. Served War of 1939-45 (American Navy Cross, 1943). Transferred to RNZN as Commander, 1945; Captain, 1952; Rear-Admiral, 1960. Chief of Naval Staff, NZ Naval Board, 1960-63; Chief of Defence Staff, New Zealand, 1963-65; Vice-Adm. 1964, retired 1965. *Recreations:* yachting, fishing, herpetology. *Address:* Picton, New Zealand. *Club:* Wellington (Wellington, NZ).

PHIPPS, Rt. Rev. Simon Wilton; *see* Lincoln, Bishop of.

PHIZACKERLEY, Ven. Gerald Robert; Archdeacon of Chesterfield, since 1978; Priest-in-charge of Ashford-in-the-Water with Sheldon, since 1978; *b*

3 Oct. 1929; *s* of John Dawson and Lilian Mabel Ruthven Phizackerley; *m* 1959, Annette Catherine Baker; one *s* one *d. Educ:* Queen Elizabeth Grammar School, Penrith; University Coll., Oxford (MA); Wells Theological Coll. Curate of St Barnabas Church, Carlisle, 1954–57; Chaplain of Abingdon School, 1957–64; Rector of Gaywood, Norfolk, 1964–78; Rural Dean of Lynn, 1968–78; Hon. Canon of Norwich Cathedral, 1975. JP Norfolk, 1972. *Address:* The Vicarage, Ashford-in-the-Water, Bakewell, Derbyshire. *T:* Bakewell 2298.

PHYSICK, John Frederick, FSA; Keeper, Department of Museum Services, Victoria and Albert Museum, since 1975; *b* 31 Dec. 1923; *s* of late Nino William Physick and Gladys (*née* Elliott); *m* 1954, Eileen Mary Walsh; two *s* one *d. Educ:* Battersea Grammar Sch. Royal Navy, 1942–46; joined Victoria and Albert Museum, as Museum Asst, Dept of Engraving, Illustration and Design, 1948; Sen. Research Asst, 1965; Asst Keeper, Dept of Public Relations and Educn, 1967; Sec. to Adv. Council, 1973–; Asst to Dir, 1974–; Member: Rochester Dio. Adv. Cttee, 1965–; RIBA Drawings Cttee, 1975; Cathedrals Adv. Cttee, 1977–81; Council for Care of Churches Monuments Sub-Cttee, 1978–. *Publications:* Catalogue of the Engravings of Eric Gill, 1963; (ed) Handbook to the Departments of Prints and Drawings and Paintings, 1964; The Duke of Wellington in caricature, 1965; Designs for English Sculpture 1680–1860, 1969; (jtly) Victorian Church Art, 1971; Five Monuments from Eastwell, 1973; (jtly) Marble Halls, 1973; Photography and the South Kensington Museum, 1975; (jtly) V&A Souvenir Guide, 1977; The Victoria and Albert Museum—the history of its building, 1982; (contrib.) Change and Decay, the Future of our Churches, 1977. *Recreations:* photography, looking at church monuments. *Address:* 49 New Road, Meopham, Kent DA13 0LS. *T:* Meopham 812301.

PICACHY, His Eminence Lawrence Trevor, Cardinal; *see* Calcutta, Archbishop of, (RC).

PICCARD, Dr Jacques; scientist; President, Foundation for the Study and Preservation of Seas and Lakes; *b* Belgium, 1922; Swiss Citizen; *s* of late Prof. Auguste Piccard (explorer of the stratosphere, in lighter-than-air craft, and of the ocean depths, in vehicles of his own design); *m* 1953, Marie Claude (*née* Maillard); two *s* one *d. Educ:* Brussels; Switzerland. Grad., Univ. of Geneva, 1946; Dip. from Grad. Inst. of Internat. Studies. Asst Prof., Univ. of Geneva, 1946–48. With his father, he participated in design and operation of the first deep diving vessels, which they named the bathyscaph (deep ship); this vessel, like its successor, operated independently of a mother ship; they first constructed the FNRS-2 (later turned over to the French Navy) then the Trieste (ultimately purchased by US Navy); Dr J. Piccard piloted the Trieste on 65 successive dives (the last, 23 Jan. 1960, was the record-breaking descent to 35,800 feet in the Marianas Trench, off Guam in the Pacific Ocean). He built in 1963, the mesoscaph Auguste Piccard, the first civilian submarine, which made, in 1964–65, over 1,100 dives carrying 33,000 people into the depths of Lake Geneva; built (with Grumman) 2nd mesoscaph, Ben Franklin, and in 1969 made 1.500 miles/30 days drift dive in Gulf Stream. Founded: Fondation pour l'Etude et la Protection de la Mer et des Lacs, 1966 (built research submersible, F. A.-FOREL, 1978); Institut International d'Ecologie, 1972. Hon. doctorate in Science, Amer. Internat. Coll., Springfield, Mass, 1962; Hon. DSc, Hofstra Univ., 1970. Holds Distinguished Public Service Award, etc. *Publications:* The Sun beneath the Sea, 1971; technical papers and a popularized account (trans. many langs) of the Trieste, Seven Miles Down (with Robert S. Dietz). *Address:* (home) 19 avenue de l'Avenir, 1012 Lausanne, Switzerland. *T:* (021) 28 80 83; (office) Institut International d'Ecologie, 1096 Cully, Switzerland. *T:* 021. 99 25 65.

PICK, Charles Samuel; Managing Director, Heinemann Group of Publishers, since 1979; *b* 22 March 1917; *s* of Samuel and Ethel Pick; *m* 1938, Hilda Beryl Hobbs; one *s* one *d. Educ:* Masonic School, Bushey. Started in publishing with Victor Gollancz, 1933; founder member, Michael Joseph Ltd, 1935. Served War, 1939–46; commnd RA, AA Command; apptd Staff Captain; served ALFSEA, India, Ceylon and Singapore. Jt Man. Director, Michael Joseph Ltd, 1959; resigned, 1962; joined William Heinemann Ltd as Man. Director, 1962; Director, Heinemann Group of Publishers, 1962; Director, Pan Books, 1968; Chairman: Secker & Warburg, 1973–80; William Heinemann, 1973–80; William Heinemann, Australia and South Africa, 1973–80; William Heinemann International, 1979; Heinemann Educational Books International, 1979; Heinemann Inc., 1980; Heinemann Distribution Ltd, 1980; Chm. and Pres., Heinemann Holdings Inc., 1980. Mem. Council, Publishers' Assoc., 1980–. *Recreations:* walking, reading, theatre. *Address:* Littlecot, Lindfield, Sussex. *T:* 2218; 2 Hyde Park Street, W2. *T:* 01-402 8043. *Club:* Savile.

PICKARD, Sir Cyril (Stanley), KCMG 1966 (CMG 1964); HM Diplomatic Service, retired; British High Commissioner in Nigeria, 1971–74; *b* 18 Sept. 1917; *s* of G. W. Pickard and Edith Pickard (*née* Humphrey), Sydenham; *m* 1941, Helen Elizabeth Strawson (*d* 1982); three *s* one *d* (and one *s* decd). *Educ:* Alleyn's Sch., Dulwich; New Coll. Oxford. 1st Class Hons Modern History, 1939. Asst Principal, Home Office, 1939. War of 1939–45: Royal Artillery 1940–41, Captain; appointment in Office of Minister of State, Cairo, 1941–44 Principal, 1943; with UNRRA in Middle East and Germany, 1944–45; transf. to Commonwealth Relations Office, 1948; Office of UK High Comr in India, New Delhi, 1950; Local Asst Sec., Office of UK High Comr, Canberra, 1952–55; Commonwealth Relations Office, Head of South Asian Dept, 1955–58; Deputy High Commissioner for the UK in New Zealand, 1958–61; Asst Under Sec. of State, CRO, 1962–66 (Acting High Commissioner in

Cyprus, 1964); British High Comr, Pakistan, 1966–71. *Recreation:* gardening. *Address:* 37A Brodrick Road, SW17.

PICKARD, Prof. Huia Masters, FDSRCS; Professor of Conservative Dentistry, University of London, 1963–74, now Emeritus; *b* 25 March 1909; *o s* of late Ernest Pickard and Sophie Elizabeth Robins; *m* 1945, Daphne Evelyn, *d* of Hugh F. Marriott; two *d. Educ:* Latymer Sch.; Royal Dental Hosp. of London Sch. of Dental Surgery; Charing Cross Hosp. MRCS, LRCP, FDSRCS. Private dental practice with H. Sumner Moore and E. W. Fish, pre-1940; EMS, East Grinstead, 1939. Served War, in RAMC, 8th Army (despatches), 1940–45. Dental practice and teaching, 1945; Dir, Dept of Conservative Dentistry, Royal Dental Hosp., and Consultant in Dental Surgery, 1955; Reader in Conservative Dentistry, London Univ., 1957–63; Dir of Dept of Restorative Dentistry, Royal Dental Hosp., 1965–74. Mem. Bd of Governors, St George's Hosp., 1969; First Pres., British Soc. for Restorative Dentistry, 1969; Pres., Odontological Section of Royal Soc. Med., 1971; Examr for Univs of London, Newcastle, Glasgow, Birmingham, Wales; also RCS. *Publications:* Manual of Operative Dentistry (4th edn), 1976; contribs: Dental Record, Brit. Dental Jl, Internat. Dental Jl. *Recreations:* gardening, sailing. *Address:* The Nuttery, Newnham, Daventry, Northamptonshire. *T:* Daventry 3561. *Club:* Army and Navy.

PICKARD, Rt. Rev. Stanley Chapman, CBE 1968; Assistant Bishop of Johannesburg since 1968; Rector of St John's, Belgravia, Diocese of Johannesburg, since 1972; Chaplain to Anglicans of Jeppe Boys High School, since 1972; *b* 4 July 1910; *s* of John Chapman and Louisa Mary Pickard, Gloucester; unmarried. *Educ:* Grammar Sch., Birmingham. Studied pharmacy, 1928–32. Dorchester Theological College, 1933–36; Deacon, 1937; Priest, 1938; Curate St Catherine's, New Cross, SE14, 1937–39; joined UMCA, 1939; Kota Kota, Nyasaland, 1939–40; Likoma Island, Nyasaland, 1940–48; Archdeacon of Msumba, Portuguese East Africa, 1949–58; Bishop of Lebombo, 1958–68; Provincial Exec. Officer, Province of S Africa, 1968–71. *Recreations:* walking, bridge. *Address:* St John's Rectory, 170 Park Street, Belgravia, Johannesburg, South Africa.

PICKAVANCE, Thomas Gerald, CBE 1965; MA, PhD; FRS 1976; Fellow, St Cross College, Oxford, since 1967; *b* 19 October 1915; *s* of William and Ethel Pickavance, Lancashire; *m* 1943, Alice Isobel (*née* Boulton); two *s* one *d. Educ:* Cowley School, St Helens; Univ. of Liverpool. BSc (Hons Phys) 1937; PhD 1940. Research Physicist, Tube Alloys Project, 1941–46; Lecturer in Physics, University of Liverpool, 1943–46; Atomic Energy Research Establishment, Harwell: Head of Cyclotron Group, 1946–54; Head of Accelerator Group, 1954–57; Deputy Head of General Physics Division, 1955–57; Dir, Rutherford High Energy Lab., SRC, 1957–69; Dir of Nuclear Physics, SRC, 1969–72. Chm., European Cttee for Future Accelerators, 1970–71. Hon. DSc, City Univ., 1969. *Publications:* papers and articles in learned journals on nuclear physics and particle accelerators. *Recreations:* motoring, travel, photography. *Address:* 3 Kingston Close, Abingdon, Oxon OX14 1ES. *T:* Abingdon 23934.

PICKEN, Dr Laurence Ernest Rowland, FBA 1973; Fellow of Jesus College, Cambridge, 1944–76, now Emeritus; *b* 1909. *Educ:* Oldknow Road and Waverley Road, Birmingham; Trinity Coll., Cambridge. BA 1931; PhD 1935; ScD 1952. Asst Dir of Research (Zoology), Cambridge Univ., 1946–66; Asst Dir of Research (Oriental Music), Cambridge Univ., 1966–76. FBA; FIBiol. Editor: Musica Asiatica, 1977–; Music from the Tang Court, 1981–. *Publications:* The Organization of Cells and Other Organisms, 1960; Folk Musical Instruments of Turkey, 1975; contribs to many learned jls. *Address:* Jesus College, Cambridge.

PICKERILL, Dame Cecily (Mary Wise), DBE 1977 (OBE 1958); Retired Surgeon; *b* 9 Feb. 1903; *d* of Rev. Percy Wise Clarkson and Margaret Ann Clarkson; *m* 1934, Henry Percy Pickerill, CBE, MD, MDS (*d* 1956); one *d. Educ:* Diocesan High School for Girls, Auckland, NZ; Otago Univ. Medical School, Dunedin, NZ (MB, ChB). House Surg., Dunedin Hosp., 1926; Asst Plastic Surgeon in Sydney, Aust., 1927–35; Specialist Plastic Surgeon, Wellington, NZ, 1935–68; retired, 1968. Licencee, with late husband, and owner of Bassam Hosp., Lower Hutt, NZ—a "Rooming-In" hospital for mother nursing of infants and small children with congenital defects requiring plastic surgery. *Publications:* contribs to medical and nursing jls and NZ Education Jl, 1980. *Recreations:* travel, gardening, camping, nature conservation, great involvement with NZ Anglican Church. *Address:* Beech Dale, 50 Blue Mountains Road, Silverstream, New Zealand. *T:* Wellington 284542.

PICKERING, Derek; *see* Pickering, Frederick Derwent.

PICKERING, Sir Edward (Davies), Kt 1977; Executive Vice-Chairman, Times Newspapers Ltd, since 1982; *b* 4 May 1912; 3rd *s* of George and Louie Pickering; *m* 1st, 1936, Margaret Soutter (marr. diss., 1947); one *d*; 2nd, 1955, Rosemary Whitton; two *s* one *d. Educ:* Middlesbrough High Sch. Chief Sub-Editor Daily Mail, 1939. Served Royal Artillery 1940–44; Staff of Supreme Headquarters Allied Expeditionary Force, 1944–45. Managing Editor: Daily Mail, 1947–49; Daily Express, 1951–57; Editor, Daily Express, 1957–62; Dir, Beaverbrook Newspapers, 1956–64; Editorial Dir, The Daily Mirror Newspapers Ltd, 1964–68, Chm., 1968–70; Director: Scottish Daily Record and Sunday Mail Ltd, 1966–69; IPC, 1966–75; Times Newspapers Holdings Ltd, 1981–82; William Collins Sons & Co. Ltd, 1981–; Pitkin

Pictorials, 1981-; Chairman: International Publishing Corporation Newspaper Div., 1968-70; IPC Magazines, 1970-74; Mirror Group Newspapers, 1975-77. Member Press Council, 1964-69, 1970- (Vice-Chm., 1976-81). Treasurer, Fédération Internationale de la Presse Periodique, 1971-75; Chm. Council, Commonwealth Press Union, 1977-. Mem. Council, Royal Opera House, Covent Garden, 1978-. *Address:* Britmore House, Donhead St Andrew, Shaftesbury, Dorset FP7 9BG. *Club:* Garrick.

PICKERING, Ven. Fred; Archdeacon of Hampstead, since 1974; *b* 18 Nov. 1919; *s* of Arthur and Elizabeth Pickering; *m* 1948, Mabel Constance Threlfall; one *s* one *d. Educ:* Preston Grammar Sch.; St Peter's Coll., Oxford; St Aidan's Theol Coll., Birkenhead. BA 1941 (PPE), MA 1945. Curate: St Andrew's, Leyland, 1943-46; St Mary's, Islington, 1946-48; Organising Sec. for Church Pastoral Aid Soc. in NE England, 1948-51; Vicar: All Saints, Burton-on-Trent, 1951-56; St John's, Carlisle, 1956-63; St Cuthbert's, Wood Green, 1963-74; Rural Dean of East Haringey, 1968-73; Exam. Chaplain to Bp of Edmonton, 1973-. *Address:* 177 Winchmore Hill Road, N21 1QN. *T:* 01-886 2680. *Club:* Sion College.

PICKERING, Frederick Derwent, (Derek Pickering), CBE 1974; DL; Chairman, Local Authorities Mutual Investment Trust, 1975-81; Member, Conference of Local and Regional Authorities of Europe, 1977-81; County Councillor, Berkshire, 1961-81; *b* 28 Nov. 1909; *s* of Frederick Owen Pickering and Emma Pickering; *m* 1935, Marjorie Champion (*née* Shotter) (*d* 1980), JP; one *s. Educ:* Bedford House Sch., Oxford. Employed in industry, 1927-43; Sudan CS, 1943-55; company dir, 1955-63. County Alderman, Berks, 1967-74; Chm., Berks CC, 1973-77; Vice-Chm., Exec. Council, ACC, 1976-78; Chm., Local Authorities Management Services and Computer Cttee, 1980-81. DL Berks, 1978. Hon. DLitt Reading, 1976. *Recreations:* cricket (now as spectator), politics (sometime Pres., Reading South, Windsor and Maidenhead Conservative Assocs). *Address:* Grimston Court, Hull Road, Dunnington, York YO1 5LE. *T:* York 489343.

PICKERING, Herbert Kitchener; Agent-General in London, Government of Province of Alberta, since Nov. 1973; *b* 9 Feb. 1915; *s* of Herbert Pickering, Hull, and Ethel Bowman, Carlisle; *m* 1963, Florence Marion Carr; two *s* two *d. Educ:* Montreal; Bishop's Univ. (Business Admin); Cornell Univ. (Hotel Admin); Michigan State Univ. (Hotel and Business Admin). Canadian National Railways: Gen. Passenger Traffic Dept, Montreal, 1930; various cities in Canada and US; served War of 1939-45, RCAF; returned to CNR; assisted in creation and management of Maple Leaf Tour Dept, 1953-59; created Sales Dept for Canadian National Hotels in Western Canada and then for System, 1960-67; Man., Bessborough Hotel, Saskatoon, 1968; Gen. Man., Jasper Park Lodge, until 1973. *Recreations:* golf, ski-ing, swimming, philately. *Address:* 37 Hill Street, W1 7FD. *T:* 01-499 3061, (home) 01-491 3588. *Clubs:* Lansdowne, East India and Sports, Wellington, Les Ambassadeurs, Curzon House, Canada.

PICKERING, Ian George Walker, VRD (with clasp) 1952; MD; FRCP 1972; Consultant in forensic psychiatry, special hospitals, Department of Health and Social Security, since 1976; *b* 24 Nov. 1915; *e s* of Geo. W. Pickering, Bradford, Yorks; *m* 1948, Jean (*d* 1975), 2nd *d* of John Bell Lowthian, MC and Bar; one *s* one *d. Educ:* Bradford Grammar Sch.; Leeds Univ. MB, ChB 1939; MD 1947; MRCP 1966; FRCPsych 1971; FFCM 1972. Various hosp. appts, 1939 and 1946-47. RNVR, 1939-46: at sea and appts RN Hosps, Plymouth and Sydney, NSW. Surgeon Lt-Comdr RNR, retd list, 1965. HM Prison Service, 1947; Senior MO, HM Prison and Borstal, Durham, 1955-63. Nuffield Travelling Fellow, 1961-62. Dir, Prison Med. Services and Inspector of Retreats for Inebriates, 1963-76; Mem. Prisons Bd, Home Office, 1967-76. Hon. Clinical Lectr in Psychiatry, Univ. of Sheffield, 1977-. Pres., British Acad. of Forensic Sciences, 1969-70; Vice-President: 2nd Internat. Congress of Social Psychiatry, London, 1969; British Assoc. of Social Psychiatry; Oxford Postgrad. Fellowship in Psychiatry, 1966-76; Chm., Dukeries Div., BMA, 1980-81; Vice-Chm., Soc. for Study of Addiction, 1967-74; Member, Executive Councils: Med. Council on Alcoholism, 1967-76; N of England Medico-Legal Soc., Newcastle upon Tyne, 1960-63. Officier de Jurade and Vigneron (*hc*), St Emilion, Aquitaine; Hon. Mem., Prichard Soc., Bristol. *Publications:* articles in professional journals. *Recreations:* travel, music, wine. *Address:* Rampton Hospital, Retford, Notts DN22 0PD. *T:* Retford 84321; (home) Drift House, Ockham Road North, East Horsley, Surrey KT24 6NU. *Clubs:* Royal Automobile, Naval.

PICKERING, John Robertson; His Honour Judge Pickering; a Circuit Judge, since 1972; *b* 8 Jan. 1925; *s* of late J. W. H. Pickering and Sarah Lilian Pickering (*née* Dixon); *m* 1951, Hilde (*widow* of E. M. Wright); one *s* two step *s. Educ:* Winchester; Magdalene Coll., Cambridge. Degree in Classics (wartime) and Law, MA. Served War, Lieut RNVR, Russia, Europe and Far East, 1942-47. Called to Bar, Inner Temple, 1949. Subseq. with Nat. Coal Bd and Dyson Bell & Co (Parliamentary Agents). Mem. Parliamentary Bar. Dep. Chm. of Pneumoconiosis, Byssinosis and Miscellaneous Diseases Benefit Bd, and Workmen's Compensation (Supplementation) Bd, 1970; apptd Dep. Chm. NE London Quarter Sessions, 1971. *Address:* 35 Eaton Terrace, SW1. *T:* 01-730 4271. *Club:* MCC.

PICKERING, Richard Edward Ingram; His Honour Judge Richard Pickering; a Circuit Judge, since 1981; *b* 16 Aug. 1929; *s* of Richard and Dorothy Pickering; *m* 1962, Jean Margaret Eley; two *s. Educ:* Birkenhead Sch.; Magdalene Coll., Cambridge (MA). Called to the Bar, Lincoln's Inn,

1953; has practised on Northern Circuit, 1955-; a Recorder of the Crown Court, 1977-81. Councillor, Hoylake UDC, 1961-64; Legal Chm., Min. of Pensions and Nat. Insurance Tribunal, Liverpool, 1967-77; pt-time Chm., Liverpool Industrial Tribunal, 1977-79; Regional Chm., Merseyside Mental Health Rev. Tribunal, 1979-81 (Legal Mem., 1967-79). *Recreations:* walking, gardening, reading. *Address:* c/o The Crown Court, Crown Square, Manchester; 5 Essex Court, Temple, EC4Y 9AH. *Club:* Athenæum (Liverpool).

PICKETT, Thomas, CBE 1972; Senior Regional Chairman, North West Area, Industrial Tribunals (England and Wales), since 1975 (Chairman for Manchester, 1972); *b* 22 November 1912; *s* of John Joseph Pickett and Caroline Pickett (*née* Brunt); *m* 1940, Winifred Irene Buckley, *yr d* of late Benjamin Buckley; no *c. Educ:* Glossop Grammar School; London University (LLB). Barrister-at-Law, Lincoln's Inn; called to Bar, 1948. Served in Army, 1939-50, retiring with permanent rank of Major. Dep. Asst Dir of Army Legal Services, 1948; Dist Magistrate, Gold Coast, 1950; Resident Magistrate, Northern Rhodesia 1955; Sen. Res. Magistrate, 1956; Acting Puisne Judge, 1960; Puisne Judge, High Courts of Northern Rhodesia, 1961-64; Zambia, 1964-69; Justice of Appeal, 1969-71, Acting Chief Justice, 1970, Judge President, Court of Appeal, 1971, Zambia. Chairman: Tribunal on Detainees, 1967; Electoral Commn (Supervisory); Delimitation Commn for Zambia, 1968; Referendum Commn, 1969; Local Govt Commn, 1970. *Recreations:* walking, swimming. *Address:* Oakmere, Chester Road, Mere, Cheshire. *T:* Bucklow Hill 830040. *Club:* Royal Over-Seas League.

PICKFORD, Frank; Under-Secretary, General Manpower Division, Department of Employment, 1970-72, retired; *b* 26 Oct. 1917; *s* of late Edwin Pickford, Bulwell, Nottingham; *m* 1944, May Talbot; two *s. Educ:* Nottingham High Sch.; St John's Coll., Cambridge. Entered Min. of Labour, 1939; Asst Private Sec. to Minister of Labour, 1941-43; Dir, London Office, Internat. Labour Office, 1951-56; Sec., NEDC, 1962-64; Under-Sec., Ministry of Labour, 1964; Asst Under-Sec. of State, Dept of Employment and Productivity, 1968-70. *Address:* 64 Westbere Road, NW2. *T:* 01-435 1207.

PICKFORD, Prof. (Lillian) Mary, DSc; FRS 1966; Special Professor of Endocrinology, University of Nottingham, since 1973; Professor, Department of Physiology, University of Edinburgh, 1966-72 (Reader in Physiology, 1952-66); retired 1972, now Emeritus Professor; *b* 14 Aug. 1902; *d* of Herbert Arthur Pickford and Lillian Alice Minnie Wintle. *Educ:* Wycombe Abbey Sch.; Bedford and University Colls, Univ. of London. BSc (1st cl., Gen.) 1924; BSc (2nd cl., Physiology Special) 1925; MSc (Physiology) 1926; MRCS, LRCP 1933; DSc London 1951. FRCPE 1977. House Physician and Casualty Officer, Stafford Gen. Infirmary, 1935; Jun. Beit Memorial Research Fellow, 1936-39; Lectr, Dept of Physiology, Univ. of Edinburgh, 1939; Personal Chair, Dept of Physiology, Univ. of Edinburgh, 1966. Fellow, University Coll., London, 1968-. *Publications:* The Central Role of Hormones, 1969; papers in Jl Physiology, British Jl Pharmacology, Jl Endocrinology. *Recreations:* walking, travel, painting. *Address:* The Hall, King Sterndale, near Buxton, Derbyshire.

PICKFORD, Prof. Mary; *see* Pickford, Prof. L. M.

PICKFORD, Prof. Ralph William; Professor of Psychology in the University of Glasgow, 1955-73, now Emeritus; *b* 11 Feb. 1903; *s* of William Pickford and Evelyn May Flower; *m* 1st, 1933, Alexis Susan Macquisten (*d* 1971); 2nd, 1971, Laura Ruth Bowyer. *Educ:* Bournemouth School and Municipal Coll.; Emmanuel Coll., Cambridge. Emmanuel College: Exhibitioner, 1924, Sen. Schol. and Internal Research Student, 1927; BA 1927, MA 1930, PhD 1932. Goldsmiths' Company's Exhibitioner, 1925; Moral Sciences Tripos, First Class, 1927. Lecturer in Psychology and Acting Head of Dept, Aberdeen Univ., 1929. Asst in Psychology Dept, 1930, Lectr, 1935, Sen. Lectr and Acting Head of Psychology Dept 1947, Glasgow Univ. DLitt (Glasgow) 1947. Hon. Psychotherapist Notre Dame Child Guidance Clinic, 1942-80, and Davidson Clinic, Glasgow, 1952-80. First Pres., Experimental Psychology Group; Chm. and then Hon. Sec. Scottish Br. Brit. Psychological Soc.; Pres. Sect. J Brit. Assoc., 1958. Vice-Pres., Internat. Assoc. of Empirical Aesthetics; Hon. Mem. Soc. Française d'Esthétique; Mem., Council of Soc. Internat. de Psychopathologie de l'Expression; Hon. Pres., Scottish Assoc. for Art and Psychopathology. FBPsS. *Publications:* Individual Differences in Colour Vision, 1951; The Analysis of an Obsessional, 1954; (with R. Kherumian), Hérédité et Fréquence des Dyschromatopsies, 1959; (with G. M. Wyburn and R. J. Hirst), The Human Senses and Perception, 1963; Pickford Projective Pictures, 1963; Studies in Psychiatric Art, 1967; Psychology and Visual Aesthetics, 1972; Monograph: The Psychology of Cultural Change in Painting, 1943; many articles on Experimental, Social and Clinical Psychology, and the Psychology of Art. *Recreations:* painting, gardening, music. *Address:* 34 Morven Road, Bearsden, Glasgow G61 3BX. *T:* 041-942 5386.

PICKLES, James; His Honour Judge Pickles; a Circuit Judge, since 1976; *b* 18 March 1925; *s* of Arthur Pickles, OBE, JP and Gladys Pickles; *m* 1948, Sheila Ratcliffe; two *s* one *d. Educ:* Worksop Coll.; Leeds Univ. (LLB); Christ Church, Oxford (MA). Called to Bar, Inner Temple, 1948 (Philip Teichman Scholar); practised at Bradford, 1949-76; a Recorder of the Crown Court, 1972-76. Councillor, Brighouse Borough Council, 1956-62. Contested

(L) Brighouse and Spenborough, 1964. Author of various radio plays. *Address:* c/o Sheffield Crown Court, Sheffield S1 1EH.

PICKTHORN, Sir Charles (William Richards), 2nd Bt *cr* 1959; *b* 3 March 1927; *s* of Rt Hon. Sir Kenneth William Murray Pickthorn, 1st Bt, and Nancy Catherine Lewis (*d* 1982), *d* of late Lewis Matthew Richards; *S* father, 1975; *m* 1951, Helen Antonia, *o d* of late Sir James Mann, KCVO; one *s* two *d*. *Educ:* Eton; Corpus Christi Coll., Cambridge (Major Schol., BA). Served RNVR, 1945–48. Called to the Bar, Middle Temple, 1952. Dir, J. Henry Schroder Wagg & Co. Ltd, 1971–79. *Recreations:* sailing, reading. *Heir: s* James Francis Mann Pickthorn, *b* 18 Feb. 1955. *Address:* Manor House, Nunney, near Frome, Somerset. *T:* Nunney 574; 3 Hobury Street, SW10. *T:* 01-352 2795.

PICKUP, Ronald Alfred; actor; *b* 7 June 1940; *s* of Eric and Daisy Pickup; *m* 1964, Lans Traverse, USA; one *s* one *d. Educ:* King's Sch., Chester; Leeds Univ. (BA); Royal Academy of Dramatic Art. Repertory, Leicester, 1964; Royal Court, 1964 and 1965–66; National Theatre, 1965, 1966–73, 1977: appearances include: Rosalind, in all-male As You Like It, 1967; Richard II, 1972; Edmund, in Long Day's Journey into Night, 1971; Cassius, in Julius Caesar, 1977; Philip Madras, in The Madras House, 1977; Norman, in Norman Conquests, Globe, 1974; Play, Royal Court, 1976; Hobson's Choice, Lyric, Hammersmith, 1981; Astrov, in Uncle Vanya, Haymarket, 1982; *films:* Three Sisters, 1969; Day of the Jackal, 1972; Joseph Andrews, 1976; 39 Steps, Zulu Dawn, 1978; Nijinsky, 1979; *television:* Dragon's Opponent, 1973; Jennie, Fight Against Slavery, 1974; The Philanthropist, Ghost Trio, The Discretion of Dominic Ayres, 1977; Memories, Henry VIII, 1978; England's Green and Pleasant Land, Christ Hero, Tropic, 1979; Life of Giuseppe Verdi, The Letter, Ivanhoe, 1981; Wagner, 1982. *Recreations:* listening to music, walking, painting.

PICOT, Jacques M. C. G.; *see* Georges-Picot.

PICTON, Jacob Glyndwr, (Glyn Picton), CBE 1972; Senior Lecturer in Industrial Economics, University of Birmingham, 1947–79; *b* Aberdare, 28 Feb. 1912; *s* of David Picton; *m* 1939, Rhiannon Mary James (Merch Megan), LRAM, ARCM (*d* 1978); one *s* one *d. Educ:* Aberdare Boys' County Sch.; Birmingham Univ. (MCom). Chance Bros Ltd, 1933–47, Asst Sec. 1945–47. Pres., W Midland Rent Assessment Panel, 1965–72 (Chm. Cttee 1973–81); Governor, United Birmingham Hosps, 1953–74 (Chm., Children's Hosp., 1956–66; Teaching Hosps Rep. Professional and Techn. Whitley Council, 1955–61; Mem., Birmingham Regional Hosp. Bd, 1958–74 (Vice-Chm. 1971–74); Mem., NHS Nat. Staff Cttee, 1964–73 (Vice-Chm. 1968–73); Chm., Birmingham Hosp. Region Staff Cttee, 1964–74; Vice-Chm., W Mids RHA, 1973–79 (Mem., 1979–82); Vice-Chm., NHS Nat. Staff Cttee (Admin. and Clerical), 1973–82; NHS Nat. Assessor (Admin), 1973. Chm., Birmingham Industrial Therapy Assoc. Ltd, 1965–79 and W Bromwich Industrial Therapy Assoc. Ltd, 1969–79; Indep. Mem., Estate Agents Council, 1967–69; Chm. of Wages Councils, 1953–; Dep. Chm., Commn of Inquiry concerning Sugar Confectionery and Food Preserving Wages Council, 1961; Chm., Commn of Inquiry concerning Licensed Residential Estabts and Restaurants Wages Council, 1963–64; sole Comr of Inquiry into S Wales Coalfield Dispute, 1965; Dep. Chm., Commn of Inquiry concerning Industrial and Staff Canteens Wages Council, 1975; Independent Arbitrator, Lock Industry, 1976–81. *Publications:* various articles and official reports. *Recreations:* music, gardening, Pembrokeshire history. *Address:* 54 Chesterwood Road, Kings Heath, Birmingham B13 0QE. *T:* 021-444 3959.

PIENKOWSKI, Jan Michal; designer and illustrator, since 1958; Art Director, Gallery Five Ltd, since 1961 (Founder Director, 1961); *b* 8 Aug. 1936; *s* of Jerzy Dominik Pieńkowski and Wanda Maria Pieńkowska. *Educ:* Cardinal Vaughan Sch., London; King's Coll., Cambridge (MA Classics and English). Art Director: J. Walter Thompson, London, 1958–59; William Collins, London, 1959–60; Art Editor, Time and Tide, London, 1960–61. Work includes graphics and surface design, posters and greeting cards, BBC children's TV, and book illustration. Kate Greenaway Medal, Library Assoc., 1972 and 1979. *Publications:* illustrator: A Necklace of Raindrops, 1968; The Kingdom under the Sea, 1971; Meg and Mog series, 1973–82 (co-designed Meg and Mog Show, 1981); Tale of a One Way Street, 1978; J. P. Fairy Tale Library, etc; illustrator/author: Concept series, 1973–80; Haunted House, 1979; Robot, 1981; Dinner Time, 1981; Gossip, 1983. *Recreations:* movies, riding, skiing, gardening, collecting illustrated books. *Address:* Oakgates, 45 Lonsdale Road, Barnes, SW13 9JR. *T:* 01-748 6269. *Club:* Polish Hearth.

PIERCE, Francis William, MA (Belfast and Dublin); Hughes Professor of Spanish, University of Sheffield, 1953–80, now Emeritus Professor; Dean of the Faculty of Arts, 1964–67; *b* 21 Sept. 1915; *s* of late Robert Pierce, JP and Catherine Ismay Pierce; *m* 1944, Mary Charlotte Una, *o d* of late Rev. J. C. Black, Asyut, Upper Egypt; three *s. Educ:* Royal Belfast Academical Institution; Queen's University, Belfast. BA, 1st Cl. Hons, Spanish studies, QUB, 1938; Postgrad. Schol., Columbia Univ., New York, 1938–39; MA, QUB, 1939; Asst Lectr in Spanish, Univ. of Liverpool, 1939–40. Dep. to Prof. of Spanish, TCD, 1940–45; MA *jure officii*, Univ. of Dublin, 1943; Hughes Lectr in Spanish, Univ. of Sheffield, 1946. Visiting Professor: Brown Univ., Providence, RI, 1968; Case Western Reserve Univ., Cleveland, O, 1968. President: Anglo-Catalan Soc., 1955–57; Assoc. of Hispanists of GB and Ireland, 1971–73. *Publications:* The Heroic Poem of the Spanish Golden Age: Selections, chosen with Introduction and Notes, 1947; Hispanic Studies:

Review and Revision, 1954; (ed) Hispanic Studies in Honour of I. González Llubera, 1959; La poesia épica del siglo de oro, 1961 (Madrid), 2nd edn 1968; The Historie of Aravcana, transcribed with introd. and notes, 1964; (ed with C. A. Jones) Actas del Primer Congreso Internacional de Hispanistas, 1964; (ed) Two Cervantes Short Novels, 1970, 2nd edn 1976; (ed) La Cristiada by Diego de Hojeda, 1971; (ed) Luís de Camões: Os Lusiadas, 1973, 2nd edn 1981; Amadis de Gaula, 1976; articles and reviews in Hispanic Review, Mod. Language Review, Bulletin of Hispanic Studies, Bulletin Hispanique, Ocidente, Estudis Romànics, Quaderni Ibero-Americani. *Address:* 16 Taptonville Crescent, Sheffield S10 5BP. *T:* Sheffield 664239.

PIERCE, Hugh Humphrey; barrister; *b* 13 Oct. 1931; *s* of Dr Gwilym Pierce, Abercynon, Glam; *m* 1958, Rachel Margaret Procter; two *s. Educ:* Clifton; King's Coll., Univ. of London. LLB Hons 1954; Pres. Faculty of Laws Soc.; Pres. Union. Called to Bar, Lincoln's Inn, 1955. Diploma Personnel Management, 1962; MIPM 1963. Army Service in Intell. Corps (Cyprus), 1955–57; Kodak Ltd, legal and personnel work, 1957–63; joined BBC, 1963, personnel and industrial relations: Admin. Officer, Local Radio, 1967–68; Local Radio Develt Manager, 1968–69; General Manager, Local Radio, 1970–74; Asst Controller, Staff Admin, 1974–78; Asst Controller, Employment Policy and Appts, 1978–80. Member: Justice; Amnesty; NACRO; Council, Howard League. *Recreations:* chamber music, narrow boats. *Address:* 68 Priory Gardens, Highgate, N6. *T:* 01-348 1737.

PIERCE, Rt. Rev. Reginald James, Hon. DD (Winnipeg), 1947; *b* 1909; *s* of James Reginald Pierce and Clara (*née* Whitehand) Plymouth; *m* 1932, Ivy Bell, *d* of Edward and Lucy Jackson, Saskatoon, Canada; one *d. Educ:* University of Saskatchewan (BA 1931); Emmanuel Coll., Saskatoon (LTh 1932); Univ. of London (BD 1942). Deacon, 1932; priest, 1934; Curate of Colinton, 1932–33; Priest-in-charge, 1933–34; Rector and Rural Dean of Grande Prairie, 1934–38; Rector of South Saanich, 1938–41; Rector of St Barnabas, Calgary, 1941–43; Canon of St John's Cathedral, Winnipeg, and Warden of St John's Coll., 1943–50; Priest-in-charge of St Barnabas, Winnipeg, 1946–50; Bishop of Athabasca, 1950–74; Acting Rector: All Saints, Victoria, BC, 1975–76; St David's, Victoria, BC, 1976–. Examining Chaplain: to Bishop of Athabasca, 1935–38; to Archbishop of Rupertsland, 1943–50. *Address:* Apt 807, 777 Blanshard Street, Victoria, BC V&W 2Q9, Canada.

PIERCE-GOULDING, Lt-Col Terence Leslie Crawford, MBE 1943; CD; Secretary, Commonwealth Press Union, since Oct. 1970; *b* 2 March 1918; *o s* of late Rev. Edward Pierce-Goulding and Christina; *m* 1964, Catherine Yvonne, *d* of John Welsh, Dunedin, NZ; one *s* one *d. Educ:* public and private schs, Edmonton, Alta. Enlisted British Army, 1940, 2nd Lieut Mddx Regt (DCO); Capt. Loyal Edmonton Regt, 1941–42; Staff Coll., 1943; GS03 (Ops), Canadian Planning Staff and HQ 1st Canadian Army, 1943–44; GSO2 (PR), HQ 21 Army Gp and BAOR, 1945–46; Sen. PRO, Central Comd HQ, 1947–48; Adviser to Perm. Canadian Delegn to UN, 1948–50; regtl and staff appts, Royal Canadian Regt and Army HQ, 1950–60; Chief Logistics Officer, UN Emergency Force (Middle East), 1962–63; Dir of Sen. Appts (Army), Canadian Forces HQ, 1963–66; Sen. Admin. Officer, Canadian Defence Liaison Staff (London), 1966–69, retd 1969. Canadian Internat. Development Agency, 1969–70. *Recreations:* golf, travel, photography, literature. *Address:* 20 Hill Rise, NW11. *T:* 01-455 2306. *Club:* Pathfinders.

PIERCY, family name of **Baron Piercy.**

PIERCY, 3rd Baron *cr* 1945, of Burford; **James William Piercy;** *b* 19 Jan. 1946; *s* of 2nd Baron Piercy and of Oonagh Lavinia, *d* of late Major Edward John Lake Baylay, DSO; *S* father, 1981. *Educ:* Shrewsbury; Edinburgh Univ. (BSc 1968). *Heir: b* Hon. Mark Edward Pelham Piercy [*b* 30 June 1953; *m* 1979, Vivien Angela, *d* of His Honour Judge Evelyn Faithfull Monier-Williams, *qv*; one *d*]. *Address:* 13 Arnold Mansions, Queen's Club Gardens, W14 9RD.

PIERCY, Hon. Joanna Elizabeth; *see* Turner, Hon. J. E.

PIERCY, Hon. Penelope Katherine, CBE 1968; Under-Secretary, Ministry of Technology, 1965–68; *b* 15 Apr. 1916; *d* of 1st Baron Piercy, CBE. *Educ:* St Paul's Girls' School; Somerville College, Oxford. War of 1939–45, various appointments, Military Intelligence. Foreign Office, 1945–47; Economist, Colonial Development Corp., 1948–54; Department of Scientific and Industrial Research, 1955–65 (Sen. Prin. Scientific Officer, 1960). CIMechE. *Address:* Southside, Hinton Martell, Wimborne, Dorset.

PIERRE, Abbé; (Henri Antoine Groués); Officier de la Légion d'Honneur, 1980; French priest; Founder of the Companions of Emmaüs; *b* Lyon, 5 Aug. 1912; 5th *c* of Antoine Groués, Soyeux. *Educ:* Collège des Jésuites, Lyon. Entered Capuchin Monastery, 1930; studied at Capuchin seminary, Crest, Drôme, and Faculté de Théologie, Lyon. Secular priest, St Joseph Basilica, Grenoble. Served war of 1939–45 (Chevalier de la Légion d'Honneur, Croix de Guerre, Médaille de la Résistance); Alsatian and Alpine fronts; Vicar of the Cathedral, Grenoble; assumed name of Abbé Pierre and joined resistance movement, 1942; Chaplain of French Navy at Casablanca, 1944; of whole Free French Navy, 1945. Elected (Indep.) to 1st Constituent Assembly of 4th French Republic, 1945; elected as candidate of Mouvement Républicain Populaire to 2nd Constituent Assembly; re-elected 1946; contested (Indep.), 1951. Président de l'Exécutif du Mouvement Universel pour une

Confédération Mondiale, 1947-51. Founded the Companions of Emmaüs, a movement to provide a roof for the "sanslogis" of Paris. *Publications:* 23 Mois de Vie Clandestine; L'Abbé Pierre vous Parle; Vers l'Homme; Feuilles Eparses; Emmaüs ou Venger l'homme. *Address:* 2 Avenue de la Liberté, Charenton-Val de Marne, France. *T:* 368.62.44.

PIERRE, Sir (Joseph) Henry, Kt 1957; CMT; FRCS; Consultant Surgeon, General Hospital, Port of Spain, Trinidad, WI, since 1950; Hon. Surgeon, Caura Tuberculosis Sanatorium, Trinidad; Hon. Surgeon, Mental Hospital, Trinidad; *b* 28 Oct. 1904; *s* of Charles Henry and Carmen M. Pierre; *m* 1939; one *s*; *m* 1962, Marjorie Boös; one *s*. *Educ:* Queen's Royal College, Trinidad. WI; St Bartholomew's Hosp., London; London Univ.; Royal Coll. of Surgeons, Edinburgh. Qualified in medicine, 1931; Casualty House Physician, St Bartholomew's Hosp., 1931; junior MO, Trinidad Medical Service, 1932; FRCSE 1939; FRCS 1959; Medical Officer, Grade A, 1945; Sen. Officer Surgeon, Gen. Hosp., San Fernando, 1945; Pres., Trinidad and Tobago Red Cross Soc.; Fellow Internat. Coll. of Surgeons, USA. Navy Meritorious Public Service Citation from US Govt, 1957; Chaconia Medal, Trinidad, 1976; Scroll of Honour, Surgery, Trinidad and Tobago Medical Assoc. Coronation Medal, 1953. *Recreations:* photography, golf, yachting, tennis, horticulture. *Address:* St Florian, Fishery Road, Bray, near Maidenhead, Berks SL6 1UN. *Clubs:* Royal Commonwealth Society (West Indian); Yacht, Union, Country, St Andrew's Golf, (Hon. mem.) Pointe-a-Pierre (Trinidad, WI).

PIERS, Sir Charles Robert Fitzmaurice, 10th Bt, *cr* 1660; Lt-Cmdr RCNVR; *b* 30 Aug. 1903; *s* of Sir Charles Piers, 9th Bt, and Hester Constance (Stella) (*d* 1936), *e d* of late S. R. Brewis of Ibstone House, Ibstone; *S* father, 1945; *m* 1936, Ann Blanche Scott (*d* 1975), *o d* of late Capt. Thomas Ferguson (The Royal Highlanders); one *s* one *d*. *Educ:* RN Colleges, Osborne and Dartmouth. Served European War, 1939-45. *Heir: s* James Desmond Piers, *b* 24 July 1947. *Address:* Duncan, British Columbia, Canada.

PIERS, Rear-Adm. Desmond William, DSC 1943; CD; RCN, retd; Agent General of Nova Scotia in the United Kingdom and Europe, 1977-79; *b* 12 June 1913; *s* of William Harrington Piers and Florence Maud Piers (*née* O'Donnell), MD; *m* 1941, Janet, *d* of Dr and Mrs Murray Macneill, Halifax, NS; one step *d*. *Educ:* Halifax County Acad.; RMC of Canada; RN Staff Coll.; Nat. Defence Coll. of Canada. Joined RCN as cadet, 1932; CO, HMC Destroyer Restigouche, and Sen. Officer, Fourth Canadian Escort Gp on N Atlantic convoy routes, 1941-43 (DSC); CO, HMC Destroyer Algonquin with Brit. Home Fleet, Scapa Flow, and participated in invasion of Normandy and convoys to N Russia, 1944-45, Comdr 1945; Exec. Officer, HMC Aircraft Carrier Magnificent (Comdr), 1947-48; Dir, Naval Plans and Ops, Naval Headquarters, Ottawa (Captain), 1949-50; Asst COS (Personnel and Admin.) to SACLANT, 1952-53; CO, HMC Cruiser Quebec, 1955-56; Sen. Canadian Offr Afloat (Atlantic), 1956-57; Comdt, RMC Canada, and Hon. ADC to the Governor General (Cdre), 1957-60; Asst Chief of Naval Staff (Plans), Naval HQ, 1960-62; Chm., Can. Def. Liaison Staff, Washington DC, and Can. Rep. on NATO Mil. Cttee (Rear-Adm.), 1962-66; retd 1967. Hon. DScMil, RMC of Canada, 1978. Freeman of City of London, 1978; KLJ 1969. *Recreations:* golf, tennis, figure skating, photography. *Address:* The Quarter Deck, Chester, Nova Scotia B0J 1J0, Canada. *T:* 902-275-4462. *Clubs:* Halifax (Halifax); Halifax Golf and Country, Royal Nova Scotian Yacht Squadron, Chester Golf (all Nova Scotia); Rideau (Ottawa).

PIGGOTT, Donald James; Director-General, British Red Cross Society, since 1980; *b* 1 Sept. 1920; *s* of James Piggott and Edith Piggott (*née* Tempest); *m* 1974, Kathryn Courtenay-Evans. *Educ:* Bradford Grammar School; Christ's College, Cambridge (MA); London School of Economics. Served Army in NW Europe and India, 1941-46. PA to Finance and Supply Director, London Transport, 1947-50; Shell-Mex and BP Ltd, 1951-58; Manager Development Div., Marketing Dept, British Petroleum Co. Ltd, 1958-73; BRCS: Dir, Internat. Affairs, 1973; Head of Internat. Div., 1975; Asst Dir-Gen. International, 1980. Mem., Central Appeals Adv. Cttee, BBC and IBA, 1980-. Mem., Open Sect., R.SocMed. *Recreations:* music, theatre. *Address:* 18 Elm Lodge, River Gardens, SW6. *T:* 01-385 5588; Beech Tree House, Tostock, Bury St Edmunds, Suffolk. *T:* Beyton 70589.

PIGGOTT, Maj.-Gen. Francis James Claude, CB 1963; CBE 1961; DSO 1945; *b* Tokyo, Japan, 11 Oct. 1910; *s* of late Maj.-Gen. F. S. G. Piggott, CB, DSO; *m* 1940, Muriel Joan, *d* of late Wilfred E. Cottam, Rotherham, Yorks; one *s* one *d*. *Educ:* Cheltenham; RMC Sandhurst. 2nd Lieut The Queen's Royal Regt, 1931; Language Officer, Japan, 1935-37; Captain, 1939; served 1939-45 in France (despatches), New Zealand, India and Burma (DSO); in Japan, UK and Egypt (OBE and Bt Lt-Col), 1946-52; attended 1st Course, Joint Services Staff Coll., 1947; Lt-Col comdg 1st Bn The Queen's Royal Regt, 1952, BAOR and Malaya; Colonel, War Office, 1954; Comd 161 Infantry Bde (TA), 1956; Dep. Director of Military Intelligence, War Office (Brigadier), 1958; Major-General, 1961; Assistant Chief of Staff (Intelligence), SHAPE, 1961-64; retired, 1964; served in Civil Service (Security), 1965-75. Col, The Queen's Royal Surrey Regt, 1964-66; Dep. Col (Surrey) The Queen's Regt, 1967-69. *Recreations:* cricket and foreign travel. *Address:* 20 St John Street, Wells, Somerset BA5 1SW. *T:* Wells 73318. *Clubs:* Army and Navy, Free Foresters.

PIGGOTT, Lester Keith, OBE 1975; jockey; *b* 5 Nov. 1935; *s* of Keith Piggott and Iris Rickaby; *m* 1960, Susan Armstrong; two *d*. Selection of races won: the Derby (8 times): 1954 (on Never Say Die); 1957 (on Crepello); 1960

(on St Paddy); 1968 (on Sir Ivor); 1970 (on Nijinsky); 1972 (on Roberto); 1976 (on Empery); 1977 (on The Minstrel); St Leger (7 times). In several seasons since 1955 he has ridden well over 100 winners a year, in this country alone; rode 4,000th winner in Britain, 1982; Champion Jockey 10 times, 1960, 1964-71 and 1981; rides frequently in France; won Prix de l'Arc de Triomphe on Rheingold, 1973, on Alleged, 1977 and 1978. Won Washington, DC, International on Sir Ivor, 1968 (first time since 1922 an English Derby winner raced in USA), on Karabas, 1969, on Argument, 1980. *Recreations:* swimming, water skiing, golf. *Address:* Florizel, Newmarket, Suffolk. *T:* Newmarket 2584.

PIGGOTT, Prof. Stuart, CBE 1972; FBA 1953; Abercromby Professor of Prehistoric Archæology, University of Edinburgh, 1946-77; *b* 28 May 1910; *s* of G. H. O. Piggott. *Educ:* Churchers Coll., Petersfield; St John's Coll., Oxford (Hon. Fellow, 1979). On staff on Royal Commn on Ancient Monuments (Wales), 1929-34; Asst Dir of Avebury excavations, 1934-38; from 1939 in ranks and later as Intelligence Officer in Army in charge of military air photograph interpretation, South-East Asia. Conducted archæological excavations in southern England and carried out research on European prehistory up to 1942; in India, 1942-45; studied Oriental prehistory. Hon. DLittHum, Columbia, 1954. Fellow of Royal Soc. of Edinburgh, and of Soc. of Antiquaries; Mem. German Archæolog. Inst., 1953; Hon. Mem. Royal Irish Acad., 1956; Foreign Hon. Member American Academy of Arts and Sciences, 1960; advisory editor, Antiquity. Trustee, British Museum, 1968-74. Travelled in Europe and Asia. *Publications:* Some Ancient Cities of India, 1946; Fire Among the Ruins, 1948; British Prehistory, 1949; William Stukeley: an XVIII Century Antiquary, 1950; Prehistoric India, 1950; A Picture Book of Ancient British Art (with G. E. Daniel), 1951; Neolithic Cultures of British Isles, 1954; Scotland before History, 1958; Approach to Archæology, 1959; (ed) The Dawn of Civilization, 1961; The West Kennet Long Barrow, 1962; Ancient Europe, 1965; Prehistoric Societies (with J. G. D. Clark), 1965; The Druids, 1968; Introduction to Camden's Britannia of 1695, 1971; (ed jtly) France Before the Romans, 1974; Ruins in a Landscape, 1977; Antiquity Depicted, 1978; (ed and contrib.) Agrarian History of England and Wales Ii, 1981; numerous technical papers in archæological jls. *Recreations:* reading, cooking, travel. *Address:* The Cottage, West Challow, Wantage, Oxon. *Club:* United Oxford & Cambridge University.

PIGOT, Maj.-Gen. Sir Robert (Anthony), 7th Bt *cr* 1764; CB 1964; OBE 1959; DL; *b* 6 July 1915; *s* of George Douglas Hugh Pigot (*d* 1959) (2nd *s* of 5th Bt) and Hersey Elizabeth Pigot (*née* Maltby) (*d* 1970); *S* uncle, 1977; *m* 1942, Honor (*d* 1966), *d* of late Capt. Wilfred St Martin Gibbon; one *s* one *d*; *m* 1968, Sarah Anne Colville, *e d* of Mr David and Lady Joan Colville, The Old Vicarage, Dorton; one *s* one *d*. *Educ:* Stowe Sch. Commissioned into the Royal Marines, 1934; served War of 1939-45 (despatches): Regimental service in RM Div. and Special Service Group; Staff appts in 3rd Commando Brigade in SE Asia; psc 1943-44; Directing Staff, Staff Coll., Camberley, 1946-47; Min. of Defence, 1953-54; Standing Group, NATO, Washington, 1954-57; Dep. Standing Gp Rep. with North Atlantic Council, Paris, 1958-59; Chief of Staff, Royal Marines, 1960-64; retd, Dec. 1964. Man. Director, Bone Brothers Ltd, 1964-66; Director: John Brown Plastics Machinery Ltd, 1965-66; Executive Appointments Ltd, 1968-70. High Sheriff, DL, Isle of Wight, 1978. *Recreations:* field sports and yachting. *Heir: s* George Hugh Pigot [*b* 28 Nov. 1946; *m* 1967, Judith (marr. diss. 1973), *er d* of late Major John Hele Sandeman-Allen, RA; one *d*]. *Address:* Yew Tree Lodge, Bembridge, Isle of Wight. *Clubs:* Royal Yacht Squadron; Bembridge Sailing.

PIGOT, Thomas Herbert, QC 1967; His Honour Judge Pigot; a Circuit Judge, since 1972; Deputy Senior Judge (non-resident), Sovereign Base Area, Cyprus; *b* 19 May 1921; *e s* of late Thomas Pigot and of Martha Ann Pigot; *m* 1950, Zena Marguerite, *yr d* of late Tom and Dorothy Gladys Wall; three *d*. *Educ:* Manchester Gram. Sch. (Schol.); Brasenose Coll., Oxford (Somerset Schol.). BA (1st cl. hons Jurisprudence) 1941; MA 1946; BCL 1947. Commissioned Welch Regt, 1942; served N Africa with Royal Lincs Regt; wounded and taken prisoner, 1943; released, 1945. Called to Bar, Inner Temple, 1947; practised in Liverpool on Northern Circuit until 1967. Mem., Bar Council, 1970. *Recreation:* golf. *Address:* Fairfields, Dunsden Green, near Reading, Berks RG4 9QD. *T:* Reading 478730; (professional) 2 Pump Court, Temple, EC4. *T:* 01-353 3106/7540. *Clubs:* White Elephant; Vincent's (Oxford); Royal Birkdale Golf; Huntercombe Golf; Harlequin FC.

PIGOTT, Sir (Berkeley) Henry (Sebastian), 5th Bt *cr* 1808; farmer; *b* 24 June 1925; *s* of Sir Berkeley Pigott, 4th Bt, and Christabel (*d* 1974), *d* of late Rev. F. H. Bowden-Smith; *S* father, 1982; *m* 1954, (Olive) Jean, *d* of John William Balls; two *s* one *d*. *Educ:* Ampleforth College. Served War with Royal Marines, 1944-45. *Recreation:* sailing (blue water). *Heir: er s* David John Berkeley Pigott [*b* 16 Aug. 1955; *m* 1981, Alison Fletcher]. *Address:* Brook Farm, Shobley, Ringwood, Hants. *T:* Ringwood 3268.

PIGOTT, Air Vice-Marshal Michael Joseph, CBE 1956; Director of Dental Services, RAF, 1954-58; retired, 1958; *b* 16 May 1904; *m* 1938, Ethel Norah, *d* of Alfred Sutherland Blackman; one *d*. *Educ:* Blackrock College, Dublin; Nat. Univ. of Ireland; Nat. Dental Hosp. of Ireland. BDS 1925; FDSRCS 1948. Joined RAF 1930. Served War of 1939-45, Bomber Command; Inspecting Dental Officer: MEAF, 1945-48, Flying Trng Comd, 1948-49, Tech. Trng Comd, 1949-50; Principal Dental Officer, Home Comd 1950-54;

Air Vice-Marshal, 1955. QHDS, 1950-58. *Address:* 18 Duck Street, Cerne Abbas, Dorchester, Dorset DT2 7LA. *T:* Cerne Abbas 538.

PIGOTT-BROWN, Sir William Brian, 3rd Bt, *cr* 1902; *b* 20 Jan. 1941; *s* of Sir John Pigott-Brown, 2nd Bt (killed in action, 1942) and Helen (who *m* 1948, Capt. Charles Raymond Radclyffe), *o d* of Major Gilbert Egerton Cotton, Priestland, Tarporley, Cheshire; *S* father, 1942. *Heir:* none. *Address:* Orchard House, Aston Upthorpe, Oxfordshire; 25 Chapel Street, SW1.

PIHL, Brig. Hon. Dame Mary Mackenzie, (Fru Mary Pihl), DBE 1970 (MBE 1958); Director, Women's Royal Army Corps, 1967-Aug. 1970, retired; *b* 3 Feb. 1916; *d* of Sir John Anderson, later 1st Viscount Waverley, PC, GCB, OM, GCSI, GCIE, FRS, and Christina Mackenzie Anderson; *m* 1973, Frithjof Pihl. *Educ:* Sutton High Sch.; Villa Brillantmont, Lausanne. Joined Auxiliary Territorial Service, 1941; transferred to Women's Royal Army Corps, 1949. Hon. ADC to the Queen, 1967-70. *Address:* Engø, 3145 Tjøme, Norway. *Club:* English-Speaking Union.

PIKE, Baroness *cr* 1974 (Life Peer), of Melton, Leics; **Irene Mervyn Parnicott Pike,** DBE 1981; Chairman, Broadcasting Complaints Commission, since 1981; *b* 16 Sept. 1918; *d* of I. S. Pike, Director, Okehampton, Devonshire. *Educ:* Hunmanby Hall; Reading University. BA Hons Economics and Psychology, 1941. Served WAAF, 1941-46. Mem., WRCC, 1955-57. Contested (C): Pontefract, 1951; Leek, Staffordshire, 1955. MP (C) Melton, Leics, Dec. 1956-Feb. 1974; Assistant Postmaster-General, 1959-63; Joint Parliamentary Under-Secretary of State, Home Office, 1963-64. Director: Watts, Blake, Bearne & Co. Ltd; Dunderdale Investments. Chairman: IBA Gen. Adv. Council, 1974-79; WRVS, 1974-81. *Recreations:* gardening, walking. *Address:* Hownam, near Kelso, Roxburgh TD5 8AL.

PIKE, Andrew Hamilton, CMG 1956; OBE 1945; Minister for Lands and Mineral Resources, Tanganyika, 1957-59, retired; *b* 26 August 1903; *s* of late Canon William Pike, Thurles, Co. Tipperary; *m* 1951, Catherine Provan Cathcart, *y d* of late Prof. E. P. Cathcart, CBE; four *s. Educ:* The Abbey, Tipperary; Trinity College, Dublin; University College, Oxford. Tanganyika: Administrative Officer (Cadet), 1927; Asst Dist Officer, 1930; Dist Officer, 1938; Dep. Provincial Comr, 1947; Provincial Comr, 1948; Senior Provincial Comr, 1951; Member for Lands and Mines, 1953. President Tanganyika Society, 1954-57; Member Editorial Board of "Tanganyika Notes and Records", until 1959. *Recreation:* historical research. *Address:* Blatchfeld, Blackheath, Guildford, Surrey GU4 8QY. *T:* Guildford 892358.

See also Rt Rev. St J. S. Pike, Sir Theodore Pike, Rt Rev. V. J. Pike.

PIKE, Edward Roy, PhD; FRS 1981; Deputy Chief Scientific Officer, Royal Signals and Radar Establishment, Malvern, since 1973; *b* 4 Dec. 1929; *s* of Anthony Pike and Rosalind Irene Davies; *m* 1955, Pamela Sawtell; one *s* two *d. Educ:* Southfield Grammar Sch., Oxford; University Coll., Cardiff (BSc, PhD; Fellow, 1982). FInstP, FIMA. Served Royal Corps of Signals, 1948-50. Fulbright Schol., Physics Dept, MIT, 1958-60; Royal Signals and Radar Estab Physics Group, 1960-: theoretical and experimental research condensed matter physics and optics; Individual Merit SPSO 1967, IM DCSO 1973. Govt assessor, SRC Physics Cttee, 1973-76. Mem. Council: Inst. of Physics, 1976-80; European Physical Soc., 1981-; Vice-Pres. for Publications and Chm., Adam Hilger, 1981-; Director, NATO Advanced Study Insts, 1973-77. Editor: Journal of Physics A, 1973-78; Optica Acta, 1978-. Nat. Science Foundn Vis. Lectr, USA, 1959; Lectures: Univ. of Rome, 1976; Univ. of Bordeaux, 1977; Simon Fraser Univ., 1978; Univ. of Genoa, 1980. Royal Society Charles Parsons medal and lecture, 1975; MacRobert award (jtly) and lecture, 1977; Worshipful Co. of Scientific Instrument Makers Annual Achievement award (jtly), 1978; Committee on Awards to Inventors award, 1980; Confrérie St-Etienne, 1980. *Publications:* (ed jtly) Photon Correlation and Light Beating Spectroscopy, 1974; (ed) High Power Gas Lasers, 1975; (ed jtly) Photon Correlation Spectroscopy and Velocimetry, 1977; numerous papers in scientific jls. *Recreations:* music, languages, squash, woodwork. *Address:* 8 Bredon Grove, Malvern, Worcs WR14 3JR. *T:* Malvern 4910.

PIKE, Air Cdre James Maitland Nicholson, CB 1963; DSO 1942; DFC 1941; RAF, retired; with Ministry of Defence, 1969-78; *b* 8 Feb. 1916; *s* of late Frank Pike, Glendarary, Achill Island, Co. Mayo, Eire, and Daphne (*née* Kenyon Stow), Worcester; *m* 1st, 1942; one *d* ; 2nd, 1955, Amber Pauline Bettesworth Hellard; one *s* one step *d* ; 3rd, 1972, Dorothy May Dawson (*née* Holland); one step *d. Educ:* Stowe; RAF Coll., Cranwell. Commnd 1937; War Service: Aden, Middle East, UK (Coastal Command), Malta and Azores. Directing staff, RAF Staff Coll., 1945-47; Group Capt. 1955; Comd RAF Station, St Mawgan and RAF Station, Kinloss, 1955-57; SASO, RAF Malta, 1958-60; Air Cdre 1961; AOC, RAF Gibraltar, 1961-62; Imperial Defence College, 1963; Air Cdre Intelligence (B), Ministry of Defence, 1964; Dir of Security, RAF, 1965-69. *Recreations:* shooting, fishing. *Address:* Glendarary, Christmas Common, Watlington, Oxford. *T:* Watlington 2350.

PIKE, Michael Edmund; HM Diplomatic Service; Ambassador to Vietnam, since 1982; *b* 4 Oct. 1931; *s* of Henry Pike and Eleanor Pike; *m* 1962, Catherine (*née* Lim); one *s* two *d. Educ:* Wimbledon Coll.; London Sch. of Econs and Polit. Science; Brasenose Coll., Oxford (MA 1956). Service in HM Armed Forces, 1950-52. Editor, Cherwell, Oxford Univ., 1954; part-time News Reporter, Sunday Express, 1954-55; Feature Writer and Film Critic, Surrey Comet, 1955-56; joined HM Foreign (now Diplomatic) Service, 1956; Third Secretary: FO, 1956-57; Seoul, 1957-59; Second Secretary: Office of

Comr Gen. for Singapore and SE Asia, 1960-62; Seoul, 1962-64; FO, 1964-68; First Sec., Warsaw, 1968-70; FCO, 1970-73; First Sec., Washington, 1973-75; Counsellor: Washington, 1975-78; Tel Aviv, 1978-82; RCDS, 1982. Pres., Union of Catholic Students of GB, 1955-56. *Recreations:* reading, running, contemplating London. *Address:* c/o Foreign and Commonwealth Office, SW1.

PIKE, Sir Philip Ernest Housden, Kt 1969; Chief Justice of Swaziland, 1970-72, retired; *b* 6 March 1914; *s* of Rev. Ernest Benjamin Pike and Dora Case Pike (*née* Lillie); *m* 2nd, 1959, Millicent Locke Staples; one *s* one *d* of 1st marriage. *Educ:* De Carteret School, and Munro Coll., Jamaica; Middle Temple, London. Barrister at Law, 1938. Crown Counsel, Jamaica, 1947-49; Legal Draftsman, Kenya, 1949-52; Solicitor General, Uganda, 1952-58; QC (Uganda) 1953; Attorney General, Sarawak, 1958-65; QC (Sarawak) 1958; Chief Justice, High Court in Borneo, 1965-68; Judge, High Court of Malawi, 1969-70, Actg Chief Justice, 1970. Coronation Medal, 1953. PNBS-Sarawak, 1965; Malaysia Commemorative Medal, 1967; PMN Malaysia 1968. *Recreations:* golf, gardening. *Address:* 30 Berg Road, Fish Hoek, Cape, South Africa.

PIKE, Rt. Rev. St John Surridge; DD *jure dig* 1958; Assistant Bishop, Diocese of Guildford, since 1963; Vicar of Holy Trinity, Botleys and Lyne, and Christ Church, Longcross (in plurality), since 1971; *b* 27 Dec. 1909; *s* of late Rev. Canon William Pike, Thurles, Co. Tipperary; *m* 1958, Clare, *d* of late William Henry Jones; one *s* one *d* (and one *s* decd). *Educ:* The Abbey, Tipperary; Bishop Foy School, Waterford; Trinity Coll., Dublin (MA). Deacon, 1932; Priest, 1934; Curate of Taney, 1932-37; Head of Southern Church Mission, Ballymacarrett, Belfast, 1937-47; SPG Missionary, Diocese of Gambia, 1947-52; Rector of St George's, Belfast, 1952-57; Commissary for Gambia in N Ireland, 1954-57; Bishop of Gambia and the Rio Pongas, 1958-63; Vicar of St Mary the Virgin, Ewshot, 1963-71. *Address:* The Vicarage, Lyne and Longcross, Chertsey, Surrey. *T:* Ottershaw 3551.

PIKE, Sir Theodore (Ouseley), KCMG 1956 (CMG 1953); *b* 1904; 3rd *s* of late Canon W. Pike, Thurles, Co. Tipperary; *m* 1934, Violet F., *d* of late Sir William Robinson, DL, JP; two *s* one *d. Educ:* The Abbey, Tipperary; Trinity Coll., Dublin; University Coll., Oxford. Colonial Administrative Service, Tanganyika, 1928-53. Governor, Somaliland Protectorate, 1953; Governor and Commander-in-Chief, Somaliland Protectorate, 1954-59. Hon. LLD (Dublin). *Address:* c/o Grindlay's Bank, 23 Fenchurch Street, EC3.

PIKE, Marshal of the Royal Air Force Sir Thomas (Geoffrey), GCB 1961 (KCB 1955; CB 1946); CBE 1944; DFC 1942 and Bar, 1942; Deputy Supreme Allied Commander, Europe, 1964-67; *b* 29 June 1906; *s* of late Capt. S. R. Pike, RA; *m* 1930, Kathleen Althea, *e d* of Maj. H. Elwell; one *s* two *d. Educ:* Bedford School; RAF Coll., Cranwell. Joined RAF, 1923. Served War of 1939-45, Directorate of Organisation, Air Ministry; commanded a Fighter Squadron, 1941; Desert Air Force, 1943-45; AOC No 11 Group Fighter Command, 1950-51; DCS, HQ Air Force Central Europe, 1951-53; Deputy Chief of the Air Staff, Dec. 1953-July 1956; Air Officer Commanding-in-Chief, Fighter Command, July 1956-Dec. 1959; Chief of the Air Staff, 1960-63. Squadron Leader, 1937; Group Captain, 1941; Air Commodore, 1944; Air Vice-Marshal, 1950; Air Marshal, 1955; Air Chief Marshal, 1957; Marshal of the RAF, 1962. DL Essex, 1973-81. Officer Legion of Merit (USA). *Address:* Little Wynters, Hastingwood, Harlow, Essex.

See also Lt-Gen. Sir William Pike.

PIKE, Rt. Rev. Victor Joseph, CB 1953; CBE 1950 (OBE 1944); DD (*hc*) 1955; Chaplain to Retired Clergy in the Rural Deanery (formerly Archdeaconry) of Sarum, since 1978; *b* 1 July 1907; *s* of late Canon William Pike, Thurles, Co. Tipperary, and Mrs William Pike (*née* Surridge); *m* 1937, Dorothea Elizabeth Frend, *d* of late Capt. W. R. Frend, Bedenham, Gosport; one *s* two *d. Educ:* Bishop Foy School, Waterford; Trinity College, Dublin; BA 1930; MA 1935 (Hon. DD 1955). Curate, Dundrum, Co. Dublin, 1930-32; CF 4th Class, Aldershot, Gibraltar, RMA Woolwich, 1932-39; Senior Chaplain, 43rd Div., 11th Armoured Div., 1940-42; DACG, 5th Corps, CMF, 1942-44 (despatches 1943); ACG, 8th Army, 1945 (despatches); DCG, MELF, 1946; ACG, Western Command, 1947-49; ACG, BAOR, 1950-51; Chaplain-General to the Forces, 1951-60 (with title of Archdeacon, 1958-60); Prebend of Fordington with Writhlington in Salisbury Cathedral, 1960; Bishop Suffragan of Sherborne, 1960-76. Hon. Canon of Canterbury, 1951-60; QHC, 1948-53; Chaplain to the Queen, Nov. 1953-June 1960. *Recreation:* Rugby. *Address:* 53 The Close, Salisbury, Wilts. *T:* Salisbury 5766. *Club:* Cavalry and Guards.

See also A. H. Pike, Rt Rev. St J. S. Pike, Sir Theodore Pike.

PIKE, Lt-Gen. Sir William (Gregory Huddleston), KCB 1961 (CB 1956); CBE 1952; DSO 1943; Chief Commander, St John Ambulance, 1969-75; *b* 24 June 1905; *s* of late Captain Sydney Royston Pike, RA, and Sarah Elizabeth Pike (*née* Huddleston); *m* 1939, Josephine Margaret, *er d* of late Maj.-Gen. R. H. D. Tompson, CB, CMG, DSO, and Mrs B. D. Tompson; one *s* two *d. Educ:* Bedford School; Marlborough Coll.; RMA Woolwich. Lieutenant RA, 20th and 24th Field Brigades, RA and "A" Field Brigade, Indian Artillery, 1925-36; Staff College, Camberley, 1937-38; Command and Staff Appointments in UK, France and Belgium, North Africa, USA and Far East, 1939-50; CRA, 1st Commonwealth Div., Korea, 1951-52; idc 1953; Director of Staff Duties, War Office, 1954-57; Chief of Staff, Far East Land Forces, Oct. 1957-60; Vice-Chief of the Imperial General Staff, 1960-63; Col Comdt

RA, 1962-70. Lieutenant of HM Tower of London, 1963-66; Commissioner-in-Chief, St John Ambulance Brigade, 1967-73. Jt Hon. Pres., Anglo-Korean Society, 1963-69. Hon. Col 277 (Argyll and Sutherland Highlanders) Regt RA (TA), 1960-67; Hon. Col Lowland Regt RA (T), 1967-70. Member Honourable Artillery Company; Chm., Lord Mayor Treloar Trust, 1976-82; Corps of Commissionaires, 1964-81 (Mem. Administrative Bd). Officer, US Legion of Merit, 1953. GCStJ 1976. *Recreations:* field sports and gardening. *Address:* Ganwells, Bentley, Hants; Rhos-y-Bayvil, Velindre, Crymych, Dyfed.

See also Marshal of the Royal Air Force Sir Thomas Pike.

PILBROW, Richard Hugh; Chairman, Theatre Projects Group of Companies, since 1957; *b* 28 April 1933; *s* of Arthur Gordon Pilbrow and Marjorie Pilbrow; *m* 1st, 1958, Viki Brinton; one *s* one *d* ; 2nd, 1974, Molly Friedel; one *d. Educ:* Cranbrook Sch.; Central Sch. of Speech and Drama. Stage Manager, Teahouse of the August Moon, 1954; founded Theatre Projects, 1957. Lighting Designer for over 200 prodns in London, New York, Paris and Moscow, incl.: Brand, 1959; Blitz, 1962; Zorba, 1968; Annie, 1978; Oklahoma!, 1980; The Little Foxes, Windy City, 1982; for Nat. Theatre Co., 1963-70, incl. Hamlet, 1963; Rosencrantz and Guildenstern are Dead, 1966; Heartbreak House, 1975. Theatrical Producer in London of prodns incl.: A Funny Thing Happened on the Way to the Forum, 1963; Cabaret, 1968; Company, 1972; A Little Night Music, 1975. Film Prod., Swallows and Amazons, 1973; TV Prod., All You Need is Love—the story of popular music, 1975; Dir, Mister, 1971. Theatre Projects Consultants have been consultants on many theatres incl. Nat. Theatre of GB, Barbican Theatre, Royal Opera House, and theatres and arts centres in Canada, Iran, Hong Kong, Saudi Arabia, Mexico, Iceland, Nigeria, Norway, USA, etc. Vice President: Assoc. of British Theatre Technicians: Nat. Youth Theatre; Co-founder, Soc. of Brit. Theatre Designers, 1975; Chm., Assoc. of Lighting Designers; Member: Drama Panel, Arts Council of GB, 1968-70; Soc. of West End Theatre; Council, London Acad. of Music and Drama. FRSA. *Publication:* Stage Lighting, 1970, 2nd edn 1979. *Recreations:* The Hebrides, cooking, dogs. *Address:* Theatre Projects Ltd, 10 Long Acre, WC2E 9LN. *T:* 01-240 5411. *Club:* Garrick.

PILCHER, Sir (Charlie) Dennis, Kt 1974; CBE 1968; FRICS; Chairman, Commission for the New Towns, 1971-78; Consultant, late Senior Partner (Partner 1930), Graves, Son & Pilcher (Chartered Surveyors); Director, Save and Prosper Group Ltd, 1970-80; *b* 2 July 1906; *s* of Charlie Edwin Pilcher, Fareham, Hants; *m* 1929, Mary Allison Aumonier, *d* of William Aumonier, London; two *d. Educ:* Clayesmore Sch. Served War: Major, RA (despatches, Normandy), 1940-45. Hemel Hempstead Development Corp., 1949-56; Bracknell Development Corp., 1956-71 (Chm. 1968-71); Dir, Sun Life Assurance Soc. Ltd, 1968-77. Pres., RICS, 1963-64; Mem., Milner Holland Cttee on London Housing, 1963-64; Vice-Pres., London Rent Assessment Panel, 1966-70; Adviser to Business Rents Directorate of DoE, 1973-77. Mem. Council, Glyndebourne Fest. Opera, 1969-. *Recreations:* opera, golf, fishing. *Address:* Brambles, Batts Lane, Mare Hill, Pulborough, West Sussex. *T:* Pulborough 2126. *Club:* Garrick.

PILCHER, Sir John (Arthur), GCMG 1973 (KCMG 1966; CMG 1957); HM Diplomatic Service, retired; Chairman: Brazil Fund, since 1975; Fleming Japan Fund, SA, since 1976; Adviser on Far Eastern Affairs, Robert Fleming & Co., since 1973; *b* 16 May 1912; *s* of late Lt-Col A. J. Pilcher; *m* 1942, Delia Margaret Taylor; one *d. Educ:* Shrewsbury; Clare Coll., Cambridge; France, Austria and Italy. Served in Japan, 1936-39; China, 1939-41; Ministry of Information and Foreign Office, 1941-48; Italy, 1948-51; Foreign Office, 1951-54; Spain (Counsellor, Madrid), 1954-59; Philippines (Ambassador), 1959-63; Assistant Under-Secretary, Foreign Office, 1963-65; Ambassador to: Austria, 1965-67; Japan, 1967-72. Dir, Foreign & Colonial Investment Trust, 1973-82. Member: Museums and Galleries Commn (formerly Standing Commission on Museums and Galleries), 1973-; Cttee, Soc. for Protection of Ancient Buildings, 1974-; Treasure Trove Reviewing Cttee, 1977-. Grand Cross (Gold) Austrian Decoration of Honour, 1966; Order of the Rising Sun, First Class, Japan, 1971; Grand Official of Order of Merit of the Italian Republic, 1977. *Address:* 33 The Terrace, SW13. *T:* 01-876 9710. *Club:* Brooks's.

PILCHER, Robin Sturtevant, MS, FRCS, FRCP; Emeritus Professor of Surgery, University of London; Professor of Surgery and Director of the Surgical Unit, University College Hospital, London, 1938-67; *b* 22 June 1902; *s* of Thorold and Helena Pilcher; *m* 1929, Mabel Pearks; one *s* one *d. Educ:* St Paul's Sch.; University Coll., London. Fellow University Coll., London. *Publications:* various surgical papers. *Address:* Swanbourne, 21 Church End, Haddenham, Bucks. *T:* Haddenham 291048.

PILDITCH, James George Christopher; Chairman: Allied International Designers, since 1963; AID (Allied International Designers) Group Ltd, since 1980; AID Research, since 1980; AID Technology, since 1980; *b* 7 Aug. 1929; *s* of Frederick Henry Pilditch and Marie-Thérèse (*née* Priest); *m* 1st, 1952, Molly (marr. diss.); one *d* ; 2nd, 1970, Anne Elisabeth W:son Johnson. *Educ:* Slough Grammar Sch.; Reading Univ. (Fine Arts); INSEAD. Nat. Service, commnd RA, 1950; Royal Canadian Artillery Reserve, 1953-56. Journalism in Canada including Maclean-Hunter Publishing Co., 1952-56; work in design offices, Orr Associates (Toronto), THM Partners (London), Jim Nash Assocs (New York), 1956-59; started Package Design Associates (later Allied International Designers), in London, 1959. FRSA; ASAID 1968. *Publications:* The Silent Salesman, 1961, 2nd edn 1973; (with Douglas Scott) The Business

of Product Design, 1965; Communication By Design, 1970; Talk About Design, 1976. *Recreations:* squash, watching the Lord's Test, travel, writing, sketching. *Address:* 62 Cadogan Square, SW1. *T:* 01-584 9279; Brookhampton House, North Cadbury, Som. *T:* North Cadbury 40225. *Clubs:* Army and Navy, MCC.

PILDITCH, Sir Richard (Edward), 4th Bt, *cr* 1929; *b* 8 Sept. 1926; *s* of Sir Philip Harold Pilditch, 2nd Bt, and Frances Isabella, *d* of J. G. Weeks, JP, Bedlington, Northumberland; *S* brother (Sir Philip John Frederick Pilditch, 3rd Bt) 1954; *m* 1950, Pauline Elizabeth Smith; one *s* one *d. Educ:* Charterhouse. Served War of 1939-45, with Royal Navy, in India and Ceylon, 1944-45. *Recreations:* shooting, fishing. *Heir: s* John Richard Pilditch, *b* 24 Sept. 1955. *Address:* 4 Fishermans Bank, Mudeford, Christchurch, Hants.

PILE, Colonel Sir Frederick (Devereux), 3rd Bt *cr* 1900; MC 1945; *b* 10 Dec. 1915; *s* of Gen. Sir Frederick Alfred Pile, 2nd Bt, GCB, DSO, MC; *S* father, 1976; *m* 1940, Pamela, *d* of late Philip Henstock; two *d. Educ:* Weymouth; RMC, Sandhurst. Joined Royal Tank Regt, 1935; served War of 1939-45, Egypt and NW Europe; commanded Leeds Rifles, 1955-56; Colonel GS, BJSM, Washington, DC, 1957-60; Commander, RAC Driving and Maintenance School, 1960-62. Secretary, Royal Soldiers' Daughters' School, 1965-71. *Recreations:* fishing, cricket, travelling. *Heir: b* Sir John Devereux Pile, *qv. Address:* Harriet House, Sedlescombe, Battle, Sussex. *T:* Sedlescombe 240. *Club:* MCC.

PILE, Sir John (Devereux), Kt 1978; Chairman, Imperial Group Ltd, 1975-80 (Group Chief Executive, 1973-75; Member, Group Policy Committee, 1971-80; Director, 1967-80); *b* 5 June 1918; 2nd *s* of Gen. Sir Frederick A. Pile, 2nd Bt, GCB, DSO, MC, and Lady Ferguson; *b* and *heir-pres.* to Sir Frederick Devereux Pile, 3rd Bt, *qv* ; *m* 1946, Katharine Mary Shafe; two *s* two *d. Educ:* Weymouth Coll., Dorset; Trinity Coll., Cambridge (MA). Service with RA, 1939-46 (Major). Joined Imperial Tobacco Group, 1946; Manager, W. D. & H. O. Wills and Wm Clarke & Son, Dublin, 1956-59; Chairman: Robert Sinclair Ltd, 1960-64; Churchmans, 1964-67; Chm. and Man. Dir, W. D. & H. O. Wills, 1968-71; Dep. Chm., Imperial Tobacco Gp Ltd, 1971-73; Dir, Nat. West. Bank, 1977-81. Member: Council, CBI, 1975-80; Council, Industry for Management Educn, 1975-80. FBIM 1973-80. Governor, London Graduate Sch. of Business Studies, 1976-80. Freeman of City of London. *Address:* Munstead, Godalming, Surrey. *T:* Godalming 4716.

PILE, Sir William (Dennis), GCB 1978 (KCB 1971; CB 1968); MBE 1944; Chairman, Board of Inland Revenue, 1976-79; *b* 1 Dec. 1919; *s* of James Edward Pile and Jean Elizabeth Pile; *m* 1948, Joan Marguerite Crafter; one *s* two *d. Educ:* Royal Masonic School; St Catharine's College, Cambridge. Served Border Regt, 1940-45. Ministry of Education, 1947-50, 1951-66; Cabinet Office, 1950; Asst Under-Sec. of State: Dept of Education and Science, 1962; Ministry of Health, 1966; Dep. Under-Sec. of State, Home Office, 1967-70; Director-General, Prison Service, 1969-70; Permanent Under-Sec. of State, DES, 1970-76. Director: Nationwide Building Soc., 1980-; Distillers' Co. Ltd, 1980-. *Address:* The Manor House, Riverhead, near Sevenoaks, Kent. *T:* Sevenoaks 54498. *Clubs:* United Oxford & Cambridge University; Hawks (Cambridge).

PILKINGTON, family name of **Baron Pilkington.**

PILKINGTON, Baron, *cr* 1968 (Life Peer), of St Helens; **Harry (William Henry) Pilkington,** Kt 1953; DL; Hon. Life President, Pilkington Brothers Ltd (Chairman, 1949-73); *b* 19 April 1905; *e s* of Richard Austin Pilkington and Hon. Hope (*née* Cozens-Hardy); *m* 1930, Rosamond Margaret Rowan (*d* 1953); one *s* one *d* (and one *d* decd); *m* 1961, Mrs Mavis Wilding. *Educ:* Rugby; Magdalene Coll., Cambridge. Joined Pilkington Brothers Ltd, 1927; Dir, 1934-80; Director of the Bank of England, 1955-72. President: Federation of British Industries, 1953-55; Council of European Industrial Federations, 1954-57; Court of British Shippers' Council, 1971-74; Chairman: Royal Commn to consider pay of Doctors and Dentists, 1957-60; Cttee on Broadcasting, 1960-62; National Advisory Council for Education for Industry and Commerce, 1956-66; Econ. Develt Cttee for the Chemical Industry, 1967-72; NW Management Centre, 1974-76; NW Regional Sports and Recreations Council, 1976-82; Mem. Council Manchester Business Sch., 1964-72; President: Assoc. of Technical Institutions, 1966-68; British Plastics Fedn, 1972-74. Chancellor, Loughborough Univ. of Technology, 1966-80. DL Merseyside (formerly Lancs), 1968; Vice Lord-Lieutenant, 1974-80. Hon. FIOB 1974. Hon. LLD: Manchester, 1959; Liverpool, 1963; Hon. DSc Loughborough, 1966; Hon. DCL Kent, 1968. Freeman, St Helens, 1968. *Recreations:* walking, gardening, tennis, cycling. *Address:* Windle Hall, St Helens, Lancs. *T:* 23423. *Club:* United Oxford & Cambridge University.

PILKINGTON, Sir Alastair; see Pilkington, Sir L. A. B.

PILKINGTON, Charles Vere; retired as Chairman, Sotheby & Co.; *b* 11 Jan. 1905; *e s* of Charles Carlisle Pilkington and Emilia (*née* Lloyd); *m* 1936, Honor Chedworth (*d* 1961), *y d* of first and last Baron Kylsant; one *s. Educ:* Eton; Christ Church, Oxford, (MA). Dir, Sotheby & Co., Fine Art Auctioneers, 1927-58, Chm. 1953-58. Member of Council, Royal Musical Assoc., 1952-58; Member Business Cttee Musica Britannica. *Recreation:* music (harpsichord). *Address:* Casal da Nora, Colares, Sintra 2710, Portugal. *T:* 2990.253. *Clubs:* Travellers'; Eça de Queiroz.

PILKINGTON, Rev. Canon Evan Matthias, MA; Chaplain to the Queen since 1969; Canon Residentiary of St Paul's Cathedral, 1976–82, now Canon Emeritus; *b* 27 Dec. 1916; *s* of Rev. Matthias Pilkington; *m* 1946, Elsie (*née* Lashley); four *s. Educ:* Worksop Coll.; Keble Coll., Oxford; Cuddesdon Theol. College. Curate of: Bottesford and Ashby, Scunthorpe, 1940; Holy Trinity, Southall, 1942; St John the Divine, Kennington, 1944; Vicar of: East Kirkby and Miningsby, Lincs, 1946; Holy Trinity, Upper Tooting, 1952; Kingston upon Thames, 1961; Canon Residentiary, Bristol Cathedral, 1968–76. *Recreations:* walking, lettering. *Address:* 14 Park Close, Bladon, Oxford OX7 1RN.

PILKINGTON, Godfrey; *see* Pilkington, R. G.

PILKINGTON, Lawrence Herbert Austin, CBE 1964; JP; Director, Pilkington Brothers Ltd, since 1935; *b* 13 Oct. 1911; 2nd *s* of Richard Austin and Hon. Hope Pilkington; *m* 1936, Norah Holden, Whitby, Ont., Canada; two *d. Educ:* Bromsgrove School; Magdalene College, Cambridge. Volunteer with Grenfell Mission, 1933–34. Joined Pilkington Brothers Limited, 1935. Chairman: Glass Delegacy, 1949–54; Glass Industry Research Assoc., 1954–58; British Coal Utilisation Research Assoc., 1963–68; Soc. of Acoustic Technology, 1963–; Member: Building Research Board, 1958–62; Wilson Cttee on Noise, 1960–63; Adv. Council on R&D for Fuel and Power, 1973–75. President, Soc. of Glass Technology, 1960–64. JP Lancs, 1942. Hon. LLD Sheffield, 1956; Hon. DSc Salford, 1970. *Publications:* mainly on glass in various technical jls. *Recreations:* sailing, climbing, amateur radio, shooting. *Address:* Coppice End, Colborne Road, St Peter Port, Guernsey, CI. *Club:* Royal Dee Yacht.

PILKINGTON, Sir Lionel Alexander Bethune, (Sir Alastair), Kt 1970; FRS 1969; Director, Pilkington Brothers Ltd, St Helens (Executive Director, 1955–71; Deputy Chairman, 1971–73; Chairman, 1973–80); Chairman, Chloride Group Ltd, since 1979; a Director of Bank of England, since 1974; Director, British Petroleum, since 1976; *b* 7 Jan. 1920; *yr s* of late Col L. G. Pilkington and of Mrs L. G. Pilkington, Newbury, Berks; *m* 1945, Patricia Nicholls (*née* Elliott) (*d* 1977); one *s* one *d* ; *m* 1978, Kathleen, *widow* of Eldridge Haynes. *Educ:* Sherborne School; Trinity Coll., Cambridge. War service, 1939–46. Joined Pilkington Brothers Ltd, Glass Manufacturers, St Helens, 1947; Production Manager and Asst Works Manager, Doncaster, 1949–51; Head Office, 1952; Sub-Director, 1953. Member: Central Adv. Council for Science and Technology, 1970–; SRC, 1972–; British Railways Bd, 1973–76; Court of Governors, Administrative Staff Coll., 1973–; Chm., Council for Business in the Community, 1982–. Pro-Chancellor, Lancaster Univ., 1980–. Hon. FUMIST, 1972; Hon. Fellow: Imperial Coll., 1974; LSE, 1980. FBIM 1971. Hon. DTech: Loughborough, 1968; CNAA, 1976; Hon. DEng Liverpool, 1971; Hon. LLD Bristol, 1979; Hon. DSc (Eng) London, 1979. Toledo Glass and Ceramic Award, 1963; Mullard Medal, Royal Soc., 1968; John Scott Medal, 1969; Wilhelm Exner Medal, 1970; Phoenix Award, 1981. *Recreations:* gardening, sailing, music. *Address:* Goldrill Cottage, Patterdale, near Penrith, Cumbria. *T:* Glenridding 263; 74 Eaton Place, SW1. *Club:* Athenæum.

PILKINGTON, Rev. Canon Peter; Headmaster, King's School, Canterbury, since 1975; Hon. Canon of Canterbury Cathedral, since 1975; *b* 5 Sept. 1933; *s* of Frank and Doris Pilkington; *m* 1966, Helen, *d* of Charles and Maria Wilson; two *d. Educ:* Dame Allans Sch., Newcastle upon Tyne; Jesus Coll., Cambridge. BA 1955, MA 1958. Schoolmaster, St Joseph's Coll., Chidya, Tanganyika, 1955–57; ordained 1959; Curate in Bakewell, Derbs, 1959–62; Schoolmaster, Eton College, 1962–75, Master in College, 1965–75. *Address:* 14 The Precincts, Canterbury, Kent. *T:* Canterbury 62963. *Club:* Athenæum.

PILKINGTON, (Richard) Godfrey; Partner and Director, Piccadilly Gallery, since 1953; *b* 8 Nov. 1918; *s* of Col Guy R. Pilkington, DSO and Margery (*née* Frost); *m* 1950, Evelyn Edith (Eve) Vincent; two *s* two *d. Educ:* Clifton; Trinity Coll., Cambridge (MA). Lieut, RA, N Africa and Central Mediterranean, 1940–46. Joined Frost & Reed, art dealers, 1947; edited Pictures and Prints, 1951–60; founded Piccadilly Gallery, 1953. Master, Fine Art Trade Guild, 1964–66; Chm., Soc. of London Art Dealers, 1974–77. *Publications:* numerous exhibn catalogues. *Recreations:* walking, boating, tennis, golf. *Address:* 45 Barons Court Road, W14 9DZ. *Clubs:* Athenæum, Hurlingham.

PILKINGTON, Dr Roger Windle; Author; *b* 17 Jan. 1915; 3rd *s* of Richard Austin Pilkington and Hon. Hope (*née* Cozens-Hardy); *m* 1937, Theodora Miriam Jaboor; one *s* one *d* ; *m* 1973, Fru Ingrid Geijer, Stockholm. *Educ:* Rugby; Freiburg, Germany; Magdalene Coll., Cambridge (MA, PhD). Research, genetics, 1937; Chm., London Missionary Soc., 1962; Chm. of Trustees, Homerton Coll., Cambridge, 1962; Chm. of Govs, Hall Sch., 1962; jt author, Sex and Morality Report, Brit. Council of Churches, 1966; Vice-Pres., River Thames Soc., 1967; Master, Glass Sellers' Co., 1967. *Publications:* Males and Females, 1948; Stringer's Folly, Biology, Man and God, Sons and Daughters, 1951; How Your Life Began, 1953; Revelation Through Science, 1954; Jan's Treasure, In the Beginning, 1955; Thames Waters, The Facts of Life, 1956; Small Boat Through Belgium, The Chesterfield Gold, The Great South Sea, The Ways of the Sea, 1957; The Missing Panel, 1958; Small Boat Through Holland, Robert Boyle: Father of Chemistry, How Boats Go Uphill, 1959; Small Boat to the Skagerrak, World Without End, The Dahlia's Cargo, Don John's Ducats, 1960; Small Boat to Sweden, Small Boat to Alsace, The Ways of the Air, Who's Who and Why, 1961; Small Boat to Bavaria, Nepomuk of the River, Boats Overland, How Boats are Navigated, 1962; The River, (with Noel Streatfeild) Confirmation and After, Facts of Life for Parents, Small Boat to Germany, The Eisenbart Mystery, 1963; Heavens Alive, Small Boat Through France, 1964; Small Boat in Southern France, Glass, 1965; Small Boat on the Thames, The Boy from Stink Alley, 1966; Small Boat on the Meuse, Small Boat to Luxembourg, 1967; Small Boat on the Moselle, 1968; Small Boat to Elsinore, 1968; Small Boat in Northern Germany, 1969; Small Boat on the Lower Rhine, 1970; Small Boat on the Upper Rhine, 1971; Waterways in Europe, 1972; The Ormering Tide, 1974; The Face in the River, 1976; contribs to Guardian, Daily Telegraph, Times, Family Doctor, Yachting World, etc. *Recreations:* inland waterways, walking. *Address:* La Maison du Côti, Mont Arthur, St Aubin, Jersey, Channel Islands. *T:* Jersey 43760.

PILKINGTON, Sir Thomas Henry Milborne-Swinnerton-, 14th Bt, *cr* 1635; Chairman, Thos & James Harrison Ltd, since 1980 (Director, since 1963); Chairman, Charente Steamship Co. Ltd, since 1977; *b* 10 Mar. 1934; *s* of Sir Arthur W. Milborne-Swinnerton-Pilkington, 13th Bt and Elizabeth Mary (she *m* 1950, A. Burke), *d* of late Major J. F. Harrison, King's Walden Bury, Hitchin; *S* father 1952; *m* 1961, Susan, *e d* of N. S. R. Adamson, Durban, South Africa; one *s* two *d. Educ:* Eton College. *Recreations:* golf, cricket, racing. *Heir: s* Richard Arthur Milborne-Swinnerton-Pilkington, *b* 4 Sept. 1964. *Address:* King's Walden Bury, Hitchin, Herts. *Club:* White's.
See also Sir J. L. Armytage, Bt.

PILL, Malcolm Thomas; QC 1978; a Recorder of the Crown Court, since 1976; *b* 11 March 1938; *s* of Reginald Thomas Pill and Anne Pill (*née* Wright); *m* 1966, Roisin Pill (*née* Riordan); two *s* one *d. Educ:* Whitchurch Grammar Sch.; Trinity Coll., Cambridge. MA, LLB, Dip. Hague Acad. of Internat. Law. Served RA, 1956–58; Glamorgan Yeomanry (TA), 1958–67. Called to Bar, Gray's Inn, 1962; Wales and Chester Circuit, 1963. 3rd Sec., Foreign Office, 1963–64. Chm., UNA (Wales) Trust, 1969–77, 1980–; Chm., Welsh Centre for Internat. Affairs, 1973–76. Chm., UK Cttee, Freedom from Hunger Campaign, 1978–. *Address:* 9 Westbourne Crescent, Whitchurch, Cardiff CF4 2BL. *T:* Cardiff 65961; Goldsmith Building, Temple, EC4Y 7BL. *T:* 01-353 7881. *Clubs:* Royal Commonwealth Society; Cardiff and County (Cardiff).

PILLAI, Sir (Narayana) Raghavan, KCIE 1946 (CIE 1939); CBE 1937; Padma Vibhushan, 1960; *b* 24 July 1898; *s* of M. C. Narayana Pillai, Trivandrum, S India; *m* 1928, Edith Minnie Arthurs (*d* 1976); two *s. Educ:* Madras Univ.; Trinity Hall, Cambridge (schol.). BA (Madras) 1st Cl. English, 1918; Natural Sciences Tripos Pt 1 (Cambridge), 1st Cl., 1921; Law Tripos Pt 2, 1st Cl., 1922; ICS 1921; various appointments under the Government of Central Provinces and the Government of India. Secretary General, Ministry of External Affairs, New Delhi, 1952–60. Hon. DLitt Kerala University, 1953. Hon. Fellow, Trinity Hall, Cambridge, 1970. *Recreation:* walking. *Address:* 1022 St James's Court, SW1. *Clubs:* Oriental, Royal Commonwealth Society; Gymkhana (New Delhi).

PILLAR, Rt. Rev. Kenneth Harold; *see* Hertford, Bishop Suffragan of.

PILLAR, Adm. Sir William (Thomas), KCB 1980; CEng, FIMechE, FIMarE; Commandant, Royal College of Defence Studies, since 1982; *b* 24 Feb. 1924; *s* of William Pillar and Lily Pillar; *m* 1946, Ursula Ransley; three *s* one *d. Educ:* Blundells Sch., Tiverton; RNEC. FIMechE 1969, FIMarE 1972. Entered RN, 1942; HMS Illustrious, 1946–48; staff RNEC, 1948–51; HMS Alert, 1951–53; HM Dockyard, Gibraltar, 1954–57; HMS Corunna, 1957–59; BEO, HMS Lochinvar, 1959–61; staff of C-in-C, SASA, Cape Town, 1961–64; HMS Tiger, 1964–65; staff of Dir of Naval Officer Appts (Eng), 1965–67; sowc 1967; Naval Ship Prodn Overseer, Scotland and NI, 1967–69; IDC 1970; Asst Dir, DG Ships, 1971–73; Captain RNEC, 1973–75; Port Adm., Rosyth, 1976–77; Asst Chief of Fleet Support, 1977–79; Chief of Fleet Support (Mem., Admiralty Bd of Defence Council), 1979–81. *Recreations:* sailing, rough gardening and fixing things. *Address:* Selwood, Zeals Row, Zeals, Warminster, Wilts. *T:* Bourton (Dorset) 840577. *Clubs:* Army and Navy; Royal Naval Sailing Association (Portsmouth).

PIM, Captain Sir Richard (Pike), KBE 1960; Kt 1945; VRD; DL; Inspector-General, Royal Ulster Constabulary, retired; National Governor for Northern Ireland, BBC, 1962–67; Member of Council, Winston Churchill Memorial Trust, 1965–69; Member, Ulster Transport Authority, 1962–64, retired; *b* Dunmurry, Co. Antrim, 1900; *yr s* of late Cecil Pim; *m* 1925, Marjorie Angel, 3rd *d* of late John ff. Young, Dungiven, Londonderry; two *s. Educ:* Lancing Coll., Sussex; Trinity College, Dublin. Served in RNVR in European War, 1914–18; Royal Irish Constabulary, 1921. Appointed to Civil Service, N Ireland, 1922; Asst Secretary, Ministry of Home Affairs (N Ireland), 1935; Staff of Prime Minister, Northern Ireland, 1938; in charge of Mr Churchill's War Room at Admiralty, 1939, and later of Map Room at Downing St; Capt. RNVR. North African Campaign (despatches). DL City of Belfast, 1957. Order of Crown of Yugoslavia; Legion of Merit, USA. *Address:* Mullagh, Killyleagh, Co. Down, Northern Ireland. *T:* Killyleagh 267.

PIMENTA, Most Rev. Simon Ignatius; *see* Bombay, Archbishop of, (RC).

PINA-CABRAL, Rt. Rev. Daniel (Pereira dos Santos) de; an Auxiliary Bishop, Diocese of Gibraltar in Europe, since 1976; *b* 27 Jan. 1924; *m* 1951, Ana Avelina Pina-Cabral; two *s* two *d. Educ:* University of Lisbon (Licentiate in Law). Archdeacon of the North in the Lusitanian Church, 1965; Suffragan Bishop of Lebombo (Mozambique), Church of the Province of Southern Africa, 1967; Diocesan Bishop of Lebombo, 1968; Canon of Gibraltar, 1976–. *Address:* Rua Prof. Damião Peres, 4l-16.-Hab. 161, 4100-Porto, Portugal. *T:* Porto 667929.

PINAY, Antoine; Médiateur, French Republic, 1973–74; leather manufacturer; *b* Department of the Rhône, 30 Dec. 1891. *Educ:* Marist Fathers' Sch., St-Chamond. Joined a tannery business there; became Mayor, 1929–; later became gen. councillor, Dept of the Loire (Pres. 1949-). Was returned to Chamber of Deputies, 1936, Ind. Radical party; Senator, 1938; elected to 2nd Constituent Assembly, 1946; then to 1st Nat. Assembly; re-elected to Nat. Assembly as an associate of Ind. Republican group; Sec. of State for Economic Affairs, Sept. 1948-Oct. 1949; in several successive ministries, July 1950-Feb. 1952, he was Minister of Public Works, Transportation, and Tourism; Prime Minister of France, March-Dec. 1952; Minister of Foreign Affairs, 1955-56; Minister of Finance and Economic Affairs, 1958-60. Served European War, 1914–18, in artillery as non-commnd officer (Croix de Guerre, Médaille Militaire). *Address:* 87 Boulevard Suchet, 75016 Paris, France.

PINCHAM, Roger James, CBE 1982; Chairman of the Liberal Party, since 1979; *b* 19 Oct. 1935; *y s* of Sam and Bessie Pincham; *m* 1965, Gisela von Ulardt (*d* 1974); one *s* two *d. Educ:* Kingston Grammar School. National Service, RAF, 1954-56. With Phillips & Drew, 1956–, Partner, 1967-76, consultant, 1976-. Contested (L) Leominster, 1970, Feb. and Oct. 1974, 1979. Liberal Party: Nat. Exec., 1974–75 and 1978–; Assembly Cttee, 1974-; Standing Cttee, 1975–; Vice-Chm., 1977-80; Jt Negotiating Cttee with SDP, and signatory to A Fresh Start for Britain, 1981. Founder Chairman: Gladstone Club, 1973–; Centre for Commercial and Industrial Policy Studies, 1976–; First Chairman: Indep. Educnl Assoc., 1974–; St James and St Vedast Schools, 1974–; Treasurer, Roma Housing Soc., 1977-80; Pres., Kingston Eisteddfod, 1978. Chm., Roger Pincham (Consultants) Ltd, 1980-. Freeman, City of London. Liveryman, Barbers' Co.; Hon. Freeman, Founders' Co.; Freeman, Co. of Watermen and Lightermen. *Publications:* (jtly) New Deal for Rural Britain, 1977; (ed) New Deal for British Farmers, 1978. *Recreations:* gardening, cricket, theatre. *Address:* 610 Seddon House, Barbican, EC2. *T:* 01-638 8154; Dutton House, Leominster, Herefordshire. *T:* Leominster 2538. *Clubs:* Reform, National Liberal, City of London, City Livery; Surrey County Cricket, Woolhope Naturalists' Field, Grange Cricket.

PINCHER, (Henry) Chapman; freelance journalist, novelist and business consultant; Assistant Editor, Daily Express, and Chief Defence Correspondent, Beaverbrook Newspapers, 1972-79; *b* Ambala, India, 29 March 1914; *s* of Major Richard Chapman Pincher, E Surrey Regt, and Helen (*née* Foster), Pontefract; *m* 1965, Constance Wolstenholme; one *s* one *d* (by previous *m*). *Educ:* Darlington Gram. Sch.; King's Coll., London (FKC 1979); Inst. Educn; Mil. Coll. of Science. Carter Medallist, London, 1934; BSc (hons Botany, Zoology), 1935. Staff Liverpool Inst., 1936-40. Joined Royal Armoured Corps, 1940; Techn SO, Rocket Div., Min. of Supply, 1943-46; Defence, Science and Medical Editor, Daily Express, 1946-73. Hon. DLitt Newcastle upon Tyne, 1979. Granada Award, Journalist of the Year, 1964; Reporter of the Decade, 1966. *Publications:* Breeding of Farm Animals, 1946; A Study of Fishes, 1947; Into the Atomic Age, 1947; Spotlight on Animals, 1950; Evolution, 1950; (with Bernard Wicksteed) It's Fun Finding Out, 1950; Sleep, and how to get more of it, 1954; Sex in Our Time, 1973; Inside Story, 1978; Their Trade is Treachery, 1981; *novels:* Not with a Bang, 1965; The Giantkiller, 1967; The Penthouse Conspirators, 1970; The Skeleton at the Villa Wolkonsky, 1975; The Eye of the Tornado, 1976; The Four Horses, 1978; Dirty Tricks, 1980; The Private World of St John Terrapin, 1982; original researches in genetics, numerous articles in scientific and agricultural jls. *Recreations:* fishing, shooting, natural history, country life; ferreting in Whitehall and bolting politicians. *Address:* The Church House, 16 Church Street, Kintbury, near Hungerford, Berks. *T:* Kintbury 58855.

PINCOTT, Leslie Rundell, CBE 1978; Vice-Chairman, Remploy Ltd, since 1979 (Director, since 1975); *b* 27 March 1923; *s* of Hubert George Pincott and Gertrude Elizabeth Rundell; *m* 1944, Mary Mae Tuffin; two *s* one *d. Educ:* Mercers' Sch., Holborn. Served War, Royal Navy, 1942-46. Broads Paterson & Co. (Chartered Accountants), 1946-50; joined Esso Petroleum Co. Ltd, 1950; Comptroller, 1958-61; Asst Gen. Manager (Marketing), 1961-65; Dir and Gen. Manager, Cleveland Petroleum Co. Ltd, 1966-68; Standard Oil Co. (NJ): Exec. Asst to Pres., and later, to Chm., 1968-70; Man. Dir, Esso Petroleum Co. Ltd, 1970-78; Director: George Wimpey & Co. Ltd, 1978–; Canada Permanent Trust Co. (UK) Ltd, 1978–; Chm., Stone-Platt Industries, 1980-82, Chief Exec. 1981-82. A Dep. Chm., 1978-79, Chm., 1979-80, Price Commn; Chairman: Hundred Gp of Chartered Accountants, 1978-79; Oxford Univ. Business Summer Sch., 1975-78; Printing Industries Sector Working Party, NEDO, 1982–. Pres., District Heating Assoc., 1977-79. Mem., BR Southern Region Bd, 1977-. Vice-Pres., English Schs Athletics Assoc., 1977–. Mem., The Pilgrims, 1971-. FCA, MInstMSM; CBIM. *Recreation:* tennis. *Address:* 6 Lambourne Avenue, Wimbledon SW19 7DW. *Clubs:* Royal Automobile, Hurlingham.

PINDLING, Rt. Hon. Lynden Oscar, PC 1976; Prime Minister and Minister of Economic Affairs of the Commonwealth of The Bahamas, since 1969; *b* 22 March 1930; *s* of Arnold Franklin and Viola Pindling; *m* 1956, Marguerite McKenzie; two *s* two *d. Educ:* Western Senior Sch., Nassau Govt High Sch.; London Univ. (LLB 1952; LLD 1970; DHL 1978). Called to the Bar, Middle Temple, 1953. Practised as Lawyer, 1952-67. Parly Leader of Progressive Liberal Party, 1956; elected to Bahamas House of Assembly, 1956, re-elected 1962, 1967, 1968, 1972 and 1977. Worked for human rights and self-determination in the Bahamas; Mem., several delegns to Colonial Office, 1956-66; took part in Constitutional Conf., May 1963; Leader of Opposition, 1964; Mem., Delegns to UN Special Cttee of Twenty-four, 1965, 1966; Premier of the Bahamas and Minister of Tourism and Development, 1967; led Bahamian Delegn to Constitutional Conf., London, 1968; to Independence Conf., 1972 (first Prime Minister after Independence). Chm., Commonwealth Parly Assoc., 1968. *Recreations:* swimming, boating, travel. *Address:* Office of the Prime Minister, Rawson Square, Nassau, Bahamas.

PINE, John Bradley; *b* 2 Dec. 1913; *yr s* of late Percival William Pine and late Maud Mary Pine (*née* Bradley); *m* 1st, 1945, Elizabeth Mary (Jayne) Hallett (*d* 1948); one *s*; 2nd, 1952, Ann Carney; one *s. Educ:* Douai School. Asst Solicitor, GWR, Eng., 1935-39; Mil. Service, Captain RAC, 1939-45; a Sen. Prosecutor, CCG, 1945-47; Resident Magistrate and Crown Counsel, N Rhodesia, 1947-49; Called to Bar, 1950; Asst Attorney Gen., Gibraltar, 1949-54; QC (Bermuda), 1955; Attorney Gen., Bermuda, 1955-57; Actg Governor of Bermuda, 1956; QC (Nyasaland), 1958; Solicitor Gen., Nyasaland, 1958-60; Minister of Justice and Attorney Gen., Nyasaland, 1960-62, when replaced by an Elected Minister under self-governing Constitution; Legal Adviser to Governor of Nyasaland, July 1963, until Independence, July 1964; Parly Draftsman, Govt of N Ireland, 1965-66; Sec., Ulster Tourist Develt Assoc., 1967; antique business, 1968-70. *Address:* Uplands, Marine Walk, Fishguard, Dyfed SA65 9DU. *T:* Fishguard 872071.

PINE, Leslie Gilbert; author and lecturer; Editor, The National Message, 1977-80 (Assistant Editor, 1975-77); Chairman, Covenant Publishing Co. Ltd, 1978-79; *b* 22 Dec. 1907; *s* of Henry Moorshead Pine, Bristol, and Lilian Grace (*née* Beswetherick); *m* 1948, Grace V. Griffin; one *s. Educ:* Tellisford House Sch., Bristol; South-West London Coll., Barnes; London Univ. (BA). Asst Editor, Burke's Landed Gentry, 1935; subseq. Editor of Burke's Peerage and Landed Gentry and other reference books and then Managing Editor, The Shooting Times, 1960-64, and Shooting Times Library, 1962-64 (resigned as unable to agree with blood sports); Director L. & G. Pine & Co. Ltd, 1964-69; Man. Ed., Internat. Who's Who of the Arab World, 1975-76. Censorship and Air Min., 1940; Min. of Labour, 1941; RAF 1942; Sqn Ldr 1945-46; served in N Africa, Italy, Greece and India (Intel. Branch). Barrister-at-Law, Inner Temple, 1953; Freeman, City of London, Liveryman of the Glaziers' Company, 1954. Prospective Parly Candidate (C) Bristol Central, 1956; contested seat, 1959; re-adopted, 1960; resigned and joined Liberal Party, 1962; Prospective Parly Candidate (L), S Croydon, 1963, resigned candidature, June 1964, disagreeing profoundly with Liberalism. Dioc. Lay Reader, London, 1939, Canterbury, 1961, St Edmundsbury and Ipswich, 1975; received into Catholic Church, 1964; reconciled to C of E, 1971. Corr. Mem. Inst. Internacional de Genealogica y Heraldica (Madrid) and of Gen. Socs in Belgium, Chile and Brazil; Gov., St And. Sch., S Croydon, 1960-64. FSA Scot., 1940; MJI, 1947 (Mem. Council, 1953-61); FJI 1957; Associate, Zool. Soc., London, 1961; FRSA 1961; Soc. of Authors, 1965; Augustan Soc., 1967; FRGS 1969; FRAS 1970. Member: RUSI; Royal Soc. St George. Has given over 1,000 lectures in Gt Britain, Ireland, Holland and USA, also series of tutorial lectures under WEA and Further Educn. Trustee and Reg. Org. Sec., Prayer Book Soc., 1976-. *Publications:* The Stuarts of Traquair, 1940; The House of Wavell, 1948; The Middle Sea, 1950, new edn, 1972; The Story of Heraldry, 1952 (4th edn 1968, Japan, USA); Trace Your Ancestors, 1953; The Golden Book of the Coronation, 1953; They Came with The Conqueror, 1954; The Story of the Peerage, 1956; Tales of the British Aristocracy, 1956; The House of Constantine, 1957; Teach Yourself Heraldry and Genealogy, 1957, 5th (enlarged) edn 1975; The Twilight of Monarchy, 1958; A Guide to Titles, 1959; Princes of Wales, 1959, new edn, 1970; American Origins, 1960, 1968; Your Family Tree, 1962; Ramshackledom, A Critical Appraisal of the Establishment, 1962; Heirs of the Conqueror, 1965; Heraldry, Ancestry and Titles, Questions and Answers, 1965; The Story of Surnames, 1965; After Their Blood, 1966; Tradition and Custom in Modern Britain, 1967; The Genealogist's Encyclopedia (USA and UK), 1969; The Story of Titles, 1969; International Heraldry, 1970; The Highland Clans, 1972; Sons of the Conqueror, 1972; The New Extinct Peerage, 1972; The History of Hunting, 1973; Compleat Family Historian, 1978; A Dictionary of Mottoes, 1983; contrib. Encyclopedia Britannica, 1974; Contributing Editor, The Augustan (USA). *Recreations:* reading, walking, gardening, travel, motoring; contributes articles to press. *Address:* Hall Lodge Cottage, Brettenham, Ipswich, Suffolk IP7 7QP. *T:* Rattlesden 402. *Clubs:* Press, Wig and Pen.

PINEAU, Christian Paul Francis, Commandeur, Légion d'Honneur; Compagnon de la Libération; Croix de Guerre (French), Médaille de la Résistance (Rosette); French Statesman and Writer; *b* Chaumont (Haute-Marne), 14 Oct. 1904; *m* 1962, Mlle Blanche Bloys; one *d* (and five *s* one *d* of previous marriages). Minister of Food and Supplies, June-Nov. 1945; General Rapporteur to Budget Commission 1945-46; Chm. Nat. Assembly Finance Commn, 1946-47; Minister of Public Works, Transport, and Tourism (Schuman Cabinet), 1947-48, also (Marie Cabinet) July-Aug. 1948, also

(Queuille Cabinet), Sept. 1948, also (Bidault Cabinet), Oct. 1949; Minister of Finance and Economic Affairs (Schuman Cabinet), Aug. 1946; Chm. Nat. Defence Credits Control Commn, 1951-55; Designated Premier, Feb. 1955; Minister for Foreign Affairs, Feb. 1956-June 1957. Holds GCMG (Hon.) Great Britain, and numerous other foreign decorations. *Publications: books for children:* Contes de je ne sais quand; Plume et le saumon; L'Ourse aux pattons verts; Cornerousse le Mystérieux; Histoires de la forêt de Bercé; La Planète aux enfants perdus; La Marelle et le ballon; La Bête à bêtises; *other publications;* The SNCF and French Transport; Mon cher député; La simple verité, 1940-45; L'escalier des ombres; Khrouchtchev; 1956: Suez, 1976; economic and financial articles; contrib. to various papers. *Address:* 55 rue Vaneau, 75007 Paris, France.

PINK, Ralph Bonner, CBE 1961; VRD 1951; JP; MP (C) Portsmouth South since 1966; *b* 30 Sept. 1912; *s* of Frank Pink and Helen Mary (*née* Mumby); *m* 1939, Marguerite Nora Bannar-Martin; one *s* one *d. Educ:* Oundle School. Portsmouth City Council, 1948-; Lord Mayor of Portsmouth, 1961-62; JP for City of Portsmouth, 1950. Knight of Order of Dannebrog (Denmark). *Recreation:* yachting. *Address:* House of Commons, SW1A 0AA. *Club:* Royal Naval and Royal Albert Yacht (Portsmouth).

PINKER, George Douglas, FRCS(Ed), FRCOG; Surgeon-Gynaecologist to the Queen, since 1973; Consulting Gynaecological Surgeon and Obstetrician, St Mary's Hospital, Paddington and Samaritan Hospital, since 1958; Consulting Gynaecological Surgeon, Middlesex and Soho Hospitals, since 1969; Consultant Gynaecologist, King Edward VII Hospital for Officers, since 1974; *b* 6 Dec. 1924; *s* of late Ronald Douglas Pinker and of Queenie Elizabeth Pinker (*née* Dix); *m* Dorothy Emma (*née* Russell); three *s* one *d* (incl. twin *s* and *d*). *Educ:* Reading Sch.; St Mary's Hosp., London Univ. MB BS London 1947; DObst 1949; MRCOG 1954; FRCS(Ed) 1957; FRCOG 1964. Late Cons. Gyn. Surg., Bolingbroke Hosp., and Res. Off., Nuffield Dept of Obst., Radcliffe Infirmary, Oxford; late Cons. Gyn. Surg., Queen Charlotte's Hosp. Arthur Wilson Orator and Turnbull Scholar, and Hon. Consultant Obstetrician and Gynaecologist, Royal Women's Hosp., Melbourne, 1972. Examiner in Obst. and Gynae.: Univs of Cambridge, Dundee, London, and FRCS Edinburgh; formerly also in RCOG, and Univs of Birmingham, Glasgow and Dublin. Sims Black Travelling Prof., RCOG, 1979; Vis. Prof., SA Regional Council, RCOG, 1980; Hon. Treas., 1970, Vice-Pres., 1980-, RCOG. Mem. Council, Winston Churchill Trust, 1979-. Mem., Editorial Bd, Modern Medicine (Obs. and Gynae.), 1976-. Mem., Blair Bell Research Soc.; FRSocMed. *Publications:* (all jtly) Ten Teachers Diseases of Women, 1964; Ten Teachers Obstetrics, 1966; A Short Textbook of Obstetrics and Gynaecology, 1967. *Recreations:* music, gardening, sailing, skiing, fell walking. *Address:* 96 Harley Street, W1N 1AF. *T:* 01-935 2292; Medley, Kingston Hill, Kingston-on-Thames, Surrey KT2 7IU.

PINKER, Rev. Martin Wallis, OBE 1957; Member, Minister's Advisory Council (Canada) on Treatment of Offenders, 1959-73, retired (Chairman, 1959-73); Chairman, Ontario Training Schools Advisory Board, 1958-63; (first) General Secretary, National Association of Discharged Prisoners' Aid Societies Inc., 1936-58; Director, Men's Division, Central After-Care Association, 1948-58; *b* 11 April 1893; 2nd *s* of late Douglas Collyer Pinker and of Amelia Jane Wallis, Reading; *m* 1922, Lilian Hannah, *o d* of late Frederick and Betsy Eccles, Blackpool; one *s* one *d. Educ:* private study; Hartley Victoria Coll., Manchester. After training for business career, served European War, 1914-18, as Lieut Lancs Fus., India. Entered Primitive Methodist Ministry: ordained, 1922; served in London, Gravesend and Lymm (Cheshire) 1924-29; released from pastoral work, 1929, to become Organising Sec. of Discharged Prisoners' Aid Soc. at Strangeways Prison, Manchester. Mem. Jt Cttee to review work of Discharged Prisoners' Aid Socs (Maxwell Cttee), 1951; Internat. Prisoners' Aid Assoc. (Vice-Pres. 1951, Pres., 1954). Visited Germany at request of UN High Commn for Refugees, 1952. Has attended meetings of Congress of Correction, in USA and Canada; Founding Hon. Sec. Commonwealth Assoc. of Prisoners' Aid Societies. *Address:* Rotary Laughlen Centre, 110 Edward Street, Toronto, Ont M5G 2A5, Canada. *Club:* Empire (Canada).

PINKERTON, Prof. John Henry McKnight; Professor of Midwifery and Gynæcology, Queen's University, Belfast, since 1963; Gynæcologist: Royal Victoria and City Hospitals, Belfast; Ulster Hospital for Women and Children; Surgeon, Royal Maternity Hospital, Belfast; *b* 5 June 1920; *s* of late William R. and Eva Pinkerton; *m* 1947, Florence McKinstry, MB, BCh, BAO; four *s. Educ:* Royal Belfast Academical Institution; Queen's Univ., Belfast. Hyndman Univ. Entrance Scholar, 1939; MB, BCh, BAO Hons; Magrath Scholar in Obstetrics and Gynæcology, 1943. Active service in HM Ships as Surg.-Lt, RNVR, 1945-47. MD 1948; MRCOG 1949; FRCOG 1960; FZS 1960; FRCPI 1977. Sen. Lectr in Obstetrics and Gynæcology, University Coll. of the West Indies, and Consultant Obstetrician and Gynæcologist to University Coll. Hosp. of the West Indies, 1953-59; Rockefeller Research Fellow at Harvard Medical Sch., 1956-57; Prof. of Obstetrics and Gynæcology, Univ. of London, at Queen Charlotte's and Chelsea Hosps and the Inst. of Obstetrics and Gynæcology, 1959-63; Obstetric Surgeon to Queen Charlotte's Hosp.; Surgeon to Chelsea Hosp. for Women. Vice-Pres., RCOG, 1977-80. *Publications:* various papers on obstetrical and gynæcological subjects. *Address:* Department of Midwifery and Gynæcology, The Institute of Clinical Science, Grosvenor Road, Belfast BT12 6BJ. *T:* Belfast 40503.

See also W. R. Pinkerton.

PINKERTON, William Ross, CBE 1977; JP; HM Nominee for Northern Ireland on General Medical Council, since 1979; a director of companies; *b* 10 April 1913; *s* of William Ross Pinkerton and Eva Pinkerton; *m* 1943, Anna Isobel Lyness; two *d.* Managing Director, H. Stevenson & Co. Ltd, Londonderry, 1941-76. Mem., Baking Wages Council (NI), 1957-74. Mem. later Chm, Londonderry/Gransha Psychiatric HMC, 1951-69; Vice-Chm., then Chm., North West HMC, 1969-72; Chm., Western Health and Social Services Board, 1972-79; Member: Central Services Agency (NI), 1972-79; NI Health and Social Services Council, 1975-79; Lay Mem., Health and Personal Social Services Tribunal, NI, 1978-. Member, New Ulster Univ. Court, 1973-, Council, 1979-. Hon. Life Governor: Altnagelvin, Gransha, Waterside, St Columb's, Roe Valley, Strabane, Foyle and Stradreagh Hosps. JP Co. Londonderry, 1965. *Recreations:* yachting, fishing. *Address:* 2 Ard-Na-Ree, The Brae, Groomsport, Co. Down, N Ireland BT19 2JL. *T:* Groomsport 525. *Club:* Royal Highland Yacht (Oban).

See also J. H. McK. Pinkerton.

PINNINGTON, Geoffrey Charles; Editor, Sunday People, 1972-82; *b* 21 March 1919; *s* of Charles and Beatrice Pinnington; *m* 1941, Beryl, *d* of Edward and Lilian Clark; two *d. Educ:* Harrow County Sch.; Rock Ferry High Sch., Birkenhead; King's Coll., Univ. of London. Served War as Air Navigator, RAF Bomber and Middle East Commands, 1940-45 (Sqdn Ldr, 1943). On staff of (successively): Middlesex Independent; Kensington Post (Editor); Daily Herald: Dep. News Editor, 1955; Northern Editor, 1957; Dep. Editor, 1958; Daily Mirror: Night Editor, 1961, Assistant Editor, 1964, Dep. Editor, 1968; Dir, Mirror Group Newspapers, 1976-82. Mem., Press Council, 1982-. *Recreations:* his family, travel, reading, theatre and the arts, amateur cine-photography. *Address:* 23 Lauderdale Drive, Richmond, Surrey TW10 7BS.

PINNOCK, Comdr Harry James, RN retd; Director, Cement Makers' Federation, since 1979; *b* 6 April 1927; *s* of Frederick Walter Pinnock and Kate Ada (*née* Shepherd); *m* 1962, Fru Inger Connie Ahgren (*d* 1978); one *d. Educ:* Sutton Valence Sch. Joined RN, 1945; Midshipman, HMS Nelson, 1945-47; Sub-Lieut/Lieut, HMS Belfast, Far East, 1948-50; RN Rhine Flotilla, 1951-52; Staff of First Sea Lord, 1952-55; Lt-Comdr, Mediterranean Minesweepers, 1955-57; HMS Ceylon, E of Suez, 1957-59; Staff of C-in-C Plymouth, 1960-61; HQ Allied Naval Forces, Northern Europe, Oslo, 1961-63; Comdr, MoD, 1964-67, retd. Cement Makers' Fedn, 1970-. *Recreations:* ski-ing, gardening, travel. *Address:* Windy Ridge, Bells Lane, Tenterden, Kent TN30 6EX. *T:* Tenterden 3025. *Club:* Army and Navy.

PINSENT, Sir Christopher (Roy), 3rd Bt *cr* 1938; Lecturer, Camberwell School of Art; *b* 2 Aug. 1922; *s* of Sir Roy Pinsent, 2nd Bt, and Mary Tirzah Pinsent (*d* 1951), *d* of Dr Edward Geoffrey Walls, Spilsby, Lincs; *S* father, 1978; *m* 1951, Susan Mary, *d* of John Norton Scorer, Fotheringhay; one *s* two *d. Educ:* Winchester College. *Heir: s* Thomas Benjamin Roy Pinsent, *b* 21 July 1967. *Address:* The Chestnuts, Castle Hill, Guildford, Surrey.

PINSENT, Roger Philip; HM Diplomatic Service, retired; *b* 30 Dec. 1916; *s* of late Sidney Hume Pinsent; *m* 1941, Suzanne Smalley; one *s* two *d. Educ:* Downside Sch.; Lausanne, London and Grenoble Univs. London Univ. French Scholar, 1938; BA Hons London, 1940. HM Forces, 1940-46; HM Diplomatic Service, May 1946; 1st Sec., HM Legation, Havana, 1948-50; HM Consul, Tangier, 1950-52; 1st Sec., HM Embassy, Madrid, 1952-53; FO, 1953-56; 1st Sec., Head of Chancery, HM Embassy, Lima (Chargé d'Affaires, 1958, 1959), 1956-59; Dep. Head of UK Delegation to the European Communities, Luxembourg, 1959-63; HM Ambassador to Nicaragua, 1963-67; Counsellor (Commercial), Ankara, 1967-70; Consul-Gen., São Paulo, 1970-73. Mem., Inst. of Linguists, 1976-79. *Recreations:* music, photography, book-binding, golf. *Address:* Cranfield Cottage, Maugersbury, Stow-on-the-Wold, Glos GL54 1HR. *T:* Stow-on-the-Wold 30992. *Clubs:* Canning; Broadway Golf; Stow on the Wold RFC.

PINSON, Barry, QC 1973; *b* 18 Dec. 1925; *s* of Thomas Alfred Pinson and Alice Cicily Pinson; *m* 1950, Miriam Mary; one *s* one *d* ; *m* 1977, Anne Kathleen Golby. *Educ:* King Edward's Sch., Birmingham; Univ. of Birmingham. LLB Hons 1945. Fellow Inst. Taxation. Mil. Service, 1944-47. Called to Bar, Gray's Inn, 1949, Bencher 1981. Trustee, RAF Museums, 1980-. *Publications:* Revenue Law, 15 edns. *Recreations:* music, photography. *Address:* 11 New Square, Lincoln's Inn, WC2. *T:* 01-242 3981.

PINTER, Lady Antonia; *see* Fraser, Antonia.

PINTER, Harold, CBE 1966; actor, playwright and director; Associate Director, National Theatre, since 1973; *b* 10 Oct. 1930; *s* of J. Pinter; *m* 1st, 1956, Vivien Merchant (marr. diss. 1980; she *d* 1982); one *s* ; 2nd, 1980, Lady Antonia Fraser, qv. *Educ:* Hackney Downs Grammar Sch. Actor (mainly repertory), 1949-57. Directed: Exiles, Mermaid, 1970; Butley, 1971; Butley (film), 1973; Next of Kin, Nat. Theatre, 1974; Otherwise Engaged, Queen's, 1975, NY 1977; The Rear Column, Globe, 1978; Close of Play, Nat. Theatre, 1979; Quartermaine's Terms, Queen's, 1981. Shakespeare Prize, Hamburg, 1970; Austrian State Prize for European Literature, 1973; Pirandello Prize, 1980; Donatello Prize, 1982. Hon. DLitt: Reading, 1970; Birmingham, 1971; Glasgow, 1974; East Anglia, 1974; Stirling, 1979; Brown, 1982. *Plays:* The Room, The Birthday Party (filmed, 1968), The Dumb Waiter, 1957; The Hothouse, 1958, (stage) 1980, (television) 1981; A Slight Ache (radio) 1958, (stage) 1961; A Night Out (radio and television), 1961, The Caretaker (filmed,

1963), 1960; Night School (television), 1960; The Dwarfs (radio), 1960, (stage), 1963; The Collection (television), 1961, (stage), 1962; The Lover (television, stage), 1963 (Italia Prize for TV); Tea Party (television), 1964; The Homecoming, 1964; Landscape (radio), 1968, (stage), 1969; Silence (stage), 1969; Old Times (stage), 1971; Monologue (television), 1972; No Man's Land (stage), 1975 (television), 1978; Betrayal (stage), 1978 (SWET Award, 1979); Family Voices (radio), 1981 (Giles Cooper Award, 1982), (stage), 1982; Victoria Station, 1982; A Kind of Alaska, 1982. *Screenplays:* The Caretaker, The Servant, 1962; The Pumpkin Eater, 1963; The Quiller Memorandum, 1966; Accident, 1967; The Birthday Party, 1968; The Go-Between, 1969; Langrishe, Go Down, 1970 (adapted for television, 1978); A la Recherche du Temps Perdu, 1972; The Last Tycoon, 1974; The French Lieutenant's Woman, 1981. *Publications:* The Caretaker, 1960; The Birthday Party, and other plays, 1960; A Slight Ache, 1961; The Collection, 1963; The Lover, 1963; The Homecoming, 1965; Tea Party, and, The Basement, 1967; Mac, 1968; Jt Editor, New Poems 1967, 1968; Landscape, and, Silence, 1969; Five Screenplays, 1971; Old Times, 1971; No Man's Land, 1975; The Proust Screenplay: A la Recherche du Temps Perdu, 1978; Poems and Prose 1941-1977, 1978; Family Voices, 1981. *Recreations:* drinking and cricket. *Address:* c/o ACTAC Ltd, 16 Cadogan Lane, SW1.

PIPER, Bright Harold, (Peter Piper), CBE 1979; Director since 1970, Chief Executive, 1973-78, Lloyds Bank Group; *b* 22 Sept. 1918; 2nd *s* of Robert Harold Piper; *m* 1st, 1945, Marjorie Joyce, 2nd *d* of Captain George Arthur; one *s* one *d*; 2nd, 1979, Leonie Mary Lane, *d* of Major C. V. Lane. *Educ:* Maidstone Grammar School. Served with RN, 1939-46. Entered Lloyds Bank, 1935: Asst Gen. Man., 1963; Jt Gen. Man., 1965; Asst Chief Gen. Man., 1968; Dep. Chief Gen. Man., 1970; Chief Gen. Man., 1973. Freeman, City of London; Liveryman, Spectacle Makers' Company. *Recreation:* sailing. *Address:* Greenways, Hawkshill Close, Esher, Surrey. *Clubs:* Overseas Bankers, Australia.

PIPER, David Towry, CBE 1969; MA, FSA; FRSL; Director, Ashmolean Museum, Oxford, since 1973; Fellow of Worcester College, Oxford, since 1973; *b* 21 July 1918; *s* of late Prof. S. H. Piper; *m* 1945, Anne Horatia Richmond; one *s* three *d. Educ:* Clifton Coll.; St Catharine's Coll., Cambridge. Served War of 1939-45: Indian Army (9th Jat Regt); Japanese prisoner-of-war, 1942-45. National Portrait Gallery: Asst-Keeper, 1946-64; Dir, Keeper and Sec., 1964-67; Dir and Marlay Curator, Fitzwilliam Museum, Cambridge, 1967-73; Fellow, Christ's College, Cambridge, 1967-73. Slade Prof. of Fine Art, Oxford, 1966-67. Clark Lectr, Cambridge, 1977-78. Mem., Royal Fine Art Commn, 1970-. Trustee: Watts Gall., 1966-; Paul Mellon Foundn for British Art, 1969-70; Pilgrim Trust, 1973-; Leeds Castle Foundn, 1981-. *Publications:* The English Face, 1957; Catalogue of the 17th Century Portraits in the National Portrait Gallery, 1963; The Royal College of Physicians; Portraits (ed G. Wolstenholme), 1964; (ed) Enjoying Paintings, 1964; The Companion Guide to London, 1964; Shades, 1970; London, 1971; (ed) The Genius of British Painting, 1975; The Treasures of Oxford, 1977; Kings and Queens of England and Scotland, 1980; (ed) Mitchell Beazley Library of Art, 1981; Artists' London, 1982; The Image of the Poet, 1982; *novels (as Peter Towry) include:* It's Warm Inside, 1953; Trial by Battle, 1959. *Address:* c/o Ashmolean Museum, Beaumont Street, Oxford. *Club:* Athenæum.

PIPER, John Egerton Christmas, CH 1972; painter and writer; Member of the Oxford Diocesan Advisory Committee, since 1950; *b* 13 Dec. 1903; *s* of late C. A. Piper, Solicitor; *m* 1935, Mary Myfanwy Evans; two *s* two *d. Educ:* Epsom Coll.; Royal College of Art. Paintings, drawings, exhibited in London since 1925; Pictures bought by Tate Gallery, Contemporary Art Society, Victoria and Albert Museum, etc.; Series of watercolours of Windsor Castle commissioned by the Queen, 1941-42; windows for nave of Eton College Chapel commissioned 1958; windows and interior design, Nuffield College Chapel, Oxford, completed, 1961; window, Coventry Cathedral, completed, 1962; windows for King George VI Memorial Chapel, Windsor, 1969; windows for Robinson Coll., Cambridge, 1981. Designed Tapestry for High Altar, Chichester Cathedral, 1966, and for Civic Hall, Newcastle upon Tyne. Designer for opera and ballet. Mem., Royal Fine Art Commn, 1959-78; a Trustee: Tate Gallery, 1946-53, 1954-61, 1968-74; National Gallery, 1967-74, 1975-78; Arts Council art panel, 1952-57. Hon. Fellow, Robinson Coll., Cambridge, 1980. Hon. ARIBA, 1957, Hon. FRIBA 1971; Hon. ARCA 1959; Hon. DLitt: Leicester, 1960; Oxford, 1966; Sussex, 1974; Reading, 1977; Wales (Cardiff), 1981. *Publications:* Wind in the Trees (poems), 1921; 'Shell Guide' to Oxfordshire, 1938; Brighton Aquatints, 1939; British Romantic Painters, 1942; Buildings and Prospects, 1949; (ed with John Betjeman) Buckinghamshire Architectural Guide, 1948; Berkshire Architectural Guide, 1949; (illus.) The Castles on the Ground by J. M. Richards, 1973; (jtly) Lincolnshire Churches, 1976; (illus.) John Betjeman's Church Poems, 1981. *Relevant publications:* John Piper: Paintings, Drawings and Theatre Designs, 1932-54 (arr. S. John Woods), 1955; John Piper, by Anthony West, 1979. *Address:* Fawley Bottom Farmhouse, near Henley-on-Thames, Oxon. *Club:* Athenæum.

PIPER, Peter; see Piper, Bright Harold.

PIPKIN, (Charles Harry) Broughton, CBE 1973; Chairman: BICC Ltd, 1977-80; Electrak International Ltd, 1982; *b* 29 Nov. 1913; *er s* of late Charles Pipkin and Charlotte Phyllis (*née* Viney), Lewisham; *m* 1941, Viola, *yr d* of Albert and Florence Byatt, Market Harborough; one *s* one *d. Educ:* Christ's

Coll., Blackheath; Faraday House. CEng, FIEE; FBIM. Various appts with BICC, 1936-73, Dep. Chm. and Chief Exec., 1973-77. War service, 1940-46: Major REME, 14th Army (despatches). President: British Non-ferrous Metals Fedn, 1965-66; Electric Cable Makers' Fedn, 1967-68; BEAMA, 1975-76. *Recreations:* travel, reading, racing. *Address:* The Old Dairy, Maugersbury, Stow-on-the-Wold, Glos. *T:* Stow-on-the-Wold 30677. *Club:* City Livery.

PIPPARD, Prof. Sir (Alfred) Brian, Kt 1975; FRS 1956; Cavendish Professor of Physics, University of Cambridge, 1971-82, now Emeritus; *b* 7 Sept. 1920; *s* of late Prof. A. J. S. Pippard; *m* 1955, Charlotte Frances Dyer; three *d. Educ:* Clifton Coll.; Clare Coll., Cambridge (Hon. Fellow 1973). BA (Cantab) 1941, MA 1945. PhD 1949; ScD 1966. Scientific Officer, Radar Research and Development Establishment, Great Malvern, 1941-45; Stokes Student, Pembroke Coll., Cambridge, 1945-46; Demonstrator in Physics, University of Cambridge, 1946; Lecturer in Physics, 1950; Reader in Physics, 1959-60; John Humphrey Plummer Prof. of Physics, 1960-71; Pres., Clare Hall, Cambridge, 1966-73. Visiting Prof., Institute for the Study of Metals, University of Chicago, 1955-56. Fellow of Clare Coll., Cambridge, 1947-66. Cherwell-Simon Memorial Lectr, Oxford, 1968-69. Pres., Inst. of Physics, 1974-76. Hughes Medal of the Royal Soc., 1959; Holweck Medal, 1961; Dannie-Heinemann Prize, 1969; Guthrie Prize, 1970. *Publications:* Elements of Classical Thermodynamics, 1957; Dynamics of Conduction Electrons, 1962; Forces and Particles, 1972; The Physics of Vibration, vol. 1, 1978, vol. 2, 1982; papers in Proc. Royal Soc., etc. *Recreation:* music. *Address:* 30 Porson Road, Cambridge.

PIRATIN, Philip; *b* 15 May 1907; *m* 1929, Celia Fund; one *s* two *d. Educ:* Davenant Foundation Sch., London, E1. Was a Member of Stepney Borough Council, 1937-49; MP (Com) Mile End Division of Stepney, 1945-50.

PIRBHAI, Count Sir Eboo; see Eboo Pirbhai.

PIRIE, Group Captain Gordon Hamish, CBE 1946; JP; DL; Deputy High Bailiff of Westminster, since 1978; Member, Westminster City Council, 1949-82 (Mayor, 1959-60; Leader of Council, 1961-69; Alderman, 1963-78; Lord Mayor, 1974-75); Chairman, Services Sound and Vision Corporation, since 1979; Director, Parker Gallery; *b* 10 Feb. 1918; *s* of Harold Victor Campbell Pirie and Irene Gordon Hogarth; *m* 1st, 1953, Margaret Joan Bomford (*d* 1972); no *c*; 2nd, 1982, Joanna, widow of John C. Hugill. *Educ:* Eton (scholar); RAF Coll., Cranwell. Permanent Commission, RAF, 1938. Served War of 1939-45: Dir of Ops, RNZAF, Atlantic and Pacific (despatches, CBE); retired as Group Captain, 1946. Comr No 1 (POW) Dist SJAB, 1960-69; Comdr St John Ambulance, London, 1969-75; Chm., St John Council for London, 1975-. A Governor of Westminster Sch., 1962-; Vice-Pres., Engineering Industries Assoc., 1966-69; Mem., Council of Royal Albert Hall, 1965-; a Trustee, RAF Museum, 1965-; Vice-Chm., London Boroughs Assoc., 1968-71; Pres., Conf. of Local and Regional Authorities of Europe, 1978-80 (Vice-Pres., 1974-75, 1977-78, 1980-); Mem. Solicitors Disciplinary Tribunal, 1975-. Contested (LNat&U) Dundee West, 1955. DL, JP Co. of London, 1962; Mem., Inner London Adv. Cttee on appointment of Magistrates, 1969-; Chm., S Westminster PSD, 1974-77. Liveryman, Worshipful Company of Girdlers. KStJ 1969. Comdr, Legion of Honour, 1960; Comdr, Cross of Merit, SMO Malta, 1971. JSM Malaysia, 1974. *Recreations:* motoring, bird-watching. *Address:* Cottage Row, Tarrant Gunville, Blandford, Dorset DT11 8JJ. *T:* Tarrant Hinton 212. *Clubs:* Carlton, Royal Air Force.

PIRIE, Henry Ward; crossword compiler, journalist and broadcaster; Sheriff (formerly Sheriff-Substitute) of Lanarkshire at Glasgow, 1955-74; *b* 13 Feb. 1922; *o surv. s* of late William Pirie, Merchant, Leith; *m* 1948, Jean Marion, *y d* of late Frank Jardine, sometime President of RCS of Edinburgh; four *s. Educ:* Watson's Coll., Edinburgh; Edinburgh Univ. MA 1944; LLB 1947. Served with Royal Scots; commnd Indian Army, 1944; Lieut, Bombay Grenadiers, 1944-46. Called to Scottish Bar, 1947. Sheriff-Substitute of Lanarkshire at Airdrie, 1954-55. OStJ 1967. *Recreations:* curling, golf, bridge. *Address:* 16 Poplar Drive, Lenzie, Kirkintilloch, Dunbartonshire. *T:* Kirkintilloch 2494.

PIRIE, Iain Gordon; Sheriff of South Strathclyde, Dumfries and Galloway at Airdrie, since 1979; *b* 15 Jan. 1933; *s* of Charles Fox Pirie and Mary Ann Gordon; *m* 1960, Sheila Brown Forbes, MB, ChB; two *s* one *d. Educ:* Harris Acad., Dundee; St Andrews Univ. (MA, LLB). Legal Asst, Stirling, Eunson & Belford, Solicitors, Dunfermline, 1958-60; Depute Procurator Fiscal, Paisley, 1960-67; Sen. Depute Procurator Fiscal, Glasgow, 1967-71; Procurator Fiscal: Dumfries, 1971-76; Ayr, 1976-79. *Recreations:* golf, tennis, reading, wine-making, playing the violin. *Address:* 56 Aytoun Road, Glasgow G41 5HE.

PIRIE, Norman Wingate, FRS 1949; *b* 1 July 1907; *yr s* of late Sir George Pirie, painter, Torrance, Stirlingshire; *m* 1931, Antoinette Patey; one *s. Educ:* Emmanuel Coll., Cambridge. Demonstrator in Biochemical Laboratory, Cambridge, 1932-40; Virus Physiologist, 1940-46, Head of Biochemistry Dept, 1947-73, Rothamsted Experimental Station, Harpenden. Vis. Prof., Indian Statistical Inst., Calcutta, 1971-. Copley Medal, 1971; Rank Prize for Nutrition, 1976. *Publications:* Food Resources: conventional and novel, 1969, 2nd edn 1976; Leaf Protein and other aspects of fodder fractionation, 1978; ed several works on world food supplies; scientific papers on various aspects of Biochemistry but especially on separation and properties of macromolecules; articles on viruses, the origins of life, biochemical engineering, and the need for greatly extended research on food production and contraception. *Address:* Rothamsted Experimental Station, Harpenden, Herts. *T:* Harpenden 63133.

PIRIE, Psyche; Consultant Design and Decoration Editor, Woman's Journal (IPC Magazines), since 1979; *b* 6 Feb. 1918; *d* of late George Quarmby; *m* 1940, James Mansergh Pirie; one *d. Educ:* Kensington High Sch.; Chelsea Sch. of Art. Air Ministry, 1940-44. Teaching, Ealing Sch. of Art and Willesden Sch. of Art, 1944-46; Indep. Interior Designer, 1946-56; Furnishing Editor, Homes and Gardens, 1956-68, Editor, 1968-78. *Recreations:* conversation, cinema, theatre, junk shops; or doing absolutely nothing. *Address:* 9 Lansdowne Walk, W11. *T:* 01-727 5294.

PIRZADA, Syed Sharifuddin, SPk 1964; Attorney-General of Pakistan, 1965-66, 1968-71 and since 1977; Adviser to the Chief Martial Law Administrator and Federal Minister, since 1978; Minister for Law and Parliamentary Affairs, since 1979; *b* 12 June 1923; *s* of Syed Vilayat Ali Pirzada; *m* 1960; two *s* two *d. Educ:* University of Bombay. LLB 1945. Secretary, Provincial Muslim League, 1946; Managing Editor, Morning Herald, 1946; Prof., Sind Muslim Law Coll., 1947-55; Advocate: Bombay High Court, 1946; Sind Chief Court, 1947; West Pakistan High Court, 1955; Supreme Court of Pakistan, 1961; Senior Advocate Supreme Court of Pakistan; Foreign Minister of Pakistan, 1966-68. Represented Pakistan: before International Tribunal on Rann of Kutch, 1965; before Internat. Ct of Justice regarding Namibia, SW Africa, 1971; Pakistan Chief Counsel before ICAO Montreal in complaint concerning overflights over Indian territory; Leader of Pakistan delegations to Commonwealth Conf. and General Assembly of UN, 1966; Mem., UN Sub-Commn on Prevention of Discrimination and Protection of Minorities, 1972- (Chm., 1968). Hon. Advisor, Constitutional Commn, 1961; Chm., Pakistan Company Law Commn, 1962; Mem., Internat. River Cttee, 1961-68; President: Pakistan Br., Internat. Law Assoc., 1964-67; Karachi Bar Assoc., 1964; Pakistan Bar Council, 1966; Inst. of Internat. Affairs. Led Pakistan Delegn to Law of the Sea Conferences, NY, 1978 and 1979, and Geneva, 1980. Member: Pakistan Nat. Gp, Panel of the Permanent Ct of Arbitration; Panel of Arbitrators and Umpires, Council of Internat. Civil Aviation Organisation; Panel of Arbitrators, Internat. Centre for Settlement of Investment Disputes, Washington; Internat. Law Commn, 1981-. Chm., Cttee of Experts constituted by Organisation of Islamic Conf. for drafting statute of the Islamic Internat. Ct of Justice, 1980. *Publications:* Pakistan at a Glance, 1941; Jinnah on Pakistan, 1943; Leaders Correspondence with Jinnah, 1944, 3rd edn 1978; Evolution of Pakistan, 1962 (also published in Urdu and Arabic); Fundamental Rights and Constitutional Remedies in Pakistan, 1966; The Pakistan Resolution and the Historic Lahore Session, 1970; Foundations of Pakistan, vol. I, 1969, vol. II, 1970; Some Aspects of Quaid-i-Azam's Life, 1978. *Recreation:* bridge. *Address:* C-37, KDA Scheme No 1, Drigh Road, Karachi, Pakistan. *Clubs:* Sind (Karachi); Karachi Boat, Karachi Gymkhana.

PISANI, Edgard (Edouard Marie Victor); Chevalier de la Légion d'honneur; Member for France, Commission of the European Communities, since 1981; *b* Tunis, 9 Oct. 1918; *s* of François and Zoë Pisani; *m* Isola Chazereau (decd); three *s* one *d. Educ:* Lycée Carnot, Tunis; Lycée Louis-le-Grand, Paris. LèsL. War of 1939-45 (Croix de Guerre; Médaille de la Résistance). Chef du Cabinet, later Dir, Office of Prefect of Police, Paris, 1944; Dir, Office of Minister of Interior, 1946; Prefect: of Haute-Loire, 1946; of Haute-Marne, 1947; Senator (democratic left) from Haute-Marne, 1954; Minister of Agriculture, 1961; (first) Minister of Equipment, 1966; Deputy, Maine et Loire, 1967-68; Minister of Equipment and Housing, 1967; Conseiller Général, Maine et Loire, 1964-73; Mayor of Montreuil Bellay, 1965-75; Senator (socialist) for Haute-Marne, 1974-81; Mem., European Parlt, 1978-79 (Pres., Econ. and Monetary Affairs Cttee). Mem., Commn on Develt Issues (Brandt Commn), 1978-80. Mem., Club of Rome, 1975. *Publications:* La région: pourquoi faire?, 1969; Le général indivis, 1974; Utopie foncière, 1977; Socialiste de raison, 1978; Défi du monde, campagne d'Europe, 1979; (contrib.) Pour la science, 1980. *Address:* (office) 200 rue de la Loi, 1049 Brussels, Belgium; (home) 8 rue Joseph Bara, 75006 Paris, France.

PITBLADO, Sir David (Bruce), KCB 1967 (CB 1955); CVO 1953; Chairman, Davies Educational Services, since 1979 (Member Council, since 1975); Comptroller and Auditor-General, 1971-76; *b* 18 Aug. 1912; *o s* of Robert Bruce and Mary Jane Pitblado; *m* 1941, Edith (*d* 1978), *yr d* of Captain J. T. and Mrs Rees Evans, Cardigan; one *s* one *d. Educ:* Strand Sch.; Emmanuel Coll., Cambridge (Hon. Fellow 1972); Middle Temple. Entered Dominions Office, 1935; Asst Private Secretary to Secretary of State, 1937-39; served in War Cabinet Office, 1942; transferred to Treasury, 1942; Under-Secretary, Treasury, 1949; Principal Private Secretary to the Prime Minister (Mr Clement Attlee, Mr Winston Churchill, and Sir Anthony Eden), 1951-56; Third Secretary, Treasury, 1960; Economic Minister and Head of Treasury Delegation, Washington, and Executive Dir for the UK, IMF and World Bank, 1961-63; Permanent Sec., Min. of Power, 1966-69, Permanent Sec. (Industry), Min. of Technology, 1969-70; Second Permanent Sec., Civil Service Dept, 1970-71. Advr on non-exec. directorships, Inst. of Dirs, 1977-81. Member: Data Protection Cttee, 1976-78; Victoria County Histories Cttee, 1974-; Finance Cttee, RPMS, 1980-; Council, SSAFA, 1976- (Hon. Treasurer). Jt Editor, The Shetland Report, 1978-. Companion Inst. of Fuel.

Address: 23 Cadogan Street, SW3; Pengoitan, Borth, Dyfed. *Club:* Athenæum.

PITCHER, Desmond Henry, CEng, FIEE, FBCS; Managing Director, Plessey Telecommunications and Office Systems, since 1978; Director, Plessey Co., since 1979; *b* 23 March 1935; *s* of George Charles and Alice Marion Pitcher; *m* ; twin *d* ; *m* 1978, Carol (*née* Rose); two *s*, and one step *s. Educ:* Liverpool Coll. of Technology. MIEEE (USA). A. V. Roe & Co., Develt Engr, 1955; Automatic Telephone and Elec. Co. (now Plessey), Systems Engr, 1958; Univac Remington Rand (now Sperry Rand Ltd), Systems Engr, 1961; Sperry Univac: Dir, Systems, 1966; Managing Dir, 1971; Vice-Pres., 1974; Dir, Sperry Rand, 1971-78, Dep. Chm., 1974-78. Man. Dir, Leyland Vehicles Ltd, 1976-78; Dir, British Leyland, 1977-78. Dir, CEI, 1979; Pres., TEMA, 1981-. *Publications:* Institution of Electrical Engineers Faraday Lectures, 1974-75; various lectures on social implications of computers and micro-electronics. *Recreations:* golf, music. *Address:* Hough Hall, Hough, Nantwich, Cheshire. *T:* Nantwich 67865. *Clubs:* Royal Birkdale Golf; Royal Liverpool Golf; Camberley Heath Golf.

PITCHER, Prof. Wallace Spencer, PhD, DSc, DIC; George Herdman Professor of Geology, 1962-81, Leverhulme Emeritus Research Fellow, since 1981, University of Liverpool; *b* 3 March 1919; *s* of Harry George and Irene Bertha Pitcher; *m* 1947, Stella Ann (*née* Scutt); two *s* two *d. Educ:* Acton Tech. Coll., Chelsea Coll. FIMM, MIG. Asst Analytical Chemist, Geo. T. Holloway & Co., 1937-39. Served War, RAMC, 1939-44. Chelsea Coll., 1944-47; Imperial College: Demonstrator, 1947-48; Asst Lectr, 1948-50; Lectr, 1950-55; Reader in Geology, King's Coll., London, 1955-62. Geological Society London: Hon. Sec., 1970-73; Foreign Sec., 1974-75; Pres., 1976-77; Pres., Section C, British Assoc., 1979. Hon. Mem., GA, 1972; Hon. Mem., RIA, 1977; Lyell Fund, 1956; Bigsby Medal, 1963; Liverpool Geol Soc. Silver Medal, 1969; Murchison Medal, 1979. *Publications:* ed (with G. W. Flinn) Controls of Metamorphism, 1965; (with A. R. Berger) Geology of Donegal: a study of granite emplacement and unroofing, 1972; (with E. J. Cobbing) Geology of Western Cordillera of Northern Peru, 1981; many papers on late Precambrian stratigraphy, tillites, Caledonian and Andean granites, structure of the Andes. *Address:* 14 Church Road, Upton, Wirral, Merseyside L49 6JZ. *T:* 051-677 6896.

PITCHERS, Christopher John; Barrister; a Recorder of the Crown Court, since 1981; *b* 2 Oct. 1942; *s* of Thomas and Melissa Pitchers; *m* 1965, Judith Stevenson; two *s. Educ:* Uppingham Sch.; Worcester Coll., Oxford. MA. Called to the Bar, Inner Temple, 1965. *Address:* The White House, Church Langton, Leics.

PITCHFORD; *see* Watkins-Pitchford.

PITCHFORD, Charles Neville; His Honour Judge Pitchford; a Circuit Judge, Wales and Chester Circuit, since 1972. Called to the Bar, Middle Temple, 1948. *Address:* Llanynant, Kennel Lane, Coed Morgan, Abergavenny, Gwent.

PITCHFORD, John Hereward, CBE 1971; President, Ricardo Consulting Engineers Ltd, since 1976 (Chairman, 1962-76); *b* 30 Aug. 1904; *s* of John Pitchford and Elizabeth Anne Wilson; *m* 1930, Teresa Agnes Mary Pensotti; one *s* two *d. Educ:* Brighton Coll.; Christ's Coll., Cambridge (MA). FEng, FIMechE (Pres. 1962). Ricardo & Co. Engineers (1927) Ltd: Test Shop Asst, 1926; Asst Research Engr, 1929; Personal Asst to Man. Dir, 1935; Gen. Man., 1939; Dir and Gen. Man., 1941; Man. and Jt Techn. Dir, 1947; Chm. and Man. Dir, 1962; Chm. and Jt Man. Dir, 1965; Chm., 1967. Pres., Fédération Internationale des Sociétés d'Ingénieurs des Techniques de l'Automobile, 1961-63; Chm., Navy Dept Fuels and Lubricants Adv. Cttee, 1964-71. Hon. Mem., Associazione Tecnica Automobile, 1958. *Publications:* papers on all aspects of internal combustion engine. *Recreations:* music, sailing. *Address:* Byeways, Ditchling, East Sussex. *T:* Hassocks 2177. *Clubs:* Athenæum, Royal Automobile.

See also Sir J. H. G. Leahy.

PITCHFORTH, Harry; General Manager, Home Grown Cereals Authority, 1974-78, retired; *b* 17 Jan. 1917; *s* of John William Pitchforth and Alice Hollas; *m* 1941, Edna May Blakebrough; one *s* one *d. Educ:* Heath Sch., Halifax; Queen's Coll., Oxford. 1st class Hons, School of Modern History, Oxford, 1939. Served War, 1940-45, Captain, RASC, and later Education Officer, 5 Guards Brigade. Ministry of Food, 1945; Principal Private Secretary, to Minister, Major G. Lloyd-George, 1952-54; seconded to National Coal Board, 1955-58; Ministry of Agriculture, Fisheries and Food: Regional Controller, 1957-61; Director of Establishments and Organisation, 1961-65; Under-Sec., HM Treasury, 1965-67; Controller of HM Stationery Office and the Queen's Printer of Acts of Parliament, 1967-69; Chief Executive, Metropolitan Water Bd, 1969-74. *Recreations:* walking, music. *Address:* 93 George V Avenue, Pinner, Mddx. *T:* 01-863 1229.

PITFIELD, (Peter) Michael, QC (Can.) 1972; Clerk of the Privy Council and Secretary to the Cabinet, Canada, Jan. 1975-June 1979, and since March 1980; *b* Montreal, 18 June 1937; *s* of Ward Chipman Pitfield and Grace Edith (*née* MacDougall); *m* 1971, Nancy Snow; one *s* two *d. Educ:* Lower Canada Coll., Montreal; Sedbergh Sch., Montebello; St Lawrence Univ. (BASc; Hon. DLitt 1979); McGill Univ. (BCL); Univ. of Ottawa (DESD). Lieut, RCNR. Read Law with Mathewson Lafleur & Brown, Montreal (associated with firm,

1958-59); called to Quebec Bar, 1962; QC (Fed.) 1972; Admin. Asst to Minister of Justice and Attorney-Gen. of Canada, 1959-61; Sec. and Exec. Dir, Royal Commn on Pubns, Ottawa, 1961-62; Attaché to Gov.-Gen. of Canada, 1962-65; Sec. and Res. Supervisor of Royal Commn on Taxation, 1963-66; entered Privy Council Office and Cabinet Secretariat of Govt of Canada, 1965; Asst Sec. to Cabinet, 1966; Dep. Sec. to Cabinet (Plans), and Dep. Clerk to Council, 1969; Dep. Minister, Consumer and Corporate Affairs, 1973. Fellow, Harvard Univ., 1974; Mackenzie King Vis. Prof., Kennedy Sch. of Govt, Harvard, 1979-80. Member: Canadian, Quebec and Montreal Bar Assocs; Can. Inst. of Public Admin; Can. Hist. Assoc.; Can. Polit. Sci. Assoc.; Amer. Soc. Polit. and Social Sci.; Internat. Commn of Jurists; Beta Theta Pi. *Recreations:* squash, ski-ing, reading. *Address:* (home) 305 Thorold Road, Ottawa, Ont, Canada; (office) Langevin Block, Wellington Street, Ottawa, Ont, Canada. *Club:* University (Montreal).

PITMAN, Edwin James George, BSc, MA, FAA; Emeritus Professor of Mathematics, University of Tasmania (Professor, 1926; retired, Dec. 1962); *b* Melbourne, 29 Oct. 1897; of English parents; *s* of late Edwin Edward Major Pitman and Ann Ungley Pitman; *m* 1932, Edith Elinor Josephine, *y d* of late William Nevin Tatlow Hurst; two *s* two *d. Educ:* South Melbourne Coll.; Ormond Coll., University of Melbourne. Enlisted Australian Imperial Forces, 1918; returned from abroad, 1919; BA with First Class Honours, Dixson scholarship and Wyselaskie scholarship in Mathematics; acting-Professor of Mathematics at Canterbury Coll., University of New Zealand, 1922-23; Tutor in Mathematics and Physics at Trinity Coll. and Ormond Coll., University of Melbourne, 1924-25; Visiting Prof. of Mathematical Statistics at Columbia Univ., NY, Univ. of N Carolina, and Princeton Univ., 1948-49; Visiting Prof. of Statistics: Stanford Univ., Stanford, California, 1957; Johns Hopkins Univ., Baltimore, 1963-64; Chicago, 1968-69; Vis. Sen. Res. Fellow, Univ. of Dundee, 1973. Fellow, Inst. Math. Statistics, 1948; FAA 1954; Vice-Pres., 1960; Mem. International Statistical Institute, 1956; Pres., Australian Mathematical Soc., 1958-59; Hon. Fellow, Royal Statistical Soc., 1965; Hon. Life Member: Statistical Soc. of Australia, 1966 (first Pitman Medal, 1978, for contribs to theory of statistics and probability); Australian Mathematical Soc., 1968. Hon. DSc Tasmania, 1977. *Publication:* Some Basic Theory for Statistical Inference, 1979. *Address:* 301 Davey Street, Hobart, Tasmania 7000, Australia.

PITMAN, Sir Hubert, Kt 1961; OBE 1953; Member of Lloyd's since 1926; Chairman, H. Pitman & Co. Ltd, London, EC; *b* 19 Aug. 1901; *yr s* of W. H. Pitman, JP, sometime one of HM's Lieutenants for the City of London; unmarried. *Educ:* Repton. Member, Corporation of London, 1929-54; one of HM's Lieutenants for City of London, 1950-; Member LCC (Cities of London and Westminster), 1955-58; Alderman, 1954-63 (Sheriff, 1959-60) City of London. Senior Past Master, Painter Stainers' Co. OStJ. Comdr Etoile Noire, France. *Recreation:* country. *Address:* 57 Porchester Terrace, W2. *T:* 01-262 6593; Danemore Park, Speldhurst, Kent. *T:* Langton 2829; 11/12 Blomfield Street, EC4. *T:* 01-588 1852. *Club:* Carlton.

PITMAN, Sir (Isaac) James, KBE 1961; MA; Charter Pro-Chancellor, Bath University; Vice-President: British and Foreign School Society; British Association for Commercial and Industrial Education; Member, National Union of Teachers; Proponent of Initial Teaching Alphabet, and its designer, for the easier learning of literacy, oracy and the language in English; *b* London, 14 Aug. 1901; *e s* of late Ernest Pitman; *g s* of late Sir Isaac Pitman; *m* 1927, Hon. Margaret Beaufort Lawson-Johnston (Order of Mercy), 2nd *d* of 1st Baron Luke of Pavenham; three *s* one *d. Educ:* Eton; Christ Church, Oxford, 2nd Class Hons Mod. Hist. Played Rugby football for Oxford v Cambridge, 1921, for England v Scotland, 1922; ran for Oxford v Cambridge, 1922; skied for Oxford v Cambridge, 1922; won Middle Weight Public Schools Boxing, 1919. Bursar, Duke of York's and King's Camp, 1933-39. Chairman, Sir Isaac Pitman and Sons Ltd, 1934-66. RAF 1940-43, Acting Sqdn Leader; Director of Bank of England, 1941-45; HM Treasury, Director of Organisation and Methods, 1943-45. MP (C) Bath, 1945-64. Formerly Chm., Royal Soc. of Teachers; Chm. of Council, Initial Teaching Alphabet Foundn and Nat. Centre for Cued Speech (for the deaf child); Life Pres., UK Fedn of ita Schs; Mem. Cttee, Nat. Foundn for Educational Res. (which conducted comparative researches into reasons for reading failure in earliest stages of learning); Mem., Cttee advising Public Trustee under Will of late George Bernard Shaw in carrying out his wishes for design and publication of a proposed British alphabet). Hon. Pres., Parly Group for World Govt; Vice-Pres., Inst. of Administrative Management, 1965-69. Hon. DLittHum Hofstra, NY; Hon. DLitt: Strathclyde and Bath. *Address:* 58 Chelsea Park Gardens, SW3 6AE. *T:* 01-352 7004; Holme Wood, Chisbridge Cross, Marlow, Bucks. *T:* High Wycombe 881260. *Clubs:* Carlton; Harlequins, Achilles.

PITOI, Sir Sere, Kt 1977; CBE 1975; MACE; Chairman, Public Services Commission of Papua New Guinea, since 1971; *b* Kapa Kapa Village, SE of Port Moresby, 11 Nov. 1935; *s* of Pitoi Sere and Laka Orira; *m* 1957, Daga Leva; two *s* three *d. Educ:* Sogeri (Teachers' Cert.); Queensland Univ. (Cert. in Diagnostic Testing and Remedial Teaching); Univ. of Birmingham, UK (Cert. for Headmasters and Administrators). Held a number of posts as teacher, 1955-57, and headmaster, 1958-68, in Port Moresby, the Gulf district of Papua, Eastern Highlands, New Britain. Apptd a District Inspector of Schools, 1968. Chm., Public Service Bd, Papua New Guinea, 1969-76. Fellow, PNG Inst. of Management. *Recreation:* fishing. *Address:* PO Box 6029, Boroko, Papua New Guinea. *Clubs:* Rotary (Port Moresby); Cheshire Home (PNG).

PITT, family name of **Baron Pitt of Hampstead.**

PITT OF HAMPSTEAD, Baron *cr* 1975 (Life Peer), of Hampstead, in Greater London and in Grenada; **David Thomas Pitt,** TC 1976; MB, ChB Edinburgh, DCH London; JP; General Practitioner, London, since 1947; *b* St David's, Grenada, WI, 3 Oct. 1913; *m* 1943, Dorothy Elaine Alleyne; one *s* two *d. Educ:* St David's RC Sch., Grenada, WI; Grenada Boys' Secondary Sch.; Edinburgh Univ. First Junior Pres., Student Rep. Council, Edinburgh Univ., 1936-37. Dist. Med. Officer, St Vincent, WI, 1938-39; Ho. Phys., San Fernando Hosp., Trinidad, 1939-41; GP, San Fernando, 1941-47; Mem. of San Fernando BC, 1941-47; Dep. Mayor, San Fernando, 1946-47; Pres., West Indian Nat. Party (Trinidad), 1943-47. Mem. LCC, 1961-64, GLC 1964-77, for Hackney (Dep. Chm., 1969-70; Chm. 1974-75). Mem. Nat. Cttee for Commonwealth Immigrants, 1965-67; Chm., Campaign Against Racial Discrimination, 1965; Dep. Chm., Community Relations Commn, 1968-77, Chm. 1977; Mem., Standing Adv. Council on Race Relations, 1977-. Mem. (part time), PO Bd, 1975-77. Chm., Shelter, 1979. JP 1966. Contested (Lab): Hampstead, 1959; Clapham (Wandsworth), 1970. Hon. DSc Univ. of West Indies, 1975; Hon. DLitt Bradford, 1977; Hon. LLD Bristol, 1977. *Recreations:* reading, watching television, watching cricket, listening to music, theatre. *Address:* 6 Heath Drive, NW3. *Clubs:* Royal Commonwealth Society, MCC.

PITT, Barrie (William Edward); author and editor of military histories; *b* Galway, 7 July 1918; *y s* of John Pitt and Ethel May Pitt (*née* Pennell); *m* 1st, 1943, Phyllis Kate (*née* Edwards); one *s* (decd); 2nd, 1953, Sonia Deirdre (*née* Hoskins) (marr. diss., 1971). *Educ:* Portsmouth Southern Grammar Sch. Bank Clerk, 1935. Served War of 1939-45, in Army. Surveyor, 1946. Began writing, 1954. Information Officer, Atomic Energy Authority, 1961; Historical Consultant to BBC Series, The Great War, 1963; Editor, Purnell's History of the Second World War, 1964; Editor-in-Chief: Ballantine's Illustrated History of World War 2, 1967 (US Book Series); Ballantine's Illustrated History of the Violent Century, 1971; Editor: Purnell's History of the First World War, 1969; British History Illustrated, 1974-78. *Publications:* The Edge of Battle, 1958; Zeebrugge, St George's Day, 1918, 1958; Coronel and Falkland, 1960; 1918 The Last Act, 1962; The Battle of the Atlantic, 1977; The Crucible of War: Western Desert 1941, 1980; Churchill and the Generals, 1981; The Crucible of War: Year of Alamein 1942, 1982; contrib. to: Encyclopaedia Britannica; The Sunday Times. *Recreations:* golf, travel. *Address:* c/o National Westminster Bank Ltd, 13 Market Place, Reading RG1 2EP. *Club:* Savage.

PITT, Desmond Gordon; Commissioner of HM Customs and Excise, since 1979; *b* 27 Dec. 1922; *s* of Archibald and Amy Pitt; *m* 1946, Barbara Irene; one *s* two *d. Educ:* Bournemouth Sch. ACCA. Officer, HM Customs and Excise, 1947; Inspector, 1958; Asst Sec., 1973; Under Sec., 1979. *Recreations:* travel, sailing. *Address:* 133 Johnstone Road, Thorpe Bay, Essex. *Club:* Thorpe Bay Yacht.

PITT, Mgr George Edward, CBE 1965; Parish Priest, St Joseph's, Wroughton, Wilts, since 1969; *b* 10 Oct. 1916; *s* of Francis Pitt and Anna Christina Oviedo. *Educ:* St Brendan's Coll., Bristol; Ven. English College, Rome. Priest, 1939; worked in Diocese of Clifton, 1940-43; joined Royal Navy as Chaplain, 1943; Principal Roman Catholic Chaplain, RN, 1963-69. Nominated a Domestic Prelate, 1963. *Recreation:* music. *Address:* 14 Wharf Road, Wroughton, Swindon, Wilts SN4 9LB. *T:* 812330. *Club:* Army and Navy.

PITT, Sir Harry (Raymond), Kt 1978; BA, PhD; FRS 1957; Vice-Chancellor, Reading University, 1964-79; *b* 3 June 1914; *s* of H. Pitt; *m* 1940, Clemency Catherine, *d* of H. C. E. Jacoby, MIEE; four *s. Educ:* King Edward's Sch., Stourbridge; Peterhouse, Cambridge. Bye-Fellow, Peterhouse, Cambridge, 1936-39; Choate Memorial Fellow, Harvard Univ., 1937-38; Univ. of Aberdeen, 1939-42. Air Min. and Min. of Aircraft Production, 1942-45. Prof. of Mathematics, Queen's Univ., Belfast, 1945-50; Deputy Vice-Chancellor, Univ. of Nottingham, 1959-62; Prof. of Pure Mathematics, Univ. of Nottingham, 1950-64. Visiting Prof., Yale Univ., 1962-63. Chm., Universities Central Council on Admissions, 1975-78. Hon. LLD: Aberdeen 1970; Nottingham 1970; Hon. DSc Reading, 1978. *Publications:* Tauberian Theorems, 1957; Measure, Integration and Probability, 1963; mathematical papers in scientific journals. *Address:* 46 Shinfield Road, Reading, Berks RG2 7BW. *T:* Reading 872962.

PITT, Terence John; Senior Advisor on Economic Development, West Midlands County Council, since 1981; *b* Willenhall, Staffs, 2 March 1937. *Educ:* Queen Mary's Sch., Walsall; Univ. of Aston, Birmingham. Head of Labour Party Research Department, 1965-74; Special Adviser to Lord President of the Council, 1974. Freelance writer and consultant on govt affairs, 1975-78; Founding Dir, Inst. of Nat. Affairs, PNG, 1978-81. *Publications:* contrib.: Nuclear Power Technology (ed Pearson), 1963; People and Parliament (ed McIntosh), 1978. *Recreation:* politics. *Address:* 27 Beck Road, E8 4RE. *T:* 01-254 1794.

PITT, William Augustus Fitzgerald Lane F.; *see* Fox-Pitt.

PITT, William Henry; MP (L) Croydon North West, since Oct. 1981; *b* 17 July 1937; *m* 1961, Janet Pitt (*née* Wearn). *Educ:* Heath Clark Sch., Croydon; London Nautical Sch.; Polytechnic of South Bank. Lighting Engineer,

1955-75; Housing Officer, Lambeth Borough Council, 1975-81. Chm., Lambeth Br., NALGO, 1979-81. Joined Liberal Party, 1959; contested (L) Croydon NW, Feb. and Oct. 1974, and 1979; first L and SDP alliance cand. to be elected MP. *Recreations:* photography, music, reading, walking. *Address:* House of Commons, SW1A 0AA; 9 Dunheved Road North, Thornton Heath, Surrey CR4 6AH. *Club:* National Liberal.

PITT-RIVERS, Dr Rosalind Venetia, FRS 1954; *b* 4 March 1907; *d* of late Hon. Anthony Morton Henley, CMG, DSO, and late Hon. Sylvia Laura Henley, OBE (*née* Stanley); *m* 1931, Captain George Henry Lane Fox Pitt-Rivers (*d* 1966); one *s. Educ:* Notting Hill High Sch.; Bedford Coll., University of London. MSc London 1931; PhD London, 1939. Head, Chemistry Division, Nat. Inst. for Medical Research, 1969-72. *Publications:* The Thyroid Hormones, 1959; The Chemistry of Thyroid Diseases, 1960; (with W. R. Trotter) The Thyroid Gland, 1964. *Address:* 23A Lyndhurst Road, Hampstead, NW3 5NX.

PITTAM, Robert Raymond; research worker; Assistant Under-Secretary of State, Home Office, 1972-79; *b* 14 June 1919; *e s* of Rev. R. G. Pittam and Elsie Emma Pittam (*née* Sale); *m* 1946, Gwendoline Lilian Brown; one *s* one *d. Educ:* Bootle Grammar Sch.; Pembroke Coll., Cambridge. MA; 1st Cl. Law Tripos. War of 1939-45: temp. Civil Servant, and service in RAOC, 1940-46. Home Office, 1946-66: Private Sec. to Home Secretary, 1955-57; Asst Sec., 1957; HM Treasury, 1966-68; CSD, 1968-72. *Recreations:* cricket, reading. *Address:* 14 Devonshire Way, Shirley, Croydon, Surrey. *Club:* Civil Service.

PITTER, Ruth, CBE 1979; CLit 1974; poetess; *b* Ilford, Essex, 7 Nov. 1897; *d* of George Pitter, Elementary Schoolmaster. *Educ:* Elementary Sch.; Coborn Sch., Bow, E. Heinemann Foundation Award, 1954; Queen's Medal for Poetry, 1955. *Publications:* First Poems, 1920; First and Second Poems, 1927; Persephone in Hades (privately printed), 1931; A Mad Lady's Garland, 1934; A Trophy of Arms, 1936 (Hawthornden Prize, 1937); The Spirit Watches, 1939; The Rude Potato, 1941; The Bridge, 1945; Pitter on Cats, 1946; Urania, 1951; The Ermine, 1953; Still By Choice, 1966; Poems 1926-66, 1968; End of Drought, 1975. *Recreation:* gardening. *Address:* 71 Chilton Road, Long Crendon, near Aylesbury, Bucks. *T:* Long Crendon 208 373.

PITTOM, L(ois) Audrey, CB 1979; retired; Under Secretary, Health and Safety Executive, Department of Employment, 1975-78; *b* 4 July 1918; *d* of Thomas Pittom and Hylda (*née* Ashby). *Educ:* Laurels Sch., Wroxall Abbey, Warwick; St Anne's Coll., Oxford (BA Hons). Inspector of Factories, 1945; Superintending Inspector, Nottingham, 1967; Dep. Chief Inspector of Factories, 1970. *Recreations:* gardening, sight-seeing in Europe. *Address:* 1 Rectory Lane, Barby, Rugby, Warwicks. *T:* Rugby 890424.

PITTS, Sir Cyril (Alfred), Kt 1968; President, British and South Asian Trade Association, since 1978; Chairman: Process Plant EDC, since 1979; Peter Brotherhood, since 1980; *b* 21 March 1916; *m* 1942, Barbara; two *s* one *d. Educ:* St Olave's; Jesus Coll., Cambridge. Chairman of ICI Companies in India, 1964-68; Chm., ICI (Export) Ltd and Gen. Manager, Internat. Coordination, ICI Ltd, 1968-78; Dir, ICI Americas Ltd, 1974-77; Dep. Chm., Ozalid Gp Holdings Ltd, 1975-77. President, Bengal Chamber of Commerce and Industry, and Associated Chambers of Commerce and Industry of India, 1967-68. Councillor, RIIA, 1968-77; Dep. Chm., London Sch. of Hygiene and Tropical Medicine. *Address:* 11 Queensmead, St John's Wood Park, NW8. *T:* 01-586 0871. *Clubs:* Oriental; Bengal (Calcutta).

PITTS CRICK, R.; see Crick, Ronald P.

PITTS-TUCKER, Robert St John, CBE 1975; *b* 24 June 1909; *e s* of Walter Greame Pitts-Tucker, Solicitor, and Frances Elsie Wallace; *m* 1942, Joan Margery, *d* of Frank Furnivall, Civil Engineer, India, and Louisa Cameron Lees; three *s* one *d. Educ:* Haileybury (Schol.); Clare Coll., Cambridge (Schol.). 1st cl. Class. Tripos, Pts I and II, 1930 and 1931. Asst Master, Shrewsbury Sch., 1931-44; Headmaster, Pocklington Sch., 1945-66; Dep. Sec. to HMC and HMA, 1966-69, Sec., 1970-74. Mem., House of Laity, Church Assembly, 1956-70; St Albans diocese: Reader; Vice-Pres. of Synod, 1976-79; Member: ER Yorks Educn Cttee, 1946-66; Herts Educn Cttee, 1974-; Vice-Chm., Yorks Rural Community Council, 1949-65; Mem., Secondary Schools Examination Council, 1954-57. Governor: Mill Hill Sch.; Haileybury; St George's, Harpenden; Mem., GBA Exec. Cttee, 1975-80. *Recreations:* tennis, country walks, listening to music, gardening. *Address:* 59 Kings Road, Berkhamsted, Herts. *Club:* Royal Commonwealth Society.

PIX WESTON, John; see Weston, J. P.

PIXLEY, Sir Neville (Drake), Kt 1976; MBE (mil.) 1944; VRD 1941; company director; *b* 21 Sept. 1905; *s* of Arthur and Florence Pixley; *m* 1938, Lorna, *d* of Llewellyn Stephens; three *d. Educ:* C of E Grammar Sch., Brisbane. FCIT. Served RANR, 1920-63; War Service, Comd Corvettes, 1939-46 (Comdr 1945). Macdonald, Hamilton & Co. (P&O agents), 1922-59, Managing Partner, 1949-59; Chm., P&O Lines of Australia, 1960-70; Director: Burns Philp & Co. Ltd, 1962-80; Mauri Brothers & Thomson Ltd, 1970-77; NSW Boards of Advice: Nat. Bank of Australasia Ltd, 1970-77; Elder Smith Goldsborough Mort Ltd, 1970-76. Chm. Australian Cttee, Lloyd's Register of Shipping, 1967-80. ADC to King George VI and to the Queen, 1951-54. Vice Chancellor, 1978-, and Receiver-Gen., 1963-, Order of St John in Australia; KStJ 1963. Chm., Royal Humane Soc. of NSW. *Recreation:* tennis. *Address:* Koiyong, 335 New South Head Road, Double Bay, Sydney, NSW 2028, Australia. *T:* 3262676. *Clubs:* Union, Australian, Imperial Service (Sydney); Queensland (Qld); Melbourne (Melbourne). *See also N. S. Pixley.*

PIXLEY, Norman Stewart, CMG 1970; MBE 1941; VRD 1927; retired company director; Dean of the Consular Corps of Queensland since 1965; Hon. Consul for the Netherlands, 1948-72; *b* Brisbane, 3 May 1898; 2nd *s* of Arthur and Florence Pixley; *m* 1931, Grace Josephine, *d* of Arthur and Grace Spencer; twin *s* one *d. Educ:* Bowen House Sch.; Brisbane Grammar School. Served in RANR, 1913-46; Comdr, RANR, retd. Councillor, National Trust of Queensland; Pres., Qld Lawn Tennis Assoc., 1948-52; Pres., Brisbane Chamber of Commerce, 1952-53; Leader of Aust. Delegn to British Commonwealth Chambers of Commerce Conf., 1951; founded Qld Div. of Navy League, 1953 (Pres. until 1969). FRHistSoc Qld 1965 (Pres. 1968-). Kt, Order of Orange Nassau, 1964. *Publications:* papers on Australian history in Jl of Royal Hist. Soc. Qld, etc. *Recreations:* tennis, yachting, golf. *Address:* 147 Sherwood Road, Toowong, Brisbane, Queensland 4066, Australia. *T:* 701150. *Clubs:* Queensland, United Service, Tattersalls, Indooroopilly Golf (all Qld). *See also Sir Neville Pixley.*

PIZEY, Admiral Sir (Charles Thomas) Mark, GBE 1957 (KBE 1953); CB 1942; DSO 1942; idc; RN retired; DL; *b* 1899; *s* of late Rev. C. E. Pizey, Mark and Huntspill, Somerset; *m* Phyllis, *d* of Alfred D'Angibau; two *d.* Served European War, 1914-18, Midshipman, Revenge, 1916-18; Lieut, 1920; HMS Danae Special Service Squadron World Cruise, 1921-22; Flag Lieut to Vice-Admiral Sir Howard Kelly, 2nd in command Mediterranean Fleet, 1929-30; Destroyer Commands Mediterranean and Home Fleets, 1930-39; War of 1939-45: Captain, 1939; Commanded HMS Ausonia, Atlantic Patrol and Convoys, 1939-40. Captain (D) 21st Destoyer Flotilla in HMS Campbell, Nore Command, Channel and North Sea Operations, 1940-42 (CB, DSO, despatches twice); commanded HMS Tyne and Chief Staff Officer to Rear-Admiral Destroyers, Home Fleet, Russian convoys, 1942-43 (bar to DSO); Director of Operations (Home) Admiralty Naval Staff, 1944-45; Chief of Staff to C-in-C Home Fleet, 1946; Imperial Defence Coll., 1947; Rear-Admiral, 1948; Chief of UK Services Liaison Staff, Australia, 1948-49; Flag Officer Commanding First Cruiser Squadron, 1950-51; Vice-Admiral, 1951; Chief of Naval Staff and Commander-in-Chief, Indian Navy, 1951-55; Admiral, 1954; Commander-in-Chief, Plymouth, 1955-58, retired. DL County of Somerset, 1962. *Address:* 1 St Ann's Drive, Burnham on Sea, Somerset.

PIZZEY, Erin Patria Margaret; see Shapiro, E. P. M.

PLACE, Rear-Adm. (Basil Charles) Godfrey, VC 1944; CB 1970; DSC 1943; Lay Observer, 1975-78; *b* 19 July 1921; *s* of late Major C. G. M. Place, DSO, MC, and late Mrs Place; *m* 1943, Althea Annington, *d* of late Harry Tickler, Grimsby; one *s* two *d. Educ:* The Grange, Folkestone; RNC, Dartmouth. Midshipman, 1939; 10th and 12th submarine flotillas, 1941-43; Lieut, 1942; Comdr, 1952; HMS Glory (801 Sqn), 1952-53; Comdg HMS Tumult, 1955-56; Exec. Officer, HMS Theseus, 1956-57; HMS Corunna, 1957-58; Captain, 1958; Chief SO to Flag Officer Aircraft Carriers, 1958-60; Deputy Director of Air Warfare, 1960-62; HMS Rothesay and Captain (D), 25th Escort Squadron, 1962-63; HMS Ganges, 1963-65; HMS Albion, 1966-67; Adm. Comdg Reserves, and Dir-Gen., Naval Recruiting, 1968-70. Chm., VC and GC Assoc., 1971-. Polish Cross of Valour, 1941. *Address:* 87 Bishop's Mansions, SW6; The Old Bakery, Corton Denham, Sherborne, Dorset.

PLAIDY, Jean; see Hibbert, Eleanor.

PLAISTER, Sir Sydney, Kt 1980; CBE 1972; FRICS; chartered quantity surveyor, since 1930; *b* 15 Jan. 1909; *s* of Herbert Plaister; *m* 1937, Coralie Fraser Steele; one *s* one *d. Educ:* Acton and Chiswick Polytechnic; College of Estate Management. Partner, L. C. Wakeman & Partners, 1942, Consultant, 1977. Chairman, Solihull Conservative Assoc., 1951-53 and 1957; West Midlands Conservative Council: Hon. Treasurer, 1967-73; Chairman, 1973-76; President, 1980-; Chairman, Midlands Central Conservative Euro-constituency Council, 1978-; Mem. Exec. Cttee, Nat. Union of Conservative Associations, 1967-82. Freeman, City of London; Liveryman, Worshipful Co. of Glaziers. *Recreations:* gardening, music, travel. *Address:* Turnpike Close, Old Warwick Road, Lapworth, Warwickshire B94 6AP. *T:* Lapworth 2792. *Club:* Carlton.

PLANT, family name of **Baron Plant.**

PLANT, Baron *cr* 1978 (Life Peer), of Benenden in the County of Kent; **Cyril Thomas Howe Plant,** CBE 1975 (OBE 1965); JP; Kt, Staffs, 27 Aug. 1910; *s* of late Sidney Plant and late Rose Edna Plant; *m* 1931, Gladys Mayers; two *s* one *d. Educ:* Leek High School. Entered Post Office, 1927; Inland Revenue Staff Federation: Asst Sec., 1944; Gen. Sec., 1960-76; Chm. of Post Office and Civil Service Sanatorium Soc., 1950-75; Mem. General Council TUC, 1964-76 (Mem. Economic, Internat. Cttees TUC, Adviser to UK Workers' Deleg. ILO, 1965-); Chm., TUC, 1976; Mem. Exec. Cttee, Public Service International, 1960-77; UK Workers' Mem. of ILO Governing Body, Nov. 1969-77. Member: NE Metrop. Hosp. Bd, 1965-68; Community Relations Commn, 1974-77; Monopolies and Mergers Commn,

1975-78; Race Relations Bd, 1976-77; Southern Water Bd, 1977-80; Chm., NI Standing Adv. Commn on Human Rights, 1976-80; Mem., Police Pay and Structure Cttee, 1977-79; Vice-Chm., British Waterways Bd, 1977-80. Chm. of Governors, Ruskin Coll., Oxford, 1967-79; Treas., London Trades Council, 1952-74; Member: Civil Service Nat. Whitley Council, 1948-76; Inland Revenue Departmental Whitley Council, 1938-76 (Chm. 1958-76); Chm. British Productivity Council, 1972-77; Vice Pres., WEA, 1981- (Treasurer, 1969-81). A Dir, LOB, 1977-80. Trustee, Brighton and Hove Enginerium, 1980-. *Recreations:* horse racing, international activity. *Address:* Longridge, 19 Montacute Road, Lewes, East Sussex. *T:* Lewes 2556. *Club:* English-Speaking Union.

PLASKETT, Maj.-Gen. Frederick Joseph, CB 1980; MBE 1966; FCIT; Director General and Chief Executive, Road Haulage Association, since 1981; *b* 23 Oct. 1926; *s* of Frederick Joseph Plaskett and Grace Mary Plaskett; *m* 1950, Heather (*née* Kington) (*d* 1982); four *d.* Commnd infantry, 1946; RASC, 1951; RCT, 1965; regimental and staff appts, India, Korea, Nigeria, Malaya, Germany and UK; Student, Staff Coll., Camberley, 1958; Jt Services Staff Coll., 1964; Instr, Staff Coll., Camberley, 1966-68; Admin. Staff Coll., Henley, 1969; RCDS, 1975; Dir of Movements (Army), 1975-78; Dir Gen., Transport and Movements (Army), 1978-81, retired. Col Comdt, RCT, 1981-. *Recreations:* shooting, fishing, sailing, gardening. *Address:* c/o National Westminster Bank Ltd, Minster Street, Salisbury, Wilts. *Clubs:* Army and Navy; Royal Automobile.

PLASTOW, David Arnold Stuart; Managing Director and Chief Executive, Vickers PLC, since 1980 (Director, since 1975); *b* Grimsby, 9 May 1932; *s* of James Stuart Plastow and Marie Plastow; *m* 1954, Barbara Ann May; one *s* one *d. Educ:* Culford Sch., Bury St Edmunds. Apprentice, Vauxhall Motors Ltd, 1950; joined Rolls-Royce Ltd, Motor Car Div., Crewe, Sept. 1958; apptd Marketing Dir, Motor Car Div., 1967; Managing Director: Motor Car Div., 1971; Rolls-Royce Motors Ltd, 1972; Gp Man. Dir, 1974-80. Regional Dir, Lloyds Bank, 1974-76; non-executive Dir, GKN, 1978-. Vice-Pres., Inst. of Motor Industry; Pres., SMMT, 1976-77, 1977-78 (Dep. Pres., 1978-79, 1979-80); Pres., Motor Industry Res. Assoc., 1978-81; Chm., Grand Council, Motor and Cycle Trades Benevolent Fund, 1976-78. Patron, Coll. of Aeronautical and Automobile Engrg, 1972-79. Member: Council, CBI; BOTB; Engineering Council; Bd of Companions, BIM (Pres. S Cheshire Br.); Council, Industrial Soc.; Council, Regular Forces Employment Assoc.; Court of Manchester Univ.; Chm. Governors, Culford Sch., 1979-. Pres., Crewe Alexandra FC, 1975-82. Liveryman, Worshipful Co. of Coachmakers & Coach Harness Makers. FRSA. Young Business Man of the Year Award, The Guardian, 1976. Hon. DSc Cranfield, 1978. *Recreations:* golf, music. *Address:* Vickers PLC, Vickers House, Millbank Tower, Millbank, SW1P 4RA. *T:* 01-828 7777. *Club:* Royal and Ancient (St Andrews).

PLATT, family name of **Baroness Platt of Writtle.**

PLATT OF WRITTLE, Baroness *cr* 1981 (Life Peer), of Writtle in the County of Essex; **Beryl Catherine Platt,** CBE 1978; Vice-Chairman, Essex County Council, since 1980; *b* 18 April 1923; *d* of Ernest and Dorothy Myatt; *m* 1949, Stewart Sydney Platt; one *s* one *d. Educ:* Westcliff High School; Girton Coll., Cambridge (MA). Technical Assistant, Hawker Aircraft, 1943-46; BEA, 1946-49. Mem., Engineering Council, 1981-. Member, Chelmsford RDC, 1958-74. Member, Essex CC, 1965-: Alderman, 1969-74; Chm., Education Cttee, 1971-80. Vice-Chairman: Technician Education Council, 1979-81; London Regional Adv. Council for Technology Education, 1975-81. Member: CNAA, 1973-79; Council, CGLI, 1974-; Cambridge Univ. Appointments Bd, 1975-79; ACC Education Cttee, 1974-80; Court of Essex Univ., 1964-, and of City Univ., 1969-78. Trustee, Homerton Coll., 1970-81. Pres., Chelmsford Engineering Soc., 1979-80. FRSA. *Recreations:* cooking, gardening, reading. *Address:* House of Lords, SW1.

PLATT, Prof. Desmond Christopher Martin; Professor of the History of Latin America, University of Oxford, and Director, Centre of Latin American Studies, since 1972; Fellow, since 1972, Senior Tutor, since 1979, St Antony's College, Oxford; *b* 11 Nov. 1934; *s* of J. W. Platt, CBE; *m* 1958, Sarah Elizabeth Russell; no *c. Educ:* Collyer's Sch., Horsham; Balliol Coll., Oxford; Stanford Univ.; St Antony's Coll., Oxford. BA 1st cl. Hist. 1958, MA, DPhil 1962, Oxon; FRHistS. Asst Principal, Min. of Aviation, 1960-61; Asst Lectr, Edinburgh Univ., 1961-62; Lectr, Exeter Univ., 1962-68; Fellow, Queens' Coll., Cambridge and Univ. Lectr in Latin American History, 1969-72; Dir, Centre of Latin Amer. Studies, Univ. of Cambridge, 1971-72; Chm., Soc. for Latin American Studies, 1973-75. Member Editorial Board: Jl of Latin American Studies; Bull. of Latin American Res. *Publications:* Finance, Trade and Politics in British Foreign Policy 1815-1914, 1968; The Cinderella Service: British Consuls since 1825, 1971; Latin America and British Trade 1806-1914, 1972; (ed) Business Imperialism: an inquiry based on British experience in Latin America before 1930, 1977. *Address:* 23 Park Town, Oxford OX2 6SN. *T:* Oxford 54908.

PLATT, Eleanor Frances, QC 1982; a Recorder of the Crown Court, since 1982; *b* 6 May 1938; *er d* of Dr Maurice Leon Platt and Sara Platt (*née* Stein), Hove, Sussex; *m* 1963; two *c. Educ:* Hove County School for Girls; University College London. LLB 1959. Called to the Bar, Gray's Inn, 1960. *Recreations:* the arts, travel, skiing. *Address:* 6 Pump Court, Temple, EC4. *T:* 01-583 6013.

PLATT, Sir Harry, 1st Bt, *cr* 1958; Kt 1948; MD (Victoria), MS (London), FRCS; Hon. FACS; Hon. FRCS (Canada); Hon. FRCSE; Hon. FDS; Professor of Orthopædic Surgery, University of Manchester, 1939-51, now Emeritus Professor; President, National Fund for Research into Crippling Diseases, since 1970; Hon. President: International Federation of Surgical Colleges (Pres., 1958-66); Société Internationale de Chirurgie Orthopédique et de Traumatologie; *b* Thornham, Lancashire, 7 Oct. 1886; *e s* of Ernest Platt; *m* 1916, Gertrude Sarah (*d* 1980), 2nd *d* of Richard Turney; one *s* four *d. Educ:* Victoria Univ. of Manchester. University Gold Medal. MB, BS (London), 1909; Gold Medal for thesis MD (Vic), 1921; Hunterian Prof. of Surgery and Pathology, RCS, 1921; post-graduate study in USA, 1913-14 (Boston, New York, etc). Captain RAMC (TF), 1915-19. Surgeon in charge of Special Military Surgical Centre (Orthopædic Hospital), Manchester. Consultant Adviser: Ministry of Health, 1940-63; Ministry of Labour, 1952-64. President: British Orthopædic Assoc., 1934-35; RCS, 1954-57; Central Council for the Disabled, 1969; Mem., Central Health Services Council, 1948-57. Member: Council, E-SU; The Pilgrims. Hon. Degrees: DM Berne, 1954; Dr, Univ. of Paris, 1966; LLD: Univs of Manchester, 1955, Liverpool, 1955, Belfast, 1955, Leeds, 1965. KStJ 1972. *Publications:* monographs and articles on orthopædic surgery, medical education, hospital organisation, etc. *Recreations:* music, travel. *Heir: s* F(rank) Lindsey Platt, Barrister-at-Law [*b* 16 Jan. 1919; *m* 1951, Johanna Laenger]. *Address:* 14 Rusholme Gardens, Platt Lane, Manchester M14 5LS. *T:* 061-224 2427. *Clubs:* Travellers'; St James's (Manchester).
See also Sir F. J. W. Williams, Bt.

PLATT, Kenneth Harry, CBE 1966 (MBE 1944); Secretary, Institution of Mechanical Engineers, 1961-76, Secretary Emeritus, 1977; *b* 14 March 1909; *m* 1956, Janet Heather Walters; one *d. Educ:* Shrewsbury School; Glasgow Univ. (BSc in Mech. Eng.). Lecturer, School of Mines, Treforest, 1936-38; Prof. of Mech. Engineering, Benares, India, 1938-39. War Service, RAOC and REME (Major), 1939-45. HM Inspectorate of Schools, 1946-48; Educn and Personnel Manager, Brush Elec. Eng. Co. Ltd, 1949-52; Instn of Mechanical Engineers, 1952-76; Dep. Secretary, 1955. *Address:* 10 Castle Close, Warwick CV34 4DB.

PLATT, Norman; Artistic Director of Kent Opera, since 1969; *b* 29 Aug. 1920; *s* of Edward Turner Platt and Emily Jane Platt; *m* 1st, 1942, Diana Franklin Clay; one *s* one *d* ; 2nd, 1963, Johanna Sigrid Bishop; one *s* two *d. Educ:* Bury Grammar Sch.; King's Coll., Cambridge (BA). Principal: Sadler's Wells Opera, 1946-48; English Opera Group, 1948; Mem. Deller Consort, and freelance singer, actor, teacher and producer in Britain and Western Europe; founded Kent Opera, 1969. Hon. DCL Kent, 1981. *Publications:* translations of numerous songs and operas, incl. L'Incoronazione di Poppea, and Don Giovanni; articles on musical subjects. *Recreations:* reading, looking at pictures. *Address:* Pembles Cross, Egerton, Ashford, Kent TN27 9EN. *T:* Egerton 406.

PLATT, Hon. Sir Peter, 2nd Bt *cr* 1959; Professor of Music, University of Sydney, since 1975; *b* 6 July 1924; *s* of Baron Platt (Life Peer), and of Margaret Irene, *d* of Arthur Charles Cannon; *S* to baronetcy of father, 1978; *m* 1948, Jean Halliday, *d* of late Charles Philip Brentnall, MC; one *s* two *d. Educ:* Abbotsholme School, Derbyshire; Magdalen Coll., Oxford; Royal College of Music. BMus 1950, MA, BLitt 1954, Oxon. Lectr and Sen. Lectr in Music, Univ. of Sydney, 1952-57; Professor of Music, Univ. of Otago, NZ, 1957-75. Served War of 1939-45 with RNVR (despatches). *Heir: s* Martin Philip Platt [*b* 9 March 1952; *m* 1971, Frances Corinne Moana, *d* of Trevor Samuel Conley; two *s* two *d*]. *Address:* 1 Ellison Place, Pymble, NSW 2073, Australia.

PLATT, Terence Charles; Assistant Under-Secretary of State and Principal Establishment and Finance Officer, Northern Ireland Office, since 1981; *b* 22 Sept. 1936; *yr s* of Bertram Reginald Platt, QPM and Nina Platt; *m* 1959, Margaret Anne Cotmore; two *s. Educ:* St Olave's and St Saviour's Grammar School; Joint Services School for Linguists; Russian Interpreter. HM Immigration Officer, 1957; Asst Principal, Home Office, 1962; Principal, 1966; Cabinet Office, 1970; Principal Private Sec. to Sec. of State for NI (Rt Hon. William Whitelaw), 1972-73; Asst Sec., Home Office, 1973-81. *Recreations:* growing roses, photography, butterflies. *Address:* c/o Northern Ireland Office, Great George Street, SW1P 3AJ.

PLATT, Rev. William James; General Secretary, British and Foreign Bible Society, 1948-60; Consultant, 1960-61; retired, 1961; *b* 2 May 1893; *s* of James and Mary Platt; *m* 1921, Hilda Waterhouse (*d* 1975); one *d. Educ:* Rivington Grammar School; Didsbury Theological College, Manchester. Methodist Missionary in West Africa, 1916-30; Chairman and General Superintendent, Methodist District of French West Africa, 1925-30; joined Bible Society Staff as Secretary for Equatorial Africa, 1930; since 1948 has travelled extensively as General Secretary of Bible Society. Chairman of Council, United Bible Societies, 1954-57. Hon. DD, Knox College, Toronto, Canada, 1954. Officer of the Order of Orange Nassau, 1954; Commander, National Order of the Ivory Coast Republic, 1964. *Publications:* An African Prophet; From Fetish to Faith; Whose World?; Three Women in Central Asia; articles in religious and missionary publications. *Address:* Flat 8, Dewstraw, 147 Lent Rise Road, Burnham, Bucks. *Club:* Royal Commonwealth Society.

PLATTS-MILLS, John Faithful Fortescue, QC 1964; Barrister; *b* 4 Oct. 1906; *s* of John F. W. Mills and Dr Daisy Platts-Mills, Karori, Wellington,

NZ; *m* 1936, Janet Katherine Cree; six *s. Educ:* Nelson College and Victoria University, NZ; Balliol College, Oxford (Rhodes Scholar). LLM (NZ), MA, BCL (1st Cl.) Oxon. MP (Lab) Finsbury, 1945-48, (Ind Lab) 1948-50. Pilot Officer, RAF, 1940; "Bevin Boy", 1944; collier, 1945. Bencher, Inner Temple, 1970. Pres., Haldane Soc.; Vice-Pres., Internat. Assoc. of Democratic Lawyers; Mem. TGWU. *Address:* Cloisters, Temple, EC4. *T:* 01-583 9526; Terrible Down Farm, Halland, E Sussex. *T:* Halland 310. *Clubs:* Athenæum; Vincent's (Oxford); Leander.

PLAXTON, Ven. Cecil Andrew; Archdeacon of Wiltshire, 1951-74, now Archdeacon Emeritus of the Diocese of Salisbury; *b* 1902; *s* of Rev. J. W. Plaxton, Wells and Langport, Somerset; *m* 1929, Eleanor Joan Elisabeth Sowerby; one *s* one *d. Educ:* Magdalen College School, Oxford; St Edmund Hall, Oxford; Cuddesdon Theological College. BA 1924, MA 1928, Oxford; Deacon, 1926; Priest, 1927; Curate of Chard, 1926-28; Curate of St Martin, Salisbury, 1928-32; Vicar of Southbroom, Devizes, 1932-37; Vicar of Holy Trinity, Weymouth, 1937-51; Rural Dean of Weymouth, 1941-51; Rector of Pewsey, 1951-65; Canon of Salisbury and Prebend of Netheravon, 1949. Officiating Chaplain to the Forces, 1932-51. *Publication:* The Treasure of Salisbury: Life and Death of St Edmund of Abingdon, 1971, repr. 1980. *Recreations:* archæology and travelling, music. *Address:* St Edmund's Way, Potterne Road, Devizes, Wilts. *T:* Devizes 3391.

PLAYER, Denis Sydney, CBE 1967; Hon. President, Newall Engineering Group, 1973 (Chairman 1962-73; Deputy Chairman, 1955); Chairman, Newall Machine Tool Co. Ltd, 1964-73; *b* 13 Nov. 1913; *s* of Sydney Player and Minnie Emma Rowe; *m* 1940, Phyllis Ethel Holmes Brown (*d* 1975); three *d. Educ:* England; Worcester Acad., Mass. Apprenticed to Newall Engrg Co. Ltd, 1930; spent a year with Federal Produce Corp., RI, before rejoining Newall Engrg on Sales side; Man. Dir, Optical Measuring Tools, 1940; formed Sales Div. for whole of Newall Engrg Gp, 1945. Joined Royal Artillery, 1939; invalided out, 1940. CEng, FIProdE, FRSA. High Sheriff of Rutland, 1970-71. *Recreations:* yachting, fishing, shooting. *Address:* Sundial Cottage, 3 Digby Drive, North Luffenham, near Oakham, Rutland, Leics. *T:* Stamford 720039. *Clubs:* Royal Automobile; Royal Ocean Racing, Royal Burnham Yacht.

PLAYER, Gary (Jim); professional golfer, since 1953; *b* Johannesburg, 1 Nov. 1935; *s* of Francis Harry Audley Player and late Muriel Marie Ferguson; *m* 1957, Vivienne, *d* of Jacob Wynand Verwey; two *s* four *d. Educ:* King Edward Sch., Johannesburg. Won first, Dunlop tournament, 1956; major championship wins include: British Open, 1959, 1968, 1974; US Masters, 1961, 1974, 1978; US PGA, 1962, 1972; US Open, 1965; S African Open, thirteen times, 1956-81; S African PGA, 1959, 1960, 1969, 1979, 1982; Australian Open, seven times, 1958-74; Tooth Gold Coast Classic, Australia, 1981; World Match Play Tournament, 1965, 1966, 1968, 1971, 1973. *Address:* Mark McCormack Agency, 58 Queen Anne Street, W1M 0DX.

PLAYFAIR, Sir Edward (Wilder), KCB 1957 (CB 1949); *b* 17 May 1909; *s* of late Dr Edward Playfair; *m* 1941, Dr Mary Lois Rae; three *d. Educ:* Eton; King's Coll., Cambridge. Inland Revenue, 1931-34; HM Treasury, 1934-46 and 1947-56 (Control Office for Germany and Austria, 1946-47); Permanent Under-Secretary of State for War, 1956-59; Permanent Sec., Ministry of Defence, 1960-61. Chairman, International Computers and Tabulators Ltd, 1961-65; Director: National Westminster Bank Ltd, 1961-79; Glaxo Hldgs Ltd, 1961-79; Tunnel Holdings Ltd, 1966-80; Equity and Law Life Assce Soc. plc, 1968-83. Governor, Imperial Coll. of Science and Technology, 1958-83 (Fellow, 1972); College Cttee of UCL, 1961-77 (Hon. Fellow, UCL, 1969); Chm., National Gallery, 1972-74 (Trustee, 1967-74). Hon. FBCS. *Address:* 12 The Vale, Chelsea, SW3 6AH. *T:* 01-352 4671. *Club:* Brooks's.

PLAYFORD, Jonathan Richard; QC 1982; *b* 6 Aug. 1940; *s* of Cecil R. B. Playford and Euphrasia J. Playford; *m* 1978, Jill Margaret Dunlop; one *s. Educ:* Eton Coll.; London Univ. (LLB). Called to the Bar, Inner Temple, 1962. *Recreations:* music, country pursuits, golf. *Address:* 2 Harcourt Buildings, Temple, EC4Y 9DB. *T:* 01-583 9020. *Clubs:* Garrick, Royal Automobile; Huntercombe Golf (Henley).

PLAYFORD, Hon. Sir Thomas, GCMG 1957; Premier, Treasurer and Minister of Immigration of S Australia, Nov. 1938-March 1965; Minister of Industry and Employment, 1946-53; Leader of the Opposition, 1965-66; MP, South Australia, 1933-66; *b* 5 July 1896; *o s* of T. Playford, Norton's Summit, SA; *gs* of late Hon. T. Playford, sometime Premier of S Australia; *m* 1928, Lorna Beaman, *e d* of F. S. Clark; one *s* two *d. Educ:* Norton Summit Public School. Engaged in primary production (fruit grower); served European War 27th Bn AIF obtaining a Commission; entered SA Parliament, 1933, as one of representatives for District of Murray; representative for Gumeracha District, 1938-68; Member of Liberal Country Party; Commissioner of Crown Lands, Minister of Repatriation and Irrigation, March 1938; succeeded Hon. R. L. Butler as Leader of Liberal Country Party, 1938. *Recreation:* horticulture. *Address:* Norton Summit, SA 5136, Australia.

PLEASENCE, Donald; actor; *b* 5 Oct. 1919; *s* of late Thomas Stanley and of Alice Pleasence; *m* 1st, 1940, Miriam Raymond; two *d* ; 2nd, 1959, Josephine Crombie (marr. diss. 1970); two *d* ; 3rd, 1970, Meira Shore; one *d. Educ:* The Grammar School, Ecclesfield, Yorkshire. Made first stage appearance at the Playhouse Theatre, Jersey, CI, May 1939; first London appearance, Twelfth Night, Arts Theatre, 1942. Served with RAF, 1942-46 (Flt Lieut); shot down

and taken prisoner, 1944. Returned to stage in The Brothers Karamazov, Lyric, Hammersmith, 1946; Huis Clos, Arts Theatre; Birmingham Repertory Theatre, 1948-50; Bristol Old Vic, 1951; Right Side Up, and Saint's Day, Arts Theatre, 1951; Ziegfeld Theatre, New York (with L. Olivier Co.), 1951; played in own play, Ebb Tide, Edinburgh Festival and Royal Court Theatre, 1952; Stratford-on-Avon season, 1953. *Other London Appearances:* Hobson's Choice, 1952; Antony and Cleopatra, 1953; The Rules of the Game, 1955; The Lark, 1956; Misalliance, 1957; Restless Heart, 1960; The Caretaker, London, 1960, New York, 1961; Poor Bitos, London and New York; The Man in the Glass Booth, St Martin's, 1967 (London Variety Award for Stage Actor of the Year, 1968), New York, 1968-69; Tea Party, The Basement, London, 1970; Reflections, Theatre Royal, Haymarket, 1980; 1970; Wise Child, NY, 1972. Many television appearances. Named Actor of the Year, 1958. *Films include:* The Beachcomber, Heart of a Child, Manuela, The Great Escape, Doctor Crippen, The Caretaker, The Greatest Story Ever Told, The Hallelujah Trail, Fantastic Voyage, Cul-de-Sac, The Night of the Generals, Eye of the Devil, Will Penny, The Mad Woman of Chaillot, Sleep is Lovely, Arthur! Arthur?, THX 1138, Outback, Soldier Blue, The Pied Piper, The Jerusalem File, Kidnapped, Innocent Bystanders, Death Line, Henry VIII, Wedding in White, The Rainbow Boys, Malachi's Cove, Mutations, Tales From Beyond the Grave, The Black Windmill, Escape to Witch Mountain, I Don't Want to be Born, Journey Into Fear, Hearts of the West, Trial by Combat, The Last Tycoon, The Passover Plot, The Eagle has Landed, Golden Rod, The Devil's Men, Tomorrow Never Comes, Telefon, Sgt Pepper's Lonely Hearts Club Band, Halloween, Power Play, Dracula, Halloween II, The Monster Club, Escape from New York. *Recreation:* talking too much. *Address:* 11 Strand on the Green, W4. *Clubs:* White Elephant, Burkes.

PLEASS, Sir Clement (John), KCMG 1955 (CMG 1950); KCVO 1956; KBE 1953; MA; retired as Governor; *b* 19 November 1901; *s* of J. W. A. Pleass, Tiverton, Devon; *m* 1927, Sybil, *d* of Alwyn Child, Gerrard's Cross; one *s. Educ:* Royal Masonic School; Selwyn College, Cambridge. Joined Colonial Administrative Service, Jan. 1924; served in Nigeria, 1924-56. Lieut-Governor, 1952-54, Governor, 1954-56, Eastern Region of Nigeria. Formerly Mem., Colonial Development Corporation. *Recreation:* golf. *Address:* Higher Barton, Malborough, near Kingsbridge, S Devon. *Club:* Royal Commonwealth Society.

PLENDERLEITH, Harold James, CBE 1959; MC 1918; BSc, PhD; FRSE; FBA 1973; FSA; FMA; Director, International Centre for the Study of the Preservation and Restoration of Cultural Property (created by UNESCO), 1959-71, now Emeritus; Vice-President, International Institute for the Conservation of Museum Objects, 1958 (President, 1965-67, Hon. Fellow 1971); Member, Directory Board of Museum Laboratories Committee, International Council of Museums; *b* 19 Sept. 1898; *s* of Robert James Plenderleith, FEIS; *m* 1926, Elizabeth K. S. Smyth (*d* 1982). *Educ:* Dundee Harris Acad.; St Andrews Univ. Keeper, Research Lab., British Museum, 1949-59. Mem., Hon. Scientific Adv. Cttee, Nat. Gallery, 1935-81 (Chm., 1944-58); Professor of Chemistry, Royal Academy of Arts, London, 1936-58. Hon. Treas. Internat. Inst. for Conservation of Museum Objects, 1950-58. Rhind Lecturer (Edinburgh) 1954. Gold Medal, Society of Antiquaries of London, 1964; Gold Medal, Univ. of Young Nam, Tae Gu, Korea, 1970; Bronze Medal, UNESCO, 1971; Conservation Service Award, US Dept of the Interior, 1976; ICCROM International Oscar, Rome, 1979. Hon. LLD St Andrews. *Publications:* The Preservation of Antiquities, 1934; The Conservation of Prints, Drawings and Manuscripts, 1937; The Preservation of Leather Bookbindings, 1946; The Conservation of Antiquities and Works of Art, 1956 (2nd edn with A. E. A. Werner, 1971); papers on allied subjects and on technical examinations of museum specimens in museum and scientific journals. *Recreations:* art and music. *Address:* Riverside, 17 Rockfield Crescent, Dundee DD2 1JF. *T:* Dundee 641552. *Club:* Athenæum.

PLENDERLEITH, Thomas Donald, RE 1961 (ARE 1951); Senior Art Master, St Nicholas Grammar School, Northwood, since 1956; *b* 11 March 1921; *s* of James Plenderleith and Georgina Ellis; *m* 1949, Joyce Rogers; one *s. Educ:* St Clement Danes; Ealing Sch. of Art; Hornsey Sch. of Art. Pilot, Bomber Command, RAF, 1941-46. Art Master, Pinner County Grammar Sch., 1948-56. Art Teacher's Diploma, 1947. *Recreations:* cricket, badminton. *Address:* 46 Sylvia Avenue, Hatch End, Mddx. *T:* 01-428 5019.

PLEVEN, René Jean; French Statesman; Compagnon de la Libération, 1943; Commandeur du Mérite Maritime, 1945; Député des Côtes-du-Nord, 1945-73; Président du Conseil Général des Côtes-du-Nord, 1949; Président du Conseil Régional de Bretagne, 1974; *b* 15 April 1901; *s* of Colonel Jules Pleven; *m* 1924, Anne Bompard (*d* 1966); two *d. Educ:* Faculté de Droit de Paris (LLD); Ecole Libre des Sciences Politiques. Company Director. Deputy chief of French Air Mission to USA, 1939. French National Committee and Comité Français de Libération Nationale (Finances, Colonies, Foreign Affairs), 1941-44; Minister: of Colonies (Provisional Government), 1944; of Finances, 1944-46; of Defence, Nov. 1949 and 1952-54; Président du Conseil, July 1950, Aug. 1951-Jan. 1952; Vice-Président du Conseil, Feb. 1951; Ministre des Affaires Etrangères, 1958; Délégué à l'Assemblée parlementaire européenne, and Chm., Liberal Gp of this Assembly, 1956-69; Ministre de la Justice, et Garde des Sceaux, 1969-73. Grand Officer Order of Leopold, 1945; Grand Cross: Le Million d'éléphants, 1949; Etoile Polaire, 1950; Orange-Nassau, 1950; Dannebrog, 1950; Nicham Alaouite, 1950; Vietnam, 1951; Order of Merit of the Republic of Italy, 1972; National Order of Ivory Coast, 1972; Order of Central African Republic, 1972; Hon GBE, 1972.

Publications: Les Ouvriers de l'agriculture anglaise depuis la guerre, 1925; Avenir de la Bretagne, 1962. *Recreation:* fishing. *Address:* 12 rue Chateaubriand, Dinan (Côtes-du-Nord), France.

PLEYDELL-BOUVERIE, family name of **Earl of Radnor.**

PLIATZKY, Sir Leo, KCB 1977 (CB 1972); Member (part-time), British Airways Board, since 1980; *b* 1919; *m* 1948, Marian Jean Elias (*d* 1979); one *s* one *d. Educ:* Manchester Grammar Sch.; City of London Sch.; Corpus Christi Coll., Oxford (Hon. Fellow, 1980). First Cl. Classical Honour Mods, 1939. Served in RAOC and REME, 1940–45 (despatches). First Cl. Philosophy, Politics and Economics, 1946. Research Sec., Fabian Soc., 1946-47; Min. of Food, 1947-50; HM Treasury, 1950-77; Under-Sec., 1967; Dep. Sec., 1971; Second Permanent Sec., 1976; Permanent Sec., Dept of Trade, 1977; retired 1979, retained for special duties, 1979-80. Director: Associated Communications Corporation Ltd, 1980-82; Central Independent Television Ltd, 1981-; Ultramar Co. Ltd, 1981-. Vis. Prof., City Univ., 1980-. FRSA. *Publication:* Getting and Spending, 1982. *Address:* 27 River Court, Upper Ground, SE1. *T:* 01-928 3667. *Club:* Reform.

PLIMMER, Sir Clifford (Ulric), KBE 1967; *b* 25 July 1905; *s* of late Arthur Bloomfield Plimmer and Jessie Elizabeth (*née* Townsend); *m* 1935, Letha May (*née* Port); three *s* (and one *s* decd). *Educ:* Scots Coll., Wellington; Victoria Univ. of Wellington. Office Junior, 1922, Wright, Stephenson & Co. Ltd (stock and station agents, woolbrokers, gen. merchants, manufrs, car dealers, insurance agents, etc), retired as Chm. and Man. Dir, 1970. Director: McKechnie Bros. (NZ) Ltd; James Smith Ltd; Tradespan NZ Ltd; owns and operates a number of sheep and cattle farms in New Zealand. Nat. Patron, Intellectually Handicapped Children's Soc. Inc.; Member: Dr Barnardos in NZ; Wellington Med. Res. Foundn. *Address:* PO Box 10218, Wellington, New Zealand. *Clubs:* Wellington; Northern, (Auckland); Hutt (Lower Hutt, NZ).

PLIMSOLL, Sir James, AC 1978; Kt 1962; CBE 1956; Governor of Tasmania, since 1982; *b* Sydney, New South Wales, 25 April 1917; *s* of late James E. and Jessie Plimsoll; unmarried. *Educ:* Sydney High School; University of Sydney. Economic Department, Bank of New South Wales, 1938-42; Australian Army, 1942-47. Australian Delegation, Far Eastern Commission, 1945-48; Australian Representative, United Nations Commission for the Unification and Rehabilitation of Korea, 1950-52; Assistant Secretary, Department of External Affairs, Canberra, 1953-59; Australian Permanent Representative at the United Nations, 1959-63; Australian High Commissioner to India and Ambassador to Nepal, 1963-65; Secretary of Dept of External Affairs, Australia, 1965-70; Australian Ambassador to USA, 1970-74, to the USSR and Mongolia, 1974-77, to Belgium, Luxembourg, and the European Communities, 1977-80; High Commissioner for Australia in UK, 1980-81; Australian Ambassador to Japan, 1981-82. KStJ 1982. *Address:* Government House, Hobart, Tasmania 7000, Australia.

PLOMLEY, (Francis) Roy, OBE 1975; writer and broadcaster; *s* of Francis John Plomley, MPS, and Ellinor Maud Wigg; *m* Diana Beatrice Wong; one *d. Educ:* King's Coll. Sch. Announcer and Producer with Internat. Broadcasting Co. (Radio Normandy, Poste Parisien, Radio Internat.), 1936-40; devised: Desert Island Discs, BBC, 1941; Hurrah for Hollywood, 1942; To Town on Two Pianos, 1944; Gala Night at the Rhubarb Room, 1948; Chairman: We Beg to Differ, 1949 (television, 1951); One Minute, Please, 1951; These Foolish Things, 1956; Round Britain Quiz, 1961; Many a Slip, 1964; produced Dinner Date with Death, first film made in UK esp. for television, 1949. Chairman: Exec. Cttee, Radio and Television Writers Assoc., 1957-59; Exec. Cttee, Radiowriters Assoc., 1960-62. Variety Club Award as BBC Radio Personality of the Year, 1979; Radio Programme of the Year Award, Television and Radio Industries Club, 1981; Broadcasting Press Guild Radio Award, 1981. *Plays:* All Expenses Paid, 1951; Devil's Highway, 1952; Half Seas Over, 1953; We'll All Be Millionaires, 1956; (with Arthur Swinson) Lock, Stock and Barrel, 1957; (with Archie Menzies) Tax Free, 1960; The First Time I Saw Paris, 1960; The Best Hotel in Boulogne, 1961; The Shiny Surface, 1963; Everybody's Making Money—Except Shakespeare, 1964; Home and Dry, 1964; (with John Allegro) The Lively Oracles, 1965; Moonlight Behind You, 1967; You're Welcome to My Wife (from the French), 1971; Just Plain Murder, 1972; Murder for Two (from the French), 1973. *Publications:* Desert Island Discs, 1975; French Dressing (novel), 1977; (ed) Desert Island Book, 1979; Days Seemed Longer, 1980; Plomley's Pick, 1982. *Recreations:* English history, French travels, painting, swimming, playing boules. *Address:* 91 Deodar Road, Putney, SW15 2NU. *Clubs:* Garrick, Savage.

PLOURDE, Most Rev. Joseph Aurèle; *see* Ottawa, Archbishop of, (RC).

PLOUVIEZ, Peter William; General Secretary, British Actors' Equity Association, since 1974; *b* 30 July 1931; *s* of Charles and Emma Plouviez; *m* 1978, Alison Dorothy Macrae; two *d* (by previous marr.). *Educ:* Sir George Monoux Grammar Sch.; Hastings Grammar Sch. Greater London Organiser, NUBE, 1955-60; Asst Sec., Equity, 1960, Asst Gen. Sec., Equity, 1964. Contested (Lab), St Marylebone bye-election, 1963; Councillor, St Pancras, 1962-65. Chm., Radio and Television Safeguards Cttee, 1974-; Sec., Fedn of Theatre Unions, 1974-; Vice-Chm., Confedn of Entertainment Unions, 1974-; Mem., Cinematograph Films Council, 1974-; Assoc. for Business Sponsorship of the Arts; Trustee: Theatres Trust, 1977-; Carl Rosa Opera. *Recreations:*

supporting (half-heartedly) Orient FC, (colour blind) painting. *Address:* 8 Harley Street, W1. *T:* 01-637 9311. *Club:* Gerry's.

PLOW, Maj.-Gen. the Hon. Edward Chester, CBE 1945; DSO 1944; CD 1950; DCL; Hon. DScMil; Canadian Army (Retired); *b* St Albans, Vermont, 28 September 1904; *s* of late John Plow and Hortense Harlow Plow (*née* Locklin); *m* 1937, Mary Nichols, *d* of late Thomas E. G. Lynch and M. Edith Lynch (*née* Nichols), Digby, NS; one *d. Educ:* Montreal schools; RMC Kingston. Commnd in RCHA, 1925; served in Canada and UK until 1939. Served War of 1939-45 (despatches twice): Italy and NW Europe; Artillery Staff Officer and Comdr; during latter part of War was Senior Artillery Officer, Canadian Army. Following the War served in various appts in Germany, Canada and the UK, and was GOC Eastern Command, Canada, 1950-58. Lieut-Governor of the Province of Nova Scotia, 1958-63. Dir, Canadian Imperial Bank of Commerce, 1963-74. Member Board of Governors: Izaak Walton Killam Hosp. for Children, Halifax; Canadian Corps of Commissionaires. Life Mem., Royal Canadian Artillery Assoc. Patron, St John Ambulance Assoc. KStJ; Comdr, Order of Orange Nassau (Netherlands). Anglican. *Address:* Locklands, RR1, Brockville, Ont, Canada. *Clubs:* Brockville Country; Halifax (Halifax).

PLOWDEN, family name of **Baron Plowden.**

PLOWDEN, Baron, *cr* 1959, of Plowden (Life Peer); **Edwin Noel Plowden,** KCB 1951; KBE 1946; Chairman, Top Salaries Review Body, since 1981 (Member, since 1977); President of TI Group (formerly Tube Investments Ltd), since 1976 (Chairman, 1963-76); Member, Ford European Advisory Council, since 1976; *b* 6 Jan. 1907; 4th *s* of late Roger H. Plowden; *m* 1933, Bridget Horatia (*see* Lady Plowden); two *s* two *d. Educ:* Switzerland; Pembroke College, Cambridge (Hon. Fellow, 1958). Temporary Civil Servant Ministry of Economic Warfare, 1939-40; Ministry of Aircraft Production, 1940-46; Chief Executive, and Member of Aircraft Supply Council, 1945-46; Vice-Chairman Temporary Council Cttee of NATO, 1951-52; Cabinet Office, 1947; Treasury, 1947-53, as Chief Planning Officer and Chairman of Economic Planning Board. Adviser on Atomic Energy Organization, 1953-54; Chairman, Atomic Energy Authority, 1954-59; Visiting Fellow, Nuffield College, 1956-64; Chm. Cttee of Enquiry: Treasury control of Public Expenditure, 1959-61; organisation of Representational Services Overseas, 1963-64; Aircraft Industry, 1964-65; Structure of Electricity Supply Industry in England and Wales, 1974-75; into CBI's aims and organisation, 1974-75; Dep. Chm., Cttee of Inquiry on Police, 1977-79; Chm., Police Complaints Bd, 1976-81; Independent Chm., Police Negotiating Bd, 1979-82. Director: Commercial Union Assurance Co. Ltd, 1946-78; National Westminster Bank Ltd, 1960-77; Chm., Equity Capital for Industry Ltd, 1976-82; Chm., CBI Companies Cttee, 1976-80; Vice-Chm., CBI Pres.'s Cttee, 1977-80. Pres., London Graduate Sch. of Business Studies, 1976- (Chm. 1964-76); Chm., Standing Adv. Cttee on Pay of Higher Civil Service, 1968-70; Member: Civil Service Coll. Adv. Council, 1970-76; Engineering Industries Council, 1976. Hon. DSc: Pennsylvania State Univ., 1958; Univ. of Aston, 1972; Hon DLitt, Loughborough, 1976. *Address:* Martels Manor, Dunmow, Essex. *T:* Great Dunmow 2141; 7 Cottesmore Gardens, W8. *T:* 01-937 4238.

See also W. J. L. Plowden.

PLOWDEN, Lady, (Bridget Horatia), DBE 1972; Chairman, Independent Broadcasting Authority, 1975-80; 2nd *d* of late Admiral Sir H. W. Richmond, KCB, and of Lady Richmond (Elsa, *née* Bell); *m* 1933, Baron Plowden, *qv* ; two *s* two *d. Educ:* Downe House. Dir, Trust Houses Forte Ltd, 1961-72. Chairman: Central Advisory Council for Education (England), 1963-66; Working Ladies Guild; Professional Classes Aid Council; Adv. Cttee for Educn of Romany and other travellers; Metropolitan Architectural Consortium for Educn, 1968-79; a Governor and Vice-Chm., BBC, 1970-75; Mem., Nat. Theatre Bd, 1976-. Mem., Houghton Inquiry into Pay of Teachers, 1974; Chm. of Governors: Philippa Fawcett Coll. of Educn, 1967-76; Robert Montefiore Comp. Sch., 1968-78; Co-opted Mem., Educn Cttee, ILEA, 1967-73; Vice-Chm., ILEA Schools Sub-Cttee, 1967-70; President: Pre-School Playgps Assoc., 1972-82; Harding House Assoc.; Nat. Assoc. of Adult Educn, 1980-. Liveryman, Goldsmiths' Co., 1979-. JP Inner London Area Juvenile Panel, 1962-71. Fellow, Royal TV Soc., 1980. Hon. LLD: Leicester, 1968; Reading, 1970; London, 1976; Hon DLitt Loughborough, 1976; DUniv Open, 1974. Hon. Fellow, College of Preceptors, 1973. *Address:* Martels Manor, Dunmow, Essex. *T:* Great Dunmow 2141; 7 Cottesmore Gardens, W8. *T:* 01-937 4238.

See also W. J. L. Plowden.

PLOWDEN, William Julius Lowthian, PhD; Director-General, Royal Institute of Public Administration, since 1978; *b* 7 Feb. 1935; *s* of Lord and Lady Plowden, *qqv* ; *m* 1960, Veronica Gascoigne; two *s* two *d. Educ:* Eton; King's Coll., Cambridge (BA, PhD); Univ. of Calif, Berkeley. Staff Writer, Economist, 1959-60; BoT, 1960-65; Lectr in Govt, LSE, 1965-71; Central Policy Review Staff, Cabinet Office, 1971-77; Under Sec., Dept of Industry, 1977-78. Hon. Prof., Dept of Politics, Univ. of Warwick, 1977-. Mem., W Lambeth DHA, 1982-. *Publication:* The Motor Car and Politics in Britain, 1971. *Address:* 49 Stockwell Park Road, SW9. *T:* 01-274 4535.

PLOWMAN, Sir (John) Anthony, Kt 1961; Judge of the High Court of Justice (Chancery Division), 1961-76, Vice-Chancellor, 1974-76; *b* 27 Dec. 1905; *e s* of late John Tharp Plowman (solicitor); *m* 1933, Vernon, 3rd *d* of late A. O. Graham, Versailles; three d. Educ: Highgate School; Gonville and Caius Coll., Cambridge. Solicitors Final (John Mackrell Prize); 1927; LLB London, 1927; LLB Cantab (1st Cl.), 1929; LLM Cantab 1956. Called to Bar, Lincoln's Inn, 1931 (Tancred and Cholmeley studentships; Buchanan Prize); QC 1954; Bencher of Lincoln's Inn, 1961. Served, 1940-45, Squadron-Leader, RAF. Member of General Council of the Bar, 1956-60. Address: Lane End, Bucks.

PLOWMAN, Hon. Sir John (Robin), Kt 1979; CBE 1970 (OBE 1949); Member of the Legislative Council, later Senator, Bermuda, 1966-82, Government Leader in the Senate, 1968-82; Minister of Government and Commercial Services, Bermuda, 1980-82; b Bermuda, 18 Sept. 1908; s of Owen and Elizabeth Plowman; m 1936, Marjorie Hardwick; two s. Educ: Bermuda and England. Member, Ealing Borough Council, 1931-35; returned to Bermuda, 1935; Bermuda Volunteer Engineers, 1939-42; Dep. Dir, Dir and later Chm. of Bermuda Supplies Commission, 1942-47; Man. Director of Holmes, Williams & Purvey Ltd, 1947-78, Chairman of Board, 1961-. Chm. or Mem. of various govt commns and bds, including Training and Employment, Ports Facilities, Transport Control and Civil Service; Minister of Organisation, 1968-77; Minister of Marine and Air Services, 1977-80. Attached to UK negotiating team for Bermuda II Civil Aviation agreement, 1977. Chm. Bd of Governors, Warwick Academy, 1946-73; Life Vice-Pres. Bermuda Olympic Assoc. and Bermuda Football Assoc. Recreations: golf, sports administration. Address: Chiswick, Paget, Bermuda. Clubs: Carlton; Royal Hamilton Dinghy and Mid-Ocean (Bermuda).

PLOWRIGHT, David Ernest; Managing Director, Granada Television Ltd, since 1981 (Joint Managing Director, 1975-81); Director: Granada International, since 1975; Granada Group, since 1981; Independent Television News, since 1981; b 11 Dec. 1930; s of William Ernest Plowright and Daisy Margaret Plowright; m 1953, Brenda Mary (née Key); one s two d. Educ: Scunthorpe Grammar Sch.; on local weekly newspaper and during National Service, Germany. Reporter, Scunthorpe Star, 1950; freelance corresp. and sports writer, 1952; Reporter, Feature Writer and briefly Equestrian Corresp., Yorkshire Post, 1954; Granada Television: News Editor, 1957; Producer, Current Affairs, 1960; Exec. Prod., Scene at 6.30, 1964; Exec. Prod., World in Action, 1966; Head of Current Affairs, 1968; Dir, 1968; Controller of Programmes, 1969-79. Chm., Network Programme Cttee, ITV, 1980-82. Dir, Independent Television Cos Assoc., 1976-. Governor, Nat. Film Sch., 1981-. Recreations: television, theatre, watching sport and messing about in a boat. Address: Granada TV Ltd, Manchester M60 9EA. T: 061-832 7211; Granada TV, 36 Golden Square, W1. T: 01-734 8080.
See also J. A. Plowright.

PLOWRIGHT, Joan Ann, (The Lady Olivier), CBE 1970; Leading actress with the National Theatre, 1963-74; Member of the RADA Council; b 28 Oct. 1929; d of William Ernest Plowright and Daisy Margaret (née Burton); m 1st, 1953, Roger Gage (marr. diss.); 2nd, 1961, (as Sir Laurence Olivier) Baron Olivier, qv; one s two d. Educ: Scunthorpe Grammar School; Laban Art of Movement Studio; Old Vic Theatre School. First stage appearance in If Four Walls Told, Croydon Rep. Theatre, 1948; Bristol Old Vic and Mem. Old Vic Co., S Africa tour, 1952; first London appearance in The Duenna, Westminster, 1954; Moby Dick, Duke of York's, 1955; season of leading parts, Nottingham Playhouse, 1955-56; English Stage Co., Royal Court, 1956; The Crucible, Don Juan, The Death of Satan, Cards of Identity, The Good Woman of Setzuan, The Country Wife (transferred to Adelphi, 1957); The Chairs, The Making of Moo, Royal Court, 1957; The Entertainer, Palace, 1957; The Chairs, The Lesson, Phoenix, NY, 1958; The Entertainer, Royale, NY, 1958; The Chairs, The Lesson, Major Barbara, Royal Court, 1958; Hook, Line and Sinker, Piccadilly, 1958; Roots, Royal Court, Duke of York's, 1959; Rhinoceros, Royal Court, 1960; A Taste of Honey, Lyceum, NY, 1960 (Best Actress Tony Award); Rosmersholm, Greenwich, 1973; Saturday, Sunday, Monday, Queen's, 1974-75; The Sea Gull, Lyric, 1975; The Bed Before Yesterday, Lyric, 1975 (Variety Club of GB Award, 1977); Filumena, Lyric, 1977 (Soc. of West End Theatre Award, 1978); Enjoy, Vaudeville, 1980; Chichester Festival: Uncle Vanya, The Chances, 1962; St Joan (Best Actress Evening Standard Award), Uncle Vanya, 1963; The Doctor's Dilemma, The Taming of the Shrew, 1972; Cavell, 1982; National Theatre: St Joan, Uncle Vanya, Hobson's Choice, opening season, 1963; The Master Builder, 1964; Much Ado About Nothing, 1967, 1968; Three Sisters, 1967, 1968; Tartuffe, 1967, 1968; The Advertisement, 1968; Love's Labour's Lost, 1968; The Merchant of Venice, 1970; A Woman Killed with Kindness, 1971; The Rules of the Game, 1971; Eden End, 1974. Directed, Rites, 1969; produced, The Travails of Sancho Panza, 1969. Films include: Moby Dick, The Entertainer, Three Sisters, The Merchant of Venice, Equus, Britannia Hospital, Brimstone and Treacle, Wagner, A Dedicated Man. Appears on TV; Daphne Laureola, 1976. Recreations: reading, music, entertaining. Address: c/o LOP Ltd, 33-34 Chancery Lane, WC2A 1EN. T: 01-836 7932.
See also D. E. Plowright.

PLOWRIGHT, Walter, CMG 1974; DVSc; FRCVS 1977; FRS 1981; Head of Department of Microbiology, Institute for Research on Animal Diseases, Compton, Berks, since 1978; b 20 July 1923; 2nd s of Jonathan and Mahala Plowright, Holbeach, Lincs; m 1959, Dorothy Joy (née Bell). Educ: Moulton and Spalding Grammar Schs; Royal Veterinary Coll., London. MRCVS 1944; DVSc (Pret.) 1964. Commissioned, RAVC, 1945-48; Colonial Service, 1950-64; Animal Virus Research Inst., Pirbright, 1964-71 (seconded E Africa, 1966-71); Prof. of Vet. Microbiology, RVC, 1971-78. J. T. Edwards Memorial Prize, 1964; R. B. Bennett Commonwealth Prize of RSA, 1972; Bledisloe Vet. Award, RASE, 1979. Publications: numerous contribs to scientific jls relating to virus diseases of animals. Recreations: gardening, travel. Address: Whitehill Lodge, Goring-on-Thames, Reading RG8 0LL. T: Goring 872891.

PLUM, Patrick; see McConville, M. A.

PLUMB, Sir (Charles) Henry, Kt 1973; DL; Member (C) The Cotswolds, European Parliament, since 1979 (Chairman, Agricultural Committee, 1979-82; Leader, European Democratic Group, since 1982); b 27 March 1925; s of Charles and Louise Plumb; m 1947, Marjorie Dorothy Dunn; one s two d. Educ: King Edward VI School, Nuneaton. National Farmers Union: Member Council, 1959; Vice-President, 1964, 1965; Deputy-President, 1966, 1967, 1968, 1969; President, 1970-79. Chm., British Agricl Council, 1975-79. Mem., Duke of Northumberland's Cttee of Enquiry on Foot and Mouth Disease, 1967-68; Pres., Warwickshire County Fedn of Young Farmers' Clubs, 1974- (Pres., Nat. Fedn of YFC); Member: Council, CBI; Council, Animal Health Trust; Liveryman, Farmers' Co.; Pres., Royal Agric. Soc. of England, 1977, Dep. Pres. 1978; Pres., Internat. Fedn of Agricl Producers, 1979-82; Hon. Pres., Ayrshire Cattle Soc.; Past Pres., Comité des Organisations Professionels Agricoles de la CEE (COPA). Director: United Biscuits Ltd; Lloyds Bank Ltd; Fisons Ltd. FRSA 1970; FRAgS 1974. DL Warwick 1977. Recreations: shooting, tennis, fishing. Address: Southfields Farm, Coleshill, Birmingham B46 3EJ. T: Coleshill 63133; 2 Queen Anne's Gate, SW1. T: 01-222 1720; 01-222 0411. Clubs: Farmers'; Coleshill Rotary (Hon. Member).

PLUMB, Sir Henry; see Plumb, Sir C. H.

PLUMB, Sir John (Harold), Kt 1982; FBA 1968; historian; Master of Christ's College, Cambridge, 1978-82; Professor of Modern English History, University of Cambridge, 1966-74; b 20 Aug. 1911; 3rd s of late James Plumb, Leicester. Educ: Alderman Newton's Sch., Leicester; University Coll., Leicester; Christ's Coll., Cambridge. BA London, 1st Class Hons History, 1933; PhD Cambridge, 1936; LittD Cambridge, 1957. Ehrman Research Fellow, King's Coll., Cambridge, 1939-46; FO, 1940-45; Fellow of Christ's Coll., 1946-, Steward, 1948-50, Tutor, 1950-59. Vice-Master, 1964-68. Univ. Lectr in History, 1946-62; Reader in Modern English History, 1962-65; Chm. of History Faculty, 1966-68, Univ. of Cambridge. Trustee of National Portrait Gallery, 1961-; Syndic of the Fitzwilliam Museum, 1960-77; Member: Wine Standards Bd, 1973-75; Council, British Acad., 1977-80; Chm., Centre of E Anglian Studies, 1979-82. FRHistS; FSA; FRSL 1969. Visiting Prof., Columbia Univ., 1960; Distinguished Vis. Prof., NYC Univ., 1971-72, 1976; Cecil and Ida Green Honors Chair, Texas Christian Univ., 1974; Dist. Vis. Prof., Washington Univ., 1977; Lectures: Ford's, Oxford Univ., 1965-66; Saposnekov, City College, NY, 1968; Guy Stanton Ford, Univ. of Minnesota, 1969; Stenton, Reading, 1972; George Rogers Clark, Soc. of the Cincinnati, 1977. Hon. For. Mem., Amer. Acad. for Arts and Sciences, 1970; Hon. Member: Soc. of Amer. Historians, 1976; Amer. Historical Assoc., 1981. Hon. DLitt: Leicester, 1968; East Anglia, 1973; Bowdoin Coll., 1974; S California, 1978; Westminster Coll., 1982. Editor, History of Human Society, 1959-; Sen. Editor to American Heritage Co. Historical Adviser, Penguin Books, 1960-; Editor, Pelican Social History of Britain, 1982-. Publications: England in the Eighteenth Century, 1950; West African Explorers (with C. Howard), 1952; Chatham, 1953; (ed) Studies in Social History, 1955; Sir Robert Walpole, Vol. I, 1956, Vol. II, 1960, both vols repr. 1972; The First Four Georges, 1956; The Renaissance, 1961; Men and Places, 1962; Crisis in the Humanities, 1964; The Growth of Political Stability in England, 1675-1725, 1967; Death of the Past, 1969; In the Light of History, 1972; The Commercialisation of Leisure, 1974; Royal Heritage, 1977; New Light on the Tyrant, George III, 1978; Georgian Delights, 1980; Royal Heritage: The Reign of Elizabeth II, 1980; contrib. to: Man versus Society in Eighteenth Century Britain, 1968; Churchill Revisited, 1969 (Churchill, the historian); Festschrift: Historical Perspectives: Essays in Honour of J. H. Plumb, 1974. Address: Christ's College, Cambridge. T: Cambridge 67641; The Old Rectory, Westhorpe, Stowmarket, Suffolk. T: Bacton 781235. Clubs: Brooks's, Beefsteak.

PLUMLEY, Rev. Prof. Jack Martin; Herbert Thompson Professor of Egyptology, University of Cambridge, 1957-77; b 2 Sept. 1910; e s of Arthur Henry Plumley and Lily Plumley (née Martin); m 1938, Gwendolen Alice Darling; three s. Educ: Merchant Taylors' Sch., London; St John's Coll., Durham (BA, Univ. Hebrew Schol., MLitt); King's Coll., Cambridge (MA). Deacon 1933; Priest 1934; Curacies, 1933-41; Vicar of Christ Church, Hoxton, 1942-45, of St Paul's, Tottenham, 1945-47; Rector and Vicar of All Saints', Milton, Cambridge, 1948-57. Associate Lectr in Coptic, Univ. of Cambridge, 1949-57; Fellow Selwyn Coll., 1957. Mem. Council of Senate, Cambridge, 1965-70. Dir of excavations on behalf of Egypt Exploration Soc. at Qasr Ibrim, Nubia, 1963, 1964, 1966, 1969, 1972, 1974, 1976; Chm., British Cttee of Internat. Critical Greek New Testament Project, 1963-. Pres., Internat. Soc. for Nubian Studies, 1978-. FSA 1966; Fellow, Inst. of Coptic Studies, United Egyptian Repub., 1966; Corresp. Mem., German Inst. of Archaeology, 1966. Recreations: music, rowing, photography, travel. Address: Selwyn College, Cambridge; 13 Lyndewode Road, Cambridge. T: Cambridge 350328.

PLUMMER, family name of Baron Plummer of St Marylebone.

PLUMMER OF ST MARYLEBONE, Baron cr 1981 (Life Peer), of the City of Westminster; **(Arthur) Desmond (Herne) Plummer;** Kt 1971; TD

1950; JP; DL; Chairman, Horserace Betting Levy Board, 1974-82; *b* 25 May 1914; *s* of late Arthur Herne Plummer and Janet (*née* McCormick); *m* 1941, Pat Holloway (Pres., Cons. Women's Adv. Cttee, Greater London Area, 1967-71); one *d. Educ:* Hurstpierpoint Coll.; Coll. of Estate Management. Served 1939-46, Royal Engineers. Member: TA Sports Bd, 1953-79; London Electricity Consultative Council, 1955-66; St Marylebone Borough Council, 1952-65 (Mayor, 1958-59); LCC, for St Marylebone, 1960-65; Inner London Educn Authority, 1964-76. Greater London Council: Mem. for Cities of London and Westminster, 1964-73, for St Marylebone 1973-76; Leader of Opposition, 1966-67 and 1973-74; Leader of Council, 1967-73. Member: South Bank Theatre Board, 1967-74; Standing Conf. on SE Planning, 1967-74; Transport Co-ordinating Council for London, 1967-69; Local Authorities Conditions of Service Adv. Bd, 1967-71; Exec. Cttee, British Section of Internat. Union of Local Authorities, 1967-74; St John Council for London, 1971-; Exec. Cttee, Nat. Union Cons. and Unionist Assocs, 1967-76; Chm., St Marylebone Conservative Assoc., 1965-66. Director: Portman Building Soc. (Vice-Chm., 1979-82; Chm., 1983-); Nat. Employers' Mutual Gen. Insurance Assoc. (Dep. Chm., 1973-); Nat. Employers' Life Assurance Assoc. Member of Lloyd's. Mem. Court, Univ. of London, 1967-77. Chairman: Epsom and Walton Downs Trng Grounds Man. Bd, 1974-82; National Stud, 1975-82; President: London Anglers' Assoc., 1976-; Thames Angling Preservation Soc., 1970-. Liveryman, Worshipful Co. of Tin Plateworkers. FAI 1948; FRICS 1970; FRSA 1974; Hon. FFAS 1966. JP, Co. London, 1958; DL Greater London, 1970. Comdr (Brother) OStJ 1980. *Publications:* Time for Change in Greater London, 1966; Report to London, 1970; Planning and Participation, 1973. *Recreations:* swimming (Capt. Otter Swimming Club, 1952-53); growing things, relaxing. *Address:* 4 The Lane, St Johns Wood, NW8 0PN. *Clubs:* Royal Automobile, MCC.

PLUMMER, (Arthur) Christopher (Orme), CC (Canada) 1968; actor; *b* Toronto, 13 Dec. 1929; *m* 1st, 1956, Tammy Lee Grimes; one *d* ; 2nd, 1962, Patricia Audrey Lewis (marr. diss. 1966); 3rd, 1970, Elaine Regina Taylor. *Educ:* public and private schs, Montreal. French and English radio, Canada, 1949-52; Ottawa Rep. Theatre; Broadway: Starcross Story, 1951-52; Home is the Hero, 1953; The Dark is Light Enough, 1954 (Theatre World Award); The Lark, 1955; J. B., 1958 (Tony nomination); Arturo Ui, 1963; Royal Hunt of the Sun, 1965-66; Stratford, Conn, 1955: Mark Antony, Ferdinand; leading actor, Stratford Festival, Canada, 1956-67: Henry V, The Bastard, Hamlet, Leontes, Mercutio, Macbeth, Cyrano de Bergerac, Benedic, Aguecheek, Antony; Royal Shakespeare Co., Stratford-on-Avon, 1961-62: Benedic, Richard III; London debut as Henry II in Becket, Aldwych and Globe, 1961 (Evening Standard Best Actor Award, 1961); National Theatre, 1971-72: Amphytrion 38, Danton's Death; Broadway musical, Cyrano, 1973 (Outer Critics Circle Award, Best Actor in a Musical); The Good Doctor, NY, 1974; Othello, NY, 1982. *Films:* Stage-Struck, 1956; Across the Everglades, 1957; The Fall of the Roman Empire, 1963; The Sound of Music, 1964; Daisy Clover, 1964; Triple Cross, 1966; Oedipus Rex, 1967; The Battle of Britain, 1968; Royal Hunt of the Sun, 1969; The Pyx, 1973; The Man Who Would Be King, 1975; Aces High, 1976; International Velvet, 1978; The Silent Partner, 1978; Hanover Street, 1979; Murder by Decree, 1980; The Disappearance, 1981; The Janitor, 1981. TV appearances, Britain, Denmark, and major N American networks, incl. Hamlet at Elsinore, BBC and Danish TV, 1964 (4 Emmy Award nominations). *Recreations:* tennis, ski-ing, piano. *Clubs:* Hurlingham; Players (New York).

PLUMMER, Christopher; see Plummer, A. C. O.

PLUMMER, Maj.-Gen. Leo Heathcote, CBE 1974; retired 1979; *b* 11 June 1923; *s* of Lt-Col Edmund Waller Plummer and Mary Dorothy Brookesmith; *m* 1955, Judyth Ann Dolby; three *d. Educ:* Canford Sch.; Queens' Coll., Cambridge. Commnd RA, 1943; War Service, N Africa, Sicily, Italy, 1943-45 (mentioned in despatches, 1945); Adjt, TA, 1947-49; Staff Coll., Camberley, 1952, Directing Staff, 1961-63; Comdt, Sudan Staff Coll., 1963-65; CO, 20 Heavy Regt, 1965-67; Col, Gen. Staff, MoD, 1967; Brig., 1967; Comdr, 1st Artillery Bde, 1967-70; Dep. Dir Manning (Army), 1971-74; Asst Chief of Staff Ops, HQ Northern Army Gp, 1974-76; Chief, Jt Service Liaison Orgn, Bonn, 1976-78. ADC to HM The Queen, 1974-76; Col Comdt, RA, 1981-. *Recreation:* gardening. *Address:* Winchelsea Farmhouse, Hastings Road, Winchelsea, East Sussex TN36 4AD. *T:* Rye 226669. *Club:* Army and Navy.

PLUMMER, Peter Edward; Deputy Director, Department for National Savings, 1972-79; *b* 4 Nov. 1919; *s* of Arthur William John and Ethel May Plummer; *m* 1949, Pauline Wheelwright; one *s* one *d. Educ:* Watford Grammar Sch. Served War, REME, 1941-46. Customs and Excise, 1936-38; Dept for National Savings, 1938-79; Principal, 1956; Assistant Sec., 1964; seconded to Nat. Giro, 1970-71; Under-Sec., 1972. *Recreations:* gardening, photography. *Address:* Old Timbers, Farm Lane, Nutbourne, Chichester, W Sussex. *T:* Emsworth 77450.

PLUMPTON, Alan, CBE 1980; BSc, CEng, FIEE; FCIBS; CBIM; FRSA; Deputy Chairman, Electricity Council, since 1981; *b* 24 Nov. 1926; *s* of late John Plumpton and of Doris Plumpton; *m* 1950, Audrey Smith; one *s* one *d. Educ:* Sunderland Technical Sch.; Durham Univ. (BSc Elec. Eng). Pupil Engr, Sunderland Corp. Elec. Undertaking, 1942; various engrg and commercial appts, NEEB, 1948-61; Dist Manager, E Monmouthshire Dist, S Wales Electricity Bd, 1961-64. Admin. Staff Coll., Henley, 1963; Dep. Chief Commercial Engr, S Wales Elec. Bd, 1964-67; Chief Commercial Engr, S

Wales Elec. Bd, 1967-72; Dep. Chm., London Elec. Bd, 1972-76, Chm., 1976-81. Liveryman, Gardeners' Co. JP Mon, 1971-72. *Recreations:* golf, gardening. *Address:* Lockhill, Stubbs Wood, Amersham, Bucks HP6 6EX. *T:* Amersham 3791. *Club:* Harewood Downs Golf.

PLUMPTRE, family name of Baron Fitzwalter.

PLUMTREE, Air Vice-Marshal Eric, CB 1974; OBE 1946; DFC 1940; Co-ordinator of Anglo-American Relations, Ministry of Defence (Air), since 1977; *b* 9 March 1919; *s* of William Plumtree, Plumbley Farm, Mosborough, Derbys, and Minnie Plumtree (*née* Wheatley); *m* 1942, Dorothy Patricia (*née* Lyall); two *s* (and one *s* decd). *Educ:* Eckington Grammar Sch. Served War of 1939-45: No 53 Army Co-op. Sqdn, 1940-41; No 241 FR Sqdn, 1942; OC No 169 FR Sqdn, 1943; Chief Instr, No 41, OTU, 1944; HQ, Fighter Command, 1945; Staff Coll., Haifa, 1946; Personal Staff Officer to C-in-C, MEAF, 1947-49; OC, No 54 (F) Sqdn, 1949-52; PSO to Chief of Air Staff, 1953-56; OC Flying Wing, Oldenburg, 1957-58; OC, Admin. Wing, Jever, 1958; JSSC, Latimer, 1959; OC, RAF Leuchars, 1959-61; Dep. Dir, Joint Planning Staff, 1962-63; IDC, 1964; Air Adviser to UK High Comr and Head of BDLS (Air), Ottawa, 1965-67; Air Cdre 1966; Dir, Air Plans, MoD (Air), 1968-69; AOC 22 Group RAF, 1970-71; Air Vice-Marshal 1971; Comdr, Southern Maritime Air Region, 1971-73; Economy Project Officer (RAF), MoD, 1973-74. Mem. Council, Ardingly Coll., 1976-. *Recreations:* gardening, most sports. *Address:* Wings Cottage, Ditchling, Sussex. *T:* Hassocks 5539. *Club:* Royal Air Force.

PLUNKET, family name of Baron Plunket.

PLUNKET, 8th Baron *cr* 1827; **Robin Rathmore Plunket;** *b* 3 Dec. 1925; *s* of 6th Baron Plunket (*d* 1938) and Dorothé Mabel (*d* 1938), *d* of late Joseph Lewis and widow of Captain Jack Barnato, RAF; *S* brother, 1975; *m* 1951, Jennifer, *d* of late Bailey Southwell, Olivenhoutpoort, S Africa. *Educ:* Eton. Formerly Captain, Rifle Brigade. *Heir:* *b* Hon. Shaun Albert Frederick Sheridan Plunket [*b* 5 April 1931; *m* 1961, Judith Ann, *e d* of late G. P. Power; one *s* one *d* ; *m* 1980, Mrs Elizabeth de Sancha]. *Address:* Rathmore, Melsetter, Zimbabwe; 39 Lansdowne Gardens, SW8.

PLUNKET GREENE, Mary, (Mrs Alexander Plunket Greene); see Quant, Mary.

PLUNKETT, family name of Baron Dunsany, of Earl of Fingall, and of Baron Louth.

PLUNKETT, Brig. James Joseph, CBE 1945; Colonel Commandant, Royal Army Veterinary Corps, 1953-59; *b* 1893; *m* 1951, Mrs Rachel Kelly, *d* of Eustace H. Bent, Lelant, Cornwall. *Educ:* Royal Dick Veterinary College. Commissioned, 1914; continuous military service. Director Army Veterinary and Remount Services, 1947-51; retired pay, 1951. *Recreation:* hunting. *Address:* Templeshanbo, near Enniscorthy, Co. Wexford, Eire. *Club:* Naval and Military.

PLUNKETT, William Joseph; Valuer and Estates Surveyor, Greater London Council, 1977-81; *b* 8 Nov. 1921; *s* of John Joseph Archer and Marjorie Martin Plunkett; *m* 1949, Gwendoline Innes Barron; two *s* five *d. Educ:* Finchley Catholic Grammar Sch.; Coll. of Estate Management. BSc(Est. Man.). FRICS. RN, 1941-46; commnd, 1942; Lt RNVR. Dep. County Valuer, Middlesex CC, 1962-65; Asst Valuer, Valuation and Estates Dept, GLC, 1965-73; Dep. Valuer and Estates Surveyor, GLC, 1973-74; Dir of Valuation and Estates Dept, GLC, 1974-77. Mem., South Bank Polytechnic Adv. Cttee on Estate Management, 1973-76; Chm., Covent Garden Officers' Steering Gp, 1977-81. Mem. General Council, RICS, 1978-80 (Pres. Planning and Develt Div., 1978-79; Chm., S London Br. Cttee, 1976-77); Pres., Assoc. of Local Authority Valuers and Estate Surveyors, 1980-81. *Publications:* articles on Compensation, Valuation and Development. *Address:* 105 Ember Lane, Esher, Surrey KT10 8EQ. *T:* 01-398 6097.

PLYMOUTH, 3rd Earl of, *cr* 1905; **Other Robert Ivor Windsor-Clive;** Viscount Windsor (UK 1905); 15th Baron Windsor (England, *cr* 1529); DL; FRSA 1953; Chairman, Reviewing Committee on Export of Works of Art, since 1982; *b* 9 October 1923; *e s* of 2nd Earl and Lady Irene Charteris, *d* of 11th Earl of Wemyss; *S* father, 1943; *m* 1950, Caroline Helen, *o d* of Edward Rice, Dane Court, Eastry, Kent; three *s* one *d. Educ:* Eton. Mem., Museums and Galls Commn (formerly Standing Commn on Museums and Galls), 1972-. DL County of Salop, 1961. *Heir:* *s* Viscount Windsor, *qv. Address:* Oakly Park, Ludlow, Salop.
See also Dr Alan Glyn.

PLYMOUTH, Bishop of, (RC), since 1955; **Rt. Rev. Cyril Edward Restieaux;** *b* 25 Feb. 1910; *s* of Joseph and Edith Restieaux. *Educ:* English Coll., Rome; Gregorian University. Ordained, 1932; Curate at Nottingham, 1933; Parish Priest at Matlock, 1936; Hon. Canon of Nottingham, 1948; Vicar-General of Nottingham, 1951; Provost and Domestic Prelate to HH Pope Pius XII, 1955. *Address:* Vescourt, Hartley Road, Plymouth PL3 5LR.

PLYMOUTH, Bishop Suffragan of, since 1982; **Rt. Rev. Kenneth Albert Newing;** *b* 29 Aug. 1923; *s* of Albert James Pittock Newing and Nellie Louise Maude Newing; unmarried. *Educ:* Dover Grammar School; Selwyn College,

Cambridge (MA); Theological College, Mirfield, Yorks. Assistant Curate, Plymstock, 1955-63; Rector of Plympton S Maurice, Plymouth, 1963-82; Archdeacon of Plymouth, 1978-82. *Address:* c/o Diocesan House, Palace Gate, Exeter, Devon EX1 1HX.

PLYMOUTH, Archdeacon of; *see* Ellis, Ven. R. G.

POANANGA, Maj.-Gen. Brian Matauru, CB 1980; CBE 1977 (OBE 1967; MBE 1962); Chief of General Staff, New Zealand Army, 1978-81, retired; *b* 2 Dec. 1924; *s* of Henare and Atareta Poananga; *m* 1949, Doreen Mary Porter (formerly QAIMNS/R); two *s* one *d. Educ:* Royal Military College, Duntroon, Australia. Graduated RMC, 1946; served BCOF, Japan, 1947-48; Commonwealth Div., Korea, 1952-53; Staff Coll., Camberley, 1957; 28 Commonwealth Inf. Bde, Malaya, 1959-61; Jt Services Staff Coll., Latimer, 1964; CO 1RNZIR, Malaysia, 1965-67; Dir of Army Training, 1968-69; Dir of Services Intelligence, 1969-70; Comdr Army Training Gp, 1970-72; RCDS, 1973; Comdr 1st (NZ) Inf. Bde Gp, 1974; NZ High Commissioner to Papua New Guinea, 1974-76; Deputy Chief of General Staff, 1977-78. *Recreations:* golf and fishing. *Address:* PO Box 397, Taupo, New Zealand. *T:* Taupo 48296. *Club:* Taupo (NZ).

POCHIN, Sir Edward (Eric), Kt 1975; CBE 1959; MA, MD, FRCP; *b* 22 Sept. 1909; *s* of Charles Davenport Pochin; *m* 1940, Constance Margaret Julia (*d* 1971), *d* of T. H. Tilly; one *s* one *d. Educ:* Repton; St John's Coll., Cambridge. Natural Science Tripos, Part I, 1st 1930, Part II (Physiology) 1st, 1931; Michael Foster Student, Strathcona Student, 1931-32; MA 1935; Gifford-Edmunds Prize, 1940; MD 1945; FRCP 1946. Mem. of Scientific Staff of MRC, 1941; Dir, Dept of Clinical Research, UCH Med. Sch., 1946-74. Horton Smith Prize, 1945; Antoine Béclère Lectr, 1979. Mem., International Commn on Radiological Protection, 1959, Chm., 1962-69, Emeritus Mem., 1977; Member: Nat. Radiological Protection Bd, 1971-82; WHO Expert Adv. Panel on Radiation; Physiological Soc., Assoc. of Physicians, Internat. Radiation Protection Assoc.; British Inst. of Radiology; Medical Research Soc.; Hon. Fellow: Royal Coll. of Radiologists; Hon. Member: British Radiological Protection Assoc.; Nippon Soc. Radiologica; British Nuclear Med. Soc.; Hospital Physicists' Assoc.; Amer. Thyroid Assoc. UK Representative, UN Scientific Cttee on Effects of Atomic Radiation, 1956-82. *Publications:* articles on thyroid disease, radiation protection and risk estimation in scientific journals. *Recreations:* trivial painting, fell walking. *Address:* c/o National Radiological Protection Board, Chilton, Didcot, Oxon. *Clubs:* Athenæum, Oriental.

POCOCK, Air Vice-Marshal Donald Arthur, CBE 1975 (OBE 1957); Director, British Metallurgical Plant Constructors Association, since 1980; *b* 5 July 1920; *s* of late A. Pocock and of E. Broad; *m* 1947, Dorothy Monica Griffiths; two *s* three *d. Educ:* Crouch End. Served War of 1939-45: commissioned, 1941; Middle East, 1941-48. Transport Command, 1948-50; commanded RAF Regt Sqdn, 1950-52; Staff Coll., 1953; Staff Officer, HQ 2nd Allied TAF, 1954-57; comd RAF Regt Wing, 1957-58; MoD, 1958-59; HQ Allied Air Forces Central Europe, 1959-62; Sen. Ground Defence SO, NEAF, 1962-63; MoD, 1963-66; Sen. Ground Defence SO, FEAF, 1966-68; ADC to the Queen, 1967; Commandant, RAF Catterick, 1968-69; Dir of Ground Defence, 1970-73; Comdt-Gen. RAF Regt, 1973-75. Gen. Man., Iran, British Aerospace Dynamics Gp, 1976-79. *Recreations:* shooting, equitation. *Address:* Brincliffe, Dence Park, Herne Bay, Kent. *T:* Herne Bay 4773. *Club:* Royal Air Force.

POCOCK, Gordon James; Chief Executive, Business Products and Systems, British Telecommunications, since 1981; *b* 27 March 1933; *s* of Leslie Pocock and Elizabeth Maud Pocock; *m* 1959, Audrey Singleton. *Educ:* Royal Liberty Sch., Romford; Keble Coll., Oxford. Joined PO, 1954; Private Sec. to Dir Gen., 1958-59; Principal, 1960-68; Asst Sec., 1968-72; Dep. Dir, 1972-76; Director: Ext. Telecommns, 1976-79; Telecommns Marketing, 1979, Sen. Dir, 1979-81. *Publications:* Corneille and Racine, 1973; Boileau and the Nature of Neo-Classicism, 1980. *Recreations:* travel, theatre, local history. *Address:* 29 Old Palace Lane, Richmond, Surrey TW9 1PQ. *T:* 01-940 7118.

POCOCK, Hugh Shellshear; formerly: Director, Associated Iliffe Press Ltd; Chairman of Iliffe Electrical Publications Ltd; Managing Editor, The Electrical Review; (formerly Editor) of The Wireless World; retired Dec. 1962; *b* 6 May 1894; 3rd *s* of late Lexden Lewis Pocock, artist; *m* 1920, Mayda, *d* of late Serab Sévian. *Educ:* Privately. Served European War, 1914-18: commissioned RE, 1915; served in Egypt, Mesopotamia, Persia, on wireless and intelligence work with rank of Capt. (despatches). Assisted in organisation of first short wave amateur transatlantic tests, 1921-22; organised first transatlantic broadcasting trials, 1923; proposed Empire Broadcasting on short wave in 1926, and urged its adoption in face of BBC opposition. Promoted and organised the National Wireless Register of technical personnel 1938, under Service auspices; CEng, FIEE; Life Senior Member of the Institute of Electrical and Electronics Engineers. Hon. Mem., British Record Soc.; Member of Honour, Union Internationale de la Presse Radiotechnique et Electronique. *Publications:* numerous articles relating to radio and electrical progress, technical and general. *Recreations:* genealogy and local history research. *Address:* 103 Boydell Court, St Johns Wood, NW8 6NH. *Clubs:* 25, Dynamicables.

POCOCK, Kenneth Walter; *b* 20 June 1913; *s* of Walter Dunsdon Pocock and Emily Marion Pocock; *m* 1939, Anne Tidmarsh; one *s* one *d. Educ:*

Canford School. United Dairies (London) Ltd, 1930; Armed Forces, 1942-46; Man. Dir, Edinburgh and Dumfriesshire Dairy Co. Ltd, 1946; Dir, United Dairies Ltd, 1948; Pres., Scottish Milk Trade Fedn, 1956-59; Dir, Unigate Ltd, 1959; Man. Dir, Unigate Ltd and United Dairies Ltd, 1963; Chm. of Milk Div., Unigate Ltd, 1968; Dep. Chm., Unigate Ltd, 1970-82; Pres., Unigate Long Service Corps (40 years), 1971-. Governor, Nat. Dairymen's Benevolent Instn (Chm., 1977-81). *Recreations:* motoring, shooting, photography, gardening. *Address:* Cedar Lodge, Marsham Lane, Gerrards Cross, Bucks SL9 8HD. *T:* Gerrards Cross 89278.

POCOCK, Leslie Frederick; Chairman, Liverpool Health Authority, since 1982; *b* 22 June 1918; *s* of Frederick Pocock and Alice Helena Pocock; *m* 1946, Eileen Horton; two *s. Educ:* Emanuel School. FCCA. Chief Accountant: London & Lancashire Insurance Co. Ltd, 1959; Royal Insurance Co. Ltd, 1966; Chief Accountant and Taxation Manager, 1971, Dep. Gp Comptroller, 1974, Royal Insurance Gp; retired 1981. *Recreations:* countryside, golf. *Address:* Farnley, Croft Drive West, Caldy, Wirral, Merseyside. *T:* 051-625 5320. *Club:* Royal Commonwealth Society.

POCOCK, Most Rev. Philip F., LLD; retired 1978. *Educ:* Univ. of Western Ontario; St Peter's Seminary, London, Can.; Catholic University of America, Washington, DC; Angelicum University, Rome. Ordination to Priesthood, 1930; Angelicum University, Rome, JCD, 1934; Professor of Moral Theology, St Peter's Seminary, 1934; consecrated Bishop of Saskatoon, 1944; Apostolic Administrator of Winnipeg, June 1951; Titular Archbishop of Apro and Coadjutor Archbishop of Winnipeg, Aug. 1951; Archbishop of Winnipeg, 1952-61; Coadjutor Archbishop of Toronto, 1961-71; Archbishop of Toronto, 1971-78. Hon. LLD: Univ. of Western Ontario, 1955; Univ. of Ottawa, 1958; Univ. of Manitoba, 1958; Assumption Univ. of Windsor, 1961; St Francis Xavier Univ., Antigonish, 1963; Hon. DD: Huron Coll., London, Ont., 1967. *Address:* 3 Woodbrook Drive, Brampton, Ont L6W 3P2, Canada.

PODDAR, Prof. Ramendra Kumar, PhD; Vice-Chancellor, Calcutta University, since 1979; *b* 9 Nov. 1930; *m* 1955, Srimati Jharna Poddar; two *s* one *d. Educ:* Univ. of Calcutta (BSc Hons Physics, MSc Physics; PhD Biophysics); Associateship Dip., Saha Inst. of Nuclear Physics. Progressively, Research Asst, Lecturer, Reader, Associate Prof., Biophysics Div., Saha Inst. of Nuclear Physics, 1953-73; Calcutta University: Prof. of Biophysics, 1973-77; Pro-Vice-Chancellor (A), 1977-79. Research experience in Univ. of California, USA, 1958-60, Purdue Univ., 1960-61, California Inst. of Technology, 1970. *Publications:* research papers in jls of internat. repute, contribs to congresses/symposia and to all-India seminars/symposia, in the fields of biophysics, incl. molecular biology and photobiology. *Address:* Senate House, University of Calcutta, Calcutta 700 073, India. *T:* 34-3467.

PODMORE, Ian Laing; Chief Executive, Sheffield City Council, since 1974; *b* 6 Oct. 1933; *s* of Harry Samuel Podmore and Annie Marion (*née* Laing); *m* 1961, Kathleen Margaret (*née* Langton); one *s* one *d. Educ:* Birkenhead School. Admitted Solicitor 1960. Asst Solicitor, Wallasey County Borough, 1960-63; Sen. Asst Solicitor, Southport Co. Borough, 1963-66; Deputy Town Clerk: Southport, 1966-70; Sheffield, 1970-74. *Recreations:* golf, gardening, watching football. *Address:* Town Hall, Sheffield S1 2HH. *T:* Sheffield 734000; 55 Devonshire Road, Sheffield S17 3NU. *T:* Sheffield 367654. *Club:* Abbeydale Golf.

POETT, Gen. Sir (Joseph Howard) Nigel, KCB 1959 (CB 1952); DSO and Bar, 1945; idc; psc; *b* 20 Aug. 1907; *s* of late Maj.-General J. H. Poett, CB, CMG, CBE; *m* 1937, Julia, *d* of E. J. Herrick, Hawkes Bay, NZ; two *s* one *d. Educ:* Downside; RMC Sandhurst. 2nd Lieut, DLI, 1927; Operations, NW Frontier, 1930-31; Adjt 2nd Bn DLI, 1934-37; GSO2, 2nd Div., 1940; GSO1, War Office, 1941-42; Comd 11th Bn DLI, 1942-43; Comdr, 5th Parachute Bde, 1943-46; served North-West Europe, 1944-45; Far East, 1945-46; Director of Plans, War Office, 1946-48; idc 1948; Dep.-Commander, British Military Mission, Greece, 1949; Maj.-General, 1951; Chief of Staff, FARELF, 1950-52; GOC 3rd Infantry Division, Middle East Land Forces, 1952-54; Dir of Military Operations, War Office, 1954-56; Commandant, Staff Coll., Camberley, 1957-58; Lt-Gen., 1958; General Officer Commanding-in-Chief, Southern Command, 1958-61; Commander-in-Chief, Far East Land Forces, 1961-63; General, 1962. Colonel, The Durham Light Infantry, 1956-65. Dir, British Productivity Council, 1966-71. Silver Star, USA. *Address:* Swaynes Mead, Great Durnford, Salisbury, Wilts. *Club:* Army and Navy.

PÖHL, Karl Otto; Grosses Verdienstkreuz des Verdienstordens der Bundesrepublik Deutschland; Governor, Deutsche Bundesbank (Vice-Chairman, 1977-79), and German Governor, International Monetary Fund and Bank of International Settlement, since 1980; *b* 1 Dec. 1929; *m* 1974; two *s* two *d. Educ:* Göttingen Univ. (Econs; Diplom.-Volkswirt). Div. Chief for Econ. Res., Munich, 1955-60; econ. journalist, Bonn, 1961-67; Mem. Exec., Fed. Assoc. of German Bank, Cologne, 1968-69; Div. Chief in Fed. Min. of Econs, Bonn, 1970-71; Dept Chief in Fed. Chancellery (Head, Dept for Econ. and Fiscal Policy), Bonn, 1971-72; Sec. of State in Fed. Min. of Finance, resp. for national and internat. monetary policy and basic issues related to fiscal and credit policy, 1972-77; Chairman: EEC Monetary Cttee, 1976-77; Deputies of Gp of Ten, 1978-80. *Publications:* miscellaneous. *Address:* Deutsche Bundesbank, Wilhelm-Epstein-strasse 14, 6000 Frankfurt, Federal Republic of Germany. *T:* Frankfurt 1581.

POITIER, Sidney, KBE (Hon.) 1974; actor, film and stage; director; *b* Miami, Florida, 20 Feb. 1927; *s* of Reginald Poitier and Evelyn (*née* Outten); *m* 1950, Juanita Hardy (marr. diss.); four *d*; *m* 1975, Joanna Shimkus; two *d*. *Educ:* private tutors; Western Senior High Sch., Nassau; Governor's High Sch., Nassau. Served War of 1941-45 with 1267th Medical Detachment, United States Army. Started acting with American Negro Theatre, 1946. *Plays include:* Anna Lucasta, Broadway, 1948; A Raisin in the Sun, Broadway, 1959; *films include:* Cry, the Beloved Country, 1952; Red Ball Express, 1952; Go, Man, Go, 1954; Blackboard Jungle, 1955; Goodbye, My Lady, 1956; Edge of the City, 1957; Band of Angels, 1957; Something of Value, 1957; The Mark of the Hawk, 1958; The Defiant Ones, 1958 (Silver Bear Award, Berlin Film Festival, and New York Critics Award, 1958); Porgy and Bess, 1959; A Raisin in the Sun, 1960; Paris Blues, 1960; Lilies of the Field, 1963 (award for Best Actor of 1963, Motion Picture Academy of Arts and Sciences); The Bedford Incident, 1965; The Slender Thread, 1966; A Patch of Blue, 1966; Duel at Diablo, 1966; To Sir With Love, 1967; In the Heat of the Night, 1967; Guess Who's Coming to Dinner, 1968; For Love of Ivy, 1968; They Call Me Mister Tibbs, 1971; The Organization, 1971; The Wilby Conspiracy, 1975; director and actor: Buck and the Preacher, 1972; A Warm December, 1973; Uptown Saturday Night, 1975; Let's Do It Again, 1976; A Piece of the Action, 1977; *director:* Stir Crazy, 1981; Hanky Panky, 1982. *Publication:* This Life (autobiography), 1980. *Address:* c/o Verdon Productions Ltd, 9350 Wilshire Boulevard, Beverly Hills, Calif 90212, USA.

POLAK, Cornelia Julia, OBE 1964 (MBE 1956); HM Diplomatic Service, retired; *b* 2 Dec. 1908; *d* of late Solomon Polak and late Georgina Polak (*née* Pozner). Foreign Office, 1925-38; Asst Archivist, British Embassy, Paris, 1938-40; Foreign Office, 1940-47; Vice-Consul, Bergen, 1947-49; Consul, Washington, 1949-51; Foreign Office, 1951-55; Consul, Paris, 1955-57; Consul, Brussels, 1957-60; Foreign Office, 1960-63; Head of Treaty and Nationality Department, Foreign Office, 1963-67; Consul General, Geneva, 1967-69, retired; re-employed at FCO, 1969-70. *Address:* 24 Belsize Court, NW3.

POLAND, Rear-Admiral Allan, CBE 1943; DSO 1918; RN, retired; *b* 1888; *s* of William Poland, Blackheath; *m* 1912, Phyllis (*d* 1968), *d* of Dr R. A. Weston, Portsmouth; one *d* (and one *s* lost in HMS Thetis, 1939). Entered Navy, 1903; served in submarines and in command of submarine flotillas, 1910-37; Senior Naval Officer, Persian Gulf, 1937-39; Commodore Commanding East Indies Station, 1938 and 1939; ADC to the King, 1939; Commodore Commanding 9th Cruiser Squadron, 1939-40; Chief of Staff to Commander-in-Chief America and West Indies, 1940-42; Senior British Naval Officer Western Atlantic (Acting Vice-Admiral), 1942; Rear-Admiral, Alexandria, 1942-45; Naval Assistant to Director of Sea Transport, 1945-47. Grand Officer, Order of Humayun (Persia); Kt Comdr Order of Phœnix (Greece). *Address:* 35 Chiltley Way, Liphook, Hants. *T:* Liphook 722359.

POLAND, Rear-Adm. Edmund Nicholas, CB 1967; CBE 1962; Vice-President, Scottish Association for the Care and Resettlement of Offenders, since 1979 (Director, 1975-79); *b* 19 Feb. 1917; 2nd *s* of late Major Raymond A. Poland, RMLI; *m* 1941, Pauline Ruth Margaret Pechell; three *s* one *d* (and one *d* decd). *Educ:* Royal Naval Coll., Dartmouth. Served at sea during Abyssinian and Palestine crises, Spanish Civil War; War of 1939-45: convoy duties, Norwegian waters; Motor Torpedo Boats, Channel and Mediterranean; Torpedo Specialist, 1943; Staff Officer Ops to Naval Force Comdr, Burma; Sqdn T. Officer, HMS Royalist; HMS Hornet, 1946; Flotilla Torpedo and Anti-Submarine Officer of Third Submarine Flotilla, HMS Montclare; Air Warfare Div., Admiralty, 1950; British Naval Staff, Washington, 1953; jssc 1955; Directorate of Tactics and Ship Requirements, Admiralty; comd RN Air Station, Abbotsinch, 1956; Nato Standing Gp, Washington; Director of Under Sea Warfare (Naval), Ministry of Defence, 1962; Chief of Staff to C-in-C Home Fleet, 1965-68; retired. Commander, 1950; Capt., 1956; Rear-Adm., 1965. Vice-Pres., Internat. Prisoners' Aid Assoc., 1978. Chm. (UK), 1979. Pres., Portia Trust, 1979. *Recreations:* golf, fishing, gardening. *Address:* Bryant's Cottage, Burgate Cross, near Fordingbridge, Hants. *Club:* New (Edinburgh).
See also R. D. Poland.

POLAND, Richard Domville, CB 1973; *b* 22 Oct. 1914; *er s* of late Major R. A. Poland, RMLI, and late Mrs F. O. Bayly-Jones; *m* 1948, Rosalind Frances, *y d* of late Surgeon-Captain H. C. Devas; one *s* one *d*. *Educ:* RN Coll., Dartmouth. Traffic Trainee, Imperial Airways, 1932; Traffic Clerk, British Continental Airways and North Eastern Airways, 1934-39. Ops Officer, Air Ministry, Civil Aviation Dept, 1939; Civil Aviation Dept Rep., W Africa, 1942-44; Private Secretary to Minister of Civil Aviation, 1944-48; Principal, 1946; Asst Secretary, 1953; Shipping Attaché, British Embassy, Washington, DC, 1957-60; Under-Secretary: Min. of Transport, 1964-70; DoE, 1970-74. Sec., Internat. Maritime Industry Forum, 1976-78. Chm., Kent Branch, CPRE, 1980. *Address:* Downs House, Blunden Lane, Yalding, Kent ME18 6JD. *T:* Maidstone 814337.
See also Rear-Admiral E. N. Poland.

POLANI, Prof. Paul Emanuel, MD, DCH; FRCP; FRCOG; FRS 1973; Prince Philip Professor of Pædiatric Research in the University of London, 1960-80, now Professor Emeritus; Director of Pædiatric Research Unit, Guy's Hospital Medical School, London, since 1960; Children's Physician and Geneticist to Guy's Hospital; Geneticist, Italian Hospital; Director, SE Thames Regional Genetics Centre, since 1976; *b* 1 Jan. 1914; first *s* of Enrico Polani and Elsa Zennaro; *m* 1944, Nina Ester Sullam; no *c*. *Educ:* Trieste, Siena and Pisa (Italy). MD (Pisa) 1938; MRCP (London) 1948; FRCP (London) 1961; FRCOG 1979. National Birthday Trust Fund Fellow in Pædiatric Research, 1948; Assistant to Director, Dept of Child Health, Guy's Hospital Medical School, 1950; Research Physician on Cerebral Palsy and Director, Medical Research Unit, National Spastic Society, 1955; Consultant to WHO (Regional Office for Europe) on Pregnancy Wastage, 1959; Consultant, Nat. Inst. Neurol. Disease and Blindness, Nat. Insts of Health, USA, 1959-61. Chm., Mutagenesis Cttee, UK, 1975-. Vis. Prof. of Human Genetics and Develt, Columbia Univ., 1977-. *Publications:* chapters in books on human genetics, mental deficiency, psychiatry and pædiatrics; papers on human genetics, cytogenetics, congenital malformations and neurological disorders of children. *Recreations:* reading, riding, ski-ing. *Address:* Little Meadow, West Clandon, Surrey. *T:* Guildford 222436. *Club:* Athenæum.

POLANYI, Prof. John Charles, CC (Canada) 1979 (OC 1974); FRS 1971; FRSC 1966; University Professor, since 1974 and Professor of Chemistry, University of Toronto, since 1962; *b* 23 Jan. 1929; *m* 1958, Anne Ferrar Davidson; one *s* one *d*. *Educ:* Manchester Grammar Sch.; Victoria Univ., Manchester (BSc, PhD, DSc). Research Fellow: Nat. Research Council, Ottawa, 1952-54; Princeton Univ., 1954-56; Univ. of Toronto: Lectr, 1956; Asst Prof., 1957-60; Assoc. Prof., 1960-62. Sloan Foundn Fellow, 1959-63; Guggenheim Meml Fellow, 1970-71, 1979-80; Sherman Fairchild Distinguished Scholar, CIT, 1982. Mem., Scientific Adv. Bd, Max Planck Inst. for Quantum Optics, Garching, Germany, 1982-. Marlow Medal, Faraday Soc., 1963; Steacie Prize for Natural Sciences, 1965; Chem. Inst. Canada Medal, 1976 (Noranda Award, 1967); Chem. Soc. Award, 1970; Henry Marshall Tory Medal, RSC, 1977; Remsen Award, Amer. Chem. Soc., 1978. Lectures: Centennial, Chem. Soc., 1965; Ohio State Univ., 1969 (and Mack Award); Reilly, Univ. of Notre Dame, 1970; Harkins Meml, Univ. of Chicago, 1971; Purves, McGill Univ., 1971; Killam Meml Schol., 1974, 1975; F. J. Toole, Univ. of New Brunswick, 1974; Philips, Haverford Coll., 1974; Kistiakowsky, Harvard Univ., 1975; Camille and Henry Dreyfus, Kansas, 1975; J. W. T. Spinks, Saskatchewan, 1976; Laird, Western Ontario, 1976; CIL Dist., Simon Fraser Univ., 1977; Gucker, Indiana Univ., 1977; Jacob Bronowski Meml, Toronto Univ., 1978; Hutchinson, Rochester Univ., 1979; Priestley, Penn State Univ., 1980; Barré, Univ. of Montreal, 1982. Hon. For. Mem., Amer. Acad. of Arts and Sciences, 1976; For. Associate, Nat. Acad. of Sciences, USA, 1978. Hon. DSc: Waterloo, 1970; Memorial, 1976; McMaster, 1977; Carleton, 1981; Harvard, 1982; Hon. LLD Trent, 1977. *Film:* Concept in Reaction Dynamics, 1970. *Publications:* (with F. G. Griffiths) The Dangers of Nuclear War, 1979; papers in scientific jls, articles on science policy and on control of armaments. *Address:* 3 Rosedale Road, Toronto M4W 2P1, Canada.

POLE; *see* Carew Pole.

POLE; *see* Chandos-Pole.

POLE, Prof. Jack Richon, PhD; FRHistS; Rhodes Professor of American History and Institutions, Oxford University, and Fellow of St Catherine's College, since 1979; *b* 14 March 1922; *m* 1952, Marilyn Louise Mitchell; one *s* two *d*. *Educ:* Oxford Univ. (BA 1949); Princeton Univ. (PhD 1953). MA Cantab 1963. FRHistS 1970. Instr in History, Princeton Univ., 1952-53; Asst Lectr/Lectr in Amer. History, UCL, 1953-63; Cambridge University: Reader in Amer. History and Govt, 1963-79; Fellow, Churchill Coll., 1963-79 (Vice-Master, 1975-78); Mem., Council of Senate, 1970-74. Vis. Professor: Berkeley, 1960-61; Ghana, 1966; Chicago, 1969. Commonwealth Fund Amer. Studies Fellowship, 1956; Fellow, Center for Advanced Study in Behavioral Sciences, 1969-70; Guest Schol., Wilson Internat. Center, Washington, 1978-79. Jefferson Meml Lectr, Berkeley, 1971; Richard B. Russell Lectr, Ga, 1981. Member: Council, Inst. for Early Amer. History and Culture, 1973-76; Acad. Européenne d' Histoire, 1981. Hon. Fellow, Hist. Soc. of Ghana. *Publications:* Abraham Lincoln and the Working Classes of Britain, 1959; Abraham Lincoln, 1964; Political Representation in England and the Origins of the American Republic, 1966 (also USA); (ed) The Advance of Democracy, USA 1967; The Seventeenth Century: the origins of legislative power, USA 1969; (ed) The Revolution in America: documents of the internal development of America in the revolutionary era, 1971 (also USA); (co-ed) The Meanings of American History, USA 1971; Foundations of American Independence, 1763-1815, 1973 (USA 1972); (Gen. Editor) American Historical Documents (ed, Slavery, Secession and Civil War), 1975; The Decision for American Independence, USA 1975; The Idea of Union, USA 1977; The Pursuit of Equality in American History, USA 1978; Paths to the American Past, 1979 (also USA); articles in Amer. Hist. Rev., William and Mary Qly, and Jl of Southern Hist. *Recreations:* cricket, painting, drawing. *Address:* 20 Divinity Road, Oxford OX4 1JL; St Catherine's College, Oxford OX1 3UJ. *Club:* Trojan Wanderers Cricket.

POLE, Sir Peter Van Notten, 5th Bt, *cr* 1791; FASA; ACIS; accountant; *b* 6 Nov. 1921; *s* of late Arthur Chandos Pole and Marjorie, *d* of late Charles Hargrave, Glen Forrest, W Australia; *S* kinsman, 1948; *m* 1949, Jean Emily, *d* of late Charles Douglas Stone, Borden, WA; one *s* one *d*. *Educ:* Guildford Grammar Sch. *Heir: s* Peter John Chandos Pole [*b* 27 April 1952; *m* 1973, Suzanne Norah, BAppSc(MT), *d* of Harold Raymond and Gwendoline Maude Hughes; one *s*]. *Address:* 5 Sandpiper Mews, 10 Perina Way, City Beach, WA 6015, Australia.

POLKINGHORNE, Rev. John Charlton, FRS 1974; Fellow, Trinity College, Cambridge, since 1954; Curate of St Michael's, Bedminster, since 1982; *b* 16 Oct. 1930; *s* of George Baulkwill Polkinghorne and Dorothy Evelyn Polkinghorne (*née* Charlton); *m* 1955, Ruth Isobel Martin; two *s* one *d. Educ:* Elmhurst Grammar Sch.; Perse Sch.; Trinity Coll., Cambridge (MA 1956; PhD 1955; ScD 1974); Westcott House, Cambridge, 1979-81. Deacon, 1981; Priest, 1982. Commonwealth Fund Fellow, California Institute of Technology, 1955-56; Lecturer in Mathematical Physics, Univ. of Edinburgh, 1956-58; Cambridge University: Lecturer in Applied Mathematics, 1958-65; Reader in Theoretical Physics, 1965-68; Prof. of Mathematical Physics, 1968-79. Curate, St Andrew's, Chesterton, 1981-82. Mem. SRC, 1975-79; Chm., Nuclear Phys. Bd, 1978-79. Chm. of Governors, Perse Sch., 1972-81. Licensed Reader, Diocese of Ely, 1975. *Publications:* (jointly) The Analytic S-Matrix, 1966; The Particle Play, 1979; Models of High Energy Processes, 1980; many articles on elementary particle physics in learned journals. *Recreation:* gardening. *Address:* 1 Nutgrove Avenue, Bedminster, Bristol. *T:* Bristol 779697.

POLLARD, Maj.-Gen. Barry; *see* Pollard, Maj.-Gen. C. B.

POLLARD, Bernard; Under Secretary, since 1979, and Director of Counter Avoidance and Evasion Division, since 1981, Board of Inland Revenue; *b* 24 Oct. 1927; *m* 1961, Regina (*née* Stone); one *s* one *d. Educ:* Tottenham Grammar Sch.; London Univ. (BSc Econ). Called to the Bar, Middle Temple, 1968. Served RAF (Flying Officer), 1949-53. Entered Tax Inspectorate, Inland Revenue, 1953; Principal Inspector of Taxes, 1969; Asst Sec., 1973. *Recreations:* reading biographies, watching cricket and National Hunt racing. *Address:* 10 Merrows Close, Northwood, Mddx HA6 2RT. *T:* Northwood 24762. *Club:* Surrey County Cricket.

POLLARD, Maj.-Gen. (Charles) Barry; National Director, Trident Trust, since 1980; *b* 20 April 1927; *s* of Leonard Charles Pollard and Rose Constance (*née* Fletcher); *m* 1954, Mary Heyes; three *d. Educ:* Ardingly Coll.; Selwyn Coll., Cambridge. Commnd, Corps of RE, 1947; served in ME, Korea and UK, 1947-58; Student, Staff Coll., Camberley, 1958; GSO 2 (Trng), HQ Eastern Comd, 1959-61; Liaison Officer, Ecole du Genie, France, 1961-63; OC 5 Field Sqdn, 1963-65; JSSC, 1965; Mil. Asst to DCOS, Allied Forces Central Europe, 1966; GSO 1 MoD, 1967; GSO 1 (DS), Staff Coll., Camberley, 1968; CRE 3 Div., 1969-71; Col GS 3 Div., 1971-72; CCRE 1st British Corps, 1972-74; RCDS, 1975; Chief Engr, BAOR, 1976-79. Col Comdt, RE, 1982-. *Recreations:* sailing, golf. *Address:* Yateley, Coombe Road, Salisbury, Wilts. *Club:* Army and Navy.

POLLARD, Sir (Charles) Herbert, Kt 1962; CBE 1957 (OBE 1946; MBE 1943); retired as City Treasurer, Kingston upon Hull, 1961; *b* 23 Oct. 1898; *s* of Charles Pollard; *m* 1922, Elsie (*d* 1970), *d* of Charles Crain; one *d* ; *m* 1971, Hilda M. Levitch. *Educ:* Blackpool. City Treasurer, Kingston upon Hull, 1929-61; formerly held appointments in Finance Depts of Blackpool and Wallasey; Fellow, Inst. of Chartered Accountants; Member Council, Inst. of Municipal Treasurers and Accountants, 1944-61 (President Inst. 1952-53); Financial Adviser to Assoc. of Municipal Corporations, 1951-61; Member several cttees and working parties arranged by government departments on various aspects of education, housing, police and local authority finance; Hon. Manager, Savings Bank, Hull Area, 1943-78. Trustee: C. C. Grundy Trust; Chamberlain Trust. Life Vice-Pres., Hanover Housing Assoc.; Mem., Nat. Savings Cttee, 1946-51; Official delegate at International Confs on aspects of local government finance (including Education) in Rome and Geneva, held under auspices of International Union of Local Authorities (prepared British paper for this) and UNESCO Licentiate, London College of Music. Hon. Treas. and Member Council, General Assembly of Unitarian and Free Christian Churches, 1959-70 (President, 1956-57); Hon. Treas., British and Foreign Unitarian Assoc. Inc., 1964-79; Member, St John Council for Lancs, 1962-72. OStJ 1962. *Publications:* contrib. to: Local Government Finance and to other local government journals. *Recreations:* music, theatre; membership of voluntary service organisations. *Address:* Hale Barns, Elloughton, Brough, N Humberside. *T:* Brough 667206. *Clubs:* Rotary (Past Pres., Hull and St Annes-on-Sea).

POLLARD, Geoffrey Samuel; Director of Finance, West Yorkshire Metropolitan County Council, since 1973; *b* 5 March 1926; *s* of Reginald Samuel Pollard and Kezia Mary (*née* Piper); *m* 1949, Estelle Mercia (*née* Smith); one *s* one *d. Educ:* Eastbourne Grammar School. IPFA, FCA. Clerical Asst, E Sussex CC, 1941-44; Accountancy Asst, Brighton Co. Borough Council, 1944-48; Techn. Asst, Tunbridge Wells Borough Council, 1948-50; Coventry County Borough Council: Sectional Accountant, 1950-52; Chief Accountant, 1952-55; Asst City Treas., 1955-57; Dep. Borough Treas., West Ham Co. Borough Council, 1957-62; Borough Treas., Swansea Co. Borough Council, 1962-68; Treas., W Glamorgan Water Bd, 1966-68; City Treas. and Jt Co-ordinator, Bradford Co. Borough Council, 1968-74. Pres., CIPFA, 1975 (Mem. Council, 1965-; Hon. Treasurer, 1978-); Pres., Soc. of Co. Borough Treasurers, 1972-73 (Mem. Exec. Cttee, 1969-74); Mem. Exec. Cttee, Soc. of County Treasurers, 1974-; Pres., Soc. of Metropolitan Treasurers, 1979-80; Chm., CIPFA Jt Cttee of Students Socs, 1972-73; Mem. Students Soc. Exec. Cttee, 1951-; Pres., NE Students Soc., CIPFA, 1972-73; Financial Adviser, Assoc. of Metrop. Authorities, 1974-; Mem., DoE Steering Gp on Regional Water Authorities Econ. and Financial Objectives (Jukes Cttee), 1972-74; Hon. Treas., Royal National Eisteddfod of Wales, 1964; Yorks Arts Assoc.: Hon. Treas., 1969-73; Hon. Auditor, 1973-; Hon. Treas., Bradford Arts

Festival, 1969-73. Hon. Editor, Telescope (Jl of CIPFA Students), 1959-71 (Sir Harry Page Merit Award 1970). *Publications:* contrib. various financial jls. *Recreations:* classical music, cricket, football, photography. *Address:* Department of Finance, West Yorkshire Metropolitan County Council, County Hall, Wakefield, W Yorks WF1 2QN. *T:* Wakefield 67111.

POLLARD, Sir Herbert; *see* Pollard, Sir C. H.

POLLARD, Prof. Sidney; Professor of Economic History, University of Bielefeld, since 1980; *b* 21 April 1925; *s* of Moses and Leontine Pollak; *m* 1949, Eileen Andrews; two *s* one *d. Educ:* London School of Economics. University of Sheffield: Knoop Fellow, 1950-52; Asst Lecturer, 1952-55; Lecturer, 1955-60; Senior Lecturer, 1960-63; Prof., 1963-80. *Publications:* Three Centuries of Sheffield Steel, 1954; A History of Labour in Sheffield 1850-1939, 1959; The Development of the British Economy, 1914-1950, 1962; The Genesis of Modern Management, 1965; The Idea of Progress, 1968; (with D. W. Crossley) The Wealth of Britain, 1086-1966, 1968; (ed) The Gold Standard and Employment Policies between the Wars, 1970; (ed, with others) Aspects of Capital Investment in Great Britain, 1750-1850, 1971; (ed) The Trades Unions Commission: the Sheffield outrages, 1971; (ed with J. Salt) Robert Owen, prophet of the poor, 1971; (ed with C. Holmes) Documents of European Economic History, vol. 1, 1968, vols 2 and 3, 1972; The Economic Integration of Europe, 1815-1970, 1974; (ed with C. Holmes) Essays in the Economic and Social History of South Yorkshire, 1977; (with Paul Robertson) The British Shipbuilding Industry 1870-1914, 1979; Peaceful Conquest, 1981; The Wasting of the British Economy, 1982; articles in learned journals in field of economics, economic history and history. *Recreations:* walking, music. *Address:* Loebellstrasse 14, D-4800 Bielefeld 1, Germany. *T:* Bielefeld 178390.

POLLEN, Sir John Michael Hungerford, 7th Bt of Redenham, Hampshire, *cr* 1795; *b* 6 April 1919; *s* of late Lieut-Commander John Francis Hungerford Pollen, RN; *S* kinsman, Sir John Lancelot Hungerford Pollen, 6th Bt, 1959; *m* 1st, 1941, Angela Mary Oriana Russi (marr. diss., 1956); one *s* one *d* ; 2nd, 1957, Mrs Diana Jubb. *Educ:* Downside; Merton Coll., Oxford. Served War of 1939-45 (despatches). *Heir: s* Richard John Hungerford Pollen [*b* 3 Nov. 1946; *m* 1971, Christianne, *d* of Sir Godfrey Agnew, *qv* ; three *s* one *d*]. *Address:* Mancr House, Rodbourne, Malmesbury, Wiltshire; Lochportain, Isle of North Uist, Outer Hebrides.

POLLEN, Peregrine Michael Hungerford; Executive Deputy Chairman, Sotheby Parke Bernet and Co., 1975-82; *b* 24 Jan. 1931; *s* of late Sir Walter Michael Hungerford Pollen, MC, JP, and of Lady Pollen; *m* 1958, Patricia Helen Barry; one *s* two *d. Educ:* Eton Coll.; Christ Church, Oxford. National Service, 1949-51. ADC to Sir Evelyn Baring, Governor of Kenya, 1955-56; Sotheby's, 1957-82: Dir, 1961; Pres., Sotheby Parke Bernet, New York, 1965-72. *Recreations:* silviculture, shooting. *Address:* Norton Hall, Mickleton, Glos. *T:* Mickleton 218. *Club:* Brooks's.

POLLEY, Denis William; computer consultant; Under Secretary, Management Support and Computers Division, Department of Health and Social Security, 1978-81, retired; *b* 11 Feb. 1921; *s* of William Henry Polley and Laura Emily (*née* Eyre); *m* 1943, Joyce Stopford; two *d. Educ:* Baines Grammar Sch., Poulton le Fylde; Lancashire Indep. Coll., Manchester. Served War, Army, RASC (Captain), 1942-47. Entered Civil Service, 1947; Asst Comr, Nat. Savings Cttee, 1947-48; HEO, Min. of Nat. Insce, 1948; Asst Sec., Computers Div., 1969; Central Computer Agency, Civil Service Dept, 1972-75; Family Support Div., DHSS, 1975-76; Under Sec., Contributions Div., DHSS, 1977-78. *Recreations:* horticulture, exploring countryside. *Address:* Inniscarra, 19 Springfarm Road, Camelsdale, Haslemere, Surrey GU27 3RH. *T:* Haslemere 2481.

POLLINGTON, Viscount; John Andrew Bruce Savile; *b* 30 Nov. 1959; *s* and *heir* of 8th Earl of Mexborough, *qv*.

POLLOCK, family name of Viscount Hanworth.

POLLOCK, Alexander; MP (C) Moray and Nairn, since 1979; advocate; *b* 21 July 1944; *s* of Robert Faulds Pollock, OBE, and Margaret Findlay Pollock; *m* 1975, Verena Francesca Gertraud Alice Ursula Critchley; one *s* one *d. Educ:* Rutherglen Academy; Glasgow Academy; Brasenose Coll., Oxford (BA Hons); Edinburgh Univ. (LLB); Perugia Univ. Solicitor, Bonar Mackenzie & Kermack, WS, 1970-73; Advocate, Scottish Bar, 1973-. PPS to Sec. of State for Scotland, 1982-. Mem., Commons Select Cttee on Scottish Affairs, 1979-82. *Recreations:* music, golf. *Address:* Drumdarrach, Forres, Moray, Scotland IV36 0DW. *Clubs:* Travellers'; New (Edinburgh); Rothes FC Social (Rothes); Royal Findhorn Yacht.

POLLOCK, David Linton; *b* 7 July 1906; *yr s* of late Rev. C. A. E. Pollock, formerly President of Corpus Christi College, Cambridge, and of Mrs G. I. Pollock; *m* 1st, 1933, Lilian Diana Turner; one *s* ; 2nd, 1950, Margaret Duncan Curtis-Bennett (*née* Mackintosh). *Educ:* Marlborough Coll.; Trinity Coll., Cambridge. Partner in the firm of Freshfields, 1938-51; served with HM Treasury, 1939-40; War of 1939-45, Commander RNVR (despatches). Member of British Government Economic Mission to Argentina, 1946. Member of Council, Royal Yachting Assoc., 1950-65. Former Director: S. Pearson & Son Ltd; National Westminster Bank Ltd; Vickers Ltd; Legal and General Assurance Soc. Ltd; Industrial and Commercial Finance Corp. Ltd.

President, Société Civile du Vignoble de Château Latour. Member of Council, Marlborough College, 1950-71. *Recreation:* sailing. *Address:* The Old Rectory, Wiggonholt, near Pulborough, West Sussex RH20 2EL. *T:* Pulborough 2531. *Clubs:* Royal Thames Yacht; Itchenor Sailing (Sussex).

POLLOCK, Ellen Clara; actress and director; President, The Shaw Society; Professor at RADA and Webber Douglas School of Acting; *m* 1st, 1929, Lt-Col L. F. Hancock, OBE, RE (decd); one *s* ; 2nd, 1945, James Proudfoot (*d* 1971). *Educ:* St Mary's College, W2; Convent of The Blessed Sacrament, Brighton. First appeared, Everyman, 1920, as page in Romeo and Juliet. Accompanied Lady Forbes-Robertson on her S. African tour, and later visited Australia as Moscovitch's leading lady. West End successes include: Hit the Deck, Hippodrome, 1927; Her First Affaire, Kingsway, and Duke of York's, 1930; The Good Companions, Her Majesty's, 1931; Too True to be Good, New, 1933; Finished Abroad, Savoy, 1934; French Salad, Westminster and Royalty, 1934; The Dominant Sex, Shaftesbury and Aldwych, 1935. Open Air Theatre: Lysistrata; As You Like It. Seasons of Shaw's plays: at Lyric, Hammersmith, 1944, and with late Sir Donald Wolfit at King's, Hammersmith, 1953; three seasons of Grand Guignol plays at The Irving and Granville, Walham Green; Six Characters in Search of an Author, New Mayfair Theatre, 1963; Lady Frederick, Vaudeville and Duke of York's, 1969-70; Ambassador, Her Majesty's, 1971; Pygmalion, Albery, 1974; Tales from the Vienna Woods, Nat. Theatre, 1976; The Dark Lady of the Sonnets, Nat. Theatre, 1977; The Woman I Love, Churchill, 1979; Country Life, Lyric, Hammersmith, 1980; Harlequinade, and Playbill, Nat. Theatre, 1980. Has acted in numerous films and TV, inc. Forsyte Saga, The Pallisers and World's End. *Productions include:* Summer in December, Comedy Theatre, 1949; Miss Turner's Husband, St Martin's, 1949; The Third Visitor, Duke of York's, 1949; Shavings, St Martin's, 1951; Mrs Warren's Profession, Royal Court, 1956; A Matter of Choice, Arts, 1967. *Recreations:* motoring, antiques and cooking. *Address:* 9 Tedworth Square, SW3. *T:* 01-352 5082.

POLLOCK, Sir George, Kt 1959; QC 1951; *b* 15 March 1901; *s* of William Mackford Pollock; *m* 1st, 1922, Doris Evelyn Main (*d* 1977); one *s* one *d* ; 2nd, 1977, Mollie (*née* Pedder), widow of J. A. Van Santen. Served Merchant Navy, 1914-18 War. Entered journalism as trainee reporter on Leamington Spa Courier; sub-editor Daily Chronicle, 1922-28; called to Bar, Gray's Inn, 1928; Bencher, 1948. Recorder of Sudbury, 1946-51. Served Army (Special Forces), 1940-44, Egypt, N Africa, Sicily and Italy (Colonel, Gen. Staff); Chief Judicial Officer, Allied Control Commn, Italy, 1944. Retired from Bar, 1954; Dir, British Employers' Confedn, 1954-65; assisted in planning and orgn of newly constituted CBI; Senior Consultant to CBI on Internat. Labour Affairs, 1965-69. Member: Governing Body, ILO, 1963-69; EFTA Consultative Cttee, 1966-69; Royal Commn on Trade Unions and Employers' Organisations. Mem. Council, Sussex Univ., 1974-77. *Publication:* Life of Mr Justice McCardie, 1934. *Address:* 62 Saffrons Court, Eastbourne, East Sussex.

POLLOCK, Sir George F(rederick), 5th Bt, *cr* 1866; Artist-Photographer since 1963; *b* 13 Aug. 1928; *s* of Sir (Frederick) John Pollock, 4th Bt and Alix l'Estom (*née* Soubiran); *S* father, 1963; *m* 1951, Doreen Mumford, *o d* of N. E. K. Nash, CMG; one *s* two *d*. *Educ:* Eton; Trinity Coll., Cambridge. BA 1953, MA 1957. 2nd Lieut, 17/21 Lancers, 1948-49. Admitted Solicitor, 1956. Hon. FRPS (Past Pres.); FIIP; FRSA. Past Chm., London Salon of Photography. *Recreation:* ski-ing. *Heir: s* David Frederick Pollock, *b* 13 April 1959. *Address:* Netherwood, Stones Lane, Westcott, near Dorking, Surrey. *T:* Dorking 885447. *Clubs:* Lansdowne, Ski Club of Great Britain; DHO (Wengen).

POLLOCK, Sir George Seymour Montagu-; 4th Bt, *cr* 1872; Lieutenant-Commander, RN (retired); *b* 14 Sept. 1900; *s* of Sir Montagu Frederick Montagu-Pollock, 3rd Bt and Margaret Angela (*d* 1959), *d* of late W. A. Bell, Pendell Court, Blechingley; *S* father, 1938; *m* 1927, Karen-Sofie, *o c* of Hans Ludvig Dedekam, of Oslo; one *s* one *d*. *Educ:* Royal Naval Colleges, Osborne and Dartmouth. Entered RN, 1913; retired, 1920; With Unilever, 1920-64. Served in RN, War of 1939-45. *Heir: s* Giles Hampden Montagu-Pollock; [*b* 19 Oct. 1928; *m* 1963, Caroline Veronica, *yr d* of Richard Russell; one *s* one *d*]. *Address:* Brooke House, Swallowcliffe, near Salisbury, Wilts. *T:* Tisbury 870220. *Club:* Special Forces.

See also Sir William Montagu-Pollock.

POLLOCK, John Denton; General Secretary, Educational Institute of Scotland, since 1975; a Forestry Commissioner, since 1978; *b* 21 April 1926; *s* of John Pollock and Elizabeth (*née* Crawford); *m* 1961, Joyce Margaret Sharpe; one *s* one *d*. *Educ:* Ayr Academy; Royal Technical Coll., Glasgow; Glasgow Univ.; Jordanhill Coll. of Education. BSc (Pure Science). FEIS 1971. Teacher, Mauchline Secondary Sch., 1951-59; Head Teacher, Kilmaurs Secondary Sch., 1959-65; Rector, Mainholm Acad., 1965-74. Chm., Scottish Labour Party, 1959 and 1971. Vice-Chm., Scottish TUC, 1980-81, Chm., 1981-82 (Mem., Gen. Council, 1975-). Member: (Annan) Cttee on Future of Broadcasting, 1974-77; Manpower Services Cttee Scotland, 1977-; Council for Tertiary Educn in Scotland, 1979-. Chm., European Cttee, World Conf. of Orgns of Teaching Profession. *Address:* 52 Douglas Road, Longniddry, East Lothian, Scotland. *T:* Longniddry 52082.

POLLOCK, Martin Rivers, FRS 1962; Professor of Biology, University of Edinburgh, 1965-76, now Emeritus; *b* 10 Dec. 1914; *s* of Hamilton Rivers Pollock and Eveline Morton Pollock (*née* Bell); *m* 1941, Jean Ilsley Paradise;

two *s* two *d*. *Educ:* Winchester Coll., Trinity Coll., Cambridge; University College Hospital, London. BA Cantab, 1936; Senior Scholar, Trinity Coll., Cambridge, 1936; MRCS, LRCP 1939; MB, BCh Cantab 1940. House Appointments at UCH and Brompton Hospital, 1940-41; Bacteriologist, Emergency Public Health Laboratory Service, 1941-45; seconded to work on Infective Hepatitis with MRC Unit, 1943-45; apppointment to scientific staff, Medical Research Council, under Sir Paul Fildes, FRS, 1945-; Head of Division of Bacterial Physiology, Nat. Inst. for Medical Research, Mill Hill (MRC), 1949-65. *Publications:* articles in British Journal of Experimental Pathology, Biochemical Journal, Journal of Microbiology, etc. *Recreation:* contemplating, planning and occasionally undertaking various forms of mildly adventurous travel, preferably through deserts. *Address:* Marsh Farm House, Margaret Marsh, Shaftesbury, Dorset SP7 0AZ. *T:* Marnhull 820479.

POLLOCK, Adm. of the Fleet Sir Michael (Patrick), GCB 1971 (KCB 1969; CB 1966); MVO 1952; DSC 1944; Bath King of Arms, since 1976; *b* 19 Oct. 1916; *s* of late C. A. Pollock and of Mrs G. Pollock; *m* 1st, 1940, Margaret Steacy (*d* 1951), Bermuda; two *s* one *d*; 2nd, 1954, Marjory Helen Reece (*née* Bisset); one step *d*. *Educ:* RNC Dartmouth. Entered Navy, 1930; specialised in Gunnery, 1941. Served War of 1939-45 in Warspite, Vanessa, Arethusa and Norfolk, N. Atlantic, Mediterranean and Indian Ocean. Captain, Plans Div. of Admiralty and Director of Surface Weapons; comd HMS Vigo and Portsmouth Sqdn, 1958-59; comd HMS Ark Royal, 1963-64; Asst Chief of Naval Staff, 1964-66; Flag Officer Second in Command, Home Fleet, 1966-67; Flag Officer Submarines and Nato Commander Submarines, Eastern Atlantic, 1967-69; Controller of the Navy, 1970-71; Chief of Naval Staff and First Sea Lord, 1971-74; First and Principal Naval Aide-de-Camp to the Queen, 1972-74. Comdr, 1950; Capt., 1955; Rear-Adm., 1964; Vice-Adm., 1968; Adm., 1970. *Recreations:* sailing, tennis, shooting, fishing, travel. *Address:* The Ivy House, Churchstoke, Montgomery, Powys SY15 6DU. *T:* Churchstoke 426.

POLLOCK, Sir William H. M.; *see* Montagu-Pollock.

POLSON, Prof. Cyril John; Professor of Forensic Medicine, University of Leeds, 1947-69, now Emeritus Professor; *b* 1901; *s* of William Polson, MB, CM, and A. D., *d* of Thomas Parker, JP, MInstCE, FRSE; *m* 1932, Mary Watkinson Tordoff (*d* 1961); one *d* ; *m* 1963, G. Mary Pullan (BSc, MB, ChB, MFCM, DObst, RCOG). *Educ:* Wrekin Coll.; Birmingham Univ. MB, ChB and MRCS, LRCP, 1924; MRCP 1926; FRCP, 1941; FRCPath, 1964; MD 1929, Birmingham. Called to the Bar, Inner Temple, 1940. Assistant Lecturer, Univ. of Manchester, 1927; Univ. of Leeds: Lecturer in Pathology, 1928; Senior Lecturer in Pathology, and Pathologist to St J. Hospital, Leeds, 1945; Hon. Member, N England Laryngological Society, 1948. Corr. Member la Société de Médecine Légale de France, 1950. Vice-President 2nd International Meeting in Forensic Medicine, NY, 1960; President: British Association in Forensic Medicine, 1962-65; British Acad. of Forensic Sciences, 1974-75; Mem., Leeds and West Riding Medico-Legal Society, 1963 (Pres. 1966); Hon. Mem., Leeds and West Riding Medico-Chirurgical Soc., 1970. A. G. Marshall Lectr, Midland Inst. of Forensic Medicine and Bd of Grad. Studies, Birmingham Univ., 1979. *Publications:* Clinical Toxicology (with M. A. Green and M. R. Lee), 2nd edn, 1969; The Scientific Aspects of Forensic Medicine, 1969, Swedish trans., 1973; The Essentials of Forensic Medicine, 3rd edn (with D. J. Gee), 1973; The Disposal of the Dead (with T. K. Marshall), 3rd edn, 1975; papers in scientific journals devoted to pathology and forensic medicine. *Recreations:* gardening, photography. *Address:* 16 Tewit Well Road, Harrogate HG2 8JE. *T:* Harrogate 503434.

POLTIMORE, 7th Baron *cr* 1831; **Mark Coplestone Bampfylde;** Bt 1641; *b* 8 June 1957; *s* of Captain the Hon. Anthony Gerard Hugh Bampfylde (*d* 1969) (*er s* of 6th Baron) and of Brita Yvonne (who *m* 2nd, 1975, Guy Elmes), *o d* of late Baron Rudolph Cederström; *S* grandfather, 1978; *m* 1982, Sally Anne, *d* of Dr Norman Miles. *Heir: uncle* Hon. David Cecil Warwick Bampfylde [*b* 3 March 1924; *m* 1950, Jean Margaret, *d* of late Lt-Col Patrick Kinloch Campbell; three *s*]. *Address:* 10 Kempsford Gardens, SW5 9LH.

POLUNIN, Nicholas, CBE 1976; MS (Yale); MA, DPhil, DSc (Oxon.); FLS; FRGS; Editor (founding), Environmental Conservation, since 1974; Convener and General Editor, Environmental Monographs and Symposia, since 1979; Secretary-General and Editor, International Conferences on Environmental Future, since 1971; President, The Foundation for Environmental Conservation, since 1975; *b* Checkendon, Oxon, 26 June 1909; *e s* of late Vladimir and Elizabeth Violet (*née* Hart) Polunin; *m* 1st, 1939, Helen Lovat Fraser (*d* 1973); one *s* ; 2nd, 1948, Helen Eugenie Campbell; two *s* one *d*. *Educ:* The Hall, Weybridge; Latymer Upper and privately; Oxford, Yale and Harvard Univs. Open Scholar of Christ Church, Oxford, 1928-32; First Class Hons Nat. Sci. Final Examination, Botany and Ecology; Goldsmiths' Senior Studentship for Research, 1932-33; Botanical tutor in various Oxford Colls, 1932-47; Henry Fellowship at Pierson Coll., Yale Univ., USA, 1933-34 (Sigma Xi); Departmental Demonstrator in Botany 1934-35, and Senior (Research) Scholar of New Coll., Oxford, 1934-36; Dept of Scientific and Industrial Research, Senior Research Award, 1935-38; Rolleston Memorial Prize, 1938; DSIR Special Investigator, 1938; Research Associate, Gray Herbarium, Harvard Univ., USA, 1936-37, and subs. Foreign Research Associate; Fielding Curator and Keeper of the Univ. Herbaria, Oxford, and Univ. Demonstrator and Lectr in Botany, 1939-47; Oxford Univ. Botanical Moderator, 1941-45; Macdonald Prof. of Botany, McGill Univ., Canada, 1947-52 (Visiting Prof., 1946-47); Research Fellow, Harvard

Univ., 1950-53; Lectr in Plant Science and Research Associate, Yale Univ., 1953-55; Project Dir, US Air Force, 1953-55, and Consultant to US Army Corps of Engineers; formerly Sen. Research Fell. and Lectr, New Coll., Oxford; Prof. of Plant Ecology and Taxonomy, Head of Dept of Botany, and Dir of Univ. Herbarium, etc., Baghdad, Iraq, Jan. 1956-58 (revolution); Founding Prof. of Botany and Head of Dept, Faculty of Science (which he established as Dean), Univ. of Ife, Nigeria, 1962-66 (revolutions, etc). Leverhulme Res. Award, 1941-43; Arctic Inst. Res. Fellowship, 1946-48; Guggenheim Mem. Fellowship, 1950-52. Haley Lectr, Acadia Univ., NS, 1950; Visiting Lectr and Adviser on Biology, Brandeis Univ., Waltham, Mass, 1953-54; Guest Prof., Univ. of Geneva, 1959-61 and 1975-76. US Order of Polaris; Marie-Victorin Medal for services to Canadian botany; FRHS. Fellow: AAAS, Arctic Inst. NA, American Geographical Soc. Member or Leader, numerous scientific expeditions from 1930, particularly in arctic or sub-arctic regions, including Spitsbergen, Lapland (3 times), Iceland, Greenland, Canadian Eastern Arctic (5 times, including confirmation of Spicer Islands in Foxe Basin north of Hudson Bay and discovery in 1946 of last major islands to be added to world map following their naming in 1949 as Prince Charles Is. and Air Force Is.), Labrador—Ungava (many times), Canadian Western Arctic (including Magnetic Pole), Alaska, summer and winter flights over geographical North Pole; subsequently in Middle East and West Africa; Ford Foundation Award, Scandinavia and USSR, 1966-67. International Botanical Congresses: VII (Stockholm, 1950); VIII (Paris, 1954); X (Edinburgh, 1964); XI (Seattle, 1969, symposium chm., etc); XII (Leningrad, 1975, Conservation Section 1st chm., etc.); XIII (Sydney, 1981). Founding Editor: Biological Conservation, 1967-74; Plant Science Monographs, 1954-78; Associate Ed., Environmental Pollution, 1969-; Mem., Adv. Bd, The Environmentalist, 1981-, and other jls. Chairman: Internat. Steering Cttee, and Editor of Proceedings, (1st) Internat. Conf. on Environmental Future, Finland, 1971; Chm. (founding), Foundn for Environmental Conservation, 1973- (subsequently consolidated and placed under Swiss federal surveillance). *Publications:* Russian Waters, 1931; The Isle of Auks, 1932; Botany of the Canadian Eastern Arctic, vol. I, Pteridophyta and Spermatophyta, 1940; (ed) vol. II, Thallophyta and Bryophyta, 1947; vol. III, Vegetation and Ecology, 1948; Arctic Unfolding, 1949; Circumpolar Arctic Flora, 1959; Introduction to Plant Geography, 1960 (subseq. Amer. and other edns); Eléments de Géographie botanique, 1967; (ed) The Environmental Future, 1972; Growth Without Ecodisasters?, 1980; Global Strategies and Prospects, 1983; (with G. A. Knox) Ecosystem Theory and Application, 1983; papers chiefly on arctic and boreal flora, phytogeography, ecology, vegetation, aerobiology, and conservation; editor of International Industry, 1943-46, and of World Crops Books, 1954-76; contrib. Encyclopædia Britannica, and some 350 other scientific papers, editorials, reviews, etc, to various jls. *Recreations:* travel and scientific exploration, nature conservation, stock-markets. *Address:* 15 chemin F.-Lehmann, 1218 Grand-Saconnex, Geneva, Switzerland. *T:* (022) 982383/84; c/o New College, Oxford. *Clubs:* Reform (life); Harvard (life), Explorers, Torrey Botanical (New York City); New England Botanical (Boston); Canadian Field Naturalists' (Ottawa).
See also O. Polunin.

POLUNIN, Oleg; Assistant Master, Charterhouse School, 1938-72; *b* 28 Nov. 1914; Russian father, British mother; *m* 1943, Lorna Mary Venning; one *s* one *d. Educ:* St Paul's Sch.; Magdalen Coll., Oxford. Served War of 1939-45, Intelligence Corps. Botanical Exploration and collecting, Nepal, 1949-52; Turkey, 1954-56; Karakoram, Pakistan, 1960; Kashmir; Iraq; Lebanon; Lecturer and Guide on Hellenic cruises and other tours, often off the beaten track. Founder member, past Chairman, and Secretary, Surrey Naturalists' Trust. *Publications:* (with A. J. Huxley) Flowers of the Mediterranean, 1965; Flowers of Europe, 1969; Concise Flowers of Europe, 1972; (with B. E. Smythies) Flowers of South West Europe, 1973; (with B. Everard) Trees and Bushes of Europe, 1976; Flowers of Greece and the Balkans, 1980. *Recreations:* travel, plant photography and collecting, pottery. *Address:* 2 Lockwood Court, Knoll Road, Godalming, Surrey.
See also N. Polunin.

POLWARTH, 10th Lord, *cr* 1690; **Henry Alexander Hepburne-Scott; TD;** DL; Vice-Lord-Lieutenant, Borders Region (Roxburgh, Ettrick and Lauderdale), since 1975; Member, Royal Company of Archers; a Scots Representative Peer, 1945-63; Chartered Accountant; *b* 17 Nov. 1916; *s* of late Hon. Walter Thomas Hepburne-Scott (*d* 1942); *S* grandfather, 1944; *m* 1st, 1943, Caroline Margaret (marr. diss. 1969), 2nd *d* of late Captain R. A. Hay, Marlefield, Roxburghshire, and Helmsley, Yorks; one *s* three *d*; 2nd, 1969, Jean, *d* of Adm. Sir Angus Cunninghame Graham of Gartmore, KBE, CB, and formerly wife of C. E. Jauncey, QC; two step *s* one step *d. Educ:* Eton Coll.; King's Coll., Cambridge. Served War of 1939-45, Captain, Lothians and Border Yeomanry. Former Partner, firm of Chiene and Tait, CA, Edinburgh; Governor, Bank of Scotland, 1966-72, Director, 1974-; Chm., General Accident, Fire & Life Assurance Corp., 1968-72; Director: ICI Ltd, 1969-72, 1974-81; Halliburton Co., 1974-; Canadian Pacific Ltd, 1975-; Sun Life Assurance Co. of Canada, 1975-. Minister of State, Scottish Office, 1972-74. Chm., later Pres., Scottish Council (Develt and Industry), 1955-72. Mem., Franco-British Council, 1981-. Chm., Scottish Nat. Orchestra Soc., 1975-79. Chancellor, Aberdeen Univ., 1966. Hon. LLD: St Andrews; Aberdeen; Hon. DLitt Heriot-Watt; DUniv Stirling. FRSE; FRSA. DL Roxburgh, 1962. Heir: *s* Master of Polwarth, *qv. Address:* Harden, Hawick, Scotland. *T:* Hawick 2069. *Clubs:* Brooks's, Pratt's; New (Edinburgh).
See also Baron Moran.

POLWARTH, Master of; Hon. Andrew Walter Hepburne-Scott; *b* 30 Nov. 1947; *s* and *heir* of 10th Lord Polwarth, *qv*; *m* 1971, Isabel Anna, *e d* of Maj. J. F. H. Surtees, OBE, MC; two *s* one *d. Educ:* Eton; Trinity Hall, Cambridge. *Address:* 72 Cloncurry Street, SW6.

POLYNESIA, Bishop in, since 1975; **Rt. Rev. Jabez Leslie Bryce;** Chairman, Pacific Conference of Churches, since 1976; *b* 25 Jan. 1935. *Educ:* St John's College, Auckland, NZ (LTh); St Andrew's Seminary, Manila, Phillipines (BTh). Deacon 1960, priest 1962, Polynesia; Curate of Suva, 1960-63; Priest-in-charge: Tonga, 1964; St Peter's Chinese Congregation, Manila, 1965-67; Archdeacon of Suva, 1967-69; Deputy Vicar-General, Holy Trinity Cathedral, Suva, 1967-72; Lectr, St John Baptist Theological Coll., Suva, 1967-69; Vicar of Viti Levu W, 1969-75; Archdeacon in Polynesia, 1969-75; Vicar-General of Polynesia, 1972-75. *Recreations:* tennis, golf. *Address:* Bishop's House, Suva, Fiji Islands. *T:* (office) 24357, (home) 23436.

POMEROY, family name of **Viscount Harberton.**

POMFRET, Surgeon Rear-Adm. Arnold Ashworth, CB 1957; OBE 1941; retired, 1957; *b* 1 June 1900; *s* of John and Eleanor Pomfret; *m* 1928, Carlene Blundstone; one *s* two *d. Educ:* Manchester Univ.; Postgraduate at London, Capetown and Oxford. MB, ChB (Manchester), 1922; DO (Oxon) 1934; DOMS (RCS&PEng), 1934. Senior Ophthalmic Specialist, RN. Last MO i/c Wei-Hai-Wei, 1940. Formerly Asst to MDG, 1944-45 and 1952-54. MO i/c RN Hospitals: Simonstown, 1946; Portland, 1948; Bermuda, 1950; MO i/c RN Hospital, Plymouth, and Command MO Plymouth, 1954-57. Gilbert Blane Medallist, 1934. Surgeon Comdr, 1934; Surgeon Captain, 1944; Surgeon Rear-Adm., 1954. QHS, 1954-57. CStJ 1957. *Recreations:* cricket, Association football. *Address:* Passlands, Forton, Chard, Somerset.
See also Lt-Gen. Sir A. C. S. Boswell.

PONCET, Jean André F.; *see* François-Poncet.

POND, Sir Desmond (Arthur), Kt 1981; MA, MD, FRCP, FRCPsych; Chief Scientist, Departments of Health and Social Security, since 1982; *b* 2 Sept. 1919; *o s* of Thomas Arthur and Ada Celia Pond; *m* 1945, Margaret Helen (*née* Jordan), MD; three *d. Educ:* John Lyon's, Harrow; St Olave's, SE1; Clare Coll., Cambridge; University College Hospital. Rockefeller Scholar, Duke Med. Sch., N Carolina, 1942-44; Sen. Lectr, Dept of Clin. Neurophysiology, Maudsley Hosp., and Cons. Psychiatrist, UCH, 1952-66; Prof. of Psychiatry, Univ. of London at London Hosp. Medical Coll., E1, 1966-82. Goulstonian Lectr, RCP, 1961; Founder Mem., Inst. of Religion and Med., 1964; Mem., Archbishop's Gp on Divorce Law ('Putting Asunder'), 1964-66; Mem., MRC, 1968-72, 1982-; H. B. Williams Vis. Prof., Australian and New Zealand Coll. of Psychiatrists, 1968; Riddell Memorial Lectr, Univ. of Newcastle, 1971. Pres., RCPsych, 1978-81. Hon. FBPsS; Hon. FRCGP. *Publications:* Counselling in Religion and Psychiatry, 1973; various, .on psychiatry and electroencephalography. *Recreations:* making music, gardens. *Address:* Welcombe, Bridford, Exeter EX6 7JA. *T:* Christow 52645.

PONSFORD, Brian David; Under Secretary and Director of Local Government Finance Policy, Department of the Environment, since 1981; *b* 23 Dec. 1938; *s* of Herbert E. Ponsford and Kathleen W. C. (*née* Parish); *m* 1966, Erica Neumark; one *s. Educ:* City of London Sch.; Corpus Christi Coll., Oxford (1st Cl. Classical Mods 1958, 1st Cl. Lit. Hum. 1960). Teacher, Westminster Sch., 1960-61; Asst Principal, Min. of Housing and Local Govt, 1961-67; Asst Private Sec. to Minister, 1964-66; Private Sec. to Minister of State, 1966-67; Principal, 1967-69; Principal, Cabinet Office, 1969-71, DoE, 1971-73; Asst Sec., DoE, 1973; Counsellor, Office of UK Perm. Representative to European Communities, 1975-78. *Recreations:* music, books, films. *Address:* 19 Hermitage Lane, NW2. *T:* 01-435 2368.

PONSONBY, family name of **Earl of Bessborough** and of **Barons de Mauley, Ponsonby of Shulbrede,** and **Sysonby.**

PONSONBY OF SHULBREDE, 3rd Baron *cr* 1930, of Shulbrede; **Thomas Arthur Ponsonby;** Deputy Chief Opposition Whip, House of Lords, since 1981; *b* 23 Oct. 1930; *o surv. s* of 2nd Baron Ponsonby of Shulbrede, and of Hon. Elizabeth Bigham, *o d* of 2nd Viscount Mersey, PC, CMG, CBE; *S* father, 1976; *m* 1st, 1956, Ursula Mary (marr. diss. 1973), *yr d* of Comdr Thomas Stanley Lane Fox-Pitt, OBE, RN; one *s* two *d* (and one *d* decd); 2nd, 1973, Maureen Estelle Campbell-Tiech, *d* of Alfred William Windsor, Reigate, Surrey. *Educ:* St Ronan's Sch.; Bryanston; Hertford Coll., Oxford. Councillor, 1956-65, Alderman, 1964-74, Royal Borough of Kensington and Chelsea; Leader, Labour Gp, 1968-73. GLC: Alderman, 1970-77; Chm. Covent Garden Cttee, 1973-75; Chm., Central Area Bd (Transport and Planning Cttees), 1973-76; Chm. of Council, 1976-77. Opposition Whip, House of Lords, 1979-81. Chairman: London Tourist Bd, 1976-80; Greater London Citizens Advice Bureaux Service Ltd, 1977-79; Age Concern Greater London, 1977-78; London Convention Bureau, 1977-; Bd of Trustees, Community Projects Foundn, 1978-; Tourism Soc., 1980-; Local Govt Trng Bd, 1981-; Galleon Trust, 1981- (Pres., Galleon World Travel Assoc. Ltd, 1977-81). Chm., Rona-Naïve Artists Ltd, 1978-. Contested (Lab) Heston and Isleworth, general election, 1959. Fabian Society: Asst Gen. Sec., 1961-64; Gen. Sec., 1964-76. Governor, London Sch. of Economics, 1970-. Patron, New Mozart Orch., 1978-. Pres., British Handball Assoc., 1981-. *Recreations:* eating, drinking, window box gardening. Heir: *s* Hon. Frederick Matthew

Thomas Ponsonby, *b* 27 Oct. 1958. *Address:* 19 Morpeth Mansions, Morpeth Terrace, SW1P 1ER. *T:* 01-828 0164.

PONSONBY, Sir Ashley (Charles Gibbs), 2nd Bt *cr* 1956; MC 1945; Adviser, J. Henry Schroder, Wagg & Co. Ltd, since 1980 (Director, 1962-80); Chairman: Colville Estate Ltd; Trans-Oceanic Trust Ltd; Vice-President, Equitable Life Assurance Society, since 1980; Director, Rowntree Mackintosh Ltd and other companies; Lord-Lieutenant of Oxfordshire, since 1980; *b* 21 Feb. 1921; *o s* of Col Sir Charles Edward Ponsonby, 1st Bt, TD, and of Hon. Winifred, *d* of 1st Baron Hunsdon; *S* father, 1976; *m* 1950, Lady Martha Butler, *yr d* of 6th Marquess of Ormonde, CVO, MC; four *s. Educ:* Eton; Balliol College, Oxford. 2nd Lieut Coldstream Guards, 1941; served war 1942-45 (North Africa and Italy, wounded); Captain 1943; on staff Bermuda Garrison, 1945-46. A Church Commissioner, 1963-80; Mem., Council of Duchy of Lancaster, 1977-. DL Oxon, 1974-80. *Heir: e s* Charles Ashley Ponsonby, *b* 10 June 1951. *Address:* Woodleys, Woodstock, Oxon. *T:* Woodstock 811422. *Clubs:* Brooks's, Pratt's.

PONSONBY, Myles Walter, CBE 1966; HM Diplomatic Service, retired; Foreign and Commonwealth Office, 1977-80; *b* 12 Sept. 1924; *s* of late Victor Coope Ponsonby, MC and Gladys Edith Ponsonby (*née* Walter); *m* 1951, Anne Veronica Theresa Maynard, *y d* of Brig. Francis Herbert Maynard, CB, DSO, MC, and of Ethel Maynard (*née* Bates); one *s* two *d. Educ:* St Aubyn's, Rottingdean; Eton College. HM Forces (Captain, KRRC), 1942-49. Entered Foreign (subseq. Diplomatic) Service, 1951; served in: Egypt, 1951; Cyprus, 1952-53; Beirut, 1953-56; Djakarta, 1958-61; Nairobi, 1963-64; Hanoi (Consul-Gen.), 1964-65; FO, 1966-69; Rome, 1969-71; FCO, 1972-74; Ambassador to Mongolian People's Republic, 1974-77. *Recreation:* gardening. *Address:* 11 Le Bourgage, Alderney, CI. *T:* Alderney 2875. *Club:* Army and Navy.

PONSONBY, Robert Noel; Controller of Music, BBC, since 1972; *b* 19 Dec. 1926; *o s* of late Noel Ponsonby, BMus, Organist Christ Church Cathedral, Oxford, and Mary White-Thomson (now Mrs L. H. Jaques, Winchester); *m* 1st, 1957, Una Mary (marr. diss.), *er d* of late W. J. Kenny; 2nd, 1977, Lesley Margaret Black, *o d* of late G. T. Black. *Educ:* Eton; Trinity Coll., Oxford. MA Oxon., Eng. Litt. Commissioned Scots Guards, 1945-47. Organ Scholar, Trinity Coll., Oxon., 1948-50; staff of Glyndebourne Opera, 1951-55; Artistic Director of the Edinburgh International Festival, 1955-60; with Independent Television Authority, 1962-64; Gen. Administrator, Scottish Nat. Orchestra, 1964-72. Director, Commonwealth Arts Festival, Glasgow, 1965. Artistic Adviser to Internat. Arts Guild of Bahamas, 1960-72. Hon. RAM 1975. FRSA 1979. *Publication:* Short History of Oxford University Opera Club, 1950. *Recreations:* fell-walking, English and Scottish painting, music. *Address:* 4 Rosslyn Court, Ornan Road, NW3 4PU. *Clubs:* Oriental; Trinity Society.

PONTECORVO, Guido, FRS 1955; FRSE 1946; FLS 1971; PhD (Edinburgh) 1941; DrAgr (Pisa) 1928; *b* Pisa, Italy, 29 Nov. 1907; *s* of Massimo Pontecorvo and Maria (*née* Maroni); *m* 1939, Leonore Freyenmuth, Frauenfeld, Switzerland; one *d. Educ:* Pisa (Classics). Ispettorato Agrario per la Toscana, Florence, 1931-38; Inst. of Animal Genetics, Univ. of Edinburgh, 1938-40 and 1944-45; Dept of Zoology, Univ. of Glasgow, 1941-44; Dept of Genetics, Univ. of Glasgow, 1945-68 (Prof. 1955-68); Mem. Res. Staff, Imperial Cancer Res. Fund, 1968-75, Hon. Consultant Geneticist, 1975-80. Jesup Lectr, Columbia Univ., 1956; Messenger Lectr, Cornell Univ., 1957; Visiting Prof., Albert Einstein Coll. Med., 1965, 1966; Vis. Lectr, Washington State Univ., 1967; Royal Society, Leverhulme Overseas Vis. Prof., Inst. of Biophysics, Rio de Janeiro, 1969 and Dept of Biology, Pahlavi Univ., 1974; Sloane Foundn Vis. Prof., Vermont, 1971; Visiting Professor: UCL, 1968-75; King's Coll., London, 1970-71; Biology Dept, Tehran Univ., 1975; Prof. Ospite Linceo, Scuola Normale Superiore, Pisa, 1976-81; L. C. Dunn Lectr, NY Blood Center, 1976; Ranan Prof., Indian Acad. of Scis, 1982-83. Pres., Genetical Soc., 1964-66; Vice-Pres., Inst. of Biology, 1969-71. For. Hon. Member: Amer. Acad. Arts and Sciences, 1958; Danish Royal Acad. Sci. and Letters, 1966; Peruvian Soc. of Medical Genetics, 1969. Hon. DSc: Leicester, 1968; Camerino, 1974; East Anglia, 1974; Hon. LLD Glasgow, 1978. Hansen Prize, Carlsberg Foundn, 1961; Darwin Medal, Royal Soc., 1978. Campano d'Oro, Pisa, 1979. *Publications:* Ricerche sull' economia montana dell' Appennino Toscano, 1933 (Florence); Trends in Genetic Analysis, 1958. Numerous papers in British, American, Swiss, French and Italian journals on genetics and high mountain botany. *Recreation:* alpine plants photography. *Address:* Flat 25, Cranfield House, 97 Southampton Row, WC1B 4HH. *T:* 01-636 9441.

PONTEFRACT, Bishop Suffragan of, since 1971; **Rt. Rev. Thomas Richard Hare;** *b* 1922; *m* 1963, Sara, *d* of Lt-Col J. E. Spedding, OBE; one *s* two *d. Educ:* Marlborough; Trinity Coll., Oxford; Westcott House, Cambridge. RAF, 1942-45, Curate of Haltwhistle, 1950-52; Domestic Chaplain to Bishop of Manchester, 1952-59; Canon Residentiary of Carlisle Cathedral, 1959-65; Archdeacon of Westmorland and Furness, 1965-71; Vicar of St George with St Luke, Barrow-in-Furness, 1965-69; Vicar of Winster, 1969-71. *Address:* 306 Barnsley Road, Wakefield WF2 6AX. *T:* Wakefield 256935.

PONTEFRACT, Archdeacon of; *see* Unwin, Ven. K.

PONTI, Signora Carlo; *see* Loren, Sophia.

PONTIFEX, Brig. David More, CBE 1977 (OBE 1965; MBE 1956); General Secretary, Army Cadet Force Association and Secretary, Combined Cadet Force Association, since 1977; *b* 16 Sept. 1922; *s* of Comdr John Weddall Pontifex, RN, and Monica Pontifex; *m* 1968, Kathleen Betsy (*née* Matheson); one *s* four *d. Educ:* Worth Preparatory Sch.; Downside Sch. Commnd The Rifle Brigade, 1942; served War, Italy (despatches); Staff Coll., Camberley, 1951; HQ Parachute Brigade, 1952-54; Kenya, 1954-56; War Office, 1956-58; Armed Forces Staff Coll., USA, 1958-59; Brigade Major, 63 Gurkha Brigade, 1961-62; CO 1st Bn Federal Regular Army, Aden, 1963-64; GSO1 2nd Div., BAOR, 1965-66; Col GS, Staff Coll., Camberley, 1967-69; Divisional Brig., The Light Div., 1969-73; Dep. Dir, Army Staff Duties, MoD, 1973-75; Dep. Comdr and COS, SE District, 1975-77, retired 1977. ADC to the Queen, 1975-77. *Address:* 68 Shortheath Road, Farnham, Surrey. *T:* Farnham 723284. *Club:* Naval and Military.

PONTIN, Sir Frederick William, (Sir Fred Pontin), Kt 1976; Founder: Pontin's Ltd, 1946; Pontinental Ltd, 1963; Chairman and Joint Managing Director of Pontin's Ltd, 1946-79, and Pontinental (HS) Ltd, 1972-79; Director, E. J. Riley Ltd, since 1981; *b* 24 Oct. 1906; *m* Dorothy Beatrice Mortimer; one *d. Educ:* Sir George Monoux Grammar Sch., Walthamstow. Began career on London Stock Exchange. Catering and welfare work for Admiralty, Orkney Is, 1939-46. Acquired: Industrial Catering Bristol, 1946; Brean Sands Holiday Village, 1946. Chief Barker, Variety Club of GB (Raising £1,000,000 for charity), 1968; Mem. Exec. Bd, Variety Club, 1968-, Pres. 1969-75, formed 15 regional cttees of club; Mem., Grand Order of Water Rats; co-opted Mem., Stars Orgn for Spastics. Mem., St John Council for Merseyside; Pres., Lancs Youth Club Assoc.; Blackpool Hotel and Catering Students Soc.; Prescot Band. Life Mem., BRCS (Hon. Vice Pres., Dorset Branch). Underwriting Mem., Lloyd's Insurance. Freeman of Christchurch, Dorset. *Recreations:* racing (owner of Specify, winner of 1971 Grand National, and Cala Mesquida, winner of 1971 Schweppes Gold Trophy); connected with Walthamstow Avenue FC for many years prior to 1939-45 war; interested in all sporting activities. *Address:* 55 Park Lane, W1. *T:* 01-499 1205. *Clubs:* Eccentric, Saints and Sinners, World Sporting (Patron); The Toffs; Bristol (Bristol).

POOLE, family name of **Baron Poole.**

POOLE, 1st Baron, *cr* 1958, of Aldgate; **Oliver Brian Sanderson Poole,** PC 1963; CBE 1945; TD; Member of Lloyd's; lately Director, S. Pearson & Son Ltd; *b* 11 Aug. 1911; *s* of late Donald Louis Poole of Lloyd's; *m* 1st, 1933, Betty Margaret Gilkison (marr. diss., 1951); one *s* three *d*; 2nd, 1952, Mrs Daphne Heber Percy (marr. diss., 1965); 3rd, 1966, Barbara Ann Taylor. *Educ:* Eton; Christ Church, Oxford. Life Guards, 1932-33; joined Warwickshire Yeomanry, 1934. Service in 1939-45 in Iraq, Syria, North Africa, Sicily and NW Europe (despatches thrice, MBE, OBE, CBE, US Legion of Merit, Order of Orange Nassau). MP (C) Oswestry Division of Salop, 1945-50. Conservative Party Organisation: Jt Hon. Treas., 1952-55; Chairman, 1955-57; Dep.-Chm., 1957-59; Jt Chm., May-Oct. 1963, Vice-Chm., Oct. 1963-Oct. 1964. Governor of Old Vic, 1948-63; a Trustee, Nat. Gallery, 1973-81. Hon. DSc City Univ., 1970. *Heir: s* Hon. David Charles Poole, [*b* 6 Jan. 1945; *m* 1st, 1967, Fiona, *d* of John Donald, London SW6; one *s*; 2nd, 1975, Philippa, *d* of Mark Reeve]. *Address:* 24 Campden Hill Gate, Duchess of Bedford Walk, W8. *Clubs:* MCC, Buck's; Royal Yacht Squadron (Cowes).
See also Sir Hugh Munro-Lucas-Tooth, Bt.

POOLE, Mrs Avril Anne Barker; Chief Nursing Officer, Department of Health and Social Security, since 1982; *b* 11 April 1934; *d* of Arthur George and Norah Heritage; *m* 1959, John Percy Poole. *Educ:* High Sch., Southampton. SRN 1955, SCM 1957, Health Visitors Cert., 1958. Asst Chief Nursing Officer, City of Westminster, 1967-69; Chief Nursing Officer, London Borough of Merton, 1969-73; Area Nursing Officer, Surrey AHA, 1974-81; Dep. Chief Nursing Officer, DHSS, 1981-82. *Address:* Ancaster House, Church Hill, Merstham, Surrey. *T:* Merstham 4332.

POOLE, Isobel Anne; Sheriff of the Lothian and Borders (travelling commission), since 1979; *b* 9 Dec. 1941; *d* of John Cecil Findlay Poole, DM Oxon, and Constance Mary (*née* Gilkes), SRN. *Educ:* Oxford High Sch. for Girls; Edinburgh Univ. (LLB). Admitted to Faculty of Advocates, 1964. Formerly Standing Jun. Counsel to Registrar Gen. for Scotland. *Recreations:* country, decorative arts, houses, gardens, friends. *Address:* 5 Randolph Place, Edinburgh EH3 7TQ. *T:* 031-225 1931.

POOLE, Rev. Canon Joseph Weston; Canon Emeritus of Coventry Cathedral, since 1977; *b* 25 March 1909; *s* of Rev. S. J. Poole and Mrs Poole (*née* Weston); *m* 1945, Esmé Beatrice Mounsey; three *s* two *d. Educ:* St George's School, Windsor; King's School, Canterbury; Jesus Coll., Cambridge (Organ Schol. and Class. Exhibnr); Westcott House, Cambridge. Curate of St Mary-at-the-Walls, Colchester, 1933; Sub-Warden of Student Movement House, 1935; Minor Canon and Sacrist of Canterbury, 1936; Precentor of Canterbury, 1937; Rector of Merstham, Surrey, 1949; Hon. Canon of Coventry, 1958, Precentor, 1958-77; Canon Residentiary, 1963-77. ChStJ, 1974. FRSCM 1977. *Recreations:* music, literature, typography. *Address:* The Limes, 21A Beauchamp Avenue, Leamington.

POOLE HUGHES, Rt. Rev. John Richard Worthington; *see* Llandaff, Bishop of.

POOLEY, Frederick Bernard, CBE 1968; PPRIBA; architect and planning consultant; Architect to Greater London Council, 1978-80, Controller of Planning and Transportation, 1974-80, and Superintending Architect of Metropolitan Buildings, 1978-80; *b* 18 April 1916; *s* of George Pooley and Elizabeth Pawley; *m* 1944, Hilda Olive Williams; three *d. Educ:* West Ham Grammar Sch.; RIBA, FRICS, FRTPI, MIStructE, FCIArb. Served war, RE, 1940-45. Deputy Borough Architect and Planning Officer, County Borough of West Ham, 1949-51; Deputy City Architect and Planning Officer, Coventry, 1951-54; County Architect and Planning Officer, Bucks, 1954-74. Major projects include: public and sch. bldg programme; scheme for public acquisition of bldgs of arch. or hist. interest for preservation and resale; new methods for assembling and servicing land; early planning work for new Milton Keynes. RIBA: Mem. Council, 1962-; Treasurer, 1972; Pres., 1973-75. *Publications:* contribs on planning, transport and architecture. *Address:* Long Ridge, Whiteleaf, Aylesbury, Bucks. *T:* Princes Risborough 6151. *Club:* Reform.

POOLEY, Peter; Fisheries Secretary, Ministry of Agriculture, Fisheries and Food, since 1982; *b* 19 June 1936; *er* (twin) *s* of late W. M. Pooley, OBE, Truro, and of Grace Lidbury; *m* 1966, Janet Mary, *er d* of Jack Pearson, Banbury; one *s* one *d. Educ:* Brentwood Sch.; Clare Coll., Cambridge (BA); Royal Tank Regt. Joined MAFF as Asst Principal, 1959; seconded to: Diplomatic Service, 1961-63 (served in Brussels) and 1979-82 (Minister (Agric.), Office of UK Perm. Rep. to EEC, Brussels); CSD, 1977-79; Under-Sec., MAFF 1979. *Address:* 24 Hurst Road, East Molesey, Surrey. *See also R. Pooley.*

POOLEY, Robin; Chief Executive, Potato Marketing Board, since 1981; *b* 19 June 1936; *yr* (twin) *s* of late W. Melville Pooley, OBE and of Grace M. Pooley (*née* Lidbury); *m* 1972, Margaret Anne, *yr d* of Jack Pearson, Banbury; one *d. Educ:* Brentwood School. Various posts, Towers & Co. Ltd, 1954-71; Gen. Manager, CWS Gp, 1971-76; Man. Dir., Buxted Poultry Ltd, 1976-81. *Recreations:* shooting, fishing (dry fly). *Address:* Potato Marketing Board, 50 Hans Crescent, Knightsbridge, SW1. *T:* 01-589 4874. *Club:* City Livery. *See also P. Pooley.*

POORE, Dennis; *see* Poore, R. D.

POORE, Sir Herbert Edward, 6th Bt, *cr* 1795; *b* April 1930; *s* of Sir Edward Poore, 5th Bt, and Amelia Guliemone; *S* father 1938. *Heir: u* Nasionceno Poore [*b* 1900; *m* Juana Borda (*d* 1943); three *s* three *d*]. *Address:* Curuzu Cuatia, Corrientes, Argentine Republic.

POORE, Prof. Martin Edward Duncan, MA, PhD; FInstBiol; FIFor; Professor of Forest Science, and Director, Commonwealth Forestry Institute, Oxford University, since 1980; Fellow, St John's College, Oxford; *b* 25 May 1925; *s* of T. E. D. Poore and Elizabeth McMartin; *m* 1948, Judith Ursula, *d* of Lt-Gen. Sir Treffry Thompson, KCSI, CB, CBE, and late Mary Emily, *d* of Rev. Canon Medd; two *s. Educ:* Trinity Coll., Glenalmond; Edinburgh Univ.; Clare Coll., Cambridge. MA, PhD Cantab.; MA Oxon. Japanese interpreter, 1943-45. Nature Conservancy, 1953-56; Consultant Ecologist, Hunting Technical Services, 1956-59; Prof. of Botany, Univ. of Malaya, Kuala Lumpur, 1959-65; Dean of Science, Univ. of Malaya, 1964-65; Lectr, Forestry Dept, Oxford, 1965-66; Dir, Nature Conservancy, 1966-73; Scientific Dir, Internat. Union for Conservation of Nature and Natural Resources, Switzerland, 1974-78. Member: Thames Water Authority; Nature Conservancy Council. FRSA; FRGS. *Publications:* papers on ecology and land use in various jls and scientific periodicals. *Recreations:* hill walking, natural history, music, gardening, photography. *Address:* Evenlode, Stonesfield, Oxon. *T:* Stonesfield 246; St John's College, Oxford OX7 2PX. *Club:* Athenæum.

POORE, Roger Dennistoun; Executive Chairman: Manganese Bronze Holdings plc (Chairman, since 1963; Director, since 1961); Norton Villiers Triumph Ltd, since 1973; Federated Trust Corporation Ltd, since 1967; The Scottish & Mercantile Investment Trust plc, since 1971 (Director, since 1965); Director, Scottish Cities Investment Trust plc, since 1953; Member Lloyd's, since 1950; *b* 19 Aug. 1916; *s* of Lt-Col Roger Alvin Poore, DSO, and Lorne Margery, *d* of Major R. J. W. Dennistoun; *m* 1949, Mrs Peta Farley; one *d. Educ:* Eton; King's College, Cambridge (MA). Served War, Royal Air Force, 1939-46 (Wing Comdr 1944). Motor racing successes, 1947-55 (British Hill Climb Champion, 1950). *Recreations:* tennis, golf, bridge. *Address:* 33 Phillimore Gardens, W8. *T:* 01-937 1384.

POPA, Pretor; Order Star of Socialist Republic of Romania; Order of Labour and other medals; Deputy Foreign Trade Minister, Romania, since 1980; *b* 20 April 1922; *m* Ileana Popa. *Educ:* Academy for High Commercial and Industrial Studies, Bucharest. Director, Ministry for Oil Extraction and Processing, 1950-66; Gen. Director, Ministry for Foreign Trade, 1966-70; Deputy Minister, Ministry for Foreign Trade, and Vice-Chairman at Chamber of Commerce, 1970-73; Ambassador of Romania to the UK, 1973-80. *Address:* Ministry for Foreign Trade, 1 University Square, Bucharest, Romania.

POPE, HH the; *see* John Paul II.

POPE, Andrew Lancelot, CMG 1972; CVO 1965; OBE 1959; HM Diplomatic Service, retired; *b* 27 July 1912; *m* 1st, 1938 (marr. diss.); 2nd,

1948, Ilse Migliarina; one *step d. Educ:* Harrow School. Served War of 1939-45 (despatches): Lieut, Royal Fusiliers, 1939; POW 1940-45. Served in Mil. Govt and Allied High Commn in Germany, 1945-56; entered Foreign (subseq. Diplomatic) Service, 1959; Counsellor, Bonn, 1962-72. Dir, Conf. Bd, NY; Dir, Gerling Global General and Reinsurance Co. Ltd. Order of Merit (Germany), 1965; Order of Merit (Bavaria), 1970; Order of Merit (Lower Saxony), 1972. *Recreations:* shooting, gardening. *Address:* Goldhill Grove, Lower Bourne, Farnham, Surrey. *T:* Farnham 21662.

POPE, Sir Barton; *see* Pope, Sir Sidney Barton.

POPE, Dudley Bernard Egerton; Naval historian and author; *b* 29 Dec. 1925; *s* of late Sydney Broughton Pope and late Alice Pope (*née* Meehan); *m* 1954, Kathleen Patricia Hall; one *d. Educ:* Ashford (Kent). Served War of 1939-45: Midshipman, MN, 1941-43 (wounded and invalided). The Evening News: naval and defence correspondent, 1944-57, Dep. Foreign Editor, 1957-59; resigned to take up full-time authorship, 1959. Counsellor, Navy Record Soc., 1964-68. Created: "Lt Ramage RN" series of historical novels covering life of naval officer in Nelson's day, 1965; series of novels portraying sea life of Yorke family, 1979. cruising trans-Atlantic and Caribbean in own yacht, doing naval historical research, 1965-. Hon. Mem., Mark Twain Soc., 1976. *Publications: non-fiction:* Flag 4, the Battle of Coastal Forces in the Mediterranean, 1954; The Battle of the River Plate, 1956; 73 North, 1958; England Expects, 1959; At 12 Mr Byng was Shot, 1962; The Black Ship, 1963; Guns, 1965; The Great Gamble, 1972; Harry Morgan's Way, 1977; Life in Nelson's Navy, 1981; *fiction: the Ramage series:* Ramage (Book Society Choice) 1965; Ramage and the Drum Beat (Book Society Alternative Choice), 1967; Ramage and the Freebooters (Book of the Month Club Alt. Choice), 1969; Governor Ramage, RN, 1973; Ramage's Prize, 1974; Ramage and the Guillotine, 1975; Ramage's Diamond, 1976; Ramage's Mutiny, 1977; Ramage and the Rebels, 1978; The Ramage Touch, 1979; Ramage's Signal, 1980; Ramage and the Renegades, 1981; Ramage's Devil, 1982; *the Yorke series:* Convoy (Book Club Associates' Choice), 1979; Buccaneer, 1981; Admiral, 1982. *Recreations:* ocean cruising, skin-diving. *Address:* c/o Peter Janson Smith Ltd, 31 Newington Green, N16 9PU. *Club:* Royal Temple Yacht.

POPE, Sir Ernle; *see* Pope, Sir J. E.

POPE, Geoffrey George, PhD, FRAeS; Assistant Chief Scientific Adviser (Projects), Ministry of Defence, since 1981; *b* 17 April 1934; *s* of Sir George Reginald Pope, *qv; m* 1961, Rosemary Frances Harnden; two *s. Educ:* Epsom Coll.; Imperial Coll., London. MSc (Eng), PhD, CEng, DIC, ACGI. Junior Technical Asst, Hawker Aircraft Ltd, 1952-53; Student, Imperial Coll., 1953-58; Royal Aircraft Establishment: Structures Dept, 1958-73 (Head, Research Div., 1969-73); Aerodynamics Dept, 1973-77 (Head, 1974-77); Gp Head, Aerodynamics, Structures and Materials Depts, 1978-79; Dep. Dir (Weapons), 1979-81. *Publications:* technical papers, mainly on structural mechanics and optimum design of structures, in ARC (R&M series) and various technical jls. *Recreations:* music, photography, walking. *Address:* 22 Rosemary Lane, Rowledge, Farnham, Surrey. *T:* Frensham 2426.

POPE, Sir George (Reginald), Kt 1967; General Manager of The Times, 1965-67; Director: Times Newspapers Ltd, 1967-76 (Deputy General Manager during 1967); Kingsway Press Ltd; *b* 25 Mar. 1902; *s* of G. J. Pope; *m* 1930, Susie A. Hendy; one *s. Educ:* Clapham Parochial Sch. The Morning Post, 1916-37; The Daily Telegraph, 1937; The Times, 1937-. Pres. of the Advertising Assoc., 1962-63. Mackintosh Medal, 1953; Publicity Club of London Cup, 1961. *Recreation:* bowls. *Address:* 57 West Drive, Cheam, Surrey. *T:* 01-642 4754. *See also G. G. Pope.*

POPE, Jeremy James Richard; Finance and Planning Director, Eldridge, Pope & Co. plc, since 1972; *b* 15 July 1943; *s* of Philip William Rolph Pope and Joyce Winifred Harcourt Pope (*née* Slade); *m* 1969, Hon. Jacqueline Best; three *s. Educ:* Charterhouse; Trinity Coll., Cambridge. Law tripos, MA. Solicitor. Joined Eldridge, Pope & Co., 1969. Chm., Smaller Firms Council, CBI, 1981-; Mem., NEDC, 1981-. Chm., Winterbourne Hosp. plc, 1981-. *Recreations:* shooting, fishing, gardening, cooking the resultant produce. *Address:* (office) Dorchester Brewery, Dorchester, Dorset DT1 1QT. *T:* Dorchester 64801; (home) Field Cottage, West Compton, Dorchester, Dorset DT2 0EY. *T:* Maiden Newton 20469.

POPE, Air Vice-Marshal John Clifford, CB 1963; CBE 1959; CEng, FIMechE; FRAeS; RAF (retired); *b* 27 April 1912; *s* of George Newcombe-Pope; *m* 1950, Christine Agnes, *d* of Alfred Hames, Chichester; one *s* two *d. Educ:* Tiverton Sch.; RAF Coll., Cranwell. Commnd, 1932; served with No 3 Sqdn, 1933, Nos 27 and 39, on NW Frontier, 1933-36. War of 1939-45; Comd RAF Station, Cleave, 1940-42; served in Egypt and Palestine, 1943-46; Asst Dir Research and Develt, Min. of Supply, 1947-50; Dir of Engineering, RNZAF, 1951-53; Comd RAF Station, Stoke Heath, 1954-57; Sen. Tech. Staff Officer, No 3 Gp Bomber Comd, 1957-59 and Flying Trng Comd, 1960-61; AOC and Comdt, RAF Technical College, 1961-63; Senior Technical Staff Officer, Transport Command, 1963-66. Life Vice-Pres., RAF Boxing Assoc. *Address:* Dilston, 47 Oxford Road, Stone, near Aylesbury, Bucks. *T:* Aylesbury 748467. *Club:* Royal Air Force.

POPE, Vice-Adm. Sir (John) Ernle, KCB 1976; *b* 22 May 1921; *s* of Comdr R. K. C. Pope, Homme House, Herefordshire. *Educ:* RN Coll., Dartmouth. Royal Navy, 1935. Served throughout War of 1939-45, in Destroyers. CO, HMS Decoy, 1962-64; Dir, Naval Equipment, 1964-66; CO, HMS Eagle, 1966-68; Flag Officer, Western Fleet Flotillas, 1969-71; C of S to C-in-C Western Fleet, 1971-74; Comdr, Allied Naval Forces, S Europe, 1974-76; Rear-Adm. 1969; Vice-Adm. 1972. Pres., Royal Naval Assoc. *Recreations:* sailing, shooting. *Address:* Homme House, Much Marcle, Herefordshire. *Club:* Army and Navy.

See also Rear-Adm. M. D. Kyrle Pope.

POPE, Rev. (John) Russell; President of Methodist Conference, 1974-75; *b* 15 Aug. 1909; 3rd *s* of George and Rhoda Pope; *m* 1939, Doreen Minette Foulkes; one *s* one d. *Educ:* Canton High Sch., and Technical Coll., Cardiff; Handsworth Theological Coll., Birmingham. Manchester and Salford Mission, 1936-39; Liverpool South Circuit, 1939-44; Manchester and Salford Mission, 1944-48; Bristol Mission, 1948-57; Nottingham Mission, 1957-59; Chm., Plymouth and Exeter Methodist District, 1959-76, retired; Second Minister, Ilfracombe Circuit, 1976-79. Preaching tours: S Africa, 1953; NSW, 1959; Bahamas, 1962; New England, 1966; two visits to Holy Land, 1964 and 1969 (second visit being Jt Leadership of Ecumenical Pilgrimage to Rome and Holy Land with Bp of Bath and Wells, and Bishop of Clifton); audience with the Pope. *Recreations:* gardening, travel. *Address:* 11 Lime Grove, Exmouth, Devon. *T:* Exmouth 78438. *Club:* National Liberal.

POPE, Sir Joseph (Albert), Kt 1980; DSc, PhD (Belfast), WhSc; Chairman, TecQuipment Group, Nottingham (Director, 1960-); *b* 18 October 1914; *s* of Albert Henry and Mary Pope; *m* 1940, Evelyn Alice Gallagher; one *s* two d. *Educ:* School of Arts and Crafts, Cambridge; King's College, London. Apprentice, Boulton & Pauls, Norwich, 1930-35. Whitworth Scholarship, 1935. Assistant Lecturer in Engineering, Queen's Univ., Belfast, 1938-44; Assistant Lecturer in Engineering, Univ. of Manchester, 1944-45; Lecturer, then Senior Lecturer, Univ. of Sheffield, 1945-49; Professor of Mechanical Engineering, Nottingham University, 1949-60; Vice-Chancellor, Univ. of Aston in Birmingham, 1969-79. Research Dir, Mirrlees Nat. Research Div., Stockport, 1960-69; Director: Mirrlees National Ltd, 1960-69; John Brown & Co. Ltd, 1970-82; Midlands Electricity Bd, 1975-80; Royal Worcester Ltd, 1979-; Chm., W Midlands Econ. Planning Council, 1977-79. Gen. Treasurer, British Assoc., 1975-82; Pres., Whitworth Soc., 1978-79; Chm., Birmingham Civic Soc., 1978-79. Hon. LLD Birmingham, 1979; Hon. DUniv Heriot-Watt, 1979; Hon. DSc: Aston, 1979; Belfast, 1980; Salford, 1980. *Publications:* papers on the impact of metals and metal fatigue published in Proc. of Inst. of Mech. Engineers and Jl of Iron and Steel Inst. *Address:* 3 Mapperley Hall Drive, Nottingham NG3 5EP. *T:* Nottingham 621146.

POPE, Rear-Adm. Michael Donald K.; see Kyrle Pope.

POPE, Very Rev. Robert William, OBE 1971; Dean of Gibraltar, 1977-82; *b* 20 May 1916; *s* of late Rev. Jonas George Pope and Marjorie Mary Pope (*née* Coates); *m* 1940, Elizabeth Beatrice Matilda (*née* Bressey); two *s* one d. *Educ:* English College, Temuco, Chile; Harvey Grammar Sch., Folkestone; Maidstone Grammar Sch.; St Augustine's Coll., Canterbury; Durham Univ. (LTh). Deacon 1939, priest, 1940, Rochester; Curate: Holy Trinity, Gravesend, 1939-41; St Nicholas, Guildford, 1942-43; Priest in charge, Peaslake, 1943-44; Chaplain, Royal Navy, 1944-71; Vicar of Whitchurch with Tufton and Litchfield, Dio. Winchester, 1971-77. Member of Sion College. Fellow, Royal Commonwealth Soc. *Address:* Woodcote, 59 Elm Hill, Motcombe, Shaftesbury, Dorset SP7 9HR. *T:* Shaftesbury 2257.

POPE, Russell; see Pope, J. R.

POPE, Sir (Sidney) Barton, Kt 1959; *b* 18 Feb. 1905; *s* of Henry Pope, Northam, W Australia; *m* 1944, Ada Lilian, d of late J. B. Hawkins; two *s* two d. *Educ:* Pulteney Grammar School, S Australia. President S Aust. Chamber of Manufacturers, 1947-49. Patron, SA Assoc. for Mental Health. *Recreations:* cricket, golf. *Address:* 8/4 Chisholm Avenue, Burnside, SA 5066, Australia. *Club:* Naval, Military and Air Force (SA).

POPE-HENNESSY, Sir John (Wyndham), Kt 1971; CBE 1959 (MBE 1944); FBA 1955; FSA; FRSL; Consultative Chairman, Department of European Paintings, Metropolitan Museum, New York, since 1977; Professor of Fine Arts, New York University, since 1977; *b* 13 Dec. 1913; *er s* of late Major-General L. H. R. Pope-Hennessy, CB, DSO, and late Dame Una Pope-Hennessy, DBE. *Educ:* Downside School; Balliol Coll., Oxford (Hon. Fellow). Joined staff of Victoria and Albert Museum, 1938. Served Air Ministry, 1939-45. Victoria and Albert Museum: Keeper, Dept of Architecture and Sculpture, 1954-66; Dir and Sec., 1967-73; Dir, British Museum, 1974-76. Slade Professor of Fine Art, Univ. of Oxford, 1956-57; Clark Professor of Art, Williams College, Mass., USA, 1961-62; Slade Professor of Fine Art, and Fellow of Peterhouse, University of Cambridge, 1964-65. Member: Arts Council, 1968-76; Ancient Monuments Bd for England, 1969-72; Dir, Royal Opera House, 1971-76. Fellow, Amer. Acad. of Arts and Scis, 1978; Corresponding Member: Accademia Senese degli Intronati; Bayerische Akademie der Wissenschaften; Hon. Academician, Accademia del Disegno, Florence; For. Mem., Amer. Philosophical Soc., 1974; Hon. Fellow, Pierpoint Morgan Library, 1975. Serena Medal of British Academy for Italian Studies, 1961; New York University Medal, 1965; Torch of Learning Award, Hebrew Univ., Jerusalem, 1977. Hon. LLD Aberdeen, 1972; Hon. Dr RCA, 1973.

Publications: Giovanni di Paolo, 1937; Sassetta, 1939; Sienese Quattrocento Painting, 1947; A Sienese Codex of the Divine Comedy, 1947; The Drawings of Domenichino at Windsor Castle, 1948; A Lecture on Nicholas Hilliard, 1949; Donatello's Ascension, 1949; The Virgin with the Laughing Child, 1949; edition of the Autobiography of Benvenuto Cellini, 1949; Paolo Uccello, 1950, rev. edn, 1972; Italian Gothic Sculpture in the Victoria and Albert Museum, 1952; Fra Angelico, 1952, rev. edn, 1974; Italian Gothic Sculpture, 1955, rev. edn 1972; Italian Renaissance Sculpture, 1958, rev. edn 1971; Italian High Renaissance and Baroque Sculpture, 1963, rev. edn 1970; Catalogue of Italian Sculpture in the Victoria and Albert Museum, 1964; Renaissance Bronzes in the Kress Collection, 1965; The Portrait in the Renaissance, 1967; Essays on Italian Sculpture, 1968; Catalogue of Sculpture in the Frick Collection, 1970; Raphael (Wrightsman lectures), 1970; (with others) Westminster Abbey, 1972; Luca della Robbia, 1980 (Mitchell Prize, 1981); The Study and Criticism of Italian Sculpture, 1980. Contributor, Apollo, etc. *Recreation:* music. *Address:* 1130 Park Avenue, New York, NY 10028, USA.

POPHAM, Maj.-Gen. Christopher John, CB 1982; Assistant Chief of Staff (Intelligence), Supreme Headquarters Allied Powers Europe, 1979-82; *b* 2 April 1927; *s* of late Gordon F. B. Popham and Dorothy A. L. Popham (*née* Yull); *m* 1950, Heather Margaret, *y* d of late Lt-Col and Mrs H. R. W. Dawson; two *s*. *Educ:* Merchant Taylors' School. Commnd Royal Engineers, 1946; served with King George V's Own Bengal Sappers and Miners, RIE and Royal Pakistan Engineers, 1946-48; UK and Germany, 1948-57; Staff Coll., 1958; Cyprus, 1959-62; OC 4 Field Sqdn, 1963-65; JSSC 1965; Mil. Asst to QMG, 1966-68; CO 36 Engineer Regt, 1968-70; CRE 4 Div., 1971-73; Comd 12 Engineer Bde, 1973-75; BGS Intelligence and Security, HQ BAOR and ACOS G-2 HQ Northern Army Group, 1976-79. FBIM. *Recreations:* music, photography, railways. *Address:* c/o Barclays Bank, High Street, Andover, Hants.

POPJÁK, George Joseph, FRS 1961; DSc (London), MD, FRSC; Professor of Biochemistry at University of California in Los Angeles, since 1968; *b* 5 May 1914; *s* of late George and Maria Popják, Szeged, Hungary; *m* 1941, Hasel Marjorie, d of Duncan and Mabel Hammond, Beckenham, Kent. *Educ:* Royal Hungarian Francis Joseph University, Szeged. Demonstrator at Department of Morbid Anatomy and Histology, University of Szeged, 1938-39; Br Council Scholar, Postgraduate Med. School of London, 1939-41; Demonstrator in Pathology, Dept of Pathology, St Thomas's Hosp. Med. School, London, 1941-43; Beit Mem. Fellow for medical research at St Thomas's Hosp. Med. School, London, 1943-47; Member scientific staff of Med. Research Council at Nat. Inst. for Med. Research, 1947-53; Director of Medical Research Council Experimental Radiopathology Research Unit, Hammersmith Hosp., 1953-62; Jt Dir, Chemical Enzymology Lab., Shell Res. Ltd, 1962-68; Assoc. Prof. in Molecular Sciences, Warwick Univ., 1965-68. Foreign member of Belgian Roy. Flemish Acad. of Science, Literature and Fine Arts, 1955; Hon. Member: Amer. Soc. of Biological Chemists, 1968; Alpha-Omega-Alpha, 1970; Mem., Amer. Acad. of Arts and Sciences, 1971. (With Dr J. W. Cornforth, FRS) CIBA Medal of Biochemical Soc., 1965 (first award); Stouffer Prize, 1967; Davy Medal, Royal Soc., 1968; Award in Lipid Chem., Amer. Oil Chem. Soc., 1977; Distinguished Scientific Achievement award, Amer. Heart Assoc., 1978. *Publications:* Chemistry, Biochemistry and Isotopic Tracer Technique (Roy. Inst. of Chemistry monograph), 1955; articles on fat metabolism in Jl Path. Bact., Jl Physiol., Biochemical Jl, etc. *Recreations:* music, modelling and gardening. *Address:* Departments of Psychiatry and Biochemistry, University of California at Los Angeles, Center for the Health Sciences, Los Angeles, Calif 90024, USA.

POPLE, John Anthony, FRS 1961; John Christian Warner University Professor of Natural Sciences (formerly Professor of Chemical Physics), Carnegie-Mellon University, Pittsburgh, USA, since 1964; *b* 31 Oct. 1925; *e s* of Herbert Keith Pople and Mary Frances Jones, Burnham-on-Sea, Som.; *m* 1952, Joy Cynthia Bowers; three *s* one d. *Educ:* Bristol Grammar School; Cambridge University, MA, PhD. Mayhew Prize, 1948, Smith Prize, 1950, Cambridge; Fellow, Trinity College, 1951-58, Lecturer in Mathematics, 1954-58, Cambridge; Superintendent of Basic Physics Division, National Physical Laboratory, 1958-64. Ford Visiting Professor, Carnegie Inst. of Technology, Pittsburgh, 1961-62. Fellow, Amer. Physical Soc., 1970; Mem., Amer. Acad. of Arts and Scis, 1971. For. Associate, Nat. Acad. of Sci., 1977. Marlow Medal, Faraday Soc., 1958; ACS Pauling Award, 1977; Awards from American Chemical Society: Langmuir, 1970; Harrison Howe, 1971; Gilbert Newton Lewis, 1973; Pittsburgh, 1975. *Publications:* High Resolution nuclear magnetic resonance, 1959; Approximate Molecular Orbital Theory, 1970; scientific papers on molecular physics and theoretical chemistry. *Recreations:* music, travel. *Address:* Carnegie-Mellon University, 5000 Forbes Avenue, Pittsburgh, Pa 15213, USA.

POPONDETTA, Bishop of, since 1977; **Rt. Rev. George Somboba Ambo,** OBE 1978; *b* Gona, Nov. 1925; *s* of late J. O. Ambo, Gona; *m* 1946, Marcella O., d of Karau; two *s* two d. *Educ:* St Aidan's College, Dogura; Newton Theological Coll., Dogura. Deacon 1955; Priest, 1958. Curate of: Menapi, 1955-57; Dogura, 1957-58; Priest in charge of Boianai, Diocese of New Guinea, 1958-63; Missionary at Wamira, 1963-69; an Asst Bishop of Papua New Guinea, 1960 (first Papuan-born Anglican Bishop). *Publication:* St John's Gospel in Ewage. *Recreations:* reading, carpentry. *Address:* PO Box 26, Popondetta, Papua New Guinea.

POPOV, Viktor Ivanovich; Soviet Ambassador to the Court of St James's, since 1980; *b* 19 May 1918; *m* Natalia Aleksandrovna Popova; two *s*. *Educ*: Moscow Inst. of History and Philosophy; Higher Diplomatic Sch. of USSR. Entered Min. of Foreign Affairs, 1954; Vietnam, 1960-61; Australia, 1967-68; UK, 1968; Ambassador on special assignments, UN and Unesco, and Rector, Diplomatic Acad. of USSR, 1968-80. Many Soviet and foreign awards. *Publications:* Anglo-Soviet Relations 1927-29; Anglo-Soviet Relations 1929-39; (jtly) History of Diplomacy series III. *Address:* Embassy of USSR, 13 Kensington Palace Gardens, W8.

POPPER, Prof. Sir Karl (Raimund), CH 1982; Kt 1965; FRS 1976; FBA 1958; PhD (Vienna), MA (New Zealand), DLit (London); Professor of Logic and Scientific Method in the University of London (London School of Economics and Political Science), 1949-69; Emeritus Professor, 1969; *b* Vienna, 28 July 1902; *s* of Dr Simon Siegmund Carl Popper, Barrister, of Vienna, and of Jenny Popper (*née* Schiff); *m* 1930, Josefine Anna Henninger; no *c*. *Educ*: University of Vienna. Senior Lecturer in Philosophy, Canterbury University College, Christchurch (Univ. of NZ), 1937-45; Reader in Logic and Scientific Method, LSE, Univ. of London, 1945-49. Fellow, Center for Advanced Study in the Behavioral Sciences, Stanford, Calif, 1956-57; Visiting Professor: Harvard (Wm James Lectures in Philosophy), 1950; Univ. of California Berkeley, 1962; Minnesota Center for Phil. of Science, 1962; Indiana Univ., 1963; Inst. for Advanced Studies, Vienna, 1964; Denver Univ., 1966; Vis. Fellow, The Salk Institute for Biological Studies, 1966-67; Kenan Univ. Prof., Emory Univ., 1969; Jacob Ziskind Vis. Prof. in Philosophy and the History of Thought, Brandeis Univ., 1969; William Evans Vis. Prof., Otago, 1973; Vis. Erskine Fellow, Canterbury, NZ, 1973; Lectures: Yale, Princeton, Chicago, Emory Univs, 1950, 1956; Eleanor Rathbone, Bristol, 1956; Annual Philos. to British Acad., 1960; Herbert Spencer, Oxford, 1961 and 1973; Shearman Meml, UCL, 1961; Farnum, Princeton, 1963; Arthur H. Compton Meml, Washington, 1965; Romanes, Oxford, 1972; Broadhead Meml, Canterbury, 1973; First Darwin, Darwin Coll., Cambridge, 1977; Tanner, Ann Arbor, 1978; Frank Nelson Doubleday, Smithsonian Inst., 1979; first Morrell Meml, York, 1981. Member: Editorial Bd: Foundations of Physics; British Jl Phil. of Science; Studi Internat. di Filosofia; Jl of Political Theory; Biologie et Logique; Board of Consulting Editors: Theory and Decision; Idea; Advisory Board: Medical Hypotheses; The Monist; Co-Editor: Ratio; Studies in the Foundations Methodology and Philosophy of Science; Methodology and Science; Rechtstheorie; Schriftenreihe Erfahrung und Denken; Library of Exact Philosophy; Ed. Correspond., Dialectica. Chairman, Phil. of Science Group, 1951-53; President: The Aristotelian Soc., 1958-59; British Society for the Phil. of Science, 1959-61; Mem. Council, Assoc. for Symb. Logic, 1951-55. Mem., Académie Internat. de Philosophie des Sciences, 1949; Hon. Mem., RSNZ, 1965; For. Hon. Mem., Amer. Acad. of Arts and Scis, 1966; Correspondant de l'Institut de France, 1974; Associate Mem., Académie Royale de Belgique, 1976; Membre d'Honneur, Académie Internationale d'Histoire des Sciences, 1977; Hon. Mem., Deutsche Akademie für Sprache und Dichtung, 1979; Membre de l'Académie Européenne des Sciences, des Arts et des Lettres (Delegn of GB), 1980; Membre de l'Institut de France, 1980; Socio Straniero dell'Accademia Nazionale dei Lincei, 1981; Ehrenmitglied, Oesterreichische Akademie der Wissenschaften, 1982. Hon. Mem., Harvard Chapter of Phi Beta Kappa, 1964; Hon. Fellow, LSE, 1972; Hon. Mem., Allgemeine Gesellschaft für Philosophie in Deutschland, 1979; Hon. Fellow, Darwin Coll., Cambridge, 1980; Hon. Research Fellow, Dept. of History & Philosophy of Science, Chelsea College, University of London, 1982. Hon. LLD: Chicago, 1962; Denver, 1966; Hon. LittD: Warwick, 1971; Canterbury, NZ, 1973; Cantab, 1980; Hon. DLitt: Salford, 1976; City Univ., 1976; Guelph, Ontario, 1978; Oxon 1982; Hon. Dr.rer.nat, Vienna, 1978; Dr. phil *hc* : Mannheim, 1978; Salzburg, 1979; Hon. Dr.rer.pol, Frankfurt, 1979; Hon. DSc Gustavus Adolphus Coll., 1981. Prize of the City of Vienna for 'Geisteswissenschaften' (mental and moral sciences) 1965; Sonning Prize, Univ. of Copenhagen, 1973; Lippincott Award, Amer. Pol. Sci. Assoc., 1976; Dr Karl Renner Prize, Vienna, 1978; Dr Leopold Lucas Prize, Univ. of Tübingen, 1981. Grand Decoration of Honour in Gold (Austria), 1976; Gold Medal for Disting. Service to Sci., Amer. Mus. of Nat. Hist., NY, 1979; Ehrenzeichen für Wissenschaft und Kunst (Austria), 1980; Order Pour le Mérite (German Fed. Rep.), 1980. *Publications:* (trans into 22 languages): Logik der Forschung, 1934, rev. edn 1966, 7th edn 1980; The Open Society and Its Enemies, 1945, 5th edn, rev. 1966, 13th impr. 1980; The Poverty of Historicism, 1957, 10th impr. 1979; The Logic of Scientific Discovery, 1959, 10th impr. 1980; On the Sources of Knowledge and of Ignorance, 1961; Conjectures and Refutations, 1963, 7th impr. 1978; Of Clouds and Clocks, 1966; Objective Knowledge, 1972, 5th impr. rev. 1979; Unended Quest: An Intellectual Autobiography, 1976, 5th impr. 1980; (with Sir John Eccles) The Self and Its Brain, 1977, 2nd impr. rev. 1981; Die beiden Grundprobleme der Erkenntnistheorie, 1979; Postscript to The Logic of Scientific Discovery, 3 vols, 1982; A Pocket Popper, 1982; The Open Universe, 1982; Quantum Theory and the Schism in Physics, 1982; contribs to: learned jls; anthologies; The Philosophy of Karl Popper, Library of Living Philosophers (ed P.A. Schilpp), 1974. *Recreation:* music. *Address:* Fallowfield, Manor Close, Manor Road, Penn, Buckinghamshire HP10 8HZ.

POPPLEWELL, Oliver Bury, QC 1969; a Recorder of the Crown Court, since 1972; *b* 15 Aug. 1927; *s* of late Frank and Nina Popplewell; *m* 1954, Catharine Margaret Storey; four *s* (and one *s* decd). *Educ*: Charterhouse (Schol.); Queens' Coll., Cambridge (Class. exhibnr). BA 1950; LLB 1951. CUCC, 1949-51. Called to the Bar, Inner Temple, 1951, Bencher, 1978. Recorder, Burton-on-Trent, 1970-71; Dep. Chm., Oxon QS, 1970-71. Chm.

and Indep. Mem., Wages Councils; Mem., Home Office Adv. Bd on Restricted Patients, 1981-. Mem. Cttee, MCC, 1971-74, 1976-78, 1980-. *Recreations:* sailing, cricket, tennis. *Address:* 2 Crown Office Row, Temple, EC4. *T:* 01-353 9337; Lime Tree Farm, Chartridge, Bucks. *T:* The Lee 356. *Clubs:* MCC; Hawks (Cambridge), Blakeney Sailing.

POPPLEWELL, Patrick John Lyon; HM Diplomatic Service, retired; *b* 2 April 1937; *s* of Geoffrey Douglas Popplewell and late Marjorie Helen (*née* Macdonald). *Educ*: Haileybury and Imperial Service Coll.; Brasenose Coll., Oxford (Hons degree Law). HM Armed Forces, 1955-57. Appointed Foreign Office, 1960; 3rd and 2nd Sec., Tokyo, 1960-65; Resident Clerk, CRO and FO, 1965-67; 1st (Press) Sec., Cairo, 1968-70; Tokyo, 1970-74; Foreign and Commonwealth Office: Trade Relations and Export Dept, 1974-76; Far Eastern Dept, 1976-77; Counsellor, Peking, 1977-78, FCO, 1978-80. *Recreation:* all aspects of Japanese Art. *Address:* Clouds Hill, Shillingstone, near Blandford Forum, Dorset. *T:* Child Okeford 263. *Club:* United Oxford & Cambridge University.

PORCHER, Michael Somerville, CMG 1962; OBE 1960; Secretary (Operations Division), Royal National Life-Boat Institution, since 1964; *b* 9 March 1921; *s* of late Geoffrey Lionel Porcher and Marjorie Fownes Porcher (*née* Somerville); *m* 1955, Mary Lorraine Porcher (*née* Tweedy); two *s*. *Educ*: Cheltenham College; St Edmund Hall, Oxford. Military Service, 1941-42. Joined Colonial Admin. Service: Sierra Leone; Cadet, 1942; Asst Dist, Comr, 1945; Dist Comr, 1951; British Guiana: Dep. Colonial Sec., 1952; Governor's Sec. and Clerk Exec. Council, 1953; Dep. Chief Sec., 1956. British Honduras: Colonial Secretary, 1960; Chief Secretary, 1961; retired, 1964. *Recreations:* fishing, shooting, sailing, riding. *Address:* Bladon, Worth Matravers, near Swanage, Dorset.

PORCHESTER, Lord; Henry George Reginald Molyneux Herbert, KCVO 1982; KBE 1976; DL; *b* 19 Jan. 1924; *o s* of 6th Earl of Carnarvon, *qv* ; *m* 1956, Jean Margaret, *e d* of Hon. Oliver Wallop, Big Horn, Sheridan Co., Wyoming, USA; two *s* one *d*. Late Lieut RHG; retired pay, 1947. Hon Col, Hampshire Fortress Regt, RE (TA) 1963-67, retaining rank of Hon. Col. Racing Manager to the Queen, 1969-. Chairman: South East Economic Planning Council, 1971-79; Agricultural Research Council, 1978-82; Game Research Assoc., 1960-67 (Vice-Pres., 1967-); Stallion Adv. Cttee to Betting Levy Bd, 1974-; President: Thoroughbred Breeders' Assoc., 1969-74 (Chm. 1964-66); RASE, 1980-81. Member: Hampshire Agriculture Exec. Cttee, 1955-65; Nature Conservancy, 1963-66; Sports Council, 1965-70 (Chm., Planning Cttee, 1965-70); Forestry Commission, 1967-70; President: Amateur Riders' Assoc., 1969-75; Hampshire County Cricket Club, 1966-68; Mem., Jockey Club, 1964- (Chm., Race Planning Cttee, 1967-). CC Hants, 1954; County Alderman, 1965-74; Vice-Chm. County Council, 1971-74, Chm., New County Council, 1973-77; Vice-Chm., CC Assoc., 1972-74 (Chm. Planning Cttee, 1968-74); Member: Basingstoke Town Develt Jt Cttee, 1960-73; Andover Town Develt Jt Cttee, 1960-65. Verderer of the New Forest, 1961-65. DL Hants 1965. High Steward of Winchester, 1977. Hon. Fellow, Portsmouth Polytech., 1976. Hon. DSc Reading, 1980. *Address:* Milford Lake House, Burghclere, Newbury, Berks RG16 9EL. *T:* Highclere 253387. *Clubs:* White's, Portland.
See also Earl of Portsmouth.

PORRITT, family name of **Baron Porritt.**

PORRITT, Baron *cr* 1973 (Life Peer), of Wanganui, NZ, and of Hampstead; **Arthur Espie Porritt,** GCMG 1967 (KCMG 1950); GCVO 1970 (KCVO 1957); CBE 1945 (OBE 1943); Bt 1963; Life Vice-President, African Medical and Research Foundation; President, Arthritis and Rheumatism Council; *b* 10 Aug. 1900; *e s* of late E. E. Porritt, VD, MD, FRCS, Wanganui, New Zealand; *m* 1st, 1926, Mary Frances Wynne, *d* of William Bond; 2nd, 1946, Kathleen Mary, 2nd *d* of late A. S. Peck and Mrs Windley, Spalding, Lincs; two *s* one *d*. *Educ*: Wanganui Collegiate School, NZ; Otago University, NZ; Magdalen College, Oxford (Rhodes Scholar); St Mary's Hospital, London. MA Oxon.; MCh Oxon. Surgeon: St Mary's Hosp.; Hosp. of St John and St Elizabeth; King Edward VII Hosp. for Officers; Royal Masonic Hosp.; Consulting Surgeon: Princess Louise Kensington Hosp. for Children; Paddington Hosps; Royal Chelsea Hosp.; Civil Consulting Surgeon to the Army, 1954-67, Emeritus, 1971; Brigadier, RAMC, 21 Army Group; Surgeon-in-Ordinary to the Duke of York; Surgeon to HM Household; a Surgeon to King George VI, 1946-52; Sergeant-Surgeon to the Queen, 1952-67; Governor-General of New Zealand, 1967-72. Dir, Sterling Winthrop and Sterling Europa. Chairman: Medical Advisory Cttee, Ministry of Overseas Develt; Medical Services Review Cttee, 1958; Red Cross Comr for NZ in UK; Chapter-Gen., Order of St John; Hunterian Soc., 1934-39 (Past Pres.); President: RCS, 1960-63; BMA, 1960-61; RSM, 1966-67; Assoc. of Surgeons of Gt Britain and Ireland; Med. Council on Alcoholism; Med. Commn on Accident Prevention; Past Master, Soc. of Apothecaries, 1964-66; Vice-Pres., Royal Commonwealth Soc.; Pres., OUAC, 1925-26; holder of 100 yards and 220 yards hurdles records at Oxford and 100 yards Oxford v. Cambridge (9 9/10 seconds); represented Oxford in Athletics, 1923-26; Finalist, Olympic 100 metres (Bronze Medallist), Paris, 1924; Captain NZ Olympic Team, Paris, 1924, Amsterdam, 1928, Manager Berlin, 1936; Mem., Internat. Olympic Cttee, British Olympic Council; Vice-Pres., British Empire and Commonwealth Games Federation. FRCS (Eng.); Fellow: Amer. Surgical Assoc.; Amer. Soc. of Clinical Surgery; French Acad. of Surgery; Hon. FRACS; Hon. FRCS (Ed.); Hon. FACS; Hon. FRCS (Glas.); Hon.

FRCS (Can.); Hon. FCS (SAf); Hon. FRCS (I); Hon. FRCP; Hon. FRACP; Hon FRCOG; Hon. FRACR; Hon. Fellow, Magdalen College, Oxford, 1961. BMA Gold Medal, 1964. Hon. LLD: St Andrews; Birmingham; New Zealand; Otago. Hon. MD Bristol; Hon. DSc Oxon. Legion of Merit (USA); KStJ. *Publications:* Athletics (with D. G. A. Lowe), 1929; Essentials of Modern Surgery (with R. M. Handfield-Jones), 1938, 6th edn 1956; various surgical articles in medical jls. *Recreations:* riding, golf, swimming; formerly athletics and Rugby football. *Heir* (to baronetcy only): *s* Hon. Jonathon Espie Porritt, *b* 6 July 1950. *Address:* 57 Hamilton Terrace, NW8. *Club:* Buck's.

PORT ELIZABETH, Bishop of, since 1975; **Rt. Rev. Bruce Read Evans;** *b* 10 Nov. 1929; *s* of Roy Leslie and Lilia Evans; *m* 1955, Joan Vanda Erlangsen; two *s* one *d*. *Educ:* King Edward Sch., Johannesburg; Univ. of the Witwatersrand, Johannesburg; Oak Hill Theological Coll., London. ACIS 1952; director of companies, 1952-54. Ordained into CofE, Southwark, 1957; Curate, Holy Trinity, Redhill, Surrey, 1957-59; Senior Curate, St Paul's, Portman Square, W1, and Chaplain to West End Business Houses in London, 1959-61; Curate-in-Charge: St Luke's, Diep River, Cape, 1962; Christ Church, Kenilworth, Cape, 1963-69; Rector of St John's, Wynberg, Cape, 1969-75. *Recreations:* formerly boxing and hockey; now painting. *Address:* Bishop's House, 14 Buckingham Road, Port Elizabeth, CP, 6001, South Africa. *T:* 39-2173. *Club:* Port Elizabeth.

PORT ELIZABETH, Assistant Bishop of; *see* Cowdry, Rt Rev. R. W. F.

PORT OF SPAIN, Archbishop of, since 1968; **Most Rev. Anthony Pantin,** CSSp; *b* 27 Aug. 1929; *s* of Julian and Agnes Pantin, both of Trinidad. *Educ:* Sacred Heart Private Sch., Belmont Boys' Intermediate Sch., St Mary's Coll., Port of Spain; Seminary of Philosophy, Montreal; Holy Ghost Missionary Coll., Dublin. Ordained Dublin, 1955; Guadeloupe, French West Indies, 1956-59; Fatima College, Port of Spain, 1959-64; Superior, St Mary's Coll., Port of Spain, 1965-68. Mem., Vatican Secretariat for Christian Unity, 1971-. Pres., Antilles Episcopal Conference, 1979-. *Address:* Archbishop's House, 27 Maraval Road, Port of Spain, Trinidad. *T:* 21103.

PORTAL, family name of **Baroness Portal of Hungerford.**

PORTAL OF HUNGERFORD, Baroness (2nd in line), *cr* 1945; **Rosemary Ann Portal;** *b* 12 May 1923; *d* of 1st Viscount Portal of Hungerford, KG, GCB, OM, DSO, MC, and Joan Margaret, *y d* of Sir Charles Glynn Welby, 5th Bt; *S* to barony of father, 1971. Formerly Section Officer, WAAF. *Heir:* sister Hon. Mavis Elizabeth Alouette Portal, *b* 13 June 1926. *Address:* West Ashling House, Chichester, West Sussex PO18 8DN.

PORTAL, Sir Francis Spencer, 5th Bt, *cr* 1901; DL; President, Portals Holdings Ltd; *b* 27 June 1903; *s* of 4th Bt and late Mary, *d* of late Colonel William Mure, Caldwell, Ayrshire; *S* father, 1955; *m* 1st, 1930, Rowena (*d* 1948), *d* of late Paul Selby, Johannesburg; two *d*; 2nd, 1950, Jane Mary, *d* of late Albert Henry Williams, OBE, Flint House, Langston, Havant, Hants, and of Mrs E. G. Selwyn, Priors Barton Cottage, Kingsgate Road, Winchester; two *s* one *d*. *Educ:* Winchester; Christ Church, Oxford; McGill Univ., Montreal. Served War of 1939-45, Captain, late Welsh Guards, Guards Armoured Division (Croix de Guerre, 2nd Class Belgium). Chm., YMCA Nat. Commn, 1968. Master, Worshipful Co. of Clothworkers, 1970. High Sheriff of Hampshire, 1963, DL Hants, 1967-. *Recreations:* miscellaneous. *Heir:* *s* Jonathan Francis Portal [*b* 13 Jan. 1953; *m* 1982, Louisa Caroline, *er d* of F. J. C. G. Hervey-Bathurst, Somborne Park, near Stockbridge, Hants]. *Address:* Burley Wood, Ashe, near Basingstoke, Hants RG25 3AG. *T:* Basingstoke 770269.

PORTAL, Admiral Sir Reginald Henry, KCB 1949 (CB 1946); DSC 1916; *b* 6 Sept. 1894; *s* of late Edward Robert Portal, JP; DL; *m* 1926, Helen, *d* of late Frederick Anderson; two *s* two *d*. Served European War, 1914-19, with RN and RNAS (DSC); War of 1939-45 (despatches, CB); comd HMS York, 1939-41; HMS Royal Sovereign, 1941-42; Asst Chief of Naval Staff (Air), 1943-44; ADC to the King, 1943; Flag Officer Naval Air Stations (Australia), 1945; Naval representative on Joint Chiefs of Staff Cttee (Australia), 1946-47; Flag Officer, Air (Home), 1947-51; retired, 1951. *Address:* Overton House, Queen Camel, Yeovil, Somerset.

PORTARLINGTON, 7th Earl of, *cr* 1785; **George Lionel Yuill Seymour Dawson-Damer;** Baron Dawson 1770; Viscount Carlow 1776; *b* 10 Aug. 1938; *er s* of Air Commodore Viscount Carlow (killed on active service, 1944) and Peggy (who *m* 2nd, 1945, Peter Nugent; she *d* 1963), *yr d* of late Charles Cambie; *S* grandfather, 1959; *m* 1961, Davina, *e d* of Sir Edward Windley, KCMG, KCVO; three *s* one *d*. *Educ:* Eton. Page of Honour to the Queen, 1953-55. Director: G. S. Yuill & Co. Ltd, Sydney, 1964; Cold Storage Holdings Ltd, London, 1965; Queensland Trading Holding Co. Ltd, Brisbane, 1967; Australian Stock Breeders Co. Ltd, Brisbane, 1966. *Heir:* *s* Viscount Carlow, *qv*. *Recreations:* fishing, ski-ing, books. *Address:* 19 Coolong Road, Vaucluse, NSW 2030, Australia. *T:* Sydney 337-3013. *Club:* Union (Sydney).

PORTEOUS, Christopher, MA; Headmaster of Eltham College, 1959-83; *b* 2 April 1921; *e s* of late Rev. Gilbert Porteous; *m* 1944, Amy Clunis, *d* of Theodore J. Biggs; one *s* three *d*. *Educ:* Nottingham High Sch. (Foundation Scholar); Emmanuel Coll., Cambridge (Senior Scholar). First Classes, with distinction, in Classical Tripos. Master of Classical Sixth, Mill Hill Sch., 1947-55; Asst Director, HM Civil Service Commission, 1955-59. FRSA. *Recreations:* travel, the countryside. *Address:* Little Thatch, Edwardstone, Suffolk.

PORTEOUS, Rev. Norman Walker, MA Edinburgh et Oxon, BD Edinburgh, DD St Andrews; *b* Haddington, 9 Sept. 1898; *yr s* of late John Dow Porteous, MA, formerly Rector of Knox Memorial Inst, Haddington, and Agnes Paton Walker; *m* 1929, May Hadwen, *y d* of late John Cook Robertson, Kirkcaldy; three *s* three *d*. *Educ:* Knox Memorial Institute, Haddington; Universities of Edinburgh, Oxford (Trinity College), Berlin, Tübingen and Münster; New Coll., Edinburgh. MA Edinburgh with 1st Class Honours in Classics; MA Oxon with 1st Class in Literæ Humaniores; BD Edinburgh with distinction in Old Testament; 1st Bursar at Edinburgh University, 1916; C. B. Black Scholar in New Testament Greek, 1920; John Edward Baxter Scholar in Classics, 1923; Ferguson Scholar in Classics, 1923; Senior Cunningham Fellow at New College and Kerr Travelling Scholar, 1927; served in army, 1917-19, commissioned 2nd Lieut, March 1918, served overseas with 13th Royal Scots; Ordained to Ministry of United Free Church of Scotland, 1929; Minister of Crossgates Church, Church of Scotland, 1929-31; Regius Professor of Hebrew and Oriental Languages in the University of St Andrews, 1931-35; Professor of Old Testament Language, Literature and Theology in the University of Edinburgh, 1935-37; Prof. of Hebrew and Semitic Languages, Univ. of Edinburgh, 1937-68; Principal of New Coll., and Dean of Faculty of Divinity, Univ. of Edinburgh, 1964-68; retd, 1968; now Emeritus Professor. Hon. DD St Andrews, 1944; Lectures: Stone, Princeton Theological Seminary, 1953; Montague Burton, Leeds, 1974. President, Soc. for Old Testament Study, 1954. *Publications:* Das Alte Testament Deutsch 23: Das Danielbuch, 1962, 3rd edn 1979 (English edition, 1965, 2nd, 1979); Living the Mystery: Collected Essays, 1967; Old Testament and History, 5 lectures in Annual of Swedish Theological Inst., vol. VIII, 1970-71; contributions to: Theologische Aufsätze Karl Barth zum 50 Geburtstag, 1936; Record and Revelation, 1938; The Old Testament and Modern Study, 1951; Peake's Commentary on the Bible, 1962. *Address:* 3 Hermitage Gardens, Edinburgh EH10 6DL. *T:* 031-447 4632.

PORTEOUS, Colonel Patrick Anthony, VC 1942; RA, retired 1970; *b* 1 Jan. 1918; *s* of late Brig.-General C. McL. Porteous, 9th Ghurkas, and late Mrs Porteous, Fleet, Hampshire; *m* 1943, Lois Mary (*d* 1953), *d* of late Maj.-General Sir H. E. Roome, KCIE; one *s* one *d*; *m* 1955, Deirdre, *d* of late Eric King; three *d*. *Educ:* Wellington Coll.; Royal Military Acad., Woolwich. BEF France, Sept. 1939-May 1940, with 6th AA Regt, RA; Dieppe, Aug. 1942 (VC); No 4 Commando, Dec. 1940-Oct. 1944; BLA June-Sept. 1944; 1st Airborne Div. Dec. 1944-July 1945; 6th Airborne Div., July 1945-March 1946; Staff Coll., Camberley, May-Nov. 1946; 16 Airborne Div. TA, Jan. 1947-Feb. 1948; 33 Airborne Lt Regt, RA, Feb. 1948-April 1949; No 1 Regular Commission Board, 1949; Instructor, RMA, Sandhurst, July 1950-July 1953; GHQ, Far East Land Forces, Singapore, Sept. 1953-July 1955; 1st Singapore Regt, RA, July-Dec. 1955; 14 Field Regt, RA, 1956-58; RAF Staff Coll., Jan. 1958-Dec. 1958; AMS, HQ Southern Comd, 1959-60; Colonel Junior Leaders Regt, RA, 1960-63; Colonel, General Staff War Office, later Ministry of Defence, 1963-66; Comdr Rheindahlen Garrison, 1966-69. *Recreation:* sailing. *Address:* Christmas Cottage, Church Lane, Funtington, W Sussex PO18 9LQ. *T:* Chichester 58315.

PORTER, Alastair Robert Wilson; Secretary and Registrar, Royal College of Veterinary Surgeons, since 1966; barrister; *b* 28 Sept. 1928; *s* of late James and Olivia Porter (*née* Duncan); *m* 1954, Jennifer Mary Priaulx Forman; two *s* one *d*. *Educ:* Irvine Royal Academy; Glasgow Academy; Merton Coll., Oxford (MA). Called to Bar, Gray's Inn, 1952. Resident Magistrate, N Rhodesia, 1954; Registrar of High Court of N Rhodesia, 1961; Permanent Secretary: Min. of Justice, N Rhodesia, 1964; Min. of Justice, Govt of Republic of Zambia, Oct. 1964. Mem., Fedn (formerly Liaison Cttee) of Veterinarians of the EEC, 1966-, Sec.-Gen., 1973-79; Vice-Chm., EEC's Adv. Cttee on Veterinary Trng, 1981-. Wooldridge Meml Lectr, BVA Congress, 1976; MacKellar Meml Lectr, Western Counties Veterinary Assoc., Tavistock, 1978; Centenary Prize Lectr, Central Vet. Soc., 1981. Hon. Mem., BVA, 1978; Hon. Associate, RCVS, 1979. *Publication:* (jtly) An Anatomy of Veterinary Europe, 1972. *Address:* 4 Savill Road, Lindfield, West Sussex. *T:* Lindfield 2001. *Club:* Caledonian.

PORTER, Alfred Ernest, CSI 1947; CIE 1942; *b* 2 Nov. 1896; *s* of F. L. Porter; *m* 1929, Nancy Florence (decd), *d* of late E. L. Melly; two *s*. *Educ:* Manchester Grammar Sch.; Corpus Christi Coll., Oxford. Manchester Regt, 1915; Machine Gun Corps, 1916; Indian Civil Service, 1922-48. *Address:* The Old Hall, Chawleigh, Chulmleigh, Devon EX18 7HH. *T:* Chulmleigh 80280.

PORTER, Sir Andrew M. H.; *see* Horsbrugh-Porter.

PORTER, Prof. Arthur, MSc, PhD (Manchester); FIEE; FRSC 1970; Professor of Industrial Engineering, and Chairman of Department, University of Toronto, Toronto, 1961-76, now Emeritus Professor; President, Arthur Porter Associates Ltd, since 1973; Associate, Hickling-Johnston Ltd, since 1980; *b* 8 Dec. 1910; *s* of late John William Porter and Mary Anne Harris; *m* 1941, Phyllis Patricia Dixon; one *s*. *Educ:* The Grammar Sch., Ulverston; University of Manchester. Asst Lecturer, University of Manchester, 1936-37;

Commonwealth Fund Fellow, Massachusetts Inst. of Technology, USA, 1937-39; Scientific Officer, Admiralty, 1939-45; Principal Scientific Officer, National Physical Laboratory, 1946; Prof. of Instrument Technology, Royal Military Coll. of Science, 1946-49; Head, Research Division, Ferranti Electric Ltd, Toronto, Canada, 1949-55; Professor of Light Electrical Engineering, Imperial College of Science and Technology, University of London, 1955-58; Dean of the College of Engineering, Saskatchewan Univ., Saskatoon, 1958; Acting Dir, Centre for Culture and Technology, Toronto Univ., 1967-68; Academic Comr, Univ. of W Ontario, 1969-71. Chairman: Canadian Environmental Adv. Council, 1972-75; Ontario Royal Commn on Electric Power Planning, 1975-80. *Publications:* An Introduction to Servomechanisms, 1950; Cybernetics Simplified, 1969; Towards a Community University, 1971; articles in Trans. Royal Society, Proc. Royal Society, Phil. Mag., Proc. Inst. Mech. Eng, Proc. IEE, Nature, etc. *Recreations:* landscape architecture, energy conservation. *Address:* Watendlath, Belfountain, Ontario L0N 1B0, Canada. *T:* (519) 927-5732; Hickling-Johnston Ltd, 415 Yonge Street, Toronto, Ont M5B 2E7, Canada. *Clubs:* Athenæum; Arts and Letters (Toronto).

PORTER, Arthur Thomas, MRSL 1979; MA, PhD; Vice-Chancellor, University of Sierra Leone, Freetown, Sierra Leone, since 1974; *b* 26 Jan. 1924; *m* 1953, Rigmor Sondergaard (*née* Rasmussen); one *s* one *d*. *Educ:* Fourah Bay Coll. (BA Dunelm) Cambridge Univ. (BA (Hist Tripos), MA); Boston Univ. (PhD). Asst, Dept of Social Anthropology, Edinburgh Univ., UK, 1951-52. Prof. of History and Head of Dept of Hist., also Dir of Inst. of African Studies, Fourah Bay Coll., 1963-64; Principal, University Coll., Nairobi, Univ. of E Africa, 1964-70; UNESCO Field Staff Officer; Educl Planning Adviser, Min. of Educn, Kenya, 1970-74. Mem. Exec. Bd, UNESCO, 1976-80. Hon. LHD Boston 1969; Hon. LLD Royal Univ. of Malta 1969. Phi Beta Kappa 1972. *Publications:* Creoledom, a Study of the Development of Freetown Society, 1963; contribs to The Times, Africa, African Affairs. *Recreation:* photography. *Address:* University of Sierra Leone, Private Mail Bag, Freetown, Sierra Leone, West Africa. *T:* 26859.

PORTER, Rt. Rev. David Brownfield; *b* 10 May 1906; *s* of Sydney Lawrence Porter and Edith Alice Porter; *m* 1936, Violet Margaret Eliot (*d* 1956); one *s*; *m* 1961, Mrs Pamela Cecil (*née* Lightfoot) (*d* 1974), widow of Neil McNeill. *Educ:* Hertford Coll., Oxford. Curate of St Augustine's, Leeds, 1929; Tutor of Wycliffe Hall, Oxford, 1931; Chaplain 1933; Chaplain of Wadham Coll., Oxford, 1934; Vicar of All Saints', Highfield, Oxford, 1935; Vicar of Darlington, 1943; Rector of St John's, Princes Street, Edinburgh, 1947-61; Dean of Edinburgh, 1954-61; Bishop Suffragan of Aston, 1962-72. Select Preacher, Oxford Univ., 1964. *Recreations:* fishing and painting. *Address:* Silver Leys, Brockhampton, near Cheltenham.

PORTER, Dorothea Noelle Naomi, (Thea Porter); fashion designer, since 1967; *b* 24 Dec. 1927; *d* of Rev. Dr M. S. Seale and Renée Seale; *m* 1953, Robert S. Porter (marr. diss. 1967); one *d*. *Educ:* Lycée français, Damascus; Fernhill Manor; Royal Holloway Coll., London Univ. Embassy wife, Beirut; fashion designer, 1967-, interior and fabric designer. *Recreations:* cooking, travelling, painting, collecting antique Islamic fabrics and objets; consulting clairvoyants. *Address:* Thea Porter Ltd, 1A Avery Row, W1. *T:* 01-499 4260. *Club:* Colony.

PORTER, Eric (Richard); actor; *b* London, 8 April 1928; *s* of Richard John Porter and Phoebe Elizabeth (*née* Spall). *Educ:* LCC and Wimbledon Technical College. First professional appearance with Shakespeare Memorial Theatre Company, Arts, Cambridge, 1945; first appearance on London stage as Dunois' Page in Saint Joan with the travelling repertory company, King's, Hammersmith, 1946; Birmingham Repertory Theatre, 1948-50; under contract to H. M. Tennant, Ltd, 1951-53. *Plays include:* The Silver Box, Lyric, Hammersmith, 1951; The Three Sisters, Aldwych, 1951; Thor, With Angels, Lyric, Hammersmith, 1951; title role in Noah, Whitehall, 1951; The Same Sky, Lyric, Hammersmith, 1952; Under the Sycamore Tree, Aldwych, 1952; season at Lyric, Hammersmith, directed by John Gielgud, 1953-plays: Richard II, The Way of the World, Venice Preserved; with Bristol Old Vic Company, 1954, and again 1955-56; parts included title roles in King Lear, Uncle Vanya, Volpone; with Old Vic Company, 1954-55: parts included Jacques in As You Like It, title role in Henry IV, Bolingbroke in Richard II, Christopher Sly in The Taming of the Shrew; Romanoff and Juliet, Piccadilly, 1956; A Man of Distinction, Edinburgh Festival and Princes, 1957; Time and Again, British tour with the Lunts, 1957, and New York in The Visit, 1958; The Coast of Coromandel, English tour, 1959; Rosmersholm, Royal Court, 1959, Comedy, 1960. (Evening Standard Drama Award as Best Actor of 1959); under contract to Royal Shakespeare Company, 1960-65; parts: Malvolio in Twelfth Night, Stratford, 1960, Aldwych, 1961; Duke in The Two Gentlemen of Verona, Stratford, 1960; Leontes in The Winter's Tale, Stratford, 1960; Ulysses in Troilus and Cressida, Stratford, 1960; Ferdinand in The Duchess of Malfi, Stratford, 1960, Aldwych, 1961; Lord Chamberlain in Ondine, Aldwych, 1961; Buckingham in Richard III, Stratford, 1961; title role in Becket, Aldwych, 1961, Globe, 1962; title role in Macbeth, Stratford, 1962; Iachimo in Cymbeline, Stratford, 1962; Pope Pius XII in The Representative, Aldwych, 1963. Stratford Season, 1964; Bolingbroke in Richard II; Henry IV in Henry IV Parts I and II; Chorus in Henry V; Richmond in Richard III; Stratford Season, 1965: Barabas in The Jew of Malta; Shylock in The Merchant of Venice; Chorus in Henry V, Aldwych, 1965; Ossip in The Government Inspector, Aldwych, 1966; Stratford Season, 1968; Lear in King Lear; Faustus in Dr Faustus (US tour, 1969); Paul Thomsen in My Little Boy-My Big Girl

(also directed), Fortune, 1969; The Protagonist, Brighton, 1971; Peter Pan, Coliseum, 1971; Malvolio, inaugural season, St George's Elizabethan Theatre, 1976. *Films:* The Fall of the Roman Empire, 1964; The Pumpkin Eater, 1964; The Heroes of Telemark, 1965; Kaleidoscope, 1966; The Lost Continent, 1968; Hands of the Ripper, Nicholas and Alexandra, Antony and Cleopatra, 1971; Hitler: the last ten days, 1973; The Day of the Jackal, 1973; The Belstone Fox, 1973; Callan, 1974; Hennessy, 1975; The Thirty-Nine Steps, 1978; Little Lord Fauntleroy, 1980; *television parts include:* Soames Forsyte in The Forsyte Saga, BBC (Best Actor Award, Guild of TV Producers and Directors, 1967); Karenin, in Anna Karenina, BBC, 1977; Alanbrooke in Churchill and the Generals, BBC, 1979; Polonius in Hamlet, BBC, 1980; Dep. Governor Danforth in The Crucible, BBC, 1981; Neville Chamberlain in Winston Churchill: The Wilderness Years, Southern, 1981. *Recreations:* walking, swimming, sailing. *Address:* c/o London Management, 235 Regent Street, W1A 2JT.

PORTER, Prof. Sir George, Kt 1972; FRS 1960; BSc (Leeds); MA, PhD, ScD, (Cambridge); FRSC; Director of the Royal Institution of Great Britain, and Fullerian Professor of Chemistry, since 1966; Honorary Professor of Physical Chemistry, University of Kent at Canterbury, since 1966; Visiting Professor: Department of Chemistry: University College, London, since 1967; Imperial College, London, since 1978; *b* 6 Dec. 1920; *o s* of late John Smith Porter and of Alice Ann Porter, Stainforth, Yorks; *m* 1949, Stella Jean Brooke, *o d* of late G. A. Brooke, Leeds, Kent, and late Mrs J. Brooke; two *s*. *Educ:* Thorne Grammar Sch,; Leeds Univ.; Emmanuel Coll., Cambridge. Ackroyd Scholar, Leeds Univ., 1938-41. Served RNVR in Western Approaches and Mediterranean, 1941-45. Cambridge: Demonstrator in Physical Chemistry, 1949-52, Fellow of Emmanuel Coll., 1952-54; Hon. Fellow, 1967; Asst Director of Research in Physical Chemistry, 1952-54. Asst Director of British Rayon Research Assoc., 1954-55. Prof. of Physical Chemistry, 1955-63, Firth Prof. of Chemistry, 1963-66, Univ. of Sheffield; Prof. of Chemistry, Royal Institution, 1963-66. Member: various cttees of DSIR and SRC, 1962-68; ARC, 1964-66; Open Univ. Council, 1969-75; Science Mus. Adv. Council, 1970-73; Council and Science Bd, SRC, 1976-80; President: Chemical Soc., 1970-72 (Pres. Faraday Div., 1973-74); Comité Internat. de photobiologie, 1968-72; Nat. Assoc. for Gifted Children, 1975-80; R&D Soc., 1977-80. Counsellor, Inst. for Molecular Sci., Okazaki, Japan, 1980. Hon. Member: NY Acad. of Sciences, 1968; Leopoldina Acad., 1970; Chemical Soc. of Japan, 1982; For. Associate, Nat. Acad. of Sciences, 1974; Corresp. Mem., Göttingen Acad. of Sciences, 1974; Mem. Pontifical Acad. of Sciences, 1974; For. Corresp. Mem., La Real Academia de Ciencias, Madrid, 1978; For. Hon. Mem., Amer. Acad. of Arts and Scis, 1979; Hon. Prof., Chinese Acad. of Scis, 1980. Lectures: Tilden, 1958; Remsen Meml, Amer. Chem. Soc., 1962; Liversidge, 1970; Theodor Förster Meml, 1975; Geoffrey Frew, Aust. Acad. of Sci. (also Geoffrey Frew Fellow), 1976; Robbins, USA, 1976; Pahlavi, Iran, 1977; Bakerian, Royal Soc., 1977; Robertson Meml, Nat. Acad. of Sciences, USA, 1978; Romanes, Oxford, 1978; Goodman, London, 1979. Trustee, British Museum, 1972-74. Hon. Fellow, Inst. of Patentees and Inventors, 1970; Hon. Freeman, Livery of Salters' Co., 1981. Hon. DSc: Utah, 1968; Sheffield, 1968; East Anglia, 1970; Durham, 1970; Leeds, 1971; Leicester, 1971; Heriot-Watt, 1971; City, 1971; Manchester, 1972; St Andrews, 1972; London, 1972; Kent, 1973; Oxon, 1974; Hull, 1980; Rio de Janeiro, 1980; Instituto Quimica de Sarria, Barcelona, 1981; DUniv. Surrey, 1970. Fairchild Dist. Scholar, California Inst. of Technology, 1974; Hitchcock Prof., Univ. of California, Berkeley, 1978. Corday-Morgan Medal, Chem. Soc., 1955; Nobel Prize (Jt) for Chemistry, 1967; Silvanus Thompson Medal, 1969; Royal Society: Davy Medal, 1971; Rumford Medal, 1978; Kalinga Prize, 1977; Faraday Medal, Chem. Soc., 1980. *Publications:* Chemistry for the Modern World, 1962; scientific papers in Proc. Royal Society, Trans. Faraday Society, etc. TV Series: Laws of Disorder, 1965-66; Time Machines, 1969-70; Natural History of a Sunbeam, 1976-77. *Recreation:* sailing. *Address:* The Royal Institution, 21 Albemarle Street, W1X 4BS. *T:* 01-409 2992. *Club:* Athenæum.

PORTER, George Barrington; MP (C) Bebington and Ellesmere Port, since 1979; *b* 11 June 1939; *s* of Kenneth William Porter and Vera Porter; *m* 1965, Susan Carolyn James; two *s* three *d*. *Educ:* Birkenhead Sch.; University Coll., Oxford (BA Hons). Admitted solicitor, 1965. Councillor: Birkenhead County Bor. Council, 1967-74; Wirral Bor., 1975-79 (Chm., Housing Cttee, 1976-77, and Educn Cttee, 1977-79). *Recreations:* golf, Rugby Union football, watching cricket, real ale. *Address:* 42 Village Road, Oxton, Birkenhead, Merseyside L43 6TY. *T:* 051-652 1006. *Clubs:* Royal Commonwealth Society, Royal Automobile; Lyceum (Liverpool); Oxton Conservative, Birkenhead Constitutional (Birkenhead); Ellesmere Port Conservative; Birkenhead Park Football, Wirral Ladies Golf, Birkenhead Squash Racquets, Oxton Cricket.

PORTER, Prof. Helen Kemp, FRS 1956; DSc; FRSC; Emeritus Professor, University of London; Hon. Fellow, Bedford College, since 1975; Scientific Adviser to the Secretary, Agricultural Research Council, 1971-72, retired (Second Secretary, 1969-71); Fellow, Imperial College of Science and Technology, 1966; *b* 10 Nov. 1899; *d* of George Kemp Archbold and Caroline E. B. Archbold (*née* Whitehead); *m* 1937, William George Porter, MD, MRCP (decd); *m* 1962, Arthur St George Huggett, FRS, DSc, MB, BS (*d* 1968). *Educ:* Clifton High School for Girls, Bristol; University of London, Research Assistant, Food Investigation Board, 1922-32; DSc London, 1932. On staff of Research Institute of Plant Physiology, Imperial Coll., 1932-59; Reader in Enzymology, University of London, Imperial College of Science and Technology, 1957-59; Prof. of Plant Physiology, Imperial Coll. of Science and Technology, London Univ., 1959-64; Dir, ARC Unit of Plant Physiology, 1959-64. Hon. ARCS 1964. *Publications:* contributions to Annals of Botany, Biochemical Journal, Journal of Experimental Botany, etc. *Recreation:* needlework. *Address:* 49e Beaumont Street, W1N 1RE. *T:* 01-935 5862.

PORTER, Ivor Forsyth, CMG 1963; OBE 1944; HM Diplomatic Service, retired; *b* 12 Nov. 1913; *s* of Herbert and Evelyn Porter; *m* 1951, Ann, *o d* of late Dr John Speares (marr. diss., 1961); *m* 1961, Katerina, *o d* of A. T. Cholerton; one *s* one *d. Educ:* Barrow Grammar Sch.; Leeds Univ. (BA, PhD). Lecturer at Bucharest Univ., 1939-40; Temp. Secretary, at Bucharest Legation, 1940-41; Raiding Forces, 1941-45 (Major). Joined Foreign (subseq. Diplomatic) Service, May 1946, as 2nd Secretary in Sen. Branch; 1st Secretary 1948; transferred to Washington, 1951; Foreign Office, 1953; UK Delegation to NATO Paris as Counsellor and Head of Chancery, 1956; Nicosia, 1959 (Deputy Head UK Mission), Deputy High Commissioner, 1961-62, Cyprus; Permanent Rep. to Council of Europe, Strasbourg, 1962-65 (with personal rank of Minister); Dep. High Commissioner, Eastern India, 1965-66; Ambassador, UK Delegn to Geneva Disarmament Conf., 1968-71 (Minister, 1967-68); Ambassador to Senegal, Guinea, Mali and Mauritania, 1971-73; later Dir, Atlantic Region, Research Dept, FCO, retired. *Publication:* The Think Trap, 1972. *Recreations:* writing, walking. *Address:* 17 Redcliffe Road, SW10. *Clubs:* Travellers', PEN.

PORTER, James Forrest; Director of the Commonwealth Institute, since 1978; *b* Frodsham, Cheshire, 2 Oct. 1928; *s* of Ernest Porter and Mary Violetta Porter; *m* 1952, Dymphna, *d* of Leo Francis Powell, London; two *d. Educ:* Salford Grammar Sch.; LSE (BSc Sociol.); Univ. of London Inst. of Educn (MA). Asst Master, St George in the East Sec. Sch., Stepney, 1948-50; Leverhulme Scholar, Univ. of London, 1950-55; Lectr in Sociol. and Educn, Worcester Coll., 1955-60; Head of Educn Dept, Chorley Coll., 1960-62; Dep. Principal, Coventry Coll., 1962-67; Principal, Bulmershe Coll. of Higher Educn, Reading, 1967-78. Director: bi-annual internat. courses on teacher educn, Brit. Council, 1975, 1977, 1979, on museums in educn, 1982; Adult Literacy Support Services Fund, 1977-. Consultant: Finland, 1976; Unesco, Paris, 1979-82; Commonwealth Fellow, Australia, 1977. Chm., World Educn Fellowship, 1979-; Member: Nat. Cttee of Inquiry into Teacher Educn and Trng (James Cttee), 1971; Educn Cttee, UGC, 1970-78; Educnl Adv. Council, IBA, 1970-80; Nat. Council for Dance Educn, 1978; Exec. Cttee, Internat. Council of Museums, 1981-; Editorial Bd, Higher Education Review, 1974-; UK Delegn to Unesco, Geneva, 1975 (Vice-Pres., Commn on Changing Role of Teacher); OECD Seminar, USA, 1976; Commonwealth Educn Ministers' Conf., Colombo, Sri Lanka, 1980; Unesco missions to Morocco and Senegal, 1982. FRSA 1978; Hon. FCP 1978. *Publications:* (ed) Rural Development and the Changing Countries of the World, 1969; (with N. Goble) The Changing Role of the Teacher, Paris 1977; regular contributor, Times Higher Educn Sup., Museum and other jls and books. *Recreations:* writing, river watching. *Address:* Commonwealth Institute, Kensington High Street, W8 6NQ. *T:* 01-602 3252; House by the Water, Bolney Avenue, Shiplake, Oxon. *T:* Wargrave 2187. *Club:* Royal Commonwealth Society.

PORTER, John Andrew, JP; Director, Anglia Building Society (formerly Anglia, Hastings and Thanet Building Society), since 1978 (Chairman, 1978-81); Partner, Porter and Cobb, as Chartered Surveyor, since 1940; *b* 18 May 1916; *s* of late Horace Augustus Porter, DFC, JP, and Vera Marion Porter; *m* 1941, Margaret Isobel Wisnom; two *d. Educ:* Radley Coll.; Sidney Sussex Coll., Cambridge (MA). Commissioned RA, TA, 1938; served War, 1939-46, Lt-Col. Dir, Kent County Building Soc., 1947 (Chm., 1965-68); Dir, Hastings and Thanet Building Soc., 1968 (Chm., 1972-78). JP Gravesham PSD, 1952, Chm., Gravesham Div., 1976-. Pres., Gravesend Cons. Assoc., 1965-77. General Commissioner of Taxes, 1970-. *Recreations:* cricket, hockey, golf. *Address:* Leaders, Hodsoll Street, near Wrotham, Kent TN15 7LH. *T:* Fairseat 822260. *Clubs:* Royal Automobile, MCC; Hawks (Cambridge).

PORTER, Prof. Joseph William Geoffrey, PhD; Director, National Institute for Research in Dairying, since 1978; *b* 22 May 1920; *s* of Joseph Henry Porter and Alice Porter; *m* 1944, Brenda Mary Matthews; one *s* one *d. Educ:* Repton Sch.; Emmanuel Coll., Cambridge (MA, PhD; Sen. Scholar, 1941). Res. Worker, Organic Chemistry Dept, Cambridge, 1942-46; Nat. Inst. for Research in Dairying: Scientific Officer, Nutrition Dept, 1946-65; Head of Nutrition Dept, 1965-77. *Publications:* Milk and Dairy Foods, 1975; papers in scientific jls on nutrition. *Recreation:* gardening. *Address:* National Institute for Research in Dairying, Shinfield, Reading, Berks RG2 9AT. *T:* Reading 883103.

PORTER, Prof. Rev. Canon Joshua Roy; Professor and Head of Department of Theology, University of Exeter, since 1962; *b* 7 May 1921; *s* of Joshua Porter and Bessie Evelyn (*née* Earlam). *Educ:* King's Sch., Macclesfield; Merton Coll., Oxford (Exhibnr); S Stephen's House, Oxford. BA: Mod. Hist. (Cl. I), Theology (Cl. I), MA Oxon. Liddon Student, 1942; Deacon 1945, Priest 1946; Curate of S Mary, Portsea, 1945-47; Resident Chaplain to Bp of Chichester, 1947-49; Hon. Chaplain, 1949-50; Examining Chaplain from 1950; Fellow, Chaplain and Lectr, Oriel Coll., Oxford, 1949-62; Tutor, 1950-62; Kennicott Hebrew Fellow, 1955; Sen. Denyer and Johnson Schol., 1958; Select Preacher: Univs of Oxford, 1953-55, Cambridge, 1957, TCD, 1958; Canon and Preb. of Wightring and Theol Lectr in Chichester Cath., 1965-; Vis. Prof., Southeastern Seminary, Wake Forest, N Carolina, 1967; Dean of Arts, Univ. of Exeter, 1968-71; Proctor in

Convocation of Canterbury for dio. of Exeter, 1964-75; for Other Univs (Canterbury), 1975-; Examining Chaplain to Bps of Peterborough, 1973-, of Truro, 1973-81, and of London, 1981-. Ethel M. Wood Lectr, Univ. of London, 1979. Mem., Adv. Council for the Church's Ministry, 1975-; Vice-Pres., Folklore Soc., 1979- (Pres., 1976-79); Pres., Soc. for OT Study, 1983-. *Publications:* World in the Heart, 1944; Moses and Monarchy, 1963; The Extended Family in the Old Testament, 1967; Proclamation and Presence, 1970; The Non-Juring Bishops, 1973; Leviticus, 1976; Animals in Folklore, 1978; The Crown and the Church, 1978; Folklore and the Old Testament, 1981; contributor to: Promise and Fulfilment, 1963; A Source Book of the Bible for Teachers, 1970; The Journey to the Other World, 1975; Tradition and Interpretation, 1979; A Basic Introduction to the Old Testament, 1980; Divination and Oracles, 1981; Folklore Studies in the Twentieth Century, 1981; The Folklore of Ghosts, 1981; Israel's Prophetic Tradition, 1982; numerous articles in learned jls and dictionaries. *Recreations:* theatre and opera, book-collecting, travel. *Address:* Queen's Building, University of Exeter, Exeter, Devon EX4 4QH. *T:* Exeter 77911; Jasin, Taddyforde, Exeter, Devon EX4 4AT. *T:* Exeter 70413; 36 Wilmington Square, WC1. *T:* 01-837 6840. *Club:* University Women's.

PORTER, Leslie; Chairman, Tesco Stores (Holdings) Ltd, since 1973 (Deputy Chairman and Managing Director, 1972-73); *b* 10 July 1920; *s* of late Henry Alfred and Jane Porter; *m* 1949, Shirley Cohen; one *s* one *d. Educ:* Holloway County Sch. Joined family textile business (J. Porter & Co), 1938. Served War: Techn. Quartermaster Sergt, 1st Bn The Rangers, KRRC, in Egypt, Greece, Crete, Libya, Tunisia, Algeria, Italy, 1939-46. Re-joined J. Porter & Co, 1946; became Managing Dir, 1955. Joined Tesco Stores (Holdings) Ltd: Dir, 1959; Asst Managing Dir, 1964; Dep. Chm., 1970. Member of Lloyd's, 1964- (John Poland syndicate). Pres., Inst. of Grocery Distribution, 1977-80. Mem. Court, Cranfield Inst. of Technology, 1977-; Dep. Chm., Bd of Governors, Tel Aviv Univ. Mem. President's Council, Hong Kong Baptist Coll. Hon. PhD (Business Management), Tel Aviv Univ., 1973. *Recreations:* golf, yachting, bridge. *Address:* 19 Chelwood House, Gloucester Square, W2 2SY. *T:* 01-262 2911. *Clubs:* City Livery; Dyrham Park County (Barnet, Herts); Coombe Hill Golf (Kingston Hill, Surrey); Frilford Heath Golf (Abingdon).

PORTER, Air Marshal Sir (Melvin) Kenneth (Drowley), KCB 1967 (CB 1959); CBE 1945 (OBE 1942); educational consultant since 1974; *b* 19 Nov. 1912; *s* of late Edward Ernest Porter and late Helen Porter; *m* 1940, Elena, *d* of F. W. Sinclair; two *s* one *d. Educ:* No. 1 School of Technical Training, Halton; RAF Coll., Cranwell. Aircraft apprentice, RAF Halton; cadetship to RAF Coll., Cranwell; commissioned, 1932; Army Co-operation Sqdn, Fleet Air Arm, 1933-36, as PO and FO; specialised on Signals, 1936-37, Flt-Lieut; Sqdn Leader, 1939. Served War of 1939-45 (despatches thrice, OBE, CBE); Chief Signals Officer, Balloon Command, 1939; DCSO and CSO, HQ No. 11 Group, 1940-42; Temp. Wing Comdr, 1941; CSO, HQ 2nd TAF, 1943-45; Temp Gp Captain, 1943; Actg Air Commodore, 1944-45; CSO, HQ Bomber Command, 1945; Air Min. Tech. Plans, 1946-47, Gp Captain, 1946; Member Directing Staff, RAF Staff Coll., Andover, 1947-49; Senior Tech. Staff Officer, HQ No. 205 Group, 1950-52; Comdg Nos 1 and 2 Air Signallers Schools, 1952-54; CSO HQ 2nd ATAF, 1954-55; CSO, HQ Fighter Command, Actg Air Commodore, 1955-58, Air Cdr, 1958; Student Imperial Defence Coll., 1959; Commandant of No 4 School of Technical Training, RAF St Athan, Glamorgan, and Air Officer Wales, 1960-61; Actg Air Vice-Marshal, 1961; Air Vice-Marshal, 1962; Director-General: Ground Training, 1961-63; of Signals (Air), Ministry of Defence, 1964-66; AOC-in-C, Maintenance Command, 1966-70; Hd of RAF Engineer Branch, 1968-70; Actg Air Marshal, 1966; Air Marshal, 1967. Dir of Tech. Educn Projects, UC Cardiff, 1970-74. Governor, Bryanston Sch., 1972. CEng 1966; FIEE; FRAeS; CBIM; FInstProdE. Officer, Legion of Merit (US), 1945. *Recreation:* reading. *Address:* c/o Lloyds Bank Ltd, Redland Branch, 163 Whiteladies Road, Clifton, Bristol BS8 8RW.

PORTER, Hon. Sir Murray (Victor), Kt 1970; Agent-General for Victoria in London, 1970-76; *b* 20 Dec. 1909; *s* of late V. Porter, Pt Pirie, SA; *m* 1932, Edith Alice Johnston, *d* of late C. A. Johnston; two *d. Educ:* Brighton (Victoria) Grammar Sch., Australia. Served War, 2nd AIF, 1941-45. MLA (Liberal) Sandringham, Victoria, 1955-70; Govt Whip, 1955-56; Asst Minister, 1956-58; Minister for: Forests, 1958-59; Local Govt, 1959-64; Public Works, 1964-70. *Recreations:* golf, swimming. *Address:* Flat 7, The Point, 405 Beach Road, Beaumaris, Victoria 3193, Australia. *Clubs:* Melbourne Cricket, Royal Melbourne Golf, Royal Automobile Club of Victoria.

PORTER, Peter Neville Frederick; freelance writer, poet; *b* Brisbane, 16 Feb. 1929; *s* of William Ronald Porter and Marion Main; *m* 1961, Jannice Henry (*d* 1974); two *d. Educ:* Church of England Grammar Sch., Brisbane; Toowoomba Grammar Sch. Worked as journalist in Brisbane before coming to England in 1951; clerk, bookseller and advertising writer, before becoming full-time poet, journalist, reviewer and broadcaster in 1968. Chief work done in poetry and English literature. *Publications:* Once Bitten, Twice Bitten, 1961; Penguin Modern Poets No 2, 1962; Poems, Ancient and Modern, 1964; A Porter Folio, 1969; The Last of England, 1970; Preaching to the Converted, 1972; (trans.) After Martial, 1972; (with Arthur Boyd) Jonah, 1973; (with Arthur Boyd) The Lady and the Unicorn, 1975; Living in a Calm Country, 1975; (jt ed) New Poetry 1, 1975; The Cost of Seriousness, 1978; English Subtitles, 1981. *Recreations:* buying records and listening to music; travelling in Italy. *Address:* 42 Cleveland Square, W2. *T:* 01-262 4289.

PORTER, Raymond Alfred James; b 14 Oct. 1896; o s of Philip and Alice Porter; m 1922, Nellie (d 1979), er d of George Edward Loveland; no c. Educ: Reigate Grammar Sch. Entered Lloyd's, 1912, Under-writing Member, 1934. Served European War, 1914-19, in Queen's Royal (West Surrey) Regt. Member, Cttee of Lloyd's, 1950-53, 1955-58, 1960-63 (Deputy Chairman of Lloyd's, 1961); Member, Cttee, Lloyd's Underwriters' Assoc., 1945-65 (Chairman, 1949-54, 1962); Chairman Joint Hull Cttee, 1958 and 1959. Member: Local Govt Management Cttee, 1964-67; Godstone RDC, 1946-60 and 1962-69 (Chairman, 1952-54); Surrey CC, 1955-58. Silver Medal for Services to Lloyd's, 1978. Address: Mashobra, Limpsfield, Oxted, Surrey. T: Oxted 2509.

PORTER, Sir Robert (Evelyn), Kt 1978; Partner, F. W. Porter & Co. (Member of the Stock Exchange of Adelaide), since 1937; b 10 July 1913; s of Frederick Windmill Porter and Clara Francis Niall Porter; m 1942, June Leah Perry, d of late Stanley W. Perry, OBE, Perth, WA. Educ: St Peter's Collegiate Sch., Adelaide, SA; Univ. of Adelaide. Served War, 2/10 Bn AIF, 1939-45, enlisted as private, 1939; commnd. 1940; Major, 1942 (mentioned in despatches); personal staff C-in-C Field Marshal Sir Thomas Blamey. Director: Standard Chartered Australia Ltd; Castalloy Ltd; Freeman Motors Ltd. Lord Mayor of Adelaide, 1968-71. President: Good Neighbour Council of SA, 1971-74; RSPCA, SA, 1956-. Past Pres. and Vice Patron: SA Polo Assoc.; (Captain SA team, Australian Polo Championships, 1952-65); SA Rugby Union (Mem. Australian team, Ceylon tour, 1938). Chm., Rothman Nat. Sports Foundn. Governor: Anti-Cancer Foundn, Univ. of Adelaide; Adelaide Festival of Arts. Consul of Belgium for SA and Northern Territory, 1949-. Chevalier, Order of the Crown, Belgium, 1959; Kt, Order of Leopold, 1969; Officer, Order of Leopold II, 1973. Recreation: golf. Address: 1 Edwin Terrace, Gilberton, SA 5081, Australia. T: 44 1455. Clubs: Adelaide, Royal Adelaide Golf (Adelaide); Melbourne (Melbourne); Royal and Ancient Golf (Scotland).

PORTER, Rt. Rev. Robert George; see Murray, Bishop of The.

PORTER, Robert Stanley, CB 1972; OBE 1959; Deputy Secretary (Chief Economist), Overseas Development Administration, Foreign and Commonwealth Office (formerly Ministry of Overseas Development), since 1980; b 17 Sept. 1924; s of S. R. Porter; m 1st, 1953, Dorothea Naomi (marr. diss. 1967), d of Rev. Morris Seale; one d; 2nd, 1967, Julia Karen, d of Edmund A. Davies. Educ: St Clement Danes, Holborn Estate, Grammar Sch.; New Coll., Oxford. Research Economist, US Economic Cooperation Administration Special Mission to the UK, 1949; British Middle East Development Division: Asst Statistical Adviser, Cairo, 1951; Statistical Adviser and Economist, Beirut, 1955; Min. of Overseas Development: Dir, Geographical Div., Economic Planning Staff, 1965; Dep. Dir-Gen. of Economic Planning, 1967; Dir-Gen. of Economic Planning, 1969. Publications: articles in Oxford Economic Papers, Kyklos, Review of Income and Wealth. Recreations: music, theatre. Address: Morland Cottage, Sheepstead, Marcham, Abingdon, Oxon. T: Frilford Heath 390458. Club: Athenæum.

PORTER, Rt. Hon. Sir Robert (Wilson), Kt 1971; PC (NI) 1969; QC (NI) 1965; County Court Judge, Northern Ireland, since 1978; b 23 Dec. 1923; s of late Joseph Wilson Porter and late Letitia Mary (née Wasson); m 1953, Margaret Adelaide, y d of late F. W. Lynas; one s one d (and one d decd). Educ: Model Sch. and Foyle Coll., Londonderry; Queen's Univ., Belfast. RAFVR, 1943-46; Royal Artillery (TA), 1950-56. Foundation Schol., Queen's Univ., 1947 and 1948; LLB 1949. Called to Bar of N Ireland, 1950. Lecturer in Contract and Sale of Goods, Queen's Univ., 1950-51; Jun. Crown Counsel, Co. Londonderry, 1960-63, Co. Down, 1964-65; Counsel to Attorney-General for N Ireland, 1963-64 and 1965; Recorder of Londonderry, 1979-81. Vice-Chairman, 1959-61, Chairman, 1961-66, War Pensions Appeal Tribunal for N Ireland. MP (U) Queen's Univ. of Belfast, 1966-69, Lagan Valley, 1969-73, Parlt of N Ireland; Minister of Health and Social Services, N Ireland, 1969; Parly Sec., Min. of Home Affairs, 1969; Minister of Home Affairs, Govt of NI, 1969-70. Recreations: gardening, golf. Address: Ardkeen, Marlborough Park North, Belfast, N Ireland BT9 6HL. T: 666761. Club: Royal Air Force.

PORTER, Prof. Rodney Robert, FRS 1964; Whitley Professor of Biochemistry, and Fellow, Trinity College, University of Oxford, since 1967; b 8 Oct. 1917; s of Joseph L. and Isobel M. Porter; m 1948, Julia Frances New; two s three d. Educ: Grammar Sch., Ashton-in-Makerfield; Liverpool and Cambridge Universities. Scientific Staff at Nat. Inst. for Medical Research, Mill Hill, NW7, 1949-60; Pfizer Prof. of Immunology, St Mary's Hospital Medical Sch., London Univ., 1960-67. Mem., MRC, 1970-74. Linacre Lectr, Cambridge Univ., 1975; Gowland Hopkins Meml Lectr, Biochem. Soc., 1977. Award of Merit, Gairdner Foundn, 1966; Ciba Medal, Biochemical Soc., 1967; Karl Landsteiner Meml Award, Amer. Assoc. of Blood Banks, 1968; (jtly) Nobel Prize for Medicine or Physiology, 1972; Royal Medal, Royal Soc., 1973. Hon. Member: Amer. Soc. of Biological Chemists, 1968; Amer. Assoc. of Immunologists, 1973; Société Française d'Immunologie, 1978; Hon. Foreign Mem., Amer. Acad. of Arts and Sciences, 1968; Foreign Associate, Amer. Nat. Acad. of Scis, 1972. Hon. FRCP, 1974; Hon. FRSE, 1976; Hon. FIBiol, 1977. Hon. DSc: Liverpool, 1973; Hull, 1975; St Andrews, 1976; Manchester, 1979; Dr hc Vrije Univ., Brussels, 1974. Publications: papers in Biochemical Journal and other learned journals. Recreation: walking. Address: Downhill Farm, Witney, Oxon.

PORTER, Thea; see Porter, D. N. N.

PORTER, Walter Stanley, TD 1950; MA (Cantab); Headmaster of Framlingham College, 1955-71; b 28 Sept. 1909; s of late Walter Porter, Rugby; m 1937, Doreen, o d of B. Haynes, Rugby; one d. Educ: Rugby Sch.; Gonville and Caius Coll., Cambridge. Assistant Master and Officer Commanding Training Corps, Trent Coll., 1933-36; Felsted Sch., 1936-43; Radley Coll., 1944-55. FRSA 1968. Recreations: travel, amateur dramatics; formerly Rugby football, hockey. Address: The Hermitage, 29 Cumberland Street, Woodbridge, Suffolk. T: Woodbridge 2340.

PORTERFIELD, Dr James Stuart; Reader in Bacteriology, Sir William Dunn School of Pathology, Oxford University, and Senior Research Fellow, Wadham College, Oxford, since 1977; b 17 Jan. 1924; yr s of late Dr Samuel Porterfield and Mrs Lilian Porterfield, Widnes, Lancs, and Portstewart, Co. Londonderry, NI; m 1950, Betty Mary Burch; one d (one s decd). Educ: Wade Deacon Grammar Sch., Widnes; King's Sch., Chester; Liverpool Univ. MB, ChB 1947, MD 1949. Asst Lectr in Bacteriology, Univ. of Liverpool, 1947-49; Bacteriologist and Virologist, Common Cold Res. Unit, Salisbury, Wilts, 1949-51; Pathologist, RAF Inst. of Pathology and Tropical Med., Halton, Aylesbury, Bucks, 1952-53; seconded to W African Council for Med. Res. Labs, Lagos, Nigeria, 1953-57; Mem. Scientific Staff, Nat. Inst. for Med. Res., Mill Hill, 1949-77; WHO Regional Ref. Centre for Arthropod-borne Viruses, 1961-65; WHO Collaborating Lab., 1965-; Ref. Expert on Arboviruses, Public Health Lab. Service, 1967-76. Chm., Arbovirus Study Gp, Internat. Cttee for Nomenclature of Viruses, 1968-78; Meetings Sec., Soc. for General Microbiology, 1972-77; Vice-Pres., Royal Soc. for Tropical Med. and Hygiene, 1980-81 (Councillor, 1973-76); Secretary and Vice-Pres., Royal Institution, 1973-78. Publications: contribs to medical and scientific jls. Recreations: fell-walking, gardening. Address: Sir William Dunn School of Pathology, South Parks Road, Oxford OX1 3RE.

PORTES, Prof. Richard David, DPhil; Professor of Economics, University of London, since 1972, and Head of Department of Economics, Birkbeck College, 1975-77 and since 1980; b 10 Dec. 1941; s of Herbert Portes and Abra Halperin Portes; m 1963, Barbara Diana Frank; one s one d. Educ: Yale Univ. (BA 1962 summa cum laude); Balliol and Nuffield Colls, Oxford (Rhodes Schol., 1962; Woodrow Wilson Fellow, 1962; Danforth Fellow, 1962; MA 1965; DPhil 1969). Official Fellow and Tutor in Econs, Balliol Coll., Oxford, 1965-69; Asst Prof. of Econs and Internat. Affairs, Princeton Univ., 1969-72. Dir d'Etudes Associé and Co-Dir, Centre d'Economie Quantitative et Comparative, Ecole des Hautes Etudes en Sciences Sociales, Paris, 1978-. Hon. Res. Fellow, UCL, 1971-72; Guggenheim Fellow, 1977-78; British Acad. Overseas Vis. Fellow, 1977-78; Res. Associate, Nat. Bureau of Econ. Res., Cambridge, Mass, 1980-; Vis. Res. Prof., Inst. for Internat. Econ. Studies, Stockholm Univ., 1973, 1974, 1976, 1978; Vis. Prof., Harvard Univ., 1977-78. Vice-Chm., Econs Cttee, SSRC, 1981- (Mem. 1980-). Member: Bd of Dirs, Soc. for Econ. Analysis (Rev. of Econ. Studies), 1967-69, 1972-80 (Sec. 1974-77); RIIA, 1973- (Res. Cttee, 1982-); Council on Foreign Relations, 1978-. Member Editorial Board: Applied Economics, 1973-; Jl of Comparative Economics, 1980-. Governor, Birkbeck Coll., 1981-82. Publications: (ed) Planning and Market Relations, 1971; The Polish Crisis, 1981; contribs to many learned jls. Recreations: opera, theatre, music, food and wine, newspapers. Address: 29 Ellington Street, N7 8PN. T: 01-607 0732.

PORTLAND, 9th Duke of, cr 1716; **Victor Frederick William Cavendish-Bentinck,** CMG 1942; Earl of Portland, Viscount Woodstock, Baron Cirencester, 1689; Marquess of Titchfield, 1716; Chairman, Bayer (UK) Ltd; Director, NUKEM Nuklear-Chemie und-Metallurgie GmbH (Germany); b 18 June 1897; s of (William George) Frederick Cavendish-Bentinck (d 1948) (ggs of 3rd Duke) and Ruth Mary St Maur (d 1953); granted, 1977, the same title and precedence that would have been due to him if his father had succeeded to the Dukedom of Portland; S brother, 1980; m 1st, 1924 (marr. diss.); one d (one s decd); 2nd, 1948, Kathleen Elsie, yr d of Arthur Barry, Montreal. Educ: Wellington Coll., Berks. Attaché HM Legation, Oslo, 1915; 2nd Lieut, Grenadier Guards, 1918; 3rd Sec., HM Legation, Warsaw, 1919; transferred to Foreign Office, 1922; attended Lausanne Conference, 1922-23; 2nd Sec., HM Embassy, Paris, 1923; HM Legation, The Hague, 1924; transferred to Foreign Office, 1925; attended Locarno Conference, 1925; 1st Sec., HM Embassy, Paris, 1928; HM Legation, Athens, 1932; HM Embassy, Santiago, 1934; transferred to Foreign Office, 1937; Asst Under-Sec. of State, 1944; Chm. Jt Intelligence Cttee of Chiefs of Staff, 1939-45, also Foreign Office Adviser to Directors of Plans, 1942-45; Ambassador to Poland, 1945-47; retired from Diplomatic Service, 1947. Pres. Council British Nuclear Forum. Grosses Verdienstkreuz (Germany). Recreations: travelling and antiques. Heir (to earldom only): kinsman Henry Noel Bentinck, Count of the Holy Roman Empire [b 2 Oct. 1919; m 1st, 1940, Pauline Ursula (d 1967), y d of late Frederick William Mellowes; one s two d; 2nd, 1974, Jenifer, d of late Reginald Hopkins]. Address: 21 Carlyle Square, SW3. T: 01-352 1258. Clubs: Turf, Beefsteak.

PORTLOCK, Rear-Admiral Ronald Etridge, CB 1961; OBE 1947; DL; retired; b London, 28 June 1908; o s of late Henry and Doris Portlock; m 1939, Angela, d of late Gerard Kirke Smith; no c. Educ: Royal Naval Coll., Dartmouth. Naval Cadet, 1922; Midshipman, 1926; Lieut-Commander, 1938; Commander, 1943; Captain, 1949; Rear-Admiral 1959. Served War of 1939-45 in HMS Ark Royal and King George V as Lieut-Commander; Admiralty as Commander. Post-war Mine Clearance in Far East, 1946-47;

Captain, HM Underwater Detection Establishment, 1950-52; Chief of Staff to C-in-C, The Nore, 1953-54; in comd HMS Newfoundland, and Flag Captain to Flag Officer; Second in Command Far East Station, 1955-56; Director of Underwater Weapons, Admiralty, 1957-58; Chief of Staff to the Commander-in-Chief, Far East Station, 1959-61, retired, 1961. ADC to the Queen, 1958. Chairman, Assoc. of Retired Naval Officers, 1965-67. DL Greater London, 1967. Royal Swedish Order of the Swords, 1954. *Address:* 1 Swan Court, Chelsea, SW3. *T:* 01-352 4390.

PORTMAN, family name of **Viscount Portman.**

PORTMAN, 9th Viscount, *cr* 1873; **Edward Henry Berkeley Portman;** Baron 1873; *b* 22 April 1934; *s* of late Hon. Michael Berkeley Portman (*d* 1959) (*yr s* of 7th Viscount), and June Charles (*d* 1947); *S* uncle, 1967; *m* 1st, 1956, Rosemary Farris (marr. diss., 1965); one *s* one *d*; 2nd, 1966, Penelope Allin; four *s*. *Educ:* Canford; Royal Agricultural College. Farmer. *Recreations:* shooting, fishing, music. *Heir: s* Hon. Christopher Edward Berkeley Portman, *b* 30 July 1958. *Address:* Clock Mill, Clifford, Herefordshire. *T:* Clifford 235. *Club:* White's.

PORTSMOUTH, 9th Earl of, *cr* 1743; **Gerard Vernon Wallop;** Viscount Lymington, Baron Wallop, 1720; Hereditary Bailiff of Burley, New Forest; Vice-Chairman, East Africa Natural Resources Research Council, since 1963; *b* 16 May 1898; *e s* of 8th Earl and Marguerite (*d* 1938), *d* of S. J. Walker, Kentucky; *S* father 1943; *m* 1st, 1920, Mary Lawrence (who obtained a divorce, 1936, and *m* 2nd, 1938, E. J. B. How), *d* of W. K. Post, Bayport, Long Island; one *s* one *d*; 2nd, 1936, Bridget (*d* 1979), *o d* of late Captain P. B. Crohan, Royal Navy, Owlpen Manor, Glos; one *s* two *d*. Served European War, 1916-19; MP (U) Basingstoke Division of Hants, 1929-34; Member of the Milk Marketing Board, July 1933; Vice-Chairman Hampshire War Agric. Cttee, 1939-47; Vice-President and Chairman Country Landowners Assoc., 1947-48. President, Electors Union, Kenya, 1953-55; MLC Kenya (Corporate Member for Agric.), 1957-60; Vice-Chairman, East African Natural Resources Research Council, 1963-. *Publications:* Git le Cœur, 1928; Ich Dien; The Tory Path, 1931; Horn, Hoof and Corn, 1932; Famine in England, 1938; Alternative to Death, 1943; British Farm Stock, 1950; A Knot of Roots (autobiog.), 1965. *Heir: s* Viscount Lymington, *qv*. *Address:* c/o Farleigh Wallop, Basingstoke, Hants. *Club:* Buck's.
See also Viscount Chelsea, Lord Porchester.

PORTSMOUTH, Bishop of, since 1975; **Rt. Rev. Archibald Ronald McDonald Gordon;** *b* 19 March 1927; *s* of late Sir Archibald Gordon, CMG, and late Dorothy Katharine Gordon, Bridge House, Gerrards Cross, Bucks. *Educ:* Rugby Sch.; Balliol Coll., Oxford (Organ Schol., MA 1950); Cuddesdon Theol. Coll. Deacon 1952; Priest 1953; Curate of Stepney, 1952-55; Chaplain, Cuddesdon Coll., 1955-59; Vicar of St Peter, Birmingham, 1959-67; Res. Canon, Birmingham Cathedral, 1967-71; Vicar of University Church of St Mary the Virgin with St Cross and St Peter in the East, Oxford, 1971-75. Fellow of St Cross Coll., Oxford, 1975. Mem., Church Assembly and General Synod, and Proctor in Convocation, 1965-71; Chm., ACCM, 1976-. *Address:* Bishopswood, Fareham, Hants PO14 1NT.

PORTSMOUTH, Bishop of, (RC), since 1976; **Rt. Rev. Anthony Joseph Emery;** *b* Burton-on-Trent, 17 May 1918. Ordained 1953. Auxiliary Bishop of Birmingham (Titular Bishop of Tamallula), 1968-76. Chm. Catholic Education Council, 1968-. *Address:* Bishop's House, Edinburgh Road, Portsmouth PO1 3HG.

PORTSMOUTH, Archdeacon of; *see* Scruby, Ven. R. V.

PORTSMOUTH, Provost of; *see* Stancliffe, Very Rev. D. S.

POSKITT, Frederick Richard, CBE 1962; *b* 15 Aug. 1900; *s* of Frederick Hardy Poskitt and Kate Penlington Spencer; *m* 1936, Margaret Embree, *e d* of Cecil E. Turner, Woolton, Liverpool; two *s* one *d*. *Educ:* Kilburn Grammar Sch.; Downing Coll., Cambridge. Asst Master, Colchester Royal Grammar Sch., 1921-25; Head of History Dept, Manchester Grammar Sch., 1926-33; Headmaster, Bolton Sch., 1933-66; Dir, Nat. Teachers' Coll., Kampala, Uganda, 1966-71. Former Member: Cttee, Headmasters' Conf.; Council, IAHM. Founder Mem., Fifty-One Soc. (BBC), 1951-60; Mem., Chief Scout's Adv. Panel, 1943-49; Chairman: SE Lancs County Scout Council, 1943-60; Bolton Lads Club, 1944-53; Oxford Br., Save the Children Fund, 1976-81; Pres., Bolton Br., Historical Assoc., 1933-66. *Recreation:* travel. *Address:* 11 Hedge End, Hensington Gate, Woodstock, Oxon OX7 1NP. *T:* Woodstock 811590. *Club:* Royal Commonwealth Society (Mem. Cttee, Oxford Br., 1974-).

POSKITT, Prof. Trevor John, DSc, PhD; Professor of Civil Engineering, Queen Mary College, University of London, since 1972; *b* 26 May 1934; *s* of late William Albert Poskitt, Worthing, and Mrs D. M. Poskitt, Lincoln; *m* 1968, Gillian Mary, *d* of L. S. Martin, MBE, Romiley, Cheshire; one *s* one *d*. *Educ:* Corby Technical Sch.; Huddersfield Technical Coll.; Univ. of Leeds; Univ. of Cambridge. HND (Mech. Eng.); BSc Leeds, PhD Cambridge, DSc Manchester; FICE, FIStructE. Apprentice Engineer to Thos. Broadbent & Sons, Huddersfield, 1949-53; Graduate Assistant, English Electric Co. Ltd, 1958-60; Whitworth Fellow, 1960-63; Lectr, 1963-71, Senior Lectr, 1971-72, in Civil Engineering, Univ. of Manchester. *Publications:* numerous on civil

engineering topics. *Recreations:* tennis, music. *Address:* Queen Mary College, Mile End Road, E1 4NS. *T:* 01-980 4811.

POSNER, Michael Vivian; Fellow of Pembroke College, Cambridge, since 1960; a Member, British Railways Board, since 1976; Chairman, Social Science Research Council, since 1979; *b* 25 Aug. 1931; *s* of Jack Posner; *m* 1953, Rebecca Posner, *qv*; one *s* one *d*. *Educ:* Whitgift Sch.; Balliol Coll., Oxford. Research Officer, Oxford Inst. of Statistics, 1953-57; Asst Lecturer, Lecturer, then Reader in Economics, Univ. of Cambridge, 1958-79; Chm., Faculty Bd of Economics, Cambridge, 1974-75. Vis. Prof., Brookings Instn, Washington, 1971-72. Director of Economics, Ministry of Power, 1966-67; Economic Adviser to Treasury, 1967-69; Economic Consultant to Treasury, 1969-71; Consultant to IMF, 1971-72; Energy Adviser, NEDO, 1973-74; Econ. Adviser, Dept of Energy, 1974-75; Dep. Chief Econ. Adviser, HM Treasury, 1975-76. Mem., Post Office Bd, 1978-79. Member: Adv. Council for Energy Conservation, 1974-; Standing Commn on Energy and the Environment, 1978-; Chm., Energy Panel, SSRC, 1978-. Mem. Council, PSI, 1978-. *Publications:* (co-author) Italian Public Enterprise, 1966; Fuel Policy: a study in applied economics, 1973; (ed) Resource Allocation in the Public Sector, 1977; (ed) Demand Management, 1978; (co-author) Energy Economics, 1981; books and articles on economics. *Recreation:* country life. *Address:* Rushwood, Jack Straw's Lane, Oxford. *T:* Oxford 63578; Pembroke College, Cambridge. *T:* Cambridge 352241. *Club:* United Oxford & Cambridge University.

POSNER, Prof. Rebecca; Professor of the Romance Languages, University of Oxford, since 1978; Fellow, St Hugh's College, Oxford, since 1978; *b* 17 Aug. 1929; *d* of William and Rebecca Reynolds; *m* 1953, Michael Vivian Posner, *qv*; one *s* one *d*. *Educ:* Somerville Coll., Oxford. MA, DPhil (Oxon); PhD (Cantab). Fellow, Girton Coll., Cambridge, 1960-63; Prof. of French Studies, Univ. of Ghana, 1963-65; Reader in Language, Univ. of York, 1965-78. Vis. Prof. of Romance Philology, Columbia Univ., NY, 1971-72. *Publications:* Consonantal Dissimilation in the Romance Languages, 1961; The Romance Languages, 1966; (with J. Orr and I. Iordan) Introduction to Romance Linguistics, 1970; (ed with J. N. Green) Trends in Romance Linguistics and Philology, 1980-82; numerous articles. *Recreations:* walking, gardening, theatre, music. *Address:* St Hugh's College, Oxford OX2 6LE. *T:* Oxford 57341; Rushwood, Jack Straw's Lane, Oxford OX3 0DN. *T:* Oxford 63578.

POSNETT, Sir Richard (Neil), KBE 1980 (OBE 1963); CMG 1976; Governor and C-in-C of Bermuda, since 1981; HM Diplomatic Service, retired; *b* 19 July 1919; *s* of Rev. Charles Walker Posnett, K-i-H, Medak, S India, and Phyllis (*née* Barker); *m* 1st; two *s* one *d*; 2nd, 1959, Shirley Margaret Hudson; two *s* one *d*. *Educ:* Kingswood; St John's Coll., Cambridge. BA 1940, MA 1947. Called to the Bar, Gray's Inn, 1951. HM Colonial Administrative Service in Uganda, 1941; Chm., Uganda Olympic Cttee, 1956; Colonial Office, London, 1958; Judicial Adviser, Buganda, 1960; Perm. Sec. for External Affairs, Uganda, 1962; Perm. Sec. for Trade and Industry, 1963; joined Foreign (subseq. Diplomatic) Service, 1964; FO, 1964; served on UK Mission to UN, NY, 1967-70; briefly HM Comr in Anguilla, 1969; Head of W Indian Dept, FCO, 1970-71; Governor and C-in-C of Belize, 1972-76; Special Mission to Ocean Island, 1977; Dependent Territories Adviser, FCO, 1977-79; British High Comr, Kampala, 1979. UK Comr, British Phosphate Comrs, 1978-81. First ascent of South Portal Peak on Ruwenzori, 1942. Pres., Kingswood Assoc., 1980. Mem., RIIA. KStJ 1972. *Publications:* articles in Uganda Journal, World Today. *Address:* Government House, Hamilton, Bermuda. *Clubs:* Ski Club of Great Britain, Royal Commonwealth Society, Achilles; West Surrey Golf; Mid-Ocean Golf; Privateers Hockey; Royal Bermuda Yacht.

POSNETTE, Prof. Adrian Frank, CBE 1976; FRS 1971; VMH 1982; Director, East Malling Research Station, Kent, 1972-79 (Deputy Director, 1969-72, and Head of Plant Pathology Section, 1957-72); *b* 11 Jan. 1914; *e s* of late Frank William Posnette and Edith (*née* Webber), Cheltenham; *m* 1937, Isabelle, *d* of Dr Montgomery La Roche, New York; one *s* two *d*. *Educ:* Cheltenham Grammar Sch.; Christ's Coll., Cambridge. MA, ScD Cantab; PhD London; AICTA Trinidad; FIBiol. Research at Imperial Coll. of Tropical Agriculture, Trinidad, 1936-37; Colonial Agric. Service, Gold Coast, 1937; Head of Botany and Plant Pathology Dept, W African Cacao Research Inst., 1944; research at East Malling Research Stn, 1949-. Vis. Prof. in Plant Sciences, Wye Coll., Univ. of London, 1971-78. *Publications:* Virus Diseases of Apples and Pears, 1963; numerous research papers in Annals of Applied Biology, Jl of Horticultural Science, Nature, Tropical Agriculture. *Recreations:* ornithology, sailing, gardening. *Address:* Walnut Tree, East Sutton, Maidstone, Kent. *T:* Maidstone 843282. *Clubs:* Farmers'; Hawks (Cambridge); Helford River Sailing.

POST, Col Kenneth Graham, CBE 1945; TD; *b* 21 Jan. 1908; *s* of Donnell Post and Hon. Mrs Post; *m* 1st, 1944, Stephanie Bonté Wood (marr. diss., 1963); one *s* two *d*; 2nd, 1963, Diane Allen; two *s*. *Educ:* Winchester; Magdalen, Oxford. London Stock Exchange, 1929-37; 2nd Lieut, RA (TA) 1937; Norway, 1940; War Office, 1941-42; Ministry of Supply, 1943-44; Ministry of Works, 1945-47; Ministry of Housing, 1956-57; Ministry of Defence, 1957-59. Member Corby New Town Development Corporation, 1955-62; Director, Civic Trust, 1957-63. *Address:* Giles Cottage, Giles Lane, Canterbury, Kent. *T:* Canterbury 66679. *Club:* Pratt's.

POSTGATE, Prof. John Raymond, FRS 1977; FInstBiol; Director, ARC Unit of Nitrogen Fixation, since 1980 (Assistant Director, 1963-80), and Professor of Microbiology, University of Sussex, since 1965; *b* 24 June 1922; *s* of Raymond William Postgate and Daisy Postgate (*née* Lansbury); *m* 1948, Mary Stewart; three *d. Educ:* Woodstock Sch., Golders Green; Kingsbury County Sch., Mddx; Balliol Coll., Oxford. BA, MA, DPhil, DSc. Research in chemical microbiology: with D. D. Woods on action of sulfonamide drugs, 1946-48, with K. R. Butlin on sulphate-reducing bacteria, 1948-59. Research on bacterial death, 1959-63, incl. Visiting Prof., Univ. of Illinois, 1962-63, working on sulphate-reducing bacteria. Visiting Prof., Oregon State Univ., 1977-78. Pres., Inst. of Biology, 1982-. *Publications:* Microbes and Man (Pelican), 1969, 2nd edn 1976; Biological Nitrogen Fixation, 1972; Nitrogen Fixation, 1978; The Sulphate-Reducing Bacteria, 1979; A Plain Man's Guide to Jazz, 1973; ed, 3 scientific symposia: regular columnist in Jazz Monthly, 1952-72; reviewer for Gramophone, 1965-; numerous scientific papers in microbiol/biochem. jls; many record reviews and articles on jazz. *Recreations:* listening to jazz and attempting to play it. *Address:* 1 Houndean Rise, Lewes, Sussex BN7 1EG. *T:* Lewes 2675.

POSTGATE, Richmond Seymour, MA; FCP; Consultant, education and broadcasting; *b* 31 Dec. 1908; *s* of Prof. J. P. Postgate, FBA and Edith Postgate; *m* 1949, Audrey Winifred Jones; one *s* two *d. Educ:* St George's Sch., Harpenden, Herts; Clare Coll., Cambridge. Editorial staff, Manchester Guardian newspaper; teaching in Public and Elementary Schools; County LEA Administration; RAFVR. In BBC: Head of School Broadcasting, etc; Director-General, Nigerian Broadcasting Corporation, 1959-61; Controller, Educnl Broadcasting, BBC, 1965-72. FCP 1973. *Recreation:* walking. *Address:* 3 Stanford Road, Faringdon, Oxon. *T:* Faringdon 20172.

POTT, Sir Leslie, KBE 1962 (CBE 1957); *b* 4 July 1903; *s* of Charles Groves Pott; *m* 1937, Norma (*d* 1978), *d* of Captain Kynaston Lyons-Montgomery, Jersey; one *s. Educ:* Manchester Grammar Sch.; Gonville and Caius Coll., Cambridge (Open Scholar). Entered Levant Consular Service, 1924; served at Casablanca, Damascus and Beirut, 1926-29; Moscow and Leningrad, 1930-35; Foreign Office, 1936-37; Piraeus and Athens, 1938-40; Consul at Baghdad, 1940-43; Foreign Office, 1943-45; Consul at Alexandria, 1946-47. Consul-General at Tabriz, 1947-50; Deputy High Commissioner for the UK at Bombay, 1950-52; Consul-General at Istanbul, 1952-55; at Marseilles, 1955-61, also to Monaco, 1957-61. Retired from HM Diplomatic Service, 1962. *Address:* Becking Spring, Hudnall Common, near Berkhamsted, Herts HP4 1QJ. *T:* Little Gaddesden 3409.

POTTER, Prof. Allen Meyers, PhD; FSS; James Bryce Professor of Politics, University of Glasgow, since 1970; *b* 7 March 1924; *s* of Maurice A. and Irene M. Potter; *m* 1949, Joan Elizabeth Yeo; two *d. Educ:* Wesleyan Univ., Conn (BA 1947, MA 1948); Columbia Univ., NY (PhD 1955). FSS 1967. Instructor, College of William and Mary, 1949-51; Lectr/Sen. Lectr, Univ. of Manchester, 1951-62; Vis. Professor, Univ. of Texas, 1960; Professor: Univ. of Strathclyde, 1963-65; Univ. of Essex, 1965-70; Pro-Vice-Chancellor, Univ. of Essex, 1969-70. Vice-Principal, Univ. of Glasgow, 1979-82. Member, US-UK Educational Commn, 1979-. Governor, Glasgow Sch. of Art, 1979-82. *Publications:* American Government and Politics, 1955, 2nd edn 1978; Organised Groups in British National Politics, 1961; articles in American and British social science jls. *Recreations:* inventing table games, abolishing committees. *Address:* Hazelwood, 2 Grove Park, Lenzie, Glasgow G66 5AH. *T:* 041-776 1599. *Clubs:* Royal Commonwealth Society; XIII (Glasgow).

POTTER, Arthur Kingscote, CMG 1957; CBE 1946; *b* 7 April 1905; *s* of late Richard Ellis Potter, Ridgewood, Almondsbury, Glos and Harriott Isabel (*née* Kingscote, of Kingscote, Glos); *m* 1950, Hilda, *d* of late W. A. Butterfield, OBE; one *d. Educ:* Charterhouse; New Coll., Oxford (BA). Entered Indian CS, 1928; posted to Burma; District Comr, 1934; Financial Adviser, Army in Burma, 1942 (despatches); Finance Secretary, Government of Burma, 1942-43; Financial Adviser (Brigadier), 11th Army Group, 1943, and Allied Land Forces, South-East Asia, 1943-44; Chief Financial Officer (Brig.), Military Administration of Burma, 1944-47; HM Treasury Representative in India, Pakistan and Burma, 1947-50; Asst Secretary, HM Treasury, 1950-56; Counsellor, UK Delegation to NATO, Paris, 1956-65. *Address:* Lower House Barns, Bepton, Midhurst, W Sussex GU29 0JB.

POTTER, Dennis (Christopher George); playwright, author and journalist (freelance since 1964); *b* 17 May 1935; *s* of Walter and Margaret Potter; *m* 1959, Margaret Morgan; one *s* two *d. Educ:* Bell's Grammar Sch., Coleford, Glos; St Clement Danes Grammar Sch.; New Coll., Oxford. Editor, Isis, 1958; BA (Hons) in PPE Oxon, 1959. BBC TV (current affairs), 1959-61; Daily Herald, feature writer, then TV critic, 1961-64; contested (Lab) East Herts, 1964; Leader writer, The Sun, Sept.-Oct. 1964, then resigned; TV Critic, Sunday Times, 1976-78. First television play, 1965. NFT retrospective, 1980. *Television plays:* Vote Vote Vote for Nigel Barton (also at Bristol Old Vic, 1968); Stand Up Nigel Barton; Where the Buffalo Roam; A Beast with Two Backs; Son of Man; Traitor; Paper Roses; Casanova; Follow the Yellow Brick Road; Only Make Believe; Joe's Ark; Schmoedipus; (adapted from novel by Angus Wilson) Late Call, 1975; Brimstone and Treacle, 1976 (not transmitted); Double Dare, 1976; Where Adam Stood, 1976; Pennies from Heaven (sextet), 1978 (BAFTA award, 1978); Blue Remembered Hills, 1979 (BAFTA award, 1980); Blade on the Feather, Rain on the Roof, Cream in my Coffee, 1980; *screenplays:* Pennies from Heaven, 1981; Brimstone and Treacle, 1982; *stage play:* Sufficient Carbohydrate, 1982. *Publications:* The

Glittering Coffin, 1960; The Changing Forest, 1962; *plays:* The Nigel Barton Plays (paperback, 1968); Son of Man, 1970; Brimstone and Treacle, 1979; *novels:* Hide and Seek, 1973; Pennies from Heaven, 1982. *Recreations:* nothing unusual, ie the usual personal pleasures, sought with immoderate fervour. *Address:* Morecambe Lodge, Duxmere, Ross-on-Wye, Herefordshire. *T:* Ross-on-Wye 3199.

POTTER, Donald Charles, QC 1972; *b* 24 May 1922; *s* of late Charles Potter, Shortlands, Kent. *Educ:* St Dunstan's Coll.; London Sch. of Economics. RAC (Westminster Dragoons), 1942-46 (Lieut); served England, NW Europe (D-day), Germany; mentioned in despatches; Croix de Guerre (France). LLB London 1947; called to Bar, Middle Temple, 1948; Bencher, Lincoln's Inn, 1979. Asst Lectr in Law, LSE, 1947-49; practised at Bar, 1950-. Chm., Revenue Bar Assoc., 1978-. *Publication:* (with H. H. Monroe) Tax Planning with Precedents, 1954. *Recreations:* farming, travel, theatre, reading. *Address:* 24 Old Buildings, Lincoln's Inn, WC2A 3UJ; Bow Cottage, East Portlemouth, Devon TQ8 8PE. *Club:* Garrick.

POTTER, His Honour Douglas Charles Loftus; a Circuit Judge (formerly Judge of County Courts), 1959-78; *b* 17 Dec. 1903; *s* of John Charles Potter, solicitor, Putney, and Caroline Annette Tidy Potter (*née* Onslow); *m* 1st, 1934, Margaret Isabel (*d* 1979), *d* of Dr William Savile Henderson, Liverpool; one *d*; 2nd, 1980, Nicole, *d* of Dr Eugene Charles Joseph Kayser, Versailles. *Educ:* Radley; Trinity Coll., Oxford (MA). Rowed in winning crew, Ladies' Plate, Henley Regatta, 1923; Half-blue, OUAC, 3 miles, 1925. Barrister, Inner Temple, 1928; SE Circuit, Herts and Essex Sessions. Served War of 1939-45 in RAFVR, 1940-45. Judge of County Courts, 1959-71, Willesden, Croydon and Kingston upon Thames. *Publications:* The Law Relating to Garages and Car Parks, 1939; The National Insurance Act, 1946, 1946. *Recreations:* walking, travel, reading, music, gardening. *Address:* 4 Longdown Road, Epsom, Surrey; 32 avenue de Saint-Cloud, 78000 Veisailles, France. *Club:* Royal Automobile.

POTTER, Ernest Frank; Director, Finance, since 1979 (Director of Finance and Corporate Planning, 1977-79), Cable & Wireless Ltd; *b* 29 April 1923; *s* of Frank William and Edith Mary Potter; *m* 1945, Madge (*née* Arrowsmith); one *s. Educ:* Dr Challoner's Grammar Sch., Amersham. FCMA, FCIS, MIMC. Commissioned Pilot and Navigator, RAF, 1941-49. Chief Accountant, Bulmer & Lumb Ltd, 1950-58; Director, Management Consulting, Coopers & Lybrand, 1959-71; British Steel Corporation, Cammell Laird Shipbuilders Ltd, 1972-77. *Recreations:* golf, squash. *Address:* Long Meadow, Gorse Hill Road, Virginia Water, Surrey GU25 4AS. *T:* Wentworth 2178. *Clubs:* Royal Air Force, Royal Commonwealth Society; Wentworth (Surrey).

POTTER, Francis Malcolm; His Honour Judge Malcolm Potter; a Circuit Judge, since 1978; *b* 28 July 1932; *s* of Francis Martin Potter and Zilpah Jane Potter; *m* 1970, Bertha Villamil; one *s* one *d. Educ:* Rugby Sch.; Jesus Coll., Oxford. Called to Bar, Lincoln's Inn, 1956. A Recorder of the Crown Court, 1974-78. *Recreation:* painting. *Address:* 5 Fountain Court, Steelhouse Lane, Birmingham B4 6DR.

POTTER, Sir Ian; see Potter, Sir W. I.

POTTER, Jeremy; see Potter, R. J.

POTTER, Maj.-Gen. Sir John, KBE 1968 (CBE 1963; OBE 1951); CB 1966; Chairman, Traffic Commissioners and Licensing Authority, Western Traffic Area, since 1973; *b* 18 April 1913; *s* of late Major Benjamin Henry Potter, OBE, MC; *m* 1st, 1943, Vivienne Madge (*d* 1973), *d* of late Captain Henry D'Arcy Medlicott Cooke; one *s* one *d*; 2nd, 1974, Mrs D. Ella Purkis; one step *s* one step *d.* Served War of 1939-45. Major-General, 1962; Colonel Comdt: RAOC, 1965-69; RCT, 1968-73. Director of Supplies and Transport, 1963-65; Transport Officer in Chief (Army), 1965-66; Dir of Movements (Army), MoD, 1966-68; retired. *Address:* Orchard Cottage, The Orchard, Freshford, Bath, Avon.

POTTER, John Herbert, MBE 1974; HM Diplomatic Service; Counsellor (Administration), Bonn, since 1981; *b* 11 Jan. 1928; *s* of Herbert George and Winifred Eva Potter; *m* 1953, Winifred Susan Florence Hall; one *d. Educ:* elementary education at various state schools. Electrical Engineering jobs, 1942-45; served HM Forces, 1945-48; GPO, 1948-53; Foreign Office, 1953-55; Commercial Attaché, Bangkok, 1955-57; FO, 1957-60; Istanbul, 1960; Ankara, 1960-64; Second Secretary, Information, 1962; Second Sec., Information, Addis Ababa, 1964; Vice-Consul, Information, Johannesburg, 1964-66; DSAO, later FCO, 1966-70; First Sec. (Administration): Brussels, 1970-74; Warsaw, 1974-76; FCO (Inspectorate), 1976-80; Counsellor (Admin.) and Consul-Gen., Moscow, 1980-81. *Recreations:* reading, languages, walking, gardening. *Address:* c/o Foreign and Commonwealth Office, SW1A 2AH.

POTTER, John McEwen, DM, FRCS; Director of Postgraduate Medical Education and Training, Oxford University, since 1972; Professorial Fellow, Wadham College, Oxford, since 1974 (Fellow, 1969; Sub-Warden, 1978-81); Hon. Consultant Neurosurgeon, Oxford Regional Health Authority and Oxfordshire Health Authority, since 1972; *b* 28 Feb. 1920; *er s* of Alistair Richardson Potter and Mairi Chalmers Potter (*née* Dick); *m* 1943, Kathleen Gerrard; three *s. Educ:* Clifton Coll.; Emmanuel Coll., Cambridge; St Bartholomew's Hosp. BA, MB, BChir Cantab, 1943; MA 1945; FRCS 1951;

MA, BM, BCh Oxon, 1963, DM 1964. Active service (Captain, RAMC), Europe, India and Burma, 1944–47. Lectr in Physiol. and Jun. Chief Asst, Surg. Professorial Unit, St Bart's Hosp., 1948–51; Graduate Asst to Nuffield Prof. of Surgery, Oxford, 1951–56; E. G. Fearnsides Scholar, Cambridge, 1954–56; Hunterian Prof., 1955; Cons. Neurosurgeon: Manchester Royal Infirmary, 1956–61; Radcliffe Infirm., Oxford, 1961–72; Vis. Prof., UCLA, 1967; Univ. of Oxford: Clin. Lectr in Neurosurgery, 1962–68, Univ. Lectr, 1968–; Mem., Gen. Bd of Faculties, 1975–; Fellow, Linacre Coll., 1967–69. Governor, United Oxford Hosps, 1973. Cairns Lectr, Adelaide, 1974. Examr for Final BM, BCh Oxon; Ext. Examr, Med. Sciences Tripos Pt II, Cambridge Univ. FRSM (Pres., Sect. of Neurol., 1975–76); Member: GMC, 1973– (Chm., Registration Cttee, 1979–); Oxfordshire HA, 1982–; Soc. of British Neurol Surgeons (formerly Hon. Sec.); Constitution Cttee, World Fedn of Neurosurgical Socs (Vice-Pres., 4th Internat. Congress of Neurol Surgery). Corres. Member: Amer. Assoc. of Neurol Surgeons; Deutsche Gesellschaft für Neurochirurgie; Sociedad Luso-Espanhola de Neurocirurgia; Hon. Mem., Egyptian Soc. of Neurol Surgeons. Publications: The Practical Management of Head Injuries, 1961, 3rd edn 1974; contrib. to books and jls on subjects relating mostly to neurology and med. educn. Recreation: fishing. Address: 47 Park Town, Oxford OX2 6SL. T: Oxford 57875; Myredykes, Newcastleton, Roxburghshire TD9 05R. Club: Kielder Working Men's.
See also R. J. Potter.

POTTER, Sir (Joseph) Raymond (Lynden), Kt 1978; Chairman, Halifax Building Society, since 1974; b 21 April 1916; s of Rev. Henry Lynden and Mabel Boulton Potter; m 1939, Daphne Marguerite, d of Sir Crawford Douglas-Jones, CMG; three s one d. Educ: Haileybury Coll.; Clare Coll., Cambridge (MA). War Service, 1939–46, Queen's Own Royal W Kent Regt, England and Middle East; GSO2 Staff Duties, GHQ, MEF; AQMG War Office. Sec., Royal Inst. of Internat. Affairs, 1947–51; joined Halifax Building Soc., 1951; Gen. Man. 1956; Chief Gen. Man., 1960–74; Dir, 1968–. Mem., Board, Warrington and Runcorn (formerly Warrington) New Town Develt Corp., 1969–. Vice Pres., Building Socs Assoc., 1981– (Mem. Council, 1965–81; Chm., 1975–77). Freeman, City of London, 1981. Life Governor, Haileybury Coll. Recreation: hill walking. Address: Oakwood, Chilbolton, Stockbridge, Hampshire SO20 6BE. T: Chilbolton 523. Club: Hawks (Cambridge).

POTTER, Malcolm; see Potter, F. M.

POTTER, Mark Howard, QC 1980; b 27 Aug. 1937; s of Prof. Harold Potter, LLD, PhD, and Beatrice Spencer Potter (née Crowder); m 1962, Undine Amanda Fay Miller; two s. Educ: Perse Sch., Cambridge (Schol.); Gonville and Caius Coll., Cambridge (Schol; BA (Law Tripos) 1960, MA 1963). National Service, 15 Med. Regt RA, 1955–57 (commnd 1956); Territorial Army, 289 Lt Parachute Regt RHA(TA), 1958–64. Asst Supervisor, Legal Studies, Gonville and Caius, Queens' and Sidney Sussex Colls, 1961–68; called to Bar, Gray's Inn, 1961; in practice, 1962–; Member: Senate of Inns of Court and Bar, 1976–79, 1982–; Senate Law Reform Cttee, 1976–; Supreme Ct Rule Cttee, 1980–. Recreations: family and sporting. Address: 6 St Mary's Grove, N1 2NT; Fountain Court, Temple, EC4 9DH. T: 01-353 7356.

POTTER, Rev. Philip Alford; General Secretary, World Council of Churches, since Nov. 1972; b 19 Aug. 1921; s of Clement Potter and Violet Peters, Roseau, Dominica, Windward Is, WI; m 1956, Ethel Olive Doreen Cousins (d 1980), Jamaica, WI. Educ: Dominica Grammar Sch.; United Theological Coll., Jamaica; London Univ. BD, MTh. Methodist Minister. Overseas Sec., British SCM, 1948–50; Superintendent, Cap Haitien Circuit, Methodist Church, Haiti, 1950–54; Sec., later Dir, Youth Dept, WCC, 1954–60; Sec. for WI and W Africa, Methodist Missionary Society, London, 1961–66; Dir, Commn on World Mission and Evangelism, and Associate Gen. Sec., WCC, 1967–72. Mem., then Chm., Youth Dept Cttee, WCC, 1948–54; Chm., World Student Christian Fedn, 1960–68. Editor: Internat. Review of Mission, 1967–72; Ecumenical Rev., 1972–. Hon. Doctor of Theology: Hamburg Univ., Germany, 1971; Geneva, 1976; Theol Inst. of Rumanian Orthodox Church, 1977; Humboldt Univ., Berlin (GDR), 1982; Hon. LLD W Indies, 1974. Publications: (with Prof. Hendrik Berkhof) Key Words of the Gospel, 1964; The Love of Power or the Power of Love, 1974; Living the Christian Year, 1981; Life in all its Fullness, 1981; chapter in Explosives Lateinamerika (ed by T. Tschuy), 1969; essays in various symposia; contrib. various jls, incl. Ecumenical Rev., Internat. Rev. of Mission, Student World. Recreations: swimming, hiking, music, geology. Address: World Council of Churches, 150 route de Ferney, PO Box 66, 1211 Geneva 20, Switzerland. T: 98.94.00.

POTTER, Sir Raymond; see Potter, Sir J. R. L.

POTTER, (Ronald) Jeremy; Group Director of Corporate Affairs, London Weekend Television, since 1979; Chairman, Hutchinson Ltd, since 1982 (Director, since 1978, Deputy Chairman 1980–82); b 25 April 1922; s of Alistair Richardson Potter and Mairi Chalmers (née Dick); m 1950, Margaret, d of Bernard Newman; one s one d. Educ: Clifton Coll.; Queen's Coll., Oxford (Neale Exhibnr, MA). Served War, Intell. Officer, Indian Army. Manager, subseq. Man. Dir, Dep. Chm., New Statesman, 1951–69; Man. Dir, Independent Television Publications Ltd, 1970–79; Chm., Independent Television Books Ltd, 1971–79. Pres., Periodical Publishers Assoc., 1978–79; Appeals Chm., Newsvendors' Benevolent Instn, 1979; Chairman: Twickenham Arts Council, 1967–68; Richard III Soc., 1971–. FRSA. Captain,

Hampstead Hockey Club, 1954–57. Publications: novels: Hazard Chase, 1964; Death in Office, 1965; Foul Play, 1967; The Dance of Death, 1968; A Trail of Blood, 1970; Going West, 1972; Disgrace and Favour, 1975; Death in the Forest, 1977; lectures: ITV: Critics and Viewers, 1975; Problems in Mass Communication, 1976. Recreations: reading, writing, Real tennis. Clubs: Garrick, MCC, Puritans Hockey.
See also J. McE. Potter.

POTTER, Ronald Stanley James; Director of Social Services, Surrey County Council, 1970–81; b 29 April 1921; e s of late Stanley Potter and Gertrude Mary Keable, Chelmsford; m 1954, Ann (Louisa Eleanor) Burnett; one s one d. Educ: King Edward VI Grammar Sch., Chelmsford. MISW. Territorial Army, 1939, War Service, 1939–47; commnd RA, 1942; Captain 1946. Area Welfare Officer, Essex CC, 1953–61; Dep. Co. Welfare Officer, Lindsey CC, 1962; County Welfare Officer: Lindsey CC, 1962–64; Herts CC, 1964–70. Dir, Watford Sheltered Workshop Ltd, 1964–70; Mem. Cttee of Enquiry into Voluntary Workers in Social Services, 1966–69; Dir, Industrial Advisers to Blind Ltd, 1969–74; Chm, SE Regional Assoc. for Deaf, 1976– (Vice-Chm., 1968–76); Member: Council of Management, RNID, 1968–71, 1976–; Nat. Jt Council for Workshops for the Blind, 1970–81; Adv. Council, Nat. Corp. for Care of Old People, 1974–77; Local Authorities Adv. Cttee on Conditions of Service of Blind Workers, 1974–81; Exec. Council, RNIB, 1975–81; Nat. Adv. Council on Employment of Disabled People, 1978–81; Dir, Remploy Ltd, 1974–. Recreations: walking, swimming, caravanning. Address: 4 New Inn Lane, Guildford, Surrey GU4 7HW. T: Guildford 504272.

POTTER, Maj.-Gen. Sir Wilfrid John; see Potter, Maj.-Gen. Sir John.

POTTER, Sir (William) Ian, Kt 1962; Stockbroker, Melbourne, Australia; b 25 Aug. 1902; s of James William Potter and Maria Louisa (née McWhinnie); m 1975; two d of former m. Educ: University of Sydney. Economist to Federal Treas., 1935–36; Commonwealth Rep. Rural Debt Adjustment Cttee, 1936; founded Ian Potter & Co., 1937; Principal Partner, 1937–67. Served RANVR, 1939–44. Member: Cttee Stock Exchange of Melbourne, 1945–62; Melbourne University Council, 1947–71; Commonwealth Immigration Planning Council, 1956–62; Victorian Arts Centre Building Cttee, 1960–78. President, Australian Elizabethan Theatre Trust, 1964–66, Chairman, 1968–; Vice-Pres., Howard Florey Inst., Melbourne. Publications: contrib. articles on financial and economic subjects to learned journals and press. Recreations: yachting, tennis, golfing. Address: 99 Spring Street, Melbourne, Victoria 3000, Australia. Clubs: Melbourne, Australian, Royal Melbourne Golf (Melbourne); The Links (NY).

POTTERTON, Homan, FSA; Director, National Gallery of Ireland, since 1980; b 9 May 1946; sixth s of late Thomas Edward Potterton and of Eileen Potterton. Educ: Kilkenny Coll.; Trinity Coll., Dublin (BA 1968, MA 1973); Edinburgh Univ. (Dip. Hist. Art 1971). FSA 1981. Cataloguer, National Gall. of Ireland, 1971–73; Asst Keeper, National Gall., London, 1974–80. Hon. Mem., National Trust Archive, Ireland, 1979–; HRHA 1982. Publications: Irish Church Monuments 1570–1880, 1975; A Guide to the National Gallery, 1976, rev. edn 1980 (German, French, Italian and Japanese edns 1977); The National Gallery, London, 1977; Reynolds and Gainsborough: themes and painters in the National Gallery, 1976; Pageant and Panorama: the elegant world of Canaletto, 1978; (jtly) Irish Art and Architecture, 1978; Venetian Seventeenth Century Painting (National Gallery Exhibn Catalogue), 1979; introd. to National Gallery of Ireland Illustrated Summary Catalogue of Paintings, 1981; (jtly) National Gallery of Ireland, 50 Pictures, 1981; contrib. Burlington Mag., Apollo, Connoisseur, and Country Life. Recreation: Pimlico. Address: National Gallery of Ireland, Merrion Square West, Dublin 2. T: Dublin 761699.

POTTINGER, Don; see Pottinger, J. I. D.

POTTINGER, John Inglis Drever, (Don Pottinger); Islay Herald of Arms, Lyon Clerk and Keeper of the Records in the Court of the Lord Lyon, since 1981; b 25 March 1919; s of Rev. William Pottinger and Janet Woodcock; m 1943, Agnes Fay Keeling. Educ: Edinburgh Coll. of Art 1937; Dip. in Drawing and Painting 1948); Edinburgh Univ. (MA Hons in Fine Art 1951). Commnd RA (Field Br.), 1939; served N Africa, Italy and Palestine, 1939–46; Captain. Falkland Pursuivant Extraordinary, 1953; Linlithgow Pursuivant Extraordinary, 1958; Unicorn Pursuivant of Arms, 1961. Freelance artist and portrait painter; many mural decorations in UK and elsewhere. Chalmers Prize, RSA, 1947. Publications: (with Sir Iain Moncreiffe of that Ilk: Simple Heraldry, 1952, revd edn 1978; Simple Custom, 1954; Blood Royal, 1956; Scotland of Old, 1961; (with Michael Grant): Greeks, 1958; Romans, 1960; (with A. V. Norman) Warrior to Soldier, 1966; (with P. Belbin) New History Atlas, 1969; (jtly) The Kings and Queens of Great Britain, 1970; (with John Stewart of Ardvorlich) Clan Cameron Map, 1971; (with I. Nicolson) Simple Astronomy, 1973; (with G. Cousins) An Atlas of Golf, 1974; (with J. Munro) Robert the Bruce Maps, 1974; (with J. T. Dunbar) The Official Tartan Map, 1976; The Clan Headquarters Flags Chart, 1977; The Official Chart of the Tower of London, 1978; World of Flags, 1981; and illustrations to many others. Recreations: etcetera. Address: 11 Ainslie Place, Edinburgh EH3 6AS. T: 031-225 6146. Club: New (Edinburgh).

POTTINGER, (William) George; b 11 June 1916; e s of late Rev. William Pottinger, MA, Orkney, and Janet Woodcock; m 1946, Margaret Rutherfurd

Clark McGregor; one *s. Educ:* George Watson's; High School of Glasgow; Edinburgh Univ.; Heidelberg; Queens' Coll., Cambridge (Major Scholar). Entered Scottish Home Dept, as Assistant Principal, 1939. Served War of 1939-45, RFA; France, N Africa, Italy (despatches), Lieut-Col RA. Principal, 1945; Private Secretary to successive Secretaries of State for Scotland, 1950-52; Asst Secretary, Scottish Home Dept, 1952; Secretary, Royal Commn on Scottish Affairs, 1952-54; Under-Secretary: Scottish Home Dept, 1959-62; Scottish Home and Health Dept, 1962-63; Scottish Development Dept, 1963-64; Scottish Office, 1964-68; Dept of Agriculture and Fisheries for Scotland, 1968-71; Secretary, Dept of Agriculture and Fisheries for Scotland, 1971. *Publications:* The Winning Counter, 1971; Muirfield and the Honourable Company, 1972; St Moritz: an Alpine caprice, 1972; The Court of the Medici, 1977; The Secretaries of State for Scotland 1926-76, 1979; Whisky Sour, 1979; The Bubble Reputation, 1981; papers and reviews. *Recreations:* squash rackets, golf, fishing. *Address:* West Lodge, Balsham, Cambs CB1 6EP. *T:* Cambridge 892958. *Club:* Savile.

POTTLE, Frederick Albert, BA Colby, MA, PhD Yale, Hon. LittD Colby, Rutgers, Hon. LHD Northwestern; Hon. LLD Glasgow; Sterling Professor of English, and Fellow Emeritus of Davenport College, Yale University; Public Orator, Yale University, 1942 and 1946; *b* Lovell, Maine, 3 Aug. 1897; *y s* of late Fred Leroy Pottle and Annette Wardwell Kemp; *m* 1920, Marion Isabel Starbird, Oxford, Maine; one *s. Educ:* Colby Coll. (*Summa cum laude*); Yale (John Addison Porter Prize). Served as private in Evacuation Hospital No 8, AEF, 1918-19; formerly Assistant Professor of English, University of New Hampshire; Editor of the Private Papers of James Boswell (succeeding the late Geoffrey Scott); Hon. member of Johnson Club; Vice-Pres., Johnson Soc., London; Pres., Johnson Soc., Lichfield, 1974; Trustee: General Theological Seminary, 1947-68; Colby Coll., 1932-59, 1966-78, Hon. Life Trustee, 1978; Messenger Lecturer, Cornell Univ., 1941; Member of Joint Commission on Holy Matrimony of the Episcopal Church, 1940-46; Guggenheim Fellow, 1945-46, 1952-53; Chancellor Academy of American Poets, 1951-71; Chairman of Editorial Cttee of Yale Editions of Private Papers of James Boswell, 1949-79; Member Provinciaal Utrechtsch Genootschap van Kunsten en Wetenschappen, 1953-; Member American Academy of Arts and Sciences, 1957-; FIAL, 1958-; Member, American Philosophical Society, 1960. Wilbur Lucius Cross Medal, Yale, 1967; William Clyde DeVane Medal, Yale, 1969; Lewis Prize, Amer. Philosophical Soc., 1975; Dist. Alumnus Award, Colby, 1977. *Publications:* Shelley and Browning, 1923; A New Portrait of James Boswell (with Chauncey B. Tinker), 1927; The Literary Career of James Boswell, 1929; Stretchers, the Story of a Hospital on the Western Front, 1929; The Private Papers of James Boswell: A Catalogue (with Marion S. Pottle), 1931; Vols 7-18 of The Private Papers of James Boswell, 1930-34; Boswell's Journal of a Tour to the Hebrides, from the Original Manuscript (with Charles H. Bennett), 1936, revised edition, 1963; Index to the Private Papers of James Boswell (with Joseph Foladare, John P. Kirby and others), 1937; Boswell and the Girl from Botany Bay, 1937; The Idiom of Poetry, 1941, revised and enlarged edition, 1946; James Boswell, the Earlier Years, 1966; Pride and Negligence, A History of the Boswell Papers, 1982; *editions of Boswell's journals:* Boswell's London Journal (1762-63), 1950; Boswell in Holland (1763-64), 1952; Boswell on the Grand Tour: Germany and Switzerland (1764), 1953; Boswell on the Grand Tour: Italy, Corsica and France, 1765 (with Frank Brady), 1955; Boswell in Search of a Wife, 1766-1769 (with Frank Brady), 1956; Boswell for the Defence, 1769-1774 (with William K. Wimsatt), 1959; Boswell: The Ominous Years, 1774-1776 (with Charles Ryskamp), 1963; Boswell in Extremes, 1776-1778 (with Charles McC. Weis), 1970; Boswell, Laird of Auchinleck, 1778-1782 (with Joseph W. Reed), 1977; Boswell, the Applause of the Jury, 1981; various articles. *Recreation:* gardening. *Address:* Edgehill Road, New Haven, Conn 06511, USA. *Clubs:* Elizabethan (New Haven); Grolier, Ends of the Earth (New York).

POTTS, Archie; Under-Secretary, and Director of Scientific and Technical Intelligence, Ministry of Defence, 1964-74; *b* 28 Dec. 1914; *s* of late Mr and Mrs A. Potts, Newcastle upon Tyne; *m* 1951, Winifred Joan Bishop, MBE, *d* of late Mr and Mrs Reginald Bishop; two *s. Educ:* University of Durham. BSc (Hons) Physics, 1935. Research in Spectroscopy, King's Coll., University of Durham, 1936-39. War of 1939-45: Operational Research in Radar and Allied Fields, Fighter Command, and N Africa and Italy, 1939-45; Hon. Sqdn Leader, RAFVR, 1943-45. Chief Research Officer, Fighter Command, 1946-51; Defence Research Staff, Min.ʼ of Defence, 1951-53; Scientific Adviser, Allied Air Forces Central Europe, 1954-56; Asst Scientific Adviser, Air Ministry, 1957; Dep. Director for Atomic Energy, Jt Intell. Bureau, 1957-63. FInstP 1945. *Recreation:* listening to music. *Address:* 3 The Keir, West Side, SW19 4UG. *T:* 01-946 7077. *Club:* Royal Air Force.

POTTS, Prof. Edward Logan Johnston, MSc; FEng; Professor of Mining, Department of Mining Engineering, University of Newcastle upon Tyne, 1951-80, now Professor Emeritus; *b* Niddrie, Midlothian, 22 Jan. 1915; *s* of Samuel Potts; *m* 1940, Edith Mary, *d* of A. Hayton, Scarborough; one *s* one *d. Educ:* Coatbridge Grammar Sch., Lanarkshire; Gosforth Grammar Sch., Newcastle upon Tyne; King's Coll., University of Durham. BSc (dist.) 1939, 1st Class Hons (Dunelm) 1940; 1st Class Colliery Manager's Certif., 1941; MSc (Dunelm) 1945. FEng 1980. Apprentice Mine Surveyor, Hazlerigg & Burradon Coal Co., Ltd, 1931-34. Asst to Chief Surveyor, Charlaw & Sacriston Collieries Co. Ltd, 1934-36; Certificated Mine Surveyor, 1936; Apprentice Mining Engineer, Wallsend & Hebburn Coal Co. Ltd, 1936-40; Cons. Mining Engineer, Northumberland, Durham, N Staffs; Surveyor to

Northern "A" Regional cttee; prepared report on Northumberland and Cumberland Reserves and output, 1944; Reader in Mining, King's Coll., University of Durham, 1947; Mining Adviser: Northumberland Coal Owners' Assoc., 1947; Mickley Associated Collieries, 1949-51; Peterlee Development Corp. on mining subsidence, 1947-72; Adviser to Kolar Gold Fields, S India, rock bursts in deep mining, 1955-70; Mem., Coal Res. Commn, EEC, 1972-. President, N of England Inst. Mining and Mech. Engineering, 1957-58. Consultant, Rock Mechanics, ICI Mond Div., Cleveland Potash Ltd, etc. Research on rock mechanics, etc; co-designer Dunelm circular fluorescent mine lighting unit, hydraulic coal plough. *Publications:* (jointly) Horizon Mining, 1953; papers on ventilation, mine lighting, strata control in Trans. Inst. Mining Eng., British Assoc. and other journals. *Recreations:* athletics, motoring. *Address:* 4 Montagu Avenue, Gosforth, Newcastle upon Tyne NE3 4HX. *T:* Newcastle 3852171.

POTTS, Francis Humphrey, QC 1971; a Recorder of the Crown Court, since 1972; *b* 18 Aug. 1931; *er s* of late Francis William Potts and Elizabeth Hannah Potts (*née* Humphrey); *m* 1971, Philippa Margaret Campbell, *d* of the late J. C. H. Le B. Croke and of Mrs J. F. G. Downes; two *s*; two step-*s. Educ:* Royal Grammar Sch., Newcastle upon Tyne; St Catherine's Society, Oxford. BA 1953, BCL 1954, MA 1957. Barrister-at-Law, Lincoln's Inn, 1955 (Tancred Student, 1953; Cholmeley Scholar, 1954), Bencher, 1979; North Eastern Circuit, 1955. *Address:* 11 King's Bench Walk, Temple, EC4. *T:* 01-353 3337. *Clubs:* Reform; County (Durham).

POTTS, Kenneth Hampson; Chief Executive, Leeds City Council, 1973-79; *b* 29 Sept. 1921; *s* of late James Potts and Martha Ann Potts; *m* 1945, Joan Daphne Wilson; two *s. Educ:* Manchester Grammar Sch.; Liverpool Univ. (LLB Hons). Solicitor. Captain, RA, 1942-46. Deputy Town Clerk, Leeds, 1965; Chief Management and Legal Officer, Leeds, 1969. Member: Yorks and Humberside Economic Planning Council; Data Protection Cttee, 1976-. *Recreations:* gardening, theatre, music, reading. *Address:* 8 Burlyn Road, Hunmanby, Filey, N Yorks YO14 0QA. *T:* Scarborough 891100.

POTTS, Peter; General Secretary, General Federation of Trade Unions, since 1977; *b* 29 June 1935; *s* of late John Peter Potts and of Margaret (*née* Combs); *m* 1st, 1956, Mary Longden (*d* 1972); two *s* one *d*; 2nd, 1974, Angela Elouise van Lieshout (*née* Liddelow); one step *s* one step *d. Educ:* Chorlton High Sch., Manchester; Ruskin Coll., Oxford; Oxford Univ. (Dip. in Econs and Pol. Science). Served RAF, 1953-55. USDAW, 1951-65; Res. Officer, Union of Tailors and Garment Workers, 1965-74; National Officer, Clerical and Supervisory Staffs, 1974-77. Member: Clothing EDC, 1970-77 (Trade Union Advisor, 1966-70); Jt Textile Cttee, NEDO, 1970-77; Trade Union Unit Trust Investors Cttee, 1977-; Trade Union Res. Unit, 1975-; Trade Union Internat. Res. and Educn Gp, 1979-; Governing Council, Ruskin Coll., 1977- (Mem. Exec. Cttee, 1977-). *Recreations:* tennis, do-it-yourself hobbies, art, listening to jazz. *Address:* Caribana, 46 Bridle Drive, Clapham, Bedford MK41 6BE. *T:* Bedford 63615.

POTTS, Robin, QC 1982; barrister; *b* 2 July 1944; *s* of William and Elaine Potts; *m* 1968, Rebeca Giwercer; one *s. Educ:* Wolstanton Grammar Sch.; Magdalen Coll., Oxford (BA, BCL). Called to the Bar, Gray's Inn, 1968. *Publication:* (contrib.) Gore-Browne on Companies, 43rd edn. *Address:* The Grange, Church Lane, Pinner, Mddx HA5 3AB. *T:* 01-866 9013.

POTTS, Thomas Edmund, ERD 1957; Company Director; *b* 23 March 1908; *s* of late T. E. Potts, Leeds; *m* 1932, Phyllis Margaret, *d* of late J. S. Gebbie, Douglas, Isle of Man; one *s. Educ:* Leeds Modern School. Joined The British Oxygen Co. Ltd, 1928. Commissioned RE, Supp. R of O, 1938; served War of 1939-45, Madras Sappers and Miners in India, Eritrea, Western Desert, Tunisia, with 4th and 5th Indian Divs (despatches, 1942 and 1943; Major); CRE 31st Indian Armoured Div., 9th Army (Lt-Col); released from active service and transferred to RARO (resigned Commission, RE, 1950). Rejoined British Oxygen Co. Ltd, London, 1945; Managing Director, African Oxygen Ltd, Johannesburg, 1947; Director, British Oxygen Co. Ltd, 1955; Group Managing Director, The British Oxygen Co. Ltd, 1958-63; UK Atomic Energy Authority: Consultant, 1968-78, a Dir, 1971-78, Radiochemical Centre; Dir, Amersham Corp., Chicago, 1968-78. Pres. South African Instn of Welding, 1951; Vice-Pres., Inst. of Welding, 1963-64. CBIM 1979. *Recreations:* golf, gardening. *Address:* Budds Oak, Primrose Lane, Holyport, Berks. *T:* Maidenhead 26887. *Clubs:* Rand (Johannesburg); Temple Golf.

POULTON, Rev. Canon John Frederick; Residentiary Canon, Norwich Cathedral, since 1979; *b* 15 June 1925; *m* 1946, Iris Joan Knighton; two *s* two *d. Educ:* King's Coll., London (BA Hons); Ridley Hall, Cambridge. Tutor, 1955-60, and Actg Principal, 1960-61, Bishop Tucker Coll., Mukono, Uganda; Dir, Church of Uganda Literature and Radio Centre, 1962-66; Res. Sec., World Assoc. of Christian Communication, 1966-68; Exec. Sec., Archbishops' Council on Evangelism, 1968-78. *Publications:* A Today Sort of Evangelism, 1972; People under Pressure, 1973; Jesus in Focus, 1975; Dear Archbishop, 1976; The Feast of Life, 1982. *Address:* 27 The Close, Norwich NR1 4DZ. *T:* Norwich 28506.

POULTON, Richard Christopher, MA; Headmaster, Wycliffe College, since 1980; *b* 21 June 1938; *e s* of Rev. Christopher Poulton and Aileen (*née* Sparrow); *m* 1965, Zara, *o d* of Prof. P. and Mrs J. Crossley-Holland; two *s* one *d. Educ:* King's Coll., Taunton; Wesleyan Univ., Middletown, Conn,

USA; Pembroke Coll., Cambridge (BA 1961, CertEd 1962, MA 1965). Asst Master: Bedford Sch., 1962-63; Beckenham and Penge Grammar Sch., 1963-66; Bryanston School: Asst Master, 1966-80; Head of History Dept, 1971-76; Housemaster, 1972-80. *Publications:* Victoria, Queen of a Changing Land, 1975; Kings and Commoners, 1977; A History of the Modern World, 1980. *Recreations:* writing, hill walking, choral music, squash. *Address:* The Headmaster's House, Wycliffe College, Stonehouse, Glos GL10 2LP. *T:* Stonehouse 3217.

POUNCEY, Denys Duncan Rivers, MA, MusB Cantab; FRCO; Organist and Master of the Choristers, Wells Cathedral, 1936-70; Conductor of Wells Cathedral Oratorio Chorus and Orchestra, 1946-66; Hon. Diocesan Choirmaster Bath and Wells Choral Association, 1946-70; *b* 23 Dec. 1906; *s* of late Rev. George Ernest Pouncey and late Madeline Mary Roberts; *m* 1937, Evelyn Cottier. *Educ:* Marlborough College; Queens' College, Cambridge. Asst to Dr Cyril Rootham, Organist and Choirmaster of St John's Coll., Cambridge, 1928-34; Organist and Choirmaster St Matthew's, Northampton, 1934-36; Founder Conductor of Northampton Bach Choir. *Address:* Longstring, 23 Ash Lane, Wells, Somerset. *T:* Wells 73200.
See also P. M. R. *Pouncey.*

POUNCEY, Philip Michael Rivers, MA; FBA 1975; a Director of Sothebys, since 1966; Hon. Keeper of Italian Drawings, Fitzwilliam Museum, since 1975; *b* 15 Feb. 1910; *s* of Rev. George Ernest Pouncey and Madeline Mary Roberts; *m* 1937, Myril Gros; two *d. Educ:* Marlborough; Queens' Coll., Cambridge (MA). Hon. Attaché, Fitzwilliam Museum, 1931-33; Assistant, National Gall., London, 1934-45; Asst Keeper, 1945-54, Dep. Keeper, 1954-66, British Museum; Visiting Professor: Columbia Univ., NY, 1958; Inst. of Fine Arts, New York Univ., 1965. *Publications:* Catalogues of Italian Drawings in the British Museum: (with A. E. Popham) XIV-XV Centuries, 1950; (with J. A. Gere) Raphael and his Circle, 1962; Lotto disegnatore, 1965; articles in Burlington Magazine, etc. *Recreation:* travel in Italy and France. *Address:* 5 Lower Addison Gardens, W14 8BG.
See also D. D. R. *Pouncey.*

POUND, Sir John David, 5th Bt *cr* 1905; *b* 1 Nov. 1946; *s* of Sir Derek Allen Pound, 4th Bt; *S* father, 1980; *m* 1st, 1968 (marr. diss.); one *s* ; 2nd, 1978, Penelope Ann, *er d* of Grahame Arthur Rayden, Bramhall, Cheshire; one *s.* Liveryman, Leathersellers' Co. *Heir:* *s* Robert John Pound, *b* 12 Feb. 1973. *Address:* 54 Lime Tree Avenue, Worthing, West Sussex.

POUNDER, Rafton John; Secretary, Northern Ireland Bankers' Association, since 1977; *b* 13 May 1933; *s* of Cuthbert C. Pounder, Gefion, Ballynahatty, Shaw's Bridge, Belfast; *m* 1959, Valerie Isobel, *d* of late Robert Stewart, MBE, Cherryvalley, Belfast; one *s* one *d. Educ:* Charterhouse; Christ's College, Cambridge. Qualified as a Chartered Accountant, 1959. Chm. Cambridge Univ. Cons. and Unionist Assoc., 1954; Ulster rep. on Young Cons. and Unionist Nat. Adv. Cttee, 1960-63; Hon. Mem., Ulster Young Unionist Council, 1963; Member: UK delegn (C) to Assembly of Council of Europe, and to Assembly of WEU, 1965-68; UK Delegn to European Parlt, Strasbourg, 1973-74; Exec. Cttee, Nat. Union of Cons. and Unionist Assocs, 1967-72; Exec. Cttee, Ulster Unionist Council, 1967-73. MP (UU) Belfast S, Oct. 1963-Feb. 1974; Mem., House of Commons Select Cttee on Public Accounts, 1970-73; Vice-Chm., Cons. Parly Party's Technology Cttee, 1970; PPS to Minister for Industry, 1970-71. Mem. CPA Delegn to: Jamaica and Cayman Is, Nov. 1966; Malawi, Sept. 1968. Hon. Secretary: Ulster Unionist Parly Party at Westminster, 1964-67; Cons. Parly Party's Power Cttee, 1969-70. Pres., Ulster Soc. for Prevention of Cruelty to Animals, 1968-74. Dir, Progressive Building Soc., 1968-77. Lay Member, General Synod of the Church of Ireland, 1966-78. *Recreations:* golf, reading, music, sailing. *Address:* Gunpoint, Coastguard Lane, Orlock, Groomsport, Co. Down.

POUNDS, Maj.-Gen. Edgar George Derek, CB 1975; Chief Executive, British Friesian Cattle Society, since 1976; Executive Committee, National Cattle Breeders' Association, since 1978; *b* 13 Oct. 1922; *s* of Edgar Henry Pounds, MBE, MSM, and Caroline Beatrice Pounds; *m* 1944, Barbara Winifred May Evans; one *s* one *d. Educ:* Reading Sch. War of 1939-45: enlisted, RM, 1940 (King's Badge, trng); HMS Kent, 1941-42 (Atlantic); commissioned as Reg. Off., Sept. 1942 (sword for drawing); HMS Berwick, 1943-44 (Atlantic and Russia). Co. Comdr, RM, 1945-51: Far East, Palestine, Malta, UK (Sniping Wing), Korea (US Bronze Star, 1950); Captain 1952. Instr, RM Officers' Trng Wing, UK, 1952-54; Adjt, 45 Commando, RM, 1954-57, Malta, Cyprus (despatches), Suez; RAF Staff Coll., Bracknell, 1958; Staff Captain, Dept of CGRM, London, 1959-60; Major 1960; Amphibious Ops Officer, HMS Bulwark, 1961-62, Kuwait, Aden, E Africa, Borneo; Corps Drafting Off., UK, 1962-64; 40 Commando RM: 2nd in Comd, 1964-65, Borneo, and CO, 1966-67, Borneo and Far East; CO, 43 Commando, RM, 1967-68, UK based; GSO1 Dept CGRM, 1969-70; Col 1970; Naval Staff, MoD, 1970-72; Comdt Commando Trng Centre, RM, 1972-73; Actg Maj.-Gen. 1973; Maj.-Gen., RM, 1974; Comdt Commanding Commando Forces, RM, 1973-76, retired. *Publications:* articles on strategy, amphibious warfare, and tactics, in professional jls and cattle breeding and dairying in farming journals. *Recreations:* hunting, target rifle shooting, boating, reading. *Address:* Langdon, Burtons Way, Chalfont St Giles, Bucks HP8 4BW. *Clubs:* Army and Navy, Farmers'.

POUNDS, Prof. Kenneth Alwyne, FRS 1980; Professor of Space Physics, and Director, X-ray Astronomy Group, University of Leicester, since 1973; *b* 17

Nov. 1934; *s* of Harry and Dorothy Pounds; *m* 1961, Margaret Mary (*née* Connell); two *s* one *d. Educ:* Salt Sch., Shipley, Yorkshire; University Coll. London (BSc, PhD). Department of Physics, University of Leicester: Asst Lectr, 1960; Lecturer, 1961; Sen. Lectr, 1969. Mem., SERC, 1981- (Chm., Astronomy, Space and Radio Bd). *Publications:* many, in Monthly Notices, Nature, Astrophysical Jl, etc. *Recreations:* cricket, music. *Address:* 12 Swale Close, Oadby, Leicester LE2 4GF. *T:* Leicester 719370.

POUNTAIN, Eric John; Group Chief Executive and Chairman of all seven divisions, since 1979 and Deputy Group Chairman, since 1982, Tarmac PLC; *b* 5 Aug. 1933; *s* of Horace Pountain and Elsie Pountain; *m* 1960, Joan Patricia Sutton; one *s* one *d. Educ:* Queen Mary Grammar Sch., Walsall. CBIM; FSVA; FFB. Joined F. Maitland Selwyn & Co., auctioneers and estate agents, 1956, joint principal, 1959; founded Midland & General Develts, 1964, acquired by John McLean & Sons Ltd, 1969; Chief Exec., John McLean & Sons, 1969, acquired by Tarmac Ltd, 1973; Chief Exec., newly formed Tarmac Housing Div., until 1979. Dir, Tarmac Ltd, 1977-. Member: Inst. of Dirs; Council, Burton upon Trent Graduate Medical Centre. Trustee, Ironbridge Museum. Chm., Haflinger Soc. of GB. *Recreations:* farming, horse breeding. *Address:* Edial House, Edial, Lichfield. *T:* Burntwood 2229.

POUT, Harry Wilfrid, CB 1978; OBE 1959; CEng, FIEE; Defence consultant, since 1980; Underwater Weapons Marconi Space and Defence Systems, Portsmouth, since 1982; *b* 11 April 1920; British; *m* 1949, Margaret Elizabeth (*née* Nelson); three *d. Educ:* East Ham Grammar Sch.; Imperial Coll., London. BSc (Eng); ACGI 1940. RN Scientific Service, 1940; Admty Signal Estab. (later Admty Signal and Radar Estab.), 1940-54; Dept of Operational Research, Admty, 1954-59; idc 1959; Head of Guided Weapon Projects, Admty, 1960-65; Asst Chief Scientific Adviser (Projects), MoD, 1965-69; Dir, Admiralty Surface Weapons Estabt, 1969-72; Dep. Controller, Guided Weapons, 1973, Guided Weapons and Electronics, 1973-75, Air Systems, 1975-79, Aircraft Weapons and Electronics, 1979-80, MoD. FCGI 1972. *Publications:* (jtly) The New Scientists, 1971; classified books; contribs to jls of IEE, RAeS, RUSI, etc. *Recreations:* mountaineering, gardening and do-it-yourself activities, amateur geology. *Address:* Oakmead, Fox Corner, Worplesdon, near Guildford, Surrey. *T:* Worplesdon 232223.

POWDITCH, Alan (Cecil Robert), MC 1944; JP; District Administrator, NW District, Kensington and Chelsea and Westminster Area Health Authority, 1974-77, retired; *b* 14 April 1912; *s* of Cecil John and Annis Maudie Powditch; *m* 1942, Barbara Leggat; one *s* one *d. Educ:* Mercers School. Entered Hospital Service, 1933; Accountant, St Mary's Hospital, W2, 1938. Served War of 1939-45, with 51st Royal Tank Regt, 1941-46. Dep. House Governor, St Mary's Hospital, 1947-50, Sec. to Bd of Governors, 1950-74. Mem. Nat. Staff Cttee (Min. of Health) 1964-72; Chm., Juvenile Panel, Gore Div., 1973-76. Mem. Council, Sue Ryder Foundn, 1977; Mem. Magistrates' Courts Cttee, 1979-81. JP Co. Middlesex 1965, supp. List 1982. *Recreations:* golf; interested in gardening when necessary. *Address:* Brentmore, Cygnet Close, Northwood, Mddx HA6 2TA.

POWELL; *see* Baden-Powell.

POWELL, Albert Edward, JP; General President of Society of Graphical and Allied Trades, 1973-82, of SOGAT '82 since 1982; *b* 20 May 1927; *s* of Albert and Mary Powell; *m* 1947, Margaret Neville; one *s* two *d. Educ:* Holy Family Elementary Sch., Morden. FIWSP. London Organiser, SOGAT, 1957, Organising Secretary, 1967. Has served on various Committees and Boards, including: past Chairman, Croydon College of Art, past Governor, London College of Printing. Chairman, Paper & Paper Products Industry Trng Bd, 1975- (Mem. Central Arbitration Cttee, 1976-); Member: TUC Printing Industries Cttee, 1971-; NEDO Printing Industries Sector Working Party, 1980-; Methods-Time Measurement Assoc., 1966-. Queen's Silver Jubilee Medal, 1977. JP Wimbledon, 1961. *Recreations:* gardening, reading (science fiction), music. *Address:* 31 Red House Lane, Bexleyheath, Kent DA6 8JF. *T:* 01-304 7480.

POWELL, Anthony Dymoke; CBE 1956; *b* 21 Dec. 1905; *o s* of late Lt-Col P. L. W. Powell, CBE, DSO; *m* 1934, Lady Violet Pakenham, 3rd *d* of 5th Earl of Longford, KP; two *s. Educ:* Eton; Balliol College, Oxford, MA; Hon. Fellow, 1974. Served War of 1939-45, Welch Regt and Intelligence Corps, Major. A Trustee, National Portrait Gallery, 1962-76. Hon. Mem., Amer. Acad. of Arts and Letters, 1977. Hon. Fellow, Mod. Lang. Assoc. of Amer., 1981. Hon. DLitt: Sussex, 1971; Leicester, 1976; Kent, 1976; Oxon, 1980; Bristol, 1982. Orders of: the White Lion, (Czechoslovakia); the Oaken Crown and Croix de Guerre (Luxembourg); Leopold II (Belgium). *Publications:* Afternoon Men, 1931; Venusberg, 1932; From a View to a Death, 1933; Agents and Patients, 1936; What's become of Waring, 1939; John Aubrey and His Friends, 1948; Selections from John Aubrey, 1949; Music of Time, 12 vol. sequence, 1951-75: A Question of Upbringing, 1951; A Buyer's Market, 1952; The Acceptance World, 1955; At Lady Molly's, 1957 (James Tait Black Memorial Prize); Casanova's Chinese Restaurant, 1960; The Kindly Ones, 1962; The Valley of Bones, 1964; The Soldier's Art, 1966; The Military Philosophers, 1968; Books do Furnish a Room, 1971; Temporary Kings, 1973 (W. H. Smith Prize, 1974); Hearing Secret Harmonies, 1975; *memoirs:* To Keep the Ball Rolling, 4 vols, 1976-82: Infants of the Spring, 1976; Messengers of Day, 1978; Faces In My Time, 1980; The Strangers All are Gone, 1982; *plays:* Afternoon Men (adapted by Riccardo Aragno), Arts Theatre Club,

1963; The Garden God, 1971; The Rest I'll Whistle, 1971. *Address:* The Chantry, near Frome, Somerset. *T:* Nunney 314. *Clubs:* Travellers', Pratt's.

POWELL, Sir Arnold Joseph Philip; *see* Powell, Sir Philip.

POWELL, Arthur Barrington, CMG 1967; Executive Director, Welsh Development Agency, since 1976; *b* 24 April 1918; *er s* of late Thomas and Dorothy Powell, Maesteg, Glam; *m* 1945, Jane, *d* of late Gen. Sir George Weir, KCB, CMG, DSO; four *s* one *d. Educ:* Cowbridge; Jesus Coll. Oxford. Indian Civil Service, 1939-47; served in Province of Bihar. Asst Princ., Min. of Fuel and Power, 1947; Princ. Private Sec. to Minister, 1949-51; Asst Sec., 1955; Petroleum Div., 1957-68; Petroleum Attaché, HM Embassy, Washington, 1962-64; Gas Div., 1968-72; Reg. Finance Div., DoI, 1972-76. *Address:* Croeslanfro House, Rogerstone, Gwent. *Club:* United Oxford & Cambridge University.

POWELL, Charles David; HM Diplomatic Service; Counsellor, United Kingdom Permanent Representation to the European Communities, since 1980; *b* 6 July 1941; *s* of Air Vice Marshal John Frederick Powell, *qv* ; *m* 1964, Carla Bonardi; two *s. Educ:* King's Sch., Canterbury; New Coll., Oxford (BA). Entered Diplomatic Service, 1963; Third Sec., FO, 1963-65; Second Sec., Helsinki, 1965-67; FCO, 1968-71; First Sec. and Private Sec. to HM Ambassador, Washington, 1971-74; First Sec., Bonn, 1974-77; FCO, 1977-80 (Counsellor, 1979; Special Counsellor for Rhodesia, 1979-80). *Recreation:* walking. *Address:* c/o Foreign and Commonwealth Office, SW1. *Club:* Turf.

POWELL, David; *see* Powell, E. D. B.

POWELL, David; *b* 1914; *s* of Edward Churton Powell and Margaret (*née* Nesfield); *m* 1941, Joan Boileau (Henderson); one *s* four *d. Educ:* Charterhouse. Served 1939-46: Lt, Kent Yeomanry RA; Captain and Major on Staff. Qualifed as Chartered Accountant, 1939, admitted, 1943; in practice, 1946-47; joined Booker McConnell Ltd, 1947; Finance Dir, 1952; Dep. Chm. 1957; Man. Dir, 1966; Chm. and Chief Exec., 1967, retired 1971; Chm., Bookers Shopkeeping Holdings, 1956-63. *Recreations:* stalking, golf, English water-colours, fishing. *Address:* The Cottage, 20 Coldharbour Lane, Hildenborough, Kent. *T:* Hildenborough 833103.

POWELL, Dewi Watkin, JP; **His Honour Judge Watkin Powell;** a Circuit Judge, since 1972; *b* Aberdare, 29 July 1920; *o s* of W. H. Powell, AMICE and of M. A. Powell, Radyr, Glam; *m* 1951, Alice, *e d* of William and Mary Williams, Nantmor, Caerns; one *d. Educ:* Penarth Grammar Sch.; Jesus Coll., Oxford (MA). Called to Bar, Inner Temple, 1949. Dep. Chm., Merioneth and Cardigan QS, 1966-71; Dep. Recorder of Cardiff, Birkenhead, Merthyr Tydfil and Swansea, 1965-71; Junior, Wales and Chester Circuit, 1968; Liaison Judge for Dyfed; Vice-Pres., South and Mid Glamorgan branch of Magistrates' Assoc. Mem. Exec. Cttee, Plaid Cymru, 1943-55, Chm., Constitutional Cttee, 1967-71; Mem. Council, Hon. Soc. of Cymmrodorion, 1965- (Chm., 1978-). Member: Court, Univ. of Wales; Court and Council, Univ. Coll. of Wales, Aberystwyth and Univ. Coll. Cardiff (and Vice-Pres., UC Cardiff); Welsh Council of Social Services; Magistrates Courts and Probation and After-Care Cttees for Co. of Dyfed. Hon. Mem., Gorsedd of Bards. JP Dyfed. *Recreations:* gardening, reading, theology, Welsh history and literature. *Address:* Crown Court, Law Courts, Cathays Park, Cardiff.

POWELL, Edward, CBE 1973; *b* 10 June 1907; *s* of Edward Churton Powell and Margaret Nesfield; *m* 1941, Patricia Florence (*née* Harris); one *s* one *d. Educ:* Shrewsbury School. Captain, Royal Marines, 1941-45. Solicitor in private practice until 1941; joined Chloride Electrical Storage Co. Ltd (now Chloride Group Ltd), 1941; Man. Dir, 1962-72; Chm., 1965-74; Hon. Pres., 1974-80. Pres., British Electrical and Allied Manufacturers' Assoc. Ltd, 1973-75. *Recreations:* landscape gardening, fishing. *Address:* Little Orchard, Mayfield, East Sussex. *T:* Mayfield 873441.

POWELL, (Elizabeth) Dilys, CBE 1974; FRSL; TV Film Critic of The Sunday Times, since 1976 (Film Critic, 1939-76); Film Critic, Punch, since 1979; *yr d* of late Thomas and Mary Powell; *m* 1st, 1926, Humfry Payne, later Director of the British School of Archæology at Athens (*d* 1936); 2nd, 1943, Leonard Russell (*d* 1974); no *c. Educ:* Bournemouth High School; Somerville College, Oxford. Editorial Staff, Sunday Times, 1928-31 and 1936-41. Lived and travelled extensively in Greece, 1931-36. Member: Bd of Governors of British Film Institute, 1948-52; Independent Television Authority, 1954-57; Cinematograph Films Council, 1965-69; President, Classical Association, 1966-67. *Publications:* Descent from Parnassus, 1934; Remember Greece, 1941; The Traveller's Journey is Done, 1943; Coco, 1952; An Affair of the Heart, 1957; The Villa Ariadne, 1973. *Address:* 14 Albion Street, Hyde Park, W2. *T:* 01-723 9807.

POWELL, Rt. Hon. Enoch; *see* Powell, Rt Hon. J. E.

POWELL, (Evan) David (Brynmor); Regional Chairman of Industrial Tribunals (Cardiff), since 1968; *b* 31 July 1927; *s* of David Harold Idris and Mary Powell; *m* 1962, Margaret Gwynne Thomas; one *s* two *d. Educ:* Swansea Grammar Sch.; Winchester Coll.; Trinity Coll., Oxford (MA); King's Coll., London (LLB). Called to the Bar, Gray's Inn, 1953; practised on Wales and Chester Circuit, 1953-68. *Address:* 14 St Michael's Road, Cardiff CF5 2AP. *T:* Cardiff 566216.

POWELL, Francis Turner, MBE 1945; Chairman, Laing & Cruickshank, Stockbrokers, 1978-80; *b* 15 April 1914; *s* of Francis Arthur and Dorothy May Powell; *m* 1940, Joan Audrey Bartlett; one *s* one *d. Educ:* Lancing College. Served War, Queen's Royal Regt (TA), 1939-45 (Major). Joined L. Powell Sons & Co. (Stockbrokers), 1932, Partner, 1939; merged with Laing & Cruickshank, 1976. Mem. Council, Stock Exchange, 1963-78 (Dep. Chm., 1976-78). *Recreations:* golf, gardening. *Address:* Tanglewood, Oak Grange Road, West Clandon, Surrey. *T:* Guildford 222698.

POWELL, Harry Allan Rose, (Tim Powell), MBE 1944; TD 1973; Chairman: Massey-Ferguson Holdings Ltd, 1970-80 (Managing Director, 1962-78); Holland and Holland Holdings Ltd; *b* 15 Feb. 1912; *er s* of late William Allan Powell and Marjorie (*née* Mitchell); *m* 1936, Elizabeth North Hickley; two *d. Educ:* Winchester; Pembroke Coll., Cambridge (MA). Joined Corn Products Ltd, 1934. Commissioned Hertfordshire Yeomanry, 1938; Staff Coll., 1942; War Office 1942; Joint Planning Staff, 1943; seconded to War Cabinet Secretariat, 1943-44; Head of Secretariat, Supreme Allied Commander, South East Asia, 1944-45 (Col). Mitchells & Butlers Ltd, 1946-49; Gallaher Ltd, 1949-52. Joined Harry Ferguson Ltd, 1952. British Inst. of Management: Fellow, 1963; Vice-Chm., 1970-77. Governor, St Thomas' Hosp., 1971-74. *Recreations:* fishing, shooting, skiing, arguing. *Address:* Ready Token, near Cirencester, Glos. *T:* Bibury 219; 12 Shafto Mews, Cadogan Square, SW1. *T:* 01-235 2707. *Clubs:* Buck's, MCC.

POWELL, Herbert Marcus, FRS 1953; BSc, MA; Professor of Chemical Crystallography, Oxford University, 1964-74, now Emeritus; *s* of William Herbert and Henrietta Powell; *m* 1973, Primrose Jean Dunn. *Educ:* St John's College, Oxford. MA Oxon 1931. Reader in Chemical Crystallography in the University of Oxford, 1944-64; Fellow of Hertford College, Oxford, 1963-74, Emeritus Fellow, 1974. *Address:* 46 Davenant Road, Oxford.

POWELL, John Alfred, MA, DPhil, CEng, FIEE, FRSE; consultant; *b* 4 Nov. 1923; *s* of Algernon Powell and Constance Elsie (*née* Honour); *m* 1949, Zena Beatrice (*née* Steventon); one *s* one *d. Educ:* Bicester County Sch.; The Queen's Coll., Oxford. No 1 Sch. of Technical Trng, RAF Halton, 1940-42. The Queen's Coll., Oxford, 1945-48. DPhil, Clarendon Lab., Oxford, 1948-51; Post-Doctorate Research Fellowship, Nat. Research Council, Ottawa, Canada, 1952-54; Marconi Research Labs, 1954-57; Texas Instruments Ltd: joined, 1957; Gen. Manager, 1959; Man. Dir, 1963; Asst Vice-Pres., TI Inc. (US), 1968; EMI Ltd: Main Bd Dir, Group Tech. Dir, 1971; Dir, Commercial Electronics, 1972; Dep. Man. Dir, 1973; Gp Man. Dir, 1974-78; Vice Chm., 1978-79. Mem., Honeywell Adv. Council, 1978-. Faraday Lectr, 1978-79. CBIM (FBIM 1974); FRSA 1975; SMIEE (US). Member: Electronic Components Bd, 1968-71; Court of Cranfield Coll. of Technology, 1968-72; Electronics Research Council, 1972-74; Cttee of Inquiry into Engrg Profession, 1977-80; Physical Scis Sub-Cttee, UGC, 1980-. Hon. Mem., BIR, 1980. *Recreations:* arts, sports, the rural scene. *Address:* Kym House, 21 Buccleuch Road, Branksome Park, Poole, Dorset BH13 6LF.

POWELL, Rt. Hon. (John) Enoch, PC 1960; MBE 1943; MA (Cantab); MP (UU) South Down, since Oct. 1974; *b* 16 June 1912; *s* of Albert Enoch Powell and Ellen Mary Breese; *m* 1952, Margaret Pamela (*née* Wilson); two *d. Educ:* King Edwards, Birmingham; Trinity College, Cambridge. Craven Scholar, 1931; First Chancellor's Classical Medallist; Porson Prizeman; Browne Medallist, 1932; BA (Cantab); Craven Travelling Student, 1933; Fellow of Trinity College, Cambridge, 1934-38; MA (Cantab) 1937; Professor of Greek in the University of Sydney, NSW, 1937-39; Pte and L/Cpl R Warwickshire Regt, 1939-40; 2nd Lieut General List, 1940; Captain, General Staff, 1940-41; Major, General Staff, 1941; Lieut-Col, GS, 1942; Col, GS, 1944; Brig. 1944; Diploma in Oriental and African Studies. MP (C) Wolverhampton SW, 1950-Feb. 1974; Parly Sec., Ministry of Housing and Local Government, Dec. 1955-Jan. 1957; Financial Secretary to the Treasury, 1957-58; Minister of Health, July 1960-Oct. 1963. *Publications:* The Rendel Harris Papyri, 1936; First Poems, 1937; A Lexicon to Herodotus, 1938; The History of Herodotus, 1939; Casting-off, and other poems, 1939; Herodotus, Book VIII, 1939; Llyfr Blegywryd, 1942; Thucydidis Historia, 1942; Herodotus (translation), 1949; Dancer's End and The Wedding Gift (poems), 1951, repr. 1976; The Social Services; Needs and Means, 1952; (jointly) One Nation, 1950; Change is our Ally, 1954; Biography of a Nation (with Angus Maude), 1955, 2nd edn 1970; Great Parliamentary Occasions, 1960; Saving in a Free Society, 1960; A Nation not Afraid, 1965; Medicine and Politics, 1966, rev. edn 1976; The House of Lords in the Middle Ages (with Keith Wallis), 1968; Freedom and Reality, 1969; Common Market: the case against, 1971; Still to Decide, 1972; Common Market: renegotiate or come out, 1973; No Easy Answers, 1973; Wrestling with the Angel, 1977; Joseph Chamberlain, 1977; A Nation or No Nation (ed R. Ritchie), 1978; numerous political pamphlets. *Address:* 33 South Eaton Place, SW1. *T:* 01-730 0988.

POWELL, Air Vice-Marshal John Frederick, OBE 1956; Warden and Director of Studies, Moor Park College, 1972-77; *b* 12 June 1915; *y s* of Rev. Morgan Powell, Limpley Stoke, Bath; *m* 1939, Geraldine Ysolda, *e d* of late Sir John Fitzgerald Moylan, CB, CBE; four *s. Educ:* Lancing; King's Coll., Cambridge (MA). Joined RAF Educnl Service at No 1 Sch. of Techn Trng, 1937; Junior Lectr, RAF College, 1938-39; RAFVR (Admin. and Special Duties) ops room duties, Coastal Comd, 1939-45 (despatches); RAF Educn Br., 1946; Sen. Instructor in History, RAF Coll., 1946-49; RAF Staff Coll., 1950; Air Min., 1951-53; Sen. Tutor, RAF Coll., 1953-59; Educn Staff, HQ,

FEAF, 1959-62; Min. of Def., 1962-64; Comd Educn Off., HQ Bomber Comd, 1964-66; OC, RAF Sch. of Educn, 1966-67; Dir of Educational Services, RAF, 1967-72; Air Commodore, 1967; Air Vice-Marshal, 1968. *Recreations:* beagling, choral music, tennis, squash. *Address:* Old Post Office, Northington, near Alresford, Hants. *T:* Alresford 2221. *Club:* Royal Air Force.

See also C. D. Powell.

POWELL, Lewis Franklin, Jr; Associate Justice of US Supreme Court, since Dec. 1971; *b* Suffolk, Va, USA, 19 Sept. 1907; *s* of Lewis Franklin Powell and Mary Lewis (*née* Gwathmey); *m* 1936, Josephine Pierce Rucker; one *s* three *d*. *Educ:* McGuire's Univ. Sch., Richmond, Va; Washington and Lee Univ., Lexington, Va (BS *magnum cum laude*, LLB); Harvard Law Sch. (LLM). Admitted to practice, Bar of Virginia, 1931; subseq. practised law; partner in firm of Hunton, Williams, Gay, Powell and Gibson, in Richmond, 1938-71. Served War, May 1942-Feb. 1946, USAAF, overseas, to rank Col; subseq. Col. US Reserve. Legion of Merit and Bronze Star (US), also Croix de Guerre with Palms (France). Member: Nat. Commn on Law Enforcement and Admin of Justice, 1965-67; Blue Ribbon Defence Panel, 1969-70. Chairman or Dir of companies. Past Chm., Richmond Public Sch. Bd, etc; Trustee: Colonial Williamsburg Inc. (also Exec. and Gen. Council); Richmond Meml Hosp.; Washington and Lee Univ., etc. Mem., Amer. Bar Assoc. (Pres. 1964-65); Fellow, Amer. Bar Foundn (Pres. 1969-71); Pres. or Mem. various Bar Assocs and other legal and social instns; Hon. Bencher, Lincoln's Inn. Holds several hon. degrees. Phi Beta Kappa, Phi Delta Phi, Omiaran Delta Kappa, Phi Kappa Sigma. Is a Democrat. *Publications:* contribs to legal periodicals, etc. *Address:* Supreme Court Building, Washington, DC 20543, USA. *Clubs:* Century, University (NYC); Commonwealth, Country Club of Virginia (Richmond, Va).

POWELL, Prof. Michael James David; John Humphrey Plummer Professor of Applied Numerical Analysis, University of Cambridge, since 1976; Professorial Fellow of Pembroke College, Cambridge, since 1978; *b* 29 July 1936; *s* of William James David Powell and Beatrice Margaret (*née* Page); *m* 1959, Caroline Mary Henderson; one *s* two *d*. *Educ:* Eastbourne Coll.; Peterhouse, Cambridge (Schol.; BA 1959; ScD 1979). Mathematician at Atomic Energy Research Estabt, Harwell, 1959-76; special merit research appt to banded level, 1969, and to senior level, 1975. George B. Dantzig prize in Mathematical Programming, 1982. *Publications:* Approximation Theory and Methods, 1981; papers on numerical mathematics, especially approximation and optimization calculations. *Recreations:* canals, golf, walking. *Address:* 134 Milton Road, Cambridge.

POWELL, Michael L., FRGS; film director; *b* Bekesbourne, near Canterbury, Kent, 30 Sept. 1905; *s* of Thomas William Powell and Mabel, *d* of Frederick Corbett, Worcester; *m* 1943, Frances, *d* of Dr J. J. Reidy, JP, MD; two *s*. *Educ:* King's Sch., Canterbury; Dulwich Coll. Hon. DLitt East Anglia, 1978. BFI Special Award (with Emeric Pressburger), 1978. Joined National Provincial Bank, 1922; Metro-Goldwyn-Mayer film co., 1925, making Mare Nostrum, in the Mediterranean, with Rex Ingram as Dir; various capacities on 2 subseq. Ingram films: Somerset Maugham's The Magician and Robert Hichens' The Garden of Allah; was brought to Elstree, 1928, by the painter and film director, Harry Lachman; worked on 3 Hitchcock silent films, incl. script of Blackmail (later made into talking film). Travelled in Albania; wrote scripts for films of Caste and 77 Park Lane; given chance to direct by Jerry Jackson, 1931; Dir Two Crowded Hours and Rynox (both melodramas of 40 mins); went on to make a dozen short features, incl. 4 for Michael Balcon at Shepherd's Bush Studios, incl. The Fire Raisers and The Red Ensign (both orig. stories by Jackson and Powell); wrote and dir The Edge of the World, on Foula, Shetland, 1936 (prod. Joe Rock); travelled in Burma, up the Chindwin; given a contract by Alexander Korda, 1938; met Emeric Pressburger, together wrote and then dir The Spy in Black, and Contraband; co-dir, Thief of Bagdad and The Lion has Wings; prod. and dir 49th Parallel (from orig. story by Pressburger); formed The Archers Company and together wrote, prod. and dir 16 films, incl. Colonel Blimp, I Know Where I'm Going, A Matter of Life and Death, Black Narcissus, The Red Shoes, all for J. Arthur Rank; returned to Korda, 1948, to make 4 films, incl. The Small Back Room and Tales of Hoffman; returned to Rank for The Battle of the River Plate (The Archers' second Royal Perf. film) and Ill Met By Moonlight; also made Rosalinda (film of Fledermaus) at Elstree; The Archers Company then broke up; since then has dir Honeymoon, Peeping Tom, The Queen's Guards, Bluebeard's Castle (Bartók opera); The Sorcerer's Apprentice (ballet film); film (for Children's Film Foundn) from a story and script by Pressburger, The Boy Who Turned Yellow; They're a Weird Mob (Aust.); Age of Consent (Aust.); Return to the Edge of the World. *In the theatre:* prod. and dir (Hemingway's) The Fifth Column, 1945; (Jan de Hartog's) The Skipper Next to God, 1947; (James Forsyth's) Heloise, 1951; (Raymond Massey's) Hanging Judge, 1955. TV Series (several episodes): Espionage and The Defenders, for Herbert Brodkin. Hon. Fellow, BAFTA. *Publications:* 200,000 Feet on Foula; Graf Spee; A Waiting Game, 1975; (with Emeric Pressburger) The Red Shoes, 1978. *Recreation:* leaning on gates. *Address:* Lee Cottages, Avening, Tetbury, Glos. *Clubs:* Savile, Royal Automobile.

POWELL, Sir Nicholas (Folliott Douglas), 4th Bt *cr* 1897; Director, since 1971; *b* 17 July 1935; *s* of Sir Richard George Douglas Powell, 3rd Bt, MC, and Elizabeth Josephine (*d* 1979), *d* of late Lt-Col O. R. McMullen, CMG; *S* father, 1980; *m* 1960, Daphne Jean, 2nd *d* of G. H. Errington, MC; one *s* one *d*. *Educ:* Gordonstoun. Lieut Welsh Guards, 1953-57. *Heir:* *s* James

Richard Douglas Powell, *b* 17 Oct. 1962. *Address:* Petrunella Coffee Estate, Box 58, Chipinga, Zimbabwe.

POWELL, Prof. Percival Hugh, MA, DLitt, Dr Phil.; Professor of German, Indiana University, since 1970; *b* 4 Sept. 1912; 3rd *s* of late Thomas Powell and late Marie Sophia Roeser; *m* 1944, Dorothy Mavis Pattison (*née* Donald) (marr. diss. 1964); two *s* one adopted *d* ; *m* 1966, Mary Kathleen (*née* Wilson); one *s*. *Educ:* University College, Cardiff (Hon. Fellow 1981); Univs of Rostock, Zürich, Bonn. 1st Class Hons German (Wales), 1933; Univ. Teachers' Diploma in Education, 1934; MA (Wales) Dist. 1936; Research Fellow of Univ. of Wales, 1936-38; Modern Languages Master, Towyn School, 1934-36; Dr Phil. (Rostock) 1938; Lektor in English, Univ. of Bonn, 1938-39; Asst Lectr, Univ. Coll., Cardiff, 1939-40; War Service, 1940-46 (Capt. Intelligence Corps); Lecturer in German, Univ. Coll., Leicester, 1946, Head of Department of German, 1954; Prof. of German, Univ. of Leicester, 1958-69. Barclay Acheson Prof. of Internat. Studies at Macalester Coll., Minn., USA, 1965-66. DLitt (Wales) 1962. British Academy award, 1963; Fritz Thyssen Foundation Award, 1964; Leverhulme Trust Award, 1968. *Publications:* Pierre Corneilles Dramen in Deutschen Bearbeitungen, 1939; critical editions of dramas of Andreas Gryphius, 1955-72; critical edn of J. G. Schoch's Comœdia vom Studentenleben, 1976; articles and reviews in English and foreign literary jls. *Recreation:* music. *Address:* Department of Germanic Languages, Ballantine Hall, Indiana University, Bloomington, Indiana 47405, USA.

POWELL, Sir Philip, Kt 1975; OBE 1957; RA 1977 (ARA 1972); FRIBA; Partner of Powell and Moya, Architects, since 1946, and Powell, Moya and Partners, since 1976; *b* 15 March 1921; *yr s* of late Canon A. C. Powell and late Mary Winnifred (*née* Walker), Epsom and Chichester; *m* 1953, Philippa, *d* of Lt-Col C. C. Eccles, Tunbridge Wells; one *s* one *d*. *Educ:* Epsom Coll.; AA Sch. of Architecture (Hons Diploma). *Works include:* Churchill Gdns flats, Westminster, 1948-62 (won in open competition); houses and flats at Gospel Oak, St Pancras, 1954 and Vauxhall Park, Lambeth, 1972; houses at: Chichester, 1950; Toys Hill, 1954; Oxshott, 1954; Baughurst, Hants, 1954; Skylon for Fest. of Britain, 1951 (won in open competition); British Pavilion, Expo 70, Osaka, Japan, 1970; Mayfield Sch., Putney, 1955; Plumstead Manor Sch., Woolwich, 1970; Dining Rooms at Bath Acad. of Art, Corsham, 1970, and Eton Coll., 1974; extensions, Brasenose Coll., Oxford, 1961, and Corpus Christi Coll., Oxford, 1969; picture gall. and undergrad. rooms, Christ Church, Oxford, 1967; Wolfson Coll., Oxford, 1974; Cripps Building, St John's Coll., Cambridge, 1967; new buildings, Queens' Coll., Cambridge, 1976; Chichester Fest. Theatre, 1962; Swimming Baths, Putney, 1967; Mental Hosp. extensions at Fairmile, nr Wallingford, 1957 and Borocourt, nr Henley-on-Thames, 1964; Hosps at Swindon, Slough, High Wycombe, Wythenshawe and Woolwich; Museum of London, 1976; London and Manchester Assurance HQ, near Exeter, 1978; NatWest Bank, Shaftesbury Ave, London, 1982. Has won numerous medals and awards for architectural work, inc. Royal Gold Medal for Architecture, RIBA, 1974. Mem. Royal Fine Art Commn, 1969-. *Recreations:* travel, listening to music. *Address:* 16 The Little Boltons, SW10 9LP. *T:* 01-373 8620; 21 Upper Cheyne Row, SW3. *T:* 01-351 3881.

POWELL, Raymond; MP (Lab) Ogmore, since 1979; *b* 19 June 1928; *s* of Albert and Lucy Powell; *m* 1951, Marion Grace Evans; one *s* one *d*. *Educ:* Pentre Grammar Sch.; National Council of Labour Colls; London School of Economics. British Rail, 1945-50; Shop Manager, 1950-66; Secretary/Agent to Walter Ridley, MP, 1967-69, voluntarily, 1969-79; Sen. Administrative Officer, Welsh Water Authority, 1969-79. Chairman: Labour Party Wales, 1977-78; S Wales Euro-Constituency Labour Party, 1979-. *Recreations:* gardening, sport, music. *Address:* 8 Brynteg Gardens, Bridgend, Mid-Glam. *T:* Bridgend 2159. *Club:* Ogmore Constituency Labour Party Social.

POWELL, Sir Richard (Royle), GCB 1967 (KCB 1961; CB 1951); KBE 1954; CMG 1946; Deputy Chairman, Permanent Committee on Invisible Exports, 1968-76; Chairman, Alusuisse (UK) Ltd and subsidiary companies, since 1969; President, Wilkinson Match Ltd, since 1981 (Chairman, 1979-80, and Director, 1971-80); *S* 30 July 1909; *er s* of Ernest Hartley and Florence Powell; unmarried. *Educ:* Queen Mary's Grammar Sch., Walsall; Sidney Sussex Coll., Cambridge (Hon. Fellow, 1972). Entered Civil Service, 1931 and apptd to Admiralty; Private Sec. to First Lord, 1934-37; Member of British Admiralty Technical Mission, Canada, and of British Merchant Shipbuilding Mission, and later of British Merchant Shipping Mission in USA, 1940-44; Civil Adviser to Commander-in-Chief, British Pacific Fleet, 1944-45; Under-Secretary, Ministry of Defence, 1946-48. Dep. Sec., Admiralty, 1948-50; Dep. Sec., Min. of Defence, 1950-56; Permanent Secretary, Board of Trade, 1960-68 (Min. of Defence, 1956-59). Dir, Philip Hill Investment Trust, 1968-81; Director: Whessoe Ltd, 1968-; Sandoz Gp of Cos, 1972- (Chm.); Clerical, Medical and General Life Assurance Soc., 1972-; BPB Industries Ltd, 1973-; Ladbroke Gp, 1980-. Pres., Inst. for Fiscal Studies, 1970-78. *Address:* 56 Montagu Square, W1. *T:* 01-262 0911. *Club:* Athenæum.

POWELL, Robert Lane B.; *see* Bayne-Powell.

POWELL, Robert William; Headmaster of Sherborne, 1950-70; retired; *b* 29 October 1909; *s* of late William Powell and Agnes Emma Powell; *m* 1938, Charity Rosamond Collard; one *s*. *Educ:* Bristol Grammar School; Christ Church, Oxford. Assistant Master, Repton, May-Dec. 1934; Assistant Master,

Charterhouse, 1935. Served War of 1939–45, 1940–45. Housemaster of Gownboys, Charterhouse, 1946–50. *Recreations:* fishing, music. *Address:* Manor Farm House, Child Okeford, near Blandford, Dorset. *T:* Child Okeford 860648.

POWELL, Roger, OBE 1976; bookbinder; *b* 17 May 1896; *er s* of late Oswald Byrom Powell and Winifred Marion Powell (*née* Cobb); *m* 1924, Rita Glanville, *y d* of late Frank and Katherine F. Harvey; one *s* twin *d. Educ:* Bedales Sch. Served European War, 1914–18: Hampshire Regt, Palestine, 1917; Flt Lt, RAF, Egypt, 1918. Poultry farming, 1921–30; studied bookbinding at LCC Central Sch., 1930–31; joined Douglas Cockerell & Son, bookbinders, 1935; Partner, 1936; opened own bindery at Froxfield, 1947. Member: Art Workers' Guild; Double Crown Club; Red Rose Guild. Has repaired and bound many early manuscripts, incunabula and other early printed books including: for Winchester (both Coll. and Cathedral); for TCD, The Book of Kells, 1953; The Book of Durrow, The Book of Armagh, The Book of Dimma (in accommod. Brit. Mus.), 1954–57; for Lichfield Cath., The St Chad Gospels, 1961–62; for RIA, The Book of Lecan, Lebor na hUidre, Leabhar Breac, The Book of Fermoy, The Cathach of St Columba, 1968–81; for Durham Cathedral, The A. II. 17 Gospels, 1976. Tooled Memorial Bindings, incl: WVS Roll of Honour, Civilian War Dead, 1939–45, in Westminster Abbey. Rolls of Honour: for RMA Sandhurst and Woolwich; Coastal Command, RAF; S Africa, India, Pakistan. Other tooled bindings, in: Brit. Mus., Victoria and Albert Mus.; in Libraries: (Bodleian, Oxford; Pierpont Morgan; Syracuse Univ.; Grolier Club, New York; Newberry, Chicago), and in private collections in Britain, Ireland and USA. Visited, to advise on book-conservation: Iceland, 1965; Florence, 1966; Portugal, 1967. Hon. For. Corresp. Mem., Grolier Club, NY. Hon. MA Dublin, 1961. *Publications:* various contribs to The Library; Scriptorium, Brussels; Eriu, Dublin, 1956–69. *Recreations:* cricket, singing, 'finding out', photography, amateur operatics and dramatics, organic cultivations, bee-keeping, golf. *Address:* The Slade, Froxfield, Petersfield, Hants GU32 1EB. *T:* Hawkley 229.

POWELL, Tim; *see* Powell, H. A. R.

POWELL, Victor George Edward; Senior Partner, Victor G. Powell Associates, Management Consultants, since 1963; Director and Chief Adviser, International Labour Organisation since 1977 (Senior Adviser, 1976); Director, Mosscare Housing Association Ltd, since 1974; *b* London, 1 Jan. 1929; *s* of George Richard Powell and Kate Hughes Powell, London; *m* 1956, Patricia Copeland Allen; three *s* one *d. Educ:* Beckenham Grammar Sch.; Univs of Durham and Manchester. BA 1st cl. hons Econs 1954, MA Econ. Studies 1957, Dunelm; PhD Manchester 1963. RN Engrg Apprentice, 1944–48. Central Work Study Dept, ICI, London, 1954; Chief Work Study Engr, Ind Coope Ltd, 1956–58; Lectr in Industrial Administration, Manchester Univ., 1959, Hon. Lectr 1959–63; Asst Gen. Manager, Louis C. Edwards & Sons Ltd, 1959–63; Chm., Food Production & Processing Ltd, 1971–74. Gen. Sec., 1970–72, Dir, 1972–73, War on Want. MBIM 1957; Mem. Inst. Management Consultants, 1968. *Publications:* Economics of Plant Investment and Replacement Decisions, 1964; Techniques for Improving Distribution Management, 1968; Warehousing, 1976; various articles. *Recreations:* music, walking. *Address:* Inglewood, Coppice Lane, Disley, Stockport, Cheshire SK12 2LT. *T:* Disley 2011. *Club:* Royal Commonwealth Society.

POWELL-COTTON, Christopher, CMG 1961; MBE 1951; MC 1945; JP; Uganda CS, retired; *b* 23 Feb. 1918; *s* of Major P. H. G. Powell-Cotton and Mrs H. B. Powell-Cotton (*née* Slater); unmarried. *Educ:* Harrow School; Trinity College, Cambridge. Army Service, 1939–45: commissioned Buffs, 1940; seconded KAR, Oct. 1940; T/Major, 1943. Apptd to Uganda Administration, 1940, and released for Mil. Service. District Commissioner, 1950; Provincial Commissioner, 1955; Minister of Security and External Relations, 1961. Landowner in SE Kent. Dir, Powell-Cotton Museum of Nat. History and Ethnography. *Address:* Quex Park, Birchington, Kent. *T:* Thanet 41836. *Club:* MCC.

POWELL-JONES, John Ernest, CMG 1974; HM Diplomatic Service; Ambassador to Switzerland, since 1982; *b* 14 April 1925; *s* of late Walter James Powell-Jones and Gladys Margaret (*née* Taylor); *m* 1st, 1949, Ann Murray (marr. diss. 1967); two *s* one *d*; 2nd, 1968, Pamela Sale. *Educ:* Charterhouse; University Coll., Oxford (1st cl. Modern Hist.). Served with Rifle Bde, 1943–46. HM Foreign (now Diplomatic) Service, 1949; 3rd Sec. and Vice-Consul, Bogota, 1950–52; Eastern and later Levant Dept, FO, 1952–55; 2nd, later 1st Sec., Athens, 1955–59; News Dept, FO, 1959–60; 1st Sec., Leopoldville, 1961–62; UN Dept, FO, 1963–67; ndc Canada 1967–68; Counsellor, Political Adviser's Office, Singapore, 1968–69; Counsellor and Consul-General, Athens, 1970–73; Ambassador at Phnom Penh, 1973–75; RCDS 1975; Ambassador to Senegal, Guinea, Mali, Mauritania and Guinea-Bissau, 1976–79, to Cape Verde, 1977–79; Ambassador and Perm. Rep., UN Conf. on Law of the Sea, 1979–82. *Recreations:* gardening, lawn tennis. *Address:* c/o Foreign and Commonwealth Office, SW1; Gascons, Gaston Gate, Cranleigh, Surrey. *T:* Cranleigh 4313. *Club:* Travellers'.

POWER, Vice-Adm. Sir Arthur (Mackenzie), KCB 1974; MBE 1952; Secretary to the Senate of the Inns of Court and the Bar, since 1975; *b* 18 June 1921; *s* of Admiral of the Fleet Sir Arthur Power, GCB, GBE, CVO; *m* 1949, Marcia Helen Gell; two *s* one *d. Educ:* Rugby. Royal Navy, 1938; served War of 1939–45 and Korean War; specialised in gunnery; Captain, 1959; ADC to

the Queen, 1968; Rear-Admiral, 1968; Adm. Supt, Portsmouth, 1968–71; Flag Officer, Spithead, 1969–71; Vice-Adm., 1971; Flag Officer Flotillas, Western Fleet, 1971–72; Flag Officer, First Flotilla, 1972–73; Flag Officer Plymouth, Port Adm. Devonport, Cmdr Central Sub Area, E Atlantic, and Cmdr Plymouth Sub Area, Channel, 1973–75. *Address:* Gunnsmead, South Road, Liphook, Hants. *Club:* Army and Navy.
See also M. G. *Power.*

POWER, Mrs Brian St Quentin; *see* Stack, (Ann) Prunella.

POWER, Eugene Barnum, Hon. KBE 1977; microphotographer, retired 1970; business executive; *b* Traverse City, Mich, 4 June 1905; *s* of Glenn Warren Power and Annette (*née* Barnum); *m* 1929, Sadye L. Harwick; one *s. Educ:* Univ. of Mich (AB 1927, MBA 1930). With Edwards Bros, Inc., Ann Arbor, Mich, 1930–38; engaged in expts with methods and uses of microfilm technique for reprodn of materials for res., 1935; Founder: Univ. Microfilms (merged with Xerox Corp. 1962), 1938; Univ. Microfilms, Ltd London, 1952; Dir, Xerox Corp., 1962–68. Organized: 1st large microfilming proj. for libraries, copying all books printed in England before 1640; Microfilms, Inc., as distbn agency, using microfilm as reprodn medium for scientific and technical materials, 1942–62; Projected Books, Inc. (non-profit corp.), for distbn of reading and entertainment materials in photog. form to physically incapacitated, 1944–70; Eskimo Art, Inc. (non-profit corp.). During War, dir. large-scale copying of important Brit. MSS in public and private archives, also enemy documents. Pres. and Chm., Power Foundn, 1968–. Special Rep. Co-ordinator of Inf. and of Library of Congress, London 1942, Office of Strategic Services, 1943–45. President: Internat. Micrographic Congress, 1964–65; Nat. Microfilm Assoc., 1946–54. Chm., Mich Co-ordinating Council for State Higher Educn; Regent, Univ. of Michigan, 1956–66. Member: Council of Nat. Endowment for the Humanities, 1968–74; Amer. Philos. Soc., 1975. Fellow, Nat. Microfilm Assoc., 1963 (Award of Merit, 1956); Fellow of Merit, Internat. Micrographic Congress, 1978; Paul Harris Fellow, Rotary Internat., 1979. Hon. Fellow: Magdalene Coll., Cambridge, 1967; Northwestern Mich Coll., 1967. Hon. LHD: St John's Univ., 1966; Univ. of Michigan, 1971. *Publications:* numerous articles on techniques and uses of microfilm. *Recreations:* swimming, sailing, fishing, hunting, music. *Address:* (home) 989 Forest Road, Barton Hills, Ann Arbor, Mich 48105, USA. *T:* (313) 662-2886; (office) 2929 Plymouth Road, Ann Arbor, Mich 48105. *T:* (313) 769-8424. *Clubs:* American; Rotary (Ann Arbor).

POWER, Sir John (Patrick McLannahan), 3rd Bt, *cr* 1924, of Newlands Manor; Chairman, Arthur Beale Ltd, London; *b* 16 March 1928; *s* of Sir Ivan McLannahan Cecil Power, 2nd Baronet, and Nancy Hilary, *d* of late Reverend J. W. Griffiths, Wentworth, Virginia Water; *m* 1st, 1957, Melanie (marr. diss. 1967), *d* of Hon. Alastair Erskine, Glenfintaig House, Spean Bridge, Invernesshire; two *s* one *d*; 2nd, 1970, Tracey (marr. diss. 1974), *d* of George Cooper, Amberley Place, Amberley, Sussex. *Educ:* Pangbourne Coll. Served RN, 1946–48, The Cunard Steamship Co. Ltd, London, 1945–58. *Recreations:* sailing, painting. *Heir:* *s* Alastair John Cecil Power, *b* 15 Aug. 1958. *Address:* Ashwick House, Dulverton, Somerset. *T:* Dulverton 488. *Clubs:* Arts, Royal Ocean Racing, Royal London Yacht; Royal Naval Sailing Association; Island Sailing.
See also Lord Cardross.

POWER, Michael George; Director, Greenwich Hospital, since 1982; *b* 2 April 1924; *s* of Admiral of the Fleet Sir Arthur Power, GCB, GBE, CVO, and Amy Isabel (*née* Bingham); *m* 1954, Kathleen Maeve (*née* McCaul); one *s* two *d* and two step *d. Educ:* Rugby Sch.; Corpus Christi Coll., Cambridge. Served War, Rifle Bde, 1942–46 (Captain); ME Centre of Arab Studies (Jerusalem), 1946–47; Colonial Admin. Service, 1947–63: District Officer: Kenya, 1948–53; Malaya, 1953–57; Kenya, 1957–63; Home Civil Service, 1963–81; Under-Sec., MoD, 1973–81. Mem., Royal Patriotic Fund Corp., 1982. *Recreations:* sailing, golf, gardening. *Address:* Wancom Way, Puttenham Heath Road, Compton, Guildford. *T:* Guildford 810470. *Club:* Army and Navy.
See also Sir A. M. *Power.*

POWER, Noel Plunkett; Hon. Mr Justice Power; Judge of the High Court, Hong Kong, since 1979; *b* 4 Dec. 1929; *s* of John Joseph Power and Hilda Power; *m* 1965, Irma Maroya; two *s* one *d. Educ:* Downlands Coll.; Univ. of Queensland (BA, LLB). Called to the Bar, Supreme Court of Queensland and High Court of Australia, 1955; Magistrate, Hong Kong, 1965–76; Pres., Lands Tribunal, Hong Kong, 1976–79. *Publications:* (ed) Lands Tribunal Law Reports, 1976–79. *Recreations:* travel, cooking, reading, tennis. *Address:* Flat 1, 11 Mansfield Road, Hong Kong. *T:* 5-96798. *Club:* Queensland (Brisbane).

POWERSCOURT, 10th Viscount *cr* 1743; **Mervyn Niall Wingfield; Baron** Wingfield, 1743; Baron Powerscourt (UK), 1885; *b* 3 Sept. 1935; *s* of 9th Viscount Powerscourt and of Sheila Claude, *d* of late Lt-Col Claude Beddington; *S* father, 1973; *m* 1962, Wendy Ann Pauline (marr. diss. 1974), *d* of R. C. G. Slazenger; one *s* one *d*; *m* 1978, Pauline, *d* of W. P. Vann, San Francisco. *Educ:* Stowe; Trinity Coll., Cambridge. Formerly Irish Guards. *Heir:* *s* Hon. Mervyn Anthony Wingfield, *b* 21 Aug. 1963.
See also Sir H. R. H. *Langrishe, Bt.*

POWIS, 6th Earl of, *cr* 1804; **Christian Victor Charles Herbert;** Baron Clive (Ire.), 1762; Baron Clive, 1794; Viscount Clive, Baron Herbert, Baron Powis,

1804; *b* 28 May 1904; 2nd *s* of Colonel Edward William Herbert, CB (*d* 1924) (*g s* of 2nd Earl of Powis) and Beatrice Anne (*d* 1928), *d* of Sir Hedworth Williamson, 8th Bt; *S* brother, 1974. *Educ:* Oundle; Trinity Coll., Cambridge (BA); University Coll., London. Barrister, Inner Temple, 1932; Private Secretary to: Governor and C-in-C, British Honduras, 1947-55; Governor of British Guiana, 1955-64. Served War of 1939-45 with RAOC, UK and India; Major, 1943. *Heir: cousin* George William Herbert [*b* 4 June 1925; *m* 1949, Hon. Katharine Odeyne de Grey, *d* of 8th Baron Walsingham, DSO, OBE; four *s* two adopted *d*]. *Address:* Powis Castle, Welshpool, N Wales. *T:* 3360. *Clubs:* Brooks's, MCC.

POWLES, Sir Guy (Richardson), KBE 1961; CMG 1954; ED 1944; first Ombudsman of New Zealand, 1962-75, Chief Ombudsman, 1975-77; *b* 5 April 1905; *s* of late Colonel C. G. Powles, CMG, DSO, New Zealand Staff Corps; *m* 1931, Eileen, *d* of A. J. Nicholls; two *s. Educ:* Wellington Coll., NZ; Victoria Univ. (LLB). Barrister, Supreme Court, New Zealand, 1929; served War of 1939-45 with NZ Military Forces, to rank of Colonel; Counsellor, NZ Legation, Washington, DC, USA, 1946-48; High Comr, Western Samoa, 1949-60, for NZ in India, 1960-62, Ceylon, 1960-62, and Ambassador of NZ to Nepal, 1960-62. President, NZ Inst. of Internat. Affairs, 1967-71. NZ Comr, Commn of the Churches on Internat. Affairs, World Council of Churches, 1971-80; Comr, Internat. Commn of Jurists, Geneva, 1975-. Race Relations Conciliator, 1971-73. Patron: Amnesty International (NZ); NZ-India Soc.; Environmental Defence Soc. Hon. LLD Victoria Univ. of Wellington, 1969. *Publications:* articles and speeches on international affairs, administrative law and race relations. *Address:* 34 Wesley Road, Wellington, NZ.

POWLETT; *see* Orde-Powlett.

POWLETT, Vice-Admiral Sir Peveril B. R. W. W.; *see* William-Powlett.

POWLETT, Rear-Adm. Philip Frederick, CB 1961; DSO 1941 (and Bar 1942); DSC 1941; DL; retired; *b* 13 Nov. 1906; *s* of late Vice-Admiral F. A. Powlett, CBE; *m* 1935, Frances Elizabeth Sykes (*née* Elwell); two *s* one *d. Educ:* Osborne and Dartmouth. War of 1939-45 (DSC, DSO and Bar; Polish Cross of Valour, 1942); in command of destroyers and corvettes, Shearwater, Blankney, Cassandra. Deputy Director of Naval Air Organisation and Training, 1950; Senior Officer, Reserve Fleet, Clyde, 1952; Captain (F), 6th Frigate Squadron, 1954-55; Director (RN), Joint Anti-Submarine School, and Senior Naval Officer, Northern Ireland, 1956-58; Flag Officer and Admiral Superintendent, Gibraltar, 1959-62; retired, 1962. DL Norfolk, 1974. *Address:* The Mill House, Lyng, Norwich, Norfolk NR9 5QZ.

POWNALL, Henry Charles, QC 1979; a Recorder of the Crown Court, since 1972; a Judge, Court of Appeal of Jersey and of Guernsey, since 1980; *b* 25 Feb. 1927; *e s* of late John Cecil Glossop Pownall, CB, and of Margaret Nina Pownall (*née* Jesson); *m* 1955, Sarah Bettine, *d* of late Major John Deverell; one *s* one *d* (and one *d* decd). *Educ:* Rugby Sch.; Trinity Coll., Cambridge; BA 1950, MA 1963; LLB 1951. Served War, Royal Navy, 1945-48. Called to Bar, Inner Temple, 1954, Bencher, 1976; joined South-Eastern Circuit, 1954. Junior Prosecuting Counsel to the Crown at the Central Criminal Court, 1964-71; a Sen. Prosecuting Counsel, 1971-79. Mem. Cttee: Orders and Medals Research Soc., 1961-69, and 1970- (Pres., 1971-75, 1977-81); Nat. Benevolent Instn, 1964-. Hon. Legal Advr, ABA, 1976-. *Publication:* Korean Campaign Medals, 1950-53, 1957. *Recreations:* travel; medals and medal ribbons. *Address:* 69 Eaton Terrace, SW1W 8TN; 2 Harcourt Buildings, Temple, EC4Y 9DB. *T:* 01-353 2112. *Clubs:* Pratt's; Hurlingham; Ebury Court.

POWNALL, Leslie Leigh, MA, PhD; Chairman, NSW Planning and Environment Commission, 1974-77, retired; *b* 1 Nov. 1921; *y s* of A. de S. Pownall, Wanganui, New Zealand; *m* 1943, Judith, *d* of late Harold Whittaker, Palmerston North. *Educ:* Palmerston North Boys' High Sch.; Victoria University College, University of Canterbury, University of Wisconsin. Asst Master, Christchurch Boys' High Sch., 1941-46; Lecturer in Geography: Christchurch Teachers' Coll., 1946-47; Ardmore Teachers' Coll., 1948-49; Auckland University College, 1949-51; Senior Lecturer in Geography, 1951-60, Prof. of Geography, 1960-61, Vice-Chancellor and Rector, 1961-66, University of Canterbury; Clerk of the University Senate, Univ. of London, 1966-74. Consultant, Inter-University Council for Higher Educn Overseas, London, 1963; Consultant to Chm. of Working Party on Higher Educn in E Africa, 1968-69. Member Meeting, Council on World Tensions on Social and Economic Development (S Asia and Pacific), Kuala Lumpur, Malaysia, 1964; Member: Central Governing Body, City Parochial Foundation, London, 1967-74 (Mem., Grants Sub-Cttee; Chm., Finance and Gen. Purposes Cttee); UK Commonwealth Scholarship Commn, 1979-80; Governor, Internat. Students Trust, London, 1967-74. *Publications:* New Zealand, 1951 (New York); geographic contrib. in academic journals of America, Netherlands and New Zealand. *Recreations:* music, literature. *Address:* c/o National Westminster Bank, Regent Street Branch, 250 Regent Street, W1A 4RY. *Clubs:* Canterbury, University (Christchurch, NZ).

POWYS, family name of **Baron Lilford.**

POYNTON, Sir (Arthur) Hilton, GCMG 1964 (KCMG 1949; CMG 1946); *b* 20 April 1905; *y s* of late Arthur Blackburne Poynton, formerly Master of University College, Oxford; *m* 1946, Elisabeth Joan, *d* of late Rev. Edmund Williams; two *s* one *d. Educ:* Marlborough Coll.; Brasenose Coll., Oxford (Hon. Fellow 1964). Entered Civil Service, Department of Scientific and Industrial Research, 1927; transferred to Colonial Office, 1929; Private Secretary to Minister of Supply and Minister of Production 1941-43; reverted to Colonial Office, 1943; Permanent Under-Secretary of State, CO, 1959-66. Mem. Governing Body, SPCK, 1967-72. Mem., Ct of Governors, London Sch. Hygiene and Tropical Med., 1965-77; Treas., Soc. Promotion Roman Studies, 1967-76; Dir, Overseas Branch, St John Ambulance, 1968-75. KStJ 1968. *Recreations:* music, travel. *Address:* Craigmillar, 47 Stanhope Road, Croydon CR0 5NS. *T:* 01-688 3729.

POYNTON, (John) Orde, CMG 1961; MD; Consulting Bibliographer, University of Melbourne, 1962-74; Fellow of Graduate House, University of Melbourne; *b* 9 April 1906; *o s* of Frederick John Poynton, MD, FRCP, and Alice Constance, *d* of Sir John William Powlett Campbell-Orde, 3rd Bt, of Kilmory; *m* 1965, Lola, *widow* of Group Captain T. S. Horry, DFC, AFC. *Educ:* Marlborough Coll.; Gonville and Caius Coll., Cambridge; Charing Cross Hospital (Univ. Schol. 1927-30). MA, MD (Cambridge); MD (Adelaide) 1948; MRCS, LRCP; Horton-Smith prize, University of Cambridge, 1940. Sen. Resident MO, Charing Cross Hosp., 1932-33; Health Officer, Fed. Malay States, 1936-37; Res. Officer Inst. for Med. Research, FMS, 1937-38, Pathologist, 1938-46; Pathologist, Inst. of Med. and Veterinary Science, S Australia, 1948-50, Director, 1950-61. Hon. LLD Melbourne, 1977. *Publications:* monographs and papers relating to medicine and bibliography. *Recreation:* bibliognostics. *Address:* 8 Seymour Avenue, Mount Eliza, Victoria 3930, Australia. *Club:* MCC.

POYNTZ, Rt. Rev. Samuel Greenfield; *see* Cork, Cloyne and Ross, Bishop of.

PRACY, Robert, FRCS; Dean of the Institute of Laryngology and Otology, University of London, since 1981; *b* 19 Sept. 1921; *s* of Douglas Sherrin Pracy and Gwendoline Blanche Power; *m* 1946, Elizabeth Patricia Spicer; one *s* two *d* (and one *s* decd). *Educ:* Berkhamsted Sch.; St Bartholomew's Hosp. Med. Coll. (MB BS 1945). LRCP 1944; MRCS, FRCS 1953. Former Captain, RAMC. House Surgeon appts, St Bartholomew's Hosp.; formerly: Registrar, Royal Nat. Throat, Nose and Ear Hosp.; Consultant Surgeon: Liverpool Regional Board, 1954; United Liverpool Hosps, 1959; Alder Hey Childrens' Hosp., 1960; Royal Nat. Throat, Nose and Ear Hosp.; Hosp. for Sick Children, Gt Ormond St; Dir, Dept of Otolaryngology, Liverpool Univ. Mem. Ct of Examnrs, RCS and RCSI. Lectures: Yearsley, 1976; Joshi, 1978; Wilde, 1979; Semon, London Univ., 1980. Pres., British Assoc. of Otolaryngologists; FRSocMed (Pres., Sect. of Laryngology, 1982-83). Hon. FRCSI 1982; Hon. Fellow: Irish Otolaryngol Assoc.; Assoc. of Otolaryngologists of India. *Publications:* (jtly) Short Textbook: Ear, Nose and Throat, 1970, 2nd edn 1974 (trans. Italian, Portuguese, Spanish); (jtly) Ear, Nose and Throat Surgery and Nursing, 1977; contribs to learned jls. *Recreations:* cabinet making, painting, engraving, reading, theatre. *Address:* Wardens Post, Moor Lane, South Newington, near Banbury, Oxon OX15 4JQ. *T:* Banbury 720433.

PRAG, Derek; Member (C) Hertfordshire, European Parliament, since 1979; *b* 6 Aug. 1923; *s* of Abraham J. Prag and Edith Prag; *m* 1948, Dora Weiner; three *s. Educ:* Bolton Sch.; Emmanuel Coll., Univ. of Cambridge (MA; Cert. of Competent Knowledge in Russian). Served War, Intelligence Corps, England, Egypt, Italy, Austria, 1942-47. Economic journalist with Reuters News Agency in London, Brussels and Madrid, 1950-55; Information Service of High Authority, European Coal and Steel Community, 1955-59; Head of Division, Jt Information Service of European Communities, 1959-65; Director, London Information Office of European Communities, 1965-73; ran own consultancy company on relations with EEC, 1973-79. European Democratic Group spokesman on Institutional Cttee. Associate Mem., RIIA, 1973-. Hon. Dir, EEC Commn, 1974. Silver Medal of European Merit, Luxembourg, 1974. *Publications:* Businessman's Guide to the Common Market, 1973; various reports on Europe's internat. role, and booklets and articles on European integration. *Recreations:* reading, theatre, music, walking, swimming, gardening. *Address:* The Euro-centre, Maynard House, The Common, Hatfield, Herts AL10 0NF. *Clubs:* Royal Automobile, English-Speaking Union, Europe House; St Anne's (Brussels).

PRAGNELL, Anthony William, CBE 1982 (OBE 1960); DFC 1944; Deputy Director-General, Independent Broadcasting Authority (formerly Independent Television Authority), since 1961; *b* 15 Feb. 1921; *s* of William Hendley Pragnell and Silvia Pragnell; *m* 1955, Teresa Mary, *d* of Leo and Anne Monaghan, Maidstone; one *s* one *d. Educ:* Cardinal Vaughan Sch., London. Asst Examiner, Estate Duty Office, 1939. Joined RAF as aircrew cadet, 1942; Navigator, Bomber Command, one tour of ops with 166 Squadron; second tour with 109 Squadron (Pathfinder Force), 1943-46. Examiner, Estate Duty Office, 1946. LLB London Univ., 1949. Asst Principal, General Post Office, 1950; Asst Secretary, ITA, 1954; Secretary, ITA, 1955. Fellow, Royal Television Soc., 1980. *Recreations:* reading, music. *Address:* Ashley, Grassy Lane, Sevenoaks, Kent. *T:* Sevenoaks 451463. *Club:* Royal Air Force.

PRAIN, Alexander Moncur, CBE 1964; Sheriff: of Perth and Angus at Perth, 1946-71; of Lanarkshire at Airdrie, 1943-46; *b* Longforgan, Perthshire, 19 Feb. 1908; 2nd *s* of A. M. Prain, JP, and Mary Stuart Whytock; *m* 1936, Florence

Margaret Robertson; one s. Educ: Merchiston Castle; Edinburgh Academy; Edinburgh Univ. Called to Scottish Bar, 1932; Army, 1940–43, Major, RAC. Recreations: fishing, reading. Address: Castellar, Crieff, Perthshire.

PRAIN, John Murray, DSO 1940; OBE 1956; TD 1943 (two Bars); DL; b 17 Dec. 1902; e s of late James Prain, Hon. LLD St Andrews University, of Kincaple by St Andrews, Fife, and late Victoria Eleanor Murray; m 1934, Lorina Helen Elspeth, o d of late Colonel P. G. M. Skene, OBE, DL, of Halyards and Pitlour, Fife; one s one d. Educ: Charterhouse; Clare Coll., Cambridge, BA 1924. Chm., James Prain & Sons Ltd, Dundee, 1945–56; Vice-Chm., Caird (Dundee) Ltd, 1956–64; Director: Alliance Trust Co. Ltd, 1946–73; 2nd Alliance Trust Co. Ltd, 1946–73; Tayside Floorcloth Co. Ltd, 1946–69; The Scottish Life Assurance Co. Ltd, 1949–72; Royal Bank of Scotland, 1955–71; William Halley & Sons Ltd; Member Scottish Committee, Industrial and Commercial Finance Corporation, 1946–55; Chairman: Jute Importers Association, 1947–49; Assoc. of Jute Spinners and Manufacturers, 1950–52; Dundee District Cttee, Scottish Board for Industry, 1948–62. Member, Jute Working Party, 1946–48; part-time Member Scottish Gas Board, 1952–56; Member Employers' Panel Industrial Disputes Tribunal, 1952–59. Member: Employers' Panel, Industrial Court, 1959–71; Industrial Arbitration Bd, 1971–72. DL for County of Fife, 1958; Served in War of 1939–45, Fife and Forfar Yeomanry (wounded, despatches, DSO); GSO(2), 1943–44; Lt-Col (AQ) RAC, OCTU, RMC Sandhurst, 1944–45; Member Queen's Body Guard for Scotland, Royal Company of Archers; Hon. President, Fife and Kinross Area Council, Royal British Legion (Scotland). Address: Long Rigg, Hepburn Gardens, St Andrews, Fife KY16 9LT. T: St Andrews 3205. Club: Royal and Ancient (St Andrews).

PRAIN, Sir Ronald (Lindsay), Kt 1956; OBE 1946; Chief Executive, 1943–68, Chairman, 1950–72, RST international group of companies; Director: Monks Investment Trust Ltd; Pan-Holding SA, and other companies; b Iquiqui, Chile, 3 Sept. 1907; s of Arthur Lindsay Prain and Amy Prain (née Watson); m 1938, Esther Pansy, d of late Norman Brownrigg, Haslemere; two s. Educ: Cheltenham Coll. Controller (Ministry of Supply): Diamond Die and Tool Control, 1940–45; Quartz Crystal Control, 1943–45. First Chairman: Agricultural Research Council of Rhodesia & Nyasaland, 1959–63; Merchant Bank of Central Africa Ltd, 1956–66; Merchant Bank (Zambia) Ltd, 1966–72; Director: Metal Market & Exchange Co. Ltd, 1943–65; San Francisco Mines of Mexico Ltd, 1944–68; Selection Trust Ltd, 1944–78; Internat. Nickel Co. of Canada Ltd, 1951–72; Wankie Colliery Co. Ltd, 1953–63; Minerals Separation Ltd, 1962–78; Foseco Minsep Ltd, 1969–80; Barclays Bank International, 1971–77. Chairman, Council of Commonwealth Mining & Metallurgical Institutions, 1961–74; President, British Overseas Mining Assoc., 1952; President, Inst. of Metals, 1960–61; Hon. Pres., Copper Develt Assoc.; Hon. Member: Metals Soc.; Amer. Inst. of Min. & Metall. Engrs. Trustee, Inst. for Archaeo-Metallurgical Studies; Pres. Council, Cheltenham College, 1972–80. ANKH Award, Copper Club, New York, 1964; Gold Medal, 1968, and Hon. Fellow, Instn of Mining and Metallurgy; Platinum Medal, Inst. of Metals, 1969. Publications: Selected Papers (4 Vols); Copper: the anatomy of an industry, 1975 (Japanese trans. 1976; Spanish trans. 1980); Reflections on an Era, 1981. Recreations: cricket, real tennis, travel. Address: Waverley, St George's Hill, Weybridge, Surrey KT13 0QJ. T: Weybridge 42776; 43 Cadogan Square, SW1X 0HX. T: 01-235 4900. Clubs: Brooks's, White's, MCC.

PRAIN, Vyvyen Alice; retired as Principal, Princess Helena College, Temple Dinsley, Herts, 1935–July 1958; b 11 Oct 1895; d of Hunter Douglas Prain and Ellen Flora Davis. Educ: Edinburgh Ladies' Coll.; Edinburgh Univ. Graduated MA (Hons) in History (second class) in 1918, having gained the Gladstone Memorial Prize for History and Political Economy, and three class medals; Trained for teaching at Cambridge Training Coll., and gained a First Class Teacher's Certificate in 1919; History Mistress at Princess Helena Coll., Ealing, 1919–24; History and Economics at Wycombe Abbey Sch., 1924–29; Principal of the Ladies' Coll., Guernsey, 1929–35. Recreations: needlework, reading, travelling. Address: Halesworth, Suffolk.

PRANKERD, Thomas Arthur John, FRCP; Professor of Clinical Haematology, 1965–79 and Dean, 1972–77, University College Hospital Medical School; Hon. Consultant Physician: University College Hospital; Whittington Hospital; b 11 Sept. 1924; s of late H. A. Prankerd, Barrister-at-Law, and J. D. Shorthose; m 1950, Margaret Vera Harrison Cripps; two s (and one s one d decd). Educ: Charterhouse Sch.; St Bartholomew's Hospital Med. Sch. MD (London) Gold Medal 1949; FRCP 1962. Jnr med. appts, St Bart's and University Coll. Hosp., 1947–60. Major, RAMC, 1948–50. Univ. Travelling Fellow, USA, 1953–54; Consultant Physician, University Coll. Hosp., 1960–65. Goulstonian Lectr, RCP, 1963; Examr, RCP, and various univs. Vis. Prof., Univ. of Perth, WA, 1972. Mem., NE Thames RHA, 1976–79. Mem. Bd of Governors, UCH, 1972–74. Publications: The Red Cell, 1961; Haematology in Medical Practice, 1968; articles in med. jls. Recreations: fishing, gardening, music. Address: Pikes, Oakford, Tiverton, Devon. T: Oakford 392.

PRASADA, Krishna, CIE 1943; JP; ICS retired; Director-General, Posts and Telegraphs, New Delhi, 1945–53; b 4 Aug. 1894; s of Pandit Het Ram, CIE; m 1911, Bishan Devi (d 1950); three s. Educ: Bareilly; New Coll., Oxford. Joined ICS 1921; Joint Magistrate and subsequently a District Magistrate in UP. Services borrowed by Government of India in 1934, when he was appointed as Postmaster-General. Led Government of India deputations to

International Tele-communications Conference, Cairo, 1938, Buenos Aires, 1952, and to International Postal Congress, Paris, 1947. Retired, 1954. Director, Rotary International, 1961–63. Recreation: tennis, Oxford Tennis Blue (1921) and played for India in the Davis Cup in 1927 and 1932. Won All India Tennis Championships. Address: D/152, East of Kailash, New Delhi 24, 65 India.

PRASHAR, Usha Kumari, (Mrs V. K. Sharma); Director, Runnymede Trust, since 1977; b 29 June 1948; d of Nauhria Lal Prashar and Durga Devi Prashar; m 1973, Vijay Kumar Sharma. Educ: Duchess of Gloucester Sch., Nairobi; Wakefield Girls' High Sch. (Head Girl, 1966–67); Univ. of Leeds (BA Hons Pol. Studies); Univ. of Glasgow (postgrad. Dip. Social Admin). Race Relations Bd, 1971–75; Asst Dir, Runnymede Trust, 1976–77. Member: Arts Council of GB, 1979–81; Study Commn on the Family; Social Security Adv. Cttee, 1980–. Trustee, Thames Help Trust. Recreations: painting, reading, country walks, squash, tennis, music. Address: c/o Runnymede Trust, 37 Gray's Inn Road, WC1. T: 01-405 7703.

PRATLEY, Clive William; Under-Secretary, Lord Chancellor's Department, since Jan. 1976; Circuit Administrator: Midland and Oxford Circuit, 1976–82; North-Eastern Circuit, since 1982; b 23 Jan. 1929; s of late F. W. Pratley and late Minnie Pratley (née Hood); m 1962, Eva, d of Nils and Kerstin Kellgren, Stockholm; one s one d. Educ: RMA Sandhurst; and after retirement from Army, at Univs of Stockholm, 1961–62, and Hull, 1962–65 (LLB Hons). Commissioned into Royal Tank Regt, 1949; Adjt, 2nd Royal Tank Regt, 1959–61; retired from active list, 1961. Entered Administrative Class of Home Civil Service as Principal, 1966; Lord Chancellor's Department: Sen. Principal, 1971; Asst Sec., 1974; Courts Administrator, NE Circuit, 1971–73; Dep. Circuit Administrator, Midland and Oxford Circuit, 1974–75. Recreations: horses, the countryside, lawn tennis, badminton, music. Address: North Eastern Circuit Office, National Westminster House, 29 Bond Street, Leeds LS1 5BQ. Club: Army and Navy.

PRATLEY, David Illingworth; Regional Director, Arts Council of Great Britain, since 1981; b 24 Dec. 1948; s of Arthur George Pratley and Olive Constance Illingworth. Educ: Westminster Abbey Choir Sch.; Westminster Sch.; Univ. of Bristol (LLB). PRO, Thorndike Theatre, Leatherhead, 1970–71; Gen. Asst, Queen's Univ. Festival, Belfast, 1971–73; Dep. Dir, Merseyside Arts Assoc., 1973–76; Dir, Greater London Arts Assoc., 1976–81. Publication: (co-ed) Culture for All, 1981. Recreations: music, theatre, art, countryside, travel. Address: 27 Kew Green, Richmond, Surrey TW9 3AA.

PRATT, family name of Marquess Camden.

PRATT, Anthony Malcolm G.; see Galliers-Pratt.

PRATT, (Arthur) Geoffrey, CBE 1981; Chairman, South Eastern Gas Region (formerly South Eastern Gas Board), 1972–82; part-time Member, British Gas Corporation, 1981–82; b 19 Aug. 1922; s of William Pratt, Willington, Co. Durham; m 1946, Ethel Luck; two s one d. Educ: King James I Grammar Sch., Bishop Auckland. CEng, FIGasE. Joined E Mids Gas Bd, 1951: Chief Engr, 1964; Dir of Engrg, 1967; Dep. Chm., S Eastern Gas Bd, 1970. Chm., Metrogas Building Soc., 1977–. Hon. Sec., IGasE, 1982– (Pres., 1974–75). Recreations: golf, squash, swimming, bridge. Address: c/o Institution of Gas Engineers, 17 Grosvenor Crescent, SW1.

PRATT, His Honour Hugh MacDonald; a Circuit Judge (formerly County Court Judge) 1947–72; b 15 Sept. 1900; o c of late Sir John William Pratt; m 1928, Ingeborg, e d of late Consul Johannes Sundfor, MBE, Haugesund, Norway; one s. Educ: Hillhead High Sch., Glasgow; Aske's Haberdashers' Sch., London; Balliol Coll., Oxford. Called to Bar, Inner Temple, 1924; practised London and Western Circuit; member General Council of the Bar; President, Hardwicke Society; contested Drake Div. of Plymouth, 1929; Dep. President War Damage (Valuation Appeals) Panel, 1946. Chairman, Devon Quarter Sessions, 1958–64. Hon. LLD Exeter, 1972. Publications: English trans. of Professor Axel Möller's International Law (Vol. I, 1931, Vol. II, 1935); trans. of various articles in Norwegian, Danish and Swedish on commercial and international law. Recreations: reading, gardening. Address: Portland Lodge, Pennsylvania, Exeter. T: Exeter 72859.

PRATT, Very Rev. John Francis, MA; Provost Emeritus, since 1978; s of late Rev. J. W. J. Pratt, Churchill, Somerset; m 1939, Norah Elizabeth (d 1981), y d of late F. W. Corfield, Sandford, Somerset; two d. Educ: Keble Coll., Oxford; Wells Theological Coll. Priest, 1937. CF, 1st KSLI, 1941–46; (despatches, 1943); SCF, Cyprus, 1946. Vicar of: Rastrick, 1946–49; Wendover, 1949–59; Reading S Mary's (with All Saints, S Saviour's, S Mark's and S Matthew's), 1959–61; Vicar of Chilton with Dorton, 1961–70; Archdeacon of Buckingham, 1961–70; Provost of Southwell, 1970–78; Priest-in-charge, Edingley with Halam, 1975–78. RD of Wendover, 1955–59; Chaplain to High Sheriff of Bucks, 1956, 1962; Examining Chaplain to Bishop of Southwell, 1971–78. Address: 42 Bickerton Road, Headington, Oxford OX3 7LS. T: Oxford 63060.

PRATT, Michael John, QC 1976; a Recorder of the Crown Court, since 1974; b 23 May 1933; o s of W. Brownlow Pratt; m 1960, Elizabeth Jean Hendry; two s three d. Educ: West House Sch., Edgbaston; Malvern Coll. LLB (Birmingham). Army service, 2nd Lieut, 3rd Carabiniers (Prince of Wales's Dragoon Guards); Staff Captain. Called to the Bar (Middle Temple), 1954.

Recreations: music, theatre, sport generally. *Address:* South Hill, 170 Oak Tree Lane, Bournville, Birmingham B30 1TX. *T:* 021-472 2213. *Clubs:* Cavalry and Guards; Birmingham Conservative.

PRATT, Prof. Peter Lynn, PhD; FInstP; CEng, FIM; Professor of Crystal Physics, Imperial College of Science and Technology, London University, since 1963; *b* 10 March 1927; *s* of late William Lynn Pratt and Margery Florence Pratt; *m* 1951, Lydia Elizabeth Anne, *y d* of late G. A. Lyon Hatton, Edgbaston; two *s. Educ:* Cheltenham Coll.; Birmingham Univ. (BSc 1948); Pembroke Coll., Cambridge (PhD 1952). FInstP 1967; FIM 1980. Res. Fellow, AERE, 1951-53; Lectr, Univ. of Birmingham, 1953-58; Reader in Physical Metallurgy, Imperial Coll., 1959-63; Dean, Royal Sch. of Mines, and Mem. Governing Body, Imperial Coll., 1977-80; Dir of Continuing Educn, Imperial Coll., 1981-. Vis. Scientist, N Amer. Aviation Centre, 1963; Vis. Prof., Univ. of Stanford, 1964. Consultant at various times to: AERE; Commonwealth Trans-Antarctic Expedn; Commonwealth Develt Corp.; indust. firms and publishing houses. Chm., Adv. Cttee on Trng and Qualification of Patent Agents, 1972-73. Sir George Beilby Gold Medal and Prize, Institute of Metals, 1964. *Publications:* (ed) Fracture, 1969; technical appendix to Longbow (by Robert Hardy), 1976; articles on materials science and engrg in learned jls. *Recreations:* toxophily (esp. the English longbow), sailing, music, motor racing, recovery of the Mary Rose and its artefacts. *Address:* 20 Westfield Road, Beaconsfield, Bucks HP9 1EF. *T:* Beaconsfield 3392.

PRATT, Rev. Ronald Arthur Frederick; *b* 27 Aug. 1886; *s* of Charles Robert and Florence Maria Pratt; *m* 1925, Margaret Elam; no *c. Educ:* Tonbridge Sch.; Gonville and Caius Coll., Cambridge. Curate of Emmanuel, West Hampstead, 1910-13; of St Matthew's, Bethnal Green, E2, 1913-21; Chaplain RN (temp.), 1917-19; Vicar of Ossington, Newark on Trent, 1921-23; Vicar of St John, Long Eaton, Derbyshire, 1923-32; Vicar of St Barnabas, Derby, 1932-35; Archdeacon of Belize, British Honduras, CA, 1935-46; Licentiate to Officiate Dio. Canterbury, 1947-62. Missionary work in the Diocese of British Honduras, 1930-31. *Address:* Barham House Nursing Home, The Street, Barham, Canterbury, Kent.

PRAWER, Prof. Siegbert Salomon, FBA 1981; Taylor Professor of German Language and Literature, University of Oxford, since 1969; Fellow of The Queen's College, Oxford, since 1969; *b* 15 Feb. 1925; *s* of Marcus and Eleonora Prawer; *m* 1949, Helga Alice (*née* Schaefer); one *s* two *d* (and one *s* decd). *Educ:* King Henry VIII Sch., Coventry; Jesus Coll. (Schol.) and Christ's Coll., Cambridge. Charles Oldham Shakespeare Scholar, 1945, MA 1950, LittD 1962, Cantab; PhD Birmingham, 1953; MA 1969, DLitt 1969, Oxon. Adelaide Stoll Res. Student, Christ's Coll., Cambridge, 1947-48; Asst Lecturer, Lecturer, Sen. Lecturer, University of Birmingham, 1948-63; Prof. of German, Westfield Coll., London Univ., 1964-69. Visiting Professor: City Coll., NY, 1956-57; University of Chicago, 1963-64; Harvard Univ., 1968; Hamburg Univ., 1969; Univ. of Calif, Irvine, 1975; Otago Univ., 1976; Pittsburgh Univ., 1977; Visiting Fellow: Knox Coll., Dunedin, 1976; Humanities Research Centre, ANU, 1980; Tauber Inst., Brandeis Univ., 1981-82. Hon. Director, London Univ. Inst. of Germanic Studies, 1966-68. Goethe Medal, 1973. Co-editor: Oxford German Studies, 1971-75; Anglica Germanica, 1973-79. *Publications:* German Lyric Poetry, 1952; Mörike und seine Leser, 1960; Heine's Buch der Lieder: A Critical Study, 1960; Heine: The Tragic Satirist, 1962; The Penguin Book of Lieder, 1964; The Uncanny in Literature (inaug. lect.), 1965; (ed, with R. H. Thomas and L. W. Forster) Essays in German Language, Culture and Society, 1969; (ed) The Romantic Period in Germany, 1970; Heine's Shakespeare, a Study in Contexts (inaug. lect.), 1970; (ed) Seventeen Modern German Poets, 1971; Comparative Literary Studies: an Introduction, 1973; Karl Marx and World Literature, 1976 (Isaac Deutscher Meml Prize, 1977); Caligari's Children: the film as tale of terror, 1980; articles on German, English and comparative literature in many specialist periodicals and symposia. *Address:* The Queen's College, Oxford.
See also Mrs R. P. Jhabvala.

PRAWER JHABVALA, Mrs Ruth; *see* Jhabvala.

PREBBLE, David Lawrence; Master, Queen's Bench Division, Supreme Court of Justice, since 1981; *b* 21 Aug. 1932; *s* of George Wilson Prebble and Margaret Jessie Prebble (*née* Cuthbertson); *m* 1959, Fiona W. Melville; three *d. Educ:* Cranleigh; Christ Church, Oxford. MA. National Service, 1950-52; commissioned in 3rd Carabiniers (Prince of Wales's Dragoon Guards); Served TA, 1952-61, City of London Yeomanry (Rough Riders) TA (Captain). Called to the Bar, Middle Temple, 1957; practised at Bar, 1957-81. *Recreations:* reading; wine and food; hounds and dogs; friends' horses; own wife and family (not necessarily in foregoing order as to precedence). *Address:* 16 Wool Road, Wimbledon, SW20. *T:* 01-946 1804. *Club:* Royal Wimbledon Golf.

PREBBLE, John Edward Curtis, FRSL; Writer; *b* 23 June 1915; *o s* of late John William Prebble, Petty Officer, RN, and Florence (*née* Wood); *m* 1936, Betty, *d* of late Ernest Golby; two *s* one *d. Educ:* Sutherland Public Sch., Saskatchewan; Latymer Upper Sch., London. Entered journalism, 1934; in ranks with RA, 1940-45; Sergeant-reporter with No 1 British Army Newspaper Unit (Hamburg), 1945-46; reporter, columnist and feature-writer for British newspapers and magazines, 1946-60; novelist, historian, film-writer and author of many plays and dramatised documentaries for radio and TV. *Publications: novels:* Where the Sea Breaks, 1944; The Edge of Darkness,

1948; Age Without Pity, 1950; The Mather Story, 1954; The Brute Streets, 1954; The Buffalo Soldiers, 1959; *short stories:* My Great Aunt Appearing Day, 1958; Spanish Stirrup, 1972; *biography:* (with J. A. Jordan) Mongaso, 1956; *history:* The High Girders, 1956; Culloden, 1961; The Highland Clearances, 1963; Glencoe, 1966; The Darien Disaster, 1968; The Lion in the North, 1971; Mutiny: Highland Regiments in Revolt, 1975. *Recreation:* serendipity. *Address:* Hill View, The Glade, Kingswood, Surrey. *T:* Mogador 832142.

PRELOG, Prof. Dr Vladimir; Professor of Organic Chemistry, Swiss Federal Institute of Technology, 1950-76; *b* 23 July 1906; *m* 1933, Kamila Vitek; one *s. Educ:* Inst. of Technology, Prague. Chemist, Prague, 1929-34; Lecturer and Professor, University of Zagreb, 1935-41. Privatdozent, Swiss Federal Inst. of Technology, Zürich, 1941; Associate Professor, 1947. Mem. Bd, CIBA-GEIGY Ltd, Basel. Vis. Prof. of Chemistry, Univ. of Cambridge, 1974. Mem. Leopoldina, Halle/Saale, 1963; Hon. Member: American Acad. of Arts and Sciences, 1960; Chem. Society, 1960; Nat. Acad. of Sciences, Washington, 1961; Royal Irish Acad., Dublin, 1971; Foreign Member: Royal Society, 1962; Acad. of Sciences, USSR, 1966; Acad. dei Lincei, Roma 1965; Istituto Lombardo, Milano, 1964; Royal Danish Acad. of Sciences, 1971; Amer. Philosophical Soc. Philadelphia, 1976; Acad. Sciences, Paris, 1981. Dr *hc* Universities of: Zagreb, 1954; Liverpool, 1963; Paris, 1963; Bruxelles, 1969. Hon. DSc: Cambridge, 1969; Manchester, 1977; Inst. Quimico Sarria, Barcelona, 1978. Davy Medal, Royal Society, 1967; A. W. Hofmann Medal, Gesell. deutscher Chem., 1967; Marcel Benoist Prize, 1965; Roger Adams Award, 1969; (jtly) Nobel Prize for Chemistry, 1975. Order of Rising Sun, Japan; Order of Yugoslav Star. *Publications:* numerous scientific papers, mainly in Helvetica chimica acta. *Address:* (office) Laboratorium für organische Chemie, ETH-Zentrum, Universitätstrasse 16, CH-8092 Zürich, Switzerland; (home) Bellariastr. 33, 8002 Zürich. *T:* CH 01 202 17 81.

PREMADASA, Ranasinghe; Member of Parliament of Sri Lanka, since 1960; Prime Minister of Sri Lanka, since 1978; also Minister of Local Government, Housing and Construction and Leader of the National State Assembly, since 1977; *b* 23 June 1924; *m* 1964, Hema Wickrematunge; one *s* one *d. Educ:* Lorenz Coll., Colombo; St Joseph's Coll., Colombo. Member, Colombo Municipal Council, 1950; Dep. Mayor of Colombo, 1955. Joined United Nat. Party and contested Ruvanwella, 1956; MHR(Colombo): 3rd Mem., 1960; 2nd Mem., 1965; 1st Mem., 1970; Nat. State Assembly (Colombo): 1st Mem., 1977-. Chief Whip, Opp. Parly Gp, in House of Reps, 1970; Dep. Leader, United Nat. Party, 1976. Has visited, as state guest or member of delegns: UK, USA, Australia, China, USSR, Japan, Singapore, Hong Kong, and several European countries, 1955-. *Publications:* 10 books in Sinhalese language. *Address:* Prime Minister's Office, Colombo, Sri Lanka. *T:* 27447.

PREMINGER, Otto (Ludwig); Producer-Director since 1928; *b* 5 Dec. 1906; *m* 1960, Hope Preminger (*née* Bryce); two *s* one *d* (one *s* one *d* are twins). *Educ:* University of Vienna (LLD). Associate Professor, Yale Univ., 1938-41. *Films:* Margin for Error, 1942; A Royal Scandal, 1944; Laura, 1944; Fallen Angel, 1945; Centennial Summer, 1945; Forever Amber, 1947; Daisy Kenyon, 1948; That Lady in Ermine, 1948; The Fan, 1949; Whirlpool, 1949; Where the Sidewalk Ends, 1950; The 13th Letter, 1950; Angel Face, 1952; The Moon is Blue, 1953; The River of No Return, 1953; Carmen Jones, 1954; Court Martial of Billy Mitchell, 1955; The Man with the Golden Arm, 1955; Saint Joan, 1957; Bonjour Tristesse, 1958; Porgy and Bess, 1959; Anatomy of a Murder, 1959; Exodus, 1960; Advise and Consent, 1961; The Cardinal, 1963; In Harm's Way, 1965; Bunny Lake is Missing, 1965; Hurry Sundown, 1967; Skidoo, 1968; Tell Me that You Love Me, Julie Moon, 1970; Such Good Friends, 1972; Rosebud, 1974; The Human Factor, 1979; *plays include:* (director) Libel, Broadway, 1936; (prod. and dir) Outward Bound, Broadway, 1938; (leading rôle and director) Margin for Error, Broadway, 1939; (prod. and dir) My Dear Children, 1940; Beverley Hills, 1940; Cue for Passion, 1940; The More the Merrier, 1941; In Time to Come, 1941; Four Twelves are 48, 1951; A Modern Primitive, 1951; (prod. and dir) The Moon is Blue, Broadway, 1951; The Trial, 1953; This is Goggle, 1958; (prod. and dir) Critic's Choice, Broadway, 1960; Full Circle, Broadway, 1973. *Publication:* Preminger: an autobiography, 1977. *Recreation:* art collector. *Address:* 129 East 64th Street, New York, NY 10021, USA. *T:* (212) 535 6001.

PRENDERGAST, (Christopher) Anthony, CBE 1981; Chairman, Dolphin Square Trust Ltd, since 1967; an Underwriting Member of Lloyd's; *b* 4 May 1931; *s* of Maurice Prendergast, AINA, and Winifred Mary Prendergast, Falmouth; *m* 1959, Simone Ruth Laski, OBE 1981, OStJ, JP, DL; one *s. Educ:* Falmouth Grammar School. Westminster City Council: Mem., 1959-; Chairman: Housing Cttee, 1962-65; Health Cttee, 1965-68; Town Planning Cttee, 1972-75, 1976-78; Gen. Purposes Cttee, 1978-80; Management Services, 1981-; Lord Mayor and Dep. High Steward of Westminster, 1968-69; High Sheriff of Greater London, 1980; Governor, Westminster Sch., 1974-; Additional Mem., GLC (Covent Garden Cttee), 1971-75; Mem., London Boroughs Trng Cttee, 1965-68; Mem., Docklands Develt Cttee, 1974. Chm., Location of Offices Bureau, 1971-79. Member: Assoc. of Metropolitan Authorities Cttee, 1976-; Nat. Jt Council (Manual Workers), 1978-. Upper Warden, Pattenmakers' Co. *Recreations:* fishing, shooting, photography. *Address:* 51 Sutherland Street, SW1V 4JX. *T:* 01-821 7653. *Clubs:* Carlton, Brooks's, Irish; MCC.

PRENDERGAST, Sir John (Vincent), KBE 1977 (CBE 1960); CMG 1968; GM 1955; CPM 1955; QPM 1963; retired; Deputy Commissioner and Director of Operations, Independent Commission Against Corruption, Hong Kong, 1973-77; *b* 11 Feb. 1912; *y s* of late John and Margaret Prendergast; *m* 1943, Enid Sonia, *yr d* of Percy Speed; one *s* one *d. Educ:* in Ireland; London Univ. (External). Local Government, London, 1930-39. War Service, 1939-46 (Major). Asst District Comr, Palestine Administration, 1946-47; Colonial Police Service, Palestine and Gold Coast, 1947-52; seconded Army, Canal Zone, on special duties, 1952-53; Colonial Police Service, Kenya, 1953-58 (Director of Intelligence and Security, 1955-58); Chief of Intelligence, Cyprus, 1958-60; Director, Special Branch, Hong Kong (retired as Dep. Comr of Police), 1960-66. Director of Intelligence, Aden, 1966-67. *Recreations:* racing, collecting first editions. *Address:* 20 Westbourne Terrace, W2 3UP. *Clubs:* East India; Hong Kong, Royal Hong Kong Jockey (Hong Kong).

PRENDERGAST, (Walter) Kieran; HM Diplomatic Service; Counsellor, Head of Chancery and Consul-General, Tel Aviv, since 1982; *b* 2 July 1942; *s* of Lt-Comdr J. H. Prendergast and Mai Hennessy; *m* 1967, Joan Reynolds; two *s* two *d. Educ:* St Patrick's College, Strathfield, Sydney, NSW; Salesian College, Chertsey; St Edmund Hall, Oxford. Turkish language student Istanbul, 1964; Ankara, 1965; FO (later FCO), 1967; 2nd Sec. Nicosia, 1969; Civil Service Coll., 1972; 1st Sec. FCO, 1972; The Hague, 1973; Asst Private Sec. to Foreign and Commonwealth Sec. (Rt Hon. Anthony Crosland, Rt Hon. Dr David Owen), 1976; UK Mission to UN, 1979 (detached for duty Jan.-March 1980 at Govt House, Salisbury). Rhodesia Medal, 1980; Zimbabwe Independence Medal, 1980. *Recreations:* family, walking, reading, sport, wine. *Address:* British Embassy, Tel Aviv, Israel.

PRENTICE, (Hubert Archibald) John, CEng; FInstP; consultant on manufacturing and management strategies to several UK and USA companies; *b* 5 Feb. 1920; *s* of Charles Herbert Prentice and Rose Prentice; *m* 1947, Sylvia Doreen Elias; one *s. Educ:* Woolwich Polytechnic, London; Salford Univ. (BSc, MSc). CEng; MRAeS 1962; FInstP 1967. Min. of Supply, 1939-56; R&D posts, res. estabts and prodn, MoD, 1956-60; Space Dept, RAE, Min. of Aviation, 1960-67; Head, Road User Characteristics Res., 1967-70, and Head, Driver Aids and Abilities Res., 1970-72, MoT; Head, Road User Dynamics Res., DoE, 1972-75; Counsellor (Sci. and Technol.), British Embassy, Tokyo, 1975-80. *Recreations:* walking, climbing. *Address:* 5 Foxhill Crescent, Camberley, Surrey GU15 1PR. *T:* Camberley 66373.

PRENTICE, Rt. Hon. Reginald Ernest; PC; JP; MP (C) Daventry, since 1979 (MP (Lab) East Ham North, May 1957-1974, Newham North East, 1974-Oct. 1977, MP (C) Newham North East, Oct. 1977-1979); *b* 16 July 1923; *s* of Ernest George and Elizabeth Prentice; *m* 1948, Joan Godwin; one *d. Educ:* Whitgift Sch.; London School of Economics. Temporary Civil Servant, 1940-42; RA, 1942-46; commissioned 1943; served in Italy and Austria, 1944-46. Student at LSE, 1946-49. BSc (Econ). Member staff of Transport and General Workers' Union, Asst to Legal Secretary; in charge of Union's Advice and Service Bureau, 1950-57; Minister of State, Department of Education and Science, 1964-66; Minister of Public Building and Works, 1966-67; Minister of Overseas Develt, 1967-69; Opposition Spokesman on Employment, 1972-74; Sec. of State for Educn and Science, 1974-75; Minister for Overseas Develt, 1975-76; Minister of State (Minister for Social Security), DHSS, 1979-81. Alderman, GLC, 1970-71. JP County Borough of Croydon, 1961. *Publications:* (jt) Social Welfare and the Citizen, 1957; Right Turn, 1978. *Recreations:* walking, golf. *Address:* Bridle Cottage, Ballards Farm Road, Croydon CR0 5RL; St Hilda's Cottage, The Green, Creaton, Northants. *Clubs:* Reform; Addington Palace Golf.

PRENTICE, Thomas, MC 1945; Chairman, Harrisons & Crosfield Ltd, since 1977; *b* 14 Oct. 1919; *s* of Alexander and Jean Young Prentice; *m* 1949, Peggy Ann Lloyd; two *s* two *d. Educ:* McLaren High Sch., Callander, Perthshire. Served Army, 1939-46. Harrisons & Crosfield (Sabah) Sdn. Bhd., Malaysia, 1947-67; Harrisons & Crosfield Ltd, 1967-. *Recreations:* golf, gardening. *Address:* Eveley, Standford, near Bordon, Hants. *T:* Passfield 228. *Club:* East India, Devonshire, Sports and Public Schools.

PRENTICE, Hon. Sir William (Thomas), Kt 1977; MBE 1945; Senior Member, Administrative Appeals Tribunal, Australia, since 1981; *b* 1 June 1919; *s* of Claud Stanley and Dorothy Prentice; *m* 1946, Mary Elizabeth, *d* of F. B. Dignam; three *s* one *d. Educ:* St Joseph's College, Hunters Hill; Sydney Univ. (BA, LLB). AIF, Middle East and New Guinea, 2-33 Inf. Bn and Staff Captain 25 Aust. Inf. Bde, Owen Stanleys and Lae Ramu campaigns; Staff Course, Duntroon, 1944; Staff Captain, 7 Aust. Inf. Bde, Bougainville campaign, 1944-45. Resumed law studies, 1946; admitted Bar, NSW, 1947; Judge, Supreme Court, PNG, 1970; Senior Puisne Judge, 1975; Deputy Chief Justice on independence, PNG, 1975, Chief Justice 1978-80. *Recreations:* bush walking, swimming, reading. *Address:* 16 Olympia Road, Naremburn, NSW 2065, Australia. *Clubs:* Tattersall's, NSW Leagues (Sydney).

PRENTICE, Dame Winifred (Eva), DBE 1977 (OBE 1972); SRN; President, Royal College of Nursing, 1972-76; *b* 2 Dec. 1910; *d* of Percy John Prentice and Anna Eva Prentice. *Educ:* Northgate Sch. for Girls, Ipswich; E Suffolk and Ipswich Hosp. (SRN); W Mddx Hosp. (SCM Pt I); Queen Elizabeth Coll., London Univ. (RNT); Dip. in Nursing, London Univ. Ward Sister: E Suffolk and Ipswich Hosp., 1936-39; Essex County Hosp., 1941-43; Nurse Tutor, King's Lynn Hosp., 1944-46; Principal Tutor, Stracathro Hosp.,

Brechin, Angus, 1947-61, Matron, 1961-72. *Publications:* articles in Nursing Times and Nursing Mirror. *Recreations:* music, amateur dramatics, gardening. *Address:* Marleish, 4 Duke Street, Brechin, Angus. *T:* Brechin 2606. *Club:* VAD Ladies.

PRESCOTT, James Arthur, CBE 1947; FRS 1951; DSc; retired; Director, Waite Agricultural Research Institute, 1938-55; Professor of Agricultural Chemistry, University of Adelaide, 1924-55, Emeritus Professor since 1956; *b* 7 Oct. 1890; *e s* of Joseph Arthur Prescott, Bolton, Lancs; *m* 1915, Elsie Mason, Accrington, Lancs; one *s. Educ:* Ecole Littré, Lille; Accrington Grammar Sch.; Manchester Univ.; Leipzig Univ. Rothamsted Experimental Station; Chief Chemist and Superintendent of Field Experiments, Bahtim Experimental Station, Sultanic Agricultural Society of Egypt, 1916-24; Chief, Division of Soils, Commonwealth Council for Scientific and Industrial Research, 1929-47. Mem. Council and Scientific Adviser, Australian Wine Research Inst., 1954-69. Hon. DAgSc Melbourne, 1956. Hon. Member: Internat. Society of Soil Science, 1964; All-Union (Soviet) Soc. of Soil Science, 1977. (Foundn) FAA 1954. *Publications:* various scientific, chiefly on soils, climatology and principles of crop production. *Address:* 6 Kinross Lodge, 2 Netherby Avenue, Netherby, SA 5062, Australia.

PRESCOTT, John Leslie; MP (Lab) Kingston upon Hull (East), since 1970; Opposition spokesman on transport, since 1979; *b* 31 May 1938; *s* of John Herbert Prescott, JP, and Phyllis Prescott; *m* 1961, Pauline Tilston; two *s. Educ:* Ellesmere Port Secondary Modern Sch.; WEA; correspondence courses; Ruskin Coll., Oxford (DipEcon/Pol Oxon); Hull Univ. (BSc Econ). Trainee Chef, 1953-55; Steward, Passenger Lines, Merchant Navy, 1955-63; Ruskin Coll., Oxford, 1963-65; Recruitment Officer, General and Municipal Workers Union (temp.), 1965; Hull Univ., 1965-68. Contested (Lab) Southport, 1966; Full-time Official, National Union of Seamen, 1968-70. Member: Select Cttee Nationalized Industries, 1973-79; Council of Europe, 1972-75; European Parlt, 1975-79 (Leader, Labour Party Delegn, 1976-79); PPS to Sec. of State for Trade, 1974-76; opposition spokesman on Transport, 1979-81; opposition front bench spokesman on Regional Affairs and Devolution, 1981-. *Publication:* Not Wanted on Voyage, 1966. *Address:* 365 Saltshouse Road, Sutton-on-Hull, North Humberside.

PRESCOTT, Sir Mark, 3rd Bt, *cr* 1938, of Godmanchester; Racehorse Trainer, in Newmarket; *b* 3 March 1948; *s* of late Major W. R. Stanley Prescott (MP for Darwen Div., 1943-51; 2nd *s* of Colonel Sir William Prescott, 1st Bt) and of Gwendolen (who *m* 2nd, 1952, Daniel Orme (*d* 1972)), *o c* of late Leonard Aldridge, CBE; *S* uncle, Sir Richard Stanley Prescott, 2nd Bt, 1965. *Educ:* Harrow. *Address:* Heath House, Moulton Road, Newmarket, Suffolk CB8 8DU. *T:* Newmarket 2117.

PRESCOTT, Brig. Peter George Addington, MC 1944; Secretary, National Rifle Association, since 1980; *b* 22 Sept. 1924; *s* of Col and Mrs John Prescott; *m* 1953, June Marian Louise Wendell; one *s* one *d. Educ:* Eton Coll.; Staff Coll. (psc 1957); Royal Coll. of Defence Studies (rcds 1973). Commnd Grenadier Guards, 1943; 2nd Armoured Bn Gren. Gds, 1944-45; comd 2nd Bn Gren. Gds, 1966-69; Comdr 51st Inf. Bde, 1970-72; Dep. Comdr NE Dist, 1974-77; Dep. Dir of Army Trng, 1977-79, retd. Chevalier, Royal Order of the Sword, Sweden, 1954. *Recreations:* sailing, painting, gardening. *Address:* The Bourne, Church Lane, Holybourne, Alton, Hants.

PRESCOTT, Westby William P.; *see* Percival-Prescott.

PRESLAND, John David; Executive Vice-Chairman, Port of London Authority, 1978-82; *b* 3 July 1930; *s* of Leslie and Winifred Presland; *m* 1969, Margaret Brewin. *Educ:* St Albans Sch.; London Sch. of Economics. BScEcon. FCA, IPFA, MBCS. Knox Cropper & Co., Chartered Accountants, 1950-58; Pfizer Ltd (various financial posts), 1958-64; Berk Ltd: Chief Accountant, 1964-67; Financial Controller, 1967-68; Dir and Financial Controller, 1968-71; Port of London Authority: Financial Controller, 1971-73; Asst Dir-Gen. (Finance), 1973-76; Exec. Dir (Finance), 1976-78. Freeman of City of London; Freeman of Company of Watermen and Lightermen of River Thames. *Recreations:* history, natural history, music. *Address:* c/o British Ports Association, Commonwealth House, 1-19 New Oxford Street, WC1A 1DZ. *Club:* Oriental.

PRESS, John Bryant, FRSL; author and poet; *b* 11 Jan. 1920; *s* of late Edward Kenneth Press and late Gladys (*née* Cooper); *m* 1947, Janet Crompton; one *s* one *d. Educ:* King Edward VI Sch., Norwich; Corpus Christi Coll., Cambridge, 1938-40 and 1945-46. Served War of 1939-45: RA, 1940-45. British Council, 1946-79: Athens, 1946-47; Salonika, 1947-50; Madras, 1950-51; Colombo, 1951-52; Birmingham, 1952-54; Cambridge, 1955-62; London, 1962-65; Paris, 1966-71 (also Asst Cultural Attaché, British Embassy); Regional Dir, Oxford, 1972-78; Literature Advr, London, 1978-79. Mem. Council, RSL, 1971-. Gave George Elliston Poetry Foundation Lectures at Univ. of Cincinnati, 1962; Vis. Prof., Univ. of Paris, 1981-82. *Publications:* The Fire and the Fountain, 1955; Uncertainties, 1956; (ed) Poetic Heritage, 1957; The Chequer'd Shade, 1958 (RSL Heinemann Award); Andrew Marvell, 1958; Guy Fawkes Night, 1959; Herrick, 1961; Rule and Energy, 1963; Louis MacNeice, 1964; (ed) Palgrave's Golden Treasury, Book V, 1964; A Map of Modern English Verse, 1969; The Lengthening Shadows, 1971; John Betjeman, 1974; Spring at St Clair, 1974; Aspects of Paris, (with illus by Gordon Bradshaw), 1975; (with Edward Lowbury and Michael Riviere) Troika, 1977; War Poets 1914-1918, 1983. Libretto, new version of

Bluebeard's Castle, for Michael Powell's colour television film of Bartók's opera, 1963. *Recreations:* travel (especially in France), theatre, opera, concerts, cinema; architecture and visual arts; watching football and cricket. *Address:* 5 South Parade, Frome BA11 1EJ.

PRESS, Dr Robert, CB 1972; CBE 1962; Deputy Secretary, Science and Technology, Cabinet Office, 1974-76, retired; Adviser in the Cabinet Office since 1976; *b* 22 Feb. 1915; *s* of William J. Press; *m* 1946, Honor Elizabeth Tapp; no *c. Educ:* Regent House Secondary Sch., Co. Down; Queen's Univ., Belfast; Trinity Coll., Dublin Univ. BSc 1936, MSc 1937 QUB; PhD 1949 Dublin. Res. Physicist, TCD, 1938-40; Physics Master, Dungannon Royal Sch., NI, 1940-41; Physicist: War Dept Research, UK, 1941-43, and in India, 1944-46; on Staff of Scientific Adviser, Army Council, 1946-48; in Dept of Atomic Energy, Min. of Supply, 1948-51. Attaché at HM Embassy, Washington, 1951-55; Head of Technical Res. Unit, MoD, 1955-59; Mem. British Delegn to Conf. for Discontinuance of Nuclear Tests, 1958-59. Dep. Chief Scientific Officer, MoD, 1960-62, Chief Scientific Officer, 1962; Asst Chief Scientific Adviser (Nuclear), MoD, 1963-66; Chief Scientific Officer, Cabinet Office, 1967-71; Dep. Sec., Cabinet Office, 1971-74; Dep. to Chief Scientific Adviser to HM Govt, 1971-74. Mem., Internat. Consultative Gp on Nuclear Energy, 1979-80. Hon. Sec., Inst. of Physics, 1966-76; Foundn Mem., Council of European Physical Soc., 1969-72; Chm., Council of Science and Technology Insts, 1978-80 (Mem. Council, 1976-). FPhysS 1950, FInstP 1961, FRSA 1967 (Mem. Council, 1971-76). *Publications:* papers in: Nature, and Proc. Royal Soc., 1938, 1941; Scientific Proc. Royal Dublin Soc., 1939; Irish Jl of Med. Science, 1941; Internat. Consultative Gp on Nuclear Energy (series), 1978-80. *Address:* 8 Ardross Avenue, Northwood, Mddx HA6 3DS. *T:* Northwood 23707. *Club:* Army and Navy.

PRESSBURGER, Emeric; Author, Film Producer; *b* 5 Dec. 1902; one *d. Educ:* Universities of Prague and Stuttgart. Journalist in Hungary and Germany, author and writer of films in Berlin and Paris; came to England in 1935; formed jointly with Michael Powell, The Archers Film Producing Company, and Vega Productions Ltd, and made the following films: Spy in Black, 1938; 49th Parallel, 1940 (USA Academy Award 1942, under American title, The Original Story of The Invaders); One of our Aircraft is Missing, 1941; Colonel Blimp, 1942; I Know Where I'm Going, 1944; A Matter of Life and Death, 1945; Black Narcissus, 1946; The Red Shoes, 1947; Small Back Room, 1948; Gone to Earth, 1949; The Tales of Hoffmann, 1951; Oh Rosalinda!!, 1955; The Battle of the River Plate, 1956; Ill Met by Moonlight, 1956. Wrote, produced, and directed first film Twice Upon a Time, 1952; wrote and produced Miracle in Soho, 1957; wrote The Boy who Turned Yellow (film). British Film Institute Special Award (with Michael Powell), 1978. *Publications:* Killing a Mouse on Sunday (novel), 1961; The Glass Pearls (novel), 1966; (with Michael Powell) The Red Shoes, 1978. *Recreations:* music, travel, and sports. *Address:* Shoemaker's Cottage, Aspall, Stowmarket, Suffolk. *Club:* Savile.

PRESSMAN, Mrs J. J.; *see* Colbert, Claudette.

PREST, Prof. Alan Richmond; Professor of Economics (with special reference to the Public Sector), London School of Economics, since 1970; *b* 1 March 1919; *s* of F. and E. A. Prest; *m* 1945, Pauline Chasey Noble; two *s* one *d. Educ:* Archbishop Holgate's Sch., York; Clare Coll., Cambridge; Christ's Coll., Cambridge. Res. Worker, Dept of Applied Economics, Cambridge, 1946-48; Rockefeller Fellow, USA, 1948-49; University Lecturer, Cambridge, 1949-64; Fellow, Christ's Coll., Cambridge, 1950-64; Tutor, 1954-55, Bursar, 1955-64, Christ's Coll.; Prof. of Economics and Public Finance, 1964-68, and Stanley Jevons Prof. of Political Economy, 1968-70, University of Manchester. Visiting Professor: Columbia Univ., New York, 1961-62; Univ. of Pittsburgh, 1969; ANU, 1971. Vis. Fellow, ANU, 1977, 1978. Mem., Royal Commn on Civil Liability and Compensation for Personal Injury, 1973-78. President, Section F, British Association, 1967; Mem., Departmental Cttee on Liquor Licensing, 1971-72. Treasurer, Royal Economic Soc., 1971-75. *Publications:* War Economics of Primary Producing Countries, 1948; The National Income of Nigeria, 1950-51, (with I. G. Stewart), 1953; Consumers' Expenditure in the UK, 1900-19, 1954; Fiscal Survey of the British Caribbean, 1957; Public Finance in Theory and Practice, 1960; Public Finance in Under-Developed Countries, 1962; (ed) The UK Economy, 1966; (ed) Public Sector Economics, 1968; Transport Economics in Developing Countries, 1969; (with N. A. Barr and S. R. James) Self-Assessment for Income Tax, 1977; Intergovernmental Financial Relations in the UK, 1978; The Taxation of Urban Land, 1981; papers in various professional journals. *Address:* 21 Leeward Gardens, Wimbledon Hill, SW19. *T:* 01-947 4492. *Club:* United Oxford & Cambridge University.

PRESTIE, Janet Miriam Taylor; *see* Caldwell, Taylor.

PRESTON, family name of Viscount Gormanston.

PRESTON, Alan; Director of Fisheries Research, Ministry of Agriculture, Fisheries and Food, since 1980; *b* 23 May 1929; *s* of Ivor Gordon Preston and Lottie May Preston (née Bentley); *m* 1952, Beatrice Patricia Smith; two *s* two *d. Educ:* Univ. of Reading (BSc (Gen.) 1950, BSc Hons Marine Zoology 1951). Nat. Service, RCS, 1953-55; 2nd Lieut 1954. Joined Fisheries Lab., Lowestoft, 1951: Head, Fisheries Radiobiol Lab., 1965-72; Dep. Dir, Fisheries Res., 1972-80. Buckland Foundation Professor, 1981. *Publications:* papers in learned jls. *Recreations:* gardening, haute cuisine, American history. *Address:*

The Hall, Oulton, Lowestoft, Suffolk. *T:* Lowestoft 65115. *Club:* Rotary (Lowestoft South).

PRESTON, Aston Zachariah, JP; Vice-Chancellor, University of the West Indies, since 1974; *b* 16 April 1925; *s* of Zachariah and Caroline Preston; *m* 1954, Barbara Marie (née Mordecai); two *s* one *d. Educ:* Univ. of London (LLB); FCA, FCCA, FCIS, FREconS. University of the West Indies: Bursar, 1956; Pro-Vice-Chancellor, 1969. Mem., Bd of Governors, Univ. of Guyana, 1967; Financial Adviser to E Africa, S Africa, Zambia and S Pacific Govts on univ. financing and develt, 1968; Chm., Shortwood Teachers' Coll., Jamaica, 1970-77; Mem., Council, ACU, 1975-79, Chm. 1981-82; Mem., Adv. Cttee, Unesco Reg. Centre for Higher Educn in Latin America and the Caribbean, 1978-; Chm., Caribbean Exams Council, 1979-. Chairman: Public Passenger Transport Bd of Control, Jamaica, 1972-74; Jamaica Omnibus Services Ltd, 1974-77, 1979-80; Jamaica State Trading Corp. Ltd, 1979-; Inst. of Internat. Relations, Trinidad, 1974; PAHO Caribbean Epidemiology Centre, Trinidad, 1975-; Bd of Directors, Workers' Savings & Loan Bank, Jamaica, 1978; Finance Cttee, Port Authority, 1980-; Finance Cttee, Air Jamaica, 1981-; Sole Comr of Enquiries into two railway accidents, 1973; Pres., Public Accounting Bd, Jamaica, 1975; Mem., Industrial Disputes Tribunal, 1977. Mem. Council, Univ. of Zambia, 1979-. Trustee, Caribbean News Agency. JP Jamaica, 1957. *Recreations:* reading, music, bridge. *Address:* Vice-Chancellor's House, University of the West Indies, Kingston, Jamaica. *T:* 92-70736.

PRESTON, (Frederick) Leslie, FRIBA; AADip; formerly Senior Partner in firm of Easton Robertson Preston and Partners, Architects; *b* 27 Nov. 1903; *m* 1927, Rita Lillian, *d* of late T. H. J. Washbourne; one *d. Educ:* Dulwich Coll.; Architectural Association Sch., London. Henry Jarvis Student, 1924; joined firm of Easton & Robertson, 1925, and engaged on: in London: Royal Horticultural Society's New Hall; Royal Bank of Canada; Metropolitan Water Board's Laboratories; in Cambridge: reconstruction of Old Library; Zoological laboratories; School of Anatomy; Gonville and Caius new buildings; in New York: British Pavilion, World's Fair, 1939. Hon. Citizen of City of New York, 1939. Served War of 1939-45, RAF, Wing Comdr, Airfield Construction Branch (despatches). *Principal works:* laboratories for Brewing Industry Research Foundation; laboratories for Coal Research Establishment, NCB, Cheltenham; Bank of England, Bristol; offices for Lloyds Bank, Plymouth; Birmingham; plans for development of Reading University: Faculty of Letters, Library, Windsor Hall, Depts of Physics and Sedimentology, Dept of Mathematics. Applied Physical Science Building, Palmer Building, Whiteknights House, Students Union, Animal Biology and Plant Sciences Buildings; additions to St Patrick's Hall and to Depts of Horticulture and Dairying, Reading Univ.; Buildings for Dulwich Coll.; office building for Salters' Co., London; Laboratories and Aquarium for Marine Biological Association, Plymouth; offices for Friends' Provident & Century Life Office, Dorking; Research Laboratories for Messrs Arthur Guinness Son & Co. (Park Royal) Ltd; University of Keele, Library; Midland Hotel, Manchester, alterations; University of Kent at Canterbury, Chemistry Laboratories, Biology Laboratories, Physics 11; Bank of England Printing Works Extension, Debden; Eagle Star Insurance Head Office, City; Plans for Aquarium, Rangoon Zoological Gardens. Member of RIBA Practice Cttee, 1951-55; Member Council of Architects' Registration Council of the UK, 1954-60. Governor of Westminster Technical College, 1957-67. Hon. DLitt, Reading, 1964. *Address:* Wichenford, Ashtead, Surrey. *Clubs:* Athenæum, Reform.

PRESTON, Geoffrey Averill; Under-Secretary (Legal), Department of Trade, since 1975; *b* 19 May 1924; *s* of George and Winifred Preston; *m* 1953, Catherine Wright. *Educ:* St Marylebone Grammar Sch. Barrister-at-Law. Served, RNVR, 1942-46. Called to Bar, Gray's Inn, 1950. Treasury Solicitor's Dept, 1952-71; Solicitor's Department: Dept of Environment, 1971-74; Dept of Trade, 1974-. *Recreations:* gardening, carpentry, chess. *Address:* Ledsham, Glaziers Lane, Normandy, Surrey. *T:* Normandy (Surrey) 2250.

PRESTON, Prof. Joseph Henry; Professor of Fluid Mechanics, University of Liverpool, 1955-76, now Emeritus; Fellow, Queen Mary College, London, since Dec. 1959; *b* 1 March 1911; *s* of William and Jean Preston, Penruddock, Cumberland; *m* 1938, Ethel Noble, Bampton, Westmorland; one *s* one *d. Educ:* Queen Elizabeth Grammar Sch., Penrith, Cumberland; Queen Mary Coll., University of London. BSc Eng London 1932; 1851 Industrial Bursary, for practical training at Short Bros Ltd, Rochester, 1932-34; PhD (Aeronautics) London 1936; Asst Lecturer, Imperial Coll., 1936-38; Officer, Aero Division, National Physical Laboratory, Teddington, 1938-46; Lecturer in Aeronautics, Cambridge Univ., 1946-54 (MA Cantab); Reader in Engineering, at Cambridge, 1955. FRAeS. *Publications:* contributor to Phil. Mag.; Journal Royal Aero. Society; Engineer; Engineering; Aero. Engineer; Aero. Quarterly; Journal of Mechanics and Applied Maths; Reports and Memoranda of the Stationery Office. *Recreation:* mountaineering. *Address:* 2 Croome Drive, West Kirby, Wirral L48 8AH. *Club:* Wayfarers (Liverpool).

PRESTON, Sir Kenneth (Huson), Kt 1959; *b* 19 May 1901; *e s* of late Sir Walter Preston, Tetbury, Glos; *m* 1922, Beryl Wilmot (decd), *d* of Sir William Wilkinson; one *s* one *d. Educ:* Rugby; Trinity Coll., Oxford. Dir, J. Stone & Co, 1925; Chm. Platt Bros, 1946; Chm. Stone-Platt Industries, 1958-67, retired; Dir, Midland Bank Ltd, 1945-76. Mem. S Area Bd, BR. Mem. British Olympic Yachting team, 1936 and 1952, Captain 1960. *Recreations:* yachting, hunting. *Address:* Ilsom, Tetbury, Gloucestershire. *T:*

Tetbury 52348. *Clubs:* Royal Yacht Squadron (Vice-Cdre, 1965-71); Thames Yacht (Vice-Cdre, 1953-56).

PRESTON, Leslie; see Preston, F. L.

PRESTON, Myles Park; schoolmaster, since 1979; HM Diplomatic Service, retired; *b* 4 April 1927; *s* of Robert and Marie Preston; *m* 1st, 1951, Ann Betten (marr. diss.); one *s* one *d*; 2nd, 1981, Joy Moore (*née* Fisher). *Educ:* Sudley Road Council Sch.; Liverpool Inst. High Sch.; Clare Coll., Cambridge. Instructor Lieut, RN, 1948-51; Asst Principal, Admty, 1951-53; CRO, 1953-54; 2nd Sec., British High Commn, New Delhi, 1954-56; 1st Sec., CRO, 1956-59; 1st Sec., Governor-General's Office and British High Commn, Lagos, 1959-62; CRO, 1962-64; 1st Sec., British High Commn, Kampala, 1964-67; Commonwealth Office and FCO, 1967-69; Counsellor and Consul-Gen., Djakarta, 1969-72; Canadian Nat. Defence Coll., 1972-73; FCO, 1973-77; Dep. Governor, Solomon Islands, 1977-78; Consul-Gen., Vancouver, 1978-79. *Address:* 20 Prince Edwards Road, Lewes, East Sussex BN7 1BE. *T:* Lewes 5809.

PRESTON, Peter John; Editor, The Guardian, since 1975; *b* 23 May 1938; *s* of John Whittle Preston and Kathlyn (*née* Chell); *m* 1962, Jean Mary Burrell; two *s* two *d*. *Educ:* Loughborough Grammar Sch.; St John's Coll., Oxford (MA EngLit). Editorial trainee, Liverpool Daily Post, 1960-63; Guardian: Political Reporter, 1963-64; Education Correspondent, 1965-66; Diary Editor, 1966-68; Features Editor, 1968-72; Production Editor, 1972-75. *Recreations:* football, films; four children. *Address:* The Guardian, 119 Farringdon Road, EC1R 3ER.

PRESTON, Sir Peter (Sansome), KCB 1978 (CB 1973); Permanent Secretary, Overseas Development Administration, Foreign and Commonwealth Office (formerly Ministry of Overseas Development), 1976-82; *b* Nottingham, 18 Jan. 1922; *s* of Charles Guy Preston, Solicitor; *m* 1951, Marjory Harrison; two *s* three *d*. *Educ:* Nottingham High School. War Service, RAF, 1942-46; Board of Trade: Exec. Officer, 1947; Higher Exec. Off., 1950; Asst Principal, 1951; Principal, 1953; Trade Comr, New Delhi, 1959; Asst Sec., 1964; idc 1968; Under-Sec., BoT later DTI, 1969-72; Dep. Sec., Dept of Trade, 1972-76. Mem., BOTB, 1975-76. *Address:* 5 Greville Park Avenue, Ashtead, Surrey. *T:* Ashtead 72099.

PRESTON, Prof. Reginald Dawson, FRS 1954; retired; Professor of Plant Biophysics, 1952-73 (now Professor Emeritus), and Head, Astbury Department of Biophysics, 1962-73, University of Leeds; Chairman, School of Biological Sciences, 1970-73; Dean of the Faculty of Science, 1955-58; *b* 21 July 1908; *s* of late Walter C. Preston, builder, and late Eliza Preston; *m* 1935, Sarah J. Pollard (decd); two *d* (one *s* decd); *m* 1963, Dr Eva Frei. *Educ:* Leeds University; Cornell University, USA. BSc (Hons Physics, Class I), 1929; PhD (Botany), 1931; 1851 Exhibition Fellowship, 1932-35; Rockefeller Foundation Fellowship, 1935-36. Lecturer, Botany Dept, Univ. of Leeds, 1936-46; Sen. Lectr, 1946-49; Reader, 1949-53. Vis. Prof. of Botany, Imperial Coll., London, 1976-79. Mem. NY Acad. Sci., 1960. Hon. Mem., Internat. Assoc. of Wood Anatomists, 1981. DSc 1943; FInstP 1944; FLS 1958; FIWSc 1960; FIAWS 1973. Editor: Proc. Leeds Phil. Soc. Sci. Sec., 1950-74; Advances in Botanical Research, 1968-77; Associate Editor, Jl Exp. Bot., 1950-77. *Publications:* Molecular Architecture of Plant Cell Walls, 1952; Physical Biology of Plant Cell Walls, 1974; about 180 articles in Proc. Roy. Soc., Nature, Ann. Bot., Biochem. Biophys Acta, Jl Exp. Bot., etc. *Recreations:* walking, climbing, music. *Address:* 117 St Anne's Road, Leeds, West Yorks LS6 3NZ. *T:* 785248.

PRESTON of Ardchattan, Robert Modan Thorne C.; see Campbell-Preston of Ardchattan.

PRESTON, Sir Ronald (Douglas Hildebrand), 7th Bt *cr* 1815; country landowner and journalist; *b* 9 Oct. 1916; *s* of Sir Thomas Hildebrand Preston, 6th Bt, OBE, and of Ella Henrietta, *d* of F. von Schickendanz; *S* father, 1976; *m* 1st, 1954, Smilya Stefanovic (marr. diss.); 2nd, 1972, Pauleen Jane, *d* of late Paul Lurcott. *Educ:* Westminster School; Trinity Coll., Cambridge (Hons History and Economics, MA); Ecole des Sciences Politiques, Paris. Served War, 1940-46, in Intelligence Corps, reaching rank of Major: Western Desert, Middle East, Italy, Austria, Allied Control Commn, Bulgaria. Reuter's Correspondent, Belgrade, Yugoslavia, 1948-53; The Times Correspondent: Vienna and E Europe, 1953-60; Tokyo and Far East, 1960-63. HM Diplomatic Service, 1963-76; retired, 1976. *Recreations:* shooting, tennis, picture frame making. *Heir: cousin* Philip Charles Henry Hulton Preston, *b* 31 Aug. 1946. *Address:* Beeston Hall, Beeston St Lawrence, Norwich NR12 8YS. *T:* Horning 630771. *Clubs:* Travellers'; Norfolk (Norwich); Tokyo (Tokyo).

PRESTON, Rev. Prof. Ronald Haydn; Professor of Social and Pastoral Theology in the University of Manchester, 1970-80, now Emeritus; *b* 12 March 1913; *o s* of Haydn and Eleanor Jane Preston; *m* 1948, Edith Mary Lindley; one *s* two *d*. *Educ:* London School of Economics, University of London; St Catherine's Society, Oxford. BSc (Econ.) 1935, Cl. II, Div. I; Industrial Secretary of Student Christian Movement, 1935-38; BA Cl. I Theology, 1940; MA 1944; MA Manchester 1974; Curate, St John, Park, Sheffield, 1940-43; Study Secretary, Student Christian Movement, 1943-48; Warden of St Anselm Hall, University of Manchester, 1948-63; Lectr in Christian Ethics, Univ. of Manchester, 1948-70; Examining Chaplain: to Bishop of Manchester, 1948-; to Bishop of Sheffield, 1971-80; Canon

Residentiary of Manchester Cathedral, 1957-71, Sub-Dean 1970-71, Hon. Canon 1971, Canon Emeritus, 1980. Editor, The Student Movement, 1943-48. *Publications:* (jointly) Christians in Society, 1939; (jointly) The Revelation of St John the Divine, 1949; Technology and Social Justice, 1971; (ed) Industrial Conflicts and their Place in Modern Society, 1974; (ed) Perspectives on Strikes, 1975; (ed) Theology and Change, 1975; Religion and the Persistence of Capitalism, 1979; (ed jtly) The Crisis in British Penology, 1980; (ed) Explorations in Theology, No 9, 1981; reviews, etc in The Guardian, Theology, etc. *Address:* 161 Old Hall Lane, Manchester M14 6HJ. *T:* 061-225 3291.

PRESTON, Col Rupert Lionel, CBE 1945; Vice-Chairman, Royal Aero Club, 1970; Secretary-General, Royal Aero Club of the United Kingdom, 1945-63; *b* 1 Nov. 1902; *s* of late Admiral Sir Lionel Preston, KCB; *m* 1st, 1932, Jean Mary (*d* 1976), *d* of late F. B. Pitcairn and of Mrs Pitcairn; 2nd, 1978, Mrs Lona Margit Chambers. *Educ:* Cheltenham College. Coldstream Guards, 1924-45. Assistant Provost Marshal, London, 1938-40; 11 Group RAF Defence Officer, 1940-43; comd RAF Regt 83 Group RAF, 1943-45 (despatches, 1945). Mem. Council Air Registration Boards, 1946-65; Vice-Pres. Fédération Aeronautique Internationale, 1961-64; AFRAeS; Vice-Patron, Guards Flying Club; Hon. Member Soc. of Licensed Aeronautical Engineers. Silver Medal of Royal Aero Club, 1964. Specialist in 17th century Seascape paintings of the Netherlands. *Publication:* 17th Century Seascape: paintings of the Netherlands, 1974. *Address:* 1 St Olaves Court, St Petersburg Place, W2 4JY. *T:* 01-727 9878. *Clubs:* Naval and Military, Cavalry and Guards; Aero Club de France; Wings (New York).

PRESTON, Simon John; Organist and Master of the Choristers, Westminster Abbey, since 1981; *b* 4 Aug. 1938. *Educ:* Canford Sch.; King's Coll., Cambridge (Dr Mann Organ Student). BA 1961, MusB 1962, MA 1964. ARCM, FRAM, Hon. FRCO. Sub Organist, Westminster Abbey, 1962-67; Acting Organist, St Albans Abbey, 1967-68; Organist and Lecturer in Music, Christ Church, Oxford, 1970-81. Conductor, Oxford Bach Choir, 1971-74. Edison Award, 1971; Grand Prix du Disque, 1979. *Recreations:* croquet, squash. *Address:* 8 The Little Cloister, Westminster Abbey, SW1P 3PL. *T:* 01-222 6222. *Club:* Athenæum.

PRESTON, Timothy William; QC 1982; barrister-at-law; a Recorder of the Crown Court, since 1979; *b* 3 Nov. 1935; *s* of Charles Frank Preston, LDS, RCS and Frances Mary, *o d* of Captain W. Peters, 5th Lancers; *m* 1965, Barbara Mary Haygarth. *Educ:* Haileybury; Jesus Coll., Oxford (BA Hons Jurisprudence, 1960). 2/Lieut 16/5 Lancers, 1955; Captain, Staffs Yeomanry, retd. Called to the Bar, Inner Temple, 1964. *Recreations:* hunting, golf. *Address:* 2 Temple Gardens, EC4Y 9AY. *T:* 01-583 6041. *Club:* Cavalry and Guards.

PRESTT, Arthur Miller, QC 1970; JP; **His Honour Judge Prestt;** a Circuit Judge (formerly Judge of County Courts), since 1971; Hon. Recorder of Manchester and Senior Circuit Judge, Manchester, since 1982; *b* 23 April 1925; *s* of Arthur Prestt and Jessie (*née* Miller), Wigan; *m* 1949, Jill Mary, *d* of late Graham Dawbarn, CBE, FRIBA, FRAeS, and of Olive Dawbarn (*née* Topham); one *s* one *d*. *Educ:* Bootham Sch., York; Trinity Hall, Cambridge (MA). Served 13th Bn Parachute Regt, NW Europe and Far East, 1944-46; Major Legal Staff, Singapore, 1946-47, War Crimes Prosecutor. Called to Bar, Middle Temple, 1949. Mental Health Review Tribunal, 1963-70; Dep. Chm., Cumberland QS, 1966-69, Chm., 1970-71. Has held various appts in Scout Assoc. (Silver Acorn, 1970); Pres., Chorley and Dist Scout Council. Pres., SW Lancs Parachute Regt Assoc. JP Cumberland, 1966. 5 years Medal, Ampleforth Lourdes Hospitalite, 1976. *Recreations:* gardening, golf. *Address:* Glebe House, Eccleston, Chorley, Lancs PR7 6LY. *T:* Eccleston (Lancs) 451397. *See also I. Prestt.*

PRESTT, Ian; Director, Royal Society for the Protection of Birds, since 1975; *b* 26 June 1929; *s* of Arthur Prestt and Jessie Prestt (*née* Miller); *m* 1956, Jennifer Ann Wagstaffe; two *d* (one *s* decd). *Educ:* Bootham School, York; Univ. of Liverpool (BSc, MSc). FIBiol. 2nd Lt, RA, 1947-49. Joined staff of Nature Conservancy, 1956; Asst Regional Officer (SW England), 1956-59; Asst to Dir-Gen. and Ornithological Officer (GB, HQ), 1959-61; Dep. Regional Officer (N England), 1961-63; PSO, Monks Wood Experimental Station, 1963-70; Dep. Dir, Central Unit on Environmental Pollution, Cabinet Office and DoE, 1970-74; Dep. Dir, Nature Conservancy Council, 1974-75. Member: Sec. of State's Adv. Cttee on Protection of Birds Acts (Eng. and Wales), 1977-; Council, Wildfowl Trust, 1976-; Chairman: Exec. Cttee, Internat. Council for Bird Preservation, 1982- (Mem., 1979-); Huntingdon Div., CPRE, 1975-. *Publications:* scientific papers in ecol and ornithol jls. *Recreations:* sketching, architecture, reading. *Address:* Stuart House, Huntingdon Road, Wyton, Huntingdon, Cambs PE17 2AD. *T:* St Ives 62760. *Club:* Athenæum. *See also A. M. Prestt.*

PRESTWOOD, Viscount; John Richard Attlee; *b* 3 Oct. 1956; *s* and *heir* of 2nd Earl Attlee, *qv*.

PRETORIA, Bishop of, since 1982; **Rt. Rev. Richard Austin Kraft;** *b* 3 June 1936; *s* of Arthur Austin Kraft and Mary Roberta Hudson Kraft; *m* 1958, Phyllis Marie Schaffer; three *s* one *d*. *Educ:* Ripon Coll., Ripon, Wisconsin, USA (BA); General Theolog. Seminary, New York (MDiv). Deacon then priest, 1961; Asst priest, St Alphege's, Scottsville, dio. Natal, 1961-63; Asst priest and Rector, St Chad's Mission, Klip River, 1963-67; Dir of Christian Education, Diocese of Zululand, 1968-76; Rector, All Saints Parish, Melmoth, 1974-76; Dir of Education Dept, Church of Province of S Africa, 1977-79; Dean and Rector, St Alban's Cathedral, Diocese of Pretoria, 1979-82. Canon, Dio. of Zululand, 1971; Canon Emeritus, 1977. *Recreation:* woodwork. *Address:* Bishop's House, 264 Celliers Street, Muckleneuk, Pretoria, 0002, S Africa. *T:* (home) (012) 443163, (office) (012) 266956.

PRETYMAN, Sir Walter (Frederick), KBE 1972; President, Usina Santa Cruz: *b* 17 Oct. 1901; *s* of Rt Hon. E. G. Pretyman and Lady Beatrice Pretyman; *m* 1st, 1929, Margaret Cunningham (*d* 1942); one *d*; 2nd, 1947, Vera de Sa Sotto Maior; two *s. Educ:* Eton; Magdalen Coll., Oxford. From 1923 onwards, industrial and agricultural activities in Brasil. Served War, with RAFVR, 1943-45; despatches, 1946; retd with rank of Sqdn Ldr. *Recreations:* fishing, shooting. *Address:* 90 Rua Mexico, Rio de Janeiro, Brazil. *T:* 232-8179. *Clubs:* White's; Gavea Golf and Country, Jockey (Rio de Janeiro).

PREVIN, André (George); conductor and composer; *b* Berlin, Germany, 6 April 1929; *s* of Jack Previn and Charlotte Epstein; *m* 1970, Mia Farrow (marr. diss. 1979), *qv*; three *s* (inc. twin *s*), three *d*; *m* 1982, Heather, *d* of Robert Sneddon. *Educ:* Berlin and Paris Conservatoires; private study with Pierre Monteux, Castelnuovo-Tedesco. Composer of film scores, 1950-62 (four Academy Awards). Music Dir, Houston Symphony Orchestra, 1967-69; Principal Conductor, London Symphony Orchestra, 1968-79, Conductor Emeritus, 1979; Music Dir, Pittsburgh Symphony Orchestra, 1976-; Guest Conductor, most major orchestras, US and Europe, Covent Garden Opera, Salzburg Festival, Edinburgh Festival, Osaka Festival; Music Dir, London South Bank Summer Festival, 1972-74. Member: Composers Guild of GB; Amer. Composers League; Dramatists League. Recording artist. Principal compositions: Cello Concerto; Guitar Concerto; Wind Quintet; Serenades for Violin; piano preludes; Symphony for Strings; overtures; Principals, Reflections (for orchestra); Every Good Boy Deserves Favour (text by Tom Stoppard); Six Songs Mezzo-Soprano (text by Philip Larkin). Annual TV series: specials for BBC; PBS (USA). *Publications:* Music Face to Face, 1971; (ed) Orchestra, 1979; *relevant publication:* André Previn, by Edward Greenfield, 1973. *Address:* c/o Harrison/Parrott Ltd, 12 Penzance Place, W11 4PA. *Club:* Garrick.

PREVOST, Captain Sir George James Augustine, 5th Bt, *cr* 1805; *b* 16 Jan. 1910; *s* of Sir Charles Thomas Keble Prevost, 4th Bart, and Beatrice Mary (*d* 1973), *o d* of Rev. J. A. Burrow of Tunstall, Kirkby Lonsdale; *S* father, 1939; *m* 1st, 1935, Muriel Emily (*d* 1939), *d* of late Lewis William Oram; one *s* one *d*; 2nd, 1940, Phyllis Catherine Mattock (from whom he obtained a divorce, 1949); 3rd, 1952, Patricia Betty Porter, Hampenden, Herts; two *s. Educ:* Repton. *Heir:* *s* Christopher Gerald Prevost [*b* 25 July 1935; *m* 1964, Dolores Nelly, *o d* of Dezo Hoffman; one *s* one *d. Address:* St Mary's, Little Petherick, Cornwall.

PREY, Hermann; baritone; *b* Berlin, 11 July 1929; *s* of Hermann Prey; *m* Barbara Pniok; one *s* two *d. Educ:* Humanistisches Gymnasium, Berlig; Staatliche Musikhochschule, Berlin. With State Opera, Wiesbaden, 1952; appearances in Germany, Vienna, (La Scala) Milan, (Metropolitan Opera) New York, Buenos Aires, San Francisco, Covent Garden, etc. Festivals include: Salzburg, Bayreuth, Edinburgh, Vienna, Tokyo, Aix-en-Provence, Perugia, Berlin. *Address:* D-8033 Krailling vor München, Fichtenstrasse 14, Federal Republic of Germany; c/o Lies Askonas, 19a Air Street, Regent Street, W1R 6LQ.

PRICA, Srdja; Member: Council of the Federation of Yugoslavia, since 1972; Council for Foreign Affairs of the Presidency of the Republic of Yugoslavia, since 1971; *b* 20 Sept. 1905; *m* 1956, Vukica Tomanović-Prica. *Educ:* University of Zagreb, Yugoslavia. Newspaperman until 1946; Director of Department, Foreign Office, Belgrade, 1947-49; Asst Min., FO, Belgrade, 1949-51; Ambassador of Yugoslavia, Paris, 1951-55; Under-Sec. of State for Foreign Affairs, Belgrade, 1955-60; Ambassador: to Court of St James's, 1960-65; to Italy, 1967-71; to Malta, 1968-72. Grand Officier, Légion d'Honneur (France); Egyptian, Italian, Norwegian, Austrian and Greek Orders. *Address:* c/o Council of the Federation of Yugoslavia, Belgrade, Yugoslavia.

PRICE, Arnold Justin, QC 1976; a Recorder of the Crown Court, since 1972; Adjudicator, Immigration Appeals, since 1970; *b* 16 Aug. 1919; *s* of late Sydney Walter Price, LLB, Solicitor, and Sophia Price (*née* Marks); *m* 1948, Ruth Corinne, *d* of Ralph and Dorothy Marks; four *d. Educ:* St Christopher's Sch., Liverpool; Kingsmead Sch., Meols; Liverpool Coll.; Liverpool Univ. Bd of Legal Studies. Served War, Royal Engrs, 42nd Inf. Div. TA (invalided), later 2nd Lieut Royal Corps Mil. Police, 42nd Inf. Div. TA. Called to Bar, Middle Temple, 1952; practised Wales and Chester Circuit; Resident Magistrate, Nyasaland, 1955; Magistrate, N Nigeria, 1957; Actg Chief Magistrate and Judge, High Court N Nigeria, 1957-60; returned to practice, Wales and Chester Circuit, 1960; Northern Circuit, 1969. CC Chester, 1963-68. *Publications:* articles on politics, agriculture and legal subjects. *Recreations:* sailing, fishing, the countryside, beekeeping. *Address:* Thicket Ford, Thornton Hough, Wirral. *T:* 051-336 4444; 16 Queen Avenue, Castle Street, Liverpool. *T:* 051-236 5072; 2 Pump Court, Temple, EC4. *T:* 01-353 3106. *Club:* Athenæum (Liverpool).

PRICE, (Arthur) Leolin, QC 1968; *b* 11 May 1924; 3rd *s* of late Evan Price and Ceridwen Price (*née* Price), Hawkhurst, Kent; *m* 1963, Hon. Rosalind Helen Penrose Lewis, *er d* of 1st Baron Brecon, PC, and of Mabel, Baroness Brecon, CBE, JP; two *s* two *d. Educ:* Judd Sch., Tonbridge; Keble Coll., Oxford (Schol.; MA). War service, 1943-46 with Army: Capt., RA; Adjt, Indian Mountain Artillery Trng Centre and Depot, Ambala, Punjab, 1946. Treas., Oxford Union, 1948; Pres., Oxford Univ. Conserv. Assoc., 1948. Tutor (part-time), Keble Coll., Oxford, 1951-59. Called to Bar, Middle Temple, 1949; Bencher, 1970-; Barrister of Lincoln's Inn, 1959. QC Bahamas, 1969. Member: Editorial Cttee, Modern Law Review, 1954-65; Bar Council Law Reform Cttee, 1969-75; Cttee, Soc. of Cons. Lawyers, 1971-; Cttee of Management, Inst. of Child Health, 1972- (Chm., 1976-). Director: Child Health Res. Investment Trust Co. plc, 1980-; Marine Adventure Sailing Trust plc, 1981-. Governor, Gt Ormond St Hosp. for Sick Children, 1972-; Mem., Falkland Islands Cttee, 1972-. Governor, Christ Coll., Brecon, 1977-. Chancellor, Diocese of Swansea and Brecon, 1982-. *Publications:* articles and notes in legal jls. *Address:* 32 Hampstead Grove, NW3 6SR. *T:* 01-435 9843; 10 Old Square, Lincoln's Inn, WC2A 3SU. *T:* 01-405 0758; Moor Park, Llanbedr, near Crickhowell, Powys NP8 1SS. *T:* Crickhowell 810443. *Club:* Carlton.

See also V. W. C. Price.

PRICE, (Benjamin) Terence; Secretary-General, Uranium Institute, since 1974; *b* 7 January 1921; *er s* of Benjamin and Nellie Price; *m* 1947, Jean Stella Vidal; one *s* one *d. Educ:* Crypt School, Gloucester; Queens' College, Cambridge (Scholar). Naval electronics res., 1942-46; Atomic Energy Research Establishment, Harwell (Nuclear Physics Division), 1947-59; Head of Reactor Development Division, Atomic Energy Estabt, Winfrith, 1959; Chief Scientific Officer, Ministry of Defence, 1960-63; Assistant Chief Scientific Adviser (Studies), Ministry of Defence, 1963-65; Director, Defence Operational Analysis Establishment, MoD, 1965-68; Chief Scientific Adviser, Min. of Transport, 1968-71; Dir of Planning and Development, Vickers Ltd, 1971-73. Chm., NEDO Mechanical Handling Sector Working Party, 1976-80. *Publication:* Radiation Shielding, 1957. *Recreations:* flying, ski-ing, making music. *Address:* Seers Bough, Wilton Lane, Jordans, Buckinghamshire. *T:* Chalfont St Giles 4589. *Club:* Athenæum.

PRICE, Rear-Adm. Cecil Ernest, CB 1978; AFC 1953; Deputy Assistant Chief of Staff (Operations), SHAPE, 1976-80, retired; *b* 29 Oct. 1921; *s* of Ernest C. Price and Phyllis M. Price; *m* 1946, Megan Morgan; one *s* one *d. Educ:* Bungay Grammar Sch. Joined Royal Navy, 1941; served as Pilot in several aircraft carriers, 1942-46; completed Empire Test Pilot School, and Test Flying, Boscombe Down, 1948-52; CO 813 Sqdn, 1953-54; Comdr 1956; CO Naval Test Sqdn, Boscombe Down, 1956-58; British Navy Staff, Washington, 1959-61; Captain 1966; idc 1970; Director: Naval Air Warfare, 1971-72; Naval Operational Requirements, 1972-73; CO RNAS, Culdrose, 1973-75; Rear-Adm. 1976. *Recreations:* golf, fishing, gardening. *Address:* Low Farm, Mendham, Harleston, Norfolk. *T:* Harleston 852676.

PRICE, Maj.-Gen. Cedric Rhys, CB 1951; CBE 1945 (OBE 1943); Principal Staff Officer to Secretary of State for Commonwealth Relations, 1959-64; ADC to the Queen, 1954-57; *b* 13 June 1905; *o s* of late Colonel Sir Rhys H. Price, KBE, CMG, Highlands, Purley Downs; *m* 1935, Rosamund, *e d* of late Arthur W. Clifford, Dursley, Glos; two *d. Educ:* Wellington College; RMA Woolwich; Trinity College, Cambridge. Commissioned Royal Engineers, 1925; served in India, 1932-38; Staff College, 1938-39; Military Assistant Secretary, offices of War Cabinet, 1940-46; Secretary, British Joint Services Mission, Washington, USA, 1946-48; Secretary, Chiefs of Staff Cttee, Ministry of Defence, 1948-50; student, Imperial Defence College, SW1, 1951; Chief of Staff to Chairman of British Joint Services Mission, Washington, 1952-54; Brigadier, General Staff, Eastern Command, 1955-56; Director of Military Intelligence, War Office, 1956-59. *Recreations:* golf, tennis, riding. *Address:* Furze Field Cottage, Hoe Lane, Peaslake, Guildford, Surrey. *T:* Dorking 730586. *Club:* Army and Navy.

PRICE, Sir Charles (Keith Napier) Rugge-, 9th Bt *cr* 1804; Supervisor Compensation, City of Edmonton; *b* 7 August, 1936; *s* of Lt-Col Sir James James Napier Rugge-Price, 8th Bt, and of Lady (Maeve Marguerite) Rugge-Price (*née* de la Pena); *S* father, 1966; *m* 1965, Jacqueline Mary (*née* Loranger); two *s. Educ:* Middleton College, Eire. 5th Regt Royal Horse Artillery, Germany and Wales, 1954-59. Actuarial Dept, William Mercers Ltd, Canada, 1959-60; Alexander and Alexander Services Ltd, Montreal, Canada, 1960-67; with Domtar Ltd, 1968-71; Manager, Tomenson Alexander Ltd, Toronto, 1971-76. *Heir:* *s* James Keith Peter Rugge-Price, *b* 8 April 1967. *Address:* 23 Lambert Crescent, St Albert, Alberta T8N 1M1, Canada.

PRICE, Christopher; MP (Lab) Lewisham West, since Feb. 1974; *b* 26 Jan. 1932; *s* of Stanley Price; *m* 1956, Annie Grierson Ross; two *s* one *d. Educ:* Leeds Grammar School; Queen's College, Oxford. Sec., Oxford Univ. Labour Club, 1953; Chm., Nat. Assoc. of Labour Student Organisations, 1955-56. Sheffield City Councillor, 1962-66; Dep. Chm., Sheffield Educn Cttee, 1963-66. MP (Lab) Perry Barr Division of Birmingham, 1966-70; PPS to Secretary of State for Education and Science, 1966-67 and 1975-76; Chm., H of C Select Cttee on Educn, Science and the Arts, 1980-. Mem., European Parlt, 1977-78. Chm., Council, Nat. Youth Bureau, 1977-80. Editor, New Education, 1967-68; Educn corresp., New Statesman, 1969-74. *Publications:* (Contrib.) A Radical Future, 1967; Crisis in the Classroom, 1968; (ed) Your

Child and School, 1968; Which Way?, 1969. *Address:* House of Commons, SW1. *T:* 01-219 3437; 30 Horniman Drive, SE23 3BP. *T:* 01-699 2335.

PRICE, Maj.-Gen. David; *see* Price, Maj.-Gen. M. D.

PRICE, Sir David (Ernest Campbell), Kt 1980; DL; MP (C) Eastleigh Division of Hampshire, since 1955; *b* 20 Nov. 1924; *o s* of Major Villiers Price; *m* 1960, Rosemary Eugénie Evelyn, *o d* of late Cyril F. Johnston, OBE; one *d. Educ:* Eton; Trinity College, Cambridge; Yale University, USA; Rosebery Schol., Eton; Open History Schol., Trinity College, Cambridge. Served with 1st Battalion Scots Guards, CMF; subsequently Staff Captain (Intelligence) HQ, 56 London Div., Trieste, 1942-46. Trin. Coll., Cambridge, BA Hons, MA. Pres. Cambridge Union; Vice-Pres. Fedn of Univ. Conservative and Unionist Assocs, 1946-48; Henry Fellow of Yale Univ., USA, 1948-49. Industrial Consultant. Held various appts in Imperial Chemical Industries Ltd, 1949-62. Parly Sec., Board of Trade, 1962-64; Opposition Front-Bench spokesman on Science and Technology, 1964-70; Parly Sec., Min. of Technology, June-Oct. 1970; Parly Sec., Min. of Aviation Supply, 1970-71; Parly Under-Sec. of State, Aerospace, DTI, 1971-72. Member: Public Accounts Cttee, 1974-75; Select Cttee on Transport, 1979-; Vice-Pres., Parly and Scientific Cttee, 1975-79 and 1982- (Vice-Chm., 1965-70, Chm., 1973-75 and 1979-82). Vice-Chairman: Cons. Arts and Heritage Cttee, 1979-81; Cons. Shipping and Ship-Building Cttee, 1979-. British Representative to Consultative Assembly of the Council of Europe, 1958-61. Director: Assoc. British Maltsters, 1966-70; T. W. Downs Ltd, 1973-; Aberdeen Cold Storage Co. Ltd, 1977-; Linear Shipping Agencies Ltd. Gen. Cons. to IIM (formerly IWM), 1973-; Cons. to Union International Ltd. Vice-Pres., IIM, 1980-. Governor, Middlesex Hospital, 1956-60. DL Hants, 1982. *Recreations:* swimming, arts and heritage, history, science, wine, cooking. *Address:* 36 Sloane Court West, SW3. *T:* 01-730 3326; Flat 2, Lepe House, Exbury, Southampton. *Club:* Beefsteak.

PRICE, David William T.; *see* Tudor Price.

PRICE, Eric Hardiman Mockford; Under Secretary, Head of Economics and Statistics Division, Department of Energy, since 1980; *b* 14 Nov. 1931; *s* of Frederick Hardiman Price and Florence Nellie Hannah Price (*née* Mockford); *m* 1963, Diana Teresa Mary Stanley Robinson; one *s* three *d. Educ:* St Marylebone Grammar Sch.; Christ's Coll., Cambridge. Econs Tripos, 1955; MA 1958. FREconS, 1956; FSS 1958. Army service, 1950-52. Supply Dept, Esso Petroleum Co. Ltd, 1955-56; Economist: Central Electricity Authority, 1956-57; Electricity Council, 1957-58; British Iron & Steel Fedn, 1958-62; Chief Economist, Port of London Authority, 1962-67; Sen. Econ. Adviser, Min. of Transport, 1966-69; Chief Econ. Adviser, Min. of Transport, 1969-71; Dir of Econs, 1971-75, Under Sec., 1972-76, Dir of Econs and Stats, 1975-76, DoE; Under Sec., Econs and Stats Div., Depts of Industry, Trade and Consumer Protection, 1977-80. Member: Soc. of Business Economists, 1961; Northern Regional Strategy Steering Gp, 1976-77; Long Range Forecasting Soc., 1980-; Vice-Chm., British Inst. of Energy Economics, 1981- (Mem., 1980-). *Publications:* various articles in learned jls on transport economics, investment, public sector industries, technological innovation in industry and regional planning. *Recreations:* tennis, squash, history, racehorse breeding. *Address:* Ranelagh, 50 Russell Road, Moor Park, Northwood, Mddx. *Club:* Moor Park Golf.

PRICE, Sir Francis (Caradoc Rose), 7th Bt *cr* 1815; barrister and solicitor; *b* 9 Sept. 1950; *s* of Sir Rose Francis Price, 6th Bt and of Kathleen June, *d* of late Norman W. Hutchinson, Melbourne; *S* father, 1979; *m* 1975, Marguerite Jean, *d* of Roy S. Trussler, Cobble Hill, BC; three *d. Educ:* Eton; Trinity College, Melbourne Univ. (Sen. Student 1971, LLB Hons 1973); Univ. of Alberta (LLM 1975); Canadian Petroleum Law Foundn Fellow, 1974-75. Admitted Province of Alberta 1976, Northwest Territories 1978, Canada. Lectr, Alberta Bar Admission Course, 1979-. *Publications:* Pipelines in Western Canada, 1975; contribs to Alberta and Melbourne Univ. Law Revs, etc. *Recreations:* cricket, skiing, squash, running, theatre. *Heir: b* Norman William Rose Price, *b* 17 March 1953. *Address:* 9677 95th Avenue, Edmonton, Alberta, Canada T6C 2A3. *Clubs:* Royal Glenora, Faculty (Edmonton).

PRICE, Sir Frank (Leslie), Kt 1966; DL; Senior Partner, Comprehensive Development Associates, since 1968; Chairman: British Waterways Board, since 1968; Eurotech (International) Ltd, since 1980; Director, Lometa Industries Ltd; *b* 26 July 1922; *s* of G. F. Price; marr. diss.; one *s* ; married again. *Educ:* St Matthias Church Sch., Birmingham; Vittoria Street Arts Sch. Elected to Birmingham City Council, 1949; Alderman, 1958-74; Lord Mayor, 1964-65. Member: Council, Town and Country Planning Assoc., 1958-; W Midlands Economic Planning Council, 1965-72; Nat. Water Council, 1975-79. Founder/Chm., Midlands Art Centre for Young People, 1960-71; Chairman: W Midlands Sports Council, 1965-69; Telford Development Corporation, 1968-71. Member: Minister of Transport's Cttee of Inquiry into Major Ports, 1961; English Tourist Board, 1976-; Pres., BAIE, 1979-. Livery Co. of Basketmakers. FSVA; FCIT. FRSA. DL Herefordshire and Worcestershire, and County of West Midlands, 1977. Freeman, City of London. *Publications:* various pamphlets and articles on planning and transport, etc. *Recreations:* painting, inland cruising. *Address:* Trafalgar House, Paradise Circus, Queensway, Birmingham B1 2BJ. *Club:* Reform.

PRICE, Geoffrey Alan, IPFA, FBIM; County Treasurer, Hampshire County Council, since 1977 (formerly Deputy County Treasurer). Formerly held appts in: Southend-on-Sea County Borough Council; Cheshire CC; Glos CC; West Sussex CC. Finance Adviser: Finance and Educn Cttees, ACC. *Address:* The Castle, Winchester SO23 8UB. *T:* Winchester 54411.

PRICE, Rt. Hon. George (Cadle), PC 1982; Prime Minister of Belize, since 1981 (Premier from 1964 until Independence, 1981); *b* 15 Jan. 1919; *s* of William Cadle Price and Irene Cecilia Escalante de Price. *Educ:* Holy Redeemer Primary Sch., Belize City; St John's Coll., Belize City. Private Sec. to late Robert S. Turton; entered politics, 1944; City Councillor, 1947-65 (Mayor of Belize City several times); founding Mem., People's United Party, 1950; Party Sec., 1950-56, Leader, 1956-; elected to National Assembly, 1954; under 1961 Ministerial System, led People's United Party to 100% victory at polls and became First Minister; under 1964 Self-Govt Constitution, title changed to Premier; has led delegns to Central American and Caribbean countries; spearheaded internationalization of Belize problem at internat. forums; addressed UN's Fourth Cttee, 1975, paving way for overwhelming victory at UN when majority of nations voted in favour of Belize's right to self-determination and territorial integrity. *Address:* Office of the Prime Minister, Belmopan, Belize.

PRICE, Prof. Harold Louis; Professor of Mathematics for Applied Science, University of Leeds, since 1968; *b* 3 Sept. 1917; *s* of Reuben Price and Annie Boltsa; *m* 1941, Gertrude Halpern; two *d. Educ:* Manchester Grammar Sch.; Sidney Sussex Coll., Cambridge; Univ. of Leeds. MA Cantab; MSc (distinction), PhD Leeds; FRAeS; FIMA. Mathematician, Rotol Airscrews Ltd, 1939-40; Aerodynamicist, Blackburn Aircraft, 1940-45; Research Mathematician, Sperry Gyroscope Co., 1945-46; Univ. of Leeds: Lectr in Applied Maths, 1946-60; Sen. Lectr, 1960-64; Prof. of Maths, 1964-68; Chm., Sch. of Mathematics, 1970-73. *Publications:* research papers on aircraft dynamics, etc. *Address:* 11 West Park Place, Leeds LS8 2EY. *T:* Leeds 664212.

PRICE, Henry Alfred, CBE 1962; Managing Director, Grove Paper Co. Ltd; *b* 3 January 1911; *s* of James Wm and Louisa Rebecca Price; *m* 1938, Ivy May Trimmer; one *s* one *d. Educ:* Holloway County School. Joined paper trade, 1927. Member LCC, 1946-52; MP (C) West Lewisham, 1950-64. *Recreations:* music and sport. *Address:* 22 Cator Road, Sydenham, SE26. *T:* 01-778 3838.

PRICE, Henry Habberley, FBA 1943; MA, BSc; Professor Emeritus, University of Oxford, and Honorary Fellow of New College; *b* 1899; *s* of H. H. Price; unmarried. *Educ:* Winchester College; New College, Oxford (Scholar). Served in Royal Air Force, 1917-19; 1st Class in Lit. Hum. 1921; Fellow of Magdalen College, 1922-24; Assistant lecturer at Liverpool University, 1922-23; Fellow and Lecturer in Philosophy at Trin. Coll., 1924-35; Univ. Lectr in Philosophy, 1932-35; Wykeham Prof. of Logic, and Fell. New Coll., 1935-59. Pres. of Soc. for Psychical Research, 1939-40 and 1960-61. Visiting Professor at Princeton University, USA, 1948; Gifford Lecturer, Aberdeen University, 1959-60; Flint Visiting Prof., Univ. of California, Los Angeles, 1962; Boutwood Lecturer, Cambridge, 1965; Sarum Lectr, Oxford, 1970-71. Hon. DLitt, Dublin, 1953; Hon. LLD, St Andrews, 1954; Hon DLitt, Univ. of Wales, 1964. *Publications:* Perception, 1932, repr. 1973; Hume's Theory of the External World, 1940; Thinking and Experience, 1953; Belief (Gifford Lectures), 1969; Essays in the Philosophy of Religion, 1972; articles in Proc. Aristotelian Society and other philosophical periodicals. *Recreations:* aviation, painting and ornithology. Founder-member of Oxford University and City Gliding Club. *Address:* 69 Jack Straw's Lane, Oxford. *T:* Oxford 68945.

PRICE, Captain Henry Ryan; racehorse trainer, since 1937; *b* 16 Aug. 1912; *m* 1946, Dorothy Audrey Dale; two *s* one *d. Educ:* Served War of 1939-45, 6th Commandos (N Staffs) (MC). Big races won include: Grand National, Champion Hurdle, Schweppes Gold Trophy (four times), Oaks Stakes, St Leger Stakes. *Recreations:* shooting, fishing, work. *Address:* Soldiers Field, Findon, Sussex BN14 0SH. *T:* Findon 2388.

PRICE, Very Rev. Hilary Martin Connop; Rector and Provost of Chelmsford, 1967-77, now Provost Emeritus; *b* 1912; *s* of late Rev. Connop Lewis Price and late Shirley (*née* Lewis); *m* 1939, Dorothea (*née* Beaty-Pownall); one *s* two *d. Educ:* Cheltenham Coll.; Queens' Coll., Cambridge (MA); Ridley Hall, Cambridge. Asst Curate, St Peter's, Hersham, Surrey, 1936-40; Sen. Chaplain, Portsmouth Cathedral, 1940-41; Asst Curate, Holy Trinity, Cambridge, 1941-46; Chaplain, RAFVR, 1943-46; Vicar, St Gabriel's, Bishopwearmouth, 1946-56; Rector and Rural Dean, Newcastle-under-Lyme, 1956-67. Prebendary of Lichfield, 1964-67. Proctor in Convocation: of York for Durham Dio., 1954-56; of Canterbury for Lichfield Dio., 1962-67. Mem., General Synod, 1970-75. *Address:* 98 St James Street, Shaftesbury, Dorset SP7 8HF. *T:* Shaftesbury 2118.

PRICE, Comdr Hugh Perceval, DSO 1940; OBE 1945; RN retired; Hydrographic Surveyor; *b* 19 May 1901; *s* of late Lt-Col Ivon Henry Price, DSO, LLD, Asst Insp.-Gen., Royal Irish Constabulary, and May Emily Kinahan; *m* 1925, Annie Grant Berry; one *s* one *d. Educ:* Monkstown Park School, Co. Dublin; Chesterfield School, Birr; RN Colleges, Osborne and Dartmouth. Entered RNC Osborne, 1915; HMS King George V, 1917; joined Surveying Service in 1925; employed on escort work and Hydrographic duties during war of 1939–45; retired list, 1946. *Recreation:* fishing. *Address:* 55 Tudor Avenue, Worcester Park, Surrey. *T:* 01-337 8966.

PRICE, Sir (James) Robert, KBE 1976; FAA 1959; Chairman of the Executive, Commonwealth Scientific and Industrial Research Organization, 1970–77; *b* 25 March 1912; *s* of Edgar James Price and Mary Katherine Price (*née* Hughes); *m* 1940, Joyce Ethel (*née* Brooke); one *s* two *d. Educ:* St Peter's Coll., Adelaide; Univ. of Adelaide (BSc Hons, MSc, DSc); Univ. of Oxford (DPhil). Head, Chemistry Section, John Innes Horticultural Inst., London, 1937–40; (UK) Min. of Supply, 1941–45; Div. of Industrial Chemistry, Council for Scientific and Industrial Research (CSIR), Australia, from 1945; CSIRO: Officer-in-Charge, Organic Chem. Section, 1960, subseq. Chief of Div. of Organic Chem.; Mem., Executive, 1966. Pres., Royal Aust. Chemical Inst., 1963–64. *Publications:* numerous scientific papers in learned jls. *Recreations:* squash; growing Australian native plants. *Address:* Yangoora, 2 Ocean View Avenue, Red Hill South, Victoria 3936, Australia. *Club:* Melbourne (Melb.).

PRICE, John Alan, QC 1980; a Recorder of the Crown Court, since 1980; a Deputy Circuit Judge, since 1975; *b* 11 Sept. 1938; *s* of Frederick Leslie Price and Gertrude Davilda Alice Price; *m* 1964, Elizabeth Myra (*née* Priest); one *s* one *d. Educ:* Stretford Grammar Sch.; Manchester Univ. (LLB Hons 1959). Called to the Bar, Gray's Inn, 1961; in practice on Northern Circuit; Head of 60 King St Chambers, Manchester, 1978–80. *Recreations:* tennis, squash, football, golf. *Address:* (home) 15 Carrwood Road, Wilmslow, Cheshire. *T:* Wilmslow 523532; (chambers) 25 Byrom House, Quay Street, Manchester. *T:* 061-834 5238; 5 Essex Court, Temple, EC4Y 9AH. *Clubs:* Northern Lawn Tennis; Wilmslow Golf; Wilmslow Rugby Union Football.

PRICE, John Lister Willis, CVO 1965; HM Diplomatic Service, retired; *b* 25 July 1915; *s* of Canon John Willis Price, Croughton, Brackley, Northants; *m* 1940, Frances Holland (marr. diss.); one *s* one *d. Educ:* Bradfield; New College, Oxford. Military Service, 1940–46 (despatches). Joined Foreign Office News Dept, 1946; apptd First Secretary, Paris, 1950; transf. to FO, 1952; to Sofia, 1956; to FO, 1959; Counsellor, Head of British Information Services, Bonn, 1962–66; IDC 1967; seconded as Dir of Information, NATO, 1967–72; retired 1972. Dir, Merseyside Develt Office in London (subseq. Merseyside CC's London Office), 1972–79. *Recreations:* ski-ing, hill walking. *Address:* 21 Sheffield Terrace, W8. *Club:* Ski Club of Great Britain.

PRICE, J(ohn) Maurice, QC 1976; *b* 4 May 1922; second *s* of Edward Samuel Price and Hilda M. Price, JP; *m* 1945, Mary, *d* of Dr Horace Gibson, DSO and bar, Perth, WA; two *s. Educ:* Grove Park Sch., Wrexham; Trinity Coll., Cambridge (MA). Served in Royal Navy, 1941–46 (Submarines, 1943–46), Lieut RNVR. Called to Bar, Gray's Inn, 1949 (Holt Schol., Holker Sen. Scholar; Bencher 1981), and to Lincoln's Inn (*ad eundem*), 1980. Mem., Senate of Inns of Court and the Bar, 1975–78. *Recreations:* fishing, opera. *Address:* Bowzell Place, Weald, Sevenoaks, Kent TN14 6NF; (chambers) 2 New Square, Lincoln's Inn, WC2A 3RU. *T:* 01-242 6201. *Club:* Flyfishers'.

PRICE, John Playfair; *b* 4 July 1905; *s* of William Arthur Price and Edith Octavia Playfair; *m* 1932, Alice Elizabeth Kendall, Boston, Mass; two *d. Educ:* Gresham School; New College, Oxford. Hon. Exhib., New Coll., Oxford; Pres. Oxford Union Society. Diplomatic and Consular posts at Peking, Nanking, Tientsin, Canton, Chinkiang, Harbin (Manchuria), Katmandu (Nepal), Gangtok (Sikkim), Los Angeles, Kansas City, Tunis, Tangier, Lisbon, Santiago (Chile), and Geneva. Additional Judge, China, 1933–37; Foreign Office, 1938; 1st Secretary of Embassy, 1943; Consul-General for Khorasan, Sistan and Persian Baluchistan, 1948; retired from Diplomatic Service, 1950. Civil Service and Foreign Service Selection and Final Selection Boards, 1950; Dir and Chm. of Exec., Central African Rhodes Centenary Exhibition, 1951–52; British Council, 1959–61. *Address:* 3 rue Pasteur, 74200 Thonon, France. *T:* (50) 71.83.96.

PRICE, Air Vice-Marshal John Walter, CBE 1979 (OBE 1973); Assistant Chief of the Air Staff (Operations), since 1982; *b* Birmingham, 26 Jan. 1930; *s* of Henry Walter Price and Myrza Price (*née* Griffiths); *m* 1956, Margaret Sinclair McIntyre, Sydney, Aust. *Educ:* Solihull Sch.; RAF Coll., Cranwell. MRAeS 1971, FBIM 1979. Joined RAF, 1948; Adjutant, No 11 (Vampire) Sqn, 1950–52; No 77 (Meteor) Sqn, RAAF, Korea, 1952–53 (mentioned in despatches, 1953); No 98 Sqn (Venoms and Vampires), 1953–54; No 2 (F) Op. Trng Unit (Vampires) and No 75 (F) Sqn (Meteors), RAAF, 1954–56; Cadet Wing Adjutant, RAF Tech. Coll., Henlow, 1956–60; RAF Staff Coll., 1960; Air Ministry (Ops Overseas), 1961–64; Comd No 110 Sqn (Sycamore and Whirlwind), 1964–66; Directing Staff, RAF Staff Coll., 1966–68; PSO to Chief of Air Staff, 1968–70; Comd No 72 (Wessex) Sqn, 1970–72; Air Warfare Course, 1973; Dep. Dir Ops (Offensive Support and Jt Warfare), MoD (Air), 1973–75; sowc 1975–76; Comd RAF Laarbruch, 1976–78; Gp Capt. Ops, HQ Strike Comd, 1979; Dir of Ops (Strike), MoD (Air), 1980–82. Governor, Solihull Sch., 1979–. *Recreations:* golf, cabinet making. *Address:* c/o Williams & Glyn's Bank, Holt's Branch, 22 Whitehall, SW1.

PRICE, Leolin; see Price, A. L.

PRICE, Leonard Sidney, OBE 1974; HM Diplomatic Service, retired 1981; Association Deputy Director, St John Ambulance in Somerset, since 1982; *b* 19 Oct. 1922; *s* of late William Price and late Dorothy Price; *m* 1958,

Adrienne Mary (*née* Wilkinson); two *s* one *d. Educ:* Central Foundation Sch., EC1. Served War, 1942–45. Foreign Office, 1939–42 and 1945–48; Chungking, later Vice-Consul, 1948; Mexico City, 1950; Rome, 1953; Vice-Consul, later Second Sec., Katmandu, 1954; FO, 1957; Consul, Split, 1960; Consul and First Sec., Copenhagen, 1963; FO, later FCO, 1967; First Sec. i/c, Kuching, 1970; Suva, 1972; Parly Clerk, FCO, 1975; Counsellor (Admin), Canberra, 1977–81. *Recreations:* carpentry, wine making. *Address:* 5 Staplegrove Manor, Taunton, Somerset TA2 6EG. *T:* Taunton 87093. *Club:* Civil Service.

PRICE, Leontyne; Opera Prima Donna (Soprano), United States. *Educ:* Public Schools, Laurel, Mississippi; Central State College, Wilberforce, Ohio. Four Saints, 1952; Porgy and Bess, 1952–54. Operatic Debut on TV, 1955, as Tosca; Concerts in America, England, Australia, Europe. Operatic debut as Madame Lidouine in Dialogues of Carmelites, San Francisco, 1957; Covent Garden, Verona Arena, Vienna Staatsoper, 1958; five roles, inc. Leonora in Il Trovatore, Madame Butterfly, Donna Anna in Don Giovanni, Metropolitan, 1960–61; Salzburg debut singing soprano lead in Missa Solemnis, 1959; Aida in Aida, Liu in Turandot, La Scala, 1960; opened season at Metropolitan in 1961 as Minnie in Fanciulla del West; opened new Metropolitan Opera House, 1966, as Cleopatra in world premiere of Samuel Barber's Antony and Cleopatra; debut Teatre Dell'Opera, Rome, in Aida, 1967; debut Paris Opera, in Aida, 1968; debut Teatro Colon, Buenos Aires, as Leonora in Il Trovatore, 1969; opened season at Metropolitan Opera, in Aida, 1969. Numerous recordings. Fellow, Amer. Acad. of Arts and Sciences. Hon. Dr of Music: Howard Univ., Washington, DC, 1962; Central State Coll., Wilberforce, Ohio, 1968; Hon. DHL, Dartmouth Univ., 1962; Hon. Dr of Humanities, Rust Coll., Holly Springs, Miss, 1968; Hon. Dr of Humane Letters, Fordham Univ., New York, 1969. Hon. Mem. Bd of Dirs, Campfire Girls, 1966. Presidential Medal of Freedom, 1966; Spingarn Medal, NAACP, 1965. Order of Merit (Italy), 1966. *Recreations:* cooking, dancing, shopping for clothes, etc, antiques for homes in Rome and New York. *Address:* c/o Columbia Artists Management Inc., 165 W 57th Street, New York, NY 10019, USA.

PRICE, Sir Leslie Victor, Kt 1976; OBE 1971; Chairman, Australian Wheat Board, since 1977 (Member since 1971); *b* Toowoomba, Qld, 30 Oct. 1920; *s* of late H. V. L. Price; *m* Lorna Collins; one *s* two *d. Educ:* Queensland Graingrowers Assoc., 1966–77; Australian Wheatgrowers Fedn, 1970–72; Mem., Queensland State Wheat Bd, 1968–77. *Recreation:* clay target shooting. *Address:* 80 Studley Park Road, Kew, Victoria 3101, Australia. *Clubs:* Queensland; Melbourne.

PRICE, (Llewelyn) Ralph, CBE 1972; Director, Honeywell, since 1971 (Chairman, 1971–81); Chairman, ML Holdings Ltd, since 1976; *b* 23 Oct. 1912; *s* of late L. D. Price, schoolmaster, and late Lena Elizabeth (*née* Dixon); *m* 1939, Vera Patricia Harrison; one *s* two *d. Educ:* Quarry Bank Sch., Liverpool. Chartered Accountant, 1935; Sec. to Honeywell Ltd, 1936; Cost Investigator, Min. of Supply, 1943–46; Dir of Manufacturing (Scotland), Honeywell Ltd, 1947; Financial Dir, Honeywell Europe, 1957; Dir, Computer Div., Honeywell, 1960; Managing Dir, Honeywell Ltd, 1965; Chm., Honeywell UK Adv. Council, 1981–. Pres., British Industrial, Measuring & Control Apparatus Manufrs Assoc., 1971–76. CBIM. *Recreations:* golf, bridge, music. *Address:* Nascot, Pinkneys Drive, Pinkneys Green, Maidenhead, Berks. *T:* Maidenhead 28270. *Clubs:* Royal Automobile; Temple Golf (Maidenhead).

PRICE, Margaret Berenice, CBE 1982; opera singer; *b* Tredegar, Wales, 13 April 1941; *d* of late Thomas Glyn Price and of Lilian Myfanwy Richards. *Educ:* Pontllanfraith Secondary Sch.; Trinity Coll. of Music, London. Debut as Cherubino in Marriage of Figaro, Welsh Nat. Opera Co., 1962; debut, in same rôle, at Royal Opera House, Covent Garden, 1963; has subseq. sung many principal rôles at Glyndebourne, San Francisco Opera Co., Cologne Opera House, Munich State Opera, Hamburg State Opera, Vienna State Opera, Lyric Opera, Chicago, Paris Opera; La Scala, Milan; Metropolitan Opera House, NY. Major rôles include: Countess in Marriage of Figaro; Pamina in The Magic Flute; Fiordiligi in Cosi Fan Tutte; Donna Anna in Don Giovanni; Konstanze in Die Entführung; Amelia in Simone Boccanegra; Agathe in Freischütz; Desdemona in Otello; Elisabetta in Don Carlo; title rôles in Aida and Norma. BBC recitals and concerts, also TV appearances. Has made recordings. Hon. FTCL. Elisabeth Schumann Prize for Lieder; Ricordi Prize for Opera; Silver Medal, Worshipful Co. of Musicians. *Recreations:* cooking, driving, reading, walking, swimming. *Address:* c/o Harrison/Parrott Ltd, 12 Penzance Place, W11 4PA.

PRICE, Maj.-Gen. (Maurice) David, CB 1970; OBE 1956; *b* 13 Feb. 1915; *s* of Edward Allan Price and Edna Marion Price (*née* Turner); *m* 1st, 1938, Ella Lacy (*d* 1971), *d* of late H. L. Day; two *s* two *d* ; 2nd, 1972, Mrs Olga Marion Oclee. *Educ:* Marlborough; RMA, Woolwich. 2nd Lt R Signals, 1935; Vice-Quartermaster-Gen., MoD (Army), 1967–70, retired. Col Comdt, Royal Corps of Signals, 1967–74. *Recreation:* fishing. *Address:* The Cross, Chilmark, Salisbury, Wiltshire. *T:* Teffont 212. *Club:* Army and Navy.

PRICE, Sir Norman (Charles), KCB 1975 (CB 1969); Member, European Court of Auditors, since 1977; Chairman, Board of Inland Revenue, 1973–76 (Deputy Chairman, 1968–73); *b* 5 Jan. 1915; *s* of Charles William and Ethel Mary Price; *m* 1940, Kathleen Beatrice (*née* Elston); two *d. Educ:* Plaistow Grammar School. Entered Civil Service as Executive Officer, Customs and

Excise, 1933; Inspector of Taxes, Inland Revenue, 1939; Secretaries' Office, Inland Revenue, 1951; Board of Inland Revenue, 1965. *Recreations:* music, history. *Address:* 40 rue Langheck, Alzingen, 5854 Luxembourg. *T:* Luxembourg 369859.

PRICE, Norman Stewart, CMG 1959; OBE 1946; *b* 9 Aug. 1907; *s* of late Lt-Col Ivon Henry Price, DSO, LLD, Asst Inspr-Gen., RIC, and May Emily (*née* Kinahan), Greystones, Ireland; *m* 1933, Rosalind Evelyn Noelle (*née* Ormsby) (*d* 1973); two *d*. *Educ:* Portora Royal School, Enniskillen; Exeter Sch.; Trinity Coll., Dublin; Queens Coll., Oxford. LLB 1929, BA Hons 1930. Cadet, Northern Rhodesia, 1930, District Officer, 1932, Provincial Comr, Northern Rhodesia, 1951-59; retired, 1959. Coronation Medal, 1953. *Recreations:* gardening; Captain Dublin University Harriers and Athletic Club, 1928-29; Half-Blue Oxford University Cross Country, 1929. *Address:* 46 Muddelhey Avenue, Knowsley Village, Prescot, Merseyside L34 0HZ. *T:* 051-546 6346.

PRICE, Rev. Peter Owen, QHC 1981; FPhS; RN; Principal Chaplain, Church of Scotland and Free Churches (Naval), Ministry of Defence, since 1981; *b* Swansea, 18 April 1930; *e s* of late Idwal Price and Florence Price; *m* 1st, 1957, Margaret Trevan (*d* 1977); three *d*; 2nd, 1982, Marilyn Lorne Campbell (*née* Murray). *Educ:* Wyggeston Sch., Leicester; Didsbury Theol Coll., Bristol. BA Open Univ. Ordained, 1960, Methodist Minister, Birmingham; entered RN as Chaplain, 1960; served: HMS Collingwood, 1960; RM, 1963-64; Staff of C-in-C Med., 1964-68; RNAS Brawdy, 1968-69; RM, 1970-73; HMS Raleigh, 1973; HMS Drake, 1974-78; BRNC Dartmouth, 1978-80. *Recreations:* Rugby refereeing, warm water sailing, music. *Address:* Ministry of Defence (N), Lacon House, Theobalds Road, WC1X 8RY. *T:* 01-430 6842.

PRICE, Peter S.; see Stanley Price.

PRICE, Ralph; see Price, L. R.

PRICE, Sir Robert; see Price, Sir J. R.

PRICE, Air Vice-Marshal Robert George; Air Officer Administration, Headquarters Strike Command, since 1981; *b* 18 July 1928; *s* of Charles and Agnes Price, Hale, Cheshire; *m* 1958, Celia Anne Mary Talamo; one *s* four *d*. *Educ:* Oundle Sch.; RAF Coll., Cranwell. 74 Sqn, 1950; Central Flying Sch., 1952; 60 Sqn, 1956; Guided Weapons Trials Sqn, 1958; Staff Coll., 1960; Bomber Comd, 1961; JSSC 1964; CO 31 Sqn, 1965; PSO to Dep. SACEUR, 1968; CO RAF Linton-on-Ouse, 1970; RCDS 1973; Dep. Dir Operations, 1974; Group Captain Flying Trng, Support Comd, 1978; Dep. Chief of Staff, Support HQ, 2nd Allied Tactical Air Force, 1979; AOA, RAF Germany, 1980. *Recreations:* golf, ski-ing, bridge. *Address:* c/o Barclays Bank, Easingwold, Yorkshire. *Club:* Royal Air Force.

PRICE, Sir Robert (John) G.; see Green-Price.

PRICE, Brig. Rollo Edward Crwys, CBE 1967; DSO 1961; *b* 6 April 1916; *s* of Eardley Edward Carnac Price, CIE; *m* 1945, Diana Budden; three *d*. *Educ:* Canford; RMC Sandhurst. Commissioned 2nd Lt in S Wales Borderers, 1936; War Service, Middle East and Italy, 1939-45; Lt-Col and seconded for service with Queen's Own Nigeria Regt, 1959-61; Col 1962; Comdr 160 Inf. Bde, 1964-67; Brig. 1968; Comdr, British Troops, Malta, 1968-69, retired. *Address:* Elsford, Netherton, near Yeovil, Somerset. *T:* Yetminster 872377. *Club:* Cardiff and County.

PRICE, Roy Kenneth, CB 1980; Under-Secretary (Legal), in office of HM Treasury Solicitor, 1972-81; *b* 16 May 1916; *s* of Ernest Price and Margaret Chapman Price (*née* Scott); *m* 1948, Martha (*née* Dannhauser); one *s* one *d*. *Educ:* Eltham Coll. Qualified as Solicitor, 1937. Town Clerk, Borough of Pembroke, and Clerk to Castlemartin Justices, 1939-40. Served War, Army, 1940-46. Officer in Charge, Legal Aid (Welfare), Northern Command, 1946 (Lt-Col). Joined HM Treasury Solicitor, as Legal Asst, 1946; Sen. Legal Asst, 1950; Asst Solicitor, 1962. Chm., Richmond Assoc., Nat. Trust; Mem. Exec. Council, RNIB. *Recreations:* gardening, theatre, travel. *Address:* 6 Old Palace Lane, Richmond, Surrey. *T:* 01-940 6685. *Club:* Law Society.

PRICE, Terence; see Price, B. T.

PRICE, Mrs Vincent; see Browne, C. E.

PRICE, Vivian William Cecil, QC 1972; *b* 14 April 1926; 4th *s* of late Evan Price, Hawkhurst, Kent; *m* 1961, Elizabeth Anne, *o c* of late Arthur and Georgina Rawlins; three *s* two *d*. *Educ:* Judd Sch., Tonbridge, Kent; Trinity Coll., Cambridge (BA); Balliol Coll., Oxford (BA). Royal Navy, 1946-49, Instructor Lieut. Called to the Bar: Middle Temple, 1954 (Bencher, 1979); Hong Kong, 1975; Singapore, 1979. Sec., Lord Denning's Cttee on Legal Educn for Students from Africa, 1960; Junior Counsel (Patents) to the Board of Trade, 1967-72; Mem., Patents Procedure Cttee, 1973. Deputy High Court Judge (Chancery Division), 1975. *Address:* Redwall Farmhouse, Linton, Kent. *T:* Maidstone 43682; New Court, Temple, EC4. *T:* 01-353 1769. *Club:* Travellers'.

See also A. L. Price.

PRICE, Walter Robert; Executive Director: Joint Ventures and African Operations, General Motors, since 1981; Overseas Assembly, North American Vehicles Overseas, since 1982; *b* 26 Feb. 1926; *m* 1951, Mary Alice Hubbard; one *s* three *d*. *Educ:* Wesleyan Univ., Middletown, Conn, USA (BA). Managing Director: General Motors Suisse, Bienne, Switzerland, 1967; General Motors Continental, Antwerp, Belgium, 1970; General Motors South African (Pty) Ltd, Port Elizabeth, S Africa, 1971; Chm. and Man. Dir, Vauxhall Motors Ltd, Luton, 1974-79; Vice Pres., General Motors Corp., 1978-. Vice Pres., SMMT, 1978-79. *Recreations:* tennis, squash, golf. *Address:* General Motors Corporation, General Motors Building, 3044 West Grand Boulevard, Detroit, Mich 48202, USA.

PRICE, Willard; explorer, naturalist, author; *b* Peterboro, Ontario, Canada, 28 July 1887; *s* of Albert Price, and Estella Martin; *m* 1st, 1914, Eugenia Reeve (*d* 1929), Willoughby, Ohio; one *s*; 2nd, 1932, Mary Selden, New York. To United States, 1901; BA, Western Reserve Univ., Cleveland, Ohio, 1909; studied New York School of Philanthropy, 1911-12; MA, Columbia University, 1914; studied Journalism New York Univ. and Columbia; editorial staff, The Survey, New York, 1912-13; editoral secretary Board of Foreign Missions, Methodist Episcopal Church, 1915-19; editor World Outlook; manager of publication of Everyland and La Nueva Democracia; director periodical department of Interchurch World Movement and supervising editor various class and travel publications; travel in 148 countries, particularly on expeditions for National Geographic Society and American Museum of Natural History, 1920-67. *Publications:* books: Ancient Peoples at New Tasks; The Negro Around the World; Study of American Influence in the Orient; Pacific Adventure; Rip Tide in the South Seas; Where Are You Going, Japan?; Children of the Rising Sun; Japan Reaches Out; Barbarian (a novel); Japan Rides the Tiger; Japan's Islands of Mystery; The Son of Heaven; Key to Japan; Roving South; Tropic Adventure; Amazon Adventure; I Cannot Rest from Travel; The Amazing Amazon; Journey by Junk; Underwater Adventure; Adventures in Paradise; Volcano Adventure; Innocents in Britain; Whale Adventure; Incredible Africa; African Adventure; The Amazing Mississippi; Elephant Adventure; Rivers I Have Known; America's Paradise Lost; Safari Adventure; Lion Adventure; Gorilla Adventure; Odd Way Round the World; Diving Adventure; The Japanese Miracle; Cannibal Adventure; Tiger Adventure; Arctic Adventure; My Own Life of Adventure; The Nile; contrib. to Spectator, Daily Telegraph, Saturday Evening Post, Encyc. Brit., etc. *Address:* 814-N Via Alhambra, Laguna Hills, Calif 92653, USA.

PRICE, Prof. William Charles, FRS 1959; Wheatstone Professor of Physics, University of London, at King's College, 1955-76, now Emeritus; *b* 1 April 1909; *s* of Richard Price and Florence Margaret (*née* Charles); *m* 1939, Nest Myra Davies; one *s* one *d*. *Educ:* Swansea Grammar Sch.; University of Wales (Swansea); Johns Hopkins University, Baltimore; Trinity Coll., Cambridge, BSc (Wales) 1930; Commonwealth Fellow, 1932; PhD (Johns Hopkins), 1934; Cambridge: Senior 1851 Exhibitioner, 1935, University Demonstrator, 1937-43, PhD (Cantab) 1937. Prize Fellow, Trinity Coll., 1938; ScD (Cantab) 1949; Meldola Medal of Inst. of Chem., 1938; Senior Spectroscopist, ICI (Billingham Div.), 1943-48; Research Associate, University of Chicago, 1946-47; Reader in Physics, University of London (King's Coll.) 1948. FKC 1970. FRIC 1944; FIP 1950. Co-editor, British Bulletin of Spectroscopy, 1950-. Hon. DSc Wales, 1970. *Publications:* research and review articles on physics and chemistry in scientific journals. *Address:* 38 Cross Way, Petts Wood, Kent. *T:* Orpington 28815.

PRICE, William Frederick Barry, OBE 1977; HM Diplomatic Service; Consul-General, Amsterdam, since 1983; *b* 12 Feb. 1925; *s* of William Thomas and Vera Price; *m* 1948, Lorraine Elisabeth Suzanne Hoather; three *s* two *d*. *Educ:* Worcester Royal Grammar Sch.; St Paul's Training Coll., Cheltenham. Served War: Armed Forces, 1944-47: commissioned Royal Warwicks, 1945; demobilised, 1947. Primary Sch. Teacher, 1948. Joined Bd of Trade, 1950; Asst Trade Comr: in Delhi, 1954; in Nairobi, 1957; Trade Commissioner, Accra, 1963; transferred to HM Diplomatic Service, 1966; 1st Sec., Sofia, 1967; seconded to East European Trade Council, 1971; Consul-Gen., Rotterdam, 1973-77; Consul, Houston, 1978-81; Counsellor (Commercial and Economic), Bangkok, 1981-82; Kuala Lumpur, 1982. *Recreation:* Proust. *Address:* c/o Foreign and Commonwealth Office, SW1. *Club:* Oriental.

PRICE, William George; Consultant, National Union of Licensed Victuallers, since 1979; *b* 15 June 1934; *s* of George and Lillian Price; *m* 1963, Joy Thomas (marr. diss. 1978); two *s*. *Educ:* Forest of Dene Technical Coll.; Gloucester Technical Coll. Staff Journalist: Three Forest Newspapers, Cinderford, until 1959; Coventry Evening Telegraph, 1959-62; Birmingham Post & Mail, 1962-66. MP (Lab) Rugby, Warks, 1966-79; PPS: to Sec. of State for Educn and Science, 1968-70; to Dep. Leader, Labour Party, 1972-74; Parliamentary Secretary: ODM, March-Oct. 1974; Privy Council Office, 1974-79. *Recreation:* sport. *Address:* 54 Kings Grove, Peckham, SE15 2NB.

PRICE, Winford Hugh Protheroe, FCA; City Treasurer, Cardiff City Council, since 1975; *b* 5 Feb. 1926; *s* of Martin Price and Doris Blanche Price. *Educ:* Cardiff High Sch. IPFA 1952; FCA 1954. Served War, RAFVR, 1944-48. City Treasurer's and Controller's Dept, Cardiff, 1942; Dep. City Treasurer, Cardiff, 1973-75. Public Works Loan Comr, 1979-. Treasurer and Financial Adviser, Council for the Principality, 1975-; Financial Adviser, Assoc. of Dist Councils Cttee for Wales, 1975-; Treasurer: The Queen's Silver

Jubilee Trust (S Glam), 1976–; Royal National Eisteddfod of Wales (Cardiff), 1978. Occasional lectr on local govt topics. *Publications:* contrib. to jls. *Recreation:* chess. *Address:* 3 Oakfield Street, Roath, Cardiff CF2 3RD. *T:* Cardiff 494635.

PRICE EVANS, David Alan; *see* Evans.

PRICE HOLMES, Eric Montagu; *see* Holmes, E. M. P.

PRICHARD, Sir Montague (Illtyd), Kt 1972; CBE 1965; MC 1944; Director: Polysius Ltd; Tozer, Kemsley & Millbourn (Holdings) Ltd, since 1976 (Deputy Chairman, since 1981); *b* 26 Sept. 1915; *s* of late George Montague Prichard; *m* 1942, Kathleen Georgana Hamill; two *s* one *d. Educ:* Felsted Sch., Essex. Served War of 1939-45 (despatches thrice, MC): Royal Engineers: Somaliland, India, Burma, Malaya and Far East, Lt-Col as CRE 20 Indian Division. R. A. Lister & Co. Ltd, 1933-53 (excluding war service), Dir, 1950-53; Perkins Engineering Group Ltd, 1953, Man. Dir, 1958, Chm., 1959-75; Dir, Massey-Ferguson Ltd (Canada), 1961-75; retired from exec. capacities, 1975. Member: British Productivity Council; BNEC, 1965-72; Founder Chairman: Nat. Marketing Council, 1963; British Industry Roads Campaign. Vice-Pres., SMMT, 1966-70; Pres., Motor Industry Res. Assoc., 1972-74. FInstMSM. *Address:* Monte Kay, Mijas, Malaga, Spain. *T:* Malaga 485085. *Club:* East India, Devonshire, Sports and Public Schools.

PRICHARD, Air Vice-Marshal Richard Augustin R.; *see* Riseley-Prichard.

PRICHARD, Air Commodore Richard Julian Paget, CB 1963; CBE 1958; DFC 1942; AFC 1941; *b* 4 Oct. 1915; *o s* of Major W. O. Prichard, 24th Regt; unmarried. *Educ:* Harrow; St Catharine's Coll., Cambridge. Entered RAF, 1937; Air Armament Sch., Eastchurch and Manby, 1937-39; Flying Instructor, South Cerney, 1939-41; No. 21 (LB) Squadron, 1942-43; Staff Coll. (psa), 1943; AEAF, 1943-45; Chief Intelligence Officer, Burma and FEAF, 1946-47; Chief Flying Instructor, RAF Coll., Cranwell, 1947-49; Ministry of Defence, 1949-52; Instructor, RAF Staff Coll., 1953-55; Station Comdr, RAF Tengah, Singapore, 1956-58. IDC, 1959; Director Air Plans, Air Ministry, 1960-63; AOC No 13 Scottish Sector, Fighter Command, 1963-64; AOC Northern Sector of Fighter Command, 1965-66; retired, 1966. US Legion of Merit, 1944. *Recreations:* tennis, fishing. *Address:* c/o Lloyds Bank Ltd, 6 Pall Mall, SW1Y 5NH. *Club:* Royal Air Force.

PRICHARD-JONES, Sir John, 2nd Bt, *cr* 1910; Captain, Reserve of Officers; *b* 20 Jan. 1913; *s* of 1st Bt and Marie, *y d* of late Charles Read; *S* father, 1917; *m* 1937, Heather, (from whom he obtained a divorce, 1950), *er d* of late Sir Walter Nugent, 4th Bt; one *s*; *m* 1959, Helen Marie Thérèse, *e d* of J. F. Liddy, 20 Laurence Street, Drogheda; one *d. Educ:* Eton; Christ Church, Oxford (BA Hons; MA). Called to Bar, Gray's Inn, 1936. *Heir: s* David John Walter Prichard-Jones, BA (Hons) Oxon, *b* 14 March 1943. *Address:* Allenswood House, Lucan, Co. Dublin.

PRICKETT, Air Chief Marshal Sir Thomas (Other), KCB 1965 (CB 1957); DSO 1943; DFC 1942; RAF retired; *b* 31 July 1913; *s* of late E. G. Prickett; *m* 1942, Elizabeth Gratian, *d* of late William Galbally, Laguna Beach, Calif, USA; one *s* one *d. Educ:* Stubbington House Sch.; Haileybury Coll. Joined RAF, 1937; commanded RAF Tangmere, 1949-51; Group Captain operations, HQ Middle East Air Force, 1951-54; commanded RAF Jever, 1954-55; attended Imperial Defence Coll., 1956; Chief of Staff Air Task Force, 1956; Director of Policy, Air Ministry, 1957-58; SASO, HQ No 1 Group, 1958-60; ACAS (Ops) Air Ministry, 1960-63; ACAS (Policy and Planning) Air Ministry, 1963-64; AOC-in-C, NEAF, Comdr British Forces Near East, and Administrator, Sovereign Base Area, 1966-67; AOC-in-C, RAF Air Support Command, 1967-68; Air Mem. for Supply and Organisation, MoD, 1968-70. *Recreations:* polo, sailing, golf. *Address:* 3 Grange House, Aldwick Grange, Bognor, Sussex. *Club:* Royal Air Force.

PRICKMAN, Air Cdre Thomas Bain, CB 1953; CBE 1945; *b* 1902; *m* 1st, Ethel Serica (*d* 1949), *d* of John Cubbon, Douglas, IOM; 2nd, 1952, Dorothy (who *m* 1946, Group Captain F. C. Read, *d* 1949), *d* of John Charles Clarke, *Educ:* Blundell's Sch. Joined RAF, 1923. Served War of 1939-45, with Fighter Command; RAF Liaison staff in Australia, 1946-48; AOA, Home Command, 1950-54; retired, 1954. *Address:* Tilsmore Cottage, Cross-in-Hand, Heathfield, Sussex TN21 0LS.

PRIDDLE, Robert John; Under Secretary, since 1977, and Head of Energy and International Policy Division, Department of Energy; *b* 9 Sept. 1938; *s* of Albert Leslie Priddle and Alberta Edith Priddle; *m* 1962, Janice Elizabeth Gorham; two *s. Educ:* King's Coll. Sch., Wimbledon; Peterhouse, Cambridge (MA). Asst Principal, Min. of Aviation, 1960, Principal 1965; Private Sec. to Minister for Aerospace, 1971-73; Asst Sec., DTI, 1973, and Dept of Energy, 1974. *Publication:* Victoriana, 1959 (2nd edn 1963). *Address:* Department of Energy, Thames House South, Millbank, SW1P 4QJ.

PRIDEAUX, Sir Humphrey (Povah Treverbian), Kt 1971; OBE 1945; President, The London Life Association Ltd, since 1973 (Director, 1964; Vice-President, 1965-72); Vice-Chairman, Morland & Co., since 1982 (Director, 1981); Director, Grindlays Holdings, since 1982; Chairman, Lord Wandsworth Foundation, since 1966; *b* 13 Dec. 1915; 3rd *s* of Walter Treverbian Prideaux and Marion Fenn (*née* Arbuthnot); *m* 1939, Cynthia, *er*

d of late Lt-Col H. Birch Reynardson, CMG; four *s. Educ:* St Aubyns, Rottingdean; Eton; Trinity Coll., Oxford (MA). Commissioned 3rd Carabiniers (Prince of Wales's Dragoon Guards) 1936; DAQMG Guards Armd Div., 1941; Instructor, Staff Coll., 1942; AQMG 21 Army Gp, 1943; AA QMG Guards Armd Div., 1944; Joint Planning Staff, War Office, 1945; Naval Staff Coll., 1948; Commandant School of Administration, 1948; Chiefs of Staff Secretariat, 1950; retired, 1953. Director, NAAFI, 1956-73 (Man. Dir, 1961-65; Chm., 1963-73); Chm., Brooke Bond Liebig Ltd, 1972-80 (Dir, 1968; Dep. Chm., 1969-71); Vice-Chm., W. H. Smith & Son Ltd, 1977-81 (Dir, 1969-77). *Recreation:* riding. *Address:* Summers Farm, Long Sutton, Basingstoke, Hants. *T:* Long Sutton 295. *Club:* Cavalry and Guards.
See also Sir J. F. Prideaux, W. A. Prideaux.

PRIDEAUX, Sir John (Francis), Kt 1974; OBE 1945; DL; Director: Arbuthnot Latham Holdings Ltd, since 1969 (Chairman, 1969-74); Dow Scandia Banking Corporation, since 1982; *b* 30 Dec. 1911; 2nd *s* of Walter Treverbian Prideaux and Marion Fenn (*née* Arbuthnot); *m* 1934, Joan, *er d* of late Captain Gordon Hargreaves Brown, MC, and Lady Pigott Brown; two *s* one *d. Educ:* St Aubyns, Rottingdean; Eton. Middlesex Yeomanry, 1933; served War of 1939-45, Colonel Q, 2nd Army, 1944. Joined Arbuthnot Latham & Co. Ltd, Merchant Bankers, 1930, Dir, 1936-69, Chm., 1964-69. Mem., London Adv. Bd, Bank of NSW, 1948-74; Director: Westminster Bank Ltd, later National Westminster Bank Ltd, 1955-81 (Chm., 1971-77); Westminster Foreign Bank Ltd, later Internat. Westminster Bank Ltd, 1955-81 (Chm., 1969-77). Chm., Cttee of London Clearing Bankers, 1974-76; Vice-Pres., British Bankers' Assoc., 1972-77. Pres., Inst. of Bankers, 1974-76. Mem., Wilson Cttee to review functioning of financial instns in the City, 1977-80. Dep. Chm., Commonwealth Develt Corp., 1960-70; Chm., Victoria League for Commonwealth Friendship, 1977-. Mem., Lambeth, Southwark and Lewisham AHA(T), 1974-82 (Commissioner, Aug. 1979-March 1980); Treasurer and Chm., Bd of Governors, St Thomas' Hosp., 1964-74; Chm., Special Trustees, St Thomas' Hosp., 1974-. Prime Warden, Goldsmiths' Company, 1972. DL Surrey 1976. Legion of Merit, USA, 1945. *Address:* Elderslie, Ockley, Surrey. *T:* Dorking 711263. *Clubs:* Brooks's, Overseas Bankers (Pres. 1976-77).
See also Sir H. P. T. Prideaux, W. A. Prideaux.

PRIDEAUX, Walter Arbuthnot, CBE 1973; MC 1945; TD 1948; *b* 4 Jan. 1910; *e s* of Walter Treverbian Prideaux and Marion Fenn (*née* Arbuthnot); *m* 1937, Anne, *d* of Francis Stewart Cokayne; two *s* two *d. Educ:* Eton; Trinity Coll., Cambridge. Solicitor, 1934. Assistant Clerk of the Goldsmiths' Company, 1939-53, Clerk 1953-75. Chm., City Parochial Foundn, 1972-80. Kent Yeomanry, 1936-48. *Recreation:* rowed for Cambridge, 1930, 1931. *Address:* 16 Tanbridge Place, Horsham, West Sussex RH12 1RY.
See also Sir H. P. T. Prideaux, Sir J. F. Prideaux.

PRIDHAM, Brian Robert; HM Diplomatic Service, retired; Centre for Arab Gulf Studies, University of Exeter; *b* 22 Feb. 1934; *s* of Reginald Buller Pridham and Emily Pridham (*née* Winser); *m* 1954, Fay Coles; three *s. Educ:* Hele's Sch., Exeter. RWAFF (Nigeria Regt), 1952-54; Foreign Office, 1954-57; MECAS, 1957-59; Bahrain, 1959; Vice-Consul, Muscat, 1959-62; Foreign Office, 1962-64; 2nd Sec., Algiers, 1964-66; 1st Sec., 1966-67; Foreign Office, 1967-70; Head of Chancery: La Paz, 1970-73; Abu Dhabi, 1973-75; Dir of MECAS, Shemlan, Lebanon, 1975-76; Counsellor, Khartoum, 1976-79; Head of Communications Ops Dept, FCO, 1979-81. *Recreations:* sailing, old roses. *Address:* c/o Barclays Bank, Exeter.

PRIDHAM, Kenneth Robert Comyn, CMG 1976; HM Diplomatic Service, retired; *b* 28 July 1922; *s* of late Colonel G. R. Pridham, CBE, DSO, and Mignonne, *d* of late Charles Cumming, ICS; *m* 1965, Ann Rosalind, *d* of late E. Gilbert Woodward, Metropolitan Magistrate, and of Mrs Woodward. *Educ:* Winchester; Oriel Coll., Oxford. Lieut, 60th Rifles, 1942-46; served North Africa, Italy, Middle East (despatches). Entered Foreign (subseq. Diplomatic) Service, 1946; served at Berlin, Washington, Belgrade and Khartoum, and at the Foreign Office; Counsellor: Copenhagen, 1968-72; FCO, 1972-74; Asst Under Sec. of State, FCO, 1974-78; Ambassador to Poland, 1978-81. Vis. Res. Fellow, RIIA, 1981-82. *Address:* c/o Lloyds Bank Ltd, 16 St James's Street, SW1. *Club:* Travellers'.

PRIEST, Prof. Robert George, MD, FRCPsych; Professor of Psychiatry, University of London and Head of Department of Psychiatry at St Mary's Hospital Medical School, since 1973; Hon. Consultant Psychiatrist, St Mary's Hospital, London, since 1973; *b* 28 Sept. 1933; *er s* of late James Priest and of Phoebe Priest; *m* 1955, Marilyn, *er d* of late Baden Roberts Baker and of Evelyn Baker; two *s. Educ:* University Coll., London and University Coll. Hosp. Med. Sch. MB, BS 1956; DPM 1963; MRCPE 1964; MD 1970; MRCPsych 1971 (Foundn Mem.); FRCPE 1974; FRCPsych 1974. Lectr in Psychiatry, Univ. of Edinburgh, 1964-67; Exchange Lectr, Univ. of Chicago, 1966; Consultant, Illinois State Psychiatric Inst., Chicago, 1966; Sen. Lectr, St George's Hosp. Med. Sch., London, 1967-73; Hon. Consultant: St George's Hosp., London, 1967-73; Springfield Hosp., London, 1967-73; Recognised Teacher, Univ. of London, 1968-; Examiner in Psychiatry, NUI, 1975-78, 1980-. Chairman: Div. of Psychiatry, Kensington and Chelsea and Westminster AHA (T), NW Dist, 1976-79; Psychiatric Adv. Sub-Cttee, NW Thames RHA, 1976-79 (Vice-Chm., Reg. Manpower Cttee, 1980-). Mem. Council (Chm. Membership Cttee), British Assoc. for Psychopharmacology, 1977-81; Pres., Soc. for Psychosomatic Res., 1980-81 (Vice-Pres., 1978-80); Mem. Council, Mental Health Section, BMA, 1978-; Fellow, Internat. Coll.

of Psychosomatic Medicine (Mem. Gov. Body and UK Delegate, 1978–81; Secretary, 1981–); Chm., Chiltern and Thames Valley Div., RCPsych, 1981–. A. E. Bennett Award, Soc. for Biol Psychiatry, USA (jtly), 1965; Doris Odlum Prize (BMA), 1968; Gutheil Von Domarus Award, Assoc. for Advancement of Psychotherapy and Amer. Jl of Psychotherapy, NY, 1970. *Publications:* Insanity: A Study of Major Psychiatric Disorders, 1977; (jtly) 7th edn, Minski's Handbook of Psychiatry, 1978; (ed jtly) Sleep Research, 1979; (ed jtly) Benzodiazepines Today and Tomorrow, 1980; chapters in: Current Themes in Psychiatry, 1978; Mental Illness in Pregnancy and the Puerperium, 1978; articles in BMJ, Brit. Jl of Psychiatry, Amer. Jl of Psychotherapy and other learned jls. *Recreations:* squash, tennis, gardening, foreign languages, nature study. *Address:* Woodeaves, 29 Old Slade Lane, Richings Park, Iver, Bucks SL0 9DY. *T:* Iver 653178.

PRIESTLAND, Gerald Francis; Religious Affairs Correspondent, BBC, 1977–82; *b* 26 Feb. 1927; *s* of late Frank Priestland and Nelly Priestland (*née* Renny); *m* 1949, Helen Sylvia (*née* Rhodes); two *s* two *d.* *Educ:* Charterhouse; New Coll., Oxford (BA). Subeditor, BBC News, 1949–54; BBC Correspondent: New Delhi, 1954–58; Washington, 1958–61; Beirut, 1961–65; Washington, 1965–70; news presenter on Radio and TV, 1970–76. Hon. Fellow, Manchester Polytechnic, 1978. *Publications:* America the Changing Nation, 1968; Frying Tonight (the Saga of Fish and Chips), 1971; The Future of Violence, 1976; Yours Faithfully, Vol. 1, 1979; Dilemmas of Journalism, 1979; (with Sylvia Priestland) West of Hayle River, 1980; Yours Faithfully, Vol. 2, 1981; Priestland's Progress, 1981. *Recreation:* trying to think of a recreation. *Address:* 4 Temple Fortune Lane, NW11 7UD. *T:* 01-455 3297.

PRIESTLEY, Prof. Charles Henry Brian, AO 1976; FAA 1954; FRS 1967; Professor of Meteorology, Monash University, Australia, 1978–80; *b* 8 July 1915; *s* of late T. G. Priestley; *m* 1946, Constance, *d* of H. Tweedy; one *s* two *d.* *Educ:* Mill Hill Sch.; St John's Coll., Cambridge. MA 1942, ScD 1953. Served in Meteorological Office, Air Ministry, 1939–46; subseq. with CSIRO, Australia; Chief of Div. of Meteorological Physics, 1946–71; Chm., Environmental Physics Res., 1971–78. David Syme Prize, University of Melbourne, 1956. Member Exec. Cttee, International Assoc. of Meteorology, 1954–60, Vice-Pres., 1967–75; Vice-Pres., Australian Acad. of Science, 1959–60; Mem., Adv. Cttee, World Meteorological Organisation, 1964–68 (Chm., 1967; Internat. Met. Orgn Prize, 1973). FRMetSoc (Hon. Life Fellow, 1978; Buchan Prize, 1950 and Symons Medal, 1967, of Society); FInstP. Hon. Mem., Amer. Met. Soc., 1978 (Rossby Medal, 1975). *Publications:* Turbulent Transfer in the Lower Atmosphere, 1959; about 60 papers in scientific journals. *Recreation:* golf. *Address:* Flat 2, 862 Malvern Road, Armidale, Vic 3143, Australia.

PRIESTLEY, Clive; Under Secretary, Management and Personnel Office, since 1982; *b* 12 July 1935; *s* of Albert Ernest and Annie May Priestley; *m* 1961, Barbara Anne, *d* of George Gerard and Ann Doris Wells; two *d.* *Educ:* Loughborough Grammar Sch.; Nottingham Univ. BA 1956; MA 1958. Nat. Service, 1958–60. Joined HM Home Civil Service, 1960; Min. of Educn, later DES, 1960–65; Schools Council, 1965–67; Harkness Commonwealth Fund Fellow, Harvard Univ., 1967–68; CSD, 1969–79; Prime Minister's Office, 1979–82 (Chief of Staff to Sir Derek Rayner); Under Sec., 1979. *Recreation:* parish life. *Address:* 67 Marlborough Place, NW8. *T:* 01-624 8691. *Club:* Army and Navy.

PRIESTLEY, John Boynton, OM 1977; MA, LittD; LLD; DLitt; Author; *b* Bradford, 13 Sept. 1894; *s* of Jonathan Priestley, schoolmaster; *m* Jacquetta Hawkes, *qv*; one *s* four *d* by previous marriages. *Educ:* Bradford; Trinity Hall, Cambridge (Hon. Fellow, 1978). Served with Duke of Wellington's and Devon Regts, 1914–19. UK Delegate to UNESCO Conferences, 1946–47; Chairman of International Theatre Conf.: Paris, 1947, Prague, 1948; Chairman British Theatre Conf., 1948; President International Theatre Institute, 1949; Member of the National Theatre Board, 1966–67. Freeman, City of Bradford, 1973. *Publications:* Brief Diversions, 1922; Papers from Lilliput, 1922; I for One, 1923; Figures in Modern Literature, 1924; The English Comic Characters, 1925; George Meredith (English Men of Letters), 1926; Talking, 1926; Adam in Moonshine, 1927; Open House, 1927; Peacock (English Men of Letters), 1927; Benighted, 1927; The English Novel, 1927; Apes and Angels, 1928; English Humour, 1928; The Good Companions, 1929 (dramatised with E. Knoblock, 1931); The Balconinny, 1929; Town Major of Miraucourt; Angel Pavement, 1930; Self-Selected Essays, 1932; Dangerous Corner, play, 1932; Faraway, 1932; Wonder Hero, 1933, The Roundabout, play, 1933; Laburnum Grove, play, 1933; English Journey, 1934; Eden End, 1934; Duet in Floodlight, play, 1935; Cornelius, play, 1935; Bees on the Boat Deck, play, 1936; They Walk in the City, 1936; Midnight on the Desert, 1937; Time and the Conways, play, 1937; I Have Been Here Before, play, 1937; People at Sea, play, 1937; The Doomsday Men, 1938; Music at Night, play, 1938; When We Are Married, play, 1938; Johnson Over Jordan, play, 1939; Rain upon Godshill, 1939; Let the People Sing, 1939; The Long Mirror, play, 1940; Postscripts, 1940; Out of the People, 1941; Goodnight, Children, play, 1942; Black-Out in Gretley, 1942; The Foreman went to France, film screenplay, 1942; They Came to a City, play, 1943; Daylight on Saturday, 1943; The Man-Power Story, 1943; British Women go to War, 1943; Desert Highway, play, 1943; How Are They At Home?, play, 1944; Three Men in New Suits, 1945; An Inspector Calls, Ever Since Paradise, plays, 1946; The Secret Dream; Bright Day, 1946; Arts under Socialism; Theatre Outlook; Jenny Villiers; The Linden Tree, play, 1947; Home is Tomorrow, play, 1948; Summer Day's

Dream, play, 1949; libretto, The Olympians, opera, 1948; Delight (essays), 1949; libretto, Last Holiday (film), 1950; Festival at Farbridge, 1951; (with Jacquetta Hawkes) Dragon's Mouth, play, 1952; The Other Place, 1953; The Magicians; Low Notes on a High Level, 1954; Mr Kettle and Mrs Moon, play, 1955; Journey Down a Rainbow (with Jacquetta Hawkes), 1955; The Glass Cage, play, 1957; Thoughts in the Wilderness, 1957; The Art of the Dramatist, 1957; Topside or the Future of England, 1958; Literature and Western Man, 1960; Saturn Over The Water, 1961; The Thirty-First of June, 1961; Charles Dickens: A Pictorial Biography, 1961; The Shapes of Sleep, 1962; Margin Released, 1962; A Severed Head (with Iris Murdoch), play, 1963; Sir Michael and Sir George, 1964; Man and Time, 1964; Lost Empires, 1965; The Moment-And Other Pieces (essays), 1966; Salt is Leaving, 1966; It's an Old Country, 1967; Trumpets Over the Sea, 1968; The Image Men, Vol. I, Out of Town, 1968, Vol. II, London End, 1968; Essays of Five Decades, ed Susan Cooper, 1969; The Prince of Pleasure and his Regency, 1969; The Edwardians, 1970; Snoggle, 1971; Victoria's Heyday, 1972; Over the Long High Wall, 1972; The English, 1973; Outcries and Asides (essays), 1974; A Visit to New Zealand, 1974; The Carfitt Crisis, 1975; Particular Pleasures, 1975; Found, Lost, Found, or the English Way of Life, 1976; The Happy Dream, 1976; English Humour, 1976; Instead of the Trees (autobiog.), 1977. *Relevant publications:* J. B. Priestley: An Informal Study of His Work, by David Hughes, 1959; J. B. Priestley: the Dramatist, by Gareth Lloyd Evans, 1964; J. B. Priestley: portrait of an author, by Susan Cooper, 1970; J. B. Priestley, by John Braine, 1978; J. B. Priestley: the last of the sages, by John Atkins, 1980, etc. *Address:* Alveston, Stratford-upon-Avon, Warwickshire.
See also Air Marshal Sir P. G. *Wykeham.*

PRIESTLEY, Mrs J. B.; *see* Hawkes, Jacquetta.

PRIESTLEY, Prof. Maurice Bertram, MA, PhD; Professor of Statistics, University of Manchester Institute of Science and Technology, since 1970 and Head of Department of Mathematics, 1973–75, 1977–78 and since 1980; *b* 15 March 1933; *s* of Jack and Rose Priestley; *m* 1959, Nancy, *d* of late Ralph and Hilda Nelson; one *s* one *d.* *Educ:* Manchester Grammar Sch.; Jesus Coll., Cambridge. BA (Wrangler, 1954), MA, DipMathStat (Cambridge); PhD (Manchester). Scientific Officer, RAE, 1955–56; Asst Lectr, Univ. of Manchester, 1957–60, Lectr, 1960–65; Vis. Professor, Princeton and Stanford Univs, USA, 1961–62; Sen. Lectr, UMIST, 1965–70; Dir, Manchester-Sheffield Sch. of Probability and Stats, and Hon. Prof. of Probability and Stats, Sheffield Univ., 1976–79. Mem. Court and Council, UMIST, 1971–74. FIMS; FSS; Mem. Council, Royal Statistical Soc., 1971–75; Mem., ISI. Editor-in-chief, Jl of Time Series Analysis, 1980–. *Publications:* Spectral Analysis and Time Series, Vols I and II, 1981; papers and articles in Jl RSS, Biometrika, Technom., Automatica, Jl of Sound and Vibration. *Recreations:* music, hi-fi and audio, golf. *Address:* Department of Mathematics, University of Manchester Institute of Science and Technology, PO Box 88, Manchester M60 1QD. *T:* 061-236 3311.

PRIESTMAN, John David; Clerk of the Parliamentary Assembly of the Council of Europe, since 1971; *b* 29 March 1926; *s* of Bernard Priestman and Hermine Bréal; *m* 1951, Nada Valić; two *s* two *d.* *Educ:* private sch. in Paris; Westminster Sch.; Merton Coll. and Christ Church, Oxford (Hon. Mods, Lit. Hum.). Served Coldstream Guards, 1944–47, Temp. Captain. Third, subseq. Second, Sec., Belgrade, 1949–53; Asst Private Sec. to Rt Hon. Anthony Eden, 1953–55; joined Secretariat, Council of Europe, 1955; Head of Sec. Gen's Private Office, 1961; Sec., Cttee of Ministers, 1966; Dep. Clerk of Parly Assembly, 1968–71. *Recreations:* off-piste Alpine ski-ing, music, competition bridge, gastronomic research. *Address:* 53 Allée de la Robertsau, 67000 Strasbourg, France. *T:* 88-354049. *Club:* Buck's.

PRIGOGINE, Prof. Ilya; Grand-Croix de l'Ordre de Léopold II, Belgium, and Commandeur de L'Ordre du Mérite, France; Professor, Université Libre de Bruxelles, since 1951; Director, Instituts Internationaux de Physique et de Chimie, since 1959; Director, Ilya Prigogine Center of Statistical Mechanics and Thermodynamics, University of Texas at Austin, since 1967; *b* 25 Jan. 1917; *m* 1961, Maria Prokopowicz; two *s.* *Educ:* Univ. of Brussels (Dr en Sciences Physiques, 1941). Prof., Dept of Chemistry, Enrico Fermi Inst. for Nuclear Studies, and Inst. for Study of Metals, Univ. of Chicago, 1961–66; Member: Académie Royale de Belgique, 1958; Royal Soc. of Sciences, Uppsala, Sweden, 1967; German Acad. Naturforscher Leopoldina, GDR, 1970; Acad. Internat. de Philosophie des Sciences, 1973. Hon. Member: Amer. Acad. of Arts and Sciences, 1960; Chem. Soc., Warsaw, 1971. Fellow, Acad. of Sciences, New York, 1962; Centennial Foreign Fellow, Amer. Chem. Soc., 1976; Foreign Associate, Nat. Acad. of Sciences, USA, 1967; Corresponding Member: Acad. of Romania, 1965; Soc. Royale des Sciences, Liège, 1967; Section of Phys. and Math., Akad. der Wissenschaften, Göttingen, 1970; Akad. der Wissenschaften, Vienna, 1971. Dr (*hc*): Newcastle upon Tyne, 1966; Poitiers, 1966; Chicago, 1969; Bordeaux, 1972; Uppsala, 1977; Liège, 1978; Aix-Marseille, 1979; Georgetown, 1980; Rio de Janeiro, 1981; Cracow, 1981; Stevens Inst. of Technology, Hoboken, 1981. Prizes: Van Laar, Société Chimique de Belgique, 1947; A. Wetrems 1950, and Annual (jtly) 1952, Acad. Royale de Belgique; Francqui, 1955; E. J. Solvay, 1965. Nobel Prize for Chemistry, 1977. Gold Medals: Swante Arrhenius, Royal Acad. of Sciences, Sweden, 1969; Cothenius, German Acad. Naturforscher Leopoldina, 1975; Rumford, Royal Soc., 1976. Bourke Medal, Chem. Soc., 1972; Medal, Assoc. for the Advancement of Sciences, Paris, 1975; Southwest Science Forum Prize, NY Acad. of Science; Karcher Medal, Amer. Crystallographic Assoc., 1978; Descartes Medal, Univ. Descartes, Paris, 1979. *Publications:* (with R. Defay)

Traité de Thermodynamique, conformément aux méthodes de Gibbs et de Donder: Vol. I, Thermodynamique Chimique, 1944 (Eng. trans. 1954); Vol. II, Tension Superficielle et Adsorption, 1951 (Eng. trans. 1965); Etude Thermodynamique des Phénomènes Irreversibles, 1947; Introduction to Thermodynamics of Irreversible Processes, New York 1954 (3rd edn 1967); (with A. Bellemans and V. Mathot) The Molecular Theory of Solutions, Amsterdam 1957; Non. Equilibrium Statistical Mechanics, 1962 (also New York); (with R. Herman) Kinetic Theory of Vehicular Traffic, New York 1971; (with P. Glansdorff) Thermodynamic Theory of Structure, Stability and Fluctuations, London and New York 1971 (also French edn); (with G. Nicolis) Self-Organization in Non Equilibrium Systems, 1977 (also New York); Dialog mit der Natur, 1979; From Being to Becoming: time and complexity in the physical sciences, 1980 (also French and German edns); (with I. Stengers) La Nouvelle Alliance: les métamorphoses de la science, 1981 (Prix du Haut Comité de la langue française, Paris, 1981) (also Italian and Yugoslavian edns). *Recreations:* art, music. *Address:* avenue Fond'Roy 67, 1180 Bruxelles, Belgium. *T:* 02/3742952.

PRIME, Prof. Henry Ashworth, CEng, FIEE; Professor of Electronic and Electrical Engineering, University of Birmingham, since 1963; *b* 11 March 1921; *s* of late E. V. Prime and Elsie (*née* Ashworth); *m* 1943, Ella Stewart Reid; one *s* one *d*. *Educ:* N Manchester High Sch.; Manchester Univ. (MSc). CEng, FIEE 1964. Scientific Officer, Admiralty Signal and Radar Estab., 1942-46; Lectr, Univ. of Liverpool, 1946-50; Sen. Lectr, Univ. of Adelaide, 1950-55; Chief Electronic Engr and Manager Control Div., Brush Elec. Engrg Co., 1955-63. Pro-Vice-Chancellor, Univ. of Birmingham, 1978-82. Vis. Professor: Univ. of Teheran, 1971; Univ. of Hanover, 1978. Member: CNAA Elec. Engrg Bd, 1970-74; Council, IEE, 1974-77, 1980-; Naval Educn Adv. Cttee, 1973-79 (Chm., 1978-79); Chm., Computing and Control Divl Bd, IEE, 1982-83. *Publications:* (contrib.) Telecommunication Satellites, ed Gatland, 1964; Modern Concepts in Control Theory, 1970; papers in scientific jls on electrical discharges, microwave interaction with ionised gases, and control systems. *Recreation:* golf. *Address:* Revelwood, 1C Plymouth Road, Barnt Green, Birmingham B45 8JE. *T:* 021-445 2545.

PRIMROSE, family name of Earl of Rosebery.

PRIMROSE, Sir John Ure, 3rd Bt, *cr* 1903, of Redholme; farming in the Argentine; *b* 15 April 1908; *er s* of Sir William Louis Primrose, 2nd Bt, and Elizabeth Caroline (*d* 1951), *d* of Hugh Dunsmuir, Glasgow; *S* father, 1953; *m* Enid, *d* of James Evans Sladen, British Columbia; one *s*. *Educ:* Rugby; Sandhurst. Lieut, QO Cameron Highlanders, 1928-33. *Heir: s* Alasdair Neil Primrose [*b* 11 Dec. 1935; *m* 1958, Elaine Noreen, *d* of E. C. Lowndes, Buenos Aires; two *s* two *d*. *Educ:* St George's College, Buenos Aires]. *Address:* Puerto Victoria, Alto Parana, Misiones, Argentina.

PRINCE, Prof. Frank Templeton, MA (Oxon); *b* Kimberley, South Africa, 13 Sept. 1912; 2nd *s* of late H. Prince and Margaret Templeton (*née* Hetherington); *m* 1943, Pauline Elizabeth, *d* of late H. F. Bush; two *d*. *Educ:* Christian Brothers' Coll., Kimberley, South Africa; Balliol Coll., Oxford. Visiting Fellow, Graduate Coll., Princeton, NJ, 1935-36. Study Groups Department, Chatham House, 1937-40. Served Army, Intelligence Corps, 1940-46. Department of English, 1946-57, Prof. of English, 1957-74, Southampton Univ.; Prof. of English, Univ. of WI, Jamaica, 1975-78. Hurst Vis. Prof., Brandeis Univ., 1978-80; Vis. Prof., Washington Univ., St Louis, 1980-81, Sana'a Univ., N Yemen, 1981-82; Visiting Fellow, All Souls Coll., 1968-69. Clark Lectr, Cambridge, 1972-73. Hon. DLitt Southampton, 1981. *Publications:* Poems, 1938; Soldiers Bathing (poems), 1954; The Italian Element in Milton's Verse, 1954; The Doors of Stone (poems), 1963; Memoirs in Oxford (verse), 1970; Drypoints of the Hasidim (verse), 1975; Collected Poems, 1979; contrib. to Review of English Studies. *Recreations:* music, etc. *Address:* 32 Brookvale Road, Southampton. *T:* Southampton 555457.

PRINCE, Harold Smith; theatrical director/producer; *b* NYC, 30 Jan. 1928; *s* of Milton A. Prince and Blanche (*née* Stern); *m* 1962, Judith Chaplin; two *d*. *Educ:* Univ. of Pennsylvania (AB 1948). Co-Producer: The Pajama Game, 1954-56 (co-prod film, 1957); Damn Yankees, 1955-57 (co-prod film, 1958); New Girl in Town, 1957-58; West Side Story, 1957-59; Fiorello!, 1959-61 (Pulitzer Prize); Tenderloin, 1960-61; A Call on Kuprin, 1961; They Might Be Giants, London 1961; Side By Side By Sondheim, 1977-78. Producer: Take Her She's Mine, 1961-62; A Funny Thing Happened on the Way to the Forum, 1962-64; Fiddler on the Roof, 1964-72; Poor Bitos, 1964; Flora the Red Menace, 1965. Director-Producer: She Loves Me, 1963-64, London 1964; Superman, 1966; Cabaret, 1966-69, London 1968; Zorba, 1968-69; Company, 1970-72, London 1972; A Little Night Music, 1973-74, London 1975 (dir. film, 1977); Pacific Overtures, 1976. Director: A Family Affair, 1962; Baker Street, 1965; Something For Everyone (film), 1970; New Phoenix Rep. prodns of Great God Brown, 1972-73, The Visit, 1973-74, and Love for Love, 1974-75; Some of my Best Friends, 1977; On the Twentieth Century, 1978; Evita, London 1978, USA 1979-80, Australia, Vienna, 1980, Mexico City, 1981; Sweeney Todd, 1979, London 1980. Directed: Amer. première of opera, Ashmedai, for New York City Opera, 1976; Girl of the Golden West, San Francisco Op., 1979; première of Kurt Weill's Silverlake, NY City Op., 1980; world première, Willie Stark, Houston Grand Opera, 1981. Co-Director-Producer, Follies, 1971-72; co-Producer-Director: Candide, 1974-75; Merrily We Roll Along, 1981. Antoinette Perry Awards for: The Pajama Game; Damn Yankees; Fiorello!; A Funny Thing Happened on the Way to the Forum; Fiddler on the Roof; Cabaret; Company; A Little Night Music;

Candide; Sweeney Todd; Evita; SWET award: Evita, 1977-78. Member: League of New York Theatres (Pres., 1964-65); Council for National Endowment for the Arts. Hon. DLit, Emerson College, 1971; Hon. Dr of Fine Arts, Univ. of Pennsylvania, 1971. Drama Critics' Circle Awards; Best Musical Award, London Evening Standard, 1955-58, 1972. *Publication:* Contradictions: notes on twenty-six years in the theatre, 1974. *Recreation:* tennis. *Address:* Suite 2410, 1270 Avenue of the Americas, New York, NY 10020, USA. *T:* 212-399-0960.

PRINCE, Maj.-Gen. Hugh Anthony, CBE 1960; retired as Chief, Military Planning Office, SEATO, Bangkok; *b* 11 Aug. 1911; *s* of H. T. Prince, FRCS, LRCP; *m* 1st, 1938, Elizabeth (*d* of Dr Walter Bapty, Victoria, BC; two *s*; 2nd, 1959, Claude-Andrée, *d* of André Romanet, Château-de-Tholot, Beaujeu, Rhône; one *s*. *Educ:* Eastbourne Coll.; RMC, Sandhurst. Commissioned, 1931; served in 6th Gurkha Rifles until 1947; The King's Regt (Liverpool), 1947. *Recreations:* golf, gardening, antiques. *Address:* 13200 Raphèle-les-Arles, France. *T:* 98.46.93.

PRINCE, Leslie Barnett, CBE 1973; MA; FCA; FCIArb; *b* 27 May 1901; *s* of Sir Alexander William Prince, KBE, and Lady Prince (*née* Edith Jonas); *m* 1st, 1924, Norah Millie (*d* 1979), *d* of Eliot Lewis, JP; one *s* two *d*; 2nd, 1980, Gerwin Sylvia Delacour Davis, MB ChB, DPM (Univ. of Cape Town), MRCPsych, *d* of Harold Delacour Davis, South Africa. *Educ:* Clifton Coll.; Magdalene Coll., Cambridge (MA). FCA 1930. Chartered Accountant; Dir, Hand in Hand Assce Co. (Commercial Union), 1934- (Chm., 1974-82; Dep. Chm., 1982-). London Chest Hospital Board, 1937-48; Hospital for Diseases of the Chest, Board of Management, 1948-61. Joint Chairman of Jewish Refugees Cttee, 1939-43; Hon. Director of Accounts, ROF, Ministry of Supply, 1944-46. Member Court of Common Council, City of London, 1950-; Chairman: Rates Finance Cttee, 1957-65; Coal and Corn and Finance Cttee, Corporation of London, 1967; Coal, Corn and Rates Finance Cttee, 1968-70; Real Estate Cttee, 1970-; Chief Commoner, City Lands and Bridge House Estates Cttee, 1971. Sheriff of City of London, 1954-55; Chm., London Court of Arbitration, 1974-77. Member Council: Metropolitan Hospital Sunday Fund, 1951-; Royal Veterinary Coll., 1971-. Deputy of Ward of Bishopsgate, 1970. Master, Worshipful Co. of Farriers, 1955-56. President: United Wards Club, 1957; Bishopsgate Ward Club, 1958. Pres., Old Cliftonian Soc., 1973-75 (Hon. Treas., 1934-73). Companion of Star of Ethiopia, 1954; Commandeur Léopold II, 1963; Order of Sacred Treasure (Japan), 1972; Order of Stor (Afghanistan), 1972. *Publication:* The Farrier and his Craft, 1980. *Recreation:* knitting. *Address:* 21 Cadogan Gardens, SW3. *T:* 01-730 0515. *Clubs:* Gresham, City Livery (Treasurer, 1966-72, and 1974-78, Pres., 1973-74), Samuel Pepys (Treasurer, 1982-).

PRINCE-SMITH, Sir (William) Richard, 4th Bt, *cr* 1911; Landowner; *b* 27 Dec. 1928; *s* of Sir William Prince-Smith, 3rd Bt, OBE, MC, and Marjorie, Lady Prince-Smith (*d* 1970); *S* father, 1964; *m* 1st, 1955, Margaret Ann Carter; one *s* one *d*; 2nd, 1975, Ann Christina Faulds. *Educ:* Charterhouse; Clare Coll., Cambridge (MA). BA (Agric.) 1951. *Recreations:* music, photography, yachting. *Heir: s* James William Prince-Smith, *b* 2 July 1959. *Address:* Augres House, Trinity, Jersey.

PRING, David Andrew Michael, CB 1980; MC 1943; Clerk of Committees, House of Commons, since 1976; *b* 6 Dec. 1922; *s* of late Captain John Arthur Pring and Gladys Pring; *m* 1962, Susan Brakspear, Henley-on-Thames; one *s* one *d*. *Educ:* King's Sch., Rochester; Magdalene Coll., Cambridge (MA). Served Royal Engineers, N Africa, Sicily, Italy, Austria, 1941-46; attached staff Governor-General, Canada, 1946. A Clerk of the House of Commons, 1948-. *Publications:* various, incl. (with Kenneth Bradshaw) Parliament and Congress, 1972. *Recreation:* living in the country. *Address:* Bushy Platt, Stanford Dingley, Berks RG7 6DY. *T:* Woolhampton 2585. *Club:* Athenæum.

PRINGLE, Air Marshal Sir Charles (Norman Seton), KBE 1973 (CBE 1967); MA, FEng, FRAeS; CBIM; Director, Society of British Aerospace Companies, since 1979; *b* 6 June 1919; *s* of late Seton Pringle, OBE, FRCSI, Dublin; *m* 1946, Margaret, *d* of late B. Sharp, Baildon, Yorkshire; one *s*. *Educ:* Repton; St John's Coll., Cambridge. Commissioned, RAF, 1941; served India and Ceylon, Air Ministry, 1946-48; RAE, Farnborough, 1949-50; attached to USAF, 1950-52; appts in UK, 1952-60; STSO No 3 Group, Bomber Comd, 1960-62, and Air Forces Middle East, 1962-64; Comdt RAF St Athan and Air Officer Wales, 1964-66; MoD, 1967; IDC, 1968. Dir-Gen. of Engineering (RAF) MoD, 1969-70; Air Officer Engineering, Strike Command, 1970-73; Dir-Gen. Engineering (RAF), 1973; Controller, Engrg and Supply (RAF), 1973-76; Sen. Exec., Rolls Royce Ltd, 1976-78; Dir, Hunting Engineering Ltd, 1976-78. Pres., RAeS, 1975-76; Vice-Chm., 1976-77, Chm., 1977-78, CEI. *Recreations:* photography, ornithology, motor sport. *Address:* 8 Strangways Terrace, W14 8NE. *T:* 01-602 3356. *Clubs:* Institute of Directors, Royal Air Force, Buck's.

PRINGLE, Dr Derek Hair, CBE 1980; FRSE; Chairman and Managing Director, Scientific and Electronic Enterprises Ltd, Livingston, since 1980; *b* 8 Jan. 1926; *s* of Robert Pringle and Lilias Dalgleish Hair; *m* 1949, Anne Collier Caw; three *s* one *d*. *Educ:* George Heriot's Sch., Edinburgh; Edinburgh Univ. (BSc 1948, PhD 1951. FInstP 1957. FRSE 1970. Res. Physicist, Ferranti Ltd, Edinburgh, 1948-59; Nuclear Enterprises Ltd: Technical Dir, 1960-76; Man. Dir, 1976-78; Chm., 1978-80. Director: Amersham Internat. Ltd, 1978-; Creative Capital Nominees Ltd, 1982-.

Member: Nat. Radiol Protection Bd, Harwell, 1969-81; Council for Applied Science in Scotland, 1981-; Univ. Court, Heriot-Watt Univ., 1968-77. Pres., Edinburgh Chamber of Commerce and Manufactures, 1979-81. Faraday Lectr, 1978-79. Hon. DSc Heriot Watt Univ., 1981. *Publications:* papers on microwave engrg, gas discharge physics and nuclear science in scientific jls. *Recreations:* golf, gardening. *Address:* Lochinver House, 75 Trinity Road, Edinburgh EH5 3JX. *T:* 031-552 4549. *Clubs:* Royal Over-Seas League, English-Speaking Union.
See also R. W. Pringle.

PRINGLE, John Martin Douglas, *b* 1912; *s* of late J. Douglas Pringle, Hawick, Scotland; *m* 1936, Celia, *d* of E. A. Carroll; one *s* two *d. Educ:* Shrewsbury Sch.; Lincoln Coll., Oxford. First Class Literae Humaniores, 1934. Editorial Staff of Manchester Guardian, 1934-39. Served War of 1939-45 with King's Own Scottish Borderers, 1940-44; Assistant Editor, Manchester Guardian, 1944-48; Special Writer on The Times, 1948-52; Editor of The Sydney Morning Herald, 1952-57; Deputy Editor of The Observer, 1958-63; Managing Editor, Canberra Times, 1964-65; Editor, Sydney Morning Herald, 1965-70. *Publications:* China Struggles for Unity, 1938; Australian Accent, 1958; Australian Painting Today, 1963; On Second Thoughts, 1971; Have Pen, Will Travel, 1973; The Last Shenachie, 1976. *Address:* 103 Riverview Road, Avalon Beach, NSW 2107, Australia.

PRINGLE, John William Sutton, MBE 1945; FRS 1954; ScD 1955; Linacre Professor of Zoology, Oxford, and Fellow of Merton College, Oxford, 1961-79; now Professor Emeritus; *b* 22 July 1912; *e s* of late John Pringle, MD, Manchester, and of Dorothy Emily (*née* Beney); *m* 1946, Beatrice Laura Wilson (*née* Gilbert-Carter); one *s* two *d. Educ:* Winchester Coll.; King's Coll., Cambridge (MA). University Demonstrator in Zoology, 1937-39; University Lecturer, 1945-59; Fellow of King's Coll., Cambridge, 1938-45; Telecommunications Research Establishment, 1939-44; Ministry of War Transport, 1944-45; Fellow of Peterhouse, Cambridge, 1945-61, Emeritus Fellow, 1961, Hon. Fellow, 1982-. Senior Tutor, 1948-57; Senior Bursar, 1957-59; Librarian, 1959-61; Reader in Experimental Cytology, Cambridge, 1959-61. Pres., Soc. for Experimental Biol., 1977-. American Medal of Freedom, 1945. *Publications:* Insect Flight, 1957; (ed) Biology and the Human Sciences, 1972; papers in Journal of Experimental Biology, Journal of Physiology, Philos. Trans. Royal Society. *Recreation:* bee-keeping. *Address:* 437 Banbury Road, Oxford OX2 8ED. *T:* 58470.

PRINGLE, Dr Mia Lilly Kellmer, CBE 1975; Founder, and Director, National Children's Bureau, 1963-81, Vice-President, since 1981; *d* of late Samuel and late Sophie Kellmer; *m* 1946, William Joseph Sommerville Pringle, BSc (*d* 1962); *m* 1969, William Leonard Hooper, MA Oxon (*d* 1980). *Educ:* schools in Vienna; Birkbeck Coll., University of London (Hon. Fellow, 1980). BA (Hons) 1944; Dip. Educ. Psychol. 1945; Fellowship, London Child Guidance Training Centre, 1945; PhD (Psych.) 1950. Teaching in Primary Schools, Middx and Herts, 1940-44; Educ. and Clin. Psychologist, Herts Child Guidance Service, 1945-50; University of Birmingham: Lecturer in Educ. Psych., 1950-54; Dep. Head, Dept of Child Study, 1954-63; Senior Lecturer in Educ. Psych., 1960-63. Member: Birmingham Educ. Cttee, 1957-63; Home Sec.'s Adv. Council on Child Care, 1966-72; Consultative Panel for Social Develt, ODM, 1968-71; Sec. of State's Adv. Cttee on Handicapped Children, 1971-; Bd of Governors, Hosp. for Sick Children, Gt Ormond Street, 1969-81; Research Consultant: on play needs, to Min. of Housing and Local Govt, 1968-73; UN Research Inst. for Social Develt, 1967-69; co-opted Mem., Islington Social Services Cttee, 1972-78; Personal Social Services Council, 1973-80 (Chm. Study Gp on A Future for Intermediate Treatment, report published 1977); Chm., Assoc. of Social Res. Orgns, 1977-81; Vice-Chairman: UK Assoc. for Internat. Year of the Child, 1978-80; Children's Cttee (apptd by Sec. of State for Health and Social Security), 1978-81; Consultant to Unicef (Europe), 1982-; Pres., Pre-school Playgroups Assoc., 1982-. Hon. DSc: Bradford, 1972; Aston, 1979; Hull, 1982. Hon. Fellow, Manchester Polytechnic; Hon. FCP. Hon. Mem., British Paediatric Assoc. FBPsS; FRSocMed; FRSA. *Publications:* The Emotional and Social Adjustment of Physically Handicapped Children, 1964; Deprivation and Education, 1965; Investment in Children (ed), 1965; Social Learning and its Measurement, 1966; Adoption-Facts and Fallacies, 1966; Caring for Children (ed), 1968; Able Misfits, 1970; The Needs of Children, 1974, 2nd edn 1980; co-author: 11,000 Seven-Year-Olds, 1966; Four Years On, 1967; Residential Child Care-Facts and Fallacies, 1967; Foster Care-Facts and Fallacies, 1967; The Community's Children, 1967; Directory of National, Voluntary Children's Organisations, 1968; The Challenge of Thalidomide, 1970; Living with Handicap, 1970; Born Illegitimate, 1971; Growing Up Adopted, 1972; Advances in Educational Psychology, vol. 2, 1973; Early Child Care and Education, 1975; Controversial Issues in Child Development, 1978; Preparation for Parenthood, 1980; Psychological Approaches to Child Abuse, 1980; A Fairer Future, 1980; papers in journals of psychology, education and child care. *Recreations:* swimming, music, theatre-going, cooking. *Address:* 68 Wimpole Street, W1. *T:* 01-935 3144. *Club:* Royal Over-Seas League.

PRINGLE, Dr Robert William, OBE 1967; BSc, PhD; FRSE; FRSC; President, Nuclear Enterprises Ltd, Edinburgh, since 1976; *b* 2 May 1920; *s* of late Robert Pringle and late Lillias Dalgleish Hair; *m* 1948, Carol Stokes; three *s* one *d. Educ:* George Heriot's Sch., Edinburgh; Edinburgh Univ. (Vans Dunlop Scholar in Natural Philosophy); Lecturer, Natural Philosophy, Edinburgh, 1945; Associate Professor of Physics, Manitoba, 1949; Prof. and Chairman of Physics, Manitoba, 1953-56. Chm. and Man. Dir, Nuclear

Enterprises Ltd, 1956-76 (Queen's Award to Industry, 1966, 1979); Dir, N Sea Assets Ltd, 1977-78. Member: Scottish Council, CBI (Cttee), 1966-72; University Court, Edinburgh Univ., 1967-75; Scottish Univs Industry Liaison Cttee, 1968-75; Bd, Edinburgh Univ. Centre for Industrial Liaison and Consultancy, 1968-; Bd, Royal Observatory (Edinburgh), 1968-79; Council, SRC, 1972-76; Bd, Astronomy, Space and Radio (SRC), 1970-72; Bd, Nuclear Physics (SRC), 1972-76; Economic Council for Scotland, 1971-75; Bd, Scottish Sch. Business Studies, 1972-; Press Cttee, Edinburgh Univ., 1977-78; Trustee: Scottish Hospitals Endowments Res. Trust, 1976-; Scottish Trust for the Physically Disabled, 1977-. Hon. Adviser, Nat. Museum of Antiquities of Scotland, 1969. FInstP 1948; Fellow, American Inst. Physics, 1950; FRSC 1955; FRSE 1964; Hon. Fellow, Royal Scottish Soc. Arts, 1972. *Publications:* papers on nuclear spectroscopy and nuclear geophysics in UK and US scientific journals. *Recreations:* golf, book-collecting, Rugby (Edinburgh, Edinburgh and Glasgow, Rest of Scotland, 1945-48). *Address:* 27 avenue Princesse Grace, Monaco. *Clubs:* Athenæum; New (Edinburgh); Yacht Club de Monaco.
See also D. H. Pringle.

PRINGLE, Lt-Gen. Sir Steuart (Robert), 10th Bt, *cr* 1683, Stichill, Roxburghshire; KCB 1982; Commandant General Royal Marines, since 1981; *b* 21 July 1928; *s* of Sir Norman H. Pringle, 9th Bt and Lady (Oonagh) Pringle (*née* Curran) (*d* 1975); *S* father, 1961; *m* 1953, Jacqueline Marie Gladwell; two *s* two *d. Educ:* Sherborne. Royal Marines: 2nd Lieut, 1946. *Heir: s* Simon Robert Pringle, *b* 6 Jan. 1959. *Address:* 76 South Croxted Road, Dulwich, SE21.

PRINZ, Gerhard, Dr jur; Chairman of the Executive Board, since 1980, and Director, since 1974, Daimler-Benz AG; *b* Solingen, 5 April 1929; *s* of Albert Prinz; *m* Renate Ebner. Joined Volkswagen, 1967; Mem., Bd of Management, Volkswagenwerk AG, 1969-73; Chm., Bd of Management, Audi-NSU, 1972-73; Director: Carl Prinz AG, Solingen; Agrippina-Vers. AG, Köln; Bertelsmann AG; Beirat Deutsche Bank AG, Braunschweig. *Address:* Daimler-Benz AG, Mercedesstrasse 136, 7000 Stuttgart 60, Federal Republic of Germany.

PRIOR, Ven. Christopher, CB 1968; Archdeacon of Portsmouth, 1969-77, Archdeacon Emeritus since 1977; *b* 2 July 1912; *s* of late Ven. W. H. Prior; *m* 1945, Althea Stafford (*née* Coode); two *d. Educ:* King's Coll., Taunton; Keble Coll., Oxford; Cuddesdon Coll. Curate of Hornsea, 1938-41; Chaplain RN from 1941, Chaplain of the Fleet, 1966-69. Served in: HMS Royal Arthur, 1941; HMHS Maine, 1941-43; HMS Scylla, 1943-44; HMS Owl, 1944-46; various ships, 1946-58; Britannia RNC, Dartmouth, 1958-61; HMS Blake, 1961-62; HM Dockyard, Portsmouth, 1963-66; QHC, 1966-69. *Recreations:* golf, walking. *Address:* Ponies End, West Melbury, Shaftesbury, Dorset SP7 0LY. *T:* Shaftesbury 811239.

PRIOR, Rt. Hon. James Michael Leathes, PC 1970; MP (C) Lowestoft Division of Suffolk since 1959; Secretary of State for Northern Ireland, since 1981; *b* 11 Oct. 1927; 2nd *s* of late C. B. L. and A. S. M. Prior, Norwich; *m* 1954, Jane Primrose Gifford, 2nd *d* of late Air Vice-Marshal O. G. Lywood, CB, CBE; three *s* one *d. Educ:* Charterhouse; Pembroke College, Cambridge. 1st class degree in Estate Management, 1950; commissioned in Royal Norfolk Regt, 1946; served in India and Germany; farmer and land agent in Norfolk and Suffolk. PPS to Pres. of Bd of Trade, 1963, to Minister of Power, 1963-64, to Mr Edward Heath, Leader of the Opposition, 1965-70; Minister of Agriculture, Fisheries and Food, 1970-72; Lord Pres. of Council and Leader of House of Commons, 1972-74; Opposition front bench spokesman on Employment, 1974-79; Sec. of State for Employment, 1979-81. A Dep. Chm., Cons. Party, 1972-74 (Vice-Chm., 1965). Chm. Aston Boats Ltd, 1968-70; Director: F. Lambert and Sons Ltd, 1958-70; IDC Group, 1968-70, 1974-79; United Biscuits (Holdings) Ltd, 1974-79; Norwich Union Adv. Bd, 1974-79; Avon Cosmetics Ltd, 1975-79; Consultant: Trust Houses Forte, 1974-79; Nickerson Gp, 1975-79. *Recreations:* cricket, tennis, golf, gardening. *Address:* Old Hall, Brampton, Beccles, Suffolk. *T:* Brampton 278; 36 Morpeth Mansions, SW1. *T:* 01-834 5543. *Clubs:* MCC; Butterflies Cricket.

PRIOR, Peter James, CBE 1980; Chairman, H. P. Bulmer Holdings Ltd, 1977-82 (H. P. Bulmer Ltd, 1973-77); Director, British Sugar Corporation, since 1969; *b* 1 Sept. 1919; *s* of Percy Prior; *m* 1957, Prinia Mary, *d* of late R. E. Moreau, Berrick Prior, Oxon; two *s. Educ:* Royal Grammar Sch., High Wycombe; London Univ. BSc(Econ). FCA, FIMC, CBIM, FIIM, FRSA. Royal Berks Regt, 1939; Intell. Corps, 1944-46 (Captain) (Croix-de-Guerre 1944). Company Sec., Saunders-Roe (Anglesey) Ltd, 1948; Consultant, Urwick, Orr & Partners, 1951; Financial Dir, International Chemical Co., 1956; Financial Dir, British Aluminium Co., 1961; Man. Dir, H. P. Bulmer Ltd, 1966. Member: English Tourist Bd, 1969-75; Midlands Electricity Bd, 1973-; Mem. Council, Brit. Inst. of Management; Chairman: Inquiry into Potato Processing Industry, 1971; Motorway Service Area Inquiry, 1977-78. Pres., Incorp. Soc. of British Advertisers' Council, 1980-. Chm. Trustees, Leadership Trust, 1975-79. Communicator of the Year Award, British Assoc. of Industrial Editors, 1982. *Publications:* Leadership is not a Bowler Hat, 1977; articles on management and leadership. *Recreations:* free-fall parachuting, flying (Vice Chm., Hereford Air Sports Centre, 1979-), motor-cycling, restoration of locomotive King George V. *Address:* Rathays, Sutton Saint Nicholas, Herefordshire HR1 3AY. *T:* Sutton Saint Nicholas 313. *Clubs:* Army and Navy, Special Forces.

PRIOR, William Johnson, CBE 1979; CEng, FIEE; CBIM; Chairman, Yorkshire Electricity Board, since 1979; Member, National Coal Board, since 1977; *b* 28 Jan. 1924; *s* of Ernest Stanley and Lilian Prior; *m* 1945, Mariel (*née* Irving); two *s* one *d*. *Educ:* Goole and Barnsley Grammar Schs. Barugh, Mexborough, Stuart Street (Manchester) and Stockport Power Stations, 1944-52; Keadby, 1952-56, Supt, 1954-56; Supt, Berkeley, 1957-58; Supt, Hinkley Point Generating Station, 1959-66; CEGB and predecessors: Asst Reg. Dir (Generation), NW Region, 1967-70; Dir (Generation), SW Region, 1970-72; Dir-Gen., SE Region, 1972-76; Mem., Electricity Council, 1976-79. *Recreation:* country walking. *Address:* Yorkshire Electricity Board, Scarcroft, Leeds LS14 3HS; Highfield House, Lime Kiln Lane, Kirk Deighton, Wetherby, W Yorks LS22 4EA. *T:* Wetherby 64434.

PRIOR-PALMER, Lucinda Jane; *see* Green, L. J.

PRIOR-PALMER, Brig. Sir Otho (Leslie), Kt 1959; DSO 1945; *b* 28 Oct. 1897; *s* of late Spunner Prior-Palmer, County Sligo, Ireland, and Merrion Square, Dublin, and Anne Leslie Gason. Kilteelagh, Co. Tipperary; *m* 1940, Sheila Mary Weller Poley (OBE 1958), Boxted Hall, Bury St Edmunds; one *s* two *d* (and one *d* by previous marr.); *m* 1964, Elizabeth, *d* of late Harold Henderson; two *s*. *Educ:* Wellington; RMC, Sandhurst. Commissioned 9th Lancers, 1916; commanded 2nd Northamptonshire Yeo., 1940-42; comd 30th Armoured Brigade, Mar.-Aug. 1942; 29th Armoured Brigade, 1942-43; 7th Armoured Brigade, 1943-45 (DSO); commanded latter during Italian Campaign; retd pay 1946, hon. rank of Brig. MP (C) Worthing Div. W Sussex, 1945-50, Worthing, 1950-64. Vice-Chm. Conservative Members' Defence Cttee, 1958-59; Past Chm. NATO Parliamentarians Defence Cttee. *Recreations:* ski-ing, sailing, all field sports, fishing. *Address:* Grange, Honiton, Devon. *T:* Broadhembury 377. *Clubs:* Royal Yacht Squadron (Cowes); Pratt's.

PRITCHARD, family name of **Baron Pritchard**.

PRITCHARD, Baron *cr* 1975 (Life Peer), of West Haddon, Northamptonshire; **Derek Wilbraham Pritchard**; Kt 1968; DL; *b* 8 June 1910; *s* of Frank Wheelton Pritchard and Ethel Annie Pritchard (*née* Cheetham); *m* 1941, Denise Arfor Pritchard (*née* Huntbach); two *d*. *Educ:* Clifton College, Bristol. Took over family business of E. Halliday & Son, Wine Merchants, 1929, Man. Dir, 1930-51. Called up in TA and served War of 1939-45; demob. as Col and joined Bd of E. K. Cole, Ltd, 1946. Joined Ind Coope Ltd, as Man. Dir of Grants of St James's Ltd, 1949, Chm., 1960-69; Chm., Victoria Wine & Co. Ltd, 1959-64. Former Director: Ind Coope Ltd, 1951; Ind Coope Tetley Ansell Ltd on merger of those companies, 1961; Allied Breweries Ltd, 1961-80 (Chm., 1968-70); Allied Breweries Investments Ltd, 1957-80; Guardian Assurance Ltd, 1960-80; Guardian Royal Exchange Assurance Ltd, 1968-80; George Sandeman Sons & Co. Ltd, 1952-80; Carreras Ltd, 1970-72 (Chm.); Dorchester Hotel Ltd, 1976-80 (Chm.); Rothmans of Pall Mall Canada Ltd, 1972-77; Rothmans of Pall Mall (Australia) Ltd, 1972-77; Rothmans of Pall Mall (Malaysia) Berhad, 1972-77; Rothmans of Pall Mall (Singapore) Ltd, 1972-77; Deltec International, 1975-77; London-American Finance Corp., 1976-78. Director: J. & W. Nicholson (Holdings) Ltd, 1952-; Midland Bank Ltd, 1968-; Samuel Montagu Ltd, 1969-; Adelaide Associates Ltd, 1970-; Rothmans International Ltd, 1972- (Chm., 1972-75); Rothmans Group Services SA, 1972-; Rothmans of Pall Mall (London) Ltd, 1980-; Rothmans Group Holdings Ltd, 1981-; Carreras Group (Jamaica) Ltd, 1972-; Paterson, Zochonis & Co. Ltd, 1977-; Philips Electronic & Associated Industries Ltd, 1978-; Templeton Investments International Inc., 1980-; Templeton Investments International Ltd, 1980-. Chairman: Dorchester Hotel Bd of Trustees, 1980-; Adv. Bd, Rembrandt-Rothmans World Gp, 1980-; Mem., Salomon Bros Adv. Bd, USA, 1980-. Dep. Chm., BNEC, 1965-66; Chm. 1966-68; Member: Nat. Inds Appts Bd, 1973-; Top Salaries Review Body, 1975-78; House of Lords EEC Cttee, 1975-79, EEC Sub-Cttee A, 1975-81; British Overseas Trade Adv. Council, 1976-; Fund Raising Cttee, RCS, 1976-; Chancellor of the Duchy of Lancaster's Cttee on Business Sponsorship of the Arts, 1980-; Amer. European Community Assoc., 1981-; President: Inst. of Directors, 1968-74; British Export Houses Assoc., 1976-; Northants Co. Branch, Royal Agricl Benevolent Instn, 1981-; Patron, Northants British Red Cross Soc., 1982- (Pres., 1975-82); Vice-President: Inst. of Export, 1976- (Pres., 1962-64); Wine and Spirit Assoc. of GB, 1964- (Pres., 1962-64); Northants Youth Club Assoc., 1965-; East of England Agricl Soc., 1974-; Co-Chm., UK-Jamaica Cttee, 1981-; Trustee: Age Action Trust, 1975-; St Giles Church, Northampton, 1976-; Patron: Northampton and County Chamber of Commerce, 1978-; Three Shires Indept Hosp., 1978-; Abbeyfield Soc. for the Aged, 1979- (Pres., 1970-79); Governor: Clifton Coll., Bristol; Nene Coll., Northampton; Lyford Cay Club, Bahamas; British Foundn for Age Research. DL Northants, 1974. *Recreations:* farming, tennis, golf, swimming, hunting (Chm., Pytchley). *Address:* West Haddon Hall, Northampton NN6 7AU. *T:* West Haddon 210.

PRITCHARD, Arthur Alan, CB 1979; JP; formerly Deputy Under Secretary of State, Ministry of Defence; *b* 3 March 1922; *s* of Arthur Henry Standfast Pritchard and Sarah Bessie Myra Pritchard (*née* Mundy); *m* 1949, Betty Rona Nevard (*née* Little); two *s* one *d*. *Educ:* Wanstead High Sch., Essex. Board of Trade, 1939. RAF Pilot, 1941-46. RAFVR, 1947-52. Joined Admiralty, 1952; Asst Sec., 1964; attended Royal College of Defence Studies, 1972; Asst Under-Sec. of State, Naval Personnel and Op. Requirements, MoD, 1972-76; seconded as Dep. Sec., NI Office, 1976-78; Secretary to the Admiralty Bd, 1978-81. JP Totton, 1981. *Recreations:* sailing, walking. *Address:* c/o Midland

Bank, Fordingbridge, Hants. *Clubs:* Royal Air Force; Lilliput Sailing (Poole).

PRITCHARD, Sir Asa Hubert, Kt 1965; Merchant, retired; President, Asa H. Pritchard Ltd, Nassau; *b* 1 Aug. 1891; *s* of William Edward Pritchard, Bahamas; *m* 1915, Maud Pauline Pyfrom (*d* 1978); two *s* two *d*. *Educ:* Queen's College, Bahamas. MHA, Bahamas, 1925-62; Deputy Speaker, 1942-46; Speaker, 1946-62. Member: Board of Education, 1930-35; Electricity Board, 1940-46; Chm., Bahamas Develt Bd, 1946. *Address:* Breezy Ridge, PO Box 6218 ES, Nassau, Bahamas.

PRITCHARD, Frederick Hugh Dalzel, CBE 1961; Secretary-General, British Red Cross Society, 1951-70; *b* 26 Aug. 1905; *e s* of Gerald William and Alice Bayes Pritchard (*née* Dalzel), Richmond, Surrey; *m* 1935, Rosamund Wright Marshall; two *d*. *Educ:* Charterhouse School; Oriel College, Oxford. Admitted Solicitor, 1931. Partner in Pritchard Sons Partington & Holland, solicitors, London, 1933. Legal Adviser, War Organisation of British Red Cross Soc. and Order of St John, 1940. Exec. Asst to Vice-Chm., British Red Cross Soc., 1948. OStJ 1942. *Address:* Denver, Bulstrode Way, Gerrards Cross, Bucks. *T:* Gerrards Cross 83483.

PRITCHARD, Rear-Adm. Gwynedd Idris, CB 1981; *b* 18 June 1924; *s* of Cyril Idris Pritchard and Lily Pritchard; *m* 1975, Mary Thérèsa (*née* Curtin); three *s* (by previous marriage). *Educ:* Wyggeston Sch., Leicester. FBIM, MNI. Joined Royal Navy, 1942; Sub-Lieut 1944; Lieut 1946; Lt-Comdr 1954; Comdr 1959; Captain 1967; Rear-Adm. 1976; Flag Officer Sea Training, 1976-78; Flag Officer Gibraltar, 1979-81; retired list, 1981. *Recreations:* riding, caravanning. *Address:* Hoofprints, Beach Road, Burton Bradstock, Dorset.

PRITCHARD, Hugh Wentworth, CBE 1969; Member of Council of Law Society, 1947-66; *b* 15 March 1903; *s* of late Sir Harry G. Pritchard; *m* 1934, Barbara Stableforth; two *s*. *Educ:* Charterhouse; Balliol College, Oxford. Admitted a solicitor, 1927; partner in Sharpe Pritchard & Co., 1928-80. Pres. Soc. of Parliamentary Agents, 1952-55; Member: Statute Law Committee, 1954-81; Committee on Administrative Tribunals and Enquiries, 1955; Council on Tribunals, 1958-70. Lay Reader, 1947. Served War of 1939-45, in England, France, Belgium and Germany; joined The Queen's as a private; commissioned in RAOC, attaining rank of Lt-Col. *Recreation:* golf. *Address:* Barton, Great Woodcote Drive, Purley, Surrey CR2 3PL. *T:* 01-660 9029.

PRITCHARD, John Michael, CBE 1962; Chief Conductor: Cologne Opera, since 1978; BBC Symphony Orchestra, since 1982 (Chief Guest Conductor, 1979-82); Music Director, Belgian Opera Nationale, since 1981; *b* 5 Feb. 1921; *s* of Albert Edward Pritchard and Amy Edith Shaylor. *Educ:* Sir George Monoux School, London; privately. Conductor: Derby String Orchestra, 1943-51; Music Staff, Glyndebourne Opera, 1947, Chorus master, 1949; Conductor, Jacques Orchestra, 1950-52; Asst to Fritz Busch, Vittorio Gui, 1950-51; Conductor Glyndebourne Festivals, 1952-77; Conductor and Musical Director, Royal Liverpool Philharmonic Orchestra, 1957-63; Musical Director, London Philharmonic Orchestra, 1962-66; Principal Conductor, 1967-77, and Musical Director, 1969-77, Glyndebourne Opera; Guest Conductor: Vienna State Opera, 1952-53, 1964-65; Covent Garden Opera, 1952-77; Edinburgh Internat. Festivals, opera and symphony concerts 1951-55, 1960-63, 1979-81; Aix-en-Provence Festival, 1963, 1981; Frankfurt Radio Orchestra, 1953; Cologne Radio Orchestra, 1953; Vienna Symphony Orchestra, 1953-55; Berlin Festival, 1954, 1964; Zürich Radio Orchestra, 1955, 1961; Santa Cecilia Orchestra, Rome, 1958, 1972, 1979; Orchestre Nationale, Brussels, 1958, 1965-67; Cracow Philharmonic Orch., 1961; Basel, Winterthur Orch., 1961, 1969; RIAS Orchestra, Berlin, 1961, 1966; Royal Philharmonic Soc., London, 1959, 1961, 1963, 1964, 1965, 1966, 1970, 1974; Wexford Festival, 1959, 1961; Oslo Philharmonic Orch., 1960, 1961, 1966, 1975; Pittsburgh Symphony Orch., 1963, 1964, and San Francisco Symphony, 1964; BBC Promenade Concerts, 1960-77; tour of Switzerland, 1962, 1966; of Australia, 1962; of Germany, 1963, 1966; with BBC Symph. Orch., 1968, 1982; tour of Jugoslavia, 1968; Georges Enesco Festival, Bucharest, 1964; Lausanne Festival, 1964; Berlin Philharmonic, 1964; New York Opera Assoc., 1964; Société Philharmonique, Brussels, 1965, 1967; Helsinki Philharmonic, 1966; Salzburg Festival, 1966; Teatro Colon, Buenos Aires, 1966; RAI Symphony Orch., Turin, 1967; Sjaellands Symphony Orch., Copenhagen, 1967-70; SABC Orchestra, Johannesburg, 1967-70; Scandinavian Tour, Glyndebourne Opera, 1967; Teatro San Carlo, Naples, 1969-70; Danish Radio Symph., 1968; Palermo Sinfonia, 1968; Munich State Opera, 1968-69; Athens Festival, 1968-70; Leipzig Gewandhaus, 1968-70; Dresden Staatskapelle, 1968-70, 1972; Berlin Radio, 1968-70, 1972; Chicago Lyric Opera, 1969, 1975, 1977, 1978; Florence Maggio Musicale, 1977, 1978, 1979; Zürich Tonhalle, 1977-78, 1979; London Philharmonic Tours: Far East, 1969; USA, 1971; Hong Kong and China, 1973; New Philharmonia Orch., Osaka, Tokyo, 1970; San Francisco Opera, 1970, 1973-74, 1976, 1977, 1979; Geneva Opera, 1971, 1974; Metropolitan Opera, NY, 1971, 1973-74, 1977-79; Yomiuri Nippon Orch., Tokyo, 1972; English Chamber Orch. Tour, Latin America, 1972; Australian Opera, Sydney, 1974, 1977; Cologne Opera, 1975, 1976, 1977-79, 1982; Philadelphia Orch., 1975, 1976, 1978; Opera Orch., Monte Carlo, 1976-78; Houston Grand Opera, 1976, 1978, 1979; Vancouver Symphony, 1978; Paris Opéra, 1979, 1981. Shakespeare Prize, Hamburg, 1975. *Recreations:* good food and wine, theatre. *Address:* c/o Basil Horsfield, Estoril (B), Avenue Princesse Grace 31, Monte Carlo.

PRITCHARD, Kenneth John, CB 1982; Director General of Supplies and Transport (Naval), Ministry of Defence, since 1981; *b* 18 March 1926; *s* of William Edward Pritchard and Ethel Mary Pritchard (*née* Cornfield); *m* 1st, 1949, Elizabeth Margaret Bradshaw (*d* 1978); two *d*; 2nd, 1979, Angela Madeleine Palmer; one *s. Educ:* Newport High Sch.; St Catherine's Coll., Oxford (BA 1951). Served Army, 1944-48; Indian Mil. Acad., Dehra Dun, 1945; served with 8th/12th Frontier Force Regt and 2nd Royal W Kent Regt. Asst Principal, Admiralty, 1951; Private Sec. to Sec. of State for Wales, 1964; Asst Sec., Min. of Aviation, 1966; RCDS, 1972; Principal Supply and Transport Officer (Naval), Portsmouth, 1978, Exec. Dir 1980. *Recreations:* squash, tennis. *Address:* Pickford House, Beckington, Som BA3 6SJ. *T:* Frome 830329.

PRITCHARD, Sir Neil, KCMG 1962 (CMG 1952); HM Diplomatic Service, retired; Ambassador in Bangkok, 1967-70; *b* 14 January 1911; *s* of late Joseph and Lillian Pritchard; *m* 1943, Mary Burroughes, Pretoria, S Africa; one *s. Educ:* Liverpool Coll.; Worcester Coll., Oxford. Dominions Office, 1933; Private Secretary to Permanent Under-Sec., 1936-38; Assistant Secretary, Rhodesia-Nyasaland Royal Commission, 1938; Secretary, Office of UK High Commissioner, Pretoria, 1941-45; Principal Secretary, Office of UK Representative, Dublin, 1948-49; Assistant Under-Secretary of State, Commonwealth Relations Office, 1951-54; Dep. UK High Commissioner: Canada, 1954-57; Australia, 1957-60; Actg Dep. Under-Sec. of State, CRO, 1961; British High Comr in Tanganyika, 1961-63; Deputy Under-Secretary of State, Commonwealth Office (formerly CRO), 1963-67. *Recreation:* golf. *Address:* Little Garth, Daglingworth, Cirencester, Glos GL7 7AQ.

PRITCHETT, Sir Victor (Sawdon), Kt 1975; CBE 1968; FRSL; Author and Critic; *b* 16 Dec. 1900; *s* of Sawdon Pritchett and Beatrice Martin; *m* Dorothy, *d* of Richard Samuel Roberts, Welshpool, Montgomeryshire; one *s* one *d. Educ:* Alleyn's School. Christian Gauss Lectr, Princeton Univ., 1953; Beckman Prof., Univ. California, Berkeley, 1962; Writer-in-Residence, Smith Coll., Mass, 1966; Vanderbilt Univ., Tenn., 1981; Visiting Professor: Brandeis Univ., Mass; Columbia Univ.; Clark Lectr, 1969. Foreign Member: Amer. Acad. and Inst., 1971; Amer. Acad. Arts and Sciences, 1971. Pres., Internat. PEN, 1974-76; Soc. of Authors, 1977-. Hon. LittD Leeds, 1972; Hon. DLitt: Columbia, 1978; Sussex, 1980. *Publications:* Marching Spain, 1928; Clare Drummer, 1929; The Spanish Virgin, 1930; Shirley Sanz, 1932; Nothing Like Leather, 1935; Dead Man Leading, 1937; You Make Your Own Life, 1938; In My Good Books, 1942; It May Never Happen, 1946; The Living Novel, 1946; Why Do I Write?, 1948; Mr Beluncle, 1951; Books in General, 1953; The Spanish Temper, 1954; Collected Stories, 1956; When My Girl Comes Home, 1961; London Perceived, 1962; The Key to My Heart, 1963; Foreign Faces, 1964; New York Proclaimed, 1965; The Working Novelist, 1965; Dublin: A Portrait, 1967; A Cab at the Door, 1968 (RSL Award); Blind Love, 1969; George Meredith and English Comedy, 1970; Midnight Oil, 1971; Balzac, 1973; The Camberwell Beauty, 1974; The Gentle Barbarian, 1977; Selected Stories, 1978; The Myth Makers, 1979; On the Edge of the Cliff, 1980; The Tale Bearers, 1980; (ed) The Oxford Book of Short Stories, 1981; (with Reynolds Stone) The Turn of the Years, 1982; Collected Stories, 1982. *Address:* 12 Regent's Park Terrace, NW1. *Clubs:* Savile, Beefsteak.

PRITTIE, family name of **Baron Dunalley**.

PRITTIE, Hon. Terence Cornelius Farmer, MBE 1945; Editor, Britain and Israel, since 1970; *b* 15 Dec. 1913; *yr s* of 5th Baron Dunalley, DSO; *m* 1946, Laura Dundas; two *s. Educ:* Cheam Sch.; Stowe; Christ Church, Oxford (MA). Butler Exhibn for Modern History, 1934. Served Rifle Bde, 1938-45 (despatches, Calais, 1940); POW, Germany, escaped 6 times (MBE). Staff, Manchester Guardian, 1945-70: Cricket Corresp., 1946; Chief Corresp. in Germany, 1946-63; Diplomatic Corresp., 1963-70. Federal Cross of Merit of West Germany, 1971. *Publications:* South to Freedom, 1946; Mainly Middlesex, 1947; (with John Kay) Second Innings, 1947; Lancashire Hot-Pot, 1948; A History of Middlesex Cricket, 1951; Germany Divided, 1960; Germany (Life Magazine World Series), 1963; Germans Against Hitler, 1964; Israel: Miracle in the Desert, 1967; Eshkol, the Man and the Nation, 1969; Adenauer: A Study in Fortitude, 1972; (with Otto Loeb) Wines of the Moselle, 1972; Willy Brandt, 1974; Through Irish Eyes, 1977; The Economic War against the Jews, 1977; The Velvet Chancellors: the history of post-war Germany, 1979; Whose Jerusalem?, 1981. *Recreations:* cricket, shooting, real tennis, lawn tennis. *Address:* 9 Blithfield Street, W8 6RH. *T:* 01-937 0164. *Clubs:* Travellers', MCC, Greenjackets.
See also Baron Dunalley.

PROBY, Sir Peter, 2nd Bt *cr* 1952; FRICS; Lord-Lieutenant of Cambridgeshire, since 1981; *b* 4 Dec. 1911; *s* of Sir Richard George Proby, 1st Bt, MC, and Betty Monica (*d* 1967), *d* of A. H. Hallam Murray; *S* father, 1979; *m* 1944, Blanche Harrison, *o d* of Lt-Col Henry Harrison Cripps, DSO; one *s* three *d* (and one *s* decd). *Educ:* Eton; Trinity College, Oxford. BA 1934. Served War of 1939-45, Captain, Irish Guards. Bursar of Eton College, 1953-71. Heir: *s* William Henry Proby, ACA [*b* 13 June 1949; *m* 1974, Meredyth Anne Brentnall; two *d*]. *Address:* Pottle Green, Elton, Peterborough.

PROBYN, Air Commodore Harold Melsome, CB 1944; CBE 1943; DSO 1917; *b* 8 Dec. 1891; *s* of late William Probyn; *m* 1920, Marjory (*d* 1961), *d* of late Francis Evance Savory. Served European War, 1914-17 (despatches, DSO); commanded: 208 (AC) Squadron, Egypt; No 2 (AC), Squadron,

Manston; 25 (Fighter) Squadron at Hawkinge; RAF School of Photography, 1932; No 22 Group, RAF, 1932-34; Senior Personnel Staff Officer, Middle East, Cairo, 1934-35; Senior Engineer Staff Officer, Middle East, Cairo, 1935-37; No 12 (Fighter) Group Royal Air Force, Hucknall, Notts, 1937; served War of 1939-45 (despatches); SASO, No 11 Fighter Group, Uxbridge, 1939-40; commanded RAF Station, Cranwell, 1940-44; retired, 1944. *Recreations:* flying, fishing, golf. *Address:* The Cottage, PO Box 61, Nyeri, Kenya. *T:* 2248. *Clubs:* Naval and Military; Nairobi (Kenya).

PROCKTOR, Patrick, RWS 1981; painter since 1962; *b* 12 March 1936; 2nd *s* of Eric Christopher Procktor and Barbara Winifred (*née* Hopkins); *m* 1973, Kirsten Bo (*née* Andersen); one *s. Educ:* Highgate; Slade Sch. (Diploma). Many one-man exhibns, Redfern Gallery, from 1963. *Publications:* One Window in Venice, 1974; Coleridge's Rime of the Ancient Mariner (new illustrated edn), 1976; A Chinese Journey (aquatint landscapes), 1980. *Recreation:* Russian ballet. *Address:* 26 Manchester Street, W1M 5PG. *T:* 01-486 1763.

PROCTER, Norma; Contralto Singer; *b* Cleethorpes, Lincolnshire, 1928. Studied under Roy Henderson and Alec Redshaw. Made first London appearance at Southwark Cathedral; debut at Covent Garden, in Gluck's Orpheus, 1961. Has sung at major British music and European festivals. Numerous concerts and recitals throughout Europe; frequent broadcasts in Britain, Holland and Germany; has made many recordings. Hon. RAM 1974. *Address:* 194 Clee Road, Grimsby, Lincolnshire; c/o Ibbs & Tillett Ltd, 450-452 Edgware Road, W2 1EG.

PROCTER, Sidney, FCIS, FIB; Director since 1978, and Group Chief Executive, since 1982, Royal Bank of Scotland Group; Director: Williams & Glyn's Bank, since 1976; Royal Bank of Scotland, since 1979; *b* 10 March 1925; *s* of Robert and Georgina Margaret Procter; *m* 1952, Isabel (*née* Simmons); one *d. Educ:* Ormskirk Grammar School. Served RAF, 1943-47. Entered former Williams Deacon's Bank, 1941; Asst General Manager, 1969; Dep. Dir, Williams & Glyn's Bank, 1970; Exec. Dir and Asst Chief Executive, 1976; Dep. Chief Executive, 1977, Chief Exec., 1978-82; Dep. Gp Man. Dir, Royal Bank of Scotland Gp, 1979-82. *Address:* c/o 24 Lombard Street, EC3V 9BA. *T:* 01-621 1210. *Club:* Overseas Bankers.

PROCTOR, David Victor; Head of Printed Books and Manuscripts Department, National Maritime Museum, since 1976; *b* 1 March 1930; *s* of Comdr Victor William Lake Proctor, RN and Marjorie Proctor (*née* Weeks); *m* 1959, Margaret Graham; three *s. Educ:* Dauntsey's Sch.; Clare Coll., Cambridge (MA; DipEd 1955); Imperial Coll., London (DIC). Shipbroking, 1953-54; Teacher: Lycée de Brest, France, 1955-56; Clifton Coll., Bristol, 1956-62; National Maritime Museum: Educn Officer, 1962-72; Sec. and Educn Officer, 1972-74; Hd of Educn and Res. Facilities, 1974-76. Chm., Gp for Educn'l Services in Museums, 1971-75; Vice-Pres., Internat. Congress of Maritime Museums, 1981- (Mem. Exec. Council, 1978-; Sec. Gen., 1972-78); Sec. Gen., Internat. Commn for Maritime Hist., 1980-. *Publications:* Child of War, 1972; contribs to jls on museums, museum educn and hist. of science. *Recreations:* sailing, piano, walking, travel, DIY. *Address:* 6 Kinveachy Gardens, SE7 8ED. *T:* 01-855 6243. *Club:* Royal Cruising.

PROCTOR, Sir Dennis; *see* Proctor, Sir P. D.

PROCTOR, Sir (George) Philip, KBE 1971 (CBE 1961); *b* 8 June 1902; *s* of late C. A. Proctor; *m* 1st, 1926, Mary Turney (*d* 1939), *d* of late K. W. Monsarrat; one *s* two *d*; 2nd, 1939, Hilary Frances, *d* of late F. S. Clark; one *s* two *d. Educ:* Cheltenham Coll., Liverpool Univ. (BEng). Joined Dunlop Gp, 1927; Manager, Dunlop (NZ) Ltd, 1936-41 (Chm. and Man. Dir, 1945-65). Chm., NZ Industrial Design Council, 1968-79; Mem., Prison Parole Bd, 1964-78; Chm., NZ Heart Foundn, 1968-78; Nat. Co-ordinator and Chm., Duke of Edinburgh Award in NZ, 1963-69. KStJ 1976. *Recreation:* fly-fishing. *Address:* Flat 5, Landscape Apartments, 123 Austin Street, Wellington 1, New Zealand. *Club:* Wellington (New Zealand).

PROCTOR, Harvey; *see* Proctor, K. H.

PROCTOR, Ian Douglas Ben, RDI 1969; FSIAD 1969; FRSA 1972; Chairman, Ian Proctor Metal Masts Ltd, 1959-78 and since 1981 (Director, since 1959); freelance industrial designer since 1950; *b* 12 July 1918; *s* of Douglas McIntyre Proctor and Mary Albina Louise Proctor (*née* Tredwen); *m* 1943, Elizabeth Anne Gifford Lywood, *d* of Air Vice-Marshal O. G. Lywood, CB, CBE; three *s* one *d. Educ:* Gresham's Sch., Holt; London University. RAFVR (Flying Officer), 1941-47. Man. Dir, Gosport Yacht Co., 1947-48; Joint Editor Yachtsman Magazine, 1948-50; Daily Telegraph Yachting Correspondent, 1950-64. Yachtsman of the Year, 1965; Council of Industrial Design Award, 1967; Design Council Awards, 1977, 1980. *Publications:* Racing Dinghy Handling, 1948; Racing Dinghy Maintenance, 1949; Sailing: Wind and Current, 1950; Boats for Sailing, 1968; Sailing Strategy, 1977. *Recreation:* sailing. *Address:* Ferry House, Duncannon, Stoke Gabriel, near Totnes, Devon. *Clubs:* Nash House; Royal Dart Yacht, Hayling Island Sailing, Aldenham Sailing.

PROCTOR, Ven. Jesse Heighton, MA (London); Archdeacon of Warwick, 1958-74, now Emeritus; Vicar of Sherbourne, Warwick, 1958-69; *b* 26 May 1908; *s* of Thomas and Sophia Proctor, Melton Mowbray; *m* 1938, Helena Mary Wood, *d* of John Thomas and Jessie Wood, Melton Mowbray; one *s*

two *d. Educ:* County Grammar Sch. of King Edward VII, Melton Mowbray; Coll. of St Mark and St John, Chelsea, Univ. of London; St Andrew's Theological Training House, Whittlesford. Asst Master, Winterbourne Sch., Croydon, 1929–32; Sen. History Master, Melton Mowbray Gram. Sch., 1932–35; Deacon 1935, Priest 1936; Chap. and Tutor, St Andrew's, Whittlesford, 1935–38; Curate, St Philip's, Leicester, 1938–39; Vicar, Glen Parva and South Wigston, and Chap., Glen Parva Barracks, Leicester, 1939–46; Precentor of Coventry Cath., 1946–58; Hon. Canon of Coventry, 1947; Chaplain, Gulson Hosp., 1953–58; Sen. Examining Chap. to Bishop of Coventry, 1947–65; Canon Theologian of Coventry, 1954–59; Vice-Pres. CMS. Governor: Univ. of Warwick, 1966–68; City of Coventry Coll. of Educn, 1966–70. Barnabas of Coventry Evening Telegraph, 1955–75. *Publications:* contrib. to Neville Gorton (SPCK), 1957. *Recreations:* study of theology and history; the countryside. *Address:* Dilkusha, Bank Crescent, Ledbury, Herefordshire HR8 1AA. *T:* Ledbury 2241.

PROCTOR, (Keith) Harvey; MP (C) Basildon, since 1979; *b* 16 Jan. 1947; *s* of Albert Proctor and Hilda Tegerdine. *Educ:* High School for Boys, Scarborough; Univ. of York. BA History Hons, 1969. Asst Director, Monday Club, 1969–71; Research Officer, Conservative 1970s Parliamentary Gp, 1971–72; Exec. Director, Parliamentary Digest Ltd, 1972–74; British Paper & Board Industry Federation: Asst Sec., 1974–78; Secretary, 1978–79; Consultant, 1979–. *Recreation:* tennis. *Address:* House of Commons, SW1. *T:* 01-219 3000.

PROCTOR, Sir Philip; *see* Proctor, Sir G. P.

PROCTOR, Sir (Philip) Dennis, KCB 1959 (CB 1946); *b* 1 Sept. 1905; *s* of late Sir Philip Proctor, KBE; *m* 1st, 1936, Dorothy Varda (*d* 1951); no *c*; 2nd, 1953, Barbara, *d* of Sir Ronald Adam, Bt, *qv*; two *s* one *d. Educ:* Falconbury; Harrow; King's Coll., Cambridge. MA, 1929; entered Min. of Health, 1929; transferred to Treasury, 1930; Third Secretary, HM Treasury, 1948–50; resigned from Civil Service; joined the firm of A. P. Moller, Copenhagen, 1950; Man. Dir, The Maersk Company Ltd, 1951–53; re-entered Civil Service, 1953; Dep. Sec., Min. of Transport and Civil Aviation, 1953–58; Permanent Sec., Min. of Power, 1958–65. Dir, Williams Hudson Ltd, 1966–71. Trustee of Tate Gallery, 1952; Chairman of the Tate Gallery, 1953–59. Hon. Fellow, King's Coll., Cambridge, 1968. *Publications:* Hannibal's March in History, 1971; Autobiography of G. Lowes Dickinson, 1973; The Experience of Thucydides, 1980. *Address:* 102 High Street, Lewes, Sussex.

PROCTOR, Sir Roderick (Consett), Kt 1978; MBE 1946; FCA; company director; *b* 28 July 1914; *s* of Frederick William Proctor and Ethel May (*née* Christmas); *m* 1st, 1943, Kathleen Mary (*née* Murphy; *d* 1978); four *s* ; 2nd, 1980, Janice Marlene (*née* Pryor). *Educ:* Hale Sch., Perth, WA; Melbourne C of E Grammar Sch., Vic. FCA 1958. Served War, 1939–45. Commenced career as chartered accountant, 1931, as Jun. Clerk with R. Goyne Miller, Perth; joined Clarke & Son, Chartered Accountants, Brisbane, Qld, 1937; Partner, 1950, Sen. Partner, 1966 (firm merged with Aust. national firm, Hungerfords, 1960); retd as Partner, 1976. *Recreations:* surfing, golf. *Address:* Unit 102, The Gardens, Alice Street, Brisbane, Qld 4000, Australia. *Clubs:* Queensland, Brisbane, United Service, Royal Queensland Golf (Brisbane); Southport Golf.

PROCTOR-BEAUCHAMP, Sir Christopher Radstock P.; *see* Beauchamp.

PROFUMO, John Dennis, CBE 1975 (OBE (mil.) 1944); 5th Baron of the late United Kingdom of Italy; *b* 30 Jan. 1915; *e s* of late Baron Albert Profumo, KC; *m* 1954, Valerie Hobson, *qv*; one *s. Educ:* Harrow; Brasenose College, Oxford, Brigadier, Chief of Staff UK Mission in Japan, 1945. MP (C) Kettering Division, Northamptonshire, 1940–45; MP (C) Stratford-on-Avon Division of Warwickshire, 1950–63; Joint Parliamentary Secretary, Ministry of Transport and Civil Aviation, Nov. 1952–Jan. 1957; Parliamentary Under-Secretary of State for the Colonies, 1957–58; Parliamentary Under-Sec. of State, Foreign Affairs, Nov. 1958–Jan. 1959; Minister of State for Foreign Affairs, 1959–60; Secretary of State for War, July 1960–June 1963. Dir, Provident Life Assoc. of London, 1975– (Dep. Chm., 1978–82). Mem., Bd of Visitors, HM Prison, Grendon, 1968–75. 1st Northamptonshire Yeomanry, 1939 (despatches). *Recreations:* shooting, gardening, DIY. *Heir: s* David Profumo [*b* 30 Oct. 1955; *m* 1980, Helen, *o d* of Alasdair Fraser]. *Club:* Boodle's.
See also Baron Balfour of Inchrye.

PROKHOROV, Prof. Alexander Mikhailovich; Physicist and Deputy Director, P. N. Lebedev Institute of Physics, Academy of Sciences of the USSR, Moscow; Editor-in-Chief, Bolshaya Sovetskaya Encyclopedia Publishing House, since 1970; *b* Atherton, Australia, 11 July 1916; *s* of Mikhail Prokhorov; *m* 1941, Galina Alexeyevna (*née* Shelepina); one *s. Educ:* Leningrad State University; Lebedev Inst. of Physics. Corresp. Mem., Academy of Sciences of the USSR (Department of General Physics and Astronomy), 1960–66, Full Mem., 1966–, Mem. Presidial Body, 1970, Academician-Secretary, 1973–. Professor, Moscow University, 1958–. Hon. Professor: Delhi Univ.; Bucharest Univ., 1971; Hon. Member: Amer. Acad. of Arts and Sciences, 1972; Acad. of Sciences of Hungary, 1976; Acad. of Sciences, German Democratic Republic, 1977. Member, Communist Party of the Soviet Union, 1950–. Awarded Lenin Prize, 1959; Nobel Prize for Physics (jointly with Prof. N. G. Basov and Prof. C. H. Townes), 1964. *Publications:*

contributions on non-linear oscillations, radiospectroscopy and quantum radio-physics. *Address:* P. N. Lebedev Institute of Physics, Academy of Sciences of the USSR, 53 Lenin Prospekt, Moscow, USSR.

PROKHOROVA, Violetta; *see* Elvin, V.

PROKOSCH, Frederic; Writer; *b* 17 May 1908; *s* of Eduard (Professor of Linguistics, Yale University) and Mathilde Prokosch. *Educ:* Yale University (PhD, 1933); King's College, Cambridge. Educated as a child in Wisconsin, Texas, Munich, Austria; travelled extensively all his life; research work in Chaucerian MSS, 1933–38 (PhD Dissertation: The Chaucerian Apocrypha). *Publications:* The Asiatics (novel), 1935; The Assassins (poems), 1936; The Seven Who Fled (novel), 1937; The Carnival (poems), 1938; Night of The Poor (novel), 1939; Death at Sea (poems), 1940; The Skies of Europe (novel), 1942; The Conspirators (novel), 1943; Some Poems of Hölderlin, 1943; Chosen Poems, 1944; Age of Thunder (novel), 1945; The Idols of the Cave (novel), 1946; The Medea of Euripides, 1947; The Sonnets of Louise Labé, 1947; Storm and Echo (novel), 1948; Nine Days to Mukalla (novel), 1953; A Tale for Midnight (novel), 1955; A Ballad of Love (novel), 1960; The Seven Sisters (novel), 1962; The Dark Dancer (novel), 1964; The Wreck of the Cassandra (novel), 1966; The Missolonghi Manuscript (novel), 1968; America, My Wilderness (novel), 1972. *Recreations:* squash racquets (Champion of France, 1938, 1939, Champion of Sweden, 1944), lawn tennis (Champion of Mallorca). *Address:* Ma Trouvaille, 06 Plan de Grasse, France. *Clubs:* Pitt (Cambridge); Yale (New York); France-Amérique (Paris).

PROLE, Lozania; *see* Bloom, Ursula.

PROOM, Major William Arthur, TD 1953; *b* 18 Dec. 1916; *s* of Arthur Henry Proom and Nesta Proom; *m* 1941, Nellie Lister; one *s* one *d. Educ:* Richmond Sch., Yorks; Keighley Technical Coll. Commnd TA, 1/6 Bn Duke of Wellington's Regt, 1938; served War: Iceland, 1940–42; REME/IEME, India and Burma, 1943–46; Major, retd. Mayor of Keighley, 1973; Member: W Yorks Metropolitan CC, 1974–81 (Chm., 1979–80); City of Bradford Metrop. Dist Council, 1975–79. Chm., NE Gas Consumers' Council, 1973–77. Hon. Rep., Officers' Assoc. *Recreations:* gardening, reading. *Address:* Thorn Bank, Occupation Lane, Exley Head, Keighley, W Yorks BD22 7LB. *T:* Keighley 605150.

PROOPS, Mrs Marjorie, OBE 1969; journalist; *d* of Alfred and Martha Rayle; *m* 1935; one *s. Educ:* Dalston Secondary Sch. Daily Mirror, 1939–45; Daily Herald, 1945–54; Daily Mirror, 1954–. Broadcaster, Television, 1960–. Member: Royal Commn on Gambling, 1976–78; Council for One Parent Families. Woman Journalist of the Year, 1969. *Publications:* Pride, Prejudice & Proops, 1975; Dear Marje, 1976. *Address:* 9 Sherwood Close, SW13.

PROPHET, Prof. Arthur Shelley, CBE 1980; DDS; DpBact; FDSRCS; FFDRCSI; Professor of Dental Surgery, University of London, since 1956, and Vice-Dean, Faculty of Clinical Sciences, University College London, since 1982 (Dean, 1980–82); *b* 11 Jan. 1918; *s* of Eric Prophet and Mabel Wightman; *m* 1942, Vivienne Mary Bell; two *s. Educ:* Sedbergh School; University of Manchester. BDS Hons (Preston Prize and Medal), 1940; Diploma in Bacteriology (Manchester), 1948; DDS (Manchester) 1950; FDSRCS 1958; FFDRCS Ireland, 1964. RNVR (Dental Branch), 1941–46; Nuffield Dental Fellow, 1946–48; Lecturer in Dental Bacteriology, University of Manchester, 1948–54; Lecturer in Dental Surgery, QUB, 1954–56; Dir of Dental Studies, 1956–74, Dean of Dental Studies, 1974–77, UCH Dental Sch.; Dean, UCH Medical Sch., 1977–80. Lectures: Charles Tomes, RCS, 1977; Wilkinson, Univ. of Manchester, 1978; Elwood, QUB, 1979. Rep. of University of London on Gen. Dental Council, 1964–. Elected Mem. Bd, Faculty of Dental Surgery, RCS, 1964–80 (Vice-Dean, 1972–73); Member: Cttee of Management, Inst. of Dental Surgery, 1963–; Dental Sub-Cttee, UGC, 1968–78; Bd of Governors, UCH, 1957–74; Camden and Islington AHA(T), 1974–82; Bloomsbury HA, 1982–. WHO Consultant, 1966; Consultant Dental Advr, DHSS, 1977–. *Publications:* contrib. to medical and dental journals. *Recreation:* golf. *Address:* 40 Ollards Grove, Loughton, Essex. *T:* 01-508 3566.

PROPPER, Arthur, CMG 1965; MBE 1945; *b* 3 Aug. 1910; 2nd *s* of late I. Propper; *m* 1941, Erica Mayer; one *d. Educ:* Owen's Sch.; Peterhouse, Cambridge (schol.). 1st class, Hist. Tripos, Pt 2. With W. S. Crawford Ltd (Advertising Agents), 1933–38, and the J. Walter Thompson Co. Ltd, 1939; Min. of Economic Warfare, 1940; transf. to Min. of Food, 1946 (subseq. to Min. of Agric., Fisheries and Food); established in Home Civil Service, 1949; Asst Sec., 1952; Mem. UK Delegn at Common Market negotiations, with rank of Under-Sec., 1962–63; seconded to Foreign Office, 1963; Counsellor (Agric.), UK Delegn to the European Communities, Brussels, and HM Embassy, Bonn, 1963–64; Under-Sec., Min. of Agriculture, Fisheries and Food, 1964–70; Common Mkt Advr, Unigate Ltd, 1970–73; Sec., Food Panel, Price Commn, 1973–76. *Recreations:* the theatre, music, buying books, visiting Scotland. *Address:* 3 Hill House, Stanmore Hill, Stanmore, Mddx. *T:* 01-954 1242. *Club:* United Oxford & Cambridge University.

PROSSER, (Albert) Russell (Garness), CMG 1967; MBE 1953; Senior Adviser (formerly Adviser), Social Development, Overseas Development Administration, 1967–80; *b* 8 April 1915; *s* of late Thomas Prosser; *m* 1957, Ruth Avalon Moore; one *s* (and one *s* decd). *Educ:* Godlys Sch.; London Sch. of Economics. Principal, Sch. of Social Welfare, Accra, 1947; Dep. Sec.,

Uganda, 1959; Permanent Secretary, Uganda, 1962; Adviser, Social Development, Kenya, 1963. Alternate UK delegate, UN Social Develt Commn, 1965-72, UK delegate, 1973-80. Associate Mem., Inst. of Develt Studies, Univ. of Sussex; External Examr Rural Develt, Univ. of Reading. Editor, Clare Market Review, 1939-40. FRSA 1974. Golden Medallion, Belgian Govt, 1962. *Recreations:* angling, gardening. *Address:* 18b Wray Park Road, Reigate, Surrey. *T:* Reigate 42792.

PROSSER, (Elvet) John; QC 1978; a Recorder of the Crown Court, since 1972; Part-time Chairman of Industrial Tribunals, since 1975; *b* 10 July 1932; *s* of David and Hannah Prosser; *m* 1957, Mary Louise Cowdry; two *d. Educ:* Pontypridd Grammar Sch.; King's Coll., London Univ. LLB. Flt Lt, RAF, 1957-59. Called to the Bar, Gray's Inn, 1956; Mem., Senate of Inns of Court and the Bar, 1980-. An Asst Boundary Comr for Wales, 1977-. *Recreations:* watching cricket and television. *Address:* 78 Marsham Court, Westminster, SW1. *T:* 01-834 9779; Hillcroft, Mill Road, Lisvane, Cardiff CF4 5XJ. *T:* Cardiff 752380. *Clubs:* East India, Devonshire, Sports and Public Schools; Cardiff and County (Cardiff).

PROSSER, Raymond Frederick, CB 1973; MC 1942; Member (part-time), Civil Aviation Authority, since 1980; *b* 12 Sept. 1919; *s* of Frederick Charles Prosser and Jane Prosser (*née* Lawless); *m* 1949, Fay Newmarch Holmes; two *s* three *d. Educ:* Wimbledon Coll.; The Queen's Coll., Oxford (1938-39 and 1946). Served Royal Artillery (Field), 1939-45 (MC, despatches): service in Egypt, Libya, India and Burma; Temp. Major. Asst Principal, Min. of Civil Aviation, 1947; Sec., Air Transport Advisory Council, 1952-57; Private Sec. to Minister of Transport and Civil Aviation, 1959, and to Minister of Aviation, 1959-61; Counsellor (Civil Aviation), HM Embassy, Washington, DC, 1965-68; Under-Sec., Marine Div., BoT, later DTI, 1968-72; Deputy Sec., Regional Industrial Organisation and Policy, DTI, later DoI, 1972-77; Principal Estabt and Finance Officer, Depts of Industry, Trade, and Prices and Consumer Protection, 1977-79, retired. Dir, European Investment Bank, 1973-77. *Address:* Juniper House, Shalford Common, Shalford, Guildford, Surrey. *T:* Guildford 66498.

PROSSER, Russell; *see* Prosser, A. R. G.

PROSSER, Thomas Vivian, CBE 1963; Chairman, T.V. Prosser & Son (Estates) Ltd; Consultant Director, Proteus-Bygging Ltd; *b* 25 April 1908; *er s* of T. V. Prosser, Liverpool; *m* 1935, Florence Minnie (Billie), 2nd *d* of W. J. Boulton, Highworth, Wilts; one *s* one *d. Educ:* Old Swan Technical Institute (now West Derby High School); College of Technology, Liverpool. Pupil of A. E. Cuddy, LRIBA, Architect, 1924. Founder, Chm. and Man. Dir, Nat Building Agency, 1964-67. Formerly: President, Liverpool Regional Fedn of Building Trades Employers, 1956; Pres., Nat. Fedn of Building Trades Employers, 1959-60. *Recreations:* gardening, reading. *Address:* Priory Cottage, 1 Mill Street, Steventon, near Abingdon, Oxon OX13 6SP. *T:* Abingdon 831219. *Club:* Lyceum.

PROSSER, William David; QC (Scotland) 1974; Vice-Dean of the Faculty of Advocates, since 1979; *b* 23 Nov. 1934; *yr s* of David G. Prosser, MC, WS, Edinburgh; *m* 1964, Vanessa, *er d* of Sir William O'Brien Lindsay, KBE, Nairobi; two *s* two *d. Educ:* Edinburgh Academy; Corpus Christi Coll., Oxford (MA); Edinburgh Univ. (LLB). Advocate, 1962; Standing Junior Counsel, Scottish Develt Dept, 1965-69; Standing Junior Counsel in Scotland, Board of Inland Revenue, 1969-74; Advocate-Depute, 1978-79. Mem., Scottish Cttee, Council on Tribunals, 1977-. *Address:* 7 Randolph Crescent, Edinburgh EH3 7TH. *T:* 031-225 2709; Netherfoodie, Dairsie, Fife. *T:* Balmullo 438. *Clubs:* New, Scottish Arts (Edinburgh).

PROTHEROE, Alan Hackford, MBE (mil.) 1980; TD 1981; Assistant Director General, BBC, since 1982; *b* 10 Jan. 1934; *s* of Rev. B. P. Protheroe and R. C. M. Protheroe; *m* 1956, Anne Miller; two *s. Educ:* Maesteg Grammar Sch., Glamorgan. FBIM. Nat. Service, 2nd Lieut The Welch Regt, 1954-56; Lt-Col, Royal Regt of Wales (TA), 1979-. Reporter, Glamorgan Gazette, 1951-53; BBC Wales: Reporter, 1957-59; Industrial Correspondent, 1959-64; Editor, News and Current Affairs, 1964-70; BBC TV News: Asst Editor, 1970-72; Dep. Editor, 1972-77; Editor, 1977-80; Asst Dir, BBC News and Current Affairs, 1980-82. During BBC career has made films and radio progs, reported wars, and travelled widely; seconded to Greek Govt to assist in reorganisation of Greek TV, 1973. Mem., Steering Cttee, EBU News Gp, 1977-; Dir, Visnews Ltd, 1982-. *Publications:* contribs to newspapers and specialist jls on industrial and media affairs. *Recreations:* writing, pistol and rifle shooting. *Address:* c/o Broadcasting House, Portland Place, W1A 1AA. *T:* 01-580 4468.

PROUD, Air Cdre Harold John Granville Ellis, CBE 1946; *b* 23 Aug. 1906; *s* of late Ralph Henry Proud, Glasgow; *m* 1937, Jenefer Angela Margaret, *d* of late Lt-Col J. Bruce, OBE, 19th Lancers; two *d.* HAC (Inf.), 1924-26; commissioned RAF, pilot, 1926; Staff Coll., 1936; served in: Mediterranean (FAA), 1928; India, 1937 and 1942; Singapore, 1949; AOC 67 (NI) Gp and Senior Air Force Officer N Ire., 1951-54; Provost Marshal and Chief of Air Force Police, 1954; retired 1956; in business, 1957-71; now domiciled in Switzerland; Mem. Council, British Residents Assoc. of Switzerland, 1973-77, Chm., 1974-75. *Address:* Appt 10, Les Libellules, 1837 Chateau d'Oex, Switzerland. *T:* (029) 46223.

PROUD, Sir John (Seymour), Kt 1978; mining engineer; director and chairman of companies; *b* 9 Aug. 1907; *s* of William James Proud and Hannah Seymour; *m* 1964, Laurine, *d* of M. Ferran. *Educ:* Univ. of Sydney (Bachelor of Engrg, Mining and Metallurgy). CEng, FIMM, FIE(Aust), M(Aust)IMM. Chm., Newcastle Wallsend Coal Co., which merged with Peko Mines NL, 1960; Chm., Peko-Wallsend Investments Ltd, then Chm., Peko-Wallsend Ltd; retd from chair, 1978; Dir/Consultant, 1978-. Chairman: Electrical Equipment Ltd (Group), 1978-82 (Dir, 1943-); Oil Search Ltd, 1978- (Dir, 1974-); Oil Co. of Australia NL, 1979-; Dir, CSR Ltd, 1974-79. Fellow of Senate, Univ. of Sydney, 1974-. Chm. Trustees, Lizard Island Foundn, 1978-; Trustee, Aust. Museum, 1971-77. *Recreations:* yachting, pastoral activity. *Address:* 9 Finlay Road, Turramurra, NSW 2074, Australia. *T:* 44-3860. *Clubs:* Union, Royal Sydney Yacht Squadron, Royal Prince Alfred Yacht, American National (Sydney).

PROUDFOOT, Bruce; *see* Proudfoot, V. B.

PROUDFOOT, Bruce Falconer; Publicity Officer, Ulster Savings Committee, 1963-69; Editor, Northern Whig and Belfast Post, 1943-63; *b* 1903; 2nd *s* of G. A. Proudfoot, Edinburgh; *m* 1928, Cecilia, *er d* of V. T. T. Thompson, Newcastle on Tyne; twin *s. Educ:* Edinburgh Education Authority's Primary and Secondary Schools. Served with Edinburgh Evening Dispatch, Galloway Gazette (Newton-Stewart) and Newcastle Daily Chronicle before joining Northern Whig, 1925. *Address:* 10 Ophir Gardens, Belfast BT15 5EP. *T:* 776368.
See also V. B. Proudfoot.

PROUDFOOT, (George) Wilfred; owner, self-service stores; consultant in distribution; *b* 19 December 1921; *m* 1950, Margaret Mary, *d* of Percy Clifford Jackson, Pontefract, Yorks; two *s* one *d. Educ:* Crook Council Sch.; Scarborough Coll. Served War of 1939-45, NCO Fitter in RAF, 1940-46. Served Scarborough Town Council, 1950-58 (Chm. Health Cttee, 1952-58). MP (C) Cleveland Division of Yorkshire, Oct. 1959-Sept. 1964; PPS to Minister of State, Board of Trade, Apr.-July 1962, to Minister of Housing and Local Govt and Minister for Welsh Affairs (Rt Hon. Sir Keith Joseph, Bt, MP), 1962-64; MP (C) Brighouse and Spenborough, 1970-Feb. 1974; Minister of State, Dept of Employment, 1970; contested (C) Brighouse and Spenborough, Oct. 1974. Man. Dir, Radio 270, 1965-. Chm., Scarborough Cons. Assoc., 1978-80; Chm., Cleveland European Constituency Cons. Assoc., 1979-. Professional hypnotist; face lifted by Dr John Williams, USA, 1978. *Publication:* The Two Factor Nation, or How to make the people rich, 1977. *Recreations:* reading, photography, caravanning, travel, walking, skiing, jogging. *Address:* 278 Scalby Road, Scarborough, North Yorkshire. *T:* Scarborough 67027. *Club:* St Stephen's Constitutional.

PROUDFOOT, Prof. (Vincent) Bruce, FSA 1963; FRSE 1979; Professor of Geography, University of St Andrews, since 1974; *b* 24 Sept. 1930; *s* of Bruce Falconer Proudfoot, *qv* ; *m* 1961, Edwina Valmai Windram Field; two *s. Educ:* Royal Belfast Academical Instn; Queen's Univ., Belfast (BA, PhD). Research Officer, Nuffield Quaternary Research Unit, QUB, 1954-58; Lectr in Geography, QUB, 1958-59, Durham Univ., 1959-67; Tutor, 1960-63, Librarian, 1963-65, Hatfield Coll., Durham; Visiting Fellow, Univ. of Auckland, NZ, 1966; Associate Prof., 1967-70, Prof., 1970-74, Univ. of Alberta, Edmonton, Canada; Acting Chm., Dept of Geography, Univ. of Alberta, 1970-71; Co-ordinator, Socio-Economic Opportunity Studies, and Staff Consultant, Alberta Human Resources Research Council, 1971-72. Chairman: Rural Geog. Study Gp, Inst. of British Geographers, 1980-; Soc. for Landscape Studies, 1979-. Lister Lectr, BAAS, 1964; Commonwealth Visiting Fellow, Australia, 1966. Hon. Editor, RSGS, 1979. *Publications:* The Downpatrick Gold Find, 1955; (with R. G. Ironside *et al*) Frontier Settlement Studies, 1974; numerous papers in geographical, archaeological and soils jls. *Recreation:* gardening. *Address:* Westgate, Wardlaw Gardens, St Andrews, Scotland KY16 9DW. *T:* St Andrews 73293.

PROUDFOOT, Wilfred; *see* Proudfoot, G. W.

PROUT, Christopher James, DPhil; Member (C) Shropshire and Stafford, European Parliament, since 1979; barrister-at-law; *b* 1 Jan. 1942; *s* of late Frank Yabsley Prout, MC and bar, and of Doris Lucy Prout (*née* Osborne). *Educ:* Sevenoaks Sch.; Manchester Univ. (BA); The Queen's Coll., Oxford (Scholar; BPhil, DPhil). Reserve Officer, 16/5 Lancers, 1970-. Called to the Bar, The Middle Temple, 1972. English-Speaking Union Fellow, Columbia Univ., NYC, 1963-64; Staff Mem., World Bank Group (UN), Washington DC, 1966-69; Leverhulme Fellow and Lectr in Law, Sussex Univ., 1969-79. Chm., Brighton Pavilion Cons. Assoc., 1979. *Publications:* contribs to symposia and articles in legal jls. *Recreations:* riding, sailing. *Address:* 54 Broad Street, Ludlow, Shropshire. *T:* Ludlow 2187. *Club:* Beefsteak.

PROVAN, James Lyal Clark; Member (C) NE Scotland, European Parliament, since 1979; farmer; *b* 19 Dec. 1936; *s* of John Provan and Jean (*née* Clark); *m* 1960, Roweena Adele Lewis; twin *s* one *d. Educ:* Ardvreck Sch., Crieff; Oundle Sch., Northants; Royal Agricultural Coll., Cirencester. Member: Tayside Regional Council, 1978-82; Tay River Purification Bd, 1978-82. Member: Agriculture and Fisheries Cttee, European Parlt, 1979- (European Democratic Gp spokesman on agricl and fisheries affairs); Environment, Consumer Affairs and Public Health Cttee, European Parlt, 1979-. Area President, Scottish NFU, 1965 and 1971; Manager, Scottish Farming News, 1966-68; Founder Vice-Chm., East of Scotland Grassland Soc.,

1972- (Chm., 1973-75). Treasurer, Perth and E Perthshire Conservative Assoc., 1975-77; Member, Lord Lieutenant's Queen's Jubilee Appeal Cttee, 1977. *Recreations:* country pursuits, sailing, flying, musical appreciation, travel. *Address:* Wallacetown, Bridge of Earn, Perth, Scotland PH2 8QA. *T:* Bridge of Earn 2243. *Clubs:* Farmers', East India, Devonshire, Sports and Public Schools; Royal Perth Golfing Society.

PROWSE, Florence Irene; *see* Calvert, F. I.

PRUDE, Mrs Walter F.; *see* de Mille, Agnes George.

PRYCE, George Terry; Managing Director, since 1978, and Chief Executive, since 1981, Dalgety Ltd; *b* 26 March 1934; *s* of Edwin Pryce and Hilda Florence (*née* Price); *m* 1957, Thurza Elizabeth Tatham; two *s* one *d*. *Educ:* Welshpool Grammar Sch.; National Coll. of Food Technol. FIFST 1972; FBIM 1976. Dir, various food cos in THF Gp, 1965-70; Asst Man. Dir, Dalgety (UK) Ltd, 1970, Man. Dir, 1971; Dir, Dalgety Ltd, 1972-; Chairman: Dalgety (UK) Ltd, 1978-; Dalgety Spillers Ltd, 1980-. Governor, National Coll. of Food Technol., 1981-. *Recreations:* sport, esp. golf; reading, music. *Address:* 89 Brookmans Avenue, Brookmans Park, Hatfield, Herts.

PRYCE, Maurice Henry Lecorney, FRS 1951; Professor of Physics, University of British Columbia, 1968-78, now Hon. Professor; *b* 24 Jan. 1913; *e s* of William John Pryce and Hortense Lecorney; *m* 1939, Susanne Margarete Born (marr. diss., 1959); one *s* three *d*; *m* 1961, Freda Mary Kinsey. *Educ:* Royal Grammar Sch., Guildford; Trinity Coll., Cambridge. Commonwealth Fund Fellow at Princeton, NJ, USA, 1935-37; Fellow of Trinity Coll., Cambridge, and Faculty Asst Lecturer, University of Cambridge, 1937-39; Reader in Theoretical Physics, University of Liverpool, 1939-45. Engaged on Radar research with Admiralty Signal Establishment, 1941-44, and on Atomic Energy Research with National Research Council of Canada, Montreal, 1944-45. University Lecturer in Mathematics and Fellow of Trinity Coll., Cambridge, 1945-46; Wykeham Professor of Physics, University of Oxford, 1946-54; Henry Overton Wills Professor of Physics, University of Bristol, 1954-64; Prof. of Physics, University of Southern California, 1964-68. Visiting Professor: Princeton Univ., NJ, USA, 1950-51; Duke Univ., NC, USA, 1958; Univ. of Sussex, 1976-77. *Publications:* various on Theoretical Physics, in learned journals. *Recreations:* lawn tennis, badminton. *Address:* Physics Department, University of British Columbia, 2075 Wesbrook Mall, Vancouver V6T 1W5, Canada; 4754 West 6th Avenue, Vancouver, BC V6T 1C5, Canada. *Club:* Athenæum.

PRYCE, Prof. Roy; Visiting Professor in Contemporary European History, European University Institute, Florence, since 1981; *b* 4 Oct. 1928; *s* of Thomas and Madeleine Pryce; *m* 1954, Sheila Rose, *d* of Rt Hon. James Griffiths, CH; three *d*. *Educ:* Grammar Sch., Burton-on-Trent; Emmanuel Coll., Cambridge (MA, PhD). MA Oxon. Research Fellow: Emmanuel Coll., Cambridge, 1953-55; St Antony's Coll., Oxford, 1955-57; Head of London Information Office of High Authority of European Coal and Steel Community, 1957-60; Head of London Inf. Office, Jt Inf. Service of European Communities, 1960-64; Rockefeller Foundn Res. Fellow, 1964-65; Dir, Centre for Contemp. European Studies, Univ. of Sussex, 1965-73; Directorate General for Information, Commission of the European Communities: Dir, 1973-78; Sen. Advr for Direct Elections, 1978-79; Chief Advr for Programming, 1979-81. Vis. Professorial Fellow, Centre for Contemporary European Studies, Univ. of Sussex, 1973-81; Vis. Prof., Coll. of Europe, Bruges, 1965-72. *Publications:* The Italian Local Elections 1956, 1957; The Political Future of the European Community, 1962; (with John Pinder) Europe After de Gaulle, 1969, German and Ital. edns 1970; The Politics of the European Community, 1973; contrib. Encycl. Brit., Jl Common Market Studies, etc. *Recreations:* gardening, collecting water colours and prints. *Address:* Stone House, Cade Street, Old Heathfield, Sussex. *Clubs:* Reform, Europe House.

PRYCE-JONES, Alan Payan, TD; book critic, author and journalist; *b* 18 Nov. 1908;*s* of late Colonel Henry Morris Pryce-Jones, CB; *m* 1934, Thérèse (*d* 1953), *d* of late Baron Fould-Springer and of Mrs Frank Wooster, Paris; one *s*; *m* 1968, Mrs Mary Jean Kempner Thorne (*d* 1969), *d* of late Daniel Kempner. *Educ:* Eton; Magdalen Coll., Oxford. Formerly Asst Editor, The London Mercury, 1928-32; subseq. Times Literary Supplement; Editor, Times Literary Supplement, 1948-59; Book critic: New York Herald Tribune, 1963-66; World Journal Tribune, 1967-68; Newsday, 1969-71; Theatre Critic, Theatre Arts, 1963-. Trustee, National Portrait Gallery, 1950-61; Director, Old Vic Trust, 1950-61; Member Council, Royal College of Music, 1956-61; Program Associate, The Humanities and Arts Program, Ford Foundation, NY, 1961-63. Served War of 1939-45, France, Italy, Austria; Lieut-Colonel, 1945. *Publications:* The Spring Journey, 1931; People in the South, 1932; Beethoven, 1933; 27 Poems, 1935; Private Opinion, 1936; Nelson, an opera, 1954; Vanity Fair, a musical play (with Robin Miller and Julian Slade), 1962. *Recreations:* music, travelling. *Address:* 46 John Street, Newport, RI 02840, USA. *Clubs:* Travellers', Garrick, Beefsteak, Pratt's; Knickerbocker, Century (New York); Artillery (Galveston, Texas).

PRYER, Eric John; Deputy Chief Land Registrar, since 1981; *b* 5 Sept. 1929; *s* of late Edward John and Edith Blanche Pryer; *m* 1962, Moyra Helena Cross; one *s* one *d*. *Educ:* Beckenham and Penge County Grammar Sch.; Birkbeck Coll., London Univ. (BA Hons). Called to the Bar, Gray's Inn, 1957. Exec. Officer, Treasury Solicitor's Dept, 1948; Legal Asst, HM Land Registry, 1959;

Asst Land Registrar, 1965; Dist Land Registrar, Durham, 1976. *Recreations:* reading, gardening. *Address:* Sprangewell, Poles Lane, Thundridge, Ware, Herts SG12 0SQ. *T:* Ware 2595.

PRYKE, Sir David Dudley, 3rd Bt *cr* 1926; *b* 16 July 1912; *s* of Sir William Robert Dudley Pryke, 2nd Bt; *S* father 1959; *m* 1945, Doreen Winifred, *er d* of late Ralph Bernard Wilkins; two *d*. *Educ:* St Lawrence Coll., Ramsgate. Liveryman Turners' Company, 1961. *Heir: b* William Dudley Pryke [*b* 18 Nov. 1914; *m* 1940, Lucy Irene, *d* of late Frank Madgett; one *s* one *d*]. *Address:* Flatholme, Brabant Road, North Fambridge, Chelmsford, Essex. *T:* Maldon 740227.

PRYN, Maj.-Gen. William John, OBE, 1973; QHS 1981; MB, BS; FRCS; Director of Army Surgery, and Consulting Surgeon to the Army, since 1982; *b* 25 Jan. 1928; *s* of late Richard Harold Cotter Pryn, FRCS, late RAMC and Una St George Ormsby (*née* Roe); *m* 1st, 1952, Alison Lynette (marr. diss.), 2nd *d* of Captain Norman Arthur Cyril Hardy, RN; two *s* one *d*; 2nd, 1982, June de Medina, *d* of Surg. Comdr Norman Bernard de Medina Greenstreet, RN; one step *s* one step *d*. *Educ:* Malvern Coll.; Guy's Hosp. Med. Sch., London Univ. (MB, BS 1951). MRCS, LRCP 1951; FRCS 1958. Trooper, 21st SAS Regt (Artists Rifles), TA, 1948-50. House appts, Gen. Hosp., Ramsgate and Royal Berks Hosp., Reading, 1951-52; commnd into RAMC, 1952; Regtl MO to No 9 Training Regt RE, 1952-53; surg. appts in mil. hosps in UK, Cyprus and N Africa, 1953-58; seconded as Surg. Registrar, Royal Postgrad. Med. Sch., Hammersmith Hosp., 1958-59; Officer i/c Surg. Div. and Consultant Surgeon to mil. hosps, Malaya, Singapore, N Borneo and UK, 1959-69; CO BMH Dhekelia, 1969-72; Sen. Consultant Surgeon in mil. hosps, UK and NI, 1972-77; Consulting Surgeon to BAOR, 1977-82. Hon. Consultant to S Dist, Kensington and Chelsea and Westminster AHA (T), 1981. Fellow, Assoc. of Surgeons of GB and Ireland, 1960. Member: Med. Cttee, Defence Scientific Adv. Council, 1982-; BMA, 1950-; Wessex Surgeons Club, 1976-; Editorial Bd, Injury, 1982-. *Publications:* (contrib.) Field Surgery Pocket Book, 1981; original articles in the Lancet and British Jl of Surgery. *Recreations:* fishing, shooting and other country pursuits, golf, tennis, sailing, gardening, joinery, house maintenance. *Address:* c/o Ministry of Defence, First Avenue House, High Holborn, WC1V 6HE.

PRYOR, John Pembro, MS; FRCS; Consultant Urological Surgeon to King's College Hospital and St Peter's Hospital, since 1975; Dean, Institute of Urology, London University, since 1978; *b* 25 Aug. 1937; *s* of William Benjamin Pryor and Kathleen Pryor; *m* 1959, Marion Hopkins; four *s*. *Educ:* Reading Sch.; King's Coll. and King's Coll. Hosp. Med. Sch. (MB, BS; AKC 1961). FRCS 1967; MS London 1971. Training appointments: Doncaster Royal Infirm., 1965-66; Univ. of Calif, San Francisco, 1968-69; King's Coll. Hosp. and St Paul's Hosp., 1971-72. Hunterian Prof., RCS, 1971. Chm. (first), British Andrology Soc., 1979-. *Publications:* articles on urology and andrology in scientific jls. *Address:* 147 Harley Street, W1N 1DL. *T:* 01-935 4444.

PUCKEY, Sir Walter (Charles), FEng. *Address:* Silverdale, Beech Drive, Kingswood, Surrey.

PUGH, Alastair Tarrant; Managing Director, British Caledonian Airways, since 1978; *b* 16 Sept. 1928; *s* of Sqdn Leader Rev. Herbert Cecil Pugh, GC, MA, and Amy Lilian Pugh; *m* 1957, Sylvia Victoria Marlow; two *s* one *d*. *Educ:* Tettenhall Coll.. Staffs; De Havilland Aeronautical Tech. Sch. FRAeS; FCIT; FRSA; CBIM. Design Dept, De Havilland Aircraft Co., 1949-52; Sen. Designer, H. M. Hobson, 1952-55; journalist, Flight, 1955-61; Channel Air Bridge, 1961-63; British United Airways, 1963-70: Planning Dir, 1968; British Caledonian Airways: Dir, R&D, 1970; Production Dir, 1973-74; Corporate Planning Dir, 1974-77; Dep. Chief Exec., 1977-78. Pres., Inst. of Freight Forwarders, 1981-82. *Recreation:* the chain-driven Frazer Nash. *Address:* England's Cottage, Sidlow Bridge, Reigate, Surrey. *T:* Reigate 43456.

PUGH, Harold Valentine, CBE 1964; Chairman, Northern Ireland Joint Electricity Authority, 1967-70, retired; *b* 18 Oct. 1899; *s* of Henry John Valentine Pugh and Martha (*née* Bott); *m* 1934, Elizabeth Mary (*née* Harwood); two *s* one *d*. *Educ:* The High Sch., Murree, India; Manchester College of Technology. Trained Metropolitan-Vickers (asst engineer erection, 1925-30). Chief Engineer, Cory Bros, 1930-35; Deputy Superintendent and later Superintendent, Upper Boat Power Station, 1935-43; Generation Engineer, South Wales Power Company, 1943-44; Deputy Chief Engineer, Manchester Corporation Electricity Dept, 1944-48; Controller, British Electricity Authority, South Wales Division, 1948; Controller, British (later Central) Electricity Authority, London Division, 1951; Chairman: Eastern Electricity Board, 1957-63; South-Eastern Electricity Board, 1963-66. Director: Aberdare Holdings, 1966-70. AMCT; FIEE; FIMechE. *Recreations:* gardening, golf. *Address:* Clontaff, Doggetts Wood Lane, Chalfont St Giles, Bucks. *T:* Little Chalfont 2330.

PUGH, Sir Idwal (Vaughan), KCB 1972 (CB 1967); Chairman, Chartered Trust Ltd, since 1979; Director: Standard Chartered Bank, since 1979; Halifax Building Society, since 1979; Chairman, Development Corporation of Wales, since 1980; *b* 10 Feb. 1918; *s* of late Rhys Pugh and Elizabeth Pugh; *m* 1946, Mair Lewis; one *s* one *d*. *Educ:* Cowbridge Grammar Sch.; St John's Coll., Oxford (Hon. Fellow, 1979). Army Service, 1940-46. Entered Min. of Civil Aviation, 1946; Alternate UK Rep. at International Civil Aviation Organisation, Montreal, 1950-53; Asst Secretary, 1956; Civil Air Attaché,

Washington, 1957-59; Under Secretary, Min. of Transport, 1959; Min. of Housing and Local Govt, 1961; Dep. Sec., Min. of Housing and Local Govt, 1966-69; Permanent Sec., Welsh Office, 1969-71; Second Permanent Sec., DoE, 1971-76. Parly Comr for Administration and Health Service Comr for England, Wales and Scotland, 1976-79. *Address:* Nant-y-Garreg, Bontddu, Gwynedd. *Club:* Brooks's.

PUGH, John Arthur, OBE 1968; HM Diplomatic Service, retired; British High Commissioner to Seychelles, 1976-80; *b* 17 July 1920; *er s* of late Thomas Pugh and Dorothy Baker Pugh; unmarried. *Educ:* Brecon Grammar Sch.; Bristol Univ. RN, 1941-45. Home CS, 1950-54; Gold Coast Admin. Service, 1955-58; Adviser to Ghana Govt, 1958-60; First Sec., British High Commn, Lagos, 1962-65; First Sec. (Economic), Bangkok, and British Perm. Rep. to Economic Commn for Asia and Far East, 1965-68; British Dep. High Comr, Ibadan, 1971-73; Diplomatic Service Inspector, 1973-76. *Recreations:* Oriental ceramics, anthropology, the sea. *Address:* Pennybrin, Hay on Wye, Hereford. *T:* Hay on Wye 820695. *Club:* Royal Commonwealth Society.

PUGH, John Stanley; Editor, Liverpool Echo, since 1978; *b* 9 Dec. 1927; *s* of John Albert and Winifred Lloyd Pugh; *m* 1953, Kathleen Mary; two *s* one *d. Educ:* Wallasey Grammar School. Editor, Liverpool Daily Post, 1969-78. *Recreation:* golf. *Address:* 26 Westwood Road, Noctorum, Birkenhead, Merseyside. *Club:* Royal Liverpool (Hoylake).

PUGH, Prof. Leslie Penrhys, CBE 1962; MA (Cantab); BSc (London), FRCVS; Emeritus Professor, Cambridge University; Professor of Veterinary Clinical Studies, Cambridge, 1951-63; Life Fellow of Magdalene Coll., Cambridge; Member, Agricultural Research Council, 1952-57; President, Royal College of Veterinary Surgeons, 1956; *b* 19 Dec. 1895; *s* of David Pugh and Emily Epton Hornby; *m* 1st, 1918, Paula Storie (*d* 1930); one *s* two *d* ; 2nd, 1933, Betty Chandley; one *s* one *d. Educ:* Tonbridge; Royal Veterinary Coll.; London Univ. MRCVS 1917, BSc (London) 1917; FRCVS, 1923 (Hon. FRCVS, 1979). General Practitioner in West Kent, 1919-50; Deputy Assistant Director of Veterinary Services (44th Home Counties Division TA), 1927; Major, 1927; Divisional Commandant Kent Special Constabulary (Sevenoaks Division), 1949. *Publication:* From Farriery to Veterinary Medicine, 1962. *Recreation:* gardening. *Address:* 69 South Cliff, Bexhill-on-Sea, East Sussex. *T:* Bexhill 212047.
See also P. D. Storie-Pugh.

PUGH, Lionel Roger Price, CBE 1975; VRD 1953; Deputy Chairman, Bridon Ltd, since 1977 (Director since 1973); Director, L. Ryan Holdings Ltd, since 1979; *b* 9 May 1916; *s* of late Henry George Pugh, Cardiff; *m* 1942, Joyce Norma Nash; one *s* one *d. Educ:* Clifton. FCA. Supply Officer, RNVR, 1938-60; war service mainly in Mediterranean, 1939-46; retired as Lt Comdr, RNR, 1960. With Deloitte & Co., 1933-47; joined Guest Keen & Bladwins Iron & Steel Co. Ltd, 1947; Dir 1955; Man. Dir 1960; Chm. 1962; Jt Man. Dir, GKN Steel, 1964. Dir, Product Co-ordination, British Steel Corp., 1967; Dep. Commercial Man. Dir, 1969; Man. Dir, Ops and Supplies, 1970; Mem., Corporate Finance and Planning, 1972; Exec. Mem., 1972-77. Pres., Iron and Steel Inst., 1973; Hon. Member: American Iron and Steel Inst. 1973; Metals Soc., 1976. Mem., Civil Aviation Council for Wales, 1962-66; part-time Mem., S Wales Electricity Bd, 1963-67. DL S Glamorgan (formerly Glamorgan), 1963-78. Gold Cross of Merit (Poland), 1942. *Address:* Brook Cottage, Bournes Green, Oakridge, Glos. *T:* Bisley 554. *Clubs:* Naval and Military; Cardiff and County; Royal Porthcawl Golf, Cirencester Golf.

PUGH, Surg. Rear-Adm. Patterson David Gordon, OBE 1968; surgeon and author; *b* 19 Dec. 1920; *o s* of late W. T. Gordon Pugh, MD, FRCS, Carshalton, and Elaine V. A. Pugh (*née* Hobson), Fort Beaufort, S Africa; *m* 1st, 1948, Margaret Sheena Fraser; three *s* one *d* ; 2nd, 1967, Eleanor Margery Jones; one *s* one *d. Educ:* Lancing Coll.; Jesus Coll., Cambridge; Middlesex Hosp. Med. Sch. MA (Cantab), MB, BChir; FRCS, LRCP. Ho. Surg., North Middlesex Hosp., 1944. RNVR, 1945; served, HMS Glasgow and HMS Jamaica, 1945-47; perm. commn, 1950; served, HMS Narvik, 1952, HMS Warrior, 1956; Consultant in Orthopaedics, RN Hospitals: Malta, 1960; Haslar, 1962; Plymouth, 1968; Sen. MO (Admin.), RN Hosp., Plymouth, 1973; MO i/c, RN Hosp., Malta, 1974-75; Surgeon Rear-Adm. (Naval Hosps), 1975-78. QHS, 1975-78. MO, Home Office Prison Dept, 1978-80. Fellow, British Orthopaedic Assoc.; FRSA. CStJ 1976. *Publications:* Practical Nursing, 16th edn 1945, to 21st edn 1969; Nelson and his Surgeons, 1968; Staffordshire Portrait Figures and Allied Subjects of the Victorian Era, 1970, enlarged edn 1981; Naval Ceramics, 1971; Heraldic China Mementos of the First World War, 1972; Pugh of Carshalton, 1973. *Recreation:* travel. *Address:* 29 Fitzroy Street, Grahamstown, Cape Province, 6140, Republic of South Africa. *T:* Grahamstown 6491.

PUGH, Peter David S.; *see* Storie-Pugh.

PUGH, Prof. Ralph Bernard, MA Oxon; DLit London; FSA; Professor of English History in the University of London, 1968-77, now Emeritus; Emeritus Fellow of St Edmund Hall, Oxford, since 1977 (Supernumerary Fellow, 1959-77; Lecturer in Administrative History, 1952-59); *b* 1 Aug. 1910; *o c* of Bernard Carr and Mabel Elizabeth Pugh, Sutton, Surrey; unmarried. *Educ:* St Paul's Sch.; Queen's Coll., Oxford. 1st Class Hons, Modern History, 1932 (BA). Asst Keeper of Public Records, 2nd Cl. 1934, 1st Cl. 1946; Dominions Office, 1940-46, Acting Principal, 1941-46. Member, Institute for Advanced Study, Princeton, NJ, 1963-64, 1969-70; Raleigh Lectr, British Acad., 1973; Fellow, Folger Shakespeare Lib., Washington, DC, 1973; British Acad. Fellow, Newberry Lib., Chicago, 1978. Wiltshire Archaeological and Nat. History Society: President, 1950-51, 1953-55; Vice-President, 1955-; Wiltshire Record Society (until 1967 Records Br. of Wilts Archaeological and Nat. History Society): Hon. Secretary and Editor, 1937-53; Chairman, 1953-67; President, 1967-; Vice-President: Selden Society, 1966-69; Nat. Trust Council, 1967-75. Editor, Victoria History of Counties of England, 1949-77. *Publications:* (ed) Abstracts of Feet of Fines for Wiltshire, Edw. I and II, 1929; (ed) Calendar of Antrobus Deeds, 1947; How to Write a Parish History, 1954; The Crown Estate, 1960; Records of the Colonial and Dominions Offices (PRO Handbooks), 1964; Itinerant Justices in English History, 1967; Imprisonment in Medieval England, 1968; (ed) Court Rolls of the Wiltshire Manors of Adam de Stratton, 1970; (ed) Calendar of London Trailbaston Trials, 1976 for 1975; (ed) Wiltshire Gaol Delivery and Trailbaston Trials, 1978; articles in Victoria County History, Cambridge History of the British Empire and in learned periodicals. *Recreation:* sight-seeing. *Address:* 67 Southwood Park, N6 5SQ. *T:* 01-340 5661. *Club:* Reform.

PUGH, Roger Courtenay Beckwith, MD; Pathologist to St Peter's Hospitals and the Institute of Urology, London, 1955-82; *b* 23 July 1917; *y s* of late Dr Robert Pugh, Talgarth, Breconshire, and of late Margaret Louise Pugh (*née* Gough); *m* 1942, Winifred Dorothy, *yr d* of late Alfred Cooper and late Margaret Cooper (*née* Evans); one *s* one *d. Educ:* Gresham's Sch., Holt; St Mary's Hospital (University of London). MRCS, LRCP 1940; MB, BS, 1941; MD 1948; MCPath. 1964; FRCPath. 1967. House Surgeon, St Mary's Hospital and Sector Hospitals, 1940-42; War Service in RAF (Mediterranean theatre), 1942-46, Sqdn Leader; Registrar, Department of Pathology, St Mary's Hospital, 1946-48; Asst Pathologist and Lecturer in Pathology, St Mary's Hospital, 1948-51; Asst Morbid Anatomist, The Hospital for Sick Children, Great Ormond Street, 1951-54. Erasmus Wilson Demonstrator, RCS, 1959, 1961; Member: Board of Governors, St Peter's Hospitals, 1961-82; Pathological Society of Great Britain and Ireland; Assoc. of Clin. Pathologists (Marshall Medal, 1982); Internat. Society of Urology; Internat. Acad. of Pathology (former Pres., British Div.); Assoc. Member British Assoc. of Urological Surgeons (St Peter's Medal, 1981); FRSocMed (former Pres., Sect. of Urology). *Publications:* (ed) Pathology of the Testis, 1976; various contributions to Pathological, Urological and Paediatric Journals. *Recreations:* gardening, photography. *Address:* 19 Manor Way, Beckenham, Kent. *T:* 01-658 6294.

PUGH, William David, CBE 1965; FIM; CBIM; FIIM; JP; Deputy Chairman, English Steel Corporation Ltd, 1965-67 (Managing Director, 1955-65); Director of Personnel, British Steel Corporation (Midland Group), 1967-70; *b* 21 Nov. 1904; *s* of late Sir Arthur and Lady Pugh; *m* 1936, Mary Dorothea Barber; one *d. Educ:* Regent Street Polytechnic; Sheffield Univ. Joined Research Dept, Vickers Ltd, Sheffield, 1926, Director, Vickers Ltd, 1962-67; Chairman: The Darlington Forge Ltd, 1957-66; Taylor Bros & Co. Ltd, 1959-66; Director: (and alternate Chairman), Firth Vickers Stainless Steels Ltd, 1948-67; High Speed Steel Alloys Ltd, 1953-68; Industrial Training Council Service, 1960-67; British Iron and Steel Corp. Ltd, 1962-67; Sheffield Boy Scouts Holdings Ltd, 1965-; Sheffield Centre for Environmental Research Ltd. Associate of Metallurgy (Sheffield University; Mappin Medallist). Hon. DMet (Sheffield), 1966. *Recreations:* gardening, golf, reading, drystone-walling. *Address:* Freebirch Cottage, Freebirch, Chesterfield, Derbyshire S42 7DQ. *T:* Baslow 3153. *Club:* Sheffield (Sheffield).

PUGH, Rt. Rev. William Edward Augustus, MA, LRAM (Singing); Hon. Assistant Bishop, diocese of Carlisle; *b* 22 July 1909; *s* of William Arthur Augustus and Margaret Caroline Pugh; *m* 1937, Freda Mary, *er d* of Charles Frederick and Susannah Merishaw; no *c. Educ:* Leeds Univ.; College of the Resurrection, Mirfield. Assistant Curate: Staveley, Derbys, 1934-37; Edwinstowe, Notts, 1937-38; Rector of Bestwood Park, Notts, 1938-44; Vicar of Sutton-in-Ashfield, Notts, 1944-55; Hon. Canon of Southwell, 1954; Vicar of East Retford, Notts, 1955-59; Rector of Harrington, 1959-62; Vicar of Cockermouth, 1962-70, and Archdeacon of West Cumberland, 1959-70; Bishop Suffragan of Penrith, 1970-79. *Recreations:* fishing, music. *Address:* 25 Brigham Road, Cockermouth, Cumbria CA13 0AX.

PUGSLEY, Sir Alfred Grenville, Kt 1956; OBE 1944; DSc; FRS 1952; FEng; Professor of Civil Engineering, University of Bristol, 1944-68, now Emeritus; Pro-Vice-Chancellor, 1961-64; *b* 8 May 1903; *s* of H. W. Pugsley, BA, FLS, London; *m* 1928, Kathleen M. Warner (*d* 1974); no *c. Educ:* Rutlish Sch.; London Univ. Civil Engineering Apprenticeship at Royal Arsenal, Woolwich, 1923-26; Technical Officer, at the Royal Airship Works, Cardington, 1926-31; Member scientific and technical staff at Royal Aircraft Establishment, Farnborough, 1931-45, being Head of Structural and Mechanical Engineering Dept there, 1941-45. Visiting Lecturer on aircraft structures at Imperial Coll., London, 1938-40. Chairman of Aeronautical Research Council, 1952-57; Member: Advisory Council on Scientific Policy, 1956-59; Tribunal of Inquiry on Ronan Point, 1968; Member of various scientific and professional institutions and cttees; President: IStructE, 1957-58; Section G, British Assoc. for Advancement of Science, 1960; a Vice-Pres., ICE, 1971-73. Hon. FRAeS 1963; Hon. FICE 1981. Hon. DSc: Belfast, 1965; Cranfield, 1978; Birmingham, 1982; Hon. DUniv Surrey, 1968. Structural Engineers' Gold Medal, 1968; Civil Engineers' Ewing Gold Medal, 1979. *Publications:* The Theory of Suspension Bridges, 1957 (2nd edn 1968); The Safety of Structures, 1966; (ed and contrib.) The Works of Isambard Kingdom

Brunel, 1976; numerous Reports and Memoranda of Aeronautical Research Council; papers in scientific journals and publications of professional engineering bodies; articles and reviews in engineering press. *Address:* 4 Harley Court, Clifton Down, Bristol BS8 3JU. *Club:* Athenæum.

PUGSLEY, Rear-Admiral Anthony Follett, CB 1944; DSO 1943; retired; *b* 7 Dec. 1901; *e s* of late J. Follett Pugsley, Whitefield, Wiveliscombe, Somerset; *m* 1931, Barbara, *d* of late J. Byam Shaw; one *s. Educ:* RN Colleges, Osborne and Dartmouth. Midshipman, 1918; Commander, 1936; Captain, 1942; Rear-Admiral, 1952; retired, 1954. Served European War from May 1918; on Upper Yangtse, 1925-27, and in command HM Ships P.40, Antelope and Westcott, 1933-36; during War of 1939-45, in command HM Ships Javelin, Fearless, Paladin; Captain (D) 14th Flotilla, Jervis (despatches thrice, DSO and bar, Greek War Cross); Assault Gp Comdr, Normandy landing, 1944 (2nd bar to DSO); Naval Force Commander in assault on Walcheren, 1944 (CB); Captain (D) 19th Flotilla (Far East), 1945-46; Directing Staff, Senior Officers War Course, 1947-48; Naval Officer in charge, Londonderry and Director (RN) Joint Anti-Submarine School, 1948-50; in command HMS Warrior, 1951; Flag Officer, Malayan Area, Dec. 1951-Nov. 1953. *Publication:* Destroyer Man, 1957. *Address:* Javelin, Milverton, Taunton, Somerset. *T:* Milverton 400355.

PULLAN, John Marshall, MChir, FRCS; Surgeon, King Edward VII Hospital; Hon. Surgeon, St Thomas' Hospital, London; late of Bolingbroke Hospital, London and Royal Masonic Hospital, London; *b* 1 Aug. 1915; *e s* of late William Greaves Pullan and of Kathleen, *d* of Alfred Marshall, Otley, Yorkshire; *m* 1940, Leila Diana, *d* of H. C. Craven-Veitch, Surgeon; one *s* three *d. Educ:* Shrewsbury; King's Coll., Cambridge; St Thomas' Hospital, London. MA Cantab (1st Cl. Nat. Sc. Tripos) 1937; MB, BChir 1940; FRCS, 1942; MChir 1945. Teacher in Surgery, Univ. of London; Examiner in Surgery, Univs of: London, 1956; Cambridge. Member: Court of Examiners, RCS, 1964; Board of Governors, St Thomas' Hospital. *Publications:* Section on Diseases of the Liver, Gall Bladder and Bile Ducts, in Textbook of British Surgery, ed Sir Henry Souttar, 1956; articles in surgical journals. *Address:* Palings, Warboys Road, Kingston Hill, Surrey. *T:* 01-546 5310; 3 Upper Wimpole Street, W1. *T:* 01-935 5873. *Clubs:* White's, Flyfishers', Boodle's.

PULLAR, Hubert Norman, CBE 1964; MA; HM Diplomatic Service, retired; *b* 26 Dec. 1914; *y s* of late William Laurence and Christine Ellen Pullar, formerly of Uplands, Bridge-of-Allan, Stirlingshire; *m* 1943, Helen Alice La Fontaine; one *s* one *d. Educ:* Trin. Coll., Glenalmond; Trin. Coll., Oxford. Entered HM Consular Service, 1938. Served in Turkey, 1938-42; USA, 1943-46; Persia, 1946-48; Morocco, 1949-52; Foreign Office, 1952-54; Finland, 1954-56; Syria, 1956; Iraq, 1957-59; Antwerp, 1960-64; HM Consul-General, Jerusalem, 1964-67; Foreign Office, 1967-68; Consul-General, Durban, 1968-71. Order of Ouissam Alouite, Morocco, 1952. CStJ 1966. Coronation Medal, 1953. *Recreations:* golf, motoring, travel. *Address:* Camelot, Ringles Cross, Uckfield, East Sussex. *T:* Uckfield 2159.

PULLÉE, Ernest Edward, CBE 1967; ARCA, ASIA, FSAE, NEAC; Chief Officer, National Council for Diplomas in Art and Design, 1967-74; retired; *b* 9 Feb. 1907; *s* of Ernest and Caroline Elizabeth Pullée; *m* 1933, Margaret Fisher, ARCA, NEAC; one *s. Educ:* St Martin's Sch., Dover; Royal Coll. of Art, London. Principal: Gloucester Coll. of Art, 1934-39; Portsmouth Coll. of Art, 1939-45; Leeds Coll. of Art, 1945-56; Leicester Coll. of Art and Design, 1956-67. Pres., Nat. Soc. for Art Educn, 1945, 1959; Chm., Assoc. of Art Instns, 1959; Mem., Nat. Adv. Coun. for Art Educn, 1959; Mem., Nat. Coun. for Diplomas in Art and Design, 1961. Hon. DA (Manchester), 1961. *Publications:* contribs to professional and academic jls. *Recreation:* travel. *Address:* 9 Fulford Park, Fulford, York YO1 4QE. *Club:* Chelsea Arts.

PULLEIN-THOMPSON, Denis; *see* Cannan, D.

PULLEN, William Reginald James, CVO 1975 (MVO 1966); LLB; FCIS; JP; Receiver-General, since 1959, Chapter Clerk since 1963 and Registrar since 1964, Westminster Abbey; *b* 17 Feb. 1922; *s* of late William Pullen and Lillian Pullen (*née* Chinn), Falmouth; *m* 1948, Doreen Angela Hebron; two *d. Educ:* Falmouth Gram. School; King's College, London; private study. Served War of 1939-45; Flt Lt, RAFVR (admin and special duties) SE Asia. Asst to Chief Accountant, Westminster Abbey, 1947; Dep. Registrar, 1951; Sec. Westminster Abbey Appeal, 1953. Westminster City Council, 1962-65; a Chm., Inner London Juvenile Ct. Freeman, Worshipful Co. of Wax Chandlers. CStJ 1981 (OStJ 1969). *Publication:* contrib. A House of Kings, 1966. *Recreations:* reading, walking, cooking. *Address:* 4b Dean's Yard, Westminster, SW1. *T:* 01-222 4023. *Clubs:* Royal Air Force, MCC.

PULLEYBLANK, Prof. Edwin George, PhD; FRSC; Professor of Chinese, University of British Columbia, since 1966; *b* Calgary, Alberta, 7 Aug. 1922; *s* of W. G. E. Pulleyblank, Calgary; *m* 1945, Winona Ruth Relyea (*decd*), Arnprior, Ont; one *s* two *d. Educ:* Central High School, Calgary; University of Alberta; University of London. BA Hons Classics, Univ. of Alberta, 1942; Nat. Research Council of Canada, 1943-46. School of Oriental and African Studies, Univ. of London: Chinese Govt School, 1946; Lectr in Classical Chinese, 1948; PhD in Classical Chinese, 1951; Lectr in Far Eastern History, 1952; Professor of Chinese, University of Cambridge, 1953; Head, Dept of Asian Studies, Univ. of British Columbia, 1968-75. Fellow of Downing Coll., Cambridge, 1955-66. *Publications:* The Background of the Rebellion of An

Lu-Shan, 1955; articles in Asia Major, Bulletin of School of Oriental and African Studies, etc. *Address:* Department of Asian Studies, University of British Columbia, Vancouver, BC V6T 1W5, Canada.

PULLICINO, Dr Anthony Alfred; *b* 14 March 1917; *s* of late Sir Philip Pullicino; *m* 1944, Edith Baker; three *s* two *d. Educ:* St Aloysius Coll., Malta; Royal Univ. of Malta; Melbourne University. BA 1939, LLD 1943, Malta; LLB Melbourne 1963. Served in Royal Malta Artillery, 1944-45 (Lieut). MLA Malta, 1951-55 (Speaker, 1951-52). Mem. Council, CPA, attending sessions in London 1952, Nairobi 1953. Practised as Solicitor, Melbourne, 1963-65; High Comr for Malta in Canberra, 1965-69; High Comr in London and Ambassador of Malta to USSR, 1970-71. *Recreation:* golf. *Address:* 191/4 Tower Road, Sliema, Malta. *Club:* Casino Maltese (Malta).

PULLING, Martin John Langley, CBE 1958 (OBE 1954); *b* 30 May 1906; *o s* of late Rev. Augustine J. Pulling and Dorothea Fremlin Key; *m* 1939, Yvonne Limborgh, Antwerp, Belgium; no *c. Educ:* Marlborough College; King's College, Cambridge (Scholar). Mech. Scis. Tripos, BA 1928; MA 1943. Various posts in radio industry, 1929-34; joined BBC Engrg Div., 1934; retired as Dep. Dir of Engrg, 1967. Was Chm. of Technical Cttee of European Broadcasting Union) responsible for development of "Eurovision" from its inception in 1952 until 1962. Chairman: The Ferrograph Co., 1968-72; Rendar Instruments Ltd, 1968-72. FIEE 1967 (MIEE 1945, AMIEE 1935); Chm., Electronics and Communications Section, IEE, 1959-60; Mem. Council, IEE, 1963-66; MITE 1966; Hon. FBKS. *Address:* 6 Cadogan House, 93 Sloane Street, SW1X 9PD. *T:* 01-235 1739. *Clubs:* Hurlingham, MCC, Anglo-Belgian.

PULLINGER, Sir (Francis) Alan, Kt 1977; CBE 1970; Chairman, Haden Carrier Ltd, 1961-79; *b* 22 May 1913; *s* of William Pullinger; *m* 1st, 1946, Felicity Charmian Gotch Hobson (decd); two *s* one *d* ; 2nd, 1966, Jacqueline Louise Anne Durin. *Educ:* Marlborough Coll.; Balliol Coll., Oxford (MA). Pres., IHVE, 1972-73; Hon. FCIBS, 1977. *Recreations:* mountaineering, sailing, beagling. *Address:* Barnhorn, Meadway, Berkhamsted, Herts. *T:* Berkhamsted 3206. *Clubs:* Alpine, Travellers'.

PULLINGER, John Elphick; His Honour Judge Pullinger; a Circuit Judge, since 1982; *b* 27 Aug. 1930; *s* of late Reginald Edward Pullinger and of Elsie Florence Pullinger; *m* 1956, Carette Maureen, *d* of late Flt Lieut and late Mrs E. D. Stephens; one *s* one *d. Educ:* Friern Barnet Grammar Sch.; Quintin Sch.; London Sch. of Econs and Pol. Science (LLB 1955). Called to the Bar, Lincoln's Inn, 1958; Sir Thomas More Bursary, 1958. Legal Sec. to Lord Shrewsbury's Commn of Enquiry into the Infantile Paralysis Fellowship, 1958-59; Dep. Judge Advocate, 1965; AJAG, 1972-82; Judge Advocate to NZ Force SE Asia, 1973-75; served on JAG's staff in Germany, Mediterranean, Near East and Far East. Member: NRA, 1979-; NSRA, 1977-; HAC, 1950-. *Publication:* The Position of the British Serviceman under the Army and Air Force Acts 1955, 1975. *Recreation:* shottist. *Address:* Mill House, Rockshaw Road, Merstham, Surrey RH1 3BZ. *T:* Merstham 2070. *Club:* Naval and Military.

PULVERTAFT, Prof. Robert James Valentine, OBE 1944; MD Cantab; FRCP; FRCPath; Emeritus Professor of Clinical Pathology, University of London (Professor, 1950-62); Visiting Professor of Pathology, Makerere University College; Visiting Professor of Pathology, University of Ibadan, W Nigeria; President Association of Clinical Pathologists, 1953; Director of Laboratories, Westminster Hospital, until 1962; Lieutenant-Colonel RAMC, 1943, serving Middle East Forces; subsequently Assistant Director of Pathology, Northern Command and MEF; lately Hon. Consultant in Pathology to the Army at Home; *b* 14 Feb. 1897; *s* of Rev. T. J. Pulvertaft and B. C. Denroche; *m* E. L. M. Costello; one *s* two *d. Educ:* Westminster School; Trinity College, Cambridge (Classical Scholar); St Thomas' Hosp. Lt 3rd Royal Sussex 1915-19; served with 4th Royal Sussex (Palestine); seconded to RFC as observer (Palestine) and pilot in 205 Squadron RAF (France); Senior Exhibitioner and Scholar, Nat. Science, Trinity College Cantab. 2nd class Part II Tripos Nat. Science (Physiology); Entrance University Scholar St Thomas' Hospital; Asst Bacteriologist, VD Dept St Thomas' Hospital; Pathologist to Units, St Thomas' Hosp., 1923-32; Plimmer Research Fellow in Pathology, 1929-32; EMS Sept.-Nov. 1939; National Institute Medical Research, 1939-40. Examiner in Pathology, Univs of Cambridge, Oxford, London, Trinity College, Dublin, National University of Ireland, Liverpool University; also for the Conjoint Board and Royal Army Medical Coll. Hon. FRSM 1972. *Publications:* Studies on Malignant Disease in Nigeria by Tissue Culture; various papers on bacteriology and pathology, particularly in relation to the study of living cells by cinemicrography. *Address:* 31 Izaak Walton Way, Chesterton, Cambridge.

PUMPHREY, Sir (John) Laurence, KCMG 1973 (CMG 1963); HM Diplomatic Service, retired; Ambassador to Pakistan (formerly High Commissioner), 1971-76; *b* 22 July 1916; *s* of late Charles Ernest Pumphrey and Iris Mary (*née* Moberly-Bell); *m* 1945, Jean, *e d* of Sir Walter Buchanan Riddell, 12th Bt; four *s* one *d. Educ:* Winchester; New College, Oxford. Served War of 1939-45 in Army. Foreign Service from 1945. Head of Establishment and Organisation Department, Foreign Office, 1955-60; Counsellor, Staff of British Commissioner-General for SE Asia, Singapore, 1960-63; Counsellor, HM Embassy, Belgrade, 1963-65; Deputy High Commissioner, Nairobi, 1965-67; British High Comr, Zambia, 1967-71.

Military Cross, 3rd Class (Greece), 1941. *Address:* Caistron, Thropton, Morpeth, Northumberland NE65 7LG.

PUNGAN, Vasile; Counsellor to the President of the Socialist Republic of Romania on Economic Affairs, since 1973; *b* 2 Nov. 1926; *m* 1952, Liliana Niță (*d* 1973); one *d*. *Educ:* Inst. of Econs, Bucharest. Dr in Econ. Scis and Univ. Prof.; Dean of Faculty, Agronomical Inst., Bucharest, 1954; Gen. Dir, Min. of Agric. and Forestry, 1955–58; Counsellor, Romanian Embassy, Washington, 1959–62; Dir and Mem. College, Min. of Foreign Affairs, 1963–66; Ambassador of Socialist Republic of Romania to Court of St James's, 1966–72. Mem., Central Cttee of Romanian Communist Party, 1972 (Alternate Mem. 1969); Mem., Grand National Assembly, 1975. Holds orders and medals of Socialist Republic of Romania and several foreign countries. *Address:* State Council, Bucharest, Romania.

PURCELL, Denis; see Purcell, J. D.

PURCELL, Prof. Edward Mills, PhD; Gerhard Gade University Professor, Harvard University, 1960–80, now Emeritus; *b* 30 Aug. 1912; *s* of Edward A. Purcell and Mary Elizabeth Mills; *m* 1937, Beth C. Busser; two *s*. *Educ:* Purdue University; Harvard University. PhD Harvard, 1938. Instructor in Physics, Harvard, 1938–40; Radiation Laboratory, Mass. Inst. of Technology, 1940–45; Associate Professor of Physics, Harvard, 1945–49; Professor of Physics, 1949–60. Senior Fellow, Society of Fellows, Harvard, 1950–71. Halley Lectr, Oxford Univ., 1982. Hon. DEng Purdue, 1953; Hon. DSci Washington Univ., St Louis, 1963. (Jointly) Nobel Prize in Physics, 1952; Nat. Medal of Science, 1979. *Publications:* Principles of Microwave Circuits, 1948; Physics for Students of Science and Engineering, 1952; Electricity and Magnetism, 1965. Papers in Physical Review, Astrophys. Jl. *Address:* 5 Wright Street, Cambridge, Mass, USA. *T:* 547–9317.

PURCELL, Harry, CBE 1982; Licensee of the New Inn, Cutnall Green, since 1972; Member (C) for Chaddesley Corbett, Hereford and Worcester County Council, since 1974; *b* 2 Dec. 1919; *s* of Charles and Lucy Purcell; *m* 1941, Eunice Mary Price; three *s* one *d*. *Educ:* Bewdley C of E Sch.; Kidderminster Coll. Joined TA, 1938; served War, 1939–46, Queen's Own Worcester Hussars; Transport Officer, Berlin, 1946–48. Carpet industry, 1949–60; self-employed, 1961–. Formerly Mem., Kidderminster Bor. Council; Mayor of Kidderminster, 1967–68. Chairman: West Mercia Police Authority, 1979–82; Police Cttee, National Assoc. of County Councils, 1977–; National Police Negotiating Bd, 1978–82; Vice-Chm., ACC, 1982–. *Recreations:* theatre, tennis, public service. *Address:* Flat 2, Holt Castle, Holt Heath, near Ombersley, Worcs. *T:* (home) Worcester 620773, (business) Cutnall Green 202.

PURCELL, (John) Denis; Metropolitan Magistrate, Clerkenwell Magistrates' Court, since 1963; *b* 7 Dec. 1913; *s* of John Poyntz Purcell and Dorothy Branston, Newark; *m* 1951, Pauline Mary, *e d* of Rev. Hiram Craven, Painswick, Glos; two *s*. *Educ:* Marlborough; Wadham College, Oxford. Called to Bar, Gray's Inn, 1938; SE Circuit; Sussex QS. Served War of 1939–45: commnd from HAC, 1939, to Shropshire Yeo., 1940; ADC to GOC-in-C, Western Command, 1941; Staff Capt., Western Command; GSO3, Italy; DAAG, HQ British Troops, Palestine. Actg Dep. Chm., London QS, 1962. *Recreations:* back-yard gardening, racing. *Address:* 1 Cheltenham Terrace, SW3. *T:* 01–730 2896.

PURCELL, Robert Michael; HM Diplomatic Service; Ambassador to Somali Democratic Republic, since 1980; *b* 22 Oct. 1923; *s* of late Lt-Col Walter Purcell and Constance (*née* Fendick); *m* 1965, Julia Evelyn, *o d* of late Brig. Edward Marsh-Kellett; two *d*. *Educ:* Ampleforth Coll. Commnd 60th Rifles (Greenjackets), 1943–47. Colonial Service, later HMOCS, Uganda, 1949–62: Dist Officer, 1949–60; Dist Comr, 1961–62; retd 1962. 1st Sec., CRO, later FCO, 1964–68; 1st Sec. (Commercial/Economic), Colombo, 1968–69; FCO, 1969–71; 1st Sec. (Aid), Singapore, 1971–73; Head of Chancery, HM Legation to the Holy See, 1973–76; Counsellor and Dep. High Comr, Malta, 1977–80. KSG 1976. *Recreation:* country life. *Address:* c/o Foreign and Commonwealth Office, SW1; Lythe House, Selborne, Hants. *T:* Selborne 231. *Club:* Naval and Military.

PURCELL, Rev. Canon William Ernest; author and broadcaster; Residentiary Canon of Worcester Cathedral, 1966–76; *b* 25 May 1909; *s* of Will and Gwladys Purcell; *m* 1939, Margaret Clegg; two *s* one *d*. *Educ:* Keble Coll., Oxford (MA); Univ. of Wales (BA); Queens Coll., Birmingham. Curate: St. John's Church, Keighley, 1938; Dover Parish Church, 1939–43; Vicar: St. Peter's, Maidstone, 1944–47; Sutton Valence, 1947–53; Chaplain, HM Borstal Instn, East Sutton, 1947–53; Religious Broadcasting Organiser, BBC Midlands, 1953–66. *Publications:* These Thy Gods, 1950; Pilgrim's Programme, 1957; Onward Christian Soldier (biog. of S. Baring Gould), 1957; A Plain Man Looks At Himself, 1962; Woodbine Willie (biog. of G. Studdert Kennedy), 1962; This Is My Story, 1963; The Plain Man Looks At The Commandments, 1966; Fisher of Lambeth (biog. of Archbp of Canterbury), 1969; Portrait of Soper (biog. of Lord Soper), 1972; British Police in a Changing Society, 1974; A Time to Die, 1979; Pilgrim's England, 1981. *Address:* 14 Conifer Close, Cumnor Hill, Oxford OX2 9HP. *Club:* National Liberal.

PURCELL, Ven. William Henry Samuel, MA; Archdeacon of Dorking, 1968–82; *b* 22 Jan. 1912; *m* 1941, Kathleen Clough, Leeds; one *s* (and one *s*

decd). *Educ:* King Edward VI School, Norwich; Fitzwilliam House, Cambridge (MA). Asst Curate, St Michael's, Headingley, Leeds, 1937; Minor Canon of Ripon Cathedral, 1940; Vicar: St Matthew, Holbeck, Leeds, 1943; St Matthew, Chapel Allerton, Leeds, 1947; St Martin's, Epsom, 1963. Rural Dean of Epsom, 1965. Hon. Canon of Ripon Cathedral, 1962; Hon. Canon of Guildford Cathedral, 1968, Canon Emeritus, 1982. *Recreations:* walking, travel. *Address:* 55 Windfield, Epsom Road, Leatherhead, Surrey KT22 8UQ. *T:* Leatherhead 75708.

PURCHAS, Rt. Hon. Sir Francis (Brooks), Kt 1974; PC 1982; **Rt. Hon. Lord Justice Purchas;** a Lord Justice of Appeal, since 1982; *b* 19 June 1919; *s* of late Captain Francis Purchas, 5th Royal Irish Lancers and late Millicent Purchas (*née* Brooks); *m* 1942, Patricia Mona Kathleen, *d* of Lieut Milburn; two *s*. *Educ:* Summerfields Sch., Oxford; Marlborough Coll.; Trinity Coll., Cambridge. Served RE, 1940–46: North Africa, 1943 (despatches); Hon. Lt-Col retd (Africa Star, Italy Star, 1939–45 Medal; Defence Medal). Allied Mil. Commission, Vienna. Called to Bar, Inner Temple, 1948, QC 1965, Bencher, 1972; practised at Bar, 1948–74; Leader, SE Circuit, 1972–74; Dep. Chm., E Sussex QS, 1966–71; Recorder of Canterbury, 1969–71 (Hon. Recorder of Canterbury, 1972–74); Recorder of the Crown Court, 1972–74; a Judge of the High Court of Justice, Family Div., 1974–82; Presiding Judge, SE Circuit, 1977–82. Comr, Central Criminal Court, 1970–71. Mem., Bar Council, 1966–68, 1969–71, 1972–74. Mem. of Livery, Worshipful Co. of Broderers, 1962. *Recreations:* shooting, golf, fishing. *Address:* Parkhurst House, near Haslemere, Surrey GU27 3BY. *T:* North Chapel 280; 1 Mitre Court Buildings, Temple, EC4Y 7BS. *T:* 01–353 5124. *Club:* Hawks (Cambridge).

PURDEN, Roma Laurette, (Laurie Purden; Mrs J. K. Kotch), MBE 1973; journalist and writer; Editor-in-Chief: Woman's Journal, since 1978; Woman & Home, since 1982; *b* 30 Sept. 1928; *d* of George Cecil Arnold Purden and Constance Mary Sheppard; *m* 1957, John Keith Kotch (*d* 1979); two *d*. *Educ:* Harecroft Sch., Tunbridge Wells. Fiction Editor, Home Notes, 1948–51; Asst Editor, Home Notes, 1951–52; Asst Editor, Woman's Own, 1952; Sen. Asst Editor, Girl, 1952–54; Editor of: Housewife, 1954–57; Home, 1957–62; House Beautiful, 1963–65; Good Housekeeping, 1965–73; Editor-in-Chief, Good Housekeeping, and Womancraft, 1973–77. Dir, Brickfield Publications Ltd, 1978–80. Magazine Editor of the Year, 1979, Soc. of Magazine Editors. *Address:* 11 Abbey Gardens, NW8 9AS.

PURDIE, Cora Gwendolyn Jean, (Wendy); see Campbell-Purdie.

PURDON, Maj.-Gen. Corran William Brooke, CBE 1970; MC 1945; CPM 1982; Commander, St John's Ambulance, Wiltshire, since 1981; *b* 4 May 1921; *s* of Maj.-Gen. William Brooke Purdon, DSO, OBE, MC, KHS, and Dorothy Myrtle Coates; *m* 1945, Maureen Patricia, *d* of Major J. F. Petrie; two *s* one *d*. *Educ:* Rokeby, Wimbledon; Campbell Coll., Belfast; RMC Sandhurst. MBIM. Commnd into Royal Ulster Rifles, 1939; service with Army Commandos, France and Germany, 1940–45; 1st Bn RU Rifles, Palestine, 1945–46; GHQ MELF, 1949–51; psc 1955; Staff, Malayan Emergency, 1956–58; Co. Comdr, 1 RU Rifles, Cyprus Emergency, 1958; CO, 1st Bn RU Rifles, BAOR and Borneo War, 1962–64; GSO1 and Chief Instructor, Sch. of Infantry, Warminster, 1965–67; Comdr, Sultan's Armed Forces, Oman, and Dir of Ops, Dhofar War, 1967–70 (Sultan's Bravery Medal, 1968 and Distinguished Service Medal for Gallantry, 1969, Oman); Comdt, Sch. of Infantry, Warminster, 1970–72; GOC, NW Dist, 1972–74; GOC Near East Land Forces, 1974–76, retired. Dep. Comr, Royal Hong Kong Police Force, 1978–81. Hon. Col, Queen's Univ. Belfast OTC, 1975–78. Pres., Army Gymnastic Union, 1973–76. CStJ 1976. *Publications:* articles in British Army Review and Infantryman. *Recreations:* physical training, swimming, collecting military pictures and military commemorative plates. *Address:* Old Park House, Devizes, Wilts. *Clubs:* Army and Navy; Hong Kong.

PURDY, Robert John, CMG 1963; OBE 1954; Bursar, Gresham's School, Holt, 1965–81; retired from HM Overseas Civil Service, 1963; *b* 2 March 1916; 2nd *s* of late Lt-Col T. W. Purdy, Woodgate House, Aylsham, Norfolk; *m* 1957, Elizabeth (*née* Sharp); two *s* one *d*. *Educ:* Haileybury College; Jesus College, Cambridge (BA). Served 1940–46 with 81 West African Division Reconnaissance Regt, 3rd and 4th Burma Campaigns (despatches, Major). Appointed to Colonial Administrative Service, Northern Nigeria, 1939; promoted Resident, 1956; Senior Resident, Staff Grade, 1957. Resident, Adamawa Province, 1956; Senior Resident, Plateau Province, 1958–61; Senior Resident, Sokoto Province, 1961–63, retd. *Recreations:* shooting, fishing, gardening. *Address:* Spratt's Green House, Aylsham, Norwich NR11 6TX. *T:* Aylsham 2147.

PURNELL, Paul Oliver, QC 1982; *b* 13 July 1936; *s* of Oliver Cuthbert Purnell and Pauline (*née* Brailli); *m* 1966, Celia Consuelo Ocampo; one *s* two *d*. *Educ:* The Oratory Sch.; Jesus Coll., Oxford (MA). Served 4th/7th Royal Dragoon Guards, 1958–62. Called to the Bar, Inner Temple, 1962. Jun. Treasury Counsel at Central Criminal Court, 1976–82. *Recreations:* windsurfing, tennis. *Address:* 3 Temple Gardens, Temple, EC4Y 9AU. *T:* 01–353 2460. *Club:* Cavalry and Guards.

PURSEGLOVE, John William, CMG 1973; Tropical Crops Specialist, Overseas Development Administration at East Malling Research Station, Kent, 1967–75; *b* 11 Aug. 1912; *s* of late Robert and Kate Purseglove; *m* 1947, Phyllis Agnes Adèle, *d* of late George and Mary Turner, Falkland Is; one *s* one d. Educ: Lady Manners Sch., Bakewell; Manchester Univ. (BSc Hons Botany); Gonville and Caius Coll., Cambridge; Imperial Coll. of Tropical Agriculture, Trinidad (AICTA). Agricultural and Sen. Agricl Officer, Uganda, 1936-52; Lectr in Tropical Agriculture, Univ. of Cambridge, 1952-54; Dir, Botanic Gardens, Singapore, 1954-57; Prof. of Botany, Imperial Coll. of Tropical Agriculture and Univ. of the West Indies, Trinidad, 1957-67. Pres., Assoc. for Tropical Biology, 1962-65. FLS 1944; FIBiol 1970. Publications: Tobacco in Uganda, 1951; Tropical Crops, Dicotyledons, 2 vols, 1968; Tropical Crops, Monocotyledons, 2 vols, 1972; (with E. G. Brown, C. L. Green and S. R. J. Robbins) Spices, 2 vols, 1981; papers on land use, ethnobotany, etc, in scientific jls and symposia vols. Recreations: gardening, natural history. Address: Walnut Trees, Sissinghurst, Cranbrook, Kent TN17 2JL. T: Cranbrook 712836.

PURSSELL, Anthony John Richard; Joint Deputy Chairman, Arthur Guinness & Sons plc, since 1981 (Managing Director, 1975-81); b 5 July 1926; m 1952, Ann Margaret Batchelor; two s one d. Educ: Oriel Coll., Oxford (BA Hons Chemistry). Managing Director: Arthur Guinness Son & Co. (Park Royal) Ltd, 1968; Arthur Guinness Son & Co. (Dublin) Ltd, 1973. Mem. IBA, 1976-81. Regional Dir, S Midlands Bd, Lloyds Bank plc. Recreations: travel, golf, sailing, books; Guinness. Address: c/o Arthur Guinness Son & Co. Ltd, 10 Albemarle Street, W1X 4AJ. T: 01-493 6747. Club: Leander (Henley).

PURVES, Dame Daphne (Helen), DBE 1979; Senior Lecturer in French, Dunedin Teachers College, 1967-73, retired (Lecturer, 1963-66); b 8 Nov. 1908; d of Irvine Watson Cowie and Helen Jean Cowie; m 1939, Herbert Dudley Purves; one s two d. Educ: Otago Girls' High Sch., Dunedin, NZ; Univ. of Otago, Dunedin (MA 1st Cl. Hons English and French). Secondary sch. teacher, 1931-40 and 1957-63. Pres., NZ Fedn of University Women, 1962-64; Internat. Fedn of University Women: Mem., Cultural Relations Cttee, 1965-68, Convener, 1968-71; 3rd Vice-Pres., 1971-74; 1st Vice-Pres., 1974-77; Pres., 1977-80. Chm., National Theme Cttee, The Child in the World, NZ Nat. Commn for Internat. Year of the Child, 1978-80; Mem., Internat. Year of the Child Telethon Trust, 1978-81; Exec. Mem., NZ Cttee for Children (IYC) Inc., 1980-. Mem., NZ Nat. Commn, Unesco, 1964-68. Vice-Pres. for Women, Global Cooperation Soc. Club, 1980. Recreations: reading, gardening, bridge, travel, public speaking. Address: 12 Grendon Court, 36 Drivers Road, Dunedin, New Zealand. T: Dunedin 779 105.

PURVES, James Grant, CMG 1971; HM Diplomatic Service, retired; b 15 May 1911; s of Alexander Murray and Elizabeth Purves; m 1947, Mary Tinsley; three s one d. Educ: Universities of St Andrews and Freiburg-im-Breisgau. Research, 1933-35; Market Research, 1935-36; Secretary, Central Council for Health Education, 1936-39; German Section, BBC, 1939-45. 1st Secretary, Foreign Service: in Berne, Warsaw, Tel Aviv, Bangkok; Consul in Luanda, Lille, Johannesburg; Counsellor, HM Embassy, Berne, 1965-67; HM Consul-General, Hamburg, 1967-71. Recreations: swimming, travel. Address: Long Roof, Walberswick, Southwold, Suffolk. T: Southwold 722242. Clubs: Royal Automobile; Anglo-German (Hamburg); Grande Société (Berne).

PURVIS, Air Vice-Marshal Henry R.; see Reed-Purvis.

PURVIS, John Robert; Member (C) Mid-Scotland and Fife, European Parliament, since 1979; Managing Director, Gilmerton Management Services Ltd, since 1973; b 6 July 1938; s of Lt-Col R. W. B. Purvis, MC, JP, and Mrs R. W. B. Purvis, JP; m 1962, Louise S. Durham; one s two d. Educ: Cargilfield, Barnton, Edinburgh; Trinity Coll., Glenalmond, Perthshire; St Salvator's Coll., Univ. of St Andrews (MA Hons). National Service, Lieut Scots Guards, 1956-58. First National City Bank, New York, 1962-69: London, 1962-63; New York, 1963-65; Milan, 1965-69; Treasurer, Noble Grossart Ltd, Edinburgh, 1969-73. Publication: (section 'Money') in Power and Manoeuvrability, 1978. Address: Gilmerton, Dunino, St Andrews, Fife, Scotland KY16 8NB. T: St Andrews 73275. Clubs: Cavalry and Guards, Farmers'; New (Edinburgh); Royal and Ancient (St Andrews).

PUSACK, George Williams, MS; Chief Executive, Mobil Oil Australia Ltd, since 1980; b 26 Sept. 1920; s of George F. Pusack and Winifred (née Williams); m 1942, Marian Preston; two s one d. Educ: Univ. of Michigan; Univ. of Pennsylvania. BSE (AeroEng), BSE (Eng.Math), MS (MechEng). Aero Engr, US Navy, 1942-45; Corporal, US Air Force, 1945-46; Mobil Corp.: Tech. Service and Research Manager, USA, 1946-53; Product Engrg Manager, USA, 1953-59; International Supply Manager, USA, 1959-69; Vice-Pres., N Amer. Div., USA, 1969-73; Regional Exec., Mobil Europe, London, 1973-76; Chm. and Chief Exec, Mobil Oil Co. Ltd, 1976-80. Trustee, Victorian State Opera Foundn. Teacher, layreader, vestryman and warden of Episcopal Church. Recreations: golf, travel. Address: 41 Clendon Road, Toorak, Victoria 3142, Australia. T: (03) 241-1634. Clubs: River Hills Country (Clover, USA); Commonwealth Golf, Royal Melbourne Golf (Melbourne).

PUSEY, Nathan Marsh, PhD; President Emeritus, Harvard University; b Council Bluffs, Iowa, 4 April 1907; s of John Marsh Pusey and Rosa Pusey (née Drake); m 1936, Anne Woodward; two s one d. Educ: Harvard University, USA. AB 1928, AM 1932, PhD, 1937. Assistant, Harvard, 1933-34; Sophomore tutor, Lawrence Coll., 1935-38; Asst Prof., history and literature, Scripps Coll., Claremont, Calif., 1938-40; Wesleyan Univ.: Asst Prof., Classics, 1940-43, Assoc. Prof., 1943-44; President: Lawrence Coll., Appleton, Wisconsin, 1944-53; Harvard Univ., 1953-71; Andrew Mellon

Foundn, 1971-75. Pres., United Bd for Christian Higher Educn in Asia, 1979-. Holds many hon. degrees from Universities and colleges in USA and other countries. Officier de la Légion d'Honneur, 1958. Publications: The Age of the Scholar, 1963; American Higher Education 1945-1970, 1978. Address: 200 East 66th Street, New York, NY 10021, USA.

PUSINELLI, (Frederick) Nigel (Molière), CMG 1966; OBE 1963; MC 1940; HM Overseas Civil Service, retired; b 28 April 1919; second s of late S. Jacques and T. May Pusinelli, Frettenham, Norfolk and Fowey, Cornwall; m 1941, Joan Mary Chaloner, d of late Cuthbert B. and Mildred H. Smith, Cromer, Norfolk and Bexhill-on-Sea, Sussex; one s one d. Educ: Aldenham School; Pembroke College, Cambridge (BA Hons in law). Commissioned RA 1939; served BEF, 1940; India/Burma, 1942-45; Major, 1942; Staff College, Quetta, 1945. Administrative officer, Gilbert and Ellice Islands Colony, 1946-57. Transferred to Aden, 1958; Dep. Financial Sec. and frequently Actg Financial Sec. till 1962; Director of Establishments, 1962-68, and Assistant High Commissioner, 1963-68, Aden and Federation of South Arabia. Member E African Currency Board, 1960-62. Salaries Commissioner various territories in West Indies, 1968-70. Chm., Overseas Service Pensioners' Assoc.; Mem., Chichester Harbour Conservancy (and its Adv. Cttee); Chairman: RYA Southern Region; Chichester Harbour Fedn of sailing clubs and yachting orgns. Publication: Report on Census of Population of Gilbert and Ellice Islands Colony, 1947. Recreation: dinghy racing. Address: Routledge Cottage, Westbourne, Emsworth, Hants PO10 8SE. T: Emsworth 2915. Clubs: Royal Commonwealth Society; Royal Yachting Assoc., Cambridge University Cruising, Emsworth Sailing.

PUTT, S(amuel) Gorley, OBE 1966; MA; Fellow, Christ's College, Cambridge, since 1968 (Senior Tutor, 1968-78; Praelector, 1976-80); Vice-President, English Association, since 1972 (Chairman, Executive Council, 1964-72); b 9 June 1913; o c of late Poole Putt and late Ellen Blake Gorley, Brixham. Educ: Torquay Grammar School; Christ's College, Cambridge; Yale University. 1st Class English Tripos Pts I and II, MA 1937, Cambridge; Commonwealth Fund Fellow, MA 1936, Yale. BBC Talks Dept, 1936-38; Warden and Sec., Appts Cttee, Queen's Univ. of Belfast, 1939-40; RNVR, 1940-46, Lieut-Comdr; Warden and Tutor to Overseas Students and Director International Summer School, Univ. Coll., Exeter, 1946-49; Warden of Harkness House, 1949-68 and Director, Div. of International Fellowships, The Commonwealth Fund, 1966-68. Visiting Professor: Univ. of Massachusetts, 1968; Univ. of the South, Sewanee, 1976; Univ. of Pisa, 1979. Member: English-Speaking Union, London Cttee, 1952-57; UK-US Educational Commn: Travel Grants Cttee, 1955-64; Cttee of Management, Inst. of US Studies, London Univ., 1965-69. Contested (L) Torquay, 1945. FRSL 1952. Cavaliere, Order of Merit of Italy, 1980. Publications: Men Dressed As Seamen, 1943; View from Atlantis, 1955; (ed) Cousins and Strangers, 1956; Coastline, 1959; Scholars of the Heart, 1962; (ed) Essays and Studies, 1963; A Reader's Guide to Henry James, 1966; The Golden Age of English Drama, 1981. Address: Christ's College, Cambridge. T: Cambridge 67641. Club: Athenæum.

PUTTICK, Richard George; Chairman, since 1974, and Chief Executive, since 1978, Taylor Woodrow Ltd; b Kingston, Surrey, 16 March 1916; e s of late George Frederick Puttick and Dorothea (née Bowerman); m 1943, Betty Grace Folbigg; two s. Educ: St Mark's, Teddington. Joined Taylor Woodrow Construction Ltd, 1940 (the Taylor Woodrow Group's largest contracting subsidiary co.); Dir, 1955; Asst Managing Dir, 1968; Dir, Taylor Woodrow Ltd, 1969; Jt Dep. Chm., 1972. Mem. Council, CBI, July 1967-Dec. 1969; Pres., NW Mddx Branch, BIM. FCIOB; CBIM; FRSA; FFB. Liveryman, Worshipful Co. of Joiners and Ceilers; Mem., Co. of Builders. Vice-Pres., Mddx Assoc. of Boys' Clubs. Recreations: music, reading, gardening, supporting sports. Address: (home) Woodlawn, Hanger Hill, Weybridge, Surrey; (office) 10 Park Street, W1Y 4DD. T: 01-499 8871.

PUTTNAM, David; film producer (self-employed); b 25 Feb. 1941; s of Leonard Arthur Puttnam and Marie Beatrix Puttnam; m 1961, Patricia Mary (née Jones); one s one d. Educ: Minchenden Grammar Sch., London. Advertising, 1958-66; photography, 1966-68; film prodn, 1968-. Producer: Melody; The Pied Piper; That'll Be The Day; Mahler; The Double Headed Eagle; Swastika; Stardust; Brother can you Spare a Dime; Lisztomania; Bugsy Malone; The Duellists (Special Jury Prize, Cannes, 1977); Midnight Express; Foxes; Chariots of Fire (four Acad. Awards, for Best Picture, Best Original Screenplay, Best Original Score and Best Costume Design, 1981; three BAFTA Awards, for Best Film, Best Costume Design and Best Supporting Actor, 1981); Local Hero. Producer of films and series for television. Dir, National Film Finance Corp.; Founder Mem., Adv. Bd, National Film Develt Fund; Member: Cinema Films Council; Governing Body, BAFTA; Amer. Acad. of Motion Picture Arts and Sciences; Governor, National Film Sch. Michael Balcon Award for outstanding contribn to British Film Industry, BAFTA, 1982. Recreations: following the fortunes of Tottenham Hotspur Football Club, going to the cinema. Address: 15 Queensgate Place Mews, SW7 5BG. T: 01-581 0238. Clubs: Turf, Chelsea Arts, Royal Geographical Society.

PUXON, (Christine) Margaret, (Mrs F. Morris Williams), QC 1982; MD, FRCOG; practising barrister, since 1954; a Deputy Circuit Judge, since 1970; b 25 July 1915; d of Reginald Wood Hale and Clara Lilian Hale; m 1955, F. Morris Williams, MBE; two s one d. Educ: Abbey Sch., Malvern Wells; Birmingham Univ. (MB, ChB; MD Obstetrics 1944). MRCS, LRCP 1942;

FRCOG 1976. Called to the Bar, Inner Temple, 1954. Gynaecological Registrar, Queen Elizabeth Hosp., Birmingham, and later Consultant Gynaecologist, Essex CC, 1942-49. Privy Council Member, Council of Pharmaceutical Soc., 1971-; Mem., Genetic Manipulation Adv. Gp, 1979-. Liveryman, Worshipful Soc. of Apothecaries, 1982-. *Publications:* The Family and the Law, 1963, 2nd edn 1971; contrib. med. and legal jls, incl. Proc. RSM, Practitioner and Solicitors' Jl. *Recreations:* cooking, travel, opera, gardening. *Address:* Number Two, 63 Fonnereau Road, Ipswich IP1 3JN. *T:* Ipswich 57275. *Clubs:* VAD Ladies; Norfolk (Norwich).

PYATT, Rt. Rev. William Allan; *see* Christchurch, Bishop of.

PYBUS, William Michael; Partner, Herbert Oppenheimer, Nathan & Vandyk, Solicitors, since 1953; Chairman: A.A.H. Ltd, since 1968; British Fuel Co., since 1968; *b* 7 May 1923; *s* of Sydney James Pybus and Evelyn Mary Pybus; *m* 1959, Elizabeth Janet Whitley; two *s* two *d. Educ:* Bedford Sch.; New College, Oxford (1st cl. hons Jurisprudence). Served War, 1942-46: commissioned 1st King's Dragoon Guards; Lieut attached XIth Hussars in Normandy (wounded); King's Dragoon Guards, Egypt, Palestine, Syria, Lebanon. Admitted Solicitor (Scott Schol.), 1950. Chairman: Inter-Continental Fuels Ltd, 1975-; Overseas Coal Developments Ltd, 1979-; Siebe Gorman Holdings Ltd, 1980- (Dir, 1972-); Dep. Chm., R. Mansell Ltd, 1980-; Director: National Westminster Bank (Outer London Region), 1977-; Coal Trade Benevolent Assoc., 1969-; Cornhill Insurance Co. Ltd, 1977-. Part-time Member: British Railways (London Midland) Bd, 1974; British Railways (Midlands and West) Bd, 1975-77; Chm., BR Midlands and N Western Bd, 1977-. Pres., Coal Industry Soc., 1976-81. Master, Pattenmakers' Co, 1972-73. FBIM, FInstM. *Recreation:* fishing. *Address:* 20 Copthall Avenue, EC2R 7JH. *T:* 01-628 9611; Beades, Old Malden Lane, Worcester Park, Surrey. *T:* 01-337 1496. *Clubs:* Cavalry and Guards, MCC.

PYE, Prof. Norman; Professor of Geography, University of Leicester, 1954-79, now Emeritus; Pro-Vice-Chancellor, 1963-66; Dean, Faculty of Science, 1957-60; Chairman of Convocation, since 1982; *b* 2 Nov. 1913; *s* of John Whittaker Pye and Hilda Constance (*née* Platt); *m* 1940, Isabella Jane (*née* Currie); two *s. Educ:* Wigan Grammar School; Manchester University. Manchester University: BA Hons Geography Class I, 1935, Diploma in Education Class I, 1936. Asst Lecturer in Geography, Manchester Univ., 1936-37 and 1938-46; Mem., Cambridge Univ. Spitsbergen Expedn. 1938. Seconded to Hydrographic Dept, Admiralty, for War Service, 1940-46. Lecturer in Geography, 1946-53, Sen. Lecturer, 1953-54, Manchester Univ. Vis. Professor: Univ. of BC, 1964; Univ. of Alberta, Edmonton, 1967, 1968, 1969, 1973, 1974, 1975, 1978; External Examnr: Univ. of E Africa, 1964-67; Univ. of Guyana, 1974-78. Hon. Editor, "Geography", 1965-80. Member Corby Development Corp., 1965-80. Governor, Up Holland Grammar Sch., 1953-74; Member: Northants CC Educn Cttee, 1956-74; Court, Nottingham Univ., 1964-79; Standing Conf. on Univ. Entrance, 1966-79; Schools Council, 1967-78. Member: Council, RMetS, 1953-56; Council, Inst. of Brit. Geographers, 1954, 1955; Council, RGS, 1967-70; Council for Urban Studies Centres, 1974-; Brit. Nat. Cttee for Geography, 1970-75; Heritage Educn Gp, 1976-; Hon. Vice-Pres., Geographical Assoc., 1979-. *Publications:* Leicester and its Region (ed and contrib.), 1972; research papers and articles in learned journals. *Recreations:* travel, oenology, music, gardening, walking. *Address:* 127 Spencefield Lane, Evington, Leicester. *T:* Leicester 415167. *Club:* Geographical.

PYKE, David Alan, MD, FRCP; Physician-in-charge, Diabetic Department, King's College Hospital, London, since 1971; *b* 16 May 1921; *s* of Geoffrey and Margaret Pyke; *m* 1948, Janet, *d* of Dr J. Gough Stewart; one *s* two *d. Educ:* Leighton Park Sch., Reading; Cambridge Univ.; University Coll. Hosp. Med. Sch., London. MD Cantab; FRCP. Junior med. appts in London and Oxford, 1945-59. Service in RAMC, 1946-48. Apptd to staff of King's Coll. Hosp., 1959. Hon. Sec.: Assoc. of Physicians of GB and Ire., 1968-73; Royal Soc. of Med., 1972-74. Registrar, Royal Coll. of Physicians of London, 1975-. *Publications:* (jt ed) Clinical Diabetes and its Biochemical Basis, 1968; (ed) Clinics in Endocrinology and Metabolism, Vol. 1, No 3, 1972; (jtly) Diabetes and its Management, 1973, 3rd edn 1978; articles in med. and sci. jls. *Recreations:* golf, opera. *Address:* 17 College Road, SE21 7BG. *T:* 01-693 2313.

PYKE, Sir Louis (Frederick), Kt 1978; ED 1946; FAIB; FAIM; Chairman and Managing Director, Costain (Aust.) Pty Ltd, 1971-77 (Managing Director, 1965-73); consultant to Meldrum & Partners, architects; *b* 21 Nov. 1907; *m* 1936, Sierlah, *d* of H. J. Cohen; two *s* one *d. Educ:* Melbourne C of E Grammar Sch. Director: Pyke Simmie, Master Builders, 1947; Union Assce, 1963-74; Costain Investments (Aust.) Pty Ltd, 1977-; Steel Deck Industries Pty Ltd, 1978-; Davis Vindin Pty Ltd, 1978-. Lt-Col, AASC. Mem., United Services Inst., 1936. Member Council: S Melbourne Tech. Sch., 1963-73; Master Builders Assoc., Vic, 1972-. Mem., Melbourne South Rotary, 1962-; Pres., Multiple Sclerosis Soc. of Vic, 1975-; Dep. Nat. Chm., Business Adv. Bd, Multiple Sclerosis Soc. of Aust., 1979-. *Recreation:* farming. *Address:* 419 Wattletree Road, East Malvern, Victoria 3145, Australia. *T:* 25 6961. *Clubs:* Naval and Military, Melbourne Cricket, Victoria Racing (Melbourne).

PYKE, Magnus, OBE 1978; PhD, CChem, FRSC, FInst Biol, FIFST, FRSE; *b* 29 Dec. 1908; *s* of Robert Bond Pyke and Clara Hannah Pyke (*née* Lewis); *m* 1937, Dorothea Mina Vaughan; one *s* one *d. Educ:* St Paul's Sch., London;

McGill Univ., Montreal; University Coll. London. BSc, PhD. Scientific Adviser's Div., Min. of Food, London, 1941-45; Nutritional Adviser, Allied Commn for Austria, Vienna, 1945-46; Principal Scientific Officer (Nutrition), Min. of Food, London, 1946-48; Distillers Co. Ltd: Dep. Manager, Yeast Research Outstation, 1949-55; Manager, Glenochil Research Station, 1955-73; Sec. and Chm. of Council, British Assoc. for the Advancement of Science, 1973-77 (Mem. Council, 1968-77; Pres. Section X, 1965). Member: (Vice-Pres.) Soc. for Analytical Chemistry, 1959-61; Council, Royal Inst. of Chemistry, 1953-56, 1962-65; Council, Royal Soc. of Edinburgh, 1961-64; Council, Soc. of Chemical Industry, 1967-69; (Chm.) Scottish Section, Nutrition Soc., 1954-55; (Vice-Pres.) Assoc. for Liberal Education, 1964-81; (Pres.) Inst. of Food Science and Technology of the UK, 1969-71; Participated in Don't Ask Me, 1974-78, Don't Just Sit There, 1979-80, Yorkshire TV. FInstBiol (Mem. Council, Scottish Sect., 1959-62); Hon. Fellow: Australian IFST, 1973; NZ IFST, 1979. DUniv Stirling, 1974; Hon. DSc: Lancaster, 1976; McGill, 1981. Pye Colour TV Award: the most promising newcomer to television, 1975; BBC Multi-Coloured Swap Shop Star Award (Expert of the Year), 1977-78. *Publications:* Manual of Nutrition, 1945; Industrial Nutrition, 1950; Townsman's Food, 1952; Automation, Its Purpose and Future, 1956; Nothing Like Science, 1957; Slaves Unaware, 1959; The Boundaries of Science, 1961; Nutrition, 1962; The Science Myth, 1962; Food Science and Technology, 1964; The Science Century, 1967; Food and Society, 1968; Man and Food, 1970; Synthetic Food, 1970; Technological Eating, 1972; Catering Science and Technology, 1973; Success in Nutrition, 1975; Butter-side Up, 1976; There and Back, 1978; Food for all the Family, 1980; Long Life, 1980; Our Future, 1980; (with P. Moore) Everyman's Scientific Facts and Feats, 1981; Six Lives of Pyke, 1981; Fun to Know about Inventions, 1981. *Recreation:* he writes a page a day and savours the consequences. *Address:* 3 St Peter's Villas, W6 9BQ. *T:* 01-748 9920. *Club:* Savage.

PYLE, Cyril Alfred; Head Master, South East London School, 1970-80; *s* of Alfred John Pyle and Nellie Blanche Pyle; *m* 1940, Jean Alice Cotten; one *s* one *d. Educ:* Shooters Hill Grammar Sch.; Univ. of London, Goldsmiths' Coll. Dep. Headmaster, Woolwich Polytechnic Secondary Sch., 1940-66; Headmaster, Bow Sch., 1966-70. Pres., London Teachers' Assoc., 1962; Chm., Council for Educnl Advance, 1964-76; Sec., Conference of London Comprehensive School Heads, 1973-79. *Recreations:* Rotary Club, motoring, gardening. *Address:* Barleyfields, Hartlip, Sittingbourne, Kent ME9 7TH. *T:* Newington 842719.

PYM, Rt. Hon. Francis Leslie, PC 1970; MC 1945; DL; MP (C) Cambridgeshire since 1961; Secretary of State for Foreign and Commonwealth Affairs, since 1982; *b* 13 Feb. 1922; *s* of late Leslie Ruthven Pym, MP, *d* of Charles Orde; *m* 1949, Valerie Fortune Daglish; two *s* two *d. Educ:* Eton; Magdalene Coll., Cambridge. Served War of 1939-45 (despatches, 1944 and 1945, MC): 9th Lancers, 1942-46; African and Italian campaigns. Contested (C) Rhondda West, 1959. Asst Govt Whip (unpaid), Oct. 1962-64; Opposition Whip, 1964-67; Opposition Dep. Chief Whip, 1967-70; Parly Sec. to the Treasury and Govt Chief Whip, 1970-73; Sec. of State for NI, 1973-74; Opposition spokesman on: agriculture, 1974-76; H of C affairs and devolution, 1976-78; Foreign and Commonwealth affairs, 1978-79; Sec. of State for Defence, 1979-81; Chancellor of the Duchy of Lancaster and Paymaster Gen., and Leader of the House of Commons, 1981; Lord Pres. of the Council and Leader of the House of Commons, 1981-82. Mem. Herefordshire County Council, 1958-61. DL Cambs, 1973. *Address:* Everton Park, Sandy, Beds. *Clubs:* Buck's, Cavalry and Guards.

PYMAN, Lancelot Frank Lee, CMG 1961; HM Diplomatic Service, retired; *b* 8 August 1910; *s* of late Dr F. L. Pyman, FRS, and of Mrs I. C. Pyman; *m* 1936, Sarah Woods Gamble. *Educ:* Dover College; King's College, Cambridge (Exhibitioner). Entered Levant Consular Service, 1933; various posts in Persia, 1933-38; Consul, Cernauti, Roumania, 1939-40; Vice-Consul, Beirut, Lebanon, 1940-41. Served with HM Forces in Levant States, 1941. Asst Oriental Secretary, HM Embassy, Tehran, Dec. 1941-44; Foreign Office, 1944-48; Consul, St Louis, Missouri, Dec. 1948-49; Oriental Counsellor, Tehran, Dec. 1949-Sept. 1952; Counsellor, British Embassy, Rio de Janeiro, 1952-53; Consul-General, Tetuan, 1953-56; Counsellor, British Embassy, Rabat, 1956-57; HM Consul-General: Zagreb, 1957-61; Basra, March-Dec. 1961; Ambassador to the Somali Republic, 1961-63; Consul-General, San Francisco, 1963-66. *Recreations:* listening to music, tennis, golf.

PYRAH, Prof. Leslie Norman, CBE 1963; retired as Senior Consultant Surgeon, Department of Urology, Leeds General Infirmary (1950-64); Hon. Director, Medical Research Council Unit, Leeds General Infirmary, 1956-64; Professor of Urological Surgery, Leeds University, 1956-64, now emeritus; *b* 11 April 1899; *s* of Arthur Pyrah; *m* 1934, Mary Christopher Batley; one *s* one *d* (and one *s* decd). *Educ:* University of Leeds; School of Medicine, Leeds. Hon. Asst Surgeon, Leeds Gen. Infirmary, 1934; Hon. Consultant Surgeon, Dewsbury Infirmary, Leeds Public Dispensary, Goole Hosp., and Lecturer in Surgery, Univ. of Leeds, 1934; Hon. Cons. Surgeon, St James' Hosp., Leeds, 1941; Surgeon with charge of Out-patients, Leeds Infirmary, 1944; Weild Lectr, Royal Faculty Physicians and Surgeons, Glasgow, 1955; Ramon Guiteras Lectr, Amer. Urological Assoc., Pittsburgh, USA, 1957; Pres., Section of Urology, Royal Soc. Med.; 1958; Litchfield Lectr, Univ. of Oxford, 1959; Hunterian Orator, RCS, 1969. Chm., Specialist Adv. Cttee in Urology, Jt Royal Colls of Surgeons of GB and Ireland, 1968-72. Pres., British Assoc. of Urological Surgeons, 1961, 1962; Pres. Leeds and W Riding Medico-

Chirurgical Soc., 1959. Mem. Council (elected), Royal College of Surgeons of England, 1960–68. Hon. Mem. Soc. Belge de Chirurgie, 1958; Corresponding Member: Amer. Assoc. of Genito-Urinary Surgeons, 1962; Amer. Soc. of Pelvic Surgeons, 1962; Australasian Soc. of Urology, 1963. St Peter's Medal (British Assoc. of Urological Surgeons) for outstanding contributions to urology, 1959; Honorary Medal, RCS, 1975. DSc (*hc*) Leeds, 1965; Hon. FRSM, 1978. *Publications:* Renal Calculus, 1979; (contrib.) British Surgical Progress, 1956; numerous contribs to British Journal of Surgery, British Journal of Urology, Proc. Royal Soc. Med., Lancet, BMJ. *Recreations:* tennis, music. *Address:* Fieldhead, Weetwood Lane, Leeds LS16 5NP. *T:* 52777; (consulting rooms) 27 Clarendon Road, Leeds LS16 5NP. *Club:* Athenæum.

PYTCHES, Rt. Rev. George Edward David; Vicar of St Andrew's, Chorley Wood, Rickmansworth, since 1977; *b* 9 Jan. 1931; 9th *c* and 6th *s* of late Rev. Thomas Arthur Pytches and late Eirene Mildred Pytches (*née* Welldon); *m* 1958, Mary Trevisick; four *d. Educ:* Old Buckenham Hall, Norfolk; Framlingham Coll., Suffolk; Univ. of Bristol (BA); Trinity Coll., Bristol. Deacon 1955, priest 1956; Asst Curate, St Ebbe's, Oxford, 1955–58; Asst Curate, Holy Trinity, Wallington, 1958–59; Missionary Priest in Chol Chol, Chile, 1959–62; in Valparaiso, Chile, 1962–68; Rural Dean, Valparaiso, 1966–70; Asst Bishop of Diocese of Chile, Bolivia and Peru, 1970–72; Vicar General of Diocese, 1971–72; Bishop in Chile, Bolivia and Peru, 1972–77. *Recreations:* collecting semi-precious stones, walking. *Address:* The Vicarage, Quickley Lane, Chorley Wood, Rickmansworth, Herts.

Q

QUANT, Mary, (Mrs A. Plunket Greene), OBE 1966; RDI 1969; Director of Mary Quant Group of companies since 1955; *b* 11 Feb. 1934; *d* of Jack and Mildred Quant; *m* 1957, Alexander Plunket Greene; one *s. Educ:* 13 schools; Goldsmiths' College of Art. Fashion Designer. Mem., Design Council, 1971–. Member: British/USA Bicentennial Liaison Cttee, 1973–; Adv. Council, V&A Museum, 1976–78. Exhibition, Mary Quant's London, London Museum, 1973–74. Maison Blanche Rex Award (US), 1964; Sunday Times Internat. Award, 1964; Piavola d'Oro Award (Italy), 1966; Annual Design Medal, Inst. of Industrial Artists and Designers, 1966. FSIA 1967. *Publication:* Quant by Quant, 1966. *Address:* 3 Ives Street, SW3. *T:* 01-584 8781.

QUANTRILL, Prof. Malcolm, RIBA; architect, author and critic; Professor of Architecture and Urban Design, University of Jordan, Amman-Jordan, since 1980; *b* Norwich, Norfolk, 25 May 1931; *s* of Arthur William Quantrill and Alice May Newstead; *m* 1971, Esther Maeve, *d* of James Brignell Dand and Winifred Dand, Chester; two *s* two *d. Educ:* City of Norwich Sch.; Liverpool Univ. (BArch); Univ. of Pennsylvania (MArch); Univ. of Wroclaw (Doc. Ing Arch). RIBA 1961. Fulbright Scholar and Albert Kahn Meml Fellow, Univ. of Pennsylvania, 1954–55; Asst Prof., Louisiana State Univ., 1955–60; Lecturer: Univ. of Wales, Cardiff, 1962–65; UCL, 1965–66; Asst to Dir, Architectural Assoc., 1966–67, Dir, 1967–69; Lectr, Univ. of Liverpool, 1970–73; Dean, Sch. of Environmental Design, Polytechnic of N London, 1973–80. Vis. Professor: Univ. of Illinois, Chicago, 1973–75; Carleton Univ., Ottawa, 1978; Gastprofessor, Technische Universität, Wien, 1975–77. Sir William Dobell Meml Lectr in Modern Art, Sydney, NSW, 1978. Plays performed: Honeymoon, 1968; Life Class, 1968 (TV); radio plays include: The Fence, 1964; Let's Get This Straight, 1977; Immortal Bite, 1982. *Publications:* The Gotobed Trilogy (novels), 1962–64; Ritual and Response in Architecture, 1974; Monuments of Another Age, 1975; On the Home Front (novel), 1977; The Art of Government and the Government of Art, 1978; Alvar Aalto—a critical study, 1982; articles in RIBA Jl, Arch. Assoc. Qly, Arch. Design, and Art Internat. *Address:* 18 Causton Road, Highgate, N6. *T:* 01-348 1064; Faculty of Engineering and Technology, University of Jordan, Amman-Jordan. *Club:* Garrick.

QUANTRILL, William Ernest; HM Diplomatic Service; Deputy Head of Personnel Operations Department, Foreign and Commonwealth Office, since 1981; *b* 4 May 1939; *s* of Ronald Frederick Quantrill and late Norah Elsie Quantrill (*née* Matthews); *m* 1964, Rowena Mary Collins; three *s* one *d. Educ:* Colston's Sch., Bristol; Hatfield Coll., Univ. of Durham (BA Hons French). Entered FO, 1962; served Brussels, Havana, Manila, Lagos and FCO, 1964–80; Head of Training Dept, FCO, 1980–81. *Recreations:* painting, wild life, travel. *Address:* c/o Foreign and Commonwealth Office, SW1A 2AH. *T:* 01-233 3000.

QU'APPELLE, Archbishop of, since 1982; **Most Rev. Michael Geoffrey Peers;** Metropolitan of Rupert's Land; *b* 31 July 1934; *s* of Geoffrey Hugh Peers and Dorothy Enid Mantle; *m* 1963, Dorothy Elizabeth Bradley; two *s* one *d. Educ:* University of British Columbia (BA Hons); Universität Heidelberg (Zert. Dolm.-Interpreter's Certificate); Trinity Coll., Toronto (LTh). Deacon 1959, priest 1960; Curate: St Thomas', Ottawa, 1959–61; Trinity, Ottawa, 1961–65; University Chaplain, Diocese of Ottawa, 1961–66; Rector: St Bede's, Winnipeg, 1966–72; St Martin's, Winnipeg, with St Paul's Middlechurch, 1972–74; Archdeacon of Winnipeg, 1969–74; Rector, St Paul's

Cathedral, Regina, 1974–77; Dean of Qu'Appelle, 1974–77; Bishop of Qu'Appelle, 1977. DD (*hc*) Trinity Coll., Toronto, 1978. *Address:* 1701 College Avenue, Regina, Saskatchewan S4P 1B8, Canada. *T:* 306-527-8606.

QUARMBY, David Anthony, PhD; FCIT; Managing Director (Buses), London Transport Executive, since 1978 (Member, LTE, since 1975); *b* 22 July 1941; *s* of Frank Reginald and Dorothy Margaret Quarmby; *m* 1968, Hilmary Hunter; four *d. Educ:* Shrewsbury Sch.; King's Coll., Cambridge (MA); Leeds Univ. (PhD, Dip. Industrial Management). Asst Lectr, then Lectr, Dept of Management Studies, Leeds Univ., 1963; Economic Adviser, Economic Planning Directorate, Min. of Transport, 1966; Dir of Operational Research, London Transport Exec., 1970; Chief Commercial and Planning Officer, LTE, 1974. Vice-Pres., Bus and Coach Council, 1981–. Member: Southwark Diocesan Bd of Finance, 1976–; Southwark Diocesan Synod, 1982–. *Publications:* Factors Affecting Commuter Travel Behaviour (PhD Thesis, Leeds), 1967; contribs to Jl of Transport Economics and Policy, Regional Studies, Enterprise Management, and to books on transport, economics and operational research. *Recreations:* music, singing. *Address:* 13 Shooters Hill Road, Blackheath, SE3 7AR. *T:* 01-858 7371.

QUARRELL, Prof. Arthur George, ARCS, DSc, PhD (London); Professor of Metallurgy, Sheffield University, 1950–76, now Emeritus; *b* 30 Oct. 1910; *m* 1934, Rose Amy Atkins; one *s* (and two *s* decd). *Educ:* College Secondary School, Swindon; Imperial College of Science and Technology. FInstP 1938; FIM 1946 (Pres., 1970–72; Hon. FIM, 1979). University of Sheffield, Department of Metallurgy: Assistant Lecturer, 1937–39; Lecturer, 1940–45. British Non-Ferrous Metals Research Association: Senior Metallurgist, Oct. 1945–March 1946; Research Manager, March 1946–Sept. 1950; Prof. of Physical Metallurgy, Sheffield Univ., 1950–55; Dean of the Faculty of Metallurgy, 1950–55, 1962–64. Pro-Vice-Chancellor of Sheffield Univ., 1958–62. Warden of Sorby Hall, Sheffield Univ., 1963–71. Hatfield Meml Lectr, 1963; Bessemer Gold Medal, 1970; Hon. Fellow, Sheffield City Polytechnic, 1970; Hon. DMet Sheffield, 1980. *Publications:* Physical Examination of Metals, 1940, 2nd edn 1961; Papers in Proc. Roy. Soc., Proc. Phys Soc., Jl Inst. Metals, Jl Iron and Steel Inst. *Recreations:* gardening and other manual activities. *Address:* 38 Endcliffe Grove Avenue, Sheffield S10 3EJ. *T:* 665857.

QUARREN EVANS, John Kerry; His Honour Judge Quarren Evans; a Circuit Judge, on South Eastern circuit, since 1980; *b* 4 July 1926; *s* of late Hubert Royston Quarren Evans, MC and of Violet Soule Quarren Evans; *m* 1958, Janet Shaw Lawson; one *s* one *d. Educ:* King Edward VII Sch., Coventry; Cardiff High Sch.; Trinity Hall, Cambridge, 1948–51 (MA, LLB). 21st Glam. (Cardiff) Bn Home Guard, 1943–44; enlisted, Grenadier Gds, 1944; commnd Royal Welch Fusiliers, 1946, from OTS Bangalore; att. 2nd Bn The Welch Regt, Burma, 1946–47; Captain 1947. Admitted solicitor, 1953; Partner: Lyndon Moore & Co., Newport, 1954–71; T. S. Edwards & Son, Newport, 1971–80; Recorder, Wales and Chester Circuit, 1974–80. *Recreations:* golf, Rugby football, music. *Address:* 2 Mount Park Crescent, Ealing, W5 2RN. *Clubs:* Denham Golf, Newport Golf.

QUARTANO, Ralph Nicholas, CEng, MIChemE; Chief Executive, The Post Office Staff Superannuation Fund, since 1974; Director, London American Energy NV, since 1981; *b* 3 Aug. 1927; *s* of late Charles and Vivienne Mary Quartano; *m* 1954, Cornelia Johanna de Gunst; two *d. Educ:* Sherborne Sch.; Pembroke Coll., Cambridge (MA). Bataafsche Petroleum Mij, 1952–58; The Lummus Co, 1958–59; Temple Press, 1959–65; Man. Director: Heywood Temple Industrial Publications, 1965–68; Engineering Chemical and Marine Press, 1968–70. The Post Office, 1971–; Sen. Dir, Central Finance, 1973–74. Mem., Engineering Council, 1981–. Sloan Fellow of London Business School. *Address:* 9 Oakcroft Road, SE13 7ED. *T:* 01-852 1607.

QUASTEL, Juda Hirsch, CC (Canada) 1970; FRS 1940; DSc London; PhD Cantab; ARCS London; FRIC; FRSC; Professor of Neurochemistry, University of British Columbia, Canada, since 1966; *b* 2 Oct. 1899; *e s* of late Jonas and Flora Quastel, Sheffield, Yorks; *m* 1st, 1931, Henrietta Jungman, MA (*d* 1973); two *s* one *d*; 2nd, 1975, Shulamit Ricardo. *Educ:* Central Secondary School, Sheffield; Imperial College of Science, London University; Trinity College, Cambridge. Commenced research in biochemistry in Cambridge University, Oct. 1921; awarded Senior Studentship by Royal Commissioners for Exhibition of 1851, 1923; Demonstrator and lecturer in biochemistry, Cambridge Univ. 1923; Fellow of Trinity College, Cambridge, 1924; Meldola Medallist 1927; Beit Memorial Research Fellow, 1928; Director of Research, Cardiff City Mental Hospital, 1929–41; Rockefeller Foundation Fellow, 1936; Director of ARC Unit of Soil Metabolism, 1941–47; Prof. of Biochemistry, McGill Univ., Montreal, 1947–66; Director: McGill-Montreal Gen. Hosp. Research Inst., 1947–65; McGill Unit of Cell Metabolism, 1965–66. Member of Council of Royal Institute of Chemistry, 1944–47; Member: Water Pollution Research Board, 1944–47; Bd of Governors, Hebrew Univ., Jerusalem, 1950; Pres., Montreal Physiological Soc., 1950; Pres. Canadian Biochemical Soc., 1963; Canadian Microbiological Soc. Award, 1965; Flavelle Medal, RSC, 1974; Gairdner Internat. Award for Med. Res., 1974. Member, British, Can. and Amer. scientific societies; Consultant, Montreal General Hosp. Leeuwenhoek Lectr, Royal Society, 1954; Bryan Priestman Lectr, Univ. New Brunswick, 1956; Kearney Foundation Lectr, Univ. Calif, 1958; Seventh Jubilee Lectr, Biochemical Soc.

UK, 1974; Royal Society Leverhulme Visiting Professor, in India, 1965-66; Vis. Prof., Nat. Hospital for Nervous Diseases (Neurology Dept), London, 1976-77. Hon. Pres., Internat. Congress of Biochem., 1979. Fellow: NY Academy of Science, 1954; Amer. Assoc. for Advancement of Science, 1964. Hon. Fellow: Japanese Pharmacological Soc., 1963; Canadian Microbiological Soc., 1965; N Pacific Soc. of Neurology and Psychiatry, 1966. Hon. Mem., Biochemical Soc. UK, 1973. Hon. DSc McGill, 1969; Hon. PhD Jerusalem, 1970. *Publications:* since 1923 mainly on subjects of biochemical interest; author and co-editor: Neurochemistry, 1955- (1963); Methods in Medical Research, Vol. 9, 1961; Chemistry of Brain Metabolism, 1962; Metabolic Inhibitors, vol. 1, 1963, vol. 2, 1964, vol. 3, 1972, vol. 4, 1973. *Address:* TRIUMF, University of British Columbia, 4004 Wesbrook Mall, Vancouver, BC V6T 1W5, Canada.

QUAYLE, Anthony; *see* Quayle, J. A.

QUAYLE, Bronte Clucas, CB 1980; OBE 1969; QC 1978; *b* 24 Oct. 1919; *s* of late Alfred Clucas Quayle and Edith Anne Quayle; *m* 1944, Joan Proctor Strickland; two *s*. *Educ:* St Peter's Coll., Adelaide; Adelaide Univ. (LLB). AIF, 1940-45. Admitted Barrister and Solicitor, Adelaide, 1948; Office of Parliamentary Counsel, Canberra, 1950-82, First Parly Counsel, 1977-81. Consulting Draftsman, Pakistan Constitution, 1962. Sitara-i-Pakistan 1962. *Recreations:* yachting, motor sport, music. *Address:* 68 Stradbroke Street, Deakin, ACT 2600, Australia. *Clubs:* Canberra Yacht, Canberra Sporting Car, Canberra Wine and Food, University House, ANU (all in Canberra).

QUAYLE, (John) Anthony, CBE 1952; Actor; *b* 7 September 1913; *s* of Arthur Quayle and Esther Quayle (*née* Overton); *m* 1947, Dorothy Hyson; one *s* two *d*. *Educ:* Rugby. First appeared on stage, 1931; acted in various London productions between then and 1939, including several appearances at Old Vic; also acted in New York. Served War of 1939-45, Royal Artillery. After 1945 became Play-producer as well as actor; produced: Crime and Punishment; The Relapse; Harvey; Who is Sylvia. Director, Shakespeare Memorial Theatre, 1948-56; *productions:* The Winter's Tale, Troilus and Cressida, Macbeth, Julius Caesar, King Lear (with John Gielgud), Richard II, Henry IV, Part I (with John Kidd), Henry V, Othello and Measure for Measure. *Stratford rôles include:* The Bastard, Petruchio, Claudius, Iago, Hector in Troilus and Cressida; Henry VIII, 1949; Antony and Henry VIII, 1950; Falstaff in Henry IV, Parts I and II, 1951; Coriolanus; Mosca in Volpone, 1952; Othello, Bottom in a Midsummer Night's Dream, Pandarus in Troilus and Cressida, 1954; Falstaff in The Merry Wives of Windsor; Aaron in Titus Andronicus, 1955. Took Shakespeare Memorial Theatre Company to Australia, 1949, 1953. *Other rôles include:* Tamburlaine, NY, 1956; A View from the Bridge, Comedy Theatre, 1956; Titus Andronicus, European tour, 1957; (also dir) The Firstborn, NY, 1958; Long Day's Journey into Night, Edinburgh Festival and London, 1958; Look After Lulu!, Royal Court, 1959; Chin-Chin, Wyndham's, 1960; The Right Honourable Gentleman, Her Majesty's, 1964; Incident at Vichy, Phœnix, 1966; Galileo, NY, 1967; Halfway Up The Tree, NY 1967; Sleuth, St Martin's, 1970, NY, 1970-71; The Idiot, National Theatre, 1970; The Headhunters, Washington, 1974; Old World, RSC, 1976-77; Do You Turn Somersaults, USA, 1977; Heartbreak House, Lord Arthur Saville's Crime, Malvern Festival, 1980; Hobson's Choice, A Coat of Varnish, Haymarket, 1982; Prospect Theatre at Old Vic: (also co-prod.) The Rivals, 1978; King Lear (as Lear), 1978. *Directed:* Lady Windermere's Fan, 1967; Tiger at the Gates, New York, 1968; Harvey, Prince of Wales, 1975; Rip Van Winkle, Washington, 1976; The Old Country, Queen's, 1978. *Films:* Saraband for Dead Lovers, Hamlet, Oh Rosalinda, Battle of the River Plate, The Wrong Man, Woman in a Dressing Gown, The Man Who Wouldn't Talk, Ice Cold in Alex, Serious Charge, Tarzan's Greatest Adventure, The Challenge, The Guns of Navarone, HMS Defiant, Lawrence of Arabia, The Fall of the Roman Empire, Operation Crossbow, A Study in Terror, Incompreso, MacKenna's Gold, Before Winter Comes, Anne of the Thousand Days, Bequest to the Nation, The Tamarind Seed, Moses the Lawgiver, Great Expectations, 21 Hours in Munich, The Eagle has Landed, The Antagonists, Masada, Dial M for Murder. *Publications:* Eight Hours from England, 1945; On Such a Night, 1947. *Club:* Special Forces.

QUAYLE, Prof. John Rodney, PhD; FRS 1978; West Riding Professor of Microbiology, University of Sheffield, since 1965; *b* 18 Nov. 1926; *s* of John Martin Quayle and Mary Doris Quayle (*née* Thorp); *m* 1951, Yvonne Mabel (*née* Sanderson); one *s* one *d*. *Educ:* Alun Grammar Sch., Mold; University Coll. of North Wales, Bangor (BSc, PhD); Univ. of Cambridge (PhD); MA Oxon. Res. Fellow, Radiation Lab., Univ. of California, 1953-55; Sen. Scientific Officer, Tropical Products Institute, London, 1955-56; Mem. Scientific Staff, MRC Cell Metabolism Res. Unit, Univ. of Oxford, 1956-63; Lectr, Oriel Coll., Oxford, 1957-63; Sen. Lectr in Biochemistry, Univ. of Sheffield, 1963-65. Vis. Res. Prof. of Gesellschaft für Strahlen und Umweltforschung, Institut für Mikrobiologie, Universität Göttingen, 1973-74; Walker-Ames Vis. Prof., Univ. of Washington, Seattle, 1981. Korrespondierendes Mitglied, Akademie der Wissenschaften, Göttingen, 1976. Ciba Medal, Biochem. Soc., 1978. *Publications:* articles in scientific jls. *Recreations:* hill-walking, gardening, bread-making. *Address:* 15 Burnt Stones Close, Sheffield S10 5TS. *T:* Sheffield 301429.

QUEBEC, Archbishop of, (RC), since 1981; **Most Rev. Louis-Albert Vachon,** CC (Canada) 1969; FRSC 1974; Officier de l'Ordre de la fidélité française, 1963; *b* 4 Feb. 1912; *s* of Napoléon Vachon and Alexandrine Gilbert. *Educ:* Laval Univ. (PhD Philosophy, 1947); PhD Theology, Angelicum,

Rome, 1949. Superior, Grand Séminaire de Québec, 1955-59; Superior General, 1960-77; Auxiliary Bishop of Quebec, 1977-81; Vice-Rector of Laval Univ., 1959-60, Rector, 1960-72. Hon. doctorates: Montreal, McGill and Victoria, 1964; Guelph, 1966; Moncton, 1967; Queen's, Bishop's and Strasbourg, 1968; Notre-Dame (Indiana), 1971; Carleton, 1971. Mem., Royal Canadian Soc. of Arts. Hon. Fellow, Royal Coll. Physicians and Surgeons of Canada, 1972. *Publications:* Espérance et Présomption, 1958; Vérité et Liberté, 1962; Unité de l'Université, 1962; Apostolat de l'universitaire catholique, 1963; Mémorial, 1963; Communauté universitaire, 1963; Progrès de l'université et consentement populaire, 1964; Responsabilité collective des universitaires, 1964; Les humanités aujourd'hui, 1966; Excellence et loyauté des universitaires, 1969. *Address:* 2 Port-Dauphin, PO Box 459, Quebec G1R 4R6. *T:* 692-3935. *Club:* Cercle Universitaire.

QUEBEC, Bishop of, since 1977; **Rt. Rev. Allen Goodings;** *b* Barrow-in-Furness, Lancs, 7 May 1925; *s* of late Thomas Jackson Goodings and Ada Tate; *m* 1959, Joanne Talbot; one *s* one *d*. *Educ:* Sir George Williams Univ. (BA); McGill Univ. (BD); Diocesan Theological Coll., Montreal (LTh; Hon. DD). Studied engineering and worked for Vickers Armstrongs (Britain) and Canadian Vickers (Montreal); studied in Montreal and ordained into Ministry of Anglican Church of Canada, 1959. Chaplain, Canadian Grenadier Guards, Montreal, 1966-69. Dean of Holy Trinity Cathedral, Quebec, 1969-77. Played Rugby Union (capped for Lancashire, 1947/8, including County Championship). *Recreations:* skiing, tennis, squash, cycling. *Address:* 29 Rue des Jardins, Quebec, PQ G1R 4L5, Canada. *T:* 694-9329. *Clubs:* Cercle Universitaire (Quebec); Mess (Royale 22nd Regiment, Quebec); Quebec Garrison (Hon. Mem.).

QUEENSBERRY, 12th Marquess of, *cr* 1682; **David Harrington Angus Douglas;** late Royal Horse Guards; Viscount Drumlanrig and Baron Douglas, 1628; Earl of Queensberry, 1633; Bt (Nova Scotia), 1668; Professor of Ceramics, Royal College of Art, since 1959; Partner, Queensberry Hunt design group; *b* 19 Dec. 1929; *s* of 11th Marquess of Queensberry and late Cathleen Mann; *S* father, 1954; *m* 1st, 1956, Mrs Ann Radford; two *d*; 2nd, 1969, Alexandra, *d* of Guy Wyndham Sich; three *s* one *d*. *Educ:* Eton. Mem. Council, Crafts Council; Pres., Design and Industries Assoc., 1976-78. *Heir:* *s* Viscount Drumlanrig, *qv*.

QUEENSLAND, NORTH, Bishop of, since 1971; **Rt. Rev. Hurtle John Lewis;** *b* 2 Jan. 1926; *s* of late Hurtle John Lewis and late Hilda Lewis. *Educ:* Prince Alfred Coll.; London Univ. (BD). ThL of ACT. Royal Australian Navy, 1943-46; Student, St Michael's House, S Aust., 1946-51; Member, SSM, 1951-; Provincial Australia, SSM, 1962-68; Prior, Kobe Priory, Japan, 1969-71. *Recreations:* rowing, horse riding. *Address:* Box 1244, Townsville, Queensland 4810, Australia. *T:* 71-2297.

QUEGUINER, Jean; Légion d'Honneur, 1970; Chairman, Chantiers Navals de l'Esterel, since 1981; Administrateur Général des Affaires Maritimes, France; Deputy Secretary-General, Inter-Governmental Maritime Consultative Organization (IMCO), 1968-77; *b* 2 June 1921; *s* of Etienne Quéguiner and Anne Trehin; *m* 1952, Marguerite Gaillard; one *s* one *d*. *Educ:* Lycée Buffon, Collège Stanislas and Faculté de Droit, Paris; Coll. of Administration of Maritime Affairs, St Malo. Docteur en Droit (maritime), Bordeaux. Head of Maritime Dist of Caen, 1953; Dep. Head of Coll. of Admin. of Maritime Affairs, 1955; Head of Safety of Navigation Section, 1963; Vice-Chm. of Maritime Safety Cttee of Inter-Govtl Maritime Consultative Organization, 1965-68. *Publications:* Législation et réglementation maritime, 1955; Le code de la mer, 1965; La croisière cotière, 1967; Le code fluvial à l'usage des plaisanciers, 1970. *Recreation:* sailing. *Address:* 20 square La-Motte-Picquet, 75015 Paris, France.

QUÉNET, Hon. Sir Vincent (Ernest), Kt 1962; Judge President of Appellate Division, High Court of Rhodesia, 1964-70, retired; *b* 14 Dec. 1906; *y s* of George Alfred Quénet, Worcester, CP, SA; *m* 1938, Gabrielle, *d* of Hon. Norman Price; three *s*. *Educ:* Worcester High Sch.; University of Cape Town. Advocate of Supreme Court of SA and Barrister-at-law, Middle Temple. Practised at Johannesburg Bar, QC; Judge of: High Court of S Rhodesia, 1952-61; Fed. Supreme Court, Federation of Rhodesia and Nyasaland, 1961-64. *Address:* Tiger Valley, Borrowdale, Salisbury, Zimbabwe. *T:* 8872813. *Clubs:* Rand (Johannesburg); Salisbury (Zimbabwe).

QUENINGTON, Viscount; Michael Henry Hicks Beach; *b* 7 Feb. 1950; *s* and *heir* of 2nd Earl St Aldwyn, *qv*; *m* 1982, Gilda Maria, *o d* of Barão Saavedra, Copacabana, Rio de Janeiro. *Educ:* Eton; Christ Church, Oxford. MA. *Address:* Williamstrip Park, Cirencester, Glos; 13 Upper Belgrave Street, SW1; Apartment 13E, 344 W 38th Street, New York, NY 10018, USA. *T:* New York 736-0203.

QUENNELL, Joan Mary, MBE 1958; *b* 23 Dec. 1923; *o c* of late Walter Quennell, Dangstein, Rogate. *Educ:* Dunhurst and Bedales Schools. War Service, WLA and BRCS. Vice-Chairman, Horsham Division Cons. Assoc., 1949 (Chairman, 1958-61); W Sussex CC, 1951-61. Served on Finance, Local Government, Selection and Education Cttees, etc; also as Governor various schools and colleges; Governor, Crawley Coll., Further Education, 1956-69; Member: Southern Reg. Council for Further Education, 1959-61; Reg. Adv. Council, Technological Education (London and Home Counties), 1959-61. MP (C) Petersfield, 1960-Sept. 1974; PPS to the Minister of Transport, 1962-64; Member: Select Cttee on Public Accounts, 1970-74; Speaker's Panel of Temporary Chairmen of House of Commons, 1970-74; Cttee of Selection, House of Commons, 1970-74; Select Cttee on European Secondary Legislation, 1973-74. Chm., EUW, Hampshire, 1978-80. JP W Sussex, 1959-80. *Recreations:* reading, gardening. *Address:* Dangstein, Rogate, near Petersfield, Hants.

QUENNELL, Peter, CBE 1973; *b* March 1905; *s* of late Marjorie and C. H. B. Quennell. *Educ:* Berkhamsted Grammar Sch.; Balliol Coll., Oxford. Editor, History To-day, 1951-79; edited The Cornhill Magazine, 1944-51. *Publications:* Poems, 1926; Baudelaire and the Symbolists, 1929, 2nd edn 1954; A Superficial Journey through Tokyo and Peking, 1932, 2nd edn 1934; Sympathy, and Other Stories, 1933; Byron, 1934; Byron: the years of fame, 1935, 3rd edn 1967; Victorian Panorama: a survey of life and fashion from contemporary photographs, 1937; Caroline of England, 1939; Byron in Italy, 1941; Four Portraits, 1945, 2nd edn 1965; John Ruskin, 1949; The Singular Preference, 1952; Spring in Sicily, 1952; Hogarth's Progress, 1955; The Sign of the Fish, 1960; Shakespeare: the poet and his background, 1964; Alexander Pope: the education of Genius 1688-1728, 1968; Romantic England, 1970; Casanova in London and other essays, 1971; Samuel Johnson: his friends and enemies, 1972; The Marble Foot (autobiog.), 1976; The Wanton Chase (autobiog.), 1980; Customs and Characters, 1982; *edited:* Aspects of Seventeenth Century Verse, 1933, 2nd edn 1936; The Private Letters of Princess Lieven to Prince Metternich, 1820-1826, 1948; Byron: selected letters and journals, 1949; H. Mayhew, Mayhew's Characters, 1951; Diversions of History, 1954; H. Mayhew, Mayhew's London, 1954; George Borrow, The Bible in Spain, 1959; H. Mayhew, London's Underworld, 1960; G. G. N. Byron, Lord Byron, Byronic Thoughts, 1960; H. de Montherlant, Selected Essays, 1960; W. Hickey, Memoirs, 1960; T. Moore, The Journal of Thomas Moore, 1964; H. Mayhew, Mayhew's Characters, 1967; Marcel Proust, 1871-1922: a centenary volume, 1971; (with H. Johnson) A History of English Literature, 1973; Vladimir Nabokov, his Life, his Work, his World, 1979; A Lonely Business: a self-portrait of James Pope-Hennessy, 1981. *Address:* 26 Cheyne Row, SW3. *Club:* White's.

QUEREJAZU CALVO, Roberto; Cross of the Chaco and Award of Military Merit (Bolivia); Bolivian Ambassador to the Court of St James's 1966-70, and to the Court of The Hague, 1966-70; *b* 24 Nov. 1913; *m* 1944, Dorothy Lewis; one *s* one *d. Educ:* Sucre Univ., Bolivia. Director of Minister's Cabinet, Legal Dept, and Political Dept, Bolivian Foreign Service, 1939-42; First Secretary, Embassy in Brazil, 1943; Secretary-General, Bolivian Delegn to UN, 1946; Bolivian Embassy, London: Counsellor, 1947; Chargé d'Affaires, 1948-52; Bolivian Rep.: to UN Conference on Tin, 1951; to Interamerican Conference for De-Nuclearization of Latin America, Mexico, 1964; Bolivian Delegate: XX UN General Assembly, 1965; 2nd Interamerican Conference Extraord., Rio de Janeiro, 1965; Under-Secretary of State for Foreign Affairs, Bolivia, 1966. Holds foreign awards. *Publications:* Masamaclay (history of Chaco War), 1966; Bolivia and the English, 1973; Llallagua (history of a mountain), 1976; Guano, Salitre, Sangre (history of the Pacific War), 1979; Adolfo Costa du Rels (biography of a diplomat and writer), 1981. *Address:* Casilla 4243, Cochabamba, Bolivia.

QUICK, Anthony Oliver Hebert; Headmaster of Bradfield College since 1971; *b* 26 May 1924; *er s* of late Canon O. C. Quick, sometime Regius Prof. of Divinity at Oxford, and late Mrs F. W. Quick; *m* 1955, Eva Jean, *er d* of late W. C. Sellar and of Mrs Hope Sellar; three *s* one *d. Educ:* Shrewsbury Sch.; Corpus Christi Coll., Oxford; Sch. of Oriental and African Studies, Univ. of London (Govt Schol.). 2nd cl. hons Mod. History, Oxford. Lieut, RNVR, serving mainly on East Indies Stn, 1943-46. Asst Master, Charterhouse, 1949-61; Headmaster, Rendcomb Coll., Cirencester, 1961-71. *Publications:* (jtly) Britain 1714-1851, 1961; Britain 1851-1945, 1967; Twentieth Century Britain, 1968. *Recreations:* walking, gardening, sailing, fishing. *Address:* Crossways, Bradfield, Reading, Berks. *T:* Bradfield 744203. *Club:* Naval.

QUICK SMITH, George William, CBE 1959; Chief Executive, latterly Vice-Chairman, and Member of National Freight Corporation, 1968-71; *b* 23 Aug. 1905; *s* of George Windsor Smith and Maud Edith (*née* Quick); *m* 1934, Ida Muriel Tinkler; no *c. Educ:* Univ. of London (LLB). Barrister-at-law, Inner Temple. FCIS; FCIT (past Vice-Pres.). Various positions in shipping, 1922-35; Sec. of various assocs and Mem. of joint negotiating and other bodies connected with road transport; British employers deleg. to various internat. confs including ILO, 1935-48; First Legal Adviser and Sec. and later Mem. of Board of British Road Services, 1948-59; Adviser on Special Projects, British Transport Commn, 1959-62; Chief Sec. and Chief Exec. of Transport Holding Co., 1962-71. Dir various road haulage and bus cos; Mem., Transport Tribunal, 1973-77; Trustee various transport benevolent funds; Master of Carmen's Co., 1967-68; Freeman of City of London. Churchwarden, All Saints Margaret Street, London, 1960-77. Mem. Governing Body, SPCK, 1967-75 (Vice-Pres., 1976-). Hon. Mem., Road Haulage Assoc., 1971. *Publications:* various books and papers on road transport and road transport law; Commentary on Transport Act 1947. *Recreations:* reading, writing, and the arts. *Address:* 6 Martello Towers, Canford Cliffs, Poole, Dorset BH13 7HX. *T:* Canford Cliffs 708127. *Club:* Royal Motor Yacht (Poole).

QUICKE, John Godolphin, CBE 1978; *b* 20 April 1922; *s* of Captain Noel Arthur Godolphin Quicke and Constance May Quicke; *m* 1953, Prudence Tinné Berthon, *d* of Rear-Adm. (E) C. P. E. Berthon; three *s* three *d. Educ:* Eton; New Coll., Oxford. Chairman, Minister of Agriculture's SW Regional

Panel, 1972-75; Pres., Country Landowners' Assoc., 1975-77; Member: SW Regional Bd, Nat. Westminster Bank Ltd, 1974-; Severn Barrage Cttee, 1978-80; Countryside Commn, 1981-. *Recreations:* reading, music, trees. *Address:* Sherwood, Newton St Cyres, near Exeter, Devon EX5 5BT. *T:* Newton St Cyres 216. *Club:* Boodle's.

QUIGLEY, William George Henry, CB 1982; PhD; Permanent Secretary, Department of Finance and Personnel, Northern Ireland, since 1982; *b* 26 Nov. 1929; *s* of William George Cunningham Quigley and Sarah Hanson Martin; *m* 1971, Moyra Alice Munn, LLB. *Educ:* Ballymena Academy; Queen's Univ., Belfast, BA (1st Cl. Hons), 1951; PhD, 1955. Apptd Asst Principal, Northern Ireland Civil Service, 1955; Permanent Secretary: Dept of Manpower Services, NI, 1974-76; Dept of Commerce, NI, 1976-79; Dept of Finance, NI, 1979-82. CBIM. *Publication:* (ed with E. F. D. Roberts) Registrum Iohannis Mey: The Register of John Mey, Archbishop of Armagh, 1443-1456, 1972. *Recreations:* historical research, reading, music.

QUILL, Colonel Raymond Humphrey, CBE 1947; DSO 1947; MVO (4th Class) 1934; Colonel (retired), Royal Marines; *b* 4 May 1897; *s* of late Maj.-General Richard Henry Quill, CB, MD; unmarried. *Educ:* Wellington Coll.; Cheltenham. Joined Royal Marines, 1914. Served European War, 1914-19. Major, RM, 1934; Lieut-Colonel, 1943; Colonel, 1944. Served War of 1939-45. ADC to the King, 1948-50; retired, 1950. Legion of Merit, USA, 1948. Fellow, British Horological Institute, 1954-. *Publication:* John Harrison: the man who found Longitude, 1967. *Recreations:* athletics, fishing, horology. *Address:* Hollington House, Woolton Hill, Newbury, Berks RG15 9XR. *T:* 01-828 3730. *Clubs:* Boodle's, Royal Thames Yacht, Royal Automobile.

QUILLEY, Denis Clifford; actor; *b* 26 Dec. 1927; *s* of Clifford Charles Quilley and Ada Winifred (*née* Stanley); *m* 1949, Stella Chapman; one *s* two *d. Educ:* Bancroft's, Woodford, Essex. First appearance, Birmingham Rep. Theatre, 1945; The Lady's not for Burning, Globe, 1949; Old Vic and Young Vic Cos, 1950-51: parts included: Fabian in Twelfth Night (on tour, Italy), Gratiano in Merchant of Venice; Revue, Airs on a Shoe String (exceeded 700 perfs), Royal Court, 1953; first leading rôle in West End as Geoffrey Morris in Wild Thyme, Duke of York's, 1955; subseq. parts incl.: Tom Wilson in Grab Me a Gondola (over 600 perfs), Lyric; Captain Brassbound, and Orlando, Bristol Old Vic; Candide, Saville; Benedick in Much Ado about Nothing, Open Air Th.; Archie Rice in The Entertainer, Nottingham Playhouse; Krogstad in A Doll's House, Brighton; Privates on Parade, Aldwych, 1977, Piccadilly, 1978 (SWET award, 1977); Deathtrap, Garrick, 1978; title rôle in Sweeney Todd, Theatre Royal Drury Lane (SWET award), 1980. Nat. Theatre, 1971-76: Aufidius (Coriolanus); Macbeth; Bolingbroke (Richard II); Caliban (The Tempest); Lopakin (Cherry Orchard); Jamie (Long Day's Journey into Night); Claudius (Hamlet); Hector (Troilus and Cressida); Bajazeth (Tamburlaine); Morell (Candida), Albery Theatre, 1977. Has played in NY, Melbourne and Sydney. *Films:* Life at the Top, Anne of the Thousand Days, Murder on the Orient Express, The Antagonists, Evil Under the Sun, Privates on Parade. *TV plays and series* incl.: Merchant of Venice; The Father; Henry IV (Pirandello); Murder in the Cathedral; Time Slip; Contrabandits (Aust.); Clayhanger; The Serpent Son; The Crucible; Gladstone, in No 10. *Recreations:* playing the piano, flute and cello, walking. *Address:* 22 Willow Road, Hampstead, NW3. *T:* 01-435 5976.

QUILTER, Sir Anthony (Raymond Leopold Cuthbert), 4th Bt, *cr* 1897; landowner since 1959; *b* 25 March 1937; *s* of Sir (John) Raymond (Cuthbert) Quilter, 3rd Bt and Margery Marianne (*née* Cooke); *S* father 1959; *m* 1964, Mary Elise, *er d* of late Colonel Brian (Sherlock) Gooch, DSO, TD; one *s* one *d. Educ:* Harrow. Is engaged in farming. *Recreations:* shooting, golf. *Heir:* *s* Guy Raymond Cuthbert Quilter, *b* 13 April 1967. *Address:* Sutton Hall, Sutton, Woodbridge, Suffolk. *T:* Shottisham 411246.

QUILTER, David (Cuthbert) Tudway; Vice Lord-Lieutenant of Somerset, since 1978; Local Director, Barclays Bank, Bristol, since 1962 (Director, Barclays Bank UK Ltd, 1971-81); *b* 26 March 1921; *o s* of Percy Cuthbert Quilter and Clare Tudway; *m* 1953, Elizabeth Mary, *er d* of Sir John Carew Pole, Bt, *qv*; one *s* two *d. Educ:* Eton. Served War of 1939-45, Coldstream Guards, 1940-46. JP London Juvenile Courts, 1959-62. Mayor of Wells, 1974-75; Chm. of Trustees, Wells Cathedral Preservation Trust, 1976-; Treasurer, Bristol Univ., 1976-; Governor, Wells Cathedral Sch., 1968-; Member: Council, Outward Bound Trust, 1959-; Garden Soc., 1973-; Life Trustee, Carnegie UK Trust, 1981-. DL 1970, High Sheriff 1974-75, Somerset. *Publication:* No Dishonourable Name, 1947. *Recreations:* gardening, music, tennis, golf, shooting. *Address:* Milton Lodge, Wells, Somerset BA5 3AQ. *T:* Wells 72168. *Club:* Boodle's.

QUIN; *see* Wyndham-Quin.

QUIN, Rt. Rev. George Alderson. *Educ:* Trinity College, Dublin (MA). Deacon, 1937, priest 1938, Down; Curate of St Jude, Ballynafeigh, Belfast, 1937-39; Dean's Vicar of St Anne's Cathedral, Belfast, 1939-41; Holywood, 1941-43; Incumbent of Magheralin, 1943-51; Vicar of Mathacarrett, 1951-58; Canon of St Anne's Cathedral, Belfast, 1955-56; Archdeacon of Down, 1956-70; Exam. Chaplain to Bishop of Down and Dromore, 1957-70; Rector of Bangor, Dio. Down, 1958-70; Bishop of Down and Dromore, 1970-80. *Address:* c/o The See House, Knockdene Park, S Belfast.

QUIN, Joyce Gwendolen; Member (Lab) South Tyne and Wear, European Parliament, since 1979; *b* 26 Nov. 1944; *d* of Basil Godfrey Quin and Ida (*née* Ritson). *Educ:* Univ. of Newcastle upon Tyne (BA French, 1st Cl. Hons); Univ. of London (MSc Internat. Relns). Research Asst, Internat. Dept, Labour Party Headquarters, Transport House, 1969-72; Lecturer in French, Univ. of Bath, 1972-76; Resident Tutor, St Mary's Coll., and Lectr in French and Politics, Univ. of Durham, 1977-79. *Publications:* articles on French and European politics in various academic jls. *Recreations:* North-East local history (Newcastle upon Tyne City Guide); music, theatre, walking, cycling. *Address:* 5 Grange Crescent, Sunderland, Tyne and Wear; European Parliament, Centre européen, Plateau du Kirchberg, Luxembourg. *T:* 43001.

QUINCE, Peter; *see* Thompson, John W. McW.

QUINE, Prof. Willard Van Orman; American author; Professor of Philosophy, 1948, and Edgar Pierce Professor of Philosophy, 1956-78, Harvard University, now Emeritus Professor; *b* Akron, Ohio, 25 June 1908; *s* of Cloyd Robert and Hattie Van Orman Quine; *m* 1st, 1930, Naomi Clayton; two *d*; 2nd, 1948, Marjorie Boynton; one *s* one *d*. *Educ:* Oberlin Coll., Ohio (AB); Harvard Univ. (AM, PhD). Harvard: Sheldon Travelling Fellow, 1932-33 (Vienna, Prague, Warsaw); Jun. Fellow, Society of Fellows, 1933-36 (Sen. Fellow, 1949-78, Chairman, 1957-58); Instructor and Tutor in Philosophy, 1936-41; Assoc. Professor of Philosophy, 1941-48; Chairman, Dept of Philosophy, 1952-53. Visiting Professor, Universidade de São Paulo, Brazil, 1942. Lieut, then Lieut-Commander, USNR, active duty, 1942-46. Consulting editor, Journal of Symbolic Logic, 1936-52; Vice-President, Association for Symbolic Logic, 1938-40; President, 1953-55; Vice-President, Eastern Division, American Philosophical Assoc., 1950, President, 1957; Member: Amer. Philos. Soc., 1957- (Councillor, 1966-68, 1982-); Acad. Internat. de Philosophie de Science, 1960. FAAAS, 1945- (Councillor, 1950-53); Fellow, Nat. Acad. of Sciences, 1977-. Corres. Member: Instituto Brasileiro de Filosofia, 1963-; Institut de France, 1978-; Corres. Fellow: British Acad., 1959-; Norwegian Acad. of Scis, 1979-; Trustee, Institute for Unity of Science, 1949-56; Syndic, Harvard University Press: 1951-53; 1954-56, 1959-60, 1962-66. George Eastman Visiting Prof., Oxford Univ., 1953-54; Vis. Professor: Univ. of Tokyo, 1959; Rockefeller Univ., 1968; Collège de France, 1969. A. T. Shearman Lecturer, University of London, 1954; Gavin David Young Lectr in Philosophy, Univ. of Adelaide, 1959; John Dewey Lectr, Columbia Univ., 1968; Paul Carus Lectr, Amer. Philos. Assoc., 1971; Hägerström Lectr, Uppsala, 1973. Member Institute for Advanced Study, Princeton, USA, 1956-57. Fellow: Centre for Advanced Study in the Behavioural Sciences, Palo Alto, California, 1958-59; Centre for Advanced Studies, Wesleyan Univ., Conn, 1965; Sir Henry Saville Fellow, Merton Coll., Oxford, 1973-74. Hon. degrees: MA Oxon, 1953; DLitt Oxon, 1970; LittD: Oberlin, 1955; Akron, 1965; Washington, 1966; Temple, 1970; Cambridge, 1978; LLD: Ohio State, 1957; Harvard, 1979; Dèsl Lille, 1965; LHD: Chicago, 1967; Syracuse, 1981; DPh Uppsala, 1980. N. M. Butler Gold Medal, 1970. *Publications:* A System of Logistic, 1934; Mathematical Logic, 1940, rev. edn 1951; Elementary Logic, 1941, rev. edn 1965; O sentido da nova logica, 1944 (São Paulo); Methods of Logic, 1950, rev. edn 1982; From a Logical Point of View, 1953, rev. edn 1961; Word and Object, 1960; Set Theory and its Logic, 1963, revised edn 1969; Ways of Paradox and Other Essays, 1966, rev. edn 1976; Selected Logic Papers, 1966; Ontological Relativity and Other Essays, 1969; Philosophy of Logic, 1970; (with J. S. Ullian) The Web of Belief, 1970; The Roots of Reference, 1974; Theories and Things, 1981; contribs to Journal of Symbolic Logic; Journal of Philosophy; Philosophical Review; Mind; Rivista di Filosofia; Scientific American; NY Review of Books; Library of Living Philosophers. *Recreation:* travel. *Address:* 38 Chestnut Street, Boston, Mass 02108, USA. *T:* 723-6754.

QUINLAN, Maj.-Gen. Henry, CB 1960; *b* 5 Jan. 1906; *s* of Dr Denis Quinlan, LRCP, LRCS (Edinburgh), of Castletownroche, Co. Cork; *m* 1936, Euphemia Nancy, *d* of John Tallents Wynyard Brooke of Shanghai, and Altrincham, Cheshire; two *s* two *d*. *Educ:* Clongowes Wood Coll., Sallins, Co. Kildare. BDS 1926; FFD RCS (1) 1964. Royal Army Dental Corps: Lieut, 1927; Captain, Dec. 1930; Major, 1937; Lieut-Colonel, Dec. 1947; Colonel, 1953; Maj.-General, Oct. 1958; Director Army Dental Service, 1958-63; QHDS 1954-64, retired; Colonel Comdt Royal Army Dental Corps, 1964-71. Officer OStJ 1958. *Address:* White Bridges, Redlands Lane, Crondall, Hants. *T:* Aldershot 850239.

QUINLAN, Michael Edward, CB 1980; Permanent Secretary, Department of Employment, since 1983; *b* 11 Aug. 1930; *s* of Gerald and Roseanne Quinlan, Hassocks; *m* 1965, Margaret Mary Finlay; two *s* two *d*. *Educ:* Wimbledon Coll.; Merton Coll., Oxford. 1st Cl. Hon. Mods, 1st Cl. LittHum. RAF, 1952-54. Asst Principal, Air Ministry, 1954; Private Sec. to Parly Under-Sec. of State for Air, 1956-58; Principal, Air Min., 1958; Private Sec. to Chief of Air Staff, 1962-65; Asst Sec., MoD, 1968; Defence Counsellor, UK Delegn to NATO, 1970-73; Under-Sec., Cabinet Office, 1974-77; Dep. Under-Sec. of State, MoD, 1977-81; seconded as Dep. Sec., HM Treasury, 1981-82. *Recreations:* cricket, squash, listening to music. *Address:* c/o Department of Employment, Caxton House, Tothill Street, SW1. *Club:* Royal Air Force.

QUINN, Prof. David Beers, DLit (QUB), PhD (London), MRIA, FRHistS; Andrew Geddes and John Rankin Professor of Modern History, University of Liverpool, 1957-76; *b* 24 April 1909; *o s* of late David Quinn, Omagh and Belfast, and Albertina Devine, Cork; *m* 1937, Alison Moffat Robertson, MA, *d* of late John Ireland Robertson, Edinburgh; two *s* one *d*. *Educ:* Clara (Offaly) No. 2 National Sch.; Royal Belfast Academical Institution; Queen's Univ., Belfast; King's Coll., University of London. University Schol., QUB, 1928-31 (1st Class Hons in Medieval and Modern History, 1931); PhD London, 1934. Asst Lecturer, 1934, and Lecturer, 1937, University College, Southampton; Lecturer in History, QUB, 1939-44; seconded to BBC European Service, 1943; Prof. of History, University College, Swansea, 1944-57; DLit (QUB), 1958. Secretary, Ulster Society for Irish Historical Studies, 1939-44; Member: Council of Hakluyt Society, 1950-54, 1957-60 (Vice-Pres., 1960-82, Pres., 1982-); Council of Royal Historical Society, 1951-55, 1956-60 (Vice-President, 1964-68); Fellow, Folger Shakespeare Lib. (Washington, DC), 1957, 1959, 1963-64; Fellow, John Carter Brown Lib., 1970, 1982; Leverhulme Res. Fellow, 1963; British Council Visiting Scholar, NZ, 1967; Hungary, 1972; Fellow, Huntington Library, 1980; Fellow, Nat. Inst. for the Humanities, 1983; Harrison Vis. Prof., Coll. of William and Mary, Williamsburg, Va, 1969-70; Visiting Professor: St Mary's Coll., St Mary's City, Md, 1976-78, 1980-82; Michigan Univ., 1979. Hon. DLitt: Newfoundland, 1964; New Univ. of Ulster, 1975; NUI, 1981; Hon. DHL St Mary's Coll., 1978; Hon. LLD Univ. of N Carolina, 1980. *Publications:* The Port Books or Petty Customs Accounts of Southampton for the Reign of Edward IV, 2 vols, 1937-38; The Voyages and Colonising Enterprises of Sir Humphrey Gilbert, 2 vols, 1940; Raleigh and the British Empire, 1947; The Roanoke Voyages, 1584-90, 2 vols, 1955; (with Paul Hulton) The American Drawings of John White, 1577-1590, 1964; (with R. A. Skelton) R. Hakluyt's Principall Navigations (1589), 1965; The Elizabethans and the Irish, 1966; Richard Hakluyt, Editor, 1967; North American Discovery, 1971; (with W. P. Cumming and R. A. Skelton) The Discovery of North America, 1972; (with N. M. Cheshire) The New Found Land of Stephen Parmenius, 1972; (with A. M. Quinn) Virginia Voyages from Hakluyt, 1973; England and the Discovery of America 1481-1620, 1974; The Hakluyt Handbook, 2 vols, 1974; (with W. P. Cumming, S. E. Hillier and G. Williams) The Exploration of North America, 1630-1776, 1974; The Last Voyage of Thomas Cavendish, 1975; North America from First Discovery to Early Settlements, 1977; (with A. M. Quinn and S. Hillier) New American World, 5 vols, 1979; Early Maryland and a Wider World, 1982; (with A. M. Quinn) English New England Voyages 1602-1608, 2 vols, 1982; contribs on Irish history and the discovery and settlement of N America in historical journals. *Address:* 9 Knowsley Road, Cressington Park, Liverpool L19 0PF. *T:* 051-427 2041.

QUINN, James Charles Frederick; film producer and exhibitor; *b* 23 Aug. 1919; *y s* of Rev. Chancellor James Quinn and Muriel Alice May (*née* MaGuire); *m* 1942, Hannah, 2nd *d* of Rev. R. M. Gwynn, BD (Sen. Fellow and Vice-Provost, TCD), and Dr Eileen Gwynn; one *s* one *d*. *Educ:* Shrewsbury Sch.; TCD (Classical Exhibnr); Christ Church, Oxford (MA; Dip. in Econ. and Polit. Sci.). Served War: 1st Bn Irish Guards, N Africa and Italy; Intell. Officer, 1943-44; Adjt, 3rd Bn, NW Europe, 1945; British Army Staff, France, and Town Major, Paris, 1945-46. Courtaulds Ltd, 1949-55. Dir, BFI, 1955-64: National Film Theatre built, London Film Festival inaugurated, and 1st Univ. Lectureship in Film Studies in UK estabd at Slade Sch. of Fine Art, University Coll., London. Council of Europe Fellowship, 1966. Chairman: Internat. Short Film Conf., 1971-78 (Life Pres., 1979); National Panel for Film Festivals, 1974-. Member: Gen. Adv. Council, BBC, 1960-64; Bd, Gardner Arts Centre, Sussex Univ., 1968-71. Trustee: Imperial War Museum, 1968-78; Grierson Meml Trust, 1975-. Invited to stand by New Ulster Movement as Indep. Unionist Parly candidate, S Down, 1968. Foreign Leader Award, US State Dept, 1962. Films: co-producer, Herostratus, 1966; Producer, Overlord, 1975. Silver Bear Award, Berlin Internat. Film Festival, 1975; Special Award, London Evening News British Film Awards, 1976. Chevalier de l'Ordre des Arts et des Lettres, France, 1979. *Publications:* Outside London, 1965; The Film and Television as an Aspect of European Culture, 1968; contrib. Chambers's Encyclopaedia (cinema), 1956-59. *Recreations:* lawn tennis, squash racquets; formerly Eton Fives. *Address:* Crescent Cottage, 108 Marine Parade, Brighton, E Sussex. *T:* Brighton 67888. *Clubs:* Cavalry and Guards; Vincent's (Oxford).

QUINN, Sheila Margaret Imelda, CBE 1978; FHA, FRCN; Regional Nursing Officer, Wessex Regional Health Authority, since 1978; *b* 16 Sept. 1920; *d* of late Wilfrid Amos Quinn and Ada Mazella (*née* Bottomley). *Educ:* Convent of Holy Child, Blackpool; London Univ. (BScEcon Hons); Royal Lancaster Infirmary (SRN 1947); Birmingham (SCM); Royal Coll. of Nursing, London (RNT). FHA 1971; FRCN 1978. Admin. Sister, then Principal Sister Tutor, Prince of Wales' Gen. Hosp., London, 1950-61; Internat. Council of Nurses, Geneva: Dir, Social and Econ. Welfare Div., 1961-66; Exec. Dir, 1967-70; Chief Nursing Officer, Southampton Univ. Hosps, 1970-74; Area Nursing Officer, Hampshire AHA (Teaching), 1974-78. UK Rep., Standing Cttee of Nurses of EEC, 1972-. Member: Council, Royal Coll. of Nursing, 1971-79 (Chm. Council, 1974-79; Dep. Pres., 1980-); Bd of Dirs, Internat. Council of Nurses, 1977-, first Vice-Pres., 1981-; Pres., EEC Adv. Cttee on Trng in Nursing, 1978-. *Publications:* Nursing and the EEC, 1980; articles, mainly on internat. nursing and EEC, in national and internat. jls. *Recreations:* boating, gardening. *Address:* Far Close, Wickham Lodge, Wickham, Fareham, Hants. *T:* Wickham 832942. *Club:* VAD Ladies.

QUINNELL, Air Commodore John Charles, CB 1943; DFC 1918; *b* 7 Jan. 1891; *er s* of late John B. Quinnell, Edenburn, Gortatlea, Co. Kerry, Ireland; *m* 1923, Atwell (*d* 1945), *d* of late James McFarlane, Fifeshire, Scotland; no *c* ; *m* 1948, Mildred Joan (*d* 1976), *widow* of Major Cyril Drummond, Cadland Fawley, Southampton, and *d* of late Horace Humphreys. *Educ:* Royal Sch., Dungannon, Co. Tyrone. Commissioned RA 1914; seconded RFC 1915; transferred RAF, 1918. Served European War, 1914–19 (despatches, DFC); RAF Staff Coll., 1924; Imperial Defence Coll., 1929; Air HQ Staff, Bagdad, 1931; AOC No 6 Auxiliary Group, 1935–38, and of No 6 Group 1939; Senior Air Staff Officer, Advanced Air Striking Force, 1939–40 (despatches); AOC a Group, RAF, 1942; retired, 1945. Pres., Solent Cruising and Racing Assoc., 1947–79, Hon. Life Pres., 1979; Chm., Solent Area Sailing Adv. Cttee. *Recreations:* shooting, yachting. *Address:* Nelson's Place, Fawley, Southampton, Hants. *T:* Fawley, Hants 891002. *Clubs:* Turf, Royal Thames Yacht; Royal Yacht Squadron.

QUINTON, Anthony Meredith, FBA 1977; President of Trinity College, Oxford, since 1978; *b* 25 March 1925; *s* of late Richard Frith Quinton, Surgeon Captain, RN, and late Gwenllyan Letitia Quinton; *m* 1952, Marcelle Wegier; one *s* one *d.* *Educ:* Stowe Sch.; Christ Church, Oxford (St Cyres Scholar; BA 1st Cl. Hons PPE 1948). Served War, RAF, 1943–46: flying officer and navigator. Fellow: All Souls Coll., Oxford, 1949–55; New Coll., Oxford, 1955–78. Delegate, OUP, 1970–76. Mem., Arts Council, 1979–81. Vis. Professor: Swarthmore Coll., Pa, 1960; Stanford Univ., Calif, 1964; New Sch. for Social Res., New York, 1976–77. Lecturer: Dawes Hicks, British Acad., 1971; Gregynog, Univ. of Wales, Aberystwyth, 1973; T. S. Eliot, Univ. of Kent, Canterbury, 1976. Pres., Aristotelian Soc., 1975–76. Governor, Stowe Sch., 1963– (Chm. Governors, 1969–75); Fellow, Winchester Coll. 1970–. Emeritus Fellow, New College, Oxford, 1980. *Publications:* Political Philosophy (ed), 1967; The Nature of Things, 1973; Utilitarian Ethics, 1973; (trans.) K. Ajdukiewicz (with H. Skolimowski) Problems and Theories of Philosophy, 1973; The Politics of Imperfection, 1978; Francis Bacon, 1980; Thoughts and Thinkers, 1982. *Recreations:* sedentary pursuits. *Address:* President's Lodgings, Trinity College, Oxford. *T:* Oxford 42888. *Clubs:* Garrick, Beefsteak.

QUINTON, John Grand; Director and Senior General Manager, Barclays Bank, since 1982; *b* 21 Dec. 1929; *s* of William Grand Quinton and Norah May (*née* Nunn); *m* 1954, Jean Margaret Chastney; one *s* one *d.* *Educ:* Norwich Sch.; St John's Coll., Cambridge (MA 1954); FIB 1964. Joined Barclays Bank, 1953: Asst Manager, Piccadilly, 1961; Dep. Principal, Staff Trng Centre, 1963; Manager, King's Cross, 1965; seconded to Min. of Health as Principal, Internat. Div. and UK Deleg., World Health Assembly, 1966; Asst Gen. Manager, 1968; Local Dir, Nottingham, 1969; Reg. Gen. Manager, 1971; Gen. Manager, 1975; Dep. Chm., Mercantile Credit Co. Ltd, 1975–79. Member: City Capital Markets Cttee, 1981–; NE Thames RHA, 1974–; Accounting Standards Cttee, 1982–; Chm., Motability Finance Ltd, 1978–; Treasurer, Inst. of Bankers, 1980–. *Recreations:* tennis, gardening, music, occasional golf. *Address:* Pine Trees, Pinner Hill, Middlesex. *T:* 01-866 9825.

QUIRK, Prof. (Charles) Randolph, CBE 1974; MA, PhD, DLit (London); Fil.Dr (Lund and Uppsala); DU (Paris); DHC (Liège); DLitt (Reading); LLD (Leicester); FBA 1975; Vice-Chancellor, University of London, since 1981; Fellow of University College London; *b* 12 July 1920; *s* of late Thomas and Amy Randolph Quirk, Lambfell, Isle of Man. *Educ:* Cronk y Voddy Sch.; Douglas High Sch., IOM; University College London. Served RAF, 1940–45. Lecturer in English, University College London, 1947–54; Commonwealth Fund Fellow, Yale Univ. and University of Michigan, 1951–52; Reader in English Language and Literature, University of Durham, 1954–58; Professor of English Language in the University of Durham, 1958–60, in the University of London, 1960–68; Quain Prof. of English Language and Literature, University Coll. London, 1968–81. Special University Lectures, London, 1960; Director: University of London, Summer School of English, 1962–67; Survey of English Usage, 1959–; Member: Senate, Univ. of London, 1970–78 (Chm., Acad. Council, 1972–75); Ct, Univ. of London, 1972–75; Council, Queen Elizabeth, Westfield and Chelsea Colleges; Admin. Board, British Inst. in Paris; Governor: British Inst. of Recorded Sound, 1975–80; E-SU, 1980–; Amer. Internat. Coll. of London, 1981–. Chairman: Cttee of Enquiry into Speech Therapy Services; British Council English Cttee, 1976–; Mem., BBC Archives Cttee, 1975–. For. Fellow, Royal Belgian Acad. of Scis, 1975. Hon. FCST; Hon. FIL. Jubilee Medal, Inst. of Linguists, 1973. *Publications:* The Concessive Relation in Old English Poetry, 1954; Studies in Communication (with A. J. Ayer and others), 1955; An Old English Grammar (with C. L. Wrenn), 1955, revised edn, 1958; Charles Dickens and Appropriate Language, 1959; The Teaching of English (with A. H. Smith), 1959, revised edn, 1964; The Study of the Mother-Tongue, 1961; The Use of English (with Supplements by A. C. Gimson and J. Warburg), 1962, enlarged edn, 1968; Prosodic and Paralinguistic Features in English (with D. Crystal), 1964; A Common Language (with A. H. Marckwardt), 1964; Investigating Linguistic Acceptability (with J. Svartvik), 1966; Essays on the English Language— Mediaeval and Modern, 1968; (with S. Greenbaum) Elicitation Experiments in English, 1970; (with S. Greenbaum, G. Leech, J. Svartvik) A Grammar of Contemporary English, 1972; The English Language and Images of Matter, 1972; (with S. Greenbaum) A University Grammar of English, 1973; The Linguist and the English Language, 1974; (with V. Adams, D. Davy) Old English Literature: a practical introduction, 1975; (with J. Svartvik) A Corpus of English Conversation, 1980; Style and Communication in the English

Language, 1982; contrib. to: Proc. 8th Internat. Congress of Linguists, 1958; Language and Society (Festschrift for Arthur M. Jensen), 1961; Proc. 9th International Congress of Linguists, 1962; English Teaching Abroad and the British Universities (ed G. Bullough), 1961; Dictionaries and that Dictionary (ed J. H. Sledd and W. R. Ebbitt), 1962; World Book Encyclopædia Dictionary (ed C. L. Barnhart), 1963; Early English and Norse Studies (Festschrift for A. H. Smith), 1963; (ed Lady Birkenhead) Essays by Divers Hands, 1969; Essays and Studies, 1970; Charles Dickens (ed S. Wall), 1970; A New Companion to Shakespeare Studies, 1971; Linguistics at Large, 1971; The Crown and the Thistle, 1979; The State of the Language, 1980; papers in linguistic and literary journals. *Address:* Senate House, Malet Street, WC1E 7HU. *T:* 01-636 8000. *Club:* Athenæum.

QUIRK, John Stanton S.; *see* Shirley-Quirk.

QVIST, Dame Frances; *see* Gardner, Dame Frances.

R

RABBI, The Chief; *see* Jakobovits, Rabbi Sir Immanuel.

RABI, Prof. Isidor Isaac, PhD; University Professor Emeritus, Columbia University, NY; Member: Naval Research Advisory Committee, since 1952; (US Member) Science Committee of United Nations, since 1954; (US Member) Science Committee of NATO, since 1958; General Advisory Committee, Arms Control and Disarmament Agency since 1962; Consultant: to General Advisory Committee, Atomic Energy Commission, since 1956 (Chairman, 1952–56, Member, since 1946); to Department of State, since 1958; etc; *b* Rymanov, Austria, 29 July 1898; *s* of David and Sheindel Rabi; *m* Helen Newmark; two *d.* *Educ:* Cornell University (BChem 1919); Columbia University (PhD, 1927). Lecturer, Physics, Columbia University, New York, 1929; then various posts, there, 1930–50, when Higgins Professor of Physics until 1964, University Professor, 1964–67. Associate Director, Radiation Laboratory, Massachusetts Institute of Technology, Cambridge, Mass, 1940–45. Mem., National Academy of Sciences; Fellow, American Physics Soc. (Pres., 1950–51). Holds numerous honorary doctorates; awarded medals and prizes, 1939 onwards, including Nobel prize in physics, 1944, Atoms for Peace Award (jointly), 1967. *Publications:* My Life and Times as a Physicist, 1960; communications to The Physical Review, 1927–; contrib. to scientific jls on magnetism, quantum mechanics, nuclear physics, and molecular beams. *Recreations:* the theatre, travel, walking. *Address:* 450 Riverside Drive, New York City, NY 10027, USA. *Clubs:* Athenæum (London); Cosmos (Washington); Century Association (New York).

RABIN, Prof. Brian Robert; Professor of Biochemistry and Head of Department of Biochemistry, University College, London, since 1970; *b* 4 Nov. 1927; *s* of Emanuel and Sophia Rabin, both British; *m* 1954; one *s* one *d.* *Educ:* Latymer Sch., Edmonton; University Coll., London. BSc 1951, MSc 1952, PhD 1956. University College, London: Asst Lectr, 1954–57; Lectr, 1957–63; Reader, 1963–67; Prof. of Enzymology, 1967–70. Rockefeller Fellow, Univ. of California, 1956–57. *Publications:* numerous in Biochem. Jl, European Jl of Biochem., Nature, Proc. Nat. Acad. Sciences US, etc. *Recreations:* travel, listening to music, carpentry. *Address:* 34 Grangewood, Potters Bar, Herts. *T:* Potters Bar 54576. *Club:* Athenæum.

RABORN, Vice-Adm. William Francis, Jr, DSM 1960; President, W. F. Raborn Company Inc., McLean, Virginia, since 1966; Director: Curtiss Wright Corporation; Avemco; E-Sys Inc.; S.A.I. Corporation; Wackenhut Corporation; *b* Decatur, Texas, 8 June 1905; *s* of William Francis, Sr, and Mrs Cornelia V. Raborn (*née* Moore); *m* 1955, Mildred T. Terrill; one *s* one *d.* *Educ:* US Naval Acad., Annapolis, Md (BS); Naval War Coll., Newport, RI. Ensign, USN, 1928; Naval Aviator, 1934; Sea duty, 1928–40; Aviation Gunnery Sch., 1940–42; Exec. Off., USS Hancock, 1943–45; Chief Staff Comdr Task Force 77, W Pacific, 1945–47; Ops Off. Comdr for Air W Coast, 1947–49; R & D Guided Missiles, 1949–50; Guided Missile Div., Office of Naval Ops, 1952–54; CO, USS Bennington, 1954–55; Asst Chief of Staff to C-in-C, Atlantic Fleet, 1955; Dir, Office of Special Projects, Polaris program, 1955; Dep. Chief, Naval Ops (Develt), 1962; retd from USN, 1963; Vice-Pres., Program management Aerojet Gen. Corp., Azusa, Calif, 1963–65; Director of Central Intelligence, USA, 1965–66; Industrial Consultant, Aerojet Gen. Corp. Silver Star, 1945; Bronze Star Medal, 1951; Commendation Medal, 1954; National Security Medal, 1966. *Address:* (home and business) 1606 Crestwood Lane, McLean, Virginia 22101, USA. *Clubs:* Army-Navy, Metropolitan (Washington, DC); Burning Tree (Bethesda, Md); Canyon Country (Palm Springs, Calif).

RABUKAWAQA, Sir Josua Rasilau, KBE 1977 (CBE 1974; MBE 1968); MVO 1970; Ambassador-at-Large for Fiji and Chief of Protocol, Fiji, since 1978; *b* 2 Dec. 1917; *s* of Dr Aisea Rasilau and Adi Mereoni Dimaicakau, Bau, Fiji; *m* 1944, Mei Tolanivutu; three *s* two *d.* *Educ:* Suva Methodist Boys' Sch.; Queen Victoria Sch.; Teachers' Trng Coll., Auckland. Diploma in Public and Social Admin. 1958. Teaching in schools throughout Fiji, 1938–52; Co-operatives Inspector, 1952. Joined Fiji Mil. Forces, 1953; attached Gloucester Regt at Warminster Sch. of Infantry and Support Weapons Wing, Netheravon; comd Mortar Platoon, Malaya, 1954–55. Subseq. Econ. Develt

Officer, Fiji, 1957; District Officer, Fiji Admin. Service, 1961; Comr, Central Div., 1968. MLC, Fiji, 1964–66; Delegate, Constitutional Conf., London, 1965; (first) High Comr for Fiji in London, 1970–76. Active worker for Scouts, Red Cross and Methodist Church Choir. Formed Phoenix Choir. Compiled manual of singing in Fijian language, 1956, and guide for Fijian pronunciation for use by Fiji Broadcasting Commn, 1967; Chm., Fijian Adv. Cttee of Fiji Broadcasting Commn, 1965–70; Chm. Bd of Examrs for High Standard Fijian and Interpreters Exams, 1965–70; Mem., Housing Authority; Mem., Educn Adv. Council. *Recreations:* cricket, Rugby football (toured NZ as player/manager for Fiji, 1967). *Address:* 6 Vunivivi Hill, Nausori, Fiji. *Clubs:* Royal Commonwealth Society; Defence, Union (Fiji).

RABY, Sir Victor Harry, KBE 1956; CB 1948; MC; Deputy Under-Secretary of State, Department of the Permanent Under-Secretary of State for Air, 1946–57, retired December 1957; *b* 1897; *s* of Harry Raby, Menheniot, Cornwall; *m* 1921, Dorothy Alys, *d* of Rodney Buzzard, Ditchling, Sussex; one *s*. *Educ:* Grey College, Bloemfontein, S Africa. Served European War, 1914–19, with London Regt (MC). *Address:* New Way, Forder Lane, Bishopsteignton, Devon.

RACE, (Denys Alan) Reg; MP (Lab) Haringey, Wood Green, since 1979; *b* 23 June 1947; *s* of Denys and Elsie Race; *m* 1972, Linda J. Freeman; one *s* one *d*. *Educ:* Sale Grammar School; Univ. of Kent. BA (Politics and Sociology), PhD (Politics). Senior Research Officer, National Union of Public Employees, 1972. *Publications:* numerous pamphlets and articles in Labour Movement press. *Address:* House of Commons, SW1. *T:* 01-219 3000.

RACE, Robert Russell, CBE 1970; FRS 1952; PhD Cantab, MRCS, FRCP; FRCPath; Director, Medical Research Council Blood Group Unit, Lister Institute, SW1, 1946–73; *b* 28 Nov. 1907; *e s* of late Joseph Dawson Race and late May Race (*née* Tweddle), Kensington; *m* 1st, 1938, Margaret Monica (*d* 1955), *d* of late J. R. C. Rotton, MVO; three *d*; 2nd, 1956, Ruth Ann Sanger, *qv. Educ:* St Paul's School; St Bartholomew's Hosp.; Trinity Hall, Cambridge. Asst Pathologist, Hosp. for Consumption and Diseases of the Chest, Brompton, 1935–37; Asst Serologist, Galton Laboratory, UCL, 1937–39; Asst Dir then Dir, Galton Laboratory Serum Unit, at Dept of Pathology, Cambridge, 1939–46. Mem., Deutsche Akademie der Naturforscher Leopoldina, 1973. Hon. MD: Univ. of Paris, 1965; Univ. of Turku, 1970. Oliver Memorial Award for Blood Transfusion, 1948; Carlos J. Finlay Medal, Republic of Cuba, 1955; Landsteiner Memorial Award, USA, jtly with Ruth Sanger, 1957; Oehlecker Medal, Deutsche Gesellschaft für Bluttransfusion, 1970; Philip Levine Award, USA, jtly with Ruth Sanger, 1970; Conway Evans Prize, Royal Soc. and RCP, 1972; Gairdner Foundn Award, Canada, jtly with Ruth Sanger, 1972. Hon. Fellow, RSM, 1974. Kruis van Verdienst, Netherlands Red Cross, 1959. *Publications:* (with Ruth Sanger) Blood Groups in Man, 1950, 6th edn, 1975; many papers in genetical and medical journals. *Address:* 22 Vicarage Road, East Sheen, SW14 8RU. *T:* 01-876 1508.

RACE, Ruth Ann; see Sanger, Dr R. A.

RACE, Steve, (Stephen Russell Race); broadcaster, musician and author; *b* Lincoln, 1 April 1921; *s* of Russell Tinniswood Race and Robina Race (*née* Hurley); *m* 1st, Marjorie Clair Leng (*d* 1969); one *d*; 2nd, Léonie Rebecca Govier Mather. *Educ:* Lincoln Sch. (now Christ's Hospital Sch.); Royal Academy of Music. FRAM 1978. Served War, RAF, 1941–46; free-lance pianist, arranger and composer, 1946–55; Light Music Adviser to Associated-Rediffusion Ltd, 1955–60; conductor for many TV series incl. Tony Hancock and Peter Sellers Shows. Appearances in radio and TV shows include: My Music, Musician at Large, A Good Read, Mainly for Pleasure, Any Questions?, Music Now; radio reviews in The Listener, 1975–80; long-playing records and commentary for Nat. Gall., London, Glasgow Art Gall. and Nat. Mus. of Wales, 1977–80. Mem. Council, Royal Albert Hall of Arts and Scis. FRSA 1975. *Principal compositions:* Nicola (Ivor Novello Award); Faraway Music; The Pied Piper; incidental music for Richard The Third, Cyrano de Bergerac, Twelfth Night (BBC); Cantatas: Song of King David; The Day of the Donkey (and other Songs of Praise for Juniors); misc. works incl. ITV advertising sound-tracks (Venice Award, 1962; Cannes Award, 1963); film scores include: Calling Paul Temple, Three Roads to Rome, Against The Tide, Land of Three Rivers. *Publications:* Musician at Large: an autobiography, 1979; My Music, 1979; Dear Music Lover, 1981. *Recreations:* reading about the past, looking at paintings, the open air. *Address:* Martins End Lane, Great Missenden, Bucks HP16 9HS. *T:* Great Missenden 4443.

RACZYNSKI, Count Edward, Dr Juris; Chairman, Polish Cultural Foundation, since 1970; Hon. President, The Polish Institute and Sikorski Museum, since 1977 (Chairman, 1966–77); Polish President-in-exile, since 1979; *b* 19 Dec. 1891; *s* of Count Edouard Raczynski and Countess Rose Potocka; *m* 1st, 1925, Joyous (*d* 1930), *d* of Sir Arthur Basil Markham, 1st Bt, and Lucy, CBE, *d* of Captain A. B. Cunningham, late RA; 2nd, 1932, Cecile (*d* 1962), *d* of Edward Jaroszynski and Wanda Countess Sierakowska; three *d*. *Educ:* Universities of Krakow and Leipzig; London School of Economics and Political Science. Entered Polish Ministry of Foreign Affairs, 1919; served in Copenhagen, London, and Warsaw; Delegate to Disarmament Conference, Geneva, 1932–34; Polish Minister accredited to the League of Nations, 1932–34; Polish Ambassador to the Court of St James's, 1934–45; Acting Polish Minister for Foreign Affairs, 1941–42; Minister of State in charge of Foreign Affairs, Cabinet of Gen. Sikorski, 1942–43; Chief Polish

Rep. on Interim Treasury Cttee for Polish Questions, 1945–47; Hon. Chief Polish Adviser, Ministry of Labour and National Service, 1952–Dec. 1956; Chairman: Polish Research Centre, London, 1940–67. Grand Officier of the Order of Polonia Restituta, Order of White Eagle, Poland, Grand Cross of the Crown of Rumania, etc. *Publications:* In Allied London: Diary 1939-45 (in Polish); In Allied London: (Wartime Diaries), (in English), 1963; Rogalin and its Inhabitants (in Polish), 1963; Pani Róża (in Polish), 1969; Book of Verse (in Polish), 1960; Memoirs of Viridianne Fiszer (translated from French to Polish), 1975; From Narcyz Kulikowski to Winston Churchill (in Polish), 1976. *Recreations:* tennis, golf, skating, ski-ing. *Address:* 8 Lennox Gardens, SW1; 5 Krakowskie Przedmieście, Warsaw, Poland.

RADCLIFFE, Anthony Frank; Keeper, Department of Sculpture, Victoria and Albert Museum, since 1979; *b* Wivenhoe, Essex, 23 Feb. 1933; *s* of Dr Walter Radcliffe and Muriel Laure Radcliffe (*née* Brée); *m* 1960, Enid Clair Cawkwell; two *s*. *Educ:* Oundle Sch.; Gonville and Caius Coll., Cambridge (MA). Victoria and Albert Museum: joined Dept of Circulation, 1958; transferred to Dept of Architecture and Sculpture, 1960; Res. Asst, Dept of Circulation, 1961–67; Personal Asst to Dir, 1967–74; Asst Keeper, Dept of Architecture and Sculpture, 1974–79. *Publications:* European Bronze Statuettes, 1966; Jean-Baptiste Carpeaux, 1968; (with J. Pope-Hennessy and T. Hodgkinson) The Frick Collection: an illustrated catalogue, III, IV, 1970; (with C. Avery) Giambologna, sculptor to the Medici, 1978; contribs to Burlington Mag., Apollo, Connoisseur, etc. *Address:* 5 Kennylands Road, Sonning Common, Reading RG4 9JR. *T:* Kidmore End 722182.

RADCLIFFE, Francis Charles Joseph; *b* 23 Oct. 1939; *s* of Charles Joseph Basil Nicholas Radcliffe and Norah Radcliffe (*née* Percy); *m* 1968, Nicolette, *e d* of Eugene Randag; one *s* two *d*. *Educ:* Ampleforth Coll.; Gonville and Caius Coll., Cambridge (MA). Called to the Bar, Gray's Inn, 1962; a Recorder of the Crown Court, 1979–82. Governor, Bar Grammar Sch., York. Mem., Assoc. of Lawyers for the Defence of the Unborn. Contested (Christian: stop abortion candidate) York, 1979; founded York Christian Party, 1981. *Recreations:* shooting, beagling, gardening, etc. *Address:* 11 King's Bench Walk, Temple, EC4Y 7EQ; 40 The Horseshoe, York.

RADCLIFFE, Hugh John Reginald Joseph, MBE 1944; Chairman, Dun and Bradstreet Ltd, 1974–76; *b* 3 March 1911; 2nd *s* of Sir Everard Radcliffe, 5th Bt; *m* 1937, Marie Therese, *d* of late Maj.-Gen. Sir Cecil Pereira, KCB, CMG; five *s* one *d*. *Educ:* Downside. Dep. Chm., London Stock Exchange, 1967–70. Kt Comdr St Silvester (Papal), 1965. *Address:* The White House, Stoke, Andover, Hants.

See also Sir S. E. Radcliffe, Bt.

RADCLIFFE, Percy; farmer; Chairman, Isle of Man Government Executive Council (Manx Cabinet), since 1981; *b* 14 Nov. 1916; *s* of Arthur and Annie Radcliffe; *m* 1942, Barbara Frances Crowe; two *s* one *d*. *Educ:* Ramsey Grammar Sch., Isle of Man. Member (Ind.) Isle of Man Govt, 1963, re-elected 1966, 1971, 1976; elected by House of Keys to be Mem. Legislative Council, 1980; Chairman: IoM Local Govt Board, 1966–76; Finance Board, 1976–81; elected by Tynwald (Govt of IoM) first Chm. of Manx Cabinet, 1981. Member: Isle of Man Agricultural Marketing Soc., 1945–75; British Horse Driving Soc., 1979–. Silver Jubilee Medal, 1977. *Address:* Kellaway, Sulby, Isle of Man. *T:* Sulby 7257.

RADCLIFFE, Sir Sebastian Everard, 7th Bt *cr* 1813; *b* 8 June 1972; *s* of Sir Joseph Benedict Everard Henry Radcliffe, 6th Bt, MC and of Marcia Anne Helen, *y d* of Major David Turville Constable Maxwell, Bosworth Hall, Husbands Bosworth, Rugby; *S* father, 1975. *Heir:* uncle Hugh John Reginald Joseph Radcliffe, *qv. Address:* Le Château de Cheseaux, 1033 Cheseaux, Vaud, Switzerland.

RADCLYFFE, Sir Charles Edward M.; see Mott-Radclyffe.

RADDA, Dr George K., MA, DPhil; FRS 1980; Fellow and Tutor in Organic Chemistry, Merton College, Oxford, since 1964; University Lecturer in Biochemistry, Oxford University, since 1966; *b* 9 June 1936; *s* of Dr Gyula Radda and Dr Anna Bernolak; *m* 1961, Mary O'Brien; two *s* one *d*. *Educ:* Pannonhalma, Hungary; Eötvös Univ., Budapest, Hungary; Merton Coll., Oxford (BSc Cl. 1, Chem., 1960; DPhil 1962). Res. Associate, Univ. of California, 1962–63; Lectr in Organic Chemistry, St John's Coll., Oxford, 1963–64. Mem., various Editorial Bds of scientific jls including: Editor, Biochemical and Biophysical Research Communications, 1977–; Man. Editor, Biochimica et Biophysica Acta, 1977–. Founder Mem., Oxford Enzyme Gp, 1970–. Colworth Medal, Biochem. Soc., 1969; Feldberg Prize, Feldberg Foundn, 1982; British Heart Foundn Prize and Gold Medal for cardiovascular research, 1982. *Publications:* articles in books and in jls of biochemistry and medicine. *Recreations:* opera, swimming, jazz. *Address:* Merton College, Oxford. *T:* Oxford 49651.

RADFORD, (Courtenay Arthur) Ralegh, FBA 1956; *b* 7 Nov. 1900; *o s* of late Arthur Lock and Ada M. Radford; unmarried. *Educ:* St George's School, Harpenden; Exeter College, Oxford. BA 1921; MA 1937; Inspector of Ancient Monuments in Wales and Monmouthshire, 1929–34; Director of the British School at Rome, 1936–39; Member of Royal Commission on Ancient Monuments in Wales and Monmouthshire, 1935–46; Member of Royal Commission on Historical Monuments (England), 1953–76; supervised excavations at Tintagel, Ditchley, Castle Dore, the Hurlers, Whithorn,

Glastonbury, Birsay and elsewhere; FSA 1928 (Vice-Pres. 1954-58; Gold Medal, 1972); FRHistS 1930; President: Prehistoric Soc., 1954-58; Roy. Archæological Inst., 1960-63; Cambrian Archæological Assoc., 1961; Soc. of Medieval Archæology, 1969-71. Hon. DLitt Glasgow, 1963; Univ. of Wales, 1963; Exeter, 1973; *Publications:* Reports on the Excavations at Tintagel, Ditchley, Whithorn, etc.; various articles on archæological subjects. *Address:* Culmcott, Uffculme, Devon EX15 3AT. *Club:* Athenæum.

RADFORD, Air Cdre Dudley Spencer, CB 1957; DSO 1944; DFC 1940; AFC 1943; *b* 21 Sept. 1910; *s* of late John Francis Radford and of Alice Radford; *m* 1943, Pamela Biddulph Corr (*née* Padley); two *d. Educ:* Bedford School. Pilot training, 1932; No III Fighter Sqdn, 1933-35; flying instructor, 1936-38; Asst Adjt No 600 City of London Sqdn, 1938; Adjutant No 616 S Riding Sqdn, 1939; OC No 8 Sqdn, Aden, 1940-41; Chief Instructor: No 1 Flying Instructors' School, 1942; No 3 Advanced Flying Unit, 1943; OC No 10 Bomber Sqdn, 1944; RN Staff College course, 1944-45; Group Capt. Trng, HQ Transport Comd, 1945-46; Officer Comdg: RAF Spitalgate, 1947; RAF Wittering, 1948; RAF Liaison Officer, S Rhodesian Govt, 1949-50; Dep. Dir Postings, Air Ministry, 1951-53; idc 1954; Dir of Tactical and Air Transport Ops, 1955-56; Commandant, Central Reconnaissance Establishment, 1957-59; retired 1959. Gen. Services Manager, H. S. A. Ltd, 1960-75, retired. Officer, Order of Leopold (Belgium), 1947. *Address:* New Road Cottage, Prestbury, Cheshire.

RADFORD, Joseph; Public Trustee, 1978-80; *b* 7 April 1918; *s* of Thomas Radford and Elizabeth Ann Radford (*née* Sanders); *m* 1976, Rosemary Ellen Murphy. *Educ:* Herbert Strutt, Belper; Nottingham Univ. Admitted solicitor, 1940. First Cl. Hons, Law Soc. Intermediate, 1937; Dist., Law Soc. Final, 1940. Served War, 1940-47, RA; 41st (5th North Staffordshire) RA; 1st Maritime Regt, RA; Staff, MELF (Major). Joined Public Trustee Office, 1949; Chief Admin. Officer, 1973-75; Asst Public Trustee, 1975-78. *Address:* 80 Cunningham Park, Harrow, Mddx HA1 4QJ.

RADFORD, Ralegh; *see* Radford, C. A. R.

RADFORD, Robert Edwin, CB 1979; Assistant Director General, St John Ambulance Association, since 1981; Deputy Secretary and Principal Finance Officer, Department of Health and Social Security, 1977-81; *b* 1 April 1921; *s* of late Richard James Radford and late May Eleanor Radford (*née* Briant); *m* 1945, Eleanor Margaret, *d* of late John Idwal Jones; one *s* one *d. Educ:* Royal Grammar Sch., Guildford. Board of Educn, 1938. Served War, Lieut, RNVR, 1940-46. Colonial Office: Asst Principal, 1947; Private Sec. to Permanent Under-Sec. of State for the Colonies, 1950-51; Principal, 1951; First Sec., UK Commn, Singapore, 1961-63; Asst Sec., Dept of Techn. Co-op., 1963; transferred to ODM, 1964; Counsellor, British Embassy, Washington, and UK Alternate Exec. Dir, IBRD, 1965-67; Under Secretary: FCO (ODA), 1973; DHSS, 1974-76. Mem., SW Surrey HA, 1982-. *Recreations:* walking, reading. *Address:* Highfield, Nether Mount, Guildford, Surrey GU2 5LL. *T:* Guildford 61822.

RADFORD, Sir Ronald (Walter), KCB 1976 (CB 1971); MBE 1947; Secretary-General, Customs Co-operation Council, since 1978; *b* 28 Feb. 1916; *er s* of late George Leonard Radford and Ethel Mary Radford; *m* 1949, Jean Alison Dunlop Strange; one *s* one *d. Educ:* Southend-on-Sea High Sch.; St John's Coll., Cambridge (Schol., Wrangler, MA). Joined ICS, 1939; Dist Magistrate and Collector, Shahabad, Bihar, 1945; on leave, prep. to retirement from ICS, 1947; Admin. Class, Home CS, and posted to HM Customs and Excise, 1947; Asst Sec., 1953; Comr, 1965; Dep. Chm., 1970; Chm., 1973-77. Chm., Civil Service and PO Lifeboat Fund, 1977-; Mem. Management Cttee, RNLI, 1977-. *Address:* 171 Avenue de Tervuren, 1040 Brussels, Belgium; 4 Thomas Close, Brentwood, Essex CM15 8BS. *T:* Brentwood 211567. *Clubs:* Reform, Civil Service, City Livery; MCC; International Château Sainte-Anne (Brussels).

RADICE, Edward Albert, CBE 1946; *b* 2 Jan. 1907; *s* of C. A. Radice, ICS and Alice Effie (*née* Murray), DSc (Econ); *m* 1936, Joan Keeling; one *s* one *d. Educ:* Winchester Coll.; Magdalen Coll., Oxford. DPhil, Oxford. Commonwealth Fund Fellow, Columbia Univ., New York, 1933-35; Assistant Professor of Economics, Wesleyan University, Middletown, Conn., 1937-39; League of Nations Secretariat, 1939; Ministry of Economic Warfare, 1940-44; HM Foreign Service, 1945-53; Min. of Defence, 1953-70 (Dir of Economic Intelligence, 1966-70); Senior Research Fellow, St Antony's Coll., Oxford, 1970-73. *Publications:* (jt) An American Experiment, 1936; Fundamental Issues in the United States, 1936; Savings in Great Britain, 1922-35, 1939; (contrib.) Communist Power in Europe 1944-1949, 1977; papers in Econometrica, Oxford Economic Papers, Economic History Review. *Address:* 2 Talbot Road, Oxford. *T:* Oxford 55573.
See also I. de L. Radice.

RADICE, Fulke Rosavo, CBE 1959; MA; late Vice-Director International Bureau of Universal Postal Union (1946-58); *b* Naples, 8 Feb. 1888; British subject; *s* of late Albert Hampden Radice, Thistleborough, NI and Adelaide Anna Teresa (*née* Visetti); *m* 1917, Katharine Stella Mary Speck (*d* 1974) *d* of late Canon J. H. Speck and Mrs Speck (*née* Dalrymple); two *s* (and one *s* killed fighting in French Maquis, 1944). *Educ:* Bedford School (Scholar); Brasenose Coll., Oxford (open scholarship in History; 2nd Cl. Hons Mods (classical), 1909; 1st Cl. Mod. History, 1911). Home Civil Service, 1911; Secretary's Office, Gen. Post Office, 1911-46. Head of Brit. Secretariat of Universal

Postal Union Congress, 1929, Head of Congress Secretariat at UPU Congresses, 1947, 1952, 1957. Served European War, 1914-18, in France, Salonica, Egypt, Italy; War of 1939-45 in Home Guard. *Publications:* The Radice Family, 1979; articles in Nineteenth Century and After, and in History. *Recreations:* rifle shooting (Oxford half blue, Oxford long range; English XX, 1909, 1910; King's Prize at Bisley, gold and silver medals, 1910; record score); Rugby football; ski-ing; freemasonry; historical studies. *Address:* 32 Jersey Avenue, Cheltenham, Glos GL52 2SZ; c/o Coutts & Co., 440 Strand, WC2. *Club:* English-Speaking Union.

RADICE, Giles Heneage; MP (Lab) Chester-le-Street, since March 1973; *b* 4 Oct. 1936. *Educ:* Magdalen Coll., Oxford. Head of Research Dept, General and Municipal Workers' Union (GMWU), 1966-73. Front Bench Spokesman on foreign affairs, 1981, on employment, 1981-. Member: Council, Policy Studies Inst., 1978-; Exec., Fabian Soc. *Publications:* Democratic Socialism, 1965; (ed jointly) More Power to People, 1968; (co-author) Will Thorne, 1974; The Industrial Democrats, 1978. *Recreations:* reading, tennis. *Address:* 40 Inverness Street, NW1.

RADICE, Italo de Lisle, CB 1969; Appointed Member, Royal Patriotic Fund Corporation, since 1969; *b* 2 March 1911; *s* of Charles Albert Radice, ICS, and Alice Effie (*née* Murray); *m* 1935, Betty Dawson; three *s* (and one *d* decd). *Educ:* Blundell's School; Magdalen College, Oxford (demy). Admitted Solicitor, 1938; Public Trustee Office, 1939; Military Government East and North Africa, Italy, and Germany, 1941-46; Treasury, 1946, Under-Secretary, 1961-68; Sec. and Comptroller General, Nat. Debt Office, 1969-76. Dir, Central Trustee Savings Bank Ltd, 1976-80. Comr for Income Tax, City of London, 1972-. Cavaliere Ufficiale dell'Ordine al Merito (Italy), 1981. *Address:* 65 Cholmeley Crescent, N6. *T:* 01-348 4122; Old Post Office, Berrick Salome, Oxford. *T:* Oxford 891100.
See also E. A. Radice.

RADJI, Parviz Camran; diplomat; Ambassador of Iran to the Court of St James's, 1976-79; *b* 1936. *Educ:* Trinity Hall, Cambridge (MA Econs). National Iranian Oil Co., 1959-62; Private Sec. to Minister of Foreign Affairs, 1962-65; Private Sec. to Prime Minister, subseq. Personal Asst, 1965-72; Special Adviser to Prime Minister, 1972-76. *Publication:* In the Service of the Peacock Throne: the diaries of the Shah's last Ambassador to London, 1983. *Address:* 85 Holland Park W11.

RADLEY-SMITH, Eric John, MS; FRCS; Surgeon: Royal Free Hospital, London; Brentford Hospital; Epsom Hospital; Neurosurgeon, Royal National Throat, Nose and Ear Hospital. *Educ:* Paston; King's College, London; King's College Hospital. MB, BS (Hons, Distinction in Medicine, Surgery, Forensic Medicine and Hygiene), 1933; MS, London, 1936; LRCP, 1933; FRCS 1935 (MRCS 1933). Served War of 1939-45, Wing Comdr i/c Surgical Div. RAFVR. Formerly: Surgical Registrar, King's Coll. Hosp.; House Surgeon, National Hosp. for Nervous Diseases, Queen Square. Examnr in Surgery, Univs of London and West Indies. Mem. Court, RCS. Mem. Assoc. of British Neurosurgeons; Fellow, Assoc. of Surgeons of Great Britain. *Publications:* papers in medical journals. *Recreations:* football and farming.

RADNOR, 8th Earl of, *cr* 1765; **Jacob Pleydell-Bouverie;** Bt 1713-14; Viscount Folkestone, Baron Longford, 1747; Baron Pleydell-Bouverie, 1765; *b* 10 Nov. 1927; *e s* of 7th Earl of Radnor, KG, KCVO, and Helen Olivia, *d* of late Charles R. W. Adeane, CB; *S* father, 1968; *m* 1st, 1953, Anne (marr. diss. 1962), *d* of Donald Seth-Smith, Njoro, Kenya and Whitsbury Cross, near Fordingbridge, Hants; two *s*; 2nd, 1963, Margaret Robin, *d* of late Robin Fleming, Catter House, Drymen; four *d. Educ:* Harrow; Trinity Coll., Cambridge (BA Agriculture). *Heir: s* Viscount Folkestone, *qv. Address:* Longford Castle, Salisbury, Wilts. *T:* Salisbury 29732.

RADO, Prof. Richard, FRS 1978; Professor of Pure Mathematics, University of Reading, 1954-71, Emeritus since 1971; Canadian Commonwealth Fellow, University of Waterloo, Ontario, 1971-72; *b* 28 April 1906; 2nd *s* of Leopold Rado, Berlin; *m* 1933, Luise, *e d* of Hermann Zadek, Berlin; one *s. Educ:* University of Berlin (DPhil); University of Göttingen; University of Cambridge (PhD). Lecturer, Sheffield Univ., 1936-47; Reader, King's College, Univ. of London, 1947-54. Vis. Prof., Calgary, Alberta, 1973. London Mathematical Society: Mem. of Council, 1948-57; Hon. Sec., 1953-54; Vice-President, 1954-56. Chm., British Combinatorial Cttee. FIMA. Dr rer. nat. *hc* Freie Univ., Berlin, 1981. Sen. Berwick Prize, London Mathematical Soc., 1972. *Publications:* articles in various journals on topics in pure mathematics; Mem. Editorial Bds of Aequationes mathematicae, Discrete Mathematics, Jl Combinatorial Theory, Combinatorica; *relevant publication:* Festschrift: Studies in Pure Mathematics, ed Prof. L. Mirsky, 1971. *Recreations:* music, reading, walking. *Address:* 14 Glebe Road, Reading RG2 7AG. *T:* 871281.

RADZINOWICZ, Sir Leon, Kt 1970; MA, LLD; FBA 1973; Fellow of Trinity College, Cambridge, since 1948; Wolfson Professor of Criminology, University of Cambridge, 1959-73, and Director of the Institute of Criminology, 1960-72; Associate Fellow, Silliman College, Yale, since 1966; Adjunct Professor of Law and Criminology, Columbia Law School, since 1966; *b* Poland, 15 Aug. 1906; *m* 1st, 1933, Irene Szereszewski (marr. diss., 1955); 2nd, 1958, Mary Ann (marr. diss. 1979), *d* of Gen. Nevins, Gettysburg, Pa, USA; one *s* one *d*; 3rd, 1979, Isolde Klarmann, *d* of late Prof. Emil and Elfriede Doernenburg, and widow of Prof. Adolph Klarmann, Philadelphia;

naturalised British subject, 1947. *Educ:* Warsaw, Paris, Geneva and Rome. University of Paris, 1924-25; Licencié en Droit, Univ. of Geneva, 1927; Doctor of Law, Rome, 1928; LLD Cambridge, 1951. Lectr, Univ. of Geneva, 1928-31; Doctor of Law, Cracow, 1929; Reported on working of penal system in Belgium, 1930; Lectr, Free Univ. of Warsaw, 1932, and Asst Prof., 1936. Came to England on behalf of Polish Ministry of Justice to report on working of English penal system, 1938; Asst Dir of Research, Univ. of Cambridge, 1946-49; Dir, Dept of Criminal Science, Univ. of Cambridge, 1949-59; Walter E. Meyer Research Prof. of Law, Yale Law Sch., 1962-63; Distinguished Prof. of Criminal Justice, John Jay Coll. of Criminal Justice, City of NY Univ., 1978-79; Vis. Prof. and Carpentier Lectr, Columbia Law Sch.; Dist. Prof. of Criminology, Rutgers Univ., 1970; Visiting Professor: Virginia Law School, 1968-; Univ. of Pennsylvania, 1970-73; Benjamin Cardozo Law Sch., Yeshiva Univ., 1979; Visitor, Princeton Inst. for Advanced Study, 1975; Overseer, Pennsylvania Law Sch. and Associate Trustee, Pennsylvania Univ., 1978-. Mem., Conseil de Direction de l'Assoc. Intern. de Droit Pénal, Paris, 1947-; Vice-Pres. Internat. Soc. of Social Defence, 1956-; Head of Social Defence Section, UN, New York, 1947-48. Mem. Roy. Commission on Capital Punishment, 1949-53; Mem. Advisory Council on the Treatment of Offenders, Home Office, 1950-63; Jt Chm., Second UN Congress on Crime, 1955; Chm. Sub-Cttee on Maximum Security in Prisons, 1967-68; Mem. Advisory Coun. on the Penal System, 1966-; first Pres., Brit. Acad. of Forensic Sciences, 1960-61; Vice-Pres., 1961-; First Chm. Council of Europe Sci. Cttee, Problems of Crime, 1963-70; Mem. Royal Commn on Penal System in Eng. and Wales, 1964-66; Consultant, President's Nat. Commn on Violence, Washington, 1968-69; Hon. Vice-Chm., Fifth UN Congress on Crime, Geneva, 1975. Hon. LLD Leicester, 1965. For. Hon. Mem., Amer. Acad. of Arts and Sciences, 1973; Hon. For. Mem., Aust. Acad. Forensic Scis, 1973; Hon. Mem., Amer. Law Inst., 1981. Coronation Medal, 1953. Chevalier de l'Ordre de Léopold, Belgium, 1930. James Barr Ames Prize and Medal, Faculty of Harvard Law School, 1950; Bruce Smith Sr award, Amer. Acad. Criminal Justice Sciences, 1976; Sellin-Glueck Award, Amer. Assoc. of Criminology, 1976. *Publications:* Sir James Fitzjames Stephen (Selden Soc. Lect.), 1957; In Search of Criminology, 1961 (Italian edn 1965; French edn 1965; Spanish edn 1971); The Need for Criminology, 1965; Ideology and Crime (Carpentier Lectures), 1966, (Italian edn 1968); The Dangerous Offender (Frank Newsam Memorial Lecture), 1968; History of English Criminal Law, Vol. I, 1948 (under auspices of Pilgrim Trust), Vols II and III, 1956, Vol. IV, 1968 (under auspices of Rockefeller Foundation); (ed with Prof. M. E. Wolfgang) Crime and Justice, 3 vols, 1971, 2nd edn 1977; (with Joan King) The Growth of Crime, 1977; (with Dr R. Hood) Criminology and the Administration of Criminal Justice: a Bibliography (Joseph L. Andrews Award, Amer. Assoc. of Law Libraries 1977), 1976; (ed) English Studies in Criminal Science, now Cambridge Studies in Criminology, 50 vols; numerous articles in English and foreign periodicals. *Address:* Trinity College, Cambridge; Rittenhouse Claridge Apartment 2416, Rittenhouse Square, Philadelphia, Pa 19103, USA. *T:* 215-546-9250. *Club:* Athenæum.

RAE, Charles Robert Angus; *b* 20 Feb. 1922; *s* of Charles E. L. Rae and Gladys M. Horsfall; *m* 1948, Philippa Neild; one *s* two *d*. *Educ:* Eton Coll.; Trinity Coll., Cambridge; London Sch. of Slavonic Studies. BA (Hons History) Cantab, 1945, MA 1948. War service in N Russia, RNVR, 1943-45. Foreign Office, 1947, service in Rome, 1950-54, Mexico City, 1957-59, Moscow, 1959-60; Private Sec. to Parly Under-Sec., 1954-57; seconded to Dept of Technical Co-operation on its formation, 1961; transf. to ODM as Asst Sec., 1964; Under Sec., 1975-79. Mem., Bd of Exec. Dirs, Inter-American Development Bank, 1979-82. Chm., Chelsham and Farleigh Parish Council, 1974-79. *Recreations:* walking, gardening. *Address:* c/o National Westminster Bank, Warlingham, Surrey.

RAE, John Malcolm, MA, PhD; Headmaster of Westminster School, since 1970; *b* 20 March 1931; *s* of late Dr L. John Rae, radiologist, London Hospital, and Blodwen Rae; *m* 1955, Daphne Ray Simpson, *d* of John Phimester Simpson; two *s* four *d*. *Educ:* Bishop's Stortford Coll.; Sidney Sussex Coll., Cambridge. MA Cantab 1958; PhD 1965. 2nd Lieut Royal Fusiliers, 1950-51. Asst Master, Harrow School, 1955-66; Dept of War Studies, King's Coll., London, 1962-65; Headmaster, Taunton School, 1966-70. Member: Council, Nat. Cttee for Electoral Reform. Council, King's Coll. London; Chm., HMC, 1977. Trustee, Imperial War Mus. JP Middlesex, 1961-66. *Publications:* The Custard Boys, 1960 (filmed 1979); (jtly, film) Reach for Glory (UN Award); Conscience and Politics, 1970; The Golden Crucifix, 1974; The Treasure of Westminster Abbey, 1975; Christmas is Coming, 1976; Return to the Winter Palace, 1978; The Third Twin: a ghost story, 1980; The Public School Revolution: Britain's independent schools, 1964-1979, 1981; articles in The Times, Encounter; columnist in Times Ed. Supp. *Recreations:* writing, swimming, children, cinema. *Address:* 17 Dean's Yard, SW1. *T:* 01-222 6904. *Clubs:* Royal Automobile; Hawks (Cambridge).

RAE, Robert Wright; Civil Service, retired; Clerk to the General Commissioners of Income Tax, Bromley and Blackheath Divisions, since 1977; *b* 27 March 1914; *s* of Walter Rae and Rachel Scott; *m* 1st, 1945, Joan McKenzie (*d* 1966); two *s* ; 2nd, 1977, Marjorie Ann Collyer. *Educ:* George Heriot's Sch., Edinburgh; Edinburgh Univ. MA 1st cl. hons. Asst Inspector of Taxes, 1936; Dep. Chief Inspector of Taxes, 1973-75; Dir Personnel, Inland Revenue, 1975-77. *Recreations:* gardening, walking. *Address:* Oak Lodge, Blackbrook Lane, Bickley, Bromley BR1 2LP. *T:* 01-467 2377.

RAE, Air Vice-Marshal Ronald Arthur R.; *see* Ramsay Rae.

RAE, Hon. Sir Wallace (Alexander Ramsay), Kt 1976; Agent-General for Queensland, in London, 1974-80; grazier, Ramsay Park, Blackall, Queensland; *b* 31 March 1914; *s* of George Ramsay Rae and Alice Ramsay Rae. *Educ:* Sydney, Australia. Served War: RAAF Coastal Command, 1939; Pilot, Flt Lt, UK, then OC Test Flight, Amberley, Qld. Mem., Legislative Assembly (Nat. Party of Australia) for Gregory, Qld, 1957-74; Minister for: Local Govt and Electricity, 1969-74; Lands and Forestry, Qld, 1974. Founder Pres., Pony Club Assoc. of Queensland. *Recreations:* bowls, golf. *Address:* The Gardens, Alice Street, Brisbane, Australia. *Clubs:* Queensland, Tattersall's (Brisbane); Longreach (Longreach).

See also Air Vice-Marshal R. A. Ramsay Rae.

RAE SMITH, David Douglas, CBE 1976; MC 1946; MA; FCA; Senior Partner, Deloitte Haskins & Sells, Chartered Accountants, 1973-82 (Partner, 1954); *b* 15 Nov. 1919; *s* of Sir Alan Rae Smith, KBE, and Lady (Mabel Grace) Rae Smith; *m* 1947, Margaret Alison Watson; three *s* one *d*. *Educ:* Radley Coll.; Christ Church, Oxford (MA). FCA 1959. Served War, RA, 1939-46: ME, N Africa and NW Europe; Captain; MC and mentioned in despatches. Chartered accountant, 1950. Hon. Treasurer, RIIA, 1961-81. Dir, Thomas Tilling Ltd, 1982-. Member: Licensed Dealers Tribunal, 1974-; Council, Radley Coll., 1966- (Chm., 1976-). *Recreations:* horse racing, golf, travel. *Address:* Oakdale, Crockham Hill, Edenbridge, Kent. *T:* Crockham Hill 220. *Club:* Gresham.

RAEBURN, David Antony; Headmaster of Whitgift School, Croydon, since 1970; *b* 22 May 1927; *e* s of late Walter Augustus Leopold Raeburn, QC; *m* 1961, Mary Faith, *d* of Arthur Hubbard, Salisbury, Rhodesia; two *s* one *d*. *Educ:* Charterhouse; Christ Church, Oxford (Schol., MA). 1st cl. hons Hon. Mods, 2nd in Greats. Nat. Service, 1949-51: Temp. Captain, RAEC. Asst Master: Bristol Grammar Sch., 1951-54; Bradfield Coll., 1955-58 (prod. Greek Play, 1955 and 1958); Senior Classics Master, Alleyn's Sch., Dulwich, 1958-62; Headmaster, Beckenham and Penge Grammar Sch., 1963-70 (school's name changed to Langley Park School for Boys, Beckenham in 1969). Schoolteacher Fellow-Commoner, Jesus Coll., Cambridge, 1980. Chm. Classics Cttee, Schs Council, 1974-80; Pres., Jt Assoc. of Classical Teachers, 1983-. FRSA 1969. *Publications:* articles on Greek play production. *Recreation:* play production (produced Cambridge Greek Play, 1980, 1983). *Address:* Haling House, 38 Haling Park Road, South Croydon CR2 6NE. *T:* 01-688 8114.

RAEBURN, Maj.-Gen. Sir Digby; *see* Raeburn, Maj.-Gen. Sir W. D. M.

RAEBURN, Prof. John Ross, CBE 1972; BSc (Agric.), PhD, MS; FRSE; FIBiol; Strathcona-Fordyce Professor of Agriculture, Aberdeen University, 1959-78; Principal, North of Scotland College of Agriculture, 1963-78; *b* 20 Nov. 1912; *s* of late Charles Raeburn and Margaret (*née* Ross); *m* 1941, Mary, *o d* of Alfred and Kathrine Roberts; one *s* three *d*. *Educ:* Manchester Grammar School; Edinburgh and Cornell Universities. Professor of Agricultural Economics, Nanking University, 1936-37; Research Officer, Oxford University, 1938-39; Ministry of Food Divisional statistician, 1939-41, Head Agricultural Plans Branch, 1941-46; Senior research officer, Oxford University, 1946-49; Reader in Agricultural Economics, London University, 1949-59. Visiting Professor, Cornell, 1950. Consultant to UN. Member: Agricultural Mission to Yugoslavia, 1951; Mission of Enquiry into Rubber Industry, Malaya, 1954; Colonial Economic Research Committee, 1949-61; Scottish Agricultural Improvement Council, 1960-71; Scottish Agricultural Develt Council, 1971-76; Verdon-Smith Committee, 1962-64; Council, Scottish Agricultural Colls, 1974-78. Hon. MA Oxford, 1946. FRSE 1961; FIBiol 1968. Vice-President, International Association of Agricultural Economists, 1964-70 (Hon. Life Mem., 1976-); President, Agric. Econ. Society, 1966-67 (Hon. Life Mem., 1981-). *Publications:* Preliminary economic survey of the Northern Territories of the Gold Coast, 1950; (jtly) Problems in the mechanisation of native agriculture in tropical African Territories, 1950; research bulletins and contributions to agricultural economic journals. *Recreations:* gardening, travel. *Address:* 30 Morningfield Road, Aberdeen AB2 4AQ.

RAEBURN, Michael Edward Norman; (4th Bt, *cr* 1923, but does not use the title); *b* 12 Nov. 1954; *s* of Sir Edward Alfred Raeburn, 3rd Bt, and of Joan, *d* of Frederick Hill; *S* father, 1977; *m* 1979, Penelope Henrietta Theodora Penn; one *s*. *Heir:* s Christopher Edward Alfred Raeburn, *b* 4 Dec. 1981. *Address:* Dewhurst Lodge, Wadhurst, East Sussex TN5 6QB.

RAEBURN, Maj.-Gen. Sir (William) Digby (Manifold), KCVO 1979; CB 1966; DSO 1945; MBE 1941; Major and Resident Governor, HM Tower of London, and Keeper of the Jewel House, 1971-79; *b* 6 Aug. 1915; *s* of late Sir Ernest Manifold Raeburn, KBE, and of Lady Raeburn; *m* 1960, Adeline Margaret (*née* Pryor). *Educ:* Winchester; Magdalene College, Cambridge (MA). Commnd into Scots Guards, 1936; comd 2nd Bn Scots Guards, 1953; Lieut-Col Comdg Scots Guards, 1958; Comdr, 1st Guards Bde Group, 1959; Comdr, 51st Infty Bde Group, 1960; Director of Combat Development (Army), 1963-65; Chief of Staff to C-in-C, Allied Forces, N Europe, 1965-68; Chief Instructor (Army), Imperial Defence College, 1968-70. Freeman of City of London, 1972. *Recreations:* ski-ing, shooting, sailing. *Address:* c/o Lloyds Bank Ltd, 6 Pall Mall, SW1. *Clubs:* Pratt's, Cavalry and Guards; Royal Yacht Squadron.

RAFAEL, Gideon; Ambassador of Israel, retired 1978; *b* Berlin, 5 March 1913; *s* of Max Rafael; *m* 1940, Nurit Weissberg; one *s* one *d*. *Educ:* Berlin Univ.

Went to Israel, 1934; Member, kibbutz, 1934-43; Jewish Agency Polit. Dept, 1943; in charge of prep. of Jewish case for JA Polit. Dept, Nuremberg War Crimes Trial, 1945-46; Member: JA Commn to Anglo-American Commn of Enquiry, 1946, and of JA Mission to UN Special Commn for Palestine, 1947; Israel Perm. Deleg. to UN, 1951-52; Alt. Rep. to UN, 1953; Rep. at UN Gen. Assemblies, 1947-66; Counsellor in charge of ME and UN Affairs, Min. for Foreign Affairs, 1953-57. Ambassador to Belgium and Luxembourg, 1957-60, and to the European Economic Community, 1959. Head, Israel Delegn to 2nd Geneva Conf. on Maritime Law, 1960; Dep. Dir-Gen., Min. of Foreign Affairs, 1960-65; Perm. Rep. to UN and Internat. Organizations in Geneva, Sept. 1965-April 1966; Special Ambassador and Adviser to Foreign Minister, 1966-67; Perm. Rep. to UN, 1967; Dir-Gen., Min. for Foreign Affairs, 1967-71; Head, Israel Delegn to UNCTAD III, 1972; Sen. Polit. Adviser, Foreign Ministry, 1972-73; Ambassador to the Court of St James's, 1973-77, and non-resident Ambassador to Ireland, 1975-77; Sen. Advr to Foreign Minister, 1977-78. *Publications:* Destination Peace: three decades of Israeli foreign policy, 1981; articles on foreign affairs in Israel and internat. periodicals. *Address:* Ministry for Foreign Affairs, Jerusalem, Israel.

RAFFERTY, Hon. Joseph Anstice, BA; FAIM, FID; Agent General for Victoria in London, since 1979; *s* of late Col Rupert A. Rafferty, DSO, and Rose Sarah Anne Rafferty; *m* 1st, 1940, Miriam K. (decd), *d* of late Frank Richards, Devonport, Tas; two *s*; 2nd, 1973, Lyn, *d* of Grace Jones, Brisbane, Qld. *Educ:* Christ Coll., Univ. of Tas (BA); Univ. of Melbourne. FAIM 1958; FID 1964. Commonwealth Public Service, 1934-45; Personnel Manager, Australian National Airways, 1945-53; Personnel Management and Indust. Relations Consultant, 1953-70 (own practice; co. dir). MP (Lib) for: Caulfield, Vic, 1955-58; Ormond, Vic, 1958-67; Glenhuntly, Vic, 1967-79; Chm. Cttees and Dep. Speaker, Victorian Legislative Assembly, 1961-65; Parly Sec. for Cabinet, 1965-70; Minister for Labour and Industry, 1970-76; Asst Minister for Educn, 1970-72; Minister for Consumer Affairs, 1972-76; Minister for Fed. Affairs, 1974-76; Minister for Transport, 1976-78; Chief Sec., 1978-79; Leader, Aust. Delegn to ILO Conf., Geneva, 1974. Pres., Melbourne Jun. Chamber of Commerce, 1950; Treasurer, Nat. Assoc. of Jun. Chambers of Commerce of Australia, 1951; Councillor: Melbourne Chamber of Commerce, 1950-76; Victorian Employers' Fedn, 1952-65. Dep. Leader, Aust. Delegn, 5th World Congress, Jun. Chamber of Commerce, Manila, 1950; Aust. Delegate, 6th World Congress, Jun. Chamber of Industry, Montreal, 1951; Delegate, 17th Triennial Congress, British Empire Chambers of Commerce, London, 1951. Mem. Council, La Trobe Univ., Vic, 1964-70; Trustee, Caulfield Racecourse Reserve, 1965-. *Recreations:* golf, swimming, walking, travel. *Address:* Flat 11, Kingston House North, Princes Gate, SW7 1LN. *T:* 01-589 7892. *Clubs:* Caledonian, Royal Automobile, East India, Devonshire, Sports and Public Schools, Royal Wimbledon Golf; Athenæum, Metropolitan Golf, MCC (Melbourne).

RAGG, Rt. Rev. Theodore David Butler; *see* Huron, Bishop of.

RAGLAN, 5th Baron, *cr* 1852; **FitzRoy John Somerset;** JP; DL; Chairman, Cwmbran New Town Development Corporation, since 1970; *b* 8 Nov. 1927; *er s* of 4th Baron and Hon. Julia Hamilton, CStJ (*d* 1971), *d* of 11th Baron Belhaven and Stenton, CIE; *S* father, 1964; *m* 1973, Alice Baily, *yr d* of Peter Baily, Great Whittington, Northumberland. *Educ:* Westminster; Magdalen College, Oxford; Royal Agricultural College, Cirencester. Captain, Welsh Guards, RARO. Crown Estate Comr, 1970-74. Chm., Agriculture and Consumer Affairs sub-cttee, House of Lords Select Cttee on the European Community, 1975-77. Mem., Cttee of Managers, UK Housing Assoc. Ltd. Pres., Pre Retirement Assoc., 1970-77. Chairman: The Courtyard Arts Trust, 1974-; Bath Preservation Trust, 1975-77; The Bath Soc., 1977-; President: Gwent Foundn Concert Soc.; Usk Civic Soc.; Usk Farmers Club; Bath Centre of Nat. Trust; S Wales Reg., NSMHC, 1971-; Mem., Distinguished Members Panel, National Secular Soc.; Patron, The Raglan Baroque Players. JP 1958, DL 1971, Gwent (formerly Monmouthshire). Farms 600 acres at Usk. *Recreation:* being mechanic to a Bugatti. *Heir: b* Hon. Geoffrey Somerset [*b* 29 Aug. 1932; *m* 1956, Caroline Rachel, *d* of Col E. R. Hill, *qv*; one *s* two *d*]. *Address:* Cefntilla, Usk, Gwent. *T:* Usk 2050. *Clubs:* Beefsteak, Bugatti Owners, Vintage Sports Car; Usk Farmers'.

RAHIMTOOLA, Habib Ibrahim, BA, LLB, FRPS (Gt Br.); Chairman: Pakistan Red Cross, 1970-73; Pakistan Government Shipping Rates Advisory Board, 1959-71; Diplomatist, Pakistan; *b* 10 March 1912; *s* of late Sir Ibrahim Rahimtoola, GBE, KCSI, CIE, and Lady Kulsum Rahimtoola (*née* Mitha); *m* Zubeida, *d* of Sir Sultan Chinoy; two *s* one *d*. *Educ:* St Xavier's School and College and Govt Law Coll., Bombay. High Commissioner for Pakistan in London, 1947-52; Ambassador for Pakistan to France, 1952-53; Governor of Sind Province, 1953-54, of Punjab Province, June-Nov. 1954; Minister for Commerce, Central Govt, Nov. 1954-Aug. 1955; Minister for Commerce and Industries, 1955-56. President: Fed. of Muslim Chambers of Commerce and Industry, New Delhi, 1947-48; Bombay Provincial Muslim Chamber of Commerce, 1944-47; Bombay Provincial Muslim League Parly Board for Local Bodies, 1945-47; Young Men's Muslim Association, 1946-47; Bombay Muslim Students' Union, 1946-47-48. Director, Rotary Club, 1944-46; Chairman Membership Committee, 1945-46, Classification Cttee, 1944-45; Member: Govt of India Food Delegation to UK and USA, 1946; Govt of India Policy Cttee on Shipping; Govt of Bombay Housing Panel; Civil Aviation Conference, Govt of India, 1947; Cttee on Trade Policy, Govt of India, 1947; Indian Delegation to Internat. Trade and Employment Conference, Geneva, 1947; alternate Leader Indian Delegation Special Cereals Conference, Paris,

1947; Delegate or Leader of Pakistan Delegations: Inter-Allied Reparations Agency, Brussels, 1947-48-49-50-51; FAO, Geneva, 1947; Dollar Talks, London, 1947; Internat. Trade and Employment Conf., Geneva, 1947; Freedom of Information Conf., Geneva, 1948; Safety of Life at Sea (1948), and Sterling Balance (1948, 1949, 1950, 1951) Confs, London; Prime Ministers' Conferences, London, 1948, 1949, 1951; Foreign Ministers' Conference, Ceylon, 1950; ILO, 1950; Commonwealth Finance Ministers' Conf., 1948-52; SE Asia Conf. on Colombo Plan, 1950; Commonwealth Talks on Japanese Peace Treaty, London, 1950; General Agreement on Tariffs and Trade Conf., 1950-52; Supply Ministers' Conf., London, 1951; UNESCO, Paris, 1953; Afro-Asian Conf., Bandung, 1955; Leader Pakistan Trade Delegation to Brit. E Africa, 1956; Leader, Flood Control Conf., New Delhi, 1956; Chm. Karachi Development Authority, 1958-60; Chm. Water Co-ordination Council, 1958-60. Chm., or Dir, numerous companies. Internat. Counsellor, Lions Internat.; Chairman: Karachi Race Club Ltd, 1958-70 (Pres., 1970-71); Pak-Japan Cultural Assoc., 1959-. District Governor 305W, Lions International, 1964-67. FRSA; FRPS. Order of Sacred Treasure, Japan. *Recreations:* photography, horse racing, golf, tennis. *Address:* Bandenawaz Ltd, Standard Insurance House, I.I. Chundrigar Road, PO Box 4792, Karachi 2, Pakistan. *T:* 221267; Kulib, KDA 1, Habib I. Rahimtoola Road, Karachi 8. *T:* 432125. *Clubs:* MCC; Sind, Boat, Gymkhana (Karachi); Willingdon (Bombay).

RAHMAN PUTRA, Tunku (Prince) Abdul; *see* Abdul Rahman Putra.

RAHTZ, Prof. Philip Arthur; Professor of Archaeology, University of York, since 1979; *b* 11 March 1921; *s* of Frederick John Rahtz and Ethel May Rahtz; *m* 1st, 1940, Wendy Hewgill Smith (*d* 1977); three *s* two *d*; 2nd, 1979, Lorna Rosemary Watts. *Educ:* Bristol Grammar Sch. MA Bristol 1964. FSA. Served RAF, 1941-46. Articled to accountant, 1937-41; photographer (Studio Rahtz), 1946-49; schoolteacher, 1950-53; archaeological consultant, 1953-63; Univ. of Birmingham: Lectr, 1963-75; Sen. Lectr, later Reader, 1975-79. *Publications:* Rescue Archaeology, 1973; Chew Valley Lake Excavations, 1978; Saxon and Medieval Palaces at Cheddar, 1979; contrib. nat. and regional jls in England, W Africa and Poland. *Recreations:* swimming, sunbathing, music, travel. *Address:* Flat 3, King's Manor, York YO1 2EP. *T:* York 29170.

RAIKES, Sir (Henry) Victor (Alpin MacKinnon), KBE 1953; *b* 19 Jan. 1901; *s* of late H. St John Raikes, CBE, KC; *m* 1940, Audrey Elizabeth Joyce, *o d* of A. P. Wilson, Repton; two *d*. *Educ:* Westminster School; Trinity Coll., Cambridge (BA). Called to Bar, Inner Temple, 1924; contested (C) Ilkeston Division of Derbyshire, 1924 and 1929; MP (C) SE Essex, 1931-45; MP (C) Wavertree Division of Liverpool, 1945-50, Garston Division of Liverpool, 1950-57 (Ind C 1957). Chm., Monday Club, 1975-78. Flight Lieut RAFVR, 1940-42. JP Derbyshire, 1927. Kt of Malta, Order of St John of Jerusalem, 1970. *Address:* 8 Gledhow Gardens, SW5. *Clubs:* Carlton, MCC.

RAIKES, Vice-Adm. Sir Iwan (Geoffrey), KCB 1976; CBE 1967; DSC 1943; Flag Officer Submarines, and Commander Submarines, Eastern Atlantic Area, 1974-76; retired 1977; *b* 21 April 1921; *s* of Adm. Sir Robert Henry Taunton Raikes, KCB, CVO, DSO, and Lady (Ida Guinevere) Raikes; *m* 1947, Cecilia Primrose Hunt; one *s* one *d*. *Educ:* RNC Dartmouth. Entered Royal Navy, 1935; specialised in Submarines, 1941; Comdr, 1952; Captain, 1960; Rear-Adm., 1970; Naval Sec., 1970-72; Vice-Adm., 1973; Flag Officer, First Flotilla, 1973-74. *Recreations:* shooting, fishing, sailing, skiing, tennis, gardening. *Address:* Aberyscir Court, Brecon, Powys. *Club:* Naval and Military.

RAIKES, Sir Victor; *see* Raikes, Sir H. V. A. M.

RAILTON, Brig. Dame Mary, DBE 1956 (CBE 1953); *b* 28 May 1906; *d* of late James and Margery Railton. *Educ:* privately. Joined FANY, 1938; commissioned in ATS, 1940; WRAC 1949; Director WRAC, 1954-57; Deputy Controller Commandant, 1961-67. *Address:* 1 Frogmore Cottages, Great Bedwyn, Marlborough, Wilts.

RAILTON, Dame Ruth, DBE 1966 (OBE 1954); Founder and Musical Director of the National Youth Orchestra and National Junior Music School, 1947-65; *b* 14 Dec. 1915; *m* 1962, Cecil Harmsworth King, *qv*. *Educ:* St Mary's School, Wantage; Royal Academy of Music, London. Director of Music or Choral work for many schools and societies, 1937-49; Adjudicator, Fedn of Music Festivals, 1946-74; Pres., Ulster Coll. of Music, 1960-; Governor, Royal Ballet School, 1966-74. Founder and Pres., Irish Children's Theatre, 1978-; Vice-Pres., Cork Internat. Fest., 1975-; Mem., Bd of Dirs, Nat. Concert Hall, Dublin, 1981-. Hon. Professor: Chopin Conservatoire, Warsaw, 1960; Conservatoire of Azores, 1972. FRAM 1956; Hon. RMCM 1959; Hon. FRCM 1965; Hon. FTCL 1969. Hon. LLD Aberdeen Univ., 1960. Harriet Cohen Medal for Bach, 1953. *Recreations:* interested in everything. *Address:* The Pavilion, Greenfield Park, Dublin 4. *T:* Dublin 695870.

RAINBIRD, George Meadus; Director, Thomson Publications Ltd, since 1969 (Deputy Chairman, 1973-77); author and publisher; *b* 22 May 1905; *s* of Leonard Rainbird and Sarah (*née* Meadus); *m* 1st, 1926, Eva Warner (marr. diss.); one *s* two *d*; 2nd, 1939, Joyce Trinder (*d* 1970); two *s* one *d*; 3rd, 1972, Lena Wickman. *Educ:* local grammar school. Founded publishing house, George Rainbird Ltd, 1951; acquired Zaehnsdorf Ltd and Wigmore Bindery Ltd, 1954-56; merged with Thomson Organization, 1965. Chairman: Thos

Nelson & Sons Ltd, 1970-75; George Rainbird Ltd, 1970-75; Rainbird Reference Books Ltd, 1970-75; Sphere Books Ltd, 1970-75; Michael Joseph Ltd, 1970-75; Westerham Press Ltd, 1972-75; Acanthus Press Ltd, 1979-; Dir, Hamish Hamilton Ltd. Chm., International Wine and Food Soc., 1964-72. *Publications:* Escape to Sunshine, 1952; A Pocket Book of Wine, 1963, (with Ronald Searle) repr. as The Subtle Alchemist, 1973; Sherry and the Wines of Spain, 1966. *Recreations:* books, gardens and wine. *Address:* The Old Parsonage, Church Street, Moreton-in-Marsh, Glos. *T:* Moreton-in-Marsh 50492; A15 Albany, W1. *T:* 01-734 0143. *Clubs:* Buck's, Saintsbury.

RAINBOW, (James) Conrad (Douglas), CBE 1979; Chairman, Sovereign Education, since 1979; *b* 25 Sept. 1926; *s* of Jack Conrad Rainbow and Winifred Edna (*née* Mears); *m* 1974, Kathleen Margaret (*née* Holmes); one *s* one *d. Educ:* William Ellis Sch., Highgate; Selwyn Coll., Cambridge (MA). Asst Master, St Paul's Sch., London, 1951-60; HM Inspector of Schools, 1960-69; Dep. Chief Educn Officer, Lancashire, 1969-74, Chief Educn Officer, 1974-79. Vis. Prof., Univ. of Wisconsin, 1979. Education Consultant: ICI, 1980-; Shell Petroleum Co. Ltd, 1980-; Advr to H of C Select Cttee on Educn, 1980-82. Consultant to British School of Brussels. *Publications:* various articles in educnl jls. *Recreations:* rowing (now as an observer), music, reading. *Address:* Freefolk House, Laverstoke, Whitchurch, Hants. *Clubs:* Royal Commonwealth Society; Leander.

RAINE, (Harcourt) Neale; Chairman, Technician Education Council, since 1976; Director, Stothert & Pitt Ltd, since 1978; *b* 5 May 1923; *s* of late Harold Raine and Gertrude Maude Healey; *m* 1947, Eileen Daphne, *d* of A. A. Hooper; one *s. Educ:* Dulwich and London. MSc (Eng) London; CEng, FIProdE, MICE, FIMC. Various appts as professional civil engr, 1947-52; Industrial Management Consultant with Production Engrg Ltd, 1953-59; Jt Man. Dir, Mycalex & TIM Ltd, 1959-63; Chief Exec., Car Div., Wilmot Breedon Ltd, 1963; Management Consultancy in assoc. with Production Engrg Ltd, 1964-65; Dep. Man. Dir, 1965, later Chm. and Man. Dir, Brico Engrg Ltd (Associated Engrg Gp); Chm., Coventry Radiator & Presswork Co. Ltd (Associated Engrg Gp), 1968-70; Man. Dir, Alfred Herbert Ltd, 1970-75. Dir, Associated Engineering Ltd and Man.-Dir of Gen. Div., 1968-70. Pres., Coventry and District Engrg Employers' Assoc., 1975-77. Governor, Lanchester Polytechnic, Coventry and Rugby, 1970-80. *Address:* Penn Lea, The Avenue, Charlton Kings, Cheltenham, Glos GL53 9BJ. *T:* Cheltenham 26185.

RAINE, Kathleen Jessie, (Mrs Madge), FRSL; poet; Co-Editor, Temenos, a Review devoted to the Arts of the Imagination; *b* 1908; *o d* of late George Raine, schoolmaster, and Jessie Raine; *m* Charles Madge (marr. diss.); one *s* one *d. Educ:* Girton College, Cambridge. Hon. DLitt: Leicester, 1974; Durham, 1979. *Publications:* Stone and Flower, 1943; Living in Time, 1946; The Pythoness, 1949; The Year One, 1952; Collected Poems, 1956; The Hollow Hill (poems), 1965; Defending Ancient Springs (criticism), 1967; Blake and Tradition (Andrew Mellon Lectures, Washington, 1962), Princeton 1968, London 1969 (abridged version, Blake and Antiquity, Princeton 1978, London 1979); (with George Mills Harper) Selected Writings of Thomas Taylor the Platonist, Princeton and London, 1969; William Blake, 1970; The Lost Country (verse), 1971 (W. H. Smith & Son Award, 1972); On a Deserted Shore (verse), 1973; Yeats, the Tarot and The Golden Dawn (criticism), 1973; Faces of Day and Night, 1973; Farewell Happy Fields (autobiog.), 1973 (French trans. as Adieu prairies heureuses, 1978; Prix du meilleur livre étranger); Death in Life and Life in Death (criticism), 1974; The Land Unknown (autobiog.), 1975 (French trans. as Le royaume inconnu, 1978), The Oval Portrait (verse), 1977; The Lion's Mouth (autobiography), 1977; David Jones and the Actually Loved and Known (criticism), 1978; From Blake to a Vision (criticism), 1979; The Oracle in the Heart, (verse), 1979; Blake and the New Age (criticism), 1979; Collected Poems, 1981; The Human Face of God, 1982; The Inner Journey of the Poet and other papers (criticism), 1982; French trans. of verse: Isis errante, 1978; Sur un rivage désert, 1978; Le Premier Jour, 1980; Spanish trans.: En una desierta orilla, 1980; contributions to literary journals. *Address:* 47 Paultons Square, SW3. *Club:* University Women's.

RAINE, Neale; *see* Raine, H. N.

RAINER, Luise; actress and painter; *b* Vienna, 12 Jan.; *d* of Heinz Rainer; *m* 1937, Clifford Odets, (*d* 1963) (from whom she obtained a divorce, 1940); *m* 1945, Robert, *s* of late John Knittel; one *d. Educ:* Austria, France, Switzerland and Italy. Started stage career at age of sixteen under Max Reinhardt in Vienna; later was discovered by Metro-Goldwyn-Mayer talent scout in Vienna; came to Hollywood; starred in: Escapade, The Great Ziegfeld, The Good Earth, Emperor's Candlesticks, Big City, Toy Wife (Frou Frou), The Great Waltz, Dramatic School; received Motion Picture Academy of Arts and Sciences Award for the best feminine performance in 1936 and 1937. One-man exhibn of paintings at Patrick Seale Gallery, SW1, 1978. US Tour in recitation of Tennyson's Enoch Arden with music by Richard Strauss, 1981-82. George Eastman Award, 1982. *Recreation:* mountain climbing. *Address:* Casa Isola, Vico Morcote, Lake Lugano, CH 6911, Switzerland. *T:* (091) 692201.

RAINEY, Dr Reginald Charles, OBE 1979; FRS 1975; Senior Principal Scientific Officer, Centre for Overseas Pest Research, Ministry of Overseas Development (formerly Anti-Locust Research Centre), 1958-78; *b* 18 June 1913; *s* of Charles Albert Rainey and Ethel May Rainey; *m* 1943, Margaret Tasman; three *s* (one *d* decd). *Educ:* Purbrook Park County High Sch., Hants;

Imperial Coll. of Science and Technology (ARCS); London Sch. of Hygiene and Trop. Med. DSc London; FIBiol. Res. biologist, Empire Cotton Growing Corp., Transvaal, 1938-40 and 1946-49; Meteorological Officer, S African Air Force, S and E Africa and ME, 1940-46; Sen. Entomologist, Desert Locust Survey, E Africa High Commn (res. and develt work on use of meteorology and aircraft in forecasting and control of desert locust invasions), 1949-58; i/c FAO Desert Locust Inf. Service (desert locust forecasting, with co-operation and support of countries concerned, in Africa and Asia), 1960-67; res. and develt work on use of meteorology and aircraft in forecasting and control of other insect pests, with co-operation and support of E African Agric. and Forestry Res. Org., Sudan Gezira Bd, Canadian Forestry Service, Agricl Aviation Res. Unit (Ciba-Geigy Ltd), Cranfield Coll. of Aeronautics, Univ. of New Brunswick, FAO, Acad. Sinica, 1967-. Pres., Royal Entomological Soc., 1979-81. Fitzroy Prize, Royal Meteorological Soc., 1971. *Publications:* Meteorology and the Migration of Desert Locusts, 1963; (ed) Insect Flight, 1975; (ed with D. L. Gunn) Migrant Pests, 1979; papers in sci. jls. *Recreations:* as above. *Address:* Elmslea, Old Risborough Road, Stoke Mandeville, Bucks. *T:* Stoke Mandeville 2493.

RAINGER, Peter, CBE 1978; FRS 1982; FEng; Deputy Director of Engineering, British Broadcasting Corporation, since 1978; *b* 17 May 1924; *s* of Cyril and Ethel Rainger; *m* 1st, 1953, Josephine Campbell (decd); two *s*; 2nd, 1972, Barbara Gibson. *Educ:* Northampton Engrg Coll.; London Univ. (BSc(Eng)). CEng, FIEE; FEng 1979. British Broadcasting Corporation: Head of Designs Dept, 1968-71; Head of Research Dept, 1971-76; Asst Dir of Engrg, 1976-78. Chairman: Professional Gp E14, IEE, 1973-76; various working parties, EBU, 1971-. Fellow, Royal Television Soc., 1969. Geoffrey Parr Award, Royal TV Soc., 1964; J. J. Thompson Premium, IEE, 1966; TV Acad. Award, Nat. Acad. of Arts and Scis, 1968; David Sarnoff Gold Medal, SMPTE, 1972. *Publications:* technical papers in IEE, Royal TV Soc. and SMPTE jls. *Recreations:* sailing, model engineering. *Address:* Applehurst, West End Avenue, Pinner, Mddx. *T:* 01-868 5166.

RAINS, Prof. Anthony John Harding, MS, FRCS; Assistant Director, British Postgraduate Medical Federation, University of London, and Postgraduate Dean, SW Thames Regional Health Authority, since 1981; Professor of Surgery in the University of London at Charing Cross Hospital Medical School, and Hon. Consultant Surgeon, Charing Cross Hospital, 1959-81; Hon. Consultant Surgeon to the Army; *b* 5 Nov. 1920; *s* of late Dr Robert Harding Rains and Mrs Florence Harding Rains; *m* 1943, Mary Adelaide Lillywhite; three *d. Educ:* Christ's Hospital School, Horsham; St Mary's Hospital, London. MB, BS London, MRCS, LRCP 1943. Ho. Surg. and Ho. Phys. St Mary's, 1943. RAF, 1944-47. Ex-Service Registrar to Mr Handfield-Jones and Lord Porritt, 1947-48. FRCS 1948; Res. Surgical Officer, Bedford County Hosp., 1948-50; Lectr in Surgery, Univ. of Birmingham, 1950-54, Sen. Lectr, 1955-59. MS (London) 1952. Hon. Consulting Surgeon, United Birmingham Hospitals, 1954-59. Dean, Inst. of Basic Med. Scis, RCS, 1976-; Chm., Med. Commn on Accident Prevention. Pres., Nat. Assoc. of Theatre Nurses, 1979-. Mem. Council and Mem. Court of Examiners, RCS. Sir Arthur Keith medal, RCS. Editor, Annals of RCS. *Publications:* (ed with Dr P. B. Kunkler) The Treatment of Cancer in Clinical Practice, 1959; Gallstones: Causes and Treatment, 1964; (ed) Bailey and Love's Short Practice of Surgery, rev. edn 1981; Edward Jenner and Vaccination, 1975; Emergency and Acute Care, 1976; Lister and Antisepsis, 1977; 1,001 Multiple Choice Questions and Answers in Surgery, 1978; articles on the surgery of the gall bladder, on the formation of gall stones, inguinal hernia and arterial disease. *Recreations:* music, country garden, painting. *Address:* British Postgraduate Medical Federation, 14 Ulster Place, NW1 5HD. *T:* 01-935 8173; 62 Chequers Lane, Walton on the Hill, Tadworth, Surrey KT20 7QD. *T:* Tadworth 2840.

RAINSFORD, Surg. Rear-Adm. (retd) Seymour Grome, CB 1955; FRCPath 1964; ARC Research Fellow, Bone and Joint Research Unit, London Hospital Medical College, since 1975; Hon. Consultant in Coagulation Disorders, Wessex Regional Hospital Board, since 1975; *b* 24 April 1900; *s* of Frederick Edward Rainsford, MD, Palmerstown Hse, Co. Dublin; *m* 1st, 1929, Violet Helen (*née* Thomas) (decd); 2nd, 1972, Caroline Mary Herschel, *d* of late Sir Denis Hill, FRCP, FRCPsych; twin *s. Educ:* St Columba's College, Co. Dublin; Trinity College, Dublin. MD 1932; ScD 1939; DPH 1937; FRCPath 1964; FRCP 1977. Joined RN as Surg. Lieut, 1922. North Persian Forces Memorial Medal, for research on Mediterranean Fever, 1933; Gilbert Blane Gold Medal for research on Typhoid Fever, 1938; Chadwick Gold Medal and Prize for research on typhoid vaccine and on blood transfusion in the Royal Navy, 1939. Surgeon Rear-Adm. 1952; Deputy Medical Director-General of the Royal Navy, 1952-55. Chevalier de la Légion d'Honneur, 1948; CStJ 1955. *Publications:* papers on typhoid fever and other tropical diseases, haematology, blood transfusion, blood clotting disorders and physiological problems concerned in diving and submarine escape, in Jl Hygiene, Lancet, BMJ, British Jl of Haematology, Jl Clin. Pathology, Thrombosis and Diathesis and Journal RN Med. Serv. *Recreations:* shooting, golf. *Address:* 14 Eggars Field, Bentley, Farnham, Surrey. *Club:* Army and Navy.

RAINWATER, Prof. (Leo) James; Professor of Physics, Columbia University, New York, since 1952; *b* 9 Dec. 1917; *s* of Leo Jasper Rainwater and Edna Eliza (*née* Teague); *m* 1942, Emma Louise Smith; three *s. Educ:* California Inst. of Technol.; Columbia Univ., NY (BS, MA, PhD). Asst in Physics, 1939-42, Instr 1946-47, Asst Prof. 1947-49, Assoc. Prof., 1949-52,

Columbia Univ.; Scientist, OSRD and Manhattan Project, 1942-46; Dir, Nevis Cyclotron Lab., 1951-53 and 1956-61; scientific research contracts with US naval research, Atomic Energy Commn and Nat. Science Foundn, 1947-. Fellow: Amer. Phys. Soc.; AAAS; IEEE; NY Acad. of Science; Optical Soc. of Amer.; Mem., Nat Acad. of Sciences. Ernest Orlando Lawrence Physics Award, US Atomic Energy Commn, 1963; (jtly) Nobel Prize for Physics, 1975. *Recreations:* classical music, environmental problems, astronomy. *Publications:* numerous articles in Phys. Review, 1946-, and other professional jls. *Address:* Physics Department, Columbia University, New York, NY 10027, USA. *T:* 212-280-3345; (home) 342 Mt Hope Boulevard, Hastings-on-Hudson, NY 10706, USA. *T:* 914-GR8-1368.

RAIS, Tan Sri Abdul J.; *see* Jamil Rais.

RAISMAN, John Michael; Chairman, since 1979, and Chief Executive, since 1978, Shell UK Ltd; *b* 12 Feb. 1929; *er s* of Sir Jeremy Raisman, GCMG, GCIE, KCSI, and Renee Mary Raisman; *m* 1953, Evelyn Anne Muirhead; one *s* three *d*. *Educ:* Dragon Sch., Oxford; Rugby Sch.; The Queen's Coll., Oxford (Jodrell Schol., BA Lit Hum). FBIM 1980. Joined Royal Dutch/Shell Group, 1953; served in Brazil, 1954-60; General Manager, Shell Panama, 1961-62; Asst to Exploration and Production Coordinator, The Hague, 1963-65; Gen. Man., Shell Co. of Turkey, 1966-69; President, Shell Sekiyu K. K. Japan, 1970-73; Head, European Supply and Marketing, 1974-77; Man. Dir, Shell UK Oil, 1977-78; Regional Coordinator, UK and Eire, Shell Internat. Pet. Co. Ltd, 1978-; Dep. Chm., Shell UK Ltd, 1978-79. Dir, Vickers Ltd, 1981-. Chairman: Adv. Council, London Enterprise Agency, 1979-; UK Oil Industry Emergency Cttee, 1980-; Council, Industry for Management Educn, 1981-. Member: Council, CBI, 1979- (Chm., CBI Europe Cttee, 1980-; Mem., President's Cttee, 1980-); Council, Inst. of Petroleum, 1979-; Council, Inst. for Fiscal Studies, 1982-; Governing Council, Business in the Community, 1982-. Governor, National Inst. of Econ. and Social Res. *Recreations:* golf, skiing, listening to music. *Address:* Netheravon House, Netheravon Road South, W4 2PY. *T:* 01-994 3731. *Clubs:* Brooks's; Royal Mid-Surrey.

RAISON, Dr John Charles Anthony, MA, MD; Specialist in Community Medicine, Wessex Regional Health Authority, since 1982; *b* 13 May 1926; *s* of late Cyril A. Raison, FRCS, Edgbaston, Birmingham, and of Ceres Raison; *m* 1951, Rosemary Padmore (marr. diss. 1982); one *s* two *d*. *Educ:* Malvern Coll.; Trinity Hall, Cambridge; Birmingham Univ. MA, MD; MFCM. Consultant Clinical Physiologist in Cardiac Surgery, Birmingham Reg. Hosp. Bd, 1962; Hon. Associate Consultant Clinical Physiologist, United Birmingham Hosps, 1963; Sen. Physiologist, Dir of Clinical Res. and Chief Planner, Heart Research Inst., Presbyterian-Pacific Medical Center, San Francisco, 1966; CSO and SPMO, Scientific Services, DHSS, 1974-78; Dep. Dir, Nat. Radiological Protection Bd, 1978-81. Vis. Consultant, Civic Hosps, Lisbon (Gulbenkian Foundn), 1962; Arris and Gale Lectr, RCS, 1965. Councillor, Southam RDC, 1955-59. FRSM. *Publications:* chapters in books, and papers in medical jls on open-heart surgery, extracorporeal circulation, intensive care, scientific services in health care, and computers in medicine. *Recreations:* gardening, theatre, beekeeping, sailing. *Address:* September Cottage, Taylor's Lane, Bosham, near Chichester, West Sussex PO18 8QQ. *T:* Bosham 572966.

RAISON, Rt. Hon. Timothy (Hugh Francis), PC 1982; MP (C) Aylesbury since 1970; Minister of State, Home Office, since 1979; *b* 3 Nov. 1929; *s* of Maxwell and late Celia Raison; *m* 1956, Veldes Julia Charrington; one *s* three *d*. *Educ:* Dragon Sch., Oxford; Eton (King's Schol.); Christ Church, Oxford (Open History Schol.). Editorial Staff: Picture Post, 1953-56; New Scientist, 1956-61; Editor: Crossbow, 1958-60; New Society, 1962-68. Member: Youth Service Develt Council, 1960-63; Central Adv. Council for Educn, 1963-66; Adv. Cttee on Drug Dependence, 1966-70; Home Office Adv, Council on Penal System, 1970-74; (co-opted) Inner London Educn Authority Educn Cttee, 1967-70; Richmond upon Thames Council, 1967-71. PPS to Sec. of State for N Ireland, 1972-73; Parly Under-Sec. of State, DES, 1973-74; Opposition spokesman on the Environment, 1975-76. Sen. Fellow, Centre for Studies in Soc. Policy, 1974-77; Mem. Council, PSI, 1978-79; Consultant, Selection Trust, 1977-79. Nansen Medal (for share in originating World Refugee Year), 1960. *Publications:* Why Conservative?, 1964; (ed) Youth in New Society, 1966; (ed) Founding Fathers of Social Science, 1969; Power and Parliament, 1979; various political pamphlets. *Recreation:* golf. *Address:* 66 Riverview Gardens, SW13. *T:* 01-748 4724. *Clubs:* Beefsteak, MCC.

RAITZ, Vladimir Gavrilovich; Chairman: Hickie Borman Grant & Co. Ltd, since 1980; US Real Estate Sales Ltd, since 1979; Holiday in Florida Ltd, since 1978; Director, Medallion Holidays, since 1976; *b* 23 May 1922; *s* of Dr Gavril Raitz and Cecilia Raitz; *m* 1954, Helen Antonia (*née* Corkrey); three *d*. *Educ:* Mill Hill Sch.; London University. BSc(Econ.), Econ. History, 1942. British United Press, 1942-43; Reuters, 1943-48; Chm., Horizon Holidays, 1949-74. Member: NEDC for Hotels and Catering Industry, 1968-74; Cinematograph Films Council, 1969-74; Ct of Governors, LSE, 1971-. Cavaliere Ufficiale, Order of Merit (Italy), 1971. *Recreations:* reading, ski-ing. *Address:* 53 St John's Avenue, SW15. *T:* 01-788 1728. *Club:* Reform.

RAJ, Prof. Kakkadan Nandanath; Fellow, Centre for Development Studies, Trivandrum, Kerala State, since 1973; *b* 13 May 1924; *s* of K. N. Gopalan and Karthiayani Gopalan; *m* 1957, Dr Sarasamma Narayanan; two *s*. *Educ:* Madras Christian Coll., Tambaram (BA (Hons), MA, in Economics); London Sch. of Economics (PhD (Econ); Hon. Fellow, 1982). Asst Editor, Associated Newspapers of Ceylon, Nov. 1947-July 1948; Research Officer, Dept of Research, Reserve Bank of India, Aug. 1948-Feb. 1950; Asst Chief, Economic Div., Planning Commn, Govt of India, 1950-53; Prof. of Economics, Delhi Sch. of Economics, Univ. of Delhi, 1953-73 (Vice-Chancellor, Univ. of Delhi, 1969-70; Nat. Fellow in Economics, 1971-73). Visiting Prof., Johns Hopkins Univ., Jan.-June, 1958; Vis. Fellow, Nuffield Coll., Oxford, Jan.-June, 1960; Corresp. Fellow, British Academy, 1972. Hon. Fellow, Amer. Economic Assoc. *Publications:* The Monetary Policy of the Reserve Bank of India, 1948; Employment Aspects of Planning in Underdeveloped Economies, 1956; Some Economic Aspects of the Bhakra-Nangal Project, 1960; Indian Economic Growth-Performance and Prospects, 1964; India, Pakistan and China-Economic Growth and Outlook, 1966; Investment in Livestock in Agrarian Economies, 1969; also articles in Economic Weekly, Economic and Political Weekly, Indian Economic Review, Oxford Economic Papers. *Address:* Nandavan, Kumarapuram, Trivandrum 695011, Kerala State, India. *T:* (home) 62409, (office) 8881-8884, 8412.

RAJAH, Hon. Arumugam Ponnu; Hon. Mr Justice Rajah; a Judge of the Supreme Court, Singapore, since 1976; *b* Negri Sembilan, Malaysia, 23 July 1911; *m* Vijaya Lakshmi; one *s* one *d*. *Educ:* St Paul's Inst., Seremban; Raffles Instn, Singapore; Oxford Univ. (BA). Barrister-at-law, Lincoln's Inn. City Councillor, Singapore: nominated, 1947-49; elected, 1949-57; MLA, Singapore, 1959-66, Chm., Public Accounts Cttee, 1959-63, Speaker, 1964-66; first High Comr for Singapore to UK, 1966-71; High Comr to Australia, 1971-73; practised law in Singapore, 1973-76. Mem. Bd of Trustees, Singapore Improvement Trust, 1949-57; Mem., Raffles Coll. Coun. and Univ. of Malaya Coun., 1955-63. *Address:* Supreme Court, Singapore; 7-D Balmoral Road, Singapore 10.

RALEIGH, Nigel Hugh C.; *see* Curtis-Raleigh.

RALLI, Sir Godfrey (Victor), 3rd Bt, *cr* 1912; TD; *b* 9 Sept. 1915; *s* of Sir Strati Ralli, 2nd Bt, MC; *S* father 1964; *m* 1st, 1937, Nora Margaret Forman (marriage dissolved, 1947); one *s* two *d*; 2nd, 1949, Jean, *er d* of late Keith Barlow. *Educ:* Eton. Joined Ralli Bros Ltd, 1936. Served War of 1939-45 (despatches), Captain, Berkshire Yeomanry RA. Director and Vice-Chairman, Ralli Bros Ltd, 1946-62; Chm., Greater London Fund for the Blind, 1962-82. *Recreations:* fishing, golf. *Heir:* s David Charles Ralli [*b* 5 April 1946; *m* 1975, Jacqueline Cecilia, *d* of David Smith; one *d*]. *Address:* Great Walton, Eastry, Sandwich, Kent CT13 0DN. *T:* Sandwich 611355. *Clubs:* White's, Flyfishers'.

RALPH, Ronald Seton, MRCS, LRCP, DPH; retired; late Consultant Pathologist Battersea and Putney Group of Hospitals; Hon. Pathologist, Eltham and Mottingham Cottage Hospital; *b* Saugor, India, 22 July 1895; *s* of late Col A. C. Ralph, DSO; *m* 1918, Marjorie, *d* of late Dr Joseph Bott, Richmond, Surrey; one *s*. *Educ:* Dover College; Guy's Hospital. Late Director of Clinical Research Assoc. Laboratories; late Clinical Pathologist, St John's Hospital, Lewisham, SE13; late Assistant Bacteriologist, Guy's Hospital, and late Physician in Charge of Diseases of the Skin, St John's Hospital, SE13. *Publications:* various on medical subjects in Lancet, Medical World, and Journal of Clinical Research. *Address:* Les Champs des Cailles, Trinity, Jersey.

RAM, Jagjivan; *b* Arrah, Bihar, 5 April 1908; *m* 1935, Indrani Devi; one *s* one *d*. *Educ:* Banaras Hindu Univ.; Calcutta Univ. (BSc). Appeared before Hammond Commn, 1936; started Agricl Lab. Movement in Bihar and formed Bihar Provincial Khet Mazdoor (Agricl Lab.) Sabha, 1937; Parly Sec., Bihar Govt, 1937-39; jailed in 1940 and 1942 and released in Oct. 1943 on med. grounds; Vice-Pres., Bihar Br. of All India TUC, 1940-46; Sec., Bihar Provincial Congress Cttee, 1940-46; Labour Minister of interim Govt, Sept. 1946-May 1952; appeared before Cabinet Mission, 1946, as accredited leader of Scheduled Castes and rep. their case. Leader, Indian Delegn to ILO Conf., Geneva, 1947; Chm., Preparatory Asia Regional Conf. of ILO, Oct.-Nov. 1947; Leader, Indian Delegn to 33rd Session of ILO Conf. 1950 (Chm. Conf.); Communication Minister, Govt of India, 1952-56; Minister for: Transport and Railway, Dec. 1956-Apr. 1957; Railways, 1957-62; Transport and Communications, 1962-63; Labour, Employment and Rehabilitation, 1966 (AN); Leader, Indian Delegn to Asian Labour Ministers' Conf., Manila, 1966; Minister of Food, Agriculture, Community Develt and Co-op., 1967-70 (also charge Min. of Labour, Employment and Rehabilitation, Nov. 1969-1970); Minister of Defence, 1970-74, 1977-79; Minister of Agriculture and Irrigation, 1974-77; Dep. Prime Minister, 1979. Leader, Indian Delegns: FAO Conf., Rome, 1967, 1974; World Food Congress, The Hague, 1970, Khartoum, 1974. Mem. Exec. Cttee, Hindustan Mazdoor Sewak Sangh, 1947-; Pres., All India Congress Cttee, 1969-71 (Mem. Cttee, 1940-77, and of its Central Parly Bd, 1950-77); Chm., Reception Cttee, 67th Session, Indian Nat. Congress, Patna, 1962; Member: Disciplinary Action Cttee of Congress Working Cttee (since constituted, to 1977); All India Congress Working Cttee, 1948-77; Central Election Cttee, 1951-56, 1961; Gen. Body, AICC, 1973-77; Gandhi Smarak Nidhi; Chairman: Central Campaign Cttee, AICC, 1974-77; Panchayati Raj Cell, AICC, 1974-77. Formed Congress for Democracy Party, Feb. 1977; Leader, Janata Party, and Leader of the Opposition, 1979-80. Chm., Indian Inst. of Public Admin, 1974-75; Mem. Governing Bodies, several colls and educnl instns. Trustee, Nehru Memorial Trust, etc. Past Pres. of several Trades Unions. Hon. Dr of Sciences, Univs of Vikram, Udaipur, Agra, and others. *Address:* 6 Krishna Menon Marg, New Delhi 110011, India. *T:* 376555.

RAM CHANDRA, CIE 1933; MBE 1919; MA (Punjab); MA (Cantab); a Trustee of The Tribune (English daily newspaper in Chandigarh), 1949-76, President of Board of Trustees, 1967-76; *b* 1 March 1889; *m* 1917; one *s* one *d*. *Educ:* Government College, Lahore (Fuller Exhibitioner); Panjab Univ. (MA English 1907; MA 1st class, Mathematics, 1908); Trinity College, Cambridge (Senior Scholar, Mathematical Tripos and Wrangler, b star, 1913); Govt of India Bd of Examrs Cert. of High Proficiency in Persian, 1915; Degree of Honour in Urdu, 1921. Assistant Professor of Mathematics, Government College, Lahore, 1908-10; joined ICS, 1913; served in Punjab as Assistant Commissioner in various districts; Colonisation Officer, 1915; Under-Secretary, 1919-21; Settlement Officer, 1921-25; Director of Land Records, 1924; Deputy Commissioner, 1925; Secretary to Punjab Government, Transferred Department, 1926-27; Home Secretary to Punjab Government, 1928; Deputy Secretary to Govt of India, Department of Education, Health, and Lands, 1928; Joint Secretary, 1932; Secretary, 1935; Member Council of State, 1935; Member, Punjab Legislative Council, 1936; Finance Secretary to Punjab Govt, 1936-37; Commissioner, 1938-39; Sec. to Punjab Govt, Medical and Local Govt Depts, 1939-41; Chief Controller of Imports, India, 1941-44; Leader of Indian Delegation to Egypt for Cotton Conference, 1943; Secretary to Government of India, Commerce Dept, 1944-45; Secretary to Govt of India, Defence Dept, 1945-46; Financial Comr, Punjab, 1946-48; Chairman, Punjab (India) Public Service Commission, 1948-53; Mem., Punjab Legislative Council (elected by Graduates' Constituency), 1954-60; Fellow of Panjab Univ., Chandigarh, 1947-68, Syndic, 1949-64; Syndic and Fellow, Punjabi Univ., Patiala, 1962-72. Chief Comr, Scouts and Guides, Punjab, 1955-68. *Recreation:* gardening. *Address:* Forest Hill, Simla 2, India. *T:* 2129.

RAMACHANDRAN, Dr Gopalasamudram Narayana, FRS 1977; Distinguished Scientist, Centre for Cellular and Molecular Biology, Hyderabad, since 1981; *b* 8 Oct. 1922; *s* of G. R. Narayana Iyer and Lakshmi Ammal; *m* 1945, Rajalakshmi Sankaran; two *s* one *d*. *Educ:* Maharaja's Coll., Ernakulam, Cochin; Indian Inst. of Science; Univ. of Madras (MA, MSc, DSc); Univ. of Cambridge (PhD). Lectr in Physics, Indian Inst. of Science, 1946-47, Asst Prof., 1949-52; 1851 Exhibn Scholar, Univ. of Cambridge, 1947-49; Prof., Univ. of Madras, 1952-70 (Dean, Faculty of Science, 1964-67); Prof. of Biophysics, 1970-78, Inst. Prof. of Mathematical Philosophy, 1978-81, Indian Inst. of Science. Dir, Univ. Grants Commn Centre of Advanced Study in Biophysics, 1962-70; part-time Prof. of Physics, Univ. of Chicago, 1967-78. Member: Physical Res. Cttee, 1959-; Nat. Cttee for Biophysics, 1961-; Bd of Sci. and Ind. Res., India, 1962-65; Council, Internat. Union of Pure and Applied Biophysics, 1969-72; Commn on Macromolecular Biophysics, 1969; Chm., Nat. Cttee for Crystallography, 1963-70; Senior Vis. Prof., Univ. of Michigan, 1965-66; Jawaharlal Nehru Fellow, 1968-70; Fogarty Internat. Schol., NIH, 1977-78. Fellow, Indian Acad. of Sciences, 1950 (Mem. Council, 1953-70; Sec., 1956-58; Vice-Pres., 1962-64); Fellow, Nat. Inst. of Sciences, 1963; FRSA 1971. Hon. Mem., Amer. Soc. of Biological Chem., 1965; Hon. Foreign Mem., Amer. Acad. of Arts and Scis; Founder Mem., Indian Acad. of Yoga, 1980; Mem., Afralasian Acad., Rome, 1982. Hon. DSc Roorkee, 1979. Bhatnagar Meml Prize, 1961; Watumull Prize, 1964; John Arthur Wilson Award, 1967; Ramanujan Medal, 1971; Maghnad Saha Medal, 1971; J. C. Bose Gold Medal and Prize of Bose Inst., 1975; Fogarty Medal, 1978; Distinguished Alumni Award, Indian Inst. of Sci., 1978; C. V. Raman Award, 1982. Editor: Current Science, 1950-58; Jl Indian Inst. of Sci., 1973-77; Member Editorial Board: Jl Molecular Biol., 1959-66; Biochimica et Biophysica Acta, 1965-72; Indian Jl Pure and Applied Physics, 1963-; Internat Jl Peptide and Protein Res., 1969-; Indian Jl Biochem. and Biophys., 1970-; Biopolymers, 1973-. *Publications:* Crystal Optics, in Handbuch der Physik, vol. 25; Molecular Structure of Collagen, in Internat. Review of Connective Tissue Research, vol. 1; Conformation of Polypeptides and Proteins, in Advances in Protein Chemistry, vol. 23; Conformation Polypeptide Chains, in Annual Reviews in Biochemistry, vol. 39; Fourier Methods in Crystallography, 1970; (ed) Advanced Methods of Crystallography; (ed) Aspects of Protein Structure; (ed) Treatise on Collagen, 2 vols, 1967; (ed) Conformation of Biopolymers, vols 1 and 2, 1967; (ed) Crystallography and Crystal Perfection; (ed) Biochemistry of Collagen. *Recreations:* Indian and Western music; detective fiction. *Address:* Centre for Cellular and Molecular Biology, Regional Research Laboratory Campus, Hyderabad 500009, India. *T:* Hyderabad 71487; Gita, 5, 10-A Main Road, Malleswaram West, Bangalore 560055. *T:* 30362.

RAMAGE, Captain Cecil Beresford, MC; *b* 17 Jan. 1895; *o s* of John Walker Ramage, Edinburgh; *m* 1921, Cathleen Nesbitt, CBE (*d* 1982); one *s* one *d*. *Educ:* Edinburgh Academy; Pembroke College, Oxford (open Classical Scholar); President Oxford Union Society. Commissioned in the Royal Scots, 1914; served Gallipoli, Egypt, Palestine, until 1919 (despatches, Order of the Nile). Contested Newcastle upon Tyne, General Election, 1922; MP (L) Newcastle upon Tyne (West Division), 1923-24; contested Southport, 1929. Barrister-at-Law, Middle Temple, 1921; subseq. Oxford Circuit. *Recreation:* golf. *Address:* 11 Dean Park Road, Bournemouth, Dorset.

RAMAGE, (James) Granville (William), CMG 1975; HM Diplomatic Service, retired; *b* 19 Nov. 1919; *s* of late Rev. George Granville Ramage and Helen Marion (*née* Middlemass); *m* 1947, Eileen Mary Smith; one *s* two *d*. *Educ:* Glasgow Acad.; Glasgow University. Served in HM Forces, 1940-46 (despatches). Entered HM Foreign Service, 1947; seconded for service at Bombay, 1947-49; transf. to Foreign Office, 1950; First Sec. and Consul at Manila, 1952-56; South-East Asia Dept, FO, 1956-58; Consul at Atlanta, Ga, 1958-62; Gen. Dept, FO, 1962-63; Consul-General, Tangier, 1963-67; High Comr in The Gambia, 1968-71; Ambassador, People's Democratic Republic of Yemen, 1972-75; Consul General at Boston, Massachusetts, 1975-77. *Recreations:* music, golf. *Address:* 4 Merton Hall Road, Wimbledon, SW19 3PP. *T:* 01-542 5492.

RAMBAHADUR LIMBU, Captain, VC 1966; HM the Queen's Gurkha Orderly Officer, since 1983; *b* Nov. 1939; *s* of late Tekbir Limbu; *m* 1st, 1960, Tikamaya Limbuni (*d* 1966); two *s*; 2nd, 1967, Purnimaya Limbuni; three *s*. Army Cert. of Educn 1st cl. Enlisted 10th Princess Mary's Own Gurkha Rifles, 1957; served on ops in Borneo (VC); promoted Sergeant, 1971; WOII, 1976; commissioned, 1977. *Publication:* My Life Story, 1978. *Recreations:* football, volley-ball, badminton, basketball. *Address:* Queen Elizabeth Barracks, Church Crookham, Aldershot, Hants GU13 0RJ. *Clubs:* VC and GC Association, Royal Society of St George (England).

RAMELSON, Baruch, (Bert); Member, Editorial Board, World Marxist Review, published in Prague, and Editor of the English edition, since 1977; *b* 22 March 1910; *s* of Jacob and Liuba Mendelson; *m* 1st, 1939, Marion Jessop (*d* 1967); 2nd, 1970, Joan Dorothy Smith; one step *s* two step *d*. *Educ:* Univ. of Alberta. 1st cl. hons LLB. Barrister and Solicitor, Edmonton, Alta, 1934-35; Internat. Bde, Mackenzie-Pappinard Bn, Spanish Civil War, 1937-39; Adjt, Canadian Bn of Internat. Bde; Tank Driver, Royal Tank Corps, 1941; captured, Tobruk, 1941; escaped Prison Camp, Italy, 1943; OCTU, Catterick, 1944-45, commnd RA 1945; served in India, 1945-46 (Actg Staff Captain Legal). Communist Party of GB: full-time Sec., Leeds, 1946-53; Sec., Yorks, 1953-65; Mem. Nat. Exec., 1953-78; Mem. Polit. Cttee, 1954-78; National Industrial Organiser, 1965-77. *Publications:* The Case for an Alternative Policy, 1977; various pamphlets and booklets; contrib. Communist (Moscow), Marxism Today, World Marxist Review. *Recreations:* travel, reading. *Address:* 160A Conisborough Crescent, Catford, SE6 2SF. *T:* 01-698 0738.

RAMGOOLAM, Dr Rt. Hon. Sir Seewoosagur, GCMG 1978; Kt 1965; PC 1971; LRCP, MRCS; MLA (Lab) for Pamplemousses-Triolet, 1959-82; Prime Minister of Mauritius, 1965-82; also Minister for Defence and Internal Security and Information and Broadcasting, 1969-82; Leader of the House, 1960-82; *b* Belle Rive, 1900; *m*; one *s* one *d*. *Educ:* Royal Coll., Curepipe; University Coll. (Fellow, 1971) and University Coll. Hosp., London. Municipal Councillor, 1940-53, 1956-60; Deputy Mayor of Port Louis, 1956; Mayor of Port Louis, 1958; entered Legislative Council, 1940; MLC, Pamplemousse-Rivière du Rempart, 1948, re-elected 1953; Mem., Executive Council, 1948-; Liaison Officer for Education, 1951-56; Ministerial Secretary to the Treasury, 1958-60; Chief Minister, 1961-65, and Minister of Finance, 1960-72; Minister for External Affairs, 1968-76. Chm., Organisation of African Unity, 1976-77; Président d'Honneur des Parlements africains, 1977; Vice-Pres., Afro-Arab Summit, 1977. Chm., Bd of Dirs, Advance. Founder and Pres., Mauritius Soc. for Prevention of Cruelty to Animals; 1st Patron, World Fedn for Protection of Animals, 1974; Richard Martin Award, RSPCA, 1981. Pres., Indian Cultural Assoc.; Hon. Fellow, All-India Inst. of Med. Scis, New Delhi, 1979; Editor, Indian Cultural Review. Hon. Citizen: Port Louis, 1969; Quatre Bonnes, 1973; Pamplemousses, 1973. Grand Croix de l'Ordre National de la République Malagasy, 1969; Médaille de l'Assemblée Nationale française, 1971; Grand Croix, Ordre National de Lion (Senegal), 1973; Grand Croix de l'Ordre du Mérite (Central African Republic), 1973; Grand Croix National de Benin (Togo), 1973; Grand Officier de la Légion d'honneur (France), 1973; Médaille de la Francophonie, 1975; Grand Croix de l'Ordre du Mérite, République Fédérale d'Allemagne, 1978. UN Prize for Outstanding Achievements in the field of Human Rights, 1973; Prix International des Relations Diplomatiques, Inst. of Diplomatic Relations, Brussels, 1980. Dr in Law *hc*, New Delhi; Hon. DCL Mauritius, 1974; Dr *hc* Aix-en-Provence, 1978. 1st Hon. Mem., African Psychiatric Assoc., 1970. *Recreations:* art and literature. *Address:* 85 Desforges Street, Port Louis, Mauritius. *T:* 20460.

RAMIN, Mme Manfred; *see* Cotrubas, I.

RAMPHAL, Sir Shridath Surendranath, AC 1982; Kt 1970; CMG 1966; QC (Guyana) 1965, SC 1966; Secretary-General of the Commonwealth, since 1975; *b* 1928; *m*. *Educ:* King's Coll., London (LLM 1952). FKC 1975; Fellow, London Sch. of Econs, 1979. Called to the Bar, Gray's Inn, 1951 (Hon. Bencher 1981). Colonial Legal Probationer, 1951; Arden and Atkin Prize, 1952; John Simon Guggenheim Fellow, Harvard Law Sch., 1962. Crown Counsel, British Guiana, 1952-54; Asst to Attorney-Gen., 1954-56; Legal Draftsman, 1956-58; First Legal Draftsman, West Indies, 1958-59; Solicitor-Gen., British Guiana, 1959-61; Asst Attorney-Gen., West Indies, 1961-62, Attorney-Gen., Guyana, 1965-73; Minister of State for External Affairs, Guyana, 1967-72; Foreign Minister and Attorney General, Guyana, 1972-73; Minister, Foreign Affairs and Justice, 1973-75; Mem., National Assembly, Guyana, 1965-75. Member: Hon. Adv. Cttee, Center for Internat. Studies, NY Univ., 1966-; Internat. Commn of Jurists, 1970-; Bd, Vienna Inst. of Develt, 1973-; Internat. Hon. Cttee, Dag Hammarskjold Foundn, 1977-; Independent (Brandt) Commn on International Development Issues, 1977-; Governing Body, Inst. Develt Studies, Univ. of Sussex, 1977-81; Ind. Commn on Disarmament and Security Issues, 1980. Chm., Selection Cttee, Third World Prize, 1979; Vice-Chm., Centre for Research on New Internat. Econ. Order, Oxford, 1977. FRSA 1981; Hon. LLD: Panjab, 1975; Southampton, 1976; St Francis Xavier, NS, 1978; Univ. of WI, 1978; Aberdeen, 1979; Surrey, 1979; Essex, 1980; Cape Coast, Ghana, 1980; London, 1981; Benin, Nigeria, 1982;

Hon. DHL, Simmons Coll., Boston, 1982; Hon. DCL Oxon, 1982. *Publications:* One World to Share: selected speeches of the Commonwealth Secretary-General 1975-79, 1979; Nkrumah and the Eighties: Kwame Nkrumah Memorial Lectures, 1980; contrib. various political, legal and other jls incl. International and Comparative Law Qly, Caribbean Qly, Public Law, Guyana Jl, Round Table, Foreign Policy, Third World Qly, RSA Jl. *Address:* Commonwealth Secretariat, Marlborough House, Pall Mall, SW1Y 5HX. *Clubs:* Athenæum, Royal Automobile, Travellers'.

RAMPTON, Sir Jack (Leslie), KCB 1973 (CB 1969); Director, London Atlantic Investment Trust, since 1981; *b* 10 July 1920; *s* of late Leonard Wilfrid Rampton and of Sylvia (*née* Davies); *m* 1950, Eileen Joan (*née* Hart); one *s* one *d. Educ:* Tonbridge Sch.; Trinity Coll., Oxford. MA. Treasury, 1941; Asst Priv. Sec. to successive Chancellors of the Exchequer, 1942-43; Priv. Sec. to Financial Sec., 1945-46; Economic and Financial Adv. to Comr-Gen. for SE Asia and to British High Comr, Malaya, 1959-61; Under-Secretary, HM Treasury, 1964-68; Dep. Sec., Min. of Technology (formerly Min. of Power), 1968-70; Dep. Sec., DTI, 1970-72; Second Permanent Sec. and Sec. (Industrial Develt), DTI, 1972-74; Perm. Under-Sec. of State, Dept of Energy, 1974-80. Dir, Sheerness Steel Co.; Special Adviser: North Sea Sun Oil Co., 1982-; Sun Exploration and Development Co. Inc., 1982-; Member: Council, Victoria League; Honeywell UK Adv. Council, 1981-; Oxford Energy Policy Club, 1978-. CBIM; CIGasE. Hon. DSc Aston, 1979. *Recreations:* gardening, games, photography, travel; Oxford Squash V (Capt.) 1939-40; Authentic, 1940. *Address:* 17 The Ridgeway, Tonbridge, Kent. *T:* Tonbridge 352117. *Clubs:* Pilgrims, Britain Australia Society, Cook Society; Vincent's (Oxford).

RAMSAY, family name of **Earl of Dalhousie.**

RAMSAY, Lord; James Hubert Ramsay; Director, Hambros Bank Ltd, 1981-82; *b* 17 Jan. 1948; *er s* and *heir* of 16th Earl of Dalhousie, *qv; m* 1973, Marilyn, *yr d* of Major David Butter, *qv;* one *s* two *d. Educ:* Ampleforth. 2nd Bn Coldstream Guards, commnd 1968-71, RARO 1971. *Heir: s* Hon. Simon David Ramsay, *b* 18 April 1981. *Address:* Dalhousie Lodge, Edzell, Angus; 3 Vicarage Gardens, W8. *Clubs:* White's, Pratt's, Turf.

RAMSAY, Sir Alexander William Burnett, 7th Bt, *cr* 1806, of Balmain (also *heir-pres* to Btcy of Burnett, *cr* 1626 (Nova Scotia), of Leys, Kincardineshire, which became dormant, 1959, on death of Sir Alexander Edwin Burnett of Leys, and was not claimed by Sir Alexander Burnett Ramsay, 6th Bt, of Balmain); *b* 4 Aug. 1938; *s* of Sir Alexander Burnett Ramsay, 6th Bt and Isabel Ellice, *e d* of late William Whitney, Woodstock, New South Wales; *S* father, 1965; *m* 1963, Neryl Eileen, *d* of J. C. Smith Thornton, Trangie, NSW; three *s. Heir: s* Alexander David Ramsay, *b* 20 Aug. 1966. *Address:* Bulbah, Warren, NSW 2824, Australia.

RAMSAY, Allan John Heppel Ramsay; HM Diplomatic Service; Counsellor and Head of Chancery, British Embassy, Baghdad, since 1980; *b* 19 Oct. 1937; *s* of Norman Ramsay Ramsay and Faith Evelyn Sorel-Cameron; *m* 1966, Pauline Therese Lescher; two *s* one *d. Educ:* Bedford Sch.; RMA Sandhurst. Served Army, 1957-70: Somerset Light Infantry, 1957-65; DLI, 1965-70. Entered FCO, 1970. *Recreations:* collecting butterflies, birdwatching. *Address:* c/o Foreign and Commonwealth Office, SW1A 2AH. *Club:* Brooks's.

RAMSAY, Arthur; *see* Ramsay, James A.

RAMSAY, Donald Allan, ScD; FRS 1978, FRSC 1966; Principal Research Officer, National Research Council of Canada, since 1968;*b* 11 July 1922; *s* of Norman Ramsay and Thirza Elizabeth Beckley; *m* 1946, Nancy Brayshaw; four *d. Educ:* Latymer Upper Sch.; St Catharine's Coll., Cambridge. BA 1943, MA 1947, PhD 1947, ScD 1976 (all Cantab). Research Scientist (Div. of Chemistry, 1947, Div. of Physics, 1949, Herzberg Inst. of Astrophysics, 1975), Nat. Research Council of Canada. Fellow, Amer. Phys. Soc., 1964; FCIC, 1970; Vice-Pres., Acad. of Science, 1975-76; Hon. Treas., RSC, 1976-79, Centennial Medal, RSC, 1982. Dr *hc* Reims, 1969. Queen Elizabeth II Silver Jubilee Medal, 1977. *Publications:* numerous articles on molecular spectroscopy and molecular structure, espec. free radicals. *Recreations:* sailing, fishing, organ playing. *Address:* 1578 Drake Avenue, Ottawa, Ontario K1G 0L8, Canada. *T:* 613-733-8899. *Club:* Leander (Henley).

RAMSAY, Henry Thomas, CBE 1960; Director, Safety in Mines Research Establishment, Ministry of Technology (formerly Ministry of Power), Sheffield, 1954-70, retired; *b* 7 Dec. 1907; *s* of Henry Thomas and Florence Emily Ramsay, Gravesend, Kent; *m* 1953, Dora Gwenllian Burgoyne Davies (*d* 1979); one *s* one *d. Educ:* Gravesend Junior Techn. Sch.; thereafter by evening study. On scientific staff, Research Labs, GEC, 1928-48; RAE, 1948-54. Chartered engineer; FInstP; FIMinE; Pres., Midland Inst. Mining Engrs, 1970-71. *Publications:* contrib. to: trans of Instn of Electrical Engrs; Jl of Inst. of Mining Engrs; other technical jls. *Recreations:* gardening, horses. *Address:* Well Farm, Lower Ansford, Castle Cary, Somerset.

RAMSAY, J(ames) Arthur, MBE 1945; FRS 1955; Fellow of Queens' College, Cambridge, 1934-76, now Hon. Fellow; Professor of Comparative Physiology, University of Cambridge, 1969-76, now Emeritus Professor (Reader, 1959); *b* 6 Sept. 1909; *s* of late David Ramsay and Isabella Rae Ramsay (*née* Garvie); *m* 1939, Helen Amelie, *d* of late Oscar Dickson

Stockholm; one *s* one *d. Educ:* Fettes College; Gonville and Caius College, Cambridge. University Demonstrator and Fellow of Queens', 1934. Major RA Coast and Anti-Aircraft Defence Experimental Establishment, 1939-45. Joint Editor, Journal of Experimental Biology, 1952-74. *Publications:* Physiological Approach to the Lower Animals, 1952; The Experimental Basis of Modern Biology, 1965; A Guide to Thermodynamics, 1972; papers in Jl of Experimental Biology. *Recreations:* mountaineering, ski-ing. *Address:* The Boxer's Croft, Achbuie 3, Abriachan, Inverness-shire. *T:* Dochgarroch 269.

RAMSAY, Cdre Sir James (Maxwell), KCMG 1978; Kt 1976; CBE 1966; DSC 1952; Governor of Queensland, since 1977; *b* 27 Aug. 1916; *s* of William Ramsay and Mary Ramsay; *m* 1945, Janet Burley; one *s* three *d. Educ:* Hutchins Sch., Hobart; RAN Coll., Jervis Bay. RAN, 1930-72: Naval Representative, London, 1964-65; NOIC, Western Australia, 1968-72; Lieut-Governor of Western Australia, 1974-77. KStJ 1977. Legion of Merit, US, 1952. *Recreations:* golf, yachting, fishing. *Address:* Government House, Brisbane, Qld 4001, Australia. *Club:* Weld.

RAMSAY, Prof. John Graham, FRS 1973; Professor of Geology, Eidgenössische Technische Hochschule and University of Zürich, since 1977; *b* 17 June 1931; *s* of Robert William Ramsay and Kathleen May Ramsay; *m* 1st, 1952, Sylvia Hiorns (marr. diss. 1957); 2nd, 1960, Christine Marden; three *d* (and one *d* decd). *Educ:* Edmonton County Grammar Sch.; Imperial Coll., London. DSc, PhD, DIC, BSc, ARCS, FGS. Musician, Corps of Royal Engineers, 1955-57; academic staff Imperial Coll., London, 1957-73: Prof. of Geology, 1966-73; Prof. of Earth Sciences, Leeds Univ., 1973-76. Vice-Pres., Société Géologique de France, 1973. Dr *hc* Rennes, 1978. *Publication:* Folding and Fracturing of Rocks, 1967. *Recreations:* chamber music, mountaineering, ski-ing. *Address:* Eidgenössische Technische Hochschule Zürich, ETH Zentrum, CH 8092 Zürich, Switzerland.

RAMSAY, Sir Neis Alexander, 12th Bt of Bamff, *cr* 1666; Farmer since 1953; Landowner and Farmer since 1959; *b* 4 Oct. 1909; *s* of Sir James Douglas Ramsay, 11th Bt, MVO, TD, JP; *S* father 1959; *m* 1st, 1940, Edith Alix Ross Hayes (marr. diss. 1950; she *d* 1979), *d* of C. F. Hayes, Linksfield, Johannesburg; 2nd, 1952, Rachel Leanore Beatrice Drummond (*d* 1982), *d* of late Colonel E. B. Urmston, CB, Glenmorven; no *c. Educ:* Winchester; Trinity College, Cambridge. Lieut 1st Gordon Highlanders, 1933-34; British South African Police, 1934-35; Lieutenant, South African Engineer Corps, 1939-45; Mining in South Africa, 1936-50; Returned to UK, 1950. *Recreations:* shooting and golf. *Heir (to feudal barony of Bamff'):* Paul Robert Warner Ramsay, yr of Bamff [*b* 30 Oct. 1945; *s* of Sir Edward Redston Warner, *qv*; assumed name of Ramsay, 1975; *m* 1979, Helen Louise Gibbon, *d* of late Lt-Col Aubrey Wynter Gibbon, OBE, Argyll and Sutherland Highlanders. *Educ:* Eton; Edinburgh Univ.; UCL]. *Address:* Bamff, Alyth, Perthshire. *T:* Alyth 2382. *Clubs:* New (Edinburgh); Royal Perth Golfing Society (Perth).

RAMSAY, Norman James Gemmill; Sheriff of South Strathclyde, Dumfries and Galloway at Kirkcudbright, Stranraer and Dumfries (formerly Dumfries and Galloway, Western Division), since 1971; *b* 26 Aug. 1916; *s* of late James Ramsay and late Mrs Christina Emma Ramsay; *m* 1952, Rachael Mary Berkeley Cox, *d* of late Sir Herbert Charles Fahie Cox; two *s. Educ:* Merchiston Castle Sch.; Edinburgh Univ. (MA, LLB). Writer to the Signet, 1939; Advocate, Scotland, 1956. War Service, RN, 1940-46; Lt (S), RNVR. Colonial Legal Service, Northern Rhodesia: Administrator-General, 1947; Resident Magistrate, 1956; Sen. Resident Magistrate, 1958; Puisne Judge of High Court, Northern Rhodesia, later Zambia, 1964-68. Mem., Victoria Falls Trust, 1950-58. *Address:* Mill of Borgue, Kirkcudbright DG6 4SY.

RAMSAY, Patrick George Alexander; Controller, BBC Scotland, since 1979; *b* 14 April 1926; *yr s* of late Rt Rev. Ronald Erskine Ramsay, sometime Bishop of Malmesbury, and of Winifred Constance Ramsay (*née* Partridge); *m* 1948, Hope Seymour Dorothy, *y d* of late Rt Rev. Algernon Markham, sometime Bishop of Grantham, and Winifred Edith Markham (*née* Barne); two *s. Educ:* Marlborough Coll.; Jesus Coll., Cambridge (MA). Served War, Royal Navy (Fleet Air Arm), 1944-46. Joined BBC as Report Writer, Eastern European Desk, Monitoring Service, 1949; Liaison Officer, US Foreign Broadcasts Information Service, Cyprus, 1951-52; Asst, Appts Dept, 1953-56; Sen. Admin. Asst, External Broadcasting, 1956-58; Admin. Officer News and Head of News Administration, 1958-64; Planning Manager, Television Programme Planning, 1964-66; Asst Controller: Programme Services, 1966-69; Programme Planning, 1969-72; Controller, Programme Services, 1972-79. Dir, Windsor Festival Soc., 1973-76. Councillor and Alderman, Royal Borough of New Windsor, 1962-67; Chm., Windsor and Eton Soc., 1971-76. FRSA. *Recreations:* fellwalking, gardening, foreign travel, history, looking in junk shops, thwarting bureaucrats. *Address:* 2A Ramsay Garden, Edinburgh EH1 2NA. *Clubs:* Naval; New (Edinburgh).

RAMSAY, Thomas Anderson; Professor of Post Graduate Medical Education, University of Warwick, since 1980; Director, Post Graduate Medical Education, Coventry Area Health Authority, Warwickshire Post Graduate Medical Centre, since 1980; *b* 9 Feb. 1920; *s* of David Mitchell Ramsay and Ruth Bramfitt Ramsay; *m* 1949, Margaret Lilian Leggat Donald; one *s* two *d. Educ:* Glasgow Univ. BSc, MB, ChB. FRCSGlas; FFCM; FRSH; MRCP. Surg. Lieut, RNVR, 1945-47. Various posts in general and clinical hospital practice (mainly paediatric and orthopaedic surg.), 1943-56; Asst, later Dep. Sen. Admin. Med. Officer, NI Hospitals Authority, 1957-58; Dep. Sen., later Sen. Admin. Med. Officer, NE Metropolitan Reg. Hospital Bd, 1958–72; Post-Grad. Dean and Prof. of Post-Grad. Med., Univ. of Aberdeen, 1972–76; Dir of Post-Grad. Med. Educn, NE Region (Scotland), 1972–76; Med. Officer, W Midlands Regional Health Authority, 1976–79. Vis. Prof. of Health Services Admin, London Sch. of Hygiene and Tropical Medicine, 1971–72; Vis. Prof., Health Services Admin., Univ. of Aston, 1979–. Mem. Bd, Faculty of Community Medicine, 1972–. Governor, London Hosp., 1965–72. *Publications*: several papers in learned jls regarding post-graduate medical educn and community medicine. *Recreations*: travel, photography. *Address*: 3 Beacon Park, Penrith, Cumbria. *T*: Penrith 5121.

RAMSAY, Sir Thomas (Meek), Kt 1972; CMG 1965; Chairman: The Kiwi International Company Ltd, Melbourne, 1967–80; joined The Kiwi Polish Co. Pty Ltd, Melbourne, 1926, Managing Director, 1956–72 (Joint Managing Director, 1945); *b* Essendon, Victoria, 24 Nov. 1907; *s* of late William Ramsay, Scotland; *m* 1941, Catherine Anne, *d* of John William Richardson, Adelaide, SA; four *s* one *d. Educ*: Malvern Grammar; Scotch Coll.; Melbourne Univ. (BSc). CMF, 1940–41 (Lieut); Asst Controller, Min. of Munitions, 1941–45. Chairman: Norwich Union Life Insurance Soc. (Aust. Bd), 1968–79; Collie (Aust.) Ltd Group, 1977–79; Industrial Design Council of Australia, 1969–76; ANZAC Fellowship Selection Cttee, 1971–78; Director: Australian Consolidated Industries Ltd Group, 1965–79; Alex Harvey Industries Group, NZ. President: Associated Chambers of Manufrs of Australia, 1962–63; Victorian Chamber of Manufrs, 1962–64; Mem., Selection Cttee (Industrial) Sir Winston Churchill Fellowships. FRHistS of Queensland, 1964; FRHistS of Victoria, 1965; FAIM; FSAScot. *Recreations*: gardening, Australian historical research. *Address*: 23 Airlie Street, South Yarra, Victoria 3141, Australia. *T*: 26 1751. *Clubs*: Athenæum, Australian, Melbourne (Melbourne).

RAMSAY-FAIRFAX-LUCY, Sir Edmund J. W. H. C.; *see* Fairfax-Lucy.

RAMSAY RAE, Air Vice-Marshal Ronald Arthur, CB 1960; OBE 1947; *b* 9 Oct. 1910; *s* of late George Ramsay Rae, Lindfield, NSW, and Alice Ramsay Rae (*née* Haselden); *m* 1939, Rosemary Gough Howell, *d* of late Charles Gough Howell, KC, Attorney General, Singapore; one *s* one *d. Educ*: Sydney, New South Wales, Australia. Served Australian Citizen Force and then as Cadet, RAAF, at Point Cook, 1930–31; transf. to RAF, 1932; flying duties in UK and Middle East with Nos 33 and 142 Sqdns until 1936; Advanced Armament Course; Armament officer in Far East, 1938–42; then Comdr RAF Tengah, Singapore; POW, 1943–45; Gp Captain in comd Central Gunnery Sch., Leconfield, Yorks, 1946; despatches, 1946. RAF Staff Coll., Andover, 1948; Dep. Dir Organisation (Estabt), Middle East; in comd RAF North Luffenham and then RAF Oakington (206 Advanced Flying Sch.); Commandant, Aircraft and Armament Exptl Estabt, Boscombe Down, 1955–57; Dep. Air Sec., Air Min., 1957–59; AOC No 224 Group, RAF, 1959–62, retd. NPFA, 1963–71. AFRAeS 1936. *Recreations*: cricket, golf, tennis, winter sports (Cresta Run and ski-ing); Pres., St Moritz Tobogganing Club). *Address*: Commonwealth Bank of Australia, 71 Aldwych, WC2; Little Wakestone, Bedham, Fittleworth, W Sussex. *Club*: Royal Air Force.

See also Hon. Sir Wallace A. R. Rae.

RAMSBOTHAM, family name of Viscount Soulbury.

RAMSBOTHAM, Brig. David John, CBE 1980 (OBE 1974); Director of Public Relations (Army), since 1982; *b* 6 Nov. 1934; *s* of Rt Rev. J. A. Ramsbotham, *qv*; *m* 1958, Susan Caroline (*née* Dickinson); two *s. Educ*: Haileybury Coll.; Corpus Christi Coll., Cambridge (BA 1957, MA 1973). Nat. Service, 1952–54; Rifle Bde, UK and BAOR, 1958–62; seconded to KAR, 1962–63; Staff Coll., 1964; Rifle Bde, Far East, 1965; Staff, 7 Armoured Bde, 1966–68; 3 and 2 Green Jackets (BAOR), 1968–71; MA to CGS (Lt-Col) 1971–73; CO, 2 RGJ, 1974–76; Staff, 4 Armd Div., BAOR, 1976–78; Comd, 39 Infantry Bde (NI), 1978–80; RCDS, 1981. *Recreations*: sailing, shooting, gardening. *Address*: Morteyn, Piddlehinton, Dorset. *T*: Piddletrenthide 378. *Club*: MCC.

RAMSBOTHAM, Rt. Rev. John Alexander; *b* 25 Feb. 1906; *s* of late Rev. Alexander Ramsbotham and of late Margaret Emily Ramsbotham; *m* 1933, Eirian Morgan Owen; three *s* two *d. Educ*: Haileybury College; Corpus Christi College, Cambridge; Wells Theological College. Travelling Secretary, 1929–30, Missionary Secretary, 1930–33, Student Christian Movement; Chaplain, 1933–34. Vice-Principal, 1934–36, Wells Theol. Coll.; Priest-Vicar Wells Cathedral, 1933–36; Warden, College of the Ascension, Selly Oak, 1936–40; Rector of Ordsall, Notts, 1941–42; Vicar of St George's, Jesmond, Newcastle on Tyne, 1942–50; Bishop Suffragan of Jarrow, 1950–58, also Archdeacon of Auckland and Canon of Durham; Bishop of Wakefield, 1958–67; Asst Bishop, Dio. Newcastle, 1968–76. *Publication*: Belief in Christ and the Christian Community, 1949. *Recreation*: music. *Address*: 13 Hextol Terrace, Hexham, Northumberland NE46 2DF. *T*: Hexham 602607.

See also Brig. D J. Ramsbotham.

RAMSBOTHAM, Hon. Sir Peter (Edward), GCMG 1978 (KCMG 1972; CMG 1964); GCVO 1976; HM Diplomatic Service, retired; Director: Lloyds Bank, since 1981; Lloyds Bank International, since 1981; Regional Director, Southern Regional Board, Lloyds Bank, since 1981; Director, Commercial Union Assurance Co., since 1981; *b* 8 Oct. 1919; *yr s* of 1st Viscount Soulbury, PC, GCMG, GCVO, OBE, MC; *b* and *heir pres.* to 2nd Viscount Soulbury,

qv; *m* 1941, Frances Blomfield; two *s* one *d. Educ*: Eton College; Magdalen College, Oxford. HM Forces, 1943–46 (despatches; Croix de Guerre, 1945). Control Office for Germany and Austria from 1947; Regional Political Officer in Hamburg; entered Foreign Service, Oct. 1948; Political Division of Allied Control Commission, Berlin, Nov. 1948; transferred to Foreign Office, 1950; 1st Secretary, 1950; Head of Chancery, UK Delegation, New York, 1953; Foreign Office, 1957; Counsellor, 1961, Head of Western Organisations and Planning Dept; Head of Chancery, British Embassy, Paris, 1963–67; Foreign Office, 1967–69 (Sabbatical year, Inst. of Strategic Studies, 1968); High Comr, Nicosia, 1969–71; Ambassador to Iran, 1971–74; Ambassador to the United States, 1974–77; Governor and C-in-C of Bermuda, 1977–80. Trustee, Leonard Cheshire Foundn, 1981–; Governor, King's Sch., Canterbury, 1981–. Hon. LLD: Akron Univ., 1975; Coll. of William and Mary, 1975; Maryland Univ., 1976; Yale Univ., 1977. KStJ 1976. *Recreations*: gardening, fishing. *Address*: East Lane, Ovington, near Alresford, Hants SO24 0RA. *T*: Alresford 2515. *Clubs*: Garrick; Metropolitan (Washington).

RAMSBURY, Bishop Suffragan of, since 1974; Rt. Rev. John Robert Geoffrey Neale, AKC; Hon. Canon of Salisbury Cathedral since 1974; *b* 21 Sept. 1926; *s* of late Geoffrey Brockman Neale and Stella Beatrice (*née* Wild). *Educ*: Felsted Sch.; King's Coll., London Univ. Served War of 1939–45: Lieut RA; Army, 1944–48. Business, G. B. Neale & Co Ltd, EC2, 1948–51. King's Coll. London, 1951–55 (Jelf Prize, 1954). Deacon, 1955, priest, 1956; Curate, St Peter, St Helier, Dio. Southwark, 1955–58. Chaplain, Ardingly Coll., Sx, 1958–63; Recruitment Sec., CACTM (ACCM), 1963–67; Archbishops' Rep. for ordination candidates, 1967–68; Canon Missioner, Dio. Guildford, Hon. Canon of Guildford Cath. and Rector of Hascombe, Surrey, 1968–74; Archdeacon of Wilts, 1974–80. *Publication*: Ember Prayer (SPCK), 1965. *Recreation*: horticulture. *Address*: Chittoe Vicarage, Bromham, Chippenham, Wilts. *T*: Bromham 850651. *Club*: Royal Commonwealth Society.

RAMSDEN, Caryl Oliver Imbert, CMG 1965; CVO 1966; *b* 4 April 1915; *s* of late Lt-Col J. V. Ramsden; *m* 1945, Anne, *d* of late Sir Charles Wickham, KCMG, KBE, DSO; one *s. Educ*: New Coll., Oxford. Served in Royal Regiment of Artillery, 1937–49; Assistant Military Attaché, Bucharest, 1947–49. Entered HM Foreign Service, 1949, retired 1967; Private Secretary to Prime Minister, 1957; Consul-General, Hanover, 1957–59; Counsellor, Rio de Janeiro, 1959; acted as Chargé d'Affaires, 1960; Counsellor, Brussels 1962. Pro-Principal (Admin), University College at Buckingham, 1975–79. Commander of the Star of Ethiopia, 1954; Commander, Order of Leopold, 1966. *Recreation*: golf. *Address*: The Old Brewery, Helperby, York YO6 2NS. *Club*: Cavalry and Guards.

RAMSDEN, Sir Geoffrey Charles Frescheville, Kt 1948; CIE 1942; *b* 21 April 1893; *s* of Colonel H. F. S. Ramsden, CBE, and Hon. Edwyna Fiennes, *d* of 17th Lord Saye and Sele, DL, JP, CC; *m* 1930, Margaret Lovell (*d* 1976), *d* of late Rev. J. Robinson; no *c. Educ*: Haileybury College; Sidney Sussex Coll., Cambridge (MA). Served in the Army, 1914–19; Capt. 1st Bn Royal Sussex Regt, NW Frontier (India) 1915–19; joined ICS 1920; Secretary Indian Tariff Board, 1923–25; Deputy Commissioner of Jubbulpore, 1926 and 1931–34, and of various other Districts; Commissioner, Jubbulpore Div., 1936 and 1941–44, and Chhatisgarh Div., 1937–40; Development Adviser to Governor, 1945; Financial Comr CP and Berar, 1941–45 and 1946–47; retd, 1948. *Recreations*: travel, photography, tennis and fishing. *Address*: Fynescourt, Grayshott, Hindhead, Surrey. *T*: Hindhead 4499. *Club*: Royal Over-Seas League.

RAMSDEN, Sir Geoffrey William P.; *see* Pennington-Ramsden.

RAMSDEN, Prof. Herbert, MA, Dr en Filosofiia y Letras; Professor of Spanish Language and Literature, University of Manchester, 1961–82, now Emeritus; *b* 20 April 1927; *s* of Herbert and Ann Ramsden; *m* 1953, Joyce Robina Hall, SRN, ONC, CMB; three *s* (incl. twin *s*) twin *d. Educ*: Sale Grammar Sch.; Univs of Manchester, Strasbourg, Madrid and Sorbonne. National Service, Inf. and Intell. Corps, 1949–51 (commnd). Travel, study and research abroad (Kemsley Travelling Fellow, etc), 1951–54; Univ. of Manchester: Asst Lectr in Spanish, 1954–57; Lectr in Spanish, 1957–61; Chm. of MA Cttee, 1964–65; Pres., Philological Club, 1966–68. *Publications*: An Essential Course in Modern Spanish, 1959; Weak-Pronoun Position in the Early Romance Languages, 1963; (ed with critical study) Azorín, La ruta de Don Quijote, 1966; Ángel Ganivet's Idearium español: A Critical Study, 1967; The Spanish Generation of 1898, 1974; The 1898 Movement in Spain, 1974; (ed with critical study) Lorca, Bodas de sangre, 1980; Pío Baroja: La busca, 1982; Pío Baroja: La busca 1903 to La Busca 1904, 1982; articles in Bulletin of Hispanic Studies, Modern Language Review, Modern Languages, etc. *Recreations*: family, hill-walking, foreign travel. *Address*: Grove House, Grove Lane, Cheadle Hulme, Cheshire. *T*: 061-439 4306.

RAMSDEN, Rt. Hon. James Edward, PC 1963; Director: Prudential Assurance Co. Ltd, since 1972 (Deputy Chairman, 1976–82); Prudential Corporation Ltd, since 1979 (Deputy Chairman, 1979–82); *b* 1 Nov. 1923; *s* of Capt. Edward Ramsden, MC, and late Geraldine Ramsden, OBE, Breckamore Hall, Ripon; *m* 1949, Juliet Barbara Anna, *y d* of late Col Sir Charles Ponsonby, 1st Bt, TD, and of Hon. Lady Ponsonby, *d* of 1st Baron Hunsdon; three *s* two *d. Educ*: Eton; Trinity College, Oxford (MA). Commnd KRRC, 1942; served North-West Europe with Rifle Brigade, 1944–45. MP (C) Harrogate, WR Yorks, March 1954–Feb. 1974; PPS to Home Secretary, Nov. 1959–Oct. 1960; Under-Sec. and Financial Sec., War

Office, Oct. 1960-Oct. 1963; Sec. of State for War, 1963-64; Minister of Defence for the Army, April-Oct. 1964. Director: UK Board, Colonial Mutual Life Assurance Society, 1966-72; Standard Telephones and Cables, 1971-81; London Clinic, 1973-. Mem., Historic Buildings Council for England, 1971-72. *Address:* Old Sleningford Hall, Ripon, North Yorks. *T:* Ripon 85229. *Clubs:* Brooks's, Pratt's.

RAMSDEN, John Michael; Editor-in-Chief, Flight, since 1981; *b* 2 Oct. 1928; *s* of John Leonard Ramsden and Edith Alexandra Ramsden; *m* 1953, Angela Mary Mortimer; one *s* one *d. Educ:* Bedford Sch.; de Havilland Aeronautical Tech. Sch. CEng, FRAeS, FSLAET. With de Havilland Aircraft Co. Ltd, 1946-55; Flight, 1955-: Air Transport Editor, 1961-64; Editor, 1964-81. Queen's Silver Jubilee Medal, 1977. *Publications:* The Safe Airline, 1976, 2nd edn 1978; Caring for the Mature Jet, 1981. *Recreations:* light-aircraft flying, water-colour painting. *Address:* 58 Fishpool Street, St Albans, Herts AL3 4RX. *Clubs:* Sloane; London School of Flying (Elstree).

RAMSDEN, Sally, OBE 1981; Director, North East Broadcasting Co. Ltd (Metro Radio), 1973-81; *d* of John Parkin and Hannah Bentley; *m* 1948, Allan Ramsden. *Educ:* Ryhope Grammar Sch.; Neville's Cross Coll., Durham (Teaching Diploma). Teacher, 1930-47; Headmistress, 1947-69; Asst. Group Officer (part time), Nat. Fire Service, 1941-45; Hon. Organiser, Citizens' Advice Bureau, 1971-73; Pres., UK Fedn of Business and Professional Women, 1972-75; Member: Women's Nat. Commn, 1972-75; Women's Internat. Year Cttee, 1974-75; VAT Tribunals, 1973-; Royal Commn on Legal Services, 1976-79; Durham PO Adv. Cttee, 1980-. *Recreations:* fly fishing, gardening, reading. *Address:* 1 Westcott Drive, Durham Moor, Durham City DH1 5AG. *T:* Durham 42989.

RAMSEY OF CANTERBURY, Baron *cr* 1974 (Life Peer), of Canterbury; **Rt. Rev. and Rt. Hon. Arthur Michael Ramsey,** PC 1956; Royal Victorian Chain, 1974; MA, BD; Hon. Fellow: Magdalene College, Cambridge, since 1952; Merton College, Oxford, since 1974; Keble College, Oxford, since 1975; St Cross College, Oxford, since 1981; *b* 14 Nov. 1904; *s* of late Arthur Stanley Ramsey, Fellow and sometime President of Magdalene Coll., Cambridge; *m* 1942, Joan, *d* of Lieut-Colonel F. A. C. Hamilton. *Educ:* Repton; Magdalene Coll., Cambridge (Scholar); Cuddesdon. 2nd Class, Classical Tripos, 1925; 1st Class, Theological Tripos, 1927; President of Cambridge Union, 1926; ordained, 1928; curate of Liverpool Parish Church, 1928-30; subwarden of Lincoln Theological Coll., 1930-36; Lecturer of Boston Parish Church, 1936-38; Vicar of S Benedict, Cambridge, 1939-40; Canon of Durham Cathedral and Professor of Divinity in Univ. of Durham, 1940-50, Emeritus Prof., 1977, Hon. Fellow, St Chad's Coll., 1980; Regius Professor of Divinity, Univ. of Cambridge, and Fellow of Magdalene Coll., 1950-52; Canon and Prebendary in Lincoln Cathedral, 1951-52; Bishop of Durham, 1952-56; Archbishop of York, 1956-61; Archbishop of Canterbury, 1961-74. Examining Chaplain to Bishop of Chester, 1932-39, to Bishop of Durham, 1940-50, and to Bishop of Lincoln, 1951-52; Select Preacher, Cambridge 1934, 1940, 1948, 1959, 1964, Oxford, 1945-46; Hulsean Preacher, Cambridge, 1969-70. Hon. Master of the Bench, Inner Temple, 1962. A President of World Council of Churches, 1961-68. Trustee, British Museum, 1963-69. Hon. degrees include: Hon. DD: Durham, 1951; Leeds, Edinburgh, Cambridge, Hull, 1957; Manchester, 1961; London, 1962; Hon. DCL: Oxford, 1960; Kent, 1966; Hon. DLitt Keele, 1967, and a number from Universities overseas. *Publications:* The Gospel and the Catholic Church, 1936; The Resurrection of Christ, 1945; The Glory of God and the Transfiguration of Christ, 1949; F. D. Maurice and the Conflicts of Modern Theology, 1951; Durham Essays and Addresses, 1956; From Gore to Temple, 1960; Introducing the Christian Faith, 1961; Canterbury Essays and Addresses, 1964; Sacred and Secular, 1965; God, Christ and the World, 1969; (with Cardinal Suenens) The Future of the Christian Church, 1971; The Christian Priest Today, 1972; Canterbury Pilgrim, 1974; Holy Spirit, 1977; Jesus and the Living Past, 1980; Be Still and Know, 1982. *Recreation:* walking. *Address:* 16 South Bailey, Durham DH1 3EE. *T:* Durham 62934.

RAMSEY, Sir Alfred (Ernest), Kt 1967; Director: Sadler & Sons, since 1974; Gola Sports, since 1975; *b* Dagenham, 1920; *m* 1951, Victoria Phyllis Answorth, *d* of William Welch. *Educ:* Becontree Heath School. Started playing for Southampton and was an International with them; transferred to Tottenham Hotspur, 1949; with Spurs (right back), 1949-51; they won the 2nd and 1st Division titles in successive seasons. Manager of Ipswich Town Football Club, which rose from 3rd Division to Championship of the League, 1955-63; Manager, FA World Cup Team, 1963-74. Played 31 times for England. Dir, Birmingham City, 1976-77, Consultant, 1977-78. *Address:* 41 Valley Road, Ipswich, Suffolk.

RAMSEY, Rt. Rev. Kenneth Venner; an Assistant Bishop, Diocese of Manchester, since 1975; *b* 26 Jan. 1909; *s* of James Ernest and Laura Rebecca Ramsey, Southsea, Hants; unmarried. *Educ:* Portsmouth Grammar Sch.; University Coll., Oxford; Manchester Univ. Curate of St Matthew, Stretford, 1933-35; Vice-Prin., Egerton Hall, Manchester, and Lectr in Christian Ethics, Manchester Univ., 1935-38; Vice-Prin., Bishop Wilson Coll., Isle of Man, 1938-39; Prin., Egerton Hall, Manchester, 1939-41; Vicar of St Paul, Peel, Little Hulton, Lancs, 1941-48; Rector of Emmanuel Church, Didsbury, Manchester, 1948-55; Hon. Canon, Manchester Cathedral, 1950-53; Proctor in Convocation and mem. Church Assembly, 1950-55; Rural Dean of Heaton, 1950-53; Bishop Suffragan of Hulme, 1953-75. *Address:* 41 Bradwell Drive, Heald Green, Cheadle, Cheshire SK8 3BX. *T:* 061-437 8612.

RAMSEY, Leonard Gerald Gwynne; Editor of The Connoisseur, 1951-72; *b* 17 March 1913; *s* of late L. B. Ramsey, London Stock Exchange; *m* 1941, Dorothy Elizabeth, *y d* of late W. J. McMillan, Belfast; one *s* one *d. Educ:* Radley College. Commissioned Oxfordshire and Buckinghamshire Light Infantry (T), 1938; invalided out of Army, 1944; on General Staff, War Office, 1941-44, and other staff appointments. Public Relations Officer, The National Trust, 1946-49; Press Officer at Board of Trade and Colonial Office, 1950-51. Member of several Committees associated with ecclesiastical art and charitable matters. FSA 1949. *Publications:* (ed) The Connoisseur Encyclopædia of Antiques, 5 vols, 1954-60; (ed. with Ralph Edwards) The Connoisseur Period Guides, 6 vols, 1956-59; Montague Dawson, marine artist, a biography, 1967; (ed with Helen Comstock) The Connoisseur's Guide to Antique Furniture, 1969. *Recreations:* historic buildings, works of art, gardening. *Address:* Half Moon House, Cumberland Street, Woodbridge, Suffolk IP12 4AX. *Club:* Light Infantry.

RAMSEY, Prof. Norman Foster; Higgins Professor of Physics, Harvard University, since 1947; Senior Fellow, Harvard Society of Fellows, since 1971; *b* 27 Aug. 1915; *s* of Brig.-Gen. and Mrs Norman F. Ramsey; *m* 1940, Elinor Stedman Jameson; four *d. Educ:* Columbia Univ.; Cambridge Univ. (England). Carnegie Fellow, Carnegie Instn of Washington, 1939-40; Assoc., Univ. of Ill, 1940-42; Asst Prof., Columbia Univ., 1942-45; Research Assoc., MIT Radiation Laboratory, 1940-43; Cons. to Nat. Defense Research Cttee, 1940-45; Expert Consultant to Sec. of War, 1942-45; Grp Leader and Assoc. Div. Head, Los Alamos Lab. of Atomic Energy Project, 1943-45; Chief Scientist of Atomic Energy Lab. at Tinian, 1945; Assoc. Prof., Columbia Univ., 1945-47; Head of Physics Dept, Brookhaven Nat. Lab., 1946-47; Assoc. Prof., Harvard Univ., 1947-50; John Simon Guggenheim Fell., Oxford Univ., 1953-54; George Eastman Vis. Prof., Oxford Univ., 1973-74; Luce Prof. of Cosmology, Mt Holyoke, 1982-83. Dir Harvard Nuclear Lab., 1948-50, 1952; Chm., Harvard Nuclear Physics Cttee, 1948-60; Science Adviser, NATO, 1958-59; Fell. Amer. Phys. Soc. and Amer. Acad. of Arts and Sciences; Nat. Acad. of Sciences; Amer. Philos. Soc.; Sigma Xi; Phi Beta Kappa; Amer. Assoc. for Advancement of Science, 1940- (Chm., Phys. Sect., 1976). Bd of Directors, Varian Associates, 1964-66; Bd of Trustees: Associated Univs; Brookhaven Nat. Lab., 1952-55; Carnegie Endowment for Internat. Peace; Univ. Research Assoc. (Pres., 1966-81, Pres. Emeritus 1981-); Rockefeller Univ., 1976-; Air Force Sci. Adv. Bd, 1948-54; Dept of Defense Panel on Atomic Energy, 1953-59; Bd of Editors of Review of Modern Physics, 1953-56; Chm. Exec. Cttee for Camb. Electron Accelerator, 1956-63; Coun. Amer. Phys. Soc., 1956-60 (Vice-Pres., 1977; Pres., 1978); Chm., Bd of Governors, Amer. Inst. of Physics, 1980-. Gen. Adv. Cttee, Atomic Energy Commn, 1960-72. Chm., High Energy Accelerator Panel of President's Sci. Adv. Cttee and AEC, 1963. Presidential Certificate of Merit, 1947; E. O. Lawrence Award, 1960; Davisson-Germer Prize, 1974; Award for Excellence, Columbia Univ. Graduate Alumni, 1980. Hon. MA Harvard, 1947; Hon. ScD Cambridge, 1953; Hon. DSc: Case Western Reserve, 1968; Middlebury Coll., 1969; Oxford, 1973. *Publications:* Experimental Nuclear Physics, 1952; Nuclear Moments, 1953; Molecular Beams, 1956; Quick Calculus, 1965; and numerous articles in Physical Review and other scientific jls. *Recreations:* tennis, ski-ing, walking, sailing, etc. *Address:* 55 Scott Road, Belmont, Mass 02178, USA. *T:* 617-484-3553, Belmont.

RAMSEY, Robert John, CBE 1977; President, Institute of Personnel Management, since 1981; *b* 16 Aug. 1921; *m* 1949, Arlette Ikor; one *s* one *d. Educ:* Royal Liberty Sch., Romford. Joined Ford Motor Co. Ltd, as student, 1937. Served War of 1939-45: RAF Air Crew, Flt-Lt, 1942-46; POW, 1944-45. Rejoined Ford Motor Co. Ltd, 1946; Industrial Relations Manager, 1958; Dir of Labour Relations, 1969-73; Dir of Indust. Relations, 1973-81. Member: CRE, 1977-82; Council, Industrial Soc., 1977-81; Employment Policy Cttee, CBI, 1975-81; Megaw Inquiry into Civil Service Pay, 1981-82. FRSA 1979; CIPM 1977. *Recreations:* reading, theatre, hill walking, boating. *Address:* 47 Eastwood Road, Leigh-on-Sea, Essex. *T:* Southend-on-Sea 72884. *Club:* Royal Air Force.

RAMSEY, Waldo Emerson W.; see Waldron-Ramsey.

RANCHHODLAL, Sir Chinubhai Madhowlal, 2nd Bt, *cr* 1913; *b* 18 April 1906; *s* of 1st Bt and Sulochana, *d* of Chunilal Khushalrai; *S* father, 1916; *m* 1924, Tanumati, *d* of late Jhaverilal Bulakhiram Mehta of Ahmedabad; three *s.* Father was only member of Hindu community to receive a baronetcy. *Heir: s* Udayan, [*b* 25 July 1929; *m* 1953, Muneera Khodadad Fozdar; one *s* three *d.* Arjuna Award, 1972]. *Address:* Shantikunj, PO Shahibaug, Ahmedabad, India. *T:* 26953. *Club:* Willingdon (Bombay).

RANDALL, Lt-Col Charles Richard, OBE 1969; TD 1947; Vice Lord-Lieutenant for the County of Bedfordshire, since 1978; *b* 21 Jan. 1920; *s* of Charles Randall and Elizabeth Brierley; *m* 1945, Peggy Dennis; one *s* one *d. Educ:* Bedford Sch. Served War, 1939-45: commissioned Bedfordshire Yeomanry, 1939. Chm., Randalls Group Ltd, 1965-. Chm., Bedfordshire County TA&VR, 1978-; Dep. Hon. Col, The Royal Anglian Regt (Bedfordshire), TAVR, 1979-. High Sheriff, Bedfordshire, 1974-75. *Recreations:* shooting, fishing, gardening. *Address:* The Rookery, Aspley Guise, Milton Keynes MK17 8HP. *T:* Milton Keynes 582188. *Clubs:* Naval and Military, MCC.

RANDALL, Rev. Canon Edmund Laurence, AM 1980; Warden, St Barnabas' Theological College, since 1964; Hon. Canon of Adelaide, since

1979; *b* 2 June 1920; *s* of Robert Leonard Randall and Grace Annie Randall (*née* Young); unmarried. *Educ:* Dulwich College; Corpus Christi College, Cambridge. BA 1941. MA 1947. Served War, 1940-45, with Royal Artillery (AA). Corpus Christi Coll., 1938-40 and 1945-47. Wells Theological College, 1947-49. Deacon, 1949; Priest, 1950. Assistant Curate at St Luke's, Bournemouth, 1949-52; Fellow of Selwyn College, Cambridge, 1952-57; Chaplain, 1953-57; Residentiary Canon of Ely and Principal of Ely Theological Coll., 1957-59; Chaplain, St Francis Theological Coll., Brisbane, 1960-64. *Recreations:* travel, motoring. *Address:* St Barnabas' Theological College, Belair, South Australia 5052, Australia. *Club:* Naval, Military and Air Force, South Australia.

RANDALL, Sir John (Turton), Kt 1962; FRS 1946; FInstP; DSc (Manchester); Honorary Professor in the University of Edinburgh; Emeritus Professor of Biophysics in the University of London, King's College; FKC 1960; *b* 23 March 1905; *o s* of late Sidney and Hannah Cawley Randall; *m* 1928, Doris Duckworth; one *s*. *Educ:* Univ. of Manchester (Graduate Res. Schol. and Prizeman, 1925; MSc 1926, DSc 1938). Res. physicist, Res. Lab of GEC Ltd, 1926-37; Warren Res. Fellow of Royal Soc. 1937-43; Hon. Mem. of the staff, Univ. of Birmingham, 1940-43; res. in Univ. of Birmingham for Admiralty, 1939-43, jt inventor (with H. A. H. Boot) of cavity magnetron; Temp. Lectr in Cavendish Laboratory, Cambridge, 1943-44; Prof. of Natural Philosophy, United Coll. of St Salvator and St Leonard, Univ. of St Andrews, 1944-46; Wheatstone Prof. of Physics, 1946-61, Prof. of Biophysics, 1961-70, Univ. of London (King's Coll.); Dir, MRC Biophysics Research Unit, 1947-70; Chm., Sch. of Biological Sciences, KCL, 1963-69. Lectr, Rockefeller Inst. for Med. Res., NY, 1956-67; Gregynog Lectr, UCW Aberystwyth, 1958; Vis. Prof. of Biophysics, Yale Univ., 1960. Awarded (with H. A. H. Boot) Thomas Gray Meml Prize of Royal Soc. of Arts (1943) for discovery of the cavity magnetron. Duddell Medallist, Physical Soc. of London, 1945; Hughes Medallist, Royal Soc. 1946; John Price Wetherill Medal of Franklin Inst. of State of Pennsylvania, 1958; John Scott Award, City of Philadelphia, 1959. FRSE 1972. *Publications:* The Diffraction of X-rays by Amorphous Solids, Liquids and Gases, 1934; (Editor) The Nature and Structure of Collagen, 1953; (Jt Editor) Progress in Biophysics, 1950-55; papers in various scientific journals on structure in glasses and liquids, the luminescence of solids, the cavity magnetron; and, since 1946, the biophysics of connective tissues, problems of fine structure, the morphogenesis of cellular organelles; and, since 1975, the scattering of neutrons, synchrotron radiation and light by various biological systems. *Address:* Department of Zoology, University of Edinburgh, West Mains Road, Edinburgh EH9 3JT; 16 Kevock Road, Lasswade EH18 1HT. *Club:* Athenæum.

RANDALL, Sir Richard (John), Kt 1964; BEcon; ACIS; Secretary to the Treasury, Commonwealth of Australia, 1966-71; *b* 13 Oct. 1906; *s* of G. Randall, Birkdale, Queensland; *m* 1945, Nora Barry, *d* of T. J. Clyne; two *s* one *d*. *Educ:* Wynnum High School; University of Sydney (BEcon, 1st cl. hons). Carnegie Research Scholar, Sydney University, 1937; Research Officer, Premier's Office, Sydney, 1937-39; Commonwealth Treasury, 1940. Served with AIF, 1941-45. *Recreations:* golf, fishing. *Address:* 5 Throsby Crescent, Narrabundah, Canberra, ACT 2604, Australia. *Clubs:* Royal Canberra Golf, Commonwealth (Canberra).

RANDALL, William Edward, CBE 1978; DFC 1944; AFC 1945; Chairman, Chubb & Son Ltd, since 1981 (Managing Director, 1971-81, Deputy Chairman, 1976-81); *b* 15 Dec. 1920; *s* of William George Randall and Jane Longdon (*née* Pannell); *m* 1st, 1943, Joan Dorothea Way; two *s* one *d*; 2nd, 1975, Iris Joyce Roads. *Educ:* Tollington Sch., London. FCII, CBIM, FRSA. Served RAF, Flt Lieut, 1941-46. Commercial Union Assce Co., 1946-50; Chubb & Sons Lock and Safe Co., 1950, Man. Dir, 1965; Dir, Chubb & Son Ltd, 1965; Dir, Metal Closures Ltd, 1976. Mem., Home Office Standing Cttee on Crime Prevention, 1967-; Chm. Council, British Security Industry Assoc., 1981-; Mem. Exec. Cttee, British Digestive Foundn, 1982-. *Recreations:* reading, gardening. *Address:* Hollydene, Fulmer Common Road, Iver, Bucks SL0 0NP. *T:* Fulmer 2254. *Club:* Athenæum.

RANDELL, Peter Neil; Secretary, Administration and Personnel, British Technology Group (National Research Development Corporation and National Enterprise Board), since 1981; *b* 18 Nov. 1933; *s* of Donald Randell and Dorothy (*née* Anthonisz); *m* 1962, Anne Loraine Mudie; one *s* one *d*. *Educ:* Bradfield Coll.; Wye Coll., Univ. of London (BSc (Agric) Hons). FCIS. Farming and other employments, Rhodesia, 1955-61; Asst to Sec., British Insulated Callenders Cables Ltd, 1962-65; Asst Sec., NRDC, 1965-73, Sec. 1973-81. *Recreations:* the outdoors, reading. *Address:* Silver Birches, 60 Park Road, Woking, Surrey. *T:* Woking 61088.

RANDLE, Prof. Philip John, MD, FRCP; Professor of Clinical Biochemistry, University of Oxford, since 1975; Fellow of Hertford College, Oxford, since 1975; *b* 16 July 1926; *s* of Alfred John and Nora Anne Randle; *m* 1952, Elizabeth Ann Harrison; three *d* (one *s* decd). *Educ:* King Edward VI Grammar Sch., Nuneaton; Sidney Sussex Coll., Cambridge (MA, PhD, MD); UCH, London. FRCP. Med. and Surg. Officer, UCH, 1951; Res. Fellow in Biochem., Cambridge, 1952-55; Univ. Lectr, Biochem., Cambridge, 1955-64; Fellow of Trinity Hall and Dir of Med. Studies, 1957-64; Prof. of Biochem., Univ. of Bristol, 1964-75. Member: Board of Governors, United Cambridge Hospitals, 1960-64; Clinical Endocrinology Cttee, MRC, 1957-64; Chm., Grants Cttee, MRC, 1975-77; Pres., European Assoc. for Study of Diabetes, 1977-80; Chm., Research Cttee, British Diabetic Assoc., 1971-78;

General Medical Council, 1967-75. Lectures: Banting, British Diabetic Assoc., 1965; Minkowski, European Assoc. for Study of Diabetes, 1966; Copp, La Jolla, 1972; Humphry Davy Rolleston, RCP, 1983. Corresp. Mem. of many foreign medical and scientific bodies. *Publications:* numerous contribs. to books and med. sci. jls on diabetes mellitus, control of metabolism and related topics. *Recreations:* travel, swimming, bricklaying. *Address:* John Radcliffe Hospital, Headington, Oxford OX3 9DU; 11 Fitzherbert Close, Iffley, Oxford OX4 4EN.

RANDOLPH, Cyril George; *b* 26 June 1899; *s* of late Felton Randolph; *m* 1927, Betty Dixey; one *d*. *Educ:* Christ's Hospital. A Man. Dir, Glyn, Mills & Co., 1941-64; Chairman: Sun Life Assurance Society, 1953-71 (Director, 1943-71); General Funds Investment Trust, 1965-73 (Director, 1964-73); Household & General Insurance Co. Ltd, 1965-71. Almoner, Christ's Hospital. *Recreation:* golf. *Address:* 3 Castle Court, Castle Hill, Farnham, Surrey. *Club:* New Zealand Golf (West Byfleet).
See also Ven. T. B. Randolph.

RANDOLPH, Denys, BSc; CEng, MRAeS, FIProdE, CBIM; Chairman: Pains Fireworks, since 1980; Woodrush Investments Ltd, since 1980; P.L.C. Peters Ltd, since 1981; Peters Jackson Ltd, since 1981; Haddon Rocking Horses, since 1981; President and Special Consultant, Wilkinson Sword Ltd, since 1980; *b* 6 Feb. 1926; *s* of late Harry Beckham Randolph and Margaret Isabel Randolph; *m* 1951, Marjorie Hales; two *d*. *Educ:* St Paul's School; Queen's Univ., Belfast (BSc). Served Royal Engineers, 1944-48 (Captain). Queen's Univ., Belfast, 1948-52; post-grad. apprenticeship, Short Bros & Harland, 1952-55; Wilkinson Sword Ltd: Prod. Engr/Prod. Dir, Graviner Div., 1955-66; Man. Dir, Hand Tools Div., 1966-69; Chm., Graviner Div., 1969-79; Chm., 1972-79; Wilkinson Match Ltd: Dir, 1974-80; Chm., 1976-79. Institute of Directors: Chm., 1976-79; Vice-Pres., 1979-; Chm., European Cttee; Mem., Policy Cttee. Past Master, Worshipful Co. of Scientific Instrument Makers, 1977; Assistant, Worshipful Co. of Cutlers, 1977. Mem. Bd, Management Research Gp, BIM. Governor, Henley Admin. Staff Coll. FRSA (Manufactures and Commerce). *Publication:* From Rapiers to Razor Blades—The Development of the Light Metals Industry (paper, RSA). *Recreations:* yachting, golf, viticulture. *Address:* The Cottages, Rush Court, Wallingford OX10 8LJ. *T:* Wallingford 36586. *Clubs:* Army and Navy, Royal Automobile, City Livery, Little Ship.

RANDOLPH, John Hugh Edward; His Honour Judge Randolph; a Circuit Judge, since 1972; *b* 14 Oct. 1913; *s* of late Charles Edward Randolph and Phyllis Randolph; *m* 1959, Anna Marjorie (*née* Thomson). *Educ:* Bradford Grammar Sch.; Leeds University. RAF, 1940-46. Called to Bar, Middle Temple, 1946; practised on NE Circuit until 1965; Stipendiary Magistrate of Leeds, 1965-71. Deputy Chairman: E Riding QS, 1958-63; W Riding QS, 1963-71. *Recreation:* golf. *Address:* 39 Park Square, Leeds LS1 2NU. *T:* Leeds 26633. *Club:* Leeds (Leeds).

RANDOLPH, Michael Richard Spencer; Editor since 1957, Director since 1967, British Reader's Digest; Deputy Executive Editor, Reader's Digest International Editions, since 1979; *b* 2 Jan. 1925; *s* of late Leslie Richard Randolph and late Gladys (*née* Keen); *m* 1952, Jenefer Scawen Blunt; two *s* two *d*. *Educ:* Merchant Taylors' Sch.; New Rochelle High Sch., NY, USA; Queen's Coll., Oxford. Served RNVR, Intell. Staff Eastern Fleet, 1944-46, Sub-Lieut. Editorial staff, Amalgamated Press, 1948-52; Odham's Press, 1952-56; Reader's Digest, 1956-; Press Mem., Press Council, 1975-. Chm., Reader's Digest Pension Trustees Ltd, 1975-; Chm., Soc. of Magazine Editors, 1973; Dir, Periodical Publishers' Assoc., 1978-; Mem. Council, British Atlantic Cttee, 1970-. Chm., Weald of Kent Preservation Soc., 1981-. *Recreations:* country life, reading. *Address:* The Cloth Hall, Smarden, Kent TN27 8QB. *Club:* Savile.

RANDOLPH, Ven. Thomas Berkeley; Archdeacon of Hereford, 1959-70, Archdeacon Emeritus, since 1970; Canon Residentiary of Hereford Cathedral, 1961-70; *b* 15 March 1904; *s* of Felton George Randolph, Barrister-at-law, and Emily Margaret Randolph, Chichester, Sx; *m* 1935, Margaret, *d* of Rev. H. C. R. F. Jenner, Vennwood, Hereford and Wenvoe, Glam; two *s* one *d*. *Educ:* Christ's Hospital; Queen's College, Oxford (Scholar). BA (2nd Class Theology) 1927; MA 1932; Cuddesdon Coll., 1927; Curate of St Mary's, Portsea, 1928-33; Chaplain (Eccles. Est.) St Paul's Cathedral, Calcutta, 1934-37; Vicar of Eastleigh, 1938-46; Vicar of St Mary the Virgin with All Saints, St Saviour's, St Mark's and St Matthew's, Reading, 1946-59. Proctor in Convocation for the Diocese of Oxford, 1950-55; Hon. Canon of Christ Church, Oxford, 1957-59; Vicar of Wellington, Hereford, 1959-61. *Address:* 14 Heatherwood, Midhurst, West Sussex. *T:* Midhurst 2765.
See also C. G. Randolph.

RANDRUP, Michael; retired; *b* 20 April 1913; *s* of Soeren Revsgaard and Alexandra Randrup, Skive, Denmark; *m* 1941, Betty Perry (*d* 1949); one *s* one *d*; *m* 1954, Florence May Dryden. *Educ:* King's School, Canterbury; Chelsea College of Aeronautics. Learned to fly, 1934; RAF, 1940-46; OC Engine Research Flight RAE, 1945; Chief Test Pilot, D. Napier & Son Ltd, 1946-60; Manager, British Aircraft Corporation, Saudi Arabia, 1966-73. Aircraft Altitude World Record, 1957; Britannia Trophy, 1958; Derry Richards Meml Trophy, 1958. *Address:* 10 Fairlawn Road, Lytham, Lancs.

RANELAGH, John O'B.; *see* O'Beirne Ranelagh.

RANFURLY, 6th Earl of, *cr* 1831; **Thomas Daniel Knox**, KCMG 1955; Baron Welles, 1781; Viscount Northland, 1791; Baron Ranfurly (UK) 1826; Chairman: Colonial Mutual Life Assurance Society Ltd (London Board), 1966–82; Inchcape Insurance Holdings Ltd; Director: Inchcape & Co. Ltd; a Member of Lloyd's, since 1947; *b* 29 May 1913; *s* of late Viscount Northland (killed in action, 1915) and Hilda, *d* of late Sir Daniel Cooper, 2nd Bt; *S* grandfather 1933; *m* 1939, Hermione, *e d* of late G. R. P. Llewellyn, Baglan Hall, Monmouth Road, Abergavenny, Mon; one *d*. *Educ:* Eton; Trinity Coll., Cambridge. ADC to Gov.-Gen. of Australia, 1936–38; served European War of 1939–45 (prisoner). Governor and C-in-C, Bahamas, 1953–56. Chairman London Scout Council, 1957–65; Chief Scout's Commissioner, Greater London, 1965–79. President, Shaftesbury Homes and "Arethusa" Training Ship, 1959–; Chairman: Madame Tussauds Ltd, 1971–80; Bd of Governors, London Clinic, 1973–; Ranfurly Library Service Ltd. Steward, Jockey Club, 1973–75. Heir: kinsman Gerald Françoys Needham Knox [*b* 4 Jan. 1929; *m* 1955, Rosemary, *o d* of late Air Vice-Marshal Felton Vesey Holt, CMG, DSO; two *s* two *d*]. *Address:* Great Pednor, Chesham, Bucks. *T:* Gt Missenden 2155. *Clubs:* White's; Jockey (Newmarket).

RANG, Prof. Humphrey Peter, DPhil; FRS 1980; Professor of Pharmacology, University College London, since 1979; *b* 13 June 1936; *s* of Charles Rang and Sybil Rang; *m* 1960, Elizabeth Harvey Clapham; one *s* three *d*. *Educ:* University Coll. Sch.; University Coll. London (MSc 1960); UCH Med. Sch. (MB, BS 1961); Balliol Coll., Oxford (DPhil 1965). J. H. Burn Res. Fellow, Dept of Pharmacol., Oxford, 1961–65; Vis. Res. Associate, Albert Einstein Coll. of Medicine, NY, 1966–67; Univ. Lectr in Pharmacol., Oxford, 1966–72; Fellow and Tutor in Physiol., Lincoln Coll., Oxford, 1967–72; Prof. of Pharmacology: Univ. of Southampton, 1972–74; St George's Hosp. Med. Sch., London, 1974–79. *Publication:* Drug Receptors, 1973. *Recreations:* sailing, music. *Address:* 1 Belvedere Drive, SW19 7BX. *T:* 01-947 7603.

RANGER, Sir Douglas, Kt 1978; FRCS; Otolaryngologist, The Middlesex Hospital, since 1950; Dean, The Middlesex Hospital Medical School, since 1974; *b* 5 Oct. 1916; *s* of William and Hatton Thomasina Ranger; *m* 1943, Betty, *d* of Captain Sydney Harold Draper and Elsie Draper; two *s*. *Educ:* Church of England Grammar Sch., Brisbane; The Middlesex Hosp. Med. Sch. MB BS 1941, FRCS 1943. Surgical Registrar, The Mddx Hosp., 1942–44. Served War, Temp. Maj. RAMC and Surgical Specialist, 1945–48 (SEAC and MELF). Otolaryngologist, Mount Vernon Hosp., 1958–74; Hon. Sec., Brit. Assoc. of Otolaryngologists, 1965–71. RCS: Mem. Court of Examiners, 1966–72; Mem. Council, 1967–72; Pres., Assoc. of Head and Neck Oncologists of GB, 1974–77. Civil Consultant in Otolaryngology, RAF, 1965–. Dir, Ferens Inst. of Otolaryngology, 1965–; Cons. Adviser in Otolaryngology, DHSS, 1971–. *Publications:* papers and lectures on otolaryngological subjects, esp. with ref. to malignant disease. *Address:* The Tile House, The Street, Chipperfield, King's Langley, Herts WD4 9BH. *T:* King's Langley 68910; 44 Wimpole Street, W1M 7DG. *T:* 01-935 3332.

RANK, Sir Benjamin (Keith), Kt 1972; CMG 1955; MS, FRCS; FRACS; FACS; Consulting Plastic Surgeon, Royal Melbourne Hospital, Repatriation Department, Victoria Eye and Ear Hospital, Queen Victoria Hospital, etc, and in Tasmania; *b* 14 Jan. 1911; *s* of Wreghitt Rank and Bessie Rank (*née* Smith); *m* 1938, Barbara Lyle Facy; one *s* three *d*. *Educ:* Scotch College, Melbourne; Ormond College, University of Melbourne. MB, BS Melbourne, 1934; Resident Medical Officer, Royal Melbourne Hospital, 1935–36; MS (Melb.), 1937; MRCS, LRCP 1938; Resident Surgical Officer, London County Council, 1938–39 (St James' Hospital, Balham); FRCS 1938; Assistant Plastic Surgeon (EMS) at Hill End (Bart's), 1939–40; AAMC, 1940–45; Officer i/c AIF Plastic Surgery Unit in Egypt, and later at Heidelberg Military Hospital, Victoria, Australia (Lt-Col); Hon. Plastic Surgeon, Royal Melbourne Hosp., 1946–66. Carnegie Fellow, 1947. Member: Dental Board of Victoria 1949–73; Joske Orator 1974; BMA State Council, 1950–60; Chm. Exec. Cttee, RACS (Pres., 1966–68); Chm., Cttee of Management, Victorian Plastic Surgery Unit (Preston Hosp.), 1966–; Mem. Bd of Management, Royal Melbourne Hosp., 1971– (Vice-Pres., 1979–). Mem., Motor Accident Bd, Victoria, 1977–; Chm., St John's Ambulance Council, Victoria, 1978–. Sir Arthur Sims Commonwealth Travelling Prof., RCS, 1958; Moynihan Lectr, 1972; Vis. Prof., Harvard Med. Sch., 1976. Syme Orator, RACS, 1976; Stawell Orator, 1977. 87th Mem., James IV Assoc. of Surgeons; Pres., British Assoc. of Plastic Surgeons, 1965. Pres., 5th Internat. Congress of Plastic Surgery, Melbourne, 1971. FRACS 1943; Hon. FACST 1952; Hon. FRCS Canada; Hon. FRCSE 1973; Hon. FACS. Hon. DSc Punjabi Univ., 1970; Hon. Member: Société Française de Chirurgie Plastique; Indian Association of Surgeons. *Publications:* (jointly) Surgery of Repair as applied to Hand Injuries, 1953. Papers in British, American and Australian Surgical Jls. *Recreations:* golf, gardening. *Address:* 12 Jerula Avenue, Mount Eliza, Victoria 3930, Australia. *Clubs:* Melbourne (Melbourne); Peninsula Golf (Vice-Pres.).

RANK, Joseph McArthur; President, Ranks Hovis McDougall Ltd, since 1981; *b* 24 April 1918; *s* of late Rowland Rank and of Margaret McArthur; *m* 1946, Hon. Moira (who *m* 1940, Peter Anthony Stanley Woodwark, killed in action, 1943; one *d*), *d* of 3rd Baron Southborough; one *s* one *d*. *Educ:* Loretto. Joined Mark Mayhew Ltd, 1936. Served RAF, 1940–46. Personal Pilot to Air C-in-C, SEAC, 1945; Jt Man. Dir, Joseph Rank Ltd 1955–65; Dep. Chm. and Chief Exec., Ranks Hovis McDougall Ltd, 1965–69, Chm., 1969–81. Pres., Nat. Assoc. of British and Irish Millers, 1957–58, Centenary Pres., 1978. Chm., Millers Mutual Assoc., 1969–; Chm. Council, British

Nutrition Foundation, 1968–69; Dir, Royal Alexandra and Albert Sch., 1952–, Chm., Governing Body, 1975–; Friend of the Royal Coll. of Physicians, 1967–; Council, Royal Warrant Holders Assoc., 1968–71. Mem., Shrievalty Assoc., 1974. First High Sheriff of East Sussex, 1974. Hon. FRCP, 1978. *Recreations:* boating, travelling. *Address:* Landhurst, Hartfield, East Sussex. *T:* Hartfield 293. *Clubs:* Royal Air Force; Sussex.

RANKEILLOUR, 4th Baron *cr* 1932, of Buxted; **Peter St Thomas More Henry Hope**; *b* 29 May 1935; *s* of 3rd Baron Rankeillour and Mary Sibyl, *d* of late Col Wilfrid Ricardo, DSO; *S* father, 1967; unmarried. *Educ:* Ampleforth College; privately. *Recreations:* hunting, shooting, boating; agricultural machinery inventor. *Heir: cousin* Michael Richard Hope [*b* 21 Oct. 1940; *m* 1964, Elizabeth Rosemary, *e d* of Col F. H. Fuller; one *s* two *d*]. *Address:* Achaderry House, Roy Bridge, West Inverness-shire. *T:* Spean Bridge 206.

RANKIN, Andrew, QC 1968; a Recorder of the Crown Court, since 1972; *b* 3 Aug. 1924; *s* of William Locke Rankin and Mary Ann McArdle, Edinburgh; *m* 1st, 1944, Winifred (marr. diss. 1963), *d* of Frank McAdam, Edinburgh; two *s* two *d* (and one *s* decd); 2nd, 1964, Veronica, *d* of George Aloysius Martin, Liverpool. *Educ:* Royal High Sch., Edinburgh; Univ. of Edinburgh; Downing Coll., Cambridge. Served War of 1939–45 (Gen. Service Medal, 1939–45 Star): Sub-Lt, RNVR, 1943. BL (Edin.) 1946; BA, 1st cl. hons Law Tripos (Cantab), 1948. Royal Commonwealth Soc. Medal, 1942; Cecil Peace Prize, 1946; Lord Justice Holker Exhibn, Gray's Inn, 1947–50; Lord Justice Holker Schol., Gray's Inn, 1950–53; Univ. Blue, Edin., 1943 and 1946 and Camb., 1948. Lectr in Law, Univ. of Liverpool, 1948–52. Called to Bar, Gray's Inn, 1950. *Publications:* (ed, 4th edn) Levie's Law of Bankruptcy in Scotland, 1950; various articles in UK and foreign legal jls. *Recreations:* swimming, travel by sea, racing (both codes), watching soccer (especially Liverpool FC). *Address:* Chelwood, Pine Walks, Prenton, Cheshire. *T:* 051-608 2987; 69 Cliffords Inn, EC4. *T:* 01-405 2932; 2 Hare Court, Temple, EC4. *T:* 01-353 0076.

RANKIN, Dame Annabelle (Jane Mary), DBE 1957; Australian High Commissioner, New Zealand, 1971–75; *b* Brisbane; *d* of Mrs A. Rankin, Brisbane, and late Col C. D. W. Rankin, former Qld MLA for many years and sometime Minister for Railways; unmarried. *Educ:* Childers and Howard State Schools, Queensland; Glennie Memorial School, Toowoomba, Queensland. Clerk in Trustee Company; State Sec., Queensland Girl Guides' Assoc. War Service: YWCA Assistant Commissioner for Queensland, attached to Australian Women's Services, 1943–46. Appointed Organiser, Junior Red Cross, Queensland, 1946. First Queensland woman to enter Federal Parliament; Senator for Queensland, 1946–71; Mem., of Public Works Cttee, 1950; Govt Whip, Senate, 1951–66; Minister of Housing, 1966–71. Mem., Parly Standing Cttee on Broadcasting, 1947; Whip of Senate Opposition, 1947; Vice-Pres, Liberal Party of Australia, Queensland Div., 1949; Mem., Australian delegn to Commonwealth Parly Assoc. Conf., Ottawa, 1952. Represented Austr. Govt at Independence Celebrations, Mauritius, 1968. *Recreations:* motoring, reading. *Address:* 79 Captain Cook Parade, Deception Bay, Qld, Australia. *Clubs:* Moreton, Lyceum (Brisbane).

RANKIN, Sir Hugh (Charles Rhys), 3rd Bt, *cr* 1898; FSAScot 1948; Member, Standing Council of the Baronetage, since 1979; Representative to District Council Perth CC (Eastern District), 1949, Perth CC 1950; Councillor for Boro' of Rattray and Blairgowrie, 1949; joined RASC as 2nd Lieut, May 1940, at age of 41 years; Captain 1940–45, India; sheep farming and is a judge of sheep at prominent shows; formerly Senior Vice-President of the Western Islamic Association; a former Vice-President of Scottish National Liberal Association; has lived during the reigns of six sovereigns; *b* 8 Aug. 1899; *er s* of Sir Reginald Rankin, 2nd Bt, and Hon. Nest Rice (*d* 1943), 2nd *d* of 6th Baron Dynevor; changed his names by Scotch law in July 1946 to above; *S* father, 1931; *m* 1932, Helen Margaret (*d* 1945), *e d* of Sir Charles Stewart, KBE, 1st Public Trustee, and *widow* of Capt. Colin Campbell, Scots Guards; *m* 1946, Robina Kelly, FSA (Scot.), SRN, Cordon Bleu (Edin.), Crieff, Perthshire. *Educ:* Harrow. Served in 1st Royal Dragoon Guards in Sinn Feinn Campaign, 1920–22 (oldest surviving mem.); ex-Pres. Clun Forest Sheep Breeders Assoc., 1928, and their representative to National Sheep Breeders Association that year; whole-time 'piece-work' shearer, in W Australia, covering area between Bunbury and Broome, 1929–31; in 1938 was a representative on committee of British sheep breeders in London appointed to petition Government *re* sheep industry. Runner-up All Britain Sheep Judging Competition (6,000 entrants), 1962. A writer on agricultural stock; expert on Highland problems; was Brit. Rep., 1937, to 1st all European Muslim Congress at Geneva; a practising Non-Theistic Theravada Buddhist since 1944, and performed Holy Buddhist Pilgrimage, Nov. 1944, the 2nd Britisher to do so; Vice-Pres. World's Buddhist Assoc., 1945. Joined Labour Party 1939 and holds extreme political views; has been a Dominion Home Ruler for Scotland, member Scottish National Party; joined Scottish Communist Party, 1945, resigned 1980; Welsh Republican Nationalist and Welsh speaker; now left-side Labour; also zealous SNP who desires an independent Red Republic of all Scotland, exc. Orkneys and Shetlands. Has made archaeological discoveries in Dumfries, 1977–. Mem. Roy. Inst. of Roy. Soc. of Arts; is Hereditary Piper of the Clan Maclaine. News of the World Kt of the Road (for courtesy in motor driving). Broadsword Champion of British Army (Cavalry), 1921. *Publications:* articles in agricultural publications, etc. *Recreations:* golf (holds an amateur record amongst golfers of Gt Britain in having played on 382 separate courses of UK and Eire), shooting, coarse fishing, hunting, motoring, cycling on mountain tracks to tops of British mountains (Pres. Rough Stuff Cycling Assoc., 1956); study of ancient track ways; bowls, tennis, archæology (wife and himself are only persons who have crawled under dwarf fir forest for last ½ mile of most northerly known section of any Roman road in Europe, terminating opposite end of Kirriemuir Golf Course), study of domestic animals, speaking on politics, especially *re* Scottish Home Rule and Highland problems. *Heir:* *nephew* Ian Niall Rankin [*b* 19 Dec. 1932; *s* of Arthur Niall Talbot Rankin and of Lady Jean Rankin, *qv* ; *m* 1959, Alexandra, *o d* of Adm. Sir Laurence Durlacher, *qv* ; one *s* one *d*]. *Address:* Carterton Cottage, Corrie Common, Lockerbie, Dumfriesshire. *T:* Boreland 263. *Clubs:* Royal and Ancient Golf (St Andrews), Burns (Dumfries).

RANKIN, James Deans, PhD; Chief Inspector, Cruelty to Animals Act (1876), Home Office, since 1976; *b* 17 Jan. 1918; *s* of late Andrew Christian Fleming Rankin and Catherine Sutherland (*née* Russell); *m* 1950, Hilary Jacqueline Bradshaw; two *d. Educ:* Hamilton Acad.; Glasgow Veterinary Coll. (MRCVS); Reading Univ. (PhD Microbiology). FIBiol. Gen. practice, 1941; Res. Officer, Min. of Agriculture and Fisheries, 1942; Principal Res. Officer, ARC, 1952; Inspector, Home Office, 1969. *Publications:* scientific contribs in standard works and in med. and veterinary jls. *Recreations:* golf, DIY. *Address:* Home Office, 50 Queen Anne's Gate, SW1H 9AT. *T:* 01-213 6269. *Club:* Farmers'.

RANKIN, Lady Jean (Margaret), DCVO 1969 (CVO 1957); Woman of the Bedchamber to Queen Elizabeth The Queen Mother, 1947-81, Extra Woman of the Bedchamber, since 1982; *b* 15 Aug. 1905; *d* of 12th Earl of Stair; *m* 1931, Niall Rankin (*d* 1965), *s* of Sir Reginald Rankin, 2nd Bt; two *s*. Governor, Thomas Coram Foundation. Order of Orange-Nassau, Netherlands, 1950. *Address:* House of Treshnish, Calgary, Isle of Mull. *T:* Dervaig 249; 3 Catherine Wheel Yard, SW1.
See also Sir Hugh C. R. Rankin, Bt.

RANKIN, Prof. Robert Alexander, MA, PhD, ScD; FRSE, FRSAMD; Professor of Mathematics, Glasgow University, 1954-82, now Professor Emeritus; Clerk of the Senate, 1971-78; *b* 27 Oct. 1915; *s* of late Rev. Prof. Oliver Shaw Rankin, DD, and late Olivia Theresa Shaw; *m* 1942, Mary Ferrier Llewellyn, *d* of late W. M. Llewellyn and late K. F. Llewellyn, JP; one *s* three *d. Educ:* Fettes; Clare Coll., Cambridge. Wrangler, 1936; Fellow of Clare College, 1939-51; Vis. Fellow, Clare Hall, 1971. Ministry of Supply (work on rockets), 1940-45; Faculty Asst Lecturer, Cambridge Univ., 1945-48; Univ. Lecturer, Cambridge, 1948-51; Asst Tutor, Clare Coll., 1947-51; Praelector, Clare Coll., 1949-51; Mason Professor of Pure Mathematics at Birmingham University, 1951-54. Mathematical Sec. and Editor of Proceedings of Cambridge Philosophical Soc., 1947-51; Hon. Pres. Glasgow Gaelic Soc., 1957-; Pres. Edinburgh Mathematical Soc., 1957-58, 1978-79. Mem., Special Cttee, Advisory Coun. on Educn in Scotland, 1959-61; Vis. Prof., Indiana Univ., 1963-64; Vice-Pres. Roy. Soc. of Edinburgh, 1960-63; Vice-Pres., Scottish Gaelic Texts Soc., 1967-; Founder Mem., and Chm., Scottish Mathematical Council, 1967-73; Chm., Clyde Estuary Amenity Council, 1969-82. Keith Prize, RSE, 1961-63. *Publications:* Matematicheskaya Teorija Dvizhenija Neupravljaemykh Raket, 1951; An Introduction to Mathematical Analysis, 1963; The Modular Group and its Subgroups, 1969; Modular Forms and Functions, 1977; papers on the Theory of Numbers, Theory of Functions, Rocket Ballistics and Gaelic Subjects in various journals. *Recreations:* hill-walking; Gaelic studies; organ music. *Address:* 10 The University, Glasgow G12 8QG. *T:* 041-339 2641; Cromla Cottage, Corrie, Isle of Arran.

RANKINE, Sir John (Dalzell), KCMG 1954 (CMG 1947); KCVO 1956; *b* 8 June 1907; *o s* of late Sir Richard Rankine, KCMG; *m* 1939, Janet Grace (*d* 1976), *d* of Major R. L. Austin, Clifton, Bristol; one *d. Educ:* Christ's College, Christchurch, New Zealand; Exeter College, Oxford. BA 1930; entered Colonial Administration Service as Cadet, Uganda, 1931; Asst Sec. East African Governor's Conference, 1939; First Asst Sec., 1942; Asst Colonial Sec., Fiji, 1942; Colonial Sec., Barbados, 1945; Chief Secretary, Kenya, 1947-51; Chairman, Development and Reconstruction Authority. British Resident, Zanzibar, 1952-54; administered Govts of Barbados and Kenya on various occasions; Governor, Western Region, Nigeria, 1954-60. KStJ 1958. Brilliant Star of Zanzibar (1st Class), 1954. *Recreations:* tennis, squash, golf. *Address:* 12A Crittles Court, Townsland Road, Wadhurst, East Sussex TN5 6BY. *T:* Wadhurst 3642. *Clubs:* Athenæum, MCC, Queen's.

RANKING, Robert Duncan; His Honour Judge Ranking; a Circuit Judge (formerly County Court Judge), since 1968; Judge of the Mayors and City of London Court, since 1980; *b* 24 Oct. 1915; *yr s* of Dr R. M. Ranking, Tunbridge Wells, Kent; *m* 1949, Evelyn Mary Tagart (*née* Walker); one *d. Educ:* Cheltenham Coll.; Pembroke Coll., Cambridge (MA). Called to Bar, 1939. Served in Queen's Own Royal W Kent Regt, 1939-46. Dep. Chm. E Sussex QS, 1962-71; Dep. Chm., Agricultural Land Tribunal (S Eastern Area), 1963. *Address:* Little Oakfield, Camden Hill, Tunbridge Wells, Kent. *T:* 27551.

RANNIE, Prof. Ian; FRCPath 1964; FIBiol 1964; Professor of Pathology (Dental School), University of Newcastle upon Tyne, 1960-81, Professor Emeritus 1981; *b* 29 Oct. 1915; *o s* of James Rannie, MA, and Nicholas Denniston McMeekan; *m* 1943, Flora Welch; two *s. Educ:* Ayr Academy;

Glasgow University. BSc (Glas), 1935; MB, ChB (Glas), 1938; BSc Hons Pathology and Bacteriology (Glas), 1939; Hutcheson Research Schol. (Pathology), 1940. Assistant to Professor of Bacteriology, Glasgow, 1940-41; Lecturer in Pathology, 1942-60, King's College, Univ. of Durham. Consultant Pathologist, United Newcastle upon Tyne Hospitals, 1948-81, Hon. Consultant 1981-. Pres., International Soc. of Geographical Pathology, 1969-72; Vice-President: Assoc. of Clinical Pathologists, 1978-80; Internat. Union of Angiology. Hon. Mem., Hungarian Arteriosclerosis Res. Soc. *Publications:* papers on various subjects in medical journals. *Recreation:* golf. *Address:* 5 Osborne Villas, Newcastle upon Tyne NE2 1JU. *T:* 813163. *Club:* East India, Devonshire, Sports and Public Schools, Sesame, Royal Over-Seas League.

RANSOM, Charles Frederick George, CMG 1956; OBE 1950; an Historian, Historical Section of Cabinet Office, since 1972; Director of the Centre for Contemporary European Studies, University of Sussex, 1973-74, Fellow of the Centre, 1968-80; *b* 9 July 1911; *s* of late Charles Edward Ransom and Elizabeth Ransom, Harrow, Middlesex; *m* 1943, Eileen Mary Emily, *d* of late Rt Rev. A. I. Greaves, Bishop Suffragan of Grimsby, DD; two *s* one *d. Educ:* Harrow CGS; University College, London (Ricardo Scholar, 1933-35). Schoolmaster and Univ. Extra-Mural Lecturer, 1936-40. Served in UK and Italy, York and Lancaster Regt (Major), 1940-46. FO 1946; First Sec., HM Embassy, Rome, 1958-61; FO Supernumerary Fellow, St Antony's Coll., Oxford, 1966-67. *Publications:* The European Community and Eastern Europe, 1973; (jtly) British Intelligence in the Second World War, vol. I, 1979, vol. II, 1981, vol. III, Part 1, 1982; articles on European affairs. *Recreations:* music, literature, gardening. *Address:* Ladyfield, Etchingham, East Sussex. *T:* 216.

RANSOME, Maj.-Gen. Robert St George Tyldesley, CB 1946; CBE 1944; MC 1940; *b* 22 June 1903; *s* of Dr A. S. Ransome; *m* 1947, Kathleen, *widow* of Brig. C. Leslie-Smith, IA. *Educ:* Winchester Coll.; Royal Military College, Sandhurst. Joined Royal Fusiliers, 1924; Instructor, Royal Military College, Sandhurst, 1935-37; Staff College, 1938-39; BEF 1939-40 (despatches, MC); Instructor, Senior Staff College, 1940; served in Mediterranean, Middle East, 1941-43; commanded 11th Battalion Royal Fusiliers, 1942. Visited Middle East, Quebec, S Africa, Yalta, Potsdam, Italy, France, etc, 1943-45; Vice-QMG to the Forces (Maj.-Gen.), 1946; idc 1947; BGS, GHQ Far East, 1948; Comdr Scottish Beach Bde (TA), 1950; Malaya, 1950 (despatches); Services Adviser, UK High Commission, Germany, 1954-55; Chief (Maj.-Gen.), Jt Services Liaison Organisation, BAOR, 1955-58, retd. Deputy Colonel, Royal Fusiliers, 1962-63. Chm., Royal Fusiliers' Old Comrades Assoc., 1960-76. *Recreations:* gardening, shooting, military history. *Address:* Wilford Cottage, Melton, Suffolk. *Clubs:* Army and Navy, MCC.

RANT, James William, QC 1980; a Recorder of the Crown Court, since 1979; *b* 16 April 1936; *s* of Harry George Rant, FZS and Barbara Rant; *m* 1963, Helen Rant, BA (*née* Adnams); two *s* two *d. Educ:* Stowe Sch.; Selwyn Coll., Cambridge (MA, LLB). Called to the Bar, Gray's Inn, 1961; pupillage with late James N. Dunlop, 1962-63; a Dep. Circuit Judge, 1975-80. *Recreations:* cookery, music, family life. *Address:* 6 Barnstaple Road, Thorpe Bay, Essex.

RAO, Calyampudi Radhakrishna, FRS 1967; Jawaharlal Nehru Professor, Indian Statistical Institute and University Professor, University of Pittsburgh, since 1976; Director, Research and Training School, Indian Statistical Institute 1964-76, and Secretary, 1972-76; *b* 10 Sept. 1920; *s* of C. D. Naidu and A. Laksmikantamma; *m* 1948, C. Bhargavi Rao; one *s* one *d. Educ:* Andhra Univ. (MA, 1st Class Maths); Calcutta Univ. (MA, 1st Class Statistics; Gold Medal); PhD, ScD, Cambridge (Hon. Fellow, King's Coll., Cambridge, 1975). Superintending Statistician, Indian Statistical Institute, 1943-49; Professor and Head of Division of Theoretical Research and Training, Indian Statistical Institute, 1949-64. Co-editor, Sankhya, Indian Jl of Statistics, 1964-72, Editor, 1972-. Member, Internat. Statistical Inst., 1951 (Mem. Statistical Educn Cttee, 1958-; Treasurer, 1962-65; Pres.-elect, 1975-77, Pres., 1977-79); Chm., Indian Nat. Cttee for Statistics, 1962-; Pres., Biometric Soc., 1974. Fellow: Indian Nat. Sci. Acad., 1953 (Vice-Pres., 1973, 1974); Inst. of Math. Statistics, USA, 1958 (Pres., 1976-77); Amer. Statistical Assoc., 1972; Econometric Soc., 1972; Indian Acad. of Sciences. Hon. Fellow: Royal Stat. Soc., 1969; Amer. Acad. of Arts and Sciences, 1975. Shanti Swarup Bhatnagar Memorial Award, 1963; Guy Medal in Silver, Royal Stat. Soc., 1965; Padma Bhushan, 1968; Meghnad Saha Gold Medal, 1969; J. C. Bose Gold Medal, 1979. Hon. DSc: Andhra; Leningrad; Athens; Osmania; Ohio State; Hon. DLitt Delhi. *Publications:* (with Mahalanobis and Majumdar) Anthropometric Survey of the United Provinces, 1941, a statistical study, 1949; Advanced Statistical Methods in Biometric Research, 1952; (with Mukherjee and Trevor) The Ancient Inhabitants of Jebal Moya, 1955; (with Majumdar) Bengal Anthropometric Survey, 1945, a statistical study, 1959; Linear Statistical Inference and its Applications, 1965; (with A. Matthai and S. K. Mitra) Formulae and Tables for Statistical Work, 1966; Computers and the Future of Human Society, 1968; (with S. K. Mitra) The Generalised Inverse of Matrices and its Applications, 1971; (with A. M. Kagan and Yu. V. Linnik) Characterization Problems of Mathematical Statistics, 1973. *Address:* Indian Statistical Institute, 7 S.J.S. Sansanwal Marg, New Delhi 110016, India; Department of Mathematics and Statistics, University of Pittsburgh, Pittsburgh, Pa 15260, USA.

RAO, Prof. Chintamani Nagesa Ramachandra, Padma Shri, 1974; FRS 1982; CChem, FRSC; Professor of Chemical Sciences, Indian Institute of

Science, Bangalore, India, since 1976; b 30 June 1934; s of H. Nagesa Rao; m 1960, Indumati; one s one d. Educ: Univ. of Mysore (DSc); Univ. of Purdue, USA (PhD). Research Chemist, Univ. of California, Berkeley, 1958-59; Lectr, Indian Inst. of Science, 1959-63; Prof., Indian Inst. of Technology, Kanpur, 1963-76, Head of Chemistry Dept, 1964-68, Dean of Research, 1969-72; Jawaharlal Nehru Fellow, 1973-75; Commonwealth Vis. Prof., Univ. of Oxford, and Fellow, St Catherine's Coll., 1974-75; Chm., Solid State and Structural Chemistry Unit and Materials Res. Laboratory, Indian Inst. of Science, Bangalore, 1976-. Member: First Nat. Cttee of Science and Technology, Govt of India, 1971-74; Science Adv. Cttee to Union Cabinet of India, 1981-. Hon. DSc Purdue, 1982; Fellow: Indian Acad. of Scis; Indian Nat. Sci. Acad.; For. Mem., Slovenian Acad. of Scis; many awards and medals, incl.: Marlow Medal of Faraday Soc. (London), 1967; Royal Soc. of Chemistry (London) Medal, 1981; Centennial For. Fellowship of Amer. Chemical Soc., 1976. Publications: Ultraviolet and Visible Spectroscopy, 1960, 3rd edn 1975; Chemical Applications of Infrared Spectroscopy, 1964; Spectroscopy in Inorganic Chemistry, 1970; Modern Aspects of Solid State Chemistry, 1970; University General Chemistry, 1973; Solid State Chemistry, 1974; Phase Transitions in Solids, 1978; Preparation and Characterization of Materials, 1981; 400 research papers. Recreations: gourmet cooking, gardening. Address: Solid State and Structural Chemistry Unit, Indian Institute of Science, Bangalore-560012, India. T: 34411.

RAO, P. V. Narasimha; Member, Lok Sabha, re-elected 1980; Minister of External Affairs, India, since 1980; b Karimnagar, Andhra Pradesh, 28 June 1921; widower; three s five d. Educ: Osmania Univ., Hyderabad; Bombay Univ.; Nagpur Univ. (BSc, LLB). Career as leader, writer, poet and administrator. Member, Andhra Pradesh Legislative Assembly, 1957-77; Minister in Andhra Pradesh Govt, 1962-71; Chief Minister of the State, 1971-73. Chm., Telugu Academy, Andhra Pradesh; Vice-Pres., Dakshin Bharat Hindi Prachar Sabha, Madras, 1972; Gen. Sec., All India Congress Cttee, 1975-76. Elected to Lok Sabha, 1972, 1977 and 1980 (from Hanamkonda, Andhra Pradesh). Has lectured on political matters in univs in USA and Federal Republic of Germany, and has visited many countries. Publications: many, including Sahasra Plan (Hindi trans.). Address: Ministry of External Affairs, New Delhi 110011, India.

RAPALLO, Rt. Rev. Edward; see Gibraltar, Bishop of, (RC).

RAPER, Vice-Adm. Sir (Robert) George, KCB 1971 (CB 1968); Director-General, Ships, 1968-May 1974; Chief Naval Engineer Officer, 1968-74; b 27 Aug. 1915; s of Major Robert George Raper and Ida Jean (née MacAdam Smith); m 1940, Frances Joan St John (née Phillips); one s two d. Educ: RNC Dartmouth; RN Engineering College, Keyham; Advanced Engineering Course RNC Greenwich. Sen. Engineer, HMS Edinburgh, 1940 until ship was sunk, 1942 (despatches); Turbine Research Section, Admiralty, 1942-45; Engineer Officer, HMS Broadsword, Battleaxe, Crossbow, 1945-47; Comdr, 1947; Engineer-in-Chief's Dept, Admiralty, 1948-51; Engr Officer, HMS Birmingham, 1952-54; lent to RCN, 1954; Technical Sec. to Engineer-in-Chief of the Fleet, 1955-57; Capt. 1957; IDC 1958; in command HMS Caledonia, 1959-61; Dep. Dir of Marine Engineering, Admiralty, 1961-63; CSO (T) to Flag Officer Sea Training, 1963-65; Dir, Marine Engineering, MoD (Navy Dept), 1966-67. FEng, FRINA; FIMechE; FIMarE (Pres. 1972); FRSA. Recreations: carpentry, walking. Address: Hollytree Farm, Moorlinch, near Bridgwater, Somerset. T: Ashcott 210510.

RAPHAEL, Chaim, CBE 1965 (OBE 1951); writer; b Middlesbrough, 14 July 1908; s of Rev. David Rabinovitch and Rachel Rabinovitch (name Hebraised by deed poll 1936); m 1934, Diana Rose (marr. diss. 1964); one s one d. Educ: Portsmouth Grammar Sch.; University Coll., Oxford (scholar). PPE 1930. James Mew Post-Grad. Schol. in Hebrew, 1931. Kennicott Fellowship, 1933-36. Cowley Lectr in Post-Biblical Hebrew, 1932-39. Liaison Officer for Internment Camps: UK 1940; Canada 1941. Adviser, British Information Services, NY, 1942-45; Dir (Economics), 1945-57; Dep. Head of Information Div., HM Treasury, 1957-59; Head of Information Division: HM Treasury, 1959-68; Civil Service Dept, 1968-69. Research Fellow, Univ. of Sussex, 1969-75. Publications: Memoirs of a Special Case, 1962; The Walls of Jerusalem, 1968; A Feast of History, 1972; A Coat of Many Colours, 1979; The Springs of Jewish Life, 1982; novels: (under pseudonym Jocelyn Davey): The Undoubted Deed, 1956; The Naked Villany, 1958; A Touch of Stagefright, 1960; A Killing in Hats, 1964; A Treasury Alarm, 1976; Murder in Paradise, 1982. Recreation: America. Address: 27 Langdale Road, Hove, East Sussex. T: Brighton 770563. Clubs: Reform, Jack's.

RAPHAEL, Prof. David Daiches, DPhil, MA; Professor of Philosophy since 1973, and Head of Department of Humanities since 1980, Imperial College, University of London (Academic Director of Associated Studies, 1973-80); b 25 Jan. 1916; 2nd s of late Jacob Raphael and late Sarah Warshawsky, Liverpool; m 1942, Sylvia, er d of late Rabbi Dr Salis Daiches and of Flora Levin, Edinburgh; two d. Educ: Liverpool Collegiate School; University College, Oxford (scholar). 1st Class, Classical Moderations, 1936; Hall-Houghton Junior Septuagint Prizeman, 1937; 1st Class, Literae Humaniores, 1938; Robinson Senior Scholar of Oriel College, Oxford, 1938-40; Passmore Edwards Scholar, 1939. Served in Army, 1940-41. Temporary Assistant Principal, Ministry of Labour and National Service, 1941-44; temp. Principal, 1944-46. Professor of Philosophy, University of Otago, Dunedin, NZ, 1946-49; Lecturer in Moral Philosophy, Univ. of Glasgow, 1949-51; Senior Lecturer, 1951-60; Edward Caird Prof. of Political and Social Philosophy,

Univ. of Glasgow, 1960-70; Prof. of Philosophy, Univ. of Reading, 1970-73. Visiting Professor of Philosophy, Hamilton Coll., Clinton, NY (under Chauncey S. Truax Foundation), and Univ. of Southern California, 1959; Mahlon Powell Lectr, Indiana Univ., 1959; Vis. Fellow, All Souls Coll., Oxford, 1967-68. Independent Member: Cttee on Teaching Profession in Scotland (Wheatley Cttee), 1961-63; Scottish Agricultural Wages Board, 1962-; Agricultural Wages Bd for England and Wales, 1972-78. Mem. Academic Adv. Cttee, Heriot-Watt Univ., Edinburgh, 1964-71; Mem. Cttee on Distribution of Teachers in Scotland (Roberts Cttee), 1965-66; Independent Member Police Advisory Board for Scotland, 1965-70; Member Social Sciences Adv. Cttee, UK Nat. Commission, UNESCO, 1966-74; Vice-Pres., Internat. Assoc. Philosophy of Law and Social Philosophy, 1971-; Pres., Aristotelian Soc., 1974-75. Academic Mem., Bd of Governors, Hebrew Univ. of Jerusalem, 1969-81, Hon. Governor 1981-. Publications: The Moral Sense, 1947; Edition of Richard Price's Review of Morals, 1948; Moral Judgement, 1955; The Paradox of Tragedy, 1960; Political Theory and the Rights of Man, 1967; British Moralists 1650-1800, 1969; Problems of Political Philosophy, 1970; (ed jtly) Adam Smith's Theory of Moral Sentiments, 1976; Hobbes: Morals and Politics, 1977; (ed jtly) Adam Smith's Lectures on Jurisprudence, 1978; (ed jtly) Adam Smith's Essays on Philosophical Subjects, 1980; Justice and Liberty, 1980; Moral Philosophy, 1981; (trans. jtly with Sylvia Raphael) Richard Price as Moral Philosopher and Political Theorist, by Henri Laboucheix, 1982; articles in jls of philosophy and of political studies. Address: Imperial College of Science and Technology, SW7 2AZ.

RAPHAEL, Frederic Michael; author; b 14 Aug. 1931; s of late Cedric Michael Raphael and of Irene Rose (née Mauser); m 1955, Sylvia Betty Glatt; two s one d. Educ: Charterhouse; St John's Coll., Cambridge (MA (Hons)). FRSL 1964. Publications: novels: Obbligato, 1956; The Earlsdon Way, 1958; The Limits of Love, 1960; A Wild Surmise, 1961; The Graduate Wife, 1962; The Trouble with England, 1962; Lindmann, 1963; Orchestra and Beginners, 1967; Like Men Betrayed, 1970; Who Were You With Last Night?, 1971; April, June and November, 1972; Richard's Things, 1973; California Time, 1975; The Glittering Prizes, 1976; short stories: Sleeps Six, 1979; Oxbridge Blues, 1980; biography: Somerset Maugham and his World, 1977; Byron, 1982; essays: Bookmarks (ed), 1975; Cracks in the Ice, 1979; screenplays: Nothing but the Best, 1964; Darling, 1965 (Academy Award); Two For The Road, 1967; Far From the Madding Crowd, 1967; A Severed Head, 1972; Daisy Miller, 1974; The Glittering Prizes, 1976 (sequence of TV plays) (Writer of the Year 1976, Royal TV Soc.); Rogue Male, 1976; (and directed) Something's Wrong (TV), 1978; School Play (TV), 1979; The Best of Friends (TV), 1979; Richard's Things, 1981; play: From The Greek, Arts, Cambridge, 1979; translations: (with Kenneth McLeish): Poems of Catullus, 1976; The Oresteia, 1978 (televised as The Serpent Son, BBC, 1979). Recreations: tennis, painting things white. Address: The Wick, Langham, Colchester, Essex CO4 5PE.

RAPHAEL, Prof. Ralph Alexander, CBE 1982; PhD, DSc (London), ARCS, DIC; FRS 1962, FRSE, FRSC; Fellow of Christ's College, and Professor of Organic Chemistry, Cambridge University, since June 1972; b 1 Jan. 1921; s of Jack Raphael; m 1944, Prudence Marguerite Anne, d of Col P. J. Gaffikin, MC, MD; one s one d. Educ: Wesley College, Dublin; Tottenham County School; Imperial College of Science and Technology. Chemist, May & Baker Ltd, 1943-46. ICI Research Fellow, Univ. of London, 1946-49; Lecturer in Organic Chemistry, Univ. of Glasgow, 1949-54; Professor of Organic Chemistry, Queen's University, Belfast, 1954-57; Regius Prof. of Chemistry, Glasgow Univ., 1957-72. Tilden Lectr, Chem. Soc., 1960, Corday-Morgan Vis. Lectr, 1963; Roy. Soc. Vis. Prof., 1967; Pedler Lectr, Chem. Soc., 1973; Pacific Coast Lectr, West Coast Univs tour from LA to Vancouver, 1979; Lady Davis Vis. Prof., Hebrew Univ. of Jerusalem, 1980. Vice-Pres. Chemical Soc., 1967-70; Mem., Academic Bd, Warwick Univ. Hon. DUniv Stirling, 1982. Meldola Medallist, RIC, 1948; Chem. Soc. Ciba-Geigy Award for Synthetic Chemistry, 1975; Davy Medal, Royal Soc., 1981. Publications: Chemistry of Carbon Compounds, Vol. IIA, 1953; Acetylenic Compounds in Organic Synthesis, 1955; papers in Journal of Chemical Society. Recreations: music, bridge. Address: University Chemical Laboratory, Lensfield Road, Cambridge CB2 1EW. T: Cambridge 66499; 4 Ivy Field, High Street, Barton, Cambs. Club: Athenæum.

RAPHOE, Bishop of, (RC), since 1982; **Most Rev. Séamus Hegarty;** b 26 Jan. 1940; s of James Hegarty and Mary O'Donnell. Educ: Kilcar National School; St Eunan's Coll., Letterkenny; St Patrick's Coll., Maynooth; University Coll., Dublin. Priest, 1966; post-grad. studies, University Coll., Dublin, 1966-67; Dean of Studies 1967-71, President 1971-82, Holy Cross College, Falcarragh. Publication: contribs to works on school administration and student assessment. Recreations: bridge, fishing. Address: Ard Adhamhnain, Letterkenny, Co. Donegal, Ireland. T: Letterkenny 21208.

RAPP, Sir Thomas (Cecil), KBE 1950; CMG 1945; MC; b Saltburn-by-the-Sea, 1893; m 1922, Dorothy, d of John Clarke; one d (and one d decd). Educ: Coatham School; Sidney Sussex College, Cambridge. Served European War (Duke of Wellington's Regiment TF), 1914-18, retiring with rank of Major; an assistant in Levant Consular Service, 1919; Acting Vice-Consul, Port Said, 1920; Vice-Consul, Cairo, 1922; Rabat, 1927; Consul, Sofia, 1931; Moscow, 1932; Zagreb, 1936; Consul-General at Zagreb, Jugoslavia, 1939-41. Captured by German armed forces and interned in Germany, 1941-43; Consul-General, Tabriz, 1943-44; Salonica, 1944-45; Minister to Albania (did not proceed), 1946; Deputy head and subsequently head of British Economic Mission to

Greece, 1946–47; Ambassador to Mexico, 1947–50; Head of British Middle East Office, Cairo, 1950–53. *Recreation:* walking. *Address:* York Cottage, Sandgate, Kent. *T:* Folkestone 38594.

RASCH, Sir Richard Guy Carne, 3rd Bt, *cr* 1903; a Member of HM Body Guard, Honourable Corps of Gentlemen-at-Arms, since 1968; *b* 10 Oct. 1918; *s* of Brigadier G. E. C. Rasch, CVO, DSO (*d* 1955); *S* uncle, 1963; *m* 1st, 1947, Anne Mary, *d* of late Major J. H. Dent-Brocklehurst; one *s* one *d*; 2nd, 1961, Fiona Mary, *d* of Robert Douglas Shaw. *Educ:* Eton; RMC, Sandhurst. Major, late Grenadier Guards. Served War of 1939–45; retired, 1951. *Recreations:* shooting, fishing. *Heir: s* Simon Anthony Carne Rasch [*b* 26 Feb. 1948. *Educ:* Eton; Royal Agric. Coll., Cirencester]. *Address:* 30 Ovington Square, SW3. *T:* 01-589 9973; The Manor House, Lower Woodford, near Salisbury, Wilts. *Clubs:* White's, Pratt's, Cavalry and Guards.

RASH, Mrs D. E. A.; *see* Wallace, Doreen.

RASHLEIGH, Sir Harry (Evelyn Battie), 5th Bt, *cr* 1831; *b* 17 May 1923; *er s* of late Captain Harry Rashleigh, JP (3rd *s* of 3rd Bt) and Jane Henrietta, *d* of late E. W. Rashleigh, Stoketon, Saltash, Cornwall; *S* kinsman 1951; *m* 1954, Honora Elizabeth Sneyd, *d* of G. S. Sneyd, The Watch House, Downderry, Cornwall; one *s* three *d*. *Educ:* Wellington Sch., Som. Served War of 1939–45, Westminster Dragoons, 1941–45; 79th Armoured Div. Experimental Wing, 1945–46. Mechanical Engineer with John Mowlem & Co. Ltd, UK, 1947–48; John Mowlem & Co. Ltd, Tanganyika, East Africa, 1948–50; Earth Moving & Construction Ltd, Tanganyika, East Africa, 1948–51; Engineer, UK, 1951–54; farming, Kampi-ya-Moto, Kenya, 1954–65; farming, Holdstrong Farm, Coryton, 1965–71, retired. *Recreations:* shooting, sailing. *Heir: s* Richard Harry Rashleigh, *b* 8 July 1958. *Address:* Stowford Grange, Lewdown, near Okehampton, Devon. *T:* Lewdown 237. *Club:* Royal Fowey Yacht.

RASHLEIGH BELCHER, John; *see* Belcher, J. R.

RASMINSKY, Louis, CC (Canada), 1968; CBE 1946; Governor, Bank of Canada, 1961–73; *b* 1 Feb. 1908; *s* of David and Etta Rasminsky; *m* 1930, Lyla Rotenberg; one *s* one *d*. *Educ:* University of Toronto; London School of Economics. Financial Section, League of Nations, 1930–39; Chairman, Foreign Exchange Control Board, Canada, 1940–51; Deputy Governor, Bank of Canada, 1956–61. Executive Director: IMF, 1946–62; International Bank, 1950–62; Alternate Governor for Canada, IMF, 1969–73. Chm. Bd of Governors, Internat. Develt Res. Centre, 1973–78. Hon. Fellow, LSE, 1960. Hon. LLD: Univ. of Toronto, 1953; Yeshiva Univ., 1965; Queen's Univ., 1967; Bishop's Univ., 1968; McMaster Univ., 1969; Trent Univ., 1972; Concordia Univ., 1975; Univ. of Western Ontario, 1978; Univ. of British Columbia, 1979; Hon. DHL Hebrew Union Coll., 1963. Outstanding Achievement Award of Public Service of Canada, 1968; Vanier Medal, Inst. of Public Admin, 1974. *Recreations:* golf, fishing. *Address:* 440 Roxborough Road, Rockcliffe Park, Ottawa, Ont. Canada. *T:* 749-7704. *Clubs:* Rideau, Cercle Universitaire d'Ottawa (Ottawa); Five Lakes (Wakefield, PQ).

RASMUSSEN, Prof. Steen Eiler; architect; Professor of Architecture, Royal Academy of Fine Arts, Copenhagen, 1938–68; *b* Copenhagen, 9 Feb. 1898; *s* of General Eiler Rasmussen; *m* 1934, Karen Margrete Schrøder; two *d*. *Educ:* Metropolitanskolen; Royal Academy of Fine Arts, Copenhagen. Three first prizes in town planning competitions, 1919. Mem. Danish Roy. Acad. of Fine Arts, 1922; Lecturer at Architectural Sch. of the Academy, 1924; Architect to Municipal Town Planning Office, Copenhagen, 1932–38. Pres. Copenhagen Regional Planning Cttee, 1945–58. Visiting Professor in USA: Massachusetts Inst. of Technology, 1953, Yale, 1954, Philadelphia, 1958, Berkeley, 1959. Lethaby Professor, Roy. College of Art, London, 1958. Designed: Tingbjerg Housing Estate, Copenhagen, 1953–; Schools, Town Hall. Hon. Corr. Member: RIBA London, Bavarian Acad. of Fine Arts, 1958; American Institute of Architects, 1962; Hon. Royal Designer for Industry, London, 1947; Hon. Dr: Technische Hochschule Munich; Univ. of Lund. *Publications:* London, the Unique City, 1937; Towns and Buildings, 1951; Experiencing Architecture, 1959. *Recreation:* to doze in a chair thinking of future books. *Address:* Dreyersvej 9, 2960 Rungsted Kyst, Denmark. *T:* 01863510.

RASUL, Syed Alay; Hon. Chairman, Federation of Bangladesh Associations, UK and Europe, since 1974; Hon. Secretary General, Standing Conference of Asian Organisations, UK, since 1970; Senior Community Relations Officer, Sheffield, since 1967; *b* 1 Feb. 1931; *s* of late Syed Ahmed Rasul and Khodeja Rasul; *m* 1956, Kamrunnessa Rasul; three *s* one *d* (and one *d* decd). *Educ:* Univ. of Aligarh, India (BA 1950); Univ. of Dacca, Bangladesh (MA 1953); Univ. of Manchester (Dipls. Adult Educn and Community Development 1963, Social Admin. 1964; Pres., Pakistan Students Soc., 1963–64); High Wycombe Coll. of Technology. NEBSS Cert., 1974; UN and Govt of Pakistan Cert. of Merit in Community Develt, 1956. Manpower Survey Officer, Pakistan Govt, 1955; E Pakistan Government: Social Welfare Organiser, 1956–60; Divl Welfare Organiser, 1960–62; Exec. Sec., Pakistan Welfare and Inf. Centre, Manchester, 1964–67. Gen. Sec., E Pakistan Conf. of Social Work, 1956–57; Hon. Vice-Chm., UK Immigrants Advisory Service, 1975–; Convenor, EEC Migrant Workers Forum, 1975–; founder Mem., Bangladesh International and Adv. Service, 1978–. Member: BBC Adv. Council for Asian Unit, 1965–70; Electricity Consumer Council, 1977–; presenter and broadcaster, Asian programme, Radio Sheffield, 1966–76. Governor, Waltheaf Comp. Sch., Sheffield, 1978–; Pres., Aligarh Muslim

Univ. Old Boys' Assoc., UK, 1981–. *Publications:* 6 special brochures; weekly column on immigration and race relations in Janomot. *Recreations:* billiards, music; visiting places and meeting people. *Address:* 2 Marchwood Road, Sheffield S6 5LD. *T:* (home) Sheffield 349506; (office) Sheffield 27232.

RATCLIFF, Antony Robin Napier; Chief General Manager, Eagle Star Group, since 1974; *b* 26 Sept. 1925; *m* 1956, Helga Belohlawek, Vienna; one *s*. *Educ:* Sutton Valence Sch. FIA 1953; ASA. Nat. Correspondent for England, Internat. Actuarial Assoc., 1965–70; Mem. Council, British Insurance Assoc., 1969–. Pres., Inst. of Actuaries, 1980–82; Vice-Pres., London Insce Inst., 1964–. Mem. Finance Cttee, Nat. Assoc. for Gifted Children. Corresponding Member: Deutsche Gesellschaft für Versicherungsmathematik; Verein zur Förderung der Versicherungswirtschaft. Hon. Treasurer, German Christ Church, London. Messenger and Brown Prize-Winner, Inst. of Actuaries, 1963. *Publications:* (jtly) Lessons from Central Forecasting, 1965; (jtly) Strategic Planning for Financial Institutions, 1974; contribs to Jl of Inst. of Actuaries, Trans of Internat. Congress of Actuaries, Jl London Insce Inst., Jl Chartered Insce Inst., Blätter der Deutschen Gesellschaft für Versicherungsmathematik. *Address:* 1 Threadneedle Street, EC2R 8BE. *T:* 01-588 1212. *Clubs:* Actuaries, Roehampton, Anglo-Austrian Society.

RATCLIFFE, Frederick William, MA, PhD; JP; University Librarian, University of Cambridge, since 1980; Fellow, Corpus Christi College, Cambridge, since 1980; *b* 28 May 1927; *y s* of late Sydney and Dora Ratcliffe, Leek, Staffs; *m* 1952, Joyce Brierley; two *s* one *d*. *Educ:* Leek High Sch., Staffs; Manchester Univ. (MA, PhD); MA Cantab. Manchester University: Graduate Res. Scholarship, 1951; Res. Studentship in Arts, 1952; Asst Cataloguer and Cataloguer, 1954–62; Sub-Librarian, Glasgow Univ., 1962–63; Dep. Librarian, Univ. of Newcastle upon Tyne, 1963–65; University Librarian, 1965–80, Dir, John Rylands University Library, 1972–80, Manchester University. Trustee, St Deiniol's Library, Hawarden, 1975–. Hon. Lectr in Historical Bibliography, Manchester Univ., 1970–80; External Prof., Dept of Library and Inf. Studies, Loughborough Univ., 1981–; Fellow, Chapter of Woodard Schools (Eastern Div.), 1981–. JP Stockport, 1972–80, Cambridge, 1981. *Publications:* many articles in learned journals. *Recreations:* book collecting, hand printing, cricket. *Address:* Cambridge University Library, West Road, Cambridge CB3 9DR. *T:* Cambridge 61441; Light Alders Farm, Light Alders Lane, Disley, Cheshire SK12 2LW. *T:* Disley 2234.

RATCLIFFE, John Ashworth, CB 1965; CBE 1959 (OBE 1947); FRS 1951; MA; Director of Radio and Space Research Station, Slough, Oct. 1960–Feb. 1966; *b* 12 Dec. 1902; *s* of H. H. Ratcliffe, Rawtenstall, Lancs; *m* 1930, Nora Disley; two *d*. *Educ:* Giggleswick School; Sidney Sussex College, Cambridge. Taught Physics at Cambridge and Research in Radio Wave Propagation, 1924–60 (War Service with Telecommunications Res. Est., Malvern); Reader in Physics, Cambridge University, 1947–60; Fellow of Sidney Sussex College, 1927–60, Hon. Fellow 1962. President: Physical Society, 1959–60; Section A, British Association, 1964; Chairman, Electronics Board, IEE, 1962–63; Vice-Pres., IEE, 1963–66, Pres., 1966. Hon. Pres., URSI; Foreign Fellow, Indian Nat. Sci. Acad. FEng, FIEEE. Hon. FInstP; Hon. FIEE; Hon. DSc Kent, 1979. Faraday Medal (IEE), 1966; Royal Medal (Roy. Soc.), 1966; Guthrie Medal (Inst. Physics), 1971; Gold Medal (RAS), 1976. *Publications:* numerous papers in scientific journals on Radio Wave Propagation. *Address:* 193 Huntingdon Road, Cambridge CB3 0DL.

RATFORD, David John Edward, CVO 1979; HM Diplomatic Service; Counsellor and Head of Chancery, Copenhagen, since 1978; *b* 22 April 1934; *s* of George Ratford and Lilian (*née* Jones); *m* 1960, Ulla Monica, *d* of Oskar and Gurli Jerneck, Stockholm; two *d*. *Educ:* Whitgift Middle Sch.; Selwyn Coll., Cambridge (1st Cl. Hons Mod. and Med. Langs). National Service (Intell. Corps), 1953–55. Exchequer and Audit Dept, 1952; FO, 1955; 3rd Sec., Prague, 1959–61; 2nd Sec., Mogadishu, 1961–63; 2nd, later 1st Sec., FO, 1963–68; 1st Sec. (Commercial), Moscow, 1968–71; FCO, 1971–74; Counsellor (Agric. and Econ.), Paris, 1974–78. Comdr, Order of the Dannebrog, Denmark, 1979. *Recreations:* music, squash, tennis. *Address:* c/o Foreign and Commonwealth Office, SW1; Käringön, Bohuslän, Sweden. *Club:* Travellers'.

RATHBONE, John Francis Warre, CBE 1966; TD 1950; Secretary of National Trust for Places of Historic Interest or Natural Beauty, 1949–68; President, London Centre of the National Trust, since 1968; *b* 18 July 1909; *e s* of Francis Warre Rathbone and Edith Bertha Hampshire, Allerton Beeches, Liverpool. *Educ:* Marlborough; New College, Oxford. Solicitor, 1934. Served War of 1939–45; AA Comd and staff (Col 1945). Dir Ministry of Justice Control Branch, CCG (British Element), 1946–49. Member Bd of Governors, UCH, 1968–74. Mem. Management Cttee, Mutual Households Assoc. Ltd; Mem., Friends of UCH. *Recreations:* music, travel. *Address:* 15 Furlong Road, N7 8LS. *T:* 01-607 4854. *Club:* Travellers'.

RATHBONE, John Rankin, (Tim Rathbone); MP (C) Lewes since Feb. 1974; *b* 17 March 1933; *s* of J. R. Rathbone, MP (killed in action 1940) and Lady Wright (*see* Beatrice Wright); *m* 1st, 1960, Margarita Sanchez y Sanchez (marr. diss. 1981); two *s* one *d*; 2nd, 1982, Mrs Susan Jenkin Stopford Sackville. *Educ:* Eton; Christ Church, Oxford; Harvard Business School. 2nd Lieut KRRC, 1951–53. Robert Benson Lonsdale & Co., Merchant Bankers, 1956–58; Trainee to Vice-Pres., Ogilvy & Mather Inc., NY, 1958–66; Chief Publicity and Public Relations Officer, Conservative Central Office, 1966–68; Director: Charles Barker Group, 1968–; Ayer Barker Ltd, 1971– (Man. Dir

1970-73; Dep. Chm., 1973-79); Charles Barker CBC, 1981-; Charles Barker Management Selection Internat., 1981-. PPS to Minister of Health, 1979-82, to Minister for Trade (Consumer Affairs), 1982-. Mem., Nat. Cttee for Electoral Reform. FRSA 1979. *Recreation:* family. *Address:* 30 Farringdon Street, EC4A 4EA. *T:* 01-236 3011. *Clubs:* Brooks's; Sussex; Society of Sussex Downsmen.

RATHBONE, Very Rev. Norman Stanley; Dean of Hereford, 1969-82, now Dean Emeritus; *b* 8 Sept. 1914; *er s* of Stanley George and Helen Rathbone; *m* 1952, Christine Olive Gooderson; three *s* two *d*. *Educ:* Lawrence Sheriff Sch., Rugby; Christ's Coll., Cambridge; Westcott House, Cambridge. BA 1936, MA 1939. St Mary Magdalen's, Coventry: Curate, 1938; Vicar, 1945; Canon Theologian, Coventry Cathedral, 1954; Canon Residentiary and Chancellor, Lincoln Cathedral, 1959. *Address:* The Daren, Newton St Margarets, Herefordshire. *T:* Michaelchurch 623.

RATHBONE, Philip Richardson; Secretary, Royal Town Planning Institute, 1960-75; *b* 21 May 1913; *s* of Herbert R. Rathbone, sometime Lord Mayor of Liverpool, and Winifred Richardson Evans, Wimbledon; *m* 1940, Angela, *d* of Captain A. B. de Beer, Liverpool; one *s* two *d*. *Educ:* Clifton Coll., Bristol; University Coll., Oxford. BA Hons Mod. History 1934. Sec., Housing Centre, London, 1935-39. Army, King's Regt, Liverpool; Personnel Selection, WO, 1939-45 (Major). Principal, Min. of Town and Country Planning, 1945-53; Sec., Royal Instn of Chartered Surveyors (Scotland), 1953-60. Hon. MRTPI, 1975. *Publications:* Paradise Merton: The Story of Nelson and the Hamiltons at Merton Place, 1973; The Angel and the Flame: the two marriages of Sir William Hamilton, 1978; A Wheelchair for all Seasons, 1981. *Recreations:* writing, Lady Hamilton. *Address:* 19 Raymond Road, SW19 4AD. *T:* 01-946 2478.

RATHBONE, Tim; *see* Rathbone, J. R.

RATHCAVAN, 1st Baron, *cr* 1953, of The Braid, Co. Antrim; **(Robert William) Hugh O'Neill,** Bt, *cr* 1929, PC (Ireland 1921, Northern Ireland 1922, Gt Brit. 1937); Hon. LLD, Queen's University Belfast; HM Lieutenant for County Antrim, 1949-59; *b* 8 June 1883; *o surv. s* of 2nd Baron O'Neill; *m* 1909, Sylvia (*d* 1972), *d* of Walter A. Sandeman of Morden House, Royston; two *s* (and one *s* decd). *Educ:* Eton; New Coll., Oxford, BA. Bar, Inner Temple, 1909; contested Stockport, 1906; MP (UU) Mid-Antrim, 1915-22, Co. Antrim, 1922-50, North Antrim, 1950-52; MP for County Antrim in the Parliament of Northern Ireland, 1921-29; first Speaker of the House of Commons of Northern Ireland, 1921-29; Chairman Cons Private Members' (1922) Committee, 1935-39; Parl. Under-Sec. of State for India and for Burma, 1939-40; late Lt North of Ireland Imperial Yeomanry; late Captain Royal Irish Rifles and Major (general list); served in European War, 1915-18, France and Palestine. *Recreations:* shooting, fishing. *Heir: s* Rt Hon. Phelim Robert Hugh O'Neill, *qv. Address:* Cleggan Lodge, Ballymena, Co. Antrim. *T:* Aughafatten 209; 28 Queen's Gate Gardens, SW7. *T:* 01-584 0358. *Clubs:* Carlton; Ulster (Belfast).
See also Hon. Sir Con D. W. O'Neill.

RATHCREEDAN, 2nd Baron, *cr* 1916; **Charles Patrick Norton,** TD; *b* 26 Nov. 1905; *er s* of 1st Baron and Marguerite Cecil (*d* 1955), *d* of Sir Charles Huntington, 1st Bart, MP; *S* father, 1930; *m* 1946, Ann Pauline, *er d* of late Surgeon Capt. William Bastian, RN; two *s* one *d*. *Educ:* Wellington Coll.; Lincoln Coll., Oxford, MA. Called to Bar, Inner Temple, 1931; admitted Solicitor, 1936; Major 4th Battalion Oxford and Buckinghamshire Light Inf., TA; served France, 1940; prisoner of war, 1940-45. Master, Founders' Co., 1970. *Recreations:* tennis, golf. *Heir: s* Hon. Christopher John Norton [*b* 3 June 1949; *m* 1978, Lavinia, *d* of A. G. R. Ormiston, Holford House, N Chailey, Sussex]. *Address:* Church Field, Fawley, Henley-on-Thames, Oxon. *T:* Henley 4160. *Clubs:* Farmers'; Leander.

RATHDONNELL, 5th Baron, *cr* 1868; **Thomas Benjamin McClintock Bunbury;** Lieutenant, RN; *b* 17 Sept. 1938; *o s* of William, 4th Baron Rathdonnell and Pamela, *e d* of late John Malcolm Drew; *S* father 1959; *m* 1965, Jessica Harriet, *d* of George Gilbert Butler, Scatorish, Bennettsbridge, Co. Kilkenny; three *s* one *d*. *Educ:* Charterhouse; Royal Naval College, Dartmouth. *Heir: s* Hon. William Leopold McClintock Bunbury, *b* 6 July 1966. *Address:* Lisvanagh, Rathvilly, County Carlow, Ireland. *T:* Carlow 55104.

RATTEE, Donald Keith, QC 1977; *b* 9 March 1937; *s* of Charles Ronald and Dorothy Rattee; *m* 1964, Diana Mary Howl; four *d*. *Educ:* Clacton-on-Sea County High School; Trinity Hall, Cambridge (MA, LLB). Called to Bar, Lincoln's Inn, 1962; Second Junior Counsel to the Inland Revenue (Chancery), 1972-77. *Recreations:* tennis, sailing, gardening. *Address:* 29 Shirley Avenue, Cheam, Surrey. *T:* 01-642 3062; 7 New Square, Lincoln's Inn, WC2. *T:* 01-405 1266. *Clubs:* Sutton Tennis and Squash (Sutton, Surrey); Walton-on-Thames Sailing (Walton-on-Thames).

RATTER, John, CBE 1945 (OBE 1944); ERD 1953; retired; Railway Adviser, World Bank, Washington DC, 1970-74; *b* 15 May 1908; *s* of George Dempster Ratter, South Shields; *m* 1937, Eileen Cail, Knaresborough, Yorkshire; two *s* one *d*. *Educ:* St Peters School, York; Durham University. BSc; MICE. Various appointments as civil engineer with London and North Eastern Railway and London Passenger Transport Board, 1929-39; War of 1939-45: served with Royal Engineers, France, Africa and Italy, and in War

Office; Deputy Director of Transportation, CMF, with rank of Colonel. Various appointments with LNE Railway and LPTB and Railway Exec., 1945-53; Chief Civil Engineer, British Transport Commission, 1953-54; Technical Adviser, BTC, 1954-58; Member: BTC, 1958-62. British Railways Board, 1963-70. Pres., Internat. Union of Railways, 1960-62. Legion of Merit (USA), 1944; Légion d'Honneur (France), 1963; Order of Merit, German Federal Republic, 1968; Comdr, Order of Leopold II, Belgium, 1969. *Address:* Old Timbers, Poole Street, Great Yeldham, Essex.

RATTLE, Simon; Principal Conductor, City of Birmingham Symphony Orchestra since Sept. 1980; Artistic Director, South Bank summer music, since 1981; *b* Liverpool, 1955; *m* 1980, Elise Ross, American soprano. Won Bournemouth John Player Internat. Conducting Comp., when aged 19. Has conducted: Bournemouth Sinfonietta; Philharmonia; Northern Sinfonia; London Philharmonic; London Sinfonietta; Los Angeles Philharmonic; Stockholm Philharmonic; Toronto Symphony, etc. Festival Hall début, 1976. Royal Albert Hall (Proms. etc.), 1976-80; Asst Conductor, BBC Scottish Symphony Orch. (début Glasgow 1976), 1977; Queen Elizabeth Hall, 1977-; Associate Conductor, Royal Liverpool Philharmonic Soc., 1977-80; Glyndebourne début, 1977; Principal Conductor, London Choral Soc., 1979; Principal Guest Conductor, Rotterdam Philharmonic, 1981-. Exclusive contract with EMI Records. *Address:* c/o Harold Holt Ltd, 134 Wigmore Street, W1H 0DJ. *T:* 01-935 2331.

RAU, Santha Rama; free-lance writer since 1945; English teacher at Sarah Lawrence College, Bronxville, NY, since 1971; *b* Madras, India, 24 Jan. 1923; *d* of late Sir Benegal Rama Rau, CIE; *m* 1st, 1952, Faubion Bowers (marr. diss. 1966); one *s* ; 2nd, Gurdon W. Wattles. *Educ:* St Paul's Girls' School, London, England; Wellesley College, Mass., USA. Feature writer for the Office of War Information, New York, USA, during vacations from college, 1942-45. Hon. doctorate: Bates College, USA, 1961; Russell Sage College, 1965; Phi Beta Kappa, Wellesley College, 1960. *Publications:* Home to India, 1945; East of Home, 1950; This is India, 1953; Remember the House, 1955; View to the South-East, 1957; My Russian Journey, 1959; A Passage to India (dramatization), 1962; Gifts of Passage, 1962; The Adventuress, 1971; Cooking of India, 1971 (2 vols); A Princess Remembers (with Maharani Gayatri Devi of Jaipur), 1976; An Inheritance (with Dhanvanthi Rama Rau), 1977. Many articles and short stories in New Yorker, Art News, Horizon, Saturday Evening Post, Reader's Digest, etc. *Address:* RR Box 200, Leedsville Road, Amenia, NY 12501, USA.

RAVEN, John Armstrong, CBE 1982; Chief Executive, Simplification of International Trade Procedures Board, since 1974 (Director, SITPRO Board, 1970-72); *b* 23 April 1920; *s* of late John Colbeck Raven; *m* 1st, 1945, Megan Humphreys (*d* 1963); one *s* one *d* ; 2nd, 1965, Joy Nesbitt; one step *d*. *Educ:* High Sch., Cardiff; Downing Coll., Cambridge (MA). Called to Bar, Gray's Inn, 1955. Dir, British Coal Exporters' Fedn, 1947-68; Section Head, Nat. Economic Develt Office, 1968-70; Dir-Gen., Assoc. of British Chambers of Commerce, 1972-74. *Recreation:* worrying. *Address:* 6 Farrance Court, Tunbridge Wells, Kent. *T:* Tunbridge Wells 24769. *Club:* Travellers'.

RAVEN, Rear-Adm. John Stanley, CB 1961; BSc, FIEE; *b* 5 Oct. 1910; *s* of Frederick William Raven; *m* 1935, Nancy, *d* of William Harold Murdoch; three *s*. *Educ:* Huddersfield College; Leeds University (BSc). Temp. RNVR Commission, 1939; transferred to RN, 1946; retired, 1965. *Recreation:* painting. *Address:* East Garth, School Lane, Collingham, Yorks.

RAVEN, Dame Kathleen, (Dame Kathleen Annie Ingram), DBE 1968; SRN 1936; SCM 1938; Chief Nursing Officer in the Department of Health and Social Security (formerly Ministry of Health), 1958-72; *b* 9 Nov. 1910; *o d* of late Fredric William Raven and late Annie Williams Mason; *m* 1959, Prof. John Thornton Ingram, MD, FRCP (*d* 1972). *Educ:* Ulverston Grammar School; privately; St Bartholomew's Hosp., London; City of London Maternity Hospital. St Bartholomew's Hospital: Night Superintendent, Ward Sister, Administrative Sister, Assistant Matron, 1936-49; Matron, Gen. Infirmary, Leeds, 1949-57; Dep. Chief Nursing Officer, Min. of Health, 1957-58. Mem. Gen. Nursing Council for England and Wales, 1950-57; Mem. Council and Chm. Yorkshire Br., Roy. Coll. of Nursing, 1950-57; Mem. Central Area Advisory Bd for Secondary Education, Leeds, 1953-57; Area Nursing Officer, Order of St John, 1953-57; Mem. Exec. Cttee Assoc. of Hospital Matrons for England and Wales, 1955-57; Mem. Advisory Cttee for Sister Tutor's Diploma, Univ. of Hull, 1955-57; Internal Examr for Diploma of Nursing, Univ. of Leeds, 1950-57; Member: Area Nurse Trg Cttee, 1951-57; Area Cttee Nat. Hosp. Service Reserve, 1950-57; Central Health Services Council, 1957-58; Council and Nursing Advisory Bd, British Red Cross Soc., 1958-72; Cttee of St John Ambulance Assoc., 1958-72; National Florence Nightingale Memorial Cttee of Great Britain and Northern Ireland, 1958-72; WHO Expert Advisory Panel on Nursing, 1961-79; a Vice-Pres., Royal Coll. of Nursing, 1972-. Civil Service Comr, 1972-80. Chief Nursing Adviser, Allied Med. Gp, 1974-. Nursing missions to Saudi Arabia and Egypt, 1972-. Hon. Freewoman, Worshipful Co. of Barbers, 1981. FRSA 1970. Officer (Sister) Order of St John, 1963. *Recreations:* painting, reading, travel. *Address:* Jesmond, Burcott, Wing, Leighton Buzzard, Bedfordshire. *T:* Wing 244; 29 Harley Street, W1. *T:* 01-580 3765. *Club:* Royal Commonwealth Society.
See also R. W. Raven.

RAVEN, Ronald William, OBE (mil.) 1946; TD; FRCS 1931; Consulting Surgeon, Westminster Hospital and Royal Marsden Hospital, since 1969; Surgeon, French Hospital, London, since 1936; Cons. Surgeon (General Surgeon) Eversfield Chest Hospital since 1937; Cons. Surgeon, Royal Star and Garter Home for Disabled Sailors, Soldiers and Airmen since 1948; *b* 28 July 1904; *e s* of late Fredric William Raven and Annie Williams Mason, Coniston. *Educ:* Ulverston Grammar School; St Bartholomew's Hospital Medical College, Univ. of London. St Bart's Hosp.: gained various prizes and Brackenbury surgical schol.; resident surgical appts, 1928–29; Demonstrator in Pathology, St Bart's Hosp., 1929–31; Registrar Statistics Nat. Radium Commn, 1931–34; jun. surgical appts, 1931–35; Asst Surg. Gordon Hosp., 1935; Asst Surg. Roy. Cancer Hosp., 1939–46, Surg. 1946–62; Jt Lectr in Surgery, Westminster Med. Sch., Univ. of London, 1951–69; Surgeon, Westminster (Gordon) Hosp., 1947–69; Sen. Surgeon, Royal Marsden Hosp. and Inst. of Cancer Research, Royal Cancer Hosp., 1962–69. Member: DHSS Standing Sub-Cttee on Cancer; DHSS Adv. Cttee on Cancer Registration. Fellow Assoc. of Surg. of GB; Mem., Internat. Soc. of Surgery; FRSM (PP, Section of Proctology, PP, Section of Oncology); Mem. Council, 1968–76, Mem. Court of Patrons, 1976–, RCS; Founder Pres., British Assoc. of Surgical Oncology (1973–77); Past (Founder) Pres., Assoc. of Head and Neck Oncologists of GB; Chm. Council, 1961–, and Chm. Exec. Cttee, 1948–61, Marie Curie Meml Foundn; Chm. Joint Nat. Cancer Survey Cttee; Vice-Pres. and Chm., Council of Epsom Coll., 1954–; late Chm., Conjoint Cttee; late Mem. Bd of Governors Royal Marsden Hosp.; formerly Mem. Council of Queen's Institute of District Nursing; Mem. (late Chm.), Cttee of Management Med. Insurance Agency; Formerly Mem. Council, Imperial Cancer Res. Fund; Founder Pres., World Fedn of Nat. Voluntary Cancer Care Assocs, 1982–. Surg. EMS, 1939; joined RAMC, 1941, and served in N Africa, Italy and Malta (despatches); o/c Surg. Div. (Lt-Col); and o/c Gen. Hosp. (Col), 1946; Lt-Col RAMC (TA); o/c Surg. Div. Gen. Hosp., 1947–53; Col RAMC (TA); o/c No 57 (Middlesex) General Hospital (TA), 1953–59; Colonel TARO, 1959–62; Hon. Colonel RAMC. OStJ 1946. Hon. Professor National Univ. of Colombia, 1949; Hon. MD Cartagena, 1949; Corr. For. Member: Soc. of Head and Neck Surgeons of USA; Roman Surg. Soc.; Soc. Surg. of Bogotá; Société de Chirurgie de Lyon; Member: Nat. Acad. Med. of Colombia; NY Acad. of Sciences; Soc. of Surgeons of Colombia; Italian Soc. Thoracic Surg.; Czechoslovak Soc. of J. E. Purkyne; Lectures: Arris and Gale, 1933; Erasmus Wilson, 1935, 1946, 1947; Malcolm Morris Meml, 1954; Blair Bell Meml, 1960; Elizabeth Matthai Endowment, Madras Univ., 1965; First W. Emory Burnett Honor, Temple Univ., USA, 1966; Edith A. Ward Meml, 1966; Gerald Townsley Meml, 1974; Bradshaw, RCS, 1975; Ernest Miles Meml, 1980; Honor, Amer. Soc. of Surg. Oncology, 1981; Honor, 1st Congress, Eur. Soc. of Surg. Oncology, Athens, 1982. Hunterian Prof., RCS, 1948; Vis. Prof. of Surgery: Ein-Shams University, Cairo, 1961; Maadi Hosp., Cairo, 1974. Surgical missions to: Colombia, 1949; Saudi Arabia, 1961, 1962, 1975, 1976; United Arab Emirates, 1975. Mem. Court, 1973–, Master, 1980–81, Worshipful Co. of Barbers. Chevalier de la Légion d'Honneur, 1952. Senior Editor, Clinical Oncology, 1979–. *Publications:* Treatment of Shock, 1942 (trans. Russian); Surgical Care, 1942, 2nd edn 1952; Cancer in General Practice (jointly), 1952; Surgical Instruments and Appliances (jointly), 1952; War Wounds and Injuries (jt editor and contrib.). 1940; chapters on Shock and Malignant Disease in Encyclopædia British Medical Practice, 1952, 1955, 1962–69, and Medical Progress, 1970–71; Handbook on Cancer for Nurses and Health Visitors, 1953; Cancer and Allied Diseases, 1955; contrib. chapters in Operative Surgery (Rob and Rodney Smith), 1956–57; Editor and contrib. Cancer (7 vols), 1957–60; Cancer of the Pharynx, Larynx and Oesophagus and its Surgical Treatment, 1958; (ed) Cancer Progress, 1960 and 1963; (ed jtly) The Prevention of Cancer, 1967; (ed) Modern Trends in Cancer, pt 1, Research Progress, part 2, Clinical Progress, 1973; (ed and contrib.) The Dying Patient, 1975 (trans. Japanese and Dutch); (ed and contrib.) Principles of Surgical Oncology, 1977; (ed and contrib.) Foundations of Medicine, 1978; papers on surgical subjects, especially relating to Cancer in British and foreign journals. *Recreations:* philately (medallist Internat. Stamp Exhibn, London, 1950), music, ceramics and pictures, travel. *Address:* 29 Harley Street, W1N 1DA. *T:* 01-580 3765; Manor Lodge, Wingrave, Aylesbury, Bucks. *T:* Aston Abbots 287; Meadow View, Coniston, Cumbria. *Clubs:* MCC, Pilgrims.
See also Dame Kathleen Raven.

RAVEN, Simon (Arthur Noël); author, critic and dramatist since 1957; *b* 28 Dec. 1927; *s* of Arthur Godart Raven and Esther Kate Raven (*née* Christmas); *m* 1951, Susan Mandeville Kilner (marriage dissolved); one *s. Educ:* Charterhouse; King's Coll., Cambridge (MA). Research, 1951–52; regular commn, King's Shropshire Light Inf., 1953–57 (Capt.): served in Kenya; resigned, 1957. Member, Horatian Society. *Publications:* novels: The Feathers of Death, 1959; Brother Cain, 1959; Doctors Wear Scarlet, 1960; Close of Play, 1962; The Roses of Picardie, 1980; An Inch of Fortune, 1980; The Alms for Oblivion sequence: The Rich Pay Late, 1964; Friends in Low Places, 1965; The Sabre Squadron, 1966; Fielding Gray, 1967; The Judas Boy, 1968; Places Where They Sing, 1970; Sound the Retreat, 1971; Come like Shadows, 1972; Bring Forth the Body, 1974; The Survivors, 1976; *short stories:* The Fortunes of Fingel, 1976; *autobiography:* Shadows on the Grass, 1982; *general:* The English Gentleman, 1961; Boys Will be Boys, 1963; Royal Foundation and Other Plays, 1965; contribs to Observer, Spectator, Punch, etc. *Plays and dramatisations for broadcasting:* BBC TV: Royal Foundation, 1961; The Scapegoat, 1964; Sir Jocelyn, 1965; Huxley's Point Counter-Point, 1968; Trollope's The Way We Live Now, 1969; The Pallisers, a serial in 26 episodes based on the six Palliser novels of Anthony Trollope, 1974, repeated 1976; Iris Murdoch's An Unofficial Rose, 1975; Sexton Blake, 1978; ABC TV: The Gaming Book, 1965; Thames TV: Edward and Mrs Simpson, a serial based on Edward VIII by Frances Donaldson, 1978, repeated 1980; Love in a Cold Climate, a dramatisation of Nancy Mitford's Pursuit of Love and Love in a Cold Climate, 1980; BBC Radio: Triad, a trilogy loosely based on Thucydides' History of the Peloponnesian War, 1965–68, repeated 1972. *Recreations:* cricket, travel, reading. *Address:* c/o Curtis Brown Ltd, 1 Craven Hill, W2 3EP. *Clubs:* Reform; MCC, Butterflies Cricket, Trogs' Cricket.

RAVENSCROFT, John Robert Parker, (John Peel); broadcaster/journalist, since 1961; *b* 30 Aug. 1939; *s* of Robert Leslie and Joan Mary Ravenscroft; *m* 1974, Sheila Mary Gilhooly; two *s* two *d. Educ:* Woodlands Sch., Deganwy, N Wales; Shrewsbury. National Service, Royal Artillery (B2 Radar Operator), 1957–59. Mill operative, Rochdale, 1959–60; office boy, Dallas, Texas, 1960–65; part-time disc-jockey, 1961–; computer programmer, 1965; Pirate Radio, London, 1967; BBC Radio 1, 1967–. *Recreations:* adoring Liverpool FC, cycling, staring out of the window. *Address:* c/o BBC Radio 1, W1A 4WW. *T:* 01-580 4468. *Clubs:* Liverpool Supporters; Eddie Grundy Fan (Sutton).

RAVENSDALE, 3rd Baron *cr* 1911; **Nicholas Mosley,** MC 1944; Bt 1781; *b* 25 June 1923; *e s* of Sir Oswald Mosley, 6th Bt (*d* 1980) and Lady Cynthia (*d* 1933), *d* of 1st Marquess Curzon of Kedleston; *S* to barony of aunt, who was also Baroness Ravensdale of Kedleston (Life Peer), 1966, and to baronetcy of father, 1980; *m* 1st, 1947, Rosemary Laura Salmond (marr. diss. 1974); three *s* one *d*; 2nd, 1974, Mrs Verity Bailey; one *s. Educ:* Eton; Balliol College, Oxford. Served in the Rifle Brigade, Captain, 1942–46. *Publications:* (as Nicholas Mosley): Spaces of the Dark, 1951; The Rainbearers, 1955; Corruption, 1957; African Switchback, 1958; The Life of Raymond Raynes, 1961; Meeting Place, 1962; Accident, 1964; Experience and Religion, 1964; Assassins, 1966; Impossible Object, 1968; Natalie Natalia, 1971; The Assassination of Trotsky, 1972; Julian Grenfell: His Life and the Times of his Death, 1888–1915, 1976; Catastrophe Practice, 1979; Imago Bird, 1980; Serpent, 1981; The Rules of the Game: Sir Oswald and Lady Cynthia Mosley 1896–1933, 1982. *Heir: s* Hon. Shaun Nicholas Mosley, *b* 5 August 1949. *Address:* Church Row Studios, 21a Heath Street, NW3. *T:* 01-435 5479.

RAVENSDALE, Thomas Corney, CMG 1951; retired; *b* 17 Feb. 1905; *s* of late Henry Ravensdale and late Lilian (*née* Corney); *m* (marriage dissolved); two *s*; *m* 1965, Mme Antoine Watteau (*née* Ricard). *Educ:* Royal Masonic Sch., Bushey, Herts; St Catharine's Coll., Cambridge. Acting Vice-Consul, Smyrna, 1928; 3rd Secretary, British Embassy, Ankara, 1929–34; 2nd Asst Oriental Sec., The Residency, Cairo, 1934–37; Vice-Consul, Bagdad, 1937–42; 1st Asst Oriental Sec., Brit. Embassy, Cairo, 1942–47; Oriental Counsellor, Cairo, 1948–51; Political Adviser, British Residency, Benghazi, 1951; Couns., Brit. Embassy in Libya, 1952–55; Ambassador to Dominican Republic, 1955–58; Insp. Foreign Service Establishments, 1958–60; Ambassador to the Republics of Dahomey, Niger, Upper Volta and the Ivory Coast, 1960–63. *Recreation:* gardening. *Address:* The Cottage, 13 rue de Penthièvre, Petit Andely, 27700 Les Andelys, France. *T:* 54-16-38 Les Andelys (Eure). *Club:* Athenæum.

RAVENSWORTH, 8th Baron *cr* 1821; **Arthur Waller Liddell,** Bt 1642; JP; *b* 25 July 1924; *s* of late Hon. Cyril Arthur Liddell (2nd *s* of 5th Baron) and Dorothy L., *d* of William Brown, Slinfold, Sussex; *S* cousin 1950; *m* 1950, Wendy, *d* of J. S. Bell, Cookham, Berks; one *s* one *d. Educ:* Harrow. Radio Engineer, BBC, 1944–50. JP Northumberland, 1959. *Heir: s* Hon. Thomas Arthur Hamish Liddell, *b* 27 Oct. 1954. *Address:* Eslington Park, Whittingham, Alnwick, Northumberland. *T:* Whittingham 239.

RAW, Rupert George, CMG 1979; UK Director, European Investment Bank, 1973–81; *b* 5 April 1912; *s* of late Captain Rupert George Raw, DSO, and late Winifred Melville (*née* Francis), later Lady Stuart-Menteth; *m* 1936, Joan Persica, *d* of Sir Alban Young, 9th Bt, KCMG, MVO; one *s* two *d. Educ:* Eton; Oxford (BA Hons History). Supplementary Reserve Scots Guards, Lt-Col; parachuted Yugoslavia. CCG, 1946–48; joined OEEC; Finance Director, 1952–55; Bank of England, 1955; Adviser to Governor, 1962–72, retired; Director of Banque Belge, 1973, resigned, 1977; Dep. Chm., Italian Internat. Bank, 1973–76, Chm. 1976–79, retired 1980. *Recreations:* tennis, skiing. *Address:* 23 Warwick Square, SW1.

RAWBONE, Rear-Adm. Alfred Raymond, CB 1976; AFC 1951; *b* 19 April 1923; *s* of A. Rawbone and Mrs E. D. Rawbone (*née* Wall); *m* 1943, Iris Alicia (*née* Willshaw); one *s* one *d. Educ:* Saltley Grammar Sch., Birmingham. Joined RN, 1942; 809 Sqdn War Service, 1943; CO 736 Sqdn, 1953; CO 897 Sqdn, 1955; CO Loch Killisport, 1959–60; Comdr (Air) Lossiemouth and HMS Ark Royal, 1961–63; Chief Staff Officer to Flag Officer Naval Air Comd, 1965–67; CO HMS Dido, 1968–69; CO RNAS Yeovilton, 1970–72; CO HMS Kent, 1972–73; Dep. ACOS (Operations), SHAPE, 1974–76. Comdr 1958; Captain 1964; Rear-Adm. 1974. *Address:* Halstock Leigh, Halstock, near Yeovil, Somerset.

RAWCLIFFE, Rt. Rev. Derek Alec; *see* Glasgow and Galloway, Bishop of.

RAWDEN-SMITH, Rupert Rawden; Metropolitan Stipendiary Magistrate, 1967–78, retired; *b* 24 Sept. 1912; *s* of late Dr Hoyland Smith; *m* 1941, Mollie Snow; one *s* one *d. Educ:* Rossall School; King's College, London University (LLB). Barrister, Middle Temple, 1939; Recorder of Sunderland, 1961–67.

Recreations: gardening, travel. *Address:* 97 Church Road, Wimbledon, SW19 5AL. *T:* 01-946 4325.

RAWES, Francis Roderick, MBE 1944; MA; *b* 28 Jan. 1916; *e s* of late Prescott Rawes and Susanna May Dockery; *m* 1940, Dorothy Joyce, *d* of E. M. Hundley, Oswestry; two *s* one *d. Educ:* Charterhouse; St Edmund Hall, Oxford. Served in Intelligence Corps, 1940-46; GSO3(I) 13 Corps; GSO1 (I) HQ 15 Army Group and MI14 WO. Asst Master at Westminster School, 1938-40 and 1946-64; Housemaster, 1947-64; Headmaster, St Edmund's School, Canterbury, 1964-78. Mem. Governing Body, Sutton Valence Sch., 1978-; Governor, Westonbirt Sch., 1979-. *Address:* Peyton House, Chipping Campden, Glos.

RAWLEY, Alan David, QC 1977; a Recorder of the Crown Court, since 1972; *b* 28 Sept. 1934; *er s* of late Cecil David Rawley and of Theresa Rawley (*née* Pack); *m* 1964, Ione Jane Ellis; two *s* one *d. Educ:* Wimbledon Coll.; Brasenose Coll., Oxford. Nat. Service, 1956-58; commnd Royal Tank Regt. Called to the Bar, Middle Temple, 1958. Dep. Chairman, Cornwall Quarter Sessions, 1971. *Address:* Lamb Building, Temple, EC4. *T:* 01-353 6381. *Clubs:* Garrick; Exeter and County (Exeter); Hampshire (Winchester).

RAWLINGS, Margaret; actress; *b* Osaka, Japan, 5 June 1906; *d* of Rev. G. W. Rawlings and Lilian Boddington; *m* 1st, 1927, Gabriel Toyne, actor (marr. diss. 1938); no *c* ; 2nd, 1942, Robert Barlow (knighted 1943; *d* 1976); one *d. Educ:* Oxford High School for Girls; Lady Margaret Hall, Oxford. Left Oxford after one year, and joined the Macdona Players Bernard Shaw Repertory Company on tour, 1927; played Jennifer in the Doctor's Dilemma and many other parts; toured Canada with Maurice Colbourne, 1929; First London engagement Bianca Capello in The Venetian at Little Theatre in 1931, followed by New York; played Elizabeth Barrett Browning, in The Barretts of Wimpole Street in Australia and New Zealand; Oscar Wilde's Salome at Gate Theatre; Liza Kingdom, The Old Folks at Home, Queen's; Mary Fitton in This Side Idolatry, Lyric; Jean in The Greeks had a word for it, Liza Doolittle in Pygmalion and Ann in Man and Superman, Cambridge Theatre, 1935; Katie O'Shea in Parnell, Ethel Barrymore Theatre, New York 1935, later at New, London; Lady Macbeth for OUDS 1936; Mary and Lily in Black Limelight, St James's and Duke of York's, 1937-38; Helen in Trojan Women, Karen Selby in The Flashing Stream, Lyric, 1938-39, and in New York; Revival of Liza in Pygmalion, Haymarket, 1939; You of all People, Apollo, 1939; A House in the Square, St Martin's, 1940; Mrs Dearth in Dear Brutus, 1941-42; Gwendolen Fairfax in the Importance of Being Earnest, Royal Command Perf., Haymarket, 1946; Titania in Purcell's Fairy Queen, Covent Garden, 1946; Vittoria Corombona in Webster's The White Devil, Duchess, 1947; Marceline in Jean-Jacques Bernard's The Unquiet Spirit, Arts, 1949; Germaine in A Woman in Love, tour and Embassy, 1949; The Purple Fig Tree, Piccadilly, 1950; Lady Macbeth, Arts, 1950; Spring at Marino, Arts, 1951; Zabina in Tamburlaine, Old Vic, 1951-52; Lysistrata in The Apple Cart, Haymarket, 1953; Countess in The Dark is Light Enough, Salisbury and Windsor Repertory, 1955; Paulina and Mistress Ford, Old Vic, 1955-56; Title Rôle in Racine's Phèdre, Theatre in the Round, London and tour, 1957-58; Sappho in Sappho, Lyceum, Edinburgh, 1961; Ask Me No More, Windsor, 1962; Title role in Racine's Phèdre, Cambridge Arts, 1963; Ella Rentheim in John Gabriel Borkman, Duchess, 1963; Jocasta in Œdipus, Playhouse (Nottingham), 1964; Gertrude in Hamlet, Ludlow Festival, 1965; Madame Torpe in Torpe's Hotel, Yvonne Arnaud Theatre, Guildford, 1965; Mrs Bridgenorth, in Getting Married, Strand, 1967; Carlotta, in A Song at Twilight, Windsor, 1968; Cats Play, Greenwich, 1973; Mixed Economy, King's Head Islington, 1977; Empress Eugénie, May Fair, 1979, trans. to Vaudeville, UK tour and Dublin Fest., 1979; Lord Arthur Saville's Crime, Malvern Fest. and tour, 1980; Empress Eugénie, Kings Lynn Fest., 1980, Cologne, Horsham, MacRobert Arts Centre, Stirling, and Pitlochry Fest., 1981; Riverside Theatre, Univ. of Coleraine, 1980, 1981; Uncle Vanya, Haymarket, 1982. *Films:* Roman Holiday; Beautiful Stranger; No Road Back; Hands of the Ripper. *Television:* Criss Cross Quiz; Somerset Maugham Hour; Sunday Break; Compact; Maigret; Planemakers; solo performance, Black Limelight, Armchair Theatre, 1969; Wives and Daughters, 1971. Innumerable broadcasts, incl. We Beg to Differ, and, Brains Trust; poetry recitals; recordings of: Keats, Gerard Manley Hopkins, Alice in Wonderland; (Marlowe Soc.) King Lear, Pericles; New English Bible Gospels. *Publication:* (trans.) Racine's Phèdre, 1961, (US, 1962). *Recreation:* poetry. *Address:* Rocketer, Rocky Lane, Wendover, Bucks. *T:* Wendover 622234. *Club:* Arts Theatre.

RAWLINS, Colin Guy Champion, OBE 1965; DFC 1941; Director of Zoos, Zoological Society of London, since 1966; *b* 5 June 1919; *s* of R. S. C. Rawlins and Yvonne Blanche Andrews; *m* 1946, Rosemary Jensen; two *s* one *d. Educ:* Prince of Wales Sch., Nairobi; Charterhouse; Queen's Coll., Oxford (BA). Served with RAF, 1939-46: Bomber Comd, NW Europe; POW, 1941-45; Sqdn-Leader. HM Overseas Civil Service, 1946-66: Administrative Officer, Northern Rhodesia (later Zambia); appointments at Headquarters and in field; Provincial Commissioner, Resident Secretary. Mem., Pearce Commn on Rhodesian Opinion, 1972. Past Pres., Internat. Union of Dirs of Zool. Gardens. FCIS 1967. *Recreations:* aviation, travel, gardening. *Address:* c/o Zoological Society of London, Regent's Park, NW1; Birchgrove, Earl Howe Road, Holmer Green, Bucks.

RAWLINS, Surg. Vice-Adm. Sir John (Stuart Pepys), KBE 1978 (OBE 1960; MBE 1956); *b* 12 May 1922; *s* of Col S. W. H. Rawlins, CB, CMG,

DSO and Dorothy Pepys Cockerell; *m* 1944, Diana Colbeck; one *s* three *d. Educ:* Wellington Coll.; University Coll., Oxford; St Bartholomew's Hospital. BM, BCh 1945; MA, FRCP, FFCM, FRAeS. Surg. Lieut RNVR, HMS Triumph, 1947; Surg. Lieut RN, RAF Inst. Aviation Med., 1951; RN Physiol Lab., 1957; Surg. Comdr RAF Inst., Aviation Med., 1961; HMS Ark Royal, 1964; US Navy Medical Research Inst., 1967; Surg. Captain 1969; Surg. Cdre, Dir of Health and Research (Naval), 1973; Surg. Rear-Adm. 1975; Dean of Naval Medicine and MO i/c, Inst. of Naval Medicine, 1975-77; Actg Surg. Vice-Adm. 1977; Medical Dir-Gen. (Navy), 1977-80. QHP 1975. Director: Deep Ocean Technology Inc.; Diving Unlimited International Ltd. Vice-Pres., Underseas Med. Soc.; Founder-Mem. European Underseas Biomed. Soc.; Fellow Aerospace Med. Soc.; FRAeS 1973; FRSM. Erroll-Eldridge Prize 1967; Sec. of US Navy's Commendation 1971; Gilbert Blane Medal 1971; Tuttle Meml Award 1973; Chadwick Medal and Prize 1975; Armstrong Lectr (Aerospace Med. Soc.), 1980; Man of the Year, British Council for Rehabilitation of the Disabled, 1964. *Publications:* papers in fields of aviation and diving medicine. *Recreations:* diving, fishing, stalking, riding. *Address:* Wey House, Standford Lane, Headley, Bordon, Hants GU35 8RH. *T:* Bordon 2830. *Clubs:* Army and Navy; Vincent's (Oxford).

RAWLINSON, family name of **Baron Rawlinson of Ewell.**

RAWLINSON OF EWELL, Baron *cr* 1978 (Life Peer), of Ewell in the County of Surrey; **Peter Anthony Grayson Rawlinson,** PC 1964; Kt 1962; QC 1959; QC (NI) 1972; *b* 26 June 1919; *o surv. s* of Lt-Col A. R. Rawlinson, OBE, and of Ailsa, *e d* of Sir Henry Mullenux Grayson, Bt, KBE; *m* 1st, 1940, Haidee Kavanagh; three *d* ; 2nd, 1954, Elaine Dominguez, Newport, Rhode Island, USA; two *s* one *d. Educ:* Downside; Christ's Coll., Cambridge (Exhibitioner 1938, Hon. Fellow 1980). Officer Cadet Sandhurst, 1939; served in Irish Guards, 1940-46; N Africa, 1943 (despatches); demobilized with rank of Major, 1946. Called to Bar, Inner Temple, 1946, Bencher, 1962; Recorder of Salisbury, 1961-62; called to Bar, Northern Ireland, 1972. Contested (C) Hackney South, 1951; MP(C) Surrey, Epsom, 1955-74, Epsom and Ewell, 1974-78. Solicitor-General, July 1962-Oct. 1964; Opposition Spokesman: for Law, 1964-65, 1968-70; for Broadcasting, 1965; Attorney-General, 1970-74; Attorney-General for NI, 1972-74; Recorder of Kingston upon Thames, 1975-; Leader, Western Circuit, 1975-82. Vice-Chm., Cons. Parly Legal Cttee, 1966; Chm., Parly Legal Cttee, 1967-70. Member of Council, Justice, 1960-62, 1964; Trustee of Amnesty, 1960-62; Member, Bar Council, 1966-68; Mem. Senate, Inns of Court, 1968, Vice-Chm., 1974; Vice-Chm., Bar, 1974-75; Chairman of the Bar and Senate, 1975-76. Hon. Fellow, Amer. Coll. of Trial Lawyers, 1973; Hon. Mem., Amer. Bar Assoc., 1976. SMO Malta. *Publications:* War Poems and Poetry today, 1943; Public Duty and Personal Faith—the example of Thomas More, 1978; articles and essays in law jls. *Recreations:* the theatre and painting. *Address:* 12 King's Bench Walk, Temple, EC4. *T:* 01-353 5892/6. *Clubs:* White's, Pratt's, MCC.

RAWLINSON, Sir Anthony Henry John, 5th Bt *cr* 1891; fashion photographer; *b* 1 May 1936; *s* of Sir Alfred Frederick Rawlinson, 4th Bt and of Bessie Ford Taylor, *d* of Frank Raymond Emmatt, Harrogate; *S* father, 1969; *m* 1st, 1960, Penelope Byng Noel (marr. diss. 1967), 2nd *d* of Rear-Adm. G. J. B. Noel, RN; one *s* one *d* ; 2nd, 1967, Pauline Strickland (marr. diss. 1976), *d* of J. H. Hardy, Sydney; one *s* ; 3rd, 1977, Helen Leone, *d* of T. M. Kennedy, Scotland; one *s. Educ:* Millfield School. Coldstream Guards, 1954-56. *Heir:* s Alexander Noel Rawlinson, *b* 15 July 1964. *Address:* Heath Farm, Guist, near Dereham, Norfolk. *Club:* Clermont.

RAWLINSON, Sir Anthony (Keith), KCB 1978 (CB 1975); Second Permanent Secretary, HM Treasury, since 1977; *b* 5 March 1926; *s* of late Alfred Edward John Rawlinson, Bishop of Derby 1936-59, and Mildred Ansley Rawlinson (*née* Ellis); *m* 1956, Mary Hill; three *s. Educ:* Maidwell Hall; Eton; Christ Church, Oxford. Eton: King's Schol., 1939, Newcastle Schol., 1944, Captain of Sch. 1944; Christ Church, Open Schol. (classics), 1944. Gren. Gds (Lieut) 1944-47. Oxford: 1st Cl. Honour Mods (classics), 1949, 2nd Cl. Lit. Hum., 1951. Entered Civil Service by open competition as Asst Principal, 1951; Min. of Labour and Nat. Service, 1951-53; transferred to Treasury, 1953; Principal, 1955; seconded to Atomic Energy Authority as Private Sec. to Chairman, 1958-60; returned to Treasury, 1960: Asst Sec., 1963; Under-Sec., 1968; Dep. Sec., 1972; Econ. Minister and Head of UK Treasury and Supply Delegn, Washington, and UK Exec. Dir, IMF and IBRD, 1972-75; Department of Industry: Dep. Sec., 1975-76; Second Permanent Sec., 1976-77. Chm., Mount Everest Foundn, 1970-71; Mem., C of E Central Bd of Finance, 1981-. *Publications:* articles and reviews in mountaineering jls. Editor, Climbers' Club Jl, 1955-59. *Recreation:* mountaineering (Pres. OU Mountaineering Club, 1949-50). *Address:* 105 Corringham Road, NW11 7DL. *T:* 01-458 3402. *Clubs:* United Oxford & Cambridge University, Alpine (Hon. Sec., 1963-66, Vice-Pres., 1972-73).

RAWLINSON, Dennis George Fielding, OBE 1978; Member Board, National Bus Company, since 1979, and Northern Regional Director, since 1974; Company Director, since 1964; *b* 3 Sept. 1919; *s* of George and Mary Jane Rawlinson; *m* 1943, Lilian Mary; one *s* one *d. Educ:* Grocers' Co.'s Sch. Army, 1939-46. Various progressive positions in omnibus industry. *Recreations:* theatre, music, golf and various lesser sports. *Address:* 62 Cleveland Avenue, Darlington, Co. Durham DL3 7HG. *T:* Darlington 61254. *Club:* Army and Navy.

RAWNSLEY, Prof. Kenneth, FRCP, FRCPsych, DPM; Professor and Head of Department of Psychological Medicine, Welsh National School of Medicine, since 1964; *b* 1926; *m* Dr Elinor Kapp; one *s* one *d* (two *s* one *d* by previous marr.). *Educ:* Burnley Grammar Sch.; Univ. of Manchester Med. Sch. MB ChB Manchester 1948; MRCP 1951; DPM Manchester 1954; FRCP 1967; FRCPsych 1971. Member, Scientific Staff of Medical Research Council, 1954-64; Registrar, Bethlem Royal and Maudsley Hosps; Pres., Royal College of Psychiatrists, 1981- (Dean, 1972-77); Vice-Provost, Welsh Nat. Sch. of Medicine, 1979-80. Hon. Consultant Psychiatrist, S Glam. AHA(T); Postgrad. Organiser and Clinical Tutor in Psychiatry, S Glam. Member, Royal Soc. Med. *Publications:* contribs to Brit. Jl Psych., Postgrad. Med. Jl, Jl Psychosom. Res., etc. *Address:* Department of Psychological Medicine, University Hospital of Wales, Heath Park, Cardiff CF4 4XN. *T:* 755944. *Club:* Athenæum.

RAWSON, Christopher Selwyn Priestley; an Underwriting Member of Lloyd's; *b* 25 March 1928; *e s* of late Comdr Selwyn Gerald Caygill Rawson, OBE, RN (retd) and late Dr Doris Rawson, MB, ChB (*née* Brown); *m* 1959, Rosemary Ann Focke; two *d. Educ:* The Elms Sch., Colwall, near Malvern, Worcs; The Nautical College, Pangbourne, Berks. Navigating Apprentice, Merchant Service, T. & J. Brocklebank Ltd, 1945-48. Sheriff of the City of London, 1961-62; Member of Court of Common Council (Ward of Bread Street), 1963-72; Alderman, City of London, (Ward of Lime Street), 1972-; one of HM Lieutenants of City of London, 1980. Chairman: Governors, The Elms Sch., Colwall, near Malvern, Worcs, 1965-; Port and City of London Health Cttee, 1967-70; Billingsgate and Leadenhall Mkt Cttee, 1972-75. Silver Medal for Woollen and Worsted Raw Materials, City and Guilds of London Institute, 1951; Livery of Clothworkers Company, 1952, Mem. Court of Assistants, 1977; Freeman, Company of Watermen and Lightermen, 1966, Mem. Ct of Assts, 1974, Master, 1982-83. Hon. Mem., London Metal Exchange, 1979. ATI 1953; AIMarE 1962. OStJ 1980. Commander: National Order of Senegal, 1961; Order of the Ivory Coast, 1962; Star of Africa, Liberia, 1962. *Recreations:* shooting, sailing. *Address:* 56 Ovington Street, SW3. *T:* 01-589 3136; 65/68 Leadenhall Street, EC3. *T:* 01-481 0012. *Clubs:* Royal London Yacht, Royal Automobile, City Livery.

RAWSON, Kenneth John, RcNC; Deputy Director, Ship Design and Chief Naval Architect (Under Secretary), Ministry of Defence, Bath, since 1979; *b* 27 Oct. 1926; *s* of late Arthur William Rawson and Beatrice Anne Rawson; *m* 1950, Rhona Florence Gill; two *s* one *d. Educ:* Northern Grammar Sch., Portsmouth; HM Dockyard Technical Coll., Portsmouth; RN Colls, Keyham and Greenwich. RCNC; CEng, FRINA. WhSch. At sea, 1950-51; Naval Construction Res. Estabt, Dunfermline, 1951-53; Ship Design, Admiralty, 1953-57; Lloyd's Register of Shipping, 1957-59; Ship and Weapons Design, MoD, Bath, 1959-69; Naval Staff, London, 1969-72; Prof. of Naval Architecture, University Coll., Univ. of London, 1972-77; Head of Forward Design, Ship Dept, Bath, 1977-79. *Publications:* Photoelasticity and the Engineer, 1953; (with E. C. Tupper) Basic Ship Theory, 1968, 2nd edn (2 vols) 1976; contrib. numerous technical publications. *Recreations:* cabinet making, wine making, gardening, walking. *Address:* Moorlands, The Street, Chilcompton, Bath BA3 4HB. *T:* Stratton-on-the-Fosse 232793.

RAWSTHORNE, Rt. Rev. John; Titular Bishop of Rotdon and an Auxiliary Bishop of Liverpool, (RC), since 1981; *b* Crosby, Merseyside, 12 Nov. 1936. Priest, 1962. Administrator, St Mary's, Highfield. *Address:* St Mary's, Highfield Street, Liverpool L3 6AA.

RAY, Hon. Ajit Nath; Chief Justice of India, Supreme Court of India, 1973-77; *b* Calcutta, 29 Jan. 1912; *s* of Sati Nath Ray and Kali Kumari Debi; *m* 1944, Himani Mukherjee; one *s. Educ:* Presidency Coll., Calcutta; Calcutta Univ. (Hindu Coll. Foundn Schol., MA); Oriel College, Oxford (MA; Hon. Fellow, 1975). Called to Bar, Gray's Inn, 1939; practised at Calcutta High Court, 1940-57; Judge, Calcutta High Court, 1957-69; Judge, Supreme Court of India, 1969-73. Pres., Governing Body, Presidency Coll., Calcutta, 1959-70; Vice-President: Asiatic Soc., 1965-67 (Hon. Treas. 1962-65); Internat. Law Assoc., 1977- (Pres., 1974-76; Pres., Indian Br., 1973-77); Indian Law Inst., New Delhi, 1973-77; Mem., Internat. Court of Arbitration, 1976-; Pres., Soc. for Welfare of Blind, Narendrapur, 1959-80; Mem., Samsad Visva-Bharati, 1961-73. *Address:* 15 Panditia Place, Calcutta 700029, India. *T:* Calcutta 475213. *Club:* Calcutta (Calcutta).

RAY, Rt. Rev. Chandu; Senior Lecturer at Haggai Institute for Advanced Leadership Training for men and women in the third world, since 1977, and co-ordinating Officer for Asian Evangelism since 1969; *b* 14 April 1912; Pakistani parentage; *m* Anita Joy (*née* Meggitt); two *s* three *d. Educ:* D. J. Sind Coll., Karachi; Bishop's Coll., Calcutta. Bursar, Bishop Cotton Sch., Simla. Deacon, 1943; Priest, 1943. Vicar, St Philip's Church, Hyderabad, 1944; Sec., British and Foreign Bible Soc. in Pakistan, 1948; Canon of Lahore Cathedral, 1954; Archdeacon of Karachi, 1956; Asst Bishop of Lahore and Bishop in Karachi, 1957; first Bishop of Karachi, 1963-69. Hon. Dr of Sacred Theology, Wycliff, Toronto; Hon. Dr of Divinity, Huron, London. Gutenberg Award, 1978. *Publications:* (trans) Old Testament in Sindhi Language, 1954; (revised 2nd edn) New Testament in Sindhi, 1955. *Recreations:* hockey, cricket, tennis. *Address:* 4 Callington Avenue, City Beach, Perth, WA 6015, Australia. *T:* 385 8753.

RAY, Cyril; *b* 16 March 1908; *e s* of Albert Benson Ray (who changed the family name from Rotenberg, 1913), and Rita Ray; *m* 1953, Elizabeth Mary,

JP, *o d* of late Rev. H. C. Brocklehurst; one *s. Educ:* elementary sch., Bury, Lancs; Manchester Gr. Sch. (schol.); Jesus Coll., Oxford (open schol.). Manchester Guardian and BBC war correspondent: 5th Destroyer Flotilla, 1940; N African Landings, 1942; 8th Army, Italy (despatches); US 82nd Airborne Div., and 3rd Army, 1944-45. UNESCO missions, Italy, Greece, East, Central and S Africa, 1945-50. Sunday Times, 1949-56 (Moscow Correspondent, 1950-52); Asst Editor, The Spectator, 1958-62; Wine Correspondent: The Director, 1958-76; The Observer, 1959-73; Punch, 1978-; Editorial Council, later Chief Consltnt, The Good Food Guide, 1968-74; Founder and past President, Circle of Wine Writers; Chm. Trustees, Albany, 1981- (Trustee, 1967-). Much occasional broadcasting, 1940-62 (The Critics, 1958-62), Southern TV, 1958-59. Hon. Life Mem., NUJ. Glenfiddich Wine and Food Writer of the Year, 1979. Freeman, City of London; Liveryman, Fan-Makers Co. Mem. Labour Party. Commendatore dell'Ordine al Merito della Repubblica Italiana, 1981 (Cavaliere 1972); Chevalier du Mérite Agricole, 1974. *Publications:* (ed) Scenes and Characters from Surtees, 1948; From Algiers to Austria: The History of 78 Division, 1952; The Pageant of London, 1958; Merry England, 1960; Regiment of the Line: The Story of the Lancashire Fusiliers, 1963; (ed) The Gourmet's Companion, 1963; (ed) Morton Shand's Book of French Wines, 1964; (ed) Best Murder Stories, 1965; The Wines of Italy, 1966 (Bologna Trophy, 1967); In a Glass Lightly, 1967; Lafite: The Story of Château Lafite-Rothschild, 1968. Editor, The Compleat Imbiber, 1956-71 (Wine and Food Soc.'s first André Simon Prize, 1964); Bollinger: the story of a champagne, 1971, rev. edn 1982; Cognac, 1973; Mouton: the story of Mouton-Rothschild, 1974; (with Elizabeth Ray) Wine with Food, 1975; The Wines of France, 1976; The Wines of Germany, 1977; The Complete Book of Spirits and Liqueurs, 1978; The Saint Michael Guide to Wine, 1978; (with C. Mozley) Ruffino: the story of a Chianti, 1979; Lickerish Limericks, with Filthy Pictures by Charles Mozley, 1979; Ray on Wine (Glenfiddich Wine Book of the Year), 1979; The New Book of Italian Wines, 1982. *Recreation:* riding. *Address:* Albany, Piccadilly, W1. *T:* 01-734 0270; 66 Regency Square, Brighton BN1 2FF. *T:* Brighton 726171. *Clubs:* Athenæum, Brooks's, MCC, Special Forces; Kildare Street and University (Dublin).

RAY, Edward Ernest; Partner, Spicer and Pegler, Chartered Accountants, since 1957; *b* 6 Nov. 1924; *s* of Walter James Ray and Cecilia May Ray; *m* 1949, Margaret Elizabeth, *d* of George Bull; two *s. Educ:* Holloway Co. Sch.; London Univ. (External) (BCom). Served RN, 1943-46. Qualified, Inst. of Chartered Accountants: Mem., 1950; FCA 1955; Council Mem., 1973; Vice Pres., 1980; Dep. Pres., 1981; Pres., 1982; Chm., London Chartered Accountants, 1972-73. *Publications:* Partnership Taxation, 1972, 2nd edn 1978; (jtly) VAT for Accountants and Businessmen, 1972; contrib. accountancy magazines. *Recreations:* walking, birdwatching, golf. *Address:* Oakbeams, 17 The Green, Southgate, N14 7EH. *T:* 01-886 4017. *Club:* City of London.

RAY, Frederick Ivor, CB 1958; CBE 1953; BSc (Eng); FIEE; Telecommunications Consultant; *b* 18 Jan. 1899; *s* of Frederick Pedder Ray; *m* 1923, Katherine (*d* 1968), *d* of Hubert Abdy Fellowes, Newbury; two *s. Educ:* Royal British Orphan Sch.; Bournemouth School; Faraday House Electrical Engineering College. Served European War, 1917-19, RE. Entered GPO Engineering Dept, 1922; Sectional Engineer, 1932-35; Telephone Manager, Scotland West, 1935-39; Telecommunications Controller, NW Region, 1939; Controller Telephones, London, 1940-44; Assistant Secretary, 1944-48; Regional Director, London, 1948-56; Director of Inland Telecommunications, 1956-61; CPU Advr on Telecommunications, 1963-67; Dir, Internat. Press Telecommunications Council, 1965-67. *Recreations:* fishing, caravanning, golf. *Address:* 22A Edward Road, Bromley, Kent. *T:* 01-464 3859.

RAY, Gordon Norton; President of the John Simon Guggenheim Memorial Foundation, since 1963; *b* New York City, 8 Sept. 1915; *s* of Jesse Gordon and Jessie Norton Ray; unmarried. *Educ:* University of Indiana (AM); Harvard Univ. (AM, PhD). Instructor in English, Harvard, 1940-42; Guggenheim Fellow, 1941-42, 1946, 1956-57. Lt, US Navy, serving aboard aircraft carriers Belleau Wood and Boxer, Pacific, 1942-46; Professor of English, 1946-60, Head of Dept, 1950-57, Vice-President and Provost, 1957-60, University of Illinois. Associate Secretary General, Guggenheim Foundn, 1960-61; Sec.-Gen., 1961-63. Rockefeller Fellow, 1948-49; Member US Educational Commn in UK, which established Fulbright program, 1948-49. Lowell Lectures, Boston, 1950; Pierpont Morgan Lib., 1982; Berg Professor, New York Univ. 1952-53; Professor of English, 1962-80, now Emeritus Professor. Advisor in literature, Houghton Mifflin Co., 1953-71. Member Commission on Trends in Education, Mod. Lang. Assoc., 1953-59, Trustee 1966-; Mem. Council, Smithsonian Instn, 1968-, Chm. 1970-; Dir and Treasurer, Amer. Council of Learned Socs, 1973-. Advisory Bd, Guggenheim Foundation, 1959-60, Trustee, 1963-; Trustee: Pierpont Morgan Library, 1970-; Rosenbach Foundn, 1972-81; New York Public Library, 1975-; Columbia Univ. Press, 1977-; Winterthur Museum, 1977-; American Trust for the British Library, 1979-. Dir, Yaddo, 1979-. Hon. LittD: Monmouth Coll., 1959; Syracuse, 1961; Duke, 1965; Illinois, 1968; Northwestern, 1974; Hon. LLD: New York, 1961; Tulane, 1963; California, 1968; Columbia, 1969; Southern California, 1974; Pennsylvania, 1978; Hon. LHD, Indiana, 1964. FRSL 1948. Fellow, Amer. Acad. of Arts and Sciences, 1962; Mem., Amer. Philosophical Soc., 1977. Joseph Henry Medal, Smithsonian Instn, 1980. *Publications:* Letters and Private Papers of Thackeray, 4 vols, 1945-46; The Buried Life, 1952; Thackeray: The Uses of Adversity, 1955; Henry James and H. G. Wells, 1958; Thackeray: The Age of Wisdom, 1958; H. G. Wells and

Rebecca West, 1974; The Illustrator and the Book in England from 1790 to 1914, 1976; The Art of the French Illustrated Book 1700-1914, 2 vols, 1982, etc; contrib. to magazines and learned jls. *Recreations:* book-collecting, travel. *Address:* (business) 90 Park Avenue, New York, NY 10016; (home) 25 Sutton Place South, New York, NY 10022, USA. *Clubs:* Athenæum (London); Harvard, Grolier (President, 1965-69), Century (New York).

RAY, Philip Bicknell, CMG 1969; Ministry of Defence 1946-76, retired; *b* 10 July 1917; *s* of late Basil Ray and Clare (*née* Everett); *m* 1946, Bridget Mary Robertson (decd); two *s* one *d. Educ:* Felsted Sch.; Selwyn Coll., Cambridge (MA). Indian Police, 1939-46. *Address:* The Cottage, Little Shoddesden, Andover, Hants.

RAY, Robin; freelance broadcaster and entertainer; *s* of Ted Ray and Sybil (*née* Olden); *m* 1960, Susan Stranks; one *s. Educ:* Highgate Sch.; RADA. West End Stage: The Changeling, 1960; Beyond the Fringe, 1964; Side by Side by Sondheim, 1978; Tomfoolery, 1980. Associate Dir, Meadowbrook Theatre, Detroit, USA, 1965; devised, directed and presented stage entertainments: 7 Deadly Sins, Salisbury Festival, 1977; Time For Lovers, Belfast, Wavendon, Harrogate and Kings Lynn, 1979. Over 400 shows for BBC Television, including series: Face The Music; The Lively Arts; Music Now; The Movie Quiz; Robin Ray's Picture Gallery; radio series dealing with classical music, BBC radios 3 and 4; reviewer for Capital Radio, 1977-. *Publications:* Time For Lovers (anthology), 1975; Robin Ray's Music Quiz, 1978; Favourite Hymns and Carols, 1982. *Recreations:* cinema, television, music. *Address:* 8 Waterloo Place, Pall Mall, SW1Y 4AW.

RAY, Satyajit; Padma Shree, 1957; Padma Bhushan, 1964; Padma Bibhushan, 1976; Indian film producer and film director since 1953; *b* 2 May 1921; *s* of late Sukumar and Suprabha Ray (*née* Das); *m* 1949, Bijoya (*née* Das); one *s. Educ:* Ballygunge Govt School; Presidency College, Calcutta. Joined British advertising firm, D. J. Keymer & Co., as visualiser, 1943; Art Director, 1950. In 1952, started first feature film, Pather Panchali, finished in 1955 (Cannes Special Award, 1956, San Francisco, best film, 1957). Left advertising for whole-time film-making, 1956. Other films: Aparajito, 1957 (Venice Grand Prix, 1957, San Francisco, best direction); Jalsaghar, 1958; Devi, 1959; Apur Sansar, 1959 (Selznick Award and Sutherland Trophy 1960); Teen Kanya (Two Daughters), 1961; Kanchanjangha, 1962; Mahanagar, 1963; Charulata, 1964; The Coward and The Holy Man (Kapurush-O-Mahapurush), 1965; The Hero (Nayak), 1965; Goopy Gyne and Bagha Byne, 1969; Days and Nights in the Forest, 1970; Pratidwandi (The Adversary), 1970; Company Limited, 1971; Distant Thunder, 1973 (Golden Bear, Berlin Film Festival, 1973); The Golden Fortress, 1974; The Middleman, 1975; The Chess Players, 1977; The Elephant God, 1979; The Kingdom of Diamonds, 1980; Pikoo, Deliverance, 1981. Founded first Film Society in Calcutta, 1947. Composes background music for own films. Hon. DLitt Oxon, 1978. *Publications:* Our Films, Their Films, 1976; film articles in Sight and Sound, Sequence; (Editor, 1961-) children's magazine Sandesh, with contributions of stories, poems. *Recreations:* listening to Indian and Western classical music, and reading science-fiction. *Address:* Flat 8, 1-1 Bishop Lefroy Road, Calcutta 20, India. *T:* 44-8747.

RAYLEIGH, 5th Baron *cr* 1821; **John Arthur Strutt;** *b* 12 April 1908; *e s* of 4th Baron Rayleigh, FRS, and late Mary Hilda, 2nd *d* of 4th Earl of Leitrim; *S* father 1947; *m* 1934, Ursula Mary (*d* 1982), *o d* of Lieut-Colonel R. H. R. Brocklebank, DSO and Charlotte Carissima, *o d* of General Sir Bindon Blood, GCB, GCVO. *Educ:* Eton; Trinity College, Cambridge. *Heir: nephew* John Gerald Strutt, *b* 4 June 1960. *Address:* Terling Place, Chelmsford, Essex. *T:* Terling 235; 01-453 3235.

RAYMER, Michael Robert, OBE 1951; Assistant Secretary, Royal Hospital, Chelsea, 1975-82; *b* 22 July 1917; surv. *s* of late Rev. W. H. Raymer, MA; *m* 1948, Joyce Marion Scott; two *s* one *d. Educ:* Marlborough College (Foundation Scholar); Jesus College, Cambridge (Rustat Schol.). BA (Hons) 1939. Administrative Officer, Nigeria, 1940-49 and 1952-55. Served in Royal W African Frontier Force, 1940-43. Colonial Sec. to Govt of the Falkland Islands, 1949-52; Prin. Estab. Officer, N Nigeria, 1954; Controller of Organisation and Establishments, to Government of Fiji, 1955-62; retired, 1962; Principal, MoD, 1962-75. *Recreation:* gardening. *Address:* The Stable House, Manor Farm, Apethorpe, Northants PE8 5DG.

RAYMOND, Sir Stanley (Edward), Kt 1967; FCIT; FBIM; *b* 10 Aug. 1913; *s* of late Frederick George and Lilian Grace Raymond; *m* 1st, 1938, Enid (*d* 1979), *d* of Capt. S. A. Buley, Polruan-by-Fowey; one *s* ; 2nd, 1982, Mrs Constance Clarke. *Educ:* Orphanage; Grammar Sch., Hampton, Mx. Entered Civil Service, 1930. Asst Sec., Soc. of Civil Servants, 1939-45. War service in Royal Artillery, 1942-45; Lieutenant-Colonel on demobilisation. London Passenger Transport Board, 1946; British Road Services, 1947; BTC, 1955; Director of Establishment and Staff, 1956; Chief Commercial Manager, Scottish Region, British Railways, 1957 and Asst Gen. Manager, 1959; Traffic Adviser, BTC, 1961; Chm. Western Railway Board, and General Manager, Western Region, British Railways, 1962-63; Member, 1963, a Vice-Chm., 1964-65, and Chm., 1965-67, British Railways Bd. Chairman: Horserace Betting Levy Bd, 1972-74; Gaming Bd for GB, 1968-77. *Recreation:* walking. *Address:* 14 Dunsford Place, Bathwick Hill, Bath BA2 6HF.

RAYMOND, William Francis, CBE 1978; FRSC; Chief Scientist (Agriculture and Horticulture), Ministry of Agriculture, Fisheries and Food,

1981-82; *b* 25 Feb. 1922; *m* 1949, Amy Elizabeth Kelk; three *s* one *d. Educ:* Bristol Grammar Sch.; The Queen's Coll., Oxford (MA). Research Officer, MRC, 1943-45; Head of Animal Science Div. and later Asst Dir, Grassland Research Inst., Hurley, 1945-72; Dep. Chief Scientist, MAFF, 1972-81. Mem., ARC, 1981-82. Sec., 8th Internat. Grassland Congress, 1960; President: Brit. Grassland Soc., 1974-75; Brit. Soc. Animal Production, 1981-82. Vis. Prof. in Agriculture, Wye Coll., 1978. *Publications:* (with Shepperson and Waltham) Forage Conservation and Feeding, 1972, 3rd edn 1978; over 120 papers in scientific jls. *Recreation:* gardening. *Address:* High Walls, Pinkneys Drive, Maidenhead, Berks SL6 6QD. *T:* Maidenhead 26660. *Club:* Farmers'.

RAYNE, family name of **Baron Rayne.**

RAYNE, Baron *cr* 1976 (Life Peer), of Prince's Meadow in Greater London; **Max Rayne,** Kt 1969; Chairman, London Merchant Securities plc, since 1960; *b* 8 Feb. 1918; *er s* of Phillip and Deborah Rayne; *m* 1st, 1941, Margaret Marco (marr. diss., 1960); one *s* two *d* ; 2nd, 1965, Lady Jane Antonia Frances Vane-Tempest-Stewart, *er d* of 8th Marquess of Londonderry; two *s* two *d. Educ:* Central Foundation Sch. and University Coll., London. Served RAF 1940-45. Chm., The Westpool Investment Trust plc, 1980-; Dir, other companies. Governor: Royal Ballet Sch., 1966-79; Yehudi Menuhin Sch., 1966-; Malvern Coll., 1966-; Centre for Environmental Studies, 1967-73; Special Trustee, St Thomas' Hosp., 1974- (Governor, 1962-74); Member: Gen. Council, King Edward VII's Hosp. Fund for London, 1966-; Council, St Thomas's Hospital Medical School, 1965-82; Council of Governors, United Med. Schs of Guy's and St Thomas's Hosps, 1982-; Internat. Council, Salk Inst., 1982-. Hon. Vice-Pres., Jewish Welfare Bd, 1966-; Chairman: London Festival Ballet Trust, 1967-75; Nat. Theatre Board, 1971-; Founder Patron, The Rayne Foundation, 1962-. Hon. Fellow: Darwin Coll., Cambridge, 1966; UCL, 1966; LSE 1974; King's Coll. Hosp. Med. Sch., 1980; UC, Oxford, 1982. Hon. FRCPsych, 1977. Hon. LLD London, 1968. Chevalier Légion d'Honneur, 1973. *Address:* 33 Robert Adam Street, W1M 5AH. *T:* 01-935 3555.

RAYNE, Edward, CVO 1977; Chairman and Managing Director of H. & M. Rayne Ltd, since 1951; Director, Debenhams Ltd, since 1975; President, Debenhams Inc., since 1976; Executive Chairman: Rayne-Delman Shoes Inc., since 1972 (President, 1961-72); Harvey Nichols, since 1979; *b* 19 Aug. 1922; *s* of Joseph Edward Rayne and Meta Elizabeth Reddish (American); *m* 1952, Phyllis Cort; two *s. Educ:* Harrow. Chairman: Fashion Multiple Div., Debenhams Ltd, 1978-; Harvey Nichols Ltd, 1978-; Lotus Ltd, 1978-. Member: Export Council for Europe, 1962-71; European Trade Cttee, 1972-; Bd of Governors, Genesco Inc., 1967-73; Franco British Council, 1980-. Chm., Incorp. Soc. of London Fashion Designers, 1960-; Pres., Royal Warrant Holders' Assoc., 1964, Hon. Treas. 1974-; President: British Footwear Manufacturers' Fedn, 1965; British Boot and Shoe Instn, 1972-79; Clothing and Footwear Inst., 1979-80. Master, Worshipful Co. of Pattenmakers, 1981. FRSA 1971. Harper's Bazaar Trophy, 1963. *Recreations:* golf and bridge (Mem., winning British team, European Bridge Championship, 1948, 1949). *Address:* 15 Grosvenor Square, W1. *T:* 01-493 2871. *Clubs:* Portland, White's, Brooks's; Travellers' (Paris).

RAYNER, Bryan Roy; Under-Secretary, Department of Health and Social Security, since 1975; *b* 29 Jan. 1932; *s* of Harold and Florence Rayner; *m* 1957, Eleanora Whittaker; one *d. Educ:* Stationers' Company's School, N8. Clerical Officer, Customs and Excise, 1948; Asst Private Sec. to Minister of Health, 1960-62; Principal, 1965; Asst Sec., 1970. *Recreations:* listening to music, gardening. *Address:* 8 West Common Drive, Haywards Heath, W Sussex RH16 2AP.

RAYNER, Sir Derek George, Kt 1973; Joint Managing Director, since 1973 and Joint Vice-Chairman, since 1982, Marks & Spencer plc; *b* 30 March 1926; *o s* of George William Rayner and Hilda Jane (*née* Rant); unmarried. *Educ:* City Coll., Norwich; Selwyn Coll., Cambridge. Fellow, Inst. Purchasing and Supply, 1970. Nat. Service, commnd RAF Regt, 1946-48. Joined Marks & Spencer, 1953; Dir, 1967. Special Adviser to HM Govt, 1970; Chief Exec., Procurement Executive, MoD, 1971-72. Mem., UK Permanent Security Commn, 1977-80. Dep. Chm., Civil Service Pay Bd, 1978-80. Member: Design Council, 1973-75; Council RCA, 1973-76. Adviser to Prime Minister on improving efficiency and eliminating waste in Government, 1979-. *Recreations:* music, food, travel. *Address:* Michael House, Baker Street, W1.

RAYNER, Edward John; British Council Representative, Brazil, since 1983; *b* 27 Feb. 1936; *s* of Edward Harold Rayner and Edith Rayner; *m* 1960, Valerie Anne Billon; one *s* one *d. Educ:* Slough Grammar Sch.; London Univ. (BSc Econs). British Council: Asst Regional Rep., Lahore, Pakistan, 1959-62; Asst Rep., Lagos, Nigeria, 1962-65; Inspector, Complements Unit, 1965-67; Head, Overseas Careers, Personnel Dept, 1967-70; Dep. Rep., Pakistan, 1970-71; Regional Dir, Sao Paulo, Brazil, 1972-75; Controller, Estabts Div., 1975-78; Secretary, 1978-82. *Recreations:* golf, tennis, theatre, music. *Address:* CRN 708/9-Bl. 3 nos 1/3, Caixa Postal 14-2336, 70,740 Brasilia DF, Brazil.

RAYNER, Most Rev. Keith; *see* Adelaide, Archbishop of.

RAYNER, Neville, JP, FRSA; Underwriting Member of Lloyd's, since 1963; General Commissioner of Income Tax, since 1965; property consultant, since

1936; *b* 1914; *m* 1941, Elsie Mary (*née* Lindley); two *s. Educ:* Emanuel Sch., SW11. Commd RAFVR(T), 1941-45. Mem., Court of Common Council, City of London, 1960-81; Sheriff of London, 1971-72. Former Mem., LCC and Wandsworth Borough Council. Director, Bedford Building Soc. Parish Clerk, Priory Church of St Bartholomew-the-Great, Smithfield; Mem., Honourable Artillery Co.; Liveryman: Painter Stainers Co.; Basketmakers Co. (Prime Warden, 1980-81); Glovers' Co. (Master, 1982-83); Playing Card Makers Co.; Co. of Parish Clerks. JP, Inner London, 1959; Dep. Chm., Greater London (SW) Valuation Appeals Court, 1950-; Pres., Greater London Council Br., Royal British Legion, 1962- (Gold Badge, 1979); Asst Dir, St John Ambulance Assoc. (Greater London); Vice-Pres., Nat. Union of Ratepayers. FRVA, FSVA, FCIArb. Past Pres., Farringdon Ward Club. Member: Magistrates Assoc.; British Olympic Assoc.; Southwark Diocesan Sites Cttee; Magic Circle; Council, Gardeners' Royal Benevolent Soc.; Council, Royal Soc. St George (Mem. Council, and Vice-Pres., City of London Br.); Luxembourg Soc.; Sheriff's Soc. EsqStJ. Order of Sacred Treasure (Japan), 1972; Star of Afghanistan, 1972; Comdr, Order of Orange-Nassau (Holland), 1972; Couronne de Chêne (Luxembourg), 1972; Comendador de la Orden del Merito Civil (Spain), 1975. *Recreations:* magic, travel, carpentry. *Address:* Old Selsfield, Turners Hill, West Sussex RH10 4PS. *T:* Copthorne 715203; 1 Montpelier Mews, SW7 1HB. *T:* 01-589 3939. *Clubs:* Guildhall, United Wards (Past Pres.), City Livery (Council), Pilgrims, Press, Anglo-Spanish, Wig and Pen.

RAYNHAM, Viscount; Charles George Townshend; *b* 26 Sept. 1945; *s* and *heir* of 7th Marquess Townshend, *qv*; *m* 1975, Hermione, *d* of Lt-Cdr R. M. D. Ponsonby and Mrs Dorothy Ponsonby; one *s* one *d. Educ:* Eton; Royal Agricultural College, Cirencester. Mem. Council, RASE. *Heir: s* Hon. Thomas Charles Townshend, *b* 2 Nov. 1977. *Address:* Raynham Hall, Fakenham, Norfolk. *T:* Fakenham 2133. *Clubs:* White's, Farmers'.

RAYNOR, Prof. Geoffrey Vincent, MA, DPhil, DSc Oxon; FRS 1959; Professor of Physical Metallurgy, University of Birmingham, 1954-81, now Emeritus; *b* 2 Oct. 1913; *y s* of late Alfred Ernest Raynor, Nottingham; *m* 1943, Emily Jean, *er d* of late Dr Geo. F. Brockless, London; three *s. Educ:* Nottingham High School; Keble Coll., Oxford, 1st cl. Hons, School of Natural Science (Chemistry), 1936, Hon. Fellow, 1972. Research Assistant, Oxford University, 1936; Departmental Demonstrator in Inorganic Chemistry, 1937-45; DSIR Senior Research Award, 1938-41. Metallurgical research for Ministry of Supply and Ministry of Aircraft Production, 1939-45; University of Birmingham: ICI Research Fellow, 1945-47; Beilby Memorial Award, 1947; Reader in Theoretical Metallurgy, 1947-49; Prof. of Metal Physics, 1949-54; Feeney Prof. of Physical Metallurgy, and Head of Dept of Physical Metallurgy and Science of Materials, 1955-69; Dean, Faculty of Science and Engineering, 1966-69; Dep. Principal, 1969-73. Vis. Prof. of Metallurgy, Chicago Univ., 1951-52; Battelle Vis. Prof., Ohio State Univ., 1962; Royal Soc. Leverhulme Vis. Prof., Witwatersrand Univ., 1974; Vis. Prof., Univ. of NSW, 1975; Canadian Commonwealth Vis. Fellowship, Queen's Univ., 1979; Leverhulme Emeritus Fellow, 1981. Vice-President: Inst. of Metals, 1953-56; Instn of Metallurgists, 1963-66, 1977-80; President: Birmingham Metallurgical Assoc., 1965-66; Keble Assoc., 1974. Fellow, New York Acad. of Science, 1961; Member several metallurgical research committees. Walter Rosenhain Medal, Inst. of Metals, 1951; Heyn Medal, Deutsche Gesellschaft für Metallkunde, 1956; Hume-Rothery Prize, Metals Soc., 1981. *Publications:* Introduction to the Electron Theory of Metals, Inst. of Metals monograph and report series, No 4, 1947; contrib. to Butterworth's scientific publications: Progress in Metal Physics, 1949, and Metals Reference Book, 1949; The Structure of Metals and Alloys (with W. Hume-Rothery), 1954; The Physical Metallurgy of Magnesium and its Alloys, 1959; scientific papers on theory of metals and alloys in Proc. Royal Soc., Philosophical Mag., Trans. Faraday Soc., and metallurgical journals. *Recreations:* rowing and sculling. *Address:* 94 Gillhurst Road, Harborne, Birmingham B17 8PA. *T:* 021-429 3176. *Club:* Athenæum.

RAZZALL, Leonard Humphrey; a Master of the Supreme Court (Taxing), 1954-81; *b* 13 Nov. 1912; *s* of Horace Razzall and Sarah Thompson, Scarborough; *m* 1936, Muriel (*d* 1968), *yr d* of late Pearson Knowles; two *s. Educ:* Scarborough High Sch. Admitted solicitor, 1935; founded firm Humphrey Razzall & Co., 1938. Served in Royal Marines, 1941-46, Staff Captain; Staff Coll., Camberley (jsc). Contested (L) Scarborough and Whitby Division, 1945. Sometime Examr in High Court practice and procedure for solicitors final examination. *Recreations:* travel, cricket, book-collecting and book-selling. *Address:* 10 Glentham Gardens, Lonsdale Road, SW13. *T:* 01-748 5733; 01-878 7859. *Clubs:* National Liberal, English-Speaking Union.

REA, family name of **Baron Rea.**

REA, 3rd Baron *cr* 1937, of Eskdale; **John Nicolas Rea,** MD; Bt 1935; General Medical Practitioner in James Wigg Group Practice, Kentish Town Health Centre, NW5, since 1968; *b* 6 June 1928; *s* of Hon. James Russell Rea (*d* 1954) (2nd *s* of 1st Baron) and Betty Marion (*d* 1965), *d* of Arthur Bevan, MD; *S* uncle, 1981; *m* 1951, Elizabeth Anne, *d* of late William Hensman Robinson; four *s. Educ:* Dartington Hall School; Belmont Hill School, Mass, USA; Dauntsey's School; Christ's Coll., Cambridge Univ.; UCH Medical School. MA, MD (Cantab); MRCGP; DPH, DCH. Research Fellow in Paediatrics, Lagos, Nigeria, 1962-65; Lecturer in Social Medicine, St Thomas's Hosp. Medical School, 1966-68. FRSocMed. *Publications:* Interactions of Infection

and Nutrition (MD Thesis, Cambridge Univ.), 1969; (jtly) Learning Teaching—an evaluation of a course for GP Teachers, 1980; articles on epidemiology and medical education in various journals. *Recreations:* music (bassoon), fishing, sailing, winter sports, walking. *Heir: s* Hon. Matthew James Rea, *b* 28 March 1956. *Address:* 48 Hungerford Road, N7 9LP. *T:* 01-607 4415.

REA, James Taylor, CMG 1958; HM Overseas Civil Service, retired; *b* 19 Oct. 1907; *s* of Rev. Martin Rea, Presbyterian Minister, and Mary Rea (*née* Fisher); *m* 1934, Catharine, *d* of Dr W. H. Bleakney, Whitman College, Walla Walla, Washington, USA; one *s* one *d. Educ:* Royal School, Dungannon; Queen's University, Belfast (BA); St John's College, Cambridge (MA). HM Colonial Administrative Service (now known as HM Overseas Civil Service) serving throughout in Malaya and Singapore, 1931-58; Principal offices held: Asst Sec., Chinese Affairs, Fedn of Malaya, 1948; Dep. Comr for Labour, Fedn of Malaya, 1949; Dep. Malayan Establishment Officer, 1950; Dep. Pres., 1952-55, Pres., 1955-58, City Council, Singapore. Retired, 1958. Chairman: Hotel Grants Adv. Cttee, NI, 1963-75; NI Training Exec., 1972-75; Down District Cttee, Eastern Health and Social Services Bd, 1974-78; Mem., NI Housing Trust, 1959-71, Vice Chm., 1970-71. Indep. Mem.: Catering Wages Council, N Ireland, 1965; Retail Bespoke Tailoring Wages Council, 1965-; Laundry Wages Council, 1965-; Shirtmaking Wages Council, 1965. Nominated Member General Dental Council, under Dentist Act, 1957, 1961-79. Mem. Downpatrick HMC, 1966-73, Chm., 1971-73. *Address:* Craigduff, Downpatrick, N Ireland. *T:* Seaforde 258.

REA, Dr John Rowland, FBA 1981; Lecturer in Documentary Papyrology, University of Oxford, since 1965; Senior Research Fellow, Balliol College, Oxford, since 1969; *b* 28 Oct. 1933; *s* of Thomas Arthur Rea and Elsie Rea (*née* Ward); *m* 1959, Mary Ogden. *Educ:* Methodist Coll., Belfast; Queen's Univ., Belfast (BA); University Coll. London (PhD). Asst Keeper, Public Record Office, 1957-61; Res. Lectr, Christ Church, Oxford, 1961-65. *Publications:* The Oxyrhynchus Papyri, Vol. XL, 1972, Vol. XLVI, 1978, also contribs to Vols XXVII, XXXI, XXXIII, XXXIV, XXXVI, XLI, XLIII; (with P. J. Sijpesteijn) Corpus Papyrorum Raineri V, 1976; articles in classical jls. *Address:* Balliol College, Oxford.

READ, Prof. Alan Ernest Alfred, MD, FRCP; Professor of Medicine and Director of Medical Professorial Unit, University of Bristol, since 1969; *b* 15 Nov. 1926; *s* of Ernest Read and Annie Lydia; *m* 1952, Enid Malein; one *s* two *d. Educ:* Wembley County Sch.; St Mary's Hosp. Med. Sch., London. House Phys., St Mary's Hosp., 1950; Med. Registrar, Royal Masonic Hosp., 1951; Mil. Service Med. Specialist, Trieste, 1952-54; Registrar and Sen. Registrar, Central Mddx and Hammersmith Hosps, 1954-60; Lectr in Medicine and Cons. Phys., University of Bristol, 1961, Reader in Medicine, 1966; Associate Prof. of Medicine, Univ. of Rochester, USA, 1967. *Publications:* Clinical Apprentice (jtly), 1948, 5th edn 1978; (jtly) Basic Gastroenterology, 1965, 3rd edn 1980; (jtly) Modern Medicine, 1975, 2nd edn 1979. *Recreations:* boating, fishing. *Address:* Riverbank, 77 Nore Road, Portishead, Bristol BS20 9JZ.

READ, Rt. Rev. Allan Alexander; *see* Ontario, Bishop of.

READ, Gen. Sir Antony; *see* Read, Gen. Sir J. A. J.

READ, Air Marshal Sir Charles (Frederick), KBE 1976 (CBE 1964); CB 1972; DFC 1942; AFC 1958; Chief of the Air Staff, RAAF, 1972-75, retired; *b* Sydney, NSW, 9 Oct. 1918; *s* of J. F. Read, Bristol, England; *m* 1946, Betty E., *d* of A. V. Bradshaw; three *s. Educ:* Sydney Grammar Sch. Former posts include: OC, RAAF Base, Point Cook, Vic., 1965-68; OC, RAAF, Richmond, NSW, 1968-70; Dep. Chief of Air Staff, 1969-72. *Recreation:* yachting. *Address:* 2007 Pittwater Road, Bayview, NSW 2104, Australia. *T:* 997-1686.

READ, Rev. David Haxton Carswell, MA, DD; Minister of Madison Avenue Presbyterian Church, New York City, USA, since 1956; regular broadcaster on: National Radio Pulpit; Thinking It Over; *b* Cupar, Fife, 2 Jan. 1910; *s* of John Alexander Read and Catherine Haxton Carswell; *m* 1936, Dorothy Florence Patricia Gilbert; one *s. Educ:* Daniel Stewart's College, Edinburgh. Edinburgh Univ.; Univs of Montpellier, Strasbourg, Paris, and Marburg; New Coll., Edinburgh. MA Edin. (first class Hons in Lit.) 1932; BD (dist. in Dogmatics) 1936. Ordained Minister of the Church of Scotland, 1936; Minister of Coldstream West Church, 1936-39. CF, 1939-45 (despatches; POW, 1940-45, Germany). Minister of Greenbank Parish, Edinburgh, 1939-49; first Chaplain, Univ. of Edinburgh, 1949-55; Chaplain to the Queen in Scotland, 1952-55. Pres., Japan Internat. Christian Univ. Foundn. Guest Lectr and Preacher in USA, Scotland, Canada, Australia. Hon. DD: Edinburgh, 1956; Yale, 1959; Lafayette Coll., 1965; Hope Coll., 1969; Knox Coll., Canada, 1979; Hon. LHD: Hobart Coll., 1972; Trinity Univ., 1972; Hon. LittD Coll. of Wooster, 1966; Hon. DHL: Japan Internat. Christian Univ., 1979; Rockford Coll. *Publications:* The Spirit of Life, 1939; The Church to Come (trans. from German), 1939; Prisoners' Quest, Lectures on Christian doctrine in a POW Camp, 1944; The Communication of The Gospel, Warrack Lectures, 1952; The Christian Faith, 1955 (NY 1956); I am Persuaded, 1961 (NY 1962); Sons of Anak, 1964 (NY); God's Mobile Family, 1966 (NY); Whose God is Dead?, 1966 (Cin); Holy Common Sense, 1966 (Tenn); The Pattern of Christ, 1967 (NY); The Presence of Christ, 1968 (NJ); Christian Ethics, 1968 (NY 1969); Virginia Woolfe Meets Charlie Brown,

1968 (Mich); Giants Cut Down To Size, 1970; Religion Without Wrappings, 1970; Overheard, 1971; Curious Christians, 1972; Sent from God, 1974; Good News in the Letters of Paul, 1975; Go and make Disciples, 1978; Unfinished Easter, 1978; The Faith is Still There, 1980; articles and sermons in Atlantic Monthly, Scottish Jl of Theology, Expository Times, etc. *Recreations:* languages; drama; travel, especially in France. *Address:* 1165 Fifth Avenue, New York, NY 10029, USA. *Club:* The Century (New York).

READ, Gen. Sir (John) Antony (Jervis), GCB 1972 (KCB 1967; CB 1965); CBE 1959 (OBE 1957); DSO 1945; MC 1941; Governor of Royal Hospital, Chelsea, 1975-81; *b* 10 Sept. 1913; *e s* of late John Dale Read, Heathfield, Sussex; *m* 1947, Sheila, *e d* of late F. G. C. Morris, London, NW8; three *d*. *Educ:* Winchester; Sandhurst. Commissioned Oxford and Bucks Lt Inf., 1934; seconded to Gold Coast Regt, RWAFF, 1936; comd 81 (WA) Div. Reconnaissance Regt, 1943; comd 1 Gambia Regt, 1944; war service Kenya, Abyssinia, Somaliland, Burma; DAMS, War Office, 1947-49; Company Comd RMA Sandhurst, 1949-52; AA&QMG 11 Armd Div., 1953-54; comd 1 Oxford and Bucks Lt Inf., 1955-57; comd 3 Inf. Bde Gp, 1957-59; Comdt School of Infantry, 1959-62; GOC Northumbrian Area and 50 (Northumbrian) Division (TA), 1962-64; Vice-Quarter-Master-General, Min. of Defence, 1964-66; GOC-in-C, Western Comd, 1966-69; Quartermaster-General, 1969-72; Comdt, Royal Coll. of Defence Studies, 1973. ADC (Gen.) to the Queen, 1971-73. Colonel Commandant: Army Catering Corps, 1966-76; The Light Division, 1968-73; Small Arms School Corps, 1969-74. President: TA Rifle Assoc.; Ex-Services Fellowship Centres, 1975-; ACF Assoc., 1982- (Chm., 1973-82). Governor: Royal Sch. for Daughters of Officers of the Army, 1966- (Chm., 1975-81); St Edward's Sch., Oxford, 1972; Special Comr, Duke of York's Royal Mil. Sch., 1974. *Address:* Brackles, Little Chesterton, near Bicester, Oxon. *T:* Bicester 2189. *Club:* Army and Navy.

READ, Sir John (Emms), Kt 1976; FCA 1947; Chairman: Central Board, Trustee Savings Bank, since 1980; United Dominions Trust, since 1981; Deputy Chairman, Thames Television Ltd, since 1981 (Director, since 1973); *b* 29 March 1918; *s* of late William Emms Read and of Daysie Elizabeth (*née* Cooper); *m* 1942, Dorothy Millicent Berry; two *s*. *Educ:* Brighton, Hove and Sussex Grammar Sch. Served Royal Navy, 1939-46 (rank of Comdr (S) RNVR); Admiral's Secretary: to Asst Chief of Naval Staff, Admty, 1942-45; to Brit. Admty Technical Mission, Ottawa, Canada, 1945-46. Ford Motor Co. Ltd, 1946-64 (Admin. Staff Coll., Henley, 1952), Dir of Sales, 1961-64; Dir, Electric and Musical Industries Ltd, 1965-; EMI Group: Jt Man. Dir, 1967; Chief Exec., 1969-79; Dep. Chm., 1973-74; Chm., 1974-79; Dep. Chm., 1979-81, Dir, 1981-, THORN EMI. Director: Dunlop Holdings Ltd; Capitol Industries-EMI Inc.; Chairman: CBI Finance & GP, 1978-; TSB Holdings Ltd, 1980-. Chm., EDC for Electronics Industry, 1977-80. Member: (part time), PO Bd, 1975-77; Engineering Industries Council, 1975-80; BOTB, 1976-79; Armed Forces Pay Review Body, 1976-; Nat. Electronics Council, 1977-80; Groupe des Présidents des Grandes Enterprises Européennes, 1977-80. Vice-Pres., Inst. of Bankers. Member: RN Film Corp., 1975-; Brighton Festival Soc. Council of Management, 1977-; Presidents' Cttee, CBI, 1977-; White Ensign Assoc. Council of Management, 1979-; Chm., Inst. of Neurology Council of Management, 1980-; Trustee, Westminster Abbey Trust, 1978-; President: Central Brighton Boys Club, 1978; Sussex Assoc. of Boys' Clubs, 1982-; Cheshire Homes, Seven Rivers, Essex, 1979-; Governor, Admin. Staff Coll., Henley, 1974. CBIM (FBIM 1974); CompIERE 1974; FRSA 1974. *Recreations:* music, arts, sports. *Address:* Muster House, 12 Muster Green, Haywards Heath, W Sussex RH16 4AG. *T:* Haywards Heath 413333. *Club:* MCC.

READ, Lt.-Gen. Sir John (Hugh Sherlock), KCB 1972; OBE 1944; retired; Adviser, West Africa Committee, since 1975; *b* 6 Sept. 1917; *s* of late Group Captain John Victor Read, Blunham, Bedfordshire, and Chacewater, Cornwall, and Elizabeth Hannah (*née* Link); *m* 1942, Mary Monica Wulfhilde Curtis, *d* of late Henry Curtis, Spofforth, Yorks, and Harrogate; two *s* one *d*. *Educ:* Bedford School; RMA Woolwich; Magdalene Coll., Cambridge. BA (Cantab.) 1939. MA (Cantab.) 1944. Commissioned 2nd Lt RE, 1937. Served UK, France, Belgium, Egypt, Palestine, Greece, Austria at regimental duty and on staff, 1939-45, and UK, Austria, Germany, Hong Kong, 1945-57; GSO1, Singapore Base Dist, 1957; CO, Training Regt, RE, 1959; IDC, 1962; Min. of Defence (War Office), 1963; Comdr, Training Bde, RE, 1963; Asst Comdt, RMA, 1966-68; Director of Military Operations, MoD, 1968-70; ACDS (Policy), MoD, 1970-71; Dir, Internat. Mil. Staff, HQ, NATO, Brussels, 1971-75. Col Comdt, Corps of Royal Engineers, 1972-77. *Recreations:* fishing, shooting, gardening. *Address:* Fullbrook Farm, Elstead, Surrey. *T:* Elstead 703312. *Club:* Travellers'.

READ, Leonard Ernest, (Nipper), QPM 1976; Security Adviser to the National Museums and Galleries, since 1978; *b* 31 March 1925; *m* 1st, 1951, Marion Alexandra Millar (marr. diss. 1979); one *d*; 2nd, 1980, Patricia Margaret Allen. *Educ:* elementary schools. Worked at Players Tobacco factory, Nottingham, 1939-43; Petty Officer, RN, 1943-46; joined Metropolitan Police, 1947; served in all ranks of CID; Det. Chief Supt on Murder Squad, 1967; Asst Chief Constable, Notts Combined Constabulary, 1970; National Co-ordinator of Regional Crime Squads for England and Wales, 1972-76. Mem. Council, British Boxing Bd of Control, 1976-. *Recreations:* cine photography, collecting club ties. *Address:* 33 Oaklands Avenue, N9 7LN.

READ, Lionel Frank, QC 1973; a Recorder of the Crown Court, since 1974; *b* 7 Sept. 1929; *s* of F. W. C. Read and Lilian Chatwin; *m* 1956, Shirley Greenhalgh; two *s* one *d*. *Educ:* Oundle Sch.; St John's Coll., Cambridge (BA Hons). Called to Bar, Gray's Inn, 1954; Bencher, 1981. *Recreations:* golf, gardening. *Address:* Cedarwood, Church Road, Ham Common, Surrey. *T:* 01-940 5247.

READ, Prof. Margaret (Helen), CBE 1949; MA (Cantab), PhD (London); *b* 5 Aug. 1889; *d* of Mabyn Read, MD, Worcester, and Isabel Margaret Lawford. *Educ:* Roedean School, Brighton; Newnham College, Cambridge. Social work in India, 1919-24; lecturing on international affairs in Gt Britain and USA, 1924-30; LSE, student of anthropology and occasional lecturer, 1930-34; Research Fellow, Internat. African Inst. and field work in N Rhodesia and Nyasaland, 1934-39; Asst Lecturer, LSE, 1937-40; Univ. of London Inst. of Educ., Prof. and Head of Dept of Educ. in Tropical Areas, 1940-55; Prof. of Educ., Univ. Coll., Ibadan, Nigeria, 1955-56; occasional Consultant to WHO, 1956-62; Consultant to Milbank Memorial Fund, New York, 1964, 1965, 1966, 1967, 1968, 1969. Vis. Prof., Cornell Univ., 1951-52, Northwestern Univ., 1955, Michigan State Univ., 1960, Yale Univ. Medical School, 1965, 1966, 1967, 1968. *Publications:* Indian Peasant Uprooted, 1931; Africans and their Schools, 1953; Education and Social Change in Tropical Areas, 1955; The Ngoni of Nyasaland, 1956; Children of their Fathers, 1959; Culture, Health and Disease, 1966; articles in Africa, Bantu Studies, Journal of Applied Anthropology, Annals of the American Academy, etc. *Recreations:* gardening, music. *Address:* 9 Paradise Walk, Chelsea, SW3. *T:* 01-352 0528.

READ, Piers Paul, FRSL; author; *b* 7 March 1941; 3rd *s* of Sir Herbert Read, DSO, MC and Margaret Read, Stonegrave, York; *m* 1967, Emily Albertine, *o d* of Evelyn Basil Boothby, *qv*; two *s* two *d*. *Educ:* Ampleforth Coll.; St John's Coll., Cambridge (MA). Artist-in-residence, Ford Foundn, Berlin, 1963-64; Sub-Editor, Times Literary Supplement, 1965; Harkness Fellow, Commonwealth Fund, NY, 1967-68. Member: Council, Inst. of Contemporary Arts, 1971-75; Cttee of Management, Soc. of Authors, 1973-76; Literature Panel, Arts Council, 1975-77. Adjunct Prof. of Writing, Columbia Univ., NY, 1980. TV plays: Coincidence, 1968; The House on Highbury Hill, 1972; The Childhood Friend, 1974; radio play: The Family Firm, 1970. *Publications:* novels: Game in Heaven with Tussy Marx, 1966; The Junkers, 1968 (Sir Geoffrey Faber Meml Prize); Monk Dawson, 1969 (Hawthornden Prize and Somerset Maugham Award); The Professor's Daughter, 1971; The Upstart, 1973; Polonaise, 1976; A Married Man, 1979; The Villa Golitsyn, 1981; *non-fiction:* Alive, 1974; The Train Robbers, 1978. *Address:* 50 Portland Road, W11 4LG.

READ, Simon Holcombe Jervis, CBE 1977; MC 1944; HM Diplomatic Service, retired 1977; Secretary, Game Farmers' Association, since 1977; *b* 7 Feb. 1922; *s* of John Dale Read and Evelyn Constance Read (*née* Bowen); *m* 1st, 1946, Bridget Elizabeth Dawson (marr. diss. 1959); two *s* one *d*; 2nd, 1960, Coelestine von der Marwitz. *Educ:* Winchester Coll. Served War: Private soldier, Essex Regt, 1940; commissioned 10th Baluch Regt, 1941; SOE and Detachment 101 (US Army), 1942, in Burma; service in Burma, Malaya, Thailand, Cambodia, Indo-China, China. Joined FCO, 1946; 3rd/2nd Sec., Singapore, Thailand, 1946-50; 1st Secretary: Hongkong, 1952-54; Iran, 1954-59; Berlin, 1959-64; UK, 1964-77. *Publication:* provisional check list of Birds of Iran (Teheran Univ.), 1958. *Recreations:* ornithology, shooting, gardening. *Address:* The Cottage, Little Chart, near Ashford, Kent. *T:* Pluckley 610. *Club:* Special Forces.

READE, Sir Clyde Nixon, 12th Bt *cr* 1661; *b* 1906; *s* of Sir George Reade, 10th Bt; *S* brother, Sir John Reade, 11th Bt, 1958; *m* 1930, Trilby (*d* 1958), *d* of Charles McCarthy. Is a Royal Arch Mason. *Address:* Box 242, Mason, Michigan 48854, USA.

READER, Dame Audrey Tattie Hinchcliff, DBE 1978 (OBE 1966); voluntary worker in several community organizations and in politics; *b* 9 Dec. 1903; *d* of William Henry Nicholls and Mabel Tattie Brimacombe Nicholls (*née* Mallett); *m* 1928, Reginald John Reader; one *d*. *Educ:* Macedon Primary Sch., Victoria; Malvern Coll., Melbourne. Housewife. Member: Victoria League for Commonwealth Friendship, Melbourne; Royal Soc. of St George. *Recreations:* reading, writing, gardening. *Address:* 68 Millewa Avenue, Chadstone, Victoria 3148, Australia. *T:* 5688716.

READER HARRIS, Dame (Muriel) Diana, DBE 1972; Headmistress, Sherborne School for Girls, Dorset, 1950-75; *b* Hong Kong, 11 Oct. 1912; *er d* of late Montgomery Reader Harris. *Educ:* Sherborne School for Girls; University of London (external student). BA 1st Class Honours (English), 1934. Asst Mistress, Sherborne School for Girls, 1934, and House Mistress, 1938. Organised Public Schools and Clubs Camps for Girls, 1937-39; in charge of group evacuated from Sherborne to Canada, 1940; joined staff of National Association of Girls' Clubs, 1943; Chm. Christian Consultative Cttee Nat. Assoc. of Mixed Clubs and Girls' Clubs, 1952-68, Vice-Pres., 1968; Chm. Outward Bound Girls' Courses, 1954-59; Mem. Council, Outward Bound Trust, 1956-64. Member: Women's Consultative Cttee, Min. of Labour, 1958-77; Women's Nat. Commn, 1976-78. Member: Dorset Educn Cttee, 1952-70; Exec. Cttee, Assoc. of Headmistresses, 1953-58, 1960 (Pres., 1964-66); Pres., Assoc. of Headmistresses of Boarding Schs, 1960-62; Member: Cttee on Agricl Colls, Min. of Agric., 1961-64; Schs Council, 1966-75. Member: Archbishop's Council on Evangelism, 1966-68; Panel on Broadcasting, Synod of C of E, 1975–; Bd, Christian Aid, 1976– (Chm., 1978–); Exec. Cttee and Assembly, BBC, 1977–. Pres., CMS, 1969-82 (Mem., 1953-82, Chm., 1960-63, Exec. Cttee). King George's Jubilee Trust: Mem., Standing Res. and Adv. Cttee, 1949; Mem., Admin. Council, 1955-67; Member: Council, 1951-62, Exec. and Council, 1976-79, Nat. Youth Orch. of GB; ITA, 1956-60; Council, Westminster Abbey Choir Sch., 1976–; Court, Royal Foundn of St Katharine, 1979– (Chm., 1981–). President: Sch. Mistresses and Governesses Benevolent Instn, 1980–; Time and Talents Assoc., 1981–; British and For. Sch. Soc., 1982–. Governor: Godolphin Sch., Salisbury, 1975–; St Michael's Sch., Limpsfield, 1975– (Chm., 1977). FRSA 1964 (Mem. Council, RSA, 1975–; Chm., 1979-81; Vice-Pres., 1981–); Mem., The Pilgrims, 1979–. Hon. FCP 1975. *Address:* 35 The Close, Salisbury, Wilts SP1 2EL. *T:* Salisbury 26889.

READHEAD, James (Templeman), 3rd Bt, *cr* 1922 (but discontinued style of Sir and the use of his title, 1965); Lieutenant late King's Own Yorkshire Light Infantry, TA; *b* 12 Feb. 1910; *s* of late Stanley Readhead, Stanhope House, Westoe, South Shields, and late Hilda Maud, *d* of Thomas John Templeman, Weymouth, Dorset; *S* uncle, 1940; *m* 1946, Hilda Rosemary, *o d* of George Henry Hudson, The Manor, Hatfield, nr Doncaster, Yorks; one *d. Educ:* Repton School. Electrical Engineer, retired. *Recreations:* various.

READING, 4th Marquess of, *cr* 1926; **Simon Charles Henry Rufus Isaacs**; Baron 1914; Viscount 1916; Earl 1917; Viscount Erleigh 1917; *b* 18 May 1942; *e s* of 3rd Marquess of Reading, MBE, MC, and of Margot Irene, *yr d* of late Percy Duke, OBE; *S* father, 1980; *m* 1979, Melinda Victoria, *yr d* of Richard Dewar, Seale, Surrey; one *d. Educ:* Eton. Lieut in 1st Queen's Dragoon Guards, 1961-64. *Heir: b* Lord Anthony Michael Rufus Isaacs, *b* 22 Sept. 1943. *Address:* 14 Shalcomb Street, SW10. *Clubs:* Cavalry and Guards, MCC.

READING, Bishop Suffragan of, since 1982; **Rt. Rev. Ronald Graham Gregory Foley;** *b* 13 June 1923; *s* of Theodore Gregory Foley and Cessan Florence Page; *m* 1944, Florence Redman; two *s* two *d. Educ:* King Edward's Grammar Sch., Aston, Birmingham; Wakefield Grammar Sch.; King's Coll., London; St John's Coll., Durham BA Hons Theol., LTh. Curate, South Shore, Blackpool, 1950; Vicar, S Luke, Blackburn, 1954; Dir of Educn, Dio. of Durham, and Rector of Brancepeth, 1960; Chaplain, Aycliffe Approved Sch., 1962; Vicar of Leeds, 1971-82; Chaplain to the Queen, 1977-82. Hon. Canon: Durham Cathedral, 1965-71; Ripon Cath., 1971-82. Dir, Yorks Electricity Bd, 1976-82. *Publication:* (jtly) Religion in Approved Schools, 1969. *Recreations:* journalism, reading detective stories, watching other people mow lawns. *Address:* Greenbanks, Old Bath Road, Sonning-on-Thames, Reading RG4 0SY. *T:* Reading 692187. *Clubs:* Royal Commonwealth Society; The Leeds (Leeds).

READWIN, Edgar Seeley, CBE 1971; retired; *b* 7 Nov. 1915; *s* of Ernest Readwin, Master Mariner and Edith Elizabeth Readwin; *m* 1940, Lesley Margaret (*née* Barker); two *s* one *d. Educ:* Bracondale Sch., Norwich. FCA. Articled Clerk, Harman & Gowen, Norwich, 1932-37; Asst Auditor, Bengal & North Western Railway, 1938-40; commnd service 14th Punjab Regt, 1941-45, PoW Far East, Singapore, Siam-Burma Railway, 1942-45; Indian Railway Accounts Service, 1945-49. Booker Group of Companies in Guyana: Asst to Accounts Controller, 1950; Finance Dir, 1951-56; Dep. Chm., 1956-62; Chm., 1962-71. Dir, West Indies Sugar Assoc., 1962-71; Finance Dir, Indonesia Sugar Study, 1971-72; Chm., Minvielle & Chastenet Ltd, St Lucia, 1973-76. Hon. Treas., Guyana Lawn Tennis Assoc., 1951-67, Pres., 1968-70, Hon. Life Vice-Pres., 1971–. *Recreations:* lawn tennis, golf, gardening, chess, bridge. *Address:* Lane End Farmhouse, Ancton Lane, Middleton-on-Sea, Sussex. *T:* Middleton-on-Sea 2131. *Clubs:* Veterans' Lawn Tennis of Great Britain; Bognor Tennis; Littlehampton Golf.

REAGAN, Ronald; President of the United States of America, since 1981; *b* Tampico, Ill, 6 Feb. 1911; *m* 1st, 1940, Jane Wyman (marr. diss. 1948); one *s* one *d* ; 2nd, 1952, Nancy Davis; one *s* one *d. Educ:* public schools in Tampico, Monmouth, Galesbury, and Dixon, Ill; Eureka Coll., Ill (AB). Sports Announcer, WHO, Des Moines, 1932-37; actor and producer, films and television, 1937-66; Host and Program Superviser, Gen. Electric Theater (TV), 1954-62; Host, Death Valley Days (TV), 1962-65. Pres., Screen Actors' Guild, 1947-52, 1959-60; Chm., Motion Picture Industry Council, 1949. Served with USAAF, 1942-45. Governor, State of California, 1967-74; Chairman, State Governors' Assoc., 1969. Republican Candidate for nomination for the Presidency, 1974. Operates horsebreeding and cattle ranch. *Publication:* Where's the Rest of Me? (autobiog.), 1965 (repr. 1981 as My Early Life). *Address:* The White House, 1600 Pennsylvania Avenue NW, Washington, DC 20500, USA; 10960 Wilshire Boulevard, Los Angeles, Calif 90024, USA.

REARDON-SMITH, Sir William; see Smith.

REASON, Dr Richard Edmund, OBE 1967; FRS 1971; Consultant, Rank Taylor-Hobson. *Address:* 5 Manor Road, Great Bowden, Leicestershire. *T:* Market Harborough 63219.

REAY, 14th Lord, *cr* 1628, of Reay, Caithness; **Hugh William Mackay;** Bt of Nova Scotia, 1627; Baron Mackay of Ophemert and Zennewijnen, Holland; Chief of Clan Mackay; Delegate to the Council of Europe and to WEU, since 1979; *b* 19 July 1937; *s* of 13th Lord Reay and Charlotte Mary Younger; *S* father, 1963; *m* 1st, 1964, Hon. Annabel Thérèse Fraser (marr. diss.

1978), *y d* of 17th Baron Lovat, *qv* ; two *s* one *d* ; 2nd, 1980, Hon. Victoria Isabella Warrender, *d* of Baron Bruntisfield, *qv* ; one *d. Educ:* Eton; Christ Church. Mem., European Parlt, 1973-79 (Vice-Chm., Cons. Gp). *Heir: s* The Master of Reay, *qv. Address:* House of Lords, SW1; Kasteel Ophemert, Ophemert, (Gld) Holland.

REAY, Master of; Aeneas Simon Mackay, *b* 20 March 1965; *s* and *heir* of 14th Lord Reay, *qv.*

REAY, Lt-Gen. Sir Alan; see Reay, Lt-Gen. Sir H. A. J.

REAY, Basil; see Reay, S. B.

REAY, Lt-Gen. Sir (Hubert) Alan (John), KBE 1981; QHP, FRCP, FRCP(Edin); Director General, Army Medical Services, since 1981; *b* 19 March 1925; *s* of Rev. John Reay; *m* 1960, Ferelith Haslewood Deane; two *s* two *d* (and one *s* decd). *Educ:* Lancing College; Edinburgh Univ. MB, DTMQH, DCH. Field Medical Services, Malaya, 1949-52 (despatches); Exchange Physician, Brooke Hosp., San Antonio, Texas, 1957; Command Paediatrician: Far East, 1962; BAOR, 1965; Adviser in Paediatrics, MoD (Army), 1968; Hon. Out-patient Consultant, Great Ormond Street Hosp., 1975-79; Postgraduate Dean and Comdt, Royal Army Med. Coll., 1977-79; DMS, HQ BAOR, 1979-81. Sec., Paediatric Section, RSocMed, 1977-79. *Publications:* paediatric articles in med. jls. *Address:* Ministry of Defence, First Avenue House, High Holborn, WC1V 6HE.

REAY, (Stanley) Basil, OBE 1957; Chairman, British Schools Lawn Tennis Association, since 1980; *b* 2 Feb. 1909; *s* of Robert and Maud Reay (*née* Cox), Stockton on Tees; *m* 1935, Beatrice Levene; one *s* one *d. Educ:* Queen Elizabeth Grammar School, Hexham; St John's College. Schoolmaster in England, 1929-32; Min. of Education, Egypt, 1932-39. Chairman Inter-Services Language Training Cttee, 1945-47. Served RAF, 1939-47, chiefly in ME (Wing Comdr, 1944). Wing Comdr, RAFVR. Sec., LTA, 1948-73; Sec. Gen., Internat. Lawn Tennis Fedn and Davis Cup Competition, 1973-76 (Hon. Sec., 1948-73; Hon. Life Counsellor, 1976–). Commandeur, Ordre de Merite Sportif (France), 1960; Gold Medal of Jerusalem (Israel); sports decorations from Yugoslavia, Brazil and others. *Recreations:* travel and sports. *Address:* Molende, Molember Road, East Molesey, Surrey. *Clubs:* Royal Automobile, RAF Reserves; All England (Wimbledon); International Lawn Tennis Clubs of Great Britain, USA, France, Italy, Sweden, Denmark, Australia, Argentina, Belgium.

REBBECK, Dr Denis, CBE 1952; JP, DL; MA, MSc, PhD, BLitt; FEng, FICE, FIMechE, FRINA, FIMarE, FCIT; *b* 22 Jan. 1914; *er s* of late Sir Frederick Ernest Rebbeck, KBE; *m* 1938, Rosamond Annette Kathleen, *e d* of late Henry Jameson, Bangor, Co. Down; four *s. Educ:* Campbell Coll., Belfast; Pembroke Coll., Cambridge. BA (Hons) Mech. Sciences Tripos, 1935; MA (Cantab) 1939; MA (Dublin) 1945; BLitt (Dublin) 1946; MSc (Belfast) 1946; PhD (Belfast) 1950; Part-time Post-grad. Research. Harland & Wolff, Ltd: Director, 1946-70; Dep. Man. Director, 1953; Man. Dir, 1962-70; Chm., 1965-66. Chm., 1972–, Dir, 1950–, Iron Trades Employers' Insurance Association Ltd and Iron Trades Mutual Insurance Co. Ltd (Vice-Chm., 1969-72); Director: Nat. Shipbuilders Security Ltd, 1952-58; Colvilles Ltd, 1963-67; Brown Brothers & Co. Ltd, 1967-68; Shipbuilding Corporation Ltd, 1963-73; National Commercial Bank of Scotland Ltd, 1965-69; Royal Bank of Scotland Ltd, 1969–; Belships Co. Ltd, 1970-76 (Chm., 1972-76); John Kelly Ltd, 1968-79 (Dep. Chm., 1968; Chm., 1969-79); Howdens Ltd, 1977-79; Norman Canning Ltd, 1977-79; Nationwide Building Soc., 1980–; Nordic Business Forum for Northern Britain Ltd, 1980–. Special Consultant, Swan Hunter Group Ltd, 1970-79; Consultant, Ellerman Travel, 1979–. Belfast Harbour Commissioner, 1962–. Member Research Council, and Chairman, Design Main Committee, British Ship Research Association, 1965-73; Pres., Shipbuilding Employers' Fedn, 1962-63; Past Chm. Warship Gp., Shipbuilding Conf.; NI Economic Council, 1965-70; Lloyd's Register of Shipping General Cttee, 1962- and Technical Cttee, 1964-76; Management Board: Engineering Employers Fedn, 1963-75; Shipbuilders & Repairers Nat. Assoc., 1966-71; Council, RINA, 1964-72; Council for Scientific R&D in NI, 1948-59; Member Inst. of Engineers and Shipbuilders in Scotland; Past Chm. and Trustee, Belfast Savings Bank; Cambridge Univ. Engineers' Assoc.; Science Masters' Assoc. (Pres. NI Branch, 1954-55); NI Grammar Schools Careers Assoc. (Pres., 1964-65); Life Mem. Brit. Assoc. for the Advancement of Science; National Playing Fields Assoc. (NI Exec. Cttee), 1952-77; Chairman: Adv. Cttee on Marine Pilotage, 1977-79; Pilotage Commn, 1979–; Member: Drummond Technical Investigation Cttee, 1955-56; Lord Coleraine's Committee to enquire into Youth Employment Services in NI, 1957-58; Sir John Lockwood's Cttee on Univ. and Higher Techn. Educn in Northern Ireland, 1963-64; Queen's Univ., Better Equipment Fund Exec. Cttee, 1951-82; Vice-Pres. of Belfast Savings Council; Visitor, Linen Industry Research Assoc., DSIR, 1954-57; President: Belfast Assoc. of Engineers, 1947-48; NI Society of Incorporated Secretaries, 1955-70; Glencraig Curative Schools, NI, 1953-70; World Ship Soc., 1978-81 (Vice Pres., 1956); Past Mem. Council IMechE; IMarE; Chm. NI Assoc., ICE, 1952-53; FEng 1979. Member: Smeatonian Soc. of Civil Engrs; Incorp. of Hammermen of Glasgow. Liveryman, Worshipful Company of Shipwrights, 1952- (Prime Warden, 1980-81). Vice-Pres., Queen's Univ. Guild, 1951-65; Board Governors Campbell Coll., Belfast, 1952-60 (Vice-Chm. 1957-60); Member of Court, New Univ. of Ulster. Mem., T&AFA for Belfast, 1947-65; Dep.-Chm. NI Festival of Britain, 1948-51; papers read before British

Association, ICE, etc; Akroyd Stuart Award, IMarE, 1943. JP County Borough of Belfast, 1949; DL County of the City of Belfast, 1960. *Recreation:* sailing. *Address:* The White House, Craigavad, Holywood, County Down, N Ireland BT18 0HE. *T:* Holywood 2294. *Clubs:* Royal Yacht Squadron, Royal Automobile, City Livery, Den Norske; Cambridge Union; Shippingklubben (Oslo); Royal Norwegian Yacht; Royal North of Ireland Yacht (Cultra, Co. Down).

REBBECK, Rear-Admiral Sir (Leopold) Edward, KBE 1956; CB 1954; retired; *b* 26 July 1901; *s* of Edward Wise Rebbeck, Bournemouth; *m* Clara Margaret Allen, *e d* of R. G. Coombe, Ceylon; two *s* two *d. Educ:* Pembroke Lodge; Royal Naval Colls Osborne and Dartmouth. Served European War in HMS Erin; HM Yacht Victoria and Albert, 1932-35; War of 1939-45; HMS Birmingham, and as Assistant Naval Attaché, USA. Commanding Officer, RN Air Station Anthorn, 1946; Fleet Engineer Officer to C in C Mediterranean, 1949. ADC to King George VI, 1951-52; ADC to the Queen, 1952; Rear-Admiral Reserve Aircraft, 1952-55, retired. Vickers Group, 1956-66. Mem., Soc. Naval Architects and Marine Engineers (New York). *Recreations:* golf, motoring. *Address:* Stubb Hill House, Iping, near Midhurst, West Sussex GU29 0PQ. *T:* Milland 238. *Clubs:* Army and Navy, Royal Automobile.

RECKITT, Lt-Col Basil Norman; TD 1946; Director, Reckitt and Colman Ltd, retired 1972 (Chairman, 1966-70); *b* 12 Aug. 1905; *s* of Frank Norman Reckitt, Architect, and Beatrice Margaret Hewett; *m* 1st, 1928, Virginia Carre-Smith (*d* 1961); three *d;* 2nd, 1966, Mary Holmes (*née* Peirce), widow of Paul Holmes, Malham Tarn, near Settle. *Educ:* Uppingham; King's Coll., Cambridge (MA). Joined Reckitt & Sons Ltd, 1927; Dir, Reckitt & Colman Ltd, 1938. 2nd Lieut, 62nd HAA Regt (TA), 1939; Bde Major, 39th AA Brigade, 1940; CO 141 HAA (M) Regt, 1942; Military Government, Germany, 1944-45. Chm. Council, 1971-80, and Pro-Chancellor, 1971-, Hull Univ. Sheriff of Hull, 1970-71. Hon. LLD, Hull University, 1967. *Publications:* History of Reckitt & Sons Ltd, 1951; Charles I and Hull, 1952; The Lindley Affair, 1972. *Recreations:* riding and walking. *Address:* Haverbrack, Milnthorpe, Cumbria LA7 7AH. *T:* Milnthorpe 3142.

REDCLIFFE-MAUD, family name of **Baron Redcliffe-Maud.**

REDCLIFFE-MAUD, Baron *cr* 1967 (Life Peer), of City and County of Bristol; **John Primatt Redcliffe Redcliffe-Maud,** GCB 1955 (KCB 1946); CBE 1942; Master of University College, Oxford, 1963-76; *b* 3 Feb. 1906; *yr s* of late John Primatt Maud, Bishop of Kensington, and late Elizabeth Diana Furse; *m* 1932, Jean, *yr d* of late J. B. Hamilton, Melrose; one *s* two *d* (and one *d* decd). *Educ:* Eton (King's Scholar); New College, Oxford (Open Classical Scholar); Harvard College, USA. Henry P. Davison Scholar from Oxford Univ. to Harvard College, 1928-29; AB Harvard, 1929; Junior Research Fellow, 1929, University College, Oxford; Fellow and Dean, 1932-39; Rhodes Travelling Fellowship to Africa, 1932; University Lecturer in Politics, 1938-39; Councillor Oxford City, 1930-36; invited by Johannesburg City Council to write municipal history of city; Tutor to Colonial Administrative Services Course, Oxford, 1937-39; Master of Birkbeck College, University of London, 1939-43; Deputy Secretary, later Second Secretary, Ministry of Food, 1941-44; Second Secretary, Office of the Minister of Reconstruction, 1944-45; Secretary, Office of Lord President of the Council, 1945; Permanent Secretary, Ministry of Education, 1945-52; Mem. Economic Planning Board, 1952-58; Permanent Secretary, Ministry of Fuel and Power, 1952-59; British Ambassador in South Africa, 1961-63 (High Commissioner, 1959-61), and High Commissioner for Basutoland, Bechuanaland Protectorate and Swaziland, 1959-63. High Bailiff of Westminster, 1967-. UK deleg. to Confs on Food and Agric., Hot Springs, 1943, UNRRA, Atlantic City, 1943, and UNESCO, 1946, 1947, 1948, 1949, 1950 (President Executive Board, 1949-50). Chm., Council, Royal Coll. of Music, 1965-73. Chairman: Local Govt Management Cttee, 1964-67; Royal Commn on Local Govt in England, 1966-69; Prime Minister's Cttee on Local Govt Rules of Conduct, 1973-74. President: RIPA, 1969-79; British Diabetic Assoc., 1977-. Hon. Fellow: New Coll., Oxford, 1964; University Coll., Oxford, 1976; Fellow, Eton Coll., 1964-76. For. Associate, Venezuelan Acad. of Scis, 1973. Hon. LLD: Witwatersrand, 1960; Natal, 1963; Leeds, 1967; Nottingham, 1968; Hon. DSocSc Birmingham, 1968. Sen. Fell., RCA, 1961; FRCM, 1964; Associate Fellow, Jonathan Edwards Coll., Yale, 1968. *Publications:* English Local Government, 1932; City Government: The Johannesburg Experiment, 1938; Chapter in Oxford and the Groups, 1934; Chapter in Personal Ethics, 1935; Johannesburg and the Art of Self-Government, 1937; Chapter in Education in a Changing World, 1951; English Local Government Reformed, 1974; Support for the Arts in England and Wales, 1976; Experiences of an Optimist (memoirs), 1981. *Address:* 221 Woodstock Road, Oxford. *T:* Oxford 55354. *Clubs:* Savile; Eton Ramblers.
See also Hon. H. J. H. Maud.

REDDAWAY, (Arthur Frederick) John, CMG 1959; OBE 1957; Director-General, Arab-British Centre, London, 1970-80; *b* 12 April 1916; *s* of Arthur Joseph Reddaway, Chartered Accountant, and Thirza May King; *m* 1945, Anthoula, *d* of Dr Christodoulos Papaioannou, Nicosia; two *s. Educ:* County High School, Ilford; University of Reading. Colonial Administrative Service, Cyprus, 1938; Imperial Defence College, 1954; Administrative Sec., Cyprus, 1957-60; Dep. Comr-General, UNRWA for Palestine Refugees, 1960-68.

Address: 19 Woodsyre, Sydenham Hill, SE26. *Club:* East India, Devonshire, Sports and Public Schools, Royal Commonwealth Society.

REDDAWAY, (George Frank) Norman, CBE 1965 (MBE 1946); HM Diplomatic Service, retired; *b* 2 May 1918; *s* of late William Fiddian Reddaway and late Kate Waterland Reddaway (*née* Sills); *m* 1944, Jean Brett, OBE; two *s* three *d. Educ:* Oundle School; King's College, Cambridge. Scholar Modern Langs, 1935; 1st Class Hons Mod. Langs Tripos Parts 1 and 2, 1937 and 1939. Served in Army, 1939-46; psc Camberley, 1944. Foreign Office, 1946; Private Sec. to Parly Under Sec. of State, 1947-49; Rome, 1949; Ottawa, 1952; Foreign Office, 1955; Imperial Defence College, 1960; Beirut, 1961; Counsellor, Office of the Political Adviser to the C-in-C, Far East, Singapore, 1965-66; Counsellor (Commercial), Khartoum, 1967-69; Asst Under-Sec. of State, FCO, 1970-74; Ambassador to Poland, 1974-78. Chm., English International, 1978-; Dir, Catalytic International, 1978-; Sec., Farmington Trust, 1978-; Trustee: Thomson Foundn, 1978-; Trinity Trust, 1980-. *Recreations:* gardening, family history. *Address:* 51 Carlton Hill, NW8. *T:* 01-624 9238. *Clubs:* Athenæum, United Oxford & Cambridge University.

REDDAWAY, John; *see* Reddaway, A. F. J.

REDDAWAY, Norman; *see* Reddaway, G. F. N.

REDDAWAY, Prof. William Brian, CBE 1971; FBA 1967; Professor of Political Economy, University of Cambridge, 1969-80; Fellow of Clare College, Cambridge, since 1938; Economic Consultant to CBI, since 1972; *b* 8 Jan. 1913; *s* of late William Fiddian Reddaway and late Kate Waterland Reddaway (*née* Sills); *m* 1938, Barbara Augusta Bennett; three *s* one *d. Educ:* Oundle Sch.; King's Coll., Cambridge; Maj. schol. natural science; 1st cl. Maths tripos, part I, 1st cl. 1st div. Economics tripos, part II; Adam Smith Prize; MA. Assistant, Bank of England, 1934-35; Research Fellow in Economics, University of Melbourne, 1936-37; Statistics Division, Board of Trade (final rank Chief Statistician), 1940-47; University Lectr in Economics, 1939-55, Reader in Applied Economics, 1957-65, Dir of Dept of Applied Economics, 1955-69, Univ. of Cambridge. Economic Adviser to OEEC, 1951-52; Visiting Economist, Center for International Studies, New Delhi, 1959-60; Vis. Lectr, Economic Develt Inst. (Washington), 1966-67; Consultant, Harvard Develt Adv. Service (in Ghana), 1967; Vis. Prof., Bangladesh Inst. of Develt Studies, 1974-75. Regional Adviser, Economic Commn for Western Asia, 1979-80. Member: Royal Commn on the Press, 1961-62; NBPI, 1967-71; Chm., Inquiry into Consulting Engineering Firms' Costs and Earnings, 1971-72. Editor, Economic Jl, 1971-76. *Publications:* Russian Financial System, 1935; Economics of a Declining Population, 1939; (with C. F. Carter, Richard Stone) Measurement of Production Movements, 1948; The Development of the Indian Economy, 1962; Effects of UK Direct Investment Overseas, Interim Report, 1967, Final Report, 1968; Effects of the Selective Employment Tax, First Report, 1970, Final Report, 1973; (with G. C. Fiegehen) Companies, Incentives and Senior Managers, 1981; articles in numerous economic journals. *Recreations:* skating, squash, walking. *Address:* 4 Adams Road, Cambridge. *T:* 350041.

REDDISH, Prof. Vincent Cartledge, OBE 1974; Professor Emeritus, Edinburgh University, 1980; industrial and scientific consultant, with business interests in the Scottish Tourist industry, since 1980; *b* 28 April 1926; *s* of William H. M. Reddish and Evelyn Reddish; *m* 1951, Elizabeth Waltho; two *s. Educ:* Wigan Techn. Coll.; London Univ. BSc Hons, PhD, DSc. Lectr in Astronomy, Edinburgh Univ., 1954; Lectr in Radio Astronomy, Manchester Univ., 1959; Royal Observatory, Edinburgh: Principal Scientific Officer, 1962; Sen. Principal Sci. Off., 1966; Dep. Chief Sci. Off., 1974; Regius Prof. of Astronomy, Edinburgh Univ., Dir, Royal Observatory, Edinburgh, and Astronomer Royal for Scotland, 1975-80. Governor, Rannoch Sch., 1981-. *Publications:* Evolution of the Galaxies, 1967; The Physics of Stellar Interiors, 1974; Stellar Formation, 1978; numerous sci. papers in Monthly Notices RAS, Nature and other jls. *Recreations:* hill walking, sailing, ornithology, do-it-yourself. *Address:* Croiscrag, Rannoch Station, Perthshire PH17 2QG. *T:* Bridge of Gaur 255.

REDDY, (Neelam) Sanjiva; President of India, 1977-82; *b* 13 May 1913; *m* Nagaratnamma; one *s* three *d. Educ:* Adyar Arts Coll., Anantapur. Andhra Provincial Congress: Sec., Congress Cttee, 1936-46; Pres., 1951-; Leader, Congress Legislature Party, 1953-; Mem. and Sec., Madras Legislative Assembly, 1946; Mem., Indian Constituent Assembly, 1947; Minister for Prohibition, Housing and Forests, Madras Govt, 1949-51; Mem., Rajya Sabha, 1952-53; Andhra Pradesh: Mem., Legislative Assembly, 1953-64; Dep. Chief Minister, 1953-56; Chief Minister, 1956-57 and 1962-64; Pres., All-India Congress Party, 1960-62; Member: Rajya Sabha, 1964-67; Lok Sabha, 1967-71, and 1977; Minister: of Steel and Mines, 1964-65; of Transport, Aviation, Shipping and Tourism, 1966-67; Speaker of Lok Sabha, 1967-69, 1977. Farmer and lemon grower in Illure. *Address:* Illure, Anantapur, Andhra Pradesh, India.

REDESDALE, 5th Baron, *cr* 1902; **Clement Napier Bertram Mitford;** Vice President, Corporate Communications Europe and Middle East, Chase Manhattan Bank NA; *b* 28 Oct. 1932; *o s* of late Hon. E. R. B. O. Freeman-Mitford, 5th *s* of 1st Baron; *S* uncle, 1963; *m* 1958, Sarah Georgina Cranston Todd; one *s* six *d. Educ:* Eton. MCAM. Joined Colin Turner (London) Ltd, 1953; joined Erwin Wasey (Advertising), 1955, Associate

Director, 1960-64. Pres., Guild of Cleaners and Launderers, 1968-70. Chm., Nat. Council of Royal Soc. of St George, 1970-75, Pres., 1975-79. Governor, Yehudi Menuhin Sch., 1973-. *Heir: s* Hon. Rupert Bertram Mitford, *b* 18 July 1967. *Address:* 2 St Mark's Square, NW1 7TP. *T:* 01-722 1965. *Club:* Lansdowne.

REDFEARN, Sir Herbert, Kt 1973; JP; DL; wire and wire goods manufacturer; Chairman, Siddall & Hilton Ltd, and all subsidiary companies, since 1972; *b* 26 Sept. 1915; *s* of Harry Reginald and Annie Elizabeth Redfearn; *m* 1942, Doris Vickerman, *y d* of Joseph Vickerman and Sarah Elizabeth Vickerman; one *s* one *d*. *Educ:* local council and technical schs. Brighouse: Borough Council, 1943-74; Alderman of Borough, 1953-74; Mayor, 1967. Chm., Brighouse and Spenborough Conservative Constituency Assoc., 1961-66, Pres., 1966-; Treas., Yorks Provincial Area Council of Conservative and Unionist Assoc., 1966-70, Chm., 1971-76. Member: Conservative Party Bd of Finance, 1966-70; Nat. Union Exec. Cttee, 1966-; Cons. and Unionist Agents': Examination Bd, 1970-; Superannuation Fund Management Cttee, 1972-79 (Trustee 1979-); Vice Chm., Nat. Union of Cons. and Unionist Assocs, 1976-77, Chm. 1978. JP W Yorks, 1956; DL W Yorks, 1977. *Recreations:* freemasonry, gardening. *Address:* Ash Lea, Woodhouse Lane, Brighouse, West Yorkshire. *Club:* Carlton.

REDFERN, Sir (Arthur) Shuldham, KCVO 1939; CMG 1945; *b* 13 June 1895; *er s* of Dr J. J. Redfern; *m* 1925, Ruth Marion Grimshaw (*d* 1972); one *s*. *Educ:* Winchester; Trinity College, Cambridge. Served European War, 1914-19, Major Royal Flying Corps and RAF, 1918; joined Sudan Political Service, 1920; successively Assistant District Commissioner in Provinces of Khartoum, Darfur, Blue Nile; Dep. Governor of Blue Nile Province, 1927; Assistant Civil Secretary, Khartoum, 1929; Commissioner Port Sudan, 1932; Governor Kassala Province, 1934; Secretary to Governor-General of Canada, 1935-45; British Council, 1947-51. Pres., English Chamber Orch. and Music Soc., 1982-. CStJ; Officer of Order of the Nile, 1925. *Publications:* articles in Canadian papers. *Recreations:* music, painting. *Address:* 32 Sheffield Terrace, W8. *T:* 01-229 1323. *Club:* Athenæum.

REDFERN, Philip; Deputy Director, Office of Population, Censuses and Surveys, 1970-82; *b* 14 Dec. 1922; *m* 1951, Gwendoline Mary Phillips; three *d*. *Educ:* Bemrose Sch., Derby; St John's Coll., Cambridge. Wrangler, Mathematical Tripos, Cambridge, 1942. Asst Statistician, Central Statistical Office, 1947; Chief Statistician, Min. of Education, 1960; Dir of Statistics and Jt Head of Planning Branch, Dept of Educn and Science, 1967.

REDFERN, Sir Shuldham; see Redfern, Sir A. S.

REDFORD, Donald Kirkman, CBE 1980; Chairman, The Manchester Ship Canal Company, since 1972 (Managing Director, 1970-80); *b* 18 Feb. 1919; *er s* of T. J. and S. A. Redford; *m* 1942, Mabel (*née* Wilkinson), Humberside, Lincs; one *s* one *d*. *Educ:* Culford Sch.; King's Coll., Univ. of London (LLB). Served, 1937-39, and War until 1945, in RAFVR (retd as Wing Comdr). Practice at the Bar until end of 1946, when joined The Manchester Ship Canal Company, with which Company has since remained; Dir, Bridgewater Estates Ltd. Chairman, Nat. Assoc. of Port Employers, 1972-74; Dep. Chm., British Ports Assoc., 1973-74, Chm. 1974-78. Member: Cttee of Management, RNLI, 1977-; Court and Council, Manchester Univ., 1977- (Dep. Treas., 1980-). *Recreations:* reading, history, sailing, golf. *Address:* North Cotes, 8 Harrod Drive, Birkdale, Southport. *T:* Southport 67406; The Manchester Ship Canal Co., Ship Canal House, King Street, Manchester M2 4WX. *T:* 061-872 2411. *Clubs:* Oriental; St James's (Manchester).

REDGRAVE, Lynn; actress; *b* 8 March 1943; *d* of Sir Michael Redgrave, *qv*; and of Rachel Kempson, *qv*; *m* 1967, John Clark; one *s* two *d*. *Educ:* Queensgate Sch.; Central Sch. of Speech and Drama. Nat. Theatre of GB, 1963-66 (Tulip Tree, Mother Courage, Hay Fever, etc); Black Comedy, Broadway 1967; The Two of Us, Slag, Zoo Zoo Widdershins Zoo, Born Yesterday, London 1968-71; A Better Place, Dublin 1972; My Fat Friend, Knock Knock, Mrs Warren's Profession, Broadway 1973-76; The Two of Us, California Suite, Hellzapoppin, US tours 1976-77; Saint Joan, Chicago and NY 1977; Twelfth Night, Amer. Shakespeare Festival, Conn, 1978; Les dames du jeudi, LA, 1981. *Films include:* Tom Jones, Girl with Green Eyes, Georgy Girl (NY Film Critics, Golden Globe and IFIDA awards, Academy nomination Best Actress), Deadly Affair, Smashing Time, Virgin Soldiers, Last of the Mobile Hotshots, Every Little Crook and Nanny, National Health, Happy Hooker, Everything You Always Wanted to Know about Sex, The Big Bus, Sunday Lovers. *USA television includes:* Co-host of nationally televised talk-show, Not For Women Only, appearances in documentaries, plays, The Muppets, Centennial, Beggarman Thief, The Seduction of Miss Leona, and series: Housecalls (CBS); Teachers Only (NBC). *Recreations:* cooking, gardening, horse riding. *Address:* PO Box 1207, Topanga, Calif 90290, USA. *T:* (213) 455-1334.

REDGRAVE, Sir Michael (Scudamore), Kt 1959; CBE 1952; Actor; *b* 20 March 1908; *s* of G. E. ("Roy") Redgrave, actor, and Margaret Scudamore, actress; *m* 1935, Rachel Kempson, *qv*; one *s* two *d*. *Educ:* Clifton Coll.; Magdalene Coll., Cambridge. MA; formerly modern language master Cranleigh Sch. Liverpool Repertory Theatre, 1934-36; Country Wife, As You Like It, Hamlet, etc, Old Vic Season, 1936-37; Richard II, School for Scandal, Three Sisters, Queen's Theatre, 1937-38; White Guard, Twelfth Night, Phœnix Theatre, 1938-39; Family Reunion, Westminster Theatre,

1939; Beggar's Opera, Haymarket Theatre, 1940; Thunder Rock, Globe Theatre, 1940; The Duke in Darkness, St James's Theatre, 1942; A Month in the Country, Parisienne, St James's Theatre, 1943; Uncle Harry, Garrick Theatre, 1944; Jacobowsky and the Colonel, Piccadilly, 1945; Macbeth, Aldwych, 1947; Macbeth, National Theatre, New York, 1948; The Father, Embassy, 1948, and Duchess, 1949; A Woman in Love, Embassy, 1949; Love's Labour's Lost, She Stoops to Conquer, A Month in the Country, Hamlet, with Old Vic Theatre Co., New, 1949-50; played Hamlet at Switzerland and Holland Festivals, also at Kronborg Castle, Élsinore, 1950; Richard II, Henry IV Parts 1 and 2, Henry V, The Tempest, Memorial Theatre, Stratford-on-Avon, 1951; solo performance of Shakespeare, Holland Festival, 1951; Winter Journey, St James's, 1952; Rockefeller Foundation Lecturer, Bristol Univ., 1952; Shylock, Antony and King Lear, Stratford-on-Avon, 1953; Antony, Princes, 1953, and Amsterdam, Brussels and Paris, 1954; Tiger at the Gates, Apollo, 1955, and Plymouth, New York, 1955; Theodore Spencer Memorial Lecturer, Harvard Univ., 1956; The Sleeping Prince, Coronet, New York, 1956; A Touch of the Sun, Saville, 1958; Hamlet and Benedick, Stratford-on-Avon, 1958; played Hamlet with Shakespeare Memorial Theatre Co., in Russia, 1958; The Aspern Papers, Queen's, 1959; The Tiger and the Horse, Queen's, 1960; solo performances of Shakespeare and of Hans Andersen, Bath Festival, 1961; The Complaisant Lover, Barrymore, NY, 1961; Uncle Vanya, Chichester Festival, 1962; Out of Bounds, Wyndham's, 1962; Uncle Vanya, Chichester Festival, 1963; joined National Theatre, 1963 (first production, Oct. 1963); Claudius in Hamlet; Uncle Vanya, Hobson's Choice, The Master Builder; A Month in the Country, Y. Arnaud and Cambridge Theatres, also Samson Agonistes (YA), 1965; The Old Boys, Mermaid, 1971; A Voyage Round My Father, Haymarket, Canada and Australia, 1972-73; The Hollow Crown, and Pleasure and Repentance, US 1973, 1974, World Tour, 1975; Shakespeare's People, S African tour, 1975; South America and Eastern Canada Tour, 1976; Denmark, British Columbia, NZ, US tours, 1977; Close of Play, Nat. Theatre, 1979; *films:* The Lady Vanishes, The Stars Look Down, Kipps, Jeannie, Thunder Rock, The Way to the Stars, Dead of Night, The Captive Heart, The Man Within, Fame is the Spur, Mourning Becomes Electra, The Browning Version, The Importance of being Earnest, The Green Scarf, Dam Busters, The Night My Number Came Up, Confidential Report, 1984, Time without Pity, The Happy Road, The Quiet American, Shake Hands with the Devil, Wreck of the Mary Deare; No, my darling daughter!, The Innocents, The Loneliness of the Long-Distance Runner, Young Cassidy, The Hill, The Heroes of Telemark, Oh What a Lovely War!, The Battle of Britain, Goodbye Mr Chips, Connecting Rooms, The Go-Between, Nicholas and Alexandra. Producer: Werther, Glyndebourne, 1966, 1969; La Bohème, Glyndebourne, 1967. Joined Royal Navy, 1941; discharged on medical grounds, 1942. President, English-Speaking Board; President, Questors Theatre; Director of Festival, Yvonne Arnaud Theatre, Guildford, 1965. FRSA; Hon. DLitt (Bristol), 1966. Commander Order of Dannebrog, 1955. *Publications:* The Seventh Man (play), 1936; Actor's Ways and Means, 1953; Mask or Face, 1958; The Aspern Papers (play), 1959; The Mountebank's Tale (novel), 1959; Circus Boy (play), 1963. *Relevant Publication:* Michael Redgrave, Actor, by Richard Findlater, 1956. *Address:* c/o Hutton Management Ltd, 194 Old Brompton Road, SW5 0AS.
See also Lynn Redgrave, Vanessa Redgrave.

REDGRAVE, Rachel, (Lady Redgrave); see Kempson, R.

REDGRAVE, Maj.-Gen. Sir Roy Michael Frederick, KBE 1979; MC 1945; FRGS; Director General, Winston Churchill Memorial Trust, since 1980; *b* 16 Sept. 1925; *s* of late Robin Roy Redgrave and Michelene Jean Capsa; *m* 1953, Caroline Margaret Valerie, *d* of Major Arthur Wellesley; two *s*. *Educ:* Sherborne Sch. Served War of 1939-45: enlisted Trooper, Royal Horse Guards, 1943; Lieut, 1st Household Cavalry Regt, NW Europe, 1944-45. GSO III Intell., HQ Rhine Army, 1950; Canadian Army Staff Coll., 1955; GSO II Ops HQ, London Dist, 1956; Recce, Sqn Ldr, Cyprus, 1959 (despatches); Mil. Assistant to Dep. SACEUR, Paris, 1960-62; JSSC 1962; Comd Household Cavalry Regt (Mounted), 1963-64; Comd Royal Horse Guards (The Blues), 1965-67; AAG PS12, MoD, 1967-68; Chief of Staff, HQ 2nd Div., 1968-70; Comdr, Royal Armoured Corps, 3rd Div., 1970-72; Nat. Defence Coll., Canada, 1973; Comdt Royal Armoured Corps Centre, 1974-75; British Comdt, Berlin, 1975-78; Comdr, British Forces, Hong Kong, and Maj.-Gen. Brigade of Gurkhas, 1978-80. Chm., Hammersmith and Fulham HA, 1981-. Mem. Council, Victoria League for Commonwealth Friendship. *Recreations:* walking, archaeology, philately. *Address:* c/o Lloyds Bank, Wareham, Dorset BH20 4LX. *Club:* Cavalry and Guards.

REDGRAVE, Vanessa, CBE 1967; Actress since 1957; *b* 30 Jan. 1937; *d* of Sir Michael Redgrave, *qv* and of Rachel Kempson, *qv*; *m* 1962, Tony Richardson, *qv* (marr. diss., 1967); two *d*. *Educ:* Queensgate School; Central School of Speech and Drama. Frinton Summer Repertory, 1957; Touch of the Sun, Saville, 1958; Midsummer Night's Dream, Stratford, 1959; Look on Tempests, 1960; The Tiger and the Horse, 1960; Lady from the Sea, 1960; Royal Shakespeare Theatre Company: As You Like It, 1961, Taming of the Shrew, 1961, Cymbeline, 1962; The Seagull, 1964; The Prime of Miss Jean Brodie, Wyndham's, 1966; Daniel Deronda, 1969; Cato Street, 1971; The Threepenny Opera, Prince of Wales, 1972; Twelfth Night, Shaw Theatre, 1972; Antony and Cleopatra, Bankside Globe, 1973; Design for Living, Phoenix, 1973; Macbeth, LA, 1974; Lady from the Sea, NY, 1976, Roundhouse, 1979. *Films:* Morgan-A Suitable Case for Treatment, 1966 (Cannes Fest. Award, Best Actress 1966); The Sailor from Gibraltar, 1967; Blow-Up, 1967; Camelot, 1967; Red White and Zero, 1967; Charge of the

Light Brigade, 1968; Isadora, 1968; A Quiet Place in the Country, 1968; The Seagull, 1969; Drop-Out, 1970; La Vacanza, 1970; The Trojan Women, 1971; The Devils, 1971; Mary, Queen of Scots, 1972; Murder on the Orient Express, 1974; Out of Season, 1975; Seven Per Cent Solution, 1975; Julia, 1976 (Academy Award, 1977; Golden Globe Award); Agatha, 1978; Yanks, 1978; Bear Island, 1978; Playing for Time, 1980; My Body, My Child, 1981. Has appeared on TV. *Publication:* Pussies and Tigers (anthology of writings of school children), 1963.

REDGRAVE, William Archibald; *b* 7 Dec. 1903; *s* of Joseph Ernest Redgrave and Rose Mabel (*née* Bradley); *m* 1st, 1925, Renée Marshall (now Renée Lady Truscott); one *d*; 2nd, 1949, Mary Crinkley; one *s* one *d*; 3rd, 1973, Elizabeth Eleanor Holbrook (solo violist); one *s* two *d*. *Educ:* Christchurch Rd Sch., Ilford; Central Sch. of Arts and Crafts; West Clapham Sch. of Art; The Old Vic, The National Gallery, The Tate Gallery. Junior clerk, insurance office, 1917; Pay-roll clerk, London Transport, 1919–40; Asst, later Music Asst, Recorded Programmes, BBC, 1940–47; long illness (TB), 1947–52; founded St Peter's Loft School of Art, St Ives, Cornwall (partnered with Peter Lanyon); returned to London, 1960; commissions in painting and sculpture; altarpiece, St Antony, Hayes, Middx; sculpture, Luminastra, Bristol; financial help from Sir Eric Truscott, Bt, to construct bronze triptych, The Event, now on loan to ILEA. *Bronze portraiture includes:* Sir Adrian Boult (Festival Hall and BBC Concert Hall), Lord Olivier (Nat. Theatre), Francis Bacon, Diana Rigg, Paul Tortelier, Henry Cooper, Margaret Barbieri, Bevis Hillier, Robert Hanson, Sydney Cowan. *Publications:* Tread and Rise, Tread and Fall, (illust. poems), 1975; Collected Poems (illust.), 1976; Residua (poems), 1980; contribs to Connoisseur, Art News. *Recreations:* violin, viola, snooker. *Address:* 23 Hungate Street, Aylsham, Norfolk. *T:* Aylsham 3487. *Clubs:* Chelsea Arts; Aylsham Ex-Service Men's.

REDGROVE, Peter William; poet; Resident Author, Falmouth School of Art, since 1966; *b* 2 Jan. 1932; *s* of Gordon James Redgrove and late Nancy Lena Cestrilli-Bell; *m* Penelope Shuttle, *qv*; one *d*; (two *s* one *d* by former marr.). *Educ:* Taunton Sch.; Queens' Coll., Cambridge. Scientific journalist and copywriter, 1954–61; Visiting Poet, Buffalo Univ., NY, 1961–62; Gregory Fellow in Poetry, Leeds Univ., 1962–65; study with John Layard, 1968–69. O'Connor Prof. of Literature, Colgate Univ., NY, 1974–75. George Rylands' Verse-speaking Prize, 1954; Fulbright Award, 1961; Poetry Book Society Choices, 1961, 1966, 1979, 1981; Arts Council Awards, 1969, 1970, 1973, 1975, 1977; Guardian Fiction Prize, 1973; Prudence Farmer Poetry Award, 1977. *Publications: poetry:* The Collector, 1960; The Nature of Cold Weather, 1961; At the White Monument, 1963; The Force, 1966; Penguin Modern Poets 11, 1968; Work in Progress, 1969; Dr Faust's Sea-Spiral Spirit, 1972; Three Pieces for Voices, 1972; The Hermaphrodite Album (with Penelope Shuttle), 1973; Sons of My Skin: Selected Poems, 1975; From Every Chink of the Ark, 1977; Ten Poems, 1977; The Weddings at Nether Powers, 1979; The Apple-Broadcast, 1981; *novels:* In the Country of the Skin, 1973; The Terrors of Dr Treviles (with Penelope Shuttle), 1974; The Glass Cottage, 1976; The Sleep of the Great Hypnotist, 1979; The God of Glass, 1979; The Beekeepers, 1980; The Facilitators, 1982; *plays:* Miss Carstairs Dressed for Blooding (play-book containing several dramatic pieces), 1976; (for radio): In the Country of the Skin, 1973; The Holy Sinner, 1975; Dance the Putrefact, 1975; The God of Glass, 1977 (Imperial Tobacco Award 1978); Martyr of the Hives, 1980 (Giles Cooper Award 1981); Florent and the Tuxedo Millions, 1982; (for television): The Sermon, 1963; Jack Be Nimble, 1980; *psychology:* The Wise Wound (with Penelope Shuttle), 1978. *Recreations:* work, photography, judo (1st Kyu Judo: Otani and Brit. Judo Assoc.), yoga. *Address:* c/o David Higham Associates, 5-8 Lower John Street, Golden Square, W1R 4HA.

REDINGTON, Frank Mitchell, MA, FIA; Chief Actuary, Prudential Assurance Co. Ltd, 1950–68, Director 1968–81; *b* 10 May 1906; *e s* of late William David and Lily Redington; *m* 1938, Katie Marianne Rosenfeld; one *s* one *d*. *Educ:* Liverpool Institute; Magdalene College, Cambridge (MA). Entered Prudential, 1928; FIA 1934; Chairman, Life Offices Association, 1956–57; President, Institute of Actuaries, 1958–60 (Gold Medal of Inst., 1968). *Publications:* contributions to Jl of Inst. of Actuaries and foreign actuarial journals. *Address:* 10 Rose Walk, St Albans, Herts. *T:* St Albans 54722.

REDMAN, Maj.-Gen. Denis Arthur Kay, CB 1963; OBE 1942; retired; Colonel Commandant, REME, 1963–68; Director, Electrical and Mechanical Engineering, War Office, 1960–63; *b* 8 April 1910; *s* of late Brig. A. S. Redman, CB; *m* 1943, Penelope, *d* of A. S. Kay; one *s* one *d*. *Educ:* Wellington Coll.; London Univ. BSc (Eng) 1st class Hons (London); FCGI, MIMechE, AMIEE. Commissioned in RAOC, 1934; served in Middle East, 1936–43; transferred to REME, 1942; Temp. Brig., 1944; DDME 1st Corps, 1951; Comdt REME Training Centre 1957–59. Graduate of Staff Coll., Joint Services Staff Coll. and Imperial Defence Coll. *Recreations:* normal. *Club:* Army and Navy.

REDMAN, Lt-Gen. Sir Harold, KCB 1953 (CB 1947); CBE 1944; *b* 25 August 1899; *s* of late A. E. Redman, Shawford, Winchester; *m* 1st, 1947, Patricia Mary (*d* 1951), *d* of late Brig. John Leslie Weston, CBE, DSO; one *d*; 2nd, 1953, Barbara Ann, *d* of late J. R. Wharton, Haffield, nr Ledbury; one *s* one *d*. *Educ:* Farnham Grammar Sch.; RMA, Woolwich. Commissioned into R Artillery, 1917; served in France and Germany, 1918 (BWM, VM); Waziristan, 1923–24 (NWF medal); Staff College, Camberley, 1929–30; transferred to KOYLI 1929; GSO 3 War Office, 1932–34; Bt Major, 1935; Brigade Major (3rd Division), 1934–36; GSO 2 Senior Officer School,

1937–38; GSO 2 Staff College, 1938–39; Bt Lt-Col 1939; War Cabinet Secretariat, 1939–40; Col 1942; Comd 7 Bn KOYLI 1940–41; Comd 151 (DLI) Infantry Bde Feb.-Dec. 1941; BGS Eighth Army, 1941–42; Comd 10 Ind. Motor Bde 1942–43; Secretary Combined Chiefs of Staff (Brig.), 1943–44; Deputy Commander French Forces of the Interior (Maj.-Gen.), Aug.-Sept. 1944; SHAEF Mission to French High Command, 1944–45; Head British Military Mission (France), 1945–46; CGS, ALFSEA, 1946–48; Director of Military Operations, War Office, 1948–51; Principal Staff Officer to Deputy Supreme Allied Commander, Europe, 1951–52; Vice-Chief of the Imperial General Staff, 1952–55; Governor and Commander-in-Chief, Gibraltar, 1955–58, retired. Director and Secretary The Wolfson Foundation, 1958–67. Col KOYLI, 1950–60. *Recreation:* gardening. *Address:* Stair House, West Lulworth, Dorset. *T:* West Lulworth 257.

REDMAN, Maurice; Chairman, Scottish Region, British Gas Corporation, since 1974; *b* 30 Aug. 1922; *s* of Herbert Redman and Olive (*née* Dyson); *m* 1960, Dorothy (*née* Appleton); two *d*. *Educ:* Hulme Grammar Sch., Oldham; Manchester Univ. BSc(Tech), 1st cl. Hons. Joined staff of Co. Borough of Oldham Gas Dept, 1943; Asst, later Dep. Production Engr, North Western Gas Bd, 1951; Chief Develt Engr, NW Gas Bd, 1957; Chief Engr, Southern Gas Bd, 1966; Dir of Engrg, Southern Gas Bd, 1970; Dep. Chm., Scottish Gas Bd, 1970; Regional Dep. Chm., Scottish Region, British Gas Corp., 1973. *Publications:* papers to Instn of Gas Engrs, Inst. of Fuel, Czechoslovak Internat. Gasification Symposium, etc. *Recreations:* gardening, music, photography. *Address:* Arington, 3 Cramond Regis, Edinburgh EH4 6LW. *T:* 031-336 6178. *Club:* New (Edinburgh).

REDMAN, Sydney, CB 1961; *b* 12 Feb. 1914; *s* of John Barritt Redman and Ann Meech; *m* 1939, Barbara Mary Grey; one *s* two *d*. *Educ:* Manchester Gram. Sch.; Corpus Christi Coll., Oxford. Asst Principal, WO, 1936; Principal Private Sec. to Secretary of State for War, 1942–44; Asst Under-Sec. of State: War Office, 1957–63; Ministry of Defence, 1963–64; Dep. Under-Sec. of State, MoD, 1964–73. Dir-Gen., Timber Trade Fedn, 1973–82. *Address:* Littlehurst, Birch Avenue, Haywards Heath, West Sussex. *T:* Haywards Heath 413738.

REDMAYNE, family name of **Baron Redmayne.**

REDMAYNE, Baron *cr* 1966 (Life Peer), of Rushcliffe; **Martin Redmayne;** Bt *cr* 1964; PC 1959; DSO 1944; DL; Deputy Chairman, House of Fraser Ltd, 1972–78; Director, The Boots Co., 1969–80; Chairman, Retail Consortium, 1971–76; *b* 16 Nov. 1910; *s* of Leonard Redmayne; *m* 1933, Anne Griffiths (*d* 1982); one *s*. *Educ:* Radley. Commanded 14th Bn The Sherwood Foresters, Italy, 1943; formed and commanded 66 Inf. Bde, 1944–45; Hon. Brig., 1945. MP (C) Rushcliffe Div. of Notts, 1950–66. A Govt Whip, 1951; A Lord Comr of the Treasury, 1953–59; Dep. Govt Chief Whip, 1955–59; Parly Sec. to Treasury and Govt Chief Whip, Oct. 1959–64; Opposition Chief Whip, Oct.-Nov. 1964. Chm., N American Adv. Gp, BOTB, 1972–76. JP Nottingham, 1946–66; DL Notts, 1954. *Recreations:* golf, fishing. *Heir:* (to Baronetcy only): *s* Hon. Nicholas Redmayne [*b* 1 Feb. 1938; *m* 1st, 1963, Ann Saunders (marr. diss. 1976); one *s* one *d*; 2nd, 1978, Mrs Christine Hewitt]. *Address:* Flat 1, 18 Hans Place, SW1X 0EP. *T:* 01-584 1525. *Club:* Buck's.

REDMAYNE, Clive; Director General Aircraft 3, Procurement Executive, Ministry of Defence, since 1981; *b* 27 July 1927; *s* of late Procter Hubert Redmayne and Emma (*née* Torkington); *m* 1952, Vera Muriel, *d* of Wilfred Toplis and late Elsie Maud Toplis; one *s* one *d*. *Educ:* Stockport Sch. BSc (Hons Maths) London External. CEng, MIMechE; MRAeS. Fairey Aviation Co.: apprentice, 1944–48; Stress Office, 1948–50; English Electric Co., Warton: Stress Office, 1950–51; A. V. Roe & Co., Chadderton: Stress Office, 1951–55; A. V. Roe & Co., Weapons Research Div., Woodford: Head of Structural Analysis, 1955–62; Structures Dept, RAE, 1962–67; Asst Director, Project Time and Cost Analysis, Min. of Technology, 1967–70; Sen. Officers' War Course, RNC, Greenwich, 1970; Asst Dir, MRCA, MoD(PE), 1970–74; Division Leader, Systems Engrg, NATO MRCA Management Agency (NAMMA), Munich, 1974–76; Chief Supt, A&AEE, Boscombe Down, 1976–78; Dir, Harrier Projects, MoD(PE), 1978–80; Director General, Future Projects, MoD(PE), 1980–81. *Recreations:* reading, chess, ski-ing, squash, sailing, caravanning. *Address:* Pennycot, 47 Old Bisley Road, Frimley, Camberley, Surrey GU16 5RE. *T:* Camberley 21610. *Clubs:* Civil Service, Caravan.

REDMOND, Sir James, Kt 1979; FEng, FIEE; Director of Engineering, BBC, 1968–78; *b* 8 Nov. 1918; *s* of Patrick and Marion Redmond; *m* 1942, Joan Morris; one *s* one *d*. *Educ:* Graeme High Sch., Falkirk. Radio Officer, Merchant Navy, 1935–37 and 1939–45; BBC Television, Alexandra Palace, 1937–39; BBC: Installation Engr, 1949; Supt Engr Television Recording, 1960; Sen. Supt Engr TV, 1963; Asst Dir of Engrg, 1967. Pres., Soc. of Electronic and Radio Technicians, 1970–75; Pres., IEE, 1978–79. Member: Council, Brunel Univ., 1980–; Council, Open Univ., 1981–. *Recreation:* golf. *Address:* 43 Cholmeley Crescent, Highgate, N6. *T:* 01-340 1611. *Club:* Athenæum.

REDMOND, Robert Spencer, TD 1953; Director and Chief Executive, National Federation of Clay Industries, since 1976; *b* 10 Sept. 1919; *m* 1949, Marjorie Helen Heyes; one *s*. *Educ:* Liverpool Coll. Served War, Army, 1939–46: commissioned The Liverpool Scottish, 1938; transferred, RASC,

1941; Middle East, Junior Staff Sch., 1943; DAQMG, HQ Special Ops (Mediterranean), 1943–45; released, rank of Major, 1946. Conservative Agent, 1947–56 (Wigan, 1947–49, Knutsford, 1949–56). Managing Dir, Heyes & Co. Ltd, Wigan, 1956–66; Ashley Associates Ltd: Commercial Manager, 1966–69; Managing Dir, 1969–70; Dir, 1970–72. Dir, Manchester Chamber of Commerce, 1969–74. MP (C) Bolton West, 1970–Sept. 1974; Vice-Chm., Cons. Parly Employment Cttee, 1972–74 (Sec., 1971–72). Pres., Alderley Edge British Legion, 1968–76; Chm. (and Founder), NW Export Club, 1958–60. *Publications:* formerly contrib. to The Director, Manchester Evening News, Bolton Evening News, FBI Review. *Address:* Ballytrent, White Edge Drive, Baslow, Bakewell, Derbyshire. *T:* Baslow 3228. *Clubs:* Army and Navy, Special Forces.

REDON, Clare Mary; see Francis, C. M.

REDPATH, John Thomas, CB 1969; MBE 1944; FRIBA; architect in private practice, since 1977; *b* 24 Jan. 1915; *m* 1st, 1939, Kate (*née* Francis) (*d* 1949); one *d*; 2nd, 1949, Claesina (*née* van der Vlerk); three *s* one *d*. *Educ:* Price's Sch.; Southern Coll. of Art. Served with RE, 1940–47. Asst Architect: Kent CC, 1936–38; Oxford City Coun., 1938–40; Princ. Asst Architect, Herts, CC, 1948–55; Dep. County Architect, Somerset CC, 1955–59; Chief Architect (Abroad), War Office, 1959–63; MPBW later DoE: Dir of Development, 1963–67; Dir Gen. of Research and Development, 1967–71; Dir Gen. of Develt, 1971–72; Dep. Ch. Exec., Property Services Agency, 1972–75; Man. Dir, Millbank Technical Services Educn Ltd, 1975–77. *Publications:* various articles in architectural jls. *Recreation:* golf. *Address:* Pines Edge, Sandy Lane, Cobham, Surrey. *Club:* Arts.

REDSHAW, Sir Leonard, Kt 1972; Member, Lloyd's General Committee, 1972–81; Director: Fillite (Runcorn) Ltd, since 1971; Silica Fillers Ltd, since 1971; consultant; *b* 15 April 1911; *s* of late Joseph Stanley Redshaw, Naval Architect; *m* 1939, Joan Mary, *d* of Wm White, London; one *s* one *d*. *Educ:* Barrow Grammar Sch.; Univ. of Liverpool. 1st cl. Hons degree in naval architecture; 1851 Exhibn Royal Comr's post grad. Schol., Master's degree. Joined the Management Staff of Vickers-Armstrongs, 1936; Asst to Shipbuilding Manager, 1950; Special Dir, 1953; when Vickers-Armstrongs (Shipbuilders) Ltd was formed he was apptd Shipbuilding Gen. Man. of Yards at Barrow-in-Furness and Newcastle, 1955; Dir, Vickers-Armstrongs (Shipbuilders) Ltd, 1956, Deputy Managing Director, 1961; Builders' Chief Polaris Exec., 1963; Man. Dir, Vickers Ltd Shipbuilding Group, 1964; Special Dir, Vickers Ltd, 1965; Dir, 1967, Asst Man. Dir, 1967–76; Chairman: Vickers Ltd Shipbuilding Group, 1967–76; Vickers Oceanics Ltd, 1972–78; Vickers Offshore Engineering Group, 1975–78; Slingsby Sailplanes, 1969–77; Brown Brothers & Co. Ltd, 1973–77; Director: Rolls Royce & Associates, Ltd, 1966–77; Shipbuilding Corp. Ltd, 1970–77; Brown Bros & Co. Ltd, 1970–77; Cockatoo Docks & Eng. Co. Pty Ltd, 1972–76. Jt Chm., Technical Cttee, Lloyd's Register of Shipping, 1972–81; Mem. Safety Cttee, Pacific Nuclear Transport Ltd (BNFL). Mem., Nat. Defence Industries Council, 1971–76; Chairman: Assoc. W European Shipbuilders, 1972–73; Warshipbuilders Cttee; President: Shipbuilders and Repairers Nat. Assoc., 1977–78; Inst of Welding, 1963–65 (Mem. Council); Welding Institute, 1977–79. FRINA; FWeldI; FEng 1976. *Publications:* British Shipbuilding-Welding, 1947; Application of Welding to Ship Construction, 1962. *Recreations:* gliding, fishing. *Address:* Netherclose, Ireleth, Askam-in-Furness, Cumbria LA16 7EZ. *T:* Dalton-in-Furness 62529.

REDSHAW, Emeritus Prof. Seymour Cunningham, DSc (Wales), PhD (London), FICE, FIStructE, FRAeS; Beale Professor and Head of Civil Engineering Department, University of Birmingham, 1950–69; Dean of Faculty of Science, 1955–57; Member of Aeronautical Research Council, 1955; a Governor of Coll. of Aeronautics, 1951–69; *b* 20 March 1906; *s* of Walter James Redshaw and Edith Marion Cunningham; *m* 1935, Mary Elizabeth Jarrold; three *s*. *Educ:* Blundell's School; University of Wales. Technical Assistant, Bristol Aeroplane Co. Ltd, 1927–31; Asst Designer General Aircraft Ltd, 1931–32; Member of Staff: Imperial College, London, 1933–35; Building Research Station, 1936–40; Boulton Paul Aircraft Ltd, 1940–50: Chief Engineer, 1945; Director, 1949. Mem. Adv. Cttee on Building Research, 1965–67; Mem. Council, Univ. of Aston, 1966–67; Chm., Acad. Adv. Cttee, and Mem. Council, Univ. of Bath, 1966. Hon. DSc: Bath, 1966; Cranfield, 1976. *Publications:* numerous papers in scientific and engineering journals. *Address:* 22 Newport Street, Brewood, Staffs. *T:* Brewood 850274.

REDWOOD, Sir Peter (Boverton), 3rd Bt *cr* 1911; Lt-Col, King's Own Scottish Borderers; *b* 1 Dec. 1937; *o s* of Sir Thomas Boverton Redwood, 2nd Bt, TD, and Ruth Mary Redwood (*née* Creighton, now Blair); *S* father, 1974; *m* 1964, Gilian, *o d* of John Lee Waddington Wood, Limuru, Kenya; three *d*. *Educ:* Gordonstoun. National Service, 1956–58, 2nd Lieut, Seaforth Highlanders; regular commn, KOSB 1959; served in UK (despatches 1972), BAOR, ME and Far East; Staff Coll., Camberley, 1970; Nat. Defence Coll., Latimer, 1978–79. *Heir:* half-*b* Robert Boverton Redwood [*b* 24 June 1953; *m* 1978, Mary Elizabeth Wright; one *d*]. *Address:* c/o National Westminster Bank Ltd, Thames House, Millbank, SW1. *Club:* Army and Navy.

REECE, Sir Alan; see Reece, Sir L. A.

REECE, Courtenay Walton; Puisne Judge, Hong Kong, 1952–61, retired; *b* 4 Dec. 1899; 3rd *s* of H. Walter Reece, KC (Barbados); *m* 1927, Rosa U. E. Parker (*d* 1956); two *d*. *Educ:* Harrison College and Codrington College,

Barbados; Jesus College, Oxford (BA). Called to Bar, Middle Temple, 1925; Police Magistrate, Barbados, 1926; Registrar, Barbados, 1931; Magistrate, Nigeria, 1938; Crown Counsel, Nigeria, 1939; Senior Crown Counsel, Nigeria, 1946; Puisne Judge, Nigeria, 1949. *Recreations:* motor-boating, swimming, carpentry, fishing. *Address:* 108 Macdonnell Road, 7th Floor, Hong Kong. *T:* 5-231705.

REECE, (Edward Vans) Paynter; a Recorder of the Crown Court, since 1980; *b* 17 May 1936; *s* of Clifford Mansel Reece and Catherine Barbara Reece (*née* Hathorn); *m* 1967, Rosamund Mary Reece (*née* Roberts); three *s* one *d*. *Educ:* Blundell's Sch.; Magdalene Coll., Cambridge (MA). Called to the Bar, Inner Temple, 1960. *Recreation:* fishing. *Address:* 2 Harcourt Buildings, Temple, EC4Y 9DB.

REECE, Sir Gerald, KCMG 1950; CBE 1943 (OBE 1937); DL; Chairman of Managers, Loaningdale Approved School, 1968–76; *b* 10 Jan. 1897; *s* of Edward Mackintosh Reece; *m* 1936, Alys Isabel Wingfield (MBE 1978, JP), *d* of Dr H. E. H. Tracy; one *s* two *d* (and one *s* decd). *Educ:* Rugby School. Commissioned Sherwood Foresters, 1915; served France and Belgium (wounded thrice); served London Scottish (Territorial) Regt, 1920–25 (non-commnd). Solicitor Sup. Court, England, 1921; entered Kenya Administrative Service, 1925; seconded as HBM's Consul for Southern Ethiopia, 1934; Senior Political Officer, Borana Province of Ethiopia, 1941; Officer in Charge, Northern Frontier of Kenya, 1939–45; Provincial Commissioner, Kenya, 1945–48; Military Governor, British Somaliland, 1948; Governor and Commander-in-Chief, Somaliland Protectorate, 1948–53. Patron, Anglo-Somali Soc., 1978–. Scottish Chm., Howard League for Penal Reform, 1961–73. Chairman: Scottish Soc. for Prevention of Vivisection, 1973–; St Andrew Animal Fund, 1974–. Hon. Sheriff, E Lothian, 1962–73; DL, E Lothian, 1971–. *Publications:* sundry papers on Somalia. *Address:* Bolton Old Manse, near Haddington, East Lothian. *T:* Gifford 351.

REECE, Sir (Louis) Alan, TC 1977; Kt 1964; CMG 1963; *b* 1906; *s* of Claud Austin Reece; *m* 1941, Erna Irmgard Meyer. *Educ:* Queen's Royal Coll., Trinidad. Secretary to the Cabinet and Permanent Secretary to the Prime Minister, Trinidad and Tobago, 1961–63, retd. Chm., Elections and Boundaries Commn; former Chairman: Trinidad and Tobago Electricity Commn; Industrial Develt Corp. *Address:* c/o 4 Hayes Street, St Clair, Port of Spain, Trinidad.

REECE, Paynter; see Reece, E. V. P.

REED, Adrian Harbottle, CMG 1981; HM Diplomatic Service, retired; Consul-General, Munich, 1973–80; *b* 5 Jan. 1921; *s* of Harbottle Reed, MBE, FRIBA, and Winifred Reed (*née* Rowland); *m* 1st, 1947, Doris Davidson Duthie (marr. diss. 1975); one *s* one *d*; 2nd, 1975, Maria-Louise, *d* of Dr and Mrs A. J. Boekelman, Zeist, Netherlands. *Educ:* Hele's Sch., Exeter; Emmanuel Coll., Cambridge. Royal Artillery, 1941–47. India Office, 1947; Commonwealth Relations Office, 1947; served in UK High Commission: Pakistan, 1948–50; Fedn of Rhodesia and Nyasaland, 1953–56; British Embassy, Dublin, 1960–62; Commonwealth Office, 1962–68; Counsellor (Commercial), and Consul-Gen., Helsinki, 1968–70; Economic Counsellor, Pretoria, 1971–73. Bavarian Order of Merit, 1980. *Address:* Old Bridge House, Uffculme, Cullompton, Devon. *T:* Craddock 40595.

REED, David; Director of Communications, Hewlett-Packard, since 1975; *b* 24 April 1945; *s* of Wilfred Reed and Elsie Swindon; *m* 1973, Susan Garrett, MA Oxon, MScEcon. *Educ:* West Hartlepool Grammar Sch. Journalist: Northern Echo, 1963–64; Imperial Chemical Industries, 1964–65; Public Relations Officer: NE Development Council, 1966–68; Vickers Ltd, 1968–70. MP (Lab) Sedgefield, Co. Durham, 1970–Feb. 1974. *Publications:* many articles in national newspapers and other jls, on regional and consumer affairs. *Recreations:* many and varied. *Address:* 34 St Andrews Road, Henley-on-Thames, Oxon RG9 1JB. *T:* Henley 3777.

REED, Edward John; Clerk to the Clothworkers' Company of the City of London, 1963–78; *b* 2 Sept. 1913; *o c* of late Edward Reed; *m* 1939, Rita Isabel Venus Cheston-Porter; one *s* one *d*. *Educ:* St Paul's School. Admitted Solicitor, 1938. Territorial Service with HAC; commnd 1940; served BEF and BAOR with 63 (WR) Medium Regt RA; Capt. 1942. Clerk to Governors of Mary Datchelor Girls' Sch., 1963–78. Vice Pres., Metropolitan Soc. for the Blind, 1979– (Chm., 1965–79); Chm., Indigent Blind Visiting Society, 1965–79; Vice-Pres., N London District, St John Ambulance, 1969–81. Mem., Court of Common Council, City of London, for Tower Ward, 1978–. Clothworkers' Co.: Liveryman, 1964; Sen. Warden, 1981; Mem., Ct of Assistants; Governor: Christ's Hosp., 1981–; City of London Freemen's Sch., 1982–. Hon. MA Leeds, 1979. CStJ 1968. Chevalier, Order of Leopold with Palm, and Croix de Guerre with Palm, Belgium, 1944. *Recreations:* sailing, photography. *Address:* 54 Hillcrest Gardens, Hinchley Wood, Esher, Surrey KT10 0BX. *T:* 01-398 3984. *Club:* City Livery.

REED, Henry; poet, radio-dramatist, translator; *b* 22 Feb. 1914; *s* of late Henry Reed and late Mary Ann Ball; unmarried. *Educ:* King Edward VI Sch., Aston, Birmingham; Birmingham Univ. (BA 1st cl. Hons Lang. and Lit., 1934; Charles Grant Robertson Scholar, 1934; MA 1936). From then on, verse and journalism. Taught for a year before call-up in 1941; served (or rather *studied*) in Army, 1941–42; transf. to Naval Intelligence, FO, 1942–45; released VJ day, 1945; recalled to Army, 1945; did not go, 1945; matter silently dropped, 1945. During war continued to write and publish verse and book-reviews; began occasional broadcasting; began writing radio-plays, 1946 (Premio della Radio Italiana, 1953), and doing much translation from Italian and French. Academic appts at Univ. of Washington, Seattle: Vis. Prof. of Poetry, winter quarter 1964; Asst Prof. of English, 1965-66; Vis. Prof. of Poetry, winter quarter 1967. Pye gold award (Soc. of Authors), 1979. *Publications:* A Map of Verona (poems), 1946, enl. edn NY 1948; Moby Dick (radio-version in prose and verse of Melville's novel), 1947; The Novel since 1939 (British Council booklet), 1947; The Lessons of the War (poems), 1970; Hilda Tablet and others, 1971; The Streets of Pompeii and other plays for radio, 1971. Numerous published translations include: Paride Rombi: Perdu and his Father (novel), 1954; Ugo Betti: Three Plays (with foreword), 1956, NY 1958; Ugo Betti: Crime on Goat Island, 1961 (staged NY 1960); Dino Buzzati: Larger than Life (novel), 1962; Balzac: Père Goriot, NY 1962; Balzac: Eugénie Grandet, NY 1964; Natalia Ginzburg: The Advertisement (play), 1969 (Nat. Theatre 1969). *Address:* c/o Messrs Jonathan Cape Ltd, 30 Bedford Square, WC1. *Club:* Savile.

REED, Jane Barbara; Editor-in-chief, Woman magazine, since 1981; 2nd *d* of William and late Gwendoline Reed, Letchworth, Herts. *Educ:* Royal Masonic Sch.; sundry further educational establishments. Worked on numerous magazines; returned to Woman's Own, 1965; Editor, 1970-79; Publisher, IPC Women's Monthly Group, 1979-81. Chairman: Editorial Cttee, Fédération International de la Presse Périodique, 1979-; Publicity Cttee, Birthright, 1979-. *Publications:* Girl About Town, 1964; (jtly) Kitchen Sink—or Swim?, 1982. *Address:* King's Reach Tower, Stamford Street, SE1.

REED, Laurance Douglas; *b* 4 Dec. 1937; *s* of Douglas Austin Reed and late Mary Ellen Reed (née Philpott). *Educ:* Gresham's Sch., Holt; University Coll., Oxford (MA). Nat. Service, RN, 1956-58; worked and studied on Continent (Brussels, Bruges, Leyden, Luxembourg, Strasbourg, Paris, Rome, Bologna, Geneva), 1963-66; Public Sector Research Unit, 1967-69. MP (C) Bolton East, 1970-Feb. 1974; PPS to Chancellor of Duchy of Lancaster, 1973-74. Jt Sec., Parly and Scientific Cttee, 1971-74; Member: Soc. for Underwater Technology; Select Cttee on Science and Technology, 1971-74. *Publications:* Europe in a Shrinking World, 1967; An Ocean of Waste, 1972; Political Consequences of North Sea Oil, 1973. *Recreations:* gardening, painting. *Address:* Water-Flag House, Isle of Soay, Inverness-shire. *T:* Soay 4. *Club:* Carlton.

REED, Leslie Edwin, PhD; CEng, MIMechE, FInstE; Chief Alkali and Clean Air Inspector, Health and Safety Executive, since 1981; *b* 6 Feb. 1925; *s* of Edwin George and Maud Gladys Reed; *m* 1947, Ruby; two *s*. *Educ:* Sir George Monoux Grammar Sch., Walthamstow; University Coll. London (BScEng, MScEng, PhD). Engineering Officer, RNVR, 1945-47; Fuel Research Station, 1950-58; Warren Spring Laboratory, 1958-70; Central Unit on Environmental Pollution, DoE, 1970-79; Head, Air and Noise Div., DoE, 1979-81. *Address:* 20 Deards Wood, Knebworth, Herts SG3 6PG. *T:* Stevenage 813272.

REED, Michael, CB 1962; *b* 7 July 1912; *s* of late Richard and Winifred Reed; *m* 1st, 1939, Marcia Jackson; two *d*; 2nd, 1950, Hermione Jeanne, *d* of late Dr P. Roux, Kimberley, SA; one *s* one *d*. *Educ:* Christ's Hospital; Jesus College, Cambridge. Entered Ministry of Health, 1935; Private Secretary to Minister, 1942-45; Under-Secretary, Ministry of Health, 1956-58, Cabinet Office, 1958-61, Ministry of Health, 1961-63; Registrar General, 1963-72 and Dir, Office of Population Censuses and Surveys, 1970-72. *Address:* 10 Fir Avenue, Hermanus, Cape, South Africa.

REED, Sir Nigel (Vernon), Kt 1970; CBE 1967 (MBE (mil.) 1945); TD 1950; Chief Justice of the Northern States of Nigeria, 1968-75; *b* 31 Oct. 1913; *s* of Vernon Herbert Reed, formerly MP and MLC New Zealand, and of Eila Mabel Reed; *m* 1945, Ellen Elizabeth Langstaff; one *s* two *d*. *Educ:* Wanganui Collegiate School, NZ; Victoria University College, NZ; Jesus College, Cambridge. LLB (NZ) and LLB (Cantab). Called to the Bar, Lincoln's Inn, 1939. Military Service, 1939-45, Lt-Col 1944. Appointed to Colonial Legal Service, 1946; Magistrate, Nigeria, 1946; Chief Magistrate, Nigeria, 1951; Chief Registrar, High Court of the Northern Region of Nigeria, 1955; Judge, High Court of the Northern Region of Nigeria, 1956; Sen. Puisne Judge, High Court of Northern Nigeria, 1964. *Address:* Old Farm Cottage, Corton, Warminster, Wilts.

REED, Oliver; *see* Reed, R. O.

REED, Philip Dunham; Corporation Director; *b* Milwaukee, Wisconsin, 16 Nov. 1899; *s* of William Dennis Reed and Virginia Brandreth Dunham; *m* 1921, Mabel Mayhew Smith; one *s* one *d*. *Educ:* University of Wisconsin (BS in Electrical Engineering); Fordham Univ. (LLB). Hon. LLD, Union Coll. and Brooklyn Poly. Inst., Hon. DEng Rensslaer Poly. Inst.; Hon. Dr of Commercial Science, New York Univ. 1950; Hon. Dr of Laws, Univ. of Wisconsin, 1950. Swarthmore Coll., 1954. With General Electric Co. (Law Dept), 1926-; Asst to Pres. and Dir, 1937-39; Chm. of Bd, 1940; resigned Chairmanship Dec. 1942 to continue war work in England; re-elected Chm. of Bd, 1945-58; Chm., Finance Cttee, General Electric Co., NY, 1945-59, Director Emeritus, 1968-. Chm. of Board: of Internat. General Electric Company, 1945 until merger with parent co., 1952; Federal Reserve Bank of NY, 1960-65. Director: American Express Co.; American Express Internat.

Banking Corp., 1958-72; US Financial, 1970-72; Otis Elevator Company, 1958-72; Kraftco Corp., 1958-70; Scott Paper Co., 1958-66; Metropolitan Life Insurance Co., 1940-73; Tiffany & Co., 1956-; Bigelow-Sanford Inc., 1959-74; Bankers Trust Co., 1966-72; Cowles Communications Inc., 1972-; Metropolitan Opera Assoc. Inc., 1945-53; Mem. Business Advisory Council for Dept of Commerce, 1940- (Vice-Chm. 1951-52); US Adv. Commn on Information, 1948-61; Member: Executive Commn, Payroll Savings Adv. Cttee for US Treasury Dept, 1946-56; Dir, Council on Foreign Relations, 1946-69; Trustee: Carnegie Endowment for Internat. Peace, 1945-53; Cttee for Economic Development (and Member Research and Policy Cttee); Member of the Visiting Cttee, Graduate School of Business Admin., Harvard Univ., 1940-60; Director, Ford Foundation Fund for Advancement of Education, 1951-53; Consultant to US Deleg., San Francisco Conf. on World Organization; Chm. US Associates (now US Council), Internat. Chamber of Commerce, 1945-Jan. 1948; mem. Exec. Cttee, US Council, ICC; Hon. Pres. Internat. Chamber of Commerce (Pres., 1949-51); Chm. US Side of Anglo-American Productivity Council, 1948-52; Vice-Chm. Eisenhower Exchange Fellowships, 1953-; Chm. Finance Cttee, 1955-56. Mem. President's Cttee on Information Activities Abroad, 1960; Mem. Cttee on the Univ. and World Affairs (Ford Foundn), 1960; Trustee of Kress Foundn, 1960-65. Entered War work, 1941, with Office of Production Management, Washington, and its successor the War Production Board (Chief of Bureau of Industry Branches responsible for organising and converting peacetime industries to war production). Went to London, July 1942, as Deputy Chief of Economic Mission headed by W. Averell Harriman; Chief of Mission for Economic Affairs, London, with rank of Minister, Oct. 1943-31 Dec. 1944. Special Ambassador to Mexico, 1958. President's Certificate of Merit Award, 1947; Comdr Légion d'Honneur (France), 1951 (Officer, 1947). *Address:* 375 Park Avenue, New York, NY 10022, USA; (home) Rye, NY. *Clubs:* University, The Links (NY City); Apawamis (Rye, NY); Blind Brook (Purchase, NY); Clove Valley Rod and Gun (Dutchess Co., NY); Bohemian (San Francisco); Mill Reef (Antigua, WI).

REED, (Robert) Oliver; actor; *b* 13 Feb. 1938; *s* of Peter and Marcia Reed; one *s* one *d*. *Educ:* Ewel Castle. Films include: Oliver, 1967; Women In Love, 1969; The Devils, 1971; Three Musketeers, 1974; Tommy, 1975; The Prince and the Pauper, 1977; Lion of the Desert, Condorman, 1981; Venom, The Next Sting, 1982. *Publication:* Reed All About Me, 1979. *Recreations:* rugby, racing. *Address:* c/o Suite 505A, Triumph House, 189 Regent Street, W1. *T:* 01-734 2466.

REED, Stanley William; Director, British Film Institute, 1964-72, Consultant on Regional Development, 1972-76; *b* 21 Jan. 1911; *s* of Sidney James Reed and Ellen Maria Patient; *m* 1937, Alicia Mary Chapman; three *d*. *Educ:* Stratford Grammar Sch.; Coll. of St Mark and St John, Chelsea. Teacher in E London schools, 1931-39. In charge of school evacuation parties, 1939-45. Teacher and Visual Aids Officer, West Ham Education Cttee, 1939-50. British Film Institute: Educn Officer, 1952-56; Sec., 1956-64. *Publications:* The Cinema, 1952; How Films are Made, 1955; A Guide to Good Viewing, 1961. Neighbourhood 15 (film, also Dir). *Recreations:* opera and exploring London's suburbs. *Address:* 54 Felstead Road, Wanstead, E11. *T:* 01-989 6021.

REED, Most Rev. Thomas Thornton, CBE 1980; MA, DLitt, ThD; *b* Eastwood, South Australia, 9 Sept. 1902; *s* of Alfred Ernest Reed, Avoca, Vic; *m* 1932, Audrey Airlie, *d* of Major Harry Lort Spencer Balfour-Ogilvy, MBE, DCM, Tannadice, Renmark, South Australia; two *d* (and one *d* decd). *Educ:* Collegiate Sch. of St Peter, Adelaide; Trinity College, University of Melbourne (Hon. Schol., BA, MA); St Barnabas' Theol. Coll., Adelaide. ThL, ATC, 1st cl. hons. Fred Johns Schol. for Biography, Univ. of Adelaide, 1950. Deacon, 1926; Priest, 1927; Curate, St Augustine's, Unley, 1926-28; Priest in Charge, Berri Mission, 1928-29; Resident Tutor, St Mark's Coll., Univ. of Adelaide, and Area Padre, Toc H, 1929-31; Asst Chaplain, Melbourne Grammar Sch., 1932-36; Rector, St Michael's, Henley Beach, 1936-44; Rector, St Theodore's, Rose Park, 1944-54; Chaplain, Australian Mil. Forces, 1939-57; Chaplain, AIF with HQ, New Guinea Force, 1944-45; Asst Tutor, St Barnabas' Coll., 1940-46; Senior Chaplain, RAAChD, HQ, C Command, South Australia, 1953-56; Editor, Adelaide Church Guardian, 1940-44; Rural Dean, Western Australia, 1944; Priest Comr, Adelaide Dio. Centenary, 1947; Canon of Adelaide, 1947-49; Archdeacon of Adelaide, 1949-53; Dean of Adelaide, 1953-57; Bishop of Adelaide, 1957-73; Archbishop of Adelaide, and Metropolitan of S Australia, 1973-75. Pres., Toc H, S Aust., 1960; Pres., St Mark's Coll., Univ. of Adelaide, 1961-74, Hon. Fellow, 1973. Hon. ThD, Australian Coll. of Theology, 1955; DLitt, Univ. of Adelaide, 1954. Chaplain and Sub Prelate of Venerable Order of St John of Jerusalem, 1965. *Publications:* Henry Kendall: A Critical Appreciation, 1960; Sonnets and Songs, 1962; (ed) The Poetical Works of Henry Kendall, 1966; A History of the Cathedral Church of St Peter, Adelaide, 1969; Historic Churches of Australia, 1978. *Recreations:* golf, research on Australian literature, heraldry, and genealogy. *Address:* 44 Jeffcott Street, North Adelaide, SA 5006, Australia. *T:* 2674841; PO Box 130, North Adelaide, SA 5006, Australia. *Clubs:* Adelaide, Naval, Military and Air Force, Royal Adelaide Golf (Adelaide).

REED-PURVIS, Air Vice-Marshal Henry, CB 1982; OBE 1972; Commandant General of the RAF Regiment and Director General of Security (RAF), since 1979; *b* 1 July 1928; *s* of late Henry Reed and of Nancy Reed-Purvis; *m* 1951, Isabel Price; three *d*. *Educ:* King James I School,

Durham; Durham Univ. BSc Hons 1950. Entered RAF, 1950; various Op. Sqdns, 1951-58; Instr, Jt Nuclear Biological and Chemical Sch., 1958-60; RMCS Shrivenham (Nuclear Sci. and Tech.), 1961; MoD Staff, 1962-64; OC No 63 Sqdn, RAF Regt, Malaya, 1964-66; Exchange Duties, USAF, 1966-69; USAF War Coll., 1969-70; OC No 5 Wing RAF Regt, 1970-72; Gp Capt. Regt, HQ Strike Comd, 1972-74, HQ RAF Germany, 1974-76; ADC to the Queen, 1974-76; Dir, RAF Regt, 1976-79. *Recreations:* golf, bridge and music. *Address:* 9 Elm Road, Great Stukeley, Huntingdon, Cambs. *T:* Huntingdon 55775. *Club:* Royal Air Force.

REEDY, Norris John; editorial consultant; *b* 1934; *s* of John Reedy; *m* 1964, Sheila Campbell McGregor; one *d. Educ:* Chorlton High Sch., Manchester; Univ. of Sheffield. Sheffield Telegraph, 1956; Sunday Times, 1961; Lancashire Evening Telegraph, 1962; Guardian, 1964; Birmingham Post: Features Editor, 1964; Sen. Asst Editor, 1968; Dep. Editor, 1973; Editor, 1974-82. Guild of British Newspaper Editors: Chm., W Midlands Region, 1979-80, Sec. and Councillor, 1980-82; Nat. Vice-Pres., 1981-82. *Recreations:* astronomy, natural history, riding, photography. *Address:* Arden Editorial, The Old Manor, Rowington, near Warwick. *T:* Lapworth 3129.

REEKIE, Henry Enfield; Headmaster of Felsted School, 1951-68; *b* Hayfield, Derbyshire, 17 Oct. 1907; *s* of John Albert Reekie and Edith Dowson; *m* 1936, Pauline Rosalind, *d* of Eric W. Seeman; one *s* three *d. Educ:* Oundle; Clare College, Cambridge. Asst Master, Felsted School, 1929, Housemaster, 1933, Senior Science Master, 1945; Headmaster, St Bees School, 1946. *Recreations:* ski-ing, gardening, travel. *Address:* Tarn House, Mark Cross, Crowborough, East Sussex. *T:* Mayfield 873100. *Club:* East India, Devonshire, Sports and Public Schools.

REES, Anthony John David; Headmaster, Blundell's School, Tiverton, Devon, since 1980; *b* 20 July 1943; *s* of Richard Frederick and Betty Rees; *m* 1967, Carol Stubbens; one *s* one *d* (and one *d* decd). *Educ:* Newcastle Royal Grammar Sch.; Clare Coll., Cambridge (Exhibr; BA 2nd Cl. Hons Geog.); PGCE 1966. Head of Economics, Harrow Sch., 1966-80. Established Notting Dale Urban Study Centre, 1972; Vis. Tutor, London Inst. of Education, 1973-. Member Executive Committee: Queen's Silver Jubilee Appeal, 1976-; and Admin. Council, Royal Jubilee Trusts, 1978-; Chm., Prince's Trust for Devon, 1981-; Member: COSIRA Cttee for Devon, 1981-; Council, Drake Fellowship, 1981-. *Publications:* articles on economics and community service in many jls incl. Economics, Youth in Society, etc. *Recreations:* hill walking, family and friends. *Address:* Blundell's School, Tiverton, Devon. *T:* Tiverton 252543.

REES, Arthur Morgan, CBE 1974 (OBE 1963); QPM 1970; DL; Chairman and County Director, St John's Staffordshire, since 1974; *b* 20 Nov. 1912; *s* of Thomas and Jane Rees, The Limes, Llangadog; *m* 1943, Dorothy Webb; one *d. Educ:* Llandovery Coll.; St Catharine's Coll., Cambridge. BA 1935, MA 1939. Metropolitan Police, 1935-41; RAF (Pilot), 1941-46 (Subst. Sqdn Ldr; Actg Wing Comdr); Metropolitan Police, 1946-57; Chief Constable: Denbighshire, 1957-64; Staffordshire, 1964-77. Life Mem., Midlands Sports Adv. Cttee, 1981; Chm., Queen's Silver Jubilee Appeal (Sport), 1976-; Mem., King George's Jubilee Trust Council, 1973-. President: Martial Arts Commn (GB); British Karate Fedn, 1982; Chairman: English Karate Council, 1982; British Taekwondo Control Bd, 1982. Trustee and Board of Governors, Llandovery College; Mem. Court, Univ. of Keele, 1981-. Founder Pres., Eccleshall Rugby Football Club, 1980-. DL Staffs, 1967. KStJ 1977 (CStJ 1969). *Recreations:* former Rugby International for Wales (14 caps), Cambridge Rugby Blue, 1933 and 1934; Chairman: Crawshays Welsh Rugby XV, 1970; Welsh Schs Hockey Internat. *Address:* The Old Vicarage, Ellenhall, Stafford. *T:* Eccleshall 850789. *Clubs:* Royal Air Force; Hawks (Cambridge).

REES, Brian, MA Cantab; Headmaster, Rugby School, since 1981; *b* 20 Aug. 1929; *s* of late Frederick T. Rees; *m* 1959, Julia (*d* 1978), *d* of Sir Robert Birley, KCMG; two *s* three *d. Educ:* Bede Grammar Sch., Sunderland; Trinity Coll., Cambridge (Scholar). 1st cl. Historical Tripos, Part I, 1951; Part II, 1952. Eton College: Asst Master, 1952-65; Housemaster, 1963-65; Headmaster: Merchant Taylors' Sch., 1965-73; Charterhouse, 1973-81. Pres., Conference for Independent Further Education, 1973-; Chm., ISIS, 1982-. Patron, UC of Buckingham, 1973-; Chm., Tormead Sch. Council. Liveryman, Merchant Taylors' Co., 1981. *Recreations:* music, painting. *Address:* School House, Rugby, Warwicks. *T:* Rugby 3465. *Clubs:* Athenæum, Savile, Beefsteak.

REES, Prof. Brinley Roderick, MA Oxon; PhD, Hon. LLD Wales; Principal, Saint David's University College, Lampeter, 1975-80; *b* 27 Dec. 1919; *s* of John David Rees and Mary Ann (*née* Roderick); *m* 1951, Zena Muriel Stella Mayall; two *s. Educ:* Christ Coll., Brecon; Merton Coll., Oxford (Postmaster). 1st Cl., Class. Hons Mods and Hon. Mention, Craven and Ireland Schols, 1946. Welch Regt, 1940-45. Asst Classics Master, Christ Coll., Brecon, 1947; Cardiff High Sch., 1947-48; Asst Lectr in Classics, University Coll. of Wales Aberystwyth, 1948-49; Lectr 1949-56; Sen. Lectr in Greek, Univ. of Manchester, 1956-58; UC Cardiff: Prof. of Greek, 1958-70; Dean of Faculty of Arts, 1963-65; Dean of Students, 1967-68; Prof. Emeritus, 1981; Univ. of Birmingham: Prof. of Greek, 1970-75; Dean of Faculty of Arts, 1973-75. Welsh Supernumerary Fellow, Jesus Coll., Oxford, 1975-76. Hon. Secretary, Classical Association, 1963-69, Vice-Pres., 1969, Pres., 1978-79. Hon. LLD Wales, 1981. *Publications:* The Merton Papyri, Vol. II (with H. I. Bell and J. W. B. Barns), 1959; The Use of Greek, 1961; Papyri from

Hermopolis and other Byzantine Documents, 1964; (with M. E. Jervis) Lampas: a new approach to Greek, 1970; Classics: an outline for intending students, 1970; Aristotle's Theory and Milton's Practice, 1972; Strength in What Remains, 1980; articles and reviews in various classical and other jls. *Address:* 4 Cranmer Court, Ely Road, Llandaff, Cardiff CF5 2JD. *T:* Cardiff 566037.

REES, Prof. Charles Wayne, DSc; FRS 1974; FRSC; Hofmann Professor of Organic Chemistry, Imperial College, London, since 1978; *b* 15 Oct. 1927; *s* of Percival Charles Rees and Daisy Alice Beck; *m* 1953, Patricia Mary Francis; three *s. Educ:* Farnham Grammar Sch.; University Coll., Southampton (BSc, PhD). Lectr in Organic Chem.: Birkbeck Coll., Univ. of London, 1955-57; King's Coll., Univ. of London, 1957-63, Reader, 1963-65; Prof. of Organic Chem., Univ. of Leicester, 1965-69; Prof. of Organic Chem., 1969-77, Heath Harrison Prof. of Organic Chem., 1977-78, Univ. of Liverpool. Visiting Prof., Univ. of Würzburg, 1968; Tilden Lectr, Chemical Soc., 1973-74. *Publications:* Organic Reaction Mechanism (8 annual vols), 1965-72; Carbenes, Nitrenes, Arynes, 1969; about 230 research papers and reviews, mostly in jls of Chemical Soc. *Recreations:* music, wine. *Address:* Department of Chemistry, Imperial College of Science and Technology, South Kensington, SW7 2AY. *T:* 01-589 5111.

REES, Sir (Charles William) Stanley, Kt 1962; TD 1949; DL; Judge of High Court of Justice, Family Division (formerly Probate, Divorce and Admiralty Division), 1962-77; *b* 30 Nov. 1907; *s* of Dr David Charles Rees, MRCS, LRCP, and Myrtle May (*née* Dolley); *m* 1934, Jean Isabel Munro Wheildon; one *s. Educ:* St Andrew's College, Grahamstown, S Africa; University College, Oxford. BA, BCL (Oxon). Called to the Bar, 1931; Bencher, Inner Temple, 1962. 2nd Lt 99th Regt AA RA (London Welsh), 1939; JAG's office in Home Commands, 1940-43; Lt-Col in charge JAG's Branch, HQ Palestine Command, 1944-45; released from military service as Hon. Lt-Col, 1945. QC 1957; Recorder of Croydon, 1961-62; Commissioner of Assize, Stafford, Dec. 1961; Dep. Chm., 1959-64, Chm., 1964-71, E Sussex QS. DL E Sussex (formerly Sussex), 1968. Chm., Statutory Cttee, Pharmaceutical Soc. of GB, 1980-81. Governor, Brighton College, 1954- (Pres., 1973-). *Recreations:* walking, gardening. *Address:* Lark Rise, Lyoth Lane, Lindfield, Sussex RH16 2QA. *Clubs:* United Oxford & Cambridge University, Sussex.

See also Harland Rees.

REES, Prof. David, FRS 1968; Professor of Pure Mathematics, University of Exeter, since 1958; *b* 29 May 1918; *s* of David and Florence Gertrude Rees; *m* 1952, Joan Sybil Cushen; four *d. Educ:* King Henry VIII Grammar School, Abergavenny; Sidney Sussex College, Cambridge. Manchester University: Assistant Lecturer, 1945-46, Lecturer, 1946-49; Cambridge University: Lecturer, 1949-58; Fellow of Downing College, Cambridge, 1950-58, Hon. Fellow, 1970-. Mem. Council, Royal Soc., 1979-81. *Publications:* papers on Algebraic topics in British and foreign mathematical journals. *Recreations:* reading and listening to music. *Address:* 6 Hillcrest Park, Exeter EX4 4SH. *T:* Exeter 59398.

REES, Dr David Allan, BSc, PhD, DSc; FRS 1981; Director, National Institute for Medical Research, Mill Hill, since 1982; *b* 28 April 1936; *s* of James Allan Rees and Elsie Bolam; *m* 1959, Myfanwy Margaret Parry Owen; two *s* one *d. Educ:* Hawarden Grammar Sch., Clwyd; University Coll. of N Wales, Bangor, Gwynedd (BSc 1956; PhD 1959). DSc Edinburgh, 1970. DSIR Res. Fellow, University Coll., Bangor, 1959, and Univ. of Edinburgh, 1960; Asst Lectr in Chem., 1961, Lectr, 1962-70, Univ. of Edinburgh; Section Manager, 1970-72, Principal Scientist, 1972-82, and Sci. Policy Exec., 1978-82, Unilever Res., Colworth Lab.; Chm., Science Policy Gp for Unilever Res., 1979-82. Associate Dir (pt-time), MRC Unit for Cell Biophysics, KCL, 1980-82. Vis. Professorial Fellow, University Coll., Cardiff, 1972-77. Colworth Medal, Biochemical Soc., 1970; Carbohydrate Award, Chemical Soc., 1970. *Publications:* various, on carbohydrate chem. and biochem. and cell biology. *Recreations:* the countryside, reading, listening to music. *Address:* The Old Vicarage, Church Lane, Riseley, Bedford MK44 1ER. *T:* Riseley 636.

REES, Dame Dorothy (Mary), DBE 1975 (CBE 1964); Member, Central Training Council, 1964-67; *b* 1898; widow. *Educ:* Elementary and Secondary Schools. Formerly: school teacher; Member of Barry Borough Council. Alderman of Glamorgan CC; former Mem. Nat. Advisory Committee for National Insurance; Member: Joint Education Committee for Wales (Chm., Technical Educn Sub-Cttee); Welsh Teaching Hospitals Board. Liaison Officer, Ministry of Food, during War of 1939-45. MP (Lab) Barry Division of Glamorganshire, 1950-51; formerly Parliamentary Private Secretary to the Minister of National Insurance. *Address:* Mor-Hafren, 341 Barry Road, Barry, S Glam.

REES, Dr (Florence) Gwendolen, FRS 1971; FIBiol; a Professor of Zoology, University of Wales, at University College of Wales, Aberystwyth, 1971-73, now Emeritus; *b* 3 July 1906; *yr d* of late E. and E. A. Rees; unmarried. *Educ:* Girls' Grammar Sch., Aberdare; UCW Cardiff. BSc 1927; PhD 1930; DSc 1942. FIBiol 1971. UCW, Aberystwyth: Lectr in Zoology, 1930-46; Sen. Lectr, 1946-66; Reader, 1966-71. Vis. Scientist, Univ. of Ghana, 1961. Research grants from Royal Soc., SRC, Shell Grants Cttee, Nat. Research Council, USA. Hon. Member: Amer. Soc. of Parasitologists, 1975; British Soc. for Parasitology, 1976. *Publications:* numerous papers on parasitology (helminthology) in scientific jls. *Recreations:* riding, amateur dramatics, the arts. *Address:* Grey Mist, North Road, Aberystwyth, Dyfed. *T:* Aberystwyth 612389.

REES, Prof. Garnet; Professor of French, 1957-79, now Emeritus Professor, University of Hull; Pro-Vice-Chancellor, 1972-74; *b* 15 March 1912; *o s* of William Garnet and Mabel Rees; *m* 1941, Dilys, *o d* of Robert and Ellen Hughes; two *d. Educ:* Pontardawe Grammar School; University College of Wales, Aberystwyth; University of Paris. BA (Wales), 1934; MA (Wales), 1937; Docteur de l'Université de Paris, 1940; Fellow of Univ. of Wales, 1937-39; Asst Lecturer in French, Univ. Coll., Aberystwyth, 1939-40. Served War of 1939-45, in Roy. Regt of Artillery (Captain, Instructor in Gunnery), 1940-45. Lecturer in French, Univ. of Southampton, 1945-46; Sen. Lecturer in French, Univ. Coll., Swansea, 1946-57. Hon. DLitt Hull, 1979. Officier des Palmes Académiques (France), 1961. Chevalier de la Légion d'Honneur, 1967. *Publications:* Remy de Gourmont, 1940; Guillaume Apollinaire, Alcools, 1975; Baudelaire, Sartre and Camus: lectures and commentaries, 1976; articles on modern French literature and bibliography in learned journals. *Recreations:* gardening and motoring. *Address:* 45 Exeter Gardens, Stamford, Lincs PE49 2RN. *T:* Stamford 3672.

REES, Geraint; *see* Rees, R. G.

REES, Gwendolen; *see* Rees, F. G.

REES, Harland, MA, MCh, FRCS; Hon. Consultant Urological Surgeon, King's College Hospital; Hon. Consultant Surgeon and Urological Surgeon, Royal Free Hospital; *b* 21 Sept. 1909; *yr s* of Dr David Charles Rees, MRCS, LRCP, and Myrtle May (*née* Dolley); *m* 1950, Helen Marie Tarver; two *s* (one *d* decd). *Educ:* St Andrew's Coll., Grahamstown, S Africa; University Coll., Oxford; Charing Cross Hospital. Rhodes Scholar, Oxford University. Served RAMC, 1942-46; OC Surgical Div. 53, Indian General Hospital. Adviser in Surgery, Siam (Thailand). Examiner in Surgery, University of Cambridge, 1963-73. *Publications:* articles and chapters in various books and journals, 1952-63. *Recreations:* walking, cultivation of trees; Rugby football, Oxford *v* Cambridge, 1932-33. *Address:* Clinic Seven, Royal Free Hospital, Pond Street, NW3. *T:* 01-794 0500; Kensworth Gorse, Kensworth, near Dunstable, Beds. *T:* Whipsnade 872411. *Club:* Vincent's (Oxford).

See also Hon. Sir C. W. S. Rees.

REES, Haydn; *see* Rees, T. M. H.

REES, Prof. Hubert, DFC 1945; PhD, DSc; FRS 1976; Professor of Agricultural Botany, University College of Wales, Aberystwyth, since 1968; *b* 2 Oct. 1923; *s* of Owen Rees and Tugela Rees, Llangennech, Carmarthenshire; *m* 1946, Mavis Hill; two *s* two *d. Educ:* Llandovery and Llanelli Grammar Schs; University Coll. of Wales, Aberystwyth (BSc). PhD, DSc Birmingham. Served RAF, 1942-46. Student, Aberystwyth, 1946-50; Lectr in Cytology, Univ. of Birmingham, 1950-58; Sen. Lectr in Agric. Botany, University Coll. of Wales, Aberystwyth, 1958, Reader 1966. *Publications:* Chromosome Genetics, 1977; articles on genetic control of chromosomes and on evolutionary changes in chromosome organisation. *Recreation:* fishing. *Address:* Irfon, Llanbadarn Road, Aberystwyth, Dyfed. *T:* Aberystwyth 3668.

REES, Hugh; *see* Rees, J. E. H.

REES, Hugh Francis E.; *see* Ellis-Rees.

REES, (John Edward) Hugh; Chartered Surveyor; *b* 8 Jan. 1928; *s* of David Emlyn Rees, Swansea; *m* 1961, Gillian Dian Milo-Jones (decd); two *s.* MP (C) Swansea, West Division, Oct. 1959-64; Assistant Government Whip, 1962-64. UK Rep., Econ. and Soc. Cttee, EEC, 1973-78. Dir, Abbey National Building Soc., 1976-. Mem., Welsh Develt Agency, 1980-. Chm., Ffynone House Sch. Trust, 1977-. Governor, Nat. Mus. of Wales. FRICS, FRVA. *Address:* Sherwood, 35 Caswell Road, Newton, Mumbles, Swansea, W Glamorgan.

REES, Very Rev. John Ivor; Dean of Bangor, since 1976; Vicar of Cathedral Parish of Bangor, since 1979; *b* 19 Feb. 1926; *o s* of David Morgan Rees and Cecilia Perrott Rees; *m* 1954, Beverley Richards; three *s. Educ:* Llanelli Gram. Sch.; University Coll. of Wales (BA 1950); Westcott House, Cambridge. Served RN, Coastal Forces and British Pacific Fleet, 1943-47. Deacon 1952, priest 1953, Dio. St David's; Curate: Fishguard, 1952-55; Llangathen, 1955-57; Priest-in-Charge, Uzmaston, 1957-59; Vicar: Slebech and Uzmaston, 1959-65; Llangollen, 1965-74; Rural Dean of Llangollen, 1970-74; Rector of Wrexham, 1974-76; Canon of St Asaph, 1975-76; Chaplain, Order of St John for County of Clwyd, 1974-76, County of Gwynedd, 1976-. SBStJ 1975, OStJ 1981. *Publication:* Monograph—The Parish of Llangollen and its Churches, 1971. *Recreations:* music and good light reading. *Address:* The Deanery, Bangor, Gwynedd LL57 1LH. *T:* Bangor 51693.

REES, Rt. Rev. Leslie Lloyd; *see* Shrewsbury, Bishop Suffragan of.

REES, Linford; *see* Rees, W. L. L.

REES, Llewellyn; *see* Rees, (Walter) L.

REES, Prof. Martin John, FRS 1979; Plumian Professor of Astronomy and Experimental Philosophy, Cambridge University, since 1973; Fellow of King's College, since 1973 (and 1969-72); Director, Institute of Astronomy, 1977-82; *b* 23 June 1942; *s* of Reginald J. and Joan Rees. *Educ:* Shrewsbury Sch.; Trinity Coll., Cambridge. MA, PhD (Cantab). Fellow, Jesus Coll., Cambridge, 1967-69; Research Associate, California Inst. of Technology, 1967-68 and 1971; Mem., Inst. for Advanced Study, Princeton, 1969-70; Visiting Prof., Harvard Univ., 1972; Prof., Univ. of Sussex, 1972-73. For. Hon. Mem., Amer. Acad. of Arts and Sciences, 1975. *Publications:* mainly articles and reviews in scientific jls. *Address:* c/o King's College, Cambridge. *T:* Cambridge 350411; (office) Cambridge 62204.

REES, Rt. Hon. Merlyn, PC 1974; MP (Lab) South Leeds since June 1963; *b* Cilfynydd, South Wales, 18 Dec. 1920; *s* of late L. D. and E. M. Rees; *m* 1949, Colleen Faith (*née* Cleveley); three *s. Educ:* Elementary Schools, S Wales and Wembley, Middx; Harrow Weald Grammar School; Goldsmiths' Coll., Univ. of London; London School of Economics; London Univ. Institute of Education. Nottingham Univ. Air Sqdn; Served RAF, 1941-46; demobilised as Sqdn Ldr. Teacher in Economics and History, Harrow Weald Grammar School, 1949-60. Organised Festival of Labour, 1960-62. Lecturer in Economics, Luton Coll. of Technology, 1962-63; contested (Lab) Harrow East, Gen. Elections 1955 and 1959 and by-election, 1959; PPS to Chancellor of the Exchequer, 1964; Parly Under-Sec. of State, MoD (Army), 1965-66; MoD (RAF), 1966-68; Home Office, 1968-70; Mem., Shadow Cabinet, 1972-74; Opposition spokesman on NI affairs, 1972-74; Sec. of State for NI, 1974-76; Home Sec., 1976-79; Shadow Home Sec., 1979-80; Opposition spokesman on Energy, 1980-. Mem., Cttee to examine operation of Section 2 of Official Secrets Act, 1971. *Publication:* The Public Sector in the Mixed Economy, 1973. *Recreation:* reading. *Address:* House of Commons, SW1. *Club:* Reform.

REES, Owen; Under Secretary, Welsh Office, since 1977, and Director, Industry Department, since 1980; *b* 26 Dec. 1934; *s* of late John Trevor and Esther Rees, Trimsaran, Dyfed; *m* 1958, Elizabeth Gosby; one *s* two *d. Educ:* Llanelli Grammar Sch.; Univ. of Manchester. BA (Econ). Bank of London and South America, 1957; regional development work in Cardiff, Birmingham and London, BoT, 1959-69; Cabinet Office, 1969-71; Welsh Office, 1971-; Asst Sec. (European Div.), 1972; Sec. for Welsh Educn, 1977-78. *Address:* 4 Llandennis Green, Cyncoed, Cardiff CF2 6JX. *T:* Cardiff 759712.

REES, Peter Magnall; a Senior Clerk, House of Lords, since 1981; *b* 17 March 1921; *s* of late Edward Saunders Rees and of Gertrude Rees (*née* Magnall); *m* 1949, Moya Mildred Carroll. *Educ:* Manchester Grammar Sch.; Jesus Coll., Oxford. Served War, RA, 1941-46 (SE Asia, 1942-45). HM Overseas Service, Nigeria, 1948; Dep. Govt Statistician, Kenya, 1956; Dir of Economics and Statistics, Kenya, 1961; HM Treasury, 1964; Chief Statistician, 1966; Under-Sec., DTI later Dept of Industry, 1973-81. Consultant, OECD, 1981. *Publications:* articles in statistical jls. *Recreations:* choral singing, music, studying architecture. *Address:* Fiddlers Green, West Clandon, Guildford, Surrey GU4 7TL. *T:* Guildford 222311. *Club:* Royal Commonwealth Society.

REES, Peter Wynford Innes, QC 1969; MP (C) Dover and Deal, since 1974 (Dover, 1970-74); Minister for Trade, since 1981; *b* 9 Dec. 1926; *s* of late Maj.-Gen. T. W. Rees, Indian Army, Goytre Hall, Abergavenny; *m* 1969, Mrs Anthea Wendell, *d* of Major H. J. M. Hyslop, late Argyll and Sutherland Highlanders. *Educ:* Stowe; Christ Church, Oxford. Served Scots Guards, 1945-48. Called to the Bar, 1953, Bencher, Inner Temple, 1976; Oxford Circuit. Contested (C): Abertillery, 1964 and 1965; Liverpool, West Derby, 1966. PPS to Solicitor General, 1972; Minister of State, HM Treasury, 1979-81. *Address:* 39 Headfort Place, SW1; Goytre Hall, Abergavenny, Gwent; 5 Church Street, St Clement's, Sandwich, Kent. *Club:* Boodle's.

REES, His Honour Richard Geraint; a Circuit Judge (formerly Deputy Chairman, Inner London Sessions), 1971-81; *b* 5 May 1907; *s* of Rev. Richard Jenkyn Rees, MA, and Apphia Mary Rees, Aberystwyth; *m* 1st, 1938, Mary Davies; one *s* ; 2nd, 1950, Margaret Grotrian; one *d. Educ:* Cardiff High School; University College of Wales, Aberystwyth; St John's College, Cambridge. LLB 1st Cl. Hons, University Coll. of Wales, 1929, BA 1st Cl. Parts I and II Law Tripos, 1930 and 1931; Barrister, Inner Temple, 1932 (Certificate of Honour). Practised on S Wales Circuit, 1934-39. Commissioned Welsh Guards, Nov. 1939; DAAG London Dist, 1943-44; Assistant Director Army Welfare Services, Lt-Col, British Army Staff, Paris, 1944-45; Despatches, Bronze Star (USA), 1946. Practised in London and on Wales and Chester Circuit, 1946-56; Metropolitan Stipendiary Magistrate, 1956-71. *Recreations:* gardening, fishing. *Address:* Fellside, 23 Heath Road, Weybridge, Surrey. *T:* Weybridge 42230.

REES, Dr Richard John William, CMG 1979; FRCPath; Head, Laboratory for Leprosy and Mycobacterial Research, and WHO Collaborating Centre for Reference and Research on *M. leprae*, National Institute for Medical Research, London, since 1969; *b* 11 Aug. 1917; *s* of William and Gertrude Rees; *m* 1942, Kathleen Harris; three *d. Educ:* East Sheen County Sch., London; Guy's Hosp., London (BSc 1939; MB, BS 1942). MRCS, LRCP 1941; MRCPath 1963, FRCPath 1964. Served War, 1942-46: Captain, RAMC Army Blood Transfusion Service, N Africa and Italy campaigns. House Surg. and Phys., Southern Hosp., Kent, 1941-42; Asst Clin. Pathologist, Guy's Hosp., 1946-49; Mem. of Scientific Staff, NIMR, 1949-69. Sec., MRC

Leprosy Cttee, 1959–; Consultant, US Japanese Co-op. Scientific Prog. on Leprosy, 1969-73. Chairman: LEPRA Med. Adv. Bd, 1963- (Mem. Exec. Cttee, 1964-); Acid Fast Club, 1960; Pres., Section of Comparative Medicine, RSM, 1975. Member: Trop. Medicine Res. Bd, 1968-72; Council, Internat. Leprosy Assoc., 1963-; 3rd WHO Expert Cttee on Leprosy, 1965; WHO IMMLEP Steering Cttee, 1974-; WHO THELEP Steering Cttee, 1977-. Almoth Wright Lectr, 1971; Erasmus Wilson Demonstration, RCS, 1973; 1st Clayton Meml Lectr, 1974; BMA Film, Silver Award, Leprosy, 1974. Mem. Editorial Boards: Leprosy Review; Internat. Jl of Leprosy; Jl of Medical Microbiology; Excerpta Medica Leprosy. Manson Medal, 1980. *Publications:* scientific papers on basic and applied studies in animals and man relevant to pathogenesis, immunology and chemotherapy of leprosy and tuberculosis. *Address:* Highfield, Highwood Hill, Mill Hill, NW7 4EU. *T:* 01-959 2021.

REES, Sir Stanley; *see* Rees, Sir C. W. S.

REES, (Thomas Morgan) Haydn, CBE 1975; JP; DL; Chairman, Welsh Water Authority, 1977-82; Member: National Water Council, 1977-82; Water Space Amenity Commission, 1977-82; *b* 22 May 1915; *y s* of late Thomas Rees and Mary Rees, Gorseinon, Swansea; *m* 1941, Marion, *y d* of A. B. Beer, Mumbles, Swansea; one *d. Educ:* Swansea Business Coll. Served War, 1939-45. Admitted solicitor, 1946; Sen. Asst Solicitor, Caernarvonshire CC, 1947; Flints County Council, 1948-65: Dep. Clerk, Dep. Clerk of the Peace, Police Authority, Magistrates Courts Cttee, and of Probation Cttee; 1966-74: Chief Exec.; Clerk of Peace (until office abolished, 1971); Clerk, Flints Police Authority (until merger with N Wales Police Authority, 1967); Clerk of Probation, Magistrates Courts, and of Justices Adv. Cttees; Clerk to Lieutenancy; Chief Exec., Clwyd CC, and Clerk, Magistrates Courts Cttee, 1974-77; Clerk to Lieutenancy and of Justices Adv. Cttee, Clwyd, 1974-77. Clerk: N Wales Police Authority, 1967-77; Theatr Clwyd Governors, 1974-77. Secretary: Welsh Counties Cttee, 1968-77; (Corresp.) Rep. Body (Ombudsman) Cttee for Wales, 1974-77; Mem., Severn Barrage Cttee, 1978-81. Asst Comr, Royal Commn on Constitution, 1969-73. Chm., New Jobs Team, Shotton Steelworks, 1977-; part-time Mem. Bd, BSC (Industry) Ltd, 1979-. Chm., N Wales Arts Assoc., 1981-. Member: Lord Chancellor's Circuit Cttee for Wales and Chester Circuit, 1972-77; Welsh Council, 1968-79; Welsh Arts Council, 1968-77; Gorsedd, Royal National Eisteddfod for Wales; Prince of Wales Cttee, 1976-79. DL Flints 1969, Clwyd 1974; JP Mold, 1977 (Dep. Chm., 1978-). *Recreations:* the arts, golf. *Address:* Cefn Bryn, Gwernaffield Road, Mold, Clwyd CH7 1RQ. *T:* Mold 2421. *Club:* Mold Golf.

REES, (Walter) Llewellyn, MA; Actor and Theatre Administrator; Director, Travelling Playhouse Ltd; Honorary President of International Theatre Institute since 1951; *b* 18 June 1901; *s* of Walter Francis Rees and Mary Gwendoline Naden; *m* 1961, Madeleine Newbury; one *s* one *d. Educ:* King Edward's School, Birmingham; Keble College, Oxford. Private Tutor, 1923-26; studied at RADA, 1926-28; Actor, 1928-40; Gen. Sec. of British Actors' Equity Assoc., 1940-46; Jt Secretary: London Theatre Council, 1940-46, Prov. Theatre Council, 1942-46; Sec. of Fed. of Theatre Unions, 1944-46; Governor of the Old Vic, 1945-47; Drama Director, Arts Council of Great Britain, 1947-49; Administrator of the Old Vic, 1949-51; Administrator of Arts Theatre, 1951-52; General Administrator, Donald Wolfit's Company, 1952-58; Chairman Executive Committee of International Theatre Institute, 1948-51; Hon. Counsellor to Council of Repertory Theatres, 1951-77. Returned to West End Stage, 1956, as Bishop of Buenos Aires in The Strong are Lonely, Theatre Royal, Haymarket; Olmeda in The Master of Santiago, Lyric Theatre, Hammersmith, 1957; Polonius in Hamlet, Bristol Old Vic, 1958; Dean of College in My Friend Judas, Arts Theatre, 1959; Mr Brandy in Settled out of Court, Strand Theatre, 1960-61; Justice Worthy in Lock Up Your Daughters, Mermaid Theatre and Her Majesty's, 1962-63; Sir Henry James in the Right Honourable Gentleman, Her Majesty's, 1964-65; Father Ambrose in The Servants and the Snow, Greenwich, 1970; Duncan in Macbeth, Greenwich, 1971; Mr Justice Millhouse in Whose Life Is It Anyway?, Savoy, 1978-79. Many film and television appearances. *Recreation:* travel. *Address:* 6 Byfeld Gardens, Barnes, SW13 9HP.

REES, William Howard Guest; Chief Veterinary Officer, State Veterinary Service, since 1980; *b* 21 May 1928; *s* of Walter Guest Rees and Margaret Elizabeth Rees; *m* 1952, Charlotte Mollie (*née* Collins); three *s* one *d. Educ:* Llanelli Grammar Sch.; Royal Veterinary Coll., London (BSc). MRCVS; DVSM. Private practice, Deal, Kent, 1952-53; joined MAFF as Veterinary Officer, 1953; stationed Stafford, 1953-66: Divl Vet. Officer, Vet. Service HQ, Tolworth, 1966-69; Divl Vet. Officer, Berks, 1969-71; Dep. Regional Vet. Officer, SE Reg., 1971-73; Regional Vet. Officer, Tolworth, 1973-76, Asst Chief Vet. Officer, 1976-80. Mem. ARC, 1980-. *Recreations:* Rugby and cricket follower, golf. *Address:* Taliesin, Paddocks Way, Ashtead, Surrey KT21 2QY. *T:* Ashtead 76522.

REES, William Hurst; Member of Lands Tribunal, since 1973; *b* 12 April 1917; *s* of Richard and Florence A. Rees; *m* 1941, Elizabeth Mary Wight; two *s* one *d. Educ:* College of Estate Management, Univ. of London (BSc Est. Man.). FRICS. Served War, RA and RE (SO2), 1940-46; Liaison Officer, Belgian Army Engrs. Lectr in Valuations, Coll. of Estate Management, 1946-48; Head of Valuation Dept, 1948-51. Principal in Private Practice as Chartered Surveyor: City of London, Richard Ellis & Son, 1951-61; East Grinstead, Sx, Turner, Rudge & Turner, 1961-73. Gov., Coll.

of Estate Management, 1965-72; Mem. Council, RICS, 1967-70; Chm. Bd of Studies in Estate Management, Univ. of London, 1970-74; Mem. Surveying Bd, Council for Nat. Academic Awards, 1969-80 (Chm., 1976-77); Hon. Mem., Rating Surveyors Assoc. Hon. Sec., BSc (Estate Management) Club, 1953-56, Pres. 1961-62. *Publications:* Modern Methods of Valuation, 1943, (jointly) 6th edn 1971; (ed) Valuations: Principles into Practice, 1980. *Recreation:* music, mainly opera. *Address:* Brendon, Carlton Road, South Godstone, Godstone, Surrey RH9 8LD. *T:* South Godstone 2109.

REES, (William) Linford (Llewelyn), CBE 1978; FRCP; FRCPsych; Emeritus Professor of Psychiatry, University of London, 1980; Consulting Physician, St Bartholomew's Hospital, since 1981; Lecturer in Psychological Medicine, St Bartholomew's Medical College, since 1958; Recognised Clinical Teacher in Mental Diseases, Institute of Psychiatry, University of London, since 1956; Chairman: University of London Teachers of Psychiatry Committee; Armed Services Consultant Advisory Board in Psychiatry, since 1979; *b* 24 Oct. 1914; *e s* of late Edward Parry Rees and Mary Rees, Llanelly, Carmathenshire; *m* 1940, Catherine, *y d* of late David Thomas, and of Angharad Thomas, Alltwen, Glam; two *s* two *d. Educ:* Llanelly Grammar School; University Coll., Cardiff; Welsh Nat. Sch. of Medicine; The Maudsley Hosp.; Univ. of London. BSc 1935; MB, BCh 1938; DPM 1940; DSc London, 1978; MRCP 1942; MD 1943; FRCP 1950; FRCPsych 1971 (Pres., 1975-78); Hon. FRCPsych 1978. David Hepburn Medal and Alfred Hughes Medal in Anatomy, 1935; John Maclean Medal and Prize in Obstetrics and Gynaecology, 1937, etc. Specialist, EMS, 1942; Dep. Med. Supt, Mill Hill Emergency Hosp., 1945; Asst Physician and Postgrad. Teacher in Clinical Psychiatry, The Maudsley Hosp., 1946; Dep. Physician Supt, Whitchurch Hosp., 1947; Regional Psychiatrist for Wales and Mon, 1948; Consultant Physician, The Bethlem Royal Hosp. and The Maudsley Hosp., 1954-66; Med. Dir, Charter Clinic, London, 1980-. Consultant Advisor in Psychiatry to RAF; WHO Consultant to Sri Lanka, 1973; Hon. Consultant, Royal Sch. for Deaf Children. Lectures to Univs and Learned Socs in Europe, USA, Asia, Australia and S America. Examiner: Diploma Psychological Medicine, RCP, 1964-69; MRCP, RCP, RCPE and RCPGlas, 1969-; MB and DPM, Univ. of Leeds, 1969-. President: Soc. for Psychosomatic Research, 1957-58; Royal Coll. of Psychiatrists, 1975-78 (Vice-Pres., 1972-75; Chm., E Anglian Region); Section of Psychiatry, RSM, 1971-72 (Vice-Pres., (Vice-Pres., 1968; Hon. Mem., 1982); BMA, 1978- (Fellow, 1981); Chm., Medico-Pharmaceutical Forum, 1982 (Vice-Chm., 1981). Treasurer, World Psychiatric Assoc., 1966- (Hon. Mem.) Member: Clinical Psychiatry Cttee, MRC, 1959-; Council, Royal Medico-Psychological Assoc. (Chm., Research and Clinical Section, 1957-63); Soc. for Study of Human Biology; Asthma Research Council; Cttee on Safety of Medicines (also Toxicity and Clinical Trials Sub-Cttee), 1971-; Psychological Medicine Group, BMA, 1967-; Bd of Advanced Med. Studies, Univ. of London, 1966-69; Higher Degrees Cttee, Univ. of London; Acad. Council Standing Sub-Cttee in Medicine, Univ. of London; Cttee of Management, Inst. of Psychiatry, Maudsley Hosp., 1968-; Council and Exec. Cttee, St Bartholomew's Hosp. Med. Coll., 1972-; Jt Policy Cttee, QMC, St Bartholomew's Hosp. and London Hosp., 1973-; Cttee on Review of Medicines (Chm., Psychotropic Drugs Sub-Cttee); Central Health Services Council; Standing Medical Adv. Cttee; Jt Consultants Cttee; Conference of Presidents of Royal Colls; GMC, 1980- (Mem., Educn Cttee, Preliminary Health Cttee and Prof. Conduct Cttee). Founder Mem., Internat. Coll. of Neuro-psychopharmacology. Hon. Mem. Learned Socs in USA, Sweden, Venezuela, East Germany, Spain and Greece. FRSM; Fellow: Eugenics Soc.; and Vice-Pres., Internat. Coll. of Psychosomatic Medicine, 1973; University Coll., Cardiff, 1980; Distinguished Fellow, Amer. Psychiatric Assoc., 1968; Hon. Fellow: Amer. Soc. of Physician Analysts; Amer. Coll. Psychiatrists; Hon. Mem., Biological Psychiatry Assoc., USA. Chm. Bd of Trustees, Stress Syndrome Foundn, 1981- (Chm., Scientific Adv. Council). Governor: The Bethlem Royal Hosp. and The Maudsley Hosp.; Med. Coll. of St Bartholomew's Hosp., 1980-. Pres., Golden Jubilee Appeal, Welsh Nat. Sch. of Med., 1980; Patron of Extend, 1976. Co-Editor, Jl of Psychosomatic Research. Liveryman: Barber Surgeons; Apothecaries. Hon. LLD Wales, 1981. Bard of Welsh Gorsedd. *Publications:* (with Eysenck and Himmelweit) Dimensions of Personality, 1947; Short Textbook of Psychiatry, 1967. Chapters in: Modern Treatment in General Practice, 1947; Recent Progress in Psychiatry, 1950; Schizophrenia: Somatic Aspects, 1957; Psychoendocrinology, 1958; Recent Progress in Psychosomatic Research, 1960; Stress and Psychiatric Disorders, 1960. Papers in: Nature, BMJ, Jl of Mental Sci., Jl of Psychosomatic Research, Eugenics Review, etc. Contribs to Med. Annual, 1958-68. *Recreations:* swimming, photography, amusing grandchildren. *Address:* Penbryn, 62 Oakwood Avenue, Purley, Surrey. *Club:* Athenæum.

REES-DAVIES, William Rupert, QC 1973; MP (C) Thanet West, since 1974 (Isle of Thanet, March 1953-1974); Barrister-at-law; *b* 19 Nov. 1916; *o s* of late Sir William Rees-Davies, KC, DL, JP, formerly Chief Justice of Hong Kong and Liberal MP for Pembroke and of late Lady Rees-Davies; *m* 1st, 1959, Jane (marr. diss. 1981), *d* of Mr and Mrs Henry Mander; two *d*; 2nd, 1982, Sharlie Kingsley. *Educ:* Eton; Trinity Coll., Cambridge; Eton Soc., Eton XI, 1934-35; Eton Victor Ludorum; Cambridge Cricket XI, 1938; Honours in History and Law. Called to Bar, Inner Temple, 1939. Commissioned HM Welsh Guards, 1939; served War of 1939-45 (discharged disabled with loss of arm, 1943). Contested (C) South Nottingham in 1950 and 1951. Cons. Leader, Select Cttee on Health and the Social Services, 1980-; Chm., Cons. Cttee on Tourism. *Recreations:* collecting pictures and antiques.

Address: 5 Lord North Street, SW1. *Clubs:* MCC; Hawks, University Pitt (Cambridge).

REES-JONES, Geoffrey Rippon, MA Oxon; Principal, King William's College, Isle of Man, 1958-79; *b* 8 July 1914; *er s* of W. Rees-Jones, BA, Ipswich; *m* 1950, Unity Margaret McConnell, *d* of Major P. M. Sanders, Hampstead; one *s* one *d. Educ:* Ipswich School (scholar); University College, Oxford (open scholar). Assistant Master, Eastbourne College, 1936-38, Marlborough College, 1938-54 (Housemaster, C2, 1946-54); Headmaster, Bembridge School, 1954-58; served War mainly in Commandos, 1940-45; Commandant, Commando Mountain Warfare School, 1943; Staff College, Camberley, 1944 (sc); Brigade Major, 4 Commando Bde, 1944-45 (despatches). *Recreations:* sailing, cricket, golf, fives; Oxford Rugby 'blue', 1933-35, Wales XV, 1934-36. *Address:* c/o King William's College, Isle of Man. *T:* Castletown 2551.

REES-MOGG, Sir William, Kt 1981; Chairman and Proprietor, Pickering & Chatto Ltd, since 1981; Director, General Electric Co., since 1981; Vice-Chairman, Board of Governors, BBC, since 1981; Chairman, Arts Council of Great Britain, since 1982; *b* 14 July 1928; *s* of late Edmund Fletcher Rees-Mogg and late Beatrice Rees-Mogg (*née* Warren), Temple Cloud, Somerset; *m* 1962, Gillian Shakespeare Morris, *d* of T. R. Morris; two *s* three *d. Educ:* Charterhouse; Balliol Coll., Oxford (Brackenbury Scholar). President, Oxford Union, 1951. Financial Times, 1952-60, Chief Leader Writer, 1955-60; Asst Editor, 1957-60; Sunday Times, City Editor, 1960-61; Political and Economic Editor, 1961-63; Deputy Editor, 1964-67; Editor, The Times, 1967-81; Mem., Exec. Bd, Times Newspapers Ltd, 1968-81; Director: The Times Ltd, 1968-81; Times Newspapers Ltd, 1978-81. Contested (C) Chester-le-Street, Co. Durham, By-election 1956; General Election, 1959. Treasurer, Institute of Journalists, 1960-63, 1966-68, Pres., 1963-64; Vice-Chm. Cons. Party's Nat. Advisory Cttee on Political Education, 1961-63. Vis. Fellow, Nuffield Coll., Oxford, 1968-72. High Sheriff, Somerset, 1978. Hon. LLD Bath, 1977. *Publications:* The Reigning Error: the crisis of world inflation, 1974; An Humbler Heaven, 1977. *Recreation:* collecting. *Address:* 3 Smith Square, SW1; The Old Rectory, Hinton Blewitt, near Bristol, Avon. *Club:* Garrick.

REES-WILLIAMS, family name of **Baron Ogmore.**

REESE, Prof. Colin Bernard, PhD, ScD; FRS 1981; Daniell Professor of Chemistry, King's College, University of London, since 1973; *b* 29 July 1930; *s* of Joseph and Emily Reese; *m* 1968, Susanne Bird; one *s* one *d. Educ:* Dartington Hall Sch.; Clare Coll., Cambridge (BA 1953, PhD 1956, MA 1957, ScD 1972). 1851 Sen. Student, 1956-58; Research Fellow: Clare Coll., Cambridge, 1956-59; Harvard Univ., 1957-58; Official Fellow and Dir of Studies in Chem., Clare Coll., 1959-73; Cambridge University: Univ. Demonstrator in Chem., 1959-63; Asst Dir of Res., 1963-64; Univ. Lectr in Chem., 1964-73. *Publications:* scientific papers, mainly in chemical jls. *Address:* Department of Chemistry, King's College, Strand, WC2R 2LS. *T:* 01-836 5454.

REESE, Surg. Rear-Adm. John Mansel, CB 1962; OBE 1953; *b* 3 July 1906; *s* of late Dr D. W. Reese, and late Mrs A. M. Reese; *m* 1946, Beryl (*née* Dunn) (*d* 1973); two *d* (and one *s* decd). *Educ:* Epsom Coll.; St Mary's Hosp. Med. Sch., London University. MRCS, LRCP 1930; DPH 1934. Entered Royal Navy, Jan. 1931; Naval Medical Officer of Health, Orkney and Shetland Comd, 1942-44; Naval MOH, Ceylon, 1944-46; Admiralty, 1947-53; Medical Officer-in-Charge RN Hospital, Plymouth, 1960-63; QHP 1960-63. Surgeon Comdr, 1943; Surgeon Captain, 1954; Surgeon Rear-Adm., 1960; retd 1963. FRSTM&H. Sir Gilbert Blane Gold Medal, 1939. Member Gray's Inn, 1953. CStJ 1961. *Address:* 4 Meldon Court, East Budleigh Road, Budleigh Salterton, Devon.

REESE, (John) Terence; bridge expert, author and journalist; *b* 28 Aug. 1913; *s* of John and Anne Reese; *m* 1970, Alwyn Sherrington. *Educ:* Bilton Grange; Bradfield Coll. (top scholar); New Coll., Oxford (top class. scholar). Worked at Harrods, 1935-36; left to follow career as bridge expert and journalist. Became bridge correspondent of the Evening News, 1948, the Observer, 1950, the Lady, 1954, and the Standard, 1981. Winner of numerous British, European and World Championships. *Publications:* The Elements of Contract, 1938; Reese on Play, 1948; The Expert Game, 1958; Play Bridge with Reese, 1960; Story of an Accusation, 1966; Precision Bidding and Precision Play, 1972; Play These Hands With Me, 1976; Bridge at the Top (autobiog.), 1977; *with Albert Dormer:* The Acol System Today, 1961; The Play of the Cards, 1967; Bridge for Tournament Players, 1969; The Complete Book of Bridge, 1973; and many others. *Recreations:* golf, backgammon. *Address:* 18a Woods Mews, Park Lane, W1. *T:* 01-629 5553. *Clubs:* Clermont, St James's; Berkshire Golf.

REEVE, Anthony; HM Diplomatic Service; Counsellor at Cairo, since 1981; *b* 20 Oct. 1938; *s* of Sidney Reeve and Dorothy (*née* Mitchell); *m* 1964, Pamela Margaret Angus; one *s* two *d. Educ:* Queen Elizabeth Grammar Sch., Wakefield; Marling Sch., Stroud; Merton Coll., Oxford (MA). Lever Brothers & Associates, 1962-65; joined HM Diplomatic Service, 1965; Middle East Centre for Arab Studies, 1966-68; Asst Political Agent, Abu Dhabi, 1968-70; First Secretary, FCO, 1970-73; First Sec., later Counsellor, Washington, 1973-78; Head of Arms Control and Disarmament Dept, FCO, 1979-81. *Recreations:* writing, gardening, music. *Address:* c/o Foreign and

Commonwealth Office, SW1. *Clubs:* United Oxford & Cambridge University; Leander (Henley-on-Thames).

REEVE, Hon. Sir (Charles) Trevor, Kt 1973; Hon. Mr Justice Reeve; a Judge of the High Court of Justice, Family Division, since 1973; *b* 4 July 1915; *o s* of William George Reeve and Elsie (*née* Bowring), Wokingham; *m* 1941, Marjorie, *d* of Charles Evelyn Browne, Eccles, Lancs. *Educ:* Winchester College; Trinity College, Oxford. Commissioned 10th Royal Hussars (PWO) 1940; served BEF, CMF (Major) 1940-44 (despatches); Staff College, Camberley, 1945. Called to Bar, Inner Temple, 1946, Bencher, 1965; Mem., Bar Council, 1950-54. QC 1965; County Court Judge, 1968; Circuit Judge, 1972. Mem., Appeals Tribunal for E Africa in respect of Commonwealth Immigration Act, 1968. *Recreations:* golf, dancing. *Address:* 95 Abingdon Road, Kensington, W8 6QU. *T:* 01-937 7530. *Clubs:* Garrick; Royal North Devon Golf (Westward Ho!); Sunningdale Golf.

REEVE, James Ernest, CMG 1982; HM Diplomatic Service; HM Minister and Consul-General, Milan, since 1980; *b* 8 June 1926; *s* of Ernest and Anthea Reeve; *m* 1947, Lillian Irene Watkins; one *s* one *d. Educ:* Bishops Stortford Coll. Vice-Consul, Ahwaz and Khorramshahr, Iran, 1949-51; UN General Assembly, Paris, 1951; Asst Private Sec. to Rt Hon. Selwyn Lloyd, Foreign Office, 1951-53; 2nd Secretary: Brit. Embassy, Washington, 1953-57; Brit. Embassy, Bangkok, 1957-59; FO, 1959-61; HM Consul, Frankfurt, 1961-65; 1st Secretary: Brit. Embassy in Libya, 1965-69; Brit. Embassy, Budapest, 1970-72; Chargé d'Affaires, Budapest, 1972; Counsellor (Commercial), East Berlin, 1973-75; Consul-Gen., Zurich and Principality of Liechtenstein, 1975-80. *Recreations:* theatre, tennis, skiing, travel. *Address:* c/o Foreign and Commonwealth Office, SW1. *Club:* Royal Automobile.

REEVE, Major-General John Talbot Wentworth, CB 1946; CBE 1941; DSO 1919; *b* 1891; *e s* of Charles Sydney Wentworth Reeve; *m* 1st, 1919, Sybil Alice (*d* 1949), 4th *d* of Sir George Agnew, 2nd Bt; one *d* (one *s* killed in North Africa, June 1942); 2nd, 1950, Mrs Marjorie Frances Wagstaff (*see* Mrs M. F. Reeve). *Educ:* Eton; Royal Military College, Sandhurst. Served European War, 1914-19 (despatches, DSO); commanded 1st Bn The Rifle Brigade, 1936-38; Commander Hong Kong Infantry Brigade, 1938-41; DAG Home Forces, 1942-43; Commander Sussex District, 1943-44; DAG, MEF, 1944-46; retd pay, 1946. *Address:* Livermere Lodge, near Bury St Edmunds, Suffolk. *T:* Honington 376. *Club:* Army and Navy.

REEVE, Mrs Marjorie Frances Wentworth, CBE 1944; TD 1950; JP; *d* of late Charles Fry, Bedford; *m* 1st, Lieutenant-Commander J. K. Laughton, Royal Navy (*d* 1925); one *s* ; 2nd, Major-General C. M. Wagstaff, CB, CMG, CIE, DSO (*d* 1934); 3rd, 1950, Major-General J. T. Wentworth Reeve, qv. Joined ATS, 1938; served with BEF, and in Middle East and BAOR; late Controller ATS. Was i/c Public Welfare Section of Control Commission for Germany (BE); Principal in Board of Trade (Overseas) till 1950; Swedish Red Cross Medal in Silver, 1950; County Director, BRCS, 1953-57; Dep. Pres. Suffolk BRCS, 1957, Hon. Vice-Pres., 1977. Badge of Honour (2nd Class) BRCS, 1970. JP (W Suffolk), 1954. *Address:* Livermere Lodge, near Bury St Edmunds, Suffolk. *T:* Honington 376. *Club:* Army and Navy.

REEVE, Hon. Sir Trevor; see Reeve, Hon. Sir C. T.

REEVES, Christopher Reginald; Deputy Chairman and Group Chief Executive, Morgan Grenfell & Co. Ltd, Bankers, since 1980; *b* 14 Jan. 1936; *s* of Reginald and Dora Reeves; *m* 1965, Stella, *d* of Patrick and Maria Whinney; three *s. Educ:* Malvern College. National Service, Rifle Bde, 1955-57. Bank of England, 1958-63; Hill Samuel & Co. Ltd, 1963-67; joined Morgan Grenfell & Co. Ltd, 1968; Dir, 1970. Director: London Board, Westpac Banking Corp. (formerly Commercial Bank of Australia Ltd) 1972-, Chm., 1976-82, Dep. Chm., 1982-; Midland and International Banks Ltd, 1976-; BICC, 1982-; Andrew Weir & Co., 1982-. Member: Adv. Panel, City University Business Sch., 1972-81 (Chm., 1979-81); Incorporated Assoc. of Preparatory Schs Adv. Cttee, 1977-; Governor: Stowe Sch., 1976-81; Dulwich College Prep. Sch., 1977-; Mermaid Theatre Trust, 1981-. *Recreations:* sailing, shooting. *Address:* c/o 23 Great Winchester Street, EC2P 2AX. *T:* 01-588 4545. *Clubs:* Boodle's; Royal Southern Yacht (Southampton).

REEVES, Marjorie Ethel, MA (Oxon), PhD (London), DLitt (Oxon); FRHistS; FBA 1974; Vice-Principal, St Anne's College, Oxford, 1951-62, 1964-67; *b* 17 July 1905; *d* of Robert J. W. Reeves and Edith Saffery Whitaker. *Educ:* The High School for Girls, Trowbridge, Wilts; St Hugh's Coll., Oxford; Westfield Coll., London. Asst Mistress, Roan School, Greenwich, 1927-29; Research Fellow, Westfield Coll., London, 1929-31; Lecturer, St Gabriel's Trng Coll., London, 1931-38; Tutor, later Fellow of St Anne's College, 1938-72, Hon. Fellow, 1973. Member: Central Advisory Council, Min. of Educn, 1947-61; Academic Planning Bd, Univ. of Kent; Academic Advisory Cttee, University of Surrey; formerly Member: Educn Council, ITA; British Council of Churches; School Broadcasting Council. Corresp. Fellow, Medieval Acad. of America, 1979. *Publications:* Growing Up in a Modern Society, 1946; (ed, with L. Tondelli, B. Hirsch-Reich) Il Libro delle Figure dell'Abate Gioachino da Fiore, 1953; Three Questions in Higher Education (Hazen Foundation, USA), 1955; Moral Education in a Changing Society (ed W. Niblett), 1963; ed, Eighteen Plus: Unity and Diversity in Higher Education, 1965; The Influence of Prophecy in the later Middle Ages: a study in Joachimism, 1969; Higher Education: demand and response (ed W. R. Niblett), 1969; (with B. Hirsch-Reich) The Figurae of

Joachim of Fiore, 1972; Joachim of Fiore and the Prophetic Future, 1976; Sheep Bell and Ploughshare, 1978; Why History, 1980; Then and There Series: The Medieval Town, 1954, The Medieval Village, 1954, Elizabethan Court, 1956, The Medieval Monastery, 1957, The Norman Conquest, 1958, Alfred and the Danes, 1959; The Medieval Castle, 1960, Elizabethan Citizen, 1961; A Medieval King Governs, 1971; Explorers of the Elizabethan Age, 1977; contributions on history in Speculum, Medieval and Renaissance Studies, Traditio, Sophia, Recherches de Théologie, etc, and on education in Times Educational Supplement, New Era, etc. *Recreations:* music, gardening, bird-watching. *Address:* 38 Norham Road, Oxford. *T:* Oxford 57039. *Club:* University Women's.

REEVES, Most Rev. Paul Alfred; *see* New Zealand, Primate and Archbishop of.

REEVES, Philip Thomas Langford, RSA 1976 (ARSA 1971); artist in etching and other mediums; Senior Lecturer, Glasgow School of Art, since 1973; *b* 7 July 1931; *s* of Herbert Reeves and Lilian; *m* 1964, Christine MacLaren; one *d*. *Educ:* Naunton Park Sch., Cheltenham. Student, Cheltenham Sch. of Art, 1947-49. Army service, 4th/7th Royal Dragoon Guards, Middle East, 1949-51. RCA, 1951-54 (ARCA 1st Cl.); Lectr, Glasgow Sch. of Art, 1954-73. Associate, Royal Soc. of Painter Etchers, 1954, Fellow 1964; RSW 1962; RGI 1981. Works in permanent collections: Arts Council; Gall. of Modern Art, Edinburgh; Glasgow Art Gall.; Glasgow Univ. Print Collection; Manchester City Art Gall.; Royal Scottish Acad.; Aberdeen Art Gall.; Paisley Art Gall.; Inverness Art Gall.; Milngavie Art Gall.; Dept of the Environment; Dundee Art Gall.; Scottish Develt Agency; Stirling and Strathclyde Univs; Contemporary Art Soc. *Recreation:* walking. *Address:* 13 Hamilton Drive, Glasgow G12 8DN. *Club:* Traverse (Edinburgh).

REFFELL, Rear-Adm. Derek Roy; Naval Task Group Commander, South Atlantic, since July 1982; *b* 6 Oct. 1928; *s* of late Edward (Roy) and Murielle Reffell; *m* 1956, Janne Gronow Davis; one *s* one *d*. *Educ:* Culford Sch., Suffolk; Royal Naval Coll., Dartmouth. MNI. Various ships at Home, Mediterranean, West Indies and Far East, 1946-63; qualified Navigating Officer, 1954; Comdr 1963; Comd HMS Sirius, 1966-67; Comdr BRNC Dartmouth, 1968-69; Captain 1970; Chief Staff Officer Plans Far East, 1970-71; Naval Staff, 1971-74; Comd HMS Hermes, 1974-76; Director Naval Warfare, 1976-78; Commodore Amphibious Warfare, 1978-79; Asst Chief of Naval Staff (Policy), 1979-82; Flag Officer Third Flotilla and Comdr Anti-Submarine Group Two, March-July 1982. Liveryman, Coachmakers Company, 1976-. *Recreation:* wine-making. *T:* Hindhead 5184.

REFSHAUGE, Maj.-Gen. Sir William (Dudley), AC 1980; Kt 1966; CBE 1959 (OBE 1944); ED 1965; Secretary-General, World Medical Association, 1973-76; Hon. Consultant to Australian Foundation on Alcoholism and Drugs of Dependence, since 1979; *b* 3 April 1913; *s* of late F. C. Refshauge, Melbourne; *m* 1942, Helen Elizabeth, *d* of late R. E. Allwright, Tasmania; four *s* one *d*. *Educ:* Hampton High Sch.; Scotch Coll., Melbourne; Melbourne University. MB, BS (Melbourne) 1938; FRCOG 1961; FRACS 1962; FRACP 1963; Hon. FRSH 1967; FACMA 1967; FRACOG 1978. Served with AIF, 1939-46; Lt-Col, RAAMC (despatches four times). Medical Supt, Royal Women's Hosp., Melbourne, 1948-51; Col, and Dep. DGAMS, Aust., 1951-55; Maj.-Gen., and DGAMS, Aust., 1955-60; QHP, 1955-64. Commonwealth Dir-Gen. of Health, Australia, 1960-73. Chairman: Council, Aust. Coll. of Nursing, 1958-60 (Chm. Educn Cttee, 1951-58); Nat. Health and MRC, 1960-73; Nat. Fitness Council, 1960-; Nat. Tuberculosis Adv. Council, 1960-; Prog. and Budget Cttee, 15th World Health Assembly, 1962; Admin., Fin. and Legal Cttee 19th World Health Assembly (Pres., 24th Assembly, 1971); Exec. Bd, WHO, 1969-70 (Mem., 1967-70). Member: Council, Aust. Red Cross Soc., 1954-60; Mem. Nat. Blood Transfusion Cttee, ARCS 1955-60; Nat. Trustee, Returned Services League Aust., 1961-73, 1976-; Mem. Bd of Management, Canberra Grammar Sch., 1963-68; Mem. Bd of Trustees, Walter and Eliza Hall Inst. of Med. Res., Melbourne, 1977-. Chm., ACT Cttee, Mem., Nat. Cttee and Mem. Nat. Exec., Sir Robert Menzies Foundn, 1979-. Hon. Life Mem., Australian Dental Assoc., 1966. Patron: Australian Sports Medicine Assoc., 1971-; ACT Br., Aust. Sports Medicine Fedn, 1980-. Leader, Commemorative Tour of Europe for 60th anniversary, RSL. Nat. Pres., 1st Pan Pacific Conf. on alcohol and drugs, 1980. *Publications:* contribs to Australian Med. Jl, NZ Med. Jl, etc. *Recreations:* bowls, rug-making, gardening. *Address:* 26 Birdwood Street, Hughes, Canberra, ACT 2605, Australia. *Clubs:* Royal Society of Medicine (London); Naval and Military, Cricket (Melbourne); Commonwealth (Canberra); Bowling (Canberra); Royal Automobile (Victoria).

REGAN, Charles Maurice; Under-Secretary, Department of Health and Social Security, 1972-79 and since 1981; *b* 31 Oct. 1925; *m* 1961, Susan (*née* Littmann) (*d* 1972); one *s* one *d*. *Educ:* Taunton Sch.; London Sch. of Economics and Political Science (BSc(Econ)). Academic research, 1950-52. Asst Principal, Min. of National Insurance, 1952; Principal Private Sec. to Minister of Pensions and National Insurance, 1962-64; Asst Sec., 1964; Treasury/Civil Service Dept, 1967-70; Under-Sec., DES, 1979-81. *Recreations:* walking, travel. *Address:* 35 Crediton Hill, NW6 1HS. *T:* 01-794 6404.

REGAN, Donald Thomas; Secretary of the Treasury, United States Treasury Department, since 1981; *b* 21 Dec. 1918; *s* of late William F. Regan and Kathleen A. Regan; *m* 1942, Ann Gordon Buchanan; two *s* two *d*. *Educ:*

Cambridge Latin Sch.; Harvard Univ. (BA). Served War, US Marine Corps, 1940-46; retd as Lt Col, Marine Corps Reserve. Merrill Lynch, Pierce, Fenner & Smith Inc., 1946-81: Vice Pres., 1959-64; Exec. Vice Pres., 1964-68; Pres., 1968-71; Chm. of Bd, 1971-80; Chm. of Bd, Merrill Lynch & Co., Inc., 1973-81. Hon. LLD: Hahnemann Med. Coll. and Hosp., 1968; Tri-State Coll., 1969; Univ. of Penn., 1972; Hon. Dr of Commercial Science, Pace Univ., 1973. Fortune magazine's Hall of Fame for business leadership, 1981. *Publication:* A View from the Street, 1972. *Recreations:* golf, reading. *Address:* United States Treasury Department, Washington, DC 20220, USA. *T:* 202-566-2533. *Clubs:* Metropolitan, Army-Navy (Washington, DC); Burning Tree (Bethesda, Md).

REGAN, Hon. Gerald Augustine, QC (Can.); MP (L) Halifax, Nova Scotia, since 1980; Secretary of State for Canada since 1981; Minister responsible for Fitness and Amateur Sport, since 1980; lawyer; *b* Windsor, NS, 13 Feb. 1929; *s* of Walter E. Regan and Rose M. Greene; *m* 1956, A. Carole, *d* of John H. Harrison; three *s* three *d*. *Educ:* Windsor Academy; St Mary's and Dalhousie Univs, Canada; Dalhousie Law Sch. (LLB). Called to Bar of Nova Scotia, 1954; QC (Can.) 1970. Formerly practising lawyer. Liberal candidate in Provincial gen. elecs, 1956 and 1960, and in Fed. gen. elec., 1962. MP for Halifax, NS, House of Commons of Canada, 1963-65; Leader, Liberal Party of Nova Scotia, 1965-80; MLA for Halifax-Needham, Provincial gen. elec., 1967, re-elected, 1970-74 and 1978; Premier of Nova Scotia, 1970-78, Leader of the Opposition 1978-80; Minister of Labour, Govt of Canada, 1980-81. Mem., NS Barristers Soc.; Chm. Exec. Cttee, Commonwealth Parly Assoc., 1973-76; Mem., Canadian Delegn, UN, 1965. *Recreations:* tennis, ski-ing. *Address:* House of Commons, Ottawa, Ontario K1A 0A6, Canada; (home) 2332 Georgina Drive, Ottawa, K2B 7M4, Canada. *Club:* Halifax (Halifax, NS).

REGINA, Archbishop of, (RC), since 1973; **Most Rev. Charles A. Halpin;** *b* 30 Aug. 1930; *s* of John S. Halpin and Marie Anne Gervais. *Educ:* St Boniface Coll. (BA); St Boniface Seminary (BTh); Gregorian Univ., Rome (JCL). Priest, 1956; Vice-Chancellor of Archdiocese of Winnipeg and Secretary to Archbishop, 1960; Officialis of Archdiocesan Matrimonial Tribunal, 1962; Chaplain to the Holy Father with title of Monsignor, 1969; ordained Bishop, Nov. 1973; installed as Archbishop of Regina, Dec. 1973. *Address:* 3225 13th Avenue, Regina, Saskatchewan S4T 1P5, Canada. *T:* (306) 352-1651.

REHNQUIST, Hon. William H.; Associate Justice, Supreme Court of the United States, since 1972; *b* 1 Oct. 1924; *s* of William Benjamin and Margery Peck Rehnquist; *m* 1953, Natalie Cornell; one *s* two *d*. *Educ:* Stanford and Harvard Univs. BA, MA 1948, LLB 1952, Stanford; MA Harvard 1949. Law Clerk for Mr Justice Robert H. Jackson, 1952-53; Partner, Phoenix, Ariz: Evans, Kitchell & Jenckes, 1953-55; Ragan & Rehnquist, 1956-57; Cunningham, Carson & Messenger, 1957-60; Powers & Rehnquist, 1960-69; Asst Attorney-Gen., Office of Legal Counsel, Dept of Justice, 1969-72. Phi Beta Kappa; Order of the Coif. *Publications:* contrib. US News and World Report, Jl of Amer. Bar Assoc., Arizona Law Review. *Recreations:* swimming, tennis, reading, hiking. *Address:* Supreme Court of the United States, Washington, DC 20543, USA. *Club:* National Lawyers (Washington, DC).

REICH, Peter Gordon, FRIN; Counsellor (Defence Research), Canberra, and Head of British Defence Research and Supply Staffs, Australia, since 1979; *b* 16 Sept. 1926; *s* of Douglas Gordon Reich and Josephine Grace Reich; *m* 1948, Kathleen, *d* of Alan and Florence Lessiter, Banstead; three *d*. *Educ:* Sutton Grammar Sch.; London Univ. (BSc). FRIN 1967 (Bronze Medal, 1967). Served RN, 1944-47. Entered Civil Service as Scientific Officer, 1952; Armament Res. Estab., 1952-54; Opl Res. Br., Min. of Transport and Civil Aviation, 1955-60; RAE, 1960-68; Asst Dir of Electronics Res. and Develt (2), Min. of Technol., 1968-70; Asst Dir of Res. (Avionics, Space and Air Traffic), Min. of Aviation Supply, 1971-73; Supt, Def. Opl Analysis Estab., MoD, 1973-76; Mem., Reliability and Costing Study Gp, MoD, 1976-79. *Publications:* papers in Jl of Inst. of Nav., and Jl of Opl Res. Soc. *Recreations:* racquet games, walking, aural pleasures. *Address:* c/o Foreign and Commonwealth Office, King Charles Street, SW1. *Club:* Commonwealth (Canberra).

REICHENBACH, Henry-Béat de F.; *see* de Fischer-Reichenbach.

REICHSTEIN, Prof. Tadeus, Dr ing chem; Ordentlicher Professor, Head of Department of Organic Chemistry, University of Basel, 1946-60, now Emeritus; *b* Wloclawek, Poland, 20 July 1897; *s* of Isidor Reichstein and Gustava Brockmann; *m* 1927, Henriette Louise Quarles van Ufford; two *d*. *Educ:* Oberrealschule and Eidgenössische Technische Hochschule, Department of Chemistry, Zürich. Assistant, ETH, Zürich, 1922-34; professor of organic chemistry, ETH, Zürich, 1934; head of department of pharmacy, University of Basel, 1938. Dr *hc* Sorbonne, Paris, 1947, Basel 1951, Geneva, 1967, ETH, Zürich, 1967, Abidjan 1967, London 1968, Leeds 1970. Marcel Benoit Prize, 1948; (jointly) Nobel Prize for Medicine, 1950; Cameron Prize, 1951; Copley Medal, Royal Soc., 1968; Dale Medal, Soc. for Endocrinology, 1975. Foreign Member: Royal Society, 1952; Linnean Society, 1974. Hon. Member: British Pteridological Soc., 1967; Amer. Fern Soc., 1974; Deutsche Botanische Gesellschaft, 1976; Schweizerische Botanische Gesellschaft, 1977. *Publications:* numerous papers. *Recreations:* botany (ferns), devoted gardener, mountain-climber. *Address:* Institut für Organische Chemie der Universität, St Johanns-Ring 19, CH 4056 Basel, Switzerland. *T:* (061) 576060.

REID, Sir Alexander (James), 3rd Bt *cr* 1897; JP; DL; *b* 6 Dec. 1932; *s* of Sir Edward James Reid, 2nd Bt, KBE, and of Tatiana, *d* of Col Alexander Fenoult, formerly of Russian Imperial Guard; *S* father, 1972; *m* 1955, Michaela Ann, *d* of Olaf Kier, *qv*; one *s* three *d*. *Educ:* Eton; Magdalene Coll., Cambridge. Nat. Certificate Agriculture (NCA). 2nd Lieut, 1st Bn Gordon Highlanders, 1951; served Malaya; Captain, 3rd Bn Gordon Highlanders (TA), retired 1964. Director: Ellon Castle Estates Co. Ltd, 1965-; Cristina Securities Ltd, 1970-; Quantock Veal Ltd, 1974-; Bellinger Bros Ltd, 1975-; Kingston Agricultural Services Ltd, 1977-. Governor, Heath Mount Prep. Sch., Hertford, 1970, Chm., 1976. JP Cambridgeshire and Isle of Ely, 1971, DL 1973. *Recreation:* shooting. *Heir: s* Charles Edward James Reid, *b* 24 June 1956. *Address:* Kingston Wood Manor, Arrington, Royston, Herts SG8 0AP. *T:* Caxton 231. *Clubs:* Farmers', Caledonian.

REID, Andrew Milton; Chairman, Imperial Tobacco Ltd, since 1979; *b* 21 July 1929; *s* of late Rev. A. R. R. Reid, DD and of Lilias Symington Tindal; *m* 1953, Norma Mackenzie Davidson; two *s*. *Educ:* Glasgow Academy; Jesus Coll., Oxford. Imperial Tobacco Management Pupil, 1952; Asst Managing Director, John Player & Sons, 1975; Director Imperial Group Ltd., 1978. Member, Tobacco Adv. Council, 1977-. *Recreations:* sailing, golf, fishing. *Address:* Parsonage Farm, Publow, Pensford, near Bristol BS18 4JD. *T:* Compton Dando 229. *Club:* Clifton (Bristol).

REID, Archibald Cameron, CMG 1963; CVO 1970; retired 1971; *b* 7 Aug. 1915; *s* of William Reid; *m* 1941, Joan Raymond Charlton; two *s* two *d*. *Educ:* Fettes; Queen's College, Cambridge. Apptd Admin. Officer, Class II, in Colony of Fiji, 1938; Admin. Officer, Class I, 1954; British Agent and Consul, Tonga, 1957-59; Sec. for Fijian Affairs, 1959-65; British Comr and Consul, Tonga, 1965-70; Dep. High Comr, Tonga, 1970-71. Engaged in Pacific History research. *Publications:* sundry articles. *Recreations:* walking, painting, golf. *Address:* 37 Kevin Avenue, Avalon Beach, NSW 2107, Australia. *T:* 918 6402.

REID, Beryl; actress; *b* 17 June 1920. *Educ:* Lady Barne House Sch.; Withington High Sch.; Levenshulme High Sch., Manchester. First stage appearance, Bridlington, 1936; on London stage, 1951; appeared in variety, numerous sketches, revues and pantomimes, 1951-64. *Plays:* The Killing of Sister George, Duke of York's, 1965, NY, 1966 (Tony Award for Best Actress); Blithe Spirit, Globe, 1970; Entertaining Mr Sloane, Royal Court, Duke of York's, 1975; National Theatre: Spring Awakening, Romeo and Juliet, 1974; Il Campiello, Counting the Ways, 1976; The Way of the World, RSC, Aldwych, 1978; Born in the Gardens, Bristol Old Vic, 1979, Globe (SWET Award), 1980. *Films include:* The Belles of St Trinians, Star, The Killing of Sister George, Entertaining Mr Sloane, No Sex Please—We're British!, Joseph Andrews, Carry On, Emmanuelle. Frequent television and radio performances, including her own series on several occasions. *Recreations:* gardening, cooking. *Address:* c/o Eric Braun Enterprises, 36 Michelham Gardens, Strawberry Hill, Twickenham TW1 4SB. *T:* 01-892 6795.

REID, Charles William, BSc (Econ); ASAA; *b* 29 May 1895; *s* of Charles and Ada Reid; *m* 1924, Gladys Ellen Edith Dudley; two *d*. *Educ:* Latymer Upper School; Holloway County School; University of London. War Office, 1914; Queen's Westminster Rifles, 1915-19 (served overseas, wounded twice). Exchequer and Audit Department, 1919-38; Exports Credit Guarantee Dept, 1938-39; Ministry of Supply, 1939-40; Ministry of Supply Mission, USA, 1940-46, Director of Requirements and Secretary-General; Ministry of Supply, Overseas Disposals, 1946-48; Dep. Financial Adviser. Control Commn, Germany, 1948-50; Min. of Works, Comptroller of Accounts, 1950-54; Under-Secretary for Finance, 1954-56; retired, 1956. Incorporated Accountant, 1926. Medal of Freedom (USA), 1947. *Recreations:* travel and sports. Athletics purple, Univ. of London; represented Great Britain in first athletics match with France, 1921. *Address:* Pynes, Edington, Bridgwater TA7 9LD. *T:* Chilton Polden 772320.

REID, Desmond Arthur; *b* 6 Feb. 1918; *s* of late Col Percy Lester Reid, CBE, DL, and late Mrs Katharine Marjorie Elizabeth Reid; *m* 1939, Anne, *d* of late Major J. B. Paget and late Mrs J. B. Paget, London SW7; one *s*. *Educ:* Eton. Joined Lloyd's, 1936, Member 1939. SRO, Irish Guards, 1939 (wounded in Normandy, 1944; Major). Returned Lloyd's, 1946. Chairman: R. K. Harrison & Co. Ltd, 1947-; Yeoman Investment Trust Ltd, 1956-; Young Companies Investment Trust Ltd, 1972-; Prudential Portfolio Management Ltd, 1975-81; Prudential Pensions Ltd, 1975- (Dir, 1970); Director: Prudential Assurance Co. Ltd, 1960-81; Drayton Premier Investment Trust Ltd, 1972-; Edger Investments Ltd, 1965-; Estate Duties Investment Trust Ltd, 1971-; General Consolidated Investment Trust Ltd, 1964- (Dep. Chm., 1978-); London & St Lawrence Investment Co. Ltd, 1956-; Moorgate Investment Co. Ltd, 1960- (Dep. Chm., 1978-); Practical Investment Co. Ltd, 1948-; Prudential Corp. Ltd, 1979-; Selection Croissance, 1970-; Pan Holding SA, 1975-; Managing Trustee, Irish Guards Common Investment Fund, 1970-. Member: Lloyd's Investment Cttee, 1971- (Chm. 1974-); Cttee of Ottoman Bank, London, 1979- (Chm. 1982-). Governor: Royal Ballet, 1973-; Royal Ballet School, 1974-. Councillor, Chelsea Bor. Council, 1945-52 (Chm. Finance Cttee, 1950-52). Chm., Inst. of Obstetrics and Gynæcology; Vice-Pres., Insurance Inst. of London; Mem., The Livery of Merchant Taylors. *Recreations:*

shooting, gardening, ballet. *Address:* 3 Belgrave Place, SW1. *T:* 01-235 6507; Burmans, Ripe, Sussex. *T:* Ripe 271. *Clubs:* White's, City of London (Chm., 1977), MCC; Travellers' (Paris).
See also Col P. F. Reid.

REID, Dougal Gordon; HM Diplomatic Service; Ambassador to Liberia, since 1980; *b* 31 Dec. 1925; *e s* of late Douglas Reid and Catherine Jean (*née* Lowson); *m* 1950, Georgina Elizabeth Johnston; one *s* (and one *s* decd). *Educ:* Sedbergh Sch.; Trinity Hall, Cambridge; LSE. Served in Royal Marines, 1944-46. Cadet, Colonial Admin. Service (later HMOCS), Sierra Leone, 1949; District Comr 1956; retd as Perm. Sec., Min. of Natural Resources, 1962. Arthur Guinness Son & Co. Ltd, 1962-63. Entered CRO, 1963; 1st Sec., Accra, 1964-65; Commonwealth Office, 1966; Accra, 1966-68 (concurrently Lomé, 1967-68); Seoul, 1968-71; FCO, 1971-74; Counsellor (Commercial) and Consul-General, Kinshasa (and concurrently at Brazzaville, Bujumbura and Kigali), 1974-77; Counsellor, New Delhi, 1977-78; Counsellor (Economic and Commercial), Singapore, 1979-80. *Recreations:* golf, music, watching sport. *Address:* c/o Foreign and Commonwealth Office, SW1A 2AL. *Clubs:* Travellers', Royal Commonwealth Society, MCC.

REID, George Newlands; freelance broadcaster and journalist since 1972; presenter of political and documentary programmes for BBC; *b* 4 June 1939; *s* of late George Reid, company director, and of Margaret Forsyth; *m* 1968, Daphne Ann MacColl; two *d*. *Educ:* Tullibody Sch.; Dollar Academy; Univ. of St Andrews (MA Hons). Pres., Students' Representative Council. Features Writer, Scottish Daily Express, 1962; Reporter, Scottish Television, 1964; Producer, Granada Television, 1965; Head of News and Current Affairs (Scottish Television), 1968. MP (SNP) Stirlingshire E and Clackmannan, Feb. 1974-1979; Member, Select Committee on: Assistance to Private Members, 1975-76; Direct Elections to European Assembly, 1976-77; Mem., British Parly Delegn to Council of Europe and WEU, 1977-79. Dir, Scottish Council Res. Inst., 1974-77. *Address:* 21 Hamilton Drive, Glasgow G12 8DN.

REID, Hon. Sir George Oswald, Kt 1972; QC (Vic) 1971; Attorney-General, Victoria, Australia, 1967-73; Barrister and Solicitor; *b* Hawthorn, Vic, 22 July 1903; *s* of late George Watson Reid and Lillias Margaret Reid (*née* Easton); *m* 1st, 1930, Beatrix Waring McCay, LLM (*d* 1972), *d* of Lt-Gen. Hon. Sir James McCay; one *d*; 2nd, 1973, Dorothy, *d* of late C. W. F. Ruttledge. *Educ:* Camberwell Grammar Sch. and Scotch Coll., Melbourne; Melbourne Univ. (LLB). Admitted to practice as Barrister and Solicitor, Supreme Ct of Vic., 1926. Has practised as Solicitor in Melbourne, 1929-. Served War, RAAF, 1940-46, Wing Comdr. MLA (Liberal) for Box Hill, 1947-52, and 1955-73. Government of Victoria: Minister without Portfolio, 1955-56; Minister of Labour and Industry and Electrical Undertakings, 1956-65; Minister: for Fuel and Power, 1965-67; of Immigration, 1967-70; Chief Secretary, March 9-Apr. 27, 1971. *Recreations:* bowls, golf, reading. *Address:* Nilja, Alexander Road, Warrandyte, Vic 3113, Australia. *Clubs:* Melbourne, Savage, Melbourne Cricket (Melbourne); Royal Automobile (Victoria).

REID, Air Vice-Marshal Sir (George) Ranald Macfarlane, KCB 1945 (CB 1941); DSO 1919; MC and bar; Extra Gentleman Usher to the Queen, 1959; Gentleman Usher to the Queen, 1952 (formerly to King George VI, 1952); *b* 25 Oct. 1893; *s* of late George Macfarlane Reid and Gertrude Macquisten, Prestwick; *m* 1934, Leslie Livermore Washburne, *d* of late Hamilton Wright, Washington, DC, USA, and *g d* of Senator William Washburne; one *s* one *d*. *Educ:* Routenburn; Malvern Coll. Regular Officer, 1914-46 in: 4th (SR) Argyll and Sutherland Highlanders; 2nd Black Watch; RFC and RAF. Served European War, 1914-18 (wounded, despatches, MC and Bar, DSO); Egypt, 1919-21; Sudan, 1927-29; RAF Staff Coll., 1930; Imperial Defence Coll., 1932; Air Attaché, British Embassy, Washington, 1933-35; AOC Halton, 1936-38; Air Officer Commanding British Forces, Aden, 1938-41; Air Officer Administration Flying Training Command; AOC 54 Group; AOC West Africa, 1944-45; retired from Royal Air Force, 1946. *Address:* 31 Sussex Square, Brighton. *Clubs:* Royal Air Force; Weld (Perth, Western Australia).

REID, George Smith; retired; Sheriff (formerly Sheriff-Substitute) of Ayr and Bute, later South Strathclyde, Dumfries and Galloway, at Ayr, 1948-76; *b* 29 Feb. 1904; *yr s* of John Mitchell Reid, manufacturer, Glasgow; *m* 1935, Marion Liddell Boyd; two *s* two *d*. *Educ:* Hutchesons' Grammar School, Glasgow; Glasgow University. MA 1925, LLB 1927. Called to Scottish Bar, 1935. *Recreation:* swimming. *Address:* 10 Wheatfield Road, Ayr. *T:* 67858.

REID, Very Rev. George Thomson Henderson, MC 1945; Chaplain to the Queen in Scotland, 1969-80, Extra Chaplain since 1980; *b* 31 March 1910; *s* of Rev. David Reid, DD; *m* 1938, Anne Guilland Watt, *d* of late Principal Very Rev. Hugh Watt, DD, Edinburgh; three *s* one *d*. *Educ:* George Watson's Boys' Coll.; Univ. of Edinburgh. MA 1932, BD 1935, Edinburgh. Served as Chaplain to 3rd Bn Scots Guards, 1940-45, Sen. Chaplain to 15th (S) Div., 1945. Minister at: Port Seton, E Lothian, 1935-38; Juniper Green, Edinburgh, 1938-49; Claremont Church, Glasgow, 1949-55; West Church of St Andrew, Aberdeen, 1955-75. Moderator of the General Assembly of the Church of Scotland, 1973-74. Hon. DD Aberdeen, 1969. *Recreations:* golf, bird-watching, painting. *Address:* 33 Westgarth Avenue, Colinton, Edinburgh.
See also Prof. J. K. S. Reid.

REID, Graham Livingstone; Director of Manpower Intelligence and Planning, Manpower Services Commission, since 1975; b 30 June 1937; s of late William L. Reid and of Louise M. Reid; m 1973, Eileen M. Loudfoot. *Educ:* Univ. of St Andrews (MA); Queen's Univ., Kingston, Canada (MA). Dept of Social and Economic Res., Univ. of Glasgow: Asst Lectr in Applied Economics, 1960, Lectr 1963, Sen. Lectr 1968, Reader 1971; Sen. Econ. Adviser and Head of Econs and Statistics Unit, Scottish Office, 1973. Vis. Associate Prof., Mich State Univ., 1967; Vis. Res. Fellow, Queen's Univ., Canada, 1969. *Publications:* Fringe Benefits, Labour Costs and Social Security (ed with D. J. Robertson), 1965; (with K. J. Allen) Nationalised Industries, 1970 (3rd edn 1975); (with L. C. Hunter and D. Boddy) Labour Problems of Technological Change, 1970; (with K. J. Allen and D. J. Harris) The Nationalised Fuel Industries, 1973; contrib. to Econ. Jl, Brit. Jl of Indust. Relations, Scot. Jl of Polit. Econ., Indust & Lab. Relns Rev. *Recreations:* golf, music. *Address:* 15 Allison Grove, SE21 7ER. *T:* 01-693 8252. *Club:* Royal Commonwealth Society.

REID, (Harold) Martin (Smith), CMG 1978; HM Diplomatic Service; Minister, British Embassy, Pretoria/Cape Town, since 1979; b 27 Aug. 1928; s of late Marcus Reid and late Winifred Mary Reid (née Stephens); m 1956, Jane Elizabeth Harwood; one s three d. *Educ:* Merchant Taylors' Sch.; Brasenose Coll., Oxford (Open Scholar). RN, 1947-49. Entered HM Foreign Service, 1953; served in: FO, 1953-54; Paris, 1954-57; Rangoon, 1958-61; FO, 1961-65; Georgetown, 1965-68; Bucharest, 1968-70; Dep. High Comr, Malawi, 1970-73; Private Sec. to successive Secs of State for NI, 1973-74; Head of Central and Southern Africa Dept, FCO, 1974-78. *Recreations:* painting and drawing; chess. *Address:* c/o Foreign and Commonwealth Office, SW1.
See also M. H. M. Reid.

REID, Sir Hugh, 3rd Bt cr 1922; farmer; b 27 Nov. 1933; s of Sir Douglas Neilson Reid, 2nd Bt, and of Margaret Brighton Young, d of Robert Young Maxtone, MBE, JP, S father, 1971. *Educ:* Loretto. Royal Air Force, 1952-56; RAFVR, 1956-78 (Flying Officer, Training Branch, 1965-78). *Recreations:* skiing, travel. *Heir:* none.

REID, Ian George; Director, Centre for European Agricultural Studies, Wye College, University of London, since 1974; b 12 May 1921; 2nd s of James John Reid and Margaret Jane Reid; m 1946, Peggy Eileen Bridgman. *Educ:* Merchant Taylors' Sch.; London Sch. of Econs (BScEcon); Christ's Coll., Cambridge (Dip. Agric.). Lectr, Reading Univ., 1945-53; Lectr, 1953-63, and Sen. Lectr, 1963-, Wye Coll. Pres., Agricultural Econs Soc., 1981-82. *Recreations:* enjoying music, gardening, art. *Address:* 20 Bridge Street, Wye, Ashford, Kent TN25 5EA. *T:* Wye (Kent) 812388. *Clubs:* Athenæum, Farmers'.

REID, Col Ivo; *see* Reid, Col P. F. I.

REID, James, OBE (mil.) 1968; VRD 1967; Director, Investments and Loans, Commission of European Communities, 1973-76; b 23 Nov. 1921; s of William Reid, MBE, and Dora Louisa Reid (née Smith); m 1949, Margaret James; two d. *Educ:* City of London Sch.; Emmanuel Coll., Cambridge (MA). Served War, RN: RNVR (Sub. Lieut), 1942-45. Served RNVR and RNR (Comdr), 1953-72. Entered Northern Ireland Civil Service, 1948 (Asst Principal); Min. of Finance, 1948-61 and 1963-73; Min. of Commerce, 1961-63; Principal, 1953; Asst Sec., 1963; Sen. Asst Sec., 1971; Dep. Sec., 1972. *Recreations:* reading, music. *Address:* 6 Avenue Guillaume, Luxembourg. *Club:* United Oxford & Cambridge University.

REID, James Robert, QC 1980; b 23 Jan. 1943; s of His Honour Judge J. A. Reid, MC and Jean Ethel Reid; m 1974, Anne Prudence Wakefield; two s one d. *Educ:* Marlborough Coll.; New Coll., Oxford (MA). Called to the Bar, Lincoln's Inn, 1965. *Recreations:* fencing, cricket. *Address:* 9 Old Square, Lincoln's Inn, WC2.

REID, John, CB 1967; Chief Veterinary Officer, Ministry of Agriculture, Fisheries and Food, 1965-70; b 14 May 1906; s of late John and Jessie Jamieson Reid, Callander, Perthshire; m 1933, Molly Russell; one d. *Educ:* McLaren High Sch., Callander; Royal (Dick) Veterinary Coll., Edinburgh. FRCVS 1971; DVSM 1931. Asst Veterinary Officer, Midlothian County Council, 1931; Asst Veterinary Officer, Cumberland County Council, 1932; Ministry of Agriculture and Fisheries: Divisional Veterinary Officer, 1938; Superintending Veterinary Officer, 1952; Ministry of Agriculture, Fisheries and Food: Regional Veterinary Officer, 1958; Deputy Chief Veterinary Officer, 1960; Director of Veterinary Field Services, 1963. Mem. ARC, 1965-70. Vice-Chm., FAO European Commn for Control of Foot-and-Mouth Disease, 1967-70; Member: Cttee of Inquiry into Veterinary Profession, 1971-75; Scientific Authority for Animals, DoE, 1976-77. *Recreations:* gardening, bird watching. *Address:* Owl's Green Cottage, Dennington, Woodbridge, Suffolk IP13 8BY. *T:* Badingham 205. *Club:* Farmers'.

REID, Dr John James Andrew, CB 1975; TD; MD, FRCP, FRCPE; Chief Medical Officer, Scottish Home and Health Department, since 1977; Hon. Consultant in Community Medicine to the Army, since 1971; b 21 Jan. 1925; s of Alexander Scott Reid and Mary Cullen Reid (née Andrew); m 1949, Marjorie Reid (née Crumpton), MB, ChB; one s four d. *Educ:* Bell-Baxter Sch.; Univ. of St Andrews. BSc 1944; MB, ChB 1947; DPH 1952; MD 1961;

Hon. DSc 1979; FRCP (Edin.) 1970; FRCP 1971; FFCM 1972. Lt-Col RAMC (TA). Hospital, Army (Nat. Service) and junior Public Health posts, 1947-55; Lectr in Public Health and Social Medicine, Univ. of St Andrews, 1955-59; Dep. County MOH, Northamptonshire, 1959-62; County MOH, Northamptonshire, 1962-67; County MOH, Buckinghamshire, 1967-72; Dep. Chief MO, DHSS, 1972-77. Member: GMC (Crown Nominee), 1973-81; Council for Post-grad. Med. Educn, 1973-77; Scottish Council for Post-grad. Med. Educn, 1977-; Scottish Health Service Planning Council, 1977-; Exec. Bd, WHO, 1973-75, 1976-79, 1980- (Vice Chm., 1977-78; Chm., 1978-79); MRC, 1977-. Formerly: WHO Fellow; Mem., Standing Med. Adv. Cttee, DHSS; Chm., Jt Sub-Cttee on Health and Welfare Services for People with Epilepsy; Vice-Chm. of Council, Queen's Inst. of District Nursing; Mem., Working Party on Medical Administrators. Vis. Prof. in Health Services Admin, London Sch. of Hygiene and Tropical Medicine, 1973-78. FRCPS (Hon.) 1980. *Publications:* papers on medical care, public health, diabetes, epilepsy, etc, in BMJ, Lancet, etc. *Address:* St Andrew's House, Edinburgh EH1 3DE.

REID, John Kelman Sutherland, CBE 1970; TD 1961; Professor of Christian Dogmatics, 1961-70, of Systematic Theology 1970-76, University of Aberdeen; b 31 March 1910; y s of late Reverend Dr David Reid, Calcutta and Leith, and of late Mrs G. T. Reid (née Stuart); m 1950, Margaret Winifrid Brookes. *Educ:* George Watson's Boys' College, Edinburgh; Universities of Edinburgh (MA and BD), Heidelberg, Marburg, Basel, and Strasbourg. MA 1st Cl. Hons Philosophy, 1933. Prof. of Philosophy in Scottish Church Coll., Univ. of Calcutta, 1935-37; BD (dist. in Theol.), 1938, and Cunningham Fellow. Ordained into Church of Scotland and inducted into Parish of Craigmillar Park, Edinburgh, 1939. CF, chiefly with Parachute Regt, 1942-46. Jt Ed. Scot. Jl Theol. since inception, 1947; Hon. Sec. Jt Cttee on New Translation of the Bible, 1949-; Prof. of Theology and Head of Department of Theology, University of Leeds, 1952-61. Hon. DD (Edinburgh), 1957. *Publications:* The Authority of Scripture, 1957; Our Life in Christ, 1963; Christian Apologetics, 1969. Translation of: Oscar Cullmann's The Earliest Christian Confessions, 1949; Baptism in the New Testament, 1952; Calvin's Theological Treatises, ed and trans. 1954; Jean Bosc's The Kingly Office of the Lord Jesus Christ, 1959; Calvin's Concerning the Eternal Pre-destination of God, ed and trans., 1961. *Address:* 1 Camus Park, Fairmilehead, Edinburgh. *Club:* Mortonhall Golf (Edinburgh).
See also Very Rev. G. T. H. Reid.

REID, Prof. John Low, DM; Regius Professor of Materia Medica, University of Glasgow, since 1978; b 1 Oct. 1943; s of Dr James Reid and Irene M. Dale; m 1964, Randa Pharaon; one s one d. *Educ:* Fettes Coll., Edinburgh; Magdalen Coll., Oxford. MA; DM; FRCP. House Officer, Radcliffe Infirmary, Oxford, and Brompton Hosp., 1967-70; Res. Fellow, RPMS, 1970-73; Vis. Fellow, Nat. Inst. of Mental Health, USA, 1973-74; Royal Postgraduate Medical School: Sen. Lectr in Clin. Pharmacol., and Consultant Physician, 1975-77; Reader in Clin. Pharmacol., 1977-78. *Publications:* Central Action of Drugs in Regulation of Blood Pressure, 1975; Lecture Notes in Clinical Pharmacology, 1982; papers on cardiovascular and neurological diseases in clinical and pharmacological journals. *Recreations:* books, gardening, jogging. *Address:* Department of Materia Medica, Stobhill General Hospital, Glasgow G21 3UW. *T:* 041-558 0111.

REID, Rt. Rev. John Robert; Assistant Bishop, Diocese of Sydney, NSW, since 1972; b 15 July 1928; s of John and Edna Reid; m 1955, Alison Gertrude Dunn; two s four d. *Educ:* Melbourne Univ. (BA); Moore Coll., Sydney (ThL). Deacon 1955, Priest 1955; Curate, Manly, 1955-56; Rector, Christ Church, Gladesville, NSW, 1956-69; Archdeacon of Cumberland, NSW, 1969-72. *Recreation:* walking. *Address:* 33 Fairfax Road, Bellevue Hill, NSW 2023, Australia. *T:* 36-3320.

REID, John (Robson); architect and consultant designer; Partner, John and Sylvia Reid, since 1951; Pageantmaster to the Lord Mayors of London, since 1972; b 1 Dec. 1925; s of late Thomas Robson Reid and Olive Reid; m 1948, Sylvia Reid (née Payne), Dip. Arch., RIBA, FSIAD; one s twin d. *Educ:* Wellingborough Grammar Sch.; Sch. of Architecture, The Polytechnic, WI (Dip. in Architecture with dist.). RIBA, FSIAD, FCIBS. Capt., Green Howards, 1944-47; Mem. HAC, 1980. *Architectural work includes:* hotels, showrooms, museums, houses and pubs: Civic Suite, Wandsworth Town Hall; Savile Room, Merton Coll., Oxford; Great Room, Grosvenor House; Dunhill Res. Lab., Inst. of Dermatology; Westminster Theatre; Lawson House, ICI, Runcorn; Heatherside Shopping Centre; Savoy Grill; Exec. Suite, British Telecoms HQ; Barbican Exhibition Halls, Corporation of City of London; *industrial design work includes:* furniture, lighting fittings, road and rail transport, carpets, textiles, civic regalia; lighting consultant for Coventry Cathedral; some-time design consultant to Thorn, Rotaflex, Stag, CMC, BR, N General Transport, PO; UNIDO consultant on industrial design in India, Pakistan, Egypt and Turkey, 1977-79. *Exhibitions:* 350th Anniversary Celebration, Jamestown, Virginia, USA, 1957; various exhibns for BR, Cardiff Corp., City of London, etc. Leader, British delegn of design educn in Soviet Union, Anglo-Soviet Cultural Exchange Treaty, 1967. Dean of Art and Design, Middx Polytechnic, 1975-78; some-time mem. of adv. cttees, Central Sch. of Art and Design, Leeds Coll. of Art and Design, Newcastle-upon-Tyne Sch. of Art and Design, Carleton Univ., Ottawa; Governor, Hornsey Coll. of Art. Lectured in Canada, Czechoslovakia, Eire, Hungary, Japan, Poland, USA, USSR. PSIAD, 1965-66; Pres., Internat. Council of Socs of Ind. Design, 1969-71; Vice-Pres., Illuminating Engrg Soc., 1969-71. RIBA

Mem., Bd of Nat. Inspection Council for Electrical Installation Contracting (Chm., 1972-73). Liveryman and Mem. Court of Assts, Worshipful Co. of Furniture Makers. Four CoID Awards; Silver Medals of 12th and 13th Milan Internat. Triennales. *Publications:* International Code of Professional Conduct, 1969; A Guide to Conditions of Contract for Industrial Design, 1971; Industrial Design in India, Pakistan, Egypt and Turkey, 1978; various articles in professional jls. *Recreations:* music, dinghy-sailing, gardening. *Address:* Arnoside House, The Green, Old Southgate, N14 7EG. *T:* 01-882 1083. *Clubs:* City Livery, Wig and Pen.

REID, Sir John (Thyne), Kt 1974; CMG 1971; *b* 15 Oct. 1903; *s* of Andrew Reid and Margaret (*née* Thyne), both born in Scotland; *m* 1929, Gladys Violet Boyd Scott, Glasgow; one *s* three *d*. *Educ:* King's Sch., Parramatta, NSW; Edinburgh Academy, Scotland. Mem., 1961-72, Vice-Chm., 1968-72, Australian Broadcasting Commn. Formerly Mem. Council, Victorian Coll. of the Arts. Hon. LLD Melbourne, 1977; Hon. DASc VIC, 1977. *Recreation:* bowls. *Address:* 4 St George's Court, 290 Cotham Road, Kew, Vic 3101, Australia. *T:* 80 4759. *Clubs:* Caledonian (London); Melbourne; Australian (Melbourne and Sydney); Rotary (Melbourne).

REID, Leslie, CBE 1978; HM Diplomatic Service, retired; Director General, The Association of British Mining Equipment Companies, since 1980; *b* 24 May 1919; *s* of late Frederick Sharples and Mary Reid; *m* 1942, Norah Moorcroft; three *d*. *Educ:* King George V Sch., Southport, Lancs. Served War of 1939-45, W Europe and SEAC, Major, XX The Lancashire Fusiliers. Board of Trade, 1947-49; Asst Trade Commissioner: Salisbury, Rhodesia, 1949-55; Edmonton, Alberta, 1955-56; Trade Comr, Vancouver, 1956-60; Principal, BoT, 1960-62; Trade Comr and Economic Advisor, British High Commn, Cyprus, 1962-64; BoT, 1964-66; 1st Sec., FCO, 1966-68; Sen. Commercial Sec., British High Commn, Jamaica, and 1st Sec., British Embassy, Port-au-Prince, Haiti, 1968-70; Commercial and Economic Counsellor, Ghana, 1970-73; Consul Gen., Cleveland, Ohio, 1973-79. *Recreations:* golf, reading, hill-walking. *Address:* Abbotswood, Guildford, Surrey GU1 1UY.

REID, Louis Arnaud, MA, PhD, DLitt; Professor Emeritus of Philosophy of Education, Institute of Education, London University (Professor 1947-62); *b* Ellon, Aberdeenshire; *s* of late Rev. A. H. Reid and late Margaret C. Miller; *m* 1920, Gladys Kate, *y d* of late W. H. Bignold; two *s*; *m* 1957, Frances Mary Holt, *d* of Denys Horton; two *step d*. *Educ:* Aberdeen Grammar School; Leys Sch., Camb.; University of Edinburgh. Studied engineering, 1913; RE 1914; discharged, 1915; 1st Cl. Hons in Mental Philosophy, 1919; medallist, English Essays; University verse prizeman; Cousin prizeman in Fine Art; medallist in Moral Philosophy; Bruce of Grangehill and Falkland prizeman in Advanced Metaphysics; Vans Dunlop scholar in Moral Philosophy; Lord Rector's prizeman; Hamilton Philosophical Fellow; Mrs Foster Watson Memorial Prizeman; Lecturer in Philosophy in University College, Aberystwyth, 1919-26; Visiting Professor Stanford University, California, 1927; Independent Lecturer in Philosophy University of Liverpool, 1926-32; Prof. of Philosophy Armstrong Coll. (now Univ. of Newcastle upon Tyne), 1932-47. Visiting Prof., Univ. of British Columbia, 1951; Vis. Prof. of Philosophy, Univ. of Oregon, 1962-63; Vis. Prof., Chinese Univ. of Hong Kong, 1966-67. Ext. Examiner, Univs of Liverpool, Sheffield, Leeds, Edinburgh, Aberdeen, Glasgow, London, Warwick, Leicester, W Indies, Hong Kong. Pres., Philosophy of Educn Soc. of GB. *Publications:* Knowledge and Truth, An Epistemological Essay, 1923; A Study in Aesthetics, 1931; Creative Morality, 1936; Preface to Faith, 1939; The Rediscovery of Belief, 1945; Ways of Knowledge and Experience, 1960; Philosophy and Education, 1961; Meaning in the Arts, 1970; articles in Mind, Hibbert, Procs of Aristotelian Soc., Philosophy, British Jl of Aesthetics, Amer. Jl of Aesthetics Educn, TES, etc. *Address:* 50 Rotherwick Road, NW11. *T:* 01-455 6850. *Clubs:* Athenæum, PEN.

REID, Prof. Lynne McArthur; S. Burt Wolbach Professor of Pathology, Harvard Medical School, since 1976; Chairman, Department of Pathology, Children's Hospital Medical Center, Boston, since 1976; *b* Melbourne, 12 Nov. 1923; *er d* of Robert Muir Reid and Violet Annie Reid (*née* McArthur). *Educ:* Wimbledon Girls' Sch. (GPDST); Janet Clarke Hall, Trinity Coll., Melbourne Univ.; Royal Melbourne Hosp. MB, BS Melb. 1946; MRACP 1950; MRCP 1951; FRACP, MRCPath (Foundn Mem.) 1964; FRCPath 1966; FRCP 1969; MD Melb. 1969. House Staff, Royal Melb. Hosp., 1946-49; Res. Fellow, Nat. Health and MRC, Royal Melb. Hosp. and Eliza Hall, 1949-51; Res. Asst, Inst. Diseases of Chest, 1951-55; Sen. Lectr founding Res. Dept of Path., Inst. Diseases of Chest, 1955; Reader in Exper. Path., London Univ., 1964; Prof. of Exper. Path., Inst. of Diseases of Chest (later Cardiothoracic Inst.), 1967-76; Hon. Lectr, UC Med. Sch., 1971-76; Hon. Consultant in Exper. Path., Brompton Hosp., 1963-76; Dean, Cardiothoracic Inst. (British Postgrad. Med. Fedn), 1973-76. 1st Hastings Vis. Prof. in Path., Univ. of California, 1965; Holme Lectr, UC Med. Sch., 1969; Walker-Ames Prof., Univ. of Washington, 1971; Neuhauser Lectr, 1976; Fleischner Lectr, 1976; Waring Prof., Stanford and Denver, 1977; Amberson Lectr, Amer. Thoracic Soc., 1978. Mem. Fleischner Soc., 1971 (Pres., 1977); 1st Hon. Fellow, Canadian Thoracic Soc., 1973; Chm., Cystic Fibrosis Res. Trust, 1974 (Mem. Med. Adv. Cttee 1964); Royal Soc. Medicine (Sect. Pathology): Vice-Pres. 1974; Standing Liaison Cttee on Sci. Aspects of Smoking and Health, 1971; Commn of European Cttees (Industrial Safety and Medicine), 1972; Mem. Bd of Governors, Nat. Heart and Chest Hosps, 1974; Manager, Royal Instn of Gt Britain, 1973 (Vice-Pres. 1974); Mem. Gov. Body, British Postgrad. Med. Fedn, 1974. *Publications:* The Pathology of Emphysema, 1967;

numerous papers in sci. jls. *Recreations:* music, travel, reading. *Address:* 75 Montrose Court, Princes Gate, SW7; Children's Hospital Medical Center, Harvard Medical School, 300 Longwood Avenue, Boston, Mass 02115, USA. *Club:* University Women's.

REID, Malcolm Herbert Marcus; Under Secretary, Department of Trade, since 1978; *b* 2 March 1927; *s* of late Marcus Reid and Winifred Stephens; *m* 1st, 1956, Eleanor (*d* 1974), *d* of late H. G. Evans, MC; four *s*; 2nd, 1975, Daphne, *e d* of Sir John Griffin, *qv. Educ:* Merchant Taylors' Sch.; St John's Coll., Oxford. Served in Navy, 1945-48 and in RNVR, 1949-53. Entered Board of Trade, 1951; Private Secretary to Permanent Secretary, 1954-57; Trade Comr in Ottawa, 1957-60; Board of Trade, 1960-63; Private Secretary to successive Prime Ministers, 1963-66; Commercial Counsellor, Madrid, 1967-71; Asst Sec., DTI, 1972-74; Under Sec., DoI, 1974-78. *Recreation:* National Hunt racing. *Address:* 71 Thurleigh Road, SW12 8TZ. *T:* 01-675 1172; Collins Cottage, Duton Hill, Essex. *T:* Great Easton 462. *Club:* United Oxford & Cambridge University.

See also H. M. S. Reid.

REID, Martin; *see* Reid, H. M. S.

REID, Sir Norman (Robert), Kt 1970; DA (Edinburgh); FMA; FIIC; Director, the Tate Gallery, 1964-79; *b* 27 December 1915; *o s* of Edward Daniel Reid and Blanche, *d* of Richard Drouet; *m* 1941, Jean Lindsay Bertram; one *s* one *d*. *Educ:* Wilson's Grammar School; Edinburgh Coll. of Art; Edinburgh Univ. Served War of 1939-46, Major, Argyll and Sutherland Highlanders. Joined staff of Tate Gallery, 1946; Deputy Director, 1954; Keeper, 1959. Fellow, International Institute for Conservation (IIC) (Secretary General, 1963-65; Vice-Chm., 1966); British Rep. Internat. Committee on Museums and Galleries of Modern Art, 1963-79; President, Penwith Society of Arts; Member: Council, Friends of the Tate Gall., 1958-79 (Founder Mem.); Arts Council Art Panel, 1964-74; Inst. of Contemporary Arts Adv. Panel, 1965-; Contemporary Art Soc. Cttee, 1965-72, 1973-77; "Paintings in Hospitals" Adv. Cttee, 1965-69; British Council Fine Arts Cttee, 1965-77 (Chm. 1968-75); Culture Adv. Cttee of UK Nat. Commn for Unesco, 1966-70; Univ. of London, Bd of Studies in History of Art, 1968; Cttee, The Rome Centre, 1969-77 (Pres. 1975-77); Adv. Council, Paul Mellon Centre, 1971-78; Council of Management, Inst. of Contemp. Prints, 1972-78; Council, RCA, 1974-77. Mem. Bd, Burlington Magazine, 1971-75. Trustee, Graham and Kathleen Sutherland Foundn, 1980-. Hon. LittD East Anglia, 1970. Officer of the Mexican Order of the Aztec Eagle. *Address:* 50 Brabourne Rise, Park Langley, Beckenham, Kent.

REID, Patrick Robert, MBE 1940; MC 1943; Managing Director, Kem Estates Ltd; *b* 13 Nov. 1910; *s* of John Reid, CIE, ICS, and Alice Mabel Daniell; *m* 1943, Jane Cabot (marr. diss. 1966); three *s* two *d*; *m* 1977, Mrs Mary Stewart Cunliffe-Lister (*d* 1978). *Educ:* Clongowes Wood College, Co. Kildare; Wimbledon College; King's College, London University. BSc (London) 1932; AMICE, 1936; Pupilage, Sir Alex Gibb & Partners, 1934-37. Served War of 1939-45, BEF, France, Capt. RASC 2nd Div., Ammunition Officer, 1939-40; POW Germany, 1940-42; Asst Mil. Attaché, Berne, 1943-46; First Sec. (Commercial), British Embassy, Ankara, 1946-49; Chief Administrator, OEEC, Paris, 1949-52. Prospective Parly Candidate (C) Dartford and Erith, 1953-55. Director, Richard Costain (Projects) Ltd, 1959-62; Dir, Richard Costain (Middle East) Ltd, 1959-62. W. S. Atkins & Partners, Consulting Engineers, 1962-63. *Publications:* The Colditz Story, 1953; The Latter Days, 1955 (omnibus edn of the two, as Colditz, 1962, televised as The Colditz Story, BBC, 1973-74); (with Sir Olaf Caroe and Sir Thomas Rapp) From Nile to Indus, 1960; Winged Diplomat, 1962; Economic Survey Northern Nigeria, 1962; My Favourite Escape Stories, 1975. *Recreations:* ski-ing, yachting, gardening. *Address:* The Well House, Eastbourne Road, Uckfield, East Sussex. *Club:* Lansdowne.

REID, Col (Percy Fergus) Ivo, OBE 1953; DL; *b* 2 Nov. 1911; *er s* of Col Percy Lester Reid, CBE, DL, JP; *m* 1940, Mary Armida, *d* of Col James Douglas Macindoe, MC; two *s* one *d*. *Educ:* Stowe; Pembroke Coll., Oxford. Joined Irish Guards, 1933; Egypt, 1936-38; served in 2nd World War, Guards Armd Div., Europe (Despatches); Staff Coll., 1945; Comdt, Guards Depot, 1950-53; Lt Col 1951; comd Irish Guards and Regt District, 1955-59; Col 1955; retd 1959. Mem., HM Bodyguard of Hon. Corps of Gentlemen at Arms, 1961-81; Harbinger, 1979-81. Northamptonshire: High Sheriff 1967; DL 1969. *Recreations:* hunting, shooting. *Address:* Hill House, Somerton, Oxford OX5 4LR. *T:* Fritwell 210. *Club:* White's.

See also D. A. Reid.

REID, Maj.-Gen. Peter Daer, CB 1981; Director, Armoured Warfare Studies, 1981; *b* 5 Aug. 1925; *s* of Col S. D. Reid and Dorothy Hungerford (*née* Jackson); *m* 1958, Catherine Fleetwood (*née* Boodle); two *s* two *d*. *Educ:* Cheltenham College; Wadham Coll., Oxford. Commissioned into Coldstream Guards, 1945; transferred Royal Dragoons, 1947; served: Germany, Egypt, Malaya, Gibraltar, Morocco; Staff Coll., 1959; Comdg Officer, The Royal Dragoons, 1965-68; student, Royal College of Defence Studies, 1973; Commander RAC, 3rd Div., 1974-76; Dir, RAC, 1976-78; Chief Exec., Main Battle Tank 80 Proj., 1979-80. Cdre, ASA. *Recreations:* sailing, skiing, fishing, bird watching. *Address:* The Border House, Cholderton, near Salisbury, Wilts. *Clubs:* Army and Navy; Royal Western Yacht; Kandahar Ski.

REID, Philip; *see under* Ingrams, R. R.

REID, Air Vice-Marshal Sir Ranald; *see* Reid, Sir G. R. M.

REID, Robert Basil, CBE 1980; FCIT; Chief Executive (railways), British Railways Board, since 1980; *b* 7 Feb. 1921; *s* of Sir Robert Niel Reid, KCSI, KCIE, ICS and Lady (A.H.) Reid (*née* Disney); *m* 1951, Isobel Jean McLachlan (*d* 1976); *one s one d. Educ:* Malvern Coll.; Brasenose Coll., Oxford (MA). Commnd Royal Tank Regt, 1941, Captain 1945. Traffic Apprentice, LNER, 1947; Goods Agent, York, 1958; Asst Dist Goods Manager, Glasgow, 1960, Dist Passenger Man., 1961, Divl Commercial Man., 1963; Planning Man., Scottish Region, 1967; Divl Man., Doncaster, 1968; Dep. Gen. Man., Eastern Region, York, 1972; Gen. Manager, Southern Reg., BR, 1974-76; Exec. Mem. for Marketing, BRB, 1977-80. Dir, British Transport Hotels Ltd, 1977-; Chm., Freightliner Co. Ltd, 1978-80. Pres., CIT, 1982-83. FInstM; CBIM. *Recreations:* golf, sailing, shooting. *Address:* 23 Edgehill Road, Purley, Surrey CR2 2ND. *T:* 01-660 5429. *Club:* Naval and Military.

REID, Dr Robert Douglas; *b* 6 Sept. 1898; *s* of John and Maud Helen Reid; unmarried. *Educ:* Wells Cathedral School; St John's College, Oxford (DPhil); Bristol University (BSc). Army 1917-19, Somerset Light Infantry in Flanders and Ireland; Assistant Master at Downside School, 1923-24; Canford School, 1924-28; Housemaster at Worksop College, 1928-33; Headmaster Kings School, Taunton, 1933-37. Somerset County Council, 1958-66; High Constable and Dep. Mayor, City of Wells. *Publications:* Cathedral Church of St Andrew at Wells; Diary of Mary Yeoman; Notes on Practical Chemistry; A Concise General Science, 1949; Houses of Mendip, 1979. *Recreations:* archæology, lawn tennis. *Address:* 8 Chamberlain Street, Wells, Somerset. *T:* 72494.

REID, Whitelaw; President and Director, Reid Enterprises; *b* 26 July 1913; *s* of late Ogden Reid and Mrs Ogden Reid; *m* 1st, 1948, Joan Brandon (marr. diss., 1959); *two s*; 2nd, 1959, Elizabeth Ann Brooks; *one s one d. Educ:* Lincoln Sch., NYC; St Paul's Sch., Concord, New Hampshire; Yale Univ. (BA). New York Herald Tribune: in various departments, 1938-40; foreign correspondent, England, 1940; Assistant to Editor, 1946; Editor (and Pres., 1953-55), 1947-55; Chm. of Bd, 1955-58; Director, 1946-65; Pres., Herald Tribune Fresh Air Fund, 1946-62, Dir 1962-. Served War of 1939-45, 1st Lieut naval aviator, USNR. Formerly Director: Farfield Foundn; Freedom House; Director: Golden's Bridge Hounds Inc., 1970-; Yale Westchester Alumni Assoc. Chm., NY State Cttee on Public Employee Security Procedures, 1956-57. Ambassador to inauguration of President Ponce, Ecuador, 1956. Member: Nat. Commn for Unesco, 1955-60; President's Citizen Advisers on the Mutual Security Program, 1956-57; Yale Alumni Board (Vice-Chm., 1962-64), Yale Univ. Council (Chm., Publications Cttee, 1965-70); Council on Foreign Relations; Nat. Inst. of Social Sciences. District Comr, Purchase Pony Club, 1964-70; Pres., New York State Horse Council (formerly Empire State Horsemen's Assoc.), 1975-80. Fellow, Pierson Coll., Yale, 1949-. *Address:* (home and office) Reid Enterprises, Ophir Farm, Purchase, New York 10577, USA. *Clubs:* Century, Overseas Press, Silurians, Pilgrims, Amateur Ski (New York); Metropolitan (Washington); St Regis Yacht; Manursing Is.

REID, Flight Lt William, VC 1943; agricultural consultant; Agriculture Adviser, The MacRobert Trust, Douneside, Tarland, Aberdeenshire, since 1950; *b* 21 Dec. 1921; *s* of late William Reid, Baillieston, Glasgow; *m* 1952, Violet Gallagher, 11 Dryburgh Gdns, Glasgow, NW1; *one s one d. Educ:* Coatbridge Secondary Sch.; Glasgow Univ.; West of Scotland Coll. of Agriculture. Student of Metallurgy, Sept. 1940; BSc (Agric.), 1949; Post-Graduate World Travelling Scholarship for 6 months, to study Agric. and Installations in India, Australia, NZ, USA and Canada, 1949-50. Joined RAF 1941; trained in Lancaster, Calif, USA. Won VC during a trip to Düsseldorf, 3 Nov. 1943, when member of 61 Squadron; pilot RAFVR, 617 Squadron (prisoner); demobilised, 1946; recalled to RAF for 3 months, Dec. 1951. Joined RAFVR, commissioned Jan. 1949, 103 Reserve Centre, Perth. Nat. Cattle and Sheep Advr, Spillers Ltd, 1959-81. *Recreations:* golf, shooting, fishing, etc. *Address:* Cranford, Ferntower Place, Crieff, Perthshire. *T:* Crieff 2462. *Club:* Royal Air Force.

REID, Sir William, Kt 1972; CBE 1962; PhD, DSc; FRSE 1952; FEng 1977; Chairman, Northern Economic Planning Council, 1970-73; *b* 20 June 1906; *o s* of late Sir Charles Carlow Reid; *m* 1935, Sheila Janette Christiana Davidson; *one s one d. Educ:* Dollar Acad.; Dunfermline High School. Early underground practical experience in coal mining attached to The Fife Coal Co. Ltd, and in the Ruhr and US. BSc (Mining and Metallurgy) 1929, and PhD (Mining) 1933, Univ. of Edinburgh. Held various mining appointments with The Fife Coal Co. Ltd, 1922-42; apptd Gen. Works Manager and Dir, 1942. Leader of Ministry of Fuel and Power Technical Mission to the Ruhr Coalfield, 1945; apptd in the Scottish Div. Nat. Coal Board, Prod. Dir, 1947, Deputy Chairman, 1950, Chairman, 1952; Board Member for Production, NCB, 1955-57; Chm., Durham Div., NCB, 1957-63; Chm., Northumberland and Durham Div., NCB, 1964-67; Regional Chm., 1967-69. Leader of NCB Technical Mission to coalfields of Soviet Union, 1956. Chm., Northern Regional Marketing Cttee, 1966. Mem., N Reg. Econ. Planning Council, 1965. Chairman: Northern Brick Co., 1968-71; Associated Heat Services (N) Ltd, 1968-71; Victor Products (Wallsend) Ltd, 1972-77; Council, Univ. of Durham, 1972-78; Northern Region, Anchor Housing Assoc., 1980-.

President: Mining Inst. of Scotland, 1951-52; IMinE, 1956-57. Hon. DCL Durham, 1970. *Publications:* numerous papers related to industry, particularly coal mining. *Address:* Norwood, Picktree Village, Washington, Tyne and Wear. *T:* Chester-le-Street 882260.

REID, William, FSA; FMA; Director, National Army Museum, since 1970; *b* Glasgow, 8 Nov. 1926; *o s* of Colin Colquhoun Reid and Mary Evelyn Bingham; *m* 1958, Nina Frances Brigden. *Educ:* Glasgow and Oxford. Commnd RAF Regt, 1946-48. Joined staff of Armouries, Tower of London, 1956. Organising Sec., 3rd Internat. Congress of Museums of Arms and Military History, London, Glasgow and Edinburgh, 1963; Sec.-Gen., Internat. Assoc. of Museums of Arms and Military History, 1969-81, Pres., 1981-; Member: British Nat. Cttee, ICOM, 1973-; Council, Chelsea Soc., 1979-. FSA 1965 (Mem. Council, 1975-76); FMA 1974. Trustee, The Tank Museum, 1970-. Hon. Member: Amer. Soc. of Arms Collectors, 1975; Indian Army Assoc., 1981. *Publications:* The Lore of Arms, 1976 (Military Book Society choice) (also trans. French, German, Danish, Italian and Swedish); contribs to Connoisseur, Guildhall Miscellany, Jl of Arms and Armour Soc. and other British and foreign jls. *Recreations:* the study of armour and arms, music, ornithology. *Address:* 66 Ennerdale Road, Richmond, Surrey. *T:* 01-940 0904. *Club:* Athenæum.

REID, William Kennedy, CB 1981; Deputy Secretary (Central Services), Scottish Office, since 1978; *b* 15 Feb. 1931; *3rd s* of late James and Elspet Reid; *m* 1959, Ann, *d* of Rev. Donald Campbell; *two s one d. Educ:* Robert Gordon's Coll.; George Watson's Coll.; Univ. of Edinburgh; Trinity Coll., Cambridge. MA 1st cl. Classics Edinburgh and Cantab. Ferguson scholar 1952; Craven scholar 1956. Nat. service, 1952-54. Min. of Educn, 1956; Asst Private Sec. to Minister, 1958-60; Cabinet Office, 1964; Private Sec. to Sec. of Cabinet, 1965-67; Asst Sec., DES, 1967; Sec., Council for Scientific Policy, 1967-72; Under Sec., 1974-78, Accountant-General, 1976-78, DES. *Address:* 11 Inverleith Terrace, Edinburgh EH3 5NS. *T:* 031-556 1089. *Club:* New (Edinburgh).

REID, William Macpherson; Sheriff of Glasgow and Strathkelvin, since 1978; *b* 6 April 1938; *s* of William Andrew Reid and Mabel McLeod; *m* 1971, Vivien Anne Eddy; *three d. Educ:* Elgin Academy; Aberdeen Univ.; Edinburgh Univ. MA; LLB. Admitted Advocate, 1963; Sheriff of Lothian and Borders, 1978. *Address:* c/o Sheriffs' Library, 149 Ingram Street, Glasgow G1 1SY.

REIDHAVEN, Viscount, (Master of Seafield;) James Andrew Ogilvie-Grant; *b* 30 Nov. 1963; *s* and *heir* of Earl of Seafield, *qv*.

REIDY, Joseph Patrick Irwin, FRCS; Consulting Plastic Surgeon, retired: Westminster Hospital, 1948-72; Stoke Mandeville Hospital, Bucks, 1951-72 (Director, Plastic Surgery, 1957-72); Oldchurch Hospital, Romford, 1946-72; Consulting Plastic Surgeon (Hon.), St Paul's Hospital, WC, 1959-72; *b* 30 October 1907; *2nd s* of late Dr Jerome J. Reidy, JP, MD, Co. Limerick and London and of Alderman Mrs F. W. Reidy, JP (*née* Dawson), Castle Dawson, Co. Derry; *m* 1943, Anne (*d* 1970), *e d* of late T. Johnson, and of late Mrs T. Johnson, County Durham; *three d*; *m* 1972, Freda M. Clout (*née* Lowe), Gosfield Hall, Essex. *Educ:* Stonyhurst College, Lancs; St John's Coll., Cambridge; London Hospital. MA (Nat. Sci. Trip.) (Cantab); MD, BCh (Cantab); FRCS. Casualty Officer and Ho. Phys., Poplar Hosp., 1932; Ho. Surg. and Casualty Officer, London Hosp., 1933; Ho. Surg., Leicester Roy. Inf., 1934; General Practitioner, 1934-37. Surgeon H. Div., Metropolitan Police, 1934-37. Hon. Dem. of Anatomy, Med. Sch., Middx Hosp., 1938; Civilian Surg., RAF Hosp., Halton, Bucks, 1939; Res. Surg. Officer; EMS, Albert Dock Hosp., 1939-40; EMS, St Andrew's Hosp., Billericay, 1940-42; Chief Asst, Plastic Surgery, St Thomas' Hosp., 1943-48. Cons. Plastic Surgeon, Essex Co. Hosp., Colchester, 1943-46; Senior Grade Surgeon, Plastic Surg. Unit, Min. of Pensions: Stoke Mandeville Hosp., Bucks, 1942-51; Queen Mary's Hosp., Roehampton, 1942-51. Consulting Plastic Surgeon: Middlesex CC, 1944-48; Nelson Hosp., Kingston, 1948-50; Metropolitan ENT Hosp., 1948-50; West Middlesex Hosp.; Lord Mayor Treloar Hosp., Alton, 1953-56. Hon. Chief MO, Amateur Boxing Association, 1948; Hon. Secretary and Treas. United Hospitals Rugby Football Club, 1957-62. Liveryman Soc. of Apothecaries; Freeman of City of London; FRSocMed; FMedSoc Lond.; Fellow Hunterian Soc.; Pres., Chiltern Medical Soc., 1958-60; Pres., Brit. Assoc. of Plastic Surgeons, 1962. Member: BMA; British Assoc. of Surgeons; Brit. Acad. of Forensic Sciences; Colchester Med. Soc. Hunterian Prof., RCS, 1957, 1968; Lecturer, London Univ., 1952; Purkinje Medal, Czechoslovak Acad. of Sciences, 1965. *Publications:* contrib. since 1944 to: Proc. Roy. Soc. Med., Medical Press, West London Medico-Chirurgical Journal, British Journal of Plastic Surgery, BMJ, Medical History 2nd World War, Monograph Plastic Surgery and Physiotherapy, Annals RCS, etc. *Recreations:* gardening, fishing. *Address:* Priory Cottage, Earls Colne, Essex. *T:* Earls Colne 2271.

REIGATE, Baron *cr* 1970 (Life Peer), of Outwood, Surrey; **John Kenyon Vaughan-Morgan;** Bt 1960; PC 1961; *b* 2 Feb. 1905; *yr s* of late Sir Kenyon Vaughan-Morgan, DL, OBE, MP and late Lady Vaughan-Morgan; *m* 1940, Emily, *d* of late Mr and Mrs W. Redmond Cross, New York City; *two d. Educ:* Eton; Christ Church, Oxford. Mem. Chelsea Borough Council, 1928; Member of London County Council for Chelsea, 1946-52; Chm. East Fulham Conservative and Unionist Assoc., 1935-38 (Pres. 1945); MP (C) Reigate Div. of Surrey, 1950-70. Parly Sec., Min. of Health, 1957; Minister of State, BoT,

1957-59. Dir, Morgan Crucible Co. Ltd, now retired. Chm. Bd of Govs, Westminster Hosp., 1963-74 (Mem., 1960). Pres., Royal Philanthropic Sch., Redhill. Dep. Chm., South Westminster Justices, now retired. Mem., Court of Assistants, Merchant Taylors Co. (Master 1970). Hon. Freeman, Borough of Reigate, 1971. Served War of 1939-45; Welsh Guards, 1940; GSO2, War Office; GSO1, HQ 21 Army Group (despatches). *Address:* 36 Eaton Square, SW1. *T:* 01-235 6506. *Clubs:* Brooks's, Beefsteak, Hurlingham.

REIHER, Frederick Bernard Carl, CMG 1982; Secretary to the Prime Minister of Papua New Guinea, since 1980; also accredited Ambassador to the Federal Republic of Germany, Belgium, the EEC, the State of Israel, and Turkey; *b* 7 Feb. 1945; *s* of William and Ruth Reiher; *m* 1974, Helen Perpetua; two *d*. *Educ:* Holy Spirit National Seminary; Univ. of Papua New Guinea (BD). Private Sec. to Minister for Finance, PNG, 1973-76. Joined Diplomatic Service, 1976; established Diplomatic Mission for PNG in London, 1977; High Comr for PNG in London, 1978-80. *Address:* Office of the Prime Minister, (Pineapple Building), Government Offices, Ward's Strip, Papua New Guinea. *Clubs:* Royal Commonwealth Society, Travellers' (Hon.); Aviat Social & Sporting, South Pacific Motor Sports, PNG Pistol.

REILLY, family name of **Baron Reilly.**

REILLY, Baron *cr* 1978 (Life Peer), of Brompton in the Royal Borough of Kensington and Chelsea; **Paul Reilly;** Kt 1967; Director: Conran Associates; The Building Trades Exhibition Ltd; Chairman, Race International Designs Ltd; Director, Design Council (formerly Council of Industrial Design), 1960-77; *b* 29 May 1912; *s* of late Prof. Sir Charles Reilly, formerly Head of Liverpool Sch. of Architecture; *m* 1st, 1939, Pamela Wentworth Foster; one *d*; 2nd, 1952, Annette Stockwell. *Educ:* Winchester; Hertford College, Oxford; London School of Economics. Salesman and Sales Manager, Venesta Ltd, 1934-36; Leader Page Editor and Features Editor, News Chronicle, 1936-40. RAC, 1940; RNVR 1941-45. Editorial Staff, Modern Plastics, New York, 1946; Co-Editor, British Plastics Encylopædia, 1947; Chief Information Officer, Council of Industrial Design, 1948; Deputy Director, 1954. Member: Council, Royal Society of Arts, 1959-62, 1963-70; Council, BTA, 1960-70; Council, RCA, 1963-81; BBC General Advisory Council, 1964-70; BNEC, 1966-70; British Railways Design Panel, 1966-, Environment Panel, 1977-; GLC Historic Buildings Cttee, 1967-; Post Office Stamp Adv. Cttee, 1967-; Design Adv. Cttee, 1970-; British Telecom Design Cttee, 1981-; British Council Fine Arts Adv. Cttee, 1970-80; Conseil Supérieur de la Création Esthétique Industrielle (France), 1971-73; Adv. Council of Science Policy Foundn, 1971-; British Crafts Centre Bd, 1972-77; Nat. Theatre Design Adv. Cttee, 1974-; Royal Fine Art Commn, 1976-81; Crafts Advisory Cttee, 1977-81 (Chief Exec., 1971-77). Chairman: Trustees, Building Conservation Trust, 1977-82; Conran Foundn, 1981-. President: Soc. of Designer-Craftsmen, 1976-; Assoc. of Art Institutions, 1977-80; World Crafts Council, 1978-80; Vice-President: ICSID, 1963-67; Modular Soc., 1968-77; London Soc., 1977-; ICA, 1979-; Rye Conservation Soc., 1980-. Governor: Hammersmith Coll. of Art and Building, 1948-67; Central Sch. of Art and Design, 1953-74; Camberwell Sch. of Art and Design, 1967-77; City of Birmingham Polytechnic, 1970-77. Mem., Ct of Governors, LSE, 1975-80. Hon. FSIA, 1959; Hon. FRIBA, 1965; Sen. Fellow, RCA, 1972; Hon. Assoc. Manchester Coll. of Art, 1963; Hon. Member, Art Workers Guild, 1961; Hon. Corresponding Mem., Svenskaslöjdforeningen, 1956. Hon. Liveryman, Furniture Makers' Co., 1980. Hon. DSc: Loughborough, 1977; Aston, 1981; Hon. Dr RCA, 1978. Comdr, Royal Order of Vasa (Sweden), 1961. Bicentenary Medal, RSA, 1963. *Publication:* An Introduction to Regency Architecture (Art and Technics), 1948. *Recreation:* looking at buildings. *Address:* 3 Alexander Place, SW7 2SG. *T:* 01-589 4031. *Club:* Arts.

REILLY, Brian Thomas; Chairman, National Panasonic (UK) Ltd, since 1979; *b* 9 Dec. 1924; *s* of Thomas Joseph and Eugene Reilly; *m* 1952, Jean Cynthia Gilbey; one *s* four *d*. *Educ:* Mount St Mary's Coll., Spinkhill, near Sheffield. Captain, KRRC, 1943-47. Various pursuits, 1947-51; Sales Man., Thomas Hedley & Co. Ltd (now Proctor & Gamble Ltd), 1951-60; Sales Dir, Man. Dir and Dep. Chm., Radio & Allied Industries Ltd (wholly owned subsid. of GEC Co. Ltd), 1960-79; Associate Dir, GEC Co. Ltd, 1976-79. *Address:* Marsham Manor, Marsham Lane, Gerrards Cross, Bucks. *T:* Gerrards Cross 82188. *Club:* Annabel's.

REILLY, Sir (D'Arcy) Patrick, GCMG 1968 (KCMG 1957; CMG 1949); OBE 1942; Chairman, Banque Nationale de Paris Ltd (formerly British and French Bank), 1969-80; *b* 17 March 1909; *s* of late Sir D'Arcy Reilly, Indian Civil Service; *m* 1938, Rachel Mary, *d* of late Brigadier-General Sir Percy Sykes, KCIE, CB, CMG; two *d*. *Educ:* Winchester; New Coll., Oxford. (1st class Hon. Mods, 1930, Lit Hum 1932), Hon. Fellow 1972. Laming Travelling Fellow, Queen's College, 1932; Fellow of All Souls College, 1932-39, 1969-; Diplomatic Service, 1933; Third Secretary, Tehran, 1935-38; Ministry of Economic Warfare, 1939-42; First Secretary, Algiers, 1943; Paris, 1944; Athens, 1945. Counsellor, HM Foreign Service, 1947; Counsellor at Athens, 1947-48; Imperial Defence College, 1949; Assistant Under-Secretary of State, Foreign Office, 1950-53; Minister in Paris, 1953-56; Dep. Under-Sec. of State, Foreign Office, Oct. 1956; Ambassador to the USSR, 1957-60; Dep. Under-Sec. of State, Foreign Office, 1960-64; Official Head of UK Delegation to UN Conference on Trade and Development, 1964; Ambassador to France, 1965-68. Pres., 1972-75, Vice-Pres., 1975-, London Chamber of Commerce and Industry. Chairman: London Chamber of Commerce Standing Cttee for Common Market countries, 1969-72; Overseas Policy Cttee, Assoc. of British Chambers of Commerce, 1970-72; London Univ. Management Cttee, British Inst. in Paris, 1970-79; Council, Bedford Coll., London Univ., 1970-75. Hon. DLitt Bath, 1982. Comdr Légion d'Honneur, 1979. *Address:* Hampden Cottage, Ramsden, Oxford OX7 3AU. *T:* Ramsden 348. *Club:* Athenæum.

REILLY, Maj.-Gen. Jeremy Calcott, DSO 1973; Commander, 4th Armoured Division, BAOR, since 1981; *b* 7 April 1934; *s* of Lt-Col J. F. C. Reilly and E. N. Reilly (*née* Moreton); *m* 1960, Julia Elizabeth (*née* Forrester); two *d* (and one *d* decd). *Educ:* Uppingham; RMA Sandhurst. Commissioned Royal Warwickshire Regt, 1954; served Egypt, Cyprus (Despatches), Ireland, Hong Kong, Germany, Borneo, BJSM Washington DC; psc 1965; Brigade Major, BAOR, 1967-69; Chief Instructor, RMA, 1969-71; CO 2nd Bn Royal Regt of Fusiliers, 1971-73 (DSO); Instructor, Staff Coll., 1974-75; Col GS (Army Deployment), MoD, 1975-77; PSO to Field Marshal Lord Carver and attached FCO (Rhodesia), 1977-79; Comdr 6 Field Force and UK Mobile Force, 1979-81. Dep. Col, RRF (Warwickshire), 1981-. *Publications:* minor articles in various jls. *Address:* St John's House, Warwick CV34 4NF. *T:* Warwick 491653.

REILLY, Noel Marcus Prowse, CMG 1958; Board Member, New Hampshire Energy Coalition, since 1980; *b* 31 Dec. 1902; *s* of late Frederick Reilly and late Ellen Prowse; *m* 1st, 1927, Dolores Albra Pratten (marr. diss., 1963); one *s* one *d*; 2nd, 1963, Dorothy Alma Rainsford. *Educ:* University Coll. Sch.; Gonville and Caius College, Cambridge (MA 1928); London Univ. (BSc Econ., 1st Cl. Hons 1946, PhD 1972). Schoolmaster, Boston, Massachusetts, USA, 1924; business in New Zealand, 1926, England, 1928; Secretary, Area Cttee for National Fitness for Oxon, Bucks, and Berks, 1938; Press Censor, Ministry of Information, 1939; Principal, HM Treasury, 1946; Economic Counsellor, Persian Gulf, 1953-59; Financial Counsellor and Dep. Head, UK Treasury Delegation, British Embassy, Washington, 1960-65; Alternate Exec. Dir for the UK, IBRD, and Affiliates, 1962-65. *Publication:* The Key to Prosperity, 1931. *Recreations:* ski-ing, windsurfing, whitewater kayaking. *Address:* North Sandwich, New Hampshire 03259, USA. *T:* 603-284-7730.

REILLY, Sir Patrick; *see* Reilly, Sir D. P.

REINDORP, Rt. Rev. George Edmund, DD; an Assistant Bishop, Diocese of London, since 1982; with BBC Radio Religious Department, since 1982; *b* 19 Dec. 1911; *s* of Rev. Hector William Reindorp and Dora Lucy (*née* George), Goodmayes, Essex; *m* 1943, Alix Violet Edington, MB, ChB, *d* of Alexander Edington, MD, and Helen Edington, Durban, Natal; three *s* one *d* (and one *d* decd). *Educ:* Felsted Sch.; Trinity Coll., Cambridge; Westcott House, Cambridge. MA Cantab, 1939. Deacon, 1937; Priest, 1938; Curate, S Mary Abbots, Kensington, 1937-39; Chaplain RNVR, 1938-46; Vicar St Stephen with St John, Westminster, 1946-57. Commissary for: Bishop of Natal, 1948-61; Bishop of New Guinea, 1956-61; Provost of Southwark and Rector of St Saviour with All Hallows, Southwark, 1957-61; Bishop of Guildford, 1961-73; Bishop of Salisbury, 1973-81. Mem., House of Lords, 1970. Chaplain, RCGP, 1965. Hon. DD Lambeth, 1961; DUniv Surrey, 1970. *Publications:* What about You?, 1956; No Common Task, 1957; Putting it Over: ten points for preachers, 1961; Over to You, 1964; Preaching Through the Christian Year, 1973. *Recreations:* ski-ing, radio and television; avoiding committees. *Address:* 28a Clarendon Gardens, W9 1AZ. *Clubs:* Ski Club of Great Britain, Kandahar.
See also Sir Humphrey Mynors, Bt.

REINERS, William Joseph; Director of Research Policy, Departments of the Environment and Transport, 1977-78, retired 1978; *b* 19 May 1923; *s* of late William and Hannah Reiners; *m* 1952, Catharine Anne Palmer; three *s* one *d*. *Educ:* Liverpool Collegiate Sch.; Liverpool Univ. RAE Farnborough, 1944-46; Min. of Works, 1946-50; Head, Building Operations and Economics Div., Building Research Station, 1950-63; Dir of Research and Information, MPBW, 1963-71; Dir of Research Requirements, DoE, 1971-77. *Publications:* various on building operations and economics. *Address:* Valais, Berks Hill, Chorleywood, Herts. *T:* Chorleywood 3293.

REINHARDT, Max; Joint Chairman, Chatto, Bodley Head and Jonathan Cape Ltd, since 1973; Chairman, Bodley Head Group of Publishers, since 1981; Chairman, Max Reinhardt Ltd and HFL (Publishers) Ltd, since 1948; *b* 30 Nov. 1915; *s* of Ernest Reinhardt and Frieda Reinhardt (*née* Darr); *m* 1st, 1947, Margaret Leighton, CBE (marr. diss. 1955; she *d* 1976); 2nd, 1957, Joan, *d* of Carlisle and Dorothy MacDonald, New York City; two *d*. *Educ:* English High Sch. for Boys, Istanbul; Ecole des Hautes Etudes Commerciales, Paris; London School of Economics. Acquired HFL (Publishers) Ltd, 1947; founded Max Reinhardt Ltd, 1948, which acquired: The Bodley Head Ltd, 1956 (Man. Dir, 1957-81); Putnam & Co., 1963. Mem. Council: Publishers' Assoc., 1963-69; Royal Academy of Dramatic Art, 1965-. *Recreations:* squash racquets, tennis, swimming, bridge. *Address:* 16 Pelham Crescent, SW7 2NR. *T:* 01-589 5527. *Clubs:* Beefsteak, Garrick, Hurlingham, Royal Automobile.

REISS, Sir John (Anthony Ewart), Kt 1967; BEM 1941; Chairman of Associated Portland Cement Manufacturers Ltd (now Blue Circle Industries), 1957-74; *b* 8 April 1909; *m* 1st, 1938, Marie Ambrosine Phillpotts; one *s* one *d*; 2nd, 1951, Elizabeth Booth-Jones (*née* MacEwan); two *d*. *Educ:* Eton. Cotton, Banking, Insurance, 1928-34. Joined Associated Portland Cement Manufacturers, 1934; Dir, 1946. Chm., Foundn for Business Responsibilities;

Pres., Aims of Industry, 1978- (Hon. Treasurer, 1967-78); Vice-Chm., CRC. *Recreations:* shooting, cricket. *Address:* Barrow House, Barrow, Oakham, Leics. *Club:* Buck's.

REISS, John Henry, OBE 1972; British Ambassador to Liberia, 1973-78, retired; *b* 26 March 1918; *s* of late Rev. Leopold Reiss and Dora Lillian (*née* Twisden-Bedford); *m* 1943, Dora Lily (*née* York); one *s* two *d. Educ:* Bradfield Coll.; St Thomas' Hosp. Served War, Army, 1939-42. Kenya Govt, 1945-59; Dir of Information, 1954-59; Commonwealth Office, 1959; Dir of Information Services: Johannesburg, 1961-63; Wellington, New Zealand, 1963-65. Foreign and Commonwealth Office, 1966-69; Dep. British Govt Representative, Antigua/St Kitts, 1969-73. *Recreations:* golf, tennis, bridge. *Address:* Flat 6, Forres, The Esplanade, Frinton-on-Sea, Essex.

REISZ, Karel; film director; *b* 21 July 1926; *s* of Joseph Reisz and Frederika; *m* 1963, Betsy Blair; three *s. Educ:* Leighton Park Sch., Reading; Emmanuel Coll., Cambridge (BA). Formerly: co-ed with Lindsay Anderson, film magazine, Sequence; worked for BFI; first Programme Dir, National Film Theatre. Co-directed, with Tony Richardson, Momma Don't Allow, 1956; produced: Every Day Except Christmas, 1957; This Sporting Life, 1960; directed: We Are the Lambeth Boys, 1958; Saturday Night and Sunday Morning, 1959; Night Must Fall, 1963; Morgan, a Suitable Case for Treatment, 1965; Isadora, 1967; The Gambler, 1975; Dog Soldiers, 1978; The French Lieutenant's Woman, 1981. *Publication:* The Technique of Film Editing (also ed), 1953. *Address:* c/o Film Contracts, 2 Lower James Street, Golden Square, W1.

REITH, Barony of (*cr* 1940); title disclaimed by 2nd Baron; *see under* Reith, Christopher John.

REITH, Christopher John; farmer; *b* 27 May 1928; *s* of 1st Baron Reith, KT, PC, GCVO, GBE, CB, TD, of Stonehaven, and Muriel Katharine, *y d* of late John Lynch Odhams; *S* father, 1971, as 2nd Baron Reith, but disclaimed his peerage for life, 1972; *m* 1969, Penelope Margaret Ann, *er d* of late H. R. Morris; one *s* one *d. Educ:* Eton; Worcester College, Oxford (MA Agriculture). Served in Royal Navy, 1946-48; farming thereafter. *Recreations:* fishing, gardening, forestry. *Heir* (*to disclaimed peerage*): *s* Hon. James Harry John Reith, *b* 2 June 1971. *Address:* Whitebank Farm, Methven, Perthshire. *T:* Methven 333.

REITH, Douglas, QC (Scotland) 1957; a Social Security (formerly National Insurance) Commissioner, since 1960; *b* 29 June 1919; *s* of William Reith and Jessie McAllan; *m* 1949, Elizabeth Archer Stewart; one *s* one *d. Educ:* Aberdeen Grammar School; Aberdeen University (MA, LLB). Became Member of Faculty of Advocates in Scotland, 1946. Served in Royal Signals, 1939-46. Standing Junior Counsel in Scotland to Customs and Excise, 1949-51; Advocate-Depute, Crown Office, Scotland, 1953-57; Pres., Pensions Appeal Tribunal (Scotland), 1958-64; Chm., Nat. Health Service Tribunal (Scotland), 1963-65. *Address:* 11 Heriot Row, Edinburgh EH3 6HP. *T:* 031-556 6966. *Club:* New (Edinburgh).

REITH, Martin; HM Diplomatic Service; Deputy High Commissioner in Malta, since 1980; *b* 6 Dec. 1935; *s* of late James Reith and of Christian (*née* Innes); *m* 1964, Ann Purves; four *s. Educ:* Royal High Sch. of Edinburgh. Served: India (Calcutta), 1957-59; Uganda, 1962-66; Scottish Office, Edinburgh, 1966-68; Australia (Canberra), 1969-72; Asst Head of Central and Southern Africa Dept, FCO, 1974-77; Commercial Sec., Beirut, 1977-78; UN Dept, FCO, 1979; Counsellor, NATO Def. Coll., Rome, 1980. *Recreations:* hill-walking, bridge, watching the Scottish literary scene. *Address:* c/o Foreign and Commonwealth Office, SW1A 2AH.

RELLIE, Alastair James Carl Euan; HM Diplomatic Service; Counsellor, Foreign and Commonwealth Office, since 1979; *b* 5 April 1935; *s* of William and Lucy Rellie; *m* 1961, Annalisa (*née* Modin); one *s* two *d. Educ:* Michaelhouse, SA; Harvard Univ., USA (BA). Rifle Bde, 1958-60. Second Sec., FCO, 1963-64; Vice-Consul, Geneva, 1964-67; First Secretary: FCO, 1967-68; (Commercial), Cairo, 1968-70; Kinshasa, 1970-72; FCO, 1972-74; (and later Counsellor), UK Mission to UN, New York, 1974-79. *Recreations:* travel, talk, newspapers. *Address:* c/o Foreign and Commonwealth Office, SW1A 2AH. *Clubs:* Greenjackets; Harvard (New York).

RELLY, Gavin Walter Hamilton; Chairman, Anglo American Corporation of South Africa Ltd, since 1983 (Deputy Chairman, 1977-82); *b* 6 Feb. 1926; *s* of Cullis Hamilton Relly and Helen Relly; *m* 1951, Jane Margaret Glenton; one *s* two *d. Educ:* Diocesan Coll., Cape Town; Trinity Coll., Oxford (MA). Joined Anglo American Corp., 1949 (Sec. to H. F. Oppenheimer and then to Sir Ernest Oppenheimer); Manager, Chm.'s Office, 1958; elected to Bd of Corp., 1965; Exec. Dir, 1966; Chm., Exec. Cttee, 1978. Chm., Hudson Bay Mining & Smelting Co. Ltd, 1970-73. *Recreations:* fishing, golf. *Address:* PO Box 61587, Marshalltown, 2107, South Africa. *T:* 638-3234. *Clubs:* Rand, Country (Johannesburg).

RELPH, Michael Leighton George; film producer, director, designer, writer; *s* of late George Relph and Deborah Relph (later Harker); *m* 1st, 1939, Doris Gosden (marr. diss.); one *s* ; 2nd, 1950, Maria Barry; one *d. Educ:* Bembridge Sch. Stage designer, 1940-50: West-end prodns include: Indoor Fireworks; The Doctor's Dilemma; Up and Doing; Watch on the Rhine; The Man Who Came to Dinner; Frieda; Saloon Bar; Old Acquaintance; Quiet Week-end; Heartbreak House; Relative Values; A Month in the Country; The Last of Summer; Love in Idleness; The White Carnation; The Petrified Forest; The Banbury Nose; They Came to a City. Began film career as apprentice, then Asst Art Dir, Gaumont British Studios; Art Dir, Warner Brothers Studios; Art Dir, Ealing Studios, 1942-45: prodns include: The Bells Go Down; Dead of Night; Champagne Charley; Nicholas Nickleby; Saraband for Dead Lovers (nominated Hollywood Oscar); Associate Producer to Michael Balcon, 1945; subseq. Producer with Basil Dearden as Dir until Dearden's death, 1972: prodns include: The Captive Heart; Kind Hearts and Coronets; The Blue Lamp (Best British Film Award, Brit. Film Acad.); Frieda; Saraband for Dead Lovers; I Believe in You (co-author); The Ship that Died of Shame; The Rainbow Jacket; The Square Ring; The Gentle Gunman; Cage of Gold; Pool of London. Director: Davy, 1957; Rockets Galore, 1958; Producer: Violent Playground; Sapphire (Best British Film Award, Brit. Film Acad.); All Night Long; The Smallest Show on Earth. Founder Dir, Allied Film Makers: produced: League of Gentlemen; Victim; Man in the Moon (co-author); Life for Ruth; The Mind Benders; Woman of Straw; Masquerade (co-author); The Assassination Bureau (also author and designer); The Man Who Haunted Himself (co-author); in charge of production, Boyd's Company, 1978-82: Scum (exec. producer), 1979; An Unsuitable Job for a Woman (co-producer), 1981. Chm., Film Prodn Assoc. of GB, 1971-76; Mem., Cinematograph Films Council, 1971-76; Governor, BFI, 1972-79 (Chm., Prodn Bd, 1972-79). *Recreations:* reading, theatre going, painting. *Address:* The Lodge, Primrose Hill Studios, Fitzroy Road, NW1 8JP. *T:* 01-586 0249.

RELTON, Stanley; HM Diplomatic Service; Counsellor (Administration), British Embassy, Brussels, since 1978; *b* 19 May 1923; *s* of José Shakespeare; four *d.* Army, 1942-47. Joined HM Diplomatic Service, 1948: Haifa, 1949; Seoul, 1950; Tokyo, 1951; FCO, 1952-53; Vice-Consul, Stuttgart, 1954-57; Bremen, 1957-59; Consul, Rotterdam, 1959-61; Budapest, 1961-64; Second Sec., Buenos Aires, 1964-68; First Sec., Algiers, 1968-71; FCO, 1971-75; First Sec., Blantyre, Malawi, 1975-78. *Recreations:* music, chess. *Address:* c/o Foreign and Commonwealth Office, SW1A 2AH.

REMEDIOS, Alberto Telisforo, CBE 1981; opera and concert singer; *b* 27 Feb. 1935; *s* of Albert and Ida Remedios; *m* 1965, Judith Annette Hosken; two *s* one *d. Educ:* studied with Edwin Francis, Liverpool. Début with Sadler's Wells Opera, 1956; sings regularly: English Nat. Opera; Royal Opera House, Covent Garden; Welsh Nat. Opera; Metropolitan NY, San Francisco, San Diego, Seattle, Australia, NZ, S Africa, Frankfurt, Bonn, France, Spain; sang Peter Grimes, Teatro Colon, Buenos Aires, 1979; also with major English orchestras. Recordings include Wagner's Ring; Tippett: A Midsummer Marriage. Queen's Prize, RCM, 1958; 1st prize, Union of Bulgarian Composers, 1963. *Recreations:* soccer, motoring, record collecting. *Address:* c/o S. A. Gorlinsky, 35 Dover Street, W1X 4NJ; 27 The Ridgeway, N14 6NX. *T:* 01-882 0599.

REMEZ, Aharon; Chairman, Airports Authority Board, Israel, since 1977; *b* 8 May 1919; *m* 1952, Rita (*née* Levy); one *s* three *d. Educ:* Herzliah Grammar Sch., Tel Aviv. Volunteered for service with RAF, and served as fighter pilot in Gt Brit. and in European theatre of war; after end of war with British Occupation forces in Germany. Mem., kibbutz Kfar Blum, 1947-. Dir Planning and of Ops and subseq. Chief of Staff, and C-in-C Israel Air Force (rank Brig.-Gen.), 1948-51; Head of Min. of Defence Purchasing Mission, USA, 1951-53; Aviation Adviser to Minister of Def., 1953-54; Mem. Bd of Dirs, Solel Boneh Ltd, and Exec. Dir, Koor Industries Ltd, 1954-59; MP (Israel Lab Party) for Mapai, 1956-57; Admin. Dir, Weizmann Inst. of Science, Rehovot, 1959-60. Dir, Internat. Co-op. Dept, Min. for Foreign Affairs, Jerusalem, 1960; Adviser on Internat. Co-operation to Min. for Foreign Affairs, also Consultant to OECD, 1964-65; Ambassador of Israel to the Court of St James's, 1965-70. Dir Gen., Israel Ports Authority, 1970-77. Chm., Nat. Council for Civil Aviation, 1960-. *Recreations:* handicrafts, sculpture. *Address:* 8 San Martin Street, The Cottages, Jerusalem, Israel.

REMNANT, family name of **Baron Remnant.**

REMNANT, 3rd Baron *cr* 1928, of Wenhaston; **James Wogan Remnant,** Bt 1917; CVO 1979; FCA; Chairman, Touche, Remnant & Co., since 1981; *b* 23 October 1930; *s* of 2nd Baron and of Dowager Lady Remnant; *S* father, 1967; *m* 1953, Serena Jane Loehnis, *o d* of Sir Clive Loehnis, *qv* ; three *s* one *d. Educ:* Eton. Partner, 1958-70, Jt Man. Dir, 1970-80, Touche Ross & Co.; Director: Australia and New Zealand Banking Group, 1969-81; National Provident Institution; Ultramar Ltd (Dep. Chm., 1981-); Union Discount Co. of London (Dep. Chm.); TR City of London (formerly City of London Brewery and Investment) Trust (Chm.); TR Energy (Chm.). Chm., Assoc. of Investment Trust Cos, 1977-79. A Church Comr, 1976-. Chm., Royal Jubilee Trusts, 1980- (Hon. Treasurer, 1972-80). FCA 1955. *Heir:* *s* Hon. Philip John Remnant [*b* 20 December 1954; *m* 1977, Caroline Elizabeth Clare, *yr d* of late Godfrey H. R. Cavendish; one *s*]. *Address:* Bear Ash, Hare Hatch, Reading RG10 9XR.

RENALS, Sir Stanley, 4th Bt, *cr* 1895; formerly in the Merchant Navy; *b* 20 May 1923; 2nd *s* of Sir James Herbert Renals, 2nd Bt; *S* brother, Sir Herbert Renals, 3rd Bt, 1961; *m* 1957, Maria Dolores Rodriguez Pinto, *d* of late José Rodriguez Ruiz; one *s. Educ:* City of London Freemen's School. *Heir:* *s* Stanley Michael Renals, *b* 14 January 1958. *Address:* 47 Baden Road, Brighton, East Sussex BN2 4DP.

RENAUD, Madeleine, (Mme Jean-Louis Barrault); Officier de la Légion d'Honneur; actress; formed Madeleine Renaud-Jean-Louis Barrault Company, 1946, Co-director and player leading parts; *b* Paris, 21 Feb. 1903; *d* of Prof. Jean Renaud; *m* 1940, Jean-Louis Barrault, *qv*. *Educ:* Lycée Racine; Conservatoire de Paris (Ier Prix de Comédie). Pensionnaire, Comédie Française, 1921–46. Has appeared in classical and modern plays, and in films. Commander des Arts et Lettres. *Publications:* novels, short stories, plays. *Address:* 18 Avenue du Président Wilson, 75116 Paris, France.

RENAULT, Mary, (pseudonym of **Mary Challans**); *b* 4 Sept. 1905; *er d* of late Dr Frank Challans, and of Clementine Mary Newsome Challans (*née* Baxter). *Educ:* Clifton High School, Bristol; St Hugh's Coll. Oxford (MA; Hon. Fellow, 1982). Radcliffe Infirmary, Oxford. Completed nursing training in 1937; returned to nursing, 1939, until end of War. FRSL 1959. *Publications:* Purposes of Love, 1939; Kind Are Her Answers, 1940; The Friendly Young Ladies, 1944; Return to Night, 1946; North Face, 1948; The Charioteer, 1953; The Last of the Wine, 1956; The King Must Die, 1958; The Bull from the Sea, 1962; The Lion in the Gateway (for children), 1964; The Mask of Apollo, 1966; Fire from Heaven, 1970 (Silver Pen Award 1971); The Persian Boy, 1972; The Nature of Alexander (biography), 1975; The Praise Singer, 1979; Funeral Games, 1981; contrib. TLS, London Rev. of Books and New York Rev. of Books. *Recreations:* conversation and dogs. *Address:* 3 Atholl Road, Camps Bay, Cape Town 8001, South Africa.

RENDALL, Archibald, OBE 1967; HM Diplomatic Service, retired; Consul General, Lille, France, 1977–81; *b* 10 Aug. 1921; *s* of late James Henry Rendall; *m* 1951, Sheila Catherine (*née* Martin); one *d. Educ:* Broughton Sch., Edinburgh. Inland Revenue Dept, 1938; served in RN, 1941–46; joined Foreign (subseq. Diplomatic) Service, 1948; Vice-Consul, Monrovia, 1948–49; Vice-Consul and 2nd Sec., Baghdad, 1950–54; FO, 1954–57; 1st Sec. (Commercial), Beirut, 1957–60; Consul (Commercial), New York, 1960–65; 1st Sec. (Commercial), Bucharest, 1965–68; FCO, 1969–72; Consul-Gen., St Louis, 1972–77. *Address:* 41 Arnison Road, East Molesey, Surrey KT8 9JR.

RENDALL, Peter Godfrey; Headmaster, Bembridge School, Isle of Wight, 1959–74; Clerk to Burford Town Council; *b* 25 April 1909; *s* of Godfrey A. H. Rendall and Mary Whishaw Rendall (*née* Wilson); *m* 1944, Ann McKnight Kauffer; two *s* one *d. Educ:* Rugby School; Corpus Christi College, Oxford. Assistant Master: Felsted School, Essex, 1931–34; Upper Canada College, Toronto, 1934–35; Felsted School, Essex, 1935–43. Served War of 1939–45, RAF, 1943–46, Flight-Lieut. Second Master, St Bees School, Cumberland, 1946–48; Headmaster Achimota School, Gold Coast, 1949–54; Assistant Master, Lancing College, 1954–59. Coronation Medal, 1953. *Recreations:* reading, gardening, carpentry, painting. *Address:* Chippings, The Hill, Burford, Oxon. *Clubs:* Royal Commonwealth Society; Oxford Union Society.

RENDALL, Philip Stanley, MBE 1964; DL; retired as Managing Director of Courtaulds Ltd (1943–61), and as Deputy Chairman (1949–61); *b* 7 July 1895; *s* of late Dr Stanley Rendall and Claire Louise Rendall; *m* 1923, Louise Gwendoline, 2nd *d* of James Calcott; two *d. Educ:* Shrewsbury. Served European War, 1914–18, in France. Joined Courtaulds Ltd, 1920; Director, 1937. Chairman, Lustre Fibres Limited, 1946–57; formerly Chairman, British Nylon Spinners Ltd, Chairman, British Celanese Ltd, 1960–61 (Vice-Chm., 1957–60). High Sheriff of Warwickshire, 1949–50. Commandant, Warwickshire Special Constabulary, retired. DL Co. Warwick, 1967. Chevalier de la Légion d'Honneur, 1957. *Recreations:* golf, tennis. *Address:* 47 Kenilworth Road, Leamington Spa. *T:* Leamington Spa 24682. *Club:* Leamington Tennis Court (Leamington).

RENDELL, Sir William, Kt 1967; General Manager, Commonwealth Development Corporation, 1953–73, retired; *b* 25 Jan. 1908; *s* of William Reginald Rendell and Hon. Janet Marion Rendell; *m* 1950, Annie Henriette Maria (*née* Thorsen). *Educ:* Winchester; Trinity Coll., Cambridge. FCA. Partner, Whinney Murray & Co., 1947–52. Mem., PLA, 1967–78. *Recreations:* shooting, fishing, gardening. *Address:* 10 Montpelier Place, SW7. *T:* 01-584 8232.

RENDLE, Michael Russel; Managing Director, British Petroleum Co. plc, since 1981; *b* 20 Feb. 1931; *s* of late H. C. R. Rendle and Valerie Patricia (*née* Gleeson); *m* 1957, Heather, *d* of J. W. J. Rinkel; two *s* two *d. Educ:* Marlborough; New College, Oxford. MA. Joined Anglo-Iranian Oil Co. (now BP), 1954; Man. Dir, BP Trinidad, 1967–70; Man. Dir, BP Australia, 1974–78; Dir, BP Trading Ltd (now BP International), 1978–; Chm., BP Chemicals Int., plc, 1981–. Mem., London Adv. Bd, Commercial Bank of Australia (now Bank of NSW), 1978–. *Recreations:* golf, music, outdoor sports, gardening. *Address:* British Petroleum Co. plc, Britannic House, Moor Lane, EC2Y 9BU. *T:* 01-920 6283. *Clubs:* Vincent's (Oxford); Australian, Melbourne, Royal Melbourne Golf (Melbourne).

RENDLE, Peter Critchfield; Under-Secretary (Principal Finance Officer), Scottish Office, 1978–80, retired; *b* Truro, 31 July 1919; *s* of late Martyn and Florence Rendle; *m* 1944, Helen Barbara Moyes; three *s. Educ:* Queen Elizabeth's Sch., Hartlebury. Clerical Officer, Min. of Transport, 1936–49. Served War, Royal Navy, 1940–46 (Lieut RNVR). Min. of Town and Country Planning, 1949; Dept of Health for Scotland, 1950–59 (Sec., Guest Cttee on Bldg Legislation in Scotland); Scottish Home and Health Dept,

1959–63 and 1972–73; Scottish Educn Dept, 1963–72; Scottish Development Dept, 1973–78 (Under Sec., Housing). Member: Legal Aid Central Cttee for Scotland, 1980–; Scottish Is Councils Cttee of Inquiry, 1982–. *Recreations:* hockey, taking photographs, gardening. *Address:* St Clair, 159 Granton Road, Edinburgh EH5 3NL. *T:* 031-552 3396.

RENDLESHAM, 8th Baron, *cr* 1806; **Charles Anthony Hugh Thellusson;** Royal Corps of Signals; *b* 15 March 1915; *s* of Lt-Col Hon. Hugh Edmund Thellusson, DSO (3rd *s* of 5th Baron); *S* uncle, 1943; *m* 1st, 1940, Margaret Elizabeth (marr. diss. 1947; she *m* 1962, Patrick P. C. Barthropp) *d* of Lt-Col Robin Rome, Monk's Hall, Glemsford; one *d* ; 2nd, 1947, Clare, *d* of Lt-Col D. H. G. McCririck; one *s* three *d. Educ:* Eton. *Heir: s* Hon. Charles William Brooke Thellusson, *b* 10 Jan. 1954. *Address:* 498 King's Road, SW10 0LE.

See also Sir William Goring, Bt.

RENÉ, (France) Albert; barrister-at-law; President of the Republic of Seychelles since 1977; *b* Mahé, Seychelles, 16 Nov. 1935; *s* of Price René and Louisa Morgan; *m* 1st, 1956, Karen Handlay; one *d* ; 2nd, 1975, Geva Adam; one *s. Educ:* St Louis Coll., Seychelles; St Moritz, Switzerland; St Mary's Coll., Southampton, England; King's Coll., Univ. of London; Council of Legal Educn, 1956; LSE, 1961. Called to Bar, 1957. Leader, Founder and Pres., Seychelles People's United Party (first effective political party and liberation movement in Seychelles), 1964; MP, 1965; Mem. in Governing Council, 1967; Mem., Legal Assembly, 1970 and 1974; Minister of Works and Land Development, 1975, Prime Minister, 1976–77. Founder, Leader and Pres., Seychelles People's Progressive Front, 1978. Advocates positive non-alignment, the development of a Seychellois-socialist society and the promotion of the Indian Ocean as a zone of peace. *Address:* President's Office, State House, Republic of Seychelles.

RENFREW, Prof. (Andrew) Colin; FBA 1980; Disney Professor of Archaeology, University of Cambridge, and Fellow of St John's College, Cambridge, since 1981; *b* 25 July 1937; *s* of late Archibald Renfrew and Helena Douglas Renfrew (*née* Savage); *m* 1965, Jane Margaret, *d* of Ven. Walter F. Ewbank, *qv* ; two *s* one *d. Educ:* St Albans Sch.; St John's Coll., Cambridge (Exhibr); British Sch. of Archaeology, Athens. Pt I Nat. Scis Tripos 1960; BA 1st cl. hons Archaeol. and Anthrop. Tripos 1962; MA 1964; PhD 1965; ScD 1976. Pres., Cambridge Union Soc., 1961; Sir Joseph Larmor Award 1961. Nat. Service, Flying Officer (Signals), RAF, 1956–58. Res. Fellow, St John's Coll., Cambridge, 1965; Bulgarian Govt School., 1966; Univ. of Sheffield: Lectr in Prehistory and Archaeol., 1965–70; Sen. Lectr, 1970–72; Reader, 1972; Prof. of Archaeology, Southampton Univ., 1972–81. Vis. Lectr, Univ. of Calif at Los Angeles, 1967. Contested (C) Sheffield Brightside, 1968; Vice-Chm., Sheffield Brightside Conserv. Assoc., 1968–72. Member: Ancient Monuments Bd for England, 1974–; Royal Commn on Historical Monuments (England), 1977–; Trustee, Antiquity Trust, 1974–; Chm., Hants Archaeol Cttee, 1974–81; a Vice-Pres., RAI, 1982–. Lectures: Dalrymple in Archaeol., Univ. of Glasgow, 1975; George Grant MacCurdy, Harvard, 1977; Patten, Indiana Univ., 1982; Harvey, New Mexico Univ., 1982. Excavations: Saliagos near Antiparos, 1964–65; Sitagroi, Macedonia, 1968–70; Phylakopi in Melos, 1974–76; Quanterness, Orkney, 1972–74; Maes Howe, 1973–74; Ring of Brodgar, 1974; Liddle Farm, 1973–74. Rivers Meml Medal, RAI, 1979. FSA 1968; FSAScot 1970. *Publications:* (with J. D. Evans) Excavations at Saliagos near Antiparos, 1968; The Emergence of Civilisation, 1972; (ed) The Explanation of Culture Change, 1973; Before Civilisation, 1973; (ed) British Prehistory, a New Outline, 1974; Investigations in Orkney, 1979; (ed) Transformations: Mathematical Approaches to Culture Change, 1979; Problems in European Prehistory, 1979; (with J. M. Wagstaff) An Island Polity, 1982; (ed) Theory and Explanation in Archaeology, 1982; articles in archaeol jls. *Recreations:* modern art, numismatics, travel. *Address:* 5A Chaucer Road, Cambridge CB2 2EB. *T:* Cambridge 357139; Department of Archaeology, Downing Street, Cambridge CB2 3DZ. *T:* Cambridge 59714. *Clubs:* Athenæum, United Oxford & Cambridge University.

RENFREW, Rt. Rev. Charles McDonald; Titular Bishop of Abula and Auxiliary to the Archbishop of Glasgow, (RC), since 1977; Vicar General of Archdiocese of Glasgow, since 1974; *b* 21 June 1929; *s* of Alexander Renfrew and Mary (*née* Dougherty). *Educ:* St Aloysius College, Glasgow; Scots College, Rome. PhL, STL (Gregorian). Ordained Rome, 1953; Assistant at Immaculate Conception, Glasgow, 1953–56; Professor and Procurator, Blairs Coll., Aberdeen, 1956–61; First Rector and founder of St Vincent's Coll., Langbank, 1961–74. Sound and television broadcasts for BBC and STV. Comdr, Order of Merit (Republic of Italy), 1982. *Publications:* St Vincent's Prayer Book, 1971; pamphlets and articles in newspapers and magazines. *Recreation:* music, especially grand and light opera. *Address:* St Joseph's, 38 Mansionhouse Road, Glasgow G41 3DN. *T:* 041-649 2228.

RENFREW, Prof. Colin; *see* Renfrew, Prof. A. C.

RENFREW, Glen McGarvie; Managing Director, Reuters Ltd, since 1981; *b* 15 Sept. 1928; *s* of Robert Renfrew and Jane Grey Watson; *m* 1954, Daphne Ann Hailey; one *s* two *d* (and one *d* decd). *Educ:* Sydney Univ., NSW, Australia (BA). Joined Reuters, London, 1952; reporting and/or management assignments in Asia, Africa and Europe, 1956–64; London management posts in computer and economic information services, 1964–70; Manager, Reuters N America, 1971–80. *Recreation:* sailing. *Address:* c/o Reuters, 85 Fleet

Street, EC4. *T:* 01-250 1122. *Clubs:* Manhasset Bay Yacht (Long Island, NY), National Press (Washington).

RENFREY, Rt. Rev. Lionel Edward William; Dean of Adelaide, since 1966; Assistant Bishop of Adelaide, since 1969; Rector of Mallala and Two Wells, since 1981; *b* Adelaide, SA, 26 March 1916; *s* of late Alfred Cyril Marinus Renfrey and Catherine Elizabeth Rose Frerichs (*née* Dickson); *m* 1948, Joan Anne, *d* of Donald Smith, Cooke's Plains, SA; one *s* five *d*. *Educ:* Unley High School; St Mark's Coll., Univ. of Adelaide; St Barnabas' Theological Coll., Adelaide. BA (First Cl. Hons English), ThL (ACT) (Second Cl. Hons). Deacon 1940, priest 1941, Dio. Adelaide; Curate, St Cuthbert's, Prospect, 1940–43; Mission Chaplain, Mid Yorke Peninsula, 1943–44; Warden, Brotherhood of St John Baptist, 1944–47; Priest-in-charge: Berri-Barmera, 1948–50; Kensington Gardens, 1950–57; Rector, St James', Mile End, 1957–63; Rural Dean, Western Suburbs, 1962–63; Organising Chaplain, Bishop's Home Mission Soc., 1963–66; Editor, Adelaide Church Guardian, 1961–66; Archdeacon of Adelaide, 1965–66; Examining Chaplain to Bishop of Adelaide, 1965–; Administrator (*sede vacante*), Diocese of Adelaide, 1974–75. OStJ 1981 (SBStJ 1969). *Publications:* Father Wise: a Memoir, 1951; Short History of St Barnabas' Theological College, 1965; What Mean Ye By This Service?, 1978; (ed) Catholic Prayers, 1980. *Recreations:* reading, golf, motoring. *Address:* 40 Pennington Terrace, North Adelaide, SA 5006, Australia. *T:* 2672597. *Club:* Royal Adelaide Golf.

RENNELL, 3rd Baron *cr* 1933, of Rodd, Herefordshire; **John Adrian Tremayne Rodd;** *b* 28 June 1935; *s* of Hon. Gustaf Guthrie Rennell Rodd (*d* 1974) (yr *s* of 1st Baron) and Yvonne Mary Rodd (*d* 1982), *d* of late Sir Charles Murray Marling, GCMG, CB; *S* uncle, 1978; *m* 1977, Phyllis, *d* of T. D. Neill; one *s* one *d*. *Educ:* Downside; RNC, Dartmouth. Served Royal Navy, 1952–62. With Morgan Grenfell & Co. Ltd, 1963–66; free-lance journalist, 1966–67; Marks of Distinction Ltd, 1968–79; Dir, Tremayne Ltd, 1980–. *Recreations:* Scotland Rugby XV, 1958–65; golf, Real tennis. *Heir:* *s* Hon. James Roderick David Tremayne Rodd, *b* 9 March 1978. *Clubs:* White's, Queen's; Sunningdale (Ascot).

RENNIE, Alexander Allan, CBE 1980; QPM 1971; Chief Constable, West Mercia Constabulary, 1975–81; *b* 13 June 1917; *s* of Charles Rennie and Susan Parsons Rennie; *m* 1941, Lucy Brunt; one *s* one *d*. *Educ:* Ellon Acad., Aberdeenshire. Armed Services, 1941–45: commnd 30 Corps Royal Northumberland Fusiliers; active service in Europe (mentioned in despatches, 1945). Joined Durham County Constab., 1937; Chief Supt, 1963; Dep. Chief Constable, Shropshire, 1963–67; Dir, Sen. Comd Course, Police Coll., Bramshill, 1967–69; Asst Chief Constable, West Mercia, 1969–72, Dep. Chief Constable, 1973–75. OStJ 1975. *Recreations:* golf, hill walking. *Address:* 14 Minter Avenue, St Andrews Gardens, Droitwich, Worcs WR9 8RP. *Club:* Special Services.

RENNIE, Sir Alfred (Baillie), Kt 1960; formerly a Federal Justice of the West Indies Federation (1958–62); *b* 18 March 1896; *s* of James Malcolm and Mary Jane Rennie; *m* 1925, Patricia Margaret O'Gorman; one *s* two *d*. *Educ:* Wolmer's School, Kingston, Jamaica; King's College, London. Lieut, British West Indies Regt, 1916–19. Called to the Bar, 1922; practised in Jamaica and Bermuda, 1922–29; Clerk of the Courts, Jamaica, 1929–33; Resident Magistrate, 1933–34; Crown Solicitor, 1934–49; Judge of Supreme Court of Jamaica, 1949–58. *Recreation:* shooting. *Address:* 65 Friary Park, Ballabeg, Isle of Man.

RENNIE, Archibald Louden, CB 1980; Secretary, Scottish Home and Health Department, since 1977; *b* 4 June 1924; *s* of John and Isabella Rennie; *m* 1950, Kathleen Harkess; four *s*. *Educ:* Madras Coll.; St Andrews University. Experimental Officer, Mine Design Dept, Admty, 1944–47; Dept of Health for Scotland, 1947–62; Private Sec. to Sec. of State for Scotland, 1962–63; Asst Sec., Scottish Home and Health Dept, 1963–69; Registrar Gen. for Scotland, 1969–73; Under-Sec., Scottish Office, 1973–77. *Recreations:* Scottish literature, sailing, gardening. *Address:* 24A Mayfield Terrace, Edinburgh EH9 1RZ. *T:* 031-667 1359. *Club:* Scottish Arts (Edinburgh).

RENNIE, Compton Alexander, CMG 1969; Nuclear Energy Consultant since 1968; *b* 12 Dec. 1915; *s* of George Malcolm Rennie, Southampton; *m* 1941, Marjorie Dorothy Pearson; no *c*. *Educ:* Sutton Valence Sch., Kent; Sidney Sussex Coll., Cambridge. Radar Officer, TRE, Malvern, 1940–45. Atomic Energy Research Establt, Harwell, 1945–59: Overseas Liaison Officer, 1955; Dep. Head, Reactor Div., 1957; Head, High Temperature Reactor Div., 1958; Atomic Energy Establt, Winfrith, Dorset, and Chief Exec. of OECD High Temperature Reactor Project (Dragon Project), 1959–68; Dir, Nuclear Power and Reactors Div., Internat. Atomic Energy Agency, Vienna, 1970–72. Ford Foundn Atoms for Peace Award, 1969. *Recreations:* golf, sailing, gardening. *Address:* 43 East Street, Wareham, Dorset BH20 4NW. *T:* Wareham 2671.

RENNIE, James Douglas Milne; Parliamentary Counsel, since 1976; *b* 2 Nov. 1931; *s* of Douglas Frederick Milne Rennie and Margaret Wilson Fleming Rennie (*née* Keanie); *m* 1962, Patricia Margaret Calhoun Watson; one *s* one *d*. *Educ:* Charterhouse; New Coll., Oxford (Schol.). 1st cl. Hon. Mods 1953; 2nd cl. Lit. Hum. 1955; 2nd cl. Jurisprudence 1957; MA. Called to Bar, Lincoln's Inn, 1958 (Cholmeley Schol.). Asst Lectr, UCW Aberystwyth, 1957; practised at Chancery Bar, 1958–65; Asst Parly Counsel, HM Treasury, 1965; Sen. Asst Parly Counsel, 1972; Dep. Parly Counsel, 1973–75. *Recreations:*

opera, travel. *Address:* 46 Holland Park, W11 3RS. *T:* 01-727 5000; Old Tythe House, Happisburgh, Norfolk. *T:* Walcot 650380.

RENNIE, John Chalmers; Town Clerk of Aberdeen, 1946–68; retired; *b* 16 April 1907; *s* of late John Chalmers Rennie, Pharmacist, Wishaw; *m* 1937, Georgina Stoddart, *d* of late Henry Bell, Engineer and Ironfounder, Wishaw; one *s*. *Educ:* University of Glasgow (BL). Town Clerk Depute, Motherwell and Wishaw, 1929–43; Town Clerk Depute, Aberdeen, 1943–46. *Recreation:* do-it-yourself. *Address:* 34 Morningfield Road, Aberdeen AB2 4AQ. *T:* Aberdeen 36904.

RENNIE, Sir John Shaw, GCMG 1968 (KCMG 1962; CMG 1958); OBE 1955; Commissioner-General, United Nations Relief and Works Agency for Palestine Refugees, 1971–77 (Deputy Commissioner-General, 1968–71); *b* 12 Jan. 1917; *s* of late John Shaw Rennie, Saskatoon, Sask, Canada; *m* 1946, Mary Winifred Macalpine Robertson; one *s*. *Educ:* Hillhead High School; Glasgow University; Balliol College, Oxford. Cadet, Tanganyika, 1940; Asst District Officer, 1942; District Officer, 1949; Deputy Colonial Secretary, Mauritius, 1951; British Resident Comr, New Hebrides, 1955–62; Governor and C-in-C of Mauritius, 1962–March 1968, Governor-General, March–Aug. 1968. Mem. Council, Royal Anthropological Inst., 1981–. Hon. LLD Glasgow, 1972. *Address:* 26 College Cross, N1 1PR; via Roma 33, 06050 Collazzone (PG), Italy. *Club:* Royal Commonwealth Society.

RENOWDEN, Very Rev. Charles Raymond; Dean of St Asaph since 1971; *b* 27 Oct. 1923; *s* of Rev. Canon Charles Renowden; *m* 1951, Ruth Cecil Mary Collis; one *s* two *d*. *Educ:* Llandysil Grammar Sch.; St David's Univ. Coll., Lampeter; Selwyn Coll., Cambridge. BA (Hons Philosophy, cl. I), Lampeter; BA, MA (Hons Theology, cl. I), Cambridge. Served War, Army, Intelligence Corps, in India and Japan, 1944–47. Cambridge Ordination Course; Deacon, 1951, Priest, 1952, Wales. Asst Curate, Hubberston, Milford Haven, 1951–55. St David's Univ. Coll., Lampeter: Lectr in Philosophy and Theology, 1955–57; Head of Dept of Philosophy, 1957–69; Sen. Lectr in Philosophy and Theology, 1969–71. *Publications:* (monograph) The Idea of Unity, 1965; New Patterns of Ministry, 1973; The Rôle of a Cathedral Today and Tomorrow, 1974; contributor to: Theology, The Modern Churchman, Church Quarterly Review, Trivium, Province. *Recreations:* music, gardening, ornithology. *Address:* The Deanery, St Asaph, Clwyd. *T:* St Asaph 583597.

RENSHAW, Sir (Charles) Maurice (Bine), 3rd Bt *cr* 1903; *b* 7 Oct. 1912; *s* of Sir (Charles) Stephen (Bine) Renshaw, 2nd Bt and of Edith Mary, *d* of Rear-Adm. Sir Edward Chichester, 9th Bt, CB, CMG; *S* father, 1976; *m* 1942, Isabel Bassett (marr. diss. 1947), *d* of late Rev. John L. T. Popkin; one *s* one *d* (and one *s* decd); *m* 2nd, Winifred May, *d* of H. F. Gliddon, Ashwater, Devon, and formerly wife of James H. T. Sheldon; three *s* three *d*. *Educ:* Eton. Served as Flying Officer, RAF (invalided). *Heir:* *s* John David Renshaw [*b* 9 Oct. 1945; *m* 1970, Jennifer, *d* of Group Captain F. Murray, RAF]. *Address:* Tam-na-Marghaidh, Balquhidder, Perthshire; Linwood, Instow, N Devon.

RENSHAW, Hon. John Brophy, AC 1979; Agent-General for New South Wales in London, since 1980; *b* 8 Aug. 1909; *s* of late J. I. Renshaw; *m* 1st, 1943 (she *d* 1964); one *s*; 2nd, 1966, Mrs M. McKay. *Educ:* Ryde Sch. Mem., Coonabarabran Shire Council, 1937–40 (Pres., 1939–40); MLA, Castlereagh, NSW, 1941–80; Assistant Minister: for Lands, 1950; for Local Govt, 1952; Minister: for Public Works, 1952, and for Local Govt, 1953–56; for Local Govt and Highways, 1956–59; Treasurer, 1959–65; Dep. Premier and Minister for Industrial Develt and Decentralisation, 1962–64; Premier of NSW, 1964–65; Leader of the Opposition, 1965–68 (resigned); Treasurer, 1976–80. *Address:* New South Wales House, 66 Strand, WC2.

RENTON, family name of **Baron Renton.**

RENTON, Baron *cr* 1979 (Life Peer), of Huntingdon in the County of Cambridgeshire; **David Lockhart-Mure Renton,** KBE 1964; TD; PC 1962; QC 1954; MA; BCL; DL; *b* 12 Aug. 1908; *s* of late Dr Maurice Waugh Renton, The Bridge House, Dartford, Kent, and Eszma Olivia, *d* of late Allen Walter Borman, Alexandria; *m* 1947, Claire Cicely (Pres., Greater London Assoc. for the Disabled), *y d* of late Walter Duncan; three *d*. *Educ:* Stubbington; Oundle; University College, Oxford. BA (Hons Jurisprudence), 1930; BCL, 1931; MA. Called to Bar, Lincoln's Inn, 1933; South-Eastern Circuit; elected to General Council of the Bar, 1939; Bencher, Lincoln's Inn, 1962, Treasurer, 1979. Commnd RE (TA), 1938; transferred to RA 1940; served throughout War of 1939–45; Capt. 1941; Major, 1943; served in Middle East, 1942–45. MP (Nat L) 1945–50, (Nat L and C) 1950–68, (C) 1968–79, Huntingdonshire; Parly Sec., Min. of Fuel and Power, 1955–57, Ministry of Power, 1957–58; Joint Parly Under-Sec. of State, Home Office, 1958–61; Minister of State, Home Office, 1961–62; Chm., Select Cttee for Revision of Standing Orders, House of Commons, 1963 and 1970; Dep. Chm., Select Cttee on H of C Procedure, 1976–78; Mem., Cttee of Privileges, 1973–79. Recorder of Rochester, 1963–68, of Guildford, 1968–71; Vice-Chm., Council of Legal Educn, 1968–70, 1971–73. Member: Senate of Inns of Court, 1967–69, 1970–71, 1975–79; Commn on the Constitution, 1971–73; Chm., Cttee on Preparation of Legislation, 1973–75. Pres., Statute Law Soc., 1980–. Pres., Royal Soc. for Mentally Handicapped Children, 1982– (Hon. Treas., 1976–78; Chm., 1978–82). President: Conservation Soc., 1970–71; Nat. Council for Civil Def., 1980–. Patron: Nat. Law Library, 1979–; Huntingdonshire Conservative Assoc., 1979–; Ravenswood Foundn, 1979–. DL

Huntingdonshire, 1962, Huntingdon and Peterborough, 1964, Cambs, 1974. Coronation and Jubilee Medals. *Recreations:* outdoor sports and games, gardening. *Address:* Moat House, Abbots Ripton, Huntingdon. *T:* Abbots Ripton 227; 22 Old Buildings, Lincoln's Inn, WC2. *T:* 01-242 8986. *Clubs:* Carlton, Pratt's.

RENTON, Gordon Pearson; Assistant Under-Secretary of State, Home Office, since 1978; *b* 12 Dec. 1928; *s* of Herbert Renton and Annie (*née* Pearson); *m* 1st, 1952, Joan Mary Lucas (marr. diss. 1971); two *s*; 2nd, 1978, Sylvia Jones. *Educ:* King Edward VII Sch., Sheffield; Lincoln Coll., Oxford (Scholar, BA Lit. Hum.). Served Royal Signals, 1951-53. Teacher, W Riding, 1953-54; Asst Principal, Home Office, 1954; Asst Private Sec. to Home Sec. and Lord Privy Seal, 1959-60; Principal, 1960; Asst Sec., 1967. *Recreations:* music, gardening, sailing. *Address:* Cornwalls, Felden Lane, Boxmoor, Herts. *T:* Hemel Hempstead 50429. *Club:* Reform.

RENTON, Air Cdre Helen Ferguson, CB 1982; Director, Women's Royal Air Force, since 1980; *b* 31 March 1931; *d* of late John Paul Renton and Sarah Graham (*née* Cook). *Educ:* Stirling High Sch.; Glasgow Univ. (MA). Joined WRAF, 1954; commnd, 1955; served in UK, 1955-60; Cyprus, 1960-62; HQ Staff, Germany, 1967; MoD Staff, 1968-71; NEAF, 1971-72; Training Comd, 1973-76; MoD Staff, 1976-78. Hon. LLD Glasgow, 1981. *Publications:* (jtly) Service Women, 1977. *Recreations:* needlework, travel, reading. *Address:* c/o Ministry of Defence, Adastral House, Theobald's Road, WC1X 8RU. *T:* 01-430 7141. *Club:* Royal Air Force.

RENTON, Ronald Timothy; MP (C) Mid-Sussex since Feb. 1974; *b* 28 May 1932; *yr s* of R. K. D. Renton, CBE, and Mrs Renton, MBE; *m* 1960, Alice Fergusson of Kilkerran, Ayrshire; two *s* three *d. Educ:* Eton Coll. (King's Schol.); Magdalen Coll., Oxford (Roberts Gawen Schol.). First cl. degree in History, MA Oxon. Joined C. Tennant Sons & Co. Ltd, London, 1954; with Tennants' subsidiaries in Canada, 1957-62; Dir, C. Tennant Sons & Co. Ltd and Managing Dir of Tennant Trading Ltd, 1964-73; Director: Silvermines Ltd, 1967-; Australia & New Zealand Banking Group, 1967-76; J. H. Vavasseur & Co. Ltd, 1971-74. Mem., BBC Gen. Adv. Council, 1982-. Contested (C) Sheffield Park Div., 1970; PPS to Rt Hon. John Biffen, MP, 1979-81; Mem., Select Cttee on Nationalised Industries, 1974-79; Vice-Chm., Cons. Parly Trade Cttee, 1974-79; Chm., Cons. Commonwealth and Overseas Council, 1982-; Vice-Pres., 1978-80, Pres., 1980-, Cons. Trade Unionists; Industry and Parlt Trust Fellowship, 1977-79. *Publications:* articles in newspapers and periodicals. *Recreations:* gardening, tennis, growing trees. *Address:* Mount Harry House, Offham, Lewes, E Sussex. *T:* Lewes 4456. *Clubs:* Brooks's, Coningsby.

RENWICK, family name of **Baron Renwick.**

RENWICK, 2nd Baron *cr* 1964, of Coombe; **Harry Andrew Renwick;** Bt 1927; Member of the Stock Exchange, associated with W. Greenwell & Co. (Partner, 1964-80); *b* 10 Oct. 1935; *s* of 1st Baron Renwick, KBE, and of Mrs John Ormiston, Miserden House, Stroud, *er d* of late Major Harold Parkes, Alveston, Stratford-on-Avon; *S* father, 1973; *m* 1965, Susan Jane, *d* of late Captain Kenneth S. B. Lucking and of Mrs Moir P. Stormonth-Darling, Lednathie, Glen Prosen, Angus; two *s. Educ:* Eton. Grenadier Guards (National Service), 1955-56. Director: General Technology Systems Ltd, 1975-; Piev Ltd, 1979-; Eurotech Developments Ltd, 1980-. Vice-Pres., British Dyslexia Assoc., 1982- (Chm., 1977-82). *Heir: s* Hon. Robert James Renwick, *b* 19 Aug. 1966. *Address:* 22 Rosslyn Hill, Hampstead, NW3 1PD. *Clubs:* White's, Turf.

RENWICK, George Russell, MA; Headmaster, Dover College, 1934-54, retired; *b* 7 Aug. 1901; *s* of George Edward Renwick and Helen Isabella Russell; *m* 1927, Isabella Alice Watkins; one *s* three *d. Educ:* Charterhouse; New College, Oxford. Assistant Master, Stowe School, 1924-25; Charterhouse, 1926-34; OUAC 1923, 1924; British Olympic Team, 1924. Councillor, Dover Borough Council, 1946-50. *Address:* The Old Parsonage, Sidlesham, near Chichester. *Club:* (former Commodore) Royal Cinque Ports Yacht (Dover).

RENWICK, Prof. James Harrison, DSc, FRCP, FRCPath; Professor of Human Genetics and Teratology, University of London, since 1979; *b* 4 Feb. 1926; *s* of late Raymond Renwick and of Edith Helen Renwick; *m* 1st, 1959, Helena Verheyden (marr. diss. 1979); one *s* one *d* ; 2nd, 1981, Kathleen Salafia. *Educ:* Sedbergh School; Univ. of St Andrews; MB ChB (commend), 1948; University Coll. London; PhD 1956, DSc 1970; FRCP 1972, MFCM 1972; FRCPath 1982. Captain RAMC, Korean war; research on genetical effects of atomic bomb, Hiroshima, 1951-53. Univ. of Glasgow, 1959, Prof. of Human Genetics, 1967-68; London Sch. of Hygiene and Tropical Medicine, 1968, Head of Preventive Teratology Unit, 1977-. Hon. Treasurer, Genetical Soc., 1960-65, Hon. Auditor, 1965-72. FRSocMed. Freeman, Co. of Stationers and Newspaper Makers. *Publications:* numerous scientific articles on mapping of genes on human chromosomes and on prevention of human congenital malformations. *Recreations:* walking, music. *Address:* 409 Gilbert House, Barbican, EC2. *T:* (home) 01-638 3332; (office) 01-637 2839.

RENWICK, Sir John, Kt 1968; JP; Consultant with Renwick & Co., Solicitors, Eckington; *b* 16 Nov. 1901; *s* of James David and Mary Beatrice Renwick; *m* 1933, Margaret Rachel, *d* of Alfred Stanley and Rachel Fawcett; one *s* one *d. Educ:* King Edward VII School, Sheffield; Sidney Sussex College,

Cambridge (MA, LLB). Admitted a Solicitor, 1927, practising, since, at Eckington, near Sheffield. Mem. Council, Law Society, 1949-72 (Pres. 1967-68); Chm., Trustee Savings Banks Inspection Cttee, 1954-76; Trustee, Sheffield Savings Bank, 1948- (Chm., 1972); Sheffield Town Trustee, 1971. Hon. LLD Sheffield, 1968. *Address:* Saint Cross, Ridgeway, Sheffield S12 3YA. *T:* Eckington (Derbyshire) 433114.

RENWICK, Sir Richard Eustace, 4th Bt *cr* 1921; *b* 13 Jan. 1938; *er s* of Sir Eustace Deuchar Renwick, 3rd Bt, and of Diana Mary, *e d* of Colonel Bernard Cruddas, DSO; *S* father, 1973; *m* 1966, Caroline Anne, *er d* of Major Rupert Milburn; three *s. Educ:* Eton. *Heir: s* Charles Richard Renwick, *b* 10 April 1967. *Address:* Whalton House, Whalton, Morpeth, Northumberland. *T:* Whalton 383. *Club:* Northern Counties (Newcastle).

RENWICK, Robin William, CMG 1980; HM Diplomatic Service; Head of Chancery, Washington, since 1981; *b* 13 Dec. 1937; *s* of Richard Renwick, Edinburgh, and the late Clarice Henderson; *m* 1965, Anne Colette Giudicelli; one *s* one *d. Educ:* St Paul's Sch.; Jesus Coll., Cambridge (1st Cl. Hons History Tripos; Newling Prize); Univ. of Paris (Sorbonne). Army, 1956-58. Entered Foreign Service, 1963; Dakar, 1963-64; FO, 1964-66; New Delhi, 1966-69; Private Sec. to Minister of State, FCO, 1970-72; First Sec., Paris, 1972-76; Counsellor, Cabinet Office, 1976-78; Head, Rhodesia Dept, FCO, 1978-80; Political Adviser to Governor of Rhodesia, 1980; Vis. Fellow, Center for Internat. Affairs, Harvard, 1980-81. *Publication:* Economic Sanctions, 1981. *Recreation:* tennis. *Address:* c/o Foreign and Commonwealth Office, SW1; British Embassy, 3100 Massachusetts Avenue NW, Washington, DC 20008, USA. *Clubs:* Hurlingham, Travellers'.

REPORTER, Sir Shapoor (Ardeshirji), KBE 1973 (OBE 1969); Consultant on Economic and Political Matters concerning Iran, since 1962; *b* 26 Feb. 1921; *s* of Ardeshirji Reporter and Shirin Reporter; *m* 1952, Assia Alexandra; one *s* one *d. Educ:* Zoroastrian Public Sch., Teheran; matriculated in Bombay (specially designed course in Political Science under Cambridge Univ. Tutors, UK). PRO, British Legation, Teheran, 1941-43; in charge of Persian Unit of All India Radio, New Delhi, 1943-45; Teaching English, Imperial Staff Coll., Teheran, 1945-48; Political Adviser, US Embassy, Teheran, 1948-54; Free-lance Correspondent, 1954-62; Economic Consultant to major British interests in Iran, 1962-73. *Publications:* English-Persian Phrases, 1945 (Delhi); Dictionary of English-Persian Idioms, 1956 (Teheran); Dictionary of Persian-English Idioms, 1972 (Teheran Univ.). *Recreations:* tennis, walking, travelling.

REPTON, Bishop Suffragan of, since 1977; **Rt. Rev. Stephen Edmund Verney,** MBE 1945; *b* 17 April 1919; 2nd *s* of late Sir Harry Verney, 4th Bt, DSO and Lady Rachel Verney (*née* Bruce); *m* 1st, 1947, Priscilla Avice Sophie Schwerdt (*d* 1974); one *s* three *d* ; 2nd, 1981, Sandra Ann Bailey. *Educ:* Harrow School; Balliol College, Oxford (MA). Curate of Gedling, Nottingham, 1950; Priest-in-charge and then first Vicar, St Francis, Clifton, Nottingham, 1952; Vicar of Leamington Hastings and Diocesan Missioner, Dio. Coventry, 1958; Canon Residentiary, Coventry Cathedral, 1964; Canon of Windsor, 1970. *Publications:* Fire in Coventry, 1964; People and Cities, 1969; Into the New Age, 1976. *Recreations:* conversation and aloneness; music, gardening, travel. *Address:* Repton House, Lea, Matlock, Derbys DE4 5JP. *Club:* English-Speaking Union.

See also L. J. Verney, Sir R. B. Verney, Bt.

RESNAIS, Alain; French film director; *b* Vannes, 3 June 1922; *s* of Pierre Resnais and Jeanne (*née* Gachet); *m* 1969, Florence Mairaux. *Educ:* Collège St François-Xavier, Vannes; Institut des hautes études cinématographiques. Assistant to Nicole Védrée for film Paris 1900, 1947-48; has directed his own films (many of which have won prizes), since 1948. Short films, 1948-59, include: Van Gogh, 1948; Guernica (jtly with Robert Hessens), 1950; Les statues meurent aussi (jtly with Chris Marker), 1952; Nuit et brouillard, 1955. Full length films include: Hiroshima mon amour, 1959; L'année dernière à Marienbad, 1961; Muriel, 1963; La guerre est finie, 1966; Je t'aime, je t'aime, 1968; Stavisky, 1974; Providence, 1977; Mon Oncle d'Amérique, 1980. *Address:* 70 rue des Plantes, 75014 Paris, France; Artmedia, 10 Avenue George V, 75008 Paris, France.

RESO, Sidney Joseph; Vice President, Exxon Corporation, since 1978; *b* 12 Feb. 1934; *s* of late James A. Reso and of J. Agnes Reso; *m* 1955, Patricia M. Armond; two *s* three *d. Educ:* Louisiana State Univ. (BS Petroleum Engrg). Joined Humble Oil & Refining Co., Houston, Texas (now Exxon Co., USA), as engineer, 1957; Australia: engrg assignments, 1961-66; managerial assignments, 1967-71; Dir, Esso Australia Ltd, Sydney, 1972; managerial assignments, USA, 1973-74; Vice-Pres., Esso Europe Inc. and Managing Dir, Esso Petroleum Co., 1975-78. Member: Supervisory Bd of Dirs, Nederlandse Aardoli Maatschappij BV, 1975-; Exec. Cttee, Oil Industry Internat. Exploration and Prodn Forum, 1975-; Director: Exxon Prodn Research Co., Houston, Texas, 1975-; Offshore Pollution Liability Assoc. Ltd (OPOL), 1975-; President and Director: Esso Exploration and Prodn Ireland, Inc., 1975; Esso Exploration and Prodn Ireland Ltd, 1975-; Rep., Exxon Corp., on Council of UK Offshore Operators Assoc. Ltd (UKOOA), 1975-. *Recreations:* tennis, photography, reading. *Address:* Exxon Corporation, 1251 Avenue of the Americas, New York, NY 10020, USA. *Clubs:* Lansdowne, Highgate Golf.

RESTIEAUX, Rt. Rev. Cyril Edward; *see* Plymouth, Bishop of, (RC).

RESTREPO-LONDOÑO, Andrés; Order of Bocaya, Colombia; Colombian Ambassador to the Court of St James's, since 1981; *b* 20 Jan. 1942; *m* 1968, Ghislaine Ibiza; one *s* three *d*. *Educ:* Universidad de Antioquia; Université de Paris (postgraduate courses, 1966). Professor and Head of Economic Dept., Univ. de Antioquia, 1967-68; Gen. Man., La Primavera chain of stores, 1969-76; Finance Man., Empresas Públicas de Medellin, 1976-79; Gen. Man., Carbones de Colombia (Colombian Coal Bd), 1979-80; Minister for Economic Develt, May 1980-March 1981. Order Sol of Peru; Order Cruzeiro do Sul, Brazil. *Publications:* Carbones Térmicos en Colombia, Bases para una Política Contractual, 1981; several articles in El Colombiano, daily newspaper of Medellin, Colombia. *Recreations:* fishing, tennis. *Address:* 76 Chester Square, SW1. *T:* 01-730 1625. *Clubs:* Travellers', Royal Automobile, Hurlingham; Bogotá Sports.

RETTIE, (James) Philip, TD 1962; Chairman: Wm Low and Co. plc, since 1980; Sea Fish Industry Authority, since 1981; *b* 7 Dec. 1926; *s* of James Rettie and Rachel Buist; *m* 1st, 1955, Helen Grant; two *s* one *d*; 2nd, 1980, Mrs Diana Harvey (*née* Ballantyne). *Educ:* Trinity College, Glenalmond. Royal Engineers, 1945-48; RE (TA), 1949-65. Wm Low & Co., 1948-; farmer, 1964-. Trustee, Tayside TSB, 1967-. Hon. Col, 117 (Highland) Field Support Squadron, RE, TAVR, 1982-. *Recreations:* shooting, gardening, hill-walking. *Address:* Wester Ballindean, Inchture, Perthshire PH14 9QS. *T:* Inchture 86337. *Club:* Caledonian.

REUTER, Prof. Gerd Edzard Harry, MA Cantab; Professor of Mathematics, Imperial College of Science and Technology, London, since 1965; *b* 21 Nov. 1921; *s* of Ernst Rudolf Johannes Reuter and Gertrud Charlotte Reuter (*née* Scholz); *m* 1945, Eileen Grace Legard; one *s* three *d*. *Educ:* The Leys School and Trinity College, Cambridge. Mem. of Dept of Mathematics, Univ. of Manchester, 1946-58; Professor of Pure Mathematics, Univ. of Durham, 1959-65. *Publications:* Elementary Differential Equations and Operators, 1958; articles in various mathematical and scientific jls. *Address:* Department of Mathematics, Imperial College of Science and Technology, SW7.

REVANS, Sir John, Kt 1977; CBE 1967 (MBE 1943); retired; *b* 7 June 1911; *s* of Thomas William Revans, MINA and Ethel Amelia Revans; *m* 1936, Eileen Parkhurst Mitchell; two *d*. *Educ:* Middlesex Hosp. Med. Sch. (Broderip Schol. in Med., Surgery and Path.; Forensic Medicine Prize, 1935); Royal Army Med. Coll. (Montefiore Prize in Surgery, 1936). London Univ. DCH 1946; FRCP 1969. Served War of 1939-45 (despatches 1941): Col Indian Med. Service, 1936-47, retd. Sen. Admin. MO, Wessex RHB, 1959-73; Regional MO, Wessex RHA, 1973-76. Adviser on hosps and health services to Royal Commn on Health, Newfoundland and Labrador, 1965-66; Member: Med. Cons. Cttee, Nuffield Provincial Hosps Trust, 1961-76; Standing Nursing Adv. Cttee, Central Health Services Council; Cttee on Gen. Practice of CHSC; Cttee on Senior Nursing Staff Structure in Hosp. Service; Cttee on Rehabilitation; Cttee on Hosp. Complaints; Central Midwives Bd, 1963-67. Vis. Prof. of Health Service Admin, Univ. of London, 1969. Mem. Council, Univ. of Southampton, 1978. Hon. LLD Southampton, 1970. Hon. FRCGP 1974. OStJ 1946. *Recreation:* sailing (RYA/DTI Yachtmaster (Offshore)). *Address:* The Triangle, Durley, Southampton SO3 2AJ. *T:* Durley 348. *Club:* Little Ship.
See also Prof. R. W. Revans.

REVANS, Prof. Reginald William, PhD; MIMinE; Founder, Action Learning Trust, 1977; *b* 14 May 1907; *s* of Thomas William Revans, Principal Ship Surveyor, Board of Trade; *m* 1st, 1932, Annida Aquist, Gothenburg (marriage dissolved, 1947); three *d*; 2nd, 1955, Norah Mary Merritt, Chelmsford; one *s*. *Educ:* Battersea Grammar School; University Coll., London; Emmanuel Coll., Cambridge. BSc London, PhD Cantab. Commonwealth Fund Fellow, Univ. of Michigan, 1930-32; Research Fellow, Emmanuel Coll., Cambridge, 1932-35; Dep. Chief Education Officer, Essex CC, 1935-45; Dir of Education, Mining Assoc. of Gt Britain, 1945-47 and NCB, 1947-50; Research on management of coalmines, 1950-55; Prof., Industrial Admin., Univ. of Manchester, 1955-65; Res. Fellow, Guy's Hosp. Med. Sch., 1965-68; External Prof., Management Studies, Leeds Univ., 1976-. Dist. Vis. Scholar, Southern Methodist Univ., USA, 1972. Hon. DSc Bath, 1969. Chevalier, Order of Leopold, Belgium, 1971. *Publications:* Report on Education for Mining Industry, 1945; Education of the Young Worker, 1949; Standards for Morale, 1964; Science and the Manager, 1965; The Theory and Practice of Management, 1965; Developing Effective Managers, 1971; (ed) Hospitals, Communication, Choice and Change, 1972; Workers' Attitudes and Motivation (OECD Report), 1972; Childhood and Maturity, 1973; Action Learning in Hospitals, 1976; The ABC of Action Learning, 1978; Action Learning, 1979; The Origins and Growth of Action Learning, 1982; various in professional magazines upon application of analytical methods to understanding of industrial morale. *Recreations:* British Olympic Team, 1928; holder of Cambridge undergraduate long jump record, 1929-62. *Address:* 8 Higher Downs, Altrincham, Cheshire. *Club:* National Liberal.
See also Sir J. R evans.

REVELSTOKE, 4th Baron *cr* 1885; **Rupert Baring;** *b* 8 Feb. 1911; *o s* of 3rd Baron and Maude (*d* 1922), *d* of late Pierre Lorillard; *S* father, 1934; *m* 1934, Flora (who obtained a divorce 1944), 2nd *d* of 1st Baron Hesketh; two *s*. *Educ:* Eton. 2nd Lt Royal Armoured Corps (TA). *Heir: s* Hon. John Baring, *b* 2 Dec. 1934. *Address:* Lambay Island, Rush, Co. Dublin, Ireland.

REVERDIN, Prof. Olivier, DrLitt; Professor of Greek, University of Geneva, since 1958; Member, Consultative Assembly of Council of Europe, 1963-74 (President, 1969-72); Deputy (Liberal) for Geneva, Swiss National Council, 1955-71, Council of States (Senate), 1971-79; *b* 15 July 1913; *m* 1936, Renée Chaponnière; one *s* one *d*. *Educ:* Geneva, Paris and Athens. LicLitt 1935. Foreign Mem., French Sch. of Archaeology, Athens, 1936-38; Attaché Swiss Legation, Service of Foreign Interests, Rome, 1941-43; Privatdocent of Greek, Univ. of Geneva, 1945-57; Parly Redactor, 1945-54; Chief Editor 1954-59, Manager 1954-67, Pres., 1972-79, Journal de Genève. Mem. 1963-80, Pres. 1968-80, Swiss National Research Council; Mem., Swiss Science Council; Pres., Fondation Hardt pour l'étude de l'antiquité classique, Geneva, 1959-; Vice-Pres., European Science Foundn, 1974-77, Mem. Exec. Council, 1977-80. *Publications:* La religion de la cité platonicienne, 1945; La guerre du Sonderbund, 1947; La Crète, berceau de la civilisation occidentale, 1960; Connaissance de la Suisse, 1966. *Address:* 8 rue des Granges, 1204 Geneva, Switzerland. *T:* 022-21-51-91.

REVIE, Donald, OBE; Manager, Al Nasr Football Club, since 1980; *b* 10 July 1927; *m* 1949, Elsie May Leonard Duncan; one *s* one *d*. *Educ:* Archibald Secondary Modern Sch., Middlesbrough, Yorks. Professional footballer with Leicester, Hull, Manchester City, Sunderland, and Leeds United, 1945-61; Player-Manager, then Manager, Leeds United Football Club, 1961-74; Manager of England Team, FA, 1974-77; National Team Coach, UAE FA, 1977-80. *Publication:* Soccer's Happy Wanderer, 1955. *Recreations:* golf, reading. *Address:* Al Nasr Club, PO Box 2226, Dubai, United Arab Emirates.

REVINGTON, Air Commodore Arthur Pethick, CB 1950; CBE 1945 (OBE 1940); retired; *b* 24 June 1901; *s* of late Cdr G. A. Revington, RN; *m* 1946, Joan (*d* 1981), widow of Cuthbert William Prideaux Selby. *Educ:* Plymouth College; RAF College, Cranwell. Served War of 1939-45 (despatches thrice); AOC No 4 Gp, 1946-47; AOC No 47 Gp, 1948-50; Sen. Air Liaison Officer, United Kingdom Service Liaison Staff, Canada, 1950-53; retired 1954. *Address:* Trescoll, Newton Ferrers, South Devon. *T:* Newton Ferrers 872465. *Clubs:* Royal Air Force; Royal Air Force Yacht.

REX, Prof. John Arderne; Director, Social Science Research Council Research Unit on Ethnic Relations, University of Aston in Birmingham, since 1979; *b* 5 March 1925; *s* of Frederick Edward George Rex and Winifred Natalie Rex; *m* 1st, 1949, Pamela Margaret Rutherford (marr. diss. 1963); two *d*; 2nd, 1965, Margaret Ellen Biggs; two *s*. *Educ:* Grey Institute High Sch. and Rhodes University Coll., S Africa. BA (S Africa), PhD (Leeds). Served War, Royal Navy (Able Seaman), 1943-45. Graduated, 1948; Lecturer: Univ. of Leeds, 1949-62; Birmingham, 1962-64; Prof. of Social Theory and Institutions, Durham, 1964-70; Prof. of Sociology, Univ. of Warwick, 1970-79. Vis. Prof., Univ. of Toronto, 1974-75. *Publications:* Key Problems of Sociological Theory, 1961; (with Robert Moore) Race Community and Conflict, 1967, 2nd edn 1973; Race Relations in Sociological Theory, 1970; Discovering Sociology, 1973; Race, Colonialism and the City, 1974; (ed) Approaches to Sociology, 1974; Sociology and the Demystification of the Modern World, 1974; (with Sally Tomlinson) Colonial Immigrants in a British City, 1979; Social Conflict, 1980; (ed) Apartheid and Social Research, 1981. *Recreations:* politics, race relations work. *Address:* Research Unit for Ethnic Relations, St Peter's College, University of Aston in Birmingham, College Road, Alum Rock, Birmingham B8 3TE.

REY, Jean; Leader, Parti réformateur-libéral de Wallonie, since 1976; Member, European Parliament, 1979-80; *b* Liège, 15 July 1902; *s* of Arnold Rey, Protestant Pastor; *m*; four *c*. *Educ:* Athénée and Univ. of Liège (Dr of Law). Advocate, Court of Appeal, Liège, 1926-58; Served War of 1939-45 (Croix de Guerre, Commem. Medal); POW, Germany, 1940-45. Councillor, Liège, 1935-58; Mem. for Liège, Chamber of Deputies, 1939-58; founder Mem., Entente Libérale Wallone; Minister of Reconstruction, 1949-50; Minister of Economic Affairs, 1954-58; Mem. EEC, 1958-67, Pres. 1967-70. Delegate; 3rd Gen. Assembly, UN, Paris, 1948; 1st Assembly, 1949 and 5th Assembly, 1953, Council of Europe; Mem., Commn to study European Problems, 1952. President: Court of Arbitration, Internat. Chamber of Commerce, 1972-77; Internat. European Movement, 1974-78. Dir. Philips Electrical Gp, 1970-73; President: Sofina, 1971-79; Papeteries de Belgique, 1973-80. Hon. DCL Oxon, 1968; Dr *hc:* Harvard; Pace Univ., NY; Drew Univ., NJ. Grand Cross, Order of the Crown; Grand Officer, Order of Leopold; Grand Cross, Order of Orange Nassau; Grand Cordon, Order of Lion of Finland; Comdr, Order of Crown of Oak; Comdr, Legion of Honour, and many other high national distinctions. *Address:* 16 rue Hovade, 4040 Tilff, Belgium.

REYES, Narciso G., Bintang Mahaputera, 1964; Order of Diplomatic Service Merit, 1972; Secretary General, Association of South-East Asian Nations, 1980-82; *b* Manila, 6 Feb. 1914; *m*. *Educ:* Univ. of Sto Tomas (AB). Mem., English Faculty, Univ. of Sto Tomas, 1935-36; Assoc. Ed., Philippines Commonweal, 1935-41; Nat. Language Faculty, Ateneo de Manila, 1939-41; Assoc. Ed., Manila Post, 1945-47; Assoc. News Ed., Evening News, Manila, 1947-48; Man. Ed., Philippine Newspaper Guild Organ, 1947-48; various advisory and UN posts, 1948-; Dir, Philippine Information Agency, 1954-55; Minister-Counsellor, Bangkok, 1956; Public Relations Dir, SEATO, 1956-58; Minister, later Amb., Burma, 1958-62; Ambassador to: Indonesia, 1962-67; London, Stockholm, Oslo, Copenhagen, 1967-70; Permanent Rep. to UN, 1970-77; Philippine Ambassador to People's Republic of China, 1977-80. Mem. various delegns and missions, incl. sessions of UN; Philippine Rep. to

UN Commn for Social Devt, 1967-72 (Vice-Chm., 1967; Chm., 1968); Special UN Rep. on Social Develt, 1968; Rep. to UN Human Rights Commn, 1970-72; Chairman: UNICEF Exec. Bd, 1972-74; UN Gen. Assembly Finance and Economic Cttee, 1971; Pres., UNDP Governing Council; Vice-Pres., UN Environment Governing Council. Outstanding Alumnus, Univ. of Sto Tomas, 1969. Dr of Laws (*hc*), Philippine Women's Univ., 1977. *Publications:* essays, poems and short stories. *Address:* 8 Lipa Road, Philamlife Homes, Quezon City, Manila, Philippine.

REYNOLD, Frederic, QC 1982; *b* 7 Jan. 1936; *s* of Henry and Regina Reynold. *Educ:* Battersea Grammar School; Magdalen College, Oxford. BA Hons Jurisprudence. Called to the Bar, Gray's Inn, 1960; commenced practice, 1963. *Publication:* The Judge as Lawmaker, 1967. *Recreations:* music, the arts, association croquet, dining out among friends. *Address:* 5 Hillcrest, 51 Ladbroke Grove, W11. *T:* 01-229 3848. *Club:* Sussex County Croquet.

REYNOLDS, Alan (Munro); painter, maker of reliefs, and printmaker; *b* 27 April 1926; *m* 1957, Vona Darby. *Educ:* Woolwich Polytechnic Art School; Royal College of Art (Scholarship and Medal). One man exhibitions: Redfern Gall., 1952, 1953, 1954, 1956, 1960, 1962, 1964, 1966, 1970, 1972, 1974; Durlacher Gall., New York, 1954, 1959; Leicester Galleries, 1958; Aldeburgh, Suffolk, 1965; Arnolfini Gall., Bristol, 1971 (graphics); Annely Juda Fine Art, 1978; Juda Rowan Gall., 1982; Thomas Agnew, Albemarle Street Gall., 1982. Work in exhibitions: Carnegie (Pittsburgh) Internat., USA, 1952, 1955, 1958, 1961; Internat. Exhibn, Rome, (awarded one of the three equal prizes), subsequently Musée d'Art Moderne, Paris, and Brussels; British Council Exhibn, Oslo and Copenhagen, 1956; Redfern Gall., 1971; Spectrum, Arts Council of GB, 1971; British Painting 1952-77, Royal Academy, 1977; Galerie Loyse Oppenheim, Nyon, Switzerland, 1977; Galerie Renée Ziegler, Zürich, 1981. Works acquired by: Tate Gall.; V&A; National Galleries of: S Aust.; Felton Bequest, Vic., Aust.; NZ; Canada; City Art Galleries of: Birmingham; Bristol; Manchester; Wakefield; Mus. of Modern Art, NY; Contemporary Art Soc.; British Council; Arts Council of GB; Rothschild Foundn; The Graves Art Gall., Sheffield; Nottingham Castle Mus.; Fitzwilliam Mus., Cambridge; Mus. of Modern Art, São Paulo, Brazil; Leeds Art Gall.; Toledo Art Gall., Ohio, USA; Barnes Foundn, USA; Oriel Coll., Oxford; Warwick Univ.; Mus. and Art Galls, Brighton and Plymouth; Texas Univ., Austin, USA; Berlin Nat. Gall.; McCrory Corp., NY. CoID Award, 1965; Arts Council of GB Purchase Award, 1967. *Relevant Publication:* The Painter, Alan Reynolds, by J. P. Hodin. 1962. *Address:* Briar Cottage, High Street, Cranbrook, Kent.

REYNOLDS, (Arthur) Graham; Keeper of the Department of Prints and Drawings, 1961-74 (of Engraving, Illustration and Design, 1959-61), and of Paintings, Victoria and Albert Museum, 1959-74; *b* Highgate, 10 Jan. 1914; *o s* of late Arthur T. Reynolds and Eva Mullins; *m* 1943, Daphne, *d* of late Thomas Dent, Huddersfield. *Educ:* Highgate School; Queens' College, Cambridge. Joined staff of Victoria and Albert Museum, 1937. Seconded to Ministry of Home Security, 1939-45. Trustee, William Morris Gallery, Walthamstow, 1972-75; Chm., Gainsborough's House Soc., Sudbury, 1977-79. Leverhulme Emeritus Fellowship, 1980-81. *Publications:* Twentieth Century Drawings, 1946; Nicholas Hilliard and Isaac Oliver, 1947, 2nd edn, 1971; Van Gogh, 1947; Nineteenth Century Drawings, 1949; Thomas Bewick, 1949; An Introduction to English Water-Colour Painting, 1950; Gastronomic Pleasures, 1950; Elizabethan and Jacobean Costume, 1951; English Portrait Miniatures, 1952; Painters of the Victorian Scene, 1953; Catalogue of the Constable Collection, Victoria and Albert Museum, 1960, rev. edn, 1973; Constable, the Natural Painter, 1965; Victorian Painting, 1966; Turner, 1969; A Concise History of Water Colour Painting, 1972; Catalogue of Portrait Miniatures, Wallace Collection, 1980. Editor of series English Masters of Black and White. Contributions to Burlington Magazine, Apollo, etc. *Address:* The Old Manse, Bradfield St George, Bury St Edmunds, Suffolk IP30 0AZ. *T:* Sicklesmere 610. *Club:* Athenæum.

REYNOLDS, Barbara, MA Cantab; BA (Hons), PhD London; author, lexicographer; Reader in Italian Studies, University of Nottingham, 1966-78; *b* 13 June 1914; *d* of late Alfred Charles Reynolds; *m* 1st, 1939, Prof. Lewis Thorpe (*d* 1977); one *s* one *d* ; 2nd, Kenneth Imeson, *qv*. *Educ:* St Paul's Girls' Sch.; UCL. Asst Lectr in Italian, LSE 1937-40. Chief Exec. and Gen. Editor, The Cambridge Italian Dictionary, 1948-81; Man. Editor, Seven, an Anglo-American Literary Review, 1980-. Mem. Coun. Senate, Cambridge Univ., 1961-62. University Lecturer in Italian Literature and Language, Cambridge, 1945-62 (Faculty Assistant Lecturer, 1940-45); Warden of Willoughby Hall, Univ. of Nottingham, 1963-69. Vis. Professor: Univ. of Calif., Berkeley, 1974-75; Wheaton Coll., Illinois, 1977-78, 1982; Trinity Coll., Dublin, 1980, 1981; Hope Coll., Mich., 1982. Hon. Reader in Italian, Univ. of Warwick, 1975-. Hon. DLitt: Wheaton Coll., Illinois, 1979; Hope Coll., Mich., 1982. Silver medal for Services to Italian culture (Italian Govt), 1964; Edmund Gardner Prize, 1964; Silver Medal for service to Anglo-Veneto Cultural relations, Prov. Admin of Vicenza, 1971; Cavaliere Ufficiale al Merito della Repubblica Italiana, 1978. *Publications:* (with K. T. Butler) Tredici Novelle Moderne, 1947; The Linguistic Writings of Alessandro Manzoni: a Textual and Chronological Reconstruction, 1950; rev. edn with introd., Dante and the Early Astronomers, by M. A. Orr, 1956; The Cambridge Italian Dictionary, Vol. I, Italian-English, 1962, Vol. II, English-Italian, 1981; (with Dorothy L. Sayers) Paradise: a translation into English triple rhyme, from the Italian of Dante Alighieri, 1962; (with Lewis Thorpe) Guido Farina, Painter of Verona, 1967; La Vita Nuova (Poems of Youth); trans. of Dante's Vita Nuova, 1969;

Concise Cambridge Italian Dictionary, 1975; Orlando Furioso, trans. into rhymed octaves of Ariosto's epic, Vol. I, 1975 (Internat. Literary Prize, Monselice, Italy, 1976) Vol. II, 1977; numerous articles on Italian literature in learned jls. *Address:* 220 Milton Road, Cambridge CB4 1LQ. *T:* Cambridge 357894. *Clubs:* University Women's, Authors'.

REYNOLDS, Sir David James, 3rd Bt, *cr* 1923; Member of Lloyd's Insurance; *b* 26 Jan. 1924; *er s* of Sir John Francis Roskell Reynolds, 2nd Bt, MBE, JP and Milicent (*d* 1931), *d* of late Major James Orr-Ewing and late Lady Margaret Orr-Ewing; *S* father 1956; *m* 1966, Charlotte Baumgartner; one *s* two *d. Educ:* Downside. Active service in Army, 1942-47, Italy, etc; on demobilisation, Captain 15/19 Hussars. *Recreation:* sport. *Heir: s* James Francis Reynolds, *b* 10 July 1971. *Address:* Blanche Pierre House, St Lawrence, Jersey, CI.

REYNOLDS, Doris Livesey, (Mrs Arthur Holmes), DSc, FRSE, FGS; Honorary Research Fellow, Bedford College, since 1962; *b* 1 July 1899; *d* of Alfred Reynolds and Louisa Margaret Livesey; *m* 1939, Arthur Holmes, FRS (*d* 1965). *Educ:* Palmer's School, Grays, Essex; Bedford College, London University. Assistant in Geology, Queen's Univ., Belfast, 1921-26; Dem. in Geology, Bedford Coll., London Univ., 1927-31; Lectr in Petrology, University Coll., London Univ., 1931-33; Lectr in Petrology, Durham Colls, Durham Univ., 1933-43. Hon. Research Fellow of the University of Edinburgh, 1943-62. Leverhulme Fellowship to investigate the geology of the Slieve Gullion volcano, 1946-48. Lyell Medallist, Geological Soc., London, 1960. *Publications:* Elements of Physical Geology, 1969; Revision for 3rd edn of Holmes Principles of Physical Geology, 1978; on the origin of granite and allied subjects in Quart. Journ. Geol Soc., Proc. Roy. Irish Acad., Roy. Soc. of Edin., Geological Magazine, etc. *Address:* 7 Tandridge Road, Hove, E Sussex.

REYNOLDS, Eric Vincent, TD 1948; MA; Headmaster of Stowe, 1949-58, retired; *b* 30 April 1904; *o s* of late Arthur John and Lily Reynolds; unmarried. *Educ:* Haileybury College; St John's College, Cambridge. Modern and Mediæval languages Tripos, Parts 1 and 2; Lector in English at University of Leipzig, 1926-27; MA 1930. Assistant Master: Rugby School, 1927-31; Upper Canada College, Toronto, 1931-32; Rugby School, 1932-49 (Housemaster, 1944-49). CO, Rugby School JTC, 1938-44. *Recreations:* ski-ing and mountaineering. *Address:* 48 Lemsford Road, St Albans, Herts AL1 3PR. *T:* 53599.

REYNOLDS, Eva Mary Barbara; see Reynolds, Barbara.

REYNOLDS, Frank Arrowsmith, OBE 1974; LLB; HM Diplomatic Service, retired; *b* 30 March 1916; *s* of late Sydney Edward Clyde Reynolds and Bessie (*née* Foster); *m* 1938, Joan Marion Lockyer; one *s* two *d. Educ:* Addey and Stanhope Sch.; London University. Army, 1941-46 (Lieut, R.E). District Officer, Tanganyika, 1950; Commonwealth Relations Office, 1952-63; First Secretary, Bombay, 1964-67; CO, later FCO, 1967-69; Consul-Gen., Seville, 1969-71; Head of Chancery, Maseru, 1971-75. *Publication:* Guide to Super-8 Photography, 1981. *Recreations:* music, sailing, photography. *Address:* 16 Walnut Way, Clacton, Essex. *Club:* Royal Bombay Yacht.

REYNOLDS, Graham; see Reynolds, A. G.

REYNOLDS, Guy Edwin K.; see King-Reynolds.

REYNOLDS, Maj-Gen. Jack Raymond, CB 1971; OBE 1945; ERD 1948; Director-General, British Equestrian Federation, since 1975; *b* 10 June 1916; *s* of Walter Reynolds and Evelyn Marion (*née* Burrows); *m* 1940, Joan Howe Taylor; one *s* one *d. Educ:* Haberdashers' Aske's. Student Apprentice, AEC Ltd, 1934. Commissioned RASC (SR), 1936. Served War of 1939-45, France, Middle East and Italy (despatches). CRASC 7th Armoured Div., 1955-57; GSO 1 War Office, 1958-60; Col GS; UK Delegn to NATO Standing Group, Washington, DC, 1960-62; DDST, Southern Command, 1962-64; Commandant, RASC Training Centre, 1964-65; Imperial Defence College, 1966; Dep. Quarter-Master-General, BAOR, 1967-68; Dir of Movements (Army), MoD, 1968-71, retired. Col Comdt, Royal Corps of Transport, 1972-78. Dir-Gen., BHS, 1971-75. FCIT. *Recreation:* shooting. *Address:* Old Mill House, Hellidon, near Daventry, Northants. *Club:* Army and Navy.

REYNOLDS, James; Judge of the High Court, Eastern Region of Nigeria, 1956-63; *b* Belfast, May, 1908; *yr s* of late James Reynolds and late Agnes Forde (*née* Cully); *m* 1946, Alexandra Mary Erskine Strain; two *s* two *d. Educ:* Belfast Roy. Acad.; Queen's Univ., Belfast. Called to Bar of N Ire., 1931; practised at N Ire Bar, 1931-40. Colonial Legal Service as Crown Counsel in Hong Kong, 1940. Prisoner-of-war in Japanese hands, 1941-45. Returned to Hong Kong, 1946; apptd District Judge, 1953. Chairman: Local Tribunal under Nat. Insce Acts, 1964; Industrial Tribunal, 1969. *Address:* 10 Church Road, Helen's Bay, Co. Down, Northern Ireland.

REYNOLDS, Joyce Maire, FBA 1982; University Lecturer in Classics (formerly Assistant Lecturer), University of Cambridge, and Fellow, Lecturer and Director of Studies in Classics, Newnham College, Cambridge, since 1951; *b* 18 Dec. 1918; *d* of William Howe Reynolds and Nellie Farmer Reynolds. *Educ:* Walthamstow County High Sch. for Girls; St Paul's Girls' Sch., Hammersmith; Somerville Coll., Oxford. Temp. Civil Servant, BoT, 1941-46; Rome Scholar, British Sch. at Rome, 1946-48; Lectr in Ancient History,

King's Coll., Newcastle upon Tyne, 1948-51. Woolley Travelling Fellow, Somerville Coll., Oxford, 1961. *Publications:* (with J. B. Ward Perkins) The Inscriptions of Roman Tripolitania, 1952; Aphrodisias and Rome, 1982; articles on Roman history and epigraphy in jls, 1951-. *Recreation:* walking. *Address:* Newnham College, Cambridge CB3 9DF. *T:* Cambridge 62273.

REYNOLDS, Dr Martin Richard Finch; Regional Medical Officer, South Western Regional Health Authority, since 1980; *b* 26 July 1943; 2nd *s* of Gerald Finch Reynolds and Frances Bertha (*née* Locke); *m* 1965, Shelagh (*née* Gray); two *d. Educ:* Newton Abbot Grammar Sch.; Univ. of Bristol. MB ChB, DPH; FFCM. House posts in medicine, surgery, infectious diseases and paediatrics, 1966-67; Dep. Med. Officer, Glos CC, 1967-70; Sen. Dep. Med. Officer, Bristol City and Asst Sen. Med. Officer, SW Regional Hosp. Bd, 1970-72; Dist Community Physician, Southmead Dist of Avon AHA (Teaching) and Med. Officer for Environmental Health, Northavon Dist Council, 1974-79; Area Med. Officer, Wilts AHA, 1979-80. *Publications:* contrib. various articles in professional jls on subjects in community medicine. *Address:* Coppinhall, 23 Church Lane, Old Sodbury, Bristol BS17 6NB. *T:* Chipping Sodbury 318075.

REYNOLDS, Michael Emanuel, CBE 1977; Chairman and Managing Director, Moorgold Ltd (trading as Susan Reynolds Books), since 1977; *b* 22 April 1931; *s* of Isaac Mark and Henrietta Rosenberg; *m* 1964, Susan Geraldine Yates; two *d. Educ:* Haberdashers' Aske's (HSC). Marks & Spencer Ltd, 1951-61; Food Controller, British Home Stores Ltd, 1961-64; Spar (UK) Ltd, 1964-77: Trading Controller, 1964-67; Chm. and Managing Dir, 1967-77; BV Intergroup Trading (IGT), 1974-77: Founder Mem., Bd of Admin.; Dir, 1974-75; Chm. and Dir, 1975-77. Dep. Chm., Apple and Pear Marketing Bd, 1980-; Chm., West One Retailers' Assoc.; Mem. Council, Oxford Street Assoc. *Recreations:* tennis, squash, bridge. *Address:* Maple Downe, Main Drive, Gerrards Cross, Buckinghamshire SL9 7PS. *T:* Gerrards Cross 87671. *Club:* Green Street Bridge.

REYNOLDS, Maj.-Gen. Michael Frank; Commander, Allied Command Europe Mobile Force (Land), 1980-June 1983; *b* 3 June 1930; *s* of Frank Reynolds and Gwendolyn Reynolds (*née* Griffiths); *m* 1955, Anne Bernice (*née* Truman); three *d. Educ:* Cranleigh Sch.; RMA, Sandhurst. Commnd Queen's Royal Regt, 1950; served Germany, Korea, Cyprus, Canada, Persian Gulf, Netherlands; *psc* 1960; GSO 1 Ops, HQ AFCENT, 1970-71; comd 2 Queen's, BAOR and Ulster, 1971-73; GSO 1 Ops, N Ireland, 1973-74; comd 12 Mech Bde BAOR, 1974-76; RCDS, 1977; Dep. Adjt Gen., BAOR, 1978-80. *Recreations:* military history, architecture, golf. *Address:* HQ ACE Mobile Force (Land), Box 2004, BFPO 105. *Club:* Army and Navy.

REYNOLDS, Peter William John, CBE 1975; Chairman, Ranks Hovis McDougall plc, since 1981; *b* 10 Sept. 1929; *s* of Harry and Gladys Victoria Reynolds; *m* 1955, Barbara Anne (*née* Johnson); two *s. Educ:* Haileybury Coll., Herts. National Service, 2nd Lieut, RA, 1948-50. Unilever Ltd, 1950-70: Trainee; Managing Dir, then Chm., Walls (Meat & Handy Foods) Ltd. Asst Gp Managing Dir, Ranks Hovis McDougall Ltd, 1971, Gp Man. Dir, 1972-81. *Recreations:* gardening, beagling. *Address:* The White House, Beamond End, Amersham, Bucks. *T:* High Wycombe 713248. *Clubs:* Naval and Military, Farmers'.

REYNOLDS, Prof. Philip Alan; DL; Vice-Chancellor, University of Lancaster, since 1980; *b* 15 May 1920; *s* of Harry Reynolds and Ethel (*née* Scott); *m* 1946, Mollie Patricia (*née* Horton); two *s* one *d. Educ:* Worthing High Sch.; Queen's Coll., Oxford (BA 1940, 1st Cl. Mod. Hist.; MA 1950). Served War, 1940-46: HAA and Staff, UK, ME and Greece; Major 1945. Asst Lectr, then Lectr in Internat. History, LSE, 1946-50; Woodrow Wilson Prof. of Internat. Politics, UCW Aberystwyth, 1950-64 (Vice-Principal, 1961-63); Prof. of Politics and Pro-Vice-Chancellor, Univ. of Lancaster, 1964-80. Vis. Professor: in Internat. Relations, Toronto, 1953; in Commonwealth History and Instns, Indian Sch. of Internat. Studies, New Delhi, 1958; Anspach Fellow, Univ. of Pa, 1971; Vis. Res. Fellow, ANU Canberra, 1977. Chm., Brit. Internat. Studies Assoc., 1976, Hon. Pres., 1981; Mem. Council, RIIA, 1975-80. DL Lancs, 1982. *Publications:* War in the Twentieth Century, 1951; Die Britische Aussenpolitik zwischen den beiden Weltkriegen, 1952 (rev. edn, 1954, as British Foreign Policy in the Inter-War Years); An Introduction to International Relations, 1971, rev. edn 1980 (Japanese edn 1977, Spanish edn 1978); (with E. J. Hughes) The Historian as Diplomat: Charles Kingsley Webster and the United Nations 1939-46, 1976; contrib. New Cambridge Mod. Hist., History, Slavonic Rev., Pol. Qly, Pol. Studies, Internat. Jl, Internat. Studies, Brit. Jl of Internat. Studies. *Recreations:* music, bridge, eating and drinking. *Address:* 8 Castle Park, Lancaster LA1 1YQ. *T:* Lancaster 63016.

REYNOLDS, Major-General Roger Clayton, CB 1944; OBE 1941; MC 1916; *b* 26 Jan. 1895; *s* of late Lewis William Reynolds and Fanny Matilda Clayton; *m* 1st, 1918, Marjorie Grace McVeagh (*d* 1938); one *s* one *d* ; 2nd, 1952, Mrs August Oddleifson, Rochester, New York, USA. *Educ:* Bradfield College; RMA, Woolwich. 1st Commission RA, Aug. 1914; served European War, 1914-18 (MC, 1914 Star); Staff College, Camberley, 1928-29; Staff Captain Chief India Independent Brigade, 1931; DAAG, AHQ, India, 1932-36; GSO 1 War Office, 1939-40; AA Brigade Comd 1941-42; comd 3rd AA Group, Bristol, 1942-44; Comd 1 AA Group London, 1944-47; retired pay, 1948. *Recreations:* Bradfield College 1st XI Soccer, cricket; RMA, 1st XI

Soccer; Staff College 1st team hockey, tennis. *Address:* The Old Orchard, Avon, New York State 14414, USA. *Club:* Army and Navy.

REYNOLDS, Seymour John Romer, MA, MB, BChir (Cambridge) 1936; MRCS, LRCP, 1935; DMRE 1938; Physician to Radiological Department, Charing Cross Hospital, 1945-76; Consultant Radiologist: Kingston Hospital Group, 1948-73; New Victoria Hospital, Kingston-upon-Thames; *b* 26 April 1911; *s* of late Russell J. Reynolds, CBE, FRCP; *m* 1939, Margaret Stuart McCombie; one *s. Educ:* Westminster School; Trinity Coll., Cambridge; Charing Cross Hosp. Med. School. Formerly: House Surgeon, House Physician and Clin. Asst at Charing Cross Hosp.; Univ. Demonstrator in Anatomy, Cambridge Univ., 1937; Radiologist: Victoria Hosp., Kingston-upon-Thames, 1939; Prince of Wales Gen. Hosp., Tottenham, 1939; Highlands Hosp.; Hackney Hosp.; Epsom Hosp. 1943; Queen Mary's Hosp., Roehampton, 1946. Dean of Charing Cross Hosp. Med. Sch., 1962-76. Mem. Bd of Governors, Charing Cross Hosp., 1962-74; Mem., Ealing, Hammersmith and Hounslow AHA, 1974-76. *Recreations:* gardening, visiting art galleries. *Address:* Camelot, Renfrew Road, Kingston Hill, Surrey. *T:* 01-942 3808.

REYNOLDS, William Oliver, OBE 1973 (MBE 1944); Chairman, Derek Crouch Construction Co., since 1976; *b* 2 Nov. 1915; *s* of Edgar Ernest Reynolds and Elizabeth Wilson Biesterfield; *m* 1944, Eleanor Gill; two *s. Educ:* Royal Grammar Sch., Newcastle upon Tyne. LNER Traffic apprentice, 1936. Served War, with Royal Engineers, 1940-46: despatches, 1942 and 1944; Lt-Col, 1944. Lt-Col, Engineer and Railway Staff Corps, RE (T&AVR IV), 1971-. Divisional Manager, London Midland, BR, 1960; Asst Gen. Manager, Scottish Region, 1964; Chief Operating Manager, BR Bd, 1968; Exec. Dir, BR Bd, 1969; Gen. Manager, Eastern Region, British Rail, 1973-76. Mem., Adv. Council, Science Mus. 1975-. FCIT. *Recreations:* fishing, golf, gardening. *Address:* Oak House, Follifoot, Harrogate, N Yorks. *Club:* Oriental.

REYNOLDS, William Vaughan; Principal, St Marylebone Literary Institute, 1965-70, retired; *b* 10 May 1908; *yr s* of late William Reynolds, MBE, editor of The Midland Daily Telegraph; *m* 1932, Gertrude Mabel, *yr d* of late Arthur Charles Flint; four *s. Educ:* King Henry VIII School, Coventry; St Edmund Hall, Oxford. First class in Final Hons School of Eng. Lang. and Lit., 1930; BLitt, 1931; MA 1934; Senior Exhibitioner, St Edmund Hall, 1930-31. Assistant Lecturer in English Literature, University of Sheffield, 1931-34; Lecturer, 1934-41. Deputy Regional Officer, Ministry of Information (NE Region), 1941-45; Sec., East and West Ridings Industrial Publicity Cttee, 1943-45. Joined staff of The Birmingham Post as Leader-writer and Editorial Asst, 1945; served in London office, 1949; Editor, 1950-64, retired. Mem. British Cttee, Internat. Press Inst., 1952-64; Pres., Rotary Club of Birmingham, 1962-63; Mem., Church Information Adv. Cttee, 1966-72. *Publications:* Selections from Johnson, 1935; articles contributed to The Review of English Studies and to Notes and Queries; literary and dramatic reviews in various periodicals and newspapers. Has broadcast frequently in Gt Britain and US. *Recreations:* motoring, cats, theatre going, and reading. *Address:* 6 Orleigh Close, Buckland Brewer, Bideford, North Devon. *T:* Horns Cross 655. *Club:* Athenæum.

REYNTIENS, Nicholas Patrick, OBE 1976; Head of Fine Art, Central School of Art and Design, London, since 1976; *b* 11 Dec. 1925; *s* of Nicholas Serge Reyntiens, OBE, and Janet MacRae; *m* 1953, Anne Bruce; two *s* two *d. Educ:* Ampleforth; Edinburgh Coll. of Art (DA). Served Scots Guards, 1943-47. St Marylebone Sch. of Art, 1947-50; Edinburgh Coll. of Art, 1950-51. Founder, Reyntiens Trust, 1970. Numerous commns for stained glass, 1950-. *Publication:* Technique of Stained Glass, 1967, 2nd edn 1977. *Address:* The Warden's Flat, The Old School, Windsor End, Beaconsfield, Bucks. *T:* Beaconsfield 6361. *Club:* Garrick.

RHEA, Alexander Dodson, III; *b* 10 May 1919; *s* of Alexander D. Rhea, Jr and Annie Rhea; *m* 1945, Suzanne Menocal; one *s. Educ:* Princeton Univ. BA Econs and Social Instns. Active service as Lt-Comdr USNR, 1941-45. Vice-Pres., Govt Employees Ins. Corp., Washington, DC, 1946-48; Treas. and Man. Dir, General Motors de Venezuela, Caracas, 1949-55; Vice-Pres., General Motors Overseas Corp., 1960-68; Regional Gp Dir, NY, 1960-66, Staff Man., 1966-67, General Motors Overseas Operations; Chm. and Man. Dir, General Motors-Holden's, Melbourne, 1968-70; Chm. and Man. Dir., Vauxhall Motors Ltd, 1970-74; Chm., General Motors Corp. European Adv. Council, 1974-77; Exec. Vice-Pres. and Dir, General Motors Overseas Corp., 1974-77. *Recreations:* reading, golf. *Address:* 1 East Sixty Six Street, New York, NY 10021, USA. *Clubs:* Knickerbocker, Metropolitan, Princeton, Colony (New York); Fort Worth, River Crest Country, Century II (Fort Worth, Texas); Melbourne (Melbourne).

RHIND, Donald, CMG 1962; OBE 1947; retired 1970; *b* 26 September 1899; *er s* of late Thomas Rhind, MRCS, LRCP; *m* 1939, Annemarie Eugenia Ludovica von Ferrari and Brunnerfeld; one *s* one *d. Educ:* Aldenham School; Bristol University (BSc). Economic Botanist, Burma, 1923-45; Civil Affairs Service, Burma (Lieutenant-Colonel), 1945; Senior Economic Botanist, Burma, 1946-47; Director of Agriculture, Ceylon, 1947-50; Secretary for Agriculture and Forestry Research, West Africa, 1951-53; Secretary for Colonial Agricultural Research, 1953-61; Adviser on Agricultural Research, Department of Technical Co-operation, 1961-64, Min. of Overseas Development, 1964-67; Agricultural Research Coordinator, SEATO, 1968-

69. FLS, FIBiol. *Publications:* The Grasses of Burma, 1945; numerous scientific papers on tropical agriculture. *Address:* 1 The Briars, Upper Richmond Road, Putney, SW15. *T:* 01-788 9512.

RHODES, family name of **Baron Rhodes.**

RHODES, Baron *cr* 1964, of Saddleworth (Life Peer); **Hervey Rhodes,** KG 1972; PC 1969; DFC and Bar; DL; *b* 12 August 1895; *s* of John Eastwood and Elizabeth Ann Rhodes; *m* 1925, Ann Bradbury; two *d. Educ:* Greenfield, St Mary's Elementary Sch.; Huddersfield Technical College; evening classes. Woollen worker pre-1914; joined King's Own Royal Lancs, 1914, commissioned, seconded to Flying Corps (wounded, DFC and Bar). Discharged from Hospital, 1921. Commenced business as woollen manufacturer. Served on Local Authority. Chairman of Urban District Council, 1944-45. Chairman, Saddleworth War Charities. Commanded 36th West Riding Bn Home Guard. Contested Royton Division of Lancs, 1945; MP (Lab) Ashton-under-Lyne, 1945-64; PPS, Min. of Pensions, 1948; Parliamentary Secretary, Board of Trade, 1950-51, 1964-67. Led all-party Parly delegns to China, 1978, 1979, 1981. Lord Lieutenant of Lancaster, 1968-71; DL Lancs, 1971. Freedom of Borough of Ashton-under-Lyne, 1965, and of Saddleworth, Yorks, 1966. KStJ 1968. Fellow, Huddersfield Polytechnic, 1976. Hon. DTech Bradford, 1966; Hon LLD Manchester, 1971. *Address:* Cribbstones, Delph, near Oldham, Lancs. *T:* Saddleworth 4500.

RHODES, Rev. Canon Cecil; Canon Residentiary of St Edmundsbury Cathedral, 1964-80; retired 1980; *b* Preston, Lancs, 5 Oct. 1910; *s* of James Rhodes; *m* 1940, Gladys, *d* of H. B. Farlie; one *s* two *d. Educ:* Preston Gram. Sch.; St Peter's Hall, Oxford; Wycliffe Hall, Oxford (MA). Deacon, 1936. Priest, 1937. Curate, St Stephen, Selly Hill, Birmingham, 1936-38; Asst Editor and Youth Sec., The Pathfinder, 1938-40; Jt Editor, Light and Life Publications, 1941-44; Diocesan Chaplain-in-charge, St Mary, Pype Hayes, Birmingham, 1940-44; Vicar: St Luke, Tunbridge Wells, 1944-49; St Augustine, Edgbaston, Birmingham, 1949-64; Birmingham Diocesan Adviser for Stewardship, 1960-64; Hon. Canon of Birmingham, 1961-64. Diocesan Dir of Lay Training, Diocese of St Edmundsbury and Ipswich, 1968-74; Chm., Diocesan Information Cttee, 1968-76. Founder and Editor, Church News, 1946-; Jt Editor, The Pilgrim, C of E youth magazine, 1949-50; regular contributor to The Birmingham Post, 1950-64; East Anglian Daily Times, 1970-78. *Recreations:* writing, books, travel. *Address:* College Gate House, Bury St Edmunds, Suffolk. *T:* Bury St Edmunds 3530.

RHODES, Rev. Clifford Oswald, MA Oxon; *b* 12 April 1911; *s* of Rev. Edward Rhodes; *m* 1941, Elizabeth, *e d* of H. R. Bowden; one *s* three *d. Educ:* The Grange Grammar Sch., Bradford; St Peter's Coll., Oxford. Journalism, 1934-37; Wycliffe Hall, Oxford, 1937-38; Curate, St Luke's Church, Wythenshawe, Manchester, 1938-40; CF 1940-45; Editor of the Record, 1946-49. Hon. Chaplain, St Bride's, Fleet Street, 1952-; Lectr, St Margaret's, Lothbury, EC2, 1954-. Licence to preach, from Oxford Univ., 1957; Rector of Somerton, 1958-81, also Priest-in-charge, Upper Heyford, Lower Heyford and Rousham, 1976-81, retired. Editor of the Church of England Newspaper, 1949-59; Director and Secretary, the Modern Churchmen's Union, 1954-60; Editor of Business, 1960-63; Account Executive, Gilbert McAllister and Partners Ltd, public relations consultants, 1963-65. Editorial Director, Harcourt Kitchin and Partners Ltd, 1964-72. *Publications:* The New Church in the New Age, 1958; Musical Instruments and the Orchestra, 1968; The Awful Boss's Book, 1968; (ed) Authority in a Changing Society, 1969; The Necessity for Love: the history of interpersonal relations, 1972; contrib. to many newspapers and periodicals and learned jls. *Recreations:* the arts and country life. *Address:* 233 Balmoral Avenue, Banbury, Oxfordshire OX16 0BB. *T:* Banbury 3425.

RHODES, Sir John (Christopher Douglas), 4th Bt, *cr* 1919; *b* 24 May 1946; *s* of Sir Christopher Rhodes, 3rd Bt, and of Mary Florence, *d* of late Dr Douglas Wardleworth; *S* father, 1964. *Heir:* br Michael Philip James Rhodes [*b* 3 April 1948; *m* 1973, Susan, *d* of Patrick Roney-Dougal; one *d*].

RHODES, John Ivor McKinnon, CMG 1971; *b* 6 March 1914; *s* of late Joseph Thomas Rhodes and late Hilda (née McKinnon); *m* 1939, Eden Annetta (née Clark); one *s* one *d. Educ:* Leeds Modern School. Exec. Officer, WO, 1933; Financial Adviser's Office, HQ British Forces in Palestine, 1938; Major 1940; Asst Comd Sec., Southern Comd, 1944; Financial Adviser, London District, 1946; Principal 1947, Asst Sec. 1959, HM Treasury; Minister, UK Mission to UN, 1966-74. Member: UN Pension Board, 1966-71; UN Cttee on Contributions, 1966-71, 1975-77; Chm., UN Adv. Cttee on Admin. and Budgetary Questions, 1971-74; Senior Adviser (Asst Sec.-Gen.) to Administrator, UNDP, 1979-80. *Recreations:* gardening, playing the electronic organ. *Address:* Quintins, Watersfield, Sussex. *T:* Bury 634.

RHODES, Marion, RE 1953 (ARE 1941); etcher, painter in water colour and oils; *b* Huddersfield, Yorks, 1907; *d* of Samuel Rhodes and Mary Jane Mallinson. *Educ:* Greenhead High School, Huddersfield; Huddersfield Art School; Leeds College of Art; The Central School of Arts and Crafts, London. Art Teachers' Certificate (Univ. of Oxford); 1930; teaching posts, 1930-67; pt-time lecturer in Art at Berridge House Training Coll., 1947-55. SGA 1936, Hon. Life Mem., 1969; FRSA 1944; Member, Manchester Acad. of Fine Art, 1955-81; Paris Salon: Honourable Mention, 1952; Bronze Medal, 1956; Silver Medal 1961; Gold Medal, 1967. Exhibited from 1934 at: Royal Academy, Royal Scottish Academy, Mall Gall., The Paris Salon, Walker Art Gall.,

Towner Art Gall., Atkinson Art Gall., Southport, Brighton, Bradford, Leeds, Manchester and other provincial Art Galls, also USA and S Africa. Etching of Jordans' Hostel and drawing of The Meeting House purchased by Contemporary Art Soc. and presented to British Museum; other works in the Print Room, BM, and Print Room, V&A; work also purchased by Bradford Corp. Art Gall., Brighouse Art Gall., Huddersfield Art Gall., Stoke-on-Trent Educn Cttee's Loan Scheme, and South London (Camberwell) Library Committee; works reproduced. Fellow, Ancient Monuments Soc.; Associate, Artistes Français, 1971-79; Hon. Mem., Tommaso Campanella Acad., Rome (Silver Medal, 1970). Cert. of Merit, Dictionary of Internat. Biography, 1972. Mem., Accademia delle Arti e de Lavoro (Parma), 1979-82; Academic of Italy with Gold Medal, 1979. *Recreations:* gardening and geology. *Address:* 2 Goodwyn Avenue, Mill Hill, NW7 3RG. *T:* 01-959 2280. *Club:* English-Speaking Union.

RHODES, Peregrine Alexander, CMG 1976; HM Diplomatic Service; Ambassador to Greece, since 1982; *b* 14 May 1925; *s* of Cyril Edmunds Rhodes and Elizabeth Jocelyn Rhodes; *m* 1st, 1951, Jane Marion Hassell (marr. diss.); two *s* one *d* ; 2nd, 1969, Margaret Rosemary Page. *Educ:* Winchester Coll.; New Coll., Oxford. Served with Coldstream Guards, 1944-47. Joined FO, 1950; 2nd Sec., Rangoon, 1953-56; Private Sec. to Minister of State, 1956-59; 1st Sec., Vienna, 1959-62; 1st Sec., Helsinki, 1962-65; FCO, 1965-68, Counsellor 1967; Inst. for Study of Internat. Organisation, Sussex Univ., 1968-69; Counsellor: Rome, 1970-73; E Berlin, 1973-75; on secondment as Under Sec., Cabinet Office, 1975-78; High Comr, Cyprus, 1979-82. *Recreations:* photography, reading. *Address:* c/o Foreign and Commonwealth Office, SW1. *Club:* Travellers'.

RHODES, Philip, FRCS, FRCOG, FRACMA; Regional Postgraduate Dean of Medical Studies, and Professor of Postgraduate Medical Education, Southampton University, since 1980; *b* 2 May 1922; *s* of Sydney Rhodes, Dore, Sheffield; *m* 1946, Mary Elizabeth Worley, Barrowden, Rutland; three *s* two *d. Educ:* King Edward VII Sch., Sheffield; Clare Coll., Cambridge; St Thomas's Hospital Medical School. BA(Cantab) 1943, MB, BChir(Cantab) 1946; FRCS 1953; MRCOG 1956; FRCOG 1964; FRACMA 1976. Major RAMC, 1948-50. Medical appointments held in St Thomas' Hosp., Folkestone, Harrogate, Chelsea Hosp. for Women, Queen Charlotte's Hosp., 1946-58; Consultant Obstetric Physician, St Thomas' Hosp., 1958-63; Prof. of Obstetrics and Gynæcol., St Thomas's Hosp. Med. Sch., Univ. of London, 1964-74, Dean, 1968-74; Dean, Faculty of Medicine, Univ. of Adelaide, 1975-77; Postgrad. Dean and Dir, Regional Postgrad. Inst. for Med. and Dentistry, Newcastle Univ., 1977-80. Member: SW Metropolitan Regional Hosp. Board, 1967-74; SE Thames Reg. Health Authority, 1974; GMC, 1979-. Mem. Steering Cttee of DHSS on management of NHS, 1971-72. Mem., Adv. Cttee, Nat. Inst. of Medical Hist., Australia, 1976. Chm., Educn Cttee, King Edward's Hosp. Fund for London, 1981-. Governor: Dulwich Coll., 1966-74; St Thomas' Hosp., 1969-74; Pembroke Sch., Adelaide, 1976-77. *Publications:* Fluid Balance in Obstetrics, 1960; Introduction to Gynæcology and Obstetrics, 1967; Reproductive Physiology for Medical Students, 1969; Woman: A Biological Study, 1969; The Value of Medicine, 1976; Dr John Leake's Hospital, 1978; articles in Jl of Obstetrics and Gynæcology of the British Empire, Lancet, Brit. Med. Jl, Med. Jl of Australia. *Recreations:* reading, gardening, photography, anthropology, sociology. *Address:* Postgraduate Department, Southampton General Hospital, Southampton SO9 4XY.

RHODES, Reginald Paul; Chairman, Southern Gas Region, since 1975; *b* 10 April 1918; *s* of Edwin Rhodes and Dorothy Lena Molyneux; *m* 1940, Margaret Frances Fish; two *s* three *d. Educ:* Merchant Taylors Sch., Northwood. Joined Gas Light & Coke Co., 1937; North Thames Gas, 1948 (Dep. Chm., 1972). Member, Co. of Pikemen, Honourable Artillery Company. FIGasE. *Recreations:* music, gardening. *Address:* Tidebrook Lodge, Royden Lane, Boldre, near Lymington, Hants SO4 8PE. *T:* Lymington 22399.

RHODES, Robert Elliott; First Prosecuting Counsel to Inland Revenue at Central Criminal Court and Inner London Crown Courts, since 1981; *b* 2 Aug. 1945; *s* of late Gilbert G. Rhodes, FCA and of Elly, who *m* 2nd, Leopold Brook, *qv* ; *m* 1971, Georgina Caroline, *d* of J. G. Clarfelt, *qv* ; two *s. Educ:* St Paul's School; Pembroke Coll., Oxford. MA. Called to the Bar, Inner Temple, 1968. Second Prosecuting Counsel to Inland Revenue at Central Criminal Court and Inner London Crown Courts, 1979. *Recreations:* opera, reading, cricket, fishing. *Address:* 114 Loudoun Road, NW8. *T:* 01-722 0818. *Club:* MCC.

RHODES, Stephen, OBE 1969; solicitor; Secretary, Association of District Councils, 1973-81; *b* 19 Jan. 1918; *s* of late Edward Hugh Rhodes, CBE, and Helen Edith Laurie Patricia Rhodes; *m* 1958, Jane, *d* of late Norman S. Bradley, Sydney, Aust.; one *s* two *d. Educ:* St Paul's Sch.; Law Society's Sch. of Law. LLB (London). Articled to Sir Cecil Oakes, CBE, Clerk of East Suffolk CC; admitted solicitor, 1941. Served RAF, 1939-46: commnd 1941; Sqdn-Ldr, 1944 (despatches). Asst Solicitor, East Suffolk CC, 1946-47; Sen. Asst Solicitor, Norfolk CC, 1947-49; Asst Sec., County Councils Assoc., 1949-59; Secretary, Rural District Councils Assoc., 1959-73; Jt Sec., Internat. Union of Local Authorities, 1975-81. Mem., Health Educn Council, 1968-74; Jt Sec., Standing Adv. Cttee on Local Authorities and the Theatre, 1975-81; Sec., Local Authorities Management Services and Computer Cttee, 1980-81. Vice-Chm., Metropolitan Region, Nat. Soc. for Mentally Handicapped

Children and Adults, 1978-. *Recreation:* wine making. *Address:* 9 Hitherwood Drive, College Road, SE19 1XA. *T:* 01-670 7520. *Clubs:* National Liberal, English-Speaking Union.

RHODES, Zandra Lindsey, DesRCA; RDI; Managing Director, Zandra Rhodes (UK) Ltd and Zandra Rhodes (Shops) Ltd, since 1975; *b* 19 Sept. 1940; *d* of Albert James Rhodes and Beatrice Ellen (*née* Twigg). *Educ:* Medway Technical Sch. for Girls, Chatham; Medway Coll. of Art; Royal Coll. of Art (DesRCA 1965). RDI 1976. With Alexander MacIntyre, set up print factory and studio, 1965; sold designs (and converted them on to cloth) to Foale and Tuffin and Roger Nelson; formed partnership with Sylvia Ayton and began producing dresses using her own prints, 1966; opened Fulham Road Clothes Shop, designing dresses as well as prints, first in partnership, 1967-68, then (Fulham Road shop closed) alone, producing first clothes range in which she revolutionised use of prints in clothes by cutting round patterns to make shapes never before used; took collection to USA, 1969; sold to Fortnum and Mason, London, through Anne Knight, 1969, then to Piero de Monzi, 1971; began building up name and business in USA (known for her annual spectacular Fantasy Shows); also started designing in jersey and revolutionised its treatment with lettuce edges and seams on the outside; with Anne Knight and Ronnie Stirling founded Zandra Rhodes (UK) Ltd and Zandra Rhodes (Shops) Ltd, opening first shop in London, 1975; others opened in Bloomingdales NY, Marshall Field, Chicago, and Harrods, London, 1976. Licensees: Wamsutta, USA, 1976 (sheets and pillowcases); CVP Designs, 1977 (patterns for the interior); Regal Rugs, USA, 1977 (rugs); Baar and Beard Inc., USA, 1978 (scarves); Sari Fabrics, 1979 (kitchen accessories); Wagner Furs, 1979 (furs); Sabrina Coats, 1979 (coats); Jack Mulqueen, USA, 1980 (printed silk dresses and blouses); Green and Makofsky, USA, 1980 (coats); Senko, Japan, 1980 (rugs and bathroom accessories); Suffola, USA, 1980 (sheets and bed accessories); Falmers, 1981 (jeans and T-shirts); Seibu, Japan, 1981 (blouses); Courtaulds, 1981 (knitted silk lingerie); Launched Zandra Rhodes Ready-to-Wear, Australia, 1979. One-man exhibitions: Oriel, Cardiff (Welsh Arts Council), 1978; Texas Gall., Houston, 1981; Otis Parsons, Los Angeles, 1981; La Jolla Museum of Contemporary Art, San Diego, 1982; ADITI Creative Power, Barbican Centre, 1982; Sch. of Art Inst., Chicago, 1982. Work represented in major costume collections: Chicago Hist. Soc.; Metropolitan Museum NY; V&A Museum; City Museum and Art Gall., Stoke-on-Trent; Bath Museum; Royal Pavilion Brighton Museum; Smithsonian Instn. Opening speaker, Famous Women of Fashion, Smithsonian Inst., Washington, 1978. Citations and commendations from USA estabs. *Relevant publications:* in English Vogue, 1978 and 1982; Architectural Digest, 1978; The Connoisseur, 1981. *Recreations:* travelling, drawing. *Address:* (studio) 64 Porchester Road, W2. *T:* (business) 01-602 1929.

RHODES JAMES, Robert Vidal; MP (C) Cambridge, since Dec. 1976; Parliamentary Private Secretary, Foreign and Commonwealth Office, since 1979; *b* 10 April 1933; *y* of late Lieut-Col W. R. James, OBE, MC; *m* 1956, Angela Margaret Robertson, *er d* of late R. M. Robertson; four *d. Educ:* private schs in India; Sedbergh Sch.; Worcester Coll., Oxford. Asst Clerk, House of Commons, 1955-61; Senior Clerk, 1961-64. Fellow of All Souls Coll., Oxford, 1965-68, 1979-; Dir, Inst. for Study of Internat. Organisation, Univ. of Sussex, 1968-73; Principal Officer, Exec. Office of Sec.-Gen. of UN, 1973-76. Kratter Prof. of European History, Stanford Univ., Calif., 1968. Consultant to UN Conf. on Human Environment, 1971-72; UK Mem., UN Sub-Commn on Prevention of Discrimination and Protection of Minorities, 1972-73. FRSL 1964; NATO Fellow, 1965; FRHistS 1973; Professorial Fellow, Univ. of Sussex, 1973. *Publications:* Lord Randolph Churchill, 1959; An Introduction to the House of Commons, 1961 (John Llewelyn Rhys Memorial Prize); Rosebery, 1963 (Royal Society Lit. Award); Gallipoli, 1965; Standardization and Production of Military Equipment in NATO, 1967; Churchill: a study in failure, 1900-39, 1970; Ambitions and Realities: British politics 1964-70, 1972; Victor Cazalet: a portrait, 1976; The British Revolution 1880-1939, vol. I, 1976, vol. II, 1977, 1 Vol. edn, 1978. (ed) Chips: The Diaries of Sir Henry Channon, 1967; (ed) Memoirs of a Conservative: J. C. C. Davidson's Memoirs and Papers, 1969; (ed) The Czechoslovak Crisis 1968, 1969; (ed) The Complete Speeches of Sir Winston Churchill, 1897-1963, 1974; contrib. to: Suez Ten Years After, 1967; Essays From Divers Hands, 1967; Churchill: four faces and the man, 1969; International Administration, 1971; The Prime Ministers, vol. II, 1975. *Address:* The Stone House, Great Gransden, near Sandy, Beds. *T:* Great Gransden 300. *Clubs:* Travellers'; Century (New York).

RHYMES, Rev. Canon Douglas Alfred; Canon Residentiary and Librarian, Southwark Cathedral, 1962-69, Hon. Canon, since 1969; Parish Priest of Woldingham, since 1976; Tutor, Southwark Ordination Course; *b* 26 March 1914; *s* of Peter Alfred and Jessie Rhymes; unmarried. *Educ:* King Edward VI School, Birmingham; Birmingham Univ.; Ripon Hall Theological College, Oxford. BA (2nd Cl. Hons 1st Div.) Philosophy 1939. Asst Curate, Dovercourt, Essex, 1940-43; Chaplain to the Forces, 1943-46; Asst Curate, Romford, Essex (in charge of St George's, Romford and St Thomas', Noak Hill), 1946-49; Priest-in-charge, Ascension, Chelmsford, 1949-50; Sacrist, Southwark Cathedral, 1950-54; Vicar, All Saints, New Eltham, SE9, 1954-62; Director of Lay Training, Diocese of Southwark, 1962-68; Vicar of St Giles, Camberwell, 1968-76. Proctor in Convocation and Mem. of Gen. Synod, 1975-. *Publications:* (part author) Crisis Booklets, Christianity and Communism, 1952; Layman's Church, 1963; No New Morality, 1964; Prayer in the Secular City, 1967; Through Prayer to Reality, 1974. *Recreations:*

theatre, conversation, country walks. *Address:* The Rectory, Woldingham, Surrey. *T:* 01-905 2192.

RHYS, family name of **Baron Dynevor**.

RHYS, Keidrych; poet and writer; editor (founder) of magazine Wales, 1937-60; *b* Bethlehem, Llandilo, 26 Dec. 1915; *m* 1st, 1939, Lynette Roberts, poet and novelist, of Buenos Aires; one *s* one *d*; 2nd, 1956, Eva Smith; one *s. Educ:* Bethlehem; Llangadog; Llandovery Grammar Sch., etc. Literary and other journalism, London, etc, 1935. Served in Army (London Welsh AA) (1939-45 medals); with Ministry of Information, London, 1943-44; War Correspondent Europe, 1944-45. Public Relations Consultant, various charities and organisations, 1950-54; Welsh columnist and correspondent, The People, 1954-60; London Editor, Poetry London-New York, 1956-60. Runs Druid Books, Antiquarian and Out-of-print Booksellers, Heath Street, Hampstead. Arts Council Award in Literature, 1969-70. Vice-President International Musical Festival and Eisteddfod; Executive Committee (writers' group); Chairman Friends of Wales Soc.; Vice-Pres. Carmarthen Arts Club; Carmarthenshire County Drama Crime and Rural Community Council. *Publications:* The Van Pool and other poems, 1941; Poems from the Forces, 1942; More Poems from the Forces, 1943; Modern Welsh Poetry, 1945; Angry Prayers, 1952; Poems; Contributor to: Wales, Times Lit. Supp., New Statesman, anthologies, and to European and American jls. *Recreations:* Welsh National affairs, lecturing, theatre. *Address:* 40 Heath Street, NW3. *T:* 01-794 2970.

RHYS WILLIAMS, Sir Brandon (Meredith), 2nd Bt, *cr* 1918; MP (C) Kensington, since 1974 (Kensington South, March 1968-1974); Member (ED) European Parliament, since 1973, elected for London South East, 1979; *b* 14 Nov. 1927; *s* of Sir Rhys Rhys Williams, 1st Bt, DSO, QC, and Lady (Juliet) Rhys Williams, DBE (*d* 1964); *S* father, 1955; *m* 1961, Caroline Susan, *e d* of L. A. Foster, Greatham Manor, Pulborough, Sussex; one *s* two *d. Educ:* Eton. Served in Welsh Guards, 1946-48 (Lt). Contested (C) Pontypridd Div., 1959, and Ebbw Vale Div., 1960 and 1964. Consultant, Management Selection Ltd, 1963-71; formerly with ICI Ltd. Asst Dir, Spastics Soc., 1962-63. Vice-Chm., European Parlt Economic and Monetary Affairs Cttee, 1973-79. *Publications:* The New Social Contract, 1967; More Power to the Shareholder?, 1969; Redistributing Income in a Free Society, 1969. *Heir: s* Arthur Gareth Ludovic Emrys Rhys Williams, *b* 9 Nov. 1961. *Address:* 32 Rawlings Street, SW3. *T:* 01-584 0636; Miskin Manor, Pontyclun, Mid Glamorgan. *T:* Llantrisant 224204. *Clubs:* White's, Pratt's; Cardiff and County (Cardiff).

RIABOUCHINSKA, Tatiana, (Mme Lichine); Ballerina of Russian Ballet; owns and operates the Lichine Ballet Academy, Beverly Hills; *b* 23 May 1916; *d* of Michael P. Riabouchinsky, Moscow (Banker), and Tatiana Riabouchinska (*d* 1935), Dancer of Moscow Imperial School of Dance; *m* 1942, David Lichine (*d* 1972); one *d. Educ:* Cour Fénelon, Paris. Trained first by her mother; then by Volinine (dancer of the Moscow Imperial Grand Theatre); then by Mathilde Kchesinska. First appeared as child dancer with Balieff's Chauve Souris in London, 1931; joined new Russian Ballet (de-Basil), 1932, and danced with them in nearly all countries of Western Europe, Australia and N and S America. Contribution to books on dancing by: Andre Levinson, Arnold L. Haskell, Irving Deakin, Rayner Heppenstall, Kay Ambrose, Prince Peter Lieven, Cyril W. Beaumont, Cyril Brahms, Adrian Stokes, A. V. Coton, Ninette de Valois, etc. *Address:* 965 Oakmont Drive, Los Angeles, Calif 90049, USA.

RIALL, Air Cdre Arthur Bookey, CBE 1956 (OBE 1953); RAF Regiment, retired; General Secretary, National Rifle Association, 1968-80; *b* 7 Dec. 1911; *o s* of late Major M. B. Riall, OBE, and Mrs S. M. Riall (*née* Lefroy); *m* 1950, Pamela Patricia Hewitt; five *s* one *d. Educ:* Charterhouse; RMC, Sandhurst. Commissioned E Yorks Regt, 1932; served in India with 1st Bn until 1939 when posted as Instr to Small Arms Sch.; Staff Coll., 1941; staff appts until Home posting, 1944; served 2nd Bn NW Europe (wounded, despatches); seconded to RAF in Iraq, for service with Iraq Levies, 1947; transf. RAF Regt, 1948; Chief Instr, RAF Regt Depot, 1951-53; commanded RAF Levies, until their disbandment, 1953-55 and RAF Regt Depot, Catterick, 1955-59; Staff appts in UK and Cyprus, 1959-62; Air Cdre, 1963; apptd Dir of Ground Defence, RAF, 1962; retd Dec. 1966, and joined staff of NRA, 1967. *Recreations:* hunting (Master, Royal Exodus Hunt, Iraq, until disbandment in 1955), target rifle shooting (rep. GB, Ireland and RAF), ornithology (Vice-Pres., RAF Ornith. Soc.). *Address:* Hill House, Ewshot, Farnham, Surrey. *Club:* Naval and Military.

RIBBANS, Prof. Geoffrey Wilfrid, MA; Kenan University Professor of Hispanic Studies, since 1978, and Chairman, Department of Hispanic and Italian Studies, since 1981, Brown University, USA; *b* 15 April 1927; *o s* of late Wilfrid Henry Ribbans and Rose Matilda Burton; *m* 1956, Magdalena Cumming (*née* Willmann), Cologne; one *s* two *d. Educ:* Sir George Monoux Grammar Sch., Walthamstow; King's Coll., Univ. of London. BA Hons Spanish 1st cl., 1948; Univ. of London Postgrad. Studentship; MA 1953. Asst Lectr, Queen's Univ., Belfast, 1951-52; Asst, St Salvator's Coll., Univ. of St Andrews, 1952-53; Univ. of Sheffield: Asst Lectr, 1953-55; Lectr, 1955-61; Sen. Lectr, 1961-63; Gilmour Prof. of Spanish, Univ. of Liverpool, 1963-78; First Director, Centre for Latin-American Studies, 1966-70; Dean, Faculty of Arts, 1977-78. Andrew Mellon Vis. Prof., Univ. of Pittsburgh, 1970-71; Leverhulme Res. Fellow, 1975. Vice-Pres., Internat. Assoc. of Hispanists,

1974–80; Pres., Anglo-Catalan Soc., 1976–78; Dir, Liverpool Playhouse, 1974–78. Editor, Bulletin of Hispanic Studies, 1964–78. Hon. Fellow, Inst. of Linguists, 1972. Corresp. Member: Real Academia de Buenas Letras, Barcelona, 1978; Hispanic Soc. of Amer., 1981. MA *ad eund.* Brown Univ., 1979. *Publications:* Catalunya i València vistes pels viatgers anglesos del segle XVIIIè, 1955; Niebla y Soledad: aspectos de Unamuno y Machado, 1971; ed, Soledades, Galerias, otros poemas, by Antonio Machado, 1975; Antonio Machado (1875–1939): poetry and integrity, 1975; B. Pérez Galdós: Fortunata y Jacinta, a critical guide, 1977; numerous articles on Spanish literature in specialised publications. *Recreations:* travel, fine art. *Address:* c/o Department of Hispanic and Italian Studies, Box E, Brown University, Providence, Rhode Island 02912, USA.

RICE; *see* Spring Rice, family name of Baron Monteagle of Brandon.

RICE, Dennis George, PhD; Social Security (formerly National Insurance) Commissioner, since 1979; *b* 27 Nov. 1927; *s* of George Henry Rice and Ethel Emily Rice; *m* 1959, Jean Beryl Wakefield; one *s. Educ:* City of London Sch.; King's Coll., Cambridge (Scholar and Prizeman; 1st Cl. Classical Tripos Pt I, Law Tripos Pt II; BA 1950, LLB 1951, MA 1955); London Sch. of Econs (PhD 1956). Called to the Bar, Lincoln's Inn, 1952. Served RAF, 1946–48. Entered J. Thorn and Sons Ltd, 1952; Dir, 1955; Man. Dir, 1956; Chm. and Man. Dir, 1958–69; in practice at Chancery Bar, 1970–79. Member: Cttee of Timber Bldg Manufrs Assoc., 1967–69; Cttee of Joinery and Woodwork Employers Fedn, 1968–69. *Publications:* Rockingham Ornamental Porcelain, 1965; Illustrated Guide to Rockingham Pottery and Porcelain, 1971; Early Derby Porcelain, 1750–1770: The Golden Years, 1983; articles on company law in legal jls and on Rockingham porcelain in art magazines. *Recreations:* history of English porcelain, gardening. *Address:* c/o Office of the Social Security Commissioners, 6 Grosvenor Gardens, Victoria, SW1W 0DH. *Club:* Reform.

RICE, Maj.-Gen. Desmond Hind Garrett, CBE 1976 (OBE 1970); Secretary, Central Chancery of the Orders of Knighthood, since 1980; *b* 1 Dec. 1924; *s* of Arthur Garrett Rice and Alice Constance (*née* Henman); *m* 1954, Denise Ann (*née* Ravenscroft); one *d. Educ:* Marlborough College. Commissioned into The Queen's Bays, 1944; psc 1954; 1st The Queen's Dragoon Guards, 1958; jssc 1963; First Comdg Officer, The Royal Yeomanry, 1967–69; Col GS 4 Div., 1970–73; BGS (MO) MoD, 1973–75; rcds 1976; Director of Manning (Army), 1977–78; Vice Adjutant General, 1978–79; Col, 1st The Queen's Dragoon Guards, 1980–. *Recreations:* field sports, skiing, gardening. *Address:* Fairway, Malacca Farm, West Clandon, Surrey. *T:* Guildford 222677. *Club:* Cavalry and Guards.

RICE, Gordon Kenneth; His Honour Judge Rice; a Circuit Judge, since 1980; *b* 16 April 1927; *m* 1967. *Educ:* Brasenose Coll., Oxford (MA). Called to the Bar, Middle Temple, 1957. *Address:* 83 Beach Avenue, Leigh-on-Sea, Essex.

RICE, Peter D.; *see* Davis-Rice.

RICE, Roderick Alexander; Executive Director, Cable & Wireless Ltd, since 1965; *b* 7 April 1922; *s* of Samuel Richard Rice and Katrine Alice Rice; *m* 1965, Monica McClean; three *s. Educ:* Brockley County Grammar Sch. Cable & Wireless Ltd: Asst Chief Accountant, 1959; Dep. Chief Accountant, 1961; Chief Accountant, 1962; Executive Director, 1965. Jordan Star of Independence, 1965. *Recreations:* bowls, cricket, gardening. *Address:* Flat 7, 5 Manor Road, Ashford, Mddx. *Clubs:* Royal Commonwealth Institute, English-Speaking Union, MCC; (Chairman) Exiles (Richmond).

RICE, Timothy Miles Bindon; writer and broadcaster; *b* 10 Nov. 1944; *s* of Hugh Gordon Rice and Joan Odette Rice; *m* 1974, Jane Artereta McIntosh; one *s* one *d. Educ:* Lancing Coll. EMI Records, 1966–68; Norrie Paramor Org., 1968–69. Lyrics for musicals (with music by Andrew Lloyd Webber): Joseph and the Amazing Technicolor Dreamcoat, 1968 (rev. 1973); Jesus Christ Superstar, 1970; Evita 1976 (rev. 1978). Lyrics for songs, 1975–, with other composers, incl. Marvin Hamlisch, Elton John, Rick Wakeman, Vangelis, Paul McCartney, Mike Batt, Francis Lai and Florrie Palmer. Founder and Director: GRRR Books, 1978–; Pavilion Books, 1981–. Presenter, TV series incl. Musical Triangles, Friday Night Saturday Morning. Film début as actor in insultingly small rôle, The Survivor, 1980. *Publications:* Heartaches Cricketers' Almanac, yearly, 1975–; (jtly) Guinness Book of British Hit Singles, 1977, 3rd edn 1981; (with Andrew Lloyd Webber), Evita, 1978; (ed) Lord's Taverners Sticky Wicket Book, 1979; (jtly) Guinness Book of Hits of the 70's, 1980; (with Andrew Lloyd Webber) Joseph and the Amazing Technicolor Dreamcoat, 1982; (jtly) Guinness Book of 500 Number One Hits, 1982; (jtly) Guinness Book of British Hit Albums, 1983. *Recreations:* cricket, history of popular music. *Address:* 196 Shaftesbury Avenue, W1. *T:* 01-836 1306. *Clubs:* MCC, Royal Automobile, Dramatists'.

RICE-OXLEY, James Keith, CBE 1981; Chairman, Merchant Navy Training Board, since 1981; *b* 15 Aug. 1920; *o s* of late Montague Keith Rice-Oxley and Margery Hyacinth Rice-Oxley (*née* Burrell), Kensington; *m* 1949, Barbara, *yr d* of late Frederick Parsons, Gerrards Cross; two *d. Educ:* Marlborough Coll.; Trinity Coll., Oxford. MA(Law). Served War of 1939–45: Wiltshire Regt; GSO III, HQ 3 Corps; GSO II, HQ Land Forces, Greece (despatches). Joined Shipping Fedn, 1947, Dir, 1965–75; Dir, Internat. Shipping Fedn, 1970–80; Dir, Gen. Council of British Shipping, 1975–80.

Chm., Nat. Sea Training Trust, 1965–80; Mem. Nat. Maritime Bd, 1965–80; Mem., Merchant Navy Welfare Bd, 1965–80; Internat. Shipowners' Chm. and British Shipowners' Rep. on Jt Maritime Commn of ILO, 1970–80; Chm., Shipowners' Gp at Internat. Labour (Maritime) Confs, 1969, 1970, 1975, 1976; a Vice-Pres., IMCO/ILO Maritime Conf., 1978. Chm., Maritime Studies Cttee, Technician Educn Council, 1980–; Mem. Industrial Tribunals (England and Wales), 1981–. Member: Council and Exec. Cttee, Dr Barnardo's, 1981–; Council, King George's Fund for Sailors, 1965–. *Recreations:* squash, tennis, ceramics. *Address:* Ox House, Bimport, Shaftesbury SP7 8AX. *T:* Shaftesbury 2741.

RICH, Sir Almeric (Frederic Conness), 6th Bt, *cr* 1791; *b* 9 Feb. 1897; *o s* of Sir Almeric E. F. Rich, 5th Bt, and Louise (*d* 1932), *d* of Hon. John Conness, Mattapan, Mass, USA; *S* father 1948. Lt RGA, 1914–19. HM Borstal Service, 1932–61. *Address:* c/o National Westminster Bank Ltd, 1 St James's Square, SW1.

RICH, Jacob Morris, MA, LLB; Hon. Consultant, South African Jewish Board of Deputies (Secretary 1939–74); *b* Longton, Stoke-on-Trent, 4 March 1897; *m* 1940, Sylvia Linken; two *d. Educ:* Hanley High School; Fitzwilliam Hall, Cambridge. Served in Palestine with Jewish Battalions of the Royal Fusiliers during European War; Secretary to the Board of Deputies of British Jews, 1926–31; Secretary of the Joint Foreign Committee of the Board of Deputies of British Jews and the Anglo-Jewish Association, 1930–31; Hon. Secretary Jewish Historical Society of England, 1924–31; Editor, The Jewish Chronicle, 1931–36. *Address:* 17 Campbell Road, Parktown West, Johannesburg, S Africa.

RICH, John Rowland, CMG 1978; HM Diplomatic Service; Ambassador to Czechoslovakia, since 1980; *b* 29 June 1928; *s* of late Rowland William Rich, Winchester, and of Phyllis Mary, *e d* of Charles Linstead Chambers, Southgate; *m* 1956, Rosemary Ann, *yr d* of late Bertram Evan Williams, Ferndown, Dorset; two *s* one *d. Educ:* Sedbergh; Clare Coll., Cambridge (Foundn Exhibnr 1948). BA 1949, MA 1954. HM Forces, 1949–51; FO, 1951–53; 3rd, later 2nd Sec., Addis Ababa, 1953–56; 2nd, later 1st Sec., Stockholm, 1956–59; FO, 1959–63; 1st Sec. (Economic) and Head of Chancery, Bahrain (Political Residency), 1963–66; FCO, 1966–69; Counsellor and Head of Chancery, Prague, 1969–72; Diplomatic Service Inspector, 1972–74; Commercial Counsellor, Bonn, 1974–78; Consul-Gen., Montreal, 1978–80. *Recreations:* motoring, walking, gardening, tennis. *Address:* c/o Foreign and Commonwealth Office, SW1. *Club:* Travellers'.

RICH, Michael Samuel, QC 1980; *b* 18 Aug. 1933; *s* of Sidney Frank Rich, OBE and Erna Babette; *m* 1963, Janice Sarita Benedictus; three *s* one *d. Educ:* Dulwich Coll.; Wadham Coll., Oxford (MA). Called to the Bar, Middle Temple, 1958. *Publication:* (jtly) Hill's Law of Town and Country Planning, 5th edn, 1968. *Recreations:* "prog-nosed" activities. *Address:* 2 Paper Buildings, Temple, EC4. *T:* 01-353 5835; 18 Dulwich Village, SE21. *T:* 01-693 1957.

RICHARD, Cliff, OBE 1980; singer, actor; *b* 14 Oct. 1940; *s* of Rodger Webb and Dorothy Webb. *Educ:* Riversmead Sch., Cheshunt. Awarded 8 Gold Discs for records: Living Doll, 1959; The Young Ones, 1962; Bachelor Boy, 1962; Lucky Lips, 1963; Congratulations, 1968; Power to all Our Friends, 1973; Devil Woman, 1976; We Don't Talk Anymore, 1979; also 27 Silver Discs. Films: Serious Charge, 1959; Expresso Bongo, 1960; The Young Ones, 1962; Summer Holiday, 1963; Wonderful Life, 1964; Finders Keepers, 1966; Two a Penny, 1968; His Land, 1970; Take Me High, 1973. Own TV series, ATV and BBC; rep. and variety seasons. Top Box Office Star of GB, 1962–63 and 1963–64. *Publications:* Questions, 1970; The Way I See It, 1972; The Way I See It Now, 1975; Which One's Cliff, 1977. *Recreations:* swimming, tennis. *Address:* c/o Peter Gormley, PO Box 46C, Esher, Surrey, KT10 9AF. *T:* Esher 67326.

RICHARD, Ivor Seward, QC 1971; Member, Commission of the European Communities, since 1981; *b* 30 May 1932; *s* of Seward Thomas Richard, mining and electrical engineer, and Isabella Irene Richard; *m* 1962, Alison Mary Imrie; one *s* one *d* (and one *s* by former marriage). *Educ:* St Michael's Sch., Bryn, Llanelly; Cheltenham Coll.; Pembroke Coll., Oxford (Wightwick Scholar; Hon Fellow, 1981). BA Oxon (Jurisprudence) 1953; MA 1970; called to Bar, Inner Temple, 1955. Practised in chambers, London, 1955–74. UK Perm. Representative to UN, 1974–79; Chm., Rhodesia Conf., Geneva, 1976. Parly Candidate, S Kensington, 1959; MP (Lab) Barons Court, 1964–Feb. 1974. Delegate: Assembly, Council of Europe, 1965–68; Western European Union, 1965–68; Vice-Chm., Legal Cttee, Council of Europe, 1966–67; PPS, Sec. of State for Defence, 1966–69; Parly Under-Sec. (Army), Min. of Defence, 1969–70; Opposition Spokesman, Broadcasting, Posts and Telecommunications, 1970–71; Dep. Spokesman, Foreign Affairs, 1971–74. Member: Fabian Society; Society of Labour Lawyers; Inst. of Strategic Studies; Royal Inst. of Internat. Affairs. *Publications:* (jt) Europe or the Open Sea, 1971; articles in various political jls. *Recreations:* playing piano, watching football matches (Chelsea), talking. *Address:* 200 Rue de la Loi, 1049 Brussels, Belgium. *T:* Brussels 735 85 46.

RICHARDS, family name of Baron Milverton.

RICHARDS, Alun; *see* Richards, R. A.

RICHARDS, Archibald Banks, CA; retired; *b* 29 March 1911; *s* of late Charles Richards and Margaret Pollock Richards; *m* 1941, Edith Janet Sinclair; one *s* one *d. Educ:* Daniel Stewart's Coll., Edinburgh. Partner, A. T. Niven & Co., Chartered Accountants, Edinburgh, 1939-69, Touche Ross & Co., Chartered Accountants (UK firm), 1964-78. Inst. of Chartered Accountants of Scotland: Mem., 1934; Mem. Council, 1968-73; Vice Pres., 1974-76; Pres., 1976-77. *Address:* 7 Midmar Gardens, Edinburgh EH10 6DY. *T:* 031-447 1942. *Clubs:* Caledonian; New (Edinburgh).

RICHARDS, Audrey Isabel, CBE 1955; FBA 1967; Hon. Fellow, Newnham College, Cambridge (Fellow, 1956); Smuts Reader in Anthropology, Cambridge University, 1961-67; *b* 1899. *Educ:* Downe House Sch.; Newnham Coll., Cambridge (MA); PhD (Lond.). Field work: in Northern Rhodesia, 1930-31, 1933-34, 1957; in Northern Transvaal, 1939-40; in Uganda, 1950-55. Lecturer in Social Anthropology, London School of Economics, 1931-33; 1935-37; Sen. Lectr in Social Anthropology, Univ. of Witwatersrand, 1939-41; Principal, Colonial Office, 1942-45; Reader in Social Anthropology, London Univ. 1946-50; Director, East African Institute of Social Research, Makerere College, Kampala, Uganda, 1950-56; Dir, Centre for African Studies, Cambridge University, 1956-67. Member: Colonial Res. Cttee, 1944-47; Colonial Social Science Res. Council, 1944-50 and 1956-62; Committee for scientific research in Africa South of Sahara, 1954-56. President: Royal Anthropological Institute, 1959-61; African Studies Assoc., 1964-65. Overseas Fellow, American Acad. of Arts and Sciences, 1974. *Publications:* Hunger and Work in a Savage Tribe, 1932; Land, Labour and Diet in N Rhodesia, 1939; (ed) Economic Development and Tribal Change, 1954 (2nd edn, 1975); Chisungu, a study of girls' initiation ceremonies in N Rhodesia, 1956; (ed) East African Chiefs, 1960; The Changing Structure of a Ganda Village, 1966; The Multi-Cultural States of East Africa, 1969; (with A. Kuper) Councils in Action, 1971; (ed) Subsistence to Commercial Farming in Buganda, 1973; (with Jean Robin) Some Elmdon Families, 1974; papers in Africa, African Studies and African Affairs. *Address:* Crawley Cottage, Elmdon, Saffron Walden, Essex. *Club:* Royal Commonwealth Society.

RICHARDS, Bertrand; see Richards, E. B. B.

RICHARDS, Sir Brooks; see Richards, Sir F. B.

RICHARDS, Charles Anthony Langdon, CMG 1958; *b* 18 April 1911; *s* of T. L. Richards, Bristol, Musician; *m* 1937, Mary Edith Warren-Codrington; two *s. Educ:* Clifton Coll.; Brasenose Coll., Oxford. Appointed Colonial CS, Uganda, 1934; Major, 7th King's African Rifles, 1939-41: duties in Mauritius, 1941-46; District Officer, Uganda, 1946-50; Commissioner for Social Development, Tanganyika, 1950-53; Commissioner for Community Development, Uganda, 1953-54; Resident, Buganda, Oct. 1954-60; Minister of Local Government, Uganda, 1960-61. *Recreation:* gardening. *Address:* The Wall House, Oak Drive, Highworth, Wilts SN6 7BP.

RICHARDS, Rev. Canon Daniel; Residentiary Canon of Llandaff Cathedral since 1949; Priest-in-charge of Merthyr Mawr and Ewenny, 1968-77; *b* 13 February 1892; *s* of John and Elizabeth Richards; *m* 1919, Hilda Roberts; one *s* (and one *s* killed 1944). *Educ:* St David's College, Lampeter, Cards. LD 1915, Mathews Scholar, 1928-29, BA and BD 1929; Curate of St Mary's Church, Court Henry, Carms, 1915-18; Curate of St Mary's Church, Burry Port, Carms, 1918-24; Rector of Llangeitho, Cards, 1924-31; Vicar of: Llangynwyd with Maesteg, 1931-66; Grouped Parish of Troedyrhiw Garth, Maesteg, 1950-60; Precentor of Llandaff Cathedral, 1961-67; SPCK Hon. Group Secretary for Dioceses of St David's, Swansea and Brecon, Llandaff and Monmouth, 1966-. Fellow of Philosophical Society of England, 1942. MTh Geneva Theol Coll., 1980; STh Lambeth Diploma of Student in Theology, 1981. *Publications:* Honest to Self (autobiog.), 1971; History of the Lampeter Society, 1972, revd edn 1982. *Address:* Llandre, 26 Brynteg Avenue, Bridgend, Mid Glamorgan. *T:* Bridgend 5117.

RICHARDS, David Gordon, FCA; Partner, Deloitte, Haskins & Sells, Chartered Accountants, since 1974; *b* 25 Aug. 1928; *s* of late Gordon Charles Richards and Vera Amy (*née* Barrow); *m* 1960, Stephanie, *er d* of late E. Gilbert Woodward, Metropolitan Magistrate and of Mrs Woodward; one *s* two *d. Educ:* Highgate Sch. FCA 1961. Articled to Harmood Banner & Co., 1945; served, 8th Royal Tank Regt, 1947-49; Partner, Harmood Banner & Co., 1955. Admitted Associate Mem. Inst. of Chartered Accountants in England and Wales, 1951 (Council, 1970; Vice-Pres., 1977-78; Dep. Pres., 1978-79; Centenary Pres., 1979-80; Mem., Gen. Purposes and Finance Cttee, 1977-; Chm., Internat. Affairs Cttee, 1980-); Member: Cttee of London Soc. of Chartered Accountants, 1966-70, 1981-82 (Chm., 1969-70); Council for Securities Industry, 1979-80; Panel on Take Overs and Mergers, 1979-80; Chm., Cons. Cttee of Accountancy Bodies, 1979-80; UK and Ireland rep. on Council, Internat. Fedn of Accountants, 1981-. Governor, Highgate Sch., 1982-. *Publications:* numerous contribs to professional press and lectures on professional topics given internationally. *Recreations:* golf, lawn tennis, sailing, reading, music. *Address:* 13 Woodsford Square, Kensington, W14 8DP. *T:* 01-602 0084; The Cardinal's Hat, Chaucers Lane, Woodstock, Oxon. *T:* Woodstock 811161. *Clubs:* Gresham; Frilford Heath Golf.

RICHARDS, Denis Edward, CMG 1981; HM Diplomatic Service, retired; Ambassador to the United Republic of Cameroon and the Republic of Equatorial Guinea, 1979-81; *b* 25 May 1923; *m* 1947, Nancy Beryl Brown; two *d. Educ:* Wilson's Grammar Sch., London; St Peter's Coll., Oxford. Lieut RNVR, 1941-46; Colonial Service (HMOCS), 1948-60: District Admin. and Min. of Finance, Ghana (Gold Coast); HM Diplomatic Service, 1960-: CRO, 1960; Karachi, 1961-63; FO (News Dept), 1964-68; Brussels (NATO), 1969; Brussels (UK Negotiating Delegn), 1970-72; Counsellor, Kinshasa, 1972-74; Consul-Gen., Philadelphia, 1974-79. *Recreations:* music, amateur dramatics. *Address:* Tresco House, Spencer Road, Birchington, Kent CT7 9EY. *T:* Thanet 45637.

RICHARDS, Denis George; author; *b* 10 Sept. 1910; *s* of late George Richards and Frances Amelia Gosland; *m* 1940, Barbara, *d* of J. H. Smethurst, Heaton, Bolton; four *d. Educ:* Owen's Sch.; Trinity Hall, Cambridge (Scholar). BA 1931 (1st Cl. in both Parts of Historical Tripos); MA 1935; Asst Master, Manchester Grammar School, 1931-39; Senior History and English Master, Bradfield Coll., 1939-41; Narrator in Air Ministry Historical Branch, writing confidential studies on various aspects of the air war, 1942-43; Sen. Narrator, 1943-47; Hon. Sqdn Ldr RAFVR, 1943-47; engaged in writing, under Air Min. auspices, an official History of the Royal Air Force in the Second World War, 1947-49; was established in Admin. Civil Service, Principal, Department of Permanent Under Secretary of State for Air, 1949-50; Principal, Morley College, 1950-65; Longman Fellow in Univ. of Sussex, 1965-68. Chm., Women's League of Health and Beauty; Governor: Milton Abbey Sch.; Purcell Sch. for Young Musicians. *Publications:* An Illustrated History of Modern Europe, 1938; Modern Europe (1919-39 section for revised edn of work by Sydney Herbert), 1940; (with J. W. Hunt) An Illustrated History of Modern Britain, 1950; (with late Hilary St G. Saunders) Royal Air Force 1939-45-an officially commissioned history in 3 volumes, 1953-54 (awarded C. P. Robertson Memorial Trophy, 1954); (with J. Evan Cruikshank) The Modern Age, 1955; Britain under the Tudors and Stuarts, 1958; Offspring of the Vic: a History of Morley College, 1958; (with Anthony Quick) Britain 1714-1851, 1961; (with J. A. Bolton) Britain and the Ancient World, 1963; (with Anthony Quick) Britain, 1851-1945, 1967; (with Anthony Quick) Twentieth Century Britain, 1968; (with A. W. Ellis) Medieval Britain, 1973; Portal of Hungerford, 1978. *Recreations:* music, pictures, golf, travel in the more civilized parts of Europe, the lighter tasks in the garden. *Address:* 16 Broadlands Road, N6. *T:* 01-340 5259. *Clubs:* Arts, Garrick, PEN.

See also W. P. Shovelton.

RICHARDS, Edgar Lynton, (Tony Richards), CBE 1971 (MBE 1954); MC 1944, Bar 1945; TD 1953; formerly partner, Moy, Vandervell & Co.; *b* 21 April 1912; *s* of late Thomas Edgar Richards, ARIBA, MICE, and Enid Marie (*née* Thomas); *m* 1937, Barbara Lebus; three *s* one *d.* Served War, 1939-45. Member: Stock Exchange, 1939-; Stock Exchange Council, 1955-68. Mem., 1965-79, Dep. Chm., 1974-79; Monopolies, later Monopolies and Mergers, Commn. Former Chm. Trustees, Amer. Museums in Britain.

RICHARDS, (Edmund) Bertrand (Bamford); His Honour Judge Bertrand Richards; a Circuit Judge since 1972; *b* 14 Feb. 1913; *s* of Rev. Edmund Milo Richards, Llewesog Hall, Denbigh; *m* 1966, Jane, *widow* of Edward Stephen Porter. *Educ:* Lancing Coll.; Corpus Christi Coll., Oxford. Served War, RA, 1940-46. Called to Bar, Inner Temple, 1941. Dep. Chm., Denbighshire QS, 1964-71. Hon. Recorder of Ipswich, 1975. *Address:* Melton Hall, near Woodbridge, Suffolk. *T:* Woodbridge 4215. *Club:* Carlton.

RICHARDS, Hon. Sir Edward (Trenton), Kt 1970; CBE 1967; Premier of Bermuda, 1972-75 (Leader, 1971; Deputy Leader, 1968-71); MP 1948-76; *b* 4 Oct. 1908; 2nd *s* of late George A. Richards and Millicent Richards, British Guiana; *m* 1940, Madree Elizabeth Williams; one *s* two *d. Educ:* Collegiate Sch.; Queen's Coll., Guyana; Middle Temple. Secondary School-teacher, 1930-43; called to Bar, 1946. Elected to House of Assembly, Bermuda, 1948; served numerous Select Cttees of Parliament; served on Commns; Member, Exec. Council (now Cabinet), 1963-75; Mem. of Govt responsible for Immigration, Labour and Soc. Security, 1968-71. Served on many Govt Boards; Chairman: Public Transportation Board; Transport Control Board. Bermuda Representative: CPA Confs, Lagos, 1962, Kuala Lumpur, 1971; Guyana's Independence Celebrations, 1966, Bahamas Independence Celebrations, 1973; Mem., Constitution Conf., 1966; Leader Bermuda Delegn, ILO Confs Geneva, 1969-71. Magistrate, 1958. Chm., Berkeley Educational Soc., 1956-72. Hon. Life Vice-Pres., Bermuda Football Assoc. Hon. LLD, Wilberforce, USA, 1960. *Recreations:* music, reading, walking. *Address:* Wilton, Keith Hall Road, Warwick East, Bermuda. *T:* 2-3645. *Clubs:* Somerset Cricket, Warwick Workman's, Blue Waters Anglers (Bermuda); Royal Hamilton Amateur Dinghy.

RICHARDS, Prof. Elfyn John, OBE 1958; FEng; FRAeS; FIMechE; Research Professor, Southampton University, and Acoustical Consultant, since 1975; *b* Barry, Glamorgan, South Wales, 28 Dec. 1914; *s* of Edward James Richards, Barry, schoolmaster, and of Catherine Richards; *m* 1941, Eluned Gwenddydd Jones (*d* 1978), Aberporth, Cardigan; three *d. Educ:* Barry County School; Univ. Coll. of Wales, Aberystwyth (BSc); St John's Coll., Cambridge (MA). DSc (Wales), 1959. Research Asst, Bristol Aeroplane Company, 1938-39; Scientific Officer, National Physical Laboratory, Teddington, 1939-45, and Secretary, various Aeronautical Research Council sub-cttees; Chief Aerodynamicist and Asst Chief-Designer, Vickers Armstrong, Ltd, Weybridge, 1945-50; Prof. of Aeronautical Engineering, 1950-64, and Founder Dir, Inst. of Sound and Vibration Research, 1963-67, Univ. of Southampton, also Aeronautical Engineering Consultant; Vice-Chancellor, Loughborough Univ., 1967-75. Member: SRC, 1970-74; Noise

Adv. Council; Noise Research Council, ARC, 1968-71; Construction Research and Adv. Council, 1968-71; Inland Transport and Develt Council, 1968-71; Gen. Adv. Council of BBC (Chm. Midlands Adv. Council, 1968-71); Cttee of Scientific Advisory Council; Wilson Cttee on Problems of Noise; Planning and Transport Res. Adv. Council, 1971-. Chm., Univs Council for Adult Educn; President: British Acoustical Soc., 1968-70; Soc. of Environmental Engrs, 1971-73. Mem. Leics CC. Hon. LLD Wales, 1973; Hon. DSc Southampton, 1973; Hon DTech Loughborough, 1975. Hon. FIOA 1978; Hon. Fellow Acoustical Soc. of America, 1980. Taylor Gold Medal, RAeS, 1949; James Watt Medal, ICE, 1963; Silver Medal, RSA, 1971. *Publications:* many reports and memoranda of Aeronautical Research Council; articles and lectures in Roy. Aeronautical Soc. *Recreations:* swimming, walking. *Address:* 6 Highfield Lane, Southampton.

RICHARDS, Sir (Francis) Brooks, KCMG 1976 (CMG 1963); DSC and Bar, 1944; *b* 18 July 1918; *s* of Francis Bartlett Richards; *m* 1941, Hazel Myfanwy, *d* of Lt-Col Stanley Price Williams, CIE; *one s one d. Educ:* Stowe School; Magdalene College, Cambridge. Served with RN, 1939-44 (Lieut-Comdr RNVR). HM Embassy: Paris, 1944-48; Athens, 1952-54; First Sec. and Head of Chancery, Political Residency, Persian Gulf, 1954-57; Assistant Private Secretary to Foreign Secretary, 1958-59; Counsellor (Information), HM Embassy, Paris, 1959-64; Head of Information Policy Dept, 1964-65, and of Jt Inf. Policy and Guidance Dept, FO/CRO, 1964-65; seconded to Cabinet Office, 1965-69; HM Minister, Bonn, 1969-71; HM Ambassador, Saigon, 1972-74; HM Ambassador, Greece, 1974-78; Dep. Sec., Cabinet Office, 1978-80; NI Office, 1980-81. Member: IISS; RIIA. Chevalier, Légion d'Honneur and Croix de Guerre (France), 1944. *Recreations:* sailing, gardening, travelling. *Address:* The Ranger's House, Farnham, Surrey. *Clubs:* Travellers', Royal Ocean Racing.

RICHARDS, Sir Gordon, Kt 1953; Racing Manager, since 1970 (Jockey, retired 1954, then Trainer, 1955-70); *b* 5 May 1904; *s* of Nathan Richards; *m* (wife died 1982); two *s.* Started life as a clerk; went as a stable apprentice to Mr Martin G. Hartigan, 1919; has headed the list of winning jockeys, 1925, 1927-29, 1931-33, 1938-40, 1942; 259 winners in 1933, breaking Fred Archer's record; passed Archer's record total of 2,749 winners, 26 April 1943; passed own record with 269 winners, 1947; rode 4000th winner 4 May 1950; broke world record with 4,500 winners 17 July 1952; final total, 4,870. Won the 1953 Derby on Pinza. Hon. Member, Jockey Club, 1970. *Publication:* My Story, 1955. *Recreations:* shooting, watching football. *Address:* Duff House, Kintbury, Berks.

RICHARDS, Very Rev. Gwynfryn; Dean of Bangor, 1962-71; Archdeacon of Bangor, 1957-62; Rector of Llandudno, 1956-62; *b* 10 Sept. 1902; *er s* of Joshua and Elizabeth Ann Richards, Nantyffyllon, Glam; *m* 1935, Margery Phyllis Evans; *one s one d. Educ:* Universities of Wales, Oxford and Boston. Scholar, Univ. Coll., Cardiff, 1918-21; BSc (Wales), 1921; Jesus Coll., Oxford, 1921-23; Certificate, School of Geography, Oxford, 1922; BA 1st Cl. Hons School of Natural Science, 1923; MA 1928. In industry (USA), 1923-25. Boston Univ. Sch. of Theology, 1926-28; STB First Cl., 1928; Scholar and Travelling Fellow, 1928-29; Oxford, 1928-29; St Michael's Coll., Llandaff, 1929-30; deacon, 1930; priest, 1931. Curate of: Llanrhos, 1930-34; Aberystwyth, St Michael, 1934-38; Rector of Llanllyfni, 1938-49; Vicar of Conway with Gyffin, 1949-56. Canon of Bangor Cathedral, 1943-62, Treas., 1943-57; Examining Chaplain to Bp of Bangor, 1944-71; Rural Dean of Arllechwedd, 1953-57. Pantyfedwen Lectr, Univ. Coll., Aberystwyth, 1967. *Publications:* Ffurfiau Ordeinio Holl Eglwysi Cymru, 1943; Yr Hen Fam, 1952; Ein Hymraniadau Annedwydd, 1963; Gwir a Diogel Obaith, 1972; Ar Lawer Trywydd, 1973; A Fynn Esgyn, Mynn Ysgol, 1980; contrib. to Journal of the Historical Society of the Church in Wales, Nat. Library of Wales Jl, Trans of Caernarvonshire Hist. Soc. *Recreations:* gardening, photography, local history. *Address:* Llain Werdd, Llandegfan, Menai Bridge, Gwynedd LL59 5LY. *T:* Menai Bridge 713429.

RICHARDS, Brigadier Hugh Upton, CBE 1943; DSO 1944; *b* 1894; *s* of J. Richards; *m* Florence Matilda (*d* 1964), *d* of J. McLeod; *one s ; m* 1966, Mrs Irene Mary Olver, *widow* of Cecil Paul Olver. Served European War, 1914-19, with Worcestershire Regiment; Lieutenant, 1917; Captain, 1931; Bt Major, 1934; Major, 1936; transfd West Yorkshire Regt, 1936; Lt-Col 1939; Col 1942; Brig. 1940; commanded 4 Bn Nigeria Regt 1933-34, Sierra Leone Bn 1939, and 3 (West African) Inf. Bde, 1940-44. Campaign Palestine, 1936 and 1938 and Burma. *Club:* Army and Navy.

RICHARDS, James Alan, OBE 1979; Agent-General for Western Australia in London, 1975-78; *b* 8 Oct. 1913; *s* of James Percival Richards and Alice Pearl Richards (*née* Bullock), Adelaide; *m* 1939, Mabel Joyce, *d* of R. H. Cooper, Riverton, S Austr.; *three s one d. Educ:* Unley High Sch.; Coll. of Business Admin, Univ. of Hawaii. Served War of 1939-45, 2nd AIF. Ampol Petroleum Ltd, 1946-75: Sales Man., South Australia, 1952-53; State Man., Western Australia, 1954-75. *Recreation:* bowls. *Address:* 4 Nuytsia Avenue, Sorrento, WA 6020, Australia.

RICHARDS, Sir James (Maude), Kt 1972; CBE 1959; FSA 1980; architectural writer, critic and historian; Editor, Architectural Review, 1937-71; Editor, Architects' Journal, 1947-49 (editorial board, 1949-61); Architectural Correspondent, The Times, 1947-71; *b* 13 Aug. 1907; 2nd *s* of late Louis Saurin Richards and Lucy Denes (*née* Clarence); *m* 1st, 1936, Margaret (marr. diss., 1948), *d* of late David Angus; (one *s* decd) one *d* ; 2nd,

1954, Kathleen Margaret (Kit), *widow* of late Morland Lewis and 2nd *d* of late Henry Bryan Godfrey-Faussett-Osborne, Queendown Warren, Sittingbourne, Kent; *one s decd. Educ:* Gresham's School, Holt; AA School of Architecture. ARIBA, AADipl 1930. Studied and practised architecture in Canada and USA, 1930-31, London and Dublin, 1931-33; Asst Editor, The Architects' Jl, 1933; The Architectural Review, 1935; Editor, Publications Div., 1942, Director of Publications, Middle East, Cairo, 1943-46, MOI; Gen. Editor, The Architectural Press, 1946. Hoffman Wood Prof. of Architecture, Leeds Univ., 1957-59. Editor, European Heritage, 1973-75. Member: exec. cttee Modern Architectural Research Gp, 1946-54; AA Council, 1948-51, 1958-61, 1973-74; Advisory Council, Inst. of Contemporary Arts, 1947-68; Architecture Council, Festival of Britain, 1949-51; British Cttee, Internat. Union of Architects, 1950-66; Royal Fine Art Commn, 1951-66; Fine Art Cttee, Brit. Council, 1954-78; Council of Industrial Design, 1955-61; Min. of Transport (Worboys) Cttee on traffic signs, 1962-63; World Soc. of Ekistics, 1965-; Council, Victorian Soc., 1965-; National Trust, 1977-; Vice-Pres. Nat. Council on Inland Transport, 1963-; Chm., Arts Council inquiry into provision for the arts in Ireland, 1974-76. Broadcaster, television and sound (regular member, BBC Critics panel, 1948-68). FRSA 1970; Hon. AILA, 1955. Chevalier (First Class), Order of White Rose of Finland, 1960; Gold Medal, Mexican Institute of Architects, 1963; Bicentenary Medal, RSA, 1971. *Publications:* Miniature History of the English House, 1938; (with late Eric Ravilious) High Street, 1938; Introduction to Modern Architecture, 1940, new edn 1970 (trans. seven langs); (with John Summerson) The Bombed Buildings of Britain, 1942; Edward Bawden, 1946; The Castles on the Ground, 1946, new enl. edn 1973; The Functional Tradition in Early Industrial Buildings, 1958; (ed) New Building in the Commonwealth, 1961; An Architectural Journey in Japan, 1963; Guide to Finnish Architecture, 1966; A Critic's View, 1970; (ed, with Nikolaus Pevsner) The Anti-Rationalists, 1972; Planning and Redevelopment in London's Entertainment Area, 1973 (Arts Council report); The Professions: Architecture, 1974; (ed) Who's Who in Architecture: from 1400 to the present day, 1977; 800 Years of Finnish Architecture, 1978; Memoirs of an Unjust Fella (autobiog.), 1980; Goa, 1981; The National Trust Book of English Architecture, 1981. *Recreations:* travel and topography. *Address:* 29 Fawcett Street, SW10. *T:* 01-352 9874. *Clubs:* Athenæum, Beefsteak.

RICHARDS, Ven. John; Archdeacon of Exeter and Canon Residentiary of Exeter Cathedral, since 1981; *b* 4 Oct. 1933; *s* of William and Ethel Mary Richards; *m* 1958, Ruth Haynes; *two s three d. Educ:* Reading School; Wyggeston Grammar School, Leicester; Sidney Sussex Coll., Cambridge (MA); Ely Theological Coll. Asst Curate, St Thomas, Exeter, 1959-64; Rector of Holsworthy with Hollacombe and Cookbury, 1964-74; RD of Holsworthy, 1970-74; Rector of Heavitree with St Paul's, Exeter, 1974-81; RD of Exeter, 1978-81. Chm. of House of Clergy, Exeter Diocesan Synod, 1979-82. *Recreations:* gardening, fishing, walking. *Address:* 12 The Close, Exeter. *T:* Exeter 75745.

RICHARDS, John Arthur; Under-Secretary, Department of Education and Science, 1973-77; *b* 23 June 1918; *s* of late Alderman A. J. Richards and Mrs Annie Richards, Dulwich; *m* 1946, Sheelagh, *d* of late Patrick McWalter and Katherine McWalter, Balla, Co. Mayo; *two s one d. Educ:* Brockley Sch.; King's Coll., London. BA, AKC, Dip. in Educn. Hon. Sec., King's Coll. Union Soc., 1939. Served War: Captain RA; Directorate of Personnel Selection, War Office, 1945-46. Temp. Third Sec., Foreign Office, 1946; Staff, Hackney Downs Grammar Sch., 1948; Ministry of Education: Asst Principal and Principal, 1949 (Jt Sec., Secondary Schs Examinations Council, 1956-57); Asst Sec. (also Dept of Educn and Science), 1963-73. Mem., Southwark Diocesan Schs Commn; Vice-Chm. of Governors, Thomas More Sch., Purley; Governor, St Joseph's Coll., Beulah Hill. *Publications:* occasional verse and contribs to journals. *Recreations:* walking, journalism, writing verse. *Address:* 14 Blacksmiths Hill, Sanderstead, Surrey CR2 9AY. *T:* 01-657 1275.

RICHARDS, Lt-Gen. Sir John (Charles Chisholm), KCB 1980; HM Marshal of the Diplomatic Corps, since 1982; *b* 21 Feb. 1927; *s* of Charles C. Richards and Alice Milner; *m* 1953, Audrey Hidson; *two s one d. Educ:* Worksop Coll., Notts. CBIM. Joined Royal Marines, 1945; 45 Commando, Malaya, 1950-52; HMS Birmingham, 1955-56; Canadian Army Staff Coll., 1959-61; 43 Commando, 1962-63; Naval staff, 1963-64; Instructor, Staff Coll., Camberley, 1965-67; 45 Commando: Aden, 1967; CO, 1968-69; GSO1 Plymouth Gp, 1969; CO 42 Commando, 1970-72; Chief of Staff, Brit. Def. Staff, Washington DC, UN Deleg., and Mem. Mil. Staff Cttee, 1972-74; Comdr 3rd Commando Bde, 1975-76; Comdt Gen., Royal Marines, 1977-81. Freeman, City of London, 1982. *Recreations:* golf, gardening. *Address:* St James's Palace, SW1.

RICHARDS, John Deacon, CBE 1978; ARSA 1974; RIBA, FRIAS; architect; Partner in Robert Matthew, Johnson-Marshall and Partners, since 1964; *b* 7 May 1931; *s* of William John Richards and late Ethel Richards; *m* 1958, Margaret Brown, RIBA, ARIAS; *one s three d. Educ:* Geelong Grammar Sch., Vic; Cranleigh Sch.; Architect. Assoc. Sch. of Arch., London (Dipl. 1954). RIBA 1955; FRIAS 1968. RE, 1955-57. Buildings include: Stirling Univ., 1965-; Royal Commonwealth Pool, Edinburgh, 1970; airport terminals, Edinburgh and Aberdeen, 1977. Member: Royal Fine Art Commn for Scotland, 1975-; Bd, Housing Corp., 1982-. Mem., Agrément Bd, 1980-. Hon. DUniv Stirling, 1976. Gold Medallist, RSA, 1972. *Recreation:* country life. *Address:* Lady's Field, Whitekirk, Dunbar, East Lothian EH42 1XS. *T:*

Whitekirk 206. *Clubs:* Scottish Arts (Edinburgh); Royal Forth Yacht (Edinburgh).

RICHARDS, Rt. Rev. John Richards, DD (Lambeth); President, St David's University College, Lampeter, 1971-77; *b* 3 March 1901; *s* of Thomas and Elizabeth Richards, Llanbadarn, Fawr, Aberystwyth; *m* 1929, Katherine Mary (*d* 1980), *d* of W. E. and M. Hodgkinson, Inglewood, St Michael's, Tenterden; one *s* one *d. Educ:* Ardwyn School, Aberystwyth; Univ. College of Wales; St Michael's College Llandaff. BA 1922 (2nd Cl. Hons Mod. Langs); MA 1955; DD 1956. Deacon, 1924; priest, 1925; Curate of Pembrey w Burry Post, 1924-27; CMS missionary in Iran, 1927-45, at Shiraz, 1927-36, at Yezd, 1938-42, at Isfahan, 1942-45; Archdeacon in Iran, 1937-45. Mem. of Near East Christian Council, 1932-38; Hon. CF, Paiforce, 1942-45; Vicar of Skewen, 1945-52, Vicar of St Catherine, Pontypridd, 1952-54; Canon of St Andrew in Llandaff Cathedral, 1949-54; Dean of Bangor, 1955-56; Vicar of St James', Bangor, and Canon of Bangor Cathedral, 1954-55; Bishop of St David's, 1956-March 1971. Pantyfedwen Lectr, UC Swansea, 1972. Mem. of Governing Body of the Church in Wales, 1948-71. Chaplain and Sub-Prelate, Order of St John, 1961. Hon. LLD Wales, 1971. *Publications:* The Religion of the Baha'is, 1932; The Open Road in Persia, 1932; Baha'ism, 1965; Under His Banner, 1973; Jesus: Son of God and Son of Man, 1974. *Address:* Lluest Wen, Llanbadarn Road, Aberystwyth SY23 1EY.

RICHARDS, Michael; Director, Samuel Montagu & Co. Ltd, since 1959; *b* 4 Oct. 1915; *s* of Frank Richards and Jenny Charlotte (*née* Levinsen); *m* 1942, Lucy Helen Quirey; three *d. Educ:* Roundhay High Sch., Leeds; Leeds Univ. (LLB). Solicitor, 1936. Partner, Ashurst, Morris Crisp & Co., Solicitors, City of London, 1936-54; Chm. and Man. Dir, Hart, Son & Co. Ltd, Merchant Bankers, 1954-60. Chm., Wood Hall Trust Ltd, 1950-82. *Recreations:* work, farming, collecting works of art. *Address:* Wood Hall, Shenley, Radlett, Herts. *T:* Radlett 6624.

RICHARDS, Prof. Owain Westmacott, FRS 1959; MA, DSc (Oxford); Professor of Zoology and Applied Entomology, Imperial College, London, 1953-67, now Emeritus; Fellow of Imperial College, 1969-80; *b* 31 Dec. 1901; 2nd *s* of H. M. Richards, MD; *m* 1st, 1931, Maud Jessie (*d* 1970), *d* of Eng. Capt. C. M. Norris, RN; two *d*; 2nd, 1972, Joyce Elinor Benson (*née* McLuckie). *Educ:* Hereford Cathedral School; Brasenose College, Oxford. Exhibitioner, 1920, and Senior Hulme Schol., Brasenose Coll.; Christopher Welch Schol., Oxford Univ., 1924. Research Asst, Dept of Entomology, Imperial College, 1927; Lecturer, 1930; Reader, 1937. Hon. Mem. Société Entomologique d'Egypte; Hon. Fellow, Royal Entomological Soc. of London; Hon. Member: Nederlandsche Entomologische Vereeniging; British Ecological Soc.; Accademia Nazionale Italiana di Entomologia. *Publications:* The Variations of Animals in Nature (with G. C. Robson), 1936; The Social Insects, 1953; Imms' General Textbook of Entomology, 10th edn (with R. G. Davies), 1977; The Social Wasps of the Americas, 1978. *Recreation:* entomology. *Address:* 89 St Stephen's Road, Ealing, W13 8JA.

RICHARDS, Prof. Peter; Dean and Professor of Medicine, St Mary's Hospital Medical School, University of London, since 1979; *b* 25 May 1936; *s* of William and Barbara Richards; *m* 1959, Anne Marie Larsen; one *s* three *d. Educ:* Monkton Combe Sch.; Emmanuel Coll., Cambridge (MA, MD); St George's Hosp. Medical Sch. (PhD). FRCP. Consultant Physician, St Peter's Hosp., Chertsey and Hon. Sen. Lectr in Medicine, St Mary's Hosp. Med. Sch., 1970-73; Sen. Lectr in medicine, St George's Hosp. Med. Sch. 1973-79. *Publications:* The Medieval Leper, 1977; (ed jtly) Clinical Medicine and Therapeutics, Vol. I, 1977, Vol. II, 1979; scientific papers esp. concerning kidney disease in Lancet, BMJ, etc. *Recreations:* walking, listening to music, Finland, social history. *Address:* St Mary's Hospital Medical School, Paddington, W2 1PG.

RICHARDS, Sir Rex (Edward), Kt 1977; DSc Oxon 1970; FRS 1959; FRIC; Warden of Merton College, Oxford, since 1969; Chancellor, Exeter University, since 1982; *b* 28 Oct. 1922; *s* of H. W. and E. N. Richards; *m* 1948, Eva Edith Vago; two *d. Educ:* Colyton Grammar School, Devon; St John's College, Oxford. Senior Demy, Magdalen College, Oxford, 1946; MA; DPhil; Fellow, Lincoln College, Oxford, 1947-64, Hon. Fellow, 1968; Research Fellow, Harvard University, 1955; Dr Lee's Prof. of Chemistry, Oxford, 1964-70; Fellow Exeter College, 1964-69; Vice-Chancellor, Oxford Univ., 1977-81; Hon. Fellow, St John's Coll., Oxford, 1968; Associate Fellow, Morse Coll., Yale, 1974-79. Dir, IBM-UK Ltd, 1978-. Member: Chemical Society Council, 1957; Faraday Society Council, 1963; Royal Soc. Council, 1973-75; Scientific Adv. Cttee, Nat. Gall., 1978-; ABRC, 1980-; Trustee: CIBA Foundn, 1978-; Nat. Heritage Memorial Fund, 1980-; Tate Gall., 1982-; Nat. Gall., 1982-. Tilden Lectr, 1962. Corday-Morgan Medal of Chemical Soc., 1954; Davy Medal, Royal Soc., 1976; Award in Theoretical Chemistry and Spectroscopy, Chem. Soc., 1977. FRIC 1970. Hon. DSc: East Anglia, 1971; Exeter, 1975; Leicester, 1978; Salford, 1979; Edinburgh, 1981; Hon. LLD Dundee, 1977. *Publications:* various contributions to scientific journals. *Recreation:* 20th century painting and sculpture. *Address:* Warden's Lodgings, Merton College, Oxford. *T:* Oxford 249651. *Club:* United Oxford & Cambridge University.

RICHARDS, (Richard) Alun; Welsh Secretary in charge of Welsh Office Agriculture Department, 1978-81; *b* 2 Jan. 1920; *s* of Sylvanus and Gwladys Richards, Llanbrynmair, Powys; *m* 1944, Ann Elonwy Mary (Nansi) Price, Morriston, Swansea; two *s. Educ:* Machynlleth County Sch.; Liverpool Univ.

(BVSc, MRCVS, 1942). Veterinary Officer with State Vet. Service, Caernarfon and Glamorgan, 1943-57; Divl Vet. Officer, HQ Tolworth and in Warwick, 1957-65; Dep. Reg. Vet. Officer (Wales), 1965-67; seconded to NZ Govt to advise on control of Foot and Mouth disease, 1967-68; Reg. Vet. Officer, HQ Tolworth, 1968-71; Asst Chief Vet. Officer, 1971-77; Asst Sec., Welsh Dept, MAFF, 1977-78; Under-Sec., 1978. *Publications:* contrib. to vet. jls. *Recreations:* gardening, fishing, shooting. *Address:* Isfryn, Llandre, Bow Street, Dyfed. *T:* Aberystwyth 828246.

RICHARDS, Rt. Rev. Ronald Edwin, MA, ThD (*jure dig*); *b* Ballarat, Vic., 25 Oct. 1908; *s* of Edward and Margaret Elizabeth Richards, Ballarat; *m* 1937, Nancy, *d* of W. E. Lloyd Green; one *d. Educ:* Ballarat High Sch.; Trinity Coll., Melbourne Univ. BA 2nd Cl Hons Phil., 1932, MA 1937; Asst Master, Ballarat C of E Gram. Sch., 1926, Malvern C of E Gram. Sch., 1927-28; deacon, 1932; priest, 1933; Curate of Rokewood, 1932-33, Priest-in-charge, 1934; Priest-in-charge, Lismore, 1934-41 and 1945-46; Chaplain AIF, 1941-45; Vicar of Warrnambool, 1946-50; Archdeacon of Ballarat, and Examining Chapl. to Bp of Ballarat, 1950-57; Vicar-Gen., 1952-57; Bishop of Bendigo, 1957-74. *Address:* Madron, 119 Dare Street, Ocean Grove, Victoria 3226, Australia. *Clubs:* Royal Automobile of Victoria (Melbourne); Barwon Heads Golf.

RICHARDS, Tony; see Richards, E. L.

RICHARDSON, family name of **Baron Richardson.**

RICHARDSON, Baron *cr* 1979 (Life Peer), of Lee in the County of Devon; **John Samuel Richardson,** 1st Bt, *cr* 1963; Kt 1960; MVO 1943; MD, FRCP; retired; President, General Medical Council, 1973-80; Hon. Consulting Physician: St Thomas' Hospital; King Edward VII's Hospital for Officers; Consultant Emeritus to the Army; Consulting Physician: Metropolitan Police, 1957-80; London Transport Board, since 1964; *b* 16 June 1910; *s* of Major John Watson Richardson, solicitor, and Elizabeth Blakeney, *d* of Sir Samuel Roberts, 1st Bt, both of Sheffield; *m* 1933, Sybil Angela Stephanie, *d* of A. Ronald Trist, Stanmore; two *d. Educ:* Charterhouse; Trinity Coll., Cambridge (Hon. Fellow, 1979). MB BChir 1936, MD 1940; MRCP 1937, FRCP 1948; FRCPE 1975. Major, RAMC (temp.), 1939; Lt-Col, RAMC (temp.), 1942. 1st asst, Med. Professorial Unit, St Thomas's Hosp., 1946; Physician to St Thomas's Hosp., 1947-75. Examiner to Univs of Cambridge, London, Manchester, NUI, RCP London and Edinburgh Conjoint Bd. President: Internat. Soc. of Internal Medicine, 1966-70 (Hon. Pres. 1970); Royal Soc. of Medicine, 1969-71 (Hon. Librarian, 1957-63; Pres., Med. Educn Sect., 1967-68); BMA, 1970-71; 2nd Congress, Assoc. Européene de Médicine Interne d'Ensemble, Bad-Godesberg, 1973 (Hon. Mem. 1974); Assoc. for the Study of Med. Educn, 1978-80 (Vice-Pres., 1974-78, Hon. Mem., 1980); Vice-President: Med. Soc. of London, 1961-63 (Hon. Fellow, 1981); Royal Coll. of Nursing, 1972-; Chairman: Jt Consultants Cttee, 1967-72; Council for Postgrad. Med. Educn in England and Wales, 1972-80; Medico-Pharmaceutical Forum, 1973-76; Armed Forces Med. Adv. Bd, MoD, 1975-80. Mem., Bd of Governors, St Thomas's Hosp., 1953-59, 1964-74. Mem. Ct, Soc. of Apothecaries, 1960- (Master, 1971-72). Lectures: Lettsomian, Med. Soc. of London, 1963; Scott Heron, Royal Victoria Hosp., Belfast, 1969; Maudsley, RCPsych, 1971; Wilkinson Meml, Inst. of Dental Surgeons, London Univ., 1976; Harveian Oration, RCP, 1978; Orator, Med. Soc. of London, 1981. Hon. Fellow: Swedish Soc. Med. Scis, 1970; RSocMed 1973; Heberden Soc., 1973; Osler Club of London, 1973; Hon. Mem., Assoc. of Clinical Tutors of GB, 1980; Hon. FPS, 1974; Hon. FRCPI 1975; Hon. FFCM 1977; Hon. FRCPsych 1979; Hon. FRCS 1980; Hon. FRCPSG 1980; Hon. FRCPE 1981. Hon. Bencher, Gray's Inn, 1974. Hon. DSc: NUI, 1975; Hull, 1981; Hon. DCL Newcastle, 1980; Hon. LLD Nottingham, 1981. CStJ 1970. Baron de Lancey Law Prize, RSM, 1978; Gold Medal, BMA, 1982; Guthrie Medal, RAMC, 1982. Editor-in-Chief, British Encyclopaedia of Medical Practice, 1970-74. *Publications:* The Practice of Medicine, 2nd edn 1960; Connective Tissue Disorders, 1963; Anticoagulant Prophylaxis and Treatment (jointly), 1965. *Heir* to baronetcy: none. *Address:* Windcutter, Lee, near Ilfracombe, North Devon EX34 8LW. *T:* Ilfracombe 63198.

RICHARDSON, Alexander Stewart, CBE 1943; BSc; *b* 17 May 1897; *e s* of late Alexander Stewart Richardson and Susan Hamilton Horsburgh; *m* 1931, Kathleen Margaret, *o d* of late Angus McColl, Inverness; one *s* one *d. Educ:* Edinburgh University. Military Service, 1916-19; Agricultural Officer, Tanganyika Territory, 1924; Senior Agricultural Officer, 1930; Deputy Director of Agriculture, Uganda, 1937; Director of Agriculture, Nyasaland, 1940-44; MLC 1940; Chairman Supply Board and Controller of Essential Supplies and Prices, 1941 and 1942; Controller of Production and Food, 1943. Member of Executive and Legislative Councils; Officer in general charge of Supplies, Prices and Distribution of Commodities; Uganda Govt Rep. on East African Production and Supply Council; Leader of East African Cotton deleg. to New Delhi, India, 1946; retired, 1947; Director of Agriculture, Uganda, 1944-47. *Recreations:* golf, shooting, fishing. *Address:* 24 Drummond Road, Inverness IV2 4NF. *T:* 33497.

RICHARDSON, Anthony; see Richardson, H. A.

RICHARDSON, Gen. Sir Charles (Leslie), GCB 1967 (KCB 1962; CB 1957); CBE 1945; DSO 1943; Chief Royal Engineer, 1972-77; *s* of late Lieutenant-Colonel C. W. Richardson, RA, and Mrs Richardson; *m* 1947, Audrey Styles (*née* Jorgensen); one *s* two *d. Educ:* Wellington College; Royal

Military Acad., Woolwich (King's Medal); Cambridge Univ. (BA). Commissioned Royal Engineers, 1928; Exhibitioner, Clare College, Cambridge, 1930, 1st Cl. Hons Mech Sciences Tripos. Served France and Belgium, 1939-40; GSO1 Plans HQ, Eighth Army, 1942; BGS Eighth Army, 1943; Deputy Chief of Staff Fifth US Army, 1943; BGS Plans, 21st Army Group, 1944; Brigade Commander, 1953-54; Commandant, Royal Military College of Science, 1955-58; General Officer Commanding Singapore District, 1958-60; Director of Combat Development, War Office, 1960-61; Director-General of Military Training, 1961-63; General Officer Commanding-in-Chief, Northern Command, 1963-65. Quartermaster General to the Forces, 1965-66; Master-General of the Ordnance, 1966-71; ADC (General) to the Queen, 1967-70. Legion of Merit (US), 1944. Col Comdt, RAOC, 1967-71. Consultant, International Computers Ltd, 1971-76. Treasurer, Kitchener Nat. Meml Fund, 1971-81; Chm., Gordon Boy's Sch., 1977-. *Address:* The Stables, Betchworth, Surrey RH3 7AA. *Club:* Army and Navy.

RICHARDSON, Brigadier (Retd) Charles Walter Philipps, DSO and Bar 1945; *b* 8 Jan. 1905; *s* of W. J. Richardson and E. C. Philipps; *m* 1st, 1932, Joan Kathleen Constance Lang (from whom he obtained a divorce, 1946); one *s* ; 2nd, 1946, Hon. Mrs Averil Diana Going; one *s. Educ:* RNC Osborne and Dartmouth; RMC Sandhurst. 2nd Lieut KOSB, 1924; served in Egypt, China and India; Bde Maj. 52nd (Lowland) Div., 1942; Comdr 6th Bn KOSB 15th (Scottish) Div., 1944-46; Colonel 1946; Comdt, Tactical Wing, School of Infantry, Warminster, 1947-48; GSO(1) Singapore District, 1948-49 (despatches, Malaya, 1948); Deputy Comdt Malay Regt, 1949; Dir Amphibious Warfare Trg, 1951; Comdr 158 Inf. Bde (TA), 1952; Brig. 1952; Dep. Comdr Lowland District, 1955-57. Retired 1957. Order of Leopold and Belgian Croix de Guerre, 1945; King Haakon Victory Medal, 1945. *Recreations:* shooting, fishing. *Address:* Quintans, Steventon, Hants. *T:* Dummer 473.

RICHARDSON, David; Director, London Office, International Labour Organisation, since 1982; *b* 24 April 1928; *s* of Harold George Richardson and Madeleine Raphaële Richardson (*née* Lebret); *m* 1951, Frances Joan Pring; three *s* one *d. Educ:* Wimbledon Coll.; King's Coll., London (BA Hons). Served in RAF, 1949. With Unilever, 1951. Inland Revenue, 1953; Min. of Labour: Asst Principal, 1956; Principal, 1960; Sec., Construction Industry Training Bd, 1964; Asst Sec., Min. of Labour, 1967; Chm., Central Youth Employment Exec., 1969; attended Royal Coll. of Defence Studies, 1971; Under Sec., Incomes Div., Dept of Employment, 1972; Dir, Safety and Gen. Gp, Health and Safety Exec., 1975-77; Sec., ACAS, 1977-81. *Recreations:* music, walking, landscape gardening. *Address:* 183 Banstead Road, Carshalton, Surrey. *T:* 01-642 1052. *Club:* Royal Air Force.

RICHARDSON, Air Vice-Marshal David William; Air Officer Commanding Maintenance Group, HQ RAF Support Command, since 1981; *b* 10 Feb. 1932; *s* of Herbert Cyril Richardson and Emily Lydia Richardson; *m* 1954, Mary Winifred Parker; two *s* one *d. Educ:* Southend Grammar Sch.; Birmingham Univ. (BSc Maths); Cranfield Inst. of Technology (MSc Eng). CEng, FIMechE, MRAeS. Joined RAF from Univ. Air Sqdn, 1953 and completed flying and technical trng; served in Fighter Comd before attending Staff Coll. 1964; Staff: HQ Middle East, 1965-67; HQ RAF Germany, 1969-71; CO, RAF Colerne, 1971-74; RCDS, 1974; AO Engrg and Supply, HQ NEAF, 1975; Dir, Engrg and Supply Policy, 1976-78; AO Engrg and Supply, HQ RAF Germany, 1978-81. *Publications:* contrib. RUSI Jl. *Recreations:* sailing, travel, gardening (the last two being more accurately described as vocational risk). *Address:* Bounds Cottage, Bidborough, Kent. *T:* Tunbridge Wells 26969. *Club:* Royal Air Force.

RICHARDSON, Sir Egerton (Rudolf), OJ 1975; Kt 1968; CMG 1959; Permanent Representative of Jamaica to the United Nations, New York, since 1981; *b* 15 Aug. 1912; *s* of James Neil Richardson and Doris Adel (*née* Burton); *m* ; one *s* one *d. Educ:* Calabar High School, Kingston, Jamaica; Oxford University. Entered Civil Service, 1933; Secretary Land Policy Co-ordinating Committee, 1943-53; Permanent Sec., Min. of Agric. and Lands, 1953-54; Under-Sec. Finance, 1954-56; on secondment, CO, London, 1953-54; Financial Secretary, Jamaica, 1956-62; Ambassador and Permanent Representative at UN, 1962-67; to USA, 1967-75; to Mexico, 1967-75; Permanent Sec., Min. of the Public Service, 1973-75. *Recreations:* swimming, golf, astronomy. *Address:* 215E 68th Street, New York, NY 10021, USA.

RICHARDSON, Elliot Lee; Partner, Milbank, Tweed, Hadley & McCloy, Washington DC, since 1980; *b* 20 July 1920; *s* of Dr Edward P. and Clara Lee Richardson; *m* 1952, Anne F. Hazard; two *s* one *d. Educ:* Harvard Coll.; Harvard Law Sch. BA 1941, LLB 1947, *cum laude.* Served with US Army, 1942-45 (Lieut): litter-bearer platoon ldr, 4th Inf. Div., Normandy Landing (Bronze Star, Purple Heart). Law clerk, 1947-49; Assoc., Ropes, Gray, Best, Coolidge and Rugg, lawyers, Boston, 1949-53 and 1955-56; Asst to Senator Saltonstall, Washington, 1953 and 1954; Asst Sec. for Legislation of Dept of Health, Educn and Welfare, 1957-59 (Actg Sec., April-July 1958); US Attorney for Massachusetts, 1959-61; Special Asst to Attorney General of US, 1961; Partner, Ropes & Gray, 1961-62 and 1963-64; Lieut Governor of Mass, 1964; Attorney General of Mass, 1966; Under Sec. of State, 1969-70; Sec. of Health, Educn and Welfare, 1970-73; Sec. of Defense, Jan.-May 1973; Attorney General of US, May-Oct. 1973, resigned; Ambassador to UK, 1975-76; Sec. of Commerce, 1976-77; Ambassador-at-large and Special Rep. of the US Pres. to the Law of the Sea Conf., 1977-80. Fellow, Woodrow

Wilson Internat. Center for Scholars, 1973-74. Holds numerous hon. degrees. *Publications:* The Creative Balance, 1976; numerous articles on law, social services and govt policy. *Address:* 1100 Crest Lane, Mclean, Va 22101, USA.

RICHARDSON, Sir Eric; *see* Richardson, Sir J. E.

RICHARDSON, Sir Frank; *see* Richardson, Sir (H.) Frank.

RICHARDSON, Maj.-Gen. Frank McLean, CB 1960; DSO 1941; OBE 1945; MD; Director Medical Services, BAOR, 1956-61; *b* 3 March 1904; *s* of late Col Hugh Richardson, DSO, and of Elizabeth Richardson; *m* 1944, Sylvia Innes, *d* of Col S. A. Innes, DSO; two *s* one *d. Educ:* Glenalmond; Edinburgh Univ. MB, ChB 1926. MD 1938. Joined RAMC, 1927; Captain 1930; Major 1936; Lt-Col 1945; Col 1949; Brig. 1956; Maj.-Gen. 1957. Honorary Surgeon to the Queen, 1957-61. Hon. Col 51 (H) Div. Dist RAMC, TA, 1963-67. Vice-Pres., Piobaireachd Soc. *Publications:* Napoleon: Bisexual Emperor, 1972; Napoleon's Death: An Inquest, 1974; Fighting Spirit: psychological factors in war, 1978; The Public and the Bomb, 1981; Mars without Venus: a study of some homosexual Generals, 1981. *Address:* c/o Williams & Glyn's Bank Ltd, Kirkland House, SW1; 4B Barnton Avenue West, Edinburgh EH4 6DE.

RICHARDSON, Prof. Frederick Denys, PhD, DSc; FRS 1968; FEng 1976; FIMM; FIChemE; Professor Emeritus and Senior Research Fellow, Department of Metallurgy, Imperial College of Science and Technology, London University, since 1976; *b* 17 Sept. 1913; *y s* of late Charles Willerton Richardson, Bombay; *m* 1942, Irene Mary, *o d* of late George E. Austin, Birkdale; two *s. Educ:* privately; University College, London (Fellow, 1971); Princeton University, USA. Commonwealth Fund Fellow, 1937-39; RNVR 1939-46; Commander, 1942; Deputy Director Miscellaneous Weapon Development, Admiralty, 1943-46; Superintending Chemist, British Iron and Steel Research Association, 1946-50; Nuffield Fellow and Director Nuffield Research Group, Imperial College, 1950-57; Prof. of Extraction Metallurgy, Imperial Coll., 1957-76. Member: Council, Iron and Steel Inst., 1962-74; InstnMM, 1961- (Pres., 1975-76); Metals Soc., 1974-; Charter Fellow, Metallurgical Soc.; American Inst. of Mining and Metallurgical Engineers, 1963. Sir George Beilby Memorial Award for researches on the thermodynamics of high temperature systems, 1956; Bessemer Gold Medal of Iron and Steel Inst. for contribs to kinetics and thermodynamics of metallurgical processes, 1968. Howe, Hatfield, May, Wernher and AIME Extractive Metallurgy and Yukawa Lectures, 1964-73. Hon. Member: Japanese Iron and Steel Inst.; Ingénieurs de Liège; Japan Inst. of Metals; Foreign Associate, Nat. Acad. of Engrg, USA, 1976. Hon. DIng, Technische Hochschule, Aachen; Hon. Dr, Liège. Gold Medal, InstnMM, 1973; Gold Medal, Amer. Soc. of Metals, 1975; Tunner Medal, Verein Eisenhütte Osterreich, 1976; Grande Medaille, Soc. Française de Métallurgie, 1977; Carl-Lueg Medal, Verein Deutscher Eisenhüttenleute, 1978. *Publications:* The Physical Chemistry of Melts in Metallurgy, 1974; papers on chemical and metallurgical research in scientific jls. *Recreations:* riding, fishing, gardening. *Address:* Imperial College, Prince Consort Road, SW7. *Club:* Royal Automobile.

RICHARDSON, George Barclay, CBE 1978; Fellow of St John's College, Oxford, since 1951; Secretary to the Delegates and Chief Executive of the Oxford University Press, since 1974; *b* 19 Sept. 1924; *s* of George and Christina Richardson; *m* 1957, Isabel Alison Chalk; two *s. Educ:* Aberdeen Central Secondary Sch. and other schs in Scotland; Aberdeen Univ.; Corpus Christi Coll., Oxford. BSc Physics and Maths, 1944 (Aberdeen); MA (Oxon) PPE 1949. Admty Scientific Res. Dept, 1944; Lieut, RNVR, 1945. Intell. Officer, HQ Intell. Div. BAOR, 1946-47; Third Sec., HM Foreign Service, 1949; Student, Nuffield Coll., Oxford, 1950; University Reader in Economics, 1969-73. Economic Advr, UKAEA, 1968-74. Member: Economic Devo lt Cttee for Electrical Engineering Industry, 1964-73; Monopolies Commn, 1969-74; Royal Commn on Environmental Pollution, 1973-74. Deleg., Oxford Univ. Press, 1971-74. *Publications:* Information and Investment, 1960; Economic Theory, 1964; articles in academic jls. *Address:* Cutts End, Cumnor, Oxford. *Club:* United Oxford & Cambridge University.

RICHARDSON, George Taylor; President, James Richardson & Sons, Limited, Winnipeg, Canada, since 1966 (Vice-President 1954); Senior Partner, Richardson Securities of Canada, since 1947; *b* 22 Sept. 1924; *s* of late James Armstrong Richardson and Muriel (*née* Sprague); *m* 1948, Tannis Maree Thorlakson; two *s* one *d. Educ:* Grosvenor Sch. and Ravenscourt Sch. Winnipeg; Univ. of Manitoba (BComm). Joined family firm of James Richardson & Sons Ltd, 1946. Chm., Pioneer Grain Co. Ltd; Chm./Dir of other cos owned by James Richardson & Sons Ltd; Vice-Pres. and Mem., Exec. Cttee, Canadian Imperial Bank of Commerce; Director: Inco Ltd; Hudson's Bay Co.; Hon. Dir, Canada's Aviation Hall of Fame. Hon. Dr of Laws, Univ. of Manitoba, 1969. Hon. Col, City of Winnipeg Air Reserve Sqdn. *Recreations:* hunting, helicopter flying. *Address:* (business) James Richardson & Sons, Limited, Richardson Building, One Lombard Place, Winnipeg R3B 0Y1, Manitoba, Canada. *T:* 988-5811. *Clubs:* Manitoba, St Charles, Winnipeg Winter (Winnipeg); Vancouver (Vancouver, BC); Royal Lake of the Woods Yacht (Ont.).

RICHARDSON, Rt. Hon. Gordon (William Humphreys), PC 1976; MBE 1944; TD 1979; Governor, Bank of England, since 1973, Member, Court of the Bank of England, since 1967; *b* 25 Nov. 1915; *er s* of John Robert and Nellie Richardson; *m* 1941, Margaret Alison, *er d* of Canon H. R. L. Sheppard; one *s* one *d. Educ:* Nottingham High School; Gonville and Caius College, Cambridge (BA, LLB); Hon. Fellow, 1977. Commnd S Notts Hussars Yeomanry, 1939; Staff Coll., Camberley, 1941; served until 1946. Called to Bar, Gray's Inn, 1946 (Hon. Bencher, 1973); Mem. Bar Council, 1951-55; ceased practice at Bar, Aug. 1955. Industrial and Commercial Finance Corp. Ltd, 1955-57; Director: J. Henry Schroder & Co., 1957; Lloyds Bank Ltd, 1960-67 (Vice-Chm., 1962-66); Legal and General Assurance Soc., Ltd, 1956-70 (Vice-Chm. 1959-70); Director: Rolls Royce (1971) Ltd, 1971-73; ICI Ltd, 1972-73; Chairman: J. Henry Schroder Wagg & Co. Ltd, 1962-72; Schroders Ltd, 1966-73; Schroders Inc. (NY), 1968-73. Chm., Industrial Develt Adv. Bd, 1972-73. Mem. Company Law Amendment Committee (Jenkins Committee), 1959-62; Chm. Cttee on Turnover Taxation, 1963. Member: Court of London University, 1962-65; NEDC, 1971-73, 1980-; Trustee, National Gallery, 1971-73. One of HM Lieutenants, City of London, 1974-. Hon. Fellow, Woolfson Coll., Cambridge, 1977. Hon. LLD Cambridge, 1979; Hon. DSc: City Univ., 1976; Aston, 1979. *Address:* Bank of England, EC2R 8AH. *T:* 01-601 4444. *Club:* Brooks's.
See also Sir John Riddell, Bt.

RICHARDSON, Graham Edmund; Rector, Dollar Academy, Clackmannanshire, 1962-75; *b* 16 July 1913; *s* of H. W. Richardson, BSc, MIEE, AMIMechE, Studland, Dorset; *m* 1939, Eileen Cynthia, *d* of Lewis Beesly, FRCSE, Brightwalton, Newbury, Berks; one *s* one *d. Educ:* Tonbridge School; Strasbourg University; Queen's College, Oxford. Asst Master, Fettes College, Edinburgh, 1935-55; Housemaster, 1946-55; Headmaster, Melville College, Edinburgh, 1955-62. Mem., Scottish Adv. Cttee, IBA, 1968-73. *Recreations:* sailing, fishing, natural history. *Address:* Sunnyholme, Studland, Dorset.

RICHARDSON, (Henry) Anthony; a Recorder of the Crown Court, since 1978; barrister; *b* 28 Dec. 1925; *er s* of late Thomas Ewan Richardson and of Jessie (*née* Preston), Batley, W Yorks; *m* 1954, Georgina (*née* Lawford), *d* of Rosamond Bedford and step *d* of Gp Captain G. R. Bedford, MB, ChB, RAF retd. *Educ:* Giggleswick Sch.; Leeds Univ. (LLB 1950, LLM 1956). Called to the Bar, Lincoln's Inn, 1951; North-Eastern Circuit; Dep. Circuit Judge, 1972-78. *Publications:* articles in legal periodical. *Recreations:* walking, swimming, listening to music. *Address:* (home) Grey Thatch, Wetherby Road, Scarcroft, Leeds LS14 3BB. *T:* Leeds 892555; (chambers) 38 Park Square, Leeds LS1 2PA. *T:* Leeds 39422.

RICHARDSON, Sir (H.) Frank, Kt 1953; *b* 1901; *s* of William Thomas and Louisa Jane Richardson; *m* 1949, Marjorie Amy Hislop; four *s* two *d. Educ:* All Saints Gram. Sch., St Kilda, Vict.; Univ. of Tasmania, Australia. Deputy Chairman: Business Board, Defence Department, Commonwealth of Australia, 1941-47; Commonwealth Disposals Commission, Australia, 1944-49. Past Chairman of various Department Stores, etc., in Australia; now Director of Proprietary companies. Life Governor, Retail Traders Assoc. of Victoria. Mem. Council, The Australian National University, 1953-76. *Recreations:* tennis, golf. *Address:* 40 Heyington Place, Toorak, Victoria 3142, Australia. *T:* 20.40.30. *Club:* Athenæum (Melbourne, Australia).

RICHARDSON, Horace Vincent, OBE 1968; HM Diplomatic Service, retired; *b* 28 Oct. 1913; *s* of late Arthur John Alfred Richardson and late Mrs Margaret Helena Jane Richardson (*née* Hooson); *m* 1942, Margery Tebbutt; two *s* one *d* (and one *d* decd). *Educ:* Abergele Grammar Sch.; King's Coll., London (LLB). Served with Army, 1940-45. LCC, 1931-35; Supreme Court of Judicature, 1935-47; FO, 1947-48; British Vice-Consul, Shanghai, 1948-50; Washington, 1950-53; 2nd Sec., Rome, 1953-56; FO, 1956-61; Consul, Philadelphia, 1961-63; FO, 1963-66; Consul, Cairo, 1966-68; 1st Sec., Washington, 1968-70; Head of Nationality and Treaty Dept, FCO, 1970-73. Rep. HM Govt at 9th and 10th Sessions of Hague Conf. of Private Internat. Law. *Recreations:* golf, gardening, tennis. *Address:* 34 Friern Barnet Lane, N11. *T:* 01-368 1983. *Clubs:* MCC, Civil Service; Turf (Cairo); Highgate Golf.

RICHARDSON, Hugh Edward, CIE 1947; OBE 1944; *b* 22 Dec. 1905; *s* of Hugh Richardson, DSO, MD, and Elizabeth, *née* McLean; *m* 1951, Huldah Rennie (*née* Walker). *Educ:* Trinity College, Glenalmond; Keble College, Oxford. Entered Indian Civil Service, 1930; SDO, Tamluk, Midnapore Dist, Bengal, 1932-34; entered Foreign and Political Service of Govt of India, 1934; APA Loralai, Baluchistan, 1934-35; British Trade Agent, Gyantse, and O-in-C British Mission, Lhasa, 1936-40; service in NWFP, 1940-42; 1st Sec. Indian Agency-General in China, Chungking, 1942-43; Dep. Sec. to Govt of India, EA Dept, 1944-45; British Trade Agent, Gyantse, and O-in-C, British Mission, Lhasa, 1946-47; Indian Trade Agent, Gyantse and Officer-in-charge, Indian Mission, Lhasa, 1947-50. Retd from ICS, 1950. *Publications:* Tibet and its History, 1962; (with D. L. Snellgrove) A Cultural History of Tibet, 1968. *Recreation:* golf. *Address:* c/o Grindlay's Bank Ltd, 13 St James's Square, SW1. *Club:* Royal and Ancient Golf (St Andrews).

RICHARDSON, Ian; actor; *b* 7 April 1934; *s* of John Richardson and Margaret Drummond; *m* 1961, Maroussia Frank; two *s. Educ:* Tynecastle; Edinburgh; Univ. of Glasgow. Studied for stage at Coll. of Dramatic Art, Glasgow (James Bridie Gold Medal, 1957). FRSAMD 1971. Joined Birmingham Repertory Theatre Co. 1958 (leading parts incl. Hamlet); joined Shakespeare Meml Theatre Co. (later RSC), 1960; rôles, Stratford and Aldwych, 1960-: Arragon in Merchant of Venice; Sir Andrew Aguecheek, 1960; Malatesti in Duchess of Malfi, 1960; Oberon in A Midsummer Night's Dream, 1961; Tranio in Taming of the Shrew, 1961; the Doctor in The Representative, 1963; Edmund in King Lear, 1964; Antipholus of Ephesus in Comedy of Errors, 1964; Herald and Marat in Marat/Sade, 1964, 1965; Ithamore, The Jew of Malta, 1964; Ford, Merry Wives of Windsor, 1964, 1966, 1969; Antipholus of Syracuse in Comedy of Errors, 1965; Chorus, Henry V, 1965; Vindice, The Revengers Tragedy, 1965, 1969; Coriolanus, 1966; Bertram, All's Well That Ends Well, 1966; Malcolm, Macbeth, 1966; Cassius, Julius Caesar, 1968; Pericles, 1969; Angelo, Measure for Measure, 1970; Buckingham, Richard III, 1970; Proteus, Two Gentlemen of Verona, 1970; Prospero, The Tempest, 1970; Richard II/Bolingbroke, Richard II, 1973; Berowne, Love's Labour's Lost, 1973; Iachimo, Cymbeline, 1974; Shalimov, Summer Folk, 1974; Ford, Merry Wives of Windsor, 1975; Richard III, 1975; tours with RSC: Europe and USSR, NY, 1964; NY, 1965; USSR, 1966; Japan, 1970; NY, 1974, 1975; Tom Wrench in musical Trelawny, Sadler's Wells, 1971-72; Professor Higgins, My Fair Lady, Broadway, 1976 (Drama Desk Award, 1976); Jack Tanner, in Man and Superman, and Doctor in The Millionairess, Shaw Festival Theatre, Niagara, Ont; The Government Inspector, Old Vic, 1979; Romeo and Juliet, Old Vic, 1979; Lolita, Broadway, 1981. *Films:* Captain Fitzroy in The Darwin Adventure, 1971; Priest in Man of la Mancha, 1972; Montgomery in Ike—the War Years, 1978; Charlie Muffin, 1979. *Television: plays:* BBC: Danton's Death, 1978; Churchill and the Generals, 1979; A Cotswold Death, Passing Through, 1981; Russian Night, Kisch-Kisch, Beauty and the Beast, 1982; Yorks TV: Salad Days, 1982; *serials:* BBC: Eyeless in Gaza, 1971; Tinker, Tailor, Soldier, Spy, 1979; Private Schulz, 1981; ITV: The Woman in White, 1982; *series:* Yorks TV: Ramsay Macdonald, in Number 10, 1982. RTS Award, 1982. *Publication:* Preface to Cymbeline (Folio Soc.), 1976. *Recreations:* music, exploring churches and castles. *Address:* c/o London Management, Regent House, 235-241 Regent Street, W1. *T:* 01-734 4192. *Club:* Garrick.

RICHARDSON, Rt. Hon. Ivor Lloyd Morgan, PC 1978; SJD; **Rt. Hon. Mr Justice Richardson;** Judge, Court of Appeal of New Zealand, since 1977; *b* 24 May 1930; *s* of W. T. Richardson; *m* 1955, Jane, *d* of I. J. Krchma; three *d. Educ:* Canterbury Univ. (LLB); Univ. of Mich (LLM, SJD). Partner, Macalister Bros, Invercargill, 1957-63; Crown Counsel, Crown Law Office, Wellington, 1963-66; Prof. of Law, Victoria Univ. of Wellington, 1967-73 (Dean of Law Faculty, 1968-71; Pro-Chancellor, 1979-); Partner, Watts & Patterson, Wellington, 1973-77. Chm., Cttee of Inquiry into Inflation Accounting, 1975-76. *Publications:* books and articles on legal subjects. *Address:* 29 Duthie Street, Wellington 5, New Zealand. *T:* 769-310. *Club:* Wellington (Wellington, NZ).

RICHARDSON, Hon. James Armstrong, PC (Can.); *b* Winnipeg, Manitoba, 28 March 1922; *s* of James Armstrong Richardson and Muriel Sprague; *m* 1949, Shirley Anne, *d* of John R. Rooper, Shamley Green, Surrey, England; two *s* three *d. Educ:* St John's, Ravenscourt, Winnipeg; Queen's Univ., Kingston, Ont. (BA). Pilot with No 10 BR Sqdn, before entering family firm of James Richardson & Sons, Ltd, Winnipeg, Oct. 1945; he was Chm. and Chief Exec. Officer of this company, but resigned to enter public life, 1968. MP (L), June 1968 (re-elected, Oct. 1972, July 1974); Minister without Portfolio, Canadian Federal Cabinet, July 1968; Minister of Supply and Services, May 1969; Minister of Nat. Defence, 1972-76; resigned from Federal Cabinet over constitutional language issue, Oct. 1976; crossed floor of House to sit as an Independent MP, 27 June 1978. *Address:* 5209 Roblin Boulevard, Winnipeg, Manitoba, Canada, R3R 0G8.
See also G. T. Richardson.

RICHARDSON, Joanna, MA Oxon; FRSL; author; *o d* of late Frederick Richardson and late Charlotte Elsa (*née* Benjamin). *Educ:* The Downs School, Seaford; St Anne's College, Oxford. Mem. Council, Royal Soc. of Literature, 1961-. *Publications:* Fanny Brawne: a biography, 1952; Rachel, 1956; Théophile Gautier: his Life and Times, 1958; Sarah Bernhardt, 1959; Edward FitzGerald, 1960; The Disastrous Marriage: a Study of George IV and Caroline of Brunswick, 1960; (ed) FitzGerald: Selected Works, 1962; The Pre-Eminent Victorian: a study of Tennyson, 1962; The Everlasting Spell: a study of Keats and his Friends, 1963; (ed) Essays by Divers Hands (trans. Royal Soc. Lit.), 1963; introd. to Victor Hugo: Choses Vues (The Oxford Lib. of French Classics), 1964; Edward Lear, 1965; George IV: a Portrait, 1966; Creevey and Greville, 1967; Princess Mathilde, 1969; Verlaine, 1971; Enid Starkie, 1973; (ed and trans.) Verlaine, Poems, 1974; Stendhal: a critical biography, 1974; (ed and trans.) Baudelaire, Poems, 1975; Victor Hugo, 1976; Zola, 1978; Keats and his Circle: an album of portraits, 1980; (trans.) Gautier, Mademoiselle de Maupin, 1981; The Life and Letters of John Keats, 1981; Letters from Lambeth: the correspondence of the Reynolds family with John Freeman Milward Dovaston 1808-1815, 1981; Paris under Siege, 1982. Contributor, BBC. Has also written for The Times, The Times Literary Supplement, Sunday Times, Spectator, New Statesman, New York Times Book Review, The Washington Post, French Studies, Modern Language Review, Keats-Shelley Memorial Bulletin, etc. *Recreations:* antique-collecting, sketching. *Address:* 55 Flask Walk, NW3. *T:* 01-435 5156.

RICHARDSON, John David Benbow, MC 1942, and Bar 1943; President, Northern Rent Assessment Panel, since 1979 (Vice-President, 1968-79); *b* 6

April 1919; *s* of His Honour Judge Thomas Richardson, OBE, and Winifred Ernestine (*née* Templer); *m* 1946, Kathleen Mildred (*née* Price-Turner); four *s*. *Educ:* Harrow; Clare Coll., Cambridge. Called to Bar, Middle Temple, 1947. Served War of 1939-45, as Captain in King's Dragoon Guards (wounded; MC and Bar). ADC to Governor of South Australia (Lt-Gen. Sir Willoughby Norrie, later Lord Norrie), 1946-47. Dep. Chm., Durham County Quarter Sessions, 1964-71, and Recorder, 1972-73. Mem., Police Complaints Bd, 1977-82. *Recreations:* fishing, gardening, golf. *Address:* Cliffe Lodge, Corbridge, Northumberland. *T:* Corbridge 2101. *Clubs:* MCC; York County Stand; Northern Counties (Newcastle upon Tyne).

RICHARDSON, Sir (John) Eric, Kt 1967; CBE 1962; PhD, DSc, BEng, CEng, FIEE, MIMechE, FBHI, FBOA, FPS; FRSA; Director, The Polytechnic of Central London, 1969-70; *b* 30 June 1905; *e surv. s* of late William and Mary Elizabeth Richardson, Birkenhead; *m* 1941, Alice May, *d* of H. M. Wilson, Hull; one *s* two *d* (and one *d* decd). *Educ:* Birkenhead Higher Elementary Sch.; Liverpool Univ. BEng 1st Cl. Hons, 1931, PhD 1933, Liverpool. Chief Lectr in Electrical Engineering, 1933-37, Head of Engineering Dept, 1937-41, Hull Municipal Technical Coll.; Principal: Oldham Municipal Technical Coll., 1942-44; Royal Technical Coll., Salford, 1944-47; Northampton Polytechnic, London, EC1, 1947-56; Dir Nat. Coll. of Horology and Instrument Technology, 1947-56; Dir of Educn, Regent Street Polytechnic, W1, 1957-69. Hon. Sec., Assoc. of Technical Insts, 1957-67, Chm., 1967-68; Pres. Assoc. of Principals of Technical Instns, 1961-62; Dep. Chm., Council for Overseas Colls of Arts, Science and Technology, 1949-62; Member: Council for Tech. Educn and Trng in Overseas Countries, 1962-73 (Chm. Technical Educn Cttee, 1971-73); and Vice-Chm. Council and Cttees, London and Home Counties Regional Adv. Council for Technol Educn, 1972-; Chm., Adv. Cttee on Educn for Management, 1961-66; Member: Governing Council of Nigerian Coll. of Art, Science and Technology, 1953-61; Council, Univ. Coll., Nairobi, 1961-70; Provisional Council, Univ. of East Africa, 1961-63; Governing Body, College of Aeronautics, Cranfield, 1956-59; Council of British Horological Institute, 1951-; Gen. Optical Council, 1959- (Chm., 1975-78); Science and Technol Cttee of CNAA, 1965-71; Electrical Engrg Bd of CNAA (Chm.); Industrial Trg Bd for Electricity Supply Industry, 1965-71; Univ. and Polytechnic Grants Cttee, Hong Kong, 1972-77; Council, RSA, 1968-78 (Chm. Exams Cttee, 1969-78, Hon. Treasurer, 1974-78); Council and Exec. Cttee, Leprosy Mission, 1970- (Chm., 1974); Council and Exec. Cttee, City and Guilds of London Inst., 1969-80 (Chm. Policy and Overseas Cttees; Vice-Chm. Technical Educn Cttee; Jt Hon. Sec., 1970-80; Vice-Pres., 1979; Hon. FCGI); Chm., Ealing Civic Soc., 1972-76. Chairman: Africa Evangelical Fellowship (SAGM), 1950-70; Nat. Young Life Campaign, 1949-64; Council, Inter-Varsity Fellowship of Evangelical Unions, 1966-69; President: Crusaders Union, 1972-; Governors of London Bible Coll., 1968- (Chm., 1970-77; Pres., 1978-); Chm., Governors, Clarendon Sch., Abergele, 1971-75. *Publications:* paper in IEE Jl (Instn Prize); various papers on higher technological education in UK and Nigeria. *Recreations:* gardening, photography. *Address:* 73 Delamere Road, Ealing, W5 3JP. *T:* 01-567 1588.

RICHARDSON, John Eric, MS; FRCS; Member, Medical Appeal Tribunal, since 1980; Surgeon: The London Hospital, 1949-81; The Royal Masonic Hospital, 1960-81; King Edward VII's Hospital for Officers, 1960-80; Prince of Wales Hospital, Tottenham, N15, 1958-65; former Consultant Surgeon to the Navy; *b* Loughborough, 24 February 1916; *s* of late C. G. Richardson, MD, FRCS; *m* 1943, Elisabeth Jean, *d* of late Rev. John Webster; one *s* one *d*. *Educ:* Clifton College; London Hospital. MB, BS London (Hons and Distinction, Pathology), 1939; MRCS, LRCP 1939. Andrew Clarke Prize, London Hosp., 1939. Resident Appointments, London Hospital and Poplar Hospital, 1939-41; Surgeon Lieut RNVR, HMS Prince of Wales (Surgical Specialist), 1941-46; Surgical Registrar, London Hosp., 1946-47; Rockefeller Travelling Fellow, 1947-48; Research Fellow in Surgery, Harvard Univ., 1947-48; Fellow in Clinical Surgery, Massachusetts Gen. Hosp., Boston, Mass, 1947-48. Surgeon, St Andrews Hosp., Dollis Hill, 1965-73. Hunterian Prof., RCS, 1953; Lettsomian Lectr, Med. Soc. of London, 1973. Pres., Med. Soc. of London, 1974-75. Examr in Surgery to Soc. of Apothecaries, London, 1959-67 and Univ. of London, 1962-63, 1965-66. Mem., Bd of Governors, London Hosp., 1964-73. *Publications:* contrib. to Lancet and BMJ on gastro-enterology and endocrine disease. *Address:* Allen's Barn, Swinbrook, Oxon OX8 4EA. *T:* Burford 2456.

RICHARDSON, Ven. John Farquhar, MA; Archdeacon of Derby, 1952-73, now Emeritus; Chaplain to The Queen, 1952-76; First Residentiary Canon of Derby Cathedral 1954-73; *b* 23 April 1905; 2nd *s* of late William Henry Richardson and Gertrude Richardson (*née* Walker); *m* 1936, Elizabeth Mary, *d* of Henry Roy Dean; one *s* two *d*. *Educ:* Winchester; Trinity Hall, Cambridge; Westcott House, Cambridge. Curate of Holy Trinity, Cambridge, 1929-32; Chaplain of Repton School, 1932-35; Curate of St Martin-in-the-Fields, 1935-36; Vicar of Christ Church, Hampstead, 1936-41; Rector of Bishopwearmouth, 1941-52; Rural Dean of Wearmouth, 1947-52. Proctor in Convocation, 1950-52; Hon. Canon of Durham, 1951-52. Vice Chm., Trent Coll., 1972-; Vice Provost, Midlands Div., Woodard Schs, 1971-80. *Recreation:* golf. *Address:* 474 Kedleston Road, Derby DE3 2NE. *T:* Derby 559135. *Clubs:* Royal Automobile; Jesters; Hawks (Cambridge).

RICHARDSON, John Flint; Chairman of Tyne and Wear County Council, 1976-77; *b* 5 May 1906; *s* of Robert Flint Richardson and Jane Lavinia; *m* 1932, Alexandra Graham; two *s*. *Educ:* Cone Street, South Shields. Councillor,

1938, Alderman, 1954, Mayor, 1960-61, South Shields; Freeman, South Shields, 1973. *Recreations:* serving people, reading. *Address:* 16 Forster Avenue, South Shields, Tyne and Wear NE34 6NL. *T:* South Shields 555784.

RICHARDSON, Josephine, (Jo Richardson); MP (Lab) Barking, since Feb. 1974; *b* 28 Aug. 1923; *d* of J. J. Richardson. Mem., Labour Party NEC, 1979-; Vice-Chairperson: Campaign for Nuclear Disarmament, 1975-; PLP Civil Liberties Gp, 1979- (Chairperson, 1975-79); Mem., Exec. Council, Nat. Council for Civil Liberties; Chairperson, Tribune Group, 1978-79 (Secretary, 1948-78; formerly Keep Left Group, then Bevan Group); Member: ASTMS; APEX. *Recreations:* politics, cooking. *Address:* House of Commons, SW1A 0AA. *T:* 01-219 5028.

RICHARDSON, Kenneth Albert; a Recorder of the Crown Court, since 1980; First Senior Prosecuting Counsel to the Crown at the Central Criminal Court, since 1981; *b* 28 July 1926; *s* of Albert Robert Richardson and Ida Elizabeth Richardson (*née* Williams); *m* 1956, Dr Eileen Mary O'Cleary, Galway; two *s* one *d* (and one *s* decd). *Educ:* Ruthin Sch.; Merton Coll., Oxford. MA (in English and Jurisprudence). Called to the Bar, Middle Temple, 1952 (Harmsworth Scholar; Bencher, 1975). Commissioned RWF, 1945 (attached 8th Punjab Regt). Junior Prosecuting Counsel to the Crown, 1967-73; Senior Prosecuting Counsel to the Crown, 1973-81. Mem., Bar Council, 1972; Senate of the Inns and Bar, 1974, 1980. *Recreations:* skiing, golf, sailing, music. *Address:* Queen Elizabeth Building, Temple, EC4. *Clubs:* Ski Club of Great Britain; Blackheath FC; Vincent's (Oxford).

RICHARDSON, Sir Leslie Lewis, 2nd Bt, *cr* 1924; Director of Companies; *b* 14 August 1915; *s* of Sir Lewis Richardson, 1st Bart, CBE, head of the firm of L. Richardson & Co. of London, Port Elizabeth, New York and Boston, and Phoebe, *o d* of Isaac Isaacs; *S* father 1934; *m* 1946, Joy Patricia, twin *d* of P. J. Rillstone, Johannesburg; two *s* one *d*. *Educ:* Harrow, Served with South African Artillery, 1940-44, in the Union and North Africa. *Heir: s* Anthony Lewis Richardson, *b* 5 Aug. 1950. *Address:* Old Vineyard, Constantia, Cape Town, 7800, South Africa. *T:* Cape Town 741176.

RICHARDSON, Group Captain Michael Oborne, RAF, retired; *b* Holmfirth, Yorks, 13 May 1908; *s* of Rev. Canon G. L. Richardson, MA, BD, and Edith Maria (*née* Ellison); *m* 1st, 1935, Nellie Marguerita (*d* 1974), *d* of Walter Ross Somervell, Elizavetgrad, Russia; one *s* one *d*; 2nd, 1979, Gwendolyn Oenone Jane Bevan, *e d* of William Stuart Rashleigh, JP, Menabilly and Stoketon, Cornwall. *Educ:* Lancing Coll.; Keble Coll., Oxford; Guy's Hospital. BA 1929; MRCS, LRCP 1938; DPH 1955; MA Oxon 1963; DPhysMed 1964. Oxford House, Bethnal Green, 1930. Commissioned RAF, 1939; served at Kenley; War Service included HQ Fighter Comd (Unit), S Africa, Western Desert, Malta, Sicily, Italy (despatches). Post-war service in Germany and Aden and comdt various hosps and Medical Rehabilitation Units; Commandant, Royal Star and Garter Home for Disabled Sailors, Soldiers and Airmen, 1967-73. OStJ 1965. *Recreation:* the countryside. *Address:* Tremethek, Penscott Lane, Tregorrick, St Austell, Cornwall. *T:* St Austell 63768. *Clubs:* Royal Air Force; Webbe.

RICHARDSON, Sir Ralph David, Kt 1947; Actor; President, National Youth Theatre, since 1959; *b* Cheltenham, Glos, 19 Dec. 1902; *s* of Arthur Richardson and Lydia Russell; *m* 1st, 1924, Muriel Hewitt (*d* 1942); no *c*; 2nd, 1944, Meriel Forbes-Robertson; one *s*. *Educ:* Xaverian Coll., Brighton; privately. Made his first appearance on the stage at Brighton, 1921; toured in the Provinces in Shakespeare Repertory for four years; joined the Birmingham Repertory Theatre in 1925; first London appearance in 1926 at the Haymarket Theatre as Arthur Varwell in Yellow Sands; season of plays at the Court Theatre in 1928; toured in South Africa in 1929; from 1930 to 1932 played two seasons at the Old Vic and two seasons at the Malvern summer theatre; Too True To Be Good at the New Theatre and For Services Rendered at the Queen's in 1933, followed by Wild Decembers and Sheppey; Eden End and Cornelius at the Duchess Theatre in 1935, and played Mercutio in Romeo and Juliet in the USA in 1936; Promise, Bees on the Boatdeck and The Amazing Dr Clitterhouse, until 1937; in 1938, The Midsummer Night's Dream and Othello at the Old Vic; Johnson over Jordan, Sept. 1939, joined Fleet Air Arm as Sub/Lieut RNVR; Lieut (A) RNVR 1940; Lt-Comdr RNVR 1941. Released from Naval Service, June 1944, to act for and direct Drama of Old Vic Theatre Company; Old Vic 1st Season, 1944-45: played Peer Gynt, Bluntschli in Arms and the Man, Uncle Vanya, Henry VII in Richard the Third, toured Germany and visited Comédie Française in Paris. Old Vic 2nd season, 1945-46: played Falstaff in Henry IV, parts 1 and 2, Bluntschli in Arms and the Man, Tiresias in Oedipus Rex, Lord Burleigh in The Critic. Visited New York for six weeks' season. Old Vic 3rd Season, 1946-47: played Cyrano in Cyrano de Bergerac, the Inspector in An Inspector Calls, Face in The Alchemist, produced Richard II (playing Gaunt); Dr Sloper in The Heiress, Haymarket, 1949; David Preston in Home at Seven, Wyndham's 1950; Vershinin in Three Sisters, Aldwych, 1951; Stratford-on-Avon Season, 1952: Macbeth, Volpone, The Tempest; The White Carnation (playing John Greenwood), Globe, 1953; A Day by the Sea, Haymarket, 1954; Sleeping Prince and Separate Tables, Australian and New Zealand Tour, 1955; The Waltz of the Toreadors (New York), 1957; Flowering Cherry, Haymarket, 1958; The Complaisant Lover, Globe, 1959; The Last Joke, 1960; The School for Scandal, Haymarket and US Tour, 1962; Six Characters in search of an Author, May Fair, 1963; The Merchant of Venice and A Midsummer Night's

Dream, South American and European Tour, 1964; Carving a Statue, Haymarket, 1964; You Never Can Tell, 1966; The Rivals, 1966, 1967; Merchant of Venice, 1967; What the Butler Saw, 1969; Home, London, 1970 (Evening Standard Best Actor Award), NY, 1971; West of Suez, 1971; Lloyd George Knew My Father, 1972-73 (Austr. tour 1973); John Gabriel Borkman, National, 1975; No Man's Land, National, 1975, NY 1976; The Kingfisher, Lyric, 1977; The Cherry Orchard, National, 1978; Alice's Boys, Savoy, 1978; The Double Dealer, National, 1978; Fruits of Enlightenment, The Wild Duck, National, 1979; Early Days, National, 1980, then Comedy, 1981, tour, USA and Canada, 1981; The Understanding, Strand, 1982; *films*: made his first film, The Ghoul, in 1933; other films include: Things to Come; The Man Who Could Work Miracles; Bulldog Drummond; South Riding; Divorce of Lady X; The Citadel; Four Feathers; Q Planes; Night of the Fire; The Silver Fleet; The Volunteer; School for Secrets; Anna Karenina, The Fallen Idol, The Heiress (Hollywood); Outcast of the Islands; Home at Seven; The Holly and the Ivy; The Sound Barrier; The Passionate Stranger; Oscar Wilde; Exodus; Spartacus; Long Day's Journey into Night; Woman of Straw; Dr Zhivago, 1965; The Wrong Box, 1966; Gordon of Khartoum, 1966; Twelfth Night, 1968; Battle of Britain, 1968; Oh! What a Lovely War, 1968; The Bed-Sitting Room, 1968; The Looking-Glass War, 1968; Mr Micawber in David Copperfield, 1969; A Run on Gold, 1969; Gingerbread House, 1971; Lady Caroline Lamb, 1972; Alice's Adventures in Wonderland, 1972; Eagle in a Cage, 1973; A Doll's House, 1973; O Lucky Man, 1973; Rollerball, 1975; Dragonslayer, 1980; Time Bandits, 1981; Invitation to the Wedding, 1982. Hon. DLitt Oxon, 1969. SWET Special Award, 1981. Order of St Olaf (Norway), 1950. *Publications:* articles in magazines and newspapers. *Recreations:* drawing, tennis. *Address:* 1 Chester Terrace, Regent's Park, NW1. *Clubs:* Athenæum, Beefsteak, Savile; Greenroom (Life Mem.).

RICHARDSON, Robert Augustus; HM Chief Inspector of Schools, Department of Education and Science, 1968-72; *b* 2 Aug. 1912; *s* of late Ferdinand Augustus Richardson and Muriel Emma Richardson; *m* 1936, Elizabeth Gertrude Williamson; one *d*. *Educ:* Royal College of Art. Schoolmaster, 1934; Headmaster, Sidcup School of Art, 1937. Served in Royal Navy, 1941-46. Principal: Folkestone Sch. of Art, 1946; Maidstone Coll. of Art, 1948. Dept of Education and Science: HM Inspector of Schools, 1958; HM Staff Inspector, 1966. ARCA 1934. *Recreations:* theatre, music. *Address:* 68 Highfield Drive, Hurstpierpoint, West Sussex. *T:* Hurstpierpoint 832186.

RICHARDSON, Rev. Canon Robert Douglas, DD, MLitt, MA; *b* 26 February 1893; *er s* of late Frederick Richardson; *m* 1929, Professor Linetta P. de Castelvecchio (*d* 1975). *Educ:* Hertford College and Ripon Hall, Oxford. Served European War, 1914-18, in RN; Curate of Stourport-on-Severn; Succentor of Birmingham Cathedral; Vicar of Four Oaks and Vicar of Harborne; Select Preacher, Cambridge University; sometime External Lectr in Biblical Studies to Univ. of Birmingham; Examining Chaplain to Bishop of Birmingham, 1932-53; Canon Emeritus of Birmingham Cathedral; Principal of Ripon Hall, Oxford, 1948-52; Rector of Boyton with Sherrington, 1952-67. *Publications:* The Conflict of Ideals in the Church of England, 1923; The Gospel of Modernism, 1933; Sectional Editor of Webster's Dictionary (1934 edn); A Revised Order of Holy Communion, 1936; Christian Belief and Practice, 1940; The Psalms as Christian Prayers and Praises, 1960; article on Luke and the Eucharistic Tradition, in Studia Evangelica, 1957, in The Gospels Reconsidered, 1960; Studies in the Origins of the Liturgy (publ. with Lietzmann's Studies in the History of the Liturgy in Mass and Lord's Supper), 1979; contrib. to various Theological Jls. *Address:* Corton Parva, near Warminster, Wilts. *T:* Codford St Mary 286.

RICHARDSON, Lt-Gen. Sir Robert (Francis), KCB 1982; CVO 1978; CBE 1975 (OBE 1971; MBE 1965); General Officer Commanding Northern Ireland, since 1982; *b* 2 March 1929; *s* of late Robert Buchan Richardson and Anne (*née* Smith); *m* 1956, Maureen Anne Robinson; three *s* one *d*. *Educ:* George Heriot's Sch., Edinburgh; RMA Sandhurst. Commnd into The Royal Scots, 1949; served in BAOR, Korea, and Middle East with 1st Bn The Royal Scots until 1960; Defence Services Staff Coll., India, 1960-61; psc 1961; GSO II MO4, MoD, 1961-64; jssc 1964; Brigade Major Aden Bde, 1967 (Despatches); GSO II ACDS (Ops), MoD, 1968-69; CO 1st Bn The Royal Scots, 1969-71; Col Gen. Staff, Staff Coll. Camberley, 1971-74; Comdr 39 Infantry Bde, Northern Ireland, 1974-75; Deputy Adjutant General, HQ BAOR, 1975-78; GOC Berlin (British Sector), 1978-80; Vice Adjutant Gen. and Dir of Army Manning, 1980-82. Col, The Royal Scots (The Royal Regt), 1980-. *Recreations:* golf and other outdoor sports. *Address:* c/o Lloyds Bank Ltd, Cox's and King's Branch, 6 Pall Mall, SW1. *Club:* Royal Scots (Edinburgh).

RICHARDSON, Ronald Frederick, CBE 1973 (MBE 1945); Deputy Chairman, Electricity Council, 1972-76; *b* 1913; *s* of Albert F. Richardson and Elizabeth Jane (*née* Sayer); *m* 1946, Anne Elizabeth McArdle; two *s*. *Educ:* Coopers' Company's School; Northampton Engineering Inst.; Polytechnic Inst.; Administrative Staff College. Served War of 1939-45: Major, Field Park Company RE, 1942-46. Callenders Cables, 1929-36; Central London Electricity, 1936-39, 1946-48; London Electricity Board, 1948-52; British Electricity Authority, 1952-57; South Western Electricity Board, 1957-63; Chm., North Western Electricity Board, 1964-71. Chm., Nat. Inspection Council for Electrical Installation Contracting, 1969-70; Dep. Chm., NW Regional Council, CBI, 1971; Member: North West Economic Planning Council, 1965-70; Adv. Council on Energy Conservation, 1974-76; (part-

time): NCB, 1975-77; Electricity Council, 1976; Price Commn, 1977-79. Member: Court of Manchester Univ., 1969-71; Council, 1970-71, Court, 1970-, Salford Univ., 1970-74; Governor, William Temple Coll., 1971-74. *Recreations:* music, the open air. *Address:* 12 Ryecotes Mead, Dulwich Common, SE21 7EP.

RICHARDSON, Dr Sam Scruton, AO 1980; CBE 1965 (OBE 1960); Foundation Principal, Canberra College of Advanced Education, since 1969; *b* 31 Dec. 1919; *s* of Samuel and Gladys Richardson; *m* 1949, Sylvia May McNeil; two *s* one *d*. *Educ:* Magnus Sch., Newark-on-Trent; Trinity Coll., Oxford (State Scholarship, 1937; BA PPE, 1940; MA 1946); Sch. of Oriental and African Studies, Univ. of London. Called to the Bar, Lincoln's Inn, 1958. Served War, 1940-46: commnd Royal Marines; Commando Bdes, Europe and Far East (despatches); demob., Temp. Major, 1946. Dist Comr, Sudan Polit. Service, 1946-53 (served in Kordofan and Darfur Provinces); Resident, Dar Masalit, 1954; HMOCS, Nigeria, 1954-67: Dist Comr, Bornu Prov., 1954-58; Comr for Native Courts in Attorney Gen.'s Chambers, N Nigeria, 1958-60; Dir, Inst. of Admin, Zaria, 1960-67; Dep. Vice-Chancellor, Ahmadu Bello Univ., Nigeria, 1962-67; Prof. of Public Admin, Mauritius, 1967-68; occasional Lectr in Islamic Law, ANU, 1971-. Chm., Aust. Conf. of Principals, 1979-80; Pres., Internat. Assoc. of Schs and Insts of Admin, 1982-; Member: Academic Adv. Council, RAN Coll., Jervis Bay, 1978-; Adv. Council, Aust. Jt Services Staff Coll., 1977-; Inst. of Admin, Papua New Guinea, 1970-; Council, ANU, 1981-; Immigration Adv. Council, 1971-74; National Standing Control Cttee on Drugs of Dependence, 1974-; Bd of Management, Aust. Inst. of Sport, 1980-; Consultant, Aust. Law Reform Commn, 1980-. Nat. Pres., Australia Britain Soc. Hon. LLD Ahmadu Bello, 1967. *Publications:* Notes on the Penal Code of N Nigeria, 1959, 3rd edn 1967; (with T. H. Williams) The Criminal Procedure Code of N Nigeria, 1963; (with E. A. Keay) The Native and Customary Courts of Nigeria, 1965; Parity of Esteem—the Canberra College of Advanced Education 1968-78, 1979; regular book revs in Canberra Times, 1970-; articles on public admin, customary law and higher educn in learned jls. *Recreations:* travel, reading, community service. *Address:* 3 Fuller Street, Deakin, ACT 2600, Australia. *T:* Canberra 81-6540; The Malt House, Wylye, Wilts BA12 0QP. *T:* Wylye 348. *Clubs:* United Oxford & Cambridge University; University and Schools (Sydney); University House (ANU, Canberra).

RICHARDSON, Sir Simon Alaisdair S.; *see* Stewart-Richardson.

RICHARDSON, Maj.-Gen. Thomas Anthony, CB 1976; MBE 1960; Secretary, Timber Growers England and Wales Ltd, since 1980 (Assistant Secretary, 1978-80); *b* 9 Aug. 1922; *s* of late Maj.-Gen. T. W. Richardson, Eaton Cottage, Unthank Road, Norwich, and late Mrs J. H. Boothby, Camberley; *m* 1945, Katharine Joanna Ruxton Roberts, Woodland Place, Bath; one *s* one *d*. *Educ:* Wellington Coll., Berks. ptsc, psc, pl, ph, p. War of 1939-45: enlisted, Feb. 1941; commissioned, RA, March 1942; Essex Yeomanry (France and Germany), 1942-45; Air Observation Post, 1945-46. Tech. Staff/G Staff, 1949-52, 1954-55, 1959-60, 1963-64; Regt duty, 1942-45, 1952-54, 1957-58, 1961-62. Instr, Mil. Coll. Science, 1955-56; CO, 7th Para, RHA, 1965-67; CRA, 2 Div., 1967-69; Dir, Operational Requirements (Army), 1969-71; Dir, Army Aviation, 1971-74; Defence and Military Advr, India, 1974-77. Col Comdt, RA, 1978. *Recreations:* sailing, skiing, fishing, shooting. *Address:* 12 Lauriston Road, Wimbledon, SW19 4TQ. *Club:* Army and Navy.

RICHARDSON, Thomas Legh; HM Diplomatic Service; Counsellor and Head of Chancery, Rome, since 1982; *b* 6 Feb. 1941; *s* of Arthur Legh Turnour Richardson and Penelope Margaret Richardson; *m* 1979, Alexandra Frazier Wasiqullah (*née* Ratcliff). *Educ:* Westminster Sch.; Christ Church, Oxford. MA (Hist.). Joined Foreign Office, 1962; seconded to Univ. of Ghana, 1962-63; FO, 1963-65; Third Sec., Dar-Es-Salaam, 1965-66; Vice-Consul (Commercial), Milan, 1967-70; seconded to N. M. Rothschild & Sons, 1970; FCO, 1971-74; First Sec., UK Mission to UN, 1974-78; FCO, 1978-80; seconded to Central Policy Review Staff, Cabinet Office, 1980-81. *Recreations:* reading, walking, travel, music. *Address:* c/o Foreign and Commonwealth Office, SW1. *Club:* United Oxford & Cambridge University.

RICHARDSON, Tony; Director, Woodfall Film Productions Ltd, since 1958; *b* 5 June 1928; *s* of Clarence Albert and Elsie Evans Richardson; *m* 1962, Vanessa Redgrave, *qv* (marr. diss., 1967); two *d*. *Educ:* Wadham College, Oxford. Associate Artistic Dir, English Stage Co., Royal Court Theatre, 1956-64. *Plays* directed or produced: Look Back in Anger, 1956; The Chairs, 1957; Pericles and Othello (Stratford), 1958; The Entertainer, 1958; A Taste of Honey, NY, 1961; Luther, 1961; Semi-Detached, 1962; Arturo Ui, 1963; Natural Affection, 1963; The Milk Train Doesn't Stop Here Any More, 1963; The Seagull, 1964; St Joan of the Stockyards, 1964; Hamlet, 1968; The Threepenny Opera, Prince of Wales, 1972; I Claudius, Queen's, 1972; Antony and Cleopatra, Bankside Globe, 1973; Lady from the Sea, New York, 1977; As You Like It, Los Angeles, 1979. *Films* directed or produced: Look Back in Anger, 1958; The Entertainer, 1959; Saturday Night and Sunday Morning (prod), 1960; Taste of Honey, 1961; The Loneliness of the Long Distance Runner (prod and dir.), 1962; Tom Jones (dir.), 1962; Girl with Green Eyes (prod), 1964; The Loved One (dir.), 1965; Mademoiselle (dir.), 1965; The Sailor from Gibraltar (dir.), 1965; Red and Blue (dir.) 1966; The Charge of the Light Brigade (dir.), 1968; Laughter in the Dark (dir.), 1969; Hamlet (dir.), 1969; Ned Kelly (dir.), 1969; A Delicate Balance, 1972; Dead Cert,

1974; Joseph Andrews, 1977; A Death in Canaan, 1978; The Border, 1981. *Recreations:* travel, tennis, birds, directing plays and films. *Address:* 1478 North King's Road, Los Angeles, Calif 90069, USA.

RICHARDSON, William, CBE 1981; DL; CEng; FRINA; Chairman: Vickers Shipbuilding and Engineering Ltd, since 1976 (Managing Director, 1969–76); Vosper Thornycroft (UK) Ltd, since 1978; Barclay Curle Ltd, since 1978; Brook Marine Ltd, since 1981; Board Member, British Shipbuilders, since incorporation 1977, and Deputy Chairman since 1981; Director, Vickers Cockatoo Dockyard Pty Ltd, Australia, since 1977; *b* 15 Aug. 1916; *s* of Edwin Richardson, marine engr, and Hannah (*née* Remington); *m* 1941, Beatrice Marjorie Iliffe; one *s* one *d*. *Educ:* Ocean Road Boys' Sch., Walney Is, Barrow-in-Furness; Jun. Techn. and Techn. Colls, Barrow-in-Furness (part-time). HNC (Dist.) Naval Architecture; HNC (1st Cl.) Mech. Engrg. CBIM 1981 (FBIM 1977); FInstD 1977. Vickers Ltd, Barrow-in-Furness: Shipbldg Apprentice, 1933–38; Techn. Dept, 1938–39; Admiralty Directorate of Aircraft Maintenance and Repair, UK and Far East, 1939–46; Vickers Ltd Barrow Shipyard: Techn. Depts, 1946–51; Asst Shipyard Manager, 1951–60; Dockside Outfitting Man., 1960–61; Dep. Shipyard Man., 1961–63; Shipyard Man., 1963–64; Dir and Gen. Man., 1964–66; Dir and Gen. Man., Vickers Ltd Naval Shipyard, Newcastle upon Tyne, 1966–68; Dep. Man. Dir, Swan Hunter & Tyne Shipbldrs Ltd, 1968–69. Director: Slingsby Sailplanes, 1969–70 (co. then incorp. into Vickers Ltd); Vickers Oceanics, 1972–77; Chm., Clark & Standfield (subsid. of Vickers Gp), 1976–; Dir, Vasper Shiprepairers, 1978–82. Dir of Trustees, 1976–, Mem. Res. Council and Office Bearer, 1976–, BSRA; Mem. Exec. Council, 1969–, Chm. Management Bd, 1976–78, SRNA; Pres. Brit. Productivity Assoc., Barrow and Dist, 1969–72; Shipbldg Ind. Rep., DIQAP, 1972–82; Mem., Shipbuilding Industry Trng Bd, 1979–82; Mem., NE Coast IES, 1967–. FRINA 1970 (AssocRINA 1950, MRINA 1955). Liveryman, Shipwrights' Co., 1978. DL Cumbria, 1982. Queen's Silver Jubilee Medal, 1977. *Publications:* papers on various aspects of UK shipbldg industry; contribs to techn. jls. *Recreations:* sailing, small-bore shooting, golf, fishing. *Address:* Hobroyd, Pennybridge, Ulverston, Cumbria LA12 7TD. *T:* Greenodd 86 226. *Clubs:* Directors'; Grange-over-Sands Golf, National Small-Bore Rifle Association, Lower Nibthwaite Anglers Ltd.

RICHARDSON, William Eric, CEng, FIEE, FBIM; Chairman, South Wales Electricity Board, 1968–77; Member, Electricity Council, 1968–77; retired 1977; *b* 21 May 1915; *o s* of William Pryor and Elizabeth Jane Richardson, Hove, Sussex; *m* (she *d* 1975); one *s*; *m* 1976, Barbara Mary Leech. *Educ:* Royal Masonic Sch., Bushey. Engineer with Brighton Corp., 1934–37; Southampton Corp., 1937–39; Norwich Corp., 1939–46; Distribution Engr with Newport (Mon) Corp., 1946–48; Area Engr with S Wales Electricity Bd, 1948–57; Area Manager, 1957–65; Chief Commercial Engr, 1965–67; Dep. Chm., 1967–68. *Recreations:* sailing, golf, gardening. *Address:* Beaumont, 92 Allt-yr-yn Avenue, Newport, Gwent. *T:* Newport (Gwent) 64388.

RICHARDSON, Sir William (Robert), Kt 1967; Chief Executive Officer, Cooperative Press Ltd, 1967–74; *b* 16 Jan. 1909; *s* of Thomas and Constance Margaret Richardson; *m* 1932, Gladys Gillians; one *s* two *d*. *Educ:* various public elem. schs, Newcastle upon Tyne; evening classes; Cooperative College. Editor, Cooperative News, 1938; Editor, Reynolds News, later changed name to Sunday Citizen, 1942–67, when paper closed. Mem. Post Office Users' Nat. Council, 1969–79. *Publications:* The CWS in War and Peace 1938–1976, 1977; A Union of Many Trades: the history of USDAW, 1979. *Recreation:* reading. *Address:* Flat 9, Linton Court, Linton Road, Hastings, E Sussex TN34 1TP. *T:* Hastings 716154.

RICHARDSON-BUNBURY, Sir (Richard David) Michael, *see* Bunbury.

RICHES, Sir Derek (Martin Hurry), KCMG 1963 (CMG 1958); Ambassador to Lebanon, 1963–67, retired; *b* 26 July 1912; *s* of late Claud Riches and Flora Martin; *m* 1942 Helen Barkley Hayes, Poughkeepsie, NY, USA; one *d*. *Educ:* University College School; University College, London. Appointed Probationer Vice-Consul, Beirut, Dec. 1934. Subsequently promoted and held various appts, Ethiopia and Cairo; Foreign Office, 1944; promoted one of HM Consuls serving in FO, 1945. Kabul, 1948 (in charge, 1948 and 1949); Consul at Jedda, 1951 (Chargé d'Affaires, 1952); Officer Grade 6, Branch A, Foreign Service and apptd Trade Comr, Khartoum, 1953. Attached to Imperial Defence College, 1955; returned to Foreign Office, 1955; Counsellor in the Foreign Office, Head of Eastern Department, 1955; British Ambassador in Libya, 1959–61; British Ambassador to the Congo, 1961–63. *Address:* 48 The Avenue, Kew Gardens, Surrey.

RICHES, Sir Eric (William), Kt 1958; MC; MS (London), FRCS; Emeritus Surgeon and Urologist to Middlesex Hospital; Hon. Consultant Urologist to Hospital of St John and St Elizabeth; formerly Consulting Urologist to the Army and to Ministry of Pensions Spinal Injury Centre; lately Urologist, St Andrew's Hospital, Dollis Hill; lately Urologist, Royal Masonic Hospital; Hon. Curator, Historical Surgical Instruments Collection, Royal College of Surgeons, 1962; *b* Alford, Lincolnshire, 29 July 1897; *s* of William Riches; *m* 1st, 1927, Annie M. S. (*d* 1952), *d* of late Dr A. T. Brand, Driffield, E Yorks; two *d*; 2nd, 1954, Susan Elizabeth Ann, *d* of late Lt-Col L. H. Kitton, MBE, MC; one *d*. *Educ:* Christ's Hospital; Middlesex Hospital. Served European War, 10th Lincoln and 11th Suffolk Regt, Capt. and Adjutant (MC); Senior Broderip Scholar and Lyell Gold Medallist, Middlesex Hospital,

1925. Past Vice-President, Royal College of Surgeons, Member of Court of Examiners, 1940–46; Hunterian Professor 1938 and 1942, Jacksonian Prizeman, 1942; Bradshaw Lecturer, 1962; Gordon-Taylor Lecturer, 1967. Hon. Fellow Royal College of Medicine, 1966, lately Hon. Librarian, ex-President Clinical Section, Section of Urology, and Section of Surgery. Past-President Medical Society of London; Lettsomian Lecturer, 1958, Orator, 1970; Senior Fellow Association of Surgeons of Great Britain and Ireland; Past President Hunterian Society, Orator, 1967; Vice-President, Internat. Soc. of Urology (Pres. XIII Congress, 1964); Hon. Fellow and Past Pres. of British Assoc. of Urological Surgeons; St Peters medallist, 1964; Member Association Française d'Urologie; Honorary Member: Urological Society of Australasia; Canadian Urological Assoc.; Swedish Urological Soc.; American Urological Assoc.; American Assoc. of Genito-Urinary Surgeons; Ramon Guitéras Lectr, 1963; Hon. Associate Mem. French Academy of Surgery, 1961; Emeritus Mem. Internat. Soc. of Surgery; Past Treas. British Journal of Surgery; Past Chm., Ed. Cttee, British Jl of Urology; Mem. of Biological and Medical Cttee, Royal Commission on Population. Visiting Professor, Urol.; University of Texas and State University of New York, 1965; Visiting Professor and Balfour Lecturer, University of Toronto, 1966. Treasurer, Christ's Hospital, and Chm., Council of Almoners, 1970–76. *Publications:* Modern Trends in Urology, Series 1, 1953, Series 2, 1960, Series 3, 1969; Tumours of the Kidney and Ureter, 1964; various articles on Surgery and Urology in Scientific journals; contributor to Text Book of Urology, British Surgical Practice, and to Encyclopædia of Urology. *Recreations:* golf, music, photography. *Address:* 23 Eresby House, Rutland Gate, SW7 1BG. *T:* 01-589 7129.

RICHES, General Sir Ian (Hurry), KCB 1960 (CB 1959); DSO 1945; *b* 27 Sept. 1908; *s* of C. W. H. Riches; *m* 1936, Winifred Eleanor Layton; two *s*. *Educ:* Univ. Coll. Sch., London. Joined Royal Marines, 1927; Major, 1946; Lt-Colonel, 1949; Colonel, 1953; Maj.-Gen., 1957; Lt-Gen. 1959; General 1961. Maj.-Gen., RM, Portsmouth Group, 1957–59; Commandant-General, Royal Marines, 1959–62; Regional Dir of Civil Defence, 1964–68; Representative Col Comdt, 1967–68. *Address:* Leith House, Old Hillside Road, Winchester, Hants.

RICHES, Rt. Rev. Kenneth, DD, STD; Assistant Bishop of Louisiana, USA, 1976–77; *b* 20 Sept. 1908; *s* of Capt. A. G. Riches; *m* 1942, Kathleen Mary Dixon, JP 1964; two *s* one *d*. *Educ:* Royal Gram. Sch., Colchester; Corpus Christi Coll., Cambridge. Curate of St Mary's, Portsea, 1932–35; St John's, East Dulwich, 1935–36; Chaplain and Librarian, Sidney Sussex Coll., Cambridge, 1936–42; Examining Chaplain to Bishops of Bradford and Wakefield, 1936; Editorial Sec., Cambridgeshire Syllabus, 1935; Editor, Cambridge Review, 1941–42; Rector of Bredfield with Boulge, Suffolk, and Dir of Service Ordination Candidates, 1942–45; Principal of Cuddesdon Theological Coll., Oxford, and Vicar of Cuddesdon, 1945–52; Hon. Canon of Portsmouth Cathedral, 1950–52; Bishop Suffragan of Dorchester, Archdeacon of Oxford and Canon of Christ Church, 1952–56; Bishop of Lincoln, 1956–74. Select Preacher: University of Cambridge, 1941, 1948, 1961, and 1963; University of Oxford, 1954–55. Mem. Archbishops' Commission on Training for the Ministry, 1942; Sec. of Theol. Commn on the Church of Faith and Order Movement. Visiting Lecturer the General Theological Seminary, New York, 1956 and 1962. Hon. Fellow: Sidney Sussex Coll., Cambridge, 1958; Lincoln Coll., Oxford, 1975; Corpus Christi Coll., Cambridge, 1975. Chm., Central Advisory Council for the Ministry, 1959–65. *Recreations:* gardening, antiques, and country life. *Address:* Little Dingle, Dunwich, Saxmundham, Suffolk. *T:* Westleton 316.

RICHINGS, Lewis David George; *b* 22 April 1920; *s* of Lewis Vincent Richings and Jessie Helen (*née* Clements); *m* 1944, Margaret Alice Hume; three *d*. *Educ:* Battersea Grammar Sch.; Devonport High Sch.; Darlington Grammar Sch.; London Sch. of Econs and Polit. Science (part-time). Served War, Army, 1939–46: commnd 2 Lieut Inf., 1940; attached 8 DLI, 1940–41; seconded 11 KAR, 1941–45; Actg Major, 1945; various postings, UK, 1945–46. MAFF, 1937–58; attached MoD, 1958; Gen. Administrator, AWRE, 1958–65; Health and Safety Br., UKAEA, 1965–70; Sec., Nat. Radiol Protection Bd, 1970–79, Dep. Dir, 1978–80. Mem., Radiol Protection and Public Health Cttee, Nuclear Energy Agency, OECD, 1966–80 (Chm., 1972–74). FRSA. *Publications:* articles in press and jls on admin and technical matters relating to common land, rural electrification, earthquakes, and radiol protection. *Recreation:* boats. *Address:* 51 Branksea Avenue, Poole, Dorset BH15 4DP. *T:* Poole 683381.

RICHLER, Mordecai; author; *b* 27 Jan. 1931; *s* of late Moses Isaac Richler and Lily Rosenberg; *m* 1960, Florence Wood; three *s* two *d*. *Educ:* Sir George Williams Univ., Montreal (left without degree). Writer-in-residence, Sir George Williams Univ., 1968–69; Vis. Prof., English Dept, Carleton Univ., Ottawa, 1972–74. Edit. Bd, Book-of-the-Month Club, NY. Canada Council Senior Arts Fellowship, 1960; Guggenheim Fellowship, Creative Writing, 1961; Governor-General's Award for Literature, 1969 and 1972; Paris Review Humour Prize, 1969. *Publications:* novels: The Acrobats, 1954; A Choice of Enemies, 1955; Son of a Smaller Hero, 1957; The Apprenticeship of Duddy Kravitz, 1959, repr. 1972 (filmed, Golden Bear Award, Berlin Film Fest., 1974; Writers Guild of America Annual Award, 1974; Academy Award nomination, 1974); The Incomparable Atuk, 1963; Cocksure, 1968; St Urbain's Horseman, 1971; Joshua Then and Now, 1980; *essays:* Hunting Tigers Under Glass, 1969; Shovelling Trouble, 1973; *autobiography:* The Street, 1972; *children's book:* Jacob Two-Two Meets the Hooded Fang, 1975; contrib. Encounter, Commentary, New York Review of Books, etc.

Recreations: poker, snooker. *Address:* Apt 80C, 1321 Sherbrooke Street W, Montreal, Quebec H3G 1J4, Canada. *T:* 514-288-2008.

RICHMAN, Stella; Chairman, White Elephant Club Ltd, since 1951; Managing Director, Stella Richman Ltd (Independent Television Production Co.); *b* 9 Nov. 1922; *d* of Jacob Richman and Leoni Richman; *m* 1st, Alec Clunes; 2nd, 1953, Victor Brusa (*d* 1965); one *s* one *d. Educ:* Clapton County Secondary Sch. for Girls. Started TV career at ATV, running Script Dept 1960; created and produced Love Story, 1963; joined Rediffusion, 1964; Exec. Head of Series (prod The Informer); Exec. Prod., award-winning Man of Our Times, Half Hour Story and Blackmail; prod first 6 plays, Company of Five, for newly formed London Weekend Television, 1968; Man. Dir, London Weekend Internat., 1969, and Controller of Programmes, London Weekend Television, 1970-71 (first woman to sit on bd of a television co.); in partnership with David Frost formed Stella Richman Productions, 1972-78: resp. for Miss Nightingale, Jennie, Clayhanger, Billy Brand, Just William. FRTS 1982. *Publications:* The White Elephant Cook Books, 1973, 1979. *Recreations:* doing absolutely nothing, herb cultivation, reading biographies, travel. *Address:* 28 Curzon Street, W1. *Clubs:* White Elephant (owner), White Elephant on the River (owner).

RICHMOND, 9th Duke of, *cr* 1675, **AND GORDON,** 4th Duke of, *cr* 1876; **Frederick Charles Gordon-Lennox;** Earl of March, Baron Settrington, Duke of Lennox, Earl of Darnley, Baron Methuen, 1675; Earl of Kinrara, 1876; Duke d'Aubigny (France), 1683-84; Hereditary Constable of Inverness Castle; Flight Lieut, RAFVR; *b* 5 Feb. 1904; *o* surv. *s* of 8th Duke and Hilda, DBE, *d* of late Henry Arthur Brassey, Preston Hall, Kent; *S* father, 1935; *m* 1927, Elizabeth Grace, *y d* of late Rev. T. W. Hudson; two *s. Educ:* Eton; Christ Church, Oxford. *Heir: s* Earl of March, *qv. Address:* Carne's Seat, Goodwood, Chichester, W Sussex; 29 Hyde Park Street, W2.
    See also Sir Alastair Coats, Bt, Lord N. C. Gordon Lennox, C. G. Vyner.

RICHMOND, Archdeacon of; *see* Burbridge, Ven. J. P.

RICHMOND, Sir Alan (James), Kt 1969; Associate Tutor, Further Education Staff College, Blagdon, Bristol, since 1982; *b* 12 Oct. 1919. Trained and employed Engineering Industry, 1938-45; London Univ., BSc(Eng) 1945, PhD 1954; Lecturer, Battersea Polytechnic, 1946-55; Head of Engineering Dept, Welsh Coll. of Advanced Technology, 1955-58; Principal, Lanchester College of Technology, Coventry, 1959-69; Director, Lanchester Polytechnic, 1970-71; Principal, Strode Coll., Street, 1972-81. FIMechE; ACIArb. Hon. DSc CNAA, 1972. *Publications:* (with W. J. Peck) Applied Thermodynamics Problems for Engineers, 1950; Problems in Heat Engines, 1957; various lectures, reviews and articles. *Recreations:* gardening, reading. *Address:* Juglans, 9 Springfield Drive, Wedmore, Som. *T:* Wedmore 712829. *Club:* Royal Commonwealth Society.

RICHMOND, Rt. Hon. Sir Clifford (Parris), PC 1973; KBE 1977; Kt 1972; Judge of the Court of Appeal of New Zealand, 1972-81, President, 1976-81; *b* 23 June 1914; *s* of Howard Parris Richmond, QC, and Elsie Wilhelmina (*née* MacTavish); *m* 1938, Valerie Jean Hamilton; two *s* one *d. Educ:* Wanganui Collegiate Sch.; Victoria and Auckland Univs. LLM (1st cl. Hons). Served War of 1939-45: 4 Field Regt 2NZEF, North Africa and Italy, 1942-45 (despatches, 1944). Partner, legal firm, Buddle Richmond & Co., Auckland, 1946-60. Judge of the Supreme Court of New Zealand, 1960-71. *Recreations:* golf, fishing. *Address:* 21 McFarlane Street, Mount Victoria, Wellington, New Zealand. *T:* 846-974. *Club:* Wellington (NZ).

RICHMOND, Rev. Canon Francis Henry Arthur, MA; Warden, Lincoln Theological College, and Canon and Prebendary of Lincoln Cathedral, since 1977; *b* 6 Jan. 1936; *s* of Frank and Lena Richmond; *m* 1966, Caroline Mary Berent; two *s* one *d. Educ:* Portora Royal School, Enniskillen; Trinity Coll., Dublin (MA); Univ. of Strasbourg (BTh); Linacre Coll., Oxford (MLitt); Wycliffe Hall, Oxford. Deacon, 1963; Priest, 1964; Asst Curate, Woodlands, Doncaster, 1963-66; Sir Henry Stephenson Research Fellow, Sheffield Univ. and Chaplain, Sheffield Cathedral, 1966-69; Vicar, St George's, Sheffield, 1969-77. Anglican Chaplain to Sheffield Univ. and Mem. Sheffield Chaplaincy for Higher Education, 1974-77. Examng Chaplain to Bishop of Lincoln; Proctor in Convocation for Lincoln, 1980; Mem., Gen. Synod Bd of Educn, 1981. *Recreations:* listening to classical music, playing piano, reading, theatre, walking. *Address:* Lincoln Theological College, The Bishop's Hostel, Lincoln LN1 3BP. *T:* Lincoln 25879.

RICHMOND, Prof. John, MD, FRCPE, FRCP; Professor of Medicine, University of Sheffield, since 1973; *b* 30 May 1926; *er s* of late Hugh Richmond and Janet Hyslop Brown; *m* 1951, Jenny Nicol, 2nd *d* of T. Nicol; two *s* one *d. Educ:* Doncaster Grammar Sch.; Univ. of Edinburgh. MB, ChB 1948; MD 1963. FRCPE 1963, FRCP 1970. House Officer, in Edinburgh hosps and Northants, 1948-49, 1952-54; RAMC, Military Mission to Ethiopia, Captain 1st Bn King's African Rifles, N Rhodesia, 1949-50; Rural Gen. Practice, Galloway, Scotland, 1950-52; Res. Fellow, Meml Sloan Kettering Cancer Center, New York, 1958-59; Sen. Lectr, later Reader in Medicine, Univ. of Edinburgh, 1963-73. Visiting Prof. of Medicine: Univ. of Florida; Makerere Univ. Med. Sch., Uganda; Univ. of Khartoum; Kuwait Univ. Censor, RCP, 1981-82. Mem., Sheffield HA, 1982-. High Constables of Edinburgh, 1961-70. *Publications:* Mem. Editorial Bd and contribs, A Companion to Medical Studies, ed R. Passmore and J. S. Robson, vols I-III;

contribs: Davidson's Principles and Practice of Medicine, ed J. G. Macleod; Abdominal Operations, ed Rodney Maingot; (jtly) The Spleen, 1973; papers in med. jls mainly on haematology and oncology. *Recreations:* gardening, photography. *Address:* Stumper Lea, 42 Stumperlowe Hall Road, Sheffield S10 3QS. *T:* Sheffield 301395.

RICHMOND, Sir John (Christopher Blake), KCMG 1963 (CMG 1959); retired; *b* 7 September 1909; *s* of E. T. Richmond, FRIBA, and M. M. Richmond (*née* Lubbock); *m* 1939, D. M. L. Galbraith; two *s* three *d. Educ:* Lancing College; Hertford College, Oxford; University College, London. Various archaeological expeditions, 1931-36; HM Office of Works, 1937-39; served War, Middle East, 1939-46; Dept of Antiquities, Palestine Govt, 1946-47; HM Diplomatic Service, Baghdad, 1947; Foreign Office, 1951; Counsellor, British Embassy, Amman, 1953-55; HM Consul-General, Houston, Texas, 1955-58; Foreign Office, 1958-59; Counsellor, British Property Commission, Cairo, 1959; HM Ambassador to Kuwait, 1961-63 (Political Agent, Kuwait, 1959-61); Supernumerary Fellow of St Antony's College, Oxford, 1963-64; Ambassador to Sudan, 1965-66; Lectr, Modern Near East History, Sch. of Oriental Studies, Univ. of Durham, 1966-74. *Publication:* Egypt 1798-1952, 1977. *Address:* 21 The Avenue, Durham City DH1 4ED.

RICHMOND, Sir John (Frederick), 2nd Bt, *cr* 1929; *b* 12 Aug. 1924; *s* of Sir Frederick Henry Richmond, 1st Bt (formerly Chm. Debenham's Ltd and Harvey Nichols & Co. Ltd), and Dorothy Agnes (*d* 1982), *d* of Frances Joseph Sheppard; *S* father 1953; *m* 1965, Mrs Anne Moreen Bentley; one *d. Educ:* Eton; Jesus Coll., Cambridge. Lt 10th Roy. Hussars; seconded Provost Br., 1944-47. *Address:* Shimpling Park Farm, Bury St Edmunds, Suffolk. *Club:* MCC.

RICHMOND, Mark Henry, PhD, ScD; FRCPath; FRS 1980; Vice-Chancellor, Victoria University of Manchester, since 1981; Member, Public Health Laboratory Service Board, since 1976; *b* 1 Feb. 1931; *s* of Harold Sylvester Richmond and Dorothy Plaistowe Richmond; *m* 1958, Shirley Jean Townrow; one *s* two *d. Educ:* Epsom College; Clare Coll., Cambridge. BA, PhD, ScD. Scientific Staff, MRC, 1958-65; Reader in Molecular Biology, Univ. of Edinburgh, 1965-68; Prof. of Bacteriology, Univ. of Bristol, 1968-81. Member: US/UK Educnl Commn, 1980-; SERC, 1981-; Chm., British Nat. Cttee for Microbiol., 1980-. *Publications:* several in microbiology and biochemistry jls. *Recreation:* hill-walking. *Address:* Victoria University of Manchester, Oxford Road, Manchester M13 9PL.

RICHMOND, Vice-Adm. Sir Maxwell, KBE 1957 (OBE 1940); CB 1954; DSO 1942; RN retired; *b* 19 Oct. 1900; *e s* of Robert Richardson Richmond and Bernadette Richmond (*née* Farrell); *m* 1929, Jessie Messervy Craig; one *s* three *d* (and one *s* decd). *Educ:* New Zealand State Schools; Westminster. Cadet Royal Navy 1918; Lieutenant 1922; specialised navigation; held various (N) posts, 1926-36. Comdr 1936; HMS Hostile in Comd, 1936-38; Staff Coll., 1939; HMS Basilisk in Comd, 1939-40; Dover Patrol, Norway and Dunkirk; Operations, Admty, 1940-41; HMS Bulldog as Sen. Officer Escort Gp, 1942, Atlantic and Russian Convoys; Capt. 1942; Chief Staff Officer to Cdre, Londonderry, 1943; HMS Milne as Capt. (D) 3rd Dest. Flot., 1944-46; Home Fleet, Russian Convoys and Flank Force, Mediterranean; Asst Chief of Supplies, Admty, 1946-48; Naval Liaison Officer, Wellington, NZ, 1948-50; Sen. Naval Officer, N Ire., 1951; Rear-Adm. 1952; Deputy Chief of Naval Personnel (Training), 1952-55; Flag Officer (Air), Mediterranean, and Flag Officer Second-in-Command, Mediterranean Fleet, 1955-Oct. 1956. Order of the Red Banner (Russian) 1942; Croix de Guerre (French) 1945. *Recreations:* sailing and tramping. *Address:* No 4 Rural Delivery, Whangarei, New Zealand. *Club:* Naval and Military.

RICHNELL, Donovan Thomas, CBE 1973; Director General, British Library Reference Division, 1974-79; *b* 3 Aug. 1911; *o s* of Thomas Hodgson Richnell and Constance Margaret Richnell (*née* Allen); *m* 1957, Renée Norma Hilton; one *s* one *d. Educ:* St Paul's School; Corpus Christi Coll., Cambridge; University Coll., London (Fellow 1975). BA, FLA. Sub-Librarian, Royal Soc. Med., 1946-49; Dep. Librarian, London Univ. Library, 1949-60; Librarian, Univ. of Reading, 1960-67; Dir, and Goldsmiths' Librarian, Univ. of London Library, 1967-74. Library Association: Mem. Council, 1962-; President 1970; Hon. Fellow 1979; Chm. of Council, Aslib, 1968-70. Member: Library Adv. Council for England, 1966-71, 1974-77; British Library Organising Cttee, 1971-73; Adv. Cttee for Scientific and Technical Information, 1970-74; British Library Bd, 1974-79; Chm., Standing Conf. of Nat. and Univ. Libraries, 1973-75. Hon. DLitt Loughborough, 1977. *Address:* 2 Queen Anne's Gardens, Bedford Park, W4.

RICHTER, Prof. Burton; Paul Pigott Professor in the Physical Sciences, Stanford University, USA, since 1980 (Professor of Physics, since 1967); *b* 22 March 1931; *s* of Abraham Richter and Fannie Pollack; *m* 1960, Laurose Becker; one *s* one *d. Educ:* Massachusetts Inst. of Technology. BS 1952, PhD (Physics) 1956. Stanford University: Research Associate, Physics, High Energy Physics Lab., 1956-60; Asst Prof., 1960-63; Associate Prof., 1963-67; full Prof., 1967. E. O. Lawrence Award, 1975; Nobel Prize for Physics (jointly), 1976. *Publications:* over 180 articles in various scientific journals. *Address:* Stanford Linear Accelerator Center, PO Box 4349, Stanford University, Stanford, California 94305, USA.

RICHTER, Sviatoslav; Hero of Socialist Labour, 1975; pianist; *b* Zhitomir, Ukraine, 20 March 1915; *m* Nina Dorliak. *Educ:* Moscow State Conservatoire. Gave first piano recital at age of nineteen and began to give concerts on a wide scale in 1942. Appeared at the Royal Albert Hall and the Royal Festival Hall, London, 1961; Royal Festival Hall, 1963, 1966, 1977, 1979. Was recently awarded Lenin Prize, and also holds the title of "Peoples' Artist of the USSR"; Order of Lenin, 1965. *Recreations:* walking, ski-ing and painting. *Address:* c/o Victor Hochhauser Ltd, 4 Holland Park Avenue, W11.

RICKARD, Prof. Peter, DPhil, PhD, LittD; Drapers Professor of French, University of Cambridge, since 1980; Fellow of Emmanuel College, Cambridge, 1953, Professorial Fellow since 1980; *b* 20 Sept. 1922; *s* of Norman Ernest Rickard and Elizabeth Jane (*née* Hosking); unmarried. *Educ:* Redruth County Grammar Sch., Cornwall; Exeter Coll., Oxford (Pt I Hons Mod. Langs (French and German), Cl. I, 1942; Final Hons Cl. I, 1948; MA 1948). DPhil Oxon 1952; PhD Cantab 1952. Served War, 1st Bn Seaforth Highlanders and Intell. Corps, India, 1942-46. Heath Harrison Travelling Scholar (French), 1948; Amelia Jackson Sen. Scholar, Exeter Coll., Oxford, 1948-49; Lectr in Mod. Langs, Trinity Coll., Oxford, 1949-52; Univ. of Cambridge: Asst Lectr in French, 1952-57, Lectr, 1957-74; Reader in French Lang., 1974-80; Mem., St John's Coll., 1952-; Tutor, Emmanuel Coll., 1954-65. *Publications:* Britain in Medieval French Literature, 1956; La langue française au XVIe siècle, 1968; (ed with T. G. S. Combe) The French Language: studies presented to Lewis Charles Harmer, 1970; (ed and trans.) Fernando Pessoa, Selected Poems, 1971; A History of the French Language, 1974; Chrestomathie de la langue française au XVe siècle, 1976; (ed with T. G. S. Combe) L. C. Harmer, Uncertainties in French Grammar, 1979; The Embarrassments of Irregularity, 1981; articles in Romania, Trans Phil Soc., Neuphilologische Mitteilungen, and Zeitschrift für Romanische Philologie. *Recreations:* travel, photography, music. *Address:* Emmanuel College, Cambridge CB2 3AP. *T:* Cambridge 65411; Upper Rosevine, Portscatho, Cornwall. *T:* Portscatho 582.

RICKARDS, Oscar Stanley Norman, CBE 1945; Grand Officer in the Order of Orange-Nassau, 1947; Haakon VII Liberty Cross, 1947; Director of Victualling, Admiralty, 1941-58; *b* 14 Nov. 1893; *s* of Thomas Rickards and Laura Rose Short; *m* 1925, Sylvia Annie Bdate; one *d*. *Educ:* University College School, Hampstead. Joined Admiralty, 1913. *Address:* Little Thresholds, Hawkshill Way, Esher, Surrey. *T:* 64914.

RICKETS, Brig. Reginald Anthony Scott; Managing Director, Irvine Development Corporation, since 1981; Director, Ayrshire Chamber of Industries, since 1981; *b* 13 Dec. 1929; *s* of Captain R. H. Rickets and Mrs V. C. Rickets (*née* Morgan); *m* 1952, Elizabeth Ann Serjeant; one *s* one *d*. *Educ:* St George's Coll., Weybridge; RMA Sandhurst. 2nd Lieut, RE, 1949; served with airborne, armoured and field engrs in UK, Cyrenaica, Egypt, Malaya, Borneo, Hong Kong and BAOR; special employment military forces Malaya, 1955-59; Staff Coll., Camberley, 1962; BM Engr Gp, BAOR, 1963-66; OC 67 Gurkha Indep. Field Sqn, 1966-68; DS Staff Coll., 1968-70; Comdt Gurkha Engrs/CRE Hong Kong, 1970-73; COS British Sector, Berlin, 1973-77; Col GS RSME, 1977-78; Chief Engr UKLF, 1978-81. *Recreation:* sailing (DTI Ocean skipper and RYA coach/examiner). *Address:* Irvine Development Corporation, Perceton House, Irvine, Ayrshire, Scotland. *Clubs:* Naval and Military; Royal Engineer Yacht (Commodore, 1979-81).

RICKETT, Sir Denis Hubert Fletcher, KCMG 1956 (CMG 1947); CB 1951; Director: Schroder International, 1974-79; De La Rue Co., 1974-77; Adviser, J. Henry Schroder Wagg & Co., 1974-79; *b* 27 July 1907; *s* of late Hubert Cecil Rickett, OBE, JP; *m* 1946, Ruth Pauline (MB, BS, MRCS, LRCP), *d* of late William Anderson Armstrong, JP; two *s* one *d*. *Educ:* Rugby School; Balliol College, Oxford. Fellow of All Souls College, Oxford, 1929-49. Joined staff of Economic Advisory Council, 1931; Offices of War Cabinet, 1939; Principal Private Secretary to Right Honourable Oliver Lyttelton, when Minister of Production, 1943-45; Personal Assistant (for work on Atomic Energy) to Rt Hon. Sir John Anderson, when Chancellor of the Exchequer, 1945; transferred to Treasury, 1947; Principal Private Secretary to the Rt Hon. C. R. Attlee, when Prime Minister, 1950-51; Economic Minister, British Embassy, Washington, and Head of UK Treasury and Supply Delegation, 1951-54; Third Secretary, HM Treasury, 1955-60, Second Secretary, 1960-68. Vice-Pres., World Bank, 1968-74. *Recreation:* music. *Address:* 30 Warwick Avenue, W9. *Clubs:* Athenæum, Brooks's.

RICKETT, Dr Raymond Mildmay Wilson, BSc, PhD, CChem, FRSC; Director, Middlesex Polytechnic, since 1972; *b* 17 March 1927; *s* of Mildmay Louis Rickett and Winifred Georgina Rickett; *m* 1958, Naomi Nishida; one *s* two *d*. *Educ:* Faversham Grammar Sch.; Medway Coll. of Technology (BSc London); Illinois Inst. of Technology (PhD). Royal Navy, 1946-48; Medway Coll. of Technology, 1953-55; Illinois Inst. of Technology, 1955-59; Plymouth Coll. of Technology, 1959; Lectr, Liverpool Coll. of Technology, 1960-62; Senr Lectr/Principal Lectr, West Ham Coll. of Technology, 1962-64; Head of Dept, Wolverhampton Coll. of Technology, 1965-66; Vice-Principal, Sir John Cass Coll., 1967-69; Vice-Provost, City of London Polytechnic, 1969-72. Chm., Cttee of Dirs of Polytechnics (Chm., London and SE Region); Mem. and past Vice-Chm., UNESCO Adv. Cttee, European Centre for Higher Educn; Member: UK Nat. Commn for UNESCO Educn Adv. Cttee; Higher Educn Review Group for NI; Inter-Univ. Council for Higher Educn Overseas; Inter-Univ. Council, W Africa Working Group; Working Group, Management of Higher Educn (Oakes Cttee); Educnl Credit Transfer Steering Cttee, DES; CNAA Sub-Cttee on Entry Qualifications (Chm.); CNAA Acad. Policy Cttee; Hong Kong 2nd Polytechnic Sub-Cttee; SE Regional Adv. Council for Tech. Educn; Enfield and Haringay AHA Nurse Educn Cttee (Chm.); Governor, Yehudi Menuhin Live Music Now Scheme; Pres., N London English-Speaking Union. *Publications:* Experimental in Physical Chemistry (jtly), 1962, new edn 1968; 2 chapters in The Use of the Chemical Literature, 1962, new edn 1969; articles on Polytechnics in the national press and contribs to learned jls. *Recreations:* cricket, theatre-going, opera. *Address:* Principal's Lodge, Trent Park, Cockfosters Road, Barnet, Herts EN4 0PS. *T:* 01-449 9012.

RICKETTS, Maj.-Gen. Abdy Henry Gough, CBE 1952; DSO 1945; DL; *b* 8 Dec. 1905; *s* of Lt-Col P. E. Ricketts, DSO, MVO, and L. C. Ricketts (*née* Morant); *m* 1932, Joan Warre, *d* of E. T. Close, Camberley; one *s* one *d*. *Educ:* Winchester. Sandhurst, 1924; Durham LI, 1925; Shanghai Defence Force, 1927; NW Frontier, India (medal and clasp), 1930; Burma "Chindit" campaign, 1944-45; Gen. Service Medal and clasp, Malaya, 1950; comd British Brigade, Korea, 1952; Comdr (temp. Maj.-Gen.), Cyprus District, 1955-56. Col, Durham LI, 1965-68; Dep. Col, The Light Infantry (Durham), 1968-70. DL Somerset, 1968. Officer, Legion of Merit (USA), 1953. *Address:* The Old Rectory, Pylle, Shepton Mallet, Som. *T:* Ditcheat 248. *Club:* Army and Navy.

RICKETTS, Michael Rodney, MA; Headmaster, Sutton Valence School, 1967-80; *b* 29 Sept. 1923; *er s* of late Rt Rev. C. M. Ricketts, Bishop of Dunwich, and of Mrs Ricketts; *m* 1958, Judith Anne Caroline Corry; two *s* two *d*. *Educ:* Sherborne; Trinity Coll., Oxford. Served War of 1939-45: in 8th Army with 60th Rifles, 1942-47. Trinity Coll., Oxford, 1947-50; Asst Master and Housemaster, Bradfield Coll., 1950-67. *Recreations:* cricket, shooting, country activities. *Address:* Church Farm, Saxlingham, Holt, Norfolk. *T:* Binham 307. *Clubs:* East India, Devonshire, Sports and Public Schools, MCC.

RICKETTS, Sir Robert (Cornwallis Gerald St Leger), 7th Bt, *cr* 1828; retired Solicitor; *b* 8 Nov. 1917; *s* of Sir Claude Albert Frederick Ricketts, 6th Bt, and Lilian Helen Gwendoline (*d* 1955), *o d* of Arthur M. Hill, late 5th Fusiliers; *S* father 1937; *m* 1945, Anne Theresa, *d* of late H. Hon. Sir Richard Stafford Cripps, PC, CH, FRS, QC; two *s* two *d*. *Educ:* Haileybury; Magdalene College, Cambridge (2nd Cl. Hons in History and Law, BA 1939, MA 1943). Served War of 1939-45 (Captain, Devon Regiment); Personal Assistant to Chief of Staff, Gibraltar, 1942-45; ADC to Lieutenant-Governor of Jersey, 1945-46. Formerly Partner in Wellington and Clifford. FRSA. Hon. Citizen, Mobile, USA, 1970. *Heir:* *s* Robert Tristram Ricketts [*b* 17 April 1946; *m* 1969, Ann, *yr d* of late E. W. C. Lewis, CB; one *s* one *d*]. *Address:* Forwood House, Minchinhampton, Glos. *TA* and *T:* Brimscombe 882160.
See also G. F. P. Mason.

RICKFORD, Richard Braithwaite Keevil, MD (London), BS, FRCS, FRCOG; Consulting Physician, Obstetric Department, St Thomas' Hospital, London, 1979-82 (Physician, 1946-79); Consulting Surgeon, Chelsea Hospital for Women, 1979-82 (Surgeon, 1950-79); Gynæcologist, Oxted Hospitals, 1952-82; formerly Dean, Institute of Obstetrics and Gynæcology; *b* 1 June 1914; *e s* of late L. T. R. Rickford; *m* 1939, Dorothy, *d* of late Thomas Lathan; three *s* (and one *s* decd). *Educ:* Weymouth College; University of London. Various surgical, obstetric and gynæcological appointments at Norfolk and Norwich Hospital and St Thomas' Hospital. Examiner to: Universities of London, Cambridge and Glasgow; Royal Coll. of Obstetricians and Gynæcologists; Conjoint Board; Central Midwives Board. *Publications:* contributions to medical journals. *Recreations:* winter sports, sailing. *Address:* 13A South Grove, Highgate, N6. *T:* 01-340 9700; Kingswear Lodge, Kingswear, Devon TQ6 0BS. *T:* Kingswear 361. *Club:* Royal Dart Yacht (Kingswear, Devon).

RICKS, Prof. Christopher Bruce, FBA 1975; Professor of English, and Fellow of Christ's College, since 1975, King Edward VII Professor of English Literature, since 1982, University of Cambridge; *b* 18 Sept. 1933; *s* of James Bruce Ricks and Gabrielle Roszak; *m* 1st, 1956, Kirsten Jensen (marr. diss.); two *s* two *d* ; 2nd, 1977, Judith Aronson; one *s* one *d*. *Educ:* King Alfred's Sch., Wantage; Balliol Coll., Oxford. 2nd Lieut, Green Howards, 1952. BA 1956, BLitt 1958, MA 1960, Oxon. Andrew Bradley Jun. Res. Fellow, Balliol Coll., Oxford, 1957; Fellow of Worcester Coll., Oxford, 1958-68; Prof. of English, Bristol Univ., 1968-75. Visiting Professor: Berkeley and Stanford, 1965; Smith Coll., 1967; Harvard, 1971; Wesleyan, 1974; Brandeis, 1977, 1981. A Vice-Pres., Tennyson Soc. Co-editor, Essays in Criticism. George Orwell Meml Prize, 1979; Beefeater Club Prize for Literature, 1980. *Publications:* Milton's Grand Style, 1963; (ed) The Poems of Tennyson, 1969; Tennyson, 1972; Keats and Embarrassment, 1974; (ed with Leonard Michaels) The State of the Language, 1980. *Address:* Christ's College, Cambridge; 18 Albert Street, Cambridge. *T:* Cambridge 353777; Lasborough Cottage, Lasborough Park, near Tetbury, Glos. *T:* Leighterton 252.

RICKS, Sir John (Plowman), Kt 1964; Solicitor to the Post Office, 1953-72; *b* 3 April 1910; *s* of late James Young Ricks; *m* 1st, 1936, May Celia (*d* 1975), *d* of late Robert William Chubb; three *s* ; 2nd, 1976, Mrs Doreen Ilsley. *Educ:* Christ's Hosp.; Jesus Coll., Oxford. Admitted Solicitor, 1935; entered Post

Office Solicitor's Department, 1935; Assistant Solicitor, Post Office, 1951. *Address:* 8 Sunset View, Barnet, Herts. *T:* 01-449 6114.

RICKUS, Gwenneth Margaret, CBE 1981; Director of Education, London Borough of Brent, since 1971; *b* 1925; *d* of Leonard William Ernest and Florence Rickus. *Educ:* Latymer Sch., Edmonton; King's Coll., Univ. of London. BA, PGCE. Teaching, 1948-53; Asst Sec., AAM, 1953-61; Education Administration: Mddx CC, 1961-65; London Borough of Brent, 1965-. Comr for Racial Equality, 1977-80. *Recreations:* golf, walking, reading, crafts, gardening, music. *Address:* Chesterfield House, 9 Park Lane, Wembley HA9 7RW. *T:* 01-903 1400.

RIDDELL, Sir John (Charles Buchanan), 13th Bt, *cr* 1628; CA; with Credit Suisse First Boston Ltd, since 1972, Director since 1975; Director: United Kingdom Provident Institution, since 1975; Northern Rock Building Society, since 1981; Deputy Chairman, Independent Broadcasting Authority, since 1981; *b* 3 Jan. 1934; *o s* of Sir Walter Buchanan Riddell, 12th Bt, and Hon. Rachel Beatrice Lyttelton (*d* 1965), *y d* of 8th Viscount Cobham; *S* father 1934; *m* 1969, Sarah, *o d* of Rt Hon. Gordon Richardson, *qv*; three *s. Educ:* Eton; Christ Church, Oxford. Contested (C): Durham NW, Feb. 1974; Sunderland S, Oct. 1974. *Heir: s* Walter John Buchanan Riddell, *b* 10 June 1974. *Address:* Hepple, Morpeth, Northumberland. *TA:* Hepple; 49 Campden Hill Square, W8. *Club:* City.
See also Sir J. L. Pumphrey.

RIDDELL, Roland William, (Ronald), MD; FRCP, FRCPE, FRCPath, FZS, FRGS; consultant clinical pathologist; Hon. Consulting Clinical Microbiologist to St John's Hospital for Diseases of the Skin, London, since 1968, and to the National Heart and Chest Hospitals, since 1980; *b* 9 Nov. 1913; *e s* of late William Henry Riddell and Ada (*née* Chamberlin), Highgate, London; *m* 2nd, 1976, Margaret Ann, *e d* of late John Geoffrey Strutt Lewis and of Mercy Eileen (*née* Mennell). *Educ:* William Ellis Sch.; St Mary's Hosp. Med. Sch., Univ. of London (BS, DipBact 1947; MD 1948). MRCS 1939; FRCPE 1951; FRCPath 1964; FRCP 1972; FZS (Science) 1960; FRGS 1980. Served War, 1939-45: Staff Scottish Comd, Pathol. Trng Unit, Edinburgh Castle Mil. Hosp. and Edin. Univ. Med. Sch., 1940; Specialist in Pathol. (attached RN), Orkney and Shetland Defences, 1942, and 112 Gen. Hosp. (21st Army Gp), Kent, 1943; Asst Dir of Pathol., AFHQ, Central Medit., 1944-45; Lt-Col RAMC. House Surg. and Casualty Off., Grimsby and Dist Hosp., Lincs, 1939; Registrar in Pathol., Royal Hosp., Montrose, Angus, 1939; Sen. Lectr and Dir, Dept of Med. Mycol., London Sch. of Hygiene and Trop. Medicine, 1946; Travelling Fellow in Microbiol., Commonwealth (Harkness) Fund of New York, Duke Univ., NC, and Columbia Univ., NY, 1948-49; Sen. Lectr, Dept of Med. Mycol., Inst. of Dermatol., 1949-68; Mem. Bd of Governors and Dir, Dept of Microbiol., St John's Hosp. for Diseases of Skin, 1950-65; Consultant Clin. Microbiologist and Chm. Inf. Cttees: Brompton Hosp., 1951-80; London Chest Hosp., 1970-80; Nat. Heart Hosp., 1972-80; Consulting Microbiologist (Mycobact.), Armed Forces of Indonesia, 1978–; Sen. Lectr in Professorial Dept of Medicine, Cardiothoracic Inst., Univ. of London, 1968-80; sometime Lectr, Royal Postgrad. Med. Sch., London, and British Council; Recog. Teacher and Examr in Bact. and Med. Mycol., Univ. of London, 1956–. Vis. Guest: Med. Council of India, 1959 (lectured at Sch. of Trop. Medicine, Calcutta, and in Madras, Bombay and Delhi); Govt of Hong Kong, 1966. Hon. Mem., Cttee on Bact. and Immun., Internat. Union Against Tuberculosis: meetings in Amsterdam, Ankara, Paris, Moscow (Chm.), Munich, New York, 1966-73. Lectured, Dept. Infect. Dis., Presbyt. Hosp., Columbia Univ., NY, 1980. Chm., Clin. Trials Org., Brit. Tuberculosis Assoc., 1958-61; Pres., London Chest Hosp. Assoc., 1981; Member: Cttee of Management, Inst. of Diseases of Chest, 1963; Leprosy Study Centre, London, 1960-80; Edit. Bd, Antimicrobial Agents and Chemotherapy, USA, 1971-74; Assoc. of Clin. Pathologists; Sen. Mem., Thoracic Soc. Mitchell Lectr, and Citation for Weber-Parkes Prize, RCP, 1974. *Publications:* (ed and contrib.) Fungus Diseases and their Treatment, 1958; (contrib.) Butterworths Medical Dictionary, 2nd edn 1978; *chapters in:* British Encyclopaedia of Medical Practice, 1951-52; Recent Advances in Clinical Pathology, 1951; Diseases of the Chest, 1952; Leprosy in Theory and Practice, 1959, 2nd edn 1964; Nomenclature of Disease, RCP, 8th edn 1959; Chest Diseases, 1963; Price's Textbook of Medicine, 1966, 1973, 1978 (10th-12th edns); Third Symposium on Advanced Medicine, 1967; Side Effects of Drugs VII, 1972; Modern Chemotherapy of Tuberculosis, 1975; contrib. British, USA, French and Indian jls. *Recreations:* music, travel, history and conservation of Royal Borough of Kensington and Chelsea. *Address:* 38 Devonshire Street, W1N 1LD; 58 Brompton Square, SW3 2AG. *T:* 01-589 1187.

RIDDELL-WEBSTER, John Alexander, MC 1943; Director, BP Oil Ltd (Deputy Managing Director, 1976-80); farmer; *b* 17 July 1921; *s* of Gen. Sir Thomas Riddell-Webster, GCB, DSO; *m* 1960, Ruth, *d* of late S. P. L. A. Lithgow; two *s* one *d. Educ:* Harrow; Pembroke Coll., Cambridge. Seaforth Highlanders (Major), 1940-46. Joined Anglo-Iranian Oil Co., 1946; served in Iran, Iraq, Bahrain, Aden; Vice-Pres. Marketing, BP Canada, 1959; Dir, Shell-Mex and BP, 1965, Man. Dir, Marketing, 1971-75; Dir, Public Affairs, Scotland, BP, 1979-81. Mem. Cttee, AA, 1980–; Mem. Exec. Cttee, Scottish Council (Develt and Industry), 1981–; Member of Council: Advertising Assoc., 1974-80; Inc. Soc. of British Advertisers, 1968-80; for Vehicle Servicing and Repair, 1972-80 (Chm., 1975); Royal Warrant Holders' Assoc. (Vice-Pres., 1979; Pres., 1980); British Road Fedn, 1971-80; Pres., Oil Industries Club, 1977-78. CBIM. *Recreations:* shooting, fishing, gardening.

Address: Lintrose, Coupar Angus, Perthshire. *T:* Coupar Angus 472. *Clubs:* New (Edinburgh); Royal Perth Golfing Society.

RIDDELSDELL, Dame Mildred, DCB 1972; CBE 1958; Second Permanent Secretary, Department of Health and Social Security, 1971-73; (Deputy Secretary, 1966-71); *b* 1 Dec. 1913; 2nd *d* of Rev. H. J. Riddelsdell. *Educ:* St Mary's Hall, Brighton; Bedford Coll., London. Entered Min. of Labour, 1936; Asst Sec., Min. of National Insurance, 1945; Under Secretary, 1950; On loan to United Nations, 1953-56; Secretary, National Incomes Commission, 1962-65; Ministry of Pensions and National Insurance, 1965, Social Security, 1966. Chm., CS Retirement Fellowship, 1974-77. *Recreation:* gardening. *Address:* 26A New Yatt Road, Witney, Oxon.

RIDDLE, Hugh Joseph, (Huseph), RP 1960; Artist; Portrait Painter; *b* 24 May 1912; *s* of late Hugh Howard Riddle and late Christine Simons Brown; *m* 1936, Joan Claudia Johnson; one *s* two *d. Educ:* Harrow; Magdalen, Oxford; Slade School of Art; Byam Shaw School of Art and others. *Recreations:* sailing, ski-ing, swimming, tennis, golf. *Address:* 18 Boulevard Verdi, Domaine du château de Tournon, Montauroux 83710, France.

RIDDOCH, John Haddow, CMG 1963; Under-Secretary, Board of Trade, 1966-69, retired; *b* 4 Feb. 1909; *s* of Joseph Riddoch, Gourock, Renfrewshire; *m* 1st, 1938, Isobel W. Russell (*d* 1972); one *s* two *d* ; 2nd, 1975, Margaret C. McKimmie. *Educ:* Greenock Acad.; Glasgow Univ. Entered Inland Revenue Dept (Inspectorate of Taxes), 1932; Asst Principal in Air Ministry (Dept of Civil Aviation), 1939; Principal, 1942; Asst Sec., Min. of Civil Aviation, 1945; Under-Sec., Min. of Transport and Civil Aviation, 1957, Min. of Aviation, 1959; United Kingdom Representative on the Council of the ICAO, 1957-62 (First Vice-Pres. of Council, 1961-62); Under-Sec., Min. of Aviation, 1962-66. *Recreations:* music, bowls, gardening. *Address:* 10 The Fairway, New Barnet, Herts EN5 1HN.

RIDEALGH, Mrs Mabel; General Secretary of Women's Co-operative Guild, 1953-63; Member, Women's Advisory Committee, British Standards Institute, 1953-63; *b* 11 Aug. 1898; *d* of M. A. Jewitt, Wallsend-on-Tyne, Northumberland; *m* 1919, Leonard, *s* of W. R. Ridealgh, Sunderland, Durham; one *s* one *d.* National Pres. Women's Co-op. Guild, 1941-42; Hon. Regional Organiser Bd of Trade (Make-do and Mend), 1942-44; MP (Lab) Ilford North, 1945-50. *Address:* 2 Eastwood Road, Goodmayes, Ilford, Essex. *T:* 01-599 8960.

RIDEOUT, Prof. Roger William; Professor of Labour Law, University College, London, since 1973; *b* 9 Jan. 1935; *s* of Sidney and Hilda Rideout; *m* 1st, 1959, Marjorie Roberts (marr. diss. 1976); one *d* ; 2nd, 1977, Gillian Margaret Lynch. *Educ:* Bedford School; University Coll., London (LLB, PhD). Called to the Bar, Gray's Inn, 1964. National Service, 1958-60; 2nd Lt RAEC, Educn Officer, 1st Bn Coldstream Guards. Lecturer: Univ. of Sheffield, 1960-63; Univ. of Bristol, 1963-64. University Coll., London: Sen. Lectr, 1964-65; Reader, 1965-73; Dean of Faculty of Laws, 1975-77. Dep. Chm., Central Arbitration Cttee. Chairman, Industrial Law Society, 1977-80. *Publications:* The Right to Membership of a Trade Union, 1962; The Practice and Procedure of the NIRC, 1973; Trade Unions and the Law, 1973; Principles of Labour Law, 1972, 4th edn 1983; (ed, with Lord Lloyd of Hampstead) Current Legal Problems. *Recreations:* fishing, gardening. *Address:* 255 Chipstead Way, Woodmansterne, Surrey. *T:* Downland 52033.

RIDGE, Anthony Hubert; Director-General, International Bureau, Universal Postal Union, Bern, 1973-74 (Deputy Director-General, 1964-73); *b* 5 Oct. 1913; *s* of Timothy Leopold Ridge and Magdalen (*née* Hernig); *m* 1938, Marjory Joan Sage; three *s* one *d. Educ:* Christ's Hospital; Jesus College, Cambridge. Asst Principal in GPO and Ministry of Home Security, 1937-42; Principal in Ministry of Home Security and GPO, 1942-47; Principal Private Sec. to PMG, Secretary to Post Office Board, 1947-49; Dep. Regional Director, London Postal Region, 1949-51; Asst Secretary, mainly in international Postal Service, 1951-60; Director of Clerical Mechanization and Buildings, and Member of Post Office Board, GPO, 1960-63. Mem., Postling Parish Council, 1979–. Governor, Christ's Hosp. *Recreations:* music, languages, transport, gardening. *Address:* Staple, Postling, Hythe, Kent. *T:* Lyminge 862315. *Clubs:* Christ's Hospital, United Oxford & Cambridge University, Cambridge Society.

RIDGERS, John Nalton Sharpe; Deputy Chairman and Treasurer, Lloyd's Register of Shipping, 1973-78; Director: Smit International (UK) Ltd, since 1974; *b* 10 June 1910; 4th *c* and *o s* of Sharpe Ridgers; *m* 1936, Barbara Mary, *o d* of Robert Cobb; five *d. Educ:* Wellington College. Entered Lloyd's, 1928; underwriting member, 1932. Member Cttee Lloyd's Underwriters' Association, 1951-61, 1964-69, Chm. 1961; Member Joint Hull Cttee, 1957-69, Dep. Chm., 1968, Chm., 1969. Mem. Cttee of Lloyd's, 1957-60, 1962-65, Dep. Chm., 1962, Chm., 1963. Director: London Trust Co. Ltd, 1963-80; Arbuthnot Insurance Services Ltd, 1974-80; Danae Investment Trust Ltd, 1975-80. *Recreations:* snooker, carpentry. *Address:* Little Watlynge, 4 Chestnut Lane, Sevenoaks, Kent TN13 3AR.

RIDGWAY, Gen. Matthew Bunker, DSC (with Oak Leaf Cluster); DSM (with 3rd Oak Leaf Cluster); Silver Star (with Oak Leaf Cluster); Legion of Merit; Bronze Star Medal (with Oak Leaf Cluster); Purple Heart; Hon. KCB 1955 (Hon. CB 1945); Chairman of The Mellon Institute of Industrial

Research 1955-60, retired; *b* 3 March 1895; *s* of Thomas Ridgway and Ruth Starbuck Bunker; *m* 1930; one *d*; *m* 1947, Mary Anthony; (one *s* decd). *Educ*: United States Military Academy, 1913-17. Inf. School (Company Officers' Course), 1924-25; Mem. Am. Electoral Commn, Nicaragua, 1927-28; Mem. Commn on Bolivian-Paraguayan boundary dispute, 1929; Inf. School (Advanced Course), 1929-30; Liaison Officer to Govt in Philippine Is, Tech. Adviser to Gov.-Gen., 1932-33; Comd and Gen. Staff School, 1933-35; Asst Chief of Staff, 6th Corps Area, 1935-36; Dep. Chief of Staff, Second Army, 1936; Army War College, 1936-37; Assistant Chief of Staff, Fourth Army, 1937-39; accompanied Gen. Marshall on special mission to Brazil, 1939; War Plans Div., War Department Gen. Staff, 1939-42; Asst Div. Comdr., 82nd Inf. Div., 1942; Comdr 1942; Comdg Gen. 82nd Airborne Div., Sicily, Italy, Normandy, 1942-44; Comdr 18th Airborne Corps, Belgium, France, Germany, 1944-45; Comdr Luzon Area Command, 1945; Comdr Medit. Theater, and Dep. Supreme Allied Comdr, Medit., 1945-46; Senior US Army Member Military Staff Cttee, UN, 1946-48; Chm. Inter-Am. Defense Bd, 1946-48; C-in-C Caribbean Command, 1948-49; Dep. Army Chief of Staff for Admin., 1949-50 (and Chm. Inter-Am. Defense Bd, 1950); Comdg Gen. Eighth Army in Korea, 1950-51; Comdr UN Comd in Far East, C-in-C of Far East Comd and Supreme Comdr for Allied Powers in Japan, 1951-52; Supreme Allied Comdr, Europe, 1952-53; Chief of Staff, United States Army, 1953-55, retired. Holds many American and foreign decorations. *Address*: 918 W Waldheim Road, Fox Chapel, Pittsburgh, Pa 15215, USA.

RIDING, George A., MA; Headmaster, Aldenham School, 1933-July 1949; *b* 1 April 1888; *s* of Daniel A. Riding and Anne Deighton; *m* Aideen Maud, *d* of T. W. Rolleston, *g d* of late Rev. Stopford Brooke; two *s*. *Educ*: Manchester Grammar School (Scholar); University of Manchester (MA Hons English Language and Literature); New College, Oxford, 1st Class Honours, Modern Languages (French and German), 1921, Heath Harrison Travelling Scholarship, 1920; President, Oxford University French Club, 1920; Assistant Master: Penarth County Sch., 1909-14; Mill Hill School, 1914-15; Rugby School, 1921-28 (Sixth Form Master); served with Northumberland Fusiliers (wounded); Registrar, King's Lancashire Military Convalescent Hospital, 1917-18; Captain in Rugby School OTC; Headmaster, Warwick School, 1928-33. Member of House of Laity, Church Assembly, 1944. Member of Council, Inc. Assoc. of Head Masters, 1942-44. Foundation Member of Hispanic Council. Member School Broadcasting Council, 1947-58; Chairman Secondary Programmes Committee, 1947-54. Chairman: Cornwall Modern Churchmen's Union, 1950; Truro Divisional Liberal Association, 1950-51; Cornwall Liberal Council, 1950; Minack Theatre Society, 1960-66; E Cornwall Society for the Mentally Handicapped, 1960-66. Carried out (with headmaster of Fettes Coll.) survey of pre-service education in Pakistan, 1951. *Publications*: Blackie's Longer French Texts; Les Trois Mousquetaires; La Bête dans les Neiges; Moral Foundations of Citizenship; contrib. to Naval Review, Spectator. *Address*: Colona, Port Mellon, Mevagissey, St Austell, Cornwall PL26 6PH. *T*: Mevagissey 3440.

RIDING, Laura, (Mrs Schuyler B. Jackson); *b* New York City, 16 Jan. 1901; American mother and naturalised (Austrian-born) father (Nathaniel S. Reichenthal); *m* 1941, Schuyler B. Jackson (*d* 1968) (American writer; poetry-editor of Time, 1938-43). *Educ*: American public schools; Cornell University. First published poems in American poetry magazines; member of group of Southern poets, The Fugitives; went to England in 1926, remaining abroad until 1939; engaging in writing and allied activities, seeking a single terminology of truth to supersede our confused terminological diversity (eg, as Editor of Epilogue, a critical miscellany); was co-operator of Seizin Press, first author of A Survey of Modernist Poetry (Robert Graves, collaborator), 1927; devoted herself to helping other poets with their work. Has since renounced poetry as humanly inadequate and concentrated on direct linguistic handling of truth-problem, studying ways to intensify people's consciousness of word-meanings; working long with husband on a book in which the principles of language and the principles of definition are brought into relation, to be entitled Rational Meaning: A New Foundation for the Definition of Words (publishing arrangements pending). Mark Rothko Appreciation Award, 1971; Guggenheim Fellowship award, 1973; Nat. Endowment for the Arts Fellowship Award (for writing of her memoirs, now in progress), 1979. *Publications include*: (as Laura Riding, until 1941, thereafter as Laura (Riding) Jackson) individual books of poems (10), from 1926; Contemporaries and Snobs, 1928; Anarchism Is Not Enough, 1928; Experts are Puzzled, 1930; Progress of Stories, 1935, new edn with additional stories, and new prefatory and supplementary material, 1982; Trojan Ending, 1937; The World and Ourselves, 1938; Collected Poems, 1938, new edn with new preface and extensive appendix 1980; Lives of Wives, 1939; The Telling (a personal evangel-complete magazine publication, Chelsea, USA), 1967, enl. edn in book form, UK 1972, USA 1973; Selected Poems: in five sets, 1970, USA 1973; Writings of 50 Years—Author's Miscellany, entire biannual issue, Chelsea (USA), autumn 1976; Description of Life, 1980; contribs to magazines. *Address*: Box 35, Wabasso, Florida 32970, USA.

RIDLER, Anne (Barbara); author; *b* 30 July 1912; *o d* of late H. C. Bradby, housemaster of Rugby School, and Violet Milford; *m* 1938, Vivian Ridler, *qv*; two *s* two *d*. *Educ*: Downe House School; King's College, London; and in Florence and Rome. *Publications*: *poems*: Poems, 1939; A Dream Observed, 1941; The Nine Bright Shiners, 1943; The Golden Bird, 1951; A Matter of Life and Death, 1959; Selected Poems (New York), 1961; Some Time After, 1972; (contrib.) Ten Oxford Poets, 1978; *plays*: Cain, 1943; The Shadow Factory, 1946; Henry Bly and other plays, 1950; The Trial of Thomas

Cranmer, 1956; Who is my Neighbour?, 1963; The Jesse Tree (libretto), 1972; The King of the Golden River (libretto), 1975; The Lambton Worm (libretto), 1978; *translations*: Italian opera libretti: Rosinda, 1973; Orfeo, 1975; Eritrea, 1975; Return of Ulysses, 1978; Orontea, 1979; Agrippina, 1981; *biography*: Olive Willis and Downe House, 1967; Editor: Shakespeare Criticism, 1919-35; A Little Book of Modern Verse, 1941; Best Ghost Stories, 1945; Supplement to Faber Book of Modern Verse, 1951; The Image of the City and other essays by Charles Williams, 1958; Shakespeare Criticism 1935-60, 1963; Poems of James Thomson, 1963; Thomas Traherne, 1966; (with Christopher Bradby) Best Stories of Church and Clergy, 1966; Selected Poems of George Darley, 1979. *Recreations*: music; the theatre; the cinema. *Address*: 14 Stanley Road, Oxford.

RIDLER, Vivian Hughes, CBE 1971; MA Oxon 1958 (by decree; Corpus Christi College); Printer to the University of Oxford, 1958-78; *b* 2 Oct. 1913; *s* of Bertram Hughes Ridler and Elizabeth Emmeline (*née* Best); *m* 1938, Anne Barbara Bradby (*see* A. B. Ridler); two *s* two *d*. *Educ*: Bristol Gram. Sch. Appren. E. S. & A. Robinson, Ltd, 1931-36. Works Manager University Press, Oxford, 1948; Assistant Printer, 1949-58. Pres., British Federation of Master Printers, 1968-69. Professorial Fellow, St Edmund Hall, 1966, Emeritus Fellow, 1978. *Recreations*: printing, theatre, cinema, cinematography. *Address*: 14 Stanley Road, Oxford. *T*: Oxford 47595.

RIDLEY, family name of **Viscount Ridley**.

RIDLEY, 4th Viscount, *cr* 1900; **Matthew White Ridley**, TD 1960; DL; Baron Wensleydale, *cr* 1900; Bt 1756; *b* 29 July 1925; *e s* of 3rd Viscount Ridley; *S* father, 1964; *m* 1953, Lady Anne Lumley, 3rd *d* of 11th Earl of Scarbrough, KG, PC, GCSI, GCIE, GCVO; one *s* three *d*. *Educ*: Eton; Balliol College, Oxford. ARICS 1951. Captain, Coldstream Guards, 1946; Bt-Col Northumberland Hussars (TA); Hon. Col, Northumberland Hussars Sqdn, Queen's Own Yeomanry, 1979-. Pres., North Eastern Housing Assoc. Ltd; Director: Northern Rock Building Society; Tyne Tees Television; Barclays Bank (NE) Ltd; Municipal Mutual Insurance. Pres., British Deer Soc., 1970-73. Mem., Layfield Cttee of Enquiry into Local Govt Finance, 1974-. Chm., N of England TA Assoc., 1980-. Chm., Newcastle Univ. Develt. Trust, 1981-; Hon. Fellow, Newcastle upon Tyne Polytechnic, 1980. JP 1957, CC 1958, CA 1963, DL 1968, Northumberland; Chm., Northumberland CC, 1967-74, Chm., new Northumberland CC, 1974-79; Pres., ACC, 1979-. Order of Merit, West Germany, 1974. *Heir*: *s* Hon. Matthew White Ridley, *b* 7 Feb. 1958. *Address*: Blagdon, Seaton Burn, Newcastle upon Tyne. *T*: Stannington 236. *Clubs*: Turf, Pratts; Northern Counties (Newcastle upon Tyne).

See also Hon. Nicholas Ridley.

RIDLEY, Arnold, OBE 1982; dramatic author, actor, and producer; *b* Bath, 7 January 1896; *s* of late William Robert Ridley and Rosa Morrish; *m* Althea Parker; one *s*. *Educ*: Bristol University. Formerly a schoolmaster; enlisted, 1915; served in ranks; was severely wounded, Somme, 1916, and discharged 1917; rejoined HM Forces Oct. 1939, served on PR Staff with acting rank of Major BEF, France, 1939-40; joined Birmingham Repertory Company, 1918, and played various parts for several seasons; later with: Plymouth Repertory Company; White Rose Players, Harrogate; Oxford Repertory Theatre Company; original Walter Gabriel in stage version of The Archers; frequent appearances on Television (Harry Crane in BBC series Starr and Co.; The Vicar in Crossroads; Private Godfrey in Dad's Army); also radio: Doughy Hood in The Archers; Crocks, 1960; The Tides of Chance, 1970; author of the following produced plays: The Brass God, 1921; The Ghost Train, 1925; The Burnett Mystery, 1926; The God o' Mud, 1926; The Wrecker (with Bernard Merivale), 1927; Keepers of Youth, 1929; The Flying Fool (with Merivale), 1929; Third Time Lucky, 1929; Recipe for Murder, 1932; Headline, 1934; Half-a-Crown (with Douglas Furber), 1934; Glory Be, 1934; Needs Must, 1938; Out Goes She (with Merivale), 1939; Peril at End House (with Agatha Christie), 1940; Happy Holiday (with Eric Maschwitz), 1954; Tabitha (with Mary Cathcart Borer), 1955; The Running Man (with Anthony Armstrong), 1955; Murder Happens, 1945; Easy Money, 1947; Trifles Light as Air (with St Vincent Troubridge), 1949; East of Ludgate Hill, 1950; The Dark Corridor (with Richard Reich), 1950; Beggar My Neighbour, 1951; You, My Guests!, 1956; Shadows on the Sand (with Borer), 1956; Geranium, 1957; Bellamy (with Anthony Armstrong), 1959; High Fidelity (with Cedric Wallis), 1964; Festive Board, 1970; The Ghost Train, revived 1976; prod the following plays: Sunshine House, Little Theatre 1933; Rude Awakening, Shilling Theatre, 1934; Flood Tide, Phœnix Theatre, 1938; Producer, Malvern Company, 1942-44. Wrote and directed film Royal Eagle, 1935; other films include: East of Ludgate Hill, 1935; Blind Justice, 1935; The Last Chance, 1936; The Seven Sinners, 1936. *Publications*: Keepers of Youth, 1929; various short stories and articles. *Recreations*: Rugby football and cricket; takes active interest in Bath Rugby Club, served as hon. match sec. several years and elected President 1950-52, and Life Member, 1963. *Address*: c/o Hughes Massie & Co., 31 Southampton Row, WC1. *Clubs*: Savage, Dramatists.

RIDLEY, Dame Betty; *see* Ridley, Dame M. B.

RIDLEY, Edward Alexander Keane, CB 1963; Principal Assistant Solicitor, Treasury Solicitor's Department, 1956-69, retired; *b* 16 April 1904; *s* of late Major Edward Keane Ridley, Dudswell House, near Berkhamsted, Herts, and late Ethel Janet Ridley, *d* of Alexander Forbes Tweedie; unmarried. *Educ*: Wellington College; Keble College, Oxford. Admitted Solicitor, 1928. Entered Treasury Solicitor's Department, 1934. Hon. RCM 1977.

Publications: Wind Instruments of European Art Music, 1975; Catalogue of Wind Instruments in the Museum of the Royal College of Music, 1982. *Recreation:* music. *Address:* c/o Coutts & Co., 440 Strand, WC2.

RIDLEY, Prof. Frederick Fernand, OBE 1978; PhD; Professor of Political Theory and Institutions, University of Liverpool, since 1965; *b* 11 Aug. 1928; *s* of late J. and of G. A. Ridley; *m* 1967, Paula Frances Cooper Ridley, *qv*; two *s* one *d. Educ:* The Hall, Hampstead; Highgate Sch.; LSE (BScEcon, PhD); Univs of Paris and Berlin. Lectr in Polit. Theory and Instns, Univ. of Liverpool, 1958–65. Vis. Professor: Graduate Sch. of Public Affairs, Univ. of Pittsburgh, 1968; Coll. of Europe, Bruges, 1975–. Manpower Services Commission: Chm., Job Creation Prog. for Merseyside, 1975–77; Vice-Chm., Special Progs Bd for Merseyside and Cheshire, 1978–. Member: Exec., Merseyside Arts (RAA), 1982–; Bd of Dirs, Merseyside Trng Ltd, 1982–. Member: Jt Univ. Council for Social and Public Admin, 1964– (Chm., 1972–74); Exec., Polit. Studies Assoc., 1967–75; Council, Hansard Soc., 1970–; Polit. Science Cttee, SSRC, 1972–76; Europ. Cttee, Internat. Inst. of Admin. Sciences, Brussels, 1973–; Public and Social Admin Bd, CNAA, 1975–82; Social Studies Res. Cttee, CNAA, 1980– (Chm.); Res. Adv. Gp, Arts Council, 1979–. Hon. Pres., Politics Assoc., 1976–81. Editor: Political Studies, 1969–75; Parliamentary Affairs, 1975–. *Publications:* Public Administration in France, 1964, 2nd edn 1969; (ed) Specialists and Generalists, 1968; Revolutionary Syndicalism in France, 1970; The Study of Government, 1975; (ed) Studies in Politics, 1975; (ed) Government and Administration in W Europe, 1979; articles and revs in academic jls. *Address:* Riversdale House, Grassendale Park, Liverpool L19 0LR. *T:* 051-427 1630.

RIDLEY, Gordon, OBE 1980; FICE, FIMunE, FInstHE; Director of Planning and Transportation, Greater London Council, 1978–80; *b* 1 Nov. 1921; *s* of Timothy Ridley and Lallah Sarah Ridley; *m* 1952, Doreen May Browning; one *s* one *d. Educ:* Selwyn Coll., Cambridge (MA). FICE 1965; FIMunE 1964; FInstHE 1966. Served War, Admiralty Signals Estab., 1941–46. Engrg appts, various local authorities, 1946–55; Bridges Br., MoT, 1955–58; AEA, 1958–63; LCC, 1963–65; engrg appts, GLC, 1965–78. *Publications:* papers on engrg topics presented to learned instns. *Recreations:* words, walking, photography. *Address:* 26 Greenacres, Preston Park Avenue, Brighton BN1 6HR. *T:* Brighton 559951.

RIDLEY, Jasper Godwin; author; *b* 25 May 1920; *s* of Geoffrey Ridley and Ursula (*née* King); *m* 1949, Vera, *d* of Emil Pollak; two *s* one *d. Educ:* Felcourt Sch.; Sorbonne, Paris; Magdalen Coll., Oxford. Certif. of Honour, Bar Finals. Called to Bar, Inner Temple, 1945. St Pancras Borough Council, 1945–49. Pres., Hardwicke Soc., 1954–55. Contested (Lab): Winchester, 1955; Westbury, 1959. Has written many radio scripts on historical subjects. FRSL 1963. *Publications:* Nicholas Ridley, 1957; The Law of Carriage of Goods, 1957; Thomas Cranmer, 1962; John Knox, 1968; Lord Palmerston, 1970 (James Tait Black Meml Prize, 1970); Mary Tudor, 1973; Garibaldi, 1974; The Roundheads, 1976; Napoleon III and Eugénie, 1979; History of England, 1981; The Statesman and the Fanatic: Thomas Wolsey and Thomas More, 1982. *Recreations:* walking, tennis, chess. *Address:* 6 Oakdale Road, Tunbridge Wells, Kent. *T:* Tunbridge Wells 22460.

RIDLEY, Michael Kershaw; Clerk of the Council, Duchy of Lancaster, since 1981; *b* 7 Dec. 1937; *s* of George K. and Mary Ridley; *m* 1968, Diana Loraine McLernon; two *s. Educ:* Stowe; Magdalene College, Cambridge. MA. FRICS. Grosvenor Estate, Canada and USA, 1965–69, London, 1969–72; Property Manager, British & Commonwealth Shipping Co., 1972–81. Mem., Adv. Panel, Greenwich Hosp., 1978–. *Recreation:* golf. *Address:* Duchy Office, Lancaster Place, Strand, WC2. *Club:* Royal Mid-Surrey Golf.

RIDLEY, Dame (Mildred) Betty, DBE 1975; MA (Lambeth) 1958; Third Church Estates Commissioner, 1972–81; a Church Commissioner, 1959–81; *b* 10 Sept. 1909; *d* of late Rt Rev. Henry Mosley, sometime Bishop of Southwell; *m* 1929, Rev. Michael Ridley (*d* 1953), Rector of Finchley; three *s* one *d. Educ:* North London Collegiate School; Cheltenham Ladies' College. Member: General Synod of Church of England, 1970–81, and its Standing Cttee, 1971–81; Central Board of Finance, 1955–79; Mem., Faculty Jurisdiction Commn, 1980–; Vice-Pres. British Council of Churches, 1954–56. *Recreations:* walking, gardening. *Address:* Little Dickers, Hannington, Basingstoke, Hants. *T:* Kingsclere 298191.

RIDLEY, Hon. Nicholas, MICE; MP (C) Cirencester and Tewkesbury Division of Gloucestershire since 1959; Financial Secretary to HM Treasury, since 1981; *b* 17 Feb. 1929; *yr s* of 3rd Viscount Ridley, CBE, TD; *m* 1st, 1950, Hon. Clayre Campbell (marr. diss. 1974), 2nd *d* of 4th Baron Stratheden and Campbell, CBE; three *d*; 2nd, 1979, Judy Kendall. *Educ:* Eton; Balliol College, Oxford. Civil Engineering Contractor, Brims & Co. Ltd, Newcastle upon Tyne, 1950–59, Director, 1954–70; Director: Heenan Group Ltd, 1961–68; Ausonia Finance, 1973–79; Marshall Andrew Ltd, 1975–79. Contested (C) Blyth, Gen. Election, 1955; PPS to Minister of Education, 1962–64; Delegate to Council of Europe and WEU, 1962–66; Parly Sec., Min. of Technology, June–Oct. 1970; Parly Under-Sec. of State, DTI, 1970; Minister of State, FCO, 1979–81. Mem., Royal Commn on Historical Manuscripts, 1967–79. *Recreations:* painting, architecture and fishing. *Address:* Old Rectory, Naunton, Cheltenham, Glos. *T:* Guiting Power 252; 50 Warwick Square, SW1. *T:* 01-828 1816.

RIDLEY, Nicholas Harold Lloyd, MD, FRCS; Hon. Consultant Surgeon, Moorfields Eye Hospital, 1971 (Surgeon, 1938–71); Hon. Consultant Surgeon, Ophthalmic Department, St Thomas' Hospital, 1971 (Ophthalmic Surgeon, 1946–71); *b* 10 July 1906; *s* of late N. C. Ridley, MB (London), FRCS, Royal Navy retired, Leicester; *m* 1941, Elisabeth Jane, *d* of late H. B. Wetherill, CIE; two *s* one *d. Educ:* Charterhouse; Pembroke Coll., Cambridge; St Thomas' Hospital, London. MB 1931, MD 1946, Cambridge; FRCS 1932. Originator in 1949 of intraocular implants. Late Hon. Ophthalmic Surgeon, Royal Buckinghamshire Hospital. Temp. Major, RAMC. Hon. Cons. in Ophthalmology to Min. of Defence (Army), 1964–71; Life Pres., Internat. Intraocular Implants Club, 1972; late Vice-Pres., Ophthalmological Soc. of UK; Mem. Advisory Panel, WHO, 1966–71; Hon. Mem., Oxford Ophthalmological Congress. Hon. Fellow International College of Surgeons, Chicago, 1952; Hon. Member: Peruvian Ophthalmic Society, 1957; Ophthalmological Society of Australia, 1963; Irish Ophthalmological Society; Amer. Intraocular Implants Soc., 1974. *Publications:* Monograph on Ocular Onchocerciasis; numerous contrib. in textbooks and medical journals on intraocular implant surgery and other subjects. *Recreation:* fly-fishing. *Address:* 53 Harley Street, W1N 1DD. *T:* 01-580 1077. *Club:* Flyfishers'.

RIDLEY, Paula Frances Cooper, JP; MA; Member, Independent Broadcasting Authority, since 1982; *b* 27 Sept. 1944; *d* of Ondrej Clyne and Ellen (*née* Cooper); *m* 1967, Frederick Fernand Ridley, *qv*; two *s* one *d. Educ:* Greenhead High Sch., Huddersfield; Kendal High Sch., Westmorland; Univ. of Liverpool. BA, MA; Lady Pres., Guild of Undergraduates. Standing Cttee of Convocation, Univ. of Liverpool, 1966–74 (Clerk of Convocation, 1972–74); Mem., Univ. Court, 1972–. Lectr in Politics and Public Admin., Liverpool Polytechnic, 1966–71; Proj. Coordinator, New Enterprise Workshops, Liverpool, 1981–82. Member: Governing Body, Stocktonwood County Primary Sch., 1970–81 (Chm., 1976–79); Liverpool Heritage Bureau, 1971–; Management Cttee, Liverpool Victoria Settlement, 1971– (Vice-Chm., 1977–); IBA Adv. Cttee for Radio in Liverpool, 1975–78; Barnardo's Intermediate Treatment Adv. Gp in Liverpool, 1980–; Council, Liverpool and Huyton Colls, 1979– (Life Governor); Cttee of Friends of Merseyside Maritime Mus., 1980–82; Hon. Sec., Merseyside Civic Soc., 1971–; Sec., Liverpool City Develt Trust, 1982–. JP Liverpool, 1977; Juvenile Panel, 1979–; Jt Cttee, Juv. Panel and Educn and Social Services Cttees, Liverpool City Council, 1981–. *Address:* Riversdale House, Grassendale Park, Liverpool L19 0LR. *T:* 051-427 1630.

RIDLEY, Philip Waller, CB 1978; CBE 1969; Director: Avon Rubber Co., since 1980; Hill Samuel Developments, since 1980; Programmed Neuro Cybernetics, since 1981; consultant to other companies; *b* 25 March 1921; *s* of Basil White Ridley and Frida (*née* Gutknecht); *m* 1942, Foye Robins; two *s* one *d. Educ:* Lewes County Grammar Sch.; Trinity Coll., Cambridge. Intelligence Corps, 1941–47 (Major); German Section, FO, 1948–51; Min. of Supply, 1951–55; BoT, 1955–56 and 1960–66; Atomic Energy Office, 1956–60; Counsellor (Commercial), British Embassy, Washington, 1966–70; Under-Sec., 1971–75, Dep. Sec., 1975–80, Dept of Industry. *Recreations:* music, gardening, ski-ing, sailing. *Address:* Old Chimneys, Plumpton Green, Lewes, East Sussex. *T:* Plumpton 890342.

RIDLEY, Sir Sidney, Kt 1953; Emeritus Fellow, St John's College, Oxford, 1969 (Fellow, 1962); Indian Civil Service, retired; *b* 26 March 1902; *s* of John William and Elizabeth Janet Ridley; *m* 1929, Dorothy Hoole; three *d. Educ:* Lancaster Royal Grammar Sch.; Sidney Sussex Coll., Cambridge. MA Cantab, MA Oxon. Joined ICS, 1926; Finance Secretary, Govt of Sind, 1936; Secretary to the Agent-General for India in South Africa, 1936–40; Chief Secretary, Govt of Sind, 1944; Commissioner: Northern Division, Ahmedabad, 1946; Central Div., Poona, 1947; Revenue Commissioner in Sind and Secretary to Government, 1947–54. Representative of W Africa Cttee in Ghana, Sierra Leone and the Gambia, 1957–60; Domestic Bursar, St John's Coll., Oxford, 1960–68. *Recreation:* golf. *Address:* Lambrook Cottage, Waytown, Bridport, Dorset. *T:* Netherbury 337. *Club:* East India.

RIDLEY, Tony Melville, PhD; CEng, FICE, FCIT; Managing Director (Railways), London Transport Executive, since 1980; *b* 10 Nov. 1933; *s* of John Edward and Olive Ridley; *m* 1959, Jane (*née* Dickinson); two *s* one *d. Educ:* Durham Sch.; King's Coll. Newcastle, Univ. of Durham (BSc); Northwestern Univ., Ill (MS); Univ. of California, Berkeley (PhD). Nuclear Power Group, 1957–62; Univ. of California, 1962–65; Chief Research Officer, Highways and Transportation, GLC, 1965–69; Director General, Tyne and Wear Passenger Transport Exec., 1969–75; Man. Dir, Hong Kong Mass Transit Rlwy Corp., 1975–80. Dir, Halcrow Fox and Associates, 1980–. Vis. Prof., Imperial Coll., London, 1981–. Pres., Light Rail Transit Assoc., 1974–. FHKIE, MITE. *Publications:* articles in transport, engrg and other jls. *Recreations:* theatre, music, international affairs, rejuvenation of Britain. *Address:* 77 Church Road, Richmond, Surrey TW10 6LX. *T:* 01-948 3898. *Clubs:* Hong Kong, Jockey (Hong Kong).

RIDLEY, William Arnold; *see* Ridley, A.

RIDLEY, Rear-Adm. William Terence Colborne, CB 1968; OBE 1954; Admiral Superintendent/Port Admiral, Rosyth, 1966–72; Chairman, Ex-Services Mental Welfare Society, since 1973; *b* 9 March 1915; *s* of late Capt. W. H. W. Ridley, RN and late Vera Constance (*née* Walker); *m* 1938, Barbara Allen; one *s. Educ:* Emsworth House; RNC, Dartmouth (Robert Roxburgh Prize); RNEC, Keyham. HMS Exeter, 1936; HMS Valiant, 1939;

HMS Firedrake, 1940 (despatches twice); E-in-C Dept Admty, 1941; HMS Indefatigable, 1944; Admty Fuel Experimental Stn, 1947; Seaslug Project Officer, RAE Farnborough, 1950; HMS Ark Royal, 1956; E-in-C Dept Admty, Dreadnought Project Team, 1958; CO, RNEC, 1962; Staff of C-in-C Portsmouth, 1964. Lt-Comdr 1944; Comdr 1947; Capt. 1957; Rear-Adm. 1966. *Recreations:* gardening, botany, caravanning, do-it-yourself. *Address:* The Green, Brompton Ralph, Taunton, Somerset. *T:* Wiveliscombe 23305.

RIDSDALE, Sir Julian (Errington), Kt 1981; CBE 1977; MP (C) Harwich Division of Essex, since Feb. 1954; *b* 8 June 1915; *m* 1942, Victoire Evelyn Patricia Bennett; one *d. Educ:* Tonbridge; Sandhurst. 2nd Lieutenant, Royal Norfolk Regiment, 1935; attached British Embassy, Tokyo, 1938-39; served War of 1939-45: Royal Norfolk Regt, Royal Scots, and Somerset Light Infantry; GSO3, Far Eastern Sect., War Office, 1941; GSO2, Joint Staff Mission, Washington, 1944-45; retired from Army with rank of Major, 1946. Contested SW Islington (C), LCC, 1949, N Paddington (C), Gen. Elec., 1951. PPS to Parly Under-Sec. of State for Colonies, 1957-58; PPS to Minister of State for Foreign Affairs, 1958-60; Parly Under-Sec. of State: for Air and Vice-President of the Air Council, 1962-64; for Defence for the Royal Air Force, Ministry of Defence, April-Oct. 1964. Chm., British Japanese Parly Group, 1964-; Vice-Chm., UN Parly Assoc., 1966-82; Mem., Select Cttee of Public Accounts, 1970-74. Leader, Parly Delegns to Japan, 1973, 1975, and annually 1977-. Member: Trilateral Commn, EEC, USA and Japan, 1973-; North Atlantic Assembly, 1979-. Dep. Chm., Internat. Triangle, USA, Japan and Europe, 1981-. Chm., Japan Soc., London, 1976-79. Master, Skinners' Co., 1970-71. Order of the Sacred Treasure, Japan. *Recreations:* tennis, chess, gardening, travelling, and sailing. *Address:* 12 The Boltons, SW10. *T:* 01-373 6159; Fiddan, St Osyth, Essex. *T:* St Osyth 367. *Clubs:* Carlton, MCC, Hurlingham; Frinton Tennis.

RIE, Lucie, CBE 1981 (OBE 1968); studio potter since 1927; *b* 16 March 1902; *d* of Prof. Dr Benjamin and Gisela Gomperz. *Educ:* Vienna Gymnasium (matriculate); Kunstgewerbe Schule. Pottery workshop: Vienna, 1927; London, 1939. Work included in V&A Museum, Fitzwilliam Museum, Cambridge Museum, Boymans-van Beuningen Museum, Stedelijk Museum, Museum of Modern Art, NY, Aust. Nat. Gall., Canberra, and other public collections in England and abroad. Exhibitions include: Arts Council retrospective, 1967; (with Hans Coper) Boymans-van Beuningen Museum, 1967; Expo '70, Osaka, 1970; (with Hans Coper) Museum of Art and Crafts, Hamburg, 1972; Hetjens Museum, Düsseldorf, 1978; retrospective, Sainsbury Centre and V&A Mus, 1981-82. Gold medals: Internat. Exhibn, Brussels, 1935; Trienniale, Milan, 1936, 1954; Internat. Exhib., Munich, 1964. Hon. Doctor, Royal College of Art, 1969.

RIFKIND, Malcolm Leslie; MP (C) Edinburgh, Pentlands, since Feb. 1974; Parliamentary Under Secretary of State, Foreign and Commonwealth Office, since 1982; *b* 21 June 1946; *yr s* of E. Rifkind, Edinburgh; *m* 1970, Edith Amalia Rifkind (*née* Steinberg); one *s* one *d. Educ:* George Watson's Coll.; Edinburgh Univ. LLB, MSc. Lectured at Univ. of Rhodesia, 1967-68. Called to Scottish Bar, 1970. Contested (C) Edinburgh, Central, 1970. Opposition front-bench spokesman on Scottish Affairs, 1975-76; Parly Under Sec. of State, Scottish Office, 1979-82. Chm., Scottish Cons. Devolution Cttee, 1976; Jt Sec., Cons. Foreign and Commonwealth Affairs Cttee, 1978; Member: Select Cttee on Europ. Secondary Legislation, 1975-76; Select Cttee on Overseas Develt, 1978-79. Hon. Pres., Scottish Young Conservatives, 1975-76. *Address:* House of Commons, SW1. *Club:* New (Edinburgh).

RIGBY, Bryan; Deputy Director-General, Confederation of British Industry, since 1978; *b* 9 Jan. 1933; *s* of William George Rigby and Lily Rigby; *m* 1978, Marian Rosamund; one *s* one *d* of a former marriage, and one step *s* one step *d. Educ:* Wigan Grammar Sch.; King's Coll., London (BSc Special Chemistry, Dip. Chem. Engrg). UKAEA Industrial Gp, Capenhurst, 1955-60; Beecham Gp, London and Amsterdam, 1960-64; Laporte Industries (Holdings) Ltd, 1964-78. *Recreations:* music, squash, golf, gardening. *Address:* Cluny, 61 Penn Road, Beaconsfield, Bucks HP9 2LW. *T:* Beaconsfield 3206. *Club:* Reform.

RIGBY, Herbert Cecil, DFC 1943, and Bar 1944; **His Honour Judge Rigby;** a Circuit Judge since 1980; Senior Partner, H. P. & H. C. Rigby, Solicitors, Sandbach, Cheshire; *b* 2 April 1917; *s* of Captain Herbert Parrot Rigby, TD; *m* 1st, 1939, Ethel Muriel Horton; two *d*; 2nd, 1949, Florence Rita Scotts; one *s. Educ:* Sandbach Sch.; Ellesmere Coll.; Liverpool Univ. (Law Faculty). Articled R. S. Rigby, Winsford. Commissioned, 7th Cheshire Regt, 1937. Served War: Expeditionary Force, France, 1939; evacuated, Dunkirk, 1940; transfer to RAF, 1941; Wings, 11 Gp, Hornchurch (Spitfires), 1942; Landing, N Africa, 1942; commanded 222 Sqdn, Invasion of France, 1944-45 (Bt Militaire de Pilote D'Avion, 1945); demobilised, 1946. Commanded 610 City of Chester Auxiliary Sqdn, 1947-49. Law Final, and admitted solicitor, 1947; a Recorder of the Crown Court, Wales and Chester Circuit, 1972-80. *Recreations:* fishing, golf, boating, gardening. *Address:* Shelbourne, New Platt Lane, Cranage, *via* Crewe, Cheshire.

RIGBY, Lt-Col Sir (Hugh) John (Macbeth), 2nd Bt, *cr* 1929; ERD and 2 clasps; Director, Executors of James Mills Ltd, retired 1977; *b* 1 Sept. 1914; *s* of Sir Hugh Mallinson Rigby, 1st Bt, and Flora (*d* 1970), *d* of Norman Macbeth; *S* father, 1944; *m* 1946, Mary Patricia Erskine Leacock; four *s. Educ:* Rugby; Magdalene Coll., Cambridge. Lt-Col RCT, retd, 1967. *Heir: s*

Anthony John Rigby [*b* 3 Oct. 1946; *m* 1978, Mary, *e d* of R. G. Oliver, Hope Green, Adlington, Macclesfield; two *s*]. *Address:* 5 Park Street, Macclesfield, Cheshire SK11 6SR. *T:* Macclesfield 613959; Casa das Palmeiras, Armação de Pêra, 8365 Alcantarilha, Algarve, Portugal. *T:* 82-32548.

RIGBY, Sir Ivo (Charles Clayton), Kt 1964; a Metropolitan Stipendiary Magistrate, since 1976; a Recorder of the Crown Court, since 1975; *b* 2 June 1911; *s* of late James Philip Clayton Rigby and late Elisabeth Mary Corbett; *m* 1st, 1938, Agnes Bothway; 2nd, Kathleen Nancy, *d* of late Dr W. E. Jones, CMG; no *c. Educ:* Magdalen College School, Oxford. Called to the Bar (Inner Temple), 1932; Magistrate, Gambia, 1935-38; Chief Magistrate, Crown Counsel, and President of a District Court, Palestine, 1938-48; Assistant Judge, Nyasaland, 1948-54; President of Sessions Court, Malaya, 1954-55; Puisne Judge, Malaya, 1956-61; Senior Puisne Judge, Hong Kong, 1961-70; Chief Justice of Hong Kong and of Brunei, 1970-73; Pres., Court of Appeal, Brunei, 1973-79. *Publications:* The Law Reports of Nyasaland, 1934-1952. *Recreations:* squash, cricket and bridge. *Address:* 8 More's Garden, Cheyne Walk, SW3. *T:* 01-352 0120. *Clubs:* Naval and Military, Hurlingham, East India, Devonshire, Sports and Public Schools, MCC; Hong Kong.

RIGBY, Sir John; see Rigby, Sir H. J. M.

RIGBY, Norman Leslie; Chairman, Allan H. Williams Ltd and associated companies, since 1981; *b* 27 June 1920; *s* of Leslie Rigby and Elsie Lester Wright; *m* 1950, Mary Josephine Calderhead; two *d* (one *s* decd). *Educ:* Cowley Sch., St Helens. Served RAF, 1939-45, War Intell. Officer to Free French Air Force. Management Trainee, Simon Engineering Group, 1946-48; Marketing Exec., Procter & Gamble Ltd, 1948-55; Marketing Dir, Macleans Ltd (Beecham Group), 1955-59; Nabisco Ltd: Marketing Dir 1959; Man. Dir 1960; Vice-Chm. 1962; Chm. 1964; Industrial Adviser, 1968-70, Co-ordinator of Industrial Advisers, HM Govt, 1969-70. Dir, 1970-80, Divisional Man. Dir, 1977-80, Spillers Ltd. Independent Mem., EDC for Agriculture, 1978-80. CBIM. *Recreations:* gardening, golf. *Address:* 38 West Common Way, Harpenden, Herts. *T:* Harpenden 5448.

RIGBY, Reginald Francis, TD 1950 and Clasp 1952; a Recorder of the Crown Court, since 1977; Partner, Rigby, Rowley Cooper & Co., Solicitors, Newcastle-under-Lyme; *b* Rudyard, Staffs, 22 June 1919; *s* of Reginald Rigby, FRIBA, FRICS, and Beatrice May Rigby, *d* of John Frederick Green, Woodbridge, Suffolk; *m* 1949, Joan Edwina, *d* of Samuel E. M. Simpson, Newcastle-under-Lyme, and of Dorothy C. Simpson; two *s. Educ:* Manchester Grammar Sch.; Victoria Univ., Manchester. Solicitor, 1947, Hons; John Peacock and George Hadfield Prizeman, Law Society Art Prize, 1962. Served War: commissioned 2nd Lieut 41 Bn, Royal Tank Corps, TA, 1939; served AFV Sch.; volunteered for maritime service: Captain in RASC motor boat companies in home coastal waters, India, Burma, Malaya and its Archipelago; demob. 1946; Major, QORR, The Staffordshire Yeomanry. Mem., Market Drayton RDC, 1966-71; Chm., Woore Parish Council, 1971-79; Hon. Sec., North Staffs Forces Help Soc.; Mem., Staffs War Pensions Cttee; Member: 1745 Assoc. and Mil. Hist. Soc.; Staffordshire Record Soc.; Lancs and Cheshire Record Soc.; Lancs and Cheshire Hist. Soc.; Cheetham Soc.; Lancs Parish Register Soc.; Shropshire and West Midlands Agricl Soc.; Pres., Uttoxeter Flyfishing Club, 1975-77; Trustee, Birdsgrove Flyfishing Club, Ashbourne. Life Mem., Clan Morrison Soc. Member, Military and Hospitaller Order of St Lazarus of Jerusalem. *Recreations:* fishing, shooting. *Address:* The Rookery, Woore, Salop CW3 9RG. *T:* Pipe Gate 414. *Clubs:* Army and Navy, Flyfishers'.

RIGG, Diana; actress; *b* Doncaster, Yorks, 20 July 1938; *d* of Louis Rigg and Bery Helliwell; *m* 1982, Archibald Stirling; one *d. Educ:* Fulneck Girls' Sch., Pudsey. Trained for the stage at Royal Academy of Dramatic Art. First appearance on stage in RADA prod. in York Festival, at Theatre Royal, York, summer, 1957 (Natella Abashwili in The Caucasian Chalk Circle); after appearing in repertory in Chesterfield and in York she joined the Royal Shakespeare Company, Stratford-upon-Avon, 1959; first appearance in London, Aldwych Theatre, 1961 (2nd Ondine and Violanta in Ondine); at same theatre, in repertory (The Devils, Becket, The Taming of the Shrew), 1961; (The Art of Seduction), 1962; Royal Shakespeare, Stratford-upon-Avon, Apr. 1962 (Helena in A Midsummer Night's Dream, Bianca in The Taming of the Shrew, Lady Macduff in Macbeth, Adriana in The Comedy of Errors, Cordelia in King Lear); subseq. appeared in the last production at the Aldwych, Dec. 1962, followed by Adriana in The Comedy of Errors and Monica Stettler in The Physicists, 1963. Toured the provinces, spring, 1963, in A Midsummer Night's Dream; subseq. appeared at the Royal Shakespeare, Stratford, and at the Aldwych, in Comedy of Errors, Dec. 1963; again played Cordelia in King Lear, 1964, prior to touring with both plays for the British Council, in Europe, the USSR, and the US; during this tour she first appeared in New York (State Theatre), 1964, in same plays; Viola in Twelfth Night, Stratford, June 1966; Heloise in Abelard and Heloise, Wyndham's, 1970, also at the Atkinson, New York, 1971; joined The National Theatre, 1972: in Jumpers, 'Tis Pity She's a Whore and Lady Macbeth in Macbeth, 1972; The Misanthrope, 1973, Washington and NY, 1975; Phaedra Britannica, 1975 (Plays and Players Award for Best Actress); The Guardsman, 1978; Pygmalion, Albery, 1974; Night and Day, Phoenix, 1978 (Plays and Players award, 1979); Colette, USA, 1982; *films include:* A Midsummer Night's Dream, Assassination Bureau, On Her Majesty's Secret Service, Julius Caesar, The Hospital, Theatre of Blood, A Little Night Music, Evil Under the Sun; *TV appearances include:* Sentimental Agent, The Comedy of Errors, The

Avengers, Married Alive, Diana (US series), In This House of Brede (US), Three Piece Suite, The Serpent Son, Hedda Gabler, The Marquise, Little Eyolf, and others. *Publication:* No Turn Unstoned, 1982. *Recreations:* reading and trying to get organized. *Address:* c/o London Management, 235 Regent Street, W1A 2JT.

RIGNEY, Howard Ernest; HM Diplomatic Service, retired; Consul-General, Lyons, 1977–82; *b* 22 June 1922; *o s* of late Wilbert Ernest and Minnie Rigney; *m* 1950, Margaret Grayling Benn; one *s*. *Educ:* Univs of Western Ontario, Toronto and Paris. BA Western Ont. 1945, MA Toronto 1947. Lectr, Univ. of British Columbia, 1946–48; grad. studies, Paris Univ., 1948–50; COI, 1953–56; CRO, 1956; Regional Information Officer, Dacca, 1957–60, Montreal, 1960–63; CRO, 1963–65; FO/CO, 1965–67; Consul (Information), Chicago, 1967–69; Dep. Consul-Gen., Chicago, 1969–71; Head of Chancery and Consul, Rangoon, 1971–73; Head of Migration and Visa Dept, FCO, 1973–77. Hon DLitt, Winston Churchill Coll., Ill, 1971. *Recreations:* opera, book-collecting, gardening, golf. *Address:* c/o Lloyds Bank Ltd, 6 Pall Mall, SW1. *Clubs:* Cercle de l'Union (Lyon), Golf Club de Lyon.

RILEY, Bridget Louise, CBE 1972; Artist; *b* 24 April 1931; *d* of John Riley and late Louise (*née* Gladstone). *Educ:* Cheltenham Ladies' College; Goldsmiths' School of Art; Royal College of Art. ARCA 1955. AICA critics Prize, 1963; Stuyvesant Bursary, 1964; Ohara Mus. Prize, Tokyo, 1972; Gold Medal, Grafik Biennale, Norway, 1980. Mem., RSA. One-man shows: London, 1962, 1963, 1969, 1971 (retrospective, at Hayward Gall.), 1976, 1981; New York, Los Angeles, 1965; New York, 1967, 1975, 1978; Hanover, 1970; Turin, Düsseldorf, Berne, Prague, 1971; Basle, 1975; Sydney, 1976; Tokyo, 1977; touring retrospective, USA, Aust. and Japan, 1978–80. Exhibited in group shows: England, France, Israel, America, Germany, Italy. Represented Britain: Paris Biennale, 1965; Venice Biennale, 1968 (awarded Chief internat. painting prize). Public collections include: Tate Gallery, Victoria and Albert Museum, Arts Council, British Council, Museum of Modern Art, New York, Museum of Modern Art, Pasadena, Ferens Art Gallery, Hull, Allbright Knox, Buffalo, USA, Museum of Contemporary Art, Chicago, Ulster Museum, Ireland, Stedelijk Museum, Berne Kunsthalle. Trustee, Nat. Gallery, 1981–. Hon. DLit Manchester, 1976.

RILEY, Harry Lister, DSc, ARCS, DIC, FRIC; Consultant; *b* 7 Sept. 1899; *s* of late Arthur Riley, Keighley, Yorks; *m* 1924, Marion, *o c* of David Belfield; two *s* one *d*. *Educ:* The Grammar School, Keighley; Imperial College of Science and Technology (Royal College of Science). Served with 9th Bn KOYLI, 1917–19. Beit Scientific Research Fellow, 1921–23; Demonstrator, and later Lecturer in Chemistry at the Royal College of Science, South Kensington, SW7, 1923–32; Professor of Inorganic and Physical Chemistry, King's Coll. (Univ. of Durham), Newcastle on Tyne, 1932–47; Hon. Secretary and Dir of Research to the Northern Coke Research Committee; Jubilee Memorial Lecturer, Society of Chemical Industry, 1938–39; Director of Chemical Research and Development, United Steel Companies Ltd, 1947–64; Dir of carbonization research, Nat. Coal Board, 1947. *Publications:* various research publications in The Journal of the Chemical Society, the Philosophical Magazine, the Geological Magazine, and the Proceedings of the Royal Society, etc. *Recreation:* golf. *Address:* 12 Willow Place, Ponteland, Newcastle upon Tyne NE20 9RL.

RILEY, Ralph, DSc; FRS 1967; Secretary, Agricultural Research Council, since 1978; *b* 23 Oct. 1924; *y c* of Ralph and Clara Riley; *m* 1949, Joan Elizabeth Norrington; two *d*. *Educ:* Audenshaw Gram. Sch.; Univ. of Sheffield. Infantry Soldier, 1943–47; Univ. of Sheffield, 1947–52; Research worker, Plant Breeding Inst., Cambridge, 1952–78; Head of Cytogenetics Dept, 1954–72; Dir, 1971–78. National Research Council/Nuffield Foundn Lectr at Canadian Univs, 1966; Special Prof. of Botany, Univ. of Nottingham, 1970–78. Fellow of Wolfson Coll., Cambridge, 1967–. William Bate Hardy Prize, Cambridge Phil. Soc., 1969. Sir Henry Tizard Meml Lectr, 1973; Holden Lectr, Univ. of Nottingham, 1975; Woodhull Lectr, Royal Instn, 1976; Bewley Lectr, Glasshouse Crops Res. Inst., 1980. Pres., Genetical Soc., 1973–75; Sec., Internat. Genetics Fedn, 1973–78; Pres., Sect. K, BAAS, 1979. For. Correspondent, Acad. d'Agriculture de France, 1981. For. Fellow, Indian Nat. Sci. Acad., 1976; For. Associate, Nat. Acad. Scis, USA, 1982. Hon. FRASE, 1980. Royal Medal, Royal Soc., 1981. Hon. DSc: Edinburgh, 1976; Hull, 1982. *Publications:* scientific papers and articles on genetics of chromosome behaviour, plant cytogenetics and evolution and breeding of crop plants especially wheat. *Address:* 1 Oslo Court, Prince Albert Road, NW8 7EN. *T:* 01-722 3868. *Club:* Athenæum.

RIMBAULT, Brig. Geoffrey Acworth, CBE 1954; DSO 1945; MC 1936; DL; Director, Army Sport Control Board, 1961–73; *b* 17 April 1908; *s* of late Arthur Henry Rimbault, London; *m* 1933, Joan, *d* of late Thomas Hallet-Fry, Beckenham, Kent; one *s*. *Educ:* Dulwich College. 2nd Lieut, The Loyal Regt (N Lancs) 1930; served: India, Waziristan, 1931–36; Palestine, 1937; Staff Coll., Camberley; N Africa, Anzio, Italy and Palestine, 1939–46; Chief Instructor, RMA Sandhurst, 1950–51; Chief of Staff, E Africa, 1952–54; comd 131 Inf. Bde, 1955–57; comd Aldershot Garrison, 1958–61. Colonel, The Loyal Regt, 1959–70. Life Vice-Pres., Surrey CCC (Pres., 1982–83). Liveryman, Mercers' Co., 1961, Master, 1970–71. DL Surrey, 1971. *Recreations:* cricket, tennis, golf, shooting. *Address:* 10 Clarke Place, Elmbridge, Cranleigh, Surrey. *T:* Cranleigh 71207. *Clubs:* Army and Navy, MCC.

RIMINGTON, Claude, FRS 1954, MA, PhD Cantab, DSc London; Emeritus Professor of Chemical Pathology, University of London; Head of Department of Chemical Pathology, University College Hospital Medical School, 1945–67; *b* 17 Nov. 1902; *s* of George Garthwaite Rimington, Newcastle-on-Tyne; *m* 1929, Soffi, *d* of Clemet Andersen, Askerøy, Lyngør, Norway; one *d*. *Educ:* Emmanuel College, Cambridge. Benn W. Levy Research Scholar, Univ. of Cambridge, 1926–28; Biochemist, Wool Industries Research Association, Leeds, 1928–30; Empire Marketing Board Senior Research Fellow, then Scientific Research Officer, Division of Veterinary Services, Govt of Union of South Africa, at Onderstepoort Veterinary Research Laboratory, Pretoria, 1931–37; Biochemist, National Institute for Medical Research, Medical Research Council, London, 1937–45. Hon. FRCP Edinburgh, 1967; Hon. Mem. Brit. Assoc. of Dermatology, 1967. Graham Gold Medal, Univ. of London, 1967. *Publications:* (with A. Goldberg), Diseases of Porphyrin Metabolism, 1962; numerous biochemical and scientific papers. *Recreations:* sailing, languages, Scandinavian literature. *Address:* Askerøy, Per Vestre Sandøy 4915, Norway.

RIMINGTON, John David; Director, Safety Policy Division, Health and Safety Executive, since 1981; *b* 27 June 1935; *s* of John William Rimington and Mabel Dorrington; *m* 1963, Stella Whitehouse; two *d*. *Educ:* Nottingham High Sch.; Jesus Coll., Cambridge (Cl. I Hons History, MA). Nat. Service Commn, RA, 1954–56. Joined BoT, 1959; seconded HM Treasury (work on decimal currency), 1961; Principal, Tariff Div., BoT, 1963; 1st Sec. (Economic), New Delhi, 1965; Mergers Div., DTI, 1969; Dept of Employment, 1970; Asst Sec. 1972 (Employment Policy and Manpower); Counsellor, Social and Regional Policy, UK perm. representation to EEC, Brussels, 1974; MSC, 1977–81; Under Sec. 1978. *Recreations:* walking, thinking, watching cricket. *Address:* 8 Alwyne Place, N1. *T:* 01-226 3522.

RIMMER, Prof. Frederick William, CBE 1980; MA (Cantab), BMus (Dunelm); FRCO; FRSAMD; Gardiner Professor of Music, University of Glasgow, 1966–80, now Emeritus Professor; Director of Scottish Music Archive, 1968–80; Organ Recitalist; *b* 21 Feb. 1914; 2nd *s* of William Rimmer and Amy Graham McMillan, Liverpool; *m* 1941, Joan Doreen, *d* of Major Alexander Hume Graham and Beatrice Cecilia Myles; two *s* one *d*. *Educ:* Quarry Bank High Sch., Liverpool. FRCO (Harding Prize), 1934; BMus (Dunelm), 1939. Served War: 11th Bn, The Lancashire Fusiliers, Middle East, 1941–45 (Maj. 1944). Selwyn Coll., Cambridge (Organ Scholar), 1946–48; Sen. Lecturer in Music, Homerton Coll., Cambridge, 1948–51; Cramb Lectr in Music, Univ. of Glasgow, 1951–56; Sen. Lectr, 1956–66, and Organist to the Univ., 1954–66. Henrietta Harvey Vis. Prof., Memorial Univ. of Newfoundland, 1977. A Dir of Scottish Opera, 1966–80; Chm., BBC's Scottish Music Adv. Cttee, 1972–77; Mem., Music Adv. Cttee, British Council, 1973–, Scottish Adv. Cttee, 1979–. Special Award for services to contemp. music in Scotland, Composers' Guild of GB, 1975. *Publications:* contrib. to: A History of Scottish Music, 1973; Companion to Scottish Culture, 1981; articles on 20th century music, in: Tempo; Music Review; Organists' Review; compositions for solo organ: Five Preludes on Scottish Psalm Tunes, Pastorale and Toccata, Invenzione e Passacaglia Capricciosa; anthems for choir and organ: Sing we merrily; Christus natus est alleluia; O Lord, we beseech thee; O Blessed God in Trinity; Five carols of the Nativity. *Recreations:* reading and gardening. *Address:* Manor Farmhouse, 6 Mill Way, Grantchester, Cambridge CB3 9NB. *T:* Cambridge 840716.

RINFRET, Hon. Gabriel-Edouard; PC (Canada) 1949; Chief Justice of Québec, 1977–80, retired; Counsel, Pepin, Le Tourneau and Associates, since 1981; *b* St-Jérôme, PQ, 12 May 1905; *s* of Rt Hon. Thibaudeau Rinfret, Chief Justice of Canada, and Georgine, *d* of S. J. B. Rolland; *m* 1929; two *s*. *Educ:* Collège Notre-Dame, Côte des Neiges, PQ; Petit Séminaire, Montréal; Collège Ste-Marie (BA with distinction); McGill Univ. (LLM with distinction); pupil of Hon. J. L. Perron. Admitted to practice, 1928; joined law office of Campbell, McMaster, Couture, Kerry and Bruneau; partner, Campbell, Weldon, MacFarlane and Rinfret, 1945. KC 1943. Sec. or Legal Adviser to various provincial govt commns of enquiry, 1934–45. Pres., Jeunesse Libérale de Montréal, 1934; Co-founder and 1st Pres., Assoc. de la Jeunesse Libérale de la Province de Québec, 1934–35; MP (L) Outremont, 1945–49, Outremont-St Jean 1949–52, House of Commons of Canada; Postmaster General in St Laurent Cabinet. A Judge of the Court of Appeal of Québec, 1952–80. Pres. or Director: Concerts Symphoniques de Montréal; Inst. Internat. de Musique; Grands Ballets Canadiens; Dominion Drama Festival (organised Montréal Festival, 1961; Pres., W Québec Region, and Mem., Nat. Exec. Cttee, 1962–68; Canadian Drama Award, 1969); Vice Pres., Conservatoire Lassalle, 1967–. Hon. LLD, Univ. of British Columbia, 1979. *Publications:* Répertoire du théâtre canadien d'expression française, vol. 1, 1975, vol. 2, 1976, vol. 3, 1977, vol. 4, 1978. *Recreations:* cabinet-work, Canadian paintings; formerly baseball, lacrosse, tennis, hockey, ski-ing. *Address:* 121 Melbourne Avenue, Town of Mount Royal, Québec, H3P 1G3, Canada.

RING, Prof. James; Professor of Physics, Imperial College of Science and Technology, since 1967; *b* 22 Aug. 1927; *s* of James and Florence Ring; *m* 1949, Patricia, *d* of Major H. J. Smith, MBE; two *s*. *Educ:* Univ. of Manchester (BSc, PhD). FInstP, FRAS. Reader in Spectrometry, Univ. of Manchester, 1957; Prof. of Applied Physics, Hull Univ., 1962. Member: IBA, 1974–81; Inquiry into Cable Expansion and Broadcasting Policy, 1982. *Publications:* numerous papers and articles in learned jls. *Recreations:* stargazing, dinghy sailing. *Address:* 8 Riverview Gardens, Barnes, SW13.

RING, Sir Lindsay (Roberts), GBE 1975; JP; Chairman, Ring & Brymer (Birchs) Ltd; Lord Mayor of London for 1975-76; *b* 1 May 1914; *y s* of George Arthur Ring and Helen Rhoda Mason Ring (*née* Stedman); *m* 1940, Hazel Doris, *d* of A. Trevor Nichols, CBE; *two s* one *d. Educ:* Dulwich Coll.; Mecklenburg, Germany. Served 1939-45, Europe and Middle East, Major RASC. Underwriting Member of Lloyd's, 1964. Fellow, Hotel and Catering Inst.; Chm., Hotel and Catering Trades Benevolent Assoc., 1962-71; Member: Bd of Verge of Royal Palaces; Gaming Bd for GB, 1977-; NI Develt Agency. Chancellor, City Univ., 1975-76. Governor, Farringtons Sch. Hon. Treasurer, Church Army Housing. Freeman, City of London, 1935; Mem. Court of Assistants, Armourers' and Brasiers' Co., Master 1972; Common Councilman, City of London (Ward of Bishopsgate), 1964-68; Alderman (Ward of Vintry), 1968; Sheriff, City of London, 1967-68; Governor, Hon. Irish Soc., 1980-. HM Lieut for City of London; JP Inner London, 1964. Hon. Col, 151 (Greater London) Regt, RCT(V). Hon. Burgess, Borough of Coleraine, NI. KStJ 1976. FCIS 1976. Hon. DSc City Univ., 1976; Hon. DLitt Ulster, 1976. Comdr, Legion of Honour, 1976; Order of Rio Branca (Brazil), 1976. *Address:* Chalvedune, Wilderness Road, Chislehurst, Kent, BR7 5EY. *T:* 01-467 3199. *Club:* City Livery.

RINGADOO, Hon. Sir Veerasamy, Kt 1975; Officier de l'Ordre National Malgache 1969; Minister of Finance, Mauritius, 1968-82; *b* 1920; *s* of Nagaya Ringadoo; *m* 1954, Lydie Vadamootoo; *one s* one *d. Educ:* Port Louis Grammar Sch.; LSE Eng. (LLB); Hon. Fellow, 1976. Called to Bar, 1949; Municipal Councillor, 1956; MLC for Moka-Flacq, 1951-67; Minister: Labour and Social Scurity, 1959-64; Education, 1964-67; Agriculture and Natural Resources, 1967-68; attended London Constitutional Conf., 1965; first MLA (Lab) for Quartier Militaire and Moka, 1967, re-elected 1976. Governor, IMF; Chm., Bd of Governors, African Development Bank and African Development Fund, 1977-78. Hon. Fellow, LSE, 1976. Hon LLD Mauritius, 1975; Hon. DLit Andhra, 1978. *Address:* Port Louis, Mauritius.

RINGROSE, Prof. John Robert, FRS 1977; FRSE; Professor of Pure Mathematics, University of Newcastle upon Tyne, since 1964; *b* 21 Dec. 1932; *s* of Albert Frederick Ringrose and Elsie Lilian Ringrose (*née* Roberts); *m* 1956, Jean Margaret Bates; *three s. Educ:* Buckhurst Hill County High School, Chigwell, Essex; St John's Coll., Cambridge (MA, PhD). Lecturer in Mathematics: King's Coll., Newcastle upon Tyne, 1957-61; Univ. of Cambridge (also Fellow of St John's Coll.), 1961-63; Sen. Lectr in Mathematics, Univ. of Newcastle upon Tyne, 1963-64. *Publications:* Compact Non-self-adjoint Operators, 1971; mathematical papers in various research jls. *Address:* School of Mathematics, The University, Newcastle upon Tyne NE1 7RU. *T:* Newcastle upon Tyne 328511.

RINGWOOD, Prof. Alfred Edward, FAA 1966; FRS 1972; Professor of Geochemistry, since 1967, Director, Research School of Earth Sciences, since 1978, Australian National University; *b* 19 April 1930; *s* of Alfred Edward Ringwood and Wilhelmena Grace Bruce Ringwood (*née* Robertson); *m* 1960, Gun Ivor Karlsson, Halsingborg, Sweden; *one s* one *d. Educ:* Hawthorn Central Sch., Melbourne; Geelong Grammar Sch.; Melbourne Univ. BSc 1950, MSc 1953, PhD 1956, Melbourne. Research Fellow, Geochemistry, Harvard Univ., 1957-58; Australian National Univ.: Sen. Res. Fellow, 1959; Sen. Fellow, 1960; Personal Prof., 1963. William Smith Lectr, Geol Soc. of London, 1973; Vernadsky Lectr, USSR Acad. of Scis, 1975; Centenary Lectr and Medallist, Chem. Soc., London, 1977; Matthew Flinders Lecture, Australian Acad. of Sci., 1978. Commonwealth and Foreign Mem., Geol Soc., London, 1967; Fellow, Amer. Geophysical Union, 1969; Vice-Pres., Australian Acad. of Science, 1971. For. Associate, Nat. Acad. of Scis of Amer., 1975; Hon. Mem., All-Union Mineralog. Soc., USSR, 1976. Mineralogical Soc. of America Award, 1967; Britannica Australia Award for Science, 1969; Rosentiel Award, Miami Univ., 1971; Werner Medaille, German Mineralogical Soc., 1972; Bowie Medal, American Geophysical Union, 1974; Day Medal, Geological Soc. of America, 1974; Mueller Medal, Aust. and NZ Assoc. for Advancement of Sci., 1975. *Publications:* Composition and Petrology of the Earth's Mantle, 1975; Safe Disposal of High Level Nuclear Reactor Wastes: a new strategy, 1978; Origin of Earth and Moon, 1979; numerous papers in learned jls dealing with nature of earth's interior, phase transformations under high pressures, origin and evolution of earth, moon, planets and meteorites, and safe immobilization of high level nuclear reactor wastes. *Recreations:* music, travel. *Address:* 3 Vancouver Street, Red Hill, Canberra, ACT 2603, Australia. *T:* Canberra 95-9929.

RINK, George Arnold, QC 1956; *b* 21 April 1902; *m* 1949, Dr Margaret Joan Suttill, *qv. Educ:* Charterhouse; University College, Oxford. 1st Cl. Hon. Mods, and Lit. Hum.; BCL; MA; half-blue for fencing. Called to Bar, 1926, and practised at the Chancery Bar from then until 1980 except for war-time service in Trading with the Enemy Br. and Mins of Food and Production; Bencher of Lincoln's Inn, 1962- (Treasurer 1978). Chm., Licensed Dealers' Tribunal, 1968-76. Mem., Senate, Inns of Court, 1973-74. Trustee of Charterhouse in Southwark, 1948-66. Board of Governors, Royal Free Hospital, 1955-64, Middlesex Hospital, 1964-70. Advisory Council, Science Policy Foundation, 1966-. Vice-Pres., Bar Musical Soc., 1977-. *Publications:* articles in professional journals. *Recreations:* reading, listening to music, walking, swimming. *Address:* 173 Oakwood Court, W14. *T:* 01-602 2143. *Club:* Athenæum.

RINK, Margaret Joan; *see* Suttill, Dr. M. J.

RINTOUL, Andrew, CBE 1965; AE; CA; Chairman: Trustee Savings Banks Central Board, 1976-80; Central Trustee Savings Bank, 1979-80; *b* 21 June 1908; *s* of Peter Rintoul, CA, and Margaret MacDonald Tulloch; *m* 1936, Margaret Bell; *one s* one *d. Educ:* Merchiston Castle Sch., Edinburgh; St John's Coll., Cambridge (BA). Chartered Accountant. Partner, Grahams, Rintoul & Co., 1936. Chm., Scottish National Trust Co. Ltd, 1938-79; Chm., Glasgow Stockholders Trust Ltd, 1938-79. Chm., Scottish Adv. Bd, Legal & General Assurance Society, 1967-78; Mem., Invest. Adv. Cttee, TSB Unit Trust, 1969-79. Trustee Savings Banks Association: Mem. Exec. Cttee, 1958-67; Dep. Chm., 1961-67; Vice-Pres., 1968-76. Hon. Pres., West of Scotland TSB, 1980-. *Recreations:* fishing, gardening, golf, shooting. *Address:* Bargaly House, Newton Stewart, Wigtownshire. *T:* Newton Stewart 2392. *Club:* Royal Air Force.

RIPLEY, Dillon; *see* Ripley, S. D.

RIPLEY, Sir Hugh, 4th Bt, *cr* 1880; former Director, John Walker & Sons Ltd, Scotch Whisky Distillers, retired 1981; *b* 26 May 1916; *s* of Sir Henry William Alfred Ripley, 3rd Bt, and Dorothy (*d* 1964), *e d* of late Robert William Daker Harley; *S* father 1956; *m* 1st, 1946, Dorothy Mary Dunlop Bruce-Jones (marr. diss. 1971); *one s* one *d*; 2nd, 1972, Susan, *d* of W. Parker, Leics; one *d. Educ:* Eton. Served in Africa and Italy with 1st Bn KSLI (despatches twice, American Silver Star); retired regular Major. *Recreations:* golf, fishing, shooting. *Heir: s* William Hugh Ripley, *b* 13 April 1950. *Address:* 20 Abingdon Villas, W8; The Oak, Bedstone, Bucknell, Salop. *Club:* Boodle's.

RIPLEY, (Sidney) Dillon, II, Hon. KBE 1979; PhD; Secretary, Smithsonian Institution, since 1964; *b* 20 Sept. 1913; *s* of Louis Arthur Ripley and Constance Baillie (*née* Rose); *m* 1949, Mary Moncrieffe Livingston; *three d. Educ:* St Paul's Sch., Concord, NH; Yale Univ. (BA 1936); Harvard Univ. (PhD 1943). Staff, Acad. of Natural Sciences, Philadelphia, 1936-39; Volunteer Asst, Amer. Museum of Natural History, New York, 1939-40; Teaching Asst, Harvard Univ., 1941-42; Asst Curator of Birds, Smithsonian Instn, 1942; OSS, 1942-45; Lectr, Curator, Associate Prof. of Zool. and Prof. of Biol., Yale Univ., 1946-64; Dir, Peabody Museum of Nat. Hist., 1959-64. Hon. Mem., Amer. Inst. of Architects, 1975-. Hon. MA Yale Univ., 1961; Hon. DHL: Marlboro Coll., 1965; Williams Coll., 1972; Hon. DSc: George Washington Univ., 1966; Catholic Univ., 1968; Univ. of Md, 1970; Cambridge Univ., 1974; Brown Univ., 1975; Trinity Coll., 1977; Hon. LLD: Dickinson Coll., 1967; Hofstra Univ., 1968; Yale Univ., 1975; Gallaudet Coll., 1981; Hon. DE Stevens Inst. of Technol., 1977. Order of White Elephant, Thailand, 1949; Officer: l'Ordre des Arts et des Lettres, France, 1975; Order of Leopold, Belgium, 1981; Commander: Order of Golden Ark, Netherlands, 1976; Order of Merit, State Council of Polish People's Republic, 1979; Order of Orange-Nassau, Netherlands, 1982; Comdr's Cross, Order of the Dannebrog, Denmark, 1976; Caballero Gran Cruz, Orden del Merito Civil, Spain, 1976. Freedom Medal, Thailand, 1949; Gold Medal: New York Zool Soc., 1966; Royal Zool Soc. of Antwerp, 1970; Thomas Jefferson Award, Amer. Soc. of Interior Designers, 1974; Medal for Distinguished Achievement, Holland Soc. of New York, 1977; F. K. Hutchinson Medal, Garden Club of America, 1979; Medal of Honor, National Soc. of Daughters of Amer. Revolution, 1981. *Publications:* The Trail of the Money Bird, 1942; Search for the Spiny Babbler, 1952; A Paddling of Ducks, 1957; A Synopsis of the Birds of India and Pakistan, 1961; (with Lynette L. Scribner) Ornithological Books in the Yale University Library, 1961; (co-ed) The Land and Wildlife of Tropical Asia, 1964, rev. edns 1971 and 1974; (with H. G. Deignan and R. A. Paynter, Jr) Check-list of Birds of the World, Vol. X (continuation of work of James L. Peters), 1964; The Sacred Grove, 1969; The Paradox of the Human Condition, 1975; Rails of the World, 1977; A Naturalist's Adventure in Nepal: search for the spiny babbler, 1978; (with Sálim Ali) Handbook of the Birds of India and Pakistan: Vol. I, 1968, rev. edn 1978; Vol. II, 1969, rev. edn 1979; Vol. III, 1969, rev. edn 1981; Vol. IV, 1970; Vol. V, 1972; Vol. VI, 1971; Vol. VII, 1972; Vol. VIII, 1973; Vol. IX, 1973; Vol. X, 1974. *Recreation:* watching ducks. *Address:* 2324 Massachusetts Avenue, NW, Washington, DC 20008, USA. *T:* (202) 232-3131. *Clubs:* Pilgrims of the US, Knickerbocker, Century Association (New York); Cosmos, Chevy Chase, Society of Cincinnati, Alibi, Metropolitan (Washington, DC).

RIPLEY, Sydney William Leonard, DL; Member, Greater London Council (Kingston-upon-Thames Borough), since 1964; *b* 17 July 1909; *o s* of late Leonard Ripley; *m* 1st, 1934, Doris Emily (from whom he obtained a divorce, 1966), *d* of late William Gray; *one s two d*; 2nd, 1972, Mrs Pida Polkinghorne. *Educ:* King's School, Canterbury; London. Served War of 1939-45, with RAF, Flight-Lieut (despatches). Contested (C) Ipswich, 1950, Watford, 1951; Chairman Malden and Coombe Conservative Assoc., 1938-49, Pres., 1950-; Vice-Pres., Kingston Division, 1955-. Formerly Chairman Leonard Ripley and Co. Ltd and other printing and outdoor advertising companies, resigned 1973. Member, Malden and Coombe Borough Council, 1938-48, formerly Chm. Finance Cttee; DL Surrey 1960; DL Greater London, 1966; JP 1959-69, CC 1946, CA 1955, Surrey (Chairman, Finance Cttee, 1962-64); Vice-Chm. Surrey CC, 1956-59; Chm. General Purposes Cttee, 1952-59; Chm. Surrey County Council, 1959-62; Mem., Surrey Jt Standing Cttee, 1959-65; County Council rep. on Metrop. Water Bd, 1956-65; County Councils Assoc., 1958-65; Surrey T&AFA, 1959-65; Governor Westminster Hosp., 1963-65; Jt Dep. Leader, Cons. Opposition, GLC, 1964-66; GLC rep. on Surrey T&AFA, 1965-68; London Tourist Board, 1965-68; Thames Water

Authority, 1975-; Chm., Open Spaces and Recreation Cttee, GLC, 1977-81. Chm., SW Regional Hosp. Bd, 1963-65. Freeman, City of London. *Recreations:* golf, swimming, tennis. *Address:* 41 Green Street, W1. *Clubs:* Brooks's, Carlton.

RIPON, Bishop of, since 1977; **Rt. Rev. David Nigel de Lorentz Young;** *b* 2 Sept. 1931; *s* of late Brig. K. de L. Young, CIE, MC; *m* 1962, Rachel Melverley Lewis (*d* 1966); one *s* one *d* ; *m* 1967, Jane Havill Collison; three *s. Educ:* Wellington Coll.; Balliol Coll., Oxford (MA). Director, Dept of Buddhist Studies, Theological Coll. of Lanka, 1964; Lecturer in Comparative Religion, Manchester Univ., 1967; Vicar of Burwell, Cambridge, 1970-75; Archdeacon of Huntingdon, 1975-77; Vicar of Great with Little and Steeple Gidding, 1975-77; Rector of Hemingford Abbots, 1977; Hon. Canon of Ely Cathedral, 1975-77. Mem., Doctrine Commn, 1978-81; Chairman: Partnership for World Mission, 1978-; Governing Body, SPCK, 1979-; Anglican Interfaith Consultants, 1981-. *Publications:* contribs to Religious Studies. *Recreations:* tennis, sailing. *Address:* Bishop Mount, Ripon, N Yorks HG4 5DP. *Club:* Royal Commonwealth Society.

RIPON, Dean of; *see* Le Grice, Very Rev. F. E.

RIPPENGAL, Derek, CB 1982; QC 1980; Counsel to Chairman of Committees, House of Lords, since 1977; *b* 8 Sept. 1928; *s* of William Thomas Rippengal and Margaret Mary Rippengal (*née* Parry); *m* 1963, Elizabeth Melrose (*d* 1973); one *s* one *d. Educ:* Hampton Grammar Sch.; St Catharine's Coll., Cambridge (MA). Called to Bar, Middle Temple, 1953 (Harmsworth schol.). Entered Treasury Solicitor's Office, 1958, after Chancery Bar and univ. posts; Sen. Legal Asst, 1961; Asst Treasury Solicitor, 1967; Principal Asst Treasury Solicitor, 1971; Solicitor to DTI, 1972-73; Dep. Parly Counsel, 1973-74, Parly Counsel, 1974-76, Law Commn. *Recreations:* music, fishing. *Address:* 16 Blacketts Wood Drive, Chorleywood, Herts. *T:* Chorleywood 2131. *Club:* Athenæum.

RIPPON, Rt. Hon. (Aubrey) Geoffrey (Frederick), PC 1962; QC 1964; MP (C) Hexham, since 1966; *b* 28 May 1924; *o s* of late A. E. S. Rippon; *m* 1946, Ann Leyland, *d* of Donald Yorke, MC, Prenton, Birkenhead, Cheshire; one *s* three *d. Educ:* King's College, Taunton; Brasenose College, Oxford (Hulme Open Exhibitioner; MA). Hon. Fellow, 1972. Secretary and Librarian of the Oxford Union, 1942; Pres. Oxford University Conservative Assoc., 1942; Chm., Federation of University Conservative Associations, 1943. Called to the Bar, Middle Temple, 1948 (Robert Garraway Rice Pupillage Prizeman), Bencher, 1979. Member Surbiton Borough Council, 1945-54; Alderman, 1949-54; Mayor, 1951-52; Member: LCC (Chelsea), 1952-61 (Leader of Conserv. Party on LCC, 1957-59); Court, Univ. of London, 1958-; Dep. Chm., British Section of the Council of European Municipalities; President: British Sect., European League for Economic Co-operation; The Enterprise Assoc.; London Mayors' Assoc., 1968-71; Surrey Mayors' Assoc., 1974-76; Admiral of the Manx Herring Fleet, 1971-74. Chm. Conservative National Advisory Committee on Local Government, 1957-59, Pres., 1972-74; Vice-Pres., Council of Europe's Local Government Conference, 1957 and 1958; Contested (C) Shoreditch and Finsbury, General Elections, 1950 and 1951; MP (C) Norwich South, 1955-64. PPS, Min. of Housing and Local Govt, 1956-57, Min. of Defence, 1957-59; Parly Sec., Min. of Aviation, 1959-61; Jt Parly Sec., Min. of Housing and Local Govt, Oct. 1961-July 1962; Minister of Public Building and Works, 1962-64 (Cabinet, 1963-64); Chief Opposition Spokesman on housing, local govt and land, 1966-68, on defence, 1968-70; Minister of Technology (incorporating Mins of Industry, Fuel and Power, Aviation and Supply), 1970; Chancellor of the Duchy of Lancaster, 1970-72; Sec. of State for the Environment (incorporating Mins of Trans., Housing, Land, Local Govt, Public Bldg and Works), 1972-74; Chief Opposition Spokesman on Foreign and Commonwealth Affairs, 1974-75. Chm., Parly Foreign and Commonwealth Affairs Cttee, 1979-81; Leader: Cons. Party Delegn to Council of Europe and WEU, 1967-70; Cons. Gp, European Parlt, 1977-79. Chairman: Dun and Bradstreet Ltd, 1976-; Britannia Arrow Hldgs, 1977-; formerly: Chm., Holland, Hannen & Cubitts; Dep. Chm., Drake & Gorham; Director: Fairey Co. Ltd; Bristol Aeroplane Co.; Hotung Estates. Mem., chartered Inst. of Arbitrators; Hon. Mem., Rating and Valuation Assoc. Knight Grand Cross, Royal Order of North Star (Sweden); Grand Cross, Order of Merit (Liechtenstein). *Publications:* (Co-author) Forward from Victory, 1943; The Rent Act, 1957; various pamphlets and articles on foreign affairs, local government and legal subjects. *Recreations:* watching cricket, travel. *Address:* Mantle Hill, Hesleyside, Hexham, Northumberland; 21 Caroline Terrace, SW1; 2 Paper Buildings, Temple, EC4. *T:* 01-353 5835. *Clubs:* Whites, Pratt's, MCC; Northern Counties, Northern Conservative and Unionist (Newcastle upon Tyne).

RISELEY-PRICHARD, Air Vice-Marshal Richard Augustin, QHS 1980; Principal Medical Officer, Royal Air Force Support Command, since 1980; *b* 19 Feb. 1925; *s* of late Dr J. A. Prichard and Elizabeth (*née* Riseley); *m* 1953, Alannah, *d* of late Air Cdre C. W. Busk, CB, MC, AFC; four *d. Educ:* Beaudesert Park; Radley Coll.; Trinity Coll., Oxford (MA, BM, BCh); St Bartholomew's Hosp., London. FFCM. Commnd RAF Med. Br., 1951; pilot trng, 1951-52; served at RAF Coll., Cranwell, 1953-56; Dep. Principal Med. Officer (Flying), HQ Transport Comd and HQ RAF Germany, 1956-63; RAF Staff Coll., 1964; SMO, British Forces, Aden, 1967; Dep. Principal Med. Officer, HQ Strike Comd, 1970-73; Commanding Officer: RAF Hosp. Wegberg, Germany, 1973-76; Princess Alexandra Hosp., Wroughton, 1977-80. *Recreations:* tennis, squash, bridge, gardening. *Address:* The Little House,

Allington, Devizes, Wilts SN10 3NN. *T:* Cannings 662. *Clubs:* Royal Air Force; All England Lawn Tennis.

RISHBETH, John, ScD; FRS 1974; Reader in Plant Pathology, University of Cambridge, since 1973; Fellow of Corpus Christi College, Cambridge, since 1964; *b* 10 July 1918; *e s* of late Prof. Oswald Henry Theodore Rishbeth and Kathleen (*née* Haddon), Cambridge; *m* 1946, Barbara Sadler; one *s* one *d. Educ:* St Lawrence Coll., Ramsgate; Christ's Coll., Cambridge. MA, PhD, ScD (Cantab). Frank Smart Prize, 1940, and Studentship, 1944, 1946, in Botany. Chemist, Royal Ordnance Factories, 1940-43; Bacteriologist, Scientific Adviser's Div., Min. of Food, 1943-45; Demonstrator in Botany, Univ. of Cambridge, 1947-49; Plant Pathologist, West Indian Banana Research Scheme, 1950-52; Lectr in Botany, Univ. of Cambridge, 1953-73. Visiting Prof. in Forest Pathology, N Carolina State Univ., 1967. Hon. Dr.agro, Royal Veterinary and Agricl Univ., Copenhagen, 1976. *Publications:* papers on: root diseases, especially of trees, caused by fungi; biological control. *Recreations:* hill walking, tennis. *Address:* 36 Wingate Way, Cambridge CB2 2HD. *T:* Cambridge 841298. *Club:* Hawks (Cambridge).

RISK, Douglas James; Sheriff of Grampian, Highland and Islands, at Aberdeen, since 1979; *b* 23 Jan. 1941; *s* of James Risk and Isobel Katherine Taylor Risk (*née* Dow); *m* 1967, Jennifer Hood Davidson; three *s* one *d. Educ:* Glasgow Academy; Gonville and Caius Coll., Cambridge (BA 1963, MA 1967); Glasgow Univ. (LLB 1965). Admitted to Faculty of Advocates, 1966; Standing Junior Counsel, Scottish Education Dept, 1975; Sheriff of Lothian and Borders at Edinburgh, 1977-79. Hon. Lectr, Faculty of Law, Univ. of Aberdeen, 1981-. *Address:* Sheriff's Chambers, Sheriff Court House, Aberdeen AB9 1AP. *T:* Aberdeen 573316. *Club:* Royal Northern and University (Aberdeen).

RISK, Thomas Neilson; Governor of the Bank of Scotland, since 1981 (Director, 1971; Deputy Governor, 1977-81); *b* 13 Sept. 1922; *s* of late Ralph Risk, CBE, MC, and of Margaret Nelson Robertson; *m* 1949, Suzanne Eiloart; four *s. Educ:* Kelvinside Academy; Glasgow Univ. Flight Lieut, RAF, 1941-46; RAFVR, 1946-53. Partner, Maclay Murray & Spens, Solicitors, 1950-81; Director: Standard Life Assurance Co. (Chm., 1969-77); British Linen Bank (Governor, 1977-); Howden Group; Merchants Trust; MSA (Britain) Ltd; Shell UK Ltd. Mem., Scottish Industrial Develt Bd, 1972-75. Trustee, Hamilton Bequest. *Address:* 10 Belford Place, Edinburgh EH4 3DH. *T:* 031-332 9425. *Clubs:* Royal Air Force; New (Edinburgh); Royal and Ancient (St Andrews); Prestwick Golf.

RISK, William Symington, CA; Chairman: Fleming & Ferguson Ltd; Mayflower Carpets Ltd; Director: Anglo Scottish Investment Trust Ltd; Hambros Industrial Management Ltd; Tectonic (Electronics) Ltd; Queen Charlotte's Hospital; *b* 15 Sept. 1909; *er s* of late William Risk and Agnes Hetherington Symington, Glasgow; *m* 1937, Isobel Brown McLay; one *s* one *d. Educ:* Glasgow Academy; Glasgow Univ.; Edinburgh Univ. (BCom). FCMA 1944, JDipMA 1969. Served War, with Admiralty, on torpedo production at RN Torpedo Factory, at Greenock and elsewhere, 1940-45. Partner, Robson, Morrow & Co., 1945-53; Managing Director: H. W. Nevill Ltd (Nevill's Bread), 1953; Aerated Bread Co. Ltd, 1956; Chm., The London Multiple Bakers' Alliance, 1958-59; Regional Dir for Southern England, British Bakeries Ltd, 1960; Industrial Consultant, Hambros Bank Ltd, 1963; Chm., Martin-Black Ltd, 1976-79. Inst. of Chartered Accountants of Scotland: Mem. Exam. Bd, 1951-55; Mem. Council, 1963-68; Pres., 1974-75; Jt Dip. in Management Accounting Services, and First Chm. of Bd, 1966; Inst. of Cost and Management Accountants: Mem. Council, 1952-70; Pres. of Inst., 1960-61; Gold Medal of Inst., for services to the Inst. and the profession, 1965. Mem. Bd of Governors, Queen Charlotte's Hosp., 1970. *Publications:* technical papers on Accountancy and Management subjects; papers to internat. Congress of Accountants (London, 1952, Paris, 1967). *Recreations:* golf, hill walking, gardening, reading. *Address:* Fenmore, Copperkins Lane, Amersham, Buckinghamshire HP6 5RA. *T:* Amersham 5172. *Clubs:* Caledonian, Oriental.

RISSON, Maj.-Gen. Sir Robert Joseph Henry, Kt 1970; CB 1958; CBE 1945 (OBE 1942); DSO 1942; ED 1948; Chairman Melbourne and Metropolitan Tramways Board, 1949-70; Chairman, National Fitness Council of Victoria, 1961-71; *b* 20 April 1901; *s* of late Robert Risson; *m* 1934, Gwendolyn, *d* of late C. A. Spurgin; no *c. Educ:* Gatton High Sch.; Univ. of Queensland. BE (Civil); FICE; FIEAust; FAIM. Served AIF, War of 1939-45: GOC 3 Div. (Australian), 1953-56; Citizen Military Forces Member Australian Military Board, 1957-58. Chief Commissioner, Boy Scouts, Victoria, 1958-63; Pres., Instn Engineers, Australia, 1962-63. OStJ 1966. *Address:* 39 Somers Street, Burwood, Victoria 3125, Australia. *Clubs:* Australian (Melbourne); Naval and Military (Melbourne); United Service (Brisbane).

RIST, Prof. John Michael, FRSC; Regius Professor of Classics, University of Aberdeen, 1980-83; Professor of Classics, University of Toronto, from Sept. 1983; *b* 6 July 1936; *s* of Robert Ward Rist and Phoebe May (*née* Mansfield); *m* 1960, Anna Thérèse (*née* Vogler); two *s* two *d. Educ:* Trinity Coll., Cambridge (BA 1959, MA 1963). FRSC 1976. Univ. of Toronto: firstly Lectr, finally Prof. of Classics, 1959-80; Chm., Grad. Dept of Classics, 1971-75. *Publications:* Eros and Psyche, Canada 1964; Plotinus: the road to reality, 1967; Stoic Philosophy, 1969; Epicurus: an introduction, 1972; (ed) The Stoics, USA 1978; On the Independence of Matthew and Mark, 1978; contrib. classical and phil jls. *Recreations:* travel, swimming, hill-walking.

Address: 107 High Street, Old Aberdeen AB2 3EN; (from Sept. 1983) University of Toronto, Toronto, Ontario M5S 1A1, Canada.

RITBLAT, John Henry, FSVA; Chairman and Managing Director, The British Land Co. Plc, since 1970; *b* 3 Oct. 1935; *m* 1960, Isabel Paja (*d* 1979); two *s* one *d. Educ:* Dulwich Coll.; London Univ.; College of Estate Management. Articles with West End firm of Surveyors and Valuers, 1952-58. Founder Partner, Conrad Ritblat & Co., Consultant Surveyors and Valuers, 1958; Man. Dir, Union Property Holdings (London) Ltd, 1969. Comr, Crown Estate Paving Commn, 1969-. *Recreations:* antiquarian books and libraries, old buildings and the countryside, squash, golf, skiing. *Address:* 10 Cornwall Terrace, Regent's Park, NW1 4QP. *T:* 01-486 4466. *Clubs:* Naval and Military, Royal Automobile, MCC, The Pilgrims.

RITCHESON, Prof. Charles Ray; Lovell Distinguished Professor of History, University of Southern California, since 1977; *b* 26 Feb. 1925; *s* of Charles Frederick and Jewell Vaughn Ritcheson; *m* 1st, 1953, Shirley Spackman (marr. diss. 1964); two *s*; 2nd, 1965, Alice Luethi; four *s. Educ:* Univs of Harvard, Zürich, Oklahoma and Oxford. DPhil (Oxon). FRHistS. Prof. and Chm. of History, Kenyon Coll., 1953-65; Chm. and Dir, Graduate Studies, Southern Methodist Univ., 1965-70; Lovell Prof. of History, Univ. of Southern Calif., 1971-74; Cultural Attaché, US Embassy, 1974-77. Chm., British Inst. of the US, 1979-81. Vice-Pres., Board of Dirs, Amer. Friends of Covent Garden; Member: Adv. Council, Ditchley Foundn; Adv. Council, UC, Buckingham. Hon. DLitt Leicester, 1976. *Publications:* British Politics and the American Revolution, 1954; Aftermath of Revolution: British policy toward the United States 1783-1795, 1969 (paperback, 1971); The American Revolution: the Anglo-American relation, 1969; (with E. Wright) A Tug of Loyalties, 1971. *Recreations:* horseback riding, swimming, opera. *Address:* 741 South Bristol Avenue, Los Angeles, Calif 90049, USA. *T:* (213)828-0926. *Clubs:* Athenæum, Beefsteak, Brooks's, Garrick.

RITCHIE, family name of **Baron Ritchie of Dundee.**

RITCHIE OF DUNDEE, 5th Baron *cr* 1905; **Harold Malcolm Ritchie;** English and Drama Teacher, Bedgebury School, Kent; *b* 29 Aug. 1919; 4th *s* of 2nd Baron Ritchie of Dundee and Sarah Ruth (*d* 1950), *d* of J. L. Jennings, MP; *S* brother, 1978; *m* 1948, Anne, *d* of late Col C. G. Johnstone, MC; one *s* one *d. Educ:* Stowe School; Trinity College, Oxford. MA 1940. Served in Middle East, Italy and Greece, Captain KRRC, 1940-46. Assistant Headmaster, Brickwall House School, Northiam, Sussex, 1952-65; Headmaster, 1965-72. *Recreations:* gardening, drama, music. *Heir:* *s* Hon. Charles Rupert Rendall Ritchie, *b* 15 March 1958. *Address:* The Garden House, Fairfield, Beckley, Rye, East Sussex. *T:* Beckley 296.

RITCHIE, Albert Edgar, CC 1975; Canadian Ambassador to the Republic of Ireland, since 1976; *b* 20 Dec. 1916; *m* ; two *s* two *d. Educ:* Mount Allison Univ., New Brunswick (BA 1938); Queen's College, Oxford (Rhodes Scholar, 1940; BA). Officer, Econ. Affairs Dept, UN, and Secretariat of Gen. Agreement on Tariffs and Trade, 1946-48; Counsellor, Office of Canadian High Comr, London, UK, 1948-52; Deputy Under-Secretary of State for External Affairs, Canada, 1964-66; Canadian Ambassador to USA, 1966-70; Under-Sec. of State for External Affairs, Canada, 1970-74; Special Advisor to Privy Council Office, Canada, 1974-76. Hon. LLD: Mount Allison Univ., 1966; St Thomas Univ., 1968. *Address:* Canadian Embassy, 4th Floor, 65-68 St Stephen's Green, Dublin 2, Ireland; 16 Carlyle Avenue, Ottawa K1S 4Y3, Ont, Canada. *Clubs:* Rideau (Ottawa); St Stephen's Green (Dublin).

RITCHIE, Alexander James Otway; Deputy Chairman, since 1977, and Chief Executive, since 1982, Grindlays Bank plc; Deputy Chairman, Grindlays Holdings, since 1978; Chairman, Union Discount Co. of London plc, since 1970; *b* 5 May 1928; *s* of Charles Henry Ritchie and Marjorie Alice Ritchie (*née* Stewart); *m* 1953, Joanna Willink Fletcher; two *s* one *d. Educ:* Stowe; St John's Coll., Cambridge (MA). Joined Glyn, Mills and Co., 1951 (Dir, 1964); Exec. Dir, Williams & Glyn's Bank, 1970; resigned Williams & Glyn's Bank, 1977, for present post. Mem., London Cttee, Ottoman Bank, 1966-; Mem., Export Guarantees Adv. Council, 1977- (Dep. Chm., 1980-81). *Recreation:* inland waterways. *Address:* Thornfield House, Vine Road, SW13 0NE. *T:* 01-876 4450. *Club:* Boodle's.

RITCHIE, Anthony Elliot, CBE 1978; MA, BSc, MD; FRSE; Secretary and Treasurer, Carnegie Trust for the Universities of Scotland, since 1969; *b* 30 March 1915; *s* of late Prof. James Ritchie; *m* 1941, Elizabeth Lambie Knox, MB, ChB, *y d* of John Knox, Dunfermline; one *s* three *d. Educ:* Edinburgh Academy; Aberdeen and Edinburgh Universities. MA (Aber), 1933; BSc 1936, with Hunter Memorial Prize. MB, ChB (Edin.) 1940. Carnegie Research Scholar, Physiology Dept, Edin. Univ., 1940-41; Asst Lectr 1941; Lectr 1942. Ellis Prize in Physiology, 1941; Gunning Victoria Jubilee Prize, 1943; MD (Edin.) with Gold Medal Thesis, 1945; senior lecturer grade, 1946. Lecturer in Electrotherapy, Edin. Royal Infirmary, 1943-48, 1972-; Chandos Prof. of Physiology, Univ. of St Andrews, 1948-69; Dean, Faculty of Science, 1961-66. Hon. Physiologist Gogarburn Nerve Injuries Hospital, 1941-46; Honeyman Gillespie Lecturer, 1944; Hon. Consultant in Electrotherapy, Scot. E Regional Hospital Board, 1950-69; Fellow Royal Soc. of Edinburgh, 1951 (Council RSE 1957-60, 1979-80; Secretary to Ordinary Meetings, 1960-65, Vice-President, 1965-66 and 1976-79; General Secretary, 1966-76); Scientific Adviser, Civil Defence, 1961-80; Adv. Cttee on Med. Research, Scotland, 1961-, Vice-Chm., 1967-69; Chairman: Scottish Cttee on Science Educn,

1970-78; Blood Transfusion Adv. Gp, 1970-80; Scottish Universities Entrance Bd, 1963-69; St Leonard's Sch., St Andrews, 1968-69; Mem., Council for Applied Science in Scotland, 1978-; Mem., British Library Bd, 1973-80; Trustee, Nat. Library of Scotland. Mem., Cttee of Inquiry into Teachers' Pay. Examiner, Chartered Soc. of Physiotherapy, Pharmaceutical Soc. of Great Britain, and RCSE. RAMC (TA) commission, 1942-44. Hon. FCSP, 1970. Hon. DSc St Andrews, 1972. *Publications:* (with J. Lenman) Clinical Electromyography, 1976; medical and scientific papers on nerve injury diagnosis and medical electronics. *Recreations:* reading, mountaineering, motor cars. *Address:* 12 Ravelston Park, Edinburgh EH4 3DX. *T:* 031-332 6560. *Clubs:* Caledonian; New (Edinburgh).

RITCHIE, Charles Stewart Almon, CC 1972; *b* 23 Sept. 1906; *s* of William Bruce Almon Ritchie, KC and Lilian Constance Harriette Ritchie (*née* Stewart), both of Halifax, Nova Scotia; *m* 1948, Sylvia Catherine Beatrice Smellie; no *c. Educ:* University of King's College; Ecole Libre des Sciences Politiques, Paris. BA, MA Oxford 1929, MA Harvard, 1930. Joined Dept of External Affairs, 3rd Sec. Ottawa, 1934; 3rd Sec., Washington, 1936; 2nd Sec., London, 1939; 1st Sec., London, 1943; 1st Sec., Ottawa, 1945; Counsellor, Paris, 1947; Asst Under-Secretary of State for External Affairs, Ottawa, 1950, Deputy Under-Secretary of State for External Affairs, 1952; Ambassador to Federal Republic of Germany, Bonn, and Head of Military Mission, Berlin, 1954; Permanent Rep. to UN, New York 1958; Ambassador of Canada to the United States, 1962; Ambassador and Permanent Representative of Canada to the North Atlantic Council, 1966-67; Canadian High Comr in London, 1967-71; Special Adviser to Privy Council, Canada, 1971-73. Hon. DCL: Univ. of King's College, Halifax, NS; McGill Univ., Montreal. Hon. Fellow, Pembroke College, Oxford. *Publications:* The Siren Years: undiplomatic diaries 1937-1945, 1974; An Appetite for Life: the education of a young diplomat, 1978; Diplomatic Passport, 1981. *Address:* Apt 10, 216 Metcalfe Street, Ottawa, Canada. *Clubs:* Brooks's, Beefsteak, Travellers'.

RITCHIE, Sir Douglas; *see* Ritchie, Sir J. D.

RITCHIE, Rear-Adm. George Stephen, CB 1967; DSC 1942; writer; retired hydrographer; *b* 30 Oct. 1914; *s* of Sir (John) Douglas Ritchie, *qv* ; *m* 1942, Mrs Disa Elizabeth Smith (*née* Beveridge); three *s* one *d. Educ:* RNC, Dartmouth. Joined RN Surveying Service, 1936; attached Eighth Army, 1942-43; served in HM Survey Ship Scott for invasion of Europe, 1944; comd HMS Challenger on scientific voyage round world, 1950-51; comd HM New Zealand Survey Ship Lachlan and NZ Surveying Service, 1953-56; comd HM Surveying Ship Dalrymple, Persian Gulf, 1959; comd HM Surveying Ship Vidal, West Indies and Western Europe, 1963-65; ADC to the Queen, 1965; Hydrographer of the Navy, 1966-71; Vis. Research Fellow, Southampton Univ., 1971-72; Pres., Directing Cttee, Internat. Hydrographic Bureau, Monaco, 1972-82. Founder's Medal, RGS, 1972; Prix Manley-Bendall, Académie de Marine, Paris, 1977; Gold Medal, Royal Inst. of Navigation, 1978. *Publications:* Challenger, 1957; The Admiralty Chart, 1967; papers on navigation and oceanography in various jls, including Developments in British Hydrography since days of Captain Cook (RSA Silver Medal, 1970). *Recreations:* Trinidad Carnival, boules, hunting. *Address:* Sharpe House, Wiveliscombe, Somerset. *Clubs:* Reform; Monte Carlo (Emeritus Mem.), Bouliste Monegasque; Explorers' (NY).

RITCHIE, Harry Parker, CMG 1966; Fiscal Adviser to Government of Falkland Islands, since 1978; *b* 3 June 1919; *s* of W. S. Ritchie; *m* 1949, Mary Grace, *née* Foster; two *s. Educ:* Royal Belfast Academical Institution; Queen's University, Belfast. Served War of 1939-45 (Captain). Administrative Cadet, Bechuanaland Protectorate, 1946; Swaziland, 1948; District Officer, 1953; seconded to Office of High Commissioner, as Assistant Secretary, 1954; Deputy Financial Secretary, Fiji, 1957, Financial Secretary, 1962-67, Minister of Finance, 1967-70; Secretary for Finance, Papua New Guinea, 1971-74. Financial and Econ. Consultant to Papua New Guinea Govt, 1974-75; Consultant on Civil Service Salaries to Govt of Tonga (report pubd 1976), to Govt of Seychelles (report pubd 1977), to Govt of Falkland Islands (reports pubd 1977, 1981); to Govt of St Helena (report pubd 1980). *Recreations:* gardening, reading. *Address:* 6 Mill Rise, Mill Lane, Bourton, Dorset.

RITCHIE, Horace David; Professor of Surgery, University of London, and Director of the Surgical Unit at The London Hospital, since 1964; *b* 24 Sept. 1920; marr. diss.; three *s. Educ:* Universities of Glasgow, Cambridge and Edinburgh. *Publications:* contribs to various scientific journals. *Address:* 44B Gore Road, E9.

RITCHIE, Sir James Edward Thomson, 2nd Bt, *cr* 1918 (2nd creation); TD 1943 (2 clasps); FRSA; Chairman M. W. Hardy & Co. Ltd, 1948-78; Director, Wm Ritchie & Son (Textiles) Ltd; Member Court of Assistants, Merchant Taylors' Co. (Master, 1963-64); *b* 16 June 1902; *s* of 1st Baronet and Ada Bevan, *d* of late Edward ap Rees Bryant; *S* father, 1937; *m* 1st, 1928, Esme Phyllis (*d* 1939), *o d* of late J. M. Oldham, Ormidale, Ascot; 2nd, 1936, Rosemary, *yr d* of late Col. Henry Streatfeild, DSO, TD; two *d. Educ:* Rugby; The Queen's, Oxford. Joined Inns of Court Regt, 1936; commissioned, 1938; served 1939-45 (CMF 1944-45), various staff and regimental appts; Lt-Col 1945; re-commissioned, 1949, to command 44 (Home Counties) Div. Provost Co. RCMP (TA); retired 1953. Co-opted Mem. Kent TA&AFA (Mem. General Purposes Cttee), 1953-68. Chm. Chatwood-Milner (formerly Milners Safe Co. Ltd), 1937-70; Director: Caledonian Insurance Co. (London Bd), 1951-67; Guardian Assurance Co. Ltd

(Local London Bd, 1967-71). Pres., Royal British Legion, Ashford (Kent) Br., 1952-75; Patron, Ashford and Dist Caledonian Society; Chm. Finance and General Purposes Cttee and joint Hon. Treas., London School of Hygiene and Tropical Medicine, Univ. of London, 1951-61; co-opted Mem. Bd of Management and Finance and Gen. Purposes Cttee, 1964-67. *Heir: half-b* William Peter Emerton Ritchie, *b* 1918. *Address:* Kirkbank House, High Halden, Ashford, Kent TN26 2JD. *T:* Ashford 85249.

RITCHIE, (James) Martin; Chairman: British Enkalon Ltd, since 1975; Haymills Holdings Ltd, since 1977; Director: Vickers Ltd; Sun Alliance and London Insurance Ltd; *b* 29 May 1917; *s* of late Sir James Ritchie, CBE and Lady Ritchie (*née* Gemmell); *m* 1939, Noreen Mary Louise Johnston; three *s. Educ:* Strathallan Sch., Perthshire. Joined Andrew Ritchie & Son Ltd, Glasgow, corrugated fibre container manufrs, 1934; Dir, 1938. TA Officer, 1938; served War of 1939-45: HAA Regt; Capt. 1941; psc 1943; DAA&QMG, MEF, Middle East, 1944-45 (Maj.). Rejoined Andrew Ritchie & Son Ltd, then part of Eburite Organisation; Man. Dir, 1950; Gen. Man., Bowater-Eburite Ltd, on merger with Bowater Organisation, 1956; Bowater Paper Corp. Ltd: Dir, 1959; Man. Dir, 1964; Dep. Chm. and Man. Dir, 1967; Chm. 1969-72. Councillor (C), South Bucks DC, 1980-. FBIM 1971; FRSA 1971. *Recreations:* golf, fishing. *Address:* The Court House, Fulmer, Bucks. *T:* Fulmer 2585. *Clubs:* Caledonian, Buck's; Denham Golf.

RITCHIE, James Walter, MC; a Managing Director, Inchcape & Co. Ltd; *b* 12 Jan. 1920; *m* 1951, Penelope June (*née* Forbes); two *s* two *d. Educ:* Ampleforth Coll.; Clare Coll., Cambridge. Gordon Highlanders, 1941-46. Smith Mackenzie & Co. Ltd, and Mackenzie (Kenya) Ltd, Nairobi, 1946-71; Dir, Inchcape & Co. Ltd, 1972-75. *Recreations:* hunting, fishing, golf. *Address:* Lockeridge Down, Lockeridge, near Marlborough, Wilts. *T:* Lockeridge 244. *Clubs:* City of London, Oriental.

RITCHIE, John, MBE 1944; Senior Master of the Supreme Court of Judicature (Queen's Bench Division), and Queen's Remembrancer, 1980-82 (Master, 1960); *b* 7 Feb. 1913; *e s* of W. Tod Ritchie, JP, Rector of Hutchesons' Grammar School, Glasgow; *m* 1936, Nora Gwendolen Margaret, *yr d* of Sir Frederic G. Kenyon, GBE, KCB, FBA; one *s* two *d. Educ:* Glasgow Academy; Magdalen College, Oxford. BA 1935; MA 1948. Called to the Bar, Middle Temple, 1935; practised in London and on South-Eastern Circuit, 1935-60; Recorder of King's Lynn, 1956-58. Served War of 1939-45 (MBE, Belgian Croix de Guerre, despatches twice): BEF 1940; BLA 1944-45; private, Royal Fusiliers, 1939; commissioned Queen's Own Cameron Highlanders, 1940; Major, 1942. Belgian Croix de Guerre, 1944. *Recreations:* painting, rose-growing, wine-tasting. *Address:* Kirkstead, Godstone, Surrey. *T:* Godstone 842335; Royal Courts of Justice, Strand, WC2. *T:* 01-405 7641. *Club:* Caledonian.

RITCHIE, Sir (John) Douglas, Kt 1941; MC; *b* 28 Nov. 1885; *s* of John Walker Ritchie, Collieston, Aberdeenshire, and Mary Souther; *m* 1913, Margaret Stephen, OBE 1946, JP, Officer of the Order of Orange-Nassau (*d* 1976), *d* of James Allan, Methlick, Aberdeenshire; one *s. Educ:* Manchester Grammar School; Manchester Univ. Served European War in France in 4th Gordon Highlanders and Tank Corps (MC); Town Clerk of Burnley, 1920-23; Solicitor to the Port of London Authority, 1923-26; Solicitor and Secretary to the Port of London Authority, 1927-38; Deputy General Manager, 1938; Gen. Manager, 1938-46; Vice-Chm., Port of London Authority, 1946-55. Mem. Aberdeen County Council, 1955-65; Pres., Dock and Harbour Authorities Assoc., 1954-56; Pres. of Burns Club of London, 1934-35; Chief Executive of London Port Emergency Cttee, 1939-46; Member of Inland Transport War Council; Col. Engineer and Railway Staff Corps RE (TA). *Recreations:* sailing, fishing. *Address:* Collieston, Aberdeenshire. *T:* Collieston 216.
See also Rear-Adm. G. S. Ritchie.

RITCHIE, Prof. J(oseph) Murdoch, PhD, DSc; FRS 1976; Eugene Higgins Professor of Pharmacology, Yale University, since 1968; *b* 10 June 1925; *s* of Alexander Farquharson Ritchie and Agnes Jane (*née* Bremner); *m* 1951, Brenda Rachel (*née* Bigland); one *s* one *d. Educ:* Aberdeen Central Secondary Sch.; Aberdeen Univ. (BSc Maths); UCL (BSc Physiol., PhD, DSc; Fellow 1978). MInstP. Res. in Radar, Telecommunications Res. Estabt, Malvern, 1944-46; University Coll. London: Hon. Res. Asst, Biophysics Res. Unit, Mill Hill, 1951-55; Asst Prof. of Pharmacology, 1956-57, Associate Prof., 1958-63 and Prof., 1963-68, Albert Einstein Coll. of Medicine, NY; Overseas Fellow, Churchill Coll., Cambridge, 1964-65; Chm., Dept of Pharmacol., 1968-74, Dir, Div. of Biol Scis, 1975-78, Yale Univ. Hon. MA Yale, 1968. *Publications:* papers on nerve and muscle physiol. and biophysics in Jl of Physiol. *Recreations:* skiing, chess. *Address:* 47 Deepwood Drive, Hamden, Conn 06517, USA. *T:* (home) (203) 777-0420; (office) (203) 785-4567. *Club:* Yale (NYC).

RITCHIE, Kenneth Gordon, CMG 1968; HM Diplomatic Service, retired; *b* 19 Aug. 1921; *s* of Walter Ritchie, Arbroath; *m* 1951, Esme Stronsa Nash. *Educ:* Arbroath High Sch.; St Andrews Univ. (MA). Joined FO, 1944; Embassy, Ankara, 1944-47; Foreign Office, 1947-49; Khorramshahr, 1949-50; Tehran, 1950-52; Djakarta, 1952-55; Foreign Office, 1955-57; Peking, 1957-62; Santiago, 1962-64; Elisabethville, 1965-66; Dep. High Commissioner, Lusaka, 1966-67; High Commissioner, Guyana, 1967-70; Head of Perm. Under-Sec.'s Dept, FCO, 1970-73; High Comr, Malawi, 1973-77.

Recreations: cinephotography, model railways. *Address:* Dalforbie, North Esk Road, Edzell, Angus.

RITCHIE, Margaret Claire; Headmistress of Queen Mary School, Lytham, since 1981; *b* 18 Sept. 1937; *d* of Roderick M. Ritchie, Edinburgh. *Educ:* Leeds Girls' High Sch.; Univ. of Leeds (BSc). Postgraduate Certificate in Education, Univ. of London. Asst Mistress, St Leonards Sch., St Andrews, 1960-64; Head of Science Dept, Wycombe Abbey Sch., High Wycombe, 1964-71; Headmistress, Queenswood Sch., 1972-81. *Address:* Queen Mary School, Clifton Drive South, Lytham St Annes, Lancs FY8 1DS.

RITCHIE, Martin; see Ritchie, J. M.

RITCHIE, Gen. Sir Neil Methuen, GBE 1951 (KBE 1945; CBE 1940); KCB 1947 (CB 1944); DSO 1917; MC 1918; retired; Director, Tanqueray Gordon & Co. (Can.) Ltd; *b* 29 July 1897; 2nd *s* of late Dugald Ritchie of Restholme, Liss, Hants; *m* 1937, Catherine, *d* of James A. Minnes, Kingston, Ontario; one *s* one *d. Educ:* Lancing; RMC, Sandhurst. 2nd Lieut The Black Watch, 1914; Lieutenant 1915; Capt. 1917; Bt Major, 1933; Major, 1934; Bt Lt-Col 1936; Lt-Col The King's Own Royal Regt 1938; Col 1939; Brigadier 1939; Acting Maj.-General 1940; Temp. Major-General 1941; Maj.-Gen. 1943; Temp. Lt-Gen. 1944; Lt-Gen. 1945; General 1947; served European War, 1914-19; France, 1915; Mesopotamia, 1916-17; Palestine, 1918 (despatches, DSO, MC); Palestine, 1938-39 (despatches); Gen. Staff Officer, 3rd Grade, War Office, 1923-27; Staff College, Camberley, 1929-30; GSO2, Northern Command, India, 1933-37; GSO1, 1939; Brigadier, General Staff, 1939; Comdr 51st Highland Division, 1940-41; Deputy Chief of Staff Middle East, 1941; Commander of 8th Army, Libya, acting rank of Lieut-General, 1941; Comd 52nd Lowland Division, 1942-43; Comd 12 Corps BLA, 1944-45; GOC-in-C Scottish Command and Governor of Edinburgh Castle, 1945-47; C-in-C, Far East Land Forces, 1947-49; Commander British Army Staff, Washington, and Military Member of Joint Services Mission 1950-51; ADC General to the King, 1948-51; retired pay, 1951. Colonel, The Black Watch (Royal Highland Regiment), 1950-52. Queen's Body Guard for Scotland. Dir Emeritus, Mercantile & General Re-insurance Co. of Canada Ltd. Virtuti Militari (Poland), 1942; Comdr Legion of Honour, Croix de Guerre (France), 1945; Kt Comdr Orange Nassau (Holland), 1945; Comdr Order of Merit (USA), 1945. KStJ 1963. *Address:* 355 St Clair Rue West, Apartment 1406, Toronto, Ontario, Canada M5P 1N9. *T:* (416) 960 6209. *Clubs:* Caledonian, I Zingari, Free Foresters; York (Toronto).

RITCHIE, Robert Blackwood; Director General, Ministry for Economic Development, Victoria, since 1981; grazier running family sheep and cattle properties, Western Victoria, since 1958; Chairman, Agricultural Investments Australia Ltd, since 1968; *b* 6 April 1937; *s* of Alan Blackwood Ritchie and Margaret Louise (*née* Whitcomb); *m* 1965, Eda Natalie Sandford Beggs; two *s* one *d. Educ:* Geelong Grammar Sch.; Corpus Christi Coll., Cambridge (MA; Rowing Blue, 1958). Exec. Mem., Graziers Assoc. of Vic, 1968-72; Mem., National Rural Adv. Council, 1974-75. Geelong Grammar School: Mem. Council, 1966-78 (Chm., 1973-78); Chief Exec., 1979-80 (during period between Head Masters). *Recreation:* sailing. *Address:* Blackwood, Penshurst, Vic 3289, Australia. *T:* (055) 765432. *Clubs:* Melbourne (Melbourne, Australia); Royal Geelong Yacht (Australia).

RITCHIE, Shirley Anne, (Mrs R. H. C. Anwyl), QC 1979; a Recorder of the Crown Court, since 1981; *b* 10 Dec. 1940; *d* of James Ritchie and Helen Sutherland Ritchie; *m* 1969, Robin Hamilton Corson Anwyl; two *s. Educ:* St Mary's Diocesan Sch. for Girls, Pretoria; Rhodes Univ., S Africa (BA, LLB). Called to the South African Bar, 1963; called to the Bar, Inner Temple, 1966. Member: Senate of Inns of Court and Bar, 1978-81; Criminal Injuries Compensation Bd, 1980-. Dep. Chm., Barristers' Benevolent Assoc., 1980-. *Recreations:* theatre, sailing. *Address:* 4 Paper Buildings, Temple, EC4Y 7EX. *T:* 01-353 3420.

RITCHIE, Major-General Walter Henry Dennison, CB 1953; CBE 1944 (OBE 1940); Life President, Earls Court & Olympia Ltd, 1974 (Chairman, Earls Court Ltd, 1967, Earls Court & Olympia Ltd, 1973); *b* 28 April 1901; *s* of Henry Montague Ritchie, Perth; *m* 1930, Gladys Stella, *d* of William Craven, Southsea; one *s* one *d. Educ:* St John's Coll., Southsea. 2nd Lieut RASC, 1925; served War of 1939-45, in France, N Africa, Italy; Maj. 1939; 15 Army Group (Brig.), 1943; DQMG to Field Marshal Alexander, Oct. 1943-Dec. 1944, to Gen. Mark Clark, Dec. 1944-May 1945; Maj.-Gen. 1953; Director of Quartering, War Office, 1953-54; Director of Supplies and Transport, War Office, 1954-57; retired. Col Comdt, RASC, 1959-64; Hon. Col 101 AER Regt, RCT, 1965-67. Freeman, City of London, 1962. Officer Legion of Merit, USA 1945. *Club:* Army and Navy.

RITCHIE-CALDER, Baron, *cr* 1966, of Balmashannar (Life Peer); **Peter Ritchie Ritchie-Calder,** CBE 1945; MA (Edinburgh) 1961; author and journalist; Senior Fellow, Center for the Study of Democratic Institutions, Santa Barbara, California, 1972-75; *b* 1 July 1906; *s* of David Lindsay Calder and Georgina Ritchie, Forfar, Angus; *m* 1927, Mabel Jane Forbes, *d* of Dr David McKail, Glasgow; three *s* two *d. Educ:* Forfar Academy. Police court reporter, Dundee Courier (1922), D. C. Thomson Press (London office, 1924, Glasgow, 1925), Daily News (1926-30), Daily Chronicle (1930), Daily Herald (1930-41). Author, scientific, social and political journalist and broadcaster (radio and television). Science Editor, News Chronicle, 1945-56. Dept of FO, 1941-45; Editorial Staff, New Statesman, 1945-58; Montague Burton

Professor of International Relations, Edinburgh University, 1961-67. Chm., Metrication Bd, 1969-72. Vis Prof., Heriot-Watt Univ., 1973-; Charles Beard lectr, Ruskin College, Oxford, 1957; Bentwich Lectr, Hebrew Univ., 1973; Brodetsky Lectr, Leeds Univ. 1973. Member Council British Association, Pres. Section X, 1955; Fell. Amer. Assoc. for Advancement of Science; Fabian Executive; Secretary of H. G. Wells' Debate, and Viscount Sankey Cttee, on New Declaration of the Rights of Man, 1940; Mem. British delegn to Unesco (Paris, 1946, Mexico City, 1947, 1966, 1968); special adviser at FAO Famine Conf. (Washington, 1946); Desert survey for Unesco, 1950; chief, special UN Mission to SE Asia, 1951; Mission (UN auspices) to Arctic, 1955; Member UN Secretariat, at Peaceful Uses of Atomic Energy Confs, 1955 and 1958, and Member WHO group on mental aspects of Atomic Energy, 1957; Consultant-Editor, UN Science and Technology Conference, Geneva, 1963; Chm. Chicago University study group on Radiation in the Environment, 1960; Special UN Mission to Congo, 1960; 2nd UN Mission to SE Asia, 1962. Chairman Association of British Science Writers, 1949-55. President: Mental Health Film Council; National Peace Council; British Sub-Aqua Club, 1971-74; Danforth Foundation Lecturer, USA, 1965. UK Commn for WHO; UK Commn for Unesco; Cons., OXFAM; Vice-Pres. Workers' Educational Assoc., 1958-68; Member: Gen. Council, Open Univ., 1969-81; Community Relations Commn, 1968-70; Council, Internat. Ocean Inst., 1970-; House of Lords Select Cttee on Sci. and Technology, 1980-; Chm., Adv. Cttee on Pollution of the Sea, 1977-; Consultant, US Librarian of Congress, 1976. Fellow, World Acad. of Arts and Science; DUniv Open, 1975; DSc York, Ont, 1976. Kalinga Internat. Award for science writing, 1960; Victor Gollanz Award for service to humanity, 1969; New York Library Jubilee Medal, 1961; WHO Med. Soc. Medal, 1974. Publications: Birth of the Future, 1934; Conquest of Suffering, 1935; Roving Commission, 1935; Lesson of London, 1941; Carry on, London, 1941; Start Planning Britain Now, 1941; Men against the Desert, 1951; Profile of Science, 1951; The Lamp is Lit, 1951; Men against Ignorance, 1953 (UNESCO); Men Against the Jungle, 1954; Science in Our Lives, 1954 (USA); Science Makes Sense, 1955; Men against the Frozen North, 1957; Magic to Medicine, 1958; Medicine and Man, 1958; Ten Steps Forward: The Story of WHO, 1958; The Hand of Life: The Story of the Weizmann Institute, 1959; The Inheritors, 1960; Agony of the Congo, 1961; Life-Savers, 1961; Common Sense about a Starving World, 1962; Living with the Atom, 1962; World of Opportunity (for United Nations), 1963; Two-Way Passage, 1964; The Evolution of the Machine, 1968; Man and the Cosmos, 1968; Leonardo and the Age of the Eye, 1970; How Long have we got?, 1972; The Pollution of the Mediterranean, 1972; Understanding Energy, 1979. Recreation: carpentry. Address: Philipstoun House, Linlithgow, W Lothian EH49 7NB. T: Philpstoun 187. Clubs: Savile; Scottish Arts, University Staff (Edinburgh); Century (New York).
See also N. D. R. Calder.

RIVERDALE, 2nd Baron, cr 1935; **Robert Arthur Balfour,** Bt 1929; DL; President, Balfour Darwins Ltd, 1969-75 (Chairman, 1961-69); b Sheffield, 1 Sept. 1901; er s of 1st Baron Riverdale, GBE; S father, 1957; m 1st, 1926, Nancy Marguerite (d 1928), d of late Rear-Adm. Mark Rundle, DSO; one s; 2nd, 1933, Christian Mary, er d of late Major Rowland Hill; one s one d. Educ: Aysgarth; Oundle. MRINA. Served with RNVR, 1940-45, attaining rank of Lt-Comdr. Joined Arthur Balfour & Co. Ltd, 1918; Dir, 1924; Man. Dir, 1949; Chm. and Man. Dir, 1957-61; Exec. Chm. 1961-69. Director: National Provincial Bank, Main Central Bd, 1964-69 (Local Bd, 1949-69); National Westminster Bank, E Region, 1969-71; Light Trades House Ltd, 1956-65; Yorkshire Television, 1967-73. The Association of British Chambers of Commerce: Mem. Exec. Council, 1950-; Vice-Pres., 1952-54; Dep. Pres., 1954-57; Pres., 1957-58; Chm., Overseas Cttee, 1953-57. President: Nat. Fedn of Engineers' Tool Manufacturers, 1951-57 (Hon. Vice-Pres., 1957-; Representative on Gauge and Tool Adv. Council, 1946-64); Sheffield Chamber of Commerce, 1950 (Jt Hon. Sec., 1957-); Milling Cutter and Reamer Trade Assoc., 1936-54 (Vice-Pres., 1954-57); Twist Drill Traders' Assoc., 1946-55; Chm., British Council, Aust. Assoc. of British Manufacturers, 1954-57 (Vice-Chm., 1957-65; Hon. Mem., 1965-); Member: Management and Tech. Cttee, High Speed Steel Assoc., 1947-65; British Nat. Cttee of Internat. Chamber of Commerce Adv. Cttee, 1957-58; Nat. Production Adv. Cttee, 1957-58; Consultative Cttee for Industry, 1957-58; Standing Cttee, Crucible and High Speed Steel Conf., 1951-64; Western Hemisphere Exports Council (formerly Dollar Exports Council), 1957-61; Governor, Sheffield Savings Bank, 1948-58 (Patron, 1958-); Master Cutler, 1946; Trustee, Sheffield Town Trust, 1958-; Town Collector, Sheffield, 1974-; Guardian of Standard of Wrought Plate within City of Sheffield, 1948-; Belgian Consul for Sheffield area, 1945-. JP, City of Sheffield, 1950-66 (Pres., S Yorks Br. Magistrates' Assoc., 1971-); DL, S Yorks (formerly WR Yorks and City and County of York), 1959-. Pres., Derwent Fly Fishing Club. Is a Churchman and a Conservative. Chevalier of Order of the Crown, Belgium, 1956; La Médaille Civique de première classe; Officier de l'Ordre de Leopold II, 1971. Recreations: yachting, yacht designing, shooting, stalking, fishing. Heir: s Hon. Mark Robin Balfour [b 16 July 1927; m 1959, Susan Ann, e d of R. P. Phillips, Sandygate, Sheffield; one s two d. Educ: Aysgarth; Trinity College School, Ontario. Company Director]. Address: Ropes, Grindleford, via Sheffield S30 1HX. T: Hope Valley 30408. Clubs: Royal Cruising; Sheffield (Sheffield).

RIVERINA, Bishop of, since 1971; **Rt. Rev. Barry Russell Hunter;** b Brisbane, Queensland, 15 Aug. 1927; s of late John Hunter; m 1961, Dorothy Nancy, d of B. P. Sanders, Brisbane; three d. Educ: Toowoomba Grammar Sch.; St Francis' Theological Coll., Brisbane; Univ. of Queensland (BA,ThL).

Assistant Curate, St Matthew's, Sherwood, 1953-56; Member, Bush Brotherhood of St Paul, Cunnamulla, Queensland, 1956-61; Rector, St Cecilia's, Chinchilla, 1961-66; Rector, St Gabriel's, Biloela, 1966-71; Archdeacon of the East, Diocese of Rockhampton, 1969-71. Recreation: music. Address: Bishop's Lodge, 127 Audley Street, Narrandera, NSW 2700, Australia. T: Narrandera 59 1177. Club: Griffith Aero (Griffith).

RIVERS, Georgia; see Clark, Marjorie.

RIVERS, Mrs Rosalind V.; see Pitt-Rivers.

RIVET, Prof. Albert Lionel Frederick, FBA 1981; Professor of Roman Provincial Studies, University of Keele, 1974-81, now Emeritus; b 30 Nov. 1915; s of Albert Robert Rivet, MBE and Rose Mary Rivet (née Bulow); m 1947, Audrey Catherine Webb; one s one d. Educ: Felsted Sch. (schol.); Oriel Coll., Oxford. BA 1938, MA 1946. FSA 1953; FSAScot 1959. Schoolmaster, 1938-39; ARP, 1939-40; mil. service, mainly in E Africa, 1940-46 (Major, Royal Signals); bookseller, 1946-51; Asst Archaeology Officer, Ordnance Survey, 1951-64; Keele University: Lectr in Classics, 1964-67; Reader in Romano-British Studies, 1967-74. Member: Royal Commn on Historical Monuments (England), 1979-; Exec. Cttee, British Sch. at Rome, 1974-. Pres., Soc. for Promotion of Roman Studies, 1977-80. Corresp. Mem., German Archaeol Inst., 1960. Editor, Procs of Soc. of Antiquaries of Scotland, 1961-64. Publications: Town and Country in Roman Britain, 1958, 2nd edn 1964; (ed) The Iron Age in Northern Britain, 1966; (ed) The Roman Villa in Britain, 1969; (with C. C. Smith) The Place-Names of Roman Britain, 1979; contribs to books, atlases, encyclopaedias and learned journals. Recreation: conversation. Address: 7 Springpool, The University, Keele, Staffs ST5 5BN.

RIVETT-CARNAC, Rev. Canon Sir (Thomas) Nicholas, 8th Bt cr 1836; Priest-in-charge, St Mark's, Kennington Oval, SE11; Rural Dean of Lambeth, since 1978; Hon. Canon of Southwark Cathedral, since 1980; b 3 June 1927; s of Vice-Admiral James William Rivett-Carnac, CB, CBE, DSC (2nd s of 6th Bt) (d 1970), and of Isla Nesta Rivett-Carnac (d 1974), d of Harry Officer Blackwood; S uncle, 1972; m 1977, Susan Marigold MacTier Copeland, d of late Harold and Adeline Copeland. Educ: Marlborough College. Scots Guards, 1945-55. Probation Service, 1957-59. Ordained, 1962. Heir: b Miles James Rivett-Carnac, Commander, RN [b 7 Feb. 1933; m 1958, April Sally, d of late Major Arthur Andrew Sidney Villar; two s one d]. Address: St Mark's Vicarage, Kennington Oval, SE11. T: 01-735 4609.

RIVETT-DRAKE, Brig. Dame Jean (Elizabeth), DBE 1964 (MBE 1947); JP; Member, Hove Borough Council, since 1966; Mayor of Hove, 1977-78; Lay Member, Press Council, 1973-78; Director, Women's Royal Army Corps, 1961-64, retd; b 13 July 1909; d of Comdr Bertram Gregory Drake and of late Dora Rivett-Drake. Served War of 1939-45 (despatches, 1946). Hon. ADC to the Queen, 1961-64. Mem., East Sussex CC, 1973-77 (Mem. Educn and Social Services Cttees, AHA). JP 1966. Address: 87 Hove Park Road, Hove, East Sussex BN3 6LN. T: Brighton 505839; c/o Barclays Bank Ltd, 92 Church Road, Hove, East Sussex. Club: English-Speaking Union.

RIVLIN, Geoffrey, QC 1979; a Recorder of the Crown Court, since 1978; b 28 Nov. 1940; s of late M. Allenby Rivlin and late May Rivlin; m 1974, Maureen Smith, violinist; two d. Educ: Bootham Sch.; Leeds Univ. (LLB). Called to the Bar, Middle Temple, 1963 (Colombos Prize, Internat. Law). NE Circuit Junior 1967. Mem., Senate of Inns of Court and the Bar, 1976-79. Address: 4 Paper Buildings, Temple, EC4Y 7EX; 2 Park Square, Leeds LS1 2NE.

RIX, Bernard Anthony, QC 1981; b 8 Dec. 1944; s of Otto Rix and Sadie Silverberg. Educ: St Paul's School, London; New College, Oxford (BA: Lit.Hum. 1966, Jur. 1968); Harvard Law School (Kennedy Scholar 1968; LLM 1969). Called to Bar, Inner Temple, 1970. Recreations: music, opera, Italy, fencing. Address: 3 Essex Court, Temple, EC4. T: 01-583 9294.

RIX, Brian Norman Roger, CBE 1977; actor-manager, 1948-77; Secretary-General, Mencap (Royal Society for Mentally Handicapped Children and Adults), since 1980; b 27 Jan. 1924; s of late Herbert and Fanny Rix; m 1949, Elspet Jeans Macgregor-Gray; two s two d. Educ: Bootham Sch., York. Stage career: joined Donald Wolfit, 1942; first West End appearance, Sebastian in Twelfth Night, St James's, 1943; White Rose Players, Harrogate, 1943-44. Served War of 1939-45, RAF and Bevin Boy. Became actor-manager, 1948; ran repertory cos at Ilkley, Bridlington and Margate, 1948-50; toured Reluctant Heroes and brought to Whitehall Theatre, 1950-54; Dry Rot, 1954-58; Simple Spymen, 1958-61; One For the Pot, 1961-64; Chase Me Comrade, 1964-66; went to Garrick Theatre, 1967, with repertoire of farce: Stand By Your Bedouin; Uproar in the House; Let Sleeping Wives Lie; after 6 months went over to latter, only, which ran till 1969; then followed: She's Done It Again, 1969-70; Don't Just Lie There, Say Something!, 1971-73 (filmed 1973); New Theatre, Cardiff, Robinson Crusoe, 1973; Cambridge Theatre, A Bit Between The Teeth, 1974; Fringe Benefits, Whitehall Theatre, 1976. Entered films, 1951: subsequently made eleven, including Reluctant Heroes, 1951, Dry Rot, 1956. BBC TV contract to present farces on TV, 1956-72; first ITV series Men of Affairs, 1973; A Roof Over My Head, BBC TV series, 1977. Presenter, Let's Go ..., BBC TV series (first ever for mentally handicapped), 1978-82; Disc Jockey (for first time) BBC Radio 2 series, 1978-80. Dir and Theatre Controller, Cooney-Marsh Group, 1977-80. Chm.,

Indep. Develt Council for People with Mental Handicap, 1981-. Hon. MA Hull, 1981. *Publication:* My Farce from My Elbow: an autobiography, 1975. *Recreations:* cricket, amateur radio (G2DQU). *Address:* 3 St Mary's Grove, Barnes Common, SW13. *T:* 01-785 9626. *Clubs:* Lord's Taverners' (Pres. 1970), MCC; Leander (Hon. Mem.).

RIX, Sir John, Kt 1977; MBE 1955; Chairman: Vosper Ltd, since 1978; Vosper Participações e Empreendimentos Ltda, since 1979; David Brown Vosper (Offshore) Ltd, since 1978; Vosper Hovermarine Ltd, since 1980; Mainwork Ltd, since 1980; David Brown Gear Industries Ltd, since 1980; Director: David Brown Finanziaria SRL, since 1981; Vosper Private Ltd, 1966-77 and since 1978; Charismarine Ltd, since 1976; *b* 1917; *s* of Reginald Arthur Rix; *m* 1953, Sylvia Gene Howe; two *s* one *d*. *Educ:* Southampton Univ. FRINA; FIMarE. Chm. and Chief Exec., Vosper Thornycroft (UK) Ltd, 1970-78; Chm., Vosper Shiprepairers Ltd, 1977-78. *Recreations:* sailing, tennis, walking. *Address:* Lower Baybridge House, Owslebury, Winchester, Hants. *T:* Owslebury 306. *Clubs:* Royal Thames Yacht, Island Sailing.

RIX, Timothy John; Chief Executive, Longman Group Ltd, since 1976; *b* 4 Jan. 1934; *s* of late Howard Terrell Rix and Marguerite Selman Rix; *m* 1st, 1960, Wendy Elizabeth Wright (marr. diss. 1967); one *d*; 2nd, 1967, Gillian Diana Mary Greenwood; one *s* one *d*. *Educ:* Radley Coll.; Clare Coll., Cambridge (BA); Yale Univ., USA. Sub-Lieut, RNVR, 1952-54. Mellon Fellow, Yale, 1957-58; joined Longmans, Green & Co. Ltd, 1958; Overseas Educnl Publisher, 1958-61; Publishing Manager, Far East and SE Asia, 1961-63; Head of English Language Teaching Publishing, 1964-68; Divl Man. Dir, 1968-72; Jt Man. Dir, 1972-76; Director: Pearson Longman Ltd, 1979-; Goldcrest Television, 1981-. Publishers Association: Chm., Trng Cttee, 1974-78; Chm., Book Develt Council, 1979-81; Vice-Pres., 1980; Pres., 1981-83. Member: Exec. Cttee, NBL, 1979-; Publishers Adv. Panel, British Council, 1978-. CBIM 1981. *Publications:* articles on publishing in trade jls. *Recreations:* reading, landscape, wine. *Address:* 24 Birchington Road, N8 8HP. *T:* 01-348 4143. *Club:* Garrick.

RIZZELLO, Michael Gaspard, OBE 1977; President, Royal Society of British Sculptors; sculptor and coin designer; *b* 2 April 1926; *s* of Arthur Rizzello and Maria Rizzello (*née* D'Angelo); *m* 1950, Sheila Semple Maguire; one *d*. *Educ:* Oratory Central Boys Sch., SW3; Royal College of Art. Military Service, 1944-48; served in India and Far East; commissioned 1945. Major Travelling Scholarship (Sculpture) and Drawing Prize, RCA, 1950. ARCA 1950; ARBS 1955; FRBS 1961; PRBS 1976; FSIAD 1978. Pres., Soc. of Portrait Sculptors, 1968. Prix de Rome (Sculpture), 1951. Sir Otto Beit Medal for Sculpture, 1961. Sculptor: National Memorial to David Lloyd George, Cardiff; Official Medals for Investiture of HRH Prince of Wales, 1969; 900th Anniversary of Westminster Abbey, 1965; Churchill Centenary Trust, 1974; Sir Thomas Beecham bust, Royal Opera House, 1979. Designer and Sculptor of coinages for over 70 countries. *Recreation:* people. *Address:* Melrose Studio, 7 Melrose Road, SW18 1ND. *T:* 01-870 8561.

ROADS, Dr Christopher Herbert; Director, Museums & Archives Development Associates Ltd, since 1977; consultant in museums and audio visual archives; *b* 3 Jan. 1934; *s* of late Herbert Clifford Roads and of Vera Iris Roads; *m* 1976, Charlotte Alicia Dorothy Mary Lothian; one *d*. *Educ:* Cambridge and County Sch.; Trinity Hall, Cambridge (MA; PhD 1961). Adviser to WO on Disposal of Amnesty Arms, 1961-62; Imperial War Museum: Keeper of Dept of Records, 1962-70; Dep. Dir-Gen. at Main Building, Southwark, 1964-79, at Duxford, Cambridge, 1976-79, HMS Belfast, Pool of London, 1978-79. Founder and Dir, Cambridge Coral/Starfish Res. Gp, 1968-; Chm., Coral Conservation Trust, 1972-; President: Cataloguing Commn, Internat. Films and TV Council, 1970-; Historical Breechloading Small Arms Assoc., 1973-; Vice President: World Expeditionary Assoc., 1971-; Duxford Aviation Soc., 1974-; English Eight Club, 1980-. Member Council: Scientific Exploration Soc., 1971-; Cambridge Univ. Rifle Assoc., 1955-; Hon. Sec., Cambridge Univ. Long Range Rifle Club, 1979-. Trustee, HMS Belfast Trust, 1970-78. Adjt, English VIII, 1964-. Churchill Fellowship, 1970. FRGS. Order of Independence, 2nd cl. (Jordan), 1977. *Publications:* The British Soldier's Firearm, 1850-1864, 1964; (jtly) New Studies on the Crown of Thorns Starfish, 1970; The Story of the Gun, 1978. *Recreations:* rifle shooting, marine and submarine exploration, hovercrafting, motorcycling, cine and still photography. *Address:* 60 Shelford Road, Trumpington, Cambridge. *T:* Cambridge 841176. *Clubs:* United Oxford & Cambridge University; Hawks (Cambridge).

ROADS, Peter George; Regional Medical Officer, South West Thames Regional Health Authority, 1973-82; *b* 14 Nov. 1917; *s* of Frank George Roads and Mary Dee Hill (*née* Bury); *m* 1949, Evelyn Clara (*née* Daniel); one *s* one *d*. *Educ:* Bedford Sch.; Univ. of London (St Mary's Hosp. Med. Sch.); Hon. Society of Inner Temple. MD (London); FFCM, Royal Colls of Physicians. Served War, in China, 1944-46. MRC, Pneumoconiosis Unit, 1949-50; Dep. MOH, etc, City and Co. of Bristol, 1956-59; MOH, Principal Sch. Med. Officer and Port Med. Officer for City and Port of Portsmouth, 1959-73; Med. Referee to Portchester Crematorium, 1959-73. Mem., Central Midwives Bd, 1964-76; Adviser on Health Services, Assoc. of Municipal Corporations, 1966-74. FRSocMed; Fellow, Soc. of Community Medicine. *Publications:* Care of Elderly in Portsmouth, 1970; Medical Importance of Open Air Recreation (Proc. 1st Internat. Congress on Leisure and Touring), 1966. *Recreations:* open air, walking, forestry, riding, ski-ing, history,

touring. *Address:* Pasture Cottage, School Lane, Dinton, near Aylesbury, Bucks HP17 8UG. *T:* Aylesbury 748504.

ROARK, Helen Wills; *b* California, 1905; *d* of Dr Clarence A. Wills (surgeon) and Catherine A. Wills; *m* 1st, 1929, Frederick Schander Moody (marr. diss. 1937); 2nd, 1939, Aidan Roark. *Educ:* Anna Head School, Berkeley, California; University of California; Phi Beta Kappa (Scholarship Society). *Publications:* three books on tennis; Mystery Book, 1939; articles in various magazines and periodicals. *Recreations:* American Lawn Tennis Championship, 1923-24-25-27-28-29 and 1931; English Lawn Tennis Championship, 1927-28-29-30-32-33-35-38; French, 1927-28-29-30; has held exhibitions of drawing and paintings at Cooling Galleries, London, 1929 (drawings); Grand Central Art Galleries, New York, 1930 (drawings), 1936 (flower paintings in oil); Berheim-Jenne Galleries, Paris, 1932 (etchings). *Clubs:* All England Lawn Tennis; Colony, West Side Lawn Tennis (New York); Burlingame Country (California).

ROB, Prof. Charles Granville, MC 1943; Professor of Surgery, East Carolina University Medical School, since 1978; *b* 4 May 1913; *s* of Joseph William Rob, OBE, MD; *m* 1941, Mary Dorothy Elaine Beazley; two *s* two *d*. *Educ:* Oundle School; Cambridge Univ.; St Thomas's Hospital. FRCS 1939; MChir Cantab, 1941. Lt-Col RAMC Surgeon, St Thomas' Hospital, 1948; Professor of Surgery, London University, 1950-60; Professor and Chm. Dept of Surgery, Univ. of Rochester, NY, 1960-78. Formerly Surgeon and Director of the Surgical Professorial Unit, St Mary's Hospital; Consultant Vascular Surgeon to the Army. *Publications:* (ed, with Rodney Smith) Operative Surgery (8 vols), 1956-57, (14 vols), 1968-69; various surgical. *Recreations:* mountaineering, ski-ing. *Address:* East Carolina University School of Medicine, Greenville, N Carolina 27834, USA. *Club:* Alpine.

ROBARTS, Basil; Director, since 1964 and Chief General Manager, 1963-75, Norwich Union Insurance Group; *b* 13 Jan. 1915; *s* of late Henry Ernest Robarts and Beatrice Katie (*née* Stevens); *m* 1941, Sheila Margaret Cooper Thwaites; one *s* one *d*. *Educ:* Gresham's Sch., Holt. Served Army, 1939-45 (Lt-Col, RA). Joined Norwich Union Life Insce Soc., 1934; Gen. Man. and Actuary, 1953. Director: Scottish Union & Nat. Insce Co., 1959; Norwich Union Life and Fire Insce Socs, 1964; Maritime Insce Co., 1968. Institute of Actuaries: Fellow (FIA), 1939; Treas., 1965-67; Gen. Commissioner of Income Tax, 1958-; Chm., British Insce Assoc., 1969-71. *Recreations:* tennis, sailing, music. *Address:* 466B Unthank Road, Norwich. *T:* Norwich 51135. *Club:* Naval and Military.

ROBARTS, David John; Director of Robert Fleming & Co. Ltd, 1944-76; Director of other companies; Chairman, Committee of London Clearing Bankers and President, British Bankers' Association, 1956-60 and 1968-70; *b* 1906; *e s* of Capt. Gerald Robarts; *m* 1951, Pauline Mary, *d* of Colonel Francis Follett, and *widow* of Clive Stoddart; three *s* one *d*. *Educ:* Eton; Magdalen College, Oxford. Dir, National Westminster Bank Ltd, to 1976 (Chm., 1969-71; Chm., National Provincial Bank Ltd, 1954-68). Church Commissioner, 1957-65. High Sheriff of Buckinghamshire, 1963. *Address:* 7 Smith Square, Westminster, SW1. *T:* 01-222 2428; Lillingstone House, Buckingham. *T:* Lillingstone Dayrell 202. *Club:* Pratt's.

ROBARTS, Eric Kirkby; *b* 20 Jan. 1908; *s* of Charles Martin Robarts and Flora Robarts (*née* Kirkby); *m* 1930, Iris Lucy Swan; five *d*. *Educ:* Bishops Stortford Coll.; Herts Inst. of Agriculture. Ran family business, C. M. Robarts & Son, until Aug. 1942. Joined Express Dairy Co. Ltd, 1942: Dir, 1947-74; Man. Dir, 1960-74; Dep. Chm., 1966; Chm., 1967-74. FRSA; FBIM. *Recreations:* hunting, shooting. *Address:* Frithcote, Watford Road, Northwood, Middx. *T:* Northwood 22533. *Club:* Farmers'.

ROBATHAN, Rev. Canon Frederick Norman, OBE 1945; MA; Hon. CF (1st Cl.); Canon Emeritus of Ely Cathedral, since 1960; *b* 4 Jan. 1896; *s* of Reverend Thomas Frederick and Edith Jane Robathan, St Andrew's College, Gorakhpur, India; *m* 1st, 1922, Renée Wells (*d* 1972) (JP 1947-53); one *s* (and one *s* decd); 2nd, 1972, Ruth Elizabeth Emma Corfe, 3rd *d* of late Canon E. C. Corfe and Mrs Emma Corfe. *Educ:* King's School, Chester; Dean Close Sch., Cheltenham; St Edmund Hall, Oxford (MA); Wycliffe Hall, Oxford. Served as Commissioned Officer, European War, 1914-19 (campaign medals), France, 1915-16. Ordained, 1921; Curate, Quarry Bank, Staffs, 1921; Priest Vicar, Truro Cathedral, 1923-25; Priest Vicar, Lincoln Cathedral, 1925-28; Chaplain HM Prison, Lincoln, 1926-28; Minor Canon and Sacrist and Junior Cardinal, St Paul's Cathedral, 1928-34; Chaplain Guy's Hosp., 1932-33; Minor Canon, Westminster Abbey, 1934-37, and Chaplain, Westminster Hospital; Rector of Hackney, 1937-45, and Chaplain East London Hospital, CF, RARO, 1923. War of 1939-45 (campaign medals); BEF 1940; Evacuation, Dunkirk, 1940; Sen. Chaplain 43 Div., 1941; Army Technical Sch., Arborfield, 1941; Sen. Chaplain Royal Garrison Church, Aldershot, 1942; Dep. Asst Chaplain-Gen. 12th Corps, 1943; Asst Chaplain-Gen. 21 Army Grp., 1944; Normandy Landings, 1944 (despatches). Vicar of Brighton, Sussex and Canon and Prebendary of Waltham in Chichester Cathedral, 1945-53; Canon Residentiary and Treasurer, Ely Cathedral, 1953-59; Vicar of Cardington, Bedford, 1959. Sen. Chaplain Army Cadet Force, Cambs, 1954-59. Councillor, Bedford RDC, 1960. Chaplain to High Sheriff of Beds., 1962; Rector of Charleton with Buckland tout Saints, Kingsbridge, S Devon, 1962-66. Hon. Priest Vicar, Truro Cathedral, 1967. Coronation Medal, 1937. *Recreations:* rowing, hockey, cricket, antiquaries. *Address:* Myrtle Court, Mevagissey, Cornwall. *T:* Mevagissey 842233.

ROBB, Prof. James Christie; Professor of Physical Chemistry since 1957 and Head of Department of Chemistry since 1981, University of Birmingham; *b* 23 April 1924; *s* of James M. Robb, Rocklands, The House of Daviot, Inverurie, Aberdeenshire; *m* 1951, Joyce Irene Morley; three *d. Educ:* Daviot School; Inverurie Academy; Aberdeen University (BSc Hons, 1945, PhD 1948); DSc Birmingham, 1954. DSIR Senior Research Award, Aberdeen, 1948–50. ICI Fellow, Birmingham Univ., 1950–51; on Birmingham Univ. staff, 1951–. A Guardian of Birmingham Assay Office, 1980–. Mem. Council, Birmingham Civic Soc., 1981–. Pres., Birmingham Rotary Club, 1982–83. *Publications:* scientific contrib. to Proc. Royal Soc., Trans. Faraday Soc., etc. *Recreations:* motoring, photography, computing. *Address:* 42 School Road, Moseley, Birmingham B13 9SN. *T:* 021–449 2610.

ROBB, William, NDA, FRSE; *b* 1885; *e s* of late William Robb, Rochsolloch, Airdrie; *m* 1924, Agnes Logan, *e d* of late Archibald Steel, Prestwick, Ayrshire; two *d. Educ:* Airdrie Academy; West of Scotland Agricultural College, Glasgow. Assist, Agriculture Department, The University of St Andrews, 1913–16 and 1919–20; War Service, Royal Engineers, 1916–19; Assistant Director, Scottish Society for Research in Plant Breeding, 1921–25; Director of Research, 1925–50, retired. *Recreation:* gardening. *Address:* c/o 7 Kaimes Road, Edinburgh EH12 6JR.

ROBBE-GRILLET, Alain, literary consultant, writer and cinéaste; Editions de Minuit, Paris, since 1955; *b* 18 Aug. 1922; *s* of Gaston Robbe-Grillet and Yvonne Canu; *m* 1957, Catherine Rstakian. *Educ:* Lycée Buffon, Paris; Lycée St Louis, Paris; Institut National Agronomique, Paris. Engineer: Institut National de la Statistique, 1945–49; Institut des Fruits et Agrumes Coloniaux, 1949–51. *Films:* L'Immortelle, 1963; Trans-Europ-Express, 1967; L'Homme qui ment, 1968; L'Eden et après, 1970; Glissements progressifs du plaisir, 1974; Le jeu avec le feu, 1975. *Publications:* Les Gommes, 1953 (The Erasers, 1966); Le Voyeur, 1955 (The Voyeur, 1959); La Jalousie, 1957 (Jealousy, 1960); Dans le labyrinthe, 1959 (In the Labyrinth, 1967); L'Année dernière à Marienbad, 1961 (Last Year in Marienbad, 1962); Instantanés, 1962 (Snapshots, and, Towards a New Novel, 1965); L'Immortelle, 1963 (The Immortal One, 1971); Pour un nouveau roman, 1964; La Maison de rendezvous, 1965; Projet pour une révolution à New York, 1970 (Project for a Revolution in New York, 1972); Glissements progressifs du plaisir, 1974; Topologie d'une cité fantôme, 1976 (Topology of a Phantom City, 1978); La Belle captive, 1976; Souvenirs du Triangle d'or, 1978; Un Régicide, 1978; Djinn, 1981. *Address:* 18 Boulevard Maillot, 92 Neuilly-sur-Seine, France. *T:* 722 31.22.

ROBBINS, family name of **Baron Robbins.**

ROBBINS, Baron *cr* 1959 (Life Peer), of Clare Market; **Lionel Charles Robbins,** CH 1968; CB 1944; FBA 1942; MA Oxon, BSc (Econ.); First Chancellor of Stirling University, 1968–78; *b* 22 Nov. 1898; *e s* of late Rowland Richard Robbins, CBE; *m* 1924, Iris Elizabeth, *d* of late A. G. Gardiner; one *s* one *d. Educ:* Southall County Sch.; Univ. Coll., London; London School of Economics. Served European War, 1916–19 (RFA); Lecturer New College, Oxford, 1924; Lecturer London School of Economics, 1925–27; Fellow and Lecturer New College, Oxford, 1927–29; Professor of Economics in the University of London; at London School of Economics, 1929–61; Chm., Financial Times, 1961–70. Chm., Cttee on Higher Education, 1961–64; Mem., Court of Governors, London School of Economics, (Chm., 1968–74). Director of the Economic Section of Offices of the War Cabinet, 1941–45; President of Royal Economic Society, 1954–55. Trustee: National Gallery, 1952–59, 1960–67, 1967–74; Tate Gall., 1953–59, 1962–67; Dir Royal Opera House, Covent Garden, 1955–80; Mem. Planning Board for Univ. of York; President British Academy, 1962–67. Member: Accademia dei Lincei, Rome; American Philosophical Society; American Acad. of Arts and Sciences; Foreign Associate, National Acad. of Education, America; Corr. Fellow, Academia Nacional de Ciencias Economicas, Argentina. Hon. DLitt (Dunelm, Exeter, Strathclyde, Sheffield, Heriot-Watt); Hon. LHD (Columbia); Hon. LLD (Cantab, Leicester, Strasbourg, CNAA); Hon. Dr of Laws, Calif; Hon. Doutor en Ciências Econòmicas e Financeiras Universidade Técnica de Lisboa; Hon. DSc (Econ.) London; Hon. DUniv: York; Stirling; Hon. Dr, RCA; Hon. DHL Pennsylvania; Hon. Fellow: Univ. Coll. London; Manchester Coll. of Science and Technology; LSE; London Grad. Sch. of Business Studies; Courtauld Inst. *Publications:* An Essay on the Nature and Significance of Economic Science; The Great Depression; Economic Planning and International Order; The Economic Basis of Class Conflict and other Essays in Political Economy; The Economic Causes of War; The Economic Problem in Peace and War, 1947; The Theory of Economic Policy in English Classical Political Economy, 1952; The Economist in the Twentieth Century and other Lectures in Political Economy, 1954; Robert Torrens and the Evolution of Classical Economics; Politics and Economics, 1963; The University in the Modern World, 1966; The Theory of Economic Development in the History of Economic Thought, 1968; The Evolution of Modern Economic Theory, 1970; Autobiography of an Economist, 1971; Money, Trade and International Relations, 1971; Political Economy Past and Present: a review of leading theories of economic policy, 1976; Against Inflation: speeches in the Second Chamber 1965–77, 1979; Higher Education Revisited, 1980; articles in Economic Jl, Economica, Lloyds Bank Review, etc. *Address:* 10 Meadway Close, NW11.

ROBBINS, Edgar Carmichael, CBE 1957; Legal Adviser to The British Broadcasting Corporation, 1959–74; *b* 22 March 1911; *s* of John Haldeman Robbins; *m* 1936, Alice Eugenia, *d* of Rev. Herbert Norman Nash; two *s* two

d. Educ: Westminster Sch.; London Univ. (LLB). Admitted a solicitor, 1933. Employed by The British Broadcasting Corporation, 1934–74, Solicitor to the BBC 1945–59. Clerk, City of London Solicitors' Company, 1976–. *Publications:* William Paston, Justice, 1932; The Cursed Norfolk Justice, 1936. *Address:* 9 Pensioners' Court, The Charterhouse, EC1. *T:* 01-250 0555. *Club:* Athenæum.

ROBBINS, Prof. Frederick C., MD; Bronze Star (US Army), 1945; President, Institute of Medicine, National Academy of Sciences, Washington, DC, since 1980; University Professor, Case Western Reserve University, since 1980 (Professor of Pediatrics, School of Medicine, 1952–80, Dean, 1966–80, now Emeritus); *b* 25 Aug. 1916; *s* of William J. Robbins and Christine Chapman Robbins; *m* 1948, Alice Havemeyer Northrop; two *d. Educ:* University of Missouri (AB); University of Missouri Medical School (BS); Harvard Medical School (MD). US Army, 1942–46; rank on discharge, Major. Various posts in the Children's Hospital, Boston, from 1940, finishing as Chief Resident in Medicine, 1948; Sen. Fellow in Virus Diseases, National Research Council, 1948–50; Research Fellow in Pediatrics, Harvard Med. Sch., 1948–50; Instr in Ped., 1950–51, Associate in Ped., 1951–52, at Harvard Medical School; Dir, Department of Pediatrics, Cleveland Metropolitan General Hospital, 1952–66. Associate, Research Div. of Infectious Diseases, the Children's Medical Center, Boston, 1950–52; Research Fellow in Ped., the Boston Lying-in Hospital, Boston, Mass, 1950–52; Asst to Children's Medical Service, Mass Gen. Hosp., Boston, 1950–52. Visiting Scientist, Donner Lab., Univ. of California, 1963–64. President: Soc. for Pediatric Research, 1961–62; Amer. Pediatric Soc., 1973–74. Member: Nat. Acad. of Sciences, 1972 (Co-Chm., Forum on Human Experimentation, 1974); Amer. Philosophical Soc., 1972; Adv. Cttee, Office of Technol. Assessment for Congress, 1973; Adv. Cttee on Med. Research, Pan American Health Organization, WHO, 1981–. First Mead Johnson Award, 1953; Nobel Prize in Physiology and Medicine, 1954; Award for Distinguished Achievement (Modern Medicine), 1963; Med. Mutual Honor Award for 1969. Hon. Dr of Science: John Carroll University, 1955; Univ. of Missouri, 1958; Univ. of North Carolina, 1979; Hon. Dr of Laws, Univ. of New Mexico, 1968. *Publications:* numerous in various jls, primarily on subject of viruses and infectious diseases. *Recreations:* music, tennis, sailing. *Address:* 7021 Oak Forest Lane, Bethesda, Maryland 20817, USA; (office) 2101 Constitution Avenue, NW, Washington, DC 20418, USA. *T:* 202/334-3300.

ROBBINS, Harold; writer; *m* Grace; one *d. Educ:* New York. Formerly sugar exporter, film publicist, film impresario, etc. *Publications:* The Dream Merchants, 1949; 79 Park Avenue, 1955; A Stone for Danny Fisher, 1955; Never Leave Me, 1956; Never Love a Stranger, 1958; Stiletto, 1960; The Carpetbaggers, 1961; Where Love Has Gone, 1964; The Adventurers, 1966; The Inheritors, 1969; The Betsy, 1971 (filmed 1978); The Pirate, 1974; The Lonely Lady, 1976; Dreams Die First, 1977; Memories of Another Day, 1979; Goodbye, Janette, 1981; Spellbinder, 1982. *Address:* c/o New English Library, Barnard's Inn, Holborn, EC1N 2JR.

ROBBINS, Jerome; Choreographer and Director; Ballet Master, New York City Ballet, since 1969 (Associate Artistic Director, 1949–59); Founder Director, Ballets: USA, 1958–61; *b* New York, 11 Oct. 1918; *s* of Harry and Lena Robbins. *Educ:* Woodrow Wilson High School, Weehawken, NJ; New York University. Studied ballet with Antony Tudor and Eugene Loring, and Modern, Spanish and oriental dance. First stage experience with Sandor-Sorel Dance Center, New York, 1937; dancer in chorus of American musicals, 1938–40; Theatre Ballet, 1940–44 (soloist 1941), London season, 1946; formed own company, Ballets: USA, 1958. Member: NY State Council on the Arts/Dance Panel, 1973–77; Nat. Council on the Arts, 1974-80. City of Paris Award, 1971; Handel Medallion, NYC, 1976; Kennedy Center Honoree, 1981, and many other awards. Hon. Degrees from Ohio Univ., 1974, City Univ. of NY, 1980. Chevalier, Order of Arts and Letters (France), 1964. *Ballets include:* (for Ballet Theater) Fancy Free, 1944; (for Concert Varieties) Interplay, 1945; (for New York City Ballet) Age of Anxiety, 1950; The Cage, 1951; Afternoon of a Faun, 1953; Fanfare, 1953; The Concert, 1956; Dances at a Gathering, 1969; In the Night, 1970; The Goldberg Variations, 1971; Watermill, 1972; Requiem Canticles, 1972; An Evening's Waltzes, 1973; Dybbuk (later The Dybbuk Variations, then renamed Suite of Dances), 1974; Concerto in G (later in G Major), 1975; Ma Mère l'Oye (later Mother Goose), 1975; Chansons Madécasses, 1975; The Four Seasons, 1979; Opus 19, The Dreamer, 1979; Rondo, 1981; Piano Pieces, 1981; The Gershwin Concerto, 1982; Four Chamber Works, 1982; (for Ballets: USA) NY Export: Opus Jazz, 1958; Moves, 1959; (for American Ballet Theater) Les Noces, 1965; (for Star Spangled Gala) Other Dances, 1976. *Musicals include:* On the Town, 1945; Billion Dollar Baby, 1946 (Donaldson award); High Button Shoes, 1947 (Donaldson and Tony awards); Miss Liberty, 1949; Call Me Madam, 1950; The King and I, 1951 (Donaldson award); Two's Company, 1952 (Donaldson award); Peter Pan, 1954; Bells Are Ringing, 1956; West Side Story, 1957 (Tony, Evening Standard, Laurel and two Academy awards); Gypsy, 1959; Fiddler on the Roof, 1964 (two Tony awards and Drama Critics' award). Has directed and choreographed films, drama and TV (inc. Peter Pan with Mary Martin, 1955 (Emmy award)). *Address:* c/o New York City Ballet, New York State Theater, Lincoln Center, New York, NY 10023, USA.

ROBBINS, John Dennis, OBE 1945; TD 1950; FCA; *b* 28 July 1915; *s* of Duncan Ross Robbins and Harriette Winifred Robbins (*née* Goodyear); *m* 1942, Joan Mary Mason; one *s* two *d. Educ:* Aldenham School. Commnd Mddx Regt (DCO), 2nd Lieut 1939, Captain 1940, Major 1941, Lt-Col 1944;

served N Africa, Italy, Palestine (OBE, despatches twice); retd as Lt-Col 1946. Partner, Kay Keeping & Co., Chartered Accountants, 1946–49; joined British Metal Corp. Ltd, 1950; Dir and Gen. Man., 1952; a Man. Dir, 1963. Amalgamated Metal Corp. Ltd: Dir 1965; Chief Exec. 1971; Exec. Dep. Chm., 1972, Chm., 1975–77; Dir, Smith & Nephew Associated Cos, 1958–. Mem., Worshipful Co. of Chartered Accountants. Freeman, City of London. *Recreations:* gardening, shooting, fly-fishing. *Address:* Orpen's Hill House, Birch, Colchester, Essex CO2 0LY. *T:* Colchester 330797. *Clubs:* Gresham, Royal Over-Seas League.

ROBBINS, Prof. Keith Gilbert; Professor of Modern History, Glasgow University, since 1980; *b* 9 April 1940; *s* of Gilbert Henry John and Edith Mary Robbins; *m* 1963, Janet Carey Thomson; three *s* one *d*. *Educ:* Bristol Grammar Sch.; Magdalen and St Antony's Colls, Oxford. MA, DPhil (Oxon). University of York: Asst Lectr in History, 1963; Lectr in Hist., 1964; Prof. of History, 1971–79, Dean of Faculty of Arts, 1977–79, UCNW, Bangor. Enid Muir Lectr, Newcastle Univ., 1981. Editor, History, 1977–; Editorial Bd, Jl of Ecclesiastical History, 1978–. *Publications:* Munich 1938, 1968; Sir Edward Grey, 1971; The Abolition of War: The British Peace Movement 1914–1919, 1976; John Bright, 1979; articles in Historical Jl, Internat. Affairs, Jl of Contemporary Hist., Jl of Ecclesiastical Hist., Jl of Commonwealth and Imperial Hist., etc. *Recreations:* music, gardening, walking. *Address:* Department of Modern History, The University, Glasgow G12 8QQ. *T:* 041-339 8855.

ROBBINS, Michael; *see* Robbins, R. M.

ROBBINS, Dr Raymond Frank; Director, Plymouth Polytechnic, since 1974; *b* 15 Feb. 1928; *s* of Harold and Elsie Robbins; *m* 1955, Eirian Meredith Edwards; two *d*. *Educ:* Grove Park Grammar Sch., Wrexham; UCW Aberystwyth. PhD 1954; FRIC 1962. Research Chemist, Monsanto Chemicals Ltd, 1954–55; Research Fellow, Univ. of Exeter, 1955–56; Lectr, Nottingham Coll. of Technology, 1956–59; Sen. Lectr, Hatfield Coll. of Technology, 1960–61; Head of Dept of Chem. Sciences, Hatfield Polytechnic, 1961–70; Dep. Dir, Plymouth Polytechnic, 1970–74. *Publications:* papers on organic chemistry in chem. jls, various reviews and articles in sci. and educnl press. *Recreations:* hill walking, sailing. *Address:* Lent Hill Cottage, Ashburton, Devon TQ13 7NW. *T:* (office) Plymouth 21312.

ROBBINS, (Richard) Michael, CBE 1976; *b* 7 Sept. 1915; *er s* of late Alfred Gordon Robbins and Josephine, *d* of R. L. Capell, Northampton; *m* 1939, Rose Margaret Elspeth, *er d* of late Sir Robert Reid Bannatyne, CB, Lindfield, Sussex; one *s* two *d*. *Educ:* Westminster Sch. (King's Schol.); Christ Church, Oxford (Westminster Schol.; MA); Univ. of Vienna. Joined London Passenger Transport Board, 1939. War service, RE (Transportation), 1939–46: Persia and Iraq, 1941–43; GHQ, MEF, 1943–44; Major, AML (Greece), 1944–45. Rejoined London Transport, 1946; Sec. to Chm., 1947–50; Sec., London Transp. Exec., 1950–55; Sec. and Chief Public Relations Off., 1955–60; Chief Commercial and Pub. Rel. Off., 1960–65; Mem., London Transport Exec., 1965–80 (Man. Dir, Rlys, 1971–78). Chm., Transport Adv. Cttee, Transport and Road Res. Lab., 1977–81. Pres., Inst. of Transport, 1975–76 (Mem. Council, 1957–60 and 1962–64; Chm., Metrop. Sect., 1962–63; Chm., Educn and Trg Cttee, 1969–72; Vice-Pres., 1972–75); Pres., Omnibus Soc., 1965; Chairman: Middx Victoria County History Council, 1963–76; Middx Local History Council, 1958–65; Internat. Metrop. Rlys Cttee, Internat. Union of Public Transport, 1976–81; Victorian Soc., 1978–81; President: London and Middx Archæol. Soc., 1965–71 (Mem. Council, 1951–56 and 1960–65); Greater London Industrial Archæol. Soc., 1969–; Rly Students Assoc., 1967–68; St Marylebone Soc., 1971–74. Dunhill lectr on industrial design, Australia, 1974. FSA 1957 (Mem. Council, 1965–67, 1970–71; Treasurer, 1971–). Governor, Museum of London, 1968– (Chm., 1979–); Trustee, London Museum, 1970–75. *Publications:* The North London Railway, 1937; 190 in Persia, 1951; The Isle of Wight Railways, 1953; Middlesex, 1953; (ed) Middlesex Parish Churches, 1955; The Railway Age, 1962; (with T. C. Barker) History of London Transport, vol. 1, 1963, vol. 2, 1974; George and Robert Stephenson, 1966, rev. edn 1981; Points and Signals, 1967; Joint Editor, Journal of Transport History, 1953–65; contribs to transport and historical jls. *Recreations:* exploring cities and suburbs, travelling abroad and in branch railway trains; concert-going. *Address:* 7 Courthope Villas, Wimbledon, SW19 4EH. *T:* 01-946 7308.

ROBENS, family name of **Baron Robens of Woldingham.**

ROBENS OF WOLDINGHAM, Baron *cr* 1961, of Woldingham (Life Peer); **Alfred Robens,** PC 1951; Chairman: Johnson Matthey & Co. Ltd, since 1971; St Regis Newspapers, Bolton, since 1975 (Director, 1976); Snamprogetti, since 1980; a Director: Times Newspapers Holdings Ltd, since 1980 (Times Newspapers Ltd, 1967–80); British Fuel Co., since 1967; AAH, since 1971; St Regis Paper Co. (NY), since 1976; Trust Houses Forte Ltd, since 1971; AMI (Europe) Ltd, since 1981; Chairman, Engineering Industries Council, since 1976; *b* 18 Dec. 1910; *s* of George and Edith Robens; *m* 1937, Eva, *d* of Fred and late Elizabeth Powell. *Educ:* Manchester Secondary Sch. Official of Union of Distributive and Allied Workers, 1935–45; Manchester City Councillor, 1942–45. MP (Lab) Wansbeck Div. of Northumberland, 1945–50, and for Blyth, 1950–60. Parliamentary Private Secretary to Minister of Transport, 1945–47; Parliamentary Secretary, Ministry of Fuel and Power, 1947–51; Minister of Labour and National Service, April–Oct. 1951. Chairman: National Coal Bd, 1961–71; Vickers Ltd, 1971–79; St Regis

Internat., 1976–81; MLH Consultants, 1971–81. A Dir, Bank of England, 1966–81. Chm. Foundation on Automation and Employment, 1962; Member: NEDC, 1962–71; Royal Commn on Trade Unions and Employers' Assocs, 1965–68. President: Advertising Assoc., 1963–68; Incorporated Soc. of British Advertisers, 1973–76; Chairman: Jt Steering Cttee for Malta, 1967; Jt Econ. Mission to Malta, 1967. Member: Council of Manchester Business School, 1964–79 (Dep. Chm., 1964–70; Chm., 1970–79); Court of Governors, LSE, 1965; Chancellor, Univ. of Surrey, 1966–77. Governor, Queen Elizabeth Training Coll. for the Disabled, 1951–; Chairman: Bd of Govs, Guy's Hosp., 1965–74; Guy's Hosp. Medical and Dental Sch., 1974–; Cttee on Safety and Health of people at their place of work, 1970–72; Fellow, Manchester Coll. of Science and Technology, 1965–; Hon. FRCR, 1975. Hon. DCL: Univ. of Newcastle upon Tyne, 1964; Manchester Univ., 1974; Hon. LLD: Leicester, 1966; London, 1971. Hon. MInstM, 1968; Hon. FIOB, 1974. Mackintosh Medal, Advertising Assoc., 1970; Albert Medal, RSA, 1977. *Publications:* Engineering and Economic Progress, 1965; Industry and Government, 1970; Human Engineering, 1970; Ten Year Stint, 1972; sundry articles to magazines, journals and newspapers. *Recreation:* gardening. *Address:* 100 High Street, Southgate, N14. *Club:* Reform.

ROBERGE, Guy, QC (Can.); Vice-President, Canadian Transport Commission, Ottawa, since 1971; *b* 26 Jan. 1915; *s* of P. A. Roberge and Irène Duchesneau; *m* 1957, Marie Raymond; one *s* one *d*. *Educ:* Laval Univ., Quebec. Called to Bar, 1937; Mem., Quebec Legislative Assembly, 1944–48; Mem., Restrictive Trade Practices Commn of Canada, 1955–57; Chm. and Chief Exec. Officer, Nat. Film Bd of Canada, 1957–66; Agent-General for Govt of PQ in UK, 1966–71. Hon. DCL, Bishop's Univ., 1967; Hon. docteur d'université, Laval Univ., 1975. *Address:* Canadian Transport Commission, Ottawa K1A 0N9, Canada. *T:* 997-0400; (home) 415 Wood Avenue, Ottawa, Ontario. *Clubs:* Quebec Garrison (Quebec City); Rideau (Ottawa).

ROBERTHALL, family name of **Baron Roberthall.**

ROBERTHALL, Baron *cr* 1969 (Life Peer), of Silverspur, Queensland, and Trenance, Cornwall; **Robert Lowe Roberthall,** KCMG 1954; CB 1950; MA; Principal Hertford College, Oxford, 1964–67; *b* New South Wales, 6 March 1901; *s* of late Edgar Hall and Rose Helen, *d* of A. K. Cullen; changed surname to Roberthall by deed poll, 1968; *m* 1932, Laura Margaret (marr. diss. 1968), *d* of G. E. Linfoot; two *d*; *m* 1968, Perilla Thyme, *d* of late Sir Richard Southwell, FRS. *Educ:* Ipswich, Qld; Univ. of Queensland; Magdalen College, Oxford. BEng, Queensland, 1922; Rhodes Scholar, 1923–26 (First in Modern Greats, 1926); Lecturer in Economics, Trinity College, 1926–47; Fellow, 1927–50; Hon. Fellow, 1958; Junior Dean, 1927; Dean, 1933–38; Bursar, 1938–39; Proproctor, 1933; Ministry of Supply, 1939–46; British Raw Materials Mission, Washington, 1942–44; Adviser, Board of Trade, 1946–47; Director Economic Section, Cabinet Office, 1947–53; Economic Adviser to HM Government, 1953–61; Advisory Dir, Unilever, 1961–71; advr to Tube Investments, 1961–76. Fellow of Nuffield College, 1938–47, Visiting Fellow, 1961–64. Mem. of Economic and Employment Commn UN, 1946–49; Chm., OEEC Gp of Economic Experts, 1955–61; UK Mem., Commonwealth Economic Cttee, 1961–67; Mem., (Franks) Commn of Inquiry into Oxford Univ., 1964–66; Chm. Exec. Cttee, NIESR, 1962–70; Chm. Select Cttee on Commodity Prices, 1976–77. Vice-Pres. Royal Economic Society (Hon. Secretary, 1948–58; President, 1958–60); Pres., Soc. of Business Economists, 1968–73, Hon. Fellow, 1973. Rede Lecturer, Cambridge University, 1962. Hon. DSc, University of Queensland. Joined SDP, 1981. *Publications:* Earning and Spending, 1934; The Economic System in a Socialist State, 1936; various articles, etc on economics. *Recreations:* walking, gardening. *Address:* 7a Carey Mansions, Rutherford Street, SW1. *T:* 01-834 7041; Quarry, Trenance, Newquay, Cornwall. *T:* St Mawgan 456. *Club:* Travellers'.

ROBERTS, family name of **Baron Clwyd.**

ROBERTS, Albert, JP; DL; MP (Lab) Normanton Division of West Riding of Yorkshire since 1951; *b* 14 May 1908; *s* of Albert Roberts and Annie Roberts (*née* Ward); *m* 1932, Alice Ashton; one *s* one *d*. *Educ:* Woodlesford School; Normanton and Whitwood Technical College, Yorks. Safety Board, Mines Inspector, 1941–51. Vice-Chm., Anglo-Spanish Parly Cttee; Chm., Anglo-South Korean Parly Group; Exec. Mem., British Group, Inter-Parly Union, 1967–. Exec. Mem., Yorkshire Area Heart Foundn. JP 1946, DL 1967, W Yorks. Order of Isabela la Catolica (Spain), 1967; Diplomatic Order of Merit, Korean Republic, 1979. *Recreations:* cricket, bowls. *Address:* Cordoba, 14 Aberford Road, Oulton-Woodlesford, near Leeds. *T:* Leeds 822303.

ROBERTS, Dr Albert, MSc, PhD; MIMinE, MIMM, AMInstCE, FGS, CEng; Head of Department of Mining Engineering, University of Nevada, 1969–75, retired 1975; *b* 25 April 1911; British; *m* 1938, May Taberner; two *s* one *d*. *Educ:* Wigan Mining and Techn. College. Mining Engr, Wigan Coal Corp., 1931–35, 1938–40; Ashanti Goldfields Corp., 1935–38; Lectr: Sunderland Techn. Coll., 1940–45; Nottingham Univ., 1945–55; Sheffield Univ., 1955; Dir, Postgraduate Sch. of Mining, Sheffield Univ., 1956–69. Ed., Internat. Jl of Rock Mechanics and Mining Sciences, 1964–68. *Publications:* Geological Structures, 1946; Underground Lighting, 1959; Mine Ventilation, 1959; Mineral Processing, 1965; Geotechnology, 1977. *Recreations:* gardening, photography, music, fishing.

ROBERTS, Allan; MP (Lab) Bootle, since 1979; *b* 28 Oct. 1943; *s* of Ernest and Anne Roberts. *Educ:* Droylesden, Little Moss Boys' County Sec. Sch.; Didsbury Coll. of Education (Teachers' Cert.); Manchester Univ. Extra-Mural Dept (CQSW). School teacher, 1967-70; at Manchester Univ., 1970-72; Social Worker and Sen. Social Worker, 1972-74; Training Officer, City of Salford Social Services Dept, 1974-76; Principal Officer (Child Care) with Salford Social Services Dept, 1976-79. *Publications:* contribs to Tribune. *Recreations:* reading, films, eating, drinking, theatre. *Address:* 45 Deepdale Avenue, Bootle, Merseyside. *Club:* Bootle Labour (Bootle).

ROBERTS, Alwyn; Director of Extra Mural Studies, University College of North Wales, Bangor, since 1979; *b* 26 Aug. 1933; *s* of late Rev. Howell Roberts and of Buddug Roberts; *m* 1960, Mair Rowlands Williams; one *s*. *Educ:* Penygroes Grammar Sch.; Univ. of Wales, Aberystwyth and Bangor (BA, LLB); Univ. of Cambridge (MA). Tutor, Westminster Coll., Cambridge, 1959; Principal, Pachhunga Meml Govt Coll., Aijal, Assam, India, 1960-67; Lectr in Social Admin, University Coll., Swansea, 1967-70; Lectr, subseq. Sen. Lectr, Dept of Social Theory and Instns, UCNW, Bangor, 1970-79. BBC National Governor for Wales, 1979-; Member: Broadcasting Council for Wales, 1974-78; Welsh Fourth TV Channel Auth., 1981-; Gwynedd CC, 1973- (Chm., Social Services Cttee 1977-); Gwynedd AHA, 1973-80; Royal Commn on Legal Services, 1976-79; Council, Royal National Eisteddfod of Wales, 1979-. *Address:* Gwynfryn, Holyhead Road, Bangor, Gwynedd LL57 2EE. *T:* Bangor 4052.

ROBERTS, Angus Thomas; Director of Litigation and Prosecution, Post Office Solicitor's Office (formerly Principal Assistant Solicitor to General Post Office), 1965-74; *b* 28 March 1913; *s* of late Edward Roberts and late Margaret (*née* Murray); *m* 1940, Frances Monica, *d* of late Frederick and late Agnes Bertha Cane; two *s*. *Educ:* Felsted School. Admitted Solicitor, 1936. Entered Post Office Solicitor's Dept, 1939. Served in Royal Navy, 1941-46 (Lieut, RNVR). Asst Solicitor to GPO, 1951. *Recreations:* golf, fishing, gardening. *Address:* Caen Cottage, Helmsdale, Sutherland, Scotland. *T:* Helmsdale 277. *Clubs:* Helmsdale Golf, Brora Golf.

ROBERTS, Ann Clwyd; *see* Clwyd, Ann.

ROBERTS, (Anthony) John; Director Counter Services, The Post Office, since 1981; *b* 26 Aug. 1944; *s* of Douglas and Margaret Roberts; *m* 1970, Diana June (*née* Lamdin); two *s*. *Educ:* Hampton Sch.; Exeter Univ. (BA Hons). FBIM. Open Entrant, Administrative Class Civil Service, The Post Office, 1967; PA to Dep. Chairman and Chief Executive, 1969-71; Principal, Long Range Planning, 1971-74; Controller Personnel and Finance, North Western Postal Board, 1974-76; Principal Private Sec. to Chairman, 1976-77; Director, Chairman's Office, 1977-80; Secretary Designate, 1980-81, Sec., 1981-82. *Recreations:* squash, golf, gardening, music. *Address:* The Post Office, Headquarters Building, St Martins-le-Grand, EC1A 1PG. *T:* 01-432 1234. *Clubs:* Weybridge Squash Rackets, Betchworth Park Golf.

ROBERTS, Arthur Loten, OBE 1971; Emeritus Professor, formerly Livesey Professor of Coal Gas and Fuel Industries, 1947-71, and Chairman of the Houldsworth School of Applied Science, 1956-70, University of Leeds; Pro-Vice-Chancellor, 1967-69; *b* 1 April 1906; *s* of Arthur James Roberts, Hull, and Alice Maude Loten, Hornsea, E Yorks; *m* 1941, Katherine Mary Hargrove; one *s* one *d*. *Educ:* Christ's Hospital; Univ. of Leeds. BSc 1928, PhD 1930, Assistant Lecturer, Lecturer, Senior Lecturer, Leeds Univ. Part-time mem. North-Eastern Area Gas Board, 1950-71; Mem. Gas Corp. Res. Cttee (formerly Gas Council Research Cttee), 1951-79; Hon. Sec. Advisory Research Cttee of Gas Council and University, 1947-71; Chm., former Joint Refractories Cttee of British Ceramic Research Assoc. and the Gas Corporation; Pres. British Ceramic Society, 1957-58; Member of Technology Sub-Cttee, UGC, 1960-69. FRIC, FInstF, Hon. Fellow Inst. Ceram., Hon. FInstGasE, Hon. FIChemE. *Publications:* numerous contributions to chemical, ceramic and fuel jls. *Recreations:* painting, pianoforte, garden. *Address:* Hillside, 6 King's Road, Bramhope, Leeds, W Yorks. *T:* Leeds 674977.

ROBERTS, Prof. Benjamin Charles, MA Oxon; Professor of Industrial Relations, London School of Economics, University of London, since 1962; *b* 1 Aug. 1917; *s* of Walter Whitfield Roberts and Mabel Frances Roberts; *m* 1945, Veronica Lilian Vine-Lott; two *s*. *Educ:* LSE; New Coll., Oxford. Research Student, Nuffield Coll., Oxford, 1948-49; Part-time Lectr, Ruskin Coll., Oxford, 1948-49; London Sch. of Economics: Lectr in Trade Union Studies, 1949-56; Reader in Industrial Relations, 1956-62; Mem. Ct of Govs, 1964-69, 1979-. Vis. Prof: Princeton Univ., 1958; MIT 1959; Univ. of Calif., Berkeley, 1965. Assoc., Internat. Inst. of Labour Studies, Geneva, 1966; Member: Council, Inst. Manpower Studies; Council, Foundn for Automation and Employment; British-N American Cttee; Nat. Reference Tribunal of Coal Mining Industry, 1970-; Council, ACAS, 1979-. Editor, British Jl of Industrial Relations, 1963-. Pres., British Univs Industrial Relations Assoc., 1965-68; Pres., Internat. Industrial Relations Assoc., 1967-73. Consultant to EEC, 1976-79. Chm., Economists' Bookshop, 1979-. *Publications:* Trade Unions in the New Era, 1947; Trade Union Government and Administration in Great Britain, 1956; National Wages Policy in War and Peace, 1958; The Trades Union Congress, 1868-1921, 1958; Trade Unions in a Free Society, 1959; (ed) Industrial Relations: Contemporary Problems and Perspectives, 1962; Labour in the Tropical Territories of the Commonwealth, 1964; (ed) Manpower Planning and Employment Trends 1966; (with L. Greyfie de Bellecombe) Collective Bargaining in African Countries, 1967; (ed) Industrial

Relations: Contemporary Issues, 1968; (with John Lovell) A Short History of the TUC, 1968; (with R. O. Clarke and D. J. Fatchet) Workers' Participation in Management in Britain, 1972; (with R. Loveridge and J. Gennard) Reluctant Militants: a study of industrial technicians, 1972; (with H. Okomoto and G. Lodge) Collective Bargaining and Employee Participation in Western Europe, North America and Japan, 1979; also Evidence to Royal Commn on Trade Unions, 1966, and Report to ILO on Labour and Automation: Manpower Adjustment Programmes in the United Kingdom, 1967. *Address:* 28 Temple Fortune Lane, NW11. *T:* 01-458 1421. *Club:* Reform.

ROBERTS, Bertie; Director, Department of the Environment (Property Services Agency), 1971-79; *b* 4 June 1919; *y s* of late Thomas and Louisa Roberts, Blaengarw, S Wales; *m* 1st, 1946, Dr Peggy Clark; one *s* ; 2nd, 1962, Catherine Matthew. *Educ:* Garw Grammar School. Entered Civil Service (HM Office of Works), 1936; HM Forces, 1942-46, Captain RAOC; leader of study on feasibility of using computers in Min. of Public Bldg and Works, 1958; formed operational computer orgn, 1962; Comptroller of Accounts, 1963; Dir of Computer Services, 1967; Head of Organisation and Methods, 1969; Dir of Estate Management Overseas, Dept of the Environment, 1971; Reg. Dir, DoE (Maj.-Gen.), British Forces Germany, 1976-79. Mem., Community Health Council (Hastings Dist), 1982-. *Recreations:* travel, music. *Address:* Fairmount, 41 Hollington Park Road, St Leonards on Sea, E Sussex. *T:* Hastings 714177. *Clubs:* Civil Service; Rotary of St Leonard's-on-Sea.

ROBERTS, Brian Richard; Editor, The Sunday Telegraph, 1966-76 (Managing Editor, 1961-66); *b* 16 Sept. 1906; *e s* of late Robert Lewis Roberts, CBE; *m* 1935, Elisabeth Franziska Dora, *er d* of late Dr Leo Zuntz, Berlin; one adopted *s*. *Educ:* Merchant Taylors' Sch.; St John's Coll., Oxford (MA); Hon. Fellow 1975. Editorial staff, Oxford Mail, 1930-33; Daily Mail, 1933-38 (Night Editor, 1936-38); Joined The Daily Telegraph, 1939 (Night Editor, 1944-57, Chief Asst Editor 1957-60). Pres., Inst. of Journalists, 1954-55; Pres., Guild of Agricultural Journalists, 1976; Mem. Governing Body, Northern Polytechnic, London, 1946-71 (Chm. 1956-71); Polytechnic of North London: Chm., Formation Cttee, 1970-71; Mem. Ct of Governors, 1971-79, Chm., 1971-74; Hon. Fellow 1981; Chm. of Council, Assoc. of Colls for Further and Higher Educn (formerly Assoc. of Technical Instns), 1964-65, Hon. Treasurer, 1967-77. Gold Medal, Inst. of Journalists, 1971; special award, National Press Awards, 1974; Queen's Jubilee Medal, 1977. *Recreation:* agriculture. *Address:* Old Foxhunt Manor, Waldron, near Heathfield, Sussex TN21 0RU. *T:* Horam Road 2618.

See also C. H. Roberts and Rev. R. L. Roberts.

ROBERTS, Sir Bryan Clieve, KCMG 1973 (CMG 1964); QC; JP; a Metropolitan Stipendiary Magistrate, since 1982; Chairman, Commonwealth Magistrates' Association, since 1979; *b* 22 March 1923; *s* of late Herbert Roberts, MA, and Doris Evelyn Clieve; *m* 1st, 1948, Pamela Dorothy Campbell (marr. diss. 1975); 2nd, 1976, Brigitte Patricia Reilly-Morrison. *Educ:* Whitgift School; Magdalen Coll., Oxford (BA Hons). Served War of 1939-45: commissioned in RA and RHA, 1941-46; active service in Normandy, Belgium, Holland and Germany, 1944-45. Called to Bar, Gray's Inn, 1950; in chambers in Temple, 1950-51; Treasury Solicitor's Dept, 1951-53. Crown Counsel, N Rhodesia, 1953-60; Dir of Public Prosecutions, N Rhodesia, 1960-61; Nyasaland: Solicitor-Gen. and Perm. Sec. to Min. of Justice, 1961; Solicitor-General, 1961-64; Minister of Justice, 1962-63; Mem., Nyasaland Legislative Council, 1961-63; Attorney-Gen. of Malawi, 1964-72; Perm. Sec. to Office of the President, Sec. to the Cabinet, and Head of Malawi Civil Service, 1965-72; Chairman: Malawi Army Council; Nat. Security and Intell. Cttee; Nat. Develt and Planning Cttee, 1966-72. Lord Chancellor's Office, 1973-82 (Under Sec., 1977-82). JP Inner London, 1975 (Dep. Chm., South Westminster Bench). Officer of the Order of Menelik II of Ethiopia, 1965; Comdr, Nat. Order of Republic of Malagasy, 1969. *Address:* 16 Ansdell Terrace, W8; Stonebarrow Lodge, Charmouth, Dorset. *Club:* Royal Commonwealth Society.

ROBERTS, Rear-Adm. Cedric Kenelm; CB 1970; DSO 1952; *b* 19 April 1918; *s* of F. A. Roberts; *m* 1940, Audrey, *d* of T. M. Elias; four *s*. *Educ:* King Edward's Sch., Birmingham. Joined RN as Naval Airman 2nd Cl., 1940; commnd Temp. Sub-Lt (A), RNVR, 1940; sunk in HMS Manchester, 1942, Malta Convoy; interned in Sahara; released, Nov. 1942; Personal Pilot to Vice-Adm. Sir Arthur Lyster, 1943; HMS Trumpeter, Russian Convoys, 1944; perm. commn as Lt RN, HMS Vindex, Pacific, 1945; CO 813 Sqdn, 1948; Naval Staff Coll., 1949; CO 767 Sqdn, 1950-51; CO 825 Sqdn, 1951-52: served Korean War; shot down, rescued by US Forces; lent to RAN as Dep. Dir, Air Warfare, 1953-55; CO, RNAS Eglinton, 1958-59; Chief Staff Officer: FONFT, 1959-61; FOAC, 1961-62; Capt., HMS Osprey, 1962-64; Capt., RNAS Culdrose, 1964-65; Chief Staff Officer (Ops), Far East Fleet, 1966-67; Flag Officer, Naval Flying Training, 1968-71; retired 1971; farmed in Somerset, 1971-79; emigrated to Australia, 1979. Comdr 1952; Capt. 1958; Rear-Adm. 1968. *Recreations:* sitting in the sun, drinking plonk, and watching the sheilas go by. *Address:* 11 Collins Street, Merimbula, NSW 2548, Australia. *T:* Merimbula 51754.

ROBERTS, Charles Stuart; CMG 1975; HM Diplomatic Service, retired; High Commissioner in Barbados, 1973-78; *b* 24 May 1918; *s* of late Charles William Roberts and of Dorothy Roberts; *m* 1946, Margaret Ethel Jones; one *s* two *d*. *Educ:* Merchant Taylors' School. Entered Colonial Office, 1936.

Naval Service (Lieut RNVR), 1940–46. Economic and Financial Adviser, Leeward Is, 1955–57; transferred to HM Diplomatic Service (Counsellor), 1966; British Govt Representative, W Indies Associated States, 1967–70; Head of Caribbean Dept, FCO, 1970–73. *Recreations:* chess, crosswords. *Address:* 10 Montacute Road, Tunbridge Wells, Kent TN2 5QR. *T:* Tunbridge Wells 25553. *Clubs:* MCC; Royal Commonwealth Society (West Indian).

ROBERTS, Christopher William; Under Secretary, Civil Aviation International Relations, Department of Trade, since 1979; *b* 4 Nov. 1937; *s* of Frank Roberts and Evelyn Dorothy Roberts. *Educ:* Rugby Sch.; Magdalen Coll., Oxford (MA). Lectr in Classics, Pembroke Coll., Oxford, 1959–60; Asst Principal, BoT, 1960; Second Sec. (Commercial), British High Commn, New Delhi, 1962–64; Asst Private Sec. to Pres. of BoT, 1964–65; Principal, 1965; Cabinet Office, 1966–68; Private Sec. to Prime Minister, 1970–73; Asst Sec., 1972; Dept of Trade, 1973–77; Under Sec., Dept of Prices and Consumer Protection, 1977–79. *Recreations:* travel, cricket, opera. *Address:* 11 Sprimont Place, SW3 3HT. *T:* 01-581 1860. *Clubs:* United Oxford & Cambridge University, MCC.

ROBERTS, Colin Henderson, CBE 1973; Secretary to Delegates of Oxford University Press, 1954–74; Fellow of St John's College, Oxford, 1934–76, Hon. Fellow, 1976; *b* 8 June 1909; *s* of late Robert Lewis Roberts, CBE; *m* 1947, Alison Muriel, *d* of Reginald Haynes and Phyllis Irene Barrow; one *d*. *Educ:* Merchant Taylors' School; St John's College, Oxford (MA). 1st Cl., Hon. Class. Mods, 1929; 1st Cl., Lit. hum. 1931; Sen. Schol., St John's Coll., 1931–34; Craven Univ. Fellow, 1932–34. Studied Berlin Univ., 1932; Univ. of Michigan, Near East Research (Egypt), 1932–34; Dept of Foreign Office, 1939–45. Lecturer in Classics, St John's College, Oxford, 1939–53; tutor, 1946–53; University Lecturer in Papyrology, 1937–48; Reader, 1948–53. Delegate of Oxford Univ. Press, 1946–53; FBA 1947–80; Visiting Mem. of Inst. for Advanced Study, Princeton, NJ, 1951–52; Sandars Reader in Bibliography, University of Cambridge, 1960–61. Schweich Lectr, British Acad., 1977. Hon. DLitt Oxon, 1975. *Publications:* An Unpublished Fragment of the Fourth Gospel, 1935; Catalogue of the Greek Papyri in the Rylands Library, Manchester, Vol. III, 1938, Vol. IV (with E. G. Turner), 1952; part editor of the Oxyrhynchus Papyri, Parts XVIII–XX, 1941–52 and XXII, 1954; The Antinoopolis Papyri, 1950; The Merton Papyri (with H. I. Bell), 1948; The Codex, 1955; The Greek Bookhand, 1955; Manuscript, Society and Belief in Early Christian Egypt, 1979. *Recreation:* gardening. *Address:* Hursey House, Broadwindsor, near Beaminster, Dorset. *T:* Broadwindsor 68281.

See also B. R. Roberts and Rev. R. L. Roberts.

ROBERTS, Cyril Alfred, CBE 1947 (MBE 1944); DL; *b* 4 June 1908; *s* of late A. W. Roberts; *m* 1932, Christine Annabel Kitson, *d* of late Hon. E. C. Kitson, Leeds; three *s* one *d*. *Educ:* Eton; Trinity Coll., Oxford. Called to the Bar, 1932, and practised until 1939. Served War of 1939–45, HM Forces, 1939–46; France, 1940; Western Desert, 1941–42; Instructor, Staff Coll., Haifa, 1943; War Office, Army Council Secretariat, 1943–45; Brigadier AG Co-ordination, 1945–46. Asst Sec., NCB, 1946–47, Under-Sec. 1947–51, Sec., 1951–59; Member of the Board, 1960–67. Dir, later Dep. Chm., Woodall-Duckham Gp Ltd, 1968–73. Chm., Inst. of Cardiology, 1967–72; Mem. Bd of Governors, Brompton Hosp., Chm. House Cttee, Nat. Heart Hosp., 1973–76. Adviser to Minister of Defence on Resettlement from the Forces, 1968–70; Mem., Armed Forces Pay Review Bd 1971–79; Chm., Heart Exploration and Research in Therapy, 1979–81. CBIM. Chm., Chichester District Council, 1981–. DL West Sussex, 1982. *Address:* Bury Gate House, Pulborough, West Sussex. *T:* Bury 440.

ROBERTS, David Arthur, CMG 1975; CVO 1979; HM Diplomatic Service; Ambassador to Lebanon, since 1981; *b* 8 Aug. 1924; *s* of late Rev. T. A. Roberts and Mrs T. A. Roberts; *m* 1st, 1951, Nicole Marie Fay (*d* 1965); two *d*; 2nd, 1968, Hazel Faith Arnot. *Educ:* Hereford Cathedral Sch.; Jesus Coll., Oxford (Scholar; BA). Served Royal Armoured Corps, 1943–46. HM Foreign Service, Dec. 1947. Served: Baghdad, 1948–49; Tokyo, 1949–51; FO, 1951–53; Alexandria, 1953–55; Khartoum, 1955–58; FO, 1958–60; Dakar, 1960–61 (Chargé d'Affairs at Bamako and at Lomé during same period); FO, 1962–63; Damascus, 1963–66; Political Agent in the Trucial States, Dubai, 1966–68; Head of Accommodation Dept, FCO, 1968–71; High Comr in Barbados, 1971–73; Ambassador to Syria, 1973–76; High Comr in Sierra Leone, 1976–77; Ambassador to the United Arab Emirates, 1977–81. *Address:* c/o Foreign and Commonwealth Office, SW1. *Club:* Reform.

See also M. H. A. Roberts.

ROBERTS, David Ewart; His Honour Judge David Roberts; a Circuit Judge, since 1982; *b* 18 Feb. 1921; *s* of John Hobson Roberts and Dorothy Roberts. *Educ:* Abingdon Sch.; St John's Coll., Cambridge. MA, LLB. Served War, 1941–46; commnd RA (Field); service in Middle East, North Africa, Italy, Yugoslavia and Germany. Called to Bar, Middle Temple, 1948. Asst Recorder, Coventry QS, 1966–71; a Recorder of the Crown Court, 1978–82. *Recreations:* aviation, golf, skiing, photography. *Address:* (home) 4 Greville Drive, Birmingham B15 2UU. *T:* 021-440 3231; (chambers) 4 Fountain Court, Birmingham B4 6DR. *T:* 021-236 3476.

ROBERTS, Rt. Rev. (David) John; Abbot of Downside, since 1974; *b* 31 March 1919; *s* of Albert Edward and Elizabeth Minnith Roberts. *Educ:* Downside School; Trinity Coll., Cambridge (MA). Royal Sussex Regt, Oct. 1939–Nov. 1945 (POW Germany, May 1940–April 1945). Entered monastery, Feb. 1946; ordained, 1951. House Master, Downside School, 1953–62; Novice

Master, 1962–66; Prior 1966–74. *Address:* Downside Abbey, Stratton-on-the-Fosse, Bath BA3 4RH.

ROBERTS, Dr Denis; *see* Roberts, Dr E. F. D.

ROBERTS, Denis Edwin, CBE 1974 (MBE 1945); Chairman, British Philatelic Trust, since 1981; *b* 6 Jan. 1917; *s* of late Edwin Roberts and of Alice G. Roberts; *m* 1940, Edith (*née* Whitehead); two *s*. *Educ:* Holgate Grammar Sch., Barnsley. Served War of 1939–45, Royal Signals, France, N Africa, Italy and Austria. Entered Post Office, Barnsley, 1933; various appts, 1933–71; Dir Postal Ops, 1971–75; Sen. Dir, Postal Services, 1975–77; Man. Dir, Posts, 1977–80. CBIM. *Address:* 302 Gilbert House, Barbican, EC2Y 8BD. *T:* 01-638 0881. *Clubs:* City of London, City Livery.

ROBERTS, Hon. Sir Denys (Tudor Emil), KBE 1975 (CBE 1970; OBE 1960); Hon. Mr Justice Roberts; Chief Justice of Hong Kong, since 1979; *b* 19 Jan. 1923; *s* of William David and Dorothy Elizabeth Roberts; (marriage dissolved; one *s* one *d*). *Educ:* Aldenham; Wadham Coll., Oxford, 1942 and 1946–49 (MA 1948, BCL 1949); served with Royal Artillery, 1943–46, France, Belgium, Holland, Germany, India (Captain); English Bar, 1950–53; Crown Counsel, Nyasaland, 1953–59; QC Gibraltar 1960; QC Hong Kong 1964; Attorney-General, Gibraltar, 1960–62; Solicitor-General, Hong Kong, 1962–66; Attorney-General, Hong Kong, 1966–73; Chief Secretary, Hong Kong, 1973–78. Hon. Bencher, Lincoln's Inn, 1978. *Publications:* Smuggler's Circuit, 1954; Beds and Roses, 1956; The Elwood Wager, 1958; The Bones of the Wajingas, 1960; How to Dispense with Lawyers, 1964. *Recreations:* cricket, walking, writing. *Address:* The Supreme Court, Hong Kong; High Point, 35 Beaucroft Lane, Colehill, Wimborne, Dorset. *Clubs:* MCC; Hong Kong (Hong Kong).

ROBERTS, Derek Harry, FRS 1980, FEng, FInstP; Director of Research, General Electric Company plc, since 1979; *b* 28 March 1932; *s* of Harry and Alice Roberts; *m* 1958, Winifred (*née* Short); one *s* one *d*. *Educ:* Manchester Central High Sch.; Manchester Univ. (BSc). MIEE. Joined Plessey Co.'s Caswell Res. Lab., 1953; Gen. Man., Plessey Semiconductors, 1967; Dir, Allen Clark Res. Centre, 1969; Man. Dir, Plessey Microelectronics Div., 1973. Member: Adv. Council for Applied R&D, 1981–; Engrg Council, 1982–. Hon. DSc Bath, 1982. *Publications:* about 20 pubns in scientific and technical jls. *Recreations:* reading, gardening. *Address:* The Old Rectory, Maids Moreton, Buckingham. *T:* Buckingham 3470.

ROBERTS, Rev. Canon Edward Eric, JP; Canon Emeritus of Southwell, since 1980; Secretary, Nottingham Council of Churches, since 1980; *b* 29 April 1911; *o s* of late Edward Thomas Roberts and Mrs Charlotte Roberts, Liverpool; *m* 1938, Sybil Mary (*née* Curren); two *d*. *Educ:* Univ. of Liverpool; St Augustine's Coll., Canterbury. Youth Officer: City of Oxford LEA, 1938–43; Wallasey GB, LEA, 1943–44; Training Officer, Church of England Youth Council, 1944–52; Southwell Diocesan Director: of Further Educn, 1952–61; of Educn, 1961–68. Canon, 1964; Canon Residentiary, Vice-Provost of Southwell Cathedral and Personal Chaplain to Bishop of Southwell, 1969–79; Ecumenical Officer, Diocese of Southwell, 1973–79. JP, City of Nottingham, 1958–. *Recreation:* photography. *Address:* 83 Woodbank Drive, Wollaton, Nottingham. *T:* Nottingham 283997.

ROBERTS, Sir (Edward Fergus) Sidney, Kt 1978; CBE 1972; Federal President, Australian Country Party, since 1969; grazier and manager of companies; *b* 19 April 1901; *s* of late E. J. Roberts. *Educ:* Scots Coll., Sydney. Gen. Manager, Ungra, Brisbane, 1957–70; owner, Boolaroo Downs, Clermont, Qld, 1928–63. United Graziers' Assoc., Qld: Mem. Council, 1948–76; Vice-Pres., 1950–52. Aust. Road Fedn: Mem., 1954–63; Nat. Pres., 1962–63. Mem. Bd, Queensland Country Life Newspaper, 1969–77; Pres., Aust. Country Party, Qld, 1967; Chm., Federal Council, ACP, 1969–74. Knighthood awarded for distinguished service to Primary Industry, Australia. *Address:* 53 Eldernell Avenue, Hamilton, Queensland 4007, Australia. *Club:* Queensland (Brisbane).

ROBERTS, Dr (Edward Frederick) Denis, FRSE 1980; Librarian, National Library of Scotland, since 1970; *b* 16 June 1927; *s* of Herbert Roberts and Jane Spottiswoode Roberts (*née* Wilkinson); *m* 1954, Irene Mary Beatrice (*née* Richardson); one *s* one *d*. *Educ:* Royal Belfast Academical Institution; Queen's University of Belfast. BA (1st cl. Hons Modern History) 1951; PhD 1955. Research Assistant, Dept of History, Queen's Univ. of Belfast, 1951–55; National Library of Scotland: Asst Keeper, Dept of Manuscripts, 1955–66; Secretary of the Library, 1966–67; Librarian, Trinity College Dublin, 1967–70; Hon. Prof., Univ. of Edinburgh, 1975. *Publication:* (with W. G. H. Quigley) Registrum Iohannis Mey: The Register of John Mey, Archbishop of Armagh, 1443–1456, 1972. *Address:* 6 Oswald Court, Edinburgh EH9 2HY. *T:* 031-667 9473. *Club:* New (Edinburgh).

ROBERTS, Rt. Rev. Edward James Keymer; *b* 18 April 1908; *s* of Rev. Arthur Henry Roberts; *m* 1941, Dorothy Frances, *d* of Canon Edwin David Bowser, Deal; three *s* one *d*. *Educ:* Marlborough; Corpus Christi Coll., Cambridge; Cuddesdon Theological Coll. BA 2nd class Theological Tripos, 1930; MA 1935; DD (*hc*) Cambridge, 1965. FRSCM 1977. Deacon, 1931; priest, 1932; Curate of All Saints, Margaret Street, 1931–35; Vice-Principal Cuddesdon Coll., 1935–39; Examining Chaplain to Bishop of Portsmouth and Commissary, Johannesburg, 1936–39; Vicar of St Matthew, Southsea, 1940–45; Curate-in-charge of St Bartholomew, Southsea, 1941–45; Examining

Chaplain to Bishop of Portsmouth, 1942-56; Proctor in Convocation, Portsmouth, 1944-49; Commissary, Northern Rhodesia, 1946-51; Hon. Canon of Portsmouth, 1947-49; Archdeacon of Isle of Wight, Vicar of Brading, Rector of Yaverland, 1949-52; Archdeacon of Portsmouth, 1952-56; Suffragan Bishop of Malmesbury, 1956-62; Examining Chaplain to Bishop of Bristol, 1959-62; Suffragan Bishop of Kensington, 1962-64; Bishop of Ely, 1964-77. Hon. Fellow, Corpus Christi Coll., Cambridge, 1964-. Select Preacher, University of Cambridge, 1966, 1978. *Recreation:* shoe cleaning. *Address:* Garden House, Tyne Hall, Bembridge, IoW. *T:* Bembridge 2645.

ROBERTS, Eirlys Rhiwen Cadwaladr, CBE 1977 (OBE 1971); Deputy Director, Consumers' Association (Which?), 1973-77 (Head of Research and Editorial Division, 1958-73); *b* 3 Jan. 1911; *d* of Dr Ellis James Roberts and Jane Tennant Macaulay; *m* 1941, John Cullen (marr. diss.); no *c. Educ:* Clapham High School; Girton College, Cambridge. BA (Hons) Classics. Sub-editor in Amalgamated Press; Military, then Political Intelligence, 1943-44 and 1944-45; Public Relations in UNRRA, Albanian Mission, 1945-47; Information Division of the Treasury, 1947-57. Chief Exec., Bureau of European Consumer Orgns, 1973-78. Mem., Royal Commn on the Press, 1974-77. Chm., European Res. into Consumer Affairs; Mem., Economic and Social Cttee of EEC, 1973- (Chm., Environment and Consumer Protection section, 1978-). *Publication:* Consumers, 1966. *Recreations:* climbing, ice-skating, reading detective novels. *Address:* 8 Lloyd Square, WC1. *T:* 01-837 2492.

ROBERTS, Emrys, CBE 1976 (MBE 1946); *b* 22 Sept. 1910; *s* of late Owen Owens Roberts and of Mary Grace Williams, both of Caernarvon; *m* 1948, Anna Elisabeth Tudor; one *d* (one *s* decd). *Educ:* Caernarfon; Aberystwyth; Gonville and Caius Coll., Cambridge; Geneva. MA (Cantab); LLB (Wales); 1st Class, Parts I and II, Law Tripos, Cambridge, 1933; 1st Class Hons, University of Wales, 1931, S. T. Evans Prize; Solicitor, 1936, 1st Class Hons, Clements Inn Prize. Squadron Leader RAF, 1941-45. Barrister, Gray's Inn, 1944. MP (L) for Merioneth, 1945-51; Member of Parliamentary Delegations to Yugoslavia, Germany, Rumania, and Sweden; Representative at Council of Europe, 1950 and 1951. Director: Tootal Broadhurst Lee Co. Ltd, English Sewing Ltd, English Calico Ltd and Tootal Ltd, 1958-75; Cambrian & General Securities Ltd, 1974-81. Chairman: Mid-Wales Develt Corp., 1968-77; Develt Bd for Rural Wales, 1977-81; Mem., Welsh Develt Agency, 1977-81; Dir, Develt Corp. of Wales, 1978-81). Mem. Court and Council, Univ. Coll. of Wales, Aberystwyth, 1972-82; Chm. of Council, Nat. Eisteddfod of Wales, 1964-67, and Hon. Counsel, 1957-74; Vice-Pres. Hon. Soc. of Cymmrodorion. *Publication:* (jointly) The Law of Restrictive Trade Practices and Monopolies. *Address:* Dwy Dderwen, Glyn Garth, Menai Bridge, Gwynedd LL59 5NP. *T:* Menai Bridge 712793.

ROBERTS, Rt. Rev. Eric Matthias; *b* 18 Feb. 1914; *s* of Richard and Jane Roberts; *m* 1944, Nancy Jane Roberts (*née* Davies); two *s. Educ:* Friars Sch., Bangor; University Coll., Bangor; St Edmund Hall, Oxon (MA); St Michael's Coll., Llandaff. Curate, Penmaenmawr, 1938-40; Sub-Warden, St Michael's Coll., Llandaff, 1940-47; Vicar: Port Talbot, 1947-56; Roath, 1956-65; Archdeacon of Margam, 1965-71; Bishop of St David's, 1971-81. ChStJ 1973. *Address:* 2 Tudor Close, Westbourne Road, Penarth, South Glamorgan.

ROBERTS, Ernest Alfred Cecil; MP (Lab) Hackney North and Stoke Newington, since 1979; *b* 20 April 1912; *s* of Alfred and Florence Roberts; *m* 1953, Joyce Longley; one *s* two *d. Educ:* St Chad's Boys' Elementary Sch., Shrewsbury. Engineer, 1925-57; Assistant General Secretary, AUEW, 1957-77. Tom Mann Gold Medal for services to trade unionism, 1943. *Publication:* Workers' Control, 1973. *Recreations:* work and politics, reading. *Address:* House of Commons, Westminster, SW1A 0AA.

ROBERTS, Sir Frank (Kenyon), GCMG 1963 (KCMG 1953; CMG 1946); GCVO 1965; Director: Hoechst (UK); Mercedes-Benz (UK); President, European Atlantic Group, since 1973 (Chairman, 1970-73); Vice-President: Atlantic Treaty Association, since 1973 (President, 1969-73); British Atlantic Committee (President, 1968-81); *b* Buenos Aires, 27 Oct. 1907; *s* of Henry George Roberts, Preston, and Gertrude Kenyon, Blackburn; *m* 1937, Celeste Leila Beatrix, *d* of late Sir Said Shoucair Pasha, Cairo, Financial Adviser to Sudan Government; no *c. Educ:* Bedales; Rugby; Trinity College, Cambridge (Scholar). Entered Foreign Office, 1930; served HM Embassy, Paris, 1932-35 and at HM Embassy, Cairo, 1935-37; Foreign Office, 1937-45; Chargé d'Affaires to Czechoslovak Govt, 1943; British Minister in Moscow, 1945-47; Principal Private Secretary to Secretary of State for Foreign Affairs, 1947-49; Deputy High Commr (UK) in India, 1949-51; Deputy-Under Secretary of State, Foreign Office, 1951-54; HM Ambassador to Yugoslavia, 1954-57; United Kingdom Permanent Representative on the North Atlantic Council, 1957-60; Ambassador: to the USSR, 1960-62; to the Federal Republic of Germany, 1963-68. Vice-Pres., German Chamber of Commerce in UK, 1974- (Pres., 1971-74); Dep. Chm., British Nat. Cttee, Internat. Chamber of Commerce, 1978-81. Mem., FCO Review Cttee on Overseas Representation, 1968-69. Pres., Anglo-German Assoc.; Vice-Pres., GB-USSR Assoc. Grand Cross, German Order of Merit, 1965. *Address:* 25 Kensington Court Gardens, W8 5QF. *Clubs:* Brooks's, Royal Automobile.

ROBERTS, Geoffrey Frank Ingleson, CBE 1978; Chairman, British Pipe Coaters Ltd; *b* 9 May 1926; *s* of late Arthur and Laura Roberts; *m* 1949, Veronica, *d* of late Captain J. Busby, Hartlepool; two *d. Educ:* Cathedral Sch., and High Sch. for Boys, Hereford; Leeds Univ. (BSc hons). FEng 1978;

FIGasE, FIChemE; FInstE. Pupil engr, Gas Light & Coke Co., and North Thames Gas Bd, 1947-50; North Thames Gas Board: Asst Engr, 1950-59; Stn Engr, Slough, 1959-61; Dept. Stn Engr, Southall Stn, 1961-66; Group Engr, Slough Group, 1966-68; Dep. Dir (Ops) Gas Council, 1968-71; Mem. for Production and Supply, Gas Council, later British Gas Corp., 1972-78; Mem. for External Affairs, British Gas Corp., 1979-81, retired. Pres., IGasE, 1980-81. *Recreations:* gardening, reading. *Address:* Berry Hill, Deepdene Drive, Dorking, Surrey. *T:* Dorking 884795.

ROBERTS, Air Cdre Sir Geoffrey Newland, Kt 1973; CBE 1946; AFC 1942; FRAeS; Company Director; *b* Inglewood, Taranaki, New Zealand, 8 Dec. 1906; *s* of Charles Oxford Roberts, England, and Hilda Marion Newland, New Zealand; *m* 1934, Phyllis Hamilton Bird; one *s* one *d. Educ:* New Plymouth Boys' High Sch., New Plymouth, Taranaki, NZ. In commerce, NZ, 1924-28; RAF, England/India, 1928-34; commerce, UK, 1935-36; commerce, NZ, 1936-39. Served War: RNZAF, NZ and Pacific (final rank Air Cdre), 1939-46. Air New Zealand, General Manager, 1946-58; Dir, 1958-65; Chm., 1965-75. Chairman: Lion Breweries Ltd Mimiwhangata Farm Park Trust Board, 1975-; Kaipara Edible Oils Refinery Ltd, 1978-; Director: MFL Mutual Fund Ltd, 1971-; Saudi NZ Capital Corp., 1980-; Anac Ltd, 1981-. Patron, Internat. Fedn of Airworthiness, 1976-. US Legion of Merit, 1944. *Relevant publication:* To Fly a Desk, by Noel Holmes, 1982. *Address:* Puketiro, No 2: RD, Wellsford, North Auckland, New Zealand. *T:* Wellsford 4311. *Clubs:* Northern, Auckland (Auckland, NZ); Rotary (Wellsford, NZ).

ROBERTS, Brig. Sir Geoffrey P. H.; *see* Hardy-Roberts.

ROBERTS, George Charles L.; *see* Lloyd-Roberts.

ROBERTS, Maj.-Gen. (George) Philip (Bradley), CB 1945; DSO 1942; MC 1941; late RTR; *b* 5 Nov. 1906; *m* 1st, 1936, Desirée (*d* 1979), *d* of Major A. B. Godfray, Jersey; two *s* two *d*; 2nd, 1980, Annie Cornelia, *d* of Lt-Col F. E. W. Toussieng, Kt of Dannebrog, and *widow* of Brig. J. K. Greenwood, OBE. *Educ:* Marlborough; RMC, Sandhurst. 2nd Lieut Royal Tank Corps, 1926; served War of 1939-45 (MC, DSO and two Bars, CB, despatches thrice); Officier Légion d'Honneur; Croix de Guerre avec palmes. Adjt 6 RTR 1939; DAQMG 7th Armed Div., Bde Maj. 4th Armed Bde, GSO II 7th Armed Div., AQMG 30 Corps, CO 3 RTR 1939-41; Comd 22nd Armed Bde, Comd 26th Armed Bde, Comd 30th Armed Bde, 1941-43; Commander 11th Armoured Div., 1943-46; Comdr 7th Armoured Div., 1947-48; Dir, Royal Armoured Corps, War Office, 1948-49; retired pay, 1949. Hon. Col Kent and County of London Yeomanry Squadron, The Royal Yeomanry Regt, T&AVR, 1963-70. JP County of Kent, 1960-70. *Address:* Greenbank, West Street, Mayfield, E Sussex; *c/o* Williams & Glyn's Bank Ltd, Kirkland House, Whitehall, SW1. *Club:* Army and Navy.

See also R. M. H. Vickers.

ROBERTS, Captain Gilbert Howland, CBE 1944; RD 1964; Royal Navy (retired); *b* 11 Oct. 1900; *s* of Colonel Sir Howland Roberts, 12th Baronet, and Elizabeth Marie La Roche; *m* 1930 (marriage dissolved); one *s* one *d*; *m* 1947, Jean Winifred Warren; one *d. Educ:* Westminster; Royal Naval Colleges, Osborne and Dartmouth. Served European War, 1916-18; specialised in gunnery, 1922; Medal of Royal Humane Society, 1922; Submarine X One, 1926; Commander, 1935; Staff of HM Tactical School, 1935-36; command HMS Fearless, 1937-38; invalided, 1938; rejoined Royal Navy, 1940; served since in HMS Excellent and on Staff of C-in-C Western Approaches as Director Tactical School (CBE, Comdr Order of Polonia Restituta); Captain, 1942. Commodore Royal Norwegian Navy, Naval Assistant to Norwegian Naval C-in-C, 1946-47 (1st class Comdr, Order of St Olaf; Officer, Legion of Honour); lent Royal Canadian Navy for duty and lecture tour, 1955; Comd HMS Vivid, RNR, 1956-64 (RD 1964). Lees-Knowles Lecturer, Military History, Cambridge Univ., 1951. CC Devon, 1957; Alderman, Torbay County Borough, 1967-74. *Relevant publication:* Captain Gilbert Roberts RN and the Anti-U-Boat School, by Mark Williams, 1979. *Recreation:* gardening. *Address:* Little Priors, Watcome, Torquay. *T:* 38919.

ROBERTS, Sir Gilbert (Howland Rookehurst), 7th Bt *cr* 1809; *b* 31 May 1934; *s* of Sir Thomas Langdon Howland Roberts, 6th Bt, CBE, and of Evelyn Margaret, *o d* of late H. Fielding-Hall; *S* father, 1979; *m* 1958, Ines, *o d* of late A. Labunski; one *s* one *d. Educ:* Rugby; Gonville and Caius Coll., Cambridge (BA 1957). CEng, MIMechE. *Heir:* *s* Howland Langdon Roberts, *b* 19 Aug. 1961. *Address:* 3340 Cliff Drive, Santa Barbara, Calif 93109, USA.

ROBERTS, Glynn S.; *see* Silyn Roberts.

ROBERTS, Gordon James, CBE 1975; JP; Chairman, Oxford Regional Health Authority, since 1978; Deputy Chairman, Commission for the New Towns, since 1978; *b* 30 Jan. 1921; *s* of Archie and Lily Roberts; *m* 1944, Barbara Leach; one *s* one *d. Educ:* Deanshanger Sch., Northants. Chm., Northants AHA, 1973-78. Member: Oxford Reg. Hosp. Bd, 1968-74; St Crispin Hosp. Management Cttee, 1965-74; Northants Exec. Council, NHS, 1954-74; E Midlands Econ. Planning Council, 1975-79; Bd, Northampton Develt Corp., 1976-. Parly Candidate (Labour), S Northants Constituency, Gen. Election, 1970. Mem., Towcester RDC, 1953-56; Mem., Northants CC, 1954-77 (Leader, 1973-77). JP Northants, 1952; Chm., Towcester Bench,

1977-. *Publication:* (with Dr O. F. Brown) Passenham-the history of a forest village, 1975. *Recreations:* music, reading, walking, local history. *Address:* 114 Ridgmont, Deanshanger, Milton Keynes, Bucks MK19 6JG. *T:* Milton Keynes 562605.

ROBERTS, Gwilym Edffrwd; MP (Lab) Cannock, since Feb. 1974; *b* 7 Aug. 1928; *s* of William and Jane Ann Roberts; *m* 1954, Mair Griffiths; no *c. Educ:* Brynrefail Gram. Sch.; UCW (Bangor). Industrial Management, 1952-57; Lecturer (Polytechnic and University), 1957-66, 1970-74. MP (Lab) South Bedfordshire, 1966-70. PPS, DoI, 1976-79. Industrial Consultant, Economic Forecasting, Market and Operational Research, 1957-. Vice-Pres., Inst. of Statisticians; Editor, Inst. of Statisticians Newsletter. *Recreations:* cricket, table tennis, journalism. *Address:* 60 Swasedale Road, Luton, Beds. *T:* 53893; 8 Main Road, Brereton, Rugeley, Staffs. *T:* Rugeley 3601.

ROBERTS, Sir Harold (Charles West), Kt 1953; CBE 1948; MC 1916; *b* 23 May 1892; *s* of T. B. and Elizabeth Roberts, Stoke-on-Trent; *m* Alice May (*d* 1979), *d* of A. T. Bourne, Trentham, Staffs; no *c. Educ:* Newcastle School; Birmingham University. Trained as a mining engineer in North Staffordshire. Served European War, in France and Italy, Middlesex Regiment, 1916-18; in India, Indian Army, 1918-19. BSc 1921. HM Inspector of Mines, 1922; senior Inspector, 1936; Chief Inspector of Training, Ministry of Fuel and Power, 1943; Deputy Chief Inspector of Mines, 1945; HM Chief Inspector of Mines, 1951-58, retired. *Recreations:* golf and walking. *Address:* 30 Greys Close, Cavendish, Suffolk.

ROBERTS, (Herbert) John, CMG 1965; a Director, Rural Development Corporation of Zambia, since 1980; *b* 22 Nov. 1919; *m* 1946, Margaret Pollard; three *s* one *d. Educ:* Holy Trinity, Weymouth; Milton, Bulawayo. Served War of 1939-45; Somaliland, Ethiopia, Burma. Elected MLC, 1954; Leader of Northern Rhodesia United Federal Party, 1959-63; Founder of National Progress Party, 1963; MP Zambia, Nat. Progress Party 1964-66, Ind. 1967-69; Min. of Labour and Mines, 1959-61; Leader of Opposition (NR), 1961-64; Leader of Opposition (Zambia), 1964-65; disbanded Nat. Progress Party, 1966. *Address:* Chanyanya Ranch, PO Box 32037, Lusaka, Zambia.

ROBERTS, Hugh Eifion Pritchard, QC 1971; **His Honour Judge Eifion Roberts;** a Circuit Judge, since 1977; *b* 22 Nov. 1927; *er s* of late Rev. and Mrs E. P. Roberts, Anglesey; *m* 1958, Buddug Williams; one *s* two *d. Educ:* Beaumaris Grammar Sch.; University Coll. of Wales, Aberystwyth (LLB); Exeter Coll., Oxford (BCL). Called to Bar, Gray's Inn, 1953; practised as a Junior Counsel on Wales and Chester Circuit, Sept. 1953-April 1971. Dep. Chairman: Anglesey QS, 1966-71; Denbighshire QS, 1970-71; a Recorder of the Crown Court, 1972-77. Formerly Asst Parly Boundary Comr for Wales; Mem. for Wales of the Crawford Cttee on Broadcasting Coverage. *Recreation:* gardening. *Address:* Maes-y-Rhedyn, Gresford Road, Llay, Wrexham, Clwyd. *T:* Gresford 2292.

ROBERTS, Ian White; HM Diplomatic Service; Counsellor, Foreign and Commonwealth Office, since 1980; *b* 29 March 1927; *s* of George Dodd Roberts and Jessie Dickson Roberts (*née* White); *m* 1956, Pamela Johnston; one *d. Educ:* Royal Masonic Sch., Bushey, Herts; Gonville and Caius Coll., Cambridge (MA 1st Cl. Hons Mod. Langs). Served Royal Air Force (Pilot Officer), 1948-50; postgrad. student, Cambridge (Scarborough Award), 1950. Joined Foreign Office, 1951-: Klagenfurt, 1952; Munich, 1954; Berlin, 1955; FCO, 1957-61; Second (later First) Secretary, Budapest, 1961-63; FCO, 1963; Bujumbura, 1965; FCO, 1965-66; Buenos Aires, 1966; FCO, 1969-74; Oslo, 1974-76; FCO, 1976. *Recreations:* music, languages, philately. *Address:* c/o Foreign and Commonwealth Office, SW1. *Clubs:* Travellers', Royal Commonwealth Society.

ROBERTS, (Ieuan) Wyn (Pritchard); MP (C) Conway since 1970; Parliamentary Under Secretary of State, Wales, since 1979; *b* 10 July 1930; *s* of late Rev. E. P. Roberts and Margaret Ann; *m* 1956, Enid Grace Williams; three *s. Educ:* Harrow; University Coll., Oxford. Sub-editor, Liverpool Daily Post, 1952-54; News Asst, BBC, 1954-57; TWW Ltd: News, Special Events and Welsh Language Programmes Producer, 1957-59; Production Controller, 1959-60; Exec. Producer, 1960-68; Welsh Controller, 1964-68; Programme Exec., Harlech TV, 1969. PPS to Sec. of State for Wales, 1970-74; Opposition Front-Bench Spokesman on Welsh Affairs, 1974-75, 1976-79. Vice-Pres., Assoc. of District Councils, 1975-79. Mem. of Gorsedd, Royal National Eisteddfod of Wales, 1966. Member, Court of Governors: Nat. Library of Wales; Nat. Museum of Wales; University Coll. of Wales, Aberystwyth, 1970-. *Recreation:* gardening. *Address:* Tan y Gwalia, Conway, Gwynedd. *T:* Tyn y Groes 371. *Clubs:* Savile; Cardiff and County (Cardiff).

ROBERTS, Dame Jean, DBE 1962; JP; DL; *m* 1922, Cameron Roberts (decd), Headmaster of Albert Senior Secondary Sch., Springburn; one *d. Educ:* Albert Sch.; Whitehill Sch. Taught at Bishopstreet School and later in a special school for handicapped children. Representative of Kingston Ward in Corp. of City of Glasgow from Nov. 1929-May 1966; DL 1964, JP 1934, Glasgow; Sen. Magistrate; held the following posts as first woman to do so: Convener of Electrical Cttee; Dep. Chm. of Corporation; Leader of the Labour Group; City Treasurer; Lord Provost of the City of Glasgow and Lord Lieut of the county of the City of Glasgow, 1960-63. Chm., Cumbernauld Develt Corp., 1965-72. Chm., Scottish National Orchestra Society, 1970-75; Member: Scottish Arts Council, 1963; Arts Council of Gt Britain, 1965-68. Since 1930: apptd by Secretary of State for Scotland to serve on many Advisory Cttees

dealing with Local Govt, Social and Economic matters in Scotland. Hon. LLD Glasgow, 1977. Order of St Olav, 1962. *Recreations:* music and public service. *Address:* 35 Beechwood Drive, Glasgow G11 7ET. *T:* 041-334 1930.

ROBERTS, Jeremy Michael Graham; QC 1982; Barrister; a Recorder of the Crown Court, since 1981; *b* 26 April 1941; *s* of Lt-Col J. M. H. Roberts and E. D. Roberts; *m* 1964, Sally Priscilla Johnson. *Educ:* Winchester; Brasenose Coll., Oxford. BA. Called to the Bar, Inner Temple, 1965. *Recreations:* racing, reading, theatre, opera. *Address:* 2 Dr Johnson's Buildings, Temple, EC4Y 7AY. *T:* 01-353 5371.

ROBERTS, Dame Joan (Howard), DBE 1978; President, Yooralla Society of Victoria, 1977-78; *b* 27 June 1907; *d* of Charles A. Norris and Rose M. A. Norris; *m* 1937, Allan Edwin Tainsh Roberts; two *s* one *d. Educ:* Presbyterian Ladies' Coll., Melbourne, Australia; Univ. of Melb. (MSc). Res. Biochemist, Dept of Pathology, Univ. of Melb., 1930-34; Biochemist, Prince Henry's Hosp., Melb., 1935-37. Yooralla Hosp. Sch. for Crippled Children: Mem. Cttee, 1948-68; Pres., 1968-77. Member: Council, Presbyterian Ladies' Coll., Melb., 1948-80; Council of Management, Rheumatism and Arthritis Assoc. of Victoria, 1979-. *Recreations:* travel, reading, classical music. *Address:* 2 Prowse Avenue, Balwyn, Vic 3103, Australia. *T:* 836-1258. *Club:* Lyceum (Melbourne).

ROBERTS, John; *see* Roberts, A. J.

ROBERTS, Rt. Rev. John; *see* Roberts, Rt Rev. D. J.

ROBERTS, John; *see* Roberts, H. J.

ROBERTS, John Alexander Fraser, CBE 1965; FRS 1963; MA Cantab; MD, DSc (Edinburgh); FRCP; FRCPsych; *b* 8 Sept. 1899; *er s* of late Robert Henry Roberts, Foxhall, Denbigh, and late Elizabeth Mary; *m* 1st, 1941, Doris, *y d* of late Herbert and Kate Hare; two *d* ; 2nd, 1975, Margaret, *d* of late Sydney and Dorothy Ralph. *Educ:* Denbigh Gram. Sch.; privately; Gonville and Caius Coll., Cambridge; Univs of Edinburgh, Wales and Bristol. 2nd Lieut Royal Welch Fusiliers, 1918-19; War of 1939-45: Surgeon-Comdr RNVR and Cons. in Med. Statistics, RN, 1942-46. Research Asst, Inst. of Animal Genetics, Univ. of Edinburgh, 1922-28; Biologist, Wool Industries Research Assoc., 1928-31; Macaulay Research Fellow, Univ. of Edinburgh, 1931-33; Dir, Burden Mental Research Dept, Stoke Park Colony, Bristol, 1933-57; Lectr in Med. Genetics, London School of Hygiene and Trop. Med., 1946-57; Consultant in Medical Genetics, Royal Eastern Counties Hosp., Colchester, 1946-80; Dir, Clinical Genetics Research Unit (MRC), Inst. of Child Health, Univ. of London, and Hon. Consultant in Med. Genetics, The Hospital for Sick Children, Gt Ormond St, 1957-64; Geneticist, Paediatric Res. Unit, Guy's Hosp. Med. Sch. and Hon. Clinical Geneticist, Guy's Hosp., 1964-81. President: Royal Anthropological Inst. of Gt Britain and Ire., 1957-59; Biometric Society (British Region), 1960-62; Section of Epidemiology and Preventive Medicine, RSM, 1960-62, Lectures: Charles West, RCP, 1961; Leonard Parsons, Univ. of Birmingham, 1963; Donald Paterson, Univ. of British Columbia (and Vis. Prof.), 1967; Lumleian, RCP, 1971. Ballantyne Prize, RCPE 1976. *Publications:* An Introduction to Medical Genetics, 1940, 7th edn 1978; papers in medical, biological and genetical journals. *Recreation:* mountain walks. *Address:* 10 Aspley Road, Wandsworth, SW18 2DB. *T:* 01-874 4826; Foxhall, Denbigh. *Club:* Athenæum.

ROBERTS, John Arthur, CEng, FIEE; Under-Secretary, Department of Energy, 1974-77; *b* 21 Dec. 1917; *s* of late John Richard and Emily Roberts; *m* 1st, 1944, Winifred Wilks Scott (*d* 1976); two *s* one *d* ; 2nd, 1977, Rosetta Mabel Price. *Educ:* Liverpool Institute; Liverpool Univ. (BEng). Apprentice, Metropolitan-Vickers Electrical Co Ltd, 1939. Served War, Royal Signals, 1940-46, Major. Sen. Lectr, Applied Science, RMA, Sandhurst, 1947-49; SSO and PSO, RAE, Farnborough, 1949-59; Head, Control and Computers Section, Applications Br., Central Electricity Generating Bd, 1959-62; Project Ldr, Automatic Control, CEGB, 1962-67; DCSO, Min. of Tech. and DTI, 1967-72; Under-Sec., DTI, 1972-74. *Address:* Gorse Hill Lane, Virginia Water, Surrey. *T:* Wentworth 2457.

ROBERTS, John Charles Quentin; Director, Great Britain-USSR Association, since 1974; *b* 4 April 1933; *s* of Hubert and Emilie Roberts; *m* 1st, 1959, Dinah Webster-Williams (marr. diss.); one *s* one *d* ; 2nd, 1982, Elizabeth Roberts (*née* Gough-Cooper). *Educ:* King's Coll., Taunton (scholar); Merton Coll., Oxford (MA). MIL 1972. Royal Air Force CSC Interpreter, 1953; Shell International Petroleum Co. Ltd, 1956; Shell Co. of E Africa Ltd: Representative, Zanzibar and S Tanganyika, 1957, Kenya Highlands, 1958; PA to Man. Dir, Shell Austria AG Vienna, 1960; Pressed Steel Co. Ltd, Oxford, 1961; Asst Master, Marlborough Coll., 1963. Chm., Organising Cttee for British Week in Siberia, 1978. Mem. Council, SSEES, Univ. of London, 1981-. *Recreations:* family, the arts, mountain walking, photography, collecting. *Address:* 52 Paultons Square, SW3. *T:* 01-352 3882. *Club:* Athenæum.

ROBERTS, John Eric, DSc (Leeds), FInstP; Emeritus Professor of Physics, University of London, 1969; Physicist to Middlesex Hospital, W1, 1946-70; Consultant Adviser in Physics, Department of Health and Social Security, 1960-71; *b* Leeds, 1907; *e s* of late James J. Roberts, Normanton, Yorks; *m* Sarah, *o d* of late Thomas Raybould, Normanton, Yorks; two *d. Educ:*

Normanton Grammar School; University of Leeds (Brown Scholar). BSc (Physics Hons), Leeds, 1928; Univ. Research Scholar, PhD 1930; Research Assistant in Physics, University of Leeds, 1930; Assistant Physicist, Royal Cancer Hospital, 1932; Senior Asst Physicist, Middlesex Hosp., 1937; Joel Prof. of Physics Applied to Medicine, Univ. of London, 1946-69; Regional Adviser, ME, Internat. Atomic Energy Agency, 1963-64. FInstP. 1938; DSc (Leeds), 1944. Pres., British Inst. of Radiology, 1951-52; Pres. Hospital Physicists Assoc., 1950-51; Editor, Physics in Medicine and Biology, 1956-60; Editor, British Jl of Radiology, 1964-67. Hon. Member: Royal Coll. of Radiologists; Hospital Physicists Assoc. *Publications:* Nuclear War and Peace, 1956; scientific papers in various journals. *Address:* Windrush, Malthouse Lane, Ludham, Great Yarmouth, Norfolk NR29 5QL. *T:* St Benets 459.

ROBERTS, Air Vice-Marshal John Frederick, CB 1967; CBE 1960 (OBE 1954); *b* 24 Feb. 1913; *y s* of late W. J. Roberts, Pontardawe; *m* 1st, 1942, Mary Winifred (*d* 1968), *d* of late J. E. Newns; one *s*; 2nd, 1976, Mrs P. J. Hull, *d* of A. Stiles. *Educ:* Pontardawe Gram. Sch., Glam. Chartered Accountant, 1936. Joined RAF, 1938; service in Middle East, 1942-45; Mem. Directing Staff, RAF Staff Coll., Bracknell, 1954-56; SASO, RAF Record Office, 1958-60; Dep. Comptroller, Allied Forces Central Europe, 1960-62; Stn Comdr RAF Uxbridge, 1963; Dir of Personal Services I, Min. of Def. (Air), 1964-65; Dir-Gen. of Ground Training (RAF), 1966-68; retd, 1968. With Deloitte & Co., Chartered Accountants, Swansea, 1969-78. Pres., Pontardawe Golf Club. *Recreations:* cricket, golf, cabinet-making. *Address:* Cefneithrym, 1 Lon Cadog, Sketty, Swansea SA2 0TS. *T:* Swansea 203763. *Clubs:* Royal Air Force, MCC.

ROBERTS, John Herbert; Director of Operations, Inland Revenue, since 1981; *b* 18 Aug. 1933; *s* of late John Emanuel Roberts and Hilda Mary Roberts; *m* 1965, Patricia Iris; one *s* three *d. Educ:* Canton High Sch.; London School of Economics (BScEcon Hons). Entered Civil Service by Open Competition as Inspector of Taxes, 1954; National Service, commnd RASC, 1955-57; returned to Inland Revenue, 1957; Principal Inspector, 1974; Sen. Principal Inspector, 1979; Under Secretary, 1981. *Recreations:* music, walking, Welsh Springers. *Address:* South West Wing, Bush House, Strand, WC2B 4RD. *T:* 01-438 6067.

ROBERTS, John Lewis; Assistant Under-Secretary of State (Supply and Organisation), Ministry of Defence (Air), since 1980; *b* 21 April 1928; *s* of Thomas Hubert and Meudwen Roberts; *m* 1952, Maureen Jocelyn (*née* Moriarty); two *s. Educ:* Pontardawe Grammar Sch.; Trinity Hall, Cambridge. BA (Hons) History. Joined Min. of Civil Aviation, 1950; Private Sec. to the Parly Sec., 1953; Principal: in Railways, then in Sea Transport; branches of MoT and Civil Aviation, 1954-59; Civil Air Attaché, Bonn Embassy, 1959-62; Defence Supply Counsellor, Paris Embassy, 1966-69; Asst Sec., Internat. Policy Div., MoD, 1971-74; Asst Under-Sec. of State (Air), MoD PE, 1974-76, (Sales), 1976-77; Asst Under-Sec. of State (Personnel), MoD (Air), 1977-80. *Recreations:* angling, sailing. *Address:* 23 Mount Ararat Road, Richmond, Surrey TW10 6PQ. *T:* 01-940 1035. *Club:* Fly Fishers'.

ROBERTS, Prof. John Morris; Vice-Chancellor and Professor, University of Southampton, since 1979; *b* 14 April 1928; *s* of late Edward Henry Roberts and late Dorothy Julia Roberts, Bath, Som.; *m* 1964, Judith Cecilia Mary, *e d* of late Rev. James Armitage and Monica Armitage; one *s* two *d. Educ:* Taunton Sch.; Keble Coll., Oxford (Schol.; Hon. Fellow, 1981). National Service, 1949-50; Prize Fellow, Magdalen Coll., Oxford, 1951-53; Commonwealth Fund Fellow, Princeton and Yale, 1953-54; Merton College, Oxford: Fellow and Tutor, 1953-79 (Hon. Fellow, 1980); Sen. Proctor, 1967-68, acting Warden, 1969-70, 1977-79. Mem., Inst. for Advanced Study, Princeton, 1960-61; Vis. Prof., Univ. of S Carolina, 1961; Sec. of Harmsworth Trust, 1962-68; Member: Council, Royal Literary Fund, 1975-; US/UK Educn Commn, 1981-. Mem., Gen. Cttee, Royal Literary Fund, 1975-. Editor, English Historical Review, 1967-77. Pres. Council, Taunton Sch., 1978-. *Publications:* French Revolution Documents, 1966; Europe 1880-1945, 1967; The Mythology of the Secret Societies, 1972; The Paris Commune from the Right, 1973; Revolution and Improvement: the Western World 1775-1847, 1976; History of the World, 1976; The French Revolution, 1978; (Gen. Editor) Purnell's History of the 20th Century; articles and reviews in learned jls. *Recreation:* music. *Address:* University of Southampton, SO9 5NH. *Club:* United Oxford & Cambridge University.

ROBERTS, Rear-Adm. John Oliver, CB 1976; Director General, British Printing Industries Federation, since 1981; *b* 4 April 1924; *er s* of J. V. and M. C. Roberts; *m* 1st, 1950, Lady Hermione Mary Morton Stuart (marr. diss. 1960; she *d* 1969); one *d*; 2nd, 1963, Honor Marigold Gordon Gray; one *s* one *d. Educ:* RN Coll., Dartmouth. Served War: Midshipman, HM Ships Renown and Tartar, 1941-43; Sub-Lt, HMS Serapis, 1943-44; Lieut, 1945; Pilot Trg, 1944-46. HMS Triumph, 1947-49; RNAS, Lossiemouth, 1949-51; Flag-Lt to FOGT, 1952; Lt-Comdr, 1953; HMAS Vengeance and Sydney, 1953-54; RNVR, Southern Air Div., 1954-56; CO, No 803 Sqdn, HMS Eagle, 1957-58; Comdr, 1958; RNAS, Brawdy, 1958-60; CO, HMS St Bride's Bay, 1960-61; Naval Staff, 1962-64; Captain, 1964; CSO, Flag Officer Aircraft Carriers, 1964-66; CO, HMS Galatea, 1966-68; Naval Staff, 1968-70; CO, HMS Ark Royal, 1971-72; Rear-Adm., 1972; Flag Officer Sea Training, 1972-74; COS to C-in-C Fleet, 1974-76; Flag Officer, Naval Air Command, 1976-78. Non-exec. Dir, Aeronautical & General Instruments Ltd, 1981-82 (Head of Marketing and Sales, Defence Systems Div., 1980-81). *Recreations:* Rugby football, cricket, athletics, sailing, skiing. *Address:* The Old Vicarage,

Aldingbourne, Chichester, W Sussex. *T:* Eastergate 3801. *Club:* East India, Devonshire, Sports and Public Schools.

ROBERTS, Dr Lewis Edward John, CBE 1978; FRS 1982; Director, Atomic Energy Research Establishment, Harwell, since 1975; Member, United Kingdom Atomic Energy Authority, since 1979; *b* 31 Jan. 1922; *s* of William Edward Roberts and Lilian Lewis Roberts; *m* 1947, Eleanor Mary Luscombe; one *s. Educ:* Swansea Grammar Sch.; Jesus Coll., Oxford (MA, DPhil). Clarendon Laboratory, Oxford, 1944; Scientific Officer, Chalk River Res. Estabt, Ont, Canada, 1946-47; AERE, Harwell, 1947, Principal Scientific Officer, 1952; Commonwealth Fund Fellow, Univ. of Calif, Berkeley, 1954-55; Dep. Head, Chemistry Div., 1966, Asst Dir, 1967, AERE. R. M. Jones Lectr, QUB, 1981. Governor, Abingdon Sch., 1978-. *Publications:* papers in qly revs and in Jl Chem. Soc., Jl Inorganic and Nuclear Chem., and IAEA pubns. *Recreations:* reading, gardening. *Address:* Atomic Energy Research Establishment, Harwell, Didcot, Oxon. *T:* Abingdon 24141.

ROBERTS, Prof. Michael, FBA 1960; Director, Institute for Social and Economic Research, Rhodes University, 1974-76; Professor of Modern History, The Queen's University, Belfast, 1954-73; Dean of the Faculty of Arts, 1957-60; *b* 21 May 1908; *s* of Arthur Roberts and Hannah Elizabeth Landless; *m* 1941, Ann McKinnon Morton; one *d. Educ:* Brighton Coll.; Worcester Coll., Oxford. Gladstone Meml Prizeman, 1931; A. M. P. Read Scholar (Oxford), 1932. Procter Vis. Fell., Princeton Univ., USA, 1931-32; Lectr, Merton Coll., Oxford, 1932-34; Asst Lectr, Univ. of Liverpool, 1934-35; DPhil, Oxford, 1935; Prof. of Modern History, Rhodes Univ., S Africa, 1935-53. Lieut, SA Int. Corps, 1942-44. British Council Representative, Stockholm, 1944-46. Public Orator, Rhodes Univ., 1951-53; Hugh Le May Vis. Fellow, Rhodes Univ., 1960-61; Lectures: A. L. Smith, Balliol Coll., Oxford, 1962; Enid Muir Meml, Univ. of Newcastle upon Tyne, 1965; Creighton in History, Univ. of London, 1965; Stenton, Univ. of Reading, 1969; James Ford special, Oxford Univ., 1973; Wiles, QUB, 1977. Hon. Fellow, Worcester Coll., Oxford, 1966; Vis. Fellow, All Souls Coll., Oxford, 1968-69; Leverhulme Faculty Fellow in European Studies, 1973; Vis. Fellow, Pomona Coll., Claremont, Calif, 1978. Vis. Fellow, Trevelyan Coll., Univ. of Durham, 1981. MRIA 1968. For. Member: Roy. Swedish Acad. of Letters, History and Antiquities; Royal Swedish Academy of Science; Hon. Mem. Samfundet för utgivande av handskrifter rörande Skandinaviens historia. FRHistS; Fil dr (*hc*) (Stockholm), 1960; DLitt (*hc*) QUB, 1977. Kungens medalj i Serafimerband (Sweden), 1981. Chevalier, Order of North Star (Sweden), 1954. *Publications:* The Whig Party, 1807-1812, 1939; (with A. E. G. Trollip) The South African Opposition, 1939-1945, 1947; Gustavus Adolphus: A History of Sweden, 1611-1632, Vol. I, 1953, Vol. II, 1958; Essays in Swedish History, 1967; The Early Vasas: A History of Sweden 1523-1611, 1968; Sweden as a Great Power 1611-1697, 1968; Sverige och Europa, 1969; Gustav Vasa, 1970; Gustavus Adolphus and the Rise of Sweden, 1973; (ed) Sweden's Age of Greatness, 1973; Macartney in Russia, 1974; The Swedish Imperial Experience 1560-1718, 1979; British Diplomacy and Swedish Politics, 1758-1773, 1980; Stormaktsupplevelse, 1980; trans. from Swedish of works by Nils Ahnlund, F. G. Bengtsson, Gunnar Wennerberg (Gluntarne), Birger Sjöberg (Fridas bok), Carl Michael Bellman (Epistles and Songs, I-III), Anna Maria Lenngren; articles in EHR, History, Historical Jl, Past and Present, Scandia, South African Archives Yearbook, etc. *Recreation:* music. *Address:* 38 Somerset Street, Grahamstown, CP, South Africa. *T:* Grahamstown 4855.

ROBERTS, Michael (Hilary Arthur); MP (C) Cardiff North West, since 1974 (Cardiff North, 1970-74); Parliamentary Under Secretary of State, Welsh Office, since 1979; *b* 1927; *s* of Rev. T. A. Roberts (formerly Rector of Neath); *m* 1952, Eileen Jean Evans; two *s* (and one *d* decd). *Educ:* Neath Grammar School; Cardiff University College. First Headmaster of the Bishop of Llandaff High School, 1963-70. An Opposition Whip, 1974-79. President: Cons. Trade Unionists, 1977-79; Assoc. of Cons. Clubs, 1980-. *Address:* Ashgrove Farm, Whitchurch, Cardiff. *Club:* Cardiff and County.

ROBERTS, Norman Stafford, MA, DPA; Headmaster, Taunton School, since Sept. 1970; *b* 15 Feb. 1926; *s* of late Walter S. Roberts, LLM and Florence E. Roberts (*née* Phythian), Calderstones, Liverpool; *m* 1965, Beatrice, *o d* of late George and Winifred Best, Donaghadee, Co. Down; one *s* two *d. Educ:* Quarry Bank High Sch., Liverpool; Hertford Coll., Oxford (Open Exhibnr, History). Served in RA, Egypt and Palestine, 1945-47 (Lieut). 2nd cl. hons PPE 1950; DipEd Oxford 1951; DPA London 1951. Asst Master, Berkhamsted Junior Sch., 1951-55; House Master, Sixth Form Master, Berkhamsted Sch., 1955-59; Walter Hines Page Scholar to USA, 1959, 1980; Senior History Master, CO CCF (Hon. Major 1965), Monkton Combe Sch., 1959-65, Housemaster 1962-65; Schoolmaster Student, Merton Coll., Oxford, 1964; Headmaster, Sexey's Sch., Bruton, 1965-70. *Recreations:* foreign travel, bridge, hockey, tennis. *Address:* Headmaster's House, Private Road, Staplegrove, Taunton, Somerset. *T:* Taunton 72588. *Club:* East India, Devonshire, Sports and Public Schools.

ROBERTS, Gen. Sir Ouvry Lindfield, GCB 1953 (KCB 1952; CB 1946); KBE 1950 (CBE 1944); DSO 1941; President of Grosvenor Laing (BC) Limited (Canada), 1955-60; formerly Director: Grosvenor/Laing (BC) Ltd; Grosvenor/Laing (Langley Park) Ltd; Grosvenor International (Canada) Ltd; Redhill Investment Corporation Ltd; Macdonald Buchanan Properties Ltd; *b* 3 April 1898; *m* 1924, Elsie Nora Eileen Webster (*d* 1955); two *s*; *m* 1955, Joyce Mary Segar, *yr d* of Eric W. Scorer, OBE, Coombe Hurst, Lincoln; two *s* one d. Educ: Cheltenham College; Royal Military Academy, Woolwich; King's Coll., Cambridge (MA). RE, commissioned 1917; Comdg 23 Ind. Div., 1943–45; Comdg 34 Ind. Corps, 1945; Vice-Adjutant-Gen. War Office, 1945–47; GOC Northern Ireland District, 1948–49; GOC-in-C Southern Command, 1949–52; Quarter-master-General to the Forces, 1952–55; ADC General to the Queen, 1952–55; Colonel Commandant, Corps of Royal Engineers, 1952–62. Administrative Officer, Univ. of BC, 1961–68. *Recreations*: cricket (Army, Quidnunc); hockey (Cambridge, Army, Wales). *Address*: Upper Field House, 105 Church Way, Iffley Village, Oxford. *T*: Oxford 779351. *Club*: MCC.

ROBERTS, Prof. Paul Harry, PhD, ScD; FRS 1979; FRAS; Professor of Applied Mathematics, University of Newcastle upon Tyne, since 1963; *b* 13 Sept. 1929; *s of* Percy Harry Roberts and Ethel Frances (*née* Mann); *m* 1959, Joyce Atkinson. *Educ*: Ardwyn Grammar Sch., Aberystwyth; University Coll. of Wales, Aberystwyth; Gonville and Caius Coll., Cambridge (George Green Student; BA, MA, PhD, ScD). FRAS 1955. Res. Associate, Univ. of Chicago, 1954–55; Scientific Officer, AWRE, 1955–56; ICI Fellow in Physics, 1956–59, Lectr in Phys, 1959–61, Univ. of Newcastle upon Tyne; Associate Prof. of Astronomy, Univ. of Chicago, 1961–63. Editor, Geophysical and Astrophysical Fluid Dynamics, 1976–. *Publications*: An Introduction to Magnetohydrodynamics, 1967; contrib. to Geophys. and Astrophys. Fluid Dyn., Jl Low Temp. Phys., Astrophys. Jl, Jl Fluid Mech., and Jl Phys. Soc. *Recreations*: playing bassoon, chess. *Address*: 7 The Orchard, Wylam, Northumberland NE41 8BS. *T*: Wylam 2709; School of Mathematics, University of Newcastle upon Tyne, Newcastle upon Tyne NE1 7RU. *T*: Newcastle 328511.

ROBERTS, Percy Charles; Chairman and Chief Executive, Mirror Group Newspapers Ltd, 1977–80; *b* 30 July 1920; *s of* late Herbert Bramwell Roberts and Alice (*née* Lang); *m* 1st, 1946, Constance Teresa Violet Butler (marr. diss. 1977); two *s*; 2nd, 1978, Pauline Moore. *Educ*: Brighton Hove and Sussex Grammar Sch. Reporter, Sussex Daily News, 1936–39. Served War of 1939–45: Sussex Yeomanry, in France and ME (Captain). Sub-Editor, Egyptian Mail, Cairo, 1946; Reporter, Mid-East Mail, Palestine, 1947; Sub-Editor: Sussex Daily News, 1948; Liverpool Daily Post, 1949; Editor, Nigerian Citizen, 1949–51; Editorial Adviser, Gen. Manager, Managing Dir, Nigerian Daily Times, 1951–60; Managing Dir, Mirror Gp Newspapers in Caribbean, 1960–62; Gen. Manager, Mirror Newspapers in Manchester, 1962–66; Dir, 1964–80, Managing Dir, 1966–80, Daily Mirror Newspapers Ltd; Vice-Chm., West of England Newspapers Ltd, 1965–69; Managing Dir, IPC Newspapers Ltd, 1968–75; Dir, Scottish Daily Record & Sunday Mail Ltd, 1969–74; Chm., Overseas Newspapers Ltd, 1969–75; Dep. Chm. and Chief Exec., Mirror Gp Newspapers Ltd, 1975–77. Dir, Reed Publishing Holdings Ltd, 1975–80; Mem., Reed Internat. UK Cttee, 1975–80. Mem., CBI Employment Policy Cttee, 1975–78. Mem. Council, CPU, 1979–. CBIM. *Address*: Merrick House, Weston-under-Penyard, near Ross-on-Wye, Herefordshire HR9 7PG. *Clubs*: Arts, Royal Automobile; Ross Rotary; Ross Golf.

ROBERTS, Sir Peter Geoffrey, 3rd Bt, *cr* 1919; *b* 23 June 1912; *yr* and *o* surv. *s of* Sir Samuel Roberts, 2nd Bt and Gladys Mary (*d* 1966), *d of* W. E. Dring, MD, Tenterden, Kent; *S father* 1955; *m* 1939, Judith Randell Hempson; one *s* four *d*. *Educ*: Harrow; Trinity College, Cambridge. Barr.-at-Law, Inner Temple, 1935. Maj. Coldstream Guards. MP (C) Ecclesall Div. of Sheffield, 1945–50; (C-L) Heeley Div. of Sheffield, 1950–66. Chairman: Newton Chambers & Co., Ltd, 1954–72; The Wombwell Management Co. Ltd, 1952–82; Hadfields Ltd, 1961–67; Sterling Silverware, 1978–81; Wellman Engineering Corp. 1952–72; Hill Woolgar plc, 1981; Director: Guardian Royal Exchange Assurance Ltd, 1960–82; Royal Bank of Scotland, 1978–82; Williams & Glyn's Bank Ltd, to 1982. Past Chm., Conservative Members' Committee on Fuel and Power; Past Pres., Soc. of British Gas Industries (Pres., 1963). Master Cutler, Sheffield, 1957. High Sheriff of Hallamshire, 1970–71. Hon. Freeman, 1972. Town Collector, 1971–74, Sheffield. *Publication*: Coal Act, 1938. *Heir*: *s* Samuel Roberts [*b* 16 April 1948; *m* 1977, Georgina, *yr d of* David Cory; two *d*]. *Address*: Cockley Cley Hall, Swaffham, Norfolk PE37 8AG. *T*: Swaffham 21308. *Clubs*: Carlton, Brooks's; Sheffield (Sheffield).

ROBERTS, Maj.-Gen. Philip; *see* Roberts, Maj.-Gen. G. P. B.

ROBERTS, Ven. Raymond Harcourt; QHC 1980; Chaplain of the Fleet and Archdeacon for the Royal Navy, since 1980; *b* 14 April 1931; *s of* Thomas Roberts and Carrie Maud Roberts. *Educ*: St Edmund Hall, Oxford (MA English); St Michael's Theol Coll., Llandaff. Deacon 1956, priest 1957, dio. of Monmouth (Curate of Bassaleg); Chaplain RNVR, 1958, RN, 1959; Destroyers and Frigates, Far East, 1959; HMS Pembroke, 1962; Dartmouth Trng Sqdn, 1963; RM Commando Course, 1965; 45 Commando, S. Arabia, 1965; RN Engrg Coll., 1967; HMS Bulwark, 1968; BRNC Dartmouth, 1970; HMS Ark Royal, 1974; Commando Trng Centre, RM, 1975; HMS Drake and HM Naval Base, Plymouth, 1979. Hon. Canon, Cathedral of Holy Trinity, Gibraltar, 1980. *Address*: Ministry of Defence, Lacon House, Theobald's Road, WC1X 8RY. *T*: 01-430 6847.

ROBERTS, Richard (David Hallam); Headmaster, King Edward's School, Witley, since 1980; *b* 27 July 1931; *s of* Arthur Hallam Roberts, Barrister-at-law, sometime Attorney-General, Zanzibar, and Ruvé Constance Jessie Roberts; *m* 1960, Wendy Ewen Mount; three *s*. *Educ*: King's Sch.,

Canterbury; Jesus Coll., Cambridge. Commissioned into RA 6th Field Regt, 1952. Asst Master, King's Sch., Canterbury, 1956; Housemaster, 1957; Head of Modern Language Dept, 1961; Senior Housemaster, 1965; Headmaster, Wycliffe Coll., Stonehouse, 1967–80. *Address*: King Edward's School, Witley, near Godalming, Surrey GU8 5SG.

ROBERTS, Rear-Adm. Richard Douglas, CB 1971; CEng; FIMechE; Rear-Admiral Engineering on staff Flag Officer Naval Air Command, 1969–72; *b* 7 Nov. 1916; *s of* Rear-Adm. E. W. Roberts and Mrs R. E. Roberts (*née* Cox); *m* 1943, Mary Norma Wright; one *s* one *d*. *Educ*: RN Dartmouth; RNEC Keyham. Frobisher, 1934; RNEC Keyham, 1935–38 (qual. Marine Eng); HM Ships: Kent, 1938–40; Exeter, 1941; Bermuda, 1942; Mauritius, 1943–45; RNEC Manadon, 1945 (qual. Aero Eng); RNAY Donibristle, 1946 (AMIMechE); RNAS Worthy Down, 1947; RNAS Yeovilton, 1948–49; Staff of Rear-Adm. Reserve Aircraft, 1949–50; Comdr, 1950; RN Staff Coll., 1951; RNAY Fleetlands, 1952–53 (Production Man.); HMS Newfoundland, 1954–56 (Engr Officer); Engr-in-Chief's Dept, Bath, 1956–60; Captain 1960; RNAY Belfast, 1961–62 (Supt); idc, 1963 (MIMechE); Dir, Fleet Maintenance, 1964–66; Dir, Naval Officer Appts (E), 1966–68; Rear-Adm. 1969. MBIM 1967. *Recreations*: sailing (RNSA, 1936), fishing; light railways; Vice Pres., Axe Vale Conservation Soc. *Club*: Army and Navy.

ROBERTS, Richard Frederick Anthony; High Commissioner for the Commonwealth of the Bahamas in London, since 1977; *b* 12 May 1932; *s of* Enoch Pedro Roberts and Gladys Raine Roberts (*née* Archer); *m* 1960, Melvern Hollis Bain; one *s* two *d*. *Educ*: St John's College. Personnel Officer, Bahamas Airways, 1963–67; Exec. Dir and Partner, Venn, Livingstone, Roberts (Public Relns), 1967–68; Personnel Dir, New Providence Develt Co. Ltd (Land Develt), March–Oct. 1968; MP Centreville, 1968–77; Parly Sec.: Min. of Finance, 1969–72; Min. of Agric., 1971–72; Minister of Agric. and Fisheries, Oct. 1972–Feb. 1973; Minister of Home Affairs, March–Dec. 1973; Minister of Agric., Fisheries and Local Govt, 1974–77. Pres., Airline Workers Union; Sec. Gen., Amalgamated Building Constructional Engrg Trade Union; Asst Gen. Sec., Bahamas Fedn of Labour; Pres. and Gen. Sec., Bahamas TUC. Progressive Liberal Party: Asst Gen. Sec.; first Vice-Chm.; Mem., Nat. Gen. Council. Mem., Adv. Cttee to Labour Bd; Chm., Maritime Bd; Mem., Broadcasting and TV Commn; Vice-Chm., Bahamas Agricl Corp. Sec., Methodist Preachers' Cttee. Asst Scout Master; Lt, Boys Brigade. Mem. Internat. Cultural Exchange. *Recreations*: fishing, reading, sports, religion. *Address*: 42 Chatsworth Road, Ealing, W5. *T*: 01-998 2413. *Clubs*: Royal Automobile, Hurlingham, Clermont.

ROBERTS, Robert Evan, CBE 1976; National General Secretary, National Council of YMCAs, 1965–75; *b* 16 July 1912; *s of* late Robert Thomas Roberts, Llanilar, Denbighshire; *m* 1939, Rhoda, *d of* late William Driver, Burnley, Lancs; one *s* one *d*. *Educ*: Cilcain, Flintshire; Liverpool. YMCA: Asst Sec.: Central YMCA Liverpool, 1933; Hornsey (N London), 1935; Asst Div. Sec., Lancs/Cheshire, 1937; Div. Sec., NW Div., 1939; Dep. Dir, YMCA Welfare Services, NW Europe, 1944–46 (despatches); Mem. 21st Army Gp, Council of Voluntary Welfare Work, 1944–46. Nat. Sec., Ireland, 1946; Sec., Personnel Dept. Nat. Council of YMCAs, London, 1948; Nat. Sec., Nat. Council of YMCAs, Wales, 1956–65; Hon. Sec/Treasurer, Assoc. of Secs of YMCAs of Gt Brit. and Ireland, 1963–65; Dep. Chm., Welsh Standing Conf. of Nat. Vol. Youth Orgs. 1963–65. Past Member: Welsh Nat. Council of Social Service; Welsh Jt Educn Cttee; Nat. Inst. of Adult Educn. Member: Nat. Council of Social Service, 1965–75; Brit. Council of Churches (and its Exec.), 1965–74; Council of Voluntary Welfare Work, 1965–75; S Cumbria Cttee, Health Council, 1982–; World Council of YMCAs (and its Finance Cttee), 1965–75; Vice-Pres., Welsh Nat. Council of YMCAs, 1975; Mem. Exec. Cttee, Age Concern, Cumbria, 1976–82 (Vice Chm., 1981–82); Chairman: Age Concern, S Lakeland, 1977–82; Job Creation Programme, Barrow and S Lakeland, 1976–80; Exec. Member: SE Lakeland Community Health Council, 1977–82; S Lakeland Voluntary Action, 1978–. Trustee, Framlington Trust, 1973–. Fellow, Royal Commonwealth Soc., 1974–. Silver Jubilee Medal, 1977. *Recreations*: fell-walking, gardening. *Address*: 5 Priory Crescent, Kents Bank, Grange over Sands, Cumbria LA11 7BL. *T*: Grange over Sands 2161.

ROBERTS, Rev. Roger Lewis, CVO 1973; MA Oxon; Chaplain, the Queen's Chapel of the Savoy, and Chaplain of the Royal Victorian Order, 1961–73; Chaplain to the Queen, 1969–81; *b* 3 Aug. 1911; 3rd *s of* late Robert Lewis Roberts, CBE; *m* 1935, Katie Agnes Mary Perryman; one *s*. *Educ*: Highgate School; Exeter College, Oxford. 1st Class Hon. Mods, 1931; 1st Class Lit. Hum., 1933; Charles Oldham Prize, 1933; BA 1933; MA 1938; Sixth Form Master, The Liverpool Institute, 1933–34; Sixth Form Master, Rugby School, 1934–40; enlisted RRA, 1940; Army Educational Corps, 1941–43 (Major). Headmaster, Blundell's Sch., 1943–47; Deacon, Exeter, 1946; Priest, St Albans, 1948; Assistant Priest, Cathedral and Abbey Church of St Alban, 1948–49. Vicar of Sharnbrook, Bedfordshire, 1949–54. Vicar of the Guild Church of All Hallows, London Wall, 1954–58, of St Botolph without Aldersgate, 1958–61. Warden, The Church of England Men's Society, 1957–61 (Gen. Sec. 1954–57, Vice-Pres. 1962–). Member of editorial staff, The Church Times, 1950–76 (Editor, 1960–68). Chaplain: Instn of Chartered Engineers, 1961–73; Worshipful Co. of Glaziers, 1967–77. *Address*: 97 Corringham Road, Golders Green, NW11. *T*: 01-455 2118. *Club*: United Oxford & Cambridge University.

See also B. R. Roberts and C. H. Roberts.

ROBERTS, Roy Ernest James, CEng, FIMechE, MIProdE; AMIBF; Managing Director, GKN Group, since 1980; *b* 14 Dec. 1928; *s* of Douglas Henry Roberts and Elsie Florence (*née* Rice); *m* 1950, Winson Madge Smith; two *s*. *Educ:* Farnham Grammar Sch.; Royal Aircraft Estabt, Farnborough (student apprentice). FBIM 1979; FInstD 1980. Management trainee, Guest, Keen and Nettlefolds, 1951-55; Asst to Directors, C. & B. Smith Ltd, 1956-57, Works Director, 1958-66, Dir and Gen. Manager, 1966-70 (C. & B. Smith was acquired by GKN, 1966); Managing Director: GKN Cwmbran Ltd, 1970-72; GKN Engineering Ltd, 1972-73; Chairman, GKN Engineering Ltd and GKN Building Supplies & Services Ltd, 1974-77; Member, main board of GKN, 1975; Group Director, GKN, with special responsibilities for engrg and construction services activities, also for interests in India, Pakistan, S Africa and the Middle East, 1977-79. Vice-Chm. Bd, Manufg Industries Div. of IMechE, 1980; Mem. (pt-time), UKAEA, 1981. FBIM 1979; FInstD 1980; FRSA 1980. *Recreations:* field sports, walking, music. *Address:* Guest, Keen and Nettlefolds plc, Group Headquarters-Operations, PO Box 55, Smethwick, Warley, West Midlands B66 2RZ. *T:* 021-558 3131. *Telex:* 336321. *Club:* Oriental.

ROBERTS, Dame Shelagh (Marjorie), DBE 1981; Industrial Relations Consultant since 1956; Member (C) London South West, European Parliament, since Sept. 1979; *b* 13 Oct. 1924; *d* of Glyn Roberts, Ystalyfera. *Educ:* St Wyburn Sch., Birkdale, Lancs. Member: Kensington Borough Council, 1953-71; GLC, 1970-81; Bd of Basildon Development Corp., 1971-75; Occupational Pensions Bd, 1973-79; Race Relations Bd, 1973-77; Panel of Industrial Tribunals, 1973-; PLA, 1976-79; Chm., National Women's Advisory Cttee of Conservative Party, 1972-75; Chm., Nat. Union of Conservative Party, 1976-77. Leader, Planning and Communications Policy Cttee, GLC, 1977-79. Co-Chm., Jt Cttee Against Racialism, 1978-80. *Publications:* (co-author) Fair Share for the Fair Sex, 1969; More Help for the Cities, 1974. *Recreation:* enjoying the sun and fresh air. *Address:* 23 Dovehouse Street, Chelsea, SW3 6JY. *T:* 01-352 3711. *Club:* Hurlingham.

ROBERTS, Sir Sidney; *see* Roberts, Sir E. F. S.

ROBERTS, Sir Stephen (James Leake), Kt 1981; Chairman, Milk Marketing Board, since 1977; *b* 13 April 1915; *s* of Frank Roberts and Annie Leake; *m* 1940, Muriel Hobbins; two *s* two *d*. *Educ:* Wellington Grammar Sch. Farmer; founded Wrekin Farmers Ltd, 1960 (Chm., 1960-77); Shropshire delegate to NFU Council, 1962-70; Mem. MMB for W Midland Region, 1966- (Vice-Chm., 1975-77). *Recreation:* football (now spectator). *Address:* Littlewath, Little Wenlock, Wellington, Telford, Shropshire TF6 5AX. *T:* Telford 504569. *Club:* Farmers'.

ROBERTS, Thomas Arnold, OBE 1962; TD 1947; FRICS; Chartered Surveyor; former Senior Partner, Richard Ellis, Chartered Surveyors, London, EC3; *b* 5 Nov. 1911; *s* of Sidney Herbert Roberts, Liverpool; *m* Kathleen Audrey Robertshaw. *Educ:* Bedford Sch. Joined Westminster Dragoons, 1932; transf. to Royal Signals, 1938. Served War, in N Africa and Italy, 1942-44. Partnership in Richard Ellis & Son, Chartered Surveyors, 1946. Surrey TA Assoc., 1950-72 (Chm., 1956-60); Hon. Col: 381 Lt Regt (TA), 1957-61; Surrey Yeomanry, 1961-68. Property Adviser to Electricity Council, 1957-73. A Church Commissioner, 1973-81. A Governor of Cranleigh Sch., 1960-73 (Chm., 1965-72). DL Surrey, 1958-73. *Recreations:* vintage and sporting motor vehicles, travel. *Address:* Purslow Hall, Clunbury, Craven Arms, Shropshire. *T:* Little Brampton 205. *Clubs:* Athenæum, Naval and Military.

ROBERTS, Thomas Somerville, JP; FCIT; Chairman, Milford Haven Conservancy Board, 1976-82; *b* Ruabon, N Wales, 10 Dec. 1911; *s* of Joseph Richard Roberts, Rhosllanerchrugog and Lily Agnes (*née* Caldwell); *m* 1st, 1938, Ruth Moira Teasdale; two *s*; 2nd, 1950, Margaret Peggy Anderson, Sunderland. *Educ:* Roath Park Elem. Sch., Cardiff; Cardiff High Sch.; Balliol Coll., Oxford (Domus Exhibnr). Traffic Apprentice, LNER, 1933; Docks Manager, Middlesbrough and Hartlepool, 1949; Chief Docks Manager: Hull, 1959; S Wales, 1962; Port Dir, S Wales Ports, 1970-75. Chm., S Wales Port Employers, 1962-75; Member: Nat. Jt Council for Port Transport Industry, 1962-75; Nat. Dock Labour Bd, 1970-75; Race Relations Bd, 1968-76. Dir, Develt Corp. for Wales, 1965-80, Vice-Pres. 1979-; Dep. Chm., Welsh Develt Agency, 1976-79. Member: Council, University Coll., Cardiff (Chm. Finance Cttee); Council, Univ. of Wales Inst. of Science and Technol.; Court, Univ. of Wales; Pwyllgor Tywysog Cymru (Prince of Wales' Cttee), 1977-81; Exec. Cttee, Welsh Environment Foundn, 1977-81. Hon. Fellow, University Coll., Cardiff, 1982. JP City of Cardiff, 1966-82. *Recreation:* TV. *Address:* Marcross Lodge, 9 Ely Road, Llandaff, Cardiff CF5 2JE. *T:* Cardiff 561153. *Club:* Cardiff and County (Cardiff).

ROBERTS, Wilfrid, JP; *b* 28 Aug. 1900; *s* of Charles and Lady Cecilia Roberts, Boothby, Brampton, Cumberland; *m* 1928, Anne Constance Jennings; three *d*. *Educ:* Gresham School; Balliol College, Oxford. MP (L) North Cumberland, 1935-50; joined Labour Party, July 1956. *Address:* Boothby, Brampton, Cumbria.

ROBERTS, Sir William (James Denby), 3rd Bt *cr* 1909; *b* 10 Aug. 1936; *s* of Sir James Denby Roberts, 2nd Bt, OBE, and of Irene Charlotte D'Orsey, yr *d* of late William Dunn, MB, CM; *S* father, 1973. *Educ:* Rugby; Royal Agricultural Coll., Cirencester. MRAC, ARICS. Farms at Strathallan Castle, and Combwell Priory, Flimwell, Wadhurst, Sussex. Founder, 1969, and owner 1969-81, Strathallan Aircraft Collection. *Recreations:* swimming and flying. *Heir: b* Andrew Denby Roberts, *b* 21 May 1938. *Address:* Strathallan Castle, Auchterarder, Perthshire. *T:* Auchterarder 2131.

ROBERTS, Wyn; *see* Roberts, I. W. P.

ROBERTS-JONES, Ivor, CBE 1975; RA 1973 (ARA 1969); sculptor; Teacher of sculpture, Goldsmiths' College School of Art, 1946-68; *b* 2 Nov. 1913; *s* of William and Florence Robert-Jones; *m* 1940, Monica Florence Booth; one *d* (one *s* decd). *Educ:* Oswestry Grammar Sch.; Worksop Coll.; Goldsmiths' Coll. Art Sch.; Royal Academy Schs. Served in RA, 1939-46; active service in Arakan, Burma. One-man Exhibitions of Sculpture: Beaux Arts Gall., 1957; Oriel, Welsh Arts Council Gall., Cardiff, 1978. Works purchased by: Tate Gallery; Arts Council of Gt Brit.; Welsh Arts Council; Beaverbrook Foundation, New Brunswick; Nat. Mus. of Wales. Public commissions: Winston Churchill, Parliament Square; Augustus John Memorial, Fordingbridge; Saint Francis, Lady Chapel, Ardleigh, Essex; Apsley Cherry Garrard, Wheathampstead; Winston Churchill, Oslo, 1975; Winston Churchill, New Orleans, 1977; Earl Attlee, Members' Lobby, House of Commons, 1979; Janus Rider (equestrian group), Harlech Castle, 1982, etc. Exhibited at: The John Moore, Leicester Galls, Royal Academy, Arts Council travelling exhibitions, Jubilee Exhibn of Modern British Sculpture, Battersea Park, 1977, etc. Work is in many private collections. Best known portraits include: Paul Claudel, Somerset Maugham, Yehudi Menuhin, The Duke of Edinburgh. *Publications:* poetry published in Welsh Review, Poets of the Forties, etc. Sculpture illustr. in British Art since 1900 by John Rothenstein; British Sculptors, 1947; Architectural Review, etc. *Recreation:* sailing. *Address:* Coppings, Cratfield, near Halesworth, Suffolk. *T:* Ubbeston 341. *Club:* Cruising Association.

ROBERTS-WEST, Lt-Col George Arthur Alston-; *see* West.

ROBERTS-WRAY, Sir Kenneth Owen, GCMG 1960 (KCMG 1949; CMG 1946); QC 1959; Legal Adviser, Commonwealth Relations Office (Dominions Office until 1947) and Colonial Office, 1945-60, retired; *b* 6 June 1899; *s* of late Captain Thomas Henry Roberts-Wray, CB, OBE, VD, RNVR, sometime ADC to King George V, and late Florence Grace Roberts-Wray; *m* 1st, 1927, Joan Tremayne Waring (*d* 1961); three *s*; 2nd, 1965, Lady (Mary Howard) Williams, *widow* of Sir Ernest Williams, JP. *Educ:* University Tutorial Coll.; RMA, Woolwich; Merton College, Oxford (1st Class Hons School of Jurisprudence). 2/Lt RA 1918; Lieutenant, 1919; retired on account of wounds, 1920. Called to Bar 1924 (Certificate of Honour); Professional Legal Clerk, Min. of Health, 1926, Asst Chief Clerk, 1929; 2nd Asst Legal Adviser, Dominions Office and Colonial Office, 1931; Asst Legal Adviser, 1943. Chairman: Law Officers Conf., WI, 1944; Judicial Advisers Confs, Uganda, 1953, Nigeria, 1956. Acting Attorney-Gen., Gibraltar, Jan.-June 1969. DCL Oxon, 1967; Hon. LLD Birmingham, 1968. *Publications:* part author of The Law of Collisions on Land, 1925; (Contrib.) Changing Law in Developing Countries (ed Anderson), 1963; Commonwealth and Colonial Law, 1966; articles on Colonial Law in legal publications. *Recreations:* golf, cinematography. *Address:* The Old Golf House, Forest Row, Sussex. *T:* Forest Row 2588; 5 King's Bench Walk, Temple, EC4. *T:* 01-353 2882/2884. *Clubs:* United Oxford & Cambridge University; Royal Ashdown Forest Golf.

ROBERTSON, family name of **Baron Robertson of Oakridge.**

ROBERTSON, Hon. Lord; Ian Macdonald Robertson, TD 1946; a Senator of the College of Justice in Scotland (with judicial title of Lord Robertson) since 1966; *b* 30 Oct. 1912; *s* of late James Robertson and Margaret Eva Wilson, Broughty Ferry, Angus, and Edinburgh; *m* 1938, Anna Love Glen, *d* of late Judge James Fulton Glen, Tampa, Florida, USA; one *s* two *d*. *Educ:* Merchiston Castle School; Balliol College, Oxford; Edinburgh University. BA Oxford (Mod. Greats), 1934; LLB Edinburgh 1937; Vans Dunlop Schol. in Law, Edinburgh 1937. Member Faculty of Advocates, 1939; Advocate-Depute, 1949-51; QC (Scot.), 1954; Sheriff of Ayr and Bute, 1961-66; Sheriff of Perth and Angus, 1966. Chairman: Medical Appeals Tribunal, 1957-63; Scottish Jt Council for Teachers' Salaries, 1965-81; Scottish Valuation Adv. Council, 1977; Member Court of Session Rules Council; UK Rep., Central Council, Internat. Union of Judges, 1974-. Formerly, External Examiner in law subjects, Aberdeen, Glasgow, Edinburgh and St Andrews Universities; Member Committee on Conflicts of Jurisdiction affecting Children, 1958; Governor of Merchiston Castle School, 1954, Chm., 1970; Assessor on Court of Edinburgh Univ., 1967-81. Chairman: Edinburgh Centre of Rural Economy; Edinburgh Centre for Tropical Veterinary Medicine; Jt Cttee, Edinburgh Sch. of Agriculture. Served War of 1939-45, 8th Bn The Royal Scots (The Royal Regt); commd 1939; SO (Capt.), 44th Lowland Brigade (15th Scottish Division), Normandy and NW Europe (despatches). *Publication:* From Normandy to the Baltic, 1945. *Recreation:* golf. *Address:* 13 Moray Place, Edinburgh EH3 6DT. *T:* 031-225 6637. *Clubs:* New, Honourable Company of Edinburgh Golfers (Captain 1970-72).

See also Sir James W. Robertson.

ROBERTSON OF OAKRIDGE, 2nd Baron *cr* 1961; **William Ronald Robertson;** Bt 1919; Member of the London Stock Exchange, since 1973; *b* 8 Dec. 1930; *s* of General Lord Robertson of Oakridge, GCB, GBE, KCMG, KCVO, DSO, MC, and Edith (*d* 1982), *d* of late J. B. Macindoe; *S* father, 1974; *m* 1972, Celia Jane, *d* of William R. Elworthy; one *s*. *Educ:* Hilton

Coll., Natal; Charterhouse; Staff Coll., Camberley (psc). Served The Royal Scots Greys, 1949-69. Mem. Salters' Co. *Heir: s* Hon. William Brian Elworthy Robertson, *b* 15 Nov. 1975. *Club:* Anglo-German Association.

ROBERTSON, Alan, OBE 1965; FRS 1964; BA; DSc; Deputy Chief Scientific Officer, ARC Unit of Animal Genetics, Edinburgh; *b* 21 Feb. 1920; *s* of late John Mouat Robertson and Annie Grace; *m* 1947, Margaret Sidney, *y d* of late Maurice Bernheim; two *s* one *d. Educ:* Liverpool Institute; Gonville and Caius College, Cambridge. Operational Research Section, Coastal Command, RAF, 1943-46. ARC Unit of Animal Genetics, Edinburgh, 1947-. Hon. Prof., Edinburgh Univ., 1967. For. Assoc., Nat. Acad. of Sci., USA, 1979. Hon. Dr rer nat Univ. of Hohenheim, 1968. Gold Medal, Royal Agric. Soc., 1958. *Publications:* papers in scientific jls. *Recreations:* gardening, tennis. *Address:* 47 Braid Road, Edinburgh EH10 6AW. *T:* 031-447 4239. *Club:* Farmers'.

ROBERTSON, Alan Murray; Director: Motherwell Bridge Ltd; Hardcastle & Co.; formerly Managing Director, BP Oil Ltd, and a Director, BP Trading Ltd; *b* 19 Dec. 1914; *s* of late Dr James R. Robertson; *m* 1st; one *s* two *d*; 2nd, Judith-Anne, *d* of late Robert Russell, Glasgow. *Educ:* St Anselm's Bakewell; Malvern; Pembroke Coll., Cambridge (MA). Joined Anglo-Iranian Oil Co., 1937 in Paris; served 1939-46 in RTR and RASC, Middle East and Italian Campaigns (despatches, Major); Anglo-Iranian representative in France, 1949-53; Gen. Man., Scottish Oils & Shell-Mex Ltd, 1955-56; Man. Dir, National Benzole Co. Ltd, 1957-63; Exec. Vice-Pres., BP Oil Corp., New York, 1968-70. *Recreations:* travel, fishing, gardening. *Address:* Shepherds Cottage, Shipton-under-Wychwood, Oxon. *Club:* Caledonian.

ROBERTSON, Prof. Sir Alexander, Kt 1970; CBE 1963; Professor of Tropical Animal Health, University of Edinburgh, 1971-78, now Emeritus Professor; Director: Veterinary Field Station, 1968-78; Centre for Tropical Veterinary Medicine, Edinburgh University, 1971-78; *b* 3 Feb. 1908; *m* 1936, Janet McKinlay; two *d. Educ:* Stonehaven Mackie Acad.; Aberdeen University; and Royal (Dick) Veterinary College, Edinburgh. MA Aberdeen, 1929; BSc Aberdeen, 1930; PhD Edinburgh, 1940; MRCVS, 1934. Demonstrator in Anatomy, Royal (Dick) Veterinary College, Edinburgh, 1934; Vet. Inspector, Min. of Agriculture, 1935-37; Sen. Lectr in Physiology, 1938-44, Prof. of Vet. Hygiene, 1944-53, William Dick Prof. of Animal Health, 1953-71, Director, 1957-63, Royal (Dick) School of Veterinary Studies, Univ. of Edinburgh; Dean of Faculty of Vet. Medicine, Univ. of Edinburgh, 1964-70. Exec. Officer for Scotland, Farm Livestock Emergency Service, 1942-47. FRSE, 1945; FRIC, 1946; FRSH, 1950; FRZSScot, 1952; Mem. Departmental Cttee on Foot and Mouth Disease, 1952-54; Pres. Brit. Vet. Assoc., 1954-55; Vice-Pres. Roy. Zoological Soc. of Scotland, 1959-; Mem. Governing Body, Animal Virus Research Inst., Pirbright, 1954-62; Member: Council Royal Coll. of Veterinary Surgeons, 1957-78 (Treasurer, 1964-67; Vice-Pres., 1967-68, 1969-70; Pres., 1968-69); Artificial Insemination Adv. Cttee for Scotland, 1958-65; ARC Tech. Adv. Cttee on Nutrient Requirements, 1959-78; Departmental Cttee of Inquiry into Fowl Pest, 1960-61; Governing Body Rowett Research Institute, 1962-77; ARC Adv. Cttee on Meat Research, 1968-73; Trustee, Internat. Laboratory for Res. in Animal Diseases, 1973-82 (Chm., 1980-81); Chairman: Sci. Adv. Panel, Pig Industry Develt Authority, 1962-68; Research Adv. Cttee. Meat and Livestock Commn, 1969-73; Vet. Adv. Panel, British Council, 1971-78; Member: FAO/WHO Expert Panel on Veterinary Educn, 1962-78; East African Natural Resources Research Council, 1963-78; Cttee of Inquiry into Veterinary Profession, 1971-75; Council, RSE, 1963-65, Vice-Pres., 1969-72; Inter Univ. Council, 1973-75. Editor, Jl of Tropical Animal Health and Production. Hon. FRCVS, 1970. Hon. Mem., World Veterinary Assoc., 1975. Hon. LLD Aberdeen, 1971; Hon. DVSc Melbourne, 1973. *Publications:* (ed) International Encyclopædia of Veterinary Medicine; numerous articles in veterinary and other scientific journals. *Recreations:* gardening, motoring, hill climbing. *Address:* 205 Mayfield Road, Edinburgh EH9 3BD. *T:* 031-667 1242. *Clubs:* Caledonian; New (Edinburgh).

ROBERTSON, Anne Elisabeth; *see* Mueller, A. E.

ROBERTSON, Prof. Anne Strachan, DLitt; FRSE; FSA, FSAScot; Titular Professor of Roman Archaeology, Glasgow University, 1974-75, retired; *d* of John Anderson Robertson and Margaret Purden. *Educ:* Hillhead High Sch.; Glasgow High Sch. for Girls; Glasgow Univ. (MA, DLitt); London Univ. (MA). FRSE 1975; FMA 1958; FRNS 1937; FSA 1958; FSAScot 1941. Glasgow University: Dalrymple Lectr in Archaeol., 1939; Under-Keeper, Hunterian Museum and Curator, Hunter Coin Cabinet, 1952; Reader in Roman Archaeol., Keeper of Cultural Collections and of Hunter Coin Cabinet, Hunterian Museum, 1964; Keeper of Roman Collections and of Hunter Coin Cabinet, 1974. Silver Medal, RNS, 1964; Silver Huntington Medal, Amer. Numismatic Soc., 1970. *Publications:* An Antonine Fort: Golden Hill, Duntocher, 1957; The Antonine Wall, 1960 (new edn 1979); Sylloge of Anglo-Saxon Coins in the Hunter Coin Cabinet, 1961; Catalogue of Roman Imperial Coins in the Hunter Coin Cabinet: Vol. 1, 1962; Vol. 2, 1971; Vol. 3, 1977; Vol. 4, 1978; Vol. 5, 1982; The Roman Fort at Castledykes, 1964; Birrens (Blatobulgium), 1975; contrib. to Britannia, Numismatic Chron., Proc. Soc. of Antiquaries of Scotland. *Recreations:* reading, writing, photography, walking, gardening. *Address:* Flat 7, 60 Partickhill Road, Glasgow G11 5AB. *T:* 041-339 6198.

ROBERTSON, Bryan Charles Francis, OBE 1961; Author, Broadcasting and Television, etc; regular contributor to The Spectator; *b* 1 April 1925; *yr s* of A. F. Robertson and Ellen Dorothy Black; unmarried. *Educ:* Battersea Grammar School. Worked and studied in France and Germany, 1947-48; Director: Heffer Gallery, Cambridge, 1949-51; Whitechapel Art Gallery, London, 1952-68. Mem. Arts Council Art Panel, 1958-61, 1980-; Mem. Contemporary Art Soc. Cttee, 1958-73. US Embassy Grant to visit United States, 1956; Lectr on art, Royal Ballet School, 1958; Ford Foundn Grant for research for writing, 1961; British Council Lecture Tour, SE Asia and Australian State Galleries, 1960. Dir, State Univ. of NY Museum, 1970-75. Since 1953 has organized major exhibitions at Whitechapel, including Turner, Hepworth, Moore, Stubbs, John Martin, Rowlandson and Gillray, Bellotto, Mondrian, de Stäel, Nolan, Davie, Smith, Malevich, Pollock, Richards, Australian Painting, Rothko, Tobey, Vaughan, Guston, Poliakof, Caro, Medley, etc. *Publications:* Jackson Pollock, a monograph, 1960; Sidney Nolan, a monograph, 1961; (jtly) Private View, 1965; (with H. Tatlock Miller) Loudon Sainthill, 1973; Edward Burra, 1978; contribs (art criticism) to London Magazine, Art News (US), Spectator, Harpers & Queen, Twentieth Century, Listener, Cambridge Review, Museums Jl, etc. *Address:* 73 Barnsbury Street, N1 1EJ. *Club:* Athenæum.

ROBERTSON, Catherine Christian, MA; Headmistress of George Watson's Ladies' College, 1926-45; *b* 10 Dec. 1886; *d* of late Alexander Robertson, Perth, and Mary Macfarlane Duncan, Edinburgh. *Educ:* privately; Perth Academy; University of Edinburgh. Graduated in Arts, with Hons in English Literature and Language, Class II, 1910; Cherwell Hall, Oxford; Diploma of Education, 1911; George Scott Travelling Scholar, 1911. Head of the English Department, Edinburgh Ladies' Coll., 1919-26; travel in America as Chautauqua Scholar of the English-Speaking Union (first Scotswoman to hold this award), 1925. President, Association of Headmistresses, Scottish Branch, 1941-42; Vice-Chairman of Council, Girls' Training Corps, Scotland, 1942. *Recreations:* walking, foreign travel, music.

ROBERTSON, Prof. Charles Martin; FBA 1967; Lincoln Professor of Classical Archæology and Art, University of Oxford, 1961-78; *b* 11 Sept. 1911; *s* of late Professor Donald Struan Robertson, FBA, FSA, and Petica Coursolles Jones; *m* 1942, Theodosia Cecil Spring Rice; four *s* two *d. Educ:* Leys School, Cambridge; Trinity College, Cambridge. BA Cambridge, 1934, MA 1947; student at British School of Archæology, Athens, 1934-36; Asst Keeper, Dept of Greek and Roman Antiquities, British Museum, 1936-48 (released for service, War of 1939-45, 1940-46); Yates Professor of Classical Art and Archæology in the Univ. of London (Univ. Coll.), 1948-61. Corresp. Mem., German Archæological Inst., 1953; Ordinary Mem., 1953; Chm., Man. Cttee, British School at Athens, 1958-68. Mem., Inst. for Advanced Study, Princeton, 1968-69. Guest Schol., J. Paul Getty Museum, Malibu, 1980. Hon. Fellow: Lincoln Coll., Oxford, 1980; UCL, 1980. Hon. DLit QUB, 1978. *Publications:* Why Study Greek Art? (Inaugural Lecture), 1949; Greek Painting, 1959; The Visual Arts of the Greeks (in The Greeks), 1962; Between Archæology and Art History (Inaugural Lecture), 1963; Crooked Connections (poems), 1970; indexes and editorial work in late Sir John Beazley's Paralipomena, 1971; For Rachel (poems), 1972; A History of Greek Art, 1975; (with Alison Frantz) The Parthenon Frieze, 1975; A Hot Bath at Bedtime (poems), 1977; The Sleeping Beauty's Prince (poem), 1977; (with John Boardman) Corpus Vasorum Antiquorum, Castle Ashby, 1978; A Shorter History of Greek Art, 1981; The Attic Black-figure and Red-figure Pottery, in Karageorghis, Excavations at Kition IV, 1981; articles, notes and reviews since 1935, in British and foreign periodicals. *Address:* 7a Parker Street, Cambridge CB1 1JL. *T:* Cambridge 311913.

ROBERTSON, Charles Robert Suttie; Member, Management Committee of The Distillers Company Ltd, since 1970; chartered accountant; *b* 23 Nov. 1920; *s* of late David Young McLellan Robertson and Doris May Beaumont; *m* 1949, Shona MacGregor Riddel, *d* of late Robert Riddel, MC, and Phyllis Mary Stewart; one *s. Educ:* Dollar Academy. Joined DCL group, 1949; appointed: Managing Director, Scottish Malt Distillers, 1960; Sec., DCL, 1966, Finance Director, 1967. *Recreations:* hill walking, golf. *Address:* 30 Murrayfield Road, Edinburgh EH12 6ER. *T:* 031-337 7786. *Club:* Army and Navy.

ROBERTSON, Sheriff Daphne Jean Black, WS; Sheriff of Glasgow and Strathkelvin, since 1979; *b* 31 March 1937; *d* of Rev. Robert Black Kincaid and Ann Parker Collins; *m* 1965, Donald Buchanan Robertson, *qv. Educ:* Hillhead High Sch.; Greenock Acad.; Edinburgh Univ. (MA); Glasgow Univ. (LLB). Admitted solicitor, 1961; WS 1977. *Recreations:* domestic. *Address:* Sheriff Court House, Glasgow G1 1SY. *Club:* New (Edinburgh).

ROBERTSON, David Lars Manwaring; JP; Director, Kleinwort, Benson, Lonsdale plc; *b* 29 Jan. 1917; *m* 1939, Pamela Lauderdale Meares; three *s. Educ:* Rugby; University Coll. Oxford. Served Welsh Guards, 1940-45. Man. Dir, Charterhouse Finance Corp. Ltd, 1945-55; joined Kleinwort, Sons & Co. Ltd, 1955; Dir, Kleinwort, Benson Ltd, 1955-81; Pres., Kleinwort Benson (Geneva) SA, 1975. Chairman: MK Electric Group plc, 1975-; MK Electric Ltd, 1980-; Provident Mutual Life Assurance Assoc., 1973-; Provident Mutual Managed Pensions Funds Ltd, 1974-; Director: Berry Bros and Rudd; The Rouse Co., Columbia, Maryland. JP Crowborough, 1971. *Recreations:* skiing, golf, fishing, shooting. *Address:* Kleinwort, Benson, Lonsdale plc, 20 Fenchurch Street, EC3P 3DB. *Clubs:* Boodle's, MCC.

ROBERTSON, Donald Buchanan, QC (Scot.) 1973; *b* 29 March 1932; *s* of Donald Robertson, yachtbuilder, Sandbank, Argyll, and Jean Dunsmore Buchanan; *m* 1st, 1955, Louise Charlotte, *d* of Dr J. Linthorst-Homan; one *s* one *d* ; 2nd, 1965, Daphne Jean Black Kincaid (*see* D. J. B. Robertson). *Educ:* Dunoon Grammar Sch.; Glasgow Univ. (LLB). Admitted Solicitor, 1954; Royal Air Force (National Service), 1954-56. Passed Advocate, 1960; Standing Junior to Registrar of Restrictive Practices, 1970-73. Member: Sheriff Court Rules Council, 1972-76; Royal Commn on Legal Services in Scotland, 1976-80; Legal Aid Central Cttee, 1982-; Chm., VAT Tribunal, 1978. Hon. Sheriff, Lothian and Peebles, 1982. FSA (Scot.) 1982. *Recreations:* shooting, numismatics, riding. *Address:* 6 Great Stuart Street, Edinburgh EH3 6AW. *T:* 031-225 1729; Cranshaws Castle, By Duns, Berwickshire. *T:* Longformacus 268. *Clubs:* New (Edinburgh); RNVR (Glasgow).

ROBERTSON, Douglas William, CMG 1947; DSO 1918; MC 1918; *b* 30 Nov. 1898; 2nd surv. *s* of late Rev. J. A. Robertson, MA; *m* 1924, Mary Eagland (*d* 1968), *y d* of late W. E. Longbottom, Adelaide; no *c*. *Educ:* George Watson's College, Edinburgh. 2nd Lt KRRC, 1917; France, 1918 (wounded, MC, DSO, despatches); Administrative Service, Uganda, 1921-50; Resident of Buganda, 1945; Secretary for African Affairs, Uganda, 1947-50, retired, 1950. *Address:* 3a Ravelston Park, Edinburgh EH4 3DX. *Club:* East India, Devonshire, Sports and Public Schools.

ROBERTSON, Eric Desmond, OBE 1964; Controller, English Services, BBC External Services, and Deputy Managing Director, External Broadcasting, 1973-74; *b* 5 Oct. 1914; *s* of late Major Frank George Watt Robertson, Indian Army, and Amy Robertson (*née* Davidson); *m* 1943, Aileen Margaret Broadhead; two *s*. *Educ:* Aberdeen Grammar Sch.; Univ. of Aberdeen. BSc (Forestry) 1934, BSc 1936, Hunter Meml Prize, 1936. Scientific Adviser, Guthrie & Co. Ltd, Malaya, 1938-39; Malayan Forest Service, Asst Conservator, 1939-40. War of 1939-45: Malaya Command, on special duty, 1940-41. Producer, Malaya Broadcasting Corp., 1941-42; Special Officer, Far Eastern Broadcasting, All India Radio, 1942-45; Malay Editor, BBC, 1945-46; Far Eastern Service Organiser, BBC, 1946-49; Asst Head of Far Eastern Service, BBC, 1949-52; Head of Far Eastern Service, BBC, 1952-58; Head of Asian Services, BBC, 1958-64; Asst Controller, Overseas Services, BBC, 1964-70; Controller, Overseas Services, BBC, 1970-73. *Publication:* The Japanese File, 1979. *Address:* Bullapit Hill, Werrington, near Launceston, Cornwall. *T:* Launceston 3373; B2 Albany, Piccadilly, W1. *T:* 01-734 3355. *Club:* Naval and Military.

ROBERTSON, Francis Calder F.; *see* Ford Robertson.

ROBERTSON, George Islay Macneill; MP (Lab) Hamilton, since 1978; *b* 12 April 1946; *s* of George Phillip Robertson and Marion I. Robertson; *m* 1970, Sandra Wallace; two *s* one *d*. *Educ:* Dunoon Grammar Sch.; Univ. of Dundee (MA Hons 1968). Res. Asst, Tayside Study, 1968-69; Scottish Res. Officer, G&MWU, 1969-70, Scottish Organiser, 1970-78. PPS to Sec. of State for Social Services, 1979; opposition spokesman on Scottish Affairs, 1979-80, on Defence, 1980-81, on Foreign and Commonwealth Affairs, 1981-. Chm., Scottish Council of Labour Party, 1977-78; Mem., Scottish Exec. of Lab. Party, 1973-79; Sec., Manifesto Gp of PLP, 1979-. Member: Bd, Scottish Develt Agency, 1975-78; Bd, Scottish Tourist Bd, 1974-76; Police Adv. Bd for Scotland, 1974-78; Council, British Atlantic Cttee. Chm., Seatbelt Survivors Club. *Publications:* contrib. management jls and trade press. *Recreations:* photography, golf. *Address:* House of Commons, SW1A 0AA. *T:* 01-219 3000; 3 Argyle Park, Dunblane, Perthshire.

ROBERTSON, (Harold) Rocke, CC (Canada) 1969; MD, CM, FRCS(C), FRCSE, FACS, FRSC; Principal and Vice-Chancellor of McGill University, 1962-70; *b* 4 Aug. 1912; *s* of Harold Bruce Robertson and Helen McGregor Rogers; *m* 1937, Beatrice Roslyn Arnold; three *s* one *d*. *Educ:* St Michael's Sch., Victoria, BC; Ecole Nouvelle, Switzerland; Brentwood College, Victoria, BC; McGill University. Montreal Gen. Hospital: rotating, 1936; pathology, 1937-38; Clin. Asst in Surg., Roy. Infirmary, Edinburgh, 1938-39; Demonstr in Anat., Middx Hosp. Med. Sch., 1939; Jun. Asst in Surg., Montreal Gen. Hosp., 1939-40; RCAMC, 1940-45; Chief of Surgery: Shaughnessy Hosp., DVA, Vancouver, 1945-59 (Prof. of Surg., Univ. of BC, 1950-59); Vancouver Gen. Hosp., 1950-59; Montreal Gen. Hosp., 1959-62 (Prof. of Surg., McGill University, 1959-62). Member: Nat. Research Coun., 1964; Science Council of Canada, 1976-82. Director: Bell Telephone Co. of Canada, 1965-; Ralston Purina Canada, 1973. Hon. DCL, Bishop's Univ., 1963; Hon. LLD: Manitoba, 1964; Toronto, 1964; Victoria, 1964; Glasgow, 1965; Michigan, 1967; Dartmouth, 1967; Sir George Williams, 1970; McGill, 1970; Hon. DSc: Brit. Columbia, 1964; Memorial, 1968; Jefferson Med. Coll., 1969; Dr de l'Univ., Montreal, 1965. FRSA 1963. *Publications:* article on wounds, Encyclopædia Britannica; numerous contribs to scientific journals and text books. *Recreations:* tennis, fishing, gardening, golf. *Address:* RR2, Mountain, Ontario K0E 1S0, Canada. *T:* 613-989-2967.

ROBERTSON of Brackla, Maj.-Gen. Ian Argyll, CB 1968; MBE 1947; MA; DL; Vice-Lord-Lieutenant, Highland Region (Nairn), since 1980; Representative in Scotland of Messrs Spink & Son, 1969-76; Chairman, Royal British Legion, Scotland, 1974-77 (Vice-Chairman, 1971-74); *b* 17 July 1913; 2nd *s* of John Argyll Robertson and Sarah Lilian Pitt Healing; *m* 1939, Marjorie Violet Isobel Duncan; two *d*. *Educ:* Winchester Coll.; Trinity Coll., Oxford. Commnd Seaforth Highlanders, 1934; Brigade Major: 152 Highland Bde, 1943; 231 Infantry Bde, 1944; GSO2, Staff College, Camberley, 1944-45; AAG, 15 Indian Corps, 1945-46; GSO1, 51 Highland Div., 1952-54; Comdg 1st Bn Seaforth Highlanders, 1954-57; Comdg Support Weapons Wing, 1957-59; Comdg 127 (East Lancs) Inf. Bde, TA, 1959-61; Nat. Defence College, Delhi, 1962-63; Comdg School of Infantry, 1963-64; Commanding 51st Highland Division, 1964-66; Director of Army Equipment Policy, Ministry of Defence, 1966-68; retd. Mem. Council, Nat. Trust for Scotland, 1972-75. DL Nairn 1973. *Recreations:* various in a minor way. *Address:* Brackla House, Nairn. *T:* Cawdor 220. *Clubs:* Army and Navy, MCC; Vincent's (Oxford).

ROBERTSON, Rear-Adm. Ian George William, CB 1974; DSC 1944; *b* 21 Oct. 1922; *s* of late W. H. Robertson, MC, and Mrs A. M. Robertson; *m* 1947, Barbara Irène Holdsworth; one *s* one *d*. *Educ:* Radley College. Joined RNVR, 1941; qual. Pilot; Sub-Lt 1943; air strike ops against enemy shipping and attacks against German battleship Tirpitz, 1944 (DSC); Lieut, RN, 1945; flying and instructional appts, 1944-53; Comdr (Air): RNAS Culdrose, 1956; HMS Albion, 1958; in comd: HMS Keppel, 1960; HMS Mohawk, 1963; RNAS Culdrose, 1965; HMS Eagle, 1970; Admiral Comdg Reserves, 1972-74; retd 1974. Comdr 1954; Captain 1963; Rear-Adm. 1972; idc 1968. Dir-Gen., Navy League, 1975-76; Scoutreach Resources Organiser, Scout Assoc., 1976-79. *Recreations:* golf, sailing. *Address:* 30 Hesper Mews, SW5 0HH. *T:* 01-373 0869. *Clubs:* Naval; Royal Mid-Surrey Golf.

ROBERTSON, Ian (Gow), MA Oxon; Keeper of Western Art, Ashmolean Museum, Oxford, and of Hope Collection of Engraved Portraits, and Fellow of Worcester College, Oxford, 1962-68; *b* Killearn, Stirlingshire, 20 Sept. 1910; *er s* of John Gow Robertson and Margaret Stewart. *Educ:* The King's School, Canterbury. Studied art at continental centres, in US and in public and private collections in UK. Assistant Keeper in Dept of Fine Art, Ashmolean Museum, 1931. Ministry of Home Security, 1939-41; served in Royal Navy, 1941-46. Senior Assistant Keeper, Ashmolean Museum, 1949. *Recreations:* gardening, listening to music. *Address:* Flat 3, 15 Gledhow Gardens, SW5.

ROBERTSON, Ian Macbeth, CB 1976; MVO 1956; JP; Secretary of Commissions for Scotland, since 1978; *b* 1 Feb. 1918; *s* of late Sheriff-Substitute J. A. T. Robertson; *m* 1947, Anne Stewart Marshall. *Educ:* Melville College; Edinburgh University. Served War of 1939-45 in Middle East and Italy; Royal Artillery and London Scottish, Captain. Entered Dept of Health for Scotland, 1946. Private Secretary to Minister of State, Scottish Office, 1951-52 and to Secretary of State for Scotland, 1952-55. Asst Secretary, Dept of Health for Scotland, 1955; Assistant Under-Secretary of State, Scottish Office, 1963-64; Under-Secretary: Scottish Development Department, 1964-65; Scottish Educn Dept, 1966-78. Mem., Williams Cttee on Nat. Museums and Galls in Scotland, 1979-81. Chm. of Governors, Edinburgh Coll. of Art, 1981-. JP Edinburgh 1978. *Address:* 8 Middleby Street, Edinburgh EH9 1TD. *T:* 031-667 3999. *Club:* New (Edinburgh).

ROBERTSON, Ian Macdonald; *see* Robertson, Hon. Lord.

ROBERTSON, James, CBE 1969; MA; FRCM; Hon. FTCL; Hon. GSM; Hon. RAM; *b* 17 June 1912; *s* of Ainslie John Robertson and Phyllis Mary Roughton; *m* 1st, 1949, Rachel June Fraser (*d* 1979); one *s* (and one *s* decd); 2nd, 1980, Oswalda Viktoria Pattrick. *Educ:* Winchester College; Trinity College, Cambridge; Conservatorium, Leipzig; Royal College of Music, London. On musical staff, Glyndebourne Opera, 1937-39; Conductor, Carl Rosa Opera, Co., 1938-39; Conductor, Canadian Broadcasting Corp., 1939-40; Air Ministry, 1940-42; RAFVR (Intelligence), 1942-46. Director, Sadler's Wells Opera Company, 1946-54; Conductor of National Orchestra of New Zealand Broadcasting Service, Sept. 1954-Nov. 1957. Conductor, Touring Opera, 1958; Adviser on Opera, Théâtre de la Monnaie, Brussels, 1960-61; Artistic and Musical Director, New Zealand Opera Co., 1962-63; Dir, London Opera Centre, 1964-77, Consultant, 1977-78; Musical Dir, Nat. Opera of NZ, 1979-81. *Recreation:* languages. *Address:* Ty Helyg, Llwynmawr, Pontfadog, Llangollen, Clwyd LL20 7BG. *T:* Glynceiriog 480.

ROBERTSON, Maj.-Gen. James Alexander Rowland, CB 1958; CBE 1956 (OBE 1949; MBE 1942); DSO 1944 (Bar 1945); DL; *b* 23 March 1910; *s* of Colonel James Currie Robertson, CIE, CMG, CBE, IMS, and Catherine Rowland Jones; *m* 1st, 1949, Ann Madeline Tosswill (*d* 1949); 2nd, Joan Wills, (*née* Abercromby), *widow* of R. L. Wills, CBE, MC. *Educ:* Aysgarth School; Epsom College, RMC, Sandhurst. Commissioned 2 Lieutenant IA, 1930, attached 1st KOYLI; posted 6th Gurkha Rifles, 1931; Instructor Sch. of Physical Training, 1936-37; Staff Coll., Quetta, July-Dec. 1941; Bde Major 1 (Maymyo) Bde, Jan.-June, 1942; Bde Major, 106 I Inf. Bde, 1942-44; Comdr 1/7 Gurkha Rifles, 1944-45; Comdr 48 Ind. Inf. Bde, 1945-47; GSO 1, Joint Staff Coll., Quetta, June-Nov., 1947; Comdr 1/6th Gurkha Rifles, 1947-48; GSO 1 Gurkha Planning Staff, March-June, 1948; GSO 1 Malaya comd, June-Nov. 1948; BGS 1948-49. GSO 1, War Office, 1950-52; Col GS, 1 Corps, Germany, 1952-54; Comdr 51 Indep. Bde, 1955-57; Commander 17 Gurkha Division Overseas Commonwealth Land Forces, and Maj.-Gen. Brigade of Gurkhas, 1958-61; GOC Land Forces, Middle East Command, 1961-63; Gurkha Liaison Officer, War Office, 1963-64, retd. Personnel Dir, NAAFI, 1964-69. Colonel, 6th Queen Elizabeth's Own Gurkha Rifles, 1961-69; Chm., 1968-80, Pres., 1980-82, Gurkha Brigade Assoc. DL Greater London, 1977. *Recreations:* fishing, sculpture, an outdoor life. *Club:* Army and Navy.

ROBERTSON, Sir James (Anderson), Kt 1968; CBE 1963 (OBE 1949; MBE 1942); QPM 1961; *b* Glasgow, 8 April 1906; *s* of James Robertson, East Haugh, Pitlochry, Perthshire and later of Glasgow, and Mary Rankin Anderson, Glasgow; *m* 1942, Janet Lorraine Gilfillan Macfarlane, Largs, Ayrshire; two *s* one *d. Educ:* Provanside Sch., Glasgow and Glasgow Univ. BL 1936. Chief Constable of Glasgow, 1960-71. Chairman: Scotland Cttee, Nat. Children's Home; Glasgow Standing Conf. of Voluntary Youth Organisations; Hon. President: Glasgow Bn Boys' Brigade. OStJ 1964. *Recreations:* golf and gardening. *Address:* 3 Kirklee Road, Glasgow G12 0RL. *T:* 041-339 4400.

ROBERTSON, James Geddes, CMG 1961; formerly Under-Secretary, Department of the Environment, and Chairman, Northern Economic Planning Board, 1965-71, retired 1971; *b* 29 Nov. 1910; *s* of late Captain A. M. Robertson, Portsoy, Banffshire; *m* 1939, Marion Mitchell Black; one *s* one *d. Educ:* Fordyce Academy, Banffshire; George Watson's College, Edinburgh; Edinburgh University. Kitchener Schol., 1928-32, MA 1st cl. Hons History (Edinburgh), 1932. Entered Ministry of Labour as Third Class Officer, 1933; Principal, 1943; on exchange to Commonwealth Dept of Labour and Nat. Service, Australia, 1947-49; Asst Sec., Min of Labour, 1956; Member of Government Delegations to Governing Body and Conference of ILO, 1956-60, and Social Cttee, Council of Europe, 1953-61; Safety and Health Dept, 1961-63; Training Department, Ministry of Labour, 1963-65. Member: Industrial Tribunals Panel, 1971-73; Northern Rent Scrutiny Bd, 1973-74; Rent Assessment Panel for Scotland, 1975-81. Served War of 1939-45, RAF 1942-45. *Address:* 12a Abbotsford Crescent, Edinburgh EH10 5DY. *T:* 031-447 4675.

ROBERTSON, Maj.-Gen. James Howden, CB 1974; Director, Army Dental Service, 1970-74; *b* 16 Oct. 1915; *s* of John and Marion Robertson, Glasgow and Creetown; *m* 1942, Muriel Edna, *d* of Alfred Jefferies, Elgin; two *s* one *d. Educ:* White Hill Sch., Glasgow; Glasgow Dental Hospital. LDS, RFPS(G) 1939; FDS, RCSE 1957. Lieut, Army Dental Corps, 1939; Captain 1940; Major 1943; Lt-Col 1954; Col 1962; Brig. 1967; Maj.-Gen. 1970. Served in UK and Norway, 1939-44, Europe, 1944-50; Senior Specialist in Dental Surgery, 1957; Middle East, 1958-61; Consultant, CMH Aldershot, 1962-67; Consulting Dental Surgeon to the Army, 1967-70. Col Comdt, RADC, 1975-80. QHDS, 1967-74. Pres., Oral Surgery Club of GB, 1975-76. OStJ 1969. *Publications:* various articles in medical and dental jls on oral and maxillo-facial surgery. *Recreations:* wildfowling, fishing, gardening. *Address:* Struan, Hethfelton Hollow, East Stoke, Dorset. *T:* Bindon Abbey 462272.

ROBERTSON, Rev. Canon James Smith; Canon Emeritus, Zambia, 1965; Secretary, United Society for the Propagation of the Gospel, 1973-June 1983; a Chaplain to the Queen, since 1980; *b* 4 Sept. 1917; *s* of Stuart Robertson and Elizabeth Mann Smith, Forfar; *m* 1950, Margaret Isabel Mina Mounsey; one *d. Educ:* Glasgow Univ.; Edinburgh Theol Coll.; London Univ. MA Glasgow 1938; PCE London 1953. Curate, St Salvador's, Edinburgh, 1940-45; Mission Priest, UMCA, N Rhodesia, 1945-50; St Mark's Coll., Mapanza, 1950-55; Chalimbana Trng Coll., Lusaka, 1955-65, Principal 1958-65; Head, Educn Dept, Bede Coll., Durham, 1965-68; Sec., Church Colls of Educn, Gen. Synod Bd of Educn, 1968-73. Chm., Conf. for World Mission, BCC, 1977-81. *Publications:* (contrib.) Education in South Africa, 1970; (contrib.) The Training of Teachers, 1972; (contrib.) Values and Moral Development in Higher Education, 1974; (contrib.) Grow or Die, 1981. *Recreations:* music, electronics, philosophy. *Address:* 5 Fitzwilliam Avenue, Kew Gardens, Richmond, Surrey. *T:* 01-940 8574.

ROBERTSON, Sir James (Wilson), KT 1965; GCMG 1957 (KCMG 1953); GCVO 1956; KBE 1948 (MBE 1931); *b* 27 Oct. 1899; *e s* of late James Robertson, Broughty Ferry, Angus and Edinburgh, and late Mrs Robertson, Glenlyon, Spylaw Bank Road, Colinton, Midlothian; *m* 1926, Nancy, *er d* of H. S. Walker, Huddersfield; one *s* one *d. Educ:* Merchiston Castle School, Edinburgh; Balliol College, Oxford. BA 1922, MA 1930; Honorary Fellow of Balliol, 1953. Oxford University Rugby XV, 1921. Officer Cadet, 1918-19; 2nd Lieutenant, Black Watch, 1919; entered Sudan Political Service, 1922; Assistant Dist Commissioner and Dist Comr, 1922-36. Jebel Aulia compensation commission, 1936. Sub-Governor White Nile Province, 1937; Dep. Governor Gezira Province, 1939; actg Governor Gezira Province, 1940-41. Asst Civil Secretary, 1941; Deputy Civil Secretary, 1942; Civil Secretary Sudan Government, 1945-53; Chairman British Guiana Constitutional Commission, 1953-54; Director, Uganda Co. Ltd, 1954-55 and 1961-69; Governor-General and Commander-in-Chief of Federation of Nigeria, 1955-60 (first Governor-General and Commander-in-Chief of the Independent Federation of Nigeria, Oct.-Nov. 1960). Comr to examine the question of Kenya Coastal Strip, Oct. 1961. Dir, Barclays Bank DCO, 1961-71. Chairman: Commonwealth Inst., 1961-68; Central Coun. Roy. Over-Seas League, 1962-67; Sudan British Pensioners' Assoc., 1961-67; Coun. for Aid to African Students, 1961-76; Pres. Overseas Service Pensioners' Assoc., 1961-71; Pres. Britain-Nigeria Assoc., 1961-81; a Governor, Queen Mary Coll., Univ. of London, 1961-74; Mem. Council, Royal Commonwealth Society for the Blind; Deputy Chairman, Nat. Cttee for Commonwealth Immigrants, 1965-68. Hon. LLD Leeds University, 1961. FRSA 1964. Wellcome Medal, Royal African Society, 1961. Order of the Nile, 4th Class, 1934. KStJ 1955. *Publication:* Transition in Africa—Memoirs, 1974. *Address:* The Old Bakehouse, Cholsey, near Wallingford, Oxon. *T:* Cholsey 651234. *Club:* Athenæum.
See also Hon. Lord Robertson.

ROBERTSON, John; *b* 3 Feb. 1913; *s* of William Robertson; *m* 1st, 1939 (marr. diss. 1977); two *s* three *d* ; 2nd, 1977, June Robertson (*d* 1978); 3rd, 1979, Mrs Sheena Lynch. *Educ:* elementary and secondary schools. Formerly District Secretary and Assistant Divisional Organizer of the Amalgamated Engineering Union, West of Scotland. Mem., Lanarkshire County Council, Motherwell and Wishaw Town Council, 1946-52. Member of Labour Party, 1943-; contested (Lab) Scotstoun Division of Glasgow, General Election, Oct. 1951; MP Paisley, (Lab) Apr. 1961-76, (SLP) 1976-79. Among the founders of the Scottish Labour Party, Jan. 1976. *Recreations:* politics, painting, bowling and Trade Union. *Address:* 25 Straiton Road, Kirkmichael, Mayble, Ayrshire. *T:* Kirkmichael 272.

ROBERTSON, Maj.-Gen. John Carnegie, Director of Army Legal Services, Ministry of Defence, 1973-76; *b* 24 Nov. 1917. *Educ:* Cheltenham Coll.; RMC, Sandhurst. Served War of 1939-45: Officer in Gloucestershire Regt (PoW, Germany, 1940). Called to the Bar, Gray's Inn, 1949. Joined Judge Advocate's Dept, 1948; served subseq. in Middle East, BAOR, East Africa and the Far East. Dep. Dir, Army Legal Services, HQ, BAOR, 1971-73. *Address:* Berry House, Nuffield, Henley-on-Thames, Oxon. *T:* Nettlebed 641740. *Clubs:* Huntercombe Golf, Senior Golfers' Soc.

ROBERTSON, John David H.; *see* Home Robertson.

ROBERTSON, Rear Adm. John Keith, FIEE, FBIM; Assistant Chief of Defence Staff (Intelligence), since 1982; *b* 16 July 1926; *s* of G. M. and J. L. Robertson; *m* 1951, Kathleen (*née* Bayntun); one *s* three *d. Educ:* RNC Dartmouth; Clare Coll., Cambridge (BA 1949). FIEE 1981; FBIM 1980. RNC Dartmouth, 1940-43; served, 1943-73 (Clare Coll., Cambridge, 1946-49): HM Ships Queen Elizabeth, Zest, Gabbard, Aisne and Decoy; Staff, RNC Dartmouth; Grad. Recruiting; Weapon Engr Officer, HMS Centaur; Comdr, RNEC Manadon; RCDS; Captain Technical Intell. (Navy), 1974-76; Captain Fleet Maintenance, Portsmouth, 1976-78; Dir, Naval Recruiting, 1978-79; Dir, Management and Support of Intelligence, MoD, 1980-82. *Recreations:* hockey, tennis, golf, wood carving. *Address:* Ministry of Defence, Whitehall, SW1A 2HB. *T:* 01-218 9000. *Clubs:* Royal Commonwealth Society; Corkscrew (Bath).

ROBERTSON, John Monteath, CBE 1962; FRS 1945; FRIC, FInstP, FRSE; MA, PhD, DSc (Glasgow); Gardiner Professor of Chemistry, University of Glasgow, 1942-70, now Professor Emeritus; Director of Laboratories, 1955-70; *b* 24 July 1900; *s* of William Robertson and Jane Monteath, of Nether Fordun, Auchterarder; *m* 1930, Stella Kennard Nairn, MA; two *s* one *d. Educ:* Perth Academy; Glasgow University. Commonwealth Fellow, USA, 1928; Member staff of Davy Faraday Laboratory of Royal Institution, 1930; Senior Lecturer in Physical Chemistry, University of Sheffield, 1939; Scientific Adviser (Chemical) to Bomber Command, 1941; Hon. Scientific Adviser to RAF, 1942. George Fisher Baker Lecturer, Cornell Univ., USA, 1951; Visiting Prof., Univ. of California, Berkeley, USA, 1958. Member, University Grants Committee, 1960-65; President, Chemical Society, 1962-64. Davy Medal, Royal Soc., 1960; Longstaff Medal, Chemical Society, 1966. Corresp. Member Turin Academy of Sciences, 1962. Hon. LLD Aberdeen, 1963; Hon. DSc Strathclyde, 1970; Paracelsus Medal, Swiss Chem. Soc., 1971. *Publications:* Organic Crystals and Molecules, 1953; papers and articles on chemical, physical, and X-ray diffraction subjects in Proc. Royal Soc., Jl of Chem. Soc., etc. *Address:* 11a Eriskay Road, Inverness IV2 3LX. *T:* Inverness 225561. *Club:* Athenæum.

ROBERTSON, John Windeler; Senior Partner, Wedd Durlacher Mordaunt; *b* 9 May 1934; *s* of John Bruce Robertson and Evelyn Windeler Robertson; *m* 1959, Jennifer-Ann Gourdou; one *s* one *d. Educ:* Winchester Coll. National Service, RNVR, 1953-55. Joined Wedd Jefferson & Co. (Members of Stock Exchange), 1955; Partner, 1961; Shareholder, Wedd Durlacher Mordaunt, 1968; Director, Wedd Durlacher Mordaunt Ltd, 1974; a Managing Partner, Wedd Durlacher Mordaunt, 1976, Senior Partner, 1979. Dep. Chm., Stock Exchange, 1976-79. *Recreations:* golf, deer stalking. *Address:* Flat 83, 55 Ebury Street, SW1. *T:* 01-730 0931. *Club:* City of London.

ROBERTSON, Lewis, CBE 1969; FRSE; industrialist and administrator; Chairman, F. H. Lloyd Holdings plc, since 1982; Director, Scottish and Newcastle Breweries plc, since 1975; *b* 28 Nov. 1922; *s* of John Farquharson Robertson and Margaret Arthur; *m* 1950, Elspeth Badenoch; three *s* one *d. Educ:* Trinity Coll., Glenalmond. Accountancy training; RAF Intelligence. Chm., 1968-70, and Man. Dir, 1965-70, Scott & Robertson Ltd; Chief Executive, 1971-76, and Dep. Chm., 1973-76, Grampian Holdings Ltd; Mem, 1975-76, Dep. Chm. and Chief Exec., Scottish Develt Agency, 1976-81. Chm. Eastern Regional Hosp. Bd (Scotland), 1960-70; Trustee (Exec. Cttee), Carnegie Trust for Univs of Scotland, 1963-; Member: Provincial Synod, Episcopal Church of Scotland, 1963- (Chm. Policy Cttee, 1974-76); (Sainsbury) Cttee of Enquiry, Pharmaceutical Industry, 1965-67; Court (Finance Convener), Univ. of Dundee, 1970-; Monopolies and Mergers Commn, 1969-76; Arts Council of GB (and Chm., Scottish Arts Council), 1970-71; Scottish Economic Council, 1977-; British Council, 1978- (Chm., Scottish Adv. Cttee); Council, Scottish Business School, 1978-. British Institute of Management: Chm., Bd for Scotland, 1981-; Mem. Council, 1982-; CBIM 1976. Trustee, Foundn for Study of Christianity and Society, 1980-. FRSE 1978. FRSA 1981. Hon. LLD Dundee, 1971. *Recreations:* enjoying music, books and things Italian. *Address:* 32 Saxe Coburg Place,

Edinburgh EH3 5BP. *T:* 031-332 5221. *Clubs:* Caledonian; New (Edinburgh).

ROBERTSON, Commandant Dame Nancy (Margaret), DBE 1957 (CBE 1953; OBE 1946); retired as Director of Women's Royal Naval Service (Dec. 1954–April 1958); *b* 1 March 1909; *er d* of Rev. William Cowper Robertson and Jessie Katharine (*née* McGregor). *Educ:* Esdaile School, Edinburgh; Paris. Secretarial work, London and Paris, 1928–39; WRNS, 1939. *Recreations:* needlework, gardening. *Address:* 14 Osborne Way, Tring, Herts. *T:* Tring 2560.

ROBERTSON, Prof. Noel Farnie, CBE 1978; BSc Edinburgh; MA Cantab; PhD Edinburgh; FRSE; Professor of Agriculture and Rural Economy, University of Edinburgh, and Principal, East of Scotland College of Agriculture, since 1969; *b* 24 Dec. 1923; *o s* of late James Robertson and Catherine Landles Robertson (*née* Brown); *m* 1948, Doreen Colina Gardner; two *s* two *d*. *Educ:* Trinity Academy, Edinburgh; University of Edinburgh; Trinity College, Cambridge. Plant Pathologist, West African Cacao Research Institute, 1946–48; Lecturer in Botany, University of Cambridge, 1948–59; Prof. of Botany, Univ. of Hull, 1959–69. Pres., British Mycol Soc., 1965. Governor: Scottish Crops Res. Inst., 1973; Plant Breeding Inst., 1966–82; Macaulay Inst. for Soil Res., 1970–. *Address:* Boghall Farmhouse, Biggar Road, Edinburgh EH10 7DX. *T:* 031-445 3194. *Club:* Farmers'.

ROBERTSON, Patrick Allan Pearson, CMG 1956; *b* 11 Aug. 1913; *s* of A. N. McI. Robertson; *m* 1st, 1939, Penelope Margaret Gaskell (*d* 1966); one *s* two *d*; 2nd, 1975, Lady Stewart-Richardson. *Educ:* Sedbergh School; King's College, Cambridge. Cadet, Tanganyika, 1936; Asst Dist Officer, 1938; Clerk of Exec. and Legislative Councils, 1945–46; Dist Officer, 1948; Principal Asst Sec., 1949; Financial Sec., Aden, 1951; Asst Sec., Colonial Office, 1956–57; Chief Sec., Zanzibar, 1958; Civil Sec., Zanzibar, 1961–64; Deputy British Resident, Zanzibar, 1963–64; retired, 1964. Associate Member, Commonwealth Parliamentary Association. Freeman, City of London. *Recreations:* golf, tennis, fishing. *Address:* Lynedale, Longcross, Chertsey, Surrey. *T:* Ottershaw 2329. *Club:* Royal Commonwealth Society.
See also Sir Simon Stewart-Richardson, Bt.

ROBERTSON, (Richard) Ross, RSA, FRBS; DA; sculptor; *b* Aberdeen, 10 Sept. 1914; *s* of Rev. R. R. Robertson; *m* Kathleen May Matts; two *d*. *Educ:* Glasgow School of Art; Gray's School of Art, Aberdeen (DA). Lectr, Gray's Sch. of Art, 1946–79. FRBS 1963 (ARBS 1951); RSA 1977 (ARSA 1969). *Recreation:* study of art. *Address:* 7 Polmuir Road, Aberdeen, Scotland AB1 2SP. *T:* Aberdeen 24197.

ROBERTSON, Robert, CBE 1967; JP; Member, Strathclyde Regional Council, since 1974; *b* 15 Aug. 1909; *s* of late Rev. William Robertson, MA; *m* 1938, Jean, *d* of late James Moffatt, MA, Invermay, Broomhill, Glasgow; one *s* one *d*. *Educ:* Forres Academy; Royal Technical Coll., Glasgow. Civil Engr, retd 1969. Mem., Eastwood Dist Council, 1952–58; Chm., Renfrewshire Educn Cttee, 1962–73; Convener, Renfrewshire County Council, 1973–75 (Mem., 1958); Mem., Convention of Scottish Local Authorities, 1975–. Chm., Sec. of State's Cttee on Supply and Trng of Teachers for Further Educn, 1962–; Chm., Nat. Cttee for Inservice Trng of Teachers, 1965–78. Mem. Scottish Council for Research in Educn, 1962–; Commercial Admin. and Profl Educn, 1960–69; Development of Industry, 1973–75. Chm., Sch. of Further Educn for training of teachers in Scotland, 1969–. Governor: Jordanhill Coll. of Educn, 1966–; Watt Memorial and Reid Kerr Colls, 1966–75, 1977–. Member: Scottish Nat. School Camps Assoc., 1975–80; Scottish Assoc. of Young Farmers' Clubs, 1975–; Glasgow Educnl Trust, 1978–; Hutchison Educnl Trust, 1978–; Council, Glasgow Coll. of Bldg and Printing, 1978–. Fellow, Educnl Inst. of Scotland (FEIS), at Stirling Univ., 1970; Hon. Warden, Co. of Renfrew, Ont., Canada, 1970. JP Renfrewshire, 1958. *Publications:* Robertson Report on: The Training of Teachers in Further Education (HMSO), 1965. *Recreations:* fishing, painting. *Address:* Castlehill, Newton Mearns, Renfrewshire. *T:* 041-639 3089; Castlehill, Maybole, Ayrshire. *T:* Dunure 337. *Clubs:* RNVR (Scotland); SV Carrick (Glasgow).

ROBERTSON, Robert Henry; Deputy High Commissioner for Australia in London, since 1981; *b* 23 Dec. 1929; *s* of James Rowland Robertson and Hester Mary (*née* Kay); *m* 1958, Jill Bryant Uther (marr. diss. 1982); two *s* one *d*. *Educ:* Geelong Church of England Grammar Sch.; Trinity Coll., Univ. of Melbourne (LLB). Third Secretary, Australian High Commn, Karachi, 1954–56; Second Sec., Mission to UN, New York, 1958–61; First Sec., later Counsellor, Washington, 1964–67; Ambassador to Jugoslavia, Romania and Bulgaria, 1971–73; Asst Sec., Personnel Br., Dept of Foreign Affairs, Canberra, 1974–75; First Asst Sec., Western Div., 1975–76, Management and Foreign Service Div., 1976–77; Ambassador to Italy, 1977–81. *Recreations:* gardening, reading, walking. *Address:* c/o Australian High Commission, Strand, WC2. *T:* 01-438 8211. *Club:* Commonwealth (Canberra).

ROBERTSON, Ronald Foote, CBE 1980; MD, FRCP, FRCPE, FRCPGlas; Physician to the Queen in Scotland, since 1977; *b* 27 Dec. 1920; *s* of Thomas Robertson and Mary Foote; *m* 1949, Dorothy Tweedy Wilkinson; two *d* (and one *d* deed). *Educ:* Perth Acad.; Univ. of Edinburgh. MB, ChB (Hons) 1945; MD (High Commendation) 1953; FRCPEdin. 1952; FRCP London 1969; FRCPGlas 1978. Consultant Physician: Leith Hosp., 1959–74; Deaconess Hosp., 1958–; Royal Infirmary of Edinburgh, 1975–. Sec., RCPEdin., 1958–

63; Vice-Pres., 1973–76; Pres., 1976–79. Principal MO, Scottish Life Assce Co., 1968–. Mem., Assoc. of Phys. of Gt Britain and Ireland. Has served on numerous NHS cttees; Mem. GMC, 1979–. Hon. Fellow, Coll. of Physicians and Surgeons, Pakistan, 1977; Hon. FACP 1978; Hon. FRCPI 1978; Hon. FRACP 1979. *Publications:* several articles in scientific jls. *Recreations:* gardening, curling, fishing. *Address:* 15 Wester Coates Terrace, Edinburgh EH12 5LR. *T:* 031-337 6377. *Clubs:* New, University Staff (Edinburgh).

ROBERTSON, Ross; *see* Robertson, R. R.

ROBERTSON, Prof. Sir Rutherford (Ness), AC 1980; Kt 1972; CMG 1968; DSc; PhD; FRS 1961; FAA; Emeritus Professor; Hon. Visitor, School of Biological Sciences, University of Sydney, since 1979; *b* 29 Sept. 1913; *o c* of Rev. J. Robertson, MA, and Josephine Robertson; *m* 1937, Mary Helen Bruce Rogerson; one *s*. *Educ:* St Andrew's Coll., NZ; Univ. of Sydney; St John's Coll., Cambridge (Hon. Fellow 1973). DSc Sydney 1961; FAA 1954. Sydney Univ. Science Res. Schol., 1934–35, Linnean Macleay Fell., 1935–36. Exhibn of 1851 Res. Schol., 1936–39; Res. at Botany Sch., Cambridge, in plant physiology, 1936–39, PhD 1939; Asst Lectr, later Lectr, Botany Sch., Univ. of Sydney, 1939–46; Sen. Res. Offr, later Chief Res. Offr, Div. of Food Preservation, CSIRO, 1946–59 (res. in plant physiol. and biochem.); Sydney University: jointly in charge of Plant Physiol. Unit, 1952–59, Hon. Res. Associate, 1954–59; Visiting Prof., Univ. of Calif, Los Angeles, 1958–59; Kerney Foundn Lectr, Univ. of Calif, Berkeley, 1959; Mem. Exec., CSIRO 1959–62; Prof. of Botany, Univ. of Adelaide, 1962–69, now Emeritus; Dir, Res. Sch. of Biol Scis, ANU, 1973–78, now Emeritus Professor (Master, University House, 1969–72). Chm., Aust. Res. Grants Cttee, 1965–69; Dep. Chm., Aust. Sci. and Tech. Council, 1977–81. Pres. Linnean Soc. of NSW, 1949; Hon. Sec. Austr. Nat. Res. Council, 1951–55; President: Australian Academy of Science, 1970–74 (Sec. Biological Sciences, 1957–58); Aust. and NZ Assoc. for the Advancement of Science, 1964–66; XIII Internat. Botanical Congress, Sydney, 1981; Corresp. Mem., Amer. Soc. of Plant Physiologists, 1953; For. Associate, US Nat. Acad. of Scis, 1962; Hon. Mem., Royal Soc. of NZ, 1971; For. Mem., Amer. Philosophical Soc., 1971; for. Hon. Mem., Amer. Acad. of Arts and Scis, 1973. Hon. DSc: Tasmania, 1965; Monash, 1970; ANU, 1979; Hon ScD Cambridge, 1969. Clarke Meml Medal, Royal Soc. of NSW, 1955; Farrer Meml Medal, 1963; ANZAAS Medal, 1968; Mueller Medal, 1970; Burnet Medal, 1975. *Publications:* (with G. E. Briggs, FRS, and A. B. Hope) Electrolytes and Plant Cells, 1961; Protons, Electrons, Phosphorylation and Active Transport, 1968; various scientific papers on plant physiology and biochemistry. *Recreations:* riding, water colours. *Address:* School of Biological Sciences, A12, University of Sydney, NSW 2006, Australia. *Clubs:* Union (Sydney); Commonwealth (Canberra).

ROBERTSON, Toby, (Sholto David Maurice Robertson), OBE 1978; Director, theatre, films and television; *b* 29 Nov. 1928; *s* of David Lambert Robertson and Felicity Douglas (*née* Tomlin); *m* 1963, Teresa Jane McCulloch (marr. diss. 1981); two *s* two *d*. *Educ:* Stowe; Trinity Coll., Cambridge (BA 1952). Formerly an actor. Dir. first prof. prodn, The Iceman Cometh, New Shakespeare, Liverpool, 1958. Dir. plays, London, Pitlochry and Richmond, Yorks, and for RSC, 1959–63. Director of over 40 prodns for Prospect Theatre Co., incl.: 1964: The Soldier's Fortune; You Never Can Tell; The Confederacy; The Importance of Being Earnest; 1965: The Square; Howard's End; The Man of Mode; 1966: Macbeth; The Tempest; The Gamecock; 1967: A Murder of No Importance; A Room with a View (Edinburgh Fest.; co-Dir for London season, 1975); 1968: Twelfth Night (also 1973, 1978); No Man's Land; The Beggar's Opera (also Edinburgh and London; for Phoenix Opera, 1972); The Servant of Two Masters (London); 1969: Edward II (also Edinburgh and London); 1970: Much Ado About Nothing (also Edinburgh); Boswell's Life of Johnson (also Edinburgh); Venice Preserved; 1971: King Lear (also 1978), and Love's Labour's Lost (Edinburgh, Australian tour, London); Alice in Wonderland (Ashcroft, Croydon); 1972: Richard III; Ivanov (also 1978); 1973: The Grand Tour (also 1978, 1979); Twelfth Night, Pericles, and The Royal Hunt of the Sun (internat. festivals, Moscow, Leningrad and Hong Kong); 1974: The Pilgrim's Progress (also Edinburgh and Round House, 1975); A Month in the Country (Chichester Fest.; London season, 1975); 1977: Hamlet (also 1979), War Music, and Antony and Cleopatra (Edinburgh, ME Fest., London); Smith of Smiths (also 1978, 1979); Buster (Edinburgh); 1978: The Lunatic, The Lover and The Poet (also 1979); 1979: Romeo and Juliet; The Government Inspector; The Padlock. Opera: for Scottish Opera, incl.: A Midsummer Night's Dream, 1972; Hermiston, 1975; Marriage of Figaro, 1977; for Opera Co. of Philadelphia: Elisir d'Amore (with Pavarotti and winner of Pavarotti competition), Dido and Aeneas, Oedipus Rex, 1982. Old Vic Co.: Hamlet, Elsinore, 1979; 1st visit by British co., China, 1980. Other productions: Next Time I'll Sing to You, Greenwich, 1980; Beggar's Opera, Lyric, Hammersmith, 1980; Pericles, NY, 1980 (OBIE Award for outstanding direction, 1981); Measure for Measure, People's Arts Theatre, Peking, 1981; The Revenger's Tragedy, NY, 1981 (Villager Award for outstanding treatment of classical text, 1982). Asst Dir, Lord of the Flies (film), 1961. Dir of more than 25 television prodns, incl.: The Beggar's Opera; Richard II; Edward II. Member: Bd, Cambridge Theatre Co., 1970–74; Bd, Prospect Productions Ltd, 1964– (Artistic Dir, Prospect Theatre Co., 1964–79); Dir, Old Vic Theatre, 1977–80, Old Vic Co., 1979–80. Drama Advr, Argo Records, 1979–; Prof. of Theatre, Brooklyn Coll., City Univ. NY, 1981–82. Lectures: Wilson Meml, Cambridge Univ., 1974; Hamlet, Athens Univ., 1978; Riksteatre, Stockholm, 1980. *Recreations:* painting, sailing, Bunburying.

Address: Lambert House, 210 Brixton Road, SW9; 216 Grand Street, Brooklyn, NY 11211, USA. *Clubs:* Garrick, Bunbury.

ROBERTSON, Prof. William Bruce, MD, FRCPath; Professor of Histopathology, St George's Hospital Medical School, since 1968; *b* 17 Jan. 1923; *s* of late William Bruce Robertson and Jessie Robertson (*née* McLean); *m* 1948, Mary Patricia Burrows; two *d. Educ:* The Academy, Forfar; Univ. of St Andrews. BSc 1944, MB ChB 1947, MD 1959; MRCPath 1963, FRCPath 1969. Junior appts, Cumberland Infirm., Carlisle, 1947-48; RAMC, E Africa, 1948-50; Registrar Pathology, Cumberland Infirm., 1950-53; Demonstr Pathology, Royal Victoria Infirm., Newcastle upon Tyne, 1953-56; Sen. Lectr Pathology, Univ. of the West Indies, Jamaica, 1956-64; Reader in Morbid Anatomy, St George's Hosp. Med. Sch., Univ. of London, 1964-68. Visiting Professor: Louisiana State Univ., New Orleans, USA, 1961-62; Katholieke Universiteit te Leuven, Belgium, 1972-73. *Publications:* scientific papers and book chapters in various med. jls and publns. *Address:* 3 Cambisgate, Church Road, Wimbledon, SW19 5AL. *T:* 01-947 6731.

ROBERTSON, Air Cdre William Duncan, CBE 1968; Royal Air Force, retired; Senior Air Staff Officer, HQ 38 Group, Royal Air Force, 1975-77; *b* 24 June 1922; *s* of William and Helen Robertson, Aberdeen; *m* 1st, 1952, Doreen Mary (*d* 1963), *d* of late Comdr G. A. C. Sharp, DSC, RN (retd); one *s* one *d* ; 2nd, 1968, Ute, *d* of late Dr R. Koenig, Wesel, West Germany; one *d. Educ:* Robert Gordon's Coll., Aberdeen. Sqdn Comdr, No 207 Sqdn, 1959-61. Gp Dir, RAF Staff Coll., 1962-65; Station Comdr, RAF Wildenrath, 1965-67; Dep. Dir, Administrative Plans, 1967; Dir of Ops (Plans), 1968; Dir of Ops Air Defence and Overseas, 1969-71; RCDS, 1971-72; SASO RAF Germany, 1972-74; SASO 46 Group, 1975. *Recreations:* golf, tennis. *Address:* Parkhouse Farm, Leigh, Surrey. *Club:* Royal Air Force.

ROBERTSON, William Walter Samuel, CBE 1957 (OBE 1950); *b* 3 July 1906; *s* of W. H. A. and A. M. Robertson (*née* Lane); *m* 1935, Kathleen Elizabeth Chawner East; one *s* two *d. Educ:* Bedford School; King's College, London. BSc (Eng.) First Class Hons, 1926. Apprenticeship to W. H. A. Robertson & Co. Ltd (Director, 1929) and to Torrington Mfg Co., USA, 1926-28. Regional Controller and Chm. of North Midland Regional Bd for Production, 1943-45; Chairman, Eastern Regional Bd for Industry, 1949-64 (Vice-Chm., 1945-49); Member Advisory Committee, Revolving Fund for Industry, 1955-58. MIMechE, 1943. High Sheriff of Bedfordshire, 1963. Governor, St Felix School, Southwold. *Recreations:* rowing, golf. *Address:* The Dale, Pavenham, Beds. *T:* Oakley 2895. *Clubs:* Caledonian; Leander (Henley-on-Thames).

ROBEY, Douglas John Brett, CMG 1960; HM Diplomatic Service, retired; *b* 7 Aug. 1914; *s* of late E. J. B. and Margaret Robey; *m* 1943, Elizabeth, *d* of late Col David D. Barrett, US Army; two *s* one *d. Educ:* Cranleigh School; St John's College, Oxford; Ecole des Sciences Politiques, Paris. BA (History); Editor of The Cherwell. Joined HM Foreign Service, 1937. Served in China, USA, Paris, Berlin, Baghdad; Consul-Gen., Chicago, 1966-69; Ambassador and Permanent UK Representative, Council of Europe, Strasbourg, 1969-74. *Publication:* The Innovator, 1945. *Recreations:* reading, writing, and the Niebelung Ring. *Address:* Allan Down House, Rotherfield, East Sussex. *T:* Rotherfield 2329. *Club:* Cercle Européen de Strasbourg (Hon. Life Pres.).

ROBEY, Edward George Haydon, BA, LLB; Barrister-at-Law; a Metropolitan Magistrate, 1954-72; *s* of late Sir George Robey, CBE, and his first wife, the late Ethel Haydon; *m* 1942, Denise (*d* 1981), *d* of late Denis Williams, Virginia Water. *Educ:* Westminster School; Jesus Coll., Cambridge. Called to Bar, Inner Temple, 1925; professional staff of Director of Public Prosecutions, 1932-50; apptd to Attorney-General's Executive for prosecution of the Major War Criminals at Nuremberg, 1945. *Publication:* The Jester and the Court, 1976. *Recreation:* music. *Address:* 11 Shrewsbury House, Cheyne Walk, SW3. *T:* 01-352 2403. *Club:* Garrick.

ROBIN, Dr Gordon de Quetteville; Director, Scott Polar Research Institute, University of Cambridge, 1958-82; Fellow since 1964 and Vice-Master, 1974-78, Darwin College, Cambridge; *b* Melbourne, 17 Jan. 1921; *s* of Reginald James Robin and Emily Mabel Robin; *m* 1953, Jean Margaret Fortt, Bath; two *d. Educ:* Wesley Coll., Melbourne; Melbourne Univ. ScD Cantab, MSc Melbourne, PhD Birmingham; FInstP. War service, RANVR: anti-submarine, 1942-44; submarine, RN, 1944-45 (Lieut). Physics Dept, Birmingham Univ.: research student, lectr, ICI Research Fellow, 1945-56; Sen. Fellow, Geophysics Dept, ANU, 1957-58. Meteorologist and Officer i/c Signy Is, South Orkneys, with Falkland Is Dependencies Survey, 1947-48; Physicist and Sen. British Mem. of Norwegian-British-Swedish Antarctic Expedn, 1949-52 (made first effective measurements of Antarctic ice thickness); further researches in Antarctic in 1959, 1967, 1969, 1974, and in Arctic, 1964, 1966, 1973; Sec., 1958-70, Pres., 1970-74, and Hon. Mem., Scientific Cttee on Antarctic Research of Internat. Council of Scientific Unions. Hon. DPhil Stockholm, 1978. Kongens Fortjensmedalje, Norway, 1952; Back Grant, RGS, 1953; Bruce Medal, RSE, 1953; Polar Medal, 1956; Patrons Medal, RGS, 1974. *Publications:* scientific reports of Norwegian-British-Swedish Antarctic Expedition (Glaciology III, 1958; Upper Winds, 1972); (ed) Annals of the IGY, Vol. 41, Glaciology, 1967; papers and articles on polar glaciology in scientific jls. *Recreations:* travel, walking. *Address:* 10 Melbourne Place, Cambridge CB1 1EQ. *T:* Cambridge 58463.

ROBIN, Ian (Gibson), FRCS; *b* 22 May 1909; *s* of Dr Arthur Robin, Edinburgh, and Elizabeth Parker; *m* 1939, Shelagh Marian (*d* 1978), *d* of late Colonel C. M. Croft; one *s* two *d. Educ:* Merchiston Castle School; Clare College, Cambridge. MA, MB, BCh Cantab 1933; LRCP 1933; FRCS 1935. Guy's Hosp.; late House Phys.; Sen. Science Schol., 1930; Treasurer's Gold Medals in Clinical Surgery and Medicine, 1933; Arthur Durham Travelling Schol., 1933; Charles Oldham Prize in Ophthalmology, 1933; Registrar and Chief Clin. Asst, ENT Dept, 1935-36; late Consulting ENT Surgeon: Royal Chest Hosp., 1939-44; Royal Northern Hosp., 1937-74; St Mary's Hosp., Paddington, 1948-74; Princess Louise (Kensington) Hosp. for Children, 1948-69; Paddington Green Children's Hosp., 1969-74; Surgeon EMS, Sector III London Area, 1939-45. Late Vice-Chm., Royal Nat. Institute for the Deaf. Member Hunterian Soc.; Council of Nat. Deaf Children's Soc.; Past Pres., Brit. Assoc. of Otolaryngologists, 1971-72; Past Pres., Laryng. Section, RSM, 1967-68; Vice-Pres., Otolog. Section, RSM, 1967-68, 1969; late Examiner for DLO of RCS of England. Lectures: Yearsley, 1968; Jobson Horne, 1969. Mem., Royal Water-Colour Soc. *Publications:* (jt) Diseases of Ear, Nose and Throat (Synopsis Series), 1957; papers in various med. treatises, jls, etc. *Recreations:* golf, gardening, sketching; formerly athletics and Rugby. *Address:* Stowe House, 3 North End, Hampstead, NW3. *T:* 01-458 2292; 86 Harley Street, W1. *T:* 01-580 3625. *Clubs:* Hawks (Cambridge); Achilles (Great Britain); Hampstead Golf.

ROBINS, Mrs Denise; *b* Whitehall Court, SW1; *m* 1st, 1918; three *d* ; 2nd, 1939, Lt-Col R. O'Neill Pearson. *Educ:* Staten Island, USA; Convent, Upper Norwood, SE. Entered Dundee Courier Office, Dundee, 1914; became a Free Lance writer, and published numerous serials and short stories; first novel published in 1924. *Publications:* 169 books including House of the 7th Cross, The Noble One, Khamsin, Dark Corridor, etc.; *historical novels:* Gold for the Gay Masters, Dance in the Dust, etc; *autobiography:* Stranger Than Fiction. *Recreations:* music, books, travel. *Address:* 15 Oathall Road, Haywards Heath, Sussex RH16 3EG. *T:* Haywards Heath 450580.

ROBINS, Group Captain Leonard Edward, CBE (mil.) 1979; AE 1958 (and 2 clasps); DL; Inspector, Royal Auxiliary Air Force, since 1973; Lord Mayor of London's personal staff, 1977-78, 1980-81 and since 1982; *b* 2 Nov. 1921; *yr s* of late Joseph Robins, Bandmaster RM, and late Louisa Josephine (*née* Kent); *m* 1949, Jean Ethelwynne (Headteacher), *d* of late Roy and Bessie Searle, Ryde, IoW. *Educ:* Singlegate, Mitcham, Surrey; City Day Continuation School, EC. Entered Civil Service, GPO, 1936; War service RAF, UK, SEAC, Ceylon, India, 1941-46; resumed with GPO, 1946; Min. of Health, 1948; Min. of Housing and Local Govt, 1962; DoE, 1970-80, retired. Airman, No 3700 (Co. of London) Radar Reporting Unit RAuxAF, 1950; Commissioned 1953, radar branch; transf. to No 1 (Co. of Hertford) Maritime HQ Unit RAuxAF, intelligence duties, 1960; OC No 1 Maritime Headquarters Unit, RAuxAF, 1969-73; Gp Capt., Inspector RAuxAF, 1973. ADC to the Queen, 1974-. Selected Air Force Mem., Greater London TAVRA, 1973- and City of London TAVRA, 1980-. Pres., Wandsworth Victim Support, 1980-. Freeman, City of London, 1976. Coronation Medal, 1953; Jubilee Medal, 1978. DL Greater London, 1978-; Representative DL, Borough of Wandsworth, 1979-. FBIM. *Recreations:* naval, military and aviation history; book hunting; kipping. *Address:* 16 Summit Way, Upper Norwood, SE19 2PU. *T:* 01-653 3173. *Club:* Royal Air Force.

ROBINS, Malcolm Owen, CBE 1978; Learned Societies Officer, Royal Society/British Academy, 1979-81; a Director, Science Research Council, 1972-78; *b* 25 Feb. 1918; *s* of late Owen Wilfred Robins and Amelia Ada (*née* Wheelwright); *m* 1944, Frances Mary, *d* of late William and Frances Hand; one *s* one *d. Educ:* King Edward's Sch., Stourbridge; The Queen's Coll., Oxford (Open Scholar in Science). MA (Oxon) 1943. On scientific staff of Royal Aircraft Establishment, 1940-57; a Div. Supt in Guided Weapons Dept, RAE, 1955-57; Asst Dir, Guided Weapons, Min. of Supply, London, 1957-58; UK Project Manager for jt UK/USA Space Research programme, and hon. Research Associate, University Coll. London, 1958-62; a Dep. Chief Scientific Officer and Head of Space Research Management Unit, Office of Minister for Science (later Dept of Educn and Science), 1962-65; Head of Astronomy, Space and Radio Div., SRC, 1965-68; a Research Planning post in Min. of Technology (later Dept of Trade and Industry), 1968-72. Vis. Prof., University Coll., London, 1974-77. FInstP 1945; FRAS 1974. *Publications:* papers on space research in scientific jls. *Recreation:* gardening. *Address:* Wychbury, Gorse Lane, Farnham, Surrey. *T:* Farnham 723186.

ROBINS, Prof. Robert Henry; Professor of General Linguistics, University of London, since 1966; Head of Department of Phonetics and Linguistics, School of Oriental and African Studies, University of London, since 1970; Member of Senate, University of London, since 1980; *b* 1 July 1921; *s* of John Norman Robins, medical practitioner, and Muriel Winifred (*née* Porter); *m* 1953, Sheila Marie Fynn. *Educ:* Tonbridge Sch.; New Coll., Oxford, 1940-41 and 1945-48, MA 1948; DLit London 1968. Served war, RAF Intelligence, 1942-45. Lectr in Linguistics, Sch. of Oriental and African Studies, London, 1948-55; Reader in General Linguistics, Univ. of London, 1955-65. Research Fellow, Univ. of California, 1951; Vis. Professor: Washington, 1963; Hawaii, 1968; Minnesota, 1971; Florida, 1975; Salzburg, 1977, 1979. Hon. Sec., Philological Soc., 1961-; President: Societas Linguistica Europea, 1974; CIPL, 1977-82 (British Rep., 1970-77). Hon. Mem., Linguistic Soc. of Amer., 1981-. *Publications:* Ancient and Mediaeval Grammatical Theory in Europe, 1951; The Yurok Language, 1958; General Linguistics: an introductory survey, 1964; A Short History of Linguistics, 1967; Diversions of Bloomsbury, 1970; Ideen-

und Problemgeschichte der Sprachwissenschaft, 1973; articles in Language, TPS, BSOAS, Lingua, Foundations of Language, Man, etc. *Recreations:* gardening, travel. *Address:* 65 Dome Hill, Caterham, Surrey CR3 6EF. *T:* Caterham 43778. *Clubs:* Athenæum; Royal Commonwealth Society.

ROBINS, William Edward Charles; Metropolitan Stipendiary Magistrate since 1971; solicitor; *b* 13 March 1924; *s* of late E. T. and late L. R. Robins; *m* 1946, Jean Elizabeth, *yr d* of Bruce and Flora Forsyth, Carlyle, Saskatchewan, Canada; one *s* one *d. Educ:* St Alban's Sch. Served War: commissioned as Navigator, RAF, 1943–47. Admitted as a Solicitor, 1948; joined Metropolitan Magistrates' Courts' service, 1950; Dep. Chief Clerk, 1951–60; Chief Clerk, 1960–67; Sen. Chief Clerk, Thames Petty Sessional Div., 1968–71. Sec., London Magistrates' Clerks' Assoc., 1953–60 (Chm. 1965–71). Member, Home Office working parties, on: Magistrates' Courts' Rules; Legal Aid; Motor Vehicle Licences; Fines and Maintenance Orders Enforcement, 1968–71; Member: Lord Chancellor's Sub-Cttee on Magistrates' Courts' Rules, 1969–70; Adv. Council on Misuse of Drugs, 1973–. Fellow Commoner, Corpus Christi Coll., Cambridge, Michaelmas 1975. *Recreations:* touring off the beaten track, music, theatre. *Address:* Bow Street Magistrates' Court, WC2.

ROBINSON, family name of **Baron Martonmere.**

ROBINSON, Sir Albert (Edward Phineas), Kt 1962; Executive Director, Anglo American Corporation of SA Ltd; Chairman: Johannesburg Consolidated Investment Company, 1971–80; Rustenburg Platinum Mines, 1971–80; Deputy Chairman, General Mining and Finance Corporation Ltd, 1953–71; *b* 30 December 1915; *s* of late Charles Phineas Robinson (formerly MP Durban, S Africa) and of late Mabel V. Robinson; *m* 1st, 1944, Mary Judith Bertish (*d* 1973); four *d* ; 2nd, 1975, Mrs M. L. Royston-Pigott (*née* Barrett). *Educ:* Durban High School; Universities of Stellenbosch, London, Cambridge and Leiden; MA (Cantab). Barrister, Lincoln's Inn. Served War of 1939–45, in Imperial Light Horse, Western Desert, N Africa, 1940–43. Member Johannesburg City Council, 1945–48 (Leader United Party in Council, 1946–47); MP (United Party), S African Parl., 1947–53; became permanent resident in Rhodesia, 1953. Director: Anglo American Corp., Zimbabwe Ltd; Founders Bldg Soc.; Director (in Zimbabwe) of Bd of Standard Bank, and (in SA) of Standard Bank Investment Corp.; Director, in Zimbabwe and South Africa, of various Mining, Financial and Industrial Companies. Chm. Central African Airways Corp., 1957–61. Member, Monckton Commission, 1960; High Commissioner in the UK for the Federation of Rhodesia and Nyasaland, 1961–63. *Recreations:* people, music and conversation. *Address:* 36 Smits Road, Dunkeld, Johannesburg, South Africa. *Clubs:* Carlton (London); Salisbury (Salisbury, Zimbabwe); City (Capetown).

ROBINSON, Alwyn Arnold; Managing Director, Daily Mail, since 1975; *b* 15 Nov. 1929. Jt Vice-Chm., Press Council, 1982–. *Address:* The Daily Mail, EC4. *T:* 01–353 6000.

ROBINSON, Arthur Alexander; computer consultant; Director of Computing, University of Wales Institute of Science and Technology, since 1976; *b* 5 Aug. 1924; *o s* of Arthur Robinson and Elizabeth (*née* Thompson); *m* 1956, Sylvia Joyce Wagstaff; two *s* one *d. Educ:* Epsom Coll.; Clare Coll., Cambridge (MA); Univ. of Manchester (PhD). English Electric Co. Ltd, 1944; Ferranti Ltd, 1950; Dir and Gen. Man., Univ. of London Atlas Computing Service, 1962; Dir, Univ. of London Computer Centre, 1968; Dir, National Computing Centre Ltd, 1969–74. *Publications:* papers in Proc. IEE. *Recreation:* gardening. *Address:* 4 Heol Ty Mawr, Pendoylan, Cowbridge, S Glamorgan.

ROBINSON, (Arthur) Geoffrey, CBE 1978; Chairman: English Industrial Estates Corporation, since 1977; Medway Ports Authority, since 1978; *b* 22 Aug. 1917; *s* of Arthur Robinson and Frances M. Robinson; *m* 1st, 1943, Patricia MacAllister (*d* 1971); three *s* one *d* ; 2nd, 1973, Hon. Mrs Treves, *d* of Rt Hon. Lord Salmon, *qv* ; three step *s* one step *d. Educ:* Lincoln Sch.; Jesus Coll., Cambridge (MA); Sch. of Oriental and African Studies, London Univ. Served War, RA, 1939–46. Solicitor, 1948; Treasury Solicitor's Dept, 1954–62; PLA, 1962–66; Man. Dir, Tees and Hartlepool Port Authority, 1966–77. Member: National Dock Labour Bd, 1972–77; National Ports Council, 1980–81; Chm., British Ports Assoc., 1982–. *Publications:* Hedingham Harvest, 1977; various articles. *Recreation:* music. *Address:* 19 Miller's Court, Chiswick Mall, W4 2PF. *T:* 01–748 2997; Salts End, Goss Hall Lane, Ash, Kent. *T:* Ash 812366. *Club:* United Oxford & Cambridge University.
See also P. H. Robinson.

ROBINSON, Arthur Napoleon Raymond; barrister; MHR for Tobago East; Chairman, Democratic Action Congress, Trinidad and Tobago, since 1971; *b* 16 Dec. 1926; *s* of late James Alexander Andrew Robinson, Headmaster, and Emily Isabella Robinson; *m* 1961, Patricia Rawlins; one *s* one *d. Educ:* Bishop's High Sch., Tobago; St John's Coll., Oxford. LLB (London); MA (PPE) Oxon. Called to Bar, Inner Temple; in practice, 1956–61, 1970–. Treas., People's Nat. Movt (governing Party) 1956; Mem. Federal Parlt, 1958; Mem. for Tobago East, 1961; Minister of Finance, 1961–66; Dep. Political Leader of Party, 1966; Actg Prime Minister (during his absence), April and Aug. 1967; Minister of External Affairs, Trinidad and Tobago, 1967–68. Member: Legal Commn on US Leased Areas under 1941 Agreement, 1959; Industrial Develt Corp., 1960; Council, Univ. of West

Indies, 1960–62. Consultant, Foundn for establishment of an Internat. Criminal Court, 1972–75, Exec. Dir, 1976–77. Mem., UN Expert Gp on Crime and the Abuse of Power, 1979. Dist. Internat. Criminal Law Award, Internat. Criminal Court Foundn, 1977. *Publications:* The New Frontier and the New Africa, 1961; Fiscal Reform in Trinidad and Tobago, 1966; The Path of Progress, 1967; The Teacher and Nationalism, 1967; The Mechanics of Independence, 1971; articles and addresses. *Address:* 21 Ellerslie Park, Maraval, Trinidad.

ROBINSON, Sir Austin; *see* Robinson, Sir E. A. G.

ROBINSON, Basil William, FBA 1981; retired; *b* 20 June 1912; *o c* of William Robinson and Rebecca Frances Mabel, *d* of Rev. George Gilbanks; *m* 1st, 1945, Ailsa Mary Stewart (*d* 1954); 2nd, 1958, Oriel Hermione Steel; one *s* one *d. Educ:* Winchester (Exhibitioner); CCC Oxford. BA 1935; MA, BLitt, 1938. Asst Keeper, Victoria and Albert Museum, 1939. Min. of Home Security, 1939–40. Served as Captain, 2nd Punjab Regt, India, Burma, Malaya, 1943–46. Deputy Keeper, V&A Museum, 1954, Keeper, Dept of Metalwork, 1966–72, Keeper Emeritus, 1972–76. Pres., Royal Asiatic Soc., 1970–73; Vice-Pres., Arms and Armour Soc., 1953; Hon. Pres., Tō-ken Soc. of Great Britain, 1967. FSA 1974. *Publications:* A Primer of Japanese Sword-blades, 1955; Persian Miniatures, 1957; Japanese Landscape Prints of the 19th Century, 1957; A Descriptive Catalogue of the Persian Paintings in the Bodleian Library, 1958; Kuniyoshi, 1961; The Arts of the Japanese Sword, 1961, 2nd edn, 1971; Persian Drawings, 1965; part-author, vols 2 and 3, Catalogue of Persian MSS and Miniatures in the Chester Beatty Library, 3 vols, 1958–62; Persian Miniature Painting, 1967; Persian Paintings in the India Office Library, 1976; (ed. and jt author) Islamic painting in the Keir Collection, 1976; Japanese Sword-fittings in the Baur Collection, 1980; Persian Paintings in the John Rylands Library, 1980; Kuniyoshi: the Warrior Prints, 1982; numerous booklets, articles and reviews on Persian and Japanese art. *Recreations:* catch singing (founder and Chairman, Aldrich Catch Club); cats. *Address:* 41 Redcliffe Gardens, SW10 9JH. *T:* 01–352 1290. *Club:* Hurlingham.

ROBINSON, Air Vice-Marshal Bruce, CB 1968; CBE 1953; Air Officer Commanding No 24 Gp, RAF, 1965–67; retired, 1967; *b* 19 Jan. 1912; *s* of late Dr G. Burton Robinson, Cannington, Somerset; *m* 1940, Elizabeth Ann Compton, *d* of Air Commodore D. F. Lucking; one *s* one *d. Educ:* King's School, Bruton. Commissioned in SR of O, The Somerset Light Infty, 1931–33; Commissioned in RAF, 1933; No 16 (Army Co-op. Sqdn), 1934–37; Specialist Engineer course, 1937–39. Served War of 1939–45: Technical duties in Fighter and Bomber Commands, UK Senior Technical Staff Officer, Rhodesian Air Training Group, 1946–48; on loan to Indian Air Force (Director of Technical Services), 1951–53; Commandant, No 1 Radio School, RAF Locking, 1953–55; Sen. RAF Officer at Wright Patterson Air Force Base, Dayton, Ohio, 1958–60; Commandant No 1 Sch. of Technical Training, RAF Halton, Bucks, 1961–63. Director of RAF Aircraft Development, Min. of Aviation, 1963–65. *Recreations:* golf, sailing, painting, writing. *Address:* Bent Hollow, Bromeswell, Woodbridge, Suffolk. *T:* Eyke 295.

ROBINSON, Rt. Rev. Christopher James Gossage, MA; *b* 10 June 1903; *s* of late Canon Albert Gossage Robinson; unmarried. *Educ:* Marlborough, Christ's Coll., Cambridge. Lecturer at St Stephen's Coll., Delhi, 1926–29; Deacon, 1929; Priest, 1930; Curate St Mary's, Portsea, 1929–31; Asst Priest, St James, Delhi, 1931–32; Vicar of St James, and Chaplain of Delhi, 1932–42; Vicar of St Thomas, New Delhi, 1942–45; Hon. Canon of Lahore Cathedral, 1944–47; Bishop of Lucknow, 1947–62; Bishop of Bombay, 1962–70. Member, Brotherhood of the Ascended Christ (formerly Cambridge Brotherhood of the Ascension), Delhi, since 1931. *Address:* Brotherhood House, 7 Court Lane, Delhi 110-054, India. *Club:* Royal Commonwealth Society.
See also Sir E. A. G. Robinson.

ROBINSON, Christopher John; Organist and Master of the Choristers, St George's Chapel, Windsor Castle, since 1974; *b* 20 April 1936; *s* of late Prebendary John Robinson, Malvern, Worcs; *m* 1962, Shirley Ann, *d* of H. F. Churchman, Sawston, Cambs; one *s* one *d. Educ:* St Michael's Coll., Tenbury; Rugby; Christ Church, Oxford. MA, BMus; FRCO; Hon. RAM. Assistant Organist of Christ Church, Oxford, 1955–58; Assistant Organist of New College, Oxford, 1957–58; Music Master at Oundle School, 1959–62; Assistant Organist of Worcester Cathedral, 1962–63; Organist and Master of Choristers, Worcester Cathedral, 1963–74. Conductor: City of Birmingham Choir, 1963–; Oxford Bach Choir, 1977–; Leith Hill Musical Festival, 1977–80. *Recreations:* watching cricket, motoring. *Address:* 23 The Cloisters, Windsor Castle, Berks.

ROBINSON, Mrs Clare; *see* Panter-Downes, M. P.

ROBINSON, Clifton Eugene Bancroft, OBE 1973; JP; a Deputy-Chairman, Commission for Racial Equality, since 1977; *b* 5 Oct. 1926; *s* of Theodore Emanuel and Lafrance Robinson; *m* (marr. diss.); one *s* three *d* ; *m* 1977, Margaret Ann Ennever. *Educ:* Kingston Technical Coll., Jamaica; Birmingham Univ.; Leicester Univ.; Lancaster Coll. of Educn. BA, DipEd. Served War, RAF, 1944–49. Teacher: Mellor Sch., Leicester, 1951–61; i/c Special Educn Unit, St Peter's Sch., Leicester, 1961–64; Dep. Headteacher, Charnwood Sch., Leicester, 1964–68; Headteacher: St Peter's Sch., Leicester, 1968–70; Uplands Sch., Leicester, 1970–77. JP Leicester, 1974. *Recreations:* music (mainly classical), walking; when there is time, gardening. *Address:*

Stable End Cottage, The Manor House, Newton Harcourt, Leicestershire LE8 0ST.

ROBINSON, (David) Duncan; Director, Yale Center for British Art, New Haven, Connecticut, Chief Executive, Paul Mellon Centre for Studies in British Art, London, and Adjunct Professor of the History of Art, Yale University, since 1981; *b* 27 June 1943; *s* of Tom and Ann Robinson; *m* 1967, Elizabeth Anne Sutton; one *s* one *d*. *Educ:* King Edward VI Sch., Macclesfield; Clare Coll., Cambridge (MA). *Yale Univ.* (Mellon Fellow, 1965-67; MA). Asst Keeper of Paintings and Drawings, 1970-76, Keeper, 1976-81, Fitzwilliam Museum, Cambridge; Fellow and Coll. Lectr, Clare Coll., Cambridge, 1975-81. Mem. Cttee of Management, and Chm., Exhibns Cttee, Kettle's Yard, Cambridge Univ., 1970-81. Member: Art Panel, Eastern Arts Assoc., 1973-81 (Chm., 1979-81); Arts Council of GB, 1981 (Mem., 1978-81, Vice-Chm., 1981, Art Panel). Organised Arts Council exhibitions: Stanley Spencer, 1976; William Nicholson, 1980. *Publications:* Companion Volume to the Kelmscott Chaucer, 1975, re-issued as Morris, Burne-Jones and the Kelmscott Chaucer, 1982; Stanley Spencer, 1979; (with Stephen Wildman) Morris & Company in Cambridge, 1980; Town, Country, Shore & Sea: English Watercolours from van Dyck to Paul Nash, 1982; catalogues; articles and reviews in Apollo, Burlington Magazine, etc. *Address:* 142 Huntington Street, New Haven, Conn 06511, USA. *T:* (203) 787 7199. *Clubs:* Athenæum; Mory's (New Haven).

ROBINSON, Derek, CBE 1979; Fellow of Magdalen College, Oxford, since 1969; Senior Research Officer, Oxford Institute of Economics and Statistics; *b* 9 Feb. 1932; *s* of Benjamin and Mary Robinson; *m* 1956, Jean Evelyn (*née* Lynch); one *s* one *d*. *Educ:* Barnsley Holgate Grammar Sch.; Ruskin Coll., Oxford; Lincoln Coll., Oxford. MA (Oxon), DipEcPolSci (Oxon). Civil Service, 1948-55. Sheffield Univ., 1959-60; Senior Research Officer, Oxford Inst. of Economics and Statistics, 1961-. Economic Adviser, Nat. Bd for Prices and Incomes, 1965-67; Sen. Economic Adviser, Dept of Employment and Productivity, 1968-70; Dep. Chm., Pay Bd, 1973-74; Chm., SSRC, 1975-78. Mem., British Library Bd, 1979-82. Chairman: Oxfordshire Dist Manpower Cttee, 1980- (Oxf. and S. Bucks, 1975-79); Cttee of Inquiry into the remuneration of members of local authorities, 1977; Chilterns Area Bd, Manpower Services Commn Special Programmes, 1978-79. *Publications:* Non-Wage Incomes and Prices Policy, 1966; Wage Drift, Fringe Benefits and Manpower Distribution, 1968; Workers' Negotiated Savings Plans for Capital Formation, 1970; (ed) Local Labour Markets and Wage Structures, 1970; Prices and Incomes Policy: the Austrian Experience (with H. Suppanz), 1972; Incomes Policy and Capital Sharing in Europe, 1973; (with J. Vincens) Research into Labour Market Behaviour, 1974; contributor to Bulletin of Oxford Univ. Inst. of Economics and Statistics; Industrial Relations Jl, etc. *Address:* 56 Lonsdale Road, Oxford. *T:* Oxford 52276. *Club:* Reform.

ROBINSON, Derek Anthony, DPhil; Keeper I, Department of Museum Services, Science Museum, London, since 1978; *b* 21 April 1942; *s* of late Charles Frederick Robinson and of Mary Margaret Robinson; *m* 1965, Susan Gibson; two *s*. *Educ:* Hymers Coll., Hull; The Queen's Coll., Oxford (BA 1963; MA, DPhil 1967). Post-doctoral Res. Fellow, Dept of Chemistry, Univ. of Reading, 1967-69; Mem. scientific staff, Molecular Pharmacology Unit of MRC, Cambridge, 1969-72; Sen. Asst in Res., Dept of Haematol Medicine, Cambridge Univ. Med. Sch., 1972-74; Science Museum: Asst Keeper I, Dept of Chem., 1974-77; Dep. Keeper (formerly Asst Keeper I), Wellcome Mus. of History of Medicine, and Sec. of Adv. Council, 1977-78. *Publications:* (contrib.) 2nd edn Acridines, ed R. M. Acheson, 1973; (contrib.) Vol. VI, The History of Technology, ed T. I. Williams, 1978; papers on heterocyclic chemistry, molecular pharmacol., and leukaemia chemotherapy, in Jl Chem. Soc., Brit. Jl Pharmacol., and Biochem. Trans. *Recreations:* cricket, travel, walking, eating Indian and Chinese food. *Address:* 3 Bedford Road, Letchworth, Herts SG6 4DJ. *T:* Letchworth 6961, (office) 01-589 3456.

ROBINSON, Most Rev. Donald William Bradley; see Sydney, Archbishop of.

ROBINSON, Sir Dove-Myer, Kt 1970; JP; MRSH; Mayor of Auckland, New Zealand, 1959-65 and 1968-80; *b* Sheffield, 15 June 1901; 6th *c* of Moss Robinson and Ida Robinson (*née* Brown); of Jewish race; *m* 1st, Bettine Williams; 2nd, Thelma Ruth Thompson; one *s* five *d*. *Educ:* primary schools in Sheffield, Manchester, London and Devonport (Auckland, NZ). Mem., Auckland City Council, 1952-59; Chm., Auckland Metropolitan Drainage Bd, 1953-55; Chm., Auckland Airport Cttee, 1959-61; Mem., Auckland Univ. Council, 1952-80; Chm., Auckland Regional Authority, 1963-65, Mem., 1963-80 (Chm. Rapid Transit Cttee, 1968-74); Sen. Vice-Pres., NZ Municipal Assoc., 1959-65 and 1968-80; President: Auckland Rugby League, 1964-; Auckland Festival Soc., 1959-65 and 1968-80. Fellow, NZ Inst. of Management, 1948, Hon. Fellow, 1974; Patron, NZ Pure Water Assoc., 1954-; Hon. Mem., Inst. Water Pollution Control. CStJ 1979. *Publications:* Utilization of Town and Country Wastes, Garbage and Sewage, 1946; Soil, Food and Health, 1947; Passenger Transport in Auckland, 1969; numerous leaflets and pubns on Pollution, Conservation, Fluoridation, Nutrition, Local and Regional Govt, Town Planning, Rapid Transit, etc. *Recreations:* golf, fishing, boating, photography, motoring, local government. *Address:* 12a Aldred Road, Remuera, Auckland 5, New Zealand. *T:* 503-693.

ROBINSON, Duncan; see Robinson, David D.

ROBINSON, Prof. Sir (Edward) Austin (Gossage), Kt 1975; CMG 1947; OBE 1944; FBA 1955; Emeritus Professor of Economics, Cambridge University since 1966 (Professor, 1950-65); Fellow of Sidney Sussex College, Cambridge, since 1931; Secretary of Royal Economic Society, 1945-70; Joint Editor of Economic Journal, 1944-70; *b* 20 Nov. 1897; *s* of late Rev. Canon Albert Gossage Robinson; *m* 1926, Joan (*see* Prof. J. V. Robinson), *d* of late Major-General Sir Frederick Maurice, KCMG, CB; two *d*. *Educ:* Marlborough College (Scholar); Christ's College, Cambridge (Scholar). BA 1921; MA 1923; RNAS and RAF (Pilot), 1917-19; Fellow of Corpus Christi Coll., Cambridge, 1923-26; Tutor to HH The Maharaja of Gwalior, 1926-28; University Lecturer, Cambridge, 1929-49; Asst Editor of Economic Journal, 1934, Joint Editor, 1944-70; Member of Economic Section, War Cabinet Office, 1939-42; Economic Adviser and Head of Programmes Division, Ministry of Production, 1942-45; Member of British Reparations Mission, Moscow and Berlin, 1945; Economic Adviser to Board of Trade, 1946; returned to Cambridge, Sept. 1946. Mem. of Economic Planning Staff, 1947-48; Treasurer of International Economic Association, 1950-59, President 1959-62; Mem. Council, DSIR, 1954-59; Dir of Economics, Min. of Power, 1967-68. Chairman: Council Nat. Inst. of Economic and Social Research, 1949-62; European Energy Advisory Commn, OEEC, 1957-60; Exec. Cttee, Overseas Develt Inst. *Publications:* The Structure of Competitive Industry, 1931; Monopoly, 1941; Economic Consequences of the Size of Nations, 1960; Economic Development of Africa South of the Sahara, 1964; Problems in Economic Development, 1965; The Economics of Education (with J. E. Vaizey), 1966; Backward Areas in Advanced Countries, 1969; Economic Development in South Asia, 1970; (ed jtly) The Economic Development of Bangladesh within a Socialist Framework, 1974; contributor to: Modern Industry and the African, 1933; Lord Hailey's African Survey, 1938; articles in Economic Journal, etc. *Address:* Sidney Sussex College, Cambridge; 62 Grange Road, Cambridge. *T:* Cambridge 357548. *Club:* Reform.
See also Rt. Rev. C. J. G. Robinson.

ROBINSON, Forbes; Principal Artist (Bass), Royal Opera House, Covent Garden, since 1954; *b* Macclesfield, 21 May 1926; *s* of Wilfred and Gertrude Robinson; *m* 1952, Marion Stubbs; two *d*. *Educ:* King's Sch., Macclesfield. St Paul's Coll., Cheltenham (teacher's trg), 1943-45. Capt. in RAEC, 1946-48. Loughborough Coll. (Hons Dipl., Phys. Educn), 1949-50; La Scuola di Canto (Scala, Milan), 1952-53. Promenade Debut, 1957. Guest artist with Dublin, Handel, Sadler's Wells, Scottish and Welsh National Opera Cos. Has sung at Festivals at Aldeburgh, Barcelona, Edinburgh, Holland, Leeds, Lucerne, Ottawa, Portugal and Schwetzingen. Has also sung in Argentina, Belgium, Canada, Denmark, France, Germany, Luxembourg, Sweden, USA, South Korea, Japan and South Africa. First British singer to sing Don Giovanni at Royal Opera House, Covent Garden, for 100 years. Hon. DLitt Loughborough, 1979. Awarded Opera Medal for 1963, for creating King Priam (Tippett). *Recreations:* walking, swimming. *Address:* 225 Princes Gardens, W3. *T:* 01-992 5498. *Club:* Savage.

ROBINSON, Frank Arnold, CBE 1980; DSc, CChem, FRSC; Director of Twyford Laboratories Ltd & Twyford Pharmaceutical Services Ltd, retired; *b* 3 Dec. 1907; *s* of Frank Robinson and Edith Robinson (*née* Jagger); *m* 1st, 1930, Margaret Olive Jones; two *s*; 2nd, 1958, Beth Clarence Smith. *Educ:* Elland Grammar Sch.; Univ. of Manchester (James Gaskill Scholar; Hon. Fellow, UMIST, 1981); BSc Tech (Hons) 1929, MSc Tech 1930, DSc 1958; Univ. of London LLB (Hons.) 1940. Laboratory of Govt Chemist, 1930-33; Research Chemist, Glaxo Laboratories Ltd, Greenford, 1933-45; Manager, Distillers Co. Research Labs, Epsom, 1945-48; Dir of Research, Allen & Hanburys Ltd, Ware, 1948-60. FRIC 1940 (now FRSC). Hon. Professorial Fellow, University Coll., Cardiff, 1967-72; Hon. DSc: Bath, 1968; Salford, 1972. Chm., Biochemical Soc., 1946, and Treas., 1952-62; Pres., Section I (Biomedical) of BAAS, 1972-73; Mem., British National Cttee for Biochemistry, 1973-78; President: Royal Inst. Chem., 1972-74 (Vice-Pres., 1961-63, 1970-72); Chemical Soc., 1975-76; 12th Congress of Assoc. Internat. d'Expertise Chimique, Cambridge, 1972; Mem., UNESCO Cttee on status of scientific researchers, 1974; Chairman: Council, Science and Technology Insts Ltd, 1975-76; Council for Environmental Science and Engineering, 1975-81; Vice-Pres., Parly and Scientific Cttee, 1978-81. Assessor, Sci. Board, SRC, 1978-81. *Publications:* Principles and Practice of Chromatography, 1941; The Vitamin B Complex, 1951; Antibiotics, 1951; Vitamin Co-Factors of Enzyme Systems, 1966; Chemists and the Law, 1967; research papers and reviews in scientific jls. *Recreations:* gardening, archæology. *Address:* 22 Walden Road, Welwyn Garden City, Herts. *T:* Welwyn Garden 24751.

ROBINSON, Geoffrey; MP (Lab) Coventry North-West, since March 1976; *b* 25 May 1938; *s* of Robert Norman Robinson and Dorothy Jane Robinson (*née* Skelly); *m* 1967, Marie Elena Giorgio; one *s* one *d*. *Educ:* Emanuel School; Cambridge and Yale Univs. Labour Party Research Assistant, 1965-68; Senior Executive, Industrial Reorganisation Corporation, 1968-70; Financial Controller, British Leyland, 1971-72; Managing Director, Leyland Innocenti, Milan, 1972-73; Chief Executive: Jaguar Cars, Coventry, 1973-75; Meriden Motor Cycle Workers' Co-op, 1978-80 (Dir, 1980-). *Recreations:* reading, squash. *Address:* House of Commons, SW1A 0AA. *T:* 01-491 4207.

ROBINSON, Geoffrey; see Robinson, A. G.

ROBINSON, Sir George (Gilmour), Kt 1955; *b* 30 Aug. 1894; *s* of George Thomas Robinson and Ada Violet Gallier; *m* 1942, Muriel Alice Fry. *Educ:*

Repton; Trinity College, Oxford. (MA). Served European War, 1914-19. Called to Bar, 1924, and practised. Resident Magistrate, Kenya, 1930-38; Puisne Judge, Northern Rhodesia, 1938-46; Puisne Judge, Nigeria, 1947-52; Chief Justice, Zanzibar, 1952-55; retired 1955. *Recreations:* shooting, golf. *Address:* The Old House, Southwold, Suffolk. *T:* 722374.

ROBINSON, Mrs Gower; *see* Bloom, Ursula.

ROBINSON, Harold George Robert, OBE 1961; FRAeS; CEng, MIEE; Director-General Research (General), Ministry of Defence (Procurement Executive), and Assistant Chief Scientific Adviser (Research), Ministry of Defence, since 1981; *b* 2 April 1924; *s* of Harold Arthur Robinson and Winifred Margaret (*née* Ballard); *m* 1955, Sonja (*née* Lapthorn); two *s. Educ:* Portsmouth Northern Grammar Sch.; Imperial Coll., London Univ.; California Inst. of Technology. WhSch 1944; BSc 1948; FCGI 1970. Joined RAE as Scientific Officer, 1948; Head of Satellite Launcher Div., Space Dept, RAE, 1961; Head of Avionics Dept, RAE, 1965-69; Head of Research Planning Div., Min. of Technology, 1969-71; Dir Gen., Aerospace Assessment and Res., DTI, 1971-74; Under-Sec., Space and Air Res., DoI, 1974-76; a Dep. Dir, RAE, 1976-81. Pres., Astronautics Commn, FAI, 1969-70 (Paul Tissandier Diploma, 1971); FRAeS 1981 (Bronze Medal, 1961). *Publications:* various scientific and technical papers, contribs to books, primarily on rocket and space research. *Recreations:* sailing, riding, painting. *Address:* 39 Crosby Hill Drive, Camberley, Surrey. *T:* Camberley 23771.

ROBINSON, Prof. Joan Violet; Professor of Economics, University of Cambridge, 1965-71, retired 1971; *b* Camberley, Surrey, 31 Oct. 1903; *d* of late Major-General Sir Frederick Maurice, KCMG, CB; *m* 1926, Sir E. A. G. Robinson, *qv*; two *d. Educ:* St Paul's Girls' School, London; Girton Coll., Cambridge. Economics Tripos, 1925; Faculty Asst Lectr in Economics, Cambridge Univ., 1931; Univ. Lectr, 1937; Reader, 1949. FBA 1958-71. *Publications:* Economics of Imperfect Competition, 1933; Essays in the Theory of Employment, 1937; Introduction to the Theory of Employment, 1937; Essay on Marxian Economics, 1942; Collected Economic Papers, Vol. I, 1951; The Rate of Interest and Other Essays, 1952; The Accumulation of Capital, 1956; Collected Economic Papers, Vol. II, 1960; Essays in The Theory of Economic Growth, 1963; Economic Philosophy, 1963; Collected Economic Papers, Vol. III, 1965; Economics: An Awkward Corner, 1966; The Cultural Revolution in China, 1969; Freedom and Necessity, 1970; Economic Heresies, 1971; (ed) After Keynes, 1973; (with John Eatwell) Introduction to Modern Economics, 1973; Collected Economic Papers, Vol. IV, 1973, Vol. V, 1979; contrib. Modern Economics, 1978; articles, etc in Economic Journal, etc. *Address:* 62 Grange Road, Cambridge. *T:* 57548.

ROBINSON, John Armstrong, CMG 1969; HM Diplomatic Service, retired; Ambassador to Israel, 1980-81; *b* 18 Dec. 1925; *m* 1952, Marianne Berger; one *s* one *d.* HM Forces, 1944-46; Foreign Office, 1949-50; Second Secretary, Delhi, 1950-52; Foreign Office, 1952-53; Helsinki, 1953-56; Second later First Secretary, Paris, 1956-58; Foreign Office, 1958-61; First Secretary in UK Delegation to European Communities, Brussels, 1962-67; Counsellor, Foreign Office, 1967; Head of European Economic Integration Dept, FCO, 1968-70; appointed Member of team of nine officials for negotiations on British entry into the Common Market, Brussels, 1970-71; Asst Under-Sec. of State, FCO, 1971-73; Ambassador to Algeria, 1974-77; Minister, Washington, 1977-80. *Address:* La Sirgarié, St Martin Laguépie, 81170 Cordes, Tarn, France.

ROBINSON, Rt. Rev. John Arthur Thomas, MA, BD, DD, PhD; Lecturer in Theology, Trinity College, Cambridge, since 1969; Fellow, and Dean of Chapel, Trinity College, since 1969; *b* 15 June 1919; *s* of Reverend Canon Arthur William Robinson, DD and Mary Beatrice Robinson; *m* 1947, Ruth (*née* Grace); one *s* three *d. Educ:* Marlborough College; Jesus and Trinity Colleges, Cambridge; Westcott House, Cambridge. BA 1942 (1st class Theology); MA 1945; PhD 1946; BD 1962; DD 1968. Curate of St Matthew, Moorfields, Bristol, 1945-48; Chaplain, Wells Theological College, 1948-51; Fellow and Dean, Clare College, Cambridge, 1951-59; Assistant Lecturer in Divinity, Cambridge University, 1953-54; Lecturer in Divinity, 1954-59; Bishop Suffragan of Woolwich, 1959-69. Examining Chaplain to Archbishop of Canterbury, 1953-59; Six Preacher, Canterbury Cathedral, 1958-68; Proctor in Convocation, 1960-70; Assistant Bishop: Diocese of Southwark, 1969-80; Diocese of Bradford, 1981-. Vis. Prof. and Noble Lectr, Harvard, 1955; Vis. Prof.: Union Theological Seminary, Richmond, VA, 1958; Univ. of South Africa, Pretoria, 1975; Univ. of Witwatersrand, 1977; McMaster Univ., Hamilton, Ont, 1982. Lectures: Reinicker, Va Seminary, 1958; Purdy, Hartford Seminary, Conn, 1964; Thorp, Cornell University, 1964; Lilley, Wabash Coll., Indiana, 1966; West, Stanford Univ., 1966; Hulsean, Cambridge, 1970; Nelson, Lancaster Univ., 1971; Owen Evans, University Coll. of Aberystwyth, 1971; Carnahan, Union Theological Seminary, Buenos Aires, 1971; Teape, Delhi, Madras and Calcutta, 1977-78; Selwyn, St John's Coll., Auckland, 1979. Hon. LCD Univ. of Southern California, 1980. *Publications:* In the End God, 1950, rev. edn 1968; The Body, 1952; Jesus and His Coming, 1957, rev. edn 1979; On Being the Church in the World, 1960, rev. edn 1977; Christ Comes In, 1960; Liturgy Coming to Life, 1960; Twelve New Testament Studies, 1962; Honest to God, 1963; Christian Morals Today, 1964; The New Reformation?, 1965; But That I Can't Believe!, 1967; Exploration into God, 1967, rev. edn 1977; Christian Freedom in a Permissive Society, 1970; The Difference in Being a Christian Today, 1972; The Human Face of God, 1973; Redating the New Testament, 1976; Can We Trust the New Testament?, 1977; Wrestling with Romans, 1979; Truth is Two-Eyed,

1979; The Roots of a Radical, 1980; Joseph Barber Lightfoot, 1981; *contrib. to:* Christian Faith and Communist Faith, 1953; Becoming a Christian, 1954; The Historic Episcopate, 1954; Jesus Christ, History, Interpretation and Faith, 1956; New Ways with the Ministry, 1960; Bishops, 1961; The Interpreter's Dictionary of the Bible (article: Resurrection in the NT), 1962; Layman's Church, 1963; The Roads Converge, 1963; The Honest to God Debate, 1963; The Authorship and Integrity of the New Testament, 1965; The Restless Church, 1966; Theologians of our Time, 1966; Theological Freedom and Social Responsibility, 1967; Sermons from Great St Mary's, 1968; The Christian Priesthood, 1970; More Sermons from Great St Mary's, 1971; Theological Crossings, 1971; Christ, Faith and History, 1972; To God be the Glory, 1973; Christ and Spirit in the New Testament, 1973; Face to Face with the Turin Shroud, 1978; Twentieth Century Pulpit, vol. 2, 1981; Debate on Disarmament, 1982; Christological Perspectives, 1982; articles in learned journals, mainly on New Testament subjects. *Address:* Trinity College, Cambridge CB2 1TQ. *T:* Cambridge 358201.

ROBINSON, Sir John Beverley, 7th Bt, *cr* 1854; *b* 3 Oct. 1913; *s* of Sir John Beverley Robinson, 6th Bt, and Constance Marie (*d* 1977), *d* of Robert W. Pentecost; *S* father 1954. *Heir: kinsman* Christopher Philipse Robinson [*b* 10 Nov. 1938; *m* 1962, Barbara Judith, *d* of Richard Duncan; two *s* (and one *s* decd)].

ROBINSON, John Foster, CBE 1968; TD; DL; Honorary President, DRG plc; *b* 2 Feb. 1909; *s* of late Sir Foster Gotch Robinson; *m* 1st, 1935, Margaret Eve Hannah Paterson (*d* 1977); two *s* two *d*; 2nd, 1979, Mrs Joan De Moraville. *Educ:* Harrow; Christ Church, Oxford. Dir, E. S. & A. Robinson Ltd, 1943, Jt Man. Dir 1948; Chm., E. S. & A. Robinson (Holdings) Ltd, 1961; Dep. Chm., The Dickinson Robinson Group Ltd, 1966, Chm., 1968-74. Director: Eagle Star Insurance Co. Ltd, 1968; National Westminster Bank Ltd (Mem., SW Regional Bd, 1969-76); Bristol & West Building Soc., 1973-. DL Glos 1972; High Sheriff, Avon, 1975. *Recreations:* shooting, fishing, golf. *Address:* Honor Farm, Failand Lane, Portbury, Bristol BS20 9SR. *T:* Pill 2108. *Clubs:* Houghton; Clifton, Bristol, Constitutional (Bristol).

ROBINSON, Sir John (James Michael Laud), 11th Bt *cr* 1660; *b* 19 Jan. 1943; *s* of Michael Frederick Laud Robinson (*d* 1971) and Elizabeth (*née* Bridge); *S* grandfather, 1975; *m* 1968, Gayle Elizabeth (*née* Keyes); two *s. Educ:* Eton; Trinity Coll., Dublin (MA, Economics and Political Science). Chartered Financial Analyst. *Heir: s* Mark Christopher Michael Villiers Robinson, *b* 23 April 1972. *Address:* Cranford, Kettering, Northants.

ROBINSON, Rev. Canon Joseph, MTh, FKC; Master of the Temple since 1980; *b* 23 Feb. 1927; *er s* of Thomas and Maggie Robinson; *m* 1953, Anne Antrobus; two *s* two *d. Educ:* Upholland Grammar Sch., Lancs; King's Coll., London. BD (1st cl. Hons); AKC (1st cl) 1951; MTh 1958; FKC 1973. Deacon, 1952; Priest, 1953; Curate, All Hallows, Tottenham, 1952-55; Minor Canon of St Paul's Cathedral, 1956-68; Sacrist, 1958-68; Lectr in Hebrew and Old Testament Studies, King's Coll., London, 1959-68; Canon Residentiary, Canterbury Cathedral, 1968-80, now Canon Emeritus; Librarian, 1968-73; Treasurer, 1972-80; Exam. Chaplain to Archbishop of Canterbury, 1968-80. Golden Lectr, 1963; St Antholin Lectr, 1964-67. Chaplain, Worshipful Co. of Cutlers, 1963-; Sub Chaplain, Order of St John of Jerusalem, 1965-. *Publications:* The Cambridge Bible Commentary on 1 Kings, 1972, 2 Kings, 1976; articles in: Church Quarterly Review, Expository Times, Church Times; many reviews in various jls. *Recreations:* reading, gardening. *Address:* The Master's House, The Temple, EC4. *T:* 01-353 8559. *Club:* Athenæum.

ROBINSON, Kathleen Marian, (Mrs Vincent F. Sherry; Kathleen M. Sherry); FRCS, FRCOG, MD; Hon. Obstetrician, and Hon. Gynæcologist, Royal Free Hospital; Hon. Obstetrician, Queen Charlotte's Hospital; *b* 25 May 1911; *d* of late James Robinson and Ruth Robinson (*née* Edmeston); *m* 1946, Vincent Francis Sherry; one *s* one *d* (and one *d* decd). *Educ:* Penrhos College, Colwyn Bay; Royal Free Hospital School of Medicine, London University. MB, BS, 1936; MRCS, LRCP 1936; MD London 1940; FRCS 1940; MRCOG 1941; FRCOG 1953. House Surgeon: Royal Free Hospital; Samaritan Hospital, Royal Marsden Hospital, Queen Charlotte's Hospital. Resident Obstetrician, Queen Charlotte's Hospital. Recognised Teacher of the London University. FRSM; FRHS. *Publications:* contributor to Queen Charlotte's Text Book of Obstetrics, also to Practical Motherhood and Parentcraft. *Recreations:* gardening, cooking, travel. *Address:* 17 Herondale Avenue, SW18 3JN. *T:* 01-874 8588.

ROBINSON, Rt. Hon. Kenneth, PC 1964; Hon. DLitt; FCIT; Chairman, Arts Council of Great Britain, 1977-82; *b* Warrington, Lancs, 19 March 1911; *s* of late Clarence Robinson, MRCS, LRCP; *m* 1941, Helen Elizabeth Edwards; one *d. Educ:* Oundle Sch. Insurance Broker at Lloyd's, 1927-40. Served War of 1939-45, RN 1941-46; Ord. Seaman, 1941; commissioned, 1942; Lieut-Comdr RNVR, 1944; served Home Fleet, Mediterranean, Far East and Pacific. Company Secretary, 1946-69. MP (Lab) St Pancras N, 1949-70; Asst Whip (unpaid), 1950-51, an Opposition Whip, 1951-54; Minister of Health, 1964-68; Minister for Planning and Land, Min. of Housing and Local Govt, 1968-69. Dir, Social Policy, 1970-72, Man. Dir (Personnel and Social Policy Div.), 1972-74, British Steel Corp.; Chm., LTE, 1975-78. Chm. of English National Opera, 1972-77. Hon. FRCGP; Hon. DLitt Liverpool, 1980. *Publications:* Wilkie Collins, a Biography, 1951; Policy for Mental Health, 1958; Patterns of Care, 1961; Look at Parliament, 1962;

Recreations: looking at paintings, reading, listening to music. *Address:* 12 Grove Terrace, NW5.

ROBINSON, Kenneth Dean, MA Oxon; General Secretary, British Herbal Medicine Association, since 1979 (Administrator, Advertising Code, since 1978); *b* 9 March 1909; *s* of late Rev. Arthur Edward and late Mary Edith Robinson; *m* 1936, Marjorie Belle Carter, Bradford, Yorks; two *s* two *d*. *Educ:* Bradford Grammar Sch.; Corpus Christi Coll., Oxford (Scholar). Classical Honour Mods Class I, Litt Hum. Class II. Sixth Form Classical Master, St Edmund's, Canterbury, 1932-34; Head of Classical Dept, Wellington College, Berks, 1934-41; Intelligence Corps, 1941-45; Asst to Director of Education, Shire Hall, Reading, Berks, 1945-46; Headmaster: Birkenhead Sch., Cheshire, 1946-63; Bradford Grammar Sch., 1963-74. Classics panel Secondary Sch. Examinations Council, 1948-50; Pres. Liverpool Br., Class. Assoc., 1958; Council, IAHM, 1949-53; HMC Cttee, 1956-60; Chm. NW Div., HMC, 1958-59; Chm. Direct Grant Cttee, HMC, 1958-59. Mem., 1967-70; Chm., NE Div., HMC, 1971-72; Chm. Op. Res. Sect. Div. XII, IAHM, 1952-60; Chm. Div. XII, IAHM, 1961-62; Mem. Council, 1962-63. Gen. Sec., British Herbal Medicine Assoc., 1979- (and Administrator, Advertising Code, 1978-). Governor, Giggleswick Sch., 1974-. Hon. Pres., Leeds/Bradford Branch, Nat. Assoc. for Gifted Children. *Publications:* (with R. L. Chambers) Septimus: a First Latin Reader, 1936; The Latin Way, 1947. *Recreations:* gardening, chess, painting, canals, country. *Address:* Lane House, Cowling, near Keighley, West Yorks BD22 0LX. *T:* Crosshills 34487.

ROBINSON, Kenneth Ernest, CBE 1971; MA, FRHistS; *b* 9 March 1914; *o s* of late Ernest and Isabel Robinson, Plumstead, Kent; *m* 1938, Stephanie, *o d* of late William Wilson, Westminster; one *s* one *d*. *Educ:* Monoux Grammar School, Walthamstow; Hertford College, Oxford (Scholar, 1st Cl. PPE; 1st Cl. Mod. Hist.; Beit Senior Schol. in Colonial History); London School of Economics. Colonial Office, 1936; Asst Sec. 1946; resigned 1948. Fellow of Nuffield Coll., and Reader in Commonwealth Govt, Oxford, 1948-57; Dir, Inst. of Commonwealth Studies and Prof. of Commonwealth Affairs, Univ. of London, 1957-65 (Hon. Life Mem., 1980-); Vice-Chancellor, Univ. of Hong Kong, 1965-72; Hallsworth Res. Fellow, Univ. of Manchester, 1972-74; Dir, Commonwealth Studies Resources Survey, Univ. of London, 1974-76. Leverhulme Res. Fellow, 1952-53; Vis. Lectr, Sch. of Advanced Internat. Studies, Johns Hopkins Univ., 1954; Carnegie Travel Grant, East, Central and S Africa, 1960; Reid Lectr, Acadia Univ., 1963; Vis. Prof., Duke Univ., NC, 1963; Callander Lectr, Aberdeen, 1979; Editor, Jl of Commonwealth Political Studies, 1961-65; Special Commonwealth Award, ODM, 1965. Member: (part-time) Directing Staff, Civil Service Selection Bd, 1951-56, Assessor Panel, 1973-77; Colonial Economic Res. Cttee, 1949-62; Colonial SSRC, 1958-62; Inter-Univ. Council for Higher Educn Overseas, 1973-79; Mem. Council: Overseas Develt Inst. 1960-65; RIIA, 1962-65; Internat. African Inst., 1960-65; African Studies Assoc., UK, 1963-65, 1978-81; ACU, 1967-68; Hong Kong Management Assoc., 1965-72; Chinese Univ. of Hong Kong, 1965-72; Univ. of Cape Coast, 1972-74; Royal Commonwealth Soc., 1974- (Dep. Chm., 1979-83); Life Mem. Ct, Univ. of Hong Kong, 1972. Governor, LSE, 1959-65. Corresp. Mem., Académie des Sciences d'Outre-Mer, Paris. Hon. LLD Chinese Univ. of Hong Kong, 1969; Hon. DLitt, Univ. of Hong Kong, 1972; DUniv Open, 1978. JP Hong Kong, 1967-72. *Publications:* (with W. J. M. Mackenzie) Five Elections in Africa, 1960; (with A. F. Madden) Essays in Imperial Government presented to Margery Perham, 1963; The Dilemmas of Trusteeship, 1965; (with W. B. Hamilton & C. D. Goodwin) A Decade of the Commonwealth 1955-64 (USA), 1966. Contrib. to Africa Today (USA), 1955; Africa in the Modern World (USA), 1955; University Cooperation and Asian Development (USA), 1967; L'Europe du XIXe et du XXe Siècle, Vol. 7 (Italy), 1968; Experts in Africa, 1980; papers in learned jls. *Address:* The Old Rectory, Church Westcote, Oxon. *T:* Shipton under Wychwood 830586; 10 St Augustine's Road, NW1. *T:* 01-485 1198. *Clubs:* Royal Commonwealth Society, United Oxford & Cambridge University, Lansdowne; Hong Kong.

ROBINSON, Lee Fisher; Chief Executive and Deputy Chairman, Turriff Construction Corporation Ltd, since 1970; Consultant, International Management Consultants, since 1972; Director and Vice-President, RTL SA, since 1977; Director and Chief Executive, RTR SA, since 1977; Director and Chairman, Ingeco Laing Ltd (UK), since 1977; *b* 17 July 1923; *m* 1st, 1944, Zelda Isobel Fisher; three *d*; 2nd, 1976, June Edna Hopkins. *Educ:* Howard Sch.; Cardiff Tech. College. CEng, MIArb. Royal Engrs, Sappers and Miners, IE, 1942-45. Turriff Const. Corp. Ltd, HBM (BCC), 1963; Man. Dir, Power Gas Corp. Ltd, 1964; Director: Davy-Ashmore Ltd, 1970; Combustion Systems (NRDC), 1972- (Chm., 1978); Redwood Internat. (UK) Ltd, 1972; Altech SA, 1976-; Protech SA, 1976-; Altech of Canada, 1976-; Danks Gowerton, 1976-; Hewlee Ltd, 1976-; BCS Ltd, 1976-; Charterhouse Strategic Development Ltd, 1976-80 (Gp Indust. Adviser, Charterhouse Gp); Altech (Canada) Ltd, 1976-; Ingeco Laing SA, 1977-; RTR (Oil Sands) Alberta, 1977-; RTR Canada Ltd, 1977-; SPO Minerals Co. Ltd, 1980-81; Thalassa (North Sea) Ltd, 1980-; Marcent Natural Resources Ltd (Man. Dir), 1980-; WGI Engineering Ltd, 1980-; Chairman: Sphere Oil Resources Ltd; Biotechna Ltd; Concorde Commodities Ltd. Chm., Warren Spring Adv. Bd; Mem. Adv. Council for Technology, 1968-69. *Publications:* Cost and Financing of Fertiliser Projects in India, 1967; various articles. *Recreations:* badminton, sailing. *Address:* Flat 3, Athenaeum Hall, Vale-of-Health, NW3 1AP. *Clubs:* East India, Devonshire, Sports and Public Schools, Wig and Pen.

ROBINSON, Leonard Keith, CBE 1981; County Chief Executive, Hampshire County Council, since 1974; Clerk of Lieutenancy since 1974; *b* 2 July 1920; *s* of Cuthbert Lawrence Robinson and Hilda Robinson; *m* 1948, Susan May Tomkinson; two *s* two *d*. *Educ:* Queen Elizabeth's Grammar Sch., Blackburn; Victoria Univ. of Manchester (LLB). Solicitor. RAFVR, 1940-46 (Navigator, Sqdn-Ldr). Asst Solicitor, City and County of Bristol, 1948-55; Dep. Town Clerk, Birkenhead Co. Borough Council, 1955-66; Town Clerk, Stoke-on-Trent City Council, 1966-73. Association of County Councils: Mem., Officers Adv. Gp, 1974- (Chm., 1977-82); Adviser, Policy Cttee, 1975-82; Adviser, Local Govt Finance Cttee, 1976-. Member: W Mids Econ. Planning Council, 1967-73; Keele Univ. Council, 1968-73; Central Cttee for Reclamation of Derelict Land, 1971-74; Quality Assce Council, BSI, 1973-77; Job Creation Programme Action Cttee for London and SE, 1976-77; District Manpower Cttee, 1980-; Adv. Council for Energy Conservation, 1982-; LAMIT, 1982-; Chm., Assoc. of County Chief Execs, 1975-77. Sec., Hillier Arboretum Management Cttee, 1977-. Trustee, Theatre Royal, Portsmouth, 1976-; Dir, Salisbury Playhouse, 1979-. *Publications:* contrib. local govt and legal jls. *Recreations:* cricket, theatre, cine photography, gardening. *Address:* Byewood, Hocombe Road, Chandler's Ford, Hampshire SO5 1SL. *Clubs:* National Liberal, MCC.

ROBINSON, Lloyd; *see* Robinson, T. L.

ROBINSON, Group Captain Marcus, CB 1956; AFC 1942 and Bar 1944; AE 1942; DL; Chairman, Robinson, Dunn & Co. Ltd and subsidiary companies, 1966-79, retired; *b* 27 May 1912; *s* of Wilson and Eileen Robinson; *m* 1st, 1941, Mrs Mary Playfair (marr. diss. 1951); 2nd, 1953, Mrs Joan E. G. O. Weatherlake (*née* Carter); one *s* one *d*. *Educ:* Rossall. Commissioned AAF, 602 Sqdn, 1934; Squadron Ldr, 1940, commanding 616 Squadron; Wing Comdr, 1943; Group Capt., 1945; re-formed 602 Squadron, 1947; Member Air Advisory Council, Air Ministry, 1952-56; Chairman Glasgow TA and AFA, 1953-56; Chairman Glasgow Rating Valuation Appeals Cttee, 1963-74 (Dep. Chm., 1958-63). A Vice-Pres., Earl Haig Fund, Scotland, 1978- (Chm., 1974-78). DL Glasgow, 1953. *Recreations:* ski-ing, sailing. *Address:* Rockfort, Helensburgh, Dunbartonshire G84 7BA. *Clubs:* Western (Glasgow), Royal Northern and Clyde Yacht (Rhu).

ROBINSON, Air Vice-Marshal Michael Maurice Jeffries, CB 1982; Secretary (Welfare) to the RAF Benevolent Fund, since 1982; *b* 11 Feb. 1927; *s* of Dr Maurice Robinson and Muriel (*née* Jeffries); *m* 1952, Drusilla Dallas Bush; one *s* two *d*. *Educ:* King's Sch., Bruton; Queen's Coll., Oxford; RAF Coll., Cranwell. psa 1961, jssc 1965. Commnd, 1948; 45 Sqdn, Malaya, 1948-51; CFS, 1953-55; OC 100 Sqdn, 1962-64; Comd, RAF Lossiemouth, 1972-74; Asst Comdt, RAF Coll., Cranwell, 1974-77; SASO No 1 Gp, 1977-79; Dir Gen. of Organisation (RAF), 1979-82, retd. Wing Comdr 1961, Gp Captain 1970, Air Cdre 1976, Air Vice-Marshal 1980. Governor, King's Sch., Bruton, 1980-. *Recreations:* golf, gardening, going to the opera. *Address:* Lloyds Bank Ltd (Cox's and King's Branch), 6 Pall Mall, SW1Y 5NH. *Club:* Royal Air Force.

ROBINSON, Sir Niall B. L.; *see* Lynch-Robinson.

ROBINSON, Nigel Francis Maltby; Metropolitan Stipendiary Magistrate, 1962-78; *b* 5 Nov. 1906; *s* of Francis George Robinson, OBE, Ilkeston, Derbyshire; *m* 1933, Flora, *d* of John McKay, Sutton, Surrey. *Educ:* Lancing; Hertford College, Oxford (MA, BCL). Called to Bar, Middle Temple, 1928; Practised Midland Circuit, 1928-62. Served Royal Artillery, 1940-45. JP and Dep. Chairman, Quarter Sessions for Derbyshire, 1958-64; JP and Dep. Chm., Nottinghamshire Quarter Sessions, 1961-66. *Address:* 42 Parkside, Vanbrugh Fields, SE3 7QG. *Clubs:* Flyfishers'; Nottingham and Nottinghamshire United Services.

ROBINSON, Oliver John; Editor, Good Housekeeping, 1947-65, Editor-in-Chief, 1965-67; *b* 7 April 1908; *s* of late W. Heath and Josephine Constance Robinson; *m* 1933, Evelyn Anne Laidler. *Educ:* Cranleigh Sch. Art Editor, Good Housekeeping, 1930; Art Editor, Nash's, 1933. Temporary commission, Queen's Royal Regt, 1941; Camouflage Development and Training Centre, 1942; Staff Officer, War Office, 1944. *Address:* 92 Charlbert Court, Eamont Street, NW8 7DA. *T:* 01-722 0723. *Club:* Savage.

ROBINSON, Oswald Horsley, OBE 1977; HM Diplomatic Service; Counsellor, Foreign and Commonwealth Office, since 1979; *b* 24 Aug. 1926; *s* of Sir Edward Stanley Gotch Robinson, CBE, FSA, FBA, and Pamela, *d* of Sir Victor Horsley, CB, FRS; *m* 1954, Helena Faith, *d* of Dr F. R. Seymour; two *s* one *d*. *Educ:* Bedales Sch.; King's Coll., Cambridge. Served RE, 1943-48. Joined FO, 1951; served: Rangoon and Maymyo, 1954; FO, 1958; Mexico and Guatemala, 1961; Quito and Bogotá, 1963; FO (later FCO), 1965; Georgetown, Guyana, 1973; Bangkok, 1976. *Recreation:* sailing. *Address:* c/o Foreign and Commonwealth Office, SW1. *Clubs:* Royal Cruising; West Mersea Yacht.

ROBINSON, Peter; Director, Tootal Ltd; *b* 18 Jan. 1922; *s* of Harold Robinson and Jane Elizabeth Robinson; *m* Lesley Anne, step-*d* of Major J. M. May, TD; two *s* two *d*. *Educ:* Prince Henry's Sch., Otley; Leeds Coll. of Technology (Diploma in Printing). Mem., Inst. of Printing; CBIM. Management Trainee, 1940-41; flying duties, RAFVR, 1942-46; Leeds Coll. of Technol., 1946-49; Asst Manager, Robinson & Sons Ltd, Chesterfield, 1949-53; Works Dir and Man. Dir, Taylowe Ltd, 1953-62; Director: Hazell

Sun, 1964; British Printing Corp., 1966-81, Man. Dir 1969-75; Chm. and Chief Exec., BPC Ltd (formerly British Printing Corp.), 1976-81. Formerly Council Mem., PIRA. *Recreations:* military history, cricket, golf. *Address:* Well End Lodge, Bourne End, Bucks. *T:* Bourne End 20187.

ROBINSON, Peter Damian; Deputy Secretary, since 1980, and Deputy Clerk of the Crown in Chancery, since 1982, Lord Chancellor's Department; *b* 11 July 1926; *s* of late John Robinson and Jill Clegg (*née* Easten); *m* 1956, Mary Katinka Bonner (*d* 1978), Peterborough; two *d. Educ:* Corby Sch., Sunderland; Lincoln Coll., Oxford. MA. Royal Marine Commandos, 1944-46. Called to Bar, Middle Temple, 1951; practised common law, 1952-59; Clerk of Assize, NE Circuit, 1959-70; Administrator, NE Circuit, 1970-74; Circuit Administrator, SE Circuit (Lord Chancellor's Dept), 1974-80. Member, Home Office Departmental Cttee on Legal Aid in Criminal Proceedings (the Widgery Cttee), 1964-66. *Recreations:* reading, the countryside. *Address:* 6 Morpeth Mansions, Morpeth Terrace, SW1. *T:* 01-828 2349.

ROBINSON, Peter David; MP (DemU) Belfast East, since 1979; Member (DemU) Belfast East, Northern Ireland Assembly, since 1982; *b* 29 Dec. 1948; *s* of David McCrea Robinson and Sheliah Robinson; *m* 1970, Iris Collins; two *s* one *d. Educ:* Annadale Grammar School; Castlereagh Further Education College. Gen. Secretary, Ulster Democratic Unionist Party, 1975-79, Dep. Leader, 1980-. Member, Castlereagh Borough Council, 1977; Deputy Mayor, 1978. *Publications:* booklets: The North Answers Back, 1970; Capital Punishment for Capital Crime, 1978; Self Inflicted, 1981; Ulster in Peril, 1981; Savagery and Suffering, 1981; (jtly) Ulster—the facts, 1982. *Address:* 16 Cooneen Way, Cregagh, Belfast BT6 0EE. *T:* Belfast 56418.

ROBINSON, Philip Henry; Director, J. Henry Schroder Wagg & Co. Ltd, since 1966; Executive Vice-President, Schroder International Ltd, since 1977 (Director, since 1973); Chairman, Schroder Leasing Ltd, since 1979; *b* 4 Jan. 1926; *s* of Arthur Robinson and Frances M. Robinson; *m* 1959, Helen Wharton (marr. diss. 1979); one *s* one *d. Educ:* Lincoln Sch.; Jesus Coll., Cambridge (Exhibr, MA); Sch. of Oriental and African Studies, London Univ.; NY Univ. Graduate Sch. of Business Admin. Member, Gray's Inn. Served with RN, 1944-47; N. M. Rothschild & Sons, 1950-54; Actg Sec., British Newfoundland Corp., Montreal, 1954-56; Asst Vice-Pres., J. Henry Schroder Banking Corp., NY, 1956-61; J. Henry Schroder Wagg & Co. Ltd, 1961; Director: J. Henry Schroder Wagg & Co. Ltd, 1966; Siemens Ltd, 1967; Schroders & Chartered Ltd Hong Kong, 1971. Managing Trustee, Municipal Mutual Insurance Ltd, 1977-. Mem., Nat. Coal Board, 1973-77. Hon. Treasurer, Nat. Council for One Parent Families, 1977-79. *Publications:* contrib. Investor's Chronicle. *Recreations:* music, walking. *Address:* 16 Smith Street, SW3. *T:* 01-730 4978; Saint-Maximin, 30700 Uzès, Gard, France. *Club:* Annabel's.

See also A. G. Robinson.

ROBINSON, Robert Henry; writer and broadcaster; *b* 17 Dec. 1927; *o s* of Ernest Redfern Robinson and Johanna Hogan; *m* 1958, Josephine Mary Richard; one *s* two *d. Educ:* Raynes Park Grammar Sch.; Exeter Coll., Oxford (MA). Editor of Isis, 1950. TV columnist, Sunday Chronicle, 1952; film and theatre columnist, Sunday Graphic, and radio critic, Sunday Times, 1956; editor Atticus, Sunday Times, 1960; weekly column, Private View, Sunday Times, 1962; film critic, Sunday Telegraph, 1965. Writer and presenter of TV programmes: Picture Parade, 1959; Points of View, 1961; Divided We Stand, 1964; The Look of the Week, 1966; Reason to Believe?, The Fifties, 1969; Chm., Call My Bluff, Ask The Family, 1967; The Book Programme, 1974; Word for Word, 1978; films for TV: Robinson's Travels – the Pioneer Trail West, 1977; From Shepherd's Bush to Simla, 1979; B. Traven: a mystery solved, 1978; Robinson Cruising, 1981; The Auden Landscape, 1982; contribs Panorama, Monitor, Meeting Point, etc; presenter of: BBC radio current affairs programme Today, 1971-74; Vital Statistics, 1974; Chm., Brain of Britain, 1973-; Chm., Stop the Week, 1974-. Pres., Johnson Soc. of Lichfield, 1982. Radio Personality of the Year: Radio Industries Club, 1973; Variety Club of GB, 1980. *Publications:* (ed) Poetry from Oxford, 1951; Landscape with Dead Dons, 1956; Inside Robert Robinson (essays), 1965; (contrib.) To Nevill Coghill from Friends, 1966; The Conspiracy, 1968; The Dog Chairman, 1982; contrib. The Times, Punch, Listener, etc. *Address:* 16 Cheyne Row, SW3; Laurel Cottage, Buckland St Mary, Somerset. *Club:* Savile.

ROBINSON, Prof. Roger James, FRCP; Professor of Paediatrics, Guy's Hospital Medical School, University of London, since 1975; *b* 17 May 1932; *s* of Albert Edward and Leonora Sarah Robinson; *m* 1962, Jane Hippisley Packham; two *s* one *d. Educ:* Poole Grammar Sch.; Balliol Coll., Oxford (Brackenbury schol.; MA, DPhil, BM, BCh). Lectr of Christ Church, Oxford, 1953; appts at Radcliffe Infirmary, Oxford, National Hosp., Queen Square, and Hammersmith Hosp., 1960-66; Visiting Prof., Harvard, 1967; Sen. Lectr, Inst. of Child Health, Hammersmith Hosp., 1967; Cons. Paediatrician, Guy's Hosp., 1971. *Publications:* Brain and Early Behaviour: development in the fetus and infant, 1969; (jtly) Medical Care of Newborn Babies, 1972; papers on paediatrics and child neurology. *Recreation:* sailing. *Address:* 60 Madeley Road, Ealing, W5 2LU. *T:* 01-998 2394.

ROBINSON, Prof. Ronald Edward, CBE 1970; DFC 1944; Beit Professor of the History of the British Commonwealth, and Fellow of Balliol College, Oxford University, since 1971; Director, University of Oxford Development

Records Project, since 1978; *b* 3 Sept. 1920; *e s* of William Edward and Ada Theresa Robinson, Clapham; *m* 1948, Alice Josephine Denny; two *s* two *d. Educ:* Battersea Grammar Sch.; St John's Coll., Cambridge. Major Scholar in History, St John's Coll., 1939; BA 1946, PhD 1949, Cantab. F/Lt, 58 Bomber Sqn, RAF, 1942-45. Research Officer, African Studies Branch, Colonial Office, 1947-49; Lectr in History, 1953-66, Smuts Reader in History of the British Commonwealth, 1966-71, Univ. of Cambridge; Tutor 1961-66, Fellow 1949-71, St John's Coll., Cambridge; Chm., Faculty Bd of Modern Hist., Oxford, 1974-76, Vice-Chm., 1979-. Inst. for Advanced Studies, Princeton, 1959-60. Mem., Bridges Cttee on Trng in Public Administration, 1961-62; Chm., Cambridge Confs on Problems of Developing Countries, 1961-70. UK observer, Zimbabwe election, 1980. *Publications:* Africa and the Victorians, 1961; Developing the Third World, 1971; articles in Cambridge History of the British Empire, Vol. III, 1959, and The New Cambridge Modern History, Vol. XI, 1963; reports on Problems of Developing Countries, 1963-71; articles and reviews in learned jls. *Recreation:* room cricket. *Address:* Balliol College, Oxford. *Clubs:* Royal Commonwealth Society; Hawks (Cambridge); Gridiron (Oxford).

ROBINSON, Stanford, OBE 1972; Orchestral, Choral and Opera Conductor; Lecturer on conducting and kindred musical subjects; *b* Leeds, 5 July 1904; *s* of James Percy and Carrie Robinson; *m* Lorely Dyer; one *d. Educ:* Stationers' Company's School; Royal College of Music, London, and abroad. British Broadcasting Corporation, 1924-66; Chorus Master until 1932, during which time formed the BBC choral activities in London, including the BBC Singers, the Choral Society, and the BBC Chorus; during the period also conducted the Wireless Orchestra extensively in all kinds of programmes, symphonic and otherwise; Conductor of BBC Theatre Orchestra, 1932-46; Music Dir Variety Dept, 1932-36; Dir Music Productions, producing and conducting all studio performances of opera besides operetta and other musical feature programmes, 1936-46; Opera Director and Associate Conductor of the BBC Symphony Orchestra, 1946-49; Conductor Opera Orch. and Opera Organiser, BBC, 1949-52. Toured Australia and New Zealand, conducting ABC and NZBC orchestras in numerous cities, 1966-67; Chief Conductor, Queensland Symphony Orchestra, 1968-69. Hon. ARCM; Hon. GSM; Emeritus FGSM, 1980. *Publications:* Orchestral Music, Brass Band Music, part songs, choral arrangements and songs. *Recreations:* gardening, photography. *Address:* Ivor Newton House, 10-12 Edward Road, Sundridge Park, Bromley, Kent BR1 3NQ; Flat 3, Belmont Court, Belmont, Dyke Road, Brighton, Sussex BN1 3TX. *T:* Brighton 202272.

ROBINSON, Stanley Scott, MBE 1944; TD 1950; Sheriff of Grampian, Highland and Islands (formerly Inverness (including Western Isles)), Ross, Cromarty, Moray and Nairn); *b* 27 March 1913; *s* of late William Scott Robinson, Engineer, and of Christina Douglas Robinson; *m* 1937, Helen Annan Hardie; three *s. Educ:* Boroughmuir Sch., Edinburgh; Edinburgh Univ. Admitted as solicitor, 1935; Solicitor in the Supreme Courts. Commissioned in TA, 1935. Served War: France and Belgium, 1939-40, Captain RA; France, Holland and Germany, 1944-45 (despatches twice); Major, RA, 1943; Lt-Col, 1948. Solicitor in gen. practice in Montrose, Angus, 1935-72 (except during war service). Hon. Sheriff of Perth and Angus, 1970-72. Mem. Council of Law Society of Scotland, 1963-72 (Vice-Pres., 1971-72); Dean, Soc. of Solicitors of Angus, 1970-72. *Publications:* contribs to Jl of Law Society of Scotland. *Recreations:* golf, bowling, military history. *Address:* Flat 3, Drumallin House, Drummond Road, Inverness. *T:* Inverness 33488. *Club:* Highland (Inverness).

ROBINSON, Stephen Joseph, OBE 1971; FRS 1976; FEng, FIEE; Managing Director, Pye TVT Ltd, since 1980; *b* 6 Aug. 1931; *s* of Joseph Allan Robinson and Ethel (*née* Bunting); *m* 1957, Monica Mabs Scott; one *s* one *d. Educ:* Sebright Sch., Wolverley; Jesus Coll., Cambridge (MA Natural Sciences). RAF, 1950-51. Mullard Res. Labs, 1954-72; MEL Div., Philips Industries (formerly MEL Equipment Co. Ltd), 1972-79; Product Dir, 1973-79. Mem. Council, Royal Soc., 1982-. *Recreations:* sailing, ski-ing. *Address:* 140 The Street, Kirtling, near Newmarket, Suffolk. *T:* Newmarket 730104.

ROBINSON, Thomas Lloyd, TD; Vice-Chairman, Legal & General Assurance Society, since 1978 (Director, 1970); Honorary Vice-President, The Dickinson Robinson Group Ltd, since 1978 (Chairman, 1974-77, Deputy Chairman, 1968); *b* 21 Dec. 1912; *s* of late Thomas Rosser Robinson and Rebe Francis-Watkins; *m* 1939, Pamela Rosemary Foster; one *s* two *d. Educ:* Wycliffe Coll. Served War, 1939-45: Royal Warwickshire Regt, 61 Div., and SHAEF; Staff Coll., Camberley. Director, E. S. & A. Robinson Ltd, 1952; Jt Managing Dir, 1958; Dep. Chm., E. S. & A. Robinson (Holdings) Ltd, 1963; Director: Bristol Waterworks Co., 1978-; Van Leer Groep Stichting, Holland, 1977-81; Chm., Legal & General Western Advisory Bd, 1972-; Chm., Council of Governors, Wycliffe Coll., 1971-. Master, Soc. of Merchant Venturers, Bristol, 1977-78. High Sheriff, Avon, 1979-80; Pres., Glos CCC, 1980-. *Recreations:* music, antiques, golf. *Address:* Lechlade, 23 Druid Stoke Avenue, Stoke Bishop, Bristol BS9 1DB. *T:* Bristol 681957. *Clubs:* Army & Navy, MCC; Royal and Ancient (St Andrews).

ROBINSON, Victor, CEng, FIChemE; Director, Davy International Projects (concerned with major multi-discipline overseas projects), since 1976; *b* 31 July 1925; *s* of Arthur Worsley Robinson and Nellie (*née* Halliwell); *m* 1948, Sadie Monica (*née* Grut); one *s* five *d. Educ:* Manchester Grammar Sch.; Cambridge Univ. (MA). Admin. Staff Coll., Henley. CEng, FIChemE 1960. Simon Carves Ltd: R&D Proj. Engrg, 1945; Technical Dir, 1961; Dir, 1964;

Man. Dir Overseas Ops and Dir, Sim-Chem Ltd and subsid. cos, 1966; Man. Dir, Turriff Taylor Ltd, 1974; Industrial Adviser, Dept of Trade (on secondment from Davy Corp. Ltd), 1978-81. *Recreation:* fell and alpine walking. *Address:* 1A The Crest, Surbiton, Surrey KT5 8JZ. *T:* 01-399 1753.

ROBINSON, Sir Wilfred (Henry Frederick), 3rd Bt, *cr* 1908; Finance Officer, Society of Genealogists, since 1980; Staff, Diocesan College School, Rondebosch, South Africa, 1950-77, Vice-Principal, 1969-77; *b* 24 Dec. 1917; *s* of Wilfred Henry Robinson (*d* 1922) (3rd *s* of 1st Bt), and Eileen (*d* 1963), *d* of Frederick St Leger, Claremont, SA; *S* uncle, Sir Joseph Benjamin Robinson, 2nd Bt, 1954; *m* 1946, Margaret Alison Kathleen, *d* of late Frank Mellish, MC, Bergendal, Gansbaai, Cape Province, SA; one *s* two *d*. *Educ:* Diocesan Coll., Rondebosch; St John's Coll., Cambridge, MA 1944. Served War of 1939-45, Devonshire Regt and Parachute Regt, Major. *Heir: s* Peter Frank Robinson, *b* 23 June 1949. *Address:* Charlotte Road, Barnes, SW13. *Clubs:* Lansdowne; Western Province Sports (Cape).

ROBINSON, Maj.-Gen. William Arthur, CB 1964; OBE 1944; MA; MD; retired; *b* 2 March 1908; *s* of late Sir William Robinson, DL, JP; *m* 1934, Sheela, *d* of J. R. Yarr, Newbury, Berks; two *s*. *Educ:* Wesley College and Trinity College, Dublin. MA, MD, 1934. MRCGP 1961. Commissioned RAMC, 1931; served in Egypt and Sudan, 1932-37; Instructor and MO Army Gas School, 1938-41; Adviser in Chemical Warfare, 1941-43; Comd 200 Fd Ambulance (Egypt, Sicily and NW Europe), 1943-44; ADMS: 3 (Brit.) Inf. Div., NW Europe, 1945-46; Lt-Col Assistant Director-General Army Medical Dept (AMD1) War Office, 1946-49; jssc 1949; OC Hospital, E Africa, 1950-51; ADMS HQ Cyrenaica Dist (Colonel, ADMS 1 Bn Div., 1951-52, ADG (AMD1), War Office, 1952-54; DDMS Malta, 1954-57; Commandant, Depot and TE RAMC, 1958-60; Major-General, 1960; Deputy Director-General, Army Medical Services, 1960-61; DDMS Southern Command, 1961; DMS, Far East Land Forces, 1963-65; QHS, 1960-65. Col Comdt, RAMC, 1966–. *Recreations:* cross-country running (sen. colours); sailing, hockey, golf. *Address:* Lechlade, Horton Heath, Eastleigh, Hants.

ROBINSON, William Good; Deputy Secretary, Department of the Civil Service, Northern Ireland, 1978-80, retired; *b* 20 May 1919; *s* of William Robinson and Elizabeth Ann (*née* Good); *m* 1947, Wilhelmina Vaughan; two *d*. *Educ:* Clones High Sch.; Queen's Univ. of Belfast (BScEcon). Served War, RAF, 1941-46 (Flt Lieut, Navigator). Entered NI Civil Service, 1938; Min. of Labour and National Insurance, NI, 1946-63; Principal, Min. of Home Affairs, NI, 1963; Asst Sec., 1967; Sen. Asst Sec., NI Office, 1973. *Recreations:* do-it-yourself, reading history. *Address:* Stormochree, 47 Castlehill Road, Belfast BT4 3GN. *T:* Belfast 63646.

ROBINSON, Rt. Rev. William James; *b* 8 Sept. 1916; *s* of Thomas Albert Robinson and Harriet Mills; *m* 1946, Isobel Morton; one *s* three *d*. *Educ:* Bishop's Univ., Lennoxville, PQ. BA in Theology; DCL (*hc*) 1973. Deacon, 1939; Priest, 1940; Asst Curate in Trenton, 1939-41; Rector of: Tweed and Madoc, 1941-46, Tweed and N Addington, 1946-47; Napanee, 1948-53; St Thomas' Church, Belleville, 1953-55; St John's Church, Ottawa, 1955-62; Church of Ascension, Hamilton, 1962-67; St George's Church, Guelph, 1967-70. Canon of Christ Church Cathedral, Hamilton, 1964-68; Archdeacon of Trafalgar (Niagara Diocese), 1968-70; Bishop of Ottawa, 1970-81; retired. *Recreations:* woodworking and gardening. *Address:* 168 Inverness Crescent, Kingston, Ontario, K7M 6N7. *T:* (613) 549-7599.

ROBINSON, William Rhys Brunel; Under Secretary, Overseas Division, Department of Employment, since 1980; *b* 12 July 1930; *s* of late William Robinson and Elizabeth Myfanwy Robinson (*née* Owen). *Educ:* Chepstow Secondary Grammar Sch.; St Catherine's Soc., Oxford (MA,BLitt). Entered Min. of Labour, 1954; Asst Private Sec. to Minister, 1958-59; Principal, Min. of Labour, 1959; Asst Sec., 1966; London Sch. of Economics, 1972-73 (MSc Industrial Relations, 1973); Asst Sec., Trng Services Agency, 1973-75; Dep. Chief Exec., Employment Service Agency, 1975-77; Under-Sec. and Dir of Establishments, Dept of Employment, 1977-80. FSA 1978. *Publications:* articles in historical jls. *Recreation:* historical research. *Address:* 7 Shere Avenue, Cheam, Surrey SM2 7JU. *T:* 01-393 3019.

ROBLES, Marisa, (Mrs Christopher Hyde-Smith); harpist; Professor of Harp: Madrid Conservatoire, since 1958; Royal College of Music, since 1971; *b* 4 May 1937; *d* of Cristobal Robles and Maria Bonilla; *m* 1968, Christopher Hyde-Smith; two *s* one *d*. *Educ:* Madrid National Sch.; Madrid Conservatoire. Recitals in Europe, Africa and America; soloist with major internat. orchestras. Hon. Royal Madrid Conservatoire 1958; Hon. RCM 1973. *Recreations:* theatre, indoor plants, family life in general. *Address:* 38 Luttrell Avenue, Putney, SW15 6PE. *T:* 01-788 3753. *Club:* Anglo-Spanish.

ROBOROUGH, 2nd Baron, *cr* 1938, of Maristow; **Massey Henry Edgcumbe Lopes;** Bt, *cr* 1805; JP; Brevet Major Reserve of Officers Royal Scots Greys; Lord-Lieutenant and Custos Rotulorum of Devon, 1958-78; *b* 4 Oct. 1903; *o s* of 1st Baron and Lady Albertha Louisa Florence Edgcumbe (*d* 1941), *d* of 4th Earl of Mount Edgcumbe; *S* father 1938; *m* 1936, Helen, *o d* of late Colonel E. A. F. Dawson, Launde Abbey, Leicestershire; two *s* (and one *d* decd). *Educ:* Eton Coll.; Christ Church, Oxford (BA). Served in Royal Scots Greys, 1925-38; served again 1939-45 (wounded). ADC to Earl of Clarendon, when Governor of Union of South Africa, 1936-37. CA Devon, 1956-74; DL 1946; Vice-Lieutenant of Devon, 1951; Member of Duchy of

Cornwall Council, 1958-68; High Steward of Barnstaple. Chairman: Dartmoor National Park, 1965-74; SW Devon Div. Educn Cttee, 1954-74; Devon Outward Bound, 1960-75; President: SW Reg., YMCA, 1958-67; Devon British Legion, 1958-68; Devon Conservation Forum, 1972-78; President, Devon, 1958-78: Magistrates Cttee; Council of St John; CPRE; Trust for Nature Conservation; Boy Scouts Assoc.; Football Assoc.; Assoc. of Youth Clubs. Governor: Exeter Univ.; Seale-Hayne, Kelly, Plymouth and Exeter Colls. Hon. Col, Devon Army Cadet Force, 1967-78. Hon. LLD Exeter, 1969. KStJ. *Heir: s* Hon. Henry Massey Lopes [*b* 2 Feb. 1940; *m* 1968, Robyn, *e d* of John Bromwich, Melbourne, Aust.; two *s* two *d*]. *Address:* Bickham Barton, Roborough, Plymouth, Devon. *T:* Yelverton 2478. *Club:* Cavalry and Guards.

ROBSON, family name of **Baroness Robson of Kiddington.**

ROBSON OF KIDDINGTON, Baroness *cr* 1974 (Life Peer), of Kiddington; **Inga-Stina Robson,** JP; Chairman, South-West Thames Regional Health Authority, 1974-82; *b* 20 Aug. 1919; *d* of Erik R. Arvidsson and Lilly A. Arvidsson (*née* Danielson); *m* 1940, Sir Lawrence W. Robson (*d* 1982); one *s* two *d*. *Educ:* Stockholm, Sweden. Swedish Foreign Office, 1939-40; Min. of Information, 1942-43. Contested (L) Eye Div., 1955 and 1959, Gloucester City, 1964 and 1966. President: Women's Liberal Fedn, 1968-69 and 1969-70; Liberal Party Org., 1970-71; Chm., Liberal Party Environment Panel, 1971-77. Chairman: Bd of Governors, Queen Charlotte's and Chelsea Hosps, 1970–; Midwife Teachers Training Coll.; Member: Cttee of Management, Inst. of Obst. and Gynaecology; Bd of Governors, University Coll. Hosp., 1966-74; Council, Surrey Univ., 1974. JP Oxfordshire, 1955. *Recreations:* sailing, skiing. *Address:* Kiddington Hall, Woodstock, Oxon.

ROBSON, Brian Ewart; Deputy Under-Secretary of State (Army), Ministry of Defence, since 1982; *b* 25 July 1926; 2nd *s* of late Walter Ewart Robson and Lily Robson; *m* 1962, Cynthia Margaret, *o d* of late William James Scott, Recife, Brazil; two *d*. *Educ:* Steyning Grammar Sch.; Varndean Sch., Brighton; The Queen's Coll., Oxford. Joined Army, 1944; commissioned Royal Sussex Regt, 1945; attached to Indian Army (Kumaon Regt), 1945-47; demobilised, 1948. Admin. Class, Home Civil Service, 1950; Asst Private Sec. to Sec. of State for Air, 1953-55; Principal, 1955; Asst Sec., 1965; Imperial Defence Coll., 1970; Ecole Nationale d'Administration, Paris, 1975; Asst Under-Sec. of State, MoD, 1976-82. *Publications:* Swords of the British Army, 1975; numerous articles in learned jls on weapons and military history. *Recreations:* military history, cricket, travel. *Address:* 17 Woodlands, Hove, Sussex BN3 6TJ. *T:* Hove 505803. *Club:* Oxford Union.

ROBSON, David Ernest Henry, QC 1980; a Recorder of the Crown Court (NE Circuit), since 1979; *b* 1 March 1940; *s* of late Joseph Robson and of Caroline Robson. *Educ:* Robert Richardson Grammar Sch., Ryhope; Christ Church, Oxford (MA). Called to the Bar, Inner Temple, 1965; NE Circuit, 1965–. Profumo Prize, Inner Temple, 1963. *Recreations:* acting, Italy. *Address:* Whitton Grange, Whitton, Rothbury, Northumberland NE65 7RL. *T:* Rothbury 20929. *Club:* County (Durham).

ROBSON, His Honour Denis Hicks, QC 1955; a County Court Judge, later a Circuit Judge, 1957-72; *b* 7 Jan. 1904; *s* of late Robert Robson, ISO, and Helen Julia, *d* of late James J. Hicks, KCSG; *m* 1931, Mary Grace (*d* 1947), *e d* of late Sir William Orpen, KBE; one *s* one *d*; *m* 1960, Hon. Elizabeth (*widow* of John Cockburn Millar), *d* of late Lord Atkin, PC. *Educ:* Douai School; Trinity Hall, Cambridge. Called to the Bar, Inner Temple, 1927; North Eastern Circuit. War of 1939-45, commissioned in RASC, 1940; Military Department of Judge Advocate General's Office, 1942-45; Major, 1944; Recorder of Doncaster, 1950-53; Recorder of Middlesbrough, 1953-57; Chm., Northamptonshire QS, 1970-71, Vice-Chm., 1960-70.

ROBSON, Donald; Director, Guinness Mahon & Co. Ltd (Chairman, 1976-78); *b* 29 Oct. 1910; *s* of Herbert William and Ida Robson; *m* 1956, Doreen Elizabeth Buzzel; two *s*. *Educ:* Malton Grammar Sch. BCom; FIB. Westminster Bank Ltd, 1927-67 (to Jt Gen. Manager, 1960); Internat. Commercial Bank Ltd, Managing Dir, 1967-76. *Recreations:* French, reading. *Address:* 32 St Mary at Hill, EC3R 8DH. *T:* 01-623 9333.

ROBSON, Dame Flora, DBE 1960; *b* South Shields, 28 March 1902; *d* of David Mather Robson and Eliza McKenzie. Royal Academy of Dramatic Art (Bronze medal). Hon. DLitt: Oxon, 1974, Durham, Wales; Hon. DLit London, 1971; Hon. Fellow: St Anne's Coll., Oxford, 1975; Sunderland Polytechnic, 1975; Order of Finland's White Rose and Finland's Lion. First appearance on stage, 1921; in All God's Chillun, 1933; Old Vic Season, 1934; Touchwood and Mary Read, Dragoon and Pirate; Close Quarters, 1935; Mary Tudor, 1936; Lady Brooke in Autumn, St Martin's Theatre; Thérèse Raquin in Guilty, Lyric Theatre, Hammersmith, 1944; Man about the House, Piccadilly; Message from Margaret, Duchess; Lady Macbeth, New York, 1948; Captain Brassbound's Conversion (Shaw), Lyric Hammersmith, 1948; Alicia Christie in Black Chiffon, Westminster, 1949; Paulina in The Winter's Tale, Phœnix, 1951; Miss Giddens in The Innocents, Her Majesty's, 1952; Sister Agatha in The Return, Duchess, 1953; Rachel in No Escape; Sarah in A Kind of Folly, Duchess, 1955; Mrs Smith in Suspect, Royal Court, 1955; Janet Holt in The House by the Lake, Duke of York's, 1956-58; Mrs Alving in Ghosts, Old Vic, 1958; Miss Tina in The Aspern Papers, Queen's, 1959; and tour, S Africa, 1960; Grace Rouarte in Time and Yellow Roses, St Martin's, 1961; Miss Moffat in The Corn is Green, in S Africa, S Rhodesia and at Flora

Robson Playhouse, Newcastle upon Tyne, 1962; tour, Close Quarters, 1963; Mrs Borkman in John Gabriel Borkman, Duchess, 1962; The Trojan Women, Edinburgh Festival, 1966; tour, Brother and Sister; Miss Prism in The Importance of Being Earnest, Haymarket, 1968; Ring Round The Moon, 1969; The Old Ladies, 1969. *Films:* Empress Elizabeth of Russia in Catherine the Great, 1933; Queen Elizabeth in Fire Over England; Mrs Blair in Farewell Again; Ellen Dean in Wuthering Heights; Mary Rider in Poison Pen; Ftata Teeta in Cæsar and Cleopatra; Sister Philippa in Black Narcissus; Nell Dawson, MP, in Frieda; Countess Von Platen in Saraband for Dead Lovers; Mary Rackham in Tall Headlines; Melita in Malta Story; The Nurse in Romeo and Juliet; Donna McKenzie in High Tide at Noon; Mrs Haggard in The Gipsy and the Gentleman; Olivia in Innocent Sinners; The Empress of China in 55 Days at Peking; Miss Gilchrist in Murder at the Gallop; Young Cassidy; Guns at Batasi; Those Magnificent Men in their Flying Machines; Seven Women; The Shuttered Room; Cry in the Wind; Eye of the Devil; Fragment of Fear; The Cellar; The Beloved; Alice in Wonderland; Dominique; Clash of the Titans. BBC TV series: Heidi, 1974; A Legacy, 1975; Mr Lollipop, 1976; The Shrimp and the Anemone, 1977; Eustace and Hilda, 1979; TV films: The Oresteia of Aeschylus, 1978; A Man called Intrepid, 1978, Les Misérables, 1978; Tale of Two Cities, 1980. *Publication:* (contrib.) My Drama School, 1977. *Relevant Publications:* Flora Robson by Janet Dunbar, 1960; Flora by Kenneth H. Barrow, 1981. *Address:* 7 Wykeham Terrace, Brighton, E Sussex BN1 3FF.

ROBSON, Vice-Adm. Sir Geoffrey; *see* Robson, Vice-Adm. Sir W. G. A.

ROBSON, Prof. Sir (James) Gordon, Kt 1982; CBE 1977; MB, ChB; FRCS; FFARCS; Professor of Anaesthetics, University of London, Royal Postgraduate Medical School, since 1964; Hon. Consultant, Hammersmith Hospital, since 1964; Consultant Adviser in Anaesthetics to Department of Health and Social Security, since 1975; Master, Hunterian Institute, Royal College of Surgeons, since 1982; *b* Stirling, Scot., 18 March 1921; *o s* of late James Cyril Robson and Freda Elizabeth Howard; *m* 1945, Dr Martha Graham Kennedy (*d* 1975); one *s. Educ:* High Sch. of Stirling; Univ. of Glasgow. FRCS 1977. RAMC, 1945-48 (Captain). Sen. Registrar in Anaesthesia, Western Inf., Glasgow, 1948-52; First Asst, Dept of Anaesthetics, Univ. of Durham, 1952-54; Cons. Anaesth., Royal Inf., Edinburgh, 1954-56; Wellcome Res. Prof. of Anaesth., McGill Univ., Montreal, 1956-64. Mem. Bd of Faculty of Anaesthetists, RCS, 1968- (Dean of Faculty, 1973-76); Mem. Council, RCS, 1973-81 (a Vice-Pres., 1977-79); Chm., Jt Cttee on Higher Trng of Anaesthetists, 1973-76; Member: AHA, Ealing, Hammersmith and Hounslow, 1974-77 (NW Met. RHB, 1971-74); Chief Scientists' Res. Cttee and Panel on Med. Res., DHSS, 1973-77; Neurosciences Bd, MRC, 1974-77; Clin. Res. Bd, MRC (Chm. Grants Cttee II), 1969-71; Mem. Council, RPMS (Vice-Chm. Academic Bd, 1973-76; Chm. 1976-80); Mem., Rock Carling Fellowship Panel, 1976-78; Vice-Chm., Jt Consultants' Cttee, 1974-79; Special Trustee, Hammersmith Hosp., 1974-77; Hon. Sec., Conf. of Med. Royal Colls and Their Faculties, UK, 1976-82; Examiner, Primary FFARCS, 1967-73; Member: Editorial Bd (and Cons. Editor), British Jl of Anaesthesia, 1965-; Edit. Bd, Psychopharmacology; Council, Assoc. of Anaesths of GB and Ire., 1973-; Physiol. Soc., 1966-; RSocMed; Cttee of AA, 1979-; Council, RCS, 1982-; Hon. Mem., Assoc. of Univ. Anaesths (USA), 1969-; Sir Arthur Sims Commonwealth Trav. Prof., 1968; Visiting Prof. to many med. centres, USA and Canada; Wesley Bourne Lectr, McGill Univ., 1965. Joseph Clover Medal and Dudley Buxton Prize, Fac. of Anaesths, RCS, 1972; Hon. FFARACS 1968; Hon. FFARCSI 1980; Hon. FDSRCS, 1979. *Publications:* on neurophysiol., anaesthesia, pain and central nervous system mechanisms of respiration, in learned jls. *Recreations:* practice of anaesthesia; golf, wet fly fishing. *Address:* Department of Anaesthetics, Royal Postgraduate Medical School, Ducane Road, W12 0HS. *T:* 01-743 2030 (ext. 264). *Clubs:* Savage; Council of Royal College of Surgeons, Denham Golf.

ROBSON, James Jeavons, CBE 1972; FICE; MIStructE; FIArb; Secretary for the Environment, Hong Kong, 1973-76; Member of Legislative Council, Hong Kong, 1969-76; in private practice, since 1976; *b* 4 July 1918; *m* 1945, Avis Metcalfe; one *s. Educ:* Constantine Coll., Middlesbrough. MICE 1948, FICE 1958; MIStructE 1946; FIArb 1969. War Service, RM, 1942-46 (Captain). Engrg Trng, Messrs Dorman Long & Co. and ICI, 1936-41; joined Colonial Engrg Service and posted to PWD, Hong Kong, 1946; Dir of Public Works, 1969. Mem. Council, ICE, 1967; Telford Premium (for paper, Overall Planning in Hong Kong), ICE, 1971. *Publications:* articles on civil engineering in Jl ICE. *Recreations:* golf, racing, gardening. *Address:* Labéjan, 32300 Mirande, France. *Clubs:* Oriental; Hong Kong, Royal Hong Kong Jockey, Royal Hong Kong Golf.

ROBSON, John Adam; HM Diplomatic Service; Ambassador to Colombia, since 1982; *b* 16 April 1930; *yr s* of Air Vice-Marshal Adam Henry Robson, CB, OBE, MC; *m* 1958, Maureen Molly, *er d* of E. H. S. Bullen, Edgware; three *d. Educ:* Charterhouse; Gonville and Caius Coll., Cambridge (Major Scholar). BA 1952, MA 1955, PhD 1958. Fellow, Gonville and Caius Coll., 1954-58; Asst Lectr, University Coll. London, 1958-60. HM Foreign Service (later Diplomatic Service), 1961; Second Sec., British Embassy, Bonn, 1962-64; Second, later First, Secretary, Lima, 1964-66; First Sec., British High Commn, Madras, 1966-69; Asst Head, Latin American Dept, FCO, 1969-73; Head of Chancery, Lusaka, 1973-74; RCDS, 1975; Counsellor, Oslo, 1976-78; Head of E African Dept, FCO, and Comr for British Indian Ocean Territory, 1979-82. *Publications:* Wyclif and the Oxford Schools, 1961; articles in

historical jls. *Address:* c/o Foreign and Commonwealth Office, Whitehall, SW1.

ROBSON, Lawrence Fendick; Member, Electricity Council, 1972-76; *b* 23 Jan. 1916; *s* of (William) Bertram Robson and Annie (*née* Fendick); *m* 1945, Lorna Winifred Jagger, Shafton, Yorks; two *s* one *d. Educ:* Rotherham Grammar Sch.; Clare Coll., Cambridge (BA). FIEE. North Eastern Electric Supply Co. Ltd, 1937; Royal Corps of Signals, 1939-45; various positions with NE and London Electricity Bds, 1948-65; Commercial Adviser, Electricity Council, 1965-72. *Recreations:* music, open air. *Address:* Millers Hill, Priestman's Lane, Thornton Dale, N Yorks.

ROBSON, Nigel John; Chairman, Grindlays Bank plc, since 1977 (Director, since 1969; Deputy Chairman, 1975-76); Member, London Committee, Ottoman Bank, since 1959; *b* 25 Dec. 1926; *s* of late Col the Hon. Harold Burge Robson, TD, DL, JP, Pinewood Hill, Wormley, Surrey, and Iris Robson (*née* Abel Smith); *m* 1957, Anne Gladstone, *yr d* of late Stephen Deiniol Gladstone and late Clair Gladstone; three *s. Educ:* Eton. Grenadier Guards, 1945-48. Joined Arbuthnot Latham & Co Ltd, Merchant Bankers, 1949, a Director, 1953, Chm., 1969-75; Dir, Arbuthnot Latham Holdings Ltd, 1969-81. *Recreations:* tennis, walking, music. *Address:* Pinewood Hill, Wormley, Godalming, Surrey. *Clubs:* Brooks's; MCC.
See also W. M. Robson.

ROBSON, Sir Thomas (Buston), Kt 1954; MBE 1919; FCA; Partner in Price Waterhouse & Co., Chartered Accountants, 1934-66; Chairman, Renold Ltd, 1967-72; *b* Newcastle upon Tyne, 4 Jan. 1896; *s* of late Thomas Robson, Langholm, Dumfriesshire, and Newcastle upon Tyne; *m* 1936, Roberta Cecilia Helen (*d* 1980), *d* of late Rev. Archibald Fleming, DD, St Columba's Church of Scotland, Pont St, SW1; two *d. Educ:* Rutherford College, Newcastle upon Tyne; Armstrong Collge, University of Durham. BA Hons. Modern History, 1920; MA 1923. Served European War, 1914-18, with British Salonika Force in Macedonia; Captain RGA; MBE, despatches 1919; articled with Sisson & Allden, Chartered Accountants, Newcastle upon Tyne, 1920; W. B. Peat gold medal in final examination of Inst. Chartered Accountants in England and Wales, 1922; joined staff of Price Waterhouse & Co., London, 1923; ACA, 1923, FCA, 1939; Mem. Council of Inst., 1941-66 (Vice-Pres. 1951-52; Pres., 1952-53); rep. Inst. at overseas mtgs of accountants; FCA (Ont.); CA (Rhodesia). Member: Committee on Amendment of Census of Production Act, Bd of Trade, 1945; Central Valuation Bd for Coal Industry, 1947; Accountancy Advisory Cttee on Companies Act, Bd of Trade, 1948-68 (Chm. 1955-68); Cttee of Inquiry into London Transport Exec., Min. of Transport and Civil Aviation, 1953; Chm. Cttees of Inquiry into Coal Distribution Costs, Min. of Fuel and Power, 1956 and Min. of Commerce, N Ireland, 1956; Mem. Advisory Cttee on Replacement of the "Queen" ships, Min. of Transport and Civil Aviation, 1959; Chm. Economic Development Cttee for Paper and Board Industry under National Economic Development Council, 1964-67. Vice-Pres. Union Européenne des Experts Comptables, Economiques et Financiers, 1963-64; Mem. Transport Tribunal, 1963-69. *Publications:* Garnsey's Holding Companies and their Published Accounts, 3rd edn, 1936; The Construction of Consolidated Accounts, 1936; Consolidated and other Group Accounts, 1st edn, 1946, 4th edn, 1969; numerous papers and addresses on professional subjects. *Recreations:* walking and reading; for many years an active worker in Boy Scout movement (Vice-Pres., Gr London Central Scout Council). *Address:* 23 Brompton Square, SW3 2AD. *T:* 01-589 6553. *Club:* Athenæum.

ROBSON, Thomas Snowdon, OBE 1970 (MBE 1964); CEng, MIEE; Director of Engineering, Independent Broadcasting Authority, since 1978; *b* 6 Aug. 1922; *s* of Thomas Henry Robson and Annie Jessie (*née* Snowdon); *m* 1951, Ruth Bramley; one *s* one *d. Educ:* Portsmouth Grammar Sch. BBC, 1941-42; RAF Techn. Br., 1942-46; EMI Research Labs, 1947-57; ITA: Engr in Charge, Black Hill, 1957-58; Sen. Engr, Planning and Construction, 1958-67; Head of Station Design and Construction, 1967-69; Asst Dir of Engrg, 1969-73; IBA, Dep. Dir of Engrg, 1973-77. *Recreations:* golf, home computing. *Address:* 3 Sleepers Hill Gardens, Winchester, Hants SO22 4NT. *T:* Winchester 68540.

ROBSON, Vice-Adm. Sir (William) Geoffrey (Arthur), KBE 1956; CB 1953; DSO 1940 (Bar 1941); DSC 1941; Lieutenant-Governor and Commander-in-Chief of Guernsey, 1958-64; *b* 10 March 1902; *s* of Major John Robson; *m* 1st, 1925, Sylvia Margaret Forrester (*d* 1968); one *s*; 2nd, 1969, Elizabeth Kathleen, *widow* of Lt-Col V. H. Holt. *Educ:* RN Colleges, Osborne and Dartmouth. Midshipman, HMS Malaya, 1918; served in Destroyers, 1922-37. Commanded Rowena, 1934; Wren, 1935-36; RN Staff Course, 1937; RAF Staff Course, 1938. Served War of 1939-45 (despatches thrice, DSO and Bar, DSC): Comd HMS Kandahar, 1939-41; Combined Operations, 1942-43; Commanded the 26th Destroyer Flotilla, 1944, in HMS Hardy; Captain of Coastal Forces (Nore), 1945; HMS Superb in command, 1945-47; Comd HMS Ganges, 1948-50; President of Admiralty Interview Board, 1950-51; Flag Officer (Flotillas), Home Fleet, 1951-53; Flag Officer, Scotland, 1952-56; Commander-in-Chief, South Atlantic, 1956-58; retd, 1958. Commander of the Order of St Olav (Norway). *Recreations:* shooting, fishing. *Address:* Amat, Ardgay, Ross-shire; Le Paradou, Forest, Guernsey. *Club:* Army and Navy.

ROBSON, William Michael; Deputy Chairman: The Standard Bank Ltd, 1965-May 1983 (Director, 1960-83); The Chartered Bank, 1974-May 1983;

Standard and Chartered Banking Group Ltd, 1974–May 1983 (Director, 1970–83); Director, Anton Underwriting Agencies Ltd, since 1977; Member of Lloyd's, since 1938; *b* 31 Dec. 1912; *e s* of late Col the Hon. Harold Burge Robson, TD, DL, JP, Pinewood Hill, Witley, Surrey and late Ysolt Robson (*née* Leroy-Lewis); *m* 1st, 1939, Audrey Isobel Wales (*d* 1964), *d* of late Maj. William Dick, Low Gosforth Hall, Northumberland; two *s* one *d* ; 2nd, 1965, Frances Mary Wyville, *d* of late James Anderson Ramage Dawson, Balado House, Kinross, and *widow* of Andrew Alexander Nigel Buchanan (he *d* 1960). *Educ:* Eton; New College, Oxford. Served War of 1939-45: with Grenadier Guards (Maj. 1944), England and Europe BAOR. A Vice-Chm., Victoria League for Commonwealth Friendship, 1962-65. Director: Booker McConnell Ltd, 1955-78 (Chm., Booker Pensions, 1957-78); United Rum Merchants Ltd, 1965-78; British South Africa Co., 1961-66 (Vice-Chm., Jt East & Central African Bd, 1956-63); Antony Gibbs & Sons (Insurance) Ltd, 1946-48, 1973-76; Antony Gibbs (Insurance Holdings), 1976-80; Antony Gibbs, Sage Ltd, 1976-80; Chm., Standard Bank Finance & Develt Corp. Ltd, 1966-73; Mem., BNEC, Africa, 1965-71 (Dep. Chm., 1970-71). High Sheriff of Kent, 1970. Liveryman, Vintners Co., 1953. Mem. Council of The Shrievalty Assoc., 1971-76. *Address:* 28 Smith Terrace, Chelsea, SW3. *T:* 01-352 2177; Hales Place, Tenterden, Kent. *T:* Tenterden 2932. *Clubs:* Brooks's, MCC, Overseas Bankers'.

See also N. J. Robson.

ROCH, John Ormond, QC 1976; a Recorder of the Crown Court since 1975; *b* 19 April 1934; *s* of Frederick Ormond Roch and Vera Elizabeth (*née* Chamberlain); *m* 1967, Anne Elizabeth Greany; three *d.* *Educ:* Wrekin Coll.; Clare Coll., Cambridge (BA, LLB). Called to Bar, Gray's Inn, 1961. *Recreations:* sailing, music. *Address:* 82 Heath Park Avenue, Cardiff CF4 3RJ. *T:* Cardiff 754031. *Clubs:* Pembrokeshire Yacht, Dale Yacht (Cardiff).

ROCH, Muriel Elizabeth Sutcliffe, BA; Headmistress, School of S Mary and S Anne, Abbots Bromley, Staffs, 1953-77; *b* 7 Sept. 1916; *d* of late Rev. Sydney John Roch, MA Cantab, Pembroke and Manchester. *Educ:* Manchester High Sch.; Bedford Coll., London; Hughes Hall, Cambridge. Teaching appointments at: Devonport High School, 1939-41; Lady Manners, Bakewell, 1941-44; Howells School, Denbigh, 1944-47; Talbot Heath, Bournemouth, 1947-53. *Recreations:* music, travel. *Address:* Northdown Cottage, Lamphey, Dyfed. *T:* Lamphey 2577.

ROCHDALE, 1st Viscount *cr* 1960; **2nd Baron 1913; John Durival Kemp,** OBE 1945; TD; DL; Deputy Chairman, Williams & Glyn's Bank Ltd, 1973-77 (Director since 1970); Director, National and Commercial Banking Group Ltd, 1971-77; President, North West Industrial Development Association; *b* 5 June 1906; *s* of 1st Baron and Lady Beatrice Egerton, 3rd *d* of 3rd Earl of Ellesmere; *S* father, 1945; *m* 1931, Elinor Dorothea Pease (CBE 1964; JP); one *s* (one *d* decd). *Educ:* Eton; Trin. Coll., Cambridge. Hons degree Nat. Science Tripos. Served War of 1939-45 (despatches); attached USA forces in Pacific with rank of Col, 1944; Temp. Brig., 1945. Hon. Col 251 (Westmorland and Cumberland Yeomanry) Field Regiment, RA, TA, late 851 (W&CY) Field Bty, RA, 1959-67. Joined Kelsall & Kemp Ltd, 1928, Chm., 1952-71; Chm., Harland & Wolff, 1971-75; Dep. Chm., West Riding Worsted & Woollen Mills, 1969-72; Director: Consett Iron Co. Ltd, 1957-67; Williams Deacon's Bank Ltd, 1960-70. President National Union of Manufacturers, 1953-56; Member: Dollar Exports Council, 1953-61; Western Hemisphere Exports Council, 1961-64; a Gov. of the BBC 1954-59; Pres., British Legion, NW Area, 1955-61; Mem. Central Transport Consultative Cttee for GB, 1953-57; Chairman: Docks and Harbours Committee of Inquiry, 1961; Cotton Board, 1957-62; National Ports Council, 1963-67; Cttee of Inquiry into Shipping, 1967-70. Mem., Textile Inst.; MInstT. Upper Bailiff, Weavers' Co., 1949-50, 1956-57. DL Cumberland, 1948. *Heir: s* Hon. St John Durival Kemp [*b* 15 Jan. 1938; *m* 1st, 1960, Serena Jane Clark-Hall (marr. diss. 1974); two *s* two *d* ; 2nd, 1976, Elizabeth Anderton]. *Address:* Lingholm, Keswick, Cumbria. *T:* Keswick 72003. *Club:* Lansdowne.

See also Sir John D. Barlow, Duke of Sutherland.

ROCHDALE, Archdeacon of; *see* Bonser, Ven. D.

ROCHE, family name of Baron Fermoy.

ROCHE, Sir David (O'Grady), 5th Bt *cr* 1838; FCA; *b* 21 Sept. 1947; *s* of Sir Standish O'Grady Roche, 4th Bt, DSO, and of Evelyn Laura, *d* of Major William Andon; *S* father, 1977; *m* 1971, Hon. (Helen) Alexandra Briscoe Frewen, *d* of 3rd Viscount Selby; one *s* one *d* (and one *s* decd). *Educ:* Wellington Coll., Berks; Trinity Coll., Dublin. *Heir: s* David Alexander O'Grady Roche, *b* 28 Jan. 1976. *Address:* Bridge House, Starbotton, Skipton, N Yorks; 36 Coniger Road, SW6. *T:* 01-736 0382. *Clubs:* Buck's; Kildare Street and University (Dublin); Royal Yacht Squadron.

ROCHE, Frederick Lloyd; Deputy Chairman and Managing Director, Conran Roche, since 1981; *b* 11 March 1931; *s* of John Francis Roche and Margaret Roche. *Educ:* Regent Street Polytechnic. DipArch, ARIBA. Architect (Schools), City of Coventry, 1958-62; Principal Develt Architect, Midlands Housing Consortium, 1962-64; Chief Architect and Planning Officer, Runcorn Develt Corp., 1964-70; Gen. Manager, Milton Keynes Develt Corp., 1970-80. Member: Environmental Bd, 1976-79; Council, RIBA, 1977. *Publications:* numerous technical articles. *Address:* Conran Roche, Norfolk House, 435 Silbury Boulevard, Central Milton Keynes MK9 3HB. *T:* Milton Keynes 663330.

ROCHE, James Michael; Director: General Motors Corporation; Pepsico Inc.; Chicago Board of Trade; New York Stock Exchange; *b* 16 Dec. 1906; *s* of Thomas E. and Gertrude Agnes (Buel) Roche; *m* 1929, Louise McMillan; two *s* one *d.* *Educ:* LaSalle Univ., Chicago. Statistician, Cadillac Motor Car Div., Chicago Sales and Service Br., 1927; Asst to Chicago Br. Man., Cadillac, 1928; Asst Regional Business Man., NY, Cadillac, 1931; Asst Man., Cadillac Business Management Dept, Detroit, 1933; Man., Nat. Business Management, Cadillac, 1935; Dir of Personnel, Cadillac, 1943; Dir of Personnel and Public Relations, Cadillac, 1949; Gen. Sales Man., Cadillac, 1950; Gen. Man. of Cadillac, 1957; General Motors Corporation: Vice-Pres., 1957; Vice-Pres., Distribution Staff, 1960; Exec. Vice-Pres., 1962; Pres. and Chief Operating Off., 1965; Chm. and Chief Exec. Officer, 1967-71. Hon. Dr of Laws: John Carrol Univ., Ohio, 1963; Fordham Univ., NY, 1966; Michigan State Univ., 1968; Eastern Michigan Univ., 1969; Hon. Dr of Science, Judson Coll., Ill, 1965; Hon. Dr of Commercial Science Niagara Univ., 1972. Kt of Malta (Amer. Chapter), 1951. *Recreations:* music, reading, fishing. *Address:* 425 Dunston Road, Bloomfield Hills, Michigan 48013, USA. *Clubs:* Detroit, Economic (Detroit); Links, University, Economic (NY); Detroit Athletic, Orchard Lake Country, Bloomfield Hills Country.

ROCHE, Hon. Thomas Gabriel, QC 1955; Recorder of the City of Worcester, 1959-71; *b* 1909; *yr s* of late Baron Roche, PC. *Educ:* Rugby; Wadham Coll., Oxford. Called to the Bar, Inner Temple, 1932. Served War of 1939-45 (Lt-Col 1944, despatches). Church Commissioner, 1961-65; Member, Monopolies Commission, 1966-69. *Address:* Chadlington, Oxford. *Club:* United Oxford & Cambridge University.

ROCHESTER, 2nd Baron, of the 4th creation, *cr* 1931, of Rochester in the County of Kent; **Foster Charles Lowry Lamb,** DL; *b* 7 June 1916; *s* of 1st Baron Rochester, CMG, and Rosa Dorothea, *y d* of late W. J. Hurst, JP, Drumaness, County Down; *S* father 1955; *m* 1942, Mary Carlisle, *yr d* of T. B. Wheeler, CBE; two *s* one *d* (and one *d* decd). *Educ:* Mill Hill; Jesus College, Cambridge. MA. Served War of 1939-45: Captain 23rd Hussars; France, 1944. Joined ICI Ltd, 1946: Labour Manager, Alkali Div., 1955-63; Personnel Manager, Mond Div., 1964-72. Pro-Chancellor, Univ. of Keele, 1976-. Chairman: Cheshire Scout Assoc., 1974-81; Governors of Chester Coll., 1974-; South and Mid-Cheshire Dist Manpower Cttee, 1980-. DL Cheshire, 1979. *Heir: s* Hon. David Charles Lamb [*b* 8 Sept. 1944; *m* 1969, Jacqueline Stamp; two *s.* *Educ:* Shrewsbury Sch.; Univ. of Sussex]. *Address:* The Hollies, Hartford, Northwich, Cheshire. *T:* Northwich 74733. *Clubs:* Reform, MCC.

See also Hon. K. H. L. Lamb.

ROCHESTER, Bishop of, since 1961; **Rt. Rev. Richard David Say,** DD (Lambeth) 1961; High Almoner to HM the Queen, since 1970; *b* 4 Oct. 1914; *s* of Commander Richard Say, OBE, RNVR, and Kathleen Mary (*née* Wildy); *m* 1943, Irene Frances (OBE 1980, JP 1960), *e d* of Seaburne and Frances Rayner, Exeter; one *s* two *d* (and one *s* decd). *Educ:* University Coll. Sch.; Christ's College, Cambridge (MA); Ridley Hall, Cambridge. Ordained deacon, 1939; priest, 1940. Curate of Croydon Parish Church, 1939-43; Curate of St Martin-in-the-Fields, London, 1943-50; Asst Sec. Church of England Youth Council, 1942-44; Gen. Sec., 1944-47; Gen. Sec. British Council of Churches, 1947-55; Church of England delegate to World Council of Churches, 1948, 1954 and 1961. Select Preacher, University of Cambridge, 1954 and University of Oxford, 1963; Rector of Bishop's Hatfield, 1955-61; Hon. Canon of St Albans, 1957-61. Domestic Chaplain to Marquess of Salisbury and Chaplain of Welfield Hospital, 1955-61; Hon. Chaplain of The Pilgrims, 1968-. Entered House of Lords, 1969. Chaplain and Sub-Prelate, Order of St John, 1961. Dep. Pro-Chancellor, Kent Univ., 1977; Governor, University Coll. Sch., 1980. Freeman of City of London, 1953. Hon. Mem., Smeatonian Soc., 1977. *Recreations:* walking, travel. *Address:* Bishopscourt, Rochester ME1 1TS. *T:* Medway 42721. *Club:* United Oxford & Cambridge University.

ROCHESTER, Dean of; *see* Arnold, Very Rev. J. R.

ROCHESTER, Archdeacon of; *see* Palmer, Ven. D. G.

ROCHESTER, Prof. George Dixon, FRS 1958; FInstP; Professor of Physics, University of Durham, 1955-73, now Professor Emeritus; *b* 4 Feb. 1908; *s* of Thomas and Ellen Rochester; *m* 1938, Idaline, *o d* of Rev. J. B. Bayliffe; one *s* one *d.* *Educ:* Wallsend Secondary Sch. and Technical Inst.; Universities of Durham, Stockholm and California. BSc, MSc, PhD (Dunelm). Earl Grey Memorial Scholar, Armstrong College, Durham University, 1926-29; Earl Grey Fellow, at Stockholm Univ., 1934-35; Commonwealth Fund Fellow at California Univ., 1935-37; Manchester University: Asst Lectr, 1937-46; Lectr, 1946-49; Sen. Lectr, 1949-53; Reader, 1953-55. Scientific Adviser in Civil Defence for NW Region, 1952-55. C. V. Boys Prizeman of the Physical Society of London, 1956; Symons Memorial Lecturer of the Royal Meteorological Soc., 1962. Member: Council CNAA, 1964-74; Council, British Assoc. for Advancement of Science, 1971-72; Council, Royal Soc., 1972-74; Chm., NE Branch, Inst. of Physics, 1972-74. Second Pro-Vice-Chancellor, Univ. of Durham, 1967-69, Pro-Vice-Chancellor, 1969-70. Methodist. Hon. DSc: Newcastle upon Tyne, 1973; CNAA, 1975; Hon. Fellow, Newcastle upon Tyne Polytechnic, 1977. *Publications:* (with J. G. Wilson) Cloud Chamber Photographs of the Cosmic Radiation, 1952; scientific papers on cosmic rays and spectroscopy. *Recreations:* gardening, TV, history of science. *Address:* 18 Dryburn Road, Durham DH1 5AJ. *T:* Durham 64796.

ROCHETA, Dr Manuel Farrajota; Military Order of Christ of Portugal; Ambassador for Portugal in Madrid, 1968–74, retired; *b* 6 Aug. 1906; *s* of Manuel and Rosa Rocheta; *m* 1933, Maria Luiza Belmarco Rocheta; one *d. Educ:* Lisbon University. Entered Diplomatic Service, 1931; Assistant Consul Hamburg, 1934; Consul Copenhagen, 1935–39; First Sec. and Chargé d'Affaires *ai*, Bucarest, 1943–45; First Sec. and Chargé d'Affaires *ai*, Dublin, 1945; First Secretary, Washington, 1946, Counsellor, 1947, Minister-Counsellor, 1950 (Chargé d'Affaires, 1 Nov. 1946–31 March 1947 and 11 Feb. 1950–6 June 1950); Asst Dir-Gen. of Political Dept, Foreign Affairs Ministry, Lisbon, 1951; Minister-Plen. and Dir-Gen. of Political Dept, Foreign Ministry, Lisbon, 1954; Minister in Bonn, 1956, Ambassador, 1956–58; Ambassador: to Rio de Janeiro, 1958–61; to the Court of St James's, 1961–68. Doctor in Law, Univ. of Bahia, Brazil. Knight Grand Cross of Royal Victorian Order, Gt Brit. (Hon. GCVO) 1955, and holds Grand Cross of several foreign orders. *Recreations:* walking and swimming. *Address:* c/o Ministry of Foreign Affairs, Lisbon, Portugal.

ROCHFORD, James Donald Henry; Admiralty Registrar of the Supreme Court, since 1973; Barrister-at-Law; *b* 8 July 1921; *e s* of Leonard Henry Rochford, DSC, DFC; *m* 1953, Elizabeth Mary Beverley Robinson, *d* of late Lt-Col B. B. Robinson, DSO; two *s* one *d. Educ:* Douai Sch., Woolhampton, Berks. Served War: Royal Navy and RNVR, 1940–47. Called to Bar, Inner Temple, 1951. *Recreation:* messing about in boats. *Address:* Studland, Stockcroft Road, Balcombe, West Sussex. *T:* Balcombe 321.

ROCHFORT, Sir Cecil Charles B.; *see* Boyd-Rochfort.

ROCKE, John Roy Mansfield; Vice-Chairman, J. Bibby & Sons, retired 1982; Director, Czarnikow Group; *b* 13 April 1918; *s* of late Frederick Gilbert Rocke and late Mary Susan Rocke; *m* 1948, Pauline Diane Berry; no *c. Educ:* Charterhouse; Trinity Coll., Cambridge (BA). War Service, Grenadier Guards, 1940–46 (Maj.). Orme & Eykyn (Stockbrokers), 1946–50; Booker McConnell Ltd, 1950–70, Dir, 1954, Vice-Chm., 1962–70. Mem., BNEC, and Chm., BNEC (Caribbean), 1965–68; Chm., Nat. Econ. Development Cttee for the Food Manufacturing Industry, 1967–71. *Address:* 22 Bruton Street, W1. *T:* 01-629 3393; Pendomer Manor, Pendomer, near Yeovil, Somerset. *Club:* Boodle's.

ROCKEFELLER, David; banker; *b* New York City, 12 June 1915; *s* of John Davison Rockefeller, Jr and Abby Greene (Aldrich) Rockefeller; *m* 1940, Margaret, *d* of Francis Sims McGrath, Mount Kisco, NY; two *s* four *d. Educ:* Lincoln School of Columbia University's Teachers College; Harvard Univ. (BS); London School of Economics; Univ. of Chicago (PhD). Sec. to Mayor Fiorello H. LaGuardia, 1940–41; Asst Regional Dir, US Office of Defense Health and Welfare Services, 1941. Served in US Army, N Africa and France, 1942–45 (Captain). Joined Chase National Bank, NYC, 1946; Asst Manager, Foreign Dept, 1946–47; Asst Cashier, 1947–48; Second Vice-Pres., 1948–49; Vice-Pres., 1949–51; Senior Vice-Pres., 1951–55; Exec. Vice-Pres., Chase Manhattan Bank (formed by merging Chase Nat. Bank and Bank of Manhattan Co.), 1955–57; Dir, 1955–81; Vice-Chm., 1957–61; Pres. and Chm., Exec. Cttee, 1961–69; Chm. of Bd, 1969–81 and Chief Exec. Officer, 1969–80; Chairman: Chase Internat. Investment Corp., 1961–81; Chase Internat. Adv. Cttee, 1980–. Chm., Rockefeller Brothers Fund Inc., 1981– (Vice-Chm., 1968–80); Trustee: Univ. of Chicago, 1947–62 (Life Trustee, 1966); Carnegie Endowment for Internat. Peace, 1947–60; Council of the Americas (Chm., 1965–70); Sleepy Hollow Restorations, 1981–; Chairman: Americas Soc.; Council on Foreign Relations; Economic Develt Council; NY Chamber of Commerce and Industry; NYC Partnership, 1979–; US Business Cttee on Jamaica, 1980–; N American Chm., Trilateral Commn; Rockefeller Center, Inc.; Mem. Exec. Cttee, Museum of Modern Art (Chm. 1962–72); Chm. Exec. Cttee, Rockefeller Univ. (Chm. 1950–75); Director: Downtown-Lower Manhattan Assoc., Inc. (Chm. 1958–75); Internat. Exec. Service Corps (Chm., 1964–68); NY Clearing House, 1971–78; Center for Inter-Amer. Relations (Chm. 1966–70); Overseas Develt Council; US-USSR Trade and Econ. Council, Inc.; Member: Harvard Coll. Bd of Overseers, 1954–60, 1962–68; Urban Develt Corp., NY State, Business Adv. Council, 1968–72; US Adv. Cttee on Reform of Internat. Monetary System, 1973–; Sen. Adv. Gp, Bilderberg Meetings; US Exec. Cttee, Dartmouth Conf.; American Friends of LSE; US Hon. Fellows, LSE; Municipal Union Financial Leaders. Hon. Mem., Commn on White House Fellows, 1964–65; Founding Mem., Business Cttee for the Arts. Director: Morningside Heights, 1947–70 (Pres., 1947–57, Chm., 1957–65); Internat. House, NY, 1940–63; Equitable Life Assce Soc. of US, 1960–65; B. F. Goodrich Co., 1956–64. Hon. Chm., Japan Soc. World Brotherhood Award, Jewish Theol Seminary, 1953; Gold Medal, Nat. Inst. Social Sciences, 1967; Medal of Honor for city planning, Amer. Inst. Architects, 1968; C. Walter Nichols Award, NY Univ., 1970; Reg. Planning Assoc. Award, 1971. Hon. LLD: Columbia Univ., 1954; Bowdoin Coll., 1958; Jewish Theol Seminary, 1958; Williams Coll., 1966; Wagner Coll., 1967; Harvard, 1969; Pace Coll., 1970; St John's Univ., 1971; Middlebury, 1974; Univ. of Liberia, 1979; Rockefeller Univ., 1980; Hon. DEng Colorado Sch. of Mines, 1974. Holds civic awards. Officer, Legion of Honour, France, 1955; Order of Merit of the Republic, Italy; Order of the Southern Cross, Brazil; Order of the White Elephant and Order of the Crown, Thailand; Order of the Cedar, Lebanon; Order of the Sun, Peru; Order of Humane African Redemption, Liberia; Order of the Crown, Belgium; National Order of Ivory

Coast. *Publications:* Unused Resources and Economic Waste, 1940; Creative Management in Banking, 1964. *Recreation:* sailing. *Address:* 30 Rockefeller Plaza, New York, NY 10112, USA. *Clubs:* Century, Harvard, River, Knickerbocker, Links, University, Recess (New York); New York Yacht.
See also L. S. Rockefeller.

ROCKEFELLER, James Stillman; Vice-President and Director: Indian Spring Land Co.; Indian Rock Corp.; Director, Cranston (RI) Print Works Co.; *b* New York, 8 June 1902; *s* of William Goodsell Rockefeller and Elsie (*née* Stillman); *m* 1925, Nancy Carnegie; two *s* two *d. Educ:* Yale University (BA). With Brown Bros & Co., NYC, 1924–30; joined National City Bank of New York (later First Nat. City Bank; now Citibank, NA), 1930; Asst Cashier, 1931; Asst Vice-Pres. 1933; Vice-Pres., 1940–48; Sen. Vice-Pres., 1948–52; Exec. Vice-Pres., 1952; Pres. and Director, 1952–59; Chairman, 1959–67. Rep. Greenwich (Conn.) Town Meeting, 1933–42. Served as Lieutenant-Colonel in US Army, 1942–46. Member Board of Overseers, Memorial Hospital for Cancer and Allied Diseases, NY; Trustee of Estate of William Rockefeller; Trustee American Museum of National History. Hon. Dir, NCR Corp. *Address:* Room 2900, 399 Park Avenue, New York, NY 10043, USA. *Clubs:* Links, Down Town Assoc., Union League, University (New York); Metropolitan (Washington, DC); Field (Greenwich, Conn).

ROCKEFELLER, Laurance Spelman, OBE (Hon.) 1971; conservationist and business executive; Director, Rockefeller Center Inc., 1936–78 (Chairman, 1953–56, 1958–66); *b* New York, 26 May 1910; *s* of John Davison Rockefeller, Jr, FRS and Abby Greene Aldrich; *m* 1934, Mary French; one *s* three *d. Educ:* Lincoln School of Teachers College; Princeton University (BA). War service, Lt-Comdr, USNR, 1942–45. Chairman: Citizens' Adv. Cttee on Environmental Quality, 1969–73 (Mem., 1973–79); Meml Sloan-Kettering Cancer Center, 1960–82 (Hon. Chm., 1982–); NY Zool Soc., 1970–75 (Hon. Chm., 1975–); Careel Bay Inc.; President: Amer. Conservation Assoc.; Jackson Hole Preserve, Inc.; Palisades Interstate Park Commn, 1970–77 (Chm. Emeritus, 1978–); Adv. Trustee, Rockefeller Bros Fund, 1982– (Chm., 1958–80; Vice-Chm., 1980–82); Charter Trustee, Princeton Univ.; Trustee: Alfred P. Sloan Foundn, 1950–82; Greenacre Foundn; Nat. Geog. Soc.; Nat. Park Foundn; Sleepy Hollow Restorations, 1975– (Chm., 1981–); Life Mem., Mass Inst. of Technology; Dir, Community Blood Council of Gtr NY; Mem., Nat. Cancer Adv. Bd, 1977–79; Chairman: Outdoor Recreation Resources Review Commn, 1958–65; Hudson River Valley Commn, 1956–66; 1965 White House Conf. on Nat. Beauty; Delegate UN Conf. on Human Environment, 1972. Holds numerous awards, medals and hon. degrees. Comdr, Royal Order of the Lion, Belgium, 1950; US Medal of Freedom, 1969. *Address:* Room 5600, 30 Rockefeller Plaza, New York, NY 10112, USA. *Clubs:* Boone and Crockett, River, Princeton, Downtown Association, Brook, New York Yacht, Links, Knickerbocker (New York City); Cosmos, Metropolitan (Washington, DC).
See also David Rockefeller.

ROCKHAMPTON, Bishop of, since 1981; **Rt. Rev. George Arthur Hearn;** *b* 17 Nov. 1935; *s* of Albert Frederick and Edith Maxham Hearn; *m* 1957, Adele Taylor; two *s* one *d. Educ:* Northcote High School; University High School; Latrobe Univ., Melbourne. ThL 1965, DipRE, ThSchol Aust. Coll. of Theology; MACE. Deacon 1964, priest 1965, Diocese of Gippsland; Curate of Traralgon, 1964–66; Vicar of Omeo, 1966–69; Rector of Wonthaggi, 1969–73; Rector of Kyabram, dio. Bendigo, 1973–77; Field Officer, Dept of Christian Education, Diocese of Melbourne, 1977–79; Dir, Gen. Bd of Religious Education, 1978–81. *Recreations:* gardening, reading, golf and music. *Address:* PO Box 116, Rockhampton, Queensland 4700, Australia. *T:* (079) 27 3188.

ROCKLEY, 3rd Baron *cr* 1934; **James Hugh Cecil;** Director: Kleinwort Benson Ltd, since 1970; Equity and Law Life Assurance Society Ltd, since 1980; *b* 5 April 1934; *s* of 2nd Baron Rockley, and Anne Margaret (*d* 1980), *d* of late Adm. Hon. Sir Herbert Meade-Featherstonhaugh, GCVO, CB, DSO; *S* father, 1976; *m* 1958, Lady Sarah Primrose Beatrix, *e d* of 7th Earl Cadogan, *qv* ; one *s* two *d. Educ:* Eton; New Coll., Oxford. Wood Gundy & Co. Ltd, 1957–62; Kleinwort Benson Ltd, 1963–. Trustee, Nat. Portrait Gall., 1981–. *Heir: s* Hon. Anthony Robert Cecil, *b* 29 July 1961. *Address:* Lytchett Heath, Poole, Dorset. *T:* Lytchett Minister 622228.

ROCKSAVAGE, Earl of; David George Philip Cholmondeley; *b* 27 June 1960; *s* and *heir* of 6th Marquess of Cholmondeley, *qv.*

RODD, family name of **Baron Rennell.**

RODDAN, Gilbert McMicking, CMG 1957; Deputy Agricultural Adviser, Department of Technical Co-operation, 1961 (to Secretary of State for Colonies, 1956); retired 1965; *b* 13 May 1906; *m* 1934, Olive Mary Wetherill; two *d. Educ:* Dumfries Academy; Glasgow and Oxford Universities; Imperial College of Tropical Agriculture, Trinidad. Colonial Service, 1930–56. *Address:* Wayland, Edinburgh Road, Peebles. *Club:* Royal Commonwealth Society.

RODDIE, Prof. Ian Campbell, TD 1967; FRCPI; Dunville Professor of Physiology, since 1964, and Pro-Vice-Chancellor, from Oct. 1983, Queen's University, Belfast; *b* 1 Dec. 1928; *s* of Rev. J. R. Wesley Roddie and Mary Hill Wilson; *m* 1958, Elizabeth Ann Gillon Honeyman (decd); one *s* three *d. Educ:* Methodist Coll., Belfast; Queen's Univ., Belfast. Malcolm Exhibnr,

1951, McQuitty Schol., 1953; BSc (1st cl. Hons Physiol.), MB BCh, BAO, MD (with gold medal), DSc; MRCPI; MRIA. Major RAMC (T&AVR); OC Med. Sub-unit, QUB OTC, retd 1968. Resident MO, Royal Victoria Hosp., Belfast, 1953-54; Queen's University, Belfast: Lectr in Physiology, 1954-60; Sen. Lectr, 1961-62; Reader, 1962-64; Dep. Dean, 1975-76, Dean, 1976-81, Faculty of Medicine. Consultant Physiologist: NI Hosps Authority, 1962-72; Eastern Health Bd, NI, 1972-. Harkness Commonwealth Fund Fellow, Washington Univ., 1960-61; Vis. Prof., Univ. of NSW, 1983-. External Examiner: Univs of Aberdeen, Baghdad, Birmingham, Bristol, Glasgow, Ireland, Jos, London, Sheffield, Southampton; RCS, RCSE, RCPGlas, RCSI. Chief Reg. Sci. Advr for Home Defence, NI, 1977-; Member: Home Defence Sci. Adv. Conf., 1977-; Eastern Area Health and Social Services Bd, NI, 1976-81; Physiol Systems Bd, MRC, 1974-76; Med. Adv. Cttee, Cttee of Vice-Chancellors and Principals, 1976-81; GMC, 1979-81; GDC, 1979-81. President: Biol Scis Sect., Royal Acad. of Medicine in Ireland, 1964-66; Ulster Biomed. Engrg Soc., 1979-; Mem. Council, Physiol Soc., 1960-69. Arris and Gale Lectr, RCS, 1962. Conway Bronze Medal, Royal Acad. of Medicine in Ireland, 1977. *Publications*: Physiology for Practitioners, 1971, 2nd edn 1975; Multiple Choice Questions in Human Physiology, 1971, 2nd edn 1977; The Physiology of Disease, 1975; papers on physiology and pharmacology of vascular, sudorific and lymphatic systems. *Recreations*: gardening, carpentry. *Address*: Seapark, Marino, Holywood, Co. Down BT18 0LH. *T*: Holywood 3212. *Club*: Royal Commonwealth Society.

RODEN, 9th Earl of, *cr* 1771; **Robert William Jocelyn**; Baron Newport, 1743; Viscount Jocelyn, 1755; a baronet of England, 1665; Captain Royal Navy; retired; *b* 4 Dec. 1909; *S* father 1956; *m* 1937, Clodagh, *d* of late Edward Kennedy, Bishopscourt, Co. Kildare; three *s*. Retired 1960. *Address*: Bryansford, Co. Down. *T*: Newcastle 23469.

RODERICK, Caerwyn Eifion; Councillor, South Glamorgan County Council, since 1980; *b* 15 July 1927; *m* 1952, Eirlys Mary Lewis; one *s* two *d. Educ*: Maes-y-Dderwen County Sch., Ystradgynlais; University Coll. of North Wales, Bangor. Asst Master, Caterham Sch., Surrey, 1949-52; Sen. Master, Chartesey Sch., LCC, 1952-54; Sen. Maths Master, Boys' Grammar Sch., Brecon, 1954-57; Method Study Engineer, NCB, 1957-60; Sen. Maths Master, Hartridge High Sch., Newport, Mon, 1960-69; Lecturer, Coll. of Educn, Cardiff, 1969-70. MP (Lab) Brecon and Radnor, 1970-79; PPS to Rt Hon. Michael Foot. Mem. Council: UC, Cardiff; UMIST; formerly Mem. Council, RCVS. *Address*: 29 Charlotte Square, Rhiwbina, Cardiff. *T*: Cardiff 68269.

RODERICK, Rev. Charles Edward Morys; Chaplain to the Queen, 1962-80; Rector of Longparish and Hurstbourne Priors, 1971-80; *b* 18 June 1910; *s* of Edward Thomas and Marion Petronella Roderick; *m* 1940, Betty Margaret Arrowsmith; two *s. Educ*: Christ's College, Brecon; Trinity College, Oxford (MA). Schoolmaster, 1932-38; training for ordination, 1938-39; ordained, 1939; Curate, St Luke's Parish Church of Chelsea, 1939-46; Chaplain to the Forces, 1940-45; Rector of Denham, Bucks, 1946-53. Vicar of St Michael's, Chester Square, London, 1953-71. HCF. *Address*: 135 Little Ann, Abbotts Ann, Andover, Hants.

RODGER, Allan George, OBE 1944; Under-Secretary, Scottish Education Department, 1959-63, retired; *b* Kirkcaldy, 7 Jan. 1902; *s* of Allan Rodger, Schoolmaster, and Annie Venters; *m* 1930, Barbara Melville Simpson; one *s* one *d. Educ*: Pathhead Primary School, Kirkcaldy; Kirkcaldy High School; Edinburgh University (MA (Hons) Maths, BSc, MEd, Dip Geog). Teacher, Viewforth School, Kirkcaldy, 1926-29; Lecturer, Moray House Training Coll. and Univ. Dept of Educ. (Edinburgh), 1929-35; HM Inspector of Schools, 1935-45, with special duties in regard to geography, special schools, and training colleges (seconded to special administrative duties in Education Dept, 1939-45); Asst Secretary, Scottish Educ. Dept, 1945-59. Served on Educational Commission for Govts of Uganda and Kenya, 1961. Chairman of various Govt Cttees on Scottish Educ. matters. *Publications*: contrib. to Jl of Educational Psychology and other educational journals. *Recreations*: reading, music. *Address*: 9 Viewpark, Milngavie, Glasgow. *T*: 041-956 6114.

RODGER, Rt. Rev. Patrick Campbell; see Oxford, Bishop of.

RODGER, Sir William (Glendinning), Kt 1978; OBE 1957; FCA (NZ), FCIS; JP; chartered accountant; *b* Glasgow, 5 June 1912; *s* of William Rodger, Eaglesham; *m* 1937, Dulcie Elizabeth, *d* of Frank Bray, Auckland, NZ; one *s* one *d. Educ*: Univ. of Auckland; Victoria Univ. of Wellington. BCom. FCA (NZ) 1935; FCIS 1936; FCAI 1937; FIANZ 1946; FNZIM 1947. Commercial appts, 1927-41; with public accountancy firm, 1945-54. Victoria Univ. of Wellington: Mem. Professorial Bd, 1951-61; Dean, Faculty of Commerce, 1953-54, 1957, and 1959-60; Sen. Lectr in Accountancy, Univ. of Auckland, 1967-77. Vis. Prof. of Business Admin (Fulbright Award), Univ. of Calif at LA, 1957-58; Vis. Prof. of Commerce, Sch. of Business, Queen's Univ., Ont, 1962-63; Vis. Lectr in Farm Management Accounting, Wye Coll., Univ. of London, 1965-66; Agricl Economist, Min. of Agriculture, 1965-66; Vis. Fellow: Centre for Continuing Educn, Univ. of Auckland, 1978-; Mitchell Coll. of Advanced Educn, Bathurst, NSW, 1978-79. Founder Mem., NZ Admin. Staff Coll., 1950-65 (Course Dir, 1953-59). Dir, Civic Trust, Auckland, 1978. President: NZ Inst. of Cost Accountants, 1955 (Maxwell Award, 1956); NZ Inst. of Management, 1957. Member: NZ Govt Co. Law Cttee, 1951-55; Jamaican Govt Sugar Industry Commn, 1966-67; Nat. Res.

Cttee, NZ Soc. of Accts, 1951-66; Nat. Exec., NZ Statistical Assoc., 1952-54; NZ Div., Chartered Inst. of Secs, 1945-66 (Nat. Pres., 1958; Wellington Pres., 1960); Wellington Br., Econ. Soc. of Aust. and NZ, 1946-50. Hon. Member: NZ Inst. of Valuers, 1952; NZ Libraries Assoc., 1978; NZ Council Mem., Royal Commonwealth Soc., 1979-; Founded Auckland Exec. Management Club 1968 (Pres., 1969-72). Treasurer, NZ Br. of Heraldry Soc., 1978-. Hon. Treas., Boy Scout Assoc., 1937-58. JP Auckland, 1946. Editor: The New Zealand Accountants Journal, 1945-47; Management Review, 1948-53. *Publications*: Balance Sheet Significance, Preparation and Interpretation, 1949; (jtly) Auditing, 1950 (3rd edn 1962); Interpretation of Financial Data and Company Reports, 1955 (2nd edn 1960); Bibliography of Accountancy, 1955; (rev. edn) Yorston's Advanced Accounting, 3 vols, 1956; Private Companies in NZ, 1956; (with Barton) NZ Company Secretary, 1957; An Introduction to Accounting Theory, 1957; Company Accounts in NZ, 1962; Estate Planning, 1964; An Introduction to Cost and Management Accounting, 1965; The Management Audit, 1966; Business Administration in Pharmacy, 1969; Management in the Modern Medical Practice, 1975; Introduction to Genealogy and Heraldry in New Zealand, 1980; The Arms of the New Zealand Society of Accountants, 1980; reports; contrib. prof. jls. *Address*: 61 Speight Road, St Heliers Bay, Auckland, New Zealand. *T*: 555 947. *Clubs*: Wellesley (Wellington); University (Auckland).

RODGERS, (Andrew) Piers (Wingate); Secretary, Royal Academy of Arts, London, since 1982; *b* 24 Oct. 1944; second *s* of Sir John Rodgers, Bt, *qv* ; *m* 1979, Marie Agathe Houette; one *s. Educ*: Eton Coll.; Merton Coll., Oxford (BA 1st Cl. Honour Mods, Prox. acc. Hertford and De Paravicini Prizes). J. Henry Schroder Wagg & Co. Ltd, London, 1967-73: Personal Asst to Chairman, 1971-73; Director, International Council on Monuments and Sites (ICOMOS), Paris, 1973-79; Consultant, UNESCO, Paris, 1979-80; Member, Technical Review Team, Aga Khan Award for Architecture, 1980; Secretary, UK Committee of ICOMOS, 1981. FRSA 1973. *Publications*: articles on protection of cultural heritage. *Recreations*: music, Islamic art. *Address*: 18 Hertford Street, W1. *T*: 01-409 3110. *Clubs*: Brooks's, Pratt's, MCC.

RODGERS, Mrs Barbara Noel, OBE 1975; Hon. Senior Research Fellow, Policy Studies Institute (formerly Centre for Studies in Social Policy), since 1975; *b* 1912; *d* of F. S. Stancliffe, Wilmslow, Cheshire; *m* 1950, Brian Rodgers; no *c. Educ*: Wycombe Abbey Sch.; (Exhibitioner) Somerville Coll., Oxford (MA). Social work and travel, 1935-39; Jt appt with Manch. and Salford Council of Social Service and Manchester Univ. (practical work Tutor and special Lectr), 1939-45. Lectr 1945, Sen. Lectr, 1955, and Reader, 1965-73, Manchester Univ.; Teaching Fellowship in Grad. Sch. of Social Work, Toronto Univ., 1948-49. Member: various wages councils, 1950-; National Assistance Bd, 1965; Supplementary Benefits Commn, 1966-76; Industrial Tribunal Panel. Served and serving on numerous voluntary welfare organisations. *Publications*: (co-author) Till We Build Again, 1948; (with Julia Dixon) Portrait of Social Work, 1960; A Follow Up Study of Manchester Social Administration Students, 1940-60, 1963; Careers of Social Studies Graduates, 1964; (co-author) Comparative Social Administration, 1968; (with June Stevenson) A New Portrait of Social Work, 1973; chapter on Comparative Studies in Social Administration, in Foundations of Social Administration (ed H. Heisler), 1977; The Study of Social Policy: a comparative approach, 1979; numerous articles in learned jls mainly on social security and social services in America, France and Canada. *Recreations*: walking, bird watching, travel. *Address*: The Old Vicarage, Goostrey, Crewe, Cheshire. *T*: Holmes Chapel 32397.

RODGERS, George; Sales Organiser, Labour Weekly, since 1980; *b* 7 Nov. 1925; *s* of George and Letitia Georgina Rodgers; *m* 1952, Joan, *d* of James Patrick and Elizabeth Graham; one *s* two *d. Educ*: St Margaret's and Holy Trinity, Liverpool; St Michael's, Sylvester, Rupert Road and Longview, Huyton. Co-operative Soc., Whiston, Lancs, 1939-43. Served War, RN, 1943-46 (War Medals, France, Germany Star). White's, Engrs, Widnes, 1946-50; with Civil Engineers: Eave's, Blackpool, 1950-53; Costain, Liverpool, 1953-54; Brit. Insulated Callender Cables, 1954-74. MP (Lab) Chorley, Feb. 1974-1979; Chm., NW Region Lab MPs, 1975-79; Prospective Parly Cand. (Lab), Nelson and Colne. Mem., Huyton UDC, 1964-74 (Chm., Educn Cttee, 1969-73; Chm., Local Authority, 1973-74); Mem. Liverpool Regional Hosp. Bd, 1967-74. *Publication*: (with Ivor Clemitson) A Life to Live: beyond full employment, 1981. *Recreations*: cycling, political history, amateur boxing (spectator). *Address*: 32 Willoughby Road, Huyton, Liverpool L14 6XB. *T*: 051-489 1913. *Club*: Labour (Huyton).

RODGERS, Gerald Fleming; HM Diplomatic Service, retired; *b* 22 Sept. 1917; *s* of Thomas Fleming Rodgers and Mary Elizabeth (*née* Gillespie); *m* 1965, Helen Lucy, *y d* of late Dr Wall, Coleshill; two *s. Educ*: Rugby; Queens' Coll., Cambridge. Served War of 1939-45, Army, 1939-46. Foreign (subseq. Diplomatic) Service, 1947; served at: Jedda, 1947-49; British Middle East Office, Cairo and Fayid, 1949-53; FO, 1953-59; Peking, 1959-61; UK Delegation to OECD, 1961-64; Djakarta, 1964-65; Counsellor, Paris, 1965-67. *Address*: Laurelcroft, North Street, Kilsby, Rugby, Warwickshire. *T*: Crick 822314.

RODGERS, Prof. Harold William, OBE 1943; FRCS 1933; Professor of Surgery, Queen's University of Belfast, 1947-73; Professor Emeritus, 1973; *b* 1 Dec. 1907; *s* of Major R. T. Rodgers; *m* 1938, Margaret Boycott; one *s* three *d. Educ*: King's College School; St Bartholomew's Hospital. St

Bartholomew's Hospital: House Surgeon, Demonstrator in Anatomy, Chief Asst, Casualty Surgeon, Senior Asst Surgeon. Served War of 1939-45, RAMC, North Africa, Italy, France; Hon. Lt.-Col. Prof. of Surgery and Head of Div. of Hosp. Care, Univ. of Ife, Nigeria, 1974-77, retd. Nuffield Medical Visitor to African Territories; WHO Vis. Prof. to India; Fellow Roy. Institute of International Affairs; Vice-Pres. Intervarsity Fellowship; FRC Soc.; Past Pres., Section of Surgery, RSM; Past President: British Society of Gastro-enterology; Christian Medical Fellowship; British Surgical Research Soc.; Past Chairman, Ct of Examiners of RCS; President: YMCA (Belfast); Hibernian CMS. District Surgeon, St John's Ambulance Brigade. Hon. MD QUB, 1981. OStJ 1968. *Publications:* Gastroscopy, 1937; general articles in surgical and medical journals. *Recreations:* painting, travel, gardening, poetry. *Address:* 47 Fordington Road, N6.

RODGERS, Sir John (Charles), 1st Bt, *cr* 1964; DL; *b* 5 Oct. 1906; *o s* of Charles and Maud Mary Rodgers; *m* Betsy, JP, East Sussex, *y d* of Francis W. Aikin-Sneath, JP, and of Louisa, *d* of Col W. Langworthy Baker; two *s*. *Educ:* St Peter's, York; Ecole des Roches, France; Keble College, Oxford (scholar). MA. Sub-Warden, Mary Ward Settlement, 1929; Lectr and Administrative Asst, Univ. of Hull, 1930; FO, 1938-39 and 1944-45; Special Mission to Portugal, December 1945; Dir, Commercial Relations Div., MOI, 1939-41; Dir, Post-War Export Trade Develt, Dept of Overseas Trade, 1941-42; Head Industrial Inf. Div., Min. of Production, 1942-44; Foundation Gov. of Administrative Staff Coll.; Exec. Council Member, Foundation for Management Education, 1959-; BBC General Advisory Council, 1946-52; Hon. Secretary Smuts Memorial Committee, 1953; Chm. Cttee on Litter in Royal Parks, 1954; Exec. Cttee of British Council, 1957-58; Governor, British Film Institute, 1958; Member Tucker Cttee on Proceedings before Examining Justices, 1957; Leader, Parliamentary Panel, and on Exec. and Coun., Inst. of Dirs, 1955-58; Vice-Chm. Exec. Cttee Political and Economic Planning (PEP), 1962-68; Exec. London Library, 1963-71. MP (C) Sevenoaks, Kent, 1950-79; PPS to Rt Hon. Viscount Eccles (at Ministries of Works, Education and Board of Trade), 1951-57; Parliamentary Sec., Bd of Trade, and Minister for regional development and employment, 1958-60. UK Delegate and Leader of the Conservatives to Parly Assembly, Council of Europe, and Vice-Pres., WEU, 1969-79; Chm., Independent Gp, Council of Europe, 1974-79; Chm., Political Affairs Cttee, 1976-79; Vice-Pres., European League for Econ. Co-operation, 1970-79; Hon. Treasurer, Europe-Atlantic Gp, 1975-. Pres., Centre Européen de Documentation et Information, 1963-66. Dep. Chm., J. Walter Thompson Co. Ltd, 1931-70; Chairman: Cocoa Merchants Ltd; British Market Research Bureau Ltd, 1933-54; Radio Luxembourg London, 1979-; dir of other cos. Mem. Council, Nat. Trust, 1978-; Vice-Chm., Heritage of London Trust, 1980-. Mem. Court: City Univ., 1969-; Brunel Univ., 1981-. President: Inst. of Practitioners in Advertising, 1967-69; Soc. for Individual Freedom, 1970-73; Inst. of Statisticians, 1971-77; Master, Worshipful Company of Masons, 1968-69; Freeman of the City of London. DL Kent 1973. CBIM; FSS; FIS; FRSA. Knight Grand Cross, Order of Civil Merit (Spain), 1965; Grand Cross of Liechtenstein, 1970; Comdr, Order of Dom Infante Henrique (Portugal), 1972; Grand Officer, Order of Leopold II (Belgium), 1978; Order of Brilliant Star (China), 1979; Kt Comdr, 1st cl., Royal Order of North Star, Sweden, 1980; Comdr, 1st cl., Order of Lion of Finland, 1980; Medal of Merit, Council of Europe, 1980. *Publications:* Mary Ward Settlement: a history, 1930; The Old Public Schools of England, 1938; The English Woodland, 1941; (jtly) Industry looks at the New Order, 1941; English Rivers, 1948; (jtly) One Nation, 1950; York, 1951; (ed) Thomas Gray, 1953; (jtly) Change is our Ally, 1954; (jtly) Capitalism-Strength and Stress, 1958; One Nation at Work, 1976; and other pamphlets. *Recreations:* travel, theatre. *Heir: s* John Fairlie Tobias Rodgers *b* 2 July 1940. *Address:* 72 Berkeley House, Hay Hill, W1. *T:* 01-629 5220; The Dower House, Groombridge, Kent. *T:* Groombridge 213. *Clubs:* Brooks's, Pratt's, Beefsteak, Royal Thames Yacht.
See also A. P. W. Rodgers.

RODGERS, Piers; *see* Rodgers, A. P. W.

RODGERS, Rt. Hon. William Thomas, PC 1975; MP Teeside, Stockton, since 1974 (Stockton-on-Tees, 1962-74) (Lab, 1962-81, SDP, since 1981); *b* 28 Oct. 1928; *s* of William Arthur and Gertrude Helen Rodgers; *m* 1955, Silvia, *d* of Hirsch Szulman; three *d*. *Educ:* Sudley Road Council Sch.; Quarry Bank High School, Liverpool; Magdalen College, Oxford. General Secretary, Fabian Society, 1953-60. Contested (Lab) Bristol West, March 1957; Parly Under-Sec. of State: Dept of Econ. Affairs, 1964-67, Foreign Office, 1967-68; Leader, UK delegn to Council of Europe and Assembly of WEU, 1967-68; Minister of State: BoT, 1968-69; Treasury, 1969-70; MoD, 1974-76; Sec. of State for Transport, 1976-79. Chm., Expenditure Cttee on Trade and Industry, 1971-74. Borough Councillor, St Marylebone, 1958-62. *Publications:* Hugh Gaitskell, 1906-1963 (ed), 1964; (jt) The People into Parliament, 1966; The Politics of Change, 1982; pamphlets, etc. *Address:* 48 Patshull Road, NW5. *T:* 01-485 9997.

RODNEY, family name of **Baron Rodney.**

RODNEY, 9th Baron *cr* 1782; **John Francis Rodney;** Bt 1764; Marketing Director, Vacuumatic Ltd, since 1959; *b* 28 June 1920; *s* of 8th Lord Rodney and Lady Marjorie Lowther (*d* 1968), *d* of 6th Earl of Lonsdale; *S* father, 1973; *m* 1952, Régine, *d* of late Chevalier Pangaert d'Opdorp, Belgium, and the late Baronne Pangaert d'Opdorp; one *s* one *d*. *Educ:* Stowe Sch., Buckingham; McGill Univ., Montreal. Served War of 1939-45 with Commandos, Burma,

1943-45 (despatches). Worked with Rootes Ltd, 1946-52, firstly as Executive Trainee, becoming Director of Rootes, Switzerland. With Vacuumatic Ltd (a member of Portals gp), 1952-: firstly Sales Manager, then Marketing Director. Past Chm., British Fedn of Printing Machinery and Supplies. *Recreations:* sailing, shooting, gardening, travelling round the world (not all recreation). *Heir: s* Hon. George Brydges Rodney, *b* 3 Jan. 1953. *Address:* 38 Pembroke Road, W8. *T:* 01-602 4391. *Clubs:* White's; Royal Yacht Squadron.

RODRIGUES, Sir Alberto, Kt 1966; CBE 1964 (OBE 1960; MBE (mil.) 1948); ED; General Medical Practitioner, Hong Kong; Senior Unofficial Member Executive Council 1964-74; Pro-Chancellor and Chairman of Executive Council, University of Hong Kong; *b* 5 November 1911; *s* of late Luiz Gonzaga Rodrigues and late Giovanina Remedios; *m* 1940, Cynthia Maria da Silva; one *s* two *d*. *Educ:* St Joseph's College and University of Hong Kong. MBBS Univ. of Hong Kong, 1934; Post graduate work, London and Lisbon, 1935-36; Medical Practitioner, 1937-40; also Medical Officer in Hong Kong Defence Force. POW, 1940-45. Medical Practitioner, 1945-50; Post graduate work, New York, 1951-52; Resident, Winnipeg Maternity Hosp. (Canada), 1952-53; General Medical Practitioner, 1953-. Member: Urban Council (Hong Kong), 1940-41; 1947-50; Legislative Council, 1953-60; Executive Council, 1960-74. Med. Superintendent, St Paul's Hospital, 1953-. Director: Jardine Securities, 1969-; Lap Heng Co. Ltd, 1970-; Hill & Shanghai Hotels Ltd, 1969-; Peak Tramways Co. Ltd, 1971-; Li & Fung Ltd, 1973; Hill Antenna and Engineering Co. Ltd, 1972-; Computer Data (Hill) Ltd, 1973-; Hill Commercial Broadcasting Co. Ltd, 1974-; Hong Kong and Shanghai Banking Corporation, 1974-. Officer, Ordem de Cristo (Portugal), 1949; Chevalier, Légion d'Honneur (France), 1962; Knight Grand Cross, Order of St Sylvester (Vatican), 1966. *Recreations:* cricket, hockey, tennis, swimming, badminton. *Address:* St Paul's Hospital Annexe, Causeway Bay, Hong Kong. *T:* 760017. *Clubs:* Hong Kong, Royal Hong Kong Jockey, Hong Kong Country, Lusitano, Recreio (all Hong Kong).

RODWELL, Daniel Alfred Hunter; QC 1982; a Recorder of the Crown Court, since 1980; *b* 3 Jan. 1936; *s* of late Brig. R. M. Rodwell, AFC, and Nellie Barbara Rodwell (*née* D'Costa); *m* 1967, Veronica Ann Cecil; two *s* one *d*. *Educ:* Munro Coll., Jamaica; Worcester Coll., Oxford, 1956-59 (BA Law). National service, 1954-56; 2/Lieut 1st West Yorks, PWO, 1955; TA, 1956-67: Captain and Adjt 3 PWO, 1964-67. Called to Bar, Inner Temple, 1960. A Deputy Circuit Judge, 1977. *Recreations:* hunting, gardening, sailing. *Address:* Roddimore House, Winslow Road, Great Horwood, Milton Keynes MK17 0N7. *T:* Winslow (Aylesbury) 2536.

ROE, Frederic Gordon, FSA, FRHistS; *b* 24 Sept. 1894; *s* of late Fred Roe, RI, RBC, and Letitia Mabel, *e d* of Sydney W. Lee; *m* 1921, Eleanor Beatrice, *o d* of late Cecil Reginald Grundy; one *d*. *Educ:* Westminster School; in Art under his father, and at the Chelsea School of Art. Joined The Connoisseur, 1913; Art Critic, 1919; Assistant Editor, 1921-32; Acting-Editor, March-June 1926; Editor, 1933; Director, Connoisseur Ltd, 1931-34; Gunner, 1212 Battery, RFA, 1917-19; Art Critic, Daily Mail, 1920 (resigned 1921); Member, Junior Art Workers' Guild, 1920-23; restored to Westminster Abbey Muniments Wren's Original designs for the restoration of the Abbey, 1927; Hon. Member Society of Pewter Collectors, 1933-; Art Critic, The Artist, 1935-36; ARP Warden (and higher grades), 1940-45; Odhams Press Book Dept, 1943-44. FRSA 1968. *Publications:* Henry Bright of the Norwich School, 1920; Charles Bentley, 1921; Dictator of the Royal Academy (Joseph Farington, RA), 1921; David Cox, 1924-original MS of this book is in the National Museum of Wales, Cardiff; Sporting Prints of the 18th and early 19th centuries, 1927; The Life and Times of King Edward the Eighth, 1937; Coronation Cavalcade, 1937; Catalogue of Paintings in the Nettlefold Collection (with C. R. Grundy), 1937-38; Etty and the Nude (with W. Gaunt), 1943; The Nude from Cranach to Etty and beyond, 1944; The Bronze Cross, 1945; Cox the Master, 1946; English Period Furniture, 1946; Rowlandson, 1947; Sea Painters of Britain, 1947-48; Old English Furniture, 1948; Clarence below the Basement (for children), 1948; English Cottage Furniture, 1949, 2nd edn, 1950, rev. edn., 1961; Britain's Birthright, 1950; Victorian Furniture, 1952; Windsor Chairs, 1953; The Victorian Child, 1959; The Georgian Child, 1961; The British Museum's Pictures (with J. R. F. Thompson), 1961; Home Furnishing with Antiques, 1965; Victorian Corners, 1968; Women in Profile: a study in Silhouette, 1970; The Hillingford Saga, 1975; Fred Roe, RI, his life and art (with a catalogue), 1978; much work in over 70 vols of The Connoisseur; also British Racehorse, Concise Encyclopædia of Antiques, etc. *Recreations:* walking, viewing, geneaological research. *Address:* 19 Vallance Road, Alexandra Park, N22 4UD. *T:* 01-888 4029.

ROE, Dame Raigh (Edith), DBE 1980 (CBE 1975); JP; Director, Airlines of Western Australia, since 1981; World President, Associated Country Women of the World, 1977-80; *b* 12 Dec. 1922; *d* of Alwyn and Laura Kurts; *m* 1941, James Arthur Roe; three *s*. *Educ:* Perth Girls' Sch., Australia. Country Women's Association: State Pres., 1967-70; National Pres., 1969-71. World Ambassador, WA Council, 1978-; Hon. Ambassador, State of Louisiana, USA, 1979-. Comr, ABC, 1978-; Nat. Dir (Aust.), Queen Elizabeth II Silver Jubilee Trust for Young Australians, 1978-. JP Western Australia, 1966. Australian of the Year, 1977; Brooch of Merit, Deutscher Landfrauenverband, Fed. Republic of Germany, 1980. *Address:* 76 Regency Drive, Crestwood, Thornlie, WA 6108, Australia. *T:* 4598765.

ROE, Air Chief Marshal Sir Rex (David), GCB 1981 (KCB 1977; CB 1974); AFC; retired 1981; *b* 1925; *m* 1948, Helen Sophie (*née* Nairn) (*d* 1981); one *s* two *d. Educ:* City of London Sch.; London University. Joined RAF 1943; trained in Canada; served with Metropolitan Fighter Sector, No 11 Group, 203 Sqn, 1950-51; Sch. of Maritime Reconnaissance, 1951-53; Central Flying School and Flying Training Units, 1953-55; Commanded RNZAF Central Flying School, 1956-58; RAF Staff College, 1959; Commanded No 204 Sqn, 1960-62; College of Air Warfare, 1962-64; SASO No 18 (Maritime) Gp, 1964-67; Stn Comdr RAF Syerston, 1967-69; Director of Flying Trng, 1969-71; RCDS, 1971; Deputy Controller Aircraft (C), MoD (Procurement Executive), 1972-74; SASO HQ Near East Air Force, 1972-76; AOC-in-C Training Comd, 1976-77; AOC-in-C, Support Command, 1977-78; Air Mem. for Supply and Organisation, 1978-81. *Recreations:* reading, Rugby football. *Address:* c/o Lloyds Bank, 6 Pall Mall, SW1. *Club:* Royal Air Force.

ROE, Rt. Rev. William Gordon; *see* Huntingdon, Bishop Suffragan of.

ROEBUCK, Roy Delville; Barrister-at-law; *b* Manchester, 25 Sept. 1929; *m* 1957, Dr Mary Ogilvy Adams; one *s. Educ:* various newspapers. Called to the Bar, Gray's Inn, 1974. Served RAF, 1948-50 (National Service). Journalist, Stockport Advertiser, Northern Daily Telegraph, Yorkshire Evening News, Manchester Evening Chronicle, News Chronicle, Daily Express, Daily Mirror and Daily Herald, 1950-66; freelance, 1966-. MP (Lab) Harrow East, 1966-70. Contested (Lab): Altrincham and Sale, 1964 and Feb. 1965; Leek, Feb. 1974. *Recreations:* ski-ing, music, reading Hansard. *Address:* 12 Brooksby Street, N1 1HA. *T:* 01-607 7057; 5 Pump Court, Temple, EC4Y 7AP. *T:* 01-353 2532.

ROEG, Nicolas Jack; film director; *b* 15 Aug. 1928; *s* of Jack Roeg and Gertrude Silk; *m* 1957, Susan, *d* of Major F. W. Stephen, MC; four *s. Educ:* Mercers Sch. Original story of Prize of Arms; Cinematographer: The Caretaker; Masque of the Red Death; Nothing But the Best; Petulia; A Funny Thing Happened on the Way to the Forum; Fahrenheit 451; Far From the Madding Crowd, etc; 2nd Unit Director and Cinematographer: Judith; Lawrence of Arabia; Co-Dir, Performance; Director: Walkabout; Don't Look Now; The Man who Fell to Earth; Bad Timing; Eureka. *Address:* Flat E, 2 Oxford and Cambridge Mansions, Old Marylebone Road, NW1. *T:* 01-262 8612.

ROFFEY, Harry Norman, CMG 1971; Assistant Secretary, Department of Health and Social Security, 1954-72, retired; *b* 2 March 1911; *s* of Henry Roffey and Ella Leggatt; *m* 1964, Florence Dickie; no *c. Educ:* Brighton Grammar Sch.; St Catharine's Coll., Cambridge (BA Hons, MA); Inst. of Education, London Univ. (Teacher's Dip.). Teaching (languages), 1935-40. Air Ministry and Foreign Office, 1940-45 (left as Wing Comdr); Min. of Health (Principal), 1946-54; Dept of Health and Social Security, 1954-72 (as Asst Sec. i/c Internat. Affairs, on the Health side). *Recreations:* foreign travel, music, etc. *Address:* 2 Sunnyside Place, Wimbledon, SW19 4SJ. *T:* 01-946 4991.

ROGAN, Very Rev. John; Provost of St Paul's Cathedral, Dundee, Diocese of Brechin, since 1978; *b* 20 May 1928; *s* of William and Jane Rogan; *m* 1953, Dorothy Margaret Williams; one *s* one *d. Educ:* Manchester Central High School; St John's Coll., Univ. of Durham. BA 1949, MA 1951; DipTheol with distinction, 1954; BPhil 1981. Education Officer, RAF, 1949-52. Asst Curate, St Michael and All Angels, Ashton-under-Lyne, 1954-57; Chaplain, Sheffield Industrial Mission, 1957-61; Secretary, Church of England Industrial Cttee, 1961-66; Asst Secretary, Board for Social Responsibility, 1962-66; Vicar of Leigh, Lancs, 1966-78; Sec., Diocesan Bd for Social Responsibility, 1967-74; Chm. 1974-78; Rural Dean of Leigh, 1971-78; Hon. Canon of Manchester, 1975-78. *Publication:* (ed jtly) Principles of Church Reform: Thomas Arnold, 1962. *Recreations:* Roman history, walking, music. *Address:* 4 Richmond Terrace, Dundee, Scotland DD2 1BQ. *T:* Dundee 68548.

ROGAN, Rev. William Henry; an Extra Chaplain to the Queen, since 1978 (Chaplain to the Queen, 1966-78); *b* 1908; *s* of late Rev. John Rogan and Christian Ann McGhie; *m* 1940, Norah Violet Henderson, Helensburgh; one *s* two *d. Educ:* Royal High Sch. of Edinburgh; Univ. of Edinburgh. MA 1928; BD 1931. Asst, St Cuthbert's Parish Church, Edinburgh, 1930-32; Minister: Whithorn Parish, 1932; St Bride's Parish, Helensburgh, 1936-50; Paisley Abbey, 1950-69; Humbie, East Lothian, 1969-74. Supt, Church of Scotland Huts and Canteens in Orkney and Shetland, 1941-42; Army Chaplain, 1943-46. Select Preacher: Glasgow Univ., 1960-65; Aberdeen Univ., 1959-66; St Andrews Univ., 1959; Convener, Church of Scotland Youth Cttee, 1965-70. Founder and formerly Chm., Soc. of Friends of Paisley Abbey. Pres., Scottish Church Soc., 1977-78. Hon. DD Edinburgh, 1963. *Recreation:* angling. *Address:* Westwood, Edinburgh Road, Lauder, Berwickshire TD2 6PA. *T:* Lauder 415.

ROGERS, Rt. Rev. Alan Francis Bright, MA; an Hon. Assistant Bishop of Peterborough, since 1975; Priest-in-Charge of Abthorpe with Slapton, since 1977; *b* 12 Sept. 1907; *s* of Thomas and Alice Rogers, London, W9; *m* 1932, Millicent Boarder; two *s. Educ:* Westminster City Sch.; King's Coll., London; Leeds Univ.; Bishop's Coll., Cheshunt. Curate of St Stephen's, Shepherds Bush, 1930-32; Holy Trinity, Twickenham, 1932-34; Civil Chaplain, Mauritius, 1934-49; Archdeacon of Mauritius, 1946-49; Commissary to Bishop of Mauritius, 1949-59; Vicar of Twickenham, 1949-54; Proctor in Convocation, 1951-59; Vicar of Hampstead, 1954-59; Rural Dean of Hampstead, 1955-59; Bishop of Mauritius, 1959-66; Suffragan Bishop of Fulham, 1966-70; Suffragan Bishop of Edmonton, 1970-75; Priest-in-Charge of Wappenham, 1977-80. MA Lambeth 1959. *Recreations:* walking, light music. *Address:* Phoenix Cottage, Blakesley, near Towcester, Northants NN12 8RB. *T:* Blakesley 860502. *Club:* Royal Commonwealth Society.

ROGERS, Allan Ralph, FGS; Member (Lab) South East Wales, European Parliament, since 1979; Vice-President, European Parliament, since 1979; *b* 24 Oct. 1932; *s* of John Henry Rogers and Madeleine Rogers (*née* Smith); *m* 1955, Ceridwen James; one *s* three *d. Educ:* University College of Swansea (BSc Hons Geology). Geologist, UK, Canada, USA, Australia, 1956-63; Teacher, 1963-65; Tutor-organiser, WEA, 1965-70, District Sec., 1970-79. *Recreations:* all sports, jazz bands. *Address:* 14 Dilwyn Avenue, Hengoed, Mid-Glamorgan, Wales. *Clubs:* New Labour (Ystrad Mynach); Workmen's (Ystrad Mynach); Penallta Colliery Rugby Football (Hengoed).

ROGERS, General Bernard William; General, United States Army; Supreme Allied Commander, Europe, since 1979; *b* 16 July 1921; *s* of late W. H. Rogers and of Mrs W. H. Rogers; *m* 1944, Ann Ellen Jones; one *s* two *d. Educ:* Kansas State Coll.; US Mil. Acad. (BS); Oxford Univ. (Rhodes Scholar; BA, MA); US Army Comd Staff Coll., Fort Leavenworth, Kansas; US Army War Coll., Carlisle Barracks, Pa. CO 3rd Bn, 9th Inf. Regt, 2nd Inf. Div., Korea, 1952-53; Comdr, 1st Battle Gp, 19th Inf., Div. COS, 24th Inf. Div., Augsburg, Germany, 1960-61; Exec. Officer to Chm., Jt Chiefs of Staff, Washington, DC, 1962-66; Asst Div. Comdr, 1st Inf. Div., Republic of Vietnam, 1966-67; Comdt of Cadets, US Mil. Acad., 1967-69; Comdg Gen., 5th Inf. Div., Fort Carson, Colo, 1969-70; Chief of Legislative Liaison, Office of Sec. to the Army, Washington, DC, 1971-72; Dep. Chief of Staff for Personnel, Dept of the Army, Washington, DC, 1972-74; Comdg Gen., US Army Forces Comd, Fort McPherson, Ga, 1974-76; Chief of Staff, US Army, Washington, DC, 1976-79. Hon. Fellow, University Coll., Oxford, 1979. Hon. LLD: Akron, 1978; Boston, 1981. *Publications:* Cedar Falls-Junction City: a Turning Point, 1974; Foreign Affairs, 1982. *Recreations:* golf, reading. *Address:* Supreme Allied Commander, Europe, Supreme Headquarters Allied Powers Europe, 7010 SHAPE, Belgium. *T:* 065-444113.

ROGERS, Surgeon Rear-Adm. (D) Brian Frederick, CB 1980; Director of Naval Dental Services, 1977-80; *b* 27 Feb. 1923; *s* of Frederick Reginald Rogers, MIMechE, MIMarE, and Rosa Jane Rogers; *m* 1946, Mavis Elizabeth (*née* Scott); one *s* two *d. Educ:* Rock Ferry High Sch.; Liverpool Univ. (LDS 1945). House Surgeon, Liverpool Dental Hosp., 1945; joined RNVR, 1946; transf. to RN, 1954; served HMS Ocean, 1954-56 and HMS Eagle, 1964-66; Fleet Dental Surg. on staff of C-in-C Fleet, 1974-77; Comd Dental Surg. to C-in-C Naval Home Comd, 1977. QHDS 1977. *Recreations:* European touring, photography, DIY. *Address:* 22 Trerieve, Downderry, Torpoint, Cornwall PL11 3LY. *T:* Downderry 526; Montana roja, Lanzarote, Canary Islands.

ROGERS, Prof. C(laude) Ambrose, FRS 1959; Astor Professor of Mathematics, University College, London, since 1958; *b* 1 Nov. 1920; *s* of late Sir Leonard Rogers, KCSI, CIE, FRS; *m* 1952, Mrs J. M. Gordon, widow of W. G. Gordon, and *d* of F. W. G. North; two *d. Educ:* Berkhamsted School; University Coll., London; Birkbeck Coll., London. BSc, PhD, DSc (London, 1941, 1949, 1952). Experimental officer, Ministry of Supply, 1940-45; lecturer and reader, University College, London, 1946-54; Prof. of Pure Mathematics, Univ. of Birmingham, 1954-58. Pres., London Mathematical Soc., 1970-72. *Publications:* Packing and Covering, 1964; Hausdorff Measures, 1970; articles in various mathematical journals. *Recreation:* string figures. *Address:* Department of Mathematics, University College, WC1E 6BT; 8 Grey Close, NW11 6QG. *T:* 01-455 8027.

ROGERS, Ven. David Arthur; Archdeacon of Craven, since 1977; *b* 12 March 1921; *s* of Rev. Canon Thomas Godfrey Rogers and Doris Mary Cleaver Rogers (*née* Steele); *m* 1951, Joan Malkin; one *s* three *d. Educ:* Saint Edward's School, Oxford (scholar); Christ's College, Cambridge (exhibitioner). BA 1947, MA 1952. War service with Green Howards and RAC, 1940-45; Christ's Coll. and Ridley Hall, Cambridge, 1945-49; Asst Curate, St George's, Stockport, 1949-53; Rector, St Peter's, Levenshulme, Manchester, 1953-59; Vicar of Sedbergh, Cautley and Garsdale, 1959-79; Rural Dean of Sedbergh and then of Ewecross, 1959-77; Hon. Canon of Bradford Cathedral, 1967. *Address:* Brooklands, Bridge End, Long Preston, Skipton, N Yorks BD23 4RA. *T:* Long Preston 334.

ROGERS, David Bryan; Deputy Secretary and Director General, Board of Inland Revenue, since 1981; *b* 8 Sept. 1929; *s* of Frank Rogers and Louisa Rogers; *m* 1955, Marjory Geraldine Gilmour Horribine; one *s* two *d. Educ:* Grove Park, Wrexham; University Coll., London (BA Classics). Inspector of Taxes, 1953; Principal Inspector, 1968; Sen. Principal Inspector, 1976; Under Sec. and Dir of Operations, Bd of Inland Revenue, 1978-81. *Recreations:* piano, organ, singing, reading. *Address:* 2 Abbotswood Close, Guildford, Surrey. *T:* Guildford 69135.

ROGERS, Rev. Edward; General Secretary, Methodist Division of Social Responsibility (formerly Christian Citizenship Department), 1950-75; *b* 4 Jan. 1909; *s* of Capt. E. E. Rogers, Fleetwood; *m* 1st, 1937, Edith May, *o d* of A. L. Sutton, Plaistow; 2nd, 1979, Lucy Eveline Howlett. *Educ:* Baines's

Poulton-Le-Fylde Grammar School; Manchester University. Kitchener Scholar, Shuttleworth Scholar, Hulme Hall, Manchester. MA (Econ. and Pol.) 1931; Hartley Coll.; BD, 1933. Methodist Circuit Minister: East London Mission, Bakewell, Birmingham (Sutton Park), Southport, 1933-50. Lectures: Fernley, 1951; Ainslie, 1952; Beckly, 1957; Peake 1971. Organising Director, Methodist Relief Fund, 1953-75; Chairman, Inter-Church Aid and Refugee Service, British Council of Churches, 1960-64; Pres., Methodist Conf., 1960; Moderator, Free Church Federal Council, 1968 (Chm., Exec., 1974-); Vice-Pres., British Council of Churches, 1971-74. Chairman: Standing Commn on Migration, 1964-70; Churches Cttee on Gambling Legislation, 1967-73; Exec. Council, UK Immigrants Adv. Service, 1970-; Community and Race Relations Unit, 1971-75; Avec Board, 1977-; Select Committee on Cruelty to Animals, 1963. *Publications:* First Easter, 1948; A Commentary on Communism, 1951; Programme for Peace, 1954; God's Business, 1957; That They Might Have Life, 1958; The Christian Approach to the Communist, 1959; Church Government, 1964; Living Standards, 1964; Law, Morality and Gospel, 1969; Search for Security, 1973; Plundered Planet, 1973; Money, 1976; Thinking About Human Rights, 1978. *Recreations:* travel, indiscriminate reading. *Address:* 49 Fernhurst Road, Croydon, Surrey CR0 7OJ. *T:* 01-656 1729.

ROGERS, Eric William Evan, DSc(Eng); FRAeS; Deputy Director (Aircraft), Royal Aircraft Establishment, Farnborough, Hants, since 1978; *b* 12 April 1925; *o s* of late W. P. Rogers, Southgate, N London; *m* 1950, Dorothy Joyce Loveless; two *s* one *d. Educ:* Southgate County Grammar Sch.; Imperial Coll., London. FCGI, DIC. Aerodynamics Div., NPL, 1945-70 (Head of Hypersonic Research, 1961); Aerodynamics Dept, RAE, 1970 (Head, 1973). *Publications:* various papers on high-speed aerodynamics and on industrial aerodynamics, in ARC (R and M series), RAeS jls and elsewhere. *Recreations:* music, philately. *Address:* 64 Thetford Road, New Malden, Surrey. *T:* 01-942 7452.

ROGERS, Frank J.; Chairman: East Midland Allied Press, since 1973 (Director, since 1971); Ansafone Corporation Ltd, since 1981; *b* 24 Feb. 1920; *s* of Percy Rogers, Stoke-on-Trent; *m* 1949; two *d. Educ:* Wolstanton Grammar School. Journalist, 1937-49; Military Service, 1940-46; Gen. Man., Nigerian Daily Times, 1949-52; Manager, Argus, Melbourne, 1952-55; Man. Dir, Overseas Newspapers, 1958-60; Dir, Daily Mirror, 1960-65; Man. Dir, IPC, 1965-70. Chm., Nat. Newspaper Steering Gp, 1970-72; Dir, Newspaper Publishers Assoc., 1971-73. Adviser on Corporate Affairs, The Plessey Co. Ltd, 1973-81. Chm., British Exec. Cttee, Internat. Press Inst., 1978-. Mem. Council and Chm., Exec. Cttee, Industrial Soc., 1976-79; Chm. Council, Industry and Parliament Trust, 1979-81. *Recreations:* motoring, golf. *Address:* Greensleeves, Loudwater Drive, Rickmansworth, Herts. *T:* Rickmansworth 75358. *Club:* Reform.

ROGERS, George Henry Roland, CBE 1965; *b* 1906; *m* ; one *s* one *d. Educ:* Willesden Elementary School; Middlesex CC Schools. A railway clerk. Member Wembley Borough Council, 1937-41. Served War of 1939-45, Royal Corps of Signals, 1942. MP (Lab) North Kensington, 1945-70; Chairman, London Group of Labour Members, 1949-54; Opposition London Whip, 1954-64; a Lord Commissioner of the Treasury, October 1964-January 1966. PPS to Min. of Supply, 1947-49 and to Minister of State for Foreign Affairs, 1950; Delegate to UN Assembly 1950; Delegate to Council of Europe and Western European Union, 1961-63. Hon. Sec. Parliamentary Painting Group, 1950-70. *Address:* 111 Kingswell Road, Ensbury Park, Bournemouth, Dorset BH10 5DG.

ROGERS, George Theodore; retired; Under-Secretary, Department of Trade, 1974-79; *b* 26 Feb. 1919; *s* of George James and late Margaret Lilian Rogers; *m* 1944, Mary Katherine Stedman; three *s* two *d. Educ:* Portsmouth Grammar Sch.; Keble Coll., Oxford (Open Schol. in Classics). Served War, Indian Infy, Burma, 1939-45. Resumed univ. educn (PPE), 1945-48; NATO Defence Coll., 1953-54. Min. of Supply/Min. of Aviation, 1948-65; Univ. Grants Cttee, 1965-68; Min. of Technology, 1968-70; DTI, 1970-74; Under-Sec., 1973. *Recreations:* gardening, travel, aviation. *Address:* 39 Sandy Lane, Cheam, Surrey SM2 7PQ. *T:* 01-642 6428.

ROGERS, Henry Augustus, OBE 1976 (MBE 1967); HM Diplomatic Service, retired; *b* 11 Dec. 1918; *s* of Henry Augustus Rogers and Evelyn Mary Rogers (*née* Casey); *m* 1947, Margaret May Stainsby; three *s. Educ:* The Fox Sch.; West Kensington Central Sch., London, W. Junior clerk with Solicitors, Wedlake Letts & Birds, Temple, prior to war. Joined RNVR, 1938; served war, 1939-45. Joined Foreign Office, 1945; Buenos Aires, 1946; Havana, 1953; Vice-Consul, Guatemala City, 1954; Vice-Consul (Comm.), Los Angeles, 1958; Second Sec. (Comm.), Belgrade, 1961; FO, 1963; Second Sec., Kaduna, 1965; First Sec., Head of Chancery and Consul, Tegucigalpa, 1967; FCO, 1971; Consul, Luanda, Angola, 1973; Consul-Gen., Brisbane, 1976-77; FCO, 1978. *Recreations:* studying the arts, classical literature and modern history, painting (the Impressionists), music. *Address:* 7 Fitzgerald Close, Silverdale Road, Eastbourne, East Sussex BN20 7EP. *T:* Eastbourne 30915.

ROGERS, Hugh Charles Innes, MA, FIMechE; Director, Avon Rubber Co., 1968-79 (Chairman, 1968-78); Vice-Chairman, Bristol and West Building Society; *b* 2 November 1904; *s* of late Hugh Innes Rogers, OBE, MIEE; *m* 1930, Iris Monica Seymour; one *s* three *d. Educ:* Marlborough; Clare College, Cambridge. Brecknell Munro & Rogers, 1926-31 (Chairman and Jt Man. Dir,

1931-41); SW Reg. Controller, Min. of Supply, 1941; SW Reg. Controller, Min. of Production and Chm. of Regional Bd, 1942-44; Dep. Controller (Production) in Admiralty, 1944-46. Imperial Tobacco Co. Ltd, Bristol: Chief Engr, 1948; Dir, 1949-67; a Dep. Chm., 1964-67; Dir, British American Tobacco Co., 1964-67. Member Bristol University Council, 1938, Chm., 1968-72. Chairman: SW Regional Housing Bd, 1952-53; SW Regional Council, FBI, 1954. High Sheriff of Avon, 1974. Hon. LLD Bristol, 1971; Hon. DSc Bath, 1971. *Recreations:* sailing, shooting, tennis, farming. *Address:* Beach House, Bitton, near Bristol BS15 6NP. *T:* Bitton 3127.

ROGERS, John Michael Thomas; QC 1979; barrister-at-law; a Recorder of the Crown Court, since 1976; *b* 13 May 1938; *s* of Harold Stuart Rogers and Sarah Joan Thomas; *m* 1971, Jennifer Ruth Platt; one *d. Educ:* Rydal Sch.; Birkenhead Sch.; Fitzwilliam House, Cambridge (MA, LLB). Schoolmaster, 1962-64; called to Bar, Gray's Inn, 1963. *Recreations:* farming, gardening. *Address:* Hengoed, Ruthin, Clwyd LL15 2DE. *T:* Ruthin 3849; 2 Dr Johnson's Building, Temple, EC4. *T:* 01-353 5371. *Clubs:* Reform; Pragmatists (Wirral); Ruthin Rugby Football; Bristol Channel Yacht.

ROGERS, Air Marshal Sir John (Robson), KCB 1982; CBE 1971; Controller, Aircraft, Ministry of Defence, since 1983; *b* 11 Jan. 1928; *s* of B. R. Rogers; *m* 1955, Gytha Elspeth Campbell; two *s* two *d. Educ:* Brentwood Sch.; No 1 Radio Sch., Cranwell; Royal Air Force Coll., Cranwell. OC 56(F) Sqdn, 1960-61; Gp Captain, 1967; OC RAF Coningsby, 1967-69; Air Commodore, 1971; Dir of Operational Requirements (RAF), 1971-73; Dep. Comdt, RAF Coll., 1973-75; RCDS, 1976; Air Vice-Marshal, 1977; Dir-Gen. of Organisation, RAF, 1977-79; AOC Training Units, RAF Support Comd, 1979-81; Air Mem. for Supply and Organisation, MoD, 1981-83. *Recreation:* motor racing. *Address:* c/o Lloyds Bank Ltd, 27 High Street, Colchester, Essex. *Club:* Royal Air Force.

ROGERS, John Willis, QC 1975; a Recorder of the Crown Court, since 1974; *b* 7 Nov. 1929; *s* of late Reginald John Rogers and late Joan Daisy Alexandra Rogers (*née* Willis); *m* 1952, Sheila Elizabeth Cann; one *s* one *d. Educ:* Sevenoaks Sch.; Fitzwilliam House, Cambridge (MA). Called to Bar, Lincoln's Inn, 1955 (Cholmeley Schol.). 1st Prosecuting Counsel to Inland Revenue, SE Circuit, 1969-75. *Recreations:* cricket, gardening, change ringing. *Address:* Carpmael Building, Temple, EC4Y 7AT. *T:* 01-353 5537. *Clubs:* Garrick, MCC, Band of Brothers.

ROGERS, Martin Hartley Guy; HM Diplomatic Service; on loan to Civil Service Selection Board, since 1979; *b* 11 June 1925; *s* of late Rev. Canon T. Guy Rogers and Marguerite Inez Rogers; *m* 1959, Jean Beresford Chinn; one *s* three *d. Educ:* Marlborough; Jesus Coll., Cambridge. CRO, 1949; 2nd Sec., Karachi, 1951-53; CRO, 1953-56 and 1958-60; seconded to Govt of Fedn of Nigeria, 1956-57; ndc 1960-61; 1st Sec., Ottawa, 1961-62; Adviser to Jamaican Min. of External Affairs, 1963; CRO, later Commonwealth Office, 1963-68; Dep. High Comr, Bombay, 1968-71, Kaduna, 1972-75; High Comr, The Gambia, 1975-79. *Recreations:* golf, bridge. *Address:* Croftside, Harrow Road East, Dorking, Surrey. *T:* Dorking 883789. *Club:* United Oxford & Cambridge University.

ROGERS, Martin John Wyndham; Chief Master, King Edward's School, Birmingham, since 1982; *b* 9 April 1931; *s* of John Frederick Rogers and Grace Mary Rogers; *m* 1957, Jane Cook; two *s* one *d. Educ:* Oundle Sch.; Heidelberg Univ.; Trinity Hall, Cambridge (MA). Henry Wiggin & Co., 1953-55; Westminster School: Asst Master, 1955-60; Sen. Chemistry Master, 1960-64; Housemaster, 1964-66; Under Master and Master of the Queen's Scholars, 1967-71; Headmaster of Malvern Coll., 1971-82. Seconded as Nuffield Research Fellow (O-level Chemistry Project), 1962-64; Salter's Company Fellow, Dept of Chemical Engrg and Chemical Technology, Imperial Coll., London, 1969. *Publications:* John Dalton and the Atomic Theory, 1965; Chemistry and Energy, 1968; (Editor) Foreground Chemistry Series, 1968; Gas Syringe Experiments, 1970; (co-author) Chemistry: facts, patterns and principles, 1972. *Address:* Vince House, King Edward's School, Birmingham B15 2UA. *T:* 021-472 0652.

ROGERS, Maurice Arthur Thorold; Secretary, Royal Institution, 1968-73; Joint Head, Head Office Research and Development Department, ICI, 1962-72; *b* 8 June 1911; *s* of A. G. L. Rogers; *g s* of Prof. J. E. Thorold Rogers; *m* 1947, Margaret Joan (*née* Craven); one *s* two *d. Educ:* Dragon Sch.; Westminster Sch.; University Coll., London. 1st Class hons BSc (Chem.) UCL 1932, PhD (Chem.) 1934. Chemist, ICI Dyestuffs Div., 1934-45; Head of Academic Relations Dept, 1946-58; Head of Head Office Research Dept, ICI, 1958-62. *Publications:* numerous papers in: Jl of Chem. Soc.; Nature; etc. *Recreations:* climbing, gardening, china restoration, conservation of countryside. *Address:* Mount Skippet, Ramsden, Oxford OX7 3AP. *T:* Ramsden 253.

ROGERS, Murray Rowland Fletcher; Member, Courts of Appeal for the Seychelles, St Helena, The Falkland Islands Colony and Dependencies, and the British Antarctic Territory, 1965-75; *b* 13 Sept. 1899; *s* of Geoffrey Pearson and Adeline Maud Rogers; *m* 1924, Dorothy Lilian Bardsley (*d* 1950); one *s* (one *d* decd). *Educ:* St Edward's School; RMC, Sandhurst; 2nd Lieut 8th Hussars, 1918-21; Liverpool Univ. (BA 1924). Schoolmaster until 1929; called to Bar, Gray's Inn, 1929; Northern Circuit until 1937; Magistrate, Nigeria, 1937-42; Chief Magistrate, Palestine, 1942-47; District Judge, Malaya, 1947-49; President Sessions Court, Malaya, 1949-52; Judge of Supreme Court,

Sarawak, N Borneo and Brunei, 1952-63, retd. *Publication:* Law Reports of the Seychelles Court of Appeal, vol 1, 1965-76, 1976. *Address:* Flat 10, 2 Mountview Road, N4. *Clubs:* Athenæum; Artists' (Liverpool).

ROGERS, Prof. Neville William, DLit London; FRSL; Professor of English, Ohio University, 1964-78, now Emeritus; *b* 5 Jan. 1908; *s* of Leonard George and Carrie Elizabeth Rogers (*née* Jennings). *Educ:* Rossall Sch.; Birkbeck Coll., London; studied French, Italian, Spanish and German privately abroad. BA Gen. 1932, BA Hons cl. II Classics, 1934, London; Phi Beta Kappa, Lambda Chapter of Ohio, 1974. Intell. Officer, RAF, Middle East and Italy, 1942-46. Asst Master, various prep. schs, 1927-32; Headmaster, Wellesley Sch., Croydon, 1932-34; Asst Master: King Edward VI Sch., Stafford, 1935-39; St Marylebone Grammar Sch., 1939-52; Leverhulme Fellow at Oxford, working on Shelley MSS, 1952-55; Sen. Res. Fellow and Lectr, Univ. of Birmingham, 1956-62; Vis. Professor: Michigan, 1959; Washington, St Louis, UCLA, 1960; Brandeis, 1962-64; Grant-in-Aid, American Council of Learned Socs for Res. in England, 1974; has lectured at many US and French univs. Has broadcast in English, Italian and French. Mem., Kennedy Scott's Philharmonic Choir, 1933-39; Founder Mem., London Philharmonic Choir (Vice-Chm. 1947-48); Mem. Cttee: British-Italian Soc., 1947-; Keats Shelley Memorial Assoc., 1946-. *Publications:* Keats, Shelley and Rome, 1949 (4th edn 1970); Shelley at Work, 1956 (2nd edn 1968); (ed with Archibald Colquhoun) Italian Regional Tales of the Nineteenth Century, 1961; (ed) The Esdaile Poems, 1966; (ed and annotated) Selected Poetry of Shelley, 1968; (ed) Complete Poetical Works of Percy Bysshe Shelley (Oxford English Texts, 4 vols), Vol I, 1802-1813, 1972, Vol. II, 1814-1817, 1975; contribs to Encycl. Britannica, Times Lit. Supp., Times Educnl Supp., Daily Telegraph, Twentieth Century, Review of English Studies, Mod. Lang. Review, Keats-Shelley Memorial Bulletin, Keats-Shelley Jl, Book Collector, Ulisse, Il Ponte, Ohio Review. *Recreations:* literature, languages, music, travel. *Address:* Vallombrosa, 45 Mound Street, Athens, Ohio 45701, USA. *Clubs:* National Liberal, Authors'.

ROGERS, Maj.-Gen. Norman A. C.; *see* Coxwell-Rogers.

ROGERS, Maj.-Gen. Norman Charles, FRCS 1949; Research Fellow, Guy's Hospital Medical School; *b* 14 Oct. 1916; *s* of Wing Comdr Charles William Rogers, RAF, and Edith Minnie Rogers (*née* Weaver); *m* 1954, Pamela Marion (*née* Rose); two *s* one *d. Educ:* Imperial Service Coll.; St Bartholomew's Hosp. MB, BS London; MRCS, LRCP 1939. Emergency Commn, Lieut RAMC, Oct. 1939; 131 Field Amb. RAMC, Dunkirk (despatches); RMO, 4th Royal Tank Regt, N Africa, 1941-42; Italy, 1942-43 (POW); RMO 1st Black Watch, NW Europe, 1944-45 (wounded, despatches twice). Ho. Surg., St Bartholomew's Hosp., 1946-47; Registrar (Surgical) Appts, Norwich, 1948-52; Sen. Registrar Appts, Birmingham, 1952-56; granted permanent commn, RAMC, 1956; surgical appts in mil. hospitals: Chester, Dhekelia (Cyprus), Catterick, Iserlohn (BAOR), 1956-67; Command Consultant Surgeon, BAOR, 1967-69; Dir, Army Surgery, 1969-73; QHS, 1969-73; Clin. Supt, 1975-81, and Consultant, 1973-81, Accident and Emergency Dept, Guy's Hosp. *Publications:* contribs on surgical subjects. *Address:* 31 Merrick Square, SE1. *T:* 01-407 3774.

ROGERS, Mrs P. E.; *see* Box, B. E.

ROGERS, Paul; actor; *b* Plympton, Devon, 22 March 1917; *s* of Edwin and Dulcie Myrtle Rogers; *m* 1st, 1939, Jocelyn Wynne (marr. diss. 1955); two *s*; 2nd, 1955, Rosalind Boxall; two *d. Educ:* Newton Abbot Grammar School, Devon. Michael Chekhov Theatre Studio, 1936-38. First appearance on stage as Charles Dickens in Bird's Eye of Valour, Scala, 1938; Stratford-upon-Avon Shakespeare Memorial Theatre, 1939; Concert Party and Colchester Rep. Co. until 1940. Served Royal Navy, 1940-46. Colchester Rep. Co. and Arts Council Tour and London Season, Tess of the D'Urbervilles, 1946-47; Bristol Old Vic, 1947-49; London Old Vic (incl. tour S Africa and Southern Rhodesia), 1949-53; also at Edinburgh, London and in USA, 1954-57; London, 1958; tour to Moscow, Leningrad and Warsaw, 1960. Roles with Old Vic include numerous Shakespearean leads. Other parts include: Sir Claude Mulhammer in The Confidential Clerk, Edinburgh Festival and Lyric, London, 1953; Lord Claverton in The Elder Statesman, Edinburgh Fest. and Cambridge Theatre, London, 1958; Mr Fox in Mr Fox of Venice, Piccadilly, 1959; Johnny Condell in One More River, Duke of York's and Westminster, 1959; Nickles in JB, Phœnix, 1961; Reginald Kinsale in Photo Finish, Saville, 1962; The Seagull, Queen's, 1964; Season of Goodwill, Queen's, 1964; The Homecoming, Aldwych, 1965; Timon of Athens, Stratford-upon-Avon, 1965; The Government Inspector, Aldwych, 1966; Henry IV, Stratford-upon-Avon, 1966; Max in The Homecoming, New York, 1967 (Tony Award and Whitbread Anglo-American Award); Plaza Suite, Lyric, 1969; The Happy Apple, Apollo, 1970; Sleuth, St Martin's, 1970, NY, 1971 and 1974; Othello, Nat. Theatre Co., Old Vic, 1974; Heartbreak House, Nat. Theatre, 1975; The Marrying of Ann Leete, Aldwych, 1975; The Return of A. J. Raffles, Aldwych, 1975; The Zykovs, Aldwych, 1976; Volpone, The Madras House, National Theatre, 1977; Eclipse, Royal Court, 1978; You Never Can Tell, Lyric, Hammersmith, 1979; The Dresser, New York, 1981, 1982; The Importance of Being Earnest, A Kind of Alaska, National, 1982. Appears in films and television. *Publication:* a Preface to Folio Soc. edition of Shakespeare's Love's Labour's Lost, 1959. *Recreations:* gardening, carpentry, books. *Address:* 9 Hillside Gardens, Highgate, N6 5SU. *T:* 01-340 2656. *Club:* Naval.

ROGERS, Rev. Percival Hallewell, MBE 1945; retired; *b* 13 Sept. 1912; *m* 1940, Annie Mary Stuart, 2nd *d* of Lt-Col James Morwood; two *s* one *d. Educ:* Brentwood School; St Edmund Hall, Oxford. BA Class II, Hons English, Oxford, 1935; Diploma in Education, 1936; MA 1946. Two terms of teaching, Westminster School; Master in charge of English, Haileybury, 1936; served War, 1940-45 (despatches twice, MBE): RA, Major; DÃA QMG; Bishop's College, Cheshunt, 1946; ordained, 1947; Asst Chaplain and English Master, Haileybury, 1947; Chaplain and English Master, 1949; Headmaster, Portora Royal Sch., Enniskillen, 1954-73; student, Internat. Acad. for Continuous Educn, Cheltenham, 1973-74; Chaplain, Gresham's Sch., Holt, 1974-75; Dean, Internat. Acad. for Continuous Educn, 1975-76; Asst Priest, Trinity Episcopal Church, New Orleans, 1976-80; Warden of Lay Readers, Dio. of Clogher, 1982. *Publications:* The Needs of the Whole Man, Systematics, 1971; Editor and contrib. to A Guide to Divinity Teaching (SPCK), 1962. *Address:* Moyglass Old School, Springfield, Co. Fermanagh, N Ireland. *T:* Springfield 200. *Clubs:* East India, Devonshire, Sports and Public Schools; Friendly Brothers (Dublin).

ROGERS, Peter Brian; Director of Finance, Independent Broadcasting Authority, since 1982; Director, Channel Four Television Company Ltd, since 1982; *b* 8 April 1941; *s* of late William Patrick Rogers and Margaret Elizabeth Rogers; *m* 1966, Jean Mary Bailey; one *s* two *d. Educ:* De La Salle Grammar Sch., Liverpool; Manchester Univ. (1st Cl. Hons BAEcon; Cobden Prize); London Sch. of Econs and Pol. Science, London Univ. (MSc Econs). Tax Officer, Inland Revenue, 1959-67; Res. Associate, Manchester Univ., 1967-68; Econ. Adviser, HM Treasury, 1968-73; Sen. Econ. Adviser, Central Policy Review Staff, Cabinet Office, 1973-74; Dir of Econ. Planning, Tyne and Wear CC (on secondment from Central Govt), 1974-76; Sen. Econ. Adviser, DoE, 1976-79; Dep. Chief Exec., Housing Corp., 1979-82. *Recreations:* woodwork, photography. *Address:* 52 St James's Avenue, Beckenham, Kent BR3 4HG. *T:* 01-650 7622.

ROGERS, Sir Philip, GCB 1975 (KCB 1970; CB 1965); CMG 1952; Chairman, Universities Superannuation Scheme, since 1977; Director: Glaxo Ltd, since 1978; Greater London Regional Board, Lloyds Bank, since 1980; *b* 19 Aug. 1914; *s* of William Edward and Sarah Jane Rogers; *m* 1940, Heather Mavis Gordon; one *s* one *d. Educ:* William Hulme's Grammar School, Manchester; Emmanuel Coll., Cambridge. Apptd to administrative class of Home Civil Service, as an Asst Principal in Colonial Office, 1936; seconded to be Private Secretary to Governor of Jamaica, Jan.-Dec. 1939; Asst Secretary, Colonial Office, 1946-53; Assistant Under-Secretary of State, Colonial Office, 1953-61; Under-Secretary, Department of Technical Co-operation, 1961-64; Dep. Sec. of Cabinet, 1964-67; Third Secretary, Treasury, 1967-68; Dep. Secretary, 1968-69, Second Permanent Secretary, 1969-70, Civil Service Dept; Permanent Secretary, DHSS, 1970-75. Chm., Bd of Management, London Sch. of Hygiene and Trop. Medicine, 1977-82. Member: SHA, Hammersmith Hosp., 1982-; Council, Outward Bound Trust, 1976- (Chm. 1976-80); Court, London Univ., 1978-; Council, Reading Univ., 1978- (Pres., 1980-). *Recreation:* gardening. *Address:* Orchard House, Wargrave, Berks RG10 8DE. *T:* Wargrave 2760. *Club:* East India.

ROGERS, Sir Philip (James), Kt 1961; CBE 1952; Chairman, Tobacco Research Council, 1963-71; *b* 1908; *s* of late James Henry Rogers; *m* 1939, Brenda Mary Sharp, CBE, *d* of late Ernest Thompson Sharp. *Educ:* Blundell's Sch. Served War (RWAFF and Intell. Corps), 1940-44. MLC, Nigeria, 1947-51; MLC, Kenya, 1957-62; Elected Representative, Kenya, East African Legislative Assembly, 1962 and 1963. President: Nig. Chamber of Commerce, 1948 and 1950 (Vice-Pres. 1947 and 1949); Nairobi Chamber of Commerce, 1957 (Vice-Pres. 1956); AAA of Nig., 1951; Dir, Nig. Elec. Corp., 1951; Governor, Nig. Coll. of Technology, 1951; Member: Nig. Exec. Cttee, Rd Transport Bd, 1948-51; Central Council Red Cross Soc. of W Africa, 1950-51; Trades Adv. Cttee, Nig., 1950-51; Wages Adv. Bd, Kenya, 1955-61; EA Industrial Council, 1954-63; EA Air Licensing Appeals Trib., 1958-60; EA Air Adv. Council, 1956-60; Kenya Road Authority, 1957-61; Provl Council, Univ. of E Africa, 1961-63; Gov. Council, Roy. Tech. Coll. of E Africa, 1957-58 (Chm. 1958/59/60). Chairman: East African Tobacco Co. Ltd, 1951-63; Rift Valley Cigarette Co. Ltd, 1956-63; EA Rd Fedn, 1954-56; Kenya Cttee on Study and Trg in USA, 1958-63; Bd of Govs, Coll. of Social Studies, 1960-63; Nairobi Special Loans Cttee, 1960-63; Af. Teachers' Service Bd, 1956-63; Council, Royal College (now University Coll., Nairobi), 1961-63; Fedn of Sussex Amenity Socs, 1968-; Trustee, Outward Bound Trust of Kenya, 1959-63; Rep. of Assoc. Chambers of Commerce & Indust. of Eastern Africa; Mem. of Industrial Tribunals, England and Wales, 1966-80. Governor, Plumpton Agric. Coll., 1967-76. Member: E Sussex Educn Cttee, 1969-75; Finance Cttee, UCL, 1972-79; Indep. Schools Careers Orgn, 1972-79; Chairman: Fedn of Sussex Amenity Socs, 1968-80; Age Concern, East Sussex, 1974-80. *Address:* Church Close, Newick, East Sussex BN8 4JZ. *T:* Newick 2210.

ROGERS, Richard George, ARA 1978; MArch; RIBA; Partner: Richard Rogers and Partners, Rogers PA Technical and Science Centre; Piano and Rogers, France; *b* 23 July 1933; four *s*; *m* Ruth. *Educ:* Architectural Assoc. (graduate, Dip.); Yale Univ. (Fulbright, Edward D. Stone, and Yale Scholar; MArch). RIBA 1967. Winner of Plateau Beaubourg internat. competition from 680 entries for Centre Pompidou Beaubourg (1 million sq. ft in Paris for Min. of Culture), 1977; winner of Lloyd's internat. competition for 600,000 sq. ft in City of London, 1978; projects include: furniture component system, Knoll Internat., USA; music res. centre for Pierre Boulez and Min.

of Cultural Affairs, Paris; B+B Factory, Como, Italy; Rogers PA Tech. and Science Centre; Cummins/Fleetguard factory, France; Electronics Factory for Reliance Controls Ltd, Swindon; Rogers PA Tech. and Science Centre, Phases 1, 2 and 3, near Cambridge, 1975; Inmos semi-conductor manufg facility, S Wales. Trustee, Tate Gallery, 1981-. Financial Times Indust. Arch. Award for Most Outstanding Indust. Bldg, 1967 (Reliance Controls, Swindon), and 1976 (Patscentre); Auguste Perret Prize, Internat. Union of Architects, 1978. Visiting Lecturer/Professor: UCLA, Yale, Princeton, Harvard, Berkeley, Cornell, McGill, Hong Kong, Aachen, Warsaw, Milan, Cambridge, Arch. Assoc. Hon. Fellow, Royal Acad. of Fine Arts at The Hague. Subject of BBC documentary, Building for Change. *Publications:* incl. contribs to Architectural Design, Global Arch., and Arch. and Urbanism. *Address:* 18 Belsize Grove, NW3 4UM. *T:* 01-722 2132.

ROGERS, Thomas Edward, CMG 1960; MBE 1945; HM Diplomatic Service, retired; *b* 28 Dec. 1912; *s* of T. E. Rogers and Lucy Jane Browne; *m* 1950, Eileen Mary, *d* of R. J. Speechley; no *c. Educ:* Bedford Sch.; Emmanuel Coll., Cambridge (Exhibnr); School of Oriental Studies, London. Selected for Indian Civil Service, 1936, and for Indian Political Service, 1941. Served in Bengal, 1937-41; in Persia and Persian Gulf, 1941-45; Political Agent, Quetta, 1947. Entered Foreign Service, 1948: FO, 1948-50; Bogota, 1950-53; jssc, 1953-54; Coun. (Comm.), Madrid, 1954-58; Coun. (Econ.), Belgrade, 1958-62; Minister (Econ.), Buenos Aires, 1963-65; Dep. UK High Comr, Canada, 1966-70; Actg High Comr, 1967-68; Ambassador to Colombia, 1970-73. Chm., Anglo-Colombian Soc., 1981-. Grand Cross of St Carlos, Colombia, 1974. *Recreation:* travel. *Address:* Chintens, Firway, Grayshott, Hants. *Club:* United Oxford & Cambridge University.

ROGERS, Thomas Gordon Parry; Director, Personnel and Europe, The Plessey Co. plc, since 1974; Chairman, Plessey Pension Trust, since 1980; Director: The Plessey Co.; Plessey GmbH; Plessey N America Corporation; Plessey France; *b* 7 Aug. 1924; *s* of late Victor Francis Rogers and Ella (*née* May); *m* 1st, 1947, Pamela Mary (*née* Greene) (marr. diss. 1973); one *s* seven *d* ; 2nd, 1973, Patricia Juliet (*née* Curtis); one *s* one *d. Educ:* West Hartlepool Grammar Sch.; St Edmund Hall, Oxford. MA; CIPM, CBIM, AMIPR; FRSA. Proctor and Gamble Ltd, 1948-54; Mars Ltd, 1954-56; Hardy Spicer Ltd, 1956-61; IBM United Kingdom Ltd, 1961-74; Director: IBM UK Holdings, 1964-74; Management Selection Ltd, 1970-78; ICL, 1977-79. Chairman: Adv. Cttee on Charitable Fund Raising, NCSS, 1970-76; Exec. Cttee, Inst. of Manpower Studies; Ind. Relations Cttee, Inst. of Directors (Mem. Council); Pres., Inst. of Personnel Management, 1975-77; Member: Council of Careers Research Adv. Centre, 1968-; Council and Exec., Industrial Participation Assoc., 1972-; CBI/BIM Panel on Management Educn, 1968-; CBI Employment Policy Cttee, 1980-; Council and Exec., IMS, 1968-; Oxford Univ. Appts Cttee, 1972-; Employment Appeal Tribunal, 1978-; Standing Commn on Pay Comparability, 1980-81; Management Bd, EEF, 1980-; E European Trade Council, 1982-; Econ. League, 1982-. *Publications:* The Recruitment and Training of Graduates, 1970; contribs to: The Director's Handbook, Management and the Working Environment, and various newspapers and jls. *Recreations:* birdwatching, golf, tennis. *Address:* St Edward's Chantry, Bimport, Shaftesbury, Dorset. *T:* Shaftesbury 2789. *Clubs:* Savile, Royal Automobile, Royal Wimbledon Golf.

ROGERS, William Pierce; Partner, law firm of Royall, Koegel, Rogers and Wells, 1961-69, and since 1973, when renamed Rogers & Wells; *b* 23 June 1913; *s* of Harrison A. and Myra Beswick Rogers; *m* 1937, Adele Langston; three *s* one *d. Educ:* Canton High School, Canton, New York; Colgate University; Cornell Law School. Law firm of Cadwalader, Wickersham and Taft, NY City, 1937; as Asst District Attorney in NY County, 1938; US Navy, 1942-46; Dist Attorney's Office in New York, 1946; Chief Counsel, Senate Investigating Cttee, 1947; Counsel, Senate Permanent Investigating Cttee, 1949; law firm of Dwight, Royall, Harris, Koegel and Caskey, offices in New York and Washington, 1950; Dep. Attorney-General, 1953; Attorney-General of the US, 1957-61; Secretary of State, USA, 1969-73. Holds several hon. degrees in Law, from Univs and Colls in the USA, 1956-60. Mem. Bar Assocs in the USA. US Representative: to 20th Session of UN General Assembly, 1965; on UN Ad Hoc Cttee on SW Africa, 1967; Mem., President's Commn on Law Enforcement and Administration of Justice, 1965-67. *Recreations:* golf, tennis, swimming. *Address:* 7007 Glenbrook Road, Bethesda, Md 20814, USA; 870 United Nations Plaza, New York, NY 10017. *Clubs:* Metropolitan (Washington); Burning Tree (Bethesda); Racquet and Tennis, The Sky (NYC); Chevy Chase (Chevy Chase).

ROGERSON, Rt. Rev. Barry; *see* Wolverhampton, Bishop Suffragan of.

ROGERSON, John; Part-time Inspector, Department of the Environment, 1973-75; *b* 9 March 1917; *s* of late Walter John Lancashire Rogerson and Anne Marion Rogerson; *m* 1972, Audrey, *d* of late Adrian and Dorothy Maitland-Heriot. *Educ:* Tonbridge Sch.; St John's Coll., Oxford (BA). Served War, 2nd Lieut, later Captain, Royal Norfolk Regt, 1940-46. Principal: Min. of Town and Country Planning, 1947-49; HM Treasury, 1949-51; Min. of Housing and Local Govt (later Dept of the Environment), 1951-73; Asst Sec., 1955; Under-Sec., 1963; retd 1973. *Recreations:* botany, archaeology, mycophagy. *Address:* 95 Ridgmount Gardens, WC1E 7AZ. *T:* 01-636 0433.

ROGG, Lionel; organist and composer; Professor of Organ and Improvisation, Geneva Conservatoire de Musique, since 1961; *b* 1936; *m* Claudine Effront; three *s. Educ:* Conservatoire de Musique, Geneva (1st prize for piano and

organ). Records include works by Alain, Buxtehude (complete organ works; Deutscher Schallplatten Preis, 1980), Couperin and Martin; also complete works of J. S. Bach (Grand Prix du Disque, 1970, for The Art of the Fugue). *Compositions:* Acclamations, 1964; Chorale Preludes, 1971; Partita, 1975. *Publication:* Eléments de Contrepoint, 1969. *Address:* Conservatoire de Musique, Place Neuve, Geneva, Switzerland.

ROIJEN, Jan Herman Van; Grand Cross, Order of Orange Nassau; Commander, Order of the Netherlands Lion; Netherlands Ambassador to the United Kingdom, 1964-70; Netherlands Ambassador to the Icelandic Republic, 1964-70; Netherlands Permanent Representative to Council of Western European Union, 1964-70; *b* Istanbul, 10 April 1905; *s* of Jan Herman van Roijen (sometime Neths Min. to USA), and (American-born) Albertina Winthrop van Roijen; *m* 1934, Anne Snouck Hurgronje; two *s* two *d. Educ:* Univ. of Utrecht. Doctor in Law, 1929. Joined Foreign Service, 1930; Attaché to Neths Legn, Washington, 1930-32; Min. of For. Affairs, 1933-36; Sec. to Neths Legn, Tokyo, 1936-39; Chief of Polit. Div. of Min. of For. Affairs, 1939. Jailed during German occupation; escaped to London, 1944. Minister without Portfolio, 1945; Minister of For. Affairs, March-July 1946; Asst Deleg. and Deleg. to UN Conf. and Assemblies, 1945-48; Ambassador to Canada, 1947-50. Leader, Neths Delegn to bring about Netherlands-Indonesian Round Table Conf., Batavia, 1949; Dep. Leader, Neths Delegn at Round Table Conf., The Hague, 1949. Ambassador to the United States, 1950-64. Leader, Neths Delegn in negotiations with Indonesia about W New Guinea, Middleburg (Va.) and New York, 1962. Holds several hon. doctorates in Laws, of Univs and Colls in USA; Gr. Cross, Order of Oak Crown, Luxembourg; Gr. Cross, Order of Falcon, Iceland; Comdr, Order of British Empire (CBE); Comdr, Order of Holy Treasure, Japan. *Recreations:* reading, theatre, golf. *Address:* Stoephoutflat, Stoeplaan 11, Wassenaar, Netherlands. *Club:* De Haagsche (The Hague).

ROKISON, Kenneth Stuart, QC 1976; *b* 13 April 1937; *s* of Frank Edward and Kitty Winifred Rokison; *m* 1973, Rosalind Julia (*née* Mitchell); two *d. Educ:* Whitgift School, Croydon; Magdalene College, Cambridge (BA 1960). Called to the Bar, Gray's Inn, 1961. *Recreation:* acting. *Address:* Ashcroft Farm, Gadbrook, Betchworth, Surrey. *T:* Dawes Green 244.

ROLAND, Nicholas; *see* Walmsley, Arnold Robert.

ROLF, Percy Henry; a Recorder of the Crown Court, since 1978; Senior Partner, Robinson Jarvis & Rolf, Solicitors, Isle of Wight, since 1964 (Partner 1948); *b* 25 Dec. 1915; *s* of Percy Algernon Rolf and Lydia Kate (*née* Arnold); *m* 1939, Cecilia Florence Cooper; one *s* one *d. Educ:* Sandown Grammar Sch.; London Univ. (LLB). Solicitor. Served War, RAF, 1940-46: Wing Comdr; Sen. Air Traffic Control Officer, Transport Comd, 1945-46. *Recreations:* golf, skiing, gardening. *Address:* Ashlake Water, Fishbourne, Isle of Wight. *T:* Wootton Bridge 882513.

ROLFE, Rear-Adm. Henry Cuthbert Norris, CB 1959; *b* 1908; *s* of Benedict Hugh Rolfe, MA Oxon; *m* 1931, Mary Monica Fox; one *s* two *d. Educ:* Pangbourne Nautical College. Joined Royal Navy, 1925. Served War of 1939-45: HMS Hermes, 1939; South-East Asia, 1944; Staff of Director of Air Warfare, Admiralty, 1947; Commanded HMS Veryan Bay, 1948; service with Royal Canadian Navy, 1949; Commanded HMS Vengeance, 1952; Commanded RN Air Station, Culdrose, 1952; Commanded HMS Centaur, 1954-56; Commanded RN Air Station, Ford, 1956-57; Asst Chief of Naval Staff (Warfare) 1957-60; Regional Director, Northern Region, Commonwealth Graves Commission, 1961-64, retd. Naval ADC to the Queen, 1957; Rear-Admiral, 1957. Liveryman, Worshipful Company of Coachmakers and Coach Harnessmakers, 1962. *Address:* 43 Nuns Road, Winchester, Hants.

ROLFE, Hume B.; *see* Boggis-Rolfe.

ROLL, family name of Baron Roll of Ipsden.

ROLL OF IPSDEN, Baron *cr* 1977 (Life Peer), of Ipsden in the County of Oxfordshire; **Eric Roll,** KCMG 1962 (CMG 1949); CB 1956; Director of the Bank of England, 1968-77; Chancellor, University of Southampton, since 1974; Chairman: S. G. Warburg & Co. Ltd, since 1974 (Deputy Chairman, 1967-74); Mercury Securities Ltd, since 1974; *b* 1 Dec. 1907; *yr s* of Mathias and Fany Roll; *m* 1934, Winifred, *o d* of Elliott and Sophia Taylor; two *d. Educ:* on the Continent; Univ. of Birmingham. BCom 1928; PhD 1930; Gladstone Memorial Prize, 1928; Univ. Research Scholarship, 1929. Prof. of Economics and Commerce, Univ. Coll. of Hull, 1935-46 (leave of absence 1939-46). Special Rockefeller Foundation Fellow, USA, 1939-41. Member, later Dep. Head, British Food Mission to N America, 1941-46; UK Dep. Member and UK Exec. Officer, Combined Food Board, Washington, until 1946; Asst Sec., Ministry of Food, 1946-47; Under-Secretary, HM Treasury (Central Economic Planning Staff), 1948; Minister, UK Delegation to OEEC, 1949. Deputy Head, United Kingdom Delegation to North Atlantic Treaty Organization, Paris, 1952; Under Secretary Ministry of Agriculture, Fisheries and Food, 1953-57; Executive Dir, International Sugar Council, 1957-59; Chm., United Nations Sugar Conf., 1958; Deputy Secretary, Ministry of Agriculture, Fisheries and Food, 1959-61; Deputy Leader, UK Delegation for negotiations with the European Economic Community, 1961-63; Economic Minister and Head of UK Treasury Delegation, Washington, 1963-64, also Exec. Dir for the UK International Monetary Fund and International Bank for Reconstruction and Development; Permanent Under-Sec. of State, Dept of Economic Affairs, 1964-66. Chm., subseq. Hon. Chm., Book Development Council, 1967-. Independent Mem., NEDC, 1971-80. Director: Times Newspapers Ltd, 1967-80; Times Newspapers Holdings Ltd, 1980-; also other Directorships. Hon. DSc Hull, 1967; Hon. DSocSci Birmingham, 1967; Hon. LLD Southampton, 1974. Grosses Goldene Ehrenzeichen mit Stern (Austria), 1979; Comdr 1st Cl., Order of the Dannebrog (Denmark). *Publications:* An Early Experiment in Industrial Organization, 1930; Spotlight on Germany, 1933; About Money, 1934; Elements of Economic Theory, 1935; Organized Labour (collaborated), 1938; The British Commonwealth at War (collaborated), 1943; A History of Economic Thought, 1954, new edn, 1972; The Combined Food Board, 1957; The World After Keynes, 1968; The Uses and Abuses of Economics, 1978; articles in Economic Jl, Economica, American Economic Review, etc. *Recreation:* reading. *Address:* D2 Albany, Piccadilly, W1. *Club:* Brooks's.

ROLL, Rev. Sir James (William Cecil), 4th Bt, *cr* 1921; Vicar of St John's, Becontree, since 1958; *b* 1 June 1912; *s* of Sir Cecil Ernest Roll, 3rd Bt, and Mildred Kate (*d* 1926), *d* of William Wells, Snaresbrook; *S* father, 1938; unmarried. *Educ:* Chigwell School, Essex; Pembroke College, Oxford; Chichester Theological College. Deacon, 1937. Curate East Ham Parish Church, 1944-58. *Heir:* none. *Address:* St John's Vicarage, 34 Castle Road, Dagenham, Essex. *T:* 01-592 5409; 82 Leighcliff Road, Leigh on Sea, Essex. *T:* Southend on Sea 76177.

ROLLO, family name of **Lord Rollo**.

ROLLO, 13th Lord *cr* 1651; **Eric John Stapylton Rollo**; Baron Dunning, 1869; JP; *b* 3 Dec. 1915; *s* of 12th Lord and Helen Maud (*d* 1928), *o c* of Frederick Chetwynd Stapylton of Hatton Hill, Windlesham, Surrey; *S* father, 1947; *m* 1938, Suzanne Hatton; two *s* one *d.* *Educ:* Eton. Served War of 1939-45, Grenadier Guards, retiring with rank of Captain. JP Perthshire, 1962. *Heir:* *s* Master of Rollo, *qv.* *Address:* Pitcairns, Dunning, Perthshire. *T:* Dunning 202.

ROLLO, Master of; Hon. David Eric Howard Rollo; *b* 31 March 1943; *s* and *heir* of 13th Lord Rollo, *qv*; *m* 1971, Felicity Anne Christian, *o d* of Lt-Comdr J. B. Lamb; three *s.* *Educ:* Eton. Late Captain Grenadier Guards. *Address:* 20 Draycott Avenue, SW3. *Clubs:* Cavalry and Guards, Turf.

ROLO, Cyril Felix, CMG 1975; OBE 1959; HM Diplomatic Service, retired; *b* 13 Feb. 1918; *s* of late I. J. Rolo and Linda (*née* Suares); *m* 1948, Marie Luise Christine (*née* Baeurle); one *s.* *Educ:* Charterhouse; Oriel Coll., Oxford (BA). Served with Armed Forces, 1940-46 (Major): Oxf. and Bucks LI, later on Gen. Staff; Western Desert, E Africa, Italy, Austria. Joined HM Foreign (subseq. Diplomatic) Service, 1946: Allied Commn for Austria, 1947-48; 2nd Sec., Rome, 1948-50; Political Adviser's Office, Berlin, 1950-52; FO, 1952-57; 1st Sec., Vienna, 1957-62; FO (subseq. FCO), 1962-76; Counsellor, 1971. *Recreations:* travel, golf, reading. *Address:* 32 Roxburghe Mansions, Kensington Court, W8 5BH. *T:* 01-937 4696. *Clubs:* Travellers'; Sunningdale Golf.

ROLPH, C. H.; *see* Hewitt, Cecil R.

ROMAIN, Roderick Jessel Anidjar; Metropolitan Magistrate, since 1972; *b* 2 Dec. 1916; *s* of late Artom A. Romain and Winifred (*née* Rodrigues); *m* 1947, Miriam, *d* of late Semtob Sequerra; one *s* one *d.* *Educ:* Malvern Coll.; Sidney Sussex Coll., Cambridge. Called to the Bar, Middle Temple, 1939. Commissioned from HAC to 27th Field Regt, RA, 1940. Served War of 1939-45; France and Belgium, also N Africa and Italy, JAG Staff, 1943-45; JA at Neuengamme War Crimes Trial. Admitted a Solicitor, 1949, in practice as Partner, in Freke Palmer, Romain & Gassman, until 1972; recalled to Bar, 1973; a Dep. Circuit Judge, 1975-78. *Recreations:* golf, gardening. *Address:* 43 Lyndale Avenue, NW2 2QB. *T:* 01-435 5913. *Club:* Garrick.

ROMANES, Professor George John, CBE 1971; PhD; Professor of Anatomy, since 1954, and Dean of Faculty of Medicine, since 1979, Edinburgh University; *b* 2 Dec. 1916; *s* of George Romanes, BSc, AMICE, and Isabella Elizabeth Burn Smith; *m* 1945, Muriel Grace Adam, Edinburgh; four *d.* *Educ:* Edinburgh Academy; Christ's College, Cambridge (BA, PhD); Edinburgh University (MB, ChB). Marmaduke Sheild Scholar in Human Anatomy, 1938-40; Demonstrator in Anatomy, Cambridge, 1939; Beit Memorial Fellow for Medical Research, Cambridge, 1944-46; Lectr in Neuroanatomy, Edinburgh, 1946; Prof. of Anatomy, Edinburgh, 1954. Commonwealth Fund Fell., Columbia Univ., NY, 1949-50. Chm., Bd of Management, Edinburgh Royal Infirmary, 1959-74. Mem. Anatomical Soc. of Gt Brit. and Ireland; Mem. Amer. Assoc. of Anatomists; Assoc. Mem. Amer. Neurological Assoc. FRSE 1955; FRCSE 1958. *Publications:* (ed) Cunningham's Textbook and Manuals of Anatomy; various papers on the anatomy and development of the nervous system in Jl of Anatomy and Jl of Comparative Neurology. *Recreations:* angling and curling. *Address:* 197 Colinton Road, Edinburgh EH14 1BJ. *T:* 031-443 1101.

ROME, Maj.-Gen. Francis David, CB 1955; CMG 1959; CBE 1949; DSO 1944; retired; *b* 11 Sept. 1905; *er s* of late Francis James Rome; *m* 1st, 1936, Sybil Parry (*d* 1979), 2nd *d* of late Lieut-Colonel Henry Carden, DCLI; no *c*; 2nd, 1980, Mrs Francesca Finlay. *Educ:* Cheltenham Coll.; RMC, Sandhurst. Commander: 111 Indian Infantry Brigade, Special Force, SEAC,

1944-45 (DSO); 3rd Parachute Bde, 1946-47; 1st Parachute Bde, 1947-48 (CBE). Served War of 1939-45, France, 1939-40, SEAC, 1943-45; Palestine, 1946-48; Malaya, 1950-51; General Officer Commanding, 16th Airborne Division (Territorial Army), 1953-56; General Officer Commanding, Berlin (British Sector), 1956-59. Colonel, The Royal Fusiliers, 1954-59. *Address:* Ferne Down, Ham, Marlborough, Wilts SN8 3RB. *T:* Inkpen 341. *Club:* Army and Navy.

ROMER, Mark Lemon Robert; a Metropolitan Stipendiary Magistrate since 1972; *b* 12 July 1927; *s* of late Rt Hon. Sir Charles Romer, OBE, and Hon. Lady Romer; *m* 1953, Philippa Maynard Tomson; one *s* two *d.* *Educ:* Bryanston; Trinity Hall, Cambridge (BA, LLB). Called to Bar, Lincoln's Inn, 1952; practised privately until 1958 when joined Govt Legal Service. *Recreations:* bird-watching, reading, music. *Address:* The Old Vicarage, Braughing, Ware, Herts. *T:* Ware 821434.

ROMILLY, family name of **Baron Romilly**.

ROMILLY, 4th Baron, *cr* 1865; **William Gaspard Guy Romilly**, Hon. MA Oxon 1943; *b* 8 March 1899; *o c* of 3rd Baron and Violet Edith, *o sister* of Sir Philip H. B. Grey Egerton, 12th Bt, and *niece* of Lord Londesborough; *S* father, 1905; *m* 1st, 1929, Hon. Diana Joan Sackville-West (marriage dissolved, 1944), *o d* of 4th Baron Sackville, KBE; 2nd, 1944, Dora (*d* 1960), *d* of late Reginald Morris; 3rd, 1966, Elizabeth, *widow* of Capt. Lionel Cecil, and *er d* of late Charles M. Clover. *Educ:* Eton; Sandhurst. Coldstream Guards, 1917-23; served in France in European War; Reserve of Officers, 1923. Rejoined Coldstream Guards, September 1939; served until 1945 and granted honorary rank of Major. Member of Malborough and Ramsbury Rural District Council, 1949-74 (Chairman, 1964-67). *Heir:* none. *Address:* Bridge House, Chilton Foliat, near Hungerford, Berks. *T:* Hungerford 2328.

ROMNEY, 7th Earl of, *cr* 1801; **Michael Henry Marsham**; Bt 1663; Baron of Romney, 1716; Viscount Marsham, 1801; *b* 22 Nov. 1910; *s* of Lt-Col the Hon. Reginald Hastings Marsham, OBE (*d* 1922) (2nd *s* of 4th Earl) and Dora Hermione (*d* 1923), *d* of late Charles North; *S* cousin, 1975; *m* 1939, Frances Aileen, *o d* of late Lt-Col James Russell Landale, IA. *Educ:* Sherborne. Served War of 1939-45, Major RA. *Heir:* *cousin* Julian Charles Marsham [*b* 28 March 1948; *m* 1975, Catriona Ann, *d* of Lt-Col Robert Christie Stewart, *qv* ; two *s*]. *Address:* Wensum Farm, West Rudham, King's Lynn, Norfolk. *T:* East Rudham 249.

ROMSEY, Lord; Norton Louis Philip Knatchbull; *b* 8 Oct. 1947; *s* and *heir* of Baron Brabourne, *qv* and of Countess Mountbatten of Burma, *qv* ; *m* 1979, Penelope Meredith Eastwood; one *s.* *Educ:* Dragon School, Oxford; Gordonstoun; University of Kent (BA Politics). Freelance film producer; recent work includes: Death on the Nile, 1977 (Associate Producer); Quatermass, 1978 (Associate Producer); Charlie Muffin, 1979 (Producer); Caleb Williams, 1980 (Producer); Oliver Twist, 1982 (Producer). Director: Capital Radio; Satellite Television plc. High Steward of Romsey, 1980-. *Heir:* *s* Hon. Nicholas Louis Charles Norton Knatchbull, *b* 15 May 1981. *Address:* Broadlands, Romsey, Hants SO5 9ZD. *T:* Romsey 517888.

RONALD, Edith, (Mrs Edmund Ronald); *see* Templeton, Mrs Edith.

RONALDSHAY, Earl of; Lawrence Mark Dundas; *b* 28 Dec. 1937; *e s* of 3rd Marquess of Zetland, *qv* ; *m* 1964, Susan, 2nd *d* of Guy Chamberlin, Shefford House, Great Shefford, and late Mrs Chamberlin; two *s* two *d.* *Educ:* Harrow School; Christ's College, Cambridge. Late 2nd Lieut, Grenadier Guards. *Heir:* *s* Lord Dundas, *qv.* *Address:* Copt Hewick Hall, Ripon, N Yorks. *T:* Ripon 3946.

RONAY, Egon; Chairman and Managing Director, Egon Ronay Organisation Ltd, since 1956; *m* 1967, Barbara Greenslade; one *s* (two *d* of previous marr.). *Educ:* School of Piarist Order, Budapest; Univ. of Budapest (LLD); Academy of Commerce, Budapest. Dip. Restaurateurs' Guild, Budapest; FHCIMA. After univ. degree, trained in kitchens of family catering concern; continued training abroad, finishing at Dorchester Hotel, London; progressed to management within family concern of 5 restaurants, of which eventually he took charge; emigrated from Hungary, 1946; Gen. Manager, Princes Restaurant, Piccadilly, then Society Restaurant, Jermyn Street, followed by 96 Restaurant, Piccadilly; opened own restaurant, The Marquee, SW1, 1952-55; started eating-out and general food, wine and tourism weekly column in Daily Telegraph and later Sunday Telegraph, 1954-60, also eating-out guide, 1957; weekly dining out column in Evening News, 1968-74. Mem. l'Académie des Gastronomes, France, 1979. *Publications:* Egon Ronay's Lucas Guide to Hotels and Restaurants, annually, 1956-; Egon Ronay's Lucas Just A Bite, annually, 1979-; Egon Ronay's Pub Guide, annually, 1980-; Egon Ronay's TWA Guide to Good Restaurants in Europe's Business Cities, annually, 1983-; various other tourist guides to Britain, to ski resorts in Europe, to Scandinavian hotels and restaurants and to eating places in Greece. *Address:* Greencoat House, Francis Street, SW1P 1DH. *T:* 01-828 6022.

ROOK, Prof. John Allan Fynes, FRSE, FRSC, FIBiol; Second Secretary, Agricultural Research Council, London, since 1981; Visiting Professor in Animal Nutrition, Wye College, University of London, since 1981; *b* 1 May 1926; *s* of Edward Fynes Rook and Annie Rook; *m* 1952, Marion Horsburgh Millar; two *s* one *d.* *Educ:* Scarborough Boys' High Sch.; University College of Wales, Aberystwyth. BSc, DSc (Wales); PhD (Glasgow). National Institute for Research in Dairying, Shinfield, Berks, 1954–65; Prof. of Agricultural Chemistry, Univ. of Leeds, 1965–70; Dir, Hannah Res. Inst., Ayr and Hannah Prof. of Animal Nutrition, Univ. of Glasgow, 1971–80. *Publications:* numerous articles in British Jl of Nutrition, Jl of Dairy Research, etc. *Recreations:* gardening, golf; shutting doors and switching off lights after other members of the family. *Address:* 52 Hanover House, Greenberry Street, NW8 7AB. *Club:* Farmers'.

ROOKE, Daphne Marie; author; *b* 6 March 1914; *d* of Robert Pizzey and Marie Knevitt; *m* 1937, Irvin Rooke; one *d. Educ:* Durban, S Africa. *Publications:* A Grove of Fever Trees, 1950; Mittee, 1951; Ratoons; The South African Twins, 1953; The Australian Twins, 1954; Wizards' Country; The New Zealand Twins, 1957; Beti, 1959; A Lover for Estelle, 1961; The Greyling, 1962; Diamond Jo, 1965; Boy on the Mountain, 1969; Double Ex!, 1970; Margaretha de la Porte, 1974; A Horse of his Own, 1976. *Recreation:* bushwalking. *Address:* 34 Bent Street, Bardouroka, NSW 2315, Australia.

ROOKE, Sir Denis (Eric), Kt 1977; CBE 1970; BSc (Eng.); FRS 1978; FEng 1979; Chairman, British Gas Corporation (formerly The Gas Council), since 1976 (Deputy Chairman, 1972–76); *b* 2 April 1924; *yr s* of F. G. Rooke; *m* 1949, Elizabeth Brenda, *d* of D. D. Evans, Ystradgynlais, Brecon; one *d. Educ:* Westminster City Sch.; Addey and Stanhope Sch.; University Coll., London (Fellow, 1972). Served with REME, UK and India, 1944–49 (Major). Joined staff of S Eastern Gas Bd as Asst Mechanical Engr in coal-tar by-products works, 1949; Dep. Man. of works, 1954; seconded to N Thames Gas Bd, 1957, for work in UK and USA on liquefied natural gas; mem. technical team which sailed in Methane Pioneer on first voyage bringing liquefied natural gas to UK, 1959; S Eastern Gas Bd's Development Engr, 1959; Development Engr, Gas Council, 1960; Mem. for Production and Supplies, 1966–71. Chm., CNAA, 1977–; Member: Adv. Council for R&D, 1972–77; Adv. Council for Energy Conservation, 1974–77; Offshore Energy Technology Bd, 1975–78; British National Oil Corp., 1976–; NEDC, 1976–80; Energy Commn, 1977–79. President: IGasE, 1975; Assoc. for Science Educn, 1981. Hon. DSc: Salford, 1978; Leeds, 1980. *Publications:* papers to Instn of Gas Engrs, World Power Conf., World Petroleum Conf., etc. *Recreations:* photography, listening to music. *Address:* 23 Hardy Road, Blackheath, SE3. *Clubs:* Athenæum, English-Speaking Union.

ROOKE, Giles Hugh, TD 1963; QC 1979; His Honour Judge Rooke; a Circuit Judge, since 1981; *b* 28 Oct. 1930; *s* of late Charles Eustace Rooke, CMG, and Irene Phyllis Rooke; *m* 1968, Anne Bernadette Seymour, *d* of His Honour Judge Perrett, *qv* ; three *s* one *d. Educ:* Stowe; Exeter Coll., Oxford (MA). Kent Yeomanry, 1951–61, Kent and County of London Yeomanry, 1961–65 (TA), Major. Called to Bar, Lincoln's Inn, 1957; practised SE Circuit, 1957–81; a Recorder of the Crown Court, 1975–81. Hon. Recorder of Margate, 1980–. *Address:* St Stephen's Cottage, Bridge, Canterbury CT4 5AH. *T:* Bridge 830298. *Club:* Carlton.

ROOKE, James Smith, CMG 1961; OBE 1949; Grand Decoration of Honour in Gold, of the Austrian Republic, 1981; Chief Executive, British Overseas Trade Board, 1972–75; HM Diplomatic Service, retired; now lecturer, Diplomatic Academy, Vienna; *b* 6 July 1916; *s* of Joseph Nelson Rooke and Adeline Mounser (*née* Woodgate); *m* 1938, Maria Theresa Rebrec, Vienna; one *s* two *d. Educ:* Workington Grammar Sch.; University College, London; Vienna Univ. Apptd to Dept of Overseas Trade, 1940. Military service, 1940–45, KRRC and AEC. Second Secretary (Commercial), British Embassy, Bogotá, 1946; UK Delegation to ITO Conf., Havana, 1947; Dep. UK Commercial Rep., Frankfurt, 1948; First Secretary (Commercial), British Embassy, Rome, 1951; Consul (Commercial), Milan, 1954; Deputy Consul-General (Commercial), New York, 1955–59; HM Counsellor (Commercial) British Embassy, Berne, 1959–63, Rome, 1963–66; Minister (Commercial), British High Commn, Canberra, 1966–68; Minister (Economic), British Embassy, Paris, 1968–72. *Recreations:* climbing, tennis, ski-ing. *Address:* 18 Wedderburn Road, NW3. *Club:* East India, Devonshire, Sports and Public Schools.

ROOKE, Brig. Vera Margaret, CBE 1980; RRC 1973; QHNS 1981; Matron-in-Chief (Army) and Director of Army Nursing Services, since 1981; *b* 21 Dec. 1924; *d* of late William James Rooke and Lily Amelia Rooke (*née* Cole). *Educ:* Girls' County Sch., Hove, Sussex. Addenbrooke's Hosp., Cambridge (SRN); Royal Alexandra Children's Hosp., Brighton (RSCN); St Helier Hosp., Carshalton (Midwifery). Joined Queen Alexandra's Royal Army Nursing Corps, 1951; appointments include: service in military hospitals, UK, Egypt, Malta, Singapore; Staff Officer in Work Study; Liaison Officer, QARANC, MoD, 1973–74; Assistant Director of Army Nursing Services and Matron: Military Hosp., Hong Kong, 1975; Royal Herbert Hosp. and Queen Elizabeth Military Hosp., Woolwich, 1976–78; Dep. Dir, Army Nursing Services, HQ UKLF, 1979–80. Lt-Col 1972, Col 1975, Brig. 1981. *Recreations:* gardening, walking, cookery, opera. *Address:* c/o Lloyds Bank Ltd, 208 Portland Road, Hove, Sussex.

ROOKER, Jeffrey William, CEng; MP (Lab) Birmingham, Perry Barr, since Feb. 1974; *b* 5 June 1941; *m* 1972, Angela. *Educ:* Handsworth Tech. Sch.; Handsworth Tech. Coll.; Warwick Univ. (MA); Aston Univ. (BScEng). CEng, FIProdE, Grad. IMechE; AMBIM. Apprentice toolmaker, King's Heath Engrg Co. Ltd, Birmingham, 1957–63; student apprentice, BLMC, 1963–64; Asst to Works Manager, Geo. Salter & Co., West Bromwich,

1964–65, Assembly Manager, 1965–67; Prodn Manager, Rola Celestion Ltd, Thames Ditton and Ipswich, 1967–70; Industrial Relations and Safety Officer, Metro-Cammell, Birmingham, 1971; Lectr, Lanchester Polytechnic, Coventry, 1972–74. Opposition spokesman on social services, 1979–80, on social security, 1980–. Mem. Council, Instn of Prodn Engrs, 1975–81. *Recreation:* full-time MP. *Address:* 14 Spiral Court, Wheelwright Road, Birmingham B24 8NU. *T:* 021-350 6186.

ROOM, Thomas Gerald, FRS 1941; Professor of Mathematics, Sydney University, 1935–68, now Emeritus; *b* 10 Nov. 1902; 2nd *s* of E. W. Room, OBE, JP; *m* 1937, Jessie, *d* of C. F. Bannerman; one *s* two *d. Educ:* Alleyn's School; St John's Coll., Cambridge (ScD). Asst Lectr, Liverpool University, 1925; Fellow of St John's College, Cambridge, 1927–29; Lecturer in Mathematics, Cambridge University, 1929–34; Visiting Prof. of Mathematics: Univ. of Washington, 1948; Univ. of Tennessee, 1949; Univ. of Sussex, 1966; Westfield Coll., Univ. of London, 1969–70; Open Univ., 1971–73. Fellow Sydney University Senate and Dean of Faculty of Science, 1952–56, 1960–65. Member Inst. for Advanced Study, Princeton, NJ, 1949 and 1957–58; Vis. Lectr, Univ. of Princeton, 1958. Pres., Austr. Mathematical Soc., 1960–62. *Publications:* Geometry of Determinantal Loci, 1939; The Sorting Process, 1966; A Background to Geometry, 1967; Miniquaternion Geometry, 1970. *Address:* High Walden, 100 Rosedale Road, St Ives, NSW 2075, Australia. *T:* (Sydney) 449-5743.

ROOME, Maj.-Gen. Oliver McCrea, CBE 1973; DL; *b* 9 March 1921; *s* of late Maj.-Gen. Sir Horace Roome, KCIE, CB, CBE, MC, DL, late Royal Engineers; *m* 1947, Isobel Anstis, *d* of Rev. A. B. Jordan; two *s* one *d. Educ:* Wellington Coll. Commissioned in Royal Engineers, 1940. Served War: UK, Western Desert, Sicily, Italy, 1939–45. Various appts, UK, Far and Middle East, Berlin, 1946–68; IDC, 1969; Director of Army Recruiting, 1970–73; Chief, Jt Services Liaison Organisation, Bonn, 1973–76; retired. Col Comdt, RE, 1979–. County Comr, Scouts, Isle of Wight, 1977–. DL Isle of Wight, 1981. *Recreations:* sailing, maritime and military history. *Address:* Lloyds Bank Ltd, 6 Pall Mall, SW1. *Clubs:* Army and Navy, Royal Ocean Racing, Royal Cruising; Royal Yacht Squadron.

ROONEY, Denis Michael Hall, CBE 1977; FEng, FIMechE, FIEE; CBIM; Industrial Consultant; Chairman, National Nuclear Corporation, 1980–81; *b* 9 Aug. 1919; *s* of Frederick and Ivy Rooney; *m* 1942, Ruby Teresa (*née* Lamb); three *s* three *d. Educ:* Stonyhurst Coll.; Downing Coll., Cambridge (MA). Served War, Royal Navy, 1941–46. Various appts with BICC Ltd, 1946–69; Balfour Beatty Ltd: Dep. Managing Dir, 1969–73; Man. Dir, 1973–77; Chm., 1975–80; BICC Ltd: Exec. Dir, 1973–80; Exec. Vice-Chm., 1978–80; Chm., BICC Internat., 1978–80; Dep. Chm., Metal Manufactures Ltd, Australia, 1978–80. Chm., SE Asia Trade Adv. Gp, BOTB, 1975–79; Member: British Overseas Trade Adv. Council, 1976–80; Overseas Projects Bd, BOTB, 1976–79; BOTB, 1979–80; Council: Export Gp for Construction Industries, 1964–80; Christian Assoc. of Business Execs, 1979–. Liveryman, Worshipful Company of Turners of London. *Publication:* contrib. (Brazilian Rlwy Electrification) IEE Jl. *Recreation:* golf. *Address:* Tor House, Station Road, Woldingham, Surrey CR3 7DA. *T:* Woldingham 3164. *Clubs:* Institute of Directors; Tandridge Golf (Oxted).

ROOT, Frederick James, CB 1952; Deputy Secretary, Ministry of Public Building and Works (previously Ministry of Works), 1959–66; *b* 2 July 1906; *s* of late Alan and Elizabeth A. Root; *m* 1941, Margaret Eleanor Barbour, *d* of late Dr G. F. Barbour Simpson, Edinburgh; two *d. Educ:* Christ's Hosp.; Merton Coll., Oxford (Open Exhibnr). Entered Civil Service, 1928; Private Secretary to successive First Commissioners of Works, 1933–37, and to successive Ministers of Works, 1940–43. *Address:* Halland, Pathfields Close, Haslemere, Surrey GU27 2BL. *T:* Haslemere 3750. *Club:* Athenæum.

ROOT, Rev. Canon Howard Eugene; Director of the Anglican Centre, Rome, since 1981; St Augustine Canon of Canterbury Cathedral, since 1980; Counsellor on Vatican Affairs to Archbishop of Canterbury, since 1981; *b* 13 April 1926; *s* of Dr Howard Root and Flora Hoskins; *m* 1952, Celia, *e d* of Col R. T. Holland, CBE, DSO, MC; two *s* two *d. Educ:* Univ. of Southern California; St Catherine's Coll. and Magdalen Coll., Oxford; Ripon Hall, Oxford. BA S Calif 1945; BA Oxon 1951; MA Oxon 1970; MA Cantab 1953. Teaching Fellow, 1945–47; Instructor, American Univ., Cairo, 1947–49; Sen. Demy, Magdalen Coll., Oxford, and Liddon Student, 1952–53. Deacon, 1953; Priest, 1954. Curate of Trumpington, 1953; Asst Lectr in Divinity, Cambridge, 1953–57; Lectr, 1957–65; Fellow, Emmanuel Coll., Cambridge, 1954–65, Chaplain, 1954–56, Dean, 1956–65; Prof. of Theology, Univ. of Southampton, 1966–81. Wilde Lectr, Oxford Univ., 1957–60; Senior Denyer and Johnson Scholar, Oxford, 1963–64; Bampton Lectr, Univ. of Oxford, 1972; Pope Adrian VI Chair, Univ. of Louvain, 1979. Exam. Chaplain to Bishops of Ripon, 1959–76, Southwark, 1964–81, Bristol, 1965–81, Winchester, 1971–81, and Wakefield, 1977–81; Commissary to Bishop in Jerusalem, 1976–. Official Anglican Observer at Second Vatican Council, 1963–65; Consultant, Lambeth Conf., 1968. Chm., Archbishops' Commn on Marriage, 1968–71; Member: Academic Council, Ecumenical Inst., Jerusalem, 1966–81; Anglican-RC Preparatory Commn, 1967–68; Archbishops' Commn on Christian Doctrine, 1967–74; Anglican-Roman Catholic Internat. Commn, 1969–81. Hon. Chaplain, Winchester Cathedral, 1966–67; Canon Theologian of Winchester, 1967–80. Mem., BBC Central Religious Adv. Cttee, 1971–75. Jt Editor, Jl of Theol Studies, 1969–74. *Recreations:* music, silence. *Address:*

Anglican Centre, Palazzo Doria, via del Corso 303, Rome, Italy; c/o Barclays Bank Ltd, Old Bank, High Street, Oxford. *Club:* Brooks's.

ROOTES, family name of **Baron Rootes.**

ROOTES, 2nd Baron *cr* 1959; **William Geoffrey Rootes;** Chairman, 1967-73, Chrysler United Kingdom (lately Rootes Motors Ltd); *b* 14 June 1917; *er s* of 1st Baron Rootes, GBE; *S* father, 1964; *m* 1946, Marian, widow of Wing Comdr J. H. Slater, AFC, and *d* of late Lt-Col H. R. Hayter, DSO; one *s* one *d. Educ:* Harrow; Christ Church, Oxford. Served War of 1939-45 in RASC (France, E Africa, Western Desert, Libya, Tunisia and Italy), demobilised, Actg Major, 1946. Rejoined Rootes Group, 1946: Man. Dir, 1962-67; Dep. Chm., 1965-67; Chm. 1967-70. Director: Rank Hovis McDougall, 1973-; Joseph Lucas Industries Ltd, 1973-. President: SMMT, 1960-61 (Hon. Officer, 1958-62, Chm. Exec. Cttee, 1972-73); Motor & Cycle Trades Benevolent Fund, 1968-70; Motor Ind. Research Assoc., 1970-71; Inst. of Motor Industry, 1973-75. Member: Nat. Adv. Council, Motor Manufrg Industry, 1964-71; Nat. Economic Development Cttee, Motor Manufacturing Industry, 1968-73; BNEC (Chm., American Cttee, 1969-71); Council, CBI, 1967-74, Europe Cttee CBI, 1972-76; Council, Inst. of Dirs, 1953-78; Council, Warwick Univ., 1968-74 (Chm., Careers Adv. Bd). Vice-Pres., Game Conservancy, 1979- (Chm., 1975-79); Mem., UK Council, WWF. County Pres., St John Ambulance, Berks. FRSA; FBIM; FIPE. *Recreations:* shooting, fishing. *Heir: s* Hon. Nicholas Geoffrey Rootes [*b* 12 July 1951; *m* 1976, Dorothy Anne Burn-Forti, *d* of Cyril Wood]. *Address:* North Standen House, Hungerford, Berks RG17 0QZ. *Clubs:* Buck's, Flyfishers'.

ROOTHAM, Jasper St John, MA; *b* 21 Nov. 1910; *s* of Dr Cyril Bradley and Rosamund Margaret Rootham; *m* 1944, Joan McClelland; one *s* one *d. Educ:* Tonbridge Sch. (Judd Schol.); St John's Coll., Cambridge (Maj. Schol.). 1st cl. Class. Tripos Pts I and II. Entered Civil Service, 1933; Min. of Agric., 1933-34; CO, 1934-36; Treasury, 1936-38; Pte Sec. to Prime Minister, 1938-39; Treasury, 1939-40; resigned to join Army, 1940; served Middle East, Balkans, Germany (despatches); demobilised, 1946 (Col); entered Bank of England as Actg Asst Adviser, 1946; Adviser to Governor, 1957; Chief of Overseas Dept, 1962; Asst to Governor, 1964; retd, 1967. Man. Dir, Lazard Bros & Co. Ltd, 1967-75; Dir, Agricultural Mortgage Corp., 1967-77 (Dep. Chm., 1973-77); Director: British Sugar Corp., 1968-80; Stanley Miller Holdings, Newcastle. *Publications:* Miss Fire, 1946; Demi-Paradise, 1960; Verses 1928-72, 1972; The Celestial City and Other Poems, 1975; Reflections from a Crag, 1978; Selected Poems, 1980; Stand Fixed in Steadfast Gaze, 1981; Affirmation, 1982. *Recreations:* music, country life. *Address:* 7 Watling Street, Corbridge, Northumberland NE45 5AG. *T:* Corbridge 2992. *Clubs:* United Oxford & Cambridge University; Northern Counties (Newcastle upon Tyne).

ROOTS, Paul John; Director of Industrial Relations, Ford Motor Co. Ltd, since 1981; *b* 16 Oct. 1929; *s* of William Earl and Helen Roots; *m* 1951, Anna Theresa Pateman; two *s* two *d. Educ:* Dormers Wells Sch.; London Sch. of Economics. Cert. in Personnel Admin. MIPM. RN, 1947-54: service in Korean War. Personnel Officer, Brush Gp, 1955; Labour Officer, UKAEA, 1956, Labour Manager, 1959; Ford Motor Co. Ltd: Personnel Manager, Halewood, 1962; Forward Planning Manager, 1966; Labour Relations Manager, 1969; Dir of Employee Relations, 1974. Vice-Pres., IPM, 1981-. Member: Council of Management, CBI Educn Foundn; CBI Working Party on the Employment of Disabled People; CBI Health and Safety Panel. *Publications:* articles in personnel management jls. *Recreations:* riding, theatre, music. *Address:* Glebe House, Great Saxham, Bury St Edmunds, Suffolk.

ROPER; *see* Trevor-Roper.

ROPER, Captain Edward Gregson, CBE 1959; DSO 1942; DSC; Capt. RN retd; *b* 12 April 1910; *s* of late John Gregson Roper, OBE; *m* 1933, Sylvia, *d* of E. F. L. Hopkins; one *d. Educ:* Oundle. Joined Royal Navy, 1928; served War of 1939-45 (DSC, DSO): Comd HMS Velox, 1940-42; Impulsive, 1942-43; Comdr, 1943; Comd 18th Destroyer Flotilla, 1944-45. Captain, 1950; Comd HMS Ocean, 1955-56; Royal Naval College, Greenwich, 1956-59; retired, 1959. *Address:* Polmayne, Rock, Cornwall.

ROPER, John Charles Abercromby, CMG 1969; MC; HM Diplomatic Service, retired; *b* 8 June 1915; *s* of late Charles Roper, MD, and of Mrs Roper; *m* 1st, 1945, Valerie Armstrong-MacDonnell (marr. diss.); two *d* ; 2nd, 1960, Kathryn, *d* of late Edgar Bibas, New York. *Educ:* Harrow; Universities of Cambridge and Princeton (Commonwealth Fellow). Served 1939-46, Scots Guards and Special Forces, Major (MC). HM Diplomatic Service, 1946; Athens, 1947-51; Foreign Office, 1951-54; Washington, 1954-59. Seconded to Min. of Defence and apptd Dep. Commandant (Civil) of NATO Defence College, Paris, 1960-62; Asst Sec., Cabinet Office, 1962-64; Counsellor, UK Deleg to OECD, 1964-70; Ambassador to Luxembourg, 1970-75. *Address:* Cavallini, Paganico, Provincia di Grosseto, Italy; Island of Hydra, Greece. *Club:* Special Forces.

ROPER, John (Francis Hodgess); MP Farnworth since 1970 (Lab and Co-op, 1970-1981, SDP, since 1981); *b* 10 Sept. 1935; *s* of Rev. Frederick Mabor Hodgess Roper and Ellen Frances (*née* Brockway); *m* 1959, Valerie Hope, *er d* of late Rt Hon. L. John Edwards, PC, OBE, MP, and Mrs D. M. Edwards; one *d. Educ:* William Hulme's Grammar Sch., Manchester; Reading Sch.; Magdalen Coll., Oxford; Univ. of Chicago. Nat. Service, commnd RNVR,

1954-56; studied PPE, Oxford, 1956-59 (Pres. UN Student Assoc., 1957; organised Univ. referendum on Nuclear Disarmament); Harkness Fellow, Commonwealth Fund, 1959-61; Research Fellow in Economic Statistics, Univ. of Manchester, 1961; Asst Lectr in Econs, 1962-64, Lectr 1964-70, Faculty Tutor 1968-70. Contested (Lab) High Peak (Derbs), 1964. PPS to Minister of State, DoI, 1978-79; opposition front bench spokesman on defence, 1979-81; Social Democrat Whip, 1981-. Vice-Chairman: Anglo-German Parly Gp, 1974-; Anglo-Benelux Parly Gp, 1979-; Chm., British-Atlantic Gp of Young Politicians, 1974-75. Council of Europe: Consultant, 1965-66; Mem., Consultative Assembly, 1973-80; Chm., Cttee on Culture and Educn, 1979-80; Mem., WEU, 1973-80; Chm., Cttee on Defence Questions and Armaments, WEU, 1977-80. Hon. Treasurer, Fabian Soc., 1976-81; Chm., Labour Cttee for Europe, 1976-80; Vice-Chm., GB East Europe Centre, 1974-. Research Adviser (part-time), DEA in NW, 1967-69. Director: Co-op. Wholesale Soc., 1969-74; Co-op Insurance Soc., 1973-74. Pres., Gen. Council, UNA, 1972-78; Mem. Council, Inst. for Fiscal Studies, 1975-; Mem. Gen. Adv. Council, IBA, 1974-79. Vice-Pres., Manchester Statistical Soc., 1971-; Trustee, Hist. of Parlt Trust, 1974-. *Publications:* (with Lloyd Harrison) Towards Regional Co-operatives, 1967; The Teaching of Economics at University Level, 1970; articles and reviews in Co-operative jls and Manchester School. *Recreations:* reading, travel. *Address:* House of Commons, SW1.

ROPER, Robert Burnell, CB 1978; Chief Land Registrar, since 1975 (Deputy Chief Land Registrar, 1973-75); *b* 23 Nov. 1921; *s* of Allen George and Winifred Roper; *m* 1948, Mary Brookes; two *s. Educ:* King's College Sch., Wimbledon; King's Coll., London. LLB (Hons) 1941. Called to Bar, Gray's Inn, 1948. Served War, RAF, 1942-46. Miners' Welfare Commn, 1946-48; Nat. Coal Bd, 1948-49; Treasury Solicitor's Dept, 1949-50; HM Land Registry, 1950-. *Publications:* (Ruoff and Roper) The Law and Practice of Registered Conveyancing, 3rd edn, 1972, 4th edn 1979; Consulting Editor on Land Registration matters for Encyclopaedia of Forms and Precedents (4th edn). *Recreations:* gardening, watching sport. *Address:* 11 Dukes Road, Lindfield, Haywards Heath, West Sussex RH16 2JH.

ROPER-CURZON, family name of **Baron Teynham.**

ROPNER, David; *see* Ropner, W. G. D.

ROPNER, Sir John (Bruce Woollacott), 2nd Bt *cr* 1952; Director, Ropner Holdings Ltd; *b* 16 April 1937; *s* of Sir Leonard Ropner, 1st Bt, MC, TD, and of Esmé, *y d* of late Bruce Robertson; *S* father, 1977; *m* 1st, 1961, Anne Melicent (marr. diss. 1970), *d* of late Sir Ralph Delmé-Radcliffe; two *d* ; 2nd, 1970, Auriol, *d* of Captain Graham Lawrie Mackeson-Sandbach, Caerllo, Llangernyw; one *s* two *d. Educ:* Eton; St Paul's School, USA. *Heir: s* Henry John William Ropner, *b* 24 Oct. 1981. *Address:* Thorp Perrow, Bedale, Yorks.

ROPNER, John Raymond; Consultant, Ropner PLC, and other companies; *b* 8 May 1903; *s* of William Ropner; *m* 1928, Joan Redhead; two *s* one *d. Educ:* Harrow; Clare College, Cambridge (BAEcon 1925). Durham Heavy Bde, RA (TA), 1922-28; joined Sir R. Ropner & Co. Ltd, 1925; Ministry of War Transport, North Western Europe, 1944-45. High Sheriff of Durham, 1958. Member, Shipping Advisory Panel, 1962. Order of Oranje-Nassau, 1947. *Recreations:* gardening, fishing; formerly golf (Cambridge blue, 1925). *Address:* The Limes, Dalton, Richmond, N Yorkshire. *T:* Teesdale 21447.

ROPNER, Sir Robert Douglas, 4th Bt, *cr* 1904; *b* 1 Dec. 1921; *o s* of Sir (E. H. O.) Robert Ropner, 3rd Bt; *S* father, 1962; *m* 1943, Patricia Kathleen, *d* of W. E. Scofield, W. Malling, Kent; one *s* one *d. Educ:* Harrow. Formerly Captain, RA. *Heir: s* Robert Clinton Ropner, *b* 6 Feb. 1949.

ROPNER, (William Guy) David, FICS; Chairman, Ropner PLC, since 1973; *b* 3 April 1924; *s* of late Sir William Guy Ropner and Lady (Margarita) Ropner; *m* 1955, Mildred Malise Hare Armitage (marr. diss. 1978); three *s* one *d. Educ:* Harrow. FICS 1953. Served War, 1942-47: 2nd Lieut RA, Essex Yeomanry; Captain 3rd Regt, RHA. Joined Sir R. Ropner and Co. Ltd, 1947; dir of various Ropner PLC gp cos, 1953-. Member: Baltic Exchange, 1949-; Lloyd's, 1952-; Gen. Cttee, Lloyd's Register of Shipping, 1961-; Pres., Gen. Council of British Shipping, 1979-80; Chairman: Deep Sea Tramp Section, Chamber of Shipping, 1970-72; Lights Adv. Cttee, GCBS, 1978-; Merchant Navy Welfare Bd, 1980-; Cleveland & Durham Industrial Council, 1980-; Director: British Shipowners Assoc., 1954-; Raisby Holdings Ltd, 1956-. *Recreations:* country and garden pursuits. *Address:* 1 Sunningdale Gardens, Stratford Road, W8 6PX. *T:* 01-937 3862. *Clubs:* City of London, Royal Automobile.

RORKE, Prof. John, CBE 1979; PhD, FRSE, FIMechE, FIMarE; Professor of Mechanical Engineering, Heriot-Watt University, since 1980; *b* 2 Sept. 1923; *s* of John and Janet Rorke; *m* 1948, Jane Craig Buchanan; two *d. Educ:* Dumbarton Acad.; Univ. of Strathclyde (BSc, PhD). Lectr, Strathclyde Univ., 1946-51; Asst to Engrg Dir, Alexander Stephen & Sons Ltd, 1951-56; Technical Manager, subseq. Gen. Man., and Engrg Dir, Wm Denny & Bros Ltd, 1956-63; Tech. Dir, subseq. Sales Dir, Man. Dir, and Chm., Brown Bros & Co. Ltd (subsid. of Vickers Ltd), 1963-78; Man. Dir, Vickers Offshore Engrg Gp, 1978; Dir of Planning, Vickers Ltd, 1979-80. *Recreations:* golf, bridge. *Address:* 3 Barnton Park Grove, Edinburgh EH3 6HG. *T:* 031-336 3044. *Club:* Bruntsfield Links Golfing Society (Edinburgh).

ROSCOE, (Edward) John (Townsend); Director, Willis Faber & Dumas Ltd, 1957-73 (Chairman, 1967-71); *b* 21 March 1913; *o s* of late Edward Gawne Roscoe and Mary Frances Roscoe, Clifton Manor, Warwicks; *m* 1st, 1940, Jean Mary Todd; one *s* two *d* ; 2nd, 1974, Jennifer Helen, *yr d* of J. R. Fawcus; three *s. Educ:* West Downs, Winchester; Marlborough Coll.; Trinity Coll., Oxford. BA, PPE. Joined Sedgwick Collins & Co., Lloyds Brokers, 1934; War Service, 1939-46; joined Willis Faber & Dumas Ltd, 1949; Underwriting Member of Lloyds, 1945. *Recreations:* foxhunting, tennis, swimming. *Address:* West Penthouse, Parkside, Knightsbridge, SW1. *T:* 01-235 8899. *Clubs:* Boodle's, City of London.

ROSCOE, Air Cdre Peter Henry, CB 1967; FCA; *b* 1912. Dept of Air Member for Personnel, 1963-67; Dir of Personnel (Ground) Min. of Defence (RAF), 1966; retired 1967. *Address:* Fairhaven, Tan-y-Bryn Road, Holyhead, Gwynedd LL65 1AR.

ROSCOE, Sir Robert Bell, KBE 1981; FASA, ABIA, ABINZ; Director, Chase-NBA Group Ltd (Australia and New Zealand), since 1969; Chairman: Melbourne Underground Rail Loop Authority, since 1971; First Federation Discount Co. Ltd, since 1975; *b* 7 August 1906; *s* of T. B. Roscoe; *m* 1931, Daphne, *d* of G. Maxwell; one *d. Educ:* Central Tech. Coll., Brisbane. Liquidator, Qld Nat. Bank Ltd, 1949; State Manager, Qld, 1951-54; Nat. Bank of Australasia: State Manager, Victoria, 1954-60; Chief Inspector, 1960-65; Sen. Chief Inspector, 1965-66; Asst Chief Manager, 1966-69. Director: Hoechst Australia Ltd; All States Commercial Bills Ltd; Oceania Capital Corp. Ltd. *Address:* 833 Burwood Road, Hawthorn East, Victoria 3123, Australia. *Club:* Australian (Melbourne).

ROSE, Sir Alec (Richard), Kt 1968; *b* 13 July 1908; *s* of Ambrose Rose; *m* 1st, 1931, Barbara Kathleen (*née* Baldwin); two *s* two *d* ; 2nd, 1960, Dorothy Mabel (*née* Walker). *Educ:* Simon Langton Boys School, Canterbury. Farming in Canada, 1928-30; Haulage Contractor, 1930-39; served RNVR, 1939-45; Market Gardener, 1945-57; Fruit Merchant, 1957-71. Member: Fruiterers Co.; Worshipful Co. of Basketmakers; Worshipful Co. of Shipwrights. Hon. Life Governor, RNLI, 1975-. Freedom of Portsmouth, 1968. Blue Water Medal, Cruising Club of America, 1969; Seamanship Medal, Royal Cruising Club. *Publication:* My Lively Lady, 1968. *Recreation:* sailing (inc. circumnavigation of world, 1968). *Address:* Woodlands Cottage, Eastleigh Road, Havant, Hants. *T:* Havant 77124. *Clubs:* City Livery; Portsmouth County, Royal Naval and Royal Albert Yacht (Portsmouth); Royal Yacht Squadron, Royal Naval Sailing Assoc., Eastney Cruising Assoc., Ocean Cruising (Admiral).

ROSE, Andrew; *see* Rose, W. A.

ROSE, Captain Arthur Martin Thomas, MC 1944; solicitor; a Recorder of the Crown Court, since 1979; *b* 22 Nov. 1918; *s* of late Stanley Arthur Rose and Hilda Mary Martin Rose (*née* Hayward); *m* 1952, Patricia Cameron (*d* 1978); two *s. Educ:* Perse Sch.; Uppingham; Trinity Hall, Cambridge (MA, LLB). Served War: commnd Royal Artillery, 1941-46 (MC, twice wounded). Partner in firm of Few & Kester, solicitors, 1949-82, Senior Partner, 1981-82. *Recreations:* sport, freemasonry. *Address:* 10 Marlborough Court, Grange Road, Cambridge CB3 9BQ. *T:* Cambridge 312726. *Clubs:* Camden Cricket; Gog Magog Golf.

ROSE, Barry Michael, FRSCM; Master of the Choir, St Paul's Cathedral, since 1977; *b* 24 May 1934; *s* of Stanley George Rose and Gladys Mildred Rose; *m* 1965, Elizabeth Mary Ware; one *s* two *d. Educ:* Sir George Monoux Grammar Sch., Walthamstow; Royal Acad. of Music (ARAM). FRSCM 1973. First Organist and Master of the Choristers, new Guildford Cathedral, 1960-74; Sub-Organist, St Paul's Cath., 1974-. Music Adviser to Head of Religious Broadcasting, BBC, 1970-. *Recreation:* running a record company (Guild Records, founded 1967). *Address:* 4 Amen Court, EC4M 7BU. *T:* 01-248 6868.

ROSE, Bernard William George, OBE 1980; MusB Cantab 1938, MA Oxon, Cantab 1944, DMus Oxon 1955, FRCO; Fellow, Organist, Informator Choristarum, Magdalen College, Oxford, 1957-81, Vice-President, 1973 and 1974, Emeritus Fellow since 1981; University Lecturer in Music, 1950-81; Choragus in the University, 1958-63; *b* Little Hallingbury, Herts, 9 May 1916; *s* of William and Jessie Rose; *m* 1939, Molly Daphne, JP, 5th *d* of D. G. Marshall, MBE, Cambridge; three *s. Educ:* Salisbury Cathedral Sch.; Royal Coll. of Music; St Catharine's Coll., Cambridge. Organ Scholar, St Catharine's, Cambridge, 1935-39; Stewart of Rannoch Scholar in Sacred Music, Cambridge, 1935-39; Organist, and Conductor to the Eaglesfield Musical Soc., The Queen's Coll., Oxford, 1939-57, Fellow, 1949. Served with 4th Co. of London Yeomanry (Sharpshooters), 1941-44, Adjutant 1942 (PoW 1943-44). Conductor, Oxford Orchestral Soc., 1971-74. Mem. Council, Royal Coll. of Organists (Pres. 1974-76). *Publications:* contrib. Proc. Roy. Mus. Assoc., 1955; various church music compositions and edns of church music; edns of Anthems of Thomas Tomkins; (ed) Early English Church Music, Vols 5, 9, 14 and 27; Hallische Händel Ausgabe, 'Susanna'; reviews in Music and Letters, articles in Musical Times. *Recreation:* carpentry. *Address:* Appleton Manor, near Abingdon, Oxon. *T:* Oxford 862919.

ROSE, Major Charles Frederick, MBE 1968; CEng, MICE, MCIT; Chief Inspecting Officer of Railways, Department of Transport, since 1982; *b* 9 July 1926; *s* of Charles James Rose and Ida Marguerite Chollet; *m* 1956, Huguette Primrose Lecoultre; one *s* one *d. Educ:* Xaverian Coll., Brighton; Royal School of Military Engineering, 1951-52 and 1957-59. Student engineer, Southern Railway Co., 1942-46; commnd RE, 1947; service with mil. railways, Palestine and Egypt, 1947-51; with a Field Sqdn in Germany, 1952-53; Engr SO, Korea, 1953-54; Instructor: Mons Officer Cadet Sch., 1954-57; Transportation Centre, Longmoor, 1959-62; OC a Field Sqdn, Germany, 1962-64; Instr, Royal Sch. of Mil. Engrg, 1964-66; Engr, RE road construction project, Thailand, 1966-68; Inspecting Officer of Railways, MoT, 1968-82. *Recreations:* cycling, walking, music, reading. *Address:* Hollybank, Shadyhanger, Godalming, Surrey GU7 2HR. *T:* Godalming 6429.

ROSE, Christine Brooke; *see* Brooke-Rose.

ROSE, Christopher Dudley Roger, QC 1974; a Recorder of the Crown Court, since 1978; *b* 10 Feb. 1937; *s* of Roger Rose and Hilda Rose, Morecambe; *m* 1964, Judith, *d* of late George and Charlotte Brand, Didsbury; one *s* one *d. Educ:* Morecambe Grammar Sch.; Repton; Leeds Univ.; Wadham Coll., Oxford. LLB and Hughes Prize, Leeds, 1957; 1st cl. hons BCL 1959, Eldon Scholar 1959, Oxon. Lectr in Law, Wadham Coll., Oxford, 1959-60; called to Bar, Middle Temple, 1960; Bigelow Teaching Fellow, Law Sch., Univ. of Chicago, 1960-61; Harmsworth Scholar, 1961; joined Northern Circuit, 1961. *Recreations:* playing the piano, listening to music, golf, travel. *Address:* 5 Essex Court, Temple, EC4Y 9AH. *T:* 01-353 4363. *Clubs:* Big Four (Manchester); Wilmslow Golf.

ROSE, Clifford; *see* Rose, F.C.

ROSE, Clifford Alan, FCIT, MIPM; Member (Personnel), British Railways Board, since 1977; *b* 31 Aug. 1929; *s* of Francis William and Edith May Rose; *m* 1953, Maureen (*née* Wallen); one *d. Educ:* Royal Grammar Sch., High Wycombe. Joined GWR as booking clerk, 1944; served in London area, West Country and S Wales; Divl Movements Manager, Cardiff, 1966; Asst Divl Manager, 1968. Movements Manager, Southern Region, 1968; Divl Manager, first of S Western, then S Eastern Div., 1970; Chief Personnel Officer of Southern Region, 1972; Exec. Dir, Personnel, BRB, 1975. Member: Advisory, Conciliation and Arbitration Service Council, 1978-; Business Educn Council, 1979-. CBIM. OStJ 1975. *Recreations:* cricket, Rugby (watching, now), gardening, walking. *Address:* 45 Durleston Park Drive, Great Bookham, Surrey KT23 4AJ. *T:* Bookham 52705. *Club:* MCC.

ROSE, Sir Clive (Martin), GCMG 1981 (KCMG 1976; CMG 1967); HM Diplomatic Service, retired; *b* 15 Sept. 1921; *s* of late Rt Rev. Alfred Carey Wollaston Rose; *m* 1946, Elisabeth Mackenzie, *d* of late Rev. Cyril Lewis, Gilston; two *s* three *d. Educ:* Marlborough College; Christ Church, Oxford. Rifle Bde, 1941-46 (Maj.; despatches): served in Europe, 1944-45; India, 1945; Iraq, 1945-46. Commonwealth Relations Office, 1948; Office of Deputy High Comr, Madras, 1948-49; Foreign Office, 1950-53; UK High Commn, Germany, 1953-54; British Embassy, Bonn, 1955; FO, 1956-59; 1st Sec. and HM Consul, Montevideo, 1959-62; FO, 1962-65; Commercial Counsellor, Paris, 1965-67; Imp. Defence Coll., 1968; Counsellor, British Embassy, Washington, 1969-71; Asst Under-Sec. of State, FCO, 1971-73; Head, British Delegn to Negotiations on Mutual Reduction of Forces and Armaments and Associated Measures in Central Europe, 1973-76; Dep. Secretary, Cabinet Office, 1976-79; UK Permanent Rep. on North Atlantic Council, 1979-82. Mem. Council, RUSI, 1981- (Vice-Chm., 1982-). FRSA 1982. *Address:* Chimney House, Lavenham, Suffolk. *T:* Lavenham 247699. *Club:* Army and Navy.

ROSE, Donald Henry Gair; HM Diplomatic Service; High Commissioner, Kiribati, since 1979; *b* 24 Sept. 1926; *m* 1950, Sheila Munro; three *s.* HM Forces, 1944-48; Scottish Office, 1948-66; Commonwealth Office, 1966; Nairobi, 1967; Tripoli, 1971; First Sec., Cairo, 1974-77; FCO, 1977-79. *Address:* c/o Foreign and Commonwealth Office, SW1.

ROSE, (Edward) Michael, CMG 1955; HM Diplomatic Service, retired; Chairman, International Division, British Council of Churches, since 1974; *b* 18 Oct. 1913; *s* of Frank Atcherley Rose and Marian Elizabeth Darling Harris; unmarried. *Educ:* Rugby; St John's College, Cambridge. Entered Diplomatic Service, 1937; served Oslo 1940, Algiers, 1944, Copenhagen 1945-48; Deputy to GOC British Sector of Berlin, 1952-55; Counsellor, Foreign Office, 1955-60; Minister, Bonn, 1960-63; Ambassador to the Congo (Leopoldville), 1963-65; Asst Under-Sec., Foreign Office, 1965-67; Dep. Sec., Cabinet Office, 1967-68. Dir, E Africa and Mauritius Assoc., 1969-80. Fellow, Center for Internat. Affairs, Harvard Univ., 1958-59. *Recreations:* golf, gardening. *Address:* 2 Godfrey Street, SW3; Ovington Grange, Clare, Suffolk. *Club:* National Liberal.

ROSE, Eliot Joseph Benn, (Jim Rose), CBE 1979; Chairman, Penguin Books, 1973-80; Director, Pearson Longman, 1974-81; *b* 7 June 1909; *s* of late Colonel E. A. Rose, CBE, and Dula, *e d* of Eliot Lewis, JP; *m* 1946, Susan Pamela Gibson; one *s* one *d. Educ:* Rugby; New College, Oxford. Served War of 1939-45, RAF, Wing-Comdr. Literary Editor, The Observer, 1948-51; Director: International Press Institute, Zürich, 1951-62; Survey of Race Relations in Britain, 1963-69; Editorial Dir, Westminster Press Ltd, 1970-74. Chm., Inter-Action Trust; Co-founder and Chm., Runnymede Trust; Mem., Cttee of Inquiry into educn of children from ethnic minority groups, 1979-81; Special Consultant to Unicef, 1981. Sidney Ball Meml Lectr,

Oxford, 1970. Legion of Merit (US). *Publication:* Colour and Citizenship, 1969. *Address:* 37 Pembroke Square, W8. *T:* 01-937 3772. *Club:* Garrick.

ROSE, Francis Leslie, CBE 1978 (OBE 1949); PhD, DSc; FRS 1957; FRSC; Consultant, Imperial Chemical Industries Ltd, since 1974; *b* 27 June 1909; *s* of late Frederick William and Elizabeth Ann Rose, Lincoln; *m* 1935, Ailsa Buckley; one *s. Educ:* City Sch., Lincoln; Univ. Coll. of Nottingham. BSc (Hons Chemistry) London, 1930; PhD London 1934; DSc Nottingham 1950. Research Chemist, ICI Ltd, 1932; Res. Manager, Pharmaceutical Div., ICI, 1954-71, Res. Fellow, 1971-74. Hon. Reader in Organic Chem., UMIST, 1959-72, Hon Fellow, 1972. Mem., later Consultant, Home Office Forensic Science Cttee, 1965-78. Former Mem., Court of Governors, Manchester University and Court of Governors, Univ. of Manchester Inst. of Science and Technology. Hon. Fellow, Manchester Polytechnic. Hon. DSc Loughborough, 1982. Gold Medal, Soc. of Apothecaries, 1948; Tilden Lecture and Medal, Chem. Soc., 1951; Medal, Soc. of Chem. Industry, 1975; Leverhulme Medal, Royal Soc., 1975. *Publications:* numerous scientific papers on chemotherapeutic themes, mainly in Jl of Chem. Soc., Brit. Jl of Pharmacol., Biochem. Jl, etc. *Recreations:* music, in particular the organ; sailing. *Address:* 27 Green Hall Mews, Parkway, Wilmslow, Cheshire SK9 1LP. *T:* Wilmslow 530499; ICI Ltd, Alderley Park, Macclesfield, Cheshire. *Club:* Athenæum.

ROSE, Dr Frank Clifford, FRCP; Physician in Charge, Department of Neurology, Charing Cross Hospital, since 1965; Consultant Neurologist, Medical Ophthalmology Unit, St Thomas' Hospital, since 1963; Principal Medical Officer, Hambro Life Assurance Co., since 1970; *b* 29 Aug. 1926; *s* of James and Clare Rose; *m* 1963, Angela Juliet Halsted; three *s. Educ:* King's Coll., London; Westminster Hosp. Med. Sch.; Univ. of California, San Francisco; Hôpital de la Salpêtrière, Paris. MB BS London; DCH; MRCS; FRCP 1971 (LRCP 1949, MRCP 1954). Medical Registrar, Westminster Hosp., 1955; Resident MO, National Hosp., Queen Square, 1957; Sen. Registrar, Dept of Neurology, St George's Hosp., 1960; Cons. Neurologist, Moor House Sch. for Speech Disorders, 1965. Chm., European Stroke Prevention Study, 1981; Pres., Assurance Med. Soc., 1983. Examr in Medicine, Univ. of London. Lettsomian Lectr, Med. Soc. London, 1979. Harold Wolff Award, Amer. Assoc. for the Study of Headache, 1981. *Publications:* Hypoglycaemia, 1965, 2nd edn, 1981; Basic Neurology of Speech, 1970, 2nd edn 1976; Physiological Aspects of Clinical Neurology, 1976; Medical Ophthalmology, 1976; Motor Neurone Disease, 1977; Clinical Neuroimmunology, 1978; Paediatric Neurology, 1979; Optic Neuritis and its Differential Diagnosis, 1979; Progress in Stroke Research, 1979; Progress in Neurological Research, 1979; Migraine: the facts, 1979; Clinical Neuroepidemiology, 1980; Animal Models of Neurological Disorders, 1980; Research Progress in Parkinson's Disease, 1981; Metabolic Disorders of the Nervous System, 1981; Progress in Migraine Research, 1981; Stroke: The Facts, 1981; Historical Aspects of the Neurosciences, 1982; Cerebral Hyposia in the Pathogenesis of Migraine, 1982; Advances in Sciolic Therapy, 1982; Advances in Migraine, 1982; Progress in Epilepsy, 1982; papers in neurological and gen. med. jls. *Recreations:* travel, wine, reading. *Address:* 35 Harley Street, W1N 1HA. *T:* 01-580 7710. *Clubs:* Savile, Royal Society of Medicine.

ROSE, Gerald Gershon, PhD; CChem; FRSC; Director, Thornton Research Centre, Shell Research Ltd, 1975-80; *b* 4 May 1921; *m* 1945, Olive Sylvia; one *s* two *d. Educ:* Hendon County Grammar Sch.; Imperial Coll. of Science and Technology (BSc, ARCS, DIC, PhD). Joined Shell Group, 1943; served in refineries, Stanlow, Trinidad, Singapore and South Africa; General Manager, Shell/BP South Africa Petroleum Refineries, 1963; Manufacturing and Supply Director, Shell/BP Service Co., 1968; Manager, Teesport Refinery, 1971. *Recreations:* golf, tennis, gardening. *Address:* The Tithe Barn, Great Barrow, Chester, Cheshire CH3 7HW. *T:* Tarvin 40623.

ROSE, Prof. Harold Bertram; Group Economic Adviser, Barclays Bank Ltd, since 1975; Professor of Finance, London Graduate School of Business Studies, since 1965 (Esmée Fairbairn Chair until 1975, then part-time); *b* 9 Aug. 1923; *s* of late Isaac Rose and Rose Rose (*née* Barnett); *m* 1st, 1949, Valerie Frances Anne Chubb (marr. diss. 1974); three *s* one *d*; 2nd, 1974, Diana Mary Campbell Scarlett; one *s* one *d. Educ:* Davenant Foundn Sch.; LSE (BCom). Served with RA in Britain, India and Burma, 1942-45 (Captain). Head of Econ. Intell. Dept, Prudential Assce Co., Ltd, 1948-58; Sen. Lectr, then Reader, in Business Finance, LSE, 1958-65; Member: Council, Consumers' Assoc., 1958-63; Central Adv. Council on Primary Educn (Plowden Cttee), 1963-65; Business Studies Cttee, SSRC, 1967-68, and Univ. Grants Cttee, 1968-69; Reserve Pension Bd, 1973-75; HM Treasury Inquiry into Value of Pensions, 1980; Special Adviser to H of C Treasury and Civil Service Cttee, 1980. Dir, Abbey National Building Soc., 1975-. *Publications:* The Economic Background to Investment, 1959; Disclosure in Company Accounts, 1963; Management Education in the 1970's, 1970; various papers in econ. and financial jls. *Address:* 33 Dartmouth Park Avenue, NW5. *T:* 01-485 7315.

ROSE, Jack, CMG 1963; MBE 1954; DFC 1942; *b* 18 Jan. 1917; *s* of late Charles Thomas Rose; *m* 1st, 1940, Margaret Valerie (*d* 1966), 2nd *d* of late Alec Stuart Budd; two *s*; 2nd, 1967, Beryl Elizabeth, 4th *d* of late A. S. Budd. *Educ:* Shooters Hill School; London University. Served RAF, 1938-46 (Wing Commander); served in fighter, fighter/bomber and rocket firing sqdns; France, 1940 and 1944; Battle of Britain; Burma, 1944-45. Joined Colonial Administrative Service, N Rhodesia, 1947; Private Secretary to Governor of Northern Rhodesia, 1950-53; seconded to Colonial Office, 1954-56;

Administrative posts, Northern Rhodesia, 1956-60; Administrator, Cayman Islands (seconded), 1960-63; Assistant to Governor, British Guiana, 1963-64 (Actg Governor and Dep. Governor for periods). Member: Professional and Technical 'A' Whitley Council for Health Services, 1965-75 (Chm., 1973-75); Gen. Whitley Council for Health Services, 1973-75. Secretary: Chartered Soc. of Physiotherapy, 1965-75; Salmon and Trout Assoc., 1975-79 (Vice-Pres., 1980-). *Recreations:* gardening, walking. *Address:* Ballymans Cottage, Broadway, Woodbury, Exeter, Devon EX5 1NY. *T:* Woodbury 32007.

ROSE, Jim; *see* Rose, E. J. B.

ROSE, Sir Julian (Day), 4th Bt *cr* 1909, of Hardwick House, and 5th Bt *cr* 1872, of Montreal; *b* 3 March 1947; 3rd and *o surv. s* of Sir Charles Henry Rose, 3rd Bt and of Phoebe, *d* of 2nd Baron Phillimore (*d* 1947); *S* father, 1966, and cousin, Sir Francis Cyril Rose, 4th Bt, 1979. *Educ:* Stanbridge School. *Address:* Hardwick House, Whitchurch-on-Thames, Oxfordshire.

ROSE, Michael; *see* Rose, Edward Michael.

ROSE, Morris James Alexander, DFC 1945; Sheriff of Grampian, Highland and Islands at Dingwall and Tain, since 1979, and at Lochmaddy, since 1981; *b* 21 Feb. 1923; *er s* of late Alexander Alistair Rose and late Eileen May McClure, Glasgow; *m* 1953, Jennifer Jane Moncrieff, *yr d* of late William Wallace Moncrieff, Troon; one *s* one *d. Educ:* Kelvinside Academy; Uppingham Sch.; Glasgow Univ. Served with RAFVR, 1941-46. Admitted to Faculty of Advocates, 1952; Sheriff of Aberdeen, Kincardine and Banff, later Grampian, Highland and Islands, at Aberdeen, 1968-79. *Recreation:* golf. *Address:* Sheriff's Chambers, Dingwall, Ross-shire.

ROSE, Paul (Bernard); Barrister-at-Law; *b* 26 Dec. 1935; *s* of Arthur and Norah Rose; *m* 1957, Eve Marie-Thérèse; two *s* one *d. Educ:* Bury Gram. Sch.; Manchester Univ.; Gray's Inn. LLB (Hons) Manch., 1956; Barrister-at-Law, 1957. Legal and Secretarial Dept, Co-op. Union Ltd, 1957-60; Lectureship, Dept of Liberal Studies, Royal Coll. of Advanced Technology, Salford, 1961-63; Barrister-at-Law, practising on SE circuit; a Dep. Circuit Judge. MP (Lab) Manchester, Blackley, 1964-79; PPS to Minister of Transport, 1967-68; Opposition Front Bench Spokesman, Dept of Employment, 1970-72. Chairman: Parly Labour Home Office Group, 1968-70; Parly Labour Employment Group, 1974-79; Campaign for Democracy in Ulster, 1965-73. Delegate to Council of Europe and WEU, 1968-69; Vice-Chm., Labour Cttee for Europe, 1977-79. Mem., Commn on Electoral Reform, 1975-. Founder Mem., SDP (Brent Area Sec., 1981-82); Prospective Parly Cand. (SDP), Northampton S, 1982-. Chm., NW Regional Sports Council, 1966-68. *Publications:* Handbook to Industrial and Provident Societies Act, 1960; Guide to Weights and Measures Act 1963, 1965; The Manchester Martyrs, 1970; Backbencher's Dilemma, 1981; The 'Moonies' Unmasked, 1981; (jt) A History of the Fenian Movement in Britain, 1982; contrib. to many periodicals on political and legal topics. *Recreations:* sport, theatre. *Address:* 10 King's Bench Walk, Temple, EC4Y 7EB.

ROSE, Prof. Richard; Director and Professor of Public Policy, Centre for Study of Public Policy, Strathclyde University, since 1976; *b* 9 April 1933; *o s* of Charles Imse and Mary Conely Rose, St Louis, Mo, USA; *m* 1956, Rosemary J., *o d* of late James Kenny, Whitstable, Kent; two *s* one *d. Educ:* Clayton High Sch., Mo; Johns Hopkins Univ., BA (Distinction, Phi Beta Kappa) comparative drama, 1953; London Sch. of Economics, 1953-54; Oxford University, 1957-60, DPhil (Lincoln and Nuffield Colls). Political public relations, Mississippi Valley, 1954-55; Reporter, St Louis Post-Dispatch, 1955-57; Lecturer in Govt, Univ. of Manchester, 1961-66; Prof. of Politics, Strathclyde Univ., 1966-82. Consultant Psephologist, The Times, Independent Television, Daily Telegraph, STV, 1964-. SSRC Fellow, Stanford Univ., 1967. Dir, ISSC European Summer Sch., 1973. Sec., Cttee on Political Sociology, Internat. Sociological Assoc., 1970-; Founding Mem., European Consortium for Political Res., 1970; Member: US/UK Fulbright Commn, 1971-75; Eisenhower Fellowship Programme, 1971. Guggenheim Foundn Fellow, 1974; Vis. Scholar, Woodrow Wilson Internat. Centre, Washington DC, 1974; Vis. Scholar, Brookings Inst., Washington DC, 1976; Vis. Prof., European Univ. Inst., Florence, 1977, 1978; Vis. Schol., Amer. Enterprise Inst., Washington, 1980. Consultant Chm., NI Constitutional Convention, 1976; Home Office Working Party on Electoral Register, 1975-77. BBC Radio 3: Man of Action, 1974. Co-Founder, British Politics Gp, 1974-; Convenor, Work Gp on UK Politics, Political Studies Assoc., 1976-; Mem. Council, Internat. Political Science Assoc., 1976-; Keynote Speaker, Aust. Inst. of Political Science, Canberra, 1978; Technical Consultant, OECD, 1980; Dir, SSRC Res. Programme, Growth of Govt, 1982-. Chm., Jl of Public Policy, 1981-. *Publications:* The British General Election of 1959 (with D. E. Butler), 1960; Must Labour Lose? (with Mark Abrams), 1960; Politics in England, 1964, 3rd edn 1980; (ed) Studies in British Politics, 1966, 3rd edn 1976; Influencing Voters, 1967; (ed) Policy Making in Britain, 1969; People in Politics, 1970; (ed, with M. Dogan) European Politics, 1971; Governing Without Consensus: an Irish perspective, 1971; (with T. Mackie) International Almanack of Electoral History, 1974, 2nd edn, 1983; (ed) Electoral Behaviour: a comparative handbook, 1974; (ed) Lessons from America, 1974; The Problem of Party Government, 1974; (ed) The Management of Urban Change in Britain and Germany, 1974; Northern Ireland: a time of choice, 1976; Managing Presidential Objectives, 1976; (ed) The Dynamics of Public Policy, 1976; (ed, with D. Kavanagh) New Trends in British Politics, 1977; (ed with J. Wiatr) Comparing Public Policies, 1977;

What is Governing?: Purpose and Policy in Washington, 1978; (ed, with G. Hermet and A. Rouquié) Elections without Choice, 1978; (with G. Peters) Can Government Go Bankrupt?, 1978; (with Ian McAllister) United Kingdom Facts, 1981; (ed with W. B. Gwyn) Britain: progress and decline, 1980; Do Parties Make a Difference?, 1980; (ed) Challenge to Governance, 1980; (ed) Electoral Participation, 1980; (ed with E. Suleiman) Presidents and Prime Ministers, 1980; Understanding the United Kingdom, 1982; (with I. McAllister) United Kingdom Facts, 1982; (ed with P. Madjwick) The Territorial Dimension in United Kingdom Politics, 1982; (ed with E. Page) Fiscal Stress in Cities, 1982; contribs to academic journals in Europe and America; trans. into many foreign languages; broadcasts on British, Irish and American politics. *Recreations:* architecture (historical, Britain: modern, America), music, writing. *Address:* Centre for the Study of Public Policy, McCance Building, Richmond Street, Glasgow G1 1XQ. *T:* 041-552 4400; Bennochy, 1 East Abercromby Street, Helensburgh, Dunbartonshire G84 7SP. *T:* Helensburgh 2164; 7430 Byron Place, Clayton, St Louis County, Mo 63105, USA. *Club:* Reform.

ROSE, (Thomas) Stuart, CBE 1974; FSIAD; Design Adviser, The Post Office, 1968-76; *b* 2 Oct. 1911; *s* of Thomas and Nellie Rose; *m* 1940, Dorothea Winifred, *d* of F. G. Ebsworth, Petrograd; two *d. Educ:* Choral Scholar, Magdalen College Sch., Oxford; Central Sch. of Arts and Crafts. Designer, Crawfords Advertising, 1934-39; free-lance graphics designer and typographer, 1946-68; Typographer, Cement and Concrete Assoc., 1946-51; Print Consultant, Fedn of British Industries, 1947-68; Art Editor, Design Magazine, 1947-53; Typographic Adviser to Postmaster General, 1962-68; Associate, Design Research Unit, industrial design partnership, 1964-68. Member: Industrial Design Cttee, FBI, 1948-65 (Chm. 1965-68); CoID Stamp Adv. Cttee, 1960-62; Post Office Stamp Adv. Cttee, 1968-76. Mem., Soc. of Industrial Artists and Designers, 1936, Pres. 1965. Governor, Central Sch. of Art and Design, 1965-74 (Vice-Chm., 1971-74). FRSA 1970. Phillips Gold Medal for Stamp Design, 1974. *Publication:* Royal Mail Stamps, 1980. *Recreations:* drawing, music, the country. *Address:* 25 Balcombe Street, NW1 6HE. *T:* 01-262 8242; Ladyland, Good Easter, Essex. *T:* Good Easter 365. *Club:* Arts (Chairman 1982-).

ROSE, (Wilfred) Andrew; chartered surveyor (Estate Management); Chairman and Managing Director, Photo-Scan International of South America Ltd; Chairman: Trinidad and Tobago Oil Co. Ltd; Eagle Enterprises, Trinidad; Director: Interstate Investment (Management) Ltd; Guyana and Trinidad Mutual Fire Insurance Co. Ltd; *b* 4 Oct. 1916; *s* of James Emmanuel Rose and Eleanora Rose; *m* 1944, Pamphylia Marcano; one *s. Educ:* Tranquility Boys' Intermediate Sch.; Queen's Royal Coll.; Imperial Coll. of Tropical Agriculture, Trinidad (DipAgr); Coll. of Estate Management, London; London University. FRICS. Agric. Technologist, Food Control Dept, during War of 1939-45. Subseq. Cane Farmers' Superintendent; Estate Manager; Housing Manager, Planning and Housing Commission, Trinidad and Tobago. Editor, Jl of Agricl Soc. of Trinidad and Tobago. Member: Roy. Soc. of Health; Agricl Soc. of Trinidad and Tobago (Life); W India Cttee; Assoc. of Professional Agrologists of Trinidad and Tobago; Professional Valuation and Land Economy Surveyors of Trinidad and Tobago; West Indies National Party; People's National Movement (several cttees). Chm., Commn of Enquiry on Road Passenger Transport. Elected Member for St Ann's, Trinidad, Federal Elections of the West Indies, 1958. Minister of Communications and Works, Federal Govt, West Indies, 1958-62 (twice acted as Dep. Prime Minister); High Commissioner for Trinidad and Tobago: in Canada, 1962-64; in UK, 1964-69, Ambassador to EEC, 1965-69, and Ambassador to UN Agencies, Europe, and Permanent Representative to GATT, 1965-68; Ambassador to Brazil, 1969-72; led West Indies delegn to various confs; Rep. of Govt, frequently abroad. Chm., Commonwealth Rhodesia Sanctions Cttee, 1968-69; Vice-Chm., UNCTAD II, New Delhi, 1968; Member: Commonwealth Telecommunications Bd, 1964-68; Commonwealth Telecommunications Council, 1968. Freeman, City of London, 1967. *Publications:* articles on agriculture in the Trinidad Press, 1942-45. *Recreations:* agriculture, horse-riding, golf. *Address:* PO Box 1041, Port of Spain, Trinidad, WI. *Clubs:* Royal Commonwealth Society; Union (Trinidad).

ROSE-MILLER, Brig. G. P.; *see* Miller.

ROSEBERY, 7th Earl of, *cr* 1703; **Neil Archibald Primrose,** DL; Bt 1651; Viscount of Rosebery, Baron Primrose and Dalmeny, 1700; Viscount of Inverkeithing, Baron Dalmeny and Primrose, 1703; Baron Rosebery (UK), 1828; Earl of Midlothian, Viscount Mentmore, Baron Epsom, 1911; *b* 11 Feb. 1929; *o surv. s* of 6th Earl of Rosebery, KT, PC, DSO, MC, and of Eva Isabel Marian (Eva Countess of Rosebery, DBE), *d* of 2nd Baron Aberdare; *S father,* 1974; *m* 1955, Alison Mary Deirdre, *d* of Ronald W. Reid, 19 Lexden Road, Colchester, Essex; one *s* four *d. Educ:* Stowe; New Coll., Oxford. DL Midlothian, 1960. *Heir: s* Lord Dalmeny, *qv. Address:* Dalmeny House, South Queensferry, West Lothian.

ROSEHILL, Lord; David John MacRae Carnegie; estate manager/owner; *b* 3 Nov. 1954; *s* and *heir* of 13th Earl of Northesk, *qv* ; *m* 1979, Jacqueline Reid, *d* of Mrs Elizabeth Reid, Sarasota, Florida, USA; one *s. Educ:* West Hill Park, Titchfield; Eton; Brooke House, Market Harborough; UCL. *Heir: s* Hon. Alexander Robert MacRae Carnegie, *b* 16 Nov. 1980. *Address:* Fair Oak, Rogate, Petersfield, Hants GU31 5HR. *T:* Rogate 508.

ROSEN, Charles; pianist; Professor of Music, State University of New York at Stony Brook; *b* New York, 5 May 1927; *s* of Irvin Rosen and Anita Gerber. *Educ:* studied piano with Mr and Mrs Moriz Rosenthal; Princeton Univ. (PhD). Début, NY, 1951. His many recordings include: first complete recording of Debussy Etudes, 1951; late keyboard works of Bach, 1969; last six Beethoven Sonatas, 1970; Beethoven's Five Piano Concerti; Diabelli Variations; also works by Liszt, Elliott Carter, Boulez, etc. Eliot Norton Prof. of Poetry, Harvard Univ., 1980. Hon. MusD Trinity Coll., Dublin, 1976; Hon. DMus Durham, 1980. *Publications:* The Classical Style, 1971; Schoenberg, 1976; Sonata Forms, 1980. *Recreations:* music, books. *Address:* c/o Basil Douglas Ltd, 8 St George's Terrace, NW1 8XJ. *T:* 01-722 7142.

ROSEN, Rabbi Jeremy, MA; Headmaster, Carmel College, since 1971; *b* 11 Sept. 1942; *s* of Rabbi Kopul Rosen and Bella Rosen; *m* 1971, Vera Giuditta Zippel; one *s* two *d. Educ:* Carmel Coll.; Pembroke Coll., Cambridge (MA); Mir Academy, Jerusalem. Minister, Bulawayo Hebrew Congregation, Rhodesia, 1966; Minister, Giffnock Hebrew Congregation, Scotland, 1968-71. *Address:* Mongewell Park, Wallingford, Oxon OX10 8BT. *T:* Wallingford 37505.

ROSENBERG HOFFMAN, Anna; *see* Hoffman, Anna Rosenberg.

ROSENBLUM, Prof. Robert; Professor of Fine Arts, New York University, USA, since 1966; *b* 24 July 1927; *m* 1977, Jane Kaplowitz; one *d. Educ:* Queens Coll., Flushing, NY (BA); Yale Univ. (MA); New York Univ. (PhD); Oxford Univ. (MA). Prof. of Art and Archaeology, Princeton Univ., USA, 1956-66; Slade Prof. of Fine Art, Oxford Univ., 1971-72. Frank Jewett Mather Award for Art Criticism, 1981. *Publications:* Cubism and Twentieth-Century Art, 1960; Transformations in Late Eighteenth Century Art, 1967; Jean-Auguste-Dominique Ingres, 1967; Frank Stella, 1971; Modern Painting and the Northern Romantic Tradition: Friedrich to Rothko, 1975; French Painting, 1774-1830 (exhibn catalogue), 1975; Andy Warhol: Portraits of the Seventies, 1979; articles in learned jls: Art Bulletin; Burlington Magazine; Jl of the Warburg and Courtauld Institutes; La Revue de l'Art, etc. *Address:* c/o Institute of Fine Arts, 1 East 78 Street, New York, NY 10021, USA. *T:* (212)-YU8-5550.

ROSENBROCK, Prof. Howard Harry, DSc, CEng; FRS 1976; FIEE, FIChemE; FInstMC; Professor of Control Engineering, since 1966, Vice-Principal, 1977-79, University of Manchester Institute of Science and Technology, (UMIST); Science Research Council Senior Fellow, since 1979; *b* 16 Dec. 1920; *s* of Henry Frederick Rosenbrock and Harriett Emily (*née* Gleed); *m* 1950, Cathryn June (*née* Press); one *s* two *d. Educ:* Slough Grammar Sch.; University Coll. London. BSc, PhD; Fellow 1978. Served War, RAFVR, 1941-46. GEC, 1947-48; Electrical Research Assoc., 1949-51; John Brown & Co., 1951-54; Constructors John Brown Ltd, 1954-62 (latterly Research Manager); ADR, Cambridge Univ., 1962-66. Mem. Council, IEE, 1966-70, Vice-Pres., 1977-78; Pres., Inst. of Measurement and Control, 1972-73; Member: Computer Bd, 1972-76; SRC Engineering Bd, 1976-78. *Publications:* (with C. Storey) Computational Techniques for Chemical Engineers, 1966; (with C. Storey) Mathematics of Dynamical Systems, 1970; State-space and Multivariable Theory, 1970; Computer-aided Control System Design, 1974; contribs Proc. IEE, Trans IChemE, Proc. IEEE, Automatica, Internat. Jl Control, etc. *Recreations:* microscopy, photography, 17th and 18th Century literature. *Address:* Manor Lodge, Mill Lane, Cheadle, Cheshire. *T:* 061-428 7482.

ROSENFELD, Alfred John, CB 1981; Deputy Secretary, since 1979, and Principal Finance Officer, since 1976, Department of Transport; *b* 27 Feb. 1922; *s* of late Ernest Rosenfeld and late Annie Jeanette Rosenfeld (*née* Samson); *m* 1955, Mary Elisabeth (*née* Prudence); two *s* one *d. Educ:* Leyton County High Sch. Entered Public Trustee Office, 1938. Served War, Fleet Air Arm, 1942-46. Min. of Civil Aviation, 1947 (later, Min. of Transport, and Dept of Environment); Private Sec. to Jt Parliamentary Sec., 1958-59; Asst Sec., 1967; Under-Sec., 1972. *Recreations:* chess, bridge, gardening. *Address:* 33 Elmfield Road, Chingford, E4 7HT. *T:* 01-529 8160.

ROSENHEAD, Prof. Louis, CBE 1954; FRS 1946; DSc (Leeds); PhD (Cantab.); Professor of Applied Mathematics, The University, Liverpool, 1933-73, now Professor Emeritus; formerly Fellow of St John's College, Cambridge; *b* 1 Jan. 1906; *s* of Abraham Rosenhead and Helen Nelson; *m* 1932, Esther Brostoff; two *s. Educ:* Leeds Central High School; The University of Leeds; St John's College, Cambridge (Strathcona Research Student); The University of Göttingen. BSc (Leeds 1st Class Hons); PhD (Leeds); Senior Research Student of the Dept of Scientific and Industrial Research, 1929; PhD (Cantab) 1930; DSc (Leeds) 1935; Senior Research Student of Royal Exhibition of 1851; Lecturer, Applied Mathematics at the University College of Swansea, 1931-33. Temporarily attached Min. of Supply, 1940-45. Mem. of various Govt Scientific Cttees, 1939-75. Pro-Vice-Chancellor, 1961-65, Public Orator, 1968-72, University of Liverpool. *Publications:* Index of Mathematical Tables, 2nd edn 1962 (part-author); Compressible Airflow; Tables, 1952 (part-author); Compressible Airflow: Graphs, 1954 (part-author); Laminar Boundary Layers, 1963 (editor); Scientific Publications in the Proceedings of the Royal Society, Proceedings of the Cambridge Philosophical Society, Monthly Notices of the Royal Astronomical Society, etc. *Address:* 30 Wheatcroft Road, Liverpool L18 9UF. *T:* 051-427 6033.

ROSENTHAL, Erwin Isak Jacob, LittD, DrPhil, MA; Reader in Oriental Studies, University of Cambridge, 1959-71, now Emeritus Reader; Fellow of Pembroke College, 1962-71, now Emeritus Fellow; *b* 18 Sept. 1904; *y s* of Moses and Amalie Rosenthal; *m* 1933, Elizabeth Charlotte Marx; one *s* one *d. Educ:* Heilbronn; Universities of Heidelberg, Munich, Berlin. Goldsmid Lectr in Hebrew, Lectr in North-Semitic Epigraphy, Head of Dept of Hebrew, University Coll., Univ. of London, 1933-36; Special Lectr, Semitic Langs and Lits, Univ. of Manchester, 1936-44, Nat. Service: RASC, 1944-45; attached FO, 1945; German Sect., FO, 1946-48. Lectr, Central Advisory Coun. for Educn, HM Forces, 1940-44; Tutor, Adult Educn, Univ. Tutorial Class, WEA, London, 1946-48 (Part-time); Univ. Lectr in Hebrew, Cambridge, 1948-59. Vis. Professor: Columbia Univ., 1967-68; El Colegio de Mexico, 1968; Leverhulme Emeritus Fellow, 1974, 1975. Pres., British Assoc. for Jewish Studies, 1977. *Publications:* Ibn Khalduns Gedanken über den Staat, 1932; Law and Religion (Vol. 3 Judaism and Christianity), 1938 (ed and contrib.); Saadya Studies, 1943 (ed and contrib.); Averroes' Commentary on Plato's Republic, 1956, 1966, 1969 (ed and trans.); Political Thought in Medieval Islam, 1958, 1962, 1968 (Spanish trans., 1967; Japanese trans., 1970); Griechisches Erbe in der jüdischen Religionsphilosophie des Mittelalters, 1960; Judaism and Islam, 1961; Islam in the Modern National State, 1965; (ed) Judaism section, in Religion in the Middle East, 1969; Studia Semitica (I: Jewish Themes; II: Islamic Themes), 1971; articles in learned jls; Festschriften. *Recreations:* music, walking, travelling. *Address:* Pembroke College and 199 Chesterton Road, Cambridge. *T:* 57648.
See also T. G. Rosenthal.

ROSENTHAL, Harold David; Editor of Opera since 1953; Lecturer and Broadcaster since 1950; *b* 30 Sept. 1917; *s* of Israel Victor Rosenthal and Leah Samuels; *m* 1944, Lillah Phyllis Weiner; one *s* one *d. Educ:* City of London School; University College, London (BA); Inst. of Education, London. Asst Editor, Opera, 1950-53; Archivist, Royal Opera House, Covent Garden, 1950-56. Member: Arts Council Patrons of Music Fund Cttee, 1960-70; Council, Friends of Covent Garden, 1962-; Chairman, Music Section, Critics' Circle of Gt Britain, 1965-67. Cavaliere Ufficiale, Order of Merit of the Republic (Italy), 1977. *Publications:* Sopranos of Today, 1956; Two Centuries of Opera at Covent Garden, 1958; A Concise Oxford Dictionary of Opera (with John Warrack), 1964, paperback edn, 1972, rev. and enl. edn, 1979; Great Singers of Today, 1966; Mapleson Memoires (ed and annotated), 1966; The Opera Bedside Book, 1965; Opera at Covent Garden, 1967; Covent Garden, 1976; (ed) Loewenberg's Annals of Opera 1597-1940, 3rd edn, 1979; Annals of Opera 1940-80, 1982; My Mad World of Opera, 1982. *Recreations:* travel, food; collecting playbills, prints, programmes, etc. *Address:* 6 Woodland Rise, N10 3UH. *T:* 01-883 4415.

ROSENTHAL, Thomas Gabriel; publisher, critic and broadcaster; Managing Director, William Heinemann International Ltd, since 1979; *b* 16 July 1935; *o s* of Erwin I. J. Rosenthal, *qv*; *m* Ann Judith Warnford-Davis; two *s. Educ:* Perse Sch., Cambridge; Pembroke Coll., Cambridge (Exhibnr, MA). Served RA, 1954-56, 2nd Lieut; subseq. Lieut Cambridgeshire Regt (TA). Joined Thames and Hudson Ltd, 1959; Man. Dir, Thames & Hudson Internat., 1966; joined Martin Secker & Warburg Ltd as Man. Dir, 1971; Dir, Heinemann Gp of Publishers, 1972-; Chairman: World's Work Ltd, 1979-; Heinemann Zsolnay Ltd, 1979-; William Heinemann Ltd, 1980-; Martin Secker & Warburg Ltd, 1980-; Kaye & Ward Ltd, 1980-; William Heinemann, Australia and SA, 1981-; Pres., Heinemann Inc., 1981-. Art Critic of The Listener, 1963-66. Chm., Soc. of Young Publishers, 1961-62; Member: Cambridge Univ. Appts Bd, 1967-71; Exec. Cttee, NBL, 1971-74; Cttee of Management, Amateur Dramatic Club, Cambridge (also Trustee); Trustee, Phoenix Trust. *Publications:* Monograph on Jack B. Yeats, 1964; (with Alan Bowness) Monograph on Ivon Hitchens, 1973; A Reader's Guide to European Art History, 1962; A Reader's Guide to Modern American Fiction, 1963; introdns to paperback edns of Theodore Dreiser's The Financier, The Titan and Jennie Gerhardt; articles in The Times, Guardian, TLS, London Magazine, Encounter, New Statesman, Jl of Brit. Assoc. for Amer. Studies, Studio Internat., DNB, etc. *Recreations:* opera, bibliomania, looking at pictures, reading other publishers' books. *Address:* c/o Martin Secker & Warburg Ltd, 54 Poland Street, W1V 3DF. *T:* 01-437 2075. *Clubs:* Garrick, Savile, MCC.

ROSEVEARE, Sir Martin (Pearson), Kt 1946; Hon. Fellow of St John's College, Cambridge, since 1952; *b* 24 April 1898; *s* of late Canon R. P. Roseveare, late Vicar of Lewisham; *m* 1921, Edith Mary Pearse (marr. diss., 1958; she *d* 1975); one *s* three *d* (and one *d* decd); *m* 1958, Olivia Margaret Montgomery. *Educ:* Marlborough College; St John's College, Cambridge (scholar). Maths Tripos, Part I, Class 1, 1919; Part II wrangler (b), 1921; Schoolmaster, Repton School, 1921-23; Haileybury College, 1923-26; Board of Education, HM Inspector of Schools, 1927; Staff Inspector of Mathematics, 1939. Lent to Ministry of Information, 1939, Ministry of Food, 1939-44 and 1946 (acting Assistant Sec., 1940, acting Principal Assistant Sec. 1942); Senior Chief Inspector, Ministry of Education, 1944-57, retired; Headmaster Mzuzu School, Nyasaland, 1957-63; Principal, Soche Hill College, Malawi, 1964-67; Schoolmaster, Marymount School, Mzuzu, Malawi, 1967-70. Served European War, RFA, Lt 1916-19, France, Belgium, Italy (wounded, despatches). *Recreations:* hockey, camping. *Address:* Box 29, Mzuzu, Malawi.

ROSEVEARE, Robert William, CBE 1977; Secretary, since 1967, Managing Director, Policy Co-ordination, since 1973, British Steel Corporation; *b* Mandalay, Burma, 23 Aug. 1924; *s* of late William Leonard Roseveare, MC and of Marjory C. Roseveare; *m* 1954, Patricia Elizabeth, *d* of Guy L. Thompson, FRCS, Scarborough; one *s* three *d. Educ:* Gresham's Sch., Holt; St John's Coll., Cambridge (MA). Served in Fleet Air Arm, 1943-46. Home Civil Service, Admin. Class, 1949. Asst Private Sec. to Minister of Fuel and Power, 1952-54; seconded to Cabinet Office, 1958-60; British Embassy, Washington, 1960-62; Asst Sec., Ministry of Power, 1964. Special Asst to Chm. of Organising Cttee for British Steel Corporation (Lord Melchett), 1966; seconded to British Steel Corporation on its formation, 1967; Dir, Admin. Services, 1969; Man. Dir, Corporate Administration, 1971. *Recreations:* hill-walking, bird-watching, singing. *Address:* Elm Tree Cottage, 22 Ox Lane, Harpenden, Herts. *T:* Harpenden 3071.

ROSIER, Air Chief Marshal Sir Frederick (Ernest), GCB 1972 (KCB 1966; CB 1961); CBE 1955 (OBE 1943); DSO 1942; RAF, retired; *b* 13 Oct. 1915; *s* of E. G. Rosier; *m* 1939, Hettie Denise Blackwell; three *s* one *d. Educ:* Grove Park School, Wrexham. Commissioned RAF, 1935; 43 (F) Sqdn, 1936-39. Served War of 1939-45 in France, UK, Western Desert and Europe. OC Horsham St Faith, 1947; exchange duties with USAF, 1948-50; Instructor at Jt Services Staff College, 1950-52; Gp Capt. Operations at Central Fighter Establishment, 1952-54; Gp Capt. Plans at Fighter Command, 1955-56; ADC to the Queen, 1956-58; idc 1957; Director of Joint Plans, Air Ministry, 1958; Chm. Joint Planning Staff, 1959-61; AOC Air Forces Middle East, 1961-63; Senior Air Staff Officer, HQ Transport Command, 1964-66; Air Officer C-in-C, RAF, Fighter Command, 1966-68; UK Mem., Permanent Military Deputies Group, Central Treaty Organisation, Ankara, 1968-70; Dep. C-in-C, Allied Forces Central Europe, 1970-73. Air ADC to the Queen, 1972-73. Mil. Advr and Dir, British Aircraft Corp. (Preston) Ltd, 1973-77; Director i/c BAC Ltd, Saudi Arabia, 1977-80. Commander, Order of Orange Nassau, 1947. *Address:* Flat 286, Latymer Court, Hammersmith, W6. *Club:* Royal Air Force.

ROSIER, Rt. Rev. Stanley Bruce; *see* Willochra, Bishop of.

ROSKELL, Prof. John Smith, MA, DPhil; FBA 1968; Professor of Medieval History, University of Manchester, 1962-79, now Professor Emeritus; *b* Norden, Rochdale, 2 July 1913; *s* of John Edmund and Lucy A. Roskell; *m* 1942, Evelyn Liddle; one *s* one *d. Educ:* Rochdale Municipal Secondary School; Accrington Grammar Sch.; University of Manchester; Balliol College, Oxford. Asst Lecturer in History, Manchester University, 1938; Lecturer, 1945; Senior Lecturer, 1950-52; Professor of Medieval History, University of Nottingham, 1952-62. President: Lancashire Parish Register Soc., 1962; Chetham Soc., 1972. Royal Navy, 1940-45; Lieut RNVR, 1942-45. *Publications:* The Knights of the Shire of the County Palatine of Lancaster (1377-1460), Chetham Society, 1937; The Commons in the Parliament of 1422, 1954; The Commons and their Speakers in English Parliaments, 1376-1523, 1965; (ed with F. Taylor) Gesta Henrici Quinti, 1975; articles in English Historical Review, Bulletin of the Institute of Historical Research, etc. *Recreation:* cricket. *Address:* 42 Barcheston Road, Cheadle, Cheshire. *T:* 061-428 4630.

ROSKILL, family name of **Baron Roskill.**

ROSKILL, Baron *cr* 1980 (Life Peer), of Newtown in the County of Hampshire; **Eustace Wentworth Roskill;** Kt 1962; PC 1971; DL; a Lord of Appeal in Ordinary since 1980; *b* 6 Feb. 1911; *y s* of late John Roskill, KC and of late Sybil Mary Wentworth, *d* of Ashton Wentworth Dilke, MP; *m* 1947, Elisabeth Wallace Jackson, 3rd *d* of late Thomas Frame Jackson, Buenos Aires; one *s* two *d. Educ:* Winchester College (exhibnr; Fellow, 1981); Exeter Coll., Oxford (exhibnr). 1st Cl. hons, Hon. Sch. of Mod. Hist. Oxford, BA 1932; MA 1936; Harmsworth Law Schol. Middle Temple, 1932; called to Bar, Middle Temple, 1933, Bencher 1961, Reader 1978, Dep. Treasurer 1979, Treasurer 1980; Hon. Bencher of The Inner Temple, 1980. Worked at Ministries of Shipping and War Transport, 1939-45. QC 1953. Dep. Chm. Hants QS, 1951-60, Chm. 1960-71; Comr of Assize (Birmingham), 1961; Judge of the High Court of Justice, Queen's Bench Division, 1962-71; a Lord Justice of Appeal, 1971-80. Vice-Chm., Parole Bd, 1967-69; Chm., Commn on Third London Airport, 1968-70. Pres., Senate of Four Inns of Court, 1972-74; Hon. Mem., 1974; Life Mem., Canadian Bar Assoc., 1974. Chairman: Average Adjusters Assoc., 1977-78; London Internat. Arbitration Trust, 1981. Hon. Fellow, Exeter College, Oxford, 1963. Hampshire: JP 1950; DL 1972. *Recreations:* music, swimming, gardening. *Address:* Heatherfield, Newtown, Newbury, Berks RG15 9DB. *T:* Newbury 40606; New Court, Temple, EC4. *T:* 01-353 8870; House of Lords, SW1. *Club:* Reform.
See also Sir Patrick Dean, Sir A. W. Roskill, O. W. Roskill, Captain S. W. Roskill.

ROSKILL, Sir Ashton (Wentworth), Kt 1967; QC 1949; MA Oxon; Chairman, Monopolies and Mergers Commission (formerly Monopolies Commission), 1965-75 (Part-time Member, 1960-65); *b* 1 Jan. 1902; *e s* of late John Roskill, KC, and Sybil Mary Wentworth, *d* of late Ashton Dilke, MP; *m* 1st, 1932, Violet Willoughby (*d* 1964), *d* of late Charles W. Waddington, CIE; one *s* one *d*; 2nd, 1965, Phyllis Sydney, *y d* of late Sydney Burney, CBE. *Educ:* Winchester; Exeter Coll., Oxford (Schol.), 1st class hons Modern History, 1923; Barrister-at-Law, Inner Temple, 1925; Certificate of Honour, Council of Legal Education. Attached War Office, Intelligence Staff, 1940-45. Bencher, Inner Temple, 1958, Treasurer, 1980; Hon. Bencher, Middle Temple, 1964. Chm., Barristers Benevolent Assoc., 1968-79. *Address:* 8 King's

Bench Walk, Temple, EC4. *T:* 01-353 2734; Heath Cottage, Newtown, Newbury, Berks. *T:* Newbury 40328. *Club:* Reform.

See also Baron Roskill, O. W. Roskill, Captain S. W. Roskill.

ROSKILL, Oliver Wentworth, FRSC, CEng, CChem, FInstChemE, CIMechE, FInstF, CBIM, FIMC; Senior Partner, O. W. Roskill Industrial Consultants, 1930-74; Chairman: O. W. Roskill & Co (Reports) Ltd, 1957-74; Roskill Information Services Ltd, 1971-74; *b* 28 April 1906; *s* of John Roskill, KC, and Sibyl Mary Wentworth, *d* of Ashton Wentworth Dilke, MP. *Educ:* Oundle Sch.; Lincoln Coll., Oxford (scholar). MA, BSc (Oxon) (1st Cl. Hons). Captain, Oxford Univ. Rugby Fives Club, 1927. Imperial Chemical Industries Ltd, 1928-30. Min. of Economic Warfare, Dep. Head, Enemy Countries Intell., 1939-41. Mem. Exec. Cttee of Political and Economic Planning (now Policy Studies Inst.), 1931, Vice-Pres., 1975; Founder Mem. Council, British Inst. of Management, 1947-53 (Chm. Inf. and Research Cttee); Mem. British Nat. Export Council, Caribbean Cttee, 1965-69; Mem. Council, Inst. of Management Consultants, 1963-74 (Pres., 1970-71). Consultant on industrial development projects to Govts of Iran, Pakistan, Malta, Fed. Govt of Rhodesia, and others. *Publications:* Founder and part author of 'Who Owns Whom' series of directories; part author of Fifty Years of Political and Economic Planning; author of monographs on economics of metals and minerals (incl. tungsten, titanium, chromium, fluorspar); contributor to many jls of learned societies (incl. Inst. Fuel, RIBA, Town Planning Inst.). *Recreations:* mountain walking, playing chamber music, choral singing, real tennis, gardening. *Address:* The Priory, Beech Hill, Reading, Berks. *T:* Reading 883146. *Clubs:* Brooks's; Woodmen of Arden; Hampton Court Tennis, Holyport Tennis, Hatfield Tennis.

See also Baron Roskill, Sir A. W. Roskill, Captain S. W. Roskill.

ROSKILL, Captain Stephen Wentworth, CBE 1971; DSC 1944; MA Cantab; LittD Cantab 1971; FBA 1971; FRHistS; late RN; Fellow of Churchill College, Cambridge, 1961, Life Fellow, 1970; *b* 1 Aug. 1903; *s* of John Henry Roskill, KC, and Sybil Mary Dilke, *d* of Ashton Wentworth Dilke, MP; *m* 1930, Elizabeth, *d* of Henry Van den Bergh; four *s* three *d.* *Educ:* RN Colleges, Osborne and Dartmouth. RN, 1917-48; Gunnery Specialist, 1928; Commander, 1938; Captain, 1944. Served at sea as Commander HMS Warspite, 1939; Naval Staff, 1939-41; Commander and Captain, HMNZS Leander, 1941-44; Senior Observer, Bikini Atomic Bomb Trials, 1946; Dep. Director of Naval Intelligence, 1946-48; invalided, 1948; Cabinet Office, Official Naval Historian, 1949-60. Officer Legion of Merit (USA). Lees Knowles Lecturer, Cambridge, 1961; Distinguished Visitor Lecturer, US Naval Academy, Annapolis, 1965; Richmond Lecturer, Cambridge, 1967; Leverhulme Res. Fellow, National Maritime Museum, 1974. Navy Records Society: Councillor, 1956-66, and 1968-70; Vice-Pres., 1966-68, 1970, Hon. Life Vice-Pres., 1976. Pres. Cambridge Br., RN Assoc., 1976. Hon. LittD Leeds, 1975; Hon. DLitt Oxon, 1980. Chesney Gold Medal, RUSI, 1975. *Publications:* The War at Sea (official history), Vol. I, 1954, Vol. II, 1957; HMS Warspite, 1957; The Secret Capture, 1959; The War at Sea, Vol. III, Part I, 1960; The Navy at War, 1960; the War at Sea, Vol. III, Part II, 1961: The Strategy of Sea Power, 1962; A Merchant Fleet in War, 1962; The Art of Leadership, 1964; Naval Policy between the Wars, Vol. I, 1968, Vol. II, 1976; Documents relating to the Naval Air Service 1908-1918, 1969; Hankey, Man of Secrets, Vol. 1, 1877-1918, 1970, Vol. 2, 1919-1931, 1972; Vol. 3, 1931-63, 1974; Churchill and the Admirals, 1977; Admiral of the Fleet Earl Beatty, 1980; numerous contribs to learned jls. *Recreations:* all country pursuits, painting. *Address:* Frostlake Cottage, Malting Lane, Cambridge. *T:* 354705. *Club:* Travellers'.

See also Baron Roskill, Sir A. W. Roskill, O. W. Roskill.

ROSLING, Peter Edward, MVO 1972; HM Diplomatic Service; Consul-General, Zagreb, since 1980; *b* 17 June 1929; *s* of Peregrine Starr and Jessie Rosling; *m* 1950, Kathleen Nuell; three *s.* *Educ:* grammar school. Served Royal Navy, 1948-50. HM Diplomatic Service, 1946-; Belgrade, Innsbruck, Cape Town, Rome (NATO Defence College), FCO. *Recreations:* walking, fishing, painting, bridge. *Address:* c/o Foreign and Commonwealth Office, SW1; British Consulate-General, Ilica 12/II, 41000 Zagreb, Yugoslavia. *T:* Zagreb 445522.

ROSOMAN, Leonard Henry, OBE 1981; RA 1969 (ARA 1960); FSA; Tutor, Royal College of Art, since 1957; *b* 27 Oct. 1913; *s* of Henry Rosoman; *m* 1963, Jocelyn (marr. diss. 1969), *d* of Bertie Rickards, Melbourne, Australia. *Educ:* Deacons Sch., Peterborough; Durham Univ. Teacher of Drawing and Painting, Reimann Sch. of Art, London, 1938-39; Official War Artist to Admiralty, 1943-45; Teacher: Camberwell Sch. of Art, London, 1947-48; (Mural Painting) Edinburgh Coll. of Art, 1948-56; Chelsea School of Art, 1956-57; Tutor, Royal Coll. of Art, 1957-. One Man Shows: St George's Gallery, London, 1946 and 1949; Roland, Browse and Delbanco Gallery, London, 1954, 1957, 1959, 1965 and 1969. Works bought by: HM Govt, Arts Council, British Council, York Art Gall., Contemporary Art Soc., Adelaide Art Gallery, V&A Museum. Executed large mural paintings for: Festival of Britain, 1951; British Pavilion, Brussels World Fair, 1958; Harewood House, 1959. FSIA; Hon. ARCA; HRSW. *Recreation:* travelling as much as possible. *Address:* 7 Pembroke Studios, Pembroke Gardens, W8. *T:* 01-603 3638.

ROSPIGLIOSI, family name of **Earl of Newburgh.**

ROSS, family name of **Baron Ross of Marnock.**

ROSS, Hon. Lord; Donald MacArthur Ross; a Senator of the College of Justice, Scotland, and Lord of Session, since 1977; *b* 29 March 1927; *s* of late John Ross, solicitor, Dundee; *m* 1958, Dorothy Margaret, *d* of late William Annand, Kirriemuir; two *d.* *Educ:* Dundee High School; Edinburgh University. MA (Edinburgh) 1947; LLB with distinction (Edinburgh) 1951. National Service with The Black Watch (RHR), 2nd Lt, 1947-49. Territorial Service, 1949-58, Captain. Advocate, 1952; QC (Scotland) 1964; Vice-Dean, Faculty of Advocates of Scotland, 1967-73; Dean, 1973-76; Standing Junior Counsel in Scotland to: Min. of Labour and Nat. Service, 1959-62; Scottish Development Dept (Highways), 1962-64; Junior Legal Assessor to Edinburgh Burgh and Dean of Guild Courts, 1958-64; Sheriff Principal of Ayr and Bute, 1972-73. Dep. Chm., Boundary Commn for Scotland, 1977-. Member: Scottish Cttee of Council on Tribunals, 1970-76; Cttee on Privacy, 1970. Mem. Court, Heriot-Watt Univ., 1978-. *Recreation:* gardening. *Address:* 33 Lauder Road, Edinburgh EH9 2JG. *T:* 031-667 5731. *Club:* New (Edinburgh).

ROSS OF MARNOCK, Baron *cr* 1979 (Life Peer), of Kilmarnock in the District of Kilmarnock and Loudoun; **William Ross;** PC 1964; MBE (mil.) 1945; MA; Lord High Commissioner, General Assembly of Church of Scotland, 1978-80; *b* 7 April 1911; *s* of W. Ross, Ayr; *m* 1948, Elizabeth Jane Elma Aitkenhead, Ayr; two *d.* *Educ:* Ayr Academy; Glasgow University. MA 1932; Schoolmaster. Served War of 1939-45, HLI, R Signals, Major; India, SACSEA. Contested Ayr Burgh, General Election, 1945; MP (Lab) Kilmarnock, Ayr and Bute, 1946-79; Secretary of State for Scotland, 1964-70, 1974-76; Opposition spokesman on Scottish Affairs, 1970-74; Mem., Labour Parly Cttee, 1970-79. Hon. Pres., Scottish Football Assoc., 1978. FEIS 1971. Hon. LLD: St Andrews, 1967; Strathclyde, 1969; Glasgow, 1978. *Recreation:* golf. *Address:* 10 Chapelpark Road, Ayr. *T:* Ayr 65673.

ROSS, Alan, CBE 1982; author, publisher and journalist; Editor of London Magazine; Managing Director, London Magazine Editions (Publishers), since 1965; *b* Calcutta, 6 May 1922; *o s* of John Brackenridge Ross, CBE and Clare, *d* of Captain Patrick Fitzpatrick, Indian Army; *m* 1949, Jennifer, *d* of Sir Geoffrey Fry, 1st and last Bt, KCB, CVO; one *s.* *Educ:* Haileybury; St John's College, Oxford. RN 1942-47; general service, Arctic and North Seas, 1942-44; Asst Staff Officer, Intelligence, 16th Destroyer Flotilla, 1944; on staff of Flag Officer, Western Germany, 1945, and Interpreter to British Naval Commander-in-Chief, Germany, 1946. British Council, 1947-50; on staff of The Observer 1950-71. Toured Australia as correspondent, with MCC, 1954-55, 1962-63; toured South Africa, 1956-57, 1964-65; toured West Indies, 1960, 1968. Atlantic Award for Literature (Rockefeller Foundation), 1946. FRSL 1971. *Publications:* The Derelict Day, 1947; Time Was Away, 1948; The Forties, 1950; The Gulf of Pleasure, 1951; Poetry 1945-50, 1951; The Bandit on the Billiard Table, 1954 (revised edition South to Sardinia, 1960); Something of the Sea, 1954; Australia 55, 1956; Abroad (ed), 1957; Cape Summer and the Australians in England, 1957; To Whom It May Concern, 1958; The Onion Man, 1959; Through the Caribbean, 1960; The Cricketer's Companion (ed), 1960; Danger on Glass Island, 1960; African Negatives, 1962; Australia 63, 1963; West Indies at Lord's, 1963; North from Sicily, 1965; Poems 1942-67, 1968; Tropical Ice, 1972; The Taj Express, 1973; (ed) London Magazine Stories 1-11, 1964-80; (ed) Living in London, 1974; Open Sea, 1975; (ed) Selected Poems of Lawrence Durrell, 1977; Death Valley and Other Poems, 1980; (ed) The Turf, 1982; Colours of War, 1983; several trans and introductions; contrib. to various jls in England and America. *Recreations:* travel, sport (played cricket and squash for Oxford University and Royal Navy), collecting pictures, racing. *Address:* 30 Thurloe Place, SW7. *Clubs:* Garrick, MCC; Vincent's (Oxford).

ROSS, Sir Alexander, Kt 1971; Chairman, United Dominions Trust Ltd, 1963-74 (Director, 1955; Vice-Chairman, 1962); Deputy Chairman, Eagle Star Insurance Co. Ltd; Chairman, Australia and New Zealand Banking Group Ltd, 1970-75; Chairman, Leighstock Ltd; Director: Whitbread Investment Trust Ltd, since 1972; Drayton Far Eastern Trust Ltd (formerly British Australian Investment Trust Ltd), since 1975; Power Components Ltd, since 1976; *b* 2 Sept. 1907; *s* of late William Alexander Ross and of Kathleen Ross; *m* 1st, 1933, Nora Bethia Burgess (*d* 1974); two *s* two *d* ; 2nd, 1975, Cynthia Alice Barton. *Educ:* Mount Albert Gram. Sch.; Auckland University Coll., Auckland, NZ. Joined Nat. Bank of NZ, 1927, and Reserve Bank of NZ on its establishment in 1934; Dep. Gov., 1948-55. Rep. NZ on numerous occasions overseas, including Sterling Area Conf. in Australia, 1954. Rep. NZ in rowing, at Empire Games, 1930; managed NZ team to Empire Games, Vancouver, 1954; NZ rowing selector for Olympic and Empire Games; Chairman: British Commonwealth Games Fedn, 1968-; Cttee for Exports to NZ, 1965-67; East European Trade Council, 1967-69; Vice-Pres., British Export Houses Assoc., 1968-71; Member: BNEC, 1965-69; NRDC, 1966-74; New Zealand Soc. (Past Pres.); Cttee of Directors, Royal Caledonian Schools, 1964-69; Council, Dominion Students' Hall Trust. Pres., Fellowship of the Motor Industry, 1971-73. Chm., Court of Advisors, St Paul's Cathedral, 1980-82. A past Governor, English-Speaking Union; Dep. Chm., Central Council, Royal Over-Seas League; Trustee, Aust. Musical Foundn. *Recreation:* walking. *Address:* c/o Mr Bryan O'Callaghan, Australia & New Zealand Banking Group Ltd, Queen and Creek Streets, Brisbane, Qld 4000, Australia. *Club:* Hurlingham.

ROSS, Alfred William, OBE 1955; MA, MIEE; Technical and Operational Research Consultant; Deputy Chief Scientist (Navy), Ministry of Defence, 1972-74; *b* 13 Sept. 1914; *m* 1946, Margaret Elizabeth Wilson; three *d.* *Educ:*

King Edward VI School, Stourbridge; Christ's Coll., Cambridge. Joined HM Signal Sch., Portsmouth, 1936. Worked on Radar during War at Admiralty Signal and Radar Establishment. Defence Research Policy Staff, Ministry of Defence, 1946-47; Chief Superintendent, Army Operational Research Group, 1951-56. Director, Naval Physical Research, MoD, 1956-68; Chief of Naval Research, MoD, 1968-72. *Publications:* scientific papers on radar, electronics and operational research. *Recreation:* golf. *Address:* 336 Fir Tree Road, Epsom Downs, Surrey KT17 3NW. *T:* Burgh Heath 56774. *Club:* Walton Heath Golf.

ROSS, Rev. Dr Andrew Christian; Senior Lecturer in Ecclesiastical History, University of Edinburgh, since 1966; Principal of New College and Dean of the Faculty of Divinity, since 1978; *b* 10 May 1931; *s* of George Adams Ross and Christian Glen Walton; *m* 1953, Isabella Joyce Elder; four *s* (one *d* decd). *Educ:* Dalkeith High Sch.; Univ. of Edinburgh (MA, BD, PhD); Union Theol Seminary, New York (STM). Served Royal Air Force, Pilot Officer, then FO, 1952-54. Ordained Minister of Church of Scotland, 1958; Minister, Church of Central Africa Presbyterian (Malâwi), 1958-65; Chm., Lands Tribunal of Nyasaland, then Malâwi Govt, 1963-65; Vice-Chm., Nat. Tenders Bd of Nyasaland, then Malâwi, 1963-65. Sen. Studentship in African History, Univ. of Edinburgh, 1965-66; Mem. Court of Univ. of Edinburgh, 1971-73, Chm. Student Affairs Cttee of the Court, 1977-80. *Publications:* chapter in: The Zambesian Past, 1965; Religion in Africa, 1965; Witchcraft and Healing, 1969; David Livingstone and Africa, 1973; Malâwi, Past and Present, 1974; introd. and ed for micro film-prodn: Life and Work in Central Africa 1885-1914, 1969; The Records of the UMCA 1859-1914, 1971; contribs to Union Qly Rev., New Left Rev., Scottish Historical Rev. *Recreation:* playing and watching soccer. *Address:* 27 Colinton Road, Edinburgh EH10 5DR. *T:* 031-447 5987. *Club:* University of Edinburgh Staff.

ROSS, Sir Archibald (David Manisty), KCMG 1961 (CMG 1953); HM Diplomatic Service, retired; Chairman: Alfa-Laval Co.; Saab (Great Britain); Scania (Great Britain), 1972-82; Datasaab, since 1975; *b* 12 Oct. 1911; *s* of late J. A. Ross, Indian Civil Service, and Dorothea, *e d* of late G. Eldon Manisty, Indian Civil Service; *m* 1939, Mary Melville, *d* of Melville Macfadyen; one *s* one *d* (and one *s* decd). *Educ:* Winchester; New College, Oxford (MA). 1st Class Hon. Mods 1932, Lit. Hum. 1934; Gaisford Greek Verse Prize, 1932; Laming Travelling Fellow, Queen's College, 1934-35. Diplomatic Service, 1936; Berlin, 1939, Stockholm, 1939-44; Foreign Office, 1944-47, Tehran, 1947-50; Counsellor, Foreign Office, 1950-53; HM Minister, Rome, 1953-56; Assistant Under Secretary of State for Foreign Affairs, 1956-60; Ambassador to Portugal, 1961-66; Ambassador to Sweden, 1966-71. Mem. Council, RASE, 1980-. Grand Cross, Order of the North Star, Sweden, 1981. *Address:* 17 Ennismore Gardens, SW7. *Clubs:* Travellers'; Leander.

ROSS, Hon. Sir Bruce; *see* Ross, Hon. Sir D. B.

ROSS, (Claud) Richard, CB 1973; MA; Vice-President, European Investment Bank, since 1978; *b* 24 March 1924; *o s* of late Claud Frederick Ross and Frances Muriel Ross, Steyning, Sussex; *m* 1954, Leslie Beatrice, *d* of Oliver Arnell and late Dr H. M. Arnell, Kitale, Kenya; two *d. Educ:* Ardingly Coll.; Hertford Coll., Oxford (Open Schol., Mod. Hist.). Served in Royal Engineers, 1942-47. 1st cl. PPE, 1950. Fellow of Hertford Coll., 1951-63; Lectr in Economics, Oxford Univ., 1951-52 and 1955-63; Economic Section, HM Treasury, 1952-55; Junior Proctor, Oxford Univ., 1958-59; Bursar, Hertford Coll., 1959-63; Prof. of Economics and Dean of Social Studies, Univ. of East Anglia, 1963-69 (Pro-Vice-Chancellor, 1964-68); Consultant, OECD, Paris, 1969-71; Dep. Sec., Central Policy Review Staff, Cabinet Office, 1971-78. Adviser, Bankers' Mission to India and Pakistan, 1960. Represented HM Treasury on OECD Working Party on Policies for Economic Growth, 1961-68. Leader, British Economic Mission to Tanzania, 1965; Member: East Anglia Economic Planning Council, 1966-69 (Dep. Chm., 1967-69); Jt Mission for Malta, 1967. *Publications:* Financial and Physical Problems of Development in the Gold Coast (with D. Seers), 1952; articles on economics. *Address:* European Investment Bank, 100 boulevard Konrad Adenauer, L-2950 Luxembourg; 2a Oliver's Wharf, 64 Wapping High Street, E1.

ROSS, Donald MacArthur; *see* Ross, Hon. Lord.

ROSS, Donald Nixon, FRCS; consultant cardiac surgeon; *b* 4 Oct. 1922; *m* 1956, Dorothy Curtis; one *d. Educ:* Boys' High Sch., Kimberley, S Africa; Univ. of Capetown (BSc, MB, ChB 1st Cl. Hons, 1946). FRCS 1949; FACC 1973; FACS 1976. Sen. Registrar in Thoracic Surgery, Bristol, 1952; Guy's Hospital: Res. Fellow, 1953; Sen. Thoracic Registrar, 1954; Cons. Thoracic Surg., 1958; Cons. Surg., National Heart Hosp., 1963, Sen. Surg., 1967, Cons. Emeritus, 1978; Dir, Dept of Surgery, Inst. of Cardiology, 1970. Order of Cedar of Lebanon, 1975; Order of Merit (1st cl.), West Germany, 1981. Hon. DSc CNAA. *Publications:* A Surgeon's Guide to Cardiac Diagnosis, 1962; (jtly) Medical and Surgical Cardiology, 1968; (jtly) Biological Tissue in Heart Valve Replacement, 1972; contrib. BMJ, Lancet, Proc. RSM, Annals Royal Coll. Surg., Amer. Jl Cardiol. *Recreations:* horseriding, gardening. *Address:* 69 Gloucester Crescent, NW1. *T:* 01-935 6191. *Clubs:* Garrick; Kimberley (SA).

ROSS, Hon. Sir (Dudley) Bruce, Kt 1962; retired; *b* 21 May 1892; *s* of William Alexander Ross and Annie Isabella Ross, Adelaide, S Australia; *m* 1st, 1920, Margaret Eleanor Waterhouse (decd); one *s* three *d*; 2nd, 1954,

Agnes Jessie Linklater. *Educ:* Queen's School, St Peter's College and University of Adelaide, S Australia. LLB (Adelaide) 1914. KC 1945. Judge of Supreme Court of S Australia, 1952-62. Pres. Law Society of S Australia, 1948-49; Vice-Pres., Law Council of Australia, 1948-49; Chancellor, Dioceses of Adelaide and Willochra, 1944-69; Grand Master, Grand Lodge of SA, 1959-64; Member Council of Governors, St Peter's Coll., Adelaide, 1948-60; Pres. Church of England Boys' Home, 1943-73; Pres., Kindergarten Union of SA, 1962-73. Served European War, 1914-18, with 5th Division, AIF. *Recreation:* bowls. *Address:* 19 Sherbourne Road, Medindie Gardens, SA 5081, Australia. *T:* 442178. *Club:* Adelaide.

ROSS, Duncan Alexander, CEng, MIEE; Chairman, South Wales Electricity Board, and Member, Electricity Council, since 1981; *b* 25 Sept. 1928; *s* of William Duncan Ross and Mary Ross; *m* 1958, Mary Buchanan Clarke Parsons; one *s* one *d. Educ:* Dingwall Academy; Glasgow Univ. (BSc Elec. Engrg). MBIM. Various engineering posts, South of Scotland Electricity Board, 1952-57; engineering, commercial and management posts, Midlands Electricity Board, 1957-72; Area Manager, South Staffs Area, 1972-75, Chief Engineer, 1975-77; Dep. Chairman, South Wales Electricity Bd, 1977-81. *Recreations:* golf, squash. *Address:* Cattraeth, Well Lane, Llanvair Discoed, near Chepstow, Gwent NP6 6LP. *T:* Penhow 400499.

ROSS, Ernest; MP (Lab) Dundee West, since 1979; *b* Dundee, July 1942; *m* ; two *s* one *d. Educ:* St John's Jun. Secondary Sch. Quality Control Engineer, Timex Ltd. Joined Labour Party, 1973; Mem., AUEW (TASS). *Address:* House of Commons, SW1.

ROSS, Rear-Adm. George Campbell, CB 1952; CBE 1945; FRGS; CEng, MIMechE; MRAeS; retired; *b* 9 Aug. 1900; *s* of late Sir Archibald Ross, KBE; *m* 1st, 1929, Alice Behrens; 2nd, 1950, Lucia Boer (marr. diss. 1969); two *d*; 3rd, 1975, Manolita Harris. *Educ:* Royal Naval Colleges, Osborne and Dartmouth. Served European War, 1914-18, Grand Fleet (HM Ships Warspite, P59, Vendetta). Engineering Courses at RN College, Greenwich, and RNE College, Keyham, 1919-21; HMS Hawkins, Flagship China Station, 1921-24; RNE Coll., Lecturer in Marine Engineering, 1924-27; HMS Effingham, Flagship East Indies Station, 1927-29; HM Dockyard, Chatham, 1929-31; HMS Rodney, Atlantic Fleet, 1931-33 (incl. Invergordon Mutiny); Comdr 1933; Asst Naval Attaché, Embassy, Tokyo, 1933-36; Liaison Officer to Japanese Flagship Asigara, Coronation Review, 1937; introduced the Oerlikon 20mm gun to the Royal Navy, 1937 (adopted in 1939 largely owing to Lord Mountbatten and the First Sea Lord, Sir Roger Backhouse); HMS Manchester, E Indies Station, 1937-39; Engineer-in-Chief's Dept, Admiralty, 1939-41; Engineer Officer, HMS Nelson, and Staff Engineer Officer to Flag Officer, Force "H", Malta Convoy, N Africa and Sicily, 1941-Aug. 1943; Capt. 1943; HMS St Angelo, Malta, as Staff Engineer Officer (D), on staff of Captain (D), Force "H", Aug. 1943-Dec. 1943 (first officer to go aboard flagship of Italian Fleet after its surrender); Aircraft Maintenance and Repair Dept, Admiralty, 1943-47; ADC to the King, 1948-49; Chief of Staff to Rear-Admiral Naval Reserve Aircraft, 1948-49; Rear-Adm. (E) 1949; Director of Aircraft Maintenance and Repair, Admiralty, 1949-53; retd, Oct. 1953. Joined Hawker Siddeley group, Nov. 1953, and retd Sept. 1965. Consultant to Grieveson Grant, Stockbrokers (1965-79), and other cos. Chairman, Combined Services Winter Sports Assoc., 1951-67. Freedom and Livery of Worshipful Company of Carmen. *Recreations:* fishing, travel, painting, writing. *Address:* 11 Redcliffe Close, Old Brompton Road, SW5. *T:* 01-373 0609. *Club:* Hurlingham.

ROSS, James, QC 1966; **His Honour Judge Ross;** a Circuit Judge (formerly a Judge of County Courts), since 1971; *b* 22 March 1913; *s* of John Stuart Ross, FRCSE; *m* 1939, Clare Margaret, *d* of Alderman Robert Cort-Cox, Stratford-on-Avon; one *d. Educ:* Glenalmond; Exeter Coll., Oxford. BA Oxon 1934. Admitted Solicitor, 1938; called to Bar, Gray's Inn, 1945. Legal Member, Mental Health Review Tribunal, Birmingham Region, 1962; Deputy Chairman, Agricultural Land Tribunal, East Midland Area, 1963; Dep. Chm. QS, Parts of Lindsey, 1968-71; Recorder of Coventry, 1968-71; Mem., Parole Bd, 1974-76. *Recreation:* sailing. *Address:* 2 Dr Johnson's Buildings, Temple, EC4. *T:* 01-353 5371. *Clubs:* Bar Yacht, Royal Yachting Association.

ROSS, James Alexander, MBE (mil.) 1944; MD, FRCSEd, FRCSGlas; Vice-President, International Federation of Surgical Colleges, 1975-81; *b* 25 June 1911; *s* of James McMath Ross and Bessie Hopper Flint; *m* 1940, Catherine Elizabeth, *d* of Clark Booth Curtis; one *s* three *d. Educ:* Merchiston Castle Sch.; Edinburgh Univ. MB ChB Ed 1934, MD Ed 1947; FRCSEd 1938, FRCSGlas 1965. Served War: RAMC, 1939-45: France, ME, Europe; then Lt-Col RAMC, RARO, 1953-55. Surgeon, Leith Hosp., 1946-61, and Royal Infirmary, Edinburgh, 1947-61; Surgeon, Eastern Gen. Hosp., 1961-76 and Edenhall Hosp., 1970-76. Hon. Sec., Royal Coll. of Surgeons of Edinburgh, 1960-68; Vice-Pres., 1971-73; Pres., RCSEd, 1973-76; Pres., Edinburgh Harveian Soc., 1977-78. Hon. Cons. Surgeon to Army in Scotland, 1970-76; Guthrie Medallist, RAMC, 1976; McCombe Lectr, 1977; Mason Brown Meml Lectr, 1978; Hutchinson Lectr, Edinburgh Univ., 1979; Mitchiner Meml Lectr, 1979. Hon. FRCSI, 1976; Hon. FRACS, 1977; Hon. Fellow: Pakistan Coll., P and S, 1976; Sri Lanka Coll. of Surgeons, 1976; Hong Kong Surgical Soc., 1976. *Publications:* Memoirs of an Army Surgeon, 1948; (jtly) Manual of Surgical Anatomy, 1964; (jtly) Behaviour of the Human Ureter, in Health and Disease, 1972; The Edinburgh School of

Surgery after Lister, 1978. *Recreations:* walking, swimming, watching cricket. *Address:* 5 Newbattle Terrace, Edinburgh EH10 4RU. *T:* 031-447 2292.

ROSS, Sir (James) Keith, 2nd Bt *cr* 1960; RD 1967; MS, FRCS; Consultant Cardiac Surgeon: Wessex Region, since 1972; King Edward VII Hospital, Midhurst, since 1979; *b* 9 May 1927; *s* of Sir James Paterson Ross, 1st Bt, KCVO, FRCS, and Marjorie Burton Townsend (*d* 1978); *S* father, 1980; *m* 1956, Jacqueline Annella Clarke; one *s* three *d. Educ:* St Paul's School; Middlesex Hospital. MB BS 1950; MS 1965; FRCS 1956. House Surgeon, Registrar, Sen. Registrar, Middlesex Hosp., 1950-67. Surgn Lieut, RNVR, 1952-54; Surg. Lt Comdr, RNR, retd 1972. Heller Fellowship, San Francisco, 1959; Registrar, Brompton Hosp., 1958, 1960. Consultant Thoracic Surgeon, Harefield Hosp., 1964-67; Consultant Surgeon, Nat. Heart Hosp., 1967-72. Hunterian Prof., RCS, 1961. *Publications:* on cardiac surgery in appropriate medical jls. *Recreations:* fly fishing, sailing, painting. *Heir:* s Andrew Charles Paterson Ross, *b* 18 June 1966. *Address:* Moonhills Gate, Beaulieu, Hants SO4 7YS. *T:* Beaulieu 612104. *Clubs:* MCC; Royal Southampton Yacht, Royal Lymington Yacht.

ROSS, Leonard Q.; *see* Rosten, L. C.

ROSS, Lewis Nathan, CMG 1974; FCA; Chartered Accountant (Fellow) in Public Practice, since 1932; company director, New Zealand; *b* 7 March 1911; *e s* of Robert and Raie Ross; *m* 1937, Ella Myrtle Burns, Melbourne, Australia; two *s* one *d. Educ:* Auckland Grammar Sch.; Univ. of Auckland. Commenced practice as CA, founding firm now known as Ross, Melville, Bridgman & Co, 1932; withdrew from partnership in 1965 to practise as consultant. Pres., Associated Chambers of Commerce of NZ, 1955-56; Chm., Govt Cttee: on PAYE taxation, 1964; to review all aspects of Central Govt Taxation in NZ, 1966-67. Pres., NZ Soc. of Accountants, 1972-73. Director: Bank of NZ (Chm.); UEB Industries Ltd; Bradbury Wilkinson (NZ) Ltd; NZ Forest Products Ltd (Chm.); Sanford Ltd; Rex Consolidated Ltd (Chm.); Mainline Corporation of NZ Ltd; NZ Sugar Co. Ltd (Chm.); Bank of Western Samoa (Chm.); John Webster Ltd. *Publications:* Taxation-Principles, Purpose and Incidence, 1964 (rev. edn 1973); Finance for Business, 1964; Accounting Problems that arise from Business Combinations, 1973; articles in Accountants' Jl and other business pubns. *Recreations:* bowls, contract bridge. *Address:* (private) 11 Rewiti Street, Orakei, Auckland, New Zealand. *T:* 547-449; (business) PO Box 881, Auckland, New Zealand. *T:* 798-665. *Club:* Northern (Auckland).

ROSS, Malcolm Keir; Headmaster of Crown Woods School, London, 1957-71; *b* 8 June 1910; *m* 1937, Isabel Munkley; two *d. Educ:* Grangefield Grammar Sch., Stockton-on-Tees; Keble Coll., Oxford. Schoolmaster: Gordonstoun, 1933-34; Haverfordwest Grammar Sch., 1934-36; Bromley Grammar Sch., 1936-40; war service with RAF, 1940-45; Warden of Village Coll., Sawston, Cambs, 1945-57. Mem., Cttee of Enquiry into conditions of service life for young servicemen, 1969. Governor, Rachel McMillan Coll. of Education. Book reviewer for The Times Educational Supplement. FRSA. *Recreations:* gardening, reading. *Address:* The Pheasantry, North Sydmonton, Newbury, Berks RG15 8JN.

ROSS, Rear-Adm. Maurice James, CB 1962; DSC 1940; retired; *b* 31 Oct. 1908; *s* of Basil James Ross and Avis Mary (*née* Wilkinson); *m* 1946, Helen Matheson McCall; one *d. Educ:* Charterhouse. Entered Royal Navy, 1927; specialised in gunnery, 1935; Comdr, 1943; Captain, 1951; Rear-Adm., 1960. *Address:* The School House, Chippenham, Ely, Cambs CB7 5PP.

ROSS, Mrs Nicholas; *see* Phillpotts, M. Adelaide Eden.

ROSS, Norman Stilliard; Assistant Under-Secretary of State, Fire Department, Home Office, 1976-79; *b* 10 April 1919; *s* of late James Ross and Mary Jane Elizabeth Ross; *m* 1946, Sarah Cahill; one *s* two *d. Educ:* Solihull Sch., Warwickshire; Birmingham Univ. (BA). Served in local govt, City of Birmingham, 1935-39. War service, Army, RAMC and RAOC, in France, Belgium, Kenya, Ceylon, Burma and India, 1939-46 (despatches, France and Belgium, 1940). Asst Principal, Min. of Fuel and Power, 1949; Home Office, 1950; Asst Private Sec. to Sec. of State, 1950-52; Principal, 1952; Asst Sec., 1963; Asst Under-Sec. of State, 1976. *Recreations:* walking, music, reading. *Address:* 27 Detillens Lane, Limpsfield, Oxted, Surrey RH8 0DH. *T:* Oxted 2579.

ROSS, Richard; *see* Ross, C. R.

ROSS, Robert, MA, FLS; Keeper of Botany, British Museum (Natural History), 1966-77; *b* 14 Aug. 1912; *e s* of Robert Ross, Pinner, Middx; *m* 1939, Margaret Helen Steadman; one *s* three *d. Educ:* St Paul's Sch.; St John's Coll., Cambridge. Asst Keeper, British Museum (Natural History), 1936; Principal Scientific Officer, 1950; Deputy Keeper, 1962. Royal Microscopical Society: Hon. Librarian, 1947-51; Hon. Editor, 1951-73; Vice-Pres., 1959-60. Administrator of Finances, Internat. Assoc. of Plant Taxonomy, 1964-69; Sec., Gen. Cttee for Plant Nomenclature, 1964-69, Chm., 1969-81. President: British Phycological Soc., 1969-71; Quekett Microscopical Club, 1974-76. *Publications:* various papers in scientific jls on botanical subjects. *Recreations:* morris dancing (Bagman, Morris Ring of England, 1946-50); walking; gardening. *Address:* The Garden House, Evesbatch, Bishop's Frome, Worcester. *T:* Bosbury 366.

ROSS, Comdr Ronald Douglas, RN; Clerk to the Worshipful Company of Vintners, since 1969; *b* 30 July 1920; *o s* of Captain James Ross, FRGS, Scottish Horse of Chengtu, Szechwan Province, China; *m* 1952, Elizabeth Mary, *er d* of Canon S. J. S. Groves; one *d. Educ:* Cargilfield; Sedbergh; RN Staff Coll. Joined Accountant Br. of RN and went to sea, 1937; war service in HM Ships Exeter, Devonshire and Tartar. Called to Bar, Middle Temple, 1950; called to the Bar, Supreme Court of Hong Kong, 1963; officiated frequently as Judge Advocate; Admiralty Prize Medal for Naval History, 1957; retired list, 1967. Mem., Wine Standards Bd, 1973. Chevalier du Sacavin d'Anjou, 1974; Citizen and Vintner, 1975. *Publications:* contribs to The Times, Scotsman, New York Times, Investors' Chronicle, Brassey's Naval Annual, etc. *Recreation:* scripophily. *Address:* Black Swan House, Kennet Wharf Lane, EC4. *T:* 01-236 1863.

ROSS, Stephen Sherlock, FRICS; MP (L) Isle of Wight, since Feb. 1974; *b* 6 July 1926; *s* of Reginald Sherlock Ross and Florence Beryl (*née* Weston); *m* 1949, Brenda Marie Hughes; two *s* two *d. Educ:* Bedford Sch. Served War of 1939-45, RN, 1944-48. Articled Nock & Joseland, Kidderminster, 1948-51; Assistant: Heywood & Sons, Stone, Staffs, 1951-53; Sir Francis Pittis & Son, Newport, IoW, 1953-57 (Partner, 1958-73). County Councillor, IoW CC, 1967-74 and 1981- (Chm. Policy and Resources Cttee, 1973-74 and 1981-; Chm., Library Cttee, 1970-74). Non Exec. Dir, Pilatus Britten/Norman, 1979-; Consultant, Lander Burfield Chartered Surveyors, London, 1981. *Recreations:* cricket; antique porcelain collector. *Address:* 47 Quay Street, Newport, Isle of Wight PO30 5BA. *T:* Newport 522215. *Club:* National Liberal.

ROSS, William; MP (UU) Londonderry, since Feb. 1974; *b* 4 Feb. 1936; *m* 1974, Christine; three *s* one *d. Recreations:* fishing, shooting. *Address:* Hillquarter, Turmeel, Dungiven, Northern Ireland. *T:* Dungiven 41428. *Club:* Northern Counties (Londonderry).

ROSS-MUNRO, Colin William Gordon, QC 1972; *b* 12 Feb. 1928; *s* of late William Ross-Munro and of Adela Chirgwin; *m* 1958, Janice Jill Pedrana; one step *d. Educ:* Lycée Français de Londres; Harrow Sch.; King's Coll., Cambridge. Served in Scots Guards and in Army Education Corps. Called to the Bar, Middle Temple, 1951. *Recreations:* tennis and travel. *Address:* (home) 1 Ralston Street, Chelsea, SW3; 2 Hare Court, Temple EC4Y 7BH.

ROSS TAYLOR, Walter; Assistant Public Trustee, 1971-73; *b* 5 Aug. 1912; *er s* of late Walter and Frances Ross Taylor; *m* 1939, Vera Julia, *y d* of Col Mackenzie Churchill, Cheltenham; two *s* one *d. Educ:* Repton Sch.; Trinity Coll., Oxford (BA). Called to Bar, 1934. Enlisted Princess Louise's Kensington Regt TA, 1938; served War of 1939-45 (despatches, 1945; Captain): commnd Suffolk Regt, 1940; transf. to RAC, 1941; served with 142 Regt RAC in N Africa, and subseq. on staff of Special Ops (Mediterranean). Entered Public Trustee Office, 1938: Chief Administrative Officer, 1966. *Recreations:* travelling, walking. *Address:* Little Court, 13 Courtmoor Avenue, Fleet, Hants.

ROSSE, 7th Earl of, *cr* 1806; **William Brendan Parsons;** Bt 1677; Baron Oxmantown 1792; *b* 21 Oct. 1936; *s* of 6th Earl of Rosse, KBE, and of Anne, *o d* of Lt-Col Leonard Messel, OBE; *S* father, 1979; *m* 1966, Alison Margaret, *er d* of Major J. D. Cooke-Hurle, Startforth Hall, Barnard Castle, Co. Durham; two *s* one *d. Educ:* Eton; Grenoble Univ.; Christ Church, Oxford. BA 1961, MA 1964. 2nd Lieut, Irish Guards, 1955-57. UN Official appointed successively: Admin. Officer, Ghana, 1963-65; Asst Resident Rep., Dahomey, 1965-68; Area Officer for Mid-West Africa, 1968-70; Asst Resident Rep., Iran, 1970-75; Dep. Resident Rep., Bangladesh, 1975-78, Algeria, 1978-80. *Heir:* s Lord Oxmantown, *qv. Address:* (home) Birr Castle, Co. Offaly, Ireland. *T:* Birr 23.
See also Earl of Snowdon.

ROSSER, Sir Melvyn (Wynne), Kt 1974; Partner in Deloitte, Haskins & Sells, Chartered Accountants; Director: Development Corporation for Wales; Welsh Regional Council, CBI; Chairman, Manpower Services Committee for Wales, since 1980; *b* 11 Nov. 1926; *s* of late David John and of Anita Rosser; *m* 1957, Margaret; one *s* two *d. Educ:* Glanmor Sch., Swansea; Bishop Gore Grammar Sch., Swansea. Chartered Accountant, qual. 1949; joined staff Deloitte & Co. (later Deloitte, Haskins & Sells), Swansea, 1950, Partner 1961; practised in Swansea, 1961-68, in Cardiff, 1968-. Director: Nat. Bus Co., 1969-72; BSC, 1972-80; Wales and Marches Telecom. Bd, 1970-80. Member: Welsh Econ. Council, 1965-68; Welsh Council, 1968-80 (Chm., 1971-80); Royal Commn on Standards of Conduct in Public Life, 1974-; Prime Minister's Adv. Cttee on Outside Business Appts, 1976-. Vice-Pres., UCW, Aberystwyth, 1977-. Mem. Gorsedd of Bards, Royal Nat. Eisteddfod of Wales. *Recreations:* music, gardening. *Address:* Corlan, 53 Birchgrove Road, Lonlas, Swansea SA7 9JR. *T:* Swansea 812286. *Clubs:* Reform; Cardiff and County (Cardiff).

ROSSETTI, Harold Ford, CB 1959; *b* 19 Feb. 1909; *s* of Gabriel Arthur Madox Rossetti and Dora Brandreth Lewis; *m* 1933, Joan, *er d* of Rev. G. H. Holley; two *s* one *d. Educ:* Bolton School; Gonville and Caius College, Cambridge. Administrative Civil Servant, 1932-69; Customs and Excise Dept, 1932-34; Min. of Labour, 1934-51; OEEC, Paris, 1951-55; Min. of Labour, 1955-63; Dept of Educn and Science, 1963-69; Director, London Office, ILO, 1970-75. *Publication:* The Darkling Plain (novel), 1936. *Address:* 30 Castle Street, Framlingham, Suffolk. *T:* Framlingham 723586.

ROSSI, Hugh Alexis Louis; MP (C) Haringey, Hornsey, since 1974 (Hornsey, 1966-74); Minister of State for Social Security and the Disabled (Department of Health and Social Security), since 1981; *b* 21 June 1927; *m* 1955, Philomena Elizabeth Jennings; one *s* four *d. Educ:* Finchley Catholic Gram. Sch.; King's Coll., Univ. of London (LLB). Solicitor with Hons, 1950; consultant in London practice. Member: Hornsey Borough Coun., 1956-65; Haringey Council, 1965-68; Middlesex CC, 1961-65. Govt Whip, Oct. 1970-April 1972; Europe Whip, Oct. 1971-1973; a Lord Comr, HM Treasury, 1972-74; Parly Under-Sec. of State, DoE, 1974; opposition spokesman on housing and land, 1974-79; Minister of State, NI Office, 1979-81. Dep. Leader, UK Delegn to Council of Europe and WEU, 1972-73 (Mem., 1970-73). Knight of Holy Sepulchre, 1966. *Publications:* Guide to the Rent Act, 1974; Guide to Community Land Act, 1975; Guide to Rent (Agriculture) Act, 1976. *Address:* House of Commons, SW1.

ROSSITER, Rt. Rev. (Anthony) Francis, OSB; Abbot of Ealing, since 1967; *b* 26 April 1931; *s* of Leslie and Winifred Rossiter. *Educ:* St Benedict's, Ealing; Sant Anselmo, Rome (LCL). Priest, 1955; Second Master, St Benedict's School, 1960-67; Vicar for Religious, Archdiocese of Westminster, 1969-; Pres., Conf. of Major Religious Superiors of England and Wales, 1970-74; Second Assistant to Abbot President of the English Benedictine Congregation, 1976-. *Address:* Ealing Abbey, W5 2DY. *T:* 01-998 2158.

ROSSITER, Hon. Sir John Frederick, KBE 1978; Agent-General for Victoria, in London, 1976-79; *b* 17 Dec. 1913; *s* of James and Sarah Rossiter; 1st, 1939, Joan Durrant Stewart (*d* 1979); one *s* two *d* ; 2nd, 1981, Heather Steer. *Educ:* Melbourne Univ. (BA 1937). Senior Lecturer in English, Royal Melbourne Inst. of Technology, 1946-55; MLA (Lib.), Brighton, Vic., 1955; Minister of Labour and Industry; Minister of Health; Chief Secretary, 1964-76. *Recreation:* golf. *Address:* 14 Pretoria Avenue, Balmoral, Sydney, NSW 2088, Australia. *Clubs:* Wig and Pen, United Oxford & Cambridge University, Les Ambassadeurs; Naval and Military (Melbourne), Melbourne CC; Elenora Golf, Sydney CC; Hon. Company of Edinburgh Golfers (Muirfield).

ROSSITER, Leonard; actor; *b* 21 Oct. 1926; *s* of John Rossiter and Elizabeth Rossiter; *m* 1972, Gillian Raine; one *d. Educ:* Liverpool Collegiate Secondary Sch. Entered theatre, 1954; 1st London appearance, Free As Air, Savoy, 1958; Broadway début, Semi-Detached, 1963. London appearances include: Volpone, Garrick, 1967; (title rôle) The Resistible Rise of Arturo Ui, Saville, 1969 (Edinburgh Festival, 1968; London Critics' Best Actor Award and Variety Club's Best Actor Award, 1969); The Heretic, Duke of York's, 1970; The Caretaker, Mermaid, 1972; The Banana Box, Hampstead Theatre Club and Apollo, 1973; Frontiers of Farce, Old Vic, 1976; Tartuffe (title rôle), Greenwich, 1976; The Immortal Haydon, one-man show, Mermaid, 1977, Greenwich, 1978; Semi Detached, Greenwich, 1979; Make and Break, Haymarket, 1980. Films: This Sporting Life; Billy Liar; The Whisperers; King Rat; More Deadly Than the Male; Oliver; 2001 Space Odyssey; Barry Lyndon; Voyage of the Damned; Rising Damp; Hotel Paradiso; Deadfall; The Wrong Box; Luther; Otley; Britannia Hospital. Television appearances. *Publications:* The Devil's Bedside Book, 1980; The Lowest Form of Wit, 1981. *Recreations:* squash, wine. *Club:* Hurlingham.

ROSSLYN, 7th Earl of, *cr* 1801; **Peter St Clair-Erskine;** Bt 1666; Baron Loughborough, 1795; *b* 31 March 1958; *s* of 6th Earl of Rosslyn, and of Athenais de Mortemart, *o d* of late Duc de Vivonne; *S* father, 1977. *Educ:* Ludgrove Sch.; Eton Coll; Bristol Univ. Metropolitan Police, 1980-. Trustee, Dunimarle Museum. *Recreations:* church music, piano. *Heir:* uncle Hon. David Simon St Clair-Erskine [*b* 18 Nov. 1917; *m* 1948, Antonia Mary (marr. diss. 1958; she *d* 1965), *o d* of late Adm. of the Fleet Sir John Donald Kelly, GCB, GCVO; one *s*]. *Address:* 30 Trigon Road, SW8. *Clubs:* White's; Clifton (Bristol).

ROSSMORE, 7th Baron, *cr* 1796; **William Warner Westenra;** *b* 14 Feb. 1931; *o s* of 6th Baron and Dolores Cecil (*d* 1981), *d* of late Lieut-Col James Alban Wilson, DSO, West Burton, Yorks; *S* father, 1958. *Educ:* Eton; Trinity Coll., Cambridge (BA). 2nd Lieut, Somerset LI. Co-founder, Coolemine Therapeutic Community, Dublin. *Recreations:* drawing, painting. *Heir:* none. *Address:* Rossmore Park, Co. Monaghan, Eire. *T:* Monaghan 81947.

ROST, Peter Lewis; MP (C) Derbyshire South-East, since 1970; *b* 19 Sept. 1930; *s* of Frederick Rosenstiel and Elisabeth Merz; *m* 1961, Hilary Mayo; two *s* two *d. Educ:* various primary schs; Aylesbury Grammar Sch. National Service, RAF, 1948-50; Birmingham Univ. (BA Hons Geog.), 1950-53. Investment Analyst and Financial Journalist with Investors Chronicle, 1953-58; firstly Investment Advisor, 1958, and then, 1962, Mem. London Stock Exchange, resigned 1977. Secretary: Cons. Parly Trade and Industry Cttee, 1972-73; Cons. Parly Energy Cttee, 1974-77; Select Cttee on Energy, 1979. Treasurer, Anglo-German Parly Gp, 1974-. FRGS (Mem. Council, 1980-). Grand Cross, Order of Merit, Germany, 1979. *Recreations:* tennis, ski-ing, gardening, antique map collecting. *Address:* Norcott Court, Berkhamsted, Herts. *T:* Berkhamsted 6123.

ROSTAL, Professor Max, CBE 1977; Professor at the Guildhall School of Music, London, 1944-58; Professor of the Master-Class, State Academy of Music, Cologne, since 1957; Professor of the Master-Class, Conservatoire, Berne, Switzerland, since 1958; *b* 7 Aug. 1905; *m* ; two *d* ; *m* 1980, Maria Busato. *Educ:* State Acad., Vienna (Prof. Rosé); State Academy, Berlin (Prof.

Flesch). Concert artist since age of 6; gave concerts in all parts of the world; at age of 23 Assistant to Prof. Flesch; Professor at State Academy of Music, Berlin, 1928-33. Lived in London, 1934-58; now residing in Switzerland. Has made various recordings for HMV, Decca, Argo, Concert Hall Soc., and Deutsche Grammophon Companies. FGSM 1945. Hon. RAM 1981. Silver Medal, State Acad. of Music, Cologne, 1965; Music Award, City of Berne, Switzerland, 1972. Bundesverdienstkreuz 1st Class, 1968, Grand Cross of Merit, 1981, German Federal Govt. *Publications:* Thoughts on the interpretation of Beethoven's Violin Sonatas, 1981; many compositions, transcriptions, arrangements, editions. *Recreations:* motoring, photography, reading. *Address:* Frikartweg 4, CH-3006 Berne, Switzerland. *T:* (0)31-431101; CH-3084, Gunten, Lake of Thun, Switzerland. *T:* (0)33-511867.

ROSTEN, Leo C., (pseudonym: **Leonard Q. Ross);** author and social scientist; *b* 11 April 1908; *s* of Samuel C. and Ida F. Rosten; *m* 1st, 1935, Priscilla Ann Mead (decd); one *s* two *d* ; 2nd, 1960, Gertrude Zimmerman. *Educ:* University of Chicago (PhD); London School of Economics (Hon. Fellow, 1975). Research Assistant, Political Science Dept, Univ. of Chicago, 1933-35; Fellow, Social Science Research Council, 1934-36; Grants from Rockefeller Foundation and Carnegie Corporation, 1938-40. Dir, Motion Picture Research Project, 1939-41. Spec. Consultant, Nat. Defense Advisory Commn, Washington, 1939; Chief, Motion Picture Div., Office of Facts and Figures, Washington, 1941-42; Dep. Dir, Office of War Information, Washington, 1942-45; Special Consultant, Sec. of War, Washington, 1945; special mission to France, Germany, England, 1945. Faculty Associate, Columbia Univ., 1953-; Lectr in Political Science, Yale Univ., 1955, New School for Social Research, NY, 1959. Ford Vis. Prof. in pol. Sci., Univ. of California (Berkeley), USA, 1960-61. Wrote film screenplays: Sleep, My Love; The Velvet Touch; Walk East on Beacon; The Dark Corner, etc. Member: Amer. Acad. of Political and Social Science; Amer. Assoc. for Advancement of Science; Nat. Acad. of Lit. and the Arts; Authors League of America; Authors Guild of America; Educnl Policies Cttee of Nat. Educnl Assoc. Phi Beta Kappa, 1929; Freedom Foundation's Award, 1955; George Polk Meml Award, 1955; Distinguished Alumnus Award, Univ. of Chicago, 1970. Hon. DHL: Univ. of Rochester, 1973; Hebrew Union Theol Coll., 1980. *Publications:* The Education of H*y*m*a*n K*a*p*l*a*n, 1937; The Washington Correspondents, 1937; The Strangest Places, 1939; Hollywood: The Movie Colony, The Movie Makers, 1941; The Dark Corner, 1945; (ed) Guide To The Religions of America, 1957; The Return of H*y*m*a*n K*a*p*l*a*n, 1959; Captain Newman, MD, 1961; The Story Behind the Painting, 1961; The Many Worlds of Leo Rosten; The Leo Rosten Bedside Book, 1965; A Most Private Intrigue, 1967; The Joys of Yiddish, 1968; A Trumpet for Reason, 1970; People I have Loved, Known or Admired, 1970; Rome Wasn't Burned in a Day, 1971; Leo Rosten's Treasury of Jewish Quotations, 1973; Dear "Herm", 1974; (ed) The Look Book, 1975; The 3.10 to Anywhere, 1976; O Kaplan! My Kaplan!, 1976; The Power of Positive Nonsense, 1977; Passions and Prejudices, 1978; (ed) Infinite Riches: Gems from a Lifetime of Reading, 1979; Silky!, 1979; King Silky!, 1980; contrib. learned journals. *Recreations:* photography; travel. *Address:* c/o Stanley Simon Associates, 70 Pine Street, NYC, USA. *Clubs:* Savile, Reform, Garrick (London); Cosmos (Washington), Chaos (New York).

ROSTOW, Prof. Eugene Victor; Sterling Professor of Law, Yale University, since 1964; Director, Arms Control and Disarmament Agency, since 1981; *b* 25 Aug. 1913; *s* of Victor A. and Lillian H. Rostow; *m* 1933, Edna B. Greenberg; two *s* one *d. Educ:* Yale Coll.; King's Coll., Cambridge (LLD 1962); Yale Law Sch. Practised law, New York, 1937-38; Yale Law Faculty, 1938-; Prof. of Law, 1944-; Dean of Law Sch., 1955-65. Asst to Asst Sec. of State Acheson, 1942-44; Asst to Exec. Sec., Econ. Commn for Europe, UN, Geneva, 1949-50; Under-Sec. of State for Political Affairs, 1966-69. Pres., Atlantic Treaty Assoc., 1973-76. Pitt Prof., Cambridge, 1959-60; Eastman Prof., Oxford, 1970-71. Dir, American Jewish Cttee, 1972-74; Chm. Exec. Cttee, Cttee on the Present Danger (Washington), 1976-81. Hon. LLD Boston, 1976. Chevalier, Legion of Honour (France), 1960; Grand Cross, Order of the Crown (Belgium), 1969. *Publications:* A National Policy for the Oil Industry, 1948; Planning for Freedom, 1959; The Sovereign Prerogative, 1962; Law, Power and the Pursuit of Peace, 1968; (ed) Is Law Dead?, 1971; Peace in the Balance, 1972; The Ideal in Law, 1978; contribs to legal and economic jls. *Address:* 208 St Ronan Street, New Haven, Conn 06511, USA. *T:* 203-776-3906; Peru, Vermont 05152, USA. *T:* 802-824-6627; Arms Control and Disarmament Agency, Washington, DC 20451, USA. *Clubs:* Century (New York); Elizabethan, Lawn (New Haven).

See also W. W. Rostow.

ROSTOW, Walt Whitman; Professor of Economics and of History, University of Texas at Austin, Texas, since 1969; *b* 7 Oct. 1916; 2nd *s* of Victor and Lillian Rostow; *m* 1947, Elspeth, *o d* of Milton J. and Harriet Vaughan Davies; one *s* one *d. Educ:* Yale (BA 1936; PhD 1940); Oxford (Rhodes Scholar). Social Science Research Council Fellow, 1939-40; Instructor, Columbia Univ., 1940-41; Office Strategic Services, 1941-45 (Army of the United States, 1943-45, Major; Legion of Merit; Hon. OBE); Assistant Chief Division German-Austrian Economic Affairs, Department of State, 1945-46; Harmsworth Professor American History, Oxford, 1946-47; Special Assistant to Executive Secretary, Economic Commission for Europe, 1947-49; Pitt Professor of American History, Cambridge, 1949-50; Professor of Economic History, Massachusetts Institute of Technology, 1950-61. Deputy Special Assistant to the President (USA) for National Security Affairs, Jan. 1961-Dec. 1961; Counselor and Chairman, Policy Planning Council, Department of

State, 1961-66; US Mem., Inter-Amer. Cttee on Alliance for Progress, 1964-66; Special Assistant to the President, The White House, 1966-69. Member: Royal Economic Society, England; American Academy of Arts and Sciences, 1957. Hon. LLD: Carnegie Inst. of Tech., Pittsburgh, 1962; Univ. Miami, 1965; Univ. Notre Dame, 1966; Middlebury Coll., 1967; Jacksonville Univ., 1974. Presidential Medal of Freedom, with distinction, 1969. *Publications:* The American Diplomatic Revolution, 1947; Essays on the British Economy of the Nineteenth Century, 1948; The Process of Economic Growth, 1952; (with A. D. Gayer and A. J. Schwartz) The Growth and Fluctuation of the British Economy, 1790-1850, 1953, new edn 1975; (with A. Levin and others) The Dynamics of Soviet Society, 1953; (with others) The Prospects for Communist China, 1954; (with R. W. Hatch) An American Policy in Asia, 1955; (with M. F. Millikan) A Proposal: Key to An Effective Foreign Policy, 1957; The Stages of Economic Growth, 1960, 2nd edn 1971; The United States in the World Arena, 1960; The Economics of Take-off into Sustained Growth (ed), 1963; View from the Seventh Floor, 1964; A Design for Asian Development, 1965; Politics and the Stages of Growth, 1971; The Diffusion of Power, 1972; How It All Began: origins of the modern economy, 1975; The World Economy: history and prospect, 1978; Getting from Here to There, 1978; Why the Poor Get Richer and the Rich Slow Down, 1980; Pre-Invasion Bombing Strategy: General Eisenhower's Decision of March 25, 1944, 1981; The Division of Europe after World War II: 1946, 1981; Europe after Stalin: Eisenhower's Three Decisions of March 11, 1953, 1982; various articles contributed to: The Economist, Economic Journal, Economic History Review, Journal of Econ. History, American Econ. Review, etc. *Address:* 1 Wild Wind Point, Austin, Texas 78746, USA. *Clubs:* Elizabethan (New Haven, Conn, USA); Cosmos (Washington, DC).

See also E. V. Rostow.

ROSTRON, Sir Frank, Kt 1967; MBE 1954; FIEE; Director, Ferranti Ltd, Hollinwood, Lancs, 1958-68; *b* 11 Sept. 1900; *s* of late Samuel Ernest and Martha Rostron, Oldham; *m* 1929, Helen Jodrell Owen; one *s* one *d. Educ:* Oldham High Sch.; Manchester Coll. of Tech. Ferranti Ltd, 1917-68. Served War of 1939-45: Electrical Engineer Officer, RAF; released with rank of Squadron Leader. President, Manchester Chamber of Commerce, 1956 and 1957. Director: National and Vulcan Boiler and General Insurance Co. Ltd, 1961-70; Aron Meters Ltd, 1961-68; McKechnie Brothers Ltd, 1966-71. Chairman: Cotton Board, 1963-67 (Independent Member, 1959); Cotton and Allied Textiles Industry Training Board, 1966-67; Textile Council, 1967-68. *Address:* 5 Brocklehurst Drive, Prestbury, Macclesfield, Cheshire SK10 4JD. *T:* Prestbury 829577.

ROSTROPOVICH, Mstislav; 'cellist; Music Director and Conductor, National Symphony Orchestra, Washington, since 1977; *b* 1927; *m* Galina Vishnevskaya, *qv*; two *d. Educ:* State Conservatoire, Moscow. Has played in many concerts in Russia and abroad from 1942; first performance of Shostakovich's 'cello concerto (dedicated to him), Edinburgh Festival, 1960. Series of concerts with London Symphony Orchestra under Gennadi Rozhdestvensky, Festival Hall, 1965 (Gold Medal); first perf. Britten's third cello suite, Aldeburgh, 1974. An Artistic Dir, Aldeburgh Festival, 1977-. Mem. Union of Soviet Composers, 1950-78. Lenin Prize, 1964. Holds 21 honorary degrees including Hon. MusD: St Andrews, 1968; Cambridge, 1975; Harvard, 1976; Yale, 1976; Oxon, 1980. Officier de la Légion d'Honneur (France), 1981. *Address:* c/o National Symphony Orchestra, J. F. Kennedy Center for the Performing Arts, Washington, DC 20566, USA.

ROTBLAT, Prof. Joseph, CBE 1965; MA, DSc (Warsaw); PhD (Liverpool); DSc (London); FInstP; Professor of Physics in the University of London, at St Bartholomew's Hospital Medical College, 1950-76, now Emeritus; Physicist to St Bartholomew's Hospital, 1950-76; *b* 4 Nov. 1908; *e s* of late Z. Rotblat, Warsaw. *Educ:* University of Warsaw, Poland. Research Fellow of Radiological Laboratory of Scientific Society of Warsaw, 1933-39; Asst Director of Atomic Physics Institute of Free Univ. of Poland, 1937-39; Oliver Lodge Fellow of Univ. of Liverpool, 1939-40; Lecturer and afterwards Senior Lecturer in Dept of Physics, Liverpool Univ., 1940-49; Director of Research in nuclear physics at Liverpool Univ., 1945-49; work on atomic energy at Liverpool Univ. and Los Alamos, New Mexico. Treasurer, St Bartholomew's Hosp. Med. Coll., 1974-76; Vice-Dean, Faculty of Sci., London Univ., 1974-76. Mem., Adv. Cttee on Med. Res., WHO, 1972-75. Ed., Physics in Medicine and Biol., 1960-72. Sec.-Gen., Pugwash Confs on Science and World Affairs, 1957-73. Pres., Hosp. Physicists' Assoc, 1969-70; Pres., British Inst. of Radiology, 1971-72. Mem. Governing Body of Stockholm Internat. Peace Res. Inst., 1966-71. Pres., Internat. Youth Sci. Fortnight, 1972-74. Vis. Prof. of Internat. Relations, Univ. of Edinburgh, 1975-76. Member, Polish Academy of Sciences, 1966; Hon. For. Mem., Amer. Acad. of Arts and Sciences, 1972. Hon. DSc Bradford, 1973. *Publications:* Progress in Nuclear Physics, 1950; (with Chadwick) Radio-activity and Radioactive Substances, 1953; Atomic Energy, a Survey, 1954; Atoms and the Universe, 1956; Science and World Affairs, 1962; Aspects of Medical Physics, 1966; Pugwash, the First Ten Years, 1967; Scientists in the Quest for Peace, 1972; Nuclear Reactors: to breed or not to breed, 1977; Nuclear Energy and Nuclear Weapon Proliferation, 1979; Nuclear Radiation in Warfare, 1981; Scientists: The Arms Race and Disarmament, 1982; papers on nuclear physics and radiation biology in Proceedings of Royal Society, Radiation Research, Nature, etc. *Recreations:* recorded music, travel. *Address:* 8 Asmara Road, West Hampstead, NW2 3ST. *T:* 01-435 1471. *Club:* Athenæum.

ROTH, Andrew; Political Correspondent, Manchester Evening News, since 1972; Director, Parliamentary Profiles, since 1955; *b* NY, 23 April 1919; *s* of Emil and Bertha Roth; *m* 1949, Mathilda Anna Friederich; one *s* one *d. Educ:* City Coll. of NY (BSS); Columbia Univ. (MA); Harvard Univ. Reader, City Coll., 1939; Res. Associate, Inst. of Pacific Relations, 1940; US Naval Intell., 1941-45 (Lieut, SG); Editorial Writer, The Nation, 1945-46; Foreign Corresp., Toronto Star Weekly, 1946-50; London Corresp., France Observateur, Sekai, Singapore Standard, 1950-60. *Publications:* Japan Strikes South, 1941; French Interests and Policies in the Far East, 1942; Dilemma in Japan, 1945 (UK 1946); The Business Background of MPs, 1959, 7th edn 1980; The MPs' Chart, 1967, 5th edn 1979; Enoch Powell: Tory Tribune, 1970; Can Parliament Decide . . ., 1971; Heath and the Heathmen, 1972; Lord on the Board, 1972; The Prime Ministers, Vol. II (Heath chapter), 1975; Sir Harold Wilson: Yorkshire Walter Mitty, 1977. *Recreations:* tennis, sketching, jazz-dancing. *Address:* 34 Somali Road, NW2 3RL. *T:* 01-435 6673; 3 Palace Chambers, Bridge Street, SW1A 2JT. *T:* 01-930 2677. *Club:* Brondesbury Cricket and Tennis.

ROTH, Prof. Klaus Friedrich, FRS 1960; Professor of Pure Mathematics (Theory of Numbers) at Imperial College of Science and Technology, since 1966; *b* 29 Oct. 1925; *s* of late Dr Franz Roth and Mathilde Roth (*née* Liebrecht); *m* 1955, Melek Khairy, BSc, PhD. *Educ:* St Paul's Sch.; Peterhouse, Cambridge; Univ. College, London (Fellow, 1979). BA (Cambridge, 1945); MSc, PhD (London, 1948, 1950). Asst Master, Gordonstoun School, 1945-46. Member of Dept of Mathematics, University College, London, 1948-66; title of Professor in the University of London conferred 1961. Visiting Lecturer, 1956-57, Vis. Prof., 1965-66, at Mass Inst. of Techn., USA. Fields Medal awarded at International Congress of Mathematicians, 1958. Foreign Hon. Mem., Amer. Acad. of Arts and Sciences, 1966. *Publications:* papers in various mathematical jls. *Recreations:* chess, cinema. *Address:* Department of Mathematics, Imperial College, Queen's Gate, SW7 5HH; 24 Burnsall Street, SW3 3ST. *T:* 01-352 1363.

ROTH, Prof. Sir Martin, Kt 1972; MD (London); FRCP; FRCPsych; DPM; Professor of Psychiatry, University of Cambridge, since March 1977; Fellow, Trinity College, Cambridge, since 1977; *b* 6 Nov. 1917; *s* of late Samuel Simon and Regina Roth; *m* 1945, Constance Heller; three *d. Educ:* University of London, St Mary's Hospital. FRCP 1958. MA Cantab. Formerly: Senior Registrar, Maida Vale, and Maudsley Hosps; Physician, Crichton Royal Hosp., Dumfries; Director of Clinical Research, Graylingwell Hosp.; Prof. of Psychological Medicine, Univ. of Newcastle upon Tyne, 1956-77. Visiting Assistant Professor, in the Department of Psychiatry, McGill University, Montreal, 1954; Consultant, WHO Expert Cttee on Mental Health Problems of Ageing and the Aged, 1958; Member: Med. Cons. Cttee, Nuffield Provincial Hosp. Trust, 1962; Central Health Services Council, Standing Med. Adv. Cttee, Standing Mental Health Adv. Cttee, DHSS, 1966-75; Scientific Adv. Cttee, CIBA Foundn, 1970-; Syndic of Cambridge Univ. Press, 1980-. Mayne Vis. Prof., Univ. of Queensland, 1968; Albert Sterne Vis. Prof., Univ. of Indiana, 1976; first Andrew Woods Vis. Prof., Univ. of Iowa, 1976. Adolf Meyer Lectr, Amer. Psychiatric Assoc., 1971. Pres., Section of Psychiatry, RSM, 1968-69; Member: MRC, 1964-68; Clinical Research Board, MRC, 1964-70; Hon. Dir, MRC Group for study of relationship between functional and organic mental disorders, 1962-67. Co-Editor, British Jl of Psychiatry, 1967. FRCPsych (Foundn Fellow; Pres., 1971-75; Hon. Fellow, 1975); Distinguished Fellow, Amer. Psychiatric Assoc., 1972; Hon. FRCPSGlas. Corresp. Mem., Deutsche Gesellschaft für Psychiatrie und Nervenheilkunde; Hon. Member: Société Royale de Médecine Mentale de Belgique; Canadian Psychiatric Assoc., 1972. Hon. Fellow: Amer. Coll. Neuropsychopharmacology; Australian and New Zealand College of Psychiatry. Burlingame Prize, Royal Medico Psychol Assoc., 1951; First Prize, Anna Monika Foundn, 1977; Paul Hoch Prize, Amer. Psychopathological Assoc., 1979; Gold Medal, Soc. of Biological Psychiatry, 1980. Hon. ScD Trinity College, Dublin, 1977. *Publications:* (with Mayer-Gross and Slater) Clinical Psychiatry, 1954, (with Slater) 3rd edn 1969; Studies in the Classification of Affective Disorders, 1977; papers on psychiatric aspects of ageing, depressive illness, schizophrenia, in various psychiatric and medical journals. *Recreations:* music, literature, conversation, travel. *Address:* Department of Psychiatry, New Addenbrooke's Hospital, University of Cambridge, Hills Road, Cambridge CB2 2QQ. *Club:* Athenæum.

ROTHA, Paul, FRSA; Film Producer and Director; Author; Journalist; Managing Director, Paul Rotha Productions Ltd, since 1941; *b* London, 3 June 1907. *Educ:* Highgate School; Slade School of Art, London. Painter and designer; Art Critic to The Connoisseur, 1927-28; specialised in the production of documentary films, starting with Empire Marketing Board; has made documentary films for Unesco, The Times, Shell-Mex, Imperial Airways, Manchester Corporation, Scottish Office, National Council of Social Service, Gas Industry, Royal National Life-Boat Institution, Central Electricity Board, National Book Council, Vickers-Armstrong, Orient Line, etc, Gold Medals for Films at Venice Film Festival (1934), Brussels Film Festival (1935) and Leipsig Film Festival (1962); British Film Academy Awards, 1947 and 1952. Visited US under auspices of Rockefeller Foundation, 1937-38, to lecture on documentary films, 1953-54; Simon Senior Research Fellow, Univ. of Manchester, 1967-68; Head of Documentary at BBC Television; Arts Council Grant, 1970. Tribute to Rotha Films and Books, Nat. Film Theatre, 1979. Producer and/or Director: The Silent Raid (feature), Life of Adolf Hitler, World Without End (co-dir), Cradle of Genius, Cat and Mouse (feature), No Resting Place (feature), The World is Rich, The Challenge of Television

(BBC), A City Speaks, Total War in Britain, Land of Promise, Children of the City, World of Plenty, Contact, To-Day We Live, Cover to Cover, The Future's in the Air, The Face of Britain, New Worlds for Old, The Fourth Estate, etc. *Publications:* The Film Till Now, 1930, new edns 1949, 1960, 1967; Celluloid; The Film To-Day, 1931; Documentary Film, 1936, new edns 1939, 1952, 1970; (with Roger Manvell) Movie Parade, 1936, new edn, 1950; (with E. Anstey and others) Shots in the Dark, 1951; (ed) Portrait of a Flying Yorkshireman, 1952; Television in the Making, 1956; Rotha on the Film, 1958; (with Basil Wright and A. Calder-Marshall) The Innocent Eye: a biography of Robert Flaherty, 1963; Documentary Diary, 1973; Richard Winnington: Film Criticism and Caricatures, 1975. *Address:* c/o John Farquharson Ltd, Bell House, Bell Yard, WC2A 2JU.

ROTHENSTEIN, Sir John (Knewstub Maurice), Kt 1952; CBE 1948; KCStG 1977; PhD (London 1931); Hon. LLD (New Brunswick 1961; St Andrews 1964); writer; Director of the Tate Gallery, 1938-64; Hon. Fellow: Worcester College, Oxford, 1963; University College London, 1976; Member: Architectural and Art Advisory Committee, Westminster Cathedral, since 1979 (of Advisory Committee on Decoration, 1953-79); Council, Friends of the Tate Gallery, since 1958; President: Friends of the Bradford City Art Gallery and Museums, since 1973; Friends of the Stanley Spencer Gallery, Cookham, since 1981; *b* London, 11 July 1901; *e s* of Sir William Rothenstein and Alice Mary, *e c* of Walter John Knewstub, of Chelsea; *m* 1929, Elizabeth Kennard Whittington, 2nd *d* of Charles Judson Smith, of Lexington, Kentucky; one *d*. *Educ:* Bedales School; Worcester College, Oxford (MA); University College, London (PhD). Assistant Professor: of Art History in the University of Kentucky, 1927-28; Department of Fine Arts, University of Pittsburgh, 1928-29; Director: City Art Gallery, Leeds, 1932-34; City Art Galleries and Ruskin Museum, Sheffield, 1933-38; Member: Executive Committee, Contemporary Art Society, 1938-65; British Council, 1938-64; Art Panel, Arts Council of Great Britain, 1943-56. Rector, University of St Andrews, 1964-67. Visiting Professor: Dept of Fine Arts, Fordham Univ., USA, 1967-68; of History of Art, Agnes Scott Coll., Ga, USA, 1969-70; Distinguished Prof., City Univ. of NY, at Brooklyn Coll., 1971, 1972; Regents' Lectr, Univ. of Calif at Irvine, 1973. Editor, The Masters, 1965-67; Hon. Editor, Museums Jl, 1959-61. Knight Commander, Mexican Order of the Aztec Eagle, 1953. *Publications:* The Portrait Drawings of William Rothenstein, 1889-1925, 1926; Eric Gill, 1927; The Artists of the 1890's, 1928; Morning Sorrow: a novel, 1930; British Artists and the War, 1931; Nineteenth Century Painting, 1932; An Introduction to English Painting, 1933; The Life and Death of Conder, 1938; Augustus John (Phaidon British Artists), 1944; Edward Burra (Penguin Modern Painters), 1945; Manet, 1945; Modern Foreign Pictures in the Tate Gallery, 1949; Turner, 1949; London's River, 1951 (with Father Vincent Turner, SJ); Modern English Painters, vol. I, Sickert to Smith, 1952, vol. II, Lewis to Moore, 1956, vol. III, Wood to Hockney, 1973; The Tate Gallery, 1958; Turner, 1960; British Art since 1900: an Anthology, 1962; Sickert, 1961; Paul Nash, 1961; Augustus John, 1962; Matthew Smith, 1962; Turner (with Martin Butlin), 1964; Francis Bacon (with Ronald Alley), 1964; Edward Burra, 1973; Victor Hammer: artist and craftsman, 1978; (ed) Sixteen Letters from Oscar Wilde, 1930; (ed) Stanley Spencer the Man: Correspondence and Reminiscences, 1979; John Nash, 1983; Fourteen Artists, 1983; *autobiography:* Summer's Lease (I), 1965; Brave Day, Hideous Night (II), 1966; Time's Thievish Progress (III), 1970; contribs to DNB. *Television:* Churchill the Painter, COI, 1968; Collection and Recollection, BBC, 1968. *Address:* Beauforest House, Newington, Dorchester-on-Thames, Oxon OX9 8AG; 8 Tryon Street, Chelsea, SW3 3LH. *Clubs:* Athenæum, Chelsea Arts (Hon. Mem.).
See also Baron Dynevor.

ROTHENSTEIN, Michael, ARA 1977; Painter and print-maker; *b* 1908; *yr s* of late Sir William Rothenstein; *m* 1936, Betty Desmond Fitz-Gerald (marr. diss., 1957); one *s* one *d*; *m* 1958, Diana, 2nd *d* of late Comdr H. C. Arnold-Forster, CMG. Retrospective exhibitions: Kunstnernes Hus, Oslo, 1969; Bradford Art Gallery, 1972; ICA, 1974. Works acquired by: Museum of Modern Art and Brooklyn Museum, New York; Tate Gallery; British Museum; Victoria and Albert Museum; Library of Congress, Washington; British Council; Arts Council; museums of: Sydney; Victoria; Dallas; Boston; Cincinnati; Lugano; etc. Exhibited: Cincinnati Biennial, 1954, 1960; Ljubljana Biennial of Graphic Art, 1957, 1961, 1963; Albertina, Vienna (Prints), 1963; Internat. Triennale, Grechen, 1961, 1964, 1967; 8th Internat. Exhibition, Lugano; 4th Internat. Print Exhibn, Tokyo, 1966; Internat. Print Biennale, Cracow, 1970-78; retrospective exhibn, Norway, 1980. Trust House Award, 1963; Gold Medal, first internat. Engraving Biennale, Buenos Aires; Prix d'Achat, Cracow Internat. Print Biennale, 1974; Grand Prix, Norwegian Internat. Print Biennale, 1976. *Publications:* Frontiers of Printmaking, 1966; Relief Printing, 1970; Suns and Moons, 1972; Seven Colours (with Edward Lucie Smith), 1975; Song of Songs (folio), 1979. *Address:* Columbia House, Stisted, Braintree, Essex. *T:* Braintree 25444.

ROTHERHAM, Air Vice-Marshal John Kevitt, CB 1962; CBE 1960; Director-General (Engineering), RAF, 1967-69; retired; *b* 28 Dec. 1910; *s* of Colonel Ewan Rotherham; *m* 1st, 1936, Joan Catherine Penrose (*d* 1940); one *d*; 2nd, 1941, Margot Susan Hayter. *Educ:* Uppingham; Exeter College, Oxford. Joined RAF with Univ. perm. commn, 1933; 17 (F) Sqdn, 1934; 605 (B) Sqdn, 1936; School of Aeronautical Engineering, Henlow, 1936; post-grad. course, Imperial Coll., 1938; 43 (M) Group, 1939; Kidbrooke, 1940; MAP 1941; 41 (M) Group, 1942; HQ Flying Training Comd, 1946; exchange posting with USAF, 1947; Air Ministry, 1948; Joint Services Staff Coll., 1951;

No 205 Group, Middle East, 1952; Air Ministry, 1954; seconded to Pakistan Air Force, 1957; Senior Technical Staff Officer, Transport Command, RAF, 1960-63; AOC No 24 (Training) Group, Technical Training Command, RAF, 1963-65; Senior Tech. Staff Officer, Bomber Command, 1965-67. AFRAeS 1949, FRAeS 1967. *Recreations:* sailing, ski-ing, golf. *Address:* South Meadow, Shore Road, Old Bosham, Chichester, Sussex PO18 8QL. *T:* Bosham 573346. *Clubs:* Royal Air Force; Island Sailing, Bosham Sailing.
See also R. J. S. McDowall.

ROTHERHAM, Leonard, CBE 1970; DSc; FRS 1963; FEng, FIEE, SFInstE, FIM, FInstP; Vice-Chancellor, Bath University, 1969-76; *b* 31 Aug. 1913; *m* 1937, Nora Mary Thompson; one *s* two *d*. *Educ:* Strutt School, Belper; University College, London. Physicist, Brown Firth Research Laboratories, 1935-46; Head of Metallurgy Dept, RAE Farnborough, 1946-50; Dir, R&D, UKAEA, Industrial Group, Risley, 1950-58. Mem. for Research, Central Electricity Generating Bd, 1958-69; Head of Research, Electricity Supply Industry and Electricity Council, 1965-69. Chm., Adv. Cttee for Scientific and Technical Information, 1970-74. Member: Defence Scientific Adv. Council, 1967-77 (Chm., 1974-77); Central Adv. Council for Science and Technology, 1968-70; Adv. Council for Energy Conservation, 1974-; Adv. Council for Applied R&D, 1976-81. Governor, Imperial Coll., 1977-. Hon. LLD Bristol, 1972; Hon. DSc Bath, 1976. Fellow UCL, 1959; Hon. Fellow, Inst. of Welding, 1965; Hon. Life Mem., American Society of Mechanical Engineers, 1963; President, Instn of Metallurgists, 1964; Inst. of Metals, 1965; Member of Council, Royal Society, 1965-66. Founder Fellow, Fellowship of Engineering, 1976 (Mem. Exec. Council, 1978-80). *Publications:* Creep of Metals, 1951; various scientific and technical papers; also lectures: Hatfield Memorial, 1961; Coal Science, 1961; Calvin Rice (of Amer. Soc. of Mech. Engrs), 1963; 2nd Metallurgical Engineering, Inst. of Metals, 1963. *Address:* Westhanger, Horningsham, Warminster, Wilts. *Club:* Athenæum.

ROTHERMERE, 3rd Viscount *cr* 1919, of Hemsted; **Vere Harold Esmond Harmsworth**; Bt 1910; Baron 1914; Chairman and Chief Executive, Associated Newspapers Group Ltd, since 1971; Chairman, Daily Mail and General Trust Ltd, since 1978; *b* 27 Aug. 1925; *s* of 2nd Viscount Rothermere and of Margaret Hunam, *d* of late William Redhead; *S* father, 1978; *m* 1957, Mrs Patricia Evelyn Beverley Brooks, *d* of John William Matthews, FIAS; one *s* two *d* (and one step *d*). *Educ:* Eton; Kent Sch., Conn, USA. With Anglo Canadian Paper Mills, Quebec, 1948-50; Associated Newspapers Ltd, 1951-; launched New Daily Mail, 1971. Trustee, Reuters; Dir, Consolidated Bathurst (Canada). Chm., Newsvendors' Benevolent Inst. Festival Appeal, 1963; Pres., Nat. Advertising Benevolent Soc., 1964; Festival Pres., 1966, Vice-Pres., 1967, Newspaper Press Fund; Chm., UK Section, Commonwealth Press Union, 1976; Pres., Printers Charitable Corp., 1974-76; Trustee, Vis-News; Pres., London Press Club, 1976-81; Patron, London Sch. of Journalism, 1980-. FRSA, FBIM. Commander: Order of Merit (Italy); Order of Lion (Finland). *Recreations:* painting, sailing, reading. *Heir: s* Hon. Harold Jonathan Esmond Vere Harmsworth, *b* 3 Dec. 1967. *Address:* New Carmelite House, Carmelite Street, EC4. *Clubs:* Boodle's, Beefsteak; Royal Yacht Squadron; Brook (New York City); Travellers' (Paris).
See also Lord Ogilvy.

ROTHERWICK, 2nd Baron *cr* 1939; **Herbert Robin Cayzer**; Bt 1924; *b* 5 Dec. 1912; *s* of 1st Baron Rotherwick; *S* father 1958; *m* 1952, Sarah-Jane (*d* 1978), *o d* of Sir Michael Nial Slade, 6th Bt; three *s* one *d*. *Educ:* Christ Church, Oxford (BA). Supplementary Reserve Royal Scots Greys, 1938; served War of 1939-45 with them in Middle East. Deputy Chairman British & Commonwealth Shipping Co. Ltd, and Director of other and associated companies. *Heir: s* Hon. (Herbert) Robin Cayzer, Lt Life Guards (T&AVR) [*b* 12 March 1954; *m* 1982, Sara, *o d* of R. J. McAlpine, Swettenham Hall, Cheshire]. *Address:* Cornbury Park, Charlbury, Oxfordshire. *T:* Charlbury 311; 10 Chelsea Square, SW3. *Club:* White's.

ROTHES, 21st Earl of, *cr* before 1457; **Ian Lionel Malcolm Leslie**; Lord Leslie 1445; Baron Ballenbreich 1457; *b* 10 May 1932; *o s* of 20th Earl of Rothes and of Beryl, *o d* of J. Lionel Dugdale; *S* father, 1975; *m* 1955, Marigold, *o d* of Sir David M. Evans Bevan, 1st Bt; two *s*. *Educ:* Eton. Sub-Lt RNVR, 1953. *Heir: s* Lord Leslie, *qv. Address:* Tanglewood, West Tytherley, Salisbury, Wilts.

ROTHMAN, Sydney; Chairman of Rothmans Tobacco (Holdings) Ltd, 1953-79 (Chairman and Managing Director, Rothmans Ltd, 1929-53); *b* 2 December 1897; *s* of Louis and Jane Rothman; *m* 1929, Jeannette Tropp; one *s* one *d*. *Educ:* Highgate School. Joined L. Rothman & Company, 1919, Partner, 1923, Rothmans Ltd. Ministry of Supply, 1941-45. *Recreation:* golf. *Address:* c/o National Westminster Bank, 227C City Road, EC4.

ROTHNIE, Sir Alan (Keir), KCVO 1980; CMG 1967; HM Diplomatic Service, retired; Director, Overseas Technical Service International Ltd, since 1980; *b* 2 May 1920; *s* of late John and Dora Rothnie, Aberdeen; *m* 1953, Anne Cadogan Harris, *d* of Euan Cadogan Harris; two *s* one *d*. *Educ:* Montrose Acad.; St Andrews University. Served RNVR, 1939-45. Entered Diplomatic Service, Nov. 1945; Foreign Office, 1945-46; 3rd Sec., HM Legation, Vienna, 1946-48; 2nd Sec., HM Embassy, Bangkok, 1949-50; FO 1951-53; 1st Sec. HM Embassy, Madrid, 1953-55; Asst Political Agent, Kuwait, 1956-58; FO, 1958-60; Middle East Centre for Arab Studies, Shemlan, 1960-62 (Charge d'Affaires, HM Embassy, Kuwait, 1961); Commercial Counsellor: HM Embassy, Baghdad, 1963-64; HM Embassy, Moscow, 1965-68; Consul-Gen.,

Chicago, 1969-72; Ambassador to Saudi Arabia, 1972-76, to Switzerland, 1976-80. Mem. Panel of Conciliators, Internat. Centre for Settlement of Investment Disputes, 1980-. Chm., Tenterden and District Branch, Kent Assoc. for the Disabled. Hon. LLD St Andrews, 1981. *Recreations:* shooting, ski-ing. *Address:* Little Job's Cross, Rolvenden Layne, Kent TN17 4PP. *Clubs:* White's, MCC.

ROTHSCHILD, family name of **Baron Rothschild.**

ROTHSCHILD, 3rd Baron, *cr* 1885; **Nathaniel Mayer Victor Rothschild;** Bt 1846; GBE 1975; GM 1944; PhD; ScD; FRS 1953; Chairman, Rothschilds Continuation, since 1976; Director, N. M. Rothschild & Sons (Chairman, 1975-76); Chairman, Biotechnology Investments Ltd, since 1981; Chairman, Royal Commission on Gambling, 1976-78; *b* 31 Oct. 1910; *e* of late Hon. (Nathaniel) Charles Rothschild, 2nd *s* of 1st Baron Rothschild; *S* uncle, 1937; *m* 1st, 1933, Barbara (divorced, 1946), *o d* of late St John Hutchinson, KC; one *s* two *d* ; 2nd, 1946, Teresa, MBE, MA, JP, *d* of late R. J. G. Mayor, CB; one *s* two *d* (and one *s* decd). *Educ:* Harrow, Trinity Coll., Cambridge. Prize-Fellow of Trinity Coll., Cambridge, 1935-39, Hon. Fellow, 1961. War of 1939-45: Military Intelligence (despatches, American Legion of Merit, American Bronze Star). Director, BOAC, 1946-58; Chm., Agricultural Res. Council, 1948-58; Assistant Dir of Research, Dept of Zoology, Cambridge, 1950-70; Vice-Chm., Shell Research Ltd, 1961-63, Chm., 1963-70; Chm., Shell Research NV, 1967-70; Director: Shell Internationale Research Mij, 1965-70; Shell Chemicals UK Ltd, 1963-70; Shell International Gas, 1969-70; Research Co-ordinator, Royal Dutch Shell Group, 1965-70; Dir Gen. and First Perm. Under-Sec., Central Policy Review Staff, Cabinet Office, 1971-74. Member: BBC General Advisory Council, 1952-56; Council for Scientific Policy, 1965-67; Central Adv. Council for Science and Technology, 1969. 4th Royal Soc. Technol. Lect., 1970; Trueman Wood Lect., RSA, 1972; Dimbleby Lecture, 1978. Hon. Fellow: Bellairs Research Inst. of McGill Univ., Barbados, 1960; Weizmann Inst. of Science, Rehovoth, 1962; Wolfson Coll., Cambridge, 1966; Inst. of Biol., 1971; Imperial Coll., 1975. Hon. DSc: Newcastle, 1964; Manchester, 1966; Technion, Haifa, 1968; City Univ., 1972; Bath, 1978; Hon. PhD: Tel Aviv, 1971; Hebrew Univ., Jerusalem, 1975; Bar-Ilan, Israel, 1980; Hon. LLD London, 1977; DUniv York, 1980. KStJ 1948. Melchett Medal, 1971; RSA Medal, 1972. *Publications:* The History of Tom Jones, a Changeling, 1951; The Rothschild Library, 1954, new edn, 1972; Fertilization, 1956; A Classification of Living Animals, 1961; The Rothschild Family Tree, 1973; Meditations of a Broomstick, 1977; You Have It, Madam, 1980; scientific papers. *Heir: s* Hon. (Nathaniel Charles) Jacob Rothschild, *qv*. *Club:* Pratt's.

ROTHSCHILD, Edmund Leopold de, TD; Director, N. M. Rothschild & Sons, since 1975 (Partner since 1946, Senior Partner, 1960-70, Chairman, 1970-75); Chairman, Straflo Ltd; *b* 2 Jan. 1916; *s* of late Lionel Nathan de Rothschild and Marie Louise Beer; *m* 1st, 1948, Elizabeth Edith Lentner (*d* 1980); two *s* two *d* ; 2nd, 1982, Anne, *widow* of J. Malcolm Harrison. *Educ:* Harrow Sch.; Trinity Coll., Cambridge. Major, RA (TA). Served France, North Africa and Italy, 1939-46 (wounded). Dep. Chairman: Brit. Newfoundland Corp. Ltd, 1963-69; Churchill Falls (Labrador) Corp. Ltd, 1966-69. Mem., Asia Cttee, BNEC, 1970-71, Chm., 1971. Trustee, Queen's Nursing Inst.; Mem. Council, Royal Nat. Pension Fund for Nurses; Pres., Assoc. of Jewish Ex-Servicemen and Women; Vice-Pres., Council of Christians and Jews. Governor, Tech. Univ. of Nova Scotia. Hon. LLD, Memorial Univ. of Newfoundland, 1961. Order of the Sacred Treasure, 1st Class (Japan), 1973. *Publication:* Window on the World, 1949. *Recreations:* gardening, fishing, shooting, cine-photography, hunting butterflies. *Address:* New Court, St Swithin's Lane, EC4P 4DU. *T:* 01-626 4356. *Clubs:* White's, Portland; Mount Royal (Montreal).
See also L. D. de Rothschild.

ROTHSCHILD, Evelyn de; Chairman, N. M. Rothschild & Sons Ltd; *b* 29 Aug. 1931; *s* of late Anthony Gustav de Rothschild; *m* 1973, Victoria Schott; two *s* one *d*. *Educ:* Harrow; Trinity Coll., Cambridge. Dep. Chm., Milton Keynes Development Corp., 1971-; Chairman: Economist Newspaper, 1972-; United Racecourses Ltd, 1977-. *Recreations:* art, racing.

ROTHSCHILD, Baron Guy (Edouard Alphonse Paul) de; Officier de la Légion d'Honneur, 1959; Director: Centro Asegurador SA, Madrid; Rothschild Continuation; Rothschild Inc., New York; *b* 21 May 1909; *s* of late Baron Edouard de Rothschild and late Baronne de Rothschild (*née* Germaine Halphen); *m* 1st, 1937, Baronne Alix Schey de Koromla (marriage dissolved, 1956; she *d* 1982); one *s* ; 2nd, 1957, Baronne Marie-Hélène de Zuylen de Nyevelt (who *m* 1st, Comte François de Nicolay); one *s* and one step *s*. *Educ:* Lycées Condorcet et Louis le Grand, Facultés de Droit et des Lettres (Licencié en Droit). Served War of 1939-45 (Croix de Guerre). Chevalier du Mérite Agricole, 1948. Associé de MM de Rothschild Frères, 1936-67; President: Compagnie du Chemin de Fer du Nord, 1949-68; Banque Rothschild, 1968-78; Société Imétal, 1975-79. Pres., Fonds Social Juif Unifié. Mem., Société d'Encouragement. *Recreation:* haras et écurie de courses, golf. *Address:* 131 East 66 Street, New York, NY, USA. *Clubs:* Nouveau Cercle, Automobile Club de France, Cercle Interallié.

ROTHSCHILD, Hon. Jacob; *see* Rothschild, Hon. N. C. J.

ROTHSCHILD, Leopold David de; Director, N. M. Rothschild & Sons Ltd, since 1970 (Partner, 1956-70); *b* 12 May 1927; *yr s* of Lionel de Rothschild

and Marie Louise Beer. *Educ:* Bishops Coll. Sch., Canada; Harrow; Trinity Coll., Cambridge. Director of Bank of England, 1970-. Chairman: English Chamber Orchestra and Music Soc. Ltd, 1963; Bach Choir, 1976; Anglo Venezuelan Soc., 1975-78. FRCM 1977. Order of Francisco de Miranda, 1st cl. (Venezuela), 1978. *Recreations:* music, sailing. *Address:* New Court, St Swithin's Lane, EC4. *T:* 01-626 4356. *Clubs:* Brooks's; Royal Yacht Squadron.
See also E. L. de Rothschild.

ROTHSCHILD, Hon. Miriam Louisa, (Hon. Mrs Miriam Lane), CBE 1982; *b* 5 Aug. 1908; *e d* of Hon. N. C. Rothschild and Rozsika de Wertheimstein; *m* 1943, Capt. George Lane, MC (marriage dissolved, 1957); one *s* three *d* (and one *s* one *d* decd). *Educ:* home. Member: Zoological and Entomological Research Coun.; Marine Biological Assoc.; Royal Entomological Soc.; Systematics Assoc.; Soc. for Promotion of Nature Reserves, etc.; Ed., Novitates Zoologica, 1938-41; Mem., Publications Cttee, Zoological Soc.; Foreign Office, 1940-42; Trustee, British Museum of Natural History, 1967-75. Mem., Amer. Acad. of Arts and Scis. Vis. Prof. in Biology, Royal Free Hosp. Hon. Fellow, St Hugh's Coll., Oxford. Hon. DSc, Oxford. Defence Medal (1940-45). *Publications:* Catalogue Rothschild Collection of Fleas (6 vols), British Museum; (with Theresa Clay) Fleas, Flukes and Cuckoos; 270 contribs to scientific jls. *Recreation:* watching butterflies. *Address:* Ashton, Peterborough. *Clubs:* Queen's, British Ornithological, Entomological.
See also Baron Rothschild.

ROTHSCHILD, Hon. (Nathaniel Charles) Jacob; Chairman, RIT and Northern plc, since 1982; *b* 29 April 1936; *e s* and *heir* of 3rd Baron Rothschild, *qv* ; *m* 1961, Serena Mary, *er d* of late Sir Philip Gordon Dunn, 2nd Bt; one *s* three *d*. *Educ:* Eton; Christ Church, Oxford. BA 1st cl. hons History. Chm., Rothschild Investment Trust Ltd, later RIT Ltd, 1971-82. *Address:* 20 St Swithin's Lane, EC4N 8AP. *T:* 01-283 5234.

ROTHSCHILD, Robert, KCMG (Hon.) 1963; Grand Officier de l'Ordre de Leopold (Belgium); Belgian Ambassador to the Court of St James's, 1973-76; *b* 16 Dec. 1911; *s* of Bernard Rothschild and Marianne von Rynveld; one *d*. *Educ:* Univ. of Brussels (DrRerPol). Entered Belgian Foreign Office: Brussels, 1937; Lisbon, 1942; Chungking, China, 1944; Shanghai, 1946, Washington, USA, 1950; Paris, NATO, 1952; Brussels, 1954; Ambassador to Yugoslavia, 1958; Head of Mission, Katanga, Congo, 1960; Brussels, 1960; Ambassador to: Switzerland, 1964; France, 1966. *Publication:* La Chute de Chiang Kai-Shek, 1973 (Paris). *Recreations:* gardening, travel. *Address:* 51 Avenue du Général de Gaulle, Bruxelles, Belgium; 43 Ranelagh Grove, SW1. *Clubs:* Travellers'; Cercle de l'Union (Paris); Cercle Gaulois (Brussels).

ROTHSTEIN, Saul; Solicitor to the Post Office, 1976-81; *b* 4 July 1920; *s* of late Simon Rothstein and late Zelda Rothstein; *m* 1949, Judith Noemi (*née* Katz); two *d*. *Educ:* Church Institute Sch., Bolton; Manchester Univ (LLB). Admitted solicitor, 1947. War service, RAF, 1941-46 (Flt-Lt). Entered Solicitor's Dept, General Post Office, 1949, Asst Solicitor, 1963; Director, Advisory Dept, Solicitor's Office, Post Office, 1972-76. *Recreations:* chamber music, walking, travel. *Address:* 9 Templars Crescent, Finchley, N3 3QR. *T:* 01-346 3701.

ROTHWELL, Margaret Irene; HM Diplomatic Service; Counsellor and Head of Training Department, Foreign and Commonwealth Office, since 1981; *b* 25 Aug. 1938; *d* of Harry Rothwell and Martha (*née* Goedecke). *Educ:* Southampton Grammar School for Girls; Lady Margaret Hall, Oxford (BA LitHum). Foreign Office, 1961; Third, later Second Secretary, UK Delegn to Council of Europe, Strasbourg, 1964; FO, 1966; Second Sec. (Private Sec. to Special Representative in Africa), Nairobi, 1967; Second, later First Sec., Washington, 1968; FCO, 1972; First Sec. and Head of Chancery, Helsinki, 1976; FCO, 1980. *Recreations:* gardening, cooking, tennis. *Address:* c/o Foreign and Commonwealth Office, SW1A 2AH.

ROTHWELL, Sheila Gwendoline; Director, Centre for Employment Policy Studies, Henley Administrative Staff College, since 1979; *b* 22 Aug. 1935; *d* of Reginald Herbert Paine and Joyce Margaret Paine; *m* 1958, Miles Rothwell (marr. diss. 1968); one *s* one *d*. *Educ:* Wyggeston Sch., Leicester; Westfield Coll., Univ. of London (BA Hons History, 1956); LSE (MScEcon Indust. Relations, 1972). Teaching and res., London, Trinidad and Barbados, 1958-68; Res. Officer/Lectr, Indust. Relations Dept, LSE, 1969-75; Asst Sec. (Negotiations), National Union of Bank Employees, 1975-76; Asst Chief Exec., Equal Opportunities Commn, 1976-78. Res. Sec. to House of Lords Select Cttee on Anti-Discrimination Bill, 1972-73. Mem., Williams Cttee on Obscenity and Film Censorship, 1978-79. Dir, British Consortium for Innovation. Mem., Henley Ct of Governors. *Publications:* Labour Turnover, 1980; contrib. Internat. Labour Rev., and Brit. Jl of Indust. Relations. *Recreations:* cinema, theatre, walking, dressmaking. *Address:* 753B Finchley Road, NW11 8DL.

ROUGIER, Maj.-Gen. Charles Jeremy; Assistant Chief of General Staff (Training), since 1982; *b* 23 Feb. 1933; *s* of late Lt-Col and of Mrs C. L. Rougier; *m* 1964, Judith Cawood Ellis; three *s* one *d*. *Educ:* Marlborough Coll.; Pembroke Coll., Cambridge (MA). Aden, 1960; Instructor, RMA Sandhurst, 1961-62; psc 1963; MA to MGO, 1964-66; comd 11 Engineer Sqn, Commonwealth Bde, 1966-68; jssc 1968; Company Comd, RMA Sandhurst, 1969-70; Directing Staff, Staff Coll., Camberley, 1970-72; CO 21 Engineer

Regt, BAOR, 1972-74; Staff of Chief of Defence Staff, 1974-77; Commandant, Royal Sch. of Military Engineering, 1977-79; RCDS 1980; COS, Headquarters Northern Ireland, 1981. *Recreations:* squash, hill walking, DIY, gardening. *Address:* c/o Lloyds Bank Ltd, 174 Fleet Road, Fleet, Hants. *Club:* Army and Navy.

ROUGIER, Richard George, QC 1972; a Recorder of the Crown Court, since 1973; *b* 12 Feb. 1932; *s* of late George Ronald Rougier, CBE, QC, and Georgette Heyer, novelist; *m* 1962, Susanna Allen Flint (*née* Whitworth); one *s. Educ:* Marlborough Coll.; Pembroke Coll., Cambridge (Exhibr, BA). Called to Bar, Inner Temple, 1956, Bencher 1979. *Recreations:* fishing, golf, bridge. *Address:* 35 St Georges Court, Gloucester Road, SW7. *T:* 01-584 9285. *Clubs:* Portland, Garrick; Rye Golf.

ROUND, Prof. Nicholas Grenville; Stevenson Professor of Hispanic Studies, in the University of Glasgow, since 1972; *b* 6 June 1938; *s* of Isaac Eric Round and Laura Christabel (*née* Poole); *m* 1966, Ann Le Vin; one *d. Educ:* Boynton CP Sch., Cornwall; Launceston Coll.; Pembroke Coll., Oxford. BA (1st cl. Hons, Spanish and French) 1959; MA 1963; DPhil 1967. Lecturer in Spanish, Queen's Univ. of Belfast, 1962-71, Reader, 1971-72; Warden, Alanbrooke Hall, QUB, 1970-72. *Publications:* Unamuno: Abel Sánchez: a critical guide, 1974; contribs to: Mod. Lang. Review, Bulletin Hispanic Studies, Proc. Royal Irish Academy, etc. *Recreations:* reading, music, all aspects of Cornwall. *Address:* Department of Hispanic Studies, The University, Glasgow G12 8QQ. *T:* 041-339 8855. *Club:* (Hon. Life Mem.) Students' Union (Belfast).

ROUS, family name of **Earl of Stradbroke.**

ROUS, Sir Stanley (Ford), Kt 1949; CBE 1943; JP; Secretary of the Football Association, 1934-61 (now Hon. Vice-President); President, Fédération Internationale de Football Associations, 1961-74 (now Hon. President); *b* 25 April 1895; *s* of George Samuel and Alice Rous; *m* 1924, Adrienne Gacon (*d* 1950). *Educ:* Sir John Leman School, Beccles; St Luke's College, Exeter. Served European War, 1914-18, in France and Palestine, 272nd Brigade RFA (East Anglian); Assistant Master, Watford Grammar School, 1921-34; Member Paddington Borough Council, 1943-47; Past Pres. Paddington and Marylebone Rotary Club: Hon. Vice-Pres., Central Council for Physical Recreation, 1974. (Chm., 1945-73). JP Paddington Div., 1950. Mem. King George's Jubilee Trust, King George VI Foundation. Vice-Pres., Arts Educn Trust; Governor, St Luke's Coll., Exeter. Liveryman Worshipful Co. of Loriners. Chevalier de l'Ordre Grand-Ducal de la Couronne de Chêne de Luxembourg; Chevalier de la Légion d'Honneur; Commendatore, Ordine Al Merito della Repubblica Italiana; Commander, Order of Ouissam Alaouite (Morocco), 1968; Grosses Verdienstkreuz des Verdienstordens der Bundesrepublik Deutschland, 1974; Olympic Diploma of Merit, IOC, 1974. Hon. Mem. UEFA, 1976. *Publications:* (jtly) The Football Association Coaching Manual, 1942; Recreative Physical Exercises and Activities for Association Football and other Games Players, 1942; A History of the Laws of Association Football, 1974; Football Worlds: a lifetime in sport (autobiog.), 1978. *Recreation:* watching a variety of sport. *Address:* 115 Ladbroke Road, W11. *T:* 01-727 4113. *Clubs:* MCC; All England Lawn Tennis and Croquet, Hurlingham.

ROUSE, Sir Anthony (Gerald Roderick), KCMG 1969 (CMG 1961); OBE 1945; HM Diplomatic Service, retired; *b* 9 April 1911; *s* of late Lt-Col Maxwell Rouse and of Mrs Rouse, Eastbourne; *m* 1935, Beatrice Catherine Ellis. *Educ:* Harrow; Heidelberg Univ. Joined HAC 1935; RA (T) 1938; 2 Lt 1940; transf. to Intelligence Corps; served MEF and CMF on staff of 3rd Corps (commendation); Lt-Col 1944. Entered Foreign Service, 1946; First Secretary (Information), Athens, 1946; Foreign Office, 1949. British Embassy, Moscow, 1952-54; Counsellor, 1955; Office of UK High Commissioner, Canberra, 1955-57; HM Inspector of Foreign Service Establishments, 1957-59; Counsellor (Information) British Embassy, Bonn, 1959-62; British Deputy Commandant, Berlin, 1962-64; HM Minister, British Embassy, Rome, 1964-66; Consul-General, New York, 1966-71. *Address:* St Ritas, Paradise Drive, Eastbourne, E Sussex.

ROUSE, Arthur Frederick, CMG 1949; *b* 25 Sept. 1910; *s* of late G. A. Rouse, Reading; *m* 1937, Helena, *y d* of late Rev. L. Klamborowski, Clare, Suffolk. *Educ:* Reading School; St John's College, Oxford. White Scholar of St John's, 1928; 1st Cl. Hons Classical Moderations, 1929; 2nd Cl. Literae Humaniores, 1932. Assistant Master Edinburgh Academy, 1932; entered Home Civil Service by competitive exam. starting as Asst Principal in Ministry of Labour, 1933; Private Sec. to Parl. Secretary, 1936-38; accompanied British Delegation to Internat. Labour Conf., 1936-37; Principal, Ministry of Labour, 1938, Asst Secretary, 1944; Dep. Chief, Manpower Division, CCG (British Element), 1945-46; UK Govt Rep. on various Internat. Cttees, 1946-49, including OEEC Manpower Cttee, Chairman of ILO European Manpower Cttee; Special Asst on Manpower to Dir-Gen. of ILO, 1949-50; Head of Latin American Immigration Field Office of ILO, 1950-51; Chairman of Beatrice Intensive Conservative Area Cttee, 1956; Senior Research Fellow, Univ. Coll. of Rhodesia and Nyasaland, 1957-62; Chairman, Wages Advisory Board for Nyasaland, 1960-62. Public administration and industrial consultant. *Recreations:* farming and travel. *Address:* Alicedale Farm, Beatrice, Zimbabwe.

ROUSE, E(dward) Clive, MBE 1946; Medieval Archæologist; Specialist in Mural and Panel Paintings; Lecturer; *b* 15 October 1901; *s* of late Edward Foxwell Rouse (Stroud, Gloucestershire and Acton, Middlesex) and late Frances Sarah Rouse (*née* Sams). *Educ:* Gresham's School; St Martin's School of Art. On leaving school studied art and medieval antiquities, 1920-21; FSA London, 1937 (Mem. of Council, 1943-44); FRSA 1968. President: Royal Archæological Institute, 1969-72 (Vice-Pres., 1965); Bucks Archæological Soc., 1969-79. Liveryman, Fishmongers' Company, 1962. Hon. MA Oxon 1969. Served War of 1939-45, RAFVR (Intelligence); Flight-Lt, 1941-45; MBE for special services at Central Interpretation Unit, Medmenham. *Publications:* The Old Towns of England, 1936 (twice reprinted); Discovering Wall Paintings, 1968 (reprinted); (jointly) Guide to Buckinghamshire, 1935; contributor to: The Beauty of Britain, 1935; Collins' Guide to English Parish Churches, 1958. Papers in Archæologia, Antiquaries' Journal, Archæological Journal, and publications of many County Archæological Societies. *Recreation:* travel. *Address:* Oakfield, North Park, Gerrards Cross, Bucks. *T:* Gerrards Cross 82595.

ROUSSEL, (Philip) Lyon, OBE 1974; FRGS; FRSA; Controller, Arts Division, British Council, since 1979; *b* 17 Oct. 1923; *s* of late Paul Marie Roussel and of Beatrice (*née* Cuthbert); *m* 1959, Elisabeth Mary, *d* of Kenneth and Kathleen Bennett; one *s* one *d. Educ:* Hurstpierpoint Coll.; St Edmund Hall, Oxford (MA, Cert. Public and Social Admin); Chelsea Sch. of Art. Served Indian Army in Parachute Regt, 1942-46 (Major). Sudan Political Service, 1950-55; Principal, War Office, 1955-56; Associated Newspapers, 1956-57; British Council, 1960–: India, 1960-67 (Regional Rep., Western and Central India, 1964-67); Dir, Scholarships, 1967-71; Rep. and Cultural Attaché, British Embassy, Belgium and Luxembourg, 1971-76; Europalia-Great Britain Festival Cttee, 1973; Cultural Attaché (Counsellor), British Embassy, Washington, 1976-79. Member: Fest. of India Cttee, 1981-82; London Adv. Cttee, Britain Salutes New York, 1981-83. *Recreations:* painting, the arts in general, tennis and a barn in Quercy. *Address:* 4 Holland Park, W11 3TG. *Clubs:* Athenæum, Travellers'.

ROUSSOS, Stavros G.; Secretary General, Ministry of Foreign Affairs, Greece, 1980-82; *b* 1918; *m* ; two *s* one *d. Educ:* Univ. of Lyons (LèsL); Univ. of Paris (LèsL, LèsScPol, LLD). Entered Greek Diplomatic Service as Attaché, Min. of Foreign Affairs, 1946; Mem., Greek Delegn to Gen. Assembly of UN, 1948 and 1954-55; Sec. to Permanent Mission of Greece to UN in New York, 1950; Consul, Alexandria, 1955; i/c Greek Consulate General, Cairo, 1956; Counsellor, 1959; Min. of Foreign Affairs, 1959-61; Mem., Perm. Delegn of Greece to EEC, Brussels, 1962; Perm. Rep. to EEC, 1969; Dir-Gen., Econ. and Commercial Affairs, Min. of Foreign Affairs, 1972; Ambassador of Greece to UK, 1974-79; Alternate Sec. Gen., Min. of Foreign Affairs, 1979-80. Grand Comdr, Order of Phoenix; Commander: Order of Belgian Crown; Order of Merit of Egypt. *Publication:* The Status of Dodecanese Islands in International Law, 1940 (Paris). *Address:* 5 Loukianou Street, Athens, Greece.

ROUTH, Augustus Crosbie; *b* 7 Aug. 1892; *s* of late Augustus Routh, Manager of Imperial Ottoman Bank, Salonica; *m* 1917, Ethel Madeline Martin (*d* 1973), The Steyne, Worthing; one *d* (and one *s* killed in action, 1941, one *d* decd). *Educ:* abroad; Edinburgh; LSE, London. Shipping Clerk, Consulate-General, Smyrna, 1910, Chief Clerk, 1920; General Consular Service, 1920; Acting Consul-General, Marseilles, Strasbourg, Milan, Genoa, and Monrovia at various dates: Consul at Istanbul, 1934; Actg Consul-Gen., Tripoli, 1935; Consul at Benghazi, 1936; Actg Consul-General, Marseilles, 1937; re-appointed Consul at Istanbul, 1938; Acting Consul-General, Antwerp, 1940; Chargé d'Affaires and Consul-General, Monrovia, Liberia, 1941; promoted Consul-General at Nice, France, 1944; HM Minister, Haiti, 1946-50; retired, 1950. Coronation Medal, 1937. *Address:* 16 Hailsham Road, Worthing, W Sussex. *T:* Worthing 49250.

ROUTH, Donald Thomas; Under Secretary, Department of the Environment, since 1978; *b* 22 May 1936; *s* of Thomas and Flora Routh; *m* 1961, Janet Hilda Allum. *Educ:* Leeds Modern Sch. Entered WO, Northern Comd, York, as Exec. Officer, 1954; Nat. Service, RN, 1954-56; Higher Exec. Officer, Comd Secretariat, Kenya, 1961-64; Asst Principal, Min. of Housing and Local Govt, 1964-66; Asst Private Sec. to Minister, 1966-67; Principal, 1967; on loan to Civil Service Selection Bd, 1971; Asst Sec., DoE, 1972; Under Sec., 1978; Regional Dir, West Midlands, 1978-81. *Address:* 2 Marsham Street, SW1.

ROUTLEDGE, Alan, CBE 1979; *b* 12 May 1919; *s* of George and Rose Routledge, Wallasey, Cheshire; *m* 1949, Irene Hendry, Falkirk, Stirlingshire; one *s* (and one *s* decd). *Educ:* Liscard High Sch., Wallasey. Served Army, Cheshire (Earl of Chester's) Yeomanry, 1939-46. Control Commn for Germany, 1946-51; Diplomatic Wireless Service of FO (now Foreign and Commonwealth Office), 1951-79: Head, Cypher and Signals Branch, 1962; Head, Commns Planning Staff, 1973; Head, Commns Ops Dept, 1979; retired FCO, 1979. *Recreations:* English history, cricket, golf. *Address:* 10 St Margaret's Close, Orpington, Kent. *T:* Orpington 23900. *Clubs:* Civil Service; Orpington Sports; Old Liscardians.

ROUTLEDGE, Rev. Canon (Kenneth) Graham; Canon Residentiary of St Paul's Cathedral, since 1982; Chancellor, Diocese of Ely since 1973, of Peterborough since 1976, and of Lichfield since 1976; Fellow, Corpus Christi College, Cambridge, since 1969; *b* 21 Sept. 1927; *s* of Edgar Routledge and late Catherine Perry; *m* 1960, Muriel, *d* of late Robert Shallcross. *Educ:*

Birkenhead Sch.; Liverpool Univ. (LLB 1st Cl. Hons 1951); Fitzwilliam Coll., Cambridge (BA 1965 Theol Tripos Pt II, MA 1969); Westcott House, Cambridge. Deacon, 1966; priest, 1967. Called to the Bar, Middle Temple, 1952 (Blackstone Entrance Scholar, Harmsworth Law Scholar, Campbell Foster Prize). HM Forces, RE and RAEC, 1945-48. Practice at Chancery Bar, Liverpool, and on Northern Circuit, 1952-63; Tutor and Lectr in Law, Liverpool Univ., 1952-63; Curate at St George's, Stockport, 1966-69; Lectr in Law, Manchester Univ., 1966-69; Corpus Christi Coll., Cambridge: Dean of Chapel, 1969-77; Lectr and Dir of Studies in Law, 1972-77; Canon Residentiary and Treasurer of Peterborough Cathedral, 1977-82. Mem., Birkenhead Bor. Council, 1960-63. Contested Birkenhead (Conservative), Gen. Election, 1959. Life Governor and Mem. Council, Haileybury and Imperial Service Coll., 1976-; Mem. Council, Westwood House Sch., Peterborough, 1979-; Fellow, Woodard Schools, 1979-. *Recreations:* Rugby, cricket, golf, bird watching, reading. *Address:* 3 Amen Court, EC4M 7BU. *Clubs:* Royal Commonwealth Society, MCC.

ROW, Hon. Sir John Alfred, Kt 1974; Sugar Cane Farmer since 1926; retd as Minister for Primary Industries, Queensland, Australia, 1963-72; *b* Hamleigh, Ingham, Qld, Aust., 1 Jan. 1905; *s* of Charles Edward and Emily Harriet Row; *m* 1st, 1929, Gladys M. (decd), *d* of late H. E. Hollins; one *d*; 2nd, 1966, Irene, *d* of late F. C. Gough. *Educ:* Toowoomba Grammar Sch., Qld; Trebonne State Sch., Qld. Mem. for Hinchinbrook, Qld Legislative Assembly, 1960-72. Mem. Victoria Mill Suppliers Cttee and Herbert River Cane Growers Exec., 1932-60. Rep. Local Cane Prices Bd, 1948-60; Dir, Co-op Cane Growers Store, 1955-60; Councillor, Hinchinbrook Shire, and Rep. on Townsville Regional Electricity Bd, 1952-63; Life Mem.: Aust. Sugar Producers' Assoc.; Herbert River Pastoral and Agricultural Assoc. *Recreations:* bowls (past Pres. and Trustee of Ingham Bowls Club), gardening. *Address:* 10 Gort Street, Ingham, Queensland 4850, Australia. *T:* Ingham 761671.

ROW, Commander Sir Philip (John), KCVO 1969 (CVO 1965; MVO 1958); OBE 1944; RN Retired; an Extra Equerry to the Queen since 1969; Deputy Treasurer to the Queen, 1958-68. *Address:* Clare Lodge, Ewshot, Farnham, Surrey.

ROWALLAN, 3rd Baron *cr* 1911; **Arthur Cameron Corbett;** *b* 17 Dec. 1919; *s* of 2nd Baron Rowallan, KT, KBE, MC, TD, and Gwyn Mervyn (*d* 1971), *d* of J. B. Grimond, St Andrews; *S* father, 1977; *m* 1st, 1945, Eleanor Mary (marr. diss. 1962), *o d* of late Captain George Boyle, The Royal Scots Fusiliers; one *s* three *d*; 2nd, 1963, April Ashley (marr. annulled, 1970). *Educ:* Eton; Balliol College, Oxford. Served War of 1939-45. Croix de Guerre (France), 1944. *Heir: s* Hon. John Polson Cameron Corbett [*b* 8 March 1947; *m* 1970, Susan Jane Dianne Green; one *s* one *d*]. *Address:* c/o Hon. John Corbett, Rowallan, Kilmarnock, Ayrshire KA3 2LP.

ROWAN, Carl Thomas; Syndicated columnist, correspondent, Chicago Sun-Times; radio and TV commentator, Post-Newsweek Broadcasting; Roving Editor, Reader's Digest; *b* 11 August 1925; *s* of Thomas B. and Johnnie B. Rowan; *m* 1950, Vivien Murphy; two *s* one *d*. *Educ:* Tennessee State University; Washburn University; Oberlin Coll.; University of Minnesota. Mem. Staff of Minneapolis Tribune, 1948-61; Dept of State, 1961-63; US Ambassador to Finland, 1963-64; Director, United States Information Agency, Washington, DC, 1964-65. Hon. DLitt: Simpson Coll., 1957; Hamline Univ., 1958; Oberlin Coll., 1962; Dr of Humane Letters: Washburn Univ., 1964; Talladega Coll., 1965; St Olaf Coll., 1966; Knoxville Coll., 1966; Rhode Island Coll., 1970; Maine Univ., 1971; American Univ., 1980; Dr of Laws: Howard Univ., 1964; Alfred Univ., 1964; Temple Univ., 1964; Atlanta Univ., 1965; Allegheny Coll., 1966; Colby Coll., 1968; Clark Univ., 1971; Notre Dame, 1973; Dr of Public Admin., Morgan State Coll., 1964; Dr of Letters: Wooster Coll., 1968; Miami Univ., 1982; Drexel Inst. of Technology; Dr of Science Georgetown Med. Sch., 1982. *Publications:* South of Freedom, 1953; The Pitiful and the Proud, 1956; Go South to Sorrow, 1957; Wait Till Next Year, 1960; Between Us Blacks, 1974. *Recreations:* tennis, golf and bowling, singing and dancing. *Address:* 3116 Fessenden Street North-West, Washington, DC 20008, USA. *Clubs:* Federal City, Indian Spring, (Washington, DC).

ROWAN-LEGG, Allan Aubrey; Vice President, Western Region, Edcom Ltd, Canada, since 1976; *b* 19 May 1912; *m* 1944, Daphne M. Ker; three *d*. Dir, Vice-Pres. and Gen. Sales Man., Interlake Fuel Oil Ltd, and Interlake Steel Products, 1955-57; Pres. and Dir, Superior Propane Ltd, Northern Propane Gas Co., 1957-63; Dir, Vice-Pres. and Gen. Man., Garlock of Canada Ltd, and Yale Rubber Mfg Co. of Canada Ltd, 1963-64; Regional Dir for Ont., Canadian Corp. for 1967 World Exhibn, 1964-67; Agent General for Ontario in UK, 1967-72; Man. Dir, Canada Permanent Mortgage Corp. and Canada Permanent Trust Co., 1973-75. Past Chm. and Pres., Art Gallery of Greater Victoria, (1980), now ex officio Mem. Board. Liveryman, Painter Stainers Co., 1969-. Freeman of City of London, 1969. Canada Centennial Medal. *Recreations:* yachting, golfing, swimming. *Address:* 1790 Glastonbury Road, Victoria, British Columbia V8P 2H3, Canada. *Clubs:* Royal Lymington Yacht (Hants); Union, Canadian Men's, Victoria Golf, Rotary (Victoria, BC); Harbourside Rotary (Director).

ROWE, Eric George, CMG 1955; *b* 30 June 1904; *s* of late Ernest Kruse Rowe; *m* 1931, Gladys Ethel, *d* of late Charles Horace Rogers, ARCA. *Educ:* Chatham House School, Ramsgate; St Edmund Hall Oxford. Assistant Master,

Queen Mary's Grammar School, Walsall, 1926-27. Entered Colonial Service, Tanganyika; Administrative Officer (Cadet), 1928; Asst District Officer, 1930; District Officer, 1940; Provincial Commissioner, 1948; Senior Provincial Commissioner, 1952; Minister for Local Government and Administration, Tanganyika, 1958; Supervisor, Overseas Services Courses, Oxford, 1959-69. *Publication:* paper in Ibis. *Recreation:* ornithology. *Address:* Manor Farm, East Hanney, Oxon. *T:* West Hanney 229. *Club:* Royal Commonwealth Society.

ROWE, Sir Henry (Peter), KCB 1978 (CB 1971); QC 1978; First Parliamentary Counsel, 1977-81; *b* 18 Aug. 1916; 3rd *s* of late Dr Richard Röhr and Olga Röhr, Vienna; *m* 1947, Patricia, *yr d* of R. W. King, London; two *s* one *d*. *Educ:* Vienna; Gonville and Caius Coll., Cambridge. War service, Pioneer Corps, RAC, Military Govt, British Troops, Berlin, 1941-46. Called to Bar, Gray's Inn, 1947. Joined Parliamentary Counsel Office, 1947; Jt Second Parly Counsel, 1973-76. Commonwealth Fund Travelling Fellowship in US, 1955; with Law Commn, 1966-68. *Recreations:* music, reading, walking. *Address:* 19 Paxton Gardens, Woking, Surrey. *T:* Byfleet 43816.

ROWE, Jeremy, CBE 1980; Chairman, London Brick Company Limited, since 1979; Deputy Chairman, Abbey National Building Society, since 1979; Chairman, Peterborough Development Corporation, since 1981; *b* 31 Oct. 1928; *s* of Charles William Dell Rowe and Alison (*née* Barford); *m* 1957, Susan Mary (*née* Johnstone); four *d*. *Educ:* Wellesley House Sch.; Uppingham Sch.; Trinity Coll., Cambridge (MA (Hons) Hist.). CBIM. English-Speaking Union Scholarship to USA, 1952. Joined London Brick Co. Ltd as trainee, 1952; Personal Asst to Chm., 1954; Dir and Sales Manager, 1963-67; Man. Dir, 1967-70; Dep. Chm. and Man. Dir, 1970-79; Chm. and Man. Dir, 1979-82; Bd Mem., Peterborough Develt Corp., 1979; Dir, West End Bd, Sun Alliance Insce Co. Ltd, 1978-. Mem., EDC for Building Ind., 1970-; Vice-Pres., Nat. Council of Building Material Producers, 1978-. *Recreations:* tennis, shooting, reading, music. *Address:* 23 Devonshire Place, W1. *T:* 01-935 4902; Woodside, Peasmarsh, near Rye, Sussex. *Clubs:* Buck's; All England Lawn Tennis.

ROWE, John Jermyn, QC 1982; Barrister; a Recorder of the Crown Court, since 1978; *b* 23 March 1936; *s* of John Rowe and late Olga Brookes Rowe (*née* Hutton); *m* 1966, Susan, *d* of Wing Comdr Walter Dring, DSO, DFC (killed in action, 1945) and of Sheila Mary Patricia (who *m* 2nd, His Honour Judge Gerrard, *qv*); two *d*. *Educ:* Manchester Grammar School; Brasenose Coll., Oxford. MA. 2nd Lieut, RA, 1954-56; called to the Bar, Middle Temple, 1960 (Harmsworth Scholar); practice on Northern Circuit; Prosecuting Counsel to the Inland Revenue, Northern Circuit, 1980-82; Mem., Gen. Council of the Bar, 1970-74; Bar Representative, Senate of the Inns of Court and the Bar, 1978-81. *Address:* 2 Pump Court, Temple, EC4. *Club:* Tennis and Racquet (Manchester).

ROWE, Norbert Edward, CBE 1944; FEng 1976; FIMechE; Vice-President, Engineering De Havilland Aircraft of Canada, 1962-66, retired, 1966; *b* 18 June 1898; *s* of Harold Arthur and Jane Rowe, Plymouth, Devon; *m* 1929, Cecilia Brown; two *s* two *d*. *Educ:* City and Guilds (Engineering) Coll. Whitworth Exhibition, 1921; BSc Eng. London, 1st Cl. Hons, 1923; Associate of City and Guilds Institute, 1923; DIC 1924; FRAeS 1944; Air Ministry; Royal Aircraft Establishment, 1924, Junior Technical Officer, 1925; Testing Establishment, Technical Officer, 1926; Senior Technical Officer, 1937; Testing Establishment, Chief Technical Officer, 1937; Headquarters, Asst Director, 1938; Ministry of Aircraft Production Headquarters, Deputy Director, Research and Develt of Aircraft, 1940; Director of Technical Development, Ministry of Aircraft Production, 1941-45; Director-General of Technical Development, 1945-46; Controller of Research and Special Developments, British European Airways Corporation (on resignation from Civil Service), 1946-51; Technical Director Blackburn and General Aircraft Ltd, E Yorks, 1952-61; Joint Managing Director of the Blackburn Aircraft Company, 1960-61; Director, Hawker Siddeley Aviation, 1961-62. Member: Air Registration Bd, 1968; ARC, 1969-72. Fellow Inst. Aeronautical Sciences of Amer., 1953; FCGI 1954. Pres. Royal Aeronautical Society, 1955-56, Hon. Fellow 1962. President: Helicopter Assoc. of GB, 1959-60; Whitworth Soc., 1974-75. Hon. Fellow, Canadian Aerospace Inst., 1965. *Address:* 22 Westfields Road, Mirfield, West Yorks WF14 9PW.

ROWE, Norman Francis; one of the Special Commissioners of Income Tax, 1950-73; Commissioner of Income Tax, St Marylebone Division, 1974; *b* 18 May 1908; *o s* of late Frank Rowe and Eva Eveline (*née* Metcalfe), Watford; *m* 1941, Suzanne Marian (marr. diss., 1964), *o d* of D. S. Richardson; one *s* ; *m* 1965, Vittoria, *yr d* of P. Cav. Tondi; one *s*. *Educ:* Sherborne. Chartered Accountant, 1931-37, retired; re-admitted, 1977; FCA. Called to Bar, Lincoln's Inn, 1940; Mem. of Western Circuit. Served War of 1939-45 (despatches); RAF, 1940-45, serving in UK, Middle East, India, Burma and Ceylon; demobilised with rank of Squadron Leader. Freeman, City of London; Liveryman, Worshipful Co. of Glaziers and Painters of Glass. *Publications:* author of Schedule C and Profits Tax sections of Simon's Income Tax, 1st edn. *Recreations:* fishing, yachting. *Address:* Darley House, Darley Road, Eastbourne, East Sussex BN20 7UH. *T:* Eastbourne 30878; Via Leonardo da Vinci 286, 55049 Viareggio, Italy. *T:* Viareggio 30248. *Clubs:* Naval and Military, Bar Yacht, Little Ship; Island Cruising.

ROWE, Norman Lester, CBE 1976; FRCS, FDSRCS; retired; formerly Consultant in Oral and Maxillo-Facial Surgery to: Westminster Hospital; Plastic & Oral Surgery Centre, Queen Mary's Hospital, Roehampton;

Emeritus Consultant to the Royal Navy and Retired Consultant to the Army; Recognised Teacher in Oral Surgery, University of London; Examiner, Royal College of Surgeons, Royal College of Surgeons of Glasgow, and RCSI; *b* 15 Dec. 1915; *s* of late A. W. Rowe, OBE and of L. L. Rowe; *m* 1938, Cynthia Mary Freeman; one *s* one *d. Educ:* Malvern College; Guy's Hospital; LRCP, LMSSA (London), HDDRCS (Edin.). Gen. Practice, 1937–41; Captain RADC, 1941–46. Formerly Senior Registrar, Plastic and Jaw Injuries Unit, Hill End Hosp., St Albans, 1947, and consultant in Oral Surgery, Plastic and Oral Surgery Centre, Rooksdown House, Park Prewett, Basingstoke, 1948–59; formerly Mem., Army Med. Adv. Bd; Mem. Bd of Faculty of Dental Surgery, RCS, 1956–74; Vice-Dean, 1967; Webb-Johnson Lectr, 1967–69; Colyer Gold Medal, 1981. Foundn Fellow, Brit. Assoc. of Oral Surgeons, Hon. Sec., 1962–68, Pres., 1969–70; Hon. Fellow, 1981 (Down's Surgical Prize Medal, 1976); Fellow Internat. Assoc. of Oral Surgeons (Sec. Gen., 1968–71); Member: BMA; BDA; Fedn Dent. Internat.; Oral Surgery Club (GB); Academia Nacional de Medicina de Buenos Aires, Argentina; Académie de Chirurgie Dentaire, Paris; Hon. Member: Egyptian Dental Assoc.; European Assoc. for Maxillo-Facial Surgery (Pres., 1974–76, Vice-Pres., 1977–82); Soc. of Amer. Oral Surgeons in Europe; Asociacion Mexicana de Cirugia Bucal; Amer. Soc. Maxillo-Facial Surgs; Canadian Assoc. of Oral and Maxillo-Facial Surgs; Emeritus Fellow, Colegio Brasileiro de Cirurgia e Traumatologia Buco-Maxilo-Facial (Le Fort Prize Medal, 1970); Hon. Fellow: Sociedad Venezolana de Cirurgia Bucal; Finnish Soc. of Oral Surgeons; Australian and New Zealand Soc. of Oral Surgeons; Assoc. Française des Chirurgiens Maxillo-Faciaux; Soc. Royale Belge de Stomatol. et de Chirurgie Maxillo-Faciale; Deutsche Gesellschaft für Mund-Kiefer und Gesichtschirugie; Soc. of Maxillo-Facial and Oral Surgeons of S Africa; Polish Stomatological Soc.; Israel Soc. of Oral and Maxillo-Facial Surgery; Hon. FDSRCPS(Glas.); Hon. FFDRCS (Irel.); Hon. FDSRCS(Edin.); Hon. FIMFT. *Publications:* Fractures of the Facial Skeleton (jtly), 1955, 2nd edn, 1968; (jtly) chapters in Plastic Surgery in Infancy and Childhood, 2nd edn, 1979; various articles in British and Foreign Medical and Dental Jls. *Address:* Brackendale, Holly Bank Road, Hook Heath, Woking, Surrey GU22 0JP. *T:* Woking 60008. *Club:* Royal Naval Medical.

ROWE, Owen John Tressider, MA; Headmaster of Epsom College, 1970–82; *b* 30 July 1922; *e s* of late Harold Ridges Rowe and Emma E. Rowe (*née* Matthews), Lymington, Hampshire; *m* 1946, Marcelle Ljufliny Hyde-Johnson; one *s* one *d. Educ:* King Edward VI School, Southampton; Exeter College, Oxford (Scholar, MA); 1st Cl. Hons in Classical Hon. Mods, 1942. Served War of 1939–45, Lieut in Roy. Hampshire Regt, 1942–45. 1st Cl. Hons in Lit Hum, Dec. 1947; Assistant Master: Royal Grammar School, Lancaster, 1948–50; Charterhouse, 1950–60 (Head of Classical Dept); Officer Comdg Charterhouse CCF, 1954–60; Headmaster of Giggleswick School, 1961–70. Governor, Welbeck College and other schs. *Address:* 8 Pine Hill, Epsom. *Club:* East India, Devonshire, Sports and Public Schools.

ROWE, Prof. Peter Noël, DSc (Eng); FEng, FIChemE; Ramsay Memorial Professor of Chemical Engineering, and Head of Department, University College London, since 1965; *b* 25 Dec. 1919; *e s* of Charles Henry Rowe and Kate Winifred (*née* Storry); *m* 1952, Pauline Garmirian; two *s. Educ:* Preston Grammar Sch.; Manchester Coll. of Technology; Imperial Coll., London. Princ. Scientific Officer, AERE, Harwell, 1958–65. Crabtree Orator, 1980. Pres., IChemE, 1981–82. Hon. DSc Brussels, 1978. *Publications:* scientific articles in Trans IChemE, Chem. Eng. Science, etc. *Address:* Pamber Green, Upper Basildon, Reading, Berks RG8 8PG. *T:* Upper Basildon 382. *Club:* Athenæum.

ROWE, Peter Whitmill, MA; Schoolteacher at Williston-Northampton School, Massachusetts, USA, since 1981; *b* 12 Feb. 1928; British; *s* of Gerald Whitmill Rowe, chartered accountant, one-time General Manager of Morris Commercials Co. Ltd; *m* 1952, Bridget Ann Moyle; two *s* one *d. Educ:* Bishop's Stortford College; St John's College, Cambridge. BA 1950; MA (Hons) 1956. VI Form History Master, Brentwood School, Essex, 1951–54; Senior History Master, Repton School, Derbys, 1954–57; Headmaster: Bishop's Stortford Coll., Herts, 1957–70; Cranbrook Sch., Kent, 1970–81. JP, Bishop's Stortford, 1968–70, Cranbrook, 1971–81. *Recreations:* literature, music, cricket, golf. *Address:* Williston-Northampton School, Easthampton, Mass, USA.

ROWE, Richard Brian; Registrar of the High Court (Family Division), since 1979; *b* 28 April 1933; *s* of Charles Albert Rowe and Mabel Florence Rowe; *m* 1959, Shirley Ann Symons; two *d. Educ:* Greenford County Grammar Sch.; King's Coll., London Univ. (LLB). National Service, RAF, 1952–54. High Court (Probate, Divorce and Admiralty Div.), 1954–66; Land Commn, 1966–69; Lord Chancellor's Office, 1969–75; Sec., High Court (Family Div.), 1975–79. *Publications:* (ed) 10th edn, Rayden on Divorce, 1967; (ed) 25th edn, Tristram and Coote's Probate Practice, 1978. *Recreations:* most sports. *Address:* High Court (Family Division), Somerset House, Strand, WC2R 1LP.

ROWE, Robert Stewart, CBE 1969; Director, Leeds City Art Gallery and Temple Newsam House, since 1958 (and also of Lotherton Hall since 1968); *b* 31 Dec. 1921; *s* of late James Stewart Rowe and late Mrs A. G. Gillespie; *m* 1953, Barbara Elizabeth Hamilton Baynes; one *s* two *d. Educ:* privately; Downing Coll., Cambridge; Richmond Sch. of Art. Asst Keeper of Art, Birmingham Museum and Art Gallery, 1950–56; Dep. Dir, Manchester City Art Galls, 1956–58. Pres., Museums Assoc., 1973–74; Member: Arts Council

of GB, 1981–; Fine Arts Adv. Cttee, British Council. Liveryman, Worshipful Co. of Goldsmiths. *Publications:* Adam Silver, 1965; articles in Burlington Magazine, Museums Jl, etc. *Recreations:* gardening, walking, reading. *Address:* Grove Lodge, Shadwell, Leeds LS17 8LB. *T:* Leeds 656365.

ROWE, Dr Roy Ernest, CBE 1977; Director General, Cement and Concrete Association, since 1977; *b* 26 Jan. 1929; *s* of Ernest Walter Rowe and Louisa Rowe; *m* 1954, Lillian Anderson; one *d. Educ:* Taunton's Sch., Southampton; Pembroke Coll., Cambridge (MA, ScD). FEng, FICE, FIStructE, FIHE. Cement and Concrete Association: Research Engineer, 1952–57; Head, Design Research Dept, 1958–65; Dir, R&D, 1966–77. Hon. Mem., Amer. Concrete Inst., 1978; For. Associate, Nat. Acad. of Engineering, USA, 1980. *Publications:* Concrete Bridge Design, 1962, 3rd impr. 1972; numerous papers in technical and professional jls. *Recreations:* fell walking, listening to music (and mutilating it on the piano). *Address:* Cornerway, 2 Sutton Avenue, Slough SL3 7AW. *T:* Slough 23645.

ROWELL, Sir John (Joseph), Kt 1980; CBE 1974; Chairman, Legal Aid Commission of Queensland, since 1978; Member, Commonwealth Legal Aid Commission, since 1980; *b* 15 Feb. 1916; *s* of Joseph Alfred Rowell and Mary Lilian Rowell (*née* Hooper), both born in England; *m* 1947, Mary Kathleen (*née* de Silva); three *s* two *d. Educ:* Brisbane Grammar School; Univ. of Queensland (BA). Served AIF, 1940–46; Captain 2/10 Fd Regt. Admitted Solicitor, 1939. Pres., Queensland Law Soc. Inc., 1964–66 (Mem. Council, 1956–67); Treas., Law Council of Aust., 1961–63 (Mem. Exec., 1960–67); Mem. Bd, Faculty of Law, Univ. of Queensland, 1959–78; Chm., Legal Assistance Cttee of Queensland, 1966–79. Chairman: Brisbane Gas Co. Ltd; Concrete Constructions (Qld) Pty Ltd; Dir of Principal Bd, Boral Ltd and Boral Resources Ltd; Chm., Boral Group of Companies in Queensland; Local Dir, City Mutual Life Assurance Soc. Ltd; Dir, Castlemaine Tooheys Ltd. Officer's Cross, Federal Republic of Germany, 1st class, 1979. *Recreations:* golf, fishing, reading. *Address:* Edgecliffe, 48 Walcott Street, St Lucia, Brisbane, Queensland, Australia. *T:* 370-9070. *Clubs:* Union, Australian (Sydney); Brisbane, United Service, Tattersall's (Brisbane); Indooroopilly Golf, South Port Golf.

ROWETT, Geoffrey Charles; Deputy Chairman, The Charterhouse Group plc, since 1981 (Managing Director, 1974–82; Group Chief Executive, 1976–82); *b* 1 Aug. 1925; *s* of Frederick Charles and Nell Rowett; *m* 1951, Joyce Eddiford; two *s. Educ:* Roundhay Sch., Leeds. Articled to Blackburns, Robson Coates & Co., Leeds and London. FCA, FCMA, JDipMA, FIMC, CBIM, FIAM. Midland Bank Executor & Trustee Co. Ltd, 1941; Royal Navy, 1943–46; Blackburns, Robson Coates & Co., 1947; Deloitte, Plender Griffiths Annan & Co., 1952; Production-Engineering SA (Pty) Ltd, 1954; P-E Consulting Group plc, 1964; Thomson Newspapers Ltd, 1965; Man. Dir, Sunday Times, 1965; Dir and Gen. Manager, Times Newspapers Ltd, 1967–72; Man. Dir, Corporate Finance, British Steel Corp., 1973. Member: Bd of Governors, St Mary's Hosp. Gp, 1970–74; Council, ICMA, 1974–82 (Vice-Pres., 1976; Pres., 1978). *Address:* 2 Eton Hall, Eton College Road, NW3 2DW. *T:* 01-586 8215; 13 Cork Terrace, Bath, Avon. *T:* Bath 21269. *Club:* Royal Automobile.

ROWLAND, David Powys; Stipendiary Magistrate, Mid Glamorgan (formerly Merthyr Tydfil), since 1961; *b* 7 Aug. 1917; *s* of late Henry Rowland, CBE, Weston-super-Mare; *m* 1st, 1946, Joan (*d* 1958), *d* of late Group Capt. J. McCrae, MBE, Weston-super-Mare; one *s* one *d* ; 2nd, 1961, Jenny (marr. diss. 1977), *d* of late Percival Lance, Swanage, and *widow* of Michael A. Forester-Bennett, Alverstoke; one *s* one *d* (and one step-*d*); 3rd, 1980, Diana, *d* of late W. H. Smith, Cannock, and *widow* of Lt-Col W. D. H. McCardie, S Staffs Regt (two step-*d*). *Educ:* Cheltenham Coll.; Oriel Coll., Oxford (BA). Lieut, Royal Welch Fusiliers, 1940–46. Called to Bar, Middle Temple, 1947. Deputy Chairman: Glamorgan QS, 1961–71; Breconshire QS, 1964–71. Mem. Nat. Adv. Council on Training of Magistrates, 1964–73. *Recreations:* fly-fishing, gardening, golf. *Address:* Trosglwyd, Dyffryn Crawnon, Llangynidr, Crickhowell, Powys. *T:* Bwlch 730635.

ROWLAND, Deborah Molly; Her Honour Judge Rowland; a Circuit Judge (formerly a County Court Judge) since 1971; *d* of Samuel and Hilda Rowland. *Educ:* Slade Sch. of Art; Bartlett Sch. of Architecture; Courtauld Inst of Fine Art. Diploma in Fine Art and Architecture. Called to the Bar, Lincoln's Inn, June 1950. *Publication:* Guide to Security of Tenure for Business and Professional Tenants, 1956. *Recreations:* music (Founder, Bar Musical Soc.), painting, sculpture. *Address:* Lincoln's Inn, WC2.

ROWLAND, Herbert Grimley; *b* 10 Feb. 1905; *s* of Frank Rowland, MRCS, LRCP, and Josephine Mary (*née* Quirke); *m* 1938, Margaret Jane Elizabeth, *yr d* of Robert Crawford Higginson and Mary Higginson; one *d. Educ:* Nautical Coll., Pangbourne; Peterhouse, Cambridge. Called to Bar, 1928; admitted Solicitor, 1933; private practice, Solicitor, 1933–40; joined Office of Solicitor of Inland Revenue, 1940; Princ. Asst Solicitor of Inland Revenue, 1961–65; Acting Solicitor of Inland Revenue, 1961; Special Commissioner of Income Tax, 1965–70. Chm., S Middlesex Rent Tribunal, 1972–76. *Recreation:* golf. *Address:* 10 Hillcrest, Durlston Road, Swanage, Dorset. *T:* Swanage 3256. *Clubs:* Bramley Golf (Surrey); Isle of Purbeck (Swanage).

ROWLAND, Air Marshal Sir James (Anthony), KBE 1977; DFC 1944; AFC 1953; BE; CEng, FRAeS, FIE(Aust); Governor of New South Wales, since 1981; *b* 1 Nov. 1922; *s* of Louis Claude Rowland and Elsie Jean

Rowland; *m* 1955, Faye Alison (*née* Doughton); one *d*. *Educ:* Cranbrook Sch., Sydney; St Paul's Coll., Univ. of Sydney (BE Aero). CEng, FRAeS 1969; FIE (Aust) 1978. Served War, Pilot, RAAF and RAF Bomber Comd, 1942-45. Sydney Univ., 1940-41 and 1946-47; Empire Test Pilots' Sch., Farnborough, 1949; Chief Test Pilot, RAAF R&D Unit, 1951-54; Staff Coll. and unit posts, incl. OC R&D, 1957-60; RAAF Mirage Mission, Paris, 1961-64; CO No 1 Aircraft Depot, 1966; Sen. Engr SO, Ops Comd, 1968-69; RCDS, 1971; Dir Gen., Aircraft Engrg, RAAF, 1972; Air Mem. for Technical Services, 1973; Chief of Air Staff, RAAF, 1975-79. Mem., Admin. Appeals Tribunal, 1979-80; Consultant, OFEMA Australia, 1980. KStJ 1981. *Publications:* contribs to professional jls. *Recreations:* surfing, reading, golf. *Address:* Government House, Sydney, NSW 2000, Australia. *T:* 233 2233. *Clubs:* United Services (Brisbane); Commonwealth (Canberra).

ROWLAND, Robert Todd, QC 1969; **His Honour Judge Rowland;** County Court Judge of Northern Ireland, since 1974; *b* 12 Jan. 1922; *yr s* of late Lt-Col Charles Rowland and Jean Rowland; *m* 1952, Kathleen, *er d* of late H. J. Busby, Lambourn, Berks; two *s*. *Educ:* Crossley and Porter Sch., Halifax, Yorks; Ballyclare High Sch.; Queen's Univ. of Belfast (LLB 1948). Called to Bar of N Ireland, 1949; Mem., Bar Council, 1967-72. Served 2nd Punjab Regt, IA, in India, Assam, Burma, Thailand, Malaya, 1942-46. Counsel to Attorney-Gen. for N Ireland, 1966-69; Sen. Crown Prosecutor for Co. Tyrone, 1969-72; Vice-Pres., VAT Tribunal for N Ireland, 1972-74. Served on County Court Rules Cttee, 1965-72 and 1975-; Chairman: War Pensions Appeal Tribunal, 1962-72; Commn of Inquiry into Housing Contracts, 1978; Member: Bd of Governors, Strathearn Sch., 1969-; Legal Adv. Cttee, Gen. Synod of Church of Ireland, 1975-. Chancellor, dioceses of Armagh, and Down and Dromore, 1978-. *Recreations:* fly-fishing, golf. *Address:* 36 Knocklofty Park, Belfast, N Ireland BT4 3NB. *Club:* Ulster (Belfast).

ROWLANDS, Edward; MP (Lab) Merthyr Tydfil, since April 1972; *b* 23 Jan. 1940; *e s* of W. S. Rowlands; *m* 1968, Janice Williams, Kidwelly, Carmarthenshire; two *s* one *d*. *Educ:* Rhondda Grammar Sch.; Wirral Grammar Sch.; King's Coll., London. BA Hons History (London) 1962. Research Asst, History of Parliament Trust, 1963-65; Lectr in Modern History and Govt, Welsh Coll. of Adv. Technology, 1965-. MP (Lab) Cardiff North, 1966-70; Parliamentary Under-Secretary of State: Welsh Office, 1969-70, 1974-75; FCO, 1975-76; Minister of State, FCO, 1976-79. Mem. of Governing Body and Exec. Cttee, Commonwealth Inst., 1980-. *Recreation:* music. *Address:* House of Commons, SW1; 5 Park Crescent, Thomastown, Merthyr Tydfil, Mid Glamorgan. *T:* Merthyr 4912.

ROWLANDS, John Kendall, FSA; Keeper, Department of Prints and Drawings, British Museum, since 1981; *b* 18 Sept. 1931; *s* of Arthur and Margaret Rowlands; *m* 1982, Lorna Jane Lowe. *Educ:* Chester Cathedral Choir Sch.; King's Sch., Chester; Gonville and Caius Coll., Cambridge. MA Cantab 1959; MA Oxon; FSA 1976. Asst Keeper, Dept of Art, City Mus. and Art Gall., Birmingham, 1956-60; Editor, Clarendon Press, Oxford, 1960-65; Asst Keeper, 1965-74, Dep. Keeper, 1974-81, Dept of Prints and Drawings, British Museum. *Publications:* David Cox Centenary Exhibition Catalogue, 1959; Graphic Work of Albrecht Dürer, 1971; Bosch, 1975; Rubens: drawings and sketches . . . , 1977; Urs Graf, 1977; Hercules Segers, 1979; Bosch, the Garden of Earthly Delights, 1979; contribs to specialist journals. *Recreation:* playing the piano and organ. *Address:* 21 St Paul's Place, N1 2QF.

ROWLANDS, (John) Martin, CBE 1980; Secretary for Civil Service, Hong Kong Government and Member of the Legislative Council, since 1978; *b* 20 July 1925; *s* of late John Walter Rowlands and of Mary Ace Maitland (*née* Roberts); *m* 1956, Christiane Germaine Madeleine Lacheny; two *d*. *Educ:* Charterhouse; Selwyn Coll., Cambridge (MA). Military service, 1943-47 (Captain, 3rd Royal Indian Artillery Field Regt, HQ XV Indian Corps, HQ ALFSEA). HMOCS, Hong Kong Admin. Service, 1952-; Dep. Dir of Urban Services, 1966-68; Principal Asst Colonial Sec., 1968-71; Dep. Sec. for Home Affairs, 1971-74; Dir of Immigration, 1974-78. *Recreations:* travel, railways, bird-watching. *Address:* Government Secretariat, Lower Albert Road, Hong Kong. *Club:* Royal Hong Kong Jockey.

ROWLANDS, Air Marshal Sir John (Samuel), GC 1943; KBE 1971 (OBE 1954); Consultant, Civil Aviation Administration, since 1981; *b* 23 Sept. 1915; *s* of late Samuel and Sarah Rowlands; *m* 1942, Constance Wight; two *d*. *Educ:* Hawarden School; University of Wales (BSc Hons). Joined RAFVR, 1939; permanent commission in RAF, 1945. British Defence Staff, Washington, 1961-63; Imperial Defence College, 1964; Royal Air Force College, Cranwell, 1965-68; First Director General of Training, RAF, 1968-70; AOC-in-C, RAF Maintenance comd, 1970-73; Asst Principal, Sheffield Polytechnic, 1974-80. *Recreations:* photography, tennis, motoring. *Address:* 45 Lyndhurst Road, Sheffield S11 9BJ. *Club:* Royal Air Force.

ROWLANDS, Maldwyn Jones, OBE 1979; FLA, FRGS, FLS; Head of Library Services (designation Museum Librarian, until 1974), British Museum (Natural History), 1965-81, retired; *b* 7 March 1918; *s* of Thomas and Elizabeth Rowlands; *m* 1941, Sybil Elizabeth Price; two *s* one *d*. *Educ:* Newtown Grammar Sch., Montgomeryshire; University Coll. London. Served in Army, 1940-46: commnd 1941 (Lieut), HQ 21 Army Gp (Staff Captain), 1944-46 (C-in-C's Cert. 1945). Asst Librarian, Science Museum Library, 1946-54; Deputy Librarian: British Museum (Natural History), 1954-63; Patent Office, 1963-65. *Recreations:* old books and bindings, Welsh

history and folk-lore. *Address:* 18 Aspen House, West Terrace, Folkestone, Kent CT20 1TH.

ROWLANDS, Martin; *see* Rowlands, J. M.

ROWLANDS, Martyn Omar, FSIAD, FPRI; Chairman, Martyn Rowlands Design Consultants Ltd, since 1960; *b* 27 July 1923; *s* of Edward and Mildred Rowlands; *m* 1st, 1951, Ann Patricia (*d* 1974); two *s* one *d*; 2nd, 1978, Mary Winifred. *Educ:* Eltham Coll.; Central Sch. of Art and Design. FSIAD 1960; FPRI 1973. Served War, RAF, 1940-45: India and Burma. Central Sch. of Art and Design, 1946-49; Head of Indust. Design, Ekco Plastics, 1954-59; started own design consultancy, 1959. Past Pres., SIAD. *Recreation:* photography. *Address:* Winchelsea House, Epping, Essex CM16 4DD. *T:* Epping 72887. *Club:* Arts.

ROWLANDSON, Sir (Stanley) Graham, Kt 1956; MBE 1943; JP 1944; FCA; Chairman, Rowlandson Organisation; Senior Partner, S. Graham Rowlandson & Co., Chartered Accountants; Chairman, The Finance & Industrial Trust Ltd; *b* 25 Aug. 1908; *s* of late H. Stanley Rowlandson, Claremont, Enfield, Middx; *m* 1938, Vera Elworthy, *d* of late Ernest Alfred Lane, Woodside Pk, N; two *s* one *d*. *Educ:* Mill Hill Sch.; Blois, France. Member, Enfield UDC, 1934-46 (Chm., 1940-42; Chm. Finance Cttee, 1937-45; Leader, Cons. Group and Council, 1937-40, 1942-45); Middlesex CC, 1942-46, 1947-51, 1959-63, CA, 1951-58, High Sheriff 1958 (Vice-Chm. Establishment Cttee 1949-51, Chm. 1951-55; Chm. Finance Cttee 1949-51, Vice-Chm. 1951-55; Dep. Leader, 1951, 1964-65; Leader, 1951-54; Vice-Chm. CC 1954-55, Chm. 1955-56; Chm. Health Cttee, 1956-61, Mem. 1961-65; Mem., Standing Jt Cttee, 1951-58, 1961-65); Mem. for Enfield, GLC, 1964-73; Chairman: Finance Cttee, GLC, 1969-73; Establishment Cttee, 1967-69; Member: Gen. Purposes Cttee, Supplies Cttee (Leader of Opposition), of GLC, 1964-67; Rep. on Local Govt Training Bd of GLC, 1967-70, Chm. Finance Cttee, 1967-70; Member: Local Govt Computer Centre, 1967-70; Exec. Coun. CCs Assoc., 1955-58; Local Authorities Management Services and Computer Cttee, 1969-70; Jt Hon. Treas., Middx Assoc., 1965-69, Vice-Pres., 1969-76, Pres., 1976-78; Vice-Chm., Home Counties N Local Govt Adv. Cttee, 1959-64; Greater London Area Local Govt Adv. Cttee, 1964-72, Dep. Chm., 1964-72; Mem., Nat. Local Govt Adv. Cttee, 1960-72; Common Councilman, City of London, for Coleman St Ward, 1961; Chm., Port and City of London Health and Welfare Cttees, 1964-67; Vice-Chm., Establishment Cttee, 1977-79, 1981-82, Chm., 1979-81; Mem., Lord Mayor and Sheriffs Cttee, 1971; Representative of Corp. on Disablement in the City Exec., 1976- and Greater London Assoc. for the Disabled, 1978-. Contested (C) N Tottenham, 1937 and 1938; Chairman: Enfield W Cons. Assoc., 1949-52; Enfield Bor. Cons. Assoc., 1952-64 (Pres. 1964-72); Pres., Enfield Town Cons. Club, 1970-; Hon. Life Pres., N Enfield Cons. Assoc., 1972-; Nat. Union of Cons. and Unionist Assocs: Vice-Chm. Home Counties N Prov. Area, 1953-54, 1961-64; Mem. Nat. Exec. Cttee, 1964-78; Mem., GP Cttee, 1972-75; Mem., Cons. Commonwealth and Overseas Council, 1972- (Hon. Treas., 1978-); Mem. Finance and GP Cttee, Greater London Area, 1964-78 (Dep. Chm., 1964-69, and 1970-71, Chm., 1972-75); Hon. Vice-Pres., 1976-; Hon. Treasurer, Primrose League, 1975-; Chm. Middx Parly and Local Govt Gps, 1953-54; Mem. Middx Exec. Council, 1951-53, 1962-63. Chm., Enfield Savings, 1940-45; Mem., Nat. Savings London Reg. Adv. Cttee, 1942-46; Mem., Admin. Council, Lord Mayor's Nat. Air Raid Distress Fund, 1940-54. Governor: Royal Nat. Orthopædic Hosp., 1948-52; Med. Coll., St Bartholomew's Hosp., 1966-; Chm., Chairmen of Reg. Hosp. Bds, 1971-74; Member: Gen. Council, King Edward's Hosp. Fund for London, 1956-; NE Met. Reg. Hosp. Bd, 1952-74 (Chm., 1956-74); Ct of Govs, London Sch. of Hygiene and Tropical Med., 1957-58; Bd of Governors: St Bartholomew's Hosp., 1957-74, London Hosp., 1960-74, Hammersmith and St Mark's Hosps, 1960-74, Moorfields Eye Hosp., 1961-79; Eastman Dental Hosp., 1974-78; Vice-Chm., Enfield Gp Hosp. Man. Cttees, 1948-53; Chairman: Appeals Cttee, St Antony's Hosp., Cheam, 1974; Funding Cttee, Inst. for the Study of Drug Dependence, 1976-80; Member: Whitley Council for Health Services, 1957-64; Nat. Cons Council on Recruitment of Nurses and Midwives, 1963-74; Inner London Exec. Council, 1971-74; Family Practitioner Cttee, City and E London Area Health Authority, 1974- (Chm. Dental Services Cttee, 1979-); Council of Fed. Superannuation Scheme for Nurses and Hospital Officers, 1965-74; Nat. Old People's Welfare Council, 1959-74; Adv. Council on Overseas Services Resettlement Bureau, 1968-79; Finance Cttee Internat. Soc. for Rehabilitation of Disabled, 1958-67 (Chm., 1964-67; Vice-Chm 1963-73, Chm., 1973-75, Brit. Cttee; Mem. Brit. Cttee, Royal Assoc. for Disability and Rehabilitation, 1977-); Nat. Baby Welfare Council, 1961-63; Exec. Cttee, Nat. Assoc. for Maternal and Child Welfare, 1977-80; Vice-Chm., Council for Professions supp. to Medicine, 1961-79 (Chm. Finance Cttee); Hon. Treasurer: Infantile Paralysis Fellowship, 1949-52 (Chm. 1952-57); Hand Crafts Adv. Assoc. for the Disabled, 1975-; Vice-Pres., Edmonton and Enfield Br., British Diabetic Assoc., 1960; Trustee: City Parochial Foundn, 1968-74, 1977-; Westminster Philanthropic Soc., 1960-75. Vice Pres., UNA, 1965-. Mem., Management Cttee, Bridgehead Housing Assoc. Ltd, 1974-75; Mem. Council, Stonham Housing Assoc. Ltd, 1975-; Trustee Stonham Meml Trust, 1978-; Chm., Roma Housing Assoc. Ltd, 1975-79; Member: Court, Univ. of Essex, 1965-74; SE Circuit Cttee, 1972-; Governor: Mill Hill Sch., 1952-58, 1961-; London Festival Ballet Trust, 1971-73; Vice-Pres., Internat. Cultural Exchange, 1964-; Mem. Council RSA, 1966-76 (Hon. Treasurer, 1971-76); Pres., Boy Scouts Assoc., Enfield Br., 1958-77; Vice-President: London Scout Council, 1956-65; Co. of Greater London N Scout Council, 1965-71 (Pres., 1971-80); Pres., Middx Table

Tennis Assoc., 1957–; Vice-Pres., Basildon Jikishin Judo Centre, 1980–; Mem. Council, Royal Warrant Holders' Assoc., 1958-59. Liveryman, Worshipful Co. of Masons (Mem. Ct of Assts; Renter Warden, 1962; Upper Warden, 1963; Master, 1964); Liveryman, Paviors' Co. (Mem., Ct of Assts, 1973–; Renter Warden, 1977; Upper Warden, 1978; Master, 1979). Coleman St Ward Club: Vice-Chm., 1965; Chm., 1966. *Recreations:* work, entertaining, racing. *Address:* Boundary House, 91-93 Charterhouse Street, EC1. *T:* 01-253 0101; 47 Lowndes Square, SW1. *T:* 01-235 2288; Harmer Green End, Digswell, Herts. *T:* Welwyn 5141. *Clubs:* United and Cecil (Mem. Cttee, 1972–); Old Millhillians (Pres. 1965-66).

ROWLEY, Sir Charles (Robert), 7th Bt *cr* 1836; *b* 15 March 1926; *s* of Sir William Joshua Rowley, 6th Bt and Beatrice Gwendoline, *d* of Rev. Augustus George Kirby; *S* father, 1971; *m* 1952, Astrid, *d* of Sir Arthur Massey, CBE; one *s* one *d. Educ:* Wellington. Heir: *s* Richard Charles Rowley, *b* 14 Aug. 1959. *Address:* 21 Tedworth Square, SW3; Naseby Hall, Northamptonshire.

ROWLEY, Frederick Allan, CMG 1978; OBE 1959; MC 1945; Major (retd); HM Diplomatic Service, retired; *b* 27 July 1922; *m* 1951, Anne Crawley; one *s* three *d. Educ:* Haig Sch., Aldershot. Served War of 1939-45: Ranks, 8th Worcs Regt (TA), 1939-40; Emergency Commnd Officer, 5th Bn, 10th Baluch Regt (KGVO), Jacob's Rifles, Indian Army, Burma Campaign (MC), June 1941-Nov. 1948. At partition of India, granted regular commn (backdated, 1942) in Worcestershire Regt, but retd (wounded), sub. Major. Joined HM Diplomatic Service, Nov. 1948: served (with brief periods in FO) in: Egypt; Ethiopia; Turkey; Burma; Singapore; Australia; Malaysia; FCO 1971-72; Under-Sec., N Ireland Office (on secondment), 1972-73; Counsellor, FCO, 1973-79. Joint Services Staff College (jssc), 1959. *Recreations:* cricket, golf. *Address:* Boxalland, Kirdford, West Sussex. *T:* Kirdford 337. *Clubs:* Boodle's, MCC, Surrey County Cricket.

ROWLEY, John Charles, CMG 1977; Director, Crown Agents Board of Management, since 1980; *b* 29 Sept. 1919; *s* of John Ernest Rowley and Edith Muriel (*née* Aldridge); *m* 1st, 1945, Pamela Hilda Godfrey (marr. diss. 1971); two *d* ; 2nd, 1972, Anne Patricia Dening; one *s. Educ:* Ilford; King's College, London (LLB 1948, Upper Second Cl. Hons). Inland Revenue, 1938-40. RAF, 1940-46, pilot, Flight-Lieut; Iceland, 1944 (despatches). Inland Revenue, 1946-64; Min. of Overseas Development, 1964-79, Head, Middle East Develt Div., Amman, Jordan, 1971-79; Crown Agents Regional Controller for Middle East, 1979-80. *Recreations:* choral singing, sailing. *Address:* 195 Broomwood Road, SW11 6JF. *T:* 01-228 5992.

ROWLEY, John Hewitt, CBE 1968; Controller, BBC, Wales, 1967-74; *b* 1917. *Educ:* University Coll. of N Wales, Bangor (BA); Jesus Coll., Oxford. ICS, 1939-47. Joined BBC, 1949; Asst Head, Central Estabt, 1949-53; Staff Admin. Officer (II), 1953-55; Staff Admin. Officer, 1955-56; Asst Controller, Staff Admin, 1956-60, Controller, 1960-67. CIPM. *Address:* 21 Lakeside, The Knap, Barry CF6 8ST.

ROWLEY, John Vincent d'Alessio; General Manager, Bracknell New Town Development Corporation, 1955-73; *b* 12 Sept. 1907; 2nd *s* of late Ven. Hugh Rowley, Archdeacon of Kingwilliamstown, S Africa; *m* 1st, 1936, Violet Maud (*d* 1969), *d* of S. H. Day, Grahamstown, S Africa; one *s* ; 2nd, 1972, Mary Hawkesworth. *Educ:* St Andrews Coll., Grahamstown; Trinity Coll., Oxford (Rhodes Schol.). BA 1929; Oxford Univ. Rugby XV, 1929. Entered Sudan Political Service, 1930; Asst District Comr and District Comr, 1930-49; seconded Sudan Defence Force, 1940-42; Dep. Gov., Kordofan Province, 1950-52; Asst Financial Sec., 1952-53; Governor, Darfur Province, 1953-55. Chm., South Hill Park Arts Centre Trust, 1979–. *Recreations:* music, gardening, golf. *Address:* The Spring, Stanford Dingley, near Bradfield, Berks. *T:* Bradfield 270. *Club:* United Oxford & Cambridge University.

ROWLEY, Sir Joshua Francis, 7th Bt, *cr* 1786; JP; Lord-Lieutenant of Suffolk, since 1978; *b* 31 Dec. 1920; *o s* of 6th Bt and Margery Frances Bacon (*d* 1977); *S* father, 1962; *m* 1959, Hon. Celia Ella Vere Monckton, 2nd *d* of 8th Viscount Galway; one *d. Educ:* Eton; Trinity College, Cambridge. Grenadier Guards, 1940-46. Deputy Secretary, National Trust, 1952-55. Chairman: W Suffolk CC, 1971-74; Suffolk CC, 1976-78; DL 1968, High Sheriff 1971, Vice Lord-Lieutenant, 1973-78, JP 1978, Suffolk. *Address:* Holbecks, Hadleigh, Ipswich, Suffolk. *T:* Hadleigh 823211. *Clubs:* Boodle's, Pratt's, MCC.

ROWLEY, Peter, MC 1944; Senior Partner, Titmuss Sainer & Webb, since 1981; Chairman, Leonard Cheshire Foundation, since 1982; *b* 12 July 1918; *s* of late Roland and Catherine Isabel Rowley; *m* 1940, Ethnea Louis Florence Mary Howard Kyan; four *d. Educ:* Wembley County Sch.; University Coll., Oxford (MA). Served War of 1939-45: Queen's Westminster Rifles, 1938-39; 14th Bn Sherwood Foresters, 1940-46; Adjt, Middle East, N Africa; Company Comdr, Italy; Bde Major 13 Bde, 1944-45; GSOII 8 Corps, 1945-46. Admitted Solicitor, Titmuss Sainer & Webb, 1950; Member, Law Society Land Law Cttee, 1970–. *Address:* 38 Devonshire Place Mews, W1N 1FJ. *T:* 01-935 1003. *Club:* Royal Automobile.

ROWLEY-CONWY, family name of **Baron Langford**.

ROWLEY HILL, Sir George Alfred; *see* Hill.

ROWLING, Rt. Hon. Wallace Edward, PC 1974; MP (Lab) for Buller, New Zealand, later for Tasman, since 1967; Prime Minister of New Zealand, 1974-75; Leader of Opposition, since 1975; *b* Motueka, 15 Nov. 1927; *s* of A. Rowling; *m* 1951, Glen Elna, *d* of Captain J. M. Reeves; two *s* one *d. Educ:* Nelson Coll. MA. Fulbright Schol., 1955-56. Formerly Asst Dir of Educn, NZ Army. Minister of Finance, 1972-74; Governor for New Zealand, IMF. Rep. NZ at annual meeting of ADB, Kuala Lumpur, 1974. Pres., Asia Pacific Socialist Orgn, 1977–. Col Comdt, NZ Army Educn Corps, 1977-82. *Recreation:* golf. *Address:* Parliament Buildings, Wellington, New Zealand; 15 Waverley Street, Richmond, New Zealand.

ROWLINSON, Prof. John Shipley, BSc, MA, DPhil Oxon; FRS 1970; FRSC; FEng 1976; FIChemE; Dr Lee's Professor of Physical Chemistry, Oxford University, since 1974; Fellow of Exeter College, since 1974; *b* 12 May 1926; *er s* of Frank Rowlinson and Winifred Jones; *m* 1952, Nancy Gaskell; one *s* one *d. Educ:* Rossall School (Scholar); Trinity College, Oxford (Millard Scholar). Research Associate, Univ. of Wisconsin, USA, 1950-51; ICI Research Fellow, Lecturer, and Senior Lecturer in Chemistry, University of Manchester, 1951-60; Prof. of Chemical Technology, London Univ. (Imperial Coll.), 1961-73. Lectures: Liversidge, Chem. Soc., 1978; von Hofmann, Gesell. Deutscher Chem., 1980; Faraday, RSC, 1983; Pres., Faraday Div., Chem. Soc., 1979-81; Hon. Treas., Faraday Society, 1968-71; Vice-Pres., Royal Instn of GB, 1974-76; Member, Sale Borough Council, 1956-59. Meldola Medal, Roy. Inst. of Chemistry, 1954; Marlow Medal, Faraday Soc., 1957. *Publications:* Liquids and Liquid Mixtures, 1959, (jtly) 3rd edn, 1982; The Perfect Gas, 1963; Physics of Simple Liquids (joint editor), 1968; (trans. jtly) The Metric System, 1969; (jtly) Thermodynamics for Chemical Engineers, 1975; (jtly) Molecular Theory of Capillarity, 1982; papers in scientific journals. *Recreation:* climbing. *Address:* 12 Pullens Field, Headington, Oxford OX3 0BU. *T:* Oxford 67507; Physical Chemistry Laboratory, South Parks Road, Oxford OX1 3QZ. *T:* Oxford 53322.

ROWNTREE, Sir Norman Andrew Forster, Kt 1970; CEng; FICE; Consultant to Allott and Lomax, Consulting Engineers, since 1979; *b* 11 March 1912; *s* of Arthur Thomas Rowntree, London, and Ethel, *d* of Andrew Forster; *m* 1939, Betty, *d* of William Arthur Thomas; two *s* one *d. Educ:* Tottenham County Sch.; London Univ. (BSc(Eng)). Consulting Engineer, 1953-64; Mem. and Dir, Water Resources Bd, 1964-73; Prof. of Civil Engineering, UMIST, 1975-79; Member: Adv. Council for Applied R&D, 1976-80; Meteorological Office Cttee, 1979-80; Commn for Commonwealth Scholarship, 1979-80; Scientific Council, Centre de Formation Internationale à la Gestion des Ressources en Eau (France), 1977-80, Hon. Vice-Pres., 1980–; Expert Adv. Cttee, State of New Jersey Water Supply Master Plan, 1976-80. Pres., Inst. of Water Engineers, 1962-63. Vice-Pres., ICE, 1972-75, Pres. 1975-76. Vis. Prof., KCL, 1972-75; Lectures: CEI Graham Clark, 1972; IMechE Hawksley, 1976. Hon. DSc City Univ. 1974. Gold Medal, Soc. Chem. Ind., 1977. *Address:* 97 Quarry Lane, Kelsall, Tarporley, Cheshire CW6 0NJ. *T:* Kelsall 51195.

ROWSE, Alfred Leslie, MA, DLitt; FBA; Emeritus Fellow of All Souls College, Oxford; *b* St Austell, Cornwall, 4 Dec. 1903. *Educ:* Elementary and Grammar Schools, St Austell; Christ Church Oxford (Douglas Jerrold Scholar in English Literature). Sen. Res. Associate, Huntington Library, Calif, 1962-69. Fellow of the Royal Society of Literature; President of the English Association, 1952; Raleigh Lecturer, British Academy, 1957; Trevelyan Lecturer, Cambridge, 1958; Beatty Memorial Lecturer, McGill University, 1963. Pres., Shakespeare Club, Stratford-upon-Avon, 1970-71. *Publications:* Politics and the Younger Generation, 1931; Mr Keynes and the Labour Movement, 1936; Sir Richard Grenville of the Revenge, 1937; Tudor Cornwall, 1941; Poems of a Decade, 1931-41; A Cornish Childhood, 1942; The Spirit of English History, 1943; Poems Chiefly Cornish, 1944; The English Spirit: Essays in History and Literature, 1944, rev. edn 1966; West Country Stories, 1945; The Use of History, 1946; Poems of Deliverance, 1946; The End of an Epoch, 1947; The England of Elizabeth, 1950; The English Past, 1951 (rev. edn, as Times, Persons, Places, 1965); Translation and completion of Lucien Romier's History of France, 1953; The Expansion of Elizabethan England, 1955; The Early Churchills, 1956; The Later Churchills, 1958; Poems Partly American, 1958; The Elizabethans and America, 1959; St Austell: Church, Town, Parish, 1960; All Souls and Appeasement, 1961; Ralegh and the Throckmortons, 1962; William Shakespeare:-A Biography, 1963; Christopher Marlowe: A Biography, 1964; A Cornishman at Oxford, 1965; Shakespeare's Southampton: Patron of Virginia, 1965; Bosworth Field and the Wars of the Roses, 1966; Poems of Cornwall and America, 1967; Cornish Stories, 1967; A Cornish Anthology, 1968; The Cornish in America, 1969; The Elizabethan Renaissance: the Life of the Society, 1971; The Elizabethan Renaissance: The Cultural Achievement, 1972; Strange Encounter (poems), 1972; The Tower of London in the History of the Nation, 1972; Westminster Abbey in the History of the Nation, 1972; Shakespeare's Sonnets: a modern edition, 1973; Shakespeare the Man, 1973; Simon Forman: Sex and Society in Shakespeare's Age, 1974; Windsor Castle in the History of the Nation, 1974; (with John Betjeman) Victorian and Edwardian Cornwall, 1974; Oxford in the History of the Nation, 1975; Discoveries and Reviews, 1975; Jonathan Swift: major prophet, 1975; A Cornishman Abroad, 1976; Brown Buck: a Californian fantasy, 1976; Matthew Arnold: poet and prophet, 1976; Shakespeare the Elizabethan, 1977; Homosexuals in History: ambivalence in society, literature and the arts, 1977; Heritage of Britain, 1977; Milton the Puritan: portrait of a mind, 1977; The Road to Oxford: poems, 1978; (ed) The Poems of Shakespeare's Dark Lady, 1978; The Byrons and

Trevanions, 1978; The Annotated Shakespeare, 3 vols (introds to vols and plays), 1978; Three Cornish Cats, 1978; A Man of the Thirties, 1979; Portraits and Views, 1979; Story of Britain, 1979; (ed) A Man of Singular Virtue: Roper's Life of Sir Thomas More, 1980; Memories of Men and Women, 1980; Shakespeare's Globe, 1980; A Life: Collected Poems, 1981; Eminent Elizabethans, 1982. *Address:* Trenarren House, St Austell, Cornwall. *Club:* Athenæum.

ROWSON, Lionel Edward Aston, OBE 1955; FRS 1973; FRCVS; Director, Cambridge and District Cattle Breeders (AI Centre), since 1942 (part-time, since 1979); Officer in Charge, Agricultural Research Council Animal Research Station, Cambridge, 1976–79; Fellow of Wolfson College, Cambridge, since 1973; *b* 28 May 1914; *s* of L. F. Rowson, LDS, and M. A. Rowson (*née* Aston); *m* 1942, Audrey Kathleen Foster; two *s* two *d. Educ:* King Edward VIth Sch., Stafford; Royal Veterinary Coll., London. MRCVS, FRCVS 1972; FRVC 1975. Engaged in general practice, 1939–42. Dep. Dir, ARC Unit of Reproductive Physiology and Biochemistry, 1955–76. Mem., Acad. Royale de Médecine de Belgique, 1977. Hon. MA Cantab, 1977. Thomas Baxter Prize, 1956; Wooldridge Meml Lecture and Medal, 1974; Dalrymple-Champneys Cup and Medal, 1975; Bledisloe Veterinary Medal, 1978. *Publications:* (jointly) Reproduction in Domestic Animals (ed H. H. Cole and P. T. Cupps); Mem. Editorial Bd, Jl of Agricultural Science. *Recreations:* shooting, cricket, thoroughbred breeding. *Address:* The Grove, Water Lane, Histon, Cambridge. *T:* Histon 2534.

ROXBEE COX, family name of **Baron Kings Norton.**

ROXBURGH, Air Vice-Marshal Henry Lindsay, CBE 1966; FRCP, FRCPE; Commandant, RAF Institute of Aviation Medicine, 1969–73; retired; *b* 5 Dec. 1909; *s* of John Roxburgh, Galston, Ayrshire and Cape Town, and Edith Mary Roxburgh (*née* Smithers), Kenilworth, Cape; *m* 1944, Hermione Babington (*née* Collard); one *s* two *d. Educ:* George Watson's College, Edinburgh; Edinburgh University. BSc 1932; PhD 1934; MB, ChB 1940; FRCPE 1966; FRCP 1972. Medical Branch, Royal Air Force, 1941–73. Service mainly at RAF Inst. of Aviation Med.: research undertaken in various aspects of aviation physiology and related subjects; apptd Prof. in Aviation Medicine, 1966. Chairman, Aero-Space Medical Panel of Advisory Gp of Aero-Space Research and Development, Paris, 1965–67. Mem., Internat. Acad. of Aviation and Space Medicine. QHS 1971–73. FRAeS 1965. *Publications:* papers in field of aviation medicine. *Recreation:* gardening. *Address:* 11 Auderville, Alderney, CI. *Club:* Royal Air Force.

ROXBURGH, Ven. James William; Archdeacon of Colchester, since 1977; *b* 5 July 1921; *s* of James Thomas and Margaret Roxburgh; *m* 1949, Marjorie Winifred (*née* Hipkiss); one *s* one *d. Educ:* Whitgift School; St Catharine's Coll., Cambridge (MA); Wycliffe Hall, Oxford. Deacon 1944, priest 1945; Curate: Christ Church and Holy Trinity, Folkestone, 1944–47; Handsworth, Birmingham, 1947–50; Vicar: S Matthew, Bootle, 1950–56; Drypool, Hull, 1956–65; Barking, 1965–77. Canon of Chelmsford, 1972–. Pro-Prolocutor, Convocation of Canterbury, 1977–. Pres. Barking Rotary Club, 1976–77. *Recreations:* travel, philately. *Address:* Uplands, Powers Hall End, Witham, Essex CM8 2HE. *T:* Witham 513447.

ROXBURGH, Vice-Adm. Sir John (Charles Young), KCB 1972 (CB 1969); CBE 1967; DSO 1943; DSC 1942 (Bar, 1945); *b* 29 June 1919; *s* of Sir (Thomas) James (Young) Roxburgh, CIE; *m* 1942, Philippa, 3rd *d* of late Major C. M. Hewlett, MC; one *s* one *d. Educ:* RNC, Dartmouth. Naval Cadet, 1933; Midshipman, 1937; Sub-Lt 1939; Lt 1941; Lt-Comdr 1949; Comdr 1952; Capt. 1958; Rear-Adm. 1967; Vice-Adm. 1970. Served in various ships, 1937–39; joined Submarine Br., 1940; served in ops off Norway, in Bay of Biscay and Mediterranean, 1940–42; comd HM Submarines H43, United and Tapir, 1942–45 in ops in Mediterranean and off Norway; HMS Vanguard, 1948–50; comd HM Submarine Turpin, 1951–53; HMS Triumph, 1955; HMS Ark Royal, 1955–56; comd HMS Contest, 1956–58; Brit. Jt Services Mission, Wash., 1958–60; comd 3rd Submarine Sqdn and HMS Adamant, 1960–61; idc 1962; Dep. Dir of Defence Plans (Navy), MoD, 1963–65; comd HMS Eagle, 1965–67; Flag Officer: Sea Training, 1967–69; Plymouth, 1969; Submarines, and NATO Comdr Submarines, E Atlantic, 1969–72, retired 1972. Chm., Grovebell Group Ltd, 1972–75. Mem. Management Cttee, The Freedom Assoc., 1978–. Pres., Royal Naval Benevolent Trust, 1978–. Co. Councillor, Surrey, 1977–81. *Recreations:* golf, sailing, walking, music. *Address:* Oakdene, Wood Road, Hindhead, Surrey. *T:* Hindhead 5600. *Club:* Army and Navy.

ROXBURGHE, 10th Duke of, *cr* 1707; **Guy David Innes-Ker;** Baron Roxburghe 1600; Earl of Roxburghe, Baron Ker of Cessford and Cavertoun, 1616; Bt (NS) 1625; Viscount Broxmouth, Earl of Kelso, Marquis of Bowmont and Cessford, 1707; Earl Innes (UK), 1837; *b* 18 Nov. 1954; *s* of 9th Duke of Roxburghe, and of Margaret Elisabeth (who *m* 1976, Jocelyn Olaf Hambro, *qv*), *d* of late Frederick Bradshaw McConnel; *S* father, 1974; *m* 1977, Lady Jane Meriel Grosvenor, *yr d* of 5th Duke of Westminster, TD; one *s* one *d. Educ:* Eton; RMA Sandhurst (Sword of Honour, June 1974); Magdalene Coll., Cambridge. BA (Land Economy) 1980. Commnd into Royal Horse Guards/1st Dragoons, 1974; RARO 1977. *Recreations:* shooting, fishing, cricket, racing, ski-ing. *Heir: s* Marquis of Bowmont, *qv. Address:* Floors Castle, Kelso. *T:* Kelso 24288. *Clubs:* Turf, White's.

ROXBY, John Henry M.; *see* Maude-Roxby.

ROY, Andrew Donald; economist; *b* 28 June 1920; *er s* of late Donald Whatley Roy, FRCS, FRCOG, and late Beatrice Anne Roy (*née* Barstow); *m* 1947, Katherine Juliet Grove-White; one *s* two *d. Educ:* Malvern Coll. (Scholar); Sidney Sussex Coll., Cambridge (Scholar). Maths Trip. Pt I 1939 and Econ. Trip. Pt II 1948, Class I hons. 1939–45: served Royal Artillery, in UK, India and Burma (8 Medium Regt). Cambridge Univ.: Asst Lecturer, 1949–51; Lecturer, 1951–64; Jun. Proctor, 1956–57; Sidney Sussex Coll.: Fellow, 1951–64; Tutor, 1953–56; Sen. Tutor, 1956–62. HM Treasury: Economic Consultant, 1962; Sen. Economic Adviser, 1964; Under-Sec. (Economics), 1969–72. Under-Sec., DTI, 1972–74, MoD, 1974–76; Chief Economic Adviser, DHSS, 1976–80. Consultant, NIESR, 1981–. *Publications:* British Economic Statistics (with C. F. Carter), 1954; articles in economic and statistical jls. *Address:* 15 Rusholme Road, Putney, SW15 3JX. *T:* 01-789 3180. *Club:* United Oxford & Cambridge University.

ROY, Prof. Arthur Douglas, FRCS, FRCSE, FRCSGlas, FRCSI; FACS; Professor of Surgery, Queen's University of Belfast, since 1973; *b* 10 April 1925; *s* of Arthur Roy and Edith Mary (*née* Brown); *m* 1st, 1954, Monica Cecilia Mary Bowley; three *d* ; 2nd, 1973, Patricia Irene McColl. *Educ:* Paisley Grammar Sch.; Univ. of Glasgow (MB, ChB, Commendation). RAMC, 1948–50; Surgical Registrar posts in Glasgow and Inverness, 1950–54; Sen. Surgical Registrar, Aylesbury and Oxford, 1954–57; Cons. Surgeon and Hon. Lectr, Western Infirmary, Glasgow, 1957–68; Foundn Prof. of Surgery, Univ. of Nairobi, 1968–72. Mem. Council, RCSE, 1979–. *Publications:* Lecture Notes in Surgery: tropical supplement, 1975; various papers on gastro-enterology, endocrine surgery, tropical medicine, etc. *Recreations:* sailing, squash, gardening. *Address:* 15 Pinehill Road, Ballycairn, Lisburn, N Ireland BT27 5TU. *T:* Drumbo 217. *Club:* Royal Commonwealth Society.

ROY, Ian; Assistant Under-Secretary of State, Home Office, 1963–72; *b* 2 Aug. 1912; *o s* of late John Roy and Annie Froude Marshall; *m* 1939, Betty Louise Blissett; one *s* two *d. Educ:* Manchester Grammar School; Peterhouse, Cambridge. Assistant Inspector of Taxes, 1935; Assistant Principal, Home Office, 1936; Private Secretary to Permanent Under-Secretary of State, 1938; to Parliamentary Under-Secretary of State, 1939–40; Asst Secretary, 1947. *Address:* Flat 47, Cholmeley Lodge, Cholmeley Park, Highgate, N6. *T:* 01-340 3143.

ROY, His Eminence Cardinal Maurice, CC (Canada) 1971; DD (Laval); DPh (Inst. Angelicum); Archbishop of Quebec, 1947–81; Primate of Canada, 1956–81; elevated to the Sacred College of Cardinals and given titular church of Our Lady of the Blessed Sacrament and the Holy Canadian Martyrs, 1965; *b* 25 Jan. 1905; *s* of late Ferdinand Roy. *Educ:* Seminary of Quebec and Laval Univ., Quebec; Collegium Angelicum, Rome; Institut catholique and Sorbonne, Paris. Priest, 1927; Professor of: Dogmatic Theology, 1930–35; Apologeticx, 1935–36; Sacramentary Theology, 1936–39; Students' Chaplain, 1936–37. Hon. Capt.–Chaplain Royal 22d Regt 1939; Hon. Major and Chief Chaplain Canadian Base Units at Aldershot, 1941; Hon. Lt-Col, Chaplain HQ First Cdn Corps (England and Italy), 1941; Sicily and Italy Campaigns, 1943; Hon. Col, Asst Prin. Chaplain 1st Cdn Army, 1944; France, Belgium, Germany, Holland campaigns, 1944–45 (despatches). Rector Grand Seminary of Quebec, 1945; Bishop of Three-Rivers, 1946; Bishop Ordinary to Cdn Armed Forces (Military Vicar), 1946. Central Commission preparatory to Council Vatican II, June 1962; Council Vatican II Commission on Sacred Theology, Dec. 1962; Sacred Congregations of the Council and of Seminaries and Universities, 1965; Chairman: Concilium De Laicis; Pontifical Commission, Justitia et Pax, Rome, OBE, 1945; Chevalier of the Legion of Honour, 1947; Commander of the Order of Leopold and Croix de Guerre with palm, 1948; Commander of the Order of Orange Nassau, Holland, 1949; Knight Grand Cross, Equestrian Order to the Holy Sepulchre of Jerusalem, 1965; Bailiff Grand Cross of Honour and Devotion, Sovereign Order of Malta, 1965. *Address:* c/o Archevêché de Québec, Case postale 459, Québec G1R 4R6, Canada.

ROY, Maurice Paul Mary; Grand Officier, Légion d'Honneur; Professor at Ecole Polytechnique, Paris, 1947–69; Président: Committee on Space Research; International Union of Theoretical and Applied Mechanics; *b* 7 Nov. 1899; *m* 1932, Maritchu Nebout; one *s. Educ:* Ecole Polytechnique; Ecole Nat. Sup. des Mines. Ingénieur Général des Mines (retd); Contrôle Technique des Chemins de Fer, 1922–35; Director General: Mechanical Industry, 1935–40; Office Nat. de la Recherche Aéronautique, 1949–62; Professor successively at French Nat. Engineering Schs (Ponts et Chaussées, Génie Rural, Aéronautique), and at Ecole Polytechnique. Membre de l'Institut (Académie des Sciences), 1949 (Pres. 1966). Foreign Member: US Nat. Acad. of Sci.; Austrian Acad. of Sci.; Hon. FRAeS. Dr *hc* Bruxelles, Aachen, Saarbrucken, Québec, Oxford. Médaille d'Or Lomonossov, USSR Acad. of Sci., 1976. *Publications:* books on Thermodynamics, Mechanics, Aviation and Propulsion; scientific and technical papers. *Recreations:* literature, golf. *Address:* 86 Avenue Niel, 75017 Paris, France. *T:* 763-01-02.

ROYCE, David Nowill; Director-General, Institute of Export, since 1980; *b* 10 Sept. 1920; *s* of late Bernard Royce and Ida Christine (*née* Nowill); *m* 1942, Esther Sylvia Yule; two *s* one *d. Educ:* Reading School; Vienna University. Served HM Forces, 1940–46. Major, Intelligence Corps, 1946; Asst Principal, Foreign Office, German Section, 1948; Foreign Service, 1949; First Secretary: Athens, 1953; Saigon, 1955; Foreign Office, 1957; Head of Chancery, Caracas, 1960; Counsellor (Commercial), Bonn, 1963; Counsellor (Commercial) and

Consul-Gen., Helsinki, 1967-68; Commercial Inspector, FCO, 1969-71; Dir for Co-ordination of Export Services, DTI, 1971-73; Under-Secretary: Overseas Finance and Planning Div., Dept of Trade, 1973-75; CRE 3 and Export Develt Divs, Dept of Trade, 1975-77; Export Develt Div., Dept of Trade, 1977-80. Mem., Inst. of Export. *Recreations:* tennis, swimming, sailing. *Address:* 5 Sprimont Place, SW3. *T:* 01-589 9148. *Club:* Travellers'.

ROYDEN, Sir Christopher (John), 5th Bt *cr* 1905; Partner, Spencer Thornton & Co., since 1974; *b* 26 Feb. 1937; *s* of Sir John Ledward Royden, 4th Bt, and of Dolores Catherine, *d* of late Cecil J. G. Coward; *S* father, 1976; *m* 1961, Diana Bridget, *d* of Lt-Col J. H. Goodhart, MC; two *s* one *d. Educ:* Winchester Coll.; Christ Church, Oxford (MA). Duncan Fox & Co. Ltd, 1960-71; Spencer Thornton & Co., 1971-. *Recreations:* fishing, shooting, gardening. *Heir: s* John Michael Joseph Royden, *b* 17 March 1965. *Address:* 9 Stanhope Gardens, SW7. *T:* 01-370 2665. *Club:* Cavalry and Guards.

ROYDS, Rev. John Caress, MA Cantab; Vicar of St James's, Northampton, since 1981; *b* 1920; 3rd *s* of Rev. Edward Thomas Hubert Royds, BA. *Educ:* Monkton Combe School, Bath; Queens' College, Cambridge. II 1 hons History, 1947. Military service with British and Indian Armies, 1940-46. Assistant master, Bryanston School, Dorset, 1947-61, House-master, 1951-61; Headmaster: General Wingate School, Addis Ababa, 1961-65; Uppingham Sch., 1965-75. Deacon, 1974; Priest, 1975; Dir of Educn for Peterborough diocese, 1976-81. *Address:* St James's Vicarage, Vicarage Road, Northampton NN5 7AX. *Club:* Royal Commonwealth Society.

ROYLE, Sir Anthony (Henry Fanshawe), KCMG 1974; MP (C) Richmond, since Oct. 1959; Chairman, Wilkinson Sword Group Ltd, since 1981; *b* 27 March 1927; *s* of Sir Lancelot Royle, KBE; *m* 1957, Shirley Worthington; two *d. Educ:* Harrow; Sandhurst. Captain, The Life Guards (Germany, Egypt, Palestine and Transjordan), 1945-48; served with 21st Special Air Service Regt (TA), 1948-51. Parliamentary Private Secretary: to Under-Sec. of State for the Colonies, 1960; to Sec. of State for Air, 1960-62; to Minister of Aviation, 1962-64; Vice-Chm., Cons. Parly Foreign Affairs Cttee, 1965-67; Tory Opposition Whip, 1967-70; Parly Under-Sec. of State for Foreign and Commonwealth Affairs, 1970-74. Vice-Chm., Cons. Party Orgn, 1979- (Chm., Internat. Office, 1979-). Mem., Assembly of Council of Europe and WEU, 1965. Director: British Match Corp., 1969-70; Sedgwick UK Ltd, 1974-; Brooke Bond Group PLC, 1974-; Wilkinson Match Ltd, 1974-81. Esteemed Family Order (1st cl.), Brunei, 1975. *Address:* 47 Cadogan Place, SW1; The Chapter Manor, South Cerney, Gloucestershire. *Clubs:* Pratt's, White's, Brooks's.
See also T. L. F. Royle.

ROYLE, Prof. Joseph Kenneth; Head of Department of Mechanical Engineering, University of Sheffield, since 1966; *b* 3 April 1924; *s* of J. Royle, Accrington, Lancs; *m* 1955, P. R. Wallwork; one *s* two *d. Educ:* Manchester University. Royal Aircraft Estabt, 1944-48; Manchester Univ., 1949-61; Vis. Assoc. Prof., MIT, 1961-62; Sen. Lectr, Univ. of Manchester Inst. of Science and Technology, 1962-64; Dept of Mech. Engrg, Univ. of Sheffield, 1964-. *Publications:* contribs to Proc. IMechE, etc. *Recreations:* gardening, music. *Address:* Anselm, Over Lane, Baslow, Derbyshire. *T:* Baslow 3149.

ROYLE, Mrs Julian A. C.; *see* Harwood, Elizabeth Jean.

ROYLE, Timothy Lancelot Fanshawe, FInstM; Chairman: Christian Weekly Newspapers, since 1979; Control Risks Group, since 1982; *b* 24 April 1931; *s* of Sir Lancelot Carrington Royle, KBE, and Barbara Rachel Royle; *m* 1959, Margaret Jill Stedeford; two *s* one *d. Educ:* Harrow; Mons Mil. Acad. FInstM 1977. Commnd 15th/19th King's Royal Hussars, 1949, Inns of Court Regt, TA, 1951-63. Joined Hogg Robinson Gp, 1951; Man. Dir. 1980-81. Mem., Church Assembly of C of E, 1966-70; Church Comr, 1966-. Chm., Lindley Lodge Educnl Trust, 1970-. *Recreations:* country pursuits, ski-ing. *Address:* Ilmington Grange, Shipston on Stour, Warwicks CV36 4NE. *T:* Ilmington 317. *Clubs:* Cavalry and Guards, MCC; St Moritz Tobogganing (St Moritz).
See also Sir A. H. F. Royle.

ROZARIO, Most Rev. Michael; *see* Dacca, Archbishop of, (RC).

ROZHDESTVENSKY, Gennadi Nikolaevich; Order of the Red Banner of Labour, 1981; Chief Conductor: Moscow Chamber Opera, since 1974; Vienna Symphony Orchestra, since 1981; *b* 4 May 1931; *m* Victoria Postnikova, concert pianist. Studied piano at Moscow Conservatoire; started conducting at 18. Conductor Bolshoi Theatre, 1956-60 (Assistant Conductor, 1951); Chief Conductor, USSR Radio and Television Symphony Orchestra, 1960-65 and 1970-74; Principal Conductor, Bolshoi Theatre, 1965-70; Chief Conductor Stockholm Philharmonic Orchestra, 1974-77; BBC Symphony Orchestra, 1978-81. Guest conductor, Europe, Israel, America. Merited Artist of the RSFSR. *Recreation:* photography. *Address:* c/o Victor Hochhauser Ltd, 4 Holland Park Avenue, W11.

RUBBRA, Arthur Alexander, CBE 1961; RDI 1977; *b* 29 Oct. 1903; *s* of Edmund James Rubbra and Mary Jane Rubbra; *m* 1930, Lilian Agnes Webster (*d* 1979); one *s. Educ:* Northampton Sch.; Bristol Univ. (BSc 1st Cl. Hons). FIMechE, FEng 1980. Rolls Royce Ltd: Chief Designer, 1940; Asst Chief Engineer, 1944; Dep. Chief Engr, 1951; Technical Dir, 1954; retd 1968. FRSA 1977; Hon. FRAeS 1977. *Recreations:* music, old buildings. *Address:* 100

Belper Road, Derby DE1 3EQ. *T:* Derby 43107.
See also Edmund Rubbra.

RUBBRA, Edmund, CBE 1960; MA Oxon; MRAM 1970; FGSM 1968; composer, pianist; Professor of Composition at Guildhall School of Music, 1961-74; Senior Lecturer in Music, Oxford University, 1947-68; Fellow, Worcester College, Oxford, 1963; *b* Northampton, 23 May 1901; *s* of Edmund James and Mary Jane Rubbra; *m* 1975, Colette Yardley. *Educ:* Northampton; University of Reading; Royal College of Music. Hon. LLD Leicester, 1959; Hon. DMus Durham, 1949; Hon. DLitt Reading, 1978. Orchestral works include: eleven symphonies; two overtures; Sinfonia Concertante for piano and orchestra; Concertos for piano, violin, and viola; Soliloquy for cello and small orchestra; Improvisation for Violin and orchestra; Improvisations on Virginal Pieces by Giles Farnaby; Variations for Brass Band; Brahms-Handel Variations scored for full orchestra. Opera, The Shadow. Chamber works include: Sonatas for violin and piano, cello and piano, oboe and piano; duo for cor anglais and piano; 2 Piano Trios; four string quartets; Lyric Movement for piano and string quartet; Phantasy for two violins and piano; Introduction and Fugue for piano; Eight Preludes for piano; Prelude and Fugue on a Theme by Cyril Scott for piano; Pezzo Ostinato for harp solo; Transformations for solo harp; Discourse for harp and 'cello; The Buddha Suite for flute, oboe and string trio; Meditazioni for recorder and harpsichord; Fantasia on a Theme of Machaut for recorder and string quartet; Notturno for four recorders; Passacaglia sopra Plusieurs Regrets for recorder and harpsichord; Sonatina for recorder and harpsichord; Fantasia on a Chord, for recorder, harpsichord and gamba; 3 works for unaccomp. violin, viola and cello. Vocal works include: 9 Motets; 7 Madrigals; Festival Gloria for double choir; 2 4-part Masses; 3-part Mass; Missa Brevis for 3-part treble choir and organ; Missa Cantuariensis for double choir; The Morning Watch for choir and orchestra; The Dark Night of the Soul for Choir and orchestra; Song of the Soul for choir, strings, harp and timpani; In die et nocte canticum for choir and orchestra; Inscape for choir, strings and harp; Veni, Creator Spiritus, for Choir and Brass; 3 Psalms for low voice and piano; Advent Cantata for baritone, choir and small orchestra; Amoretti for tenor and string quartet; 5 Spenser Sonnets for tenor and string orchestra; 4 Medieval Latin Lyrics for baritone and string orchestra; The Jade Mountain, five songs for harp and voice; Magnificat and Nunc Dimittis for choir and organ; Te Deum for choir, solo, and orchestra; Cantata, in Honorem Mariae Matris Dei, for choir, boys' voices, soprano and alto soli, and orchestra; Ode to the Queen for Voice and orchestra; Tenebrae settings for unaccompanied choir; Two Sonnets by William Alabaster for voice, viola and piano; Cantata Pastorale for voice, recorder, harpsichord and cello; Autumn for 3-part female choir and piano; The Beatitudes for 3-part female choir unaccompanied; Anthems: Up O my soul; And when the Builders; Lord, with what care; This Spiritual House Almighty God shall inhabit; Blessed is He; Prayer for the Queen; motet, How shall my tongue express?; 3 Greek folk songs; The Givers for 4-part unaccompanied choir; Cantata di camera Crucifixus pro nobis; Te Deum for 8-part unaccompanied choir; Lauda Sion, for unaccompanied double choir; Agnus Dei, for 4-part unaccompanied choir; Creature-Songs to Heaven, for 3-part treble voices, piano and strings; numerous songs. *Publications:* Counterpoint: A Survey; Holst: A monograph; ed Casella, The Evolution of Music, rev. and enl. edn; Collected Essays on Gustav Holst. *Address:* Lindens, Bull Lane, Gerrards Cross, Bucks SL9 8RU. *T:* Gerrards Cross 84650.
See also A. A. Rubbra.

RUBENS, Bernice Ruth; writer and director of documentary films, since 1957; *b* 26 July 1928; *m* 1947, Rudi Nassauer; two *d. Educ:* University of Wales, Cardiff (BA, Hons English; Fellow 1982). Followed teaching profession, 1950-55. American Blue Ribbon award for documentary film, Stress, 1968. *Publications:* Set on Edge, 1960; Madame Sousatzka, 1962; Mate in Three, 1965; The Elected Member, 1969 (Booker Prize, 1970); Sunday Best, 1971; Go Tell the Lemming, 1973; I Sent a Letter to my Love, 1975; The Ponsonby Post, 1977; A Five Year Sentence, 1978; Spring Sonata, 1979; Birds of Passage, 1981. *Recreation:* plays piano and 'cello. *Address:* 89 Greencroft Gardens, NW6 3LJ. *T:* 01-328 1415.

RUBIN, Kenneth Warnell; His Honour Judge Rubin; a Circuit Judge since 1972; *b* 8 March 1920; *s* of late Albert Reginald Rubin and late Mary Eales Rubin; *m* 1948, Jeanne Marie Louise de Wilde; one *s* two *d. Educ:* King's College Sch., Wimbledon; King's Coll., London (LLB). Served HM Forces, 1939-45. Called to Bar, Gray's Inn, 1948. *Address:* Tyrrellswood, Shere Road, West Horsley, Surrey. *T:* East Horsley 2848.

RUBINSTEIN, Arthur, Hon. KBE 1977; pianist; *b* Lodz, Poland, 28 January 1887; *m* 1932, Aniela Mlynarska; two *s* two *d. Educ:* under Joachim, Prof. Heinrich Barth, Robert Kahn and Max Bruch. Gave many concerts in Russia, Poland, Germany, Austria; made first appearance in Spain in 1915, followed by 120 concerts in Spain alone; later in Latin America, where made 13 tours; since 1924 has toured Europe extensively; again in US, 1937, and became American Citizen. Toured Far East. Since 1945, every year, has made tours in US and all Western Europe (but refused to play in Germany, 1914-). In 1961 gave 10 recitals at Carnegie Hall, New York, in 4 weeks' time, all for 10 different charities. Appeared Festival Hall, London, 1954, 1955, 1956, 1957, 1960, 1962, 1963, 1965, 1968, 1969, 1970, 1972. US Medal of Freedom, 1976; holds several foreign Orders. Doctor *hc :* Yale Univ.; Brown Univ.; Northwestern Univ.; Hon. Member: Acad. Santa Cecilia, Rome; Acad. of Brazil; Gold Medal, Beethoven, Roy. Phil. Society. *Publications:* My Young Years,

1973; My Many Years, 1980. *Address:* 22 square de l'avenue Foch, 75116 Paris, France.

RUBINSTEIN, Hilary Harold; Joint Chairman, A. P. Watt Ltd (Literary Agents), since 1965; *b* 24 April 1926; *s* of H. F. and Lina Rubinstein; *m* 1955, Helge (*née* Kitzinger); three *s* one *d. Educ:* Cheltenham Coll.; Merton Coll., Oxford (MA). Editorial Dir, Victor Gollancz Ltd, 1952-63; Special Features Editor, The Observer, 1963-64; Dep. Editor, The Observer Magazine, 1964-65. Mem. Council, ICA, 1976-. Founder-editor, The Good Hotel Guide (published in USA as Europe's Wonderful Little Hotels and Inns), 1978-. *Publication:* The Complete Insomniac, 1974. *Recreations:* hotel-watching, reading in bed. *Address:* 61 Clarendon Road, W11 4BR. *T:* 01-727 9550. *Club:* Garrick.
See also M. B. Rubinstein.

RUBINSTEIN, Michael Bernard; Senior Partner with Rubinstein Callingham, Solicitors, since 1976; *b* 6 Nov. 1920; *s* of late H. F. Rubinstein and Lina (*née* Lowy); *m* 1955, Joy Douthwaite; two *s* two *d. Educ:* St Paul's Sch. Admitted solicitor, 1948. Served War, RE (TA), 1939, and RA; Captain 1945. Sen. Partner, Rubinstein, Nash & Co., 1969; on merging of two firms, Sen. Partner in Rubinstein Callingham. Mem., Lord Chancellor's Cttee on Defamation, 1971-74. Trustee: Soc. for Promotion of New Music, 1967-; Areopagitica Educnl Trust, 1979-. Occasional TV and radio broadcasting. *Publications:* (ed and contrib.) Wicked, Wicked Libels, 1972; Rembrandt and Angels (monograph), 1982; contrib. legal jls. *Recreations:* ruminating, practising. *Address:* 6 Raymond Buildings, Gray's Inn, WC1R 5BZ. *T:* 01-242 8404. *Club:* Garrick.
See also H. H. Rubinstein.

RUBINSTEIN, Prof. Nicolai, FBA 1971; FRHistS; Professor of History, Westfield College, London University, 1965-78, now Emeritus; *b* 13 July 1911; *s* of Bernhard and Irene Rubinstein; *m* 1954, Ruth Kidder Olitsky. *Educ:* Univs of Berlin and Florence. LittD Florence. Lectr, UC Southampton, 1942-45; Lectr, 1945-62, Reader, 1962-65, Westfield Coll., Univ. of London. Corresp. Mem., Accad. Toscana La Colombaria, 1976. Serena Medal, British Acad., 1974. *Publications:* The Government of Florence under the Medici 1434-94, 1966; (ed) Florentine Studies: politics and society in Renaissance Florence, 1968; Gen. Editor, Letters of Lorenzo de'Medici and ed vol. 3, 1977, and vol. 4, 1981; articles in Jl of Warburg and Courtauld Insts, Italian Studies, Archivio Storico Italiano, Rinascimento, etc. *Address:* 16 Gardnor Mansions, Church Row, NW3. *T:* 01-435 6995.

RUBNER, Ben; General Secretary, Furniture, Timber and Allied Trades Union, since 1976; *b* 30 Sept. 1921; *s* of Charles and Lily Rubner; *m* 1952, Amelia Sonia Bagnari; one *s* one *d. Educ:* Mansford Street Central Sch., Bethnal Green, E2. Apprentice cabinet maker, 1935; Mem. Cttee, Trade Union Br., 1937. Served war in armed forces, Royal Corps of Signals: N Africa, Italy, Sicily, 1941-46. Shop Steward, Sec., Chm. and Convenor, London Furniture Workers Shop Stewards Council, 1947-52; NUFTO: London Dist Cttee, 1954; Gen. Exec. Council, 1958; London Dist Organiser, 1959. Nat. Trade Organiser, 1963; Asst Gen. Sec., FTAT, 1973-76. British TUC: London Delegate, 1955-58; full-time Officer Deleg., 1974-77. *Recreations:* music (opera, light and grand), chess, table tennis, swimming. *Address:* 116 Arcadian Gardens, Wood Green, N22 5AE. *T:* 01-888 6956. *Club:* Cambridge and Bethnal Green Old Boys.

RUBYTHON, Eric Gerald, CBE 1978; Member of Aerospace Board, British Aerospace, since 1977 (Deputy Chief Executive of Aircraft Group, 1977-82); *b* 11 Feb. 1921; *s* of Reginald Rubython and Bessie Rubython; *m* 1943, Joan Ellen Mills. Joined Hawker Aircraft Ltd, 1948; Co. Sec., 1953; Exec. Dir, 1959; Dir and Gen. Man., 1960; Divl Dir and Gen. Man., Hawker Blackburn Div., 1963; Hawker Siddeley Aviation: Commercial Dir, 1965; Dir and Gen. Manager, 1970; Chm. and Man. Dir, 1977. *Recreations:* golf, gardening. *Address:* Brayfield, Wonersh Park, Wonersh, near Guildford, Surrey. *T:* Guildford 892018.

RUCK, Peter Frederick C.; *see* Carter-Ruck.

RUCK KEENE, John Robert, CBE 1977 (MBE 1946); TD 1950; Secretary General, Royal Society of Chemistry, 1980-81; *b* 2 Jan. 1917; *s* of late Major Robert Francis Ruck Keene, OBE, and Dorothy Mary (*née* Chester); *m* 1951, Beryl Mary Manistre; two *s. Educ:* Eton; Trinity Coll., Cambridge (BA 1938, MA 1955). Commissioned TA, Oxford and Bucks LI, 1939; served UK and NW Europe, 1939-45 (Major 1944, MBE 1946). First appointment with Chemical Society, 1946; General Secretary, 1947-80, when the Royal Society of Chemistry was formed by unification under Royal Charter of The Chemical Society and The Royal Institute of Chemistry, 1 June 1980. Hon. FRSC, 1982. *Address:* Chenies Cottage, 8 Copperkins Grove, Amersham, Bucks HP6 5QD. *T:* Amersham 7123.

RUCKER, Sir Arthur Nevil, KCMG 1942; CB 1941; CBE 1937; Chairman of Stevenage New Town Corporation, 1962-66 (Vice-Chairman, 1956-62); *b* 20 June 1895; *o s* of late Sir Arthur Rucker, FRS, and Lady Rucker of Everington House, nr Newbury; *m* 1922, Elsie Marion Broadbent; two *s* two *d. Educ:* Marlborough; Trinity College, Cambridge. Served European War (12th Suffolk Regiment, Lieutenant), 1915-18; entered Civil Service as Assistant Principal, 1920; Private Secretary to successive Ministers of Health, 1928-36; Director of Establishments and Public Relations, Ministry of Health,

1937-39; Principal Private Secretary to Prime Minister, 1939-40; seconded for special duties, 1941, returned to Ministry of Health as Deputy Secretary, 1943; Deputy Director-General, IRO, 1948. Deputy Agent-General of the UN Korean Reconstruction Agency, 1951; Member Commonwealth War Graves Commission, 1956-69. Hon. LLD Wales, 1965. Korean Order of Diplomatic Merit, Heung-in Medal, 1974. *Address:* Manor Farm House, Yattendon, Berks. *T:* Hermitage 201205. *Club:* Athenæum.

RUDD-JONES, Derek, CBE 1981; PhD; Director, Glasshouse Crops Research Institute, Littlehampton, Sussex, since 1971; Member, British Crop Protection Council, since 1968; *b* 13 April 1924; 2nd *s* of late Walter Henry Jones and late Doris Mary, *er d* of H. Rudd Dawes; *m* 1948, Joan, 2nd *d* of late Edward Newhouse, Hong Kong, and Malvern, Worcs; two *s* one *d. Educ:* Whitgift; Repton; Emmanuel Coll., Cambridge. BA, MA, PhD (Cantab); FIBiol. Agricultural Research Council, postgrad. student, Botany Sch., Univ. of Cambridge, 1945-48; Plant Pathologist, E African Agric. and Forestry Research Org., Kenya, 1949-52; Nat. Research Council, Postdoctoral Fellow, Univ. of Saskatchewan, Saskatoon, Canada, 1952-53. ICI Ltd, Akers Research Laboratory, The Frythe, Welwyn, Herts, 1953-56; Jealott's Hill Research Station, Bracknell, Berks, 1956-59; Scientific Adviser to Sec., Agricl Research Council, 1959-71; Foundn Chm., British Crop Protection Council, 1968-72; Pres., Section K, BAAS, 1981-82; formerly Mem., Adv. Cttee on Pesticides and Other Toxic Chemicals; Vis. Fellow, Univ. of Southampton, 1975-. *Publications:* scientific papers in Nature, Annals Applied Biol., Jl Experimental Botany, etc. *Recreations:* gardening, riding, fly-fishing. *Address:* Bignor Park Cottage, near Pulborough, West Sussex RH20 1HQ. *Club:* Farmers'.

RUDDEN, Prof. Bernard (Anthony), PhD; Professor of Comparative Law, University of Oxford, since 1979; Fellow of Brasenose College, Oxford, since 1979; *b* 21 Aug. 1933; *s* of John and Kathleen Rudden; *m* 1957, Nancy Campbell Painter; three *s* one *d. Educ:* City of Norwich Sch.; St John's Coll., Cambridge. MA Cantab and Oxon; PhD Wales. Solicitor. Fellow and Tutor, Oriel Coll., Oxford, 1965-79. *Publications:* Soviet Insurance Law, 1966; co-author or editor of: The Law of Mortgages, 1967; Source-Book on French Law, 1973 (2nd edn 1978); Basic Community Laws, 1980; The Law of Property, 1982; contrib. periodical pubns. *Address:* Brasenose College, Oxford. *T:* Oxford 48641. *Club:* United Oxford & Cambridge University.

RUDDEN, James; Advisory Head Teacher on Secondary Reorganisation, ILEA, 1976-78; President: National Association of Head Teachers, 1971; London Head Teachers Association, 1969; Metropolitan Catholic Teachers Association, 1964; *b* 11 Dec. 1911; *s* of Bernard and Mary Rudden; *m* 1937, Eileen Finlay; one *s* four *d. Educ:* Carlisle Grammar Sch.; St Mary's Coll., Twickenham. BSc (Special, Geo.) (London Univ.); Teacher's Cert. (London Univ.). Asst Teacher, Carlisle, 1933-47; served War, RAF Educn Officer, 1940-45. First Head: St Cuthbert's Sec. Mod. Sch., Carlisle, 1948-52; St Thomas More Sec. Mod. Sch., Tottenham, 1952-59; Bishop Thomas Grant Comprehensive Sch., Streatham, 1959-75. External Examnr for BEd, Avery Hill Coll. Chairman: London Comprehensive Head Teachers Conf., 1974-75; Southwark Diocesan Schs Commn; Governing Body of Schs Council; Adv. Council for Supply and Trng of Teachers. KSG 1969. *Publications:* numerous articles on educnl topics in educational and national press. *Recreation:* indulgence in retirement pursuits. *Address:* 5 The Gorse, Rissington Road, Bourton-on-the-Water, Glos. *T:* Bourton-on-the-Water 21052.

RUDÉ, Prof. George Frederick Elliot; Professor of History, Concordia University, Montreal, since 1970; *b* 8 Feb. 1910; *s* of Jens Essendrop Rude, Norway, and Amy Geraldine Elliot Rude, England; *m* 1940, Doreen, *d* of J. W. De la Hoyde, Dublin; no *c. Educ:* Shrewsbury Sch.; Trinity Coll., Cambridge. Dr of Letters (Adelaide), 1967. Taught at: Stowe Sch., Bucks, 1931-35; St Paul's Sch., London, 1936-49; Sir Walter St John's Sch., London, 1950-54; Holloway Sch., London, 1954-59; Univ. of Adelaide: Sen. Lectr in History, 1960-63; Prof. of History, 1964-67; Prof. of History, Flinders Univ., SA, 1968-70; Leverhulme Vis. Prof., Univ. of Tokyo, Sept.-Nov. 1967; Vis. Prof., Univ. of Stirling, 1968; Vis. Prof. Fellow, Univ. of Sussex, 1979-82; Vis. Prof., Coll. of William and Mary, Williamsburg, USA, 1980-81. Mem., Australian Research Grants Cttee, 1969. Alexander Prize, Roy. Hist. Soc., 1955. FRHistSoc. 1957; Fellow, Australian Acad. of Humanities, 1963. *Publications:* The Crowd in the French Revolution, 1959; Wilkes and Liberty, 1962; Revolutionary Europe 1783-1815, 1964; The Crowd in History, 1964; (ed) The Eighteenth Century 1715-1815, 1965; (ed) Robespierre, 1967; (with E. J. Hobsbawm) Captain Swing, 1969; Paris and London in the 18th Century, 1970; Hanoverian London 1714-1808, 1971; Debate on Europe 1815-1850, 1972; Europe in the Eighteenth Century, 1972; Robespierre, 1975; Protest and Punishment, 1978; Ideology and Popular Protest, 1980; contribs to Eng. Hist. Review, Eng. Econ. Hist. Review, Revue Historique, Past and Present, etc. *Recreations:* swimming, reading, public speaking. *Address:* Concordia University, Sir George Williams Campus, Montreal, PQ, Canada; The Oast House, Hope Farm, Beckley, Rye, Sussex TN31 6TU.

RUDGARD, Ven. Richard Cuthbert, OBE 1944; TD 1950; Rector of Ellisfield and Farleigh Wallop, Basingstoke, 1960-74, and of Dumme, 1968-74; Archdeacon of Basingstoke and Canon of Winchester, 1958-71; now Archdeacon Emeritus; *b* 28 Dec. 1901; *e s* of Canon R. W. and Mrs E. M. Rudgard; *m* 1st, 1933, Mary M. McLean (decd); one *s*; 2nd, 1939, Maisie M. Cooke. *Educ:* Radley College; St Augustine's College, Canterbury. With

Melanesian Mission, 1922-33. Assistant Priest, Heene, Worthing, 1934; Rector of Newbold Pacey with Moreton Morrell, 1936-45; Rector of Eversley, 1946-60; Rural Dean of Odiham, 1953-59. War of 1939-45 (despatches thrice); Chaplain to the Forces, TA, 1939; SCF 1st Armoured Division, 1942, N Africa; DACG 13 Corps, 1943, Sicily and Italy; Personal Chaplain to Chaplain General, 1944-46. DACG (TA) Southern Command, 1947-56. Hon. Chaplain to the Queen, 1954-56. *Recreations:* riding and tennis. *Address:* Clevedale Cottage, 22 Christchurch Road, Winchester SO23 9SS. *T:* Winchester 61419.

RUDKIN, Walter Charles, CBE 1981; Director of Economic and Logistic Intelligence, Ministry of Defence, since 1982; *b* 22 Sept. 1922; *e s* of Walter and Bertha Rudkin; *m* 1950, Hilda Mary Hope; two *s*. *Educ:* Carre's Grammar Sch., Sleaford; UC Hull. BSc (Econ) London. Served with RAF, 1942-46. Lectr, Dept of Econs and Econ. History, Univ. of Witwatersrand, 1948-52. Entered Min. of Defence, 1954; various appts, incl. Hong Kong, 1956-59; Junior Directing Staff, Imperial Defence Coll., 1962-64; Cabinet Office, 1968-71; Dir of Economic Intelligence, MoD, 1973-81. *Recreation:* fishing. *Address:* 85 Kingsway, Petts Wood, Orpington, Kent BR5 1PW. *T:* Orpington 22603. *Club:* Royal Commonwealth Society.

RUDMAN, Michael Edward; theatre director and producer; Associate Director, National Theatre, since 1979 (Director, Lyttelton Theatre, 1979-81); *b* Tyler, Texas, 14 Feb. 1939; *s* of M. B. Rudman and Josephine Davis; *m* 1963, Veronica Anne Bennett (marr. diss. 1981); two *d*. *Educ:* St Mark's Sch., Texas; Oberlin Coll. (BA *cum laude* Govt); St Edmund Hall, Oxford (MA). Pres., OUDS, 1963-64. Asst Dir and Associate Producer, Nottingham Playhouse and Newcastle Playhouse, 1964-68; Asst Dir, RSC, 1968; Artistic Director: Traverse Theatre Club, 1970-73; Hampstead Theatre, 1973-78 (Theatre won Evening Standard Award for Special Achievement, 1978). *Plays directed* include: Nottingham Playhouse: Changing Gear, Measure for Measure, A Man for All Seasons, 1965; Julius Caesar, She Stoops to Conquer, Who's Afraid of Virginia Woolf, Death of a Salesman, Moll Flanders (own musical version), 1966; Long Day's Journey into Night, 1967; Lily in Little India, 1968; RSC Theatreground: The Fox and the Fly, 1968; Traverse Theatre: Curtains (transf. Open Space, 1971), Straight Up (transf. Piccadilly, 1971), A Game called Arthur (transf. Theatre Upstairs, 1971), Stand for my Father, (with Mike Wearing) A Triple Bill of David Halliwell plays, 1970; The Looneys, Pantagleize, 1971; Carravagio Buddy, Tell Charlie Thanks for the Truss, The Relapse, 1972; Hampstead Theatre: Ride across Lake Constance, A Nightingale in Bloomsbury Square, 1973; The Black and White Minstrels, The Show-off, The Connection, The Looneys, 1974; Alphabetical Order (transf. May Fair), 1975; Clouds, 1977; Cakewalk, Beyond a Joke, Gloo-Joo (transf. Criterion), 1978; National Theatre: For Services Rendered (televised, 1980), Death of a Salesman, 1979; Thee and Me, The Browning Version and Harlequinade, 1980; The Second Mrs Tanqueray, 1981; West End: Donkeys Years, Globe, 1976; Clouds, Duke of York's, 1978; Taking Steps, Lyric, 1980; New York: The Changing Room, 1973; Hamlet, 1976; *plays produced or co-produced* include: Traverse Theatre: As Time Goes By, Do It, Lay By, 1971; Flowers, 1972; Hampstead Theatre: Dusa, Fish, Stas and Vi, 1976 (also May Fair, 1977); Abigail's Party, 1977; Bodies, 1978; Translations (also National), 1981; National Theatre: Watch on the Rhine, On the Razzle, 1981. Founder Mem., Jt Equity Cttee (to reform British and American Equity in the matter of free exchange of artists), 1980-. Director: Hampstead Theatre, 1979-; Tres-Tex Oil and Gas, 1981-. *Recreations:* golf, Tottenham Hotspur. *Address:* c/o Peter Murphy Esq., Curtis Brown Group, 1 Craven Hill, W2. *T:* 01-262 1011. *Clubs:* Royal Automobile; Dyrham Park Country, Vanderbilt Raquet, Cumberland Lawn Tennis.

RUDOE, Wulf; CB 1975; *b* 9 March 1916; *m* 1942, Ellen Trilling; one *s* one *d*. *Educ:* Central Foundation School; Peterhouse, Cambridge (Open Schol. and Research Schol.). Mathematics Tripos Pt III, 1938, Distinction. Royal Aircraft Establishment, 1939. Operational Research, RAF, 1939-45. Operational Research in Building Industry, Min. of Works, 1946-48, Principal Scientific Officer 1948; Board of Trade, Statistician 1948, Chief Statistician 1952; Dir of Statistics and Research, DHSS (formerly Min. of Health), 1966-76; Asst Sec., Price Commn, 1976-79; Adviser to Govt of Ghana, 1980-81. Fellow Inst. of Statisticians; Mem. Council, 1962-78, Hon. Treasurer, 1965-74, Vice-Pres., 1974-75 and 1976-77, Roy. Statistical Soc. *Recreations:* walking, travel, languages. *Address:* 72 North End Road, NW11. *T:* 01-455 2890.

RUE, Dr (Elsie) Rosemary, CBE 1977; Regional Medical Officer, Oxford Regional Health Authority, since 1973; *b* 14 June 1928; *d* of Harry and Daisy Laurence; divorced; two *s*. *Educ:* Sydenham High Sch.; Univ. of London; Oxford Univ. Med. School. MB, BS, FRCP, DCH, FRCPsych, FFCM. Gen. Practitioner, 1952-58; Public Health Service, 1958-65; Hospital Service, 1965-73; SAMO, Oxford RHB, 1971. *Publications:* papers on gen. practice, women in medicine, ward design, community hosps, health services, individuals requiring security. *Address:* 2 Stanton St John, Oxford. *T:* Oxford 64861.

RUEGGER, Paul J.; Swiss diplomat and jurist; *b* 14 August 1897; *s* of Prof. J. Ruegger; *m* 1st, 1932, Countess Isabella Salazar y Munatones (*d* 1969); 2nd, 1971, Marquise Isabella Francesca Fossi. *Educ:* College Lucerne; Univs of Lausanne, Munich, and Zürich (Doctor of Law). Attaché at Swiss Foreign Office and Sec. Swiss Advisory Cttee for League of Nations and post-war problems, 1918; Secretary of the Swiss Delegation to the League of Nations,

1920-25 (technical adviser, 1923-25); Sec. Swiss Delegation to Internat. Econ. Conf. of Genoa, 1922; Asst Prof. of Internat. Law, Univ. of Geneva, 1922-24; Legal Adviser to Swiss Delegation Conference for control of trade of arms, etc., 1925; Deputy Registrar Permanent Court of International Justice, 1926-28; Counsellor Swiss Legation in Rome, 1929-31; Head of Political Office Foreign Affairs Dept in Berne, 1931-33; 1st Counsellor of the Swiss Legation in Paris, 1933-36; Swiss Minister in Rome, 1936-42; Swiss Minister to Great Britain, 1944-48. Head of the Swiss Delegation for establishment of a Convention between Switzerland and UN on diplomatic privileges and immunities of UNO establishments in Switzerland; member of Swiss Deleg. to last League of Nations Assembly, Geneva, 1946; President Internat. Committee of Red Cross, 1948-55, Chm. 1968-; Chm. ILO Committee on Forced Labour, 1956-60. Prof. of Human Rights, Univ. of Strasbourg, 1964. Member of: Perm. Court of Arbitration, 1948-; Curatorium of Acad. of Internat. Law, at The Hague; Inst. of Internat. Law, 1967-69 (1st Vice-Pres., 1967-69; Hon. Mem., 1979); Commissions of Conciliation: between Switzerland and USA; between Switzerland and Spain; between France and the Netherlands; between Sweden and Denmark (Chm.); UN Nansen Medal Award Cttee, UN High Commn for Refugees, 1958-78. Ambassador, 1957; Chm. Swiss Deleg. to UN Conf. on Law of the Sea, Geneva, 1958 and 1960, and to UN Confs on Diplomatic Relations and Immunities, Vienna, 1961; on Consular Relations and Immunities, Vienna, 1963; on Law of Treaties, Vienna, 1968 and 1969; Chm. Cttee of UN Atomic Energy Agency, Vienna, on Civil Liability and Internat. Responsibility for Nuclear Hazards, 1959-62; Chm. ILO Arbitral Commn, Ghana-Portugal, 1961-62; Pres., prep. UN Conf., 1964, and of conf. of plenipotentiaries, New York, on transit trade of land-locked countries, 1965; Chm., Study Gp on Labour and Trade Union Situation in Spain, 1968-69. Hon. Pres., Acad. Mondiale pour la Paix, Nice, 1978. Gold Medal, Red Cross Internat. Cttee, and other Red Cross awards; Grand Cross of Merit, SMO Malta, 1949. *Publications:* The Nationality of Corporations in International Law, 1918; Terms of Civil Law in International Law, 1920; The Responsibility of States for Crimes committed on their Territory, 1923; The Practice of International Conciliation Committees, 1929; Foreign Administration as Institutional Function of Intercourse between States, 1934; The Economic Foundations of International Law, 1931; Switzerland's Economy and the British Empire, 1946; The Juridical Aspects of the Organisation of the International Red Cross, 1953; Swiss Neutrality and European Integration, 1953; Notes of the International Responsibility of States for Nuclear Hazards, in Mélanges Séféréades, 1961; Introduction to Max Huber's Denkwürdigkeiten, and book on Max Huber, 1974; Le Rôle Actuel et Futur des Commissions Internationales d'Enquête, 1980, etc. *Address:* Villa il Pino, 267 Via Bolognese, Florence, Italy; Palazzo Fossi, 16 Via de'Benci, Florence, Italy. *Club:* Circolo dell' Unione (Florence).

See also Baron Armstrong.

RUETE, Dr jur. Hans Hellmuth; Ambassador of the Federal Republic of Germany at the Court of St James's, 1977-79; *b* 21 Dec. 1914; *s* of Prof. Dr med. Alfred E. Ruete and Margarita (*née* Bohnstedt); *m* 1948, Ruth (*née* Arfsten); one *s* two *d*. *Educ:* Univs of Kiel, Lausanne, Marburg, Tokyo (Political Science and Law). Doctor's Degree in Law. Judge at Ministry of Justice in Hesse, 1949-50; then at Federal Min. of Justice; Federal Foreign Office, 1952-; Tokyo, 1952-56; Bonn, 1956-60 (Head of Russian Desk); Center for International Affairs, Harvard Univ., 1960-61; Consul-Gen., Calcutta, 1961-64; Dept for Eastern Affairs, Bonn, 1964-70; Ambassador: Paris, 1970-72; Warsaw, 1972-77. *Publication:* Der Einfluss des abendländischen Rechts auf die Rechtsentwicklung in China und Japan, 1940. *Recreations:* music, literature, theatre. *Address:* Petersbergstrasse 64, 5300 Bonn-Bad Godesberg, Federal Republic of Germany.

RUFF, William Willis, CBE 1973; DL; Clerk of the Surrey County Council, 1952-74; Member, Parliamentary Boundary Commission for England, since 1974; *b* 22 Sept. 1914; *s* of late William Ruff, Whitby, Yorks; *m* 1939, Agnes, *d* of late Howard Nankivell; two *s*. *Educ:* Durham School. Served War of 1939-45: Royal Signals, North Africa and India, 1940-45; Capt., 1942; Maj., 1943. Asst Solicitor: Scarborough Corp., 1937; Heston and Isleworth Corp., 1938; Surrey County Council: Asst Solicitor, 1939; Senior Asst Solicitor, 1947; Asst Clerk, 1948; Deputy Clerk, 1951. Chm., Soc. of Clerks of Peace and of Clerks of County Councils, 1969-72. DL Surrey, 1964. *Recreations:* music, watching cricket. *Address:* 3 Brympton Close, Ridgeway Road, Dorking, Surrey. *T:* Dorking 882406.

RUFFLE, Mary, (Mrs Thomas Ruffle); *see* Dilnot, Mary.

RUGAMBWA, HE Cardinal Laurean; *see* Dar-es-Salaam, Archbishop of, (RC).

RUGBY, 2nd Baron, *cr* 1947, of Rugby; **Alan Loader Maffey;** farmer and inventor; *b* 16 April 1913; *s* of 1st Baron Rugby, GCMG, KCB, KCVO, CSI, CIE, and Dorothy Gladys, OBE 1919 (*d* 1973), *d* of late Charles Lang Huggins, JP, Hadlow Grange, Buxted; *S* father, 1969; *m* 1947, Margaret, *d* of late Harold Bindley; three *s* two *d* (and one *s* decd). *Educ:* Stowe. Served War of 1939-45, RAF. Inventor, Foldgate Herd Handler (RASE Silver Award, 1974). Mem. Court of Assistants, Saddlers' Co. (Master, 1978-79). *Heir: s* Hon. Robert Charles Maffey [*b* 4 May 1951; *m* 1974, Anne Penelope, *yr d* of late David Hale; two *s*]. *Address:* Grove Farm, Frankton, near Rugby, Warwicks.

RUGG, Sir (Edward) Percy, Kt 1959; JP; Councillor for Royal Borough of Kensington and Chelsea, Greater London Council, 1964-70; Leader of Conservative Party, on the Council, 1964-66; Chairman of Council, 1967-68; Councillor for Chelsea, LCC (Alderman, 1958-61; Leader of Conservative Party, on the LCC 1959-65); *b* 14 Jan. 1906; *s* of Albert Henry and Louise Rugg; *m* 1933, Elizabeth Frances Symes; two *s* one *d. Educ:* Leys Sch. Solicitor, 1929. Hertfordshire County Council, 1940-45. Chairman: Hertford Division Conservative Association, 1948-52; Ware Rural District Council, 1949-54; Junior Carlton Club Political Council, 1954-57; Commercial Law and International Arbitration Committee of British National Committee of International Chamber of Commerce, 1957-; Gen. Purposes Cttee, GLC, 1969-70; Heathrow Airport Consultative Cttee, 1969-70; President: East Herts Conservative Assoc., 1961-81; Chelsea Conservative Assoc., 1974-. Member: London Tourist Bd, 1968-69; BTA, 1969-. Fellow, Game Conservancy, 1977-. JP, Herts, 1949-; DL Greater London, 1967-82. Dep. Kt Pres., Hon. Soc. of Knights of Round Table; Friend, RCP, 1973-. OStJ 1980. *Recreation:* fishing. *Address:* 97 Rivermead Court, Hurlingham, SW6. *T:* 01-736 3996; 31 High Street, Sandwich, Kent. *T:* Sandwich 613018. *Clubs:* City Livery, Hurlingham; Royal St George's, Sandwich.

RUGGE-PRICE, Sir C. K. N.; *see* Price.

RUGGLES-BRISE, Captain Guy Edward, TD, DL; Associate, Brewin, Dolphin & Co., Stockbrokers; *b* 15 June 1914; *s* of late Col Sir Edward Archibald Ruggles-Brise, 1st Bt, MC, TD, DL, JP, MP, and Agatha, *e d* of J. H. Gurney, DL, JP, Keswick Hall, Norfolk; *b* and *heir pres.* of Sir John Ruggles-Brise, Bt, *qv; m* 1940, Elizabeth, *o d* of James Knox, Smithstone House, Kilwinning, Ayrshire; three *s. Educ:* Eton. Captain 104th (Essex Yeo.) Field Bde RHA (TA), No 7 Commando. Served War of 1939-45 (PoW). Vice-Chm., Pony Riding for the Disabled Trust, Chigwell, Essex, 1969. DL 1967, High Sheriff 1967, Essex. *Recreations:* field sports. *Address:* Housham Tye, Harlow, Essex. *T:* Matching 236; Ledgowan Lodge, Achnasheen, Ross-shire. *T:* Achnasheen 245; (business) 5 Giltspur Street, EC1. *Clubs:* Cavalry and Guards, City of London.

RUGGLES-BRISE, Col Sir John Archibald, 2nd Bt, *cr* 1935; CB 1958; OBE (mil.) 1945; TD; JP; Lord-Lieutenant of Essex, 1958-78; Pro-Chancellor, University of Essex, 1964-79; *b* 13 June 1908; *er s* of Colonel Sir Edward Archibald Ruggles-Brise, 1st Bt, MC, TD, DL, JP, MP, and Agatha (*d* 1937), *e d* of J. H. Gurney, DL, JP, of Keswick Hall, Norfolk; *S* father, 1942. *Educ:* Eton. Served AA Comd, 1939-45 (comd 1st 450 Mixed HAA Regt, and 2nd AA Demonstration and User Trials Regt); formed and comd 599 HAA Regt, 1947. Member of Lloyd's. Pres., CLA, 1957-59; Church Comr, 1959-64; Chm., Council of the Baronetage, 1958-63. Patron, Essex Agricl Soc., 1970-78. DL 1945, JP 1946, Vice-Lieutenant, 1947, Co. Essex. Hon. Freeman of Chelmsford. Governor of Felsted and Chigwell Schools, 1950-75. DUniv Essex, 1980. KStJ. *Recreation:* shooting. *Heir:* *b* Capt. Guy Edward Ruggles-Brise, *qv. Address:* Spains Hall, Finchingfield, Essex. *T:* Great Dunmow 810266. *Club:* Carlton.

RUHFUS, Dr Jürgen; Commander's Cross, Order of Merit, Federal Republic of Germany, 1978; Hon. KBE, 1978; Ambassador of the Federal Republic of Germany to the Court of St James's, since 1980; *b* 4 Aug. 1930; *m* ; three *d. Educ:* Universities of Munich and Münster; Univ. of Denver, Colo, USA. Joined Federal Foreign Office, Bonn, 1955; Consulate General: Geneva, 1956-57; Dakar, 1958-59; Embassy, Athens, 1960-63; Dep. Spokesman of Federal Foreign Office, 1964, Official Spokesman, 1966; Ambassador to Kenya, 1970-73; Asst Under-Secretary, Federal Foreign Office, 1973-76; Adviser on Foreign Policy and Defence Affairs to Federal Chancellor Helmut Schmidt, 1976-80. *Recreations:* golf, tennis, skiing, hunting. *Address:* 23 Belgrave Square, SW1. *T:* 01-235 5033.

RUIZ SOLER, Antonio, (Antonio); Cross of the Order of Isabella the Catholic, 1951; Comdr Order of Civil Merit, 1964; Spanish dancer; Director, Ballet Nacional Español; *b* Seville, 4 November 1921. Studied at the Realito Dance Academy. First stage appearance at the age of eight; subsequently toured North and South America Southern and Western Europe, and Scandinavia. First stage appearance in Great Britain, Edinburgh Festival, 1950; London début, Cambridge Theatre, 1951. Golden Medal, Fine Arts, 1952. Formed Ballet Company, 1953; début in Generalife Theatre, Granada, presenting his Ballet in Europe, S and N America. Has also appeared in many festivals in Spain. Appearances with Ballet in London: Stoll, 1954; Palace, 1956; Coliseum, 1958; Royalty, 1960; Drury Lane, 1963; Coliseum, 1975. Gala perf. in Washington to President Kennedy, Ed Sullivan Show in New York, appearances Europe, 1963. Festivals of Spain, 1964-65; Madrid Season, 1965; N Amer. tour, 1965; Ed Sullivan Show, 1965. Appears on TV. Gold Medal, Swedish Acad. of Dancing, 1963; Medal of Min. of Information and Tourism, Madrid, 1963; Golden Medal, Spanish Inst., NY, 1979. *Address:* Coslada 7, Madrid, Spain.

RUMBLE, Captain John Bertram, RN (retired); Director General, Royal Over-Seas League, since 1979; *b* 30 Oct. 1928; *s* of late Major Rumble and of Mrs Rumble; *m* 1953, Jennifer, *d* of late Col. R. H. Wilson, MC, CMG, and Ella Wilson; one *s* three *d. Educ:* Hordle House Sch.; Sherborne Sch. FBIM 1980, FIIM 1980. Special Entry Cadet into Royal Navy, 1946; ADC (Lieut) to Governor of Malta, 1952-53; specialised in Communications, 1954; HMS Maidstone, 1955-56; Staff, BRNC Dartmouth, 1956-57; Exchange Service with RCN, 1957-59; Signal Officer, HMS Ark Royal, 1959-61;

Comdr 1962; RN sc 1963; CO HMS Torquay, 1964-65; Staff Communications Officer to C-in-C EASTLANT, 1966-67; Exec. Officer, HMS Hermes, 1967-69; Captain 1970; Staff Dir, Gen. Weapons, 1970-71; CO HMS Fearless, 1974-75; Asst Chief of Staff Communications (as Cdre), C-in-C SOUTH, 1976-77; MoD (Intelligence), 1977-79. Younger Brother, Trinity House, 1977; Mem. Council, Mayfair, Piccadilly and St James's Assoc., 1979-. *Recreations:* shooting, sailing, fishing, gold leaf gilding. *Address:* 88 Wroughton Road, SW11. *T:* 01-223 9413; 2 Salterns View, Keyhaven, Hants. *T:* Milford-on-Sea 3462. *Clubs:* Farmers', Royal Navy of 1765 and 1785; Keyhaven Yacht.

RUMBLE, Peter William; Under-Secretary, Department of the Environment, since 1977; *b* 28 April 1929; *s* of Arthur Victor Rumble and Dorothy Emily (*née* Sadler); *m* 1953, Joyce Audrey Stephenson; one *s* one *d. Educ:* Harwich County High Sch.; Oriel Coll., Oxford (BA). Entered Civil Service, 1952; HM Inspector of Taxes, 1952; Principal, Min. of Housing and Local Govt, 1963; Asst Sec., Dept of the Environment, 1972. *Recreation:* music. *Address:* 11 Hillside Road, Cheam, Surrey SM2 6ET. *T:* 01-643 1752.

RUMBOLD, Sir Algernon; *see* Rumbold, Sir H. A. F.

RUMBOLD, Mrs Angela Claire Rosemary, CBE 1981; MP (C) Merton, Mitcham and Morden, since June 1982; *b* 11 Aug. 1932; *d* of Harry Jones, *qv* ; *m* 1955, John Marix Rumbold; two *s* one *d. Educ:* Notting Hill and Ealing High Sch.; King's Coll., London. Founder Member, National Assoc. for the Welfare of Children in Hospital, and National Chairman, 1974-76. Royal Borough of Kingston upon Thames: Councillor, 1974; Dep. Leader, 1976; Chairman: Education Cttee, 1978-79; Policy and Resources Cttee, 1979-81. Chairman: Educn Cttee, Assoc. of Metropolitan Authorities, 1979-80; Council, Local Educn Authorities, 1979-80. Member, Doctors and Dentists Review Body, 1979-82. Governor: Coombe Lodge Further Education Staff College, 1980-; Nat. Foundn for Educational Research, 1979-. *Recreations:* swimming, theatre, reading. *Address:* 18 Park Road, Surbiton, Surrey KT5 8QD.

RUMBOLD, Sir Anthony; *see* Rumbold, Sir H. A. C.

RUMBOLD, Sir (Horace) Algernon (Fraser), KCMG 1960 (CMG 1953); CIE 1947; *b* 27 Feb. 1906; *s* of late Colonel William Edwin Rumbold, CMG; *m* 1946, Margaret Adél, *d* of late Arthur Joseph Hughes, OBE; two *d. Educ:* Wellington College; Christ Church, Oxford. Assistant Principal, India Office, 1929; Private Sec. to Parliamentary Under-Secretaries of State for India, 1930-33, and to Permanent Under-Secretary of State, 1933-34; Principal, 1934; Asst Sec., transferred to Commonwealth Relations Office, 1947; Deputy High Commissioner in the Union of South Africa, 1949-53; Asst Under Sec. of State, 1954-58; Dep. Under Sec. of State, 1958-66; retired, 1966. Chm. Cttee on Inter-Territorial Questions in Central Africa, 1963; Advr, Welsh Office, 1967. Dep. Chm., Air Transport Licensing Bd, 1971-72. Mem. Governing Body, SOAS, 1965-80, Hon. Fellow, 1981. Pres., Tibet Soc. of the UK, 1977-. *Publication:* Watershed in India 1914-1922, 1979. *Address:* Shortwoods, West Clandon, Surrey. *T:* Guildford 222757. *Club:* Travellers'.

RUMBOLD, Sir (Horace) Anthony (Claude), 10th Bt, *cr* 1779; KCMG 1962 (CMG 1953); KCVO 1969; CB 1955; HM Diplomatic Service, retired; *b* 7 March 1911; *s* of Right Hon. Sir Horace Rumbold, 9th Bt, GCB, GCMG, MVO, and Etheldred, Lady Rumbold, CBE (*d* 1964), 2nd *d* of Sir Edmund Fane, KCMG; *m* 1st, 1937, Felicity Ann (marr. diss. 1974), *yr d* of late Lt-Col F. G. Bailey and late Lady Janet Bailey, Lake House, Salisbury, Wilts; one *s* three *d* ; 2nd, 1974, Mrs Pauline Graham, *d* of late Hon. David Tennant and of Hermione Baddeley, *qv. Educ:* Eton; Magdalen College, Oxford (BA). Fellow, Queen's Coll., Oxford, 1933. Third Sec. in the Foreign Office, 1935; transferred to Washington, 1937; Second Secretary, 1940; transferred to Foreign Office, 1942; served on staff of Resident Minister, Mediterranean, 1944; First Sec., 1945; transferred Prague, 1947; transferred to Foreign Office as Counsellor, 1949; transferred to Paris as Counsellor, 1951; appointed Principal Private Secretary to Foreign Secretary, 1954; Assistant Under-Secretary of State, Foreign Office, 1957; British Minister in Paris, 1960-63; Ambassador to Thailand and UK Representative on the Council of SEATO, 1965-67; Ambassador to Austria, 1967-70. Commander of the Order of St Olaf, 1955; Grand Cross of Order of Merit, Austria, 1969. *Heir:* *s* Henry John Sebastian Rumbold [*b* 24 Dec. 1947; *m* 1978, Mrs Holly Berry, *d* of late Dr A. Whitfield Hawkes and of Mrs Alistair Cooke]. *Address:* Var House, Stinsford, Dorchester, Dorset. *T:* Dorchester 62644. *Club:* Travellers'.

RUMBOLD, Jack Seddon, QC (Zanzibar) 1963; President of the Industrial Tribunals, England and Wales, since 1979; *b* 5 March 1920; *s* of William Alexander Rumbold and Jean Lindsay Rumbold (*née* Mackay), Christchurch, NZ; *m* 1st, 1949, Helen Suzanne, *d* of Col J. B. Davis, Wanganui, NZ; two *d* ; 2nd, 1970, Veronica Ellie Hurt (*née* Whigham). *Educ:* St Andrew's Coll., NZ; Canterbury Univ., NZ (LLB 1940); Brasenose Coll., Oxford (Rhodes Schol.; BCL 1948). Served Royal Navy, Lieut RNZNVR, 1941-45 (despatches). Called to Bar, Inner Temple, 1948; Crown Counsel, Kenya, 1957, Sen. Crown Counsel, 1959; Attorney General, Zanzibar, 1963; Legal Adviser, Kenya Govt, 1964-65; Academic Director, British Campus of Stanford Univ., USA, 1966-72; Chairman of Industrial Tribunals (part-time), 1968; (full-time) 1972; Regional Chairman (London South), 1977.

Recreations: books, music; formerly cricket (Oxford Blue). *Address:* 21 Chipstead Street, SW6 3SR. *T:* 01-736 2484. *Clubs:* United Oxford & Cambridge University, MCC.

RUNACRES, Eric Arthur; *b* 22 Aug. 1916; *s* of Arthur Selwyn Runacres and Mildred May Dye; *m* 1950, Penelope Jane Elizabeth Luxmoore; one *s* one *d. Educ:* Dulwich College; Merton College, Oxford. 1st cl. hons Lit. Hum. 1939. Commissioned Royal Engineers, Oct. 1939; served UK, Malta, Middle East, India, 1939-46 (Major). J. & P. Coats Ltd, 1946-48. Entered HM Foreign Service, 1948; First Secretary, 1951-53. British Productivity Council, 1954-71 (Deputy Director, 1959-71, and Secretary, 1962-71); Vice-Chm., OECD, Cttee on National Productivity Centres, 1960-66; Exec. Director, Commonwealth Agricultural Bureaux, 1973-77; Consultant, Industrial Facts & Forecasting Ltd, 1978-. *Recreations:* European thought and literature; gardening. *Address:* Meadow View, Stud Green, Holyport, Maidenhead, Berks SL6 2JG. *T:* Maidenhead 24828. *Club:* Naval and Military.

RUNCIE, Most Rev. and Rt. Hon. Robert Alexander Kennedy; *see* Canterbury, Archbishop of.

RUNCIMAN, family name of Viscount Runciman of Doxford.

RUNCIMAN OF DOXFORD, 2nd Viscount, *cr* 1937; **Walter Leslie Runciman,** OBE 1946; AFC; AE; DL; Bt 1906; Baron Runciman, 1933, of Shoreston; Director, Walter Runciman & Co. Ltd and other cos; *b* 26 Aug. 1900; *er s* of 1st Viscount Runciman of Doxford, PC, and Hilda (*d* 1956), MP (L) St Ives, 1928-29, *d* of J. C. Stevenson; *S* father 1949; *m* 2nd, 1932, Katherine Schuyler, *y d* of late Wm R. Garrison, New York; one *s. Educ:* Eton (King's Scholar); Trinity College, Cambridge (Scholar). Director, 1932, Dep. Chm., 1962-71, Lloyds Bank Ltd. Chm., North of England Shipowners Association, 1931-32 and 1970-71; Chairman of Council, Armstrong College, University of Durham, 1935-37; Director-General of British Overseas Airways Corporation, 1940-43; Air Commodore and Air Attaché, Tehran, 1943-46. Pres. Chamber of Shipping of the UK, and Chm. General-Council of British Shipping, 1952; Mem. Air Transport Advisory Council, 1946-54, Vice-Chm., 1951-54; President, RINA, 1951-61; Mem. Shipping Advisory Panel, 1962. Chairman: Cttee on Horticultural Marketing, 1955-56; Trustees, Nat. Maritime Museum, 1962-72; Adv. Cttee on Historic Wreck Sites, 1973-; British Hallmarking Council, 1974-. Cdre, RYS, 1968-74. Pres., Iran Soc., 1979-. Hon. Elder Brother of Trinity House. Hon. Mem., Hon. Co. of Master Mariners. DL Northumberland, 1961. Hon. DCL, Durham. *Recreations:* sailing, shooting. *Heir: s* Hon. Walter Garrison Runciman, *qv. Address:* 46 Abbey Lodge, Park Road, NW8; Doxford, Chathill, Northumberland. *Clubs:* Brooks's; Royal Yacht Squadron.

See also Hon. Sir Steven Runciman.

RUNCIMAN, Hon. Sir Steven; (James Cochran Stevenson), Kt 1958; FBA 1957; FSA 1964; MA; *b* 7 July 1903; 2nd *s* of 1st Viscount Runciman of Doxford, PC. *Educ:* Eton (King's Schol.); Trinity College, Cambridge (Schol.). Fellow of Trinity College, Cambridge, 1927-38 (Hon. Fellow 1965); Lecturer at the University of Cambridge, 1932-38; Press Attaché, British Legation, Sofia, 1940; British Embassy, Cairo, 1941; Professor of Byzantine Art and History in Univ. of Istanbul, 1942-45; Rep. Brit. Council in Greece, 1945-47. Lectures: Waynflete, Magdalen Coll., Oxford, 1953-54; Gifford, St Andrews, 1960-62; Birkbeck, Trinity Coll., Cambridge, 1966; Wiles, Queen's Univ., Belfast, 1968; Robb, Auckland, 1970; Regents', Los Angeles, California, 1971; Weir, Cincinnati, 1973. Alexander White Prof., Chicago, 1963. Mem. Advisory Council, Victoria and Albert Museum, 1957; Chairman: Anglo-Hellenic League, 1951-67; Nat. Trust for Greece, 1977-; Trustee: British Museum, 1960-67; Scottish Nat. Museum of Antiquities, 1972-77; Hon. Vice-Pres., RHistS; Vice-Pres., London Library; Chairman: Scottish Ballet Adv. Council; Curatorial Cttee, Nat. Trust for Scotland. Pres. British Inst. of Archæology at Ankara, 1960-75. For. Mem., American Philosophical Soc.; Corresp. Mem. Real Academia de Historia, Madrid. Hon. MRIA 1979. Hon. LittD Cambridge, 1955; Hon. LLD Glasgow, 1955; Hon. DLitt: Durham, 1956; St Andrews, 1969; Oxon, 1971; Birmingham, 1973; Hon. LitD London, 1966; Hon. DPhil Salonika, 1951; Hon. DD Wabash, USA, 1962; Hon. DHL Chicago, 1963; Hon. DHum Ball State Univ., 1973. Knight Commander, Order of the Phœnix (Greece), 1961. *Publications:* The Emperor Romanus Lecapenus, 1929; The First Bulgarian Empire, 1930; Byzantine Civilization, 1933; The Medieval Manichee, 1947; A History of the Crusades, Vol. I, 1951 (illustrated edn, as The First Crusade, 1980), Vol. II, 1952, Vol. III, 1954; The Eastern Schism, 1955; The Sicilian Vespers, 1958; The White Rajahs, 1960; The Fall of Constantinople, 1453, 1965; The Great Church in Captivity, 1968; The Last Byzantine Renaissance, 1970; The Orthodox Churches and the Secular State, 1972; Byzantine Style and Civilisation, 1975; The Byzantine Theocracy, 1977; Mistra, 1980; contributions to various historical journals. *Address:* Elshieshields, Lockerbie, Dumfriesshire DG11 1LY. *Club:* Athenæum.

RUNCIMAN, Hon. Walter Garrison, FBA 1975; Chairman, Walter Runciman & Co. Ltd and subsidiary companies, since 1976; Fellow, Trinity College, Cambridge, since 1971; *b* 10 Nov. 1934; *o s* and *heir* of 2nd Viscount Runciman of Doxford, *qv*.; *m* 1963, Ruth, *o d* of late Joseph Hellmann and Dr Ellen Hellmann, Johannesburg; one *s* two *d. Educ:* Eton (Oppidan Schol.); Trinity Coll., Cambridge (Schol.; Fellow, 1959-63, 1971-). National Service, 1953-55 (2/Lt, Grenadier Guards); Harkness Fellow, 1958-60; joined Walter Runciman & Co. Ltd, 1964; part-time Reader in Sociology, Univ. of Sussex,

1967-69; Visiting Lectr in Sociology, Harvard Univ., 1970; Vis. Fellow, Nuffield Coll., Oxford, 1979-. Treas., Child Poverty Action Gp, 1972-; Mem., SSRC, 1974-79. Mem., Gen. Policy Cttee, Gen. Council of British Shipping, 1977-. *Publications:* Plato's Later Epistemology, 1962; Social Science and Political Theory, 1963, 2nd edn 1969; Relative Deprivation and Social Justice, 1966, 2nd edn 1972; Sociology in its Place, and other essays, 1970; A Critique of Max Weber's Philosophy of Social Science, 1972; A Treatise on Social Theory: vol. I, 1983; articles in academic jls. *Address:* 36 Carlton Hill, NW8 0JY. *Club:* Brooks's.

RUNCORN, Prof. Stanley Keith, FRS 1965; Professor of Physics and Head of the School of Physics, University of Newcastle upon Tyne, since 1963, and in the University of Durham (King's College), 1956-63; *b* 19 November 1922; *s* of W. H. Runcorn, Southport, Lancs; unmarried. *Educ:* King George V Sch., Southport; Gonville and Caius Coll., Cambridge. ScD 1963. Radar Research and Devel. Establishment (Min. of Supply), 1943-46; Asst Lecturer, 1946-48, and Lecturer, 1948-49, in Physics, Univ. of Manchester; Asst Dir of Research in Geophysics, Cambridge Univ., 1950-55; Research Geophysicist, Univ. of California at Los Angeles, 1952 and 1953; Fellow of Gonville and Caius Coll., Cambridge, 1948-55; Visiting Scientist, Dominion Observatory, Ottawa, 1955; Vis. Prof. of Geophysics: Cal. Inst. of Tech., 1957; Univ. of Miami, 1966; Pa State Univ., 1967; Florida State Univ., 1968; UCLA, 1975; J. Ellerton Becker Senior Visiting Fellow, Australian Academy of Science, 1963; Res. Associate, Mus. of N Arizona, 1957-72; Rutherford Memorial Lectr (Kenya, Tanzania and Uganda), 1970; Halley Lectr, Oxford Univ., 1972-73; Hitchcock Foundn Prof., Univ. of California, Berkeley, 1981. Mem., NERC, 1965-69. Pres., Section A (Phys. and Maths), British Assoc., 1980-81. For. Mem., Indian Nat. Acad. of Science, 1980; Mem., Pontifical Acad. of Sciences, 1981. Napier Shaw Prize, Royal Met. Soc., 1959; Charles Chree Medal and Prize, Inst. of Physics, 1969; Vetlesen Prize, 1971. Hon. DSc: Utrecht, 1969; Ghent, 1971; Paris, 1979; Bergen, 1980. *Publications:* scientific papers. *Recreations:* usual. *Address:* University of Newcastle upon Tyne, Newcastle upon Tyne NE1 7RU.

RUNDALL, Sir Francis (Brian Anthony), GCMG 1968 (KCMG 1956; CMG 1951); OBE 1944; Ambassador to Japan, 1963-67; *b* 11 Sept. 1908; *s* of late Lieutenant-Colonel Charles Frank Rundall, CMG, DSO; *m* 1935, Mary, *d* of late Frank Syrett, MD; one *s* one *d. Educ:* Marlborough College; Peterhouse, Cambridge. Entered General Consular Service, 1930; served in Antwerp, Colon, Panama, Boston, Barcelona, Piraeus; Consul, New York, 1944; transferred Foreign Office, 1946; HM Inspector of Foreign Service Establishments, 1949-53. Chief Administrative Officer, UK High Commission in Germany during 1953; Consul-General in New York, 1953-57; Ambassador to Israel, 1957-59; Deputy Under-Secretary of State, Foreign Office, 1959-63. *Address:* Lime Tree Cottage, Church Oakley, Basingstoke, Hants. *T:* Basingstoke 780217. *Club:* Travellers'.

RUNDLE, Christopher John Spencer; HM Diplomatic Service; First Secretary, Tehran, since 1981; *b* 17 Aug. 1938; *s* of Percy William and Ruth Rundle (*née* Spencer); *m* 1970, Qamar Said. *Educ:* Cranbrook Sch.; St John's Coll., Cambridge (MA). Served HM Forces, 1957-59. Central Asian Res. Centre, 1962-63; joined Diplomatic Service, 1963; Tehran, 1967-68; Oriental Sec., Kabul, 1968-70; FCO, 1970-75; seconded to Cabinet Office, 1975-77; First Sec., FCO, 1977-81. *Recreations:* sports, television, foreign films and literature. *Address:* c/o Foreign and Commonwealth Office, SW1A 2AH.

RUNDLE, David John; Director, British Institute of Florence, since 1981; *b* 21 July 1938; *s* of Richard Norman Rundle and Ivy Evelyn Rundle (*née* Cole); *m* 1963, Charlotte Fallenius (marr. diss. 1979); two *s. Educ:* Tavistock Sch., Devon; Jesus Coll., Cambridge (BA, MA); Univ. of Leeds (DipEd, MTEFL 1965). Lektor for British Centre, Sweden, 1961-63; Tutor, English Language Centre, Hove, 1963-64; joined British Council career service, 1965; seconded to Zambian Min. of Educn, Lusaka, 1965-67; Education Officer, Amman, Jordan, 1967-70; Director of Studies, Milan, 1970-75; Regional Director: E Midlands, 1975-79; Munich, 1979-81; on leave of absence, 1981-. *Publications:* An English Medium Course for Zambia, 1967; articles on cultural diplomacy and teaching of English. *Recreations:* theatre, tennis, gardening, travel, writing. *Address:* Via Santo Spirito 15, Florence, Italy. *T:* (055) 291978.

RUNDLE, John Louis, AM 1981; Agent-General for South Australia, since 1980; *b* 11 Jan. 1930; *s* of late J. A. Rundle; *m* Elizabeth Phillipa, *d* of John P. Little, Melbourne; one *s* one *d. Educ:* Rostrevor Coll. Formerly Senior Partner, J. C. Rundle & Co., and Rundle, Parsons & Partners; Former Chairman: J. C. Rundle Holdings Pty Ltd; Seacliff Investments Pty Ltd; Thevenard Hotel Pty Ltd; former Director: Commonwealth Accommodation & Catering Service Ltd; Mallen & Co. Ltd; Commercial & Domestic Finance Ltd. Former Member: Nat. Employers Ind. Council (Dep. Chm., 1979-80); Confed. of Aust. Industry (Mem. Bd, 1978-80); State Develt Council, SA; Ind. Relations Adv. Council, SA; Adv. Curriculum Bd, SA; Council, Royal AA of SA. Pres., Junior Chambers, Adelaide, 1957, SA, 1958, Australia, 1959; Vice-Pres., JCI, 1960, 1963, Exec. Vice-Pres., 1964, World Pres., 1965, Pres. Senate, 1966; Councillor, Adelaide Chamber of Commerce, 1956-57, 1961-72, Vice-Pres., 1968-70, Dep. Pres., 1970-72; Vice-Pres., Chamber of Commerce & Industry, SA, 1973-75, Dep. Pres., 1975-77, Pres. 1977-79 (Chm., Commerce Div., 1973, 1974; Chm., Ind. Matters Cttee); Exec. Mem., Aust. Chamber of Commerce, 1980. Councillor: Red Cross Soc., SA Div., 1957-63 (Chm., Junior Red Cross, 1961-62); Burnside City Council, 1962-64;

President: Assoc. of Indep. Schools of SA, 1972-75; Nat. Council of Indep. Schools, 1975-77; Chm., Bd of Governors, Rostrevor Coll., 1967-77. *Address:* South Australia House, 50 Strand, WC2N 5LW. *Clubs:* East India, Royal Automobile; Stock Exchange (Pres., 1979-80), Naval Military and Air Force, Tattersall's (Adelaide); Royal Automobile (Melbourne); Clipper (USA).

RUOFF, Theodore Burton Fox, CB 1970; CBE 1962; Chief Land Registrar, 1963-75; *b* 12 April 1910; *s* of late Percy Ruoff and late Edith Crane; *m* 1947, Marjorie Alice, *er d* of late George Mawson, Worthing; no *c. Educ:* Clarence School, Weston-super-Mare; King Edward VI School, Bury St Edmunds. Admitted as a solicitor, 1933; 2nd class Hons; Hertfordshire Law Society prizeman; Nuffield Fellowship in Australia and New Zealand, 1951-52; Senior Land Registrar of HM Land Registry, 1958. (Founder) Mem., Council, Soc. for Computers and Law, 1974-80; Consultant, Oyez Computers Ltd, 1975; Mem., Law Society's Special Cttee on Computer Services, 1976; Special Adviser on Conveyancing to Royal Commn on Legal Services, 1976-79. Editor, Computers and Law, 1978-82. *Publications:* An Englishman Looks at the Torrens System, 1957; Concise Land Registration Practice, 1959; Rentcharges in Registered Conveyancing, 1961; Land Registration Forms, 1962; Curtis and Ruoff's The Law and Practice of Registered Conveyancing (2nd edn, 1965); (with R. B. Roper) Ruoff and Roper's Registered Conveyancing, 1972, 4th edn 1979; Searching without Tears: The Land Charges Computer, 1974; The Solicitor and the Silicon Chip, 1981; (Gen. Ed.) Fourmat Legal Directory, 1981; regular contribs to Australian Law Jl, Law Soc.'s Gazette, Solicitors' Jl. *Recreations:* sketching, indifferent golf, gardening. *Address:* Flat One, 83 South Hill Park, Hampstead, NW3 2SS. *T:* 01-435 8014. *Clubs:* Travellers', MCC.

RUPERT'S LAND, Metropolitan of; *see* Qu'Appelle, Archbishop of.

RUPERT'S LAND, Bishop of, since 1970; **Rt. Rev. Barry Valentine,** MA, BD, LTh, DD; *b* 26 Sept. 1927; *s* of Harry John Valentine and Ethel Margaret Purkiss; *m* 1952, Mary Currell Hayes; three *s* one *d. Educ:* Brentwood Sch.; St John's Coll., Cambridge; McGill Univ., Montreal. Curate, Christ Church Cath., Montreal, 1952; Incumbent, Chateauguay-Beauharnois, 1954; Dir, Religious Educn, Dio. Montreal, 1957; Rector of St Lambert, PQ, 1961; Exec. Officer, Dio. Montreal, 1965; Dean of Montreal, 1968; Bishop Coadjutor of Rupert's Land, 1969; Chancellor, St John's Coll., Winnipeg, 1970. Hon. DD: St John's Coll., Winnipeg, 1969; Montreal Dio. Theol Coll., 1970. *Recreations:* music, theatre, walking, reading; over-aged and bibulous cricket. *Address:* Anglican Centre, 935 Nesbitt Bay, Winnipeg, Manitoba R3T 1W6, Canada. *T:* 204-453-6248. *Clubs:* Winnipeg Squash Racquet; Taverners Cricket.

RUPP, Rev. Prof. Ernest Gordon, MA, DD; FBA 1970; Dixie Professor of Ecclesiastical History, and Fellow of Emmanuel College, University of Cambridge, 1968-77, now Emeritus; Principal, Wesley House, Cambridge, 1967-74; *b* 7 Jan. 1910; *m* 1938, Marjorie Hibbard; one *s. Educ:* Owen's School, EC; King's College, London (BA); Wesley House, Cambridge (MA, BD 1946, DD Cantab 1955); Universities of Strasbourg and Basel. Methodist Minister, Chislehurst, Kent, 1938-46; Wesley House, Cambridge, 1946-47; Richmond College, Surrey, 1947-52; Birkbeck Lectr, Trinity Coll., Cambridge, 1947; Lecturer in Divinity, Cambridge Univ., 1952-56; Prof. of Ecclesiastical History, Univ. of Manchester, 1956-67. President of the Methodist Conference, 1968-69; Mem., Central Cttee of World Council of Churches, 1969. Hon. Fellow: Fitzwilliam College, 1969; King's Coll., London, 1969. Hon. DD: Aberdeen; Manchester, 1979; Hon. Dr Theol, Paris. *Publications:* Studies in the English Protestant Tradition, 1947; Luther's Progress to the Diet of Worms, 1951; The Righteousness of God (Luther studies), 1953; Some Makers of English Religion, 1957; The Old Reformation and the New, 1967; Patterns of Reformation, 1969; Just Men, 1977; Thomas More, 1978. *Address:* 42 Malcolm Place, King Street, Cambridge.

RUSBRIDGE, Brian John; Secretary, Local Authorities' Conditions of Service Advisory Board, since 1973; Secretary: to all Local Authority National Councils; Burnham Committees for Teachers; Police Negotiating Board; Fire Brigades; Probation Service; Whitley Councils for New Towns Staffs and for Industrial Estates Corporations; Adviser to the States of Jersey and Guernsey; *b* 10 Sept. 1922; *s* of late Arthur John and Leonora Rusbridge, Appleton, Berks; *m* 1951, Joyce, *d* of late Joseph Young Elliott, Darlington; two *s. Educ:* Willowfield Sch., Eastbourne; Univ. of Oxford Dept of Social and Admin. Studies (Dip. Social Admin.). Served War of 1939-45, Lieut RNVR. Personnel Manager, Imperial Chemical Industries (Teesside), 1949; British Railways Board: Dir of Industrial Relations, 1963; Divisional Manager, London, 1970. Companion, Inst. of Personnel Management; Mem., Chartered Inst. of Transport. *Recreations:* walking, gardening. *Address:* 19 Beauchamp Road, East Molesey, Surrey KT8 0PA. *T:* 01-979 4952.

RUSBY, Vice-Adm. Sir Cameron, KCB 1979; MVO 1965; Deputy Supreme Allied Commander, Atlantic, 1980-82; *b* 20 Feb. 1926; *s* of Captain Victor Evelyn Rusby, CBE, RN (Rtd), and Mrs Irene Margaret Rusby; *m* 1948, Marion Elizabeth Bell; two *d. Educ:* RNC, Dartmouth. Midshipman 1943; specialised in communications, 1950; CO HMS Ulster, 1958-59; Exec. Officer, HM Yacht Britannia, 1962-65; Dep. Dir, Naval Signals, 1965-68; CO HMS Tartar, 1968-69; Dep. ACOS (Plans and Policy), staff of Allied C-in-C Southern Europe, 1969-72; Sen. Naval Off., WI, 1972-74; Rear-Adm. 1974; ACDS (Ops), 1974-77; Vice-Adm. 1977; Flag Officer Scotland and N Ireland,

1977-79. *Recreations:* sailing, equitation. *Address:* c/o Bank of Scotland, 70 High Street, Peebles EH45 8AQ. *Club:* Army and Navy.

RUSBY, Norman Lloyd, MA, DM Oxon, FRCP; Consulting Physician: London Hospital since 1970 (Physician, 1946-70); London Chest Hospital since 1970 (Physician, 1936-70); King Edward VII Hospital, Midhurst; Benenden Chest Hospital (Civil Service); Civil Consultant in Diseases of the Chest to the Royal Navy; *b* 26 October 1905; *s* of Dr Edward L. M. Rusby, Streatham and Katharine Helen Rusby (*née* Wright); *m* 1941, Elizabeth, *e d* of F. A. Broadhead, FRIBA, Nottingham; three *s. Educ:* Lancing College; St John's College, Oxford; St Thomas's Hospital. BA (Hons) Oxon, 1928, MA 1931; DM 1941; BM; BCL. Res. appts, St Thomas' Hosp.; Res. MO and Registrar, London Chest Hosp., 1934-36; Medical Registrar and Tutor, British Postgraduate Medical School, Hammersmith, 1937-39. Member Standing Advisory Committee on Tuberculosis to Min. of Health, 1940-44; Editor of Tubercle, 1938-44; Physician, EMS, 1939; RAMC Med. specialist, 21 Army Gp, 1944-45; Officer i/c Med. Div., ME Chest Unit, 1945-46; Local Brigadier, Consulting Physician Middle East Land Forces, 1946. Nuffield visitor to East Africa, 1950, 1953. Lecturer for British Council: Poland, 1959; Malta, 1966; Nepal, India and Afghanistan, 1973. Examiner in Medicine: Univ. of London, 1951-56; Univ. of Cambridge, 1957-60; Univ. of W Indies, 1967; RCP, 1962-68. Councillor, RCP, 1964-66; Mitchell Lecturer, RCP, 1967. Member: Attendance Allowance Bd; Council, Chest, Heart and Stroke Assoc. (Vice-Chm., 1957-77); Council, British Heart Foundn; Assoc. of Physicians of Gt Britain and Ireland; Thoracic Society; Hon. Mem., Brit. Thoracic Assoc. Mem., Board of Governors: Hospitals for Diseases of the Chest, 1962-67; London Hospital, 1967-70. *Publications:* (jtly) Recent Advances in Respiratory Tuberculosis, 4th and 5th edns, (ed jtly) 6th edn 1968; contributions to various journals, chiefly on diseases of the chest. *Address:* 21 Windmill Hill, Hampstead, NW3. *T:* 01-794 6889. *Clubs:* United Oxford & Cambridge University, MCC.

RUSH, (Edward Antisell) Michael (Stanistreet); His Honour Judge Rush; a Circuit Judge, since 1980; *b* 27 March 1933; *s* of Edward Antisell Evans Rush and Karen (*née* Kröyer, Copenhagen). *Educ:* St John's Sch., Leatherhead; Queen's Univ., Belfast; Inns of Court Sch. of Law. Pres., Inns of Court Students' Union, 1958; called to the Bar, Lincoln's Inn, 1958 (Sir Thomas More Scholar). Commissioned, Grenadier Guards, 1958-61. Oxford Circuit, 1961-71 (Junior, 1966); Midland and Oxford Circuit, 1972-80. A Recorder of the Crown Court, 1978-80. *Address:* 2 Harcourt Buildings, Temple, EC4Y 9DB.

RUSH, Most Rev. Francis Roberts; *see* Brisbane, Archbishop of, (RC).

RUSH, Michael; *see* Rush, E. A. M. S.

RUSHBROOKE, Prof. G(eorge) Stanley, MA, PhD; FRS 1982; FRSE; Professor of Theoretical Physics, University of Newcastle upon Tyne, 1951-80; Head of Department of Theoretical Physics, 1965-80; Deputy Head, School of Physics, 1972-80; *b* 19 January 1915; *s* of George Henry Rushbrooke and Frances Isobel Rushbrooke (*née* Wright), Willenhall, Staffs; *m* 1949, Thelma Barbara Cox (*d* 1977). *Educ:* Wolverhampton Grammar School; St John's College, Cambridge. Schol. St John's Coll., Camb., 1933-37; Research Asst, Bristol Univ., 1938-39; Senior DSIR award and Carnegie Teaching Fellowship, 1939-44, UC Dundee, Univ. of St Andrews; Lectr in Mathematical Chemistry, The Univ., Leeds, 1944-48; Sen. Lectr in Theoretical Physics, Oxford, Univ. and Lecturer in Mathematics, University Coll., Oxford, 1948-51. Leverhulme Emeritus Fellow, 1981. Visiting Prof., Dept of Chemistry, Univ. of Oregon, USA, 1962-63; Vis. Prof. of Physics and Chemistry, Rice Univ., Houston, 1967. *Publications:* Introduction to Statistical Mechanics, 1949; research papers in scientific journals. *Recreations:* hillwalking, birdwatching. *Address:* 46 Belle Vue Avenue, Newcastle upon Tyne NE3 1AH.

RUSHFORD, Antony Redfern, CMG 1963; HM Diplomatic Service, retired; Deputy Legal Adviser (Senior Grade, Assistant Under-Secretary of State), Foreign and Commonwealth Office, 1969-82; constitutional advisor to Government of St Kitts and Nevis, since 1982; Special Legal Adviser, Government of St Lucia, 1982; escalated to FCO for special duties, 1982; *m* 1975, June Jeffery Wells; one step *s* one step *d. Educ:* Taunton School; Trinity College, Cambridge. RAFVR, 1943-47, Sqdn Ldr, 1946. Admitted a Solicitor, 1944 (removed from roll at own request, 1957). BA, LLB 1948; MA 1951; Student, Inner Temple, 1957. Colonial Office: Legal Asst, 1949-54; Senior Legal Assistant, 1954-60; Assistant Legal Adviser, 1960-66; Legal Counsellor, FCO (formerly CO), 1966-69. Crown Counsel, Uganda, 1954-. Mem., Edit. Adv. Bd, Small Island Area Studies, Inst. of Internat. Law and Econ. Develt, 1977-. OStJ (Hon. Legal Counsellor to Order, 1978-). Foundn Mem. Exec. Council, Royal Commonwealth Soc. for the Blind, 1969-81. *Address:* 12 Chester Row, Belgravia, SW1W 9JH. *T:* 01-730 2811.

RUSHTON, William George; actor, author, cartoonist and broadcaster; *b* 18 Aug. 1937; *s* of John and Veronica Rushton; *m* 1968, Arlene Dorgan; three *s. Educ:* Shrewsbury Sch. Founder/Editor, Private Eye, 1961. Stage début in The Bed-sitting Room, by Spike Milligan, Marlowe Theatre, Canterbury, 1961; Gulliver's Travels, Mermaid, 1971, 1979; Pass the Butler, by Eric Idle, Globe, 1982; *films:* Nothing but the Best, 1963; Those Magnificent Men in their Flying Machines, 1964, and several others; *television* includes: That Was the Week that Was, 1962; Up Sunday, 1975-78; Celebrity Squares, 1979-80;

numerous Jackanory progs; *radio* includes: I'm Sorry I Haven't a Clue, 1976-82; much other broadcasting in UK and Australia. *Publications:* written and illustrated: William Rushton's Dirty Book, 1964; How to Play Football: the art of dirty play, 1968; The Day of the Grocer, 1971; The Geranium of Flüt, 1975; Superpig, 1976; Pigsticking: a joy for life, 1977; The Reluctant Euro, 1980; The Filth Amendment, 1981; illustrations for many others. *Recreations:* losing weight, gaining weight, parking. *Address:* 9 Wallgrave Road, SW5. *T:* 01-370 2826. *Clubs:* Tatty Bogle's, Lord's Taverners, Surrey CC.

RUSHWORTH, Dr (Frank) Derek; Headmaster, Holland Park School, London, since 1971; *b* 15 Sept. 1920; *s* of late Frank and Elizabeth Rushworth, Huddersfield; *m* 1941, Hamidah Begum, *d* of Justice S. Akhlaque Hussain, Lahore, and late Edith (*née* Bayliss), Oxford; three *d. Educ:* Huddersfield Coll.; St Edmund Hall, Oxford (Schol.; BA 1942, MA 1946); Doctorate of Univ. of Paris (Lettres), 1947. Served 6th Rajputana Rifles, Indian Army, 1942-45 (Major); began teaching, 1947; Head of Modern Languages: Tottenham Grammar Sch., 1953; Holland Park Sch., 1958; Head of Shoreditch Sch., London, 1965. Chairman: Associated Examining Board, French Committee, 1964-74; Schools Council, 16+ Examination Feasibility Study (French), 1971-75. *Publications:* Our French Neighbours, 1963, 2nd edn 1966; French text-books and language-laboratory books; articles in French Studies, Modern Languages, also educnl jls. *Recreation:* photography. *Address:* 25c Lambolle Road, NW3 4HS. *T:* 01-794 3691.

RUSK, Dean, KBE (Hon.) 1976; Professor of International Law, University of Georgia School of Law, Athens, Georgia, since 1971; *b* 9 February 1909; *s* of Robert Hugh Rusk and Frances Elizabeth Clotfelter; *m* 1937, Virginia Foisie; two *s* one *d. Educ:* Davidson College, North Carolina; St John's College, Oxford. Associate Prof. of Government and Dean of Faculty, Mills Coll., 1934-40; US Army, 1940-46; Special Asst to Secretary of War, 1946; US Dept of State, 1947-51; Asst Sec. of State for UN Affairs, 1949; Dep. Under Sec. of State, 1949-50; Asst Sec. of State for Far Eastern Affairs, 1950-51; Sec. of State, 1961-69; President, The Rockefeller Foundation, 1952-61, Distinguished Fellow, 1969-. Hon. Fellow, St John's Coll., Oxford, 1955. Hon. LLD: Mills Coll., Calif, 1948; Davidson Coll., 1950; Univ. of Calif, 1961; Emory Univ., Georgia, 1961; Princeton Univ., NJ, 1961; Louisiana State Univ. 1962; Amherst Coll., 1962; Columbia Univ., 1963; Harvard Univ., 1963; Rhode Island Univ., 1963; Valparaiso Univ., 1964; Williams Coll., 1964; Univ. of N Carolina, 1964; George Washington Univ., 1965; Oberlin Coll., 1965; Maryville Coll., 1965; Denver Univ., 1966; Erskine Coll., 1967. Hon. DCL Oxford, 1962; Hon. LHD: Westminster Coll., 1962; Hebrew Union Coll., 1963; Hardin-Simmons Univ., 1967. Cecil Peace Prize, 1933. Legion of Merit (Oak Leaf Cluster). *Address:* 1 Lafayette Square, 620 Hill Street, Athens, Ga 30601, USA.

RUSSELL; *see* Hamilton-Russell.

RUSSELL, family name of Duke of Bedford, Earl Russell, Baron Ampthill, Baron de Clifford, Baron Russell of Killowen and Baron Russell of Liverpool.

RUSSELL, 4th Earl *cr* 1861; **John Conrad Russell;** Viscount Amberley, 1861; *b* 16 Nov. 1921; *er s* of 3rd Earl Russell, OM, FRS, and Dora Winifred, MBE, *d* of late Sir Frederick Black, KCB; *S* father, 1970; *m* 1946, Susan Doniphan (marr. diss. 1954), *d* of late Vachel Lindsay; one *d* (and one *d* decd). *Educ:* Beacon Hill Sch., 1927-34; Dartington Hall Sch., 1934-39; University of California, Los Angeles, 1939-41; Harvard University, 1941-43. Served War of 1939-45, in RNVR, 1943-46; Temp. Admin. Asst, FAO of the United Nations, Washington, DC, 1946-47; temp. Admin. Asst, HM Treasury, 1947-49. Took his seat in the House of Lords, 12 May 1976. *Heir: half-brother* Hon. Conrad Sebastian Robert Russell [*b* 15 April 1937; *m* 1962, Elizabeth Franklin, *e d* of Horace Sanders; two *s*]. *Address:* Carn Voel, Porthcurno, near Penzance, Cornwall.

RUSSELL OF KILLOWEN, Baron *cr* 1975 (Life Peer), of Killowen, Co. Down; **Charles Ritchie Russell,** PC 1962; Kt 1960; a Lord of Appeal in Ordinary, 1975-82; *b* 12 Jan. 1908; *s* of Francis Xavier, Baron Russell of Killowen, Lord of Appeal in Ordinary (*s* of Charles, Baron Russell of Killowen, Lord Chief Justice of England) and Mary Emily Ritchie (*d* of 1st Baron Ritchie of Dundee, former Chancellor of Exchequer); *m* 1933, Joan Elisabeth (*d* 1976), *d* of late Dr J. A. Torrens, MD, FRCP; two *s* one *d* ; *m* 1979, Elizabeth Cecilia, *widow* of His Honour Judge Laughton-Scott, QC. *Educ:* Beaumont; Oriel College, Oxford. Called to Bar, Lincoln's Inn, 1931; QC 1948; Bencher, 1952; Treasurer, 1972. Army, 1939-45; RA (Airborne) (despatches, French Croix de Guerre with star). Attorney-General to the Duchy of Cornwall, 1951-60; Judge of Chancery Division, High Court of Justice, 1960-62; a Lord Justice of Appeal, 1962-75. President, Restrictive Practices Court, 1961-62 (Member, 1960-62). *Recreation:* golf. *Address:* Orchard House, Sheepdown, Petworth, West Sussex. *T:* Petworth 42657. *Club:* Garrick.

RUSSELL OF LIVERPOOL, 3rd Baron *cr* 1919; **Simon Gordon Jared Russell;** *b* 30 Aug. 1952; *s* of Captain Hon. Langley Gordon Haslingden Russell, MC (*d* 1975) (*o s* of 2nd Baron), and of Kiloran Margaret, *d* of late Hon. Sir Arthur Jared Palmer Howard, KBE, CVO; *S* grandfather, 1981. *Educ:* Charterhouse; Trinity Coll., Cambridge; INSEAD, Fontainebleau,

France. *Heir: b* Adam Mark Haslingden Russell, *b* 23 Oct. 1957. *Address:* Ash Farm, Stourpaine, Blandford, Dorset.

RUSSELL, Alan; *b* 5 Dec. 1910; *s* of late Hon. Cyril Russell; *m* 1st, 1937, Grace Evelyn Moore (decd); one *d* ; 2nd, 1944, Jean Patricia, *widow* of Wing Comdr J. R. Cridland, AAF, and *d* of late Stafford Croom Johnson, JP; one step *s* one *s. Educ:* Beaumont. Joined Helbert Wagg & Co. Ltd, 1929. Served War of 1939-45, in Army, London Scottish, Lt-Col, attached US Army, Europe, 1941-45. Director: Helbert Wagg & Co. Ltd, 1946-62; District Bank Ltd, 1948-70; Alexanders Discount Co. Ltd, 1948-79; IBM United Kingdom Ltd, 1956-79; Legal & General Assurance Society Ltd, 1958-76; J. Henry Schroder & Co. Ltd, 1960-62; United Molasses Co. Ltd, 1962-66; J. Henry Schroder Wagg & Co. Ltd, 1962-70; Turner & Newall Ltd, 1962-75; Schroders Ltd, 1963-70; Yorkshire Bank Ltd, 1965-79; National Westminster Bank Ltd, 1968-79. *Address:* 23 Park Lane, Aldeburgh, Suffolk.

RUSSELL, Alan Keith; Special Advisor UNCTAD, Head of the Division for West Africa, Commission of the European Communities, since 1982; *b* 22 Oct. 1932; *s* of Keith Russell and Gertrude Ann Russell; *m* 1959, Philippa Margaret Stoneham; two *s* one *d. Educ:* Lincoln and Nuffield Colls, Oxford, 1953-58. BA, MA Econ. and Pol. Sci., 1962; DPhil Edwardian Econ. and Pol. Hist. Oxon, 1962. Colonial Office, 1959-62; ODM, 1962-65; FCO, 1st Sec., Aid, Malawi, 1966-68; CS Coll., 1969-71; Head of Internat. and European Dept, ODA, 1972-75; Head of Div./Special Advisor, Commn of European Communities (DG VIII), 1976-80; Dir, Inter University Council for Higher Educn Overseas, 1980-81. *Publications:* ed, The Economic and Social History of Mauritius, 1962; Liberal Landslide: the General Election of 1906, 1973; contrib. Edwardian Radicalism, 1974; articles on commodity trade and development; poems and ballads. *Recreations:* gardening, travelling, services for the mentally handicapped. *Address:* 11 Holly Lodge Gardens, Highgate, N6 6AA.

RUSSELL, Albert Muir Galloway, QC (Scot.) 1965; Sheriff of Grampian, Highland and Islands (formerly Aberdeen, Kincardine and Banff) at Aberdeen and Stonehaven, since 1971; *b* 26 Oct. 1925; *s* of Hon. Lord Russell; *m* 1954, Margaret Winifred, *o d* of T. McW Millar, FRCS(E), Edinburgh; two *s* two *d. Educ:* Edinburgh Academy; Wellington College; Brasenose College, Oxford. BA (Hons) Oxon, 1949; LLB (Edin.), 1951. Lieut, Scots Guards, 1944-47. Member of Faculty of Advocates, 1951-. *Recreation:* golf. *Address:* Easter Ord House, Skene, Aberdeenshire. *T:* Aberdeen 740228. *Club:* Royal Northern (Aberdeen).

RUSSELL, Alexander William; Under Secretary, Management and Personnel Office (formerly Civil Service Department), since 1979; *b* 16 Oct. 1938; *s* of William and Elizabeth W. B. Russell (*née* Russell); *m* 1962, Elspeth Rae (*née* Robertson). *Educ:* Royal High Sch., Edinburgh; Edinburgh Univ. (MA Hons); Manitoba Univ. (MA). Assistant Principal, Scottish Development Dept, 1961-64; Private Sec. to Parliamentary Under Secretary of State, Scottish Office, 1964-65; Principal, Regional Development Div. and Scottish Development Dept, 1965-72; Principal Private Sec. to Secretary of State for Scotland, 1972-73; Asst Secretary: Scottish Development Dept, 1973-76; Civil Service Dept, 1976-79. *Address:* c/o Drummonds Branch, Royal Bank of Scotland, Trafalgar Square, SW1.

RUSSELL, Anna; International Concert Comedienne; *b* 27 Dec. 1911; *d* of Col C. Russell-Brown, CB, DSO, RE, and Beatrice M. Tandy; single. *Educ:* St Felix School, Southwold; Royal College of Music, London. Folk singer, BBC, 1935-40; Canadian Broadcasting Corp. programmes, 1942-46; Radio interviewer, CBC, 1945-46; Debut, Town Hall, New York, as concert comedienne, 1948; Broadway show, Anna Russell and her Little Show, 1953; Towns of USA, Canada, Great Britain, Australia, New Zealand, the Orient and South Africa, 1948-60. Television, Radio Summer Theatre, USA; recordings, Columbia Masterworks. Resident in Australia, 1968-75. Mayfair Theatre, London, 1976. *Publications:* The Power of Being a Positive Stinker (NY); The Anna Russell Song Book. *Recreation:* gardening. *Address:* No 16, 1148 W Huntington Drive, Arcadia, Calif 91006, USA. *Club:* Zouta International (USA, Toronto Branch, Internat. Mem.).

RUSSELL, Sir Archibald (Edward), Kt 1972; CBE 1954; FRS 1970; Joint Chairman, Concorde Executive Committee of Directors, 1965-69; Vice-Chairman, BAC-Sud Aviation Concorde Committee, 1969-70, retired; *b* 30 May 1904; *m* ; one *s* one *d. Educ:* Fairfield Secondary Sch.; Bristol Univ. Joined Bristol Aeroplane Co. Ltd, 1926; Chief Technician, 1931; Technical Designer, 1938; Chief Engineer, 1944; Dir, 1951; Tech. Dir, 1960-66; Chm., British Aircraft Corporation, Filton Div., 1967-69 (Man. Dir, 1966-67). Wright Bros Memorial Lecture, Washington, 1949; 42nd Wilbur Wright Memorial Lecture, London, 1954; RAeS British Gold Medal, 1951; David Guggenheim Medal, 1971; Hon. DSc Bristol, 1951. CEng; FIAeS; Hon FRAeS 1967. *Publications:* papers in R&M Series of Aeronautical Research Cttee and RAeS Journal. *Address:* Glendower House, Clifton Down, Bristol BS8 3BP. *T:* Bristol 739208.

RUSSELL, Rev. Arthur Colin, CMG 1957; ED; MA; *b* 1906; *e s* of late Arthur W. Russell, OBE, WS; *m* 1939, Elma (*d* 1967), *d* of late Douglas Strachan, Hon. RSA; three *d. Educ:* Harrow; Brasenose College, Oxford. Barrister-at-law, Inner Temple. Cadet, Gold Coast (now Ghana), 1929; Asst Dist Comr, 1930; Dist Comr, 1940; Judicial Adviser, 1947; Senior, 1951; Regional Officer, 1952; Permanent Sec., Min. of Education and Social

Welfare, 1953; Governor's Secretary, 1954; Chief Regional Officer, Ashanti, 1955-57, retd. Trained for the Ministry, 1957-59; Ordained (Church of Scotland), 1959; Parish Minister, Aberlemno, 1959-76; retd. District Councillor, Angus District, 1977. *Publication:* Stained Glass Windows of Douglas Strachan, 1972. *Address:* Aberlemno, Forfar, Angus. *T:* Aberlemno 265.

RUSSELL, Audrey; *see* Russell, M. A.

RUSSELL, Barbara Winifred, MA; Headmistress, Berkhamsted School for Girls, 1950-July 1971; *b* 5 Jan. 1910; *er d* of Lionel Wilfred and Elizabeth Martin Russell. *Educ:* St Oran's School, Edinburgh; Edinburgh University; Oxford University, Dept of Education. History Mistress, Brighton and Hove High School, 1932-38; Senior History Mistress, Roedean School, 1938-49. *Recreations:* reading, gardening, travel. *Address:* 1 Beech Road, Thame, Oxon. *T:* Thame 2738. *Club:* East India, Devonshire, Sports and Public Schools.

RUSSELL, Brian Fitzgerald, MD, FRCP; Consulting Physician, formerly Physician, Department of Dermatology, The London Hospital (1951-69); Consulting Physician, formerly Physician, St John's Hospital for Diseases of the Skin (1947-69); formerly Civilian Consultant in Dermatology to the Royal Navy (1955-69); past Dean, Institute of Dermatology; *b* 1 Sept. 1904; *s* of Dr John Hutchinson Russell and Helen Margaret (*née* Collingwood); *m* 1932, Phyllis Daisy Woodward; three *s* one *d*. *Educ:* Merchant Taylors' School. MD (London) 1929; FRCP 1951; DPH (Eng.) 1943. Medical First Asst, London Hosp., 1930-32; general medical practice, 1933-45; Dermatologist, Prince of Wales's Hosp., Tottenham, 1946-51; Asst Physician, Dept of Dermatology St Bartholomew's Hosp., 1946-51. President: St John's Hosp. Dermatological Soc., 1958-60; Dermatological Sect., RSM, 1968-69 (Hon. Mem., 1977); Corr. Mem.: American Dermatological Soc.; Danish Dermatological Soc. *Publications:* St John's Hospital for Diseases of the Skin, 1863-1963, 1963; (with Eric Wittkower) Emotional Factors in Skin Diseases, 1953; Section on Dermatology in Price's Medicine (ed by Bodley Scott), 1973. *Recreation:* rustication. *Address:* 24 St John's Close, Saffron Walden, Essex CB11 4AR.

RUSSELL, Cecil Anthony Francis; Director of Intelligence, Greater London Council, 1970-76; *b* 7 June 1921; *s* of late Comdr S. F. Russell, OBE, RN retd and late Mrs M. E. Russell (*née* Sneyd-Kynnersley); *m* 1950, Editha May (*née* Birch); no *c*. *Educ:* Winchester Coll.; University Coll., Oxford (1940-41, 1945-47). Civil Service, 1949-70: Road Research Lab., 1949-50; Air Min., 1950-62; Dep. Statistical Adviser, Home Office, 1962-67; Head of Census Div., General Register Office, 1967-70. FSS. *Recreation:* ocean sailing. *Address:* Pagan Hill, Whiteleaf, Princes Risborough, Bucks. *T:* Princes Risborough 3655. *Clubs:* Cruising Association; Royal Lymington Yacht.

RUSSELL, Sir Charles Ian, 3rd Bt, *cr* 1916; partner in Charles Russell & Co., Hale Court, Lincoln's Inn, WC2; Captain, RHA (despatches); *b* 13 March 1918; *s* of Captain Sir Alec Charles Russell, 2nd Bt, and Monica (who *m* 2nd, 1942, Brig. John Victor Faviell, CBE, MC; she *d* 1978), *d* of Hon. Sir Charles Russell, 1st Bt; *S* father, 1938; *m* 1947, Rosemary, *er d* of late Sir John Prestige; one *s* one *d*. *Educ:* Beaumont College; University College, Oxford. Admitted Solicitor, 1947. *Recreation:* golf. *Heir: s* Charles Dominic Russell, *b* 28 May 1956. *Address:* Hidden House, Sandwich, Kent. *Clubs:* Garrick, Army and Navy; Royal St George's.

RUSSELL, David Sturrock W.; *see* West-Russell.

RUSSELL, Rev. David Syme, CBE 1982; MA, DD, DLitt; General Secretary, Baptist Union of Great Britain and Ireland, 1967-82; *b* 21 Nov. 1916; second *s* of Peter Russell and Janet Marshall Syme; *m* 1943, Marion Hamilton Campbell; one *s* one *d*. *Educ:* Scottish Baptist Coll., Glasgow; Trinity Coll., Glasgow; Glasgow Univ. (MA, BD, DLitt, Hon. DD); Regent's Park Coll.; Oxford Univ. (MA, MLitt). Minister of Baptist Churches: Berwick, 1939-41; Oxford, 1943-45; Acton, 1945-53. Principal of Rawdon Coll., Leeds, and lectr in Old Testament languages and literature, 1953-64; Joint Principal of the Northern Baptist College, Manchester, 1964-67. Moderator, Free Church Federal Council, 1974-75. Pres., European Baptist Fedn, 1979-81. Mem., Central Cttee, WCC, 1968-; Vice-Pres., BCC, 1981-. *Publications:* Between the Testaments, 1960; Two Refugees (Ezekiel and Second Isaiah), 1962; The Method and Message of Jewish Apocalyptic, 1964; The Jews from Alexander to Herod, 1976; Apocalyptic: Ancient and Modern, 1978; Daniel (The Daily Study Bible), 1981; In Journeyings Often; contrib. to Encyc. Britannica, 1963. *Recreation:* woodwork. *Address:* 40 Northumbria Drive, Henleaze, Bristol BS9 4HP. *T:* Bristol 623660.

RUSSELL, Donald Andrew Frank Moore, FBA 1971; Fellow and Tutor, St John's College, Oxford since 1948; Reader in Classical Literature, Oxford, since 1978; *b* 13 Oct. 1920; *s* of Samuel Charles Russell (schoolmaster) and Laura Moore; *m* 1967, Joycelyne Gledhill Dickinson. *Educ:* King's College Sch., Wimbledon; Balliol Coll., Oxford (MA). Served War: Army (R Signals and Intelligence Corps), 1941-45. Craven Scholar, 1946; Lectr, Christ Church, Oxford, 1947; Fellow of St John's Coll., 1948; Dean, 1957-64; Tutor for Admissions, 1968-72. Co-editor, Classical Quarterly, 1965-70. *Publications:* Commentary on Longinus, On the Sublime, 1964; Ancient Literary Criticism (with M. Winterbottom), 1972; Plutarch, 1972; (with N. G. Wilson) Menander Rhetor, 1981; Criticism in Antiquity, 1981; articles and reviews in classical periodicals. *Address:* 47 Woodstock Road, Oxford. *T:* Oxford 56135.

RUSSELL, Dorothy Stuart, MD (London); MA (Oxon); ScD (Cantab); LLD (Glasgow); DSc (McGill); FRCP; retired 1960; Director of Bernhard Baron Institute of Pathology, London Hospital; Professor of Morbid Anatomy in University of London, 1946-60, Emeritus Professor, 1960; Hon. Fellow: Girton College, Cambridge; St Hugh's College, Oxford; *b* 27 June 1895; 2nd *d* of late Philip Stuart Russell, Sydney, NSW, and Alice Louisa, *d* of William Cave. *Educ:* Perse High School for Girls, Cambridge; Girton College, Cambridge; London Hospital. Natural Sciences Tripos, Part I, Class I, 1918; Gilchrist Studentship, Girton College, 1918; Sutton Prize in Pathology and Clinical Obstetrics and Gynæcology Prize, London Hospital, 1921; Junior Beit Fellow, 1923-26, attached to Bernhard Baron Institute of Pathology, London Hospital, and subsequently with grants from Medical Research Council; Rockefeller Travelling Fellow, 1928-29, at Boston, Mass, and Montreal; Medical Research Council, Scientific Staff, 1933-46. Attached to Nuffield Dept of Surgery, Oxford, 1940-44; returned to London Hospital, Oct. 1944. John Hunter Medal and Triennial Prize, Royal College of Surgeons, 1934, for work on the kidney and the brain; Oliver-Sharpey Prize, RCP, 1968, for research. Hon. FRCPath 1973. *Publications:* Tumours of the Nervous System; papers in pathology to various journals. *Address:* Holcombe End, Westcott, Dorking, Surrey.

RUSSELL, Rev. Prof. Edward Augustine; Principal, Union Theological College, Belfast, since 1981; Professor of New Testament (originally at Presbyterian College, Belfast), since 1961; *b* 29 Nov. 1916; *s* of William Russell and Annie (*née* Sudway); *m* 1st, 1948, Emily Frances Stevenson (*d* 1978); two *s* one *d*; 2nd, 1979, Joan Evelyn Rufli (*née* Craig). *Educ:* Royal Belfast Academical Instn; London Univ. (BA, BD, MTh); Magee UC, 1942-43; Presbyterian Coll., Belfast, 1943-44, 1945-46; New Coll., Edinburgh, 1944-45. Research at Göttingen Univ. Ordained to Ministry of Presbyterian Church in Ireland, 1948; Minister: Donacloney, 1948-53; Mountpottinger Churches, 1953-61. External Examiner, Glasgow Univ., 1968, 1972-73; extra-mural Lectr, QUB, 1972-. Vis. Prof., Southwestern Univ., Memphis, 1980. Member of various clerical associations. Editor, Irish Biblical Studies, 1979-. Hon. DD Presbyterian Theol Faculty of Ireland, 1966. *Publications:* contribs to Studia Evangelica VI, Berlin 1973; Ministry and the Church, 1977; Studia Biblica vol. II, Sheffield 1980; Studia Evangelica VII, Berlin 1982. *Recreations:* music, golf, painting, languages, bird-watching. *Address:* 14 Cadogan Park, Belfast BT9 6HG.

RUSSELL, Sir (Edward) Lionel, Kt 1962; CBE 1953; *b* 8 May 1903; *s* of Edward and Kate Russell, Bristol. *Educ:* Clifton College; Christ's College, Cambridge. Lecturer in English, Univ. of Lund, Sweden, 1925-31; Assistant Master, Charterhouse, 1932-35; Asst Director of Education, Liverpool, 1935-38; Asst Education Officer, Birmingham, 1938-46; Chief Education Officer, Birmingham, 1946-68. Member: Univ. Grants Cttee, 1954-63; Council for Nat. Academic Awards, 1964-70; Nat. Cttee for Commonwealth Immigrants, 1965-68; Chairman: Inquiry into Adult Educn in England and Wales, 1969-73; Centre for Educnl Develt Overseas, 1970-74; Nat. Adv. Council on Educn for Industry and Commerce, 1975-77; Youth Employment Service Training Bd, 1970-75. Pres., Assoc. of Chief Education Officers, 1955-57. Chm., Bristol Folk House, 1977-80. Hon. ACT Birmingham, 1962; Hon. DEd CNAA, 1969; Hon. DLitt Warwick, 1974; Hon. LLD Birmingham, 1975. *Address:* 24 Tyndall's Park Road, Bristol BS8 1PY. *T:* Bristol 37121. *Club:* Athenæum.

RUSSELL, Edward Walter, CMG 1960; MA Cantab, PhD Cantab; Professor of Soil Science, Reading University, 1964-70, now Professor Emeritus; *b* Wye, Kent, 27 Oct. 1904; *e s* of late Sir (Edward) John Russell, OBE, FRS; *m* 1933, Margaret, *y d* of late Sir Hugh Calthrop Webster; one *s* two *d*. *Educ:* Oundle; Gonville and Caius College, Cambridge. Soil Physicist, Rothamsted Experimental Station, Harpenden, 1930-48; Reader in Soil Science, Oxford Univ., 1948-55; Director, East African Agriculture and Forestry Research Organisation, 1955-64. Member: Scientific Council for Africa, 1956-63; Agricultural Research Council of Central Africa, 1959-64. FInstP; FIBiol; FIAgrE. Hon. Member: British Soc. of Soil Science (Pres., 1968-70); Internat. Soc. of Soil Science. For. Corr. Mem., French Acad. of Agriculture, 1969. Hon. Councillor, Consejo Superior de Investigaciones Cientificas, Madrid, 1970. Hon DSc Univ. of East Africa, 1970. *Publications:* 8th, 9th and 10th Editions of Soil Conditions and Plant Growth; contrib. on physics and chemistry of soils to agricultural and soil science journals. *Address:* 31 Brooklyn Drive, Emmer Green, Reading, Berks RG4 8SR. *T:* Reading 472934.

RUSSELL, Edwin John Cumming, FRBS 1978; sculptor; *b* 4 May 1939; *s* of Edwin Russell and Mary Elizabeth Russell; *m* 1964, Lorne McKean (sculptor; commnd by the Queen for her personal silver wedding gift to Prince Philip—Prince Philip riding polo pony); two *d*. *Educ:* Brighton Coll. of Art and Crafts; Royal Academy Schs (CertRAS). *Works:* Crucifix, pulpit, St Paul's Cathedral, 1964; St Catherine, Little Cloister, Westminster Abbey, 1966; St Michael, Chapel of St Michael and St George, St Paul's Cath., 1970; Suffragette Memorial, Westminster, 1970; Silver Jubilee Sundial, Nat. Maritime Mus., 1979; Bishop, Wells Cathedral, 1980. Royal Academy Gold Medal for Sculpture, 1960. *Recreation:* philosophy. *Address:* Lethendry, Polecat Valley, Hindhead, Surrey GU26 6BE. *T:* Hindhead 5655.

RUSSELL, Sir Evelyn (Charles Sackville), Kt 1982; Chief Metropolitan Stipendiary Magistrate, 1978-82; *b* 2 Dec. 1912; *s* of late Henry Frederick Russell and late Kathleen Isabel, *d* of Richard Morphy; *m* 1939, Joan, *er d* of Harold Edward Jocelyn Camps; one *d*. *Educ*: Douai School; Château de Mesnières, Seine Maritime, France. Hon. Artillery Co., 1938. Served War of 1939-45, Royal Artillery, in UK, N Africa, Italy and Greece. Called to the Bar, Gray's Inn, 1945 (Hon. Bencher 1980); Metropolitan Stipendiary Magistrate, 1961. *Recreations*: tennis, racing. *Address*: The Gate House, Coopersale, Epping, Essex. *T*: Epping 72568. *Club*: Garrick.

RUSSELL, Francis Mark; Chairman since 1975, and Chief Executive since 1972, B. Elliott & Co. plc; Chairman, Goldfields Industrial Corporation, Johannesburg, since 1975; *b* 26 July 1927; *s* of W. Sidney and Beatrice M. Russell; *m* 1950, Joan Patricia Ryan; two *s* three *d*. *Educ*: Ratcliffe Coll., Leicester; Clare Coll., Cambridge (MA). CBIM. Palestine Police, 1946-48; Director: S. Russell & Sons Ltd, 1959; B. Elliott & Co. Ltd, 1967; Chief Executive, Goldfields Industrial Corporation, 1969; Dep. Chm., B. Elliott & Co. Ltd, 1971. *Recreations*: golf, gardening. *Address*: Welders Wood, Welders Lane, Chalfont St Peter, Bucks SL9 8TT. *T*: Chalfont St Giles 4559. *Clubs*: Boodle's; Denham Golf.

RUSSELL, Sir Frederick (Stratten), Kt 1965; CBE 1955; DSC; DFC; FRS 1938; BA Cantab; Secretary to Marine Biological Association of the United Kingdom and Director of the Plymouth Laboratory, 1945-65, retd; *b* Bridport, 3 Nov. 1897; *y s* of late William Russell, MA Oxon, Newquay, and late Lucy Binfield, *d* of Henry Newman, Liverpool; *m* 1923, Gweneth, MBE (*d* 1979), *d* of late John and late Mary Barnhouse Moy Evans; one *s*. *Educ*: Oundle School; Gonville and Caius College, Cambridge (Hon. Fellow 1965). Served European War, RNAS and RAF, 1916-18 (DSC, DFC, French Croix de Guerre avec Palme); Interallied Belgian Coast Defence Committee, 1919; Assistant Director of Fisheries Research to Government of Egypt, 1922-23; on scientific staff of Marine Biological Association's Laboratory, Plymouth, Devon, 1924-65; Great Barrier Reef Expedition, 1928-29; served War of 1939-45 as Wing Comdr on Air Staff Intelligence, 1940-45. Colonial Fisheries Advisory Cttee, 1945-61; Min. Overseas Devlt Fisheries Advisory Panel, 1961-; National Oceanographic Council, 1950-65; Chairman, Advisory Panel on biological research to Central Electricity Generating Board, 1962-75; Trustee, Nat. Maritime Museum, 1965-72; Pres. Devonshire Association, 1953. Editor: Journal of Marine Biological Association, 1945-65; Advances in Marine Biology, 1962-. Hon. FIBiol. 1981. Hon. LLD Glasgow, 1957; Hon. DSc: Exeter, 1960; Birmingham, 1966; Bristol, 1972. Coronation Medal. Linnean Soc. Gold Medal, 1961. For. Mem. Roy. Danish Acad.; Hon. Member: Physiological Soc.; Challenger Soc.; Fisheries Soc. of British Isles. *Publications*: The Seas (with C. M. Yonge), 1928; The Medusae of the British Isles, 1953, vol. II, 1970; The Eggs and Planktonic Stages of British Marine Fishes, 1976; numerous scientific publications on biology of marine plankton invertebrates and fishes, in scientific journals, and on marine biology in Britannica Book of The Year, 1949-70. *Recreations*: angling, sketching. *Address*: Thames Bank, Thames Road, Goring-on-Thames, Reading RG8 9AH. *T*: Goring 873848.

RUSSELL, George; Managing Director, Alcan Aluminium (UK) Ltd, since 1981; *b* 25 Oct. 1935; *s* of William H. Russell and Frances A. Russell; *m* 1959, Dorothy Brown; three *d*. *Educ*: Gateshead Grammar Sch.; Durham Univ. (BA Hons). Vice President and General Manager: Welland Chemical Co. of Canada Ltd, 1968; St Clair Chemical Co. Ltd, 1968; Man. Dir, Alcan UK Ltd, 1976; Asst Man. Dir, Alcan Aluminium (UK) Ltd, 1977-81; Chairman: Luxfer Holdings Ltd, 1976; Alcan UK Ltd, 1978; Dir, Alcan Aluminiumwerke GmbH, Frankfurt. Visiting Professor, Univ. of Newcastle upon Tyne, 1978. Member: Board, Northern Sinfonia Orchestra, 1977-; Northern Industrial Development Board, 1977-; Washington Development Corporation, 1978-; IBA, 1979-; Board, Civil Service Pay Research Unit 1980-81; Megaw Inquiry into Civil Service Pay, 1981-. *Recreations*: tennis, badminton, bird watching. *Address*: 46 Downshire Hill, NW3 1NX. *T*: 01-435 7742.

RUSSELL, Sir George Michael, 7th Bt, *cr* 1812; *b* 30 Sept. 1908; *s* of Sir Arthur Edward Ian Montagu Russell, 6th Bt, MBE and late Aileen Kerr, *d* of Admiral Mark Robert Pechell; *S* father, 1964; *m* 1936, Joy Frances Bedford, *d* of late W. Mitchell, Irwin, Western Australia; two *d*. *Educ*: Radley, Berkshire, England. *Heir*: half-*b* Arthur Mervyn Russell, *b* 7 Feb. 1923.
See also Baron Broughshane.

RUSSELL, Gerald Francis Morris, MD, FRCP, FRCPE, FRCPsych, DPM; Professor of Psychiatry, Institute of Psychiatry, University of London, and Physician, Bethlem Royal and Maudsley Hospital, since 1979; *b* Grammont, Belgium, 12 Jan. 1928; 2nd *s* of late Maj. Daniel George Russell, MC, and late Berthe Marie Russell (*née* De Boe); *m* 1950, Margaret Taylor, MB, ChB; three *s*. *Educ*: Collège St Jean Berchmans, Brussels; George Watson's Coll., Edinburgh (Dux); Univ. of Edinburgh (Mouat Schol. in Practice of Physic). MD (with commendation), 1957. RAMC Regimental Med. Off., Queen's Bays, 1951-53; Neurological Registrar, Northern Gen. Hosp., Edin., 1954-56; MRC Clinical Res. Fellow, 1956-58; Inst. of Psychiatry, Maudsley Hospital: 1st Asst, 1959-60; Senior Lectr, 1961-70; Dean, 1966-70; Bethlem Royal and Maudsley Hospital: Physician, 1961-70; Mem. Bd of Governors, 1966-70; Prof. of Psychiatry, Royal Free Hosp. Sch. of Medicine, 1971-79. Chm., Educn Cttee, Royal Medico-Psychological Assoc., 1970 (Mem. Council, 1966-71); Sec. of Sect. of Psychiatry, Roy. Soc. Med., 1966-68; Member

Editorial Boards: British Jl of Psychiatry, 1966-71; Psychological Medicine, 1970-; Jl Neurology, Neurosurgery and Psychiatry, 1971-75; Medical Education, 1975-. Mem. European Soc. for Clinical Investigation, 1968-72. Corr. Fellow, Amer. Psychiatric Assoc., 1967; 1942 Club, 1978-. *Publications*: contrib. to Psychiatrie der Gegenwart, vol. 3, 1975; Anorexia Nervosa (ed R. Vigersky), 1977; Textbook of Medicine (ed J. B. Wyngaarden and L. H. Smith), 1979; articles in med. jls on psychiatry, disorders of eating, education and neurology. *Recreations*: roses, language, music, swimming. *Address*: The Institute of Psychiatry, De Crespigny Park, SE5.

RUSSELL, His Honour Henry Stanway; a Circuit Judge (formerly County Court Judge), 1965-80; *b* 27 April 1910; *s* of William Stanway Russell and late Dorothy Sophia Taylor; *m* 1937, Norah Patricia Knight Tapson; two *d*. *Educ*: Haileybury College; Merton College, Oxford. Called to Bar Inner Temple, 1934; Western Circuit, 1934. 1st Derbyshire Yeomanry RAC (Lieut). Served Tunisia and Italy, 1942-44. Capt., Judge Advocate General's Dept., 1945; Dep. Chm., Cornwall QS, 1963-71. *Address*: Field Farm House, Bibury, Cirencester, Glos.

RUSSELL, James Francis Buchanan, QC (NI) 1968; **His Honour Judge Russell**; County Court Judge of Northern Ireland, since 1978; *b* 7 July 1924; *e s* of John Buchanan Russell and Margaret Bellingham Russell; *m* 1946, Irene McKee; two *s* one *d* (and one *d* decd). *Educ*: King's Sch., Worcester; St Andrews Univ.; Queen's Univ., Belfast (LLB). Served Royal Air Force, 1941-47. Called to Bar, NI, 1952; Crown Prosecutor: Co. Fermanagh, 1970; Co. Tyrone, 1974; Co. Londonderry, 1976. Bencher, Inn of Court, N Ireland, 1972-78, Treasurer, 1977. Member, Standing Advisory Commn on Human Rights, 1974-78; Chairman, War Pensions Appeal Tribunal, N Ireland, 1970-82. *Recreations*: golf, gardening. *Address*: 5 Grey Point, Helen's Bay, Co. Down, Northern Ireland. *T*: Helen's Bay 852249. *Clubs*: Royal Air Force; Royal Belfast Golf, Ulster (Belfast).

RUSSELL, Prof. James Knox, MD; ChB; FRCOG; Emeritus Professor of Obstetrics and Gynæcology, University of Newcastle upon Tyne, since 1982; Dean of Postgraduate Medicine, 1968-77; Consulting Obstetrician, Princess Mary Maternity Hospital; Consultant Gynæcologist, Royal Victoria Infirmary, Newcastle upon Tyne, since 1956; *b* 5 Sept. 1919; *s* of James Russell, Aberdeen; *m* 1944, Cecilia V. Urquhart, MD, DCH, *o d* of Patrick Urquhart, MA; three *d*. *Educ*: Aberdeen Grammar School; University of Aberdeen. MB, ChB 1942, MD 1954, Aberdeen; MRCOG 1949; FRCOG 1958. Served War, 1943-46, as MO in RAF, UK and Western Europe. First Assistant to Prof. of Obstetrics and Gynæcology, Univ. of Durham, 1950; Senior Lecturer in Obstetrics and Gynæcology, Univ. of Durham, 1956; Consultant Obstetrician, Princess Mary Maternity Hosp., 1956; Consultant Gynæcologist, Royal Victoria Infirmary, Newcastle upon Tyne, 1956. Hon. Obstetrician, MRC Unit on Reproduction and Growth; Examiner in Obstetrics and Gynæcology, Univs of London, Birmingham, Aberdeen, Liverpool, RCOG, CMB, Tripoli and Kuala Lumpur; Presiding Examiner, CMB, Newcastle upon Tyne; Consultant in human reproduction, WHO. Commonwealth Fund Fellow 1962. Visiting Professor: New York, 1974; South Africa, 1978; Kaula Lumpur, 1980. *Publications*: Teenage Pregnancy: Medical, Social and Educational Aspects, 1982; various papers, editorials and articles on obstetrical and gynæcological subjects to learned journals, newspapers and magazines. *Recreations*: writing, gardening, curing and smoking bacon, eels, salmon, etc. *Address*: Newlands, Tranwell Woods, Morpeth, Northumberland NE61 6AG. *T*: Morpeth 55666. *Club*: Royal Over-Seas League.

RUSSELL, John, CBE 1975; Art critic, since 1974, Chief Art Critic, since 1982, The New York Times; *b* 1919; *o s* of Isaac James Russell and Harriet Elizabeth Atkins; *m* 1st, 1946, Alexandrine Apponyi (marr. diss., 1950); one *d*; 2nd, 1956, Vera Poliakoff (marr. diss., 1971); 3rd, 1975, Rosamond Bernier. *Educ*: St Paul's Sch.; Magdalen Coll., Oxford (MA). Hon. Attaché, Tate Gall., 1940-41; MOI, 1941-43; Naval Intell. Div., Admty, 1943-46. Regular contributor, The Sunday Times, 1945-, art critic, 1949-74. Mem. art panel, Arts Council, 1958-68. Organised Arts Council exhibns: Modigliani, 1964, Rouault, 1966 and Balthus, 1968 (all at Tate Gallery); Pop Art (with Suzi Gablik), 1969 (at the Hayward Gallery); organised Vuillard exhibn (Toronto, Chicago, San Francisco), 1971. Frank Jewett Mather Award (College Art Assoc.), 1979. Grand Medal of Honour (Austria), 1972; Officier de l'Ordre des Arts et des Lettres, 1975. TV scripts for arts programmes. *Publications*: books include: Shakespeare's Country, 1942; British Portrait Painters, 1945; Switzerland, 1950; Logan Pearsall Smith, 1950; Erich Kleiber, 1956; Paris, 1960; Seurat, 1965; Private View (with Bryan Robertson and Lord Snowdon), 1965; Max Ernst, 1967; Henry Moore, 1968; Ben Nicholson, 1969; Pop Art Redefined (with Suzi Gablik), 1969; The World of Matisse, 1970; Francis Bacon, 1971; Edouard Vuillard, 1971; The Meanings of Modern Art, 1981. *Recreations*: reading, writing, Raimund (1790-1836). *Address*: c/o The New York Times, 229 West 43rd Street, New York, NY 10036, USA. *Clubs*: Travellers'; Century, Knickerbocker (New York).

RUSSELL, John Harry; Chairman and Chief Executive, Duport Ltd, since 1981; *b* 21 Feb. 1926; *s* of Joseph Harry Russell and Nellie Annie Russell; *m* 1951, Iris Mary Cooke; one *s* one *d*. *Educ*: Halesowen Grammar Sch. FCA; FBIM. War Service, RN. Joseph Lucas Ltd, 1948-52; Vono Ltd (Duport Gp Co.), 1952-59; Standard Motors Ltd, 1959-61; rejoined Duport Gp, 1961: Man. Dir, Duport Foundries Ltd, 1964; Dir, Duport Parent Bd, 1966; Chm., Burman & Sons Ltd (formerly part of Duport), 1968-72; Chief Exec., Duport

Engrg Div., 1972-73; Dep. Gp Man. Dir, 1973-75; Gp Man. Dir, 1975-80, Dep. Chm., 1976-81, Duport Ltd. Non-exec. Dir, Birmingham Local Bd, Barclays Bank Ltd, 1976-. Liveryman, Worshipful Co. of Glaziers and Freeman and Citizen of London, 1976. *Recreations:* reading, music, antiques. *Address:* 442 Bromsgrove Road, Hunnington, Halesowen, West Midlands B62 0JL.

RUSSELL, John Lawson; Commissioner for Local Administration in Scotland, 1978-82; *b* 29 May 1917; *er s* of late George William Russell and Joan Tait Russell; *m* 1946, Rachel Essington Howgate; three *s. Educ:* Central School and Anderson Inst., Lerwick; Edinburgh Univ. (BL). Enrolled Solicitor. Served Royal Scots, Royal Artillery, Gordon Highlanders and 30 Commando, 1939-46 (despatches). Assistant Secretary, Assoc. of County Councils in Scotland, 1946-49; Depute County Clerk: West Lothian, 1950-57; Caithness, 1957-58; County Clerk: Caithness, 1958-67; Aberdeen, 1967-75; Chief Executive, Grampian Region, 1974-77. Member, Countryside Commission for Scotland, 1978-82. *Recreations:* sailing, hill-walking, camping, photography. *Address:* 39 Salisbury Terrace, Aberdeen AB1 6QG. *T:* Aberdeen 23595.

RUSSELL, Sir John (Wriothesley), GCVO 1968 (KCVO 1965); CMG 1958; HM Diplomatic Service, retired; Chairman, Elf Aquitaine UK (Holdings), since 1981; *b* 22 Aug. 1914; *s* of late Sir Thomas Russell Pasha, KBE, CMG; *m* 1945, Aliki Diplarakos, Athens, Greece; one *s* one *d. Educ:* Eton; Trinity Coll., Cambridge (MA). Entered HM Diplomatic Service, 1937; 3rd Sec.: Foreign Office, 1937, Vienna, 1937, Foreign Office, 1938, Moscow, 1939; 2nd Sec., Washington, 1942; 1st Sec.: Warsaw, 1945, Foreign Office, 1948; First Dir-Gen., Brussels Treaty Orgn, London, 1948. Rome, 1950; Counsellor, 1953, and Dir Gen. British Information Services, New York; Counsellor, HM Embassy, Teheran, 1956-59; Foreign Office Spokesman (Head of News Dept, Foreign Office) 1959-62; Ambassador: to Ethiopia, 1962-66; to Brazil, 1966-69; to Spain, 1969-74. Foreign Affairs Adviser, Rolls Royce Ltd, 1974-79. Montagu Burton Vis. Prof. of International Relations, Univ. of Edinburgh, 1980. Chm., Anglo-Spanish Soc., 1980. Joint Master, West Street Foxhounds, 1960-. Coronation Medal, 1953. Order of the Throne, Iran; Order of the Star of Ethiopia; Order of the Southern Cross, Brazil. *Address:* 80 Chester Square, SW1W 9DU. *T:* 01-730 3355; The Vine Farm, Northbourne, Kent. *T:* Deal 4794. *Clubs:* Beefsteak, White's, Garrick.

See also Sir H. R. B. Boothby, Bt.

RUSSELL, Ken; film director since 1958; *b* 3 July 1927. Merchant Navy, 1945; RAF, 1946-49. Ny Norsk Ballet, 1950; Garrick Players, 1951; free-lance photographer, 1951-57; Film Director, BBC, 1958-66; free-lance film director, 1966; *Films:* Elgar; Bartok; Debussy; Henri Rousseau; Isadora Duncan; Delius; Richard Strauss; French Dressing; The Billion Dollar Brain; Women in Love; The Music Lovers; The Devils; The Boy Friend; Savage Messiah; Mahler; Tommy; Lisztomania; Valentino; Clouds of Glory; Altered States; *opera:* The Rake's Progress, Florence, 1982. *Recreation:* music.

RUSSELL, Mrs Leonard; *see* Powell, (E.) Dilys.

RUSSELL, Hon. Leopold Oliver, CBE 1970 (OBE 1944); TD; Chairman, Cement Makers' Federation, since 1979; *b* 26 Jan. 1907; 4th *s* of 2nd Baron Ampthill, GCSI, GCIE; *m* 1935, Rosemary Wintour (marr. diss., 1954); no *c. Educ:* Eton. Weekly newspaper publishing company, 1925-38; served War of 1939-45, 5th Battalion Beds and Herts Regiment TA; Gen. Staff appts HQ 18th Div., Eastern Command, South-Eastern Command, GHQ Home Forces, HQ 21st Army Group, and CCG; released with rank of Brigadier; Asst Sec. to Board of Trade, 1946-47; Dir, British Institute of Management, 1947-56. Dir-Gen., Cement and Concrete Assoc., 1958-77. Chm. 1976-80. Chm., E Anglian RHA, 1973-78; Member: Bd of Governors, Nat. Hosps for Nervous Diseases, 1963-76; E Anglian Regional Hosp. Bd, 1972-73. *Address:* 17 Onslow Square, SW7. *T:* 01-589 0891; The Old Rectory, Kettlebaston, Ipswich, Suffolk. *T:* Bildeston 740314. *Clubs:* Brooks's, Buck's, Beefsteak, Pratt's.

RUSSELL, Sir Lionel; *see* Russell, Sir E. L.

RUSSELL, Mark; *see* Russell, R. M.

RUSSELL, Martin Guthrie, CBE 1970; Children's Division, Home Office, later Department of Health and Social Security, 1964-74; *b* 7 May 1914; *s* of William James Russell and Bessie Gertrude Meades; *m* 1951, Moira May Eynon, *d* of Capt. Richard Threlfell; one *d. Educ:* Alleyn's School; Sidney Sussex Coll., Cambridge (MA). Asst Principal, Home Office, 1937; Asst Private Sec. to Lord Privy Seal, 1942; Principal, Home Office, 1942; seconded to Treasury, 1949-51 and 1952-54; Asst Sec. 1950; Estabt Officer, 1954, Dep. Chm., 1960-64, Prison Commn. In charge of Interdepartmental Social Work Gp, 1969-70. *Recreations:* gardening, enjoying retirement. *Address:* 4 Camden Road, Sutton, Surrey SM1 2SH. *T:* 01-642 5090. *Club:* United Oxford & Cambridge University.

RUSSELL, (Muriel) Audrey, MVO 1976; broadcaster, radio and television; *o d* of late John Strangman Russell and Muriel Russell (*née* Metcalfe), Co. Dublin; unmarried. *Educ:* privately, in England, and France. Trained Central School of Speech and Drama. First stage appearance in London in Victoria Regina, Lyric, 1937. National Fire Service, 1939-42; joined war-time staff,

BBC, 1942; accredited BBC war correspondent overseas, 1944-45; news reporter, BBC 1946-51. Commentaries on State occasions have included: Funeral of King George VI at Windsor; the Coronation of Queen Elizabeth II in Westminster Abbey; Royal weddings: Princess Elizabeth; Princess Margaret; Princess Alexandra; Duke of Kent; Princess Anne; Prince Charles, Prince of Wales (for CBC); Funeral of Sir Winston Churchill in St Paul's; Royal Silver Wedding, 1972; Silver Jubilee, 1977; opening of Humber Bridge, 1981. BBC Commentator, 1953-: on Commonwealth Tours of the Queen and Duke of Edinburgh to Bermuda, NZ, Australia, Uganda, Malta, Canada, Nigeria, India, Pakistan, Ghana, Sierra Leone, Tanganyika; visits of Queen Elizabeth the Queen Mother to Central and E Africa; State Visits include: Oslo, 1955; Stockholm, 1956; Lisbon, Paris, Copenhagen, USA, 1957; Amsterdam, 1958; Nepal, Iran, Italy, 1961; W Germany, 1965; Austria, 1969; France, 1972. Royal Maundy Distribution broadcasts, 1952-78; numerous TV appearances in connection with history, art, and Royal occasions. FRSA. Freeman of City of London, 1967. *Recreations:* painting in oils, and visiting art galleries. *Address:* 117 Kenilworth Court, SW15.

RUSSELL, Hon. Sir Patrick; *see* Russell, Hon. Sir T. P.

RUSSELL, Prof. Peter Edward Lionel Russell, DLitt; FBA 1977; (surname formerly Wheeler); King Alfonso XIII Professor of Spanish Studies, Oxford, 1953-81; *b* 24 Oct. 1913; *er s* of Hugh Bernard Wheeler and late Rita Muriel (*née* Russell), Christchurch, NZ. *Educ:* Cheltenham College; Queen's College, Oxford. First Class Final Honour School of Modern Langs 1935; DLitt 1981. Lecturer of St John's College, 1937-53 and Queen's College, 1938-45. Enlisted, 1940; commissioned (Intelligence Corps) Dec. 1940; Temp. Lt-Col, 1945; specially employed in Caribbean, W Africa and SE Asia, 1942-46. Fellow of Queen's College, 1946-53, and Univ. Lectr in Spanish Studies, 1946-53; Fellow of Exeter Coll., 1953-81, Emeritus Fellow, 1981; Norman Maccoll Lectr, Cambridge, 1969; Vis. Prof., Univ. of Virginia, 1982. Member: Portuguese Academy of History, 1956; Real Academia de Buenas Letras, Barcelona, 1972; UGC Cttee on Latin-American Studies in British Univs, 1962-64. FRHistS. *Publications:* As Fontes de Fernão Lopes, 1941 (Coimbra); The English Intervention in Spain and Portugal in the Time of Edward III and Richard II, 1955; Prince Henry the Navigator, 1960; (with D. M. Rogers) Hispanic Manuscripts and Books in the Bodleian and Oxford College Libraries, 1962; (ed) Spain: a Companion to Spanish Studies, 1973; Temas de la Celestina y otros estudios (del Cid al Quijote), 1978; articles and reviews in Modern Language Review, Medium Aevum, Bulletin of Hispanic Studies, etc. *Recreations:* photography and travel. *Address:* 23 Belsyre Court, Woodstock Road, Oxford OX2 6HU. *T:* Oxford 56086. *Club:* United Oxford & Cambridge University.

RUSSELL, Most Rev. Philip Welsford Richmond; *see* Cape Town, Archbishop of.

RUSSELL, Robert Christopher Hamlyn, CBE 1981; formerly Director, Hydraulics Research Station, Department of the Environment (formerly Ministry of Technology), 1965-81; *b* Singapore, 1921; *s* of Philip Charles and Hilda Gertrude Russell; *m* 1950, Cynthia Mary Roberts; one *s* two *d. Educ:* Stowe; King's Coll., Cambridge. Asst Engineer: BTH Co., Rugby, 1944; Dunlop Rubber Co., 1946; Sen. Scientific Officer, later PSO, then SPSO, in Hydraulics Research Station, 1949-65. Visiting Prof., Univ. of Strathclyde, 1967. *Publications:* Waves and Tides, 1951; papers on civil engineering hydraulics. *Address:* 29 St Mary's Street, Wallingford, Oxfordshire. *T:* Wallingford 37323.

RUSSELL, (Robert) Mark, CMG 1977; HM Diplomatic Service; Ambassador to Turkey, since 1983; *b* 3 Sept. 1929; *s* of Sir Robert E. Russell, CSI, CIE; *m* 1954, Virginia Mary Rogers; two *s* two *d. Educ:* Trinity Coll., Glenalmond; Exeter Coll., Oxford (MA). Hon. Mods cl. 2, Lit. Hum. cl. 1. Royal Artillery, 1952-54; FO, 1954-56; 3rd, later 2nd Sec., HM Legation, Budapest, 1956-58; 2nd Sec., Berne, 1958-61; FO, 1961-65; 1st Sec., 1962; 1st Sec. and Head of Chancery, Kabul, 1965-67; 1st Sec., DSAO, 1967-69; Counsellor, 1969; Dep. Head of Personnel (Ops) Dept, FCO, 1969-70; Commercial Counsellor, Bucharest, 1970-73; Counsellor, Washington, 1974-78, and Head of Chancery, 1977-78; Asst Under Sec. of State, FCO and Dep. Chief Clerk and Chief Inspector, HM Diplomatic Service, 1978-82. *Recreations:* travel, music, golf. *Address:* c/o Foreign and Commonwealth Office, SW1. *Clubs:* Royal Commonwealth Society; New (Edinburgh).

RUSSELL, Prof. Roger Wolcott; Vice Chancellor, and Professor of Psychobiology, Flinders University of South Australia, 1972-79, now Emeritus Professor; *b* 30 Aug. 1914; *s* of Leonard Walker and Sadie Stanhope Russell, Worcester, Mass, USA; *m* 1945, Kathleen Sherman Fortescue; one *s* one *d. Educ:* Worcester (Mass, USA) Public Schools; Clark Univ. (Livermore Schol., Clark Fellow in Psychology); BA 1935, MA 1936; Peabody Coll. (Payne Schol.); University of Virginia (Du Pont Research Fellow); PhD 1939; DSc Univ. of London, 1954. Instructor in Psychology: Univ. of Nebraska, 1939-41, Michigan State Coll., 1941; Research Psychologist, USAF Sch. of Aviation Medicine, 1941-42; Officer USAF, 1942-46; Asst Prof. in Psychol., Univ. of Pittsburgh, 1946-47; Assoc. Prof. of Psychol., Univ. of Pittsburgh and Res. Fellow in Neurophysiol., Western Psychiatric Inst., 1947-49; Fulbright Advanced Research Schol. and Director, Animal Research Lab., Institute of Psychiatry, Univ. of London, 1949-50; Prof. of Psychology and Head of Dept of Psychol., University Coll., London 1950-57 (on leave of absence, 1956-57); Dean of Advanced Studies, Indiana Univ., 1966-67 (Prof.

and Chm. Dept of Psychology, 1959-66); Vice Chancellor, Academic Affairs, and Prof. of Psycho-Biology and of Clinical Pharmacology and Therapeutics, Univ. of Calif., Irvine, 1967-72. Member: Australian Vice-Chancellors' Cttee, 1972-79; Bd of Dirs, Australian-American Educnl Foundn, 1972-79; Commonwealth Educnl R&D Cttee, 1974-79. Visiting Professor: (of Pharmacology) Sch. of Medicine, UCLA, 1976-77; Dept of Psychology, Univ. of Reading, 1977; Dept of Psychology, Univ. of Stockholm, 1977; (of Pharmacology) Sch. of Medicine, UCLA, 1980, 1981. Executive Sec. of the American Psychological Assoc., 1956-59, Board of Directors, 1963-65, Pres. Div. 1, 1968-69; Mem., USPHS Advis. Cttee in Psychopharmacology, 1957-63, 1967-70, 1981-; Member: Nat. Research Coun. (USA), 1958-61, 1963-65, 1967-71; Army Sci. Adv. Panel (USA), 1958-66; Sec.-Gen. Internat. Union of Psychological Science, 1960-66 (Vice-Pres., 1966-69; Pres., 1969-72; Mem. Exec. Cttee, 1972-80); Aust.-Amer. Educn Foundn Vis. Prof., Dept of Psychol., Univ. of Sydney, 1965-66; Vis. Erskine Fellow, Univ. of Canterbury, NZ, 1966. Member, Scientific and Professional Socs in Europe, USA, Australia. FACE 1972; FASSA 1973. Hon. DSc: Newcastle, NSW, 1978; Flinders, 1979. Bronze Star Medal (USA), 1945. Army Commendation Medal (USA), 1946. *Publications*: (ed) Frontiers in Psychology, 1964; (ed) Frontiers in physiological Psychology, 1966; (ed) Matthew Flinders: The Ifs of History, 1979; research papers on neurochemical bases of behaviour, experimental psycho-pathology, physiological, child and social psychology, psychopharmacology. *Recreations*: writing, farming. *Address*: The Flinders University of South Australia, Bedford Park, SA 5042, Australia. *T*: Adelaide 275-3911; Kindra, Box 55, Aldinga, SA 5173, Australia. *T*: Adelaide (085) 56-5011.

RUSSELL, Rudolf Rosenfeld; a Recorder of the Crown Court, since 1980; *b* 5 Feb. 1925; *s* of Robert and Johanna Rosenfeld; *m* 1952, Eva Maria Jaray; one *s*. *Educ*: Bryanston Sch.; Worcester Coll., Oxford (MA). Service in RAF, 1943-46. Called to the Bar, Middle Temple, 1950. *Recreations*: walking, music, skiing. *Address*: Devereux Chambers, Devereux Court, Temple, WC2. *T*: 01-353 7534.

RUSSELL, Terence Francis; Sheriff, North Strathclyde, and Grampian, Highland and Islands, since 1981; *b* 12 April 1931; *s* of Robert Russell and Catherine Cusker Russell; *m* 1965, Mary Ann Kennedy; two *d*. *Educ*: Glasgow Univ. (BL). Qualified as Solicitor, 1955; practised in Glasgow, 1955-58 and 1963-81; Solicitor in High Court, Bombay, 1958-63. *Recreations*: gardening, painting. *Address*: Larchmont, Ganavan, Oban, Argyll PA34 4AA. *T*: Oban 65308.

RUSSELL, Thomas, CMG 1980; CBE 1970 (OBE 1963); HM Overseas Civil Service, retired; Representative of the Cayman Islands in UK; *b* 27 May 1920; *s* of Thomas Russell, OBE, MC and Margaret Thomson Russell; *m* 1951, Andrée Irma Désfossés; one *s*. *Educ*: Hawick High Sch.; St Andrews Univ.; Peterhouse, Cambridge. MA St Andrews; Dip. Anthrop. Cantab. War Service, Cameronians (Scottish Rifles), 1941; 5th Bn (Scottish), Parachute Regt, 1943; served in N Africa and Italy; POW, 1944; Captain 1945; OC Parachute Trng Company, 1946. Cambridge Univ., 1946-47. Colonial Admin. Service, 1948; District Comr, British Solomon Is Protectorate, 1948; Asst Sec., Western Pacific High Commn, Fiji, 1951; District Comr, British Solomon Is Protectorate, 1954-56; seconded Colonial Office, 1956-57; Admin. Officer Class A, 1956; Dep. Financial Sec., 1962; Financial Sec., 1965; Chief Sec. to W Pacific High Commn, 1970-74; Governor of the Cayman Islands, 1974-81. FRAI. *Publications*: monographs in Oceania, Jl of Polynesian Society. *Recreations*: anthropology, archaeology. *Address*: 6 Eldon Drive, Frensham Road, The Bourne, Farnham, Surrey. *Club*: Royal Commonwealth Society.

RUSSELL, Hon. Sir (Thomas) Patrick, Kt 1980; **Hon. Mr Justice Russell;** Judge of the High Court of Justice (Queen's Bench Division), since 1980; Presiding Judge, Northern Circuit, since 1983; *b* 30 July 1926; *s* of late Sidney Arthur Russell and Elsie Russell; *m* 1951, Doreen (Janie) Ireland; two *d*. *Educ*: Urmston Grammar Sch.; Manchester Univ. (LLB). Served in Intelligence Corps and RASC, 1945-48. Called to Bar, Middle Temple, 1949; Bencher, 1978; QC 1971; Leader, Northern Circuit, 1978-80; Mem. Senate, Inns of Court and Bar, 1978-80. Prosecuting Counsel to the Post Office (Northern Circuit), 1961-70; Asst Recorder of Bolton, 1963-70; Recorder of Barrow-in-Furness, 1970-71; a Recorder of the Crown Court, 1972-80. Mem., Lord Justice James Cttee on Distribution of Criminal Business, 1973-76. Pres., Manchester and Dist Medico-Legal Soc., 1978-79; Vice-Pres., Lancs CCC, 1980. *Recreation*: cricket. *Address*: Royal Courts of Justice, WC2; Oakfield, 65 Crofts Bank Road, Urmston, Manchester M31 1UB. *T*: 061-748 2004.

RUSSELL, William Robert; Vice-President, Australian British Trade Association, since 1980 (Chairman, 1967-72 and 1975-77; Deputy Chairman, 1972-74 and 1977-80); Chairman: New Zealand/UK Chamber of Commerce and Industry, since 1979; Bank of New Zealand (London Board), since 1981; *b* 6 Aug. 1913; *s* of William Andrew Russell and Mary Margaret Russell; *m* 1940, Muriel Faith Rolfe; one *s* one *d*. *Educ*: Wakefield Road Central, East Ham. Served War of 1939-45: Mine-Sweeping and Anti-Submarine vessels; Commissioned, 1942; appointed to command, 1943. Joined Shaw Savill & Albion Co. Ltd, 1929; Director, 1958-; Manager, 1959; Gen. Manager, 1961; Dep. Chm., 1966; Chm. and Man. Dir, 1968-73. Chm., London Bd, Bank of NZ, 1981- (Dir, 1968-). Chm., Council of European and Japanese Nat. Shipowners Assocs, 1969-71 and 1973-75; Chm., Aust. and NZ Adv. Cttee to BOTB, 1975-77, Dep. Chm., 1977-79. Mem., Tandridge Dist Council,

1978-82. *Recreations*: gardening, golf. *Address*: Westland, Uvedale Road, Limpsfield, Oxted, Surrey. *T*: Oxted 3080. *Clubs*: Naval, Directors.

RUSSELL-DAVIS, John Darelan, FRICS; chartered surveyor, retired; *b* 23 Dec. 1912; *s* of Edward David Darelan Davis, FRICS, and Alice Mildred Russell; *m* 1938, Barbarina Elizabeth Graham Arnould; one *s* one *d*. *Educ*: Stowe Sch.; Germany; Coll. of Estate Management, London. FRICS 1934. Served War, HAC, 1939; commnd RA, 1940; Captain 1942; mentioned in despatches, 1945. Partner, C. P. Whiteley & Son, Chartered Surveyors, 1938; Sen. Partner, Whiteley, Ferris & Puckridge, and Kemsley, Whiteley & Ferris, City of London, 1948-72. Mem., Lands Tribunal, 1972-77. Royal Instn of Chartered Surveyors: formerly Mem. Council (twice); Chm., City branch, 1959; Hon. Treasurer, Benevolent Fund. Mem., East Grinstead UDC, 1957-60 (Vice-Chm., 1960). Sec., Merston Deanery Synod, 1978. Formerly: Mem. Council, Wycombe Abbey Sch.; Governor, Christ's Hosp.; Trustee, Cordwainer and Bread Street Foundn; Mem. Court, Turners Co. (Renter-Warden, 1975). *Recreations*: gardening, motoring, Somerset and Dorset countryside. *Address*: Church Cottage, Queen Camel, Yeovil, Somerset BA22 7NX. *T*: Marston Magna 850419. *Clubs*: Army and Navy; Somerset CCC.

See also D. R. Davis.

RUSSELL-SMITH, Dame Enid (Mary Russell), DBE 1953; MA; Principal of St Aidan's College, Durham University, 1963-70; Hon. part-time Lecturer in Politics since 1964; *b* 3 March 1903; *d* of late Arthur Russell-Smith, of Hartfield, Sussex. *Educ*: St Felix Sch., Southwold, Suffolk; Newnham Coll., Cambridge. Modern Languages Tripos (French and German). Entered Civil Service as Assistant Principal in Ministry of Health, 1925. Deputy Secretary, Ministry of Health, 1956-63. Co-opted Mem., Teesside (later Cleveland) Educn Cttee, 1968-75; Chairman: Sunderland Church Commn., 1971; Durham County Conservation Trust, 1973-75; St Paul's Jarrow Develt Trust, 1975-80. Associate Fellow, Newnham College, 1956-72, Hon. Fellow, 1974. *Publication*: Modern Bureaucracy: the Home Civil Service, 1974. *Address*: 3 Pimlico, Durham DH1 4QW. *Club*: University Women's.

RUSSELL VICK, Arnold Oughtred; His Honour Judge Russell Vick; *see* Vick.

RUSSO, Sir Peter (George), Kt 1964; CBE 1953 (OBE 1939); JP; Barrister-at-Law; Minister of Housing and Economic Development, Gibraltar Council, 1964-68; *b* 1899; *s* of George Russo; *m* 1926, Margot, *d* of late John A. Imossi, Gibraltar; one *d*. Mem. various Govt bodies and cttees; Dir of several local cos; Trustee, John Mackintosh Foundation; past Chm. City Council, former Mem. Exec. Council, Gibraltar. JP Gibraltar, 1947-. *Address*: 2 Red Sands Road, Gibraltar. *T*: Gibraltar 5622. *Club*: Royal Gibraltar Yacht (past Cdre).

RUSTON, Rev. Canon (Cuthbert) Mark; Vicar, Holy Sepulchre with All Saints (The Round Church), Cambridge, since 1955; Hon. Chaplain to The Queen, since 1980; *b* 23 Aug. 1916; *s* of Samuel Montague Ruston and Florence Mary Ruston, MBE. *Educ*: Tonbridge Sch.; Jesus Coll., Cambridge (Lady Kaye Schol. 1937; BA 1939, MA 1940); Ridley Hall, Cambridge. Curate, St John's, Woking, 1940-42; Chaplain: Cheltenham Coll., 1942-51; Jesus Coll., Cambridge, 1951-53; Emmanuel Coll., Cambridge, 1953-54. *Recreation*: inland waters cruising. *Address*: 37 Jesus Lane, Cambridge CB5 8BW. *T*: Cambridge 357931. *Club*: Royal Commonwealth Society.

RUTHERFORD, Prof. Andrew; Regius (Chalmers) Professor of English Literature, University of Aberdeen, since 1968; *b* Helmsdale, Sutherland, 23 July 1929; *s* of Thomas Armstrong Rutherford and Christian P. Rutherford (*née* Russell); *m* 1953, Nancy Milroy Browning, *d* of Dr Arthur Browning and Dr Jean G. Browning (*née* Thomson); two *s* one *d*. *Educ*: Helmsdale Sch.; George Watson's Boys' Coll.; Univ. of Edinburgh; Merton Coll., Oxford. MA Edinburgh Univ., First Cl. Hons Eng. Lang. and Lit., James Elliott Prize, and Vans Dunlop Schol., 1951; Carnegie Schol., 1953; BLitt Oxford, 1959. Commnd Seaforth Hldrs, 1952; served with Somaliland Scouts, 1952-53; 11th Bn Seaforth Hldrs (TA), 1953-58. Asst Lectr in English, Univ. of Edinburgh, 1955; Lectr, 1956-64; Vis. Assoc. Prof., Univ. of Rochester (NY), 1963; University of Aberdeen: Sen. Lectr, 1964; Second Prof. of English, 1965-68; Mem. Court, 1978; Dean, Faculty of Arts and Soc. Scis, 1979; Vice-Principal, 1982. Lectures: Byron Foundn, Nottingham Univ., 1964; Chatterton, British Acad., 1965; Stevenson, Edinburgh Univ., 1967; Byron Soc., 1973. Chm., English Bd, CNAA, 1966-73; Pres., Internat. Assoc. of Univ. Profs of English, 1977-80. Mem., BBC Gen. Adv. Council, 1979. British Council lecture tours in: India, Greece, Italy, Colombia, Austria, Luxembourg, Malta, Belgium. *Publications*: Byron: A Critical Study, 1961; (ed) Kipling's Mind and Art, 1964; (ed) Byron: The Critical Heritage, 1970; (ed) 20th Century Interpretations of A Passage to India, 1970; (ed) Kipling, A Sahibs' War and other stories, 1971; (ed) Kipling, Friendly Brook and other stories, 1971; The Literature of War, 1979; articles in learned journals. *Recreation*: shooting. *Address*: Department of English, Taylor Building, King's College, Aberdeen AB9 2UB; 150 Hamilton Place, Aberdeen AB2 4BB. *T*: Aberdeen 23868. *Club*: Royal Northern (Aberdeen).

RUTHERFORD, Herman Graham, CBE 1966; QPM 1957; DL; Chief Constable of Surrey, 1956-68; retired, 1968; *b* 3 April 1908; *m* 1940, Dorothy Weaver; three *s* one *d*. *Educ*: Grammar School, Consett, County Durham. Metropolitan Police, 1929-45; Chief Constable: of Oxfordshire, 1945-54; of

Lincolnshire, 1954–56. Barrister, Gray's Inn, 1941. Served Army, Allied Military Government, 1943-45, Lt-Colonel. DL Surrey, 1968. *Recreation:* sailing. *Address:* Hankley Farm, Elstead, Surrey. *T:* Elstead 702200; Milina, Volos, Greece.

RUTHERFORD, Thomas, CBE 1982; Chairman, North Eastern Electricity Board, since 1977; *b* 4 June 1924; *s* of Thomas and Catherine Rutherford; *m* 1950, Joyce Foreman; one *s* one *d. Educ:* Tynemouth High Sch.; King's Coll., Durham Univ. BSc(Hons); CEng, FIEE. Engrg Trainee, subseq. Research Engr, A Reyrolle & Co. Ltd, Hebburn-on-Tyne, 1943-49; North Eastern Electricity Bd: various engrg and commercial appts, 1949-61; Personal Asst to Chm., 1961-63; Area Commercial Engr, then Area Engr, Tees Area, 1964-69; Dep. Commercial Man., 1969-70; Commercial Man., 1970-72; Chief Engr, 1972-73; Dep. Chm., 1973-75; Chm., SE Electricity Board, 1975-77. *Address:* 76 Beach Road, Tynemouth, Tyne and Wear. *T:* North Shields 571775.

RUTHVEN; *see* Hore-Ruthven, family name of Earl of Gowrie.

RUTHVEN OF CANBERRA, Viscount; Patrick Leo Brer Hore-Ruthven; *b* 4 Feb. 1964; *s* and *heir* of 2nd Earl of Gowrie, *qv.*

RUTLAND, 10th Duke of, *cr* 1703; **Charles John Robert Manners,** CBE 1962; Marquess of Granby, 1703; Earl of Rutland, 1525; Baron Manners of Haddon, 1679; Baron Roos of Belvoir, 1896; Captain Grenadier Guards; *b* 28 May 1919; *e s* of 9th Duke and Kathleen, 3rd *d* of late F. J. Tennant; *S* father, 1940; *m* 1946, Anne Bairstow Cumming (marr. diss. 1956), *e d* of late Major Cumming Bell, Binham Lodge, Edgerton, Huddersfield; one *d*; *m* 1958, Frances Helen, *d* of Charles Sweeny and of Margaret, Duchess of Argyll; two *s* one *d* (and one *s* decd). *Educ:* Eton; Trinity Coll., Cambridge. Owns 18,000 acres; minerals in Leicestershire and Derbyshire; picture gallery at Belvoir Castle. Chairman: E Midlands Economic Planning Council, 1971-74; Leicestershire County Council, 1974-77. *Heir: s* Marquis of Granby, *qv. Address:* Belvoir Castle, Grantham; Haddon Hall, Derby.
See also Marquess of Anglesey, Sir R. G. M. Throckmorton, Bt, Earl of Wemyss.

RUTT, Rt. Rev. Cecil Richard; *see* Leicester, Bishop of.

RUTTER, Prof. Arthur John; Emeritus Professor and Senior Research Fellow, Imperial College, University of London (Professor of Botany, 1967-79 and Head of Department of Botany and Plant Technology, 1971-79); *b* 22 Nov. 1917; *s* of late W. Arthur Rutter, CBE, FRIBA and Amy, *d* of William Dyche, BA, Cardiff; *m* 1944, Betsy Rosier Stone (*d* 1978); two *s* one *d. Educ:* Royal Grammar Sch., Guildford; Imperial Coll. of Science and Technology. ARCS, BSc, PhD, FIBiol. Mem., ARC team for selection of oil-seed crops and develt selective herbicides, 1940-45; Asst Lectr, Imperial Coll., 1945, Lectr 1946; Reader in Ecology, Univ. of London, 1956. Vis. Prof., Univ. of the Panjab, W Pakistan, 1960-61. *Publications:* papers, mainly in Annals of Botany, Jl of Ecology, Jl of Applied Ecology on water relations of plants, forest hydrology and effects of atmospheric pollution on trees. *Recreations:* gardening, walking. *Address:* Fairseat, Bagshot Road, Knaphill, Woking, Surrey. *T:* Brookwood 3347.

RUTTER, John Cleverdon; His Honour Judge Rutter; a Circuit Judge, since 1972; *b* 18 Sept. 1919; 2nd *s* of late Edgar John Rutter; *m* 1951, Jill, *d* of Maxwell Duncan McIntosh; one *s* one *d. Educ:* Cardiff High Sch.; Univ. Coll., of SW of England, Exeter (Open Schol.); Keble Coll., Oxford. MA Oxon; LLB London. Royal Artillery, 1940-45; commnd 1941; served overseas. Called to the Bar, Lincoln's Inn, 1948; practised Wales and Chester Circuit, 1948-66, Stipendiary Magistrate for City of Cardiff, 1966-71. A Legal Member, Mental Health Review Tribunal for Wales Region, 1960-66. An Assistant Recorder of: Cardiff, 1962-66; Merthyr Tydfil, 1962-66; Swansea, 1965-66; Dep. Chm., Glamorgan QS, 1969-71. *Recreations:* golf, reading. *Address:* Law Courts, Cardiff. *T:* Cardiff 45931.

RUTTER, Air Vice-Marshal (Retd) Norman Colpoy Simpson, CB 1965; CBE 1945; idc; jssc; psa; Sen. Tech. Staff Officer, Bomber Command, 1961-65; *b* 1909; *s* of Rufus John Rutter; *m* 1936, Irene Sophia, *d* of late Colonel A. M. Lloyd; one *s* one *d.* Air Cdre, 1957; Air Officer Commanding and Commandant of the Royal Air Force Technical College, Henlow, 1959-61. CEng, FIMechE; FRAeS. *Address:* 37 Meadow Road, Pinner, Mddx.

RUTTER, Trevor John, OBE 1976; Assistant Director General, The British Council, since 1981; *b* 26 Jan. 1934; *s* of late Alfred and Agnes Rutter; *m* 1959, Josephine Henson; one *s. Educ:* Monmouth Sch.; Brasenose Coll., Oxford (BA). National Service, Army, 1955-57. British Council, Indonesia, W Germany (Munich), London, 1959-66; First Secretary, Foreign Office, 1967; British Council, 1968-: Representative: Singapore, 1968-71; Thailand, 1971-75; Deputy Head, Home Division, 1975-76; Head: Far East Dept, 1977; Educnl Contracts Dept, 1978-79; Home Div., 1980. *Address:* West House, West Street, Wivenhoe, Essex CO7 9DE. *T:* Wivenhoe 2562.

RUTTLE, His Honour Henry Samuel; a Circuit Judge (formerly Judge of County Courts), 1959-81; *b* 10 Nov. 1906; *yr s* of late Michael Ruttle, Portlaw, Co. Waterford, Ireland; *m* 1st, 1943, Joyce Mayo Moriarty (*d* 1968), *yr d* of late J. O. M. Moriarty, Plymouth; one *s* two *d* ; 2nd, 1978, Mary

Kathleen Scott, *d* of late F. T. Scott, Wimbledon. *Educ:* Wesley College, Dublin and Trinity College, Dublin. BA (Moderatorship in Legal and Political Science) and LLB, 1929; LLD 1933; MA 1950. Called to the Bar, Gray's Inn, 1933; practised in Common Law: London and Western Circuit. Served War of 1939-45: RAFVR, 1940-45; Squadron Leader. Deputy Judge Advocate Judge Advocate General's Office. Resumed practice at Bar, 1945. Member of Church Assembly, 1948-55; Mem., General Council of the Bar, 1957-59; Deputy Chairman Agricultural Land Tribunal (SW Area), 1958-59. JP, Co. Surrey, 1961. Mem., County Court Rules Cttee, 1969-81 (Chm., 1978-81). Jt Editor, The County Court Practice, 1973-. *Recreations:* Rugby football (Leinster Inter-Provincial, 1927; Captain London Irish RFC, 1935-36; Middlesex County); fly-fishing. *Address:* West Lodge, West Side, Wimbledon Common, SW19.

RYAN, Arthur James, CBE 1953; Regional Director, London Postal Region, 1949-60, retired; *b* 10 Oct. 1900; *e s* of late Stephen James Ryan, Little Common, Bexhill on Sea, Sx; *m* 1926, Marjorie, *y d* of late George James Dee; two *d. Educ:* City of London College and privately. Clerk, Headquarters, GPO London, 1918; Asst Surveyor, GPO, Class II, 1926, Class I, 1935; served in N Wales, Eastern Counties, South Western District; Chief Superintendent, then Assistant Controller, 1936, Controller (Mails and Transport), 1941, London Postal Region; Assistant Secretary, Min. of Fuel and Power (on loan), 1941; Dep. Regional Director, London Postal Region, 1944; Member of Post Office Board, 1950. Freeman, City of London. *Recreations:* golf, gardening. *Address:* Daymer Cottage, Cooden Drive, Bexhill-on-Sea, East Sussex. *T:* Cooden 2277.

RYAN, (Christopher) Nigel (John), CBE 1977; Director of Programmes, Thames Television, 1980-82; *b* 12 Dec. 1929; *s* of late Brig. C. E. Ryan, MC, RA. *Educ:* Ampleforth Coll.; Queen's Coll., Oxford (MA). Joined Reuters, London, 1954; Foreign Corresp., 1957-60; joined Independent Television News, 1961, Editor, 1968-71, Editor and Chief Executive, 1971-77; Vice-Pres., NBC News, America, 1977-80. Silver Medal, Royal Television Soc., 1970; Desmond Davis Award, 1972. *Publications:* trans. novels from French by Georges Simenon and others. *Address:* 28 St Petersburgh Place, W2.

RYAN, Sir Derek Gerald, 3rd Bt, *cr* 1919; *b* 9 July 1922; *s* of Sir Gerald Ellis Ryan, 2nd Bt, and Hylda Winifryde Herapath; *S* father 1947; *m* 1st, 1947, Penelope Anne Hawkings (marr. diss. 1971); one *s* three *d* ; 2nd, 1972, Katja, *d* of Ernst Best. *Educ:* Harrow. Served War of 1939-45. Lieut Grenadier Guards, 1941-45. *Heir: s* Derek Gerald Ryan, Junior, *b* 25 March 1954. *Address:* 6228 Eltville, Nikolausstrasse 11, W Germany. *T:* 06123-5333.

RYAN, Most Rev. Dermot; *see* Dublin, Archbishop of, and Primate of Ireland, (RC).

RYAN, Gerard Charles, QC 1981; *b* 16 Dec. 1931; *er s* of Frederick Charles Ryan, Hove, and Louie Violet Ryan (*née* Ball); *m* 1960, Sheila Morag Clark, *er d* of Sir James Clark Cameron, *qv* ; two *s. Educ:* Clayesmore Sch.; Brighton Coll.; Pembroke Coll., Cambridge. MA. Served RA, 1955-57 (Lieut). Called to the Bar, Middle Temple, 1955. *Publication:* (with A. O. B. Harris) Outline of the Law of Common Land, 1967. *Recreations:* gardening, natural history, walking. *Address:* 13 Westmoreland Place, SW1; 2 Harcourt Buildings, Temple, EC4. *T:* 01-353 8415.

RYAN, (James) Stewart; Principal Assistant Solicitor, Department of the Environment, 1975-78; *b* 9 Sept 1913; *o s* of late Philip F. Ryan and Bridget Ryan; *m* 1939, Rachel Alleyn; two *s Educ:* Beaumont Coll.; Balliol Coll., Oxford (BA). Called to Bar, Inner Temple, 1939. War service, 1939-46, Oxford and Bucks Light Infantry, War Office, DAAG, Major 1944. Joined Govt Legal Service, 1946; Asst Solicitor, Min. of Housing and Local Govt, 1957, later DoE. *Address:* 28 Manor Road, Henley-on-Thames RG9 1LU. *T:* Henley-on-Thames 3345. *Club:* Leander (Henley).
See also S. K. O'Malley.

RYAN, John; Management consultant and lecturer; *b* 30 April 1940; *m* 1964, Eunice Ann Edmonds; two *s. Educ:* Lanark Grammar School; Glasgow University. Member, National Association of Labour Student Organisations, 1958-62; formerly Youth Organiser, Lanark City Labour Party; Member, Executive Committee, North Paddington Labour Party, 1964-66. Contested (Lab) Buckinghamshire South, 1964; MP (Lab) Uxbridge, 1966-70. Member, Fabian Society, 1961; Dir, Tribune Publications Ltd, 1969-. Mem., Inst. of Marketing; Associate Member: Market Res. Soc.; BIM. *Recreations:* golf, walking.

RYAN, Rt. Rev. Joseph Francis, DD, JCD; *b* Dundas, Ontario, 1 March 1897; *s* of Wm Ryan and Ellen Manion. *Educ:* St Mary's Sch., Hamilton; St Jerome's Coll., Kitchener; St Augustine's Seminary, Toronto; Appolinaris Univ., Rome, Italy. Ordained 1921; Asst Priest, St Mary's Cathedral, Hamilton, 1921-25; Rector, 1925; First Rector of new Cathedral of Christ the King, Hamilton, 1933; Administrator of diocese after serving several years as Chancellor; Bishop of Hamilton, 1937-73. *Address:* St Joseph's Motherhouse, PO Box 155, Hamilton, Ontario L8N 3A2, Canada.

RYAN, Nigel; *see* Ryan, C. N. J.

RYAN, Stewart; *see* Ryan, J. S.

RYAN, Thomas; County Councillor, South Yorkshire, since 1973 (Chairman, 1977-78); *b* 26 Sept. 1911; *s* of John Ryan and Bridget (*née* Griffin); *m* 1939, Phoebe (*née* Taylor); two *s*. *Educ:* Netherfield Lane Council Sch.; WEA (adult educn); Sheffield Univ. (2 days per week part-time). Coal miner, Aldwarke Main Colliery, at age of 14; life-long NUM Mem.; NUM Sec., Aldwarke Main Colliery, 1955-62, when Colliery closed; transf. to Denaby Main Colliery, 1962; NUM Pres., 1962; resigned, then elected NUM Sec., 1963-68, when Colliery closed and merged with Cadeby Colliery; underground worker, Cadeby, 1968-71; NUM Sec., Cadeby, 1971-73; elected Sec. again but took redundancy, 1973; retd. Councillor, Rawmarsh UDC, 1960-74 (Chm., 1969); County Councillor, W Riding, 1972-73. Silver Jubilee Medal, 1977. *Recreation:* country walks. *Address:* 24 Hawke Close, Manor Farm Estate, Rawmarsh, Rotherham, S Yorks. *T:* Rawmarsh 2581. *Clubs:* Rawmarsh Trades, Rawmarsh Labour.

RYAN PRICE, Henry; *see* Price, H. R.

RYBCZYNSKI, Tadeusz Mieczyslaw, FIB; Economic Adviser, Lazard Brothers & Co Ltd, and Director, Lazard Securities Ltd, since 1969; *b* 21 May 1923; *s* of Karol Rybczynski and Helena (*née* Sawicka); *m* 1951, Helena Perucka; one *d*. *Educ:* primary and secondary schs, Lwow, Poland; LSE, Univ. of London (BCom, MScEcon). FIB 1966. Lloyds Bank, 1949-53; Lazard Brothers & Co. Ltd, 1954-. Vis. Professor: Univ. of Surrey, 1968-74; City Univ., 1974-. Chm., Soc. of Business Economists, 1962-75. Member: Monopolies and Mergers Commn, 1978-81; Council of Management and Exec. Cttee, NIESR, 1968- (also Governor); Council, REconS, 1969-74 (Treasurer, 1976-); Governing Body, Trade Policy Res. Centre, 1968-; Cttee, Foreign Affairs Club, 1968-; Adv. Bd in Banking and Finance, Univ. of Aston Management Centre, 1973-; Court, Brunel Univ., 1976-. *Publications:* (contrib.) Comparative Banking, ed H. W. Auburn, 1960 (3rd edn 1969); (contrib.) Long Range Planning, Paris and New York, 1967; (ed jtly and contrib.) The Economist in Business, 1967; (contrib.) Readings in International Economics, ed R. E. Caves and H. Johnson, 1968; (ed and contrib.) Value Added Tax-the UK position and the European experience, 1969; (contrib.) Money in Britain 1959-69, ed R. Croome and H. Johnson, 1970; (contrib.) Problems of Investment, ed Sir Robert Shone, 1971; (contrib.) Users of Economics, ed G. D. N. Worswick, 1972; (ed) A New Era in Competition, 1973; (ed and contrib.) The Economics of the Oil Crisis, 1976; (contrib.) Financial Management Handbook, 1977; articles in serious jls, and in academic and bank revs. *Recreations:* music, ballet, history, international affairs, travel. *Address:* 2 Windyridge Close, Parkside Avenue, SW19 5HB. *T:* 01-946 7363. *Club:* Reform.

RYBURN, Rev. Hubert James, CMG 1959; MA (Oxon and NZ), BD (Union); *b* 19 April 1897; *s* of Very Rev. Robert Middelton Ryburn and Anna Jane Steadman; *m* 1st, 1931, Jocelyn Maud Dunlop (*d* 1980), *d* of Prof. F. W. Dunlop; two *s* two *d* ; 2nd, 1981, Isabella Paterson May. *Educ:* Otago University; Oxford University; Union Theological Seminary, NY. Rhodes Scholar, 1921-24. Ordained a minister of the Presbyterian Church of New Zealand, 1926; Minister: Bay of Islands, 1926-29; St Andrews', Dunedin, 1929-41; Master of Knox College, Dunedin, 1941-63. Member: Council of Otago University, 1946-71, Pro-Chancellor, 1954-55, Chancellor, 1955-70; Senate of Univ. of NZ, 1948-61. Hon. LLD (Otago). *Publication:* Te Hemara, James Hamlin, 1980. *Recreation:* fishing. *Address:* 15 Cornwall Street, Dunedin, New Zealand. *T:* 42-032.

RYCROFT, Sir Richard Newton, 7th Bt, *cr* 1784; *b* 23 Jan. 1918; *yr s* of Sir Nelson Edward Oliver Rycroft, 6th Bt, and Ethel Sylvia (*d* 1952), *d* of late Robert Nurton, Odcombe, Yeovil; *S* father 1958; *m* 1947, Ann, *d* of late Hugh Bellingham-Smith, Alfriston, Sussex, and Mrs Harvey Robarts; two *d*. *Educ:* Winchester; Christ Church, Oxford (BA). Served War of 1939-45: Bedfordshire and Hertfordshire Regt, on special service work in Balkans (Major, despatches); Knight's Cross of Royal Order of Phœnix with Swords (Greece). *Heir: uncle* Henry Richard Rycroft, OBE, DSC, Comdr RN retd [*b* 28 Dec. 1911; *m* 1941, Penelope Gwendolen, *d* of late Lt-Col C. S. B. Evans-Lombe; one *s* three *d*]. *Address:* Winalls Wood House, Stuckton, Fordingbridge, Hampshire. *T:* Fordingbridge 2263.
See also Viscount FitzHarris.

RYDBECK, Olof; Royal Order of the Star of the North, Sweden; Commissioner-General, United Nations Relief and Works Agency, since 1979; *b* Djursholm, 15 April 1913; *s* of Oscar Rydbeck and Signe Olson; *m* 1940, Monica Schnell; one *s* one *d*. *Educ:* Univ. of Uppsala, Sweden (BA 1934, LLB 1939). Attaché, Min. for Foreign Affairs, 1939; Berlin, 1940; Ankara, 1941; Stockholm, 1942; Second Sec., 1943; Washington, 1945-50 (First Sec., 1946); Bonn, 1950; Head of Press Sect., Min. for For. Affairs, 1952; Dir Gen., Swedish Broadcasting Corp., 1955-70; Perm. Rep. to UN, 1970-76; Rep. of Sweden to Security Council, 1975-76; Special Rep. of Sec. Gen. on Western Sahara, 1976; Ambassador of Sweden to the UK, 1977-79. Chairman: Adv. Cttee on Outer Space Communications, UNESCO, 1966-70; Working Gp on Direct Broadcast Satellites, UN Cttee on Peaceful Uses of Outer Space, 1969-75; Cttee of Trustees, UN Trust Fund for S Africa, 1970-75; Prep. Cttee, World Food Conf., 1974; Second Cttee, 30th Gen. Assembly, 1975. Chairman: Assoc. of Royal Swedish Nat. Defence Coll., 1957-70; Internat. Broadcasting Inst., Rome, 1967-70; Hon. Pres., EBU, 1964-. Pres., 1961-64). Member: Central Cttee, Swedish Red Cross; Nat. Swedish Preparedness Commn for Psychol. Defence, 1954-70 (Vice Chm., 1962-70); Royal Swed. Acad. of Music, 1962-. Member Boards: Swed. Inst., 1953-55; Amer.-Swed. News

Exchange, 1953-55; Swed. Tourist Traffic Assoc., 1953-55; Stockholm Philharmonic Soc., 1955-62; Swed. Central News Agency, 1967-70; Swed. Inst. of Internat. Affairs, 1967-. Order of: White Rose, Finland; Falcon, Iceland; Dannebrog, Denmark; Verdienstkreutz, Fed. Republic of Germany. *Recreations:* music, equitation. *Address:* UNRWA Headquarters, VIC, PO Box 800, A-1400 Vienna, Austria.

RYDEN, Kenneth, MC and Bar 1945; DL; *b* 15 Feb. 1917; *s* of Walter and Elizabeth Ryden; *m* 1950, Catherine Kershaw (*née* Wilkinson); two *s*. *Educ:* Queen Elizabeth's Grammar School, Blackburn. FRICS; FRVA. Served War of 1939-45 (MC and Bar, despatches 1945): RE, attached Royal Bombay Sappers and Miners, India, Assam and Burma, 1940-46, retd (Captain). Articled pupil and prof. trng, 1936-39; Min. of Works: Estate Surveyor, 1946-47; attached UK High Commns, India and Pakistan, 1947-50; Sen. Estate Surveyor, Scotland, 1950-59. Founder and Sen. Partner, Kenneth Ryden & Partners (Chartered Surveyors) Edinburgh, Glasgow and London, 1959-74, retd, Consultant 1974-80. Chm., Scottish Br. Chartered Auctioneers and Estate Agents' Institute, 1960-61; Mem., Edinburgh Valuation Appeal Cttee, 1965-75, 1981-. Mem. Bd, Housing Corp., 1972-76. Master, Co. of Merchants of City of Edinburgh, 1976-78; Liveryman, Chartered Surveyors' Co. DL City of Edinburgh, 1978. *Recreations:* fishing, golf, Scottish art. *Address:* 19 Belgrave Crescent, Edinburgh EH4 3AJ. *T:* 031-332 5893. *Club:* New (Edinburgh).

RYDER, family name of **Earl of Harrowby** and of **Baron Ryder of Eaton Hastings.**

RYDER OF EATON HASTINGS, Baron *cr* 1975 (Life Peer), of Eaton Hastings, Oxfordshire; **Sydney Thomas Franklin, (Don), Ryder,** Kt 1972; Industrial Adviser to the Government, since 1974; Chairman, National Enterprise Board, 1975-77; *b* 16 Sept. 1916; *s* of John Ryder; *m* 1950; one *s* one *d*. *Educ:* Ealing. Editor, Stock Exchange Gazette, 1950-60; Jt Man. Dir, 1960-61, Sole Man. Dir, 1961-63, Kelly Iliffe Holdings, and Associated Iliffe Press Ltd; Dir, Internat. Publishing Corp., 1963-70; Man. Dir, Reed Paper Gp, 1963-68; Chm. and Chief Executive, Reed International Ltd, 1968-75; Dir, MEPC Ltd, 1972-75. Member: British Gas Corp., 1973-78; Reserve Pension Bd, 1973-; Council and Bd of Fellows, BIM, 1970-; Court and Council, Cranfield Inst. of Technology, 1970-74; Council, UK S Africa Trade Assoc., 1974-; Nat. Materials Handling Centre (Pres., 1970-77); Council, Industrial Soc., 1971-; NEDC, 1976-77. Vice-Pres., RoSPA, 1973-. *Recreations:* sailing, chess. *Address:* 12-18 Grosvenor Gardens, SW1W 0DW.

RYDER OF WARSAW, Baroness *cr* 1979 (Life Peer), of Warsaw in Poland and of Cavendish in the County of Suffolk; **(Sue Ryder);** CMG 1976; OBE 1957; Founder and Social Worker, Sue Ryder Foundation for the Sick and Disabled of all Age Groups; *b* 3 July 1923; *d* of late Charles and Elizabeth Ryder; *m* 1959, Geoffrey Leonard Cheshire, *qv* ; one *s* one *d*. *Educ:* Benenden Sch., Kent. Served War of 1939-45 with FANY and with Special Ops Executive. Co-Founder, Mission for the Relief of Suffering; Trustee, Cheshire Foundn. Hon. LLD: Liverpool, 1973; Exeter, 1980; London, 1981; Hon. DLitt Reading, 1982. Holds Officer's Cross of Order of Polonia Restituta, Poland, 1965; Medal of Yugoslav Flag with Gold Wreath and Diploma, 1971; Golden Order of Merit, Polish People's Republic, 1976; Order of Smile (Poland), 1980. *Publications:* Remembrance (annual leaflet of the Sue Ryder Foundation); And the Morrow is Theirs (autobiog.), 1975. *Address:* Sue Ryder Home, Cavendish, Suffolk CO10 8AY.

RYDER, Eric Charles, MA, LLB; Barrister; Professor of English Law in the University of London (University College) 1960-82; *b* 28 July 1915; *er s* of late Charles Henry Ryder, solicitor, Hanley, Staffs, and of Ellen Miller; *m* 1941, Nancy Winifred Roberts; no *c*. *Educ:* Hanley High School; Gonville and Caius College, Cambridge (scholar). BA (Law Tripos Parts I and II, 1st Cl.), 1936; LLB (1st Cl.) 1937; MA 1940; Tapp Law Scholar, Gonville and Caius College, 1937; called to Bar, Gray's Inn, 1937; practice at Chancery Bar. Ministry of Food, 1941-44; Lecturer in Law, King's College, Newcastle upon Tyne, 1944; Dean of Faculty of Law, Univ. of Durham, 1947-60; Professor of Law, Univ. of Durham (King's College), 1953-60. Practised as conveyancing counsel, Newcastle upon Tyne, 1944-53. *Publications:* Hawkins and Ryder on the Construction of Wills, 1965; contrib. to legal periodicals. *Address:* 19 Langton Avenue, Whetstone, N20. *T:* 01-445 1588.

RYDER, Peter Hugh Dudley, MBE 1944; Managing Director, Thomas Tilling Ltd, 1957-68; *b* 28 April 1913; *s* of Hon. Archibald Dudley Ryder and Eleanor Frederica Fisher-Rowe; *m* 1940, Sarah Susannah Bowes-Lyon; two *s* one *d*. *Educ:* Oundle School. Provincial Newspapers Ltd, Hull and Leeds, 1930-33; Illustrated Newspapers Ltd, 1933-39; seconded from TA to Political Intell. Dept of FO, 1939-45 (Lt-Col 1944); Jt Man. Dir, Contact Publications Ltd, 1945; Man. Dir, Daimler Hire Ltd, 1950; Commercial Dir, James A. Jobling & Co. Ltd, Sunderland, 1953; Chairman: James A. Jobling & Co. Ltd, 1957-62 and 1967-68; Heinemann Gp of Publishers Ltd, 1961-68; Director: District Bank Ltd, 1961-69; Cornhill Insce Co. Ltd, 1965-68. Mem. Council, BIM, 1966-69 (Mem. Bd of Fellows, 1968-69); Mem. Bd of Govs, Ashridge Management Coll., 1968. *Recreations:* home life, many forms of sport and games. *Address:* Hillside House, Baldhoon, Isle of Man. *T:* Laxey 787.

RYDER, Richard Andrew, OBE 1981; Political Secretary to the Prime Minister, 1979-81; *b* 4 Feb. 1949; *s* of Richard Stephen Ryder, JP, DL, and Margaret MacKenzie; *m* 1981, Caroline, *o d* of Sir David Stephens, *qv*. *Educ:*

Radley; Magdalene Coll., Cambridge. BA Hons History, 1971. Manager, Private Office of Leader of the Opposition, 1975-79. Contested (C) Gateshead East, Feb. and Oct. 1974. Director and Partner, Great Bradley Farms. *Recreations:* shooting, football and reading.

RYDER, Richard Hood Jack Dudley; Senior Clinical Psychologist, Warneford Hospital, Oxford, since 1970; *b* 3 July 1940; *s* of D. C. D. Ryder; *m* 1974, Audrey Jane Smith; one *s* one *d. Educ:* Cambridge Univ. (MA); Edinburgh Univ. (DCP). ABPsS. Univ. Fellow, Columbia Univ., NY, 1963-64. Member: Oxford Regional Adolescent Service, 1971-; Oxford AHA Professional Adv. Cttee (Psychiatric Sector), 1974-; DHSS Health Adv. Service, 1977-78. Royal Society for Prevention of Cruelty to Animals: Council Mem., 1972-; Vice-Chm., 1976; Chm., 1977-79; Chm. Political Cttee, 1980; founding mem. of Animal Experimentation Adv. Cttee, 1972, Chm. 1981-; Wildlife Adv. Cttee, 1972-; Legal Adv. Cttee, 1977. Founding Member: Jt Adv. Cttee on Pets in Society, 1974; Cttee on Reform of Animal Experimentation, 1977-; Farm Animal Welfare Coordinating Exec., 1977; Gen. Election Coordinating Cttee on Animal Protection, 1978. Director: RSPCA Trading Ltd, 1976; Internat. Soc. for Protection of Animals, 1978. Chm. Oxford Br., Clinical Div., British Psychological Soc.; Member: BPsS Cttee on Standard for Psychological Research and Teaching involving Animals, 1981-; Working Party on Private Practice, 1982-; Liberal Party Home and European Affairs Panels, 1981-. UK Delegate, Eurogroup for Animal Welfare, 1980; Chm., Liberal Animal Welfare Gp, 1981-; Mem. Cttee, Liberal Ecology Gp. Pres., British Union for Abolition of Vivisection, 1981-; Patron: Internat. Primate Protection League; Free Range Egg Assoc. Broadcaster and writer on psychological and animal protection subjects; author, RSPCA's Declaration Against Speciesism, 1977. *Publications:* Speciesism, 1970; (contrib.) Animals Men and Morals, 1971; The Extensive Use of Animals in Non-Medical Research, 1972; Pets Are Good for People, 1974; Scientific Cruelty for Commercial Profit, 1974; Victims of Science: the use of Animals in Research, 1975; Speciesism: the Ethics of Vivisection, 1975; (contrib.) Animal Rights and Human Obligations, 1976; (jtly) Experiments on Living Animals, 1976; (contrib.) Animal Marking, 1978; (ed) Animal Rights—a Symposium, 1979. *Recreations:* medieval furniture, hot baths, ancestors. *Address:* c/o Warneford Hospital, Oxford. *Clubs:* Royal Over-Seas League, National Liberal.

RYDER, Captain Robert Edward Dudley, VC 1942; RN (retired); *b* 16 Feb. 1908; *s* of late Col C. H. D. Ryder, CB, CIE, DSO; *m* 1941, Hilare Myfanwy Green-Wilkinson (*d* 1982); one *s* one *d. Educ:* Hazelhurst, Frant; Cheltenham College. Entered RN 1926; commanded Yacht Tai Mo Shan, 1933-34, on passage from Hong-Kong to Dartmouth; a member of British Graham Land Expedition to the Antarctic, 1934-37, in command of the Research Yacht Penola (Polar Medal with Clasp); commanded Naval forces in attack on St Nazaire, March 1942 (VC); took part in attack on Dieppe, Aug. 1942 (despatches); retd list, 1950. MP (C) Merton and Morden, 1950-55. *Publications:* The Attack on St Nazaire, 1947; Coverplan, 1953. *Address:* c/o Lloyds Bank, Cox's & King's Branch, 6 Pall Mall, SW1.

RYDILL, Prof. Louis Joseph, OBE 1962; RCNC; Professor of Naval Architecture, University College London, since 1981; *b* 16 Aug. 1922; *s* of Louis and Queenie Rydill; *m* 1949, Eva (*née* Newman); two *d. Educ:* HM Dockyard Sch., Devonport; RNEC Keyham; RNC Greenwich; Royal Corps of Naval Constructors. FEng, FRINA (Gold Medallist). Asst Constructor, 1946-52; Constructor, 1952-62, incl. Asst Prof. of Naval Architecture, RNC Greenwich, 1953-57; Chief Constructor, 1962-72, incl. Prof. of Naval Architecture, RNC Greenwich and UCL, 1967-72; Asst Dir Submarines, Constructive, 1972-74; Dep. Dir Submarines (Polaris), 1974-76; Dir of Ship Design and Engrg (formerly Warship Design), MoD, 1976-81. Hon. Res. Fellow, UCL, 1974. Silver Jubilee Medal, 1977. *Recreations:* literature, theatre, jazz and other music. *Address:* The Lodge, Entry Hill Drive, Bath, Avon. *T:* Bath 27888.

RYDON, Prof. Henry Norman, DSc, PhD (London), DPhil (Oxon), FRSC; Professor of Chemistry, University of Exeter, 1957-77, now Emeritus; Deputy Vice-Chancellor, 1973-75; Public Orator, 1976-77; *b* 24 March 1912; *o s* of late Henry William Rydon and Elizabeth Mary Anne (*née* Salmon); *m* 1st, 1937, Eleanor Alice Tattersall (*d* 1968); one *d* ; 2nd, 1968, Lovis Elna Hibbard (*née* Davies). *Educ:* Central Foundation Sch., London; Imperial Coll., London. BSc (London), 1931; PhD (London), 1933; DSc (London), 1938; DPhil (Oxon), 1939. Demonstrator in Organic Chemistry, Imperial College, London, 1933-37; Demonstrator in Chemistry, Birkbeck College, London, 1933-37; 1851 Exhibition Senior Student, Oxford University, 1937-40; Chemical Defence Experimental Station, Porton, 1940-45; Member Scientific Staff, Medical Research Council, Lister Institute, 1945-47; Reader in Organic Chemistry, Birkbeck Coll., London, 1947-49; Asst Prof. and Reader in Organic Chemistry, Imperial Coll., London, 1949-52; Professor of Chemistry and Director of the Chemical Laboratories, Manchester College of Science and Technology, 1952-57. Member Council: Chem. Society, 1947-50, 1951-52, 1954-57, 1964-67; Roy. Inst. of Chemistry, 1955-58, 1959-62, 1963-66, 1971-73; Soc. of Chemical Industry, 1961-63; Regional Scientific Adviser for Civil Defence, Home Office, 1951-52, 1955-57. Member: Chemical Defence Adv. Bd, MoD, 1955-66; Scientific Adv. Council, MoD, 1960-63. Hon. DSc Exeter, 1981. Meldola Medal, Roy. Inst. of Chemistry, 1939; Harrison Memorial Prize, Chem. Soc., 1941. *Publications:* papers in Jl of Chem. Soc. and other scientific jls, 1933-. *Recreations:* travel, gardening

and motoring. *Address:* Stadmans, Dunsford, Exeter EX6 7DD. *T:* Christow 52532.

RYKWERT, Prof. Joseph, MA (Cantab), DrRCA; Lecturer in Architecture, University of Cambridge, since 1980; *b* 5 April 1926; *s* of Szymon Rykwert and Elizabeth Melup; *m* 1st, 1960 (marr. diss. 1967); 2nd, 1972, Anne-Marie Sandersley; one *s* one *d. Educ:* Charterhouse; Bartlett Sch. of Architecture; Architectural Assoc. Lectr, Hochschule für Gestaltung, Ulm, 1958; Librarian and Tutor, Royal Coll. of Art, 1961-67; Prof. of Art, Univ. of Essex, 1967-80. Fellow, Inst. for Arch. and Urban Studies, NY, 1969-71; Sen. Fellow, Council of Humanities, Princeton Univ., 1971; Visiting Professor: Institut d'Urbanisme, Univ. of Paris, 1974-76; Princeton Univ., 1977; Andrew Mellon Vis. Prof., Cooper Union, NY, 1977; Slade Prof. of Fine Art, Cambridge Univ., 1979-80. Vis. Fellow, Darwin Coll., Cambridge, 1979-80. Sen. Fellow, Center for the Advanced Studies in the Visual Arts. Nat. Gall. of Art, Washington. Mem., Comité Internat. des Critiques d'Architecture. Mem. Commn, Venice Biennale, 1974-; Co-editor, Lotus, 1974-. *Publications:* The Golden House, 1947; (ed) The Ten Books of Architecture, by L. B. Alberti, 1955; The Idea of a Town, 1963, 2nd edn 1976; Church Building, 1966; On Adam's House in Paradise, 1972; (ed) Parole nel Vuoto, by A. Loos, 1972; The First Moderns, 1980; The Necessity of Artifice, 1981; contrib. Arch. Rev., Burlington Mag., Lotus. *Recreations:* rare. *Address:* Faculty of Architecture and History of Art, University of Cambridge, 1 Scroope Terrace, Cambridge CB2 1PX. *T:* Cambridge 69501. *Club:* Savile.

RYLAND, Sir (Albert) William (Cecil), Kt 1973; CB 1965; Chairman, Post Office Corporation, 1971-77; *b* 10 Nov. 1913; *s* of late A. E. Ryland, OBE; *m* 1946, Sybil, *d* of late H. C. Wookey; one *s* one *d. Educ:* Gosforth County Grammar School. Assistant Traffic Superintendent, GPO, 1934; Asst Surveyor, GPO, 1938. Served War of 1939-45 in Royal Engineers (Postal Section), Middle East and Central Mediterranean. Principal, GPO, 1949; Principal Private Secretary to PMG, 1954; Asst Secretary, GPO, 1955; Director of Establishments and Organisation, GPO, 1958; Director of Inland Telecommunications, GPO, 1961-65; Dep. Director-General, 1965-67; Man. Dir, Telecommunications, GPO, 1967-69; PO Corporation: Jt Dep. Chm. and Chief Exec., 1969-70; Acting Chm., 1970-71. Adviser: to Republic of Ireland Posts and Telegraphs Review Gp, 1978-79; to Deloitte, Haskins and Sells, 1981-. Mem., Standing Cttee on Pay Comparability, 1979-80. CompIEE; FBIM; Hon. CGIA. *Address:* 13 Mill View Gardens, Croydon CR0 5HW. *T:* 01-656 4224. *Clubs:* Reform, City Livery, MCC.

RYLAND, Charles Mortimer Tollemache S.; *see* Smith-Ryland.

RYLAND, Judge John, CIE 1946; RIN (retired); Judge for British Columbia, 1969; retired; *b* 31 March 1900; *s* of late W. J. Ryland, Surbiton; *m* 1938, Lucy Lenore, *d* of J. W. Bryden, Victoria, BC; two *s. Educ:* King's College School; HMS Conway. *Address:* Royston, BC V0R 2V0, Canada.

RYLAND, Sir William; *see* Ryland, Sir A. W. C.

RYLANDS, George Humphrey Wolferstan, CBE 1961; MA; Fellow of King's College, Cambridge; Sometime Dean, Bursar, College Lecturer, and Director of Studies; University Lecturer in English Literature (retd); *b* 23 October 1902; *s* of Thomas Kirkland Rylands. *Educ:* Eton (King's Scholar); King's Coll., Cambridge (Scholar). Chm. of Directors and Trustees of the Arts Theatre, Cambridge, 1946-82; Governor of the Old Vic, 1945-78; Chm. of Apollo Soc., 1946-72. Member: Cheltenham Coll. Council, 1946-76; Council of RADA. Directed Hamlet with Sir John Gielgud, 1945; LP Recordings of the Shakespeare canon and the English Poets, for the British Council. Hon. LittD Cambridge, 1976. *Publications:* Words and Poetry, 1928; Shakespeare the Poet (in a Companion to Shakespeare Studies), 1934; Poems; The Ages of Man, a Shakespeare Anthology, 1939; Shakespeare's Poetic Energy (British Academy Lecture, 1951). *Address:* King's College, Cambridge. *T:* Cambridge 350411. *Club:* Athenæum.

RYLE, Kenneth Sherriff, CBE 1964; MC 1945; Secretary to the Church Commissioners for England, 1969-75; *b* 13 April 1912; *s* of Herbert Ryle, CVO, OBE; *m* 1941, Jean Margaret Watt; one *s* one *d. Educ:* Cheltenham Coll. Chartered Accountant, 1936; Queen Anne's Bounty, 1936-48. Served in RA, 1940-45: India, Persia, Middle East, Sicily, Italy, Germany; Captain 1944. Church Commissioners, 1948- (Dep. Sec., 1964-69). *Recreation:* golf. *Address:* 47 Albyfield, Bickley, Kent. *T:* 01-467 6319. *Club:* Chislehurst Golf.

RYLE, Sir Martin, Kt 1966; FRS 1952; Professor of Radio Astronomy, Cambridge, 1959-82, now Emeritus; Director, Mullard Radio-Astronomy Observatory, Cambridge, 1957-82; Astronomer Royal, 1972-82; *b* 27 Sept. 1918; *s* of late Prof. J. A. Ryle, MD, FRCP, and Mrs Miriam Ryle (*née* Scully); *m* 1947, Ella Rowena Palmer; one *s* two *d. Educ:* Bradfield Coll.; Christ Church, Oxford. Telecommunications Research Establishment, 1939-45; ICI Fellowship, Cavendish Laboratory, Cambridge, 1945-48; University Lecturer in Physics, Cambridge, 1948-58; Reader, 1958-59; Fellow, Trinity Coll., Cambridge, 1949-. Foreign Member: Royal Danish Acad. of Scis and Letters, 1968; Russian Academy of Sciences, 1971; For. Associate, US Nat. Acad. of Scis, 1975; Hon. Life Mem, NY Acad. of Scis, 1975; Mem., Pontifical Acad. of Scis, Vatican, 1975. Hon. DSc: Strathclyde, 1968; Oxford, 1969; Hon. Dr Nicholas Copernicus Univ., Poland, 1973. Hughes Medal, 1954, Royal Medal, 1973, Royal Soc.; Gold Medal, Royal Astronomical Soc., 1964; Henry

Draper Medal, Nat. Academy of Sciences (US), 1965; Nobel Prize for Physics (jtly), 1974. *Publications:* papers in: Proc. Roy. Soc., Proc. Physical Soc., Monthly Notices of Roy. Astronomical Soc. *Recreation:* sailing. *Address:* 5a Herschel Road, Cambridge. *T:* 56670.

RYLEY, Air Vice-Marshal Douglas William Robert, CB 1956; CBE 1944; retired, 1962; *b* 11 November 1905; *y s* of late Lachlan Macpherson Ryley, OBE, Ichapur, India and Palta, Bournemouth; *m* 1932, Madeline Doreen, *d* of late William Lloyd-Evans, Postlip, Glos; one *d*. *Educ:* Bedford School; RAF College, Cranwell. Commissioned in RAF 1925; India, 1929-34; Air Armament School, 1935; HQ RAF Far East, 1937; Woolwich Arsenal, 1939; UK Tech. Mission, USA, 1941; UK Tech. Mission, Canada, 1943; Ordnance Board, 1944; Superintendent EE Pendine, 1945; OC 10 S of TT, 1947; STSO No. 3 Group, 1948; AOC and Comdt, RAF Tech. Coll., Henlow, 1949; STSO HQ Coastal Comd, 1952; Dir of Armament Engineering, Air Min., 1954; Dir of Guided Weapons Engineering, Air Min., 1957; AOA, HQ Maintenance Command, 1958. *Recreations:* golf and shooting. *Address:* Foresters, Over Wallop, Stockbridge, Hants.

RYMAN, Prof. Brenda Edith, (Mrs Harry Barkley), MA, PhD; FRSC; FRCPath; Professor of Biochemistry, Charing Cross Hospital Medical School, University of London, since 1972, and Mistress of Girton College, Cambridge, since 1976; *b* 6 Dec. 1922; *d* of William Henry Ryman and Edith Florence Terry; *m* 1948, Dr Harry Barkley, BSc, FRCP, FRCPath (*d* 1978); one *s* one *d*. *Educ:* Colston Girls' Sch., Bristol; Cambridge Univ. (BA, MA); Birmingham Univ. (PhD). Royal Free Hospital Medical School: Asst Lectr in Biochemistry, 1948-51; Lectr, 1952-61; Sen. Lectr, 1961-69; Reader, 1970-72. *Publications:* many scientific, in jls such as Biochem. Jl, European Jl of Biochem., FEBS Letters, Biochim. et Biophys. Acta, Advances in Enzymology, Jl of Clin. Path., Nature. *Recreations:* foreign travel, athletic pursuits, gardening. *Address:* 54 Primrose Gardens, Hampstead, NW3 4TP. *T:* 01-722 1627.

RYMAN, John; MP (Lab) Blyth, since Oct. 1974; *b* 7 Nov. 1930. *Educ:* Leighton Park; Pembroke College, Oxford. Inns of Court Regt (TA), 1948-51. Called to the Bar, Middle Temple, 1957. Harmsworth Law Scholar. Mem. Council, Assoc. of the Clergy, 1976-. *Recreation:* Horses. *Address:* House of Commons, SW1A 0AA; Lowstead, Wark, Hexham, Northumberland.

RYMER-JONES, Brig. John Murray, CBE 1950 (OBE 1941); MC 1917, and Bar 1918; QPM 1959; retired as Assistant Commissioner Metropolitan Police (1950-59); Secretary, Drinking Fountain Association, 1959-76; Committee Member, Royal Humane Society, 1957-77; *b* 12 July 1897; *s* of late John and Lilian Rymer-Jones; *m* 1930, Gertrude Alice Wobey; one *s* two *d*. *Educ:* Felsted School; RMA, Woolwich. Commissioned RFA 1916; served European War: France and Flanders, 1916-18; Army of Rhine, 1919. Ireland, 1920-21 with KORR (Lancaster); Plebiscite, Upper Silesia, 1921; HQ British Army in Egypt, 1921-25; HQ Shanghai Defence Force, 1927-28; Company Commander and Instructor, RMA, Woolwich, 1929-33; retired as Captain, RA. Joined Metropolitan Police as Chief Inspector, 1934; Superintendent, 1935; Chief Constable, 1936; Inspector-General and Brigadier commanding Palestine Police, 1943-46. Commander Metropolitan Police, 1946-50. Area Comr, St John Ambulance, North Kent, 1963-66. Commander of St John of Jerusalem, 1952; Chevalier, Légion d'Honneur, 1950; *Recreations:* talking and music. *Address:* Lion House Lodge, High Halden, Kent. *T:* High Halden 538. *Club:* Army and Navy.

RYMILL, Hon. Sir Arthur (Campbell), Kt 1954; MLC, South Australia, 1956-75; Chairman, Advertiser Newspapers Ltd; Director, The Bank of Adelaide, 1953-80 (Chairman, 1953-79); Member of Principal Board, Australian Mutual Provident Society, 1964-80; Director of public companies in South Australia; *b* 8 Dec. 1907; *s* of late Arthur Graham Rymill, North Adelaide; *m* 1934, Margaret Earle, *d* of Roland Cudmore; two *d*. *Educ:* Queen's Sch. and St Peter's Coll., Adelaide; Univ. of Adelaide. Barrister and Solicitor, 1930. Mem. Adelaide City Council, 1933-38, 1946-64; Lord Mayor of Adelaide, 1950-54. Pres., S Australian Liberal and Country League, 1953-55; First Pres., Nat. Trust of S Australia; Vice-Pres., Aust. Elizabethan Theatre Trust, 1954-63; Mem., Found. Bd of Govs, Adelaide Festival of Arts; Vice-Pres., Adelaide Children's Hosp. Won Australasian Unlimited Speedboat Championship, 1933; rep. S Austr. in Australasian Polo Championships, 1938 and 1951. Served War of 1939-45, 2nd AIF: enlisted Private, 2/7th Field Regt, later commissioned. *Recreations:* farming, violin playing, golf. *Address:* 39 Jeffcott Street, North Adelaide, SA 5006, Australia. *T:* 267 2477. *Clubs:* Adelaide (Adelaide); Melbourne (Melbourne); Royal Adelaide Golf, Royal SA Yacht Squadron.

RYRIE, Sir William (Sinclair), KCB 1982 (CB 1979); Permanent Secretary, Overseas Development Administration, Foreign and Commonwealth Office, since 1982; *b* 10 Nov. 1928; *s* of Rev. Dr Frank Ryrie and Mabel Moncrieff Ryrie (*née* Watt); *m* 1st, 1953, Dorrit Klein (marr. diss. 1969); two *s* one *d*; 2nd, 1969, Christine Gray Thomson; one *s*. *Educ:* Mount Hermon Sch., Darjeeling; Heriot's Sch., Edinburgh; Edinburgh Univ. MA 1st cl. hons History, 1951. Nat. Service, 1951-53: Lieut, Intell. Corps, Malaya, 1952-53 (despatches). Colonial Office, 1953; seconded to Uganda, 1956-58; Principal 1958; transf. to Treasury, 1963; Asst Sec., internat. monetary affairs, 1966-69; Principal Private Sec. to Chancellor of Exchequer, 1969-71; Under-Sec., Public Sector Gp, HM Treasury, 1971-75; Econ. Minister and Head of UK

Treasury and Supply Delegn, Washington, and UK Exec. Dir, IMF and IBRD, 1975-79; 2nd Perm. Sec. (Domestic Economy Sector), HM Treasury, 1980-82. *Recreations:* photography, walking, music. *Address:* Overseas Development Administration, Eland House, Stag Place, SW1E 5DH. *Club:* Reform.

S

SAATCHI, Charles; Director, Saatchi & Saatchi Co., since 1970; *b* 9 June 1943; *m* 1973, Doris Lockhart. *Educ:* Christ's Coll., Finchley. Associate Director, Collett Dickenson Pearce, 1966-68; Director, Cramer Saatchi, 1968-70. *Address:* 80 Charlotte Street, W1.

SABATINI, Lawrence John; retired; Assistant Under Secretary of State, Ministry of Defence, 1972-79; *b* 5 Dec. 1919; *s* of Frederick Laurence Sabatini and Elsie May Sabatini (*née* Friggens); *m* 1947, Patricia Dyson; one *s* one *d*. *Educ:* Watford Grammar School. Joined HM Office of Works, 1938. Army service, 1940-46: commnd in RTR, 1943: service in NW Europe with 5 RTR. Asst Principal, Min. of Works, 1947; Asst Private Sec. to Minister of Works, 1948-49; Principal, 1949; Principal Private Sec. to Ministers of Defence, 1958-60; Asst Sec., MoD, 1960; Defence Counsellor, UK Delegn to NATO, on secondment to Diplomatic Service, 1963-67. *Recreations:* gardening, photography, music. *Address:* 44a Batchworth Lane, Northwood, Mddx HA6 3DT. *T:* Northwood 23249. *Club:* MCC.

SABBEN-CLARE, Ernest E., MA Oxon, BA London; Information Officer to University of Oxford, 1970-77; *b* 11 Aug. 1910; *s* of late Mr and Mrs J. W. Sabben-Clare; *m* 1938, Rosamond Dorothy Mary Scott; two *s* one *d*. *Educ:* Winchester Coll. (schol.); New College, Oxford (schol.). 1st cl. Mod. Hist., Oxford, 1932. Asst Master, Winchester Coll., 1932-34; Asst Dist Officer, Tanganyika, 1935-40; seconded Colonial Office, 1940-47; Lt, 10th Essex Bn Home Guard; Colonial Attaché, British Embassy, Washington, and Comr, Caribbean Commn, 1947-49; Nigerian Govt, 1950-55; Permanent Sec., Min. of Commerce, 1953-55; 1st cl. French, London Univ. (external), 1954; Asst Master, Marlborough Coll., 1955-60, Under-Master from 1957; Headmaster, Bishop Wordsworth's School, Salisbury, 1960-63; Headmaster, Leeds Grammar Sch., 1963-70. Chairman of Governors: Bramcote Sch., Scarborough, 1970-80; Badminton Sch., 1981-. Editor, Wilts Archaeological and Natural History Magazine, 1956-62. *Publication:* (ed jtly) Health in Tropical Africa during the Colonial Period, 1980. *Recreations:* caravanning, gardening. *Address:* 4 Denham Close, Abbey Hill Road, Winchester SO23 7BL. *Club:* Athenæum.

SABIN, Professor Albert B.; Distinguished Research Professor of Biomedicine, Medical University of South Carolina, Charleston, SC, 1974-82, now Emeritus Professor; Consultant to World Health Organization, since 1969; *b* 26 Aug. 1906; *s* of Jacob Sabin and Tillie Krugman; *m* 1935, Sylvia Tregillus (*d* 1966); two *d*; *m* 1967, Jane Blach Warner (marr. diss. 1971); *m* 1972, Heloisa Dunshee de Abranches. *Educ:* New York Univ. (MD). Ho. Phys., Bellevue Hosp., NY, 1932-33; Nat. Research Council Fellow, Lister Inst., London, 1934; Rockefeller Inst. for Med. Research, NY, 1935-39; Associate Prof. of Research Pediatrics, Univ. of Cincinnati, 1939-43; active duty, US Army, 1943-46 (Legion of Merit, 1945); Prof. of Research Pediatrics, Univ. of Cincinnati Coll. of Medicine and The Children's Hosp. Research Foundn, 1946-60, Distinguished Service Prof., 1960-71, Emeritus 1971-. Pres., Weizmann Inst. of Science, Israel, 1970-72. Fogarty Scholar, NIH, 1973. Mem. Nat. Acad. of Sciences of the USA; Fellow, Amer. Acad. of Arts and Sciences; Mem. and Hon. Mem. of various Amer. and foreign societies; Hon. Member: Royal Acad. of Med. of Belgium; British Paediatric Association. Holds hon. degrees; awards include: Feltrinelli Prize ($40,000) of Accad. Naz. dei Lincei, Rome, 1964; Lasker ($10,000) Prize for Clinical Medicine Research, 1965. Gold Medal, Royal Soc. of Health, 1969; National Medal of Science (USA), 1970; Statesman in Medicine Award (USA), 1973. Hon. FRSH London. *Publications:* numerous papers on pneumococcus infection, poliomyelitis, encephalitis, virus diseases of nervous system, toxoplasmosis, sandfly fever, dengue, other topics relating to various infectious diseases and virus-cancer relationships. *Recreations:* reading and music. *Address:* Sutton Towers, Apt 1001, 3101 New Mexico Avenue NW, Washington, DC 20016, USA.

SABIN, Howard Westcott; Legal Adviser to Associated Newspapers Group Ltd since 1972; *b* 19 Oct. 1916; *s* of John Howard Sabin and Octavia Roads (*née* Scruby); *m* 1st, 1942, Joan Eunice Noble (marr. diss. 1959); two *s* one *d*; 2nd, 1959, Janet Eileen Baillie. *Educ:* Shrewsbury; St John's Coll., Cambridge; MA (Hons in History and Law). Lieut, RNVR, 1939-46 (despatches 1944). Called to the Bar, Middle Temple, 1946. Dep. Chm., Bedfordshire QS, 1968-72; Assistant Recorder, Portsmouth, 1966, Bournemouth, 1967. Counsel for Post Office (Midland Circuit), 1964. *Recreations:* golf, swimming, music. *Address:* 40 Wynnstay Gardens, W8 6UT. *T:* 01-937 9247. *Club:* Hadley Wood Golf.

SABINE, Neville Warde, CMG 1960; CBE 1957; *b* 6 April 1910; *s* of late John William Sabine; *m* 1954, Zoë Margherita Bargna; two *d. Educ:* Manchester Grammar School; Brasenose College, Oxford. BA Hons. (Oxon) 1934. Colonial Service (Colonial Audit Dept) 1934; served Gold Coast, Malaya, Uganda, Leeward Islands, and N Borneo. Served War of 1939-45: Gold Coast Regt, 1939-40; Singapore RA (V), 1940-42; British Military Administration, Malaya, 1945-46. Auditor-General, Ghana, 1954-64; Secretary, Central Bd of Finance of Church of England, 1964-75. Sec., Soc. of Sussex Downsmen, 1976. *Recreations:* bridge and tennis. *Address:* 11 Windlesham Road, Brighton BN1 3AG. *T:* Brighton 732157.

SABINE, Peter Aubrey, DSc, FRSE, FRSA, FIMM, FGS; Deputy Director (Chief Scientific Officer, Chief Geologist), Institute of Geological Sciences, since 1977; *b* 29 Dec. 1924; *s* of Bernard Robert and Edith Lucy Sabine; *m* 1946, Peggy Willis Lambert, MSc, FBCS; one *s. Educ:* Brockley County Sch.; Chelsea Polytechnic; Royal Coll. of Science, London. BSc, ARCS (1st Cl. Geol.; Watts medal) 1945; PhD 1951, DSc 1970 (London). Apptd Geological Survey of Gt Britain as Geologist, 1945; Geological Museum, 1946-50; in charge Petrographical Dept, Geol Survey and Museum, 1950, Chief Petrographer, 1959; Asst Dir, S England and Wales, 1970; Chief Geochemist, 1977; Dep. Dir, 1977-. Sec., Geol Soc. of London, 1959-66, Vice-Pres., 1966-67 (Lyell Fund, 1955); Member Council: Geologists' Assoc., 1966-70; Mineralogical Soc., 1950-53; Instn of Mining and Metallurgy, 1976-80; Member: Dept of Industry Chem. and Mineral Research Requirements Bd, 1973-; IUGS Commn on Systematics of Igneous Rocks, 1969-; EEC Cttees on minerals and geochemistry; Chm., Sub-Cttee on geochem. and cosmochem. of British Nat. Cttee for Geology, 1977-. Chief UK Deleg. to IUGS, 1980-. Visitor, Royal Instn, 1979-. FMSA. *Publications:* Chemical analysis of igneous rocks (with E. M. Guppy), 1956; numerous scientific contribs in Mem. Geol. Surv., Qly Jl Geol. Soc., Mineral. Mag., Phil. Trans Roy. Soc., etc. *Recreations:* gardening, geneaology. *Address:* 19 Beaufort Road, Ealing, W5 3EB. *T:* 01-997 2360. *Clubs:* Athenæum; Geological Society's.

SABITI, Most Rev. Erica; *b* 1903; *m* 1934, Geraldine Kamuhigi; four *s* three *d. Educ:* Mbarara High Sch.; King's Coll., Budo; Makerere Coll. Teacher, 1920-25 and 1929-30; training in education, 1925-29; training for Ministry, 1931-32; ordained, 1933; Bishop of Ruwenzori, 1960-72; Bishop of Kampala, 1972-74; Archbishop of Uganda, Rwanda, Burundi and Boga Zaire, 1966-74. *Address:* PO Box 134, Mbarara, Uganda.

SACHER, Michael Moses, Vice-Chairman, since 1972 (Joint, since 1982) and Joint Managing Director, since 1971, Marks & Spencer plc; *b* 17 Oct. 1917; *e s* of late Harry and Miriam Sacher; *m* 1938, Audrey Glucksman; three *s* two *d. Educ:* St Paul's Sch.; New Coll., Oxford (MA). RASC, 1940-46: served Western Desert; psc Haifa 1943; Liaison Gen. Leclerc's HQ Free French, N Africa; Allied Armies in Italy. Marks & Spencer, 1938-39 and 1946-: Alt. Dir, 1954-62; full Dir, 1962-; Asst Man. Dir, 1967-71. Director: St Michael Finance Ltd; Marks & Spencer Pension Trust Ltd; Marks & Spencer Canada Inc. Mem. Jewish Agency Exec. and Governor of Jewish Agency, 1971-; Jt Pres., Jt Israel Appeal (UK); Dir and Mem. Council, Weizmann Inst. Foundn; Vice-Pres., Jewish Colonization Assoc.; Governor: Hebrew Univ. of Jerusalem; Weizmann Inst.; Reali Sch., Haifa; Vice-Pres. and Mem. Admin. Cttee, Jewish Nat. Fund for Gt Britain and Ireland (Past Pres.); Chm., Keren Hayesod Discretionary Trust; Director: Brit Olim Soc. Ltd, Israel; and Mem. Bd of Management, Jewish Nat. Fund Charitable Trust. Hon. Vice-Pres., Zionist Fedn of GB. Trustee, Nat. Gall., 1982-. FRSA; FRPSL. *Publications:* various philatelic monographs. *Recreation:* philately. *Address:* Michael House, Baker Street, W1A 1DN. *T:* 01-935 4422.

See also Earl of Antrim, M. J. Gilbert.

SACHS, Michael Alexander Geddes; Partner in Slater, Heelis & Co., Solicitors, Manchester, since 1962; a Recorder of the Crown Court, since 1980; *b* 8 April 1932; *s* of Dr Joseph Sachs, MB, ChB, DPH, and Mrs Ruby Mary Sachs; *m* 1957, Patricia Mary (*née* Conroy); two *s* two *d* (and one *s* decd). *Educ:* Sedbergh; Manchester Univ. (LLB 1954). Admitted solicitor, 1957. Pres., Manchester Law Soc., 1978-79; Chm., Greater Manchester Legal Services Cttee, 1977-81; Member: No 7 (NW) Area, Legal Aid Cttee, 1966-80 (Chm., 1975-76); Council, Law Soc., 1979- (Chm., Standing Cttee on Criminal Law, 1982-); Court, Univ. of Manchester, 1977-. KSS 1980. *Recreations:* golf, travelling in France and Ireland, Manchester United Football Club. *Address:* Delamer House, Delamer Road, Bowdon, Altrincham, Cheshire WA14 2NQ. *T:* 061-928 0353.

SACKVILLE, family name of **Earl De la Warr.**

SACKVILLE, 6th Baron, *cr* 1876; **Lionel Bertrand Sackville-West;** *b* 30 May 1913; *s* of late Hon. Bertrand George Sackville-West, *y b* of 4th Baron and Eva Adela Mabel Inigo (*d* 1936), *d* of late Maj.-Gen. Inigo Richmond Jones, CB, CVO; *S* cousin, 1965; *m* 1st, 1953, Jacobine Napier (*d* 1971), widow of Captain John Hichens, RA, and *d* of J. R. Menzies-Wilson; five *d*; 2nd, 1974, Arlie, Lady de Guingand. *Educ:* Winchester; Magdalen Coll., Oxford. Formerly Capt. Coldstream Gds; served War, 1939-42 (POW). Member of Lloyd's. [*Heir:* b Hugh Rosslyn Inigo Sackville-West, MC [*b* 1 Feb. 1919; *m* 1957, Bridget Eleanor, *d* of Capt. Robert Lionel Brooke Cunliffe, *qv*; two *s* three *d*]. *Address:* Knole, Sevenoaks, Kent.

SACKVILLE-WEST, family name of **Baron Sackville.**

SACKWOOD, Dr Mark; Regional Medical Officer, Northern Regional Health Authority, since 1973; *b* London, 18 Jan. 1926; *s* of Philip and Frances Sackwood; *m* 1953, Anne Harper Wilson; one *s* two *d. Educ:* King's Coll., London; Westminster Hosp. Med. School. MB, BS, FFCM, LRCP, MRCS, DPH, DR.COG. Various hosp. appts, South of England, 1949-58; mil. service, Far East, 1951-53; subseq. admin. med. appts, Middlesbrough and Newcastle upon Tyne, incl. Dep. Sen. Admin. MO with Newcastle RHB, 1968-73. *Recreations:* walking, reading, music. *Address:* 11 The Chesters, Beaumont Park, Whitley Bay, Tyne and Wear. *T:* Whitley Bay 527401.

SADIE, Stanley (John), CBE 1982; writer on music; Music Critic for The Times, 1964-81, thereafter freelance; Editor: The Musical Times, since 1967; The New Grove Dictionary of Music and Musicians (1980), since 1970; Master Musicians series, since 1976; *b* 30 Oct. 1930; *s* of David Sadie and Deborah (*née* Simons); *m* 1st, 1953, Adèle Bloom (*d* 1978); two *s* one *d*; 2nd, 1978, Julie Anne Vertrees; one *d. Educ:* St Paul's Sch.; Gonville and Caius Coll., Cambridge Univ. (MA, PhD, MusB). Prof., Trinity Coll. of Music, London, 1957-65. Writer and broadcaster on musical subjects, *circa* 1955-; Editor of many edns of 18th-century music, *circa* 1955-. Member: Council, Royal Musical Assoc.; Internat. Musicological Soc.; American Musicological Soc.; Critics' Circle. Hon. RAM 1981; Hon. DLitt Leicester, 1981. FRSA 1982. *Publications:* Handel, 1962; Mozart, 1966; Beethoven, 1967; Handel, 1968; (with Arthur Jacobs) Pan Book of Opera/The Opera Guide, 1964, new edn 1969; Handel Concertos, 1973; Mozart (The New Grove Biographies), 1982; contrib.: The Musical Times, Gramophone, Opera, Music and Letters, Musical Quarterly, Proc. Roy. Musical Assoc. *Recreations:* watching cricket, drinking (mainly wine and coffee), bridge, reading. *Address:* 12 Lyndhurst Road, NW3 5NL. *T:* 01-435 2482.

SADLER, Joan; Principal, Cheltenham Ladies' College, since 1979; *b* 1 July 1927; *d* of Thomas Harold Sadler and Florence May Sadler. *Educ:* Cambridgeshire High Sch.; Univ. of Bristol (BA Hons (History); DipEd). Downe House, Cold Ash, Newbury, Berks: Asst History teacher, 1950-56; Head of History Dept, 1956-58; Heriots Wood School, Stanmore, Mddx: Head of History Dept, 1958-68; Sen. Mistress, 1966-68; Headmistress, Howell's School, Denbigh, 1968-79. Hon. Freewoman: City of London; Drapers' Co., 1979. *Recreations:* music, theatre, reading. *Address:* The Ladies' College, Cheltenham, Glos. *Club:* Royal Over-Seas League.

SADLER, John Stephen, CBE 1982; Finance Director, John Lewis Partnership Ltd, since 1971; Member, Monopolies and Mergers Commission, since 1973; *b* 6 May 1930; *s* of Bernard and Phyllis Sadler; *m* 1952, Ella (*née* McCleery); three *s. Educ:* Reading Sch.; Corpus Christi Coll., Oxford (BA). Board of Trade, 1952-54; Treasury, 1954-56; Board of Trade, 1956-60; British Trade Commissioner, Lagos, Nigeria, 1960-64; Board of Trade, 1964-66. John Lewis Partnership Ltd, 1966-. *Recreations:* golf, boating. *Address:* Riverlea, The Warren, Mapledurham, Reading RG4 7TQ. *T:* Reading 472684. *Club:* Winter Hill Golf.

SAGAN, Françoise, pen-name of Françoise Quoirez; authoress; *b* France, 21 June 1935; *y c* of Paul Quoirez; *m* 1958, Guy Schoeller (marr. diss. 1960); *m* 1962, Robert James Westhoff; one *s. Educ:* convent and private school. Published first novel at age of 18. Has written some songs and collaborated in scheme for ballet Le Rendez-vous Manqué, produced Paris and London, 1958. *Publications:* (all trans. into Eng., usually French title): Bonjour Tristesse, 1954; Un Certain Sourire, 1956 (filmed, 1958); Dans un mois, dans un an, 1957 (Eng. trans. Those Without Shadows, 1958); Aimez-vous Brahms . . . . 1959 (Eng. trans. 1960); Château en Suède (play), 1960; Les Violons, parfois . . . (play), 1961; La Robe Mauve de Valentine (play), 1963; Bonheur, impair et passe (play), 1964; Toxique . . . (tr. 1965); La Chamade, 1965 (tr. 1966) (film, 1970); Le Cheval Evanoui (play), 1966; L'Echarde, 1966; Le Garde du cœur, 1968 (tr., The Heart-Keeper, 1968); Un peu de soleil dans l'eau froide, 1969 (tr., Sunlight and Cold Water, 1971); Un piano dans l'herbe (play), 1970; Des bleus a l'âme, 1972 (tr., Scars on the Soul, 1974); Zaphorie (play), 1973; Lost Profile, 1976; Silken Eyes (short stories), 1977; The Unmade Bed, 1978; Le Chien Couchant, 1980; La femme fardée, 1981 (tr., The Painted Lady, 1982). *Address:* c/o Editions Flammarion, 26 rue Racine, 75006 Paris, France.

SAGITTARIUS; *see* Katzin, Olga.

SAINER, Leonard; Consultant, Titmuss, Sainer & Webb, Solicitors; *b* 12 Oct. 1909; *s* of Archer and Sarah Sainer. Chairman: Sears Holdings Ltd; British Shoe Corporation Ltd; Lewis Investment Trust Ltd; Selfridges Ltd; Mappin & Webb Ltd; Shaw & Kilburn Ltd; Sears Engineering Ltd; Sears Industries Inc. (USA); Butler Footwear Hldgs Inc. (USA); United Real Property Trust Ltd; Dir, First National Finance Corp. Ltd. *Address:* (business) 40 Duke Street, W1; (home) 15 Chesterfield House, South Audley Street, W1.

SAINSBURY, family name of **Baron Sainsbury.**

SAINSBURY, Baron, *cr* 1962, of Drury Lane (Life Peer); **Alan John Sainsbury;** Joint President of J. Sainsbury Ltd, since 1967 (Chairman, 1956-67); *b* 13 Aug. 1902; *er s* of John Benjamin and Mabel Miriam Sainsbury; *m* 1st, 1925, Doreen Davan Adams (marr. diss. 1939); three *s*; 2nd, 1944, Anne Elizabeth Lewy; one *d. Educ:* Haileybury. Joined Grocery and Provision Firm of J. Sainsbury, Ltd (founded by his grandparents), 1921. Served on many war-time consultative committees of Ministry of Food; Member Williams'

Committee on Milk Distribution, 1947-48; Member: Food Research Advisory Cttee, 1960-70 (Chm., 1965-70); NEDC Cttee for the Distributive Trades, 1964-68; Exec. Cttee, PEP, 1970-76; House of Lords Select Cttee on the European Communities, 1978-81; Chm., Cttee of Inquiry into Relationship of Pharmaceutical Industry with National Health Service, 1965-67. President: Multiple Shops' Fedn, 1963-65; The Grocers' Inst., 1963-66; Internat. Assoc. of Chain Stores, 1965-68; The Royal Inst. of Public Health and Hygiene, 1965-70; Pestalozzi Children's Village Trust, 1963-; Distributive Trades Educn and Trng Council, 1975-; a Vice-President, Assoc. of Agriculture, 1965-73; Royal Society for the Encouragement of Arts, Manufactures and Commerce, 1962-66; Mem., Court of Univ. of Essex, 1966-76; Governor, City Literary Inst., 1967-69; Chairman of Trustees: Overseas Students Adv. Bureau; Uganda Asian Relief Trust, 1972-74; Vice-President: World Development Movement; Internat. Voluntary Service, 1977-81; Parly Gp for World Govt, 1982-. Liberal candidate, Sudbury Div. of Suffolk, Gen. Elections of 1929, 1931 and 1935. Joined Labour Party, 1945, SDP, 1981. Hon. Fellow, Inst. of Food Sci, and Technology. *Address:* J. Sainsbury Ltd, Stamford House, Stamford Street, SE1.
See also Sir J. D. Sainsbury, Hon. T. A. D. Sainsbury.

SAINSBURY, Anya, (Lady Sainsbury); *see* Linden, Anya.

SAINSBURY, Edward Hardwicke; TD 1945; Solicitor and Senior Partner (formerly Partner), Dawson, Hart & Co., Uckfield, since 1963; District Notary Public, Uckfield, since 1965; *b* 17 Sept. 1912; *e s* of Henry Morgan Sainsbury, and *g s* of James C. Hardwicke, a pioneer of technical and other education in S Wales; *m* 1946, Ann, 2nd *d* of late Kenneth Ellis, Tunbridge Wells; one *s* one *d*. *Educ:* Cardiff High School; University of S Wales and Monmouth. Solicitor in private practice, 1935; commissioned (TA) 1936; Prosecuting Solicitor, Cardiff, 1938, Sen. Pros. Solicitor, 1939. Served War of 1939-45; Adjutant, 77th HAA Regt, 1940; comd 240 HAA Battery Gibraltar, 1944; demobilised Nov. 1945. Hong Kong: Asst Crown Solicitor, 1946; commissioner for revision of the laws of Hong Kong, 1947; magistrate, 1948; registrar, High Court, 1949; sen. magistrate, Kowloon, 1951; Barrister, Inner Temple, 1951; Land Officer and crown counsel, Hong Kong, 1952; legal draftsman, Nigeria, 1953; Principal Legal Draftsman, Fed. of Nigeria, 1958. President, Commonwealth Parliamentary Assoc., Southern Cameroons, 1959-63. Judge, High Court of Lagos, 1960-63, and of Southern Cameroons, 1961-63 (Speaker, House of Assembly, 1958-63, Chm., Public Service Commn, 1961-63, Southern Cameroons). *Publication:* (jointly) Revised Laws of Hong Kong, 1948. *Recreations:* squash (a memory), golf. *Address:* Little Gassons, Fairwarp, Uckfield, East Sussex. *T:* Nutley 2100.

SAINSBURY, Sir John (Davan), Kt 1980; Chairman, J. Sainsbury Ltd, since 1969 (Vice-Chairman, 1967-69; Director, since 1958); Director, Royal Opera House, Covent Garden, since 1969; *b* 2 Nov. 1927; *e s* of Baron Sainsbury, *qv* ; *m* 1963, Anya Linden, *qv* ; two *s* one *d*. *Educ:* Stowe School; Worcester College, Oxford (Hon. Fellow 1982). Director: The Economist, 1972-80; Royal Opera House Trust, 1974-. Jt Hon. Treas., European Movement, 1972-75, a Pres., 1975-. Member: Council, Retail Consortium, 1975-79; Nat. Cttee for Electoral Reform, 1976-; President's Cttee, CBI, 1982-. Chm., Friends of Covent Garden, 1969-81; Trustee: Nat. Gall., 1976-; Westminster Abbey Trust, 1977-; Tate Gall., 1982-. Fellow, Inst. of Grocery Distribution, 1973-. *Address:* c/o Stamford House, Stamford Street, SE1 9LL. *T:* 01-921 6000. *Club:* Garrick.
See also Hon. T. A. D. Sainsbury.

SAINSBURY, Richard Eric, CBE 1964; *b* 15 Sept. 1909; 2nd *s* of E. A. Sainsbury and F. W. Sainsbury (*née* Hill), Trowbridge, Wilts; *m* 1936, Margaret (*née* Horne); one *s*. *Educ:* Lewisham School, Weston-super-Mare; Bristol University. Grad. in Engineering, 1932; time-study with J. Lucas, 1934; subseq. with various firms; Ministry of Aircraft Production, 1940, Deputy Director, 1943; Joint Services Staff College, 1947; Director Instrument and Radio Production, Ministry of Supply, 1950; Imperial Defence College, 1959; Director, Guided Weapons Production, 1960; Dir-Gen., Electronics and Weapons Prodn, Min. of Aviation, 1964-66; Min. of Technology, 1967-70, Min. of Aviation Supply, 1970-71; Dir Gen., Telecommunications, MoD, 1971-72. Dir, Aeromaritime Ltd, Hounslow, 1973-75. Coronation Medal, 1953. *Recreations:* walking, reading, skiing. *Address:* 6 Blenheim Drive, Oxford OX2 8DG. *T:* Oxford 56029.

SAINSBURY, Sir Robert, Kt 1967 (for services to the arts); Joint President, J. Sainsbury Ltd; *b* 24 Oct. 1906; *s* of late John Benjamin Sainsbury and late Mable Miriam (*née* Van den Bergh); *m* 1937, Lisa Ingeborg (*née* Van den Bergh; second cousin); one *s* two *d* (and one *d* decd). *Educ:* Haileybury Coll.; Pembroke Coll., Cambridge (MA). ACA, 1930, FCA, 1935. Joined J. Sainsbury Ltd, 1930; Dir, 1934; Jt Gen. Man., 1938; Dep. Chm., 1956; Chm. 1967; Jt Pres., 1969. Formerly Mem. Art Panel of Arts Council; Mem., Mngt Cttee, Courtauld Inst. of Art, Univ. of London, 1979-82. Trustee, Tate Gall., 1959-73 (Vice-Chm. 1967, Chm., 1969); Mem. Vis. Cttee to Primitive Art Dept, Metropolitan Museum of Art, NY; Hon. Treasurer, Inst. of Med. Social Workers, 1948-71; Governor, St Thomas' Hospital, 1939-68. Hon. Dr RCA, 1976; Hon. LittD East Anglia, 1977. *Address:* 5 Smith Square, SW1. *T:* 01-222 7252.

SAINSBURY, Hon. Timothy Alan Davan; MP (C) Hove, since Nov. 1973; Parliamentary Private Secretary to Secretary of State for the Environment, since 1979; Director, J. Sainsbury Ltd, since 1962; *b* 11 June 1932; *y s* of Baron

Sainsbury, *qv* ; *m* 1961, Susan Mary Mitchell; two *s* two *d*. *Educ:* Eton; Worcester Coll., Oxford (MA; Hon. Fellow 1982). Chm., Council for the Unit for Retail Planning Information Ltd, 1974-79. Mem. Council, RSA, 1981-. *Address:* House of Commons, SW1A 0AA.
See also Sir J. D. Sainsbury.

SAINT, Sir (Sidney) John, Kt 1950; CMG 1946; OBE 1942; BSc, PhD (London); MSc (Reading); CChem; FRSC; Director, Sugar Technological Laboratory, Barbados, 1949-63, retd; *b* 16 Sept. 1897; *m* 1923, Constance Elizabeth Hole; two *s* one *d*. *Educ:* Beaminster Grammar School; Reading University. Served with RFC and RAF, 1916-19; Salter's Research Fellow, 1920-22; Lecturer in Agricultural Chemistry, Leeds University, 1922-27; Chemist, Department of Agriculture, Barbados, 1927-37; Director of Agriculture Barbados, 1937-49; Chm., BWI Sugar Cane Breeding Station, 1937-49; Competent Authority and Controller of Supplies, Barbados, 1939-46; Pres., Barbados Technologists Assoc., 1939-42, 1950-63; Gen. Chm., Internat. Soc. of Sugar Cane Technologists, 1950-53; Chairman: Barbados Public Service Commn, 1952-57; Barbados Development Bd, 1956-59; Interim Federal Public Service Commn, 1956-59. Pres. Museum and Hist. Soc., 1946-59. MEC, 1947-61; PC (Barbados), 1961-63. Hon. Freeman, City of Bridgetown, Barbados, 1963. *Publications:* numerous papers on soils, manuring of tropical crops and sugar technology. *Address:* Selwyn, St George's Lane, Hurstpierpoint, Sussex. *T:* Hurstpierpoint 832335.

SAINT, Dr Stafford Eric, CVO 1956; Medical Practitioner, 1931-70; *b* 13 April 1904; *s* of late Sir Wakelin Saint; *m* 1931, Isabel Mary Fulford; two *s* one *d*. *Educ:* King's School, Ely; The London Hospital. MRCS Eng., LRCP Lond., 1926. *Address:* 28 The Uplands, Gerrard's Cross, Bucks SL9 7JG.

ST ALBANS, 13th Duke of, *cr* 1684; **Charles Frederic Aubrey de Vere Beauclerk,** OBE 1945; Earl of Burford and Baron of Heddington, 1676; Baron Vere, 1750; Hereditary Grand Falconer of England; Hereditary Registrar, Court of Chancery; Chairman, Amalgamated Developers Group; *b* 16 Aug. 1915; *s* of Aubrey Topham Beauclerk and Gwendolen, *d* of late Sir Frederic Hughes; *S* kinsman, 1964; *m* 1st, Nathalie Chatham (who obtained a divorce, 1947), *d* of late P. F. Walker; one *s* ; 2nd, 1947, Suzanne Marie Adele, *d* of late Emile William Fesq, Mas Mistral, Vence, AM, France; three *s* one *d*. *Educ:* Eton; Magdalene Coll., Cambridge (MA). Served War of 1939-45 in Infantry, Military Intelligence and Psychological Warfare; Col, Intelligence Corps. Controller Inf. Services, Allied Commn for Austria, 1946-50. Central Office of Information: Chief Books Editor, 1951-58; Chief Films Production Officer, 1958-60; Dir, Films Div., 1960-64. Pres., Fedn of Industrial Develt Assocs; Vice-Pres., Ancient Monuments Soc.; Governor General, Royal Stuart Soc.; Pres., Shakespearian Authorship Soc. *Heir:* s Earl of Burford, *qv*. *Address:* 432 Palais de la Scala, Monte Carlo, Monaco. *Club:* Brooks's.

ST ALBANS, Bishop of, since 1980; **Rt. Rev. John Bernard Taylor;** *b* 6 May 1929; *s* of George Ernest and Gwendoline Irene Taylor; *m* 1956, Linda Courtenay Barnes; one *s* two *d*. *Educ:* Watford Grammar Sch.; Christ's Coll., Cambridge; Jesus Coll., Cambridge. MA Cantab. Vicar of Henham and Elsenham, Essex, 1959-64; Vice-Principal, Oak Hill Theological Coll., 1964-72; Vicar of All Saints', Woodford Wells, 1973; Archdeacon of West Ham, 1975-80. Examining Chaplain to Bishop of Chelmsford, 1962-80. *Publications:* A Christian's Guide to the Old Testament, 1966; Evangelism among Children and Young People, 1967; Tyndale Commentary on Ezekiel, 1969. *Address:* Abbey Gate House, St Albans, Herts AL3 4HD.

ST ALBANS, Dean of; *see* Moore, Very Rev. P. C.

ST ALBANS, Archdeacon of; *see* Norfolk, Ven. E. M.

ST ALDWYN, 2nd Earl, *cr* 1915, of Coln St Aldwyns; **Michael John Hicks Beach,** GBE 1980 (KBE 1964); TD 1949; PC 1959; JP; Bt 1619; Viscount St Aldwyn, 1906; Viscount Quenington, 1915; Vice Lord-Lieutenant, of Gloucestershire, since 1981; *b* 9 Oct. 1912; *s* of Visc. Quenington, Roy. Glos. Hussars Yeo. (*d* 1916; *o s* of 1st Earl) and Marjorie (*d* 1916), *d* of late H. Dent Brocklehurst, Sudeley Castle, Gloucs; *S* grandfather, 1916 (his father having been killed in action a week previously); *m* 1948, Diana Mary Christian, DStJ (she *m* 1st, 1939, Major Richard Patrick Pilkington Smyly, MC; marriage annulled, 1942), *o d* of late Henry C. G. and Mrs Mills; three *s*. *Educ:* Eton; Christ Church, Oxford. Major Royal Glos Hussars Yeomanry, 1942. Parliamentary Secretary, Ministry of Agriculture and Fisheries, 1954-58; Captain of the Honorable Corps of Gentlemen-at-Arms and Govt Chief Whip, House of Lords, 1958-64 and 1970-74; Opposition Chief Whip, House of Lords, 1964-70 and 1974-78. DL 1952, Glos. GCStJ 1978; Chancellor, Order of St John, 1978– (Vice-Chancellor, 1969-78). *Heir:* s Viscount Quenington, *qv*. *Address:* Williamstrip Park, Cirencester, Gloucestershire. *T:* Coln St Aldwyns 226; 13 Upper Belgrave Street, SW1. *T:* 01-235 8464. *Clubs:* Carlton, Pratt's, Beefsteak; Royal Yacht Squadron.
See also Sir Richard Keane, Bt.

ST ANDREWS, Earl of; George Philip Nicholas Windsor; *b* 26 June 1962; *s* of HRH the Duke of Kent and HRH the Duchess of Kent.
See under Royal Family.

ST ANDREWS AND EDINBURGH, Archbishop of, (RC), since 1951; **His Eminence Cardinal Gordon Joseph Gray,** MA (Hon.) St Andrews;

Hon. DD St Andrews, 1967; *b* 10 August 1910; 2nd *s* of Francis William and Angela Gray. *Educ:* Holy Cross Acad., Edinburgh; St John's Seminary, Wonersh. Assistant-Priest, St Andrews, 1935-41; Parish Priest, Hawick, 1941-47; Rector of Blairs College, Aberdeen (Scottish National Junior Seminary), 1947-51. Cardinal, 1969. Member Pontifical Congregation: for Evangelization of Peoples; for Divine Worship; Mem., Pontifical Commn for Social Communications. Hon. FEIS, 1970. DUniv. Heriot-Watt, 1981. *Address:* St Bennet's, 42 Greenhill Gardens, Edinburgh EH10 4BJ. *T:* 031-447 3337.

ST ANDREWS AND EDINBURGH, Bishop Auxiliary of, (RC); *see* Monaghan, Rt Rev. James.

ST ANDREWS, DUNKELD AND DUNBLANE, Bishop of, since 1969; **Rt. Rev. Michael Geoffrey Hare Duke;** *b* 28 Nov. 1925; *s* of late A. R. A. Hare Duke, Civil Engineer; *m* 1949, Grace Lydia Frances McKean Dodd; one *s* three *d. Educ:* Bradfield Coll.; Trinity Coll., Oxford. BA 1949, MA 1951. Sub-Lt, RNVR, 1944-46. Deacon, 1952; Priest, 1953; Curate, St John's Wood Church, 1952-56; Vicar, St Mark's, Bury, 1956-62; Pastoral Dir, Clin. Theol. Assoc., 1962-64; Vicar, St Paul's, Daybrook, and Pastoral Consultant to Clin. Theol. Assoc., 1964-69; OCF, E Midland Dist HQ, 1968-69. Chm., Scottish Assoc. for Mental Health, 1978-. Mem. Editorial Bd, Contact Magazine, 1962-79. *Publications:* (jointly): The Caring Church, 1963; First Aid in Counselling, 1968; Understanding the Adolescent, 1969; The Break of Glory, 1970; Freud, 1972; Good News, 1976; Stories, Signs and Sacraments in the Emerging Church, 1982. Contributor to: Expository Times, Blackfriars, New Christian, Church Quarterly Review, Church Times, Contact. *Address:* Bishop's House, Fairmount Road, Perth PH2 7AP. *T:* Perth 21580.

ST ANDREWS, DUNKELD AND DUNBLANE, Dean of; *see* Shone, Very Rev. J. T.

ST ARNAUD, Diocese; amalgamated with diocese of Bendigo, 1977.

ST ASAPH, Bishop of, since 1982; **Rt. Rev. Alwyn Rice Jones;** *b* 25 March 1934; *s* of John Griffith and Annie Jones, Capel Curig, Caernarvonshire; *m* 1968, Meriel Anne Thomas; one *d. Educ:* Llanrwst Grammar School, Denbighshire; St David's Coll. Lampeter (BA Hons Welsh 1955); Fitzwilliam House, Cambridge (BA 1957 Theology Tripos, MA 1961); St Michael's Coll., Llandaff. Deacon 1958, priest 1959, Bangor Cathedral; Asst Curate, Llanfairisgaer, 1958-62; Secretary for SCM in N Wales Colleges and SCM in schools, 1962-65; Director of Education, Diocese of Bangor, 1965-75; Chaplain, St Winifred's School, Llanfairfechan, 1965-67; Diocesan Warden of Ordinands, 1970-75; Vicar of Porthmadog, dio. Bangor, 1975-79; Exam. Chaplain to Archbishop of Wales, 1970-79; Hon. Canon, Bangor Cathedral, 1974-78, Preb. of Llanfair, 1978-79; Dean of Brecon Cathedral, 1979-82. Mem., IBA Panel of Religious Advisers and Welsh Cttee, IBA, 1972-76; Asst Tutor in Religious Education, UCNW, Bangor, 1973-76. *Recreations:* music and walking. *Address:* Esgobty, St Asaph, Clwyd, Deeside LL17 0TW. *T:* St Asaph 583503.

ST ASAPH, Dean of; *see* Renowden, Very Rev. C. R.

ST AUBYN, family name of **Baron St Levan.**

ST AUBYN; *see* Molesworth-St Aubyn.

ST BONIFACE, Archbishop of, (RC), since 1974; **Most Rev. Antoine Hacault,** STD; *b* Bruxelles, Manitoba, 17 Jan. 1926. *Educ:* Sainte-Marie Elem. Sch., Bruxelles; St Boniface Coll. (BA 1947); St Boniface Major Seminary; Angelicum Univ., Rome (STD 1954). Priest, 1951; Prof. of Theology, St Boniface Major Seminary, 1954-64; Auxiliary Bishop of St Boniface and Titular Bishop of Media, 1964; also Rector, St Boniface College, 1967; Bishop Coadjutor of St Boniface, 1972. Member: Vatican Secretariat for Non-Believers, 1973-; Vatican Secretariat for promoting Christian Unity, 1976-; Pres., Canadian Episcopal Commn for Ecumenism. *Address:* Archbishop's Residence, 151 Cathedral Avenue, St Boniface, Manitoba R2H 0H6, Canada.

SAINT BRIDES, Baron *cr* 1977 (Life Peer), of Hasguard, Dyfed; **John Morrice Cairns James,** PC 1968; GCMG 1975 (KCMG 1962; CMG 1957); CVO 1961; MBE 1944; King of Arms of the Most Distinguished Order of St Michael and St George, since 1975; *b* 30 April 1916; *s* of late Lewis Cairns James and Catherine, *d* of John Maitland Marshall; *m* 1st, 1948, Elizabeth Margaret Roper Piesse (*d* 1966); one *s* two *d*; 2nd, 1968, Mme Geneviève Sarasin. *Educ:* Bradfield; Balliol Coll., Oxford. Dominions Office, 1939; served Royal Navy and Royal Marines, 1940-45; released as Lieut-Col. Asst Sec., Office of UK High Comr in S Africa, 1946-47; Head of Defence Dept, Commonwealth Relations Office, 1949-51, and of Establishment Dept, 1951-52; Dep. High Comr for the UK, Lahore, 1952-53; attended Imperial Defence Coll., 1954; Dep. High Comr for UK in Pakistan, 1955-56; Asst Under-Sec. of State, Commonwealth Relations Office, 1957. Dep. High Comr for UK in India, 1958-61; British High Comr in Pakistan, 1961-66; Dep. Under Sec. of State, CO, 1966-68; Permanent Under-Sec. of State, CO, March-Oct. 1968; British High Commissioner: in India, 1968-71; in Australia, 1971-76. Vis. Fellow, Political Sci. Dept, Chicago Univ., 1978-79; Fellow, Center for Internat. Affairs, Harvard Univ., 1979-80; Distinguished Vis.

Fellow, S Asian Reg. Studies Dept, Univ. of Pa, 1980-81; Distinguished Diplomat-in-Residence, For. Policy Res. Inst., Philadelphia, 1980-81 (took part, as mem. FPRI team, with the Lady Saint Brides, in talks at Zvinigorod with Soviet Inst. for the USA and Canada, Dec. 1981); Vis. Scholar, Univ. of Texas at Austin, 1982. Leon Lectr, Univ. of Pa, 1980; lectured for E-SU, Council on World Affairs and Council for For. Relns in fourteen US cities, 1979-82. *Publications:* articles on internat. affairs in learned US jls incl. Internat. Security, and Orbis. *Recreation:* exploring the fallibility of contemporary statesmen. *Address:* Cap Saint-Pierre, 83990 Saint Tropez, France. *T:* (94) 97-14-75. *Clubs:* Oriental; Harvard (NY).

ST CLAIR, family name of **Lord Sinclair.**

ST CLAIR, Malcolm Archibald James, farmer; *b* 16 Feb. 1927; *o s* of late Maj.-Gen. George James Paul St Clair, CB, CBE, DSO and late Charlotte Theresa Orme Little; *m* 1955, Mary-Jean Rosalie Alice, *o d* of Wing-Comdr Caryl Liddell Hargreaves, Broadwood House, Sunningdale; two *s* one *d. Educ:* Eton. Served with Royal Scots Greys, 1944-48. Formerly Hon. Sec. to Sir Winston Churchill. Contested (C) Bristol South-East, 1959; MP (C) Bristol South-East, 1961-63. Lt Col Comdg, Royal Gloucestershire Hussars (TA), 1967-69. High Sheriff Glos, 1972. *Address:* Upton House, Tetbury, Glos. *Club:* White's.

ST CLAIR-ERSKINE, family name of **Earl of Rosslyn.**

ST CLAIR-FORD, Capt. Sir Aubrey, 6th Bt, *cr* 1793; DSO 1942; RN, retired; *b* 29 Feb. 1904; *e s* of late Anson and Elsie St Clair-Ford; *S* cousin 1948; *m* 1945, Anne, *o d* of Harold Christopherson, Penerley Lodge, Beaulieu, Hants; one *s* one *d. Educ:* Stubbington House; RNC, Osborne and Dartmouth. Served War of 1939-45 (despatches, DSO and bar); Korean War of 1950-53 (despatches, Officer, Legion of Merit, US). *Heir: s* James Anson St Clair-Ford [*b* 16 March 1952; *m* 1977, Jennifer Margaret, *yr d* of Cdre Robin Grindle]. *Address:* Corner House, Sandle Copse, Fordingbridge, Hants. *Club:* Army and Navy.

See also Maj.-Gen. Sir Peter St Clair-Ford.

ST CLAIR-FORD, Maj.-Gen. Sir Peter, KBE 1961 (CBE 1953); CB 1954; DSO 1943 and Bar 1944; idc; psc; General Secretary of the Officers' Association, 1963-66; *b* 25 Nov. 1905; *s* of late Anson St Clair-Ford and Elsie (*née* Adams); unmarried. *Educ:* Dover College; Royal Military College, Sandhurst. Commissioned into KOYLI, 1925; Somaliland Camel Corps, 1932-39; France, 1939; Staff College, Camberley, 1940 (psc); various Staff appts, UK, 1940-43; Comd 1 Bn KOYLI, 1943-44, Italy and Palestine; Comd 3 Inf. Bde, 1944-46, Italy and Palestine; Comd 129 Inf. Bde (TA), 1947-48; BGS Southern Command (UK), 1948-49; Imperial Defence College (idc), 1950; BGS, FARELF, 1951-52; Training Adviser to Pakistan Army, 1952-54; Commander 1 Federal Division, Malaya, 1954-57; Deputy Chief of Staff, Headquarters Allied Land Forces Central Europe, 1958-60; retd, 1960. *Recreations:* golf, racing. *Address:* Cotswold Lodge, Littlestone, New Romney, Kent. *T:* New Romney 2368. *Club:* East India, Devonshire, Sports and Public Schools.

See also Capt. Sir Aubrey St Clair-Ford, Bt.

ST CYRES, Viscount; John Stafford Northcote; *b* 15 Feb. 1957; *s* and *heir* of 4th Earl of Iddesleigh, *qv. Educ:* Downside Sch.; RAC Cirencester. *Address:* Shillands House, Upton Pyne Hill, Exeter, Devon EX5 5EB.

ST DAVIDS, 2nd Viscount, *cr* 1918; **Jestyn Reginald Austen Plantagenet Philipps;** Baron Strange of Knokin, 1299; Baron Hungerford, 1426; Baron de Moleyns, 1445; Bt 1621; Baron St Davids, 1908; Founder and Patron, Pirate Club, Floating Youth Club for Boys and Girls; *b* 19 Feb. 1917; *s* of 1st Viscount and Elizabeth Frances (Baroness Strange of Knokin, Baroness Hungerford and Baroness de Moleyns), *d* of late Hon. Paulyn F. C. Rawdon-Hastings, of The Manor House, Ashby-de-la-Zouch; *S* father, 1938, and to baronies of mother; *m* 1938, Doreen Guinness (marr. diss., 1954; she *d* 1956), *o d* of Captain Arthur Jowett, Toorak, Australia; one *s* four *d*; *m* 1954, Elisabeth Joyce, *e d* of Dr E. A. Woolf, Hove, Sussex (marr. diss., 1959); *m* 1959, Evelyn Marjorie, *d* of late Dr J. E. G. Harris, Bray, Berks. *Educ:* Eton; Trinity Coll., Cambridge. *Heir: s* Hon. Colwyn Jestyn John Philipps [*b* 30 Jan. 1939; *m* 1965, Augusta Victoria Correa Larrain, *d* of late Don Estantislao Correa Ugarte; two *s*]. *Address:* 15 St Mark's Crescent, Regent's Park, NW1.

ST DAVIDS, Bishop of, since 1982; **Rt. Rev. George Noakes;** *b* 13 Sept. 1924; *s* of David John and Elizabeth Mary Noakes; *m* 1957, Jane Margaretta Davies. *Educ:* Tregaron Secondary School; University Coll. of Wales, Aberystwyth (BA); Wycliffe Hall, Oxford. Curate of Lampeter, 1950-56; Vicar: Eglwyswrw, 1956-59; Tregaron, 1959-67; Dewi Sant, Cardiff, 1967-76; Rector of Aberystwyth, 1976-79; Canon of St Davids Cathedral, 1977-79; Archdeacon of Cardigan, 1979-82; Vicar of Llanychaearn, 1980-82. *Recreations:* cricket and angling. *Address:* Llys Esgob, Abergwili, Carmarthen, Dyfed SA31 2JG. *T:* Carmarthen 6597.

ST DAVID'S, Dean of; *see* Bowen, Very Rev. L.

ST EDMUNDSBURY, Provost of; *see* Furnell, Very Rev. R.

ST EDMUNDSBURY AND IPSWICH, Bishop of, since 1978; **Rt. Rev. John Waine;** b 20 June 1930; s of William and Ellen Waine; m 1957, Patricia Zena Haikney; three s. Educ: Prescot Grammar Sch.; Manchester Univ. (BA); Ridley Hall, Cambridge. Deacon 1955, Priest 1956; Curate of St Mary, West Derby, 1955-58; Curate in Charge of All Saints, Sutton, 1958-60; Vicar of Ditton, 1960-64; Vicar of Holy Trinity, Southport, 1964-69; Rector of Kirkby, 1969-75; Bishop Suffragan of Stafford, 1975-78. Recreations: caravanning, music, gardening. Address: Bishop's House, 4 Park Road, Ipswich IP1 3ST. Club: Royal Air Force.

ST GEORGE, Air Vice-Marshal Douglas Fitzclarence, CB 1974; CBE 1971; DFC; AFC; RNZAF, retd; b Nelson, NZ, 7 Sept. 1919; s of D. St George; m 1953, Patrine, d of J. Darrow; two s. Educ: Auckland Grammar Sch., NZ. Served War, Royal New Zealand Air Force, 1938-45. Comdg Flying Wing, RNZAF, Ohakea, 1953-56; exchange duty, RAAF, Aust., 1956-58; Comdg Ohakea, 1958-60; Dir ops, RNZAF, 1961-63; Rep. of NZ Mil. Advisers, HQ of SEATO, Bangkok, 1963-65; AOC comdg Training Gp, 1966-67; IDC, 1968; Air Mem. for Personnel, HQ of RNZAF, 1969-70; Dep. Chief of the Air Staff, NZ, 1970-71; Chief of the Air Staff, NZ, 1971-74. Address: 84 Barton Road, Heretaunga, New Zealand.

ST GEORGE, Sir Robert Alan, 7th Bt, cr 1766; now Religious Lay Brother; b 20 March 1900; s of Sir Theophilus John St George, 6th Bt, and Florence Emma, d of late John Venderplank, Natal; S father, 1943. Educ: St Charles Coll., Maritzburg. Served RAF, 1918; War of 1939-45, Middle East (prisoner). Heir: b Rev. Denis Howard St George, b 6 Sept. 1902. Address: Nazareth House, 82 South Ridge Road, Durban, Natal, South Africa.

ST GERMANS, 9th Earl of, cr 1815; **Nicholas Richard Michael Eliot;** Baron Eliot, 1784; Major, Duke of Cornwall's Light Infantry; b 26 Jan. 1914; er s of 8th Earl of St Germans, KCVO, OBE, and of Helen Agnes Post (d 1962) (d of Lady Barrymore and late Arthur Post, New York, USA); S father 1960; m 1st, 1939, Helen Mary (marr. diss., 1947), d of late Lt-Col Charles Walter Villiers, CBE, DSO, and late Lady Kathleen Villiers; one s one d; 2nd, 1948, Mrs Margaret Eleanor Eyston (marr. diss., 1959), o d of late Lt-Col William Francis George Wyndham, MVO; 3rd, 1965, Mrs Mary Bridget Lotinga, d of late Sir Shenton Thomas and of Lady Thomas, SW7. Educ: Eton. Joined Duke of Cornwall's Light Infantry, 1937. Served War of 1939-45: attached Royal Armoured Corps. Heir: s Lord Eliot, qv. Address: Les Arcs, Chemin du Signal, 1807, Blonay, Vaud, Switzerland.

See also Earl of Shelburne.

ST GERMANS, Bishop Suffragan of, since 1979; **Rt. Rev. Brother Michael Fisher,** SSF (**Reginald Lindsay Fisher**); b 6 April 1918; s of Reginald Watson Fisher and Martha Lindsay Fisher. Educ: Clapham Central School; Bolt Court; Westcott House, Cambridge. Member, Society of St Francis, 1942. Deacon 1953, priest 1954, dio. Ely; Licence to officiate: Diocese of Ely, 1954-62; Newcastle, 1962-67; Sarum, 1967-79. Minister Provincial, SSF, 1967-79. MA Lambeth, 1978. Recreations: poetry, music, cinema; people. Address: 32 Falmouth Road, Truro, Cornwall TR1 2HX. T: Truro 3190.

ST HELENA, Bishop of, since 1979; **Rt. Rev. Edward Alexander Capparis Cannan;** b 25 Dec. 1920; s of Alexander and Mabel Capparis; m 1941, Eunice Mary Blandford; three s. Educ: St Marylebone Grammar School; King's College, London (BD, AKC). Served RAF, 1937-46 (despatches). Deacon 1950, priest 1951, dio. Salisbury; Curate, Blandford Forum, Dorset, 1950-53. Chaplain, RAF, 1953-74: RAF Cosford, 1953-54; Padgate, 1954-57; HQ 2 Gp, Germany, 1957-58; Lecturer, RAF Chaplains' Sch., 1958-60; RAF Gan, Maldive Islands, 1960-61; RAF Halton, 1961-62; Hereford, 1962-64; Khormaksar, Aden, 1964-66; Vice-Principal, RAF Chaplains' School, 1966-69; Asst Chaplain-in-Chief, 1969-74; Far East Air Force, Singapore, 1969-72; HQ Training Comd, 1972-73; Principal, RAF Chaplains' Sch., 1973-74; Hon. Chaplain to the Queen, 1972-74; Chaplain, St Margaret's Sch., Bushey, 1974-79. Recreations: gardening, house maintenance, photography. Address: Bishopsholme, Island of St Helena, South Atlantic Ocean.

ST HELENS, 2nd Baron cr 1964; **Richard Francis Hughes-Young;** b 4 Nov. 1945; s of 1st Baron St Helens, MC, and Elizabeth Agnes (d 1956), y d of late Captain Richard Blakiston-Houston; S father, 1980. Educ: Nautical College, Pangbourne. Heir: none. Address: 10 Rivermill House, Grosvenor Road, SW1.

ST JOHN, family name of Baron St John of Bletso, and of **Viscount Bolingbroke.**

ST JOHN OF BLETSO, 21st Baron cr 1558; **Anthony Tudor St John; Bt** 1660; practising solicitor in Cape Town; b 16 May 1957; s of 20th Baron St John of Bletso, TD, and of Katharine, d of late A. G. von Berg; S father, 1978. Educ: Diocesan College, Rondebosch, Cape; Univ. of Cape Town (BSocSc 1977, BA (Law) 1978); Univ. of S Africa (BProc 1982); London Univ. Publication: articles: Quality of Life: Survey on the Squatter Community in the Cape, 1977. Recreations: golf, tennis, surfing and skiing; bridge. Heir: cousin Edmund Oliver St John, WS [b 13 Oct. 1927; m 1959, Elizabeth Frances, o d of Lt-Col H. R. Nicholl; one s two d]. Address: By-The-Sea, Weston Road, Kalk Bay, Cape, 7975, South Africa. T: 881963; (to Oct. 1983) c/o London House, Mecklenburgh Square, WC1. T: 01-837 8888. Clubs: Royal Cape Golf, Western Province Sports.

ST JOHN, Oliver Beauchamp, CEng, FRAeS; Chief Scientist, Civil Aviation Authority, 1978-82; b 22 Jan. 1922; 2nd s of late Harold and Ella Margaret St John; m 1945, Eileen (née Morris); three s. Educ: Monkton Combe Sch.; Queens' Coll., Cambridge (MA); London Univ. (External) (BSc). Metropolitan Vickers, Manchester, 1939; Royal Aircraft Estabt, Farnborough, from 1946, on automatic control of fixed-wing aircraft and helicopters; Supt, Blind Landing Experimental Unit, RAE, Bedford, 1966; Director of Technical Research & Development, CAA, 1969-78. Queen's Commendation for Valuable Services in the Air, 1956. Recreations: mountaineering, skiing, antiques. Address: The Old Stables, Manor Farm Barns, East Hagbourne OX11 9ND. T: Didcot 818437. Clubs: Alpine, Swiss Alpine.

ST JOHN, Maj.-Gen. Roger Ellis Tudor, CB 1965; MC 1944; b Hexham on Tyne, 4 Oct. 1911; s of late Major B. T. St John, Craigveigh, Aboyne, Aberdeenshire; m 1943, Rosemary Jean Douglas Vickers, Englefield Green, Surrey; one s three d. Educ: Wellington College; RMC Sandhurst. Joined Fifth Fusiliers, 1931; served War of 1939-45 (despatches, MC), in Hong Kong, UK and NW Europe; Bde Major 11 Armoured Div., 1944-45; GSO 2 Instructor Camberley Staff Coll., 1945-46; AA and QMG 1st Division, Tripoli, 1948-50; comd 1st Bn Royal Northumberland Fusiliers, 1953-55 (despatches), Mau Mau Rebellion; AMS Mil. Secretary's Branch, War Office, 1955-57; Comdr 11 Inf. Bde Group, BAOR, 1957-60; Asst Comdt, Camberley Staff Coll., 1960-62; Comdr, British Army Staff, Military Member, British Defence Staffs, and Military Attaché, Washington, 1963-65; President, Regular Army Commissions Board, 1965-67; retired, 1967. Colonel, Royal Northumberland Fusiliers, 1965-68. Personnel Adminr, Urwick, Orr and Partners Ltd, Management Consultants, 1967-73. Address: Harelaw, Gorse Hill Road, Virginia Water, Surrey. Club: Army and Navy.

ST JOHN PARKER, Michael, MA (Cantab); Headmaster, Abingdon School, Oxfordshire, since 1975; b 21 July 1941; s of Rev. Canon J. W. Parker; m 1965, Annette Monica Ugle; two s two d. Educ: Stamford Sch.; King's Coll., Cambridge. Asst Master: Sevenoaks Sch., 1962-63; King's Sch., Canterbury, 1963-69; Winchester Coll., 1969-75; Head of History Dept, Winchester Coll., 1970-75. Member: Council, Hansard Soc., 1972-; Marsh Cttee on Politics and Industry, 1978-79. Governor: St Helen's Sch.; Christ Church Cathedral Sch. Publications: The British Revolution—Social and Economic History 1750-1970, 1972; various pamphlets and articles. Recreations: old buildings, music, books. Address: Lacies Court, Abingdon, Oxfordshire. T: Abingdon 20163.

ST JOHN-STEVAS, Rt. Hon. Norman Antony Francis, PC 1979; FRSL 1966; MP (C) Chelmsford, since Oct. 1964; Chancellor of the Duchy of Lancaster, Leader of the House of Commons, and Minister for the Arts, 1979-81; author, barrister and journalist; b London, 18 May 1929; o s of late Stephen Spiro Stevas, civil engineer and company director, and late Kitty St John O'Connor; unmarried. Educ: Ratcliffe; Fitzwilliam, Cambridge; Christ Church, Oxford; Yale. Scholar, Clothworkers Exhibnr, 1946, 1947; BA (Cambridge) (1st cl. hons in law), 1950, MA 1954; President, Cambridge Union, 1950; Whitlock Prize, 1950; MA 1952, BCL 1954 (Oxon); Sec. Oxford Union, 1952. Contested (C) Dagenham, Gen. Election, 1951; Barrister, Middle Temple, 1952; Blackstone and Harmsworth schol., 1952; Blackstone Prize, 1953. Lecturer, Southampton University, 1952-53, King's Coll., London, 1953-56, tutored in jurisprudence, Christ Church, 1953-55, and Merton, 1955-57, Oxford. Founder member, Inst. of Higher European Studies, Bolzano, 1955; PhD (Lond.) 1957; Yorke Prize, Cambridge Univ., 1957; Fellow Yale Law School, 1957; Fulbright Award, 1957; Fund for the Republic Fellow, 1958; Dr of Sc. of Law (Yale), 1960; Lecture tours of USA, 1958-68. Regents' Prof., Univ. of California at Santa Barbara, 1969. Legal Adviser to Sir Alan Herbert's Cttee on book censorship, 1954-59; joined The Economist, 1959, to edit collected works of Walter Bagehot and became legal, ecclesiastical and political correspondent. Deleg., Council of Europe and WEU, 1967-71; Parly Under-Sec. of State, DES, 1972-73; Min. of State for the Arts, DES, 1973-74; Sec., Cons. Parly Home Affairs Cttee, 1969-72; Vice-Chm., Cons. Parly N Ireland Cttee, 1972-; Mem. Executive, Cons. Parly 1922 Cttee, 1971-72 and 1974; Vice Chm., Cons. Group for Europe, 1972-75; Mem. Shadow Cabinet, 1974-79, and Opposition Spokesman on Educn, 1975-78, Science and the Arts, 1975-79; Shadow Leader of the House, 1978-79; Member: Cons. Nat. Adv. Cttee on Policy, 1961; Fulbright Commission, 1961; Parly Select Cttee: on Race Relations and Immigration, 1970-72; on Civil List, 1971-. Founder Mem., Christian-Social Inst. of Culture, Rome, 1969; Hon. Sec., Fedn of Cons. Students, 1971-73, Hon. Vice-Pres. 1973. Editor The Dublin (Wiseman) Review, 1961. Vice Pres., Les Amis de Napoléon III, 1974; Mem., Académie du Second Empire, 1975. Presidential Fellow, Aspern Inst., 1980. Silver Jubilee Medal, 1977. SBStJ. Commendatore, Order of Merit (Italian Republic), 1965. GCKLJ 1976 (KSLJ 1963). Publications: Obscenity and the Law, 1956; Walter Bagehot, 1959; Life, Death and the Law, 1961; The Right to Life, 1963; Law and Morals, 1964; The Literary Works of Walter Bagehot, vols I, II, 1966, The Historical Works, vols III, IV, 1968, The Political Works, vols V, VI, VII, and VIII, 1974, The Economic Works, vols IX, X and XI, 1978; The Agonising Choice, 1971; Pope John Paul II, his travels and mission, 1982; contrib. to: Critical Quarterly, Modern Law Review, Criminal Law Review, Law and Contemporary Problems, Twentieth Century, Times Lit. Supp., Dublin Review. Recreations: reading, talking, listening (to music), travelling, walking, appearing on television, sleeping. Address: 34 Montpelier Square,

SW1. *T:* 01-589 3001. *Clubs:* White's, Garrick, Pratt's, Arts (Hon. Mem., 1980).

ST JOHN WILSON, Colin Alexander; *see* Wilson.

ST JOHN'S (Newfoundland), Archbishop of, (RC), since 1979; **Most Rev. Alphonsus Liguori Penney;** *b* 17 Sept. 1924; *s* of Alphonsus Penney and Catherine Penney (*née* Mullaly). *Educ:* St Bonaventure's Coll., St John's, Newfoundland; University Seminary, Ottawa (LPh, LTh). Assistant Priest: St Joseph's Parish, St John's, 1950-56; St Patrick's Parish, St John's, 1956; Parish Priest: Marystown, Placentia Bay, Newfoundland, 1957; Basilica Parish, St John's, 1969. Prelate of Honour, 1971. Bishop of Grand Falls, Newfoundland, 1972. Co-Chm., Episcopal Commn for Religious Education, Canadian Conf. of Catholic Bishops, 1975. Hon. LLD, Memorial Univ. of Newfoundland, 1980. Confederation Medal, 1967. *Recreations:* walking, golf. *Address:* Basilica Residence, PO Box 37, St John's, Newfoundland A1C 5H5, Canada. *T:* 709-726-3660.

ST JOHN'S (Transkei and South Africa), Bishop of, since 1980; **Rt. Rev. Godfrey William Ernest Candler Ashby;** *b* 6 Nov. 1930; *s* of William Candler Ashby and Vera Fane Ashby (*née* Hickey); *m* 1957, Valerie Hawtree; four *s* two *d. Educ:* King's School, Chester; King's Coll., London (BD, AKC, PhD). Deacon 1955, priest 1956; Assistant Curate: St Peter, St Helier, Morden, 1955-57; Clydesdale Mission, 1958; Priest-in-charge, St Mark's Mission, 1958-60; Subwarden, St Paul's Coll., Grahamstown, 1960-65; Rector of Alice and Lectr, Federal Theological Seminary, 1966-68; Sen. Lecturer, Old Testament and Hebrew, Rhodes Univ., Grahamstown, 1969-75; Assoc. Professor, 1974-75; Overseas Visiting Scholar, St John's Coll., Cambridge, 1975; Dean and Archdeacon, Cathedral of St Michael and St George, Grahamstown, 1976-80. *Publications:* Theodoret of Cyrrhus as Exegete of the Old Testament, 1970; articles in theological jls. *Recreation:* ornithology. *Address:* Bishopsmead, PO Box 163, Umtata, Transkei. *T:* Umtata 2427.

ST JOHNSTON, Colin David; Director, Ocean Transport and Trading Ltd, since 1974; *b* 6 Sept. 1934; *s* of Hal and Sheilagh St Johnston; *m* 1958, Valerie Paget; three *s* one *d. Educ:* Shrewsbury Sch.; Lincoln Coll., Oxford (Modern History degree). Booker McConnell Ltd, 1958-70; Ocean Transport and Trading Ltd, 1970-; non-Executive Director, FMC Ltd, 1981-. Mem. Council: Royal Commonwealth Society for the Blind, 1967-; Industrial Soc., 1981-. *Recreations:* music, Victorian commemorative pottery, squash. *Address:* 30 Fitzroy Road, NW1 8TY. *T:* 01-722 5932. *Club:* MCC.

ST JOHNSTON, Kerry; Chairman and Chief Executive, Overseas Containers Ltd, since 1982; *b* 30 July 1931; *s* of George Eric St Johnston and Viola Rhona Moriarty; *m* 1st, 1960, Judith Ann Nichols; two *s* one *d* ; 2nd, 1980, Charlotte Ann Taylor. *Educ:* Summer Fields, Oxford; Eton Coll.; Worcester Coll., Oxford (MA Jurisprudence). Joined Ocean Steamship Co. Ltd, 1955, Man. Dir 1963; Overseas Containers Ltd: Founder Dir, 1965; Commerical Dir, 1966; Jt Man. Dir, 1969; Dep. Chm., 1973; Pres. and Chief Exec. Officer, Private Investment Co. for Asia (PICA), SA, Singapore, 1977-82. *Recreations:* fishing, shooting, racing. *Address:* Flat 5, 53 Drayton Gardens, SW10 9RX. *T:* 01-373 3947. *Club:* Boodle's.

ST JOHNSTON, Colonel Sir (Thomas) Eric, Kt 1967; CBE 1952 (OBE 1945); QPM 1958; MA Cantab; Member of Lloyd's; Director, Group 4 Total Security; Chairman, Weller-King Ltd; security consultant; *b* 7 Jan. 1911; *s* of late T. G. St Johnston, Edgbaston, Warwicks; *m* 1st, 1937, Joan (marr. diss. 1969; she *d* 1974); one *s* two *d* ; 2nd, 1969, M. E. Jameson Till (marr. diss. 1979); 3rd, 1980, Elizabeth Condy (*née* Thomas). *Educ:* Bromsgrove School, Worcestershire; Corpus Christi, Cambridge. Late RA (TA), 1929-35; employed in rank of Colonel for special duties, War Office, 1943, and as Head of Public Safety section, G5 Div., SHAEF, 1944; member staff of King's Camp, 1932 *et seq* ; employed on civil staff at New Scotland Yard, 1932-35; Barrister, Middle Temple, 1934; Metropolitan Police College, 1935 (winner of Baton of Honour); Inspector, Metropolitan Police, 1936-40; Chief Constable of Oxfordshire, 1940-44, of Durham County, 1944-50, of Lancashire, 1950-67; HM Chief Inspector of Constabulary for England and Wales, 1967-70. Visited USA as guest of US Government, 1953; Visiting Lecturer, Univ. of California, 1953; Visiting Lectr to Israeli Police, 1955; British Council Lecturer in Australia and New Zealand, 1966; idc, 1957; invited by Govt of Victoria, Australia to examine and report on efficiency of Police Force in the State, 1970-71. Dir of Admin, Spencer Stuart & Associates Ltd, 1971-75. Freeman of City of London; Liveryman: Vintners' Company, 1956; Gunmakers' Co., 1979; Chevalier de Tastevin, 1965. Chairman, Christian Police Trust Corp. Ltd, 1954-67. Dep. Chm., Sail Training Assoc., 1968-73. Pres., 1978-, and Endowment Trustee, Bromsgrove School. Pres., Assoc. of Lancastrians in London, 1982-83. Hon. Col 33rd (Lancs and Cheshire) Signal Regt (V), 1967-70. Hon. MA Manchester, 1961. Mem., Chapter Gen., Order of St John, 1968-69; KStJ 1966 (CStJ, 1960). Legion of Honour and Croix de Guerre (France). *Publications:* One Policeman's Story, 1978; contrib. to Police periodicals in UK, and USA. *Recreations:* shooting, fishing and sailing. *Address:* Old Swan House, Great Rissington, Glos. *T:* Bourton-on-the-Water 20776. *Clubs:* Buck's, Naval and Military, MCC.

ST JOSEPH, Prof. John Kenneth Sinclair, CBE 1979 (OBE 1964); FBA 1978; Professor of Aerial Photographic Studies, University of Cambridge, and Professorial Fellow of Selwyn College, 1973-80, Professor Emeritus since 1980; *b* 1912; *s* of late John D. St Joseph and of Irma Robertson (*née* Marris); *m* 1945, Daphne Margaret, *d* of late H. March, Worcester; two *s* two *d. Educ:* Bromsgrove Sch.; Selwyn Coll., Cambridge (Scholar). BA 1934, PhD 1937, MA 1938, LittD 1976. Harkness Scholar, 1934; Goldsmiths' Company Senior Student, 1935-37; DSIR Sen. Research Award, 1936-37; Fellow, Selwyn Coll., Cambridge, 1939-, Lectr in Natural Sciences and Dean, 1939-62; Tutor, 1945-62; Librarian, 1946-62; Vice Master, 1974-80; Univ. Demonstrator in Geology, 1937-45; Operational Research, Min. of Aircraft Production, 1942-45; Univ. Lectr in Geology, 1945-48; Leverhulme Research Fellow, 1948-49; Curator in Aerial Photography at Cambridge, 1948-62; Dir in Aerial Photography, 1962-80. Has undertaken aerial reconnaissance and photography, in aid of research, over the United Kingdom, Ireland, Denmark, the Netherlands and Northern France. Governor, Stratton Sch., Biggleswade, 1952-64; Hon. Corresp. Mem., German Archæological Inst., 1964-; Member: Council for British Archaeology, 1944-; Ancient Monuments Bd (England), 1969-; Royal Commn on Historical Monuments (England), 1972-81; Vice-Pres., Soc. for Promotion of Roman Studies, 1975-; Hon. Vice-Pres., Royal Archaeological Inst., 1982-. Lectures: Chatwin Meml, Birmingham, 1969; David Murray, Glasgow Univ., 1973; Kroon, Amsterdam Univ., 1981. Cuthbert Peek Award, RGS, 1976; President's Award, Inst. of Incorporated Photographers, 1977. FGS 1937; FSAScot 1940; FSA 1944; Hon. ScD, Trinity Coll., Dublin; Hon. LLD, Dundee; Dr *hc* in Maths and Science, Amsterdam. *Publications:* The Pentameracea of the Oslo Region, 1939; chapters in The Roman Occupation of SW Scotland (ed S. N. Miller), 1945; Monastic Sites from the Air (with M. C. Knowles), 1952; Medieval England, an aerial survey (with M. W. Beresford), 1958, 2nd rev. edn, 1979; (ed) The Uses of Air Photography, 1966, 2nd rev. edn 1977; The Early Development of Irish Society (with E. R. Norman), 1970; papers in learned jls on fossil Silurian Brachiopoda, and on aerial photography and archæology, especially of Roman Britain. *Recreations:* gardening, lumbering. *Address:* Selwyn College, Cambridge CB3 9DQ. *T:* Cambridge 62381; Histon Manor, Cambridge CB4 4JJ. *Club:* Explorers' (NY).

ST JUST, 2nd Baron, *cr* 1935, of St Just in Penwith; **Peter George Grenfell;** *b* 22 July 1922; *s* of 1st Baron and Florence (*d* 1971), *e d* of late George W. Henderson; *s* father, 1941; *m* 1st, 1949, Leslie (marriage dissolved, 1955), *d* of late Condé Nast, New York; one *d* ; 2nd, 1956, Maria Britneva; two *d. Educ:* Harrow. Served War, 1941-46, 60th Rifles. *Address:* 9 Gerald Road, SW1. *T:* 01-730 7621; Wilbury Park, Newton Tony, near Salisbury, Wilts. *T:* Cholderton 664. *Clubs:* White's, House of Lords Yacht.

SAINT LAURENT, Yves (Henri Donat Mathieu); couturier; *b* 1 Aug. 1936; *s* of Charles Mathieu and Lucienne-Andrée Saint Laurent. *Educ:* Lycée d'Oran. Designer for Christian Dior, 1954-60; Dir, Société Yves Saint Laurent, 1962-. Costume designer for several plays, ballets and films. *Publication:* La Vilaine Lulu, 1967. *Address:* (office) 5 avenue Marceau, 75016 Paris; (home) 55 rue de Babylone, 75007 Paris, France.

ST LEGER, family name of Viscount **Doneraile.**

ST LEONARDS, 4th Baron *cr* 1852; **John Gerard Sugden;** *b* 3 Feb. 1950; *s* of Arthur Herbert Sugden (*g g s* of 1st Baron) (*d* 1958) and of Julia Sheila, *d* of late Philip Wyatt; *S* kinsman, 1972. *Heir: uncle* Dr Edward Charles Sugden, *b* 24 July 1902.

ST LEVAN, 4th Baron *cr* 1887; **John Francis Arthur St Aubyn,** DSC 1942; DL; Bt 1866; landowner and company director; *b* 23 Feb. 1919; *s* of 3rd Baron St Levan, and of Hon. Clementina Gwendolen Catharine Nicolson, *o d* of 1st Baron Carnock; *S* father, 1978; *m* 1970, Susan Maria Marcia, *d* of late Maj.-Gen. Sir John Kennedy, GCMG, KCVO, KBE, CB. *Educ:* Eton Coll.; Trinity Coll., Cambridge (BA). Admitted a Solicitor, 1948. High Sheriff of Cornwall, 1974; DL Cornwall, 1977. Pres., Cornwall Br., CPRE, 1975. FRSA 1974. *Publication:* Illustrated History of St Michael's Mount, 1974. *Recreation:* sailing. *Heir: br* Hon. (Oliver) Piers St Aubyn, MC [5 July 1920; *m* 1948, Mary, *e d* of late Bailey Southwell; two *s* one *d*]. *Address:* St Michael's Mount, Marazion, Cornwall. *Clubs:* Brooks's; Royal Yacht Squadron.

ST OSWALD, 4th Baron, *cr* 1885; **Rowland Denys Guy Winn,** MC 1951; DL; Vice-Chairman of Central and Eastern European Commission of the European Movement; Chairman, Crabtree Denims Ltd; *b* 19 Sept. 1916; *s* of 3rd Baron St Oswald and Eva (*d* 1976), *d* of Charles Greene; *S* father 1957; *m* 1st, 1952, Laurian (from whom he obtained a divorce, 1955), *o d* of Sir Roderick Jones, KBE; 2nd, 1955, Marie Wanda (*d* 1981), *y d* of late Sigismund Jaxa-Chamiec, Zorawia, Warsaw; no *c. Educ:* Stowe Sch.; Universities of Bonn and Freiburg. Reuter's Corresp. for Spain, 1935; Daily Telegraph Corresp. and War Corresp., 1936 (condemned to death, Sept. 1936); Corresp. in Middle East, 1938, in Balkans 1939. Enlisted Army, 1939; served Middle East (8th King's Royal Hussars), 1941-44; Far East, 1945 (despatches). Resided Spain, 1946-50. Volunteered to serve in Korea, 1950; 8th King's Roy. Irish Hussars, 1950-51. Contested (C) Dearne Valley Div., 1955; adopted as Conservative candidate, Pudsey Div., 1957; Mem., European Parlt, 1973-79; contested (C) Yorkshire West, European Parlt, 1979. A Lord-in-Waiting to the Queen, 1959-62; Jt Parly Sec. to Min. of Agriculture, Fisheries and Food, 1962-64. Chairman, Mid-Yorkshire Conservative Assoc., 1965; President: W Riding of Yorks Playing Fields Assoc., 1970-; British Assoc. Industrial Editors, 1964-70; Yorks Region Nat. Soc. Mentally Handicapped Children; Yorkshire Area Young Conservatives; Ackworth, Upton,

Hemsworth and Wrangbrooke Branches, British Legion; Vice-President: W Riding British Legion; Anglo-Polish Soc., 1969. Trustee and Pres., Northern Cttee of Cheshire Foundn Homes for the Sick. Pres., Soc. of Yorkshiremen in London, 1960-61; Pres. Huddersfield Branch, Coldstreamers' Assoc.; Patron of Wakefield Trinity Football Club; Pres., Yorkshire Agric. Soc., 1968. Hon. Col 150 (Northumbrian) Regt RCT (V), 1967-. DL West Riding, Yorks, 1962. Croix de Guerre and Order of Leopold (Belgium), 1951; Légion d'Honneur and Croix de Guerre (France), 1945; Grand Cross, Order of Polonia Restituta, 1977; Grand Cross of Isabel la Católica (Spain), 1980. *Publications:* Lord Highport Dropped at Dawn, 1949; My Dear, it's Heaven, 1950; Carmela, 1954 (USA 1955). *Recreations:* talking and writing to friends. *Heir:* b Capt. Hon. Derek Edward Anthony Winn [b 9 July 1919; m 1954, Denise Eileen Charlotte, o d of Wilfrid Haig Loyd; one s one d]. *Address:* Nostell Priory, Wakefield, W Yorks. *T:* Wakefield 862394; White Lodge, Gilston Road, SW10. *T:* 01-373 3660. *Clubs:* Cavalry and Guards, Garrick, Press, Special Forces, Beefsteak, Pratt's.

ST PAUL'S, Dean of; *see* Webster, Very Rev. A. B.

ST VINCENT, 7th Viscount (*cr* 1801); **Ronald George James Jervis;** b 3 May 1905; o surv. s of 6th Viscount and Marion Annie (d 1911), d of James Brown, JP, Orchard, Carluke, Scotland; S father, 1940; m 1945, Phillida, o d of Lt-Col R. H. Logan, Taunton; two s one d. *Educ:* Sherborne. JP Somerset, 1950-55. *Heir:* s Hon. Edward Robert James Jervis [b 12 May 1951; m 1977, Victoria Margaret, o d of Wilton J. Oldham, St Peter, Jersey; one d]. *Address:* Les Charrieres, St Ouen, Jersey, CI.

ST VINCENT FERRERI, Marquis of; *see* San Vincenzo Ferreri.

SAINTONGE, Rolland A. A. C. de; *see* Chaput de Saintonge.

SAINTY, John Christopher; Reading Clerk, House of Lords, since 1974; b 31 Dec. 1934; s of late Christopher Lawrence Sainty and Nancy Lee Sainty (née Miller); m 1965, Elizabeth Frances Sherlock; three s. *Educ:* Winchester Coll.; New Coll., Oxford (MA). FSA; FRHistS. Clerk, Parlt Office, House of Lords, 1959; seconded as Private Sec. to Leader of House and Chief Whip, House of Lords, 1963; Clerk of Journals, House of Lords, 1965; Res. Asst and Editor, Inst. of Historical Research, 1970. *Publications:* Treasury Officials 1660-1870, 1972; Officials of the Secretaries of State 1660-1782, 1973; Officials of the Boards of Trade 1660-1870, 1974; Admiralty Officials 1660-1870, 1975; Home Office Officials, 1782-1870, 1975; Colonial Office Officials 1794-1870, 1976; (with D. Dewar) Divisions in the House of Lords: an analytical list 1685-1857, 1976; articles in Eng. Hist. Rev., Bull. Inst. Hist. Research. *Address:* 22 Kelso Place, W8 5QG. *T:* 01-937 9460.

SAKHAROV, Dr Andrei Dimitrievich; Member, Academy of Sciences of USSR, since 1953; b 21 May 1921; m 2nd, 1971, Elena Bonner; one s one d. *Educ:* Moscow State Univ. Joined P. N. Lebedev Physics Inst. as physicist, 1945; worked with Dr Igor Tamm on nuclear fusion. Member: Amer. Acad. of Arts and Sciences, 1969-; Nat. Acad. of Sciences, 1972-; Foreign Associate, Acad. des Sciences, 1981-. Eleanor Roosevelt Peace Award, 1973; Cino del Duca Prize, 1974; Reinhold Niebuhr Prize, Chicago Univ., 1974; Nobel Peace Prize, 1975; Fritt Ord Prize, 1980. *Publications:* Progress, Peaceful Co-existence and Intellectual Freedom, 1968; Sakharov Speaks, 1974; My Country and the World, 1975; Alarm and Hope, 1979; scientific works, etc. *Address:* Academy of Sciences of USSR, Leninsky prospekt 14, Moscow, USSR; Flat 3, 214 Gagarin prospekt, Sherpinki 2, Gorky, USSR.

SAKZEWSKI, Sir Albert, Kt 1973; FCA; FASA; chartered accountant; Founder, Sir Albert Sakzewski Foundation; Chairman: Avanis Pty Ltd; Blend Investments Pty Ltd; Commercial Finance Pty Ltd; Queensland Securities Pty Ltd; Southern Cross Products Pty Ltd; b Lowood, Qld, 12 Nov. 1905; s of O. T. Sakzewski, Lowood and Brisbane; m 1935, Winifred May (d 1972), d of W. P. Reade; two s. *Educ:* Ipswich High Sch., Qld. Founder and Sen. Partner, A. Sakzewski & Co./Court & Co., Chartered Accountants, 1929-76. Chairman: Qld Bd of Advice, Custom Credit Corp. Ltd, 1964-78; Rover Mowers (Aust) Pty Ltd, 1966-77; Dir, Oswald-Sealy (Australia) Pty Ltd. Chm. and Govt Nominee, Totalisator Admin Bd of Qld, 1962-81. Dir, Nat. Heart Foundn (Queensland Div.), 1960-76 (Chm., Building Appeal, 1978). Past Pres., Australian Amateur Billiards Council; Member: Aust./Britain Soc.; Nat. Trust of Qld; Aust. Ballet Foundn; Qld Art Gall. Foundn; Royal Nat. Agricl & Industrial Assoc. of Qld. *Recreations:* horse racing and breeding (administrator (Tattersall's) 1935-, owner 1941-); golf, billiards (Australian Amateur Billiards Champion, 1932, with a then Australian Record break of 206), snooker; Qld Amateur Billiards Champion 6 times; Qld Amateur Snooker Champion 8 times. *Address:* (home) Ilya Lodge, 1 Rossiter Parade, Hamilton, Qld 4007, Australia; (office) National Bank House, 255 Adelaide Street, Brisbane, Qld 4000, Australia; GPO Box 11, Brisbane, 4001. *Clubs:* Royal Commonwealth Society; Brisbane, Tattersall's (Trustee; Life Mem.) (Brisbane); Tattersall's (Sydney); Queensland Turf, Tattersall's Racing (Life Mem.), Brisbane Amateur Turf (Life Mem.), Ipswich Amateur Turf, Gold Coast Turf, Rockhampton Jockey (Life Mem.); Albion Park Trotting; Gabba Greyhound Racing; Royal Queensland Golf, Brisbane Golf, Southport Golf; Huntington Country.

SALAM, Professor Abdus, Sitara-i-Pakistan, 1959; Order of Nishan-i-Imtiaz, Pakistan, 1979; PhD; FRS 1959; Professor of Theoretical Physics at the Imperial College of Science and Technology in the University of London

since 1957; Director, International Centre for Theoretical Physics, Trieste, since 1964; b 29 Jan. 1926. *Educ:* Govt Coll., Lahore, Pakistan (MA); St John's Coll., Camb. (BA, PhD). Fellow, St John's Coll., Cambridge, 1951-56 (Hon. Fellow, 1972); Professor of Mathematics, Government College, Lahore, 1951-54; Lecturer in Mathematics, University of Cambridge, 1954-56. Sci. Advr to Pres. of Pakistan, 1961-74. Has made contributions to the theory of elementary particles. Mem., UN Adv. Cttee on Science and Technology, 1964-75 (Chm., 1971-72); Vice-Pres., IUPAP, 1972-78. Fellow, Royal Swedish Acad. of Sciences, 1970; For. Mem., USSR Acad. of Scis, 1971. Hon. DSc: Panjab University, Lahore, Pakistan, 1957; Edinburgh, 1971. Hopkins Prize, Cambridge Philosophical Soc., 1957; Adams Prize, Cambridge Univ., 1958; Maxwell Medal and Prize, IPPS, 1961; Hughes Medal, Royal Society, 1964; Atoms for Peace Award, 1968; Oppenheimer Prize and Medal, 1971; Guthrie Medal and Prize, IPPS, 1976; Matteuci Medal, Accad. Naz. di XL, Rome, 1978; John Torrence Tate Medal, Amer. Inst. of Physics, 1978; Royal Medal, Royal Society, 1978; (jtly) Nobel Prize for Physics, 1979; Einstein Medal, UNESCO, Paris, 1979; Josef Stefan Medal, Josef Stefan Inst., Ljubljana, 1980; Gold Medal for outstanding contrib. to physics, Czechoslovak Acad. of Scis, Prague, 1981; Peace Medal, Charles Univ., Prague, 1981. *Address:* Imperial College of Science and Technology, Prince Consort Road, SW7; International Centre for Theoretical Physics, PO Box 586, 34100 Trieste, Italy. *Club:* Athenæum.

SALAMAN, Myer Head, MD; Research Pathologist, Royal College of Surgeons, 1968-74; b 2 August 1902; e s of Redcliffe N. Salaman, MD, FRS and Nina Salaman; m 1926, Esther Polianowsky; one s three d. *Educ:* Clifton College; Bedales School; Trinity College, Cambridge; London Hospital Medical College. Natural Science Tripos Pts I and II, Cambridge, 1921-25; London Hosp.: Clinical training, 1927-30; House Appts, 1931-32; Research on Viruses, 1932-34, and Lister Inst. (Junior Beit Mem. Fellow) 1935-38; Cancer Research, St Bartholomew's Hosp., 1939; Asst Pathologist, Emergency Public Health Service, 1940-42; Cancer and Virus Research, Strangeways Lab., 1942-43; Temp. Major, RAMC, 1943-46. Engaged in Cancer Research at the London Hospital, 1946-48; Dir, Dept of Cancer Research, London Hosp. Med. Sch., 1948-67; engaged in Cancer Research at RCS, 1968-74. MA 1926, MD 1936 Cantab; MRCS, LRCP, 1930; Dipl. Bact. London, 1936. FRSocMed. *Publications:* papers on virus diseases, and on cancer, in Jour. Pathology and Bacteriology, Proc. Roy. Soc. (B), Brit. Jl Cancer, etc. *Recreation:* walking. *Address:* 23 Bisham Gardens, Highgate, N6. *T:* 01-340 1019. *Club:* Athenæum.

See also Prof. H. B. Barlow.

SALAS, Rafael Montinola; Executive Director (with rank of Under-Secretary-General), United Nations Fund for Population Activities, since 1971 (Sen. Consultant to Administrator of UNDP, 1969; Director UNFPA, 1969); Secretary-General, 1984 International Conference on Population; b Bago, Negros Occidental, Philippines, 7 Aug. 1928; s of Ernesto Salas and Isabel Montinola; m 1967, Carmelita J. Rodriguez; two s. *Educ:* Coll. of Liberal Arts, Univ. of the Philippines (Associate in Arts (AA) with high honours, 1950; AB magna cum laude, 1953); Coll. of Law, Univ. of the Philippines (LLB cum laude 1953); Littauer Center of Public Admin. (MPA), Harvard Univ., 1955. Mem., Philippine Bar, 1953. Professorial Lectr in: Polit. Sci. and Economics, Univ. of the Philippines, 1955-59; Economics, Grad. Sch., Far Eastern Univ., 1960-61; Law, Univ. of the Philippines, 1963-66 (Asst. Vice-Pres., 1962-63, Mem., Board of Regents, 1966-69, of the Univ.). Philippine Positions: Nat. Economic Council: Exec. Officer (with Cabinet rank), 1960-61; Exec. Dir (with Cabinet rank), 1961; Actg Chm., 1966, 1968. Gen. Manager, the Manila Chronicle, 1963-65; Asst to the President, Meralco Securities Corp., 1963-65. Action Officer, Nat. Rice and Corn Sufficiency Programme, 1967-69 (of vital importance to "Green Revolution"); Nat. Projects Overall Co-ordinator and Action Officer, 1966-69; Exec. Sec. of Republic of the Philippines, 1966-69 (office 2nd to President in executive powers). Holds numerous hon. degrees. Holds foreign Orders. *Publications:* People: an international choice, 1976; International Population Assistance: the first decade, 1979. *Recreation:* reading. *Address:* United Nations, New York 10017, USA.

SALE, Geoffrey Stead; Director of Studies, RMA, Sandhurst, Camberley, 1967-71; b 6 Aug. 1907; s of Frederic W. R. Sale, Solicitor, Carlisle, and Ivy I. Davidson; m 1938, Olivia Jean Bell-Scott (d 1950), Edinburgh; one s three d. *Educ:* Berkhamsted School; Lincoln College, Oxford (MA). Diploma in Education; Assistant Master and Housemaster, Fettes College, Edinburgh, 1931-46; Headmaster, King's School, Bruton, 1946-57; Headmaster, Rossall School, 1957-67. Captain TA (General List). Member, House of Laity, Church Assembly, 1960-70. FRSA 1953. *Publication:* Four Hundred Years a School (History of King's School). *Recreations:* walking, photography, writing. *Address:* Low House, Brackenthwaite, Cockermouth, Cumbria CA13 9UX. *T:* Lorton 642.

SALE, Richard; Headmaster of Brentwood School, 1966-81; b 4 Oct. 1919; e s of late Richard and Rachel Sale; m 1943, Elizabeth Thérèse Bauer; four s one d. *Educ:* Repton Sch. (Schol.); Oriel Coll., Oxford. Commissioned, KSLI, 1940; served War of 1939-45: Canada and Normandy; demobilised, rank of Major, 1946. Asst Master, Repton Sch., 1946-61; Housemaster of The Priory, 1953-61; Headmaster, Oswestry School, Shropshire, 1962-66. President: Arthur Dunn Cup; Old Reptonian Soc.; Essex Co. Football Assoc. FRSA 1969. *Recreations:* cricket (Oxford Blue; Warwickshire, 1939, 1946, 1947; Derbyshire, 1949-54), golf, fives (Oxford Blue), and other games.

Address: Whitegates, Ballygate, Beccles, Suffolk. *T:* Beccles 714486. *Clubs:* MCC; Vincent's (Oxford).

SALES, William Henry, BSc (Econ.) Hons. London; Chairman, Yorkshire (late NE) Division of the National Coal Board, 1957-67, retired (Member, National Coal Board, 1953-57); *b* 26 April 1903. *Educ:* pit; Fircroft; London School of Economics. Miners' Welfare Scholarship. Varied career: pit; boys' clubs; WEA Lecturer; schoolmaster. Dep. Labour Director, East Midlands Division, NCB, 1947-51; Deputy Chairman, North-Western Division, 1951-53. Chm. Church of England Industrial Council, 1967-71. Hon. Fellow, LSE, 1960. *Publications:* various papers in Economic and Sociological Journals. *Address:* Handley Cross, Cantley, Doncaster, S Yorks.

SALFORD, Bishop of, (RC), since 1964; **Rt. Rev. Thomas Holland,** DSC 1944; DD (Gregorian); *b* 11 June 1908; *s* of John Holland and Mary (*née* Fletcher). *Educ:* Upholland; Valladolid; Rome. PhD Valladolid, 1929; DD Gregorian, Rome, 1936. Taught theology: Spain, 1936-41; Lisbon, 1941-43. Chaplain, RN, 1943-46; Port Chaplain, Bombay, 1946-48; CMS, 1948-56; Secretary to Apostolic Delegate, 1956-60; Coadjutor Bp of Portsmouth, 1960-64. Privy Chamberlain to the Pope, 1958. Member of Vatican Secretariat for Promoting Christian Unity, 1961-74, for Unbelievers, 1965-73; Mem., Vatican Synod, 1974. Hon. DLitt Salford, 1980. *Publication:* Great Cross, 1958. *Address:* Wardley Hall, Worsley, Manchester M28 5ND. *T:* 061-794 2825.

SALFORD, Auxiliary Bishop of, (RC); *see* Burke, Rt Rev. Geoffrey.

SALINGER, Jerome David; American author; *b* New York City, 1919; *m* ; one *s* one *d. Educ:* Manhattan public schools; Military Academy, Paris. Served with 4th Infantry Division, US Army, 1942-46 (Staff Sergeant). Travelled in Europe, 1937-38. Started writing at age of 15; first story published, 1940. *Publications:* The Catcher in the Rye, 1951; For Esme-with Love and Squalor, 1953; Franny and Zooey, 1962; Raise High the Roof Beam, Carpenters and Seymour: an Introduction, 1963. *Address:* c/o Harold Ober Associates, 40 East 49th Street, New York, NY 10017, USA.

SALINGER, Pierre (Emil George); Politician, Journalist; Paris Bureau Chief, American Broadcasting Company, since 1979; *b* San Francisco, 14 June 1925; *s* of Herbert and Jehanne Salinger; *m* 1st; one *s* one *d* ; 2nd, 1957, Nancy Brook Joy (marr. diss., 1965); 3rd, 1965, Nicole Gillmann, Paris, France; one *s. Educ:* Lowell High School, San Francisco; State Coll., San Francisco; Univ. of San Francisco. Served War, 1942-45, with US Navy. With San Francisco Chronicle, 1942-55; Guest Lectr, Mills Coll., Calif, 1950-55; Press Officer, Democratic Presidential Campaign (Calif), 1952; West Coast Editor, Contributing Editor, Collier's Magazine, 1955-56; Investigator, Senate Labor Rackets Cttee, 1957-59; Press Sec. to President Kennedy (when Senator), 1959-61, and to President of the United States, 1961-64; appointed to serve as a US Senator, 4 Aug. 1964-2 Jan. 1965; Roving Editor, L'Express, Paris, 1973-78. Vice Pres.: Continental Airlines, Continental Air Services, 1965-68. Trustee, Robert F. Kennedy Meml Foundn; Chm., Bd of Trustees, American Coll. in Paris. Mem., Legion of Honour, 1978; US Navy and Marine Corps Medal, 1946. *Publications:* articles on county jail conditions in California, 1953; A Tribute to John F. Kennedy, Encyclopedia Britannica, 1964; With Kennedy, 1966; A Tribute to Robert F. Kennedy, 1968; For the Eyes of the President Only, 1971; Je suis un Americain, 1975; La France et le Nouveau Monde, 1976; America Held Hostage—the secret negotiations, 1981. *Address:* 248 rue de Rivoli, 75001 Paris, France.

SALISBURY, 6th Marquess of, *cr* 1789; **Robert Edward Peter Cecil;** DL; Baron Cecil, 1603; Viscount Cranborne, 1604; Earl of Salisbury, 1605; Captain Grenadier Guards; High Steward of Hertford since 1972; *b* 24 Oct. 1916; *s* of 5th Marquess of Salisbury, KG, PC, FRS, and Elizabeth Vere (*d* 1982), *e d* of late Lord Richard Cavendish, PC, CB, CMG; *S* father, 1972; *m* 1945, Marjorie Olein (Mollie), *d* of Captain Hon. Valentine Wyndham-Quin, *qv* ; four *s* one *d* (and one *s* decd). MP (C) Bournemouth West, 1950-54. Pres., Monday Club, 1974-81. DL Dorset, 1974. *Heir: s* Viscount Cranborne, *qv. Address:* Manor House, Cranborne, Dorset; Hatfield House, Hatfield, Herts.
See also Lord David Cecil, Dowager Duchess of Devonshire.

SALISBURY, Bishop of, since 1982; **Rt. Rev. John Austin Baker;** *b* 11 Jan. 1928; *s* of George Austin Baker and Grace Edna Baker; *m* 1974, Gillian Mary Leach. *Educ:* Marlborough; Oriel Coll., Oxford (B Litt, MA). Asst Curate, All Saints', Cuddesdon, and Lectr in Old Testament, Cuddesdon Theol Coll., 1954-57; Priest 1955; Asst Curate, St Anselm's, Hatch End, and Asst Lectr in NT Greek, King's Coll., London, 1957-59; Official Fellow, Chaplain and Lectr in Divinity, Corpus Christi Coll., Oxford, 1959-73, Emeritus Fellow, 1977; Lectr in Theology, Brasenose and Lincoln Colls, Oxford, 1959-73; Hebrew Lectr, Exeter Coll., Oxford, 1969-73; Canon of Westminster, 1973-82; Treas., 1974-78; Sub-Dean and Lector Theologiae, 1978-82; Rector of St Margaret's, Westminster, and Speaker's Chaplain, 1978-82. Governor of Pusey House, Oxford, 1970-78; Exam. Chaplain to Bp of Oxford, 1960-78, to Bp of Southwark, 1973-78; Governor: Westminster Sch., 1974-; Ripon Coll., Cuddesdon, 1974-80; Westminster City Sch., 1978-; Trustee, Harold Buxton Trust, 1973-79; Dorrance Visiting Prof., Trinity Coll., Hartford, Conn, USA, 1967; Visiting Prof., King's Coll., London, 1974-77; Hulsean Preacher, Univ. of Cambridge, 1979. Chm., Defence Theol Working Party, C of E Bd for Social Responsibility, 1980-82; Member: CofE Doctrine

Commn, 1967-76, 1977-81; Faith and Order Advisory Gp, CofE Bd for Mission and Unity, 1976-81. *Publications:* The Foolishness of God, 1970; Travels in Oudamovia, 1976; The Living Presence of Westminster Abbey, 1977; The Whole Family of God, 1981; contrib. to: Man: Fallen and Free (ed Kemp), 1969; Thinking about the Eucharist (ed Ramsey), 1972; Church Membership and Intercommunion (ed Kent and Murray), 1973; What about the New Testament? (ed Hooker and Hickling), 1975; Man and Nature (ed Montefiore), 1975; Studia Biblica I, 1978; Religious Studies and Public Examinations (ed Hulmes and Watson), 1980; Believing in the Church, 1981; *translations:* W. Eichrodt, Theology of the Old Testament, vol. 1 1961, vol. 2 1967; T. Bovet, That They May Have Life, 1964; J. Daniélou, Theology of Jewish Christianity, 1964; H. von Campenhausen, Ecclesiastical Authority and Spiritual Power, 1969; H. von Campenhausen, The Formation of the Christian Bible, 1972; J. Daniélou, Gospel Message and Hellenistic Culture, 1973; (with David Smith) J. Daniélou, The Origins of Latin Christianity, 1977. *Recreations:* music, walking. *Address:* South Canonry, The Close, Salisbury, Wilts SP1 2EN.

SALISBURY, Dean of; *see* Evans, Very Rev. S. H.

SALISBURY, Harrison Evans; *b* 14 Nov. 1908; *s* of Percy Pritchard Salisbury and Georgiana Evans Salisbury; *m* 1st, 1933, Mary Hollis (marr. diss.); two *s* ; 2nd, 1964, Charlotte Young Rand. *Educ:* Univ. of Minnesota (AB). United Press, 1930: London Manager, 1943; Foreign Editor, 1945. New York Times: Moscow Corresp., 1949-54; National Editor, 1962; Asst Man. Editor, 1964-69; Associate Editor and Editor Opposite-Editorial Page, 1970-73. Pres., Amer. Acad. and Inst. of Arts and Letters, 1975-77. Pres., Authors' League, 1980-. Pulitzer Prize, International Correspondence, 1955. Holds hon. doctorates. *Publications:* Russia on the Way, 1946; American in Russia, 1955; The Shook-up Generation, 1958; To Moscow-And Beyond, 1960; Moscow Journal, 1961; The Northern Palmyra Affair, 1962; A New Russia?, 1962; Russia, 1965; Orbit of China, 1967; Behind the Lines-Hanoi 1967; The Soviet Union-The 50 Years, 1967; The 900 Days, the Siege of Leningrad, 1969; The Coming War Between Russia and China, 1969; The Many Americas Shall Be One, 1971; The Eloquence of Protest: voices of the seventies, 1972; To Peking-and Beyond, 1973; The Gates of Hell, 1975; Black Night, White Snow: Russia's Revolutions 1905-1917, 1978; Russia in Revolution 1900-1930, 1978; The Unknown War, 1978; Without Fear or Favor: The New York Times and its times, 1980; A Journey for Our Times, 1983. *Address:* Box 70, Taconic, Conn, USA. *Clubs:* Century Association (New York); National Press (Washington, DC).

SALISBURY, John; *see* Caute, J. D.

SALISBURY-JONES, Maj.-Gen. Sir (Arthur) Guy, GCVO 1961 (KCVO 1953); CMG 1949; CBE 1945; MC; DL; Extra Equerry to the Queen since 1962; *b* 4 July 1896; *s* of late Arthur Thomas Salisbury-Jones; *m* Hilda, *widow* of Maj. Guy Yerburgh, Irish Guards, and *d* of Rt Hon. Sir Maurice de Bunsen, Bt, PC, GCMG, GCVO, CB; one *s* one *d. Educ:* Eton. Joined Coldstream Guards, 1915; served European War, 1914-18 (twice wounded, MC and Bar); student at Ecole Spéciale Militaire, St Cyr, 1920-21; Liaison Officer in Syria, 1924-26; Jebel Druze Campaign, 1925-26 (French Croix de Guerre); China, 1927; Staff College, 1932-34; Staff London District, 1935-38; commanded 3rd Battalion Coldstream Guards, in Palestine, 1938-39 (despatches); served in Syria, Italian Somaliland, Greece and Crete, 1939-41 (despatches); was Head of Military Mission to South Africa, 1941-44; Supreme HQ Allied Exped. Force, 1944-45; Head of British Military Mission to France and Military Attaché, Paris, 1946-49; ADC to the King, 1948-49; retired, 1949; HM Marshal of the Diplomatic Corps, 1950-61. Chm., Franco-British Soc., 1963-67. Wine Grower; Pres., English Vineyards Assoc., 1967-81. DL Hampshire, 1965. Order of Red Banner USSR, Order of White Lion Czechoslovakia, Grand Officier Legion of Honour, Croix de Guerre. *Publication:* So Full a Glory-A Life of Marshal de Lattre de Tassigny, 1954. *Address:* Mill Down, Hambledon, Hants. *T:* Hambledon 475. *Clubs:* Cavalry and Guards, Pratt's, Leander.
See also Baron Saye and Sele.

SALK, Jonas Edward, BS, MD; Fellow and Director, Salk Institute for Biological Studies, 1963-75, Fellow and Founding Director since 1975; Adjunct Professor of Health Sciences in Departments of Psychiatry, Community Medicine, and Medicine, University of California at San Diego, since 1970; *b* New York, 28 Oct. 1914; *s* of Daniel B. Salk; *m* 1st, 1939, Donna Lindsay (marr. diss. 1968); three *s* ; 2nd, 1970, Françoise Gilot. *Educ:* NY University College of Medicine; Coll. of New York City (BS). Fellow, NY Univ. Coll. of Medicine, 1935-40; Mount Sinai Hosp., NYC, 1940-42; Nat. Research Council Fellow, Sch. of Public Health, Univ. of Michigan, 1942-43, Research Fellow in Epidemiology, 1943-44, Research Assoc., 1944-46, Asst Professor, 1946-47; Assoc. Prof. of Bacteriology, 1947-49, and Director of Virus Research Laboratory, 1947-63, School of Medicine, Univ. of Pittsburgh; Research Prof., 1949-54. Consultant in epidemic diseases to: Sec. of War, 1944-47, Sec. of Army, 1947-54; Commonwealth Professor of Experimental Medicine, 1957-62 (Professor of Preventive Med., Sch. of Med., Univ. of Pittsburgh, USA, and Chairman of the Department, 1954-57). Vis. Prof.-at-Large, Pittsburgh, 1963. Specialist in polio research; developed antipoliomyelitis vaccine, 1955. Member: Amer. Epidemiological Soc., Soc. of Amer. Bacteriologists, etc. Fellow: Amer. Public Health Assoc., Amer. Soc. for Advancement of Science. US Medal of Freedom, 1977. *Publications:* Man Unfolding, 1972; The Survival of the Wisest, 1973; (with Jonathan Salk)

World Population and Human Values: A New Reality, 1981. *Address:* The Salk Institute, PO Box 85800, San Diego, Calif 92138, USA.

SALMON, family name of **Baron Salmon**.

SALMON, Baron *cr* 1972 (Life Peer), of Sandwich, Kent; **Cyril Barnet Salmon**, PC 1964; Kt 1957; a Lord of Appeal in Ordinary, 1972-80; *b* 28 Dec. 1903; *s* of late Montagu Salmon; *m* 1st, 1929, Rencie (*d* 1942), *d* of late Sidney Gorton Vanderfelt, OBE; one *s* one *d*; 2nd, 1946, Jean, Lady Morris, *d* of late Lt-Col D. Maitland-Makgill-Crichton. *Educ:* Mill Hill; Pembroke College, Cambridge. BA 1925; called to Bar, Middle Temple, 1925; QC 1945; Bencher 1953; Treasurer, 1972. Recorder of Gravesend, 1947-57; Judge of High Court of Justice, Queen's Bench Division, 1957-64; a Lord Justice of Appeal, 1964-72. Chairman: Royal Commission on the Working of the Tribunals of Inquiry (Evidence) Act, 1921, 1966; Royal Commission on Standards of Conduct in Public Life, 1974-76. Commissioned Royal Artillery, 1940. 8th Army HQ Staff, 1943-44. JP (Kent), 1949. Commissioner of Assize, Wales and Chester Circuit, 1955. Captain of the Royal St George's, Sandwich, 1972-73. Commissary of Cambridge Univ., 1979-. Governor of Mill Hill School. Hon. Fellow, Pembroke College, Cambridge. Hon. DCL Kent, 1978; Hon. LLD Cambridge, 1982. *Recreations:* golf, fishing. *Address:* Manwood House, Sandwich, Kent. *T:* Sandwich 612244. *Clubs:* Athenæum, Brooks's.
See also A. G. Robinson.

SALMON, Brian Lawson, CBE 1972; Chairman, J. Lyons & Co. Ltd, 1972-77 (Director, 1961-77, Joint Managing Director, 1967-69, Deputy Chairman, 1969-71); *b* 30 June 1917; *s* of Julius Salmon; *m* 1946, Annette Wilson Mackay; two *s* one *d*. *Educ:* Grenham Hse; Malvern Coll. Chm., Cttee on Sen. Nursing Staff Structure, 1963-66. Vice-Chm., Bd of Governors, Westminster Hosp. Gp, 1963-74; Chairman: Camden and Islington AHA, 1974-77; Supply Bd Working Gp, DHSS, 1977-78. *Recreations:* theatre, ballet, food and wine. *Address:* 34 Kingston House North, Princes Gate, SW7 1LN.
See also N. L. Salmon.

SALMON, Air Vice-Marshal Sir Cyril John Roderic; *see* Salmon, Air Vice-Marshal Sir Roderic.

SALMON, Geoffrey Isidore Hamilton, CBE 1954; President, J. Lyons & Co. Ltd, 1972-77 (Chairman, 1968-72); *b* 14 Jan. 1908; *s* of Harry Salmon and Lena (*née* Gluckstein); *m* 1936, Peggy Rica (*née* Jacobs); two *s* one *d*. *Educ:* Malvern Coll.; Jesus Coll., Cambridge (BA). Hon. Catering Adviser to the Army, 1959-71. *Address:* 10 Stavordale Lodge, Melbury Road, W14 8LW. *T:* 01-602 3425.

SALMON, Dame Nancy (Marion); *see* Snagge, Dame Nancy.

SALMON, Neil Lawson; consultant; Director, Allied Breweries, 1978-81; *b* 17 Feb. 1921; *s* of Julius and Mimi Salmon; *m* 1944, Yvonne Hélène Isaacs; one *s* one *d*. *Educ:* Malvern Coll., Malvern; Institut Minerva, Zürich. Trainee, J. Lyons & Co. Ltd, 1938-41. Served War (Army), 1941-46. Gen. Manager, J. Lyons & Co., 1947; Chm., Glacier Foods Ltd, 1962; Dir, J. Lyons & Co., 1965; Jt Managing Dir, 1969; Gp Managing Dir, 1969; Dep. Chm. and Man. Dir, 1972; Chm., 1977-78; Dep. Chm., 1978-81. Member: Restrictive Practices Court, 1971; Monopolies and Mergers Commn, 1980-. CBIM. *Recreations:* opera, ballet, theatre, wine. *Address:* c/o Eldon House, 1 Dorset Street, W1H 3FB. *T:* 01-487 3461. *Club:* Savile.
See also B. L. Salmon.

SALMON, Air Vice-Marshal Sir Roderic, KBE 1968 (OBE 1945); CB 1959; RAF; *b* 21 Aug. 1911; *s* of Edmund Frederick and Edna Salmon; *m* 1939, Hilda (*née* Mitchell); one *s* two adopted *d*. *Educ:* Howard Gardens High School, Cardiff; City of Cardiff Technical College. Commissioned in Royal Air Force, 1935; No 2 Squadron, 1936; No 70 Squadron, 1936-38; Air Ministry, Directorate of Movements, 1939-43; Second Tactical Air Force (Senior Movements Staff Officer), 1944-46 (despatches); RAF Staff College (Student), 1946; CO No 33 Maintenance Unit, 1947; No 57 Maintenance Unit, 1947-49; Member of the Directing Staff, Joint Services Staff College, 1949-51; Head of Logistics Planning, HQ Allied Air Forces, Central Europe, 1951-53; CO No 16 Maintenance Unit, 1953-54; Imperial Defence College, 1955: HQ No 40 Group (Operations Staff), 1956-59; Director of Equipment (A), Air Ministry, 1959-62; Senior Air Staff Officer, HQ Maintenance Command, 1962-64; Dir-Gen. of Equipment (RAF), MoD, 1964-68; retd 1968. Sec., Dio. of St Edmundsbury and Ipswich, 1968-80. *Recreations:* gardening, fishing. *Address:* Damer Close, Little Bealings, Woodbridge, Suffolk. *T:* Ipswich 622408.

SALMON, Thomas David; Assistant to Speaker's Counsel, House of Commons, since 1980; *b* 1 Nov. 1916; *s* of late Rev. Thomas Salmon and Isabel Salmon (*née* Littleton), North Stoneham, Hants; *m* 1950, Morris Patricia Reyner Turner, Ilford, Essex; one *s* two *d*. *Educ:* Winchester Coll.; Christ Church, Oxford (MA). Served War of 1939-45: Captain 133 Field Regt RA (despatches). Temp. Asst Principal, Cabinet Office, 1946. Admitted Solicitor, 1949; entered Treasury Solicitor's Dept, 1951; transf. to Bd of Trade, 1966; Under-Sec. (Legal), Solicitors' Dept, Depts of Industry and Trade, 1974-80, retired. *Recreations:* walking, study of history and languages, gardening. *Address:* Tenures, 23 Sole Farm Road, Great Bookham, Surrey KT23 3DW. *T:* Bookham 52837.

SALMON, Very Rev. Thomas Noel Desmond Cornwall; Dean of Christ Church, Dublin, since 1967; *b* Dublin, 5 Feb. 1913; *s* of Francis Allen Cornwall Salmon, BDS, and Emma Sophia, *d* of Dr Hamilton Jolly, Clonroche, Co. Wexford; unmarried. *Educ:* privately; Trinity College, Dublin; BA 1935, MA, BD. Deacon 1937; Priest 1938. Curate Assistant: Bangor, Co. Down, 1937-40; St James' Belfast, 1940-42; Larne, Co. Antrim, 1942-44; Clerical Vicar, Christ Church Cathedral, 1944-45; Curate Assistant, Rathfarnham, Dublin, 1945-50; Incumbent: Tullow, Carrickmines, 1950-62; St Ann, Dublin, 1962-67. Asst Lectr in Divinity School, TCD, 1945-63; Examining Chaplain to Archbishop of Dublin, 1949-. *Recreations:* in younger days Rugby football (Monkstown FC Dublin) and swimming; now walking, gardening and reading. *Address:* 13 Merlyn Park, Ballsbridge, Dublin 4. *T:* 694780.

SALMON, Col William Alexander, OBE 1956; Assistant Ecclesiastical Secretary to Lord Chancellor, 1964-77, and to Prime Minister, 1964-77, retired; *b* 16 Nov. 1910; *o s* of late Lt-Colonel W. H. B. Salmon, late IA; *m* 1939, Jean Barbara Macmillan (*d* 1982), *o d* of late J. V. Macmillan, DD, OBE (Bishop of Guildford, 1934-49); one *s* two *d*. *Educ:* Haileybury College; RMC, Sandhurst. Commissioned 2nd Lt HLI 1930; ADC to Governor of Sind, 1936-38. Served during War of 1939-45: France, 1939; Middle East, Italy, Greece, Bde Major, 1942; GSO2 HQ Aegean Force, 1943; CO, 2nd Bn Beds and Herts Regt, 1945-46. CO, 2nd Bn Royal Irish Fusiliers, 1946-47; GSO1 (Trng), HQ Scottish Command, 1947-49; Chief of Staff to Lt-Gen. Glubb Pasha, HQ Arab Legion, 1950-53; CO 1st Bn HLI, 1953-55; Col, GS (O and T Div.) SHAPE, 1957-59; AQMG (QAE2), The War Office, 1959-62; AAG (AG14), The War Office, 1962-63; retd 1963. Life Governor, Haileybury and Imperial Service Coll., 1965-. Hashemite Order of El Istiqlal (2nd Cl.), 1953. *Recreations:* shooting, fishing, gardening. *Address:* Little Thorpe, 220 Forest Road, Tunbridge Wells, Kent TN2 5HS. *T:* Tunbridge Wells 26562. *Club:* Army and Navy.

SALMON, Sir Walter (Hans), Kt 1982; Chairman of Rea Brothers Ltd, Merchant Bank, since 1950; Chairman, Canal-Randolph Corporation, since 1959; *b* 16 April 1906; *s* of Henry Salomon and Rena (*née* Oppenheimer); *m* 1935; one *s* one *d*. *Educ:* Oberreal, Eppendorf, Hamburg; Hamburg Univ. FIB 1964. Member of Lloyd's, 1958; Member of Baltic Exchange, 1957; Founder and Treas., Young Enterprise, 1963; Vice-Pres., Cambridge Settlement; Freeman, City of London; Master, Pattenmakers' Co., 1977-78; Member: Luso-Brazilian Council; Hudson Institute, 1976; 1001 Club (World Wildlife), 1973. Has lectured widely on economic and financial matters. Comdr, Southern Cross of Brazil, 1971. Officer's Cross (1 Cl.) of the Order of Merit of the Federal Republic of Germany, 1979. *Publications:* One Man's View, 1973; numerous newspaper articles. *Recreations:* yachting, ski-ing, art, bridge, snooker. *Address:* Castlemaine House, 21-22 St James's Place, SW1A 1NH. *T:* 01-493 1273. *Clubs:* Reform, City Livery, Canning House 1001, Hurlingham; Wentworth Golf; Norddeutscher Regatta-Verein Hamburg; Poole Harbour and Royal Torbay Yacht.

SALOP, Archdeacon of; *see* Jeffery, Ven. R. M. C.

SALT, Sir Anthony (Houlton), 6th Bt *cr* 1869; Chairman, Williams de Broe Hill Chaplin & Co. (Stockbrokers), since 1981 (Director, since 1968); *b* 15 Sept. 1931; *s* of Sir John Salt, 4th Bt, and Stella Houlton Jackson (*d* 1974); *S* brother, 1978; *m* 1957, Prudence Meath Baker; four *d*. *Educ:* Stowe. Member of the Stock Exchange, 1957; Partner, Hill Chaplin & Co. (Stockbrokers), 1957. *Heir:* *b* Patrick MacDonnell Salt [*b* 25 Sept. 1932; *m* 1976, Ann Elizabeth Mary, *d* of late Dr T. K. MacLachlan]. *Address:* Dellow House, Ugley Green, Bishop's Stortford, Herts. *T:* Bishop's Stortford 813141. *Club:* City of London.

SALT, Mrs Emmaline Juanita, CBE 1975; JP; *b* 22 Jan. 1910; *d* of Willie Southcombe Propert and Edith Mary (*née* Bacon); *m* 1934, William Edward Salt (*d* 1982); two *d*. *Educ:* Colston's Girls' Sch.; Bristol Univ. (MA Econ). Bristol City Councillor, 1938-41; Member: Central Council of Probation and After-Care Cttees, 1960- (Chm., 1968-71, Vice-Pres., 1979-); Home Secretary's Adv. Council for Probation and After-Care, 1961-77; Chm., Avon Probation and After-Care Cttee, 1974-77. Dep. Sec., SW Regional Cttee for Educn in HM Forces, 1941-45; sometime lecturer for WEA. JP Bristol, 1946-. *Recreations:* grandchildren, walking, opera, history. *Address:* 1 Heathercliffe, Goodeve Road, Sneyd Park, Bristol BS9 1PN. *T:* Bristol 681208.

SALT, George, FRS 1956; ScD; Fellow of King's College, Cambridge, since 1933; Reader in Animal Ecology, University of Cambridge, 1965-71, now Emeritus; *b* Loughborough, 12 Dec. 1903; *s* of late Walter Salt and Mary Cecilia (*née* Hulme); *m* 1939, Joyce Laing, Newnham Coll. and Stockton-on-Tees; two *s*. *Educ:* Crescent Heights Collegiate Inst., Calgary; Univ. of Alberta (BSc); Harvard Univ. (SM, SD); Univ. of Cambridge (PhD, ScD). National Research Fellow, Harvard Univ., 1927-28; Entomologist, Imperial Inst. Entom, 1929-31; Royal Soc. Moseley Research Student, 1932-33; Univ. Lectr in Zoology, Cambridge, 1937-65; Fellow of King's Coll., Cambridge, 1933-, Dean, 1939-45, Tutor for Advanced Students, 1945-51. Visiting Prof. Univ. of California, Berkeley, 1966. On biological expedns in NW Canada and Rocky Mts, Cuba, Republic of Colombia, E Africa, Pakistan. *Publications:* The Cellular Defence Reactions of Insects, 1970; papers in scientific jls on insect parasitism and ecology. *Recreations:* mountaineering, gardening, calligraphy and palaeography. *Address:* King's College, Cambridge; 21 Barton Road, Cambridge. *T:* Cambridge 355450.

SALT, Sir (Thomas) Michael (John), 4th Bt, *cr* 1899; *b* 7 Nov. 1946; *s* of Lt-Col Sir Thomas Henry Salt, 3rd Bt, and Meriel Sophia Wilmot, *d* of late Capt. Berkeley C. W. Williams and Hon. Mrs Williams, Herringston, Dorchester; *S* father 1965; *m* 1971, Caroline, *er d* of Henry Hildyard; two *d*. *Educ:* Eton. *Heir: b* Anthony William David Salt [*b* 5 Feb. 1950; *m* 1978, Olivia Anne, *yr d* of Martin Morgan Hudson; one *s*]. *Recreations:* cricket, shooting. *Address:* Shillingstone House, Shillingstone, Dorset. *Club:* Boodle's.

SALTER, Harry Charles, DFC 1945; Director of the Financing of the Community Budget, Commission of the European Communities, since 1973; *b* 29 July 1918; *er s* of late Harry Arnold Salter and of Irene Beatrice Salter; *m* 1946, Anne Hooper (marr. diss. 1980); one *d*. *Educ:* St Albans Sch. Entered Ministry of Health, 1936. Served War, Royal Artillery, 1939-46 (despatches, DFC). Asst Sec., Min. of Health, 1963; Under-Sec., DHSS, 1971-73. *Recreations:* golf, chess, bridge, walking. *Address:* 66c Avenue de Tervuren, 1040 Brussels. *T:* 7335713.

SALTER, Vice-Admiral Jocelyn Stuart Cambridge, CB 1954; DSO 1942 (Bar 1951); OBE 1942; *b* 24 Nov. 1901; *s* of late Henry Stuart Salter, of Messrs Lee, Bolton & Lee (Solicitors); *m* 1935, Joan (*d* 1971), *d* of late Rev. C. E. C. de Coetlogon, of the Indian Ecclesiastical Establishment; one *s* one *d*. *Educ:* Royal Naval Colleges, Osborne and Dartmouth. Joined Royal Navy, 1915; Midshipman, 1917; served European War in HMS Ramillies, Grand Fleet, 1917-19; Lieut 1923; Comdr 1937; Comd HMS Foresight in Force H, and in Home Fleet, 1941-42; Capt. 1942. Comd 16th Dest. Flotilla, 1944-45; Comd RN Air Station, Sembawang, Singapore, 1945-47; Comd HMS Jamaica, 1950-51 (served with UN Fleet in Korean waters); served on staff of SHAPE, 1951; ADC, 1951; Rear-Admiral, 1952; Vice-Admiral, 1954; Flag Officer, Malta, and Admiral Superintendent HM Dockyard, Malta, 1952-54; Admiral Superintendent HM Dockyard, Portsmouth, 1954-57; retired, 1957. Mem., Court of Assistants, Haberdashers' Company, Warden, 1958, 1963, 1968, Master, 1970. Norwegian Haakon VII Liberty Cross, 1946; United States Bronze Star medal, 1950. *Address:* Folly House, Hambledon, Hampshire. *T:* Hambledon 732. *Club:* Naval and Military.

SALTER DAVIES, Roy Dicker; *see* Davies.

SALTHOUSE, Edward Charles, PhD; CEng, MIEE; Master of University College, Durham, since 1979; Dean of the Faculty of Science, since 1982; *b* 27 Dec. 1935; *s* of Edward Salthouse, MBE, and Mrs Salthouse (*née* Boyd); *m* 1961, Denise Kathleen Margot Reid; two *s*. *Educ:* Campbell Coll., Belfast; Queen's University of Belfast (BSc, PhD). Lecturer in Electrical Engrg, Univ. of Bristol, 1962-67; University of Durham: Reader in Elec. Engrg Science, 1967-79; Chairman, Board of Studies in Engrg Science, 1976-79. *Publications:* papers on electrical insulation in Proc. IEE and other appropriate jls. *Recreations:* travel by train, photography. *Address:* The Master's House, The Castle, Durham DH1 3RL. *T:* Durham 65481.

SALTHOUSE, Leonard; Assistant Under Secretary of State, Ministry of Defence, since 1977; *b* 15 April 1927; *s* of late Edward Keith Salthouse and Dorothy Annie (*née* Clark); *m* 1950, Kathleen May (*née* Spittle); one *s* one *d*. *Educ:* Queen Elizabeth Grammar Sch., Atherstone, Warwickshire; University Coll. London (BScEcon). Home Civil Service: Asst Principal, Min. of Fuel and Power, 1950-55; Principal, Air Min., then Min. of Defence, 1955-66; Asst Sec., 1966-77. *Recreations:* gardening, music. *Address:* Orchard House, Orchehill Avenue, Gerrards Cross, Bucks SL9 8QF. *T:* Gerrards Cross 83677.

SALTON, Prof. Milton Robert James, FRS 1979; Professor and Chairman of Microbiology, New York University School of Medicine, since 1964; *b* 29 April 1921; *s* of Robert Alexander Salton and Stella Salton; *m* 1951, Joy Marriott; two *s*. *Educ:* Univ. of Sydney (BSc Agr. 1945); Univ. of Cambridge (PhD 1951, ScD 1967). Beit Meml Res. Fellow, Univ. of Cambridge, 1950-52; Merck Internat. Fellow, Univ. of California, Berkeley, 1952-53; Reader, Univ. of Manchester, 1956-61; Prof. of Microbiology, Univ. of NSW, Australia, 1962-64. Docteur en Médecine, *Dhc*, Université de Liège, 1967. *Publications:* Microbial Cell Walls, 1960; The Bacterial Cell Wall, 1964; Immunochemistry of Enzyme and their Antibodies, 1978; β-Lactam Antibiotics, 1981. *Address:* Department of Microbiology, New York University School of Medicine, 550 First Avenue, New York, NY 10016, USA. *Club:* United Oxford & Cambridge University.

SALTOUN, Lady (20th in line) *cr* 1445, of Abernethy; **Flora Marjory Fraser;** Chief of Clan Fraser; *b* 18 Oct. 1930; *d* of 19th Lord Saltoun, MC, and Dorothy, *e d* of Sir Charles Welby, 5th Bt; *S* father, 1979; *m* 1956, Captain Alexander Ramsay of Mar, Grenadier Guards retd, *o s* of late Adm. Hon. Sir Alexander Ramsay, GCVO, KCB, DSO, and The Lady Patricia Ramsay, CI, VA, CD; three *d*. *Heiress: d* Hon. Katharine Ingrid Mary Isabel Fraser [*b* 11 Oct. 1957; *m* 1980, Captain Mark Malise Nicolson, Irish Guards]. *Address:* Cairnbulg Castle, Fraserburgh, Aberdeenshire AB4 5TH.

SALTZMAN, Charles Eskridge, OBE (Hon.) 1943; DSM 1945 (US); Legion of Merit (US) 1943; Limited Partner, Goldman, Sachs & Co. (investment banking) since 1956; *b* 19 Sept. 1903; *s* of Maj.-Gen. Charles McKinley Saltzman and Mary Saltzman (*née* Eskridge); *m* 1st, 1931, Gertrude Lamont (marr. diss.); one *s* ; 2nd, 1947, Cynthia Southall Myrick (marr. diss.); two *d* (one *s* decd); 3rd, 1978, Clotilde McCormick (*née* Knapp). *Educ:* Cornell

Univ.; US Mil. Acad.; Magdalen College, Oxford University. BS (US Mil. Acad.); BA, MA (Rhodes Scholar) (Oxford Univ.). Served as 2nd Lt, Corps of Engrs, US Army, 1925-30; commissioned 1st Lieut, NY National Guard, 1930; Lieutenant-Colonel 1940; on active duty in US Army, 1940-46, serving overseas, 1942-46; Brigadier-General 1945; relieved from active duty, 1946; Maj.-Gen. AUS (Retd). With NY Telephone Co., 1930-35; with NY Stock Exchange, 1935-49 (Asst to Exec. Vice-Pres., later Sec. and Vice-Pres.). Asst Sec. of State, 1947-49; Partner Henry Sears & Co., 1949-56; Under-Sec. of State for Admin., 1954-55. Former Dir, Continental Can Co. and A. H. Robins Co., Inc. President: English-Speaking Union of the US, 1961-66 (now Hon. Director); Assoc. of Graduates, US Mil. Academy, 1974-78 (Emeritus Trustee); Mem. Pilgrims of the United States. Hon. Mem., Soc. of the Cincinnati. Member, Director, or Trustee of many boards, societies and religious, philanthropic and educational institutions. Holds foreign decorations. *Address:* (home) 30 E 62nd Street, New York, NY 10021, USA. *T:* (212) 759-5655; (office) 55 Broad Street, New York, NY 10004. *T:* (212) 676-8000. *Clubs:* Century Association, Recess, River, Union, University (New York); Metropolitan (Washington).

SALUSBURY-TRELAWNY, Sir J. B.; *see* Trelawny.

SAMARAKOON, Neville Dunbar Mirahawatte; Hon. Mr Justice Samarakoon; Chief Justice, Democratic Socialist Republic of Sri Lanka, since 1977; *b* 22 Oct. 1919; *s* of Alfred Charles Warnabarana Wickremasinghe Samarakoon and Rajapaksa Wasala Mudiyanselage Chandrawati Mirahawatte Kumarihamy; *m* 1949, Mary Patricia Mulholland; one *s* two *d*. *Educ:* Trinity Coll., Kandy; University Coll., Colombo; Law Coll., Colombo. Enrolled as Advocate, 1945; Crown Counsel, Attorney-General's Dept, 1948-51; reverted to Private Bar, 1951; QC 1968. Member: Bar Council, 1964-77; Disciplinary Bd for Lawyers 1971-74, 1976, 1977. Chairman: Judicial Service Commn, 1978-; Council of Legal Educn. *Address:* 129 Wijerama Mawatha, Colombo 7, Sri Lanka. *T:* Colombo 95364.

SAMARANCH, Juan Antonio; President, International Olympic Committee, since 1980; *b* 17 July 1920; *s* of Francisco Samaranch and Juana Torello; *m* 1955, Maria Teresa Salisachs Rowe; one *s* one *d*. *Educ:* Instituto Superior Estudios de Empresas, Barcelona; German College; Higher Inst. of Business Studies, Barcelona. Industrialist, Bank Consultant; Pres., Barcelona Diputacion, 1975; Ambassador to USSR and to People's Republic of Mongolia, 1977-80. Hon. Pres., Spanish Fedn of Roller Skating; Hon. Vice-Pres., Internat. Roller-Skating Fedn; Mem., Spanish Olympic Cttee, 1954 (Pres., 1967-70); Nat. Deleg. for Physical Educn and Sport; International Olympic Committee: Mem., 1966; Chief of Protocol, 1968-75; Mem., Exec. Bd, 1970-78 and 1979-; Vice-Pres., IOC, 1974-78; Mem., Commn for Press and Public Relations, 1967-72; President: Press Commn, 1972-; Commn for Olympic Movement, 1981-; Commn for Olympic Solidarity, 1981-. Holds numerous decorations. *Publications:* Deporte 2000, 1967; Olympic Review. *Recreation:* philately. *Address:* Avenida Pau Casals, 24 Barcelona-21, Spain. *T:* 209-07-22; International Olympic Committee, Château de Vidy, 1007 Lausanne, Switzerland. *T:* 253271.

SAMBROOK, Gordon Hartley; Member, Board, since 1978, and Chairman and Group Executive, General Steels Group, since 1980, British Steel Corporation; *b* 9 Jan. 1930; *m* 1956, Patricia Joan Mary Havard; one *s*. *Educ:* Sheffield Univ. (BA(Hons), DipEd). Graduate Apprentice, Utd Steel Cos, 1954; Rolling Mill Manager, Steel Peech and Tozer, 1956-68; British Steel Corporation: Works Manager, Rotherham, 1968-72, General Manager, 1972; Dir, Tinplate Gp, 1973-75; Man. Dir, Personnel, 1975-77; Man. Dir, Commercial, 1977-80. Chm., Allied Steel & Wire (Hldgs) Ltd, 1981-. *Address:* 3 The Briars, Sarratt, Herts WD3 6AU. *T:* Kings Langley 67833.

SAMMAN, Peter Derrick, MD, FRCP; Physician to Dermatological Department, Westminster Hospital, 1951-79, and St John's Hospital for Diseases of the Skin, 1959-79; Consultant Dermatologist, Orpington and Sevenoaks Hospitals, 1951-77; Dean, Institute of Dermatology, 1965-70; *b* 20 March 1914; *y s* of Herbert Frederick Samman and Emily Elizabeth Savage; *m* 1953, Judith Mary Kelly; three *d*. *Educ:* King William's Coll., IOM; Emmanual Coll., Cambridge; King's Coll. Hosp., London. BA (Nat. Scis. Tripos), 1936; MB, BChir Cantab 1939; MRCP 1946; MA, MD Cantab 1948; FRCP 1963. House Surg., King's Coll. Hosp., 1939; Sqdn Ldr, RAFVR, 1940-45; House Phys. and Registrar, King's Coll. Hosp., 1946; Sen. Dermatological Registrar and Tutor in Dermatology, United Bristol Hosps, 1947-48; Sen. Registrar, St John's Hosp. for Diseases of the Skin, 1949-50. FRSocMed; Mem. Brit. Assoc. of Dermatology; Hon. Mem., Dermatological Soc. of S Africa. *Publications:* The Nails in Disease, 1965, 3rd edn 1978; chapters in Textbook of Dermatology (ed Rook, Wilkinson and Ebling), 1968; (jtly) Tutorials in Postgraduate Medicine: Dermatology, 1977; various articles in med. jls. *Recreation:* gardening. *Address:* 18 Sutherland Avenue, Orpington, Kent. *T:* Orpington 20839.

SAMPLES, Reginald McCartney, CMG 1971; DSO 1942; OBE 1963; HM Diplomatic Service, retired; Assistant Director, Royal Ontario Museum, since 1978; *b* 11 Aug. 1918; *o s* of late William and Jessie Samples; *m* 1947, Elsie Roberts Hide; two *s* one step *d*. *Educ:* Rhyl Grammar Sch.; Liverpool Univ. (BCom). Served, 1940-46; RNVR (Air Branch); torpedo action with 825 Sqn against German ships Scharnhorst, Gneisenau and Prinz Eugen in English Channel (wounded, DSO); Lieut (A). Central Office of Information (Economic Editor, Overseas Newspapers), 1947-48. CRO (Brit. Inf. Services,

India), 1948; Economic Information Officer, Bombay, 1948-52; Editor-in-Chief, BIS, New Delhi, 1952; Dep.-Dir, BIS, New Delhi, 1952-56; Dir, BIS, Pakistan (Karachi), 1956-59; Dir, BIS, Canada (Ottawa), 1959-65, OBE; Counsellor (Information) to Brit. High Comr, India, and Dir, BIS, India (New Delhi), 1965-68; Asst Under-Sec. of State, Commonwealth Office, 1968; Head of British Govt Office, and Sen. British Trade Comr, Toronto, 1969; Consul-Gen., Toronto, 1974-78. *Recreations:* tennis, watching ballet. *Address:* Royal Ontario Museum, 100 Queen's Park, Toronto, Ont M5S 2C6, Canada; Apartment 1105, 44 Jackes Avenue, Toronto, Ontario M4T 1E5, Canada. *Clubs:* Naval; York, Queens (Toronto).

SAMPSON, Anthony (Terrell Seward); writer and journalist; *b* 3 Aug. 1926; *s* of Michael Sampson and Phyllis, *d* of Sir Albert Seward, FRS; *m* 1965, Sally, *d* of Dr P. G. Bentlif, Jersey, and of Mrs G. Denison-Smith, Islip, Oxon; one *s* one *d. Educ:* Westminster School; Christ Church, Oxford. Served with Royal Navy, 1944-47; Sub-Lieut, RNVR, 1946. Editor of Drum Magazine, Johannesburg, 1951-55; Editorial staff of The Observer, 1955-66, Chief American Corresp., 1973-74. Contributing Editor, Newsweek, 1977-; Editorial Conslt, The Brandt Commn, 1978-79. Associate Prof., Univ. of Vincennes, Paris, 1968-70. *Publications:* Drum, a Venture into the New Africa, 1956; The Treason Cage, 1958; Commonsense about Africa, 1960; (with S. Pienaar) South Africa: two views of Separate Development 1960; Anatomy of Britain, 1962; Anatomy of Britain Today, 1965; Macmillan: a study in ambiguity, 1967; The New Europeans, 1968; The New Anatomy of Britain, 1971; The Sovereign State: the secret history of ITT, 1973; The Seven Sisters, 1975 (Prix International de la Presse, Nice, 1976); The Arms Bazaar, 1977; The Money Lenders, 1981; The Changing Anatomy of Britain, 1982. *Recreation:* vertical gardening. *Address:* 27 Ladbroke Grove, W11. *T:* 01-727 4188, 01-221 5738; Quarry Garden, Wardour, Wilts. *T:* Tisbury 870407. *Club:* Beefsteak.

SAMSOVA, Galina; a Principal Dancer, Sadler's Wells Royal Ballet, since 1980; Teacher with the company in the Royal Ballet and Royal Ballet School; *b* Stalingrad, 1937; *d* of a Byelorussian; *m* 1st, Alexander Ursulia; 2nd, André Prokovsky. *Educ:* the Ballet Sch., Kiev (pupil of N. Verekundova). Joined Kiev Ballet, 1956 and became a soloist; Canadian Ballet, 1961; created chief rôle in Cendrillon, Paris 1963 (Gold Medal for best danseuse of Paris Festival). Ballerina, Festival Ballet, 1964-73; headed the group of André Prokovsky, The New London Ballet, (disbanded in 1977, revived for 3 new productions, The Theatre Royal, York, 1979); has danced principal rôles in Sleeping Beauty, Nutcracker, Giselle, and other classical ballets; danced in Europe, Far East and USA. *Address:* Royal Ballet School, 155 Talgarth Road, W14.

SAMUEL, family name of **Viscounts Bearsted** and **Samuel** and **Baron Samuel of Wych Cross.**

SAMUEL, 3rd Viscount *cr* 1937, of Mount Carmel and of Toxteth, Liverpool; **David Herbert Samuel;** Sherman Professor of Physical Chemistry, since 1967, and Director, Center for Neurosciences and Behavioral Research, since 1978, Weizmann Institute, Rehovot, Israel; *b* 8 July 1922; *s* of 2nd Viscount Samuel, CMG, and of Hadassah, *d* of Judah Goor (Grasovsky); *S* father, 1978; *m* 1st, 1950, Esther Berelowitz (marr. diss. 1957); one *d*; 2nd, 1960, Rinna Dafni (*née* Grossman) (marr. diss. 1978); one *d*; 3rd, 1980, Veronika Engelhardt Grimm. *Educ:* Balliol Coll., Oxford (MA 1948); Hebrew Univ. (PhD 1953). Served War of 1939-45 (despatches); Captain RA, in India, Burma and Sumatra. Member of Isotope Dept, Weizmann Inst. of Sci., Rehovot, Israel, 1949-; Sherman Prof. of Physical Chemistry and Head, Chemistry Gp, Science Teaching Dept, 1967-. Post-doctoral Fellow, Chem. Dept, UCL, 1956; Res. Fellow, Chem. Dept, Harvard Univ., 1957-58; Res. Fellow, Lab. of Chemical Biodynamics (Lawrence Radiation Lab.), Univ. of California, Berkeley, 1965-66; Visiting Professor: Sch. of Molecular Scis, Univ. of Warwick, 1967; MRC Neuroimmunology Unit, Zoology Dept, UCL, 1974-75. Member: Adv. Bd, Bat-Sheva de Rothschild Fountn for Advancement of Science in Israel, 1970-; Bd, US-Israel Educnl (Fulbright) Foundn, 1969-74 (Chm., 1974-75); Bd, Israel Center for Scientific and Technol Information, 1970-74; Scientific Adv. Cttee and Bd of Trustees of Israel Center for Psychobiol., 1973-; Acad. Adv. Cttee, Everyman's (Open) Univ., 1976-; Bd of Govs, Bezalel Acad. of Arts and Design, 1977-; Council, Israel Chemical Soc., 1977-; Internat. Brain Res. Org. (IBRO), 1977-; Israel Exec. Cttee, America-Israel Cultural Foundn, 1978-; Bd of Governors, Tel Aviv Museum, 1980-; Cttee on Teaching of Chemistry, IUPAC, 1981-. *Publications:* more than 200 papers, reviews and parts of collective volumes on isotopes, physical chemistry, reaction mechanisms, neurochemistry, psychopharmacology, behavior and science teaching. *Heir: b* Hon. Dan Judah Samuel [*b* 25 March 1925; *m* 1st, 1957, Nonni (Esther) (marr. diss. 1977), *d* of late Max Gordon, Johannesburg; one *s* two *d*; 2nd, 1981, Heather, *d* of Angus and Elsa Cumming, Haywards Heath]. *Address:* Weizmann Institute of Science, Rehovot, Israel. *T:* 054-83117.

SAMUEL OF WYCH CROSS, Baron *cr* 1972 (Life Peer), of Wych Cross, Sussex; **Harold Samuel,** Kt 1963; FRICS; Hon. Fellow: Magdalene College, Cambridge, 1961; University College, London, 1968; Chairman, The Land Securities Investment Trust Ltd; President, The Central London Housing Trust for the Aged; *b* London, 23 April 1912; *s* of late Vivian and Ada Samuel; *m* 1936, Edna Nedas; two *d* (and one *d* decd). *Educ:* Mill Hill School; College of Estate Management. Dir, Railway Sites Ltd (British Rail), 1962-65. Member: Covent Garden Market Authority, 1961-74; Special (Rebuilding) Cttee, RICS, 1962-76; Land Commn, 1967-70; Reserve Pension Bd, 1974;

Crown Estate Comrs Regent St Cttee. Member: Court of The City Univ.; Court of Univ. of Sussex; Court of Univ. Coll. of Swansea; Court of Patrons, RCS; a Vice-Pres., British Heart Foundation; Trustee, Mill Hill Sch. *Recreations:* swimming, horticulture. *Address:* 75 Avenue Road, Regent's Park, NW8 6JD; Wych Cross Place, Forest Row, East Sussex RH18 5JJ. *Club:* East India, Devonshire, Sports and Public Schools.

SAMUEL, Adrian Christopher Ian, CMG 1959; CVO 1963; *b* 20 Aug. 1915; *s* of late George Christopher Samuel and Alma Richards; *m* 1942, Sheila, *er d* of late J. C. Barrett, Killiney, Co. Dublin; three *s* one *d. Educ:* Rugby Sch.; St John's Coll., Oxford. Entered HM Consular Service, 1938; served at Beirut, Tunis and Trieste. Served War, 1940-44, in Royal Air Force. Returned to HM Foreign Service and served at HM Embassies in Ankara, Cairo and Damascus; First Secretary, 1947; Counsellor, 1956; Principal Private Secretary to the Secretary of State for Foreign Affairs, Oct. 1959-63; Minister at HM Embassy, Madrid, 1963-65; resigned 1965. Director: British Chemical Engrg Contractors Assoc., 1966-69; British Agrochemicals Assoc., 1972-78; Dir-Gen., Groupement Internat. des Assocs Nats de Fabricants de Pesticides (GIFAP), 1978-79. *Recreations:* golf, shooting and reading. *Address:* The Laundry House, Handcross, near Haywards Heath, West Sussex RH17 6HQ. *T:* Handcross 400717. *Club:* Garrick.

SAMUEL, Herbert Dawkin; Director of Greenwich Hospital, Admiralty, 1959-64, retired; *b* 21 Jan. 1904; *o s* of Alfred Samuel, Llanelly; *m* 1936, Evelyn Mary, *d* of Col H. J. Barton, RE; two *s. Educ:* Clifton Coll.; Merton Coll., Oxford; Heidelberg University. 1st cl. Hons. Mod. Langs; Laming Fellow, Queen's Coll., Oxford, 1925-27. Entered Consular Service, 1927; Actg Vice-consul, Genoa, 1927, Paris, 1929. Asst Master: Repton School, 1930; Harrow School, 1931; Dist. Inspector, Bd of Education, 1938. Entered Admiralty as Principal, 1939; Under-Secretary, 1956. Coronation Medal, 1953. *Address:* 25 Storrs Close, Bovey Tracey, Devon TQ13 9HR.

SAMUEL, Sir Jon (Michael Glen), 5th Bt, *cr* 1898; Chairman, Electric Auto Corporation (USA), since 1978; *b* 25 Jan. 1944; *o s* of Sir John Oliver Cecil Samuel, 4th Bt, and of Charlotte Mary, *d* of late R. H. Hoyt, Calgary, Canada; *S* father, 1962; *m* 1st, 1966, Antoinette Sandra, *d* of late Captain Antony Hewitt, RE, 2nd SAS Regt, and of Mrs K. A. H. Casson, Frith Farm, Wolverton, Hants; two *s*; 2nd, 1982, Mrs Elizabeth Ann Molinari, *y d* of Major R. G. Curry, Bournemouth, Dorset. *Educ:* Radley; London Univ. Director: Enfield Automotive, 1967-70; Advanced Vehicle Systems Ltd, 1971-78. *Recreations:* motor racing, water ski-ing. *Heir: s* Anthony John Fulton Samuel, *b* 13 Oct. 1972. *Address:* Box No 904, Freeport, Grand Bahama.

SAMUEL, Hon. Peter Montefiore, MC 1942; TD 1951; Banker; Director, Hill, Samuel Group (Deputy Chairman, 1935-82); Chairman: Dylon International Ltd, since 1958; Hill Samuel & Co. (Ireland) Ltd, since 1964; *b* 9 Dec. 1911; second *s* of 2nd Viscount Bearsted and Dorothea, *e d* of late E. Montefiore Micholls; *d* and *heir-pres.* to 3rd Viscount Bearsted, *qv*; *m* 1st, 1939, Deirdre du Barry (marr. diss. 1942); 2nd, 1946, Hon. Elizabeth Adelaide Pearce Serocold, *d* of late Baron Cohen, PC; two *s* one *d. Educ:* Eton; New College, Oxford (BA). Served Warwickshire Yeo, Middle East and Italy, 1939-45. Director: Shell Transport & Trading Co. Ltd, 1938-82; Samuel Properties Ltd, 1961- (Chm., 1982-); Mayborn Products Ltd (Chm.), 1946-; Trades Union Unit Trust Managers Ltd, 1961-; Norcros Ltd, 1961-77; Computer and Systems Engineering Ltd (Chm.), 1971-77; General Consolidated Investment Trust Ltd, 1975-. President, Norwood Home for Jewish Children, 1962-79; Hon. Treas., Nat. Assoc. for Gifted Children, 1968-81; Chm. Council, Royal Free Hospital of Medicine, 1973-82 (Mem., 1948-). *Recreations:* golf, fishing, shooting. *Address:* Flat 12, Rutland Court, SW7 1BN. Farley Hall, Farley Hill, near Reading, Berkshire RG7 1UL. *T:* Eversley 733242. *Club:* White's.

SAMUEL, Richard Christopher; HM Diplomatic Service; Deputy High Commissioner and Minister, New Delhi, since 1982; *b* Edinburgh, 8 Aug. 1933. *Educ:* Durham Sch.; St John's Coll., Cambridge (BA). Royal Navy, 1952-54. FO, 1957-58; Warsaw, 1958-59; Rome, 1960-63; FO, 1963; Private Sec. to Parly Under-Sec. of State, 1965-68; Hong Kong, 1968-69; 1st Sec. and Head of Chancery: Singapore, 1969-71; Peking, 1971-73; Counsellor, Washington, 1973-76; Head of Far Eastern Dept, FCO, 1976-79; Counsellor (Commercial), Moscow, 1980-82. *Recreations:* music, science fiction. *Address:* c/o Foreign and Commonwealth Office, SW1A 2AL.

SAMUELS, Sir Alexander, Kt 1963; CBE 1956; JP, FRSA, FCIT, MIMechE; Member, (part-time) British Waterways Board, 1966-75, and Covent Garden Market Authority, 1961-75; *b* 15 Sept. 1905. *Educ:* Elementary Sch. Mem., Shoreditch Borough Council, 1945-61; Chairman: London and Home Counties Traffic Advisory Cttee, 1946-61; Special Enquiry into London Traffic Congestion, 1951; Working Party for Car Parking, 1953; Cttee for Speed limit Enquiry, 1954; Special Survey Cttee on use of Parking Meters, 1956; London Travel Cttee, 1958; Operations Group of the Transport Co-ordinating Council for London, 1966; Dep. Chm., Nat. Road Safety Advisory Council, 1965-66; Vice-Pres., London Accident Prevention Council, 1956; Mem., Departmental Cttee on Road Safety, 1957-64; Adviser to the Minister of Transport on London Traffic Management, 1961-65, on Road Traffic, 1965-66. *Recreation:* golf. *Address:* Redcroft, 19 Hartsbourne Avenue, Bushey Heath, Herts. *T:* 01-950 1162. *Club:* Reform.

SAMUELS, David Jessel T.; *see* Turner-Samuels.

SAMUELS, John Edward Anthony, QC 1981; Joint Chairman, Inner London Education Authority Disciplinary Tribunals, since 1977; Alternate Chairman, Burnham Cttee, since 1981; *b* 15 Aug. 1940; *s* of late Albert Edward Samuels, solicitor, Reigate, Surrey, and of Mrs Sadie Beatrice Samuels; *m* 1967, Maxine Robertson, JP; two *s. Educ:* Charterhouse; Perugia; Queens' Coll., Cambridge (MA). Second Lieut, Queen's Royal Regt (TA), 1959; Lieut, Queen's Royal Surrey Regt (TA), 1961-67; RARO 1967. Chairman, Cambridge Univ. United Nations Assoc., 1962. Mansfield Schol., Lincoln's Inn, 1963; called to Bar, Lincoln's Inn, 1964; South Eastern Circuit. Co-opted Mem., ILEA Education Cttee, 1964-67. Governor, Brixton College of Further Education, 1964-67. Member: Richmond, Twickenham and Roehampton HA, 1982-; Kingston and Richmond Family Practitioners Cttee, 1982-. *Publications:* contributor to Halsbury's Laws of England, 4th edn. *Recreation:* serendipity. *Address:* 3 Hare Court, Temple, EC4Y 7BJ. *T:* 01-583 4555. *Club:* Athenæum.

SAMUELS, Prof. Michael Louis; Professor of English Language, University of Glasgow, since 1959; *b* 1920; *s* of late Harry Samuels, OBE, MA, barrister-at-law, and of Céline Samuels (*née* Aronowitz), London; *m* 1950, Hilary, *d* of late Julius and Ruth Samuel, Glasgow; one *d. Educ:* St Paul's School; Balliol College, Oxford. Domus Exhibitioner in Classics, Balliol College, Oxford, 1938-40 and 1945-47; MA 1947 (First Class Hons English Lang. and Lit.). Worked for Air Ministry (Maintenance Command), 1940-45. Research Fellow, University of Birmingham, 1947-48; Assistant in English Language, University of Edinburgh, 1948-49; Lecturer in English Language, Univ. of Edinburgh, 1949-59. *Publications:* Linguistic Evolution, 1972; articles and reviews in Trans Philological Soc., Medium Aevum, Review of English Studies, Archivum Linguisticum, English Studies, English and Germanic Studies. *Address:* 4 Queen's Gate, Dowanhill, Glasgow G12 9DN. *T:* 041-334 4999.

SAMUELSON, Sir (Bernard) Michael (Francis), 5th Bt *cr* 1884; *b* 17 Jan. 1917; *s* of Sir Francis Henry Bernard Samuelson, 4th Bt, and Margaret Kendall (*d* 1980), *d* of H. Kendall Barnes; *S* father, 1981; *m* 1952, Janet Amy, *yr d* of Lt-Comdr L. G. Elkington, RN retd, Chelsea; two *s* two *d. Educ:* Eton. Served War of 1939-45 with RA and Leicestershire Regt (despatches). *Heir:* *s* James Francis Samuelson, *b* 20 Dec. 1956. *Address:* Hollingwood, Stunts Green, Herstmonceux, East Sussex.

SAMUELSON, Prof. Paul A.; Institute Professor, Massachusetts Institute of Technology, 1966; *b* Gary, Indiana, 15 May 1915; *m* 1938, Marion Crawford (*d* 1978); four *s* two *d. Educ:* Univs of Chicago (BS) and Harvard (MA, PhD). SSRC Predoctoral Fellow, 1935-37; Soc. of Fellows, Harvard, 1937-40; Guggenheim Fellow, 1948-49; Ford Faculty Research Fellow, 1958-59; Hoyt Vis. Fellow, Calhoun Coll., Yale, 1962; Carnegie Foundn Reflective Year, 1965-66. MIT: Asst Prof. of Econs, 1940; Assoc. Prof. of Econs, 1944; Staff Mem., Radiation Lab., 1944-45; Prof. of Econs, 1947; Prof. of Internat. Economic Relations (part-time), Fletcher Sch. of Law and Diplomacy, 1945. Consultant: to Nat. Resources Planning Bd, 1941-43; to Rand Corp., 1948-75; to US Treasury, 1945-52, 1961-; to Johnson Task Force on Sustained Prosperity, 1964; to Council of Econ. Advisers, 1960-; to Federal Reserve Bd, 1965-; to Congressional Budget Office, 1974-. Economic Adviser to Senator, Candidate and President-elect John F. Kennedy, informal adviser to President Kennedy. Member: War Prodn Bd and Office of War Mobilization and Reconstruction, 1945; Bureau of the Budget, 1952; Adv. Bd of Nat Commn on Money and Credit, 1958-60; Research Adv. Panel to President's Nat. Goals Commn, 1959-60; Research Adv. Bd Cttee for Econ. Develt, 1960; Nat. Task Force on Econ. Educn, 1960-61; Sen. Advr, Brookings Panel on Econ. Activity. Contrib. Editor and Columnist, Newsweek. Lectures: Stamp Meml, London, 1961; Wicksell, Stockholm, 1962; Franklin, Detroit, 1962; Gerhard Colm Meml, NYC, 1971; Davidson, Univ. of New Hampshire, 1971; 12th John von Neumann, Univ. of Wisconsin, 1971; J. Willard Gibbs Lecture, Amer. Mathematical Soc., 1974. 1st Sulzbacher Distinguished Lectr, Colombia Law Sch., 1974; John Diebold Lectr, Harvard Univ., 1976. Corresp. Fellow, British Acad., 1960; Fellow: Amer. Philosoph. Soc.; Econometric Soc. (Mem. Council; Vice-Pres. 1950; Pres. 1951); Member: Amer. Acad. Arts and Sciences; Amer. Econ. Assoc. (Pres. 1961; Hon. Fellow, 1965); Phi Beta Kappa; Commn on Social Sciences (NSF), 1967-; Internat. Econ. Assoc. (Pres. 1965-68; Hon. Pres. 1968-); Nat. Acad. of Sciences, 1970-; Omicron Delta Epsilon, Bd of Trustees (Internat. Honor Soc. in Econ.). Hon. Fellow, LSE. David A. Wells Prize, Harvard, 1941; John Bates Clark Medal, Amer. Econ. Assoc., 1947; Medal of Honor, Univ. of Evansville, 1970; Nobel Prize in Econ. Science, 1970; Albert Einstein Commemorative Award, 1971. Hon. LLD: Chicago, 1961; Oberlin, 1961; Boston Coll., 1964; Indiana, 1966; Michigan, 1967; Claremont Grad. Sch., 1970; New Hampshire, 1971; Keio, Tokyo, 1971; Harvard, 1972; Gustavas Adolphus Coll., 1974; Univ. of Southern Calif, 1975; Univ. of Rochester, 1976; Univ. of Pennsylvania, 1976; Emmanuel Coll., 1977. Hon. DLitt: Ripon Coll., 1962; Northern Michigan Univ., 1973; Hon DSc: E Anglia, 1966; Massachusetts, 1972; Rhode Is., 1972; Hon. LHD: Seton Hall, 1971; Williams Coll., 1971; Stonehill Coll., 1978; Dhc Université Catholique de Louvain, Belgium, 1976. *Publications:* Foundations of Economic Analysis, 1947, enlarged edn. 1982; Economics, 1948, 11th edn 1980 (trans. 24 langs); (jtly) Linear Programming and Economic Analysis, 1958 (trans. French, Japanese); Readings in Economics, 1955; The Collected Scientific Papers of Paul A. Samuelson (ed J. E. Stiglitz), vols I and II, 1966, vol. III (ed R. C. Merton), 1972, vol. IV (ed H. Nagatani and K. Crowley),

1977; co-author, other books in field, papers in various jls, etc. *Recreation:* tennis. *Address:* Department of Economics, Massachusetts Institute of Technology E52-383, Cambridge, Mass 02139, USA. *T:* 617-253-3368. *Club:* Belmont Hill (Mass).

SAMUELSON, Sydney Wylie, CBE 1978; Chairman and Chief Executive, Samuelson Film Service Group of Companies; *b* 7 Dec. 1925; 2nd *s* of G. B. and Marjorie Samuelson; *m* 1949, Doris (*née* Magen); three *s. Educ:* Irene Avenue Council Sch., Lancing, Sussex. Served RAF, 1943-47. From age 14, career devoted to various aspects of British film industry: cinema projectionist, 1939-42; Asst Film Editor, 1943; Asst Film Cameraman, Cameraman and Dir of Documentary Films, 1947-59; founded company to service film and TV prodn organisations, supplying cameras and other technical equipment, with purchase of first camera, 1954; continued filming as technician on locations throughout world until 1959, when activities concentrated on expanding Samuelson Film Service Group. Permanent Trustee and currently Chm. Bd of Management, BAFTA (Vice-Chm. Film, 1971-73, Chm. of Council, 1973-76); Member: Exec. Cttee, Cinema and Television Veterans (Pres., 1980-81); Exec. Council, Cinema and TV Benevolent Fund (Trustee, 1982-); Brit. Soc. of Cinematographers (Governor, 1969-79; 1st Vice-Pres., 1976-77). Chm., Akim (Israel Assoc. for Rehabilitation of Mentally Handicapped). Associate Mem., Amer. Soc. of Cinematographers. Hon. Fellow, Brit. Kinematograph Sound and TV Soc., 1970. Brit. Soc. of Cinematographers award for Outstanding Contribution to Film Industry, 1967. *Recreations:* collecting recorded film music, vintage motoring, jogging (finished 13,006th London Marathon 1982). *Address:* 303-315 Cricklewood Broadway, NW2 6PQ.

SAN VINCENZO FERRERI, 8th Marquis of, **Alfio Testaferrata Ghàxaq** (Marquis Testaferrata); *b* 1911; *s* of Daniel Testaferrata Bonici Ghàxaq and Agnese (*d* 1941), *d* of Baroncino Nicola Galea di San Marciano; *S* father, 1945. *Educ:* Stonyhurst College, Blackburn; University Coll., Oxford. Sometime Mem., Cttee of Privileges of Maltese Nobility; Member Royal Numismatic Society; Membre de la Société suisse de Numismatique. Hereditary Knight of the Holy Roman Empire; Patrician of Rome, Messina, and Citta di Castello. *Address:* 29 Villegaignon Street, Mdina, Malta, GC. *T:* Rabat 674139. *Club:* Casino Maltese (Valletta).

SANCTUARY, Gerald Philip; Legal Adviser and Regional and Local Affairs Officer, Royal Society for Mentally Handicapped Children and Adults (Mencap), since 1979; *b* 22 Nov. 1930; *s* of late John Cyril Tabor Sanctuary, MD and of Maisie Toppin Sanctuary (*née* Brooks); *m* 1956, Rosemary Patricia L'Estrange, Dublin; three *s* two *d. Educ:* Bryanston Sch.; Law Soc.'s Sch. of Law. National Service Pilot, 1953-55; Asst Solicitor, Kingston, 1955-56; Partner in Hasties, Solicitors, Lincoln's Inn Fields, 1957-62; Field Sec., Nat. Marriage Guidance Council, 1963-65, Nat. Secretary 1965-69; Exec. Dir, Sex Information and Educn Council of US, 1969-71; Sec., Professional and Public Relations, The Law Soc., 1971-78; Exec. Dir, Internat. Bar Assoc., 1978-79. Editor, Law Soc. series: It's Your Law, 1973-. Regular broadcaster on radio. *Publications:* Marriage Under Stress, 1968; Divorce - and After, 1970, 2nd edn 1976; Before You See a Solicitor, 1973; contrib., Moral Implications of Marriage Counseling, 1971; Vie Affective et Sexuelle, 1972; Loss Prevention Manual, 1978; The English Legal Heritage, 1979. *Recreation:* amateur drama. *Address:* 100 Fishpool Street, St Albans, Herts.

SANDARS, George Edward Russell, CMG 1951; MBE 1933; *b* 19 Oct. 1901; *s* of Rev. Canon George Russell Sandars and Mary Lambart Wyld; *m* 1937, Vera Margaret Molyneux-Seel; no *c. Educ:* Winchester; New College, Oxford. Joined Sudan Political Service, 1924; Private Secretary to Governor General, 1933-37; Sudan Agent in Cairo, 1941-45; Governor of Blue Nile Province, 1948-51. Sec., Inst. of Brewing, 1951-64. *Address:* Red Cottages, Dogmersfield, Basingstoke, Hants. *T:* Fleet 4801. *Club:* Athenæum.

SANDARS, Prof. Patrick George Henry; Professor of Experimental Physics, Oxford University, since 1978; *b* 29 March 1935; *s* of P. R. and A. C. Sandars; *m* 1959, P. B. Hall; two *s. Educ:* Wellington Coll.; Balliol Coll., Oxford (MA, DPhil). Weir Junior Research Fellow, University Coll., and ICI Research Fellow, Clarendon Laboratory, Oxford, 1960-63; Tutorial Fellow, Balliol Coll., and Univ. Lectr, Oxford Univ., 1964-72; Reader in Physics, Oxford Univ., 1972-77. Junior Proctor, Oxford Univ., 1971-72. *Address:* 3 Hawkswell Gardens, Oxford. *T:* Oxford 58535.

SANDBACH, Prof. Francis Henry, FBA 1968; Fellow of Trinity College, Cambridge, since 1927; *b* 23 Feb. 1903; *s* of late Prof. F. E. and Ethel Sandbach; *m* 1932, Mary Warburton Mathews; one *s* one *d* (and one *s* decd). *Educ:* King Edward's Sch., Birmingham; Trinity Coll., Cambridge. Browne Schol., 1922; Craven Schol., 1923; Chancellor's Medallist, 1925; Charles Oldham Class. Schol., 1925. Asst Lectr, Manchester Univ., 1926-28; Lectr in Classics, Univ. of Cambridge, 1929-67; Brereton Reader in Classics, 1951-67; Prof. of Classics, 1967-70. Junior Proctor, 1940-41; Trinity Coll.: Lecturer in Classics, 1929-63; Tutor, 1942-52; Sen. Tutor, 1952-56. For. Mem., Kungl. Vetenskaps- och- Vitterhets- Samhället i Göteborg. *Publications:* (some jointly): Plutarch's Moralia, vol. ix, 1961, vol. xi, 1965, vol. xv, 1969; Plutarchus Moralia, vol. vii, 1967; Menandri Reliquiae Selectae, 1972; Menander: a commentary, 1973; The Stoics, 1975; The Comic Theatre of Greece and Rome, 1977; articles in class. jls. *Address:* 2 Hedgerley Close, Cambridge CB3 0EW. *T:* 353152.

SANDBANK, Charles Peter; Head of BBC Research Department, since 1978; *b* 14 Aug. 1931; *s* of Gustav and Clare Sandbank; *m* 1955, Audrey Celia (*née* Schonfield); one *s* two *d. Educ:* Bromley Grammar Sch.; London Univ. (BSc, DIC). CEng, FIEE, FInstP. Prodn Engr, 1953-55, Develt Engr, 1955-60, Brimar Valve Co.; Develt Section Head, STC Transistor Div., 1960-64; Head of Electron Devices Lab., 1964-68, Manager, Communication Systems Div., 1968-78, Standard Telecommunication Laboratories. Mem. Council, IEE, 1978-81 (Chm., Electronics Divisional Bd, 1979-80); Chm., EBU High Definition TV Cttee. *Publications:* Optical Fibre Communication Systems, 1980; papers and patents (about 100) on semiconductor devices, integrated circuits, solid-state bulk effects, compound semiconductors, micro-waves, electron-phonon interactions, navigational aids, electro-optics and broadcasting technology. *Recreations:* boatbuilding, sailing, film-making, music, garden-watching. *Address:* Grailands, Beech Road, Reigate, Surrey RH2 9NA. *T:* (office) Mogador 832361.

SANDBERG, Michael Graham Ruddock, CBE 1982 (OBE 1977); JP; Chairman: The Hongkong and Shanghai Banking Corporation, Mercantile Bank Ltd, since 1977; The British Bank of the Middle East, since 1980; *b* 31 May 1927; *s* of Gerald Arthur Clifford Sandberg and Ethel Marion Sandberg; *m* 1954, Carmel Mary Roseleen Donnelly; two *s* two *d. Educ:* St Edward's Sch., Oxford. 6th Lancers (Indian Army) and King's Dragoon Guards, 1945. Joined The Hongkong and Shanghai Banking Corp., 1949: service in Hong Kong, Japan and Singapore; Gen. Manager, 1971; Exec. Dir, 1972; Dep. Chm., 1973. Mem. (unofficial), Exec. Council of Hong Kong, 1978-. JP (Hong Kong), 1972-; Steward, Royal Hong Kong Jockey Club, 1972-, Chm., 1981-; Treasurer, Univ. of Hong Kong, 1977. *Recreations:* horse racing, bridge, cricket, horology. *Address:* c/o The Hongkong and Shanghai Banking Corporation, 1 Queen's Road Central, Hong Kong. *T:* 5-8228333. *Clubs:* Cavalry and Guards, Carlton, MCC, Surrey CCC.

SANDELSON, Neville Devonshire; MP Hillingdon, Hayes and Harlington, since 1974 (Hayes and Harlington, June 1971-1974) (Lab, 1971-81, SDP, since 1981); Barrister-at-Law; *b* Leeds, 27 Nov. 1923; *s* of late David I. Sandelson, OBE, and Dora Sandelson, (*née* Lightman); *m* 1959, Nana Karlinski, Neuilly sur Seine, France; one *s* two *d. Educ:* Westminster School; Trinity College, Cambridge; MA. Called to Bar, Inner Temple, 1946; for some years director of local newspaper and book publishing cos and producer of TV documentary programmes until resuming practice at Bar, 1964. Mem. London County Council, 1952-58; junior Whip of majority group. Travelled extensively in USA, Middle East, Europe. Contested Ashford (Kent) 1950, 1951 and 1955; Beckenham (by-election) 1957; Rushcliffe 1959; Heston & Isleworth 1966; SW Leicester (by-election) 1967; Chichester 1970. Founder Mem., SDP; Parly spokesman on NI, 1981-82; Vice-Chm., All-Party Productivity Gp; Sec., All-Party Theatre Gp; Jt Sec., British-Greek Parly Gp; Sec., British Gibraltar Parly Gp; Mem. Exec. Cttee, Parly Afghanistan Support Gp. Promoted, as a Private Mem's Bill, the Matrimonial Proceedings (Polygamous Marriages) Act, 1972. Mem., SDP Nat. Organisation Sub-Cttee; Vice-Chm., Assoc. for a Social Democratic Europe; Member: Council, Nat. Cttee for Electoral Reform; Cttee, SDP Campaign for Electoral Reform; Exec. Cttee, Wider Share Ownership Council; founder Mem., Manifesto Gp (Treas., 1975-80). Member: GMWU; Social Democratic Lawyers Assoc. Mem. Ct, Brunel Univ., 1975-81. *Address:* 1 Hare Court, Temple, EC4; House of Commons, SW1. *T:* 01-219 4592. *Club:* Reform.

SANDERS, Christopher Cavania, RA 1961 (ARA 1953); RP 1968; ARCA 1928; artist-painter; *b* near Wakefield, 25 Dec. 1905; *s* of Alfred B. Sanders; *m* 1931, Barbara L. Stubbs (ARCA 1928) (*d* 1967), *d* of Francis F. Stubbs, Isleworth and Felpham; two *s* two *d. Educ:* Ossett Grammar Sch.; Wakefield Sch. of Art; Leeds Coll. of Art; Royal Coll. of Art. Gold Medallist, Paris Salon, 1955. *Address:* 2 Tudor Gardens, Slough, Berks SL1 6HJ.

SANDERS, Cyril Woods, CB 1959; Lord of the Manor of Kavenham-Stoke-Wereham and Wretton in Norfolk; *b* 21 Feb. 1912; *er s* of Cyril Sturgis Sanders and Dorothy (*née* Woods); *m* 1944, Kate Emily Boyes, *qv*; one *s* three *d. Educ:* St Paul's Sch.; Queen's Coll., Oxford. BA Oxon 1934, Lit. Hum. Joined General Post Office as Assistant Principal, 1934; transferred to Board of Trade, 1935; retired from Dept of Trade and Industry (formerly Bd of Trade) as Under-Secretary, 1972. *Recreations:* walking, sailing, painting. *Address:* 41 Smith St, Chelsea, SW3. *T:* 01-352 8053; Giles Point, Winchelsea, Sussex. *T:* Winchelsea 431; Canower, Cashel, Connemara, Eire. *Clubs:* Ski Club of Gt Britain; Island Cruising (Devon).

SANDERS, Donald Neil; Deputy Governor and Deputy Chairman of Board, Reserve Bank of Australia, since 1975; *b* Sydney, 21 June 1927; *s* of L. G. Sanders; *m* 1952, Betty Elaine, *d* of W. B. Constance; four *s* one *d. Educ:* Wollongong High Sch.; Univ. of Sydney (BEc). Commonwealth Bank of Australia, 1943-60; Australian Treasury, 1956; Bank of England, 1960; Reserve Bank of Australia, 1960-: Supt, Credit Policy Div., Banking Dept, 1964-66; Dep. Manager, Banking Dept, 1966-67; Res. Dept, 1967-70; Aust. Embassy, Washington DC, 1968; Chief Manager: Securities Markets Dept, 1970-72; Banking and Finance Dept, 1972-74; Adviser and Chief Manager, Banking and Finance Dept, 1974-75. *Address:* Reserve Bank of Australia, 65 Martin Place, Box 3947 GPO, Sydney, NSW 2001, Australia.

SANDERS, Sir Harold (George), Kt 1963; MA, PhD; Deputy Chairman, University Grants Committee, 1964-67 (Member, 1949-55); *b* 9 Oct. 1898; *s* of W. O. Sanders, JP, Wollaston, nr Wellingborough; *m* 1923, Kathleen

Penson Plunkett (*d* 1973); one *s* one *d. Educ:* Wellingborough School; St John's College, Cambridge. Assistant (Physiology), Animal Nutrition Inst., School of Agriculture, Cambridge, 1922-29; University Lecturer (Agriculture), Cambridge, 1929-44; Fellow, St John's College, Cambridge, 1938-44; Executive Officer, Herts War Agricultural Executive Committee, 1941-44; Prof. of Agriculture, Reading Univ., 1945-54; Chief Scientific Adviser (Agriculture) to Ministry of Agriculture, Fisheries and Food, 1955-64. Served European War, 1917-19, 2nd Lt RFA (France). *Publications:* An Outline of British Crop Husbandry, 1939, 3rd edn, 1958; (with G. Eley) Farms of Britain, 1946. *Address:* Duckmire, Wollaston, Wellingborough, Northants NN9 7SH. *Club:* Farmers'.

SANDERS, John Derek; Organist and Master of the Choristers, Gloucester Cathedral, since 1967; *b* 26 Nov. 1933; *s* of Alderman J. T. Sanders, JP, CA and Mrs E. M. Sanders (*née* Trivett); *m* 1967, Janet Ann Dawson; one *s* one *d. Educ:* Felsted Sch., Essex; Royal Coll. of Music; Gonville and Caius Coll., Cambridge. ARCM 1952; FRCO 1955; MusB 1956; MA 1958. Dir of Music, King's Sch., Gloucester, and Asst Organist, Gloucester Cathedral, 1958-63; Organist and Master of the Choristers, Chester Cathedral, 1964-67. Dir of Music, Cheltenham Ladies' Coll., 1968-. Conductor: Gloucestershire Symphony Orchestra, 1967-; Gloucester Choral Soc., 1967-. Conductor of Three Choirs Festival, 1968, 1971, 1974, 1977 and 1980. *Publications:* Festival Te Deum, 1962; Soliloquy for Organ, 1977; Toccata for Organ, 1979. *Recreations:* gastronomy, travelling. *Address:* 7 Miller's Green, Gloucester GL1 2BN. *T:* 24764.

SANDERS, John Leslie Yorath; HM Diplomatic Service, retired; Ambassador to Panama, 1978-80; *b* 5 May 1929; *s* of late Reginald Yorath Sanders and Gladys Elizabeth Sanders (*née* Blything); *m* 1953, Brigit Mary Lucine Altounyan; one *s* two *d. Educ:* Dulwich Coll. Prep. Sch.; Cranleigh School. Nat. Service in HM Forces (RA), 1948-50; entered HM Foreign Service, 1950; FO, 1950-52; MECAS, Lebanon, 1953; Damascus, 1954-55; Bahrain, 1955-56; Vice-Consul, Basra, 1956-60; Oriental Sec., Rabat, 1960-63; FO, 1964-67; 1st Sec., Beirut, 1968-70; 1st Sec. and Head of Chancery, Mexico City, 1970-73; Counsellor, Khartoum, 1973-75; Counsellor, Beirut, 1975-76; Dir of Res., FCO, 1976-78. *Recreations:* conservation/restoration of furniture, sailing, music. *Address:* Town Yeat, High Nibthwaite, Ulverston, Cumbria.

SANDERS, Sir John Reynolds M.; *see* Mayhew-Sanders, Sir J. R.

SANDERS, Kate Emily Tyrrell, (Mrs C. W. Sanders); *see* Boyes, K. E. T.

SANDERS, Peter Basil; Director, Equal Opportunities Division, Commission for Racial Equality, since 1977; *b* 9 June 1938; *s* of Basil Alfred Horace Sanders and Ellen May Sanders (*née* Cockrell); *m* 1961, Janet Valerie (*née* Child); two *s* one *d. Educ:* Queen Elizabeth's Grammar Sch., Barnet; Wadham Coll., Oxford (MA, DPhil). Administrative Officer, Basutoland, 1961-66; Research in Oxford for DPhil, 1966-70; Officer, Min. of Defence, 1971-73; Race Relations Bd: Principal Conciliation Officer, 1973-74; Dep. Chief Officer, 1974-77. *Publications:* Lithoko: Sotho Praise-Poems (ed jtly and trans. with an Introd. and Notes), 1974; Moshoeshoe, Chief of the Sotho, 1975. *Address:* 28 Queensdown Road, E5. *T:* 01-986 7627.

SANDERS, Sir Robert (Tait), KBE 1980; CMG 1974; HMOCS; Secretary to the Cabinet, Government of Fiji, 1970-79; *b* 2 Feb. 1925; *s* of late A. S. W. Sanders and Charlotte McCulloch; *m* 1951, Barbara, *d* of G. Sutcliffe; three *s. Educ:* Canmore Public Sch., Dunfermline; Dunfermline High Sch.; Fettes Coll., Edinburgh; Cambridge Univ. (Major Open Classical Schol., Pembroke Coll., 1943; John Stewart of Rannoch Schol. in Latin and Greek, 1947; 1st cl. Hons, Pts I and II of Classical Tripos); London Sch. of Economics. Served War, 1943-46: Lieut, 1st Bn the Royal Scots, India and Malaya. Sir Arthur Thomson Travelling Schol., 1948; Sir William Browne Medal for Latin Epigram, 1948. MA (Cantab) 1951. Joined HM Overseas Civil Service, Fiji, as Dist Officer, 1950; Sec. to Govt of Tonga, 1956-58; Sec., Coconut Commn of Enquiry, 1963; MLC, Fiji, 1963-64; Sec. for Natural Resources, 1965-67; Actg Sec. Fijian Affairs, and Actg Cmn. Native Lands and Fisheries Commn, 1967; MEC, Fiji, 1967; Sec. to Chief Minister and to Council of Ministers, 1967; apptd Sec. to Cabinet, 1970, also Sec. for Foreign Affairs, 1970-74, Sec. for Home Affairs, 1972-74 and Sec. for Information, 1975-76. Fiji Independence Medal, 1970. *Publications:* Interlude in Fiji, 1963; articles in Corona, jl of HMOCS. *Recreations:* golf, music, hill-walking. *Address:* Greystones Lodge, Broich Terrace, Crieff. *Club:* Royal Scots (Edinburgh).

SANDERS, Roger Benedict; Metropolitan Stipendiary Magistrate, since 1980; *b* 1 Oct. 1940; *s* of Maurice Sanders, JP, FRIBA, and Lilian (*née* Stone); *m* 1969, Susan, *er d* of Simon Brenner and Phyllis (*née* Lee); two *s* (one *d* decd). *Educ:* Highgate School. Co-founder, Inner Temple Debating Soc., 1961, Chm. 1962. Called to the Bar, Inner Temple, 1965; South Eastern Circuit; Chm., Inner London Juvenile Courts, 1980-; Mem., Legal Cttee, Inner London Juvenile Panel, 1982-. Chairman, Walker School Assoc. (Southgate), 1976, 1977; Schools' Debating Assoc. Judge, 1976, 1978, 1981; Mem., Haringey Schools Liaison Group, 1979. *Recreations:* opera, model railways, collecting things. *Address:* Tower Bridge Magistrates' Court, Tooley Street, SE1. *T:* 01-407 4232. *Club:* Players' Theatre.

SANDERS, Terence Robert Beaumont, CB 1950; TD; DL; b 2 June 1901; yr s of late Robert Massy Dawson Sanders, Charleville Park, Co. Cork, and Hilda Beaumont, Buckland Court, Surrey; m 1st, 1931, Marion (d 1961), er d of late Colonel A. W. Macdonald, DSO, Spean Bridge: five s; 2nd, 1965, Deborah, y d of late Daniel C. Donoghue of Philadelphia. Educ: Eton; Trinity Coll. Cambridge. Fellow of CCC, Cambridge, 1924, Estates Bursar, 1935, Life Fellow, 1945; sometime Univ. Lectr in Engineering, Cambridge Univ. Commissioned TA, 1923, RA; Capt. 1928, Maj. 1939; Herts Yeo. 1939-42. Min. of Supply, 1944; Asst Chief Engineer, Armament Design and later Principal Dir of Tech. Development (Defence); demobilised, 1945, with rank of Colonel. Entered Scientific Civil Service, 1946, retd 1951. Engrg Advr to BSI, 1952-72, closely associated with work of Internat. Orgn for Standardization; Chm., ISO/STACO, 1964-72. Mem., S-E Gas Bd, 1961-69. Chm., Buckland Sand and Silica Co. Ltd, 1951-78; Dir, GHP Gp, 1962-76. Rowed in Univ. Boat Race, 1922; won Henley Stewards' Cup, 1922, 1923, 1924; Grand, 1929; Olympic IVs, 1924; Hon. Treas., CUBC, 1928-39. FICE, FIMechE, FInstW. High Sheriff, Surrey, 1967; DL Surrey, 1967. *Publication:* Centenary History of Boat Race. *Recreations:* rowing, shooting, farming. *Address:* Slough House, Buckland, Surrey. *Club:* Leander.

SANDERSON OF AYOT, 2nd Baron cr 1960, title disclaimed by the heir, Dr Alan Lindsay Sanderson, 1971.

SANDERSON, Sir Bryan; see Sanderson, Sir F. P. B.

SANDERSON, Charles Denis; HM Diplomatic Service; Counsellor, Caracas, since 1979; b 18 Dec. 1934; s of Norman and Elsie Sanderson; m 1960, Mary Joyce Gillow; one s two d. Educ: Bishopshalt Sch., Hillingdon, Mddx; Pembroke Coll., Oxford (MA). National Service, 1953-55; Oxford, 1955-58; British Petroleum Co. Ltd, 1958-64; Second, later First Secretary, Commonwealth Relations Office, 1964-67; First Sec., Kingston, and concurrently, Haiti, 1967-70; Acting Consul, Port au Prince, 1969; First Sec., Head of Chancery and Consul, Panama, 1970-73; First Sec., FCO, 1973-75; Consul (Commercial), British Trade Development Office, New York, 1975-77; Dep. Consul General and Director Industrial Development, New York, 1977-79. *Address:* c/o Foreign and Commonwealth Office, SW1. *Clubs:* Royal Commonwealth Society; Altamira Tennis (Caracas).

SANDERSON, Sir (Charles) Russell, Kt 1981; Partner, Chas. P. Sanderson, Wool and Yarn Merchants, Melrose, since 1958; company director; b 30 April 1933; s of Charles Plummer Sanderson and Martha Evelyn Gardiner; m 1958, Frances Elizabeth Macaulay; two s two d. Educ: St Mary's Sch., Melrose; Trinity Coll., Glenalmond; Scottish Coll. of Textiles, Galashiels; Bradford Coll. (now Bradford Univ.). Commnd Royal Signals, 1952; served: 51 (Highland) Inf. Div. Signal Regt TA, 1953-56, KOSB TA, 1956-58. Chairman, Roxburgh, Selkirk and Peebles Cons. and Unionist Assoc., 1970-73; Scottish Cons. Unionist Association: Chm. Central and Southern Area, 1974-75; Vice-Pres. 1975-77; Pres. 1977-79; Vice-Chm. Nat. Union of Cons. Assocs, 1979-81 (Mem. Exec. Cttee, 1975-); Chm. Exec. Cttee, Nat. Union of Cons. Assocs, 1981-; Member: Cons. Party Policy Cttee, 1979-; Standing Adv. Cttee of Parly Candidates, 1979- (Vice-Chm. with responsibility for Europe, 1980-81). Deacon, Galashiels Manufrs Corp., 1976; Chm., Eilden Housing Assoc., 1978-82; Governor: St Mary's Sch., Melrose, 1977-; Scottish Coll. of Textiles, 1980-; Mem. Council, Trinity Coll., Glenalmond, 1982-; Comr, Gen. Assembly of Ch. of Scotland, 1972. *Recreations:* golf, amateur operatics (Past Pres., Producer and Mem. Melrose Amateur Operatic Soc.). *Address:* Becketts Field, Bowden, Melrose, Roxburgh TD6 0ST. T: St Boswell's 22736. *Clubs:* Caledonian; Hon. Co. of Edinburgh Golfers (Muirfield); Luffness New Golf.

SANDERSON, Sir (Frank Philip) Bryan, 2nd Bt, cr 1920; Lt-Comdr RNVR; b 18 Feb. 1910; s of Sir Frank Bernard Sanderson, 1st Bt, and Amy Edith (d 1949), d of David Wing, Scarborough; S father 1965; m 1933, Annette Irene Caroline (d 1967), d of late Col Korab Laskowski, Warsaw, (g d of General Count de Castellaz); two s one d. Educ: Stowe; Pembroke College, Oxford. Served War of 1939-45 with Fleet Air Arm. A Member of Lloyd's. Chairman, Humber Fishing and Fish Manure Co., Hull. *Recreation:* shooting. *Heir:* s Frank Linton Sanderson [b 21 Nov. 1933; m 1961, Margaret Ann, o d of John C. Maxwell; two s three d]. *Address:* Lychgate Cottage, Scaynes Hill, Haywards Heath, West Sussex RH17 7NH. *Club:* Carlton.

SANDERSON, George Rutherford, CBE 1978; Administering Officer, The Kennedy Scholarships and Knox Fellowships, Association of Commonwealth Universities, 1979-82; b 23 Nov. 1919; er s of late George Sanderson and Edith Mary Sanderson, Blyth, Northumberland; m 1947, Jean Cecilia, d of late James C. McDougall, Chesterfield, Derbyshire; two s. Educ: Blyth Grammar Sch.; Univ. of London (BA 1st Cl. Hons French and Italian). War Service, 1940-46: RA, Malta and Egypt (Major). British Council, 1949-79: Actg Dir, Anglo Argentine Cultural Inst., La Plata, Argentina, 1949; Dir, Tucuman, Argentina, 1950-52; Asst Rep., Santiago, Chile, 1952-58; Dep. Area Officer, Oxford, 1958-62; Reg. Dir, and Dir Anglo Argentine Cultural Assoc., Rosario, Argentina, 1962-66; Asst Rep., Buenos Aires, 1966-69; Reg. Dir, and Dir Anglo Brazilian Cultural Soc., São Paulo, Brazil, 1969-72; Dir, Drama and Music Dept, and Dep. Controller, Arts Div., 1973; Educnl Attaché, British Embassy, Washington, 1973-76; Rep., British Council, Spain, and Cultural Attaché, British Embassy, Madrid, 1976-79. *Recreations:* art, reading. *Address:* Leafield House, Holton, Oxford. T: Wheatley 2526. *Club:* Athenæum.

SANDERSON, John Ellerslie, CB 1980; Adviser to the Department of Transport on appointments in the ports industry, 1982; b 19 March 1922; yr s of late Joseph Sanderson and Daisy (née Beeman); m 1941, Joan Ethel, y d of late H. H. Mitchell, Bromley, Kent; three s. Educ: Portsmouth Grammar Sch. Entered Civil Service in 1947 and joined Min. of Transport, 1952. On loan to Intergovernmental Maritime Consultative Organisation, 1959-61; Asst Sec., Min. of Transport, 1963; Under-Sec., Ports Directorate, DoE, 1971-76, and Dept of Transport, 1976-82. *Recreation:* music. *Address:* 54 Victoria Street, Englefield Green, Egham, Surrey. T: Egham 33359.

SANDERSON, Captain Lancelot, CIE 1942; RIN, retired; Captain, RN Emergency List; b 1889; s of late Herbert Elsworth Sanderson; m 1919, Anna St John, d of late William Sloane; two d. Educ: HMS Worcester. Joined RIN 1911; served European War, 1914-19; Surveyor-in-Charge, Marine Survey of India, 1935-39; Naval Officer-in-Charge, Calcutta, 1939-43; Chief of Personnel, Naval Headquarters, New Delhi, 1944-45; retired 1946. *Address:* 19 Elm Grove, Saffron Walden CB10 1NA. T: Saffron Walden 23405.

SANDERSON, Very Rev. Roy; see Sanderson, Very Rev. W. R.

SANDERSON, Sir Russell; see Sanderson, Sir C. R.

SANDERSON, Rt. Rev. Wilfrid Guy; b 17 Aug. 1905; s of late Wilfrid E. Sanderson; m 1934, Cecily Julia Mary Garratt (d 1982); one s two d. Educ: Malvern College; Merton College, Oxford (MA). Ordained, 1931; Curate at S Farnborough, Hants, till 1934; Priest-in-charge of St Aidan's, Aldershot, 1934-37; Vicar of All Saints, Woodham, Surrey, 1937-46; Vicar of All Saints, Alton, Hants, 1946-54; Rector of Silverton, Devon, 1954-59; Archdeacon of Barnstaple, 1958-62; Rector of Shirwell, 1959-62; Suffragan Bishop of Plymouth, 1962-72. *Address:* 3 Hinton Close, Hinton St George, Somerset TA17 8SH. T: Crewkerne 73846.

SANDERSON, Very Rev. (William) Roy; Parish Minister at Stenton and Whittingehame, 1963-73; Extra Chaplain to the Queen in Scotland, since 1977 (Chaplain, 1965-77); b 23 Sept. 1907; er s of late Arthur Watson Sanderson, Leith, and late Ethel Catherine Watson, Dundee; m 1941, Annie Muriel Easton, Glasgow; three s two d. Educ: Cargilfield Sch.; Fettes Coll.; Oriel Coll., Oxford; Edinburgh University. BA 1929, MA 1933, Oxon. Ordained, 1933. Asst Minister, St Giles' Cath., Edin., 1932-34; Minister: at St Andrew's, Lochgelly, 1935-39; at the Barony of Glasgow, 1939-63. Moderator: Glasgow Presbytery, 1958; Haddington and Dunbar Presbytery, 1972-74; Convener of Assembly Cttees: on Religious Instruction of Youth, 1950-55; on Deaconesses, 1956-61; Panel of Doctrine, 1960-65; on Gen. Administration, 1967-72. Convener of Business Cttee and Leader of General Assembly of the Church of Scotland, 1965-66, 1968-72. Moderator of Gen. Assembly of the Church of Scotland, May 1967-May 1968. Chm., BBC Scottish Religious Advisory Committee, 1961-71; Member Central Religious Advisory Cttee of BBC and ITA, 1961-71. Governor, Fettes Coll., Edinburgh, 1967-76. Hon. DD Glasgow, 1959. *Publication:* Responsibility (Moderatorial address), 1967. *Recreations:* cooking, reading. *Address:* 1a York Road, North Berwick, East Lothian. T: North Berwick 2780.

SANDFORD, 2nd Baron, cr 1945, of Banbury; **Rev. John Cyril Edmondson**, DSC 1942; Conservative Peer in House of Lords, since 1959; a Church Commissioner, since 1982; b 22 Dec. 1920; e s of 1st Baron Sandford; S father, 1959; m 1947, Catharine Mary Hunt; two s two d. Educ: Eton Coll.; Royal Naval Coll., Dartmouth; Westcott House, Cambridge. Served War of 1939-45: Mediterranean Fleet, 1940-41; Home Fleet, 1942; Normandy Landings, 1944 (wounded); Mediterranean Fleet, HMS Saumarez, 1946 (wounded). Staff of RN Coll., Dartmouth, 1947-49; HMS Vengeance, 1950; HMS Cleopatra, 1951-52; Staff Commander-in-Chief Far East, 1953-55; Commander of Home Fleet Flagship, HMS Tyne, 1956; retired 1956. Ordained in Church of England, 1958; Parish of St Nicholas, Harpenden, 1958-63; Exec. Chaplain to Bishop of St Albans, 1965-68. Opposition Whip, House of Lords, 1966-70; Parly Sec., Min. of Housing and Local Govt, June-Oct. 1970; Parliamentary Under-Secretary of State: DoE, 1970-73; DES, 1973-74. Dir, Ecclesiastical Insurance Office, 1978-. Chm., Cttee to review the condition and future of National Parks in England and Wales, 1971. Chairman: Hertfordshire Council of Social Service, 1969-70; Church Army, 1969-70; Community Task Force, 1975-82; Standing Conf. of London and SE Regional Planning Authorities, 1981-; Mem., Adv. Council on Penal Reform, 1968-70. President: Anglo-Swiss Soc., 1974-; Council for Environmental Educn, 1974-; Assoc. of District Councils, 1980; Offa's Dyke Assoc., 1980; Countrywide Holidays Assoc., 1982-; Vice-Pres., YHA, 1979-. Hon. Fellow, Inst. of Landscape Architects. *Heir:* s Hon. James John Mowbray Edmondson [b 1 July 1949; m 1973, Ellen Sarah, d of Jack Shapiro, Toronto; one d]. *Address:* 6 Smith Square, Westminster, SW1. T: 01-222 5715. *Club:* Ski Club of Gt Britain.

SANDFORD, Arthur; Clerk of the County Council and Chief Executive, Nottinghamshire County Council, since 1978; b 12 May 1941; s of Arthur and Lilian Sandford; m 1963, Kathleen Entwistle; two d. Educ: Queen Elizabeth's Grammar Sch., Blackburn; University Coll., London (LLB Hons (Upper 2nd Class)). Preston County Borough Council: Articled Clerk to Town Clerk, 1962-65; Asst Solicitor, 1965-66; Sen. Asst Solicitor, 1966-68; Asst Solicitor, Hants CC, 1969-70; Nottinghamshire County Council: Second Asst Clerk, 1970-72; First Asst Clerk, 1972-74; Dep. Dir of Admin, 1973-75; Dir of Admin, 1975-77; Dep. Clerk and County Sec., 1977-78. *Recreations:* football, gardening. *Address:* Fairford House, 66 Loughborough Road, Bunny, Nottingham. *T:* Nottingham 212440. *Club:* Royal Over-Seas League.

SANDFORD, Prof. Cedric Thomas; Professor of Political Economy, University of Bath, since 1965, and Director of Bath University Centre for Fiscal Studies, since 1974; *b* 21 Nov. 1924; *s* of Thomas Sandford and Louisa (*née* Hodge); *m* 1945, Evelyn Belch; one *s* one *d*. *Educ:* Manchester Univ. (BAEcon 1948, MAEcon 1949); London Univ. (BA History (external) 1955). Undergraduate, Manchester Univ., 1942-43 and 1946-48; RAF, 1943-46 (Pilot). Graduate Research Schol., Univ. of Manchester, 1948-49; Lectr, Burnley Municipal Coll., 1949-60; Sen. Lectr, subseq. Head of General and Social Studies Dept, Bristol Coll. of Science and Technology, 1960-65; Head of Sch. of Humanities and Social Sciences, Univ. of Bath, 1965-68, 1971-74, 1977-79. Visiting Prof., Univ. of Delaware, USA, 1969; Vis. Fellow, ANU, 1981. Mem., Meade Cttee on Reform of Direct Tax System, 1975-78; Conslt, Fiscal Div., OECD, 1976-79. *Publications:* Taxing Inheritance and Capital Gains (Hobart Paper 32, IEA), 1965, 2nd edn 1967; Economics of Public Finance, 1969, 2nd edn 1978; Realistic Tax Reform, 1971; Taxing Personal Wealth, 1971; National Economic Planning, 1972, 2nd edn 1976; Hidden Costs of Taxation, 1973; (jtly) An Accessions Tax, 1973; (jtly) An Annual Wealth Tax, 1975; (sen. editor, and jt author) Case Studies in Economics (3 vols), 1971, 2nd edn 1979; (jtly) Grants or Loans?, 1980; (jtly) The Costs and Benefits of VAT, 1981; (jtly) Tax Policy-Making in the United Kingdom, 1982; The Economic Framework, 1982; numerous articles in wide range of learned jls. *Recreations:* gardening, fishing, violin-playing. *Address:* 10 Summerhill Road, Bath BA1 2UR. *T:* Bath 26049.

SANDFORD, Sir Folliott Herbert, KBE 1949; CMG 1944; Registrar of Oxford University, and Fellow, New College, Oxford, 1958-72; *b* 28 Oct. 1906; *s* of late W. C. Sandford, Barrister-at-Law; *m* 1935, Gwendoline Alexander Masters (*d* 1977); *m* 1982, Mrs Peggy Young (*née* Odgear). *Educ:* Winchester; New Coll., Oxford (1st Class Greats, 1st Class Law); Geneva. Entered Air Ministry, 1930; Principal Private Secretary to successive Secretaries of State (Viscount Swinton, Sir Kingsley Wood, Sir Samuel Hoare, and Sir Archibald Sinclair), 1937-40; attached to RAF Ferry Command, Montreal, 1941-42; Secretary, Office of Resident Minister, West Africa, 1942-44; Assistant Under-Secretary of State, Air Ministry, 1944-47; Deputy Under-Secretary of State, Air Ministry, 1947-58. Master, Skinners' Company, 1975-76. Hon. Fellow, New Coll. and Wolfson Coll., Oxford, 1972. Hon. DCL Oxon, 1973. *Address:* Damsel's Mill, Painswick, Glos. *Club:* Reform.

SANDFORD, Herbert Henry, OBE 1963; DFM 1942; Member for St Marylebone, Greater London Council, since 1976; Opposition Member of Transport Committee, since 1981; Opposition Spokesman: GLC Staff Committee, since 1982; Staff and General Committee, ILEA, since 1982; *b* 19 Nov. 1916; *s* of Herbert Charles Sandford and Grace Ellen (*née* Onley); *m* 1st, 1938, Irene Lucy (*née* Porter) (marr. diss. 1944); 2nd, 1948, Jessie Irene (*née* Gray). *Educ:* Minchendon Secondary Sch., Southgate. Served War, Pathfinder Sqdns, RAF, 1939-45. Elected to St Marylebone Metrop. Bor. Council, 1953; Chm., Works Cttee. City of Westminster: Councillor, Lords Ward, 1964-68; Alderman, 1968-78; Dep. Leader of Council, 1975-76; Chairman: Traffic Cttee, 1964-67; Highways and Traffic Cttee, 1967-68; Highways Cttee, 1971-72 (Vice-Chm., 1969-71); Highways and Works Cttee, 1972-75; special sub-cttee of Highways and Town Planning Cttees on redevelt of Piccadilly Circus, 1972-76; Member: Policy Cttee, 1972-74; Town Planning Cttee, 1971-; Road Safety Cttee, 1972-74; Road Safety Adv. Cttee, 1974-76; Co-ord. Cttee, 1974-75; Housing Management Cttee, 1975-77; London Transport Passenger Cttee, 1974-76; Covent Garden Cttee, 1977-81; Thames Water Regional Land Drainage Cttee, 1978-. Greater London Council: Chm., Central Area Planning Cttee, 1977-81; Mem., Public Services Safety Cttee, 1977-81. Dir, Grove End Housing Assoc., Ltd, 1976-. Chairman: St Marylebone Sea Cadet Corps, 1953; St Marylebone Boy Scouts Assoc., 1958-64. Treasurer, Wiltons Music Hall Trust, 1982. Governor, St John's Hosp. for Skin Diseases, 1973-76. *Recreations:* golf, bridge, Yoga. *Address:* 5 Elmfield House, Carlton Hill, NW8 9XB. *T:* 01-624 9694. *Clubs:* Royal Air Force, Pathfinder.

SANDFORD, Jeremy; writer, journalist, musician, performer; *s* of Christopher Sandford, owner/director of the Golden Cockerel Press, and Lettice Sandford, wood engraver, craft worker; *m* 1956, Nell Dunn; three *s*. *Educ:* Eton; Oxford. Dir, The Cyrenians; Exec., Gypsy Council; Sponsor: Shelter; The Simon Community. Editor, Romano Drom (gypsy newspaper). Screen Writers' Guild of Gt Britain Award, 1967, 1971; Prix Italia prize for TV drama, 1968; Critics Award for TV drama, 1971. *Publications:* Synthetic Fun, 1967; Cathy Come Home, 1967; Whelks and Chromium, 1968; Edna the Inebriate Woman, 1971; Down and Out in Britain, 1971; In Search of the Magic Mushrooms, 1972; Gypsies, 1973; Tomorrow's People, 1974; Prostitutes, 1975; Smiling David, 1975; Virgin of the Clearways, 1977. *Recreations:* painting, music, travel, mountain exploration, riding, wandering, windsurfing, wondering, festivals, getting to know British people. *Address:* 7 Earls Court Square, SW5. *Club:* Chelsea Arts.

SANDFORD, Kenneth Leslie, CMG 1974; barrister; *b* 14 Aug. 1915; *s* of Albert Edgar Sandford and Barbara Ivy (*née* Hill); *m* 1946, Airini Ethel Scott Sergel; one *s* one *d* (and one *d* decd). *Educ:* King's Coll., Auckland, NZ; Auckland University Coll. LLB 1938. Served War: 34 Bn (NZ), rank of Captain, 1940-45. Barrister and Solicitor, 1939-72; Crown Solicitor

(Hamilton), 1950-72; Chm., Accident Compensation Commn (NZ), 1972-80. *Publications:* Dead Reckoning, 1955; Dead Secret, 1957; Mark of the Lion, 1962. *Recreation:* cricket (Pres. NZ Cricket Council, 1971-73). *Address:* 144 Lucerne Road, Remuera, Auckland, New Zealand. *Club:* Wellington (NZ).

SANDFORD, Rear-Adm. Sefton Ronald, CB 1976; *b* 23 July 1925; *s* of Col H. R. Sandford and Mrs Faye Sandford (*née* Renouf); *m* 1st, 1950, Mary Ann Prins (*d* 1972); one *s*; 2nd, 1972, Jennifer Rachel Newell; two *d*. *Educ:* St Aubyns, Rottingdean, 1934-38; Royal Naval Coll., Dartmouth, 1939-42. Served War: went to sea, July 1942; commanded HMMTB 2017, Lieut, 1946-47; ADC to Comdr British Forces, Hong Kong (Lt-Gen. Sir Terence Airey), 1952-53; commanded HMS Teazer (rank Comdr), 1958; Staff of Imperial Defence Coll., 1963-65; comd HMS Protector, Captain, 1965-67; Naval Attaché, Moscow, 1968-70; comd HMS Devonshire, 1971-73; ADC to the Queen, 1974; Flag Officer, Gibraltar, 1974-76. A Younger Brother of Trinity House, 1968. *Recreations:* cricket, sailing, fishing. *Address:* Dolphins, Rue de St Jean, St Lawrence, Jersey, Channel Islands. *T:* Jersey 62200. *Clubs:* Marylebone Cricket (MCC); Royal Yacht Squadron (Cowes).

SANDFORD SMITH, Richard Henry, FCIS; Chairman, Eastern Gas Region (formerly Eastern Gas Board), 1970-73; *b* 29 March 1909; *s* of late Dr H. Sandford Smith; *m* 1936, Dorothy Hewitt, *y d* of late Rev. J. F. Hewitt; one *s*. *Educ:* Haileybury Coll. London Stock Exchange, 1926. Qualified as Chartered Secretary and awarded Sir Ernest Clarke Prize, 1932. Joined Gas Light & Coke Co., 1932; Sec., SE Gas Corp. Ltd, 1939-49; Sec., SE Gas Bd, 1949-56 (Dep. Chm., 1956-69). *Recreations:* theatre, golf, gardening. *Address:* 60 The Marlowes, St John's Wood Park, NW8. *Club:* Savile.

SANDHURST, 5th Baron, *cr* 1871; **(John Edward) Terence Mansfield,** DFC 1944; Managing Director, Leslie Rankin Ltd, Jersey; *b* 4 Sept. 1920, *er s* of 4th Baron Sandhurst, OBE, and Morley Victoria (*née* Upcher; *d* 1961); *S* father 1964; *m* 1947, Janet Mary, *er d* of late John Edward Lloyd, NY, USA; one *s* one *d*. *Educ:* Harrow. Served RAFVR, 1939-46: Bomber Command (as Navigator and Bombing Leader): 149 Sqdn, 1941; 419 (RCAF) Sqdn, 1942; 12 Sqdn, 1943-45. 1946-55: Metropolitan Special Constabulary 'C' Div., Sergeant, 1949-52; long service medal, 1955. Hon. ADC to Lieutenant-Governor of Jersey, 1969-74. *Recreation:* golf. *Heir: s* Hon. Guy Rhys John Mansfield [*b* 3 March 1949; *m* 1976, Philippa St Clair, *er d* of Digby Verdon-Roe, 06 Le Cannet; one *s*; one *d*. *Educ:* Harrow; Oriel Coll., Oxford (MA). Called to Bar, Middle Temple, 1972]. *Address:* Les Sapins, St Mary, Jersey, CI. *Clubs:* Royal Air Force; MCC, Pathfinder; United (Jersey).
See also Earl of Macclesfield.

SANDILANDS, family name of **Baron Torphichen.**

SANDILANDS, Sir Francis (Edwin Prescott), Kt 1976; CBE 1967; Chairman since 1972 (Vice-Chairman, 1968-72), and Director since 1965, Commercial Union Assurance Co. Ltd; *b* 11 December 1913; *s* of late Lieut-Col Prescott Sandilands, DSO, RM, and late Gladys Baird Murton; *m* 1939, Susan Gillian Jackson; two *s*. *Educ:* Eton; Corpus Christi College, Cambridge (Hon. Fellow, 1975). MA 1938. Served War of 1939-45, Royal Scots Fusiliers and General Staff, UK and NW Europe (Lt-Col; despatches). Joined Ocean Accident and Guarantee Corporation Ltd, 1935, Manager, 1955; General Manager, then Chief General Manager Commercial Union Assurance Co. Ltd, 1958-72; Chairman: Royal Trust Company of Canada, 1974-; Director: ICI Ltd; Trafalgar House Ltd; Kleinwort, Benson, Lonsdale Ltd; Plessey Co. Ltd; Royal Opera House; Chm., Royal Opera House Trust; Trustee, British Museum; Mem., Royal Fine Art Commn, 1980-; Chairman: London Salvage Corps, 1962-63; British Insurance Assoc., 1965-67; Pres., Insurance Inst. of London, 1969-70. Chm., Govt Cttee of Enquiry on Inflation and Company Accounts, 1974-75; Cttee on Invisible Exports, 1975-; Member: BOTB, 1976-; Adv. Cttee, Queen's Award to Industry. Treas., UCL, 1973-81 (Hon. Fellow, 1981). Commander de l'Ordre de la Couronne (Belgium), 1974. *Address:* 53 Cadogan Square, SW1. *T:* 01-235 6384; Thackers, Geldeston, near Beccles, Suffolk. *T:* Kirby Cane 226.

SANDLER, Prof. Merton, MD, FRCP, FRCPath; Professor of Chemical Pathology, Institute of Obstetrics and Gynaecology, University of London, since 1973; Consultant Chemical Pathologist, Queen Charlotte's Maternity Hospital, since 1958; *b* 28 March 1926; *s* of Frank Sandler and late Edith (*née* Stein), Salford, Lancs; *m* 1961, Lorna Rosemary, *d* of late Ian Michael and Sally Grenby, Colindale, London; two *s* two *d*. *Educ:* Manchester Grammar Sch.; Manchester Univ. (MB ChB 1949; MD 1962). FRCPath 1970 (MRCPath 1963); FRCP 1974 (MRCP 1955). Jun. Specialist in Pathology, RAMC (Captain), 1951-53. Research Fellow in Clin. Path., Brompton Hosp., 1953-54; Lectr in Chem. Path., Royal Free Hosp. Sch. of Med., 1955-58; Recognized Teacher in Chem. Path., 1960-; extensive examining experience for various Brit. and for. univs and Royal Colls; Mem. Standing Adv. Cttee, Bd of Studies in Path., Univ. of London, 1972-76 (also Mem. Chem. Path. Sub-Cttee, 1973-); Chm., Academic Bd, 1972-73, Bd of Management, 1975-, Inst. of Obst. and Gyn.; Governor: Brit. Postgrad. Med. Fedn, 1976-78; Queen Charlotte's Hosp. for Women, 1978-; Council Mem. and Meetings Sec., Assoc. of Clin. Pathologists, 1959-70; Mem. Council, Collegium Internat. Neuro-Psychopharmacologicum, 1982-. Various offices in: RSM, incl. Pres. Section of Med. Exper. Med. and Therapeutics, 1979-80; Brit. Assoc. for Psychopharm., incl. Pres., 1980-; British Assoc. for Postnatal Illness (Pres., 1980-); For. Corresp. Mem., Amer. Coll. of Neuropsychopharm., 1975-;

office in many other learned socs and grant-giving bodies, incl. Med. Adv. Councils of Migraine Trust, 1975-80, Schizophrenia Assoc. of Gt Brit., 1975-78; Chm. and Sec., Biol Council Symposium on Drug Action, 1979, and organiser or Brit. rep. on org. cttees of many nat. and internat. meetings. Jt Editor: British Jl of Pharmacology, 1974-80; Clinical Science, 1975-77; Jl of Neural Transmission, 1979-; Jl of Psychiatric Research, 1982-, and present or past Mem. Editorial Bds of 17 other sci. jls; eponymous lectures to various learned socs; provision of Nat. Monoamine Ref. Laboratory Service, 1976-. Anna Monika Internat. Prize (jtly), for Res. on Biol Aspects of Depression, 1973; Gold Medal, Brit. Migraine Assoc., 1974. *Publications*: Mental Illness in Pregnancy and the Puerperium, 1978; The Psychopharmacology of Aggression, 1979; Enzyme Inhibitors as Drugs, 1980; Amniotic Fluid and its Clinical Significance, 1980; The Psychopharmacology of Alcohol, 1980; The Psychopathology of Anticonvulsants, 1981; (jointly): The Adrenal Cortex, 1961; The Thyroid Gland, 1967; Advances in Pharmacology, 1968; Monoamine Oxidases, 1972; Serotonin—New Vistas, 1974; Sexual Behaviour: Pharmacology and Biochemistry, 1975; Trace Amines and the Brain, 1976; Phenolsulphotransferase in Mental Health Research, 1981; Tetrahydroisoquinolines and 3-Carbolines, 1982; Progress towards a Male Contraceptive, 1982; numerous research pubns on aspects of biologically-active monoamine metabolism. *Recreations*: reading, listening to music, lying in the sun. *Address*: 27 St Peter's Road, Twickenham, Mddx TW1 1QY. *T*: 01-892 8433. *Club*: Athenæum.

SANDON, Viscount; Dudley Danvers Granville Coutts Ryder, TD; Chairman, International Westminster Bank Ltd, since 1977; a Deputy Chairman, National Westminster Bank Ltd, since 1971 (Director since 1968); Chairman: Powell Duffryn Group, since 1981 (Director since 1976); National Westminster Unit Trust Managers Ltd, since 1979; Deputy Chairman, Coutts and Co. since 1970 (Managing Director, 1949); Director, United Kingdom Provident Institution, since 1955 (Deputy Chairman, 1956-64); Chairman, National Biological Standards Board, since 1973; *b* 20 Dec. 1922; *er s* of 6th Earl of Harrowby, *qv*; *m* 1949, Jeannette Rosalthé, *yr d* of late Captain Peter Johnston-Saint; one *s* one *d*. *Educ*: Eton. Lt-Col RA. OC 254 (City of London) Field Regt, RA (TA), 1962-64. Served War of 1939-45: 59 Inf. Div., 5 Para. Bde, in NW Europe (wounded); India and Java (political offr), 56 Armoured Div., 1941-45. Dir, National Provincial Bank, 1964-69; Chm., Olympia Group, 1971-73; Dir, Sheepbridge Engrg Ltd, 1977-79; Chm., Orion Bank Ltd, 1979-81; Director: Orion Pacific Ltd, 1980-81; Orion Pension Trustees Co. Ltd, 1980-81. Mem. Kensington Borough Council, 1950-65, Kensington and Chelsea BC 1965-71. Hon. Treasurer: Family Welfare Assoc., 1951-65; Central Council for the Care of Cripples, 1953-60; South Kensington Conservative Association, 1953-56; Pres., Wolverhampton SW Conservative and Unionist Assoc., 1959-68. General Commissioner for Income Tax, 1954-71; Member: Lord Chancellor's Adv. Investment Cttees, for Court of Protection, 1965-77, for Public Trustee, 1974-77; Inst. Internat. d'Etudes Bancaires, 1976-; Trilateral Commn, 1980-. Manager, Fulham and Kensington Hosp. Group, 1953-56; Chairman: Inst of Psychiatry, 1965-73; Board of Governors Bethlem Royal and Maudsley Hospitals, 1965-73; Deputy Chairman: Teaching Hospitals Assoc.; London Postgraduate Cttee, 1968-69; Trustee, Psychiatry Research Trust, 1982-; Member: Bd of Govs of Univ. of Keele, 1956-68; Exec. Cttee London area Conservative Assoc., 1949-50; Council, Timber Growers' Organisation, 1961-62. Pres., Staffordshire Soc., 1957-59 (Hon. Treas., 1947-51). Mem., Ct of Assts, Goldsmiths Co., 1972-77. Mem., Trilateral Commn, 1980-. *Heir*: *s* Hon. Dudley Adrian Conroy Ryder [*b* 18 March 1951; *m* 1977, Sarah Nichola Hobhouse Payne, *d* of Captain Anthony Payne]. *Address*: 5 Tregunter Road, SW10. *T*: 01-373 9276; Sandon Hall, Stafford. *T*: Sandon 338; Burnt Norton, Campden, Glos. *T*: Evesham 840358.

SANDOVER, Sir (Alfred) Eric, Kt 1967; MC 1916; Chairman, Swan Portland Cement, 1956-77, retired; *b* 11 Feb. 1897; *s* of Alfred Sandover, MBE, and Rosalind Sandover; *m* 1923, Kathleen Barber, OBE, *d* of Maj.-Gen. G. W. Barber, CMG, DSO; two *s* one *d*. *Educ*: St Peter's Coll., Adelaide. Served European War, 1914-18: E Surrey Regt; 6th Sherwood Foresters, Somme, 1916; served War of 1939-45: 44 Bn AIF and on Staff, Land HQ, Australian Army. Mem. Cttee, Employers' Fedn of Australia, 1950-; Mem. Cttee, Chamber of Commerce of Australia, 1935-; Past Pres., Hardware Assoc. of Australia; Patron, Mentally Incurable Children Assoc.; Business Adviser, Ngala Mothercraft Home, etc. Mem. Shire Coun. of Peppermint Grove for 25 years. *Recreations*: riding horses (formerly MFH West Australian Hunt Club); golf, swimming, deep-sea fishing, etc. *Address*: 29 Leake Street, Peppermint Grove, West Australia 6011. *T*: 3-2101. *Clubs*: (Past Pres.) Weld, (Past Pres.) Naval, Military and Air Force, Karrinyup Golf, West Australian Turf, WA Hunt, etc. (all Perth).

SANDREY, John Gordon, FRCS; Consultant Surgeon, St Peter's Hospital for Stone; Consultant Urologist to the Royal Navy, etc; *b* 20 May 1903; *m* 1932, Eulie Barbara Johnston; one *d*. *Educ*: Sydney, Australia; MB, ChM Sydney, 1926; MRCS, LRCP, 1929; FRCS 1930. Temporary Surgeon-Captain RNVR, 1940-46. Mem. de la Soc. Internat. d'Urol.; FRSocMed. Formerly Surgical Registrar, Royal Prince Alfred Hospital, Sydney, and Resident Surgical Officer, St Mark's and St Peter's Hospital. *Publications*: contributions to medical journals from 1943. *Address*: 134 Walton Street, SW3.

SANDWICH, 10th Earl of, *cr* 1660; Viscount Hinchingbrooke and Baron Montagu of St Neots, 1660 [Disclaimed his Peerages for life, 24 July 1964]; *see under* Montagu, A. V. E. P.

SANDYS, *see* Duncan-Sandys.

SANDYS, 7th Baron, *cr* 1802; **Richard Michael Oliver Hill;** DL; Captain of the Yeomen of the Guard (Deputy Government Chief Whip), 1979-82; Landowner; *b* 21 July 1931; *o s* of late Lt-Col the Lord Sandys and of Lady Sandys; *S* father, 1961; *m* 1961, Patricia Simpson Hall, *d* of late Captain Lionel Hall, MC. *Educ*: Royal Naval College, Dartmouth. Lieutenant in The Royal Scots Greys, 1950-55. A Lord in Waiting, 1974; an Opposition Whip, 1974-79. FRGS. DL Worcestershire, 1968. *Heir*: cousin, Marcus Tufton Hill, *b* 13 March 1931. *Address*: Ombersley Court, Droitwich, Worcestershire. *T*: Worcester 620220. *Club*: Cavalry and Guards.

SANER, Robert Morton; *see* Morton-Saner.

SANGER, Frederick, CH 1981; CBE 1963; PhD; FRS 1954; on staff of Medical Research Council, 1951-Sept. 1983; *b* 13 Aug. 1918; *s* of Frederick Sanger, MD, and Cicely Sanger; *m* 1940, M. Joan Howe; two *s* one *d*. *Educ*: Bryanston; St John's College, Cambridge. BA 1939; PhD 1943. From 1940, research in Biochemistry at Cambridge University; Beit Memorial Fellowship for Medical Research, 1944-51; at MRC Lab. of Molecular Biol., Cambridge, 1961-83; Fellowship at King's College, Cambridge, 1954. For. Hon. Mem., Amer. Acad. of Arts and Sciences, 1958; Hon. Mem. Amer. Society of Biological Chemists, 1961; Foreign Assoc., Nat. Acad. of Sciences, 1967. Hon. DSc: Leicester, 1968; Oxon, 1970; Strasbourg, 1970. Corday-Morgan Medal and Prize, Chem. Soc., 1951; Nobel Prize for Chemistry, 1958, (jointly) 1980; Alfred Benzon Prize, 1966; Royal Medal, Royal Soc., 1969; Sir Frederick Gowland Hopkins Meml Medal, 1971; Gairdner Foundation Annual Award, 1971, 1979; William Bate Hardy Prize, Cambridge Philosophical Soc., 1976; Hanbury Meml Medal, 1976; Copley Medal, Royal Soc., 1977; Horwitz Prize, Albert Lasker Award, 1979; Biochem. Analysis Prize, German Soc. Clin. Chem., 1980. *Publications*: papers on Chemistry of Insulin and Nucleic Acid Structure in Biochemical and other journals. *Address*: (to Sept. 1983) MRC Laboratory of Molecular Biology, Hills Road, Cambridge CB2 2QH. *T*: Cambridge 248011; Far Leys, Fen Lane, Swaffham Bulbeck, Cambridge CB5 0NJ.

SANGER, Dr Ruth Ann, (Mrs R. R. Race), FRS 1972; Director, Medical Research Council Blood Group Unit, since 1973 (Member of Scientific Staff since 1946); *b* 6 June 1918; *yr d* of late Rev. Hubert Sanger and late Katharine M. R. Sanger (*née* Cameron), Urunga, NSW; *m* 1956, Robert Russell Race, *qv*; no *c*. *Educ*: Abbotsleigh, Sydney; Sydney and London Univs. BSc Sydney 1939, PhD London 1948. Scientific Staff of Red Cross Blood Transfusion Service, Sydney, 1940-46. Hon. Member: Sociedad de Hematología del Instituto Mexicano del Seguro Social; Deutsche Gesellschaft für Bluttransfusion; Toronto Antibody Club; Norwegian Soc. of Immunohaematology; Internat. Soc. of Blood Transfusion. Landsteiner Memorial and Philip Levine Awards, USA (jtly with R. R. Race); Gairdner Foundn Award, Canada; Oliver Meml Award for Blood Transfusion, British Red Cross, 1973. *Publications*: (with R. R. Race) Blood Groups in Man, 1950, 6th edn, 1975; many papers in genetical and med. jls. *Address*: 22 Vicarage Road, East Sheen, SW14 8RU. *T*: 01-876 1508; MRC Blood Group Unit, Wolfson House, 4 Stephenson Way, NW1 2HE.

SANGSTER, John Laing; Assistant Director, Foreign Exchange Division, Bank of England, 1980-82; *b* 21 Nov. 1922; *s* of Albert James Laing Sangster and Ottilie Elizabeth Ritzdorff; *m* 1952, Mary Louise Fitz-Alan Stuart; two *s*. *Educ*: Emanuel Sch., London; Emmanuel Coll., Cambridge (BA). Joined Bank of England, 1949; Adviser, Foreign Exchange, 1965; Deputy Chief Cashier, 1975; Chief Adviser, 1979. *Recreations*: touring, walking, bird watching. *Address*: c/o Bank of England, EC2R 8AH. *Clubs*: Overseas Bankers'; Thames Rowing; Leander (Henley on Thames).

SANGSTER, Robert Edmund; *b* 23 May 1936; *o c* of Mr Vernon Sangster and Mrs Sangster. *Educ*: Repton Coll. Owner of: The Minstrel (won Derby, 1977); Alleged (won Prix de l'Arc de Triomphe, 1977, 1978); Detroit (won Prix de l'Arc de Triomphe, 1980); Beldale Ball (won Melbourne Cup, 1980); Our Paddy Boy (won Australian Jockey Club Cup, 1981); Golden Fleece (won Derby, 1982); Assert (won Irish Sweeps Derby, 1982). *Recreation*: golf. *Address*: The Nunnery, Douglas, Isle of Man. *T*: Douglas 23351. *Club*: Jockey.

SANKEY, John Anthony; HM Diplomatic Service; High Commissioner in Tanzania, since 1982; *b* 8 June 1930; *o s* of Henry and Ivy Sankey; Plumstead, London; *m* 1958, Gwendoline Winifred Putman; two *s* two *d*. *Educ*: Cardinal Vaughan Sch., Kensington; Peterhouse, Cambridge (Robert Slade Schol.; Classical Tripos Parts 1 and 2, Class 1; MA). Colonial Office: Asst Principal, 1953; Principal, 1958; First Sec., UK Mission to United Nations, 1961; Foreign Office, 1964; Dep. High Comr, Guyana, 1968; Counsellor, Singapore, 1971; NATO Defence Coll., Rome, 1973; Dep. High Comr, Malta, 1973-75; Counsellor, The Hague, 1975-79. Govr, British Sch. in the Netherlands, 1975-79; Head of Central African Dept and Special Counsellor for African Affairs, FCO, 1979-82. *Address*: Foreign and Commonwealth Office, SW1. *Clubs*: Athenæum; Dar-Es-Salaam Yacht; Gymkhana.

SANSBURY, Rt. Rev. (Cyril) Kenneth, MA Cantab; Hon. DD (Trinity College, Wycliffe College, Toronto); Priest-in-Charge of St Mary in the Marsh, Diocese of Norwich, since 1973; Honorary Minor Canon of Norwich Cathedral, since 1974; *b* 21 Jan. 1905; *s* of late Cyril J. Sansbury; *m* 1931, Ada

Ethelreda Mary, *d* of late Captain P. B. Wamsley; one *s* two *d. Educ:* St Paul's School; Peterhouse, Cambridge; Westcott House, Cambridge. 2nd cl. Classical Tripos, 1926; 1st cl. Theological Tripos, Pt I 1927 and Pt II 1928. Curate of St Peter's, Dulwich Common, 1928-31 and Wimbledon, 1931-32; SPG Missionary, Numazu, Japan, 1932-34; Prof. at Central Theological Coll. and British Chaplain at St Andrew's, Tokyo, 1934-41; Chaplain to HM Embassy, Tokyo, 1938-41; Chaplain, RCAF, 1941-45; Warden, Lincoln Theological Coll., 1945-52; Canon and Prebendary of Asgarby in Lincoln Cathedral, 1948-53; Warden, St Augustine's College, Canterbury (Central College of the Anglican Communion), 1952-61; Hon. Canon, Canterbury Cathedral, 1953-61; Bishop of Singapore and Malaya, 1961-66; Asst Bishop, dio. London, 1966-73. Gen. Sec., British Council of Churches, 1966-73. *Publications:* Truth, Unity and Concord, 1967; Combating Racism, 1975. *Address:* 67C The Close, Norwich NR1 4DD. *Club:* Royal Over-Seas League.

SANSOM, Lt-Gen. Ernest William, CB 1943; DSO 1919; CD; *b* 18 Dec. 1890; *m* 1st, 1917, Eileen Curzon-Smith (*d* 1927); two *d* ; 2nd, 1930, Lucy Aymor Waddell (*d* 1974); one *d. Educ:* Public schools, New Brunswick; Commercial Coll., Fredericton, NB; Univ. of Toronto; Staff Coll., Camberley, Surrey. Joined 71st York Regt, Canadian Militia, 1906; Lieut, 1907; Canadian Expeditionary Force during European War, 1914-19; Commanded 16th Canadian Machine Gun Company, 2nd Bn and 1st Bn Canadian Machine Gun Corps; Permanent Active Militia, from 1920; Organised and Commanded Royal Canadian Machine Gun Brigade until 1923; Army Staff College, Camberley, 1924-25; GSO2, Halifax, NS, 1926-27; GSO2, Defence HQ, Ottawa, 1928-30; AA and QMG, Military District No 12, 1931-34; GSO1, Military District No 4, Montreal, 1935-36; Director of Military Training for Canada, 1937-39; proceeded overseas 1939 with 1st Canadian Division as AA and QMG; Commanded 2nd Inf. Bde and served as DAG at Canadian Military HQ, London, July-Nov., 1940; Commanded 3rd Canadian Div., 1940-41; 5th Canadian Armoured Division, 1941-43; 2nd Canadian Corps, 1943-44; returned to Canada, Feb. 1944, on sick leave; Inspector-General Canadian Army Overseas, Jan. 1945; retired, May 1945. Hon. ADC to Governor-General of Canada, 1948. Progressive-Conservative candidate York-Sunbury general election, June 1945 (defeated), also by-election 1947. Past President: Fredericton Soc. of St Andrew; Fredericton Br., Royal Canadian Legion; Life Mem., Canadian Rehabilitation Council for Disabled; Dir, St John Ambulance Assoc.; Hon. Vice Pres., United Empire Loyalists Assoc. of Canada. KStJ 1978. *Recreations:* fishing, shooting and gardening. *Address:* Fredericton, New Brunswick E3B 4X3, Canada. *Club:* Fredericton Garrison (Hon. Pres.).

SANTA CRUZ, Marqués de, *cr* 1569; **José Fernandez Villaverde y Roca de Togores;** Grand Cross of Carlos III; Grand Cross of Isabel La Catolica; Grand Cross of Merito Naval; Knight of Calatrava; Spanish Ambassador to Court of St James's, 1958-72; Councillor of State, May, 1972; *b* 4 April 1902; *s* of Raimundo F. Villaverde, Marqués de Pozo Rubio and Angela, Marquesa de Pozo Rubio, Grandee of Spain; *m* 1942, Casilda de Silva y Fernandez de Henestrosa, Marquesa de Santa Cruz, Duquesa de San Carlos; three *s* one *d. Educ:* privately in Madrid; University of Madrid; New College, Oxford. Entered Diplomatic Service, 1921; Attaché: London, 1921, Rome, 1923; Secretary Legation: Vienna, 1927, Stockholm, 1933, London, 1934; Minister-Counsellor Embassy, London, 1944; Minister: Copenhagen, 1948, The Hague, 1950. Chm. Spanish Delegn, 7th Session The Hague Conf. on Private Internat. Law, 1951; Ambassador to Cairo, 1953; Under Secretary of State for Foreign Affairs, 1955. Representative of Spain on Exec. Council of Latin Union, 1955; Spanish Deleg. to 11th and 12th Gen. Assembly of UN, 1956 and 1957, Permanent Counsellor of State, 1972-; Chm. of Spanish Delegn to XLVI Conf. of Inter-Parly Union, 1957. Hon. Fellow, New College, Oxford 1959. Holds several foreign decorations. *Recreations:* riding, shooting, golf. *Heir:* *s* Alvaro Villaverde, Marqués del Viso; *b* 3 Nov. 1943. *Address:* San Bernardino 14, Madrid 8, Spain. *Clubs:* Beefsteak; White's; Nuevo (Madrid).

SANTA CRUZ, Victor (Rafael Andrés), GCVO (Hon.) 1965; Ambassador of Chile to the Court of St James's, 1959-70; *b* 7 May 1913; *s* of Don Gregorio Santa Cruz and Doña Matilde Serrano; *m* 1937, Doña Adriana Sutil Alcalde; two *s* two *d. Educ:* Stonyhurst; Instituto Nacional, Chile. Law degree, Chile, 1937; Prof. of Civil Law, in Chile, 1941; elected MP, Chilean Parliament, 1945. *Recreation:* golf. *Address:* Zapallar, V Region, Chile. *Club:* Beefsteak.

SANTER, Rt. Rev. Mark; *see* Kensington, Area Bishop of.

SAOUMA, Edouard; Director-General of the Food and Agriculture Organization of the United Nations, Rome, since 1976; agricultural engineer and international official; *b* Beirut, Lebanon, 6 Nov. 1926; *m* Inés Forero; one *s* two *d. Educ:* St Joseph's University Sch. of Engineering, Beirut; Ecole Nat. Supérieure d'Agronomie, Montpellier, France. Director: Tel Amara Agric. Sch., 1952-53; Nat. Centre for Farm Mechanization, 1954-55; Sec. Gen., Nat. Fedn of Lebanese Agronomists, 1955; Dir-Gen., Nat. Inst. for Agric. Research, 1957-62; Mem. Gov. Bd, Nat. Grains Office, 1960-62; Minister of Agric., Fisheries and Forestry, 1970. Food and Agric. Organization of UN: Dep. Regional Rep. for Asia and Far East, 1962-65; Dir, Land and Water Develt Div., 1965-75; Dir-Gen., 1976. Grand'Croix, Order of the Cedar, Lebanon; Said Akl Prize, Lebanon; Chevalier du Mérite Agricole, France; Grand'Croix, Ordre National du Tchad; Grand'Croix, Ordre Nat. du Ghana; Grand'Croix, Ordre National de Haute Volta; Gran Cruz al Mérito Agrícola of Spain. Dr

(*hc*): Universidad Nacional Agrarià, Peru; Agric. Univ. La Molina, Peru; Univ. of Seoul, Republic of Korea; Univ. of Uruguay; Univ. of Indonesia; Univ. of Warsaw; Univ. of the Philippines; Punjab Agricultural Univ.; Faisalabad Agricultural Univ., Pakistan; Gödöllő Univ., Hungary. Accademico Corrispondente, Accademià Nazionale di Agricultura, Italy. *Publications:* technical publications on agriculture. *Address:* Food and Agriculture Organization of the United Nations, Via delle Terme di Caracalla, Rome 00100, Italy. *T:* 5797.

SAPPER, Alan Louis Geoffrey; General Secretary, Association of Cinematograph, Television and Allied Technicians, since 1969; *b* 18 March 1931; *y s* of late Max and Kate Sapper; *m* 1959, Helen Rubens; one *s* one *d. Educ:* Upper Latymer Sch.; Univ. of London. Botanist, Royal Botanic Gardens, Kew, 1948-58; Asst Gen. Sec., 1958-64, Dep. Gen. Sec., 1967-69, Assoc. of Cinematograph, Television and Allied Technicians; Gen. Sec., Writers' Guild of Great Britain, 1964-67. Mem. General Council, Trades Union Congress, 1970- (Chm. 1982). President: Confedn of Entertainment Unions, 1970; Internat. Fedn of Audio-Visual Workers, 1974; Sec., Fedn of Film Unions, 1968; Treas., Fedn of Broadcasting Unions, 1968; Member: British Copyright Council, 1964; Cinematograph Films Council, 1970; Wilson Interim Action Cttee on Film Industry, 1977-. Governor: BFI, 1974-; Nat. Film School, 1980-; Hammersmith Hosp., 1965-72; Ealing Coll. of Higher Educn. Chm., League for Democracy in Greece. *Publications:* articles, short stories; stage plays, On Licence, Kith and Kin; TV play, The Return, 1961. *Recreations:* taxonomic botany, hill walking, politics and human nature. *Address:* 19 Lavington Road, West Ealing, W13 9NN. *T:* 01-567 4900.

See also L. J. Sapper.

SAPPER, Laurence Joseph; General Secretary, Association of University Teachers, 1969-83; *b* 15 Sept. 1922; *s* of late Max and Kate Sapper; *m* 1951, Rita Jeski; one *d. Educ:* Univ. of London (External Student). LLB. Called to Bar, Lincoln's Inn, 1950. Churchill Fellow, 1966. Min. of Agric. and Fisheries, 1939-41 and 1946-51; Educn Instructor, RAF, 1941-46; Private Sec. to Minister of Agriculture, 1948-50; Asst Sec., Instn of Professional Civil Servants, 1951-56; Dep. Gen. Sec., Post Office Engrg Union, 1956-69. Mem. Council, Brunel Univ., 1964-; Mem., NW Met. Regional Hosp. Board, 1965-71. *Publications:* Your Job and the Law, 1969; (with G. Socrates) SI Units and Metrication, 1969; papers, articles, broadcasts. *Recreations:* astronomy, writing, law reform. *Address:* 35 Waldeck Road, W13 8LY. *T:* 01-997 1251.

See also A. L. G. Sapper.

SARAGAT, Giuseppe; President of the Italian Republic, 1964-71; a Life Senator; President, Social Democratic Party, 1975-76, and since 1976; *b* 19 Sept. 1898; *s* of Giovanni Saragat and Ernestina Stratta; *m* 1922, Giuseppina Bollani (*d* 1961); one *s* one *d. Educ:* University of Economic and Commercial Science, Turin. Served European War, 1915-18 (Lieut); joined Italian Socialist Party, 1924; Member, Exec. Office, Italian Socialist Party, 1925; left Italy for Vienna, Paris and south of France during fascist period, 1926-43; imprisoned by Nazi occupation authorities in Rome, escaped, 1943; Minister without portfolio, 1944; Italian Ambassador in Paris, 1945-46; Pres., Constituent Assembly, 1946; founded Italian Workers Socialist Party (later called Social Democratic Party), 1947; Deputy Prime Minister, 1947-48; Member of Parliament, 1948-64; Deputy Prime Minister and Minister of Merchant Marine, 1948; Deputy Prime Minister, 1954-57; Chm., Standing Cttee for Foreign Affairs, Chamber of Deputies, 1963; Minister of Foreign Affairs, 1963-64. Secretary, Social Democratic Party, 1949-54, 1957-64, and in 1976. *Publications:* L'umanesimo marxista, 1944; Socialismo e libertà, 1944; Per la difesa delle classi lavoratrici, 1951; Il problema della pace, 1951; L'unità socialista, 1956; Per una politica di centrosinistra, 1960; Quaranta anni di lotta per la democrazia, 1965. *Address:* c/o Partito Socialista Democratico, Via Santa Maria in Via 12, 00187 Rome, Italy.

SARAJČIĆ, Ivo; President, Board for Foreign Policy and International Relations, National Assembly of Croatia, since 1978; *b* 10 March 1915; *s* of Ivan and Elizabeth Sarajčić; *m* 1944, Marija Godlar; three *s. Educ:* Univ. of Philosophy, Zagreb. Participated in War of Liberation from (beginning) 1941 (Partizan Remembrance Medal); held various prominent political positions. Subsequently: Secretary, Presidium of Nat. Assembly of Croatia; Editor-in-Chief of Borba; Asst Minister of Educn; Dir of Information Office of Yugoslav Govt; MEC, Croatia; also Mem. Central Cttee of League of Communists of Croatia, Mem. Federal Assembly, Mem. Council for Foreign Affairs and Internat. Relations. Yugoslav Diplomatic Service, 1959; Ambassador to Austria, 1960-63; Asst Sec. of State for Foreign Affairs, 1963-66; Ambassador to London, 1966-70; Dir, Inst. for Developing Countries, Zagreb, 1970-78. *Address:* National Assembly of Croatia, (Sabor SRH), 41000 Zagreb, Radićev trg 6, Yugoslavia.

SAREI, Alexis Holyweek, CBE 1981; PhD; High Commissioner for Papua New Guinea, in London, 1980-late 1983; *b* 25 March 1934; *s* of late Joseph Nambong and Joanna Mota; *m* 1972, Claire Dionne; three *s* three *d* (all adopted). *Educ:* PNG Primary to Tertiary, 1949-66; Rome Univ., 1968-71 (PhD Canon Law). RC Priest, 1966-72; Secretary to Chief Minister, PNG, 1972-73; District Comr, 1973-75; Advisor to Bougainville people, 1975-76; Premier of North Solomons Provincial Govt, 1976-80. PNG Independence Medal 1977. Successor to his uncle, Gregory Moah, as Chief of Clan, Petisuun. *Publication:* The Practice of Marriage Among the Solos, Buka Island, 1974. *Recreations:* music, sketching, golf, swimming, sports. *Address:* Papua New

Guinea High Commission, 14 Waterloo Place, SW1R 4AR. *T:* 01-930 0922-6. *Clubs:* Finchley Golf; Hurlingham (Hon. Member).

SARELL, Captain Richard Iwan Alexander, DSO 1939; RN retd; *b* 22 Feb. 1909; *s* of late Philip Charles Sarell; *m* 1961, Mrs Ann Morgan (*née* Keenlyside). *Educ:* Royal Naval Coll., Dartmouth. Entered RNC Dartmouth, 1922; Comdr 1943; Capt. 1948; specialised in Gunnery, 1934; DSO for action against enemy submarines while in command of HMS Broke, 1939; despatches, 1943. Naval Attaché, Moscow and Helsinki, 1949-51; student Imperial Defence Coll., 1952; Defence Research Policy Staff, 1954; retd 1957. *Recreation:* fishing. *Address:* 43 Rivermead Court, Ranelagh Gardens, SW6 3RX.

SARELL, Sir Roderick (Francis Gisbert), KCMG 1968 (CMG 1958); KCVO 1971; HM Diplomatic Service, retired; *b* 23 Jan. 1913; *y s* of late Philip Charles Sarell, HM Consular Service and of Ethel Ida Rebecca, *d* of late John Dewar Campbell; *m* 1946, Pamela Muriel, *d* of late Vivian Francis Crowther-Smith; three *s. Educ:* Ashdown House, Sussex; Radley; Magdalen College, Oxford. HM Consular Service, 1936; Vice-Consul, Persia, 1937; Italian East Africa, 1939; Iraq, 1940; 2nd Secretary, Addis Ababa, 1942; 1st Secretary, HM Foreign Service, 1946; Rome, Bucharest, 1946; Foreign Office, 1949; Acting Counsellor, 1952; Counsellor and Consul-General, Rangoon, 1953; Consul-General, Algiers, 1956-59; Head of Southern Dept, Foreign Office, 1959-61, General Dept, 1961-63; Ambassador: to Libya, 1964-69; to Turkey, 1969-73. Coronation medal, 1953. *Recreations:* swimming, ski-ing, walking. *Address:* The Litten, Hampstead Norreys, Newbury, Berks RG16 0TD. *T:* Hermitage 201274. *Clubs:* Oriental, Royal Over-Seas League; Leander.

SARGAN, Prof. John Denis, FBA 1981; Professor of Econometrics, London School of Economics and Political Science, since 1964; *b* 23 Aug. 1924; *s* of H. and G. A. Sargan; *m* 1953, Phyllis Mary Millard; two *s* one *d. Educ:* Doncaster Grammar Sch.; St John's Coll., Cambridge. Asst. Lectr, Lectr and Reader, Leeds Univ., 1948-63; Reader, LSE, 1963-64. *Address:* 119 Highfield Way, Rickmansworth, Herts.

SARGANT, Sir (Henry) Edmund, Kt 1969; President of the Law Society, 1968-69; Partner in Radcliffes and Co., 1930-71, and Senior Partner for twenty years; *b* 24 May 1906; *s* of Rt Hon. Sir Charles Henry Sargant, Lord Justice of Appeal, and Amelia Julia Sargant, RRC; *m* 1st, 1930, Mary Kathleen Lemmey (*d* 1979); one *s* ; 2nd, 1981, Evelyn Noel (*née* Arnold-Wallinger). *Educ:* Rugby School; Trinity College, Cambridge (MA). 3rd Cl. Hons Solicitors' final examination; admitted 1930. Served War of 1939-45 in RAF, Provost and Security Branch; (W Africa; Middle East; Acting Wing Comdr). Member, Council, Law Society, 1951-75; Chm., Disciplinary Cttee of Architects Registration Council, 1964, 1965, 1966. Master, Worshipful Co. of Merchant Taylors, 1954. *Address:* 902 Keyes House, Dolphin Square, SW1V 3LX. *Club:* United Oxford & Cambridge University.
See also Hon. Mr Justice Nourse.

SARGANT, Thomas, OBE 1966; JP; Founder Secretary, Justice (British Section of International Commission of Jurists), 1957-82; *b* 17 Aug. 1905; *s* of Norman Thomas Carr Sargant and Alice Rose Walters; *m* 1st, 1929, Marie Hlouskova; two *d* ; 2nd, 1942, Dorothy Lattimer; one *s. Educ:* Highgate School. Founder Mem., Nat. Cttee of Common Wealth, 1941-45. Pioneered campaign for Parliamentary Commissioner. Mem. Council, NACRO. Chm. of Governors, Sydenham Sch., 1956-60. Hon. LLM, QUB, 1977. *Publications:* These Things Shall Be, 1941, 2nd edn; articles in legal jls. *Recreations:* playing the piano, travel, helping prisoners. *Address:* 88 Priory Gardens, N6. *T:* 01-348 7530, (office) 01-405 6018.
See also Prof. A. N. Allott, Prof. N. E. S. McIntosh, W. W. Sargant.

SARGANT, William Walters, MA, MB Cantab, FRCP, Hon. FRCPsych, DPM; Hon. Consulting Psychiatrist, St Thomas' Hospital; Physician in charge of Department of Psychological Medicine, St Thomas' Hospital, London, 1948-72; *b* 1907; *s* of Norman T. C. Sargant, Highgate; *m* 1940, Margaret Heriot Glen. *Educ:* Leys School; St John's College, Cambridge. Geraldine Harmsworth Schol., St Mary's Hosp., 1928; Asst to Medical Professorial Unit, St Mary's Hosp., 1932-34; MO and Phys., Maudsley Hosp., 1935-49; Rockefeller Travelling Fellowship and Research Fellow, Harvard Medical Sch., USA, 1938-39; Asst Clinical Dir Sutton Emergency Hosp., 1939-47; Visiting Prof. of Neuropsychiatry, Duke Univ. Med. Sch., USA, 1947-48; Registrar Royal Medico-Psychological Assoc., 1951-71; Actg Dean, Royal Coll. of Psychiatrists, 1971; Pres., Section of Psychiatry, Royal Society of Medicine, 1956-57; Examiner in Psychological Medicine, Conjoint Board of England, 1960-63; Associate Secretary, World Psychiatric Assoc., 1961-66 (Hon. Mem., 1972). Hon. Mem., Canadian, and Hon. Corres. Mem., Indian and Portuguese Psychiatric Assocs. Lectures: Ernest Parsons Memorial, Amer. Soc. of Biological Psychiatry, 1964; Herman Goldham Internat., New York Coll. of Med., 1964; Watson Smith, RCP, 1966; Maudsley, RMPA, 1968; Belisle Memorial, Michigan, 1968. Taylor Manor Hosp. Award, 1971; Starkey Meml Prize, Royal Soc. of Health, 1973. *Publications:* Physical Methods of Treatment in Psychiatry, 1944, 5th edn, 1972; Battle for the Mind, 1957; The Unquiet Mind, 1967; The Mind Possessed, 1973; Various papers on psychiatric topics, in medical jls. *Recreation:* (formerly) Barbarians RFC, St Mary's Hosp. RFC (Capt.) and Middlesex Co. RFC. *Address:* 19 Hamilton Terrace, NW8. *Club:* Savage.
See also Thomas Sargant.

SARGEANT, Frank Charles Douglas, CMG 1972; HM Diplomatic Service, retired 1977; *b* 7 Nov. 1917; *s* of late John Sargeant and Anna Sargeant; *m* 1946, Joan Adene Bickerton; one *s* one *d. Educ:* Lincoln; St Catharine's Coll., Cambridge. MA Cantab, Natural Sciences. Cadbury Bros. Ltd, 1939. Served War: Army, 1939-46; Lt-Col, Royal Signals. Imperial Chemical Industries Ltd, 1947-48. HM Diplomatic Service: Curacao, 1948; The Hague, 1951; Kuwait, 1954; Foreign Office, 1957 (First Sec. 1958); First Sec., Head of Chancery and Consul, Mogadishu, 1959; First Sec. (Commercial) Stockholm, 1962-66; First Sec., Head of Chancery, Colombo, and Consul for the Maldive Islands, 1967; Counsellor, 1968; Consul-General, Lubumbashi, 1968-70; Dep. High Comr, Dacca, 1970-71; Sen. Officers' War Course, RN Coll., Greenwich, 1971-72; Consul Gen., Lyons, 1972-77 (Doyen of the Consular Corps). *Recreations:* shooting, fishing. *Address:* c/o Lloyds Bank, Jersey, Channel Islands.

SARGEANT, Ven. Frank Pilkington; Archdeacon of Bradford, since 1977; *b* 12 Sept. 1932; *s* of John Stanley and Grace Sargeant; *m* 1958, Sally Jeanette McDermott; three *s* two *d. Educ:* Boston Grammar School; Durham Univ., St John's Coll. and Cranmer Hall (BA, Dip Theol); Nottingham Univ. (Diploma in Adult Education). National Service Commission, RA (20th Field Regt), 1955-57. Assistant Curate: Gainsborough Parish Church, 1958-62; Grimsby Parish Church, and Priest-in-Charge of St Martin's, Grimsby, 1962-67; Vicar of North Hykeham and Rector of South Hykeham, 1967-73; Residentiary Canon, Bradford Cathedral, 1973-77. *Recreations:* cricket, oil painting, games and simulations; special interest, adult education. *Address:* 11 Carlton Drive, Bradford BD9 4DL. *T:* Bradford 45747.

SARGEAUNT, Henry Anthony, CB 1961; OBE 1949; Scientific Consultant, United Nations, 1968; *b* 11 June 1907; *o s* of Lt-Col Henry Sargeaunt and Norah Ierne Carden; *m* 1939, Winifred Doris Parkinson; two *s* one *d. Educ:* Clifton Coll.; University Coll., Reading (London Univ.); Cambridge Univ. Rhodes Research Grant, 1939-42; served with HM Forces, 1944-46: France, 1944; Staff Capt. with 21 Army Group, 1944; Supt Operational Research Group (ORG) (W&E), Min. of Supply, 1946; Supt, Army ORG, 1947-50; Dep. Scientific Adviser, 1950-52, Scientific Adviser, to Army Council, 1952-55; Asst Scientific Adviser to Supreme Allied Commander in Europe, Sept. 1955-57; Dep. Science Adviser, NATO, 1958-59; re-apptd Scientific Adviser to Army Council, 1959; Dep. Chief Scientist (B), War Office, 1960-62; Chief Scientific Adviser, Home Office, 1962-67. *Recreations:* yachting, horse-racing, bird-watching. *Address:* 4 Arnewood Court, Sway, Lymington, Hants.

SARGENT, Rev. Canon Alexander, MA; Archdeacon of Canterbury, 1942-68, and Canon Residentiary of Canterbury Cathedral, 1939-68; Hon. Canon, 1968, Canon Emeritus, 1974; *b* 9 May 1895; *s* of Frederick George Sargent and Florence Crundall. *Educ:* King's School, Canterbury; St Edmund Hall, Oxford; Cuddesdon Theological Coll. Deacon, 1919; Priest, 1920; Curate of St Margarets-at-Cliffe, 1919; of All Saints, Maidstone, 1921; Chaplain of Cuddesdon Theological College, 1923; Sub-Warden of St Paul's College, Grahamstown, 1927; Resident Chaplain to the Archbishop of Canterbury, 1929-39; Archdeacon of Maidstone, 1939-42; Commissary to the Bishop of Grahamstown, 1931; Six Preacher in Canterbury Cathedral, 1933; Select Preacher, Univ. of Oxford, 1949-51. *Address:* Starr's House, The Precincts, Canterbury, Kent. *T:* Canterbury 65960.

SARGENT, Sir Donald, KBE 1961; CB 1951; Chairman: Civil Service Retirement Fellowship, 1968-74; Society of Pension Consultants, 1970-81; Vice-Chairman, Hospital Saving Association, since 1970; *b* 11 Dec. 1906; *s* of late S. G. Sargent; *m* 1944, Dorothy Mary, *d* of late E. Raven, CB; one *s. Educ:* King Edward's School, Birmingham; Trinity College, Cambridge. BA (Classical Tripos, 1st Cl.), 1928. Asst Principal, GPO, 1929; Private Sec. to Director General, 1935-37; Principal, 1937; Home Office, ARP Dept, 1938-41; Principal Private Secretary to PMG, 1941-44; Asst Sec., GPO, 1944; Dep. Chief Administrative Officer, CCG, 1946-47; idc, 1948; Director of Personnel and Accommodation, GPO 1949-53; Director of Postal Services, 1953-55; Deputy Director General, 1955-59; Secretary, National Assistance Bd, 1959-66; Sec., Supplementary Benefits Commn, and Dep. Sec., Min. of Social Security, 1966-68. Dir, Abbeyfield Soc., 1968-70. *Recreations:* mountaineering, sailing, music. *Address:* 1 Croham Valley Road, Croydon, Surrey. *T:* 01-657 4023. *Clubs:* United Oxford & Cambridge University; MCC.

SARGENT, Prof. John Richard; Group Economic Adviser, Midland Bank Ltd, since 1974; Visiting Professor of Economics, London School of Economics, since 1981; *b* 22 March 1925; *s* of John Philip Sargent and Ruth (*née* Taunton); *m* 1st, 1949, Anne Elizabeth Haigh (marr. diss. 1980); one *s* two *d* ; 2nd, 1980, Hester Mary Campbell. *Educ:* Dragon Sch., Oxford; Rugby Sch.; Christ Church, Oxford (MA). Fellow and Lectr in Econs, Worcester Coll., Oxford, 1951-62; Econ. Consultant, HM Treasury and DEA, 1963-65; Prof. of Econs, Univ. of Warwick, 1965-73 (Pro-Vice-Chancellor, 1971-72), Hon. Prof., 1974-81. Member: Doctors and Dentists Rev. Body, 1972-75; Armed Forces Pay Rev. Body, 1972-; Channel Tunnel Adv. Gp, 1974-75; SSRC, 1980-. Editor, Midland Bank Rev., 1974-. *Publications:* British Transport Policy, 1958; articles in Econ. Jl, Oxf. Inst. of Stats Bull., Oxf. Econ. Papers, Qly Jl of Econs, and in vols of conf. papers etc. *Recreation:* work. *Address:* Albion Lodge, 8 Furlong Road, N7 8LS. *Club:* Reform.

SARGENT, Prof. Roger William Herbert; Courtaulds Professor of Chemical Engineering, Imperial College, since 1966; *b* 14 Oct. 1926; *s* of Herbert Alfred Sargent and May Elizabeth (*née* Gill); *m* 1951, Shirley Jane Levesque (*née* Spooner); two *s*. *Educ:* Bedford Sch.; Imperial Coll., London. BSc, ACGI, PhD, DSc, DIC; FEng, FIChemE, FIMA. Design Engineer, Société d'Air Liquide, Paris, 1951-58; Imperial College: Sen. Lectr, 1958-62; Prof. of Chem. Engrg, 1962-66; Dean, City and Guilds Coll., 1973-76; Head of Dept of Chem. Engrg and Chem. Technology, 1975-. Pres., Instn of Chem. Engrs, 1973-74. Fellow, Fellowship of Engineering, 1976; Hon. FCGI 1977. *Publications:* contrib.: Optimization and Design, 1972; Numerical Methods for Constrained Optimization, 1974; Optimization in Action, 1976; contribs to: Trans. Instn Chem. Engrs, Chem. Engrg Sci., Génie Chimique, Computer Jl, Jl of Optimization Theory and Applications, Internat. Jl of Control, Automatica, etc. *Address:* Mulberry Cottage, 291A Sheen Road, Richmond, Surrey TW10 5AW. *T:* 01-876 9623.

SARGENT, Sir (Sidney) Donald; *see* Sargent, Sir Donald.

SARGENT, Prof. Wallace Leslie William, FRS 1981; Ira S. Bowen Professor of Astronomy, California Institute of Technology, since 1981; *b* 15 Feb. 1935; *s* of Leslie William Sargent and Eleanor (*née* Dennis); *m* 1964, Anneila Isabel Cassells, PhD; two *d*. *Educ:* Manchester Univ. (BSc Hons, MSc, PhD). Research Fellow in Astronomy, California Inst. of Tech., 1959-62; Sen. Research Fellow, Royal Greenwich Observatory, 1962-64; Asst Prof. of Physics, Univ. of California, San Diego, 1964-66; Asst Prof. of Astronomy, Calif Inst. Tech., 1966-68, Associate Prof., 1968-71; Professor, 1971-81; Executive Officer for Astronomy, 1975-81. Fellow, American Acad. of Arts and Sciences, 1977. Warner Prize, American Astronomical Soc., 1968. *Publications:* many papers in learned jls. *Recreations:* reading, gardening, oriental carpets, watching professional sports. *Address:* Astronomy Dept 105-24, California Institute of Technology, Pasadena, Calif 91125, USA. *T:* 213-356-4055; 400 South Berkeley Avenue, Pasadena, Calif 91107, USA. *T:* 213-795-6345. *Club:* Athenæum (Pasadena).

SARGINSON, Edward William; retired from Civil Service, 1976; with Confederation of British Industry until 1982; *b* 22 May 1919; *s* of Frederick William and Edith Sarginson; *m* 1944, Olive Pescod; one *s* one *d*. *Educ:* Barrow-in-Furness Grammar School. Entered Civil Service, War Office, 1936; served Infantry, 1939-46; Principal, Min. of Supply, 1955; Asst Sec., Min. of Aviation, 1965; Asst Under Sec. of State, MoD(PE), 1972-76. *Recreation:* hill walking. *Address:* 41 Kendall Avenue South, Sanderstead, Surrey. *T:* 01-660 4476.

SARGISON, Phillip Harold, MBE 1946; Director-General of Royal Ordnance Factories (Finance and Procurement), Ministry of Defence, 1977-80; *b* 4 Feb. 1920; *s* of Ernest and Ethel Sargison; *m* 1945, Doreen (*née* Rowley); one *s* one *d*. *Educ:* De La Salle Coll., Salford. Apptd to War Office, 1938. Served War of 1939-45, HM Forces, 1940-47 (attained rank of Major). Various War Office appts in UK and British Army of the Rhine, 1947-64; Dep. Dir, Civil Service Pay Research Unit, 1964-67; Ministry of Defence: Dir of Accounts, 1967-73; Dep. Dir Gen. of Defence Accounts, 1974-76. *Recreations:* music, literature. *Address:* 2 Reynard Close, Bickley, Kent BR1 2AB. *T:* 01-467 1477. *Club:* East India, Devonshire, Sports and Public Schools.

SARILA, HH Maharaja Mahipal Singh, ju Deo, Maharaja of, CSI 1939; *b* 11 Sept. 1898; *m* 1919, *d* of Landlord of Basela, UP; five *s* three *d*. *Educ:* Daly Coll., Indore. Invested with Ruling Powers, 1919; State Delegate to the First and Second Indian Round Table Conferences, London 1931 and 1932. Late Secretary, General Council and Working Committee, Daly College, Indore. 2nd *s* succeeded, 1942, as HH Maharajadhiraja of Charkhari, UP. *Recreations:* is a keen sportsman and good tennis player and has won tournaments. *Heir:* *s* Raja Bahadur Narendra Singh ju deo, [Indian Ambassador to Switzerland. *Educ:* Mayo Coll., Ajmer, India; Magdalene Coll., Cambridge]. *Address:* Mahipal Niwas Palace, Sarila State, Bundel Khand, UP, India. *TA:* Maharaja Sarila State, India. *Clubs:* National Liberal; Delhi Gymkhana (New Delhi).

SARNOFF, Robert W.; Chairman of Board, RCA Corporation, 1970-76 (Chief Executive Officer, 1968-75); Director: Manufacturers Hanover Trust Co., 1967; New York Stock Exchange, 1972; American Home Products Corporation, 1969; American Arbitration Association, 1955; Economic Development Council of New York City, 1972; *b* 2 July 1918; *s* of late David and Lizette Hermant Sarnoff; *m* 1974, Anna Moffo; three *d* by two former *m*. *Educ:* Phillips Acad.; Harvard Univ. (BA). Ensign, USN, 1942, Lieut 1945. Publisher's asst, Des Moines Register and Tribune, then joined staff of Look Magazine; joined Nat. Broadcasting Co. (subsid. of RCA), 1948: Vice-Pres. 1951; Dir, 1953; Pres. and Chief Executive Officer, 1955; Chm. 1958; Dir, RCA, 1957; Chief Operating Officer, RCA, 1966 and Pres., 1966-71. Trustee or cttee member many organisations, etc. Hon. Fellow, Royal Television Soc. 1973; Fellow, Imperial Coll. of Science and Technology, 1973. Holds numerous hon. degrees and various foreign awards.

SARRAUTE, Nathalie; writer; *b* Ivanovo, Russia, 18 July 1900; *d* of Ilya Tcherniak and Pauline Chatounowski; *m* 1925, Raymond Sarraute; three *d*. *Educ:* Sorbonne; Ecole de Droit de Paris; Oxford. *Publications:* Tropismes, 1939 (trans. Tropisms, 1964); Portrait d'un inconnu, 1948 (Portrait of a Man Unknown, 1959); Martereau, 1953 (trans. 1964); L'Ere du soupçon, 1956 (The

Age of Suspicion, 1964); Le Planétarium, 1959 (The Planetarium, 1962); Les Fruits d'or, 1963 (The Golden Fruits, 1965) (Prix international de Littérature, 1964); Entre la vie et la mort, 1968 (Between Life and Death, 1969); Vous les entendez?, 1972 (Do You Hear Them?, 1973); "disent les imbéciles", 1976 ("fools say", 1977); L'usage de la parole, 1980; (*plays*): Le Silence, Le Mensonge, 1967 (Silence and The Lie, 1969); Isma, 1970; C'est beau, 1973 (It is Beautiful, 1978); Elle est là, 1978; Collected Plays (in translation), 1980. *Address:* 12 avenue Pierre I de Serbie, 75116 Paris, France. *T:* 720.58.28.

SARUM, Archdeacon of; *see* McCulloch, Ven. Nigel S.

SASKATCHEWAN, Bishop of, since 1970; **Rt. Rev. Hedley Vicars Roycraft Short;** *b* 24 Jan. 1914; *s* of Hedley Vicars Short and Martha Hallam Parke; *m* 1953, Elizabeth Frances Louise Shirley; one *s* four *d*. *Educ:* Trinity College, Univ. of Toronto (BA, LTh, BD). Deacon, 1943, priest, 1944, Assistant Curate St Michael and All Angels, Toronto; Junior Chaplain, Coventry Cathedral, England, 1946-47; Lecturer, Trinity Coll., Toronto, 1947-51; Dean of Residence, 1949-51; Rector, Cochrane, Ont, 1951-56; Rector, St Barnabas, St Catharines, Ont, 1956-63; Canon, Christ's Church Cathedral, Hamilton, Ont, 1962; Dean of Saskatchewan, 1963-70. Member of General Synod, 1955-; Examining Chaplain successively to Bishops of Moosonee, Niagara and Saskatchewan. Pres. Council, Coll. of Emmanuel and St Chad, Saskatoon, 1974-80; Chm., Natonum Community Coll., Prince Albert, 1974-76; Chancellor, 1975-80, Hon. Fellow, 1980, Univ. of Emmanuel Coll. Hon. DD Trinity Coll., Toronto, 1964. *Publication:* (contrib.) Eucharistic Dimensions, 1977. *Recreations:* music, sketching, reading. *Address:* Bishopsthorpe, 427 21st Street W, Prince Albert, Saskatchewan S6V 4J5, Canada. *T:* 763-5534, (office) 763-2455.

SASKATOON, Bishop of, since 1981; **Rt. Rev. Roland Arthur Wood;** *b* 1 Jan. 1933; *s* of Cyril Arthur Wood and Evelyn Mae Wood (*née* Cave); *m* 1959, Elizabeth Nora (*née* Deacon); one *s* two *d*. *Educ:* Bishop's Univ., Lennoxville, Quebec (BA 1956, LST 1958). Deacon, May 1958, priest, Dec. 1958; Asst Curate, St Matthew's, Winnipeg, 1958-61; Rector, Christ Church, Selkirk, 1961-64; Assistant Priest, St John's Cathedral, Saskatoon, 1964-67; Rector, Holy Trinity Church, Yorkton, 1967-71; Dean, St John's Cathedral, Saskatoon, 1971-81. Hon. DD, Coll. of Emmanuel and St Chad, Saskatoon, 1979. *Recreation:* model railroading. *Address:* 1104 Elliott Street, Saskatoon, Saskatchewan S7N 0V3, Canada. *T:* 306-653-0890.

SATCHELL, Edward William John, CEng, FIEE, FIERE, RCNC; Director of Engineering (Ships), 1973-76; *b* 23 Sept. 1916; *s* of Horsey John Robert Satchell and Ethel Satchell (*née* Chandler); *m* 1941, Stella Grace Cook; one *d*. *Educ:* Esplanade House Sch., Southsea; Royal Dockyard Sch., Portsmouth; RNC, Greenwich. Electrical Apprentice, Portsmouth Dockyard, 1932; Probationary Asst Electrical Engr, 1936; Asst Electrical Engr, 1939; Electrical Engr, 1943; Suptg Electrical Engr, 1955. Served with British Naval Mission in USA, 1951-53. Warship Electrical Supt, Scotland, 1958-61; Dep. Admty Repair Manager, Malta, 1961-64; Dep. Elec. Engrg Manager, Devonport, 1964-66; Asst Dir of Electrical Engineering, 1966; Dep. Dir of Elec. Engrg, 1970; Head of RN Engrng Service, 1973-75; Dep. Head, RCNC (L), 1975-76; retired 1976. *Recreations:* reading, gardening, bird watching. *Address:* 6 Badminton Gardens, Bath BA1 2XS. *T:* Bath 26974.

SATOW, Rear-Adm. Derek Graham, CB 1977; Chairman, Bath and Wells Diocesan Board of Finance, since 1981; *b* 13 June 1923; *y* *s* of late Graham F. H. Satow, OBE, and of Evelyn M. Satow (*née* Moore); *m* 1944, Patricia E. A. Penaliggon; two *d*. *Educ:* Oakley Hall Sch.; Haileybury Coll.; Royal Naval Engineering Coll. CEng, FIMechE, FIMarE. HMS Ceylon, 1945-46; RNC, Greenwich, 1946-48; HMS Duke of York, 1948-49; RAE Farnborough, 1949-51; HMS Newcastle, 1951-53 (despatches, 1953); Naval Ordnance and Weapons Dept, Admiralty, 1953-59; Dir of Engineering, RNEC, 1959-62; HMS Tiger, 1962-64; Asst and Dep. Dir of Marine Engineering, MoD, 1964-67; IDC, 1968; Captain, RNEC, 1969-71; Dir, Naval Officer Appointments (Eng), MoD, 1971-73; Chief Staff Officer, Technical, later Engineering, to C-in-C Fleet, 1974-76; Dep. Dir-Gen., Ships, MoD, 1976-79; Chief Naval Engr Officer, 1977-79. Comdr, 1955; Captain, 1964; Rear-Adm., 1973.

SATTERTHWAITE, Rt. Rev. John Richard; *see* Gibraltar in Europe, Bishop of.

SATTERTHWAITE, Lt-Col Richard George, OBE 1961; Director and General Secretary, National Playing Fields Association, since 1972; *b* 8 April 1920; *s* of R. E. Satterthwaite and A. M. Elers; *m* 1949, Rosemary Ann, *d* of Gen. Sir Frank Messervy, KCSI, KBE, CB, DSO; three *s* (one *d* decd). *Educ:* Rugby Sch.; RMC Sandhurst. 2nd Lieut, 19th King George V's Own Lancers, 1939; served India, Burma, Malaya; transf. to 17th/21st Lancers, 1949; comd 17th/21st Lancers, 1959-61; retd 1962. National Playing Fields Assoc., 1969. Mem., Sports Council, 1980-. *Recreations:* cricket, golf. *Address:* 4 Wardo Avenue, SW6. *T:* 01-731 2752. *Club:* MCC.

SAUGMAN, Per Gotfred; Knight of the Order of Dannebrog; Chairman since 1972, and Managing Director since 1954, Blackwell Scientific Publications Ltd, Oxford; *b* 26 June 1925; *s* of Emanuel A. G. Saugman and Esther (*née* Lehmann); *m* 1950, Patricia (*née* Fulford); two *s* one *d* (and one *s* decd). *Educ:* Gentofte Grammar Sch.; Commercial Coll., Copenhagen. Bookselling and publishing training in Denmark, Switzerland and England, 1941-49; Sales

Manager, Blackwell Scientific Publications Ltd, 1952; Director, University Bookshops (Oxford) Ltd, 1963; Mem. Board, B. H. Blackwell Ltd, 1964; Chairman: William George's Sons Ltd, Bristol, 1965; Blackwell North America, Inc., 1975; Ejnar Munksgaard Publishers Ltd, Copenhagen, 1967; Kooyker Boekhandel Leiden, 1973. Member Council: International Publishers' Assoc., 1976–79; Publishers' Assoc. of GB and Ireland, 1977–82; President, Internat. Group of Scientific, Technical and Medical Publishers, 1977–79. Chairman, Oxford Round Table, 1953–55; Hon. Mem., British Ecological Soc., 1960–; Governor: Oxford Polytechnic, 1972–; Dragon Sch., Oxford, 1975–. Fellow, St Cross Coll., Oxford, 1978; Hon. MA Oxford, 1978; Hon. Fellow, Green Coll., Oxford, 1981. *Recreations:* reading, art— English watercolours, golf. *Address:* Sunningwood House, Lincombe Lane, Boars Hill, Oxford OX1 5DZ. *T:* Oxford 735503. *Clubs:* Athenæum, Royal Automobile; Frilford Golf (Oxford).

SAUL, Prof. Samuel Berrick, PhD; Vice Chancellor, University of York, since 1979; *b* 20 Oct. 1924; *s* of Ernest Saul and Maud Eaton; *m* 1953, Sheila Stenton; one *s* one *d. Educ:* West Bromwich Grammar Sch.; Birmingham Univ. (BCom 1949, PhD 1953). National Service, 1944–47 (Lieut Sherwood Foresters). Lectr in Econ. History, Liverpool Univ., 1951–63; Edinburgh University: Prof. of Econ. History, 1963–78; Dean, Faculty of Social Sciences, 1970–75; Vice Principal, 1975–77; Actg Principal, 1978. Rockefeller Fellow, Univ. of Calif (Berkeley), and Columbia Univ., 1959; Ford Fellow, Stanford Univ., 1969–70. Vis. Prof., Harvard Univ., 1973. Hon. LLD York, Toronto, 1981. *Publications:* Studies in British Overseas Trade 1870–1914, 1960; The Myth of the Great Depression, 1969; Technological Change: the US and Britain in the 19th Century, 1970; (with A. S. Milward) The Economic Development of Continental Europe 1780–1870, 1973; (with A. S. Milward) The Development of the Economies of Continental Europe 1850–1914, 1977. *Recreations:* fell walking, brass rubbing, music. *Address:* Vice Chancellor's House, Spring Lane, Heslington, York YO1 5DZ. *T:* York 413601.

SAULL, Rear-Adm. Keith Michael, CB 1982; Chief of Naval Staff, Royal New Zealand Navy, since 1980; *b* 24 Aug. 1927; *s* of Harold Vincent Saull and Margaret Saull; *m* 1952, Linfield Mabel (*née* Barnsdale); two *s* one *d. Educ:* Altrincham Grammar Sch.; HMS Conway. Royal Navy, 1945–50; transferred to Royal New Zealand Navy, 1951; commanded HMNZ Ships: Kaniere, Taranaki, Canterbury, 1956–71; Naval Attaché, Washington DC, 1972–75; RCDS 1976; Commodore, Auckland, 1978. *Recreations:* golf, fishing. *Address:* 49 Clutha Avenue, Khandallah, Wellington, New Zealand. *T:* 792-555.

SAULTER, Paul Reginald; Chief Executive, Manchester Chamber of Commerce and Industry, since 1981; *b* 27 Aug. 1935; *s* of Alfred Walter Saulter and Mabel Elizabeth Oliver. *Educ:* Truro Sch.; University Coll., Oxford. MA. Admin. Asst, Nat. Council of Social Service, 1960–63; Sen. Asst and Principal, CEGB, 1963–65; Dep. Head, Overseas Div., BEAMA, 1965–69; Dir, Internat. Affairs, ABCC, 1969–73; Sec.-Gen., British Chamber of Commerce in France, 1973–81. Secretary: For. Trade Working Gp, ORGALIME, 1967–69; Council of British Chambers of Commerce in Continental Europe, 1977–80. *Recreations:* walking, music, theatre. *Address:* Ship Canal House, King Street, Manchester M60 8AH. *T:* 061-832 5574. *Club:* St James's (Manchester).

SAUMAREZ, family name of **Baron de Saumarez.**

SAUNDERS, Albert Edward, CMG 1975; OBE 1970; HM Diplomatic Service, retired; Ambassador to the United Republic of Cameroon and the Republic of Equatorial Guinea, 1975–79; *b* 5 June 1919; *s* of late Albert Edward and Marie Marguerite Saunders; *m* 1945, Dorothea Charlotte Mary Whittle; one *s* one *d. Educ:* yes. Westminster Bank Ltd, 1937. Royal Navy, 1942–45: last appt, Asst Chief Port Security Officer, Middle East. Apptd to British Embassy, Cairo, 1938 and 1945; Asst Information Officer, Tripoli, 1949; Asst Admin. Officer, Athens, 1951; Middle East Centre for Arabic Studies, 1952; Third Sec., Office of UK Trade Comr, Khartoum, 1953; Third Sec. (Information), Beirut, 1954; POMEF, Cyprus, 1956; FO, 1957; Second Sec. (Oriental), Baghdad, 1958; FO, 1959; Vice-Consul, Casablanca, 1963; Second Sec. (Oriental), Rabat, 1963; Consul, Jerusalem, 1964; First Sec., FO, 1967; Chancery, Baghdad, 1968; Head of Chancery and Consul, Rabat, 1969; Counsellor and Consul General in charge British Embassy, Dubai, 1972; Chargé d'Affaires, Abu Dhabi, 1972 and 1973; RN War Coll., Greenwich, 1974, sowc, 1975. *Recreation:* iconoclasm (20th Century). *Address:* c/o National Westminster Bank Ltd, 30 Wellington Street, Aldershot, Hants GU11 1EB. *Club:* Royal Commonwealth Society.

SAUNDERS, Andrew Downing; Chief Inspector of Ancient Monuments and Historic Buildings, Department of the Environment, since 1973; *b* 22 Sept. 1931; *s* of Lionef Edward Saunders; *m* 1961, Hilary Jean (*née* Aikman); two *s* one *d. Educ:* Magdalen Coll. Sch., Oxford; Magdalen Coll., Oxford (MA). FSA. Joined Ancient Monuments Inspectorate, 1954; Inspector of Ancient Monuments for England, 1964. Vice-President: Cornwall Archaeol Soc.; Hendon and Dist Archaeol Soc.; Member: Adv. Cttee on Historic Wrecks; Cttee, Soc. for Medieval Archaeology; British and Exec. Cttees, Internat. Council of Monuments and Sites; Cttee for Aerial Photography, Cambridge Univ.; Cttee of Fortress Study Gp; Council for British Archaeology. *Publications:* ed jtly and contrib., Ancient Monuments and their Interpretation, 1977; excavation reports, articles on castles and artillery

fortification in various archæological and historical jls. *Address:* 9 Somerset Road, New Barnet, Herts. *T:* 01-449 7101. *Club:* Athenæum.

SAUNDERS, Basil; Director-General, Association of Special Libraries and Information Bureaux, 1978–80; *b* 12 Aug. 1925; *s* of late Comdr J. E. Saunders, RN and Marjorie Saunders; *m* 1957, Betty Smith; two *s* four *d. Educ:* Merchant Taylors'; Wadham Coll., Oxford (MA). FIPR. Sub-Lt, RNVR, 1944–46. Assistant d'Anglais, Collège de Tarascon, 1950–51; Writer, General Electric Co. (USA), 1952–53; PRO, BIM, 1954–57; Public Relations Exec., Pritchard, Wood and Partners, 1957–63; Head of Public Relations Services, Wellcome Foundn Ltd, 1963–78; Public Relations Officer, Arts Council, 1981. *Publications:* Crackle of Thorns (verse), 1968; short stories in magazines and on radio; backpagers in Manchester Guardian; reviews, articles, etc. *Recreation:* throwing things away. *Address:* 18 Dartmouth Park Avenue, NW5 1JN. *T:* 01-485 4672. *Club:* Savile.

SAUNDERS, Christopher John, MA; Headmaster, Eastbourne College, since 1981; *b* 7 May 1940; *s* of R. H. Saunders and G. S. Saunders (*née* Harris); *m* 1973, Cynthia Elizabeth Stiles; one *s* one *d. Educ:* Lancing Coll.; Fitzwilliam Coll., Cambridge (MA); CertEd Wadham Coll., Oxford. Assistant Master, Bradfield College, 1964–80 (Housemaster, 1972–80). Mem. Council, FA. *Recreations:* soccer (Oxford Blue 1963), cricket (Oxford Blue 1964), theatre, people. *Address:* Headmaster's House, Eastbourne College, Eastbourne, East Sussex BN21 4JX. *Clubs:* MCC, Free Foresters; Hawks (Cambridge).

SAUNDERS, Christopher Thomas, CMG 1953; Professorial Fellow, Sussex European Research Centre (until 1978, Centre for Contemporary European Studies), University of Sussex, since 1973; *b* 5 Nov. 1907; *s* of Thomas Beckenn Avening Saunders, clergyman, and Mary Theodora Slater; *m* 1947, Cornelia Jacomijntje Gielstra; one *s. Educ:* Craig School, Windermere; St Edward's School; Christ Church, Oxford. BA 1929; MA 1932; University of Liverpool: Social Survey of Merseyside, 1930–33; University of Manchester: Economic Research Dept, 1933–35; Joint Committee of Cotton Trade Organisations, Manchester, 1935–40; Cotton Control, 1940–44; Combined Production and Resources Board, Washington, 1944–45; Min. of Labour, 1945–47; Central Statistical Office, 1947–57; Dir, Nat. Inst. of Econ. and Social Research, 1957–64; Economist, UN Econ. Commn for Europe, 1965–72. *Publications:* Red Oxford (with M. P. Ashley), 1929; Social Survey of Merseyside (collaborated in), 1934; Seasonal Variations in Employment, 1936; From Free Trade to Integration?, 1975; Winners and Losers, 1977; Engineering in Britain, West Germany and France, 1978; (ed) East and West in the Energy Squeeze, 1980; (with D. Marsden) Pay Inequalities in the European Community, 1981; (ed) East-West-South: Economic Interactions Between Three Worlds, 1981; (ed) The Political Economy of New and Old Industrial Countries, 1981; articles in Economic Jl, Jl of Roy. Statistical Soc., The Manchester School. *Recreations:* walking and other forms of travel; painting. *Address:* Sussex European Research Centre, University of Sussex, Brighton BN1 9RF. *Club:* Reform.

SAUNDERS, Dame Cicely (Mary Strode), DBE 1980 (OBE 1967); FRCP; Medical Director, St Christopher's Hospice, since 1967; *b* 22 June 1918; *d* of Gordon Saunders and Mary Christian Knight; *m* 1980, Prof. Marian Bohusz-Szyszko, *s* of Antoni Bohusz-Szyszko, Wilno, Poland. *Educ:* Roedean Sch.; St Anne's Coll., Oxford; St Thomas's Hosp. Med. Sch.; Nightingale Sch. of Nursing. SRN 1944; MB, BS, 1957; MA 1960 (BA (war degree) 1945). FRCP 1974 (MRCP 1968); FRCN 1981. Founded St Christopher's Hospice, 1967 (St Christopher's has been a Registered Charity since 1961 and was opened as a Hospice in 1967). Mem., MRC, 1976–79; Dep. Chm., Attendance Allowance Bd, 1979. AIMSW 1947; Hon. DSc Yale, 1969; Dr of Medicine, Lambeth, 1977; DUniv Open, 1978; Hon. LLD Columbia, NY, 1979; DHL Jewish Theological Seminary of America, 1982. Gold Medal, Soc. of Apothecaries of London, 1979. Templeton Foundation Prize, 1981. *Publications:* Care of the Dying, 1960, 2nd edn 1977; (ed) The Management of Terminal Disease, 1978; (ed jtly) Hospice: the living idea, 1981; various papers on terminal care. *Recreations:* music, bird watching, Polish art. *Address:* St Christopher's Hospice, 51–53 Lawrie Park Road, Sydenham, SE26 6DZ. *T:* 01-778 9252.

SAUNDERS, David William; Parliamentary Counsel, since 1980; *b* 4 Nov. 1936; *s* of William Ernest Saunders and Lilian Grace (*née* Ward); *m* 1963, Margaret Susan Rose Bartholomew. *Educ:* Hornchurch Grammar Sch.; Worcester Coll., Oxford (MA). Admitted solicitor, 1964. Joined Office of Parly Counsel, 1970; Dep. Parly Counsel, 1978–80. *Recreations:* golf, bridge. *Address:* 2 West Warwick Place, SW1V 2DH. *T:* 01-828 8296. *Club:* United Oxford & Cambridge University.

SAUNDERS, Prof. Derek William; Professor of Polymer Physics and Engineering, Cranfield Institute of Technology, since 1967; Director, Science and Engineering Research Council/Department of Industry Teaching Company Scheme, since 1981; *b* 4 Dec. 1925; *s* of Alfred and Elizabeth Hannah Saunders; *m* 1949, Mahalah Harrison; three *s* two *d. Educ:* Morley Grammar Sch.; Imperial Coll., Univ. of London. PhD, ARCS, FInstP, FPRI, FIM. Building Res. Stn, Garston, 1945–47; British Rubber Producers Res. Assoc., 1947–51; Royal Instn, 1951–54; British Rayon Res. Assoc., 1954–60; Cranfield Inst. of Technology: Sen. Lectr 1960, subseq. Reader; Head of Materials Dept, 1969–81; Pro-Vice-Chancellor, 1973–76. Chm. Council, Plastics Inst., 1973–75; Chm. Council, Plastics and Rubber Inst., 1975–76;

Mem. Harpur Trust (Bedford Charity), 1968-. *Publications:* chapters in several books on polymeric materials; sci. papers in various learned jls. *Address:* 64 De Parys Avenue, Bedford. *T:* Bedford 53869.

SAUNDERS, Ernest Walter, FInstM; Managing Director, Arthur Guinness & Sons plc, since 1981; *b* 21 Oct. 1935; *m* 1963, Carole Ann Stephings; two *s* one *d. Educ:* Emmanuel Coll., Cambridge (MA). Man. Dir, Beecham Products Internat., and Dir, Beecham Products, 1966-73; Chm., European Div., Great Universal Stores, 1973-77; Pres., Nestlé Nutrition SA, and Mem. Management Cttee, Nestlé SA, Vevey, Switzerland, 1977-81. *Recreation:* skiing. *Address:* c/o Arthur Guinness & Sons plc, 10 Albemarle Street, W1X 4AJ. *T:* 01-493 6747. *Club:* Carlton.

SAUNDERS, Henry George Boulton; Organist and Choirmaster to the Hon. Society of Benchers at Gray's Inn; Organist and Master of the Choir to the Household Division; Area Inspector of Schools, Surrey County Council, 1962-78; *b* Devonport, Feb. 1914; *m* 1943, Kathleen Mary, *d* of Major S. Brandle, MC, London; one *s* two *d. Educ:* Grammar Sch., Kilburn; Royal Acad. of Music (Thomas Threlfall Organ Scholar). DMus Durham; BMus Durham and London; Grad. Royal Schs of Music, London, 1935; FRCO (La Fontaine prize, 1935); FRAM; Worshipful Company of Musicians Silver Medal, 1937; Organist and Choirmaster at St Saviour's, Hampstead, 1934-35; Music Master Trinity County Sch., Wood Green, 1935-46; Inspector of Secondary Schs, City of Leicester, 1946-62. *Publication:* Read and Sing, 1959. *Recreation:* gardening. *Address:* Court Farm, Pebworth, Stratford-upon-Avon, Warwicks CV37 8XW. *T:* Stratford 720428.

SAUNDERS, Air Chief Marshal Sir Hugh (William Lumsden), GCB 1953 (KCB 1950; CB 1943); KBE 1945 (CBE 1941); MC, DFC; MM; *b* 1894; *s* of Frederick William Saunders, Transvaal; *m* 1923, Phyllis Margaret (*d* 1980), *d* of Major P. W. Mabbett, Bidborough, Kent; one *s* (and one *s* decd). *Educ:* Marist Brothers' School, Johannesburg. Served European War, 1914-19, with Witwatersrand Rifles and South African Horse; transf. RFC 1917; Group Capt. 1939; Air Commodore, 1941; temp. Air Vice-Marshal, 1942; Air Marshal, 1947; Air Chief Marshal, 1950; Chief of Air Staff, New Zealand, 1939-41; AOC, No. 11 Group, Fighter Command, 1942-44; Director-General of Postings, Air Ministry, 1944-45; Air Marshal Commanding RAF Burma, 1945-46; AOC-in-C, Bomber Command, 1947; Air Council Member for Personnel, 1947-49; Inspector-General of the RAF, 1949-50; Commander-in-Chief Air Forces Western Europe, Jan.-April 1951. Air Deputy to Supreme Allied Commander Europe, 1951-53; Special Air Adviser to Royal Danish Air Force, 1954-56; Chief Co-ordinator of Anglo-American hospitality activities in UK, 1956-59. A Vice-Chm., Nat. Savings Cttee, 1956-70. Order of Polonia Restituta, 2nd Class (Poland); Commander Order of Merit (US); Officier Légion d'Honneur (France); Grand Cross of Dannebrog (Denmark). *Address:* c/o Barclays Bank International, 68 Knightsbridge, SW1X 7LW.

SAUNDERS, James; playwright; *b* Islington, 8 Jan. 1925; *s* of Walter Percival Saunders and Dorcas Geraldine (*née* Warren); *m* 1951, Audrey Cross; one *s* two *d. Educ:* Wembley County Sch.; Southampton Univ. *Plays:* Moonshine, 1955; Alas, Poor Fred, The Ark, 1959; Committal, Barnstable, Return to a City, 1960; A Slight Accident, 1961; Double Double, 1962; Next Time I'll Sing to You, The Pedagogue, Who Was Hilary Maconochie?, 1963; A Scent of Flowers, Neighbours, 1964; Triangle, Opus, 1965; A Man's Best Friend, The Borage Pigeon Affair, 1969; After Liverpool, 1970; Games, Savoury Meringue, 1971; Hans Kohlhaas, 1972; Bye Bye Blues, 1973; The Island, 1975; Bodies, 1977; Birdsong, 1979. *Stage adaptations :* The Italian Girl, 1968; The Travails of Sancho Panza, 1969; A Journey to London, 1975; Player Piano, 1978; Random Moments in a May Garden, 1980; The Girl in Melanie Klein, 1980; *television:* Watch Me I'm a Bird, 1964; Bloomers, 1979 (series); television adaptations of works by D. H. Lawrence, Henry James, H. E. Bates and R. F. Delderfield; *screenplay:* Sailor's Return. *Address:* c/o Margaret Ramsay Ltd, 14a Goodwin's Court, St Martin's Lane, WC2.

SAUNDERS, Sir John (Anthony Holt), Kt 1972; CBE 1970; DSO 1945; MC 1944; formerly Chairman and Chief Manager, Hongkong and Shanghai Banking Corporation, 1962-72; *b* 29 July 1917; *s* of late E. B. Saunders; *m* 1942, Enid Mary Durant Cassidy; two *d. Educ:* Bromsgrove Sch. Joined The Hongkong and Shanghai Banking Corp., 1937. War Service, 1940-45; OCTU Sandhurst (Belt of Honour); N Africa, Sicily and Italy. Lived in Hong Kong 1950-72; MEC Hong Kong Govt, 1966-72. Chm. of Stewards, Royal Hong Kong Jockey Club, 1967-72. Hon. DSocSc (Hong Kong) 1969. Comdr. Order of Prince Henry the Navigator (Portugal), 1966. *Address:* The Dairy House, Maresfield Park, Uckfield, East Sussex. *Clubs:* MCC, Oriental.

SAUNDERS, Maj.-Gen. Kenneth, CB 1979; OBE 1970; Paymaster in Chief and Inspector of Army Pay Services, 1975-79, retired; *b* 1 Jan. 1920; *m* 1953, Ann Lawrence Addison; one *s. Educ:* Lancastrian Sch., Shrewsbury. Enlisted King's Shropshire LI, 1939; commnd Royal Welch Fus., 1940; served in France, Belgium, Holland and Germany (despatches 1945); various staff appts, NW Europe and Far East, 1945-52; transf. to RAPC, 1952; Staff Paymaster: WO 1962-63; HQ Div./Malaya, 1965-67; MoD, 1967-70; Chief Paymaster: MoD, 1970-71; 1 British Corps, 1971-72; Dep. Paymaster in Chief, 1972-75; Maj.-Gen. 1975; Col Comdt, RAPC, 1979-. *Recreations:* fishing, travel. *Address:* 31 Prestonville Court, Dyke Road, Brighton BN1 3UG. *T:* Brighton 28866.

SAUNDERS, Kenneth Herbert; Chief Architect, Commission for the New Towns, since 1976; *b* 5 April 1915; *s* of William James Saunders and Anne Elizabeth Baker; *m* 1940, Kathleen Bettye Fortune (*d* 1981); one *s* one *d. Educ:* elementary sch., Worthing; Sch. of Art, Worthing; Brighton Coll. of Art. ARIBA 1940. Served War: RA Iraq and Persia; OCTU Bengal Sappers and Miners, India and Burma; Major RE ALFSEA, SORE II, 1940 (mentioned in despatches). Articled pupil, 1933; Dept of Architecture, Bor. of Worthing, 1936; City Architect's Dept, Portsmouth, 1937-39, 1946-49; Crawley Develt Corporation: Architect, 1949; Sen. Architect, 1952; Asst Chief Architect, 1958; Commission for New Towns: Asst Chief Architect, 1962; Exec. Architect, 1965; Manager (Crawley), 1978-80. *Recreations:* architecture, buildings. *Address:* Longthorpe, 22 Goffs Park Road, Crawley, West Sussex. *T:* Crawley 21334.

SAUNDERS, Sir Owen (Alfred), Kt 1965; FRS 1958; MA, DSc; Hon. FIMechE; FInstP; FInstF; FRAeS; Hon. FCGI; Life Member of ASME; Emeritus Professor of Mechanical Engineering, University of London, Imperial College (Professor, 1946; Head of Department, 1946-65; Pro-Rector, 1964-67, Acting Rector, 1966-67); Vice-Chancellor, University of London, 1967-69; *b* 24 September 1904; *s* of Alfred George Saunders and Margaret Ellen Jones; *m* 1st, 1935, Marion Isabel McKechney (*d* 1981); one *s* two *d* ; 2nd, 1981, Mrs Daphne Holmes. *Educ:* Emanuel School; Birkbeck College, London; Trinity College, Cambridge (Senior Scholar). Scientific Officer, Dept of Scientific and Industrial Research, 1926; Lecturer in Applied Mathematical Physics, Imperial College, 1932; Clothworkers' Reader in Applied Thermodynamics, Univ. of London, 1937; on loan to Directorate of Turbine Engines, MAP, 1942-45. Dean, City and Guilds Coll., 1955-64. Past Pres., IMechE; Mem., ITA, 1964-69; President: British Flame Research Cttee; Section G, British Assoc., 1959; Chm. Council, Royal Holloway Coll., 1971-. Founder Fellow, Fellowship of Engineering, 1976. Honorary Member: Yugoslav Acad., 1959-; Japan Soc. of Mechanical Engrs, 1960-; ASME, 1961-; For. Assoc., Nat. Acad. of Engrg, USA, 1979. Hon. DSc Strathclyde, 1964. Melchett medallist, Inst. of Fuel, 1962; Max Jakob Award, ASME, 1966. Hon. Mem., Mark Twain Soc., 1976. *Publications:* The Calculation of Heat Transmission, 1932; An Introduction to Heat Transfer, 1950; various scientific and technical papers in Proceedings of Royal Society, Phil. Mag., Physical Society, Engineering, and the Institutions. *Recreations:* music, golf. *Address:* Oakbank, Sea Lane, Middleton, Sussex. *T:* Middleton 2966. *Club:* Athenæum.

SAUNDERS, Sir Peter, Kt 1982; Chairman and Managing Director: Peter Saunders Properties; Peter Saunders Ltd; Peter Saunders Theatres Ltd; Volcano Productions Ltd; Director: Kroy Investments Ltd; Hampdale Ltd; West End Theatre Managers Ltd; Dominfast Investments Ltd; Duke of York's Theatre Ltd; Theatre Investment Fund Ltd (Vice-Chairman); Theatre Investment Finance Ltd; *b* 23 Nov. 1911; *s* of Ernest and Aletta Saunders; *m* 1st, 1959, Ann Stewart (*d* 1976); no *c;* 2nd, 1979, Catherine Baylis (Kate Boyle); no *c. Educ:* Oundle Sch.; Lausanne. Film cameraman, film director, journalist and press agent; served War of 1939-45 (Captain); started in theatrical production, 1947; has presented over 100 plays incl. The Mousetrap, which has run for more than 30 years (world's longest ever run, Dec. 1971); other West End productions include: Fly Away Peter; The Perfect Woman; Breach of Marriage; My Mother Said; The Hollow; Witness for the Prosecution; The Manor of Northstead; Spider's Web; The Water Gipsies; The Bride and the Bachelor; Subway in the Sky; Verdict; The Trial of Mary Dugan; The Unexpected Guest; A Day in the Life Of; And Suddenly it's Spring; Go Back For Murder; You Prove It; Fit To Print; Rule of Three; Alfie; The Reluctant Peer; Hostile Witness; Every Other Evening; Return Ticket; Arsenic and Old Lace; Justice Is A Woman; As You Like It; Oh Clarence!; On A Foggy Day; The Jockey Club Stakes; Move Over Mrs Markham; Lover; Cockie; Double Edge; A Murder is Announced; The Family Reunion; Cards On The Table; in 1971 acquired Volcano Productions Ltd., whose productions include No Sex Please, We're British; The Mating Game; Lloyd George Knew My Father; At The End Of The Day; Touch Of Spring; Betzi; operated repertory at Royal Artillery Theatre, Woolwich, 1951, and at Prince of Wales Theatre, Cardiff, 1956; has produced more than 1500 programmes for Radio Luxembourg; owns Vaudeville Theatre and controls St Martin's; an original Dir, Yorkshire Television; Mem. consortium awarded London Gen. Radio Station by IBA, which became Capital Radio, 1973. Vice-Pres., Actors' Benevolent Fund, 1972-; Mem. Exec. Council, SWET, 1954- (Pres. 1961-62 and 1967-69); Mem. Council, Theatrical Managers' Assoc., 1958-64; Pres., Stage Golfing Soc., 1963; Pres., Stage Cricket Club, 1956-65. Silver Heart award, Variety Club of GB, 1955. *Publications:* The Mousetrap Man (autobiog.), 1972; Scales of Justice (play), 1978. *Recreations:* cricket, chess, bridge, photography, music of George Gershwin, telephoning. *Address:* Vaudeville Theatre Offices, 10 Maiden Lane, WC2E 7NA. *T:* 01-240 3177.

SAUNDERS, Raymond; Secretary, British Museum (Natural History), since 1976; *b* 24 July 1933; *s* of late Herbert Charles Saunders and Doris May (*née* Kirkham-Jones); *m* 1959, Shirley Marion (*née* Stringer); two *s. Educ:* Poole Grammar Sch. WO, 1950; Air Min., 1956; Min. of Land and Natural Resources, 1966; Land Commn, 1967; Treasury, 1968; CSD, 1969. *Recreations:* reading biographies, gardening, sport (now mainly as spectator). *Address:* c/o British Museum (Natural History), Cromwell Road, SW7.

SAUNDERS, Prof. Wilfred Leonard, CBE 1982; FLA; Director, University of Sheffield Postgraduate School of Librarianship and Information Science,

1963-82, now Professor Emeritus; *b* 18 April 1920; *s* of Leonard and Annie Saunders; *m* 1946, Joan Mary Rider; two *s*. *Educ:* King Edward's Grammar Sch. for Boys, Camp Hill, Birmingham; Fitzwilliam House, Univ. of Cambridge (MA). FLA 1952. Served War: France, 1940; N Africa, 1942-43; Italy, 1943-46; Captain Royal Signals. Library Asst, Birmingham Reference Library, 1936-39; Dep. Lib., Inst. of Bankers, 1948-49; Lib., Univ. of Birmingham Inst. of Educn, 1949-56; Dep. Lib., Univ. of Sheffield, 1956-63; 12 months' secondment to UNESCO as Expert in Educnl Documentation, Uganda, 1962; Univ. of Sheffield: Prof. of Librarianship and Inf. Science, 1968; Dean, Faculty of Educnl Studies, 1974-77. Vis. Prof., Pittsburgh Univ. Grad. Sch. of Library and Inf. Sciences, 1968; Commonwealth Vis. Fellow, Australia, 1969; (1st) Elsie O. and Philip Sang Internat. Lectr, Rosary Grad. Sch. of Library Science, USA, 1974. UK Rep., Internat. Fedn for Documentation/Training of Documentalists Cttee, 1966-70; Hon. Consultant, E Africa Sch. of Librarianship, Makerere Univ., 1967-73; overseas consultancy and adv. missions. Pres., Library Assoc., 1980; Member: Council, ASLIB, 1965-71, 1972-78; British Council, 1970- (Mem., Libraries Adv. Panel, 1970-; Chm. 1975-81); Bd of Librarianship, CNAA, 1966-79; Library Adv. Council (England), 1970-73; Adv. Cttee, British Library Ref. Div., 1975-80; *ad hoc* Cttee on Educn and Trng (Gen. Inf. Prog.), UNESCO, 1978-; Chairman: Jt Consultative Cttee of Library Assoc., Aslib, SCONUL, Soc. of Archivists and IInfSc, 1980-81; Library and Information Services Council (formerly Library Adv. Council for Eng.), 1981-. Hon. FIInfSc 1977. *Publications:* (ed) The Provision and Use of Library and Documentation Services, 1966; (ed) Librarianship in Britain Today, 1967; (with H. Schur and Lisbeth J. Pargeter) Education and Training for Scientific and Technological Library and Information Work, 1968; (ed) University and Research Library Studies, 1968; (with W. J. Hutchins and Lisbeth J. Pargeter) The Language Barrier: a study in depth of the place of foreign language materials in the research activity of an academic community, 1971; (ed) British Librarianship Today, 1977; Guidelines for Curriculum Development in Information Studies, 1978; jl articles and res. reports. *Recreations:* gardening, walking, listening to music, book collecting. *Address:* 12 Whiteley Wood Road, Sheffield S11 7FE. *Club:* National Liberal (non-political mem.).

SAUNDERS-JACOBS, Brig. John Conrad, CBE 1945; DSO 1944; Indian Army, retired; *b* 12 Nov. 1900; *s* of George Saunders-Jacobs; *m* 1930, Sylvia, *e d* of Col H. Drury Shaw, DSO; one *d*. *Educ:* University College, London; RMC, Sandhurst. Joined Royal Garhwal Rifles in India, 1921; Co. comd, RMC, Sandhurst, 1937-38; Bt Major, 1938; War of 1939-45: GSO1, NWF, India, 1941-42; bn, bde and actg div. comdr, Middle East, Italy and Greece, 1942-46. Staff Coll., Quetta, 1934-35; Imperial Defence Coll., London, 1946; Asst Comdt, Staff Coll., Quetta, 1947; GHQ India, Dir of Mil. Operations, Delhi, 1947; retired Indian Army, 1948. FO UK delegate to UN Special Cttee on the Balkans, 1948; Official mil. historian, Cabinet Office, 1949-50; export agent, London, 1950-53; RO II, War Office, 1954; landscape gardener, 1955-57; govt service in Mins of Defence, Aviation and Technology, 1958-71. *Recreations:* walking, gardening, current affairs. *Address:* Firlands, West Chiltington, Pulborough, West Sussex. *T:* West Chiltington 3197.

SAUNDERS WATSON, Comdr Leslie Michael Macdonald, RN (retired); DL; President, Historic Houses Association, since 1982 (Deputy President, 1978-82); *b* 9 Oct. 1934; *s* of Captain L. S. Saunders, DSO, RN (retd), and Elizabeth Saunders (*née* Culme-Seymour); *m* 1958, Georgina Elizabeth Laetitia, *d* of Adm. Sir William Davis, *qv*; two *s* one *d*. *Educ:* Eton; BRNC, Dartmouth. Joined Royal Navy, 1951; specialised in Communications (Jackson Everett Prize); Comdr 1969; retired, 1971, on succession to Rockingham Castle Estate. Chairman: Historic Houses Assoc. Tax and Parliamentary Cttee, 1975-; Northamptonshire Assoc. Youth Clubs, 1977-; Heritage Educn Year, 1977; Corby Community Adv. Gp, 1979-; Ironstone Royalty Owners Assoc., 1979-; Vice-Chm., Northamptonshire Small Industries Cttee, 1974-79; Member: Executive and Taxation Cttees, CLA, 1975-; British Heritage Cttee, 1978-; Northamptonshire Branch, CLA, 1981-; Director: Lamport Hall Preservation Trust, 1978-; English Sinfonietta, 1980. Chm., Governors Lodge Park Comprehensive Sch., 1977-; Trustee, Oakham Sch., 1975-77. High Sheriff, 1978-79, DL 1979-, Northamptonshire. *Recreations:* sailing, music. *Address:* Rockingham Castle, Market Harborough, Leicestershire LE16 8TH. *T:* Rockingham 770240/770326. *Club:* Naval and Military.

SAUVAGNARGUES, Jean Victor; Commander, Légion d'Honneur, Croix de Guerre avec palme (1939-45); Hon. GCMG 1976; Commander of the National Order of Merit; French Ambassador; former Foreign Minister; *b* Paris, 2 April 1915; *s* of Edmond Sauvagnargues and Alice Caplan; *m* 1948, Lise Marie L'Evesque; two *s* two *d*. *Educ:* Higher Normal Sch.; Dip., Political Science Sch.; Univ. (German) (Agrégé). Attaché, Embassy, Bucharest, 1941. Served War with Free French Forces, 1943 (Army, June 1944-May 1945). Cabinet of: the High Commn, Beirut, 1943; M Massigli, 1944; Gen. de Gaulle, 1945-46; Specialist on German questions, Quai d'Orsay, 1947-55; Cabinet of M Pinay, 1955. In negotiations about the Saar, Jan.-June 1956. Ambassador to: Ethiopia, 1956-60; Tunisia, 1962-70. Director, African and Middle-Eastern Affairs, Min. of Foreign Affairs, 1960-62. Ambassador to the Federal Republic of Germany, Bonn, 1970-74; Minister for Foreign Affairs, France, 1974-76; Ambassadeur de France, 1976; Ambassador to UK, 1977-81. *Address:* 14 avenue Pierre 1er de Serbie, 75116 Paris, France.

SAUVE, Hon. Jeanne, PC (Can.) 1972; MP (L) for Montreal Laval-les-Rapides (formerly Montreal-Ahuntsic), Canada, since 1972; Speaker of the

House of Commons, since 1980; *b* 26 April 1922; *d* of Charles Albert Benoit and Mrs Anna Vaillant; *m* 1948, Hon. Maurice Sauvé; one *s*. *Educ:* Notre-Dame du Rosaire Convent, Ottawa; Ottawa Univ.; Paris Univ. Journalist; Founder, Youth Movements Fedn, 1947; Asst to Dir of Youth Section, UNESCO, Paris, 1951; Union des Artistes, Montreal: Mem., Admin. Council, 1961-72; Deleg. to Film and TV Writers Congress, Moscow, 1968; Vice-Pres., 1968-70; Sec. Gen., Fédération des Auteurs et des Artistes du Canada, 1966-72; Minister of State for Science and Technol., 1972-74; Minister of the Environment, 1974-75; Minister of Communications, 1975-79; Advisor to Sec. of State for External Affairs for relations with the French-speaking world, 1978. Pres., Canadian Inst. of Public Affairs, 1964 (Vice-Pres., 1962-64); Founding Mem., Inst. of Political Res., 1972; Member: Centennial Commn, 1967; Admin. Council, YMCA, 1969-72. Hon. DSc New Brunswick, 1974; Hon. LLD Calgary, 1982. *Recreations:* cultivating flowers and plants, reading, tennis. *Address:* Room 222-N, Centre Block, House of Commons, Ottawa, Ont K1A 0A6, Canada. *T:* (613) 992-5042.

SAUZIER, Sir (André) Guy, Kt 1973; CBE 1959; ED; retired General Overseas Representative of Mauritius Chamber of Agriculture, 1959-79; Minister Plenipotentiary, Mauritius Mission to EEC, 1972-79; *b* 20 Oct. 1910; *s* of J. Adrien Sauzier, Mauritius; *m* 1936, Thérèse, *d* of Henri Mallac; six *s* two *d*. *Educ:* Royal Coll., Mauritius. Served War of 1939-45; late Major, Mauritius TF. A nominated Member of the Legislative Council, Mauritius, 1949-57; Member, Mauritius Political Delegn to the UK, 1955; Minister of Works and Communications, 1957-59. Represented Mauritius at the Coronation, 1953. *Address:* c/o Glen House, Stag Place, SW1E 5AQ. *Clubs:* Athenæum; Cercle Royal Gaulois (Brussels).

SAVA, George; (George Alexis Milkomanovich Milkomane); Author and Consulting Surgeon; *b* 15 Oct. 1903; *s* of Col Ivan Alexandrovitch and Countess Maria Ignatiev; *nephew* of Prince Alexander Milkomanovich Milkomane; *m* 1939, Jannette Hollingdale; two *s* two *d*. *Educ:* Public Schools in Bulgaria and Russia. Entered Russian Imperial Naval Academy in 1913; after the Revolution studied in various medical schools, Univ. of Paris, Florence, Rome, Munich, Berlin and Bonn; domiciled in this country since 1932; further medical education at Manchester, Glasgow and Edinburgh; naturalised British subject in 1938; Research scholarships in medicine and surgery, University of Rome, Libero Docente (Professorship) of Univ. of Rome, 1954. Grand Chev. of the Crown of Bulgaria; Commendatore dell' Ordine al Merito Della Repubblica Italiana, 1961. *Publications: autobiog. medical:* The Healing Knife, 1937; Beauty from the Surgeon's Knife, 1938; A Surgeon's Destiny, 1939; Donkey's Serenade, 1940; Twice the Clock Round, 1941; A Ring at the Door, 1941; Surgeon's Symphony, 1944; They come by Appointment, 1946; The Knife Heals Again, 1948; The Way of a Surgeon, 1949; Strange Cases, 1950; A Doctor's Odyssey, 1951; Patients' Progress, 1952; A Surgeon Remembers, 1953; Surgeon Under Capricorn, 1954; The Lure of Surgery, 1955; A Surgeon at Large, 1957; Surgery and Crime, 1957; All this and Surgery too, 1958; Surgery Holds the Door, 1960; A Surgeon in Rome, 1961; A Surgeon in California, 1962; Appointments in Rome, 1963; A Surgeon in New Zealand, 1964; A Surgeon in Cyprus, 1965; A Surgeon in Australia, 1966; Sex, Surgery, People, 1967; The Gates of Heaven are Narrow, 1968; Bitter-Sweet Surgery, 1969; One Russian's Story, 1970; A Stranger in Harley Street, 1970; A Surgeon and his Knife, 1978; Living with your Psoriasis (essays), 1978; *political and historical books:* Rasputin Speaks, 1941; Valley of Forgotten People, 1942; The Chetniks, 1943; School for War, 1943; They Stayed in London, 1943; Russia Triumphant, 1944; A Tale of Ten Cities, 1944; War Without Guns, 1944; Caught by Revolution, 1952; *novels:* Land Fit for Heroes, 1945; Link of Two Hearts, 1945; Gissy, 1946; Call it Life, 1946; Boy in Samarkand, 1950; Flight from the Palace, 1953; Pursuit in the Desert, 1955; The Emperor Story, 1959; Punishment Deferred, 1966; Man Without Label, 1967; Alias Dr Holtzman, 1968; City of Cain, 1969; The Imperfect Surgeon, 1969; Nothing Sacred, 1970; Of Guilt Possessed, 1970; A Skeleton for My Mate, 1971; The Beloved Nemesis, 1971; On the Wings of Angels, 1972; The Sins of Andrea, 1972; Tell Your Grief Softly, 1972; Cocaine for Breakfast, 1973; Return from the Valley, 1973; Sheilah of Buckleigh Manor, 1974; Every Sweet Hath Its Sour, 1974; The Way of the Healing Knife, 1976; Mary Mary Quite Contrary, 1977; Crusader's Clinic, 1977; Pretty Polly, 1977; No Man is Perfect, 1978; A Stranger in his Skull, 1979; Secret Surgeon, 1979; Crimson Eclipse, 1980; also wrote numerous novels as George Borodin. *Recreations:* tennis, golf, riding, aviation. *Address:* c/o A. P. Watt Ltd, 26/28 Bedford Row, WC1R 4HL.

SAVAGE, Albert Walter, CMG 1954; Director-General (retired), Colonial Civil Aviation Service; *b* 12 June 1898; *s* of William Albert Savage, Wheathampstead, Herts; *m* 1923, Lilian Marie Gertrude Storch; one *s* one *d*. *Educ:* Northern Polytechnic, Northampton Institute and Sheffield University. Apprentice, Grahame White Flying School, 1914-16. Served European War, 1914-18, RFC, 1916 to end of war. Aeronautical Inspection Directorate, Air Ministry, UK 1921-34, India, 1934-36; seconded to Egyptian Govt as Chief Technical Inspector, Civil Aviation Dept, Cairo, 1936-46; Colonial Civil Aviation Service, 1946-; Director of Civil Aviation, W Africa, 1946-49; Director-General of Civil Aviation, Malaya/Borneo territories, 1949-54; Civil Aviation Adviser, Government of Jordan, 1954-55; Director of Civil Aviation, Leeward and Windward Islands, 1956-60. Director of Civil Aviation, Sierra Leone, 1961-62. *Recreations:* golf, tennis and squash. *Address:* White Cottage, 29 Wrestwood Avenue, Willingdon, Eastbourne. *T:* Eastbourne 53708.

SAVAGE, Anthony, CB 1980; Chief Executive, Intervention Board for Agricultural Produce, 1972-80; *b* 23 Aug. 1920; *s* of late Edmund Savage and Dorothy Mary (*née* Gray); *m* 1945, Heather Mary (*née* Templeman); one *s* three *d. Educ:* Johnston Sch., Durham. Entered Min. of Agriculture, 1937. War Service, Royal Artillery, 1939-46: Middle East, Italy and NW Europe, 1940-46; commnd 1943; despatches 1945. Asst Principal, MAFF, 1947; Principal, 1951; Cabinet Office, 1951-53; Asst Sec., 1961; Regional Controller, E Midland Region, 1964-69; Head of Land Drainage Div., 1969-71; Under-Sec., 1972. *Address:* 112 Powys Lane, Palmers Green, N13 4HR. *T:* 01-886 0839.

SAVAGE, Sir Ernest (Walter), Kt 1979; FCA; company director; *b* 24 Aug. 1912; *s* of Walter Edwin Savage and Constance Mary Sutton; *m* 1938, Dorothy Winifred Nicholls; one *s* one *d. Educ:* Brisbane Grammar School; Scots Coll., Warwick, Qld. In public practice as chartered accountant, 1940-76; retd as Sen. Partner of Coopers & Lybrand, Queensland. Chairman, Bank of Queensland, 1960-; board member of several other public companies and statutory bodies. Institute of Chartered Accountants in Australia: Mem. Queensland State Council, 1951-74 (Chm. three years); Nat. Council, 1961-73; Aust. Pres., 1968-70; elected Life Member, 1978. Hon. Consul for Norway at Brisbane, 1950-76. Member: Bd of Governors, Cromwell Univ. Coll., 1950-77 (Chm. 1958-67); Faculty of Commerce and Economics, Univ. of Queensland, 1960-67; Bd of Advanced Education (Finance Cttee 1974, Chm. 1978-). Knight 1st class, Order of St Olav (Norway), 1966. *Recreation:* brick and concrete work. *Address:* 12 Mount Ommaney Drive, Jindalee, Brisbane, Queensland 4074, Australia. *T:* 07-376.1086. *Clubs:* Queensland, Brisbane (Brisbane).

SAVAGE, Rt. Rev. Gordon David, MA; *b* 14 April 1915; *s* of Augustus Johnson Savage and Louisa Hannah Atkinson; *m* 1st, Eva Louise, *y d* of H. J. Jessen, Copenhagen; one *s* two *d* ; 2nd, Ammanda Lovejoy; one *s. Educ:* Reading Sch.; Tyndale Hall, Bristol; St Catherine's, Oxford. MA Oxon, 1949. Was a Librarian before ordination, 1932-37; deacon, 1940, priest, 1941; Chaplain, Lecturer and Tutor, Tyndale Hall, Bristol, 1940-44; General Secretary Church Society, London, 1945-52; Curate-in-Charge of the City Church, Oxford, 1948-52; Proctor in Convocation, 1951-61; Vicar of Marston, Oxford, 1952-57; Archdeacon of Buckingham and Vicar of Whitchurch, Bucks, 1957-61; Suffragan Bishop of Buckingham, 1960-64; Bishop of Southwell, 1964-70. Mem., Imperial Constantinian Military Order of St George. *Address:* Hinton House, Peterchurch, Hereford HR2 0SH.

SAVARESE, Signora Fernando; *see* Elvin, Violetta.

SAVERNAKE, Viscount; Thomas James Brudenell-Bruce; *b* 11 Feb. 1982; *s* and *heir* of Earl of Cardigan, *qv.*

SAVILE, family name of **Earl of Mexborough.**

SAVILE, 3rd Baron, *cr* 1888; **George Halifax Lumley-Savile;** DL; JP; *b* 2 Jan. 1919; *s* of 2nd Baron and Esme Grace Virginia (*d* 1958), *d* of J. Wolton; *S* father, 1931. *Educ:* Eton. Served in 1939-45 War in Duke of Wellington's Regiment, and attached Lincolnshire Regiment during the Burma Campaigns. DL W Yorks, 1954. Is Patron of two livings. Owns about 18,000 acres. JP Borough of Dewsbury, 1955. CStJ 1982. *Recreations:* music and shooting. *Heir: b* Hon. Henry Leoline Thornhill Lumley-Savile [*b* 2 Oct. 1923; *m* 1st, 1946, Presiley June (marr. diss. 1951), *o d* of Major G. H. E. Inchbald, Halebourne House, Chobham, Surrey; one *s* ; 2nd, 1961, Caroline Jeffie (*d* 1970), *o d* of Peter Clive, California, USA, and Elizabeth Clive, 58 Queens' Gate, SW7; 3rd, 1972, Margaret, *widow* of Peter Bruce; three *s* (triplets). Served War of 1939-45, in Grenadier Guards, Italy (wounded)]. *Address:* Gryce Hall, Shelley, Huddersfield. *T:* Huddersfield 602774; Walshaw, Hebden Bridge, Yorks. *T:* Hebden Bridge 842275. *Club:* Brooks's.

SAVILE, Jimmy, OBE 1971; TV and radio personality; *b* 31 Oct. 1926. *Educ:* St Anne's, Leeds. Man of many parts but best known as a voluntary helper at Leeds Infirmary, Broadmoor Hospital, and Stoke Mandeville where he raised ten million pounds to rebuild the National Spinal Injuries Centre. Hon. KCSG (Holy See), 1982; Bronze and Gold medals, SMO, St John of Jerusalem. *Publications:* As It Happens (autobiog.), 1975; Love is an Uphill Thing (autobiog.), 1975; God'll Fix It, 1978. *Recreations:* running, cycling, wrestling. *Address:* c/o General Infirmary, Leeds LS1 3EX. *T:* Leeds 432 799.

SAVILL, David Malcolm, QC 1969; a Recorder of the Crown Court, since 1972; *b* 18 Sept. 1930; *s* of late Lionel and of Lisbeth Savill; *m* 1955, Mary Arnott (*née* Eadie), JP, *d* of late Lady Hinchcliffe and step *d* of late Hon. Sir (George) Raymond Hinchcliffe; one *s* two *d. Educ:* Marlborough Coll.; Clare Coll., Cambridge. 2nd Lieut Grenadier Guards, 1949-50. BA (Hons) Cambridge, 1953. Called to the Bar, Middle Temple, 1954; Mem., Senate of Inns of Court and the Bar, 1976; Master of the Bench, 1977; Chancellor, diocese of Bradford, 1976-; Leader, NE Circuit, 1980-. Chm., Adv. Cttee on Conscientious Objectors, 1978-. *Recreations:* cricket, golf, gardening. *Address:* The Priory, Knaresborough, North Yorks HG5 8HX. *T:* Harrogate 862309. *Clubs:* MCC; Leeds (Leeds).

SAVILL, Colonel Kenneth Edward, CVO 1976; DSO 1945; DL; Member, HM Bodyguard of Hon. Corps of Gentlemen at Arms, 1955-76 (Lieutenant, 1973-76; Standard Bearer, 1972-73); *b* 8 August 1906; *o s* of Walter Savill,

Chilton Manor, Alresford and May, *d* of Major Charles Marriott; *m* 1935, Jacqueline (*d* 1980), *o d* of Brig. John Salusbury Hughes, MC; two *d* (and one *d* decd). *Educ:* Winchester College; RMC Sandhurst. Commissioned, 12th Royal Lancers, 1926; 1st King's Dragoon Guards, 1936; The Queen's Bays, 1947. Served War of 1939-45, France, 1939-40; N Africa and Italy, 1943-45. Comd 12th Green Howards (TA), 1943; comd 12th Royal Lancers, 1944-45; comd Queen's Bays, 1947-50; Col 1950; retd 1953. Chm., The Sunnygama Co. Ltd, 1957; Dir, Mid Southern Water Co., 1964-77. CC Hampshire, 1961-74; High Sheriff of Hampshire, 1961; DL Hampshire, 1965. Col, 1st The Queen's Dragoon Guards, 1964-68. *Address:* Chilton Manor, Alresford, Hants. *T:* Preston Candover 246. *Club:* Cavalry and Guards.

SAVILLE, Prof. John; Emeritus Professor of Economic and Social History, University of Hull; *b* 2 April 1916; *o s* of Orestes Stamatopoulos, Volos, Greece, and Edith Vessey (name changed by deed poll to that of step-father, 1937); *m* 1943, Constance Betty Saunders; three *s* one *d. Educ:* Royal Liberty Sch.; London Sch. of Economics. 1st Cl. Hons BSc (Econ) 1937. Served War, RA, 1940-46; Chief Scientific Adviser's Div., Min. of Works, 1946-47; Univ. of Hull, 1947-82. Mem., British Communist Party, 1934-56; Chm., Oral Hist. Soc., 1976-; Vice-Chm., and then Chm., Soc. for Study of Labour Hist., 1974-82; Mem. Exec. Cttee and Founder-Mem., Council for Academic Freedom and Democracy, 1971-81, Chm. 1982-; Chm., Economic and Social Hist. Cttee, SSRC, 1977-79. Trustee, Michael Lipman Trust, 1977-. *Publications:* Ernest Jones, Chartist, 1952; Rural Depopulation in England and Wales 1851-1951, 1957; numerous articles; Co-Editor: (with E. P. Thompson) Reasoner and New Reasoner, 1956-59; (with Asa Briggs) Essays in Labour History, 1960, 1971, 1977; (with Ralph Miliband) Socialist Register (annual, 1964-); (with Joyce M. Bellamy) Dictionary of Labour Biography, 1972-. *Recreations:* working for socialism, looking at churches. *Address:* 152 Westbourne Avenue, Hull HU5 3HZ. *T:* Hull 43425.

SAVILLE, Mark Oliver, QC 1975; *b* 20 March 1936; *s* of Kenneth Vivian Saville and Olivia Sarah Frances Gray; *m* 1961, Gillian Whitworth Gray; two *s. Educ:* St Paul's Primary Sch., Hastings; Rye Grammar Sch.; Brasenose Coll., Oxford (BA, BCL). Nat. Service, 2nd Lieut Royal Sussex Regt, 1954-56; Oxford Univ., 1956-60 (Vinerian Schol. 1960); called to Bar, Middle Temple, 1962. *Recreation:* sailing. *Address:* 4 Essex Court, Temple, EC4Y 9AJ. *T:* 01-583 9191.

SAVIN, Lewis Herbert, MD, MS, London (University Medal in Ophthalmology), MRCP, FRCS; retired; Fellow, King's College, London, 1953; Hunterian Professor Royal College of Surgeons of England, 1943; FRSM (Member Council Ophthalmic Section, 1943; Vice-President 1955); *b* 1901; *e s* of late Lewis Savin, MRCS, Yunnan, and of late Kate C. Savin; *m* 1931, Mary Helen, *e d* of late Walter Griffith, Wimbledon; two *s* one *d. Educ:* Christ's Hosp.; King's Coll., London; King's Coll. Hosp (Warneford Entrance Scholarship, Warneford and Barry Prizes). House Physician and House Surg. to the City of London Hosp. for Diseases of Heart and Lungs, 1924; 1st Assistant Medical Officer to St Marylebone Hospital, 1927; Medical Superintendent Seamen's Hospital, Greenwich, 1928; House Surgeon to Royal Eye Hospital, 1923; afterwards clinical assistant, pathologist, assistant Surgeon, Surgeon, Senior Surgeon, Royal Eye Hospital, SE1, resigning 1956. Ophthalmic Surgeon, Metropolitan Hospital, 1929-34; Consulting Ophthalmic Surgeon, Maudsley Hospital, 1937-39; Consulting Ophthalmic Surgeon to the LCC General Hospitals, 1936-48, and to Whipps Cross Hospital, 1931-47; Ophthalmologist to Horton War Hospital (Ministry of Health Emergency Medical Service), 1939-47; Consulting Ophthalmic Surgeon, King's College Hospital, 1966 (Asst Ophthalmic Surgeon, 1931; Senior Ophthalmic Surgeon, 1945-66). Hon. Secretary Ophthalmological Soc. of UK, 1937-39 (Member Council, 1939-42; Vice-President, 1957); Emeritus Lecturer in Ophthalmology, King's Coll. Hosp. Med. Sch.; Examr under Conjoint Examining Bd for DOMS Part I, 1941-46; Examiner in DO, 1949; Staff Examiner in Ophthalmology, Univ. of London, 1952. Vice-Pres. sect. of ophth. Roy. Soc. Med., 1956-57; President Faculty of Ophthalmologists, 1957. *Publications:* Medical and Ophthalmic contributions to Lancet, British Journal of Ophthalmology (The Effect of Aluminium and its Alloys on the Eye: a Report presented to Vision Committee of Medical Research Council, 1947), and Transactions of Ophthalmological Society of the United Kingdom. *Address:* 149 Eastcote Road, Pinner, Mddx HA5 1EX. *T:* 01-866 1581.

SAVORY, Hubert Newman, MA, DPhil Oxon, FSA; Keeper of Archæology, National Museum of Wales, Cardiff, 1956-76; *b* 7 Aug. 1911; *s* of William Charles Newman Savory and Alice Amelia (*née* Minns); *m* 1949, Priscilla Valerie Thirkell; four *s* two *d. Educ:* Magdalen College Sch., Oxford; St Edmund Hall, Oxford Univ. BA Oxon 1934 (Lit. Hum. 1st Cl.); DPhil Oxon 1937; Randall MacIver Student in Iberian Archæology, 1936-38. Assistant, 1938, Asst Keeper, 1939, Dept of Archæology, National Museum of Wales. Chm., Royal Commn on Ancient Monuments (Wales), 1979- (Mem., 1970-); Mem., Ancient Monuments Board for Wales; Pres., Cambrian Archæological Assoc., 1975-76; Chm., Glamorgan Gwent Archæological Trust, 1975-. Conducted excavations of various Welsh cromlechs, round barrows, hill-forts, etc. Served War of 1939-45, in Army, 1940-45. *Publications:* Spain and Portugal: The Prehistory of the Iberian Peninsula, 1968; Guide Catalogues of the Early Iron Age Collections, 1976, and the Bronze Age Collections, 1980, National Museum of Wales; contrib. to Proc. of Prehistoric Soc.; Archæologia Cambrensis, etc. *Recreations:* walking, gardening. *Address:* 31 Lady Mary Road, Cardiff. *T:* Cardiff 753106.

SAVORY, Sir Reginald (Charles Frank), Kt 1972; CBE 1965; Chairman of Directors, R. Savory Ltd, Building Contractors, since 1933; *b* 27 May 1908; *s* of Frank and Margaret Savory, Auckland, NZ; *m* 1935, Fai-Ola, *o c* of Ernest Vaile, Auckland; two *d. Educ:* Auckland Grammar Sch. Past Chm., Bd of Governors, Council of Auckland Technical Institutes; Member: Auckland Harbour Bd (Chm., 1961-71); Auckland City Council, 1953-62, Drainage Bd, 1956-62, and Chamber of Commerce, 1961-71. Pres., NZ Harbours Assoc., 1963-67; Past Pres., NZ Technical Assoc.; Life Mem. (Past Pres.) NZ Builders' Fedn; FIOB (Gt Britain) 1959. *Recreations:* boating, fishing, golf, bowls; watching Rugby football. *Address:* 452 Remuera Road, Auckland 5, New Zealand. *T:* 545-428. *Clubs:* Auckland (Auckland); NZ Royal Yacht Squadron.

SAVOURS, Dale Norman C.; *see* Campbell-Savours.

SAW, Prof. Ruth Lydia; Professor Emeritus in Aesthetics, University of London, 1964; *b* 1 August 1901; *d* of Samuel James and Matilda Louisa Saw (*née* Horner). *Educ:* County School for Girls, Wallington, Surrey; Bedford College, University of London. Lecturer in Philosophy, Smith Coll., Northampton, Mass., USA, 1927-34; Lecturer in Philosophy: Bedford College, 1939-44; Birkbeck College, 1939-46, Reader in Philosophy, 1946-61; Prof. of Aesthetics in Univ. of London, 1961-64, and Head of Dept of Philosophy, Birkbeck Coll. British Society of Aesthetics: Founder Mem. and Chm. Council, 1960; Vice-Pres., 1963; Pres., 1969; Pres., Aristotelian Soc., 1965. *Publications:* The Vindication of Metaphysics, 1951; Leibniz, 1954; Aesthetics, 1970; sections (William of Ockham, Leibniz), in A Critical History of Western Philosophy. Contrib. to Proc. Aristotelian Soc., Philosophy, Brit. Jl of Aesthetics. *Recreations:* gardening, the theatre; interested in illuminated manuscripts, early gardening and botany books. *Address:* 72 Grosvenor Avenue, Carshalton, Surrey. *T:* 01-647 8898. *Club:* Women's Farm and Garden.

SAWBRIDGE, Henry Raywood, CBE 1960; retired from HM Foreign Service, 1964; Deputy Director, Centre of Japanese Studies, University of Sheffield, 1964-66; *b* 1 Nov. 1907; 2nd *s* of Rev. John Edward Bridgman Sawbridge; *m* 1947, Lilian, *d* of late William Herbert Wood; one *s* one *d. Educ:* Eton; Trinity Coll., Oxford. Entered HM Consular Service, 1931, and served in Japan, Korea and at FO; served with Australian Forces, 1943; HM Consul-General, Yokohama, 1949; Chargé d'Affaires, Korea, 1950; HM Consul-General, Geneva, 1953; Counsellor at Foreign Office, 1960. Coronation Medal, 1953. *Recreations:* shooting, fishing. *Address:* The Moorings, Kingsgate, Kent. *Club:* Travellers'.

SAWERS, David Richard Hall; Under-Secretary, Departments of the Environment and Transport, since 1977; *b* 23 April 1931; *s* of late Edward and of Madeline Sawers; unmarried. *Educ:* Westminster Sch.; Christ Church, Oxford (MA). Research Asst to Prof. J. Jewkes, Oxford Univ., 1954-58; Journalist, The Economist, 1959-64; Vis. Fellow, Princeton Univ., 1964-65; Econ. Adviser, Min. of Aviation and of Technology, 1966-68; Sen. Econ. Adviser, Min. of Technology, Aviation Supply, and DTI, 1968-72; Under-Sec., Depts of Industry, Trade and Prices and Consumer Protection, 1972-76. *Publications:* (with John Jewkes and Richard Stillerman) The Sources of Invention, 1958; (with Ronald Miller) The Technical Development of Modern Aviation, 1968. *Recreations:* listening to music, looking at pictures, gardening. *Address:* 26 Groveway, SW9 0AR.

SAWERS, Maj.-Gen. James Maxwell, CB 1974; MBE 1953; Managing Director, Services Kinema Corporation, 1975-81; *b* 14 May 1920; *s* of late Lt-Col James Sawers, Woking, Surrey; *m* 1945, Grace, *d* of Joseph William Walker, Tynemouth; two *s* one *d. Educ:* Rugby; RMA Woolwich. 2nd Lieut, Royal Signals, 1939. Served War of 1939-45 in W Africa and Burma. Lt-Col, 1960; Brig., 1966; BGS, MoD, 1966-68; Comd Corps Royal Signals, 1st British Corps, 1968-69; attended IDC, 1970; Signal Officer in Chief, 1971-74. Col Comdt, Royal Signals, 1974-79; Hon. Col, 71 (Yeomanry) Signal Regt, 1977-. psc, jssc, idc. CBIM. Managing Trustee: Soldiers' Widows Fund; Single Soldiers' Dependants Fund; Chm., Army Benevolent Fund Bucks Appeals Cttee; Chm., Chalfont Centre for Epilepsy. *Recreations:* sailing, skiing, gardening, golf, photography. *Address:* Holly Lodge, Keepers Lane, Hyde Heath, Amersham, Bucks. *T:* Chesham 783367. *Club:* Army and Navy.

SAWKO, Prof. Felicjan, DSc; Professor of Civil Engineering, Liverpool University, since 1967; *b* 17 May 1937; *s* of Czeslaw Sawko and Franciszka (*née* Nawrot); *m* 1960, Genowefa Stefania (*née* Bak); four *s* one *d. Educ:* Leeds Univ. (BSc Civil Engrg, 1958; MSc 1960; DSc 1973). Engr, Rendel Palmer & Tritton, London, 1959-62; Lectr, Leeds Univ., 1962-67, Reader 1967. Henry Adams Award, IStructE, 1980. *Publications:* (ed) Developments in Prestressed Concrete, Vols 1 and 2, 1968; (with Cope and Tickell) Numerical Methods for Civil Engineers, 1981; some 60 papers on computer methods. *Recreations:* travel, bridge, numismatics. *Address:* 9 Harthill Road, Liverpool L18 6HU. *T:* 051-724 2726.

SAWYER, John Stanley, MA; FRS 1962; Director of Research, Meteorological Office, 1965-76; *b* 19 June 1916; *s* of late Arthur Stanley Sawyer and Emily Florence Sawyer (*née* Frost); *m* 1951, Betty Vera Beeching (*née* Tooke), widow; one *d. Educ:* Latymer Upper Sch., Hammersmith; Jesus Coll., Cambridge. Entered Meteorological Office, 1937. Mem., NERC, 1975-81. Pres., Commn for Atmospheric Sciences, World Meteorological Organisation, 1968-73 (IMO Prize, 1973); Pres., Royal Meteorological Soc.,

1963-65 (Hugh Robert Mill Medal 1956, Buchan Prize 1962, Symons Medal 1971). *Publications:* Ways of the Weather, 1958; scientific papers largely in Quart. Jl Roy. Met. Soc. *Address:* Ivy Corner, Corfe, Taunton, Somerset. *T:* Blagdon Hill 612.

SAWYERR, Rev. Prof. Canon Harry Alphonso Ebun, CBE 1963 (MBE 1954); Grand Commander, Order of the Star of Africa (Liberia), 1971; Tutor, 1974-80, and Vice-Principal, 1975-80, Codrington College (Acting Principal, 1979-80); Visiting Lecturer on West African Indigenous Religious Thought Forms, United Theological College of the West Indies, Kingston, Jamaica, and St John's Vianney, Roman Catholic Seminary, Tunapuna, Trinidad, since 1975; *b* 16 Oct. 1909; *s* of Rev. Obrien Alphonso Dandeson Sawyerr and Mrs Cleopatra Florence Omodele Sawyerr; *m* 1935, Edith Kehinde Lavinia Edwin; one *d. Educ:* Prince of Wales Sch.; Fourah Bay Coll.; St John's Coll., Durham. BA 1933; MA 1936; MEd 1940. Fourah Bay Coll.: Tutor 1933-45; Lectr 1948-52; Chaplain 1948-56; Sen. Lectr 1952-62; Vice-Principal 1956-58 and 1964-68; Prof. of Theology, 1962-74; Principal, 1968-74; Vice-Chancellor, Univ. of Sierra Leone, 1970-72 (Acting Vice-Chancellor, 1968; Pro-Vice-Chancellor, 1968-70). Sec., Theological Advisers Board, Province of W Africa, 1952-58; Member: World Council of Churches Commn on Faith and Order, 1962-75; Permanent Cttee, Assoc. Internationale pour Etude des Religions Préhistoriques et Ethnologiques, 1976-. Select Preacher, UC Ibadan, 1961; Chm., Board of Teacher Trng, 1960-63; Pres., Milton Margai Trng (now Teachers) Coll., 1960-69; Leader, Sierra Leone Delegn to 3rd Commonwealth Educn Conf., 1964; Mem., Public Service Commn, 1968-69. Editor: Aureol Pamphlets, 1957-74; Sierra Leone Bulletin of Religion, 1962-68; Select Preacher: Fourah Bay Coll., UC Sierra Leone, 1964; Service of Re-interment of Bishop Adjayi Crowther (ob 1891), Christ Church Cathedral, Lagos, 1971; Univ. of Ghana, 1974; Service commemorating 150th Anniversary of Landing of 1st Bishop of Barbados, William Hart Coleridge, DD, St Michael's Cath., Barbados, 1975; Lectr, Provincial Clergy Sch., Church of the Province of WI, 1975; Leader of week of prayer for Christian Unity, Trinidad and Tobago, 1975; Conductor of Clergy Retreats, Diocese of Trinidad and Tobago, 1976 and 1977, Dio. of Guyana, 1978, Dio. of Antigua, 1979; Leader of Laity Seminar on Evangelism, Trinidad, 1978; Consultant: Second Assembly Caribbean Conf. of Churches, 1977; Methodist Consultation on Evangelism in a Pluralist Society, 1980; Mem., Arts and Gen. Studies Faculty Cttee, Univ. of W Indies, 1978. 1st Prize, Thomas Cochrane Essay Comp., 1960. Sierra Leone Independence Medal, 1961. Hon. DD Durham, 1970. Knight of Mark Twain, 1978. *Publications:* Creative Evangelism, 1968; (with W. T. Harris) The Springs of Mende Belief and Conduct, 1968; God: Ancestor or Creator?, 1970; (contrib.) Biblical Revelation and Traditional Beliefs (ed K. Dickson and P. Ellingworth), 1969; (contrib.) Religion in a Pluralist Society (ed J. Pobee), 1976; articles in Scottish Jl of Theology, Church Quarterly, East Asia Jl of Theology, Internat. Review of Missions, Numen, Sierra Leone Bulletin of Religion, W African Jl of Educn, African Theological Jl, Caribbean Jl of Religious Studies; Caribbean Jl of African Studies. *Recreations:* motor driving, walking, gardening.

SAXON, David Stephen, PhD; President, University of California at Berkeley, since 1975; *b* 8 Feb. 1920; *s* of Ivan Saxon and Rebecca Moss; *m* 1940, Shirley Goodman; six *d. Educ:* Massachusetts Institute of Technology (BS 1941; PhD 1944). Massachusetts Institute of Technology: Res. physicist, Radiation Lab., 1943-46; Philips Labs, 1946-47. Univ. of California: Mem. of Faculty, 1947-75; Prof. of Physics, 1958-75; Chm. of Dept, 1963-66; Dean of Physics and Sciences, 1966-69; Exec. Vice-Chancellor, 1968-; Univ. Provost, 1974-75. Guggenheim Fellow, 1956-57 and 1961-62; Fulbright grant, 1961-62. Vis. Prof., Univ. of Paris, 1961-62; Vis. scientist, Centre d'Etudes Nucléaires, France, 1968-69; Vis. Research Fellow, Merton Coll., Oxford, 1981; consultant to research organisations, 1948-. Special research into theoretical physics: nuclear physics, quantum mechanics, electromagnetic theory and scattering theory. Member: Amer. Phys. Soc.; Amer. Assoc. Physics Teachers; Amer. Inst. Physics; Scientific Adv. Cttee for Ford Motor Co., 1979-; Corp. of MIT, 1977-. Hon. LHD: Hebrews Union Coll., 1976; Univ. of Judaism, 1977; Hon. LLD Univ. of Southern California, 1978; Hon. ScD Univ. of British Columbia, 1980. Royal Order of the Northern Star (Nordstjärnan), 1979. *Publications:* Elementary Quantum Mechanics, 1968; The Nuclear Independent Particle Model (with A. E. S. Green and T. Sawada), 1968; Discontinuities in Wave Guides (with Julian Schwinger), 1968; Physics for the Liberal Arts Student (with William B. Fretter), 1971. *Address:* President's Office, 714 University Hall, University of California, Berkeley, Calif 94720, USA.

SAY, Rt. Rev. Richard David; *see* Rochester, Bishop of.

SAYCE, Roy Beavan, FRICS; MRAC; Director, Rural Planning Services, Didcot, since 1980; *b* 19 July 1920; *s* of Roger Sayce, BScAgric, NDA, and Lilian Irene Sayce; *m* 1949, Barbara Sarah (*née* Leverton); two *s. Educ:* Culford; Royal Agricultural Coll. (MRAC). FRICS 1949. Univ. of London, 1938-40. Served War, Intell., RAFVR, 1940-46. Agricultural Land Service: Asst Land Comr, Chelmsford, 1949-50; Sen. Asst Land Comr, Norwich, 1950-63; Divl Land Comr, Oxford, 1963-71; Reg. Surveyor, Land Service, Agric. Devic. Devel and Adv. Service, Bristol, 1971-76; Chief Surveyor, Land Service, Agric. Devel and Adv. Service, MAFF, 1977-80. Royal Instn of Chartered Surveyors: Mem., Gen. and Divl Councils, 1970-80; Divl Pres., Land Agency and Agriculture Div., 1973-74. Chm., Farm Buildings Information Centre, 1980-. Governor, Royal Agric. Coll., Cirencester, 1975-

(Silver Medal, 1948). FRSA 1975; Hon. Mem., Central Assoc. of Agricl Valuers, 1978. *Publications:* Farm Buildings, 1966; (contrib.) Walmsley's Rural Estate Management, 1969; contrib. professional jls. *Recreations:* golf, non-professional writing. *Address:* 13 Haywards Close, Wantage, Oxon OX12 7AT. *T:* Wantage 4836. *Clubs:* Farmers', Civil Service.

SAYE AND SELE, 21st Baron *cr* 1447 and 1603; **Nathaniel Thomas Allen Fiennes;** DL; *b* 22 September 1920; *s* of Ivo Murray Twisleton-Wykeham-Fiennes, 20th Baron Saye and Sele, OBE, MC, and Hersey Cecilia Hester, *d* of late Captain Sir Thomas Dacres Butler, KCVO; *S* father, 1968; *m* 1958, Mariette Helena, *d* of Maj.-Gen. Sir Guy Salisbury-Jones, *qv*; three *s* one *d* (and one *s* decd). *Educ:* Eton; New College, Oxford. Served with Rifle Brigade, 1941-49 (despatches twice). Chartered Surveyor. Partner in firm of Laws and Fiennes. DL Oxfordshire, 1979. Fellow, Winchester Coll., 1967-. *Heir: s* Hon. Richard Ingel Fiennes, *b* 19 August 1959. *Address:* Broughton Castle, Banbury, Oxon. *T:* Banbury 2624.
See also Very Rev. Hon. O. W. Fiennes.

SAYEED, Dr Abul Fatah Akram, OBE 1976; FRSM; General Medical Practitioner in Leicester, since 1963; President, Standing Conference of Asian Organizations in UK; Vice-President, Overseas Doctors' Association in UK, since 1979; *b* Bangladesh, 23 Nov. 1935; *s* of late Mokhles Ahmed, school teacher; registered British; *m* 1959, Hosne-ara Ali, *d* of M. S. Ali; two *s* one *d. Educ:* St Joseph's Sch., Khulna; Dacca Univ. MB, BS 1958. Editor, Dacca Med. Coll. Jl and Magazines, 1957-58; Lit. Sec., Students Union. Went to USA, 1960; resident in Britain from 1961. Mem. Staff, Leicester Royal Infirmary; Member: Leics Local Medical Cttee, 1977-; Leics Family Practitioners Cttee, 1982. Co-founder, Nat. Fedn of Pakistani Assocs in GB, 1963; Adviser, NCCI, 1965-68; Founder Member: Leicester Council for Community Relations, 1965 (now Mem. Exec. Cttee); British-Bangladesh Soc.; Mem., Community Relations Commn, 1968-77; Pres., Standing Conference of Asian Orgs in UK, 1977- (Chm., 1973-77, Vice-Chm., 1970-73); Mem., E Midlands Adv. Cttee, CRE, 1978-; Mem., Stop Rickets Campaign (Chm. Leicester Campaign); Life Mem., Pakistan Soc.; Pres., Pakistan Assoc., Leics, 1965-71. Mem., BBC Asian Programme Adv. Cttee, 1972-77. Special interest in problems of Asians; initiated study of problems of second generation Asians (CRE report Between Two Cultures); Gen. Sec., Overseas Doctors Assoc., 1975-77 (Founder Cmn., 1975, Sponsor Chm., 1975); attended First World Conf. on Muslim Educn, Mecca, 1977; has done much work with disaster funds, etc. *Publications:* (ed jtly) Asian Who's Who, 1975-76, 2nd edn 1978; contribs on socio-med. aspects of Asians in Britain to various jls. *Recreations:* gardening, photography, stamp collecting. *Address:* Ramna, 2 Mickleton Drive, Leicester LE5 6GD. *T:* Leicester 416703. *Club:* National Liberal (non-political member).

SAYER, Vice-Adm. Sir Guy (Bourchier), KBE 1959; CB 1956; DSC 1943; retired as Flag Officer Commanding Reserve Fleet (1958-59); *b* 2 January 1903; 3rd *s* of late William Feetham and late Edith Alexandra Sayer, E Finchley, London, N; *m* 1925, Sylvia Rosalind Pleadwell, *d* of late Maj.-Gen. R. C. Munday, CB, RAF, and late Mrs Olive Munday, Hartley, Plymouth, Devon; twin *s. Educ:* Cholmeley House, Highgate; RN Colleges Osborne and Dartmouth. Naval Cadet, 1916; Midshipman, 1920; Sub-Lieut, 1923; Lieut-Comdr, 1933; Comdr Dec. 1937; Capt. 1944; Rear-Adm., 1953. Vice-Controller of the Navy and Director of Naval Equipment, Admiralty, 1953-56; Flag Officer, Home Fleet Training Squadron, 1956-57; Vice-Adm. 1957; retired, 1959. *Publication:* The History of HMS Vernon, 1929. *Recreations:* estate maintenance, walking. *Address:* Old Middle Cator, Widecombe-in-the-Moor, Devon. *T:* Widecombe 228.

SAYER, Guy Mowbray, CBE 1978; JP; Director: World Shipping and Investment Co. Ltd, Hong Kong, since 1977; World Finance International Ltd, Bermuda, since 1977; World Maritime Ltd, Bermuda, since 1977; *b* 18 June 1924; *yr s* of late Geoffrey Robley and Winifred Lily Sayer; *m* 1951, Marie Anne Sophie, *o d* of late Henri-Marie and Elisabeth Mertens; one *s* two *d. Educ:* Mill Mead Prep. Sch.; Shrewsbury School. FIB 1971. Royal Navy, 1942-46. Joined Hongkong & Shanghai Banking Corp., 1946; service in London, China, Japan, Malaysia, Burma and Hong Kong; Gen. Man. 1969; Exec. Dir 1970; Dep. Chm. 1971; Chm., 1972-79 (now Mem., London Adv. Cttee, 1979-). Chairman: Hongkong Bank of Calif., San Francisco, 1972-77; Mercantile Bank Ltd, 1973-77; Director: Internat. Commercial Bank Ltd, London, 1969-77; Mercantile Credits Ltd, Sydney, 1971-77. Treas., Hong Kong Univ., 1972-77. Member: Exchange Fund Adv. Cttee, Hong Kong, 1971-77; London Adv. Cttee, British Bank of the Middle East, 1980-. MLC, 1973-74, MEC, 1974-77, Hong Kong. JP Hong Kong, 1971. Governor, Suttons Hosp. in Charterhouse. Hon. LLD Hong Kong, 1978. *Recreations:* golf, walking. *Address:* 5 Pembroke Gardens, W8. *T:* 01-602 4578. *Clubs:* MCC; Royal Wimbledon Golf; West Sussex Golf; Hong Kong, Shek O Country (Hong Kong).

SAYER, John Raymond Keer, MA; FBIM; Principal, Banbury School, since 1973; *b* 8 Aug. 1931; *s* of Arthur and Hilda Sayer; *m* 1955, Ilserose (*née* Heyd); one *s* one *d. Educ:* Maidstone Grammar Sch.; Brasenose Coll., Oxford (Open Scholar; MA). FBIM 1979. Taught languages, 1955-63; Dep. Head, Nailsea Sch., Somerset, 1963-67; Headmaster, Minehead Sch., Somerset, 1967-73. Chairman: Reform of Assessment at Sixteen-Plus, 1972-75; PUBANSCO publishing gp, 1975-; Jt Council of Heads, 1981; Pres., Secondary Heads Assoc., 1979-80 (Editor, SHA Headlines, 1978-79); Press and Publications Officer, Headmasters' Assoc., 1977-79 (Chm., External Relations Cttee,

1974-77). Member: Exec., UCCA, 1975-; Schools Panel, CBI, 1975-; Heads Panel, TUC, 1975-80; National Adv. Council on Educn for Industry and Commerce, 1974-77. *Publications:* (ed) The School as a Centre of Enquiry, 1975; (ed) Staffing our Secondary Schools, 1980; frequent contribs on educnl topics to learned jls and symposia. *Recreation:* postal history. *Address:* 8 Northmoor Road, Oxford OX2 6UP. *T:* Oxford 56932.

SAYERS, Prof. Bruce McArthur, PhD, CEng, FIEE; Professor of Electrical Engineering Applied to Medicine, since 1968, and Head of the Department of Electrical Engineering since 1979, Imperial College of Science and Technology; *b* 6 Feb. 1928; *s* of John William McArthur Sayers and Mabel Florence Sayers (*née* Howe); *m* 1951, Ruth Woolls Humphery. *Educ:* Melbourne Boys' High School; Univ. of Melbourne (MSc); Imperial College, Univ. of London (PhD, DIC). Biophysicist, Baker Med. Research Inst. and Clinical Research Unit, Alfred Hosp., Melbourne, 1949-54; Imperial College, London: Research Asst, 1955-56; Philips Elec. Ltd Research Fellow, 1957; Lectr, 1958; Senior Lectr, 1963; Reader, 1965. Pres., Section of Measurement in Medicine, Royal Soc. of Medicine, 1971-72; Hon. Consultant, Royal Throat, Nose and Ear Hosp.. 1974-; UK rep., Bio-engineering Working Group, EEC Cttee for Med. Res., 1976-80; Temp. Adviser, WHO, 1970-76, 1981-; former Visiting Prof., Univs of Melbourne, Rio de Janeiro, McGill, Toronto. Travelling Lectr: Nuffield Foundn-Nat. Research Council, Canada, 1971; Inst. of Electron. and Radio Engrs, Australia, 1976. Hon. Foreign Mem., Medico-Chirurgical Soc. of Bologna, 1965; Hon. Member, Eta Kappa Nu (USA), 1980. *Publications:* papers, mainly on biomedical signals and control systems, epidemiology, cardiology and audiology. *Recreations:* literary pattern analysis; painting. *Address:* Department of Electrical Engineering, Imperial College, SW7 2BT. *T:* 01-589 5111; The Beeches, Gravelly Hill, Caterham, Surrey CR3 6ES. *T:* Caterham 42156.

SAYERS, Sir Edward (George), Kt 1965; CMG 1956; MD, Hon. DSc, FRCP, FRACP, Hon. FACP, Hon. FRCPE, FRS (NZ); DTM&H; Formerly Dean of the Medical Faculty and Professor of Therapeutics, University of Otago, New Zealand, 1959-67; *b* 10 Sept. 1902; *s* of Henry Hind Sayers; *m* 1st, 1928, Jane Lumsden, *d* of Wm Grove, MD; two *s* four *d*; 2nd, Patricia Dorothy, *d* of Gordon Coleman. *Educ:* Christ's College, Christchurch; Otago University; Otago Medical School, 1920-24; MB, ChB (NZ), 1924. House Physician, Wellington Hospital, 1925; Student and House Physician, London Sch. of Tropical Medicine, DTM&H 1926; Medical Missionary, British Solomon Is, 1927-34; MRCP 1935. Consulting Physician, Auckland (NZ), 1935-39; FRACP 1938. Served War of 1939-45, Middle East and Pacific, 1939-44; OC Medical Div. 1st NZ Gen. Hosp., Egypt and Greece; Cons. Physician NZ Forces in Pacific; OC 4 New Zealand Gen. Hosp. (Colonel); Cons. Physician, Auckland, NZ, 1945-59; Pres. RACP, 1956-58. Chm. NZ Med. Council, 1956-64; Mem. NZ Med. Research Council, 1956-67; Chm., Scientific Cttee, Nat. Heart Foundn of NZ, 1968-79. Col Comdt, Royal NZMC, 1963-67. Pres., NZ Branch, BMA, 1963; Fellow Christ's College (NZ); Mem. Council, Univ. of Otago, 1959-67. FRCP 1949; Hon. FACP, 1957; Hon. FRCPE, 1960; FRS (NZ), 1961; Hon. DSc Otago, 1975. Cilento Medal for distinguished work in Pacific, 1940. Legion of Merit (USA), 1944, KStJ. *Publications:* articles in med. jls. *Recreation:* fishing. *Address:* 27A Henry Street, Maori Hill, Dunedin, New Zealand. *Club:* Fernhill (Dunedin).

SAYERS, Eric Colin, CBE 1981; FCA; Chairman, Duport Ltd, 1973-81; *b* 20 Sept. 1916; *s* of Alfred William and Emily Clara Sayers; *m* 1940, Winifred Bristow; two *d. Educ:* Acton County Grammar School. JDipMA, CBIM. Joined Duport Ltd, 1956; Director, 1962; Managing Director, 1966-75. Director: Ductile Steels PLC, 1973-; International Timber Corp. PLC, 1977-; Durapipe Internat. Ltd, 1979-81. Part-time Member, Midlands Electricity Board, 1973-81; Member: Council of CBI, 1975-81 (Chm. Energy Policy Cttee, 1975-81); Government's Advisory Council on Energy Conservation, 1977-79; Energy Commn, 1977-79; Birmingham Cttee of Inst. of Directors, 1974-. Pres., Birmingham and W Midlands Soc. of Chartered Accountants, 1971-72; Inst. of Chartered Accountants in England and Wales: Council Member, 1966-; Vice-Pres., 1976; Dep. Pres., 1977; Pres., 1978. Treas., Univ. of Aston in Birmingham, 1976-. *Recreations:* golf, fishing, winemaking. *Address:* 73 Silhill Hall Road, Solihull, West Midlands B91 1JT. *T:* 021-705 3973. *Club:* Carlton.

SAYERS, Prof. James, MSc, PhD Cantab; Professor of Electron Physics, University of Birmingham, 1946-72; *b* 2 Sept. 1912; *s* of late J. Sayers; *m* 1943, Diana Ailsa Joan Montgomery; two *s* one *d. Educ:* Ballymena Academy; University of Belfast; St John's College, Cambridge. Fellow of St John's College, Cambridge, 1941-46. Research for Admiralty in Univ. of Birmingham, 1939-43, on micro-wave radar; Member of British Group of Atomic Scientists transferred to work on the US Manhattan Project, 1943-45. Award by the Royal Commission on Awards to Inventors, 1949. British delegate to Internat. Scientific Radio Union, Zürich, 1950. Life Fellow, Franklin Inst. of State of Pennsylvania. John Price Wetherill Medallist, for discovery in Physical Science, 1958. *Publications:* papers in Proc. Royal Soc., Proc. Phys. Soc., and in the reports of various Internat. Scientific Conferences, on Upper Atmosphere Physics and the Physics of Ionized Gases. *Recreations:* gardening, photography. *Address:* Edgewood Gables, The Holloway, Alvechurch, Worcestershire. *T:* Redditch 64414.

SAYERS, (Matthew Herbert) Patrick, OBE 1945; MD; FRCPath; Major-General (retired), late Army Medical Services; formerly Consulting

Pathologist, Employment Medical Advisory Service, Department of Employment and Health and Safety Executive, 1967-75; Hon. Physician to HM The Queen, 1965-67; Director of Army Pathology and Consulting Pathologist to the Army, 1964-67; *b* 17 Jan. 1908; *s* of late Herbert John Ireland Sayers, Musician, and late Julia Alice Sayers (*née* Tabb); *m* 1935, Moira, *d* of Robert Dougall; two *s* one *d*. *Educ:* Whitgift School; St Thomas's Hospital, London. MRCS, LRCP 1932; MB, BS London 1933; MD London 1961; FCPath 1964. Commissioned Lieutenant RAMC, 1935; served India and Far East, 1936-46: Asst Dir of Pathology, HQ 14th Army, 1943-44; Dep. Dir of Pathology, Allied Land Forces, SE Asia, 1945. Asst Dir-Gen., War Office, 1948; OC The David Bruce Laboratories, 1949-52 and 1955-61; Asst Dir of Pathology, Middle East Land Forces, 1953-55; Editor, Journal RAMC, 1955-61; Dep. Dir of Pathology, Far East Land Forces, 1961-64. CStJ 1968. *Publications:* contribs (jtly) to scientific jls on scrub typhus, immunology and industrial medicine. *Recreations:* gardening, music, cricket, field sports. *Address:* High Trees, Walmer, Kent. *T:* Deal 63526. *Clubs:* Army and Navy; MCC.

SAYERS, Richard Sidney, FBA 1957; Emeritus Professor of Economics with special reference to Money and Banking, University of London (Cassel Professor of Economics, 1947-68); *b* 1908; *s* of S. J. Sayers; *m* 1930, Millicent Hodson; one *s* one *d*. *Educ:* St Catharine's Coll., Cambridge. Asst Lectr in Economics, London Sch. of Economics, 1931-35; Lectr in Economics, Exeter, Corpus Christi and Pembroke Colleges, Oxford, 1935-45; Fellow of Pembroke College, Oxford, 1939-45; Ministry of Supply, 1940-45; Economic Adviser, Cabinet Office, 1945-47. Member: Radcliffe Committee on the Working of the Monetary System, 1957-59; OECD Cttee on Fiscal Measures, 1966-68; Monopolies Commission, 1968. Pres. Section F, Brit. Assoc., 1960; Vice-Pres., Brit. Academy, 1966-67; Pres., Economic Hist. Soc., 1972-74; Vice-Pres., Royal Econ. Soc., 1973-. Hon. Fellow: St Catharine's Coll., Cambridge; LSE; Inst. of Bankers. Hon. DLitt Warwick, 1967; Hon. DCL Kent, 1967. *Publications:* Bank of England Operations, 1890-1914, 1936; Modern Banking, 1938 (7th edn 1967); American Banking System, 1948; (ed) Banking in the British Commonwealth, 1952; (jt editor with T. S. Ashton) Papers in English Monetary History, 1953; Financial Policy, 1939-45, 1956; Central Banking after Bagehot, 1957; Lloyds Bank in the History of English Banking, 1957; (ed) Banking in Western Europe, 1962; (ed) Economic Writings of James Pennington, 1963; A History of Economic Change in England, 1880-1939, 1967; Gilletts in the London Money Market, 1867-1967, 1968; The Bank of England 1891-1944, 1976.

SAYLES, Prof. George Osborne, LittD, DLitt, LLD; FBA 1962; MRIA; *b* 20 April 1901; *s* of Rev. L. P. Sayles and Margaret Brown, Glasgow; *m* 1936, Agnes, *d* of George Sutherland, Glasgow; one *s* one *d*. *Educ:* Ilkeston Grammar Sch.; Glasgow Univ.; University Coll., London. Open Bursar, Ewing Gold Medallist, First Cl. Hons History, Glasgow Univ., 1923; Carnegie Res. Schol., University Coll., London, 1923-24. Asst. 1924, Lectr, 1925 and Sen. Lectr, 1934-45, in History, Glasgow Univ.; Leverhulme Res. Fellow, 1939; Professor of Modern History in the Queen's University, Belfast, 1945-53; Burnett-Fletcher Professor of History in the Univ. of Aberdeen, 1953-62; first Kenan Prof. of History, New York Univ., 1967; Vis. Prof., Louvain Univ., Belgium, 1951; Woodward Lectr, Yale Univ., USA, 1952; Fellow, Folger Library, Washington, 1960-61; Corr. Fellow, American Soc. for Legal History, 1971; Hon. Fellow, Medieval Acad. of America, 1980. Vis. Mem., Inst. for Advanced Study, Princeton, NJ, 1969. Hon. LittD Trinity Coll. Dublin, 1965; Hon. LLD Glasgow, 1979. James Barr Ames Medal, Fac. of Law, Harvard Univ., 1958. Vice-Pres., Selden Soc., London, 1953. Chm. Advisory Cttee, Official War History of Northern Ireland, 1949; Member: Commission Internationale pour l'Histoire des Assemblées d'Etats; Advisory Historical Committee, Official Histories of War (Gt Brit.), 1950; Irish Manuscripts Commn, Dublin, 1949; Scottish Cttee on History of Scottish Parliament, 1937; Council of Stair Soc. (Scotland). Intelligence Officer (voluntary) to District Commissioner for Civil Defence SW Scotland, 1939-44; HG Glasgow, 12th Bn 1940. *Publications:* Author, Editor or Joint Editor (with H. G. Richardson) of: The Early Statutes, 1934; Rotuli Parliamentorum Anglie Hactenus Inediti, 1935; Select Cases in Court of King's Bench: under Edward I (3 vols), 1936-39; Edward II (1 vol.), 1956; Edward III (2 vols), 1958, 1965; Richard II, Henry IV, Henry V (1 vol.), 1972; Select Cases in Procedure without Writ, 1943; Parliaments and Councils of Medieval Ireland, 1947; Medieval Foundations of England, 1948, 3rd edn 1964, American edn, 1950; Irish Parliament in the Middle Ages, 1952, 2nd edn 1964; The Irish Parliament in 1782, 1954; Fleta, vol I, 1955, vol II, 1972; Parliaments and Great Councils in Medieval England, 1961; Governance of Medieval England, 1963; The Administration of Ireland, 1172-1377, 1964; Law and Legislation in Medieval England, 1966; The King's Parliament of England, 1974; Documents on the Affairs of Ireland before the King's Council, 1979; The English Parliament in the Middle Ages, 1981; Scripta Diversa, 1982; articles and reviews in Eng. Hist. Review, Scot. Hist. Review, Law Quarterly Review, Proc. RIA, etc. *Recreations:* travel, motoring. *Address:* Warren Hill, Crowborough, East Sussex. *T:* 61439.

SCADDING, John Guyett, MD (London), FRCP; Emeritus Professor of Medicine in the University of London; Hon. Consulting Physician, Brompton and Hammersmith Hospitals; *b* 30 August 1907; *e s* of late John William Scadding and Jessima Alice Guyett; *m* 1940, Mabel Pennington; one *s* two *d*. *Educ:* Mercers' School; Middlesex Hospital Medical School, University of London. MRCS, LRCP, 1929; MB, BS (London), 1930. Resident appts, Middx Hosp., Connaught Hosp., Walthamstow, and Brompton Hosp.,

1930-35; MRCP 1932; MD (London, Univ. gold medal), 1932; First Asst, Dept of Med., Brit. Postgrad. Med. Sch., 1935; FRCP 1941; RAMC 1940-45 (Lt-Col, O i/c Med. Div.); Phys., Hammersmith Hosp., Postgrad. Med. Sch. of London, 1946-72; Physician, Brompton Hosp., 1939-72; Inst. of Diseases of the Chest: Dean, 1946-60; Dir of Studies, 1950-62; Prof. of Medicine, 1962-72; Hon. Cons. in Diseases of the Chest to the Army at Home, 1953-72 (Guthrie Medal, 1973). Visiting Professor: Univ. Oklahoma, 1963; Stanford Univ. and Univ. Colorado, 1965; McMaster Univ., 1973; Univ. Manitoba, 1974; Univ. Chicago, 1976; Dalhousie Univ., 1977. Mem. Central Health Services Council, and Standing Medical Advisory Cttee, 1954-66; Mem. Clinical Research Board, 1960-65. Royal College of Physicians: Bradshaw Lectr, 1949; Mitchell Lectr, 1960; Tudor Edwards Lectr, 1970; Lumleian Lectr, 1973; Councillor, 1949-52; Censor, 1968-70; Second Vice-Pres., 1971-72; Moxon Medal, 1975; Lettsomian Lectr, Med. Soc. of London, 1955. Editor, Thorax, 1946-59. President: British Tuberculosis Assoc., 1959-61; Section of Medicine, RSM, 1969-71; Thoracic Soc., 1971-72. Dr *hc* Reims, 1978. *Publications:* Sarcoidosis, 1967; contributions to textbooks and articles, mainly on respiratory diseases, in medical journals. *Recreations:* music, pottering about. *Address:* 18 Seagrave Road, Beaconsfield, Bucks HP9 1SU. *T:* Beaconsfield 6033. *Club:* Athenæum.

SCALES, Prunella, (Prunella Margaret Rumney West); actress; *d* of John Richardson Illingworth and Catherine Scales; *m* 1963, Timothy Lancaster West, *qv*; two *s*. *Educ:* Moira House, Eastbourne; Old Vic Theatre School, London; Herbert Berghof Studio, New York (with Uta Hagen). Repertory in Huddersfield, Salisbury, Oxford, Bristol Old Vic, etc; seasons at Stratford-on-Avon and Chichester Festival Theatre, 1967-68; plays on London Stage include: The Promise, 1967; Hay Fever, 1968; It's a Two-Foot-Six-Inches-Above-The-Ground-World, 1970; The Wolf, 1975; Breezeblock Park, 1978; Make and Break, 1980; An Evening with Queen Victoria, 1980; The Merchant of Venice, 1981; Quartermaine's Terms, 1981; *television:* Fawlty Towers, 1975-79; Grand Duo, The Merry Wives of Windsor, 1982; *films* include: The Wicked Lady, 1982; frequent broadcasts, readings, poetry recitals and fringe productions. Has directed plays at Bristol Old Vic, Arts Theatre, Cambridge, Billingham Forum, Almost Free Theatre, London and Playhouse, Nottingham, and taught at several drama schools. *Recreation:* growing vegetables. *Address:* c/o Jeremy Conway, 8 Cavendish Place, W1. *Club:* BBC.

SCANLON, family name of **Baron Scanlon**.

SCANLON, Baron *cr* 1979 (Life Peer), of Davyhulme in the County of Greater Manchester; **Hugh Parr Scanlon;** President, Amalgamated Union of Engineering Workers, 1968-78; Member, British Gas Corporation, 1976-82; *b* 26 Oct. 1913; *m* 1943, Nora; two *d*. *Educ:* Stretford Elem. Sch.; NCLC. Apprentice, Instrument Maker, Shop Steward-Convener, AEI, Trafford Park; Divisional Organiser, AEU, Manchester, 1947-63; Member: Exec. Council, AEU, London, 1963-67; TUC Gen. Council, 1968-78; TUC Econ. Cttee, 1968-78. Member: NEDC, 1971-; Metrication Bd, 1973-78; NEB, 1977-79; Govt Cttee of Inquiry into Teaching of Maths in Primary and Secondary Schs in England and Wales, 1978-; Chm., Engineering Industry Training Bd, 1975-82. Vice-Pres., Internat. Metalworkers' Fedn, 1969-78; Pres., European Metal Workers' Fedn, 1974-78. *Recreations:* golf, swimming, gardening. *Address:* 23 Seven Stones Drive, Broadstairs, Kent. *Club:* Eltham Warren Golf.

SCANNELL, Vernon, FRSL; free-lance author, poet and broadcaster, since 1962; *b* 23 Jan. 1922. *Educ:* elementary schools; Leeds Univ. Served with Gordon Highlanders (51st Highland Div.), ME and Normandy, 1940-45; Leeds Univ. (reading Eng. Lit.), 1946-47; various jobs incl. English Master at Hazelwood Prep. Sch., 1955-62. Southern Arts Assoc. Writing Fellowship, 1975-76; Vis. Poet, Shrewsbury Sch., 1978-79; Res. Poet, King's Sch. Canterbury, Michaelmas Term 1979. FRSL 1960. Granted a civil list pension, 1981, for services to literature. *Publications: novels:* The Fight, 1953; The Wound and the Scar, 1953; The Big Chance, 1960; The Face of the Enemy, 1961; The Shadowed Place, 1961; The Dividing Night, 1962; The Big Time, 1965; The Dangerous Ones, 1970; A Lonely Game (for younger readers), 1979; *poetry:* The Masks of Love, 1960 (Heinemann Award, 1960); A Sense of Danger, 1962; (ed, with Ted Hughes and Patricia Beer) New Poems: a PEN anthology, 1962; Walking Wounded: poems 1962-65, 1968; Epithets of War: poems 1965-69, 1969; Mastering the Craft (Poets Today Series), 1970; (with J. Silkin) Pergamon Poets, No 8, 1970; Selected Poems, 1971; The Winter Man: new poems, 1973; The Apple Raid and other poems, 1974 (Cholmondeley Poetry Prize, 1974); The Loving Game, 1975 (also in paperback); Not Without Glory: poets of World War II, 1976; New and Collected Poems 1950-80, 1980; Winterlude and other poems, 1982; *criticism:* How to Enjoy Poetry, 1982; *autobiography:* The Tiger and the Rose, 1971; A Proper Gentleman, 1977. *Recreations:* listening to radio (mainly music), drink, boxing (as a spectator), films, reading. *Address:* Flat 2, 28 Spencer Place, Leeds LS7 4BR. *T:* Leeds 625287.

SCARASCIA-MUGNOZZA, Carlo; Vice-President, Commission of the European Communities, 1972-77; *b* Rome, 19 Jan. 1920. Mem., Italian Chamber of Deputies, for Lecce-Brindisi-Taranto, 1953; Vice-Pres., Christian Democrat Parly Gp, 1958-62; Leader, Italian Delegn to UNESCO, 1962; Secretary of State: for Educn, 1962-63; for Justice, June 1963-Dec. 1963; Mem., European Parliament, 1961, Chm., Political Cttee, 1971-72.

SCARBOROUGH, Prof. Harold, CBE 1976; Visiting Professor, Department of Medicine, University of Maiduguri, Nigeria, and Acting Chief Medical Director, University of Maiduguri Teaching Hospital, 1979-82; *b* 27 March 1909; British; unmarried. *Educ:* Bridlington School, Yorks; Edinburgh University; St Mary's Hospital Medical School; Harvard University. Clinical Tutor, Royal Infirmary of Edinburgh and Assistant, Dept of Therapeutics, Edinburgh Univ., 1933-38; Beit Memorial Research Fellow and Demonstrator in Pharmacology, Edinburgh Univ., 1938-39; Beit Memorial Research Fellow, Medical Unit, St Mary's Hosp., London, 1945-47; Rockefeller Travelling Fellow at Harvard Medical School, 1947-48; Reader in Medicine, University of Birmingham, 1949-50; Prof. of Medicine in Welsh Nat. Sch. of Medicine, Univ. of Wales, 1950-70; formerly: Dir, Med. Unit, Cardiff Royal Infirmary; Chm., Div. of Medicine, United Cardiff Hosps; Prof. of Medicine and Dean of the Faculty of Medicine, Ahmadu Bello Univ., Zaria, Nigeria, 1970-76; Visiting Professor of Medicine: Garyounis Univ., Libya, 1978-79; Faculty of Health Sciences, Univ. of Ilorin, Nigeria, 1978-79. *Publications:* (part author) Textbook of Physiology and Biochemistry, 1950; papers in BMJ, Lancet, Quart. Jl Med., and other medical and scientific journals. *Recreations:* gardening, the theatre. *Address:* 1d-Dwejra, Geronimo Abos Street, Lija, Republic of Malta.

SCARBROUGH, 12th Earl of, *cr* 1690; **Richard Aldred Lumley,** DL; Viscount Lumley (Ire.), 1628; Baron Lumley, 1681; Viscount Lumley, 1690; *b* 5 Dec. 1932; *o s* of 11th Earl of Scarbrough, KG, PC, GCSI, GCIE, GCVO, and Katharine Isobel, Dowager Countess of Scarbrough, DCVO (*d* 1979), *d* of late R. F. McEwen; *S* father, 1969; *m* 1970, Lady Elizabeth Ramsay, *d* of Earl of Dalhousie, *qv* ; two *s* one *d*. *Educ:* Eton; Magdalen College, Oxford. 2nd Lt 11th Hussars, 1951-52; formerly Lt Queen's Own Yorkshire Dragoons. ADC to Governor and C-in-C, Cyprus, 1956. Hon. Col, 1st Bn The Yorkshire Volunteers, 1975-. Mem. Council, Univ. of Sheffield, 1974-79. DL S Yorks, 1974. *Heir: s* Viscount Lumley, *qv. Address:* Sandbeck Park, Maltby, Rotherham, S Yorks S66 8PF. *T:* Doncaster 742210. *Clubs:* White's, Pratt's; Jockey (Newmarket).

SCARFE, Prof. Francis Harold, CBE 1972 (OBE 1965); MA, DLit; FRSL; author; Director, British Institute in Paris, 1959-78, and Professor of French in the University of London, 1965-78, now Professor Emeritus; *b* 18 September 1911; *s* of John James Scarfe and Margaret Ingham Dobson; *m* 1938, Margarete M. Geisler; one *s*. *Educ:* Universities of Durham, Cambridge and Paris. RAOC and RAEC, 1941-46; Lt-Col, 1945. Supervisor of Studies and Secretary, Extension Lectures Committee, University of Oxford, 1946-47; Senior Lecturer in French, University of Glasgow, 1947-59. Chevalier des Arts et Lettres. Prix de l'Ile St Louis, 1967. Chevalier de la Légion d'Honneur, 1978. *Publications: poetry:* Inscapes, 1940; Poems and Ballads, 1941; Underworlds, 1950; *criticism:* Auden and After, 1942; W. H. Auden, 1949 (Monaco); The Art of Paul Valéry, 1954; La vie et l'œuvre de T. S. Eliot, 1964 (Paris); *editions:* Baudelaire, 1961; Chénier, 1961; André Chénier, his Life and Work, 1965; *novels:* Promises, 1950; Single Blessedness, 1951; Unfinished Woman, 1954; various translations. *Address:* 433 Banbury Road, Oxford OX2 8ED. *T:* Oxford 58127.

SCARFE, Gerald; artist; *b* 1 June 1936. *Educ:* scattered (due to chronic asthma as a child). Punch, 1960; Private Eye, 1961; Daily Mail, 1966; Sunday Times, 1967; cover artist to illustrator, Time Magazine, 1967; animation and film directing for BBC, 1969-. Has taken part in exhibitions: Grosvenor Gall., 1969 and 1970; Pavillon d'Humour, Montreal, 1967 and 1971; Expo '70, Osaka, 1970. One-man exhibitions of sculptures and lithographs: Waddell Gall., New York, 1968 and 1970; Grosvenor Gall., 1969; Vincent Price Gall., Chicago, 1969; National Portrait Gall., 1971. Animated film for BBC, Long Drawn Out Trip, 1973 (prizewinner, Zagreb); Designer and Dir, animated sequences in film, The Wall, 1982. *Publications:* Gerald Scarfe's People, 1966; Indecent Exposure (ltd edn), 1973; Expletive Deleted: the life and times of Richard Nixon (ltd edn), 1974. *Recreations:* drawing, painting and sculpting. *Address:* 10 Cheyne Walk, SW3.

SCARLETT, family name of **Baron Abinger.**

SCARLETT, James Harvey Anglin; His Honour Judge Scarlett; a Circuit Judge, since 1974; *b* 27 Jan. 1924; *s* of Lt-Col James Alexander Scarlett, DSO, RA, and Muriel Scarlett, *d* of Walter Blease; unmarried. *Educ:* Shrewsbury Sch.; Christ Church, Oxford (MA). Barrister-at-law. Served War, Royal Artillery (Lieut), 1943-47. Called to the Bar, Inner Temple, 1950. A Recorder of the Crown Court, 1972-74. Malayan Civil Service, 1955-58. *Recreation:* fell walking. *Address:* Chilmington Green, Great Chart, near Ashford, Kent TN23 3DP. *Club:* Athenæum; Athenæum (Liverpool); Border County (Carlisle).

SCARLETT, Hon. John Leopold Campbell, CBE 1973; Deputy to Health Service Commissioner, 1973-76; *b* 18 Dec. 1916; 2nd *s* of 7th Baron Abinger and Marjorie, *d* of John McPhillamy, Bathurst, NSW; *m* 1947, Bridget Valerie, *d* of late H. B. Crook; two *s* one *d*. *Educ:* Eton; Magdalene Coll., Cambridge (MA). Served War of 1939-45, France, Madagascar, Burma (despatches); 2nd Lieut 1940; Major 1944, RA. House Governor, London Hosp., 1962-72. *Address:* Bramblewood, Castle Walk, Wadhurst, Sussex TN5 6DB. *T:* Wadhurst 2642. *Club:* Royal Automobile.

SCARLETT, Sir Peter (William Shelley Yorke), KCMG 1958 (CMG 1949); KCVO 1955; *b* 30 March 1905; *s* of late William James Yorke Scarlett,

Fyfield House, Andover; *m* 1934, Elisabeth, *d* of late Sir John Dearman Birchall, TD, MP, Cotswold Farm, Cirencester; one *s* three *d*. *Educ:* Eton; Christ Church, Oxford. Apptd to Foreign Office as a Third Secretary, 1929; Cairo, 1930; Bagdad, 1932; Lisbon, 1934; promoted a Second Secretary, 1934; acted as Chargé d'Affaires, Riga, 1937 and 1938. Attached to representative of Latvia at coronation of King George VI, 1937; Brussels, 1938; promoted actg First Sec., 1940; captured by enemy forces, 1940; returned to UK and resumed duties at Foreign Office, 1941; Paris, 1944; Allied Forces Headquarters, Caserta, 1946; Counsellor, Foreign Office, 1947; Inspector of HM Diplomatic Service Establishments, 1950; British Permanent Representative on the Council of Europe, Strasbourg, 1952; HM Ambassador to Norway, 1955; HM Minister to the Holy See, 1960-65, retired. Chairman, Cathedrals Advisory Committee, 1967-81. *Address:* 35 Tivoli Road, Cheltenham, Glos. *Club:* Carlton.

SCARMAN, family name of **Baron Scarman.**

SCARMAN, Baron *cr* 1977 (Life Peer), of Quatt in the county of Salop; **Leslie George Scarman,** PC 1973; Kt 1961; OBE 1944; a Lord of Appeal in Ordinary, since 1977; *b* 29 July 1911; *s* of late George Charles and Ida Irene Scarman; *m* 1947, Ruth Clement Wright; one *s*. *Educ:* Radley College; Brasenose College, Oxford. Classical Scholar, Radley, 1925; Open Classical Scholar, Brasenose Coll., 1930; Hon. Mods 1st cl., 1932; Lit. Hum. 1st cl., 1934; Harmsworth Law Scholar, Middle Temple, 1936, Barrister, 1936; QC 1957. A Judge of the High Court of Justice, Probate, Divorce, and Admiralty Div., later Family Div., 1961-73; a Lord Justice of Appeal, 1973-77. Chairman: Law Commn, 1965-73; Council of Legal Educn, 1973-76. Chm., Univ. of London Court, 1970-81 (Dep. Chm., 1966-70); Chancellor, Univ. of Warwick, 1977-. Vice-Chm., Statute Law Cttee, 1967-72. Pres., Senate of Inns of Court and Bar, 1976-79. Mem. Arts Council, 1968-70, 1972-73; Vice-chm., ENO, 1976-81. Pres., RIPA, 1981-. Hon. Fellow: Brasenose College, Oxford, 1966; Imperial Coll., Univ. of London, 1975. Hon. LLD: Exeter, 1965; Glasgow, 1969; London, 1971; Keele, 1972; Freiburg, 1973; Warwick, 1974; Bristol, 1976; Manchester, 1977; Kent, 1981; Hon. DCL: City, 1980; Oxon, 1982. RAFVR, 1940-45; Chm., Malcolm Clubs, RAF. Order of Battle Merit (Russia), 1945. *Publications:* Pattern of Law Reform, 1967; English Law— The New Dimension, 1975. *Recreations:* gardening, walking. *Address:* 12 Wellington Court, SW1X 7PL. *Club:* Athenæum.

SCARR, John Geoffrey Fearnley; *b* 12 July 1910; 2nd *s* of late William Harcourt Scarr and Lydia (*née* Harrop); *m* 1945, Dorothy Edna Terry; two *d*. *Educ:* King's School, Ely; Trinity College, Cambridge (MA Hons, LLB). Called to the Bar, Lincoln's Inn, 1935; practised Northern Circuit and Lancashire Palatine Court. Served throughout War of 1939-45: Far East and War Office; major. Colonial Service; Resident Magistrate and Coroner, N Rhodesia, 1953; Chief Judicial Comr, Western Pacific High Commn Territories, 1959; Judge of the Supreme Court, Nassau and Bahamas, 1961-65; Acting Chief Justice on several occasions; Chancellor Dio. Nassau and the Bahamas, 1962-64; Deputy Chairman, Bahamas Constituencies Commn, 1964; Legal Staff of Law Commn, 1965-66, and of Foreign Compensation Commn, 1970-75; Mem., Oxford Dio. Pastoral Cttee, 1978-. Mem., South Oxfordshire DC, 1978-. *Publications:* The Law and Practice of Land Registration, Northern Rhodesia Law Reports, 1949-54; contrib. to legal journals. *Recreations:* golf, music, sailing, painting. *Address:* Littlegate, Shiplake, Henley-on-Thames, Oxon. *T:* Wargrave 2201. *Club:* Royal Nassau Sailing.

SCARSDALE, 3rd Viscount *cr* 1911; **Francis John Nathaniel Curzon;** Bt (Scotland) 1636, (England) 1641; Baron Scarsdale 1761; late Captain, Scots Guards; *b* 28 July 1924; *o s* of late Hon. Francis Nathaniel Curzon, 3rd *s* of 4th Baron Scarsdale, and late Winifred Phyllis (*née* Combe); *S* cousin, 1977; *m* 1st, 1948, Solange (marr. diss. 1967, she *d* 1974), *yr d* of late Oscar Hanse, Mont-sur-Marchienne, Belgium; two *s* one *d* ; 2nd, 1968, Helene Gladys Frances, *o d* of late Maj. William Ferguson Thomson, Kinellar, Aberdeenshire; two *s*. *Educ:* Eton. *Recreations:* piping, photography. *Heir: s* Hon. Peter Ghislain Nathaniel Curzon, *b* 6 March 1949. *Address:* Kedleston Hall, Derby. *T:* Derby 840386. *Club:* County (Derby).

SCATCHARD, Vice-Adm. John Percival, CB 1963; DSC 1941; first Bar, 1944; second Bar, 1945; *b* 5 Sept. 1910; *s* of Dr James P. Scatchard, MB, BS, Tadcaster, Yorks; *m* 1943, Edith Margaret Niven; one *d*. *Educ:* Aysgarth School, Yorkshire; RNC Dartmouth. Joined RN, 1924; served War of 1939-45, in HMS Kashmir-Garth and Termagent; Captain (D) Portsmouth, 1951-52; Captain 5th Destroyer Squadron, 1957-58; Director Naval Equipment, Admiralty, 1959-60; Commandant, Joint Services Staff College, Latimer, Bucks, 1960-62; Flag Officer, Second-in-Command, Far East Fleet, 1962-64; retd list, 1964. *Recreations:* riding, gardening, sailing. *Address:* Reachfar, Warsash, near Southampton, Hants.

SCHAFFTER, Ernest Merill James; Secretary, Royal Aeronautical Society, 1973-82 (Deputy Secretary, 1970-73); Director, Engineering Sciences Data Unit Ltd; *b* 1922; *er s* of late Dr Charles Merill Schaffter and of Bertha Grace Brownrigg, of the CMS in Isfahan, Iran; *m* 1951, Barbara Joy, *o c* of Alfred Bennett Wallis and Hilda Frances Hammond; three *d*. *Educ:* Trent Coll., Nottinghamshire; King's Coll., Cambridge. BA 1950, MA 1955. Served War: RAF, as Pilot with Coastal and Transport Command, Flt Lt, 1941-46. De Havilland Aircraft Co., Hatfield, as Aerodynamicist and Engr, 1950-54; Marshall's Flying Sch., Cambridge, as Engr, 1954-60; Marshall of Cambridge

(Eng) Ltd, as Personal Asst to Chief Designer and later as Design Office Manager, 1960-70. Freeman, GAPAN, 1978. FRAeS, AFAIAA, AFCASI, FBIM. *Address:* 43 Speldhurst Road, W4 1BX. *T:* 01-995 0708. *Clubs:* Royal Air Force, Les Ambassadeurs.

SCHALLY, Dr Andrew Victor; Chief of Endocrine and Polypeptide Laboratories since 1962, and Senior Medical Investigator since 1973, Veterans Administration Medical Center, New Orleans; Professor of Medicine, Department of Medicine, Tulane University School of Medicine, New Orleans, since 1967 (Associate Professor, 1962-67); *b* Wilno, Poland, 30 Nov. 1926; US Citizen (formerly Canadian Citizen); *s* of Casimir and Maria Schally; *m* 1st, 1956, Margaret White (marr. diss.); one *s* one *d*; 2nd, 1976, Ana Maria Comaru. *Educ:* Bridge of Allan, Scotland (Higher Learning Cert.); London (studied chemistry); McGill Univ., Montreal, Canada (BSc Biochem., 1955; PhD Biochem., 1957). Res. Assistant: Dept of Biochem., Nat. Inst. for Med. Res., MRC, Mill Hill, 1949-52; Endocrine Unit, Allan Meml Inst. for Psych., McGill Univ., Montreal, 1952-57; Baylor University Coll. of Medicine, Texas Med. Center: Res. Associate, Dept of Physiol., 1957-60; Asst Prof. of Physiol., Dept of Physiol., and Asst Prof. of Biochem., Dept of Biochem., 1960-62. Member: Endocrine Soc., USA; Amer. Chem. Soc.; AAAS; Soc. of Biol Chemists; Amer. Physiol Soc.; Soc. for Experimental Biol. and Med.; Internat. Soc. for Res. in Biol. of Reprodn; Internat. Brain Res. Org.; Nat. Acad. of Med., Mexico; Nat. Acad. of Scis (US). Hon. Member: Internat. Family Planning Res. Assoc., Inc.; Chilean Endocrine Soc.; Mexican Assoc. for Study of Human Fertility and Reprodn; Mexican Soc. of Nutrition and Endocrinol.; Acad. of Med. Sciences of Cataluna and Baleares; Endocrine Soc. of Madrid; Polish Soc. of Internal Med.; Endocrine Soc. of Ecuador; Endocrine Soc. of Peru. Dr *hc* State Univ. of Rio de Janeiro, 1977; Rosario, Argentina, 1979; Univ. Peruana Cayetano Heredia, Lima, 1979; Univ. Nat. de San Marcos, Lima, 1979; MD *hc*: Tulane, 1978; Cadiz, 1979; Univ. Villareal-Lima, 1979; Copernicus Med. Acad., Cracow, 1979; Chile, 1979; Buenos Aires, 1980; Salamanca, 1981; Hon. DSc McGill, 1979. Nobel Prize in Physiology or Medicine, 1977. Veterans Administration: William S. Middleton Award, 1970; Exceptional Service Award and Medal, 1978. Van Meter Prize, Amer. Thyroid Assoc., 1969; Ayerst-Squibb Award, US Endocrine Soc., 1970; Charles Mickle Award, Faculty of Med., Univ. of Toronto, 1974; Gairdner Foundn Internat. Award, Toronto, 1974; Edward T. Tyler Award, 1975; Borden Award, Assoc. of Amer. Med. Colls, 1975; Albert Lasker Basic Med. Res. Award, 1975; Laude Award 1975, Spanish Pharmaceutical Soc., 1977; Medal of Scientific Merit, Fed. Univ. of Ceara, Brazil, 1977; 1st Dip. of Merit of St Luke, Foundn of Social Pioneers, Rio de Janeiro, 1977. Mem. Editorial Bd, Proc. of Society for Experimental Biology and Medicine, 1973-. *Publications:* (compiled and ed with William Locke) The Hypothalamus and Pituitary in Health and Disease, 1972; over 1200 other pubns (papers, revs, books, abstracts). *Address:* Room 103, Building 3, Veterans Administration Medical Center, 1601 Perdido Street, New Orleans, La 70146, USA. *T:* (504) 589-5230.

SCHAPERA, Prof. Isaac, MA (Cape Town) 1925; PhD (London) 1929; DSc (London) 1939; FBA 1958; FRSSAf 1934; Emeritus Professor, University of London (London School of Economics), 1969; *b* Garies, South Africa, 23 June 1905; 3rd *s* of late Herman and Rose Schapera. *Educ:* S African Coll. Sch., Cape Town; Universities of Cape Town and London. Prof. of Social Anthropology, Univ. of Cape Town, 1935-50; Prof. of Anthropology, Univ. of London (LSE), 1950-69, now Emeritus; Hon. Fellow, 1974. Many anthropological field expeditions to Bechuanaland Protectorate, 1929-50. Chairman Association of Social Anthropologists of the British Commonwealth, 1954-57; President, Royal Anthropological Inst., 1961-63. Hon. DLitt Cape Town, 1975; Hon. LLD Witwatersrand, 1979. *Publications:* The Khoisan Peoples of South Africa, 1930; A Handbook of Tswana Law and Custom, 1938; Married Life in an African Tribe, 1940; Native Land Tenure in the Bechuanaland Protectorate, 1943; Migrant Labour and Tribal Life, 1948; The Ethnic Composition of Tswana Tribes, 1952; The Tswana, 1953; Government and Politics in Tribal Societies, 1956; Praise Poems of Tswana Chiefs, 1965; Tribal Innovators, 1970; Rainmaking Rites of Tswana Tribes, 1971; Kinship Terminology in Jane Austen's Novels, 1977; Editor: Western Civilization and the Natives of South Africa, 1934; The Bantu-speaking Tribes of South Africa, 1937; David Livingstone's Journals and Letters, 1841-56 (6 vols), 1959-63; David Livingstone: South African Papers 1849-1853, 1974; contrib. to many learned journals. *Address:* 457 White House, Albany Street, NW1 3UP.

SCHAPIRO, Prof. Leonard Bertram, CBE 1980; LLB; FBA 1971; Professor of Political Science, with Special Reference to Russian Studies, London School of Economics and Political Science, University of London, 1963-75, now Emeritus; Honorary Fellow, 1980; *b* Glasgow, 22 April 1908; *s* of Max Schapiro and Leah (*née* Levine); *m* 1st, 1943, Isabel Margaret (marr. diss. 1976), *d* of late Don Salvador de Madariaga; no *c*; 2nd, 1976, Roma Thewes, *d* of late Dr C. Sherris. *Educ:* St Paul's Sch.; University Coll., London (Fellow, 1973). Called to Bar, Gray's Inn, 1932; practised at Bar, London and Western Circuit, 1932-39; BBC Monitoring Service, 1940-42; War Office, 1942-45; Intell. Div., German Control Commn, 1945-46 (Maj.); practised at Bar, 1946-55; Dept of Politics, LSE, 1955-75. Member: Res. Bd, Inst. of Jewish Affairs; Council, Keston Coll. Chairman, Editorial Board: Government and Opposition; Soviet Jewish Affairs; Mem., Editorial Board, Soviet Survey; Vice-Pres., Nat. Council for One Parent Families, 1976-. For. Hon. Mem., Amer. Acad. of Arts and Sciences, 1967. *Publications:* The Origin of the Communist Autocracy, 1955, 2nd edn 1976; The Communist Party of the Soviet Union, 1960, 2nd edn 1970; The Government and Politics of Soviet Russia, 1965, 7th edn 1977; Rationalism and Nationalism in Russian Nineteenth Century Political Thought, 1967; trans. (with critical essay) Turgenev's Spring Torrents, 1972; Totalitarianism, 1972; Turgenev: his life and times, 1979; (ed jtly) The Soviet Worker, 1981; numerous contribs to learned jls, symposia, Encyclopædia Britannica, etc. *Recreations:* music, looking at paintings. *Address:* c/o London School of Economics and Political Science, Houghton Street, WC2. *Club:* Reform.

SCHAPIRO, Meyer; University Professor, Columbia University, 1965-73, now Emeritus Professor; *b* Shavly, Lithuania, 23 Sept. 1904; *s* of Nathan Menahem Schapiro and Fege Edelman; *m* 1928, Dr Lillian Milgram; one *s* one *d*. *Educ:* Boys' High Sch., Brooklyn; Columbia University. PhD Columbia, 1929. Columbia University: Lectr, Dept of Art History and Archæology, 1928; Asst Prof., 1936; Assoc. Prof., 1948; Prof., 1952; University Prof., 1965. Visiting Lecturer: Institute of Fine Arts, NY University, 1931-36; New School for Social Research, NY, 1938-50; Vis. Prof.: Univ. of London, 1947, 1957; Univ. of Jerusalem, 1961; Messenger Lectr, Cornell Univ., 1960; Patten Lectr, Indiana Univ., 1961; Charles Eliot Norton Prof., Harvard Univ., 1966-67; Slade Prof. of Fine Art, Oxford Univ., 1968; Vis. Lectr, Collège de France, 1974. Guggenheim Fellow, 1939, 1943; Fellow: Amer. Acad. of Arts and Sciences, 1952; Inst. for Advanced Study in Behavioral Sciences, Palo Alto, 1962-63; Amer. Philosophical Soc., 1969; Mediaeval Acad., 1970; Amer. Inst. of Arts and Letters, 1976. Bd of Editors: Jl of History of Ideas; Semiotica; Dissent. Award for Distinction, Amer. Council of Learned Socs, 1960; Mitchell Prize, 1979. *Publications:* The Romanesque Sculpture of Moissac, 1931; Van Gogh, 1950; Cézanne, 1952; The Parma Ildefonsus, 1964; Words and Pictures, 1973; Selected Papers, vol. I, Romanesque Art, 1976, vol. II, Modern Art, 1978; vol. III, Late Antique, Early Christian and Medieval Art, 1980; articles in collective books and in Art Bulletin, Gazette des Beaux-Arts, Jl Warburg and Courtauld Insts, Jl History of Ideas, Jl Architectural Historians, Kritische Berichte, Amer. Jl Sociology, Partisan Review, Encounter, etc. *Address:* 279 West 4th Street, New York, NY 10014, USA.

SCHAWLOW, Prof. Arthur Leonard, PhD; J. G. Jackson - C. J. Wood Professor of Physics, Stanford University, since 1961; *b* Mt Vernon, New York, 5 May 1921; *s* of Arthur Schawlow and Helen Schawlow (*née* Mason); *m* 1951, Aurelia Keith Townes; one *s* two *d*. *Educ:* Univ. of Toronto, Canada. BA 1941, MA 1942, PhD 1949. Postdoctoral Fellow and Research Associate, Columbia Univ., 1949-51; Research Physicist, Bell Telephone Laboratories, 1951-61; Visiting Assoc. Prof., Columbia Univ., 1960. Hon. DSc: Ghent, 1968; Bradford, 1980; Hon. LLD, Toronto, 1970. Ballantine Medal, Franklin Inst., 1962; Liebmann Prize, Inst. of Electrical and Electronic Engrs, 1963; Thomas Young Medal and Prize (GB), 1963; California Scientist of the Year, 1973; Ives Medal, Optical Soc. of America, 1975; Marconi Internat. Fellowship, 1977; (jtly) Nobel Prize in Physics, 1981. *Publications:* (with C. H. Townes) Microwave Spectroscopy, 1955; many contribs to learned journals. *Recreation:* jazz music. *Address:* Department of Physics, Stanford University, Stanford, California 94305, USA. *T:* (415) 497-4356.

SCHEEL, Walter; President of the Federal Republic of Germany, 1974-79; *b* 8 July 1919; *m* 1969, Dr Mildred Scheel; one *s* two *d* (and one *s* of previous *m*). *Educ:* Reform Gymnasium, Solingen. Served in German Air Force, War of 1939-45. At one time head of market research organization. Mem. of Bundestag, 1953-74; Federal Minister for Economic Co-operation, 1961-Oct. 1966, Vice-President of Bundestag, 1967-69; Vice-Chancellor and Foreign Minister, 1969-74. Former Mem., Landtag North Rhine Westphalia. Chm., Free Democrats, 1968-74. *Publications:* Konturen einer neuen Welt, 1965; Reden und Interviews, 1-5, 1972-79; Vom Recht des anderen, 1977; Die Zukunft der Freiheit, 1979. *Address:* Lindenallee 23, D 5000 Köln 51, West Germany.

SCHEMBRI, His Honour Carmelo; Chief Justice of Malta and President of the Constitutional Court, Court of Appeal and Court of Criminal Appeal, since 1981; *b* 2 Sept. 1922; *s* of Joseph Schembri and Lucia (*née* Tabone Adami); *m* 1949, Helen (*née* Holland); six *s* five *d*. *Educ:* The Lyceum, Malta; Royal Univ. of Malta (LLD 1946). Called to the Bar, 1947; elected Mem., Malta Legislative Assembly (Nationalist Party), 1950; Dep. Speaker and Chm., Cttees until dissolution of Assembly, 1951; returned to Parliament in General Election, 1951 and re-elected Dep. Speaker and Chm. Cttees; Minister of Educn, 1952-53; Asst Crown Counsel and Officer i/c Inland Revenue Dept, Gozo, 1954-62; Magistrate: for Gozo, 1962-68; Malta, 1968-78; Judge of Superior Courts, 1978-81. Coronation Medal 1953. *Recreations:* football, woodwork, collecting match boxes. *Address:* 2 Holland Court, Bisazza Street, Sliema, Malta; Chief Justice's Chambers, Law Courts, Malta. *T:* 38569. *Club:* Union (Malta).

SCHERER, Prof. Jacques, DèsL; Professor, University of Paris-III, since 1979; *b* 24 Feb. 1912; *s* of Maurice Scherer and Madeleine Franck; *m* 1965, Colette Bié. *Educ:* Ecole Normale Supérieure; Sorbonne Univ., Paris (Agrégé des Lettres, Docteur ès Lettres). Prof. of French Literature, Univ. of Nancy, 1946-54; Prof. of French Literature and Theatre, Sorbonne Univ., 1954-73; Marshal Foch Prof. of French Literature and Fellow of All Souls Coll., Univ. of Oxford, 1973-79. *Publications:* L'expression littéraire dans l'œuvre de Mallarmé, 1947; La dramaturgie classique en France, 1950; La dramaturgie de Beaumarchais, 1954; Le 'Livre' de Mallarmé, 1957 (new edn 1977); Structures de Tartuffe, 1966; Sur le Dom Juan de Molière, 1967; Le cardinal et l'orang-outang, essai sur Diderot, 1972; Théâtre du XVIIe siècle, 1975; Grammaire de Mallarmé, 1977; Racine et/ou la cérémonie, 1982. *Address:* 11 rue de la Colonie, 75013 Paris, France.

SCHERGER, Air Chief Marshal Sir Frederick (Rudolph Williams), KBE 1958 (CBE 1950); CB 1954; DSO 1944; AFC 1940; *b* 18 May 1904; *o s* of Frederick H. Scherger and Sarah (*née* Chamberlain), Ararat, Victoria, Australia; *m* 1st, 1929, Thelma Lilian Harricks (*d* 1974); one *d*; 2nd, 1975, Mrs J. Robertson. *Educ:* Ararat High School; Royal Military College, Australia. Grad. Dec. 1924; seconded to RAAF Jan. 1925; completed flying course, Dec. 1925. Various flying training and squadron appts, 1926-35; RAF Staff Coll. Course, 1935; RAF attachments, 1936; Director of Training, RAAF, 1937-40; AOC No 10 Group, RAAF, 1943-44; AOC 1st TAF, RAAF, 1945-46; idc, 1946; Deputy Chief of Air Staff, RAAF, 1947-51; Head Australian Joint Services Staff, Washington, 1951-52; Air Officer Commanding, RAF, Malaya, 1953-54; Air Member for Personnel, RAAF, 1955-57; CAS, RAAF, 1957-61; Chairman, Chiefs of Staff, 1961-66. Chairman: Australian Nat. Airlines Commn, 1966-75; Commonwealth Aircraft Corp. Pty Ltd, 1968-74; Mono Pumps (Aust.), 1970-82; Pipe Line Engrg Aust. Ltd; Director: Associated Broadcasting Services, 1973-80; Plessey (Pacific) Ltd, 1966-81; International Computers Ltd, 1969-81. *Recreations:* golf, shooting, motoring. *Address:* 45 Stephens Street, North Balwyn, Vic 3104, Australia. *Clubs:* Melbourne, Naval and Military (Melbourne).

SCHIEMANN, Konrad Hermann Theodor, QC 1980; *b* 15 Sept. 1937; *s* of Helmuth and Beate Schiemann; *m* 1965, Elisabeth Hanna Eleonore Holroyd-Reece; one *d*. *Educ:* King Edward's Sch., Birmingham; Pembroke Coll., Cambridge (Schol.; MA, LLB). Called to Bar, Inner Temple, 1962; Junior Counsel to the Crown, Common Law, 1978-80. Chairman: of panel conducting Examinations in Public of North-East Hants and Mid Hants Structure Plans, 1979; also of panel conducting Examination in Public of Merseyside Structure Plan, 1980. *Recreations:* music, reading. *Address:* 4 and 5 Gray's Inn Square, Gray's Inn, WC1R 5AY. *T:* 01-404 5252; *Telex:* Gralaw G8953743.

SCHILD, Heinz Otto, FRS 1966; MD, PhD, DSc; FIBiol; Professor of Pharmacology, University of London, at University College, 1961-73, Emeritus Professor, 1973; *b* Fiume, 18 May 1906; *s* of Hermann Schild and Thekla (*née* Spiegel); *m* 1938, Mireille Madeleine Haquin; three *d*. *Educ:* Universities of Munich, Berlin and Edinburgh. MD Munich, 1931; PhD Edinburgh, 1935; DSc London, 1950. Assistant, Pharmacology Dept, Univ. of Edinburgh, 1936; Demonstrator, 1937, Lecturer, 1942, Reader, 1945, Dept of Pharmacology, University Coll., London; Dean, Faculty of Med. Sciences, University Coll., 1964-67; Hon. Fellow UCL, 1982. Vis. Prof., NY State Univ., 1968. Mem., WHO Visiting Team of Medical Scientists to SE Asia, 1952. Examiner, Univs of Leeds, Liverpool, Oxford, Edinburgh, West Africa, West Indies, Makerere College. Schmiedeberg Plakette Deutsche Pharmak. Ges., 1977; Hon. Mem., British Pharmacol Soc.; Sen. Mem., British Immunol. Soc.; Hon. Mem., European Histamine Res. Soc. Wellcome Gold Medal, British Pharmacol Soc., 1981. *Publications:* Applied Pharmacology, 1980; papers in Journal of Physiology, British Journal of Pharmacology, Immunology, Lancet, Nature. *Recreation:* walking slowly. *Address:* Mole Ridge, St Mary's Road, Leatherhead, Surrey. *T:* Leatherhead 373773.

SCHILLER, Prof. Dr Karl; Member of Deutscher Bundestag, 1965-72; Professor of Political Economy, University of Hamburg, and Director of Institute for Foreign Trade and Overseas Economy, 1947-72; Member, Ford European Advisory Council, since 1976; *b* 24 April 1911; *s* of Carl and Maria Schiller; *m*; one *s* three *d*. *Educ:* Univs of Kiel, Frankfurt, Berlin, Heidelberg. Research Asst, Institut für Weltwirtschaft, Kiel, 1935-39; Lectr, Univ. of Kiel, 1945-46; Rector, Univ. of Hamburg, 1956-58. Senator for Economic Affairs and Transportation, Hamburg, 1948-53; Mem., Bürgerschaft Hamburg, 1949-57; Senator for Economics, West Berlin, 1961-65; Federal Minister of Economics, 1966-71, of Economics and Finance, 1971-72. Pres., EDESA, 1973-79. *Publications:* Sozialismus und Wettbewerb, 1955; Neuere Entwicklungen in der Theorie der Wirtschaftspolitik, 1958; Zur Wachstumsproblematik der Entwicklungsländer, 1960; Der Okonom und die Gesellschaft, 1964; Reden zur Wirtschaft und Finanzpolitik (10 vols), 1966-72, etc. *Address:* 2112 Jesteburg, Reindorferstrasse 84, West Germany.

SCHILLING, Prof. Richard Selwyn Francis, CBE 1975; MD (London); DSc (London); FRCP; FFCM, FFOM; DPH; DIH; Professor of Occupational Health, London School of Hygiene and Tropical Medicine, University of London, 1960-76, now Emeritus, Hon. Fellow 1979; Director, TUC Centenary Institute of Occupational Health, 1968-76; *b* 9 Jan. 1911; *s* of late George Schilling and of Florence Louise Schilling, Kessingland, Suffolk; *m* 1937, Heather Maude Elinore Norman; one *s* two *d*. *Educ:* Epsom College; St Thomas' Hospital. Obstetric house physician, St Thomas' Hosp., 1935; house physician, Addenbrooke's Hosp., Cambridge, 1936; Asst Industrial MO, ICI (metals) Ltd, Birmingham, 1937; Medical Inspector of Factories, 1939-42. Served War of 1939-45, Captain RAMC, France and Belgium, 1939-40. Sec. Industrial Health Research Board of Med. Research Council, 1942-46; Nuffield Fellow in Industrial Health, 1946-47; Reader in Occupational Health, Univ. of Manchester, 1947-56; WHO Consultant, 1956-69. Lectures: Milroy, RCP, 1956; Mackenzie, BMA, 1956; Cantor, RSA, 1963; C.-E. A. Winslow, Yale Univ., 1963; Ernestine Henry, RCP, 1970. Former Vice-Pres., Perm. Commn, Internat. Assoc. Occupational Health. Former President: Assoc. of Industrial Medical Officers; British Occupational Hygiene Soc.;

Occup. Med. Sect. of Roy. Soc. Med. Member: Committee of Inquiry into Trawler Safety, 1968; Royal Commn on Civil Liability and Compensation for Personal Injury, 1973-78. Hon. FRSM 1976. FRSA 1964. *Publications:* (ed) Modern Trends in Occupational Health, 1960; (ed) Occupational Health Practice, 1973, 2nd edn 1980; original papers on Byssinosis (respiratory disease of textile workers) and other subjects in occupational health in BMJ, Lancet, Brit. Jl of Industrial Medicine, and foreign journals. *Recreations:* fishing, gardening. *Address:* 46 Northchurch Road, N1. *T:* 01-254 4379.

SCHLESINGER, Arthur (Meier), Jr; writer; educator; Schweitzer Professor of the Humanities, City University of New York since 1966; *b* Columbus, Ohio, 15 Oct. 1917; *s* of late Arthur Meier and of Elizabeth Bancroft Schlesinger; *m* 1st, 1940, Marian Cannon (marr. diss. 1970); two *s* two *d*; 2nd, 1971, Alexandra Emmet; one *s*. *Educ:* Phillips Exeter Acad. AB (Harvard), 1938; Henry Fellow, Peterhouse, Cambridge, 1938-39. Soc. of Fellows, Harvard, 1939-42; US Office of War Information, 1942-43; US Office of Strategic Services, 1943-45; US Army, 1945. Mem. Adlai Stevenson Campaign Staff, 1952, 1956. Professor of History, Harvard University, 1954-61 (Associate, 1946-54); Special Assistant to President Kennedy, 1961-63. Film Reviewer: Show, 1962-65; Vogue (US), 1966-70; Saturday Review, 1977-80; Amer. Heritage, 1981. Member of Jury, Cannes Film Festival, 1964. Holds Hon. Doctorates, 1950-. Mem. of numerous Socs and Instns. Pulitzer Prize: History, 1946; Biography, 1966; Nat. Book Award for Biog., 1966 (for A Thousand Days: John F. Kennedy in the White House), 1979 (for Robert Kennedy and His Times); Nat. Inst. of Arts and Letters, Gold Medal for History, 1967. *Publications:* Orestes A. Brownson: a Pilgrim's Progress, 1939; The Age of Jackson, 1945; The Vital Center, 1949, (in UK) The Politics of Freedom, 1950; The General and the President (with R. H. Rovere), 1951; (co-editor) Harvard Guide to American History, 1954; The Age of Roosevelt: I: The Crisis of the Old Order, 1957; II: The Coming of the New Deal, 1958; III: The Politics of Upheaval, 1960; Kennedy or Nixon, 1960; The Politics of Hope, 1963; (ed with Morton White) Paths of American Thought, 1963; A Thousand Days: John F. Kennedy in the White House, 1965; The Bitter Heritage: Vietnam and American Democracy 1941-1966, 1967; The Crisis of Confidence: ideas, power & violence in America, 1969; (ed with F. L. Israel) History of American Presidential Elections, 1971; The Imperial Presidency, 1973; (ed) History of US Political Parties, 1973; Robert Kennedy and His Times, 1978; articles to magazines and newspapers. *Address:* (office) 33 W 42nd Street, New York, NY 10036, USA. *T:* 790-4261. *Clubs:* Century (New York), Federal City (Washington).

SCHLESINGER, Bernard, OBE 1946; MA, MD, FRCP; Consulting Physician to University College Hospital, Hospital for Sick Children, Great Ormond Street, and Royal Northern Hospital; originally Consulting Paediatrician to the Army; now retired; *b* 23 Nov. 1896; *s* of late Richard Schlesinger; *m* 1925, Winifred Henrietta, *d* of late H. Regensburg, London; two *s* one *d* (and two *d* decd). *Educ:* Uppingham; Emmanuel Coll., Cambridge. Served European War, 1914-18 as a Private, and in War of 1939-45, as Brigadier, Consulting Physician, NW Army and Central Command, India Command. Fell. of Assoc. of Physicians, Brit. Pædiatric Assoc. (Pres., 1953-54); Fell., Roy. Soc. of Med. (Pres., Pædiatric Sect, 1960-61). Milroy Lectr, 1938. Dawson Williams Prize, 1961. *Publications:* numerous articles and books on Diseases of Children and Researches on Rheumatism. *Recreation:* gardening. *Address:* Oliver's Cottage, Boxford, near Newbury, Berks. *T:* Boxford 206. *Club:* Sloane.

See also *J. R. Schlesinger.*

SCHLESINGER, John Richard, CBE 1970; film director; Associate Director, National Theatre, since 1973; *b* 16 Feb. 1926; *s* of Bernard Schlesinger, qv. *Educ:* Uppingham; Balliol Coll., Oxford (BA; Hon. Fellow 1981). Directed: *films:* for Monitor and Tonight (BBC TV), 1958-60; Terminus, for British Transport Films, 1960; A Kind of Loving, 1961; Billy Liar, 1962-63; Darling, 1964-65; Far from the Madding Crowd, 1966; Midnight Cowboy, 1968-69; Sunday, Bloody Sunday, 1971; contrib. Visions of Eight, 1973; Day of the Locust, 1973; Marathon Man, 1975-76; Yanks, 1978; Honky Tonk Freeway, 1980; *plays:* Timon of Athens, and Days in the Trees, for RSC, 1964-66; I and Albert, Piccadilly, 1972; Heartbreak House, 1975, and Julius Caesar, 1977, for Nat. Theatre; Les Contes d'Hoffmann, 1980, for Covent Garden; True West, for Nat. Theatre, 1981. Soc. of TV and Film Academy Award for Best Director, also Director's Guild of America Award and an American Oscar, for Midnight Cowboy; Golden Lion Award, Venice Film Festival 1961, for Terminus; Golden Bear Award, Berlin Film Festival 1962, for A Kind of Loving; New York Critics Award, for Darling; Soc. of TV and Film Academy Award for Best Director and David di Donatello Award, for Sunday, Bloody Sunday, 1972; David di Donatello Special Award, 1980; SWET Award for Les Contes d'Hoffmann, 1981; Shakespeare Prize, FVS Foundn of Hamburg, 1981. *Recreations:* gardening, travel, music, antiques. *Address:* c/o Michael Oliver, Berger Oliver & Co., 40 Piccadilly, W1. *T:* 01-734 7421.

SCHMIDT, Helmut H. W.; Member of Bundestag, Federal Republic of Germany, 1953-62, and since 1965; Leader of the Opposition, Bundestag, since 1982; *b* 23 Dec. 1918; *s* of Gustav L. and Ludovica Schmidt; *m* 1942, Hannelore Glaser; one *d*. *Educ:* Univ. of Hamburg. Diplom-Volkswirt, 1948. Manager of Transport Administration, State of Hamburg, 1949-53; Social Democratic Party: Member, 1946-; Chm., Parly Gp, 1967-69; Vice-Chm. of Party, 1968-; Senator (Minister) for Domestic Affairs in Hamburg, 1961-65; Minister of Defence, 1969-72; Minister of Finance and Econs, 1972; Minister of Finance, 1972-74; Chancellor, Federal Republic of Germany, 1974-82. Hon LLD: Newberry Coll., S Carolina, 1973; Johns Hopkins Univ., 1976; Hon. DCL Oxford, 1979; Hon. Doctorate: Harvard, 1979; Sorbonne, 1981. *Publications:* Defence or Retaliation, 1962; Beiträge, 1967; Balance of Power, 1971; Auf dem Fundament des Godesberger Programms, 1973; Bundestagsreden, 1975; Kontinuität und Konzentration, 1975; Als Christ in der politischen Entscheidung, 1976; (with Willy Brandt) Deutschland 1976— Zwei Sozialdemokraten im Gespräch, 1976; Der Kurs heisst Frieden, 1979; Pflicht zur Menschlichkeit, 1981. *Recreations:* sailing, chess, playing the organ. *Address:* Deutscher Bundestag, Görresstrasse 15, Bundeshaus, 5300 Bonn, West Germany.

SCHMITTHOFF, Clive Macmillan, Dr jur, LLD; barrister; Visiting Professor of Law at University of Kent at Canterbury, since 1971; Visiting Professor of International Business Law at City University, since 1971; *b* 24 March 1903; *s* of Hermann and Anna Schmitthoff; *m* 1940, Twinkie (Ilse) (*née* Auerbach). *Educ:* Univs of Berlin and London. Dr jur Berlin 1927; LLM 1936, LLD 1953, London. Called to Bar, Gray's Inn, 1936. Lectr, 1948-58, Sen. Lectr, 1958-63, Principal Lectr, 1963-71, City of London Polytechnic. Served HM Army, 1940-45: Normandy, War Office, CCG, Warrant Officer (France and Germany Star, Def. and War medals). Vis. Prof., Louisiana State Univ., 1964, 1965; Legal Adviser to UN, 1966; Vis. Prof., Univ. of Manitoba Law Sch., 1966, 1967, 1978; Gresham Prof. in Law, 1976-. Vice-President: Assoc. of Law Teachers, 1965-; Inst. of Export, 1979-; Founder and Gen. Editor, Journal of Business Law, 1957-. Hon. Professor of Law: Ruhr Univ., Bochum, 1968; Univ. of Kent, 1978; Hon. Djur Marburg and Berne, 1977; Hon. DLitt Heriot-Watt, 1978; Hon. LLD Kent, 1982. Grand Cross of Merit, German Fed. Republic, 1974. *Publications:* The English Conflict of Laws, 1945, 3rd edn 1954; The Export Trade, 1948, 7th edn 1980; The Sale of Goods, 1951, 2nd edn 1966; ed, Palmer's Company Law, 1959-, 23rd edn 1982; ed, Charlesworth's Mercantile Law, 1960-, 14th edn 1983; Commercial Law in a Changing Economic Climate, 1977, 2nd edn 1981; contrib. many legal jls, UK and abroad. *Recreations:* history, literature, music, modern art. *Address:* 29 Blenheim Road, Bedford Park, W4 1ET.

SCHMOLLER, Hans Peter, RDI 1976; typographer; *b* 9 April 1916; *o c* of Dr Hans Schmoller and Marie (*née* Behrend); *m* 1st, 1947, Dorothée Wachsmuth (*d* 1948); one *d*; 2nd, 1950, Tatyana Kent; one *s*. *Educ:* Kaiser-Friedrich-Sch., Berlin-Charlottenburg. Left sch. soon after Hitler came to power, 1933; served apprenticeship as compositor, studying calligraphy and typography privately, 1933-37; Morija Printing Works, Morija, Basutoland (now Lesotho), 1938-46; Asst to Oliver Simon at Curwen Press, London, 1947-49; joined Penguin Books Ltd, as Typographer, 1949; Head of Production, 1956-76; Dir, 1960-76; Consultant, 1976-80. Has served on book design juries in Britain, Germany and USA; lectured in England and abroad; participated in internat. book design projects. Mem. Council, RSA, 1979- (FRSA, 1977). Francis Minns Memorial Award, 1974. Gold medal, Internat. Book Design Exhibn, Leipzig, 1971. Corresp. Mem., Bund Deutscher Buchkünstler (Fed. Germany), 1965. *Publications:* Mr Gladstone's Washi, 1983; contributor to: Essays in the History of Publishing: Longman 1724-1974 (ed Asa Briggs); The Times, TLS, Penrose Annual, Signature, Imprimatur, Philobiblon; ed, The Officina Bodoni 1923-1977, German edn 1979, English and Italian edns 1980. *Recreations:* book-collecting, paper-chasing, peregrinating. *Address:* Steading, Down Place, Windsor, Berks SL4 5UG. *T:* Maidenhead 23565. *Clubs:* Arts; Double Crown (Pres. 1968-69).

SCHNEIDER, Rt. Hon. Lancelot Raymond A.; *see* Adams-Schneider.

SCHNEIDER, Dr William George, OC 1977; FRS 1962; FRSC 1951; Research Consultant, National Research Council of Canada, Ottawa, since 1980 (President, 1967-80); *b* Wolseley, Saskatchewan, 1 June 1915; *s* of Michael Schneider and Phillipina Schneider (*née* Kraushaar); *m* 1940, Jean Frances Purves; two *d*. *Educ:* University of Saskatchewan; McGill University; Harvard University. BSc 1937, MSc 1939, University of Saskatchewan; PhD (in physical chem.), 1941, McGill Univ. Research physicist at Woods Hole Oceanographic Inst., Woods Hole, Mass, USA, 1943-46 (US Navy Certificate of Merit, 1946). Joined Nat. Research Council, Division of Pure Chemistry, Ottawa, 1946; Vice-President (Scientific), 1965-67. Chemical Inst. of Canada Medal, 1961, Montreal Medal, 1973; Henry Marshall Tory Medal, RSC, 1969. Hon. DSc: York, 1966; Memorial, 1968; Saskatchewan, 1969; Moncton, 1969; McMaster, 1969; Laval, 1969; New Brunswick, 1970; Montreal, 1970; McGill, 1970; Acadia, 1976; Regina, 1976; Ottawa, 1978; Hon. LLD: Alberta, 1968; Laurentian, 1968. *Publications:* (with J. A. Pople and H. J. Bernstein) High Resolution Nuclear Magnetic Resonance, 1959; scientific papers in chemistry and physics research jls. *Recreations:* tennis, ski-ing. *Address:* 133 Blenheim Drive, Ottawa, Ontario K1A 5B7, Canada.

SCHNEIDERHAN, Frau Wolfgang; *see* Seefried, Irmgard.

SCHNYDER, Félix; Ambassador of Switzerland to the United States, 1966-75; *b* 5 March 1910; Swiss; *s* of Maximilian Schnyder and Louise (*née* Steiner); *m* 1941, Sigrid Bucher; one *d*. *Educ:* University of Berne. Barrister, 1938; activities in private enterprise, 1938-40; joined Federal Political Dept, 1940; assigned to Swiss Legation in Moscow, 1947-49; Counsellor of Legation, Head of Swiss Delegation in Berlin, 1949-54; First Counsellor, Swiss Legation in Washington, 1954-57; Swiss Minister in Israel, 1957; Permanent Observer for Switzerland at UN in New York, 1958-61; Swiss Delegate to Technical Assistance Cttee; Swiss Delegate to Exec. Board of UNICEF (Chm. 1960);

UN High Comr for Refugees, 1961-65. President: Swiss Nat. Cttee for UNESCO, 1976-80; Swiss Foreign Policy Assoc., 1976-. *Recreations:* ski-ing, mountaineering, reading (history and politics), chess and bridge. *Address:* Via Navegna 25, 6648 Minusio-Locarno, Switzerland.

SCHOFIELD, Alfred, FCBSI; Director, Leeds Permanent Building Society; General Commissioner for Income Tax, Leeds district, since 1971; *b* 18 Feb. 1913; *s* of James Henry and Alice Schofield; *m* 1939, Kathleen Risingham; one *d*. *Educ:* Queen Elizabeth's Grammar Sch., Wakefield. Apptd General Manager, Leeds Permanent Bldg Soc., 1967; retd, 1973; Pres., 1975-78. Trustee, 1969-, Dep. Chm., 1973-, Sutton Housing Trust; Dir, Leeds Bd, Royal Insce Co. Ltd, 1967-. *Recreation:* orchid growing. *Address:* The Cottage, Rudding, Harrogate, N Yorks HG3 1DH. *T:* Harrogate 872037.

SCHOFIELD, Prof. Andrew Noel, MA, PhD (Cantab); CEng, FICE; Professor of Engineering, Cambridge University, since 1974; Fellow of Churchill College, Cambridge, 1963-66 and since 1974; *b* 1 Nov. 1930; *s* of Rev. John Noel Schofield and Winifred Jane Mary (*née* Eyles); *m* 1961, Margaret Eileen Green; two *s* two *d*. *Educ:* Mill Hill Sch.; Christ's Coll., Cambridge. John Winbolt Prize, 1954. Asst Engr, in Malawi, with Scott Wilson Kirkpatrick and Partners, 1951. Cambridge Univ.: Demonstrator, 1955, Lectr, 1959, Dept of Engrg. Research Fellow, California Inst. of Technology, 1963-64. Univ. of Manchester Inst. of Science and Technology: Prof. of Civil Engrg, 1968; Head of Dept of Civil and Structural Engrg, 1973. Rankine Lecture, ICE British Geotechnical Soc., 1980. Chm., Sub-Cttee on Centrifuges, Int. Soc. for Soil Mech. and Foundn Engrg, 1982-. US Army Outstanding Civilian Service Medal, 1980. *Publications:* (with C. P. Wroth) Critical State Soil Mechanics, 1968; papers on soil mechanics and civil engrg. *Address:* 14 Hills Avenue, Cambridge CB1 4XA. *T:* Cambridge 247551.

SCHOFIELD, Bertram, CBE 1959; MA, PhD, LittD; Keeper of Manuscripts and Egerton Librarian, British Museum, 1956-61; *b* 13 June 1896; *m* 1928, Edith (*d* 1981), *d* of Arthur William and Edith Emily Thomas; one *s* two *d*. *Educ:* University Sch., Southport; University of Liverpool (Charles Beard and University Fellow); Sorbonne, Ecole des Chartes and Ecole des Hautes Etudes, Paris; Emmanuel College, Cambridge (Open Research Student). Served European War, with Roy. Wilts Yeomanry, 1917-19. Asst Keeper, Dept of MSS, British Museum, 1922; Deputy-Keeper, 1947; Keeper, 1956. Seconded to Min. of Economic Warfare, 1940-42, and for special duties with Inter-Services Intelligence and Combined Ops, HQ, 1942-44. Member: Bd of Studies in Palæography, University of London; Committee of Inst. of Historical Research, 1951-61; Council of Royal Historical Society, 1956-59; Canterbury and York Society; Vice-Pres. British Records Assoc., 1956-61; Governor: North London Collegiate School and Camden High Sch. for Girls, 1955-64. *Publications:* Muchelney Memoranda (Somerset Record Soc.), 1927; (with A. J. Collins) Legal and Manorial Formularies, 1933; The Knyvett Letters, 1949; contrib. to Musical Quarterly, Music Review, Music and Letters. British Museum Quarterly, Studies presented to Sir Hilary Jenkinson, 1957; Musik in Geschichte und Gegenwart, etc. *Recreations:* gardening and music. *Address:* 4 Farm Close, Kidlington, Oxford. *T:* Kidlington 4110.

SCHOFIELD, Vice-Adm. Brian Betham, CB 1949; CBE 1943; *b* 11 Oct. 1895; *s* of Thomas Dodgshon Schofield and Margaret Annie Bradley; *m* 1st, 1922, Doris Sibyl Ambrose (marr. diss., 1941); one *s* (and one *s* decd); 2nd, 1941, Norah Kathleen Handley (*née* Beatty) (*d* 1946); 3rd, 1946, Grace Mildred Seale; two *d*. *Educ:* RN Colleges, Osborne and Dartmouth. Midshipman, 1913 (Dogger Bank action); Lieut-Comdr 1925; Comdr 1931; Capt., 1938; Rear-Admiral, 1947; Vice-Adm., 1950; Naval Attaché at The Hague and Brussels, 1939-40; commanded HMS King George V, 1945-46; despatches, 1946. Retired list, 1950. King George VI Coronation medal. Officer of Legion of Merit (USA). *Publications:* The Royal Navy Today, 1960; The Russian Convoys, 1964; British Seapower, 1967; The Rescue Ships (with L. F. Martyn), 1968; The Loss of the Bismarck, 1972; The Attack on Taranto, 1973; Operation Neptune, 1974; The Arctic Convoys, 1977; Navigation and Direction, 1977. *Address:* Holme, Lower Shiplake, Henley-on-Thames, Oxon. *T:* Wargrave 2809.

SCHOFIELD, (Edward) Guy; FJI; Journalist; *b* 10 July 1902; *s* of Frank Garside Schofield and Fanny Atkinson; *m* 1st, Norah Ellett (*d* 1935); one *d*; 2nd, Ellen Clark (*d* 1977). *Educ:* Leeds Modern School. Leeds Mercury, 1918-25; Daily Dispatch, Manchester, 1925-27; Evening Chronicle, Manchester, 1929-30; Chief Sub-Editor, Evening Standard, London, 1931-38; Editor: Yorkshire Evening News, 1938-42; The Evening News, London, 1942-50; Daily Mail, London, 1950-55; Director: Associated Newspapers Ltd, 1947-55; United Newspapers Ltd, 1960-79; Sheffield Newspapers Ltd, 1963-79; Yorkshire Post Newspapers Ltd, 1969-82. Member of Press Council, 1953-55; Chairman British Committee, International Press Institute, 1953-55; Director of Publicity, Conservative Party Headquarters, 1955-57. *Publications:* The Purple and the Scarlet, 1959; Crime Before Calvary, 1960; In the Year 62, 1962; Why Was He Killed?, 1965; The Men that Carry the News, 1975. *Address:* Pear Tree Cottage, Sinnington, York YO6 6RZ. *Club:* National Liberal.

SCHOFIELD, Grace Florence; Regional Nursing Officer to the South West Thames Regional Health Authority, 1974-82, retired; *b* 24 Feb. 1925; *d* of Percy and Matilda Schofield. *Educ:* Mayfield Sch., Putney; University College Hosp. (SRN, SCM); Univ. of London (Dip. in Nursing); Royal College of Nursing (Dip. in Nursing Admin. (Hosp.)). Asst Matron, Guy's

Hosp., 1960-61; Dep. Matron, Hammersmith Hosp., 1962-66; Matron, Mount Vernon Hosp. Northwood, and Harefield Hosp., Harefield, 1966-69; Chief Nursing Officer, University Coll. Hosp., 1969-73. *Address:* 42 Briarwood Road, Stoneleigh, Epsom, Surrey.

SCHOLEFIELD, Charles Edward, QC 1959; *b* 15 July 1902; *e s* of Edward Scholefield, Castleford, Yorks; *m* 1966, Catherine Heléne (formerly Childs), *o d* of Reginald and Marguerite Blyth; one step *s* ; one step *d. Educ:* St Peter's School, York. Admitted a Solicitor, 1925; Barrister, Middle Temple, 1934; North Eastern Circuit. Served in Royal Army Pay Corps, 1940-45; Captain, 1943-45. Chm., Council of Professions supplementary to Medicine, 1966-73. Master of the Bench of the Middle Temple, 1966. *Publications:* (ed) 11th and 12th edns, Lumley's Public Health. *Recreations:* cricket and Rugby football (watching only now); Sherlock Holmes Society of London; Society of Yorkshiremen in London (Past Chairman). *Address:* Gray's Inn Chambers, Gray's Inn, WC2. *T:* 01-242 5226; 18 Aymer Road, Hove, East Sussex.

SCHOLES, Alwyn Denton; Senior Puisne Judge, Hong Kong, 1970-71 (Acting Chief Justice, 1970); *b* 16 Dec. 1910; *s* of Denton Scholes and Mrs Scholes (*née* Birch); *m* 1939, Juliet Angela Ierne Pyne; one *s* four *d. Educ:* Cheltenham College; Selwyn College, Cambridge. Legal Tripos Parts I and II, Cantab, 1932, 1933; MA 1933. Called to the Bar, 1934; practised at the Bar in London and on Midland Circuit, 1934-38; apptd District Magistrate, Gold Coast, 1938; Acting Crown Counsel and Solicitor General, Gold Coast, 1941; apptd Magistrate, Hong Kong, 1948; First Magistrate: Kowloon, 1949; Hong Kong, 1949. Appointed District Judge, Hong Kong, 1953, Puisne Judge, Hong Kong, 1958. Comr, Supreme Ct of State of Brunei, 1964-67, 1968-71. Pres. or Mem., Hong Kong Full Ct of Appeal, on occasions, 1949-71. Member: Sidmouth Parochial Church Council, 1972-82; Ottery Deanery Synod, 1973-82. *Recreations:* walking, swimming, gardening. *Address:* West Hayes, Convent Road, Sidmouth, Devon EX10 8RL. *Clubs:* Royal Commonwealth Society; Rock Sailing.

SCHOLES, Gordon Glen Denton; MHR for Corio (Victoria), since 1967; Shadow Minister for Defence, since 1977; *b* 7 June 1931; *s* of Glen Scholes and Mary Scholes; *m* 1957, Della Kathleen Robinson; two *d. Educ:* various schs. Loco-engine driver, Vic Railways, 1949-67. Councillor, Geelong City, 1965-67; Pres., Geelong Trades Hall Council, 1965-66. House of Representatives: Chm. cttees, 1973-75; Speaker, 1975-76. Amateur Boxing Champion (Heavyweight), Vic, 1949. *Recreations:* golf, reading. *Address:* 11 Lascelles Avenue, Geelong West, Vic 3218, Australia. *T:* 213083.

SCHOLES, Hubert, CB 1977; Specialist Adviser to House of Commons Employment Committee, since 1981; *b* 22 March 1921; *s* of late Hubert Scholes and Lucy (*née* Carter); *m* 1949, Patricia Caldwell; one *s. Educ:* Shrewsbury Sch.; Balliol Coll., Oxford. Served RA, 1940-45. Asst Principal, Min. of Fuel and Power, 1946; Principal, 1950; Ministry of Housing and Local Govt, 1956-57; Principal Private Sec. to Minister of Power, 1959-62; Asst Sec., 1962; Under-Sec., Min. of Power, subseq. Min. of Technol., DTI and Dept of Industry, 1968-78; a Comr of Customs and Excise, 1978-81. *Address:* 5A Lancaster Avenue, Farnham, Surrey. *T:* Farnham 723992.

SCHOLES, Joseph, CB 1945; OBE 1918; *b* 4 Sept. 1889; *s* of John Scholes, Radcliffe, Lancs; *m* 1915, Edna Horrocks (*d* 1981). *Educ:* Manchester Grammar School; Trinity College, Cambridge. Wrangler, Mathematical Tripos, 1911; entered GPO through Higher Division, 1912; Assistant Director of Vegetable Supplies, Ministry of Food, 1916-20; Postmaster-Surveyor, Glasgow, 1936; Regional Director, GPO 1939; Principal Officer to Regional Commissioner, Ministry of Home Security, 1940-43; Assistant Director-General (Personnel) GPO, 1946-49; retired. *Address:* Church Orchard, North Newton, Bridgwater, Somerset. *T:* North Petherton 662338.

SCHOLES, Mary Elizabeth, SRN; Chief Area Nursing Officer, Tayside Health Board, since 1973; *b* 8 April 1924; *d* of late John Neville Carpenter Scholes and Margaret Elizabeth (*née* Hines). *Educ:* Wyggeston Grammar Sch. for Girls, Leicester; Leicester Royal Infirmary and Children's Hosp. (SRN 1946;) Guy's Hosp., London (CMB Pt I Cert. 1947); Royal Coll. of Nursing, London (Nursing Admin (Hosp.) Cert. 1962). Leicester Royal Infirmary and Children's Hospital: Staff Nurse, 1947-48; Night Sister, 1948-50; Ward Sister, 1950-56; Night Supt, 1956-58; Asst Matron, 1958-61; Asst Matron, Memorial/Brook Gen. Hosp., London, 1962-64; Matron, Dundee Royal Infirm. and Matron Designate, Ninewells Hosp., Dundee, 1964-68; Chief Nursing Officer, Bd of Management for Dundee Gen. Hosps and Bd of Man. for Ninewells and Associated Hosps, 1968-73. Pres., Scottish Assoc. of Nurse Administrators, 1973-74. Member: Scottish Bd, Royal Coll. of Nursing, 1965-70; Gen. Nursing Council for Scotland, 1966-70, 1979-; Standing Nursing and Midwifery Cttee, Scotland, 1971-74 (Vice-Chm., 1973-74); UK Central Council for Nursing, Midwifery and Health Visiting, 1980-; Chm., Scottish National Bd for Nursing, Midwifery and Health Visiting, 1980-. *Recreations:* travel, gardening, music. *Address:* Tayside Health Board, PO Box 75, Vernonholme, Riverside Drive, Dundee DD1 9NL. *T:* Dundee 645151. *Club:* Royal Commonwealth Society.

SCHOLEY, David Gerald, CBE 1976; Joint Chairman, S. G. Warburg & Co. Ltd, Bankers, since 1980; a Director, Bank of England, since 1981; *b* 28 June 1935; *s* of Dudley and Lois Scholey; *m* 1960, Alexandra Beatrix, *d* of Hon. George and Fiorenza Drew, Canada; one *s* one *d. Educ:* Wellington Coll., Berks; Christ Church, Oxford. Joined S. G. Warburg & Co. Ltd, 1965, Dir

1967, Dep. Chm., 1977; Director: Mercury Securities Ltd, 1969 (Dep. Chm., 1980-); Orion Insurance Co. Ltd, 1963; Stewart Wrightson Holdings Ltd, 1972-81; Union Discount Co. of London, Ltd, 1976-81. Mem., Export Guarantees Adv. Council, 1970-75, Dep. Chm. 1974-75; Chm., Construction Exports Adv. Bd, 1975-78; Mem., Cttee on Finance for Industry, NEDO, 1980-. Governor, Wellington Coll., 1977. *Address:* Heath End House, Spaniards Road, NW3 7JE. *T:* 01-455 4795.

SCHOLEY, Robert, CBE 1982; Deputy Chairman, since 1976, Member and Chief Executive, since 1973, British Steel Corporation; *b* 8 Oct. 1921; *s* of Harold and Eveline Scholey; *m* 1946, Joan Methley; two *d. Educ:* King Edward VII Sch. and Sheffield Univ. Associateship in Mech Engrg. United Steel Companies, 1947-68; British Steel Corporation: (following nationalisation) Dir, Rotherham Div., Midland Gp, 1968; Dir, Steelworks Gp, Special Steels Div., 1970; Managing Dir: Ops (London), 1972; Strip Mills Div., 1972. *Recreations:* outdoor life, history of the arts. *Address:* The Coach House, Much Hadham, Herts. *T:* Much Hadham 2908.

SCHOLTE, Lieut-Col Frederick Lewellen, OBE (mil.) 1919; FIMechE; late RFC; retired Consulting Engineer; *b* 1890; *m* Hilda May (*d* 1969), *d* of James Gardner, Skelmorlie, Ayrshire; one *s* two *d. Educ:* Highgate School. *Address:* 6 Alvanley Court, Finchley Road, NW3. *T:* 01-435 5685. *Clubs:* Royal Automobile, Royal Air Force.

SCHOLTENS, Sir James (Henry), KCVO 1977 (CVO 1963); consultant; Director, Office of Government Ceremonial and Hospitality, Department of the Prime Minister and Cabinet, Canberra, 1973-80, retired; Extra Gentleman Usher to the Queen, since 1981; *b* 12 June 1920; *s* of late Theo F. J. Scholtens and late Grace M. E. (*née* Nolan); *m* 1945, Mary Maguire, Brisbane; one *s* five *d. Educ:* St Patrick's Marist Brothers' Coll., Sale, Vic. Served War, RAAF, 1943-45. Joined Aust. Public Service, 1935; PMG's Dept, Melbourne, 1935; Dept of Commerce, Melb., 1938; transf. to Dept of Commerce, Canberra, 1941; Dept of Prime Minister, Canberra: Accountant, 1949; Ceremonial Officer, 1954; Asst Sec., Ceremonial and Hospitality Br., 1967. Dir of visits to Australia by the Sovereign and Members of the Royal Family, Heads of State, Monarchs and Presidents, and by Heads of Govt and Ministers of State. *Address:* 74 Boldrewood Street, Turner, Canberra, ACT 2601, Australia. *T:* 48 6639. *Clubs:* Canberra, Southern Cross, National Press (Canberra); Royal Automobile of Australia (Sydney).

SCHON, family name of **Baron Schon.**

SCHON, Baron *cr* 1976 (Life Peer), of Whitehaven, Cumbria; **Frank Schon,** Kt 1966; Chairman, National Research Development Corporation, 1969-79 (Member, 1967-79); *b* 18 May 1912; *o s* of Dr Frederick Schon and Henriette (*née* Nettel); *m* 1936, Gertrude Secher; two *d. Educ:* Rainer Gymnasium, Vienna II; University of Prague; University of Vienna (studied law externally). Co-founder: Marchon Products Ltd, 1939; Solway Chemicals Ltd, 1943; Chm. and Man. Dir of both until May 1967; Dir, Albright & Wilson Ltd, 1956-67; Non-exec. Dir, Blue Circle Industries Ltd (formerly Associated Portland Cement Manufacturers Ltd), 1967-82. Mem. Council, King's College, Durham, 1959-63; Mem. Council, 1963-66, Mem. Court, 1963-78, Univ. of Newcastle upon Tyne. Chm. Cumberland Development Council, 1964-68; Member: Northern Economic Planning Council, 1965-68; Industrial Reorganisation Corp., 1966-71; Adv. Council of Technology, 1968-70; part-time Mem., Northern Gas Bd, 1963-66. Hon. Freeman of Whitehaven, 1961. Hon. DCL Durham, 1961. *Recreations:* golf, reading. *Address:* Flat 82, Prince Albert Court, 33 Prince Albert Road, NW8 7LU. *T:* 01-586 1461.

SCHOTZ, Benno, RSA 1937; RGI 1977; artist-sculptor; Queen's Sculptor in Ordinary for Scotland, since 1963; *b* 1891; *s* of Jacob Schotz; *m* 1927, Milly Stelmach; one *s* one *d. Educ:* Pärnu, Estonia; Glasgow. BSc 1965. Head of Sculpture and Ceramics Departments, Glasgow School of Art, 1938-61. Originally studied engineering at Darmstadt and Glasgow Royal Technical Coll.; then took up sculpture; at Glasgow Art School; first one-man show in 1926 at Reid and Lefevre's in Glasgow; second 1929; first London one-man show at the Lefevre Galleries, 1930; one-man show in Dundee, 1935, Edinburgh, 1945, Jerusalem and Haifa Municipal Galleries, 1954-55; Edinburgh Festival, 1955; Royal Fine Art Institute Rooms, Glasgow, 1957; Exhibitions: by Arts Council of Great Britain (Scottish Cttee) in Edinburgh, Aberdeen, Dundee, Perth, Stirling, 1962; Glasgow, 1963; New Charing Cross Gall, 1968; by Scottish Arts Council, Edinburgh and Aberdeen, 1971; represented in Public Galleries in Glasgow, Edinburgh, Aberdeen, Perth, Dundee, Paisley, Stoke-on-Trent, Belfast, Jerusalem, Tel-Aviv and New Zealand; modelled many personalities in the arts and politics; Bust of Keir Hardie in House of Commons, 1956. Has a number of carvings on buildings in Glasgow and elsewhere; sculpture groups in churches and schools; 23 foot high Group Town Centre piece in Glenrothes; statue of Rob Roy, Stirling, 1975, etc. Freedom, City of Glasgow, 1981. Hon. FRIAS 1969; Hon. President: Glasgow Group, 1970; Royal Glasgow Inst. of Fine Arts, 1973. Hon. Mem., RBS, 1980. Hon. LLD Strathclyde, 1969. *Address:* 2 Kirklee Road, Glasgow G12 0TN. *T:* 041-339 9963. *Club:* Glasgow Art (Glasgow).

SCHOUVALOFF, Alexander, MA; Curator, Theatre Museum, Victoria and Albert Museum, since 1974; *b* 4 May 1934; *s* of Paul Schouvaloff (professional name Paul Sheriff) and Anna Schouvaloff (*née* Raevsky); *m* 1st, Gillian Baker; one *s* ; 2nd, 1971, Daria Chorley (*née* de Mérindol). *Educ:* Harrow Sch.; Jesus

Coll., Oxford (MA). Asst Director, Edinburgh Festival, 1965-67; Dir, North West Arts Assoc., 1967-74; Director: Rochdale Festival, 1971; Chester Festival, 1973. Sec. Gen., Société Internat. des Bibliothèques et des Musées des Arts du Spectacle, 1980-. BBC Radio plays: Summer of the Bullshine Boys, 1981; No Saleable Value, 1982. FRSA. Cross of Polonia Restituta, 1971. *Publications:* Place for the Arts, 1971; Summer of the Bullshine Boys, 1979; (with Victor Borovsky) Stravinsky on Stage, 1982. *Recreations:* staying afloat. *Address:* 59 Lyndhurst Grove, SE15. *T:* 01-703 3671. *Club:* Garrick.

SCHRAM, Emil; Chairman of Board, Peru Trust Co.; *b* Peru, Indiana, 23 November 1893; *s* of Emil Alexander Schram and Katharine Graf; *m* 1914, Mabel Miller (decd); three *s*; *m* 1971, Margaret Beauchamp Percy. *Educ:* Peru High School. Book-keeper, J. O. Cole, Peru, Ind., 1910-15; manager Hartwell Land Trust, Hillview, Ill., 1915-33; Chairman National Drainage Assoc., 1931-33; chief, drainage, levee and irrigation div., Reconstruction Finance Corp., 1933-36; Director, 1936-41; Chm., 1939-41; President, New York Stock Exchange, 1941-51; Director: Cities Service Co.; Associates Investment Co.; Home Insce Co.; Indiana National Bank; CTS Corp. Valley Farms, Inc.; Hon. Mem. Business Council. Hon. degrees: Dr of Law: New York Univ.; Univ. of Vermont; Franklin College; Indiana Univ. *Recreations:* golf and fishing. *Address:* Hillcrest, RR1, Peru, Ind 46970, USA. *T:* 473 9100. *Club:* Columbia (Indianapolis).

SCHRAM, Prof. Stuart Reynolds; Professor of Politics (with reference to China) in the University of London, School of Oriental and African Studies, since 1968; *b* Excelsior, Minn, 27 Feb. 1924; *s* of Warren R. Schram and Nada Stedman Schram; *m* 1972, Marie-Annick Lancelot; one *s*. *Educ:* West High Sch., Minneapolis, Minn; Univ. of Minnesota (BA, 1944); Columbia Univ. (PhD 1954). Dir, Soviet and Chinese Section, Centre d'Etude des Relations Internationales, Fondation Nationale des Sciences Politiques, Paris, 1954-67; Head, Contemporary China Inst., SOAS, 1968-72. *Publications:* Protestantism and Politics in France, 1954; La théorie de la "révolution permanente" en Chine, 1963; The Political Thought of Mao Tse-Tung, 1963, rev. edn 1969; Le marxisme et l'Asie 1853-1964, 1965, rev. and enl. English edn 1969; Mao Tse-tung, 1966; Authority, Participation and Cultural Change in China, 1973; *translations:* Mao Ze-dong, Une étude de l'éducation physique, 1962; Mao Tse-tung, Basic Tactics, 1966; Mao Tse-tung, Unrehearsed, 1974. *Recreations:* concert- and theatre-going, walking in the country, fishing. *Address:* 4 Regal Lane, NW1.

SCHREIBER, Mrs Gaby, FSIAD; General Consultant Designer for Industry; specialist in Colour Consultancy and Interiors; Adviser on purchases of works of art; Chairman, Gaby Schreiber & Associates; *d* of Gunther George Peter Wolff; *m* Leopold Schreiber (*d* 1961). *Educ:* studied art and stage and interior design in Vienna, Florence, Berlin and Paris. Interior Design Consultant to: William Clark & Sons Ltd, NI, 1981-; National Westminster Bank Ltd; Westminster Foreign Bank, Brussels, 1972-73; Chm.'s offices, GHP Gp Ltd, 1974; Pres.'s offices, Gulf Oil-Eastern Hemisphere, 1973-74; Lythe Hill Hotel, Haslemere, Surrey; Anglo-Continental Investment & Finance Co. and Continental Bankers Agents, London; Myers & Co.; Peter Robinson Ltd; David Morgan, Cardiff; W Cumberland Hosp.; Newcastle Regnl Hosp. Bd; Fine Fare Ltd (Queensway Store, Crawley); Gen. Consultant and Designer to: Cunard Steamship Co. Ltd (QE2); Zarach Ltd; Marquess of Londonderry; Crown Agents; Allen and Hanbury (Surgical Engineering) Limited; BOAC (whole fleet of aeroplanes, 1957-63); Divs of Dunlop Rubber Gp; Bartrev Gp of Cos; Hawker Siddeley Aviation Ltd (for the Queen's Flight and RAF); Rank Organisation Ltd; Design Consultant on Plastics to Marks & Spencer Ltd. Yachts: Sir Gerard d'Erlanger; Whitney Straight, and others. Designed Exhibn Stands in Britain, Europe and USA. Member CoID, 1960-62 (Mem. Design Awards Cttee, 1961); Judge on Indep. Panel, to select Duke of Edinburgh's Prize for Elegant Design, 1960 and 1961. Fellow, Soc. of Industrial Artists and Designers (Past Chm., Consultant Designers Gp and Internat. Relations Cttee; Mem. Council; UK delegate at Gen. Assembly of Internat. Council of Soc. of Ind. Design, Venice, 1961); Mem., Panel of Judges for newspaper and magazine competitions on ind. design. Has broadcast and appeared on TV. *Publications:* her work has appeared in internat. books and jls on design. *Recreations:* gardening, farming, golf, arts and crafts. *Address:* 9 Eaton Square, SW1. *T:* 01-235 4656.

SCHREIBER, Mark Shuldham; Editorial Staff of The Economist, since 1974, lobby correspondent, since 1976; *b* 11 Sept. 1931; *s* of late John Shuldham Schreiber, DL, Marlesford Hall, Suffolk and Maureen Schreiber (*née* Dent); *m* 1969, Gabriella Federica, *d* of Conte Teodoro Veglio di Castelletto Uzzone; two *d*. *Educ:* Eton; Trinity Coll., Cambridge. Nat. Service in Coldstream Guards, 1950-51. Fisons Ltd, 1957-63; Conservative Research Dept, 1963-67; Dir, Conservative Party Public Sector Research Unit, 1967-70; Special Advr to the Govt, 1970-74; Special Adviser to Leader of the Opposition, 1974-75; Member: Royal Ordnance Factories Bd, 1972-74; Govt Computer Agency Council, 1973-74; Countryside Commn, 1980-. Mem., East Suffolk CC, 1968-70. *Recreation:* thinking the unthinkable. *Address:* Marlesford Hall, Woodbridge, Suffolk. *T:* Wickham Market 310; 5 Kersley Street, SW11. *Clubs:* Turf, Pratt's.

SCHREYER, Rt. Hon. Edward Richard, CC (Canada) 1979; CMM 1979; CD 1979; Governor-General and Commander-in-Chief of Canada, since Jan. 1979; *b* Beausejour, Man., 21 Dec. 1935; *s* of John and Elizabeth Schreyer, members of a pioneer family of the district; *m* 1960, Lily, *d* of Jacob Schulz,

MP; two *s* two *d*. *Educ:* United Coll., Winnipeg; St John's Coll., Winnipeg, Univ. of Manitoba (BA, BEd, MA). While at university served as 2nd Lieut, COTC, Royal Canadian Armored Corps, 1954-56. Member, Legislative Assembly of Manitoba, 1958; re-elected, 1959 and 1962; MP: for Springfield, 1965, for Selkirk, 1968; chosen as Leader of New Democratic Party in Manitoba, 1969, and resigned seat in House of Commons; MLA for Rossmere and Premier of Manitoba, 1969; re-elected MLA, 1977, becoming Leader of the Opposition. Prof. of Political Science and Internat. Relns, St John's Coll., Univ. of Manitoba, 1962-65. Member, Commonwealth Parly Assoc., Interparly Union, 1960-78. Chancellor and Principal Companion of the Order of Canada, 1979; Chancellor and Commander of the Order of Military Merit, 1979. Vanier Award as Outstanding Young Canadian, 1975. *Recreations:* curling, golf, canoeing. *Address:* Rideau Hall, Ottawa, Ontario, K1A 0A1, Canada.

SCHRIEFFER, Prof. John Robert, PhD; Professor of Physics, University of California, Santa Barbara, since 1980; *b* Oak Park, Ill, 31 May 1931; *s* of John Henry Schrieffer and Louise Anderson; *m* 1960, Anne Grete Thomsen; one *s* two *d*. *Educ:* MIT(BS); Univ. of Illinois (MS, PhD). Nat. Sci. Foundn Fellow, Univ. of Birmingham, and Niels Bohr Inst. for Theoretical Physics, Copenhagen, 1957-58; Asst Prof., Univ. of Chicago, 1957-59; Asst Prof., Univ. of Illinois, 1959-60, Associate Prof., 1960-62; Univ. of Pennsylvania: Mem. Faculty, 1962-79; Mary Amanda Wood Prof. of Physics, 1964-79. Guggenheim Fellow, Copenhagen, 1967. Member: Nat. Acad. Scis; Amer. Acad. of Arts and Scis; Amer. Philos. Soc.; Amer. Phys Soc. Hon. ScD: Technische Hoschschule, Munich, 1968; Univ. of Geneva, 1968; Univ. of Pennsylvania, 1973; Illinois Univ., 1974; Univ. of Cincinnati, 1977. Buckley Prize, Amer. Phys Soc., 1968; Comstock Prize, Nat. Acad. Scis, 1968; (jtly) Nobel Prize for Physics, 1972; John Ericsson Medal, Amer. Soc. of Swedish Engineers, 1976. *Publications:* Theory of Superconductivity, 1964; articles on solid state physics and chemistry. *Recreations:* painting, gardening, wood working. *Address:* Department of Physics, University of California, Santa Barbara, Calif 93106, USA.

SCHRODER, Ernest Melville, CMG 1970; *b* 23 Aug. 1901; *s* of Harold Schroder and Florence L. A. Schroder (*née* Stimson); *m* 1928, Winsome Dawson; two *s* one *d*. *Educ:* Newcastle (NSW) High Sch.; Newcastle Techn. College. Chief Chemist: Kandos Cement Co., Sydney, 1927-30; Australian Cement Ltd, Geelong, 1930-44; Man. Dir, Adelaide Cement Ltd, Adelaide, 1944-68, Chm., 1970-77; Dir, Quarry Industries Ltd, 1965-77. Pres., SA Chamber of Manufacturers, 1963-64, 1964-65; Vice-Pres., Assoc. Chamber of Manufrs of Aust., 1964-65; Pres., Cement and Concrete Assoc. of Aust., 1953-54, 1960-61; State Cttee Mem., CSIRO, 1954-71; Mem., CSIRO Adv. Council, 1955-61. FRACI; AIEAust; MAIMM; FAIM. *Recreation:* gardening. *Address:* 23 Coreega Avenue, Springfield, South Australia 5062. *T:* Adelaide 796452. *Club:* Adelaide.

SCHULTZ, Sir Leo, (Joseph Leopold), Kt 1966; OBE 1945; Member, Kingston upon Hull District Council, since 1973; *b* 4 Feb. 1900; *s* of Solomon Schultz; *m* 1928, Kate, *d* of George Pickersgill; one *s*. *Educ:* Hull. Alderman, City of Kingston upon Hull, 1962-74. Chm., Humberside Local Govt Reorganisation Jt Cttee, 1973; Mem., Humberside County Council, 1973-76. *Recreation:* cricket. *Address:* 6 Newland Park, Kingston upon Hull HU5 2DW. *T:* Hull 42253.

SCHULTZ, Prof. Theodore W., PhD; Charles L. Hutchinson Distinguished Service Professor of Economics, University of Chicago, since 1952; *b* 30 April 1902; *s* of Henry E. Schultz and Anna Elizabeth Weiss; *m* Esther Florence Werth; one *s* two *d*. *Educ:* South Dakota State Coll. (BS); Univ. of Wisconsin (MS, PhD). Iowa State College: Faculty of Economics, 1930-43; Head, Dept of Economics and Sociology, 1934-43; University of Chicago: Prof. of Economics, from 1943; Chairman, Dept of Economics, 1946-61. Hon. LLD: Grinnell Coll. 1949; Michigan State 1962; Illinois 1968; Wisconsin 1968; Catholic Univ. of Chile 1979; Dijon 1981. Francis A. Walker Medal, Amer. Econ. Assoc., 1972; Leonard Elmhirst Medal, Internat. Agricl Econ. Assoc., 1976; Nobel Prize for Economic Science, 1979. *Publications:* Redirecting Farm Policy, 1943; Agriculture in an Unstable Economy, 1945; The Economic Organization of Agriculture, 1953; The Economic Value of Education, 1963; Transforming Traditional Agriculture, 1964; Economic Growth and Agriculture, 1968; Investment in Human Capital: role of education and research, 1971; Human Resources: policy issues and research opportunities, 1972; (ed) Distortions of Agricultural Incentives, 1978; Investing in People: the economics of population quality, 1981. *Address:* 5620 South Kimbark Avenue, Chicago, Illinois 60637, USA. *T:* (312) 493-6083.

SCHUMANN, Maurice; Chevalier de la Légion d'Honneur; Compagnon de la Libération; Croix de Guerre 1939-45); Senator from the Department of the Nord, since 1974; Vice-President of the Senate, since 1977; Member, Académie Française, since 1974; writer and broadcaster; *b* Paris, 10 April 1911; *s* of Julien Schumann and Thérèse Michel; *m* 1944, Lucie Daniel; three *d*. *Educ:* Lycées of Janson-de-Sailly and Henry IV; Faculty of Letters, Univ. of Paris (Licencié ès Lettres). Attached to l'Agence Havas in London and later Paris, 1935-39; Chief Official Broadcaster, BBC French Service, 1940-44; Liaison Officer with Allied Expeditionary Forces at end of war; Mem. Provisional Consultative Assembly, Nov. 1944-July 1945; Deputy for Nord, 1945-67 and 1968-73; Mem. Constituent Assemblies, Oct. 1945-May 1946 and June-Nov. 1946. Chm., Popular Republican Movement (MRP); Deputy of this group, 1945-73 (Pres., 1945-49; Hon. Pres., 1949-); Dep. Minister for Foreign Affairs,

1951-54; Pres., For. Affairs Cttee of Nat. Assembly, 1959; Minister of State (Prime Minister's Office), April-May 1962; Minister of State, in charge of scientific res. and atomic and spacial questions, 1967-68; Minister of State for Social Affairs, 1968-69; Minister for Foreign Affairs, 1969-73. Has been Pres. of various organisations, incl. Internat. Movement for Atlantic Union, 1966-. Hon. LLD: Cantab, 1972; St Andrews, 1974. *Publications:* Le Germanisme en marche, 1938; Mussolini, 1939; Les problèmes Ukrainiens et la paix européenne, 1939; Honneur et Patrie, 1945; Le vrai malaise des intellectuels de gauche, 1957; La Mort née de leur propre vie: essai sur Péguy, Simone Weil et Gandhi, 1974; Un Certain 18 Juin, 1980 (Prix Aujourd'hui); *novels:* Le Rendezvous avec quelqu'un, 1962; Les Flots roulant au loin, 1973; La Communication, 1974; Angoisse et Certitude, 1978 (Grand Prix de Littérature Catholique); Le Concerto en Ut Majeur, 1982; chapters in: Mazarin, 1960; Talleyrand, 1962; Clemenceau, 1974; many articles etc (under pseudonym of André Sidobre) to L'Aube (Paris daily), Le Temps présent and La Vie catholique, etc. *Address:* 53 avenue du Maréchal-Lyautey, Paris 16e, France.

SCHUSTER, Sir (Felix) James (Moncrieff), 3rd Bt, cr 1906; OBE 1955; TD; Senior Partner, Sheppards and Chase, 1970-75, retired; b 8 January 1913; o s of Sir Victor Schuster, 2nd Bt, and Lucy, d of W. B. Skene, Pitlour-Halyards, Fife; S father, 1962; m 1937, Ragna, er d of late Direktor Sundo, Copenhagen; two d. *Educ:* Winchester. Served War of 1939-45, with The Rifle Brigade (Middle East and Combined Operations). Lt-Col comdg London Rifle Brigade. Rangers (RB), TA, 1952; Bt-Colonel, 1955. Hon. Col, 5th Bn Royal Green Jackets, 1970-75. *Heir:* none. *Address:* Piltdown Cottage, Piltdown, Uckfield, East Sussex TN22 3XB. *T:* Newick 2916. *Clubs:* Naval and Military, Lansdowne.

SCHUSTER, Sir James; see Schuster, Sir F. J. M.

SCHUSTER, Rt. Rev. James Leo; Rector of Swellendam, Archdeacon of Riversdale, since 1980; b 18 July 1912; s of Rev. Harold Vernon Schuster and Elsie Jane (née Roberton); m 1951, Ilse Henriette Emmy Gottschalk; three s two d (and one s decd). *Educ:* Lancing; Keble Coll., Oxford. Deacon, 1937; Priest, 1938; Asst Missioner, Clare Coll. Mission, Rotherhithe, 1937-38; Chaplain St Stephen's House, Oxford, 1938-40; CF (EC), 1940-46; wounded, 1942; despatches, 1943. Chaplain, St Stephen's House, Oxford, 1946-49; Principal St Bede's Coll., Umtata, 1949-56; Bishop of St John's, 1956-79. *Address:* PO Box 285, Swellendam, 6740, South Africa.

SCHWARTZ, George Leopold, BA, BSc (Econ.); Deputy City Editor Sunday Times, Economic Adviser Kemsley Newspapers, 1944-61; writer of Sunday Times economics column, 1961-71; b 10 Feb. 1891; s of late Adolph George Schwartz, Philadelphia; m 1927, Rhoda Lomax (d 1966). *Educ:* Varndean Sch; St Paul's Coll., Cheltenham; London School of Economics. Teacher, LCC, 1913; Secretary London Cambridge Economic Service, 1923; Cassel Lecturer in University of London, 1929. Editor Bankers' Magazine, 1945-54. Hon. Fellow, London School of Economics. *Publications:* (with F. W. Paish) Insurance Funds and their Investment, 1934; Bread and Circuses, 1959; articles and pamphlets. *Recreation:* detesting government. *Address:* 28 Spencer Drive, N2. *T:* 01-455 7423. *Club:* Reform.

SCHWARZ, Rudolf; CBE 1973; Conductor Laureate, Northern Sinfonia of England (formerly Northern Sinfonia Orchestra, Newcastle upon Tyne), since 1982 (Principal Guest Conductor, 1973-82); b 29 April 1905; Austrian (British subject, 1952); m 1950, Greta Ohlson; one s (and one step d and one step s). *Educ:* Vienna. Conductor, Opera House, Düsseldorf, 1923-27; Conductor, Opera House, Karlsruhe, 1927-33; Musical Director, Jewish Cultural Organisation, Berlin, 1936-41; Conductor, Bournemouth Municipal Orchestra, 1947-51; Conductor, City of Birmingham Symphony Orchestra, 1951-57; Chief Conductor of the BBC Symphony Orchestra, 1957-62; Principal Conductor, Northern Sinfonia Orchestra, Newcastle upon Tyne, 1964-73; Guest Conductor, Bergen Orchestra, Norway, 1964-71; Principal Guest Conductor, Bournemouth Symphony Orchestra, 1970-79. Hon. RAM; Hon. GSM; DMus (hc) Newcastle upon Tyne, 1972. *Address:* 24 Wildcroft Manor, SW15 3TS.

SCHWARZ-BART, André; French writer; b Metz, Lorraine, France, 1928; 2nd s of parents from Poland; m Simone Schwarz-Bart. *Educ:* self-educated; Sorbonne. Joined French Resistance at 15. Has worked in a factory and in Les Halles, Paris, while writing. *Publications:* Le Dernier des Justes, 1959 (Prix Goncourt, 1959; Eng. trans., 1960); (with Simone Schwarz-Bart) Un plat de porc aux bananes vertes, 1967 (Jerusalem Prize, 1967); A Woman Named Solitude, 1973. *Address:* c/o Editions du Seuil, 27 rue Jacob, 75261 Paris Cedex 06, France.

SCHWARZENBERGER, Prof. Georg; Professor of International Law in the University of London, 1962-75, now Emeritus; Dean, Faculty of Laws, University College, London, 1965-67 (Vice-Dean, 1949-55 and 1963-65); Director, London Institute of World Affairs since 1943; Barrister-at-Law, Gray's Inn, since 1955; b 20 May 1908; o s of Ludwig and Ferry Schwarzenberger; m 1931, Suse Schwarz; one s. *Educ:* Karls-Gymnasium, Heilbronn aN; Univs of Heidelberg, Frankfurt, Berlin, Tübingen, Paris and London. Dr Jur. (Tübingen) 1930; PhD (London) 1936. Sec. London Inst. of World Affairs (formerly New Commonwealth Inst.) 1934-43; Lectr in Internat. Law and Relations, University Coll., London, 1938-45; Sub-Dean and Tutor, Faculty of Laws, 1942-49; Reader in Internat. Law, 1945-62.

Co-Editor (with G. W. Keeton) of: The Library of World Affairs, 1946-; The Year Book of World Affairs, 1947-; Current Legal Problems, 1948-72. Member, Permanent Finnish-Netherlands Conciliation Commission. Hon. LLD Dalhousie, 1979. *Publications:* The League of Nations and World Order, 1936; Power Politics: A Study of World Society (1st edn 1941, 3rd edn 1964); International Law and Totalitarian Lawlessness, 1943; International Law as Applied by International Court and Tribunals, 1945 (Vol. I, 3rd edn 1957, Vol. II, 1968, Vol. III, 1976); A Manual of International Law, 1947 (6th edn (with E. D. Brown) 1976); The Fundamental Principles of International Law, Hague Academy of Internat. Law (Recueil, Vol. 87), 1955; The Legality of Nuclear Weapons, 1958; The Frontiers of International Law, 1962; The Inductive Approach to International Law, 1965; The Principles and Standards of International Economic Law, Hague Acad. of Internat. Law (Recueil, Vol. 117), 1966; Foreign Investments and International Law, 1969; International Law and Order, 1971; The Dynamics of International Law, 1976. *Recreations:* gardening, swimming. *Address:* 4 Bowers Way, Harpenden, Herts. *T:* Harpenden 3497.

SCHWARZKOPF, Elisabeth; Opera and Concert Singer; b 9 Dec. 1915; o d of Gymnasial-direktor Friedrich Schwarzkopf and Elisabeth (née Fröhlich); m Walter Legge (d 1979). *Educ:* High School for Music, Berlin. Sang at Vienna State Opera, Royal Opera House, Covent Garden, La Scala, Milan, 1948-64 (inc. inauguration Piccolo Teatro della Scala, 1955), Metropolitan Opera, NY, San Francisco Opera, Bayreuth, Aix-en-Provence (first Cigale d'Or, 1974), and other internat. festivals. Made film, Der Rosenkavalier, 1961. Mem., Royal Swedish Acad. for Arts and Sciences; Hon. mem., Accad. S Cecilia, Roma; Corres. mem., Bayerischer Akad. der Künste. MusD (hc) Cambridge, 1976; Hon. Dr Amer. Univ. Washington, DC, 1982. Lilli Lehmann Medal, Salzburg, 1950; first Premio Orfeo d'oro, Mantua; Lily Pons Medal, Paris; Hugo Wolf Verein Medal, Vienna, 1973. Grosse Verdienstkreuz, Germany, 1974; 1st class Order of Dannebrog, Denmark. Hon. RAM. *Publication:* (ed) On and Off the Record: a memoir of Walter Legge, 1982. *Recreations:* music, theatre, tennis, gardening, ski-ing, mountain walking.

SCHWEITZER, Prof. Miguel; Ambassador of Chile to the Court of St James's, since 1980; b 22 July 1940; s of Miguel Schweitzer and Cora Walters; m 1964, Maria Luisa Fernandes; two s one d. *Educ:* The Grange School, Santiago (preparatory and secondary schooling); Law School, Univ. of Chile (law degree). Doctorate in Penal Law, Rome, 1964-65; Professor of Penal Law: Law Sch., Univ. of Chile, 1966; High Sch. of Carabineros (Police), 1968, 1970 and from 1974; Director, Dept of Penal Sciences, Univ. of Chile, 1974-76; Chile's Alternate Representative with the Chilean Delegn to UN, 1975, 1976, 1978; Ambassador on special missions, 1975-; Chilean Delegate to OAS, 1976-78. *Publications:* El Error de Derecho en Materia Penal (Chile), 1964; Sull elemento soggettivo nel reato di bancarotta del l'imprenditore (Rome), 1965; Prospectus for a Course on the Special Part of Penal Law (USA), 1966. *Recreations:* music, reading, golf, tennis, Rugby. *Address:* 92 Eaton Place, SW1. *T:* 01-235 1047. *Clubs:* Temple Golf; Prince of Wales Country (Santiago).

SCHWEITZER, Pierre-Paul; Grand Officier de la Légion d'Honneur; Croix de Guerre (1939-45); Médaille de la Résistance avec rosette; Inspecteur Général des Finances Honoraire, 1974; Chairman: Compagnie de Participations et d'Investissements Holding SA, Luxembourg, since 1975; Société Financière Internationale de Participations, Paris, since 1976; Compagnie Monégasque de Banque, Monaco, since 1978; b 29 May 1912; s of Paul Schweitzer and Emma Munch; m 1941, Catherine Hatt; one s one d. *Educ:* Univs of Strasbourg and Paris; Ecole Libre des Sciences Politiques. Joined French Treasury as Inspecteur des Finances, 1936; Dep. Dir for Internat. Finance, French Treasury, Paris, 1946; Alternate Exec. Dir, IMF, Washington, 1947; Sec.-Gen. for European Economic Cooperation in the French Administration, Paris, 1948; Financial Counsellor, French Embassy, Washington, 1949; Director, Treasury, Paris, 1953; Dep. Governor of the Banque de France, Paris, 1960-63; Inspecteur Général des Finances, 1963; Man. Dir and Chm. Exec. Bd, IMF, 1963-73. Chm., Bank of America International, Luxembourg, 1974-77; Director: Banque Pétrofigaz, Paris, 1974- (Chm., 1974-79); Robeco Gp, Rotterdam, 1974-82; Adv. Dir, Bank of America, NY, 1974-77, and Unilever NV, Rotterdam, 1974-. Hon. LLD: Yale, 1966; Harvard 1966; Leeds, 1968; New York, 1968; George Washington Univ., 1972; Wales, 1972; Williams, 1973. *Address:* 19 rue de Valois, 75001 Paris, France. *T:* 261.48.85.

SCHWINGER, Prof. Julian, AB, PhD; University Professor, University of California at Los Angeles, since 1980 (Professor of Physics, 1972-80); b 12 Feb. 1918; s of Benjamin Schwinger and Belle Schwinger (née Rosenfeld); m 1947, Clarice Carrol. *Educ:* Columbia University. Nat. Research Council Fellow, 1939-40; Research Associate, University of California at Berkeley, 1940-41; Instructor, later Assistant Professor, Purdue University, 1941-43; Member Staff: Radiation Laboratory, MIT, 1943-46; Metallurgy Laboratory, University of Chicago, 1943; Associate Professor of Physics, Harvard University, 1945-47, Prof., 1947-72, Higgins Prof. of Physics, 1966-72. Writer and presenter of series Understanding Space and Time, BBC (jt Univ. of Calif and Open Univ. prodn). Member, Board of Sponsors, Bulletin of the Atomic Scientists. Member: Nat. Acad. of Scis; Amer. Acad. of Arts and Scis; Amer. Phys. Soc.; Amer. Assoc. for Advancement of Science; NY Acad. of Sciences; Bd of Sponsors, Amer. Fedn of Scientists; Royal Instn of GB; Civil Liberties Union. Guggenheim Fellow, 1970. Awarded Nobel Prize for Physics (with R. Feynman and S. Tomonaga), 1965; many other awards and medals. Hon.

DSc: Purdue, 1961; Harvard, 1962; Columbia, 1966; Brandeis, 1973; Gustavus Adolphus Coll., 1975; Hon. LLD City Univ. of NY, 1972. *Publications:* Quantum Electrodynamics (editor), 1958; (with D. Saxon) Discontinuities in Wave Guides, 1968; Particles and Sources, 1969; Quantum Kinematics and Dynamics, 1970; Particles, Sources and Fields, vol I, 1970, vol II, 1973. *Recreations:* tennis, swimming, ski-ing, driving, and being one of the world's worst pianists. *Address:* Department of Physics, University of California at Los Angeles, Calif 90024, USA; 10727 Stradella Court, Los Angeles, Calif 90024.

SCLATER, Prof. John George, PhD; FRS 1982; Director, Massachusetts Institute of Technology, of the Joint Program in Oceanography and Oceanographic Engineering with Woods Hole Oceanographic Institution, since 1981; *b* 17 June 1940; *s* of John George Sclater and Margaret Bennett Glen; *m* 1968, Fredrica Rose Felcyn; two *s*. *Educ:* Carlekemp Priory School; Stonyhurst College; Edinburgh Univ. (BSc); Cambridge Univ. (PhD 1966). Research Scientist, Scripps Instn of Oceanography, 1965; Assoc. Professor, MIT, 1972; Professor, 1977. Fellow Geological Soc. of America; Fellow Amer. Geophysical Union. Rosenstiel Award in Oceanography, 1979. *Recreations:* running, swimming, golf. *Address:* Department of Earth and Planetary Sciences, 54-826 Massachusetts Institute of Technology, Cambridge, Mass 02139, USA. *T:* 617-253-1980.

SCLATER-BOOTH, family name of **Baron Basing**.

SCOBLE, (Arthur William) John; Chairman, Economic Planning Board, South West Region (Bristol), 1965-71, retired; *er s* of Arthur Scoble; *m* 1935, Constance Aveline, *d* of Samuel Robbins; three *d*. Min. of Nat. Insce, 1945-50; jssc 1950; Min. of Works, 1951-59; UN, Buenos Aires, 1960-61; Min. of Works, 1962-64; Dept of Economic Affairs, 1965-70; Dept of the Environment, 1970-71, 1972-73. Chm., Agricl Housing Adv. Cttee, 1977-. Dir, Bath Preservation Trust, 1973-74. Regional Advisor, Employment Fellowship, 1975-79. Clerk to Bathampton Council, 1980-. *Address:* Cross Deep, Bathampton Lane, Bath BA2 6ST. *T:* Bath 60525.

SCOFIELD, (David) Paul, CBE 1956; Actor; *b* 21 Jan. 1922; *s* of Edward H. and M. Scofield; *m* 1943, Joy Parker (actress); one *s* one *d*. *Educ:* Varndean Sch. for Boys, Brighton. Theatre training, Croydon Repertory, 1939; London Mask Theatre School, 1940. Shakespeare with ENSA, 1940-41; Birmingham Repertory Theatre, 1942; CEMA Factory tours, 1942-43; Whitehall Theatre, 1943; Birmingham Repertory, 1943-44-45; Stratford-upon-Avon, 1946-47-48. Mem., Royal Shakespeare Directorate, 1966-68. Associate Dir, Nat. Theatre, 1970-71. London theatres: Arts, 1946; Phoenix, 1947; Adventure Story, and The Seagull, St James's, 1949; Ring Round the Moon, Globe, 1950; Much Ado About Nothing, Phœnix, 1952; The River Line, Edin. Fest., Lyric (Hammersmith), Strand, 1952; John Gielgud's Company, 1952-53: Richard II, The Way of the World, Venice Preserved, etc; A Question of Fact, Piccadilly, 1953-54; Time Remembered, Lyric, Hammersmith, New Theatre, 1954-55; Hamlet, Moscow, 1955; Paul Scofield-Peter Brook Season, Phœnix Theatre, 1956; Hamlet, The Power and the Glory, Family Reunion; A Dead Secret, Piccadilly Theatre, 1957; Expresso Bongo, Saville Theatre, 1958; The Complaisant Lover, Globe Theatre, 1959; A Man For All Seasons, Globe Theatre, 1960, New York, 1961-62; Coriolanus and Love's Labour's Lost, at Shakespeare Festival Season, Stratford, Ont., 1961; King Lear: Stratford-on-Avon, Aldwych Theatre, 1962-63, Europe and US, 1964; Timon of Athens, Stratford-on-Avon, 1965; The Government Inspector, also Staircase, Aldwych, 1966; Macbeth, Stratford-on-Avon, 1967, Russia, Finland, 1967, Aldwych, 1968; The Hotel in Amsterdam, Royal Court, 1968; Uncle Vanya, Royal Court, 1970; Savages, Royal Court and Comedy, 1973; The Tempest, Wyndhams, 1975; Dimetos, Comedy, 1976; The Family, Royal Exchange, Manchester, and Haymarket, 1978; *National Theatre:* The Captain of Kopenick, The Rules of the Game, 1971; Volpone, The Madras House, 1977; Amadeus, 1979; Othello, 1980; Don Quixote, 1982. *Films:* The Train, 1964; A Man for All Seasons, 1966 (from the play); Bartleby, King Lear, 1971; Scorpio, 1973; A Delicate Balance, 1974. Hon. LLD Glasgow, 1968; Hon. DLit Kent, 1973. Shakespeare prize, Hamburg, 1972. *Relevant Publication:* Paul Scofield, by J. C. Trewin, 1956. *Address:* The Gables, Balcombe, Sussex. *T:* 378. *Club:* Athenæum.

SCOFIELD, Paul; *see* Scofield, (D.) P.

SCOON, Sir Paul, GCMG 1979; OBE 1970; Governor General of Grenada, since 1978; *b* 4 July 1935; *m* 1970, Esmai Monica (*née* Lumsden); two step *s* one step *d*. *Educ:* St John's Anglican Sch., Grenada; Grenada Boys' Secondary Sch.; Inst. of Education, Leeds; Toronto Univ. BA, MEd. Teacher, Grenada Boys' Secondary Sch., 1953-67. Chief Educn Officer, 1967-68, Permanent Sec., 1969, Secretary to the Cabinet, 1970-72, Grenada; Dep. Director, Commonwealth Foundn, 1973-78. Governor, Centre for Internat. Briefing, Farnham Castle, 1973-78; Vice-Pres., Civil Service Assoc., Grenada, 1968; Co-founder and former Pres., Assoc. of Masters and Mistresses, Grenada. *Recreations:* reading, tennis. *Address:* Governor General's House, St George's, Grenada. *T:* 2401.

SCOONES, Major-General Sir Reginald (Laurence), KBE 1955 (OBE 1941); CB 1951; DSO 1945; late Royal Armoured Corps; Director, The Brewers' Society, 1957-69; *b* 18 Dec. 1900; *s* of late Major Fitzmaurice Scoones, Royal Fusiliers; *m* 1933, Isabella Bowie, *d* of John Nisbet, Cumbrae Isles, Scotland; one *d*. *Educ:* Wellington College; RMC, Sandhurst. 2nd Lt

R Fus., 1920; transferred Royal Tank Corps, 1923; attd Sudan Defence Force, 1926-34; Adj. 1 RTR, 1935; GSO3 Mobile Div., 1938; served War of 1939-45, Middle East and Burma; Brigade Major, Cavalry Brigade, Cairo, 1939; GSO2 Western Desert Corps, 1940; CO 42 RTR, 1941; GSO1 War Office, 1941; Brig. Dep. Dir Military Trng, 1942; Comdr, 254 Tank Brigade, Burma, 1943; Dep. Dir Military Trng, 1945; Asst Kaid, Sudan Defence Force, 1947-50; Maj.-Gen. 1950; Major-General Commanding British Troops Sudan and Commandant Sudan Defence Force, 1950-54. *Address:* 7 Court Royal Mansions, 1 Eastern Terrace, Brighton BN2 1DJ. *T:* Brighton 697141.

SCOPES, Sir Leonard Arthur, KCVO 1961; CMG 1957; OBE 1946; *b* 19 March 1912; *s* of late Arthur Edward Scopes and Jessie Russell Hendry; *m* 1938, Brunhilde Slater Rolfe; two *s* two *d*. *Educ:* St Dunstan's College; Gonville and Caius College, Cambridge (MA). Joined HM Consular Service, 1933; Vice-Consul: Antwerp, 1933, Saigon, 1935; Canton, 1937; Acting Consul, Surabaya, 1941; Vice-Consul, Lourenço Marques, 1942; Consul, Skoplje and Ljubljana, 1945; Commercial Secretary, Bogota, 1947; Assistant in United Nations (Economic and Social) Department of Foreign Office, 1950; Counsellor, Djakarta, 1952; Foreign Service Inspector, 1954; HM Ambassador to Nepal, 1957-62; HM Ambassador to Paraguay, 1962-67; Mem., UN Jt Inspection Unit, Geneva, 1968-71. *Recreation:* retirement. *Address:* Salcombe, Devon.

SCORER, Philip Segar; a Recorder of the Crown Court, since 1976; *b* 11 March 1916; *s* of Eric W. Scorer and Maud Scorer (*née* Segar); *m* 1950, Monica Smith; one *s* three *d*. *Educ:* Repton. Admitted Solicitor, 1938; London County Council Legal Dept, 1938-40. Served War, Army (Royal Signals: War Office, SHAEF and BAS, Paris), 1940-46. Solicitors' Dept, New Scotland Yard, 1947-51; Partner in Burton & Co., Solicitors, Lincoln, 1952-; Clerk of the Peace, City of Lincoln, 1952-71; Under-Sheriff of Lincolnshire, 1954-; Pres., Under Sheriffs Assoc., 1978-. *Address:* Stonebow, Lincoln LN2 1DA. *T:* Lincoln 23215. *Club:* National Liberal.

SCORGIE, Mervyn Nelson, OBE 1980; Member of Greater London Council for City of London and Westminster South 1973-81; Chairman, Industry and Employment Committee, Greater London Council, 1977-81; *b* 21 Oct. 1915; 2nd *s* of late Robert Lind Scorgie and Elsie Ida Mary Scorgie. *Educ:* King Edward VI Sch., Southampton; LSE (BScEcon Hons 1946). Qual. pharmaceutical chemist, 1938. Called to the Bar, Middle Temple, 1948. Abbott Labs, Queenborough, Kent, 1949-64: Man. Dir, 1954-64. Mem. GLC, for Cities of London and Westminster, 1970-73; Opposition spokesman, ILEA Finance Sub-Cttee, 1970-. Vice-Chm., SE Area Provincial Council, Conservative Party, 1965-71; Chm., SE Area Cons. Polit. Centre, 1967-70; National Chm., Cons. Polit. Centre, 1972-75 (Vice-Chm., 1969-72); Pres., Faversham Cons. Assoc., 1975- (Chm., 1967-70); Vice-Chm., Cities of London and Westminster Cons. Assoc., 1972-75. Cons. Parly Candidate, Neath, 1964. Governor: Parliament Hill Sch., 1971-79; Pimlico Sch., 1973-; William Ellis Sch., 1975-. Governor, Royal Festival Ballet, 1980-. ILEA Rep., Sir William Boreman's Foundn of Drapers Co.; Liveryman, Fletchers Co. Freeman, City of London, 1974. *Recreations:* reading, theatre, bridge, racing. *Address:* 1018A Kings House, St James Court, Buckingham Gate, SW1E 6BT. *T:* 01-834 5455. *Clubs:* Carlton (Mem., Political Cttee, 1969-79), St Stephen's Constitutional.

SCORRER, Aileen Mona, CBE 1953; Chief Inspector, Children's Department, Home Office, 1950-65; *b* 26 Feb. 1905; *d* of late G. H. Scorrer, Sussex, and late Mina Scorrer (*née* Drury). *Educ:* Huyton College, Liverpool; Royal Holloway College, London. *Address:* The Glade, Mead Road, Chislehurst, Kent BR7 6AD. *T:* 01-467 5370.

SCOTHORNE, Prof. Raymond John, BSc, MD Leeds; MD Chicago; FRSE; FRCSGlas; Regius Professor of Anatomy, University of Glasgow, since 1972; *b* 1920; *s* of late John Scothorne and of Lavinia Scothorne; *m* 1948, Audrey, *o d* of late Rev. Selwyn and Winifred Gillott; one *s* two *d*. *Educ:* Royal Grammar School, Newcastle upon Tyne; Universities of Leeds and Chicago, BSc (Hons) 1st cl. (Leeds), 1941; MD (Chicago), Rockefeller Student, 1941-43; MB (Hons) 1st cl. (Leeds), 1944; MD (with Distinction) (Leeds), 1951. Demonstrator and Lecturer in Anatomy, 1944-50, Univ. of Leeds; Sen. Lecturer in Anatomy, 1950-60, Univ. of Glasgow; Prof., Univ. of Newcastle upon Tyne, 1960-72. Hon. Sec., Anat. Soc. of Great Britain and Ireland, 1967-71, Pres., 1971-73; Fellow, British Assoc. of Clinical Anatomists; Mem., Med. Sub-Cttee, UGC, 1967-76. Hon. Mem., Assoc. des Anatomistes. Struthers Prize and Gold Medal in Anatomy, Univ. of Glasgow, 1957. Anatomical Editor, Companion to Medical Studies. *Publications:* chapter on Peripheral Nervous System in Hamilton's Textbook of Anatomy, 2nd edn, 1975; chapters on Early Development, on Tissue and Organ Growth and on the Nervous System in Companion to Medical Studies, 2nd edn, 1976; chapter on Development and Structure of Liver in Pathology of Liver, 1979; chapter on Respiratory System in Cunningham's Textbook, 12th edn, 1981; papers on embryology, histology and tissue transplantation. *Address:* Department of Anatomy, University of Glasgow, Glasgow G12 8QQ; Southernknowe, Linlithgow, West Lothian. *T:* Linlithgow 2463.

SCOTLAND, James, CBE 1975; MA, LLB, MEd, FEIS; FRSA; Principal, Aberdeen College of Education, 1961-Aug. 1983; *b* 1917; *s* of Duncan Anderson Scotland and Mary Emmerson; *m* 1944, Jean Cowan; two *s*. *Educ:* Whitehill Sch., Glasgow; Glasgow Univ. MA 1939; BL 1940; LLB 1943; MEd 1949. Served RA, N Africa and Italy, 1940-46. Commandant, Arts and

Modern Studies Wing, Formation College, Central Mediterranean Forces, 1945-46. Lectr in History, Jordanhill Coll. of Educn, 1949-50; Principal Lectr in Educn, 1950-61. Member: Scottish Council for Research in Educn, 1951-55; Scottish Certificate of Education Examination Board, 1964-73; General Teaching Council for Scotland, 1965-83 (Chm., 1976-79); Consultative Cttee on Curriculum, 1965-71; Police Advisory Council for Scotland, 1965-; Senatus, Univ. of Aberdeen, 1965-83; Schools Broadcasting Council for Scotland, 1965-79; Pres., Scottish Community Drama Assoc., 1964-69; Governor, Scottish Police College, 1965-; Hon. Sec., Standing Conf. on Studies in Educn, 1967-82; Chm., Cttee of Principals in Scottish Colleges of Educn, 1965-67, 1971-73, 1981-83; Vice Chm. Jt Cttee of Colleges of Educn in Scotland, 1971-73, 1981-83; Scottish Consultative Cttee, CRE, 1982-; Drama Cttee, Scottish Arts Council, 1982-. *Publications:* Modern Scotland, 1953; Our Law, 1955; The History of Scottish Education, two vols, 1970; (jtly) The Management of Innovation, 1970; Doctrines of the Great Educators, 1979; chapters in: Scottish Education Looks Ahead, 1969; The Education of Teachers, 1973; Education in Europe, 1974; various articles in professional jls; author of many plays on stage, radio and television. *Recreation:* theatre. *Address:* Aberdeen College of Education, Hilton Place, Aberdeen AB9 1FA; (private) 1 Woodburn Avenue, Aberdeen AB1 8JQ. *Club:* Royal Scots (Edinburgh).

SCOTT, family name of **Earl of Eldon.**

SCOTT; *see* Hepburne-Scott, family name of Lord Polwarth.

SCOTT; *see* Montagu Douglas Scott, family name of Duke of Buccleuch.

SCOTT, Alan James, CBE 1982; MLC; Secretary for Transport, Hong Kong Government, since 1982; *b* 14 Jan. 1934; *s* of Rev. Harold James Scott and Phyllis Mary Barbara Scott; *m* 1st, 1958, Mary Elizabeth *(d* 1969), *d* of William Harold Victor Ireland and Ivy Elizabeth Ireland; one *s* two *d* ; 2nd, 1971, Joan, *d* of Charles Harold Hall and Jennie Corinne Hall; one step *s* two step *d. Educ:* King's Sch., Ely; Cambridge Univ. (BA Classics and Social Anthropology). Suffolk Regt, Italy and Germany, 1952-54. HMOCS, 1958-: Fiji: Dist Officer, 1958; Estabt Officer, 1960; Registrar, Univ. of S Pacific, 1968; Controller, Organisation and Estabts, 1969; Hong Kong: Asst Financial Sec., 1971; Principal Asst Financial Sec., 1972; Sec. for Civil Service, 1973; MLC 1976-; Sec. for Housing, and Chm., Hong Kong Housing Authority, 1977; Sec. for Information, 1980. President: Fiji AAA, 1964-69; Hong Kong AAA, 1978-. *Recreations:* athletics, music, tennis. *Address:* Government Secretariat, Hong Kong; San Pietro a Dame, Cortona, Arezzo, Italy. *Clubs:* Farmers'; Ladies Recreation (Hong Kong).

SCOTT, Prof. Alastair Ian, FRS 1978; FRSE 1981; Professor of Organic Chemistry, Edinburgh University, since 1980 (Forbes Professor, 1980-81), and Davidson Professor of Chemistry and Biochemistry, Texas A & M University, since 1981; *b* 10 April 1928; *s* of William Scott and Nell Florence *(née* Newton); *m* 1950, Elizabeth Wilson *(née* Walters); one *s* one *d. Educ:* Glasgow Univ. (BSc, PhD, DSc). Postdoctoral Fellow, Ohio State Univ., 1952-53; Technical Officer, ICI (Nobel Div.), 1953-54; Postdoctoral Fellow, London and Glasgow Univs, 1954-57; Lectr, Glasgow Univ., 1957-62; Professor: Univ. of British Columbia, 1962-65; Univ. of Sussex, 1965-68; Yale Univ., 1968-77; Texas A&M Univ., 1977-80. Lectures: Karl Folkers, Wisconsin Univ., 1964; Burger, Virginia Univ., 1975; Benjamin Rush, Pennsylvania Univ., 1975; 5 colls, Mass, 1977; Andrews, NSW Univ., 1979. Hon. MA, Yale Univ., 1968; Corday-Morgan Medallist, Chemical Soc., 1964; Ernest Guenther Medallist, Amer. Chem. Soc., 1976. *Publications:* Interpretation of Ultraviolet Spectra of Natural Products, 1964; (with T. K. Devon) Handbook of Naturally Occurring Compounds, 1972; numerous pubns in learned jls. *Recreations:* music, gardening. *Address:* Department of Chemistry, University of Edinburgh, King's Buildings, West Mains Road, Edinburgh EH9 3JJ. *T:* 031-667 1081 ext. 3403; Texas A & M University, College Station, Texas 77843, USA.

SCOTT, Prof. Alexander Whiteford, CBE 1960; Professor of Chemical Engineering, University of Strathclyde, Glasgow, 1955-71; Hon. Engineering Consultant to Ministry of Agriculture, Fisheries and Food, 1946-62; *b* 28 January 1904; *s* of Alexander Scott, Glasgow; *m* 1933, Rowena Christiana *(d* 1970), *d* of John Craig, Glasgow; one *s. Educ:* Royal College of Science and Technology, Glasgow. BSc, PhD, ARCST, Glasgow. Pres., Instn of Engineers and Shipbuilders in Scotland, 1975-76 and 1976-77. FIMechE, FIChemE, Hon. FCIBS. Hon. LLD Strathclyde, 1980. *Address:* 9 Rowallan Road, Thornliebank, Glasgow G46 7EP. *T:* 041-638 2968.

SCOTT, Anthony Douglas, TD 1972; Chief Executive and Director, Council for Small Industries in Rural Areas, since 1981; *b* 6 Nov. 1933; *o s* of Douglas Ernest and Mary Gladys Scott; *m* 1962, Irene Robson; one *s* one *d. Educ:* Gateshead Central Technical Secondary Sch. Articled to Middleton & Middleton, also J. Stanley Armstrong, Chartered Accountants, Newcastle upon Tyne, 1952-57; National Servi*ee,* WO Selection Bd, 1957-59; Accountant with Commercial Plastics Ltd, 1959; joined ICI Ltd (Agricl Div), 1961; seconded by ICI to Hargreaves Fertilisers Ltd, as Chief Accountant, 1966; ICI Ltd (Nobel Div.) as Asst Chief Acct, 1970; seconded by ICI to MoD as Dir-Gen. Internal Audit, 1972-74. Dir of Consumer Credit, Office of Fair Trading, 1974-80. Chm., Teesside Soc. of Chartered Accts, 1969-70; Mem. Cttee, London Chartered Accountants, 1974-79. Chm., Jt Working Party on Students' Societies (ICAE&W), 1979-80. *Publications:* Accountants Digests

on Consumer Credit Act 1974, 1980; Estate Agents Act 1979, 1982. *Recreations:* antiquary, walking, gardening; TA (Major, Parachute Regt (TA), 1959-). *Address:* 33 Barlings Road, Harpenden, Herts. *T:* Harpenden 63067.

SCOTT, Audrey; *see* Scott, M. Audrey.

SCOTT, Sir Bernard (Francis William), Kt 1979; CBE 1974; TD; FIMechE; FEng; Deputy Chairman: Lloyds Bank, since 1980 (Director, since 1975); Lloyds Bank UK Management, since 1980; Vice-Chairman, Lloyds Bank International, since 1980 (Director, since 1978); Director: Boots Co., since 1976; Thomas Tilling Ltd, since 1979; Grindlays Bank, since 1981; *b* Kings Norton, 19 Nov. 1914; *s* of Francis William Robert Scott and Agnes Edith Kett; *m* 1st, 1942, Charlotte Kathleen (marr. diss. 1980), *d* of Charles and Charlotte Laidlow, Monkseaton; one *s* two *d* ; 2nd, 1980, Nicole Henriette, *d* of Gustave and Sophy Douchet, Douai. *Educ:* Bishop Vesey's Grammar Sch.; Epsom College. FRSA. Served War of 1939-45 (despatches, 1944): mobilised as TA Officer in 45th Bn Royal Warwicks Regt, 1939; Major, RA, 1946. Joined Joseph Lucas Ltd as apprentice, 1931; Personal Asst to Oliver Lucas, 1936; Sales Dir, Joseph Lucas (Electrical) Ltd, 1947; Vice-Chm. and Gen. Man., CAV Ltd and dir of various Lucas subsids at home and abroad, 1959; Dir, Joseph Lucas (Industries) Ltd, 1968; Dep. Chm., 1969-73, Man. Dir, 1972-74, Chm., 1974-80, Lucas Industries Ltd. Mem., Export Council for Europe, 1966-71; Chm., European Components Service (BNEC), 1967-71; President: Birmingham Chamber of Commerce, 1972-73 (Vice-Pres. 1970); Motor Industry Res. Assoc. Council, 1975-77; Engineering Industries Council, 1975-81; Vice-President: ABCC; Instn of Motor Industry, 1976; EEF, 1976-80; Member: Council, CBI, 1974-; British Overseas Trade Bd, 1973-77; British Overseas Trade Adv. Council, 1975-77; Nat. Defence Industries Council, 1976-80; Council, SMM&T, 1971 (Exec. Cttee, 1974, Vice-Pres., 1976-80; Pres., 1980-81); Council on Internat. Development, 1977-79. Trustee: Anglo-German Foundn for Study of Industrial Society, 1978-; Duke of Edinburgh Award Scheme, 1980-; Chm., Berks Council Boys' Clubs, 1950-70; Vice-Chm., Nat. Assoc. of Boys' Clubs, 1974; Pres., Birmingham Fedn of Boys' Clubs, 1977-81. Hon LLD Birmingham, 1977; Hon. DSc Aston in Birmingham, 1979. Belgian Croix de Guerre, 1945; Chevalier, Order of Leopold with palm, 1945. *Recreations:* sailing, gardening. *Address:* Grove Corner, Grove Road, Lymington, Hants. *T:* Lymington 78154. *Clubs:* Boodle's; Royal Lymington Yacht; Cercle de l'Union Interalliée.

SCOTT, Dame Catherine Margaret Mary; *see* Scott, Dame M.

SCOTT, Sir (Charles) Hilary, Kt 1967; *b* Bradford, 27 March 1906; *s* of late Lieutenant-Colonel C. E. Scott and Mrs M. E. M. Scott, of Bradford; *m* 1932, Beatrice Margery, *d* of late Reverend Canon Garrad; one *s* two *d. Educ:* Sedbergh Sch. Articled with Wade & Co., Bradford. Qual. as Solicitor (Class 2 Hons) 1930; Partner Slaughter & May, London, 1937-74. Served in RNVR, 1940-45 (Lieut-Comdr); President of the Law Society, 1966-67 (Mem. Council, 1948-71; Vice-Pres. 1965-66); Member: Nat. Film Finance Corp., 1948-70 (Chm. 1964-69); Jenkins Cttee on Company Law, 1959-62; Panel of Judges of The Accountant Awards for company accounts, 1961-69; London Adv. Bd of Salvation Army, 1968-82; Noise Adv. Council, 1971-75; Council, Royal Sch. of Church Music; Chm., Cttee on Property Bonds and Equity-linked Life Assurance, 1971-73. Trustee, Glyndebourne Arts Trust, 1961-76. Director: Tarmac Ltd, 1968-76; Equity & Law Life Assurance Society Ltd, 1955-81; London Board, Bank of Scotland, 1966-76. FRSA. *Recreations:* travel, music. *Address:* Knowle House, Bishop's Walk, Addington, Surrey CR0 5BA. *T:* 01-654 3638.
See also M. Audrey Scott, G. M. C. Thornely.

SCOTT, Sir (Charles) Peter, KBE 1978 (OBE 1948); CMG 1964; HM Diplomatic Service, retired; Chairman: Council of International Social Service of Great Britain, since 1979; Council of Anglo-Norse Society, since 1979; *b* 30 Dec. 1917; *er s* of late Rev. John Joseph Scott and late Dorothea Scott *(née* Senior); *m* 1954, Rachael, *yr d* of C. W. Lloyd Jones, CIE; one *s* two *d. Educ:* Weymouth Coll.; Pembroke Coll., Cambridge. Indian Civil Service: Probationer, 1939; appointed to Madras Presidency, 1940; Asst Private Sec. to Viceroy, 1946-47. Entered HM Diplomatic Service, 1947, Second Sec., Tokyo, 1948; First Sec., 1949; Foreign Office, 1950; Private Sec. to Gen. Lord Ismay at NATO, Paris, 1952; First Sec., Vienna, 1954; First Sec. at British Information Services, NY, 1956; Counsellor and Consul-General, Washington, 1959; Student at IDC, 1962; Head of UK Mission to European Office of the United Nations, Geneva, 1963; Minister at HM Embassy, Rome, 1966-69; Temp. Vis. Fellow at Centre for Contemporary European Studies, Univ. of Sussex, 1969-70; Asst Under-Sec. of State, FCO, 1970-75; Ambassador to Norway, 1975-77. Private Sec., 1978-79, Treasurer, 1979-81, to HRH Prince Michael of Kent. *Recreations:* walking, and such as offer. *Address:* Flat 15, Priory Mansions, 90 Drayton Gardens, SW10 9RG. *T:* 01-370 2389. *Club:* United Oxford & Cambridge University.

SCOTT, Ven. Claud Syms; Archdeacon of Suffolk, 1962-70, Archdeacon Emeritus, 1970; Vicar of Hoxne with Denham St John, 1962-70; *b* 31 Aug. 1901; *s* of Claud Syms and Margaret Elizabeth Scott; *m* 1930, Grace Maud Savery. *Educ:* Brentwood Sch.; Trinity Coll., Oxf. BA 1923, MA 1927. Deacon, 1926; Priest, 1927; Asst Curate, St Luke, Bedminster, 1926-30; Curate-in-charge, All Hallows Conventional District, Ipswich, 1930-38; Vicar of Exning with Landwade, 1938-54; Rural Dean of Newmarket, 1946-54;

Hon. Canon of St Edmundsbury, 1953; Rector of Stradbroke with Horham and Athelington, 1954-58; Rector of St Mary Stoke, Ipswich, 1958-62; Rural Dean of Ipswich, 1958-Dec. 1961. Master, Worshipful Company of Armourers and Brasiers, 1951. *Address:* 68 Lowestoft Road, Reydon, Southwold, Suffolk. *T:* Southwold 723485.

SCOTT, Prof. Dana Stewart, FBA 1976; University Professor of Computer Science and Mathematical Logic, Carnegie-Mellon University, since 1981; *b* Berkeley, Calif, 11 Oct. 1932; *m* 1959, Irene Schreier; one *d. Educ:* Univ. of Calif, Berkeley (BA); Princeton Univ. (PhD). Instructor, Univ. of Chicago, 1958-60; Asst Prof., Univ. of Calif, Berkeley, 1960-63; Associate Prof. and Prof., Stanford Univ., 1963-69; Prof., Princeton, 1969-72; Prof. of Mathematical Logic, Oxford Univ., 1972-81. Visiting Prof., Amsterdam, 1968-69; Guggenheim Fellow, 1978-79. *Publications:* papers on logic and mathematics in technical jls. *Address:* Department of Computer Science, Carnegie-Mellon University, Schenley Park, Pittsburgh, Pa 15213, USA.

SCOTT, Sir David; *see* Scott, Sir W. D. S.

SCOTT, David; *b* 6 Sept. 1916; *er s* of late Sir Basil Scott and late Gertrude, MBE, 2nd *d* of Henry Villiers Stuart of Dromana, MP; *m* 1951, Hester Mary, MA, *y d* of late Gilbert Ogilvy of Winton and Pencaitland; one *s* three *d. Educ:* Stowe; New College, Oxford (MA). War Service 1939-45: Argyll and Sutherland Highlanders (SR), Reconnaissance Corps and Highland Light Infantry; T/Capt., 1941; Asst to Political Adviser for Khuzistan, Iran, 1944; Actg Vice Consul, Ahwaz, 1944-45. Clerk, House of Commons, 1946; Deputy Principal Clerk, 1962; Clerk of Standing Cttees, 1966-70; Clerk of Select Cttees, 1970-73; Clerk of Private Bills, an Examiner of Petitions for Private Bills and Taxing Officer, House of Commons, 1974-77; retired 1977. *Recreation:* fishing. *Address:* Glenaros, Aros, Isle of Mull. *T:* Aros 337; 6a Stafford House, Maida Avenue, W2. *T:* 01-723 8398. *Clubs:* Pratt's; New, Puffin's (Edinburgh).

SCOTT, Ven. David; Archdeacon of Stow, since 1975; Vicar of Hackthorn with Cold Hanworth, since 1975; also Priest-in-charge of North and South Carlton, since 1978; *b* 19 June 1924; *m* ; two *c. Educ:* Trinity Hall, Cambridge (BA 1950, MA 1954); Cuddesdon Theological College. Deacon 1952, priest 1953, dio. Portsmouth; Curate of St Mark, Portsea, 1952-58; Asst Chaplain, Univ. of London, 1958-59; PC, Old Brumby, 1959-66; Vicar of Boston, Lincs, 1966-75; Rural Dean of Holland East, 1971-75; Surrogate, 1972-75; Canon and Prebendary of Lincoln Cathedral, 1971. *Address:* The Vicarage, Hackthorn, Lincoln LN2 3PF.

SCOTT, Sir David (Aubrey), GCMG 1979 (KCMG 1974; CMG 1966); HM Diplomatic Service, retired 1979; Chairman, Ellerman Lines plc, since 1982; Director: Barclays Bank International Ltd; Mitchell Cotts Group; Consultant, Delta Group; Chairman, Royal Over-Seas League, since 1981; *b* 3 Aug. 1919; *s* of late Hugh Sumner Scott and of Barbara E. Scott, JP; *m* 1941, Vera Kathleen, *d* of late Major G. H. Ibbitson, MBE, RA; two *s* one *d. Educ:* Charterhouse; Birmingham University (Mining Engrg). Served War of 1939-45, Royal Artillery, 1939-47; Chief Radar Adviser, British Military Mission to Egyptian Army, 1945-47, Major. Appointed to CRO, 1948; Asst Private Secretary to Secretary of State, 1949; Cape Town/Pretoria, 1951-53; Cabinet Office, 1954-56; Malta Round Table Conf., 1955; Secretary-General, Malaya and Caribbean Constitutional Confs, 1956; Singapore, 1956-58; Monckton Commn, 1960; Dep. High Comr, Fedn of Rhodesia and Nyasaland, 1961-63; Imperial Defence College, 1964; Dep. High Comr, India, 1965-67; British High Comr in Uganda, and Ambassador (non-resident) to Rwanda, 1967-70; Asst Under-Sec. of State, FCO, 1970-72; British High Comr to New Zealand, and Governor, Pitcairn Is., 1973-75; HM Ambassador to Republic of S Africa, 1976-79. *Publication:* Ambassador in Black and White, 1981. *Recreations:* music, birdwatching. *Address:* Wayside, Moushill Lane, Milford, Surrey. *Clubs:* Royal Over-Seas League, PEN.

See also J. B. Unwin.

SCOTT, Sir David John Montagu Douglas, KCMG 1941 (CMG 1935); OBE 1919; *b* 7 March 1887; *s* of Adm. Lord Charles Scott, GCB; *m* 1918, Dorothy Charlotte Drummond (*d* 1965); one *s* (killed during the War, 1941); *m* 1970, Valerie Finnis, VMH, *d* of late Comdr Striker Finnis. *Educ:* Eton; Christ Church, Oxford. Joined 3rd Batt. the Royal Scots, 1906; entered the Foreign Office, 1911; served in France, Flanders and Salonika, 1914-18 (wounded, despatches, Legion of Honour, OBE); re-joined Foreign Office, 1919; Assistant Under-Secretary of State for Foreign Affairs, 1938-44; Deputy Under-Secretary of State in the Foreign Office, 1944; retired, 1947. *Recreations:* gardening, fishing, looking at pictures. *Address:* The Dower House, Boughton House, Kettering, Northants. *T:* Kettering 82279.

SCOTT, Donald; *see* Scott, W. D.

SCOTT, Prof. Douglas, RDI 1974; FSIAD; Profesor Titular, Universidad Nacional Autonoma de Mexico, 1977-80; Profesor and Presidente de la Carrera, Universidad Anahuac, Mexico, 1977-80; *b* 4 April 1913; *s* of Edward Scott and Lilian Scott; *m* 1939, Kathleen Tierney; one *s* one *d. Educ:* Central Sch. of Art and Design, London (trained as silversmith and jeweller). Joined Osler & Faraday, 1929, and subseq. other lighting cos, as designer and illuminating engr; Raymond Loewy's London Office, 1936-39; opened own office, 1946; MSIAD 1946, elected FSIAD 1960. Lectr, Central Sch. of Art and Design, 1945: founded Industrial Design course, first in UK, 1946; started

postgrad. course; trained Mexican designers from Universidad Nacional Autonoma de Mexico, and helped set up course. Designed for many clients in UK, Europe and USA. Profesor Honorario, Universitario Autonoma de Guadalajara, Mexico, 1977. Wash basin designed for Ideal Standard, Italy, on perm. exhibn in Museum of Modern Art, New York. Gold Medal for Design, Instituto Mexicano de Comercio Exterior, Mexico, 1973; three Design Council awards. *Publications:* (with James Pilditch) The Business of Product Design, 1964; articles in periodicals. *Recreations:* listening to music, gardening, walking, photography. *Address:* 12 Lentune Way, Lymington, Hants SO4 9PF. *T:* Lymington 77311.

SCOTT, Prof. Douglas Frederick Schumacher; Professor of German in the University of Durham (late Durham Colleges), 1958-75, now Emeritus Professor; *b* Newcastle under Lyme, Staffs, 17 Sept. 1910; *o s* of Frederick Scott and Magdalena (*née* Gronbach); *m* 1942, Margaret (*d* 1972), *o d* of late Owen Gray Ellis, Beaumaris, Anglesey, and Helen (*née* Gibbs); two *d. Educ:* Queen Mary's Grammar School, Walsall, Staffs; Dillman-Realgymnasium Stuttgart, Germany; University of Tübingen, Göttingen (Dr phil.); University College, London (MA). Part-time Assistant, German Dept, University Coll., London, 1935-37; Lecturer in charge German Dept, Huddersfield Technical Coll., 1937-38; Lecturer in German, King's Coll., Newcastle, 1938-46; released for service with Friends' Ambulance Unit, 1940-46; Lecturer in German, King's Coll., London, 1946-49; Reader and Head of Dept of German, The Durham Colls, 1949-58. *Publications:* Some English Correspondents of Goethe, 1949; W. v. Humboldt and the Idea of a University, 1960; Luke Howard: his correspondence with Goethe and his continental journey of 1816, 1976; articles and reviews on German lit. and Anglo-German literary relations in various English and German journals. *Recreations:* music, travel. *Address:* 6 Fieldhouse Terrace, Durham DH1 4NA. *T:* Durham 64518. *Club:* Penn.

SCOTT, Douglas Keith, (Doug Scott); President, Alpine Climbing Group, since 1976; *b* Nottingham, 29 May 1941; *s* of George Douglas Scott and Edith Joyce Scott; *m* 1962, Janice Elaine Brook; one *s* two *d. Educ:* Cottesmore Secondary Modern Sch.; Mundella Grammar Sch., Nottingham; Loughborough Teachers' Trng Coll. (Teaching Certificate). Began climbing age of 12, British crag climbing, and most weekends thereafter; visited the Alps age of 16 and every year thereafter; first ascent, Tarso Teiroko, Tibest Mts, Sahara, 1965; first ascents, Cilo Dag Mts, SE Turkey, 1966; first ascent, S face Koh-i-Bandaka (22,500 ft), Hindu Kush, Afghanistan, 1967; first British ascent, Salathé Wall, El Capitain, Yosemite, 1971; 1972: Spring, Mem., European Mt Everest Expedn to SW face; Summer, first ascent, E Pillar of Mt Asgard, Baffin Island Expedn; Autumn, Mem., British Mt Everest Expedn to SW face; 1974: first ascent, Changabang; first ascent, SE spur, Pic Lenin (23,500 ft); reached summit of Mt Everest, via SW face, with Dougal Haston, as Members, British Everest Expedn, 24th Sept. 1975; first Alpine ascent of S face, Mt McKinley (20,320 ft), via new route, British Direct, with Dougal Haston, 1976; first ascent, East Face Direct, Mt Kenya, 1976; first ascent, Ogre (23,900 ft), Karakoram Mountains, 1977; first ascent, N Ridge route, Kangchenjunga (28,146 ft), without oxygen, 1979; first ascent, N Summit, Kussum Kangguru, 1979; first ascent, N Face, Nuptse, 1979; Alpine style, Kangchungtse (25,066 ft), 1980; E Pillar, Shivling, 1981; Chamlang (24,000 ft), North Face to Centre Summit, 1981; first ascent, Pungpa Ridge (7445 m), 1982; Xixabangma South Face (26,291 ft), 1982. *Publications:* Big Wall Climbing, 1974 (N America, 1974); contrib. to Alpine Jl, Amer. Alpine Jl and Mountain Magazine. *Recreations:* mountaineering; active Rugby Union player, Nottingham Moderns Rugby Football Club. *Address:* Pasture Lane, Hesket Newmarket, Wigton, Cumbria. *T:* Caldbeck 303. *Clubs:* Alpine; Alpine Climbing Group; Nottingham Climbers'.

SCOTT, Col Sir Douglas Winchester, 2nd Bt *cr* 1913; *b* 4 Feb. 1907; *s* of Admiral Sir Percy Scott, KCB, KCVO, LLD, 1st Bt, and Roma, *e d* of Sir Frederic Dixon Hartland, 1st Bt; S father, 1924; *m* 1933, Elizabeth Joyce, 2nd *d* of W. N. C. Grant, Lyne Place, Virginia Water, Surrey; two *s* one *d. Educ:* Harrow; RMC Sandhurst. Comd 3rd Hussars, 1944; Comd 9th Lancers, 1947; Hon. Col 3rd Hussars, 1955-58; Col Queen's Own Hussars, 1962-65. Treasurer Thomas Coram Foundation, 1958, Vice-Pres. 1970. *Heir: s* Anthony Percy Scott [*b* 1 May 1937; *m* 1962, Caroline Teresa Anne, *er d* of Edward Bacon; two *s* one *d*]. *Address:* Pine Trees, West Strand, West Wittering, Chichester, Sussex. *Club:* Cavalry and Guards.

SCOTT, Sir Edward Arthur Dolman, 8th Bt, *cr* 1806; resident in South Australia; *b* 14 Dec. 1905; *e s* of Sir Douglas Edward Scott, 7th Bt, and Florence Ada, *d* of W. Wilderman; S father 1951; *m* ; one *d. Educ:* Reading Grammar School. *Heir: b* Douglas Francis Scott, *b* 6 Aug. 1907.

SCOTT, Most Rev. Edward Walter, CC 1978; Archbishop, and Primate of All Canada, since 1971; *b* Edmonton, Alberta; *s* of Tom Walter Scott and Kathleen Frances Ford; *m* 1942, Isabel Florence Brannan; one *s* three *d. Educ:* Univ. of British Columbia; Anglican Theological Coll. of BC. Vicar of St Peter's, Seal Cove, 1943-45; SCM Secretary, Univ. of Manitoba, 1945-59; Staff of St John's Coll., Winnipeg, 1947-48; Rector: St John the Baptist, Fort Garry, 1949-55; St Jude's, Winnipeg, 1955-60; Dir, Diocesan Council for Social Service, Diocese of Rupertsland, and Priest Dir of Indian Work, 1960-64; Associate Sec., Council for Social Service, Anglican Church of Canada, 1964-66; Bishop of Kootenay, 1966-71. Moderator of Executive and Central Cttees, WCC, 1975-83. Hon. DD: Anglican Theol Coll., BC; Trinity Coll., Toronto, Montreal Dio. Coll.; Wycliffe Coll., Toronto; Huron Coll., Ont.; United Theol Coll., Montreal; Hon. DCL St John's Coll., Winnipeg;

Hon. STD Thorneloe Coll., Ont. *Recreation:* carpentry. *Address:* 600 Jarvis Street, Toronto, Ontario M4Y 2J6, Canada.

SCOTT, Sir Eric, Kt 1965; OBE 1958; Federal President, The Pharmacy Guild of Australia (formerly Federated Pharmaceutical Service Guild of Australia), 1947-71; *b* 11 Dec. 1891; *s* of W. G. Scott, Hawthorn, Victoria, Aust.; *m* 1914, Eva Caroline (*d* 1968), *d* of R. J. Poulton; one *s* two *d* ; *m* 1971, Peggy Vane, *d* of C. V. Lansell. *Educ:* Wesley College, Melbourne, Victoria. Pharmaceutical Chemist, 1927. State President, Federated Pharmaceutical Service Guild of Australia (Victorian Branch), 1931-47; President, Pharmaceutical Society of Victoria, 1955-60; Chm., Drug Res. Appeal Cttee, 1972; Mem., Commonwealth and State Pharmaceutical Benefits Committees under National Health Act, 1954-. Hon. Mem., Pharmaceutical Society of Great Britain, 1970. *Recreations:* golf, gardening, cooking. *Address:* Woorak, 64 Heyington Place, Toorak, Victoria 3142, Australia. *T:* 20-4883. *Clubs:* Commonwealth (Canberra); Royal Automobile of Victoria, Athenæum (Melbourne).

SCOTT, Ethleen Mary, MA; retired as Principal of St Aidan's College, University of Durham, (1961-63); *b* 25 Nov. 1896; *d* of Rev. H. R. Scott, MA, DD, and Jennie Hill Scott. *Educ:* Walthamstow Hall, Sevenoaks, Kent; Royal Holloway College, University of London. BA Hons in French, Cl. I 1919; MA (with dist.) 1923; LRAM 1919; ARCM 1942. French Mistress, Queen Elizabeth's Girls' Grammar School, Barnet, 1921-25; Lecturer in French, Royal Holloway College, 1925-28; Lecturer in French, Durham Colleges in the University of Durham, 1928-47; Principal of St Aidan's Society, 1947-61. *Recreations:* music, gardening. *Address:* Whitegates, Westbere, Canterbury, Kent.

SCOTT, Frank, (Francis Reginald), CC 1967; QC (Quebec) 1961; FRSC 1947; Emeritus Professor of Law and Poet; *b* Quebec, PQ, 1 Aug. 1899; *s* of Archdeacon Frederick George and Amy Scott; *m* 1928, Marian Mildred Dale; one *s. Educ:* Quebec High School; Bishop's College, Lennoxville, PQ (BA 1919); Magdalen College, Oxford (Rhodes Scholar, BA 1922, BLitt 1923); McGill University, Montreal (BCL 1927). Practised law one year, then became full-time teacher, McGill Faculty of Law, 1928; Dean of Faculty, 1961-64. Vis. Professor: Toronto 1953; Michigan State Univ., 1957; French Canada Studies Program, McGill, 1967-71; Dalhousie, 1969-71. Co-founder and past-Pres., League for Social Reconstruction; Mem., Nat. Exec., Canadian Inst. of Internat. Affairs, 1935-50; Nat. Chm., Co-operative Commonwealth Fedn Party, 1942-50; Chm., Legal Research Cttee, Canadian Bar Assoc., 1954-56; Mem., Royal Commn on Bilingualism and Biculturalism, 1963-71. Delegate to British Commonwealth Labour Parties Conferences, London 1944 and Toronto 1947; adviser to Govt of Saskatchewan at Constitutional Confs, 1950 and 1960; UN Technical Assistance Resident Rep. to Burma, 1952. Chm., Canadian Writers' Conf., 1955. Co-editor: McGill Fortnightly Review, 1925-27; The Canadian Mercury, 1928; Canadian Forum, 1936-39; Preview, 1942-45; Northern Review, 1945-47. Counsel in several civil liberties cases, Supreme Court of Canada, 1956-64. Corresp. Fellow, British Acad., 1978. Hon. For. Mem., Amer. Acad. of Arts and Sciences, 1967; Guggenheim Fellowship, 1940. Hon. degrees: Dalhousie; Manitoba; Queen's; British Columbia; Saskatchewan; Osgoode Hall; Sir George Williams; Montreal; Toronto; McGill; Laval; Windsor; Bishop's; York; Carleton; Simon Fraser. Guarantor's Prize for Poetry, Chicago, 1944; Lorne Pierce Medal, Royal Soc. of Canada, 1964; Molson Award, Canada Council, 1967. *Publications:* (*poetry*): Overture, 1945; Events and Signals, 1954; The Eye of the Needle, 1957; (*trans.*) Poems of Garneau and Hébert, 1962; Signature, 1964; Selected Poems, 1966; Trouvailles, 1967; The Dance is One, 1973; (*trans.*) Poems of French Canada, 1977 (Canada Council Award for Translation, 1978); Collected Poems (Governor General's Award for Poetry), 1982; (ed, with A. J. M. Smith): New Provinces: poems of several authors, 1936; The Blasted Pine: an anthology of satire, irreverent and disrespectful verse, 1957, rev. edn 1967; (*prose*): (jtly) Social Planning for Canada, 1935; Canada Today, Her National Interests and National Policy, 1938; (jtly) Democracy Needs Socialism, 1938; (jtly) Make This Your Canada, 1943; (jtly) Canada after the War, 1943; Civil Liberties and Canadian Federalism, 1959; (jtly) Quebec States Her Case, 1964; Essays on the Constitution: aspects of Canadian law and politics, 1977 (Governor-General's Award for Non-fiction, 1978). *Address:* 451 Clarke Avenue, Westmount, Quebec H3Y 3C5, Canada. *Clubs:* McGill Faculty, University, International PEN (all Montreal).

SCOTT, George Barclay; Chairman, North Western Region, British Gas Corporation, since 1982; *b* 10 Aug. 1928; *s* of late Joseph Scott and Margaret Gardner Crawford Barclay Scott; *m* 1955, Janette Margaret Forrester Lindsay; one *s* one *d* (twins). *Educ:* Whitehill Senior Secondary School, Glasgow; Univ. of Strathclyde. BSc (Hons) Mech. Eng. Scottish Gas Board: Distribution Engineer, 1962-70; Member of Board, 1970-72; Dir of Distribution and Service, 1970-73; British Gas Corporation: Commercial Dir, Scottish Region, 1973-74; Dep. Chairman, North Western Region, 1974-82. Pres., Instn of Gas Engineers, 1982-83. *Recreations:* gardening, golf, walking, music. *Address:* The Belfry, Chapel Drive, Hale Barns, Altrincham, Cheshire WA15 0BL. *Club:* St James's (Manchester).

SCOTT, Sir George (Edward), Kt 1967; CBE 1963 (OBE 1941); KPM; Chief Constable of the West Riding Constabulary, 1959-68, and of the West Yorkshire Constabulary, 1968-69, retired; *b* 6 June 1903; *s* of late Frederick William Scott; *m* 1926, Lilian, *d* of Matthew Brown, Norwich; one *s* one *d.* *Educ:* City of Norwich School. Joined Norwich City Police, as Cadet, 1918;

Dep. Chief Constable, Norwich, 1933-36; Chief Constable: Luton, 1936-44; Newcastle upon Tyne, 1944-48; Sheffield, 1948-59. Vice-President: Royal Life Saving Soc.; RoSPA. King's Police Medal, 1949; KStJ 1966 (CStJ 1957). *Recreation:* golf. *Address:* White Lodge, Barham Close, Weybridge, Surrey. *Club:* St John.

SCOTT, George Edwin; author, television commentator, broadcaster, journalist; Head of UK Offices, Commission of the European Communities, since 1979; *b* 22 June 1925; *s* of late George Benjamin Scott and Florence Hilda Scott; *m* 1947, Shelagh Maud Isobel Maw; two *s* one *d. Educ:* Middlesbrough High School; New College, Oxford. Northern Echo, 1941-42; Yorkshire Post, 1942-43; RNVR, 1943-46; New College, Oxford, 1946-48 (Founder and Editor of Oxford Viewpoint); Daily Express, 1948-53; Truth, 1953-57 (Deputy Editor, 1954; Editor, 1954-57, when ceased publication); The Economist, 1970-74; Editor, The Listener, 1974-79. Contested (L) Middlesbrough East, March 1962, Middlesbrough West, June 1962, Wimbledon, 1964. Chm., Political Div., Liberal Party, 1962-63. Mem., Panorama team, 1958-59; Chairman/Interviewer: TWW, 1959-67; Rediffusion, 1966-68; Tyne-Tees, 1970-74; Presenter, The Editors, BBC, 1976-79. *Publications:* Time and Place (auto-biographical), 1956; The RCs, 1967; Reporter Anonymous, 1968; Rise and Fall of the League of Nations, 1973; contrib. column, Liberal View, Daily Mirror, 1962-64; contribs to Punch and other jls. *Recreations:* theatre, cricket and watching others gardening. *Address:* 20 Kensington Palace Gardens, W8 4QQ. *T:* 01-727 8090. *Club:* Reform.

SCOTT, Prof. George Ian, CBE 1968; FRCSE; FRCPE; FRSE; Surgeon Oculist to the Queen in Scotland, 1965-78; Professor of Ophthalmology, University of Edinburgh, 1954-72, now Emeritus Professor; Ophthalmic Surgeon, Royal Infirmary, Edinburgh, 1953-72, now Hon. Ophthalmic Surgeon; *b* 15 March 1907; *s* of late George John Scott; *m* 1946, Maxine, *d* of late A. D. Vandamm; one *s. Educ:* Edinburgh Acad.; Univ. of Edinburgh. MA 1929; MB, ChB 1933; FRCS Edin. 1937; FRS Edin. 1954. Served War of 1939-45, RAMC; Command Ophthalmologist, Scottish Command, 1939; Mem. Advisory Ophthalmic Panel, Ministry of Supply, 1941; Consultant Ophthalmologist, MEF, 1942; Brig. RAMC, 1942. Asst Ophthalmic Surgeon, Royal Infirmary, Edinburgh, 1946; Mem. Vision Cttee, MRC, 1946; Visiting Consultant, Western General and Bangour Hosps, 1949; Consultant in Neuro-Ophthalmology to Department of Neuro-Surgery, Edinburgh, 1954. Member, International Council of Ophthalmology, 1963-70; Past President: Faculty of Ophthalmologists; RCSE; Ophthalmological Soc. of UK; Member Association of British Neurologists; FRSoc.Med. (former Vice-President Section of Ophthalmology); Hon. Col RAMC. *Publications:* papers in British Journal of Ophthalmology, Nature, Lancet, British Medical Journal, British Journal of Radiology, Proc. Roy. Soc. Med., Trans. Ophthalmological Soc., United Kingdom, and The American Journal of Ophthalmology. *Address:* 4 Moray Place, Edinburgh EH3 6DS. *T:* 031-225 6943. *Clubs:* Army and Navy; New (Edinburgh).

SCOTT, Dr Graham Alexander; Deputy Chief Medical Officer, Scottish Home and Health Department, since 1975; *b* 26 Nov. 1927; *s* of Alexander Scott and Jessie Scott; *m* 1951, Helena Patricia Margaret Cavanagh; two *s* one *d. Educ:* Daniel Stewart's Coll., Edinburgh; Edinburgh Univ. (MB, ChB). FRCPE, FFCM, DPH. RAAMC, 1951-56 (Dep. Asst Dir, Army Health, 1st Commonwealth Div., Korea, 1953-54). Sen. Asst MO, Stirling CC, 1957-62, Dep. County MO, 1962-65; Scottish Home and Health Department: MO, 1965-68; SMO, 1968-74; PMO, 1974-75. *Recreations:* curling and walking. *Address:* 2 Garden Terrace, Easter Park Drive, Edinburgh EH4 6JR. *T:* 031-336 7025. *Club:* Royal Commonwealth Society.

SCOTT, Rev. G(uthrie) Michael; Anglican priest, Diocese of Chichester, since 1950; *b* 30 July 1907; *s* of Rev. Perceval Caleb Scott and Ethel Maud (*née* Burn); unmarried. *Educ:* King's College, Taunton; St Paul's College, Grahamstown, S Africa; Chichester Theological College. Ordained, 1930; Curate St Mary, Slaugham, Sussex, 1930-32; St Stephen's, Gloucester Rd, S Kensington, 1932-34. Domestic Chaplain to Bishop of Bombay, 1935-37; Chaplain, St Paul's Cathedral, Calcutta, 1937-38; Kasauli, 1938-39. Enlisted RAF 1940, invalided 1941. Returned to S Africa, 1943; St Alban's Coloured Mission and Chaplain St Joseph's Orphanage, Johannesburg, 1943-46; General License: Diocese of Johannesburg, 1946-50, Chichester, 1950-. In 1947 appealed to United Nations on behalf of two tribes of SW African Mandated Territory; attended sessions of General Assembly at Chiefs' request and was granted hearing by Fourth Cttee 1949, 1950 and 1955; Question referred to International Court of Justice. Took part in formation of Africa Bureau, 1952. Nagaland Peace Mission, 1964-66. Hon. Canon, St George's Cathedral, Windhoek, Namibia, 1975. Grand Companion, Order of Freedom (Zambia), 1968. Hon. STD General Theological Seminary, NY, 1972. *Publications:* Shadow over Africa, 1950; Attitude to Africa (Penguin), 1951; African Episode, 1954; Orphans' Heritage, 1958; A Time to Speak (autobiography), 1958; The Nagas in Search of Peace, 1966; Voices for Life (UN World Population Year), 1974; A Search for Peace and Justice (biog.), 1980; No Faith without Doubt, 1981; What Have We To Defend?, 1982. *Recreations:* walking, reading, sailing, theatre, etc. *Address:* c/o Lloyds Bank, 6 Pall Mall, SW1.

SCOTT, Hardiman; see Scott, J. P. H.

SCOTT, Sir Hilary; see Scott, Sir C. H.

SCOTT, Sir Ian Dixon, KCMG 1962 (CMG 1959); KCVO 1965; CIE 1947; *b* Inverness, 6 March 1909; *s* of Thomas Henderson Scott, OBE, MICE, and Mary Agnes Dixon, Selkirk; *m* 1937, Hon. Anna Drusilla Lindsay, *d* of 1st Baron Lindsay of Birker, CBE, LLD; one *s* four *d. Educ:* Queen's Royal College, Trinidad; Balliol College, Oxford (MA); London School of Economics. Entered Indian Civil Service, 1932; Indian Political Service, 1935; Assistant Director of Intelligence, Peshawar, 1941; Principal, Islamia College, Peshawar, 1943; Deputy Private Secretary to the Viceroy of India, 1945-47. Dep. Dir of Personnel, John Lewis & Co. Ltd, 1948-50. Appointed to Foreign Service, 1950; First Secretary, Foreign Office, 1950-51; British Legation, Helsinki, 1952; British Embassy, Beirut, 1954; Counsellor, 1956; Chargé d'Affaires, 1956, 1957, 1958; idc 1959; Consul-General, then Ambassador to the Congo, 1960-61; Ambassador to Sudan, 1961-65, to Norway, 1965-68. Chm., Clarksons Holidays Ltd, 1972-73 (Dir, 1968-73). Chm., Suffolk AHA, 1973-77; Member: Council, Dr Barnardo's, 1970- (Chm., 1972-78); Bd of Governors, Felixstowe Coll., 1971- (Chm., 1972-78); Chm., Indian Civil Service (retd) Assoc., 1977-. *Publication:* Tumbled House, 1969. *Recreation:* sailing. *Address:* Ash House, Alde Lane, Aldeburgh, Suffolk.

SCOTT, Prof. Ian Richard, PhD; Barber Professor of Law in the University of Birmingham, since 1978; Director, Institute of Judicial Administration, since 1975; *b* 8 Jan. 1940; *s* of Ernest and Edith Scott; *m* 1971, Ecce Cole; two *d. Educ:* Geelong Coll.; Queen's Coll., Univ. of Melbourne (LLB); King's Coll., Univ. of London (PhD). Barrister and Solicitor, Supreme Court of Victoria. *Recreation:* law. *Address:* Faculty of Law, University of Birmingham, Birmingham B15 2TT. *T:* 021-472 1301.

SCOTT, Jack, (Peter), Hardiman; Chief Assistant to Director General BBC, 1975-80; *b* King's Lynn, 2 April 1920; *s* of Thomas Hardiman Scott and Dorothy Constance Smith; *m* 1st, 1942, Sheilah Stewart Roberts (marr. diss.); two *s*; 2nd, Patricia Mary (Sue) Windle. *Educ:* Grammar Sch.; privately. Northampton Chronicle and Echo series, 1939; then various provincial newspapers; Associated Press, and finally Hants and Sussex News, when began freelance broadcasting, 1948. Joined BBC; Asst News Editor Midland Region, 1950; gen. reporting staff, London, 1954; various foreign assignments, incl. Suez war; BBC's first Polit. Corresp., 1960; subseq. first Polit. Editor until 1975. Member: Study Gp on Future of Broadcasting in Zimbabwe, 1980; Broadcasting Complaints Commn, 1981-. Pres., Suffolk Poetry Soc., 1979-. *Publications:* Secret Sussex, 1949; (ed) How Shall I Vote?, 1976; *poems:* Adam and Eve and Us, 1946; When the Words are Gone, 1972; *novels:* Within the Centre, 1946; The Lonely River, 1950; Text for Murder, 1951; Operation 10, 1982; contribs to: TV and Elections, 1977; BBC Guide to Parliament, 1979; Politics and the Media, 1980. *Recreations:* poetry, paintings, listening to music, conservation, East Anglia. *Address:* 4 Butchers Lane, Boxford, Colchester, Essex. *T:* Boxford (Suffolk) 210320.

SCOTT, Prof. James Alexander; Regional Medical Officer, Trent Regional Health Authority, since 1973; Special Professor of Health Care Planning, Nottingham University, since 1974; *b* 3 July 1931; *s* of Thomas Scott, MA Oxon and Margaret L. Scott; *m* 1957, Margaret Olive Slinger, BA, SRN; one *s* two *d. Educ:* Doncaster Grammar Sch.; Trinity Coll., Dublin Univ. BA 1953; MB, BCh, BAO 1955; MA, MD 1965; FFCM 1974. Pathologist, Sir Patrick Dun's Hosp., Dublin, 1957-59; Registrar in Clinical Pathology, United Sheffield Hosps, 1959-61; Trainee, later Asst and Principal Asst Sen. MO, Sheffield RHB, 1961-70; Sen. Lectr in Community Medicine, Nottingham Univ., 1967-71; Sen. Admin. MO, Sheffield RHB, 1971-73. Chm., English Regional MOs Gp, 1978-80; Pres., Hospital Cttee, EEC, 1980-; Mem., Public Health Lab. Service Bd. QHP, 1980-. *Publications:* contrib. Lancet. *Recreation:* stamp collecting. *Address:* 5 Slayleigh Lane, Sheffield S10 3RE. *T:* Sheffield 302238; La Gardelle, 24260 Le Bugue, Dordogne, France.

SCOTT, James Archibald, MVO 1961; Under-Secretary, Scottish Economic Planning Department, since 1976; *b* 5 March 1932; *s* of late James Scott, MBE, and of Agnes Bone Howie; *m* 1957, Elizabeth Agnes Joyce Buchan-Hepburn; three *s* one *d. Educ:* Dollar Acad.; Queen's Univ. of Ont.; Univ. of St Andrews (MA Hons). RAF aircrew, 1954-56. Asst Principal, CRO, 1956; served in New Delhi, 1958-62, and UK Mission to UN, New York, 1962-65; transf. to Scottish Office, 1965; Private Sec. to Sec. of State for Scotland, 1969-71; Asst Sec., Scottish Office, 1971. *Recreations:* music, golf. *Address:* 38 Queen's Crescent, Edinburgh EH9 2BA. *T:* 031-667 8417. *Club:* Travellers'.

SCOTT, J(ames) M(aurice), OBE 1945; MA; Author and explorer; *b* 13 Dec. 1906. *Educ:* Fettes College; Clare College, Cambridge. *Publications:* Gino Watkins, 1935; Land of Seals, 1949; Bright Eyes of Danger, 1950; Hudson of Hudson's Bay, 1950; Other Side of the Moon, 1950; Snowstone, 1950; Vineyards of France, 1950; Captain Smith and Pocahontas, 1953; Man Who Made Wine, 1953; Heather Mary, 1953; Sea-wyf and Biscuit, 1955; White Magic, 1955; Choice of Heaven, 1959; The Tea Story, 1964; The Book of Pall Mall, 1965; Dingo, 1966; The Devil You Don't, 1967; In a Beautiful Pea-Green Boat, 1968; The White Poppy, 1968; From Sea to Ocean, 1969; A Walk Along the Appenines, 1973; Boadicea, 1975; Icebound, 1977; Red Hair and Moonwater: Arctic short stories, 1980; The Private Life of Polar Exploration, 1982. *Recreations:* mountain walking, sailing. *Address:* Thatched Cottage, Yelling, Huntingdon, Cambs.

SCOTT, James Steel, MD, FRCSEd; Professor of Obstetrics and Gynæcology, University of Leeds, since 1961; *b* 18 April 1924; *s* of late Dr Angus M. Scott and late Margaret Scott; *m* 1958, Olive Sharpe; two *s. Educ:* Glasgow Academy; University of Glasgow. MB, ChB 1946. Service in RAMC, 1947-49. MRCOG 1953. Obstetric Tutor, Liverpool University, 1954; Lecturer, 1958; Senior Lecturer, 1960. MD, FRCSEd 1959. *Publications:* contrib. to Lancet, Brit. Med. Jl, Jl of Obst. and Gynæc. of Brit. Empire, Amer. Jl of Obstetrics and Gynæcology. *Recreation:* sailing. *Address:* 24 Long Causeway, Leeds LS16 8EQ.

SCOTT, Sir James (Walter), 2nd Bt, *cr* 1962; DL; one of HM Body Guard, Hon. Corps of Gentlemen-at-Arms, since 1977; *b* 26 Oct. 1924; *e s* of Col Sir Jervoise Bolitho Scott, 1st Bt, and Kathleen Isabel, *yr d* of late Godfrey Walter, Maidanger, Basingstoke; *S* father 1965; *m* 1951, Anne Constantia, *e d* of late Lt-Col Clive Austin, Roundwood, Micheldever, Hants; three *s* one *d* (and one *d* decd). *Educ:* Eton. Lt-Col The Life Guards, formerly Grenadier Guards, retired 1969. Served War of 1939-45: NW Europe, 1944-45. Palestine, 1945-46; ADC to Viceroy and Gov.-Gen. of India, 1946-48; Malaya, 1948-49; Cyprus, 1958, 1960, 1964; Malaysia, 1966. Underwriting Member of Lloyd's. Master, Mercers' Co., 1976. Councillor, Hants CC, 1973-. DL 1978, High Sheriff 1981-82, Hants. *Heir: s* James Jervoise Scott [*b* 12 Oct. 1952; *m* 1982, Mrs Judy Lyndon-Skeggs, *d* of Brian Trafford]. *Address:* Rotherfield Park, Alton, Hampshire GU34 3QL. *T:* Tisted 204. *Clubs:* Cavalry and Guards, Farmers'.

SCOTT, Sir John A. G.; *see* Guillum Scott.

SCOTT, Prof. John Fraser; Vice-Chancellor, La Trobe University, Melbourne, since 1977; *b* 10 Oct. 1928; *s* of Douglas Fraser Scott and Cecilia Louise Scott; *m* 1956, Dorothea Elizabeth Paton Scott; one *s* three *d. Educ:* Bristol Grammar Sch.; Trinity Coll., Cambridge. MA, FIS. Research Asst, Univ. of Sheffield, 1950-53; Asst, Univ. of Aberdeen, 1953-55; Lectr in Biometry, Univ. of Oxford, 1955-65; Univ. of Sussex: Reader in Statistics, 1965-67; Prof. of Applied Statistics, 1967-77; Pro-Vice-Chancellor, 1971-77. Visiting Consultant in Statistics: Nigeria, 1961, 1965; Sweden, 1969; Kuwait, 1973, 1976; Iraq, 1973; Malaysia, 1976. Reader, Church of England, 1971-77; Examining Chaplain to Bp of Chichester, 1974-77; Diocesan Lay Reader, Anglican Dio. of Melbourne, 1977-. Chairman: Jt Cttee on Univ. Statistics; AVCC Working Party on Attrition; Mem., Grad. Careers Council of Aust. Mem., ABC Victorian State Adv. Cttee, 1978-81. Editor, Applied Statistics, 1971-76. *Publications:* The Comparability of Grade Standards in Mathematics, 1975; papers in JRSS, Lancet, BMJ, Chemistry and Industry, Statistician, etc. *Recreations:* wine, women and song; canals. *Address:* La Trobe University, Bundoora, Victoria 3083, Australia. *T:* 478 3122. *Club:* Melbourne.

SCOTT, John James; Assistant Managing Director, Industrial Engines (Sales) Ltd, Elbar Group, since 1980; *b* 4 Sept. 1924; *s* of late Col John Creagh Scott, DSO, OBE and Mary Elizabeth Marjory (*née* Murray of Polmaise); *m* 1st, Katherine Mary (*née* Bruce); twin *d*; 2nd, Heather Marguerite (*née* Douglas Brown); 3rd, June Rose (*née* Mackie); twin *s. Educ:* Radley (Schol.); Corpus Christi Coll., Cambridge (Schol.); National Inst. for Medical Research, London. War Service, Captain, Argyll and Sutherland Highlanders, 1944-47. BA 1st cl. hons Nat. Sci. Tripos, Pts I and II, 1950, MA 1953, Cantab; PhD London 1954. Senior Lectr in Chem. Pathology, St Mary's Hosp., 1955-61; Mem. Editorial Bd, Biochem. Jl, 1956-61; Mem. Cttee of Biochem. Soc., 1961; Vis. Scientist, Nat. Insts of Health, Bethesda, Md, 1961. Entered Diplomatic Service, 1961; Office of Comr Gen. for SE Asia, Singapore, 1962; Office of Political Adviser to C-in-C, Singapore, 1963; FO, 1966; Counsellor, Rio de Janeiro and Brasilia, 1971; seconded to NI Office as Asst Sec., Stormont, 1974-76; Asst Under-Sec., FCO, 1978-80. Francis Bacon Prize, Cambridge, 1950. *Publications:* papers in Biochem. Jl, Proc. Royal Soc. and other learned jls. *Recreations:* botany, photography, music. *Address:* The Cottage, South Rauceby, Sleaford, Lincs NG34 7QG. *T:* South Rauceby 254. *Clubs:* Carlton; Leander (Henley-on-Thames); Hawks (Cambridge); Ski Club of GB.

SCOTT, Kenneth Bertram Adam, CMG 1980; HM Diplomatic Service; Ambassador to Yugoslavia, since 1982; *b* 23 Jan. 1931; *s* of late Adam Scott, OBE, and Lena Kaye; *m* 1966, Gabrielle Justine (*d* 1977), *d* of R. W. Smart, Christchurch, New Zealand; one *s* one *d. Educ:* George Watson's Coll., Edinburgh; Edinburgh Univ. MA Hons 1952. Foreign Office, 1954; Third Sec., Moscow 1956; Second Sec., (Commercial), Bonn, 1958; FO, 1961; First Sec., Washington, 1964; Head of Chancery and Consul, Vientiane, 1968; Counsellor and Head of Chancery, Moscow, 1971; Sen. Officers' War Course, RNC, Greenwich, 1973; Dep. Head, Personnel Ops Dept, FCO, 1973; Counsellor and Head of Chancery, Washington, 1975; Head of E European and Soviet Dept, FCO, 1977; Minister and Dep. UK Perm. Rep. to NATO, 1979-82. *Address:* c/o Foreign and Commonwealth Office, SW1. *Club:* New (Edinburgh).

SCOTT, Laurence Prestwich; Chairman of the Manchester Guardian & Evening News Ltd, 1949-73; *b* 10 June 1909; *s* of John Russell and Alice Olga Scott; *m* 1939, Constance Mary Black (*d* 1969); two *s* one *d*; *m* 1970, Jessica Mary Crowther Thompson; one *s. Educ:* Rugby; Trinity College, Cambridge. Director, Anglia Television Group Ltd, 1958-80; Dir, Press Assoc. and Reuters, 1948-55, 1956-60. Mem., Council of Manchester University, 1946-70 (Dep. Chm., 1957-70). *Address:* Redes House, Siddington, Macclesfield, Cheshire.

SCOTT, M. Audrey; Headmistress of the Perse School for Girls, Cambridge, 1947-67, retired; *b* 22 Oct. 1904; *d* of late Lieutenant-Colonel C. E. Scott, solicitor, and Mrs M. E. M. Scott, Bradford. *Educ:* Queen Margaret's School, Scarborough (now at Escrick); Newnham College, Cambridge. Teaching at Benenden School, Kent, 1926-29; Atherley School, Southampton, 1929-31; Edgbaston Church College, 1931-40; Thornbury Grammar School, Glos, 1941-43; Headmistress, Yeovil High School, Jan. 1944-Aug. 1947. Association of Headmistresses: Exec. Cttee, 1956-62; Chm., Foreign and Commonwealth Education Cttee, 1960-62; Pres., Six Counties Branch, 1959-61. *Publication:* The First Hundred Years 1881-1981: a history of the Perse School for Girls, 1981. *Address:* 14 Storey's Way, Cambridge. *T:* 355030.
See also Sir Hilary Scott.

SCOTT, Dame Margaret, (Dame Catherine Margaret Mary Denton), DBE 1981 (OBE 1977); Founding Director of the Australian Ballet School, 1964-81; *b* 26 April 1922; *d* of John and Marjorie Douglas-Scott; *m* 1953, Prof. Derek Ashworth Denton, FAA, FRACP; two *s*. *Educ:* Parktown Convent, Johannesburg, S Africa. Sadler's Wells Ballet, London, 1940-43; Principal: Ballet Rambert, London and Australia, 1944-49; National Ballet, Australia, 1949-50; Ballet Rambert, and John Cranko Group, London, 1951-53; private ballet teaching, Australia, 1953-61; planned and prepared the founding of the Aust. Ballet Sch., 1962-64. *Recreations:* music, theatre, garden. *Address:* 816 Orrong Road, Toorak, Melbourne, Vic 3142, Australia. *T:* 241-2640. *Club:* Alexandra (Melbourne).

SCOTT, Maurice FitzGerald; Official Fellow in Economics, Nuffield College, Oxford, since 1968; *b* 6 Dec. 1924; *s* of Colonel G. C. Scott, OBE and H. M. G. Scott; *m* 1953, Eleanor Warren (*née* Dawson); three *d*. *Educ:* Wadham Coll., Oxford (MA); Nuffield Coll., Oxford (BLitt). Served RE, 1943-46. OEEC, Paris, 1949-51; Paymaster-General's Office (Lord Cherwell), 1951-53; Cabinet Office, 1953-54; NIESR, London, 1954-57; Tutor in Economics and Student of Christ Church, Oxford, 1957-68; NEDO, London, 1962-63; OECD, Paris, 1967-68. *Publications:* A Study of U.K. Imports, 1963; (with I. M. D. Little and T. Scitovsky) Industry and Trade in Some Developing Countries, 1970; (with J. D. MacArthur and D. M. G. Newbery) Project Appraisal in Practice, 1976; (with R. A. Laslett) Can We get back to Full Employment?, 1978; (with W. M. Corden and I. M. D. Little) The Case against General Import Restrictions, 1980. *Recreation:* walking. *Address:* 11 Blandford Avenue, Oxford OX2 8EA. *T:* Oxford 59115. *Club:* Political Economy (Oxford).

SCOTT, Rev. Michael; *see* Scott, Rev. G. M.

SCOTT, Sir Michael, KCVO 1979 (MVO 1961); CMG 1977; HM Diplomatic Service, retired; *b* 19 May 1923; *yr s* of late John Scott and Kathleen Scott; *m* 1st, 1944, Vivienne Sylvia Vincent-Barwood (marr. diss. 1967); three *s*; 2nd, 1971, Jennifer Slawikowski (*née* Cameron Smith), widow of Dr George J. M. Slawikowski. *Educ:* Dame Allan's School; Durham Univ. Durham Light Infantry, 1941; 1st Gurkha Rifles, 1943-47. Colonial Office, 1949; CRO, 1957; First Secretary, Karachi, 1958-59; Deputy High Commissioner, Peshawar, 1959-62; Counsellor and Director, British Information Services in India, New Delhi, 1963-65; Head of E and Central Africa Dept, FCO, 1965-68; Counsellor, British High Commn, Nicosia, 1968-72; RCDS, 1973; Ambassador to Nepal, 1974-77; High Comr in Malawi, 1977-79; High Comr in Bangladesh, 1980-81. *Address:* 87A Cornwall Gardens, SW7 4AY. *T:* 01-589 6794. *Clubs:* Oriental, Royal Commonwealth Society.

SCOTT, Sir Michael Fergus M.; *see* Maxwell Scott.

SCOTT, Maj.-Gen. Michael Frederick, JP; Farmer; *b* 25 Oct. 1911; *s* of Col F. W. Scott, Romsey, Hants; *m* 1961, Laila Wallis (*née* Tatchell). *Educ:* Harrow. Apprenticed as Mechanical Engr to John I. Thornycroft Co. Basingstoke, 1932-35; commnd Lieut, RAOC, 1935; transf. REME 1942. Served: India, 1938-44; Palestine, 1947-48; Germany, 1951-54; Cyprus, 1955-58. Inspector, REME, 1960-63; Commandant Technical Group, REME, 1963-65 (retd); Col Comdt, REME, 1968-73. CEng; FIMechE. JP Somerset, 1967. *Recreations:* sailing, shooting, country pursuits. *Address:* Parsonage Farm, South Barrow, Yeovil, Somerset. *T:* North Cadbury 40417. *Club:* Royal Ocean Racing.

SCOTT, Michael John; Programme Controller, Granada TV, since 1979; *b* 8 Dec. 1932; *s* of Tony and Pam Scott; *m* 1956, Sylvia Hudson; one *d*. *Educ:* Latymer Upper Sch., Hammersmith; Clayesmore, Iwerne Minster, Dorset. National Service, RAOC, 1951-53. Stagehand with Festival Ballet, and film extra, 1954; TV production trainee, Rank Organization, 1955; Granada TV: joined as floormanager, 1956; Programme Director, 1957; Producer/Performer, daily magazine programme, 1963-65; Presenter, Cinema, 1965-68; Executive Producer, local programmes, 1968-73; World in Action interviewer, and producer/performer of other programmes, 1974-75; Executive Producer and Reporter, Nuts and Bolts of the Economy, 1975-78; Dep. Programme Controller, 1978-79. *Recreations:* watching the box, jogging, a 1932 Lagonda, a garden. *Address:* Flat 1, 39 Gloucester Walk, W8. *T:* 01-937 3962; Flat 1, Scottish Life House, Bridge Street, Manchester. *T:* 061-832 9061.

SCOTT, Most Rev. Moses Nathanael Christopher Omobiala, Commander of the Rokel, 1974; CBE 1970; Hon. DD Durham; *b* 18 Aug. 1911; *s* of late Christopher Columbus Scott, Hastings Village, Sierra Leone, and Cleopatra Eliza Scott, York Village; *m* 1941, Cordelia Elizabeth Deborah Maddy, Gloucester Village; three *s* two *d*. *Educ:* CMS Grammar School and Fourah Bay Coll., Freetown, Sierra Leone. Deacon 1943; Priest, 1946. Curate of: Lunsar, 1943-44; Yongro, Bullom, 1944-46; Missionary-in-charge of Makeni, 1946-48, of Bo, 1948-50; studied at London College of Divinity for DipTheol, 1950-51; Curate of Grappenhall, Cheshire, 1951-53; returned to Bo, 1954; Priest in charge, Bo District, 1954-57 (Educn Sec. to the Diocese, 1955-61); Archdeacon of Missions, Sierra Leone, 1957-59; Archdeacon of Bonthe and Bo, 1959-61; Bishop of Sierra Leone, 1961-81; Archbishop of West Africa, 1969-81. Hon. DD Durham, 1962. *Recreations:* playwriting, croquet. *Address:* c/o PO Box 128, Freetown, Sierra Leone.

SCOTT, Nicholas Paul, MBE 1964; JP; MP (C) Chelsea, since Oct. 1974; Parliamentary Under Secretary of State, Northern Ireland Office, since 1981; *b* 1933; *e s* of late Percival John Scott; *m* 1st, 1964, Elizabeth Robinson (marr. diss. 1976); one *s* two *d*; 2nd, 1979, Hon. Mrs Cecilia Anne Tapsell, *d* of Baron Hawke, *qv*. *Educ:* Clapham College. Served Holborn Borough Coun., 1956-59 and 1962-65; contested (C) SW Islington, 1959 and 1964; MP (C) Paddington S, 1966-Feb. 1974; PPS to: Chancellor of the Exchequer, Rt Hon. Iain Macleod, 1970; Home Sec., Rt. Hon. Robert Carr, 1972-74; Parly Under-Sec. of State, Dept of Employment, 1974; Opposition spokesman on housing, 1974-75; Mem., 1922 Exec. Cttee, 1978-81; Dir, London Office, European Cons. Gp in European Parlt, 1974. Nat. Chm., Young Conservatives, 1963; Chm., Conservative Parly Employment Cttee, 1979-81 (Vice-Chm., 1967-72). Chairman: Westminster Community Relations Council, 1967-72; Paddington Churches Housing Assoc., 1970-76; British Atlantic Gp Younger Politicians, 1970-73; Nat. Pres., Tory Reform Gp. Dep. Chm., British Caribbean Assoc.; Mem. Council, Community Service Volunteers; Governor, British Inst. of Human Rights; Dep. Chm., Youthaid, 1977-79. Mem., Cttee, MCC, 1972-75. Churchwarden, St Margaret's, Westminster, 1971-73. Man. Dir, E. Allom & Co., 1968-70; Chm., Creative Consultants Ltd, 1969-79; Director: A. S. Kerswill Ltd, 1970-; Eastbourne Printers Ltd, 1970-; Juniper Studios Ltd, 1970-; Midhurst White Holdings Ltd, 1977-78; Bonusbond Hldgs Ltd, 1980-81; Bonusplan Ltd, 1977-81; Cleveland Offshore Fund Inc., 1970-; Throgmorton Securities Ltd, 1970-74; Ede & Townsend, 1977-80; Learplan Ltd, 1978-; Consultant: Campbell-Johnson Ltd, 1970-76; Roulston & Co. Inc., 1970-78; Lombard North Central Ltd, 1971-74; Clevebourne Investments Ltd, 1974-76; Claremont Textiles Ltd, 1974-76; Procter & Gamble Ltd, 1974-78; Hill & Knowlton (UK) Ltd, 1981-; VSO, 1974-76; Council, Bank Staff Assocs, 1968-77. Mem., GAPAN, 1979-. JP London, 1961. *Recreations:* cricket, tennis, golf, flying. *Address:* House of Commons, SW1A 0AA. *Clubs:* Pratt's, Buck's, MCC.

SCOTT, Sir Oliver (Christopher Anderson), 3rd Bt, of Yews, Westmorland, *cr* 1909; Hon. Consultant, Institute of Cancer Research, Sutton, since 1974; Radiobiologist, 1954-66. Director, British Empire Cancer Campaign Research Unit in Radiobiology, 1966-69; *b* 6 November 1922; *s* of Sir Samuel H. Scott, 2nd Bt and Nancy Lilian (*née* Anderson); *S* father 1960; *m* 1951, Phoebe Ann Tolhurst; one *s* two *d*. *Educ:* Charterhouse; King's College, Cambridge. Clinical training at St Thomas' Hosp., 1943-46; MRCS, LRCP, 1946; MB, BCh, Cambridge, 1946; MD Cambridge, 1976; Surgeon-Lieutenant RNVR, 1947-49. Dir, Provincial Insurance Co., 1955-64. Vice-Pres., British Cancer Council, 1972-78 (Chm., Finance Cttee, 1970-72); Mem. Council, Cancer Res. Campaign, 1978-. High Sheriff of Westmorland, 1966. *Publications:* contributions to scientific books and journals. *Recreations:* skiing and walking. *Heir:* s Christopher James Scott, *b* 16 Jan. 1955. *Address:* 31 Kensington Square, W8. *T:* 01-937 8556. *Club:* Brooks's.

SCOTT, Oliver Lester Schreiner; Physician-in-Charge, Skin Department, Charing Cross Hospital, since 1957; Consultant Dermatologist, South West Metropolitan Regional Hospital Board, since 1951; *b* London, 16 June 1919; *s* of Ralph Lester Scott, FRCSE, and Ursula Hester Schreiner; *m* 1943, Katherine Ogle Branfoot; two *d*. *Educ:* Diocesan College, Cape Town; Trinity College, Cambridge; St Thomas's Hospital, London. MRCS, LRCP 1942; MA, MB, BChir, (Cantab) 1943; MRCP (London) 1944. FRCP 1964. Med. Specialist, RAF Med. Branch, 1943-46. Dir, Medical Insurance Agency, 1976-. Hon. Treasurer: Royal Medical Foundn of Epsom Coll.; Royal Soc. of Medicine; Pres., British Assoc. of Dermatologists, 1982. Chevalier, l'Ordre National du Mérite, France. *Publications:* section on skin disorders in Clinical Genetics, ed A. Sorsby; medical articles in Lancet, British Journal of Dermatology, etc. *Recreation:* fishing. *Address:* 114 Harley Street, W1. *T:* 01-935 0621; South Lodge, South Side, Wimbledon Common, SW19. *T:* 01-946 6662.

SCOTT, Paul Henderson, CMG 1974; writer; HM Diplomatic Service, retired 1980; *b* 7 Nov. 1920; *s* of Alan Scott and Catherine Scott (*née* Henderson), Edinburgh; *m* 1953, Beatrice Celia Sharpe; one *s* one *d*. *Educ:* Royal High School, Edinburgh; Edinburgh University (MA). HM Forces, 1941-47 (Major RA). Foreign Office, 1947-53; First Secretary, Warsaw, 1953-55; First Secretary, La Paz, 1955-59; Foreign Office, 1959-62; Counsellor, Havana, 1962-64; Canadian National Defence College, 1964-65; British Deputy Commissioner General for Montreal Exhibition, 1965-67; Counsellor and Consul-General, Vienna, 1968-71; Head of British Govt Office, 1971, Consul-Gen., 1974-75. Montreal; Research Associate, IISS, 1975-76; Asst Under Sec., FO (negotiator on behalf of EEC Presidency for negotiations with USSR, Poland and East Germany), 1977; Minister and Consul-General, Milan, 1977-80. Chm., Adv. Council for the Arts in

Scotland, 1981–; Dep. Chm., Saltire Soc.; Member: Council, Nat. Trust for Scotland; Assoc. for Scottish Literary Studies; Scots Language Soc.; Cockburn Assoc. Grosse Goldene Ehrenzeichen, Austria, 1969. *Publications:* 1707: The Union of Scotland and England, 1979; (ed with A. C. Davis) The Age of MacDiarmid, 1980; Walter Scott and Scotland, 1981; (ed) Walter Scott's Letters of Malachi Malagrowther, 1981; (ed) Andrew Fletcher's United and Separate Parliaments, 1982; articles and book reviews esp. in Economist, Scotsman and Sunday Standard. *Recreations:* ski-ing, sailing. *Address:* 33 Drumsheugh Gardens, Edinburgh. *T:* 031-225 1038. *Club:* New (Edinburgh).

SCOTT, Rev. Dr Percy; Warden of Hartley Hall, Manchester, 1973–77, retired; *b* 14 Nov. 1910; *s* of Herbert and Emma Scott; *m* 1937, Christa Schleining; one *s* two *d*. *Educ:* Lincoln City School; London and Marburg Universities. Richmond College, London, 1931–35; Marburg, 1935–37; Minister at: Exeter, 1937–39; Stockton-on-Tees, 1939–45; Leeds, 1945–47; Tutor in Systematic Theology at Hartley Victoria College, 1947–73; Member, Faculty of Theology, Manchester Univ., 1953–77, Principal, Hartley Victoria Coll., Manchester, 1959–73. *Publications:* John Wesley's Lehre von der Heiligung, 1938; (trans.) Day by Day we Magnify Thee (Luther), 1950; other translations from German; signed reviews in The Expository Times and London Quarterly; articles. *Recreation:* sport. *Address:* 53 Alexandra Road South, Manchester M16 8GH. *T:* 061-226 7311. *Club:* Rotarian (Manchester South).

SCOTT, Sir Peter; see Scott, Sir C. P.

SCOTT, Peter Denys John, QC 1978; *b* 19 April 1935; *s* of John Ernest Dudley Scott and Joan G. Steinberg; *m* 1976, Hilary Mary Forsyth. *Educ:* Monroe High Sch., Rochester, NY, USA; Balliol Coll., Oxford (BA Hons). Second Lieut, RHA, Lieut (TA), National Service, 1955. Called to the Bar, Middle Temple (Harmsworth Scholar), 1960; Standing Counsel: to Dir. Gen. of Fair Trading, 1973–78; to Dept of Employment, 1974–78. Chm., Tower Hamlets Law Centre, 1978. Mem., Senate and Bar Council, 1981–82. *Recreations:* walking, theatre. *Address:* 4 Eldon Road, W8. *T:* 01-937 3301.

SCOTT, Peter Hardiman; see Scott, J. P. H.

SCOTT, Sir Peter (Markham), Kt 1973; CBE 1953 (MBE 1942); DSC 1943; Artist; Chancellor, Birmingham University, since 1974; Chairman, World Wildlife Fund (International); Hon. Director: Wildfowl Trust; Survival Anglia Ltd; Lt-Comdr RNVR, retired; *b* 14 Sept. 1909; *s* of Captain Robert Falcon Scott, CVO, RN, and Kathleen Bruce (she *m* 2nd, 1922, Edward Hilton Young, later 1st Baron Kennet, PC, GBE, DSO, DSC, who *died* 1960; she *died* 1947); *m* 1st, 1942, Elizabeth Jane (marr. diss. 1951), *d* of David Howard; one *d*; 2nd, 1951, Philippa, *d* of late Comdr F. W. Talbot-Ponsonby, RN; one *s* one *d*. *Educ:* Oundle; Trinity College, Cambridge (MA); Munich State Academy; Royal Academy Schools, London. Exhibited paintings Royal Acad. since 1933; held Exhibitions of oil paintings at Ackermann's Galleries, Bond Street, also New York; specialises in bird-painting and portraits; lectures and nature feature programmes on television. Won international 14-foot Dinghy Championship for Prince of Wales Cup, 1937, 1938, and 1946. Represented Great Britain at Olympic Games, 1936 in single-handed sailing (bronze medal). Served in destroyers in Battle of Atlantic, and Light Coastal Forces in Channel, 1939–45 (despatches thrice, MBE, DSC and Bar). President: Soc. of Wildlife Artists, 1964–78; Fauna and Flora Preservation Soc., 1981–; Glos Assoc. of Youth Clubs; Internat. Yacht Racing Union, 1955–69; Vice-President: British Gliding Assoc.; Inland Waterways Assoc.; Camping Club of Great Britain; Bristol Gliding Club; Chairman: Species Survival Commn, IUCN, 1963–80; Gloucestershire Trust for Nature Conservation; British Butterfly Conservation Soc.; Olympic Yachting Committee, 1947–48; Internat. Jury for Yachting, Olympic Games: 1956, Melbourne; 1960, Naples; 1964, Japan; Member Council, Boy Scout Assoc.; Winston Churchill Meml Trust. Rector, Aberdeen Univ., 1960–63. Admiral, Manx Herring Fleet, 1962–65. Explored unmapped Perry River area in Canadian Arctic, May-August 1949; Leader of ornithological expeditions to Central Highlands, Iceland, to mark wild geese, 1951, 1953; Expeditions to Australasia Galapagos Is, Seychelles and Antarctic (thrice). Gliding: International Gold Badge, 1958; International Diamond badge, 1963; National Gliding Champion, 1963; Chm., British Gliding Assoc., 1968–70. Hon. Fellow, UMIST, 1974. Hon. LLD: Exeter, 1963; Aberdeen, 1963; Birmingham, 1974; Bristol, 1975; Hon. DSc Bath, 1979; Guelph, 1981. Cherry Kearton Medal, RGS, 1967; Albert Medal, RSA, 1970; Bernard Tucker Medal, BOU, 1970; Arthur Allen Medal, Cornell Univ., 1971; Gold Medal, NY Zoological Soc., 1975; IUCN John Phillips Medal, 1981; World Wildlife Fund Twentieth Anniversary Special Award, 1981. Icelandic Order of the Falcon, 1969; Commander, Dutch Order of Golden Ark, 1976; Internat. Pahlavi Environment Prize (UN), 1977. *Publications:* Morning Flight, 1935; Wild Chorus, 1938; The Battle of the Narrow Seas, 1945; Portrait Drawings, 1949; Key to Wildfowl of the World, 1949 (Coloured Key, 1958); Wild Geese and Eskimos, 1951; (with James Fisher) A Thousand Geese, 1953; (with Hugh Boyd) Wildfowl of the British Isles, 1957; The Eye of the Wind (autobiography), 1961; (with Philippa Scott) Animals in Africa, 1962; (with the Wildfowl Trust) The Swans, 1972; Fishwatchers' Guide to West Atlantic Coral Reefs, 1972; Observations of Wildlife, 1980; Illustrated Lord Kennet's A Bird in the Bush, Michael Bratby's Grey Goose and Through the Air, Paul Gallico's The Snow Goose, Adventures Among Birds, Handbook of British Birds, Vol. III, Jean Delacour's

Waterfowl of the World. *Recreations:* exploring, bird-watching, fish-watching, yacht racing, gliding. *Address:* New Grounds, Slimbridge, Glos. *Clubs:* Royal Thames Yacht; Royal Yacht Squadron; Explorers (New York).

SCOTT, Prof. Richard; Professor of General Practice, University of Edinburgh, 1963–79, now Emeritus; *b* 11 May 1914; *s* of Richard Scott and Beatrice Scott (*née* Aitken); *m* 1938, Mary Ellen Maclachlan; three *s* two *d*. *Educ:* Beath High Sch.; Edinburgh Univ. MB, ChB 1936; MD (with commendation) 1938; Lewis Cameron Postgrad. Prize, 1938; DPH Edin. 1946 (class medal); FRCGP 1967; MRCPE 1971; MCFP (Can) 1972. General Practice, 1936–39. War Service, 1939–46 (Lieutenant-Colonel RAMC). Lecturer in Public Health and Social Medicine, Edin. Univ., 1946; Sen. Lectr and Dir General Practice Teaching Unit, 1951; subseq. Reader in General Practice. Mem. Foundn Steering Cttee, Coll. of GPs 1951; James Mackenzie Lectr, 1964; Albert Warder Lectr, RSM, 1967. Hon. Sec. Scottish Council, RCGP, 1952–68. Consultant and Technical Advisor, WHO. FRCPE 1979. *Publications:* Contrib. to scientific and medical jls. *Address:* 24 Fountainhall Road, Edinburgh EH9 2LW. *T:* 031-667 4244.
See also R. J. D. Scott.

SCOTT, Sheriff Richard John Dinwoodie; Sheriff of Grampian, Highland and Islands, at Aberdeen and Stonehaven, since 1977; *b* 28 May 1939; *s* of Prof. Richard Scott, *qv*; *m* 1969, Josephine Moretta Blake; two *d*. *Educ:* Edinburgh Academy; Univ. of Edinburgh (MA, LLB) (Vans Dunlop Schol. in Evidence and Pleading, 1963). Lektor in English, British Centre, Sweden, 1960–61; Tutor, Faculty of Law, Univ. of Edinburgh, 1964–72; admitted to Faculty of Advocates, 1965; Standing Jun. Counsel to Min. of Defence (Air) in Scotland, 1968–77. Hon. Lectr, Univ. of Aberdeen, 1980–. *Publications:* various articles in legal jls. *Address:* Sheriff's Chambers, Aberdeen AB9 1AP.

SCOTT, Richard Rashleigh Folliott, QC 1975; Attorney General of the Duchy of Lancaster, since 1980; *b* 2 Oct. 1934; *s* of Lt-Col C. W. F. Scott, 2/9th Gurkha Rifles and Katharine Scott (*née* Rashleigh); *m* 1959, Rima Elisa, *d* of Salvador Ripoll and Blanca Korsi de Ripoll, Panama City; two *s* two *d*. *Educ:* Michaelhouse Coll., Natal; Univ. of Cape Town (BA); Trinity Coll., Cambridge (BA, LLB). Bigelow Fellow, Univ. of Chicago, 1958–59. Called to Bar, Inner Temple, 1959, Bencher, 1981. Chm. of the Bar, 1982–83 (Vice-Chm., 1981–82). *Recreations:* hunting, tennis, bridge; formerly Rugby (Cambridge Blue, 1957). *Address:* The Old Rectory, Foscote, Buckingham. *T:* Buckingham 3142; 11 Old Square, Lincoln's Inn, WC2. *T:* 01-405 5243.

SCOTT, Robert, CBE 1976; Director, Polytechnic, Wolverhampton, 1969–77, retired; *b* 7 July 1913; 2nd *s* of H. Scott, Westhoughton, Bolton; *m* 1940, Dorothy M. Howell, Westhoughton; one *s* one *d*. *Educ:* Hindley and Abram Grammar Sch., Lancs; Univ. of Liverpool; St John's Coll., Cambridge (Wrangler; MA). BSc 1st cl. hons 1934, DipEd 1937, Liverpool; BA Cantab, 1936; FIMA. Asst Master, Newton-le-Willows Grammar Sch., 1937–41; Army and WO Staff, 1941–46; Scientific Civil Service at RMCS Shrivenham, 1946–54; Vice-Principal, Bolton Techn. Coll., 1954–57; Principal, Wolverhampton and Staffs Coll. of Technology, 1958–69. *Recreations:* motoring, reading. *Address:* 4 Wrekin Lane, The Wergs, Wolverhampton WV6 8UL. *T:* Wolverhampton 752107.

SCOTT, Col Robert Edmond Gabriel, MBE 1959; MC 1953; Director General, Engineering Industries Association, since 1981; *b* 3 Aug. 1920; *s* of Edmond James and Lilian Kate Scott; *m* 1942, Anna Maria Larkin; two *s*. *Educ:* Roan, Greenwich. Commissioned into Durham Light Inf., 1942; regimental service with this regt in Western Desert, Italy, Korea and Rhine Army, 1942–52; Staff duties, MoD and Eastern Comd, 1952–56; service with W African Frontier Force, 1956–60 (comd inf. batt., Home Service, 1960–66; seconded to Diplomatic Service, as Defence Adviser, Lagos, 1966–70; Dep. Comd, W. Midland Dist, 1970–72; retired, 1972. Engineering Industries Association: Export Sec. and Dep. Dir, 1973–77; Dir, 1977–81. *Recreations:* rough shooting, country pursuits, philately. *Address:* Melsbury, 13 Sandhurst Road, Wokingham, Berks RG11 3JG. *T:* Wokingham 738426. *Club:* Army and Navy.

SCOTT, Robin; see Scutt, R. H.

SCOTT, Ronald, OBE 1981; musician; *b* 28 Jan. 1927. *Educ:* Jews' Infant Sch., Aldgate, E1; Benthal Road Elementary Sch., N16; Central Foundation Sch., Cowper St, E1. Musician (Tenor Saxophone), 1943–. Opened Ronnie Scott's Club, 1959 (Director, with Pete King). *Publication:* (with Michael Hennessey) Some of My Best Friends are Blues, 1979. *Recreation:* motor sport. *Address:* 47 Frith Street, W1. *T:* 01-439 0747. *Club:* just his own.

SCOTT, Sheila (Christine), OBE 1968; aviator; lecturer; actress; writer; *b* 27 April 1927; *d* of Harold R. Hopkins, Worcester, and Edith Hopkins (*née* Kenward); *m* 1945, Rupert Leaman Bellamy (marr. diss. 1950). *Educ:* Alice Ottley School, Worcs. VAD, RN, 1945; acting, 1946–59, with Repertory Companies at Watford, Aldershot and Windsor; small parts in films, TV and West End Stage. Started flying, 1959; obtained British and USA commercial licences; Racing Pilot: first race won 1960 national air races (De Havilland Trophy, etc); Holder of 100 World Class Records (Aviation), incl. Round the World in class CIc and in open feminine classes; London to Capetown and Capetown to London; N Atlantic (western and eastern crossings direct);

S Atlantic, Brazil to W Africa; has flown solo three times round world, including first world flight via North Pole in a light aircraft, 1971; winner of many air races; won female Light Aircraft prize, Transatlantic Air Race London-New York May 1969; won Ford Woman's Prize, London-Sydney Air Race, Dec. 1969. Founder and 1st Gov., Brit. Section, Ninety Nines Inc., 1964. Founder British Balloon and Airships Club. Life Mem. and Hon. Diploma, Academia Romana vel Sodalitis Quirinale. Silver Award of Merit, Brit. Guild of Air Pilots and Navigators, 1966, Liveryman, 1968; Isabella D'Este Award (Italy), 1966; Silver Medal, Royal Aero Club, 1967, Gold Medal, 1972; Harmon Trophy, USA, 1967; Britannia Trophy, 1968. *Publications:* I Must Fly, 1968; On Top of the World, 1973; Barefoot in the Sky, 1974. *Recreation:* sailing. *Address:* c/o Ravenscroft, Highcliffe Lane, Turnditch, Derbyshire DE5 2EA. *T:* Ripley 89362. *Club:* Naval and Military.

SCOTT, Sir Terence Charles Stuart M.; *see* Morrison-Scott.

SCOTT, Prof. Thomas Frederick McNair, MA Cantab, MD Cantab, MRCS; FRCP; Professor of Paediatrics since 1974, and Co-Director of Ambulatory Paediatrics since 1975, Hahnemann Medical College and Hospital (Co-ordinator of Ambulatory Care Teaching, 1974-75); Senior Physician, The Children's Hospital of Philadelphia, 1940-69, now Physician Emeritus; *b* 18 June 1901; *e s* of Robert Frederick McNair Scott, MB, ChB (Edin.), and Alice Nystrom; *m* 1936, Mary Dwight Baker, PhD (Radcliffe), *o d* of late Clarence Dwight Baker, Wisconsin, USA; one *s* one *d. Educ:* Cheltenham College; Caius College, Cambridge (Scholar). Natural Science Tripos Pt I Class I, Part II (Physiology) Class II; Junior University Entrance Scholarship to St George's Hospital, 1924; Brackenbury Prize in Medicine, 1926; Qualified conjoint board, 1927; MRCP 1928; FRCP 1953; MD (Cantab) 1938; Casualty Officer, House Surgeon, House Physn, Resident Obst. Asst, Medical Registrar, at St George's Hospital, 1927-29; House Physician Queens Hospital for Children, 1930; Research Fellow of Medicine, Harvard University, Mass, USA, 1930-31; Instructor in Pædiatrics Johns Hopkins University, Baltimore, Md, USA, 1931-34; Assistant Resident Physician at Hospital of Rockefeller Institute for Medical Research, New York, USA, working on Virus diseases, 1934-36; Assistant Physician i/c of Children's Out-patients, Lecturer in Children's Diseases, at St George's Hospital, SW1, Assistant Physician at Queens Hospital for Children, E2, 1936-38; Prof. of Pediatrics, Temple Univ. Med. Sch., Philadelphia, 1938-40; Research Prof. of Pediatrics, Univ. of Pennsylvania, 1940-66, Prof. of Paediatrics, 1966-69, now Emeritus. Corp. medal, Hahnemann Med. Coll., 1978. Elected Faculty Mem., Medical Students' Honor Soc. (AOA), 1981. *Publications:* Papers on Cytology and Blood diseases, Lead poisoning in children, Virus diseases of the central nervous system, Herpetic stomatitis in children, Virus diseases of the skin. *Address:* 426 South 26th Street, Philadelphia, Pa 19146, USA; Department of Paediatrics, Hahnemann Medical College and Hospital, 230 North Broad Street, Philadelphia, Pa 19102, USA.

SCOTT, Sir Walter, 4th Bt, *cr* 1907; DL; *b* 29 July 1918; *s* of Sir Walter Scott, 3rd Bt, and Nancie Margot, *d* of S. H. March; *S* father, 1967; *m* 1945, Diana Mary, *d* of J. R. Owen; one *s* one *d. Educ:* Eton; Jesus College, Cambridge. Served 1st Royal Dragoons, 1939-46; Temp. Major, 1945. JP East Sussex, 1963; DL East Sussex, 1975. *Recreations:* field sports. *Heir:* *s* Walter John Scott, *b* 24 Feb. 1948. *Address:* Newhouse Farm, Chalvington, Hailsham, Sussex.

See also Duke of Hamilton and Brandon.

SCOTT, William Clifford Munro, MD; Consulting Psychiatrist, Montreal Children's Hospital, and Montreal General Hospital; *b* 11 March 1903; *o s* of late Rev. Robert Smyth Scott and late Katherine Munro Hopper; *m* 1934, Emmy Luise (marr. diss.), *er d* of late Hugo Böcking; two *s* ; *m* 1970, Evelyn Freeman Fitch. *Educ:* Parkdale Collegiate, Toronto; University of Toronto. BSc (Med.), MD (Tor.), DPM (London), LMSSA. James H. Richardson Fellow, Department of Anat., 1922-24; Lectr in Anat. and Physiol., Margaret Eaton Sch. of Phys. Educ., Toronto, 1923-25; Post-Grad. Educ. in Psychiatry: Johns Hopkins Med. Sch., 1928-29; Boston Psychopathic Hosp., Harvard Univ. Med. Sch., 1929-30; Commonwealth Fund Fellow, Dept of Psychiatry, Harvard Univ., 1930-33; studied at Nat. Hosp., Queen Sq., London, 1931-32, and at Inst of Psycho-Analysis, London, 1931-33. Staff positions Maudsley Hosp., 1933-35, Cassel Hosp., 1935-38; private practice, 1938-. EMS Psychiatrist, Min. of Health, London, Sheffield and S Wales, 1939-46; Psychiatric Cons. to St Dunstan's, 1945. Mem. Cttee of Management, Inst. of Psychiatry (Univ. of London), 1951-53; Med. Dir London Clinic of Psycho-Analysis, 1947-53; Senior Psychotherapist, Bethlem Royal Hosp. and Maudsley Hosp., 1948-54; Teacher Inst. of Psychiatry (Univ. of London), 1948-54; Associate Professor in charge of Training in Psycho-Analysis, Department of Psychiatry, McGill University, Montreal, 1954-59; Post-Grad. Teacher (Psychiatry and Psycho-Analysis), 1945-. Chm. Psychotherapy and Social Psychiatry Section, Roy. Medico-Psychological Assoc., 1952-54; Pres. Brit. Psycho-Analytical Soc., 1953-54; Mem. Bd Dirs, Inst. of Psycho-Analysis, 1947-54 (Chm. 1954); Director of Canadian Inst. of Psycho-Analysis, 1965-67. FRCPsych; FBPsS; ex-Chm. Med. Sect. and Mem. Council, Brit. Psychological Soc.; ex-Mem. Cttee Sect. Psychiatry; Roy. Soc. Med.; Amer. Psychiatric Assoc.; Vice-Pres., Psychiatric Sect., BMA, 1952 and 1955; ex-Asst Ed. Internat. Jl Psycho-Analysis; ex-Asst Ed., Brit. Jl Med. Psychology. Mem., Montreal AAA. *Publications:* chiefly in Brit. Jl of Med. Psychol. and Internat. Jl of Psycho-Analysis. *Recreations:* people and books. *Address:* 1260 Dr Penfield, Montreal, Quebec, Canada H3G 1B6.

SCOTT, Rear-Adm. Sir (William) David (Stewart), KBE 1977; CB 1974; Chief Polaris Executive, 1976-80; *b* 5 April 1921; *y s* of Brig. H. St G. Scott, CB, DSO and Ida Christabel Trower Scott (*née* Hogg); *m* 1952, Pamela Dorothy Whitlock; one *s* two *d. Educ:* Tonbridge. Naval Cadet, 1938; comd HM Submarines: Umbra, 1944; Satyr, 1945; Andrew, 1953; Thermopylae, 1955; comd HM Ships: Gateshead, 1951; Surprise, 1960; Adamant, 1963; Fife, 1969; Chief of British Navy Staff, Washington, UK Rep. to SACLANT, and Naval Attaché to USA, 1971-73; Deputy Controller, Polaris, 1973-76; Comdr 1956; Captain 1962; Rear-Adm. 1971. FInstD 1979. *Address:* c/o Lloyds Bank Ltd, 6 Pall Mall, SW1.

SCOTT, (William) Donald, CBE 1968; MA (Oxon); BSc (Yale); *b* 22 May 1903; *s* of late Reverend William Scott and Sara Jane (*née* Platt); *m* 1928, Muriel Barbara, *d* of late Louis F. Rothschild, NYC; two *s* one *d. Educ:* Taunton Sch., Taunton; Univ. College, Oxford (open scholar); Yale University, USA (Henry P. Davison Scholar). Hercules Powder Co., USA and Rotterdam, 1926-28; British Paint & Lacquer Co., Cowley, Oxford, 1928-35; ICI Ltd: Nobel Div., 1935-41; Dyestuffs Div., 1941-43; Southern Sales Region, Dep. Regional Manager, 1943-45; Regional Manager, 1945-51; Billingham Div., Jt Man. Dir, 1951-55; Main Board Director, 1954-65. Director, 1952-60, and Chairman, 1956-60, Scottish Agricultural Industries Ltd; Chm., Home Grown Cereals Authority, 1965-68; Director: Canadian Industries Ltd, 1957-62; Glaxo Group Ltd, 1965-68; Laporte Industries Ltd, 1965-68. Mem., Western Hemisphere Exports Council, 1961-64. FRSA 1968. *Recreations:* cricket, golf. *Address:* 42 Cumberland Terrace, Regent's Park, NW1 4HP.

SCOTT, Rev. W(illiam) G.; *see* Gardiner-Scott.

SCOTT, William (George), CBE 1966; ARA 1977; painter; *b* 15 Feb. 1913; *e s* of William John and Agnes Scott; *m* 1937, Hilda Mary Lucas; two *s. Educ:* Enniskillen; Belfast Sch. of Art; Roy. Acad. Schools, London. Hon. Dr RCA, 1975; Hon. DLit: Belfast, 1976; Dublin, 1977. *Exhibitions:* Leger Gall., 1942, 1944, 1946; Leicester Gall., 1948, 1951; Hanover Gall., 1953, 1956, 1961, 1963, 1965, 1967; Martha Jackson Gall., NY, 1954, 1958, 1973; Venice Biennale, 1958; VIth Sao Paulo Biennial, 1953 and 1961, Brazil; Tate Gall., 1972; Gimpel Fils Gall., 1974, 1980; Martha Jackson Gall., NY, 1974; Moos Gall., Toronto, 1975; Kasahara Gall., Japan, 1976; Arts Council, Ulster (retrospective), 1979; War Paintings 1942-46, Imperial War Mus., 1981; in British Council Exhibns in Europe; *works exhibited in:* Tate Gall.; Victoria and Albert Museum; Paris; New York; Toledo, USA; S Africa; Canada; Australia; S America. *Address:* 13 Edith Terrace, Chelsea, SW10. *T:* 01-352 8044.

SCOTT, William Wootton; Under Secretary, Scottish Development Department, Edinburgh, since 1978; *b* 20 May 1930; *s* of Dr Archibald C. Scott and Barbara R. Scott; *m* 1958, Margaret Chandler, SRN; three *s* one *d. Educ:* Kilmarnock Academy; Dollar Academy; Glasgow Univ. (MA, 1st Cl. Hons History). National Service in Royal Artillery, 1952-54. Assistant Principal, 1954, Principal, 1958, Min. of Transport and Civil Aviation; Principal Private Sec. to Minister of Transport, 1965-66; Asst Sec., 1966; Regional Controller (Housing and Planning), Northern Regional Office of DoE, 1971-74; joined Scottish Development Dept, 1974. *Publications:* occasional historical notes. *Recreations:* historical research, music, gardening, reading. *Address:* 26 Braid Hills Road, Edinburgh EH10 6HY. *T:* 031-447 7232. *Club:* Royal Commonwealth Society.

SCOTT-BARRETT, Lt-Gen. Sir David (William), KBE 1976 (MBE 1956); MC 1945; GOC Scotland and Governor of Edinburgh Castle, 1976-79; Executive Director, Arbuthnot Securities, since 1980; Chairman, Army Cadet Force Association, 1982; *b* 16 Dec. 1922; 2nd *s* of late Brig. Rev. H. Scott-Barrett, CB, CBE; *m* 1948, Marie Elise, *d* of late Norman Morris; three *s. Educ:* Westminster School. Commnd Scots Guards, 1942; served NW Europe, 3rd Armd Bn Scots Guards; GSO3 Gds Div., 1948; Co. Comdr 2nd Bn Malaya, 1951; GSO2, 1st Div., 1955; DS Camberley, 1961; Comdt Gds Depot, 1963; GSO1, 4th Div. BAOR, 1965; comd 6 Inf. Bde BAOR, 1967; idc 1970; GOC Eastern District, 1971-73; GOC Berlin, 1973-75. Col Comdt, Scottish Div., 1976-79; Hon. Col, 205 (Scottish) Gen. Hosp. RAMC, TAVR, 1981-. *Address:* The White House, Littlewick Common, Knaphill, Woking, Surrey. *T:* Brookwood 4198. *Club:* Cavalry and Guards.

SCOTT BLAIR, George William, MA (Oxon), DSc (London); FRSC; FInstP; *b* 23 July 1902; *s* of late James and Jessie Scott Blair; *m* 1927, Margaret Florence Riddelsdell; no *c. Educ:* Charterhouse; Trinity College, Oxford. Ten years on Research Staff at Rothamsted Experimental Station; sometime Fellow on Rockefeller Foundation at University of Cornell; Head of Chemistry, later Physics Department National Institute for Research in Dairying, University of Reading, 1937-67; retired. Herbert Freundlich Medal, Deutsche Rheol. Ges., 1954; Poiseuille Gold Medal, Internat. Soc. of Biorheology, 1969; Gold Medal, Brit. Soc. of Rheology, 1970. Membre d'honneur, Groupe français de Rhéologie, 1970. *Publications:* An Introduction to Industrial Rheology, 1938; A Survey of General and Applied Rheology, 1943, 2nd edn 1949; Measurements of Mind and Matter, 1950; (ed) Foodstuffs: their Plasticity, Fluidity, and Consistency, 1953; (with Prof. M. Reiner) Agricultural Rheology, 1957; Elementary Rheology, 1969; An Introduction to Biorheology, 1974; many papers in various scientific journals, 1925-81. *Recreations:* music, modern languages, philosophy of science. *Address:* Grist Cottage, Iffley, Oxford. *T:* Oxford 777462.

SCOTT-BOWDEN, Maj.-Gen. Logan, CBE 1972 (OBE 1964); DSO 1944; MC 1944 and Bar 1946; *b* 21 Feb. 1920; *s* of late Lt-Col Jonathan Scott-Bowden, OBE, TD, and Mary Scott-Bowden (*née* Logan); *m* 1950, Helen Jocelyn, *d* of late Major Sir Francis Caradoc Rose Price, 5th Bt, and late Marjorie Lady Price; three *s* three *d. Educ:* Malvern Coll.; RMA Woolwich. Commissioned Royal Engineers, 1939; served in War of 1939-45: Norway, 1940; Adjt, 53rd (Welsh) Div. RE, 1941; Liaison Duties in Canada and USA, 1942; Normandy Beach Reconnaissance Team (Major), 1943; OC 17 Fd Co RE, NW Europe, 1944; psc 1945; Singapore, Burma (Bde Maj. 98 Indian Inf. Bde), Palestine, Libya, 1946-51; Korea, 1953; jssc 1956; Arabia, 1958-60 (Lt-Col 1959); CRE 1st Div., BAOR, 1960; Head, UK Land Forces Planning Staff, 1963; Asst Dir, Def. Plans MoD (Col), 1964; Comd Trg Bde RE (Brig.), 1966; Nat. Defence Coll. (India), 1969; Comd Ulster Defence Regiment, 1970-71; Head of British Defence Liaison Staff, India, 1971-74, retd 1974. Col Comdt RE, 1975-80. *Recreations:* riding, ski-ing, sailing, shooting and travel. *Address:* c/o Lloyds Bank Ltd, 6 Pall Mall, SW1A 2AH.

SCOTT-BROWN, Walter Graham, CVO 1945; BA (Hon. Nat. Sci. Tripos), MD, BCh Cambridge; FRCS, FRCSE; Consulting Surgeon, Throat, Nose and Ear Department, Royal Free Hospital, and late Surgeon and Lecturer Royal National Throat, Nose and Ear Hospital; late Consulting Aurist and Laryngologist at East Grinstead Cottage Hospital and at the Maxillo-facial unit; and Lecturer to University of London; Fellow Royal Society Medicine and Member Otological and Laryngological Section; Fellow Medical Society of London; formerly engaged in consulting practice in London as oto-rhino-laryngologist; *e s* of late George A. Brown; *m* 1926, Margaret Affleck, *d* of G. K. Bannerman, High Wycombe; one *s* three *d. Educ:* Corpus Christi College, Cambridge; St Bartholomew's Hospital, London. Served European War, 1916-18 (despatches, wounded); France and Italy T Battery RHA and Captain and Adjutant 14th Brigade RHA 1918; Exhibitioner Corpus Christi College, Cambridge, 1919; Shuter Scholar St Bartholomew's Hospital, 1922; House Surgeon and Clinical Assistant in Ear, Nose and Throat Dept St Barts; Copeman Medallist for Scientific Research, Cambridge, 1932; Dorothy Temple Cross Research Fellowship (travelling), 1932, Berlin, Vienna, Stockholm, Copenhagen, etc. *Publications:* Allergic affections of the Nose, 1945; (ed and contrib.) Diseases of the Ear, Nose and Throat, 2nd edn 1965; Methods of Examination in Ear, Nose and Throat, 1953; Broncho-oesophageal fistula, Cavernous sinus thrombosis: a fatal complication of minor facial sepsis, and other scientific and clinical publications. *Recreations:* fishing, painting. *Address:* Littledown, Monkwood, near Alresford, Hants SO24 0HB. *T:* Ropley 2314.

See also Earl of Orkney.

SCOTT-ELLIOT, Aydua Helen, CVO 1970 (MVO 1958); FSA; retired 1970; *b* 1909; *d* of late Lewis Alexander Scott-Elliot and of Princess Eydua Odescalchi. *Educ:* St Paul's Girls' School and abroad. Temp. Asst Civilian Officer, Admty, 1941-46; Keeper of Prints and Drawings, Royal Library, Windsor Castle, 1944-69. *Publications:* articles in Burlington Magazine, Apollo, etc. *Recreation:* gardening. *Address:* Shaldon, Station Road, Mayfield, East Sussex. *T:* Mayfield 872079. *Club:* University Women's.

SCOTT ELLIOT, Major-General James, CB 1954; CBE 1945 (OBE 1940); DSO 1943, Bar 1944; HM Lieutenant of the County of Dumfries, 1962-67; *b* 6 Nov. 1902; *s* of late Lt-Col W. Scott Elliot, DSO and Marie Theresa Scott Elliot (*née* Lyon); *m* 1st, 1932, Cecil Margaret Du Buisson; one *s* two *d*; 2nd, 1971, Mrs Fay Courtauld. *Educ:* Wellington College; Sandhurst. 2nd Lieut KOSB, 1923; Capt. Argyll and Sutherland Highlanders, 1936; psc 1937-38; Major, 1940; served in Egypt, China, India, Malta, Palestine. War of 1939-45: France, N Africa, Sicily, Italy; Temp. Lt-Col 1941; Temp. Brig. 1944; despatches, 1945; Germany, 1946-47; War Office, 1948-49; Maj.-Gen., 1954; GOC 51st (Highland) Division and Highland Dist, 1952-56; retd, 1956. Colonel King's Own Scottish Borderers, 1954-61. President: Dumfries and Galloway Natural History and Antiquarian Soc., 1962-65; Soc. of Antiquaries of Scotland, 1965-67; Brit. Soc. of Dowsers, 1966-75. *Publication:* Dowsing One Man's Way, 1977. *Address:* 14 King Street, Emsworth, Hants PO10 7AZ. *T:* Emsworth 2401. *Club:* Army and Navy.

SCOTT-ELLIS, family name of **Baron Howard de Walden.**

SCOTT FOX, Sir (Robert) David (John), KCMG 1963 (CMG 1956); HM Diplomatic Service, retired; *b* 20 June 1910; *yr s* of late Judge John Scott Fox, KC, and late Agnes Maria Theresa, *d* of Hermann Hammer; *m* 1951, Brigitte, *d* of Pierre Taton; three *d. Educ:* Eton; Christ Church, Oxford; Fellow Queen's College. Entered HM Diplomatic Service, 1934. Served Berlin, 1937; Prague, 1937-39; Rio de Janeiro, 1940-44; Foreign Office, 1944-49; Counsellor at Jedda, 1949-51; Chargé d'Affaires there in 1949 and 1950; transferred to Ankara, Counsellor, 1951; Chargé d'Affaires there, 1951, 1952, 1953 and 1954; Minister (Economic and Social Affairs) to UK Delegation to UN, 1955-58; Minister to Roumania, 1959-61; Ambassador to Chile, 1961-66; Ambassador to Finland, 1966-69. Special Rep. of the Sec. of State for Foreign and Commonwealth Affairs, 1970-75. Grand Cross, Chilean Order of Merit, 1965; Order of the Finnish Lion, 1969. *Publication:* Mediterranean Heritage, 1978. *Address:* 47 Eaton Terrace, SW1. *T:* 01-730 5505. *Club:* Travellers'.

SCOTT-HOPKINS, Major Sir James (Sidney Rawdon), Kt 1981; Member (C) European Parliament, since 1973, elected for Hereford and Worcester, 1979; *b* 29 Nov. 1921; *s* of late Col R. Scott-Hopkins, DSO, MC and late

Mrs Scott-Hopkins; *m* 1946, Geraldine Elizabeth Mary Hargreaves, CBE; three *s* one *d. Educ:* Eton; Oxford. Army, 1939-50; farming, 1950-59. MP (C) North Cornwall, 1959-66, Derbyshire West, Nov. 1967-1979; Joint Parliamentary Secretary, Ministry of Agriculture, Fisheries and Food, 1962-64. European Parliament: Dep. Leader Cons. Gp and Spokesman on Agric., 1973-79; Vice-Pres., 1976-79; Chm., European Democratic Gp, 1979-82. *Recreations:* riding, shooting. *Address:* 602 Nelson House, Dolphin Square, SW1. *Club:* Carlton.

See also T. J. Smith.

SCOTT-JAMES, Anne Eleanor, (Lady Lancaster); journalist; *b* 5 April 1913; *d* of R. A. Scott-James and Violet Brooks; *m* 1st, 1944, Macdonald Hastings; one *s* one *d*; 2nd, 1967, Sir Osbert Lancaster, *qv. Educ:* St Paul's Girls' Sch.; Somerville Coll., Oxford (Class. Schol.). Editorial staff of Vogue, 1934-41; Woman's Editor, Picture Post, 1941-45; Editor, Harper's Bazaar, 1945-51; Woman's Editor, Sunday Express, 1953-57; Woman's Adviser to Beaverbrook Newspapers, 1959-60; Columnist, Daily Mail, 1960-68; freelance journalist, broadcasting, TV, 1968-. Member: Council, RCA, 1948-51, 1954-56; Council, RHS, 1978-82. *Publications:* In the Mink, 1952; Down to Earth, 1971; Sissinghurst: The Making of a Garden, 1975; (with Osbert Lancaster) The Pleasure Garden, 1977; The Cottage Garden, 1981. *Recreations:* reading, gardening, travelling looking at churches and flowers. *Address:* Rose Cottage, Aldworth, Reading, Berks.

SCOTT-MALDEN, (Charles) Peter, CB 1966; Member, Transport Tribunal, since 1978; *b* 29 June 1918; *e s* of late Gilbert Scott Scott-Malden and Phyllis Dorothy Scott-Malden (*née* Wilkinson); *m* 1941, Jean Honor Chamberlain Silver, *yr d* of late Lt-Col J. P. Silver, CBE, DSO, RAMC; two *s* two *d. Educ:* Winchester Coll. (Schol.); King's College, Cambridge (major Scholar). Entered Ministry of Transport, 1939. War of 1939-45; RAMC 1940-41; Glider Pilot Regiment, 1942-45. Min. of Transport (later DoE): Asst Sec., 1949; Under-Sec., 1959; Dep. Sec., 1968, retired, 1976. Mem., Management Cttee, Hanover Housing Assoc. *Recreations:* music, golf. *Address:* 23 Burdon Lane, Cheam, Surrey. *T:* 01-642 7086.

SCOTT-MALDEN, Air Vice-Marshal (Francis) David (Stephen), DSO 1942; DFC 1941; RAF (Retd); *b* 26 Dec. 1919; *s* of late Gilbert Scott Scott-Malden and Phyllis Dorothy Wilkinson; *m* 1955, Anne Elizabeth Watson; two *s* two *d. Educ:* Winchester Coll. (Scholar; Goddard Scholar, 1938); King's Coll., Cambridge (Scholar, Sir William Browne Medal for Greek Verse, 1939). Joined Cambridge University Air Squadron, Nov. 1938; called up into RAFVR as Pilot Officer, Oct 1939; flying on operations, 1940-42, as Pilot Officer, Flight Lt, Squadron Leader, and Wing Comdr (DFC and Bar, DSO, Norwegian War Cross; Commander, Order of Orange Nassau, 1945). Visited International Youth Assembly at Washington, DC, as rep. of English Universities, and toured USA as member of United Nations delegation, Sept.-Nov. 1942. RAF Selection Board (Dep. Pres.), 1946; on staff of RAF College, 1946-48; Central Fighter Establishment, 1948; RAF Staff Coll., Bracknell, 1951; psa; RAF Flying Coll., 1954-55; pfc; Jt Planning Staff, Min. of Defence, 1955-57; Group Capt. 1958; Imperial Defence College, 1957-59; idc. Dep. Dir Plans, Air Ministry, 1959-61; Air Cdre 1962; Air Vice-Marshal, 1965. Department of Transport, 1966-78. *Recreations:* shooting, fishing, sailing. *Address:* 41 Friars' Quay, Colegate, Norwich. *T:* Norwich 22496.

SCOTT-MALDEN, Peter; see Scott-Malden, C. P.

SCOTT-MILLER, Commander Ronald, VRD 1942; RNVR (Retired); *b* 1 Nov. 1904; *s* of late Colonel Walter Scott-Miller, DL; *m* 1932, Stella Louise Farquhar, *d* of late Farquhar Deuchar, Shortridge Hall, Northumberland. *Educ:* Aldro School, Eastbourne; Uppingham. Joined London Division, RNVR, as Midshipman, 1924; War of 1939-45 (despatches): HMS Dunedin, Northern Patrol, 1939; HMS London, Atlantic, Russian Convoys, 1940-43; Combined Operations, Mediterranean, NW Europe, 1943-45. Commander, 1943; retired, 1946. MP (C) King's Lynn Division of Norfolk, 1951-59; Parliamentary Private Secretary: to Financial Secretary to Treasury, Dec. 1953-July 1954; to Minister of Transport, 1954-56; to Minister of Pensions and National Insurance, 1956-59. Trustee of Uppingham School, 1954-59. Freeman of the City of London, and Liveryman of Worshipful Company of Butchers, 1926. US Legion of Merit (Legionaire), 1943. *Recreations:* shooting, sailing. *Address:* c/o Barclays Bank International, Oceanic House, 1 Cockspur Street, SW1Y 5BG. *Club:* Naval.

SCOTT-MONCRIEFF, William; Under-Secretary for Finance (Health), Department of Health and Social Security, 1977-82; *b* 22 Aug. 1922; *s* of Major R. Scott-Moncrieff and Mrs R. Scott-Moncrieff; *m* 1950, Dora Rosemary Knollys; two *d. Educ:* Trinity Coll., Glenalmond; Emmanuel Coll., Cambridge (BA Mech. Sciences). Served RE, 1941-65 (Lt-Col); DHSS (formerly Min. of Social Security), 1965-82. *Recreations:* golf, fishing. *Address:* Combe Cottage, Chiddingfold, Surrey. *T:* Wormley 2937.

SCOTT-SMITH, Catharine Mary, MA Cantab; Principal of Beechlawn Tutorial College, Oxford, 1966-71, retired; *b* 4 April 1912; *d* of Edward Montagu Scott-Smith and Catharine Lorance (*née* Garland). *Educ:* Wycombe Abbey School, Bucks; Girton College, Cambridge. Classics Mistress: St Katharine's School, Wantage, 1933-37; Godolphin School, Salisbury 1937-41; Classics Mistress and house-mistress, Headington School, Oxford, 1941-47, Second Mistress, 1946-47; Classics Mistress and house-mistress, Wycombe

Abbey School, Bucks, 1947-55. Second Mistress, 1951-54; Headmistress of Westonbirt School, Tetbury, Gloucestershire, 1955-64. Member Council: Berkhamsted School for Girls; Berkhamsted School; Mem. Exec. Cttee, GBGSA, 1975-78. Pres., Wycombe Abbey School Seniors, 1974-79. *Address:* Graystones, Fairlight, Hastings, East Sussex. *T:* Pett 3071. *Club:* University Women's.

SCOTT WHYTE, Stuart; *see* Whyte, J. S. S.

SCOTT WRIGHT, Dr Margaret; Dean of Faculty of Nursing, University of Calgary, since 1979; *b* 10 Sept. 1923; *d* of Ebenezer Wright and Margaret Greig Masson. *Educ:* Wallington County Grammar Sch.; Univ. of Edinburgh; St George's and Queen Charlotte's Hosps, London. MA Hons Hist., PhD and Dipl. Med. Services Admin, Edinburgh; SRN and SCM. Research Asst, Unilever Ltd, 1947-50; Staff Nurse and Sister, St George's Hosp., London, 1953-57; Boots Research Fellow in Nursing, Dept of Social Medicine, Univ. of Edinburgh, 1957-61; Rockefeller Fellow, USA, 1961-62; Deputy Matron, St George's Hosp., 1962-64; Matron, Middlesex Hosp., 1965-68; Dir, Dept of Nursing Studies, Univ. of Edinburgh, 1968-71; Prof. of Nursing Studies, Univ. of Edinburgh, 1972-76; Dir and Prof. of Sch. of Nursing, Dalhousie Univ., Nova Scotia, 1976-79. Second Vice-Pres., Internat. Council of Nurses, 1973-77. Silver Jubilee Medal, 1977. *Publications:* Experimental Nurse Training at Glasgow Royal Infirmary, 1963; Student Nurses in Scotland, 1968. *Recreations:* walking, music, reading, travel. *Address:* Faculty of Nursing, University of Calgary, Calgary, Alberta, Canada. *Clubs:* University Women's; Calgary University.

SCOULLER, (John) Alan; Assistant General Manager, Group Industrial Relations, Midland Bank, since 1975; *b* 23 Sept. 1929; *e s* of late Charles James Scouller and Mary Helena Scouller; *m* 1954, Angela Geneste Ambrose; two *s* five *d.* *Educ:* John Fisher Sch., Purley. Army service, Queen's Own Royal W Kent Regt, 1948-58 (Captain). Joined Unilever as management trainee, 1958; Personnel Man., Wall's Ice Cream, 1959-62; Domestos, 1963-66; Holpak, 1966-68; Commercial Plastics and Holpak, 1968-69; left Unilever to join Commn on Industrial Relations, 1969; Dir of Industrial Relations until 1973, full-time Comr, 1973-74. Mem., Employment Appeal Tribunal, 1976-. *Address:* Shortlands, 32 Sollershott West, Letchworth, Herts. *T:* Letchworth 2781.

SCOURFIELD, Edward Grismond Beaumont D.; *see* Davies-Scourfield.

SCOWEN, Sir Eric (Frank), Kt 1973; MD, DSc, LLD; FRCP, FRCS, FRCPE; FRCPath; Director, Medical Professorial Unit, 1955-75; Physician to St Bartholomew's Hospital, 1946-75; Professor of Medicine, University of London, 1961-75 (Reader in Medicine, 1938-61); *b* 22 April 1910; *s* of late Frank Edward Scowen and Eleanor Betsy (*née* Barnes) (*d* 1969). *Educ:* City of London School; St Bartholomew's Hospital Medical College. St Bartholomew's Hospital: House Physician, 1931, Second Assistant, 1933, to Medical Professorial Unit; Baly Research Fell. in Clin. Med., 1933; First Asst to Med. Professorial Unit, 1935; Asst Dir of Med. Prof. Unit, and Asst Phys, 1937; Rockefeller Research Fell. to Columbia Univ., New York, 1937. Chairman: Council, Imperial Cancer Research Fund, 1967-82 (Vice-Pres., 1982); Cttee on Safety of Drugs, 1969- (Mem., 1963); British Pharmacopœia Commission, 1963-69; Cttee on Safety of Medicines, 1970-80; Cttee on the Review of Medicines, 1975-78; Poisons Bd (Home Office), 1976-. Chm. Council, Sch. of Pharmacy, Univ. of London, 1979-. *Publications:* various in medical and scientific journals. *Address:* 44 Lincoln's Inn Fields, WC2A 3PX. *T:* 242 0200. *Club:* Athenæum.

SCRAGG, Air Vice-Marshal Sir Colin, KBE 1963 (CBE 1953; MBE 1940); CB 1960; AFC 1942, Bar to AFC 1949; retired; *b* 8 Sept. 1908; *s* of late Lt A. Scragg, KRRC; *m* 1932, Phyllis Kathleen Rayner, Southampton; one *s* two *d.* *Educ:* King Edward VI School, Southampton. No 1 (Fighter) Squadron, 1931-34; served in a succession of flying training schools, including 34 FTS Canada, until 1943; War of 1939-45, Comd No 166 (Bomber) Squadron, 1944-45 (pow, Germany). Transport Command Development Unit, 1946-49; Dep. Director, Operational Requirements, Air Min., 1950-53, Director, 1955-58; idc 1954; AOC No 23 Training Group, 1958-60; Deputy Controller Aircraft (RAF), Ministry of Aviation, 1960-64. Order of Orange Nassau (Netherlands), 1945. *Address:* Wedgwood, Pine Walk, Chilworth, Southampton. *T:* Southampton 769110.

SCREECH, Prof. Michael Andrew, FBA 1981; Fielden Professor of French Language and Literature in the University of London, since 1971; *b* 2 May 1926; 3rd *s* of Richard John Screech, MM and Nellie Screech (*née* Maunder); *m* 1956, Ursula Anne Grace (*née* Reeve); three *s.* *Educ:* Sutton High Sch., Plymouth; University Coll. London (BA 1950; Fellow, 1982); University of Montpellier, France. DLitt (Birmingham), 1958. Other Rank, Intelligence Corps (Far East), 1944-48. Asst, UCL, 1950-51; Birmingham Univ.: Lectr, 1951-58; Sen. Lectr., 1959-61; Reader, UCL 1961-66; Vis. Prof., Univ. of Western Ontario, 1964-65; Personal Chair of French, UCL, 1966; Vis. Prof., Univ. of New York, Albany, 1968-69; Johnson Prof., Inst. for Research in the Humanities, Wisconsin, USA, 1978-79; Vis. Fellow, All Souls, Oxford, 1981. Member: Cttee, Warburg Inst., 1970; Comité d'Humanisme et Renaissance, 1971. *Publications:* The Rabelaisian Marriage, 1958; L'Evangélisme de Rabelais, 1959; Tiers Livre de Pantagruel, 1964, repr. 1975; Les epistres et évangiles de Lefèvre d'Etaples, 1964; (with John Jollife) Les Regrets et autres oeuvres poëtiques (Du Bellay), 1966, repr. 1975; Marot

évangélique, 1967; (contrib.) The Art of Criticism, ed P. H. Nurse, 1969; Gargantua, 1970; (ed reprints) Le Nouveau Testament de Lefèvre d'Etaples, 1970; F. de Billon: Le Fort inexpugnable de l'Honneur du Sexe Femenin, 1970; Opuscules d'Amour par Héroet et autres divins poëtes, 1970; Amyot: Les œuvres morales et meslées de Plutarque, 1971; (contrib., with Ruth Calder) Humanism in France, ed A. Levi, 1971; (contrib.) Colloquia Erasmiana Turonensia, ed J. C. Margolin, 1972; La Pantagruéline Prognostication, 1975; (contrib.) Classical Influences in Europe AD 1500-1700, ed R. A. Bolgar, 1976; (contrib.) Réforme et Humanisme, ed J. Boisset, 1978; Rabelais, 1980; Ecstasy and the Praise of Folly, 1980; articles on Renaissance and Reformation in: Bibliothèque d'Humanisme et Renaissance, Etudes rabelaisiennes, Jl of Warburg Inst., Bulletins des Colloques de Loches, L'Esprit Créateur, etc. *Recreation:* walking. *Address:* 5 Swanston-field, Whitchurch-on-Thames RG8 7HP. *T:* Pangbourne 2513.

SCRIMGEOUR, James, CMG 1959; OBE 1944; *b* 8 June 1903; *s* of late Alexander Carron Scrimgeour and Helen May Scrimgeour (*née* Bird); *m* 1928, Winifred, *d* of late Stephen Ward Giles; one *s.* *Educ:* Loretto School; Clare College, Cambridge. Member of Stock Exchange, 1929-69. Auxiliary Air Force, 1938-45; Air staff, Air Ministry, 1942-45. Senior Partner, J. & A. Scrimgeour, 1949-69; Chm., Hume Holdings Ltd, 1953-75; Dir, MEPC Ltd, 1946-69 (Vice Chm., 1965-69). Orig. Mem., Council of White Ensign Assoc., 1958-75. *Address:* c/o Royal Bank of Scotland, Burlington Gardens, W1. *Clubs:* Turf; Hawks (Cambridge).

SCRIMSHAW, Frank Herbert; *b* 25 Dec. 1917; *s* of late John Leonard Scrimshaw and Jessie Scrimshaw (*née* Sewell), Lincoln; *m* 1950, Joan Olive, *d* of Leslie Stephen Paskall, Felixstowe; one *s.* *Educ:* The City Sch., Lincoln; University Coll., Nottingham. BSc London. Joined Scientific Civil Service, 1939; various posts at RAE, Farnborough, and Blind Landing Experimental Unit, RAF Martlesham Heath, 1939-58; Dir of Scientific Research (Electronics), Min. of Aviation, 1959-61; RRE, Malvern: Head of Guided Weapons Group, 1961-65; Head of Mil. and Civil Systems Dept, 1965-67; Dir Gen., Electronics R&D, Min. of Technology, later MoD, 1967-72; Dep. Dir, RAE, Farnborough, 1972-78, retired. *Address:* 53 Feoffees Road, Somersham, near Huntingdon, Cambs. *T:* Ramsey (Cambs) 840143.

SCRIVEN, Wilton Maxwell; Director General, South Australian Department of the Premier and Cabinet, since 1981; *b* 10 Dec. 1924; *m* 1948, Marjorie Reta Shaw; two *s* two *d.* *Educ:* Univ. of Adelaide. BSc; MIEAust. Flying Officer RAAF; served with RAF Sqdn 622 Mildenhall, 1943-45. Engr, PMG's Dept, 1946-64; Regional Dir, Dept of Trade, 1965-66; Chm., Australian Industrial Research and Develt Grants Bd, 1967-68; Dir of Industrial Develt, S Australian Govt, 1969-76; Agent General for S Australia in London, 1977-80. *Recreations:* tennis, golf, flute. *Address:* 7 Knightsbridge Road, Leabrook, SA 5068, Australia. *Clubs:* Adelaide Rotary; Royal Wimbledon Golf.

SCRIVENER, Anthony Frank Bertram, QC 1975; a Recorder of the Crown Court, since 1976; *b* 31 July 1935; *s* of Frank Bertram Scrivener and Edna Scrivener; *m* 1964, Irén Becze; one *s* one *d.* *Educ:* Kent Coll., Canterbury; University Coll. London (LLB). Called to Bar, Gray's Inn, 1958. Lectr in Law, Ghana, 1959-61; practice as Junior, 1961-75. *Recreations:* tennis, chess, cricket. *Address:* 4 Willow Dene, Uxbridge Road, Pinner, Mddx HA5 3LT. *T:* 01-868 7678; 8 New Square, Lincoln's Inn, WC2A 3QP.

SCRIVENER, Ronald Stratford, CMG 1965; HM Diplomatic Service, retired; Executive Director, British Soviet Chamber of Commerce, since 1977; *b* 29 Dec. 1919; *s* of Sir Patrick Scrivener, KCMG; *m* 1st, 1947, Elizabeth Drake-Brockman (marr. diss., 1952); 2nd, 1962, Mary Alice Olga Sofia Jane Hohler, *d* of late Squadron-Leader Robert Charlton Lane; two step-*s* two step-*d.* *Educ:* Westminster School; St Catharine's College, Cambridge. Served with Royal Air Force Volunteer Reserve, 1940-45. Appointed HM Diplomatic Service, Dec. 1945. Served in Berlin, Buenos Aires, Vienna, Caracas, Berne, Bangkok; Ambassador to: Panama, 1969-70; Czechoslovakia, 1971-74; Asst Under-Sec. of State, FCO, 1974-76. *Recreations:* travel, fishing. *Address:* 72 Bedford Gardens, W8. *Clubs:* White's, Beefsteak.

SCRIVENOR, Sir Thomas (Vaisey), Kt 1960; CMG 1956; *b* 28 Aug. 1908; *e s* of late John Brooke Scrivenor, ISO, formerly Dir of Geological Survey, Malaya; *m* 1934, Mary Elizabeth Neatby; one *s* three *d.* *Educ:* King's School, Canterbury; Oriel College, Oxford (MA). Temp. Assistant Principal, Colonial Office, 1930-33; Assistant District Officer, Tanganyika, 1934-37; Assistant District Commissioner, Palestine, 1937-43; Assistant Lt-Governor, Malta, 1943-44; Principal, Colonial Office, 1944-46; Principal Asst Sec., Palestine, 1946-48; Civil Service Comr, Nigeria, 1948-53; Deputy High Commissioner for Basutoland, the Bechuanaland Protectorate, and Swaziland, 1953-60. Sec. to Exec. Council of Commonwealth Agric. Bureaux, 1961-73. *Address:* Vine Cottage, Minster Lovell, Oxon. *T:* Asthall Leigh 620.

SCROGGIE, Alan Ure Reith, CBE 1973 (OBE 1961); QPM 1968; one of HM's Inspectors of Constabulary 1963-75; *b* 1912; *s* of late Col W. R. J. Scroggie, CIE, IMS, Callander, Perthshire; *m* 1940, Shiela Catherine, *d* of late Finlay Mackenzie, Elgin, Morayshire; two *s.* *Educ:* Cargilfield Preparatory Sch.; Fettes Coll.; Edinburgh Univ. (BL). Joined Edinburgh City Police, 1930; Asst Chief Constable of Bucks, 1947-53; Chief Constable of Northumberland, 1953-63. OStJ 1955. *Recreations:* golf, fishing, shooting. *Address:* Fowler's Cottage, Abercrombie, by St Monan's, Fife. *Clubs:* Royal and Ancient (St Andrews); Golf House (Élie).

SCRUBY, Ven. Ronald Victor, MA; Archdeacon of Portsmouth, since 1977; *b* 23 Dec. 1919; 6th *s* of late Thomas Henry Scruby and late Florence Jane Scruby, Norwood Green, Southall, Middx; *m* 1955, Sylvia Tremayne Miles, *e d* of late Rear-Adm. Roderic B. T. Miles, Trotton, Sussex; two *s* one *d. Educ:* Southall Technical Coll.; Trinity Hall, Cambridge. Engineering Apprentice, London Transport, 1936-39. Royal Engineers, 1939-45; Capt. 1943. Trinity Hall, Cambridge, 1945-48; Cuddesdon Coll., Oxford, 1948-50. Asst Curate, Rogate, Sussex, 1950-53; Chaplain, King Edward VII Hosp., Midhurst, 1950-53; Chaplain, Saunders-Roe, Osborne, E Cowes 1953-58; Vicar of Eastney, Portsmouth, 1958-65; Rural Dean of Portsmouth, 1960-65; Archdeacon of the Isle of Wight, 1965-77. *Recreations:* rowing, walking. *Address:* Victoria Lodge, 36 Osborne Road, Fareham, Hants PO16 7OS. *T:* Fareham 280101.

SCRUTTON, (Thomas) Hugh, CBE 1967; *b* 8 June 1917; *s* of late Rev. Canon Tom Burton Scrutton and Lesley Hay; *m* 1st, 1941, Helen Greeves (who obtd a divorce, 1952); one *d;* 2nd, 1960, Elizabeth Quayle. *Educ:* Charterhouse; King's Coll., Cambridge (MA). Temporary Asst Keeper, Print Room, British Museum, 1946; Asst, 1947, and Director, 1948, Whitechapel Art Gallery; Director: Walker Art Gallery, Liverpool, 1952-70; Nat. Galls of Scotland, Edinburgh, 1971-77, retired; Penwith Galleries, St Ives, 1978-80. Pres., Museums Assoc., 1970-71. Hon. DLitt Liverpool, 1971. *Address:* Gwelmor, Venton Road, St Ives, Cornwall. *T:* Penzance 795735.

SCRYMGEOUR, Lord; Alexander Henry Scrymgeour-Wedderburn; *b* 5 June 1949; *s* and *heir* of 11th Earl of Dundee, *qv; m* 1979, Siobhan Mary, *d* of David Llewellyn, Gt Somerford, Wilts; one *s* one *d. Educ:* Eton. Page of Honour to the Queen, 1964-65. Contested (C) Hamilton, by-election May 1978. *Heir: s b* 20 June 1982. *Address:* Coultra Farm House, Newport-on-Tay, Fife. *T:* Gauldry 258.

SCRYMGEOUR-WEDDERBURN, family name of **Earl of Dundee.**

SCULLARD, Geoffrey Layton, OBE 1971; HM Diplomatic Service, retired; Head of Accommodation and Services Department, Foreign and Commonwealth Office, 1978-80; *b* 5 July 1922; *s* of late William Harold Scullard and late Eleanor Mary Scullard (*née* Tomkin); *m* 1945, Catherine Margaret Pinington; three *d. Educ:* St Olave's Grammar Sch. Joined Foreign Office, 1939. Served War (RAF Signals), 1942-46. Diplomatic service at: Stockholm, Washington, Baghdad, Los Angeles, Moscow. *Recreations:* fishing, golf. *Address:* 20 Ennismore Avenue, Guildford, Surrey GU1 1SR. *T:* Guildford 39915. *Club:* Bramley Golf.

SCULLARD, Howard Hayes, FBA 1955; FSA; Professor Emeritus of Ancient History in the University of London; *b* 9 Feb. 1903; *s* of late Rev. Professor Herbert H. Scullard and Barbara Louise Scullard (*née* Dodds). *Educ:* Highgate School; St John's Coll., Cambridge (Scholar). First Class Classical Tripos Part II, 1926; Thirlwall Prize, Cambridge, 1929; MA Cambridge, PhD London, 1930. Classical Tutor, New College, London, 1926-35; Reader, 1935-59, Professor of Ancient History, 1959-70, King's College, London. A Governor of New College, London, 1930-80; Vice-Pres., Soc. for the Promotion of Roman Studies; former Mem. Council, British Acad. and of Royal Numismatic Soc.; Actg Dir, Inst. of Classical Studies, London, 1964. FKC, 1970. *Publications:* Scipio Africanus in the Second Punic War, 1930; A History of the Roman World from 753 to 146 BC, 1935, 4th edn 1980; (edited with H. E. Butler) Livy book XXX, 1939, 6th edn 1953; (Joint Editor of and contrib. to) The Oxford Classical Dictionary, 1949, Editor (with N. G. L. Hammond) of new edn, 1970; Roman Politics, 220-150 BC, 1951, 2nd edn 1973; (rev.) F. B. Marsh, A History of the Roman World from 146 to 30 BC, 1953, 3rd edn 1962; From the Gracchi to Nero, 1959, 5th edn 1982; (rev. jtly) J. C. Stobbart: The Grandeur that was Rome, 1961; (ed) Atlas of the Classical World, 1959 and Shorter Atlas of the Classical World, 1962 (Dutch, French and Spanish translations); The Etruscan Cities and Rome, 1967 (Italian translation, 1969, 2nd edn, 1977); Scipio Africanus: Soldier and Politician, 1970; The Elephant in the Greek and Roman World, 1974; A History of Rome (rev. and rewritten edn of Prof. M. Cary's book, 1935), 1975; Roman Britain: Outpost of the Empire, 1979; Festivals and Ceremonies of the Roman Republic, 1981; (Gen. Editor of series) Aspects of Greek and Roman Life, over 40 Vols to date; Annual Survey of Roman history in The Year's Work in Classical Studies, 1937-48, and of ancient history in Annual Bulletin of Historical Literature, 1949-73; articles and reviews in Journal of Roman Studies, Classical Review, Encyclopædia Britannica, etc. *Recreation:* golf. *Address:* 6 Foscote Road, Hendon, NW4. *Club:* Athenæum.

SCUPHAM, John, OBE 1961; retired as Controller of Educational Broadcasting, British Broadcasting Corporation, 1963-65; *b* 7 Sept. 1904; *s* of Roger Scupham and Kate Whittingham; *m* 1932, Dorothy Lacey Clark; one *s* one *d. Educ:* Market Rasen Gram. Sch.; Emmanuel Coll., Cambridge (Scholar). BA 1st Cl., History, 1926, 1st Cl. English, 1927 (Cantab). Various teaching posts, 1927-46. Joined staff of BBC as Educn Officer, 1946; Head of Educational Broadcasting, 1954. Member, Central Advisory Council for Education (England), 1961-63; Member, Church of England Board of Education 1960-72. President, Educational Section of British Association, 1965-66. Mem. Council, Open Univ., 1969-78. DUniv, Open Univ., 1975. *Publications:* Broadcasting and the Community, 1967; The Revolution in Communications, 1970; Open Learning, 1976. *Recreations:* reading, gardening. *Address:* 26 Crabtree Lane, Harpenden, Herts. *T:* Harpenden

3223.

See also A. R. H. Glover.

SCURR, Dr Cyril Frederick, CBE 1980; MVO 1952; FRCS, FFARCS; Consultant Anaesthetist, Westminster Hospital, since 1949; Hon. Anaesthetist, Hospital of SS John and Elizabeth, since 1952; *b* 14 July 1920; *s* of Cyril Albert Scurr and Mabel Rose Scurr; *m* 1947, Isabel Jean Spiller; three *s* one *d. Educ:* King's Coll., London; Westminster Hosp. MB, BS. Served War of 1939-45: RAMC, 1942-47, Major, Specialist Anaesthetist. Faculty of Anaesthetists: Mem. Bd, 1961-77; Dean, 1970-73; Mem. Council, RCS, 1970-73; Pres., Assoc. of Anaesthetists of GB and Ireland, 1976-78; Mem. Health Services Bd, 1977-80; Chm., Scientific Programme, World Congress of Anaesthetists, London, 1968; Pres., Anaesthetics Section, RSocMed, 1978-79; Mem. Adv. Cttee on Distinction Awards, 1973-; Vice-Chm., Jt Consultants Cttee, 1979-81; past Member: Cttee, Competence to Practise; Standing Med. Adv. Cttee, DHSS. Frederick Hewitt Lectr, RCS, 1971; Dudley Buxton Prize, RCS, 1977. Fellow, RSocMed; Hon. FFARCSI 1977. *Publication:* Scientific Foundations of Anaesthesia, 1970, 3rd edn 1982. *Recreations:* photography, gardening. *Address:* Fairlight, Totteridge Common, N20 8NJ. *T:* 01-445 7188.

SCUSE, Dennis George, MBE 1957; TD 1946; Joint Chairman and Managing Director, Character Marketing Ltd, since 1978; Managing Director, Dennis Scuse Ltd, PR, TV and Radio Consultants, since 1976; *b* 19 May 1921; *yr s* of late Charles H. and Katherine Scuse; *m* 1948, Joyce Evelyn, *yr d* of late Frank and Frances Burt; one *s. Educ:* Park Sch., Ilford; Mercers' Sch., London. Joined Martins Bank, 1937. TA (RA), 1938; mobilised, Sept. 1939. Served War, commissioned 78th (HyAA) Regt, RA, 1940. Air Defence of Gt Britain, 1940-41; Command Entertainment Officer, Ceylon Army Comd, 1942; subseq. 65th (HyAA) Regt, in MELF and CMF, 1943-44; joined Army Broadcasting Service, CMF: commanded stations in Bari, Rome and Athens, 1945-46; demobilised, Sept. 1946. Joined Overseas Div. BBC and seconded to War Office for Forces Broadcasting Service in Benghasi and Canal Zone; Chief Programme Officer, 1947-48; Asst Dir, British Forces Network, Germany, 1949-50; Dir, 1950-57. Introduced "Two-Way Family Favourites", 1952-57; Sen. Planning Asst, BBC-TV, 1958-59; Chief Asst (Light Entertainment), BBC-TV, 1960; Chief Asst (TV), BBC New York Office, Sept. 1960; BBC Rep. in USA, July 1962; Gen. Manager, BBC-TV Enterprises, 1963-72, and BBC Radio Enterprises, 1968-72. Trident Management Ltd, 1972; Man. Dir, Trident Internat. TV Enterprises Ltd, 1972-76. *Publications:* numerous articles on broadcasting, television programme exports, etc. *Recreations:* wine making, watching television. *Address:* 2 York House, Courtlands, Sheen Road, Richmond, Surrey. *T:* 01-948 4737. *Club:* Royal Greenjackets.

SCUTT, Robin Hugh, CBE 1976; Vice-Chairman, Covent Garden Video Productions, since 1980; Director: National Video Corporation, since 1980; Lella Productions plc, since 1980; *b* Sandgate, Kent, 24 Oct. 1920; *s* of late Rev. A. O. Scutt, MA and Freda M. Scutt (*née* Palmer); *m* 1st, 1943, Judy Watson (marr. diss. 1960); two *s;* 2nd, 1961, Patricia A. M. Smith. *Educ:* Fonthill; Bryanston; Jesus Coll., Cambridge (MA Mod. Lang.). Served Intell. Corps, 1941-42 (invalided out). BBC Eur. Service (French Section), 1942; BBC TV Outside Broadcasts Producer, 1955; BBC Paris Rep., 1958; Gen. Man., Trans Europe Television, 1962; rejoined BBC TV Outside Broadcasts, 1963; Asst Head of BBC TV Presentation (BBC1), 1966; Controller: BBC Radio 1 and 2, 1967-68; BBC 2, 1969-74; Development TV, 1974-77; Dep. Man. Dir, BBC TV, 1977-80. Dir, LWT, 1981-; Chm., Saxon Radio, Bury St Edmunds; Dir, Suffolk Group Radio plc. Trustee, Internat. Inst. of Communications; Fellow, Royal TV Soc., 1978, and Gold Medallist, 1980. *Recreations:* music, theatre, gardening. *Address:* The Abbey Cottage, Cockfield, Suffolk. *Club:* Garrick.

SEA-LION; *see* Bennett, Captain G. M.

SEABORG, Glenn Theodore; University Professor of Chemistry, University of California, Berkeley, since 1971; *b* 19 April 1912; *s* of Herman Theodore and Selma Erickson Seaborg; *m* 1942, Helen Lucille Griggs; four *s* two *d. Educ:* Univ. of Calif, Los Angeles (BA); Univ. of Calif, Berkeley (PhD). University of California, Berkeley: Res. Associate (with Prof. Gilbert N. Lewis), Coll. of Chem., 1937-39; Instr, Dept of Chem., 1939-41, Asst Prof., 1941-45, Prof., 1945-71; Chancellor, 1958-61; Lawrence Berkeley Laboratory: Associate Dir, 1954-61, and 1972-; Dir, Nuclear Chem. Div., 1946-58, and 1972-75; Head, Plutonium Chem. Metall. Lab., Univ. of Chicago, 1942-46; Chm., US Atomic Energy Commn, 1961-71. Member, US Delegns to: 3rd (Chm.) and 4th (Chm. and Pres.) UN Internat. Confs on Peaceful Uses of Atomic Energy, Geneva, 1964 and 1971; 5-15th annual Gen. Confs of Internat. Atomic Energy Agency, 1961-71; USSR, for signing of Memorandum on Cooperation in the Field of Utilization of Atomic Energy for Peaceful Purposes (Chm.), 1963; USSR, for signing of Limited Test Ban Treaty, 1963. Member: Nat. Council on Marine Resources and Engineering Development, 1966-71; Nat. Aeronautics and Space Council, 1961-71; Fed. Council for Science and Tech., 1961-71; Pres.'s Cttee on Manpower, 1964-69; Fed. Radiation Council, 1961-69; Nat. Sci. Bd, Nat. Sci. Foundn, 1960-71; Pres.'s Science Adv. Cttee, 1959-61; 1st Gen. Adv. Cttee, US Atomic Energy Commn, 1946-50; Commn on the Humanities, 1962-65; Scientific Adv. Bd, Robert A. Welch Foundn, 1957-; Bd of Dirs, Nat. Educnl TV and Radio Centre, 1958-64, 1967-70; Bd of Dirs, World Future Soc., 1969-; Nat. Programming Council for Public TV, 1970-72; Bd of Governors, Amer.-

Swedish Hist. Foundn, 1972–; Steering Cttee, Chem. Educn Material Study (Chm.), 1959–74; Nat. Cttee on America's Goals and Resources, Nat. Planning Assoc., 1962–64; Electoral Coll. Hall of Fame for Great Americans, 1969–; Council on Foreign Relations, 1965–; Bd of Trustees: Pacific Science Centre Foundn, 1962–; Science Service, 1965– (Pres., 1966–); Amer.-Scandinavian Foundn, 1968–; Educnl Broadcasting Corp., 1970–73; Amer. Assoc. for the Advancement of Science (Pres. 1972, Chm. 1973); Amer. Chem. Soc. (Pres., 1976); Chm. Bd, Swedish Council of America, 1978–. Mem. and Hon. Mem., Fellow and Hon. Fellow, numerous scientific and professional socs and instns, Argentina, German Dem. Republic, German Fed. Republic, Poland, Spain, Sweden, UK, USA, USSR. Holds over 45 hon. doctorates from univs and colls. Named one of America's 10 Outstanding Young Men, 1947. Awards (1947–) include: Nobel Prize for Chemistry (jtly), 1951; Perkin Medal (Amer. Sect. Soc. Chem. Ind.), 1957; USAEC Enrico Fermi Award, 1959; Priestley Meml Award, 1960; Franklin Medal (Franklin Inst. of Philadelphia), 1963; Award in Pure Chem., 1947, Charles Lathrop Parsons Award, (Amer. Chem. Soc.), 1964; Chem. Pioneer Award, 1968, Gold Medal Award, (Am. Inst. of Chemists), 1973; Arches of Science Award (Pacific Science Centre, Seattle), 1968; John R. Kuebler Award, Alpha Chi Sigma, 1978; Priestley Medal, Amer. Chem. Soc., 1979; Officer, French Legion of Honour, 1973. Co-discoverer of: nuclear energy source isotopes Pu-239 and U-233; elements (1940–74): 94, plutonium; 95, americium; 96, curium; 97, berkelium; 98, californium; 99, einsteinium; 100, fermium; 101, mendelevium; 102, nobelium; element 106. Publications: (jtly) The Chemistry of the Actinide Elements, 1958; The Transuranium Elements (Silliman Lectures), 1958; (jtly) Elements of the Universe, 1958; Man-made Transuranium Elements, 1963; (jtly) Education and the Atom, 1964; (jtly) The Nuclear Properties of the Heavy Elements, 1964; (jtly) Oppenheimer, 1969; (jtly) Man and Atom, 1971; Nuclear Milestones, 1972; (ed) Transuranium Elements—Products of Modern Alchemy, 1978; Kennedy, Khrushchev and the Test Ban, 1981; contrib. numerous papers on nuclear chem. and nuclear physics, transuranium elements, high energy nuclear reactions and educn in Physical Rev., Jl Amer. Chm. Soc., Annual Rev. of Nuclear Science, etc. Recreations: golf, reading, hiking. Address: (business) Lawrence Berkeley Laboratory, University of California, Berkeley, Calif 94720, USA; (home) 1154 Glen Road, Lafayette, Calif 94549, USA. Clubs: Faculty (Univ. Calif, Berkeley); Commonwealth Club of California, Bohemian (San Francisco); Chemists (NY); Cosmos, University (Washington).

SEABORN, Most Rev. Robert Lowder; Bishop Ordinary (Anglican) to the Canadian Forces, since 1980; b 9 July 1911; s of Rev. Richard Seaborn and Muriel Kathleen Reid; m 1938, Mary Elizabeth Gilchrist; four s one d. Educ: Univ. of Toronto Schs; Trinity Coll., Univ. of Toronto (MA); Oxford Univ. Deacon, 1934; Priest, 1935; Asst Curate, St Simon's, Toronto, 1934–36; Asst Curate, St James's Cathedral, Toronto, 1937–41; Rector, St Peter's, Cobourg, Ont., 1941–48; Chaplain, Canadian Army, 1942–45 (Padre Canadian Scottish Regt); Dean of Quebec and Rector of Parish of Quebec, 1948–57; Rector, St Mary's, Kerrisdale, Vancouver, BC, 1957–58; Asst Bishop of Newfoundland, 1958–65, Coadjutor, June-Dec. 1965; Bishop of Newfoundland, 1965–75, of Eastern Newfoundland and Labrador, 1975–80; Archbishop of Newfoundland and Metropolitan of Ecclesiastical Province of Canada, 1975–80. Croix de Guerre avec étoile de vermeil (French), 1945. DD, (jure dignitatis), Trinity Coll., 1948; DCL (hc), Bishop's Univ., 1962; Hon. LLD Meml Univ. of Newfoundland, 1972. Publication: Faith in our Time, 1963. Recreations: camping, golf. Address: 247 Lake Street, Cobourg, Ont K9A 1R6, Canada.

SEABORNE DAVIES, David Richard; see Davies, D. R. S.

SEABROOK, Air Vice-Marshal Geoffrey Leonard, CB 1965; b 25 Aug. 1909; s of late Robert Leonard Seabrook; m 1949, Beryl Mary (née Hughes); one s one d. Educ: King's Sch., Canterbury. Commissioned in RAF (Accountant Branch), 1933; served in: Middle East, 1935–43; Bomber Command, 1943–45; Transport Command, 1945–47; Iraq, 1947–49; Signals Command, 1949–51; Air Ministry Organisation and Methods, 1951–53; Home Command Group Captain Organisation, 1953–56; Far East Air Force, 1957–59; idc 1960; Director of Personnel, Air Ministry, 1961–63; Air Officer Administration, HQ, RAF Tech. Trg Comd, 1963–66; retired June 1966. Air Cdre 1961; Air Vice-Marshal, 1964. Head of Secretarial Branch, Royal Air Force, 1963–66. FCA 1957 (Associate, 1932). Recreations: sailing, tennis, golf. Address: Long Pightle, Piltdown, Uckfield, E Sussex. T: Newick 2322. Clubs: Royal Air Force; Walton and Frinton Yacht; Piltdown Golf.

SEABROOK, John, CMG 1970; AFC 1918; ED 1947; JP; Founder Chairman, Seabrook Fowlds Ltd, Auckland, NZ, 1919–70; Chairman, Amalgamated Pacific Industries Ltd, 1970–73; b 6 Jan. 1896; e s of Albert David Seabrook and Marion May Seabrook; m 1926, Doreen Mary Alexina Carr, d of Charles Edward and Rose Louise McKenzie Carr, Auckland; one s one d. Educ: Auckland Grammar School. Served RFC, France, 1916–17; RAF, Middle East, 1918 (Captain). Returned to NZ, 1919, and founded Seabrook Fowlds Ltd. Served RNZAF, 1940–44 (Group Captain). Mem. Board of Trustees, NZ Inst. for Blind for 24 years; Dir, NZ National Airways, 1952–61; Dep. Chm., Blinded Servicemen's Trust Board; Mem., Nature Conservation Council, Wellington; Mem., Hauraki Gulf Maritime Park Board; Pres., Auckland Inst. and Museum, 1961–63. Recreations: yachting, gardening. Address: 146 Orakei Road, Remuera, Auckland 5, NZ. T: 52735. Club: Royal Air Force.

SEABROOKE, George Alfred; Director, The Polytechnic, Wolverhampton, since 1977; b 8 Dec. 1923; s of late John Arthur Seabrooke and Elsie Seabrooke; m 1945, Evelyn Sargent; two s. Educ: Keighley Boys' Grammar Sch.; Bradford Technical Coll.; Stoke-on-Trent Tech. Coll.; King's Coll., London Univ. FBIM 1978. National Service, 1946–48. Post Office Engrg Dept, 1940–50; Estate Duty Office, Comrs of Inland Revenue, 1950–56; SW London Coll. of Commerce, 1956–60; Trent Polytechnic, Nottingham (and precursor Colls), 1960–73; Dep. Dir, NE London Polytechnic, 1974–77. Publications: Air Law, 1964; contrib. learned jls. Recreations: music, cricket, rugby. Address: The Polytechnic, Wolverhampton, West Midlands. T: Wolverhampton 27371.

SEABY, Wilfred Arthur; retired museum official; Director, Ulster Museum (previously Belfast Museum and Art Gallery), 1953–70; Numismatic Section, Department of Technology and Local History, 1970–73; b 16 Sept. 1910; y s of late Allen W. Seaby, sometime Prof. of Art, Univ. of Reading; m 1937, Nora, d of late A. E. Pecover, Reading; two s one d. Educ: Wycliffe College; Reading University, College of Art. Dip. Museums Assoc., 1939. Served War of 1939–45, Royal Air Force, 1940–46 (Flt-Lt). B. A. Seaby Ltd, 1927–30; Reading, Birmingham, and Taunton Museums, 1931–53. FSA 1948. Hon. MA QUB, 1971. Recreation: water colour painting. Address: 36 Ladbrook Road, Solihull, West Midlands.

SEAFIELD, 13th Earl of, cr 1701; **Ian Derek Francis Ogilvie-Grant;** Viscount Seafield, Baron Ogilvy of Cullen, 1698; Viscount Reidhaven, Baron Ogilvy of Deskford and Cullen, 1701; b 20 March 1939; s of Countess of Seafield (12th in line) and Derek Studley-Herbert (who assumed by deed poll, 1939, the additional surnames of Ogilvie-Grant; he d 1960); S mother, 1969; m 1st, 1960, Mary Dawn Mackenzie (marr. diss., 1971), er d of Henry Illingworth; two s; 2nd, 1971, Leila, d of Mahmoud Refaat, Cairo. Educ: Eton. Recreations: shooting, fishing, tennis. Heir: s Viscount Reidhaven, qv. Address: Old Cullen, Cullen, Banffshire. T: Cullen 40221. Club: White's.

SEAGA, Rt. Hon. Edward Philip George, PC 1982; Prime Minister of Jamaica, and Minister of Finance and Planning, Mining and Energy, and Culture, since 1980; MP for Western Kingston, since 1962; Leader of the Jamaica Labour Party, since 1974; b 28 May 1930; s of late Philip Seaga and of Erna (née Maxwell); m 1965, Marie Elizabeth (née Constantine) (Miss Jamaica, 1964); two s one d. Educ: Wolmers Boys' Sch., Kingston, Jamaica; Harvard Univ., USA (BA Social Science, 1952). Did field research in connection with Inst. of Social and Econ. Res., University Coll. of the West Indies (now Univ. of the WI), Jamaica, on develt of the child, and revival spirit cults, by living in rural villages and urban slums; proposed estabt of Unesco Internat. Fund for Promotion of Culture, 1971, and is founding mem. of its Administrative Council. Nominated to Upper House (Legislative Council), 1959 (youngest mem. in its history); Asst Sec., Jamaica Labour Party, 1960–62, Sec., 1962; Minister of Develt and Social Welfare, 1962–67; Minister of Finance and Planning, 1967–72; Leader of Opposition, 1974–80. Director: Consulting Services Ltd, to 1979; Capital Finance Co. Ltd, to 1979. Hon. LLD Miami, 1981. Grand Collar, and Golden Mercury Internat. Award, Venezuela, 1981; Gold Key Award, Avenue of the Americas, NYC, 1981; Grand Cross, Order of Merit of Fed. Rep. of Germany, 1982. Religion Anglican. Publications: The Development of the Child; Revival Spirit Cults. Recreations: classical music, reading, shooting, hockey, football, cricket, tennis, swimming. Address: (office) Jamaica House, Kingston, Jamaica, West Indies. T: 927-7854; (home) Vale Royal, Kingston. Clubs: Kingston Cricket, Jamaica Gun (Jamaica).

SEAGER, family name of **Baron Leighton of Saint Mellons.**

SEAGER, Ven. Edward Leslie; Archdeacon of Dorset, 1955–74, Archdeacon Emeritus of Salisbury Cathedral since 1975; b 5 Oct. 1904; s of William Seager, Chaddesley Corbett, Worcs; unmarried. Educ: Bromsgrove Sch.; Hatfield College, Durham. Foundation Scholar, Hatfield College, 1923; BA, Jenkyn's Scholar, 1926; Diploma in Theology, 1928; MA, 1931. Deacon, 1928, priest, 1929, Newcastle upon Tyne; Chaplain, Wellington School, 1931–39. War of 1939–45, CF, 1937–46; SCF, 1942–45; DACG, 1945–46; HCF, 1946–. Vicar of Gillingham, Dorset, 1946–79, and of Fifehead Magdalen, 1966–79; Team Vicar in Gillingham Team Ministry, 1979; Rural Dean of Shaftesbury, 1951–56; Canon and Prebendary of Shipton in Salisbury Cathedral, 1954–68; Examining Chaplain to Bishop of Salisbury, 1968; Canon and Prebendary of Gillingham Major, 1968–79, Canon Emeritus, 1979–; RD of Blackmore Vale, 1975–79. Governor of Milton Abbey School, 1956–; Chairman of Governors, Gillingham School, 1959–. Publication: Day unto Day, 1932. Recreations: scouting, golf. Club: East India, Devonshire, Sports and Public Schools.

SEAGER, Major Ronald Frank, RA, retired; Executive Director, RSPCA, 1971–78 (Secretary, 1966–71); Advisory Director, International Society for Protection of Animals; b 27 May 1918; s of Frank Seager and Lilias K. (née Parr); m 1941, Josephine, d of Rev. R. M. Chadwick; one s one d. Educ: St Albans School. Royal Artillery (HAC), 1939; commnd, 1941; Italy, 1944–45; seconded Royal Pakistan Artillery, 1949–50; served Korean War, 1953–54; Perm. Pres. Courts Martial, Eastern Command, 1960–63. Joined RSPCA, 1963. Recreations: golf, gardening. Address: Beech Cottage, Newlands, Sherborne, Dorset. T: 3037.

SEAGROATT, Conrad; barrister-at-law; a Recorder of the Crown Court, since 1980; b 17 Aug. 1938; s of E. G. Seagroatt, Solicitor of the Supreme

Court, and Barbara C. Seagroatt; *m* Cornelia Mary Anne Verdegaal; three *d*. *Educ:* Solihull Sch., Warwicks; Pembroke Coll., Oxford (MA Hons). Admitted Solicitor of the Supreme Court, 1967; called to the Bar, Gray's Inn, 1970; Mem., Senate of the Inns of Court and the Bar, 1980. *Recreations:* running, hockey, squash. *Address:* 1 King's Bench Walk, Temple, EC4Y 7DB. *T:* 01-353 8436.

SEAL, Dr Barry Herbert; Member (Lab) Yorkshire West, European Parliament, since 1979; *b* 28 Oct. 1937; *s* of Herbert Seal and Rose Anne Seal; *m* 1963, Frances Catherine Wilkinson; one *s* one *d. Educ:* Heath Grammar Sch., Halifax; Univ. of Bradford (MSc, PhD); European Business Sch., Fontainebleau. CEng, MIChemE; FBIM. Served RAF, 1955-58. Lab. Asst, finally Chem. Engr, ICI Ltd, 1958-64; Develt Engr, subseq. Div. Chem. Engr, Murex Ltd, 1964-68; Sen. Engr, BOC Internat., 1968-71; Principal Lectr in Systems, Huddersfield Polytechnic, 1971-79; consultant on microprocessors. Parly Candidate (Lab), Harrogate, 1974; Leader, Bradford Met. Dist Council Labour Gp, 1976-79. *Publications:* papers on computer and microprocessor applications. *Recreations:* squash, driving, reading. *Address:* 5 Paddock Close, Wyke, Bradford, West Yorks. *T:* Bradford 671888.

SEAL, Richard Godfrey, FRCO; Organist of Salisbury Cathedral, since 1968; *b* 4 Dec. 1935; *s* of William Godfrey Seal and Shelagh Seal (*née* Bagshaw); *m* 1975, Dr Sarah Helen Hamilton; two *s. Educ:* New Coll. Choir Sch., Oxford; Cranleigh Sch., Surrey; Christ's Coll., Cambridge (MA). FRCO 1958. Asst Organist: St Bartholomews the Great, London, 1960-61; Chichester Cathedral (and Dir of Music, Prebendal Sch.) Sussex, 1961-68. *Address:* 5 The Close, Salisbury, Wilts. *T:* Salisbury 6828. *Club:* Crudgemens (Godalming).

SEALE, Douglas (Robert); Producer (Stage); *b* 28 Oct. 1913; *s* of Robert Henry Seale and Margaret Seale (*née* Law). *Educ:* Rutlish. Studied for stage at Royal Academy of Dramatic Art and became an actor. First appeared as Starling in The Drums Begin, Embassy, 1934; subseq. in Repertory. Served in Army, 1940-46, commissioned in Royal Signals. Joined Shakespeare Memorial Theatre Company, Stratford-on-Avon season's 1946 and 1947. From 1948 produced at Birmingham Repertory Theatre, at The Bedford, Camden Town (under Donald Wolfit), and again at Birmingham where he became Director of Productions, 1950. Later Productions include: Figaro and Fidelio, Sadler's Wells; Shaw's Caesar and Cleopatra at Birmingham Rep. Theatre, 1956 (later presented at Théâtre Sarah Bernhardt, Paris, and Old Vic). Season 1957: The Tempest, at Univ. of BC, Vancouver; King John, Stratford-on-Avon; Richard III, Old Vic; Trilogy of Henry VI, Old Vic; Season 1958; The World of the Wonderful Dark, for first Vancouver Festival; King Lear, Old Vic; Much Ado about Nothing, Stratford-on-Avon. Old Vic productions as Associate Director, 1958: Julius Caesar; Macbeth; 1959: Molière's Tartuffe; Pinero's The Magistrate; Dryden-Davenant-Purcell version of Shakespeare's The Tempest; St Joan; She Stoops to Conquer, 1960, Landscape with Figures, by Cecil Beaton, Dublin Festival, 1960: King John, Festival Theatre, Stratford, Ontario, 1960; Director of tours in Russia and Poland for Old Vic Theatre Co., 1961: prod. The Importance of Being Earnest, New York, 1962; The Comedy of Errors, Henry V, Stratford, Connecticut, 1963; Regent's Prof., Univ. of Calif. at Santa Barbara, Jan.-June 1965; Artistic Director, Center Stage, Baltimore, Maryland, USA, 1965-67; directed and acted, Meadowbrook Theater, Rochester, Mich, 1968; co-producing Director, Goodman Theater, Chicago, 1969-72 (productions incl.: Soldiers, Marching Song, Heartbreak House (Jefferson award), The Tempest, Twelfth Night, own musical adaptation of Lady Audley's Secret); directed and acted in Lady Audley's Secret, Washington and New York, 1972; Giovani, in Pirandello's Henry IV, New York, 1973; directed: King Lear, Marin Shakespeare Festival, San Francisco; Doll's House and Look Back in Anger, Cleveland, Getting Married, New Haven, 1973; Sorin in The Seagull, Seattle; Artistic Dir, Philadelphia Drama Guild, 1974-80; The Last Few Days of Willie Callendar, Philadelphia, 1979; Summer, Philadelphia, 1980; directed at Shaw Festival, Ont.: Too True to be Good, 1974; Caesar and Cleopatra, 1975; Lady Audley's Secret, 1978; Dir, The Winslow Boy, NY, 1980, and tour; acted in: Frankenstein, NY, 1980; The Dresser, NY, 1981. Has also produced for TV. Hon. DFA Washington Coll., Md, 1967. Mensa Annual Achievement Award, 1979. *Address:* Apt 14c, One University Place, New York, NY 10003, USA. *Club:* Players (NY).

SEALE, Sir John Henry, 5th Bt, *cr* 1838; RIBA; *b* 3 March 1921; *s* of 4th Bt; *S* father, 1964; *m* 1953, Ray Josephine, *d* of Robert Gordon Charters, MC, Christchurch, New Zealand; one *s* one *d. Educ:* Eton; Christ Church, Oxford. Served War of 1939-45: Royal Artillery, North Africa and Italy; Captain, 1945. ARIBA 1951. *Heir: s* John Robert Charters Seale, *b* 17 Aug. 1954. *Address:* Slade, Kingsbridge, Devon TQ7 4BL. *T:* Loddiswell 226.

SEALES, Peter Clinton; Chief Executive, Sea Fish Industry Authority, since 1982; *b* 1 Nov. 1929; *s* of James Seales, Solicitor, and Angela Seales; *m* 1955, Bernadette Rogers; one *d* (and one *d* decd). Called to the Bar, King's Inns, 1953. Group Marketing Dir, Raleigh Industries Ltd, 1962-74; Dir, E Midlands Electricity Board, 1972-74; Man. Dir, Potterton International, and Chm. overseas subsidiaries in France, Belgium, Germany, Holland and Japan, 1974-76; International Marketing Dir, Ever Ready Holdings, 1977; Chm., PSL Associates 1978-. *Publications:* various articles on commercial matters. *Recreations:* daughter's riding, sailing, music. *Address:* 78 Northumberland Road, Leamington Spa, Warwickshire. *T:* Leamington Spa 315624. *Clubs:*

White Elephant, Wig and Pen, Institute of Directors; Leamington Real Tennis.

SEAMAN, Christopher; Principal Guest Conductor, Utrecht Symphony Orchestra, since 1979; Conductor and Artistic Advisor, Gelders Orchestra, Arnhem, since 1980; *b* 7 March 1942; *s* of late Albert Edward Seaman and of Ethel Margery Seaman (*née* Chambers). *Educ:* Canterbury Cathedral Choir Sch.; The King's Sch., Canterbury; King's Coll., Cambridge. MA, double first cl. Hons in Music; ARCM, ARCO. Principal Timpanist, London Philharmonic Orch., 1964-68 (Mem., LPO Bd of Dirs, 1965-68); Asst Conductor, 1968-70; Principal Conductor, 1971-77, BBC Scottish Symphony Orchestra; Princ. Conductor and Artistic Dir, Northern Sinfonia Orch., 1974-79. Freelance Conductor, appearing in New Zealand, Italy and many parts of the United Kingdom, 1970-71; has also appeared as Guest Conductor in Germany, Italy, Holland, Norway, Spain, Czechoslovakia, Portugal and all parts of UK. FGSM 1972. *Recreations:* people, reading, walking; New Testament Greek. *Address:* 2 The Paddox, Banbury Road, Oxford OX2 7PN. *T:* Oxford 58771.

SEAMAN, Dick; *see* Seaman, R. J.

SEAMAN, Edwin de Grey; Chairman, Edwin Seaman Farms Ltd; *b* 27 Aug. 1908; *s* of Edwin de Grey Seaman and Catherine Anne Farrow (*née* Sayer); *m* 1940, Eileen Purdy (*d* 1980); two *d. Educ:* Glebe House Sch., Hunstanton; Cheltenham Coll., Glos. Started farming 90 acres in Norfolk, 1929; marketing Fatstock for Norfolk Farmers, 1933, and extended to importing from Canada and Ireland; imported 300 pedigree Holstein Friesian cattle from Canada and founded Canadian Holstein Friesian Association, 1946. Joined NFU, 1944; became Delegate to Nat. Council, 1949. Chm., Working Party which produced a scheme for Fatstock Scheme, 1952; (with Lord Netherthorpe) founded Fatstock Marketing Corp., 1953 (which became FMC Ltd, 1963) (Vice-Chm. 1972, Dep. Chm., 1974-75). Founded Seaman's Cream Dairies Ltd, 1963; extended to five counties and sold to Milk Marketing Bd, 1963. During War of 1939-45 was Member: Agricl Exec. Cttee; Milk Production Cttee; Special Police Auxiliary and Home Guard, also Air Training Corps (ATC). Member: Royal Agricultural Soc. of England; Royal Norfolk Agricultural Soc. Freeman, City of London, 1962. *Recreations:* farming (3000 acres), fishing, shooting, and his work. *Address:* Rising Lodge, South Wootton, King's Lynn, Norfolk PE30 3PD. *T:* Kings Lynn 671079. *Clubs:* Farmers', Smithfield; Refley Society (King's Lynn).

SEAMAN, Gilbert Frederick, AO 1981; CMG 1967; Chairman, State Bank of South Australia, since 1963; Deputy Chairman, Electricity Trust of SA, since 1970; Trustee, Savings Bank of SA, 1973-81; *b* 7 Sept. 1912; *s* of Eli S. Seaman, McLaren Vale, South Australia; *m* 1935, Avenal Essie Fong; one *s* one *d. Educ:* University of Adelaide. BEc, Associate of University of Adelaide, 1935, High School Teacher, Port Pirie and Unley, 1932-35; South Australian Public Service, 1936-41; Seconded to Commonwealth of Australia as Assistant Director of Manpower for SA, 1941-46; Economist, SA Treasury, 1946-60; Under Treasurer for SA, 1960-72. *Address:* 27 William Street, Hawthorn, SA 5062, Australia. *T:* 271-4271.
See also Sir K. D. Seaman.

SEAMAN, Sir Keith (Douglas), KCVO 1981; OBE 1976; Governor of South Australia, 1977-82; *b* 11 June 1920; *s* of late E. S. and E. M. Seaman; *m* 1946, Joan, *d* of F. Birbeck; one *s* one *d. Educ:* Unley High Sch.; Univ. of Adelaide (BA, LLB). South Australian Public Service, 1937-54; RAAF Overseas HQ, London, 1941-45, Flt-Lieut. Entered Methodist Ministry, 1954: Renmark, 1954-58; Adelaide Central Methodist Mission, 1958-77 (Supt, 1971-77). Sec., Christian Television Assoc. of S Australia, 1959-73; Mem. Executive, World Assoc. of Christian Broadcasting, 1963-70; Director, 5KA, 5AU and 5RM Broadcasting Companies, 1960-; Chm., 5KA, 5AU and 5RM, 1971-77. Mem., Australian Govt Social Welfare Commn, 1973-76. KStJ 1978. *Recreations:* reading, gardening. *Address:* Victor Harbor, South Australia 5211, Australia. *Club:* Adelaide.
See also G. F. Seaman.

SEAMAN, Reginald Jaspar, (Dick Seaman); Director of Information, Department of Employment, 1978-80; *b* 19 March 1923; *o s* of Jaspar and Flora Seaman, Wandsworth; *m* 1950, Marian, *o d* of Henry and Ethel Sarah Moser. *Educ:* West Hill Elem. Sch., Wandsworth, SW18. Served War, 1940-46, RAF aircrew. Entered Civil Service as Post Office Messenger, 1937; Clerical Officer, HM Treasury, 1950; Asst Inf. Officer, Treasury, 1959-61; Inf. Officer, MAFF, 1961-64; Sen. Inf. Officer, DEA, 1964-67; Principal Inf. Officer, 1967-69; Chief Press Officer, DEP, 1969-72; Chief Inf. Officer, Northern Ireland Office, 1972-78. Silver Jubilee Medal, 1977. *Recreations:* orchids, horticulture (Vice Chm., Caterham Horticultural Soc.). *Address:* 9 Ninehams Road, Caterham, Surrey.

SEARBY, Philip James, CBE 1981; Secretary, since 1976, and Authority Finance and Programmes Officer, since 1971, UK Atomic Energy Authority; *b* 20 Sept. 1924; *s* of Leonard James and Lillian Mary Searby; *m* 1955, Mary Brent Dudley; two *s. Educ:* Bedford Sch.; Wadham Coll., Oxford (MA). Entered Civil Service, Min. of Nat. Insurance, 1949; Prime Minister's Statistical Branch, 1951; Private Sec. to Paymaster Gen. (Lord Cherwell), 1952; Principal, Atomic Energy Office, 1954. Joined UK Atomic Energy Authority, 1956; Dep. Gen. Sec., Harwell, 1959; Principal Economics and Programmes Officer, 1965. St Albans Diocesan Reader, 1950. *Recreation:*

gardening. *Address:* 35 Wordsworth Road, Harpenden, Herts AL5 4AG. *T:* Harpenden 60837. *Club:* United Oxford & Cambridge University.

SEARCY, Philip Roy, OBE 1966; Australian Consul-General, Los Angeles, 1971–75; *b* Adelaide, South Australia, 15 April 1914; *s of* Herbert Leslie Searcy and Mary Ellen MacGregor; *m* 1946, Mary Elizabeth Gavan Duffy; four *d.* *Educ:* Collegiate School of St Peter, Adelaide; Adelaide University. Royal Australian Air Force, 1940; Air Operations, Europe, 1941; Prisoner of War, Germany, Nov. 1941–45. Joined Australian Govt Trade Commissioner Service, 1955; Australian Govt Trade Commissioner, Calcutta, 1956; Commercial Counsellor, Singapore, 1957; Australian Govt Senior Trade Commissioner: London, 1958–62; Tokyo, 1962–65; Hong Kong, 1966–70. *Address:* The Bridge, Gundaroo, NSW 2620, Australia. *Clubs:* Naval and Military (Melbourne); Tokyo; Shek O, Hong Kong.

SEARLE, Rear-Adm. (retd) Malcolm Walter St Leger, CB 1955; CBE 1945; *b* 23 Dec. 1900; *s of* late Sir Malcolm W. Searle, Wynberg, S Africa; *m* 1930, Betty Margaret, *d of* late Dr H. R. Crampton; one *s* two *d.* *Educ:* RN Colleges Osborne and Dartmouth. Entered RN 1914; served European War, 1914–19; Comdr 1936; served War of 1939–45; Capt. 1943; Commodore, RN Barracks, Portsmouth, 1951; Rear-Adm. 1952; Deputy Chief of Naval Personnel, 1953–55; retired, 1956. *Address:* Lindens, Kithurst Park, Storrington, Pulborough, West Sussex RH20 4JH.

SEARLE, Ronald William Fordham, AGI; Artist; *b* Cambridge, 3 March 1920; *s of* late William James Searle and of Nellie Hunt; *m* 1st, Kaye Webb (marr. diss. 1967); one *s* one *d*; 2nd, 1967, Monica Koenig. *Educ:* Cambridge School of Art. Humorous work first published in Cambridge Daily News and Granta, 1935–39. Served with 287 Field Co. RE, 1939–46; captured by the Japanese at fall of Singapore, 1942; Prisoner of War in Siam and Malaya, 1942–45; Allied Force HQ Port Said Ops, 1946. Began contributing widely to nat. publications from 1946; creator of the schoolgirls of St Trinians, 1941 (abandoned them in 1953); Cartoonist to Tribune, 1949–51; to Sunday Express, 1950–51; Special feature artist, News Chronicle, 1951–53; Weekly Cartoonist, News Chronicle, 1954; Punch Theatre artist, 1949–62; Contributor, New Yorker. Designer of commemorative medals for the French Mint, since 1974; *Awards:* Art Dirs Club, Philadelphia, Medal, 1959; Nat. Cartoonists Soc. of America, Awards, 1959, 1960, 1966; Art Dirs Club, LA, Medal, 1959; Gold Medal, III Biennale Tolentino, 1965; Prix de la Critique Belge, 1968; Médaille de la ville d'Avignon, 1971; Prix d'Humour du Festival d'Avignon, 1971; Grand Prix de l'Humour noir "Grandville", 1971–; Prix Internationale Charles Huard de dessin de presse, 1972. *One Man Exhibitions:* Batsford Gall., 1947; Leicester Galls, 1948, 1950, 1954, 1957; New York, 1959, 1963, 1969, 1976; Hannover, Tolentino (Italy), Stuttgart, Berlin, 1965; Bremerhaven, Basle, Linz, 1966; Galerie La Pochade, Paris, 1966, 1967, 1968, 1969, 1971; Galerie Gurlitt, Munich, 1967, 1968, 1969, 1970, 1971, 1973, 1976; Grosvenor Gall., London, Brussels, 1968; Frankfurt, 1969; Konstanz, Würzburg, 1970; Salzburg, 1971; Lausanne, Poncey, 1972; Paris, Vienna, 1973; Lausanne, 1974; Paris, 1975; Berlin, Hannover, Stuttgart, Mainz, Recklinghausen, New York, Stuttgart, Paris, 1976; Brussels, London, Paris, 1977; London, Vienna, Lausanne, Berlin, 1978; Graz, Tübingen, Salzburg, 1979; Bonn, Heidelberg, 1980; Rizzoli Gall., NY, Gal. Bartsch & Chariau, Munich, 1981. *Works in permanent collections:* V&A, BM, Imperial War Museum; Bibliothèque Nat., Paris; Kunsthalle, Bremen; Wilhelm-Busch Museum, Hanover; Stadtmuseum, Munich; Art Museum, Dallas, Texas; Staatliche Mus., Berlin-Dahlem. *Films based on the characters of St Trinian's:* The Belles of St Trinian's, 1954; Blue Murder at St Trinian's, 1957; The Pure Hell of St Trinian's, 1960; The Great St Trinian's Train Robbery, 1966; The Wildcats of St Trinian's, 1980. *Films designed:* John Gilpin, 1951; On the Twelfth Day, 1954 (Acad. Award Nomination); Energetically Yours (USA), 1957; Germany, 1960 (for Suddeutschen RTV); The King's Breakfast, 1962; Those Magnificent Men in their Flying Machines (Animation Sequence), 1965; Monte Carlo or Bust (Animation Sequence), 1969; Scrooge (Animation Sequence), 1970; Dick Deadeye, 1975. *Publications:* Forty Drawings, 1946; Le Nouveau Ballet Anglais, 1947; Hurrah for St Trinian's!, 1948; The Female Approach, 1949; Back to the Slaughterhouse, 1951; John Gilpin, 1952; Souls in Torment, 1953; Rake's Progress, 1955; Merry England, etc, 1956; A Christmas Carol, 1961; Which Way Did He Go, 1961; Searle in the Sixties, 1964; From Frozen North to Filthy Lucre, 1964; Pardong M'sieur, 1965; Searle's Cats, 1967; The Square Egg, 1968; Take one Toad, 1968; Baron Munchausen, 1960; Hello-where did all the people go?, 1969; Hommage à Toulouse-Lautrec, 1969; Secret Sketchbook, 1970; The Addict, 1971; More Cats, 1975; Drawings from Gilbert and Sullivan, 1975; The Zoodiac, 1977; Ronald Searle (Monograph), 1978; The King of Beasts, 1980; The Big Fat Cat Book, 1982; *in collaboration:* (with D. B. Wyndham Lewis) The Terror of St Trinian's, 1952; (with Geoffrey Willans) Down with Skool, 1953; How to be Topp, 1954; Whizz for Atomms, 1956; The Compleet Molesworth, 1958; The Dog's Ear Book, 1958; Back in the Jug Agane, 1959; (with Kaye Webb) Paris Sketchbook, 1950 and 1957; Looking at London, 1953; The St Trinian's Story, 1959; Refugees 1960, 1960; (with Alex Atkinson) The Big City, 1958; USA for Beginners, 1959; Russia for Beginners, 1960; Escape from the Amazon!, 1964; (with A. Andrews & B. Richardson) Those Magnificent Men in their Flying Machines, 1965; (with Heinz Huber) Haven't We Met Before Somewhere?, 1966; (with Kildare Dobbs) The Great Fur Opera, 1970; (with Irwin Shaw) Paris! Paris!, 1977. *Address:* c/o Tessa Sayle, 11 Jubilee Place, SW3 3TE. *T:* 01-352 4311. *Club:* Garrick.

SEARS, Raymond Arthur William, QC 1975; a Recorder of the Crown Court, since 1977; *b* 10 March 1933; *s of* William Arthur and Lillian Sears; *m* 1960, Adelaide Sadler (marr. diss. 1981); one *s* one *d.* *Educ:* Epsom Coll.; Jesus Coll., Cambridge. BA 1956. Called to Bar, Gray's Inn, 1957. *Recreations:* watching horse-racing; gardening. *Address:* 1 Chalk Paddock, Chalk Lane, Epsom, Surrey. *Club:* Royal Automobile.

SEATON, Colin Robert; Circuit Administrator, South Eastern Circuit, since 1982; Barrister-at-Law; *b* 21 Nov. 1928; 2nd *s of* late Arthur William Robert Seaton and of Helen Amelia Seaton (née Stone); *m* 1952, Betty (née Gosling); two *s.* *Educ:* Wallington County Grammar Sch. for Boys; Worcester Coll., Oxford. BA 1953; MA 1956. Royal Air Force, 1947–49. Called to Bar, Inner Temple, 1956 (Profumo Prize, 1953, 1954); Schoolmaster for LCC (now GLC), 1953–57; Solicitor's Dept, Ministries of Health and Housing and Local Govt, also Dept of the Environment, 1957–71; Sec. (Master) of Nat. Industrial Relations Court, 1971–74; Circuit Administrator, Northern Circuit (Under-Sec.), 1974–82. *Publication:* Aspects of the National Health Service Acts, 1966. *Recreations:* golf, reading. *Address:* Tree Tops, The Drive, Coulsdon, Surrey. *T:* 01-668 5538. *Club:* Civil Service.

See also M. J. Seaton.

SEATON, Prof. Michael John, FRS 1967; Professor of Physics, Department of Physics and Astronomy, University College London, since 1963; *b* 16 Jan. 1923; *s of* Arthur William Robert Seaton and Helen Amelia Seaton; *m* 1st, 1943, Olive May (*d* 1959), *d of* Charles Edward Singleton; one *s* one *d* ; 2nd, 1960, Joy Clarice, *d of* Harry Albert Balchin; one *s.* *Educ:* Wallington Co. Sch., Surrey; University Coll., London (Fellow, 1972). BSc 1948, PhD 1951, London. Dept of Physics, UCL: Asst Lectr, 1950; Lectr, 1953; Reader, 1959; Prof., 1963. Chargé de Recherche, Institut d'Astrophysique, Paris, 1954–55; Univ. of Colorado, 1961; Fellow-Adjoint, Jt Inst. for Laboratory Astrophysics (Nat. Bureau of Standards and Univ. of Colorado), Boulder, Colo, 1964–. Pres., RAS, 1979–81. Dr *hc*, Observatoire de Paris; Hon. DSc QUB, 1982. *Publications:* papers on atomic physics and astrophysics in various jls. *Address:* 51 Hall Drive, Sydenham, SE26 6XL. *T:* 01-778 7121.

See also C. R. Seaton.

SEAWARD, Colin Hugh; HM Diplomatic Service; Consul-General, Rio de Janeiro, since 1980; *b* 16 Sept. 1926; *s of* late Sydney W. Seaward and of Molly W. Seaward; *m* 1st, 1949, Jean Bugler (decd); three *s* one *d* ; 2nd, 1973, Judith Margaret Hinkley; two *d.* *Educ:* RNC, Dartmouth. Served Royal Navy, 1944–65. Joined HM Diplomatic Service, 1965; served: Accra, 1965; Bathurst (Banjul), 1966; FO, 1968; Rio de Janeiro, 1971; Prague, 1972; FCO, 1973; RNC, Greenwich (sowc), 1976; Counsellor (Econ. and Comm.), Islamabad, 1977–80. *Address:* c/o Foreign and Commonwealth Office, SW1A 2AH.

SEBAG-MONTEFIORE, Harold Henry; Barrister-at-law; Deputy Circuit Judge; *b* 5 Dec. 1924; *e s of* late John Sebag-Montefiore and Violet, *o c of* late James Henry Solomon; *m* 1968, Harriet, *o d of* Benjamin Harrison Paley, New York; one step *d.* *Educ:* Stowe; Lower Canada Coll., Montreal; Pembroke Coll., Cambridge (MA). Served War of 1939–45, RAF. Called to Bar, Lincoln's Inn, 1951. Contested (C) North Paddington, Gen. Elec., 1959; Chm., Conservative Party Candidates Assoc., 1960–64. Member: LCC, 1955–65; GLC, for Cities of London and Westminster, 1964–73, First Chm., Arts and Recreation Cttee, 1968–73; Sports Council, 1972–74. Pres., Anglo-Jewish Assoc., 1966–71. Freeman, City of London, and Liveryman, Spectacle Makers' Co. Trustee: Nat. Theatre Foundn; Internat. Festival of Youth Orchestras; Whitechapel Art Gall.; Mem., Cttee of Honour: RAH Centenary; "Fanfare for Britain", Montefiore Hosp. (NY) Centenary. Chevalier, Légion d'Honneur, 1973. *Publications:* book reviews and articles on Polo under *nom-de-plume* of "Marco II". *Address:* 7B Vicarage Gate, W8; 2 Paper Buildings, Temple, EC4. *T:* 01-353 5835. *Clubs:* Carlton, Hurlingham, Pegasus (Pres.), 1979).

SEBASTIAN, Rear-Admiral (Retired) Brian Leonard Geoffrey, CB 1948; *b* 7 Feb. 1891; *s of* late Lewis Boyd Sebastian, Barrister-at-Law, and late Harriet M. Lennartson, Karlstad, Sweden; *m* 1927, Cicely Grace, *e d of* Dr F. W. Andrew, Hendon; one *d.* *Educ:* Osborne, Dartmouth and Greenwich Colleges; RN Engineering College, Keyham. Joined RN Coll., Osborne, with first term of new scheme, 1903; various appts at sea as junior officer; qualified in Engineering, 1914. Served in various ships during European War; Comdr (E) 1925; various appointments till 1936; Capt. (E) 1937; Squadron EO Home Fleet, in charge of RN Aircraft Training establishment, Newcastle-under-Lyme, and RN Eng. Coll., Keyham; Rear-Adm. (E) 1944; Deputy Head of British Admiralty Technical Mission, Ottawa; Staffs of C-in-C Rosyth and Plymouth, 1948; retired, 1948. *Address:* Flat 3, Weyside, Farnham, Surrey GU9 7RH. *T:* Farnham 722705.

SEBRIGHT, Sir Hugo Giles Edmund, 14th Bt, *cr* 1626; *b* 2 March 1931; *s of* Lt-Col Sir Giles Edward Sebright, 13th Bt, CBE, and of Margery Hilda, *d of* late Admiral Sir Sydney Robert Fremantle, GCB, MVO; *S* father 1954; *m* 1st, 1952, Deirdre Ann (marr. diss. 1964), *d of* Major Vivian Lionel Slingsby Bethell, late Royal Artillery; one *s* ; 2nd, 1965, Mrs Sheila Mary Howard Hervey. *Heir:* *s* Peter Giles Vivian Sebright [*b* 2 Aug. 1953; *m* 1977, Regina Maria, *d of* Francis Steven Clarebrough, Melbourne; one *s*].

SECCOMBE, Hugh Digorie, CBE 1976; Chairman, Seccombe Marshall & Campion Ltd, 1962–77; *b* 3 June 1917; *s of* Lawrence Henry Seccombe, CBE and Norah (née Wood); *m* 1947, Eirene Rosemary Banister, *d of* Richard

Whittow and Eirene, and *widow* of Lieut P. C. McC. Banister, DSC, RN; one *s* one *d. Educ:* Stowe; Sidney Sussex Coll., Cambridge (BA 1938, MA 1942). RNVR, 1939-50; retd, Lt-Comdr. Joined Seccombe Marshall & Campion, 1938; Dir, 1947. Chm., YWCA Central Club, 1971-. Fellow, Inst. of Bankers, 1964. *Recreations:* gardening, fishing, shooting, hill-walking. *Address:* Sparkes Place, Wonersh, Guildford, Surrey GU5 0PH. *T:* Guildford 893296; Benmore Lodge, Isle of Mull, Argyllshire. *T:* Aros 351. *Club:* Army and Navy.

SECOMBE, Sir Harry (Donald), Kt 1981; CBE 1963; Actor, Comedian and Singer; *b* 8 Sept. 1921; *m* 1948, Myra Joan Atherton, Swansea; two *s* two *d. Educ:* Dynevor School, Swansea. Served with Royal Artillery, 1939-46. Windmill Theatre, 1947-48: General Variety since 1948. Appearances include: at London Palladium, 1956, 1958, 1959, 1961, 1966; in Roy. Command Perfs, 1955, 1957, 1958, 1963, 1966, 1969, 1975, 1978; (musical) Pickwick, Saville, 1963; (musical) The Four Musketeers, Drury Lane, 1967; The Plumber's Progress, Prince of Wales, 1975. Radio: Goon Show, 1949-60, and special performance of Goon Show for 50th Anniversary of BBC, 1972. Television: BBC, ITV, CBS (New York), Yorkshire TV, 1950-. Films: Davy, for Ealing Films, 1957; Jetstorm, 1959; Bed-Sitting Room, 1968; Mr Bumble in Oliver!, 1968; Bjornsen in Song of Norway, 1969; Rhubarb, 1969; Doctor in Trouble, 1970; The Magnificent Seven Deadly Sins, 1971; Sunstruck, 1972. Has made recordings for HMV, 1953-54, Philips Records, 1955-80, Celebrity Records, 1980-. FRSA 1971. *Publications:* Twice Brightly, 1974; Goon for Lunch, 1975; Katy and the Nurgla, 1978; Welsh Fargo, 1981. *Recreations:* film photography, literature, travel, golf, cricket. *Address:* 46 St James's Place, SW1. *T:* 01-629 2768. *Clubs:* Savage, Royal Automobile, Lord's Taverners, Variety Club of Great Britain.

SECONDÉ, Sir Reginald (Louis), KCMG 1981 (CMG 1972); CVO 1968 (MVO 1957); HM Diplomatic Service, retired; Ambassador to Venezuela, 1979-82; *b* 28 July 1922; *s* of late Lt-Col Emile Charles Secondé and Doreen Secondé (*née* Sutherland); *m* 1951, Catherine Penelope, *d* of late Thomas Ralph Sneyd-Kynnersley, OBE, MC and late Alice Sneyd-Kynnersley; one *s* two *d. Educ:* Beaumont; King's Coll., Cambridge. Served, 1941-47, in Coldstream Guards: N Africa and Italy (despatches); Major. Entered Diplomatic Service, 1949; UK Delegn to the UN, New York, 1951-55; British Embassy: Lisbon, 1955-57; Cambodia, 1957-59; FO, 1959-62; British Embassy, Warsaw, 1962-64; First Secretary and later Political Counsellor, Rio de Janeiro, 1964-69; Head of S European Dept, FCO, 1969-72; Royal Coll. of Defence Studies, 1972-73; Ambassador to Chile, 1973-76, to Romania, 1977-79. Comdr, Order of the Southern Cross (Brazil), 1968. *Recreations:* gardening, shooting. *Address:* Wamil Hall, near Mildenhall, Suffolk. *T:* Mildenhall 714160. *Club:* Cavalry and Guards.

SECRETAN, Lance H.; consultant and entrepeneur; University and business lecturer; Director, Manpower Ltd; President: Photographic Collections Inc.; North American Trilium Inc.; *b* 1 Aug. 1939; *s* of late Kenyon and Marie-Therese Secretan; *m* 1961, Gloria Christina; two *d* (and one *d* decd). *Educ:* Los Cocos, Argentina; Italia Conti, London; St Peters, Bournemouth; Univ. of Waterloo, Canada; Univ. of Southern California (MA in International Relations, *cum laude*); Doctoral cand., LSE. Toronto Stock Exchange, 1958-59; Office Overload Co. Ltd, 1959-67; Man. Dir, Manpower Ltd Gp of Cos, UK, Ireland, Middle East and Africa, 1967-81. FRSA 1981. *Publication:* How to be an Effective Secretary, 1972. *Recreations:* skiing, cycling, walking, playing guitar, writing poetry, interesting people. *Address:* PO Box 277, RR2, Caledon East, Ontario L0N 1E0, Canada; 25a Bryanston Square, W1H 7FI. *Clubs:* White Elephant; University (Toronto).

SEDDON, Dr John; Aeronautical Consultant; *b* 29 Sept. 1915; *m* 1940, Barbara Mary Mackintosh; one *s* two *d. Educ:* Leeds Modern Sch.; Univ. of Leeds. BSc 1937, PhD 1939; DSc Bristol, 1982. Scientific Officer, RAE, Farnborough, 1939-55; Harkness Fund Fellow, California Inst. of Technology, 1955-56; Head of Experimental Supersonics, RAE, Farnborough, 1957-59; Supt, Tunnels II Div., RAE, Bedford, 1959-66; Dir, Scientific Research (Air), Min. of Technology, 1966-68; Dir-Gen. Research, Aircraft, MoD, 1969-75. Res. Fellow and Consultant, Univ. of Bristol, 1976-82. *Publications:* papers on air intakes and other aerodynamic subjects, in ARC Reports and Memoranda Series and other scientific media. *Recreations:* music, golf. *Address:* 7 Vicarage Hill, The Bourne, Farnham, Surrey. *T:* Farnham 723680.

SEDDON, Richard Harding, PhD; RWS, ARCA; artist and writer; *b* 1 May 1915; *s* of Cyril Harding Seddon; *m* 1946, Audrey Madeline Wareham. *Educ:* King Edward VII School; Roy. Coll. of Art; Univ. of Reading (PhD 1946). Demonstrator in Fine Art, Univ. of Reading, 1941; Extra-Mural Staff Tutor in Fine Art, Univ. of Birmingham, 1947; Director, Sheffield City Art Galleries, 1948-63; Curator, Ruskin Collection, 1948-63; Dir of Art History and Liberal Studies, Sch. of Design and Furniture, Buckinghamshire Coll. of Higher Educn, 1963-80. Hon. Advisory Panel, Hereford Art Galls, 1948; Arts Council Selection Bd (Art Students Exhib.), 1947; Pres. Ludlow Art Soc, 1947-67; Hon. Member: Sheffield Soc. of Artists; Oxford Folk Art Soc.; Sheffield Photographic Soc.; Mem., Oxford Bureau for Artists in War-time, 1940; Chm. Selection Cttee, Nottingham Artists Exhibition, 1953; Guest Speaker Educational Centres Association Annual Conference, 1951; West Riding Artists Exhibition Selection Committee, 1956; Northern Young Artists Exhibition Selection Committee, 1958; Member Sheffield Univ. Court; Sheffield Diocesan Advisory Cttee, 1948. Exhibitor at: RA; NEAC;

RI; RBA; Internat. Artists; Architectural Assoc.; RIBA; National Gallery (War Artists) 1943; Leicester Galleries; Redfern Galleries. Official acquisitions: V. & A. Museum, 1939; Pilgrim Trust, 1942; Imperial War Museum (War Artists), 1943, 1956 (ten paintings); Graves Gall., Sheffield, 1943 and 1956; Atkinson Gall., Southport, 1953; Reading Art Gall., 1956; Leeds Education Cttee Collection, 1956. Extra Mural and Univ. Extension lectr on art to Univs of Oxford, Birmingham, London and Sheffield, 1948-; initiated Sheffield Conference on Nation's Art Treasures, 1958; FMA, 1951-74; Mem. Yorkshire Fed. Museums and Art Galls, 1948 (Committee 1952 and 1957, President, 1954-55, Vice-President, 1955-56); Secretary Yorks Museums Regional Fact Finding Committee, 1959; National Art Collections Fund Rep. for Yorks, 1954-63; Hon. Adviser to Co. of Cutlers in Hallamshire, 1950-64; Dep. Chm., Sheffield Design Council for Gold, Silver and Jewelry Trades, 1960; Mem. BBC '51 Soc., 1960; Mem. Govg Council, Design and Res. Centre, 1960; Mem. Art Adv. Cttee Yorks Area Scheme for Museums and Art Galleries, 1963; Art Critic: Birmingham Post, 1963-71; Yorkshire Post, 1974-; Jl Fedn of British Artists, 1975-; Mem. Recognised Panel of London Univ. Extension Lectrs, 1964; ARWS, 1972, Mem. Council and Hon. Treasurer, 1976; RWS 1976; Hon. Mem., Mark Twain Soc., USA, 1976. War Service with RAOC Field Park, France, 1940 (King's Badge); facilities by War Office Order to make war drawings in Maginot Line, 1940. *Publications:* The Technical Methods of Paul Nash (Memorial Vol.), 1949; The Artist's Vision, 1949; The Academic Technique of Oil Painting, 1960; A Hand Uplifted (war memoirs), 1962; Art Collecting for Amateurs, 1964; (ed) Dictionary of Art Terms, 1981; Articles on fine art for Jl of Aesthetics (USA), Burlington Magazine, Apollo, The Studio, The Connoisseur, Arch. Review, The Artist, The Antique Collector and daily press; lectures on art in England and abroad; criticisms; book reviews; broadcasts. *Recreation:* gardening. *Address:* 6 Arlesey Close, Putney, SW15 2EX. *T:* 01-788 5899.

SEDGEMORE, Brian Charles John; barrister-at-law; Researcher, Granada Television, since 1980; *b* 17 March 1937; *s* of Charles John Sedgemore, fisherman; *m* 1964, Mary Audrey Reece; one *s. Educ:* Newtown Primary Sch.; Heles Sch.; Oxford Univ. (MA). Diploma in public and social administration. Called to Bar, Middle Temple, 1966. RAF, 1956-58; Oxford, 1958-62. Administrative Class, Civil Service, Min. of Housing and Local Govt, 1962-66 (Private Sec. to R. J. Mellish, MP, then Junior Minister of Housing, 1964-66). Practising barrister, 1966-74. MP (Lab) Luton West, Feb. 1974-1979; PPS to Tony Benn, MP, 1977-78. Prospective Parly Cand. (Lab) Hackney S and Shoreditch, 1982-. *Publications:* The How and Why of Socialism, 1977; Mr Secretary of State (fiction), 1979; The Secret Constitution, 1980; contributor to Tribune, one time contributor to Britain's top satirical magazine. *Recreation:* sleeping on the grass. *Address:* 28 Studley Road, Luton. *T:* Luton 23512; Flat 57, Belvedere Court, Upper Richmond Road, Putney, SW15. *T:* 01-789 1680.

SEDGMAN, Francis Arthur; Lawn Tennis Champion: Australia, 1949, 1950; America, 1951, 1952; Wimbledon, 1952; Professional Tennis Player since 1953; Proprietor, Sedgman's Squash Centre; Director: Flex-Straw (A/Asia) Pty Ltd; Princes Port Pty Ltd; Peninsula Squash Courts Pty Ltd; Highmont Hotel Pty Ltd; Tennis Camps of Australia Pty Ltd; *b* Victoria, Australia, 29 Oct. 1927; *m* 1952, Jean Margaret Spence; four *d. Educ:* Box Hill High School, Vic, Australia. First played in the Australian Davis Cup team, 1949. With Kenneth McGregor, won the Australian, French, English and American doubles titles in the same year (1951), the only pair ever to do so. *Publication:* Winning Tennis, 1955. *Recreation:* golfing. *Address:* 28 Bolton Avenue, Hampton, Victoria 3188, Australia. *T:* 98 6341. *Clubs:* All England Tennis and Croquet; Melbourne Cricket (Melbourne); Kooyong Tennis; Grace Park Tennis; Victoria Amateur Turf, Victoria Racing; Southport Yacht; Woodlands Golf.

SEDGWICK, Mrs A. R. M.; *see* Milkina, Nina.

SEDGWICK, Patrick Cardinall Mason, CMG 1965; *b* 8 March 1911; 2nd *s* of late William Francis Mason Sedgwick, Goudhurst, Kent; *m* 1943, Beth Mannering, Thompson, *e d* of late Frederick Mannering Thompson, St Kilda, Victoria, Australia; three *s* one *d. Educ:* St Lawrence Coll., Ramsgate; Brasenose Coll., Oxford (BA Hons); Queens' College, Cambridge. Colonial Admin. Service: Cadet Officer, Hong Kong, 1935; seconded Malayan Civil Service, Dec. 1941-Feb. 1942; Attaché, British Embassy, Chungking, 1942-43; Hong Kong Planning Unit, CO, London, 1944-45; various Govt Posts in Hong Kong, including Principal Assistant Colonial Secretary, Estabt Officer, Chm. Urban Council, and Dir of Commerce and Industry; Comr of Labour and Mines, 1955-65; MEC and MLC, of Hong Kong up to June 1965; Dir, Hong Kong Govt Office, London, 1965-69; Salaries Commissioner: St Helena, 1971; Falkland Islands and Mauritius, 1972. *Recreations:* sailing, gardening. *Address:* Ringden Wood, Flimwell, Sussex. *T:* Flimwell 431. *Clubs:* Bewl Valley Sailing; Hong Kong, Royal Hong Kong Yacht (Hong Kong).

SEDOV, Leonid I.; 5 Orders of Lenin, Hero of Socialist Labour, USSR; Professor, Moscow University, since 1937; Chief of Department of Hydrodynamics, since 1941; Member, USSR Academy of Sciences; *b* 14 Nov. 1907; *m* 1931, Galya Tolstova; one *s* one *d. Educ:* Moscow University. Chief Engineer, Associate Chief lab., N.E. Zhukovsky Aerohydrodynamic Inst., Moscow, 1930-47; Vice-President, International Astronautical Federation, 1962-80 (Pres., 1959-61); Internat. Astronautical Acad., 1980-. Hon. Member: American Academy of Arts and Sciences; Internat. Astronautical Acad.;

Serbian Academy, Belgrade; Tech. Academy, Finland; For. Associate, Acad. of Sciences, Paris; Academia Leopoldina. Hon. doctorates from many foreign universities. Medal of Obert; State Prize; Chaplygin Prize; Lomonosov Prize; Lyapunov Medal; Guggenheim Award; Van Allen Award. Commandeur de la Légion d'Honneur (France). *Publications:* Theory of Plane Flow of Liquids, 1939; Plane Problems of Hydrodynamics and Aerodynamics, 1950, 1966; Similarity and Dimensional Methods in Mechanics, 1944, 1951, 1953, 1957, 1960, 1965, 1967, 1977; Introduction into the Mechanics of Continua, 1962; Mechanics of Continuous Media, 2 vols, 1970, 1973, 1976; Thoughts about Science and Scientists, 1980; numerous articles. *Address:* Moscow University, Zone U, kv 84 Leninskie Gory, Moscow B-234, USSR.

SEEAR, family name of **Baroness Seear.**

SEEAR, Baroness *cr* 1971 (Life Peer), of Paddington; **Beatrice Nancy Seear;** formerly Reader in Personnel Management, University of London, The London School of Economics, retired 1978, Hon. Fellow, 1980; Visiting Professor of Personnel Management, The City University; *b* 7 Aug. 1913; *d* of late Herbert Charles Seear and Beatrice Maud Catchpole. *Educ:* Croydon High Sch.; Newnham Coll., Cambridge; London Sch. of Economics and Political Science. BA (Cambridge Hist. Tripos). Personnel Officer, C. & J. Clark Ltd, shoe manufacturers, 1936-46; seconded as Mem. (pt-time), staff of Production Efficiency Bd at Min. of Aircraft Production, 1943-45; Teacher at London School of Economics, 1946-78. Member: Hansard Soc. Commn on Electoral Reform, 1975-76; Top Salaries Review Body, 1971-. Chairman: Nat. Council for the Single Woman and her Dependents; Council, Morley Coll. President: BSI, 1974-77; Women's Liberal Fedn, 1974; Fawcett Soc.; Inst. of Personnel Management, 1977-79. Mem. Council, Industrial Soc. Hon. LLD Leeds, 1979. *Publications:* (with P. Jephcott and J. H. Smith) Married Women Working, 1962; (with V. Roberts and J. Brock) A Career for Women in Industry?, 1964; Industrial Social Services, 1964; The Position of Women in Industry, 1967; The Re-Entry of Women into Employment, 1971. *Recreations:* travel, gardening. *Address:* The Garden Flat, 44 Blomfield Road, W9. *T:* 01-286 5701. *Club:* Royal Commonwealth Society.

SEEBOHM, family name of **Baron Seebohm.**

SEEBOHM, Baron *cr* 1972 (Life Peer), of Hertford; **Frederic Seebohm,** Kt 1970; TD; psc; Lt-Col (Retd); *b* 18 Jan. 1909; *s* of late H. E. Seebohm, Poynders End, Hitchin, Herts; *m* 1932, Evangeline, *d* of late Sir Gerald Hurst, QC; one *s* two *d. Educ:* Leighton Park School; Trinity Coll., Cambridge. Joined Staff of Barclays Bank Ltd, 1929; Director: Barclays Bank Ltd, 1947-79 (Dep. Chm., 1968-74); Barclays Bank International Ltd, 1951-79 (formerly Barclays Bank DCO) (Vice-Chm., 1955-59, Dep. Chm., 1959-65, Chm., 1965-72; Vice-Chm., Barclays Bank SA, 1968-73); Friends' Provident Life Office, 1952-79 (Chm., 1962-68); ICFC, 1969-80 (Chm., 1974-79); Finance for Industry Ltd, 1974-80 (Chm., 1974-79); Finance Corp. for Industry Ltd, 1974-80 (Chm., 1974-79). Chairman: Joseph Rowntree Memorial Trust, 1966-81; London House, Seebohm Cttee on Local Authority and Allied Personal Social Services, 1965-68; Export Guarantees Adv. Council, 1967-72; President: Age Concern; Nat. Inst. for Social Work; Royal African Soc. Mem., Overseas Develt Inst. (Chm., 1972-77). Governor: London School of Economics; Haileybury Imperial Service Coll., 1970; Fellow, Inst. of Bankers (Pres., 1966-68). Served with Royal Artillery, 1939-45 (despatches). High Sheriff, Herts, 1970-71. Hon. LLD Nottingham, 1970; Hon. DSc Aston, 1976. Bronze Star of America, 1945. *Recreations:* gardening, painting. *Address:* 28 Marsham Court, Marsham Street, SW1. *T:* 01-828 2168; Brook House, Dedham, Colchester, Essex. *T:* Colchester 3372. *Clubs:* Carlton, Royal Commonwealth Society; Hurlingham.

SEEFRIED, Irmgard Maria Theresia; Austrian opera and concert singer; Kammersängerin at Vienna State Opera since 1943; *b* Koengetried, Bavaria; *m* 1948, Wolfgang Schneiderhan; two *d. Educ:* Augsburg Conservatory, Germany. First engagement under von Karajan, at Aachen, Germany, 1940. Concert tours all over the world; appeared: Metropolitan Opera, New York; Covent Garden, London; La Scala, Milan; also festivals at Salzburg, Lucerne, Edinburgh, San Francisco. Honorary Member: Boston Symphony Orch.; Vienna Philharmonic Orch. Hon. Mem., Austrian-German Culture Soc., 1980. Recipient various Mozart Medals; Lilly-Lehmann Medal; Golden Cross of merit for Culture and Science; Decoration of Chevalier I, Denmark; Grosses Verdienstkreuz des Verdienstordens der Bundesrepublik Deutschland, 1968; Schubert Medal; Hugo Wolf Medal; Culture Prize, Luxemburg; Culture Prize, Donauwörth, Germany, 1979; Gold Medal of Honour, Vienna, 1979; Werner Egg Prize, 1979; Silver Decoration of merit, Austria, 1979; Gold Burgher Medal, Bad Wörishofen, 1980. *Publications:* articles on Mozart, Bartók, Hindemith, Hugo Wolf. *Address:* Vienna State Opera, Austria.

SEELY, family name of **Baron Mottistone.**

SEELY, Sir Nigel (Edward), 5th Bt *cr* 1896; Chief Executive, Dancer Fitzgerald Sample International; *b* 28 July 1923; *s* of Sir Victor Basil John Seely, 4th Bt and of Sybil Helen, *d* of late Sills Clifford Gibbons; *S* father, 1980; *m* 1949, Loraine, *d* of late W. W. Lindley-Travis; three *d. Educ:* Stowe. *Heir: half-b* Victor Ronald Seely [*b* 1 Aug. 1941; *m* 1972, Annette Bruce, *d* of Lt-Col J. A. D. McEwen]. *Address:* The Colonnades, 34 Porchester Square, W2. *Clubs:* Buck's; Royal Solent.

SEENEY, Leslie Elon Sidney, OBE 1978; Director General (formerly General Secretary), National Chamber of Trade, since 1971; *b* 19 Jan. 1922; *s* of Sidney Leonard and Daisy Seeney, Forest Hill; *m* 1947, Marjory Doreen Greenwood, Spalding; one *s. Educ:* St Matthews, Camberwell. RAFVR, 1941-46 (Flt Lt, Pilot). Man. Dir, family manufrg business (clothing), 1946-63, with other interests in insce and advertising. Mem., West Lewisham Chamber of Commerce, 1951, subseq. Sec. and Chm.; Delegate to Nat. Chamber of Trade, 1960; joined NCT staff, 1966. *Publications:* various articles. *Recreations:* reading, writing, travel, photography. *Address:* 16 Barn Close, Southcote, Reading, Berks. *T:* Reading 55478.

SEENEY, Noel Conway; Commissioner of Stamp Duties, Queensland, since 1975; *b* 7 April 1926; *s* of Percy Matthew Mark Seeney and Wilhelmina Augusta Zanow; *m* 1949, Valrae Muriel Uhlmann; two *d. Educ:* Teachers' Coll., Brisbane; Univ. of Queensland (BCom). Assoc. Accountancy, Assoc. Coll. of Preceptors, London. Teacher, 1944; Dep. Principal, Secondary Sch., 1960; Principal 1964; Official Sec., Office of Agent-General for Qld in London, 1969; Agent-General for Qld in London, 1973. *Recreations:* golf, tennis. *Address:* 2nd Floor, State Government Building, Anzac Square, 202 Adelaide Street, Brisbane, Qld 4000, Australia. *T:* Brisbane 229-4143. *Clubs:* Tattersall's (Brisbane); Indooroopilly Golf.

SEERS, Dudley, CMG 1975; Fellow, Institute of Development Studies, University of Sussex, since 1972 (Director, 1967-72, Director MPhil course, 1975-77); *b* 11 April 1920; *s* of late George Clarence Seers and of Mabel Edith Seers (*née* Hallett); *m* 1943, Patricia Hindell; one *s* three *d. Educ:* Rugby Sch.; Pembroke Coll., Cambridge. Served Royal Navy, 1941-45. PM's Office, New Zealand Govt, 1945-46; Res. Off. (later Lectr and Sen. Lectr in Economic Statistics) Oxford Univ., 1946-53 and 1954-55; Mem. Min. of Health Cttee on Housebuilding Costs, 1949-50; Economist, UN Headqrs, 1953-54; Statistical Adviser to Barbados, Leeward and Windward Isles, 1955-57; Chief, Survey Section, UN Econ. Commn for Latin America, 1957-61; Vis. Prof., Yale Univ., 1961-63; Dir, Economic Develt Div., UN Econ. Commn for Africa, 1963-64; Leader, UN Economic Mission to Zambia, 1964; Director-General, Economic Planning Staff, Ministry of Overseas Development, 1964-67. Also consultant for Govts of Burma, Fiji, Ghana, Jamaica, Kenya, Malaysia, Malta, Portugal, Sri Lanka, Trinidad, Uganda, for World Bank, ILO, OECD, and UN. Member: Editorial Bd, Jl of Develt Studies; World Development; SSRC panel on N Sea Oil, 1975; OECD team on Japan's social science policy, 1975; Council, Royal Econ. Soc., 1975-78; Chm., WUS Chile Awards Cttee, 1974-78; Pres., European Assoc. of Develt Insts, 1975-78. Leader: ILO Missions to Colombia, 1970, Sri Lanka, 1971, 1978, Nigeria, 1979; Commonwealth Team on Rehabilitation of Uganda, 1979. Order of Boyacá, Colombia, 1970. *Publications:* (ed) Cuba: The Economic and Social Revolution, 1964; (ed) Development in a Divided World, 1971; (ed) Crisis in Planning, 1972; (ed) Underdeveloped Europe: Studies in Core-Periphery Relations, 1979; (ed) European Studies in Development, 1979; (ed) Integration and Unequal Development: the Experience of Western Europe, 1980; Dependency Theory: a critical re-assessment, 1981; (ed) The Second Enlargement of the EEC: Integration of Unequal Partners, 1982; (ed) The Crisis of the European Regions, 1982; contribs to: The Theory and Design of Economic Development (ed Adelman and Thorbecke), 1966; The Teaching of Development Economics (ed Martin and Knapp), 1967; Crisis in the Civil Service (ed Thomas), 1968; Africa and the World, 1969; Unfashionable Economics: Essays in Honour of Lord Balogh (ed Streeten), 1970; The Labour Government's Economic Record (ed Beckerman), 1972; Redistribution with Growth (ed Chenery), 1974; Employment, Income Distribution and Development Strategy: Essays in Honour of Hans Singer (ed Cairncross), 1975; Population and its Problems (ed Parry), 1976; Statistical Needs for Development, 1977; North Sea Oil: The Application of Development Theories, 1977; Transnational Capitalism and National Development, 1979; Development and Change—special issue in honour of Kurt Martin, 1979; The Relevance of Economic Theories to Present-Day Society (ed Feinstein), 1980; Econ. Jl; Oxford Econ. Papers; Social and Econ. Studies; Jl of Development Studies; Bulletin of IDS. *Recreations:* skiing, teasing bureaucrats. *Address:* Broadacres Farm, Chiddingly, near Lewes, East Sussex. *T:* Chiddingly 617, (office) Brighton 606261.

SEFTON, family name of **Baron Sefton of Garston.**

SEFTON OF GARSTON, Baron *cr* 1978 (Life Peer), of Garston in the County of Merseyside; **William Henry Sefton;** Chairman, North West Economic Planning Council, since 1975; Vice-Chairman, Warrington and Runcorn Development Corporation, since 1981 (Chairman, Runcorn Development Corporation, 1974-81); *b* 5 Aug. 1915; *s* of George and Emma Sefton; *m* 1940, Phyllis Kerr. *Educ:* Duncombe Road Sch., Liverpool. Joined Liverpool CC, 1953, Leader 1964; Chm. and Leader, Merseyside CC, 1974-77, Opposition Leader, 1977-79. Joined Runcorn Develt Corp., 1964, Dep. Chm. 1967. Member: New Towns Commn, 1978-; SSRC, 1978-. *Recreations:* gardening, woodwork. *Address:* House of Lords, SW1.

SEGAL, family name of **Baron Segal.**

SEGAL, Baron *cr* 1964, of Wytham (Life Peer); **Samuel Segal,** MRCS, LRCP; MA Oxon; Deputy Speaker, and Deputy Chairman of Committees, House of Lords, since 1973; *b* 2 April 1902; *e s* of late Professor M. H. Segal, MA; *m* 1934, Molly, *o d* of Robert J. Rolo, OBE, Alexandria, Egypt; two *d* (one *s* decd). *Educ:* Royal Grammar Sch., Newcastle upon Tyne (Scholar);

Jesus Coll., Oxford (Exhibitioner); Westminster Hosp. (Scholar). Casualty Surgeon and HP Westminster Hospital; Senior Clinical Assistant, Great Ormond Street Children's Hospital. Served on various LCC Hospital Committees. Contested (Lab) Tynemouth, 1935, Aston (Birmingham) By-Election, May 1939. Joined RAFVR Medical Branch, Oct. 1939; served in Aden 1940, Western Desert 1941, Syrian Campaign 1941; attached Greek Air Force, 1941; Squadron Leader, 1942; Sen. Med. Officer RAF Naval Co-operation Group in Mediterranean, 1942; on Headquarters Staff Middle East, 1943-44; on Air Min. Med. Staff, 1944-45; travelled extensively on RAF Medical duties throughout North and East Africa, Iraq, Persian Gulf, India, etc.; Regional MO, Min. of Health, 1951-62. MP (Lab) for Preston, 1945-50; Member Parly Delegations: to Austria, 1946; to Nigeria, Cameroons, Gold Coast, Sierra Leone and Gambia, 1947; to Egypt, 1947; Hungary, 1965; Cyprus, 1965; Bahrain, Aden, 1966; Malawi, 1966 (Leader); Hong Kong, Singapore and S Vietnam, 1968; Caribbean, 1974 (Leader); UK delegate, Inter-Parly Union Conf., Tokyo 1974, London 1975. Mem. FO Mission to Persia, 1947. Chairman: British Assoc. for the Retarded; Council, Anglo-Israel Assoc., 1968-80; Dolphin Square Tenants Assoc., 1973-77; Oxford Soc. in London, 1976-; Anglo-Israel Archaeological Assoc., 1976-; Jesus Coll. Assoc., London Branch, 1976-80; London Old Novocastrian Assoc., 1981-82; Hon. Treasurer: Anglo-Iranian Parly Gp, 1970-; Nat. Soc. for Mentally Handicapped Children, 1978- (Chm., 1965-78); Member: Home Office Adv. Cttee on Service Parly Candidates; Council, Oxford Society; President: NI Region, Nat. Soc. for Mentally Handicapped Children, 1977-; Oxford-Paddington Passenger Assoc.; The Haven Foundn; Trustee, Celebrities' Guild of GB, 1980-; Vice-Pres., Music Therapy Charity Ltd; Patron, Oxford Diocesan Assoc. for the Deaf. Life Governor, Manchester Coll., Oxford, Visitor 1972-; Governor, Carmel Coll. Hon. Fellow, Jesus College, Oxford, 1966. *Recreation:* getting lost. *Address:* 2 Park Town, Oxford OX2 6TB. *T:* Oxford 513322; 208 Frobisher House, Dolphin Square, SW1V 3LL. *T:* 01-828 7172.

SEGAL, Graeme Bryce, DPhil; FRS 1982; Reader in Mathematics, Oxford University, since 1978; Fellow of St Catherine's College, since 1966; *b* 21 Dec. 1941; *s* of Reuben Segal and Iza Joan Harris; *m* 1962, Desley Rae Cheetham (marr. diss. 1972). *Educ:* Sydney Grammar School; Univ. of Sydney (BSc 1962); Univ. of Cambridge; Univ. of Oxford (MA, DPhil 1967). Junior Res. Fellow, Worcester Coll., Oxford, 1964-66; Junior Lectr in Mathematics, Oxford Univ., 1965-66. Mem., Inst. for Advanced Study, Princeton, 1969-70. Editor, Topology, 1970-. *Publications:* articles in learned jls. *Address:* 2 Abberbury Road, Iffley, Oxford. *T:* Oxford 777027.

SEGAL, Prof. Judah Benzion, MC 1942; FBA 1968; Professor of Semitic Languages in the University of London, School of Oriental and African Studies, 1961-79; now Emeritus; *b* 21 June 1912; *s* of Prof. Moses H. Segal and Hannah Leah Segal; *m* 1946, Leah (*née* Seidemann); two *d*. *Educ:* Magdalen College School, Oxford; St Catharine's College, Cambridge. Jarrett Schol., 1932; John Stewart of Rannoch Schol., in Hebrew, 1933; 1st Cl. Oriental Langs Tripos, 1935; Tyrwhitt Schol. and Mason Prizeman, 1936; BA (Cambridge), 1935; MA 1938. Colours, Cambridge Univ. Boxing Club, 1935, 1936. Mansel Research Exhibitioner, St John's Coll., Oxford, 1936-39; James Mew Schol., 1937; DPhil (Oxon.), 1939. Deputy Assistant Director, Public Security, Sudan Government, 1939-41; served War of 1939-45, GHQ, MEF, 1942-44, Captain; Education Officer, British Military Administration, Tripolitania, 1945-46. Head of Dept of Near and Middle East, Sch. of Oriental and African Studies, 1961-68; Visiting Lectr, Ain Shams Univ., Cairo, 1979; Res. Fellow, Hebrew Univ., Jerusalem, 1980; Leverhulme Emeritus Fellowship, S India, 1981; Principal, Leo Baeck Coll., 1982-; Dir, Jewish Chronicle Trust. Mem., Council of Christians and Jews; President: North Western Reform Synagogue; British Assoc. for Jewish Studies, 1980. Freedom, City of Urfa, Turkey, 1973. *Publications:* The Diacritical Point and the Accents in Syriac, 1953; The Hebrew Passover, 1963; Edessa, 1970; Aramaic Texts From North Saqqara, 1982; articles in learned periodicals. *Recreations:* walking, meditation. *Address:* 17 Hillersdon Avenue, Edgware, Mddx. *T:* 01-958 4993.

SEGOVIA, Andrés; Marquis of Salobreña, 1981; Spanish concert-guitarist; *b* Spain 18 Feb. 1894; *m* 1962, Emilia; one *s* (and one *s* one *d* by former marr.). Brought up in Granada; has been playing the guitar since the age of ten; first came to England as a young man; has often returned on concert tours since 1952; has had many pupils and has taught at Santiago de Compostela and Academy Chigi, Siena, and other schools; has adapted works of Bach, Haydn, Mozart and other classical composers for the guitar; has had many works composed especially for him by Casella, Castelnuovo-Tedesco, De Falla, Ponce, Roussel, Tansman, Turina, Villa-Lobos and others. Mem., Spanish Royal Acad. of Fine Arts, 1978. Hon. DMus Oxon, 1972. Gold Medal for Meritorious Work (Spain), 1967. *Publications:* Segovia: an autobiography of the years 1893-1920, 1920, 1977; (with George Mendoza) Segovia: My Book of the Guitar, 1979. *Address:* c/o Ibbs & Tillett, 450-452 Edgware Road, W2 1EG.

SEGRE, Prof. Emilio; Grande Ufficiale, Merito della Repubblica (Italy); Professor of Physics, University of California, Berkeley, 1946-72, now Emeritus; *b* 1 Feb. 1905; *s* of Giuseppe Segrè and Amelia Treves-Segrè; *m* 1936, Elfriede Spiro (*d* 1970); one *s* two *d*; *m* 1972, Rosa Mines Segrè. *Educ:* University of Rome, Italy. Asst Prof. of Physics, Rome, 1929-35; Dir, Physics Inst., Univ. of Palermo, Italy, 1936-38; Research Associate and Lectr, Univ. of Calif., Berkeley, 1938-42; Group Leader, Los Alamos Scientific Lab.,

1942-46. Hon. Prof. S Marcos Univ., Lima, 1954; Prof. of Nuclear Physics, Univ. of Rome, 1974-75. Hon. DSc Palermo, 1958; Hon. Dr Tel Aviv Univ. Nobel laureate (joint) for physics, 1959. Member: Nat. Acad. Sciences, USA, 1952; Accad. Nazionale Lincei, Roma, 1959; Heidelberg Akad. der Wissenschaften; Amer. Phil. Soc.; Amer. Acad. of Arts and Sciences; Indian Acad. of Sciences. *Publications:* Nuclei and Particles, 1964, new edn 1977; Enrico Fermi, Physicist, 1970; contrib. to Physical Review, Proc. Roy. Soc. London, Nature, Nuovo Cimento. *Recreations:* mountaineering and fishing. *Address:* 3802 Quail Ridge Road, Lafayette, Calif 94549, USA; Department of Physics, University of California, Berkeley, Calif 94720. *Club:* University of California Faculty (Berkeley).

SEIFERT, Robin (also known as **Richard**); JP; FRIBA; Principal R. Seifert and Partners, Architects, since 1934; *b* 25 Nov. 1910; *s* of William Seifert; *m* 1939, Josephine Jeanette Harding; two *s* one *d*. *Educ:* Central Foundation Sch., City of London; University College, London (DipArch), Fellow, 1971. Commenced architectural practice, 1934. Corps of Royal Engineers, 1940-44; Indian Army, 1944-46; Hon. Lt-Col, 1946; Certif. for Meritorious Services Home Forces, 1943. Returned to private practice, 1948. Designed: ICI Laboratories, Dyestuffs Div., Blackley, Manchester; The Times Newspapers building, Printing House Square; Centre Point, St Giles Circus; Drapers Gardens, Nat. West. Bank Tower, City; The Royal Garden Hotel, Kensington; Tolworth Towers, Surbiton; Guiness Mahon Bank, Gracechurch Street; HQ of ICT, Putney; Kellogg House, Baker Street; Dunlop House, King Street, St James's; BSC Res. Labs, Middlesbrough; Britannia Hotel; Park Tower Hotel; London Heathrow Hotel; Sobell Sports Centre; ATV Centre, Birmingham; International Press Centre; Metropolitan Police HQ, Putney; Wembley Conference Centre; Princess Grace Hospital, Marylebone Road; Princess Grace Hospital, Windsor; The Pirate Castle, Camden; British Rail HQ Offices, Euston Station. Member: MoT Road Safety Council, 1969 (now disbanded); Home Office Cttee of Management, Housing Assoc. for Discharged Offenders; (part-time) British Waterways Bd, 1971-74; Council, RIBA, 1971-74. FRSA 1976. Liveryman, Glaziers' Co. City of London. JP Barnet, 1969. *Recreations:* chess, violin. *Address:* Eleventrees, Milespit Hill, Mill Hill, NW7. *T:* 01-959 3397. *Clubs:* Army and Navy, City Livery, Arts.

SEIGNORET, Eustace Edward; High Commissioner for Trinidad and Tobago in London, since 1977; *b* 16 Feb. 1925; *m* ; two *s* one *d*. *Educ:* Howard Univ., Washington; Univ. of Wales, Bangor. BSc. Agricultural Officer, Dept of Agriculture, Trinidad and Tobago, 1953-58; West Indies Fedn Public Service, 1958-62; Asst Sec., Trinidad and Tobago Public Service, 1962; First Sec., 1962-65, Counsellor, 1965-68, Trinidad and Tobago Perm. Mission to UN; Dep. High Comr in London, 1969-71; Perm. Rep. to UN, 1971-75. *Address:* Trinidad and Tobago High Commission, 42 Belgrave Square, SW1X 8NT. *T:* 01-245 9351.

SEKYI, Henry Van Hien; Permanent Representative of Ghana to the United Nations, 1979-80; *b* 15 Jan. 1928; *s* of W. E. G. Sekyi, MA London, BL, and Lily Anna Sekyi (*née* Cleland); *m* 1958, Maria Joyce Sekyi (*née* Tachie-Menson); one *s* one *d*. *Educ:* Adisadel Coll., Cape Coast; Univ. of Ghana; King's Coll., Cambridge; LSE. BA London 1953; BA Cantab 1955. Third Sec., Second Sec., and First Sec., in succession, Ghana Embassy, Washington, DC, USA, 1958-61; First Sec., later Counsellor, Ghana Embassy, Rome, 1961-62; Director, Min. Foreign Affairs, 1962-65, in charge of Divisions of: Eastern Europe and China; Middle East and Asia; UN Affairs; Personnel and Administration; Acting Principal Sec., Min. of Foreign Affairs, 1965-66; Ghana High Comr to Australia, 1966-70; Ghana Ambassador to Italy, 1970-72; High Comr in UK, 1972-75; Supervising Dir, Political Dept, Min. of Foreign Affairs, Ghana, 1975-76, Senior Principal Secretary 1976-79. *Recreations:* classics, music, Africana and gymnastics. *Address:* c/o Ministry of Foreign Affairs, Accra, Ghana.

SELBORNE, 4th Earl of, *cr* 1882; **John Roundell Palmer;** DL; Baron Selborne, 1872; Viscount Wolmer, 1882; Treasurer, Bridewell Royal Hospital (King Edward's School, Witley), since 1972; *b* 24 March 1940; *er s* of William Matthew, Viscount Wolmer (killed on active service, 1942), and of Priscilla (who *m* 1948, Hon. Peter Legh, now 4th Baron Newton, *qv*), *d* of late Captain John Egerton-Warburton; *S* grandfather, 1971; *m* 1969, Joanna Van Antwerp, *yr d* of Evan Maitland James, *qv* ; three *s* one *d*. *Educ:* Eton; Christ Church, Oxford (MA). Vice-Chm., Apple and Pear Develt Council, 1969-73; Member: Hops Mkting Bd, 1972-82 (Chm., 1978-82); Agricl Res. Council, 1975- (Vice-Chm., 1980-). Hampshire County Council, 1967-74. JP Hants 1971-78; DL Hants 1982. *Heir:* s Viscount Wolmer, *qv*. *Address:* Temple Manor, Selborne, Alton, Hants. *T:* Bordon 3646. *Club:* Brooks's.

SELBY, 4th Viscount, *cr* 1905; **Michael Guy John Gully;** Director: Kames Fish Farming Ltd; Ledger Selby Ltd; Computer Time Services Ltd; Verden Properties Ltd; Partner, Fisher and Co., chartered accountants; *b* 15 Aug. 1942; *s* of 3rd Viscount and of Veronica, *er d* of late J. George and of Mrs Briscoe-George; *S* father, 1959; *m* 1965, Mary Theresa, *d* of late Capt. Thomas Powell, London, SW7; one *s* one *d*. *Educ:* Harrow. ACA, ATII. *Recreations:* shooting, fishing, sailing. *Heir:* s Hon. Edward Thomas William Gully, *b* 21 Sept. 1967. *Address:* Ardfern House, by Lochgilphead, Argyll PA31 8QN.

SELBY, Bishop Suffragan of, since 1972; **Rt. Rev. Morris Henry St John Maddocks;** *b* 28 April 1928; *s* of late Rev. Canon Morris Arthur Maddocks and Gladys Mabel Sharpe; *m* 1955, Anne Sheail; no *c*. *Educ:* St John's Sch.,

Leatherhead; Trinity Coll., Cambridge; Chichester Theological Coll. BA 1952, MA 1956, Cambridge. Ordained in St Paul's Cathedral, London, 1954. Curate: St Peter's, Ealing, 1954-55; St Andrews, Uxbridge, 1955-58; Vicar of: Weaverthorpe, Helperthorpe and Luttons Ambo, 1958-61; S Martin's on the Hill, Scarborough, 1961-71. Co-Chm., Churches' Council for Health and Healing, 1975-82. *Publications:* The Christian Healing Ministry, 1981; The Christian Adventure, 1983. *Recreations:* golf, music, painting. *Address:* Greenriggs, 8 Bankside Close, Upper Poppleton, York YO2 6LH. *T:* York 795342. *Club:* Ganton Golf (Yorkshire).

SELBY, Harry; *b* 18 May 1913; *s* of Max Soldberg and Annie (*née* Saltman); *m* 1937, Jeannie McKean Reid; one *s. Educ:* Queen's Park Secondary, Glasgow. Served War of 1939-45: Private, Highland Light Infantry, June 1940; Royal Corps of Signals, March 1941; released Dec. 1945. Lectured through Nat. Council of Labour College. Mem., Glasgow Corp., 1972-74. MP (Lab) Glasgow, Govan, Feb. 1974-79. *Address:* House 5, 70 Kennishead Avenue, Glasgow GL6 8RJ. *T:* 041-649 7169.

SELBY, Sir Kenneth, Kt 1970; FCMA, FCCA, CBIM, FIQ; Chairman, Bath & Portland Group Ltd, 1969-82; *b* 16 Feb. 1914; *s* of Thomas William Selby; *m* 1937, Elma Gertrude, *d* of Johnstone Sleator; two *s. Educ:* High School for Boys, Worthing. Managing Director, Bath & Portland Group Ltd, 1963-81. Governor, Wells Cathedral Sch., 1976-; Mem., Ct and Council, Chm. Council, 1975-, Pro Chancellor, 1975-, Bath Univ. Chm., Air Travel Reserve Fund Agency, 1975-. *Address:* Hartham Park, Corsham, Wilts. *T:* Corsham 713176. *Clubs:* Reform; Savages (Bristol).

SELBY, Ralph Walford, CMG 1961; HM Diplomatic Service, retired; *b* 20 March 1915; *e s* of late Sir Walford Selby, KCMG, CB, CVO; *m* 1947, Julianna Snell; three *d. Educ:* Eton; Christ Church, Oxford. Entered HM Diplomatic Service, Sept. 1938; served in Foreign Office until Oct. 1939. Enlisted in Army and served with Grenadier Guards, March 1940-Feb. 1945, when returned to Foreign Office; seconded to Treasury for service in India as First Secretary in Office of High Commissioner for UK, Sept. 1947; transferred to The Hague, 1950; returned to FO, 1953-56; transf. to Tokyo as Counsellor, 1956, to Copenhagen in 1958, to Djakarta in 1961, to Warsaw in 1964; Chargé d'Affaires in 1958, 1959, 1960, 1961, 1962, 1964, 1965, 1969, 1970; Consul-Gen., Boston, 1966-69; Minister, British Embassy, Rome, 1969-72; Ambassador to Norway, 1972-75. *Recreation:* sports as available. *Address:* Mengeham House, Mengham Lane, Hayling Island, Hants PO11 9JX. *Clubs:* MCC; Royal Yacht Squadron (Cowes).

SELBY, Rear-Adm. William Halford, CB 1955; DSC 1942; *b* 29 April 1902; *s* of E. H. Selby; *m* 1926, Hilary Elizabeth Salter (*d* 1960); two *d*; *m* 1961, Mrs R. Milne. *Educ:* Royal Naval Colleges, Osborne and Dartmouth. Entered Royal Navy, 1916; Midshipman, HMS Royal Oak, Black Sea and Dardanelles, 1920; Sub.-Lt HMS Vendetta and HMY Victoria and Albert, 1924. Destroyers, Medit and China Station between 1927 and 1936; Naval Staff Coll., 1939; War of 1939-45: in comd HMS Wren, Mashona (despatches), Onslaught (despatches). Capt. 1943; Chief of Staff, Londonderry, 1944-45; Capt. 'D' Third Flotilla in comd HMS Saumarez, 1946-47; Dep. Dir Ops Div., Admty, 1948-50; Capt-in-Charge, Simonstown, 1950-52; Rear-Adm. 1953; Head of British Naval Mission to Greece, 1953-55; retired, 1956. *Address:* The Old Cottage, Chittoe, Chippenham, Wilts.

SELBY WRIGHT, Very Rev. Ronald (William Vernon); *see* Wright.

SELDON, Arthur; economist and writer; Advisory Director, Institute of Economic Affairs, since 1981; *b* 29 May 1916; *m* Audrey Marjorie, *d* of Wilfred Willett and Eileen Willett (*née* Stenhouse); three *s. Educ:* Dempsey St Elementary Sch., Stepney; Raine's Foundation Sch. (State Scholar); LSE. BCom 1937 (1st cl. hons). Editor, Store, 1946-49; economist in industry, 1949-1960; Editorial Dir, Inst. of Economic Affairs, 1959-81. Chm., Liberal Party Cttee on the Aged, 1948-49; Mem., BMA Cttee on Health Financing, 1968-70; Adviser, Australian Cabinet Cttee on Welfare, 1968; Mem Bd, Mont Pélerin Soc., 1980-; Founder Trustee, Social Affairs Unit, 1980. Founder Editor, Jl of Economic Affairs, 1980. *Publications:* Advertising in a Free Society (with Lord Harris of High Cross), 1959; Pensions for Prosperity, 1960; Choice of Welfare (with Lord Harris of High Cross), 1963, 4th edn 1978; Everyman's Dictionary of Economics (with F. G. Pennance), 1965, 2nd edn 1976; After the NHS, 1968; The Great Pensions Swindle, 1970; (contrib.) The Burden of Government, 1972; Charge, 1977. *Recreations:* work, cricket, opera, parties for all-party non-conformists. *Address:* The Thatched Cottage, Godden Green, Sevenoaks, Kent. *T:* Sevenoaks 61499.

SELDON TRUSS, Leslie; author; *b* 1892; *s* of George Marquand Truss and Ann Blanche, *d* of Samuel Seldon, CB; *m* 1st, 1918, Gwendolen, *d* of Charles Kershaw, Cooden Mount, Sussex; one *d*; 2nd, 1925, Kathleen Mary (*d* 1981), *d* of Charles Hornung, of Oaklands, Hookwood, Surrey; one *s* one *d. Educ:* Lieut Scots Guards, Special Reserve, 1915-19; Major Home Guard, 1940-44. *Publications:* Gallows Bait, 1928; The Stolen Millionaire, 1929; The Man Without Pity, 1930; The Hunterstone Outrage, 1931; Turmoil at Brede, 1932; Mr Coroner Presides, 1932; They Came by Night, 1933; The Daughters of Belial, 1934; Murder Paves the Way; Escort to Danger, 1935; Draw the Blinds; Rooksmiths, 1936; The Man who Played Patience; She Could Take Care; Footsteps Behind Them, 1937; Foreign Bodies, 1938; The Disappearance of Julie Hints, 1940; Sweeter for his Going, Where's Mr Chumley?, 1949; Ladies Always Talk, 1950; Never Fight a Lady, 1951; Death of No Lady, 1952;

Always Ask a Policeman, 1953; Put Out The Light, The High Wall, 1954; The Long Night, The Barberton Intrigue, 1956; The Truth About Claire Veryan, 1957; In Secret Places, 1958; The Hidden Men, 1959; One Man's Death, 1960; Seven Years Dead, 1961; A Time to Hate, 1962; Technique for Treachery, 1963; Walk a Crooked Mile, 1964; The Town That Went Sick, 1965; Eyes at the Window, 1966; The Bride That Got Away, 1967; The Hands of the Shadow, 1968; The Corpse That Got Away, 1969; under *pseudonym* of George Selmark, Murder in Silence, 1939; various short stories and serials. *Recreations:* anything but writing. *Address:* Dale Hill House, Ticehurst, Sussex. *T:* Ticehurst 251.

SELF, Hugh Michael, QC 1973; a Recorder of the Crown Court, since 1975; *b* 19 March 1921; *s* of Sir (Albert) Henry Self, KCB, KCMG, KBE; *m* 1950, Penelope Ann, *d* of late John Drinkwater, poet and dramatist and Daisy (*née* Kennedy), violinist; two *d. Educ:* Lancing Coll.; Worcester Coll., Oxford (BA). Royal Navy, 1942-46, Lieut RNVR 1946. Called to Bar, Lincoln's Inn, 1951, Bencher, 1980. *Recreations:* golf, walking in England, literature. *Address:* 59 Maresfield Gardens, Hampstead, NW3 5TE. *T:* 01-435 8311. *Club:* Savile.

See also Prof. P. J. O. Self.

SELF, Prof. Peter John Otter; Professor of Public Administration, University of London, since 1963; *b* 7 June 1919; *s* of Sir (Albert) Henry Self, KCB, KCMG, KBE; *m* 1st, 1950, Diana Mary Pitt (marr. diss.); 2nd, 1959, Elaine Rosenbloom Adams (marr. diss.); two *s*; 3rd, 1981, Sandra Guerita Gough (*née* Moiseiwitsch). *Educ:* Lancing Coll.; Balliol Coll., Oxford (MA). Editorial staff of The Economist, 1944-62; Extra-mural Lectr, London Univ., 1944-49; Lectr in Public Administration, LSE, 1948-61; Reader in Political Science, LSE, 1961-63. Dir of Studies (Administration), Civil Service Dept, 1969-70. Mem. Exec. and Coun., 1954, Vice-Chm. Exec., 1955, Chm. Exec., 1961-69, Chm. Council, 1979-; Town and Country Planning Assoc.; Member: SE Regional Economic Planning Coun., 1966-79; Council, RIPA; Hon. Mem., RTPI. *Publications:* Regionalism, 1949; Cities in Flood: The Problems of Urban Growth, 1957; (with H. Storing) The State and the Farmer, 1962; Administrative Theories and Politics, 1972; Econocrats and the Policy Process, 1976; Planning the Urban Region, 1982; numerous articles on administration, politics and planning. *Recreations:* walking, golf, story-telling. *Address:* 17 Temple Street, Brill, Bucks. *T:* Brill 237443. *Club:* Reform.

See also H. M. Self.

SELIGMAN, Henry, OBE 1958; PhD; President, EXEC AG, Basle, since 1975; Scientific Consultant (part-time) to International Atomic Energy Agency, Vienna, since 1969; Scientific Adviser to various industries, since 1970; *b* Frankfurt am Main, 25 Feb. 1909; *s* of Milton Seligman and Marie (*née* Gans); *m* 1941, Lesley Bradley; two *s. Educ:* Universities of Lausanne and of Zürich. Staff, DSIR, Cavendish Lab., Cambridge, 1942-43. Joined British-Canadian Research Project at Montreal, 1943, Chalk River, Ontario, 1944-; Staff, Brit. Atomic Energy Project, 1946; Head of Isotope Div., Atomic Energy Research Establishment, Harwell, UK, 1947-58; Dep. Dir Gen., Dept of Research and Isotopes, Internat. Atomic Energy Agency, Vienna, 1958-69. Austrian Decoration for Science and Art, 1979. Editor-in-Chief: Scientific Jl; Internat. Jl of Applied Radiation and Isotopes, 1973-. *Publications:* papers on: physical constants necessary for reactor development; waste disposal; production and uses of radioisotopes; contrib. scientific journals. *Address:* Scherpegasse 8/6/3, 1190 Vienna, Austria. *T:* Vienna 323225.

SELIGMAN, Madron; *see* Seligman, R. M.

SELIGMAN, Sir Peter (Wendel), Kt 1978; CBE 1969; BA; CEng; FIMechE; *b* 16 Jan. 1913; *s* of late Dr Richard Joseph Simon Seligman and of Hilda Mary Seligman; *m* 1937, Elizabeth Lavinia Mary Wheatley; two *s* four *d. Educ:* King's Coll. Sch., Wimbledon; Harrow Sch.; Kantonschule, Zürich; Caius Coll., Cambridge. Joined APV Co. Ltd, as Asst to Man. Dir, 1936; appointed Dir, 1939; Man. Dir, 1947; Dep. Chm., 1961; Chm., APV Holdings Ltd, 1966-77. Director: St Regis International Ltd, 1973- (Vice-Chm., 1981); Eibis International Ltd, 1980-; Bell Bryant Pty Ltd, 1976-80; St Regis ACI Pty Ltd, 1980-. Mem., Engineering Industries Council, 1975-77. Chm., Nat. Ski Fedn of GB, 1977-81. *Recreations:* ski-ing, yachting, carpentry. *Address:* Dagmar House, Birmingham Road, Cowes, IoW. *Clubs:* Athenæum; Royal Yacht Squadron; Hawks (Cambridge); Ski of Great Britain (Invitation Life Mem.); Kandahar Ski (Chm., 1972-77).

See also R. M. Seligman.

SELIGMAN, (Richard) Madron; Member (C) Sussex West, European Parliament, since 1979; *b* 10 Nov. 1918; 4th *s* of late Dr Richard Seligman, FCGI, FIM, and Hilda Mary (*née* MacDowell); *m* 1947, Nancy-Joan, *d* of Julian Marks; three *s* one *d. Educ:* Rokeby Sch., Wimbledon; Harrow Sch.; Balliol Coll., Oxford (BA Hons) PPE). Oxford Univ. ski team, 1938-39; President, Oxford Union, 1940. Served war, 6th Armoured Divisional Signals, N Africa and Italy, 1941-46, Major 1945. Director, APV (Holdings) Ltd, Crawley, Sussex, 1972; Chm., Incinerator Company, Eaton Socon, 1960-; Dir, Fluor (GB) Ltd, 1968-. *Recreations:* tennis, skiing, piano, sailing. *Address:* Micklepage House, Nuthurst, near Horsham, Sussex. *T:* Lower Beeding 259. *Clubs:* Royal Thames Yacht, Royal Institute of International Affairs, MCC.

See also Sir Peter Seligman.

SELKIRK, 10th Earl of, *cr* 1646; **George Nigel Douglas-Hamilton**, KT 1976; PC 1955; GCMG 1959; GBE 1963 (OBE 1941); AFC; AE; QC(Scot.), 1959; late Gp Capt. Auxiliary Air Force; Scottish Representative Peer, 1945-63; *b* Merly, Wimborne, Dorset, 4 Jan. 1906; 2nd *s* of 13th Duke of Hamilton and Brandon; *S* to earldom of father under terms of special remainder, 1940; *m* 1949, Audrey Durell, *o d* of late Maurice Drummond-Sale-Barker and of Mrs H. S. Brooks. *Educ:* Eton; Balliol College, Oxford, MA; Edinburgh University, LLB. Admitted to Faculty of Advocates, 1935; Commanded 603 Squadron AAF, 1934-38; Captain, 44th Co., Boys' Brigade, 1932-38; Member of Edinburgh Town Council, 1935-40; Commissioner of General Board of Control (Scotland), 1936-39; Commissioner for Special Areas in Scotland, 1937-39. Served War of 1939-45 (OBE, despatches twice). A Lord-in-Waiting to the Queen, 1952-53 (to King George VI, 1951-52); Paymaster-General, Nov. 1953-Dec. 1955; Chancellor of the Duchy of Lancaster, Dec. 1955-Jan. 1957; First Lord of the Admiralty, 1957-Oct. 1959; UK Commissioner for Singapore and Comr Gen. for SE Asia, 1959-63; also UK Council Representative to SEATO, 1960-63; Chm., Cons. Commonwealth Council, 1965-72. Freeman of Hamilton. President: National Ski Fedn of Great Britain, 1964-68; Anglo-Swiss Society, 1965-74; Building Societies Assoc., 1965-82; Royal Soc. for Asian Affairs, 1966-76; Assoc. of Independent Unionist Peers, 1967-79. Chm., Victoria League, 1971-77. Hon. Chief, Saulteaux Indians, 1967. Hon. Citizen of the City of Winnipeg and of the Town of Selkirk in Manitoba. *Heir presumptive: nephew* Alasdair Malcolm Douglas-Hamilton [*b* 10 Sept. 1939; *m* 1965, Angela Kathleen, 2nd *d* of John Molony Longley; two *s* two *d*]. *Address:* Rose Lawn Coppice, Wimborne, Dorset. *T:* Wimborne 883160; 60 Eaton Place, SW1. *T:* 01-235 6926. *Clubs:* Athenæum, Caledonian; New (Edinburgh).

SELLARS, John Ernest, CEng; FIMA; MRAeS; Chief Officer, Business Education Council, since 1974; *b* 5 Feb. 1936; *s* of Ernest Buttle Sellars and Edna Grace Sellars; *m* 1958, Dorothy Beatrice (*née* Morrison); three *d*. *Educ:* Wintringham Grammar Sch., Grimsby; Manchester Univ. (BSc, MSc). Research Engineer, English Electric (GW) Ltd, 1958-61; Lectr, Royal College of Advanced Technology (now Univ. of Salford), 1961-67; Head of Mathematics, Lanchester College of Technology, Coventry, 1967-71; Head of Computer Science, Lanchester Polytechnic, Coventry/Rugby, 1971-74. *Publications:* papers on mathematics, computer science and business educn. *Recreation:* walking. *Address:* 306 Cassiobury Drive, Watford, Herts WD1 3AW. *T:* Watford 33055. *Club:* Reform.

SELLERS, Norman William Malin, VRD; **His Honour Judge Sellers**; a Circuit Judge, since 1974; *b* 29 Aug. 1919; *e s* of late Rt Hon. Sir Frederic Sellers, MC, and of Grace (*née* Malin); *m* 1946, Angela Laurie, *er d* of Sidney Jukes, Barnet; four *d*. *Educ:* Merchant Taylors' Sch., Crosby; Silcoates Sch., Wakefield; Hertford Coll., Oxford (MA). Officer, RNVR, 1940-45 (despatches, HMS Nelson, 1942); Lt Cdr 1953, comd HMS Mersey. Called to Bar, Gray's Inn, 1947; Northern Circuit; Asst Recorder of Blackpool, 1962-71; Recorder of Crown Court, 1972-74. Contested (L) Crosby Div. of Lancs, 1964. *Recreation:* sailing. *Address:* Hillside, Lower Road, Longridge, Preston PR3 2YN. *T:* Longridge 3222. *Clubs:* Bar Yacht, Ribble Cruising.

SELLERS, Robert Firth, ScD; MRCVS; Director, Animal Virus Research Institute, Pirbright, since 1979; *b* 9 June 1924; *s* of Frederick Sellers and Janet Walkinshaw Shiels; *m* 1951, Margaret Peterkin; one *s* one *d*. *Educ:* Christ's Hospital; Gonville and Caius Coll., Cambridge (MA, ScD); Royal (Dick) School of Veterinary Studies, Edinburgh (PhD, BSc). Served War, Royal Artillery, 1943-46. Research Institute (Animal Virus Diseases), Pirbright, 1953-58; Wellcome Research Laboratories, Beckenham, 1958-62; Instituto Venezolano de Investigaciones Cientificas, Venezuela, 1962-64; Animal Virus Research Institute, Pirbright, 1964-, Dep. Dir, 1964-79. J. T. Edwards Meml Medal, 1976. *Publications:* papers on animal viruses in scientific jls. *Recreation:* archaeology. *Address:* 4 Pewley Way, Guildford, Surrey GU1 3PY.

SELLORS, Patrick John Holmes, FRCS; Surgeon-Oculist to the Queen, since 1980; Surgeon, King Edward VIIth Hospital for Officers, since 1975; Ophthalmic Surgeon: St George's Hospital since 1965; Croydon Eye Unit since 1970; *b* 11 Feb. 1934; *s* of Sir Thomas Holmes Sellors, *qv*; *m* 1961, Gillian Gratton Swallow; two *s* one *d*. *Educ:* Rugby Sch.; Oriel Coll., Oxford; Middlesex Hosp. Med. School. MA Oxon; BM, BCh Oxon 1958; FRCS 1965. Registrar, Moorfields Eye Hosp., 1962-65; recognised teacher in Ophthalmology, St George's Hosp., 1966. Surgeon-Oculist to HM Household, 1974-80. Sec. to Ophthalmic Soc. of UK, 1970-72; Examr for Diploma of Ophthalmology, 1974-77; Member: Council, Faculty of Ophthalmologists, 1977-; Council, Gen. Optical Council, 1978-. Vice-Pres., Med. Defence Union, 1977-. *Publications:* articles in BMJ and Trans OSUK. *Recreations:* gardening, golf. *Address:* 149 Harley Street, W1N 2DE. *T:* 01-935 4444.

SELLORS, Sir Thomas Holmes, Kt 1963; DM, MCh; FRCP; FRCS; Consultant Surgeon, London Chest Hospital, since 1934; Emeritus Thoracic Surgeon, Middlesex Hospital, since 1947; Consultant Surgeon, National Heart and Harefield Hospitals, since 1957; Consulting Surgeon, Aylesbury Group of Hospitals; *b* 7 April 1902; *s* of Dr T. B. Sellors; *m* 1st, Brenda Lyell (*d* 1928); 2nd, 1932, Dorothy Elizabeth Chesshire (*d* 1953); one *s* one *d*; 3rd, 1955, Marie Hobson. *Educ:* Loretto School; Oriel Coll., Oxford, Hon. Fellow 1973. BA Oxon 1923, MA 1927; MRCS, LRCP 1926; BM, BCh Oxon 1926; G.

H. Hunt Travelling Scholarship, Univ. of Oxford, 1928; MCh 1931, DM 1933. Held various appts in London hosps; FRCS 1930; Member of Council, RCS, 1957-73, Vice-Pres., 1968-69, President 1969-72; FRCP 1963; Chairman of Joint Consultants Committee, 1958-67; President: Thoracic Society, 1960; Soc. of Thoracic Surgeons of Great Britain and Ireland, 1961-62; BMA, 1972; Royal Med. Benevolent Fund; Pres., Internat. Soc. Surg., 1977-79, Pres. Congress 1977; Chm. Council, British Heart Foundn. Surgeon to Royal Waterloo and Queen Mary's Hospitals; Regional Adviser in Thoracic Surgery, 1940-45. Hunterian Prof. RCS, 1944; Chm., Hunterian Trustees (Trustee, 1978). Lectures: Carey Coombs, Univ. of Bristol, 1956; G. A. Gibson, RCPE, 1959; Strickland Goodall, Society Apothecaries, 1960; Entwhistle Meml and W. W. Hamburger, Chicago, 1961; St Cyre's, 1965; Grey-Turner, Internat. Soc. Surg., 1967; Gordon-Taylor, RCS, 1968; Tudor Edwards Meml, RCS, 1968; Bradshaw, RCS, 1969; Colles, RCSI, 1975. Hunterian Orator, RCS, 1973. Examiner in Surgery, Univ. of Oxford. Member: Acad. of Medicine, Rome; Royal Acad. of Medicine, Belgium; Membre d'Honneur, Europe Cardiol. Soc.; Hon. Fellow: Amer. Coll. Surgeons, 1971; Coll. of Med., S Africa; RCSE, 1972; RCSI; Faculty of Dental Surgeons, RCS, 1974. MD (*hc*) Groningen, 1964; Hon. DSc Liverpool, 1970; Hon. MS Southampton, 1972; BMA Gold Medal, 1979; Médaille de la Reconnaissance Française. Officer of the Order of Carlos Finlay, Cuba. *Publications:* Surgery of the Thorax, 1933. Editor and contributor in current text books. Articles in English and foreign medical publications. *Recreations:* water-colour painting, gardening. *Address:* Spring Coppice Farm, Speen, Aylesbury, Bucks. *T:* Hampden Row 379.
See also P. J. H. Sellors.

SELLS, Sir David (Perronet), Kt 1980; *b* 23 June 1918; *s* of late Edward Perronet Sells; *m* 1948, Beryl Cecilia, *er d* of late C. E. W. Charrington, MC; three *s*. *Educ:* Sandroyd Sch.; Repton Sch.; Christ Church, Oxford. Commissioned, Coldstream Guards, 1941; active service, N Africa and Italy. Called to Bar, Inner Temple, 1947. Chairman: Cambridgeshire Conservative and Unionist Assoc., 1962-67; Eastern Area Conservative Council, 1968-71 (Pres., 1975-78); Conservative Council for Europ. Constit. of Cambs, 1978-; Mem. Executive Cttee, Nat. Union of Conservative and Unionist Assocs, 1965-81; Chairman: Conservative Central Council and Conservative Party Conf., 1977-78. A Governor, Swinton Conservative Coll., 1970-. *Recreations:* fishing, painting, shooting. *Address:* Tadlow House, Tadlow, Royston, Herts SG8 0EL. *T:* Wrestlingworth 228. *Clubs:* Savile, Carlton.

SELLY, Susan, (Mrs Clifford Selly); *see* Strange, S.

SELSDON, 3rd Baron, *cr* 1932, of Croydon; **Malcolm McEacharn Mitchell-Thomson**; Bt 1900; banker; *b* 27 Oct. 1937; *s* of 2nd Baron Selsdon (3rd Bt, *cr* 1900), DSC; *S* father, 1963; *m* 1965, Patricia Anne, *d* of Donald Smith; one *s*. *Educ:* Winchester College. Sub-Lieut, RNVR. Deleg. to Council of Europe and WEU, 1972-78. EEC Adviser, Midland Bank Group, 1979-; Chm., Committee for Middle East Trade (COMET), 1979-. Chm., Greater London and SE Regional Council for Sport and Recreation, 1977-. *Recreations:* rackets, squash, tennis, lawn tennis, cricket, ski-ing, sailing. *Heir:* *s* Hon. Callum Malcolm McEacharn Mitchell-Thomson, *b* 7 Nov. 1969. *Address:* 33 Cadogan Lane, SW1. *T:* 01-235 8692. *Club:* MCC.

SELVON, Samuel Dickson; author since 1954; *b* Trinidad, West Indies, 20 May 1923; *m* 1st, 1947, Draupadi Persaud; one *d*; 2nd, 1963, Althea Nesta Daroux; two *s* one *d*. *Educ:* Naparima College, Trinidad. Wireless Operator, 1940-45; Journalist, 1946-50; Civil Servant, 1950-53. Fellow, John Simon Guggenheim Memorial Foundn (USA), 1954 and 1968; Travelling Schol., Soc. of Authors (London), 1958; Trinidad Govt Schol., 1962. Humming Bird Medal (Trinidad), 1969. *Publications:* A Brighter Sun, 1952; An Island is a World, 1954; The Lonely Londoners, 1956; Ways of Sunlight, 1957; Turn Again Tiger, 1959; I Hear Thunder, 1963; The Housing Lark, 1965; The Plains of Caroni, 1970; Those Who Eat the Cascadura, 1972; Moses Ascending, 1975; contribs to London Magazine, New Statesman and Nation, Sunday Times, also Evergreen Review (USA). *Recreations:* tennis, swimming, gardening, cooking. *Address:* c/o Davis-Poynter Ltd, 11 Bolt Court, Fleet Street, EC4A 3DQ.

SELWAY, Air Marshal Sir Anthony (Dunkerton), KCB 1961 (CB 1952); DFC 1940; Registrar and Secretary of the Order of the Bath, 1968-79 (Gentleman Usher of the Scarlet Rod, 1964-68); *b* 20 Feb. 1909; *s* of C. J. Selway, CVO, CBE, TD; *m* 1936, Patricia Graham, *d* of Col. P. C. MacFarlane, Ballagan, Strathblane, Stirlingshire; one *s* one *d*. *Educ:* Highgate School; Cranwell. No 1 Squadron, Tangmere, 1929; Central Flying School, 1932-34; Middle East Command, 1936-42 (despatches); Flying Trg Comd, 1942-44; Fighter Comd, 1944-45; Burma and Far East, 1945-48; Joint Services Staff Coll., 1948; Air Ministry, 1948-51; Commandant, Central Flying School, 1951-53; Air Attaché, Paris, 1953-Nov. 1955; Comdr, RAF Staff, British Joint Services Mission (USA), 1955-58; AOC No 18 Group Coastal Command, and Air Officer, Scotland 1958-60; C-in-C FEAF, 1960-62; AOC-in-C, RAF Coastal Command, 1962-65; Group Capt. 1942; Air Cdre 1951; Air Vice-Marshal, 1955; Air Marshal, 1961; retired, 1965. *Address:* c/o Williams & Glyn's Bank Ltd, 22 Whitehall, SW1. *Clubs:* Royal Air Force, White's.

SELWYN, John Sidney Augustus, OBE 1962 (MBE 1939); HM Diplomatic Service, retired; *b* 17 Oct. 1908; *s* of Rev. A. L. H. Selwyn; *m* 1932, Cicely Georgina Armour (marr. diss.); one *s* one *d* (and one *d* decd); *m* 1952, Janette

Bruce Mullin (d 1968); one s; m 1971, Sonja Fischer; one d. Educ: St Lawrence College, Ramsgate; Royal Military Coll., Sandhurst. Entered the Indian Police, 1928. Served in NWF Campaigns, 1930, 1937 and 1941. Major, 12th Frontier Force Regt, active service in Burma, 1942-46, Allied Control Commission, Germany, 1946-48. Entered Foreign Service, 1948. Served in Bucharest, Lisbon, London, Lima, Santos, Beirut; Consul-General: Berlin, 1963; Strasbourg, 1964-68; Vice-Consul, Calais, 1969-73. Recreation: walking. Address: Erlaufstrasse 35/2/6, A-2344 Maria Enzersdorf-Südstadt, Austria. Club: Civil Service.

SEMEGA-JANNEH, Bocar Ousman, MBE 1954; High Commissioner for The Gambia in London and Ambassador to Western Germany, Belgium, Sweden, Switzerland, France and Austria, 1971-80, to The Holy See, 1979-80; b 21 July 1910; s of late Ousman Semega-Janneh, merchant and late Koumba Tunkara, The Gambia; m 1936, and other Muslim marriages; several c. Educ: Mohammedan Primary Sch.; Methodist Boys' High School. Air Raid Warden, Bathurst, 1939-45. Gambia Surveys Dept: Surveys Asst 1931; Surveyor 1937; Sen. Surveyor 1948; Dir 1953; retd 1966. Gambian High Comr, Senegal, 1967; Ambassador to Mauritania, Mali, Guinea and Liberia, and High Comr, Sierra Leone, 1969; rep. Gambia at Gen. Assembly of UN, 1968-; rep. at meetings of Ministers of Foreign Affairs and Heads of State and Govt of members of Organisation of African Unity, 1968-. Rep. Gambia, triennial Survey Officers' Conf., Cambridge, 1955-65. Boy Scout, 1925; District Scout-master, 1938-42; Chief Comr of Scouts, The Gambia, 1947-66 (Silver Acorn 1954). Bathurst City Council: Councillor, 1951; Dep. Chm., 1957; Chm., 1960; first Mayor 1965; resigned 1967. Vice-Pres. 1955-56, Pres. 1957-67, Gambia Football Assoc.; formerly: Mem. Kombo Rural Authority; Governor, Gambia High Sch.; Actg Mem. Gambia Oilseeds Marketing Bd; Mem. Bathurst Colony Team and Town Planning Bd; Mem. Consultative Cttee for foundation of Constitution; Mem., Mohammedan Sch. Man. Cttee. Grand Officer, Order of Merit: Senegal, 1971; Mauritania, 1971; Officer of Republic of The Gambia. Recreations: football, cricket, golf, lawn tennis (singles champion, Gambia, 1932-50). Address: 15 Hagan Street, Banjul, Republic of the Gambia.

SEMENOV, Prof. Nikolai Nikolaevich; Orders of Lenin; State awards; Director, Institute of Chemical Physics of the USSR Academy of Sciences since 1931; Professor, Moscow State University; b 16 April 1896; s of a state employee; m Lidiya Grigorievna Scherbakova; one s one d. Educ: Leningrad State University. Chief of Electronic Phenomena Laboratory of Physico-Technical Institute in Leningrad, 1920; Assistant Professor and then Professor, Leningrad Polytechnic Institute, 1920-41. (Jointly) Nobel Prize for Chemistry, 1956. Foreign Member: Royal Society, 1958; Acad. of Sciences of French Inst., 1978-; Member: USSR Academy of Sciences, 1932-; Chem. Soc. of England, 1949-; Naturalists' Soc., Leopoldina (Halle DDR), 1959; Amer. Chem. Soc., 1976; Hon. Fellow: Indian Academy of Sciences, 1959; Hungarian Academy of Sciences, 1961; New York Academy of Sciences, 1962; Roumanian Acad. Sci., 1965; Czechoslovakian Acad. Sci., 1965; Roy. Soc. of Edinburgh, 1966; For. Associate, Nat. Acad. of Sciences (USA), 1963; Corresp. Member: Akademie der Wissenschaften, Berlin, DDR, 1966; Bulgarian Acad. of Sciences, 1969; Hon. DSc: Oxford, 1960; Bruxelles, 1962; London, 1965; Hon. DrSci: Milan, 1964; Prague, 1965; Budapest, 1965; Humboldt-Universität zu Berlin, 1973; Vroclav Univ., 1976. Publications: several textbooks and scientific monographs, notably: Chain reactions, 1934 (Russia), 1935 (Oxford); Some Problems on Chemical Kinetics and Reactivity, 1954 (Russia), enlarged 2nd edn 1958 (Russia), (Eng. trans. 1959); Science and Community, 1973 (Russia); numerous articles in the field of chemical physics. Address: Vorobyevskoye chaussée 2-B, Institute of Chemical Physics, Moscow 117977, USSR.

SEMKEN, John Douglas, CB 1980; MC 1944; Legal Adviser to the Home Office, 1977-83; b 9 Jan. 1921; s of Wm R. Semken and Mrs B. R. Semken (née Craymer); m 1952, Edna Margaret, yr d of T. R. Poole; three s. Educ: St Albans Sch.; Pembroke Coll., Oxford (MA, BCL). Solicitor's articled clerk, 1938-39. Commnd in Sherwood Rangers Yeo., 1940; 1st Lieut 1941, Captain 1942, Major 1944; 8th Armd Bde, N Africa, 1942-43; Normandy beaches to Germany, 1944. Called to Bar, Lincoln's Inn, 1949; practised at Chancery Bar, 1949-54; joined Legal Adviser's Br., Home Office, 1954; Mem., Criminal Law Revision Cttee, 1980-. Silver Star Medal (USA), 1944. Address: 2 The Ridgeway, Mill Hill, NW7 1RS. T: 01-346 3092. Clubs: Athenæum; Lawrenny Yacht.

SEMMENCE, Dr Adrian Murdoch; Civil Service Medical Adviser, Management and Personnel Office (formerly Civil Service Department), since 1979; b 5 April 1926; s of Adrian George Semmence, MA, and Henrietta Scorgie (née Murdoch), MA; m 1949, Joan, d of Hugh and Bobbie Wood; four s one d. Educ: Robert Gordon's Coll., Aberdeen; Univ. of Aberdeen (MB, ChB 1953; MD 1957); Univ. of London (MSc 1972); DObstRCOG 1954, FRCGP 1972, DIH 1972. Served War, RN, 1943-47. House Physician, Aberdeen Royal Inf. and Aberdeen Maternity Hosp., 1953-54; general practice: E Yorks, 1954-60; Berks, 1960-76; Nuffield Travelling Fellow, 1969-70; Unit of Clinical Epidemiology, Univ. of Oxford, 1970-76; Occupational Health Service, Basingstoke Dist. Hosp., 1973-76; Principal MO, CSD, 1976-79. Publications: papers on general medicine, occupational health and epidemiology. Address: Tilbury House, Petty France, SW1H 9EV. T: 01-213 6046; Stone Cottage, Steventon, Abingdon OX13 6RZ. T: Abingdon 831527. Club: Athenæum.

SEMPER, Very Rev. Colin (Douglas); Provost of Coventry Cathedral, since 1982; b 5 Feb. 1938; s of William Frederick and Dorothy Anne Semper; m 1962, Janet Louise Greaves; two s. Educ: Lincoln School; Keble College, Oxford (BA); Westcott House, Cambridge. Curate of Holy Trinity with St Mary, Guildford, 1963-66; Recruitment and Selection Sec., ACCM, 1966-69; Head of Religious Programmes, BBC Radio, and Deputy Head of Religious Broadcasting, BBC, 1969-82. Recreations: travel, reading modern novels, canals. Address: Provost's Lodge, Priory Row, Coventry, West Midlands CV1 5ES. T: Coventry 27597.

SEMPER, Dudley Henry; Puisne Judge, Jamaica, 1954-63, retired; b St Kitts, BWI, 14 Nov. 1905; s of late D. H. Semper, ISO, and Helen Semper; m 1937, Aileen Malone; one d. Educ: Antigua Grammar School; West Buckland School, North Devon. Called to Bar, Gray's Inn, 1927; practised at Bar of Leeward Islands, 1928-32; Colonial Service, 1933; Actg District Magistrate, Registrar Supreme Court, St Kitts-Nevis, 1934; District Magistrate, St Kitts-Nevis, 1935; Crown Attorney, St Kitts-Nevis, 1939; Actg Attorney General, Leeward Islands, 1943-44; Officer administering Govt of St Kitts-Nevis, intermittently 1943-44; Resident Magistrate, Jamaica, 1944. Recreations: shooting, fishing. Address: Bracebridge, 50 Cliff Road, Worlebury, Weston-super-Mare, Avon. Club: Royal Commonwealth Society.

SEMPILL, family name of **Lady Sempill** (née Forbes-Sempill).

SEMPILL, Lady (20th in line, of the Lordship cr 1489); **Ann Moira Sempill** (née Forbes-Sempill); b 19 March 1920; d of 19th Lord Sempill, AFC; S father, 1965; m 1st, 1941, Captain Eric Holt (marr. diss., 1945); one d; 2nd, 1948, Lt-Col Stuart Whitemore Chant, OBE, MC (who assumed by decree of Lyon Court, 1966, the additional surname of Sempill), now Chant-Sempill; two s. Educ: Austrian, German and English Convents. Served War, 1939-42 (Petty Officer, WRNS). Heir: s The Master of Sempill, qv. Address: East Lodge, Druminnor, Rhynie, Aberdeenshire; 15 Onslow Court, Drayton Gardens, SW10.
See also Hon. Sir Ewan Forbes of Brux, Bt.

SEMPILL, Master of; Hon. James William Stuart Whitemore Sempill; Manager, TWS Public Relations Company, Johannesburg, since 1981; Regional Manager, Argus of Ayr Ltd; b 25 Feb. 1949; s and heir of Lady Sempill, qv, and of Lt-Col Stuart Whitemore Chant-Sempill; m 1977, Josephine Ann Edith, e d of J. Norman Rees, Johannesburg; one s. Educ: The Oratory School; St Clare's Hall, Oxford (BA Hons History, 1971); Hertford Coll., Oxford. Gallagher Ltd, 1972-80; PA to Managing Director, Sentinel Engineering Pty Ltd, Johannesburg, 1980-81. Address: 76 21st Street, Parkhurst, Johannesburg, 2173, South Africa. Clubs: Vincent's, Carlton (Oxford); Wanderers' (Johannesburg).

SEMPLE, Prof. Andrew Best, CBE 1966; VRD 1953; QHP 1962; Professor of Community and Environmental Health (formerly of Public Health), University of Liverpool, 1953-77, now Professor Emeritus; b 3 May 1912; m 1941, Jean (née Sweet); one d. Educ: Allan Glen's School, Glasgow; Glasgow Univ. MB, ChB 1934, MD 1947, DPH 1936, Glasgow. FFCM 1972. Various hospital appointments, 1934-38; Asst MOH and Deputy Medical Superintendent, Infectious Diseases Hosp., Portsmouth, 1938-39; Asst MOH and Asst School Medical Officer, Blackburn, 1939-47 (interrupted by War Service); Senior Asst MOH, Manchester, 1947-48; Deputy MOH, City and Port of Liverpool, 1948-53, MOH and Principal Sch. Med. Officer, 1953-74; Area MO (teaching), Liverpool AHA, 1974-77. Served War of 1939-46; Surgeon Commander, RNVR; Naval MOH, Western Approaches, Malta and Central Mediterranean. Chm. Council and Hon. Treasurer, RSH, 1963. Publications: various regarding infectious disease, port health, hygiene, etc. Address: Kelvin, 433 Woolton Road, Gateacre, Liverpool L25 4SY. T: 051-428 2081.

SEMPLE, Andrew Greenlees; Under Secretary, and Principal Finance Officer, Property Services Agency, Department of the Environment, since 1980; b 16 Jan. 1934; s of late William Hugh Semple and Madeline, d of late E. H. Wood, Malvern, Worcs; m 1961, Janet Elizabeth, d of late H. R. G. Whates and of Mrs Whates, Ludlow, Salop; one s one d. Educ: Winchester Coll.; St John's Coll., Cambridge (MA). Entered Min. of Transport and Civil Aviation, 1957; Private Sec. to Permanent Sec., 1960-62; Principal, 1962; Asst Sec., 1970; Private Sec. to successive Secs of State for the Environment, 1972-74; Under Sec., DoE, 1976. Recreations: walking, reading, gardening. Address: 83 Burbage Road, SE24 9HB. T: 01-274 6550. Club: Dulwich Squash.

SEMPLE, John Greenlees, MA, PhD, MRIA; University Professor of Mathematics, King's College, London, 1936-69, now Emeritus; b 10 June 1904; s of James Semple, 240 Ravenhill Road, Belfast; m 1936, Daphne Caroline, d of Professor F. H. Hummel, Queen's University, Belfast; one s one d. Educ: Royal Belfast Academical Institution; Queen's University, Belfast, MA; St John's College, Cambridge (Philip Bayliss Student); Wrangler b star, Rayleigh Prize, 1929, Fellowship of St John's College, 1931; lecturer Edinburgh University, 1929; Professor of Pure Mathematics at Queen's University, Belfast, 1930-36. Publications: (with L. Roth) Introduction to Algebraic Geometry, 1949; (with G. T. Kneebone) Algebraic Projective Geometry, 1952; Algebraic Curves, 1959; (with J. A. Tyrrell) Generalized Clifford Parallelism, 1971; various papers in Cambridge Philosophical Society,

London Mathematical Society, Royal Irish Academy, Royal Society, London, etc. *Recreations:* reading, gardening, golf. *Address:* 3 Elm Road, Redhill, Surrey. *T:* Redhill 61142.

SEMPLE, John Laughlin; Under Secretary (Housing), Department of the Environment for Northern Ireland, since 1979; *b* 10 Aug. 1940; *s* of late James E. Semple and of Violet E. G. Semple; *m* 1970, Maureen Anne Kerr; *two s one d. Educ:* Campbell Coll., Belfast; Corpus Christi Coll., Cambridge (MA). BScEcon London. Joined Home CS as Asst Principal, Min. of Aviation, 1961; transf. to NI CS, 1962; Asst Principal, Mins of Health and Local Govt, Finance, and Health and Social Services, 1962-65; Dep. Principal, Min. of Health and Social Services, 1965; Principal: Min. of Finance, 1968; Min. of Community Relations, 1970-72; Asst Sec. (Planning), Min. of Develt, 1972; Asst Sec. (Housing), DoE, 1977-79. *Recreations:* golf, tennis, gardening.

SEMPLE, Prof. Stephen John Greenhill, MD, FRCP; Professor of Medicine, The Middlesex Hospital Medical School, since 1970; *b* 4 Aug. 1926; *s* of late John Edward Stewart and Janet Semple; *m* 1961, Penelope Ann, *y d* of Sir Geoffrey Aldington, *qv* ; three *s. Educ:* Westminster; London Univ. MB, BS, 1950, MD 1952, FRCP 1968. Research Asst, St Thomas' Hosp. Med. Sch., 1952; Jun. Med. Specialist, RAMC, Malaya, 1953-55; Instr, Med. Sch., Univ. of Pennsylvania, USA, 1957-59; St Thomas' Hosp. Medical Sch.: Lectr, 1959; Sen. Lectr, 1961; Reader, 1965; Prof. in Med., 1969. *Publications:* Disorders of Respiration, 1972; articles in: Lancet, Jl Physiol. (London), Jl Applied Physiol. *Recreations:* tennis, music. *Address:* White Lodge, Claremont Park Road, Esher, Surrey. *T:* Esher 65057. *Club:* Queen's.

SEMPLE, William David Crowe; Director of Education, Lothian Region, since 1974; *b* 11 June 1933; *s* of George Crowe and late Helen Davidson Semple (*née* Paterson); *m* 1958, Margaret Bain Donald; one *s* one *d. Educ:* Glasgow Univ.; Jordanhill Coll. of Educn; London Univ. BSc Hons, DipEd. Educn Officer, Northern Rhodesia, 1958-64; Zambia: Dep. Chief Educn Officer, 1964-66; Chief Educn Officer, 1966-67; Actg Dir of Techn. Educn, 1967-68; Edinburgh: Asst Dir of Educn, 1968-72; Depute Dir of Educn, 1972-74. *Publications:* contrib. Scottish Geog. Magazine. *Recreations:* gardening, reading, gastronomy. *Address:* 15 Essex Park, Edinburgh EH4 6LH. *T:* 031-339 6157.

SEN, Prof. Amartya Kumar, FBA 1977; Drummond Professor of Political Economy, Oxford University, since 1980 (Professor of Economics, 1977-80); Fellow of All Souls College, since 1980; *b* 3 Nov. 1933; *s* of late Dr Ashutosh Sen, Dacca, and of Amita Sen, Santiniketan, India; *m* 1st, 1960, Nabaneeta Dev (marr. diss. 1975); two *d* ; 2nd, 1978, Eva Colorni; one *s* one *d. Educ:* Calcutta Univ.; Cambridge Univ. MA, PhD. Educ. Prof. of Economics, Jadavpur Univ., Calcutta, 1956-58; Trinity Coll., Cambridge: Prize Fellow, 1957-61; Staff Fellow, 1961-63; Professor of Economics: Delhi Univ., 1963-71 (Chm., Dept of Economics, 1966-68); LSE, 1971-77; Fellow, Nuffield College, Oxford, 1977-80 (Associate Mem., 1980). Hon. Dir, Agricultural Economics Research Centre, Delhi, 1966-68 and 1969-71. Vis. Prof.: MIT, 1960-61; Univ. of Calif. at Berkeley, 1964-65; Harvard Univ., 1968-69; Andrew D. White Professor-at-large, Cornell Univ., 1978-. Chm., UN Expert Gp Meeting on Role of Advanced Skill and Technology, New York, 1967; Vice-Pres., Econometric Soc. (Fellow 1968); Mem. Council, Royal Economic Soc.; Pres., Development Studies Assoc., 1980-82. Foreign Hon. Mem., Amer. Acad. of Arts and Sciences, 1981; Hon. Mem., Amer. Econ. Assoc., 1981. Hon. Fellow, Inst. of Social Studies, The Hague, 1982. Hon. DLitt Saskatchewan, 1980. *Publications:* Choice of Techniques: an aspect of planned economic development, 1960 (3rd edn, 1968); Growth Economics, 1970; Collective Choice and Social Welfare, 1971; On Economic Inequality, 1973; Employment, Technology and Development, 1975; Poverty and Famines: an essay on entitlement and deprivation, 1981; (ed with Bernard Williams) Utilitarianism and Beyond, 1982; articles in various jls in economics, philosophy and political science. *Address:* All Souls College, Oxford OX1 4AL. *T:* Oxford 722251.

SEN, Shri Binay Ranjan, Padmabibhusan 1970; CIE 1944; ICS; Director-General of the United Nations Food and Agriculture Organisation, Rome, 1956-67; *b* 1 Jan. 1898; *s* of Dr K. M. Sen; *m* 1931, Chiroprova Chatterjee. *Educ:* Calcutta and Oxford Universities. Secretary to Govt of Bengal, Political and Appointment Departments, and Press Officer, 1931-34; District Magistrate, Midnapore, 1937-40; Revenue Secretary to Government of Bengal, 1940-43; Director of Civil Evacuation, Bengal, 1942-43; Relief Commissioner, 1942-43; Director-General of Food, Government of India, 1943-46; Sec. to Food Dept, Govt of India, 1946; Minister of the Embassy of India, at Washington, 1947-50; Indian Ambassador to: Italy and Yugoslavia, 1950-51; US and Mexico, 1951-52; Italy and Yugoslavia, 1952-55; Japan, 1955-56. Member Indian Delegation to General Assembly of United Nations, 1947; India's Rep. to United Nations Security Council, 1947; Agriculture Sec. to Govt of India, 1948; Head of Jt Mission of FAO and ECAFE (Economic Commn for Asia and the Far East) in Far East to study Agricultural Development plans; Head of Ind. Deleg. to: ECOSOC (Economic and Social Council of the UN), 1949 and 1953; Annual Conf. of FAO, 1949, and FAO Coun., 1950, 1951, 1953. Hon. Fellow, St Catherine's Coll., Oxford. Several Hon. degrees and decorations, incl. Kt Comdr Piani Ordinis, and Kt Grand Cross Ordinis Sancti Silvetri Papae. *Address:* 14/2 Palm Avenue, Calcutta 19, India.

SEN, K. Chandra; late Indian CS; *b* 5 Oct. 1888; *s* of Durgadas Sen and Mokshada Sundari Devi; *m* 1916, Lilavati Das-Gupta; one *s* two *d. Educ:* Hindu Sch., Calcutta; Presidency College, Calcutta; Trinity Hall, Cambridge (BA in Moral Sciences Tripos, 1913). Joined Indian Civil Service, 1913; Assistant Collector, Bombay Presidency, 1913-21; service in Judicial department of Government of Bombay since 1921; acted as a puisne judge of Bombay High Court, various times 1934-38; Secretary to Government of Bombay, Legal Department and Remembrancer of Legal Affairs, 1935-37; Additional Judge of High Court, 1939-41; Judge, High Court of Bombay, 1941-48; Pres. Industrial Court, Bombay, 1948-53; Pres. Bombay Co-op, Revenue, and Sales Tax Tribunals, between 1953 and 1959; Constitutional Adviser to Govt of West Bengal and Chm., State Law Commn, 1959-64; Chm., Police Commn, W Bengal, and Mem. Hindu Religious Endowments Commn, 1960-62. *Address:* A-12, Sea Face Park, Bombay 26, India. *T:* 82-4368.

SEN, Prof. Satyendra Nath, MA, PhD (Econ) London; Chairman, Board of Governors, Indian Institute of Technology, Kharagpur, since 1981; President, Calcutta Local Board and Member, Central Board of Directors, State Bank of India, since 1979; Vice-Chancellor, 1968-76, Professor of Economics, 1958-76, Calcutta University; *b* April 1908. Visited UK and other parts of Europe, 1949-51; Vis. Prof., Princeton and Stanford Univs (sponsored Ford Foundn), 1962-63; subseq. Dean, Faculties of Arts and Commerce, and Head of Dept of Econs, Calcutta University. Mem. Bd of Trustees: Indian Museum, Calcutta; Victoria Memorial, Calcutta; Mahajati Sadan, Calcutta; Mem. Research Programmes Cttee, Planning Commn, Govt of India (Chm. East Regional Cttee); Mem. Pay Commn, Govt of W Bengal, 1967-69; Discussion Leader, Section on Medium and Longterm Credit, Internat. Conf. on Agricultural Credit, Lahore (FAO and ECAFE), 1956; Mem. Industrial Tribunal adjudicating dispute between United Bank of India Ltd and its employees, 1954-55. Mem., Nat. Co-operative Union, Delhi; Vice-Pres., State Co-operative Union, W Bengal. Mem. Adv. Cttee of Vice-Chancellors, New Delhi, and Chm., Cttee on salary scales of univ. and coll. teachers, 1974, Univ. Grants Commn; Pres., Assoc. of Indian Univs, 1976; Mem., Central Adv. Commn on Educn, Govt of India, 1976. *Publications:* Central Banking in Undeveloped Money Markets, 1952; The City of Calcutta: a socio-economic survey, 1954-55 to 1957-58, 1960; The Co-operative Movement in West Bengal, 1966; (with T. Piplai) Industrial Relations in Jute Industry in West Bengal, 1968. *Address:* 18c Lake View Road, Calcutta, West Bengal, 700029, India.

SENDALL, Bernard Charles, CBE 1952; Deputy Director-General, Independent Broadcasting Authority (formerly Independent Television Authority), 1955-77; *b* 30 April 1913; *s* of late William Sendall, Malvern, Worcestershire; *m* 1963, Barbara Mary, *d* of late Ambrose Coviello, DCM, FRAM. *Educ:* Magdalen College, Oxford; Harvard University. Entered Civil Service in the Admiralty, 1935; Principal Private Secretary to Minister of Information 1941-45; Controller (Home), Central Office of Information, 1946-49; Controller, Festival of Britain Office, 1949-51; Assistant Secretary, Admiralty, 1951-55. *Publication:* Independent Television in Britain, vol. 1, 1982. *Address:* 144 Montagu Mansions, W1.

SENIOR, (Alan) Gordon, CBE 1981; CEng, FICE, FIStructE; in private practice as a Consulting Engineer since 1980; Founder Director, Ansen Offshore Consultants Ltd and McMillan Sloan & Partners; *b* 1 Jan. 1928; *s* of late Oscar Senior and Helen Senior (*née* Cooper); *m* 1st, 1955, Sheila Lockyer (marr. diss. 1961); 2nd, 1968, Lawmary Mitchell (marr. diss. 1978); one *s. Educ:* Normanton Grammar School; Leeds Univ. (BSc 1948, MSc 1949). J. B. Edwards (Whyteleafe) Ltd, 1949-51; Oscar Faber & Partners, Consulting Engineers, 1951-54; W. S. Atkins & Partners, Consulting Engineers, 1954-80: Technical Dir, 1967; Man. Dir of Atkins Research and Development, 1972; Director, W. S. Atkins & Partners, 1976. Member, Navy Dept Advisory Cttee on Structural Steels, 1967-71; Mem., Engineering Bd, SERC, 1974-78; Chm., Transport and Civil Engineering Cttee, SERC, 1974-78; Chm., Marine Technology Management Cttee, SERC, 1980-; Mem., Ship and Marine Technology Requirements Bd, and Chm., Marine Technology Cttee, 1976-81; Member: Maritime Technology Cttee, 1981-; Programme Cttee, Offshore Energy Technology Bd, 1978-. Vice-Pres. and Chm. of Council, Soc. for Underwater Technology, 1979-81. *Publications:* (co-author) Brittle Fracture of Steel Structures, 1970; papers on welding, fatigue and design of steel structures. *Recreations:* food and wine, travel, water ski-ing. *Address:* 31 Wolsey Road, Esher, Surrey KT10 8NT. *T:* Esher 62728. *Club:* Athenæum.

SENIOR, Derek; free-lance writer; *b* 4 May 1912; *s* of Oliver and Sally G. Senior; *m* 1st, 1942, Edith Frances Bentley; one *s* two *d* ; 2nd, 1959, Helen Elizabeth Mair; one *d. Educ:* six elementary schools; Manchester Grammar Sch.; Balliol Coll., Oxford (BA). Joined editorial staff of Manchester Guardian, 1937; turned free-lance, 1960. Member, Royal Commission on Local Government in England, 1966-69. Mem., Basildon Develt Corp., 1975-79. Hon. MRTPI (Hon. AMTPI 1956). *Publications:* Guide to the Cambridge Plan, 1956; Your Architect, 1964; The Regional City, 1966; Memorandum of Dissent from Redcliffe-Maud Report, 1969; Skopje Resurgent, 1971; numerous planning publications. *Recreations:* gardening, arguing. *Address:* Birling House, Birling, Maidstone, Kent. *T:* West Malling 842229.

SENIOR, Sir Edward (Walters), Kt 1970; CMG 1955; Chairman, Ransome Hoffman Pollard Ltd, 1953-72; Chairman, George Senior & Sons Ltd, since 1930 (Managing Director, 1929); *b* 29 March 1902; *s* of Albert Senior; *m* 1928, Stephanie Vera Heald; one *s* one *d. Educ:* Repton School; Sheffield University. Vice-Consul for Sweden, in Sheffield, 1930; RA, TA, Major, 1938; General Director of Alloy and Special Steels, Iron and Steel Control, 1941; Director, Steel Division of Raw Materials Mission, Washington, DC, 1942; Controller of Ball and Roller Bearings, 1944; British Iron and Steel Federation: Commercial Dir, 1949-61; Dir, 1961-62; Dir-Gen., 1962-66; retd, Dec. 1966; Exec. Chm., Derbyshire Stone Ltd, 1967-68; Dep. Chm., Tarmac Derby Ltd, 1968-71. Master of Cutlers' Company of Hallamshire in County of York, 1947; Vice-President of the Sheffield Chamber of Commerce, 1948; Chairman of Steel Re-Armament Panel, 1951. FBIM, 1971. JP Sheffield, 1937-50. *Recreations:* normal country activities. *Address:* Hollies, Church Close, Brenchley, Tonbridge, Kent TN12 7AA. *T:* Brenchley 2359. *Clubs:* Naval and Military; Sheffield (Sheffield).

SENIOR, Gordon; *see* Senior, A. G.

SENIOR, Olive Edith, JP, SRN; Regional Nursing Officer, Trent Regional Health Authority, since Nov. 1973; *b* 26 April 1934; *d* of Harold and Doris Senior, Mansfield, Notts. *Educ:* Harlow Wood Orthopaedic Hosp., 1949-52; St George's Hosp., Hyde Park Corner, 1952-56; City Hosp., Nottingham (Pt I, CMB 1956); Nottingham Univ. (HV Cert. 1957, MPhil 1978). Health Visitor, Notts CC, 1958-60; St George's Hosp., London (Ward Sister), 1960-63; S Africa, June-Dec. 1963; Forest Gate Hosp., London (SCM), 1964; St Mary's Hosp., Portsmouth (Asst Matron/Night Supt), 1964-66; NE Metropolitan Regional Hosp. Bd (Management Services), 1966-71; Chief Nursing Officer, Nottingham and Dist. Hosp. Management Cttee, 1971-73. Secretary of State Fellow, 1973. JP Nottingham Guildhall, 1973. *Publications:* An Analysis of Nurse Staffing Levels in Hospitals in the Trent Region (1977 Data), 1978; Dependency and Establishments, 1979; contrib. to Nursing Times (Determining Nursing Establishments). *Address:* Trent Regional Health Authority, Fulwood House, Old Fulwood Road, Sheffield S10 3TH. *T:* Sheffield 306511. *Club:* Nottingham Univ. (Nottingham).

SENIOR, Ronald Henry, DSO 1940, Bar 1943; TD; *b* 3 July 1904; *e s* of Lawrence Henry Senior and Emmadonna Shuttleworth, *d* of Reverend J. S. Holden, Aston-on-Trent, Derbyshire; *m* 1932, Hon. Norah Marguerite Joicey, *e d* of 2nd Baron Joicey; two *d. Educ:* Cheltenham College. Chairman, Nat. Assoc. of Port Employers, 1954-59. Joined TA 1924; served France, 1940; Middle East; Sicily, NW Europe. Hon. Rank Brigadier. *Recreation:* golf. *Address:* 110 Eaton Square, SW1. *Club:* Carlton.

SENIOR, William Hirst, CB 1964; Deputy Secretary (Agriculture), Dept of Agriculture and Fisheries for Scotland, 1958-66; *b* 24 August 1904; *o s* of Capt. Arthur Senior and Sarah G. G. Binns, Batley, Yorks; *m* 1930, Olive Kathleen (*d* 1978), *e d* of William Henry Killick, Shawford, Hampshire; two *s* three *d. Educ:* Bradford Grammar School; Reading University. BSc London 1926; MSc Reading 1929. Research Scholar, Reading Univ., 1926-28. Joined Dept of Agriculture for Scotland, 1929; Advisory Officer on Farm Economics, 1933; Principal, 1941; Secretary of Balfour of Burleigh Cttee on Hill Sheep Farming in Scotland, 1941-44; Asst Secretary, 1946; FRSE 1947; Under-Secretary, 1958. Mem., Agricultural Research Council, 1959-66. Chairman, Scottish Agricultural Improvement Council, 1960-66; Mem., Small Industries Council for Scotland. Pres., Agricl Econs Soc., 1963-64. Governor, Rannoch Sch. *Recreations:* varied. *Address:* Manse Wood, Innerwick, Dunbar, East Lothian. *Club:* Royal Commonwealth Society.

SENOUSSI, Badreddine; Officer, Order of Ouissame Alaouite, Morocco; Ambassador of the Kingdom of Morocco to the Court of St James's, 1977-80; *b* 30 March 1933; *m* 1958; three *s. Educ:* Univ. of Bordeaux, France (Lic. (MA) en Droit); Univ. Mohamed V Rabat, Morocco (Lic. ès Lettres). Counsellor, High Cherifian Tribunal, 1956; in charge of: State Min. of Public Functions, Mar. 1957; Nat. Defense Min., Mar.-Sept. 1958; Gen. Sec., Tobacco Management, Oct. 1958-Feb. 1963; Chief, Royal Cabinet, 1963-64; Under-Sec. of State for Commerce, Industry, Mines and Merchant Navy, Dec. 1964-June 1965; Under-Sec. of State for Admin. Affairs, June 1965-Feb. 1966; Post and Telecommunications Minister, Feb. 1966-Mar. 1970; Benslimane Dep., Mem. Representative Chamber, Aug. 1970; Youth, Sports and Social Affairs Minister, Mar. 1970-Aug. 1971; Ambassador of Kingdom of Morocco: in Washington, Sept 1971-Dec. 1974; in Teheran, Mar. 1974-Sept. 1976. Holds many foreign honours. *Address:* 238 Boulevard Zarktouni, Casablanca, Morocco. *Clubs:* Les Ambassadeurs, Mark's.

SENSI, His Eminence Cardinal (Giuseppe M.); *b* 27 May 1907. Ordained, 1929; Sec. of Apostolic Nunciature in Roumania, 1934-38; Secretary and Auditor of Apostolic Nunciature in Switzerland, 1938-46; Councillor of Apostolic Nunciature in Belgium, 1946-47; Chargé d'Affaires of the Holy See in Prague, 1948-49; Councillor in the Secretariat of State of His Holiness, 1949-53; Permanent Observer of the Holy See at UNESCO in Paris, 1953-55; apptd Nuncio Apostolic to Costa Rica, May 1955, and consecrated Titular Archbishop of Sardi, July 1955; Apostolic Delegate to Jerusalem, 1957; Apostolic Nuncio to Ireland, 1962-67; Apostolic Nuncio to Portugal, 1967-76; Cardinal, 1976. Hon. Mem., Accademia Cosentina, 1976. *Address:* Piazza S Calisto 16, 00153 Rome, Italy.

SEOUL, (Korea), Bishop of, since 1965; **Rt. Rev. Paul Chun Hwan Lee,** CBE 1974; *b* 5 April 1922; unmarried. *Educ:* St Michael's Theological Seminary, Seoul; St Augustine's College, Canterbury. Deacon, 1952 (Pusan Parish); Priest, 1953 (Sangju and Choungju Parish). Director of Yonsei University, Seoul, 1960-, Chm., Bd of Trustees, 1972-, Hon. DD 1971. Chairman: Christian Council of Korea, 1966-67; Christian Literature Soc. of Korea, 1968-; Korean Bible Soc., 1972- (Vice-Pres., 1969-72); Nat. Council of Churches in Korea, 1976-. Hon. LLD Korea, 1978. *Recreation:* reading. *Address:* 3 Chong Dong, Seoul 100, Korea. *T:* 725-6157.

SEPEKU, Rt. Rev. John; *see* Dar-es-Salaam, Bishop of.

SERBY, John Edward, CB 1958; CBE 1951; FRAeS; Consultant; *b* 15 March 1902; *m* 1933, Clarice Lilian (*née* Hawes); one *d. Educ:* Haberdashers' Aske's School; Emmanuel College, Cambridge (BA). Junior Scientific Officer, Admiralty, 1927-30; Scientific Officer, RAE, 1930-38; Headquarters, MAP, 1938-50; Deputy Director, Royal Aircraft Establishment, Farnborough, 1950-54; Dir-Gen. of Guided Weapons, Min. of Aviation, 1954-61. Dep. Controller Guided Weapons, Ministry of Aviation, 1961-63. *Recreation:* gardening. *Address:* Overwey, Bishopsmead, Farnham, Surrey. *T:* Farnham 713526.

SERGEANT, (Herbert) Howard, MBE 1978; Founder, and Editor, Outposts (quarterly poetry magazine), since 1944; *b* 6 May 1914; *s* of Edwin Sergeant and Edith Alice Sergeant (*née* Crowther); *m* 1954, Jean Crabtree; one *s* three *d. Educ:* Hull Grammar Sch.; Hull Coll. of Commerce, and privately. FCCA, FCIS, MBIM, FSCA. Dist Chief Accountant, Broadcast Relay Services, 1935-41; Travelling Accountant, Air Min., 1941-48; Co. Sec. and Accountant, Jordan & Sons Ltd, 1949-54; Co. Sec. and Gp Accountant, E. Austin & Sons (London) Ltd, 1954-63; Lectr, Norwood Tech. Coll., 1963-65; Sen. Lectr, Wandsworth Tech. Coll., 1965-68; Sen. Lectr, 1969-72, Head of Sch. of Management, 1972-78, Brooklands Tech. Coll., Weybridge; Creative Writing Fellow, Queen Mary's Coll., Basingstoke, 1978-79. Dorothy Tutin Award, 1980; Henry Shore Award, 1980. *Publications:* poetry: The Leavening Air, 1946; The Headlands, 1954; Selected Poems, 1980; Travelling Without a Valid Ticket, 1982; *criticism:* The Cumberland Wordsworth, 1950; Tradition in the Making of Modern Poetry, 1952; A Critical Survey of South African Poetry (Cape Town), 1958; compiled selections from the poetry of Milton, 1953, and from Milton and Wordsworth, 1970; ed *anthologies of poetry:* For Those Who Are Alive, 1946; An Anthology of Contemporary Northern Poetry, 1947; These Years (for schools), 1950; (jtly) New Poems, a PEN anthology, 1953; (jtly) Mavericks, 1957; Commonwealth Poems of Today, 1967; New Voices of the Commonwealth, 1968; Poems from Hospital, 1968; Universities' Poetry 8, 1968; Poetry from Africa, 1968; Poetry from Australia, 1969; The Swinging Rainbow, for children, 1969; Poetry from India, 1970; Poetry of the 1940s, 1970; Happy Landings, for children, 1971; Evans Book of Children's Verse, 1972; African Voices, 1973; For Today and Tomorrow, 1974; Poetry South East I, 1976; New Poems 1976/77, a PEN anthology, 1976; Two Continents Book of Children's Verse, 1977; Candles and Lamps, 1979; Poems from The Medical World, 1979; How Strong the Roots, 1981; The Gregory Awards Anthology 1981-82, 1982; ed (jtly) annual Borestone Mountain Poetry Award anthologies, Best Poems of 1949-76. *Recreations:* walking, writing, poetry workshops. *Address:* 72 Burwood Road, Walton-on-Thames, Surrey KT12 4AL. *T:* Walton-on-Thames 40712. *Clubs:* PEN, Society of Authors, Poetry Society; Ver Poets (St Albans) (Vice Pres.).

SERGEANT, Patrick; City Editor, Daily Mail, since 1960; *b* 17 March 1924; *s* of George and Rene Sergeant; *m* 1952, Gillian Anne Wilks, Cape Town; two *d. Educ:* Beaumont Coll. Served as Lieut, RNVR, 1945. Asst City Editor, News Chronicle, 1948; Dep. City Editor, Daily Mail, 1953. Founded Euromoney, and Managing Dir, 1969-; Dir, Associated Newspapers Group, 1971-. Wincott Award, Financial Journalist of the Year, 1979. *Publications:* Another Road to Samarkand, 1953; Money Matters, 1967; Inflation Fighters Handbook, 1976. *Recreations:* skiing, tennis, swimming, talking. *Address:* One The Grove, Highgate Village, N6 6JU. *T:* 01-340 1245. *Clubs:* Royal Automobile, Annabelle's; Cumberland Lawn Tennis.

SERGENT, René Edmond, Hon. KBE 1973; Officier de la Légion d'Honneur, 1952; *b* 16 January 1904; *s* of Charles Sergent and Emma Duvernet; *m* 1931, Monique Schweisguth; three *s* three *d. Educ:* Lycée Janson-de-Sailly, Paris, France; Ecole Polytechnique. Sub-Lieut, Artillery, 1925; Assistant, Inspection Générale des Finances, 1929; Financial Controller, Nat. Socs of Aeronautical Construction, 1937; Direction du Commerce Extérieur, 1940; Pres., French Economic and Financial Deleg. to Control Commission, Berlin, 1945; Financial Attaché, French Embassy, London, 1947; Asst Sec.-Gen. for Economics and Finance, NATO, 1952; Secretary-Gen. of OEEC, Paris, 1955; Vice-Prés. Délégué, Syndicat Général de la Construction Electrique, 1960; Président, Groupement des Industries de la Construction Electrique, 1969-75. *Address:* 1 Boulevard de Beauséjour, 75016 Paris, France. *T:* 288 3031.

SERIES, Sir Emile; *see* Seriès, Sir J. M. E.

SERIES, Prof. George William, FRS 1971; Professor of Physics, University of Reading, 1968. Emeritus 1982; *b* 22 Feb. 1920; *s* of William Series and Alice (*née* Crosthwaite); *m* 1948, Annette (*née* Pepper); three *s* one *d. Educ:* Reading Sch.; St John's Coll., Oxford. MA 1946, DPhil 1950, DSc 1969, Oxford. Served with Friends' Ambulance Unit, 1942-46. Open Schol., Oxford, 1938; 1st cl. hons Physics, Oxford, 1947; Nuffield Research Fellow,

1950. University Demonstrator, Oxford, 1951; St Edmund Hall, Oxford: Lectr, 1953; Fellow, 1954; Emeritus Fellow, 1969. William Evans Vis. Prof., Univ. of Otago, 1972; Raman Vis. Prof. Indian Acad. of Sci., 1982-83. Hon. Editor, Jl of Physics B (Atomic and Molecular Physics), 1975-79; Editor, Europ. Jl Physics, 1980. William F. Meggers Award, Opt. Soc. Amer., 1982. *Publication:* Spectrum of Atomic Hydrogen, 1957. *Recreation:* family. *Address:* J. J. Thomson Physical Laboratory, Whiteknights, Reading RG6 2AF. *T:* Reading 875123.

SERIES, Sir (Joseph Michel) Emile, Kt 1978; CBE 1974; FCIS, FAIA, FSCA, FREconS; Chairman and General Manager, Flacq United Estates Ltd and WEAL Group (West East Ltd), since 1968; *b* 29 Sept. 1918; *s* of late Emile Series and Julie (*née* Langlois); *m* 1942, Rose-Aimée Jullienne; two *s* two *d*. *Educ:* Royal Coll., Mauritius; London Univ. MCom Delhi Commercial Univ., 1967. FBIM; FCCS 1958. Accounts Dept, General Electric Supply Co. of Mauritius Ltd, 1936-52 (final position, Chief Acct); Chief Acct and Econ. Adviser, Union Flacq Sugar Estate Ltd and Flacq United Estates Ltd, 1952-61; Manager, Union Flacq Sugar Estate Ltd, 1961-68. Chairman: Alcohol & Molasses Co. Ltd; City & Beach Hotels (Mauritius) Ltd; Compagnie Mauricienne de Commerce Ltd. Director: Maur. Commercial Bank Ltd; Reinsurance Co. of Maur. Ltd; Maur. Oil Refineries Co. Ltd; La Nouvelle Quincaillerie Mauricienne Ltd; Anglo-Maur. Assurance Society Ltd; Maur. Farms Ltd, and other cos in Mauritius. Past President: Maur. Chamber of Agriculture; Maur. Sugar Industry Research Inst. Member: Maur. Sugar Producers' Assoc.; Maur. Sugar Syndicate; Amer. Management Assoc., New York; National Assoc. of Accts, New York. FRSA. Chevalier de l'Ordre National du Mérite (France), 1978. *Recreations:* sailing, shooting, photography, classical music, horse racing. *Address:* Flacq United Estates Ltd, Union Flacq, Mauritius. *T:* 532-583 and 535535. *Clubs:* Dodo, Mauritius Turf, Grand'Baie Yacht (Mauritius).

SERJEANT, Graham Roger, CMG 1981; MD; FRCP; Director, Medical Research Council Laboratories, Jamaica, since 1974; *b* 26 Oct. 1938; *s* of Ewart Egbert and Violet Elizabeth Serjeant; *m* 1965, Beryl Elizabeth, *d* of Ivor Edward King, *qv. Educ:* Sibford Sch., Banbury; Bootham Sch., York; Clare Coll., Cambridge (BA 1960, MA 1965); London Hosp. Med. Sch.; Makerere Coll., Kampala. MB BChir 1963, MD 1971, Cantab; MRCP 1966, FRCP 1977. House Physician: London Hosp., 1963-64; Royal United Hosp., Bath, 1965-66; RPMS, 1966; Med. Registrar, University Hosp. of WI, 1966-67; Wellcome Res. Fellow, Dept of Medicine, Univ. of WI, 1967-71; Medical Research Council: Mem., Scientific Staff, Abnormal Haemoglobin Unit, Cambridge, 1971-72; Epidemiology Res. Unit, Jamaica, 1972-74. Hon. Prof. Faculty of Medicine, Univ. of WI, 1981. *Publications:* The Clinical Features of Sickle Cell Disease, 1974; numerous papers on the nat. hist. of sickle cell disease, in med. jls. *Recreation:* squash. *Address:* Medical Research Council Laboratories, University of the West Indies, Mona, Kingston 7, Jamaica, WI. *T:* (809) 927-0687. *Club:* Liguanea (Kingston).

SERJEANT, Robert Bertram; Sir Thomas Adams's Professor of Arabic since 1970, and Director, Middle East Centre, since 1965, University of Cambridge; *b* 23 March 1915; *er s* of R. T. R. and A. B. Serjeant; *m* Marion Keith Serjeant (*née* Robertson), MB, ChB; one *s* one *d. Educ:* Edinburgh; Trinity Coll., Cambridge. Vans Dunlop Schol. 1935; Visit to Syria, 1935; MA 1st Cl. Hons Semitic Langs, Edinburgh Univ., 1936; PhD Cambridge 1939; Tweedie Fellow Edinburgh, 1939; Studentship, SOAS, for research in S Arabia, 1940; Governor's Commn in Aden Prot. G Guards, 1940-41. Attached Mission 106. Lectr, SOAS, 1941; Seconded to BBC Eastern Service, 1942; Editor, Arabic Listener, 1943-45; Min. of Inf., Editor Arabic pubns, 1944. Colonial Research Fell., in Hadramawt, 1947-48; Reader in Arabic, 1948; Research in S Arabia and Persian Gulf, 1953-54; in N Nigeria, Minister of Education's mission to examine instruction in Arabic, 1956; Sec. of State for Colonies' mission to examine Muslim Education in E Africa, 1957; Inter-University Council's Advisory Delegation on University of N Nigeria, 1961; Research in Trucial States, Yemen, Aden, 1963-64 and 1966; Professor of Arabic, 1955-64, Middle East Department, SOAS, University of London; Lectr in Islamic History, ME Centre, Univ. of Cambridge, 1964-66, Reader in Arabic Studies, 1966-70. Member: ME Comd Expedition to Socotra, 1967; Cambridge expedn to San'a' and N Yemen, 1972. Member: Royal Soc. for Asian Affairs; Royal Asiatic Soc.; Corresp. Mem., Arab Acad., Cairo, 1976. Lawrence of Arabia Meml Medal, RCAS, 1974; Sir Richard Burton Meml Medal, RAS, 1981. Co-editor, Arabian Studies, 1973-. *Publications:* Cat. Arabic, Persian & Hindustani MSS in New College, Edinburgh, 1942; Materials for a History of Islamic Textiles, 1942-51; Prose and Poetry from Hadramawt, I, 1950; Saiyids of Hadramawt, 1957; Portuguese off the South Arabian Coast, 1961; The South Arabian Hunt, 1976; (ed with R. Lewcock) San'a': an Arabian Islamic city, 1981; articles in BSOAS, JRAS, Le Muséon, Rivista d. Studi Orientali, Islamic Culture, etc. *Address:* Faculty of Oriental Studies, Sidgwick Avenue, Cambridge.

SERKIN, Rudolf, Presidential Medal of Freedom, 1963; Director, Curtis Institute of Music, Philadelphia, Pa, 1968-76, Head of Piano Department, 1939-76; *b* 28 March 1903; *s* of Mordko Serkin and Augusta Schargel; *m* 1935, Irene Busch; two *s* four *d. Educ:* Vienna, Austria. Concert Pianist: Début, Vienna, 1915; USA since 1933; New York Philharmonic with Arturo Toscanini, 1936. President of Marlboro School of Music, Marlboro, Vermont. Mem., Nat. Council on the Arts, USA; Fellow, Amer. Acad. of Arts and Scis; Hon. Member: Accademia Nationale di Santa Cecilia; Verein Beethoven Haus, Bonn; Philharmonic-Symphony Soc. of NY. Dr *hc* : Curtis Inst., Philadelphia;

Temple Univ., Philadelphia; Univ. of Vermont; Williams Coll., Williamstown, Mass; Oberlin Coll.; Rochester Univ.; Harvard; Marlboro Coll. Kennedy Center Honors, 1981. Orden pour le Mérite für Wissenschaften und Künste, W Germany, 1981. *Address:* RFD 3, Brattleboro, Vermont 05301, USA.

SEROTA, family name of **Baroness Serota.**

SEROTA, Baroness, *cr* 1967 (Life Peer), of Hampstead in Greater London; **Beatrice Serota,** JP; Chairman, Commission for Local Administration, 1974-82; Governor, BBC, 1977-82; *b* 15 Oct. 1919; *m* 1942, Stanley Serota, BSc (Eng), FICE; one *s* one *d. Educ:* John Howard School; London School of Economics (BSc (Econ)); Hon. Fellow, 1976. Member: Hampstead Borough Council, 1945-49; LCC for Brixton, 1954-65 (Chm., Children's Cttee, 1958-65); GLC for Lambeth, 1964-67 (Chief Whip). Baroness in Waiting, 1968-69; Minister of State (Health), Dept of Health and Social Security, 1969-70. Member: Adv. Council in Child Care, and Central Training Council in Child Care, 1958-68; Adv. Council on Treatment of Offenders, 1960-64; Longford Cttee on "Crime—A Challenge to us all", 1964; Royal Commn on Penal System, 1964-66; Latey Cttee on Age of Majority, 1965-67; Adv. Council on Penal System, 1966-68, 1974-79 (Chm., 1976-79); Seebohm Cttee on Organization of Local Authority Personal Social Services, 1966-68; Community Relations Commn, 1970-76; BBC Complaints Commn, 1975-77. Pres., Volunteer Centre. JP Inner London (West Central Division). Peerage conferred for services to children. *Recreations:* crochet, gardening, collecting shells. *Address:* The Coach House, 15 Lyndhurst Terrace, NW3.

SERPELL, Sir David Radford, KCB 1968 (CB 1962); CMG 1952; OBE 1944; Member, British Railways Board, 1974-82; *b* 10 Nov. 1911; 2nd *s* of Charles Robert and Elsie Leila Serpell, Plymouth; *m* 1st, Ann Dooley (marr. diss.); three *s* ; 2nd, Doris Farr. *Educ:* Plymouth Coll.; Exeter Coll., Oxford; Univ. of Toulouse (DèsL); Syracuse University, USA; Fletcher School of Law and Diplomacy, USA. (Fell.) Imp. Economic Cttee, 1937-39; Min. of Food, 1939-42; Min. of Fuel and Power, 1942-45; Under-Sec., HM Treasury, 1954-60; Dep. Sec., MoT, 1960-63; Second Sec., BoT, 1963-66; Second Permanent Sec., 1966-68; Second Sec., Treasury, 1968; Permanent Secretary: MoT, 1968-70; DoE, 1970-72. Private Sec. to Parly Sec., Ministry of Food, 1941-42; Principal Private Sec. to Minister of Fuel and Power, 1942-45. Chairman: Nature Conservancy Council, 1973-77; Ordnance Survey Review Cttee, 1978-79; Cttee on the Review of Railway Finances, 1982; Member: NERC, 1973-76; Council, National Trust, 1973-80. *Recreations:* walking, golf. *Address:* 25 Crossparks, Dartmouth, Devon TQ6 9HP. *T:* Dartmouth 2073. *Club:* United Oxford & Cambridge University.

SERVAN-SCHREIBER, Jean-Jacques; engineer, journalist, author, politician; *b* Paris, 13 Feb. 1924; *s* of late Emile Servan-Schreiber, journalist, and of Denise Bresard; *m* 1960, Sabine de Fouquières; four *s. Educ:* Lycée Janson-de-Sailly, Paris; Lycée de Grenoble; Ecole Polytechnique. Served as fighter pilot, Free French Air Force, World War II. Diplomatic Editor of Le Monde, 1948-53; Founder and Director of weekly news-magazine, L'Express, 1953-69. Deputy for Lorraine, French National Assembly, 1970-78; Minister of Reforms, June 1974. Pres., Region of Lorraine, 1976-78. President: Radical Party, 1971-79; "Paris Group", 1979; World Center (micro-electronics and human develt), 1981. Holds military cross for valour. *Publications:* Lieutenant en Algérie, 1957 (Lieutenant in Algeria); Le défi américain, 1967 (The American Challenge); Le Manifeste Radical, 1970 (The Radical Alternative); Le Défi mondial, 1980 (The World Challenge). *Address:* 49 boulevard de Courcelles, 75008 Paris, France.

SERVICE, Alastair Stanley Douglas; General Secretary, Family Planning Association, since 1980; writer and publisher; *b* 8 May 1933; *s* of Douglas William Service and Evelyn Caroline (*née* Sharp); *m* 1959, Louisa Anne (*née* Hemming), *qv* ; one *s* one *d. Educ:* Westminster Sch.; Queen's Coll., Oxford. Midshipman, RNR, 1952-54. Director: McKinlay, Watson and Co. Ltd, Brazil, USA and London, 1959-64 (export finance); Seeley, Service and Co. Ltd (publishers), 1965-79; Municipal Journal Ltd, 1970-78. Hon. Parly Officer: Abortion Law Reform Assoc., during passage of Abortion Act, 1964-67; Divorce Law Reform Union, during passage of Divorce Reform Act, 1967-69; Chm., Birth Control Campaign, during passage of NHS (Family Planning) Amendment Act, 1972, and NHS Reorganisation Act, 1973 (made vasectomy and contraception available free from NHS); involved in other parly campaigns, incl.: Town and Country Amenities Act, 1974; Children's Act, 1975; Public Lending Right for Authors; One-Parent Families. Member: cttees, FPA, 1964- (Mem. Nat. Exec. Cttee, 1972-79, Chm., 1975-79); Health Educn Council (Sec. of State appointee), 1976- (Vice-Chm., 1979-); Cttee, Nat. Council for One-Parent Families, 1979-; Cttee, Victorian Soc., 1976-; Cttee, Family Forum, 1981-. *Publications:* A Birth Control Plan for Britain (with Dr John Dunwoody and Dr Tom Stuttaford), 1972; The Benefits of Birth Control—Aberdeen's Experience, 1973; Edwardian Architecture and its Origins, 1975; Edwardian Architecture, 1977; The Architects of London from 1066 to Present Day, 1979; London 1900, 1979; (with Jean Bradbery) Megaliths of Europe, 1979; Lost Worlds, 1981; Edwardian Interiors, 1982; series editor, The Buildings of Britain, and author, Anglo-Saxon and Norman vol., 1982; articles in Arch. Rev., Arch. Assoc. Qly, Guardian, etc. *Recreations:* looking at buildings, opera, squash et al. *Address:* 75 Flask Walk, NW3.

SERVICE, Louisa Anne, JP; Joint Chairman, The Municipal Group of Companies, since 1976; *d* of late Henry Harold Hemming, OBE, MC, and of Alice Louisa Weaver, OBE; *m* 1959, Alastair Stanley Douglas Service, *qv*; one *s* one *d*. *Educ*: private and state schs, Canada, USA and Britain; Ecole des Sciences Politiques, Paris; St Hilda's Coll., Oxford (BA and MA, PPE). Export Dir, Ladybird Appliances Ltd, 1957-59; Municipal Journal Ltd and associated cos: Financial Dir, 1966; Dep. Chm., 1974; Chm., Merchant Printers Ltd, 1975-80; Dir, Brintex Ltd, 1965-; Dir, Glass's Guides Services Ltd, 1971, Dep. Chm. 1976-81, Chm., 1982-. Mem., Dept of Trade Consumer Credit Act Appeals Panel, 1981-. JP Inner London Juvenile Courts, 1969; Chm., Hackney Juvenile Court, 1975-82, Westminster Juvenile Ct, 1982; JP Inner London (5) PSD, 1980-; Chm., Exec. Cttee, Inner London Juvenile Courts, 1977-79; Mem., working party on re-org. of London Juvenile Courts, 1975; Vice-Chm., Paddington Probation Hostel, 1976-. Corres. mem., SDP Policy Gp on Citizens' Rights, 1982-. Chm. Council, Mayer-Lismann Opera Workshop; Hon. Sec., Women's India Assoc. of UK, 1967-74. Dir, Arts Club Ltd, 1981. *Publications*: articles on a variety of subjects. *Recreations*: travel, and attractive and witty people including my family. *Address*: c/o The Municipal Journal Ltd, 178-202 Great Portland Street, W1N 6NH. *T*: 01-637 2400. *Club*: Arts.
See also J. H. Hemming.

SESSFORD, Rt. Rev. George Minshull; *see* Moray, Ross and Caithness, Bishop of.

SETH, Prof. George; Professor of Psychology, 1958-71, Head of Department of Psychology, 1946-71, The Queen's University, Belfast; now Professor Emeritus; *b* 23 April 1905; *s* of George Seth and Jane Steven Loudon; *m* 1936, May, *er d* of John Dods, Edinburgh, and Lily Anderson; three *s* one *d*. *Educ*: Royal High School and University of Edinburgh. MA (Edin.) 1928; BEd (Edin.) 1930; PhD (Edin.) 1933. Assistant in Psychology, Edinburgh University and University Psychological Clinic, 1930-34; Research Fellow, Yale Univ., USA, 1934-35; Lecturer in Education, University College, Cardiff, and Psychologist, Cardiff Child Guidance Clinic, 1935-46; Senior Psychologist, Welsh Board of Health, (Evacuation Service), 1941-45. Vans Dunlop Scholar (Psychology), Edinburgh, 1930-33; Rockefeller Fellow, USA, 1935-36. Fellow, British Psychological Soc., President, 1967, Vice-Pres., 1968; President, Psychology Section, British Association, 1961. Member: Psychology Bd, CNAA, 1968-75; N Ireland Council for Educnl Research. Hon. Fellow, Psychological Soc. of Ireland, 1970, Lectr 1975. *Publications*: (with Douglas Guthrie) Speech in Childhood, 1934; articles in various psychological and educational jls. *Address*: 24 Osborne Park, Belfast BT9 6SN.

SETON, Lady, (Alice Ida), CBE 1949; Group Officer, WRAF, retired; *d* of late P. C. Hodge, Port Elizabeth, South Africa; *m* 1923, Capt. Sir John Hastings Seton, 10th Bt (from whom she obtained a divorce, 1950); one *s* (*see* Sir Robert Seton, 11th Bt) one *d*. Joined WAAF as Assistant Section Officer, 1939. *Address*: 3 Maddison Close, Teddington, Mddx.

SETON, Anya, (Anya Seton Chase); Author; *b* as British subject, New York City, USA; *d* of late Ernest Thompson Seton and late Grace Gallatin Thompson Seton. *Educ*: private tutors in England. *Publications*: (in USA, UK and 20 foreign countries) My Theodosia, 1941; Dragonwyck, 1944; The Turquoise, 1946; The Hearth and the Eagle, 1948; Foxfire, 1951; Katherine, 1954; The Mistletoe and Sword (juvenile), 1956; The Winthrop Woman, 1958; Washington Irving (juvenile), 1960; Devil Water, 1962; Avalon, 1966; Green Darkness, 1972; Smouldering Fires (juvenile), 1975. *Recreations*: swimming, croquet, bridge, cooking. *Address*: Binney Lane, Old Greenwich, Conn 06870, USA. *Clubs*: (Hon.) Pen and Brush (New York); PEN.

SETON, Sir (Christopher) Bruce, 12th Bt *cr* 1663, of Abercorn; farmer; *b* 3 Oct. 1909; *s* of Charles Henry Seton (*d* 1917) and Mrs V. A. Neilson (*d* 1973), Greys, Kelvedon, Essex; *S* cousin, 1969; *m* 1939, Joyce Vivian, *e d* of late O. G. Barnard, Stowmarket; two *s* two *d*. *Educ*: Marlborough; Univ. of Cambridge (BA Agric. 1931). Farming since 1931. *Heir*: *s* Iain Bruce Seton [*b* 27 Aug. 1942; *m* 1963, Margaret Ann, *o d* of Walter Charles Faulkner; one *s* one *d*]. *Address*: Bay Laurel, Thorrington Road, Great Bentley, Colchester, Essex. *T*: Colchester 250723.

SETON, Lady, (Julia), VMH; (Julia Clements, professionally); author, speaker, international floral art judge; flower arrangement judge for RHS and National Association of Flower Arrangement Societies; *d* of late Frank Clements; *m* 1962, Sir Alexander Hay Seton, 10th Bt, of Abercorn (*d* 1963); no *c*. *Educ*: Isle of Wight; Zwicker College, Belgium. Organised and conducted first Judges' School in England at Royal Horticultural Society Halls; has since conducted many other courses for judges all over Britain. VMH, RHS, 1974. *Publications*: Fun with Flowers; Fun without Flowers; 101 Ideas for Flower Arrangement; Party Pieces; The Julia Clements Colour Book of Flower Arrangements; Flower Arrangements in Stately Homes; Julia Clements' Gift Book of Flower Arranging; Flowers in Praise; The Art of Arranging a Flower, etc. *Address*: 122 Swan Court, SW3. *T*: 01-352 9039. *Clubs*: Women's Press, Anglo-Belge.

SETON, Sir Robert (James), 11th Bt, *cr* 1683; *b* 20 April 1926; *s* of Captain Sir John Hastings Seton, 10th Bt and Alice (*see* Lady Seton), *d* of Percy Hodge, Cape Civil Service; *S* father 1956; unmarried. *Educ*: HMS Worcester (Thames Nautical Training College). Midshipman RNVR (invalided), 1943-

44. Banker, with Hong Kong and Shanghai Banking Corpn, 1946-61 (retd). *Heir*: *kinsman* James Christall Seton [*b* 21 Jan. 1913; *m* 1939, Evelyn, *d* of Ray Hafer]. *Address*: c/o The Hong Kong and Shanghai Banking Corporation, 99 Bishopsgate, EC2P 2LA.

SETON-WATSON, Prof. George Hugh Nicholas, CBE 1981; DLitt; FBA 1969; Professor of Russian History, School of Slavonic and East European Studies, University of London, since 1951; *b* 15 Feb. 1916; *er s* of late Prof. Robert William Seton-Watson and late Mrs Seton-Watson; *m* 1947, Mary Hope, *d* of late G. D. Rokeling, lately of Ministry of Education; three *d*. *Educ*: Winchester; New College, Oxford. DLitt Oxon, 1974. Was attached to British Legations in Roumania and Yugoslavia, 1940-41; served Special Forces GHQ, Middle East, 1941-44. Fellow and Praelector in Politics, University Coll., Oxford, 1946-51. Mem. Council, RIIA, 1952-. Vis. Prof., Columbia Univ., 1957-58; Fellow, Center for Advanced Study in the Behavioural Sciences, Stanford, Calif., 1963-64; Vis. Fellow, ANU, Canberra, 1964; Visiting Professor: Indiana Univ., 1973; Washington Univ., Seattle, 1973. Mem. Res. Council Center for Strategic and Internat. Studies, Georgetown Univ., 1975-79, 1982-. *Publications*: Eastern Europe between the Wars, 1945; The East European Revolution, 1950; The Decline of Imperial Russia, 1952; The Pattern of Communist Revolution, 1953; Neither War Nor Peace, 1960; The New Imperialism, 1961; Nationalism and Communism (Essays, 1946-63); The Russian Empire, 1801-1917, 1967; The "Sick Heart" of Modern Europe, 1976; Nations and States, 1977; The Imperialist Revolutionaries, 1978; (ed jtly with C. Seton-Watson, L. Boban, M. Gross, B. Krizman, D. Sepic) R. W. Seton-Watson and the Yugoslavs: correspondence 1906-1941 (2 vols), 1976; (with C. Seton-Watson) The Making of a New Europe: R. W. Seton-Watson and the last years of Austria-Hungary, 1981. *Recreations*: travel, ornithology. *Address*: 8 Burghley Road, Wimbledon Common, SW19. *T*: 01-946 0861. *Club*: Athenæum.

SETSHOGO, Boithoko Moonwa; Founding Partner and Managing Director, Media Productions (Pty) Ltd, Gaborone, since 1980; *b* Serowe, 16 June 1941; *m* 1971, Jennifer Tlalane; two *d*. *Educ*: Moeng Coll.; Univ. of Botswana, Lesotho and Swaziland (BA). District Officer, Kanye, 1969-70; First Sec., High Commn, London, 1970-72; Clerk to the Cabinet, 1972-73; Under-Sec., Min. of Commerce and Industry, 1973-75; High Comr of Botswana in London, 1975-78; Dir of Inf. and Broadcasting, 1978-80. *Address*: PO Box 20645, Bontleng, Gaborone, Botswana.

SETTRINGTON, Lord; Charles Henry Gordon-Lennox; *b* 8 Jan. 1955; *s* and *heir* of Earl of March and Kinrara, *qv*; *m* 1976, Sally, *d* of late Maurice Clayton and of Mrs Denis Irwin. *Educ*: Eton. *Address*: Goodwood House, Chichester, West Sussex.

SEUFFERT, Stanislaus, QC 1965; Special Divorce Commissioner and Deputy Judge, 1967-75; Barrister-at-Law, retired 1975; *b* Johannesburg, 15 May 1899; *e s* of late Philip Seuffert and Marie Winefride Seuffert (*née* Brennan); *m* 1st, Alice, widow of George Jackson (*née* McCarthy); 2nd, Norma (*née* Klerck), widow of Maj.-Gen. Pienaar, CB, DSO; one *s* one *d*. *Educ*: Marist Brothers, Johannesburg; Stonyhurst Coll., Lancashire. Served World War, Middx Regt, 1917. Barrister, Middle Temple, 1925, Bencher, 1970. Mem. Senate, Four Inns of Court, 1970-74. First Chm., Guild of Catholic Artists, 1929; Chm. Catholic Prisoners' Aid Soc., 1938-60; Hon. Treas. and Sec., Soc. of Our Lady of Good Counsel, 1935-58. Contested (Lab) East Grinstead, 1935; Borough Councillor, Fulham, 1934-49; Dep. Civil Def. Controller, Fulham, and Leader of Council, 1939-44; Chm. Fulham Food Control Committee, 1939-46; Mayor of Fulham 1944-45. KHS Grand Cross, 1955; Kt of Order of St Gregory (Papal), 1962. *Publications*: annotations: Matrimonial Causes Act, 1937; Local Govt Act, 1949; Adoption Act, 1950. Handbook of Matrimonial Causes. *Recreations*: playgoing, reading. *Address*: 2 Gaywood Court, 42 Hawthorne Road, Bickley, Bromley BR1 2HN. *T*: 01-467 6427.

SEVER, (Eric) John; MP (Lab) Birmingham Ladywood, since Aug. 1977; *b* 1 April 1943; *s* of Eric and Clara Sever. *Educ*: Sparkhill Commercial School. Travel Executive with tour operator, 1970-77. PPS to the Solicitor General, 1978-79. *Recreations*: theatre, cinema, reading. *Address*: 14 Brookfield Precinct, Birmingham B18 7BU. *T*: 021-236 8057.

SEVERIN, (Giles) Timothy; author, traveller and historian; *b* 25 Sept. 1940; *s* of Maurice Watkins and Inge Severin; *m* 1966, Dorothy Virginia Sherman (marr. diss. 1979); one *d*. *Educ*: Tonbridge School; Keble Coll., Oxford. MA, BLitt. Commonwealth Fellow, USA, 1964-66. Expeditions: led motorcycle team along Marco Polo route, 1961; R Mississippi by canoe and launch, 1965; Brendan Voyage from W Ireland to N America, 1977; Sinbad Voyage from Oman to China, 1980-81. *Publications*: Tracking Marco Polo, 1964; Explorers of the Mississippi, 1967; The Golden Antilles, 1970; The African Adventure, 1973; Vanishing Primitive Man, 1973; The Oriental Adventure, 1976; The Brendan Voyage, 1978; The Sindbad Voyage, 1982. *Address*: Courtmacsherry, Co. Cork, Eire. *T*: Bandon 46127. *Club*: United Oxford & Cambridge University.

SEVERN, David; *see* Unwin, David Storr.

SEVERNE, Air Vice-Marshal John de Milt, MVO 1961; OBE 1968; AFC 1955; Captain of the Queen's Flight, since 1982; *b* 15 Aug. 1925; *s* of late Dr A. de M. Severne, Wateringbury, Kent; *m* 1951, Katharine Veronica, *d* of late

Captain V. E. Kemball, RN (Retd); three d. *Educ:* Marlborough. Joined RAF, 1944; Flying Instr., Cranwell, 1948; Staff Instr. and PA to Comdt CFS, 1950-53; Flt Comdr No 98 Sqdn, Germany, 1954-55; Sqdn Comdr No 26 Sqdn, Germany, 1956-57; Air Min., 1958; Equerry to Duke of Edinburgh, 1958-61; psa 1962; Chief Instr No 226 Operational Conversion Unit (Lightning), 1963-65; jsse 1965; Jt HQ, ME Comd, Aden, and Air Adviser to the South Arabian Govt, 1966-67; Dirg Staff, Jt Services Staff Coll., 1968; Gp Captain Organisation, HQ Strike Comd, 1968-70; Stn Comdr, RAF Kinloss, 1971-72; RCDS 1973; Comdt, Central Flying School, RAF, 1974-76; Air Cdre Flying Training, HQ RAF Support Comd, 1976-78; Comdr, Southern Maritime Air Region, Central Sub-Area Eastern Atlantic Command, and Plymouth Sub-Area Channel Command, 1978-80. ADC to The Queen, 1972-73. Governor: Shapwick CP Sch., 1981-; Millfield, 1982-. Pres., SW Area, RAFA, 1981-. Won Kings Cup Air Race, British Air Racing Champion, 1960. Pres., RAF Equitation Assoc., 1976-79 (Chm. 1973); Chm., Combined Services Equitation Assoc., 1977-79 (Vice-Chm., 1976). Chevalier, Legion of Honour, 1960; Order of Tri Shakti (Nepal), 1960. *Address:* The Queen's Flight, RAF Benson, Oxon OX9 6AA. *Club:* Royal Air Force.

SEWARD, Guy William, QC 1982; FRVA; *b* 10 June 1916; *s* of late William Guy Seward and Maud Peacock; *m* 1946, Peggy Dearman. *Educ:* Stationers' Sch. Called to the Bar, Inner Temple, 1956. FRVA 1948. Chairman: Examination in Public, Devon Structure Plan, 1980; E Herts Health Authority, 1982-; Member: Mid-Herts HMC, 1966-70; Napsbury HMC, 1970-74 (Chm., 1972-74); Bd of Governors, UCH, 1970-74; Herts AHA, 1974-82 (Vice Chm., 1980-82). *Publications:* (jtly) Enforcement of Planning Control, 1956; (jtly) Local Government Act, 1958; Howard Roberts Law of Town and Country Planning, 1963; (jtly) Rent Act, 1965; (jtly) Land Commission Act, 1967; (jtly) Leasehold Reform, 1967. *Recreations:* National Health Service, gardening. *Address:* 2 Mitre Court Buildings, Temple, EC4Y 7BX. *T:* 01-353 4844. *Club:* Garrick.

SEWARD, William Richard, RCNC; General Manager, HM Dockyard, Portsmouth, 1975-79, retired; *b* 7 Feb. 1922; *s* of William and Gertrude Seward, Portsmouth; *m* 1946, Mary Deas Ritchie; one d. *Educ:* Portsmouth Dockyard Techn. Coll.; RNC Greenwich; Royal Corps of Naval Constructors. Asst Constructor, HM Dockyard, Rosyth, 1945-47; Constructor, Naval Construction Dept, Admty, 1947-58; Admty Constructor Overseer, Birkenhead, 1958-63; Chief Constructor, MoD (N), 1963-70; Prodn Man., HM Dockyard, Chatham, 1970-73, Gen. Manager, 1973-75. *Recreations:* reading, music, caravanning, walking. *Address:* Willowfalls Cottage, 166A London Road West, Bath BA1 7QU. *Club:* Civil Service.

SEWELL, Sir (John) Allan, Kt 1977; ISO 1968; company director; *b* 23 July 1915; *s* of George Allan Sewell and Francis Doris Sewell; *m* 1st, 1939, Thelma Edith Buchholz (d 1965); one *s* one d; 2nd, 1978, Yoko Fukano, d of I. Fukano, Kyoto, Japan. *Educ:* Brisbane Grammar Sch. Fellow Inst. of Municipal Admin. Dir of Local Govt, 1948-60; Under Treasurer of Qld, 1960-70; Auditor-General of Qld, 1970-78; Chm., State Govt Insurance Office, Qld, 1979-81. *Recreation:* game fishing. *Address:* 63 Ryans Road, St Lucia, Brisbane, Queensland, Australia. *Clubs:* Queensland (Brisbane); Cairns Game Fishing (Cairns); Moreton Bay Game Fishing (Brisbane).

SEWELL, Thomas Robert McKie; HM Diplomatic Service, retired; international grains consultant; *b* 18 Aug. 1921; *s* of late O. B. Fane Sewell and late Frances M. Sewell (née Sharp); *m* 1955, Jennifer Mary Sandeman; one d (and one d decd). *Educ:* Eastbourne Coll.; Trinity Coll., Oxford (Schol., Heath Harrison Prize, MA); Lausanne and Stockholm Univs (Schol.). HM Forces, 1940-45 (despatches); Major. Entered Foreign Service, 1949; Second Sec., Moscow, 1950-52; FO, 1952-55; First Sec., 1954; Madrid, 1955-59; Lima, 1959-61; Chargé d'Affaires, 1960; FO, 1961-63; Counsellor and Head of Chancery, Moscow, 1964-66; Diplomatic Service Rep. at IDC, 1966; Head of Associated States, West Indies and Swaziland Depts, Commonwealth Office, 1967-68; Head of N American and Caribbean Dept, FCO, 1968-70; Asst Sec., MAFF, 1970-81; UK Rep. to Internat. Wheat Council, 1972-81. *Recreations:* ski-ing, inland waterways cruising. *Address:* c/o Barclays Bank, 16 Whitehall, SW1. *Clubs:* Farmers', Airborne.

SEXTON, Maj.-Gen. (Francis) Michael, CB 1980; OBE 1966; Bursar and Fellow, St Peter's College, Oxford, since 1980; *b* 15 July 1923; *s* of Timothy Sexton and Catherine Regan; *m* 1947, Naomi, d of Bertram Alonzo Middleton and Dorothy May Middleton; one *s* one d. *Educ:* Wanstead County High Sch.; Birmingham Univ. Commnd RE, 1943; Royal Bombay Sappers and Miners, India and Burma, 1943-46; RE units, UK, Egypt and Cyprus, 1946-53; Dept of Mines and Surveys, Canada, 1953-56; Asst Dir, MoD, 1964-65; Dep. Dir, Ordnance Survey, 1966-70; Chief Geographic Officer, SHAPE, Belgium, 1970-73; Brig. (Survey), 1973-77; Dir of Military Survey and Chief of Geographic Section of GS, MoD, 1977-80. Mem., Panel of Indep. Inspectors, 1980-. MA Oxon, 1980. *Recreations:* interested in most ball games. *Address:* St Peter's College, Oxford. *T:* Oxford 48436. *Clubs:* Army and Navy, MCC; Geographical.

SEYLER, Athene, CBE 1959; Actress on the London stage; *b* London, 31 May 1889; *d* of Clara Thies and Clarence H. Seyler; *m* 1st, James Bury Sterndale-Bennett; one d; 2nd, Nicholas James Hannen, OBE (d 1972). *Educ:* Coombe Hill School; Bedford College. Gold Medallist, Royal Academy of Dramatic Art, 1908; first appearance on the stage at Kingsway Theatre, 1909; specialised

in comedy acting; served on the Drama Panel of CEMA, 1943 and subsequently of the Arts Council of Great Britain. Pres. of RADA, 1950; Pres. of Theatrical Ladies Guild. Principal successes as Madame Ranevska in The Cherry Orchard, Fanny Farrelli in Watch on the Rhine, the Duchess of Berwick in Lady Windermere's Fan, Vita Louise in Harvey, Mrs Malaprop in The Rivals, The Nurse in Romeo and Juliet. Has appeared in films, 1932-. Hon. Treasurer of British Actors Equity Association, 1944. *Publication:* The Craft of Comedy, 1944. *Recreations:* walking, talking. *Address:* Coach House, 26 Upper Mall, Hammersmith, W6.

SEYMOUR, family name of Marquess of Hertford and Duke of Somerset.

SEYMOUR, Lord; John Michael Edward Seymour, ARICS; *b* 30 Dec. 1952; *s* and *heir* of 18th Duke of Somerset, *qv*; *m* 1978, Judith-Rose, *d* of J. F. C. Hull, *qv*; one *s*. *Educ:* Eton. *Heir: s* Hon. Sebastian Edward Seymour, *b* 3 Feb. 1982. *Address:* Maiden Bradley, Warminster, Wilts. *Club:* MCC.

SEYMOUR, Derek Robert Gurth, MA; Headmaster of Bloxham School, 1965-82; *b* 4 Sept. 1917; *s* of G. Haco Seymour; *m* 1940, Betty, *d* of late Lt-Col S. H. Little; two *s*. *Educ:* Trinity Coll., Cambridge. BA 1939; MA 1943. Head of Chemistry, Junior Housemaster, St John's School, Leatherhead, 1939-44; Asst Master, Head of Science, i/c RAF Section, CCF; Housemaster, Marlborough College, 1944-65. Seconded as Head of Chemistry and House Tutor, Cranbrook Sch., Sydney, 1951-52. Examr and Chief Examr in A and S Level Chemistry, Southern Univs Jt Bd, 1955-63. *Address:* 16 Salterns Point, Salterns Way, Lilliput, Poole, Dorset BH14 8LN. *T:* Canford Cliffs 700476.

SEYMOUR, Lady Katharine, DCVO 1961 (CVO 1939); Extra Woman of the Bedchamber to Queen Elizabeth the Queen Mother since 1960 (Woman of the Bedchamber to the Queen (now Queen Elizabeth the Queen Mother), 1937-60); First Woman of the Bedchamber to Queen Mary, 1927-30 (on marriage became Extra Woman of the Bedchamber, 1930-53); *b* 25 Feb. 1900; 3rd *d* of 3rd Duke of Abercorn; *m* 1930, Sir R. H. Seymour, KCVO (d 1938); one *s* one d (and one d decd). *Address:* 25 Regnum Court, North Walls, Chichester, West Sussex. *T:* Chichester 784871.

SEYMOUR, Lynn, CBE 1976; Ballerina; Artistic Director, Ballet of the Bavarian State Opera, Munich, 1978-80; *b* Wainwright, Alberta, 8 March 1939; *d* of E. V. Springbett; *m* 1st, 1963, Colin Jones, photo-journalist (marr. diss.); 2nd, 1974, Philip Pace; three *s*. *Educ:* Vancouver; Sadler's Wells Ballet School. Joined Sadler's Wells Ballet Company, 1957; Deutsche Oper, Berlin, 1966. *Roles created:* Adolescent, in The Burrow, Royal Opera House, 1958; Bride, in Le Baiser de la Fée, 1960; Girl, in The Invitation, 1960; Young Girl, in Les Deux Pigeons, 1961; Principal, in Symphony, 1963; Principal, in Images of Love, 1964; Juliet, in Romeo and Juliet, 1964; Albertine, BBC TV, 1966; Concerto, 1966; Anastasia, 1966; Flowers, 1972; A Month in the Country, 1976; mother, in Fourth Symphony, 1977; Mary Vetsera, in Mayerling, 1978; Take Five; Side Show. *Other appearances include:* Danses Concertantes; Solitaire; La Fête Etrange; Sleeping Beauty; Swan Lake, Australasia, 1958-59, London, 1959; Giselle (title-role), 1960; Cinderella, London, 1961; Das Lied von der Erde, 1966; The Four Seasons, 1975; Voluntaries, 1976; Manon, Sleeping Beauty, Dances at a Gathering, The Concert, Pillar of Fire, Romeo and Juliet (Tudor, Nureyev and Cranks), Las Hermañas, Moor's Pavane, Auriole, Apollon, Le Corsaire, Flower Festival, La Sylphide (Sylph and Madge). *Choreography for:* Rashomon, 1976; The Court of Love, 1977; Intimate Letters, 1978; Mae and Polly; Boreas; Tattooed Lady. *Address:* Royal Opera House, Covent Garden, WC2.

SEYMOUR, Commander Sir Michael Culme-, 5th Bt, *cr* 1809; Royal Navy (retired); *b* 26 April 1909; *o s* of Vice-Admiral Sir M. Culme-Seymour, 4th Bt, and Florence Agnes Louisa (d 1956), *y d* of late A. L. Nugent; S father, 1925; *m* 1948, Lady (Mary) Faith Nesbitt, *er d* of 9th Earl of Sandwich; one *step-d* (two *s* decd). Succeeded Rev. Wentworth Watson to the Rockingham Castle estates, 1925, and transferred them to his nephew, Cmdr L. M. M. Saunders Watson, RN, 1967; is a farmer and a landowner. ADC to Governor-General of Canada, 1933-35; served War of 1939-45 (despatches); served Imperial Defence College, 1946-47; retired from RN 1947. JP Northants, 1949; Mem. Northants CC 1948-55; DL Northants, 1958-71; High Sheriff of Northants, 1966. Bledisloe Gold Medal for Landowners, 1972. *Heir to baronetcy:* cousin Mark Charles Culme-Seymour [*b* 20 Dec. 1910; *m* 3rd, 1956, Patricia June (marr. diss. 1966), widow of G. E. Ansell and *d* of late Charles Reid-Graham; one *s* two *d*; 4th, 1973, Mary Darrall, *d* of Leander Armistead Riely and widow of Philip Kidd]. *Address:* Wytherston, Powerstock, Bridport, Dorset. *T:* Powerstock 211. *Club:* Brooks's.

SEYMOUR, Air Commodore Roland George, CB 1961; CBE 1945; RAF, retired; *b* 16 May 1905; *s* of William and Jeannie Seymour; *m* 1942, Dorothy Beatrice Hutchings (d 1980); two *s*. *Educ:* Christ's Hospital. Pilot Officer, RAF, Jan. 1929, psc 1942; Actg Air Commodore, 1945, as Dep. to Air Officer i/c Administration, Mediterranean Allied Air Forces; Air Commodore, 1958; served in: Iraq, 1930-32; N Africa and Italy, 1942-45; Singapore, 1952-54; Deputy Assistant Chief of Staff (Logistics), Supreme HQ Allied Powers Europe, 1961-63. Legion of Merit (USA), 1946. *Address:* c/o Williams & Glyn's Bank Ltd, Lawrie House, Victoria Road, Farnborough GU15 7PA.

SEYMOUR, Rosalind; see Wade, R. (H.).

SEZNEC, Prof. Jean J., FBA 1960; Marshal Foch Professor of French Literature, Oxford, 1950-72; *b* 18 March 1905; *s* of Jean Seznec and Pauline Le Férec. *Educ:* Ecole Normale Supérieure, Paris. Fellow, French School of Archaeology, Rome, 1929-31; Univ. Lecturer, Cambridge, 1931-33; Prof., Lycée of Marseilles, 1933-34; Prof., French Inst., Florence, 1934-39, Asst Director, 1939; Assoc. Professor, Harvard University, 1941-46, Professor, 1946, Smith Professor of the French and Spanish Languages, 1947-50. Mary Flexner Lecturer, Bryn Mawr, 1955; Lord Northcliffe Lecturer, London, 1958; Dillon Visiting Prof., Harvard University, 1958. Mem., Adv. Council, V&A Museum, 1970-. Hon. DLitt: Harvard, 1961; St Andrews, 1972. Officier de la Légion d'Honneur, 1957; Comdr de l'Ordre National du Mérite, 1973. *Publications:* La Survivance des Dieux Antiques, 1940; L'Episode des Dieux dans la Tentation de Saint Antoine, 1940; Nouvelles Etudes sur la Tentation de Saint Antoine, 1949; Essais sur Diderot et l'Antiquité, 1958; John Martin en France, 1964; Un tableau de Paris au milieu du XVIIIe siècle, 1974; (joint) Fragonard, Drawings for Ariosto, 1945; Diderot, Salons, Vol. I, 1957, 2nd edn 1975; Vol. II, 1960; Vol. III, 1963; Vol. IV, 1967; contributions to: French Studies, Jl of Warburg and Courtauld Institutes, Romanic Review, Gazette des Beaux Arts, etc. *Address:* 1 Stanton Harcourt, Oxford.

SHACKLE, Prof. George Lennox Sharman, FBA 1967; Brunner Professor of Economic Science in the University of Liverpool, 1951-69, now Professor Emeritus; *b* 14 July 1903; *s* of Robert Walker Shackle, MA (Cambridge) and of Fanny Shackle (*née* Sharman); *m* 1st, 1939, Gertrude Courtney Susan Rowe (*d* 1978); two *s* one *d* (and one *d* decd); 2nd, 1979, Catherine Squarey Gibb (*née* Weldsmith). *Educ:* The Perse School, Cambridge; The London School of Economics; New College, Oxford. BA (London) 1931; Leverhulme Research Schol., 1934; PhD (Econ) (London), 1937; DPhil (Oxford), 1940. Oxford University Institute of Statistics, 1937; University of St Andrews, 1939; Admiralty and Cabinet Office; Sir Winston Churchill's Statistical Branch, 1939; Economic Section of Cabinet Secretariat, 1945; Reader in Economic Theory, Univ. of Leeds, 1950. F. de Vries Lecturer, Amsterdam, 1957; Visiting Professor: Columbia University, 1957-58; of Economics and Philosophy, Univ. of Pittsburgh, 1967; Keynes Lectr, British Acad., 1976. Mem. Council, Royal Economic Society, 1955-69; Pres., Section F, BAAS, 1966. Fellow of Econometric Society, 1960. Hon. DSc NUU, 1974; Hon. DSocSc Birmingham, 1978. *Publications:* Expectations, Investment, and Income, 1938, 2nd edn 1968; Expectation in Economics, 1949, 2nd edn, 1952; Mathematics at the Fireside, 1952 (French edn 1967); Uncertainty in Economics and Other Reflections, 1955; Time in Economics, 1957; Economics for Pleasure, 1959, 2nd edn 1968 (paperback, 1962; also foreign editions); Decision, Order and Time in Human Affairs, 1961 (2nd edn 1969; also foreign editions); A Scheme of Economic Theory, 1965 (also Portuguese edn); The Nature of Economic Thought, 1966 (also Spanish edn); The Years of High Theory, 1967; Expectation, Enterprise and Profit, 1970 (Spanish edn 1976); Epistemics and Economics, 1973 (Spanish edn 1976); An Economic Querist, 1973 (Spanish edn 1976); Keynesian Kaleidics, 1974; Imagination and the Nature of Choice, 1979; (ed and contrib.) Uncertainty and Business Decisions, 1954, 2nd edn, 1957; The Theory of General Static Equilibrium, 1957; A New Prospect of Economics, 1958; On the Nature of Business Success, 1968; articles in Chambers's Encyclopædia, 1950, 1967, Internat. Encyclopedia of the Social Sciences, 1968, and in other books; sixty or more main articles in learned jls. *Address:* Rudloe, Alde House Drive, Aldeburgh, Suffolk IP15 5EE. *T:* Aldeburgh 2227 and 2003.

SHACKLETON, family name of **Baron Shackleton.**

SHACKLETON, Baron *cr* 1958 (Life Peer), of Burley; **Edward Arthur Alexander Shackleton,** KG 1974; PC 1966; OBE 1945; an Adviser to RTZ Corporation (formerly Deputy Chairman); Director, RTZ Development Enterprises; Chairman, Anglesey Aluminium Ltd; *b* 15 July 1911; *s* of late Sir Ernest Shackleton, CVO, OBE; *m* 1938, Betty Homan; one *d* (and one *s* decd). *Educ:* Radley College, Magdalen College, Oxford (MA). Surveyor, Oxford University Expedition to Sarawak, 1932; first ascent of Mt Mulu; Organiser and Surveyor, Oxford University Expedition to Ellesmereland, 1934-35; Lecture tours in Europe and America; BBC talks producer, MOI. Served War of 1939-45, 1940-45; RAF Station Intelligence Officer, St Eval; Anti-U-Boat Planner and Intelligence Officer, Coastal Command; Naval and Military Intelligence, Air Ministry; Wing Cdr (despatches twice, OBE). Contested (Lab) Epsom, General Election, and Bournemouth by-election, 1945; MP (Lab), Preston (by-election), 1946-50, Preston South, 1950-55. Parliamentary Private Secretary to Minister of Supply, 1949-50; Parliamentary Private Sec. to Foreign Sec., March-Oct. 1951 (to Lord President of the Council, 1950-51); Minister of Defence for the RAF, 1964-67; Mission to S Arabia, 1967; Minister Without Portfolio and Deputy Leader, House of Lords, 1967-68; Lord Privy Seal, Jan.-April, 1968; Paymaster-General, April-Oct. 1968; Leader of the House of Lords, April 1968-70; Lord Privy Seal, Oct. 1968-1970; Minister in charge, Civil Service Dept, Nov. 1968-70; Opposition Leader, House of Lords, 1970-74. Sen. Executive and Director, J. Lewis Patnership, 1955-64; Exec. Dir, RTZ Corp. Ltd, 1974-75. Chairman: Adv. Council on Oil Pollution, 1962-64; Political Honours Scrutiny Committee, 1976-; Economic Survey of Falkland Is, 1976 (updated 1982); East European Trade Council, 1977-; Mem. Council, Industrial Soc. BOTB, 1975-78; President: British Assoc. of Industrial Editors, 1960-64; ASLIB, 1963-65; Royal Geographical Society, 1971-74 (formerly Vice-Pres.); Parly and Scientific Cttee, 1976-80 (formerly Vice-Pres.); British Standards Inst., 1977-80. Vice-Pres., YHA. Governor: London Chest Hosps, 1947-51; Imperial Coll. of Science, 1950-53; Mem. Council, SSAFA, 1951-55. Hon. Elder Brother, Trinity Hse, 1980. Cuthbert Peek Award (Royal Geographical Society), 1933; Ludwig Medallist (Munich Geog. Soc.), 1938. Pres., Arctic Club, 1960. FBIM. Hon. LLD Univ. of Newfoundland, 1970; Hon. DSc Warwick, 1978. *Publications:* Arctic Journeys; Nansen, the Explorer; (part-author) Borneo Jungle; Review of UK Anti-Terrorist Legislation, 1978; articles, broadcasts, etc. on geographical and political subjects and personnel and general administration. *Address:* c/o RTZ Corporation, 6 St James's Square, SW1Y 4LD. *T:* 01-930 2399.

SHACKLETON, Keith Hope; artist and naturalist; President, Society of Wildlife Artists, since 1975; Chairman, Artists League of Great Britain; *b* 16 Jan. 1923; *s* of W. S. Shackleton; *m* 1951, Jacqueline Tate; two *s* one *d*. *Educ:* Oundle. Served RAF, 1941-46. Civil Pilot and Dir, Shackleton Aviation Ltd, 1948-63; natural history programmes for television, 1964-68; joined naturalist team aboard MS Lindblad Explorer, 1969. Pres., Royal Soc. of Marine Artists, 1973. Member: RGS; Zool Soc. of London; NZ Antarctic Soc. *Publications:* Tidelines, 1951; Wake, 1953; Wild Animals in Britain, 1959; illustrations for books. *Recreations:* small Boat Sailing, exploration field work. *Address:* 28 Ladbroke Square, W11 3NB. *T:* 01-727 7320. *Club:* Itchenor Sailing.

SHACKLETON, Robert, MA, DLitt Oxon; FSA, FRSL; FBA 1966; Marshal Foch Professor of French Literature, University of Oxford, and Fellow of All Souls College, since 1979; Lyell Reader in Bibliography, University of Oxford, 1983-84; *b* 25 Nov. 1919; *e s* of Albert Shackleton and Emily (*née* Sunderland); unmarried. *Educ:* Todmorden Grammar School; Oriel College, Oxford (Scholar). 1st class, Hon. School of Modern Languages, 1940. Military Service, Royal Signals, 1940-45. Candidate (L), Blackburn, Gen. Elec., 1945. Lectr, Trinity Coll., Oxford, 1946-49; Fellow, Brasenose Coll., 1946-79, now Emeritus Fellow (Librarian, 1948-66, Sen. Dean, 1954-61, Vice-Principal, 1963-66); Lectr in French, Oxford Univ., 1949-65; Reader in French literature, Oxford Univ., 1965-66; Bodley's Librarian, Oxford, 1966-79; Chm., Cttee on Oxford Univ. Libraries, 1965-66. Visiting Professor: Dept of French and Italian, Univ. of Wisconsin, 1968; Folger Inst., Washington, 1981; Vis. Fellow, Humanities Res. Centre, ANU, 1980. Lectures: Zaharoff, Oxford Univ., 1970; Foundation, Birkbeck Coll., 1971; Tredegar, RSL, 1972; Moses Tyson Meml, Manchester Univ., 1976. Delegate, Oxford Univ. Press, 1972-82. Trustee, St Deiniol's Library, Hawarden, 1980-. Chairman: Adv. Cttee for Brotherton Coll., Leeds Univ., 1970-; Academic Adv. Cttee, Voltaire Foundn, 1978-. Corresp. Member: Acad. de Bordeaux, 1954; Acad. Montesquieu (Bordeaux), 1956 (Prix Montesquieu, 1956); Acad. de Béarn, 1982; President, Society for French Studies, 1959-60; Member, Editorial Board: French Studies, 1960- (Gen. Ed., 1965-67); Archives internationales d'histoire des idées, 1962-; Clarendon Edition of Locke, 1974-; Nouvelles de la République des Lettres, 1981-. Pres., Internat. Comparative Lit. Assoc., 1964-67; Pres., Internat. Soc. for 18th Century Studies, 1975-79. Hon. Member: Soc. d'Histoire Littéraire de la France; Assoc. Internat. de Bibliophilie; Australasian and Pacific Soc. for 18th Century Studies; Soc. Univ. Studi di Lingua e Letteratura Francese; Hungarian Acad. of Sciences, 1979; For. Hon. Mem., Amer. Acad. of Arts and Sciences; Hon. For. Corresp. Mem., Grolier Club, NY. Hon. Fellow, Oriel Coll., Oxford, 1971; Hon. Professorial Fellow, UCW, 1972-81; Assoc. Fellow, Silliman Coll., Yale Univ., 1972. Hon. Dr Univ. Bordeaux, 1966; Hon. LittD: Univ. of Dublin, 1967; Manchester, 1980. Médaille de la Ville de Paris, 1978; Medal, Univ. of Pisa, 1979; John Brademas Inaugural Award, NY Univ., 1981. Chevalier de la Légion d'Honneur, 1982. *Publications:* Editor: Fontenelle, Entretiens sur la pluralité des mondes, 1955; Montesquieu, a critical biography, 1961 (French translation, 1976); The Encyclopédie and the Clerks (Zaharoff lect.), 1970; (ed jtly) The Artist and Writer in France, 1975; articles in learned jls, Encyclopædia Britannica, etc. *Recreations:* book-collecting, foreign travel. *Address:* All Souls College, Oxford OX1 4AL. *T:* Oxford 722 251; 12 Norham Gardens, Oxford OX2 6QB. *T:* Oxford 513594. *Clubs:* Athenæum, United Oxford & Cambridge University; Grolier (New York); Elizabethan (Yale).

SHACKLETON, Prof. Robert Millner, BSc, PhD; FRS 1971; FGS; Hon. Research Professor, Open University, since 1977, Senior Research Fellow since 1979; Professor of Geology, University of Leeds, 1962-75, now Emeritus; Director, Research Institute of African Geology, University of Leeds, 1966-75; *b* 30 Dec. 1909; *m* 1st, 1934, Gwen Isabel Harland; one *s* two *d*; 2nd, 1949, Judith Wyndham Jeffreys (marr. diss. 1978); one *s* one *d*. *Educ:* Sidcot School; University of Liverpool. BSc (Hons) 1931, PhD 1934, Liverpool; Beit Fellow, Imperial College, 1932-34; Chief Geologist to Whitehall Explorations Ltd in Fiji, 1935-36; on teaching staff, Imperial College, 1936-40 and 1945-48; Geologist, Mining and Geological Dept, Kenya, 1940-45; Herdman Professor of Geology, University of Liverpool, 1948-62. Royal Society Leverhulme Vis. Prof., Haile Sellassie I Univ., 1970-71. Vice-Pres., Geolog. Soc. of London, 1966. Murchison Medal, 1970. *Publications:* Mining and Geological Dept of Kenya Reports 10, 11, 12; papers in geological journals, etc. *Address:* Greylag House, 46 High Street, Odell, Bedfordshire MK43 7BB. *T:* (home) Bedford 721112; (office) Milton Keynes 653735.

SHACKLETON BAILEY, D. R.; *see* Bailey.

SHACKLOCK, Constance, OBE 1971; LRAM 1940; FRAM 1953; International Opera and Concert Singer; Professor, Royal Academy of Music, since 1968; *b* 16 April 1913; *e d* of Randolph and Hilda Shacklock, Nottingham; *m* 1947, Eric Mitchell (*d* 1965). *Educ:* Huntingdon Street Secondary School, Nottingham; RAM. Principal mezzo-soprano, Covent

Garden, 1946-56. Outstanding rôles: Carmen, Amneris (Aida), Octavian (Der Rosenkavalier), Brangaene (Tristan und Isolde). Guest artist: Wagner Society, Holland, 1949; Berlin State Opera, 1951; Edinburgh Festival, 1954; Berlin Festival, 1956; Teatro Colon, Buenos Aires, 1956; Bolshoi Theatre, Moscow, 1957; Kirov Theatre, Leningrad, 1957; Elizabethan Theatre Trust, Sydney, 1958; Liège Opera, 1960; London production of The Sound of Music, 1961-66. President: English Singers and Speakers, 1978-79; Royal Acad. of Music, 1979-80. *Recreations:* gardening, reading, tapestry. *Address:* Royal Academy of Music, Marylebone Road, NW1; East Dorincourt, Kingston Vale, SW15 3RN.

SHAFFER, Peter Levin; playwright; critic; *b* 15 May 1926; *s* of Jack Shaffer and Reka Shaffer (*née* Fredman). *Educ:* St Paul's School, London; Trinity College, Cambridge. Literary Critic, Truth, 1956-57; Music Critic, Time and Tide, 1961-62. Awards: Evening Standard Drama Award, 1958; New York Drama Critics Circle Award (best foreign play), 1959-60. *Stage Plays:* Five Finger Exercise, prod. Comedy, London, 1958-60, and Music Box Theatre, New York, 1960-61; (double bill) The Private Ear (filmed 1966) and The Public Eye, produced, Globe, London, 1962, Morosco Theater, New York 1963 (filmed 1972); The Merry Roosters Panto (with Joan Littlewood and Theatre Workshop) prod. Wyndham's Theatre, Christmas, 1963; The Royal Hunt of the Sun, Nat. Theatre, Chichester Festival, 1964, The Old Vic, and Queen's Theatres, 1964-67, NY, 1965-66 (filmed 1969); Black Comedy, Nat. Theatre, Chichester Fest., 1965, The Old Vic and Queen's Theatres, 1965-67; as double bill with White Lies, NY, 1967, Shaw, 1976; The White Liars, Lyric, 1968; The Battle of Shrivings, Lyric, 1970; Equus, Nat. Theatre, 1973-74, NY, 1976, Albery Theatre, 1976-77 (NY Drama Critics' and Antoinette Perry Awards) (filmed 1977); Amadeus, Nat. Theatre, 1979 (Evening Standard Drama Award, Plays and Players Award, London Theatre Critics Award), NY, 1980 (Antoinette Perry Award), Her Majesty's, 1981. Plays produced on television and sound include: Salt Land (ITV), 1955; Balance of Terror (BBC TV), 1957; The Prodigal Father (Radio), etc. *Recreations:* music, architecture. *Address:* c/o London Management, 235/241 Regent Street, W1A 2JT.

SHAFTESBURY, 10th Earl of, *cr* 1672; **Anthony Ashley-Cooper;** Bt 1622; Baron Ashley 1661; Baron Cooper of Paulet, 1672; *b* 22 May 1938; *o s* of Major Lord Ashley (*d* 1947; *e s* of 9th Earl of Shaftesbury, KP, PC, GCVO, CBE) and of Françoise Soulier; *S* grandfather, 1961; *m* 1st, 1966, Bianca Maria (marr. diss. 1976), *o d* of late Gino de Paolis; 2nd, 1976, Christina Eva, *o d* of Ambassador Nils Montan; two *s*. *Educ:* Eton; Christchurch, Oxford. Chm., London Philharmonic Orchestra Council, 1966-80. Hon. Citizen, South Carolina, USA, 1967. Patron of seven livings. *Recreations:* ski-ing, music, shooting. *Heir: s* Lord Ashley, *qv*. *Address:* St Giles, Wimborne, Dorset BH21 5NH. *T:* Cranborne 312. *Clubs:* Pratt's, Turf.
See also Viscount Head.

SHAGARI, Alhaji Shehu Usman Aliyu; President of Nigeria and Commander-in-Chief of the Armed Forces, since 1979; *b* April 1925; *s* of Magaji Aliyu; *m* 1946; three *s* three *d*. *Educ:* Middle Sch., Sokoto; Barewa Coll., Kaduna; Teacher Trg Coll., Zaria. Teacher of science, Sokoto Middle Sch., 1945-50; Headmaster, Argungu Sen. Primary Sch., 1951-52; Sen. Visiting Teacher, Sokoto Prov., 1953-58. Entered politics as Mem. Federal Parl., 1954-58; Parly Sec. to Prime Minister, 1958-59; Federal Minister: Economic Develt, 1959-60; Establishments, 1960-62; Internal Affairs, 1962-65; Works, 1965-66; Sec., Sokoto Prov. Educl Develt Fund, 1966-68; State Comr for Educn, Sokoto Province, 1968-70; Fed. Comr for Econ. Develt and Reconstruction, 1970-71; for Finance, 1971-75. Mem., Constituent Assembly, Oct. 1977-; Mem., Nat. Party of Nigeria. *Publications:* (poetry) Wakar Nijeriya, 1948; Dan Fodia, 1978; (collected speeches) My Vision of Nigeria, 1981. *Recreations:* Hausa poetry, reading, farming, indoor games. *Address:* State House, Lagos, Nigeria.

SHAKERLEY, Sir Geoffrey (Adam), 6th Bt *cr* 1838; Director, Photographic Records Ltd, since 1970; *b* 9 Dec. 1932; *s* of Sir Cyril Holland Shakerley, 5th Bt, and of Elizabeth Averil (MBE 1955), *d* of late Edward Gwynne Eardley-Wilmot; *S* father, 1970; *m* 1st, 1962, Virginia Elizabeth (*d* 1968), *d* of W. E. Maskell; two *s*; 2nd, 1972, Lady Elizabeth Georgiana, *d* of late Viscount Anson and Princess Georg of Denmark; one *d*. *Educ:* Harrow; Trinity College, Oxford. *Heir: s* Nicholas Simon Adam Shakerley, *b* 20 Dec. 1963. *Address:* 56 Ladbroke Grove, W11 2PB.

SHAKESPEARE, John William Richmond, MVO 1968; HM Diplomatic Service; Counsellor, British Embassy, Lisbon, since 1979; *b* 11 June 1930; *s* of late Dr W. G. Shakespeare; *m* 1955, Lalage Ann, *d* of late S. P. B. Mais; three *s* one *d*. *Educ:* Winchester; Trinity Coll., Oxford (Scholar, MA). 2nd Lieut Irish Guards, 1949-50. Lectr in English, Ecole Normale Supérieure, Paris, 1953-54; on editorial staff, Times Educational Supplement, 1955-56 and Times, 1956-59; entered Diplomatic Service, 1959; Private Sec. to Ambassador in Paris, 1959-61; FO, 1961-63; 1st Sec., Phnom-Penh, 1963-64; 1st Sec., Office of Polit. Adviser to C-in-C Far East, Singapore, 1964-66; Dir of British Information Service in Brazil, 1966-69; FCO, 1969-73; Counsellor and Consul-Gen., Buenos Aires, 1973-75; Chargé d'Affaires, Buenos Aires, 1976-77; Head of Mexico and Caribbean Dept, FCO, 1977-79. Officer, Order of Southern Cross (Brazil), 1968. *Recreations:* tennis, sailing, bicycling, gardening, sun-bathing, music (very light), poetry. *Address:* c/o Foreign and Commonwealth Office, SW1A 2AH.

SHAKESPEARE, Sir William (Geoffrey), 2nd Bt *cr* 1942; General Practitioner, Aylesbury, and Clinical Assistant, Mental Subnormality, Manor House Hospital, Aylesbury; *b* 12 Oct. 1927; *s* of Rt Hon. Sir Geoffrey Hithersay Shakespeare, 1st Bt, and Aimée Constance (*d* 1950), *d* of Walter Loveridge; *S* father, 1980; *m* 1964, Susan Mary, *d* of A. D. Raffel, Colombo, Ceylon; two *s*. *Educ:* Radley; Clare Coll., Cambridge (BA Hons Nat. Scis, MA 1957); St George's Hospital. MB BChir Camb. 1958; DCH Eng. 1961. Boston Children's Hosp., USA, 1963-64; Paediatric Registrar, Stoke Mandeville Hosp., 1964-66. Mem., Snowdon Working Party, Integration of Handicapped, 1974-76. Vice-Pres., Physically Handicapped & Able-Bodied (PHAB), 1977-. Member BMA. *Heir: s* Thomas William Shakespeare, *b* 11 May 1966. *Address:* Manor Cottage, Stoke Mandeville, Bucks. *Club:* MCC.

SHAMOYA, Leonard Hantebele; High Commissioner for Zambia, 1975-77; *b* 20 Dec. 1936; *s* of Chiyupa Shamoya and Kavumbu Shamoya; *m* 1964; two *s* three *d*. *Educ:* London Univ. (BA); Brunel Univ. (MTech). RCM, Zambia: Secretarial Asst, 1964-67; Personnel Officer, 1967-69; Chief Personnel Officer, 1969-75. Director: Bank of Zambia, 1964-75; Zambia Trade Fair, 1966-68 and 1970-75; Zambia Nat. Building Soc., 1974-75; Shell and BP, 1975. Mayor, City of Ndola, 1966-68 and 1970-75; Constituency Sec., UNIP, 1970-75. *Recreations:* football, sports. *Address:* c/o Ministry of Foreign Affairs, PO Box RW69, Lusaka, Zambia.

SHAMS-UD DOHA, Aminur Rahman; Minister for Foreign Affairs, Government of the People's Republic of Bangladesh, since 1982; *b* 1929; *m* ; two *s*; *m* 1981, Wajiha Moukaddem. *Educ:* Calcutta and Dacca Univs (BSc Hons; BA). Commnd 2nd Lieut, Pakistan Artillery, 1952; Sch. of Artillery and Guided Missiles, Ft Sill, Okla, USA, 1957-58; Gen. Staff Coll., Quetta, 1962; GS Inf. Bde HQ, 1963; RMCS, Shrivenham, 1964-65; Sen. Instr, Gunnery, 1965; GS GHQ, 1965-66, retired. Editor and Publisher, Inter-Wing, Rawalpindi, 1968-71; Gen. Sec., Awami League, Rawalpindi, 1969-71, and Mem. Working Cttee; Ambassador of Bangladesh to: Yugoslavia and Roumania, 1972-74; Iran and Turkey, 1974-77; High Comr for Bangladesh in UK, 1977-82; Minister for Information, Bangladesh, March-June 1982. Member and Leader of Bangladesh delegns to numerous internat., Islamic and Commonwealth meetings. Associate Mem., Inst. of Strategic Studies, London. C-in-C's Commendation, 1964; several military awards and decorations. Order of the Lance and Flag, Cl. 1 (Yugoslavia). *Publications:* Arab-Israeli War, 1967; The Emergence of South Asia's First Nation State; Aryans on the Indus (MS). *Recreations:* sport (selected for London Olympics, 1948), writing, gardening. *Address:* Ministry of Foreign Affairs, Government of People's Republic of Bangladesh, Segunbagicha, Dacca; Farm View, Indra Road, Tejgaon, Dacca 15, Bangladesh. *Clubs:* Grosvenor House, Royal Automobile, Hurlingham; Dacca; Chittagong; Diplomatic (Belgrade); Imperial, Iran (Tehran); etc.

SHAND, Major Bruce Middleton Hope, MC 1940, and Bar 1942; Vice Lord Lieutenant, East Sussex, since 1974; Chairman, Ellis, Son & Vidler Ltd, Wine Merchants, London and Hastings, since 1970; *b* 22 Jan. 1917; *s* of late P. Morton Shand; *m* 1946, Rosalind Maud, *d* of 3rd Baron Ashcombe; one *s* two *d*. *Educ:* Rugby; RMC, Sandhurst. 2nd Lieut 12th Royal Lancers, 1937; Major 1942; wounded and PoW 1942; retd 1947. Exon, Queen's Bodyguard of the Yeomen of the Guard, 1971, Ensign, 1978-. Joint or Acting Master, Southdown Fox Hounds, 1956-75. DL Sussex, 1962. *Recreations:* hunting, gardening. *Address:* The Laines, Plumpton, near Lewes, East Sussex BN7 3AJ. *T:* Plumpton 890248. *Club:* Cavalry and Guards.
See also E. R. M. Howe.

SHAND, Rt. Rev. David Hubert Warner; Coadjutor Bishop and Bishop of the Southern Region, Diocese of Melbourne, since 1978; *b* 6 April 1921; *s* of late Rev. Canon Rupert Warner Shand and Madeleine Ethel Warner Shand; *m* 1946, Muriel Jean Horwood Bennett; one *s* three *d*. *Educ:* The Southport Sch., Queensland; St Francis' Theological Coll., Brisbane (ThL, 2nd Cl. Hons); Univ. of Queensland (BA, 2nd Cl. Hons). Served War, AIF, 1941-45: Lieut, 1942. St Francis' Coll., Brisbane, 1946-48. Deacon, 1948; Priest, 1949; Asst Curate, Lutwyche. Served in Parishes: Moorooka, Inglewood, Nambour, Ipswich; Org. Sec., Home Mission Fund, 1960-63; Rural Dean of Ipswich, 1963-66; Dio. of Brisbane: Chaplain CMF, 1950-57; Vicar, Christ Church, South Yarra, 1966-69; St Andrew's, Brighton, 1969-73; Rural Dean of St Kilda, 1972-73; Dio. of Melbourne: consecrated Bishop, St Paul's Cathedral, Melbourne, Nov. 1973; Bishop of St Arnaud, 1973-76 (when diocese amalgamated with that of Bendigo); Vicar of St Stephen's, Mt Waverley, 1976-78. Chairman: Gen. Bd of Religious Educn, 1974; Diocesan Dept of Christian Educn, 1978; C of E Free Kindergarten Council, 1978. *Recreation:* carpentry. *Address:* 5 Bates Street, East Malvern, Victoria 3145, Australia.

SHAND, John Alexander Ogilvie; Chairman of Industrial Tribunals (Birmingham Region), since 1981; a Recorder of the Crown Court, since 1981; *b* 6 Nov. 1942; *s* of late Alexander Shand and Marguerite Marie Shand; *m* 1965, Patricia Margaret (*née* Toynbee); two *s* one *d*. *Educ:* Nottingham High Sch.; Queens' Coll., Cambridge (MA, LLB; Chancellor's Medal for Law 1965). Called to the Bar, Middle Temple, 1965 (Harmsworth Scholarship); practised on Midland and Oxford Circuit (Birmingham), 1965-71 and 1973-81 (Dep. Circuit Judge, 1979); Fellow and Tutor, Queens' Coll., Cambridge, 1971-73. Chancellor, Dio. Southwell, 1981-. *Publications:* (with P. G. Stein) Legal Values in Western Society, 1974; contrib. various articles in Cambridge Law Jl. *Address:* 15 Monmouth Drive, Sutton Coldfield, West Midlands B73 6JG. *T:* 021-354 9652.

SHANKAR, Pandit Ravi; Presidential Padma Vibhushan Award, 1980; musician and composer; *b* 7 April 1920. Studied with brother Uday Shankar in Paris, 1930, with Ustad Allaudin Khan in Maihar, 1936. Music Dir, All-India Radio, 1949-56; music and choreography for ASIAD 82 (Asian Games, New Delhi, 1982). Fellow, Sangeet Natak Akademi, 1977 (President's Award, 1962); Member, Nat. Acad. for Recording Arts and Sciences, 1966. Has received hon. doctorates in letters and arts from California, 1968; Colgate, NY, 1972; Rabindra Bharati, Calcutta; Benares Hindu Univ. *Compositions:* Indian ragas; music for ballet and films; Concertos for sitar and orch., No 1, 1971, No 2, 1981. *Publication:* My Music My Life, 1968. *Recreations:* films, people. *Address:* c/o Basil Douglas Ltd, 8 St George's Terrace, NW1 8XJ.

SHANKLAND, Sir Thomas (Murray), Kt 1960; CMG 1955; JP; Deputy-Governor, Western Region, Nigeria, 1954-57; retired; Chairman, London Board of Public Service Commission, Western Region, Nigeria, 1957-61; *b* 25 Aug. 1905; *y s* of late W. C. Shankland, MBE, Barrister-at-Law, and late E. B. Shankland; *m* 1931, Margaret Crawford Goudie; one *d. Educ:* Felsted School; Queens' College, Cambridge (BA). Administrative Officer, Class IV, Nigeria, 1929; Food and Price Controller, Nigeria, 1944-45; Director of Supplies, Nigeria, 1946-47; Secretary, Western Provinces, Nigeria, 1949; Civil Secretary, Western Region, Nigeria, 1951; Chairman, Constituency Delimitation Commn, WR Nigeria, 1959. Mem. Jt CC, Moray and Nairn, 1958-70. JP Morayshire 1960. *Recreation:* golf. *Address:* Ardlarig, Grantown-on-Spey, Morayshire. *T:* Grantown-on-Spey 2160. *Clubs:* East India, Devonshire, Sports and Public Schools, MCC.

SHANKS, Ernest Pattison, CBE 1975; QC (Singapore) 1958; Deputy Bailiff of Guernsey, 1973-76; *b* 11 Jan. 1911; *e s* of late Hugh P. Shanks and Mary E. Shanks; *m* 1st, 1937, Audrey E. Moore; one *s*; 2nd, 1947, Betty Katherine Battersby; two *s* one *d. Educ:* Mill Hill Sch.; Downing Coll., Cambridge (MA); Inner Temple; Staff Coll., Camberley. Called to the Bar, Inner Temple, 1936; N Eastern Circuit. SRO, Mddx Regt, 1939-44: Princess Louise's Kensington Regt, France (despatches); Sicily, Italy, 1944; Staff Coll., Camberley, 1944-46; Sen. Legal Officer, Schleswig-Holstein, Milit. Govt, Germany, 1946; Lt-Col RARO, 1946. Colonial Legal Service: Dist Judge, Trengganu, Malaya, 1946; Singapore: Dist Judge and First Magistrate, 1947; Crown Counsel and Solicitor-Gen.; Attorney-Gen. and Minister of Legal Affairs, 1957-59. HM Comptroller, Guernsey, 1960; HM Procureur, 1969. *Address:* Le Petit Mas, Clos des Fosses, St Martin's, Guernsey. *T:* Guernsey 38300. *Clubs:* Old Millhillians (Pres., 1979-80), Royal Commonwealth Society; Royal Channel Islands Yacht.

SHANKS, Michael James; Director: BOC International, since 1976; Henley Centre for Forecasting, Environmental Resources, since 1977; P-E International, since 1977; Chairman: Datastream, since 1977; George Bassett (Holdings), since 1982 (Director, since 1977); Chairman, National Consumer Council, since 1977; *b* 12 April 1927; *s* of Alan James Shanks and Margaret Lee; *m* 1st, 1953, Elizabeth Juliet Richardson (*d* 1972); three *s* one *d*; 2nd, 1973, Patricia Jaffé (*née* Aspin). *Educ:* Blundell's Sch.; Balliol Coll., Oxford (MA). Lectr in Econs, Williams Coll., Mass, 1950-51; Labour Corresp., Financial Times, 1954-57; Industrial Editor, Financial Times, 1957-64; Economic Corresp., Sunday Times, 1964-65; Industrial Adviser, DEA, 1965-66; Industrial Policy Coordinator, DEA, 1966-67; Economic Adviser, Leyland Motors, 1967-68; Dir of Marketing Services and Economic Planning, British Leyland Motor Corp., 1968-71; Chief Executive, Finance & Planning, British Oxygen, 1971-72, Dir, Group Strategy, Jan.-June 1973; Dir Gen. for Social Affairs, EEC, 1973-76. Dir, Royal Ordnance Factories, 1977-80. Vis. Prof., Brunel Univ., 1973-; Vis. Fellow, Univ. of Lancaster, 1969-. Hon. Treas., Fabian Soc., 1964-65; Member: Cttee of Management, Science Policy Foundn, 1968-73; Adv. Council, Business Graduates Assoc., 1968-73; Editorial Bd, Times Management Library, 1968-73; Exec. Cttee, Warwick Univ. Centre of Industrial and Business Studies, 1968-73; Wilton Park Academic Council, 1967-; Council, Soc. of Business Economists, 1968-73; Electrical Engrg EDC, 1965-73; Employment Appeal Tribunal, 1976-; NEDC, 1977-81; Council, Soc. for Long-Range Planning, 1971-73; Council, Foundn for Management Educn, 1971-; Council, Centre for Studies in Soc. Policy, 1974-78; Council, Inst. of Directors, 1976-77; European Adv. Council, Tenneco Inc., 1980-. FBIM 1972. *Publications:* The Stagnant Society, 1961; (with John Lambert) Britain and the New Europe, 1962; (ed) The Lessons of Public Enterprise, 1963; The Innovators, 1967; The Quest for Growth, 1973; European Social Policy, To-day and To-morrow, 1977; Planning and Politics, 1978; What's Wrong with the Modern World, 1978; pamphlets, contribs to symposia, learned jls, etc. *Recreations:* reading, gardening, travelling. *Address:* Clapton Revel, Wooburn Moor, High Wycombe, Bucks.

SHANN, Sir Keith (Charles Owen), Kt 1980; CBE 1964; retired Australian public servant and diplomat; *b* 22 Nov. 1917; *s* of late F. Shann, Melbourne; *m* 1944, Betty, *d* of late C. L. Evans; two *s* one *d. Educ:* Trinity Grammar Sch., Kew, Vic; Trinity Coll., Melbourne Univ. (BA). Commonwealth Treasury Dept, 1939; Dept of Labour and Nat. Service, 1940; joined Dept of External Affairs: 2nd Sec., UN Div., 1946; 1st Sec., Acting Counsellor i/c UN Div., 1948; Aust. Mission to UN, New York, 1949-52; Head, UN Branch, 1952-55; Head, Americas and Pacific Branch, 1955; Minister, later Ambassador, to the Philippines, 1955-59; External Affairs Officer, London, 1959-62; Ambassador to Indonesia, 1962-66; First Asst Sec., 1966-70, Dep.

Sec., 1970-74, Dept of External (later Foreign) Affairs; Ambassador to Japan, 1974-77; Chm., Aust. Public Service Board, 1977-78. Dir, Mount Isa Mines Ltd, 1978-; Chm., Burns Philp Trustee Co. (Canberra), 1982-. Vice-Chm., Aust.-Japan Foundn, 1977-. Mem. Delegns to UN Gen. Assembly, Paris, 1948, 1951, NY 1949, 1950, 1952, 1953, 1957, 1967, 1974; Aust. Observer Bandoeng Conf., 1955; *Rapporteur*, UN Special Cttee on Hungary, 1957; Leader, Aust. Delegn to Develt Assistance Cttee of OECD, 1966-67, 1968-69; Commonwealth Observer, Zimbabwe Elections, 1980. *Recreations:* golf, gardening, music. *Address:* 11 Grey Street, Deakin, Canberra 2600, Australia. *Clubs:* Commonwealth (Canberra); Melbourne Cricket, Royal Canberra Golf.

SHANNON, 9th Earl of, *cr* 1756; **Richard Bentinck Boyle;** Viscount Boyle, Baron of Castle-Martyr, 1756; Baron Carleton (GB), 1786; late Captain Irish Guards; Chairman, Foundation for Science and Technology; Director, Committee of Directors of Research Associations; Director of companies; Secretary and Treasurer, Federation of European Industrial Co-operative Research Organisations; *b* 23 Oct. 1924; *o s* of 8th Earl of Shannon; *S* father, 1963; *m* 1st, 1947, Catherine Irene Helen (marr. diss., 1955), *d* of the Marquis Demetrio Imperiali di Francavilla; 2nd, 1957, Susan Margaret (marr. diss. 1979), *d* of late J. P. R. Hogg; one *s* two *d. Educ:* Eton College. A Dep. Speaker and Dep. Chm. of Cttees, House of Lords, 1968-78. Vice-President: Inland Waterways Assoc.; Brit. Hydromechanics Research Assoc.; Pres., Kent Br., BIM; Hon. Pres., Foundn for Education of Underachieving and Dyslexic. Pres., Architectural Metalwork Assoc., 1966-74; Vice-Pres., Aslib, 1974. FRSA, FBIM, MBHI. *Heir: s* Viscount Boyle, *qv. Address:* Palace Chambers, Bridge Street, SW1A 2JY. *T:* 01-930 0777. *Club:* White's.

SHANNON, Alastair; journalist; Foreign News department, Daily Telegraph and Morning Post, 1937-71; *b* Hawick, 1894; *o s* of late Rev. J. W. Shannon and Agnes, *d* of Rev. Alexander Renton; *m* 1920, Betty, *d* of Rev. A. Russell; one *s* one *d. Educ:* George Watson's College and University, Edinburgh. Served Flanders, 1915; Commission, Nov. 1915; Mesopotamia Relieving Force; Prisoner of War in Turkey, Apr. 1916 to Nov. 1918; joined Staff of Morning Post, 1919; Editor Madras Mail, 1921-23; rejoined Morning Post, 1924; Foreign Editor, Morning Post, 1928-37. *Publications:* Morning Knowledge, 1920; The Black Scorpion, 1926. *Address:* 1 Highpoint, Lyonsdown Road, New Barnet, Herts. *T:* 01-440 3593.

SHANNON, Godfrey Eccleston Boyd, CMG 1951; Assistant Under-Secretary of State, in the Commonwealth Office, 1956-68, retired 1968; *b* 14 Dec. 1907; *s* of late W. B. Shannon. *Educ:* Wellington; St John's College, Cambridge. Appointed to Dominions Office, 1930; visited Australia and New Zealand, as Private Sec., with 10th Duke of Devonshire, 1936; Official Sec., UK High Commissioner's Office, New Zealand, 1939-41; served on UK Delegation to various international conferences in London, Geneva, New York, Chicago and Moscow, 1944-48, to UNCTAD, 1964, and to Commonwealth Finance Ministers' meetings, Jamaica, Montreal and Trinidad, 1965-67; Deputy United Kingdom High Commissioner in Canada, 1948-50, in Calcutta, 1952-56. Member, Cttee for Exports: to Canada, 1964-68; to Australia, 1965-68. Renter Warden, Dyers' Co., 1967-68, Prime Warden, 1968-69. *Address:* 18 Lamont Road, SW10 0JE. *T:* 01-351 1585. *Clubs:* Travellers'; Bengal (Calcutta).

SHAPCOTT, Sidney Edward, CEng, FIEE, FInstP; *b* 20 June 1920; *s* of late Percy Thomas and Beatrice Shapcott; *m* 1943, Betty Jean Richens; two *s* one *d. Educ:* Hele's School, Exeter; King's College, London. BSc. Joined Air Defence Experimental Establishment, 1941; various appointments in Min. of Supply and Min. of Aviation, 1941-62; DCSO, 1963; Dir of Projects, ESRO, 1963-65; Min. of Defence, Navy Dept, 1965-75; CSO, 1968; Dep. Dir, Admiralty Surface Weapons Establishment, 1968-72; Dir, Underwater Weapon Projects, Admiralty Underwater Weapons Establishment, Portland, 1972-75; Dir-Gen., Airborne Weapons and Electronic Systems, MoD, 1976-80. *Recreations:* travel, cinephotography. *Address:* 26 Southcote Way, Tylers Green, High Wycombe, Bucks. *T:* High Wycombe 813401.

SHAPIRO, Erin Patria Margaret; Founder of first Shelter for Battered Wives and their children, 1971; therapeutic consultant and fund-raiser, Women's Aid Ltd; *b* 19 Feb. 1939; *d* of Cyril Edward Antony Carney and Ruth Patricia Balfour-Last; *m* 1st, 1961, John Leo Pizzey (marr. diss. 1979); one *s* one *d*; 2nd, 1980, Jeffrey Scott Shapiro. *Educ:* St Antony's; Leweston Manor, Sherborne, Dorset. Somewhat chequered career as pioneering attracts frequent clashes with the law; appearances at such places as Acton Magistrates Court and the House of Lords could be considered milestones in the fulfilment of a career dedicated to defending women and children. *Publications:* Scream Quietly or the Neighbours Will Hear, 1974 (paperback), 2nd edn 1978; (autobiog.) Infernal Child, 1978; The Slut's Cookbook, 1981; (with Jeff Shapiro) Prone to Violence, 1982; Erin Pizzey Collects, 1983. *Recreations:* wine, books, travel. *Address:* 535 Cordova Road, Suite No 467, Santa Fe, New Mexico 87501, USA. *Club:* Women's Aid (Refuge for Battered Wives, Bristol).

SHAPLAND, Maj.-Gen. Peter Charles, CB 1977; MBE 1960; MA; Planning Inspector, Department of the Environment, since 1980; *b* 14 July 1923; *s* of late F. C. Shapland, Merton Park, Surrey; *m* 1954, Joyce Barbara Shapland (*née* Peradon); two *s. Educ:* Rutlish Sch., Merton Park; St Catharine's Coll., Cambridge. Served War: commissioned Royal Engineers, 1944; QVO Madras Sappers and Miners, Indian Army, 1944-47. Served United Kingdom, Middle

East (Canal Zone) and Cyprus, 1948-63. Attended Staff Coll., 1952; jssc, 1960. Lt-Col, 1965; comd in Aden, 1965-67; Brig., Dec. 1968; comd 30 Engineer Bde. Attended Royal Coll. of Defence Studies, 1971. Dep. Comdr and Chief of Staff, HQ SE Dist, 1972-74; Maj.-Gen. 1974; Dir, Volunteers Territorials and Cadets, MoD (Army), 1974-78, retired. Hon. Col, 73 Engineer Regt, TA, 1979-; Col Comdt, RE, 1981-. Chm., Combined Cadet Forces Assoc., 1982-; Pres., Instn of Royal Engrs, 1982-. *Publications:* contribs to Royal Engineers' Jl. *Recreations:* sailing, swimming, golf. *Address:* c/o Williams & Glyn's Bank Ltd, Holts Branch, Kirkland House, Whitehall, SW1A 2EB. *Clubs:* Royal Ocean Racing, Lansdowne; Royal Engineer Yacht (Chatham).

SHAPLAND, Sir William (Arthur), Kt 1982; Chairman, Blackwood Hodge plc, since 1964 (non-executive Director, 1946-55, Executive Director, 1955-64, Group Managing Director, 1964-78); Trustee, Bernard Sunley Charitable Foundation; *b* 20 Oct. 1912; *s* of late Arthur Frederick Shapland and of Alice Maud (*née* Jackson); *m* 1943, Madeline Annie (*née* Amiss); two *d. Educ:* Tollington Sch., Muswell Hill. Incorporated Accountant, 1936; Chartered Accountant, 1946. Allan Charlesworth & Co, Chartered Accountants, London, Cambridge and Rangoon: Clerk, 1929-36; Manager, 1936-46; Partner, 1946-55. Waynflete Fellow, Magdalen Coll., Oxford, 1981. Hon. FRCS 1978. OStJ 1981. *Recreations:* golf, gardening, travel. *Address:* (home) 44 Beech Drive, N2 9NY. *T:* 01-883 5073; (office) 25 Berkeley Square, W1A 4AX. *T:* 01-629 9090.

SHARKEY, Colum John, MBE 1973; HM Diplomatic Service; Ambassador to Honduras, since 1981 and non-resident Ambassador to El Salvador, since 1982; *b* 9 June 1931; *s* of late Andrew Sharkey and late Sarah Josephine Sharkey (*née* Whelan); *m* 1962, Olivia Anne (*née* Brassil); two *s* one *d.* Commonwealth Relations Office, 1954; served in New Delhi, 1955, Calcutta, 1956-58; Second Secretary: Dacca, 1959-61; Melbourne, 1962-66; Montevideo, 1967-68 (joined HM Diplomatic Service, 1968); First Sec. and Consul, Asuncion, 1969; First Sec., Montevideo, 1971; seconded to Dept of Trade, 1972-74; Consul, Vancouver, 1974-78; Consul-Gen., Bilbao, 1978-81. *Recreations:* reading, swimming, golf. *Address:* c/o Foreign and Commonwealth Office, SW1.

SHARMA, Usha Kumari, (Mrs V. K. Sharma); see Prashar, U. K.

SHARMA, Vishnu Datt; Senior Supervisor, Ealing Community Relations Council; Member, Executive Committee, National Council for Civil Liberties (Race Relations Officer, 1979-80); *b* 19 Oct. 1921; *s* of late Pandit Girdhari Lal Kaushik and Shrimati Ganga Devi; *m* 1960, Krishna Sharma; one *d. Educ:* High Sch. in India. Came to UK from India, 1957; worked in factories until 1967; apptd Mem. Nat. Cttee for Commonwealth Immigrants (by the Prime Minister, Rt Hon. Harold Wilson); twice elected Gen. Sec. of Indian Workers' Assoc., Southall, 1961-63 and 1965-67, and once Pres., 1977-79; Nat. Organiser, Campaign Against Racial Discrimination (later Vice-Chm.); Gen. Sec., Exec. Sec. and again Gen. Sec., Jt Council for the Welfare of Immigrants, 1967-77; Vice-Chm., Steering Cttee, Anti-Nazi League. Mem., Adv. Cttee BBC, Asian Magazine. Has attended five internat. confs on migrant workers and race relns. *Recreations:* cinema, watching television, sight-seeing, etc. *Address:* 43 Lady Margaret Road, Southall, Mddx UB1 2PJ. *T:* 01-843 0518.

SHARMAN, Peter William; Director since 1974 and Chief General Manager since 1975, Norwich Union Insurance Group; *b* 1 June 1924; *s* of William Charles Sharman and Olive Mabel (*née* Burl); *m* 1946, Eileen Barbara Crix; one *s* two *d. Educ:* Northgate Grammar Sch., Ipswich; Edinburgh Univ. MA 1950; FIA 1956. War service as Pilot, RAF. Joined Norwich Union Insce Gp, 1950; Gen. Man. and Actuary, 1969. Chairman: Life Offices' Assoc., 1977-78; British Insurance Assoc., 1982-. *Recreations:* tennis, badminton, golf. *Address:* 21 Eaton Rd, Norwich NR4 6PR. *T:* Norwich 52130.

SHARMAN, Thomas Charles, OBE 1960; HM Diplomatic Service, retired; *b* 12 April 1912; *s* of Thomas Sharman and Mary Ward; *m* 1935, Paulette Elisabeth Padioleau; one *d. Educ:* Long Eaton County Secondary Sch.; Clare Coll., Cambridge. HM Consular Service, 1934; Paris, 1935; Saigon, 1937; Milan, 1939; British Embassy, Lisbon, 1940, and Moscow, 1945; HM Foreign Service, 1945; Batavia, 1946; Sao Paulo, 1947; Superintending Trade Consul, New Orleans, 1949; HM Consul, Luanda, 1952, Consul (Commercial) Hamburg, 1953; Counsellor (Commercial) Lisbon, 1960; Consul-General, Atlanta, Georgia, USA, 1965-68; Consul-General, Oporto, 1968-70. *Address:* 103 Résidence Jeanne Hachette, 60000 Beauvais, France.

SHARP, family name of Baroness Sharp.

SHARP, Baroness (Life Peer) *cr* 1966, of Hornsey; **Evelyn (Adelaide) Sharp,** GBE 1961 (DBE 1948); President, London and Quadrant Housing Trust, since 1977 (Chairman, 1973-77); *b* 25 May 1903; *d* of Reverend Charles James Sharp, Vicar of Ealing, Middlesex, to 1935. *Educ:* St Paul's Girls' School; Somerville College, Oxford. Entered Administrative Class of Home Civil Service, 1926. Perm. Sec., Min. of Housing and Local Govt, 1955-66. Mem., Independent Broadcasting Authority (formerly ITA), 1966-73. Hon. DCL Oxon, 1960; Hon. LLD: Cantab, 1962; Manchester, 1967; Sussex, 1969. *Recreation:* pottering. *Address:* The Old Post Office, Lavenham, Sudbury, Suffolk. *Club:* University Women's.

SHARP, Alastair George, MBE 1945; QC 1961; DL; **His Honour Judge Sharp;** a Circuit Judge (formerly Judge of County Courts), since 1962; Liaison Judge, Durham County Magistrates Courts, since 1972; *b* 25 May 1911; *s* of late Alexander Sharp, Advocate in Aberdeen, and of late Mrs Isabella Sharp, OBE; *m* 1940, Daphne Sybil, *d* of late Maj. Harold Smithers, RGA, and late Mrs Connor; one *s* two *d. Educ:* Aberdeen Grammar School; Fettes; Clare College, Cambridge (Archdeacon Johnson Exhibitioner in Classics). BA 1933, 1st Class Hons Classical Tripos Part II, Aegrotat Part I. Boxed Cambridge Univ., 1931-32; Cambridge Union Debating Team in America, 1933. On staff of Bonar Law College, Ashridge, 1934-35; Barrister, Middle Temple, 1935; Harmsworth Law Scholar; North Eastern Circuit, 1936. Dep. Chm. of Agricultural Land Tribunal, Northern Area, 1958-62; Asst Recorder of Huddersfield, 1958-60; Recorder of Rotherham, 1960-62; Dep. Chm., N Riding Yorks QS, 1959-65; Dep. Chm., 1965-70, Chm., 1970-71, Durham QS. Chm., Washington New Town Licensed Premises Cttee, 1966-78; Jt Pres., Council of Circuit Judges, 1979. Commissioned, The Gordon Highlanders, Feb. 1939; served War of 1939-45: Staff Coll., 1943; 2nd Bn The London Scottish, 1943; Gen. Staff, War Office, 1944-45, Temp. Major. Governor, Sherburn Hosp. Charity, 1972-. DL Co. Durham, 1973. *Recreations:* golf, gardening, music, hill walking, fishing. *Address:* 49 South Street, Durham DH1 4QP; The Old Kennels, Tomintoul, Banffshire. *Clubs:* Durham County; Brancepeth Castle Golf.

See also Baron Mackie of Benshie, Sir R. L. Sharp.

SHARP, Sir Angus; see Sharp, Sir W. H. A.

SHARP, Derek Joseph; British Council Representative, Italy, since 1981; *b* 12 June 1925; *s* of Joseph Frank Sharp and Sylvia May (*née* Allen); *m* 1957, Hilda Francesca Cernigoj; two *s. Educ:* Preston Grammar School; Queen's Coll., Oxford; MA, DipEd. Lectr, British Inst., Milan, 1956-58; British Council, 1958; served Indonesia, Bristol, Bangkok, Addis Ababa, Pretoria and London, 1958-77; Controller, Africa and Middle East Div., 1977-81. *Address:* British Council, Via Quattro Fontane 20, 00184 Rome, Italy.

SHARP, Sir Edward Herbert, 3rd Bt *cr* 1922; *b* 3 Dec. 1927; *s* of Sir Herbert Edward Sharp, 2nd Bt, and Ray Alice Mary, *d* of Frederick George Bloomfield, Ealing; *S* father 1936; *m* 1949, Beryl Kathleen, *d* of L. Simmons-Green, Shirley, Warwicks; two *s* one *d. Educ:* Haileybury. *Heir: s* Adrian Sharp, *b* 17 Sept. 1951. *Address:* PO Box 749, Manzini, Swaziland.

SHARP, Eric, CBE 1980; Chairman since 1980 and Chief Executive since 1981, Cable and Wireless Ltd; *b* 17 Aug. 1916; *s* of Isaac and Martha Sharp; *m* 1950, Marion (*née* Freeman); one *s* one *d* (and one *d* decd). *Educ:* London School of Economics (BScEcon Hons). CBIM. Served Army, 1940-46, Staff Captain SOIII Southern Comd, 1944. Principal, Min. of Power, 1948; UK Delegate, Coal and Petroleum Cttee of OEEC, 1948-50; Vice-Chm., Electricity Cttee, OEEC, 1951-54; Sec. to Herbert Cttee of Inquiry into Electricity Supply Industry, 1955-56; British Nylon Spinners Ltd, 1957-64; Director, ICI Fibres Ltd, 1964-68; Mem. Board, Monsanto Europe, 1969; Resident USA, Mem. Management Bd, 1970-72; Dep. Chm., 1973-74, Chm., 1975-81, Monsanto Ltd; Chm., Polyamide Intermediates Ltd, 1975-81. Chm., Chemical Industry Safety and Health Council, 1977-79; Pres., Chemical Industries Assoc., 1979-80; part-time Mem., London Electricity Bd, 1969-78; Member: EDC for Chemical Industry, 1980-82; Central Electricity Generating Board, 1980-. *Recreations:* music, wine, gardening. *Address:* c/o Cable and Wireless Ltd, Mercury House, Theobalds Road, WC1. *Club:* Athenæum.

SHARP, Sir George, Kt 1976; OBE 1969; JP; DL; Chairman, Glenrothes Development Corporation, since 1978 (Vice-Chairman, 1973-78); commercial manager, since 1969; *b* 8 April 1919; *s* of Angus Sharp and Mary S. McNee; *m* 1948, Elsie May Rodger, *o d* of David Porter Rodger and Williamina S. Young; one *s. Educ:* Thornton Public Sch.; Buckhaven High Sch. Engine driver, 1962; PRO, 1962-69. Fife Council: Mem., 1945-75; Chm., Water and Drainage Cttee, 1955-61; Chm., Finance Cttee, 1961-72; Convener, 1972-75; Convener, Fife Regional Council, 1974-78. Managing Trustee, Municipal Mutual Insurance Co. Ltd, 1979-. President: Assoc. of County Councils, 1972-74; Convention of Scottish Local Authorities, 1975-78. Chairman: Kirkcaldy Dist Council, 1958-75; Fife and Kinross Water Bd, 1967-75; Forth River Purification Bd, 1955-67 and 1975-78; Scottish River Purification Adv. Cttee, 1967-75; Scottish Tourist Consultative Council, 1979-. Vice-Chm., Forth Road Bridge Cttee, 1972-. Member: Scottish Water Adv. Cttee, 1962-69; Cttee of Enquiry into Salmon and Trout Fishing, 1963; Scottish Valuation Adv. Cttee, 1972; Cttee of Enquiry into Local Govt Finance, 1974-76; Scottish Develt Agency, 1975-; Royal Commn on Legal Services in Scotland, 1978-80. Dir, Grampian Television, 1975-. JP Fife, 1975; DL Fife, 1978. *Recreation:* golf. *Address:* Strathlea, 56 Station Road, Thornton, Fife. *T:* Thornton 347.

SHARP, Lt-Col Granville Maynard, MA (Cantab); *b* 5 Jan. 1906; *s* of Walter Sharp, Cleckheaton, Yorks; *m* 1935, Margaret, *d* of Dr J. H. Vincent, Wembley Hill; two *d. Educ:* Cleckheaton Grammar School; Ashville College, Harrogate; St John's College, Cambridge, MA (Hons) (Economics). Lecturer in Economics at West Riding Technical Institutes, 1929-34; Chairman, Spenborough Housing and Town Planning Committee, 1935-40; Hon. Secretary, Spen Valley Divisional Labour Party, 1936-39; Battery Capt. 68 Anti-Tank Regt RA, 1939-42; Staff Capt. and DAQMG Belfast Area, 1942-43; Senior British Staff Officer, Economics Section, Allied Control

Commission, Italy, 1943-44; Chief Economics and Supply Officer, Military Govt, Austria, 1944-45. MP (Lab) for Spen Valley Div. of West Riding of Yorks, 1945-50; PPS Min. of Civil Aviation, 1946; Chairman, Select Cttee of Estimates Sub-Cttee, 1946-48; Parliamentary Private Sec. to Minister of Works, 1947-50. Keymer Parish Councillor, 1969- (Vice-Chm., 1976-80); CC E Sussex, 1970-74; CC W Sussex, 1973- (Chm., Rts of Way Cttee, 1974-); Mem., Mid-Sussex DC, 1973-76. *Recreations:* swimming, singing, scything, Sussex Downs. *Address:* 31 Wilmington Close, Hassocks, West Sussex. *T:* Hassocks 2294.

SHARP, Henry Sutcliffe, FRCS; Honorary Consulting Surgeon, Ear, Nose and Throat Department: Hospital for Sick Children, Great Ormond Street; Charing Cross Hospital; Putney Hospital; *b* 23 June 1910; *s* of late Alexander Sharp, CB, CMG; *m* 1st, 1948, Muiriel Oliver; two *s*; 2nd, 1964, Elizabeth Plant; one *s*. *Educ:* Haileybury College; Caius Coll., Cambridge; St Thomas's Hosp. BA, MB, ChB (Cantab); FRCS 1939. House Surgeon and Chief Asst, Ear, Nose and Throat Dept, St Thomas's Hosp., 1935. Major RAMC, 1940-45. FRSocMed; Member and past Hon. Sec. of Sections of Laryngology and Otology; Corresp. Mem., Excerpta Medica, Amsterdam. *Publications:* various articles concerning otolaryngology in Jl of Laryngology, Lancet, and Brit. Jl of Surgery. *Recreations:* golf, squash rackets. *Address:* 82 Wildwood Road, NW11. *T:* 01-458 3937.

SHARP, Dr John; Headmaster of Rossall School, since 1973; *b* 18 Dec. 1927; *o s* of late Alfred and May Sharp, North Ives, Oxenhope, Keighley; *m* 1950, Jean Prosser; one *s* two *d*. *Educ:* Boys' Grammar Sch., Keighley; Brasenose Coll., Oxford. BSc, MA, DPhil Oxon. RAF Educn Br., 1950-52; research at Oxford, 1952-54; Asst Master, Marlborough Coll., 1954-62; Senior Chemistry Master, 1956-62; Senior Science Master, 1959-62; Headmaster, Christ Coll., Brecon, 1962-72. Co-opted Mem., Oxford and Cambridge Schools Examn Bd, 1966-74; Selected Mem., Breconshire Educn Cttee, 1966-72; Co-opted Mem., Lancs Educn Cttee, 1974-81; Divisional Chm., HMC, SW 1971 and NW 1977-78. *Publications:* contrib. Anal. Chim. Acta. *Recreations:* fishing, photography, roses and shrubs. *Address:* The Hall, Rossall School, Fleetwood, Lancs FY7 8JW. *T:* Fleetwood 3849. *Club:* East India, Devonshire, Sports and Public Schools.

SHARP, J(ohn) M(ichael) Cartwright; Secretary of Law Commission, 1968-78; *b* 11 Aug. 1918; *s* of W. H. Cartwright Sharp, KC, and Dorothy (*née* Shelton). *Educ:* Rossall Sch.; Lincoln Coll., Oxford. Royal Artillery, 1940-46. Called to Bar, Middle Temple, 1947. Lord Chancellor's Office, 1951-65; Legal Sec. to Law Officers, 1965; Asst Solicitor, Law Commn, 1966. *Recreations:* travel, reading. *Address:* 15 Bolton Gardens, SW5. *T:* 01-370 1896. *Clubs:* Reform, Beefsteak.

SHARP, Kenneth Johnston, TD 1960; Head of the Government Accountancy Service and Accountancy Adviser to the Department of Industry, since 1975; *b* 29 Dec. 1926; *s* of Johnston Sharp and late Ann Sharp (*née* Routledge); *m* 1955, Barbara Maud Keating; one *s*. *Educ:* Shrewsbury Sch.; St John's Coll., Cambridge (MA). ACA 1955, FCA 1960. Partner, Armstrong, Watson & Co., Chartered Accountants, 1955-75. Indian Army, 1945-48; TA, 251st (Westmorland and Cumberland Yeo.) Field Regt RA, 1948-62; 2nd-in-Comd, 1959-62. Inst. of Chartered Accountants: Mem. Council, 1966-; Vice-Pres., 1972-73; Dep. Pres., 1973-74; Pres., 1974-75. Master, Co. of Chartered Accountants in England and Wales, 1979-80. Mem., Governing Body, Shrewsbury Sch., 1976-. JP Carlisle, 1957-73. *Publications:* The Family Business and the Companies Act 1967, 1967; articles in professional accountancy press. *Recreations:* sailing, canal cruising, gardening. *Address:* Hopefield, Somerton, Somerset TA11 7NG. *T:* Somerton 72104. *Clubs:* United Oxford & Cambridge University, Royal Automobile.

SHARP, Brig. Mainwaring Cato Ensor, CBE 1945; *b* 1 March 1897; *s* of late Rev. Cato Ensor Sharp; *m* 1949, Betty Yolande Constance, *o d* of late Col M. H. Knaggs, CMG. *Educ:* Trinity College School, Port Hope; RMC, Kingston, Canada. Commissioned, 1915, 5th RI Lancers; transfd Leinster Regt 1916; S Lanc. Regt 1922. Staff College, Camberley, 1928-29; retired, 1935; Insurance Broker, 1937-39; rejoined, 1939; Lt-Col 1941; Brig. 1944. Served European War and War of 1939-45 (despatches twice). Director of Maintenance, Control Commission, Germany, 1946-51; employed by War Office, 1951-58. Croix de Guerre (France); Officer, Legion of Merit (USA). *Recreations:* golf, ornithology. *Address:* 11 Maple Road, Walberton, Arundel, West Sussex. *T:* Yapton 551563.

SHARP, Margery; novelist and playwright; *m* 1938, Major G. L. Castle, RA. *Educ:* Streatham Hill High School; London University. French Honours BA. *Publications:* Rhododendron Pie; Fanfare for Tin Trumpets; The Flowering Thorn; Four Gardens; The Nymph and the Nobleman; Sophy Cassmajor; Meeting at Night (play); The Nutmeg Tree, 1937 (play: USA 1940, England 1941, filmed as Julia Misbehaves, 1948); The Stone of Chastity, 1940; Cluny Brown, 1944 (filmed 1946); Britannia Mews, 1946 (filmed 1949); The Foolish Gentlewoman, 1948 (Play, London, 1949); Lise Lillywhite, 1951; The Gipsy in the Parlour, 1953; The Tigress on the Hearth, 1955; The Eye of Love, 1957; The Rescuers, 1959; Something Light, 1960; Martha in Paris, 1962; Martha, Eric and George, 1964; The Sun in Scorpio, 1965; In Pious Memory, 1968; Rosa, 1969; The Innocents, 1971; The Faithful Servants, 1975; *books for children:* Miss Bianca, 1962; The Turret, 1964 (USA 1963); Miss Bianca in the Salt Mines, 1966; Lost at the Fair, 1967; Miss Bianca in the Orient, 1970; Miss Bianca in the Antarctic, 1971; Miss Bianca and the Bridesmaid, 1972; The Magical Cockatoo, 1974; The Children Next Door, 1974; Bernard the Brave, 1976; Summer Visits, 1977; *short stories:* The Lost Chapel Picnic, 1973. *Address:* c/o William Heinemann Ltd, 15-16 Queen Street, W1X 8BE.

SHARP, Michael Cartwright; *see* Sharp, J. M. C.

SHARP, Sir Milton Reginald, 3rd Bt, *cr* 1920; Capt. REME, TA; *b* 21 Nov. 1909; *s* of Sir Milton Sharp, 2nd Bt, and Gertrude (*d* 1940), *d* of John Earl, of London; *S* father, 1941; *m* 1951, Marie-Louise de Vignon, Paris. *Educ:* Shrewsbury; Trinity Hall, Cambridge.

SHARP, Hon. Mitchell William, PC (Can.); Commissioner, Northern Pipeline Agency, since 1978; *b* 11 May 1911; *s* of Thomas Sharp and Elizabeth (*née* Little); *m* 1938, Daisy Boyd (decd); one *s*; *m* 1976, Jeannette Dugal. *Educ:* University of Manitoba; London School of Economics. Statistician, Sanford Evans Statistical Service, 1926-36; Economist, James Richardson & Sons Ltd, 1937-42; Officer, Canadian Dept of Finance, Ottawa, 1942-51; Director Economic Policy Division, 1947-51; Associate Deputy Minister, Canadian Dept Trade and Commerce, 1951-57; Dep. Minister, 1957-58; Minister, 1963-65; elected to Canadian House of Commons, 1963; Minister of Finance, 1965-68; Sec. of State for External Affairs, 1968-74; Pres., Privy Council, 1974-76; Govt Leader in House of Commons, 1974-76; MP for Eglinton, 1976-78, resigned. Vice-Pres., Brazilian Traction, Light & Power Co., Toronto, 1958-62. Hon. LLD: Univ. of Manitoba, 1965; Univ. of Western Ontario, 1977; Hon. DrSocSci Ottawa, 1970. *Recreations:* music, walking, skating. *Address:* PO Box 1605, Station B, Ottawa, Ont K1P 5A0, Canada. *T:* 593-7466.

SHARP, Rear-Adm. Philip Graham, CB 1967; DSC 1942; Director General, International Union of Air Pollution Prevention Associations; *b* 23 Nov. 1913; *e s* of late Rev. Douglas Simmonds Sharp; *m* 1940, Dilys Mary Aldwyth, *er d* of late David Roberts, Welford-on-Avon, Warwicks; one *s*. *Educ:* Northampton Sch.; Tynemouth High Sch. Sub-Lt, RNVR, 1937; War Service in destroyers; Capt. 1956; comdg HMS Defender, 1956-58; NATO, 1958-60; Capt. of Fleet, Home Fleet, 1960-62; comdg HMS Centaur 1962-63; Cdre RN Barracks, Portsmouth, 1963-65; Rear-Adm. 1965; Flag Officer Sea Training, Portland, 1965-67; retired 1967. ADC to the Queen, 1965. Past President: Inter-Allied Confedn of Reserve Officers; Reserve Forces Assoc. *Recreations:* golf, fishing, music, model-making. *Address:* Dolphin House, Old Shoreham Road, Hove, East Sussex. *T:* Brighton 736545. *Clubs:* Naval and Military, Brighton and Hove Golf.

SHARP, Sir Richard (Lyall), KCVO 1982; CB 1977; Ceremonial Officer, Management and Personnel Office (formerly Civil Service Department), 1977-82; *b* 27 March 1915; *s* of late Alexander Sharp, Advocate, Aberdeen, and late Mrs Isabella Sharp, OBE; *m* 1950, Jean Helen, *er d* of late Sir James Crombie, KCB, KBE, CMG, and of Lady Crombie; two *s* two *d* (and one *d* decd). *Educ:* Fettes Coll.; Aberdeen Univ.; Clare Coll., Cambridge. MA with 1st Class Hons Classics, Aberdeen 1937; BA with 1st Class in Classical Tripos, Cambridge 1939. Served Royal Northumberland Fusiliers, 1939-45 (POW, Singapore and Siam, 1942-45). Principal, HM Treasury, 1946; Private Sec. to Chancellor of Exchequer, 1948-50 and to Minister of State for Economic Affairs, 1950; UK Treasury and Supply Delegn, Washington, 1952-56; Asst Sec., 1954; IDC, 1961; Under-Secretary: Nat. Bd for Prices and Incomes, 1966-68; HM Treasury, 1968-77. *Recreations:* playing the viola, gardening. *Address:* Home Farm House, Briston, Melton Constable, Norfolk. *T:* Melton Constable 0445.

See also Baron Mackie of Benshie, A. G. Sharp.

SHARP, Robert Charles, CMG 1971; Director of Public Works, Tasmania, 1949-71; *b* 20 Sept. 1907; *s* of Robert George Sharp and Gertrude Coral (*née* Bellette); *m* 1st, 1935, Margaret Fairbrass Andrewartha (*d* 1975); one *d*; 2nd, 1978, Marie, widow of Alan C. Wharton, St Albans, Herts. *Educ:* Univ. of Tasmania. BE 1929. Bridge Engr, Public Works, 1935. Enlisted RAE (Major): comd 2/4 Aust. Field Sqdn RAE, 1942; 1 Aust. Port Mtce Co. RAE, 1943; HQ Docks Ops Gp, 1944. Chief Engr, Public Works, 1946; State Co-ordinator of Works, 1949-71. *Recreation:* golf. *Address:* 129 Sandpit Lane, St Albans, Herts AL4 0BP; 594 Sandy Bay Road, Hobart, Tasmania 7005, Australia. *T:* Hobart 344.612. *Clubs:* Athenæum, Kingston Beach Golf.

SHARP, Thomas; Department of Industry, since 1979; *b* 19 June 1931; *s* of William Douglas Sharp and Margaret Sharp (*née* Tout); *m* 1962, Margaret Lucy Hailstone; two *d*. *Educ:* Brown Sch., Toronto; Abbotsholme Sch., Derbs; Jesus Coll., Oxford. BoT and DTI (with short interval HM Treasury), 1954-73; Counsellor (Commercial), British Embassy, Washington, 1973-76; Dept of Trade, 1976-79. *Address:* 41 Hall Drive, SE26 6XL. *T:* 01-778 8776.

SHARP, Sir (William Harold) Angus, KBE 1974; QPM 1969; *b* Auckland, 1915. *Educ:* Cathedral Grammar School, Christchurch. Graduated Imperial Defence College, 1966. Joined New Zealand Police Force, 1937; Commissioner of Police, 1970; retd NZ Police, 1975; Commissioner, Police and Prisons Dept, Western Samoa, 1977-78. *Address:* Rural Delivery 4, Rotorua, New Zealand.

SHARP, William Johnstone; Controller and Chief Executive, Her Majesty's Stationery Office and Queen's Printer of Acts of Parliament, since 1981; *b* 30

May 1926; *s* of Frederick Matthew and Gladys Evelyn Sharp; *m* 1952, Joan Alice Clark, MBE, *d* of Arnold and Violet Clark. *Educ:* Queen Elizabeth Grammar Sch., Hexham; Emmanuel Coll., Cambridge (MA). Army Service, Reconnaissance Corps, Durham LI and Staff, 1944–48. Entered Min. of Transport, 1949; Private Sec. to Perm. Sec., 1951–53; Principal, Min. of Civil Aviation, 1953; Asst Sec., Min. of Transport, 1962; Under-Sec., DoE, 1970; Controller of Supplies, PSA, 1976–80. *Recreations:* music, the Turf. *Address:* 43 Friars Quay, Norwich NR3 1ES. *T:* Norwich 24258; 23a Lee Terrace, Blackheath, SE3. *T:* 01-852 3222.

SHARPE, Brian Sidney; Director, Charles Barker Lyons, since 1980; *b* 12 Feb. 1927; *s* of S. H. Sharpe and Norah Sharpe; *m* 1967, Susan Lillywhite; two *s*. *Educ:* Haberdashers' Aske's Sch., Hampstead; Guildhall Sch. of Music and Drama. Royal Fusiliers (att. Forces Broadcasting Service), 1945–48; BBC: Announcer, Midland Region, 1955; Television Presentation, 1956; Producer, African Service, External Services, 1957; Senior Producer: Overseas Talks and Features, 1965; The Financial World Tonight, Radio 4, 1974; Money Programme, Sept.–Dec. 1979. On secondment as Exec. Dir, City Communications Centre, 1976–79. *Publications:* How Money Works (with A. Wilson), 1975; several articles on corporate and other forms of communication. *Recreations:* offshore fishing, music. *Address:* 26 Hallam Road, Godalming, Surrey GU7 3HW. *T:* Godalming 21551.

SHARPE, Sir Frank (Victor), Kt 1978; CMG 1972; OBE (mil.) 1943; ED 1942; Australian representative, Bell Helicopter Company, Fort Worth, USA, 1955–72; Helicopter Consultant to Bell Helicopter Australia Pty Ltd, Brisbane International Airport, 1972–74; Avocado consultant and farm adviser since 1946; Director of several companies; *b* 21 Jan. 1903; *s* of Frederick Robert Sharpe, Avening, Glos, and Elizabeth Matilda Glassop, Sydney (third generation); *m* 1947, Millicent Adelaide Gardner; one *s* one *d*. *Educ:* Rudd's Clayfield Coll.; Queensland Univ. Became dir, family merchant tool business, 1923 (Chm. and Man. Dir and sole proprietor, 1946–). Commissioned Aust. Army, 1921 (Militia); served War of 1939–45, AIF, Australia and SW Pacific; Lt-Col, retd 1955. Built and operated first commercial broadcasting station in Queensland, 1929. FAIM; Fellow, Australian Inst. Dirs. JP Brisbane 1947. *Recreations:* flying, farming, amateur radio. *Address:* 138 Adelaide Street, Clayfield, Brisbane, Qld 4011, Australia. *T:* 262.4842. *Clubs:* Athenæum (Melbourne); Queensland, Brisbane, United Service, Royal Queensland Yacht Squadron, Royal Queensland Aero, Queensland Turf, Tattersalls (Brisbane).

SHARPE, Hon. Sir John (Henry), Kt 1977; CBE 1972; JP; MP; Minister of Marine and Air Services, Bermuda, since 1980; *b* 8 Nov. 1921; *s* of Harry Sharpe; *m* 1948, Eileen Margaret, *d* of George Morrow, BC, Canada; one *s* one *d*. *Educ:* Warwick Acad., Warwick, Bermuda; Mount Allison Commercial Coll., Sackville, New Brunswick. Served War of 1939–45: Pilot Officer, with Bomber Comd, NW Europe, RCAF, attached RAF. Chm., Purvis Ltd (Importers), Bermuda. MHA for Warwick, Bermuda, 1963–; Minister of Finance, 1968–75; Dep. Leader of Govt, 1971–75; Premier of Bermuda, 1975–77, resigned; Minister of Transport, May–Dec. 1980. Formerly Member several Parliamentary Select Cttees, and of Bd of Educn, Bermuda; also Dep. Chm., Central Planning Authority and Defence Bd. Delegate to Constitutional Conf., London, 1966. Mem., War Veterans Assoc., Bermuda; Warden, Anglican Church. *Address:* Uplands, Harbour Road, Warwick West, Bermuda.

SHARPE, John Herbert S.; *see* Subak-Sharpe.

SHARPE, Sir Reginald (Taaffe), Kt 1947; QC; *b* 20 November 1898; *o s* of late Herbert Sharpe, Lindfield, Sussex; *m* 1st, 1922, Phyllis Maude (marr. diss. 1929), *d* of late Major Edward Whinney, Haywards Heath, Sussex; one *d* (and one *d* decd); 2nd, 1930, Eileen Kate (*d* 1946), *d* of Thomas Howard Usherwood, Christ's Hospital, Sussex; 3rd, 1947, Vivien Travers (*d* 1971), *d* of late Rev. Herbert Seddon Rowley, Wretham, Norfolk; 4th, 1976, Mary Millicent, *d* of late Maj.-Gen. Patrick Barclay Sangster, CB, CMG, DSO, Roehampton. *Educ:* Westminster School. Served European War: enlisted in Army, 1916; 2nd Lieut Grenadier Guards (SR), Jan. 1917; Lt, 1918; served with 2nd Bn in France (wounded). Called to Bar at Gray's Inn, Easter, 1920. Went South-Eastern Circuit and Sussex Sessions. Judge of High Court, Rangoon, 1937–48; Director of Supply, Burma (at Calcutta), 1942–44; Trustee of Rangoon University Endowment Fund, 1946–48; KC Feb. 1949; HM Comr of Assize: Western and Northern Circuits, 1949; Midland and Western Circuits, 1950; South-Eastern Circuit, 1952; North-Eastern Circuit, 1954; Birmingham October Assize, 1954; Midland Circuit, 1960. Special Comr for Divorce Causes, 1948–67. Chm., Nat. Health Service Tribunal for England and Wales, 1948–71. Deputy Chairman QS: E Sussex, 1949–69; W Kent, 1949–62; Kent, 1962–69; Mddx, 1963–65 (Asst Chm. 1951–63); Mddx area of Greater London, 1965–71; Asst Chm., W Sussex QS, 1950–70; Dep. Chm., Hailsham Petty Sessional Div., 1950–57 and 1959–70 (Chm., 1957–58). Mem. Standing Jt Cttee for E Sussex, 1958–65, for W Sussex, 1953–65. Mem., Nat. Arbitration Tribunal, 1951, and of Industrial Disputes Tribunal, 1951; Chairman, 1951–54, of Joint Council, and Independent Chairman, 1955–57, of Conciliation Board set up by Assoc. of Health and Pleasure Resorts and the Musicians' Union; Sole Commissioner to hold British Honduras Inquiry at Belize, March 1954; Chm., Departmental Cttee on Summary Trial of Minor Offences in Magistrates' Courts, 1954–55. Mem., Governing Body, Westminster Sch., 1955–. JP East Sussex. *Address:* The Old Post Office,

Rushlake Green, Sussex. *T:* Rushlake Green 830253. *Club:* East India, Devonshire, Sports and Public Schools.

SHARPE, Thomas Ridley; novelist; *b* 30 March 1928; *s* of Rev. George Coverdale Sharpe and Grace Egerton Sharpe; *m* 1969, Nancy Anne Looper; three *d*. *Educ:* Lancing College; Pembroke Coll., Cambridge (MA). National service, Royal Marines, 1946–48. Social worker 1952; teacher 1952–56, photographer 1956–61, in S Africa; Lecturer in History, Cambridge Coll. of Arts and Technology, 1963–71; full time novelist, 1971–. *Publications:* Riotous Assembly, 1971; Indecent Exposure, 1973; Porterhouse Blue, 1974; Blott on the Landscape, 1975; Wilt, 1976; The Great Pursuit, 1977; The Throwback, 1978; The Wilt Alternative, 1979; Ancestral Vices, 1980. *Recreations:* gardening, photography. *Address:* c/o Martin Secker & Warburg Ltd, 54 Poland Street, W1V 3DF.

SHARPE, William, OBE 1967; HM Diplomatic Service, retired; Overseas Relations Adviser, Potato Marketing Board, since 1979; *b* 9 Dec. 1923; *s* of late William Joseph Sharpe and of Phoebe Irene (*née* Standen); *m* 1959, Marie-Antoinette Rodesch; one *s*. *Educ:* High Sch., Chichester; London Univ. BA (Hons), MA, BSc Econ (Hons). Served RAF, 1943–47. Joined Foreign (subseq. Diplomatic) Service, 1947; Foreign Office 1947–52; Cologne and Bonn, 1952–54; Leopoldville, 1954–57; UK Mission to UN, New York, 1957–61; Foreign Office, 1961–66; Milan, 1966–70; FCO, 1971–72; Kuwait, 1972–75; Consul-Gen., Berlin, 1975–78. *Recreations:* reading, music, golf. *Address:* 15 Regis Avenue, Aldwick Bay, Bognor Regis, Sussex PO21 4HQ.

SHARPE, William James, CBE 1967 (OBE 1950); Director of Communications, Foreign and Commonwealth Office (formerly Foreign Office), 1965–69, retired; *b* 3 Jan. 1908; *s* of James Sharpe; *m* 1940, Doreen Winifred Cockell; three *s*. *Educ:* Aldershot Grammar School, 1927–39: Merchant Navy; Marconi International; Marine Communications Company. Commissioned Royal Corps of Signals, 1940; Served in France and South East Asia; Lt-Col 1945. Diplomatic Wireless Service, 1947; Deputy Director of Communications, 1959. *Address:* The Mount, Tingewick, Buckingham. *T:* Finmere 291.

SHARPLES, family name of **Baroness Sharples.**

SHARPLES, Baroness *cr* 1973 (Life Peer); **Pamela Sharples;** *b* 11 Feb. 1923; *o d* of late Lt-Comdr K. W. Newall and of Violet (who *m* 2nd, Lord Claud Hamilton), GCVO, CMG, DSO); *m* 1st, 1946, Major R. C. Sharples, MC, Welsh Guards (later Sir Richard Sharples, KCMG, OBE, MC, assassinated 1973); two *s* two *d*; 2nd, 1977, Patrick D. de Laszlo (*d* 1980). *Educ:* Southover Manor, Lewes; Florence. WAAF, 1941–46. Occupation, farming. Mem., Review Body on Armed Forces Pay, 1979–81. Dir, TVS. *Recreations:* sailing, riding, tennis, golf. *Address:* Byron's Chambers, Albany, Piccadilly, W1. *T:* 01-434 2621; Knapp House, Gold Street, Stalbridge, Dorset. *T:* Stalbridge 62327.

SHARPLES, Florence Elizabeth; National General Secretary, Young Women's Christian Association of Great Britain, since 1978; *b* 27 May 1931; *d* of late Flying Officer Albert Sharples, RAFVR, and Kathleen (*née* Evans). *Educ:* Alice Ottley Sch., Worcester; Homerton Coll., Cambridge (Teachers' Cert.); King's Coll., London (Cert. Prof. in Religious Knowledge). Head of Religious Education: Bruton Sch. for Girls, Somerset, 1953–57; Loughton High Sch., Essex, 1957–60; Housemistress, Headington Sch., Oxford, 1960–66; Headmistress, Ancaster House, Bexhill, Sussex, 1966–78. Former Mem., New Philharmonia Chorus. *Recreation:* the theatre. *Address:* The Forge, Aston Upthorpe, Oxon.

SHARPLEY, Ven. Roger Ernest Dion; Archdeacon of Hackney and Vicar of Guild Church of St Andrew, Holborn, since 1981; *b* 19 Dec. 1928; *s* of Frederick Charles and Doris Irene Sharpley; unmarried. *Educ:* Dulwich College; Christ Church, Oxford (MA); St Stephen's House, Oxford. Deacon, 1954; Priest, 1955; Curate of St Columba, Southwick, 1954–60; Vicar of All Saints', Middlesbrough, 1960–81; Curate-in-charge, St Hilda with St Peter, Middlesbrough, 1964–72; RD of Middlesbrough, 1970–81; Canon and Prebendary of York Minster, 1974–81; Priest-in-charge, St Aidan, Middlesbrough, 1979–81. *Recreations:* hill and country walking. *Address:* St Andrew's Vicarage, 5 St Andrew Street, EC4A 3AB. *T:* 01-353 3544.

SHARROCK, Prof. Roger Ian; Professor of English Language and Literature, University of London, King's College, 1968–81, now Emeritus; *b* Robin Hood's Bay, 23 Aug. 1919; *s* of Arthur and Iva France Sharrock; *m* 1940, Gertrude Elizabeth Adams, *d* of Edgar Leenie Adams, Bradford; one *s* two *d*. *Educ:* Queen Elizabeth's Sch., Wakefield; St John's Coll., Oxford (Open Exhibr). 1st cl. Hon. Sch. of Eng. Lang. and Lit., 1943; BLitt 1947. Served with King's Own Yorks LI, 1939–41; Nat. Buildings Record, 1942–44; Asst Master, Rugby Sch., 1944–46; Lectr, Univ. of Southampton, 1946; Reader, 1962; Prof. of English, Univ. of Durham, 1963. Editor, Durham Univ. Jl, 1964–68; Fulbright Vis. Prof., Univ. of Virginia, 1972; Warton Lectr of British Academy, 1972; Trustee, Dove Cottage Trust and Wordsworth Rydal Mount Trust; Chm., English Assoc., 1972–79. Gen. Editor, Oxford Bunyan. *Publications:* Songs and Comments, 1946; John Bunyan, 1954; (ed) Selected Poems of Wordsworth, 1958; (ed) Bunyan, The Pilgrim's Progress, 1960; (ed) Bunyan, Grace Abounding, 1962; (ed) Selected Poems of Dryden, 1963; (ed) Keats, Selected Poems and Letters, 1964; The Pilgrim's Progress,

1966; (ed) Oxford Standard Authors Bunyan, 1966; Solitude and Community in Wordsworth's Poetry, 1969; (ed) Pelican Book of English Prose, 1970; (ed) Casebook on Pilgrim's Progress, 1976; (ed) English Short Stories of Today, 1976; (ed) The Holy War, 1980; contrib. Encycl. Britannica, Essays in Criticism, Mod. Lang. Review, Review of English Studies, Tablet, etc. *Recreations:* walking, chess. *Address:* 12 Plough Lane, Purley, Surrey. *T:* 01-660 3248. *Club:* United Oxford & Cambridge University.

SHARWOOD-SMITH, Sir Bryan (Evers), KCMG 1955 (CMG 1950); KCVO 1956; KBE 1953; ED; Governor, Northern Nigeria, 1954-57 (Lieut-Governor, and President Northern House of Chiefs, 1952-54); retd 1957; *b* 5 Jan. 1899; *s* of late Edward Sharwood Smith; *m* 1st, 1926; one *d* ; 2nd, 1939, Winifred Joan, *d* of late Thomas and Winifred Mitchell; two *s* one *d. Educ:* Newbury School; Aldenham School, Herts (Platt Schol.). Elected to Open Classical Schol., Emmanuel College, Cambridge, 1916, but entered army (RFC), 1917; served France, Rhine and North West Frontier India, 1917-20. Assistant Master St Cuthbert's Preparatory School, Malvern, 1920. Entered Colonial Administrative Service, 1920; served in British Cameroons, 1920-27, Nigeria, 1927-57. Military Service, 1940-42; Resident, 1942; Resident, Kano, Nigeria, 1950-52; and President of Northern Region House of Assembly, 1950-52. Acting Chief Commissioner, Northern Provinces, Sept.-Dec. 1950. *Publication:* But Always as Friends, 1969. *Address:* 47 Cooden Drive, Bexhill, East Sussex. *Club:* Royal Air Force.

SHATTOCK, Rear-Adm. Ernest Henry, CB 1955; OBE 1943; Consultant for Manufacturing Licences; Director, Filtration Specialists Ltd; *b* 22 October 1904; *s* of late Ernest Mark Shattock and late Evelyn Mabel (*née* Byrde); *m* 1958, Oz Armstrong; one *s* three *d* (of previous *m*). *Educ:* Osborne; Dartmouth. Entered Osborne, 1918; specialised in flying, 1927; Commander, 1938; Captain, 1943; Rear-Admiral, 1953. Served War of 1939-45; Chief of Staff to Flag Officer Naval Air Pacific, 1944-46; Director Naval Air Warfare Division, 1946-49; commanded HMS Glory, 1949-50. Directing Captain, Senior Officers' War College, 1951; Flag Officer, Malaya, Nov. 1953-April 1956; retired list, 1956. Naval ADC to the Queen, 1953. *Publications:* An Experiment in Mindfulness, 1958; Mind Your Body, 1978; A Manual of Self-Healing, 1982. *Recreations:* music, magic. *Address:* The Mill House, Newark, Ripley, Surrey. *T:* Ripley 3020.

SHATTOCK, John Swithun Harvey, CMG 1952; OBE 1946; HM Diplomatic Service, 1947-67; *b* 21 Nov. 1907; *s* of late Rev. E. A. Shattock, Kingston St Mary, Nr Taunton; unmarried. *Educ:* Westminster School; Christ Church, Oxford. Entered ICS, 1931; served in Bengal, 1931-36; Under Sec., Govt of India (Defence Dept), 1936-39; joined Indian Political Service, 1939; served in Kathiawar, Baroda, and Kashmir Residencies, 1939-44; Dep. Sec. to Crown Representative (Political Dept), New Delhi, 1944-46; Chief Minister, Chamba State, 1946-47; apptd HM Diplomatic Service, 1947; served in UK High Commission, New Delhi, 1947-49; Head of Far Eastern Dept, Foreign Office, London, 1950-51; Head of China and Korea Dept, FO 1951; FO Rep. at Imperial Defence Coll., London, 1952; Head of China and Korea Dept, FO, 1953; Counsellor, British Embassy, Belgrade, Dec. 1953-Nov. 1955; Political Representative, Middle East Forces, Cyprus, Jan. 1956-Nov. 1958. Deputy to UK Permanent Representative on North Atlantic Council, Paris, 1959-61; Minister, UK Delegation to Disarmament Conference, Geneva, 1961-63; FO, 1963-67. *Recreation:* travel. *Address:* St Mary's Cottage, Kingston St Mary, near Taunton, Somerset; Grindlay's Bank Ltd, 13 St James's Square, SW1. *Club:* Travellers'.

SHATWELL, Prof. Kenneth Owen; Emeritus Professor in the University of Sydney; New South Wales Liaison Officer (Recruitment) for Government of Hong Kong, since 1962; *b* 16 Oct. 1909; *m* 1936, Betty, *d* of Thomas Rae Hogarth, Tasmania; one *s* one *d* (and one *d* decd). *Educ:* Lincoln College, Oxford. Served War of 1939-45: Lieut RANVR, on active service in Atlantic and Pacific. Prof. of Law and Dean of the Faculty of Law, Univ. of Tasmania, 1934-47; Challis Prof. of Law, Univ. of Sydney, 1947-74; Dean of the Faculty of Law, Univ. of Sydney, 1947-73; Dir, Inst. of Criminology, Sydney Univ., 1962-74. Vis. Prof., The Queen's Univ., Belfast, 1951; Australian Comr, S Pacific Commn, 1950-52; Sen. Research Fellow, Yale Univ., 1958-59, 1962; Visiting Professor: New York Univ. Law School Summer Workshop on Contracts, 1962; Temple Univ. Law School, 1968. Aust. Mem., Permanent Court of Arbitration under the Hague Convention, 1960-; Ministerial Cnsltnt to NSW Dept of Corrective Services, and Mem., NSW Corrective Services Adv. Council, 1972-79. FASSA. *Publications:* various articles in legal jls. *Recreation:* criminology. *Address:* 36 Chilton Parade, Turramurra, NSW 2074, Australia. *T:* Sydney 48-1189. *Clubs:* Athenæum; Tasmanian (Hobart).

SHAUGHNESSY, family name of **Baron Shaughnessy.**

SHAUGHNESSY, 3rd Baron, *cr* 1916, of Montreal; **William Graham Shaughnessy;** Vice-President, Canada Northwest Energy Ltd, Calgary, since 1969 (Director, since 1955); Director, Arbor Capital Resources Inc., Toronto, since 1972; *b* 28 March 1922; *s* of 2nd Baron and Marion (*d* 1936), *d* of late R. K. Graham, Montreal; *S* father, 1938; *m* 1944, Mary Whitley, *o d* of late John Whitley, Copthorne House, Letchworth; two *s* two *d. Educ:* Bishop's Univ., Lennoxville, Canada; BA 1941; MSc Columbia Univ., NY, 1947. Trustee, The Last Post Fund Inc., Canada. Major, Canadian Grenadier Guards, R of O. *Heir: s* Hon. Patrick John Shaughnessy, *b* 23 Oct. 1944. *Address:* 23

Albemarle Street, W1X 3HA. *Clubs:* Cavalry and Guards; Ranchmen's (Calgary); University (Montreal).

SHAVE, Kenneth George, CEng, FIMechE; Member, London Transport Executive, 1967-73, retired; *b* 25 June 1908; *s* of George Shave and Frances Larkin; *m* 1935, Doris May Stone; one *s* one *d. Educ:* St Paul's School. Apprenticed London General Omnibus Company, 1925; Rolling Stock Engineer, East Surrey Traction Company, 1930; London Transport: Asst Divisional Engineer, 1935; Divisional Engineer, 1948; Rolling Stock Engineer, 1956; Chief Mechanical Engineer, 1965. *Recreations:* golf, bridge, gardening. *Address:* 5 St Katherine's Road, Henley on Thames, Oxon RG9 7PJ. *T:* Henley 3379.

SHAW; *see* Byam Shaw.

SHAW, family name of **Baron Craigmyle** and **Baron Kilbrandon.**

SHAW, Alan Frederick, CBE 1977; JP; Chairman, Intervention Board for Agricultural Produce, 1974-80; farmer since 1946; *b* 5 March 1910; *s* of Walter Frederick and Bessie Florence Shaw; *m* 1946, Angela Dearden (*née* Burges); one step *s. Educ:* Dulwich College. J. & J. Colman, Norwich, 1927-31; own business, gravel extraction, 1931-39. War Service: BEF, 1939-40; Middle East, 8th Army, 1941-43; 2nd Army, 1944-45; Lt-Col, RE. Vice-Pres. and Dep. Pres., NFU, 1968-70; Mem. Barker Cttee on Contract Farming, 1971-72; Mem. Intervention Bd, 1972-74; Dir, Nat. Seed Develt Organisation Ltd, 1971-80; Mem., UK Seeds Exec., 1972-78; Mem. Council, Nat. Inst. Agric. Botany, 1971-80. JP Lincs, 1963. *Recreations:* golf; music (especially opera). *Address:* The Old Vicarage, Horbling, near Sleaford, Lincs. *T:* Sleaford 240563. *Clubs:* Farmers', Royal Automobile.

SHAW, Arnold John; *b* 12 July 1909; *s* of Solomon and Rachel Shaw; *m* 1935, Elizabeth Solomons; one *d. Educ:* Trafalgar Sq. (LCC) Primary Sch.; Coopers' Company's Sch.; Univ. of Southampton. BA (Hons) London, 1930. Entered teaching profession, 1932. Member: Stepney Borough Coun., 1934-48; Ilford Borough Coun., 1952-64 (Alderman, 1963-64); Redbridge, London Borough Coun., 1964-68, 1971-74. Contested (Lab) Ilford South, 1964; MP (Lab) Ilford South, 1966-70, Redbridge, Ilford South, Feb. 1974-1979; PPS to Minister for Housing and Construction, 1977-79. *Recreation:* gardening. *Address:* 2a Claybury Broadway, Ilford, Essex.

SHAW, Rev. Arthur; *see* Shaw, Rev. B. A.

SHAW, Sir Barry; *see* Shaw, Sir C. B.

SHAW, Rev. (Bernard) Arthur; Chairman of the Chester and Stoke on Trent District of the Methodist Church, 1962-80; President of the Methodist Conference, 1977-78; *b* 12 Sept. 1914; *s* of John and Lillie Shaw; *m* 1944, Alma Kirk (*d* 1977); two *s* one *d. Educ:* Queen Elizabeth Grammar Sch., Wakefield; Lancaster Royal Grammar Sch.; Richmond Coll. (Theological: London Univ.), Surrey. Filton, Bristol, 1941-43; RAF Chaplain, 1943-46; Stoke on Trent, 1946-51; Hinde Street Methodist Church, London Univ. Methodist Chaplaincy, 1951-57; Leeds Mission, 1957-62. DUniv Keele, 1977. *Recreations:* gardening, cricket. *Address:* 4 Buckingham Close, Wistaston, Crewe, Cheshire CW2 8JE. *T:* Crewe 68484.

SHAW, Prof. Bernard Leslie, FRS 1978; Professor of Chemistry, University of Leeds, since 1971; *b* Springhead, Yorks, 28 March 1930; *s* of Thomas Shaw and Vera Shaw (*née* Dale); *m* 1951, Mary Elizabeth Neild; two *s* (and one *s* decd). *Educ:* Hulme Grammar Sch., Oldham; Univ. of Manchester (BSc, PhD). Sen. DSIR Fellow, Torry Research Station, Aberdeen, 1953-55; Scientific Officer, CDEE, Porton, 1955-56; Technical Officer, ICI Ltd, Akers Research Labs, Welwyn, 1956-61; Lectr, Reader, and Prof., Univ. of Leeds, 1962-. Visiting Professor, Univ. of Western Ontario, 1969; Carnegie Mellon Univ., 1969. Member: Chem. Soc. Cttees; SERC (formerly SRC) Chem. Cttee, 1975-78, 1981- (and Inorganic Panel, 1977-78); Tilden Lectr and Prizewinner, 1975; Chem. Soc. Medal and Prize for Transition Metal Chem., 1975. *Publications:* Transition Metal Hydrides, 1967; (with N. Tucker) Organotransition Metal Chemistry, and Related Aspects of Homogeneous Catalysis, 1973; numerous original papers and reviews in chem. jls. *Recreations:* squash, tennis, pottery, music, walking, gardening. *Address:* School of Chemistry, The University of Leeds, Leeds LS2 9JT. *T:* Leeds 31751.

SHAW, Sir Bernard (Vidal), Kt 1957; *b* 28 April 1891; *s* of late Bernard Vidal Shaw; *m* 1929, Katharine Ceceley, *d* of Arthur Stanley Colls. *Educ:* St Paul's School. Indian Police, 1910-23; called to Bar, Gray's Inn, 1923; entered Colonial Service (Kenya), 1925; Resident Magistrate, 1928; Relieving President, District Court, Kenya, 1936; President, 1941; Chairman, Awqaf Commission, 1939-40; Puisne Judge, Supreme Court of Palestine, 1945-48. Chairman, North Midland District Valuation Board, 1950-55; Chm., Medical Appeal Tribunals, 1952-64; Sen. Puisne Judge, Cyprus, 1955-57. *Publications:* Kenya Law Reports, 1927-30 (Collator and Editor), and 1931-32 (Editor). *Recreation:* tennis. *Address:* 45 Rivermead Court, SW6 3RX. *T:* 01-736 1644. *Clubs:* Athenæum; Hurlingham.

SHAW, Brian Piers; Chairman and Managing Director, Furness Withy & Co. Ltd, since 1979 (Managing Director since 1977); *b* 21 March 1933; *s* of Percy Augustus Shaw; *m* 1962, Penelope Reece; three *s. Educ:* Wrekin Coll.; Corpus

Christi Coll., Cambridge (MA). National Service (2nd Lieut, Cheshire Regt), 1951-53. Called to Bar, Gray's Inn, 1957. Joined Pacific Steam Navigation Co., Liverpool, 1957; Company Secretary, 1960; Company Sec., Royal Mail Lines, London, 1961-67; Dir, Royal Mail Lines, 1968-; Manager, Furness Withy & Co., 1969-73; Chairman, Shaw Savill & Albion Co., 1973-; Director: Furness Withy & Co., 1973-; other Furness Withy Group cos; Overseas Containers Ltd, 1972-80; Nat. Bank of NZ, 1973-77 (London Board, 1977-80; Chm., London Adv. Cttee, 1980-); Grindlays Bank, 1977-; Orient Overseas Container (Holdings) Ltd, 1980-. Mem. Gen. Policy Cttee, Gen. Council of British Shipping; Asst to Court, Worshipful Co. of Shipwrights; Chm., Council of European and Japanese Nat. Shipowners' Assocs (CENSA), 1979-; Pres., New Zealand Soc., 1979-80. *Recreations:* golf, cricket, music. *Address:* 5 Alleyn Park, Dulwich, SE21 8AU. *T:* 01-670 3012.

SHAW, Very Rev. Charles Allan; Dean of Ely, since 1982; *b* 16 Feb. 1927; *s* of Henry and Anne Shaw. *Educ:* Bolton School; Christ's Coll., Cambridge (MA 1952); Westcott House, Cambridge. Assistant Master, Tonbridge School, 1949; ordained, 1951; Curate of Swinton, Manchester, 1951-54; Chaplain and Asst Master, Malvern Coll., 1954-58; Vicar of St Ambrose, Pendleton, 1958-62; Domestic Chaplain to Bishop of Birmingham and Succentor of Birmingham Cathedral, 1962-67; Dean of Bulawayo, 1967-75; Archdeacon of Bulawayo, 1969-75; Vicar General of Matabeleland, 1972-75; Residentiary Canon and Precentor of Hereford Cathedral, 1975-82. *Recreations:* theatre, music and people. *Address:* The Deanery, Ely, Cambs CB7 4DN. *T:* Ely 2432. *Club:* Junior Carlton.

SHAW, Sir (Charles) Barry, Kt 1980; CB 1974; QC 1964; Director of Public Prosecutions for Northern Ireland, since 1972; *b* 12 April 1923; *s* of late Ernest Hunter Shaw and Sarah Gertrude Shaw, Mayfield, Balmoral, Belfast; *m* 1964, Jane (*née* Phillips). *Educ:* Inchmarlo House, Belfast; Pannal Ash Coll., Harrogate; The Queen's Univ. of Belfast (LLB). Served War: commissioned RA, 97 A/Tk Regt RA, 15th (Scottish) Div., 1942-46. Called to Bar of Northern Ireland, 1948; called to Bar, Middle Temple, 1970. *Address:* Royal Courts of Justice, Belfast, Northern Ireland BT1 3NX.

SHAW, Prof. C(harles) Thurstan, CBE 1972; Professor of Archaeology, University of Ibadan, 1963-74; *b* 27 June 1914; 2nd *s* of late Rev. John Herbert Shaw and Grace Irene (*née* Woollatt); *m* Gilian Ione Maud, *e d* of late Edward John Penberthy Magor and Gilian Sarah (*née* Westmacott); two *s* three *d*. *Educ:* Blundell's Sch.; Sidney Sussex Coll., Cambridge; Univ. of London Inst. of Education. 1st cl. hons Arch. and Anthrop. Tripos 1936, MA, PhD Cantab; DipEd London. FRAI 1938; FSA 1947. Curator, Anthropology Museum, Achimota Coll., Gold Coast, 1937-45; Cambs Educn Cttee, 1945-51; Cambridge Inst. of Educn, 1951-63. Vis. Prof., Northwestern Univ., USA, 1969; Vis Lecturer: Harvard, 1975; Yale, 1979; Calgary, 1980. Founder and Editor: W African Archaeological Newsletter, 1964-70; W African Jl of Archaeology, 1971-75. Mem. Perm. Council, Internat. Union of Pre- and Proto-historic Sciences, 1965-74; Vice-Pres., Panafrican Congress on Prehistory and Study of Quaternary, 1966-77; Mem. Council, Univ. of Ibadan, 1969-71. Vis. Fellow, Clare Hall, Cambridge, 1973; Vis. Res. Prof. Ahmadu Bello Univ., 1975-78; Dir of Studies, Archaeology and Anthrop., Magdalene Coll., Cambridge, 1976-79. Hon. DSc Univ. of Nigeria, 1982. Amaury Talbot Prize, Royal Anthrop. Inst., 1970 and 1978. Onuna-Ekwulu Ora of Igbo-Ukwu, 1972. *Publications:* Excavation at Dawu, 1961; Archaeology and Nigeria, 1964; (with J. Vanderburg) Bibliography of Nigerian Archaeology, 1969; (ed) Nigerian Prehistory and Archaeology, 1969; Igbo-Ukwu: an account of archaeological discoveries in eastern Nigeria, 2 vols, 1970; Discovering Nigeria's Past, 1975; Why 'Darkest' Africa?, 1975; Unearthing Igbo-Ukwu, 1977; Ancient People and Places: Nigeria, 1978; numerous articles on African archaeology and prehistory in jls. *Recreations:* walking, music. *Address:* Silver Ley, 37 Hawthorne Road, Stapleford, Cambridge CB2 5DU. *T:* Cambridge 842283. *Clubs:* Athenæum; Explorers' (New York).

SHAW, Prof. Charles Timothy; Professor of Mining and Head of Department of Mineral Resources Engineering, Royal School of Mines, since 1980; *b* 4 Oct. 1934; *s* of Charles John and Constance Olive Shaw (*née* Scotton); *m* 1962, Tuulike Raili Linari-Linholm; one *s* two *d*. *Educ:* Univ. of Witwatersrand (BSc(Mining) 1956); McGill Univ. (MSc(Applied) (Mineral Exploration) 1959). Mine Manager's, Mine Overseer's and Mine Surveyor's Certs of SA; S African Professional Engineer. Johannesburg Consolidated Investment Co. Ltd (JCI): numerous positions at various levels, 1960-67; Head of Computer Div., 1967-70; Manager, 1970-72 (as such an appointed dir of 14 cos incl. Consolidated Murchison Ltd and Alternate Dir of 9 cos); Consulting Engr, Consolidated Murchison Ltd, Randfontein Estates Gold Mining Co. (Wits.) Ltd and Shangani Mining Corp. (Zimbabwe), 1972-74; Consulting Engr and Alternate Dir, Rustenburg Platinum Mines Ltd, 1974-76; Chief Consulting Engr and Alternate Dir, Johannesburg Consolidated Investment Co. Ltd, also Man. Dir, Western Areas Gold Mining Co. Ltd, 1976-77; Associate Prof., Virginia Polytechnic Inst. and State Univ., 1977-80. Rep. for JCI on Technical Adv. Cttee of SA Chamber of Mines, 1974-77; Alternate Mem. for Gold Producers Cttee, 1976-77. Mem. Council, InstnMM, 1981-. *Publications:* (with J. R. Lucas) The Coal Industry: Industry Guides for Accountants, Auditors and Financial Executives, 1980; papers both in technical literature and in house at Johannesburg Consolidated Investment Co. Ltd. *Recreations:* golf, mining history. *Address:* Department of Mineral Resources Engineering, Royal School of Mines, SW7 2BP. *T:* 01-589 5111.

SHAW, Colin Don; Director of Television, Independent Broadcasting Authority, since 1977; *b* 2 Nov. 1928; *s* of late Rupert M. Shaw and Enid F. Shaw (*née* Smith); *m* 1955, Elizabeth Ann, *d* of Paul Bowker; one *s* two *d*. *Educ:* Liverpool Coll.; St Peter's Hall, Oxford (MA). Called to the Bar, Inner Temple, 1960. Nat. Service, RAF, 1947-49. Joined BBC as Radio Drama Producer, North Region, 1953; Asst, BBC Secretariat, 1957-59; Asst Head of Programme Contracts Dept, 1959-60; Sen. Asst, BBC Secretariat, 1960-63; special duties in connection with recruitment for BBC2, 1963; Asst Head of Programmes, BBC North Region, 1963-66; various posts in TV Programme Planning, ending as Head of Group, 1966-69; Secretary to the BBC, 1969-72, Chief Secretary, 1972-76. Mem., Arts Council of GB, 1978-80 (Chairman: Arts Council Research Adv. Gp, 1978-80; Housing the Arts Cttee, 1979-80; Touring Cttee, 1980). Governor, E-SU of the Commonwealth, 1976-; Chm., Bd of Governors, Hampden House Sch., 1972-77. FRSA 1978. *Publications:* several radio plays and a stage-play for children. *Recreations:* going to the theatre, reading. *Address:* Lesters, Little Ickford, Aylesbury, Bucks. *T:* Ickford 225. *Club:* United Oxford & Cambridge University.

SHAW, David; General Secretary, Independent Television Companies Association, since 1981; *b* 19 Oct. 1936; *s* of Thomas Young Boyd Shaw and Elizabeth Shaw; *m* 1961, Margaret Esmé Bagnall; one *s* one *d*. *Educ:* Univ. of Birmingham (BA (Hons) Geography); Univ. of Sussex (Adv. Dip. Educnl Technology). Education Officer in Royal Air Force, final rank Sqdn Ldr, 1960-76; Training Adviser to North Western Provincial Councils, 1976-78; Gen. Sec., BAAB, 1978-81. Represented Great Britain in Athletics (3000 metres steeplechase), 1958; British Universities Cross-Country Champion, 1959. *Recreations:* reading, hill-climbing, sketching. *Address:* (business) Independent Television Companies Association, 56 Mortimer Street, W1N 7DG. *Club:* Royal Air Force.

SHAW, Prof. David Aitken, FRCP, FRCPE; Professor of Clinical Neurology since 1976, and Dean of Medicine since 1981, University of Newcastle upon Tyne; *b* 11 April 1924; *s* of John James McIntosh Shaw and Mina Draper; *m* 1960, Jill Parry; one *s* two *d*. *Educ:* Edinburgh Academy; Edinburgh Univ. MB ChB (Edin) 1951; FRCP (Edin.) 1968; FRCP (Lond.) 1976. Served as Lieut RNVR, 1943-46. Hospital appts, Edinburgh Royal Infirmary, 1951-57; Lectr, Inst. of Neurology, Univ. of London, 1957-64; Mayo Foundation Fellow, 1962-63; Sen. Lectr, Univ. of Newcastle upon Tyne, 1964-76; Public Orator, Univ. of Newcastle upon Tyne, 1976-79. *Publications:* (with N. E. F. Cartlidge) Head Injury, 1981; chapters in books and scientific articles in medical jls. *Recreations:* golf and fishing. *Address:* 4 Adderstone Crescent, Newcastle upon Tyne NE2 2HH. *T:* Newcastle upon Tyne 814146.

SHAW, Dr Dennis Frederick, CBE 1974; Fellow of Keble College, since 1957, Professorial Fellow, 1978; Keeper of Scientific Books, Bodleian Library, Oxford, since 1975; *b* 20 April 1924; 2nd *s* of Albert Shaw and Lily (*née* Hill), Teddington; *m* 1949, Joan Irene, *er d* of Sidney and Maud Chandler; one *s* three *d*. *Educ:* Harrow County Sch.; Christ Church, Oxford. BA 1945, MA 1950, DPhil 1950. FInstP 1971; FZS. Jun. Sci. Officer, MAP, 1944-46; Res. Officer in Physics, Clarendon Lab., Oxford, 1950-57, Sen. Res. Officer 1957-64; Univ. Lectr in Physics, Oxford, 1964-75. Vis. Prof. of Physics and Brown Founln Fellow, Univ. of the South, Tennessee, 1974. Mem., Oxford City Council, 1963-67; Chm., Oxford City Civil Emergency Cttee, 1966-67; Member: Home Office Sci. Adv. Council, 1966-78; Home Defence Sci. Adv. Cttee, 1978-; Hebdomadal Council, 1980-; Chairman: Oxford Univ. Delegacy for Educnl Studies, 1969-73; Home Office Police Equipment Cttee, 1969-70; Home Office Police Sci. Develt Cttee, 1971-74. Member: Amer. Phys. Soc., 1957; NY Acad. of Scis, 1981. Almoner, Christ's Hosp., 1980-. *Publications:* An Introduction to Electronics, 1962, 2nd edn 1970; A Review of Oxford University Science Libraries, 1977, 2nd edn 1981; papers in sci. jls. *Recreations:* riding, gardening, enjoying music. *Address:* Keble College, Oxford. *T:* Oxford 59201. *Club:* United Oxford & Cambridge University.

SHAW, Rev. Douglas William David; Professor of Divinity, University of St Andrews, since 1979; *b* 25 June 1928; *s* of William David Shaw and Nansie Smart. *Educ:* Edinburgh Acad.; Loretto; Ashbury Coll., Ottawa; Univs of Cambridge and Edinburgh. MA (Cantab), BD (Edin.), LLB (Edin.). WS. Practised law as Partner of Davidson and Syme, WS, Edinburgh, 1953-57. Ordained Minister of Church of Scotland, 1960; Asst Minister, St George's West Church, Edinburgh, 1960-63; Official Observer of World Alliance of Reformed Churches at Second Vatican Council, Rome, 1962. Dean, Faculty of Divinity, and Principal, New College, University of Edinburgh, 1974-78, Lectr in Divinity, 1963-79. *Publications:* Who is God? 1968, 2nd edn 1970; The Dissuaders, 1978; trans. from German: F. Heyer: The Catholic Church from 1648 to 1870, 1969; various articles in theological jls. *Recreations:* squash (Scottish Amateur Champion, 1950-51-52), golf. *Address:* St Mary's College, St Andrews, Fife. *T:* St Andrews 76161. *Clubs:* New (Edinburgh); Luffness New; Edinburgh Sports.

SHAW, Frank Howard, MBE 1945; TD; MA; JP; Headmaster, King's College School, Wimbledon, 1960-75; *b* 13 June 1913; *s* of E. H. Shaw; *m* 1950, Harriette Alice, *d* of late His Honour Robert Peel; one *s* two *d*. *Educ:* Altrincham Grammar School; Hertford College, Oxford. Asst master: King's Coll. School, 1935-39; Marlborough College (and Housemaster), 1939-52; first Headmaster of Pakistan Air Force Public School, Murree Hills, 1952-58; Principal, Aden Coll., Aden, 1958-60. Chm., HMC, 1972. Served War of

1939-45 in Devonshire Regt; Jt Planning Staff, 1943-45. Lt-Col. JP, SW London, 1966-76. *Publications:* textbooks for teaching of English in Pakistan. *Recreation:* golf. *Address:* Medstead House, Medstead, near Alton, Hants. *T:* Alton 62195. *Clubs:* East India, Devonshire, Sports and Public Schools, MCC.

SHAW, Dr Gavin Brown, CBE 1981; FRCP, FRCPE, FRCPGlas; Consultant Physician, Southern General Hospital, Glasgow, since 1956; *b* 24 May 1919; *s* of Gavin Shaw and Christian Douglas Cormack; *m* 1943, Margaret Mabon Henderson; one *s* two *d. Educ:* Glasgow Academy; Glasgow Univ., 1936-42 (BSc, MB ChB). President, Students' Representative Council, 1940-41. House Phys. to Sir J. W. McNee, 1942; Temporary Surg.-Lieut, RNVR, 1942-45; Asst Phys., Southern Gen. Hosp., Glasgow, 1948-56. Royal College of Physicians and Surgeons of Glasgow: Hon. Sec., 1957-65; Visitor, 1977-78; Pres., 1978-80. Mem., West Regional Hosp. Bd, 1971-74; Chairman: Greater Glasgow Med. Adv. Cttee, 1973-76; Jt Cttee for Higher Med. Trng, 1979-81; Specialty Adviser in Medicine, W of Scotland Post-Graduate Cttee, 1971-. Mem., GMC, 1982. Hon. FACP 1979; Hon. FRCPI 1979; Hon. FRCPsych 1980; Hon. FRCGP 1980. *Publications:* jt ed, Cardiac Resuscitation and Pacing, 1964; occasional contributor to BMJ, Brit. Heart Jl, Lancet, Practitioner, Amer. Heart Jl. *Recreations:* walking, gardening, bird watching and one-time sailor, listening to music, reading. *Address:* 4 Horseshoe Road, Bearsden, Glasgow G61 2ST. *T:* 041-942 4553. *Clubs:* Royal Scottish Automobile; College, Glasgow University.

SHAW, Rev. Geoffrey Norman; Principal, Wycliffe Hall, Oxford, since 1979; *b* 15 April 1926; *s* of Samuel Norman Shaw and Maud Shaw; *m* 1948, Cynthia Brown; one *s* two *d. Educ:* Holgate Grammar Sch., Barnsley; Jesus Coll., Oxford (MA); Wycliffe Hall, Oxford. Asst Curate, St Mary, Rushden, 1951-54; Vicar of St Paul, Woking, 1954-62; Rector of St Leonards-on-Sea, Sussex, 1962-68; Asst Master, Ecclesfield Grammar Sch., Sheffield, 1968-69; Head of Religious Educn and Classics, Silverdale Sch., Sheffield, 1969-72; Vice-Principal, Oak Hill Theol Coll., Southgate, 1972-79. *Recreations:* caravanning, tennis, music. *Address:* The Principal's Lodge, 2 Norham Gardens, Oxford OX2 6PW. *T:* Oxford 57539.

SHAW, George Anthony Theodore, CBE 1965; *b* 25 Oct. 1917; *s* of late G. E. Shaw, CMG, OBE, LLB; *m* 1st, Suzanne Alexandra Barber (marr. diss.), *d* of late H. C. Barber; one *s* one *d*; 2nd, Joan Margaret, *d* of late Rev. N. M. Livingstone, DCL, RN; two *d. Educ:* Marlborough Coll.; Clare Coll., Cambridge (MA). Intell. Corps, Army, 1941-46, Indian Civil Service, 1944-45; HM Overseas Civil Service, 1940-67: Malaya, Singapore, Sarawak, Brunei, Malaysia; State Sec., Sarawak, 1963-67; Milton Keynes Develt Corp., 1967-74; Severn Trent Water Auth., 1974-79. Order of Star of Sarawak (PNBS), 1966. *Recreations:* wide. *Address:* Wynford, Barnes Lane, Milford-on-Sea, Lymington, Hants. *Club:* Royal Lymington Yacht.

SHAW, George N. B.; *see* Bowman-Shaw.

SHAW, Giles; *see* Shaw, J. G. D.

SHAW, Dr Ian James, CMG 1979; OBE 1965; Assistant Chief Scientific Adviser (Studies), 1974-79, and Director, Defence Operational Analysis Establishment, 1977-79, Ministry of Defence; *b* 8 April 1919; *s* of Livingstone and Myrtle Shaw; *m* 1949, Audrey Jean Spalding; two *s. Educ:* Auckland UC, NZ (BSc); Cambridge Univ (BA, PhD). Joined Scientific Civil Service (Army Dept), 1950; transf. to MoD, 1958. *Recreations:* woodwork, gardening, baiting bureaucrats. *Address:* Woodilee, Mellersh Hill Road, Wonersh Park, Guildford, Surrey. *T:* Guildford 892436.

SHAW, Irwin; writer (US); *b* New York, 27 Feb. 1913; *s* of William Shaw and Rose (*née* Tompkins); *m* 1939, Marian Edwards (marr. diss.); one *s. Educ:* Brooklyn College (AB). Served War of 1939-45 in US Army. *Publications: plays:* Bury the Dead, 1936; The Gentle People, 1939; Quiet City, 1939; Retreat to Pleasure, 1941; Sons and Soldiers, 1943; The Assassin, 1945; Children From Their Games, 1963; *short stories:* Sailor Off the Bremen, 1940; Welcome to the City, 1942; Act of Faith, 1946; Mixed Company, 1952; Tip on a Dead Jockey, 1957; Love on a Dark Street, 1965; Whispers in Bedlam, 1972; God was Here, But He Left Early, 1973; Collected Stories, (in US, Five Decades), 1978; *novels:* The Young Lions, 1948; The Troubled Air, 1951; Lucy Crown, 1956; Two Weeks in Another Town, 1960; Voices of a Summer Day, 1965; Rich Man, Poor Man, 1970; Evening in Byzantium, 1973; Nightwork, 1975; Beggarman, Thief, 1977; The Top of the Hill, 1979; Bread upon the Waters, 1981; Acceptable Losses, 1982; *travel:* In the Company of Dolphins, 1962; Paris! Paris!, 1976. *Address:* c/o Hope Leresche & Sayle, 11 Jubilee Place, SW3 3TE.

SHAW, James John Sutherland, CB 1970; Chairman, Civil Service Appeal Board, 1973-77 (Deputy Chairman, 1972-73); *b* 5 Jan. 1912; *s* of Robert Shaw and Christina Macallum Sutherland; *m* 1947, Rosamond Chisholm Sharman; no *c. Educ:* Ardrossan Academy, Ayrshire; Glasgow and London Universities. Glasgow University: MA 1st Class Hons History, 1932, PhD 1935; Lecturer in History, 1936-40. Served War with RAF, 1940-45, Navigator, AC2 to Sqdn Leader (despatches). Senior Lecturer in History, Glasgow Univ., 1945-46; HM Treasury, 1946-68: Principal, Asst Sec., Under-Sec.; Under-Sec., 1968-69, Dep. Sec., 1969-72, CSD. OECD Consltnt on Greek CS, 1973; Chm., Internat. Commn on Reform, Sudan CS, 1973-74; consultant to Commn on Structure and Functions, Ghana CS, 1974, to States of Jersey on

Jersey CS, 1975. *Recreations:* talking, walking and gardening. *Address:* North Field, Neaves Lane, Stradbroke, Eye, Suffolk IP21 5JP. *T:* Stradbroke 535.

SHAW, Prof. John Calman, CA; Johnstone Smith Professor of Accountancy, University of Glasgow, since 1977; *b* 10 July 1932; *m* 1960, Shirley Botterill; three *d. Educ:* Strathallan Sch.; Edinburgh Univ. BL; FCMA, MBCS, JDipMA. Qualified Chartered Accountant, 1955. National Service, RAF, 1955-57. Resumed accountancy career in London; became a partner in Edinburgh accountancy firm of Graham, Smart & Annan (now Deloitte, Haskins & Sells), 1960, where, under terms of his appt at Glasgow Univ., he continues to practise. Vice-Pres., Inst. of Chartered Accountants of Scotland, 1981-. Commander of The Priory of Scotland of Most Venerable Order of St John, 1970; CStJ. *Publications:* ed, Bogie on Group Accounts (3rd edn), 1973; The Audit Report, 1980; numerous articles in Accountant's Magazine and Accounting and Business Research and Accountancy, etc. *Recreations:* opera, theatre, walking. *Address:* 29 Abercromby Place, Edinburgh EH3 6UE. *T:* 031-557 2111. *Clubs:* Caledonian; New (Edinburgh); Western (Glasgow).

SHAW, John Dennis Bolton, MVO 1961; HM Diplomatic Service, retired; *b* 5 July 1920; *er s* of William Bolton Shaw and Margaret Bolton Shaw, Manchester; *m* 1955, Isabel Lowe; two *s. Educ:* Manchester Grammar Sch.; Balliol Coll., Oxford (MA). Served War: in North Africa, Italy and India, Lieut RA and RWAFF, 1940-46. Colonial Office, 1948-55; District Comr and Dep. Financial Sec., Sierra Leone, 1955-57; Commonwealth Relations Office, 1957-58 and 1962-65; Karachi, 1958-61; Washington, 1961-62; apptd Counsellor, 1962; Nairobi, 1965-67; Counsellor for Trusteeship Affairs, UK Mission to the UN, 1967-71; Head of Gibraltar and General Dept, FCO, 1971-73; Ambassador to Somali Democratic Republic, 1973-76; Dep. High Comr, Kuala Lumpur, 1976-77. *Recreations:* travel, archaeology, music. *Address:* c/o Foreign and Commonwealth Office, King Charles Street, SW1.

SHAW, (John) Giles (Dunkerley); MP (C) Pudsey since Feb. 1974; Parliamentary Under Secretary of State, Department of the Environment, since 1981; *b* Nov. 1931; *y s* of Hugh D. Shaw; *m* Dione Patricia Crosthwaite Ellison; one *s* two *d. Educ:* Sedbergh Sch.; St John's Coll., Cambridge (MA). President of the Union, Cambridge, 1954. Past Rural District Councillor; served on Flaxton RDC, 1957-64. Marketing Dir, Confectionery Div., Rowntree Mackintosh Ltd, 1970-74. Contested (C) Kingston upon Hull West, 1966. Parly Under-Sec. of State, Northern Ireland, 1979-81. Mem. House of Commons Select Cttee on Nationalised Industries; Vice-Chm., Cons. Prices and Consumer Affairs Cttee; Joint-Sec., All Party Wool Textile Group; Treasurer Yorks Cons. Members' Group, 1974-79. *Recreations:* ornithology, fishing, tennis. *Address:* 20 Parkside, Horsforth, Leeds; House of Commons, SW1.

SHAW, Sir John J. K. B.; *see* Best-Shaw.

SHAW, John Michael, MC 1940; QC 1967; Barrister-at-Law; Regional Chairman of Industrial Tribunals, since 1972; *b* 14 Nov. 1914; *yr s* of late M. J. Shaw (killed in action, 1916); *m* 1940, Margaret L. *yr d* of Robert T. D. Stoneham, CBE; two *s* two *d. Educ:* Rugby; Worcester Coll., Oxford. Called to the Bar, Gray's Inn, 1937. Served War of 1939-45 (Major): commissioned Royal Fusiliers, 1940. *Recreations:* fishing, gardening. *Address:* South Knighton House, South Knighton, near Newton Abbot, Devon.

SHAW, Sir John Valentine Wistar, KCMG 1947 (CMG 1942); Kt 1946; *b* 1894; *m* 1926, Josephine Mary, *yr d* of Joseph Simpson, Horsehay, Shropshire; two *s. Educ:* Repton School. Served with Royal Engineers, 1914-19, in France and Palestine (despatches). Colonial Administrative Service, Gold Coast, 1921-35; Palestine, 1935-40; Colonial Sec. Cyprus, 1940-43 (despatches, CMG); Chief Sec. Palestine, 1943-46; Governor and C-in-C Trinidad and Tobago, 1947-50; retired, 1950. Attached War Office, 1950-54; Chairman, Commission of Inquiry into Industrial dispute and riots, Sierra Leone, 1955. *Address:* 2 White Close, Winchelsea, Sussex. *T:* Winchelsea 283.

SHAW, Max S.; *see* Stuart-Shaw.

SHAW, Sir Michael (Norman), Kt 1982; JP; DL; MP (C) Scarborough, since 1974 (Scarborough and Whitby, 1966-74); *b* 9 Oct. 1920; *s* of late Norman Shaw; *m* 1951, Joan Mary Louise, *o d* of Sir Alfred L. Mowat, 2nd Bt; three *s. Educ:* Sedbergh. Chartered Accountant. MP (L and C) Brighouse and Spenborough, March 1960-Oct. 1964; PPS: to Minister of Labour, 1962-63; to Sec. of State, Dept of Trade and Industry, 1970-72; to Chancellor of the Duchy of Lancaster, 1973. Mem., UK Delegn to European Parlt, 1974-79. FCA. JP Dewsbury, 1953; DL W Yorks, 1977. *Address:* Duxbury Hall, Liversedge, W Yorkshire. *T:* Heckmondwike 402270. *Club:* Carlton.

SHAW, Neil McGowan; Group Managing Director, Tate & Lyle Ltd, London, since 1980; Director: Texaco Canada Inc.; Touche Remnant North American Trust; Americare Corporation; *b* 31 May 1929; *s* of Harold LeRoy Shaw and Fabiola Marie Shaw; *m* 1952, Audrey Robinson (marr. diss.); two *s* three *d. Educ:* Knowlton High Sch.; Lower Canada Coll., Canada. Trust Officer, Crown Trust Co., Montreal, 1947-54; Merchandising Manager, Canada & Dominion Sugar Co., Montreal, 1954-66; Vice Pres., Canada & Dominion Sugar Co., Toronto, 1967-72; Pres. and Dir, Redpath Industries

Ltd, 1972-80. *Recreations:* sailing, skiing. *Address:* 10 Sydney Place, SW7 3NL. *Clubs:* Toronto (Toronto); Mount Royal (Montreal).

SHAW, Sir Robert, 7th Bt *cr* 1821; Design Engineer, T. Lamb, McManus & Associates Ltd, Calgary, Alberta; *b* Nairobi, Kenya, 31 Jan. 1925; *s* of Sir Robert de Vere Shaw, 6th Bt, MC, and Joan (*d* 1967), *d* of Thomas Cross; *S* father, 1969; *m* 1954, Jocelyn, *d* of late Andrew McGuffie, Swaziland; two *d. Educ:* Harrow; Univs of Oklahoma and Missouri, USA. RN, 1943-47 (Lieut RN retd). BS Civil Eng. Oklahoma, 1962; MS Civil Eng. Missouri, 1964; Professional Engineer, Alberta; Mem. Engineering Inst. of Canada. *Recreation:* sailing. *Heir: n* Charles de Vere Shaw, *b* 1 March 1957. *Address:* 234 40th Avenue SW, Calgary, Alberta T2S 0X3, Canada. *Club:* Alberta United Services Inst. (Calgary, Alberta).

SHAW, Dr Robert Macdonald, CB 1968; Deputy Chief Medical Officer, Department of Health and Social Security (formerly Ministry of Health), 1965-77; *b* 16 Sept. 1912; *s* of late Peter Macdonald and late Ellen Shaw; *m* 1941, Grace Helen Stringfellow; two *s* one *d. Educ:* Mill Hill School; Victoria Univ. of Manchester. Miscellaneous hospital appointments, etc, 1936-39. Emergency Commission, RAMC, 1939-45. Asst County MOH, Essex, 1945-48; Department of Health and Social Security (formerly Ministry of Health), 1948-77. QHP 1971-74. *Address:* The Lodge, Tor Bryan, Ingatestone, Essex CM4 9HN.

SHAW, Sir Roy, Kt 1979; Secretary General of the Arts Council of Great Britain since July 1975; *b* 8 July 1918; *s* of Frederick and Elsie Shaw; *m* 1946, Gwenyth Baron; five *s* two *d. Educ:* Firth Park Grammar School, Sheffield; Manchester Univ. BA(Hons). Newspaper printing department 'copy-holder', 1937; newspaper publicity, 1938; Library Asst, Sheffield City Library, 1939; Cataloguer, Manchester Univ. Library, 1945; Organizing Tutor, WEA, 1946; Adult Educn Lectr, Leeds Univ., 1947; Warden, Leeds Univ. Adult Educn Centre, Bradford, 1959; Professor and Dir of Adult Educn, Keele Univ., 1962. Vis. Prof., Centre for Arts, City Univ., London. Hon DLitt City, 1978; DUniv Open, 1981. *Publications:* contrib. chapters to: Trends in English Adult Education, 1959; The Committed Church, 1966; Your Sunday Paper, 1967; over 100 articles on adult education, mass media and cultural policy. *Recreations:* reading, going to theatres, films, concerts and art galleries, swimming, watching the best of television—and sometimes, for clinical reasons, the worst. *Address:* 48 Farrer Road, N8 8LB. *Club:* Arts.

SHAW, Roy Edwin; Council Member, London Borough of Camden, since 1964; *b* 21 July 1925; *s* of Edwin Victor and Edith Lily Shaw. Hampstead Borough Council, 1956-62; St Pancras Borough, 1962-65; Camden Borough Council: Chm., Planning Cttee, 1967-68; Chm., Finance Cttee, 1971-74; Chief Whip and Dep. Leader, 1965-73; Leader, 1975-82. Vice-Chm., AMA; Dep. Chm. and Leader of Labour Party, London Boroughs Assoc. Part-time Mem., London Electricity Bd; Member: Transport Users Consultative Cttee for London, 1974-80; Adv. Cttee on Local Govt Audit, Consult. Council on Local Govt Finances. *Recreations:* listening to music; entertaining attractive women. *Address:* Town Hall, Euston Road, NW1 2RU. *T:* 01-278 4444. *Club:* Talacre Social (Kentish Town).

SHAW, Sir Run Run, Kt 1977; CBE 1974; President, Shaw Organisation, since 1963; *b* 14 Oct. 1907; *m* 1932, Lily Wong Mee Chun; two *s* two *d.* Left China for Singapore and began making films and operating cinemas, 1927; left Singapore for Hong Kong and built Shaw Movietown, making and distributing films, 1959. Pres., Hong Kong Red Cross Soc., 1972-. Chairman: Hong Kong Arts Festival, 1974-; Bd of Governors, Hong Kong Arts Centre, 1978-; Hong Kong Television Broadcasts Ltd (TVB), 1980-. Mem. Council, Chinese Univ. of Hong Kong, 1977-. Hon. LLD Hong Kong Univ., 1980. *Recreations:* shadow-boxing, golf. *Address:* Shaw House, Lot 220 Clearwater Bay Road, Kowloon, Hong Kong. *T:* 3-298371. *Clubs:* Hong Kong Country, Hong Kong, Royal Hong Kong Golf, Royal Hong Kong Jockey (Hong Kong).

SHAW, Rt. Hon. Sir Sebag, Kt 1968; PC 1975; a Lord Justice of Appeal, 1975-81; *b* 28 Dec. 1906; 2nd *s* of Henry and Marie Shaw; *m* 1928, Sally (*d* 1982); one *s.* Called to Bar, Gray's Inn, 1931, Bencher 1967. QC 1962. Acting Deputy Chairman, County of London Sessions, 1949; Recorder of Ipswich, 1958-68; Prosecuting Counsel, Board of Trade, 1959-62; Leader, SE Circuit, 1967-68; Judge of Queen's Bench Division, High Court of Justice, 1968-75. Member: Interdepartmental Cttee on Court of Criminal Appeal, 1964-65; Bar Council, 1964-68; Parole Bd, 1971-74, Vice-Chm., 1973-74. Fellow UCL, 1970-. *Publication:* Law of Meetings, 1947. *Address:* 69 Wynnstay Gardens, W8. *T:* 01-937 4907.

SHAW, Sinclair, QC (Scotland) 1950; Sheriff Principal of Edinburgh, the Lothians and Peeblesshire and Sheriff of Chancery, 1966-73; *b* South Africa; *m* 1948, Denise Fanny (Mem. French Resistance, 1941-45, Médaille de la Résistance; Croix de Guerre avec Palme; Chevalier Légion d'Honneur), *e d* of Dr Charles Mantoux and Dr Dora Mantoux; no *c. Educ:* Stewart College; Edinburgh Univ. Called to Scots Bar, 1936. Chairman Scottish Council of Labour Party, 1947. Member New Towns Committee (Chm. Lord Reith) apptd by Govt to work out principles to be followed in building new towns, 1945-46. Contested (Lab): Moray and Nairn, 1945, S Aberdeen, 1951. Advocate-Depute, 1945-51; Sheriff Substitute of Fife, 1959-66. *Address:* 5 Randolph Cliff, Edinburgh EH3 7TZ. *T:* 031-225 4445; La Diane, 32 Rue des Eveuses, 78120 Rambouillet, France. *T:* 041.76.06.

SHAW, Sydney Herbert, CMG 1963; OBE 1958; *b* 6 Nov. 1903; 2nd *s* of John Beaumont and Gertrude Shaw; *m* 1930, Mary Louise, *e d* of Ernest Lewin Chapman; one *s* one *d. Educ:* King's College School; Royal School of Mines, London University. BSc Hons 1st cl. Mining Engineering, 1925 and Mining Geology, 1926; MSc (Birm.) 1937; PhD (Lond.) 1949. Geophys. prospecting N and S Rhodesia, 1926-28; Imperial Geophys. Experimental Survey, Aust., 1928-30; geophys. prospecting, Cyprus, 1930. Demonstrator, Geolog. Dept, Roy. Sch. of Mines, 1931; Lectr in Geology, Birmingham Univ., 1932-37; Govt Geologist, Palestine, 1937-48 (seconded as Dep. Controller Heavy Industries, Palestine, 1942-45); Colonial (later Overseas) Geological Surveys, London, 1949, Deputy Director, 1950, Dir, 1959-65; Head, Overseas Div., Inst. of Geological Sciences, 1965-68. Geological Adviser, Colonial Office (subseq. Dept of Tech. Co-op., then Min. of Overseas Develt), 1959-68. Retd, 1968. FIMM (Pres., 1968-69); FGS. *Publications:* scientific papers in various jls. *Recreation:* gardening. *Address:* Bisham Edge, Stoney Ware, Marlow, Bucks. *T:* Marlow 4951.

SHAW, Thomas Richard, CMG 1960; HM Diplomatic Service, retired; *b* 5 Sept. 1912; *s* of Colin R. and Ida L. Shaw, Bolton, Lancs; *m* 1939, Evelyn Frances Young; four *s. Educ:* Repton; Clare Coll., Cambridge. Appointed probationer vice-consul at Istanbul, Nov. 1934; transferred to Bushire, December 1937; acting Consul, Grade 2, Tientsin, 1938-39; transferred to Trieste, Jan. 1940, to Leopoldville, Oct. 1940, to Elisabethville, 1942; served at Casablanca, 1943; vice-consul, Rabat, Dec. 1943; appointed one of HM vice-consuls serving in Foreign Office, 1944; promoted to consul, 1945; transferred to Bremen as consul, 1949; Deputy Consul-General, New York, 1953; actg Consul-General, 1953; Consul-General, Izmir, 1955; Inspector of Foreign Service Establishments, 1957, Senior Inspector, 1961; Ambassador to the Republics of Niger, Upper Volta and the Ivory Coast, 1964-67 (also to the Republic of Dahomey, 1964-65); Minister, Tokyo, 1967-69; Ambassador to Morocco, 1969-71. *Address:* Upton, Harrow Road West, Dorking, Surrey.

SHAW, Thurstan; *see* Shaw, C. T.

SHAW, Prof. William V., MD; Professor of Biochemistry, University of Leicester, since 1974; *b* Philadelphia, Pennsylvania, 13 May 1933. *Educ:* Williams Coll., Williamstown, Mass (BA Chemistry 1955); Columbia Univ., New York (MD 1959). Diplomate: Amer. Bd of Med. Examrs, 1960; Amer. Bd of Internal Med., 1968 (Examiner, 1970). Appts, Presbyterian Hosp., New York, Nat. Heart Inst., Bethesda, Maryland, and Columbia Univ., New York, until 1966; Asst Prof. of Medicine, Columbia Univ., New York, 1966-68; University of Miami School of Medicine, Miami, Florida: Associate Prof. of Medicine and Biochemistry, 1968-73; Chief, Infectious Diseases, 1971-74; Prof. of Medicine, 1973-74. Vis. Scientist, MRC Lab. of Molecular Biology, Cambridge, Eng., 1972-74. Member: MRC Cell Biology and Disorders Bd, 1976-80 (Bd Chm. and Mem. Council, 1978-80); Science Council, Celltech Ltd, 1980-; Lister Inst. Sci. Adv. Council, 1981-. Member: Amer. Soc. for Clinical Investigation, 1971; Infectious Disease Soc. of Amer., 1969; Amer. Soc. of Biol Chemists; Biochem. Soc. (UK); Amer. Soc. for Microbiology; Soc. for Gen. Microbiology (UK). Has held research grants and awards in microbial biochemistry and molecular biology from NIH, MRC, SRC and Wellcome Trust. *Publications:* contribs to professional works and jls. *Address:* Department of Biochemistry, University of Leicester, University Road, Leicester LE1 7RH. *T:* Leicester 551234.

SHAW-STEWART, Sir Houston (Mark), 11th Bt *cr* 1667; MC 1950; TD; Vice-Lord-Lieutenant, Strathclyde Region (Eastwood, Renfrew and Inverclyde Districts), since 1980; *b* 24 April 1931; *s* of Sir Guy Shaw-Stewart, 9th Bt, MC, and Diana (*d* 1931), *d* of late George Bulteel; *S* brother, 1980; *m* 1982, Lucinda Victoria, *yr d* of Alexander Fletcher, Old Vicarage, Wighill, near Tadcaster. *Educ:* Eton. Joined Coldstream Guards, 1949; served as 2/Lt Royal Ulster Rifles, Korea, 1950 (MC); joined Ayrshire Yeomanry, 1952; retired, 1969. Member of the Royal Company of Archers, Queen's Body Guard for Scotland. Joint Master, Lanark and Renfrewshire Foxhounds, 1974-79. DL Renfrewshire, 1970. *Recreations:* hunting, shooting and racing. *Heir: kinsman* Donald Erskine Stewart [*b* 1905; *m* 1936, Ailsa Violet Annie (*d* 1970), *d* of John Forbes; one *s*]. *Address:* Ardgowan, Inverkip, Renfrewshire. *T:* Wemyss Bay 521226. *Clubs:* White's, Turf, Pratt's; Greenock (Greenock).

SHAWCROSS, family name of **Baron Shawcross.**

SHAWCROSS, Baron, *cr* 1959 (Life Peer), of Friston; **Hartley William Shawcross,** PC 1946; GBE 1974; Kt 1945; QC 1939; Chancellor, University of Sussex, since 1965; Special Adviser, Morgan Guaranty Trust of New York, since 1965 (Chairman, International Advisory Council, 1967-74); Director, Hawker Siddeley Group, 1968-82, now Consultant; Director, The Observer, since 1981; *b* 4 Feb. 1902; *s* of John Shawcross, MA, and Hilda Shawcross; *m* 1st, 1924, Rosita Alberta Shyvers (*d* 1943); 2nd, 1944, Joan Winifred Mather (*d* 1974); two *s* one *d. Educ:* Dulwich Coll.; abroad. Certificate of Honour for 1st place in Bar Final; called to Bar, Gray's Inn, 1925 (Bencher, 1939); practised on Northern Circuit. Sen. Law Lectr, Liverpool Univ., 1927-34. Chm., Enemy Aliens Tribunal, 1939-40; left practice at Bar for War Service, 1940; Chief Prosecutor for UK before Internat. Military Tribunal at Nuremberg. Asst Chm. of E Sussex QS, 1941; Recorder of Salford, 1941-45; Dep. Regional Comr, South-Eastern Region, 1941; Regional Comr, North-Western Region, 1942-45; Recorder of Kingston-upon-Thames, 1946-61;

retired from practice at Bar, 1958. MP (Lab) St Helens, 1945-58; Attorney-General, 1945-51; Pres., BoT, April-Oct. 1951. A Principal Deleg. for UK to Assemblies of UN, 1945-49; a UK Mem., Permanent Court of Arbitration at The Hague, 1950-67. Independent Chm., Kent District Coal Mining Board, 1940-45; Chairman: Catering Wages Commn, 1943-45; Bar Council, 1952-57; Royal Commn on the Press, 1961-62; MRC, 1961-65; Internat. Law Section of British Inst. of Internat. and Comparative Law; Justice (British Br. of Internat. Commn of Jurists), 1956-72; Panel on Take-overs and Mergers, 1969-80; Press Council, 1974-78; ICC Commn on Unethical Practices, 1976. President: Rainer Foundn (formerly London Police Court Mission), 1951-71; British Hotels and Restaurants Assoc., 1959-71. Member: Home Secretary's Adv. Council on Treatment of Offenders, 1944-45; Council, Internat. Law Assoc., 1958-74; Exec. Cttee, Internat. Commn of Jurists, 1959. Hon. Member: Bar Council; Amer. and New York Bar Assoc.; Fellow, Amer. Bar Foundn. Director: Shell Transport and Trading Co., 1961-72; EMI Ltd, 1965-81; Rank-Hovis-McDougall Ltd, 1965-79; Caffyns Motors Ltd, 1965-; Morgan et Cie International SA, 1966-77; Morgan et Cie SA, 1967-; Times Newspapers Ltd, 1967-74; Upjohn & Co Ltd, 1967-76 (Chm.); Birmingham Small Arms Co. Ltd, 1968-73 (Chm., 1971-73); European Enterprises Development Co. SA, 1970-78 (Chm., 1973-78); Chairman: Dominion Lincoln Assurance Co. Ltd, 1969-76; Thames Television Ltd, 1969-74; London and Continental Bankers, 1974-80 (now Consultant); Chm. Bd of Governors, Dulwich Coll.; Member: Court, London Univ., 1958-74; Council and Exec. Cttee, Sussex Univ., 1959- (Pro-Chancellor, 1960-65); Council, Eastbourne Coll., 1965-70. Hon. FRCS 1981; Hon. FRCOG 1978. Hon. Degrees from Universities of Bristol, Columbia, Hull, Lehigh, Liverpool, London, Massachusetts (Ann Arbor), Michigan, Sussex. JP Sussex, 1941-68. Chm., Soc. of Sussex Downsmen, 1962-75. Knight Grand Cross, Imperial Iranian Order of Homayoon, 1st Cl., 1974. *Recreations:* sailing, riding. *Address:* Friston Place, Sussex BN20 0AH. *Clubs:* White's, Buck's; Travellers' (Paris); Royal Cornwall Yacht (Falmouth); Royal Yacht Squadron (Cowes); New York Yacht (US).

SHAWE-TAYLOR, Desmond (Christopher), CBE 1965; Music Critic, The Sunday Times, since 1958; *b* 29 May 1907; *s* of Frank Shawe-Taylor and Agnes Ussher. *Educ:* Shrewsbury Sch.; Oriel Coll., Oxford. Literary and occasional musical criticism, New Statesman, etc until 1939. Served War of 1939-45 with the Royal Artillery. Music Critic, New Statesman, 1945-58; Guest Music Critic, New Yorker, 1973-74. *Publications:* Covent Garden, 1948; (with Edward Sackville-West, later Lord Sackville), The Record Guide (with supplements and revisions, 1951-56). *Recreations:* travel, croquet, gramophone. *Address:* Long Crichel House, Wimborne, Dorset. *T:* Tarrant Hinton 250; 15 Furlong Road, N7. *T:* 01-607 4854. *Club:* Brooks's.

SHAWYER, Robert Cort, MA, PhD; *b* 9 Oct. 1913; *e s* of late Arthur Frederic Shawyer, sometime Gen. Manager, Martins Bank; *m* 1939, Isabel Jessie Rogers; two *d. Educ:* Charterhouse; Corpus Christi Coll., Oxford; Birkbeck Coll., Univ. of London. Bank of England, 1935-37. Commissioned RAEC, 1938 (Lt-Col 1945). Princ., Min. of Nat. Insce, 1948; Admty, 1951; Asst Sec., 1957; seconded to NATO, 1960; Nat. Def. Coll., Canada, 1961-62; Commonwealth Office, 1967; Consul-Gen., Buenos Aires, 1967-70; FCO, Cultural Relations Dept, 1970-72; retired. FRGS. *Publications:* articles in professional, etc, jls. *Recreation:* archaeology. *Address:* Southfield, 3 South Road, Taunton, Somerset; (winter) Apartamentos Damara, Calpe, Spain. *Clubs:* Army and Navy; Royal Commonwealth Society (Bristol).

SHEA, Michael Sinclair MacAuslan, PhD; Press Secretary to the Queen, since 1978; *b* 10 May 1938; *s* of late James Michael Shea and of Mary Dalrymple Davidson MacAuslan, North Berwick; *m* 1968, Mona Grec Stensen, Oslo; two *d. Educ:* Gordonstoun Sch.; Edinburgh Univ. (MA, PhD Econs). FO, 1963; Inst. of African Studies, Accra, Ghana, 1963; FO, 1964; Third, later Second Sec., CRO, 1965; Second, later First Sec. (Econ.), Bonn, 1966; seconded to Cabinet Office, 1969; FO, 1971; Head of Chancery, Bucharest, 1973; Dep. Dir Gen., Brit. Inf. Services, New York, 1976. *Publications:* Britain's Offshore Islands, 1981; Maritime England, 1981; Tomorrow's Men, 1982; (as Michael Sinclair): Sonntag, 1971; Folio Forty-One, 1972; The Dollar Covenant, 1974; A Long Time Sleeping, 1976; The Master Players, 1978. *Recreation:* writing, sailing. *Address:* Buckingham Palace, SW1. *T:* 01-930 4832.

SHEA, Patrick, CB 1972; OBE 1961; Director, Unico Finance Ltd, since 1976; *b* 1908; *s* of Patrick Shea and Mary Catherine Shea (*née* McLaughlin); *m* 1941, Eithne, *d* of Michael and Mary J. MacHugh, Balmoral, Belfast; two *s* one *d. Educ:* High Sch., Clones; Abbey Sch., Newry. Entered Northern Ireland Civil Service, 1926; Asst Sec., Min. of Finance, 1963; Perm. Sec., Min. of Education for N Ireland, 1969-73. Chm., Enterprise Ulster, 1973-79. Mem. Senate, QUB, 1973-. Hon. Mem., Royal Soc. of Ulster Architects, 1971. Trustee, Ulster Sports and Recreations Trust, 1975. FRSA 1977. *Publications:* (play) Waiting Night (prod. Abbey Theatre, Dublin), 1957; Voices and the Sound of Drums (autobiog.), 1981. *Recreation:* occasional writer. *Address:* 6 Edenvale Park, The Green, Dunmurry, Belfast BT17 0EJ. *T:* Belfast 616293. *Club:* (Pres. 1961-62) Ulster Arts (Belfast).

SHEALS, Dr John Gordon, Keeper of Zoology, British Museum (Natural History), since 1971; *b* 19 Dec. 1923; *o s* of late John Joseph Sheals and Anne (*née* Ffoulkes); *m* 1945, Blodwen M. Davies (*d* 1972); two *s. Educ:* Caernarvon County Sch.; UC North Wales; Glasgow Univ. BSc, PhD, FIBiol. Asst Lectr, West of Scotland Agricultural Coll., Glasgow, 1948-56;

Asst Advisory Entomologist, Min. of Agric., Fisheries and Food, 1956-58; Asst Keeper, 1958-68, and Dep. Keeper, 1968-71, Dept of Zoology, British Museum (Natural History). Mem. Council, Freshwater Biological Assoc., 1976-; Trustee, Percy Sladen Meml Fund, 1978-. *Publications:* (with G. O. Evans and D. Macfarlane) The Terrestrial Acari of the British Isles: Introduction and Biology, 1961; papers on taxonomy and ecology of mites in scientific jls. *Recreation:* music. *Address:* 6 The Mount, Rickmansworth, Herts. *T:* Rickmansworth 77250.

SHEARER, Rt. Hon. Hugh Lawson, PC 1969; MP South-east Clarendon, since 1976 (South Clarendon, 1967-76); Deputy Prime Minister of Jamaica, and Minister of Foreign Affairs and Foreign Trade, since 1980; President, Bustamante Industrial Trade Union, since 1979; *b* 18 May 1923. *Educ:* St Simons Coll., Jamaica. Journalist on weekly newspaper, Jamaica Worker, 1941-44, subseq. Editor. Apptd Asst Gen. Sec., Bustamante Industrial TU, 1947, Island Supervisor, 1953-67, Vice-Pres., 1960-79 (on leave of absence, 1967-72). Mem. Kingston and St Andrew Corp. Council, 1947; MHR for West Kingston, 1955-59; MLC (now Senator), 1962-67; Leader of Govt Business in Senate, 1962-67; Prime Minister of Jamaica, 1967-72; Minister of Defence and of External Affairs, 1967-72; Leader of the Opposition, 1972-74; Leader, Jamaica Labour Party, 1967-74. Hon. Dr of Laws, Howard Univ., Washington, DC, 1968. *Address:* House of Representatives, Kingston, Jamaica.

SHEARER, Rt. Hon. Ian Hamilton; *see* Avonside, Rt Hon. Lord.

SHEARER, Janet Sutherland; *see* Avonside, Lady.

SHEARER, Magnus MacDonald; JP; Lord Lieutenant of Shetland since 1982; Managing Director, J. & M. Shearer Ltd (Est. 1919), since 1960; *b* 27 Feb. 1924; *s* of late Lt-Col Magnus Shearer, OBE, TD, JP, and of Flora MacDonald Stephen; *m* 1949, Martha Nicolson Henderson, *d* of late Captain John Henderson, DSM, and late Martha Nicolson; one *s. Educ:* Anderson Educational Institute, Shetland; George Watson's Coll., Edinburgh. Served RN in Atlantic, Mediterranean and Far East, 1942-46. 2nd Lieut, RA (TA), 1949; Captain, TARO, 1959. Hon. Consul: for Sweden in Shetland and Orkney, 1958-; for Federal Republic of Germany in Shetland, 1972-. Mem., Lerwick Harbour Trust, 1960-75 (Chm., 1967-72); Hon. Sec., RNLI Lerwick Branch, 1968-; Mem. Lerwick Town Council, 1963-69; JP 1969, DL 1973, Shetland. Knight 1st Class, Royal Order of Vasa (Sweden), 1969. *Recreations:* reading, bird watching and ships. *Address:* Birka, Cruester, Bressay, Shetland ZE2 9EL. *T:* Bressay 363.

SHEARER, Moira, (Mrs L. Kennedy); Lecturer; Director, Border Television, 1977-82; *b* Dunfermline, Fifeshire, 17 Jan. 1926; *d* of Harold King; *m* 1950, Ludovic Kennedy, *qv*; one *s* three *d. Educ:* Dunfermline High School; Ndola, N Rhodesia; Bearsden, Scotland. Professional training: Mayfair Sch.; Legat Sch.; Sadler's Wells School. Début with International Ballet, 1941; joined Sadler's Wells Ballet, 1942, during following ten years danced all major classic roles and full repertoire of revivals and new ballets; first ballerina rôle in Sleeping Beauty, 1946; created rôle of Cinderella, 1948; Titania in Old Vic production of A Midsummer Night's Dream (Edin. Festival, 1954, and tour of US and Canada); American tours with Sadler's Wells Ballet, 1949, 1950-51. Toured as Sally Bowles in I am a Camera, 1955; joined Bristol Old Vic, 1955; played in Man of Distinction, Edin. Fest., 1957; played Madame Ranevskaya in The Cherry Orchard, Royal Lyceum, Edin., 1977; Judith Bliss in Hay Fever, Royal Lyceum, 1978. Recorded: Thomas Hardy's Tess of the D'Urbervilles, 1977; Muriel Spark's The Ballad of Peckham Rye, BBC Radio 4, 1982. Member: Scottish Arts Council, 1971-73; BBC Gen. Adv. Council, 1970-77. Toured US, lecturing on history of ballet, March-April 1973; regular lecturing in England and Wales. Lectured and gave recitals on three world cruises, Queen Elizabeth II. Poetry and prose recitals, Edinburgh Festivals, 1974 and 1975. *Films:* Ballerina in The Red Shoes (première, 1948); Tales of Hoffmann, 1950; Story of Three Loves, 1952; The Man Who Loved Redheads, 1954; Peeping Tom, 1960; Black Tights, 1961. *Address:* 3 Upper Dean Terrace, Edinburgh EH4 1NU.

SHEARER, Thomas Hamilton, CB 1974; a Controller, Royal Opera House Development Land Trust, since 1981; *b* 7 Nov. 1923; *o s* of late Thomas Appleby Shearer, OBE; *m* 1945, Sybil Mary Robinson, Stratford-on-Avon; one *s* one *d. Educ:* Haberdashers' Aske's, Hatcham; Emmanuel Coll., Cambridge (open exhibition in English). Served RAF, 1942-45 (despatches). Entered Air Ministry, as Asst Principal, 1948; Principal, 1951; Sec. to Grigg Cttee on Recruitment to Armed Forces, 1958; Asst Sec., 1959; transf. Min. of Public Building and Works, 1963; student, IDC, 1965; Under-Sec., 1967; Dir of Establishments, MPBW, 1967-70, DoE, 1970; Dir of Personnel Management, DoE, 1970-72; Dep. Chief Exec. II, PSA, DoE, 1972-73; Deputy Secretary, 1973-81. Chairman: Maplin Develt Authority, 1974-77; British Channel Tunnel Company, 1975-77; Location of Offices Bureau, 1980. *Recreations:* opera, claret. *Address:* 9 Denny Crescent, SE11. *T:* 01-587 0921.

SHEARER, Rev. W(illiam) Russell; *b* 12 Oct. 1898; *s* of Henry S. and Jessie A. Shearer; *m* 1934, Phyllis Mary Wigfield. *Educ:* Harrogate Grammar School; Leeds University; Wesley House, Cambridge. Served European War, 1914-18, in Tank Corps. Since 1923 has been Methodist Minister at: Tunstall, Staffs; Manchester; Muswell Hill; Sutton, Surrey; Hanley. Chairman, Stoke-on-Trent Methodist District, 1943-50; Chairman, Birmingham Methodist

District, 1950-63. Pres. of Methodist Conference, 1954-55; Moderator, National Free Church Federal Council, 1959-60. Pres. UK Bd, Hope Union, 1960-74. *Address:* 32 Layton Lane, Shaftesbury, Dorset SP7 8EY. *T:* Shaftesbury 2678. *Club:* National Liberal.

SHEARLOCK, Very Rev. David John; Dean of Truro, since 1982; *b* 1 July 1932; *s* of Arthur John Shearlock and Honora Frances Hawkins; *m* 1959, Jean Margaret Marr; one *s* one *d. Educ:* Univ. of Birmingham (BA); Westcott House, Cambridge. Assistant Curate: Guisborough, Yorks, 1957-60; Christchurch Priory, Hants, 1960-64; Vicar: Kingsclere, 1964-71; Romsey Abbey, 1971-82; Diocesan Director of Ordinands (Winchester), 1977-82; Hon. Canon of Winchester, 1978-82. *Recreations:* model railways; music. *Address:* The Deanery, Lemon Street, Truro, Cornwall TR1 2PE. *T:* Truro 2661.

SHEARMAN, Rt. Rev. Donald Norman; see Grafton, NSW, Bishop of.

SHEARMAN, Sir Harold (Charles), Kt 1965; MA; Chairman, Greater London Council, 1964-66; Member for Lewisham, 1964-67; Chairman: Inner London Education Cttee, 1964-65; Further and Higher Educn Sub-Cttee, 1964-67; *b* 14 March 1896; *e s* of late Rev. C. E. P. Shearman and late Mary Charlotte Shearman; *m* 1924, Frances Mary (*d* 1982), *d* of late Henry Jameson, Hamsterley, Co. Durham; one *s. Educ:* Sulgrave National School; Magdalen College School, Brackley; Wolsingham Grammar School; St Edmund Hall, Oxford (1st Class, Modern History, 1922). Elementary Teacher, Durham, 1912-15. Served European War, 1914-18, Private RAMC, and Flying Officer (Observer) RAF, 1916-19. Contested (Lab) Isle of Wight, 1922. Tutor-organiser in Bedfordshire, WEA and Cambridge Extra Mural Board, 1927-35; Education Officer, WEA, 1935-45; Academic Adviser Tutorial Classes, Univ. of London, 1946-61. Member (Deptford) LCC 1946-65 (Chairman Education Cttee, 1955-61); Chairman: LCC, 1961-62; SE Gas Consultative Council, 1963-66; Member: UK delegation, UNESCO Conf., New Delhi, 1956; Committee on Higher Education (1961-63) and other Govt and Educational Cttees; Mem., Commonwealth Scholarships Commn, 1964-68; Pres. School Journey Assoc. of London, 1962-71. Chairman: Metropolitan Exam. Bd (Cert. of Sec. Educn), 1963-72; South Bank Polytechnic, 1970-75 (Hon. Fellow, 1976); Gov. Body, Kidbrooke Sch.; Southfields Sch.; Coombe Lodge Further Educn Coll., 1960-; Rachel Macmillan Coll. of Educn; Garnett College; Member: Court, Brunel Univ.; Univ. of London: Senate, 1966-70; King's College Delegacy; Sch. of Pharmacy, 1960-. DL Greater London, 1967-76. *Address:* 109 Blagdon Road, New Malden, Surrey.

SHEARMAN, Prof. John Kinder Gowran, PhD; FBA 1976; Chairman, Department of Art and Archaeology, Princeton University, since 1979; *b* 24 June 1931; *s* of Brig. C. E. G. Shearman; *m* 1957, Jane Dalrymple Smith; one *s* three *d. Educ:* St Edmund's, Hindhead; Felsted; Courtauld Inst., London Univ.; BA, PhD 1957. Lectr, Courtauld Inst., 1957-67; Research Fellow, Inst. for Advanced Study, Princeton, 1964; Reader, Courtauld Inst., 1967-74, Prof. of the History of Art, 1974-79 (Dep. Dir, 1974-78). Mem., Accademia del Disegno, Florence, 1979. Serena Medal, British Acad., 1979. *Publications:* Andrea del Sarto, 1965; Mannerism, 1967, 4th edn 1977; Raphael's Cartoons, 1972; Catalogue of the Early Italian Paintings in the Collection of HM the Queen, 1982; contribs to British, French, German, American jls. *Recreations:* sailing, music. *Address:* 5 Yar Quay, St Helen's, Isle of Wight. *Clubs:* Bembridge Sailing, Island Sailing (Cowes).

SHEEHAN, Harold Leeming, MD, DSc, FRCP, FRCOG, FRCPath; Professor of Pathology, University of Liverpool, 1946-65 (Professor Emeritus since 1965); *b* 4 Aug. 1900; *s* of Dr P. Sheehan, Carlisle; *m* 1934, E. S. G. Potter; no *c. Educ:* University of Manchester. Demonstrator and Lecturer in Pathology, University of Manchester, 1927-34; Rockefeller Medical Fellow in USA, 1934-35; Director of Research, Glasgow Royal Maternity Hosp., 1935-46; Hon. Lecturer in Pathology, Univ. of Glasgow, 1943-46. Served in RAMC, 1939-45; Colonel, Deputy Director of Pathology, AFHQ, Italy, 1945 (despatches, TD). Hon. Member: Fac. Med., Univ. of Chile; Fac. Med., Univ. of Concepcion; Hon. Fellow, Amer. Assoc. Obst. Gyn.; Hon. Member: Soc. Roy. Belge Gyn. Obst.; Soc. Chil. Obst. Gyn.; Soc. Argent. Neurol.; Soc. Med. Hop. Paris; Socs Endocrinology: Chile, Argentine, Roumania, Hungary. Foreign Corresp., Acad. Nat. Med., France. Hon. MD Szeged (Hungary). *Publications:* papers on pathology, endocrinology and renal physiology in various med. jls. *Address:* 18 Knowsley Road, Liverpool L19 0PG. *T:* 051-427 2936.

SHEEHY, Patrick; Chairman, BAT Industries, since 1982 (Vice-Chairman, 1981-82); *b* 2 Sept. 1930; *s* of Sir John Francis Sheehy, CSI and Jean Newton Simpson; *m* 1964, Jill Patricia Tindall; one *s* one *d. Educ:* Australia; Ampleforth Coll., Yorks. Served Irish Guards, 1948-50; rank on leaving 2nd Lieut. Joined British-American Tobacco Co., 1950, first appt in Nigeria; Ghana, 1951; Reg. Sales Manager, Nigeria, 1953; Ethiopian Tobacco Monopoly, 1954; Marketing Dir, Jamaica, 1957; General Manager: Barbados, 1961; Holland, 1967; Dir, 1970-81, Chm., 1976-81, British-American Tobacco Co.; Dir, 1976-, Mem., Chm's Policy Cttee, 1976-, Chm., 1976-81, BAT Industries; Director: Molins Ltd, 1976-; Batus Inc., 1979-82. Mem. Council, CBI, 1980-. *Recreations:* golf, reading. *Address:* BAT Industries plc, Windsor House, 50 Victoria Street, SWIH 0NL. *T:* 01-222-7979.

SHEEN, Hon. Sir Barry (Cross), Kt 1978; **Hon. Mr Justice Sheen;** a Judge of the High Court of Justice, Queen's Bench Division, since 1978; *b* 31 Aug.

1918; 2nd *s* of late Ronald Sheen, FCA, St John's Wood; *m* 1946, Diane, *d* of late C. L. Donne, MD; three *s. Educ:* Haileybury College, Hill School (USA); Trinity Hall, Cambridge (MA). Served in RNVR, 1939-46; Commanding Officer, HMS Kilkenzie, 1943-45. Called to Bar, Middle Temple, 1947, Master of the Bench, 1971; Member Bar Council, 1959-63; QC 1966. Junior Counsel to Admiralty, 1961-66; a Recorder of the Crown Court, 1972-78. On Panel of Wreck Comrs (Eng.) under Merchant Shipping Acts, 1966-78; Mem., Panel of Lloyd's Arbitrators in Salvage Cases, 1966-78, Appeal Arbitrator, 1977-78; Arbiter under London Fisheries Convention, 1967. Life Governor, Haileybury. *Recreations:* bridge, golf. *Address:* Royal Courts of Justice, WC2; 16 Parkside Gardens, Wimbledon Common, SW19. *T:* 01-946 8534. *Club:* Royal Wimbledon.

SHEERIN, John Declan; a Recorder of the Crown Court, since 1979; *b* 29 Nov. 1932; *s* of John Patrick Sheerin and Agnes Mary Sheerin; *m* 1958, Helen Suzanne (*née* LeRoux); two *s* two *d. Educ:* Wimbledon Coll.; London Sch. of Econs and Polit Science (LLB 1954). Admitted solicitor, 1957. Served RAF, 1958-60 (Flying Officer). Partner, Greene & Greene, 1962-. *Recreation:* golf. *Address:* Kings Hall Farmhouse, Rougham, Bury St Edmunds, Suffolk IP30 9LG. *T:* Beyton 70309. *Club:* Flempton Golf.

SHEERMAN, Barry John; MP (Lab) Huddersfield East, since 1979; *b* 17 Aug. 1940; *s* of Albert William Sheerman and Florence Sheerman (*née* Pike); *m* 1965, Pamela Elizabeth (*née* Brenchley); one *s* three *d. Educ:* Hampton Grammar Sch.; Kingston Technical Coll.; LSE. BSc (Economics) Hons; MSc Hons. Chemical worker, laboratory assistant, technical sales trainee, etc., 1958-61; Lectr, Univ. Coll. of Swansea, 1966-79. Chairman: Parly Adv. Cttee on Transport Safety, 1981-; PLP Trade Cttee, 1981-; Mem., Public Accounts Cttee, 1981-; Sec., All Party Media Gp. *Publications:* various. *Address:* House of Commons, SW1A 0AA. *Clubs:* Mansel Working Men's (Gowerton); Friendly and Trades (Huddersfield).

SHEFFIELD, 8th Baron; see under Stanley of Alderley, 8th Baron.

SHEFFIELD, Bishop of, since 1980; **Rt. Rev. David Ramsay Lunn;** *b* 1930. *Educ:* King's College, Cambridge (BA 1953, MA 1957); Cuddesdon College, Oxford. Deacon 1955, priest 1956, Newcastle upon Tyne; Curate of Sugley, 1955-59; N Gosforth, 1959-63; Chaplain, Lincoln Theological College, 1963-66; Sub-Warden, 1966-70; Vicar of St George, Cullercoats, 1970-75, Rector, 1975-80; Rural Dean of Tynemouth, 1975-80. *Address:* Bishopscroft, Snaithing Lane, Sheffield, S Yorks S10 3LG.

SHEFFIELD, Provost of; see Curtis, Very Rev. W. F.

SHEFFIELD, Archdeacon of; see Paton, Ven. M. J. M.

SHEFFIELD, Maj.-Gen. John, CB 1967; CBE 1961; Commandant of the Star and Garter Home, Richmond, 1975-77, a Governor, since 1977; *b* 28 April 1910; *s* of late Major W. G. F. Sheffield, DSO, and Mrs C. G. A. Sheffield (*née* Wing); *m* 1936, Mary Patience Vere (*née* Nicoll); one *s* one *d* (and one *s* decd). *Educ:* Winchester; RMA, Woolwich. Commd, 1930; served RA and RHA; transferred RAOC, 1939. Served War of 1939-45: BEF, 1939-40; MEF, 1944-48. Egypt, 1954-56; Cyprus, 1959-62; Comdr Base Organization, RAOC, 1964-67. Col Comdt, RAOC, 1970-74. *Recreations:* athletics (British Olympic Team, 1936), golf, sailing, numismatics. *Address:* Tuns Arch House, Odiham, Hants. *T:* Odiham 2436. *Club:* Royal Automobile.

SHEFFIELD, John V.; Chairman: Norcros Ltd, 1956-81; Atlantic Assets Trust Ltd, since 1972; *b* 11 Nov. 1913; *y s* of Sir Berkeley Sheffield, 6th Bt; *m* 1st, 1936, Anne (*d* 1969), *d* of Sir Lionel Faudel-Phillips, 3rd Bt; one *s* three *d*; 2nd, 1971, Mrs France Crosthwaite, *d* of Brig.-Gen. Goland Clarke. *Educ:* Eton; Magdalene College, Cambridge (MA). Private Secretary to Minister of Works, 1943-44; Chm., Portals Ltd, 1968-78. Chm., BEC, 1980-. High Sheriff of Lincolnshire, 1944-45. *Address:* New Barn House, Laverstoke, Whitchurch, Hants RG28 7PF. *T:* Whitchurch (Hants) 3187. *Club:* White's.

SHEFFIELD, Sir Reginald (Adrian Berkeley), 8th Bt *cr* 1755; Chairman, Aylesford Holdings Ltd, since 1979; Director, Normanby Estate Co. Ltd, and other companies; Member of Lloyd's, since 1977; *b* 9 May 1946; *s* of Edmund Charles Reginald Sheffield, JP, DL (*d* 1977) and of Nancie Miriel Denise, *d* of Edward Roland Soames; *S* uncle, 1977; *m* 1st, 1969, Annabel Lucy Veronica (marr. diss.), *d* of T. A. Jones; two *d*; 2nd, 1977, Victoria, *d* of late R. C. Walker, DFC; two *d. Educ:* Eton. Member of Stock Exchange, 1973-75. *Heir:* uncle John V. Sheffield, *qv. Address:* Estate Office, Normanby, Scunthorpe, S Humberside DN15 9HS. *T:* Scunthorpe 720618. *Club:* White's.

SHEHADIE, Sir Nicholas (Michael), Kt 1976; OBE 1971; Managing Director, Nicholas Shehadie Pty Ltd, since 1959; *b* 15 Nov. 1926; *s* of Michael and Hannah Shehadie; *m* 1957, Dr Marie Roslyn Bashir; one *s* two *d. Educ:* Sydney. Elected Alderman, City of Sydney, Dec. 1962; Dep. Lord Mayor, Sept. 1969-Sept. 1973; Lord Mayor of Sydney, Sept. 1973-Sept. 1975. Director: Rothmans Pall Mall (Aust.) Ltd; Wormald International Ltd; Mercantile Credits Ltd; Chm., Special Broadcasting Services. Rugby Union career: Captained NSW and Australia; played 30 Internationals and 6 overseas tours; Pres., Aust. Rugby Football Union; Mem., Barbarians'. *Recreations:* Rugby, golf, surfing, horse racing. *Address:* 118 Old Canterbury Road,

Lewisham, Sydney, NSW, Australia. *Clubs:* Randwick Rugby, Tattersall's (Sydney).

SHELBOURNE, Philip; Chairman, Britoil plc, since 1982; *b* 15 June 1924; *s* of late Leslie John Shelbourne. *Educ:* Radley Coll.; Corpus Christi Coll., Oxford (MA); Harvard Law School. Called to Bar, Inner Temple. Barrister specialising in taxation, 1951-62; Partner, N. M. Rothschild & Sons, 1962-70; Chief Exec., Drayton Corp., 1971-72; Chm., Drayton Gp and Drayton Corp., 1973-74; Chm. and Chief Exec., Samuel Montagu & Co., 1974-80; Chm. and Chief Exec., BNOC, 1980-82. *Recreation:* music. *Address:* Britoil plc, Stornoway House, Cleveland Row, SW1A 1DH. *Club:* Brooks's.

SHELBURNE, Earl of; Charles Maurice Petty-Fitzmaurice; *b* 21 Feb. 1941; *s* and *heir* of 8th Marquess of Lansdowne, *qv* ; *m* 1965, Lady Frances Eliot, *o d* of 9th Earl of St Germans, *qv* ; two *s* two *d*. *Educ:* Eton. Page of Honour to The Queen, 1956-57. Served with Kenya Regt, 1960-61; with Wiltshire Yeomanry (TA), amalgamated with Royal Yeomanry Regt, 1963-73; Pres., Wiltshire Playing Fields Assoc., 1965-74; Wiltshire County Councillor, 1970-; Vice-Chm., Finance Sub-Cttee, WCC, 1977-79; Chm., Performance Review Panel, WCC, 1977-81; Mem., South West Economic Planning Council, 1972-77; Chairman: Working Committee Population & Settlement Pattern (SWEPC), 1972-77; Calne and Chippenham RDC, 1972-73; North Wiltshire DC, 1973-76; President: Wiltshire Assocs Boys Clubs and Youth Clubs, 1976-; North-West Wiltshire District Scout Council, 1977-. Contested (C), Coventry North East, 1979. *Heir:* *s* Viscount Calne and Calstone, *qv*. *Address:* Bowood House, Calne, Wiltshire SN11 0LZ. *T:* Calne 813343; Flat 2, 99 Lexham Gardens, W8. *T:* 01-370 3159. *Clubs:* Turf, White's.

SHELDON, Hon. Sir Gervase; *see* Sheldon, Hon. Sir J. G. K.

SHELDON, Harold; County Councillor; *b* 22 June 1918; *s* of Charles Edwin Sheldon and Lily Sheldon (*née* Taylor); *m* 1941, Bessie Sheldon (*née* Barratt); two *s* one *d*. HM Forces, 1939-45 (Sgt; wounded D Day landings). Local Government: elected Batley Borough Council, 1953; Mayor of Batley, 1962-63; W Yorkshire County Council, 1973- (Chm., May 1976-May 1977); re-elected 1977, 1981. *Recreation:* Sports Council. *Address:* 5 Norfolk Avenue, Carlton Grange, Batley, West Yorkshire. *T:* Batley 473619.

SHELDON, John Denby; General Secretary, Civil Service Union, since 1982; *b* 31 Jan. 1941; *s* of Frank and Doreen Sheldon; *m* 1976; two *s*. *Educ:* Wingate County Primary and West Leeds High School. Oxford Univ. Diploma in Social Studies. Post Office Engineer, 1957-68; student, Ruskin Coll., 1968-70; full time Trade Union Official, Instn of Professional Civil Servants, 1970-72; National Officer, Civil Service Union, 1972-78; Deputy Gen. Sec., 1978-82. *Recreations:* cricket; Rugby League as spectator; family; representing the working man. *Address:* 2 Wincroft Road, Reading, Berks RG4 7HH. *T:* Reading 477810.

SHELDON, Hon. Sir (John) Gervase (Kensington), Kt 1978; **Hon. Mr Justice Sheldon;** a Judge of the High Court, Family Division, since 1978; Presiding Judge, Western Circuit, since 1980; *b* 4 Oct. 1913; *s* of John Henry Sheldon, MD, DPH, and Eleanor Gladys Sheldon, MB, BS; *m* 1st, 1940, Patricia Mary Mardon; one *s* ; 2nd, 1960, Janet Marguerite Seager; two *s* one *d*. *Educ:* Winchester Coll.; Trinity Coll., Cambridge (MA; 1st Cl. Hons Law). Barrister-at-Law, called Lincoln's Inn, 1939 (Cert. of Honour, Cholmeley Schol.), Bencher, 1978. Served RA (TA), 1939-45 (despatches twice): Egypt, N Africa, Italy; Major, RA, 1943. A Circuit Judge (formerly a County Court Judge), 1968-78. *Recreation:* family and home. *Address:* Hopton, Churt, Surrey GU10 2LD. *T:* Frensham 2035. *Club:* United Oxford & Cambridge University.

SHELDON, Rt. Hon. Robert (Edward), PC 1977; MP (Lab) Ashton-under-Lyne, since 1964; *b* 13 Sept. 1923; *m* 1st, 1945, Eileen Shamash (*d* 1969); one *s* one *d* ; 2nd 1971, Mary Shield. *Educ:* Elementary and Grammar Schools; Engineering Apprenticeship; Technical Colleges in Stockport, Burnley and Salford. Engineering diplomas; external graduate, London University. Contested Withington, Manchester, 1959; Chm., Labour Party Economic Affairs and Finance Group, 1967-68; Opposition Front Bench Spokesman on Civil Service and Machinery of Govt, also on Treasury matters, 1970-74; Minister of State, CSD, March-Oct. 1974; Minister of State, HM Treasury, Oct. 1974-June 1975; Financial Sec. to the Treasury, 1975-79; Opposition front bench spokesman on Treasury matters, 1981-; Member: Public Accounts Cttee, 1965-70, 1975-79; Public Expenditure Cttee (Chm. Gen. Sub-Cttee), 1972-74; Select Cttee on Treasury and Civil Service, 1979-81 (Chm., Sub-Cttee); Mem., Fulton Cttee on the Civil Service, 1966-68. Chm., NW Gp of Labour MPs, 1970-74. Dir, Manchester Chamber of Commerce, 1964-74, 1979-. *Recreations:* various crafts. *Address:* 27 Darley Avenue, Manchester M20 8ZD; 2 Ryder Street, SW1.

SHELDON, Sir Wilfrid (Percy Henry), KCVO 1959 (CVO 1954); Physician-Pædiatrician to the Queen, 1952-71; Consulting Pædiatrician, King's College Hospital; Consulting Physician, Hospital for Sick Children, Great Ormond Street; Hon. Fellow of Royal Society of Medicine; *b* 23 Nov. 1901; *s* of John Joseph Sheldon, FLS; *m* 1927, Mabel Winifred Netherway; three *d*. *Educ:* King's College, London; King's College Hospital. MB, BS (Honours Anatomy and Medicine), 1921; MD London 1925. FRCP 1933; FAAP 1966; FRCOG 1972; MMSA, 1972. *Publications:* Acute Rheumatism

following Tonsillitis, 1931; Amyoplasia Congenita, 1932; Congenital Pancreatic Lipase Deficiency, 1964; Text Book of Diseases of Infancy and Childhood, 8th edn, 1962. *Recreations:* golf, gardening. *Address:* Little Coombe, Warren Cutting, Kingston, Surrey. *T:* 01-942 0252.

SHELFORD, Cornelius William, DL; retired; *b* 6 July 1908; *s* of William Heard Shelford and Maud Ethel Shelford, Horncastle, Sharpthorne, Sussex, and Singapore; *m* 1934, Helen Beatrice Hilda Schuster; one *s* two *d*. *Educ:* private tutor and Trinity College, Cambridge. Chartered Accountant, 1934; Partner, Rowley Pemberton & Co., 1940 (retd 1960); Chm., Mills & Allen Ltd, 1964 (retd 1969); Chm., London County Freehold & Leasehold Properties Ltd, 1964 (retd 1970). East Sussex CC, 1952 (CA, 1957; Chm., 1964-67; Chm., Finance Cttee, 1970-74); High Sheriff of Sussex, 1954; DL Sussex, 1968-. *Recreations:* travelling, walking, gardening. *Address:* Chailey Place, near Lewes, E Sussex BN8 4DA. *T:* Newick 2881. *Club:* Carlton.

SHELLEY, Charles William Evans; Charity Commissioner, 1968-74; *b* 15 Aug. 1912; *s* of George Shelley and Frances Mary Anne Shelley (*née* Dain); *m* 1939, Patricia May Dolby; three *d* (and one *d* decd). *Educ:* Alleyn's Sch., Dulwich; Fitzwilliam House, Cambridge. Called to Bar, Inner Temple, 1937; practised at the Bar, to 1940. Served in Army: first in RAPC and later in Dept of Judge Advocate-General, rank Major, 1940-47. Joined Charity Commn as Legal Asst, 1947; Sen. Legal Asst, 1958; Dep. Comr, 1964. *Recreations:* English literature, listening to music, mountaineering. *Address:* Pen y Bryn, Llansilin, Oswestry, Salop. *T:* Llansilin 273. *Club:* Camping.

SHELLEY, Sir John (Richard), 11th Bt *cr* 1611; (professionally Dr J. R. Shelley); general medical practitioner; Partner, Drs Shelley, Newth and Doddington (formerly Durstan-Smith, Shelley and Newth), Health Centre, South Molton, Devon, since 1974; *b* 18 Jan. 1943; *s* of John Shelley (*d* 1974), and of Dorothy, *d* of Arthur Irvine Ingram; *S* grandfather, 1976; *m* 1965, Clare, *d* of Claud Bicknell, *qv* ; two *d*. *Educ:* King's Sch., Bruton; Trinity Coll., Cambridge (BA 1964, MA 1967); St Mary's Hosp., London Univ. MB, BChir 1967; DObstRCOG 1969; MRCGP 1978. Partner in Drs Harris, Barkworth, Savile, Shelley and Gurney, Eastbourne, Sx, 1969-74. Member: Exeter Diocesan Synod for South Molton Deanery, 1976-79; BMA; CLA; NFU. *Heir:* *b* Thomas Henry Shelley [*b* 3 Feb. 1945; *m* 1970, Katherine Mary Holton; three *d*]. *Address:* Molford House, 27 South Street, South Molton, Devon EX36 4AA. *T:* South Molton 3101.

SHELLEY, Ursula, MD, FRCP; retired 1971; Physician to Royal Free Hospital's Children's Department, 1940-71 (Assistant Physician, 1935-40), to Princess Louise (Kensington) Hospital for Children, 1944-71 (Assistant Physician, 1937-44), and to Queen Elizabeth Hospital for Children, 1946-71; *b* 11 Apr. 1906; *d* of Frederick Farey Shelley, FIC, and Rachel Hicks Shelley, MB, BS. *Educ:* St Paul's Girls' School; Royal Free Hospital School of Medicine. MB, BS Lond., Univ. Gold Medal, 1930; MD Lond., 1932; FRCP 1948. Examiner: Coll. of Physicians, 1960-70; Univ. of London, 1965-70. Pres., Nat. Assoc. of Nursery Matrons, 1963-75; Vice-Pres., Nat. Assoc. of Family Life and Child Care. Member: Medical Women's Fedn, 1936-; British Pædiatric Assoc., 1946. Liveryman, Worshipful Soc. of Apothecaries; Freeman of City of London, 1950. *Publications:* numerous articles in medical journals. *Recreations:* gardening, lion dogs. *Address:* 15 Hyde Park Gate, SW7 5DG. *T:* 01-584 7941.

SHELTON, Shirley Megan, (Mrs W. T. Shelton); Editor, Woman and Home magazine, 1978-82; *b* 8 March 1934; *d* of Lt-Col T. F. Goodwin; *m* 1960, William Timothy Shelton; one *s* two *d*. *Educ:* various institutions. Home Editor, Woman and Home, 1970-75; Assistant Editor, 1975-78. *Recreations:* working, cooking, and family life. *Address:* 59 Croftdown Road, NW5 1EL. *T:* 01-485 4936.

SHELTON, William Jeremy Masefield, MA Oxon; MP (C) Lambeth, Streatham, since 1974 (Clapham, 1970-74); Parliamentary Under Secretary of State, Department of Education and Science, since 1981; *b* 30 Oct. 1929; *s* of late Lt-Col R. C. M. Shelton, MBE, St Saviour's, Guernsey, and Mrs R. E. P. Shelton (*née* Coode), London Place, Oxford; *m* 1960, Anne Patricia, *o d* of John Arthur Warder, *qv* ; one *s* one *d*. *Educ:* Radley Coll.; Tabor Academy, Marion, Mass; Worcester Coll., Oxford; Univ. of Texas, Austin, Texas. Colman, Prentis & Varley Ltd, 1952-55; Corpa, Caracas, Venezuela, 1955-60; Managing Director: CPV (Colombiana) Ltd, Bogota, Colombia, 1960-64; CPV (International) Ltd, 1967-74 (Dir, 1964); Grosvenor Advertising Ltd, 1969-74 (Dir, 1964); Chm., Fletcher, Shelton, Delaney & Reynolds Ltd, 1974-. Member for Wandsworth, GLC, 1967-70; Chief Whip, on ILEA, 1968-70. PPS to Minister of Posts and Telecommunications, 1972-74; PPS to Rt Hon. Margaret Thatcher, MP, 1975. *Recreations:* golf, reading, painting. *Address:* 27 Ponsonby Terrace, SW1. *T:* 01-821 8204; The Manor House, Long Crendon, Bucks. *T:* Long Crendon 208748. *Club:* Carlton.

SHENFIELD, Barbara Estelle; Chairman, Women's Royal Voluntary Service, since 1981 (Vice Chairman, 1976-81); *d* of George and Jane Farrow, Bearwood, Staffs; *m* 1st, Flt-Lt Gwilym Ivor Lewis, RAF (killed in action); one *s* ; 2nd, Arthur A. Shenfield; one *s*. *Educ:* Langley High Sch., Worcs; Univ. of Birmingham (Hons Social and Political Science). Lectr in Soc. Studies, Univ. of Birmingham, 1945-56; Lectr, Dept of Econs and Soc. Studies, Bedford Coll., London Univ., 1959-65; Academic Dir, UC at Buckingham, 1972-73. Visiting Professor: Michigan State Univ., 1960;

Temple Univ., Philadelphia, 1974; Distinguished Vis. Prof., Rockford Coll., Ill, 1969-71, 1974. Consultant, US Dept of Labor, 1964; Dir, PEP Study of Co. Bds' Soc. Responsibilities, 1965-68. Member: UK Govt Cttee on Local Taxation, 1965-66; UK Govt Cttee on Abuse of Welfare Services, 1971-73. Chm., Nat Exec., Nat. Old People's Welfare Council (now Age Concern), 1971-73. *Publications:* Social Policies for Old Age, 1957; The Social Responsibilities of Company Boards, 1971; The Organisation of a Voluntary Service, 1972; monographs and articles on gerontological and other social subjects. *Recreations:* gardening, music, viticulture. *Address:* The Dower House, Old Windsor, Berks SL4 2HL. *T:* Windsor 54982; 27 Sloane Court West, SW3. *T:* 01-730 3781.

SHEPHARD, George Clifford, CBE 1979; retired as NCB Board Member for Industrial Relations, 1969-80, now Consultant; Member, Paul Finet Foundation, since 1974; *b* 2 Aug. 1915; British; *m* 1942, Mollie Dorothy Mansfield; one *s* (one *d* decd). *Educ:* Chesterfield Grammar School. Bolsover Colliery Co. Ltd, Head Office, 1933-40. Served in Army, N Africa, various Comd HQs, 1940-45, commnd 1942. Official, National Union of Mineworkers, 1945-69. Director, 1969-80: Coal Products Div., NCB; Associated Heat Services Ltd; Compower Ltd; British Investment; former Dir, Inst. of Occupational Medicine. Member: CBI Cttees; ECSC. Jt Hon. Sec., Coal Industry Social Welfare Organisation; Chm., Mineworkers' Pension Scheme. Editor, various bulletins and tracts. FCIS, ACWA, ACMA, CBIM. *Recreations:* golf, music. *Address:* 27 Chiswick Quay, Hartington Road, W4. *T:* 01-995 7137. *Club:* Grimsdyke Golf.

SHEPHARD, Air Cdre Harold Montague, CBE 1974 (OBE 1959); Provost Marshal (RAF) and Director of Security, 1971-74, retired; *b* 15 Aug. 1918; *s* of late Rev. Leonard B. Shephard and Lilian (*née* Robinson), Wanstead, Essex; *m* 1939, Margaret Isobel (*née* Girdlestone); one *s* one *d. Educ:* St John's, Leatherhead. Metropolitan Police (CID), 1937-41. Served War, RAF, 1941; commissioned for Provost duties, 1943. Seconded Public Safety Br., Control Commn, Germany, 1945; Wing Comdr, SIB, BAFO, 1947-50; OC, RAF Police Sch., 1951-52; then DAPM, Hong Kong; PMI, Air Ministry; Command Provost Marshal, Cyprus; OC, 4 RAF Police District; PM4, Air Ministry; Comdt, RAF Police Depot, Debden, 1963-64; CPM, FEAF, 1964-67; Comdt, Police Depot, 1967-69; Comd Provost and Security Officer, RAF Germany, 1969-71; Air Cdre, 1971. MBIM. *Recreations:* watching all sports, reading, trying to understand the French. *Address:* Le Moulin de Sourreau, Montcaret, 24230 Vélines, Dordogne, France; 2 Castle Close, Castle Hedingham, Essex. *Clubs:* Royal Air Force, Kennel.

SHEPHEARD, Major-General Joseph Kenneth, CB 1962; DSO 1943, and Bar, 1945; OBE 1949; *b* 15 Nov. 1908; *s* of late J. D. Shepheard, Poole and Bournemouth; *m* 1939, Maureen, *d* of late Capt. R. McG. Bowen-Colthurst, Oak Grove, County Cork; three *d. Educ:* Monmouth School; RMA Woolwich; Christ's Coll., Cambridge (BA Hons). Commissioned RE, 1928; served in India with King George V's Own Bengal Sappers and Miners, 1933-38; served in France with BEF as Adjt 4 Div. RE, 1939-40; Staff College, Camberley, 1940; Bde Major 161 (Essex) Inf. Bde in UK, Sierra Leone and Western Desert, 1940-41; Bde Major 18 Indian Inf. Bde in Iraq, 1941; GSO1 4 Indian Div. in N Africa and Italy, 1942-44; Comd 6 Assault Regt RE, Normandy to Baltic, 1944-46; JSSC, Latimer, Bucks, 1947; GSO1, FarELF, 1948-49; Staff Officer to Dir of Operations, Malaya, 1950; Comd 27 Fd Enrg Regt and CRE 6 Armd Div., 1951-53; Defence Research Policy Staff, 1953-56; Imperial Defence Coll., 1957; CCRE 1 (Br.) Corps in Germany, 1958-60; Chief of Staff, Northern Comd, 1960-62; Chief Engineer, Northern Army Group and BAOR, 1962-64. Col Comdt, RE, 1967-72. Gen. Sec., The Officers' Assoc., 1966-74. *Address:* Comfrey Cottage, Fields Farm Lane, Layer-de-la-Haye, Colchester, Essex.

SHEPHEARD, Sir Peter (Faulkner), Kt 1980; CBE 1972; PPRIBA, MRTPI, PPILA; Architect, town planner and landscape architect in private practice since 1948 (Shepheard, Epstein & Hunter); Professor of Architecture and Environmental Design, Graduate School of Fine Arts, University of Pennsylvania, since 1971; *b* 11 Nov. 1913; *s* of Thomas Faulkner Shepheard, FRIBA, Liverpool; *m* 1943, Mary Bailey; one *s* one *d. Educ:* Birkenhead Sch.; Liverpool Sch. of Architecture. BArch. (1st Cl. Hons) Liverpool, 1936; Univ. Grad. Scholar in Civic Design, 1936-37. Asst to Derek Bridgwater, 1937-40; Min. of Supply, Royal Ordnance Factories, 1940-43; Min. of Town and Country Planning: technical officer, first on Greater London Plan (Sir Patrick Abercrombie's staff), later on research and master plan for Stevenage New Town, 1943-47. Dep. Chief Architect and Planner, Stevenage Develt Corp., 1947-48. Vis. Prof., Landscape Architecture, 1959 and 1962-71, and Dean of Fine Arts, 1971-79, Univ. of Pennsylvania. Member: Nat. Parks Commn, 1966-68; Countryside Commn, 1968-71; Royal Fine Art Commn, 1968-71; Environmental Bd, 1977-. Artistic Advr, Commonwealth War Graves Commn, 1977-. Works include: housing and schools for GLC and other authorities; Landscape of part of Festival of Britain South Bank Exhibition, London, 1951; Master plan and buildings for University of Lancaster; work for the Universities of Keele, Liverpool, Oxford, and Ghana, and for Winchester College. Mem. Council of RIBA, 1950-75 (Pres., 1969-71); President: Architectural Association, 1954-55; Inst. of Landscape Architects, 1965-66. RIBA Distinction in Town Planning, 1956. Hon. FRAIC; Hon. FAIA. *Publications:* Modern Gardens, 1953; Gardens, 1969; various articles, lectures and broadcasts on architecture and landscape; drawings and illustrations of architecture and other things; illustr. A Book of Ducks, and Woodlands Birds (King Penguins). *Recreations:* music and poetry; drawing,

gardening and the study of natural history. *Address:* 60 Kingly Street, W1R 6EY. *T:* 01-734 8577. *Clubs:* Athenæum, Savile.

SHEPHEARD, Sir Victor (George), KCB 1954 (CB 1950); Director: William Denny & Brothers Ltd, Shipbuilders and Engineers, Dumbarton, 1959-63; Marinite Ltd, 1961-73; Director of Research, British Ship Research Association, 1959-63; *b* 21 March 1893; *e s* of late V. G. Shepheard, Shortlands, Kent; *m* 1924, Florence, *d* of late Capt. James Wood, Bridgwater. *Educ:* HM Dockyard School, Devonport; Royal Naval Coll., Greenwich. Royal Corps of Naval Constructors, 1915; Constructor Lieut, Grand Fleet, 1915-17; present at Battle of Jutland. Professor of Naval Architecture, RN College, Greenwich, 1934-39; Chief Constructor, 1939-42; Asst Director of Naval Construction, 1942-47; Deputy Director 1947-51; Director of Naval Construction, Admiralty, and Head of RCNC, 1951-58. Member Council Royal Inst. of Naval Architects, 1944-, Vice-Pres. 1952-, Hon. Vice-Pres., 1961, Treasurer, 1960-69; FEng 1976. Hon. Vice-Pres., Soc. for Nautical Research; Member: Admty Adv. Cttee on Structural Steel; Cttee on application of Nuclear Power to Marine Purposes, 1961-63; HMS Victory Advisory Technical Cttee. Hon. Fell., NEC Inst.; Mem., Smeatonian Soc. of Civil Engineers, Pres., 1976; Liveryman of Worshipful Company of Shipwrights, Prime Warden, 1968; Board of Governors Cutty Sark Society; formerly Trustee, Nat. Maritime Museum. Froude Gold Medal for services to Naval Architecture and Shipbuilding, 1963. Chev. de la Légion d'Honneur, 1947. *Publications:* various papers to Professional Institutions. *Recreations:* gardening, music. *Address:* Manor Place, Manor Park, Chislehurst, Kent. *T:* 01-467 5455.

SHEPHERD, family name of **Baron Shepherd.**

SHEPHERD, 2nd Baron, *cr* 1946, of Spalding; **Malcolm Newton Shepherd;** PC 1965; Deputy Chairman, Sterling Group of Companies, since 1976; Chairman: Packaging Council, since 1978; National Bus Company, since 1979; *b* 27 Sept. 1918; *s* of 1st Baron Shepherd, PC, and Ada Newton (*d* 1975); *S* father, 1954; *m* 1941, Allison Wilson Redmond; two *s. Educ:* Lower Sch. of John Lyon; Friends' Sch., Saffron Walden. War of 1939-45: commissioned RASC, 1941; served in Desert, N Africa, Sicily, Italy. Deputy Opposition Chief Whip, House of Lords, 1960. Member Parly Labour Party Exec., 1964; Deputy Speaker, House of Lords, subseq. Opposition Chief Whip, 1964; Captain of the Hon. Corps of Gentlemen-at-Arms and Government Chief Whip, House of Lords, 1964-67; Minister of State, FCO, 1967-70; Deputy Leader of the House of Lords, 1968-70; Opposition Dep. Leader, House of Lords, 1970-74; Lord Privy Seal and Leader, House of Lords, 1974-76, resigned. First Chm., CS Pay Res. Unit Bd, 1978-81; Chm., MRC, 1978-82. *Recreation:* golf. *Heir:* *s* Hon. Graeme George Shepherd, *b* 6 January 1949. *Address:* 29 Kennington Palace Court, Sancroft Street, SE11. *T:* 01-582 6772. *Clubs:* Singapore, Tanglin, Royal Singapore Golf (Singapore).

SHEPHERD, Archie; HM Diplomatic Service, retired; Counsellor and Head of Migration and Visa Department, Foreign and Commonwealth Office, 1977-80; *b* 2 Nov. 1922; *s* of William Shepherd and Edith (*née* Browning); *m* 1959, Dorothy Annette Walker; one *s. Educ:* Torquay Grammar Sch. Prison Commission, 1939; served War, RAF, 1942-46. Foreign Office, 1949: Asst Political Agent and Vice Consul, Muscat, 1951-53; FO, 1954-55; Second Sec., UK Delegn to United Nations, Geneva, 1956-57; HM Consul: Warsaw, 1958-60; Rabat, 1960-62; FO, 1963-67; Consul, Cape Town, 1968-72; First Sec. (Commercial), Beirut, 1973-75. *Recreations:* tennis, gardening. *Address:* 9 Oaks Way, Kenley, Surrey. *T:* 01-660 1299. *Clubs:* Civil Service, Royal Commonwealth Society.

SHEPHERD, Rear-Adm. Charles William Haimes, CB 1972; CBE 1968 (OBE 1958); *b* 10 Dec. 1917; *s* of William Henry Haimes Shepherd and Florence (*née* Hayter); *m* 1940, Myra Betty Joan Major; one *s. Educ:* Public Central Sch., Plymouth; HMS Fisgard and RNC Greenwich. Entered RN as Artificer Apprentice, 1933; specialised Engrg Officer, 1940; served War of 1939-45 in HMS: Repulse; Hero; Royal Sovereign; Gambia (RNZN); Staff of C-in-C Pacific (Sydney); R&D, Guided Weapons, 1946-49 and 1954-58 incl. Flotilla Eng Officer 3rd Trng Flotilla (HMS Crispin), 1949-51; Sen. Officers War Course, 1961-62; Tech. Dir, UK Polaris Weapon System, 1962-68; Dir Project Teams (Submarines), and Dep. Asst Controller (Polaris), MoD (Navy), 1968-71; Dep. Controller (Polaris), MoD, 1971-73. Sub-Lt 1940; Lieut 1941; Lt-Comdr 1949; Comdr 1952; Captain 1960; Rear-Adm. 1970; retired 1974. Cttee mem., Plymouth Albion RFC. *Recreations:* Do-it-yourself, sailing. *Address:* 5 Underhill Road, Stoke, Plymouth PL3 4BP. *T:* Plymouth 556888. *Clubs:* Royal Western Yacht; Royal Plymouth Corinthian Yacht.

SHEPHERD, Colin; MP (C) Hereford, since Oct. 1974; *b* 13 Jan. 1938; *s* of late T. C. R. Shepherd, MBE; *m* 1966, Louise, *d* of late Lt-Col E. A. M. Cleveland, MC. *Educ:* Oundle; Caius Coll., Cambridge; McGill Univ., Montreal. RCN, 1959-63. Marketing Dir, Haigh Engineering Co. Ltd, 1963-. Jt Sec., Cons. Parly Agr. Fish. and Food Cttee, 1975-79. Vice-Chm., 1979-; Mem., Select Cttee on H of C Services, 1979-; Sec., Cons. Parly Hort. Sub-Cttee, 1976-. *Address:* House of Commons, SW1A 0AA; Manor House, Ganarew, near Monmouth, Gwent. *T:* Symonds Yat 890220. *Club:* Naval Officers.

SHEPHERD, David; see Shepherd, R. D.

SHEPHERD, Eric William, CB 1967; *b* London, 17 May 1913; *s* of late Charles Thomas Shepherd; *m* 1938, Marie Noele Carpenter; two *d. Educ:* Hackney Downs School; The Polytechnic, Regent Street. BSc 1st Class Hons (Maths and Physics) London 1932. Entered Post Office as Executive Officer, 1932. Served War of 1939-45, with Royal Engineers (Postal Section), 1940-46. Principal, Post Office, 1948; Treasury, 1949-52; Asst Accountant General, Post Office, 1952; Dep. Comptroller and Accountant General, 1953; Assistant Secretary, 1956; Director of Finance and Accounts, 1960; Senior Director, 1967-73. *Recreations:* music, especially choral singing, golf. *Address:* 2 Arkley View, Arkley, Barnet, Herts. *T:* 01-449 9316.

SHEPHERD, Geoffrey Thomas, CBE 1979; FIMechE, FIEE; Chairman, Midlands Electricity Board, since 1972; part-time Member Central Electricity Generating Board, since 1977; *b* 1922; *s* of Thomas Henry and Louise Shepherd; *m* Irene Wilkes; one *d. Educ:* King Edward's Sch., Birmingham; Coll. of Technology, Birmingham. BSc (Eng). GEC Ltd, Witton; City of Birmingham Electricity Supply Dept; British Electricity Authority (several positions in Power Stations); Nuclear Ops Engr, CEGB, 1958-61; Asst Regional Dir (Western Div.), 1962-65; South of Scotland Electricity Bd, 1965, becoming Dir of Engineering, 1968; Dep. Chm., LEB, 1969-72. Chm., Worcestershire Cttee, VSO, 1975-81. CBIM. Vice Pres., IEE, 1978-81. *Recreations:* fair weather sailing, railways. *Address:* Avon Reach, Church Street, Wyre Piddle, Pershore, Worcs. *T:* Pershore 3076.

SHEPHERD, George Anthony; HM Diplomatic Service; Counsellor, British High Commission, New Delhi, since 1982; *b* 8 Sept. 1931; *m* 1961, Sarah Eirlys Adamson; one *s* two *d. Educ:* Blundell's School; RMA Sandhurst. Served 4th Royal Tank Regt, in Egypt and BAOR, 1951-57; Trucial Oman Scouts, 1957-59; 2nd RTR, 1959-60; Durham Univ., 1960-61; Federal Regular Army, Aden, 1961-64; 2nd RTR, 1965; Asst Defence Adviser, British High Commission, Lagos, 1967-69; retd as Major RTR, 1969. 1st Secretary, FCO, Bahrain, Dubai and Islamabad, 1969-82. Life Member, Fauna Preservation Soc., 1964. *Publications:* Arabian Adventure, 1961; Flight of the Unicorns, 1964. *Recreations:* walking, bird watching, poetry. *Address:* c/o Foreign and Commonwealth Office, SW1. *Club:* Army and Navy.

SHEPHERD, James Rodney; Under-Secretary, Department of Industry, since 1980; *b* 27 Nov. 1935; *s* of Richard James Shepherd and Winifred Mary Shepherd. *Educ:* Blundell's; Magdalen Coll., Oxford (PPE; Diploma in Statistics). National Inst. of Economic and Social Res., 1960-64; Consultant to OECD, 1964; HM Treasury, 1965-80 (Under-Sec., 1975-80). *Publications:* articles in technical jls. *Address:* 32 Addison Grove, Bedford Park, W4. *T:* 01-995 7577.

SHEPHERD, John Alan; HM Diplomatic Service; Counsellor and Head of Chancery, Office of the UK Permanent Representative to the European Economic Community, Brussels, since 1982; *b* 27 April 1943; *s* of William (Mathieson) Shepherd and (Elsie) Rae Shepherd; *m* 1969, Jessica Mary Nichols; one *d. Educ:* Charterhouse; Selwyn Coll., Cambridge (MA); Stanford Univ., Calif (MA). Merchant Navy, 1961; HM Diplomatic Service, 1965-: CO, 1965-66; MECAS, Lebanon, 1966-68; 3rd Sec., Amman, 1968-70; 2nd Sec., Rome, 1970-73; 1st Secretary: FCO, 1973-76; The Hague, 1977-80; Office of UK Rep. to EEC, Brussels, 1980-82. *Recreations:* hills, birds, books, maps, squash, tennis, music. *Address:* c/o Foreign and Commonwealth Office, King Charles Street, SW1.

SHEPHERD, John Dodson, CBE 1979; Regional Administrator, Yorkshire Regional Health Authority, 1977-82, retired; *b* 24 Dec. 1920; *s* of Norman and Elizabeth Ellen Shepherd; *m* 1948, Marjorie Nettleton; one *s* two *d. Educ:* Barrow Grammar School. FCIS, FHA. RAF, 1940-46: N Africa, Italy, Middle East, 1943-46. Asst Sec., Oxford RHB, 1956-58; Dep. Sec., Newcastle upon Tyne HMC, 1958-62; Sec., East Cumberland HMC, 1962-67; Sec., Liverpool RHB, 1967-73; Reg. Administrator, Mersey RHA, 1973-77. Pres., Inst. of Health Service Administrators, 1977-78 (Mem. Council, 1969-78). *Recreations:* golf, music. *Address:* 14 Leconfield Garth, Follifoot, Harrogate HG3 1NF. *T:* Harrogate 870520. *Clubs:* Harrogate Golf, Harrogate Rotary.

SHEPHERD, Dame Margaret (Alice), DBE 1964 (CBE 1962); Chairman, Haigh Engineering Co. Ltd, Ross-on-Wye; *b* 1910; *d* of Percy S. Turner, Redcourt, Pyrford; *m* 1935, Thomas Cropper Ryley Shepherd (*d* 1975); three *s* one *d. Educ:* Wimbledon, Lausanne and London Univ. Chairman: Conservative and Unionist Women's National Advisory Cttee, 1960-63; National Union of Conservative and Unionist Assocs, 1963-64; Conservative Political Centre National Advisory Cttee, 1966-69; Pres., Nat. Union of Conservative and Unionist Assocs, 1972-73. Member: House of Laity, Gen. Synod of C of E, 1980-; Cathedrals Adv. Commn for England, 1981-. *Recreations:* swimming, gardening. *Address:* Moraston House, Bridstow, Ross-on-Wye, Herefordshire. *T:* Ross-on-Wye 62370.

SHEPHERD, Air Vice-Marshal Melvin Clifford Seymour, CB 1975; OBE 1953; Chief Executive, Wine and Spirit Trades Benevolent Society, since 1980; *b* 22 Oct. 1922; *s* of Clifford Charles Golding Shepherd and Isabella Davidson Shepherd (*née* Kemp); *m* 1949, Patricia Mary Large; one *s. Educ:* in South Africa. Commnd SAAF 1942; war service N Africa, Sicily, Burma, 1942-45; joined RAF, 1947; comd No 73 (F) Sqdn Malta, 1950-53 psa 1954; Chief Ops Officer, Western Sector UK, 1954-57; Comdr No 15 MU Wroughton, 1957-60; Air Min. Air Plans, 1960-63; Dirg Staff, Jt Services

Staff Coll., 1963-65; Chief Ops Officer, Far East Comd, 1966; ACOS (Intell.) 2ATAF, 1967-69; comd RAF Binbrook, 1969-72; SASO No 38 Gp, 1972-74; Dir of Ops (Air Defence and Overseas), 1974-75; AOA Strike Command, 1976-78. *Recreations:* golf, shooting, fishing, reading. *Address:* 12 Albert Grove, Wimbledon. *Club:* Royal Air Force.

SHEPHERD, Sir Peter (Malcolm), Kt 1976; CBE 1967; DL; FCIOB; Chairman: Shepherd Building Group Ltd, since 1958; Construction Industry Training Board, 1973-76; *b* 18 Oct. 1916; *s* of Alderman Frederick Welton Shepherd and Mrs Martha Eleanor Shepherd; *m* 1940, Patricia Mary Welton; four *s. Educ:* Nunthorpe and Rossall Schs. Chairman: Wool, Jute and Flax ITB, 1964-74; Jt Cttee, Textile ITBs, 1966-74. Mem. Council, CBI, 1976-. Inst. of Building: Pres., 1964-65; Mem., Nat. Council, 1956-; Vice-Chm., Professional Practice Bd, 1975- (Chm. 1963-75); Mem., Bd of Bldg Educn, 1957-75 (Chm. 1965-68). British Inst. of Management: Mem., Nat. Council, 1965-71; Mem., Bd of Fellows, 1969-73; Founder Chm., Yorks and N Lincs Adv. Bd, 1969-71. Mem., President's Consult. Cttee, Nat. Fedn of Building Trades Employers, 1956-; Pres., York Assoc., 1952-53; Chm., Yorks Sect., Fedn of Civil Eng Contractors, 1953-54. Member: (founder) Technician Educn Council, 1973-79; UK Adv. Council on Educn for Management, 1960-66. Member: Co. of Merchant Adventurers of City of York; York Rotary Club. Formerly Chm., Round Table, York. Governor, St Peter's Sch., York. DL N Yorks, 1981. FCIOB; CBIM; Hon. DSc Heriot-Watt; DUniv York, 1981. *Recreation:* sailing. *Address:* Galtres House, Rawcliffe Lane, York. *T:* York 24250. *Clubs:* Royal Yachting Association; Filey Sailing.

SHEPHERD, Richard Charles Scrimgeour; MP (C) Aldridge-Brownhills, since 1979; *b* 6 Dec. 1942; *s* of Alfred Reginald Shepherd and Davida Sophia Wallace. *Educ:* LSE; Johns Hopkins Univ. (Sch. of Advanced Internat. Studies). Director: Shepherd Foods (London) Ltd, 1970-; Partridges of Sloane Street Ltd, 1972-. Mem., SE Econ. Planning Council, 1970-74. Underwriting Mem. of Lloyds, 1974-. Mem., Treasury and Civil Service Select Cttee, 1979-; Cons. Parly Industry Cttee, 1980-81; Sec., Cons. Parly European Cotttee, 1980-81. *Recreations:* book collecting; searching for the Home Service on the wireless. *Address:* 14 Addison Road, W14. *T:* 01-603 7108. *Clubs:* Carlton, Beefsteak, Chelsea Arts.

SHEPHERD, (Richard) David, OBE 1980; artist; *b* 25 April 1931; *s* of Raymond Oxley Shepherd and Margaret Joyce Shepherd (*née* Williamson); *m* 1957, Avril Shirley Gaywood; four *d. Educ:* Stowe. Art trng under Robin Goodwin, 1950-53; started career as aviation artist (Founder Mem., Soc. of Aviation Artists). Frequent worldwide trips for aviation and paintings for Services. Exhibited, RA, 1956; began painting African wild life, 1960. First London one-man show, 1962; painted 15 ft reredos of Christ for army garrison church, Bordon, 1964; 2nd London exhibn, 1965; Johannesburg exhibns, 1966 and 1969; exhibn, Tryon Gall., London, 1978; Collins Artist in Africa (publ.), 1967. Painted: HE Dr Kaunda, President of Zambia, 1967; HM the Queen Mother for King's Regt, 1969; HE Sheikh Zaid of Abu Dhabi, 1970; 3rd London exhibn, 1971. BBC made 50-minute colour life documentary, The Man Who Loves Giants, for worldwide TV, 1970; auctioned 5 wildlife paintings in USA and raised sufficient to purchase Bell Jet Ranger helicopter to combat game poaching in Zambia, 1971; painted Tiger Fire (raised £127,500 for Operation Tiger), 1973. Hon. DFA, Pratt Inst., New York, for services to wildlife conservation through his painting, 1971; Order of the Golden Ark, Netherlands, for services to wildlife conservation (Zambia, Operation Tiger, etc), 1973. *Publications:* Artist in Africa, 1967; (autobiog.) The Man who Loves Giants, 1975. *Recreations:* conservation of wildlife (on Adv. Panel, Brit. Nat. Appeal World Wildlife Fund; preservation of steam locomotives, railways, etc (purchased two main line steam locomotives, full working order, Black Prince 92203 and Green Knight 75029, 1967; Chm., E Somerset Rlwy, Cranmore, Som., incl. Victorian station, track, 7 locomotives, 7 coaches, etc; open to public, 1974. Reg. charity no. 271589). *Address:* Winkworth Farm, Hascombe, Godalming, Surrey. *T:* Hascombe 220.

SHEPHERD, Prof. William Morgan, DSc (London); Professor of Theoretical Mechanics in Faculty of Engineering, University of Bristol, 1959-71, Emeritus, 1971; *b* 19 Dec. 1905; *s* of Charles Henry and Elizabeth Shepherd; *m* 1932, Brenda Coulson; two *d. Educ:* Wellington School; University College of the South West, Exeter; University College, London. Asst lecturer and lecturer in mathematics, University College of North Wales, Bangor, 1928-35; Lecturer in mathematics in Faculty of Engineering, University of Bristol, 1935-44; Reader in Elasticity, University of Bristol, 1944-59; Head of Department of Theoretical Mechanics, 1951-71. *Publications:* various publications, mainly on applied mathematics, in Proceedings of the Royal Society and other scientific journals. *Recreations:* gardening, cricket. *Address:* 1 Thorpe Lodge, Cotham Side, Bristol BS8 5TJ. *T:* Bristol 426284.

SHEPHERD, William Stanley; *b* 1918; *s* of W. D. Shepherd; *m* 1942, Betty, *d* of late T. F. Howard, MP for Islington South, 1931-35; two *s*. Served in Army, War of 1939-45. A managing director of businesses which he has established; MP (C) for Cheadle Division of Cheshire, 1950-66 (Bucklow Division of Cheshire, 1945-50); Member of the Select Committee on Estimates; Joint Hon. Sec. Conservative Parliamentary Committee in Trade and Industry, 1945-51. Joined SDP, 1982. Hon. Mem., Valuers Institution. FREconS. *Address:* (office) 77 George Street, W1. *T:* 01-935 0753; (home) 33 Queens Grove, St John's Wood, NW8. *T:* 01-722 7526. *Club:* Savile.

SHEPPARD, Rt. Rev. David Stuart; see Liverpool, Bishop of.

SHEPPARD, Francis Henry Wollaston; General Editor, Survey of London, since 1954; *b* 10 Sept. 1921; *s* of Leslie Alfred Sheppard, *qv*; *m* 1st, 1949, Pamela Gordon Davies (*d* 1954); one *s* one *d*; 2nd, 1957, Elizabeth Fleur Lees; one *d*. *Educ:* Bradfield; King's Coll., Cambridge (MA); PhD London. FRHistS. Asst Archivist, West Sussex CC, Chichester, 1947-48; Asst Keeper, London Museum, 1948-53. Mayor of Henley on Thames, 1970-71; Pres., Henley Symphony Orchestra, 1973-76. Visiting Fellow, Leicester Univ., 1977-78; Alice Davis Hitchcock Medallion of Soc. of Architectural Historians of Gt Britain, 1966. *Publications:* Local Government in St Marylebone 1688-1835, 1958; London 1808-1870: The Infernal Wen, 1971; Brakspear's Brewery, Henley on Thames, 1779-1979, 1979; (ed) Survey of London, Vols XXVI-XL, 1956-80. *Recreation:* music. *Address:* 55 New Street, Henley on Thames, Oxon RG9 2BP. *T:* Henley on Thames 4658.

SHEPPARD, Leslie Alfred, MA; FSA; Deputy Keeper of Printed Books, British Museum, 1945-53; *b* 9 Jan. 1890; *o s* of late Alfred Sheppard, Keynsham; *m* 1918, Dorothy (*d* 1979), *y d* of late Rev. H. Ewbank, St John's, Ryde; two *s*. *Educ:* Merrywood School, Bristol; St Catharine's College, Cambridge. Served with 1st British Red Cross Unit attached to Italian Army, 1915-19; entered British Museum, 1919; worked on Catalogue of books printed in XVth cent., now in BM, vols vi, viii-x; catalogued incunabula of Bodleian Library, Oxford, 1955-70. Member of Council of Bibliographical Society, 1936-46. *Publications:* A Fifteenth-Century Humanist, Francesco Filelfo, 1935; The Printers of the Coverdale Bible, 1935; Printing at Deventer in the XVth Century, 1943; A New Light on William Caxton and Colard Mansion, 1952; and other articles and reviews in Transactions of Bibliographical Society, Gutenberg Jahrbuch, and elsewhere. Translated Memoirs of Lorenzo da Ponte, 1929. *Address:* The Bishops House, 55 New Street, Henley-on-Thames, Oxon RG9 2BP. *T:* Henley 4658.
See also F. H. W. Sheppard.

SHEPPARD, Tan Sri Dato Mervyn Cecil ffranck, PSM (Malaysia) 1969; DPMS 1982; DJPD (Malaysia), 1967; JMN (Malaysia), 1963; CMG 1957; MBE 1946; ED 1947; Vice-President and Editor, Malaysian Branch, Royal Asiatic Society; *b* 1905; *s* of late Canon J. W. ff. Sheppard; *m* 1940, Rosemary, *d* of late Major Edward Oakeley; one *d*. *Educ:* Marlborough; Magdalene Coll., Cambridge (MA). Cadet, Federated Malay States, 1928; Private Sec. to Chief Sec., 1929. Interned by Japanese, 1942-45; Major, FMS Volunteer Force, retd 1946. Director of Public Relations, 1946; District Officer, Klang, 1947-50; British Adviser, Negri Sembilan, 1952; Head of the Emergency Food Denial Organisation, Federation of Malaya, 1956. First Keeper of Public Records, 1957-62, and Director of Museums, 1958-63, Federation of Malaya. Hon. Curator, Nat. Museum, Kuala Lumpur. Panglima Setia Mahkota, 1969; Dato Jasa Purba Di-Raja, Negri Sembilan, 1967; Dato Paduka Mahkota Selangor, 1982. *Publications:* Taman Indera, 1972; The Living Crafts of Malaysia, 1978; Memoirs of an Unorthodox Civil Servant, 1979. *Address:* Flat 7C, Crescent Court, Brickfields, Kuala Lumpur, Malaysia. *Club:* United Oxford & Cambridge University.

SHEPPARD, Prof. Norman, FRS 1967; Professor of Chemical Sciences, University of East Anglia, Norwich, since 1964; *b* 16 May 1921; *s* of Walter Sheppard and Anne Clarges Sheppard (*née* Finding); *m* 1949, Kathleen Margery McLean; two *s* one *d* (and one *s* decd). *Educ:* Hymers Coll., Hull; St Catharine's Coll., Cambridge. BA Cantab 1st cl. hons 1943; PhD and MA Cantab 1947. Vis. Asst Prof., Pennsylvania State Univ., 1947-48; Ramsay Memorial Fellow, 1948-49; Senior 1851 Exhibn, 1949-51; Fellow of Trinity Coll., Cambridge and Asst Dir of Research in Spectroscopy, Cambridge Univ., 1957-64. *Publications:* scientific papers on spectroscopy in Proc. Roy. Soc., Trans. Faraday Soc., Jl Chem. Soc., Spectrochimica Acta, etc. *Recreations:* architecture, classical music, walking. *Address:* 5 Hornor Close, Norwich NR2 2LY. *T:* Norwich 53052.

SHEPPARD, Sir Richard (Herbert), Kt 1981; CBE 1964; RA 1972 (ARA 1966); FRIBA 1944 (ARIBA 1936); Founder and now Consultant to Sheppard Robson, Architects, whose work includes universities, schools and technical colleges, industrial and commercial buildings; *b* 2 July 1910; *e s* of William Sheppard and Hilda (*née* Kirby-Evans); *m* 1st, 1938, Jean Shufflebotham, ARIBA, MRTPI (*d* 1974); one *s* one *d*; 2nd, 1976, Marjorie Head. *Educ:* Bristol Grammar School; Architectural Association School of Architecture, Bedford Square. Hons Diploma, Architectural Assoc. 1935; foreign travel, 1935-37. Principal commissions include: City Univ., London; Brunel Univ., Uxbridge; Churchill College, Cambridge (competition), 1959; Collingwood College, Univ. of Durham; Campus West, Welwyn Garden City; Manchester Polytechnic; and other educnl and commercial bldgs. Vice-Pres. RIBA, 1969-70. Hon. DTech Brunel, 1972. *Publications:* Building for the People, 1945; Prefabrication and Building, 1946, etc; also technical articles. *Recreation:* looking at the work of others. *Address:* 6 Robin's Nest Hill, Little Berkhamsted, Herts. *T:* Cuffley 5066.

SHEPPARD, William Vincent, CBE 1963; Deputy Chairman, National Coal Board, 1971-75 (Member, 1967-76); Chairman, PD/NCB (Consultants) Ltd, 1975; *b* 15 Nov. 1909; *s* of late Dr H. P. Sheppard; *m* 1938, Nancy F. Watson; two *s* one *d*. *Educ:* Cheltenham College; Birmingham University (BSc (Hons) Min.). Mining Student with Bolsover Colliery Co. Ltd, 1931-35, Safety Officer to Co., 1935-37; Under Manager, Creswell Colliery, 1937; Manager, Rufford Colliery, 1938; Mining Devel. Engr, No 4 Area, East Midlands Div., NCB, 1947; Area Gen. Man., No 1 Area, East Midlands Div., NCB, 1948; Dir-Gen. of Reconstruction, NCB, 1957-60; Dir-Gen. of Production, NCB, 1960-67. Dir, Wide Range Engineering Services Ltd, 1976-. Past-Pres., Southern Counties Inst. of Instn of Mining Engineers; Hon. FIMinE. CStJ 1957. *Recreations:* gardening, model-making, Rugby football (County Cap, Glos). *Address:* Langshott Manor, Horley, Surrey. *T:* Horley 2282.

SHEPPARD FIDLER, Alwyn G.; see Fidler.

SHEPPERD, Alfred Joseph; Chairman and Chief Executive, The Wellcome Foundation Ltd, since 1977; *b* 19 June 1925; *s* of Alfred Charles Shepperd and Mary Ann Williams; *m* 1950, Gabrielle Marie Yvette Bouloux; two *d*. *Educ:* Archbishop Tenison's Sch.; University Coll., London (BSc Econ). Rank Organisation, 1949; Selincourt & Sons Ltd, 1963; Chamberlain Group, 1965; Managing Director, Keyser Ullmann Industries Ltd, 1967; Dir, Keyser Ullmann Ltd, 1967; Financial Dir, Laporte Industries Ltd, 1971, Wellcome Foundation Ltd, 1972; Dir, Anglia Maltings (Holdings) Ltd, 1972-. *Address:* Court Mead, 6 Guildown Avenue, Guildford, Surrey GU2 5HB. *Clubs:* Athenæum, Naval, Oriental.

SHEPPERSON, Prof. George Albert; William Robertson Professor of Commonwealth and American History, University of Edinburgh, since 1963; *b* 7 Jan. 1922; *s* of late Albert Edward Shepperson and Bertha Agnes (*née* Jennings); *m* 1952, Joyce Irene (*née* Cooper); one *d*. *Educ:* King's Sch., Peterborough; St John's Coll., Cambridge (Schol.; 1st Class Hons: English Tripos, Pt I, 1942; Historical Tripos, Pt II, 1947); 1st Cl. CertEd (Cantab), 1948. Served War, commnd Northamptonshire Regt, seconded to KAR, 1942-46. Edinburgh University: Lectr in Imperial and American History, 1948, Sen. Lectr, 1960, Reader, 1961; Dean of Faculty of Arts, 1974-77. Visiting Professor: Roosevelt and Chicago Univs, 1959; Makerere Coll., Uganda, 1962; Dalhousie Univ., 1968-69; Lectures: Herskovits Meml, Northwestern Univ., 1966 and 1972; Livingstone Centenary, RGS, 1973; Soc. of the Cincinnati, State of Virginia, 1976; Sarah Tryphena Phillips, in Amer. Lit. and Hist., British Acad., 1979; Rhodes Commem., Rhodes Univ., 1981. Chairman: British Assoc. for American Studies, 1971-74; Mungo Park Bicentenary Cttee, 1971; David Livingstone Documentation Project, 1973-; Commonwealth Inst., Scotland, 1973-. Jt Editor, Oxford Studies in African Affairs, 1969-. *Publications:* Independent African: John Chilembwe, 1958, 3rd edn 1969; David Livingstone and the Rovuma, 1964; many articles and chapters in learned jls, collaborative vols and encycs. *Recreations:* theatre; collecting African and Afro-American documents. *Address:* 23 Ormidale Terrace, Edinburgh EH12 6DY. *T:* 031-337 4424. *Club:* Royal Commonwealth Society.

SHER, Samuel Julius; QC 1981; *b* 22 Oct. 1941; *s* of Philip and Isa Phyllis Sher; *m* 1965, Sandra Maris; one *s* two *d*. *Educ:* Athlone High Sch., Johannesburg; Univ. of the Witwatersrand (BComm, LLB); New Coll., Oxford (BCL). Called to the Bar, Inner Temple, 1968. *Recreation:* tennis. *Address:* 12 Constable Close, NW11 6TY. *T:* 01-455 2753.

SHERBORNE, 7th Baron, *cr* 1784; **Charles Dutton;** *b* 13 May 1911; *e s* of 6th Baron, DSO and Ethel Mary (*d* 1949), *e d* of late William Baird; *S* father, 1949; *m* 1943, Joan Molesworth (*d* 1982), *d* of Sir James Dunn, 1st Bt, and widow of John Anthony Jenkinson. *Educ:* Stowe. Finance Dept, Hosp. Saving Assoc., mid-thirties; Prize Dept, Min. of Economic Warfare, 1939-40; Ferry Pilot, ATA, 1940-45. Member: Northleach RDC, 1947-57; Gloucestershire CC, 1955-64. *Heir: cousin* Ralph Stawell Dutton, *qv*. *Address:* Lodge Park, Aldsworth, Cheltenham, Glos. *T:* Windrush 296. *Club:* White's.
See also Sir John Dutton Clerk.

SHERBORNE, Bishop Suffragan of, since 1976; **Rt. Rev. John Dudley Galtrey Kirkham;** Canon and Prebendary of Salisbury Cathedral, since 1977; *b* 20 Sept. 1935; *s* of Canon Charles Dudley Kirkham and Doreen Betty Galtrey. *Educ:* Lancing Coll.; Trinity Coll., Cambridge (BA 1959, MA 1963). Commnd, Royal Hampshire Regt and seconded to 23 (K) Bn, King's African Rifles, 1954-56. Trinity Coll., Cambridge, 1956-59; Westcott House, 1960-62; Curate, St Mary-Le-Tower, Ipswich, 1962-65; Chaplain to Bishop of Norwich, 1965-69; Priest in Charge, Rockland St Mary w. Hellington, 1967-69; Chaplain to Bishop of New Guinea, 1969; Asst Priest, St Martin in the Fields and St Margaret's, Westminster, 1970-72; Domestic Chaplain to Archbishop of Canterbury, 1972-76; Canterbury Diocesan Director of Ordinands, 1972-76. Serving Brother Chaplain of the Order of St John of Jerusalem. Croix d'Argent de Saint-Rombaut, 1973. *Recreations:* skiing, walking, wood-work, reading. *Address:* Little Bailie, Sturminster Marshall, Wimborne, Dorset. *Clubs:* Army and Navy, Ski of Great Britain, Kandahar.

SHERBORNE, Archdeacon of; see Ward, Ven. E. J. G.

SHERBROOKE, Archbishop of, (RC), since 1968; **Most Rev. Jean-Marie Fortier;** *b* 1 July 1920. *Educ:* Laval University, Quebec. Bishop Auxiliary, La Pocatière, PQ, 1961-65; Bishop of Gaspé, PQ, 1965-68. Elected Pres., Canadian Catholic Conference, 1973-75. *Publication:* contrib. to Dictionnaire d'Histoire et de Géographie. *Address:* 130 rue de la Cathédrale, Sherbrooke, PQ J1H 4M1, Canada. *T:* 569-6070.

SHERBROOKE-WALKER, Col Ronald Draycott, CBE 1961; TD 1945; TA (retired); Director of Securicor (Wales and South West) Ltd, 1965-72 (of Securicor Ltd, 1945-65); *b* 1 April 1897; *s* of Rev. George Sherbrooke Walker, sometime Rector of March, Cambs; *m* 1925, Ruth Bindley, *d* of William Allen Bindley, Edgbaston. *Educ:* Sherborne. Chartered Accountant, 1923. Served European War, 1914-19; Lieut Dorset Regt and RFC. Lieut to Major 8th Bn Middx Regt TA, 1925-31. Served War of 1939-45: Lieut-Col, Middx Regt and attached RAF Regt. Mem. Middx T&AFA, 1930-63 (Vice-Chm. 1951-56); Comdt Middx Army Cadet Force, 1948-54; Vice-Chm. Army Cadet Force Assoc., 1956-66 (Vice-Pres., 1966-); Mem. Amery Cttee, 1956-57; Mem. TA Advisory Cttee, 1956-64; Governor Cadet Training Centre, Frimley Park, 1959-79. FCA. DL Middx, 1947-65; Vice-Lieutenant, Middx, 1963-65; DL Greater London, 1965-76. *Publications:* Khaki and Blue, 1952; contrib. to various jls. *Recreation:* gardening. *Address:* 22 Bathwick Hill, Bath BA2 6EW. *Club:* Lansdowne (Bath).

SHERCLIFF, Prof. John Arthur, FRS 1980; Hopkinson and ICI Professor of Applied Thermodynamics, University of Cambridge, and Fellow of Trinity College, since 1980; *b* 10 Sept. 1927; *s* of William Shercliff and Marion Prince Shercliff (*née* Hoult); *m* 1955, Daphne Margaret Llewellyn; two *s* one *d*. *Educ:* Manchester Grammar Sch.; Trinity Coll., Cambridge (MA, PhD); Harvard Univ. (SM). A. V. Roe & Co. Ltd, Manchester, 1949-51; Demonstrator, 1954-57, Lectr, 1957-64, Dept of Engrg, Univ. of Cambridge; Founding Prof., Prof. and Head of Dept of Engrg Science, (new) Univ. of Warwick, 1964-80; Visiting Professor: MIT, 1960-61; California Inst. of Technology, 1968. *Publications:* The Theory of Electromagnetic Flow Measurement, 1962; A Textbook of Magnetohydrodynamics, 1965; Vector Fields, 1977; various papers on magnetohydrodynamics, etc, in Jl of Fluid Mechanics, and others. *Recreation:* oil painting. *Address:* Trinity College, Cambridge; 158 Huntingdon Road, Cambridge.

SHERFIELD, 1st Baron, *cr* 1964; **Roger Mellor Makins,** GCB 1960 (KCB 1953); GCMG 1955 (KCMG 1949; CMG 1944); DL; Chancellor of Reading University, since 1970; Chairman: Wells Fargo Ltd, since 1972; Lindemann Trust Fellowship Committee; Director, Badger Ltd, since 1981; President, Centre for International Briefing; Member of Council, Royal Albert Hall; *b* 3 Feb. 1904; *e s* of late Brigadier-General Sir Ernest Makins, KBE, CB, DSO; *m* 1934, Alice, *e d* of late Hon. Dwight F. Davis; two *s* four *d*. *Educ:* Winchester; Christ Church, Oxford. First Class Honours in History, 1925; Fellow of All Souls College, 1925-39 and 1957-; called to Bar, Inner Temple, 1927; Foreign Office, 1928; served Washington, 1931-34, Oslo, 1934; Foreign Office, 1934; Assistant Adviser on League of Nations Affairs, 1937; Sec. Intergovernmental Cttee on Refugees from Germany, 1938-39; Adviser on League of Nations Affairs, 1939; Acting First Secretary, 1939; Acting Counsellor, 1940; Adviser to British Delegation, International Labour Conference, New York, 1941; served on Staff of Resident Minister in West Africa, 1942; Counsellor, 1942; Asst to Resident Minister at Allied Force Headquarters, Mediterranean, 1943-44; Minister at British Embassy, Washington, 1945-47; UK rep. on United Nations Interim Commission for Food and Agriculture, 1945; Asst Under-Sec. of State, FO, 1947-48, Dep. Under-Sec. of State, 1948-52; British Ambassador to the United States, 1953-56; Joint Permanent Secretary of the Treasury, 1956-59; Chairman: UKAEA, 1960-64; Hill, Samuel Group, 1966-70; Dir, Times Publishing Co. Ltd, 1964-67. Chairman: Finance for Industry Ltd, 1973-74; Finance Corp. for Industry Ltd, 1973-74; Industrial & Commercial Finance Corp., 1964-74; Estate Duties Investment Trust, 1966-73; Ship Mortgage Finance Co., 1966-74; Technical Develt Capital, 1966-74; A. C. Cossor, 1968-82; Raytheon Europe Internat. Co., 1970-82, and other companies. Pres., BSI, 1970-73. Vice-Chm., The Ditchley Foundn. 1965-74 (Chm., 1962-65). Chm., Governing Body and Fellow of Imperial Coll. of Science and Technology, 1962-74. Fellow, Winchester College, 1962-79 (Warden, 1974-79). Chm., Marshall Aid Commemoration Commn, 1965-73. Trustee, The Times Trust, 1968-73. DL Hants, 1978. Hon. Student, Christ Church, Oxford, 1973; Hon. FICE 1964; Hon. DCL Oxford; Hon. DLitt Reading; Hon. LLD: Sheffield; London; Hon. DL North Carolina; and other American universities and colleges. Benjamin Franklin Medal, RSA, 1982. *Publication:* (ed) Economic and Social Consequences of Nuclear Energy, 1972. *Recreations:* shooting, gardening. *Heir:* *s* Hon. Christopher James Makins [*b* 23 July 1942; *m* 1976, Wendy Cortesi]. *Address:* 81 Onslow Square, SW7; Ham Farm House, Ramsdell, near Kingsclere, Hants. *Clubs:* Pratt's, MCC.

See also Baron Milford.

SHERGOLD, Harold Taplin, CMG 1963; OBE 1958 (MBE 1945); served in Foreign and Commonwealth Office (formerly Foreign Office), 1954-80; *b* 5 Dec. 1915; *s* of late Ernest Henry Shergold; *m* 1949, Bevis Anael, *d* of late William Bernard Reid; no *c*. *Educ:* Peter Symonds' School, Winchester; St Edmund Hall, Oxford; Corpus Christi Coll., Cambridge. Asst Master, Cheltenham Grammar Sch., 1937-40. Joined Hampshire Regt, 1940; transferred to Intelligence Corps, 1941; served in Middle East and Italy, 1941-46 (despatches). Joined Foreign Office, 1947; served in Germany, 1947-54. *Address:* 1 Ancaster Court, Queens Road, Richmond, Surrey TW10 6JJ. *T:* 01-948 2048.

SHERIDAN, Cecil Majella, CMG 1961; *b* 9 Dec. 1911; *s* of late J. P. Sheridan, Liverpool, and Mrs Sheridan (*née* Myerscough), Preston, Lancs; *m* 1949, Monica, *d* of H. F. Ereaut, MBE, Jersey, CI; two *s* one *d*. *Educ:* Ampleforth College, York. Admitted Solicitor, England, 1934; called to Bar, Innner Temple, 1952. Practised as solicitor in Liverpool (Messrs Yates, Sheridan & Co.), 1934-40. Served in RAFVR, General Duties Pilot, 1940-46; resigned with hon. rank of Squadron Leader. Joined Colonial Legal Service, 1946; Crown Counsel and Dep. Public Prosecutor, Malayan Union, 1946-48; Legal Adviser, Malay States of Pahang, Kelantan, Trengganu and Selangor and Settlement of Penang, 1948-55; Legal Draftsman, Fedn of Malaya, 1955-57; Solicitor-General, Fedn of Malaya, 1957-59; Attorney-General, Fedn of Malaya, 1959-63; Attorney-General, Malaysia, retd. Mem. (Fedn of Malaya) Inter-Governmental Cttees for Borneo Territories and Singapore, 1962-63; Chm. Traffic Comrs, E Midland Traffic Area, 1965-81, Dep. Chm., 1981-; Pres., British Assoc. of Malaysia 1964-65. Chm., Malaysia Housing Soc., 1964-65. Hon. PMN (Malaysia), 1963. Associate Mem., Commonwealth Parly Assoc. (UK Branch). *Address:* 18 Private Road, Sherwood, Nottingham NG5 4DB. *Clubs:* East India, Devonshire, Sports and Public Schools; Nottinghamshire.

SHERIDAN, Peter, QC 1977; *b* 29 May 1927; *s* of Hugo and Marie Sheridan. *Educ:* eight schools; Lincoln Coll., Oxford Univ. BA Hons, 1950. Called to the Bar, Middle Temple, 1955. *Recreations:* motor cars, archery. *Address:* 17 Brompton Square, SW3. *T:* 01-584 7850; Pile Oak Lodge, Donhead St Andrew, Wilts. *T:* Donhead 484.

SHERIDAN, Roderick Gerald, OBE 1978; MVO 1968; HM Diplomatic Service, retired; Consul-General, Barcelona and Andorra, 1977-80; *b* 24 Jan. 1921; *s* of late Sir Joseph Sheridan; *m* 1943, Lois Mary (*née* Greene); one *s* one *d*. *Educ:* Downside Sch.; Pembroke Coll., Cambridge. Served War, Coldstream Guards, N Africa and Italy, 1940-46. HM Overseas Colonial Service: Zanzibar and Cyprus, 1946-60; retd as District Comr, Nicosia; HM Diplomatic Service, 1960-: First Sec., Cyprus, 1960-63; Foreign Office, 1964-66; First Sec., Brasilia, 1966-69; FO, 1969-70; Head of Chancery, Oslo, 1970-73; First Sec., Algeciras, 1973-77. *Recreations:* tennis, golf, skiing. *Address:* Torret 28, San Luis, Menorca, Spain. *T:* (971) 36 64 39.

SHERLOCK, Dr Alexander; Member (C) South West Essex, European Parliament, since 1979; Member of Environment Committee (European Democratic (Conservative) Leader) and Development Committee; medical practitioner; *b* 14 Feb. 1922; *s* of Thomas Sherlock, MM, and Evelyn M. Sherlock (*née* Alexander); *m* 1st, 1945, Clarice C. Scarff; one *s* two *d*; 2nd, 1976, Eileen Hall; one step *d*. *Educ:* Magdalen College Sch., Oxford; Stowmarket Grammar Sch.; London Hospital. MB BS (Hons) 1945. Ho. Phys., Ho. Surg., London Hosp.; RAF, 1946-48; Medical Practitioner, Felixstowe, and Consultant/Adviser to many organisations in matters of occupational health, safety and welfare. Called to the Bar, Gray's Inn, 1961. Member: Felixstowe UDC, 1960-74; E Suffolk CC, 1966-74; Suffolk CC, 1974-; Chairman, Fire and Public Protection Cttee, 1977-. OStJ 1974. *Recreation:* gardening. *Address:* 58 Orwell Road, Felixstowe IP11 7PS. *T:* Felixstowe 4503. *Club:* Royal Air Force.

SHERLOCK, Sir Philip (Manderson), KBE 1967 (CBE 1953); Secretary, Association of Caribbean Universities Foundation Inc., since 1979; *b* Jamaica, 25 Feb. 1902; *s* of Rev. Terence Sherlock, Methodist Minister, and Adina Sherlock; *m* 1942, Grace Marjorye Verity; two *s* one *d*. *Educ:* Calabar High Sch., Jamaica. Headmaster, Wolmer's Boys' Sch., Jamaica, 1933-38; Sec., Inst. of Jamaica, 1939-44; Educn Officer, Jamaica Welfare, 1944-47; Dir, Extra-Mural Dept, University Coll. of West Indies, 1947-60, also Vice-Principal, University Coll. of W Indies, 1952-62; Pro-Vice-Chancellor, Univ. of West Indies, 1962, Vice-Chancellor, 1963-69; Sec.-Gen., Assoc. of Caribbean Univs & Res. Insts, 1969. Hon. LLD: Leeds, 1959; Carleton, 1967; St Andrews, 1968; Hon. DCL, New Brunswick, 1966; Hon. DLitt: Acadia, 1966; Miami, 1971; Univ. of WI, 1972. *Publications:* Anansi the Spider Man, 1956; (with John Parry) Short History of the West Indies, 1956; Caribbean Citizen, 1957; West Indian Story, 1960; Three Finger Jack, 1961; Jamaica, A Junior History, 1966; West Indian Folk Tales, 1966; West Indies, 1966; Land and People of the West Indies, 1967; Belize, a Junior History, 1969; The Iguana's Tail, 1969; West Indian Nations, 1973; Ears and Tails and Common Sense, 1974; Shout for Freedom, 1976; Norman Manley, a biography, 1980; educational books and articles. *Recreations:* reading, writing, cooking. *Address:* University of Miami, PO Box 248073, Coral Gables, Florida 33124, USA. *Club:* National Liberal.

SHERLOCK, Prof. Dame Sheila (Patricia Violet), DBE 1978; MD; FRCP; FRCPEd; Professor of Medicine, University of London, at the Royal Free Hospital School of Medicine, since 1959; *b* 31 March 1918; *d* of late Samuel Philip Sherlock and Violet Mary Catherine Beckett; *m* 1951, David Geraint James, *qv*; two *d*. *Educ:* Folkestone County Sch.; Edinburgh Univ. Ettles Scholar, 1941; Beit Memorial Research Fellow, 1942-47; Rockefeller Fellow, Yale University, USA, 1948. Physician and Lecturer in Medicine, Postgraduate Medical School of London, 1948-59; Bradshaw Lecturer, RCP, 1961; Rolleston Lecturer, RCP, 1968; Lumleian Lecturer, RCP, 1978. RCP: Councillor, 1964-68; Censor, 1970-72; Senior Censor and Vice-Pres., 1976-77. Mem. Senate, Univ. of London, 1976-81. Hon. Member: Gastro-enterological Societies of America, 1963, Australasia, 1965, Mexico, 1968, Czechoslovakia, 1968, Yugoslavia, 1981; Assoc. of Amer. Physicians, 1973; Assoc. of Alimentary Systems, 1973. Hon. FACP; Hon. FRCP (C); Hon. FRCP (I). Hon. DSc City Univ. of NY; Hon. MD: Lisbon, 1981; Oslo, 1981; Hon. LLD Aberdeen, 1982. William Cullen Prize, 1962 (shared); Jimenez-Diaz Prize, 1980; Thannhauser Prize, 1980. *Publications:* Diseases of the Liver and Biliary System, 6th edn, 1981; papers on liver structure and function in various medical journals, since 1943. *Recreations:* cricket, travel. *Address:* 41 York Terrace East, NW1 4PT. *T:* 01-486 4560.

SHERMAN, Sir Louis, (Sir Lou Sherman), Kt 1975; OBE 1967; JB; Chairman, Housing Corporation, 1977-80; Deputy Chairman, Harlow Development Corporation. Initiated Lea Valley Regional Park Authority. JP Inner London Area. *Recreations:* politics, reading, talking. *Club:* Reform.

SHERRARD, Michael David, QC 1968; a Recorder of the Crown Court, since 1974; *b* 23 June 1928; *er s* of late Morris Sherrard and Ethel Sherrard; *m* 1952, Shirley (C. B. Piper, writer), *d* of late Maurice and Lucy Bagrit; two *s. Educ:* King's Coll., London. LLB 1949. Called to Bar, Middle Temple, 1949, Bencher 1977, Mem. Senate, 1977-80. Mem., SE Circuit, 1950. Mem., Winn Cttee on Personal Injury Litigation, 1966; Mem. Council and Exec. Cttee, Justice, British Section, Internat. Commn of Jurists, 1974-; Dept of Trade Inspector, London Capital Group, 1975-77; Chm., Normansfield Hosp. Inquiry, 1977-78; Comr for trial of local govt election petitions (under Representation of the People Act 1949), 1978-80. *Recreations:* oil painting, listening to opera. *Address:* 2 Crown Office Row, Temple, EC4. *T:* 01-583 2681; 14 Burgess Hill, Hampstead, NW2. *T:* 01-435 7828.

SHERRIN, Ned, (Edward George Sherrin); film, theatre and television producer, director and writer; *b* Low Ham, Som, 18 Feb. 1931; *s* of late T. A. Sherrin and D. F. Sherrin (*née* Drewett). *Educ:* Sexey's Sch., Bruton; Exeter Coll., Oxford; Gray's Inn. Produce: ATV, Birmingham, 1955-57; BBC TV, 1957-66 (prod. and dir. That Was The Week That Was). Produced films: The Virgin Soldiers (with Leslie Gilliat) 1968; Every Home Should Have One, 1969; (with Terry Glinwood) Up Pompeii, 1971; Up the Chastity Belt, 1971; Girl Stroke Boy, 1971; Rentadick, 1971; Up the Front, 1972; The National Health, 1972; TV plays (with Caryl Brahms) include: Little Beggars; Benbow was his Name; Take a Sapphire; The Great Inimitable Mr Dickens; Feydeau Farces; plays (with Caryl Brahms): No Bed for Bacon; Cindy-Ella or I Gotta Shoe, 1962-63; The Spoils, 1968; Nicholas Nickleby, 1969; Sing a Rude Song, 1970; Fish out of Water, 1971; Liberty Ranch, 1972; Nickleby and Me, 1975; Beecham, 1980; The Mitford Girls, 1981; directed: Come Spy with Me, Whitehall, 1967; (and appeared in) Side by Side by Sondheim, Mermaid, 1976, NY 1977; Only in America (with D. Yakir), Roundhouse, 1980; Noël, Goodspeed, USA, 1981. TV appearances include: Song by Song, BBC and Yorkshire TV series; Quiz of the Week, BBC; The Rather Reassuring Programme, BBC; We Interrupt this Week, PBS, NY. Governor, BFI, 1980-. Guild of TV Producers and Directors' Awards; Ivor Novello Award, 1966. *Publications:* (with Caryl Brahms) Cindy-Ella or I Gotta Shoe, 1962; Rappell 1910, 1964; Benbow was his Name, 1967; Ooh la! la! (short stories), 1973; After You Mr Feydeau, 1975; many songs. *Address:* c/o Margaret Ramsay Ltd, 14a Goodwin's Court, WC2. *T:* 01-240 0691.

SHERRY, Mrs Vincent; see Robinson, Kathleen M.

SHERSBY, (Julian) Michael; MP (C) Hillingdon, Uxbridge, since 1974 (Uxbridge, Dec. 1972-1974); *b* Ickenham, 17 Feb. 1933; *s* of William Henry and Elinor Shersby; *m* 1958, Barbara Joan, *d* of John Henry Barrow; one *s* one *d. Educ:* John Lyon Sch., Harrow-on-the-Hill. Mem., Paddington Borough Council, 1959-64; Mem., Westminster City Council, 1964-71; Deputy Lord Mayor of Westminster, 1967-68. Chm., Uxbridge Div. Young Conservatives, 1951-52; Conservative and Unionist Party Organisation, 1952-58; Sec., Assoc. of Specialised Film Producers, 1958-62; Dir, British Industrial Film Assoc., 1962-66; Dir, British Sugar Bureau, 1966-77, Dir-Gen., 1977-; Sec., UK Sugar Industry Assoc., 1978. PPS to Minister of Aerospace and Shipping, DTI, 1974; Jt Sec., Conservative Party Parly Industry Cttee, 1972-74; Chairman: Cons. Party Trade Cttee, 1974-76 (Vice-Chm., 1977-79); Cons. Party Parly Food Sub-Cttee, 1979-; Vice-Chairman: Cons. Party Parly Environment Cttee, 1979-; Cons. Party Parly Small Businesses Cttee, 1979-80; Member: CPA Delegn to Caribbean, 1975; British Parly delegn to UN, 1978; CPA Delegn to Falkland Islands, 1981; promoted Private Member's Bills: Town and Country Amenities Act, 1974; Parks Regulation (Amendment) Act, 1974; Stock Exchange (Completion of Bargains) Act, 1976; Gaming (Amendment) Act, 1980; Copyright Act (1956) Amendment Act, 1982. Jt Sec., Parly and Scientific Cttee, 1977-80, Vice Pres., 1980-. Mem. Court, Brunel Univ., 1975-; Pres., Abbeyfield Uxbridge Soc., 1975-. *Recreation:* sailing. *Address:* Anvil House, Park Road, Stoke Poges, Bucks. *T:* Farnham Common 4548. *Club:* Conservative (Uxbridge).

SHERSTON-BAKER, Sir Humphrey Dodington Benedict, 6th Bt, *cr* 1796; *b* 13 Oct. 1907; *s* of Lt-Col Sir Dodington Sherston-Baker, 5th Bt, and Irene Roper (*d* 1950), *yr d* of Sir Roper Parkington; *S* father, 1944; *m* 1938, Margaret Alice (Bobby) (marriage dissolved, 1953), *o d* of H. W. Binns, 9 Campden Street, W, and Blythburgh, Suffolk; one *s* three *d. Educ:* Downside; Christ's College, Cambridge. *Heir: s* Robert George Humphrey Sherston-Baker, *b* 3 April 1951. *Address:* 22 Frognal Court, NW3 5HP.

SHERWIN, Frederick George James, CB 1967; Chief Inspector, Board of HM Customs and Excise, 1963-69, retired; *b* 3 Sept. 1909; *s* of J. F. Sherwin and H. E. Sherwin, Woolston, Hants; *m* 1966, Margaret Dorothea Snow, *d* of Thomas L. H. Snow, Gidea Park, Essex; one *s. Educ:* Gosport Secondary Sch.; HM Dockyard Sch., Portsmouth. Civil Servant; entered Customs and Excise, 17 Feb. 1930. *Recreations:* gardening, walking. *Address:* 10 Maytree Avenue, Findon Valley, Worthing, West Sussex BN14 0HJ. *T:* Findon 3145.

SHERWIN-WHITE, Adrian Nicholas, MA; FBA 1956; Reader in Ancient History, University of Oxford, 1966-79; Fellow and Tutor of St John's College, Oxford, 1936-79, Fellow Emeritus 1979; Keeper of the Groves, 1970; *b* 1911; *s* of H. N. Sherwin-White, Solicitors' Dept of LCC. *Educ:* Merchant Taylors' School; St John's College, Oxford (Derby Scholar, 1935; Arnold Historical Essay Prize, 1935; MA, 1937). War Service in RN and Admiralty, 1942-45. Conington Prize, 1947. Sarum Lecturer, Oxford Univ., 1960-61; Gray Lecturer, Cambridge Univ., 1965-66; Special Lectr, Open Univ., 1973-81. Pres., Soc. for Promotion of Roman Studies, 1974-77. Corresp. Fellow, Bayerische Akademie der Wissenschaften, 1977. *Publications:* Roman Citizenship, 1939, enlarged edn 1973; Ancient Rome (Then and There Series), 1959; Roman Society and Roman Law in the New Testament, 1963; Historical Commentary on the Letters of Pliny the Younger, 1966; Racial Prejudice in Imperial Rome, 1967; Roman Foreign Policy in the East 167BC—AD1, 1982; ed Geographical Handbook Series, Admiralty; contrib. Jl Roman Studies. *Recreations:* watching horses and growing hardy plants. *Address:* St John's College, Oxford. *T:* Frilford Heath 390496.

SHERWOOD, Bishop Suffragan of, since 1975; **Rt. Rev. Harold Richard Darby;** *b* 28 Feb. 1919; *s* of late William and Miriam Darby; *m* 1949, Audrey Elizabeth Lesley Green; two *s* three *d. Educ:* Cathedral School, Shanghai; St John's Coll., Durham (BA). Military service, 1939-45; Durham Univ., 1946-50. Deacon 1950; priest 1951; Curate of Leyton, 1950-51; Curate of Harlow, 1951-53; Vicar of Shrub End, Colchester, 1953-59; Vicar of Waltham Abbey, 1959-70; Dean of Battle, 1970-75. Central Chaplain to Mothers' Union, 1978-. *Recreation:* vintage cars. *Address:* Applegarth, Halam, Notts. *T:* Southwell 814041.

SHERWOOD, (Robert) Antony (Frank), CMG 1981; Assistant Director-General, British Council, 1977-81, retired; *b* 29 May 1923; *s* of Frank Henry Sherwood and Mollie Sherwood (*née* Moore); *m* 1953, Margaret Elizabeth Simpson; two *s* two *d. Educ:* Christ's Hospital; St John's Coll., Oxford (BA 1949, MA 1953). War service, RAF, 1942-46. Apptd to British Council, 1949; Lectr, Turkey, 1949-50; Asst Dir, Ibadan, Nigeria, 1950-55; Lectr, Syria, 1955-56; Fellowships Dept, 1957; Asst Rep., Uganda, 1957-59; Representative: Somaliland Protectorate, 1959-60; Somali Republic, 1960-63; Dir, Commonwealth Dept, 1963-66; Dep. Controller, Home Div., 1966-69; Representative, Nigeria, 1969-72; Controller, Africa and Middle East Div., 1972-77. *Recreations:* reading, walking, current affairs, sport, theatre, gardening. *Address:* 18 Rivermount Gardens, Guildford, Surrey GU2 5DN. *T:* Guildford 38277.

SHERWOOD, Prof. Thomas, FRCP, FRCR; Professor of Radiology, University of Cambridge, since 1978; Fellow of Girton College, Cambridge, 1982; *b* 25 Sept. 1934; *m* 1961, Margaret Gooch; two *s* one *d. Educ:* Frensham Heights Sch.; Guy's Hospital, London. MA; DCH. Consultant Radiologist, Hammersmith Hospital and St Peter's Hospital, 1969-77. *Publications:* Uroradiology, 1980; papers in medical and radiological jls, 1964-. *Recreations:* music, reading and writing. *Address:* Department of Radiology, Addenbrooke's Hospital, Hills Road, Cambridge CB2 2QQ. *T:* Cambridge 45171.

SHESTOPAL, Dawn Angela, (Mrs N. J. Shestopal); see Freedman, D. A.

SHETH, Pranlal; Director: Abbey Life Assurance Co. Ltd, since 1974; Ambassador Life Assurance Co. Ltd, since 1980; Abbey Life Assurance (Ireland) Ltd, since 1981; Legal Director, Hartford Europe Group of Companies, since 1977; *b* 20 Dec. 1924; *s* of Purashotam Virji Sheth and Sakarben Sheth; *m* 1951, Indumati Sheth; one *s* one *d.* Called to the Bar, Lincoln's Inn, 1962. Journalist, Kenya, 1943-52; Chm., Nyanza Farmers' Cooperative Soc., 1954-60; Mem., Central Agriculture Bd, Kenya, 1963-66; Dep. Chm., Asian Hosp. Authority, 1964-66; Mem., Economic Planning and Develt Council, Kenya, 1964-66. Group Sec., Abbey Life Gp of Cos, 1971; Chief Editor, Gujarat Samachar Weekly, 1972-73; Mem., N Metropolitan Conciliation Cttee, Race Relations Bd, 1973-77; a Dep. Chm., CRE, 1977-80; Trustee, Project Fullemploy (Charitable Trust), 1977-; Vice-Patron, UK Assoc., Internat. Year of the Child, 1978-80. Fellow, Inst. of Directors, 1977; FBIM 1980. Mem., Court of Governors, Polytech. of N London, 1979-. *Address:* (home) 70 Howberry Road, Edgware, Mddx. *T:* 01-952 2413; (business) Abbey Life House, 1/3 St Paul's Churchyard, EC4M 8AR. *T:* 01-248 9111.

SHEVILL, Rt. Rev. Ian (Wotton Allnutt), AO 1976; MA (Sydney); *b* 11 May 1917; *s* of Erson James Shevill; *m* 1st, 1959, Dr June (*d* 1970), *d* of Basil Stephenson, Worthing; two *s* ; 2nd, 1974, Ann, *d* of A. Brabazon, Winton, Queensland. *Educ:* Scot's Coll., Sydney; Sydney Univ.; School of Oriental and African Studies, London Univ.; Moore Theological Coll., Sydney, BA, 1939, MA, 1945, Sydney; ThL, ThD, 1953, Moore Theol Coll. Deacon, 1940; Priest, 1941; Curate of St Paul, Burwood, 1940-45; Organising Secretary of the Australian Board of Missions, for Province of Queensland, 1946-47; Education Secretary, Society for the Propagation of Gospel, 1948-51; Bishop of North Queensland, 1953-70; Secretary, United Society for the Propagation of the Gospel, 1970-73; Asst Bishop, Diocese of London, 1971-73; Bishop of Newcastle, NSW, 1973-77. *Publications:* New Dawn in Papua, 1946; Pacific Conquest, 1948; God's World at Prayer, 1951; Orthodox and other Eastern Churches in Australia, 1964; Half Time, 1966; Going it with God, 1969.

Address: 13 Cottesmore Street, Fig Tree Pocket, Brisbane, Qld 4069, Australia. *Club:* Athenæum.

SHEWAN, Henry Alexander, CB 1974; OBE (mil.) 1946; QC (Scotland) 1949; Commissioner of Social Security (formerly National Insurance), 1955-81 (part time 1979-81); *b* 7 November 1906; *s* of late James Smith Shewan, Advocate in Aberdeen; *m* 1937, Ann Fraser Thomson (*d* 1977), Aberdeen; two *s. Educ:* Robert Gordon's Coll., Aberdeen; Aberdeen Univ.; Emmanuel College, Cambridge. Advocate, 1933. Served War of 1939-45, RAF, 1940-45, Sqdn Leader. Member Scottish Medical Practices Cttee, 1948-55; Member Court of Session Rules Council, 1948-55; Dep. Chm. Panel of Arbiters and Referee under Coal Industry Nationalisation Act, 1949-55; Chm., Medical Appeal Tribunal National Insurance (Industrial Injuries) Act, 1950-55; Chairman General Nursing Council for Scot., 1960-62. Referee under Child Benefit Act 1975, 1976-79. *Address:* 7 Winton Loan, Edinburgh EH10 7AN. *T:* 031-445 3239. *Clubs:* New (Edinburgh); Honourable Company of Edinburgh Golfers (Muirfield).

SHIACH, Sheriff Gordon Iain Wilson; Sheriff of Lothian and Borders, at Linlithgow, since 1979; *b* 15 Oct. 1935; *o s* of late Dr John Crawford Shiach, FDS, QHDS, and of Florence Bygott Wilson; *m* 1962, Margaret Grant Smith; two *d. Educ:* Lathallan Sch.; Gordonstoun Sch.; Edinburgh Univ. (MA, LLB); Open Univ. (BA Hons). Admitted to Faculty of Advocates, 1960; practised as Advocate, 1960-72; Tutor, Dept of Evidence and Pleading, Univ. of Edinburgh, 1963-66; Clerk to Rules Council of Court of Session, 1963-72; Standing Jun. Counsel in Scotland to Post Office, 1969-72; Sheriff of Tayside, Central and Fife, at Dunfermline, 1972-79. *Recreations:* orienteering, calligraphy, classical guitar. *Address:* Sheriffs' Chambers, Sheriff Court House, Court Square, Linlithgow EH49 7EQ. *Club:* New (Edinburgh).

SHIELD, Leslie, TD; DL; a Recorder of the Crown Court, since 1980; *b* 8 May 1916; *s* of Tom Shield and Annie Maud Shield; *m* 1941, Doris Leather; one *s. Educ:* Cowley Sch., St Helens; Univ. of Liverpool (LLB 1936, LLM 1938). Qualified solicitor, 1939, admitted 1945. Served War, 1939-46: commnd 5th Bn Prince of Wales' Volunteers (S Lancs) Regt; demob., Major. Entered into gen. practice as solicitor, 1946. DL Merseyside, 1976. *Recreations:* gardening (particular interest, orchids), music. *Address:* 185 Higher Lane, Rainford, St Helens, Merseyside WA11 8NF. *T:* Rainford 2708.

SHIELDS, John Sinclair; *b* 4 Feb. 1903; *s* of Rev. W. H. Shields and Margaret Louisa (*née* Sinclair); *m* 1st, 1924, Norah Fane Smith; three *d* ; 2nd, 1963, Mrs Noreen Moultrie, widow of Comdr John Moultrie. *Educ:* Charterhouse; Lincoln Coll., Oxford (MA). Headmaster: Wem Grammar School, 1934-47; Queen Mary's School, Basingstoke, 1947-56; Headmaster, Peter Symonds' School, Winchester, 1957-63; Vice-Pres. Classical Assoc., 1958; Mem., Broadcasting Cttee, 1960. *Recreation:* golf. *Address:* North End House, Hursley, Winchester, Hants.

SHIELDS, (Leslie) Stuart, QC 1970; a Recorder of the Crown Court, since 1972; *b* 15 May 1919; *m* 1941, Maureen Margaret McKinstry; two *s* two *d* (and one *s* decd). *Educ:* St Paul's School; Corpus Christi College, Oxford. Paid Local Serjeant, Oxford and Buckinghamshire Light Infantry, 1945-47. Called to the Bar, Middle Temple, 1948; Bencher, 1977. Mem., Criminal Injuries Compensation Bd, 1981-. *Recreation:* music. *Address:* Devereux Chambers, Devereux Court, Temple, WC2R 3JJ.

SHIELDS, Sir Neil (Stanley), Kt 1964; MC 1946; management consultant and company director; Director: Central and Sheerwood PLC; Chesham Amalgamations and Investments Ltd; Newton Chambers & Co. PLC; Sheerwood Corporate Services Ltd; The Sheerwood Trust Ltd; Trianco Group Ltd; Chairman: Holcombe Holdings PLC; The Standard Catalogue Company Ltd; Trianco Redfyre Ltd; Chairman, Commission for New Towns, since 1982 (Member, since 1981); *b* 7 September 1919; *o s* of late Archie Shields and Mrs Hannah Shields; *m* 1970, Gloria Dawn Wilson. Member of Honourable Artillery Company 1939-. Served in Royal Artillery, 1939-46; commnd 1940; Major 1943. Prospective candidate (C) North St Pancras 1947 and contested by-election, 1949. Chairman: Camden Conservative Cttee, 1965-67; Hampstead Conservative Assoc., 1954-65 (Vice-Chm., 1951-54); Hon. Treas. 1965-67; National Union of Conservative and Unionist Assocs: Chm. of London Area, 1961-63 (Vice-Chm. 1959-61); Mem. of National Executive, 1955-59, 1961-67, 1968-69; Hampstead Borough Council: Mem. 1947-65; Deputy Leader, 1952-61; Chm. of Works Cttee, 1951-55; Chm. of Finance Cttee, 1955-59. Mem. Council, Aims of Industry. *Recreations:* reading, music, walking, motoring, wining and dining. *Address:* 12 London House, Avenue Road, NW8 7PX. *T:* 01-586 4155. *Clubs:* Carlton, HAC.

SHIELDS, Prof. Robert, MD, FRCS, FRCSE; Professor of Surgery since 1969, and Dean of the Faculty of Medicine since 1982, University of Liverpool; Consultant Surgeon, Royal Liverpool Hospital and Broadgreen Hospital, since 1969; *b* 8 Nov. 1930; *o s* of late Robert Alexander Shields and Isobel Dougall Shields; *m* 1957, Grace Marianne Swinburn; one *s* two *d. Educ:* John Neilson Institution, Paisley; Univ. of Glasgow. MB, ChB 1953 (Asher-Asher Medal and MacLeod Medal); MD (Hons and Bellahouston Medal) 1965; FRCSE 1959; FRCS 1966. House appts, Western Infirmary, Glasgow, 1953-54; RAMC, Captain attached 1 Bn Argyll and Sutherland Highlanders, 1954-56; RAMC (TA), Major (Surg. Specialist) attached 7 Bn A & S H, 1956-61. Hall Fellow, Univ. of Glasgow, 1957-58; Mayo Foundn Fellow,

1959-60; Lectr in Surgery, Univ. of Glasgow, 1960-63; Sen. Lectr and Reader in Surgery, Welsh Nat. Sch. of Medicine, 1963-69. Member: Surgical Research Soc. (Hon. Sec. 1972-76 and Pres. 1983-); British Soc. of Gastroenterology; Internat. Surgical Gp; Gen. Medical Council, 1982-; Assoc. of Surgs of GB and Ire. (Mem. Council 1966-69); Cell Bd, MRC, 1974-77; Liverpool AHA(T) (Chm. Area/Univ. Liaison Cttee), 1974-78; Mersey RHA, 1982-; Editorial Bd of Brit. Jl of Surgery, 1970-, and of Gut, 1969-76. Marjorie Budd Prof., Univ. of Bristol, 1983. Former Visiting Prof., Univs of Toronto, Virginia, Witwatersrand, Rochester (NY), Hong Kong, and Examiner in Surgery, Univs of Glasgow, Edinburgh, Dundee, Leicester, Sheffield, Lagos, Amman, Riyadh, Malta. Moynihan Medal (Assoc. of Surgs of GB and Ire.). *Publications:* (ed jtly): Surgical Emergencies II, 1979; Textbook of Surgery, 1983; contribs to medical and surgical jls relating to surgery and gastroenterology. *Recreations:* sailing and walking. *Address:* 81 Meols Drive, West Kirby, Wirral L48 5DF. *T:* 051-632 3588. *Club:* Army and Navy.

SHIELDS, Maj.-Gen. Ronald Frederick, OBE 1943; BSc (Eng); CEng; FIEE; *b* 4 November 1912; *s* of late John Benjamin Frederic Shields, Chichester; *m* 1944, Lorna, *d* of late Frederick Murgatroyd, Manchester; one *s* one *d. Educ:* Portsmouth Grammar School. Lieut RAOC 1936. Served War of 1939-45 in Middle East and NW Europe; transferred to REME, 1942; Staff College Camberley, 1945; MELF, 1948-51; AQMG, HQ Northern Comd, 1952-55; War Office, 1956-59; REME Training Centre, 1959-62; DEME, HQ, BAOR, 1962-65; Comdt, Technical Group, REME, 1965-68; retd 1968. Col, 1955; Brig. 1962; Maj.-Gen. 1965. Col Comdt, REME, 1968-73. *Address:* 58 Petersfield Road, Midhurst, West Sussex.

SHIELDS, Ronald McGregor Pollock; Managing Director, Associated Newspapers Group Ltd, since Dec. 1970; *b* 30 July 1921; *s* of Thomas Shields and Beatrice Gordon; *m* 1948, Jacqueline (*née* Cowan); one *s* one *d. Educ:* Swanage Grammar Sch.; London Univ. (BSc (Econ)). Served War of 1939-45, Royal Artillery. Joined Associated Newspapers Gp, 1948; spent several years in various depts of the Co. and a year at Associated Rediffusion in charge of Audience Research. Set up the research co. National Opinion Polls, and was made Advertisement Dir of Associated Newspapers, 1963. Director: AmLaw Publishing Corp. (USA); Associated Investments (Furniture) Ltd; Associated Investments Harmsworth Ltd; Consolidated-Bathurst Ltd (Canada); Blackfriars Oil Co.; Blox Services Ltd; Bouverie Investments No 2 Ltd; Burton Reproductions Ltd; Continental Daily Mail SA (France); Copthall Developments Ltd; Crowvale Properties Ltd; Daily Mail Ltd; Euromoney Publications Ltd; Greenwall Warehousing; Harmsworth Holdings Ltd (Canada); Harmsworth Press Ltd; Harmsworth Publications Ltd; Harmsworth Publishing Ltd; London Cab Co.; John M. Newton & Sons Ltd; NOP Market Research Ltd; Piccadilly Theatre Ltd; Purfleet Deep Wharf & Storage; G. T. Rackstraw Ltd; Retail Audits Ltd; Soho Weekly News Inc. (USA); Southern Television; Taylor Brothers; Transport Group (Holdings) Ltd; Weekend Publications Ltd; Wyndhams Theatres Ltd. FSS. *Recreations:* golf, the theatre. *Address:* New Carmelite House, Carmelite Street, EC4. *T:* 01-353 6000.

SHIELDS, Stuart; see Shields, L. S.

SHIELL, James Wyllie, BSc, FICE, FIWES; Consultant, R. H. Cuthbertson & Partners, Consulting Engineers, Edinburgh; *b* 20 Aug. 1912; *yr s* of late George Douglas Shiell, farmer, Rennieston, Jedburgh and Janet Gladstone Wyllie; *m* 1941, Maureen Cameron Macpherson Hunter, *d* of late Thomas Hunter, Leeds; two *s. Educ:* Jedburgh Grammar and Kelso High Schools; Edinburgh Univ. Municipal Engrg posts in Edinburgh, Southampton, Sunderland and Leeds, 1934-39; Sen. Engr on Staff of J. D. & D. M. Watson, Consulting Engrs, Westminster, 1939-43 and 1945-47; Civil Engr on wartime service with Admty, 1943-45; Sen. Engr, Min. of Agriculture, 1947-49; Engrg Inspector, Dept of Health for Scotland, 1949-62; Dep. Chief Engr, Scottish Development Dept, 1962-68; Chief Engr, Scottish Development Dept, 1968-75. Mem. Amenity Cttee set up by Sec. of State for Scotland under Hydro-Electric (Scotland) Develt Acts. Hon. FInstWPC. *Recreations:* bowling, photography. *Address:* 25 Mortorhall Road, Edinburgh EH9 2HS. *T:* 031-667 8528.

SHIERLAW, Norman Craig; Senior Partner, N. C. Shierlaw & Associates (Stock and Sharebrokers), since 1968; *b* 17 Aug. 1921; *s* of Howard Allison Shierlaw and Margaret Bruce; *m* 1944, Patricia Yates; two *d. Educ:* Pulteney Grammar Sch., Adelaide; St Peter's Coll., Adelaide; Univ. of Adelaide (BE). Assoc. Mem. Australian Inst. Mining and Metallurgy; FSASM; Mining Manager's Certificate. War Service, AIF, 1941-45 (War Service medals). Mining Engr with North Broken Hill Ltd, 1949-58; Sharebroker's Clerk, 1959-60; Partner, F. W. Porter & Co. (Sharebrokers), 1960-68. Director: Australian Development Ltd, 1959-; Poseidon Ltd, 1968-77; North Flinders Mines Ltd, 1969-77; Nobelex NL, 1974-. FAIM 1971. *Recreations:* golf, tennis. *Address:* N. C. Shierlaw & Associates, 28 Grenfell Street, Adelaide, SA 5000, Australia. *T:* Adelaide 51-7468. *Clubs:* Royal Automobile (Sydney); Naval, Military and Air Force, Stock Exchange, Kooyonga Golf (Adelaide); West Australian (Perth).

SHIFFNER, Sir Henry David, 8th Bt, *cr* 1818; Company Director; *b* 2 Feb. 1930; *s* of Major Sir Henry Shiffner, 7th Bt, and Margaret Mary, *er d* of late Sir Ernest Gowers, GCB, GBE; *S* father, 1941; *m* 1st, 1949, Dorothy Jackson (marr. diss. 1956); one *d* (and one *d* decd); 2nd, 1957, Beryl (marr. diss. 1970), *d* of George Milburn, Saltdean, Sussex; one *d*; 3rd, 1970, Joaquina Ramos Lopez. *Educ:* Rugby; Trinity Hall, Cambridge. *Heir: cousin* George Frederick Shiffner [*b* 3 August 1936; *m* 1961, Dorothea Helena Cynthia, *d* of late T. H. McLean; one *s* one *d*]. *Club:* Royal Automobile.

SHILLINGFORD, Prof. John Parsons, MD (Harvard and London), FRCP, FACC; Sir John McMichael Professor of Cardiovascular Medicine, Royal Postgraduate Medical School, London University, 1976–79, now Emeritus Professor (Director, Cardiovascular Research Unit, and Professor of Angiocardiology, 1966–76); Hon. Medical Director, British Heart Foundation; *b* 15 April 1914; *s* of Victor Shillingford and Ethel Eugenie Parsons; *m* 1947, Doris Margaret Franklin; two *s* one *d. Educ:* Bishops Stortford; Harvard Univ.; London Hosp. Med. Sch. Rockefeller Student, Harvard Med. Sch., 1939–42; House appts, Presbyterian Hosp., New York, and London Hosp., 1943–45; Med. First Asst, London Hosp., 1945–52; Sen. Lectr Royal Postgrad. Med. Sch., 1958–62. Pres., Sect. Experimental Med., Royal Soc. Med., 1968; Sec., Brit. Cardiac Soc., 1963–70; Chm. Org. Cttee, Sixth World Congress Cardiology, 1970; Lumleian Lectr, RCP, 1972. Member: Assoc. Physicians Gt Brit.; Med. Res. Soc.; Med. Soc. London; Royal Soc. Med.; Comité Recherche Médicale, EEC; various cttees, Brit. Heart Foundn. Hon. Mem.: Hellenic Cardiac Soc.; Cardiac Soc. of Yugoslavia; Polish Cardiac Soc.; Cardiological Soc. of India; French Cardiac Soc.; Corr. Mem., Australian Cardiac Soc.; Fellow, Amer. Coll. of Cardiology; Hon. FACP; Editor, Cardiovascular Research. Visiting Prof., Australian Heart Foundn, 1965; lectured extensively in Europe, USA, S America, Africa, Middle East. James Berry Prize, RCS. *Publications:* numerous scientific papers, mainly on heart disease and coronary thrombosis. *Recreation:* sailing. *Address:* 6 Hurlingham Court, Ranelagh Gardens, SW6 3SH. *T:* 01-736 6746; Forbes, Harbour Road, Old Bosham, West Sussex. *T:* Bosham 3060. *Clubs:* Athenæum, Hurlingham.

SHILLINGFORD, Romeo Arden Coleridge, MBE 1977; High Commissioner for the Commonwealth of Dominica, in London, since 1978; concurrently non-resident Ambassador to France, Spain, Belgium, West Germany and EEC Commission, Brussels; *b* 11 Feb. 1936; *s* of Stafford Shillingford and Ophelia Thomas, step *d* of Hosford Samuel O'Brien and *d* of Clarita (*née* Hunt), Roseau, Dominica; *m* 1st, Evelyn Blanche Hart; one *s* one *d* ; 2nd, Maudline Joan Green; three *s. Educ:* Wesley High Sch., Roseau Boys' Sch., Dominica; grammar school; School of Law. Member, Hon. Soc. Inner Temple. Joined Dominican Civil Service, 1957, after brief period as solicitor's clerk; junior clerk, various Govt Depts, Dominica, 1957-59; Clerk of Court, then Chief Clerk, Magistrates' Office, 1960–61; joined staff, Eastern Caribbean Commn, London, on secondment from Dominican CS, 1965; served variously as Migrants' Welfare Officer, Students' Officer, Asst Trade Sec. and PA to Comr, 1968-71; Admin. Asst, Consular and Protocol Affairs, 1973–78 (actg Comr, several occasions, 1975–78). Past Member, numerous cttees and ad hoc bodies for West Indian Immigrant Welfare and Education; Dep. Chm., Bd of Governors, W Indian Students' Centre, 1970-75, Chm., 1976-79; Member, West India Cttee (Vice-Pres. 1979-). Liaison Officer, Victoria League for Commonwealth Friendship; Founder-Mem. and Vice-Chm., Jaycees (Dominica Jun. Chamber of Commerce). *Recreations:* cricket, collecting authentic folk music, swimming. *Address:* Dominica High Commission, 10 Kensington Court, W8 5DL. *T:* 01-937 9522, 01-937 0051.

SHILLINGTON, Courtenay Alexander Rives, CB 1953; CVO 1972; VRD 1941; DL; Commodore, RNVR, retired 1954; *b* 18 Mar. 1902; *s* of Thomas Courtenay Shillington, Glenmachan Tower, Belfast, and Bertha Wydown Hall, Charlottesville, Virginia, USA; one *d. Educ:* Bilston Grange; Rugby. Entered RNVR, Sub-Lt, 1924; ADC to: Duke of Abercorn, Northern Ireland, 1927-45; Earl Granville, Governor of Northern Ireland, 1945-52; Lord Wakehurst, Governor of Northern Ireland, 1952-64; Lord Erskine of Rerrick, Governor of NI, 1964-67; Lord Grey of Naunton, Governor of NI, 1967-73. Served War of 1939-45, in RN as Capt. RNVR, 1939-46; Comdr, Auxiliary Patrol, Scapa, 1939; Dep. Chief of Staff and Naval Liaison Officer to Field Marshal Lord Gort, Governor of Malta, 1942; Chief of Staff to Sen. Naval Officer, Persian Gulf, 1942; Naval Officer in Charge, Bahrain, 1943-45. DL County Down, 1956. *Recreation:* motor sport. *Address:* Glenganagh Farm Cottage, Groomsport, Bangor, County Down, Northern Ireland. *Clubs:* Naval and Military; Ulster Automobile (Belfast).

SHILLINGTON, Sir (Robert Edward) Graham, Kt 1972; CBE 1970 (OBE 1959; MBE 1951); DL; Chief Constable, Royal Ulster Constabulary, 1970-73; *b* 2 April 1911; *s* of Major D. Graham Shillington, DL, MP, and Mrs Louisa Shillington (*née* Collen); *m* 1935, Mary E. R. Bulloch (*d* 1977), Holywood, Co. Down; two *s* one *d. Educ:* Sedbergh Sch., Yorks; Clare Coll., Cambridge. Royal Ulster Constabulary: Officer Cadet, 1934; 3rd Class District Inspector, 1934; 2nd Class District Inspector, 1936; 1st Class District Inspector, 1944; County Inspector, 1953; Commissioner, Belfast, 1961; Deputy Inspector General (Deputy Chief Constable), 1969-70. Formerly Chm., Belfast Voluntary Welfare Soc. DL Co. Down, 1975. King's Coronation Medal, 1937; Queen's Coronation Medal, 1953; Police Long Service and Good Conduct Medal, 1955. *Recreations:* golf, gardening. *Address:* Ardeevin, 184 Bangor Road, Holywood, Co. Down. *T:* Holywood 3471. *Clubs:* Royal Belfast Golf, Royal County Down Golf.

SHILLITO, Charles Henry; Under-Secretary, Ministry of Agriculture, Fisheries and Food, 1974-82; *b* 8 Jan. 1922; *s* of Charles Cawthorne and

Florence Shillito; *m* 1947, Elizabeth Jean (*née* Bull); two *d. Educ:* Hugh Bell Sch., Middlesbrough. Clerk, Min. of Agriculture and Fisheries, 1938; War Service, Lieut RNVR, 1941-46; Principal, MAFF, 1957; Asst Sec. 1966; Section Head, Nat. Econ. Devolt Office, 1966-69 (on secondment). *Recreations:* gardening, nautical pursuits. *Address:* 62 Downs Road, Coulsdon, Surrey CR3 1AB. *T:* Downland 53392.

SHILLITO, Edward Alan, CB 1964; retired Civil Servant; *b* 13 May 1910; *s* of late Rev. Edward and Mrs Annie Shillito, Buckhurst Hill, Essex; *m* 1934, Dorothy Jean, *d* of late Robert J. Davies, Buckhurst Hill, Essex; two *s* three *d. Educ:* Chigwell School; Oriel College, Oxford (Exhibitioner). Litt Hum 2nd Class, 1933. Customs and Excise, 1934-36; HM Treas., 1936-57; Under-Secretary, 1951; Admiralty, and MoD, 1957-69; Dir, Greenwich Hosp., 1969-71; a Gen. Comr of Income Tax, 1972-82. Imperial Defence College course, 1953. *Recreations:* music, lacrosse (Oxford Univ., 1931-33. *Address:* 8 Baldwins Hill, Loughton, Essex. *T:* 01-508 1988.

SHIMELD, Kenneth Reeve, CB 1978; Permanent Secretary, Department of the Civil Service (NI), 1976-81; *b* 5 Nov. 1921; *s* of Augustus John and Gertrude Shimeld; *m* 1949, Brenda, *d* of George and Millicent Barnard; two *d. Educ:* Coatham Sch.; Univ. of Durham (BA). Pres., Durham Univ. Union. Served Royal Signals, 1941-46. Asst Principal, Min. of Finance, NI Civil Service, 1949; Asst Sec. 1957; Sen. Asst Sec., Min. of Commerce, 1963; Director of Works, Min. of Finance, 1969, Second Secretary, 1971. *Recreations:* music, cricket, reading, horse-racing.

SHINDLER, George John, QC 1970; **His Honour Judge Shindler;** a Circuit Judge, since 1980; *b* 27 Oct. 1922; *yr s* of late Dr Bruno and Mrs Alma Schindler; *m* 1955, Eva Muller; three *s. Educ:* RPS and University Coll. Sch., Hampstead. Served in Royal Tank Regt, NW Europe, 1942-47. Called to Bar, Inner Temple, 1952; Bencher 1978. Standing Counsel to Inland Revenue at Central Criminal Court and all London sessions, 1965-70; a Recorder of the Crown Court, 1972-80. *Recreations:* theatre, music, reading, watching soccer and cricket, travel. *Address:* c/o Queen Elizabeth Building, Temple, EC4Y 9BS. *T:* 01-353 6453. *Clubs:* MCC; Glaziers.

SHINNIE, Prof. Peter Lewis; Professor of Archæology, in the University of Calgary, 1970-80, now Emeritus; *b* 1915; *s* of late Andrew James Shinnie, OBE; *m* 1st, 1940, Margaret Blanche Elizabeth Cloake; two *s* one *d* ; 2nd, Ama Nantwi. *Educ:* Westminster Sch.; Christ Church, Oxford. Served War with RAF, 1939-45. Temp. Asst Keeper, Ashmolean Museum, 1945; Asst Commissioner for Archæology, Sudan Government, 1946; Commissioner for Archæology, Sudan Govt, 1948; Director of Antiquities, Uganda, 1956; Prof. of Archæology: Univ. of Ghana, 1958-66; Univ. of Khartoum, 1966-70. FSA. *Publications:* Excavation at Soba, 1955; Medieval Nubia, 1954; Ghazali: A Monastery in Northern Sudan, 1960; Meroe-Civilization of the Sudan, 1967; The African Iron Age, 1971; Debeira West, 1978; (with R. J. Bradley) The Capital of Kush, 1980; articles in Journal of Egyptian Archæology, Sudan Notes and Records, Kush. *Recreations:* reading, photography, travelling in Greece. *Address:* Department of Archæology, University of Calgary, Calgary, T2N 1H4 Canada. *T:* 403-284-5227. *Club:* Athenæum.

SHINWELL, family name of **Baron Shinwell.**

SHINWELL, Baron *cr* 1970 (Life Peer), of Easington, Durham; **Emanuel Shinwell,** CH 1965; PC 1945; *b* London, 18 October 1884. MP (Lab) Linlithgow, 1922-24 and 1928-31, Seaham Div. of Durham, 1935-50, Easington Div. of Durham, 1950-70; Financial Secretary, War Office, 1929-30; Parliamentary Secretary to Department of Mines, 1924 and 1930-31; Minister of Fuel and Power, 1945-47; Secretary of State for War, 1947-50; Minister of Defence, 1950-51. Was Chairman and Member, National Executive Labour Party; Chairman, Parly Labour Party, 1964-67. Hon. DCL Durham, 1969. *Publications:* The Britain I Want, 1943; When the Men Come Home, 1944; Conflict without Malice, 1955; The Labour Story, 1963; I've Lived Through It All, 1973; Lead with the Left, 1981. *Address:* House of Lords, SW1.

SHIPWRIGHT, Sqdn Ldr Denis E. B. K., FRSA; psa; RAFRO (retired); Established Civil Servant (Telecomm. PO); Production and Administration, Gaumont British Picture Corporation, and Gainsborough Pictures; Director Cinephonic Music Co. Ltd; KStJ; *b* London, 20 May 1898; *y s* of late T. J. Shipwright and Adelina de Lara, OBE; *m* 1918, Kate (marriage dissolved, 1926; she *d* 1954), *o d* of late Sir Edward Hain, St Ives, Cornwall; one *s* two *d* ; *m* 1947, Margaret (*d* 1977), *o d* of late Robert Edgar Haynes, Woking, Surrey. *Educ:* France; University College, Oxford. Joined the Army as a private at the age of 16, 1914; despatch rider, 1915; wounded and crashed whilst flying in France in RFC; Flight Comdr, 1918; Capt. Royal 1st Devon Yeomanry, and North Devon Hussars; Capt. R of O RE, TA, to Apr. 1939; then Pilot Officer RAFVR; Flt Lt Nov. 1939; Sqdn Ldr 1940; passed out of RAF Staff College, 1940; served in France, 1940 (despatches, 1939-43 Star); Special Mission to Gibraltar, 1942. Air ED 1944. Obtained Flight Cert., Europa Airship Ops, 1982. Middle Temple, 1920; MP (C) Penryn and Falmouth, 1922-23; Representative on the Film Producers Group, Federation of British Industries; Adviser to the British Films Advancement Council; Member of the Kinematograph Advisory Committee; Life Member of the Commonwealth Parliamentary Association. Member: Nat. Trust for Scotland, 1979-; Surrey Special Constabulary, 1950; Company of Veteran Motorists, 1953; Order of Knights of Road, 1953; Civil Service Motoring Assoc.;

Brooklands Soc.; British Unidentified Flying Object Research Assoc.; British Soc. for the Turin Shroud; Edinburgh Internat. Fest. Soc. and Guild; Sir Harry Lauder Soc., Portobello; De Havilland Moth Club; Fairoaks Flight Centre; Life Mem., Woking and Dist Scottish Assoc., 1982. Chm. NE Surrey Gp, Contact UFO Research Investigation Assoc. Voluntary Driver, Surrey County Council Hospitals Car and Ambulance Service; Governor, Royal Hosp. and Home for Incurables. British Motor Racing Driver: Brooklands (winner 24th 100 mph Long Handicap); Speed Trials; Hill Climbs. Major, 11th (HG) Battalion, Queen's Royal Regt, 1953. Officer, Ministry of Agriculture and Food, Guildford, 1954. *Recreations:* flying, music. *Publication:* The Unforgiving Minute (autobiog.), 1982-83. *Address:* Plym Lea, Triggs Lane, Woking, Surrey GU22 0EH. *T:* Woking 61736. *Clubs:* British Racing Drivers (Life Mem., and Life Mem., Silverstone Marshals Team), Royal Automobile; Oxford University Yacht (Oxford); Woking Conservative (Woking).

SHIRER, William Lawrence; broadcaster, journalist; author; *b* Chicago, 23 Feb. 1904; *s* of Seward Smith Shirer; *m* 1931, Theresa Stiberitz; two *d. Educ:* Coe College. DLitt (Hon.). Légion d'Honneur. *Publications:* Berlin Diary, 1941; End of a Berlin Diary, 1947; The Traitor, 1950; Mid-Century Journey, 1953; Stranger Come Home, 1954; The Challenge of Scandinavia, 1955; The Consul's Wife, 1956; The Rise and Fall of The Third Reich, 1960; The Rise and Fall of Adolf Hitler, 1961; The Sinking of the Bismarck, 1962; The Collapse of the Third Republic, 1970; Twentieth Century Journey: A Memoir of a Life and the Times, 1976; Gandhi, a Memoir, 1979. *Recreations:* walking, sailing. *Address:* Box 487, Lenox, Massachusetts 01240, USA. *Club:* Century (New York).

SHIRLEY, family name of **Earl Ferrers.**

SHIRLEY, Philip Hammond; retired; *b* 4 Oct. 1912; *s* of Frank Shillito Shirley and Annie Lucy (*née* Hammond); *m* 1st, 1936, Marie Edna Walsh (*d* 1972); one *s* one *d* ; 2nd, 1973, Norma Jones. *Educ:* Sydney Church of England Grammar School (Shore). Qualified in Australia as Chartered Accountant, 1934; with Peat Marwick Mitchell & Co., Chartered Accountants, London, 1937-49; with Unilever from 1951; Dep. Chief Accountant, 1951-52; Chief Accountant, 1952-58; Chm. Batchelors Foods Ltd 1958-61; Mem. BTC (Oct. 1961-Nov. 1962); Mem. BR Bd, 1962-67 (Vice-Chm. Bd, 1964-67); Dep. Chm., Cunard Steamship Co., 1968-71; Chief Commissioner of Public Transport, NSW, 1972-75. *Recreation:* golf. *Address:* Flat 5, 2a Telopea Street, Wollstonecraft, NSW 2065, Australia.

SHIRLEY, Mrs Stephanie; see Shirley, Mrs V. S.

SHIRLEY, Mrs (Vera) Stephanie, (Steve), OBE 1980; FBIM, FBCS; Chairman, F International Group, since 1962; *b* 16 Sept. 1933; *d* of late Arnold Buchthal and of Mrs Margaret Brook (formerly Buchthal, *née* Schick); *m* 1959, Derek George Millington Shirley; one *s. Educ:* Sir John Cass Coll., London. BSc (Spec.) London 1956. FBIM 1980; FBCS 1971. PO Res. Stn, Dollis Hill, 1951-59; CDL (subsid. of ICL), 1959-62; F International Ltd and its overseas subsids, 1962-. Vice Pres. (Professional), British Computer Soc., 1979-82; Member: Computer, Systems and Electronics Requirements Bd, 1979-81; Electronics and Avionics Requirements Bd, 1981-. Consulting Editor on information processing, J. Wiley & Sons, 1978-. *Publications:* articles in prof. jls, reviews, proc. of confs, and papers. *Recreation:* sleep. *Address:* c/o F International Ltd, Chesham House, Berkhamsted, Herts HP4 2HA. *Clubs:* Institute of Directors, Europe House.

SHIRLEY-QUIRK, John Stanton, CBE 1975; bass-baritone singer; *b* 28 Aug. 1931; *s* of Joseph Stanley and Amelia Shirley-Quirk; *m* 1st, 1955, Patricia Hastie (*d* 1981); one *s* one *d* ; 2nd, 1981, Sara V. Watkins; one *s. Educ:* Holt School, Liverpool; Liverpool University. Violin Scholarship, 1945; read Chemistry, Liverpool Univ., 1948-53; BSc (Hons), 1952; Dipl. in Educ 1953; became professional singer, 1961. Officer in Education Br., RAF, 1953-57. Asst Lectr in Chemistry, Acton Technical Coll., 1957-61; Lay-clerk in St Paul's Cathedral, 1961-62. First Appearance Glyndebourne Opera in Elegy for Young Lovers, 1961; subseq. 1962, 1963. Sang in first performance of Curlew River, 1964, The Burning Fiery Furnace, 1966, The Prodigal Son, 1968, Owen Wingrave, 1970, Death in Venice, 1973, Confessions of a Justified Sinner, 1976, The Ice Break, 1977. Has sung in Europe, Israel, Australia, etc. First American tour, 1966; Australian tour, 1967; first appearance Metropolitan Opera, NY, 1974. Has made numerous recordings: operas, songs, cantatas, etc. Mem. Court, Brunel Univ., 1977-. Hon. RAM 1972; Hon. DMus Liverpool, 1976; DUniv Brunel, 1981. Liverpool Univ. Chem. Soc. Medal, 1965; Sir Charles Santley Meml Gift, Worshipful Co. of Musicians, 1969. *Recreations:* trees, canals, clocks. *Address:* The White House, 82 Heath End Road, Flackwell Heath, Bucks. *T:* Bourne End 21325.

SHOCK, Maurice; Vice-Chancellor of Leicester University, since 1977; *b* 15 April 1926; *o s* of Alfred and Ellen Shock; *m* 1947, Dorothy Donald; one *s* three *d. Educ:* King Edward's Sch., Birmingham; Balliol Coll., Oxford (MA); St Antony's Coll., Oxford. Served Intell. Corps, 1945-48. Lectr in Politics, Christ Church and Trinity Colls, Oxford, 1955-56; Fellow and Praelector in Politics, University Coll., Oxford, 1956-77; Estates Bursar, 1959-74; Sen. Treasurer, Oxford Union Soc., 1954-72; Member: Franks Commn of Inquiry into the University of Oxford, 1964-66; Hebdomadal Council, Oxford Univ., 1969-75; Chm., Univ. Authorities Panel, 1980-. Vis. Prof. of Govt, Pomona Coll., 1961-62, 1968-69. Mem., SSRC, 1981-. *Publications:* The Liberal

Tradition, 1956; articles on politics and recent history. *Recreations:* gardening, theatre. *Address:* Knighton Hall, Leicester LE2 3WG. *T:* Leicester 706677.

SHOCKLEY, Dr William (Bradford); Medal of Merit (US) 1946; Alexander M. Poniatoff Professor of Engineering Science, Stanford University, 1963-75, Professor Emeritus 1975; Executive Consultant, Bell Telephone Laboratories, 1965-75; *b* 13 Feb. 1910; *s* of William Hillman Shockley and May (*née* Bradford); *m* 1933, Jean Alberta Bailey; two *s* one *d* ; *m* 1955, Emmy I. Lanning. *Educ:* Calif. Inst. of Technology (BS); Mass Inst. Tech. (PhD). Teaching Fellow, Mass. Inst. Tech., 1932-36; Mem. Technical Staff, Bell Teleph. Laboratories, 1936-42 and 1945-54; Director Transistor Physics Department, 1954-55. Dir of Research, Anti-submarine Warfare Ops Research Gp, US Navy, 1942-44; Expert Consultant, Office of Secretary of War, 1944-45. Visiting Lectr, Princeton Univ., 1946; Scientific Advisor, Policy Council, Jt Research and Development Bd, 1947-49; Visiting Prof., Calif. Inst. Tech., 1954; Dep. Dir and Dir of Research, Weapons Systems Evaluation Gp, Dept of Defense, 1954-55; Dir, Shockley Semiconductor Lab. of Beckman Instruments, Inc., 1955-58; Pres. Shockley Transistor Corp., 1958-60; Director, Shockley Transistor, Unit of Clevite Transistor, 1960-63; Consultant, 1963-65. Member: US Army Science Advisory Panel, 1951-63, 1964-; USAF Science Advisory Board, 1959-63; National Academy of Science, 1951-; Sigma Xi; Tau Beta Pi. Inducted into Inventors' Hall of Fame, 1974; more than 90 US Patents. Inventor of junction transistor; research on energy bands of solids, ferromagnetic domains, plastic properties of metals, theory of grain boundaries, order and disorder in alloys; semi-conductor theory and electromagnetic theory; mental tools for sci. thinking, ops res. on human quality statistics. Fellow AAAS. Hon. DSc: Pennsylvania, 1955; Rutgers 1956; Gustavus Adolphus Coll., 1963. Morris Liebmann Prize, 1951, Medal of Honour, 1980, IEEE. Air Force Citation of Honour, 1951; O. E. Buckley Prize (Amer. Physical Soc.), 1953; US Army Cert. of Appreciation, 1953; Comstock Prize (Nat. Acad. of Science), 1954; Wilhelm Exner Medal (Oesterreichischer Gewerberein), 1963; Holley Medal (Amer. Soc. Mech. Engrs), 1963. (Jt) Nobel Prize in Physics, 1956; Caltech Alumni Distinguished Service Award, 1966; NASA Certificate of Appreciation (Apollo 8), 1969; Public Service Group Achievement Award, NASA, 1969. *Publications:* Electrons and Holes in Semiconductors, 1950; Mechanics (with W. A. Gong), 1966; (ed) Imperfections of Nearly Perfect Crystals; over 100 articles in sci. and tech. jls. *Recreations:* mountain climbing, swimming, sailing. *Address:* 797 Esplanada Way, Stanford, Calif 94305, USA. *Clubs:* Cosmos, University (Washington, DC); Bohemian (San Francisco); Stanford Faculty; Palo Alto Yacht.

SHOENBERG, Prof. David, MBE 1944; FRS 1953; Professor of Physics, Cambridge University and Head of Low Temperature Physics Group, Cavendish Laboratory, 1973-78, now Emeritus; Life Fellow of Gonville and Caius College; *b* 4 Jan. 1911; *s* of Isaac and Esther Shoenberg; *m* 1940, Catherine Felicitée Fischmann; one *s* two *d. Educ:* Latymer Upper School, W6; Trinity College, Cambridge (Scholar). PhD 1935; Exhibition of 1851 Senior Student, 1936-39; Research in low temperature physics, 1932-, in charge of Royal Soc. Mond Laboratory, 1947-73; Univ. Lectr in Physics, 1944-52; Univ. Reader in Physics, 1952-73; UNESCO Adviser on Low Temperature Physics, NPL of India, 1953-54. Guthrie Lectr, 1961; Mellon Prof., Univ. of Pittsburgh, 1962; Gauss Prof., Univ. of Göttingen, 1964; Visiting Professor: Univ. of Maryland, 1968; Univ. of Toronto, 1974; Univ. of Waterloo, 1977; Rutherford Meml Lectr, India and Sri Lanka, 1980. Hon. Foreign Mem., Amer. Acad. of Arts and Sciences, 1982. Dr (*hc*) Univ. of Lausanne, 1973. Fritz London Award for Low Temperature Physics, 1964. *Publications:* Superconductivity, 1938, revised edn, 1952; Magnetism, 1949; scientific papers on low temperature physics and magnetism. *Address:* 2 Long Road, Cambridge; c/o Cavendish Laboratory, Madingley Road, Cambridge CB3 0HE. *T:* Cambridge 66477.

SHOLL, Hon. Sir Reginald (Richard), Kt 1962; MA, BCL, Oxon; MA Melbourne; QC; Legal consultant and company director, Melbourne and Queensland; *b* 8 Oct. 1902; *e s* of late Reginald Frank and Maud Sholl (*née* Mumby), Melbourne; *m* 1st, 1927, Hazel Ethel (*d* 1962), *yr d* of late Alfred L. and Fanny Bradshaw, Melbourne; two *s* two *d* ; 2nd, 1964, Anna Campbell, widow of Alister Bruce McLean, Melbourne, and *e d* of late Campbell Colin and Edith Carpenter, Indiana, USA. *Educ:* Melbourne Church of England Grammar Sch.; Trinity Coll., Univ. of Melbourne; New Coll., Oxford. 1st Cl. Final Hons and exhibn, Sch. of Classical Philology, and Wyselaskie Schol. in Classical and Comparative Philology and Logic, Melbourne Univ., 1922; Rhodes Schol., Victoria, 1924; 1st Cl. Final Hons, School of Jurisprudence, Oxford, 1926, Bar Finals, London, 1926 and BCL, Oxford, 1927; Official Law Fellow, Brasenose Coll., Oxford, 1927. Called to Bar, Middle Temple, 1927; journalist, London, 1927; Tutor in Classics, Melbourne Univ., 1928-29; Lectr in law, 1928-38; Barrister, Melbourne, 1929-49; admitted to Bars of NSW and Tasmania, 1935. Served Aust. Army, 1940-44; Capt. retd. Chm. various Commonwealth Bds of Inquiry into Army contracts, 1941-42; KC Vic. and Tas., 1947, NSW 1948; Justice of the Supreme Court of Victoria, 1950-66; Australian Consul-Gen. in New York, 1966-69; Chm., Western Australian Parly Salaries Tribunal, 1971-75. Consultant: to Russell, Kennedy & Cook, solicitors, Melbourne; to Nat. Trustees Executors and Agency Co. of Australasia Ltd. Trustee, Nat. Gall. of Vic., 1950-63, Dep. Chm. 1958; Pres. ESU (Vic. Br.) 1961-66; Fed. Chm., ESU in Aust., 1961-63, 1969-73; Trustee, Northcote Trust Fund, 1978-; Member: Aust. Bd of Trustees, Northcote Children's Emigration Fund for Aust., 1950-; Bd US Educnl Foundn in Aust., 1961-64; Archbishop-in-Council, Dio. Melbourne, 1958-66, 1969-79;

Advocate of Diocese of Melbourne, 1969-79; Mem. Councils: Trinity Coll., Melbourne, 1939-66; C of E Grammar Sch., Melbourne, 1960-66; Peninsula Sch., Mt Eliza, 1960-63; Toorak Coll., 1969-71; C of E Girls' Grammar Sch., Melbourne, 1969-75. Pres. Somers Area, Boy Scouts Assoc. (Vic. Br.), 1955-64, 1972-76; Member: State Exec. Boy Scouts Assoc., 1958-66, (Vice-Pres., 1964-66); Nat. Council Australian Boy Scouts Assoc., 1959-69, 1975-; Cttee, Overseas Service Bureau (Australia), 1970-71; Foundn Dir, Winston Churchill Memorial Trust in Australia, 1965-66, Dep. Nat. Chm., 1969-75, Dep. Nat. Pres., 1975-81; Chm., Nat. Fellowship Cttee, 1965-66, 1969-75; Mem., Victoria Cttee, Duke of Edinburgh's Award in Australia, 1964-66; Chairman, Vict. Supreme Court Rules Cttee, 1960-66; Chm., Royal Commn, Western Australia Inquiry into the airline system, 1974-75. Stawell Orator, 1970; Fellow, Trinity Coll., Melbourne, 1981. *Publications:* contrib. to legal periodicals. *Recreations:* lawn tennis, golf, bowls, sailing, gardening; formerly football (Melbourne Univ. blue) and lacrosse (Oxford half-blue). *Address:* 97 Gibraltar Drive, Isle of Capri, Queensland 4217, Australia. *Clubs:* Melbourne, Australian (Melbourne); Peninsula Country (Victoria); Queensland (Brisbane); Melbourne Cricket (1918-), Southport Golf, Southport Yacht (Qld).

SHOLOKHOV, Mikhail Aleksandrovich; Order of Lenin (twice); novelist; Deputy to Supreme Soviet of USSR since 1946; Member: Communist Party of Soviet Union, 1932; CPSU Central Committee, 1961; Academy of Sciences, USSR, 1939; Praesidium, Union of Soviet Writers, 1954; Nobel Prize for Literature, 1965; Hon. LLD, St Andrews; *b* 24 May 1905; *m* Maria Petrovna Sholokhova. First published in 1923. *Publications:* Woman with Two Husbands, 1925; The Heart of Alyoshka, 1925; Stories of the Don, 1926; And Quiet Flows the Don (4 vols), 1928-40 (State Prize, 1940); Virgin Soil Upturned, 1932-33, 2nd vol., 1959 (Lenin Prize, 1960); Collected Works, vols 1-8, 1959-62; They Fought for their Country, 1966; One Man's Destiny, 1967; My Homeland, 1970; At the Bidding of the Heart (articles), 1970; The Deathless Trumpeter, 1973; The Path, 1973; Stories, 1975; Stories of the Don, 1976; Publicists, 1979; Collected Works, 1979. *Address:* Union of Soviet Writers, Ulitsa Vorovskogo 52, Moscow, USSR; Stanitsa Veshenskaya, Rostor Region, USSR.

SHONE, Very Rev. John Terence; Dean of the United Diocese of St Andrews, Dunkeld and Dunblane, since 1982; Rector, St Saviour, Bridge of Allan, since 1969; Priest in Charge, St John's, Alloa, since 1977 and St James', Dollar, since 1981; *b* 15 May 1935; *s* of late Arthur Shone and of E. B. Shone; *m* 1958, Ursula Ruth Buss; three *s. Educ:* St Dunstan's College; Selwyn Coll., Cambridge (BA 1958, MA 1962); Lincoln Theological Coll. Deacon 1960, priest 1961, London; Curate, St Pancras Parish Church, 1960-62; Chaplain, St Andrew's Cathedral, Aberdeen, 1962-65; Chaplain to Anglican Students, Aberdeen, 1962-68; Lectr, Aberdeen Coll. of Education, 1965-68; Exam. Chaplain to Bishop of Aberdeen, 1966-68; Vicar, St Andrew and St Luke, Grimsby, 1968-69; Chaplain, Stirling Univ., 1969-80; Canon, St Ninian's Cathedral, Perth, 1980-82. *Address:* 21 Fountain Road, Bridge of Allan, Stirling FK9 4AT. *T:* Bridge of Allan 832368.

SHONE, Sir Robert Minshull, Kt 1955; CBE 1949; Visiting Professor, The City University, since 1967; Director, M and G Group Ltd; *b* 27 May 1906; *s* of Robert Harold Shone. *Educ:* Sedbergh School; Liverpool University (MEng); Chicago Univ. (MA Economics). Commonwealth Fellow, USA, 1932-34; Lecturer, London School of Economics, 1935-36; British Iron and Steel Federation, 1936-39 and 1946-53, Director 1950-53; Iron and Steel Control, 1940-45, Gen. Dir, 1943-45; Executive Member, Iron and Steel Board, 1953-62; Joint Chairman, UK and ECSC Steel Committee, 1954-62; Dir-Gen., Nat. Economic Develt Council, 1962-66; Research Fellow, Nuffield Coll., Oxford, 1966-67; Special Prof., Nottingham Univ., 1971-73. Dir, A. P. V. Holdings Ltd, 1969-75; Rank Organisation, 1968-78. Hon. Fellow, LSE. Pres., Soc. of Business Economists, 1963-68. *Publications:* Problems of Investment, 1971; Price and Investment Relationships, 1975; contributions to: Some Modern Business Problems, 1937; The Industrial Future of Great Britain, 1948; Large Scale Organisation, 1950; Models for Decision, 1965; Britain and the Common Market, 1967; Financial Management Handbook, 1978; articles in journals. *Recreation:* golf. *Address:* 7 Windmill Hill, Hampstead, NW3. *T:* 01-435 1930.

SHOOTER, Prof. Reginald Arthur, CBE 1980; Emeritus Professor of Medical Microbiology, London University, since 1981; *b* 1916; *s* of Rev. A. E. Shooter, TD and M. K. Shooter; *m* 1946, Jean Wallace, MB, ChB; one *s* three *d. Educ:* Mill Hill Sch.; Caius Coll., Cambridge; St Bartholomew's Hosp. BA 1937; MB, BChir 1940; MRCS, LRCP 1940; MA 1941; MD 1945; MRCP 1961; FRCP 1968; FRCS 1977; FRCPath 1963 (Vice-Pres., 1971-74). After various Hosp. appts became Surgeon Lieut, RNVR. Appointments at St Bartholomew's Hospital from 1946; Rockefeller Travelling Fellow in Medicine, 1950-51; Reader in Bacteriology, 1953-61, Prof. of Medical Microbiology, 1961-81, Univ. of London; Bacteriologist to St Bartholomew's Hosp., 1961-81 and Dean, Medical Coll., 1972-81. Member: City and E London AHA (T), 1974-81; Public Health Laboratory Service Bd, 1970-82; Gloucester HA, 1982-; Chm., Dangerous Pathogens Adv. Gp, 1975-81. Governor: St Bartholomew's Hosp., 1972-74; Queen Mary Coll., 1972-81; Trustee, Mitchell City of London Trust, 1958-82; Mem. Court, City Univ., 1972-81. Asst Editor, British Jl of Exp. Pathology, 1953-58; Hon. Editor, RSocMed, 1960-65. *Publications:* books, and articles in medical journals. *Recreations:* archaeology, gardening, fishing. *Address:* Eastlea, Back Edge Lane, The Edge, Stroud, Glos GL6 6PE. *T:* Painswick 812408.

SHOPPEE, Prof. Charles William, FRS 1956; FAA 1958; Emeritus Professor of Chemistry, University of Sydney; *b* London, 24 Feb. 1904; *er s* of J. W. and Elizabeth Shoppee, Totteridge; *m* 1929, Eileen Alice West; one *d. Educ:* Stationers' Company's Sch.; Univs of London and Leeds. PhD, DSc (London); MA, DPhil (Basle). Sen. Student of Royal Commn for Exhibition of 1851, 1926-28; Asst Lecturer and Lecturer in Organic Chemistry, Univ. of Leeds, 1929-39; Rockefeller Research Fellow, Univ. of Basle, 1939-45; Reader in Chemistry, Univ. of London, at Royal Cancer Hosp., 1945-48; Prof. of Chemistry, Univ. of Wales, at University Coll., Swansea, 1948-56; Prof. of Organic Chemistry, Univ. of Sydney, 1956-70; Foundation Welch Prof. of Chemistry, Texas Tech. Univ., 1970-75. Visiting Professor of Chemistry: Duke Univ., N Carolina, USA, 1966; Univ. of Georgia, USA, 1966; Univ. of Mississippi, USA, 1968; Hon. Professorial Fellow in Chem., Macquarie Univ., 1976-79; Hon. Vis. Prof. of Organic Chem., La Trobe Univ., 1980-. *Publications:* Scientific papers in Jl Chem. Soc. and Helvetica Chimica Acta. *Recreations:* bowls, music, bridge. *Address:* Unit 1, 75 Normanby Road, Kew, Vic 3101, Australia. *T:* 80 2644. *Club:* Royal Automobile of Victoria.

SHORE, Bernard Alexander Royle, CBE 1955; FRCM, FTCL, Hon. RAM, ARCM; retired as HM Inspector of Schools, Staff Inspector for Music (1948-59); Co-President, first International Conference for Music in Education, Brussels, 1954; viola player; formerly Professor of the Viola at RCM and Music Advisor, Rural Music Schools Association; *b* 17 March 1896; *s* of Arthur Miers Shore and Ada Alice (née Clark); *m* 1922, Olive Livett Udale; two *d. Educ:* St Paul's School, Hammersmith; Royal College of Music (studied organ under Sir Walter Alcock). Served European War, 1914-18: enlisted in Artists Rifles, 1915, France; commissioned, 2nd Rifle Bde (wounded); seconded to RFC. Returned to RCM: studied viola under Arthur Bent and later with Lionel Tertis. Joined Queen's Hall Orchestra, 1922; first appearance as Soloist, Promenade Concert, 1925; Principal Viola, BBC Symphony Orchestra, 1930-40. War of 1939-45: RAF, 1940; Squadron Leader, 1942; demobilised, 1946. Adviser on Instrumental Music in Schools, Min. of Educn, 1946-47. *Publications:* The Orchestra Speaks, 1937; Sixteen Symphonies, 1947; article on Lionel Tertis for DNB 1971-1980. *Recreations:* sketching, the viola. *Address:* Flat 6, 3 Palmeira Square, Hove, East Sussex.

See also A. J. U. Nicholas.

SHORE, Dr Elizabeth Catherine, CB 1980; Deputy Chief Medical Officer, Department of Health and Social Security, since 1977; *b* 1927; *d* of Edward Murray Wrong and Rosalind Grace Smith; *m* 1948, Rt Hon. Peter David Shore, *qv* ; one *s* two *d* (and one *s* decd). *Educ:* Newnham Coll., Cambridge; St Bartholomew's Hospital. MRCP, MRCS, FFCM, DRCOG. Medical Civil Service from 1962. *Recreations:* reading, cookery, swimming in rough seas. *Address:* c/o Department of Health and Social Security, Alexander Fleming House, Elephant and Castle, SE1.

SHORE, Jack; Head of Chester School of Art, since 1960; President, Royal Cambrian Academy of Art, since 1977; *b* 17 July 1922; *s* of Frank and Maggie Shore; *m* 1970, Olive Brenda Williams; one *s* one *d. Educ:* Accrington and Manchester Schools of Art. Lectr, Blackpool School of Art, 1945-60. RCamA 1962 (ARCamA 1961). Jubilee Medal, 1977. *Recreations:* gardening, enjoyment of music. *Address:* 11 St George's Crescent, Queens Park, Chester CH4 7AR. *T:* Chester 20099.

SHORE, Rt. Hon. Peter (David), PC 1967; MP (Lab) Tower Hamlets, Stepney and Poplar, since 1974 (Stepney, 1964-74); *b* 20 May 1924; *m* 1948, Elizabeth Catherine Wrong (*see* E. C. Shore); one *s* two *d* (and one *s* decd). *Educ:* Quarry Bank High Sch., Liverpool; King's Coll., Cambridge. Political economist. Joined Labour Party, 1948; Head of Research Dept, Labour Party, 1959-64. Member of Fabian Society. Contested (Lab) St Ives, Cornwall, 1950, Halifax, 1959. PPS to the Prime Minister, 1965-66; Jt Parly Sec.: Min. of Technology, 1966-67; Dept of Economic Affairs, 1967; Sec. of State for Economic Affairs, 1967-69; Minister without Portfolio, 1969-70; Dep. Leader of House of Commons, 1969-70; Opposition Spokesman on Europe, 1971-74; Sec. of State for Trade, 1974-76; Sec. of State for the Environment, 1976-79; Opposition Spokesman on Foreign Affairs, 1979-80, on Treasury and Economic Affairs, 1980-. *Publication:* Entitled to Know, 1966. *Recreation:* swimming. *Address:* House of Commons, SW1; 23 Dryburgh Road, SW15.

SHORROCK, James Godby; Barrister-at-Law; Recorder of Barrow-in-Furness, 1963-71; *b* 10 Dec. 1910; *s* of late William Gordon Shorrock, JP, Morland, Westmorland; *m* 1936, Mary Patricia, *d* of late George Herbert Lings, Burnage, Manchester; two *s* two *d. Educ:* Clifton; Hertford College, Oxford. Called to Bar, Inner Temple, 1934. Served War of 1939-45: Major RA (TA) and Judge Advocate General's Department. Dep. Chm., Westmorland QS, 1955-71. Legal Member, Mental Health Review Tribunal, 1960-63; Legal Chm., Manchester City Licensing Planning Cttee, 1964. *Recreations:* walking, fishing, gardening.

SHORT, family name of **Baron Glenamara.**

SHORT, David Somerset, MD, FRCP, FRCPE; Physician to the Queen in Scotland, since 1977; Consultant Physician, Aberdeen Royal Infirmary, since 1960; *b* 6 Aug. 1918; *s* of Latimer James Short, MD, DPH, Bristol, and Mabel Annie Wood, SRN, Nottingham; *m* 1948, Joan Anne McLay, BSc, MB, ChB,

Cardiff; one s four d. *Educ:* Bristol Grammar Sch.; Cambridge Univ.; Bristol Royal Hospitals. MD 1948; PhD 1957; FRCP 1964; FRCPE 1966. Served with RAMC, 1944–47; Registrar, Southmead Hosp., Bristol, 1947–49; Sen. Registrar, National Heart Hosp. and London Hosp., 1950–54; Lecturer in Medicine, Middlesex Hosp., 1955–59. *Publications:* contribs to medical journals, mainly on cardiovascular and pulmonary diseases. *Recreations:* walking, music. *Address:* 48 Victoria Street, Aberdeen, Scotland AB9 2PL. *T:* Aberdeen 645853.

SHORT, Rt. Rev. Hedley Vicars Roycraft; *see* Saskatchewan, Bishop of.

SHORT, Rev. John, MA (Edinburgh); PhD (Edinburgh); Hon. DD (St Andrews); Minister of St George's United Church, Toronto, Canada, 1951–64; *b* Berwickshire, 27 March 1896; *m* 1st; one s one d; 2nd, 1939, Anneliese, 2nd d of Dr C. J. F. Bechler, Danzig; two s. *Educ:* Edinburgh University. Trained for a business career but attracted by religious convictions to the Christian ministry; began to study for same just before the war of 1914–18, joined army and served for 3 years and 6 months; commenced studies at Edinburgh; graduated MA. First class honours in Philosophy; awarded John Edward Baxter Scholarship in Philosophy for 3 years; received University Diploma in Education and Medal; trained for Teacher's Certificate; awarded Doctorate in Philosophy for a thesis on the Philosophic Character of English XIVth Century Mysticism; medallist in class of Moral Philosophy, in Metaphysics; Prizeman in Psychology; trained in Scottish Congregational College for Ministry under Principal T. Hywel Hughes, DLitt, DD; called to Bathgate E. U. Congregational Church, 1924; Minister of Lyndhurst Road Congregational Church, Hampstead, 1930–37. Minister of Richmond Hill Congregational Church, Bournemouth, 1937–51; Chairman of the Congregational Union of England and Wales, 1949–50. Mason: 3° Home Lodge Amity, Poole, Dorset, 18° Downend Chapter Rose Croix, Gloucester, 1953; affiliated Ashlar Lodge, 247 GRC, Toronto, 1952; 32° Moore Sovereign Consistory, Hamilton, Ont, 1964; 33° Supreme Council A&ASR, Dominion of Canada (Hon. Inspector Gen.), 1967. DD (hc): St Andrews Univ., 1950; McMaster Univ., Hamilton, Ontario, 1964. *Publications:* Can I Find Faith?, 1937; All Things are Yours (book of sermons), 1939; The Interpreter's Bible Exposition of I Corinthians; Triumphant Believing, 1952. *Recreations:* gardening, reading, and travel. *Address:* 162 Coldstream Avenue, Toronto M5N 1X9, Canada. *T:* 489-8614.

SHORT, Rt. Rev. Kenneth Herbert; Anglican Bishop to the Australian Forces (Army, Navy and Air Force), since 1979; an Assistant Bishop, Diocese of Sydney (Bishop of Parramatta), since 1982; *b* 6 July 1927; s of Cecil Charles Short and Joyce Ellen Begbie; *m* 1950, Gloria Noelle Funnell; one s two d. *Educ:* Moore Theological Coll. (ThL and Moore Coll. Dipl.). Commissioned AIF, 1946; with BCOF, 1946–48; theological training, 1949–52; ordained Anglican Ministry, 1952; Minister in Charge, Provisional Parish of Pittwater, 1952–54; with CMS in Tanzania, E Africa, 1955–64; Chaplain, Tabora 1955, Mwanza 1955–59; first Principal, Msalato Bible School, 1961–64; Gen. Secretary, CMS NSW Branch, 1964–71, including Sec. for S America. Canon of St Andrew's Cathedral, Sydney, 1970–75; Exam. Chaplain to Archbishop of Sydney, 1971–; Rector of St Michael's, Vaucluse, 1971–75; Archdeacon of Wollongong and Camden, 1975–79; Chaplain General (CE), Australian Army, 1979–81; Bishop in Wollongong, Diocese of Sydney, 1975–82. *Publication:* Guidance, 1969. *Recreations:* fishing, reading, walking. *Address:* 5 Keith Place, Baulkham Hills, NSW 2153, Australia. *T:* (02) 6399878.

SHORT, Sir Noel (Edward Vivian), Kt 1977; MBE 1951; MC 1945; Speaker's Secretary, House of Commons, 1970–82; *b* 19 Jan. 1916; s of late Vivian A. Short, CIE, Indian Police, and late Annie W. Short; *m* 1st, 1949, Diana Hester Morison (d 1951); one s; 2nd, 1957, Karin Margarete Anders; one s one d. *Educ:* Radley College; RMA Sandhurst. Commissioned Indian Army, 1936; joined 6th Gurkha Rifles, 1937. Active service: NW Frontier of India, 1937, 1940–41; Assam and Burma, 1942, 1944–45; New Guinea, 1943–44; Malaysia, 1950–51, 1952–53, 1956–57. Staff College, 1946–47; jssc, 1953; Comdr, 63 Gurkha Bde, Malaysia, 1960–61; Comdr, 51 Infty Bde, Tidworth, 1962–63. Principal, Home Office, 1964–70. Col, 6th Queen Elizabeth's Own Gurkha Rifles, 1978–. *Publications:* contribs: Jl of RUSI; Army Quarterly. *Recreations:* ski-ing, photography. *Club:* Travellers'.

SHORT, Mrs Renee; MP (Lab) Wolverhampton North-East, since 1964; *m* ; two d. *Educ:* Nottingham County Grammar Sch.; Manchester Univ. Freelance journalist. Member: Herts County Council, 1952–67; Watford RDC, 1952–64; West Herts Group Hosp. Management Cttee; former Chm. Shrodell's Hosp., Watford. Governor: Watford Coll. of Technology; Watford Grammar Sch. Contested (Lab) St Albans, 1955, Watford, 1959. TGWU sponsored Member of Parliament. Member: Delegation to Council of Europe, 1964–68; Expenditure Cttee, 1970–79 (Chm., Social Services and Employment Sub-Cttee); Chm., Select Cttee on Social Services, 1979–; Chm., Parly and Scientific Cttee, 1982–; Vice-Chm., Parly East-West Trade Gp, 1968–; Chm., Anglo-GDR Parly Gp; Sec., Anglo-Soviet Parly Gp; Pres., British-Romanian Friendship Assoc. Mem., Nat. Exec. Cttee of Labour Party, 1970–81. National President: Nursery Schools Assoc.; Campaign for Nursery Educn. Mem., Roundhouse Theatre Council; Chm., Theatres' Advisory Council, 1974–80. *Publication:* The Care of Long Term Prisoners, 1979. *Address:* House of Commons, SW1A 0AA.

SHORT, Prof. Roger Valentine, FRS 1974; FRSE 1974; FRCVS 1976; Professor of Reproductive Biology, Monash University, Australia, since 1982;

b 31 July 1930; s of F. A. and M. C. Short, Weybridge; *m* 1958, Dr Mary Bowen Wilson (marr. diss. 1981); one s three d ; *m* 1982, Dr Marilyn Bernice Renfree. *Educ:* Sherborne Sch.; Univs of Bristol (BVSc, MRCVS), Wisconsin (MSc) and Cambridge (PhD, ScD). Mem., ARC Unit of Reproductive Physiology and Biochemistry, Cambridge, 1956–72; Fellow, Magdalene Coll., Cambridge, 1962–72; Lectr, then Reader, Dept of Veterinary Clinical Studies, Cambridge, 1961–72; Dir, MRC Unit of Reproductive Biology, Edinburgh, 1972–82. Hon. Prof., Univ. of Edinburgh, 1976–82. *Publications:* (ed, with C. R. Austin) Reproduction in Mammals, vols 1–8, 1972–80; (ed, with D. T. Baird) Contraceptives of the Future, 1976; contrib. Jl Endocrinology, Jl Reproduction and Fertility, Jl Zoology. *Recreations:* gardening, wildlife. *Address:* Department of Physiology, Monash University, Clayton, Victoria 3168, Australia.

SHORTIS, Maj.-Gen. Colin Terry, CBE 1980 (OBE 1977; MBE 1974); Commander, British Military Advisory and Training Team, Zimbabwe, since 1982; *b* 18 Jan. 1934; s of late Tom Richardson Shortis and Marna Evelyn Shortis (*née* Kenworthy); *m* 1957, Sylvia Mary, o d of H. C. A. Jenkinson; two s two d. *Educ:* Bedford School. Enlisted Army 1951; 2nd Lieut Royal Fusiliers, 1953; transf. to Dorset Regt, 1955; served Hong Kong, Korea, Suez Canal Zone, Sudan, BAOR, Aden, Singapore and British Guiana, 1953–63; Instructor, Sch. of Infantry, 1964–65; Staff Coll., 1966; Co. Comdr, 1st Devonshire and Dorset, 1967–73; served Malta, NI, Belize, Cyprus, BAOR, CO 1974–77; Directing Staff, Staff Coll., 1977; Comdr, 8 Infantry Brigade, 1978–80; RCDS 1981. *Recreations:* sailing, manual work. *Address:* c/o Barclays Bank, 137 Brompton Road, SW3 1QF. *Club:* Army and Navy.

SHORTT, Maj.-Gen. Arthur Charles, CB 1951; OBE 1945; psc; *b* 2 April 1899; s of Charles William Shortt and Grace Evelyn Mary (*née* Skey); *m* 1st, 1927, Loraine (*née* Thomas), one d ; 2nd, 1945, Nella (*née* Exelby). *Educ:* St Lawrence College; King's College, Cambridge; RMA Woolwich, 2nd Lt, RE, 1916. Served European War, 1914–18, in France and Belgium; 1st KGO Sappers and Miners, India, 1919–22; Gold Coast Survey Dept, 1924–27; Instructor, RMA Woolwich, 1927–30; Adjutant, Trng Bn RE, 1933–37; GS02 War Office, 1937–39. Staff College, Minley, 1939. War of 1939–45: Military Assistant to C-in-C, BEF 1940; Director of Technical Training, 1943; France and Germany, 1944–45. Military Attaché, Athens, 1947–49; Director of Military Intelligence, 1949–53; Chief Liaison Officer on UK Service Liaison Staff, Australia, 1953–56; Retired pay, 1956; Director of Public Relations, War Office, 1956–61; Col Comdt, Intelligence Corps, 1960–64. Mem. Governing Body, St Lawrence Coll., 1962–80. Officer, Legion of Honour (France), 1950. *Recreation:* numismatics. *Address:* Bolnore, Hayward's Heath, Sussex. *T:* 51386.

SHORTT, Colonel Henry Edward, CIE 1941; FRS 1950; LLD 1952; Colonel IMS, retired; formerly Professor of Medical Protozoology, University of London, and Head of Department of Parasitology, London School of Hygiene and Tropical Medicine; *b* 15 April 1887; *m* 1921, Eleanor M. Hobson; one s one d. *Educ:* Univ. of Aberdeen. MB, ChB 1910; MD 1936; DSc 1938; KHP 1941–44; Inspector-Gen. of Civil Hospitals and Prisons, Assam, 1941–44; retired, 1944. President, Royal Society of Tropical Medicine and Hygiene, 1949–51; Technical Expert under Colombo Plan in E Pakistan, 1952–55. Straits Settlements Gold Medal, 1938; Kaisar-i-Hind Gold Medal, 1945; Laveran Prize, 1948; Mary Kingsley medal, 1949; Darling medal and prize, 1951; Stewart prize, 1954; Manson Medal, 1959; Gaspar Vianna Medal, 1962. *Publications:* over 130 scientific papers. *Recreations:* shooting and fishing. *Address:* Rivenhall, 39 Lenten Street, Alton, Hants. *T:* Alton 83252.

SHOTTON, Prof. Edward; Professor of Pharmaceutics, University of London, 1956–77, now Emeritus; *b* 15 July 1910; s of Ernest Richard and Maud Shotton; *m* 1943, Mary Constance Louise Marchant; one d. *Educ:* Smethwick (Junior) Technical School; Birkbeck College, University of London. Pharmaceutical Chemist (PhC), 1933; BSc (London), 1939; PhD (London), 1955; Hon. ACT (Birmingham), 1961. FRIC 1949. Pharmaceutical research and development work at Burroughs, Wellcome & Co., Dartford, 1939–48. Sen. Lecturer in Pharmaceutics, Univ. of London, 1948–56. Chairman, British Pharmaceutical Conference, 1966. *Publications:* (with K. Ridgway) Physical Pharmaceutics, 1974; research papers, mainly in Jl of Pharmacy and Pharmacology. *Recreations:* gardening, cricket, fly-fishing. *Address:* 10 Winston Gardens, Berkhamsted, Herts. *T:* Berkhamsted 6402. *Club:* Athenæum.

SHOTTON, Prof. Frederick William, MBE 1945; MA, ScD; FRS 1956; FEng 1976; FGS; FIMinE; MIWES; Professor of Geology, University of Birmingham, 1949–74, Emeritus Professor 1975 (Pro-Vice-Chancellor and Vice-Principal, 1965–71); *b* 8 Oct. 1906; s of F. J. and Ada Shotton, Coventry; *m* 1930, Alice L. Linnett; two d. *Educ:* Bablake, Coventry; Sidney Sussex College, Cambridge. Wiltshire Prizeman and Harkness Scholar, Cambridge, 1926–27. Assistant Lecturer and Lecturer, University of Birmingham, 1928–36; Lecturer, Cambridge University, 1936–45. Served War of 1939–45, MEF and 21 Army Group, 1940–45. Prof. of Geology, Sheffield Univ., 1945–49. Mem., NERC, 1969–72. Pres., Geological Soc., 1964–66, Vice-Pres., 1966–68. Founder Fellow, Fellowship of Engineering, 1976. Hon. Mem., Royal Irish Acad., 1970. Prestwich Medal, Geological Soc. of London, 1954; Stopes Medal, Geologists' Assoc., 1967. *Publications:* (ed and contrib.) British Quaternary Studies, 1977; numerous scientific. *Recreations:* archæology and natural history; gardening. *Address:* 111 Dorridge Road, Dorridge, West Midlands B93 8BP. *T:* Knowle 2820.

SHOVELTON, Prof. David Scott, FDSRCS; Professor of Conservative Dentistry, since 1964, and Director of the Dental School, 1974-78, University of Birmingham; Consultant Dental Surgeon, Birmingham Area Health Authority (Teaching), since 1974; *b* 12 Sept. 1925; *s* of Leslie Shovelton, LDSRCS, and Marion de Winton (*née* Scott); *m* 1949, Pearl Holland; two *s. Educ:* The Downs Sch., Colwall; King's Sch., Worcester; Univ. of Birmingham (BSc, LDS, BDS). House Surg., Birmingham Dental Hosp., 1951; gen. dental practice, Evesham, Worcs, 1951; Dental Officer, RAF, 1951-53; Lectr in Operative Dental Surg., Univ. of Birmingham, 1953-60, Sen. Lectr, 1960-64. Vis. Asst Prof. of Clin. Dentistry, Univ. of Alabama, 1959-60. Cons. Dental Surg., United Birmingham Hosps, 1960-74, and Birmingham Reg. Hosp. Bd, 1962-74. Pres., British Soc. for Restorative Dentistry, 1970-71 (Vice-Pres., 1968-70 and 1971-72). Consultant, Commn on Dental Practice, Fedn Dentaire Internat., 1972-79; Member: Gen. Dental Council, 1974-; Birmingham Area Health Authority (Teaching), 1973-79; Cttee of Management, Sch. for Dental Therapists, 1977-80; Jt Cttee for Higher Trng in Dentistry, 1979- (Chm., Specialist Adv. Cttee in Restorative Dentistry, 1979-). Ext. Examnr in dental subjects, univs and colls, 1968-. *Publications:* Inlays, Crowns and Bridges (jtly), 1963 (3rd edn 1978); articles in med. and dental jls, 1957-. *Recreations:* music, photography, gardening and caravanning. *Address:* 86 Broad Oaks Road, Solihull, West Midlands B91 1HZ. *T:* 021-705 3026. *Club:* Royal Air Force.

SHOVELTON, (Walter) Patrick, CB 1976; CMG 1972; FCIT; Director General, The General Council of British Shipping, since 1978; Member, British Airports Authority, since 1982; *b* 18 Aug. 1919; *s* of late S. T. Shovelton, CBE, and M. C. Kelly, cousin of Patrick and Willie Pearse; *m* 1st, 1942, Marjorie Lucy Joan Manners (marr. diss. 1967); one *d* ; 2nd, Helena Richards, 3rd *d* of D. G. Richards, *qv. Educ:* Charterhouse; Keble Coll., Oxford (scholar of both). Rep. Oxford Univ. at Eton Fives. Served in RA and RHA, 1940-46; DAAG, War Office, 1945-46. Entered Administrative Civil Service as Asst Principal, Min. of Transport, 1946; Principal 1947; Admin. Staff College, 1951; Private Sec. to Secretary of State for Co-ordination of Transport, Fuel and Power, 1951-53; Asst Sec., 1957; transferred to Min. of Aviation, 1959; IDC, 1962; Under Secretary, 1966; transferred to Min. of Technology, 1966, and to DTI, 1970; Mem., UK Negotiating Team for entry into EEC, 1970-72; Deputy Secretary: DTI, 1972-74; Dept of Prices and Consumer Protection, 1974-76; Dept of Trade, 1976-78. Led UK Negotiating Team for Bermuda 2, 1977. Mem., Council, CIT, 1982-. Brancker Meml Lectr, Inst. of Transport, 1979. *Recreations:* golf, gardening, reading, snooker. *Address:* Long Marling, Down Lane, Frant, East Sussex. *Clubs:* Royal Ashdown Forest Golf, Hampstead Golf, Seniors' Golf, Jesters.

SHRAPNEL, Norman; Parliamentary Correspondent of the Guardian, 1958-75; *b* 5 Oct. 1912; *yr s* of Arthur Edward Scrope Shrapnel and Rosa Brosy; *m* 1940, Mary Lilian Myfanwy Edwards; two *s. Educ:* King's School, Grantham. Various weekly, evening and morning newspapers from 1930; Manchester Guardian (later the Guardian) from 1947, as reporter, theatre critic and reviewer; contributor to various journals. Political Writer of the Year Award (the Political Companion), 1969. *Publications:* A View of the Thames, 1977; The Performers: politics as theatre, 1978; The Seventies, 1980. *Recreations:* walking, music. *Address:* 27A Shooters Hill Road, Blackheath, SE3. *T:* 01-858 7123.

SHREWSBURY, Bishop Suffragan of, since 1980; **Rt. Rev. Leslie Lloyd Rees;** *b* 14 April 1919; *s* of Rees Thomas and Elizabeth Rees; *m* 1944, Rosamond Smith; two *s. Educ:* Pontardawe Grammar Sch.; Kelham Theological College. Asst Curate, St Saviour, Roath, 1942; Asst Chaplain, HM Prison, Cardiff, 1942; Chaplain, HM Prison: Durham, 1945; Dartmoor, 1948; Vicar of Princetown, 1948; Chaplain, HM Prison, Winchester, 1949; Chaplain General of Prisons, Home Office Prison Dept, 1962-80. Chaplain to the Queen, 1971-80. Hon. Canon of Canterbury, 1966-80, of Lichfield, 1980-. Freeman, City of London. *Recreations:* music, brass bands. *Address:* Athlone House, 68 London Road, Shrewsbury SY2 6PG.

SHREWSBURY, Bishop of, (RC), since 1980; **Rt. Rev. Joseph Gray,** DCL; *b* 20 Oct. 1919; *s* of Terence Gray and Mary Gray (*née* Alwill). *Educ:* St Patrick's Coll., Cavan, Eire; St Mary's Seminary, Oscott, Birmingham; Dunboyne House, St Patrick's Coll., Maynooth, Eire; Pontifical Univ. of St Thomas Aquinas, Rome. Priest, 1943; Asst Priest, Sacred Heart, Aston, Birmingham, 1943-48; Dunboyne House, 1948-50 (Licentiate in Canon Law, 1950); Sec. to Archbp of Birmingham, 1950-55. Diocesan Chancellor, Birmingham, 1951-69; Pontifical Univ., 1959-60 (Doctorate in Canon Law, 1960); Vicar-Gen., Birmingham, 1960-69; Parish Priest, St Michael's, Birmingham, 1955-69. Papal Chamberlain, 1960; Domestic Prelate, 1966. Episcopal Ordination, Cathedral of Christ the King, Liverpool, Feb. 1969; Titular Bishop of Mercia and Auxiliary Bishop of Liverpool, 1969-80. Pres., Liturgy Commn of Bishops' Conf. of England and Wales, 1976-. *Recreations:* music, reading, travel. *Address:* Bishop's House, Eleanor Road, Birkenhead L43 7QW. *T:* 051-653 3600.

SHREWSBURY, Auxiliary Bishop of, (RC); *see* Brewer, Rt. Rev. John.

SHREWSBURY AND WATERFORD, 22nd Earl of, *cr* 1442 and 1446; **Charles Henry John Benedict Crofton Chetwynd Chetwynd-Talbot;** Baron Talbot, 1733; 7th Earl Talbot, Viscount Ingestre, 1784; Premier Earl on the Rolls of England and Ireland, Hereditary Great Seneschal or Lord High Steward of Ireland; farmer; *b* 18 Dec. 1952; *s* of 21st Earl of Shrewsbury and Waterford, and of Nadine, *yr d* of late Brig.-Gen. C. R. Crofton, CBE; *S* father, 1980; *m* 1974, Deborah, *o d* of Noel Hutchinson; two *s* one *d. Educ:* Harrow. Pres., Burslem Festival. *Recreations:* hunting, racing, shooting. *Heir: s* Viscount Ingestre, *qv. Address:* Forton Hall, Newport, Salop TF10 8BY.

SHRIMSLEY, Anthony; political journalist; *b* 12 June 1934; *s* of John Shrimsley and Alice Shrimsley, London; *m* 1961, Yvonne Ann, *d* of Harry and Gertrude Ross; one *s* one *d. Educ:* William Ellis Sch., Highgate, and elsewhere. Press Assoc., 1950; Edgware Post, 1951; RAF, 1952-54; Littlehampton Gazette; Reporter, Manchester Evening News, 1955, Polit. Corresp., 1959; Polit. Corresp., later Polit. Editor, Sunday Mirror, 1962-69; Polit. Editor, The Sun, 1969; Polit. Editor, Daily Mail, 1973, Asst Editor, 1975; Asst Editor, The Sun, and political adviser, News Group Newspapers, 1976-79; Editor-in-Chief, Now! Magazine, 1979-81. Chm., Parly Lobby Journalists, 1975-76; Mem., BBC Consultative Gp on Business and Ind. Affairs, 1976-78. *Publications:* The First Hundred Days of Harold Wilson, 1965; The New Establishment, 1978. *Recreation:* sailing. *Address:* 64 Salmon Street, NW9. *T:* 01-205 0234. *Club:* Reform.
See also Bernard Shrimsley.

SHRIMSLEY, Bernard; Editor, The Mail on Sunday, 2 May-4 July 1982; Vice-Chairman, The Mail on Sunday Ltd, 2 April-4 July 1982; *b* 13 Jan. 1931; *er s* of John and Alice Shrimsley, London; *m* 1952, Norma Jessie Alexandra, *d* of Albert and Maude Porter, Southport; one *d. Educ:* Kilburn Grammar School. Press Association, 1947; Southport Guardian, 1948; RAF, 1949-51; Daily Mirror, 1953; Dep. Northern Editor, Sunday Express, 1958; Northern Editor, Daily Mirror, 1963, subseq. Asst Editor, Asst Publicity Dir; Editor, Liverpool Daily Post, 1968; Dep. Editor, The Sun, 1969; Assoc. Editor, News of the World, 1972; Editor, The Sun, 1972; Editor, News of the World, and Dir, News Group Newspapers, 1975-80. *Publication:* The Candidates, 1968. *Address:* 100 Campden Hill Road, W8. *Club:* Reform.
See also Anthony Shrimsley.

SHRIVER, (Robert) Sargent; Lawyer; Senior Partner, Fried, Frank, Harris, Shriver & Jacobson, since 1971; *b* Westminster, Md, 9 Nov. 1915; *s* of Robert Sargent and Hilda Shriver; *m* 1953, Eunice Mary Kennedy; four *s* one *d. Educ:* parochial schools, Baltimore; Canterbury School, New Milford, Conn.; Yale College; Yale University. BA (*cum laude*) 1938; LLB 1941; LLD 1964. Apprentice Seaman, USNR, 1940; Ensign, 1941. Served War of 1941-45: Atlantic and Pacific Ocean Areas aboard battleships and submarines; Lt-Comdr, USNR. Admitted to: New York Bar, 1941; Illinois Bar, (retd) 1959; US Supreme Court, 1966; District of Columbia Bar, 1971. With legal firm of Winthrop, Stimson, Putnam & Roberts, NYC, 1940-41; Asst Editor, Newsweek, 1945-46; associated with Joseph P. Kennedy Enterprises, 1946-48; Asst Gen. Man., Merchandise Mart, 1948-61; President: Chicago Bd of Educn, 1955-60; Catholic Interracial Council of Chicago, 1954-59; Dir, Peace Corps, Washington, 1961-66; Dir, Office of Economic Opportunity and Special Asst to Pres. Johnson, 1964-68; US Ambassador to France, 1968-70. Vice-Presidential candidate (Democrat), Nov. 1972. Democrat; Roman Catholic. *Address:* 600 New Hampshire Avenue NW, Washington, DC 20037, USA.

SHRUBSOLE, Alison Cheveley, CBE 1982; Principal, Homerton College, Cambridge, since 1971; Fellow of Hughes Hall, Cambridge, since 1974; *b* 7 April 1925; *d* of Rev. Stanley and Mrs Margaret Shrubsole. *Educ:* Milton Mount Coll.; Royal Holloway Coll.; Inst. of Education. BA Hons London; MA Cantab; Postgraduate Cert. in Educn. FCP. Teaching in schools in South London, 1946-50; Lectr and Sen. Lectr, Stockwell Coll., 1950-57; Principal: Machakos Training Coll., Kenya, 1957-62; Philippa Fawcett Coll., London SW16, 1963-71. *Publications:* articles in TES, THES, Dialogue, Learning for Teaching. *Recreations:* music, architecture, travel, mountaineering, gardening, cooking. *Address:* Principal's House, Homerton College, Cambridge. *T:* Cambridge 245931. *Club:* English-Speaking Union.

SHTEREV, Kiril; Order of Georgi Dimitrov; Order of Narodna Republica Bulgaria, 2nd Degree; Ambassador of the People's Republic of Bulgaria to the Court of St James's, since 1980; *b* 17 Feb. 1918; *s* of Shteriu Georgiev Gotchev and Dobra Shtereva; *m* 1945, Anna Shtereva; two *d. Educ:* Univ. of Sofia (degree in Economics). Joined Min. of Foreign Affairs, Sofia, 1947; Secretary: Bulgarian Embassy, Prague, 1950-54; Min. of Foreign Affairs, Sofia, 1954-56; Counsellor, Bulgarian Delegn to UN, 1956-59; Counsellor and Chargé d'Affaires, Bulgarian Embassy, Washington, 1959-63; Counsellor and Head of Dept, Min. of For. Affairs, Sofia, 1963-67; Ambassador to Ottawa, 1967-71; Head of State Protocol, Sofia, 1971-73; Ambassador to Teheran, 1973-79; Ambassador, Min. of For. Affairs, Sofia, 1979-80. Foreign Orders awarded by Govts of Czechoslovakia, Egypt, Ethiopia and Afghanistan. *Recreations:* reading, collection of postage stamps. *Address:* 29 Hyde Park Gate, SW7. *T:* 01-589 4694.

SHUCKBURGH, Sir (Charles Arthur) Evelyn, GCMG 1967 (KCMG 1959; CMG 1949); CB 1954; HM Diplomatic Service, retired; Chairman, Executive Committee, British Red Cross Society, 1970-80; Chairman, Council, 1976-80 (Vice-Chairman, 1980-81); Member, Standing Commission,

International Red Cross, since 1974 (Chairman, 1977-81); *b* 26 May 1909; *e s* of late Sir John Shuckburgh, KCMG, CB; *m* 1937, Nancy Brett, 2nd *d* of 3rd Viscount Esher, GBE; two *s* one *d*. *Educ:* Winchester; King's College, Cambridge. Entered Diplomatic Service, 1933; served at HM Embassy, Cairo, 1937-39; seconded for service on staff of UK High Comr in Ottawa, 1940; transferred to Buenos Aires, 1942; Chargé d'Affaires there in 1944; First Secretary at HM Embassy, Prague, 1945-47. Head of South American Department, FO, 1947-48; Western Dept, 1949-50; Western Organizations Dept, 1950-51; Principal Private Secretary to Secretary of State for Foreign Affairs, 1951-54; Assistant Under-Secretary, Foreign Office, 1954-56; Senior Civilian Instructor, IDC, 1956-58; Asst Sec.-Gen. (Polit.) of NATO, Paris, 1958-60; Dep. Under-Sec., FO, 1960-62; Perm. Brit. Rep. to N Atlantic Council, in Paris, 1962-66; Ambassador to Italy, 1966-69. Dir, Commercial Union Assurance, 1971-80. Chm., N Home Counties Regional Cttee, National Trust, 1975-79. *Address:* High Wood House, Watlington, Oxon.

SHUCKBURGH, Sir Charles Gerald Stewkley, 12th Bt, *cr* 1660; TD; DL; JP; Major, late 11th (City of London Yeomanry) LAA; *b* 28 Feb. 1911; *s* of 11th Bt and Honour Zoë, OBE (*d* 1979), *d* of Neville Thursby, of Harlestone, Northamptonshire; *S* father, 1939; *m* 1st, 1935, Remony (*d* 1936), *o d* of late F. N. Bell, Buenos Aires; 2nd, 1937, Nancy Diana Mary (OBE 1970), *o d* of late Capt. Rupert Lubbock, RN; one *s* two *d*. *Educ:* Harrow; Trinity College, Oxford. JP 1946, DL 1965, Warwickshire; High Sheriff, Warwickshire, 1965. *Heir: s* Rupert Charles Gerald Shuckburgh [*b* 12 Feb. 1949; *m* 1976, Judith, *d* of W. G. Mackaness; one *s*]. *Address:* Shuckburgh, Daventry. *TA:* Daventry. *T:* Daventry 2523. *Club:* Bath.

SHUCKBURGH, Sir Evelyn; *see* Shuckburgh, Sir C. A. E.

SHUFFREY, Ralph Frederick Dendy, CVO 1981; Deputy Under-Secretary of State and Principal Establishment Officer, Home Office, since 1980; *b* 9 Dec. 1925; *s* of Frederick and late Mary Shuffrey; *m* 1953, Sheila, *d* of late Brig. John Lingham, CB, DSO, MC, and Juliet Judd; one *s* one *d*. *Educ:* Shrewsbury; Balliol Coll., Oxford. Served Army, 1944-47 (Captain). Entered Home Office, 1951; Private Sec. to Parly Under-Sec. of State, 1956-57; Private Sec. to Home Sec., 1965-66; Asst Sec., 1966-72; Asst Under-Sec. of State, 1972-80. *Address:* 21 Claremont Road, Claygate, Surrey. *T:* Esher 65123. *Club:* Reform.

SHULMAN, Drusilla Norman; *see* Beyfus, Drusilla N.

SHULMAN, Milton; writer, journalist, critic; *b* Toronto; *s* of late Samuel Shulman, merchant, and of Ethel Shulman; *m* 1956, Drusilla Beyfus, *qv*; one *s* two *d*. *Educ:* Univ. of Toronto (BA); Osgoode Hall, Toronto. Barrister, Toronto, 1937-40. Armoured Corps and Intelligence, Canadian Army, 1940-46 (despatches, Normandy, 1945); Major. Film critic, Evening Standard and Sunday Express, 1948-58; book critic, Sunday Express, 1957-58; theatre critic, Evening Standard, 1953-; TV critic, Evening Standard, 1964-73; columnist, social and political affairs, Daily Express, 1973-75; film critic, Vogue Magazine, 1975-. Executive producer and producer, Granada TV, 1958-62; Asst Controller of Programmes, Rediffusion TV, 1962-64. Regular panel mem., Stop the Week, BBC Radio 4. IPC Award, Critic of the Year, 1966. *Publications:* Defeat in the West, 1948; How To Be a Celebrity, 1950; The Ravenous Eye, 1973; The Least Worst Television in the World, 1973; *children's books:* Preep, 1964; Preep in Paris, 1967; Preep and The Queen, 1970; *novel:* Kill Three, 1967; *novel and film story:* (with Herbert Kretzmer) Every Home Should Have One, 1970. *Recreations:* modern art, history, tennis. *Address:* 51 Eaton Square, SW1. *T:* 01-235 7162. *Club:* Hurlingham.

SHULTZ, George Pratt; Secretary of State, United States of America, since July 1982; *b* New York City, 13 Dec. 1920; *s* of Birl E. Shultz and Margaret Pratt; *m* 1946, Helena Maria O'Brien; two *s* three *d*. *Educ:* Princeton Univ., 1942 (BA Econ); Massachusetts Inst. of Technology, 1949 (PhD Industrial Econ). Served War, US Marine Corps, Pacific, 1942; Major, 1945. Faculty, MIT, 1948-57; Sen. staff economist, President's Council of Economic Advisers, 1955-56 (on leave, MIT); Univ. of Chicago, Graduate Sch. of Business: Prof. of Industrial Relations, 1957-62; Dean, 1962-69; Prof. of Management and Public Policy, Stanford Univ., Graduate Sch. of Business, 1974. Secretary of Labor, 1969-July 1, 1970; Dir, Office of Management and Budget, 1970-72; Secretary of the Treasury, 1972-74; Exec. Vice-Pres., Bechtel Corp., 1974-75, Pres. 1975-79; Vice-Chm., Bechtel Group, 1980; Pres., Bechtel Group Inc., San Francisco, 1981-82. Chm., President's Economic Policy Adv. Bd, 1981-82. Director: General Motors Corp.; Dillon, Read & Co. Inc. Hon. Dr of Laws: Notre Dame Univ., 1969; Loyola Univ., 1972; Pennsylvania, 1973; Rochester, 1973; Princeton, 1973; Carnegie-Mellon Univ., 1975. *Publications:* Pressures on Wage Decisions, 1951; The Dynamics of a Labor Market (with C. A. Myers), 1951; Management Organization and the Computer (with T. A. Whisler), 1960; Strategies for the Displaced Worker (with Arnold R. Weber), 1966; Guidelines, Informal Controls, and the Market Place (with Rober Z. Aliber), 1966; Workers and Wages in the Urban Labor Market (with Albert Rees), 1970; Economic Policy Beyond the Headlines (with Kenneth W. Dam), 1978. *Recreations:* golf, tennis. *Address:* (office) Secretary of State, 2201 C Street NW, Washington, DC 20520, USA. *T:* (202) 632-4910; (home) Bethesda, Md, USA.

SHUTE, Prof. Charles Cameron Donald, MD; Professor of Histology, Cambridge University, since 1969; Fellow of Christ's College, Cambridge,

since 1957; *b* 23 May 1917; *s* of late Cameron Deane Shute; *m* 1st, 1947, Patricia Cameron (*d* 1952), *d* of F. H. Doran; 2nd, 1954, Lydia May (Wendy) (*née* Harwood) (marr. diss. 1980); one *s* three *d*; 3rd, 1980, Rosemary Gay Robins. *Educ:* Eton; King's Coll., Cambridge; Middlesex Hosp., London. MA, MB, BChir Cambridge, 1945; MD Cambridge 1958. Resident posts at Middlesex Hosp., 1945-47; RAMC (otologist), 1947-49; Demonstrator and Lectr in Anatomy, London Hosp. Med. Coll., 1951; Univ. Demonstrator and Lectr, Cambridge, 1952-69; Univ. Reader in Neuroanatomy, Cambridge, 1969. *Publications:* The McCollough Effect, 1979; papers in biological jls. *Recreation:* Egyptology. *Address:* Milton House, Christ's Pieces, Cambridge. *T:* Cambridge 62035.

SHUTE, John Lawson, CMG 1970; OBE 1959; Member: Council of Egg Marketing Authorities of Australia, 1970-79; Egg Marketing Board of New South Wales, 1970-79; Director, Arthur Yates & Co. Pty Ltd, 1970-80; *b* Mudgee, NSW, 31 Jan. 1901; *s* of J. Shute, Mudgee; *m* 1937, Constance W. M., *d* of J. Douglas; two *s*. *Educ:* Parramatta High Sch. Asst Sec., Primary Producers' Union, NSW, 1923-33; Gen.-Sec., 1933-42; Sec., Federated Co-operative Bacon Factories, 1927-42; Member: NSW Dairy Products Bd, 1934-46; Commonwealth Air Beef Panel, 1962; Dir, Commonwealth Dairy Produce Equalisation Cttee, 1941-46; 1st Sec. Aust. Dairy Farmers' Fedn, 1942; Mem. Exec. and Asst Sec., Empire Producers' Conf., 1938; Mem. Special Dairy Industry Cttee apptd by Commonwealth Govt, 1942; Dep. Controller, Meat Supplies, NSW, 1942-46. Chairman: Aust. Meat Bd, 1946-70; Aust. Cttee of Animal Production, 1947-70; Aust. Cattle and Beef Research Cttee, 1960-66; Belmont-Brian Pastures Res. Cttee, 1962-76; Aust. Meat Research Cttee, 1966-70; Aust. Frozen Cargo Shippers' Cttee, 1967-70; Member: Export Development Council, 1958-66; Overseas Trade Publicity Cttee, 1955-70; Australia Japan Business Co-operation Cttee, 1962-70; Industry Co-operative Programme, FAO, 1973-78 (Chm., Working Gp on Integrated Meat Develt, 1975-78); NSW Rural Reconstruction Bd, 1942-71. Life Mem., Rural Youth Orgn of NSW, 1961. Life Mem., Australia-Britain Soc., 1979; Hon. Life Mem., Australian Veterinary Assoc., 1970-. Mem., Worshipful Co. of Butchers, 1950. Freedom, City of London, 1951. *Recreations:* Rugby Union (former Internat. rep.), cricket. *Address:* 5/2 Woonona Avenue, Wahroonga, NSW 2076, Australia. *Clubs:* Commercial Travellers' (NSW); Eastwood Rugby Union (NSW).

SHUTTLE, Penelope (Diane); writer and poet; *b* 12 May 1947; *d* of Jack Frederick Shuttle and Joan Shepherdess Lipscombe; *m* Peter Redgrove, *qv*; one *d*. *Educ:* Staines Grammar Sch.; Matthew Arnold County Secondary Sch., Mddx. Radio plays: The Girl who Lost her Glove, 1975 (Jt 3rd Prize Winner, Radio Times Drama Bursaries Comp., 1974); The Dauntless Girl, 1978. Poetry recorded for Poetry Room, Harvard Univ. Arts Council Awards, 1969 and 1972; Greenwood Poetry Prize, 1972; E. C. Gregory Award for Poetry, 1974. *Publications: novels:* An Excusable Vengeance, 1967; All the Usual Hours of Sleeping, 1969; Wailing Monkey Embracing a Tree, 1974; Rainsplitter in the Zodiac Garden, 1976; Mirror of the Giant, 1979; *poetry:* Nostalgia Neurosis, 1968; Midwinter Mandala, 1973; Photographs of Persephone, 1973; Autumn Piano, 1973; Songbook of the Snow, 1973; Webs on Fire, 1977; The Orchard Upstairs, 1981; *with Peter Redgrove:* The Hermaphrodite Album (poems), 1973; The Terrors of Dr Treviles (novel), 1974; The Wise Wound (psychology), 1978. *Recreations:* listening to music, Hatha Yoga, walking. *Address:* c/o David Higham Associates Ltd, 5-8 Lower John Street, Golden Square, W1R 4HA.

SHUTTLEWORTH, 5th Baron *cr* 1902, of Gawthorpe; **Charles Geoffrey Nicholas Kay-Shuttleworth;** Bt 1850; Partner, Burton, Barnes & Vigers, Chartered Surveyors, since 1977; *b* 2 Aug. 1948; *s* of 4th Baron Shuttleworth, MC, and of Anne Elizabeth, *er d* of late Col Geoffrey Phillips, CBE, DSO; *S* father, 1975; *m* 1975, Mrs Ann Mary Barclay, *d* of James Whatman; three *s*. *Educ:* Eton. Dir, Burnley Building Soc., 1978- (Vice-Chm., 1982-). Chairman: Lancs Small Industries Cttee, COSIRA, 1978-; Lancs Youth Clubs Assoc., 1980-. ARICS. *Heir: s* Hon. Thomas Edward Kay-Shuttleworth, *b* 29 Sept. 1976. *Address:* 14 Sloane Avenue, SW3 3JE; Leck Hall, Carnforth, Lancs. *Clubs:* Brooks's, MCC.

SIBBALD, Maj.-Gen. Peter Frank Aubrey, CB 1982; OBE 1972; Director of Infantry, since 1980; *b* 24 March 1928; *s* of Major Francis Victor Sibbald, MBE, MM, BEM, and Mrs Alice Emma Hawking, The Hoe, Plymouth; *m* 1957, Margaret Maureen Entwistle; one *s* one *d*. *Educ:* ISC, Haileybury. Commnd, 1948; served with 1 KOYLI, 1948-53; Malayan Emergency, 1948-51 (mentioned in despatches); Korea, 1953-54; Kenya Emergency, 1954-55; Instr, Sch. of Inf., 1955-57; psc 1961; Aden, 1965-66; Bde Maj., 151 Inf. Bde, 1962-64; jssc 1964; GSO2 HQ FARELF, 1966-68; CO 2 LI, 1968-71; Col GS HQ BAOR, 1972; Comdr 51 Inf. Bde, 1972-74; Div. Brig., Light Div., 1975-77; GOC NW District, 1977-80. Dep. Col, Light Infantry (Yorks), 1977-80; Col Comdt, The Light Div., 1980-; First Vice-Pres., Eighth Army Veterans' Assoc. FBIM. *Recreations:* game shooting, fishing, squash, swimming. *Address:* Lloyds Bank, 8 Royal Parade, Plymouth, Devon. *Club:* Army and Navy.

SIBERRY, John William Morgan; Under-Secretary, Welsh Office, 1964-73, retired; Secretary to Local Government Staff Commission for Wales, and NHS Staff Commission for Wales, 1973-75; *b* 26 Feb. 1913; *s* of late John William and Martha (*née* Morgan) Siberry; *m* 1949, Florence Jane Davies; one *s* one *d*. *Educ:* Porth County School, Rhondda; Univ. Coll. Cardiff. Entered Civil Service as Asst Principal, Unemployment Assistance Board (later Nat.

Assistance Board), 1935; Principal, 1941; Asst Sec., 1947; transferred to Min. of Housing and Local Govt as Under-Sec., 1963; Welsh Secretary, Welsh Office and Office for Wales of the Ministry of Housing and Local Government, 1963-64. Chm., Working Party on Fourth Television Service in Wales, 1975. *Recreation:* golf. *Address:* Northgates, Pwllmelin Road, Llandaff, Cardiff CF5 2NG. *T:* Cardiff 564666. *Club:* Cardiff and County.

SIBLEY, Antoinette, CBE 1973; Prima Ballerina, The Royal Ballet, Covent Garden, retired; *b* 27 Feb. 1939; *d* of Edward G. Sibley and Winifred M. Sibley (*née* Smith); *m* 1964, M. G. Somes, CBE (marr. diss. 1973); *m* 1974, Panton Corbett; one *s* one *d*. *Educ:* Arts Educational Sch. and Royal Ballet Sch. 1st performance on stage as Student with Royal Ballet at Covent Garden, a swan, Jan. 1956; joined company, July 1956. Leading role in: Swan Lake, Sleeping Beauty, Giselle, Coppelia, Cinderella, The Nutcracker, La Fille Mal Gardée, Romeo & Juliet, Harlequin in April, Les Rendezvous, Jabez & the Devil (created the role of Mary), La Fête Etrange, The Rakes Progress, Hamlet, Ballet Imperial, Two Pigeons, La Bayadère, Symphonic Variations, Scènes de Ballet, Lilac Garden, Daphnis & Chloe, The Dream (created Titania), Laurentia, Good Humoured Ladies, Aristocrat in Mam'zelle Angot, Façade, Song of the Earth, Monotones (created role), Jazz Calendar (created Friday's Child), Enigma Variations (created Dorabella), Thais (created pas de deux), Anastasia (created Kshessinska), Afternoon of a Faun, Triad (created the Girl), Pavanne, Manon (created title role), Soupirs (created pas de deux), L'invitation an voyage (created), Impromptu (created pas de deux). *Film:* The Turning Point, 1978. *Relevant publications:* Sibley and Dowell, by Nicholas Dromgoole and Leslie Spatt, 1976; Antoinette Sibley, 1981, photographs with text by Mary Clarke. *Recreations:* doing nothing; opera and books. *Address:* Royal Opera House, WC2.

SICH, Sir Rupert (Leigh), Kt 1968; CB 1953; Registrar of Restrictive Trading Agreements, 1956-73; *b* 3 Aug. 1908; *s* of late A. E. Sich, Caterham, Surrey; *m* 1933, Elizabeth Mary, *d* of late R. W. Hutchison, Gerrards Cross; one *s* one *d*. *Educ:* Radley College; Merton College, Oxford. Called to Bar, Inner Temple, 1930. Board of Trade Solicitor's Dept, 1932-48; Treasury Solicitor's Dept, 1948-56. *Recreations:* J. S. Bach; gardening. *Address:* Norfolk House, The Mall, Chiswick, W4. *T:* 01-994 2133. *Clubs:* United Oxford & Cambridge University, MCC.

SIDDALL, Norman, CBE 1975; FEng; Member, National Coal Board, since 1971, Deputy Chairman 1973-82, Chairman since 1982; *b* 4 May 1918; *m* 1943; two *s* one *d*. *Educ:* King Edward VII School, Sheffield; Sheffield Univ. (BEng). National Coal Board: Production Manager, No 5 Area, East Midlands Div., 1951-56; General Manager, No 5 Area, East Midlands Div. 1956-57; General Manager, No 1 Area, East Midlands Div., 1957-66; Chief Mining Engineer, 1966-67; Dir Gen. of Production, 1967-71. Chartered Engineer; FRSA; FIMinE; FBIM; 1st Vice-Chm., Organising Cttee, World Mining Congress, 1977; Member: Midland Counties Institution of Engineers (Silver Medal, 1951; Past President); Amer. Inst. Mining Engrs. National Association of Colliery Managers: Silver Medal, 1955; Bronze Medal, 1960; Coal Science Lecture Medal, 1972; CGLI Insignia Award in Technology (*hc*), 1978; Instn Medal, IME, 1982. Hon. DSc Nottingham, 1982. Colliery Managers Certificate. *Publications:* articles in professional journals. *Address:* c/o National Coal Board, Hobart House, Grosvenor Place, SW1. *T:* 01-235 2020.

SIDDELEY, family name of **Baron Kenilworth.**

SIDDELEY, Randle; *see* Kenilworth, 4th Baron.

SIDDIQUI, Dr Salimuzzaman, MBE 1946; Tamgha-i-Pakistan 1958; Sitara-i-Imtiaz (Pakistan) 1962; Hilal-e-Imtiaz, 1980; FRS 1961; DPhil; Hon DMed; Director, H. E. J. Research Institute of Chemistry, University of Karachi, since 1966; *b* 19 Oct. 1897. *Educ:* Lucknow; MAO College, Aligarh, UP; University College, London; Univ. of Frankfurt-on-Main. Returned to India, 1928; planned and directed Research Inst. at Ayurvedic and Unani Tibbi Coll., Delhi, 1928-40. Joined Council of Scientific and Industrial Research (India): Organic Chemist, 1940; Actg Dir of Chemical Laboratories, 1944. Director of Scientific and Industrial Research, Pakistan, 1951; Director and Chairman of Pakistan Council of Scientific and Industrial Research, 1953-66; Chairman, Nat. Science Council, 1962-66; Pres., Pakistan Acad. of Sciences, 1968. A chemist, working on the chemistry of natural products; has led the promotion of scientific and industrial research in Pakistan; has rep. Pakistan at internat. scientific confs. etc. Gold Medal, Russian Acad.; President's Pride of Performance Medal (Pakistan), 1966. Elected Mem., Vatican Acad. of Sciences, 1964. Hon. DSc. *Address:* Director, H.E.J. Research Institute of Chemistry, University of Karachi, Karachi, Pakistan. *T:* 463414.

SIDDONS, Arthur Harold Makins, MChir Cantab; FRCS; FRCP; Hon. Consulting Surgeon, St George's Hospital; *b* 17 Jan. 1911; *s* of late A. W. Siddons, Housemaster, Harrow School; *m* 1st, 1939, Joan Richardson Anderson (*née* McConnell) (*d* 1949); one *s* one *d*; 2nd, 1956, Eleanor Mary Oliver (*née* Hunter) (*d* 1970); 3rd, 1971, Margaret Christine Beardmore (*née* Smith). *Educ:* Harrow; Jesus College, Cambridge; St George's Hospital. MB, BCh Cantab 1935. Surgeon, St George's Hospital, 1941; Consultant General and Thoracic Surgeon, St George's Hosp. and others, 1948-76. Served RAF Medical Branch, 1942-46. Member of Court of Examiners, Royal College of Surgeons of England, 1958-63. *Publications:* Cardiac Pacemakers, 1967;

sections on lung surgery in various textbooks. *Recreations:* travel, gardens. *Address:* Robin Hey, Tilford Road, Farnham, Surrey GU9 8HX. *T:* Farnham 715667.

SIDEBOTHAM, John Biddulph, CMG 1946; MA Cantab; retired as Assistant Secretary, Colonial Office (1941-54); *b* 23 Nov. 1891; *er s* of late Rev. Frederick William Gilbert Sidebotham, MA, Rector of Weeting, Norfolk; *m* 1st, 1917, Hilda, *d* of late F. Haviland; one *d*; 2nd, 1941, Mary, *d* of late A. Blascheck; 3rd, 1971, Audrey (*née* Sidebotham), widow of Major D. B. Williams. *Educ:* King's School, Canterbury; Gonville and Caius Coll., Cambridge (Stanhope Exhibitioner, Open Class Exhibitioner, Scholar). 1st cl. theolog. tripos, pt 1, 1914; BA 1914, MA 1920; 2nd Lieut Home Counties RE (TF), 1914; Lieut 1916; served in France, 1914-15 (wounded); Inland Revenue, Somerset House, 1920; transferred to Colonial Office as asst prin. under reconstruction scheme, Dec. 1922; sec. managing cttee, Bureau of Hygiene and Tropical Diseases, 1925; sec., East African guaranteed loan advisory cttee, 1927; pte sec. to Parliamentary Under-Sec. of State for Dominion Affairs, 1928; pte sec. Permt Under-Sec. for the Colonies, 1929, principal, 1930; accompanied Permt Under-Secretary of State for the Colonies (Sir J. Maffey) to W Indies, 1936. Visited St Helena, 1939 and 1955; also visited Ceylon, Borneo, Sarawak, Hong Kong, Fiji and Mauritius. Mem. managing cttee of Bureau of Hygiene and Tropical Diseases, 1941-73. *Address:* Nantwatcyn, Cwmystwyth, Aberystwyth, Dyfed SY23 4AG. *T:* Pontrhydygroes 217.

SIDEBOTTOM, Edward John; a Chief Inspector, Department of Education and Science, 1973-80 (Divisional Inspector, 1969-73); *b* 1918; *s* of late Ernest Sidebottom, Wylam, Northumberland; *m* 1949, Brenda Millicent, *d* of late Alec H. Sadler, Wandsworth. *Educ:* Queen Elizabeth Grammar School, Hexham; Hatfield College, Durham (BSc). Entered Iraq Government education service, 1939; lecturer, Leavesden Green Emergency Training College, 1946; County Youth Organiser for Hampshire, 1947; HM Inspector of Schools, 1949-80. Sec. to Albemarle Cttee on the Youth Service in England and Wales, 1958-59; seconded as first Principal, Nat. Coll. for the Training of Youth Leaders, 1960-64. Chm., Jt Curriculum and Training Group (Mental Handicap), 1981-. *Address:* 3 Queen's Court, Marlborough Road, West Cliff, Bournemouth, Dorset.

SIDEY, Air Marshal Sir Ernest (Shaw), KBE 1972; CB 1965; MD, ChB, FFCM, DPH; Director-General, Chest, Heart and Stroke Association, since 1974; *b* 2 Jan. 1913; *s* of Thomas Sidey, Alyth, Perthshire; *m* 1946, Doreen Florence, *y d* of late Cecil Ronald Lurring, Dalkey, Ireland; one *d* (and one *d* decd). *Educ:* Morgan Acad., Dundee; St Andrews Univ. Commissioned in RAF, 1937. Served in Burma Campaign during War of 1939-45. Recent appts include: Chief, Med. Adv. Staff, Allied Air Forces Central Europe, 1957-59; PMO: Flying Trg Comd, 1961-63; Middle East Comd, 1963-65; Transport Command, 1965-66; DDGMS, RAF, 1966-68. PMO, Strike Command, 1968-70; DGMS, RAF, 1971-74. QHS 1966-74. Governor, Royal Star and Garter Home, 1974-. *Recreations:* racing, golf, bridge. *Address:* Callums, Tugwood Common, Cookham Dean, Berks. *T:* Marlow 3006. *Club:* Royal Air Force.

SIDEY, John MacNaughton, DSO 1945; Director, P&O Steam Navigation Co., 1970-77; retired; *b* 11 July 1914; *e c* of John and Florence Sidey; *m* 1941, Eileen, *o d* of Sir George Wilkinson, 1st Bt, KCVO; one *s* (one *d* decd). *Educ:* Exeter School. Served War, 1939-45, with Royal Tank Regiment and Westminster Dragoons, finishing as Lt-Col commanding 22nd Dragoons. Mem., Southern Area Board, BTC, 1955-61 (Chm. Jan.-Dec. 1962); part-time Mem., British Railways Bd, 1962-68; Chm., Eastern Region Bd, British Railways, 1963-65. Council Mem. and Chm., Transport Policy Cttee, CBI, 1967-79; Mem., Nat. Docks Labour Bd, 1977-. Pres., London Chapter, Nat. Defence Transportation Assoc. of America, 1961-62. *Recreations:* fishing, gardening, golf. *Address:* Acre Holt, Golf Club Road, Woking, Surrey GU22 0LS. *T:* Woking 4788.

SIDEY, Thomas Kay Stuart, CMG 1968; Managing Director, Wickliffe Press Ltd, since 1962; Barrister and Solicitor, NZ, since 1932; *b* 8 Oct. 1908; *s* of Sir Thomas Kay Sidey; *m* 1933, Beryl, *d* of Harvey Richardson Thomas, Wellington, NZ; one *s* one *d*. *Educ:* Otago Boys' High School; Univ. of Otago (LLM; Hon LLD, 1978). Served War of 1939-45 (despatches): 2nd NZEF; 4 years, Middle East and Italy, rank of Major. Dunedin City Council, 1947-50, 1953-65, 1968-; Dep. Mayor, 1956-59, 1968-77; Mayor, 1959-65; Univ. of Otago Council, 1947-, Pro-Chancellor, 1959-70, Chancellor, 1970-76. Past President: Dunedin Chamber of Commerce; Automobile Assoc., Otago; Otago Trustee Savings Bank; NZ Library Assoc.; Otago Old People's Welfare Council; Otago Boys' High Sch. Old Boys' Soc. *Recreations:* fishing, boating, ski-ing. *Address:* 16 Tolcarne Avenue, Dunedin, New Zealand. *T:* 775-694. *Club:* Dunedin (Dunedin, NZ).

SIDGWICK, Rear-Admiral John Benson, CB 1945; RN retd; late Deputy Engineer-in-Chief, Admiralty. Served European War, 1914-18; Engineer Captain, 1936; Engineer Rear-Admiral, 1942.

SIDMOUTH, 7th Viscount *cr* 1805; **John Tonge Anthony Pellew Addington;** *b* 3 Oct. 1914; *s* of 6th Viscount Sidmouth and of Gladys Mary Dever, *d* of late Thomas Francis Hughes; *S* father, 1976; *m* 1940, Barbara Mary, *d* of Bernard Rochford, OBE; two *s* five *d*. *Educ:* Downside School (Scholar); Brasenose Coll., Oxford (Scholar). Colonial Service, E Africa,

1938-54. Director, Joseph Rochford & Sons Ltd and other cos. Mem. Council and Chm. Glasshouse Cttee, Nat. Farmers Union, 1962-69; Member: Agricultural Research Council, 1964-74; Central Council for Agricultural Cooperation, 1970-73. Trustee, John Innes Charity, 1974. Chm. of Governing Body, Glasshouse Crops Research Inst., 1981-. Knight of Malta, 1962. *Recreations:* sailing, gardening. *Heir: s* Hon. Christopher John Addington [*b* 10 April 1941; *m* 1963, Clio Mona, *o d* of John Peristiany]. *Address:* Highway Manor, near Calne, Wilts SN11 8SR. *T:* Hilmarton 390; 16 Westminster Palace Gardens, Artillery Row, SW1P 1RL. *T:* 01-222 2445.

SIDNEY, family name of **Viscount De L'Isle.**

SIDNEY-WILMOT, Air Vice-Marshal Aubrey, CB 1977; OBE 1948; Director of Legal Services (Royal Air Force), 1970-79; a Chairman of Industrial Tribunals, since 1979; *b* 4 Jan. 1915; *s* of Alfred Robert Sidney-Wilmot and Harriet Sidney-Wilmot; *m* 1968, Ursula Hartmann; one *s* by former marriage. *Educ:* Framlingham College. Admitted Solicitor, 1938, practised, 1938-40. Commnd in Administrative Br., RAF, 1940; transf. to Office of JAG, 1942; DJAG (Army and RAF), Far East, 1948-50; transf. to Directorate of Legal Services (RAF), 1950; Dep. Dir of Legal Services (RAF), 1969. *Recreations:* travel, swimming, gardening. *Address:* Grove Cottage, Great Horkesley, Colchester, Essex CO6 4AG. *Club:* Royal Air Force.

SIDWELL, Martindale, FRAM; FRCO; Organist and Choirmaster, Hampstead Parish Church, since 1946; Organist and Director of Music, St Clement Danes (Church of the RAF), since 1957; Conductor, Hampstead Choral Society, since 1946; Conductor, Martindale Sidwell Choir, since 1956; Professor of Organ, Royal Academy of Music, since 1963; Director, Founder and Conductor, London Bach Orchestra, since 1967; *b* 23 Feb. 1916; *s* of John William Sidwell, Little Packington, Warwicks, and Mary Martindale, Liverpool; *m* 1944, Barbara Anne (*née* Hill) (pianist, harpsichordist and Prof. of Piano, Royal Coll. of Music, under the name Barbara Hill); two *s. Educ:* Wells Cathedral Sch., Somerset; Royal Academy of Music. Sub-Organist, Wells Cathedral, 1932. Served War of 1939-45, Royal Engineers. Organist, Holy Trinity Church, Leamington Spa, and Director of Music, Warwick School, 1943, also at same time Conductor of Royal Leamington Spa Bach Choir; Prof., RSCM, 1958-66. Mem. Council, Royal Coll. of Organists, 1966-. Harriet Cohen Bach Medal, 1967. Frequent broadcasts as Conductor and as Organ Recitalist, 1944 -. *Address:* 1 Frognal Gardens, Hampstead, NW3. *T:* 01-435 9210. *Club:* Savage.

SIE, Sir Banja T.; *see* Tejan-Sie.

SIEFF, family name of **Baron Sieff of Brimpton** and of Sieff barony (extinct).

SIEFF OF BRIMPTON, Baron *cr* 1980 (Life Peer), of Brimpton in the Royal County of Berkshire; **Marcus Joseph Sieff;** Kt 1971; OBE 1944; Chairman, Marks and Spencer plc, since 1972; Joint Managing Director, since 1967; *b* 2 July 1913; *yr s* of late Baron Sieff; *m* 1st, 1937, Rosalie Fromson (marr. diss., 1947); one *s*; 2nd, 1951, Elsa Florence Gosen (marr. diss., 1953); 3rd, 1956, Brenda Mary Beith (marr. diss., 1962); one *d*; 4th, 1963, Mrs Pauline Lily Moretzki (*née* Spatz); one *d. Educ:* Manchester Grammar School; St Paul's; Corpus Christi College, Cambridge (BA), Hon. Fellow, 1975. Served War 1939-45, Royal Artillery. Joined Marks & Spencer Ltd, 1935; Dir, 1954; Asst Man. Dir, 1963, Vice-Chm., 1965; Dep. Chm., 1971. Mem., BNEC, 1965-71 (Chm., Export Cttee for Israel, 1965-68). Vice-Pres., Joint Israel Appeal. Vice Pres., Policy Studies Institute (formerly PEP) Exec., 1975-; Pres., Anglo-Israel Chamber of Commerce, 1975-. Mem. Bd of Trustees, Police Foundn, 1980-. Patron, RCS, 1977. Hambro Award, Businessman of the Year, 1977; Aims National Free Enterprise Award, 1978; B'nai B'rith Internat. gold medallion for humanitarianism, 1982. *Address:* Michael House, Baker Street, W1A 1DN.

See also Hon. D. D. Sieff, Hon. M. D. Sieff.

SIEFF, Hon. David Daniel; Director, Marks & Spencer plc, since 1972; *b* 22 March 1939; *s* of Baron Sieff of Brimpton, *qv*, and late Rosalie Cottage; *m* 1962, Jennifer Walton; two *s. Educ:* Repton. Joined Marks & Spencer, 1957; Alternate Director, 1968; Full Director, 1972 (Director of Personnel, 1968-72 and 1975-78). Chairman, North Metropolitan Conciliation Cttee of Race Relations Board, 1969-71; Vice-Chm., Inst. of Race Relations, 1971-72; part-time Member, National Freight Corp., 1972-78; Member Council: Industrial Soc., 1976-; Policy Studies Inst. (formerly PEP), 1976-; Governor, Weizmann Inst. of Science, Rehovot, Israel, 1978-. Trustee, Glyndebourne Arts Trust, 1971-. Pres., Racehorse Owners Assoc., 1975-78; Member, Jockey Club, 1977-. *Address:* Michael House, 47 Baker Street, W1A 1DN. *T:* 01-935 4422. *Club:* Saints and Sinners.

SIEFF, Joseph Edward; Hon. President, Marks & Spencer Ltd, since 1979 (Assistant Managing Director, 1946; Joint Managing Director, 1963-72; Vice-Chairman, 1963, Deputy Chairman, 1965, Chairman, 1967-72, President, 1972-79); *b* 28 Nov. 1905; *s* of Ephraim Sieff, Manchester; *m* 1929, Maisie, *d* of Dr Sidney Marsh; two *d*; *m* 1952, Louis, *d* of William Ross; one *s* one *d. Educ:* Manchester Grammar School; Manchester University. Joined Marks & Spencer Ltd, 1933. Chairman Joint Israel Appeal, 1961-65, President 1965-. Hon. President, Zionist Federation of Great Britain and Ireland, 1974- (Vice-Pres., 1965-74). Governor, Manchester Grammar School, 1974-.

Address: Michael House, Baker Street, W1A 1DN. *T:* 01-935 4422. *Club:* Savile.

SIEFF, Hon. Michael David, CBE 1975; Director, Marks & Spencer, 1950-78 (Joint Managing Director, 1971-76; Joint Vice-Chairman, 1972-76); *b* 12 March 1911; *er s* of late Baron Sieff; *m* 1st, 1932, Daphne Madge Kerin Michael (marr. diss. 1975); one *s*; 2nd, 1975, Elizabeth Pitt; one *s* one *d. Educ:* Manchester Grammar School. Served War of 1939-45, Col RAOC 1944; Hon. Col, TA, 1956. Joined Marks & Spencer Ltd, 1929; Asst Man. Dir, 1965-71. Member: European Trade Cttee, British Overseas Trade Bd, 1974-; British Overseas Trade Adv. Council, 1975-; Pres., British Overseas Trade Gp for Israel, 1979- (Chm., 1972-78); Vice-Chm., Anglo-Israel Chamber of Commerce, 1969-. Founder Fellow and Mem. Council, Royal Post-Grad. Med. Sch. (Hammersmith Hosp.), 1972. *Address:* Michael House, Baker Street, W1A 1DN. *T:* 01-935 4422.

See also Baron Sieff of Brimpton.

SIEGBAHN, Prof. Kai Manne Börje; Professor of Physics, University of Uppsala, since 1954; *b* 20 April 1918; *s* of Manne Siegbahn and Karin Siegbahn (*née* Högbom); *m* 1944, Anna-Brita (*née* Rhedin); three *s. Educ:* Univ. of Uppsala (BSc 1939; Licentiate of Philosophy 1942); Univ. of Stockholm (Dr of Philosophy 1944). Research Associate, Nobel Inst. of Physics, 1942-51; Prof. of Physics, Royal Inst. of Technology, Stockholm, 1951-54. Member: Roy. Swedish Acad. of Sci.; Roy. Swedish Acad. of Engrg Scis; Roy. Soc. of Sci.; Roy. Acad. of Arts and Sci. of Uppsala; Roy. Physiographical Soc. of Lund; Societas Scientiarum Fennica; Norwegian Acad. of Sci.; Roy. Norwegian Soc. of Scis and Letters. Hon. Mem. Amer. Acad. of Arts and Scis; Membre de Comité des Poids et Mesures, Paris; Pres., Internat. Union of Pure and Applied Physics (IUPAP). Dr of Science, *hc* : Durham, 1972; Basel, 1980; Liège, 1980; Upsala Coll., East Orange, NJ, 1982. Lindblom Prize, 1945; Björkén Prize, 1955, 1977; Celsius Medal, 1962; Sixten Heyman Award, 1971; Harrison Howe Award, 1973; Maurice F. Hasler Award, 1975; Charles Frederick Chandler Medal, 1976; Torbern Bergman Medal, 1979; Pittsburgh Award of Spectroscopy, 1982. (Jtly) Nobel Prize for Physics, 1981. *Publications:* Beta- and Gamma-Ray Spectroscopy, 1955; Alpha-, Beta- and Gamma-Ray Spectroscopy, 1965; ESCA—Atomic, Molecular and Solid State Structure Studied by Means of Electron Spectroscopy, 1967; ESCA Applied to Free Molecules, 1969; around 400 scientific papers. *Recreations:* tennis, skiing and music. *Address:* Institute of Physics, University of Uppsala, Box 530, S-751 21 Uppsala, Sweden. *T:* 018/13 94 60.

SIEGERT, Air Vice-Marshal Cyril Laurence, CB 1979; CBE 1975; MVO 1954; DFC 1944; AFC 1954; General Manager, Marine-Air Systems Ltd; *b* 14 March 1923; *s* of Lawrence Siegert and Julia Ann Siegert; *m* 1948, Shirley Berenice Dick; two *s* two *d. Educ:* Fairlie High School; St Kevin's Coll., Oamaru; Victoria Univ. of Wellington. Joined RNZAF, 1942; served in UK with Nos 299 and 190 Sqdns; on loan to BOAC, 1945-47; Berlin airlift, 1949; NZ, 1952-54; NZ Defence Staff, Washington, 1954-56; RAF Staff Coll., 1957; NZ, 1958-62; Comdt, RNZAF's Command and Staff Sch., 1962; RAF Coll. of Air Warfare, 1963; Singapore, 1963-65; CO, No 3 Battlefield Support Sqdn and RNZAF Transport Wing, 1965-69; AOC RNZAF Ops Group, 1969-70; IDC 1970; RNZAF Air Staff, 1971; Chief of Staff, ANZUK Joint Force HQ, Singapore, 1971-73; Dep. Chief of Defence Staff (Policy), 1973-76; Chief of Air Staff, RNZAF, 1976-79. *Recreations:* fishing, tramping, gardening. *Address:* 46 Wyndrum Avenue, Lower Hutt, New Zealand. *Clubs:* Wellesley, United Services (Wellington).

SIEGHART, Paul; law reformer, international arbitrator and consultant, writer and broadcaster; Chairman, Executive Committee, Justice (British Section of International Commission of Jurists), since 1978; *b* 22 Feb. 1927; *s* of Ernest and Marguerite Alexander Sieghart; *m* 1st, 1954, Rosemary (*d* 1956), *d* of Comdr C. E. Aglionby, DSO, RN; one *s* one *d*; 2nd, 1959, Felicity Ann, *d* of A. M. Baer; one *s* one *d. Educ:* Harrow; Berkhamsted Sch.; University Coll. London. FRSA; FCIArb. Called to the Bar, Gray's Inn, 1953; retired from practice, 1966. Chm., Professions Jt Working Party on Statutory Registration of Psychotherapists, 1975-81; Member: Home Office Data Protection Cttee, 1976-78; Gpe de Bellerive, Geneva, 1977-; Gorleben Internat. Rev., 1978-79; Commn for Internat. Justice and Peace of England and Wales, 1976-80; Council, Catholic Union of GB, 1981-. Founder, Council for Sci. and Society, 1972 (Vice-Chm., 1972-78); Governor, British Inst. of Human Rights, 1974-; Trustee: European Human Rights Foundn, 1980-; The Tablet Trust, 1976-; Monteverdi Trust, 1980-; Justice Educnl and Res. Trust, 1981-; Tavistock Clinic Foundn, 1982-. Jt recipient, Airey Neave Meml Scholarship for research into freedom under national laws, 1981. Lectures: Cantor, RSA, 1977; Lucas, RCP, 1981; Shaw Meml, Oxford, 1981. Draftsman: Right of Privacy Bill 1970; Rehabilitation of Offenders Act 1974. Freeman, City of London. *Publications:* (ed) Chalmers' Sale of Goods, 13th edn 1957, 14th edn 1963; (with J. B. Whalley) Slaughterhouses, 1960; Privacy and Computers, 1976; The International Law of Human Rights, 1982; contribs to learned jls. *Recreations:* travel, music, ski-ing, sailing, shooting. *Address:* 6 Gray's Inn Square, WC1R 5AZ. *T:* 01-405 1351. *Clubs:* Brooks's; Bar Yacht.

SIEPMANN, Charles Arthur, MC; BA; Professor Emeritus, New York University, since 1967; Professor, Sarah Lawrence College, New York, 1968-71; *b* 10 Mar. 1899; *s* of Otto and Grace Florence Siepmann; *m* 1940, Charlotte Tyler; one *s* two *d. Educ:* Clifton Coll. (scholar); Keble Coll. Oxford (scholar). Served European War, 1917-18; Oxford, 1919-21; Brown

Shipley and Co., 1922-24; housemaster and education officer, HM Borstal Instns, Feltham and Rochester, 1924-27; joined BBC, 1927; Dir of Talks, 1932-35, of Regional Relations, 1935-36, of Programme Planning, 1936-39; University Lecturer, Harvard University, 1939-42. Office of War Information, 1942-45, as Consultant, and, latterly, Deputy Director of its San Francisco Office; Professor of Education, New York Univ., 1946-67. Delivered television courses, Communication and Educn, and Communication and Society, 1967-68. *Publications:* Radio in Wartime; Radio's Second Chance; Radio, TV and Society; TV and our School Crisis; Educational TV in the United States. *Recreations:* walking, reading. *Address:* RFD Box 70, Newfane, Vermont 05345, USA; 21 Matlock Court, Kensington Park Road, W11.

SIEVE, James Ezekiel Balfour, PhD, FCA; *b* 31 July 1922; *s* of Isaac and Rachel Sieve; *m* 1953, Yvonne Manley; two *s. Educ:* London Sch. of Economics. BSc Econ, PhD. With Urwick Orr & Partners, 1950-54; Aquascutum & Associated Cos Ltd, 1954-68, Finance Dir, 1957-68; Metal Box Ltd, 1968, Finance Dir, 1970-80; Hacker Young, Chartered Accountants, 1981-. Governor, Home Farm Trust (residential care of mentally handicapped), 1974-; Member: Tax Reform Cttee, 1975-; Nat. Freight Consortium, 1982- (Nat. Freight Corp., later Nat. Freight Co., 1977-82). *Publication:* Income Redistribution and the Welfare State (with Adrian Webb), 1971. *Recreation:* relaxing with family. *Address:* 56 Hampstead Lane, NW3 7JP.

SIGMON, Robert Leland; lawyer; *b* Roanoke, Va, 3 April 1929; *s* of Ottis Leland Sigmon and Aubrey Virginia (*née* Bishop); *m* 1963, Marianne Rita Gellner. *Educ:* Univ. of Virginia; Sorbonne; London Sch. of Economics. BA, DrJur. Member of the Bar: US Supreme Court; Court of Appeals, Second and District of Columbia Circuits; Virginia; District of Columbia. Chairman, Exec. Cttee, Pilgrims Soc. of Gt Britain, 1977-; Director and Founder Mem., Associates of the Victoria and Albert Museum; Mem., Council of Management, British Inst. of Internat. and Comparative Law; Trustee, American Sch. in London; Vice-Chm., Mid-Atlantic Club of London, 1977-; Vice-President: European-Atlantic Group, 1978-; Exec. Cttee, American Soc. in London (Chm. 1974); Member: Amer. Soc. of Internat. Law; Selden Soc.; Guild of St Bride's Church, Fleet Street; Ends of the Earth. Chevalier du Tastevin. *Publications:* contribs to legal periodicals. *Recreations:* collecting antiquarian books, oenology. *Address:* 2 Plowden Buildings, Middle Temple, EC4Y 9AS. *T:* 01-583 4851. *Club:* Reform.

SIGNORET, Simone (pseudonym of **Simone Henriette Charlotte Montand**); actress; *b* Wiesbaden, 25 March 1921; *d* of Jean Kaminker and Louise (*née* Signoret); *m* 1947, Yves Allegret (marriage dissolved, 1950), motion picture director; one *d* ; *m* 1950, Yves Montand, actor and singer. *Educ:* Cours Sicard, Paris. Worked as a teacher and typist before becoming actress. Films include: Dédée d'Anvers, La Ronde, Casque d'Or, Thérèse Raquin, La Mort en ce Jardin, Room at the Top (Oscar), Adua e le Compagne, Term of Trial, Ship of Fools, The Deadly Affair, Games, The Seagull, L'Aveu, Le Chat (Best Actress Award, Berlin Film Festival, 1971), La Veuve Couderc, Les Granges brûlées, Rude journée pour la reine, La Chair de l'Orchidée, The Adolescent, Madame Rosa; Chère inconnue, 1980. Has also appeared on the stage (including Lady Macbeth, Royal Ct, London 1966), and on television. Has won many awards in France, USA, England, etc, including Oscar of Acad. of Motion Picture Arts and Sciences for best actress, 1960. *Publication:* Nostalgia Isn't What It Used to Be (autobiog.), 1978. *Address:* 15 Place Dauphine, 75001 Paris, France.

SIGURDSSON, Niels P.; Ambassador of Iceland; *b* Reykjavik, 10 Feb. 1926; *s* of Sigurdur B. Sigurdsson and Karitas Einarsdóttir; *m* 1953, Olafia Rafnsdóttir; two *s* one *d. Educ:* Univ. of Iceland (Law). Joined Diplomatic Service 1952; First Sec., Paris Embassy, 1956-60; Dep. Permanent Rep. to NATO and OECD, 1957-60; Dir, Internat. Policy Div., Min. of Foreign Affairs, Reykjavik, 1961-67; Delegate to UN Gen. Assembly, 1965; Ambassador and Permanent Rep. of Iceland to N Atlantic Council, 1967-71. Ambassador: to Belgium and EEC, 1968-71; to UK, 1971-76; to Fed. Republic of Germany, 1976-78; Ministry of Foreign Affairs, Reykjavik, 1979-. *Recreations:* swimming, riding. *Address:* Laugarasvegur 19, Reykjavik, Iceland.

SIKRI, Sarv Mittra; *b* 26 April 1908; *s* of late Dr Nihal Chand; *m* 1937, Mrs Leila Sikri; two *s. Educ:* Trinity Hall, Cambridge (BA). Barrister-at-Law (Lincoln's Inn). Started practice in Lahore High Court, 1930; Asst Advocate Gen., Punjab, 1949; Advocate Gen., Punjab, 1951-64; Judge, Supreme Ct of India, 1964-71; Chief Justice of India, 1971-73. Chm., Railway Accidents Enquiry Cttee, 1978-80; Chm., Jammu and Kashmir Enquiry Cttee, 1979-80. Alternate rep., UN Cttee on Codification and Develt of Internat. Law, 1947; Legal Adviser to Min. of Irrigation and Power, Govt of India, 1949; Mem. Internat. Law Assoc. Cttee on Internat. Rivers, 1955; Mem., Indian Law Commn, 1955-58. Delegate to: Law of the Sea Conf., Geneva, 1958; World Peace Through Law Conf., Tokyo, 1961, Athens, 1963; Accra Assembly, Accra, 1962. Pres., Indian Br. of Internat. Law Assoc., 1971-73; Member: Indian Commn of Jurists; Univ. Grants Commn, 1979-82; Chm., Sir Ganga Ram Hosp. Trust; Hon. Mem., Acad. of Political Sci., NY; Vice-Pres., Delhi Public School Soc. *Recreations:* golf, tennis, bridge. *Address:* 3 Nizam-ud-din East, New Delhi 110013, India. *T:* 692327. *Clubs:* Delhi Golf, Delhi Gymkhana (both in New Delhi).

SILBERSTON, Prof. (Zangwill) Aubrey; Professor of Economics, Imperial College of Science and Technology, University of London, since 1978, and Head of Department of Social and Economic Studies, since 1981; *b* 26 Jan. 1922; *s* of Louis and Polly Silberston; *m* 1945, Dorothy Marion, *d* of A. S. Nicholls; one *s* one *d. Educ:* Hackney Downs Sch., London; Jesus Coll., Cambridge. Econs Tripos Pt II, Cambridge, 1946. Courtaulds Ltd, 1946-50; Kenward Res. Fellow in Industrial Admin., St Catharine's Coll., Cambridge, 1950-53; University Lectr in Economics, Cambridge, 1953-71; Fellow, 1958-71, Dir of Studies in Econs, 1965-71, St John's Coll., Cambridge; Chm., Faculty Bd of Econs and Politics, 1966-70; Official Fellow in Econs, 1971-78, and Dean, 1972-78, Nuffield Coll., Oxford. Member: Monopolies Commn, 1965-68; Board of British Steel Corp., 1967-76; Departmental Cttee on Patent System, 1967-70; Economics Cttee, SSRC, 1969-73; Royal Commn on the Press, 1974-77; Management Cttee, SSRC, 1977-79; Economic Adviser, CBI, 1972-74. Vis. Prof., Queensland Univ., 1977; Sec.-Gen., Royal Economic Soc., 1979-. *Publications:* Education and Training for Industrial Management, 1955; (with George Maxcy) The Motor Industry, 1959; (in collaboration with C. Pratten and R. M. Dean) Economies of Large-scale Production in British Industry, 1965; (in collaboration with K. H. Boehm) The Patent System, 1967; (with C. T. Taylor) The Economic Impact of the Patent System, 1973; (ed, with Francis Seton) Industrial Management: East and West, 1973; (with A. Cockerill) The Steel Industry, 1974; articles in Econ. Jl, Bulletin of Oxford Inst. of Statistics, Oxford Economic Papers, Jl of Royal Statistical Society. *Recreations:* music, ballet. *Address:* 53 Prince's Gate, SW7 2PG. *T:* 01-589 5111. *Club:* Travellers'.

SILK, Ven. David; *see* Silk, Ven. R. D.

SILK, Dennis Raoul Whitehall; Warden of Radley College, since 1968; *b* 8 Oct. 1931; 2nd *s* of late Rev. Dr Claude Whitehall Silk and of Mrs Louise Silk; *m* 1963, Diana Merilyn, 2nd *d* of W. F. Milton, Pitminster, Somerset; two *s* two *d. Educ:* Christ's Hosp.; Sidney Sussex Coll., Cambridge (Exhibr). BA (History) Cantab. Asst Master, Marlborough Coll., 1955-68 (Housemaster, 1957-68). *Publications:* Cricket for Schools, 1964; Attacking Cricket, 1965. *Recreations:* antiquarian, literary, sporting (Blues in cricket (Capt. Cambridge Univ. CC, 1955) and Rugby football). *Address:* The Warden's House, Radley College, Abingdon, Oxon. *T:* Abingdon 20585. *Clubs:* East India, Devonshire, Sports and Public Schools; Hawks (Cambridge).

SILK, Ven. (Robert) David; Archdeacon of Leicester, since 1980; *b* 23 Aug. 1936; *s* of Robert Reeve Silk and Winifred Patience Silk; *m* 1957, Joyce Irene Bracey; one *s* one *d. Educ:* Gillingham Grammar School; Univ. of Exeter (BA Hons Theology 1958); St Stephen's House, Oxford. Deacon 1959, priest 1960, Rochester; Curate: St Barnabas, Gillingham, 1959-63; Holy Redeemer, Lamorbey, 1963-69; Priest-in-Charge of the Good Shepherd, Blackfen, 1967-69; Rector of Swanscombe, 1969-75; Rector of Beckenham, St George, 1975-80; Team Rector of the Holy Spirit, Leicester, 1982-. Proctor in Convocation, 1970-; Prolocutor of Lower House of Convocation of Canterbury, 1980-; Member of Liturgical Commission, 1976-. *Publications:* Prayers for Use at the Alternative Services, 1980; Compline—an Alternative Order, 1980. *Recreations:* Richard III, tennis, squash. *Address:* 13 Stoneygate Avenue, Stoneygate, Leicester. *T:* Leicester 704441.

SILK, Robert K.; *see* Kilroy-Silk.

SILKE, Hon. William James; Hon. Mr Justice Silke; Justice of Appeal, Supreme Court of Hong Kong, since 1981; *b* 21 Sept. 1929; *s* of William Joseph Silke and Gertrude (*née* Delany). *Educ:* Dominican Convent, Wicklow; Xavier Sch., Donnybrook; King's Inns, Dublin. Called to Irish Bar (South Eastern Circuit, Leinster Bar), 1955; Magistrate, North Borneo/Malaysia, 1959; Registrar, High Court in Borneo (Sabah-Sarawak), 1965; Puisne Judge, 1966; retired Malaysianisation, 1969; Hong Kong: Magistrate, 1969; President, Tenancy Tribunal, 1971; Acting Asst Registrar, High Court, 1972; President, Lands Tribunal, 1974; Judge, District Court, 1975; Judicial Commissioner, State of Brunei, 1978; Judge of the High Court, 1979. *Recreations:* horse racing/breeding, music, travel. *Address:* Supreme Court, Hong Kong. *T:* 5-259899. *Clubs:* Stephen's Green (Dublin); Royal Sabah Turf (Sabah, Malaysia); Hong Kong, Royal Hong Kong Jockey (Hong Kong).

SILKIN, 2nd Baron, *cr* 1950, of Dulwich [Disclaimed his peerage for life, 1972]; *see under* Silkin, Arthur.

SILKIN, Arthur; Lecturer in Public Administration, Civil Service College, Sunningdale, 1971-76, on secondment from Department of Employment; retired 1976; *b* 20 Oct. 1916; *e s* of 1st Baron Silkin, PC, CH; *S* father, 1972, as 2nd Baron Silkin, but disclaimed his peerage for life; *m* 1969, Audrey Bennett. *Educ:* Dulwich College; Peterhouse, Cambridge. BA 1938; Diploma in Govt Administration, 1959. Served 1940-45, Royal Air Force (A and SD Branch), Pilot Officer, 1941, subsequently Flying Officer. Entered Ministry of Labour and National Service, 1939; formerly 2nd Secretary, British Embassy, Paris. First Secretary: High Commissioner's Office, Calcutta, 1960-61; British Embassy, Dakar, May 1962-Mar. 1964; British Embassy, Kinshasa, 1964-66. *Publications:* contrib. to Public Administration, Political Qly. *Address:* Cuzco, 33 Woodnook Road, SW16. *T:* 01-677 8733.
See also Rt Hon. J. E. Silkin, Rt Hon. S. C. Silkin.

SILKIN, Rt. Hon. John Ernest, PC 1966; MP (Lab) Lewisham, Deptford, since 1974 (Deptford, July 1963-1974); *b* 18 March 1923; *y s* of 1st Baron Silkin, PC, CH; *m* 1950, Rosamund John (actress), *d* of Frederick Jones; one *s. Educ:* Dulwich College; University of Wales (Hon. Fellow, University College, Cardiff, 1981); Trinity Hall, Cambridge. BA 1944; LLB 1946; MA 1949. Royal Navy, 1941-46. Admitted a Solicitor, 1946. Contested (Lab): St Marylebone, 1950; West Woolwich, 1951; South Nottingham, 1959. Govt Chief Whip, 1966-69; Dep. Leader, House of Commons, 1968-69; Minister of Public Building and Works, 1969-70; Minister for Planning and Local Govt, DoE, 1974-76; Minister of Agric., Fisheries and Food, 1976-79; Opposition spokesman on industry, 1979-80, on defence and disarmament, 1981-; Shadow Leader of House of Commons, 1980-. *Address:* 83-91 Victoria Street, SW1. *T:* 01-222 8191. *Clubs:* Garrick, Royal Automobile.
See also Arthur Silkin, Rt Hon. S. C. Silkin.

SILKIN, Jon; poet; *b* 2 Dec. 1930; *s* of Dona Rubenstein and Joseph Silkin, solicitor (retd); three *s* one *d* (and one *s* decd); *m* Lorna Tracy (American writer and co-editor of Stand). *Educ:* Wycliffe Coll.; Dulwich Coll.; Univ. of Leeds. BA Hons Eng. Lit. 1962. Journalist, 1947; Nat. Service, teaching in Educn Corps, Army; subseq. six years as manual labourer, London and two years teaching English to foreign students. Founded magazine Stand, 1952. Several poetry-reading tours, USA; Vis. Lectr, Denison Univ., Ohio; taught at Writers' Workshop, Univ. of Iowa, 1968-69; Visiting writer: for Australian Council for the Arts, 1974; College of Idaho, Caldwell, 1978; Mishkenot Sha'ananim, Jerusalem, 1980; Bingham Vis. Poet, Univ. of Louisville, 1981; Elliston Poet-in-Residence, Univ. of Cincinnati, 1983. C. Day Lewis Fellowship, 1976-77. Vis. Speaker, World Congress of Poets, Korea, 1979, Madrid, 1982. *Publications:* The Peaceable Kingdom, 1954, reprint 1976; The Two Freedoms, 1958; The Re-ordering of the Stones, 1961; Nature with Man, 1965 (Geoffrey Faber Meml Prize, 1966); (with Murphy and Tarn) Penguin Modern Poets 7, 1965; Poems New and Selected, 1966; Killhope Wheel, 1971; Amana Grass, 1971; Out of Battle: the poetry of the Great War, 1972; (ed) Poetry of the Committed Individual, 1973; The Principle of Water, 1974; The Little Time-keeper, 1976; (ed) Penguin Book of First World War Poetry, 1979; (ed with Peter Redgrove) New Poetry, 1979; The Psalms with Their Spoils, 1980; Selected Poems, 1980. *Recreation:* travelling. *Address:* 19 Haldane Terrace, Newcastle upon Tyne NE2 3AN. *T:* Newcastle upon Tyne 812614.

SILKIN, Rt. Hon. Samuel Charles, PC 1974; QC 1963; MP (Lab) Southwark, Dulwich, since 1974 (Camberwell, Dulwich, Oct. 1964-1974); *b* 6 March 1918; 2nd *s* of 1st Baron Silkin, PC, CH; *m* 1941, Elaine Violet (*née* Stamp); two *s* two *d. Educ:* Dulwich College (Schol.); Trinity Hall, Cambridge (schol.), BA (1st cl. hons Parts I and II of Law Tripos; Law Studentship, 1939). Called to Bar, Middle Temple, 1941 (Cert. of Honour 1940, Harmsworth Law Schol., 1946), Bencher 1969. Served War of 1939-45, Lt-Col RA (despatches). Member, Royal Commission on the Penal System for England and Wales, 1965-66. Chairman: Parly Labour Party's Group on Common Market and European Affairs, 1966-70; Select Cttee on Parly Privilege, 1967; Leader, UK Delegn to Assembly of Council of Europe, 1968-70; Chm. Council of Europe Legal Cttee, 1966-70; Opposition front-bench spokesman on Law Officer matters, 1970-74; Attorney General, 1974-79. Recorder of Bedford, 1966-71. Chm., Waterlow Publishers Ltd, 1981-; Dir, BPCC plc, 1981-, Dep. Chm. 1982-. Society of Labour Lawyers: Foundn Mem.; Chm., 1964-71; Vice Pres., 1971-. Governor, Royal Bethlem and Maudsley Hosps, 1970-74; Chm., British Inst. of Human Rights, 1972-74; Pres., Alcohol Educn Centre, 1973-. Mem., CIArb., 1979-. MacDermott Lectr, QUB, 1976. Hon. Freeman, London Borough of Southwark, 1982. Hon. Mem., Amer. Bar Assoc., 1976-. *Address:* House of Commons, SW1; Lamb Building, Temple, EC4.
See also Arthur Silkin, Rt Hon. J. E. Silkin.

SILLARS, James; Managing Director, Scoted Ltd, since 1980; *b* Ayr, 4 Oct. 1937; *s* of Matthew Sillars; *m* 1st, 1957; one *s* one *d*; 2nd, 1981, Mrs Margo MacDonald, *qv. Educ:* Newton Park Sch., Ayr; Ayr Academy. Former official, Fire Brigades Union; Past Member Ayr Town Council and Ayr County Council Educn Cttee; Mem., T&GWU. Head of Organization and Social Services Dept, Scottish TUC, 1968-70. Full-time Labour Party agent, 1964 and 1966 elections. MP (Lab) South Ayrshire, March 1970-1976, (SLP) 1976-79. Among the founders of the Scottish Labour Party, Jan. 1976. Especially interested in education, social services, industrial relations, development policies. *Publications:* Labour Party pamphlets on Scottish Nationalism; Tribune Gp pamphlet on Democracy within the Labour Party. *Recreations:* reading, camping, tennis, swimming. *Address:* Scoted, 14 Stafford Street, Edinburgh EH3 7AU.

SILLARS, Margo; *see* MacDonald, M.

SILLERY, William Moore; Headmaster, Belfast Royal Academy, since 1980; *b* 14 March 1941; *s* of William and Adeline Sillery; *m* 1963, Elizabeth Margaret Dunwoody; two *d. Educ:* Methodist Coll., Belfast; St Catharine's Coll., Cambridge. Head of Modern Languages, Belfast Royal Academy, 1968, Vice-Principal 1974, Deputy Headmaster 1976. *Recreations:* golf, bridge. *Address:* Ardmore, 15 Saintfield Road, Belfast BT8 4AE. *T:* Belfast 645260. *Club:* Belvoir Park (Belfast).

SILLITOE, Alan; Writer since 1948; *b* 4 March 1928; *s* of Christopher Archibald Sillitoe and Sylvina (*née* Burton); *m* 1959, Ruth Fainlight; one *s* one *d. Educ:* various elementary schools in Nottingham. Raleigh Bicycle Factory, 1942; wireless operator, RAF, 1946-49. Lived in France and Spain, 1952-58. FRGS; Hon. Fellow, Manchester Polytechnic, 1977. *Publications:* Saturday Night and Sunday Morning (Authors' Club Award for best first novel of 1958; filmed, 1960, play, 1964); The Loneliness of the Long Distance Runner, 1959 (Hawthornden Prize; filmed, 1962); The General, 1960 (filmed 1967 as Counterpoint); The Rats and Other Poems, 1960; Key to the Door, 1961; The Ragman's Daughter, 1963 (filmed 1972); Road to Volgograd (travel), 1964; A Falling Out of Love (poems), 1964; The Death of William Posters (novel), 1965; A Tree on Fire (novel), 1967; The City Adventures of Marmalade Jim (children), 1967; Love in the Environs of Voronezh (poems), 1968; Guzman, Go Home (stories), 1968; (with Ruth Fainlight) All Citizens are Soldiers (play), 1969 (based on Lope de Vega, Fuente Ovejuna; first perf. Theatre Royal, Stratford, 1967); This Foreign Field (first perf. Roundhouse, 1970); A Start in Life (novel), 1970; Travels in Nihilon (novel), 1971; Raw Material (novel), 1972; Men, Women and Children (stories), 1973; The Flame of Life (novel), 1974; Storm and Other Poems, 1974; Barbarians and other poems, 1974; Mountains and Caverns (selected essays), 1975; The Widower's Son (novel), 1976; Big John and the Stars (children), 1977; Pit Strike (TV play), 1977; Three Plays: The Slot Machine (first perf. as This Foreign Field), The Interview (perf. Almost Free, 1978), Pit Strike, 1978; The Incredible Fencing Fleas (children), 1978; The Story teller (novel), 1979; Snow on the North Side of Lucifer (poems), 1979; Marmalade Jim at the Farm (children), 1980; The Second Chance (stories), 1981; Her Victory (novel), 1982. *Recreation:* travel. *Address:* 21 The Street, Wittersham, Kent. *Club:* Savage.

SILLITOE, Leslie Richard, OBE 1977; JP; General Secretary, Ceramic and Allied Trades Union, 1975-80, now Life Member; *b* 30 Aug. 1915; *s* of Leonard Richard Sillitoe and Ellen (*née* Sutton); *m* 1939, Lucy (*née* Goulding); two *d. Educ:* St George's and St Giles' Sch., Newcastle, Staffs; Stoke-on-Trent School of Art. Modeller and mouldmaker on leaving school. Served War, Royal Artillery, sen. non-commnd officer, 1939-46. Ceramic and Allied Trades Union: General President, 1961-63; Organiser, 1963; Asst Gen. Sec., 1967. Dep. Chm., Ceramics, Glass and Mineral Products Industry Trng Bd, 1977-; Chm., Nat. Jt Council for Ceramic Industry, 1975-81. Chm., N Staffs Manpower Cttee, 1975-; Life Mem., N Staffs Trades Council (Pres., 1963-81); Member: Staffs Develt Assoc.; N Staffs Medical Inst.; Staffordshire Soc.; Pottery & Glass Benevolent Inst. (Vice-Pres., 1980-); N Staffs Community Health Council, 1975-; Staffordshire War Pensions Cttee, 1980-; Council, Univ. of Keele, 1976-; BBC Local Radio Council, 1978-81; Mem. Bd of Management, and Custodian Trustee, N Staffs Trustee Savings Bank; Vice-President: N Staffs District WEA, 1976-; Muscular Dystrophy N Staffs Gp, 1978-; Pres., Staffordshire Lads and Dads Assoc., 1981-82, Vice-Pres. 1982-; Sec. and Treas., Ceramic Ind. Welfare Soc., 1971-81. Mem., Stoke-on-Trent District Council, 1953- (Vice-Chm., Museums Cttee); Lord Mayor, Stoke-on-Trent, 1981-82, Dep. Lord Mayor 1982-83. Governor: St Peters High Sch., Penkhull, 1975-; Cauldon Coll. of Further Educn, Stoke-on-Trent, 1976-; Thistley Hough High Sch., Penkhull, 1982-. Mem., W Midland TAVRA, 1979-; Chm., Friends of the Staffordshire Regt (N Staffs), 1982-. Territorial Efficient Service Medal, 1944. JP Stoke-on-Trent 1963-. *Publication:* foreword to The History of the Potters Union, 1977. *Recreations:* walking, photography, swimming. *Address:* 19 Sillitoe Place, Penkhull, Stoke-on-Trent ST4 5DQ. *T:* Stoke-on-Trent 47866.

SILLS, Beverly, (Mrs P. B. Greenough); Director, New York City Opera, since 1979; former leading soprano, New York City Opera and Metropolitan Opera; *b* 25 May 1929; *d* of late Morris Silverman and of Sonia Bahn; *m* 1956, Peter B. Greenough; one *s* one *d. Educ:* Professional Children's Sch., NYC; privately. Vocal studies with Estelle Liebling, piano with Paulo Gallico. Operatic debut, Philadelphia Civic Opera, 1947; San Francisco Opera, 1953; New York City Opera, 1955; Vienna State Opera, 1967; Teatro Colon, Buenos Aires, 1968; La Scala, Milan, 1969; Teatro San Carlo, Naples, 1970; Royal Opera, Covent Garden, London, 1970; Deutsche Oper, W Berlin, 1971; NY Metropolitan Opera, 1975, etc. Repeated appearances as soloist with major US symphony orchestras; English orchestral debut with London Symphony Orch., London, 1971; Paris debut, orchestral concert, Salle Pleyel, 1971. Repertoire includes title roles of Norma, Manon, Lucia di Lammermoor, Maria Stuarda, Daughter of Regiment, Anna Bolena, Traviata, Lucrezia Borgia, Thais, Louise; Cleopatra in Giulio Cesare, Elizabeth in Roberto Devereux, Tales of Hoffmann, Elvira in Puritani, Rosina in Barber of Seville, Norina in Don Pasquale; created title role, La Loca, San Diego Opera, 1979. Subject of BBC-TV's Profile in Music (Nat. Acad. of TV Arts and Sciences Emmy Award, 1975); other TV includes: Sills and Burnett at the Met, 1976; Hostess/Commentator for Young People's Concerts, NY Philharmonic, 1977; Moderator/Hostess, Lifestyles with Beverly Sills, 1976, 1977 (Emmy 1978). Hon. DMus: Temple Univ., 1972; New York Univ., 1973; New England Conservatory, 1973; Harvard Univ., 1974. Woman of the Year, Hasty Pudding Club, Harvard, 1974. *Publication:* Bubbles: a self-portrait, 1976. *Recreations:* fishing, bridge. *Address:* c/o Edgar Vincent Associates, 124 East 40 Street, New York, NY 10016, USA. *T:* 212-687-5105. PL 2-3020.

SILSOE, 2nd Baron *cr* 1963; **David Malcolm Trustram Eve,** Bt 1943; QC 1972; Barrister, Inner Temple, since 1955; *b* 2 May 1930; *er* twin *s* of 1st Baron Silsoe, GBE, MC, TD, QC, and Marguerite (*d* 1945), *d* of late Sir Augustus Meredith Nanton, Winnipeg; *S* father, 1976; *m* 1963, Bridget Min, *d* of Sir Rupert Hart-Davis, *qv*; one *s* one *d. Educ:* Winchester; Christ Church,

Oxford (MA); Columbia Univ., New York. 2nd Lt, Royal Welch Fusiliers, 1949-50; Lieut, Queen Victoria's Rifles (TA), 1950-53. Bar Auditor, Inner Temple, 1965-70; Bencher, 1970. *Recreation:* ski-ing. *Heir: s* Hon. Simon Rupert Trustram Eve, *b* 17 April 1966. *Address:* Neals Farm, Wyfold, Reading, Berks RG4 9JB. *Club:* Ski of Great Britain.

SILVER, Prof. Peter H. S.; *see* Spencer-Silver.

SILVER, Prof. Robert Simpson, CBE 1967; FRSE; FIMechE; FInstP; James Watt Professor of Mechanical Engineering, University of Glasgow, 1967-79; *b* Montrose, Angus, 13 March 1913; *s* of Alexander Clark Silver and Isabella Simpson; *m* 1937, Jean McIntyre Bruce, *er d* of Alexander and Elizabeth Bruce (*née* Livingstone); two *s. Educ:* Montrose Academy; University of Glasgow. MA, 1932; BSc (1st Class Hons Nat. Phil) 1934; PhD 1938; DSc 1945. Research Physicist, ICI (Explosives), 1936-39; Head of Research, G. & J. Weir Ltd, 1939-46; Asst Director, Gas Research Board, 1947-48; Director of Research, Federated Foundries Ltd, 1948-54; Chief Designer, John Brown Land Boilers Ltd, 1954-56; Chief of Development and Research, G. & J. Weir Ltd, 1956-62 (Director 1958-); Prof. of Mech. Engrng, Heriot-Watt Coll. (now Univ.), 1962-66. FInstP 1942; MIMechE 1953; FRSE 1963. Foreign Associate, Nat. Acad. of Engineering, USA, 1979. Unesco Prize for Science, 1968. *Publications:* An Introduction to Thermodynamics, 1971; papers on physics and engineering, with special emphasis on thermo-dynamics, desalination, combustion, phase-change, and heat transfer; also on philosophy of science and education; a few poems, as Robert Simpson. *Recreations:* fishing, music, theatre, Scottish history and affairs. *Address:* Oakbank, Tobermory, Isle of Mull. *T:* Tobermory 2024. *Club:* Royal Scottish Automobile (Glasgow).

SILVERLEAF, Alexander, CB 1980; FEng; FRINA; FICE; FCIT; Co-ordinator, International Transport Group (INTRA), since 1981; *b* 29 Oct. 1920; *m* 1950, Helen Marion Scott; two *d. Educ:* Kilburn Grammar Sch., London; Glasgow Univ. (BSc 1941). Wm Denny and Bros Ltd, Shipbuilders, Dumbarton, 1937-51: Student apprentice, 1937-41; Head, Design Office, 1947-51; National Physical Laboratory, 1951-71: Superintendent, Ship Div., 1962-67; Dep. Dir, 1966-71; Dir, Transport and Road Res. Lab., 1971-81. Hon. FIHE. *Publications:* papers in Trans. Royal Instn Naval Architects and other technical jls. *Address:* 64 Fairfax Road, Teddington, Mddx. *T:* 01-977 6261. *Club:* Athenæum.

SILVERMAN, Julius; MP (Lab) Birmingham, Erdington, 1945-55 and since 1974 (Birmingham, Aston, 1955-74); Barrister-at-law; *b* Leeds, 8 Dec. 1905; *s* of Nathan Silverman; *m* 1959, Eva Price. *Educ:* Central High School, Leeds (Matriculated). Entered Gray's Inn as student in 1928; called to Bar, 1931; joined Midland Circuit, 1933, practised in Birmingham; Birmingham City Councillor, 1934-45; contested Moseley Division, 1935. *Address:* House of Commons, SW1.

SILVERWOOD-COPE, Maclachlan Alan Carl, CBE 1959; FCA 1960; ATII 1978; Chartered Accountant; HM Diplomatic Service, retired; *b* 15 Dec. 1915; *s* of late Alan Lachlan Silverwood-Cope and late Elizabeth Masters; *m* 1st, 1940, Hilkka (*née* Halme) (marr. diss. 1970); one *s* one *d*; 2nd, 1971, Jane (*née* Monier-Williams); one *s* one *d. Educ:* Malvern College. ACA 1939. HM Forces, 1939-45 (Major, RA). Foreign (later Diplomatic) Service, 1939-: served as 3rd Sec., Stockholm, 1945-50; 1st Sec., Washington, 1951 and 1956-57; Tokyo, 1952-55; Copenhagen, 1960-64; Counsellor, Buenos Aires, 1966-68; FCO, 1968-71. Finance appts with Aspro-Nicholas Ltd, 1971-78. Home Front Medal (Finland), 1940; Freedom Cross (Norway), 1945. *Recreations:* tennis, bridge, music. *Address:* Brock Hill Cottage, Winkfield Row, Berks RG12 6LS. *T:* Winkfield Row 882746.

SILVESTER, Frederick John; MP (C) Manchester, Withington, since Feb. 1974; Senior Associate Director, J. Walter Thompson; *b* 20 Sept. 1933; *s* of William Thomas Silvester and Kathleen Gertrude (*née* Jones); *m* 1971, Victoria Ann, *d* of James Harold and Mary Lloyd Davies; two *d. Educ:* Sir George Monoux Grammar Sch.; Sidney Sussex Coll., Cambridge. Called to the Bar, Gray's Inn, 1957. Teacher, Wolstanton Grammar School, 1955-57; Political Education Officer, Conservative Political Centre, 1957-60. Member, Walthamstow Borough Council, 1961-64; Chairman, Walthamstow West Conservative Association, 1961-64; MP (C) Walthamstow West, Sept. 1967-70; an Opposition Whip, 1974-76. Vice-Chm., Cons. Employment Cttee, 1976-79; PPS to Sec. of State for Employment, 1979-81, to Sec. of State for NI, 1981-. *Address:* House of Commons, SW1A 0AA.

SILYN ROBERTS, Air Vice-Marshal (retired) Glynn, CB 1959; CBE 1949; AFC 1939; *b* 2 April 1906; *s* of late R. Silyn Roberts, MA, and Mrs M. Silyn Roberts, MBE, BA. *Educ:* Bangor. Permanent Commission, RAF, 1930; No. 2 Squadron, 1930-32; Home Aircraft Depot 1932; Experimental Flying Dept, RAE, 1935; Aircraft Depot, Iraq, 1939; Chief Technical Officer, Empire Central Flying Sch., 1942; Dep. Dir Technical Development, MAP, 1943 (despatches); Director of Aircraft Research and Development, MAP, 1945; Commanding Officer, Experimental Flying Dept, RAE, 1947; Sen. Technical Staff Officer, No. 2 Group, Jan. 1949; Dep. Dir Military Aircraft Research and Development, Min. of Supply, Dec. 1949; Principal Dir of Aircraft Research and Development, Min. of Supply, 1955; Sen. Technical Staff Officer, Bomber Command, 1956; Dir-Gen. of Engineering, Air Min., 1958-61; retd, Nov. 1961. MSc, CEng, FRAeS. *Recreations:* fishing, shooting (Hon. Life Vice-Pres. RAF Small Arms Assoc.). *Address:* c/o Williams &

Glyn's Bank Ltd, Kirkland House, 22 Whitehall, SW1. *Clubs:* Royal Air Force, Naval and Military.

SIM, David, CMG 1946; retired; Deputy Minister of National Revenue for Customs and Excise, Canada, 1943-65; *b* Glasgow, Scotland, 4 May 1899; *s* of David Sim, and Cora Lilian Angus; *m* 1924, Ada Helen Inrig (*d* 1958); one *s* one *d*; *m* 1960, Winnifred Emily Blois. *Educ:* Haghill Public School, Glasgow; Kitchener-Waterloo Collegiate. Served European War, Canadian Army in Canada and Overseas with the 1st Canadian Infantry Battalion (wounded at Passchendaele). Bank of Nova Scotia, 1919-25; Waterloo Trust & Savings Co., 1926; Secretary to Minister of National Revenue, 1927-33; Commissioner of Excise, 1933-43; Administrator of Alcoholic Beverages, 1942-45; Administrator of Tobacco, 1942-46; Dir Commodity Prices Stabilization Corporation; Member of External Trade Advisory Cttee and Nat. Joint Council of the Public Service of Canada; Member, Board of Broadcast Governors, 1966-. Past President: Rotary Club; Canadian Club. Mem. Canadian delegation to: 1st Session of Preparatory Cttee for Internat. Conf. on Trade and Employment, London, 1946; 2nd Session of Preparatory Cttee for UN Conf. on Trade and Employment, Geneva, 1947. General Service, Victory, Jubilee and Coronation Medals. *Recreations:* golf, fishing, curling, reading. *Address:* 1833 Riverside Drive, Apt 616, Ottawa, Ontario, Canada. *Club:* Royal Ottawa Golf.

SIM, John Mackay, MBE 1945; Deputy Chairman, Inchcape & Co. Ltd, 1975-82 (Deputy Chairman/Managing Director, 1965-75); *b* 4 Oct. 1917; *s* of William Aberdeen Mackay Sim and Zoe Sim; *m* 1st, Dora Cecilia Plumridge Levita (*d* 1951); two *d*; 2nd, Mrs Muriel Harvard (Peggie) Norman. *Educ:* Glenalmond; Pembroke Coll., Cambridge (MA). Lieut RA, 1940, Captain 1942; served NW Europe (despatches). Smith Mackenzie & Co. Ltd (East Africa), 1946-62, Chm. 1960-62; Dir, subseq. Man. Dir, Inchcape & Co. Ltd, 1962. *Recreation:* gardening. *Address:* 6 Bryanston Mews West, W1H 7FR. *T:* 01-262 7673; Stone Lacey, Aston Sandford, near Aylesbury, Bucks. *T:* Haddenham (Bucks) 291217. *Club:* MCC.

SIMCOCK, Rev. Canon James Alexander; Canon Residentiary and Treasurer of Truro Cathedral 1951-74; Canon Emeritus, since 1974; *b* 19 Dec. 1897; *m* 1923, Mary Dorothy, *d* of Rev. T. R. Pennington; one *s. Educ:* Egerton Hall, Manchester. Deacon, 1922; Priest, 1923; Curate of St Luke, Weaste, 1922-24; Milnrow, 1924-27; Incumbent of St Mark, Chadderton, 1927-31; Rector of St Mark, Newton Heath, 1931-33; Organising Secretary, Church of England Children's Soc., for Dioceses of Bath and Wells, Exeter and Truro, and Curate of St Martin, Exminster, 1933-36; Rector of Calstock, 1936-43; Surrogate, 1939-; Vicar of St Gluvias with Penryn, 1943-51. Rural Dean of S Carnmath, 1946-49; Hon. Canon of St Germoe in Truro Cathedral, 1948-51. *Address:* 25 Kemp Close, Truro, Cornwall TR1 1EF. *T:* Truro 79277. *Club:* Royal Over-Seas League.

SIMCOX, Richard Alfred, CBE 1975 (MBE 1956); Hon. Member of the British Council; *b* 29 March 1915; *s* of Alfred William and Alice Simcox; *m* 1951, Patricia Elisabeth Gutteridge; one *s* two *d. Educ:* Gonvillé and Caius Coll., Cambridge. BA Class. Tripos. Served with N Staffs Regt, 1939-43; British Council from 1943: Rep. in Jordan, 1957-60; in Libya, 1960; in Jordan (again), 1960; Cultural Attaché, British Embassy, Cairo, 1968-71; British Council Representative, Iran, 1971-75. Governor, Gabbitas-Thring Educnl Trust. *Recreations:* gardening, philately. *Address:* Little Brockhurst, Lye Green Road, Chesham, Bucks. *T:* Chesham 783797.

SIME, His Honour William Arnold, CMG 1982; MBE 1946; QC 1957; a Circuit Judge, 1972-81; *b* 8 Feb. 1909; *s* of William Sime, Wepener, OFS, South Africa, and Bedford, and Charlotte Edith Sime; *m* 1938, Rosemary Constance, *d* of Dr Cleaton Roberts, West Byfleet, Surrey; two *d. Educ:* Grahamstown, CP; Bedford School; Balliol College, Oxford. Called to the Bar, Inner Temple, 1932 (Master of the Bench, 1964); Recorder: Grantham, 1954-57, 1958-63; Great Grimsby, 1963-71; City of Birmingham, 1971; a Senior Puisne Judge, Cyprus, 1957-58; Senior Judge (non-resident) of the Sovereign Base Areas, Cyprus, 1960-82. Served War of 1939-45 with RAF; Wing Comdr. *Recreations:* golf, cricket (captained Bedfordshire CCC, 1931-33, captained Nottinghamshire CCC, 1947-50, Pres., 1975-77); Rugby (captained Bedford RUFC, 1932-37); racing (Chm., Nottingham Racecourse Co.). *Address:* Witsend, Wymeswold, Leicestershire; 6 King's Bench Walk, Temple, EC4.

SIMENON, Georges; Novelist; *b* Liège, Belgium, 13 February 1903; *s* of Désiré Simenon and Henriette Brull; *m* Denise Ouimet; three *s* (and one *d* decd). *Educ:* Collège St Servais, Liège, Belgium. His books are translated into 55 Languages and have been published in 39 countries. *Publications:* 212 novels, including the 80 titles of the Maigret series; autobiographical works: Letter to my Mother, 1976; Un Homme comme un autre, 1975; Des traces de pas, 1975; Les petits hommes, 1976; Vent du nord vent du sud, 1976; Un banc au soleil, 1977; De la cave au grenier, 1977; A l'abri de notre arbre, 1977; Tant que je suis vivant, 1978; Vacances obligatoires, 1978; La main dans la main, 1978; Au-delà de ma porte-fenêtre, 1978; Je suis resté un enfant de choeur, 1979; A quoi bon jurer?, 1979; Point-virgule, 1979; Le prix d'un homme, 1980; On dit que j'ai soixante quinze ans, 1980; Quand vient le froid, 1980; Les libertés qu'il nous reste, 1980; La femme endormie, 1981; Jour et nuit, 1981; Destinées, 1981; Mémoires Intimes suivis du livre du Marie-Jo, 1981. *Address:* Secretariat de Georges Simenon, avenue du Temple 19B, 1012 Lausanne, Switzerland. *T:* 33 39 79; 155 avenue de Cour, 1007 Lausanne.

SIMEON, Sir John Edmund Barrington, 7th Bt, *cr* 1815; Civil Servant in Department of Social Welfare, Provincial Government, British Columbia, retired 1975; lately in Real Estate business; *b* 1 March 1911; *s* of Sir John Walter Barrington Simeon, 6th Bt, and Adelaide Emily (*d* 1934), *e d* of late Col Hon. E. A. Holmes-à-Court; *S* father 1957; *m* 1937, Anne Robina Mary Dean; one *s* two *d*. *Educ:* Eton; Christ Church, Oxford. Motor business, 1931-39. Served with RAF, 1939-43; invalided, rank of Flight Lt, 1943. Civil Servant, Ministry of Agriculture, 1943-51. Took up residence in Vancouver, Canada, 1951. *Recreations:* sailing, painting. *Heir:* s Richard Edmund Barrington Simeon, PhD Yale; Associate Professor of Political Science, Queen's Univ., Kingston, Ont [*b* 2 March 1943; *m* 1966, Agnes Joan, *d* of George Frederick Weld; one *s* one *d*]. *Address:* c/o National Westminster Bank Ltd, Newport, Isle of Wight; 1704 Wolfe Street, North Vancouver, BC V7M 2Z1, Canada.

SIMEON, John Power Barrington, OBE 1978; HM Diplomatic Service; HM Consul-General, Hamburg, since 1981; *b* 15 Nov. 1929; *o s* of late Cornwall Barrington Simeon and Ellaline Margery Mary (*née* Le Poer Power, Clonmel, Co. Tipperary); *m* 1970, Carina Renate Elisabeth Schüller; one *s*. *Educ:* Beaumont Coll.; RMA, Sandhurst. Commnd 2nd Lieut Royal Corps of Signals, 1949; Lieut 1951; resigned, 1952; RARO, 1953-. Ferrous and non-ferrous metal broker, London and Europe, 1953-57; *Rank Organisation:* served in Germany, Thailand, Singapore, India, ME, N Africa, Hong Kong and London, 1957-65; HM Diplomatic Service, 1965-: First Sec. (Commercial): Colombo, 1967; Bonn, 1968-70; First Sec., and sometime Actg High Comr, Port of Spain, 1970-73; FCO, 1973-; Dep. High Comr and Head of Post, Ibadan, Nigeria, 1975-79. Counsellor, 1978; Consul-Gen., Berlin, 1979-81. *Recreations:* travel, photography, shooting, riding. *Address:* c/o Foreign and Commonwealth Office, King Charles Street, SW1A 2AH. *Clubs:* Anglo-German (Hamburg); Royal Burnham Yacht, Norddeutscher Regatta Verein (Hamburg), Hamburg Polo.

SIMEONE, Reginald Nicola; Authority Personnel Officer, United Kingdom Atomic Energy Authority, since 1976; *b* 12 July 1927; *s* of Nicola Francisco Simeone, FCIS, and Phyllis Simeone (*née* Iles); *m* 1954, Josephine Frances, *d* of late Robert Hope and of Marjorie Hope; two *s*. *Educ:* Raynes Park Grammar Sch.; St John's Coll., Cambridge (Schol.; MA). Instr Lieut, Royal Navy, 1947-50; Admiralty: Asst Principal, 1950-55: Private Sec. to Sir John Lang (Perm. Sec.), 1954-55; Principal, 1955-59: Gen. Finance Br., 1955-57; Private Sec. to Mr Christopher Soames (Parly Sec.) (now Lord Soames), 1957-58; Military Br., 1958-59. UKAEA: Finance Br., 1959-61; Economics and Programmes Br., 1961-65; Senior Staff, 1965-: Chief Personnel Officer, AWRE, Aldermaston, 1965-69; Estabt Officer, London, 1969-70; AEA Principal Estabts Officer, 1970-76. *Recreations:* travel and music. *Club:* United Oxford & Cambridge University.

SIMEONS, Charles Fitzmaurice Creighton, MA; Consultant: Environmental Control, Market and Behavioural Studies, Health and Safety at Work, Communications with Government, technical programmes for conferences; Director, Action Learning Trust; *b* 22 Sept. 1921; *s* of Charles Albert Simeons and Vera Hildegarde Simeons; *m* 1945, Rosemary (*née* Tabrum); one *s* one *d*. *Educ:* Oundle; Queens' Coll., Cambridge. Royal Artillery with 8th Indian Div., 1942-45. Man. Dir, supplier to photographic industry, 1957-70. MP (C) Luton, 1970-Feb. 1974. Chm., Luton Cons. Assoc., 1960-63. Pres., Luton, Dunstable and District Chamber of Commerce, 1967-68; District Gov., Rotary International, 1967-68; Chm. of cttees raising funds for disabled and cancer research; Mem., Nat. Appeals Cttee, Cancer Res. Campaign, 1977-78. Chm., Adv. Cttee, Rotary Internat. Bd on Environmental Research and Resources, 1973-74; Vice Pres., Nat. Industrial Material Recovery Assoc.; Mem. Inst. of Environmental Sciences; Mem., Internat. Cttee, Water Pollution Control Federation, Washington, DC; Mem. Council, Smaller Business Assoc., 1974-76; Chm., Central Govt Cttee, Union of Independent Cos. Hon. Mem., Inst. of Water Pollution Control. Liveryman: Worshipful Co. of Feltmakers (and Asst to Court); Guild of Freemen of City of London. FIWM; FRSA. Pres., Old Oundelian Club, 1976-77. JP Luton, 1959-74. *Publications:* Energy Research in Western Europe, 1976; Coal: its role in tomorrow's technology, 1978; Water as a Source of Energy, 1980. *Recreations:* watching football, cricket, gardening. *Address:* 21 Ludlow Avenue, Luton, Beds. *T:* Luton 30965. *Club:* City Livery.

SIMINOVITCH, Prof. Louis, OC 1980; FRS 1980; FRSC 1965; Chairman, Department of Medical Genetics, since 1974 and University Professor, since 1976, University of Toronto; *b* Montreal, PQ, 1 May 1920; *s* of Nathan Siminovitch and Goldie Watchman; *m* 1944, Elinore, *d* of late Harry Faierman; three *d*. *Educ:* McGill Univ. (BSc 1941, PhD 1944; Arts and Sci. schol. 1939, Sir William McDonald schol. 1940, Anne Molson prize in Chem. 1941). With NRC at Ottawa and Chalk River, Ont., 1944-47; NRC Studentship and Fellowship, 1947-49; with Centre Nat. de la Recherche Scientifique, Paris, 1949-53; Nat. Cancer Inst. Canadian Fellowships, 1953-55; Connaught Med. Res. Labs, Univ. of Toronto, 1953-56. Head of Div. of Biolog. Research, Ontario Cancer Inst., Toronto, 1963; Chm., Dept of Med. Cell Biology, Univ. of Toronto, 1966-73. Founding Mem. and Pres., Editorial Bd, Science Forum, 1966-79; Pres., Canadian Cell Biology Soc., 1967. Member: Bd of Dirs, Nat. Cancer Inst. of Canada, 1975- (Pres., 1982); Nat. Bd of Dirs, Canadian Cancer Soc., 1981-; Bd, Ontario Cancer Treatment and Res. Foundn, 1979-; Scientific Adv. Cttee, Connaught Res. Inst., 1980-; Alfred P. Sloan, Jr, Selection Cttee, General Motors Cancer Res. Foundn,

1980. Editor: Cell; Somatic Cell Genetics; Jl de Microscopie et de Biologie Cellulaire; Annales de Microbiologie; Jl of Molecular and Cellular Biology; Jl Cancer Surveys (London). Jubilee Silver Medal, 1977; Flavelle Gold Medal, RSC, 1978; Univ. of Toronto Alumni Assoc. Award, 1978; Izaak Walton Killam Meml Prize, 1981; Gairdner Foundn Wightman Award, 1981. Has specialised in the study of bacterial and somatic cell genetics. Hon. degrees: Memorial Univ., Newfoundland, 1978; McMaster Univ., 1978. *Publications:* many contribs to scientific and learned journals. *Address:* The Hospital for Sick Children, 555 University Avenue, Toronto, Ont. MG5 1X8, Canada; 106 Wembley Road, Toronto, Ont., Canada.

SIMKINS, Charles Anthony Goodall, CB 1968; CBE 1963; *b* 2 March 1912; *s* of Charles Wyckens Simkins; *m* 1938, Sylvia, *d* of Thomas Hartley, Silchester, Hants; two *s* one *d*. *Educ:* Marlborough; New Coll., Oxford (1st Class Hons Mod. Hist.). Barrister, Lincoln's Inn, 1936; served 1939-45 as Captain, Rifle Bde (POW); attached War Office (later MoD), 1945-71. *Address:* The Cottage, 94 Broad Street, near Guildford, Surrey. *T:* Guildford 572456. *Clubs:* Naval and Military, MCC.

SIMMONDS, Prof. Kenneth Royston; Professor of International Law in the University of London, at Queen Mary College, since 1976; Dean of the Faculty of Law, Queen Mary College, since 1980; *b* 11 Nov. 1927; *s* of Frederick John Simmonds and Maude (*née* Coxhill); *m* 1958, Gloria Mary (*née* Tatchell); one *s* one *d*. *Educ:* Watford Grammar Sch.; Exeter Coll., Oxford. BA, MA, DPhil (Oxon). Amelia Jackson Sen. Fellow, Exeter Coll., Oxford, 1951-53. Director, British Inst. of Internat. and Comparative Law, 1965-76, Hon. Dir, 1976-. Gen. Editor, International and Comparative Law Qly, 1966-; Editor, Common Market Law Review, 1967-; Gen. Editor, Encyclopedia of European Community Law, 1972-; Mem. Editorial Cttee, British Year Book of International Law, 1967-. Visiting Professor McGill Univ., 1963; Univ. of Wyoming, 1969; Free Univ. of Brussels, 1972 and 1973; Univ. of Amsterdam, annually, 1979-. Mem., Legal Adv. Cttee, British Council, 1966-; Chm., UK Nat. Cttee of Comparative Law, 1973-76; Pres., Internat. Assoc. of Legal Science, 1975-76. Chevalier, l'Ordre de Mérite, 1973. *Publications:* Resources of the Ocean Bed, 1970; New Directions in the Law of the Sea, 1974; (ed) Legal Problems of an Enlarged European Community, 1972; (Gen. Editor) Encyclopedia of European Community Law, 1972-; (ed) Sweet and Maxwell's European Community Treaties, 1972, 4th edn 1980; Cases on the Law of the Sea, 1976-; (ed, with C. M. Schmitthoff) International Economic and Trade Law, 1976; Legal Problems of Multinational Corporations, 1978; (ed, with R. M. Goode) Commercial Operations in Europe, 1978; Multinational Corporations Law, 1979; numerous articles in Internat. and Comparative Law Qly, Common Market Law Rev., Europarecht. *Recreations:* travel (espec. in the Americas), classical music, cats. *Address:* The Oast Barn, Bell's Forstal, Throwley, near Faversham, Kent.

SIMMONDS, Kenneth Willison, CMG 1956; FRSA; *b* Carmacoup, Douglas, Lanarkshire, 13 May 1912; *s* of late William Henry Simmonds, Civil Servant, and late Ida, *d* of John Willison, Acharn, Killin, Perthshire; *m* 1st, 1939, Ruth Constance Sargant (marr. diss. 1974); two *s*; 2nd, 1974, Mrs Catherine Clare Lewis, *y d* of late Col F. J. Brakenridge, CMG, Chew Magna. *Educ:* Bedford Sch.; Humberstone Sch.; St Catharine's Coll., Cambridge (MA). District Officer, Colonial Administrative Service, Kenya, 1935-48; Deputy Financial Secretary, Uganda, 1948-51; Financial Secretary, Nyasaland Protectorate, 1951-57; Chief Secretary, Aden, 1957-63. Exhibited paintings: Southern Arts Open Field, 1972-73; Royal Acad., 1973, 1974, 1977, 1978; Royal West of England Acad., 1976, 1978; Bladon, Andover (one-man show), 1977; Westward Open, 1977, 1979; Royal Bath and West, 1979 (awards); group and collective exhbns. *Address:* North Close, Milverton, Taunton, Somerset TA4 1QZ. *T:* Milverton 400235.

SIMMONDS, Sir Oliver Edwin, Kt 1944; CEng; FRAeS; President, E. F. G. Ltd, Nassau, Bahamas; *b* 1897; *e s* of Rev. F. T. Simmonds; *m* 1st, 1922, Gladys Evelyn Hewitt (*d* 1977); one *s* two *d*; 2nd, 1979, Mrs Sheila Grace Kingham, widow of A. Colin Kingham. *Educ:* Taunton; Magdalene College, Cambridge (Exhibnr; Mech. Sci. Tripos). Aerodynamic research, RAE (jt author first res. report on Supersonic flight); gave over 1000 lectures on future of civil aviation, 1922-35; joined Supermarine Aviation Works, 1924; responsible (with late R. J. Mitchell) for design Supermarines S4, S5, and S6 (Schneider Trophy Winners, 1927 and 1929; from which Spitfire was subseq. developed), invented and patented interchangeable wings for aircraft (Simmonds Spartan biplane); formed Simmonds Aircraft Ltd, 1928 (produced Spartan landplanes and seaplanes), Simmonds Aerocessories Ltd, 1931, Simmonds Aerocessories Inc. NY (now Simmonds Precision Inc., NY Stock Exchange), Aerocessoires Simmonds SA Paris, 1936, Melbourne 1937, Montreal 1946. Chm., Air Transport Cttee, FBI. MP (U) Birmingham Duddeston, 1931-45. Founder-Pres. ARP Inst.; Chm., Parly ARP Cttee, 1938; led delegn to Berlin to study German ARP. Mem. Exec., 1922 Cttee, 1938-45; Chm. Govt Cttee on Brick Industry, 1941-42. Developed and patented electronic fuel gauge Pacitron. Moved to Bahamas, 1948; built Balmoral Club (now Balmoral Beach Hotel); Founder Pres., Friends of the Bahamas, 1954; Founder Pres., Bahamas Employers Confdn, 1966-68. Vice-Pres., RAeS, 1945-47. *Address:* PO Box 1480, Nassau, Bahamas. *Club:* Royal Thames Yacht.

SIMMONDS, Posy; cartoonist, The Guardian, since 1977; *b* 9 Aug. 1945; *d* of Reginald A. C. Simmonds and Betty Cahusac; *m* 1974, Richard Hollis. *Educ:* Queen Anne's Sch., Caversham; L'Ecole des Beaux Arts, Paris; Central Sch. of Art and Design, London (BA Art and Design). Bear cartoon in the

Sun, 1969-79; freelance illustrator/cartoonist for various publications incl. Sunday Times, Observer, Cosmopolitan, Woman's Own. Exhibitions of drawings at The Workshop. Cartoonist of the Year: Granada TV/What The Papers Say, 1980; British Press Awards, 1981. *Publications:* Bear Book, 1969; Mrs Weber's Diary, 1979; True Love, 1981; Pick of Posy, 1982. *Address:* c/o A. D. Peters & Co. Ltd, 10 Buckingham Street, WC2N 6BU. *T:* 01-839 2556.

SIMMONDS, Richard James; Member (C) Midlands West, European Parliament, since 1979; farmer and breeder of Jersey cattle; consultant surveyor; *b* 2 Aug. 1944; *s* of Reginald A. C. Simmonds and Betty Cahusac; *m* 1967, Mary (*née* Stewart); one *s* two *d. Educ:* Trinity Coll., Glenalmond. Councillor, Berkshire CC (Chm. of Environment, Property, Transport, and Development Cttees), 1973-79. National Vice-Chm. of Young Conservatives, 1973-75; Founding Vice-Chm. of Young European Democrats, 1974; Personal Asst to Rt Hon. Edward Heath, 1973-75; PPS to Sir James Scott-Hopkins, Leader of European Democratic Gp, European Parlt, 1979-82. Chm. of Governors, Berkshire Coll. of Agriculture, 1979-. *Publications:* The Common Agricultural Policy—a sad misnomer, 1979; An A to Z of Myths and Misunderstandings of the European Community. *Recreation:* resisting bureaucracy. *Address:* Woodlands Farm, Cookham Dean, Berkshire SL6 9PJ. *Clubs:* Carlton, United & Cecil, Ancient Britons, Tamworth.
See also Posy Simmonds.

SIMMONS, Fr Eric, CR; Superior of the Community of the Resurrection, Mirfield, Yorkshire, since May 1974; *b* 1930. *Educ:* Univ. of Leeds. BA (Phil) 1951. Coll. of the Resurrection, Mirfield, 1951; deacon, 1953, priest, 1954; Curate of St Luke, Chesterton, 1953-57; Chaplain, University Coll. of N Staffordshire, 1957-61; licensed to officiate: Dio. Wakefield, 1963-65 and 1967-; Dio. Ripon, 1965-67; Warden and Prior of Hostel of the Resurrection, Leeds, 1966-67; subseq. Novice Guardian, looking after young Community members; the Community is an Anglican foundation engaged in evangelism and teaching work, based in Yorkshire but with houses in Southern Africa. *Address:* House of the Resurrection, Mirfield, West Yorks WF14 0BN. *T:* Mirfield 494318.

SIMMONS, Ernest Bernard, QC (Seychelles) 1949; *b* 7 Sept. 1913; *o s* of Bernard Simmons and Ethel (*née* Booth); *m* 1940, Edna Muriel Tomlinson; one *s* three *d.* Barrister-at-Law, Gray's Inn, 1936; Asst Attorney-Gen., Gibraltar, 1946; Attorney-Gen., Seychelles, 1949; Judge of the Supreme Court, Mauritius, 1952-58; Judge of the High Court, Tanganyika, 1958-61; retired. *Address:* The Gate House, 27 Middleton Road, Brentwood, Essex.

SIMMONS, Guy Lintorn, MVO 1961; HM Diplomatic Service; Consul-General, Montreal, since 1982; *b* 27 Feb. 1925; *s* of late Captain Geoffrey Larpent Simmons, RN and Frances Gladys Simmons (*née* Wright); *m* 1951, Sheila Jacob; three *d. Educ:* Bradfield Coll.; Oriel Coll., Oxford. RAF, 1943-46; CRO, 1949; 2nd Sec., British High Commn: Lahore, 1950; Dacca, 1952; CRO, 1954-58 and 1964-66; 1st Sec.: Bombay, 1958; New Delhi, 1961; Commercial Counsellor: New Delhi, 1966-68; Cairo, 1968-71; Head of Trade Policy Dept, FCO, 1971-73; Diplomatic Service Inspectorate, 1973-76; Commercial Counsellor, Copenhagen, 1975-79; Consul-Gen., Karachi, 1979-82. *Recreations:* fishing, riding, amateur dramatics. *Address:* c/o Foreign and Commonwealth Office, SW1. *Clubs:* Oriental, Royal Commonwealth Society.

SIMMONS, Jack; Professor of History, University of Leicester, 1947-75, now Professor Emeritus and Hon. Archivist; Pro-Vice-Chancellor, 1960-63; Public Orator, 1965-68; *b* 30 Aug. 1915; *o c* of Seymour Francis Simmons and Katharine Lillias, *d* of Thomas Finch, MB, Babbacombe, Devon. *Educ:* Westminster Sch.; Christ Church, Oxford. Beit Lectr in the History of the British Empire, Oxford Univ., 1943-47. FSA. Mem., Adv. Council, Science Museum, 1969-; Chm., Nat. Railway Museum Cttee, York; Leicestershire Archæological and Historical Society: Hon. Editor, 1948-61; Pres. 1966-77. Chm., Leicester Local Broadcasting Council, 1967-70. Jt Editor, The Journal of Transport History, 1953-73. Editor: A Visual History of Modern Britain; Classical County Histories. *Publications:* African Discovery: An Anthology of Exploration (edited with Margery Perham), 1942; Southey, 1945; Edition of Southey's Letters from England, 1951; Journeys in England: an Anthology, 1951; Parish and Empire, 1952; Livingstone and Africa, 1955; New University, 1958; The Railways of Britain: an Historical Introduction, 1961; Transport, 1962; Britain and the World, 1965; St Pancras Station, 1968; Transport Museums, 1970; A Devon Anthology, 1971; (ed) Memoirs of a Station Master, 1973; Leicester Past and Present (2 vols), 1974; (ed) Rail 150: The Stockton and Darlington Railway and What Followed, 1975; The Railway in England and Wales, 1830-1914, Vol. 1, 1978; A Selective Guide to England, 1979; Dandy Cart to Diesel: the National Railway Museum, 1981. *Address:* c/o Department of History, The University, Leicester LE1 7RH. *Club:* Reform.

SIMMONS, Jean; film actress; *b* London, 31 Jan. 1929; *m* 1950, Stewart Granger, *qv* (marr. diss. 1960); one *d* ; *m* 1960, Richard Brooks; one *d. Educ:* Orange Hill Sch.; Aida Foster School of Dancing. First film appearance in Give Us the Moon, 1942; minor parts in Cæsar and Cleopatra, The Way to the Stars, etc., 1942-44; since then has appeared in numerous British films, including: Great Expectations, Black Narcissus, Hungry Hill, Uncle Silas, Hamlet, So Long at the Fair, The Blue Lagoon, Trio, Adam and Evalyn, Clouded Yellow; The Grass is Greener, 1960; Life at the Top, 1965; Say Hello

to Yesterday, 1971; began American film career, 1950; American films include: Androcles and the Lion, Young Bess, The Actress, Desirée, Footsteps in the Fog, Guys and Dolls, This Could be the Night, Spartacus, Elmer Gantry, All the Way Home; Divorce, American Style, 1967; The Happy Ending, 1970; Thornbirds, 1982; television includes: Down at the Hydro, 1982. Musical: A Little Night Music, Adelphi, 1975. *Address:* c/o A. Morgan Maree, Jr & Assoc., Inc., 6363 Wilshire Boulevard, Los Angeles, California 90048, USA.

SIMMONS, Robert, CMG 1954; CBE 1943; MRCVS; *b* 10 Dec. 1894; *m* 1923, Mary Dickinson Waugh; one *d. Educ:* Dunfermline High School; Royal Dick Veterinary College, Edinburgh. Served European War, 1914-19; Fife and Forfar Yeomanry, King's Own Scottish Borderers, Royal Scots. Entered Colonial Service, 1923; Director of Veterinary Services: Uganda, 1938; Nigeria, 1944. Adviser to Secretary of State, Colonial Office, 1948-55, retired. *Publications:* contributions to scientific journals. *Recreation:* golf. *Address:* Lindores, Summerfield, Dunbar, Scotland. *T:* Dunbar 63781.

SIMMONS, William Foster, CMG 1963; MB, ChM; FRACGP 1969; General Practitioner, 1919-66, retired; *b* 9 May 1888; *s* of William Alfred Simmons, JP, Vaucluse, NSW; *m* 1919, Edna Kathleen Millicent Goode; two *d* (and two *s* decd). *Educ:* Sydney Boys' High School; Sydney University. Served European War, Australian Imperial Force, AAMC, 1914-19 (Major). Asst Hon. Physician, 1925, Hon. Consultant Physician, 1954, St George Hospital; Hon. Treasurer, Federal Council of BMA in Australia, 1946-62; Mem. Nat. Health and Medical Research Council, 1943-63. Chm. Medical Research Adv. Cttee, 1957-64; Dir Australasian Medical Publishing Co., 1946-74. Fellow, AMA, 1964 (Dir, AMA Services, NSW Ltd; Vice Pres., NSW Branch, AMA, 1980). Foundation Fellow, Aust. Coll. Gen. Practitioners, Oct. 1965. Awarded Gold Medal, BMA in Australia, 1961. *Recreations:* football and rowing (retired many years); gardening. *Address:* 78 Wentworth Road, Vaucluse, NSW 2030, Australia. *T:* 337-1770.

SIMMS, Most Rev. George Otto, DD; MRIA 1957; *b* 4 July 1910; 3rd *s* of John F. A. Simms, Crown Solicitor, County Tyrone, and Mrs Simms, Combermore, Lifford, County Donegal; *m* 1941, Mercy Felicia, *o d* of Brian James Gwynn, Temple Hill, Terenure, Dublin; three *s* two *d. Educ:* St Edmund's School, Hindhead; Cheltenham College; Trinity College, Dublin; Scholar, 1930; Moderator in Classics, and History and Political Science, 1932; Berkeley Medallist; Vice-Chancellor's Latin Medallist; Theological Exhibnr; Hon. Fellow, 1978. MA 1935; BD 1936; PhD 1950; DD (*jure dignitatis*, Dublin), 1952; DD (*hc* Huron), 1963; Hon. DCL Kent, 1978. Deacon, 1935; Priest, 1936; Curate-asst, St Bartholomew's Church, Dublin, 1935-38; Chaplain Lincoln Theol. Coll., 1938-39; Dean of Residence, Trinity Coll., Dublin, 1939-52; Asst Lectr to Archbishop King's Prof. of Divinity, Dublin Univ., 1939-52; Chaplain-Secretary, Church of Ireland Training Coll., 1943-52; Hon. Clerical Vicar, Christ Church Cathedral, Dublin, 1937-52; Dean of Cork, 1952; Bishop of Cork, Cloyne, and Ross, 1952-56; Archbishop of Dublin and Primate of Ireland, 1956-69; also Bishop of Glendalough and Bishop of Kildare; Archbishop of Armagh and Primate of All Ireland, 1969-80. Member Governing Body, University College, Cork, 1953-57; President, The Leprosy Mission, 1964-. Hon. DLitt New Univ. of Ulster, 1981. *Publications:* joint-editor (with E. H. Alton and P. Meyer), The Book of Kells (fac. edn), Berne, 1951; For Better, 1951; The Book of Kells: a short description, 1950; The Bible in Perspective, 1953; contributor, The Book of Durrow (fac. edn), 1960; Memoir of Michael Lloyd Ferrar, 1962; Christ within Me, 1975; Irish Illuminated Manuscripts, 1980; In My Understanding, 1982; articles in Hermathena, Theology, and Dublin Magazine, JTS; contrib. to New Divinity, Booklore, Search. *Address:* 62 Cypress Grove Road, Dublin 6. *T:* Dublin 905594.

SIMOGUN, Sir Petar, Kt 1981; MBE 1971; BEM 1945; a Chief of Arapesh Clan; landowner; engaged in business and farming, Dagua, Papua New Guinea; *b* 1900; *s* of Hajuta Matahek and Samare Mainoken; *m* 1946, Berta Barai; three *s* seven *d* (and two *s* decd). Self-educated. Plantation worker, Manup Is, Manus Prov., 1920-34; Police Force, 1936-42; Coastwatcher with RAN, 1942-45 (War Service Medals); Supervisor, Angau, 1945-46; Police Force, 1946-47; business promotion, development and organisation of food and cash crops, transport, etc, Dagua Area, 1947-; instrumental in starting Oil Palm industry, Hoskins, 1967-77. One of first 3 New Guineans nominated to Legislative Council, 1951-60; Mem., PNG House of Assembly, 1960-65; Vice Pres., But-Boikin Local Govt Council, 1957-59. Coronation Medal, 1953. *Recreation:* hunting. *Address:* N. V. Urip, c/o Catholic Mission, Dagua, via Wewak, East Sepik Province, Papua New Guinea.

SIMON, family name of **Viscount Simon,** of **Baron Simon of Glaisdale** and of **Baron Simon of Wythenshawe.**

SIMON, 2nd Viscount, *cr* 1940, of Stackpole Elidor; **John Gilbert Simon,** CMG 1957; *b* 2 Sept. 1902; *o s* of 1st Viscount Simon, PC, GCSI, GCVO, and of Ethel Mary (*d* 1902), *d* of Gilbert Venables; *S* father, 1954; *m* 1930, James Christie, *d* of William Stanley Hunt; one *s* one *d. Educ:* Winchester; Balliol College, Oxford (Scholar). With Ministry of War Transport, 1940-47. Man. Dir, 1947-58, Dep. Chm., 1951-58, Peninsular and Oriental Steam Navigation Co. Chm., PLA, 1958-71; Mem., Nat. Ports Council, 1967-71. President: Chamber of Shipping of UK, 1957-58; Inst. of Marine Engineers, 1960-61; RINA, 1961-71; British Hydromechanics Res. Assoc., 1968-80. Officer Order of Orange Nassau, Netherlands. *Heir:* *s* Hon. Jan David Simon [*b* 20 July 1940; *m* 1969, Mary Elizabeth Burns, Sydney; one *d*]. *Address:* 26 Strand Court, Topsham, Exeter EX3 0AZ.

SIMON OF GLAISDALE, Baron *cr* 1971 (Life Peer), of Glaisdale, Yorks; **Jocelyn Edward Salis Simon**, PC 1961; Kt 1959; DL; a Lord of Appeal in Ordinary, 1971-77; *b* 15 Jan. 1911; *s* of Frank Cecil and Claire Evelyn Simon, 51 Belsize Pk, NW3; *m* 1st, 1934, Gwendolen Helen (*d* 1937), *d* of E. J. Evans; 2nd, 1948, Fay Elizabeth Leicester, JP, *d* of Brig. H. G. A. Pearson; three *s*. *Educ:* Gresham's School, Holt; Trinity Hall, Cambridge (Exhibitioner). Called to Bar, Middle Temple, 1934 (Blackstone Prizeman). Served War of 1939-45; commissioned RTR, 1939; comd Spec. Service Sqn, RAC, Madagascar, 1942; Burma Campaign, 1944; Lieut-Col. 1945. Resumed practice at Bar, 1946; QC 1951. MP (C) Middlesbrough West, 1951-62; Mem. of the Royal Commission on the Law relating to Mental Illness and Mental Deficiency, 1954-57. Jt Parly Under-Sec. of State, Home Office, 1957-58; Financial Sec. to the Treasury, 1958-59; Solicitor-General, 1959-62. President, Probate, Divorce and Admiralty Div. of the High Court of Justice, 1962-71. Elder Brother, Trinity House, 1975. Hon. Fellow, Trinity Hall, Cambridge, 1963. DL NR (now North) Yorks, 1973. *Publications:* Change is Our Ally, 1954 (part); Rule of Law, 1955 (part); The Church and the Law of Nullity, 1955 (part). *Address:* Midge Hall, Glaisdale Head, Whitby, North Yorks.

SIMON OF WYTHENSHAWE, 2nd Baron, *cr* 1947, of Didsbury; **Roger Simon**; *b* 16 Oct. 1913; *S* father, 1960 (but does not use the title and wishes to be known as Roger Simon); *m* 1951 (Anthea) Daphne May; one *s* one *d*. *Educ:* Gresham's School; Gonville and Caius College, Cambridge. *Heir: s* Hon. Matthew Simon, *b* 10 April 1955. *Address:* Oakhill, Chester Avenue, Richmond, Surrey.

See also B. Simon.

SIMON, Prof. Brian; Emeritus Professor of Education, University of Leicester; *b* 26 March 1915; *yr s* of 1st Baron Simon of Wythenshawe and Shena D. Potter; *m* 1941, Joan Home Peel; two *s*. *Educ:* Gresham's Sch., Holt; Schloss Schule, Salem; Trinity Coll., Cambridge; Inst. of Educn, Univ. of London. MA. Pres., Nat. Union of Students, 1939-40; Royal Corps of Signals, GHQ Liaison Regt (Phantom), 1940-45; teaching Manchester and Salford schs, 1945-50; Univ. of Leicester: Lectr in Educn, 1950-64; Reader, 1964-66; Professor, 1966-80; Dir, Sch. of Educn, 1968-70, 1974-77. Chairman: History of Educn Soc., 1976-79; Internat. Standing Conf. for Hist. of Educn, 1979-82; Pres., British Educn Res. Assoc., 1977-78. Editor, Forum (for discussion of new trends in educn), 1958-; Jt Editor, Students Library of Education, 1966-77. Dr *hc* Cath. Univ. of Leuven, 1980. DUniv Open Univ., 1981. *Publications:* A Student's View of the Universities, 1943; Intelligence Testing and the Comprehensive School, 1953; The Common Secondary School, 1955; (ed) New Trends in English Education, 1957; (ed) Psychology in the Soviet Union, 1957; Studies in the History of Education 1780-1870, 1960; (ed, with Joan Simon) Educational Psychology in the USSR, 1963; (ed) The Challenge of Marxism, 1963; (ed) Non-streaming in the Junior School, 1964; Education and the Labour Movement 1870-1920, 1965; (ed) Education in Leicestershire 1540-1940, 1968; (with D. Rubinstein) The Evolution of the Comprehensive School 1926-66, 1969 (revised edn 1973); (with Caroline Benn) Half-Way There: Report on the British Comprehensive School Reform, 1970 (revised edn 1972); Intelligence, Psychology and Education, 1971 (revised edn 1978); (ed) The Radical Tradition in Education in Britain, 1972; The Politics of Educational Reform 1920-1940, 1974; (ed with Ian Bradley) The Victorian Public School, 1975; (with Maurice Galton) Inside the Primary Classroom, 1980; Progress and Performance in the Primary Classroom, 1980; (ed with William Taylor) Education in the Eighties, the central issues, 1981; (ed with John Willcocks) Research and Practice in the Primary Classroom, 1981. *Address:* 11 Pendene Road, Leicester LE2 3DQ. *T:* Leicester 705176.

SIMON, Prof. Herbert A(lexander), PhD; Richard King Mellon University Professor of Computer Science and Psychology, Carnegie-Mellon University, since 1967; *b* 15 June 1916; *s* of Arthur Simon and Edna Merkel Simon; *m* 1937, Dorothea Pye; one *s* two *d*. *Educ:* University of Chicago (BA, PhD). Staff member, Internat. City Managers' Assoc., 1936-39; Study Director, Bureau of Public Admin., Univ. of California (Berkeley), 1939-42; Asst Prof. to Professor, Illinois Inst. of Technology, 1942-49 (Head, Dept of Pol. and Social Sci., 1947-49); Professor of Administration, Carnegie-Mellon Univ., 1949-67 (Associate Dean, Graduate Sch. of Industrial Admin., 1957-73). Mem., Nat. Acad. of Scis, 1967 (Mem. Council, 1978-81). Hon. degrees: DSc: Case Inst. of Technol., 1963; Yale, 1963; Marquette, 1981; LLD: Chicago, 1964; McGill, 1970; Michigan, 1978; Pittsburgh, 1979; FilDr, Lund, 1968; DrEconSci, Erasmus (Rotterdam), 1973. Hon. Prof., Tianjin Univ., 1980. Nobel Prize in Economics, 1978; Dist. Sci. Contrib. Award, Amer. Psych. Assoc., 1969; Turing Award, Assoc. for Computing Machinery, 1975. *Publications:* Administrative Behavior, 1947, 3rd edn 1976; Models of Man, 1957; (with J. G. March) Organizations, 1958; The New Science of Management Decision, 1960, rev. edn 1977; The Sciences of the Artificial, 1969, 2nd edn 1981; (with A. Newell) Human Problem Solving, 1972; Models of Discovery, 1977; (with Y. Ijiri) Skew Distributions and the Sizes of Business Firms, 1977; Models of Thought, 1979; Models of Bounded Rationality (2 vols), 1982; other books, and articles in sci. jls. *Recreations:* walking, piano, painting. *Address:* Department of Psychology, Carnegie-Mellon University, Pittsburgh, Pa 15213, USA. *T:* 412-578-2787. *Clubs:* University (Pittsburgh); Cosmos (Washington).

SIMON, Neil; playwright; *b* NYC, 4 July 1927; *s* of Irving and Mamie Simon; *m* 1st, 1953, Joan Baim (decd); two *d*; 2nd, 1973, Marsha Mason. *Educ:* De Witt Clinton High Sch.; entered Army Air Force Reserve training programme as an engineering student at New York University; discharged with rank of corporal, 1946. Went to New York Offices of Warner Brothers Pictures to work in mail room. Hon. LHD Hofstra Univ., 1981. *Screenplays include:* After The Fox (produced 1966); The Heartbreak Kid, 1973; The Prisoner of 2nd Avenue, 1975; The Sunshine Boys, 1976; Murder by Death, 1976; The Goodbye Girl, 1977; The Cheap Detective, 1978; California Suite, 1979; Chapter Two, 1979; Seems Like Old Times, 1980; Only When I Laugh, 1981; I Ought to be in Pictures, 1982. *Plays produced:* Come Blow Your Horn, 1961 (publ. 1961); (jtly) Little Me, 1962 (publ. 1979), revival, 1982; Barefoot in the Park, 1963 (publ. 1964); The Odd Couple, 1965 (publ. 1966); (jtly) Sweet Charity, 1966 (publ. 1966); The Star-Spangled Girl, 1966 (publ. 1967); Plaza Suite, 1968 (publ. 1969); (jtly) Promises, Promises, 1968 (publ. 1969); Last of the Red Hot Lovers, 1969 (publ. 1970), Criterion, 1979; The Gingerbread Lady, 1970 (publ. 1971); The Prisoner of Second Avenue, 1971 (publ. 1972); The Sunshine Boys, 1972 (publ. 1973); The Good Doctor, 1973 (publ. 1974); God's Favorite, 1974 (publ. 1975); California Suite, 1976 (publ. 1977); Chapter Two, 1977 (publ. 1978); (jtly) They're Playing Our Song, 1978 (publ. 1980); Ought To Be In Pictures, 1980 (publ. 1981); Fools, 1981 (publ. 1982). *Address:* c/o A. DaSilva, 521 Park Avenue, New York, NY 10021, USA.

SIMON, Roger; see Simon of Wythenshawe barony.

SIMON, Prof. Ulrich Ernst, DD; Professor of Christian Literature, 1972-80, Dean, 1978-80, King's College, London; *b* 21 Sept. 1913; *s* of James and Anna Simon; *m* 1949, Joan Edith Raynor Westlake; two *s* one *d*. *Educ:* Grunewald Gymnasium, Berlin; King's Coll., London. BD, MTh, DD, FKC. Ordained in Church of England, 1938; Univ. Lectr, 1945; Reader, 1960. *Publications:* Theology of Crisis, 1948; Theology of Salvation, 1953; Heaven in the Christian Tradition, 1958; The Ascent to Heaven, 1961; The End is not Yet, 1964; Theology Observed, 1966; A Theology of Auschwitz, 1967 (paperback 1978); The Trial of Man, 1973; Story and Faith, 1975; Sitting in Judgment, 1978. *Recreations:* gardening, chamber music, walking. *Address:* 22 Collingwood Avenue, N10 3ED. *T:* 01-883 4852.

SIMON, William Edward; Chairman of Boards of Wesray Corp. and Gibson Greeting Cards Inc.; Member of the Board of Directors: Citibank and Citicorp; Xerox Corporation; Dart & Kraft, Inc.; Halliburton Co. Power Corp., Canada; United Technologies; President, John M. Olin Foundation; *b* 27 Nov. 1927; *s* of Charles Simon and Eleanor Kearns; *m* 1950, Carol Girard; two *s* five *d*. *Educ:* Newark Academy, NJ; Lafayette Coll. (BA). Joined Union Securities, NYC 1952, Asst Vice-Pres. and Manager of firm's Municipal Trading Dept, 1955; Vice Pres., Weeden & Co., 1957-64; Sen. Partner, Salomon Brothers, NYC, 1964-72. Dep. Sec., US Treasury Dept, and Administrator, Federal Energy Office, 1973-74; Secretary of the Treasury, May 1974-Jan. 1977. Finance Chm., Amer. Inst. for Public Service; Chm., Bd of Dirs, Nat. Energy Foundn; Chm., Wilson Council, Woodrow Wilson Internat. Center of Scholars; Pres., US Olympic Cttee (former Treasurer); Member: Nat. Bd of Dirs, Boys' Club of America; Nat. Adv. Cttee, Amer. Family Soc.; Nat. Industrial Adv. Council (OIC); Bd of Dirs and Exec. Cttee, Internat. Rescue Cttee; Adv. Bd, Center for Strategic and Internat. Studies, Georgetown Univ.; Nat. Co-Chm., Interracial Council for Business Opportunity. Trustee: Lafayette Coll.; Georgetown Univ.; Hudson Inst.; Nat. Executive Service Corps. Hon. Dr of Laws: Lafayette Coll., 1973; Pepperdine Univ., 1975; Hon. DCL Jacksonville Univ., 1976; Hon. PhD Tel Aviv, 1976; Hon. Scriptural Degree, Israel Torah Res. Inst., 1976; Hon. DSc New England Coll., 1977. *Publications:* A Time for Truth, 1978; A Time for Action, 1980. *Address:* Wesray Corp., 330 South Street, CN 1975, Morristown, NJ 07960, USA; Sand Spring Road, New Vernon, NJ 07976, USA. *Clubs:* River, Links, Union League, Pilgrims of US (New York, NY); Maidstone (East Hampton, NY); Federal City, Alfalfa, Burning Tree (Washington, DC); Chevy Chase (Chevy Chase, Md); Balboa Bay (Calif); Morris County Golf (Convent Station, NJ).

SIMONET, Henri François; Member, Belgian Parliament, since 1966; Mayor of Anderlecht, since 1966; *b* Brussels, 10 May 1931; *m* 1960, Marie-Louise Angenent; one *s* one *d*. *Educ:* Univ. Libre de Bruxelles (DenD, DèsSc); Columbia Univ., USA. Assistant, Univ. Libre de Bruxelles, 1956-58, now Prof.; Financial Adv., Inst. Nat. d'Etudes pour le Développement du Bas-Congo, 1958-59; Legal Adv., Commn of Brussels Stock Exchange, 1956-60; Dep. Dir, Office of Econ. Programming, 1961; Director of Cabinet: of Min. of Econ. Affairs and Power, 1961-65; of Dep. Prime Minister responsible for co-ordination of Econ. Policy, 1965; Minister of Econ. Affairs, 1972; Vice-Pres., Commn of the European Communities, 1973-77; Foreign Minister, Belgium, 1977-80; Sec. of State, Brussels Regional Economy, 1977-79. Commander, Order of Leopold. *Publications:* various books and articles on economics, financial and political topics. *Address:* 1 Avenue des Crocus, 1070 Brussels, Belgium.

SIMONS, (Alfred) Murray; HM Diplomatic Service; Head of UK Delegation to Negotiations on Mutual Reduction of Forces and Armaments and Associated Measures in Central Europe, at Vienna, since 1982, with personal rank of Ambassador; *b* 9 Aug. 1927; *s* of late Louis Simons and of Fay Simons; *m* 1975, Patricia Jill, *d* of late David and May Barclay, Westbury on Trym, Bristol; two *s*. *Educ:* City of London Sch.; Magdalen Coll., Oxford (MA).

FO, 1951; 3rd Sec., Moscow, 1952-55; FO, 1955-56; Columbia Univ., 1956; 2nd Sec., Bogota, 1957; 1st Sec., Office of Comr-Gen. for SE Asia, Singapore, 1958-61; FO, 1961-64; 1st Sec., British High Commn, New Delhi, 1964-68; FCO, 1968-71; Counsellor, 1969; British Embassy, Washington, 1971-75; Head of SE Asia Dept, FCO, 1975-79; Consul General, Montreal, 1980-82. *Recreations:* tennis, theatre. *Address:* c/o Foreign and Commonwealth Office, SW1.

SIMPLE, Peter; *see* Wharton, Michael B.

SIMPSON, Alan, MA, DPhil Oxon, LHD, LLD; President and Professor of History, Vassar College, Poughkeepsie, NY, 1964-77; *b* Gateshead, Durham, England, 23 July 1912; *s* of George Hardwick Simpson and Isabella Simpson (*née* Graham); *m* 1938, Mary McQueen McEldowney, Chicago Heights, Ill; one *s* two *d*. *Educ:* Worcester Coll., Oxford (BA); Merton Coll., Oxford (MA, DPhil); Harvard Univ. (Commonwealth Fellow). Served War of 1939-45, RA, Major. Sen. Lectr in Modern British History and American History, Univ. of St Andrews, and Lectr in Constitutional Law, Law Sch., University Coll., Dundee, 1938-46; Asst Prof. of History, Univ. of Chicago, 1946-54; Associate Prof., 1954-59; Thomas E. Donnelley Prof. of History and Dean of the College, Univ. of Chicago, 1959-64. Member Board of Trustees: Colonial Williamsburg; Salve Regina Coll., Newport; Old Dartmouth Hist. Soc.; Mem., Amer. Antiquarian Soc.; Former Member: Council of the Inst. of Early Amer. History and Culture, Williamsburg, Va, 1957-60; Midwest Conf. of British Historians (Co-Founder, Sec., 1954-61); Commn on Academic Affairs and Bd of Dirs, Amer. Council on Educn; Commn on Liberal Learning, Assoc. of Amer. Colls; Hudson River Valley Commn. *Publications:* (Co-Editor) The People Shall Judge: Readings in the Formation of American Policy, 1949; Puritanism in Old and New England, 1955; The Wealth of the Gentry, 1540-1660: East Anglian Studies, 1961; (Co-Editor with Mary Simpson): Diary of King Philip's War by Benjamin Church, 1975; I Too Am Here: a selection of letters of Jane Welsh Carlyle, 1976; (with Mary Simpson) Mark Twain's Great-Niece: the story of Jean Webster. *Address:* Yellow Gate Farm, Little Compton, RI, USA. *Club:* Century (New York).

SIMPSON, Alan; author and scriptwriter since 1951 (in collaboration with Ray Galton, *qv*); *b* 27 Nov. 1929; *s* of Francis and Lilian Simpson; *m* 1958, Kathleen Phillips (*d* 1978). *Educ:* Mitcham Grammar Sch. *Television:* Hancock's Half Hour, 1954-61; Comedy Playhouse, 1962-63; Steptoe and Son, 1962-, US TV Version, Sanford and Son, 1971-; Galton-Simpson Comedy, 1969; Clochemerle, 1971; Casanova, 1974; Dawson's Weekly, 1975; The Galton and Simpson Playhouse, 1976; *films:* The Rebel, 1960; The Bargee, 1963; The Wrong Arm of the Law, 1963; The Spy with a Cold Nose, 1966; Loot, 1969; Steptoe and Son, 1971; Steptoe and Son Ride Again, 1973; Den Siste Fleksnes (Norway), 1974; *theatre:* Way Out in Piccadilly, 1966; The Wind in the Sassafras Trees, 1968; Albert och Herbert, Sweden, 1981. Awards: Scriptwriters of the Year, 1959 (Guild of TV Producers and Directors); Best TV Comedy Series (Steptoe and Son, 1962/3/4/5 (Screenwriters Guild)); John Logie Baird Award (for outstanding contribution to Television), 1964; Best Comedy Series (Steptoe and Son, Dutch TV), 1966; Best Comedy Screenplay, Screenwriters Guild, 1972. *Publications:* (jointly with Ray Galton, *qv*): Hancock, 1961; Steptoe and Son, 1963; The Reunion and Other Plays, 1966; Hancock Scripts, 1974. *Recreations:* Hampton FC (Pres.), fishing. *Address:* c/o RSO Management Ltd, 67 Brook Street, W1. *T:* 01-629 9121.

SIMPSON, Alan; a Recorder of the Crown Court, since 1975; *b* 17 April 1937; *s* of William Henry Simpson and Gladys Simpson; *m* 1965, Maureen O'Shea; one *s* one *d*. *Educ:* Leeds Grammar Sch.; Corpus Christi Coll., Oxford (MA). Called to the Bar, Inner Temple, 1962. Prosecuting Counsel to DHSS, North Eastern Circuit, 1977-. *Recreations:* music, books, sport (especially cricket and boxing). *Address:* The Keep, 41 Colton Road, Whitkirk, Leeds LS15 9AA. *T:* Leeds 605448. *Club:* St Anne's (Leeds).

SIMPSON, Alfred Henry; Hon. Mr Justice Simpson; Chief Justice of Kenya, since 1982; *b* 29 Oct. 1914; *s* of John Robertson Simpson, Dundee; *m* 1941, Hilda Corson Rodgers; one *d*. *Educ:* Grove Academy; St Andrews University; Edinburgh University. MA St Andrews, 1935; LLB Edinburgh, 1938 and Solicitor. Served in RASC, 1940-46, Middle East and Italy; Military Mission to the Italian Army and Allied Commission, Austria. Legal Officer, BMA, Cyrenaica, 1946-48. Member of the Faculty of Advocates, 1948. Crown Counsel, Singapore, 1948-56; Legal Draftsman, Gold Coast, 1956; Solicitor-General, Ghana, 1957, then Puisne Judge, Supreme Court, 1957-61; Puisne Judge, Combined Judiciary of Sarawak, North Borneo and Brunei, 1962; Senior Puisne Judge, Fedn of Malaysia High Court in Borneo, 1964; Reader, Faculty of Law, ANU, Canberra, 1965; Barrister-at-Law, NSW, 1967; Puisne Judge, High Court of Kenya, 1967-82. *Publication:* (with others) The Laws of Singapore, revised edn, 1955. *Recreation:* golf. *Address:* PO Box 30041, Nairobi, Kenya. *Clubs:* Royal Commonwealth Society; Royal Canberra Golf.

SIMPSON, Alfred Moxon, AC 1978; CMG 1959; Chairman: Simpson Holdings Ltd; SA Telecasters Ltd; *b* 17 Nov. 1910; *s* of late A. A. Simpson, CMG, CBE; *m* 1938, Elizabeth Robson Cleland; one *s*. *Educ:* St Peter's College; University of Adelaide, (BSc). Associate (Commerce) of Univ. of Adelaide, 1940. Pres. Adelaide Chamber of Commerce, 1950-52; Sen. Vice-Pres. Associated Chambers of Commerce of Aust., 1953-55; Pres. SA Chamber

of Manufrs, 1956-58; Pres. Associated Chambers of Manufrs of Aust., 1957-58. Director: Adelaide Steamship Co. Ltd; Bank of Adelaide, 1952-79; Elder Smith Goldsbrough Mort Ltd, 1954-81; QBE Insurance Group Ltd. Mem. Hulme Cttee on Rates of Depreciation, 1956. *Recreations:* carpentry, ski-ing. *Address:* 31 Heatherbank Terrace, Stonyfell, SA 5066, Australia. *T:* 31 12 85. *Clubs:* Adelaide, Mt Lofty Ski (Adelaide); Melbourne (Melbourne); Union (Sydney).

SIMPSON, Prof. (Alfred William) Brian, DCL; JP; Professor of Law, University of Kent, since 1973; *b* 17 Aug. 1931; *s* of Rev. Canon Bernard W. Simpson and Mary E. Simpson; *m* 1st, 1954, Kathleen Anne Seston (marr. diss. 1968); one *s* one *d*; 2nd, 1969, Caroline Elizabeth Ann Brown; one *s* two *d*. *Educ:* Oakham Sch., Rutland; The Queen's Coll., Oxford (MA 1958, DCL 1976). Nat. Service with RWAFF, 1950-51. Junior Research Fellow, St Edmund Hall, Oxford, 1954-55; Fellow and Tutor, Lincoln Coll., Oxford, 1955-73. Dean: Faculty of Law, Univ. of Ghana, 1968-69; Faculty of Social Sciences, Univ. of Kent, 1975-78; Visiting Professor: Dalhousie Univ., 1964; Univ. of Chicago, 1979, 1980, 1982; Hon. Dep. District Attorney, Denver City, 1982. Member, Deptl Cttee on Obscenity and Film Censorship, 1977-79. JP Canterbury and St Augustine's, 1968-. *Publications:* Introduction to the History of the Land Law, 1961; ed, Oxford Essays in Jurisprudence, 2nd Ser., 1973; A History of the Common Law of Contract, 1975; articles in legal jls. *Recreation:* gardening. *Address:* Forbury, 47 New Dover Road, Canterbury, Kent CT1 3DP. *T:* Canterbury 52395.

SIMPSON, Anthony Maurice Herbert, TD 1973; Member (C) Northamptonshire, European Parliament, since 1979; *b* 28 Oct. 1935; *y s* of late Lt-Col Maurice Rowton Simpson, OBE, TD, DL and Mrs Renée Claire Simpson; *m* 1961, Penelope Gillian, *d* of late Howard Dixon Spackman; one *s* two *d*. *Educ:* Rugby; Magdalene College, Cambridge. BA 1959, LLB 1961, MA 1963. Leics and Derbys (PAO) Yeomanry, 1956-59; 21st SAS Regt (Artists Rifles) (V), 1959-68; 23rd SAS Regt (V), 1968-74; Major 1968. Called to Bar, Inner Temple, 1961; practised Midland and Oxford Circuit, 1961-75; Mem., Legal Service of European Commn, Brussels, 1975-79; Quaestor of the European Parlt, 1979. Contested (C) West Leicester, Feb. and Oct. 1974. Common Market Law Editor, Current Law, 1965-72. *Recreations:* walking, travelling. *Address:* Bassets, Great Glen, Leicestershire. *T:* Great Glen 2386; Avenue Michel-Ange 57, 1040 Brussels, Belgium. *T:* (02) 736-4219. *Club:* Leicestershire (Leicester).

SIMPSON, Athol John Dundas, OBE 1976; Director, Crown Agents for Oversea Governments and Administrations, since 1978; *b* 4 May 1932; *s* of John Simpson and Helen Murray Simpson (*née* Cubie); *m* 1956, Ricki Ellen Carter; one *s* two *d*. *Educ:* Reigate Grammar Sch. Joined Crown Agents, 1950; served, Royal Air Force, 1951-53; Crown Agents' Representative in E Africa, 1965-69; seconded as Managing Director, Millbank Technical Services (Iran) Ltd, 1973-77; returned to Bd appt as Director of Marketing and Development with Crown Agents, Nov. 1977. *Recreations:* Rugby football, golf, reading. *Address:* 12 Lower Sloane Street, SW1. *T:* 01-730 1473. *Club:* Travellers'.

SIMPSON, Prof. Brian; *see* Simpson, Prof. A. W. B.

SIMPSON, Prof. (Cedric) Keith, CBE 1975; MA Oxon, MD London (Path.), FRCP; FRCPath; DMJ; Professor and Head of Department of Forensic Medicine to University of London, 1962-72, Professor Emeritus, since 1972 (Reader, 1946-62); Head of Department of Forensic Medicine, Guy's Hospital Medical School; *b* 20 July 1907; *s* of Dr George Herbert Simpson, Brighton, Sussex; *m* 1st, Mary McCartney Buchanan (*d* 1955); one *s* two *d*; 2nd, 1956, Jean Anderson Scott Dunn (*d* 1976; 3rd, 1982, Janet (*née* Hazell), widow of Dr Gavin Thurston, CBE. *Educ:* Brighton and Hove Grammar School, Sussex; University of London. Guy's Hospital Medical School: Gold Medallist (Golding-Bird) in Bacteriology, 1927; Beaney Prizeman, 1927; Gull Scholar and Astley Cooper Student, 1932; Lecturer in Pathology, 1932-37; Lecturer in Forensic Medicine, 1937-47; Lecturer in Forensic Med., Oxford Univ., 1961-73. Examiner in Forensic Medicine to Univs: London, 1945; St Andrews, 1948; Leeds, 1950; NUI, 1952-64; Wales, 1954; Oxford, 1957; Glasgow, 1964. Member, Home Office Scientific Advisory Council. Harvard Associate in Police Science, 1952; Medallist, Strasbourg University, 1954; President: Medico-Legal Society, 1961; British Assoc. in Forensic Medicine, 1966; British Council Lecturer, France 1954, Denmark 1961, India 1974. Corresponding Member: Société de Médicine Légale; Amer. Acad. of Forensic Sciences; Spanish and Italian Socs of Legal Medicine. Hon. MD, Ghent; Hon. LLD Edinburgh, 1976. *Publications:* Forensic Medicine, 1947 (8th edn, 1978; awarded RSA Swiney Prize, 1958); Modern Trends in Forensic Medicine, 1953 (2nd edn 1967); Doctor's Guide to Court, 1962 (2nd edn 1966); (ed) Taylor's Principles and Practice of Medical Jurisprudence, 12th edn, 1965; The Investigation of Violence, 1978; 40 Years of Murder (autobiog.), 1978; contrib. to medical and scientific journals. *Address:* Department of Forensic Medicine, Guy's Hospital, SE1. *T:* 01-407 0378; Dancers End Lodge, Tring, Herts. *Club:* Athenæum.

SIMPSON, Charles Valentine George; former Director: Wigham Poland Midlands Ltd; Walker, Moate, Simpson & Co. Ltd, Birmingham, since 1960; Wigham-Richardson and Bevingtons (Midlands) Ltd; *b* 14 Feb. 1900; 2nd *s* of Alexander Simpson, Ayrshire; *m* ; two *s* one *d*; 2nd, Muriel Edwina, *e d* of Rev. Edwin Jones, Montgomeryshire; one *s*. *Educ:* Tindal Street Elementary Sch., Birmingham. RMLI, 1915-19; RNVR, 1939-45, rank of Lt-Comdr; served China, Med., Iceland, Germany. Councillor, Birmingham,

1935, Alderman, 1949-74; Chairman, Airports Cttee, 1950, Public Works Cttee, 1966-68; Lord Mayor, City of Birmingham, 1968-69. President: RN Assoc., City of Birmingham; Handsworth Wood Residents Assoc.; Birmingham Br., RNLI; County Pres., Birmingham Royal British Legion; Vice-Pres., Birmingham Bn, Boys' Brigade; Life Mem., Court of Governors, Birmingham Univ. Successfully inaugurated appeal, 1969, for a new lifeboat to be called City of Birmingham. *Recreations:* bowls, foreign travel (preferably by caravan). *Address:* 16 Knowle Wood Road, Dorridge, W Midlands B93 8JJ. *T:* Knowle 2427.

SIMPSON, Commander Cortlandt James Woore, CBE 1956; DSC 1945; retired 1961; *b* 2 Sept. 1911; *s* of late Rear-Admiral C. H. Simpson, CBE, and, Edith Octavia (*née* Busby); *m* 1st, Lettice Mary Johnstone; 2nd, Ann Margaret Cubitt (*née* Tooth); 3rd, Joan Mary Watson; one *d. Educ:* St Ronans, Worthing; RN College, Dartmouth; London Univ. (BSc Engineering, Hons). Joined RN (Dartmouth), 1925; Lieut, 1934. Served War of 1939-45 in Home and Mediterranean Fleets; Commander, 1948. Summer expeditions to Greenland, 1950, 1951; Leader of British North Greenland Expedition, 1952-54. Polar Medal, 1954; Royal Geographical Society, Founder's Medal, 1955. *Recreations:* mountaineering, sailing, walking. *Publication:* North Ice, 1957. *Address:* Garden House, Bruisyard, Saxmundham, Suffolk. *Club:* Alpine.

SIMPSON, Prof. David Rae Fisher; Research Professor at The Fraser of Allander Institute, University of Strathclyde, since 1980; *b* 29 Nov. 1936; *s* of David Ebenezer Simpson and Roberta Muriel Wilson; *m* 1980, Barbara Dianne Goalen, *d* of Mrs G. Inglis, Edinburgh one *s* (and one step *s* one step *d*). *Educ:* Skerry's Coll.; Edinburgh and Harvard Univs. MA 1st cl. hons Econs Edinburgh; PhD Econs Harvard. Instr in Econs, Harvard Univ., 1963-64; Assoc. Statistician, UN Hdqtrs, NY, 1964-65; Res. Officer, Econ. Res. Inst., Dublin, 1965-67; Lectr in Polit. Economy, UCL, 1967-69; Sen. Lectr in Econs, Univ. of Stirling, 1969-74; Prof. and Dir, Fraser of Allander Inst., Univ. of Strathclyde, 1975-80. Contested (SNP) Berwick and E Lothian Division, 1970 and Feb. 1974. *Publications:* Problems of Input-Output Tables and Analysis, 1966; General Equilibrium Analysis, 1975; The Political Economy of Growth, 1982; articles in Econometrica, Rev. Econs and Statistics, Scientific American. *Recreations:* golf, tennis, walking. *Address:* 11 Kingsburgh Road, Edinburgh.

SIMPSON, David Richard Salisbury; Director, Action on Smoking and Health, since 1979; *b* 1 Oct. 1945; *s* of Richard Salisbury Simpson and Joan Margaret Simpson (*née* Braund). *Educ:* Merchiston Castle School, Edinburgh. ACA 1969; FCA 1979 (but resigned from Institute, 1981). Teacher at Cadet College, Hasan Abdal, West Pakistan, 1963-64 (VSO). Peat, Marwick, Mitchell & Co., Chartered Accountants, 1964-72; Scottish Director, Shelter, Campaign for the Homeless, 1972-74; Director, Amnesty International (British Section), 1974-79. Sundry journalism, broadcasting and public lectures. Consultant, Internat. Union Against Cancer Special Project on Smoking and Cancer (responsibility for Indian Sub-Continent), 1980-. *Publications:* contribs to national newspapers and magazines on housing, human rights and smoking and health. *Recreations:* friends, reading, music, hill-walking, Orkney. *Address:* c/o ASH, 5-11 Mortimer Street, W1. *T:* 01-637 9843.

SIMPSON, Lt-Col (Retd) David Sackville Bruce; Chief Executive, Civil Service Catering Organisation, since 1981; *b* 18 March 1930; *s* of Henry and Violet Simpson; *m* 1956, Margaret Elizabeth Goslin; two *s* three *d. Educ:* Brockley Grammar Sch.; Westminster Technical Coll. MHCIMA. Regular Officer, Army Catering Corps (retd in rank of Lt-Col), 1950-75; Principal Education Catering Organiser, Inner London Education Authority, 1975-81. *Recreations:* golf, squash. *Address:* 65 Gally Hill Road, Church Crookham, Hants. *T:* Fleet 3754.

SIMPSON, Dennis Charles; business consultant; Counsellor, Welsh Development Agency, since 1981; *b* 24 Oct. 1931; *s* of late Arthur and Helen Simpson; *m* 1964, Margery Bruce Anderson; three *s* one *d. Educ:* Manchester Univ. (BA). FInstPS. 2nd Lieut Royal Signals, 1952-54; commercial appts, Philips Electrical Industries, 1956-63; Group Purchasing Manager: STC Ltd, 1963-66; Rank Organisation, 1966-69; Gen. Man., Cam Gears (S Wales) Ltd, 1969-72; Industrial Dir for Wales, Dept of Industry, 1972-75; Industrial Dir for Wales, Welsh Office, 1975-76. Chairman: Spencer Harris Ltd, 1976-81; Grainger Hydraulics Ltd, 1976-81; Wellfield Engineering, 1976-81; Dir, Beechwood Holdings, 1976-81. *Recreations:* golf, bridge, reading war histories. *Address:* 9 Langland Bay Road, Langland, Swansea, West Glamorgan. *T:* Swansea 66648. *Club:* Langland Bay Golf.

SIMPSON, Edward Hugh, CB 1976; Deputy Secretary, Department of Education and Science, since 1973; *b* 10 Dec. 1922; *o s* of Hugh and Mary Simpson, of Brookfield, Ballymena, Co. Antrim; *m* 1947, Gladys Rebecca, *er d* of Samuel and Elizabeth Gibson, Ernevale, Kesh, Co. Fermanagh; one *s* one *d. Educ:* Coleraine Academical Institution; Queen's Univ., Belfast; Christ's Coll., Cambridge (Scholar). Dept of the Foreign Office, 1942-45; Min. of Education, 1947-50 and 1952-56; HM Treasury, 1950-52; Commonwealth Fund Fellow, USA, 1956-57; Private Sec. to Lord President of Council and Lord Privy Seal, 1957-60; Dep. Dir, Commonwealth Educn Liaison Unit, 1960-62; Sec., Commonwealth Educn Conf., New Delhi, 1962; Asst Sec., DES, 1962-68; Under-Sec., Civil Service Dept, 1968-71, DES,

1971-73. *Address:* 40 Frays Avenue, West Drayton, Mddx UB7 7AG. *T:* West Drayton 43417.

SIMPSON, Ernest Smith, CEng, FIMechE; Chairman since 1973, and Managing Director since 1966, Jonas Woodhead & Sons Ltd, Leeds; *b* 7 Nov. 1921; *s* of Leonard and Gladys Simpson; *m* 1961, Janet (*née* Wright); one *s* one *d. Educ:* Leeds City School of Commerce; Hendon Technical Coll. Junior draughtsman, Woodhead Group, 1936; Director of Holding Company, Woodhead Group, 1964. Member, Monopolies Commission, 1978-81. MSAE. *Recreations:* golf, painting. *Address:* Green Trees, Ling Lane, Scarcroft, Leeds, W Yorkshire LS14 3HT. *T:* Leeds 892986.

SIMPSON, Esther Eleanor, MD, FRCP, FFCM, DPH, DCH; former Senior Principal Medical Officer, Department of Education and Science, and Department of Health and Social Security, retired 1979; *b* 28 May 1919. *Educ:* Kendal High Sch.; London Univ. Medical Officer, London County Council, then to Province of Natal Centre, Inst. of Child Health; joined Medical Br., Min. of Education, 1961. *Recreations:* music, reading, walking. *Address:* 19 Belsize Lane, NW3 5AG. *T:* 01-794 4400.

SIMPSON, Ffreebairn Liddon, CMG 1967; General Manager, Central Water Authority, Mauritius, 1976-78; *b* 11 July 1916; *s* of late James Liddon Simpson and of Dorothy (*née* Blyth); *m* 1947, Dorina Laura Magda, MBE (*née* Ilieva); one *s. Educ:* Westminster School; Trinity College, Cambridge. HM Diplomatic/Foreign Service, 1939-48; HM Treasury, 1948-50; Administrative Officer, Gold Coast, 1950-55; Dep. Colonial Sec., Mauritius, 1955; Perm. Secretary: Min. of Works and Internal Communications, 1961; Premier's Office, 1966; Sec. to the Cabinet, Mauritius, 1967-76. *Recreations:* reading, philately. *Address:* c/o Hong Kong & Shanghai Banking Corporation, 9 Waterloo Place, SW1Y 4BE. *Club:* United Oxford & Cambridge University.

SIMPSON, General Sir Frank (Ernest Wallace), GBE 1953 (KBE 1947); KCB 1951 (CB 1944); DSO 1940; Chief Royal Engineer, 1961-67; Governor of Royal Hospital, Chelsea, 1961-69; *b* 21 March 1899; *s* of late Major Robert Wallace Simpson, MC; *m* 1934, Charlotte Dulcie Margaret Cooke; two *d. Educ:* Bedford School; Royal Military Academy, Woolwich; Trinity Hall, Cambridge. Commissioned in Royal Engineers, 1916; Lt-Col 1939; Col 1942; Maj.-Gen. 1944; Lt-Gen. 1946; Gen. 1950; served European War of 1914-18, France and Belgium (despatches, British War Medal, Victory Medal); Afghanistan and NW Frontier, 1919 (Medal with clasp); France, 1939-40 (DSO, 1939-45 Star, Defence Medal); Vice CIGS, 1946-48; GOC-in-C, Western Command, UK, 1948-51; Commandant, Imperial Defence College, 1952-54. ADC General to the King, 1951-52, to the Queen, 1952-54; retired pay, 1954; Mem. Eastern Electricity Board, 1954-63; Colonel Commandant: Royal Pioneer Corps, 1950-61; RE, 1954-67. Adviser to West Africa Cttee, 1956-66; Dir, United Services Trustee, 1961-69. JP Essex, 1955-61; DL Essex, 1956-65. Kt Gr Officer, Order of Orange-Nassau (with Swords), 1947. *Address:* 5 Northfields Close, Bath, Avon. *Clubs:* Naval and Military; MCC; Bath and County (Bath).

SIMPSON, Gordon Russell, DSO 1944 and Bar 1945; MVO 1979; TD; stockbroker; Partner, Bell, Cowan & Co. (now Bell, Lawrie, Macgregor & Co.), 1938-82; *b* 2 Jan. 1917; *s* of A. Russell Simpson, WS; *m* 1943, Marion Elizabeth King (*d* 1976); two *s. Educ:* Rugby School. Served with 2nd Lothians and Border Horse, 1939-46 (comd 1944-46). Chm., Edinburgh Stock Exchange, 1961-63; Chm., Scottish Stock Exchange, 1965-66; Pres., Council of Associated Stock Exchanges, 1971-73; Dep. Chm., Stock Exchange, 1973-78. Chm., General Accident Fire & Life Assurance Corporation Ltd, 1979- (Dir, 1967-). Brigadier, Queen's Body Guard for Scotland (Royal Company of Archers). Mem. Court, Stirling Univ., 1980-; Comr, Queen Victoria Sch., 1982-. *Recreations:* music, ski-ing, archery. *Address:* Erskine House, 68/73 Queen Street, Edinburgh EH2 4AE. *Club:* New (Edinburgh).

SIMPSON, Maj.-Gen. Hamilton Wilkie, CB 1945; DSO 1940; late Royal Marines; *b* 1895. 2nd Lt Royal Marines, 1913; served European War, 1914-18; War of 1939-45 (DSO); retired list, 1946. *Address:* Briar Dene, Wellswood Avenue, Torquay, Devon TQ1 2QE.

SIMPSON, Henry George, CBE 1980 (OBE 1968); Controller of Housing and Technical Services to Greater London Council, 1974-82; *b* 27 April 1917; *s* of late William James and late Alice Simpson; *m* 1938, Gladys Lee; one *s. Educ:* Enfield Grammar School. FIH, FSVA. War Service 1940-46, Royal Fusiliers. Dir of Housing and Property Services, London Borough of Lambeth, 1962-72; Dir-Gen., Northern Ireland Housing Exec., 1972-74. FRSA. *Recreations:* gardening, hi-fi, clay pigeon shooting. *Address:* 19 Abbotswood, Guildford, Surrey, GU1 1UX.

SIMPSON, Ian; Principal, St Martin's School of Art, London, since 1972; *b* 12 Nov. 1933; *s* of Herbert William and Elsie Simpson; *m* 1958, Joan (*née* Charlton) (marr. diss. 1982); two *s* one *d; m* 1982, Birgitta Willcocks (*née* Bredde). *Educ:* Bede Grammar Sch., Sunderland; Sunderland Coll. of Art; Royal Coll. of Art. ARCA 1958. Freelance artist and illustrator, 1958-63; Hornsey Coll. of Art: Lectr, 1963-66; Head, Dept of Visual Research, 1966-69; Head, Dept of Co-ordinated Studies, 1969-72. Exhibited various exhibns, Britain, USA, etc; one-man exhibn, Cambridge, 1975, Durham, 1977. Mem. Council, CNAA, 1974-80 (Chm., Fine Art Bd, 1976-81). Pres., Nat.

Soc. for Art Educn, 1976. *Publications:* Eyeline, 1968; Drawing: seeing and observation, 1973; Picture Making, 1973; Guide to Painting and Composition, 1979; *Television Programmes:* Eyeline (10 programmes), 1968, 1969; Picture Making (10 programmes), 1973, 1976; Reading the Signs (5 programmes), 1977-78. *Recreations:* reading, music. *Address:* St Martin's School of Art, 107-109 Charing Cross Road, WC2H 0DU. *T:* 01-437 0611.

SIMPSON, James Joseph Trevor, KBE (Hon.) 1965 (CBE 1957); (forename James added by deed poll, 1965); Chairman and Managing Director, James Simpson & Co. Ltd; retired as Chairman, Uganda Development Corporation, Ltd (1952-64); *b* 9 Jan. 1908; 2nd *s* of late Lieut-Colonel Herbert Simpson, OBE, MC, and of Mrs Henrietta Augusta Simpson; *m* 1940, Enid Florence (*née* Danzelman) (*d* 1979). *Educ:* Ardingly College, Sussex. Branch Manager, Vacuum Oil Co., Nakuru, Nairobi, Dar es Salaam, Mombasa, Kampala, 1932-46; General Manager, The Uganda Company Ltd, 1947-52; President, Uganda Chamber of Commerce, 1941, 1946-50. Member: Uganda Executive Council, 1952-55; Uganda Legislative Council, 1950-58 (Chm. Representative Members Organization 1951-58); E African Legislative Assembly, 1957-60, 1962-63; E African Railways and Harbours, Transport Advisory Council, 1948-61; E African Industrial Council, 1947-61; Uganda Electricity Bd, 1955-60; East African Airways Corporation, 1958-73; Minister of Economic Affairs, Uganda, 1962-63. *Recreation:* bridge. *Address:* PO Box 48816, Nairobi, Kenya; c/o PO Box 4343, Kampala, Uganda. *Clubs:* Muthaiga, Nairobi (Kenya).

SIMPSON, Ven. John Arthur; Archdeacon of Canterbury and Canon Residentiary of Canterbury Cathedral, since 1981; *b* 7 June 1933; *s* of Arthur Simpson and Mary Esther Simpson; *m* 1968, Ruth Marian (*née* Dibbens); one *s* two *d*. *Educ:* Cathays High School, Cardiff; Keble Coll., Oxford (BA, 2nd cl. Mod. History 1956, MA 1960); Clifton Theological Coll. Deacon 1958, priest 1959; Curate: Leyton, 1958-59; Christ Church, Orpington, 1959-62; Tutor, Oak Hill Coll., Southgate N14, 1962-72; Vicar of Ridge, Herts, 1972-79; Director of Ordinands and Post-Ordination Training, Diocese of St Albans, 1975-81; Hon. Canon of St Albans Cathedral, 1977-79; Residentiary Canon, St Albans, and Priest-in-charge of Ridge, 1979-81. *Recreations:* travel, theatre, opera. *Address:* 29 The Precincts, Canterbury, Kent CT1 2EP. *T:* Canterbury 63036.

SIMPSON, John (Cody Fidler-); Diplomatic Editor, BBC-TV, since 1982; *b* 9 Aug. 1944; *s* of Roy Simpson Fidler-Simpson and Joyce Leila Vivienne Cody; *m* 1965, Diane Jean Petteys, El Cajon, California; two *d*. *Educ:* St Paul's School; Magdalene Coll., Cambridge (MA). Reporter, BBC Radio News, 1970; BBC correspondent, Dublin, 1972; Common Market correspondent (based in Brussels), 1975; Southern Africa correspondent (based in Johannesburg), 1977; Diplomatic correspondent, BBC Television News, 1978; BBC Political Editor, 1980; Presenter and Correspondent, BBC-TV News, 1981. Monte Carlo TV Festival award for best news report of 1979. *Publications:* (ed jtly) The Best of Granta, 1966; novels: Moscow Requiem, 1981; A Fine And Private Place, 1983. *Recreations:* books, music, travel, and praising Suffolk. *Address:* BBC Television Centre, Wood Lane, W12. *T:* 01-743 8000.

SIMPSON, John Ferguson, FRCS; Consulting Surgeon to Ear, Nose and Throat Department, St Mary's Hospital, retired; formerly Civil Consultant, Ministry of Aviation; *b* 10 Oct. 1902; *s* of late Col P. J. Simpson, DSO, FRCVS, Maidenhead; *m* 1947, Winifred Beatrice Rood; one *s* one *d*. *Educ:* Reading Sch.; St Mary's Hosp. FRCS 1929; MRCS, LRCP 1926. Formerly: Lectr in Diseases of the Ear, Nose and Throat, Univ. of London; Specialist in Otorhino-laryngology, RAF; Hon. Surg. Royal Nat. Throat, Nose and Ear Hosp. FR.SocMed (ex-President Section of Otology; Hon. Life Mem., Section of Laryngology). Liveryman, Farriers' Co. *Publications:* A Synopsis of Otorhinolaryngology (jointly), 1957; chapters: Operative Surgery, 1957; ENT Diseases, 1965. *Recreations:* entomology; formerly Rugby football. *Address:* Waverley Cottage, Upton Grey, Basingstoke, Hants RG25 2RA. *T:* Long Sutton 433.

SIMPSON, John Liddle, CMG 1958; TD 1950; QC 1980; *b* 9 Oct. 1912; *s* of late James Simpson; *m* 1st, 1939, Nellie Lavender Mussett (*d* 1944); 2nd, 1959, Ursula Vaughan Washington (*née* Rigby). *Educ:* George Watson's Coll.; Edinburgh Univ. (MA, DLitt). Barrister, Middle Temple, 1937. Served War of 1939-45; GSO1, 1945. Principal, Control Office for Germany and Austria, 1946; Senior legal assistant, FO (German Section), 1948; transferred to Foreign (now Diplomatic) Service and promoted Counsellor, 1954; Legal Counsellor, FO, 1954-59 and 1961-68; Legal Adviser, United Kingdom Mission to the United Nations, New York, 1959-61; Dep. Legal Adviser, 1968-71, Second Legal Adviser, 1971-72, FCO; returned to practice, 1973; elected alternate Pres. of Arbitral Tribunals, Internat. Telecommunications Satellite Org., 1974 and 1976. Mem., Dubai/Sharjah Boundary Court of Arbitration, 1978-81; Chm., UNESCO Appeals Bd, 1980-. Freeman, City of London, 1976. *Publications:* Germany and the North Atlantic Community: A Legal Survey (with M. E. Bathurst), 1956; International Arbitration: Law and Practice (with Hazel Fox), 1959; articles and notes in legal journals. *Address:* 5 Paper Buildings, Temple, EC4Y 7HB. *T:* 01-353 8494; 137a Ashley Gardens, Thirleby Road, SW1P 1HN. *T:* 01-834 4814.

SIMPSON, Keith; *see* Simpson, Cedric K.

SIMPSON, Kenneth John, CMG 1961; HM Diplomatic Service, retired; *b* 5 Feb. 1914; *s* of Bernard and Ann Simpson, Millhouses, Sheffield; *m* 1939, Harriet (Shan) Hughes; three *s*. *Educ:* Downing College, Cambridge. Entered HM Foreign (now Diplomatic) Service, 1937; lastly Consul-Gen., Hanoi and Stuttgart, Inspector, Diplomatic Service and Counsellor, FCO. *Address:* 76 Wood Ride, Petts Wood, Kent. *T:* Orpington 24710.

SIMPSON, Malcolm Carter; Director of Finance, Leeds City Council, since 1978; *b* 15 June 1929; *s* of Arthur and Rhoda Simpson; *m* 1st, 1952, Doreen Patricia Wooler; two *d*; 2nd, 1980, Andrea Gillian Blythe. *Educ:* Stanningley Council Sch. DPA; CIPFA. Employed by Leeds CC for whole of working life, 1943-: Asst Dir of Finance, 1968; Dep. Dir of Finance, 1973. *Recreations:* golf, bridge. *Address:* 52 Long Causeway, Adel, Leeds LS16 8LE. *T:* Leeds 670479.

SIMPSON, Oliver, CB 1977; MA, PhD, FInstP; Chief Scientist, Deputy Under-Secretary of State, Home Office, since 1974; *b* 28 Oct. 1924; *y s* of late Sir George C. Simpson, KCB, FRS, and Dorothy (*née* Stephen); *m* 1946, Joan, *d* of late Walter and Maud Morgan; one *s* (and one *s* decd). *Educ:* Highgate Sch.; Trinity Coll., Cambridge. War Service: Admiralty Research Laboratory, Teddington, on submarine detection, 1944-46. Research Scholar, 1946-49, Fellow of Trinity Coll., Cambridge, 1949-53; Asst Prof. of Physics, Univ. of Michigan, USA, 1949-52; Imperial Chemical Industries Fellow in Dept. of Theoretical Chemistry, Cambridge, 1952-53; joined Services Electronics Research Laboratory, Admity, 1953, Head of Solid State Physics, 1956-63; Supt. Basic Physics Div., Nat. Physical Laboratory, 1964-66; Dep. Dir, Nat. Physical Laboratory, 1966-69; Under-Sec., Cabinet Office, 1969-74. *Publications:* articles in scientific jls on infra-red detectors, semiconductors, fluorescence and standards of measurement. *Address:* 4 Highbury Road, Wimbledon, SW19. *T:* 01-946 3871. *Club:* Athenæum.

SIMPSON, Peter Miller, RDI 1974; FSIA; company director; Director: Bute Looms Ltd, since 1973; Bute Fabrics Ltd, since 1977; *b* 5 April 1921; *s* of David Simpson and Annie Simpson; *m* 1964, Orma Macallum; one *s* one *d*. *Educ:* Perth High Sch.; Dundee Coll. of Art (DA 1950). MSIA 1956, FSIA 1974. Study and work, USA, 1950-53. Mem. Scottish Cttee, Design Council. Governor, Duncan of Jordanstone Coll. of Art, Dundee, 1978-. *Recreations:* gardening, pottery, walking. *Address:* 35 Lovers Lane, Scone, Perth. *T:* Perth 51573. *Clubs:* Caledonian; Arts (Edinburgh).

SIMPSON, Ven. Rennie, MVO 1974; MA Lambeth 1970; Archdeacon of Macclesfield, since 1978; Rector of Gawsworth, since 1978; Chaplain to the Queen, since 1982; *b* 13 Jan. 1920; *o s* of late Doctor Taylor Simpson and late May Simpson, Rishton; *m* 1949, Margaret, *er d* of late Herbert Hardy and Olive Hardy, South Kirkby; one *s* one *d*. *Educ:* Blackburn Tech. Coll.; Kelham Theol Coll. Curate of S Elmsall, Yorks, 1945-49; Succentor of Blackburn Cath., 1949-52; Sacrist and Minor Canon of St Paul's Cath., 1952-58, Hon. Minor Canon, 1958-, Jun. Cardinal, 1954-55, Sen. Cardinal, 1955-58; Vicar of John Keble Church, Mill Hill, 1958-63; Precentor, 1963-74, Acting Sacrist, 1973-74, Westminster Abbey; Canon Residentiary, 1974-78, Vice-Dean, 1975-78, Chester Cathedral. Chaplain, RNVR, 1953-55; Dep. Chaplain, Gt Ormond St Hosp., 1954-58; Asst Chaplain, 1956-64, Officiating Chaplain, 1964-, Sub-Prelate, 1973-, Order of St John of Jerusalem; Deputy Priest to the Queen, 1956-67; Priest-in-Ordinary to the Queen, 1967-74. Life Governor, Imperial Cancer Research Fund, 1963. Liveryman of Waxchandlers' Co. and Freeman of City of London, 1955. Jt Hon. Treas., Corp. Sons of the Clergy, 1967-74; Governor: King's School, Chester, 1974-78; King's Sch., Macclesfield, 1979-. *Recreations:* football, cricket, theatre. *Address:* The Rectory, Gawsworth, Macclesfield, Cheshire SK11 9RP. *T:* North Rode 201.

SIMPSON, Rt. Hon. Dr Robert, PC (N Ireland) 1970; *b* 3 July 1923; *er s* of Samuel and Agnes Simpson, Craigbilly, Ballymena; *m* 1954, Dorothy Isobel, *d* of Dr Robert Strawbridge, MA, DD, and Anne Strawbridge; two *s* one *d*. *Educ:* Ballymena Academy; Queen's University, Belfast. MB, BCh, BAO, 1946; Founder Mem., RCGP; LRCPI (Occupational Medicine), 1980. House Surgeon, Belfast City Hosp., 1947; Resident Anaesthetist, Royal Infirmary, Leicester, 1948; GP, Ballymena, Co. Antrim, 1949-; Medical Correspondent, Belfast Telegraph and Leicester Mercury; Medical Representative, NI, Europ Assistance; Medical Officer, Flexibox Ltd, Ballymena, Northern Dairies Ltd. Founder Chm., Ballymena Round Table, 1951. NI Deleg. to CPA Conf. in NZ and Australia, 1965. Minister of Community Relations, N Ireland, 1969-71; MP (U) Mid-Antrim, Parlt of N Ireland, 1953-72. Director, John Atkinson & Co., etc. *Publications:* contribs to newspapers and magazines on medical, country and travel subjects. *Recreations:* the country, writing, music, France, food, travel. *Address:* Random Cottage, Craigbilly, Ballymena, Co. Antrim. *T:* Ballymena 3105. *Club:* Royal Over-Seas League.

SIMPSON, Robert Wilfred Levick, DMus; composer; BBC Music Producer, 1951-80; *b* Leamington, Warwickshire, 2 March 1921; *s* of Robert Warren Simpson (British) and Helena Hendrika Govaars (Dutch); *m* 1946, Bessie Fraser (*d* 1981); *m* 1982, Angela Musgrave. *Educ:* Westminster City Sch.; studied with Herbert Howells. DMus (Dunelm) 1952. Holder of: Carl Nielsen Gold Medal (Denmark), 1956; Medal of Honor of Bruckner Soc. of America, 1962. Mem., British Astronomical Assoc.; FRAS. *Compositions:* Symphonies: No 1, 1951 (recorded); No 2, 1956; No 3, 1962 (recorded); No 4, 1972; No 5, 1972; Nos 6 and 7, 1977; No 8, 1981; Piano Concerto, 1967; Violin

Concerto, 1959; String Quartets: No 1, 1952 (recorded); No 2, 1953; No 3, 1954; No 4, 1973; No 5, 1974; No 6, 1975; No 7, 1977; No 8, 1979; No 9, 1982; Piano Sonata, 1946; Variations and Finale on a Theme of Haydn, for piano, 1948; Allegro Deciso, for string orchestra (from String Quartet No 3); Canzona for Brass, 1958 (recorded); Variations and Fugue for recorder and string quartet, 1959; Incidental Music to Ibsen's The Pretenders, 1965; Trio for clarinet, cello and piano, 1967; Quintet for clarinet, and strings, 1968 (recorded); Energy, Symphonic Study for brass band (test piece for 1971 World Championship); Incidental Music to Milton's Samson Agonistes, 1974; *Media morte in vita sumus* (Motet for choir, brass, and timpani), 1975; Quartet for horn, violin, cello and piano, 1976; Volcano, for brass band, 1979 (test piece for Nat. Championship, 1979); Sonata for two pianos, 1980; Quintet for double basses, clarinet and bass clarinet, 1981; The Four Temperaments, for brass band, 1982. *Publications:* Carl Nielsen, Symphonist, 1952, rev. edn 1977; The Essence of Bruckner, 1966; The Proms and Natural Justice, 1981; numerous articles in various jls and three BBC booklets (Bruckner and the Symphony, Sibelius and Nielsen, and The Beethoven Symphonies); contrib. to: Encycl. Brit.; Musik in Geschichte und Gegenwart; (ed) The Symphony (Pelican), 1966. *Recreation:* astronomy. *Address:* Cedar Cottage, Chearsley, Aylesbury, Bucks HP18 0DA. *T:* Long Crendon 208436.

SIMPSON, Robin Muschamp Garry, QC 1971; a Recorder of the Crown Court, since 1976; *b* 19 June 1927; *s* of Ronald Maitland Simpson, actor and Lila Maravan Simpson (*née* Muschamp); *m* 1st, 1956, Avril Carolyn Harrisson; one *s* one *d*; 2nd, 1968, Mary Faith Laughton-Scott; one *s* one *d*. *Educ:* Charterhouse; Peterhouse, Cambridge (BA). Called to Bar, Middle Temple, 1951, Bencher, 1979. Former Mem., Surrey and S London Sessions; Member: Central Criminal Court Bar Mess; SE Circuit. Appeal Steward, British Boxing Bd of Control. *Recreations:* riding, fox-hunting, sailing. *Address:* 9 Drayton Gardens, SW10. *T:* 01-373 3284. *Club:* Garrick.

SIMPSON, S(amuel) Leonard, MA, MD (Cambridge); FRCP; Chairman: S. Simpson, Ltd; Simpson (Piccadilly) Ltd; Daks-Simpson Ltd; President: Simpson Imports Inc.; Daks USA Inc., New York; Daks (Canada) Ltd, Montreal; Consultant in Industrial Psychology; Hon. Consulting Endocrinologist, St Mary's Hospital, London; *s* of late Simeon Simpson; *m* 1940, Heddy Monique, Baroness de Podmaniczky; one *d. Educ:* Westminster City School; Downing Coll., Cambridge. 1st Class Hons, Nat. Sci. Tripos, Pts I and II Physiology. Post-grad. research in Mayo Clinic, USA, Charitée Hosp., Berlin and Lister Institute, London. Member: Council, CBI (Past Mem., Grand Council of FBI); Council, Nat. Inst. of Industrial Psychology; British Nat. Council for Rehabilitation; Commonwealth Migration Council; Council, British Soc. of Endocrinology (Founder Mem.); Academic Cttee, Inst. of Social Psychiatry; Council, Inst. for Scientific Study of Delinquency; Hon. Mem. Endocrinological Socs of Argentine, Chile, France; Past Pres., Endocrine Section, RSocMed; Adv. Counsellor, English-Speaking Union, 1976-. Humphrey Davy Rolleston Lectr, RCP, 1974. Life Mem., Brit. Horse Soc.; Founder and Chm. Jermyn Street Assoc., 1978. Jt Founder, Walter Hagen Annual Award Trophy (in collab. with Golf Writers' Assoc. of USA), 1961, awarded Trophy, 1976. *Publications:* Major Endocrine Disorders, 1938, 3rd edn, 1959; contrib. Hutchison's Index of Therapeutics, Rolleston's Encyclopædia of Medical Practice, Endocrine Section of Price's Medicine, 1956, Endocrine Section of Medical Annual and Chambers's Encyclopædia; papers in Proc. Roy. Soc. Med., etc. *Recreations:* golf, painting, boxing (Capt. Cambridge Univ. 1922). *Address:* 28 Hyde Park Gate, SW7. *T:* 01-589 3671. Grouselands, Colgate, West Sussex. *Clubs:* Carlton, Simpson Services (Pres. and Founder); Machine Gun Corps Officers (Hon. Mem.); Sunningdale Golf (Sunningdale); Cowdray Park Polo; The Guards Polo.

SIMPSON, William James; Chairman, Health and Safety Commission, since 1974; *b* Falkirk, 20 May 1920; *s* of William Simpson and Margaret Nimmo; *m* 1942, Catherine McEwan Nicol; one *s. Educ:* Victoria Sch. and Falkirk Techn. Sch., Falkirk. Served War of 1939-45, Argyll and Sutherland Highlanders (Sgt). Apprenticed to moulding trade, 1935; returned to foundry, 1946. Mem. Nat. Exec. Council, Amalgamated Union of Foundry Workers, 1955-67; Gen. Sec., AUEW (Foundry Section), 1967-75. Mem. Nat. Exec. Cttee of Labour Party, 1962-; Chm. of Labour Party, 1972-73; Member: Race Relations Board; Ct of Inquiry into Flixborough explosion, 1974; Chm., Adv. Cttee on Asbestos, 1976-79. *Publication:* Labour: The Unions and the Party, 1973. *Address:* 35 Fielding Road, Bedford Park, Chiswick, W4. *T:* 01-995 9677.

SIMPSON, William Wynn, OBE 1967; MA; FRSA; Hon. Life Vice-President, International Council of Christians and Jews, since 1981 (Hon. Chairman, 1978); *b* 11 July 1907; *m* 1933; one *s* one *d. Educ:* King Edward VI Grammar School, Camp Hill, Birmingham; Birmingham University; Wesley House and Fitzwilliam College, Cambridge. Asst Minister, Leysian Mission, London, 1929-32; Oxford Methodist Circuit, 1932-33; External Student, Jews' College, London and research into contemp. Jewish problems, 1933-35; Minister Amhurst Park Methodist Church, N London, 1935-38; General Secretary: Christian Council for Refugees, 1938-42; Council of Christians and Jews, 1942-74. Vice-President: Greater London Assoc. for the Disabled; Pestalozzi Children's Village Trust. Mem., Soc. for Old Testament Study; Sec., London Soc. for Study of Religion. *Publications:* Readings in the Old Testament, 1932; Youth and Antisemitism, 1938; Christians and Jews Today (Beckly Social Service Lecture), 1942; (with A. I. Polack) Jesus in the Background of History, 1957; Jewish Prayer and Worship, 1965; Mini-

Commentary on Pentateuch (Jerusalem Bible), 1969; Light and Rejoicing: a Christian's understanding of Jewish worship, 1976; pamphlets and articles on various aspects Jewish-Christian relations. *Recreation:* being alive. *Address:* 13 Woodside Road, Northwood, Mddx HA6 3QE. *Club:* Athenæum.

SIMPSON-JONES, Peter Trevor, CBE 1971; Président d'Honneur, Société Française des Industries Lucas, since 1980 (Président-Directeur Général, 1957-80); *b* 20 March 1914; *s* of Frederick Henry Jones and Constance Agnès Simpson; *m* 1948, Marie-Lucy Sylvain; one *s* one *d. Educ:* Royal Navy School. British Chamber of Commerce, France: Vice-Pres., 1967-68 and 1970-72; Pres., 1968-70. Chevalier de la Légion d'Honneur, 1948, Officier 1973. *Recreation:* yachting. *Address:* 50 rue du Château, 92 Boulogne-sur-Seine, France. *T:* 825-01-20. *Clubs:* Special Forces; Polo (Paris).

SIMPSON-ORLEBAR, Michael Keith Orlebar, CMG 1982; HM Diplomatic Service; Minister, HM Embassy, Rome, since 1980; *b* 5 Feb. 1932; *s* of Aubrey Orlebar Simpson, Royal Artillery and Laura Violet, *d* of Captain Frederick Keith-Jones; *m* 1964, Rosita Duarte Triana; two *s* one *d. Educ:* Eton; Christ Church, Oxford (MA). 2nd Lieut, KRRC, 1950-51. Joined Foreign Service, 1954; 3rd Sec., Tehran, 1955-57; FO, 1957-62; Private Sec. to Parly Under-Sec. of State, 1960-62; 1st Sec. (Commercial) and Consul, Bogotá, 1962-65; seconded to Urwick, Orr and Partners Ltd, 1966; FO, 1966-68; 1st Sec., Paris, 1969-72; Counsellor (Commercial), Tehran, 1972-76; Head of UN Dept, FCO, 1977-80. *Recreations:* gardening, fishing. *Address:* c/o Foreign and Commonwealth Office, SW1A 2AH. *Club:* Travellers'.

SIMS, Prof. Geoffrey Donald, OBE 1971; FEng 1980; Vice-Chancellor, University of Sheffield, since 1974; *b* 13 Dec. 1926; *s* of Albert Edward Hope Sims and Jessie Elizabeth Sims; *m* 1949, Pamela Audrey Richings; one *s* two *d. Educ:* Wembley County Grammar School; Imperial College of Science and Technology, London. Research physicist, GEC, 1948-54; Sen. Scientific Officer, UKAEA, 1954-56; Lecturer/Senior Lecturer, University College, London, 1956-63; University of Southampton: Prof. and Head of Dept of Electronics, 1963-74; Dean, Faculty of Engrg, 1967-70; Senior Dep. Vice-Chancellor, 1970-72. Consultant to various companies and to Department of Education and Science, 1957-; Consulting Editor, Chapman & Hall Ltd. Member: Council, British Association for the Advancement of Science, 1965-69 (Chm., Sheffield Area Council, 1974-); EDC for Electronics Industry, 1966-75; Adv. Cttee for Scientific and Technical Information, 1969-74; CNAA Electrical Engineering Bd, 1970-73; Planning Cttee for British Library, 1971-73 (Chm., British Library R&D Adv. Cttee, 1975-81); Adv. Council, Science Museum, 1972-; British Nat. Cttee for Physics, 1972-78; Royal Soc. Cttee on Sci. Information, 1972-81; Electronics Res. Council, 1973-74; Annan Cttee on Future of Broadcasting, 1974-77; Naval Educn Adv. Cttee, 1974-79; Trent RHA, 1975-; British Council Engrg and Tech. Adv. Cttee, 1976- (Chm.); Interim Action Cttee on British Film Industry, 1977-81; EEC Adv. Cttee on Scientific and Technical Trng, 1977-81; Univs Council for Adult and Continuing Educn, 1978- (Chm., 1980-); CNAA, 1979-; Liaison Cttee on Highly Qualified Technol Manpower, 1979-82; Council, Nat. Inst. of Adult Educn, 1980-; SRC, later SERC Engrg Bd, 1980-; Inter Univ. and Polytechnic Council, 1981- (IUC and Exec. Cttee, 1974-81); Cttee for Internat. Co-operation in Higher Educn, 1981-; EEC Adv. Cttee on Programme Management, 1981-; BBC Engrg Adv. Cttee, 1981- (Chm.). UK rep. on Perm. Cttee of Conf. of European Rectors, 1981-. Chairman of Governors: Southampton College of Technology, 1967-69; Southampton Sch. of Navigation, 1972-74; Fellow, Midland Chapter, Woodard Schools, 1977-. FIEE 1963; FIERE 1966; FCGI 1980. Hon. DSc Southampton, 1979. Founder Mem., 1966, Reviews Editor, 1969-, Jl of Materials Science Bd. *Publications:* Microwave Tubes and Semiconductor Devices (with I. M. Stephenson), 1963; Variational Techniques in Electromagnetism (trans.), 1965; numerous papers on microwaves, electronics and education in learned jls. *Recreations:* golf, travel, music. *Address:* The Vice-Chancellor's Office, Sheffield University, Sheffield S10 2TN. *Clubs:* Athenæum; Sheffield (Sheffield).

SIMS, Monica Louie, OBE 1971; MA, LRAM, LGSM; Controller, BBC Radio 4, since 1978; *d* of late Albert Charles Sims and Eva Elizabeth Preen, both of Gloucester. *Educ:* Girls' High School, Gloucester; St Hugh's College, Oxford. Tutor in Literature and Drama, Dept of Adult Educn, Hull Univ., 1947-50; Educn Tutor, Nat. Fedn of Women's Institutes, 1950-53; BBC Sound Talks Producer, 1953-55; BBC Television Producer, 1955-64; Editor of Woman's Hour, BBC, 1964-67; Head of Children's Programmes, BBC TV, 1967-78. *Address:* 97 Gloucester Terrace, W2.

SIMS, Roger Edward, JP; MP (C) Chislehurst since Feb. 1974; *b* 27 Jan. 1930; *s* of late Herbert William Sims and of Annie Amy Savidge; *m* 1957, Angela Mathews; two *s* one *d. Educ:* City Boys' Grammar Sch., Leicester; St Olave's Grammar Sch., London. MInstM. National Service, 1948-50. Coutts & Co., 1950-51; Campbell Booker Carter Ltd, 1951-62; Dept Man., Dodwell & Co. Ltd, 1962-; Dir, Inchcape International Ltd, 1981-. Contested (C) Shoreditch and Finsbury, 1966 and 1970; PPS to Home Sec., 1979-. Mem., Central Exec. Cttee, NSPCC, 1982-. Mem. Chislehurst and Sidcup UDC, 1956-62; JP Bromley, 1960-72 (Dep. Chm. 1970-72); Chm., Juvenile Panel, 1971-72. *Recreations:* swimming; music, especially singing (Mem. Royal Choral Soc. from 1950). *Address:* 68 Towncourt Crescent, Petts Wood, Orpington, Kent BR5 1PJ. *T:* Orpington 25676; House of Commons, SW1A 0AA.

SIMSON, Michael Ronald Fraser, OBE 1966; Secretary of the National Corporation for the Care of Old People, 1948-73; *b* 9 Oct. 1913; *er s* of Ronald Stuart Fraser Simson and Ethel Alice Henderson; *m* 1939, Elizabeth Joan Wilkinson; one *s. Educ:* Winchester Coll.; Christ Church, Oxford. OUAFC 1936 and 1937. Asst Master, West Downs Sch., 1938-40; RNVR, 1941-46; Asst Sec., Nat. Fedn of Housing Socs, 1946-48. Member: Min. of Labour Cttee on Employment of Older Men and Women, 1953-55; Cttee on Local Authority and Allied Personal Social Services (Seebohm Cttee), 1966-68; Supplementary Benefits Commn, 1967-76; Adv. Cttee on Rent Rebates and Rent Allowances, 1973-75, resigned 1975; Personal Social Services Council, 1973-78. *Recreations:* gardening, interested in all forms of sport. *Address:* Summerhill, Kingsdon, Somerton, Somerset. *T:* Ilchester 840858.

SINATRA, Francis Albert, (Frank); singer, actor, film producer, publisher; *b* Hoboken, New Jersey, USA, 12 Dec. 1915; *s* of late Natalie and Martin Sinatra; *m* 1st, 1939, Nancy Barbato (marr. diss.); one *s* two *d* ; 2nd 1951, Ava Gardner (marr. diss.); 3rd, 1966, Mia Farrow (marr. diss.); 4th, 1976, Barbara Marx. *Educ:* Demarest High School, New Jersey. Started in radio, 1936; then became band singer with orchestras. First appearance in films, 1943. *Films include:* From Here to Eternity (Oscar for best supporting actor, 1953), Anchors Aweigh, On the Town, The Tender Trap, High Society, Guys and Dolls, The Man with the Golden Arm, Johnny Concho, The Joker is Wild, Kings Go Forth, Some Came Running, A Hole in the Head, Ocean's 11, The Devil at Four O'Clock, Sergeants Three, Manchurian Candidate, Come Blow Your Horn, Four for Texas, Robin and the Seven Hoods, None But the Brave, Marriage on the Rocks, Von Ryan's Express, Assault on a Queen, The Naked Runner, Tony Rome, The Detective, Lady in Cement, Dirty Dingus Magee, The First Deadly Sin. Owner music publishing companies, etc. Jean Hersholt Humanitarian Award, 1971. *Publications:* composed numerous popular songs. *Address:* Sinatra Enterprises, Goldwyn Studios, 1041 N Formosa, Los Angeles, Calif 90046, USA.

SINCLAIR; *see* Alexander-Sinclair.

SINCLAIR, family name of **Earl of Caithness, Viscount Thurso, Baron Pentland,** and **Baron Sinclair of Cleeve.**

SINCLAIR, 17th Lord, *cr* 1449 (Scotland); **Charles Murray Kennedy St Clair,** MVO 1953; Major, late Coldstream Guards; Extra Equerry to Queen Elizabeth the Queen Mother since 1953; Lord-Lieutenant, Dumfries and Galloway Region (District of Stewartry), since 1982 (Vice-Lord-Lieutenant, 1977-82); Member Queen's Body Guard for Scotland (Royal Company of Archers); *b* 21 June 1914; *o s* of 16th Lord Sinclair, MVO, and Violet (*d* 1953), *d* of Col J. Murray Kennedy, MVO; *S* father, 1957; *m* 1968, Anne Lettice, *yr d* of Sir Richard Cotterell, 5th Bt, CBE; one *s* two *d. Educ:* Eton; Magdalene Coll., Cambridge. Served War of 1939-45, Palestine, 1939 (wounded, despatches). Retired as Major Coldstream Guards, 1947. Portcullis Pursuivant of Arms, 1949-57; York Herald, 1957-68, retired. A Representative Peer for Scotland, 1959-63. DL Kirkcudbrightshire, 1969. *Heir: s* Master of Sinclair, *qv. Address:* Knocknalling, Dalry, Castle Douglas, Kirkcudbrightshire, Scotland. *T:* 221. *Club:* New (Edinburgh).

SINCLAIR, Master of; Hon. Matthew Murray Kennedy St Clair; *b* 9 Dec. 1968; *s* and *heir* of 17th Lord Sinclair, *qv.*

SINCLAIR OF CLEEVE, 2nd Baron *cr* 1957, of Cleeve, Somerset; **Lt-Col John Robert Kilgour Sinclair,** OBE 1963 (MBE 1954); *b* 3 Nov. 1919; *s* of 1st Baron Sinclair of Cleeve, KCB, KBE, and of Mary Shearer, *d* of late Robert Shearer Barclay (May, Lady Sinclair of Cleeve); *S* father, 1979; *m* 1950, Patricia, *d* of late Major Lawrence Hellyer; one *s* two *d. Educ:* Winchester Coll.; RMC Sandhurst. Commissioned QO Cameron Highlanders, 1939; served BEF, War of 1939-45 (despatches, POW); regimental duty, 1945-51; HQ BAOR, 1951-54; French Staff Coll., 1954-55; regtl duty, 1955-57; War Office (DAAG), 1957-59; regtl duty, 1959-60; Lt-Col 1960; Military Attaché, Leopoldville, 1960-63; Office of Dep. Supreme Allied Commander Europe, SHAPE, 1964-66; MoD (Office of Defence Services Secretary), 1967-69; retired, 1969. *Recreations:* field sports, pony club, gardening. *Heir: s* Hon. John Lawrence Robert Sinclair, *b* 6 Jan. 1953. *Address:* Toppinghoe Hall, Hatfield Peverel, Essex CM3 2EX. *T:* Chelmsford 380862.

SINCLAIR, Alexander Riddell; HM Diplomatic Service, retired; reemployed in Foreign and Commonwealth Office Library, since 1977; *b* 28 Aug. 1917; *s* of Henry W. Sinclair and Mary Turner; *m* 1948, Alice Evelyn Nottingham; three *d. Educ:* Greenock High School. DipCAM. Inland Revenue, 1935-37; Admty, 1938-47 (Comdr RNVR, 1945-46); 2nd Sec., HM Embassy, Moscow, 1947-48; Vice-Consul: Detroit, 1949; Mosul, 1950; FO, 1952; 1st Secretary, HM Embassy: Saigon, 1953-56; Amman, 1957-58; FO, 1959; 1st Sec. (Cultural), Budapest, 1962; FO, 1964; 1st Secretary (Information): Beirut, 1967-70; Rome, 1970-71; Consul-Gen., Genoa, 1972-76. Silver Jubilee Medal, 1977. *Publications:* literary articles in learned jls. *Recreations:* reading, book browsing, walking. *Address:* 7 Berry Walk, Ashtead, Surrey KT21 1BT. *Club:* Civil Service.

SINCLAIR, Andrew Annandale; author; Managing Director, Lorrimer Publishing, Timon Films, since 1967; *b* 21 Jan. 1935; *m* 1960, Marianne, *d* of Mr and Mrs Arsène Alexandre; *m* 1972, Miranda, *o d* of Mr and Hon. Mrs George Seymour; two *s. Educ:* Eton Coll.; Trinity Coll., Cambridge (BA,

PhD); Harvard. Harkness Fellow of the Commonwealth Fund, 1959-61; Dir of Historical Studies, Churchill Coll., Cambridge, 1961-63; Fellow of American Council of Learned Societies, 1963-64; Lectr in American History, University Coll., London, 1965-67. Dir/Writer Mem., ACTT. FRSL 1973; Fellow Soc. of American Historians, 1974. Somerset Maugham Literary Prize, 1966. *Film:* (dir) Under Milk Wood, 1971. *Publications:* The Breaking of Bumbo, 1958; My Friend Judas, 1959; The Project, 1960; Prohibition, 1962; The Hallelujah Bum, 1963; The Available Man: Warren E. Harding, 1964; The Better Half, 1964; The Raker, 1965; Concise History of the United States, 1966; Gog, 1967; The Greek Anthology, 1967; Adventures in the Skin Trade, 1968; The Last of the Best, 1969; Guevara, 1970; Magog, 1972; Dylan Thomas: poet of his people, 1975; The Surrey Cat, 1976; The Savage, 1977; Jack: the biography of Jack London, 1977; A Patriot for Hire, 1978; John Ford, 1979; The Facts in the Case of E. A. Poe, 1979; Corsair, 1981; The Other Victoria, 1981. *Recreations:* old cities, old movies. *Address:* 15 Hanover Terrace, Regent's Park, NW1.

SINCLAIR, Clive Marles; Chairman: Sinclair Research Ltd, since 1979; Sinclair Browne Ltd, since 1981; *b* 30 July 1940; *s* of George William Carter Sinclair and Thora Edith Ella (*née* Marles); *m* 1962, Ann (*née* Trevor Briscoe); two *s* one *d. Educ:* Boxgrove Prep. Sch., Guildford; Highgate; Reading; St George's Coll., Weybridge. Editor, Bernards Publishers Ltd, 1958-61; Chm., Sinclair Radionics Ltd, 1962-79. Vis. Fellow, Robinson Coll., Cambridge, 1982-. Chm.; British Mensa, 1980-. *Publications:* Practical Transistor Receivers, 1959; British Semiconductor Survey, 1963. *Recreations:* music, poetry, mathematics, science. *Address:* The Stone House, 3 Madingley Road, Cambridge. *T:* Cambridge 353726. *Club:* Carlton.

SINCLAIR, Prof. David Cecil; Emeritus Professor, University of Western Australia; Director of Postgraduate Medical Education, Queen Elizabeth II Medical Centre, Western Australia, 1975-80; *b* 28 Aug. 1915; *s* of Norman James Sinclair and Annie Smart Sinclair; *m* 1945, Grace Elizabeth Simondson, Melbourne, Vic.; one *s* one *d. Educ:* Merchiston Castle Sch.; St Andrews University. MB, ChB (Commendation) St Andrews, 1937; MD (Hons and Rutherford Gold Medal) St Andrews, 1947; MA Oxon, 1948; DSc Western Australia, 1965. Served in RAMC, 1940-46: AMF, 1943-45; Head of Physiology Sect., Aust. Chem. Warfare Research and Experimental Stn, 1943-44; Dep. Chief Supt, Aust. Field Experimental Stn, 1944-45. Sen. Res. Off., Dept of Human Anatomy, Oxford, 1946-49; Univ. Demonstrator in Anatomy, Oxford, 1949-56; Lectr in Anatomy, Pembroke Coll., Oxford, 1950-56; Lectr in Anatomy, Ruskin Sch. of Fine Art, 1950-56; first Prof. of Anatomy, Univ. of W Australia, 1957-64, Dean of Med. Sch., 1964; Regius Prof. of Anatomy, Univ. of Aberdeen, 1965-75. FRCSE 1966. *Publications:* Medical Students and Medical Sciences, 1955; An Introduction to Functional Anatomy, 1957 (5th edn 1975); A Student's Guide to Anatomy, 1961; Cutaneous Sensation, 1967, Japanese edn 1969; Human Growth after Birth, 1969 (3rd edn 1978); Muscles and Fascia (section in Cunningham's Anatomy), 11th edn, 1972, 12th edn, 1981; Basic Medical Education, 1972; The Nerves of the Skin (section in Physiology and Pathophysiology of the Skin, ed Jarrett), 1973; Growth, section in Textbook of Human Anatomy (ed Hamilton), 1976; Mechanisms of Cutaneous Sensation, 1981; papers on chemical warfare, neurological anatomy, experimental psychology, medical education; Editor, Jl of Anatomy, 1970-73. *Recreations:* reading, writing, photography, chess problems. *Address:* Four Winds, Barclay Park, Aboyne AB3 5JF.

SINCLAIR, Ernest Keith, CMG 1966; OBE 1946; DFC 1943; Commissioner, Australian Heritage Commission, 1976-81; Associate Commissioner, Industries Assistance Commission, 1974-81; Director: Australian Paper Manufacturers Ltd; *b* 13 November 1914; 2nd *s* of Ernest and Florence Sinclair, Victoria, Australia; *m* 1949, Jill, *d* of John and Muriel Nelder, Pangbourne; one *s. Educ:* Melbourne High School, Australia. Literary staff, The Age, 1932-38; Served War of 1939-45, RAF, 1940-45 (despatches, 1944). Associate Editor, The Age, Melbourne, 1946-59, Editor, 1959-66. Consultant to Dept of Prime Minister and Cabinet, 1967-74 and 1977- (to Prime Minister of Australia, 1967-72). Dep. Chm., Australian Tourist Commn, 1969-75 (Mem. 1966). Director: Australian Assoc. Press, 1959-66 (Chm., 1965-66); Gen. Television Corp. (Melbourne), 1959-66; Member: Australian Council, Internat. Press Inst., 1959-66; Schools Bd for the Humanities, Victoria Inst. of Colleges, 1969-72 (Chm.); Library Council of Victoria, 1966-78 (Dep. Pres., 1969-78); Council, Royal Historical Soc. of Victoria; Observer, Nat. Capital Planning Cttee, 1967-72; Dep. Chm., Building Trustees Library Council, Nat. Museum and Sci. Museum of Victoria, 1976-78. *Recreations:* gardening, reading. *Address:* 138 Toorak Road West, South Yarra, Victoria 3141, Australia. *T:* 267-1405. *Clubs:* Press (London); Melbourne (Melbourne).

SINCLAIR, Rear-Adm. Erroll Norman, CB 1963; DSC 1944; retired; *b* 6 Mar. 1909; *s* of late Col John Norman Sinclair, RHA; *m* 1940, Frances Elinor Knox-Gore; two *s. Educ:* RNC Dartmouth. Served HMS Cairo, 1936-38; HMS Gallant, 1938-40 (Dunkirk); in comd HMS Fortune, 1940, HMS Antelope, 1941-43, N African Landings; in comd HMS Eskimo, 10th Destroyer Flotilla, 1943-45 (DSC); First Lieut, RN Barracks, Chatham, 1946, Comdr 1946; Exec. Officer, RN Air Station, Eglinton, 1947; Staff Officer Ops to C-in-C, S Atlantic Station, Simonstown, and UK Liaison Officer to S Af. Naval Forces, until 1951. In comd HMS St Kitts, 5th Destroyer Sqdn, Home Fleet, 1951-53; Capt. 1952; Pres. Second Admiralty Interview Board, 1953-54; Naval Attaché at Ankara, Teheran and Tel Aviv, 1955; Capt. (D)

4th Destroyer Sqdn, HMS Agincourt, 1957-59; in comd HMS Sea Eagle and Sen. Naval Officer N Ireland, and Naval Director, Joint A/S School, Londonderry, 1959-61; Flag Officer, Gibraltar, and Admiral Superintendent, HM Dockyard, Gibraltar, also NATO Commander of Gibraltar sub areas, 1962-64; retd list, 1964; Naval Regional Officer (North), 1964-68. *Address:* Island Cottage, Wittersham, Kent. *T:* Wittersham 354. *Club:* Rye Golf.

SINCLAIR, Maj.-Gen. George Brian, CBE 1975; FIHE; Engineer-in-Chief (Army), 1980-83; *b* 21 July 1928; *s* of Thomas S. Sinclair and Blanche Sinclair; *m* 1953, Edna Margaret Richardson; two *s* one *d. Educ:* Christ's College, Finchley; RMA Sandhurst. Commissioned, Royal Engineers, 1948; served UK, BAOR, Korea, and Christmas Island, 1948-66; Directing Staff, Staff College, Camberley, 1967-69; CRE, Near East, 1970-71; Col GS, HQ 1st British Corps, 1972-74; Nat. Defence Coll., India, 1975; Commandant Royal School of Military Engineering, 1976-77; BGS, Military Operations, MoD, 1978-80. *Recreations:* hill walking, running, bird watching and discussion. *Address:* 6 Prospect Row, Brompton, Gillingham, Kent. *T:* Medway 42364. *Club:* Army and Navy.

SINCLAIR, Sir George (Evelyn), Kt 1960; CMG 1956; OBE 1950; engaged in political work in United Kingdom and overseas, since 1960; *b* Cornwall, 6 November 1912; 2nd *s* of late F. Sinclair, Chynance, St Buryan, Cornwall; *m* 1st, 1941, Katharine Jane Burdekin (*d* 1971); one *s* three *d* ; 2nd, 1972, Mary Violet, widow of George Lester Sawday, Saxmundham, Suffolk. *Educ:* Abingdon School; Pembroke College, Oxford. MA (Oxon). Entered Colonial Administrative Service, 1936; appointed to Gold Coast Administration; Asst District Comr, 1937. Military service, 1940-43. District Commissioner, Gold Coast, 1943; seconded to Colonial Office, 1943-45; Sec. to Commn on Higher Education in West Africa, 1943-45; returned to Gold Coast, 1945; Senior Assistant Colonial Secretary, 1947; Principal Assistant Secretary, 1950; Regional Officer, Trans-Volta Togoland Region, 1952; Deputy Governor, Cyprus, 1955-60; retired, 1961. MP (C) Dorking, Surrey, Oct. 1964-1979. Member, Parly Select Committees on: Procedure, 1965-66; Race Relations, 1969-70; Overseas Aid, 1969-70; Race Relations and Immigration, 1970-74; Members Interests, 1975; Abortion Act (Amendment) Bill; Joint Secretary: Cons. Parly Commonwealth Affairs Cttee, 1966-68; Cons. Parly Educn Cttee, 1974-79, Vice-Chm., 1974; Member: Wimbledon Borough Council, 1962-65; Intermediate Technology Develt Gp (Vice-Pres., 1966-79; Dir, 1979-82); Nat. Exec. Cttee, UNA (UK Branch), 1968-70; Council, Overseas Services Resettlement Bureau; Council of PDSA, 1964-70; Council, Christian Aid, 1973-78; Steering Cttee, UN/FPA World Conf. of Parliamentarians on population and develt, 1978; Vice-Chm., Family Planning Assoc., 1979-; Consultant, UN Fund for Population Affairs, 1979-. Trustee: Runnymede Trust, 1969-75; Human Rights Trust, 1971-74; Physically Handicapped and Able Bodied (Trustee), 1973-81; Wyndham Place Trust. Chm., Bd of Governors, Abingdon School, 1971-79; Mem., Bd of Governors, Felixstowe Coll., 1980-; Chm., Assoc. of Governing Bodies of Independent Schools, 1979- (Mem., 1973-); Mem., Direct Grant Jt Cttee; Mem., Indep. Schools Jt Council, 1979-, Chm. 1980-. *Recreations:* golf, sailing, shooting. *Address:* Carlton Rookery, Saxmundham, Suffolk; South Minack, Porthcurno, Cornwall. *Clubs:* Athenæum, Royal Commonwealth Society; Aldeburgh Golf, Aldeburgh Yacht.

SINCLAIR, Hugh Macdonald, DM, MA, BSc, FRCP, LMSSA; Director, International Institute of Human Nutrition, since 1972; Fellow, Magdalen College, Oxford, 1937-80, now Emeritus Fellow (Vice-President, 1956-58); *b* Duddingston House, Edinburgh, 4 Feb. 1910; 2nd *s* of late Col H. M. Sinclair, CB, CMG, CBE, RE, and late Rosalie, *d* of Sir John Jackson, CVO, LLD; unmarried. *Educ:* Winchester (Senior Science Prize); Oriel College, Oxford. First Cl. Hons Animal Physiology, 1932; Gotch Prize, 1933; Senior Demy, Magdalen College, 1932-34; University Coll. Hosp. 1933-36 (Gold and Silver Medals for Clinical Medicine); Radcliffe Schol. in Pharmacology, 1934; Radcliffe Travelling Fellow, 1937-38; Rolleston Prize, 1938. University Demonstrator and Lectr in Biochemistry, Oxford, 1937-47; Director, Oxford Nutrition Survey, 1942-47; Hon. Nutrition Consultant (with rank of Brig.), CCG, 1945-47; Lectr in Physiology and Biochemistry, Magdalen College, Oxford, 1937-76; Reader in Human Nutrition and Dir, Lab. of Human Nutrition, Oxford, 1951-58; Vis. Prof. in Food Science, Univ. of Reading, 1970-80. Lectures: Cutter, Harvard, 1951; Schuman, Los Angeles, 1962; Golden Acres, Dallas, 1963. Member: Physiological Soc.; Biochemical Soc.; Med. Research Soc.; Soc. for Experimental Biology; Soc. Philomathique; Fellow: Chem. Soc.; Inst. Biol.; Amer. Public Health Soc.; Hollywood Acad. Med. Master, Apothecaries Co., 1967-68. Hon. DSc Baldwin-Wallace, USA, 1968. US Medal of Freedom with Silver Palm; Officer of Order of Orange Nassau, Holland. Editor-in-Chief, Internat. Encyclopedia of Food and Nutrition (24 vols), 1969-. *Publications:* papers on Human Nutrition and on Brain Metabolism in scientific and med. jls; Use of Vitamins in Medicine, in Whitla's Pharmacy, Materia Medica and Therapeutics (13th edn), 1939; Vitamins in Treatment, in Modern Therapeutics (Practitioner Handbooks), 1941; Nutrition, in Aspects of Modern Science, 1951; A Short History of Anatomical Teaching in Oxford (with A. H. T. Robb-Smith), 1950; (ed) The Work of Sir Robert McCarrison, 1953; (with McCarrison) Nutrition and Health, 1953 and 1961; (with Prof. Jelliffe) Nicholl's Tropical Nutrition, 1961; (with F. C. Rodger) Metabolic and Nutritional Eye Diseases, 1968; (with D. Hollingsworth) Hutchison's Food and Principles of Nutrition, 1969; (with G. R. Howat) World Nutrition and Nutrition Education, 1980; articles on med. educn. *Recreations:* tennis, cricket, and gardening. *Address:* International Nutrition Foundation, High Street, Sutton Courtenay, Oxon

OX14 4AW. *T:* Sutton Courtenay 246; Lady Place, Sutton Courtenay, Oxon. *Clubs:* Athenæum, MCC.

SINCLAIR, Ian David; Chairman and Director, Canadian Pacific Enterprises Ltd; *b* Winnipeg, 27 Dec. 1913; *s* of late John David Sinclair and late Lillian Sinclair; *m* 1942, Ruth Beatrice, *d* of Robert Parsons Drennan, Winnipeg; two *s* two *d. Educ:* public schs, Winnipeg; Univ. of Manitoba (BA Econs 1937); Manitoba Law School (LLB 1941). Barrister, Guy Chappell & Co., Winnipeg, 1937-41; Lectr in Torts, Univ. of Manitoba, 1942-43; joined Canadian Pacific Law Dept as Asst Solicitor, Winnipeg, 1942; Solicitor, Montreal, 1946; Asst to General Counsel, 1951; General Solicitor, 1953; Vice-Pres. and Gen. Counsel, 1960; Vice-Pres., Law, 1960; Vice-Pres., Dir and Mem. Exec. Cttee, Canadian Pacific Rly Co., 1961; Pres., CPR Co., 1966; Chief Exec. Officer, CPR Co., 1969; Chm. and Chief Exec. Officer, Canadian Pacific Ltd, 1972-81. Hon. Dr of Laws, Manitoba, 1967. *Address:* 20 King Street West, 7th Floor, Toronto, Ont M5H 1C4, Canada. *T:* (416) 360-3533. *Clubs:* Rideau (Ottawa); Mount Royal, Canadian Railway, Canadian, Canadian Chamber of Commerce, Montreal Board of Trade (Montreal).

SINCLAIR, Rt. Hon. Ian (McCahon), PC 1977; MHR; Minister for Defence, Government of Australia, since 1982; Deputy Leader, National Country Party of Australia, since 1971; *b* 10 June 1929; *s* of George McCahon Sinclair and Gertrude Hazel Sinclair; *m* 1st, 1956, Margaret Tarrant (*d* 1967); one *s* two *d* ; 2nd, 1970, Rosemary Fenton; one *s. Educ:* Knox Grammar Sch., Wahroonga, NSW; Sydney Univ. BA, LLB. Mem. Legislative Council, NSW, 1961-63; MHR for New England, 1963-; Minister for: Social Services, 1965-68; Shipping and Transport, 1968-71; Trade and Industry (Asst Minister), 1966-71; Primary Industry, 1971-72; Leader of House for Opposition, 1972-75; Country Party spokesman for Defence, Foreign Affairs, Law and Agriculture, 1973; Opposition spokesman on Agriculture, 1974-75; Minister for Agriculture and Minister for N Australia, Nov.-Dec. 1975; Govt Leader in the House of Representatives, 1975-82; Minister for Primary Industry, 1975-80; Minister for Communications, 1980-82. *Address:* Parliament House, Canberra, ACT 2600, Australia. *T:* (062) 726661. *Clubs:* Australian, American, Union (Sydney); Tamworth; Killara Golf.

SINCLAIR, Sir Ian (McTaggart), KCMG 1977 (CMG 1972); QC 1979; HM Diplomatic Service; Legal Adviser, Foreign and Commonwealth Office, since 1976; *b* 14 Jan. 1926; *s* of late John Sinclair, company director; *m* 1954, Barbara Elizabeth (*née* Lenton); two *s* one *d. Educ:* Merchiston Castle Sch. (Scholar); King's Coll., Cambridge; BA 1948, LLB 1949 (1st cl. hons). Served Intelligence Corps, 1944-47. Called to the Bar, Middle Temple, 1952; Bencher, 1980. Asst Legal Adviser, Foreign Office, 1950-56; Legal Adviser, HM Embassy, Bonn, 1957-60; Asst Legal Adviser, FO, 1960-64; Legal Adviser, UK Mission to the UN, New York, and HM Embassy, Washington, 1964-67; Legal Counsellor, FCO, 1967-71; Dep. Legal Advr, FCO, 1971-72; Second Legal Advr, FCO, 1973-75. Has been Legal Adviser to UK delegn at numerous internat. confs, incl. Geneva Conf. on Korea and Indo-China, 1954, and Brussels negotiations for UK entry into the EEC, 1961-63; Dep. Chm., UK delegn to Law of Treaties Conf., Vienna, 1968-69; Legal Adviser to UK delegn on negotiations for UK entry into EEC, 1970-72; Member: Bureau of European Cttee on Legal Co-operation, Council of Europe, 1979-81; Panel of Conciliators, Annex to Vienna Convention on Law of Treaties, 1981-; Internat. Law Commn, 1981-. Mem., Committee of Management: British Inst. of Internat. and Comparative Law, 1976-; Inst. of Advanced Legal Studies, 1980-. *Publications:* Vienna Convention on the Law of Treaties, 1973; articles in British Yearbook of International Law, International and Comparative Law Qly and other legal jls. *Recreations:* golf, fishing, watching sea-birds. *Address:* c/o Foreign and Commonwealth Office, SW1. *Club:* Athenæum.

SINCLAIR, Isabel Lillias, (Mrs J. G. MacDonald), QC (Scotland) 1964; Sheriff of Lothian and Borders (formerly Roxburgh, Berwick, and Selkirk), 1968-79, now Honorary Sheriff; *d* of William Sinclair, Glasgow, and Isabella (*née* Thomson), Glasgow; *m* 1938, J. Gordon MacDonald, BL, Solicitor, Glasgow. *Educ:* Shawlands Academy; Glasgow Univ.; Edinburgh Univ. MA 1932; BL 1946. Worked as a newspaper-woman from 1932. Admitted to Faculty of Advocates, Edinburgh, 1949. Sheriff-Substitute of Lanarkshire at Airdrie, 1966-68. *Address:* 6 St Vincent Street, Edinburgh EH3 6SH. *T:* 031-556 4806. *Club:* Royal Scottish Automobile (Glasgow).

SINCLAIR, John, MBE 1958; JP; DL; Lord Lieutenant of Caithness, 1965-73; *b* 24 March 1898; *s* of John Sinclair and Margaret Gray Sinclair; unmarried. *Educ:* Miller Academy, Thurso. Served RNVR, 1916-19. Member of Thurso Town Council, 1929-63; Bailie (Magistrate), 1932-48; Provost, 1948-61; Free Burgess of the Burgh of Thurso, 1966. Hon. Sheriff Substitute, 1948; JP 1941, DL 1965, Caithness. Order of Founder of Salvation Army, 1968. Gold Medal, RNLI, 1971. *Recreations:* music, fishing. *Address:* 20 Millers Lane, Thurso. *T:* Thurso 2481.

SINCLAIR, Sir John (Rollo Norman Blair), 9th Bt, *cr* 1704; *b* 4 Nov. 1928; *s* of Sir Ronald Norman John Charles Udny Sinclair, 8th Bt, TD, and Reba Blair (Company Comdt, Auxiliary Territorial Service, 1938-41), *d* of Anthony Inglis, MS, Lismore, Ayrshire; *S* father 1952. *Educ:* Wellington College. Lt Intelligence Corps, 1948-49. Director: The Lucis Trust, 1957-61; The Human Development Trust, 1970-; The Gatekeeper Trust, 1982-; Natural Health Foundn, 1982-. *Publications:* The Mystical Ladder, 1968; The Other Universe, 1972. *Heir: cousin* Patrick Robert Richard Sinclair [*b* 21 May 1936;

m 1974, Susan Catherine Beresford, *e d* of Geoffrey Clive Davies; one *s*]. *Address:* (Seat) Barrock House, Wick, Caithness.
See also Baroness Masham of Ilton.

SINCLAIR, Air Vice-Marshal Sir Laurence (Frank), GC 1941; KCB 1957 (CB 1946); CBE 1943; DSO 1940 (and Bar, 1943); *b* 1908; *m* 1941, Valerie, *d* of Lt-Col Joseph Dalton White; one *s* one *d*. *Educ:* Imperial Service Coll.; RAF Coll. Cranwell. Comd No 110 Sqdn in 1940; Comd RAF Watton, 1941; Comd Tactical Light Bomber Force in North Africa and Italy, 1943-44; ADC to King George VI, 1943-44; subsequently Sen. Air Staff Officer, Balkan Air Force; commanded No 2 Light Bomber Group (Germany), 1948-49; Assistant Commandant RAF Staff College, 1949-50; Commandant, Royal Air Force College Cranwell, 1950-52; Commandant, School of Land/Air Warfare, Old Sarum, Wiltshire, 1952-53; Asst Chief of the Air Staff (Operations), 1953-55; Comdr British Forces, Arabian Peninsula, 1955-57; Commandant Joint Services Staff College, 1958-60, retired from RAF. Controller of Ground Services, Min. of Aviation, 1960-61; Controller, Nat. Air Traffic Control Services, Min. of Aviation, and MoD, 1962-66. Legion of Merit (American), 1943; Legion of Honour, 1944; Partisan Star (Yugoslavia). *Address:* Haines Land, Great Brickhill, Bletchley, Bucks.

SINCLAIR, Sir Leonard, Kt 1955; *b* 9 June 1895; *s* of John and Mary Sinclair, Broughton, Salford, Lancs; *m* 1926, Mary Levine; one *d*. *Educ:* Higher Grade School, Broughton, Salford, Lancs. Past Chm. Esso Petroleum Co. Ltd, 1951-58 (Dir, 1943-58). *Recreations:* golf, gardening. *Address:* Marlow, Deans Lane, Tadworth, Surrey. *T:* Tadworth 3844. *Club:* Royal Automobile.

SINCLAIR, Michael; *see* Shea, M. S. MacA.

SINCLAIR, Sir Ronald Ormiston, KBE 1963; Kt 1956; President, Court of Appeal: for the Bahamas and for Bermuda, 1965-70; for British Honduras, 1968-70; Chairman, Industrial Tribunals (England and Wales), 1966-69; *b* 2 May 1903; *yr s* of Rev. W. A. Sinclair, Auckland, NZ; *m* 1935, Ellen Isabel Entrican; two *s*. *Educ:* New Plymouth Boys' High School, NZ; Auckland University College, NZ; Balliol College, Oxford. Barrister and Solicitor of Supreme Court of New Zealand, 1924; LLM (NZ) (Hons) 1925; Administrative Service, Nigeria, 1931; Magistrate, Nigeria, 1936; Resident Magistrate, Northern Rhodesia, 1938; Barrister-at-Law, Middle Temple, 1939; Puisne Judge, Tanganyika, 1946; Chief Justice, Nyasaland, 1953-55; Vice-President, East African Court of Appeal, 1956-57, Pres., 1962-64; Chief Justice of Kenya, 1957-62. *Address:* 158 Victoria Avenue, Remuera, Auckland, New Zealand.

SINCLAIR-LOCKHART, Sir Muir (Edward), 14th Bt *cr* 1636 (NS); retired sheep farmer; *b* 23 July 1906; 3rd *s* of Sir Robert Duncan Sinclair-Lockhart, 11th Bt and Flora Louisa Jane Beresford Nation (*d* 1937), *d* of Captain Edward Henry Power; *S* brother, 1970; *m* 1940, Olga Ann, *d* of Claude Victor White-Parsons; one *s* one *d*. *Recreation:* hunting (harrier). *Heir: s* Simon John Edward Francis Sinclair-Lockhart [*b* 22 July 1941; *m* 1973, Felicity Edith, *d* of late I. L. C. Stewart, NZ; twin *s* one *d*]. *Address:* Camnethan, RD 10, Feilding, New Zealand.

SINDALL, Adrian John; HM Diplomatic Service; Counsellor, Head of Chancery and Consul-General, British Embassy, Amman, since 1979; *b* 5 Oct. 1937; *s* of Stephen Sindall and Clare Mallet; *m* 1st, 1958; one *s* one *d*; 2nd, 1978, Jill Margaret Cowley. *Educ:* Battersea Grammar Sch. FO, 1956-58; ME Centre for Arab Studies, 1958-60; Third Sec. (Commercial), Baghdad, 1960-62; Second Sec., British Embassy, Rabat, 1962-67; First Secretary: FCO, 1967-70; Beirut, 1970-72; First Sec. and Head of Chancery, British Embassy, Lima, 1972-76; FCO, 1976-79. *Address:* c/o Foreign and Commonwealth Office, SW1A 2AH.

SINDELL, Marion Harwood; Chief Executive, Equal Opportunities Commission, since 1979; *b* 23 June 1925; *d* of Arthur Barrett Sindell and Ethel Maude Sindell. *Educ:* Lincoln Girls' High Sch.; St Hilda's Coll., Oxford (MA). Solicitor. Deputy Town Clerk: Workington, 1959-64; Nuneaton, 1964-66; Town Clerk, Goole, 1966-74; Chief Exec., Boothferry Bor. Council, 1974-79. *Address:* Equal Opportunities Commission, Overseas House, Quay Street, Manchester M3 3HN. *T:* 061-833 9244.

SINDEN, Donald Alfred, CBE 1979; actor; *b* 9 Oct. 1923; *s* of Alfred Edward Sinden and Mabel Agnes (*née* Fuller), Sussex; *m* 1948, Diana, *d* of Daniel and Muriel Mahony; two *s*. *Educ:* Webber-Douglas Sch. of Dramatic Art. First appearance on stage, 1942, in Charles F. Smith's Co., Mobile Entertainments Southern Area; Leicester Repertory Co., 1945; Memorial Theatre Co., Stratford upon Avon, 1946 and 1947; Old Vic and Bristol Old Vic, 1948; The Heiress, Haymarket, 1949-50; Bristol Old Vic, 1950; Red Letter Day, Garrick, 1951. Under contract to Rank Organisation, 1952-60, appearing in 23 films including The Cruel Sea, Doctor in the House, etc. Returned to theatre, appearing in Odd Man In, St Martin's, 1957; Peter Pan, Scala, 1960; Guilty Party, St Martin's, 1961; Royal Shakespeare Co., playing Richard Plantagenet in Henry VI (The Wars of the Roses), Price in Eh?, etc, 1963 and 1964; British Council tour of S America in Dear Liar and Happy Days, 1965; There's a fly in my Soup, Globe, 1966; Lord Foppington in The Relapse, RSC, Aldwych, 1967; Not Now Darling, Strand, 1968; RSC, Stratford, 1969 and Aldwych, 1970 playing Malvolio; Henry VIII; Sir Harcourt Courtly in London Assurance, revived at New Theatre, 1972, tour of the USA, 1974 (Drama Desk

Award); In Praise of Love, Duchess, 1973; Stockmann in An Enemy of the People, Chichester, 1975; Habeas Corpus, USA, 1975; Benedick in Much Ado About Nothing, King Lear, RSC, Stratford, 1976, Aldwych, 1977 (Variety Club of GB Stage Actor of 1976; Evening Standard Drama Award, Best Actor, 1977); Shut Your Eyes and Think of England, Apollo, 1977; Othello, RSC, Stratford, 1979, Aldwych, 1980; Present Laughter, Vaudeville, 1981 (TV film, 1981); Uncle Vanya, Haymarket, 1982; *television series include:* Our Man from St Marks; Two's Company; Discovering English Churches; Never the Twain, 1981; has appeared in many films. Assoc. Artist, RSC, 1967-. Member: Council, British Actors Equity Assoc., 1966-77; Council, RSA, 1972; Adv. Council, V&A Museum, 1973-80; Arts Council Drama Panel, 1973-77; Leicestershire Educn Arts Cttee, 1974-; BBC Archives Adv. Cttee, 1975-78; London Acad. of Music and Dramatic Art Council, 1976-; Kent and E Sussex Reg. Cttee, National Trust, 1978-; Arts Council of GB, 1982-; Chairman: British Theatre Museum Assoc., 1971-77; Theatre Museum Adv. Council, 1973-80; Pres., Fedn of Playgoers Socs, 1968-; Vice-Pres., London Appreciation Soc., 1960-. FRSA 1966. *Publication:* A Touch of the Memoirs (autobiog.), 1982. *Recreations:* theatrical history, French history, architecture, ecclesiology, genealogy, serendipity, London. *Address:* 60 Temple Fortune Lane, NW11; Rats Castle, Isle of Oxney, Kent. *Clubs:* Garrick (Trustee, 1980-), Beefsteak, MCC.

SINGER, Alfred Ernst; Chairman: Cannon Assurance Ltd; Wholesale Vehicle Finance Ltd; Aregon Ltd; Director: Equity Capital for Industry Ltd; Gestetner Holdings Ltd; Guinness Mahon Holdings Ltd; *b* 15 Nov. 1924; *s* of late Dr Robert Singer and Mrs Charlotte Singer; *m* 1951, Gwendoline Doris Barnett; one *s* one *d*. *Educ:* Halesowen Grammar Sch. FCCA, FBCS. Served War of 1939-45: Army, 1943-47. Subseq. professional and exec. posts with: Callingham, Brown & Co, Bunzl Pulp & Paper Ltd, David Brown Tractors Ltd; Rank Xerox Ltd, 1963-70 (Dir, 1967); Tesco Stores (Holdings) Ltd, 1970-73 (Dep. Managing Dir); Man. Dir (Giro), PO Corpn, 1973-76; Chairman: PO Staff Superannuation Fund, 1977-79; Long Range Planning Soc., 1970-73; Council, Assoc. of Certified Accountants, 1972-81 (Vice-Pres., 1979-80); Member: Cttee for Industrial Technologies, DTI, 1972-76; National Economic Develt Council: Chm., Electronic Computers Sector Working Party; Member: Electronics EDC; Food and Drink Manufacturing Industry EDC, 1976-77. Governor, Centre for Environmental Studies, 1979- (Chm., 1981-). *Address:* 7 Bacon's Lane, South Grove, Highgate Village, N6 6BL. *T:* 01-340 0189. *Clubs:* Athenæum, MCC.

SINGER, Aubrey Edward; Deputy Director-General, and Managing Director, Television, BBC, since 1982; *b* 21 Jan. 1927; *s* of Louis Henry Singer and Elizabeth (*née* Walton); *m* 1949, Cynthia Hilda Adams; one *s* three *d*. *Educ:* Giggleswick; Bradford Grammar School. Joined film industry, 1944; directed various films teaching armed forces to shoot; worked extensively in Africa, 1946-48; worked on children's films in Austria, 1948-49; joined BBC TV Outside Broadcasts, 1949; TV Producer Scotland, 1951; BBC New York Office, 1953; returned to London as Producer, 1956; produced many scientific programmes; Asst Head of Outside Broadcasts, 1959; Head of Science and Features, 1961; Head of BBC TV, 1967; Controller, BBC 2, 1974-78; Man. Dir, BBC Radio, 1978-82. Chm., Soc. of Film and Television Arts, 1971-73. Fellow, Royal TV Soc., 1978, a Vice-Pres., 1982-. *Recreations:* walking, talking, archery. *Address:* 11 Trevanion Road, W14. *T:* 01-603 7340.

SINGER, Harold Samuel; a Recorder of the Crown Court, since 1981; *b* 17 July 1935; *s* of Ellis and Minnie Singer; *m* 1966, Adèle Berenice Emanuel; one *s* two *d*. *Educ:* Salford Grammar School; Fitzwilliam House, Cambridge. BA Cantab. Called to the Bar, Gray's Inn, 1957. *Recreations:* music, oil painting, books, photography, golf. *Address:* 6 Okeover Road, Salford M7 0JX. *T:* 061-792 2876; 460 The Royal Exchange, Cross Street, Manchester M2 7EW. *T:* 061-832 9082.

SINGER, Harry Bruce, TD 1955; FCA; Senior Partner, Singer & Partners, Chartered Accountants, since 1968; *b* 21 June 1921; *er s* of Geoffrey and Agnes Singer; *m* 1945, Betty Alison Brittan; one *s*. *Educ:* Cathedral Sch., Hereford. FCA 1960 (Mem., 1953). Served War: commnd 99th (London Welsh) HAA Regt, RA, 1941; served in UK and NW Europe; Instr, Sch. of AA Artillery, 1945; joined 281 (Glam Yeomanry) Field Regt, RA (TA), 1947; in comd, 1959-62. Pres., S Wales Soc. of Chartered Accountants, 1970-71; Inst. of Chartered Accountants in England and Wales: Mem. Council, 1973-; Vice Pres., 1979-80; Dep. Pres., 1980-81; Pres., 1981-82. Liveryman, Worshipful Co. of Chartered Accountants, 1978; Freeman, City of London, 1978. *Recreations:* golf, foreign travel, Rugby football (originally as player). *Address:* 8 Windsor House, Castle Court, Cardiff CF1 1DG. *Clubs:* Army and Navy; Cardiff and County, Cardiff Golf (Cardiff).

SINGER, Isaac Bashevis; writer; *b* Poland, 14 July 1904; *s* of Pinchos Menacheim Singer and Bathsheba Singer (*née* Zylberman); *m* 1940, Alma Haimann; one *s*. *Educ:* Tachkemoni Rabbinical Seminary, Warsaw. Worked for publishing firms, Poland, 1926-35; with Jewish Daily Forward, NY, 1935-. Fellow: Jewish Acad. of Arts and Scis; Amer. Acad. and Inst. of Arts and Letters, NY; Mem., Amer. Acad. of Arts and Sciences, Boston; Nat. Book Award, 1970, 1974; Nobel Prize for Literature, 1978. DHL Hebrew Union Coll., LA, 1963. *Publications:* The Family Moskal, 1950; Satan in Goray, 1955; Gimpel the Fool and Other Stories, 1957; The Magician of Lublin, 1959; The Spinoza of Market Street, 1961; The Slave, 1962; Short Friday, 1964; Zlateh the Goat and Other Stories, 1966; In My Father's Court, 1966; The Manor,

1967; The Seance, 1968; The Estate, 1969; A Friend of Kafka and Other Stories, 1970; A Day of Pleasure (for children), 1970; Enemies, A Love Story, 1972; Crown of Feathers, 1973; When Shlemiel Went to War and Other Stories, 1974; Passions, 1976; Shosha, 1979; Old Love, 1980; The Collected Stories of Isaac Bashevis Singer, 1982. *Address:* 209 West 86th Street, New York, NY 10024, USA. *T:* 212-877-5968.

SINGER, Norbert, PhD, FRSC; Director, Thames Polytechnic, since 1978; *b* 3 May 1931; *s* of late Salomon Singer and late Mina Korn; *m* Brenda Margaret Walter, *e d* of Richard and Gladys Walter, Tunbridge Wells, Kent. *Educ:* Highbury County School; Queen Mary Coll., London. BSc, PhD, CChem, FRIC. Research Chemist and Project Leader, Morgan Crucible Co. Ltd, 1954–57; Lecturer, Senior Lectr, Principal Lectr and Dep. Head of Department, Dept of Chemistry, Northern Polytechnic, 1958–70; Head of Dept of Life Sciences 1971–74, Professor of Life Sciences 1972–74, Polytechnic of Central London; Asst Director, then Dep. Director, Polytechnic of North London, 1974–78. *Publications:* research papers in electrochemistry, theoretical chemistry and surface chemistry in scientific jls. *Recreations:* squash, work. *Address:* 8 Crescent Road, Chingford, E4 6AT. *T:* 01-529 8539.

SINGER, Very Rev. Samuel Stanfield; Dean of Diocese of Glasgow and Galloway, since 1974; Rector of Holy Trinity, Ayr, since 1975; *b* 1920; *m* 1942, Helen Audrey Naughton, *o c* of Rev. and Mrs Michael William Naughton; three *s* one *d. Educ:* Trinity College, Dublin (BA 1942, MA 1961). Deacon 1943, priest, 1944. Dio. Down; Curate of Derriaghy, 1943–45; Minor Canon of Down Cathedral and Curate of Down, 1945–46; Curate of Wirksworth, 1946–49; Vicar of Middleton-by-Wirksworth, 1949–52; Rector: St George, Maryhill, Glasgow, 1952–62; All Saints, Jordanhill, Glasgow, 1962–75; Synod Clerk and Canon of Glasgow, 1966–74. *Address:* 12 Barns Terrace, Ayr, Ayrshire.

SINGH, Kanwar N.; *see* Natwar-Singh.

SINGH, Khushwant; Padma Bhushan, 1974; Member of Parliament, India, since 1980; Editor-in-chief, The Hindustan Times and Contour, New Delhi, since 1980; Barrister-at-Law; *b* Feb. 1915; *m* Kaval (*née* Malik); one *s* one *d. Educ:* Univ. of London (LLB); called to Bar. Practising Lawyer, High Court, Lahore, 1939–47; Min. of External Affairs, of India; PRO Ottawa and London, 1947–51; UNESCO, 1954–56. Visiting Lectr: Oxford (Spalding Trust); USA: Rochester, Princeton, Hawaii, Swarthmore; led Indian Delegn to Writers' Conf., Manila, Philippines, 1965; Guest Speaker at Montreal 'Expo 67'. Has written for many nat. dailies and foreign jls: New York Times; Observer and New Statesman (London); Harper's (USA); Evergreen Review (USA); London Magazine. Editor, The Illustrated Weekly of India, Bombay, 1969–78; Chief Editor, New Delhi, 1979–80; increased circulation of Illustrated Weekly of India from 80,000 to 410,000 in 9 yrs. *Broadcasting and Television:* All India Radio, BBC, CBC; LP recordings. Awards include: from Punjab Govt: 5,000 rupees and Robe of Honour, for contrib. to Sikh literature; Mohan Singh Award: 1,500 rupees for trans. of Sikh hymns, etc. *Publications: Sikh History and Religion:* The Sikhs, 1953; A History of the Sikhs: vol. i, 1469–1839, 1964; vol. ii, 1839–1964, 1967; Ranjit Singh, Maharajah of the Punjab, 1780–1839, 1963; Fall of the Kingdom of the Punjab; Sikhs Today; (ed) Sunset of the Sikh Empire, by Dr Sita Ram Kohli (posthumous); Hymns of Nanak The Guru. *Fiction:* The Mark of Vishnu and other stories, 1951; Train to Pakistan, 1956; I Shall Not Hear the Nightingales, 1961; *stories:* The Voice of God and other stories; Black Jasmine and other stories; A Bride for the Sahib and other stories. (*Co-author*): Sacred Writing of the Sikhs; (with Arun Joshi) Shri Ram: a biog., 1969; (with Satindra Singh) Ghadr Rebellion; (with Suneet Veer Singh) Homage to Guru Gobind Singh; *miscellaneous:* Love and Friendship (editor of anthology); Khushwant Singh's India—collection of articles (ed Rahul Singh); Shri Ram—a biography; *translations:* Umrao Jan Ada, Courtesan of Lucknow, by Mohammed Ruswa (with M. A. Husaini); The Skeleton (by Amrita Pritam); Land of the Five Rivers; I Take This Woman, by Rajinder Singh Bedi; Iqbal's Dialogue with Allah (Shikwah and Jawab-e-Shikwah); We Indians. *Recreation:* bird watching. *Address:* 49E Sujan Singh Park, New Delhi 110003, India. *T:* 690159. *Clubs:* Authors'; Imperial Gymkhana (New Delhi); Bombay Gymkhana (Bombay 1).

SINGH, Mota, QC 1978; **His Honour Judge Singh;** a Circuit Judge, since 1982; *b* 26 July 1930; *s* of Dalip Singh and Harnam Kaur; *m* 1950, Swaran Kaur; two *s* one *d. Educ:* Duke of Gloucester Sch., Nairobi, Kenya; Hon. Soc. of Lincoln's Inn. Called to the Bar, 1956. Left school, 1947; Solicitor's Clerk, Nairobi, 1948–54; Lincoln's Inn, London, 1954–56; Advocate, High Court of Kenya, 1957–65; Alderman, City of Nairobi, 1958–63; Vice-Chm., Kenya Justice; Sec., Law Soc. of Kenya, 1963–64. A Deputy Circuit Judge, 1976–82; a Recorder of the Crown Court, 1979–82. Member: London Rent Assessment Panel, 1965–67; Race Relations Bd, 1968–77. Hon. LLD; Guru Nanak Dev Univ., Amritsar, 1981. *Recreation:* reading. *Address:* Cedarwood, 3 Somerset Road, Wimbledon SW19 5JU. *T:* 01-947 5610.

SINGH, Preetam, QC 1976; *b* 1 Oct. 1914; *s* of Waryam Singh and late Balwant Kaur; *m* 1934, Rattan Kaur (*née* Bura); three *s* one *d. Educ:* A. V. High Sch., Mombasa, Kenya; King's Coll., London. Called to the Bar, Gray's Inn, 1951; Mem. Bar Council and Senate of Inns of Court. Dep. Official Receiver, Kenya, 1960–64; Barrister, N Eastern Circuit, 1964–77; Advocate: Supreme Court, Kenya; High Court (Punjab and Haryana), India. Member: Commn for Racial Equality, 1977–78; BBC Adv. Cttee on Asian

programmes, 1979–. Contested (L) Hallam (Sheffield), 1970. Hon. LLD Punjab, 1977. *Recreations:* hunting, politics, religion, Indian classical music. *Address:* 129 Trinity Road, SW17 7HJ. *T:* 01-672 1762, (office) 01-242 9228. *Club:* Liberal.

SINGH, Sardar Swaran; President, Indian Council of World Affairs; *b* 19 Aug. 1907. *Educ:* Government College, Lahore; Lahore Law College. MSc (Physics) 1930; LLB 1932. Elected to Punjab Legislative Assembly, 1946; Punjab State Government: Minister for Development, Food and Civil Supplies, 1946–47; Member, Partition Committee, 1947; Minister: of Home, General Administration, Revenue, Irrigation and Electricity, 1947–49; of Capital Projects and Electricity, 1952; for Works, Housing and Supply, 1952–57, Govt of India; Member, Upper House of Indian Legislature, 1952–57; Member, Lower House of Indian Legislature, 1957; Minister: for Steel, Mines and Fuel, 1957–62; for Railways, 1962–63; for Food and Agriculture, 1963–64; for Industry and Supply, 1964; for External Affairs, 1964–66; Foreign Minister, 1970–74, Minister of Defence, 1966–70 and 1974–75. Has led many Indian delegations to the United Nations, its agencies, foreign countries and international conferences. *Address:* c/o Indian National Congress, 5 Dr Rajendra Prasad Road, New Delhi, India.

SINGH BAHADUR, Maharawal Shri Sir Lakshman, GCIE 1947; KCSI 1935; *b* 7 March 1908; *S* father as Maharawal of Dungarpur, 1918; title no longer recognised by the Government of India, 1971; *m* grand-daughter of Raja Saheb of Bhinga, and *d* of Lieut-Col His late Highness Maharajadhiraj Sir Madan Singh Bahadur, KCSI, KCIE, of Kishengarh (wife decd); four *s* four *d. Educ:* Mayo Coll., Ajmer. Visited England, Scotland, Switzerland, France, and other European countries, 1927; invested with full ruling powers, 1928; Mem., Standing Cttee of Chamber of Princes, 1931–47; one of the select Princes chosen by his order to meet Cabinet Mission, 1946; elected Mem., Rajya Sabha, 1952–58; Leader, Rajasthan Assembly Swatantra Party and Leader of Opposition, 1962; Leader of Assembly Swatantra Party, Leader of SVD, and Leader of Opposition, 1967; President: Swatantra Party in Rajasthan, 1961–69; All–India Kshatriya Mahasabha, 1962–. Patron: Rajputana Cricket Assoc.; Cricket Club of India; Mem., MCC; captained Rajputana XI against MCC and Australian XI on four occasions. Is a keen naturalist and is interested in agriculture and study of wild life. *Address:* Udai Bilas Palace, Dungarpur, Rajasthan, India.

See also Maharaja of Bikaner.

SINGHANIA, Sir Padampat, Kt 1943; President of the JK Organisation, India; *b* 1905; *s* of late Lala Kamlapat Singhania; *m* Srimati Anusiya Devi; four *s* one *d. Educ:* Home. A pioneer of Cotton, Rayon, Nylon, Jute, Woollen Textiles, Sugar, Aluminium, Steel and Engineering, Plastic, Strawboard, Paper, Chemicals, Oil Industries, Shipping, Cement, Tyres and Tubes, Dry Cell Batteries, Banking; Patron, large number of social, educational, political, and literary institutions. Founder of the Merchants' Chamber of UP; ex-Pres. of Federation of Indian Chambers of Commerce and Industry; ex-Pres., Employers' Assoc. of Northern India; Member 1st Indian Parliament, 1947–52, and many government and semi-govt bodies; formerly Chairman, Board of Governors, IIT Kanpur. Dr of Letters, Kanpur Univ., 1968. *Recreations:* riding, music, buildings, and studies. *Address:* Kamla Tower, Kanpur 208001, India. *TA:* Laljuggi, Kanpur. *T:* 69854, 51147 and 62988. *Telex* KP215.

SINGHATEH, Alhaji Sir Farimang (Mohamadu), GCMG 1966; JP; Governor-General of The Gambia, 1965–70; *b* 30 Nov. 1912; *m* 1939; three *s* six *d* (and two *s* one *d* decd). *Educ:* Armitage Secondary School, Georgetown, The Gambia. Career as Druggist and Chemist. *Address:* 48 Grant Street, Banjul, The Gambia.

SINGHJI BAHADUR, Dr Karni; *see* Bikaner, Maharaja of.

SINGLETON, Sir Edward (Henry Sibbald), Kt 1975; solicitor; Member of Council, The Law Society, 1961–80 (Vice-President of the Society, 1973, President, 1974); *b* 7 April 1921; *s* of W. P. Singleton, Colwall, and Florence, *d* of Sir Francis Sibbald Scott, 5th Bt; *m* 1943, Margaret Vere Hutton; three *s* one *d. Educ:* Shrewsbury; BNC, Oxford. MA 1946. Served War, as Pilot, Fleet Air Arm, 1941–45. Solicitor, 1949; Partner in Macfarlanes, 1954, consultant 1977. Chm., Solicitors' Law Stationery Soc. Ltd, 1980–. Dir, Abbey National Bldg Soc. and various cos. Mem., Council for the Securities Industry, 1978–. Trustee: Fleet Air Arm Museum; Temple Bar Trust; Westminster Hospital. FCIArb 1982. *Recreation:* relaxing. *Address:* 57 Victoria Road, W8 5RH. *T:* 01-937 2277. *Clubs:* City of London; Vincent's (Oxford).

SINGLETON, Norman, CB 1966; Deputy Chairman, Central Arbitration Committee; Arbitrator and Mediator, Advisory, Conciliation and Arbitration Service; *b* 21 March 1913; *s* of Charles and Alice Singleton, Bolton, Lancs; *m* 1936, Cicely Margaret Lucas, Claverdon, Warwick; one *s* two *d. Educ:* Bolton School; Emmanuel College, Cambridge. Min. of Labour, 1935; Under-Secretary: Civil Service Pay Research Unit, 1956–60; Min. of Labour (now Dept of Employment), 1960–69; Sec., 1969–72, Dep. Chm., 1973–74, Commn on Industrial Relns. *Publication:* Industrial Relations Procedures, 1976. *Address:* 34 Willoughby Road, Hampstead, NW3. *T:* 01-435 1504.

SINHA, 3rd Baron *cr* 1919, of Raipur; **Sudhindro Prosanno Sinha;** Chairman and Managing Director, MacNeill and Barry Ltd, Calcutta; *b* 29 Oct. 1920; *s* of Aroon Kumar, 2nd Baron Sinha (*s* of Satyendra Prasanna, 1st Baron Sinha, the first Indian to be created a peer) and Nirupama, *yr d* of Rai

Bahadur Lalit Mohan Chatterjee; *S* father, 1967; *m* 1945, Madhabi, *d* of late Monoranjan Chatterjee, Calcutta; one *s* two *d* (and one *s* decd). *Educ:* Bryanston School, Blandford. *Heir:* s Hon. Sushanto Sinha, *b* 1953. *Address:* 7 Lord Sinha Road, Calcutta, India.

SINKER, Rt. Rev. George; *b* 5 May 1900; *s* of Rev. R. Sinker; *m* 1924, Eva Margaret Madden; two *s* two *d. Educ:* Rossall School; Brasenose College, Oxford. CMS Missionary, Kandy, Ceylon, 1921; ordained, 1924; Bannu, NWFP, India, 1924; Peshawar, 1932; Headmaster, Bishop Cotton School, Simla 1935; Canon of Lahore Cathedral, 1944; Gen. Sec. Bible Society, India and Ceylon, 1947; Bishop of Nagpur, 1949-54; Asst Bp of Derby, 1954-62; Vicar of Bakewell, 1955-62; Provost of Birmingham Cathedral and Asst Bishop of Birmingham, 1962-72. *Publications:* Jesus Loved Martha, 1949; What was Jesus doing on the Cross?, 1952; His Very Words, 1953. *Recreations:* reading, writing. *Address:* 5 Vicars' Close, Lichfield. *T:* Lichfield 53947.

SINKER, Rev. Canon Michael Roy; Canon Emeritus of Lincoln Cathedral, 1969; *b* 28 Sept. 1908; 3rd *s* of late Rev. Francis Sinker, sometime Vicar of Ilkley; *m* 1939, Edith Watt Applegate; one *s* two *d. Educ:* Haileybury; Clare College, Cambridge (MA); Cuddesdon College, Oxford. Curate of Dalston, Cumberland, 1932-34; Chaplain to South African Church Railway Mission, 1935-38; Curate of Bishop's Hatfield 1938-39; Vicar of Dalton-in-Furness, 1939-46; Vicar of Saffron Walden, 1946-63; Hon. Canon of Chelmsford Cathedral, 1955-63; Rural Dean of Saffron Walden, 1948-63; Archdeacon of Stow, 1963-67; Rector of St Matthew, Ipswich, 1967-77. *Address:* 8 White Horse Way, Westbury, Wilts.

SINNATT, Maj.-Gen. Martin Henry; Chief of Staff to Live Oak, Shape, since 1981; *b* 28 Jan. 1928; *s* of Dr O. S. Sinnatt and Mrs M. H. Sinnatt (*née* Randall); *m* 1957, Susan Rosemary Clarke; four *d. Educ:* Hitchin Grammar School; Hertford College, Oxford (1 Year Army Short Course); RMA Sandhurst. Commissioned RTR, 1948; served Germany, Korea, UK, Hong Kong, 1948-58; psc 1959; Aden, 1959-62; Germany and UK, 1962-64; MA to C-in-C AFNE, Norway, 1964-66; jssc 1967; Germany and UK, 1967-69; CO 4 RTR, BAOR, 1969-71; Nat. Defence Coll., 1971-72; Comdr RAC, 1 (BR) Corps, BAOR, 1972-74; Dir Operational Requirements MoD, 1974-77; rcds 1978; Dir, Combat Development (Army), 1979-81. *Publications:* articles in military jls. *Recreations:* medieval history, gardening and swimming; also, when time and finances permit, skiing and golf. *Address:* c/o Barclays Bank, 201 Church Road, Hove, East Sussex BN3 2AH. *Club:* Army and Navy.

SINNOTT, Ernest; Chairman, South Eastern Electricity Board, 1966-74; *b* 10 March 1909; *s* of John Sinnott and Emily (*née*) Currie; *m* 1934, Simone Marie (*née* Petitjean); two *s. Educ:* Salford Grammar School. City Treasurer's Dept, Salford, 1924-31; City Accountant's Dept, Chester, 1931; Borough Treasurer's Dept, Warrington, 1931-32; Dep. Borough Treasurer, Middleton 1932-35, Worthing 1935-37; Borough Treasurer, Worthing, 1937-48; Chief Accountant, SE Electricity Bd, 1948-62, Dep. Chairman, 1962-66. Chartered Accountant (hons) 1935; FIMTA (Collins gold medal), 1932, now IPFA; Pres. 1956-57. *Publications:* (jointly) Brown's Municipal Book-keeping and Accounts; contribs to learned journals on local government finance. *Recreations:* music, reading and walking. *Address:* Little Court, West Parade, Worthing, West Sussex.

SIRS, William, JP; General Secretary, Iron and Steel Trades Confederation, since 1975; *b* 6 Jan. 1920; *s* of Frederick Sirs and Margaret (*née* Powell); *m* 1941, Joan (*née* Clark); one *s. Educ:* Middleton St Johns, Hartlepool; WEA. Steel Industry, 1937-63; Iron and Steel Trades Confedn: Organiser, 1963; Divisional Officer, Manchester, 1970; Asst Gen. Sec., 1973. Member: Iron and Steel Industry Trng Bd, 1973; TUC Gen. Council, 1975-; Trade Union Steel Industry Cons. Cttee, 1973- (Chm., 1975-) and Jt Accident Prevention Adv. Cttee, 1973; Employment Appeal Tribunal, 1976-; Jt Sec., Jt Industrial Council for Slag Industry, 1973; Exec. Mem., Paul Finet Foundn, European Coal and Steel Community, 1974; Hon. Sec. (British Section), Internat. Metalworkers Fedn, 1975. Mem., Management Cttee, BSC (Industry) Ltd, 1975-. Mem. RIIA, 1973. JP Hartlepool, Co. Durham, Knutsford, Cheshire, 1963. *Recreations:* sailing, squash, swimming, running. *Address:* Swinton House, 324 Gray's Inn Road, WC1X 8DD. *T:* 01-837 6691.

SISSON, Charles Hubert; writer; Joint Editor, PN Review; *b* 22 April 1914; *s* of late Richard Percy Sisson and Ellen Minnie Sisson (*née* Worlock); *m* 1937, Nora Gilbertson; two *d. Educ:* University of Bristol, and in France and Germany. Entered Ministry of Labour as Assistant Principal, 1936; HM Forces, in the ranks, mainly in India, 1942-45; Simon Senior Research Fellow, 1956-57; Dir of Establishments, Min. of Labour, 1962-68; Dir of Occupational Safety and Health, Dept of Employment, 1972. FRSL 1975. Hon. DLitt Bristol, 1980. *Publications:* An Asiatic Romance, 1953; Versions and Perversions of Heine, 1955; The Spirit of British Administration, 1959; The London Zoo (poems), 1961; Numbers (poems); Christopher Homm, 1965; Art and Action, 1965; The Discarnation (poem), 1967; Essays, 1967; Metamorphoses (poems), 1968; English Poetry 1900-1950, 1971; The Case of Walter Bagehot, 1972; In the Trojan Ditch (poems), 1974; The Poetic Art, 1975; The Corridor (poem), 1975; (ed) The English Sermon, Vol. II 1650-1750, 1976; David Hume, 1976; Anchises (poems), 1976; (ed) Selected Poems of Jonathan Swift, 1977; The Avoidance of Literature, 1978; Exactions (poems), 1980; (ed) Autobiographical and Other Papers of Philip Mairet,

1981; Selected Poems, 1981; *translations:* Catullus, 1966; The Poem on Nature, 1976; Some Tales of La Fontaine, 1979; The Divine Comedy, 1980. *Address:* Moorfield Cottage, The Hill, Langport, Somerset. *T:* Langport 250845.

SISSON, Sir Roy, Kt 1980; CEng, FRAeS; Chairman, Smiths Industries Ltd, since 1976; *b* 17 June 1914; *s* of Bernard Sisson and Violet (*née* Hagg); *m* 1943, Constance Mary Cutchey; two *s* two *d. Educ:* Regent Street Polytechnic. De Havilland Aircraft Co. Ltd, 1933-37; Flight Engineer and Station Engineer, BOAC, 1944-47; BOAC rep. at de Havilland Aircraft Co., 1948; Smiths Industries: joined, 1955; Divl Dir, 1964; Chief Exec., Aviation Div., 1966; Managing Dir, 1973; Chm., 1976 (Chief Exec., 1976-81). Pres., SBAC, 1973-74. FBIM. *Recreations:* sailing, tennis. *Address:* Gustard Wood House, Gustard Wood, near Wheathampstead, Herts. *Club:* Royal Dart Yacht.

SITWELL, Rev. Francis Gerard, OSB, MA; *b* 22 Dec. 1906; *s* of late Major Francis Sitwell and Margaret Elizabeth, *d* of late Matthew Culley, Coupland Castle, Northumberland. *Educ:* Ampleforth; St Benet's Hall, Oxford. Received Benedictine Habit, 1924; Professed, 1925; Priest, 1933; Assistant Master at Ampleforth, 1933-39; Assistant Procurator at Ampleforth, 1939-47; Subprior of Ampleforth, 1946-47; Master of St Benet's Hall, Oxford, 1947-64; Priest of Our Lady and St Wilfrid, Warwick Bridge, Carlisle, 1966-69. *Publications:* Walter Hilton, Scale of Perfection, (trans. and ed); St Odo of Cluny; Medieval Spirituality; articles in Ampleforth Journal, Downside Review, Clergy Review, Month, etc. *Address:* Ampleforth Abbey, York YO6 4EN.

SITWELL, Sir Sacheverell, 6th Bt *cr* 1808; *b* Scarborough, 15 Nov. 1897; *s* of Sir George Sitwell, 4th Bt, and Lady Ida Emily Augusta Denison (*d* 1937), *d* of 1st Earl of Londesborough; *S* brother, 1969; *m* 1925, Georgia (*d* 1980), *yr d* of Arthur Doble, Montreal; two *s. Educ:* Eton College. High Sheriff of Northamptonshire, 1948-49. Freedom of City of Lima (Peru), 1960; Benson Silver Medal, RSL, 1981. *Publications:* Southern Baroque Art, 1924; All Summer in a Day, 1926; The Gothick North, 1929; Mozart, 1932; Life of Liszt, 1936; Dance of the Quick and the Dead, 1936; Conversation Pieces, 1936; La Vie Parisienne, 1937; Narrative Pictures, 1937; Roumanian Journey, 1938; Old Fashioned Flowers, 1939; Mauretania, 1939; Poltergeists, 1940; Sacred and Profane Love, 1940; Valse des Fleurs, 1941; Primitive Scenes and Festivals, 1942; The Homing of the Winds, 1942; Splendours and Miseries, 1943; British Architects and Craftsmen, 1945; The Hunters and the Hunted, 1947; The Netherlands, 1948; Selected Poems, 1948; Morning, Noon, and Night in London, 1948; Spain, 1950, new edn 1975; Cupid and the Jacaranda, 1952; Truffle Hunt with Sacheverell Sitwell, 1953: Portugal and Madeira, 1954; Denmark, 1956; Arabesque and Honeycomb, 1957; Malta, 1958; Bridge of the Brocade Sash, 1959; Journey to the Ends of Time; Vol. I, Lost in the Dark Wood, 1959; Golden Wall and Mirador, 1961; The Red Chapels of Banteai Srei, 1962; Monks, Nuns and Monasteries, 1965; Forty-eight Poems (in Poetry Review), 1967; Southern Baroque Revisited, 1968; Gothic Europe, 1969; For Want of the Golden City, 1973; An Indian Summer, an hundred recent poems, 1982; and 15 books of Poetry, 1918-36, with a further 40 small books of Poems, 1972-76. *Recreation:* 'Westerns'. *Heir:* s Sacheverell Reresby Sitwell [*b* 15 April 1927; *m* 1952, Penelope, *yr d* of late Col Hon. Donald Alexander Forbes, DSO, MVO; one *d*]. *Address:* Weston Hall, Towcester, Northants. *Club:* Beefsteak.

SIXSMITH, Maj.-Gen. Eric Keir Gilborne, CB 1951; CBE 1946; *b* 15 Oct. 1904; 2nd *s* of Charles Frederick Gilborne Sixsmith, Barry; *m* 1941, Rosemary Aileen, 4th *d* of Rev. Frederick Ernest Godden; two *s* one *d. Educ:* Harrow; RMC, Sandhurst. Commissioned The Cameronians (Scottish Rifles), 1924; Adjutant 1st Battalion, 1933-34; Staff College, Quetta, 1935-36. Served War of 1939-45; Bde Maj. 2 Inf. Bde, 1939-40; GSO1, 51st Highland Division, 1941-42; Commander 2nd Bn Royal Scots Fusiliers, Italy (wounded), 1944; commanded 2nd Bn Cameronians (Scottish Rifles), 1944; Deputy Director Staff Duties, War Office, 1945-46; Brigade Commander, India, 1946-47; Deputy Director Personnel Administration, War Office, 1947-50; idc 1951; Chief of Staff, Hong Kong, 1952; Chief of Staff, Far East Land Forces, 1952-54; Commanding 43 (Wessex) Infantry Division (TA) 1954-57; Assistant Chief of Staff (Organisation and Training) Supreme Headquarters, Allied Powers Europe, 1957-61, retired. *Publications:* British Generalship in the Twentieth Century, 1970; Eisenhower as Military Commander, 1973; Douglas Haig, 1976. *Recreations:* gardening, music. *Address:* Riversleigh, Langport, Somerset. *T:* Langport 250435. *Club:* Army and Navy.
See also P. G. D. Sixsmith.

SIXSMITH, (Philip) Guy (Dudley); Stipendiary Magistrate for Mid Glamorgan, 1966-75; *b* 5 Nov. 1902; *s* of late C. F. G. Sixsmith, Barry, Glam; *m* 1933, Alice Mary (JP Glam), *d* of C. J. Birch; one *d* (one *s* decd). *Educ:* Barry County Sch.; Harrow; Lincoln Coll., Oxford (MA). Assistant master, Shanghai Cathedral School for Boys, 1929-35; called to the Bar, Inner Temple, 1936; Wales and Chester Circuit. Served War of 1939-45, gazetted 2nd Lt Cameronians (Scottish Rifles), 1940; Middle East and Paiforce, 1940-45. Deputy Judge Advocate (Major), 1942-45 and at War Crime Trials in Germany, 1946-48; Stipendiary Magistrate: Cardiff, 1948-66; Pontypridd, 1966-75; Dep. Chm., Glam QS, 1966-71. Chairman: Cardiff Rent Tribunal, 1947-48; Glam and Gwent Br., Oxford Soc.; Glamorgan Branch, Council for Protection of Rural Wales, 1967-69; Monmouth Diocesan Schools Cttee, 1968-70; Hon. Pres., Soc. of Stipendiary Magistrates of England and Wales (Chm., 1967-75); Pres., D. C. Jones Challenge Cup for Best Kept Village in Vale of Glamorgan, 1970-72 (Chm., 1967-69). Pres., Cardiff E District Scout

Council, 1967-81 (Silver Acorn for services to scouting). Vice-Pres., E Glam and Mon Br., Magistrates' Assoc. (Chm., 1954-66). Member: Council, Magistrates' Assoc., 1952-71; Monmouth Diocesan Board of Finance; Governing Body, and Representative Body, Church in Wales; Court of Governors, University Coll. Cardiff; Court, University of Wales; Exec. Cttee, Council for Protection of Rural Wales, 1967-73; Exec. Cttee, Monmouth and Llandaff Housing Assoc., 1970-81 (Chm., 1975-77). *Recreation:* procrastination. *Address:* 3 Chapel Lane, Sutton Courtenay, near Abingdon, Oxfordshire OX14 4AN. *T:* Sutton Courtenay 7430. *Club:* National Liberal.

See also Maj.-Gen. E. K. G. Sixsmith.

SKAN, Peter Henry O.; *see* Ogle-Skan.

SKEAT, Theodore Cressy, BA; Keeper of Manuscripts and Egerton Librarian, British Museum, 1961-72; *b* 15 Feb. 1907; *s of* Walter William Skeat, MA; *m* 1942, Olive Martin; one *s*. *Educ:* Whitgift School, Croydon; Christ's College, Cambridge. Student at British School of Archaeology, Athens, 1929-31; Asst Keeper, Dept. of Manuscripts, British Musuem, 1931; Deputy Keeper, 1948. FBA, 1963-80. *Publications:* (with H. I. Bell) Fragments of an Unknown Gospel, 1935; (with H. J. M. Milne) Scribes and Correctors of the Codex Sinaiticus, 1938; The Reigns of the Ptolemies, 1954; Papyri from Panopolis, 1964; Catalogue of Greek Papyri in the British Museum, vol. VII, 1974; articles in papyrological journals. *Address:* 63 Ashbourne Road, W5 3DH. *T:* 01-998 1246.

SKEATES, Basil George; Under Secretary, Department of the Environment, since 1980; *b* 19 May 1929; *s of* George William Skeates and Florence Rachel Skeates; *m* 1957, Irene Margaret (*née* Hughes); four *s*. *Educ:* Hampton Grammar Sch. RIBA 1955. Mil. Service with RE, W Africa, 1947-49. Architect with LCC schs and special works, 1949-61; Principal Architect: NE Metrop. Reg. Hosp. Bd, 1961-64; MPBW, 1964-71; Superintending Architect, CSD, 1971-73; Asst Dir, Architectural Services, PSA, 1973-75; Dir of Works, PO Services, 1975-80; Dir of Def. Services II, DoE, 1980-. *Publications:* articles in prof. and technical jls. *Recreation:* designing and making things. *Address:* Department of the Environment/PSA, Whitgift Centre, Wellesley Road, Croydon, Surrey CR9 3LY. *T:* 01-686 8710.

SKEEN, Brig. Andrew, OBE 1945; psc†; *b* 1906; *s of* late Gen. Sir Andrew Skeen, KCB, KCIE, CMG; *m* 1939, Honor St Quintin Beasley (*d* 1975); one *s* one *d*. *Educ:* Wellington College; Sandhurst. 2nd Lt R Berkshire Regt, 1926; Bde Maj., 1939; Lt-Col 1941; Brig., 1943. Served, 1939-45: France, N Africa, Middle East, India and Burma (despatches); retd 1947. Chairman, Industrial Boards; Member, Rhodesian Tourist Board. Life Vice-President, Manicaland Development and Publicity Assoc. Commissioner, Rhodesian Forestry Commission. Mem., Umtali-Odzi Road Council; Chm., Vumba Town Planning Authority. High Comr for Rhodesia in London, July-Nov. 1965. MP for Arundel, Rhodesian Parlt, 1965-74. Independence Commemorative Decoration, Rhodesia, 1971. *Publication:* Prelude to Independence, 1966. *Address:* 75 Forest Glade, Tokai, Cape Town, 7945, Republic of South Africa. *T:* (021)75 6204; c/o Standard Bank, Box 57, Cape Town.

SKEET, Muriel Harvey; Health Services adviser and consultant, World Health Organisation Headquarters and other international agencies and organisations, since 1978; *b* 12 July 1926; *y d of* late Col F. W. C. Harvey-Skeet, Suffolk. *Educ:* privately; Endsleigh House; Middlesex Hosp. SRN, MRSH; FRCN. Gen. Nursing Trg at Middx Hosp., 1946-49; also London Sch. of Hygiene and Tropical Med. Ward Sister and Admin. Sister, Middx Hosp., 1949-60; Field Work Organiser, Opl Res. Unit, Nuffield Provincial Hosps Trust, 1961-64. Res. Org., Dan Mason Nursing Res. Cttee of Nat. Florence Nightingale Memorial Cttee of Gt Britain and N Ire., 1965-70; Chief Nursing Officer and Nursing Advr, BRCS, and St John in Jerusalem and BRCS Jt Cttee, 1970-78. WHO Res. Consultant, SE Asia, 1970; European Deleg. and First Chm. of Bd of Commonwealth Nurses' Fed., 1971. Leverhulme Fellowship, 1974-75. Member: Hosp. and Med. Services Cttee, 1970; Ex-Services War Disabled Help Cttee, 1970; British Commonwealth Nurses War Memorial Fund Cttee and Council, 1970; Council of Management of Nat. Florence Nightingale Memorial Cttee, 1970; Council of Queen's Inst. of District Nursing, 1970; Royal Coll. of Nursing and Nat. Council of Nurses; RSM, 1980. Fellow RCN, 1977. *Publications:* Waiting in Outpatient Departments (Nuffield Provincial Hospitals Trust), 1965; Marriage and Nursing (Dan Mason NRC), 1968; Home from Hospital (Dan Mason NRC), 1970; Home Nursing, 1975; Manual: Disaster Relief Work, 1977; Back to Our Basic Skills, 1977; Health needs Help, 1977; (jtly) Health Auxiliaries in the Health Team, 1978; Self Care for the People of Developing Countries, 1979; Discharge Procedures, 1980; Notes on Nursing 1860 and 1980, 1980; Emergency Procedures and First Aid for Nurses, 1981; The Third Age, 1982; various articles in professional jls. *Recreations:* music, opera, painting, reading. *Address:* 17 Chemin François Lehmann, 1218 Grand Saconnex, Geneva, Switzerland. *T:* Geneva 98.40.38; Oakford House, Nether Stowey, Som. *T:* Nether Stowey 303. *Clubs:* Arts, VAD Ladies.

SKEET, Trevor Herbert Harry; MP (C) Bedford since 1970; Barrister, Writer and Consultant; *b* 28 Jan. 1918; British; *m* 1958, Elizabeth Margaret Gilling (*d* 1973); two *s*. *Educ:* King's College, Auckland; University of New Zealand, Auckland (LLB). Served War of 1939-45, with NZ Engineers (sergeant); 2nd Lieut, NZ Anti-Aircraft (Heavy); Sub-Lieutenant, NZ Roy.

Naval Volunteer Reserve; demobilised, 1945. Formerly Barrister and Solicitor of Supreme Court of New Zealand; Barrister, Inner Temple, 1947. Has considerable experience in public speaking. Contested (C): Stoke Newington and Hackney, North, Gen. Election, 1951; Llanelly Div. of Carmarthenshire, Gen. Election, 1955; MP (C) Willesden East, 1959-64. Formerly associated with Commonwealth and Empire Industries Assoc.; Mem. Council, Royal Commonwealth Soc., 1952-55, and 1956-69. Vice-Chm., Cons. Party Power Cttee, 1959-64; Energy Cttee, 1974-77; Chairman: Oil Sub-Cttee, 1959-64; Cons. Party Trade Cttee, 1971-74; Cons. Party Middle East Cttee (Foreign and Commonwealth Affairs), 1973-78; Secretary: All-Party Cttee on Airships, 1971-78; All-Party Gp on Minerals, 1971- (Co-Chm., 1979); Vice-Chm., British-Japanese and British-Brazilian Gps; Sec., British-Nigerian Gp. Mem., Econ. Cttee, Machine Tool Trades Association for several years; Member Technical Legislation Cttee, CBI. *Publications:* contrib. to numerous journals including New Commonwealth and Mining World, on oil, atomic energy, metals, commodities, finance, and Imperial and Commonwealth development. *Address:* (home) The Gables, Milton Ernest, Bedfordshire MK44 1RS. *T:* Oakley 2307; 1 Harcourt Buildings, Temple, EC4. *T:* 01-353 2214. *Clubs:* Army and Navy, Royal Commonwealth Society.

SKEFFINGTON, family name of **Viscount Massereene and Ferrard.**

SKEFFINGTON-LODGE, Thomas Cecil; *b* 15 Jan. 1905; *s of* late Thomas Robert Lodge and late Winifred Marian Skeffington; unmarried. *Educ:* privately; Giggleswick and Westminster Schools. For some years engaged in Advertising and Publicity both in London and the North of England; later did Public Relations and administrative work in the Coal Trade as Northern Area Organiser for the Coal Utilisation Council, in which he served Cttees of Coal Trade in North-East, North-West and Yorkshire; on the outbreak of war, became a Mines Dept official; then volunteered for the Navy; from early 1941 a Naval Officer. Mem., Parly Delegn, Nüremberg Trials. Lecture tour in USA under auspices of Anglo-American Parly Gp, 1949. MP (Lab) Bedford, 1945-50; contested (Lab) York, 1951, Mid-Bedfordshire, 1955; Grantham, 1959; Brighton (Pavilion), March 1969; Personal Asst to Chm., Colonial Development Corp., 1950-52. Mem. of post-war Parly Delegns to Eire, Belgium, Luxembourg and USA; formerly Mem., Parly Ecclesiastical Cttee, and served on Parochial Church Council, St Margaret's, Westminster. Past-Pres. and Chm., Pudsey Divisional Labour Party; Pres., Brighton and Hove Fabian Soc.; Member: Labour Party many years; Socialist Christian Movement (Vice-Pres.); IPU; Exec. Cttee, Brighton and Hove Br. UNA; German-British Christian Fellowship (past Chm.); Union of Shop, Distributive and Allied Workers; Conservation Soc.; CPRE (Chm., Brighton Dist Cttee, Sussex Branch); RSPB; Georgian Group; Friends of the Lake District; Amnesty Internat.; British-Soviet Friendship Soc.; Anglo-German Assoc.; Anglo-Belgian Assoc.; former Chm., Socialist Christian League and Parly Socialist Christian Group. *Recreations:* travel, gardening, politics and associating Christianity with them, in the hope of erecting fairer national and international living conditions for mankind. *Address:* 5 Powis Grove, Brighton, East Sussex. *T:* Brighton 25472. *Club:* Savile.

SKELHORN, Sir Norman John, KBE 1966; QC 1954; a Recorder of the Crown Court, 1977-81; Director of Public Prosecutions, 1964-77; *b* Glossop, Derbyshire, 10 Sept. 1909; *s of* late Rev. Samuel and late Bertha Skelhorn; *m* 1937, Rosamund, *d of* late Prof. James Swain, CB, CBE; no *c*. *Educ:* Shrewsbury School. Called to Bar, Middle Temple, 1931, Master of the Bench, 1962. Member of Western Circuit; employed in Trading with the Enemy Dept (Treasury and Board of Trade), 1940-42; in Admiralty, 1942-45, latterly as head of Naval Law Branch. Recorder, Bridgwater, 1945-54; Plymouth, 1954-62; Portsmouth, 1962-64. Chairman, Isle of Wight County Quarter Sessions, 1951-64. Member, Departmental Cttee on Probation Service, 1959-61; Appointed Member of Home Secretary's Advisory Council on Treatment of Offenders, 1962; Member Home Secretary's: Probation Advisory and Training Board, 1962-73; Criminal Law Revision Cttee, 1964-80. *Publication:* Public Prosecutor: the Memoirs of Sir Norman Skelhorn, Director of Public Prosecutions, 1964-1977, 1981. *Clubs:* Athenæum, Royal Automobile.

SKELLERUP, Sir Valdemar (Reid), Kt 1979; CBE 1973; Chairman and Joint Managing Director, Skellerup Industries Ltd, since 1961; *b* 22 Dec. 1907; *s of* George Waldemar Skjellerup and Elizabeth Skjellerup; *m* 1933, Marion Caroline Bates; one *s* three *d*. *Educ:* Ashburton High Sch.; Canterbury University Coll. *Address:* 110 North Parade, Shirley, Christchurch 1, New Zealand. *T:* 852-245.

SKELMERSDALE, 7th Baron *cr* 1828; **Roger Bootle-Wilbraham;** a Lord in Waiting (Government Whip), since 1981; *b* 2 April 1945; *o s* of 6th Baron Skelmersdale, DSO, MC, and Ann (*d* 1974), *d of* late Percy Cuthbert Quilter; *S* father, 1973; *m* 1972, Christine Joan, *o d of* Roy Morgan; one *s* one *d*. *Educ:* Eton; Lord Wandsworth Coll., Basingstoke; Somerset Farm Institute; Hadlow Coll. VSO (Zambia), 1969-71; Proprietor, Broadleigh Gardens, 1972; Man. Dir, Broadleigh Nurseries Ltd, 1973-81; Vice-Chm., Co En Co, 1979-81. President: Somerset Trust for Nature Conservation, 1980-; British Naturalists Trust, 1980-. *Recreations:* gardening, reading, bridge playing. *Heir:* *s* Hon. Andrew Bootle-Wilbraham, *b* 9 Aug. 1977. *Address:* Barr House, Bishops Hull, Taunton, Somerset. *T:* Taunton 70655.

SKELTON, Rt. Rev. Kenneth John Fraser; *see* Lichfield, Bishop of.

SKELTON, Rear-Adm. Peter, CB 1956; *b* 27 Dec. 1901; *s* of Peter John and Selina Frances Skelton; *m* 1928, Janice Brown Clark; two *d. Educ:* RN Colleges, Osborne and Dartmouth; Trinity Hall, Cambridge. Cadet, 1915; Midshipman, HMS Valiant, 1918; Commander, 1936; Capt. 1944; Rear-Adm., 1953. Served War of 1939-45, as Staff Officer in HMS Aurora, later at Admiralty in Torpedo Division; Commander and Actg Capt. in HMS Royal Sovereign, 1942; Director of Trade Div., Admiralty, 1944; Supt of Torpedo Experimental Establishment, 1946; Sen. Naval Officer, Persian Gulf, 1949; Captain of Dockyard, Portsmouth, 1951; Admiral Superintendent, Rosyth, 1953-56; retired. Bucks CC, 1958. *Recreations:* golf, tennis, shooting. *Address:* Craigie Barns, Kippen, Stirlingshire.

SKELTON, Robert William; Keeper, Indian Department, Victoria and Albert Museum, since 1978; *b* 11 June 1929; *s* of John William Skelton and Victoria (*née* Wright); *m* 1954, Frances Aird; three *s. Educ:* Tiffin Boys' Sch., Kingston-upon-Thames. Joined Indian Section of Victoria and Albert Museum, 1950; Asst Keeper, 1960; Dep. Keeper, 1972; Nuffield Travelling Fellow in India, 1962. Mem. Council, Royal Asiatic Soc., 1970-73, 1975-78; Trustee, Asia House Trust (London), 1977-. *Publications:* Indian Miniatures from the XVth to XIXth Centuries, 1961; Rajasthani Temple Hangings of the Krishna Cult, 1973; (jtly) Islamic Painting and Arts of the Book, 1976; (jtly) Indian Painting, 1978; (jtly) Arts of Bengal, 1979; (jtly) The Indian Heritage, 1982; various contribs to art periodicals and conf. proc., 1956-. *Recreations:* chamber music, walking. *Address:* 10 Spencer Road, South Croydon CR2 7EH. *T:* 01-688 7187.

SKELTON, Prof. Robin, FRSL; author; Professor of English, since 1966, and Chairman of Department of Creative Writing, 1973-76, University of Victoria, British Columbia; *b* 12 Oct. 1925; *o s* of Cyril Frederick William and Eliza Skelton; *m* 1957, Sylvia Mary Jarrett; one *s* two *d. Educ:* Pocklington Grammar Sch., 1936-43; Christ's Coll., Cambridge, 1943-44; Univ. of Leeds, 1947-51. BA 1950, MA 1951. Served RAF 1944-47. Asst Lectr in English, Univ. of Manchester, 1951; Lectr, 1954. Managing Dir, The Lotus Press, 1950-52; Examiner for NUJMB, 1954-58; Chm. of Examrs in English, 'O' Level, 1958-60; Co-founder and Chm., Peterloo Gp, Manchester, 1957-60; Founding Mem. and Hon. Sec., Manchester Inst. of Contemporary Arts, 1960-63; Centenary Lectr at Univ. of Massachusetts, 1962-63; Gen. Editor, OUP edn of Works of J. M. Synge, 1962-68; Associate Prof. of English, Univ. of Victoria, BC, 1963-66. Visiting Prof., Univ. of Michigan, Ann Arbor, 1967; Dir, Creative Writing Programme, Univ. of Victoria, 1967-73; Founder and co-Editor, Malahat Review, 1967-71, Editor 1972-83. Mem. Bd of Dirs, Art Gall. of Greater Victoria, BC, 1968-69, 1970-73; Dir, Pharos Press, 1972-; Editor, Sono Nis Press, 1976-. FRSL 1966. Chm., Writers' Union of Canada, 1982 (first Vice-Chm., 1981). *Publications: poetry* Patmos and Other Poems, 1955; Third Day Lucky, 1958; Two Ballads of the Muse, 1960; Begging the Dialect, 1960; The Dark Window, 1962; A Valedictory Poem, 1963; An Irish Gathering, 1964; A Ballad of Billy Barker, 1965; Inscriptions, 1967; Because of This, 1968; The Hold of Our Hands, 1968; Selected Poems, 1947-67, 1968; An Irish Album, 1969; Georges Zuk, Selected Verse, 1969; Answers, 1969; The Hunting Dark, 1971; Two Hundred Poems from the Greek Anthology, 1971; A Different Mountain, 1971; A Private Speech, 1971; Remembering Synge, 1971; Three for Herself, 1972; Musebook, 1972; Country Songs, 1973; Timelight, 1974; Georges Zuk: The Underwear of the Unicorn, 1975; Callsigns, 1976; Because of Love, 1977; Landmarks, 1979; Collected Shorter Poems 1947-1977, 1981; Limits, 1981; De Nihilo, 1982; Zuk, 1982; *prose:* John Ruskin: The Final Years, 1955; The Poetic Pattern, 1956; Cavalier Poets, 1960; Poetry (in Teach Yourself series), 1963; The Writings of J. M. Synge, 1971; J. M. Synge and His World, 1971; The Practice of Poetry, 1971; J. M. Synge (Irish Writers series), 1972; The Poet's Calling, 1975; Poetic Truth, 1978; Spellcraft, 1978; They Call It The Cariboo, 1980; Talismanic Magic, 1983; *drama:* The Paper Cage, 1982; *edited texts:* J. M. Synge: Translations, 1961; J. M. Synge, Four Plays and the Aran Islands, 1962; J. M. Synge, Collected Poems, 1962; Edward Thomas, Selected Poems, 1962; Selected Poems of Byron, 1965; David Gascoyne, Collected Poems, 1965; J. M. Synge, Riders to the Sea, 1969; David Gascoyne, Collected Verse Translations (with Alan Clodd), 1970; J. M. Synge, Translations of Petrarch, 1971; Jack B. Yeats, Collected Plays, 1971; *anthologies:* Leeds University Poetry, 1949, 1950; Viewpoint, 1962; Six Irish Poets, 1962; Poetry of the Thirties, 1964; Five Poets of the Pacific Northwest, 1964; Poetry of the Forties, 1968; The Cavalier Poets, 1970; Six Poets of British Columbia, 1980; *symposia:* The World of W. B. Yeats (with Ann Saddlemyer), 1965; Irish Renaissance (with David R. Clark), 1965; Herbert Read: a memorial symposium, 1970. *Recreations:* book collecting, art collecting, making collages, stone carving, philately. *Address:* 1255 Victoria Avenue, Victoria, BC, Canada. *T:* (604) 592-7032.

SKEMP, Prof. Joseph Bright, MA Cantab, PhD Edinburgh; Emeritus Professor of Greek, in the University of Durham; *b* 10 May 1910; *s* of late Thomas William Widlake Skemp, solicitor and local government officer, and Caroline (*née* Southall); *m* 1941, Ruby James; no *c. Educ:* Wolverhampton Grammar School; Gonville and Caius College, Cambridge. Unofficial Drosier Fellow, Gonville and Caius College, Cambridge, 1936-47; Warden of Refugee Club and Asst Sec. to Refugee Cttee, Cambridge, 1940-46; Sec., Soc. for the Protection of Science and Learning, 1944-46; Lecturer in Greek and Latin, Univ. of Manchester, 1946-49; Reader in Greek, Univ. of Durham (Newcastle Div.), 1949-50; Prof. of Greek, Univ. of Durham, 1950-73; Vis. Prof., Univ. of Alexandria, 1977. Editor, Durham University Journal, 1953-57; Joint Editor, Phronesis, 1955-64. *Publications:* The Theory of Motion in Plato's Later Dialogues, 1942 (enlarged 1967); Plato's Statesman, 1952; The Greeks and the Gospel, 1964; Plato (supplementary vol. periodical Greece and Rome), 1976. *Recreations:* walking, history of railways. *Address:* 10 Highsett, Hills Road, Cambridge CB2 1NX. *T:* Cambridge 68292; 4 Heol y Dwr, Abergynolwyn, Tywyn, Gwynedd.

SKEMP, Terence Rowland Frazer, CB 1973; Counsel to the Speaker, since 1980; Barrister-at-Law; *b* 14 Feb. 1915; *s* of Frank Whittingham Skemp and Dorothy Frazer; *m* 1939, Dorothy Norman Pringle; one *s* two *d. Educ:* Charterhouse; Christ Church, Oxford. Called to Bar, Gray's Inn, 1938. Served War, Army, 1939-46. Entered Parliamentary Counsel Office, 1946; Parliamentary Counsel, 1964; Second Parly Counsel, 1973-80. *Address:* 997 Finchley Road, NW11.

SKEMPTON, Prof. Alec Westley, DSc London 1949; FRS 1961; FEng; FICE; Professor of Civil Engineering in the University of London (Imperial College) 1957-81, now Emeritus; Senior Research Fellow, Imperial College, since 1981; *b* 4 June 1914; *o c* of late A. W. Skempton, Northampton, and Beatrice Edridge Payne; *m* 1940, Mary, *d* of E. R. Wood, Brighouse, Yorks; two *d. Educ:* Northampton Grammar School; Imperial College, University of London (Goldsmiths' Bursar). Building Research Station, 1936-46; University Reader in Soil Mechanics, Imperial College, 1946-54; Professor of Soil Mechanics, Imperial College, 1955-57. Vice-Pres., 1974-76 (Member Council, 1949-54), Institute Civil Engineers; Pres., Internat. Soc. Soil Mechanics and Foundn Eng, 1957-61; Chm. Jt Cttee on Soils, Min. of Supply and Road Research Bd, 1954-59; Mem., Cathedrals Advisory Cttee, 1964-70; Mem., NERC, 1973-76; President: Newcomen Soc., 1977-79; Smeatonian Soc., 1981. Hitchcock Foundn Prof., Univ. of Calif, Berkeley, 1978; Lectures: Copenhagen, Paris, Harvard, Univ. of Illinois, Oslo, Stockholm, Madrid, Florence, Sydney, Quebec, Mexico City, Tokyo, Berkeley; Special Lectr, Architectural Assoc. 1948-57; Vis. Lectr Cambridge Univ. School of Architecture, 1962-66; Consultant to Binnie & Partners, John Mowlem & Co., etc. For. Associate, Nat. Acad. of Engineering, USA, 1976. Hon. DSc: Durham, 1968; Aston, 1980; Chalmers, 1982. Ewing Medal, 1968; Lyell Medal, 1972; Dickinson Medal, 1974; Karl Terzaghi Award, 1981; IStructE Gold Medal, 1981. Silver Jubilee Medal, 1977. *Publications:* Early Printed Reports in the Institution of Civil Engineers, 1977; (with C. Hadfield) William Jessop, Engineer, 1979; John Smeaton, FRS, 1981; numerous papers on soil mechanics, engineering geology and history of construction. *Recreations:* field and archive research on 18th cent. civil engineering and engineers, croquet. *Address:* Imperial College, SW7. *T:* 01-589 5111; 16 The Boltons, SW10. *T:* 01-370 3457. *Clubs:* Athenæum, Hurlingham.

SKERMAN, Ronald Sidney, CBE 1974; Director, Prudential Corporation plc, since 1980 (Group Chief Actuary, 1979); *b* 1 June 1914; *s* of S. H. Skerman; *m* 1939, Gladys Mary Fosdike; no *c. Educ:* Hertford Grammar School. FIA. Actuarial Trainee with Prudential, 1932; Chief Actuary, 1968-79. Pres., Inst. Actuaries, 1970-72; Chm., Life Offices Assoc., 1973-74; Chm., British European Insurance Cttee, 1972-82; Mem., Royal Commn on Civil Liability, 1973-78. Gold Medal, Inst. of Actuaries, 1980. *Publications:* contrib. Jl Inst. Actuaries. *Recreations:* walking, travel, music. *Address:* 30 Springfields, Broxbourne, Herts EN10 7LX. *T:* Hoddesdon 63257.

SKEWIS, (William) Iain, PhD; Chief Executive, Development Board for Rural Wales, since 1977; *b* 1 May 1936; *s* of John Jamieson and Margaret Middlemass Skewis; *m* 1963, Jessie Frame Weir; one *s* one *d. Educ:* Hamilton Academy; Univ. of Glasgow (BSc, PhD). MCIT. British Rail, 1961-63; Transport Holding Co., 1963-66; Highlands and Islands Development Bd, 1966-72; Yorkshire and Humberside Development Assoc., 1973-77. *Recreation:* soccer. *Address:* Rock House, The Square, Montgomery, Powys SY15 6RA. *T:* Montgomery 276.

SKIDELSKY, Prof. Robert Jacob Alexander, DPhil; FRHistS, FRSL; Professor of International Studies, Warwick University, since 1978; *b* 25 April 1939; *s* of Boris Skidelsky and Galia Sapelkin; *m* 1970, Augusta Mary Clarissa Hope; two *s* one *d. Educ:* Brighton Coll.; Jesus Coll., Oxford (BA and MA Mod. Hist.; DPhil). FRHistS 1973; FRSL 1978. Res. Fellow: Nuffield Coll., Oxford, 1965-68; British Acad., 1968-70; Associate Prof. of History, Sch. of Advanced Internat. Studies, Johns Hopkins Univ., Washington, DC, 1970-76; Head, Dept of History, Philosophy and Eur. Studies, Polytechnic of N London, 1976-78. *Publications:* Politicians and the Slump, 1967; English Progressive Schools, 1969; Oswald Mosley, 1975, 2nd edn 1980; (ed) The End of the Keynesian Era, 1977; (ed, with Michael Holroyd) William Gerhardie's God's Fifth Column, 1981; contrib. Encounter, Spectator, TLS, New Soc. *Recreations:* opera, ballet, cinema, squash, tennis, table tennis. *Address:* 32 Great Percy Street, WC1X 9QR. *T:* 01-278 4051. *Club:* Naval and Military.

SKILBECK, Dunstan, CBE 1957; MA Oxon; FIBiol; Principal, Wye College, University of London, 1945-68; Hon. Fellow, Wye College; *b* 13 June 1904; 2nd *s* of late Clement Oswald Skilbeck, FSA, and Elizabeth Bertha Skilbeck; *m* 1934, Elspeth Irene Jomini, *d* of late Edward Carruthers, MD, and Mary Carruthers; two *s* one *d. Educ:* University College School, London; St John's College, Oxford. Agricultural Economics Res. Inst., University of Oxford, 1927-30; Univ. Demonstrator in School of Rural Economy, University of Oxford; Director of St John's College Farm; Lecturer and Tutor in Rural Economy, St John's College, Oxford, 1930-40. Served with RAF Home and Middle East, Air Staff HQ, Middle East, 1940-45; as Wing Comdr, appointed Asst Director, Middle East Supply Centre (Food Production), 1942-45 (despatches). Vice-Chm. Imperial Coll. of Tropical Agric., 1958-60; Liaison Officer to Minister of Agriculture, for SE England, 1952-60; Mem., Ghana Commn on Univ. Educn., 1961; Chairman: Collegiate Council, Univ. of London, 1962-65 (Mem., Senate, 1959-68); Canterbury Diocesan Adv. Cttee, 1970-81. Member Council: Voluntary Service Overseas, 1964-68; England and Wales Nature Conservancy, 1968-73; Vice-Chm., CPRE, 1974-80, Vice-Pres., 1980-. Trustee, Ernest Cook Trust, 1966-. Liveryman, Worshipful Co. of Fruiterers, 1960. *Publications:* contribs to scientific and agricultural jls. *Address:* Mount Bottom, Elham, near Canterbury, Kent. *T:* Elham 258.

SKILLINGTON, William Patrick Denny, CB 1964; a Deputy Secretary, Department of the Environment (formerly Ministry of Public Building and Works), 1966-73; Housing Commissioner, for Clay Cross UDC, 1973-74; *b* 13 Feb. 1913; *s* of late S. J. Skillington, Leicester; *m* 1941, Dorin Kahn, Sydney, Australia; two *d. Educ:* Malvern College; Exeter College, Oxford. BA 1935, MA 1939, Oxford. Articled to Clerk of Leicestershire CC, 1936-39. Commissioned in R Welch Fusiliers (SR), 1933; served War of 1939-45 (despatches); regimental officer in France and Belgium, and on staff in Sicily, Italy and Greece; AA and QMG; Lt-Col. Entered Min. of Works as Principal, 1946; Asst Sec., 1952; Under-Sec. (Dir of Establishments), Min. of Public Building and Works, 1956-64; Asst Under-Sec. of State, Home Office, 1964-66. *Address:* 95a S Mark's Road, Henley-on-Thames, Oxon. *T:* Henley 3756. *Clubs:* United Oxford & Cambridge University; Phyllis Court (Henley).

SKINGSLEY, Air Vice-Marshal Anthony Gerald; Assistant Chief of Staff, Plans and Policy, Supreme Headquarters Allied Powers in Europe, 1980-82; *b* 19 Oct. 1933; *s* of Edward Roberts Skingsley; *m* 1957, Lilwen; two *s* one *d. Educ:* St Bartholomew's, Newbury; Cambridge Univ. (BA, MA). Commissioned RAFVR 1954, RAF 1955; several flying appointments, then Flt Comdr 13 Sqdn, 1961-62; OC Ops Sqdn, RAF Akrotiri, 1962-63; RAF Staff Coll., Bracknell, 1964; OC 45 Sqdn, RAF Tengah, Singapore, 1965-67; jssc Latimer, 1968; RAF Project Officer for Tornado in MoD, 1968-71; OC 214 Sqdn, RAF Marham, 1972-74; Station Comdr, RAF Laarbruch, Germany, 1974-76; Hon. ADC to the Queen, 1976-78; Asst Chief of Staff, Offensive Ops, HQ 2nd ATAF, 1977; RCDS 1978; Director of Air Staff Plans, MoD, 1978-80. Mem., Allgemeine Rheinlaendische Industrie Gesellschaft, 1975. *Recreations:* travel, off-shore sailing, music, walking. *Address:* c/o National Westminster Bank, 30 Market Place, Newbury, Berks. *Club:* Royal Air Force.

SKINNARD, Frederick William; Retired as Registrar and External Director of Examinations, the Institute of Optical Science (1951-59); *b* 8 March 1902; *s* of late F. W. Skinnard, bookplate designer and engraver, Plymouth; *m* 1st, 1931, Muriel M. Lightfoot (*d* 1959); 2nd, 1960, Greta Cory Anthony. *Educ:* Devonport High School; Borough Road Training College, Isleworth. Taught under LCC Education Authority, 1922-24; from 1924 to 1945 served in Willesden schools where his pioneer work in citizenship training and local survey work attracted much attention. Lecturer to teachers' courses in England and abroad. Invited to tour the USA in 1937, and while there and in Canada made a special study of labour problems. Earliest political experience gained in the Union of Democratic Control under the late E. D. Morel. A member of the Labour Party since 1924; served on Harrow and Hendon Divisional Executives and as Vice-Pres.; MP (Lab) Harrow East, 1945-50; member of the Executive of Middlesex Federation of Labour Parties; Chairman Middlesex Labour Joint Consultative Committee. Visited Jamaica, 1946; Member Parliamentary Delegn to W Africa, 1947; Member Labour Party's Advisory Cttee on Imperial Affairs; Lecturer and writer on Colonial Problems; Mem. of Fabian Soc., NUT, Roy. Soc. of Teachers. Pres., Harrow Fifty Club. Hon. Fellow Inst. Optical Science, 1957. *Publications:* Willesden Memorandum, in The Extra School Year; Leaving Papers for Senior Schools (privately printed, 1934 and 1935); Co-editor of Education for Citizenship in the Elementary School, 1935; The Juvenile Delinquent and the Community (The World's Children), 1946; Training and Function of the Ophthalmic Optician, 1950; contrib. reviews on French literature and continental history to Books & Bookmen. *Recreations:* gardening and youth club work. *Address:* 4 Hawthorn Avenue, Bude, Cornwall EX23 8PT. *T:* Bude 3468.

SKINNER, Prof. Andrew Forrester, MA, BSc, PhD (St Andrews); MA (Columbia); FEIS; Professor of Education, Ontario College of Education, University of Toronto, 1954-70, now Emeritus Professor; *b* 21 May 1902; *s* of Alexander H. and Jessie F. Skinner, Kingskettle, Scotland; *m* 1932, Elizabeth Balmer Lockhart, Manchester. *Educ:* Bell-Baxter School, Cupar, Fife; University of St Andrews. MA, BSc, 1st Cl. Hons Maths and Phys Sci., 1925; Carnegie Research Fellow in Chemistry, PhD, 1928; Commonwealth Fund Fellow, Columbia, New York, 1929-31 (Educ. MA); Teacher in various schools, 1931-37; Asst Dir of Education, Co. of Aberdeen, 1937-39; Principal Lecturer in Methods, Dundee Trg Coll., 1939-41; Prof. of Education, Univ. of St Andrews, and Principal, Dundee Trg Coll., 1941-54. Vis. Prof. Ontario Coll. of Educ., Univ. of Toronto, 1950 and 1954; Visiting Professor: E. Tennessee State Coll., 1951, State Univ. of Iowa, 1951-52; Univ. of British Columbia, 1962; Univ. of Victoria, 1964; Queen's Univ., Kingston, 1971. Former Member: Scottish Council for Research in Education; Scottish Universities Entrance Bd; School Broadcasting Council for Scotland; Mem., Bd of Directors, Comparative Education Soc. of USA; Mem. Exec., Comparative and Internat. Educn Soc. of Canada, Vice-Pres., 1968-69, Pres., 1969-70, now Hon. Mem. *Publications:* (Booklet) Scottish Education in Schools, 1942; (Booklet) Introductory Course on Education in Scotland, 1944; Citizenship

in the Training of Teachers, 1948; Teachers' Heritage: an introduction to the study of education, 1979; articles in Jl of Amer. Chem. Soc.; Trans. Chem. Soc.; Scottish Educnal Jl; The Year Book of Education; Educnal Forum: Educational Record of Quebec; The American People's Encyclopedia; Canadian and International Education; Canadian Education and Research Digest. *Recreations:* golf, gardening and walking. *Address:* 296 Ferry Road, Edinburgh EH5 3NP. *T:* 031-552 4907.

SKINNER, Burrhus Frederic; Emeritus Professor, Harvard University, since 1975; *b* Susquehanna, 20 March 1904; *s* of William Arthur Skinner and Grace (née Burrhus); *m* 1936, Yvonne Blue; two *d. Educ:* Hamilton Coll.; Harvard Univ. AB Hamilton 1926; MA 1930, PhD 1931, Harvard. Res. Fellow NRC, Harvard, 1931-33; Jr Fellow, Harvard Soc. Fellows, 1933-36; Minnesota Univ.: Instr Psychol., 1936-37; Asst Prof., 1937-39; Assoc. Prof., 1939-45; conducted war research sponsored by Gen. Mills, Inc., 1942-43; Guggenheim Fellow, 1944-45; Prof. Psychol., Chm. Dept, Indiana Univ., 1945-48; Harvard Univ.: William James Lectr, 1947; Prof. Psychol., 1948-57; Edgar Pierce Prof., 1958-75. FRSA; Member: Brit. and Swedish Psychol Socs; Amer. Psychol Assoc.; AAAS; Nat. Acad. Sci.; Amer. Acad. Arts and Scis; Amer. Phil Soc.; Phi Beta Kappa; Sigma Xi. Holds numerous hon. degrees; has won many awards. *Publications:* Behavior of Organisms, 1938; Walden Two, 1948; Science and Human Behavior, 1953; Verbal Behavior, 1957; (with C. B. Ferster) Schedules of Reinforcement, 1957; Cumulative Record, 1959, rev. 1961; (with J. G. Holland) The Analysis of Behavior, 1961; The Technology of Teaching, 1968; Contingencies of Reinforcement: A Theoretical Analysis, 1969; Beyond Freedom and Dignity, 1971; About Behaviorism, 1974; Particulars of My Life, 1976; The Shaping of a Behaviorist, 1979; Notebooks, 1980; Skinner for the Classroom, 1982. *Address:* 11 Old Dee Road, Cambridge, Mass 02138, USA. *T:* 864-0848.

SKINNER, Dennis Edward; MP (Lab) Bolsover since 1970; Miner at Glapwell Colliery; *b* 11 Feb. 1932; good working-class mining stock; *m* 1960; one *s* two *d. Educ:* Tupton Hall Grammar Sch.; Ruskin Coll., Oxford. Miner, 1949-70. Mem., Nat. Exec. Cttee of Labour Party, 1978-. Pres., Derbyshire Miners (NUM), 1966-70; Pres., NE Derbs Constituency Labour Party, 1968-71; Derbyshire CC, 1964-70; Clay Cross UDC, 1960-70. *Recreations:* tennis, cycling, walking. *Address:* House of Commons, SW1; 86 Thanet Street, Clay Cross, Chesterfield, Derbyshire. *T:* Clay Cross 863429. *Clubs:* Miners' Welfares in Derbyshire; Bestwood Working Men's.

SKINNER, Ernest Harry Dudley, CBE 1957; Member, Colonial Development Corporation, 1958-60; *b* 1892; *m* 1921, Edith Lilian Stretton; one *s* one *d. Educ:* private school. Entered service of Bank of England, 1911; for several years acted as Private Secretary to Governor, Rt Hon. M. C. Norman, DSO (later Lord Norman); Deputy Secretary, 1932; Asst to Governors, 1935-45; General Manager to Finance Corporation for Industry from its formation in 1945 until 1948. Chm., Northern Div., NCB, 1948-50; Chairman, Durham Division, National Coal Board, 1950-57. Mem. of Council, OStJ for County Durham, 1951-57. Member, Newcastle Regional Hospital Board, 1958-59. Vice-Pres., NE Div., Northern Counties ABA, 1954-59. JP Durham County, 1957-59. *Address:* Perrins House, Moorlands Road, Malvern, Worcs WR14 2TZ.

SKINNER, Hon. Sir Henry (Albert), Kt 1980; **Hon. Mr Justice Skinner;** a Judge of the High Court of Justice, Queen's Bench Division, since 1980; *b* 20 May 1926; *s* of Albert and Emma Mary Skinner; *m* 1949, Joan Weston Cassin; two *d. Educ:* Wyggeston Grammar Sch., Leicester; St John's Coll., Oxford. RNVR, 1944-47. Called to Bar, Lincoln's Inn, 1950 (Cholmeley Scholar), Bencher, 1973; QC 1965. A Recorder, 1966-75 (Recorder of Leicester, 1966-71; Hon. Recorder, 1972-80); a Circuit Judge, 1975-80. Dep. Chm., Notts QS, 1966-69; Chm., Lincolnshire (Lindsey) QS, 1968-71 (Dep. Chm., 1963-67). Mem. Parole Bd, 1970-73. Leader, Midland and Oxford Circuit, 1973-75. Treasurer, Univ. of Leicester, 1976-80. Hon. LLD Leicester, 1982. *Recreations:* gardening, walking, listening to music. *Address:* 18 Pendene Road, Leicester LE2 3DQ. *T:* Leicester 704092.

SKINNER, James John, QC; **Hon. Mr Justice Skinner;** Chief Justice of Malawi, since 1970; *b* 24 July 1923; *o* *s* of late William Skinner, Solicitor, Clonmel, Ireland; *m* 1950, Regina Brigitte Reiss; three *s* two *d. Educ:* Clongowes Wood Coll.; Trinity Coll., Dublin; King's Inns, Dublin. Called to Irish Bar, 1946; joined Leinster Circuit; called to English Bar, Gray's Inn, 1950; called to Bar of Northern Rhodesia, 1951; QC (Northern Rhodesia) 1964; MP (UNIP) Lusaka East, 1964-68; Minister of Justice, 1964-65; Attorney-General, 1965-69 (in addition, Minister of Legal Affairs, 1967-68); Chief Justice of Zambia, March-Sept. 1969. Grand Comdr, Order of Menelik II of Ethiopia, 1965. *Recreation:* reading. *Address:* c/o The High Court, PO Box 30244, Chichiri, Blantyre 3, Malawi; 65 Castlenau, SW13. *T:* 01-748 1228. *Club:* Irish.

SKINNER, Joyce Eva, CBE 1975; Academic Secretary, Universities' Council for the Education of Teachers, since 1979; *b* 20 Sept. 1920; *d* of Matthew and Ruth Eva Skinner. *Educ:* Christ's Hosp.; Girls' High Sch., Lincoln; Somerville Coll., Oxford. BA 1941, MA 1945. Bridlington Girls' High Sch., 1942-45; Perse Girls' Sch., 1946-50; Keswick Sch., 1950-52; Homerton Coll., Cambridge, 1952-64; Vis. Prof., Queen's Coll., NY, 1955-56; Principal, Bishop Grosseteste Coll., Lincoln, 1964-74; Dir, Cambridge Inst. of Educn, 1974-80. Fellow, Hughes Hall, Cambridge, 1974. Hon. Fellow, Coll. of

Preceptors, 1971. *Recreations:* walking, reading, conversation. *Address:* 10 Natal Road, Cambridge CB1 3NS. *T:* Cambridge 240484.

SKINNER, Sir Keith; *see* Skinner, Sir T. K. H.

SKINNER, Martyn; *b* 1906; *s* of late Sir Sydney Skinner; *m* 1938, Pauline Giles; three *s* one *d* (and one *s* one *d* decd). *Educ:* two well-known Public Schools; Magdalen College, Oxford (no degree taken). Hawthornden prize, 1943; Heinemann Award, 1947; Runner-up, Barley Championship, Brewers' Exhibition, 1949. *Publications:* Sir Elfadore and Mabyna, 1935; Letters to Malaya I and II, 1941; III and IV, 1943; V, 1947; Two Colloquies, 1949; The Return of Arthur, 1966; Old Rectory (Prologue), 1970; Old Rectory (The Session), 1973; Old Rectory (Epilogue), 1977; (with R. C. Hutchinson) Two Men of Letters, 1979. *Address:* Fitzhead, Taunton, Somerset. *T:* Milverton 400337.

SKINNER, Most Rev. Patrick James, CJM; *b* 1904. *Educ:* St Bonaventure's College, St John's; Holy Heart Seminary, Halifax; Eudist Seminary, Gros Pin, PQ; Laval University, Quebec. Priest, 1929; consecrated, as Auxiliary to Archbishop of St John's, Newfoundland, 1950; Archbishop of St John's, Newfoundland, 1951-79. *Address:* The Deanery, St Patrick's Parish, Patrick Street, St John's, Newfoundland A1E 2S7.

SKINNER, Prof. Quentin Robert Duthie, FBA 1981; Professor of Political Science, University of Cambridge, since 1978; Fellow of Christ's College, Cambridge, since 1962; *b* 26 Nov. 1940; 2nd *s* of late Alexander Skinner, CBE, and Winifred Skinner; *m* 1979, Susan Deborah Thorpe James; one *d*. *Educ:* Bedford Sch.; Gonville and Caius Coll., Cambridge (BA 1962, MA 1965). Lecturer in History, Univ. of Cambridge, 1967-78. Visiting Fellow, Research Sch. of Social Science, ANU, 1970; Institute for Advanced Study, Princeton: Mem., School of Historical Studies, 1974-75; longer-term Mem., School of Social Science, 1976-79. Lectures: Gauss Seminars, Princeton Univ., 1979; Carlyle Vis. Lectr, Univ. of Oxford, 1980-81; Lewin Lectr, Washington Univ., 1982. *Publications:* Philosophy, Politics and Society, Series 4 (ed jtly and contrib.), 1972; The Foundations of Modern Political Thought, Vol. 1, The Renaissance, 1978; Vol. 2, The Age of Reformation, 1978 (Wolfson Prize, 1979); Machiavelli, 1981. *Address:* c/o Christ's College, Cambridge CB2 3BU. *T:* Cambridge 67641.

SKINNER, Sir Thomas (Edward), KBE 1976; JP; Chairman: New Zealand Shipping Line, since 1973; The Shipping Corporation of New Zealand Ltd, since 1973; Container Terminals Ltd, since 1975; *b* 18 April 1909; *s* of Thomas Edward Skinner and Alice Skinner; *m* 1942, Mary Ethel Yardley; two *s* one *d*. *Educ:* Bayfield District Sch. Pres., NZ Fedn of Labour, 1963-79. Chm., St John Ambulance Trust Bd, Auckland, 1973-, KStJ 1970. JP New Zealand, 1943. *Recreations:* racing, boating, fishing. *Address:* 164 Kohimarama Road, St Heliers, Auckland 5, New Zealand. *T:* 587-571. *Clubs:* Avondale Jockey (New Zealand); Auckland Branch, International Lions.

SKINNER, Sir (Thomas) Keith (Hewitt), 4th Bt *cr* 1912; Director: International Publishing Corporation Ltd, since 1970; Reed International, since 1980; Chairman and Chief Executive, IPC Business Press Ltd, since 1969, and other companies; *b* 6 Dec. 1927; *s* of Sir (Thomas) Gordon Skinner, 3rd Bt, and Mollie Barbara (*d* 1965), *d* of Herbert William Girling; *S* father, 1972; *m* 1959, Jill, *d* of Cedric Ivor Tuckett; two *s*. *Educ:* Charterhouse. Managing Director, Thomas Skinner & Co (Publishers) Ltd, 1952-60; also Director, Iliffe & Co Ltd, 1958-65; Director, Iliffe-NTP Ltd; Chm., Industrial Trade Fairs Holdings Ltd, 1977-. *Recreations:* publishing, shooting, fishing, gardening, golf. *Heir: s* Thomas James Hewitt Skinner, *b* 11 Sept. 1963. *Address:* Long Acre, West Clandon, Surrey; Wood Farm, Reydon, near Southwold, Suffolk. *Clubs:* Royal Automobile; Aldeburgh Golf.

SKINNER, Thomas Monier, CMG 1958; MBE; MA Oxon; Company Chairman; *b* 2 Feb. 1913; *s* of Lt-Col and Mrs T. B. Skinner; *m* 1st, 1935, Margaret Adeline (*née* Pope) (*d* 1969); two *s*; 2nd, 1981, Elizabeth Jane Hardie, *d* of late Mr and Mrs P. L. Hardie. *Educ:* Cheltenham Coll.; Lincoln Coll., Oxford. Asst District Officer (Cadet), Tanganyika, 1935; Asst District Officer, 1937; District Officer, 1947; Senior Asst Secretary, East Africa High Commission, 1952; Director of Establishments (Kenya), 1955-62, retired 1962. Member, Civil Service Commission, East Caribbean Territories, 1962-63; Chairman, Nyasaland Local Civil Service Commission, 1963; Salaries Commissioner, Basutoland, The Bechuanaland Protectorate and Swaziland, 1964. Reports on Localisation of Civil Service, Gilbert and Ellice Islands Colony and of British National Service, New Hebrides, 1968. *Recreation:* fishing. *Address:* Blackaton, Gidleigh, Chagford, near Newton Abbot, Devon.

SKIPPER, David John; Headmaster, Merchant Taylors' School, Northwood, since 1982; *b* 14 April 1931; *s* of Herbert G. and Edna Skipper; *m* 1955, Brenda Ann Williams; three *s* one *d*. *Educ:* Watford Grammar Sch.; Brasenose Coll., Oxford (2nd Cl. Hons Nat. Science (Chemistry)). Royal Air Force (Short Service Commn) (Education), 1954-57; Assistant Master: Radley Coll., 1957-63; Rugby Sch., 1963-69; Headmaster, Ellesmere Coll., Shropshire, 1969-81. *Recreations:* squash, hillwalking, drawing, music. *Address:* Headmaster's House, Merchant Taylors' School, Sandy Lodge, Northwood, Mddx HA6 2AT. *T:* Northwood 21850. *Club:* East India, Devonshire, Sports and Public Schools.

SKIPWITH, Sir Patrick Alexander d'Estoteville, 12th Bt, *cr* 1622; The Editor, Bureau de Recherches Géologiques et Minières, Jiddah, since 1973; *b* 1 Sept. 1938; *o s* of Grey d'Estoteville Townsend Skipwith (killed in action, 1942), Flying Officer, RAFVR, and Sofka, *d* of late Prince Peter Dolgorouky; *S* grandfather, 1950; *m* 1st, 1964, Gillian Patricia (marr. diss. 1970), *d* of late Charles F. Harwood; one *s* one *d*; 2nd, 1972, Ashkhain, *d* of Bedros Atikian, Calgary, Alta. *Educ:* Harrow; Dublin (MA); London (DIC, PhD). With Ocean Mining Inc., in Tasmania, 1966-67, Malaysia, 1967-69, W Africa, 1969-70; with Min. of Petroleum and Mineral Resources, Saudi Arabia, 1970-71 and 1972-73. *Heir: s* Alexander Sebastian Grey d'Estoteville Skipwith, *b* 9 April 1969. *Address:* c/o BRGM, PO Box 1492, Jiddah, Kingdom of Saudi Arabia. *Clubs:* Travellers', Zanzibar, Chelsea Arts.

SKONE JAMES, Edmund Purcell; barrister; *b* 14 June 1927; *s* of Francis Edmund Skone James and Kate Eve Skone James; *m* 1952, Jean Norah Knight; one *s* one *d*. *Educ:* Westminster Sch.; New Coll., Oxford (MA). Served RASC, 2nd Lieut, 1946-48. Called to the Bar, Middle Temple, 1951; Bencher, Middle Temple, 1977. Mem., Whitford Cttee to Consider the Law on Copyright and Designs, 1973 (Report 1977). *Publication:* Copinger and Skone James on Copyright, 9th edn 1958-12th edn 1980. *Recreations:* gardening, walking, reading fiction. *Address:* 5 New Square, Lincoln's Inn, WC2A 3RJ. *T:* 01-405 6430.

SKUTSCH, Prof. Otto; Professor of Latin, University College London, 1951-72, now Emeritus Professor; *b* 6 Dec. 1906; *yr s* of Latinist Franz Skutsch and Selma Dorff; *m* 1938, Gillian Mary, *e d* of late Sir Findlater Stewart, GCB, GCIE, CSI; one *s* three *d*. *Educ:* Friedrichs-Gymnasium, Breslau; Univs of Breslau, Kiel, Berlin, Göttingen. DrPhil, Göttingen, 1934; Asst Thesaurus Linguae Latinae, 1932; Sen. Asst, Latin Dept, Queen's Univ., Belfast, 1938; Asst Lectr, Lectr, Sen. Lectr, Univ. of Manchester, 1939, 1946, 1949; Guest Lectr, Harvard Univ., 1958, Loeb Fellow, 1973; Vis. Andrew Mellon Prof. of Classics, Univ. of Pittsburgh, 1972-73, 1981; Guest Mem., Inst. for Advanced Study, Princeton, 1963, 1968, 1974; Vice-Pres., Soc. for Promotion of Roman Studies; For. Mem., Kungl. Vetenskaps- och Vitterhets- Samhället i Göteborg. *Publications:* Prosodische and metrische Gesetze der Iambenkürzung, 1934; Studia Enniana, 1968. Articles in classical journals, etc. *Address:* 3 Wild Hatch, NW11. *T:* 01-455 4876.

SKYRME, Stanley James Beresford, CBE 1975; Director, National Bus Company, 1972-78 (Chief Executive, 1972-76); Chairman, Lancashire United Transport Ltd, 1977-81; *b* 4 May 1912; *s* of late John Skyrme and late Kate Weeks; *m* 1938, Stephanie Mary Jay; one *s*. *Educ:* Norwich Sch. Served with cos in Tilling & BET Bus Gps, 1931-66; Exec. Dir, BET Group, 1966-68; Chm., SE Region, Nat. Bus Co., 1969-70; Dir of Manpower, Nat. Bus Co., 1971; Directorships of various Gp Cos, 1966-71; Past Pres., Confedn of British Road Passenger Transport Operators. FCIT. *Publications:* various papers for professional insts and assocs. *Recreations:* reading, gardening, walking. *Address:* 17 St Andrews Gardens, Church Road, Worthing, Sussex.

SKYRME, Sir (William) Thomas (Charles), KCVO 1974; CB 1966; CBE 1953; TD 1949; JP; Secretary of Commissions, 1948-77, retired; Vice-President, Magistrates' Association of England and Wales, since 1981 (Member of Council, since 1974; Deputy Chairman, 1977-79; Chairman, 1979-81); *b* 20 March 1913; *s* of Charles G. Skyrme, Hereford, and of Katherine (*née* Smith), Maryland, USA; *m* 1st, 1938, Hon. Barbara Suzanne Lyle (marr. diss. 1953), *yr d* of 1st Baron Lyle of Westbourne; one *s* two *d*; 2nd, 1957, Mary, *d* of Dr R. C. Leaning. *Educ:* Rugby School; New College, Oxford (MA); Universities of Dresden and Paris. Called to the Bar, Inner Temple, 1935. Practised in London and on Western Circuit. Served War of 1939-45 in Royal Artillery in Middle East, North Africa and Italy (wounded twice). Lt-Col. Secretary to the Lord Chancellor, 1944. Governor and Member of Committee of Management of Queen Mary's Hosp., London, 1938-48. Mem., Magistrates' Courts Rule Cttee, 1950-66; Chm., Interdepartmental Working Party on Legal Proceedings against Justices and Clerks, 1960; Mem., Interdepartmental Cttee on Magistrates Courts in London, 1961; Life Vice-Pres., Commonwealth Magistrates' Assoc., 1979 (Pres., 1970-79); Chm., Commonwealth Magistrates' Confs, London, 1970, Bermuda, 1972, Nairobi, 1973, Kuala Lumpur, 1975, Tonga, 1976, Jamaica, 1977, Oxford, 1979; Vice-Chm., Adv. Cttee on Training of Magistrates, 1974-80. Hon. Life Mem., Justices' Clerks' Soc., 1979-. A General Comr of Income Tax, 1977-; Broadcasting Complaints Comr, 1981-; Mem., Top Salaries Review Body, 1981-. Freeman of City of London, 1970; HM Lieut for City of London, 1977-. FRGS. JP (Oxfordshire), 1948, (London), 1952, (Gloucestershire), 1976. *Publications:* The Changing Image of the Magistracy, 1979; contribs to legal jls. *Recreations:* travel; rifle shooting (captained Oxford University, 1934). *Address:* Elm Barns, Blockley, Gloucestershire; Casa Larissa, Klosters, Switzerland. *Clubs:* Garrick; Royal Solent Yacht.
See also Sir J. G. Waterlow, Bt.

SLABBERT, Dr Frederik Van Zyl; MP (Progressive Federal Party) Claremont, since 1974; Leader of the Official Opposition, South African Parliament, since 1979; *b* 2 March 1940; *s* of Petrus Johannes and Barbara Zacharia Slabbert; *m* 1965, Marié Jordaan; one *s* one *d*. *Educ:* Univ. of Stellenbosch. BA, BA (Hons), MA 1964, DPhil 1967. Lectr in Sociology, Stellenbosch Univ., 1964-68; Senior Lecturer: Rhodes Univ., 1969; Stellenbosch Univ., 1970-71; Cape Town Univ., 1972-73; Prof. of Sociology, Univ. of the Witwatersrand, 1973-74. *Publications:* South African Society: its central perspectives, 1972; (jtly) South Africa's Options: strategies for sharing power, 1979; contributions to: Change in Contemporary South Africa, 1975; Explorations in Social Theory, 1976; various SPROCAS (Study Project of a Christian in an Apartheid Society) publications. *Recreations:* jogging, swimming, squash, chess. *Address:* PO Box 1475, Cape Town, 8000, South Africa. *T:* Cape Town 45-8311.

SLACK, Prof. Geoffrey Layton, CBE 1974 (OBE 1944); TD 1946; Emeritus Professor, University of London, since 1977; Professor of Community Dental Health, 1976-77 (formerly Professor of Dental Surgery, 1959-76). The London Hospital Medical College; *b* 27 March 1912; *er s* of late Charles Garrett Slack and Gertrude Wild, Southport; *m* Doreen Percival Ball, *d* of late Walter Knight Ball and Mary Percival, Birkdale; two *d. Educ:* Preparatory school, Croxton and Terra Nova; Leys School, Cambridge. LDS (with distinction) Univ. of Liverpool, 1934; DDS Northwestern Univ., Chicago, 1947; FDSRCS, 1948; Nuffield Fellow, 1949; Dipl. in Bacteriology, Manchester Univ. 1950; FFDRCSI 1978; FDSRCPS (Glas) 1979. Private practice, 1934-39, 1945-46; House Surg., Liverpool Dental Hosp. 1934. TA, RASC, 1934-39; served in RASC, 1939-45; Major, DADST (T) Eastern Comd HQ, 1941-43; Lieut-Col ADST (T) HQ Second Army, 1943-44; Lieut-Col ADST (T) HQ 21 Army Gp, 1944-45; demobilized 1945. Lectr in Preventive Dentistry, Univ. of Liverpool, 1948-51; Sen. Lectr, 1951-59; Head of Dept of Preventive and Children's Dentistry, 1948-59; Consultant Dental Surgeon 1948-59, United Liverpool Hosps; Dean of Dental Studies, The London Hosp. Med. Coll. Dental Sch., 1965-69. Mem., Central Health Services Council, 1969-80; Mem., 1956-80, Chm., 1974-80, Standing Dental Adv. Cttee to DHSS; Mem. General Dental Council, 1974-79; Consultant Adviser, DHSS, 1974-77; Vice-Chm. Dental Health Cttee, British Dental Assoc., 1959. Hon. Dir, MRC Dental Epidemiology Unit, 1971-77, Hon. Consultant 1977-; Hon. Consultant in Dental Surgery to the Army, 1975-77; Civilian Consultant in Community Dentistry to the RAF, 1975-. Mem. Board of Faculty of Dental Surgery, RCS, 1961-77 (Vice-Dean, 1968-69, Dean, 1971-74); Governor: The London Hosp. Med. Coll., 1963-69; The London Hospital, 1963-69. WHO Consultant, 1963-78. Fellow Am. College of Dentists, 1963; Guest Mem., Académie Dentaire, 1968-. RCS John Tomes Prize, 1960-62; RCS Charles Tomes Lectr, 1965. Hon. Dr of Odontology, Goteborg, 1974. *Publications:* (part-author) Dental Health, 1957; World Survey of Teaching Methods in Children's Dentistry, 1958; (with T. H. Melville) Bacteriology for Dental Students, 1960; (part-author) Demand and Need for Dental Care (Report to Nuffield Foundation), 1968; (part-author) Child Dental Health, 1969; (jt author) GSS Adult Dental Health in England and Wales in 1968, 1970; (ed) Dental Public Health, 1973, 2nd rev. edn, 1981; many contribs to medical and dental journals. *Recreations:* golf, sailing, contemplation; formerly hockey (played Lancashire 1933-39, 1945-52 (57 Caps), North of England, 1935-39, 1945-52, England XI 1938-39). *Address:* 1 Treesdale Close, Birkdale, Southport PR8 2EL. *T:* Southport 64007. *Clubs:* Union (Southport), Royal Birkdale Golf, Royal Liverpool Golf.

SLACK, His Honour George Granville; a Circuit Judge (formerly a County Court Judge), 1966-81; *b* 11 July 1906; *s* of George Edwin and Amy Beatrice Slack; *m* 1st, 1935, Ella Kathleen (*d* 1957), *d* of Henry Alexander Eason; one *d* ; 2nd, 1958, Vera Gertrude, *d* of Reginald Ackland Spencer; one *s* one *d. Educ:* Accrington Grammar School; London University. BA (Hons History) 1926; LLB 1929; LLM 1932. Called to Bar, Gray's Inn, 1929. Served RAFVR, 1943-46. Judge of Croydon County Court, 1969-75, of Willesden County Court, 1976-81. Contested (L): Twickenham, 1945; Dewsbury, 1950; Chairman: London Liberal Party, 1947-48, 1950-53; Liberal Party Organisation, 1956-57. Sec., Acton Baptist Church, 1954-77. Chm., West Gp Housing Soc. Ltd (West Haven), 1961-. *Publications:* Slack on War Damage, 1941; Liabilities (War Time Adjustment) Act, 1941; Liability for National Service, 1942. *Address:* 10 Baronsmede, Ealing, W5. *T:* 01-567 8164. *Club:* National Liberal.

SLACK, John Kenneth Edward, TD 1964; **His Honour Judge John Slack;** a Circuit Judge, since 1977; *b* 23 Dec. 1930; *o s* of late Ernest Edward Slack, formerly Chief Clerk Westminster County Court, and late Beatrice Mary Slack (*née* Shorten), Broadstairs; *m* 1959, Patricia Helen, MA Cantab, *o d* of late William Keith Metcalfe, Southport; two *s. Educ:* University College Sch., Hampstead; St John's Coll., Cambridge (MA). Admitted Solicitor, 1957; Partner, Freeborough Slack & Co., 1958-76; Mem. No 1 (later No 14) Legal Aid Area, 1966-69; Deputy Registrar, County Courts, 1969-72; a Recorder of the Crown Court, 1972-77; Pres., Wireless Telegraphy Appeals Tribunal, 1974-77. Captain Club Cricket Conf., 1962-66; Captain Bucks County Cricket Club, 1967-69 (Minor County Champions 1969); Active Vice-Pres., Club Cricket Conf., 1969-77, Pres., 1978. Chm. Council, University Coll. Sch., 1980- (Mem., 1974-). *Recreations:* cricket (Cambridge Blue 1954); golf. *Address:* c/o Crown Court, Aylesbury, Bucks. *Clubs:* MCC; Hawks (Cambridge); Beaconsfield Cricket, Beaconsfield Golf.

SLACK, Rev. Dr Kenneth, MBE 1946; Minister, Kensington United Reformed Church, since 1982; Moderator, Free Church Federal Council, 1983-84; *b* 20 July 1917; *s* of late Reginald Slack and late Nellie (*née* Bennett); *m* 1941, Barbara Millicent Blake; two *s* one *d. Educ:* Wallasey Grammar School; Liverpool Univ., 1937; Westminster College, Cambridge. Ordained to ministry of Presbyterian Church of England, 1941. Minister, St Nicholas', Shrewsbury, 1941-45. Chaplain, RAFVR, 1942-46, serving Air Command, South East Asia, 1943-46 (MBE). Minister, St James's,

Edgware, 1946-55; General Secretary, 1955-65, British Council of Churches; Minister, St Andrew's Church, Cheam, 1965-67; Minister of the City Temple, London, 1967-75; Moderator, Gen. Assembly, United Reformed Church, 1973-74; Dir, Christian Aid Div., British Council of Churches, 1975-82. Member: Adv. Cttee, Conf. of European Churches, 1960-67; WCC's Commn on Inter-Church Aid, Refugee and World Service, 1975-82. Vice-President, Churches' Council for Health and Healing and United Soc. for Christian Literature. Chm., Editorial Board, New Christian, 1965-70. Select Preacher, Cambridge, 1961, Oxford, 1982. Hon. LLD Southampton, 1971. *Publications:* The Christian Conflict, 1960; The British Churches Today, 1961, 2nd edn 1970; Despatch from New Delhi, 1962; Is Sacrifice Outmoded?, 1966; Uppsala Report, 1968; Martin Luther King, 1970; George Bell, 1971; Praying the Lord's Prayer Today, 1973; New Light on Old Songs, 1975; Nairobi Narrative, 1976. *Recreations:* reading, fell-walking. *Address:* The Manse, Allen Street, Kensington, W8 6BL. *T:* 01-937 8826; 3 High Busk, Blue Hill Road, Ambleside. *T:* Ambleside 3670.

SLACK, Timothy Willatt, MA; Director of Wiston House Foreign and Commonwealth Office Conference Centre (incorporating Wilton Park Conferences), Wiston House, Steyning, W Sussex; *b* 18 April 1928; *yr s* of Cecil Moorhouse Slack, MC, and late Dora Willatt, Beverley, Yorks; *m* 1957, Katharine, 2nd *d* of Walter Norman Hughes, MA, and Jean Sorsbie, Chepstow, Mon.; one *s* three *d. Educ:* Winchester Coll.; New Coll., Oxford. Hons PPE, 1951. Asst, Lycée de Rennes, France, 1951; Asst master, the Salem School, Baden, Germany, 1952; Assistant master, Repton School, 1953-59; Headmaster of Kambawsa College, Taunggyi, Shan State, Burma, 1959-62; Headmaster, Bedales Sch., 1962-74. Chairman, Society of Headmasters of Independent Schools, 1968-70. Dep. Dir, Wiston House Conf. Centre, 1975-77. Contested (L) Petersfield, Feb. and Oct. 1974. *Address:* Hamlet House, Hambledon, Portsmouth PO7 6RY.
See also W. W. Slack.

SLACK, William Willatt, MA, MCh, BM, FRCS; Surgeon to the Queen, since 1975; Consultant Surgeon, Middlesex Hospital (and Senior Lecturer in Surgery, Middlesex Hospital Medical School), since 1962; also Surgeon: Hospital of St John and St Elizabeth, since 1970; King Edward VII Hospital for Officers, since 1975; *b* 22 Feb. 1925; *s* of Cecil Moorhouse Slack, MC, and Dora Slack (*née* Willatt); *m* 1951, Joan, 4th *d* of late Lt-Col Talbot H. Wheelwright, OBE; two *s* two *d. Educ:* Winchester Coll.; New Coll., Oxford; Middlesex Hosp. Med. Sch. Ho. Surg., Surgical Registrar and Sen. Surgical Registrar, Mddx Hosp., 1950-59; Jun. Registrar, St Bartholomew's Hosp., 1953; Fulbright Scholar, R. & E. Hosp., Univ. of Illinois, Chicago, 1959. *Publications:* various surgical articles in med. jls and textbooks. *Recreations:* skiing, gardening; Oxford blue for Association football, 1946. *Address:* 18 Upper Wimpole Street, W1M 7TB. *T:* 01-486 1191; 22 Platts Lane, NW3. *T:* 01-435 5887.
See also T. W. Slack.

SLADE; see Mitford-Slade.

SLADE, (Sir) Benjamin Julian Alfred, (7th Bt *cr* 1831, but does not use the title); Chairman: Shirlstar Container Transport Ltd; Shirlstar Container Brokers Ltd; Maunsel Grange Estates Ltd; Director: Wickwell Ltd (Jersey); Shirlstar Norway SA; Shirlstar Conteneurs France SARL; Shirlstar Container Transport GmbH; Talentree Ltd (Inter Comex Ltd); Hoistlight Transport Ltd; Via Nova Properties Ltd; Mercantile Trade Bank Ltd, Antigua; National Bank of Hong Kong Ltd, Antigua; *b* 22 May 1946; *s* of Sir Michael Slade, 6th Bt and Angela (*d* 1959), *d* of Captain Orlando Chichester; *S* father, 1962; *m* 1977, Pauline Carol, *er d* of Major Claude Myburgh. *Educ:* Millfield Sch. Mem., Worshipful Co. of Ironmongers. Freeman, City of London, 1979. *Recreations:* hunting, shooting, racing, polo, bridge. *Heir:* kinsman Gerald Gordon Slade [*b* 27 Oct. 1899; *m* 1952, Netta Kathleen, *d* of Richard Edward Lloyd Maunsell, CBE]. *Address:* 164 Ashley Gardens, Emery Hill Street, SW1. *T:* 01-828 2809; Maunsel, North Newton, Bridgwater, Somerset; (office) 7/9 Swallow Street, Piccadilly, W1. *T:* 01-439 8361; *Telex:* 917760. *Clubs:* Turf, Mytton's, Institute of Directors.

SLADE, Rt. Hon. Sir Christopher John, Kt 1975; PC 1982; **Rt. Hon. Lord Justice Slade;** a Lord Justice of Appeal, since 1982; *b* 2 June 1927; *s* of late George Penkivil Slade, KC, and Mary Albinia Alice Slade; *m* 1958, Jane Gwenllian Armstrong Buckley; one *s* three *d. Educ:* Eton (Scholar); New Coll., Oxford (Scholar). Eldon Law Scholar, 1950. Called to Bar, Inner Temple, 1951; in practice at Chancery Bar, 1951-75; QC 1965; Bencher, Lincoln's Inn, 1972; Attorney General, Duchy of Lancaster and Attorney and Serjeant Within the County Palatine of Lancaster, 1972-75; a Judge of the High Ct, Chancery Division, 1975-82; a Judge of Restrictive Practices Ct, 1980-82, Pres., 1981-82. Member: Gen. Council of the Bar, 1958-62, 1965-69; Senate of Four Inns of Court, 1966-69; Lord Chancellor's Legal Educn Cttee, 1969-71. Master, Ironmongers' Co., 1973. *Address:* Royal Courts of Justice, Strand, WC2. *Club:* Garrick.

SLADE, Julian Penkivil; author and composer since 1951; *b* 28 May 1930; *s* of G. P. Slade, KC. *Educ:* Eton College; Trinity College, Cambridge (BA). Went to Bristol Old Vic Theatre School, 1951; wrote incidental music for Bristol Old Vic production of Two Gentlemen of Verona, 1952; joined Bristol Old Vic Co. as musical director, 1952. Wrote and composed Christmas in King St (with Dorothy Reynolds and James Cairncross) Bristol, 1952; composed music for Sheridan's The Duenna, Bristol, 1953; transferred to

Westminster Theatre, London, 1954; wrote and composed The Merry Gentleman (with Dorothy Reynolds), Bristol, 1953; composed incidental music for The Merchant of Venice (1953 Stratford season). Wrote musical version of The Comedy of Errors for TV, 1954, and for Arts Theatre, London, 1956; wrote (with Dorothy Reynolds) Salad Days, Bristol, 1954, Vaudeville, London, 1954, Duke of York's, 1976; Free as Air, Savoy, London, 1957; Hooray for Daisy!, Bristol, 1959, Lyric, Hammersmith, 1960; Follow that Girl, Vaudeville, London, 1960; Wildest Dreams, 1960; Vanity Fair (with Alan Pryce-Jones and Robin Miller), Queen's Theatre, London, 1962; Nutmeg and Ginger, Cheltenham, 1963; Sixty Thousand Nights (with George Rowell), Bristol, 1966; The Pursuit of Love, Bristol, 1967; composed music for songs in: As You Like It, Bristol, 1970; A Midsummer Night's Dream and Much Ado About Nothing, Regent's Park, 1970; adapted A. A. Milne's Winnie The Pooh, Phoenix Theatre, 1970, 1975; (music and lyrics) Trelawny, Bristol, then London West End, 1972; Out of Bounds (book, music and lyrics, based on Pinero's The Schoolmistress), 1973; composed incidental music for Nancy Mitford's Love in a Cold Climate, Thames TV, 1980; played and sang for solo record album of own songs, Looking for a Piano, 1981. Publications: Nibble the Squirrel (children's book), 1946; music of: The Duenna, 1954; Salad Days, 1954; Free as Air, 1957; Follow That Girl, 1967; Trelawny, 1974. Recreations: drawing, going to theatres and cinemas, listening to music. Address: 3 Priory Walk, SW10. T: 01-370 4859.

SLADE, Leslie William; Agent General for Western Australia in London, 1978-82; b 17 July 1915; s of Leonard Barrington Slade and Gwendoline (née Fraser); m 1942, Marion Joan, d of V. J. Devitt, Perth, WA; one d decd. Educ: Scotch Coll., Melbourne, Australia. Accountant, Myer Emporium Ltd, Melbourne, 1933-39; served RAN (Lieut-Comdr), 1939-46; Proprietor of import/export business, Perth, WA, 1947-61; Export Consultant, W Australian Govt, Perth, 1962-68; Official Rep., Govt of W Australia for Far East, Tokyo, 1968-78. Freedom of City of London, 1978. Recreations: golf, cricket, fishing, sailing. Address: Unit 8, Kyamala, 19 Broome Street, Mosman Park, WA 6012, Australia. Clubs: East India; West Australian Cricket Association, Royal Perth Yacht, Nedlands Golf (Perth); Tokyo (Tokyo).

SLANE, Viscount; Alexander Burton Conyngham; b 30 Jan. 1975; s and heir of Earl of Mount Charles, qv.

SLANEY, Prof. Geoffrey, FRCS; Barling Professor, Head of Department of Surgery, Queen Elizabeth Hospital, Birmingham, since 1971; Hon. Consultant Surgeon: United Birmingham Hospitals and Regional Hospital Board, since 1959; Royal Prince Alfred Hospital, Sydney; b 19 Sept. 1922; er s of Richard and Gladys Lois Slaney; m 1956, Josephine Mary Davy; one s two d. Educ: Brewood Grammar Sch.; Univs of Birmingham, London and Illinois, USA. MB, ChB (Birmingham) 1947, FRCS 1953, MS (Ill) 1956, ChM (Birmingham) 1961. Ho. Surg. and Surgical Registrar, Gen. Hosp. Birmingham, 1947-48. Captain RAMC, 1948-50. Surgical Registrar, Coventry, London and Hackney Hosps, 1950-53; Surgical Registrar, Lectr in Surgery and Surgical Research Fellow, Queen Elizabeth Hosp., Birmingham, 1953-59; Hunterian Prof., RCS, 1961-62; Prof. of Surgery, Univ. of Birmingham, 1966-. Member: London Adv. Group to Sec. of State, DHSS, 1980-81; Res. Liaison Gp, DHSS, 1979-; Midlands Med. Appeals Tribunal, 1964-. External Examr in Surgery to Univs of: Newcastle upon Tyne, London, Cambridge, Oxford, Liverpool, Nat. Univ. of Ireland, Lagos, Zimbabwe, and Licentiate Cttee, Hong Kong; Advisor in Surgery, Univs of Bristol and London. Richardson Meml Lectr, Massachusetts Gen. Hosp., Boston, USA, 1975; Visiting Professor: Durban, Cape Town, Witwatersrand, 1970; Sir Logan Campbell and RACS, NZ, 1977; Univ. of Calif and Cedars-Sinai Hosp., LA, 1978; Pearce Gould, Middlesex Hosp., 1980; McIlrath Guest, Sydney, 1981. Mem. Council, RCS, 1975-; Member: Moynihan Chirurgical Club; James IV Assoc. of Surgeons; Internat. Surgical Gp; Surgical Research Soc.; Internat. Soc. of Cardio-Vascular Surgeons; Vascular Surgical Soc., GB (Pres., 1974-75); Chm., Assoc. of Profs of Surgery of GB and Ireland, 1979-82. Mem. Council, Univ. of Zimbabwe, 1973-. Fellow: RSM; Assoc. of Surgeons GB and Ire. (Mem. Council, 1966-76, Treasurer, 1970-76). Hon. Life Mem., Los Angeles Surgical Soc. Jacksonian Prize and Medal, RCS, 1959; Pybus Meml Medal, 1978. Publications: Metabolic Derangements in Gastrointestinal Surgery (with B. N. Brooke), 1967 (USA); numerous contribs to med. and surg. jls. Recreations: fishing and family. Address: 23 Aston Bury, Edgbaston, Birmingham B15 3QB. T: 021-454 0261.

SLATCHER, William Kenneth, CVO 1975; HM Diplomatic Service; High Commissioner in Guyana and non-resident Ambassador to Suriname, since 1982; b 12 April 1926; s of John William and Ada Slatcher; m 1948, Erica Marjorie Konigs; one s one d. Educ: St John's Coll., Oxford (MA). Royal Artillery, 1950-57; HM Diplomatic Service, 1958: Peking, 1959-60; Tokyo, 1961-63; Paris, 1965-68; New Delhi, 1968-71; Tokyo, 1974-77; Consul-Gen., Osaka, 1977-80; Head of Consular Dept, FCO, 1980-82. Order of Sacred Treasure (Japan), 1975. Recreations: travelling, oriental art and history, reading. Address: c/o Foreign and Commonwealth Office, SW1A 2AL. Club: Royal Commonwealth Society.

SLATER, Bill; see Slater, W. J.

SLATER, Duncan, CMG 1982; HM Diplomatic Service; Ambassador to Oman, since 1981; b 15 July 1934; m 1972, Candida Coralie Anne Wheatley; one s two d. Joined FO, 1958; Asst Polit. Agent, Abu Dhabi, 1962-66; First Secretary: Islamabad, 1966; New Delhi, 1966-68; Head of Chancery, Aden,

1968-69; FO, 1969; Special Asst to Sir William Luce, 1970-71; First Sec., UK Representation to EEC, Brussels, 1973-75; UK Resident Rep. to IAEA and UK Perm. Rep. to UNIDO, Vienna, 1975-78; on staff of Government House, Salisbury, Dec. 1979-April 1980; Counsellor and Head of Chancery, Lagos, 1978-81. Recreations: walking, sailing, skiing, studying Islamic art. Address: c/o Foreign and Commonwealth Office, SW1.

SLATER, Prof. Edward Charles, ScD; FRS 1975; Professor of Physiological Chemistry, University of Amsterdam, The Netherlands, since 1955; b 16 Jan. 1917; s of Edward Brunton Slater and Violet Podmore; m 1940, Marion Winifred Hutley; one d. Educ: Melbourne Univ. (BSc, MSc); Cambridge Univ. (PhD, ScD). Biochemist, Australian Inst. of Anatomy, Canberra, Aust., 1939-46; Research Fellow, Molteno Inst., Univ. of Cambridge, UK, 1946-55. Member: Royal Netherlands Acad. of Science and Letters, 1964; Hollandsche Maatschappij van Wetenschappen, 1970; Hon. Mem., Amer. Soc. of Biological Chemists, 1971; Foreign Corresp., Académie Royale de Méd., Belgium, 1973; Hon. Member: Academie Nacional de Ciencias Exactas, Fisicas y Naturales, Argentina, 1973; Japanese Biochemical Soc., 1973; For. Mem., Royal Swedish Acad. of Sciences, 1975. Publications: about 300 contrib. to learned jls. Recreations: yachting, skiing. Address: Elger 9, 1141CC, Monnickendam, The Netherlands. T: (house) 02995-1450, (work) 020-522 2150.

SLATER, Eliot Trevor Oakeshott, CBE 1966; MA, MD Cantab; PhD London; FRCP; b 28 Aug. 1904; 2nd s of Gilbert Slater, MA, DSc; m 1st, 1935, Lydia (marriage dissolved), d of Leonid Pasternak; two s two d; 2nd, 1946, Jeanie Fyfe Foster. Educ: Leighton Park; Cambridge University; St George's Hospital. Medical Officer, Maudsley Hospital, 1931-39; with Rockefeller Fellowship studied in Munich and Berlin, 1934-35; MRC Research grant, 1935-37; Clinical Director, Sutton Emergency Hosp., 1939-45; Physician in Psychological Medicine, National Hosp., Queen Sq., WC1, 1946-64; Dir, MRC Psychiatric Genetics Unit, 1959-69. Mem. Royal Commn on Capital Punishment, 1949. Hon. Fellow, Amer. Psychiatric Assoc.; Ehrenmitglied, Deutsche Gesellschaft für Psychiatrie. Hon. LLD Dundee, 1971. Hon. FRCPsych, 1973; Hon. FRSocMed, 1976; Hon. Fellow, St John's Coll., Cambridge, 1981. Editor-in-chief, British Journal of Psychiatry, 1961-72. Publications: Introduction to Physical Methods of Treatment in Psychiatry (with W. Sargant), 1946; Patterns of Marriage (with M. Woodside), 1951; Psychotic and Neurotic Illness in Twins, 1953; Clinical Psychiatry (with W. Mayer-Gross and M. Roth), 1969; The Ebbless Sea (poems), 1968; The Problem of the Reign of King Edward III (1596): a statistical approach (thesis), 1981. Papers on genetical and psychiatric subjects. Recreations: Shakespeare studies, painting. Address: 128a Castelnau, SW13 9ET.
See also P. M. Oppenheimer.

SLATER, Gordon Charles Henry, CMG 1964; CBE 1956; Director, Branch Office in London of International Labour Office, 1964-70; Under-Secretary, Ministry of Labour, in the Overseas Department, 1960-64, retired; b 14 Dec. 1903; s of Matthew and Florence Slater; m 1928, Doris Primrose Hammond; one s one d. Entered Ministry of Labour, 1928, as Third Class Officer; Assistant Secretary, Organisation and Establishments, 1945, Disabled Persons Branch, 1949; Secretary of National Advisory Council on Employment of Disabled Persons, 1949-56; Sec. of Piercy Committee on Rehabilitation of Disabled, 1953-56; Under-Sec., Ministry of Labour, 1958. Member Governing Body, ILO, 1961-64; UK Govt delegate, IL Conf., 1961-64. Mem. Berkshire CC, 1970-81, Vice-Chm., 1977-79. Address: White House, Altwood Road, Maidenhead, Berks. T: Maidenhead 27463.

SLATER, Gordon James Augustus; HM Diplomatic Service, retired; High Commissioner, Honiara, Solomon Islands, 1978-82; b 8 July 1922; s of William Augustus Slater and Edith Garden; m 1st, 1952, Beryl Ruth Oliver (marr. diss. 1968); one s one d; 2nd, 1976, Gina Michelle Lambert; one d. Educ: Sydney, Australia. Foreign and Commonwealth Office (formerly Commonwealth Relations Office), 1958-. Recreations: sailing, diving, golf. Address: 56 Searchwood Road, Warlingham, Surrey.

SLATER, James Derrick, FCA; b 13 March 1929; o s of Hubert and Jessica Slater; m 1965, Helen Wyndham Goodwyn; two s two d. Educ: Preston Manor County Sch. Accountant and then Gen. Man. to a gp of metal finishing cos, 1953-55; Sec., Park Royal Vehicles Ltd, 1955-58; Dep. Sales Dir, Leyland Motor Corp. Ltd, 1963; Chm., Slater Walker Securities Ltd, 1964-75; Dir, BLMC, 1969-75. FCA 1963 (ACA 1953). Publications: Return to Go, 1977; for children: Goldenrod, 1978; A. Mazing Monsters, 1979; Grasshopper and the Unwise Owl, 1979; The Boy Who Saved Earth, 1979. Recreations: chess, backgammon, golf, table tennis. Address: High Beeches, Blackhills, Esher, Surrey.

SLATER, John Fell, CMG 1972; Assistant Secretary, HM Treasury, since 1968; b 3 July 1924; s of J. Alan Slater, FRIBA, and Freide R. Slater (née Flight); m 1951, Susan Baron; two s two d (and one d decd). Educ: Abinger Hill Preparatory Sch.; Leighton Park Sch.; New Coll., Oxford (BA). Recreations: fly-fishing, photography. Address: 50 Cathcart Road, SW10. T: 01-352 8686.

SLATER, Kenneth Frederick, CEng, FIEE; Director, Admiralty Surface Weapons Establishment, since 1978; b 31 July 1925; s of Charles Frederick and Emily Gertrude Slater; m 1965, Marjorie Gladys Beadsworth, Northampton. Educ: Hull Grammar Sch.; Manchester Univ. BSc Tech (Hons). Admiralty

Signal Estab. Extension, 1943–46; RRE, 1949–63; UK Mem., NATO Air Defence Planning Team, 1964; Supt, Radar Div., RRE, 1965–68; Asst Dir of Electronics R&D, Min. of Technology, 1968–70, Dir, 1970–71; Head of Ground Radar Gp, 1971–75, of Electronics Gp, 1975, of Applied Physics Dept, and Dep. Dir, 1976, RRE; Head of Military and Civil Systems Dept and Dep. Dir, RSRE, 1977. *Publications*: specialist contribs on Radar to Encyclopaedia Britannica and Encyclopaedic Dictionary of Physics; technical articles. *Recreations*: photography, music. *Address*: Four Winds, Portsdown Hill Road, Cosham, Portsmouth, Hants PO6 1BE. *T*: Cosham 375437.

SLATER, Leonard, CBE 1976; JP; DL; *b* 23 July 1908; *s* of S. M. Slater, Oldham, and Heysham, Lancs; *m* 1943, Olga Patricia George; two *s*. *Educ*: Hulme Grammar School, Oldham; St Catharine's College, Cambridge (MA). British Guiana Exped. 1929; Research at Cambridge, 1930–32; MA 1932. Lecturer in Geography, Univ. of Rangoon, 1932–37; Geography Master, Repton School, 1937. Served War, 1940–45; RE (Survey) in UK, India and SE Asia; Lieut-Col, 1944 and Hon. Lieut-Col, 1946. Univ. of Durham: Geography Dept, Lectr, 1939; Reader, 1948; Pro-Vice-Chancellor, 1969–73; Master, University Coll., Durham, 1953–73. Mem. Peterlee Develt Corp., 1956–63; Chairman: Durham Hosp. Management Cttee, 1961–73; Durham AHA, 1973–77; Mem., Newcastle Regional Hosp. Bd, 1965–69 and 1971–74. JP 1961, DL 1978, Durham. *Publications*: articles in geographical periodicals. *Recreation*: travel. *Address*: 8 Farnley Ridge, Durham DH1 4HB. *T*: Durham 63319. *Club*: Pathfinders'.

SLATER, Richard Mercer Keene, CMG 1962; *b* 27 May 1915; *s* of late Samuel Henry Slater, CMG, CIE; *m* 1939, Barbara Janet Murdoch; four *s*. *Educ*: Eton; Magdalene Coll., Cambridge. Indian Civil Service (Punjab Commission), 1939–47; joined HM Diplomatic Service, 1947; served in Karachi (on secondment to Commonwealth Relations Office), Lima, Moscow, Rangoon and Foreign Office; Ambassador to Cuba, 1966–70; High Comr in Uganda and Ambassador to Rwanda, 1970–72; Asst Under-Sec. of State, FCO, 1973. Adviser to Commercial Union Assurance Co., 1973–81. Chm., Hampshire Br., CPRE, 1974–. *Address*: Vicary's, Odiham, Hants.

SLATER, Admiral Sir Robin L. F. D.; *see* Durnford-Slater.

SLATER, William John, (Bill Slater), OBE 1982; Director of Physical Education, University of Birmingham, since 1970; Member, Sports Council, since 1974; *b* 29 April 1927; *s* of John Rothwell Slater and Ethel May Slater; *m* 1952, Marion Warr; two *s* two *d*. *Educ*: Clitheroe Royal Grammar Sch.; Carnegie Coll. of Physical Educn (Dip. in Phys. Educn); Univ. of Birmingham (BSc). Dep. Dir, Crystal Palace Nat. Sports Centre, 1963–64; Dir of Phys. Educn, Univ. of Liverpool, 1964–70 (Warden, McNair Hall, 1966–69). Member: Central Adv. Council for Educn (Newsom Cttee), 1961–63; Cttee of Enquiry into Association Football (Chester Cttee), 1966–68; Exec. Cttee, Internat. Council of Sport and Physical Educn, 1980–. Chairman: Cttee of Advrs, Sports Aid Foundn, 1978–; Management Cttee, Lilleshall Nat. Sports Centre, 1979–; West Midlands Council for Sport and Recreation, 1979–. Wolverhampton Wanderers Football Club, 1951–62; rep. England in Association Football, 1951–60; Olympic Games, Helsinki, 1952; World Cup (Assoc. Football), Sweden, 1958. Footballer of the Year, 1960. *Recreations*: games and sports of all kinds. *Address*: 55 Green Meadow Road, Birmingham B29 4DD. *T*: 021-475 1858.

SLATTERY, Rear-Adm. Sir Matthew (Sausse), KBE 1960; Kt 1955; CB 1946; FRAeS 1946; *b* 12 May 1902; 3rd *s* of late H. F. Slattery, one-time Chairman of National Bank Ltd; *m* 1925, Mica Mary, *d* of Col G. D. Swain, CMG; two *s* one *d*. *Educ*: Stonyhurst Coll.; RN Colls, Osborne and Dartmouth. Joined RN, 1916; Director Air Material, Admiralty, 1939–41; commanded HMS Cleopatra, 1941–42; appointed Director-General of Naval Aircraft Development and Production, Ministry of Aircraft Production, 1941, and Chief Naval Representative, 1943; Vice-Controller (Air) and Chief of Naval Air Equipment at Admiralty, and Chief Naval Representative on Supply Council, Ministry of Supply, 1945–48; retd list, Royal Navy, 1948. Vice-Chm., Air Requirements Bd, 1960–74. Man. Dir, Short Brothers & Harland, Ltd, 1948–52, Chm. and Man. Dir, 1952–60; Chairman: (SB Realisations) Ltd, 1952–60; Bristol Aircraft Ltd, 1957–60; Dir Bristol Aeroplane Co. Ltd, 1957–60. Special Adviser to Prime Minister on Transport of Middle East Oil, 1957–59; Dir National Bank Ltd, 1959–60, 1963–69; Chairman: BOAC, 1960–63; BOAC-Cunard Ltd, 1962–63; R. & W. Hawthorn, Leslie & Co., 1966–73. Commander Legion of Merit (USA). DSc(*hc*) Queen's Univ., Belfast, 1954. *Recreations*: country pursuits. *Address*: Harvey's Farm, Warninglid, West Sussex.

SLATYER, Prof. Ralph Owen, AO 1982; FRS 1975; Professor, Institute of Advanced Studies, Australian National University, Canberra, since 1967; *b* 16 April 1929; *s* of Thomas Henry and Jean Slatyer; *m* 1953, June Helen Wade; one *s* two *d*. *Educ*: Univ. of Western Australia. BSc (Agric.), MSc, DSc. CSIRO Res. Scientist, subseq. Chief Res. Scientist, 1951–67. Member: Australian Res. Grants Cttee, 1969–72; Nat. Capital Planning Cttee, 1973–76; Australian Science and Technology Council, 1975–77; Aust. Nat. Commn for Unesco, 1975–78 (Chm., 1976–78); Australian Ambassador to Unesco, 1978–81. President: Ecol Soc. of Austr., 1969–71; Unesco Man and the Biosphere Programme, 1977–81; Unesco World Heritage Cttee, 1981–82; ICSU Sci. Cttee on problems of the envt, 1982–; Chm., Aust. Biol. Resources Study, 1981–; Mem., Policy Adv. Cttee and Bd of Management, Aust. Centre for Internat. Agricl Res., 1981–. Fellow, Austr. Acad. Sci., 1967. Edgeworth

David Medal, 1960; Austr. Medal of Agric. Sci., 1968. For. Associate, US Nat. Acad. of Sciences, 1976; Hon. For. Mem., Amer. Acad. of Arts and Scis, 1981. *Publications*: (with I. C. McIlroy) Practical Microclimatology, 1961 (Russian edn 1964); Plant-Water Relationships, 1967 (Russian edn 1970); (ed with R. A. Perry) Arid Lands of Australia, 1969; (ed jtly) Photosynthesis and Photorespiration, 1971; (ed) Plant Response to Climatic Factors, 1974; papers in learned jls. *Recreations*: ski-ing, bushwalking. *Address*: 10 Tennyson Crescent, Forrest, ACT 2603, Australia.

SLAUGHTER, Frank Gill, MC; MD, FACS; novelist (self-employed); physician and surgeon (retd); *b* Washington, USA, 25 Feb. 1908; *s* of Stephen Lucius Slaughter and Sallie Nicholson Gill; *m* 1933, Jane Mundy; two *s*. *Educ*: Duke Univ. (AB); Johns Hopkins (MD). Served War, 1942–46 (MC): Major to Lt-Col, US Army Med. Corps. Intern, asst resident, and resident surgeon, Jefferson Hosp., Roanoke, Va, 1930–34; practice, specializing in surgery, Jacksonville, Fla, 1934–42; retired, 1946; Lectr, W. Colston Leigh, Inc., NY City, 1947–49. Res. Diplomate, Amer. Bd of Surgery. Mem., Sons of Amer. Revolution. Presbyterian (Elder). Hon. DHL Jacksonville Univ., 1978. *Publications*: That None Should Die, 1941; Spencer Brade, MD, 1942; Air Surgeon, 1943; Battle Surgeon, 1944; A Touch of Glory, 1945; In a Dark Garden, 1946; The New Science of Surgery, 1946; The Golden Isle, 1947; Sangaree, 1948; Medicine for Moderns, 1948; Divine Mistress, 1949; The Stubborn Heart, 1950; Immortal Magyar, 1950; Fort Everglades, 1951; The Road to Bithynia, 1951; East Side Genial, 1952; The Galileans, 1953; Storm Haven, 1953; The Song of Ruth, Apalachee Gold, 1954; The Healer, Flight from Natchez, 1955; The Scarlet Cord, 1956; The Warrior, 1956; Sword and Scalpel, 1957; The Mapmaker, 1957; Daybreak, 1958; The Thorn of Arimathea, 1958; The Crown and the Cross, 1959; Lorena, 1959; The Land and the Promise, 1960; Pilgrims in Paradise, 1960; Epidemic, 1961; The Curse of Jezebel, 1961; David: Warrior and King, 1962; Tomorrow's Miracle, 1962; Devil's Harvest, 1963; Upon This Rock, 1963; A Savage Place, 1964; The Purple Quest, 1965; Constantine: The Miracle of the Flaming Cross, 1965; Surgeon, USA, 1966; God's Warrior, 1967; Doctor's Wives, 1967; The Sins of Herod, 1968; Surgeon's Choice, 1969; Countdown, 1970; Code Five, 1971; Convention, MD, 1972; Life blood, 1974; Stonewall Brigade, 1975; Plague Ship, 1977; Devil's Gamble, 1978; The Passionate Rebel, 1979; Gospel Fever, 1980; Doctor's Daughter, 1981. *Recreations*: boating, hiking, reading. *Address*: 5051 Yacht Club Road, Jacksonville, Fla 32210, USA. *T*: 904-389-7677. *Club*: Timuquana Country (Jacksonville, Fla).

SLAUGHTER, Giles David, MA; Headmaster, University College School, since 1983; *b* 11 July 1937; *s* of Gerald Slaughter and Enid Lillian Slaughter (*née* Crane); *m* 1965, Gillian Rothwell Shepherd; three *d*. *Educ*: Royal Masonic School; King's College, Cambridge. MA. Pierrepont School, Frensham, 1961–65; Campbell College, Belfast, 1965–68; Stockport Grammar School, 1968–70; Housemaster, Ormiston House, 1970–73; Headmaster, Solihull School, 1973–82. *Recreations*: gardening, cricket, golf, theatre. *Address*: 5 Redington Road, Hampstead, NW3 7QX. *Club*: East India, Devonshire, Sports and Public Schools.

SLAUGHTER, James Cameron, CMG 1963; Executive Adviser, Brisbane City Council, 1967–71 (Town Clerk and City Administrator, 1940–67); *b* 16 Aug. 1902; *s* of late Ernest E. Slaughter; *m* 1927, Ida M. Taylor; one *s* one *d*. *Educ*: Normal School, Brisbane. Trustee, City Debt Redemption Fund, 1940; Chm., Lang Park Trust, 1959; Town Clerk: Bundaberg City Coun., 1936–40; Coolangatta Town Coun., 1927–36; Shire Clerk: Gatton Shire Coun.; Inglewood Shire Coun.; Chief Clerk, Ithaca Town Council. AASA; FIMA. *Recreations*: bowls, fishing. *Clubs*: Johnsonian and Tattersalls; Rugby League, Booroodabin Bowling.

SLEDGE, Ven. Richard Kitson; Archdeacon of Huntingdon and Rector of Hemingford Abbots, since 1978; *b* 13 April 1930; *s* of Sydney Kitson and Mary Sylvia Sledge; *m* 1958, Patricia Henley (*née* Sear); one *s* two *d* (and one *s* decd). *Educ*: Epsom College; Peterhouse, Cambridge (MA). Curate of Emmanuel, Plymouth, 1954–57; Curate-in-charge of St Stephen's, Exeter, 1957–63; Rector of Dronfield, 1963–78. *Address*: The Rectory, Hemingford Abbots, Huntingdon, Cambs PE18 9AN. *T*: St Ives 69856.

SLEEMAN, (Stuart) Colin; His Honour Judge Sleeman; a Circuit Judge, since 1976; *s* of Stuart Bertram Sleeman and Phyllis Grace (*née* Pitt); *m* 1944, Margaret Emily, *d* of late William Joseph Farmer; two *s* one *d*. *Educ*: Clifton Coll.; Merton Coll., Oxford (BA 1936, MA 1963). Called to the Bar, Gray's Inn, 1938; Bencher, 1974. World War II: Admin. Officer, Prize Dept, Min. of Economic Warfare, 1939–40; Lt-Col 16th-5th Lancers; Staff Captain: RAC Wing, Combined Trng Centre, 1941; 6th Armoured Div., 1942; Adjt, RAC Range, Minehead, 1942–44; Asst Judge Advocate Gen., HQ Allied Land Forces, SE Asia, 1945. London Corresp., Scottish Law Rev., 1949–54; a Recorder, 1975–76. *Publications*: The Trial of Gozawa Sadaichi and Nine Others, 1948; (with S. C. Silkin) The 'Double Tenth' Trial, 1950. *Recreations*: travel, genealogy. *Address*: West Walls, Cotmandene, Dorking, Surrey RH4 2BL. *T*: Dorking 883616; 1 Gray's Inn Square, WC1R 5AA. *T*: 01-404 0763.

SLEIGHT, Sir John Frederick, 3rd Bt, *cr* 1920; *b* 13 April 1909; *s* of Major Sir Ernest Sleight, 2nd Bt and Margaret (*d* 1976), *d* of C. F. Carter, JP, The Limes, Grimsby; *S* father 1946; *m* 1942, Jacqueline Margaret Mundell, *widow* of Ronald Mundell and *o d* of late Major H. R. Carter of Brisbane, Queensland; one *s*. *Heir*: *s* Richard Sleight [*b* 27 May 1946; *m* 1978,

Marie-Thérèse, *o d* of O. M. Stepan, Bromley, Kent]. *Address:* c/o National Westminster Bank Ltd, 58 High Street, Watford, Herts.

SLEIGHT, Prof. Peter, MD (Cantab), DM (Oxon), FRCP; Field-Marshal Alexander Professor of Cardiovascular Medicine in the University of Oxford, and Fellow of Exeter College, Oxford, since 1973; *b* 27 June 1929; *s* of William and Mary Sleight, Boston Spa, Yorks; *m* 1953, Gillian France; two *s. Educ:* Leeds Grammar Sch.; Gonville and Caius Coll., Cambridge; St Bartholomew's Hosp., London. Ho. Phys. and Ho. Surg., Med. and Surg. Professorial Units, Bart's, 1953; Sen. Registrar, St George's Hosp., London, 1959-64; Bissinger Fellow, Cardiovascular Research Unit, Univ. of California, San Francisco, 1961-63; MRC Scientific Officer, Depts of Physiology and Medicine, Univ. of Oxford, 1964-66; Consultant Physician, Radcliffe Infirmary, Oxford, 1966-73; Visiting Prof., Univ. of Sydney (Warren McDonald Sen. Overseas Fellow of Aust. Heart Foundn), 1972-73; Hon. Prof. of Medicine, Federal Univ. of Pernambuco, 1975. Mem. Council, Internat. Soc. of Hypertension. Chm., ASH. Mem. Editorial Bd, British Heart Jl; Editor, Jl of Cardiovascular Res. Young Investigators Award, Amer. Coll. of Cardiology, 1963. *Films:* Control of Circulation; History of Hypertension (Medal, BMA Scientific Film Competition, 1981). *Publications:* Modern Trends in Cardiology, 1976; (ed) Arterial Baroreceptors and Hypertension, 1981; contribs on nervous control of the circulation and hypertension in: Circulation Research; Jl Physiol. *Recreations:* sailing, golf, travel. *Address:* Wayside, 32 Crown Road, Wheatley, Oxon. *Club:* Royal Air Force.

SLEIGHTHOLME, Derek; Member of Tyne and Wear County Council, since 1974 (Chairman, 1975-76); *b* 4 June 1935; *s* of George Henry Sleightholme and Evelyn Sleightholme; *m* 1957, Norma; one *s* one *d. Educ:* Washington Glebe. RAF, 1953-57; miner, 1957-75. Former Member, Washington Develt Corp. *Recreations:* sport, agriculture. *Address:* 28 Woburn, Biddick Village, Washington NE38 7JX. *Club:* Celtic (Washington).

SLEMON, Air Marshal Charles Roy, CB 1946; CBE 1943; retired from RCAF, 1964; *b* Winnipeg, Manitoba, Canada, 7 November 1904; *s* of Samuel Slemon and Mary Bonser; *m* 1935, Marion Pamela Slemon, Bowmanville, Ont; one *s* two *d. Educ:* University of Manitoba (BSc). Lieut COTC (Army), Canada, 1923; Cadet Royal Canadian Air Force, 1923; Royal Air Force Staff College Course, England, 1938; Senior Air Staff Officer at Western Air Command Headquarters, Canada, 1939-41; commanded Western Air Command, Canada, for 5 months in 1941; Director of Operations at RCAF HQ Ottawa, 1941-42; Senior Air Staff Officer, No. 6 (RCAF) Bomber Group, England, 1942-44; Air Vice-Marshal, 1945; Deputy AOC-in-C, RCAF Overseas, March 1945; Commanded Canadian Air Forces preparing for the Pacific, 1945; Air Council Member for Supply and Organization, 1946; Air Council Member for Operations and Training, 1947-48; AOC Trg Comd, RCAF, 1949-53; Chief of the Air Staff, Canada, 1953-57; Dep. C-in-C, N American Defence Comd (Canada-USA), 1957-64, retd. Exec. Vice-Pres., US Air Force Acad. Foundn Inc., 1964-81. Hon. LLD (Univ. of Manitoba), 1953; Hon. DMSc (RMC), Kingston, Ont, 1965. USA Legion of Merit, 1946; French Legion of Honour and Croix de Guerre with Palm, 1947. *Recreations:* golf, swimming. *Address:* 8 Thayer Road, Broadmoor Heights, Colorado Springs, Colorado 80906, USA.

SLEVIN, Brian Francis Patrick, CMG 1975; OBE 1973; QPM 1968; CPM 1965; *b* 13 Aug. 1926; *s* of late Thomas and Helen Slevin; *m* 1972, Constance Gay, *e d* of Major Ronald Moody and Amy Moody; one *s. Educ:* Blackrock Coll., Ireland. Palestine Police, 1946-48; Hong Kong Police, 1949-79; Directing Staff, Overseas Police Courses, Metropolitan Police Coll., Hendon, London, 1955-57; Director, Special Branch, 1966-69; Sen. Asst Comr of Police, Comdg Kowloon Dist, 1969-70; Dir, Criminal Investigation Dept, 1971; Dep. Comr of Police, 1971, Comr of Police, 1974-79, Hong Kong; retired 1979. *Recreations:* walking, golf, reading, painting. *Address:* Lantau Lodge, 152 Coonanbarra Road, Wahroonga, Sydney, NSW 2076, Australia. *T:* 48661. *Clubs:* East India, Royal Automobile; Hong Kong, Royal Hong Kong Golf, Royal Hong Kong Jockey (Hong Kong).

SLIGO, 10th Marquess of, *cr* 1800; **Denis Edward Browne;** Baron Mount Eagle, 1760; Viscount Westport, 1768; Earl of Altamont, 1771; Earl of Clanricarde, 1543 and 1800 (special remainder); Baron Monteagle (UK), 1806; *b* 13 Dec. 1908; *er s* of late Lt-Col Lord Alfred Eden Browne, DSO (5th *s* of 5th Marquess) and late Cicely, *d* of Edward Wormald, 15 Berkeley Square, W; *S* uncle, 1952; *m* 1930, José Gauche; one *s. Educ:* Eton. *Heir: s* Earl of Altamont, *qv. Address:* c/o Messrs Trower, Still and Keeling, 5 New Square, Lincoln's Inn, WC2.
See also Baron Brabourne.

SLIM, family name of **Viscount Slim.**

SLIM, 2nd Viscount *cr* 1960, of Yarralumla and Bishopston; **John Douglas Slim,** OBE 1973; Vice-President and Managing Director: Boyden International Ltd; F. O's. (Trade Advisory Services) Ltd; Chairman, Peek Holdings Ltd; *b* 20 July 1927; *s* of Field Marshal the 1st Viscount Slim, KG, GCB, GCMG, GCVO, GBE, DSO, MC, and of Aileen, *d* of Rev. J. A. Robertson, MA, Edinburgh; *S* father, 1970; *m* 1958, Elisabeth, *d* of Arthur Rawdon Spinney, CBE; two *s* one *d. Educ:* Prince of Wales Royal Indian Military College, Dehra Dun. Emergency Commn, Indian Army, 6 Gurkha Rifles, 1945-48; Argyll and Sutherland Highlanders, 1948; Staff. Coll.,

Camberley, 1961; Brigade Major, HQ Infantry Bde (TA), 1962-64; JSSC 1964; GSO2, HQ Middle East Command, 1966-67; Lt-Col 1967; Comdr, 22 Special Air Service Regt, 1967-70; GSO1 (Special Forces) HQ UK Land Forces, 1970-72; retired 1972. President, Burma Star Association, 1971. Chm., Britain-Australia Soc., 1978-. *Heir: s* Hon. Mark William Rawdon Slim, *b* 13 Feb. 1960. *Address:* c/o Lloyds Bank Ltd, 6 Pall Mall, SW1. *Clubs:* White's, Special Forces.

SLIMMINGS, Sir William Kenneth MacLeod, Kt 1966; CBE 1960; *b* 15 Dec. 1912; *s* of George and Robina Slimmings; *m* 1943, Lilian Ellen Willis; one *s* one *d. Educ:* Dunfermline High School. Chartered Accountant: Partner in Thomson McLintock & Co., Chartered Accountants, London, etc, 1946-78. Member: Committee of Inquiry on the Cost of Housebuilding, 1947-53; Committee on Tax-paid Stocks, 1952-53; Committee on Cheque Endorsement, 1955-56; Performing Right Tribunal, 1963-77; Crown Agents Tribunal, 1978-82; Chairman: Board of Trade Advisory Committee, 1957-66; Review Bd for Govt Contracts, 1971-81; Accounting Standards Cttee, 1976-78. Member: Council, Inst. Chartered Accountants of Scotland, 1962-66 (Pres., 1969-70); Scottish Tourist Bd, 1969-76; Review Body on Doctors' and Dentists' Pay, 1976-. Independent Chm., Cement Makers' Fedn, 1977-80. Hon. DLitt, Heriot-Watt, 1970. *Recreation:* gardening. *Address:* (business) 70 Finsbury Pavement, EC2A 1SX. *T:* 01-638 2777; (home) 62 The Avenue, Worcester Park, Surrey. *T:* 01-337 2579. *Club:* Caledonian.

SLINGER, William; *b* 27 Oct. 1917; *yr s* of late William Slinger and Maud Slinger, Newcastle, Co. Down; *m* 1944, Muriel, *o d* of late R. J. Johnston, Belfast; three *d. Educ:* Methodist Coll., Belfast; Queen's Univ., Belfast (BComSc). Entered Northern Ireland Civil Service, 1937; Private Secretary: to Minister of Labour, 1942-43 and 1945-46; to Minister of Public Security, 1944; Sec. to Nat. Arbitration Tribunal (NI), 1946-48; Principal, Min. of Labour and Nat. Insurance, Industrial Relations Div., 1954-60; Asst Sec. and Head of Industrial Relations Div., 1961-69; Sec., Dept of Community Relations, 1969-75; Dep. Sec., Dept of Educn for NI, 1975-77. CBIM. *Recreations:* gardening, walking. *Address:* Cairnfield, Circular Road, Belfast BT4 2GD. *T:* Belfast 768240. *Clubs:* East India, Devonshire, Sports and Public Schools; Civil Service (N Ireland).

SLIVE, Prof. Seymour; Gleason Professor of Fine Arts at Harvard University since 1973; Director, Fogg Art Museum, since 1975; *b* Chicago, 15 Sept. 1920; *s* of Daniel Slive and Sonia (née Rapoport); *m* 1946, Zoya Gregorovna Sandomirsky; one *s* two *d. Educ:* Univ. of Chicago. BA 1943; PhD 1952. Served US Navy, Lieut, CO Small Craft, 1943-46. Instructor in Art History, Oberlin Coll., 1950-51; Asst Prof. and Chm. of Art Dept, Pomona Coll., 1952-54; Asst Prof. 1954-57, Assoc. Prof. 1957-61, Prof., 1961-73, Chm. of Dept 1968-71, Fine Arts, Harvard Univ.; Exchange Prof., Univ. of Leningrad, 1961. Ryerson Lectr, Yale, 1962. Slade Prof. of Fine Art, Univ. of Oxford, 1972-73. Trustee, Solomon R. Guggenheim Foundn, 1978-. FAAAS 1964. For. Mem., Netherlands Soc. of Sciences, 1971. Hon. MA Harvard, 1958; Hon. MA Oxford, 1972. Officer, Order of Orange Nassau, 1962. *Publications:* Rembrandt and His Critics: 1630-1730, 1953; Drawings of Rembrandt, 1965; (with J. Rosenberg) Dutch Art and Architecture: 1600-1800, 1965, 2nd edn (with J. Rosenberg and E. H. ter Kuile), 1978; Frans Hals, 3 vols, 1970-74; Jacob van Ruisdael, 1981; contribs to learned jls. *Address:* 1 Walker Street Place, Cambridge, Mass 02138, USA.

SLOAN, Andrew Kirkpatrick; Deputy Chief Constable, Lincolnshire, since 1981; *b* 27 Feb. 1931; *s* of Andrew Kirkpatrick Sloan and Amelia Sarah (née Vernon), Kirkcudbright; *m* 1953, Agnes Sofie Storvik, Trondheim, Norway; three *d. Educ:* Kirkcudbright Acad.; Dumfries Acad.; Open Univ. (BA). Joined RN as boy seaman, 1947; served at home and abroad in cruisers and submarines, and worked in industry in Norway, 1947-55; joined W Riding Constab., 1955; apptd to CID, 1963; Det. Sgt, Barnsley, 1964; Det. Insp., Reg. Crime Squad, Leeds, 1966; Det. Chief Insp., Goole and Pontefract, 1969; Det. Supt, Reg. Crime Squad, Wakefield, 1970; Chief Supt, Toller Lane Div., Bradford, 1975; Asst Chief Constable, Operations, Lincolnshire Police, 1976-79; National Co-ordinator, Regional Crime Squads of England and Wales, 1979-81. *Recreations:* reading, travel, walking, conversation. *Address:* Police HQ, Nettleham, Lincoln. *Club:* Chief Constables.

SLOAN, Norman Alexander, QC (Scot.) 1953; Legal Adviser, British Shipbuilders, 1978-81; *b* 27 Jan. 1914; *s* of George Scott Sloan and Margaret Hutcheson Smith; *m* 1944, Peggy Perry (*d* 1982); two *s* one *d. Educ:* Glasgow Academy; Glasgow University (BL). Solicitor, 1935; Admitted to Faculty of Advocates, 1939; Served in RNVR 1940-46. Lecturer in Industrial Law, Edinburgh University, 1946-51; Standing Counsel to Department of Health for Scotland, 1946-51; Advocate-Depute, 1951-53. Director: The Shipbuilding Employers' Federation, 1955-68; Shipbuilders and Repairers Nat. Assoc., 1968-72; Swan Hunter Group Ltd, 1973-77; Swan Hunter Shipbuilders Ltd, 1973-78. *Recreation:* golf. *Address:* Edenvale, 6 High Park, Morpeth, Northumberland NE61 2SS. *T:* Morpeth 55218.

SLOANE, Maj.-Gen. John Bramley Malet, CB 1967; CBE 1962 (OBE 1951); DL; Director of Manning (Army), Ministry of Defence, 1964-67; retired; *b* 17 Sept. 1910; *m* 1939, Marjorie (née Crowley); three *s.* Late Argyll and Sutherland Highlanders. DL Beds, 1976. *Recreations:* golf, walking. *Address:* Jordans, Newton Blossomville, near Turvey, Beds. *T:* Turvey 392. *Club:* Army and Navy.

SLOANE, Prof. Peter James, PhD; Head of Department of Economics and Management, Paisley College, since 1975; *b* 6 Aug. 1942; *s* of John Joseph Sloane and Elizabeth (*née* Clarke); *m* 1969, Avril Mary Urquhart; one *s. Educ:* Cheadle Hulme Sch.; Univ. of Sheffield (BAEcon Hons 1964); Univ. of Strathclyde (PhD 1966). Asst Lectr in Pol. Econ., Univ. of Aberdeen, 1966-67, Lectr in Pol. Econ., 1967-69; Lectr in Indust. Econs, Univ. of Nottingham, 1969-75; Economic Adviser, Unit for Manpower Studies, Dept of Employment (on secondment), 1973-74. Vis. Prof. (Commonwealth Fellow), Faculty of Business, McMaster Univ., Canada, 1978. Mem., SSRC, 1979-. *Publications:* (with B. Chiplin) Sex Discrimination in the Labour Market, 1976; (ed) Women and Low Pay, 1980; (with H. C. Jain) Equal Employment Issues, 1981; (with B. Chiplin) Tackling Discrimination, 1982; papers on changing patterns of working hours and on sport in the market; articles in learned jls, incl. Econ. Jl, Economica, Applied Econs, Bull. Econ. Res., Jl of Econ. Studies, Scottish Jl of Pol. Econ., British Jl of Indust. Relations, Indust. Relations Jl, Internat. Labour Rev., and Internat. Jl of Social Econs. *Recreation:* sport. *Address:* Garden Cottage, Church Street, Kilbarchan, Renfrewshire, Scotland PA10 2JJ. *T:* Kilbarchan 2452. *Clubs:* Royal Commonwealth Society; Bowfield Country (Renfrewshire).

SLOGGETT, Jolyon Edward, CEng, FRINA, FIMarE, FICS; Consultant to Marine and Offshore Industries; *b* 30 May 1933; *s* of Edward Cornelius Sloggett and Lena May (*née* Norton); *m* 1970, Patricia Marjorie Iverson Ward; two *d. Educ:* John Lyon Sch.; Univ. of Glasgow (BSc). CDipAF. William Denny & Brothers Ltd, Leven Shipyard, Dumbarton, 1951-57 and 1959-60. Served, Royal Navy, TA Sub Lieut (E), RNVR, 1957-58; Houlder Brothers & Co. Ltd, 1960-78, Director, 1972-78; Man. Dir, Offshore, British Shipbuilders Corp., 1978-81; Dir, Vickers Shipbuilding Group, 1979-80; Chm., Vickers Offshore (Projects & Development) Ltd, 1979-81. Liveryman, Shipwrights' Co. *Recreations:* gardening, woodwork. *Address:* Annington House, Steyning, West Sussex BN4 3WA. *T:* Steyning 812259.

SLOMAN, Albert Edward, CBE 1980; DPhil; Vice-Chancellor of University of Essex, since 1962; *b* Launceston, Cornwall, 14 Feb. 1921; *y s* of Albert Sloman; *m* 1948, Marie Bernadette, *d* of Leo Bergeron, Cognac, France; three *d. Educ:* Launceston Coll., Cornwall; Wadham Coll., Oxford (Pope Exhibitioner, 1939). Mediæval and Mod. Langs, 1941; MA (Oxon and Dublin); DPhil (Oxon). Served War of 1939-45 (despatches): night-fighter pilot with 219 and 68 squadrons; Flight-Lieut. Lecturer in Spanish, Univ. of California, Berkeley, USA, 1946-47; Reader in Spanish, in charge of Spanish studies, Univ. of Dublin, 1947-53; Fellow TCD, 1950-53; Gilmour Professor of Spanish, University of Liverpool, 1953-62; Dean, Faculty of Arts, 1961-62. Editor of Bulletin of Hispanic Studies, 1953-62. Reith Lecturer, 1963. Chairman, Dept of Education State Studentship Cttee (Humanities), 1965-; Vice-Chm., Cttee of Vice-Chancellors and Principals of UK Univs, 1979-81, Chm., 1981-; Chm., Overseas Research Students Fees Support Scheme, 1980-; Member: Council of Europe Cttee for Higher Educn and Research, 1963-72; Inter-univ. Council for Higher Educn Overseas, 1964-; Conf. of European Rectors and Vice-Chancellors, 1965- (Pres., 1969-74); Admin. Bd, Internat. Assoc., of Univs, 1965-75; Internat. Assoc. of Universities, 1970- (Vice-Pres.); Economic and Social Cttee, EEC, 1973-. Chm. Bd of Governors, Centre for Inf. on Lang. Teaching and Res., 1979-; Mem. Bd of Governors, Guyana Univ., 1966-. Hon. Doctorate, Nice, 1974. *Publications:* The Sources of Calderón's El Príncipe constante, 1950; The Dramatic Craftsmanship of Calderón, 1958; A University in the Making, 1964. Articles and reviews in Modern Language Review, Bulletin of Hispanic Studies, Hispanic Review, Romance Philology and other journals. *Recreation:* travel. *Address:* The University of Essex, Colchester. *Club:* Savile.

SLOMAN, Mrs (Margaret) Barbara; Under Secretary, Management and Personnel Office (formerly Civil Service Department), since 1975; *b* 29 June 1925; *d* of Charles and Margaret Pilkington-Rogers; *m* 1950, Peter Sloman, *qv*; one *s* one *d. Educ:* Cheltenham Ladies' Coll.; Girton Coll., Cambridge. BA Hons Classics. Asst Principal, Treasury, 1947, Principal 1954-65; Asst Sec., DES, 1965-69; Asst Sec., Civil Service Dept, 1970-75. *Address:* Management and Personnel Office, Whitehall, SW1A 2AZ.

SLOMAN, Peter; Principal Administrative Officer (Schools), London Borough of Newham, since 1980; *b* Oct. 1919; *s* of H. N. P. Sloman and Mary Sloman (*née* Trinder); *m* 1950, Margaret Barbara (*see* M. B. Sloman); one *s* one *d. Educ:* Winchester Coll.; New Coll., Oxford. War Service (RA), 1939-46. Home Civil Service, 1946-74; Under-Secretary, 1968; Min. (later Dept) of Education; Treasury; Ministries of Defence, Land and Natural Resources, Housing and Local Govt; idc 1960; Educn Officer, AMA, 1974-79. *Address:* 26 Glebe Road, SW13 0EA.

SLOSS; *see* Butler-Sloss.

SLOT, Peter Maurice Joseph; His Honour Judge Slot; a Circuit Judge, since 1980; *b* 3 Dec. 1932; *s* of Joseph and Marie Slot; *m* 1962, Mary Eiluned Lewis; two *s* three *d. Educ:* Bradfield Coll.; St John's Coll., Oxford (MA). Called to Bar, Inner Temple, 1957. A Recorder of the Crown Court, 1974-80. *Recreations:* golf, madrigals, argument. *Address:* The Red House, Betchworth, Surrey RH3 7DR. *T:* Betchworth 2010. *Club:* Walton Heath Golf.

SLYNN, Hon. Sir Gordon, Kt 1976; an Advocate-General, Court of Justice of the European Communities, since 1981; *b* 17 Feb. 1930; *er s* of late John Slynn and of Edith Slynn; *m* 1962, Odile Marie Henriette Boutin. *Educ:* Sandbach Sch.; Goldsmiths' Coll.; Trinity Coll., Cambridge (Sen. Schol.; MA, LLB; Sub-Lector, 1956-61). Commnd RAF, 1951-54. Called to Bar, Gray's Inn, 1956, Bencher, 1970. Jun. Counsel, Min. of Labour, 1967-68; Jun. Counsel to the Treasury (Common Law), 1968-74; Leading Counsel to the Treasury, 1974-76. Recorder of Hereford, 1971; a Recorder, and Hon. Recorder of Hereford, 1972-76; QC 1974; a Judge of the High Ct of Justice, QBD, 1976-81. Pres., Employment Appeal Tribunal, 1978-81. Lecturer in Air Law, LSE, 1958-61; Vis. Prof. in Law, Univ. of Durham, 1981-. Chief Steward of Hereford, 1978- (Dep. Chief Steward, 1977-78). Hon. Vice-Pres., Union Internat. des Avocats, 1976- (Vice-Pres., 1973-76); Governor, Internat. Students' Trust, 1979-; Mem., Internat. Soc. of Barristers, USA; Hon. Member: Canadian Bar Assoc.; Georgia Trial Lawyers' Assoc.; Florida Defense Lawyers' Assoc. Hon. Fellow, UC at Buckingham, 1982. Mem. Ct, Broderers Company. Chevalier du Tastevin. *Publications:* contribs Halsbury's Laws of England, Atkins' Court Forms. *Address:* Court of Justice of the European Communities, Kirchberg, Luxembourg. *Club:* Beefsteak.

SLYTH, Arthur Roy, CB 1966; OBE 1957; *b* 30 May 1910; *s* of Thomas Slyth; *m* 1938, Anne Mary Muir Grieve (*d* 1973). *Educ:* Lincoln School. Entered Exchequer and Audit Department, 1929; Dep. Sec., 1961; Sec., 1963-73. *Recreation:* golf. *Address:* 4 Broadlands Road, N6 4AS. *T:* 01-340 2366.

SMAILES, Prof. Arthur Eltringham, MA, DLit London; Emeritus Professor of Geography in the University of London; Professor of Geography at Queen Mary College, 1955-73; *b* Haltwhistle, Northumberland, 23 March 1911; *o s* of John Robert and Mary Elizabeth Smailes; *m* 1937, Dorothy Forster; one *d. Educ:* Grammar School of Queen Elizabeth, Hexham; University College, London. BA (London) with First Cl. Hons in Geography, 1930, MA 1933, DLit 1965. Lecturer, University College, London, from 1931 and Reader in Geography, 1950-53; Head of Department of Geography, Queen Mary College, University of London, 1953-73. Geographer Consultant, Middlesbrough Survey and Plan, 1944-45. Hon. Secretary, Inst. of British Geographers, 1951-62, Pres., 1970. Chm., Internat. Geog. Union Commn on Processes and Patterns of Urbanisation, 1972-76. Circuit Steward, West London Mission, Kingsway Hall, 1965-69. Research Medal, RSGS, 1964. *Publications:* The Geography of Towns, 1953; North England, 1960. Various articles in geographical and town planning journals. *Address:* Department of Geography, Queen Mary College, Mile End Road, E1 4NS.

SMAILES, George Mason; retired barrister; *b* 23 Jan. 1916; *s* of late Thomas and Kate Smailes; *m* 1939, Evelyn Mabel Jones; one *s* two *d. Educ:* The Leys Sch., Cambridge; Leeds Univ. (LLB); Metropolitan Police College. Solicitor's articled clerk, 1933-37; Station Inspector, Metropolitan Police, 1937-47; served RAF, 1944-45. Called to Bar, Gray's Inn, 1946; practised on North-Eastern Circuit, 1947-67; acted as Deputy County Court Judge and Deputy and Asst Recorder of various boroughs, 1961-68. Part-time legal member of tribunals: Mental Health Review, 1960-67; National Insurance, Local, 1962-65; Medical Appeal (Industrial Injuries), 1965-67; Industrial, 1966-67; Regional Chm. of Industrial Tribunals, Leeds, 1967-82. Associate, Wellington Dist Law Soc. (NZ). *Recreations:* listening to music, gardening. *Address:* 24 Liverpool Street, Masterton, New Zealand. *T:* Masterton 84610. *Club:* Leeds (Leeds).

SMALE, John Arthur, CBE 1953; AFC 1919; Technical consultant, Marconi's Wireless Telegraph Co. Ltd, 1957-62, retd; *b* 16 Feb. 1895; *s* of Charles Blackwell and Ann Smale; *m* 1920, Hilda Marguerita Watts; one *d* (one *s* killed on active service, RAF, 1941). *Educ:* Wycliffe Coll., Stonehouse; Bristol Univ. (BSc). Apprentice British Thompson Houston, Rugby, 1914; served European War, 1914-18, in RNAS; RAF, 1918-19. Engineer, Marconi's Wireless Telegraph Co. Ltd, 1919-29; Cable & Wireless Ltd, 1929-57, retired (Asst Engineer-in-Chief, 1935-48; Engineer-in-Chief, 1948-57). Chairman Cyprus Inland Telecommunications Authority, 1955-60, retired. FIEE 1941; Chairman, Radio Section of IEE, 1953; FIEEE 1958. *Recreations:* sport, music. *Address:* Cotswold, 21 Ilex Way, Goring-By-Sea, W Sussex BN12 4UZ.

SMALL, (Charles) John; Deputy Secretary-General of the Commonwealth, since April 1978; Canadian economist; *b* Chengtu, Szechuan, China, 19 Dec. 1919; *s* of Rev. and Mrs Walter Small; *m* 1946, Jean McNeel; four *d. Educ:* Ontario Agricultural Coll. (BSA); Univ. of Toronto (BA). LLD *hc* Univ. of Guelph, 1975. Royal Canadian Navy service, 1941-46, in N Atlantic, Mediterranean, Normandy and Australia. Mem., Dept of Trade and Commerce, 1949-56; serving in The Hague as Commercial Sec. (Agriculture), 1950-55; Dept of External Affairs, 1955-; Chinese studies at Univ. of Toronto, 1956-57; seconded to Dept of Trade and Commerce, and apptd Canadian Govt Trade Comr, Hong Kong, 1958-61; Ottawa, 1961-63; Counsellor, Canadian High Commn, Karachi, 1963-65; Perm. Rep. of Canada to OECD, Paris, concurrently Canadian observer, Council of Europe, Strasbourg, 1965-69; Amb. to Pakistan, 1969-72, concurrently Amb. to Afghanistan; Amb. to People's Repub. of China, 1972-76, concurrently to Socialist Repub. of Viet-Nam, 1975-76. Member: RIIA; CIIA; Agricl Inst. of Canada. *Recreations:* tennis, golf, swimming. *Address:* Commonwealth Secretariat, Marlborough House, Pall Mall, SW1Y 5HX. *Clubs:* Royal Automobile, Royal Commonwealth Society, Royal Over-Seas League, Belfry.

SMALL, Prof. John Rankin; Professor and Head of Department of Accountancy and Finance, Heriot-Watt University, since 1967; *b* 28 Feb. 1933; *s* of David and Annie Small; *m* 1957, Catherine Wood; one *s* two *d. Educ:* Harris Academy, Dundee; Dundee Sch. of Econs. BScEcon London; FCCA, FCMA, JDipMA. Dunlop Rubber Co., 1956-60; Lectr, Univ. of Edinburgh, 1960-64; Sen. Lectr, Univ. of Glasgow, 1964-67; Dean of Faculty of Econ. and Social Studies, Heriot-Watt Univ., 1972-74; Vice-Principal, Heriot-Watt Univ., 1974-78. Dir, Edinburgh Instruments Ltd; Mem. Adv. Bd, Douglas Llambias Associates Ltd, Scotland, 1979-. Pres., Assoc. of Certified Accountants, 1982 (Mem. Council, 1971-); Chm., Educn Cttee, Internat. Fedn of Accountants. *Publications:* (jtly) Introduction to Managerial Economics, 1966; (contrib.) Business and Accounting in Europe, 1973; articles in accounting and financial jls on accounting and financial management. *Recreation:* golf. *Address:* 39 Caiystane Terrace, Edinburgh EH10 6ST. *T:* 031-445 2638. *Club:* Caledonian.

SMALL, Very Rev. Robert Leonard, CBE 1975 (OBE 1958); DD; Minister of St Cuthbert's Parish Church, Edinburgh, 1956-75; Chaplain to the Queen in Scotland, 1967-75, Extra Chaplain since 1975; *b* N Berwick, 12 May 1905; *s* of Rev. Robert Small, MA, and Marion C. McEwen; *m* 1931, Jane Hay McGregor; three *s* one *d. Educ:* N Berwick High Sch.; Edinburgh Univ.; New Coll., Edinburgh. MA 1st cl. hons Classics; Sen. Cunningham Fellowship; studied in Rome, Berlin and Zurich; DD 1957. Ordained, 1931, to St John's, Bathgate; W High Church, Kilmarnock, 1935-44; Cramond Church, Edinburgh 1944-56. Convener: C of S Cttee on Huts and Canteens for HM Forces, 1946-58; Cttee on Temperance and Morals, 1958-63; Social and Moral Welfare Bd, 1963-64; Stewardship and Budget Cttee, 1964-69; Mem., Scottish Adv. Cttee on Treatment of Offenders; Regional Chaplain (Scotland), Air Trng Corps; Hon. Vice-Pres., Boys' Brigade; awarded Silver Acorn by Chief Scout, 1978. Warrack Lectr on Preaching, 1959. Guest Preacher: Knox Church, Dunedin, 1950; Fifth Ave., Presbyterian Church, NY, 1960; St Stephen's Presbyterian Church, Sydney, 1962, 1971, 1976, 1981; Scots Church, Melbourne, 1971, 1976, 1979. Moderator of the General Assembly of the Church of Scotland, 1966-67; First Chm., Scottish Parole Bd, 1967-73; Chm., Parkinson's Disease Soc., Edinburgh; Chm., Age Concern, Scotland, 1980-. TV Series, What I Believe, 1970. *Publications:* With Ardour and Accuracy (Warrack Lectures), 1959; No Uncertain Sound (Scholar as Preacher Series), 1964; No Other Name, 1966; contribs to The Expository Times. *Recreations:* boating, walking; formerly Association football (Edinburgh Univ. Blue, captained team, 1927-28; played as amateur for St Bernard's FC, 1928-29; capped *v* England (Amateur), 1929). *Address:* 5 Craighill Gardens, Edinburgh EH10 5PY. *T:* 031-447 4243. *Club:* Royal Over-Seas League.

SMALLEY, Beryl, FBA 1963; MA Oxon; PhD Manchester; History Tutor, 1943-69, Vice-Principal, 1957-69, Emeritus Fellow, St Hilda's College, Oxford; *b* 3 June 1905; *d* of Edgar Smalley. *Educ:* Cheltenham Ladies' College; St Hilda's College, Oxford. Assistant Lecturer, Royal Holloway College, 1931-35; Research Fellow, Girton College, 1935-40; Temporary Assistant in Dept of Western MSS, Bodleian Library, 1940-43. Ford's Lecturer, Oxford, 1966-67. Hon. DLitt Southampton, 1974. *Publications:* The Study of the Bible in the Middle Ages, 1952; English Friars and Antiquity, 1960; The Becket Conflict and the Schools, 1973; Historians in the Middle Ages, 1974; Studies in Medieval Thought from Abelard to Wyclif, 1982; in Recherches de théologie ancienne et médiévale; Mediaeval and Renaissance Studies, etc. *Recreations:* walking, swimming, travel. *Address:* 5c Rawlinson Road, Oxford. *T:* Oxford 59525. *Club:* University Women's.

SMALLEY, Rev. Canon Stephen Stewart; Canon Residentiary and Precentor of Coventry Cathedral, since 1977; *b* 11 May 1931; *s* of Arthur Thomas Smalley and May Elizabeth Selina Smalley; *m* 1974, Susan Jane Paterson; one *s. Educ:* Jesus Coll., Cambridge (MA, PhD); Eden Theological Seminary, USA (BD). Assistant Curate, St Paul's, Portman Square, London, 1958-60; Chaplain of Peterhouse, Cambridge, 1960-63; Lectr and Sen. Lectr in Religious Studies, Univ. of Ibadan, Nigeria, 1963-69; Lectr in New Testament, Univ. of Manchester, 1970-77, Sen. Lectr, 1977 (also Warden of St Anselm Hall, 1972-77). Mem., C of E Doctrine Commn, 1981-. Mem., Studiorum Novi Testamenti Soc., 1965-. *Publications:* Building for Worship, 1967; Heaven and Hell (Ibadan), 1968; The Spirit's Power (Achimota), 1972; ed, Christ and Spirit in the New Testament, 1973; John: Evangelist and Interpreter, 1978; numerous articles in learned jls, incl. New Testament Studies, Novum Testamentum, Jl of Biblical Lit. *Recreations:* literature, music, drama, travel. *Address:* 35 Morningside, Coventry CV5 6PD. *T:* Coventry 75446; Hadrians, Bourton-on-the-Hill, Moreton-in-Marsh, Gloucestershire. *T:* Blockley 700564.

SMALLMAN, Barry Granger, CMG 1976; CVO 1972; HM Diplomatic Service; High Commissioner to Jamaica, and non-resident Ambassador to Haiti, since 1982; *b* 22 Feb. 1924; *s* of late C. Stanley Smallman, CBE, ARCM, and Ruby Marian Granger; *m* 1952, Sheila Knight; two *s* one *d. Educ:* St Paul's School; Trinity College, Cambridge (Major Scholar, MA). Served War of 1939-45, Intelligence Corps, Australia 1944-46. Joined Colonial Office, 1947; Assistant Private Secretary to Secretary of State, 1951-52; Principal, 1953; attached to United Kingdom Delegation to United Nations, New York, 1956-57, 1958, 1961, 1962; seconded to Government of Western Nigeria, Senior Assistant Secretary, Governor's Office, Ibadan, 1959-60; transferred to CRO, 1961; British Deputy High Comr in Sierra Leone, 1963-64; British Dep. High Comr in NZ, 1964-67; Imp. Defence Coll., 1968; FCO, 1969-71; Counsellor and Consul-Gen., British Embassy, Bangkok, 1971-74; British

High Comr to Bangladesh, 1975-78; Resident Diplomatic Service Chm., Civil Service Selection Bd, 1978-81. *Recreations:* tennis, golf, making and listening to music, light verse, bird watching. *Address:* c/o Foreign and Commonwealth Office, SW1; Little Shepherds, Cranbrook, Kent. *T:* Cranbrook 713494.

SMALLPEICE, Sir Basil, KCVO 1961; Chartered Accountant and Air/Sea Transport Executive; *b* 18 Sept. 1906; *s* of late Herbert Charles Smallpeice, Banker; *m* 1931, Kathleen Ivey Singleton Brame (*d* 1973), *d* of late Edwin Singleton Brame; *m* 1973, Rita Burns, *yr d* of late Major William Burns. *Educ:* Shrewsbury. Articled to Bullimore & Co., Chartered Accts, 1925-30. Accountant of Hoover Ltd, 1930-37; Chief Accountant and later Sec. of Doulton & Co. Ltd, 1937-48; Dir of Costs and Statistics, British Transport Commission, 1948-50; BOAC: Financial Comptroller, 1950-56; Member of Board, 1953-63; Deputy Chief Executive, 1954-56; Man. Dir, 1956-63; Chm., Nat. Jt Council for Civil Air Transport, 1960-61; Man. Dir, BOAC-Cunard Ltd, from its inception in 1962 till end of 1963; Administrative Adviser in HM Household, 1964-80; Chairman: Cunard Steam-Ship Co. Ltd, 1965-71 (Dir, 1964; a Dep. Chm., 1965); Cunard Line Ltd, 1965-71; Cunard-Brocklebank, 1967-70; Cunard Cargo Shipping, 1970-71; ACT (Australia)/Australian Nat. Line Co-ordinating Bd, 1969-79; Associated Container Transportation (Australia), 1971-79; a Dep. Chm., Lonrho Ltd, April 1972-May 1973; Director: Martins Bank Ltd, 1966-69; London Local Bd, Barclays Bank, 1969-74. Member Council: Inst. of Chartered Accountants, 1948-57; Inst. of Transport, 1958-61; Brit. Inst. of Management, 1959-64 and 1965-75 (Chm., 1970-72; a Vice-Pres., 1972-); Pres., Inst. of Freight Forwarders, 1977-78. Mem., Cttee for Exports to the US, 1964-66. Chairman: The English Speaking Union of the Commonwealth, 1965-68; Leatherhead New Theatre Trust, 1966-74; Air League, 1971-74. Pioneers Award for contribs to develt of containerization, Containerization Inst., NY, 1981. *Publications:* various articles in the 1940s on the development of industrial and management accounting; Of Comets and Queens (autobiog.), 1981. *Recreations:* gardening, golf. *Address:* Bridge House, Leigh Hill Road, Cobham, Surrey. *T:* Cobham 5425. *Clubs:* Athenæum, Boodle's; Melbourne (Melbourne, Vic).

SMALLWOOD, Anne Hunter, CMG 1976; Commissioner, Board of Inland Revenue, 1973-81; *b* 20 June 1922; *d* of Martin Wilkinson McNicol and Elizabeth Straiton Harper; *m* 1972, Peter Basil Smallwood (*d* 1977). *Educ:* High Sch. for Girls, Glasgow; Glasgow Univ. Entered Inland Revenue, 1943; Dep. Comptroller (Scotland), 1956-58; Min. of Land and Natural Resources, 1964-66; Min. of Housing and Local Govt, 1966; Under-Sec., Inland Revenue, 1971-73. *Address:* 10C Eldon Grove, NW3 5PT. *Club:* United Oxford & Cambridge University.
See also G. P. McNicol.

SMALLWOOD, Air Chief Marshal Sir Denis (Graham), GBE 1975 (CBE 1961; MBE 1951); KCB 1969 (CB 1966); DSO 1944; DFC 1942; idc; jssc; psc; aws; FRSA; FRAeS; Military Adviser to Chairman and Chief Executive, Aircraft Group, British Aerospace, since 1977; *b* 13 Aug. 1918; *s* of Frederick William Smallwood, Moseley, Birmingham; *m* 1940, Frances Jeanne, *d* of Walter Needham; one *s* one *d. Educ:* King Edward VI School, Birmingham. Joined Royal Air Force, 1938. Served War of 1939-45, Fighter Command. Group Captain, 1957; commanded RAF Guided Missiles Station, Lincs, 1959-61; AOC and Commandant, RAF Coll. of Air Warfare, Manby, 1961-62; ACAS (Ops), 1962-65; AOC No 3 Gp, RAF Bomber Comd, 1965-67; SASO, Bomber Comd, 1967-68, Strike Comd, 1968-69; AOC-in-C, NEAF, Comdr, British Forces Near East, and Administrator, Sovereign Base Area, Cyprus, 1969-70; Vice-Chief of the Air Staff, 1970-74; C-in-C, RAF Strike Command, 1974-76, and C-in-C, UK Air Forces, 1975-76. ADC to the Queen, 1959-64. Pres., Air League, 1981-. *Address:* The Flint House, Owlswick, Bucks. *Clubs:* Royal Air Force, Arts, Les Ambassadeurs.

SMALLWOOD, John Frank Monton; a Church Commissioner, since 1966 (Board of Governors and General Purposes Committee); *b* 12 April 1926; *s* of Frank Theodore and Edith Smallwood; *m* 1952, Jean Margaret Lovell; one *s* two *d. Educ:* City of London Sch.; Peterhouse, Cambridge, 1948-51 (MA Classics). Served RAF, 1944-48 (Japanese translation and interrogation). Joined Bank of England, 1951; Private Sec. to Governors, 1959-62; Adviser, 1967; Auditor, 1969; Dep. Chief Accountant, 1974-79. Church Assembly/General Synod, 1965- (Standing Cttee, 1971-); numerous *ad hoc* Cttees, etc, over years; Central Bd of Finance, 1965- (Dep. Vice-Chm. 1972-82); Anglican Consultative Council, 1975-83 (Trinidad, 1976, Lambeth Conf., 1978, Canada, 1979, Newcastle, 1981). A Trustee: City Parochial Foundn, 1969- (Vice-Chm. 1977; Chm., 1981-); Lambeth Palace Library, 1978-. Member: Southwark Dio. Bd of Finance, 1962- (Chm. 1975-); Southwark Ordination Course Council, 1960-74 (Vice-Chm., 1980-); Lee Abbey Council, 1969-74. *Recreations:* family, music, cathedrals, old churches, historic houses, gardens. *Address:* Downsview, Brockham Lane, Brockham, Betchworth, Surrey RH3 7EL. *T:* Betchworth 2032.

SMART, (Alexander Basil) Peter; HM Diplomatic Service; Counsellor and Head of Chancery, Canberra, since 1977, and Deputy High Commissioner, since 1981; *b* 19 Feb. 1932; *s* of late Henry Prescott Smart and Mary Gertrude Todd; *m* 1955, Joan Mary Cumming; three *s* (incl. twin *s*). *Educ:* Ryhope Grammar Sch., Co. Durham. Commnd RAEC, 1951; Supervising Officer, Educn, Gibraltar Comd, 1951-52; entered HM Foreign (later Diplomatic) Service, 1953; Vice Consul, Duala, 1955; Polit. Office, ME Forces, Cyprus, 1956; 2nd Sec. (Information), Seoul, 1959; News Dept, FO, 1964; Head of

Chancery, Rangoon, 1968; FCO, 1971; Head of Communications Technical Services Dept, 1975. *Recreations:* wild nature, the arts; looking and listening. *Address:* c/o Foreign and Commonwealth Office, SW1A 2AL.

SMART, Andrew, CB 1981; Director, Royal Signals and Radar Establishment, Malvern, since 1978; *b* 12 Feb. 1924; *s* of late Mr and Mrs William S. Smart; *m* 1949, Pamela Kathleen Stephens; two *s* two *d*. *Educ:* Denny; High Sch. of Stirling; Glasgow Univ. MA 1944. TRE Malvern, 1943; Science 2 Air Min., 1950-53; Guided Weapons Gp, RRE, Malvern, 1953-70 (Head, 1968-70); Dep. Dir (Scientific B), DOAE, 1970; RAE, Farnborough: Head of Weapons Gp, 1972; Head of Weapons Dept, 1973; Dep. Dir (W), 1974-77. *Recreations:* gardening, caravanning. *Address:* Hill Orchard, Shelsey Drive, Colwall, Malvern, Worcs. *T:* Colwall 40664.

SMART, Prof. (Arthur David) Gerald, FRTPI; Professor of Urban Planning in University of London, since 1975 (Head of Bartlett School of Architecture and Planning, University College London, 1975-80); *b* 19 March 1925; *s* of Dr A. H. J. Smart and A. O. M. Smart (*née* Evans); *m* 1955, Anne Patience Smart (*née* Baxter); two *d*. *Educ:* Rugby Sch.; King's Coll., Cambridge; Polytechnic of Central London. MA, DipTP; ARICS, FRSA. Served in The Rifle Brigade, 1943-47 (Captain). Appts in local govt (planning), London, NE England, E Midlands, 1950-63; County Planning Officer, Hants CC, 1963-75; Member: Planning Adv. Gp, 1964-65, Cttee on Public Participation in Planning, 1968-69, Min. of Housing and Local Govt; Planning and Transportation Res. Adv. Council, DoE, 1975-79; Working Party on alternative uses of Historic Buildings, Historic Bldgs Council and BTA, 1979-81. *Publications:* articles, conf. papers, in professional and other jls. *Recreations:* sailing, ornithology, music, walking. *Address:* University College London, Gower Street, WC1E 6BT. *T:* 01-387 7050; 10 Harewood Green, Keyhaven, Lymington, Hants SO4 0QZ. *T:* Milford-on-Sea 5475; 5 Charmouth Court, Kings Road, Richmond, Surrey TW10 6EW. *T:* 01-940 7355. *Clubs:* Athenæum; Keyhaven Yacht (Lymington).

SMART, Edwin; *see* Smart, L. E.

SMART, Professor Sir George (Algernon), Kt 1978; MD, FRCP; Director, British Postgraduate Medical Federation, 1971-78, retired; *b* 16 Dec. 1913; *er s* of A. Smart, Alnwick, Northumb; *m* 1939, Monica Helen Carrick; two *s* one *d*. *Educ:* Uppingham; Durham Univ., BSc 1935, MB, BS 1937. MD 1939 (Durham); MRCP 1940, FRCP 1952. Commonwealth Fund Fellow, 1948-49. Lectr in Med., Univ. of Bristol, 1946-50; Reader in Medicine, Univ. of Durham, 1950-56; Prof. of Medicine, Univ. of Newcastle upon Tyne, 1968-71 (Post-graduate Sub-Dean, 1962-68, Dean of Medicine, 1968-71). Censor, 1965-67, Senior Censor and Senior Vice-Pres., 1972-73, RCP. Chairman: Review Bd for Overseas Qualified Practitioners, GMC, 1979-82; Cttee of Management, and Med. and Survival Cttee, RNLI, 1979-. *Publications:* contrib. to Price's Textbook of Medicine, and Progress in Clinical Medicine (Daley and Miller); (ed) Metabolic Disturbances in Clinical Medicine, 1958; (co-author) Fundamentals of Clinical Endocrinology, 1969, 2nd edn 1974. *Recreation:* photography. *Address:* Taffrail, Crede Lane, Old Bosham, Chichester, Sussex PO18 8NX.

SMART, Gerald; *see* Smart, A. D. G.

SMART, Henry Walter, CB 1966; formerly Director of Savings, GPO (1958-68); *b* 7 Sept. 1908; *m*; two *s*. *Educ:* Sir Thomas Rich's School, Gloucester. *Address:* Knapp Cottage, Sheepscombe, Stroud, Glos. *T:* Painswick 812091.

SMART, Sir Jack, Kt 1982; CBE 1976; JP; Leader, Wakefield Metropolitan District Council, since 1973; *b* 25 April 1920; *s* of James and Emily Smart; *m* 1941, Ethel King; one *d*. *Educ:* Altofts Colliery Sch. Miner, 1934-59; Branch Sec., Glasshoughton Colliery, NUM, 1949-59; Mem., Castleford Municipal Borough Council, 1949-74; Mayor of Castleford, 1962-63; Mem., Wakefield Metropolitan Dist Council, 1973-; Chm., Assoc. of Metropolitan Authorities, 1977-78, 1980-81, 1981-82, 1982-83; Leader of the Opposition Group, AMA, 1979-80. Chairman: Wakefield AHA, 1977-81; Wakefield DHA, 1982-; Mem., Layfield Cttee of Enquiry into Local Govt Finance, 1974-76. JP Castleford, 1960. *Recreations:* golf, music. *Address:* Churchside, Weetworth, Pontefract Road, Castleford, West Yorks. *T:* Castleford 554880.

SMART, Jack; *see* Smart, R. J.

SMART, (Louis) Edwin, JD; Chairman, President and Chief Executive Officer, Trans World Corporation, since 1978; Chairman of the Board, Hilton International Co., since 1978; *b* 17 Nov. 1923; *s* of Louis Edwin Smart and Esther Guthery; *m* 1st, 1944, Virginia Alice Knouff; one *s* one *d*; 2nd, 1964, Jeanie Alberta Milone; one *s*. *Educ:* Harvard Coll. (AB magna cum laude 1947); Harvard Law Sch. (JD magna cum laude 1949). Admitted to NY Bar, 1950; Associate, Hughes, Hubbard & Ewing, NYC, 1949-56; Partner, Hughes, Hubbard & Reed, NYC, 1957-64; Pres., Bendix Internat. and Dir, Bendix Corp. and foreign subsids, 1964-67; Sen. Vice Pres., Trans World Airlines Inc., 1967-76, Vice Chm. 1976, Chm. of Bd and Chief Exec. Officer 1977-78. Director: Southern Natural Resources, Inc.; ACF Industries, Incorp.; The Continental Corp. *Address:* (office) 605 Third Avenue, New York, NY 10158, USA. *T:* (212) 557-5300; (home) 535 E 86th Street, New York, NY

10028; Coakley Bay, Christiansted, St Croix 00820, Virgin Islands. *Clubs:* Presidents, Marco Polo, Sky (NYC); St Croix Yacht.

SMART, Ninian; *see* Smart, R. N.

SMART, Peter; *see* Smart, A. B. P.

SMART, (Raymond) Jack; non-executive Director, Marshall Sons & Co. Ltd, since 1982; *b* 1 Aug. 1917; *s* of Frank Smart and Emily Rose Smart; *m* 1942, Jessie Alice Tyrrell; one *s* one *d*. *Educ:* Redhill Technical Coll. (HNC). Apprentice Prodn Engr, Lanston Monotype Corp., 1933-38; Aeronautical Inspection Directorate, Air Min., 1939-40; Rotol Airscrews/Dowty Rotol, 1940-59: successively Chief Inspector, Prodn Controller, Works Manager; Man. Dir, British Light Steel Pressings (subsidiary of Rootes Motors Ltd), 1960-65; British Leyland (formerly BM Corp.): Man. Dir, Truck Div., 1966-72; Gp Managing Dir, 1972-76; Gp Exec. Dir and Dep. Man. Dir, 1976-79; Man. Dir, Aveling Barford Holdings Ltd, 1979-80. *Recreations:* Rugby Union, gardening. *Address:* 228 Heyhouses Lane, St Annes, Lancs FY8 3RG. *T:* St Annes 724571.

SMART, Maj.-Gen. Robert Arthur, CBE 1958; FRCP; Chief Medical Officer, Esso Petroleum Co., 1975-79, Senior Medical Officer, 1972-75; *b* 29 April 1914; *s* of Arthur Francis Smart and Roberta Teresa Farquhar; *m* 1947, Josephine von Oepen; one *d*. *Educ:* Aberdeen Gram. Sch.; Aberdeen University. MB, ChB 1936; DPH (Eng.) 1948; MRCP 1965, FRCP 1977. Lt, RAMC, 1936; Capt. 1937; Maj. 1946; Lt-Col 1951; Col 1960; Brig. 1964; Maj.-Gen. 1967. Served in Palestine, Egypt, Western Desert, Eritrea, France and Germany, 1939-45; N Africa and E Africa, 1951-55; Asst Dir of Army Health, E Africa, 1952-55; Leader, Royal Society's Internat. Geophysical Year Expedn to Antarctica, 1956-57; Dep. Chief Med. Off., Supreme HQ Allied Powers Europe, 1960-62; Dep. Dir of Army Health, BAOR, 1962-64; Dir of Army Health, MoD, 1964-68; DMS, FARELF, 1968-70; DMS, BAOR, 1970-71; DDMS, HQ Army Strategic Comd, 1971-72, retired 1972. Polar Medal, 1958. QHS 1968-72. *Address:* 186 Forest Avenue, Aberdeen AB1 6UY. *Clubs:* Army and Navy, Caledonian.

SMART, Prof. (Roderick) Ninian; Professor of Religious Studies, University of Lancaster, since 1967, and concurrently Professor of Religious Studies, University of California, Santa Barbara, since 1976; *b* 6 May 1927; *s* of late Prof. W. M. Smart, FRSE, and Isabel (*née* Carswell); *m* 1954, Libushka Clementina Baruffaldi; one *s* two *d*. *Educ:* Glasgow Academy; The Queen's College, Oxford. Army service with Intelligence Corps, 1945-48, 2nd Lt, Captain, 1947; overseas service in Ceylon. Oxford: Mods (shortened), Class II, 1949; Lit. Hum. Class I, 1951; BPhil 1954; LHD Loyola. Asst Lecturer in Philosophy, Univ. Coll. of Wales, Aberystwyth, 1952-55, Lecturer, 1955; Vis. Lecturer in Philosophy, Yale Univ., 1955-56; Lecturer in History and Philosophy of Religion, Univ. of London, King's College, 1956-61; H. G. Wood Professor of Theology, University of Birmingham, 1961-66. Pro-Vice-Chancellor, Univ. of Lancaster, 1969-72. Lectures: Banaras Hindu Univ., Summer; Teape, Univ. Delhi, 1964; Gifford, Univ. of Edinburgh, 1979-80; Visiting Professor: Univ. Wisconsin, 1965; Princeton and Otago, 1971; Queensland, 1980; Univ. of Cape Town, 1982. First Gen. Sec., Inst. of Religion and Theology, 1973-77, Pres., 1980-; Pres., British Assoc. History of Religions, 1981-. *Publications:* Reasons and Faiths, 1958; A Dialogue of Religions, 1960; Historical Selections in the Philosophy of Religion, 1962; Philosophers and Religious Truth, 1964; Doctrine and Argument in Indian Philosophy, 1964; The Teacher and Christian Belief, 1966; The Yogi and the Devotee, 1968; Secular Education and the Logic of Religion, 1968; The Religious Experience of Mankind, 1969; Philosophy of Religion, 1970; The Concept of Worship, 1972; The Phenomenon of Religion, 1973; The Science of Religion and the Sociology of Knowledge, 1973; Mao, 1974; A Companion to the Long Search, 1977; The Phenomenon of Christianity, 1979; Beyond Ideology, 1982; contrib. to Mind, Philosophy, Philosophical Quarterly, Review of Metaphysics, Religion, Religious Studies. *Recreations:* cricket, tennis, poetry. *Address:* Department of Religious Studies, University of Lancaster, Bailrigg, Lancaster LA1 4YG. *Club:* Athenæum.

SMART, William Norman H.; *see* Hunter Smart.

SMEALL, James Leathley, MA, JP; Principal, Saint Luke's College, Exeter, 1945-72; *b* 16 June 1907; *s* of late William Francis Smeall, MB, BCh (Edin.), and Ethel Mary Leathley; *m* 1936, Joan Rachel Harris; one *d*. *Educ:* Sorbonne; Queens' College, Cambridge (Scholar). Class I English Tripos, Class II Division 1 Anthropological and Archæological Tripos; Assistant Master, Merchiston, 1929-30; Staff, Royal Naval College, Dartmouth, 1930-34; Housemaster, Bradfield College, 1934-36; Head of the English Department, Epsom College, 1936-39; Headmaster, Chesterfield Grammar School, 1939-45; Commissioned RAFVR, 1941-44. Mayor of Exeter, 1965-66; Chm., Exeter Civic Soc., 1972-. Governor: Exeter Sch.; King's Coll., Taunton. *Publication:* English Satire, Parody and Burlesque, 1952. *Recreations:* gardening and travel. *Address:* Follett Orchard, Topsham, Exeter. *T:* Topsham 3892.

SMEDDLES, Thomas Henry; Chief General Manager, Royal Insurance Group, 1963-69; *b* 18 Dec. 1904; *s* of late T. H. Smeddles; *m* 1931, Dorothy Boardman; one *s*. Joined The Liverpool & London & Globe Insurance Co. Ltd, 1924. *Recreations:* gardening, sailing, golf. *Address:* 6 Abbotts Close, Abbotts Ann, Andover, Hants.

SMEDLEY, (Frank) Brian, QC 1977; a Recorder of the Crown Court, since 1972; Barrister-at-Law; *b* 28 Nov. 1934. *Educ:* West Bridgford Grammar Sch.; London Univ. LLB Hons, 1957. Called to the Bar, Gray's Inn, 1960; Midland Circuit; Mem., Senate of the Inns of Court and the Bar, 1973–77. *Recreations:* travel, music. *Address:* The Barn, Wellingore, Lincolnshire. *T:* Lincoln 810386; 4 Hale Court, Lincoln's Inn, WC2. *T:* 01-242 4552. *Club:* Garrick.

SMEDLEY, George; *see* Smedley, R. R. G. B.

SMEDLEY, Sir Harold, KCMG 1978 (CMG 1965); MBE 1946; HM Diplomatic Service, retired; British High Commissioner in New Zealand, and concurrently Governor of Pitcairn Island, 1976–80; High Commissioner in Western Samoa (non-resident), 1977–80; *b* 19 June 1920; *s* of late Dr R. D. Smedley, MA, MD, DPH, Worthing; *m* 1950, Beryl Mary Harley Brown, Wellington, New Zealand; two *s* two *d. Educ:* Aldenham School; Pembroke College, Cambridge. Served War of 1939–45, Royal Marines. Entered Dominions Office (later Commonwealth Relations Office), 1946; Private Secretary to Permanent Under-Secretary of State, 1947–48; British High Commissioner's Office: Wellington, NZ, 1948–50; Salisbury, Southern Rhodesia, 1951–53; Principal Private Sec. to Sec. of State for Commonwealth Relations, 1954–57; Counsellor, British High Comr's Office: Calcutta, 1957; New Delhi, 1958–60; British High Comr in Ghana, 1964–67; Ambassador to Laos, 1967–70; Asst Under-Sec. of State, FCO, 1970–72; Sec. Gen., Commn on Rhodesian opinion, 1971–72; High Comr in Sri Lanka, and Ambassador to Republic of Maldives, 1972–75. Dep. Chm., London Bd, Bank of NZ, 1981– (Mem., 1980-). Dep. Chm., Victoria League, 1981–. *Address:* Sherwood, Oak End Way, Woodham, Weybridge, Surrey KT15 3DX. *Clubs:* United Oxford & Cambridge University, Royal Commonwealth Society.

SMEDLEY, (Roscoe Relph) George (Boleyne); Barrister; Counsellor, HM Diplomatic Service, retired; *b* 3 Sept. 1919; *o s* of late Charles Boleyne Smedley and Aimie Blaine Smedley (*née* Relph); *m* 1st, 1947, Muriel Hallaway Murray (*d* 1975), *o d* of late Arthur Stanley Murray; one *s* ; 2nd, 1979, Margaret Gerrard Gourlay, *o c* of late Augustus Thorburn Hallaway and *widow* of Dr John Stewart Gourlay. *Educ:* King's Sch., Ely; King's Coll., London (LLB). Called to Bar, Inner Temple. Artists Rifles TA; commnd S Lancs Regt, 1940; Indian Army, 1942–46 (Captain); Foreign Office, 1937 and 1946; Foreign Service (subseq. Diplomatic Service): Rangoon, 1947; Maymyo, 1950; Brussels, 1952; Baghdad, 1954; FO, 1958; Beirut, 1963; Kuwait, 1965; FCO, 1969; Consul-Gen., Lubumbashi, 1972–74; British Mil. Govt, Berlin, 1974–76; FCO 1976; Head of Nationality and Treaty Dept, 1977–79. Part-time appointments: Legal Mem., Mental Health Review Tribunal; Adjudicator under Immigration Act 1971; Inspector, Planning Inspectorate, Depts of the Environment and Transport; Mem., No 2 Dip. Service Appeal Bd. *Address:* Garden House, Whorlton, Barnard Castle, Co. Durham DL12 8XQ. *T:* Teesdale 27381. *Clubs:* Royal Automobile, Royal Over-Seas League.

SMEDLEY, Susan M.; *see* Marsden-Smedley.

SMEETON, Vice-Adm. Sir Richard Michael, KCB 1964 (CB 1961); MBE 1942; FRAeS 1973; DL; aerospace and defence consultant; *b* 24 Sept. 1912; *s* of Edward Leaf Smeeton and Charlotte Mildred Leighton; *m* 1940, Maria Elizabeth Hawkins; no *c. Educ:* RNC, Dartmouth. 800 Squadron i/c HMS Ark Royal, 1940–41; Assistant Naval Attaché (Air), Washington, DC, 1941–43; staff of Admiral Nimitz, USN 1943–44; Air Plans Officer, British Pacific Fleet, 1944–45; Captain (Air) Med., 1952–54; Imperial Defence College, 1955; Captain, HMS Albion, 1956–57; Director of Plans, Admiralty, 1958–59; Flag Officer Aircraft Carriers, 1960–62; NATO Deputy Supreme Allied Commander, Atlantic, 1962–64; Flag Officer, Naval Air Command, 1964–65. Rear-Admiral, 1959; Vice-Admiral, 1962. Retired Nov. 1965, at own request. Dir and Chief Exec., Soc. of British Aerospace Cos, 1966–79; Sec., Defence Industries Council, 1970–79. Mem. Council, Inst. of Dirs. DL Surrey 1976. *Address:* St Mary's Cottage, Shamley Green, Guildford, Surrey GU5 0SP. *T:* Guildford 893478. *Club:* Army and Navy.

SMELLIE, Kingsley Bryce Speakman; Professor Emeritus of Political Science, London School of Economics, since 1965; Professor, 1949–65, Hon. Fellow, 1977; *b* 22 Nov. 1897; *o s* of late John and Elizabeth Smellie; *m* 1931, Stephanie, *o d* of late A. E. Narlian. *Educ:* Mrs Bolwell, 15 Mall Road, Hammersmith; Latymer Upper School, Hammersmith; St John's College, Cambridge. Served European War, 1914–18, as private in London Scottish. Staff of London School of Economics, 1921–65. Laura Spelman Rockefeller Student in USA (Harvard Law School), 1925–26; Research Assistant, propaganda research unit of BBC, 1940; temp. principal: Ministry of Home Security, 1940–42, Board of Trade, 1942–45. *Publications:* The American Federal System, 1928; A Hundred Years of English Government, 1937; Civics, 1939; Reason in Politics, 1939; Our Two Democracies at Work, 1944; A History of Local Government, 1946; Why We Read History, 1948; British Way of Life, 1955; Great Britain since 1688, 1962. *Address:* 24 Parkside Gardens, SW19 5EU. *T:* 01-946 7869.

SMELLIE, Prof. R(obert) Martin S(tuart), PhD, DSc; FRSE 1964; FIBiol; Cathcart Professor of Biochemistry, since 1966, Director of the Biochemical Laboratories, since 1972, University of Glasgow; *b* Rothesay, Bute, 1 April 1927; *s* of Rev. W. T. Smellie, OBE, MA and Jean (*née* Craig); *m* 1954, Florence Mary Devlin Adams, MB, ChB; two *s. Educ:* Dundee High Sch.;

Glasgow Acad.; Univ. of St Andrews (BSc 1947); Univ. of Glasgow (PhD 1952; DSc 1963). FIBiol 1964. National Service, 1947–49: commnd Royal Scots Fusiliers; served with 2nd Bn Royal Scots and at CDEE, Porton. University of Glasgow: Asst Lectr in Biochemistry, 1949–52; Beit Memorial Res. Fellow, 1952–53; Lectr in Biochem., 1953–55 and 1956–59, Sen. Lectr, 1959–63; Reader in Molecular Biol., 1963–65. Res. Fellow, NY Univ. Coll. of Med., 1955–56. Biochemical Society: Mem. Cttee, 1967–71; Symposium Organiser, 1970–75. Member: EMBO, 1964; MRC Physiol. Systems and Disorders Bd, 1977; Brit. Biophys. Soc., 1968; Brit. Assoc. for Cancer Res., 1961; Soc. for Endocrinology, 1968; Council, Trinity Coll., Glenalmond, 1976; Governor, Glasgow Academicals War Meml Trust, 1976–79. Hon. Gen. Sec., RSE, 1976. *Publications:* A Matter of Life: DNA, 1969; (contrib.) The Biochemistry of the Nucleic Acids, 8th edn 1976, 9th edn 1981; (ed) Biochemical Society Symposia Nos 31–41; papers in scientific jls on nucleic acid biosynthesis and hormone control mechanisms. *Recreations:* fishing, walking, music, foreign travel. *Address:* 39 Falkland Street, Glasgow G12 9QZ. *T:* 041-334 4255. *Club:* New (Edinburgh).

SMETHAM, Andrew James, MA; Headmaster, Wandsworth School, London, since 1974; *b* 22 Feb. 1937; *s* of Arthur James Smetham and Eunice (*née* Jones); *m* 1964, Sandra Mary (*née* Owen); two *s. Educ:* Vaynor and Penderyn Grammar Sch., Cefn Coed, Breconshire; King's Coll., Univ. of London (BA (Hons German) 1959, DipEd 1964, MA (Educn) 1968). Assistant Master: Wandsworth Sch., 1960–66; Sedgehill Sch., 1966–70; Dep. Headmaster, Holloway Sch., 1970–74. *Recreations:* music, walking. *Address:* 170 Court Lane, SE21 7ED. *T:* 01-693 3696.

SMETHURST, Richard Good, MA; Director, Department for External Studies, University of Oxford, since 1976; Professorial Fellow of Worcester College, Oxford; *b* 17 Jan. 1941; *s* of Thomas Good Smethurst and Madeleine Nora Foulkes; *m* 1964, Dorothy Joan (*née* Mitchenall); two *s* two *d. Educ:* Liverpool Coll.; Worcester Coll., Oxford; Nuffield Coll., Oxford. Webb Medley Jun. Schol. 1962; BA 1st Cl. 1963; MA Oxon. Research Fellow, Inst. for Commonwealth Studies, Oxford, 1966 (Consultant, UN/FAO World Food Program); Fellow and Tutor in Economics, St Edmund Hall, Oxford, 1966–67; Fellow and Tutor in Economics, Worcester Coll., Oxford, and Univ. Lectr in Economics, 1967–76; Economic Adviser, HM Treasury, 1969–71; Policy Adviser, Prime Minister's Policy Unit, 1975–76. Member: Adv. Council for Adult and Continuing Educn, DES, 1977–; Monopolies and Mergers Commn, 1978–; Governor: Liverpool Coll.; St Michael's Coll., Tenbury. *Publications:* Impact of Food Aid on Donor Countries (with G. R. Allen), 1967; contribs to New Thinking About Welfare, 1969; Economic System in the UK, 1977, 2nd edn 1979; New Directions in Adult and Continuing Education, 1979; contrib. Jl of Development Studies, Studies in Adult Education. *Recreations:* walking, gardening, good food. *Address:* Beckett House, Wallingford Street, Wantage, Oxfordshire OX12 8AZ. *T:* Wantage 4334.

SMETHURST, Stuart Wilson; Director, City of Birmingham Polytechnic, 1970–79; *b* 22 Sept. 1923; *s* of Herbert Stuart Smethurst and Eliza (*née* Wilson); *m* 1954, Pamela Marguerite Soames; two *s* one *d. Educ:* Hull Grammar Sch.; University Coll., Hull. MSc; FIMA. Scientific Civil Service, 1944–45; posts in educn in Hull, Sunderland, Bradford and Leeds, 1946–70. Member: Educn Adv. Council, IBA, 1975–80; Council, CNAA, 1973–78. *Publications:* scientific papers in technical jls. *Address:* 7 Clifton Road, Parkstone, Poole, Dorset. *T:* Poole 743674.

SMETTEM, Colin William; Chairman, North Eastern Region, British Gas Corporation, 1973–76; *b* 1 June 1916; *s* of William Home Smettem and Agnes Grace; *m* 1945, Sylvia Elisabeth (*née* Alcock); two *s* two *d. Educ:* Scarborough High Sch. Solicitor (Hons). Asst Solicitor, Scarborough Corp., 1938. Served War, 1939–45: UK, India, Assam; GII at Tactical Trng Centre, India Command, 1944. Asst Town Clerk, Wallasey, 1948; Solicitor, North Western Gas Bd, 1950; Commercial Manager, North Western Gas Bd, 1961, and Mem. Bd, 1965–68; Dep. Chm., Eastern Gas Bd, 1968. *Recreation:* DIY. *Address:* The Rookery, Tinwell, via Stamford, Lincs PE9 3UJ. *T:* Stamford 53168. *Club:* Naval and Military.

SMIETON, Dame Mary Guillan, DBE 1949; MA Oxon; Permanent Secretary, Ministry of Education, 1959–63, retired; *b* 5 Dec. 1902; *d* of John Guillan Smieton, late librarian and bursar Westminster Coll., Cambridge, and of Maria Judith Toop. *Educ:* Perse Sch., Cambridge; Wimbledon High Sch.; Bedford Coll., London (1 year) (Hon. Fellow, 1971); Lady Margaret Hall. Assistant Keeper, Public Record Office, 1925–28; Ministry of Labour and National Service, 1928–46; on loan to Home Office as General Secretary, Women's Voluntary Services, 1938–40, and to UN as Director of Personnel, 1946–48; Deputy Secretary, Ministry of Labour and National Service, 1955–59 (Under-Secretary, 1946–55). UK representative, Unesco Executive Board, 1962–68. Trustee, British Museum, 1963–73; Chm., Bedford Coll. Council, 1964–70. Member: Advisory Council on Public Records, 1965–73; Standing Commn on Museums and Galleries, 1970–73; Vice Pres., Museums Assoc., 1974–77. Hon. Fellow, Lady Margaret Hall, Oxford, 1959. *Address:* 14 St George's Road, St Margaret's on Thames, Middlesex. *T:* 01-892 9279. *Club:* United Oxford & Cambridge University.

SMIJTH-WINDHAM, Brig. William Russell, CBE 1946; DSO 1942; *b* 21 Oct. 1907; *s* of late Arthur Russell Smijth-Windham; *m* 1934, Helen Teresa, *d* of late Brig. H. Clementi Smith, DSO; one *s* three *d. Educ:* Wellington

College; Royal Military Academy, Woolwich. Commissioned Royal Corps of Signals, 1927; Mount Everest Expedition, 1933 and 1936; Mohmand Ops, 1935; Army Revolver VIII, 1937-39; British Pistol VIII, 1939. Served War of 1939-45, Greece and Crete, 1941; Western Desert and Tunisia, 1942-43; France and Germany, 1944-45 (despatches); British Mil. Mission to Greece during Greek Civil War, 1948-49; Chief Signal Officer, Eastern Command, 1957-60, retd 1960; ADC to the Queen, 1957-60. FIEE. *Recreations:* shooting, sailing. *Address:* Icentown House, Pitney, Langport, Somerset. *T:* Langport 250525.

SMILEY, Sir Hugh Houston, 3rd Bt, *cr* 1903; late Grenadier Guards; JP; Vice Lord-Lieutenant of Hampshire, 1973-82; *b* 14 Nov. 1905; *s* of 2nd Bt and Valerie (*d* 1978), *y d* of late Sir Claude Champion de Crespigny, 4th Bt; *S* father, 1930; *m* 1933, Nancy, *er d* of E. W. H. Beaton; one *s. Educ:* Eton; RMC, Sandhurst. Served with 1st Bn Grenadier Guards NW Europe, 1944-45. JP 1952, DL 1962, Hampshire; High Sheriff, 1959. Hon. Secretary Jane Austen Society, 1953- (Chm., 1969-). *Heir: s* Lt-Col John Philip Smiley [*b* 24 Feb. 1934; *m* 1963, Davina Elizabeth, *e d* of late Denis Griffiths; two *s* one d. *Educ:* Eton; RMA, Sandhurst; Lt-Col Grenadier Guards]. *Address:* Ivalls, Bentworth, Alton, Hants GU34 5JU. *T:* Alton 63193. *Club:* Cavalry and Guards.

SMILEY, Prof. Timothy John, PhD; Knightbridge Professor of Philosophy, University of Cambridge, since 1980; Fellow of Clare College, Cambridge, since 1955; *b* 13 Nov. 1930; *s* of Prof. M. T. Smiley and Mrs T. M. Smiley (*née* Browne); *m* 1955, Benita Mary Bentley; four *d. Educ:* Ardwyn Grammar Sch., Aberystwyth; Ampleforth Coll.; Fribourg Univ.; Clare Coll., Cambridge (BA 1952, Math. Tripos; MA, PhD 1956). Holt Scholarship, Gray's Inn, 1954; called to the Bar, 1956. Pilot Officer, RAFVR, 1954. Scientific Officer, Air Min., 1955-56; Clare Coll., Cambridge: Res. Fellow, 1955-59; Asst Tutor, 1959-65; Sen. Tutor, 1966-69; Asst Lectr in Phil., Cambridge Univ., 1957-62, Lectr, 1962-79. Vis. Professor: Cornell Univ., 1964; Univ. of Virginia, 1972; Yale Univ., 1975. *Publications:* (with D. J. Shoesmith) Multiple-conclusion Logic, 1978; articles in phil and math. jls. *Recreation:* orienteering. *Address:* Clare College, Cambridge. *T:* Cambridge 247106.

SMIRK, Sir (Frederick) Horace, KBE 1958; Emeritus Professor, University of Otago, Dunedin, New Zealand (Professor of Medicine, 1940-61); Director, Wellcome Research Institute, 1962-68, engaged in honororary research 1969-76; *b* 12 December 1902; *s* of Thomas Smirk and Betsy Ann (*née* Cunliffe); *m* 1931, Aileen Winifrede, *d* of Rev. Arthur Bamforth and Martha Bamforth; three *s* one d. *Educ:* Haslingden Gram. Sch.; Univ. of Manchester. Gaskill mathematical schol., 1919; MB, ChB 1st Cl. Hons 1925; MD Gold Medallist, 1927; FRCP 1940; FRACP (Hon.) 1940. Med. Registrar, Manchester Royal Infirmary, 1926-29; RMO 1929; Dickenson Travelling Scholar, University of Vienna, 1930; Beit Memorial Fell., successively Asst Depts of Pharmacology, and Medicine, Univ. Coll. London, 1930-34; Prof. of Pharmacology and Physician Postgrad. Dept, Egyptian Univ., 1935-39. Visiting Prof., Brit. Postgrad. Med. Sch., London, 1949; McIlraith Visiting Prof., Roy. Prince Alfred Hosp., Sydney, 1953; Holme Lectr Univ. Coll. Hosp. Med. Sch., 1949; Alexander Gibson Lectr, Edinburgh Coll. of Physicians, 1956; Dr N. D. Patel Inaugural lecture, Bombay, 1959; Member Board of Censors, later Senior Censor, 1940-58; Vice-President RACP, 1958-60; Chairman Clinical Reseach Committee, 1942-, Psychiatric Research Cttee, 1957-60; Mem. Council Med. Research Council of NZ, 1944-60; Mem. Expert Cttee on Hypertension and Ischaemic Heart Disease, of WHO; Life Member, New York Acad. of Science, 1961; formerly Councillor, International Society of Cardiology (Mem. Hypertension Research Sub-Cttee); Hon. overseas Mem. Assoc. of Physicians of GB, 1967. Hon. DSc: Hahnemann Coll., Pa, 1961; Otago, 1975. Gairdner Foundn International Award for Research in Medicine, 1965. *Publications:* Hypotensive Drugs, 1956; Arterial Hypertension, 1957; jointly: Modern Trends in Geriatrics, 1956, Current Therapy, 1956, Annual Reviews of Medicine, 1955; Antihypertensive Agents, 1967; contrib. to med. jls, mainly on disorders of the heart. *Recreations:* reading, writing, travel. *Address:* 68 Cannington Road, Dunedin, New Zealand. *T:* 741.046. *Club:* Fernhill (Dunedin).

SMIRNOVSKY, Mikhail Nikolaevich; Soviet Ambassador to the Court of St James's, 1966-73; non-resident Ambassador to Malta, 1967-73; *b* 7 Aug. 1921; *m* Liudmila A.; one *s* two d. *Educ:* Moscow Aviation Institute. Mem. Soviet Foreign Service, 1948; Assistant, 1955, Deputy Head of American Div., Ministry for Foreign Affairs, 1957-58; Counsellor, 1958, Minister-Counsellor, Soviet Embassy in Washington, 1960-62; Head of US Div. and Mem. Collegium, Ministry for Foreign Affairs, 1962-66. Member: Central Auditing Commn of CPSU, 1966-76; Soviet Delegations to several International Conferences. *Address:* Ministry of Foreign Affairs, 32-34 Smolenskaya Sennaya Ploshchad, Moscow, USSR.

SMITH; *see* Abel Smith and Abel-Smith.

SMITH; *see* Buchanan-Smith.

SMITH; *see* Delacourt-Smith.

SMITH; *see* Gordon-Smith.

SMITH; *see* Hamilton-Smith, family name of Baron Colwyn.

SMITH; *see* Hornsby-Smith.

SMITH; *see* Llewellyn Smith and Llewellyn-Smith.

SMITH; *see* Macdonald-Smith.

SMITH; *see* Nowell-Smith.

SMITH; *see* Spencer Smith and Spencer-Smith.

SMITH; *see* Stewart-Smith.

SMITH; *see* Stuart-Smith.

SMITH; *see* Walker-Smith.

SMITH; *see* Wenban-Smith.

SMITH, family name of **Earl of Birkenhead, Viscount Hambleden, Barons Bicester, Kirkhill** and **Smith.**

SMITH, Baron *cr* 1978 (Life Peer), of Marlow in the County of Buckinghamshire; **Rodney Smith,** KBE 1975; MS, FRCS; Hon. Consulting Surgeon: St George's Hospital London, 1978; Royal Prince Alfred Hospital, Sydney, NSW; Wimbledon Hospital; Examiner in Surgery, University of London; External Examiner in Surgery, Universities of Cambridge, Birmingham and Hong Kong; former Advisor in Surgery to Department of Health and Social Security; Hon. Consultant in Surgery to the Army, 1972, Emeritus Consultant, 1980; *b* 10 May 1914; *o s* of Dr Edwin Smith and Edith Catherine (*née* Dyer); *m* 1st, 1938, Mary Rodwell (marr. diss. 1971); three *s* one d; 2nd, 1971, Susan Fry. *Educ:* Westminster Sch.; London Univ. (St Thomas's Hospital). MB, BS London, MRCS, LRCP 1937; FRCS 1939; MS London 1941. Surgical Registrar, Middlesex Hospital, 1939-41; Surgeon RAMC, 1941-45; appointed Surgeon, St George's Hospital 1946. Royal College of Surgeons: Hunterian Professor, 1947 and 1952; Arris and Gale Lecturer, 1959; Jacksonian Prizewinner, 1951; Penrose May Tutor in Surgery, 1957-63; Dean, Inst. of Basic Medical Sciences, 1966-71; Mem., Ct of Examiners, 1963-69, Chm. Feb.-July 1969; Mem. Council, 1965-; Pres., 1973-77; Mem. Ct of Patrons; Hunterian Orator, 1975. President: Brit. Assoc. Surg. Oncologists; Harveian Soc., 1965; Pancreatic Soc., GB and Ire., 1976; Roy. Soc. Med., 1978-80; London Med. Orchestra. Chairman: ASCAB; Conf. of Med. Roy. Coll. UK, 1976-78; Armed Forces Med. Adv. Bd, 1980-. Member: Council, Brit. Empire Cancer Campaign; Exec., Internat. Fedn Surg. Colls. Trustee, Wolfson Foundn; Governor, Motability. Vis. Lectr to S Africa Assoc. of Surgeons, 1957; McIlrath Guest Prof. in Surgery, Royal Prince Alfred Hosp., Sydney, NSW, 1966; Vis. Prof., Surg. Unit, Univ. of Illinois, Chicago, 1978; Visiting Professor of Surgery: Jackson Univ., Miss, 1979; Johns Hopkins Hosp., Baltimore, 1979; Flint Univ., Mich, 1979. Lectures: First Datuk Abdul Majid Ismail Oration and Gold Medal, Malaysian Assoc. of Surgeons, 1972; Robert Whitmarsh Oration, Providence, 1972; Cheselden, St Thomas's Hosp., 1975; Philip Mitchiner, 1976; Balfour, Toronto, 1976; Colles, RCSI, 1976; Faltin (and Medal), Helsinki, 1976; Bradshaw, RCP, 1977; Sir Robert Bradlaw, Faculty of Dental Surgery, RCS, 1978; Sir Ernest Finch Meml, Sheffield, 1978; Telford Meml, Manchester, 1978; Annual Oration Med. Soc. of London, 1978; Sir William MacEwen Meml, Glasgow, 1978; Eisenberg, Boston, 1978; Judd, Minneapolis, 1979. Hon. Member: Soc. of Grad. Surgeons of LA County Hosp., 1965; Finnish Surgical Soc., 1976; Surgical Res. Soc., 1976; Surgical Soc. of Phoenix, Arizona; Soc. Surg. Alimentary Tract; Hellenic Surg. Soc.; Kentucky Surg. Soc., 1979. Hon. Fellow: Amer. Assoc. Surg.; Assoc. Clin. Anat.; Surgical Res. Soc., 1977; Assoc. of Surgeons of France, 1979; Philadelphia Acad. of Surg., 1979; Acad. de Chirurgie de Paris, 1981; Hon. FRACS 1957; Hon. FRCSEd 1975; Hon. FACS 1975; Hon. FRCSCan 1976; Hon. FRCSI 1976; Hon. FRCS S Africa 1976; Hon. FDS; Hon. FRSocMed 1981; Hon. FRCSGlas 1982. Hon. DSc: Exeter, 1974; Leeds, 1976; Hon. MD Zürich Univ., 1979. Biennial Prize, Internat. Soc. of Surgery, 1975; Gimbernat Surg. Prize, Surg. Soc. of Barcelona, 1980; Gold Medal, BMA, 1982. Hon. Freeman, Worshipful Co. of Barbers. *Publications:* Acute Intestinal Obstruction, 1947; Surgery of Pancreatic Neoplasms, 1951; Progress in Clinical Surgery, 1953, 1961, 1969; (ed with C. G. Rob) Operative Surgery (8 Vols) 1956-57 (14 Vols) 1968-69; Surgery of the Gallbladder and Bile Ducts, 1965; Clinical Surgery (Vols 1-14), 1965-67; papers in learned journals on pancreatic surgery, general abdominal surgery, intestinal obstruction. *Recreations:* music, cricket, golf, bridge. *Address:* 149 Harley Street, W1N 2DE. *T:* 01-935 4444. *Clubs:* MCC; Temple Golf.

SMITH, Agnes Lawrie Addie, (Laura); Sheriff of Glasgow and Strathkelvin, since 1982; *b* 17 June 1947; *d* of late William Smith and of Mary Marshall Smith McClure. *Educ:* Hamilton Acad.; Glasgow Univ. (LLB 1967). Admitted Solicitor, 1969; called to the Scottish Bar, 1976. Solicitor, private practice, 1969-71; Procurator Fiscal Depute, 1971-75. *Recreations:* painting, various sports.

SMITH, Alan; Chartered Mining Engineer; Research Group, Department of Industry, since 1980; *b* 19 Jan. 1930; *s* of John Smith and Alice (*née* Williams); *m* 1958, Adele Marguerite (*née* Buckle); two *s* two d. *Educ:* Rossall; St Catherine's Soc., Oxford. BSc Leeds 1957. MIMinE 1958. NCB, 1957-64; Principal Sci. Officer, Min. of Power, 1964; Sci. Counsellor, HM Embassy,

Paris, 1965-70; Cabinet Secretariat, 1970-71; DTI, 1971-73; Dept of Industry, 1973-74; Sci. and Technol. Counsellor, HM Embassy, Washington, 1975-77; Head of Sci. and Technol. Div., OECD, 1977-80. De Laune Lectr, Apothecaries' Soc., 1980. *Publications:* learned articles on steam engines. *Recreation:* engineering history. *Address:* 63 Leopold Road, SW19 7JG.

SMITH, Sir Alan, Kt 1982; CBE 1976; DFC 1941, and Bar 1942; DL; President, Dawson International plc, since 1982; *b* 14 March 1917; *s* of Alfred and Lilian Smith; *m* 1st, 1943, Margaret Stewart Todd (*d* 1971); three *s* two *d* ; 2nd, 1977, Alice Elizabeth Moncur. *Educ:* Bede College, Sunderland. Self employed, 1931-36; Unilever Ltd, 1937-39; RAF, 1939-45; Man. Dir, Todd & Duncan Ltd, 1946-60; Chm. and Chief Exec., Dawson International, 1960-82. DL Kinross, 1967. *Recreations:* sailing, swimming. *Address:* Ardgairney House, Cleish, by Kinross, Scotland. *T:* Cleish Hills 265. *Club:* Lansdowne.

SMITH, Alan Guy E.; *see* Elliot-Smith.

SMITH, Alastair Macleod M.; *see* Macleod-Smith.

SMITH, Sir Alex; *see* Smith, Sir Alexander M.

SMITH, Prof. Alexander Crampton (Alex. Crampton Smith); Nuffield Professor of Anaesthetics, Oxford University, 1965-79; *b* 15 June 1917; *s* of William and Mary Elizabeth Crampton Smith; *m* 1953, Marjorie (*née* Mason); three *s* ; two *d* by a former marriage. *Educ:* Inverness Royal Acad.; Edinburgh University. Edinburgh Univ., 1935-41. Served War of 1939-45 (Croix de Guerre, despatches), RNVR, 1942-46. Consultant Anaesthetist, United Oxford Hospitals, 1951; Clinical Lectr in Anaesthetics, Oxford Univ., 1961. FFARCS 1953; MA Oxon 1961. Civilian Consultant Anaesthetist to Royal Navy, 1968. Mem. Bd, Faculty of Anaesthetists, 1965-80. Mem. Trustees, Nuffield Medical Benefaction, 1973. *Publications:* Clinical Practice and Physiology of Artificial Respiration (with J. M. K. Spalding), 1963; contribs to anaesthetic, medical and physiological jls. *Recreations:* sailing, fishing. *Address:* 10 Horwood Close, Headington, Oxford OX3 7RF. *T:* Oxford 69593.

SMITH, Sir Alexander Mair, (Sir Alex), Kt 1975; Director of various companies; *b* 15 Oct. 1922; *s* of late John S. and Anne M. Smith; *m* 1956, Doris Neil (*née* Patrick) (*d* 1980); three *d. Educ:* Univ. of Aberdeen. MA (Maths and Nat. Phil.), PhD, FInstP. Physicist, UKAEA, 1952-56; Head of Advanced Research, Rolls Royce Ltd, 1956-67; Dir and Chief Scientist, Rolls Royce & Associates Ltd, 1967-69; Dir, Manchester Polytechnic, 1969-81. Chairman: Cttee of Dirs of Polytechnics, 1974-76; Schools Council, 1975-78; Member: UGC, 1974-76; BBC Gen. Adv. Council, 1978-81; Council, RSA, 1979-; Patron, Educnl Inst. of Design, Craft and Technology, 1977-. *Publications:* papers in learned jls. *Recreation:* golf. *Address:* 33 Parkway, Wilmslow, Cheshire. *T:* Wilmslow 522011. *Club:* Athenæum.

SMITH, Sir (Alexander) Rowland, Kt 1944; formerly Chairman and Managing Director, Ford Motor Co. Ltd; formerly Director, National Provincial Bank Ltd; Ex-Member, UK Atomic Energy Authority and National Research Corp.; *b* Gillingham, Kent, 25 Jan. 1888; *s* of late Alexander James Frederick Smith, Gillingham, Kent; *m* 1913, Janet Lucretia (*d* 1972), *d* of late George Henry Baker, Gillingham, Kent; one *s* one *d. Educ:* Mathematical School, Rochester. Freeman, City of London; Livery Cos: Glaziers (Past Master); Coachmakers and Coach Harness Makers; Member: Ministry of Aircraft Production Mission to USA, 1941; Ministry of Pensions Standing Advisory Cttee on Artificial Limbs, 1948; Cttee on Procedure for ordering Civil Aircraft, 1948. FIB; FRSA; CEng; FIMechE; Fell. Inst. of Bankers. *Recreation:* sailing. *Address:* The Manor House, Maresfield, W Sussex. *Clubs:* Athenæum; Royal Southern Yacht.

SMITH, Prof. Alwyn, PhD; Professor of Epidemiology and Social Oncology, University of Manchester, since 1979; *b* 9 Nov. 1925; *s* of Ernest Smith and Constance Barbara Smith; *m* 1950, Doreen Preston; one *s* one *d. Educ:* Queen Mary's Sch., Walsall; Birmingham Univ. MB, PhD; FRCP 1970; FRCGP 1973; FFCM 1974. Served War, RM, 1943-46. Res. Fellow in Social Medicine, Birmingham Univ., 1952-55; WHO Vis. Lectr, Univ. of Malaya, 1956-58; Lectr, Univ. of St Andrews, 1959-61; Sen. Lectr, Univ. of Edinburgh, 1961-66; First Dir, Social Paediatric Res. Gp, Glasgow, 1966-67; Prof. of Community Medicine, Univ. of Manchester, 1967-79. Pres., FCM, 1981-. *Publications:* Genetics in Medicine, 1966; The Science of Social Medicine, 1968; (ed) Cancer Control, 1979; (ed) Recent Advances in Community Medicine, 1982; papers on epidemiological subjects in Lancet, British Jl of Epidemiol., etc. *Recreations:* music, bird watching, fishing. *Address:* 66 Kingston Road, Manchester M20 8SB. *T:* 061-434 1395.

SMITH, Andreas W.; *see* Whittam Smith.

SMITH, Dame Annis Calder; *see* Gillie, Dame A. C.

SMITH, Anthony David; Director, British Film Institute, since 1979; *b* 14 March 1938; *s* of Henry and Esther Smith. *Educ:* Brasenose Coll., Oxford (BA). BBC TV Current Affairs Producer, 1960-71; Fellow, St Antony's Coll., Oxford, 1971-76. Bd Mem., Channel Four Television Co., 1980-. *Publications:* The Shadow in the Cave: the broadcaster, the audience and the state, 1973, 2nd edn 1976; British Broadcasting, 1974; The British Press since

the War, 1976; Subsidies and the Press in Europe, 1977; The Politics of Information, 1978; Television and Political Life, 1979; The Newspaper: an international history, 1979; Newspapers and Democracy, 1980; Goodbye Gutenberg—the newspaper revolution of the 1980's, 1980; The Geopolitics of Information, 1980. *Address:* Albany, Piccadilly, W1V 9RP. *T:* 01-734 5494; Bridge Cottage, Old Minster Lovell, Oxford OX8 5RN. *T:* Asthall Leigh 629. *Club:* British Academy of Film and Television Arts.

SMITH, Anthony (John Francis); writer, broadcaster; *b* 30 March 1926; 2nd *s* of Hubert Smith (formerly Chief Agent, National Trust) and Diana Watkin; *m* 1956, Barbara Dorothy Newman; one *s* two *d. Educ:* Dragon School, Oxford; Blundell's School, Devon; Balliol College, Oxford. MA Oxon., 1951. Served with RAF, 1944-48. Oxford University, 1948-51. Manchester Guardian, 1953 and 1956-57; Drum, Africa, 1954-55; Science Correspondent, Daily Telegraph, 1957-63. Scientific Fellow of Zoological Society. Glaxo Award for Science Writers, 1977; Cherry Kearton Medal and Award, RGS, 1978. TV series include: Balloon Safari, Balloons over the Alps, Great Zoos of the World, Great Parks of the World, Wilderness; radio series include A Sideways Look, 1977-. *Publications:* Blind White Fish in Persia, 1953; Sea Never Dry, 1958; High Street Africa, 1961; Throw Out Two Hands, 1963; The Body, 1968; The Seasons, 1970; The Dangerous Sort, 1970; Mato Grosso, 1971; Beside the Seaside, 1972; Good Beach Guide, 1973; The Human Pedigree, 1975; Animals on View, 1977; Wilderness, 1978; A Persian Quarter Century, 1979. *Recreations:* travel, lighter-than-air flying. *Address:* 9 Steele's Road, NW3. *T:* 01-722 4928.

SMITH, Ven. (Anthony Michael) Percival; Archdeacon of Maidstone, since 1979; Diocesan Director of Ordinands, since 1980; *b* 5 Sept. 1924; *s* of Kenneth and Audrey Smith; *m* 1950, Mildred Elizabeth; two *d. Educ:* Shrewsbury; Gonville and Caius Coll., Cambridge (MA); Westcott House Theological Coll. Served Army, Rifle Brigade, 1942-46. Cambridge, 1946-48; Westcott House, 1948-50. Deacon 1950, priest 1951; Curate, Holy Trinity, Leamington, 1950-53; Domestic Chaplain to Archbishop of Canterbury, 1953-57; Vicar of All Saints, Upper Norwood, 1957-66; Vicar of Yeovil, 1966-72; Prebendary of Wells Cathedral, 1968-72; RD of Murston, 1968-72; Vicar of St Mildred's, Addiscombe, Croydon, 1972-80; Hon. Canon of Canterbury Cathedral, 1980-. *Recreations:* reading, walking. *Address:* Archdeacon's House, Charing, Ashford, Kent TN27 0LU. *T:* Charing 2294.

SMITH, Anthony Robert; Director of Statistics and Research, Department of Health and Social Security, since 1976; *b* 29 March 1926; *s* of late Ernest George Smith and Mildred Smith (*née* Murphy); *m* 1949, Helen Elizabeth Mary Morgan; two *d. Educ:* De La Salle Coll., Pendleton; Peterhouse, Cambridge; London Sch. of Economics (BScEcon). Royal Marines and Army, 1944-47. Admiralty (Asst Statistician), 1950; various Admty appts, 1950-64; Head of Naval Manpower Div. and Defence Manpower Studies Unit, 1964-68; Chief Statistician, Treasury, 1968; Civil Service Dept, 1968-76. Under-Sec., 1970; Chm., Manpower Planning Study Gp, 1967-70; Member: Council of Manpower Soc., 1970-75 (Hon. Vice-Pres., 1975-); Council of Inst. of Manpower Studies, 1968-; Nat. Cttee of Inst. of Personnel Management, 1972-79; Consultant, Organisation for Economic Co-operation and Development, 1970-78. FIPM 1975. *Publications:* Models of Manpower Systems (ed), 1970; Manpower and Management Science (with D. J. Bartholomew), 1971; (ed) Manpower Planning in the Civil Service, 1976; Corporate Manpower Planning, 1980; contributor to: books and jls concerned with statistics, operational research, personnel administration, management, psychology and public administration. *Recreation:* dabbling in plant and animal cultivation. *Address:* 16 Carlton Road, Redhill, Surrey. *T:* Redhill 62258.

SMITH, Anthony Thomas, QC 1977; a Recorder of the Crown Court, since 1977; *b* 21 June 1935; *s* of Sydney Ernest Smith and Winston Victoria Smith; *m* 1959, Letitia Ann Wheldon Griffith; one *s* two *d. Educ:* Northampton, Stafford, and Hinckley Grammar Schs; King's Coll., Cambridge (Exhibnr; MA). Called to the Bar, Inner Temple, 1958. Flying Officer, RAF, 1958-60. *Recreations:* music, reading, hunting, farming. *Address:* Skeffington House, Skeffington, Leics. *T:* Billesdon 445.

SMITH, Arnold Cantwell, CH 1975; *b* 18 Jan. 1915; *m* 1938, Evelyn Hardwick Stewart; two *s* one *d. Educ:* Upper Canada Coll., Toronto; Lycée Champoléon, Grenoble; Univ. of Toronto; Christ Church, Oxford (Rhodes Scholar for Ont) BA Toronto, 1935; BA (Juris) Oxon 1937 (MA 1968); BCL 1938. Editor, The Baltic Times, Tallinn, Estonia, and Assoc. Prof. of Polit. Econ., Univ. of Tartu, Estonia, 1939-40; Attaché, British Legation, Tallinn, 1940; Attaché, British Embassy, Cairo, 1940-43; part-time Lectr in Polit. Sci. and Econs, Egyptian State Univ., Cairo, 1940-42; transf. to Canadian Diplomatic Service, 1943; Sec., Canadian Legation, Kuibyshev, USSR, 1943; Sec., Canadian Embassy, Moscow, 1943-45; Dept of External Affairs, Ottawa, 1946-47; Assoc. Dir, Nat. Def. Coll. of Canada, Kingston, Ont, 1947-49; Mem. Canadian Delegns to various UN Confs, 1947-51; Alternate Perm. Deleg. of Canada to UN Security Coun. and Atomic Energy Commn, 1949-50; Counsellor, Canadian Embassy, Brussels, and Head of Canadian Delegn to Inter-Allied Reparations Agency, 1950-53; Special Asst to Sec. of State for External Affairs, 1953-55; Internat. Truce Comr in Indochina, 1955-56; Canadian Minister to UK, 1956-58; Canadian Ambassador to UAR, 1958-61; Canadian Ambassador to USSR, 1961-63; Asst Under-Sec. of State for External Affairs, Ottawa, 1963-65; Secretary-General of the Commonwealth, 1965-75; Lester B. Pearson Prof. of Internat. Affairs,

Carleton Univ., Ottawa, 1975–81. Chairman: North-South Inst.; Hudson Inst. of Canada; Internat. Peace Acad., NY; Hon. Pres., Canadian Mediterranean Inst., 1981–; Trustee: Hudson Inst., Croton, NJ, 1976–81; Cambridge Univ. Commonwealth Trust, 1982–; Life Vice-Pres., Royal Commonwealth Soc. Hon. Fellow, Lady Eaton Coll., Trent Univ. R. B. Bennett Commonwealth Prize, RSA, 1975. Hon. LLD: Ricker Coll., 1964; Queen's Univ., Kingston, Ont, 1966; Univ. of New Brunswick, 1968; Univ. of BC, 1969; Univ. of Toronto, 1969; Leeds Univ., 1975; Trent Univ., 1979; Hon. DCL: Michigan, 1966; Oxon, 1975; Bishop's Univ., 1978. Zimbabwe Independence Medal, 1980. *Publications:* Stitches in Time—the Commonwealth in World Politics, 1981; reports; articles in learned jls. *Recreations:* fishing, reading, travelling, farming in France. *Address:* 300 Queen Elizabeth Driveway, Townhouse Five, Ottawa, Ont K1S 3M6, Canada. *T:* (613) 235.3073; (summer) Aux Anjeaux, Gavaudun, 47150 Monflanquin, France. *T:* (53) 711316. *Clubs:* Athenæum; Cercle Universitaire (Ottawa).

SMITH, Arnold Terence, MBE 1963; HM Diplomatic Service, retired; *b* 7 Oct. 1922; *s* of Thomas Smith and Minnie Louisa (*née* Mole); *m* 1944, Mary James, Preston, Yorks; one *s* one *d. Educ:* Christ Church, Dover; Coll. of Technol., Dover. Enlisted HM Forces, Army, 1939; served War, 1939–45; released, 1947. Joined CRO, 1948; Attaché, Karachi, 1952–56; Second Sec., Madras, 1956–60; CRO, 1960–61; First Sec., Kuala Lumpur, 1961–65; Consul, Oslo, 1965–69; FCO, 1969–73; Head of Chancery, Mbabane, 1973–77; Head of Admin., Nairobi, 1977–78; Counsellor, Lagos, Nigeria, 1978–80. *Recreations:* hiking, gardening, golf, swimming. *Address:* Weghill, Chipstead Park, Sevenoaks, Kent TN13 1DP. *T:* Sevenoaks 451979.

SMITH, Ven. Arthur Cyril, VRD 1955; MA; Archdeacon of Lincoln, 1960–76, now Archdeacon Emeritus; Rector of Algarkirk, 1960–76, now Canon Emeritus; *b* 26 Jan. 1909; *s* of late Arthur Smith and of Margaret Ryde, Manchester; *m* 1940, Patricia Marion Greenwood, *d* of late Lt-Col Ranolf Nelson Greenwood, MC, and Beatrice Marion, *d* of late Rev. Llewellyn L. Montford Bebb, DD; two *s* two *d. Educ:* St John's College, Winnipeg, Canada; Sheffield University; Westcott House, Cambridge. Curate of: Keighley, 1934–36; Bishop's Hatfield, 1936–40. Chaplain RNVR, 1940; HMS Hawkins, 1940–41; 13th Destroyer Flotilla Gibraltar, 1941–43; HMS Eaglet, 1943–44; Senior Chaplain, Liverpool 1945–46. Rector, South Ormsby Group of Parishes, 1946–60; Rural Dean, Hill North, 1955; Canon and Prebendary of Centum Solidorum, 1960. Member: Standing Cttee, House of Clergy, Church Assembly, 1966–70; General Synod, 1970–76; Inspections Cttee, Adv. Council for Churches Ministry, 1967. Church Comr, 1968. *T:* Ecclesiastical Insurance Office Ltd. *Publications:* The South Ormsby Experiment, 1960; Deaneries: Dead or Alive, 1963; Team and Group Ministry, 1965; contributor: to Mission and Communication, 1963; to Theology; to The Caring Church, 1964. *Address:* Farthings, Church End, Great Rollright, Chipping Norton, Oxon OX7 5RX. *T:* Hook Norton 737769. *Club:* Army and Navy.

SMITH, Sir Arthur (Henry), Kt 1968; Chairman, United Africa Co. Ltd, 1955–69; Director of Unilever Ltd, 1948–69; retired; *b* 18 Jan. 1905; *s* of Frederick Smith; *m* 1930, Dorothy Percy; two *s. Educ:* Bolton School. Specialised in Company's interests in French and Belgian Africa, incl. several years' residence in those territories. Econ. Adviser to Brit. Govt's Econ. Mission to French W Africa, 1943. Officer, Legion of Honour, 1957 (Cross 1951); Commander, National Order of the Ivory Coast, 1969. *Recreations:* reading, theatre. *Address:* The Coach House, 31 Withdean Road, Brighton, East Sussex.

SMITH, Arthur Norman E.; *see* Exton-Smith.

SMITH, Prof. Austin Geoffrey; Hives Professor of Thermodynamics, University of Nottingham, and Head of Department of Mechanical Engineering, since 1960; *b* 22 Aug. 1918; *s* of James Austin Smith and Olive Smith; *m* 1960, Vera Margaret Kennard; no *c. Educ:* Gillingham County School for Boys. Royal Scholar, Imperial College, London, 1937–40. Research engineer, Blackburn Aircraft Co., 1940–42; Engineer, Power Jets Ltd, 1942–46; Senior Scientific Officer and Principal Scientific Officer, National Gas Turbine Establishment, 1946–52; Reader in Gas Turbines, Imperial College, London, 1952–57; Professor of Aircraft Propulsion, The College of Aeronautics, 1957–60. *Publications:* many papers in the field of thermodynamics, heat transfer and aerodynamics. *Address:* Pinfold Close, Church Street, Bramcote, Nottingham NG9 3HD. *T:* Nottingham 258397.

SMITH, Basil Gerald P.; *see* Parsons-Smith.

SMITH, Basil Gerrard, TD 1950; *b* 29 January 1911; *m* 1938, Marjorie Elizabeth Artz; one *s* two *d. Educ:* Epsom College, Surrey; Merton College, Oxford (MA). Solicitor (England), 1938. War Service, 1939–46; Hon. Lt-Col. District Judge, Pahang, 1946; joined Colonial Legal Service, 1946; District Judge: Selangor, 1947; Perak, 1948; President, Sessions Court: Ipoh, 1949; Georgetown, Penang, 1950; Barrister (Gray's Inn), 1950; Federal Counsel and Deputy Public Prosecutor, 1953; Asst Legal Draftsman, 1954; Actg Legal Draftsman, 1955; Judge, Supreme Court, Federation of Malaya, 1956–60; Attorney-General, Southern Cameroons, 1960–61; Legal Adviser to the UK Commissioner, Malta, 1962–64; Legal Asst, Solicitor's Dept, Post Office, 1964, Senior Legal Assistant, 1967–69; Treasury Solicitor's Office, 1969–77; Adjudicator, Immigration Act, 1977–81. Law Reviser, Kiribati and Tuvalu, 1970, 1976, 1980 and 1981. *Address:* 7 Langley Grove, New Malden, Surrey

KT3 3AL. *T:* 01-949 4366.
See also S. A. Goldstein.

SMITH, Brian, OBE 1975; HM Diplomatic Service; Counsellor (Commercial), Bonn, since 1982; *b* 15 Sept. 1935; *s* of Charles Francis Smith and Grace Amelia (*née* Pope); *m* 1956, Joan Patricia Rivers; one *s* two *d. Educ:* Hull Grammar School. Foreign Office, 1952; HM Forces, 1954–57; Bahrain, 1957; Doha, 1959; Vice-Consul, Luxembourg, 1960, Casablanca, 1962; Tehran, 1964; Berne, 1967; FCO, 1969; Kampala, 1973; Tehran, 1975; FCO, 1977; New York 1979. *Recreations:* riding, photography, music, handicrafts. *Address:* c/o Foreign and Commonwealth Office, SW1A 2AH.

SMITH, Ven. Brian John; Archdeacon of Wilts and Vicar of Bishop's Cannings, All Cannings and Etchilhampton, since 1980; *b* 21 Sept. 1933; *s* of Stanley and Doris Jessie Smith; *m* 1965, Jean Margaret, *d* of Frank and Beryl Hanning; one *s* two *d. Educ:* St Marylebone Grammar School; Mill Hill School; St John's Coll., Durham; Salisbury Theological Coll. Army, 1952–55; professional photographer, 1956–62. Ordained, 1965; Curate of All Saints', Whitstable, 1965–69; Vicar of Woodford, Wilsford and Durnford, and Religious Drama Adviser to Diocese of Salisbury, 1969–76; Vicar of Mere, West Knoyle and Maiden Bradley, 1976–80; RD of Heytesbury, 1977–80; Non-residentiary Canon, Salisbury Cath., 1980–. Member: Council of RADIUS (Religious Drama Soc. of GB), 1971–76; various cttees, Diocese of Salisbury, 1969–. Author of a number of plays. *Publication:* contrib. to Religious Drama. *Recreations:* drama, photography, caravanning, canals. *Address:* The Vicarage, Bishop's Cannings, Devizes, Wiltshire SN10 2LD. *T:* Cannings 650.

SMITH, Brian Percival, CEng, FIProdE, FIM; CBIM; independent business consultant; Member, Civil Aviation Authority, since 1981; *b* 3 Oct. 1919; *s* of Percival Smith and Hilda Judge; *m* 1943, Phoebe (Tina) Ginno; one *s. Educ:* Erith, Woolwich; London Univ. (BSc). Apprentice, 1936–41, Manager, 1941–46, Royal Ordnance Factories; Gen. Manager, Cumbrian Tool Co., 1946–49; PA Management Consultants: Consultant, 1949–59; Dir, R&D, 1959–66; Man. Dir, 1966–72; Chm. of Bd, 1972–76. Mem., Design Council, 1975–80; Vice-Pres., Royal Soc. of Arts, 1976–80. Prof. of Design Management, RCA, 1977–81. Member Council: BIM, 1972–74; Instn of Prod. Engrs, 1972– (Pres., 1973–74). *Publications:* Leadership in Management, 1968; Bureaucracy in Management, 1969; Management Style, 1973; Going into Europe, Why and How, 1975; The Morality and Management of Design, 1977. *Recreations:* painting, writing, listening to music. *Address:* 4 Cliff Road, Eastbourne, East Sussex BN20 7RU. *T:* Eastbourne 31870.

SMITH, Brian Stanley, FSA, FRHistS; Secretary, Royal Commission on Historical Manuscripts, since 1982; *b* 15 May 1932; *s* of late Ernest Stanley Smith and Dorothy (*née* Palmer); *m* 1963, Alison Margaret Hemming; two *d. Educ:* Bloxham; Keble College, Oxford (Holroyd Scholar). MA 1957. FSA 1972, FRHistS 1980. Assistant Archivist, Worcestershire, 1956–58, Essex, 1958–60, Gloucestershire, 1961–68; County Archivist, Gloucestershire, 1968–79; Asst Sec., Royal Commn on Historical Manuscripts, 1980–81. Part-time Editor, Victoria County History of Gloucestershire, 1968–70; Editor, 1971–79, Vice-Pres., 1980–, Bristol and Gloucestershire Archaeological Soc. Chm., Soc. of Archivists, 1979–80. Lay Mem., Gloucester Diocesan Synod, 1972–76. *Publications:* History of Malvern, 1964, 2nd edn 1978; (with Elizabeth Ralph) History of Bristol and Gloucestershire, 1972, 2nd edn 1982; The Cotswolds, 1976; History of Bloxham School, 1978; articles in learned jls on local history and archives. *Recreations:* mountaineering, gardening. *Address:* Midwoods, Shire Lane, Cholesbury, Tring, Herts HP23 6NA.

SMITH, Maj.-Gen. Sir Brian W.; *see* Wyldbore-Smith.

SMITH, Brian William, PhD, FIEAust; Director, Royal Melbourne Institute of Technology, since 1979; *b* 24 June 1938; *s* of William Lyle Smith and Grace Ellen Smith; *m* 1961, Josephine Peden; two *d* (one *s* decd). *Educ:* Univ. of Melbourne (BEng); Univ. of Cambridge (PhD). MIEE, SMIREE Aust. Australian Paper Manufacturers Ltd, 1964–70; Consolidated Electronic Industries Ltd, 1971–73; Head, School of Electrical Engineering, 1973–77, Dean, Faculty of Engineering, 1977–79, Royal Melbourne Inst. of Technology. *Recreations:* golf, model railway. *Address:* 32 Banoon Road, Eltham, Victoria, Australia. *T:* 4396141. *Clubs:* Greenacres Golf, Melbourne Cricket.

SMITH, Bryan Crossley, CBE 1982; CEng, FIGasE; Member for Marketing, British Gas Corporation, 1977–82; *b* 28 Feb. 1921; *s* of Frank Riley Smith and Fanny Smith; *m* 1948, Patricia Mabbott; one *s* one *d. Educ:* Hipperholme Grammar Sch.; Bradford Technical Coll. CEng, FIGasE 1944. Articled pupil to John Corrigan, 1941; Operating Engr, Humphreys & Glasgow, 1944; Works Engr, Middlesbrough Corp. Gas Dept, 1948; N Eastern Gas Board: Asst Works Manager, Huddersfield, 1952; Engr and Man., Dewsbury, 1956; Group Sales Man., Wakefield, 1961; Conversion Man., 1966; Dep. Commercial Man., 1968; Chief Service Man., Gas Council, 1970; Service Dir, British Gas Corp., 1973. Senior Vice-Pres., IGasE, 1980–81. *Recreations:* golf, gardening. *Address:* Heron Path House, Wendover, Aylesbury, Bucks HP22 6NN. *T:* Wendover 622742.

SMITH, Sir Bryan Evers S.; *see* Sharwood Smith.

SMITH, Campbell (Sherston); retired; *b* 24 April 1906; *s* of Herbert Smith and Carlotta Amelia Smith (*née* Newbury); *m* 1st, 1936, Leonora Florence Beeney (marr. diss., 1948); one *s*; 2nd, 1948, Gwenllian Elizabeth Anne Williams (marr. diss., 1963); one *s*; 3rd, 1964, Barbara Irene Winstone. *Educ:* City of London School. General Departmental Manager, Keith Prowse & Co. Ltd, 1932, Director and General Manager, 1936. Squadron Leader, RAF, 1939-45 (Defence Medal). Assistant Managing Director, Keith Prowse & Co. Ltd, 1945, Managing Director, 1951-54. Director, Performing Right Society, 1951-54; Managing Director, Mechanical Copyright Protection Society, 1945-57; Director of MEEC Productions Ltd, 1953-62; Administrator of the Arts Theatre Club, 1954-62. Man. Dir, Campbell Williams Ltd, 1960-75. *Recreation:* theatre. *Address:* 32 Wordsworth Road, Worthing, West Sussex. *Clubs:* Garrick, Arts Theatre.

SMITH, Catharine Mary S.; *see* Scott-Smith.

SMITH, Maj.-Gen. Sir Cecil (Miller), KBE 1951 (CBE 1944; OBE 1941); CB 1947; MC; CEng, MIMechE; psc; late RASC; *b* 17 June 1896; *s* of John Smith, Dromore, Co. Down; *m* 1930, Isabel Buswell; two *d*. *Educ:* Royal Belfast Academical Institution; Royal Military College, Sandhurst; Staff College, Camberley. Served European War, 1914-19, ASC and Royal Inniskilling Fusiliers. France and Belgium, 1916-18 (wounded, MC, two medals); Served War, 1939-45: ME, 1939-44; NW Europe, 1944-45; Maj.-Gen., 1943; DQMG, ME/AE, 1943-44; DACOS, SHAEF, 1944-45; Maj.-Gen. in charge of Administration, Northern Command, 1945-47; Chief of Staff, Northern Command, 1947-48; Director of Supplies and Transport, War Office, 1948-51; retired pay, 1951. Col Comdt, RASC, 1950-60. Chm. Ulster Society in London, 1964-73. Commander, Legion of Merit, US; Officier de la Légion d'Honneur (France). *Address:* Crosh, Southfield Place, Weybridge, Surrey. *T:* Weybridge 42199.

SMITH, Sheriff Charles; Sheriff of Glasgow and Strathkelvin, since 1982; *b* 15 Aug. 1930; *s* of Charles Smith and Mary Allen Hunter or Smith; *m* 1959, Janet Elizabeth Hurst; one *s* one *d*. *Educ:* Kinnoull Primary Sch.; Perth Academy; St Andrews University. MA, LLB. Solicitor 1956. Practised in Perth, 1956-82; Temporary Sheriff, 1977-82. Hon. Tutor, Dept of Law, Dundee Univ. Main. Council, Law Soc. of Scotland, 1977-82. *Recreations:* tennis, golf. *Address:* c/o Sheriff Court, Ingram Street, Glasgow G1 1SY. *T:* 041-552 3434. *Club:* Western (Glasgow).

SMITH, Charles Edward Gordon, CB 1970; MD, FRCP, FRCPath; Dean, London School of Hygiene and Tropical Medicine, since 1971; *b* 12 May 1924; *s* of late John A. and Margaret Smith, Lundin Links, Fife; *m* 1948, Élsie, *d* of late S. S. McClellan, Lorton, Cumberland; one *s* two *d*. *Educ:* Forfar Academy; St Andrews University. MB, ChB (with commendation) 1947; MD (with hons and Singapore Gold Medal) 1956. House Surgeon and Physician, Cumberland Infirmary, Carlisle, 1947-48; HM Colonial Medical Service, 1948-57; Clinical appts Malacca, Kuala Lumpur, 1949-51; Virologist, Inst. for Med. Research, Kuala Lumpur, 1952-57; Sen. Lectr in Bacteriology, London Sch. of Hygiene and Trop. Med., 1957-61; Reader in Virology, London Sch. of Hygiene and Trop. Med., 1961-64; Director, Microbiological Research Estab., MoD, 1964-70. Chairman: Public Health Lab. Service Bd, 1972-; Independent Commn on the Onchocerciasis Control Programme, 1979-81. A Wellcome Trustee, 1972-. Pres., Royal Soc. of Tropical Medicine and Hygiene, 1975-77; Pres., Assoc. of Schs of Public Health in the European Region, 1979-81 (Pres.-elect 1977-79); Vice-Pres., Zoological Soc. of London, 1974-76, 1978-82. Chalmers Medal, Royal Soc. of Trop. Med. and Hygiene, 1961; Stewart Prize, BMA, 1973; Tulloch Award, Dundee, 1982. Hon. DSc St Andrews, 1975. *Publications:* papers mainly on tropical diseases and third world development. *Recreations:* gardening, golf. *Address:* London School of Hygiene and Tropical Medicine, Keppel Street, WC1E 7HT. *Clubs:* Savile; Bramshaw Golf; New Zealand Golf (West Byfleet).

SMITH, Prof. C(harles) Holt, CBE 1955; MSc; FIEE; Professor of Instrument Technology, Royal Military College of Science, Shrivenham, 1949-68, now Emeritus; (seconded to the Indian Government for four years from 1st January, 1956, as Dean of the Institute of Armament Studies); *b* 27 Aug. 1903; *s* of Charles Smith and Emily (*née* Holt); *m* 1928, Gracie Alexandra Macdonald (*née* Livingstone); one *s* one *d*. *Educ:* Bolton Grammar School; Manchester University. Peel Connor Telephone Works, 1924-26; Royal Aircraft Establishment, Farnborough, 1926-30 and 1938-40. British Broadcasting Corporation, 1930-38. Telecommunications Research Establishment: Malvern, 1940-42; Defford, 1944-46; Malvern, 1946-49. Assistant Director of Directorate of Communications Development, Ministry of Supply, 1942-44. *Recreations:* bridge, fishing, shooting. *Address:* 37 Queens Park Avenue, Bournemouth, Dorset BH8 9LH. *T:* 527525.

SMITH, Charles Nugent C.; *see* Close-Smith.

SMITH, Prof. (Christopher) Colin; Professor of Spanish, University of Cambridge, since 1975; *b* 17 Sept. 1927; *s* of Alfred Edward Smith and Dorothy May Berry; *m* 1954, Ruth Margaret Barnes; three *d* (one *s* decd). *Educ:* Varndean Grammar Sch., Brighton; St Catharine's Coll., Cambridge (MA, PhD). BA 1st cl. hons 1950. Dept of Spanish, Univ. of Leeds: Asst Lectr 1953; Lectr 1956; Sen. Lectr 1964; Sub-Dean of Arts, etc, 1963-67; Cambridge Univ.: Univ. Lectr in Spanish, 1968; Fellow, St Catharine's Coll., 1968-, Professorial Fellow, 1975-, Tutor 1970; Chm. Faculty of Mod. and Med. Langs, 1973. General Editor, Modern Language Review, 1976-81 (Hispanic

Editor, 1974-81). *Publications:* Spanish Ballads, 1964; (ed) Poema de mio Cid, 1972, Spanish edn, 1976; Collins' Spanish-English, English-Spanish Dictionary, 1971, Spanish edn 1972; Estudios cidianos, 1977; (with A. L. F. Rivet) Place-names of Roman Britain, 1979; contrib. Bull. Hispanic Studies, Mod. Lang. Rev., Bull. Hispanique, etc. *Recreations:* theatre, opera, squash, natural history (especially entomology), archaeology. *Address:* 56 Girton Road, Cambridge. *T:* Cambridge 276214.

SMITH, Christopher Patrick Crawford, MA; *b* Edinburgh, 9 May 1902; *s* of late George Smith; unmarried. *Educ:* Dulwich College; Trinity College, Oxford (Scholar, First in Classical Moderations, and First in Literae Humaniores). Assistant Master, Rugby School, 1926-38; Warden of Trinity College, Glenalmond, 1938-48; Headmaster of Haileybury, 1948-63. Chairman, Headmasters' Conference, 1961-62. *Address:* Windrush, St Andrews, Fife.

SMITH, Sir Christopher Sydney Winwood, 5th Bt, *cr* 1809; *b* 20 Sept. 1906; *s* of Sir William Sydney Winwood Smith, 4th Bt, and Caroline, *o d* of James Harris, County Cork; *S* father 1953; *m* 1932, Phyllis Berenice, *y d* of late Thomas Robert O'Grady, Grafton, New South Wales, and County Waterford, Ireland; three *s* two *d*. *Heir: s* Robert Sydney Winwood Smith, *b* 1939. *Address:* Junction Road, via Grafton, New South Wales 2460, Australia.

SMITH, Claude C.; *see* Croxton-Smith.

SMITH, Clifford Bertram Bruce H.; *see* Heathcote-Smith.

SMITH, Colin; *see* Smith, Christopher C.

SMITH, Colin; International Executive Director, National Anti-Vivisection Society Ltd, since 1981; *b* 4 July 1941; *s* of Henry E. Smith and A. E. Smith. *Educ:* Upton House Sch., London. Asst Sec., National Anti-Vivisection Soc., 1962-71, Gen. Sec., 1971-81. Hon. Sec., Internat. Assoc. Against Painful Experiments on Animals, 1969-; Dir, American Fund for Alternatives to Animal Res., 1977-. Mem., Hon. Nederlandse Laureat van de Arbeid, 1981. Editor, Animals' Defender and Anti-Vivisection News, 1967-72. *Publications:* Progress without Pain, 1973; Animal Experiments: steps towards reform, 1975; Moral and Social Aspects of Vivisection, 1981; numerous contribs to med. and scientific jls on the anti-vivisection case. *Recreations:* music, travel, gardening. *Address:* 51 Harley Street, W1N 1DD. *T:* 01-580 4034; (home) 29 College Place, St Albans, Herts.

SMITH, Cyril, MBE 1966; MP (L) Rochdale, since Oct. 1972; Liberal Chief Whip, 1975-76; Managing Director, Smith Springs (Rochdale) Ltd, since 1963; *b* 28 June 1928; unmarried. *Educ:* Rochdale Grammar Sch. for boys. Civil Service, 1944-45; Wages Clerk, 1945-48; Liberal Party Agent, Stockport, 1948-50; Labour Party Agent, Ashton-under-Lyne, 1950-53, Heywood and Royton 1953-55; rejoined Liberal Party, 1967. Newsagent (own account), 1955-58; Production Controller, Spring Manufacturing, 1958-63; founded Smith Springs (Rochdale) Ltd, 1963. Councillor, 1952-66, Alderman, 1966-74, Mayor, 1966-67, Co. Borough of Rochdale (Chm., Education Cttee, 1966-72); Councillor, Rochdale Metropolitan DC, 1973-75. A Dep. Pro-Chancellor, Lancaster Univ., 1978-. OStJ 1976. *Publications:* Big Cyril (autobiog.), 1977; Industrial Participation, 1977. *Recreations:* music (listener), reading, charitable work, local government. *Address:* 14 Emma Street, Rochdale, Lancs. *T:* Rochdale 48840.

SMITH, Cyril Robert, OBE 1945; consultant and lecturer; *b* 28 Dec. 1907; *s* of late Robert Smith and Rose Smith (*née* Sommerville); *m* 1933, Margaret Jane Kathleen Gwladys Hughes; two *s*. *Educ:* Whitgift; Queen Mary's Coll., Univ. of London. Served in Army, Europe, N Africa, 1939-45 (despatches, OBE; Col). Entered PO as Asst Traffic Supt Telephones, 1927; Asst Inspector, Telephone Traffic PO Headquarters, 1930; Asst Surveyor, Postal Services, 1935; Asst Principal, PO Headquarters, 1936; Asst Postal Controller, 1941; Instructor, PO Management Training Centre, 1954; Postal Controller, 1955; Asst Sec. i/c of Central Organisation and Methods Br., PO Headquarters, 1958; Director, Computer Development, 1965-67; Dir, National Data Processing, GPO, 1967-68. UN Advisor to Greek Govt on computers in public service, 1971-74. FBCS; FBIM. *Publications:* various papers on computer matters in Computer Jl, etc. *Address:* 64 Copse Avenue, West Wickham, Kent. *T:* 01-777 1100.

SMITH, Cyril Stanley, MSc, PhD; Secretary to Social Science Research Council, since 1975; *b* 21 July 1925; *s* of Walter and Beatrice May Smith; *m* 1968, Eileen Cameron; two *d* (by first marr.). *Educ:* Plaistow Municipal Secondary Sch.; London Sch. of Economics. HM Forces, Dorset Regt, 1943-47. Univ. of Birmingham, 1950-51; Univ. of Sheffield, 1951-52; Dulwich Coll. Mission, 1952-56; Nat. Coal Board, 1956-61; Univ. of Manchester, 1961-71; Civil Service Coll., 1971-75. Visiting Prof., Univ. of Virginia, 1965; Academic Visitor, Nuffield Coll., Oxford, 1980-81. British Nat. Expert, European Poverty Prog., 1977-. Mem., Sec. of State's Cttee on Inequalities in Health, DHSS, 1977-80. Chm., British Sociological Assoc., 1972-74; Pres., Sociol. Sect., British Assoc., 1979. *Publications:* Adolescence, 1968; (sen. author) The Wincroft Youth Project, 1972; (ed jtly) Society and Leisure in Britain, 1973; numerous articles on youth, leisure and developments in social science. *Recreations:* gardening, domestic technology. *Address:* Social Science Research Council, 1 Temple Avenue, EC4Y 0BD.

SMITH, Dan; see Smith, T. D.

SMITH, Prof. David; see Smith, Prof. N. J. D.

SMITH, David, PhD, FInstPet; Chairman and Managing Director, Esso Chemical Ltd, since 1978; *b* 18 July 1927; *s* of Walter and Annie Smith; *m* 1951, Nancy Elizabeth (*née* Hawley); two *s* three *d*. *Educ:* Burton Grammar School; Univ. of Sheffield. BSc, PhD. Lectr in Fuel Technology and Chemical Engineering, Univ. of Sheffield, 1951-55; Esso Research Ltd, 1955-65; Dir, Products Research Div., Esso Research and Engineering, USA, 1966-68; Marketing Dir and Man. Dir, Esso Chemical Ltd, 1968-71; Vice-Pres., Essochem Europe Inc., Brussels, 1971-73; Vice-Pres., Exxon Chemical Inc., USA, 1973-78. *Recreation:* golf. *Address:* Meadowlands, Stockbridge Road, Winchester, Hants SO22 5JH. *T:* Winchester 64880. *Clubs:* MCC; Royal Southampton Yacht.

SMITH, David Arthur, QC 1982; a Recorder of the Crown Court, since 1978; *b* 7 May 1938; *s* of Arthur Heber Smith and Marjorie Edith Pounds Smith; *m* 1967, Clementine Smith (*née* Urquhart); two *s*. *Educ:* Lancing College; Merton Coll., Oxford (MA Hons Jurisprudence). Called to Bar, Middle Temple, 1962; Official Principal of Archdeaconry of Hackney, 1973. Wine Treasurer, Western Circuit, 1980-. *Publications:* John Evelyn's Manuscript on Bees from Elysium Britannicum, 1966; Bibliography of British Bee Books, 1979. *Recreations:* bees (Sec. of Internat. Bee Research Assoc., 1963-), books, canals, Rossini. *Address:* 3 Pump Court, Temple, EC4Y 7AJ. *T:* 01-353 0711.

SMITH, David Arthur George, JP; Headmaster of Bradford Grammar School, since 1974; *b* 17 Dec. 1934; *o s* of Stanley George and Winifred Smith, Bath, Somerset; *m* 1957, Jennifer, *e d* of John and Rhoda Anning, Launceston, Cornwall; one *s* two *d*. *Educ:* City of Bath Boys' Sch.; Balliol Coll., Oxford. MA, Dip. Ed (Oxon). Assistant Master, Manchester Grammar Sch., 1957-62; Head of History, Rossall School, 1963-70; Headmaster, The King's School, Peterborough, 1970-74. JP West Yorks, 1975. *Publications:* (with John Thorn and Roger Lockyer) A History of England, 1961; Left and Right in Twentieth Century Europe, 1970; Russia of the Tsars, 1971. *Recreations:* writing, tennis, cricket. *Address:* Bradford Grammar School, Bradford, West Yorks. *T:* Bradford 45461.

SMITH, David Buchanan; Sheriff of North Strathclyde at Kilmarnock, since 1975; *b* 31 Oct. 1936; *s* of William Adam Smith and Irene Mary Calderwood Hogarth; *m* 1961, Hazel Mary Sinclair; two *s* one *d*. *Educ:* Paisley Grammar Sch.; Glasgow Univ. (MA); Edinburgh Univ. (LLB). Advocate, 1961; Standing Junior Counsel to Scottish Educn Dept, 1968-75. Trustee, The Scottish Curling Museum Trust, 1980-. *Publications:* Curling: an illustrated history, 1981; articles in Scots Law Times, Juridical Rev. and newspapers. *Recreations:* Scottish legal history, curling, music. *Address:* 72 South Beach, Troon, Ayrshire. *T:* Troon 312130; Sheriff's Chambers, Sheriff Court House, Kilmarnock. *T:* Kilmarnock 20211.

SMITH, Prof. David Cecil, FRS 1975; Sibthorpian Professor of Rural Economy, Oxford University, since 1980; Fellow of St John's College, Oxford, since 1980; *b* 21 May 1930; *s* of William John Smith and Elva Emily Smith; *m* 1965, Lesley Margaret Mollison Mutch; two *s* one *d*. *Educ:* Colston's Sch., Bristol; St Paul's Sch., London; Queen's Coll., Oxford (Browne Schol., MA, DPhil). Christopher Welch Res. Schol., Oxford, 1951-54; Swedish Inst. Schol., Uppsala Univ., 1951-52; Browne Res. Fellow, Queen's Coll., Oxford, 1956-59; Harkness Fellow, Univ. Calif, Berkeley, 1959-60; Univ. Lectr, Dept Agric., Oxford Univ., 1960-74; Royal Soc. Res. Fellow, Wadham Coll., 1964-71; Tutorial Fellow and Tutor for Admissions, Wadham Coll., Oxford, 1971-74; Melville Wills Prof. of Botany, 1974-80, and Dir of Biological Studies, 1977-79, Bristol Univ. Vis. Prof., Univ. Calif, Los Angeles, 1968. Chairman: NERC Aquatic Life Scis Cttee, 1978-81; SERC Biol Scis Cttee, 1981-; Subject Area Rev. Cttee in Biol. Sci., London Univ., 1982-; Member: NERC Terrestrial Life Scis Cttee, 1975-78; ARC Plants and Soils Cttee, 1976-; Consultative Bd, JCO for Res. in Agric. and Food, 1981-; ARC, 1982-; Royal Soc. Assessor, ARC, 1978-80. President: British Lichen Soc., 1972-74; British Mycological Soc., 1980; Soc. for Experimental Biol., 1983- (Vice-Pres., 1981); Vice-Pres., Royal Society, 1978-80. Editor and Trustee, New Phytologist, 1965-. *Publications:* various articles on symbiosis, in New Phytol., Proc. Royal Soc., Biol. Rev., etc. *Address:* The Old Dog, 18 School Road, Kidlington, Oxford OX5 2HB. *T:* Kidlington 3126.

SMITH, David Douglas R.; see Rae Smith, D. D.

SMITH, David Dury H.; see Hindley-Smith.

SMITH, David Grahame G.; see Grahame-Smith.

SMITH, Air Vice-Marshal David H.; see Harcourt-Smith.

SMITH, David Iser, CVO 1977; BA; Official Secretary to the Governor-General of Australia, since 1973; Secretary of the Order of Australia, since 1975; *b* 9 Aug. 1933; *s* of W. M. Smith; *m* 1955, June F., *d* of M. A. W. Forestier; three *s*. *Educ:* Scotch Coll., Melbourne; Melbourne Univ.; Australian National Univ., Canberra (BA). Entered Aust. Public Service, 1954; Dept of Customs and Excise, Melb., 1954-57; Trng Officer, Dept of the Interior, Canberra, 1957-58; Private Sec. to Minister for the Interior and Minister for Works, 1958-63; Exec. Asst to Sec., Dept of the Interior, 1963-66; Exec. Officer (Govt), Dept of the Interior, 1966-69; Sen. Adviser, Govt Br., Prime Minister's Dept, 1969-71; Sec., Federal Exec. Council, 1971-73; Asst Sec., Govt Br., Dept of the Prime Minister and Cabinet, 1972-73. Attached to The Queen's Household, Buckingham Palace, June-July 1975. Dist Comr, Capital Hill Dist, Scout Assoc. of Australia, 1971-74. CStJ 1974. *Recreations:* music, reading. *Address:* Government House, Canberra, ACT 2600, Australia. *T:* 81.1211. *Club:* Commonwealth (Canberra).

SMITH, Ven. David James; Archdeacon of Lindisfarne, since 1981; Vicar of Felton, since 1982; *b* 14 July 1935; *s* of Stanley James and Gwendolen Emie Smith; *m* 1961, Mary Hunter Moult; one *s* one *d*. *Educ:* Hertford Grammar School; King's College, London (AKC). Assistant Curate: All Saints, Gosforth, 1959-62; St Francis, High Heaton, 1962-64; Long Benton, 1964-68; Vicar: Longhirst with Hebron, 1968-75; St Mary, Monkseaton, 1975-81. *Recreations:* fell walking, reading science fiction. *Address:* Felton Vicarage, Morpeth, Northumberland NE65 9HP. *T:* Felton 263.

SMITH, David MacLeish, DSc; FRS 1952; retired; *b* 1900; *s* of David T. Smith, Elgin, Scotland; *m* 1941, Doris Kendrick; no *c*. *Educ:* Blairgowrie High School; Glasgow University (DSc 1932). College Apprentice with Metropolitan Vickers Elect. Co. Ltd, Trafford Park, Manchester, 1920, and remained with that co. and its successor AEI Ltd, until 1966. Hon. LLD, Glasgow, 1967. MIMechE 1938; FRAeS 1949; FEng 1976. *Publications:* Journal Bearings in Turbomachinery, 1969; various technical papers. *Address:* Rostherne Flat 2, Cavendish Road, Bowdon, Cheshire WA14 2NU.

SMITH, Hon. Sir David (Stanley), Kt 1948; *b* 11 Feb. 1888; *s* of Rev. J. Gibson Smith; *m* 1st, 1915, Eva Jane (*d* 1917), *d* of late Duncan Cumming; one *d*; 2nd, 1923, Margaret Elizabeth (*d* 1954), *d* of Richard Wayne Gibbs; one *s*. *Educ:* Wellington Coll.; Victoria Univ. Coll., Wellington (LLM). Barrister, Solicitor and Notary Public; American non-national member of the Permanent Commission under the Treaty of Conciliation between the United States of America and Peru, 11 Feb. 1933; Chairman of Commission on Native Affairs, New Zealand, 1934; Member of Council of Victoria University College, 1939-45; Chairman of Royal Commission on Licensing of Alcoholic Liquors, 1945-46; Chancellor, Univ. of NZ, 1945-61; Judge of Supreme Court of NZ, 1928-48 (temp. Judge, 1949-50); retired 1948; Mem. Bd Dirs, US Educl Foundn in NZ, 1948-70. Chm. NZ Bd of Trade, 1950-59. Ex-Mem. Council of Internat. Bar Assoc. Hon. DCL Oxford, 1948; Hon. LLD Univ. of New Zealand, 1961. *Address:* 10 Sefton Street, Wellington 1, NZ. *Club:* Wellington (Wellington).

SMITH, Denis M.; see Mack Smith.

SMITH, Derek Cyril; Under-Secretary, Export Credits Guarantee Department, since 1974; *b* 29 Jan. 1927; *s* of Albert Cyril and Edith Mary Elizabeth Smith; *m* 1st, 1949, Ursula Kulich (marr. diss. 1967); two *d*; 2nd, 1967, Nina Munday; one *s*. *Educ:* Pinner Grammar Sch.; St Catherine's Soc., Oxford. BA Mod. History 1951. Asst Principal, Min. of Materials, 1952-55; BoT, 1955-57: Asst Private Sec., Minister of State; Private Sec., Parly Sec.; Principal, ECGD, 1958-67; Asst Sec., BoT and DTI, 1967-72: Sec. to Lord Cromer's Survey of Capital Projects Contracting Overseas; Asst Sec., ECGD, 1972-74. *Recreations:* walking, reading, model-building. *Address:* c/o Export Credits Guarantee Department, PO Box 272, Aldermanbury House, Aldermanbury Square, EC2.

SMITH, Derek Edward H.; see Hill-Smith.

SMITH, Derek Frank; Counsellor (Overseas Development), Washington, and Alternate Executive Director of the World Bank, since 1979; *b* 11 Feb. 1929; *s* of Frank H. and late Rose V. Smith; *m* 1954, Anne Carpenter; one *s* one *d*. *Educ:* Chatham House Sch., Ramsgate. Served RAF, 1947-49. Colonial Office, 1949-66: Sec., Develt and Welfare Org. in WI, 1956-58; transf. to Min. of Overseas Develt, 1966; Financial Adviser, British Develt Div. in the Caribbean, 1966-68; Asst Sec., 1972; Head of Southern African Develt Div., 1972-75. *Address:* 3100 Massachusetts Avenue, Washington, DC 20008, USA; 3 The Close, Montreal Park, Sevenoaks, Kent TN13 2HE. *T:* Sevenoaks 52534. *Club:* Bretton Woods (Maryland).

SMITH, Maj.-Gen. Desmond; see Smith, Maj.-Gen. J. D. B.

SMITH, Dodie, (wrote under the name of C. L. Anthony up to 1935); Dramatist and Novelist; *b* 3 May 1896; *d* of Ernest Walter Smith and Ella Furber; *m* 1939, Alec Macbeth Beesley. *Educ:* St Paul's School for Girls. Studied at Royal Academy of Dramatic Art; on the stage for several years; gave up the stage and became a buyer at Heal and Son, Tottenham Court Road; wrote Autumn Crocus in 1930; produced Lyric Theatre, 1931; gave up business, 1931; wrote Service, 1932; produced Wyndham's Theatre, 1932; wrote Touch Wood, 1933; produced Theatre Royal, Haymarket, 1934; wrote Call It A Day, 1935; produced Globe Theatre, 1935; Bonnet Over the Windmill; produced New Theatre, 1937; wrote Dear Octopus, 1938; produced Queen's Theatre, 1938, revived Theatre Royal, Haymarket, 1967; wrote Lovers and Friends, 1942; prod. Plymouth Theatre, New York, 1943; Letter from Paris (adapted from novel, The Reverberator, by Henry James), Aldwych, 1952; wrote I Capture the Castle, 1952 (adapted from own novel of same name), prod. Aldwych Theatre, 1953; wrote These People-Those Books, 1957; prod. Leeds, 1958; wrote Amateur Means Lover, 1956; prod.

Liverpool, 1961. *Publications: Plays by C. L. Anthony:* Autumn Crocus; Service; Touch Wood; *Plays by Dodie Smith:* Call It A Day; Bonnet Over the Windmill; Dear Octopus; Lovers and Friends; Letter from Paris; I Capture the Castle; *novels:* I Capture the Castle, 1949 (US 1948); The New Moon with the Old, 1963 (US 1963); The Town in Bloom, 1965 (US 1965); It Ends with Revelations, 1967 (US 1967); A Tale of Two Families, 1970 (US 1970); The Girl from the Candle-lit Bath, 1978; *children's books:* The Hundred and One Dalmatians, 1956 (US 1957); The Starlight Barking, 1967 (US 1968); The Midnight Kittens, 1978; *autobiography:* Look Back With Love, 1974; Look Back With Mixed Feelings, 1978; Look Back With Astonishment, 1979. *Recreations:* reading, music, dogs, donkeys. *Address:* The Barretts, Finchingfield, Essex. *T:* Great Dunmow 810260.

SMITH, Donald Charles; a Master of the Supreme Court of Judicature (Chancery Division), 1969–73; *b* 23 Jan. 1910; *o s* of Charles Frederic Smith and Cecilia Anastasia Smith (*née* Toomey); *m* 1941, Joan Rowsell, twin *d* of Richard Norman Rowsell Blaker, MC. *Educ:* Stonyhurst College. Articled, Peacock & Goddard, Gray's Inn, 1927–31; admitted Solicitor, 1932; Solicitor with Thorold, Brodie & Bonham-Carter, Westminster, 1931–34; Legal Staff of Public Trustee Office, 1934–39; joined Chancery Registrars' Office, 1939; Chancery Registrar, 1952; Chief Registrar, 1963; first Chancery Registrar to be appointed a Master. Pres., Stonyhurst Assoc., 1969. Served in RNVR, Fleet Air Arm, 1943–46; Lieut, 1944–46. *Publications:* (Revising Editor) Atkin's Encyclopaedia of Court Forms, 1st edn, (Advisory Editor) 2nd edn; contribs to Law Jl. *Recreations:* cricket, walking, theatre, philately. *Address:* Reading Hall, Denham, Eye, Suffolk IP21 5DR. *T:* Eye 870500. *Club:* MCC.

SMITH, Ven. Donald John; Archdeacon of Suffolk, since 1975; Hon. Canon of St Edmundsbury and Ipswich, since 1973; *b* 10 April 1926; *m* 1948, Violet Olive Goss; two *s* one *d*. *Educ:* Clifton Theological Coll. Asst Curate: Edgware, 1953–56; St Margaret's, Ipswich, 1956–58; Vicar of St Mary, Hornsey Rise, Islington, 1958–62; Rector of Whitton, Ipswich, 1962–75; Rector of Redgrave cum Botesdale with The Rickinghalls, 1975–79. HCF 1964. *Publications:* A Confirmation Course, 1974; Covenanting for Disunity, 1981. *Recreations:* driving, foreign travel, chess, collecting Meerschaum and antiques, drama, reading, photography, gardening, caravanning, good food, dining out, pastoral reorganisation, redundant churches. *Address:* Starlings, Yoxford, Suffolk. *T:* Yoxford 387.

SMITH, Donald MacKeen; Agent General of Nova Scotia, in London, since 1980; *b* 26 Nov. 1923; *s* of Leonard Vernard and Lena Smith (*née* MacKeen); *m* 1949, Helen Elizabeth, *d* of late Lt-Col David Guildford; three *d*. *Educ:* Halifax Public Schs; King's College Sch.; Dalhousie Univ., Nova Scotia. Served Canadian Armored Corps, 1942–45; 18th Armored Car Regt, 1944–45. J. E. Morse and Co. Ltd, Halifax: salesman, 1946; Vice-Pres., Director, 1951; Pres., 1956–. Pres. Tea Council of Canada, 1975–78; Vice-Pres. and Dir, Tea and Coffee Assoc. of Canada, 1960–78. Member, Executive Council of Nova Scotia, 1960–69; MLA Nova Scotia (Halifax Citadel), 1960–70; Minister of Mines, Minister in Charge of Liquor Control Act, 1960–69. Mem., Rotary Club. *Recreations:* swimming, sailing, fishing, walking. *Address:* Nova Scotia House, 14 Pall Mall, SW1. *T:* 01-930 6864; Sunnywood Road, Head of St Margaret's Bay, Halifax County, Nova Scotia, Canada. *Clubs:* East India, Devonshire, Sports and Public Schools; Royal Automobile; Saraguay; Halifax; Royal Nova Scotia Yacht Squadron.

SMITH, Douglas Alexander; Commissioner of Inland Revenue, 1968–75; *b* 15 June 1915; *m* 1941, Mary Eileen Lyon; one *s* one *d*. *Educ:* Glasgow High Sch.; Glasgow Univ. MA, BSc 1937. Entered Inland Revenue, 1938; Asst Secretary: Inland Revenue, 1952–59; Office of Minister for Science, 1959–61; Under-Sec., Medical Research Council, 1964–67. *Recreations:* hockey, golf, bridge, gardening. *Address:* 66 Eastwick Drive, Great Bookham, Surrey. *T:* Bookham 54274. *Club:* Civil Service.

SMITH, Douglas Boucher, CB 1982; Deputy Secretary, Department of Employment, since 1979; *b* 9 June 1932; *m* 1956, Mary Barbara Tarran. *Educ:* Leeds Modern Sch.; Leeds Univ. Entered Ministry of Labour, 1953; successively: Private Sec. to Minister of Labour, 1967–68; to First Sec. of State and Sec. of State for Employment and Productivity, 1968–70; to Sec. of State for Employment, 1970–71; Chief Conciliation Officer, 1971–74, Under Secretary: Dept. of Employment, 1974–77; Cabinet Office, 1977–79. *Address:* 17 Dundas Close, Bracknell, Berkshire. *T:* Bracknell 54573. *Club:* Athenæum.

SMITH, Dudley (Gordon); MP (C) Warwick and Leamington, since 1968 (Brentford and Chiswick, 1959–66); *b* 14 Nov. 1926; *o s* of late Hugh William and Florence Elizabeth Smith, Cambridge; 1st marr. diss.; one *s* two *d*; *m* 2nd, 1976, Catherine Amos, *o d* of late Mr and Mrs Thomas Amos, Liverpool. *Educ:* Chichester High Sch., Sussex. Worked for various provincial and national newspapers, as journalist and senior executive, 1943–66; Asst News Editor, Sunday Express, 1953–59. Vice-Chm. Southgate Conservative Assoc., 1958–59; CC Middlesex, 1958–65. Chief Whip of Majority Group, 1961–63. A Divl Dir, Beecham Group, 1966–70; Dir, Sterling Health Services Ltd, 1974–76; Management Consultant. Contested (C) Camberwell-Peckham, General Election, 1955. PPS to Sec. for Tech. Co-operation, 1963–64; an Opposition Whip, 1965–66; an Opposition Spokesman on Employment and Productivity, 1969–70; Parliamentary Under-Secretary of State: Dept of Employment, 1970–74; (Army) MoD, 1974; UK delegate to Council of Europe and WEU, 1979–. Vice Chm., Parly Select Cttee on Race Relations

and Immigration, 1974–79. Promoted Town and Country Planning (Amendment) Act, 1977, as a private member. A Vice-Pres., District Councils' Assoc. Chm., Wilderness Foundn (UK), 1980–. Governor, Mill Hill Sch.; Chm., United & Cecil Club, 1975–80. *Publications:* Harold Wilson: A Critical Biography, 1964; etc. *Recreations:* books, travel, music, wild life and wilderness preservation. *Address:* Church Farm, Weston-under-Wetherley, Warwicks. *T:* Marton 632 352.

SMITH, Dugal N.; *see* Nisbet-Smith.

SMITH, Dr Edgar Charles B.; *see* Bate-Smith.

SMITH, His Honour Edgar Dennis; a Circuit Judge (South-Eastern Circuit), 1972–79; *b* 29 Jan. 1911; *yr s* of late George Henry Smith; *m* 1950, Mary, *yr d* of late Captain T. Drewery, MN; two *s*. *Educ:* Queen Mary's School, Walsall; Birmingham University (LLM). Lord Justice Holker (Holt) Scholar, Gray's Inn, 1933. Called to Bar, Gray's Inn, 1935. Practised in London and on Oxford Circuit. Served War of 1939–45: Special Investigation Branch, Royal Military Police, 1940–46; Assistant Provost-Marshal, Special Investigation Branch, 1945. Headquarters Commissioner The Scout Association, 1947–58 (Silver Wolf, 1956); Mem. Council, The Scout Association, 1964– (Chm., Cttee of the Council, 1968–74). Dep. Chm., Agricultural Land Tribunal, S Eastern Region, 1959–63; Dep. Chm., Staffs QS, 1961–63; Metropolitan Stipendiary Magistrate, 1963–72; Chm., Inner London Juvenile Courts, 1968–72. Hon. Technical Advr, Central Council of Probation and After-Care Cttees, 1968–74. Liveryman, Fletchers' Co., 1975. *Publications:* (ed) The County Court Pleader; (Sen. Asst Ed.) Foa's Law of Landlord and Tenant (8th edn); various other legal works. *Recreations:* travel, music, theatre. *Address:* Chilham House, Pulborough, West Sussex RH20 2AE. *T:* Pulborough 2616.

SMITH, Maj.-Gen. Sir Edmund Hakewill; *see* Hakewill Smith.

SMITH, Edward John Gregg, CB 1982; Deputy Secretary, Ministry of Agriculture, Fisheries and Food, since 1979; *b* 1 Oct. 1930; *o s* of late Major J. W. Smith and Mrs V. H. E. Smith; *m* 1956, Jean Margaret Clayton; one *s* two *d*. *Educ:* Churcher's Coll., Petersfield; Queens' Coll., Cambridge (MA). FRGS. MAFF, 1953–68: Private Sec. to Minister, 1964–66; Head of Economic Policy Div., 1966–68; Principal Private Sec. to Lord President of Council and Leader of House of Commons, 1968–70; returned to MAFF: Head of Meat Div., 1970–71; Under-sec., 1971–74, 1976–79; Under-Sec., Cabinet Office, 1974–76. Mem., ARC, 1979–; Mem., Guildford Diocesan Synod, 1976–. *Recreations:* choral music, Christian activities. *Address:* The Holme, Oakfield Road, Ashtead, Surrey. *T:* Ashtead 72311. *Club:* Reform.

SMITH, Emma; Author; *b* 1923; *m* 1951, Richard Stewart-Jones (*d* 1957); one *s* one *d*. *Publications:* Maidens' Trip, 1948 (awarded John Llewellyn Rhys Memorial Prize, 1948); The Far Cry, 1949 (awarded James Tait Black Memorial Prize, 1949); Emily, 1959; Out of Hand, 1963; Emily's Voyage, 1966; No Way of Telling, 1972; The Opportunity of a Lifetime, 1978. *Address:* c/o Curtis Brown, 1 Craven Hill, W2.

SMITH, Dame Enid Mary R. R.; *see* Russell-Smith.

SMITH, Sir Eric; *see* Smith, Sir J. E.

SMITH, Eric John R.; *see* Radley-Smith.

SMITH, Eric Norman, CMG 1976; HM Diplomatic Service, retired; British High Commissioner in The Gambia, 1979–81; *b* 28 Jan. 1922; *s* of Arthur Sidney David Smith; *m* 1955, Mary Gillian Horrocks. *Educ:* Colfe's Sch., London. Served War, Royal Corps of Signals, 1941–46. Foreign Office, 1947–53; HM Embassy, Cairo, 1953–55; UK Delegn to the UN, New York, 1955–57; FO, 1957–60; HM Embassy, Tehran, 1960–64; FO, 1964–68; British Information Services, New York, 1968–71; FCO, 1971–75; Singapore, 1975–79. *Recreations:* music, photography. *Address:* Kilsby, Llanwrtyd Wells, Powys LD5 4TL.

SMITH, E(rnest) Lester, DSc; FRS 1957; formerly Consultant, Glaxo Laboratories, Greenford; *b* 7 August 1904; *s* of Lester and Rose Smith; *m* 1931, Winifred R. Fitch; no *c*. *Educ:* Wood Green County School; Chelsea Polytechnic. Joined Glaxo Laboratories, 1926, as first post after graduation. Various posts in development, Fine Chemical Production (Head), then Biochemical Research. Shared responsibility for production of penicillin during War of 1939–45; isolation of vitamin B_{12} accomplished, 1948. *Publications:* Vitamin B_{12} (in series of Biochemical Monographs), 1960, 3rd edn 1965. Numerous research papers in various scientific journals, 1927–. *Recreation:* horticulture. *Address:* Quarry Wood, 23 Grange Road, Hastings, East Sussex TN34 2RL.

SMITH, Sir Ewart; *see* Smith, Sir Frank Ewart.

SMITH, Maj.-Gen. Sir (Francis) Brian W.; *see* Wyldbore-Smith.

SMITH, Prof. (Francis) Graham, FRS 1970; Professor of Radio Astronomy, Manchester University, 1964–74 and since 1981; Director, Nuffield Radio Astronomy Laboratories, since 1981; *b* 25 April 1923; *s* of Claud Henry and Cicely Winifred Smith; *m* 1945, Dorothy Elizabeth (*née* Palmer); three *s* one *d. Educ:* Epsom Coll.; Rossall Sch.; Downing Coll., Cambridge. Nat. Sci. Tripos, Downing Coll., 1941-43 and 1946-47; PhD Cantab 1952. Telecommunications Research Estab., Malvern, 1943-46; Cavendish Lab., 1947-64; 1851 Exhibr 1951-52; Warren Research Fellow of Royal Soc., 1959-64; Fellow of Downing Coll., 1953-64, Hon. Fellow 1970; Dir-Designate, 1974-75, Dir, 1976-81, Royal Greenwich Observatory. Vis. Prof. of Astronomy, Univ. of Sussex, 1975. Sec., Royal Astronomical Soc., 1964-71, Pres., 1975-77. *Publications:* Radio Astronomy, 1960; (with J. H. Thomson) Optics, 1971; Pulsars, 1977; papers in Monthly Notices of RAS, Nature and other scientific jls. *Recreations:* sailing, walking. *Address:* Nuffield Radio Astronomy Laboratories, Jodrell Bank, Macclesfield, Cheshire SK11 9DL; Old School House, Henbury, Macclesfield, Cheshire SK11 9PH.

SMITH, Rev. Francis Taylor; Minister of St Paul's Parish Church, Dunfermline, since 1964; *b* 22 Jan. 1933; *s* of James William Smith and Jeannie Moir Catto Cockburn; *m* 1957, Jean Millar Wallace; three *s* one *d. Educ:* Aberdeen Grammar Sch.; Aberdeen Univ. (MA); Christ's Coll., Aberdeen (Licence to Preach). Student Assistant: Queen's Cross Church, Aberdeen, 1954-56; North Church, Aberdeen, 1956-57; Sen. Asst, Govan Old Church, Glasgow, 1957-58; Parish Minister, Aberlour, Banffshire, 1958-64. Chaplain, Dunfermline and West Fife Hosp., 1964-; Moderator of Presbytery, 1973-74. Councillor, Banff CC, 1964; Chairman, West Fife Local Health Council, 1975-; Vice-Pres., Assoc. of Scottish Local Health Councils, 1978-79, Pres., 1980, 1981; Crown Lay Nominee, General Medical Council, 1979-. Governor, Aberlour Orphanage, 1964. *Recreations:* work, music, fishing, shooting, reading. *Address:* St Paul's Manse, 6 Park Avenue, Dunfermline, Fife KY12 7HX. *T:* Dunfermline 21124.

SMITH, Sir (Frank) Ewart, Kt 1946; MA; FRS 1957; FEng; Hon. FIMechE; FIChemE; a past Deputy Chairman, Imperial Chemical Industries, Ltd; *b* 31 May 1897; *s* of late Richard Sidney Smith; *m* 1924, Kathleen Winifred (*d* 1978), *d* of late H. Rudd Dawes; one *d* (one *s* decd). *Educ:* Christ's Hospital; Sidney Sussex College, Cambridge (Scholar, 1st Class Mech. Science Tripos, John Winbolt Prizeman). War service, 1916-19, RA; ICI Ltd, Billingham Works in various engineering and managerial posts, 1923-42; chief engineer, 1932-42; Chief Engineer and Supt of Armament Design, Ministry of Supply, 1942-45; Formerly Member: Advisory Council on Scientific Policy; Scientific Advisory Council of Ministry of Works and Ministry of Fuel and Power; British Productivity Council, Cttee on Scientific Manpower; Chairman, National Health Service Advisory Council for Management Efficiency (England and Wales), etc. Hon. Fellow Sidney Sussex College; Hon. Member, City and Guilds of London Institute; Hon. FIMS; Hon. Associate, Univ. of Aston. James Clayton Prize, IMechE. American Medal of Freedom with Palm, 1946. *Publications:* various technical papers. *Recreations:* cabinet making, gardening. *Address:* Parkhill Cottage, Sandy Lane, Watersfield, Pulborough, W Sussex. *T:* Bury 354.

SMITH, Frank William G.; *see* Glaves-Smith.

SMITH, Frederick Llewellyn, CBE 1964; MSc, DPhil, CEng, FIMechE; *b* 25 July 1909; *s* of late James Brooksbank Smith; *m* 1943, Alice Mary McMurdo; one *s* two *d. Educ:* Rochdale High Sch.; Univ. of Manchester; Balliol Coll., Oxford. Joined Rolls-Royce Ltd, 1933; Dir, 1947; Group Man. Dir, Automotive and subsidiary cos, 1970; Chm., Rolls-Royce Motors Ltd, 1971; retired 1972. Pres. Soc. of Motor Manufacturers & Traders Ltd, 1955-56. Mem. Nat. Research Development Corp., 1959-73. Pres., Motor Industry Research Assoc., 1963-65. *Address:* 4 Raglan Close, Reigate, Surrey RH2 0EU.

SMITH, Prof. Frederick Viggers; Professor of Psychology, University of Durham, 1950-77, now Emeritus; *b* Hamilton, New South Wales, 24 Jan. 1912; *s* of Frederick Thomas Smith and Agnes (*née* Viggers); unmarried. *Educ:* Newcastle (NSW) High School; Sydney and London Universities. BA 1938, MA 1941, Lithgow Schol., Sydney; PhD London 1948. FBPsS, 1950 (Pres., British Psychological Society, 1959-60). Research Office, Dept of Educ., NSW, 1936; Lecturer in Psychology, The Teachers' Coll., Sydney, 1938; Lectr, Birkbeck Coll., Univ. of London, 1946; Lectr, Univ. of Aberdeen, 1948. Visiting Prof., Cornell Univ., USA, 1957, Christchurch and Wellington Univs, NZ, 1960. Consultant, Council of Europe Sub-Cttee on Crime Problems, 1973; Unesco Consultant, Univ. of Riyadh, 1973. Hon. Research Associate, Univ. of Newcastle, NSW, 1980. *Publications:* The Child's Point of View (Sydney), 1946 (under pseudonym Victor Southward); Explanation of Human Behaviour (London), 1951, 1960; Attachment of the Young: Imprinting and Other Developments, 1969; Purpose in Animal Behaviour, 1971; papers to psychol and philosophical journals. *Recreations:* mountain walking, swimming, photography, music, golf. *Address:* 9 The Helm, Voyager Close, Shoal Bay, Port Stephens, NSW 2315, Australia.

SMITH, Sir Gengoult; *see* Smith, Sir Harold G.

SMITH, Geoffrey Ellrington Fane, CMG 1955; Senior Provincial Commissioner, Northern Rhodesia, 1951-55, retired; Colonial Office, 1956-61, Department of Technical Co-operation (later Ministry of Overseas Development), 1961-66; *b* 1903; *m* 1933, Olga Smith. *Educ:* King Edward VI Grammar School, Louth; Lincoln College, Oxford. Cadet, Northern Rhodesia, 1926-29; District Officer, 1929; Provincial Commissioner, Northern Rhodesia, 1947-51. *Address:* 26 Vincent Road, Stoke D'Abernon, Cobham, Surrey.

SMITH, Sir Geoffrey J.; *see* Johnson Smith.

SMITH, Geoffrey M.; *see* Maitland Smith.

SMITH, Vice-Adm. Sir Geoffrey T.; *see* Thistleton-Smith.

SMITH, Prof. George, MBE 1945; FRSE 1979; Regius Professor of Surgery, University of Aberdeen, since 1962; *b* 4 June 1919; *s* of John Shand Smith and Lilimina Myles Mathers Smith; *m* 1951, Vivienne Marie Tuck, BA, Wooster, Ohio, USA, *d* of Rev. Robert Sidney Tuck, DD; two *s* one *d. Educ:* Grove Academy; Queen's College, Univ. of St Andrews. MB, ChB (St Andrews) 1942; MD (Hons) 1957, ChM (Hons) 1959; DSc (Glasgow) 1964; FRFP&S (Glasgow) 1949; FRCS (Edinburgh) 1949; FACS 1958; FACCP 1963; FInstBiol 1963. Commonwealth Fund Fellow, 1949-51 (Johns Hopkins and Western Reserve Medical Schools). Formerly Reader in Cardiovascular Surgery, Univ. of Glasgow. Dean of Medicine, Aberdeen Univ., 1974-76; Dir. Inst. of Environmental and Offshore Med., 1975-78. Chm., NE Region Med. Postgrad. Cttee; Civil Consultant in surgery to RN; Governor: Robert Gordon's Coll.; Amer. Coll. of Chest Physicians. *Publications:* (ed jtly) Resuscitation and Cardiac Pacing, 1965; The Biology of Affluence, 1972; The Staphylococci; (ed) Proceedings, 6th International Congress on Hyperbaric Medicine, 1979; sections in books and various papers, mainly on cardiovascular, respiratory, bacteriological and educnl topics. *Recreations:* sailing, gardening, golf. *Address:* Cairn-Cot, 21 Cairn Road, Bieldside, Aberdeenshire AB1 9AL. *T:* Aberdeen 867556. *Clubs:* Naval; RNVR (Glasgow).

SMITH, George; formerly Director-General of Ordnance Factories (Finance), 1972-76; *b* 13 Dec. 1914; *s* of George Smith and Catherine Annie Smith (*née* Ashby); *m* 1939, Alice May Smith; two *s. Educ:* Alderman Newton's Sch., Leicester. FCCA. Various posts in industry, 1929-40; joined Min. of Supply, 1940, various posts in Royal Ordnance factories, 1940-52; Asst Dir of Ordnance Factories (Accounts), 1952; Civil Asst, ROF Woolwich, 1958; Dir of Ordnance Factories (Accounts), 1962. *Recreations:* gardening, walking, bowls. *Address:* 14 Blenheim Gardens, Sanderstead, Surrey. *T:* 01-657 5826.

SMITH, George Neil; HM Diplomatic Service; Consul-General, Zürich and Principality of Liechtenstein, since 1980; *b* 12 July 1936; *s* of George Smith and Ena (*née* Hill); *m* 1956, Elvi Vappu Hämäläinen; one *s* one *d. Educ:* King Edward VII Sch., Sheffield. Joined HM Foreign (subseq. Diplomatic) Service, 1953; served RAF, 1954-56; Foreign Office, 1957; Rangoon, 1958-61; 2nd Sec., Berne, 1961-65; Diplomatic Service Administration, 1965-66; 1st Sec., CO, 1966-68; British Mil. Govt, Berlin, 1969-73; FCO, 1973-77; Counsellor (Commercial), Helsinki, 1977-80. *Recreations:* music, tennis. *Address:* c/o Foreign and Commonwealth Office, SW1. *Club:* Royal Commonwealth Society.

SMITH, George William Q.; *see* Quick Smith.

SMITH, Gerard Thomas Corley, CMG 1952; HM Diplomatic Service, retired; *b* 30 July 1909; *s* of late Thomas and Nina Smith; *m* 1937, Joan Haggard; one *s* three *d. Educ:* Bolton Sch.; Emmanuel Coll., Cambridge. Gen. Consular Service, 1931; has served in Paris, Oran, Detroit, La Paz, Milan, St Louis, New York, Brussels, and at various times in the Foreign Office. Became 1st Sec. and Consul, on appt as Labour Attaché to Embassy in Brussels 1945; Counsellor UK Deleg. to UNO at New York and UK Alternate Rep. on UN Economic and Social Council, 1949-52; Press Counsellor, Brit. Embassy, Paris, 1952-54; Labour Counsellor, Brit. Embassy, Madrid, 1954-59; British Ambassador: to Haiti, 1960-62; to Ecuador, 1962-67. Sec. Gen., Charles Darwin Foundn for the Galapagos Islands, 1972-82. Grand Officer, Order of Merit (Ecuador), 1980. *Recreations:* music, mountains, birds. *Address:* Greensted Hall, Chipping Ongar, Essex. *Club:* Travellers'.

SMITH, Sir Gilbert; *see* Smith, Sir T. G.

SMITH, Sir Gordon; *see* Smith, Sir W. G.

SMITH, Gordon E.; *see* Etherington-Smith.

SMITH, Gordon Edward C.; *see* Connell-Smith.

SMITH, Graham; *see* Smith, F. G.

SMITH, Sir Guy B.; *see* Bracewell-Smith.

SMITH, Prof. Hamilton Othanel; Professor of Microbiology, Johns Hopkins University School of Medicine, Maryland, USA, since 1973; *b* 23 Aug. 1931; *s* of Bunnie Othanel Smith and Tommie Harkey Smith; *m* 1957, Elizabeth Anne Bolton; four *s* one *d. Educ:* Univ. of Illinois; Univ. of California (AB); Johns Hopkins Univ. Sch. of Medicine (MD). Research Associate, Dept of Human Genetics, Univ. of Michigan, 1964-67; Asst Prof. of Microbiology, 1967-69, Associate Prof. of Microbiology, 1969-73, Johns Hopkins Univ. Sch. of Medicine. During sabbatical leave in Zürich, worked in collaboration with Prof. Dr M. L. Birnstiel, Inst. für Molekularbiologie II der Univ. Zürich, July 1975-June 1976. Nobel Prize in Medicine (jtly), 1978. *Publications:* A restriction enzyme from Hemophilus influenzae: I. Purification and general properties (with K. W. Wilcox), in Jl Mol. Biol. 51, 379, 1970; A restriction enzyme from Hemophilus influenzae: II. Base sequence of the recognition site (with T. J. Kelly), in Jl Mol. Biol. *51*, 393, 1970. *Recreations:* piano, classical music. *Address:* Department of Molecular Biology and Genetics, Johns Hopkins University School of Medicine, 725 N Wolfe Street, Baltimore, Maryland 21205, USA. *T:* (301) 955-3650.

SMITH, Colonel Sir (Harold) Gengoult, Kt 1934; VD; JP; FRCPE, LRCP and SE, LRFP and SG; Chairman of Royal Visit (1949) Committee of Melbourne; *b* 25 July 1890; *s* of Hon. Louis Laurence Smith and Marion Higgins; *m* 1933, Cynthia Mary (decd), *d* of Sir Norman E. Brookes; one *s* one *d*. *Educ:* Melbourne Church of England Gram. Sch.; Melbourne and Edinburgh Univs; Royal College of Surgeons, Edinburgh. Australian Military Forces, 1907-47; Lt-Col Brighton Rifles (seconded), 2nd Dragoon Guard (Res. Regt), 1915, 2nd Lt; Served France, 1915-16; Qualified Royal College of Surgeons, 1917; House Surgeon, Royal Edinburgh Infirmary, 1917; Medical Clinical Asst, 1923-24; Comd Balcombe Casualty Clearing Station, 1941; CO 111th Australian General Hospital, 1944; elected Melbourne City Council, 1921; Lord Mayor, 1931-32, 1932-33 and 1933-34; Chairman Victorian and Melbourne Centenary Celebrations Council, 1934-35. Formerly: President Children's Cinema Council; Patron, Partially Blinded Soldiers' Assoc.; Chm. Exhibition Trustees; Zoological Board of Victoria; Board of Eye and Ear Hospital; Board of Infectious Diseases Hospital; Council of Old Colonists' Homes; Chairman of Public Works Cttee. *Recreations:* fox-hunting (Oaklands Hounds), golf, fishing, shooting, travelling. *Clubs:* Athenæum, Peninsula Country (Melbourne); Victoria Racing.

SMITH, Prof. Harry, PhD, DSc; FRCPath; FRS 1979; FIBiol; Professor and Head, Department of Microbiology, University of Birmingham, since 1965; *b* 7 Aug. 1921; *s* of Harry and Annie Smith; *m* 1947, Janet Mary Holmes; one *s* one *d*. *Educ:* Northampton Grammar Sch.; University Coll. (of London) at Nottingham. BPharm, BScChem (1st Cl. Hons), PhD, DSc London. Analyst, Boots Pure Drug Co., Nottingham, 1942-45; Asst Lectr, then Lectr, Dept of Chemistry, UCL at Nottingham, 1945-47; Microbiological Research Establishment, Porton: Sen. Scientific Officer, 1947; Principal Sci. Officer, 1951; Sen. Prin. Sci. Officer (Research Merit), 1956; Dep. Chief Sci. Officer (Res. Merit), 1964. Visiting Professor: Dept of Bacteriology, Univ. of Calif, Berkeley, USA, 1964, UCLA, 1972; (summer) Dept of Microbiol., Univ. of Washington, Seattle, USA, 1977, Univ. of Michigan, Ann Arbor, 1981. Society for General Microbiology: Mem. Council, 1960-64; Meetings Sec., 1964-68; Treas., 1968-75; Pres., 1975-78; Treas., Fedn of Europ. Microbiol Socs, 1975-82; Mem. Cttee, Path. Soc. of Gt Britain and Ire., 1975-80. *Publications:* over 250 papers in jls and books, mainly on mechanisms of microbial (bacterial, viral and fungal) pathogenicity. *Recreation:* farming 52 hectares, Melton Mowbray, Leics. *Address:* Department of Microbiology, University of Birmingham, PO Box 363, Birmingham B15 2TT. *T:* 021-472 1301 (ext. 3124). *Club:* Athenæum.

SMITH, Lt-Col Harry Cyril, CBE 1945 (OBE 1919); MC 1917; Russian Order of St Anne (2nd Class) 1920; *b* 1888; *s* of late Arthur B. Smith, Birmingham; *m* 1st, 1920, Catherine Koulikoff, Petrograd (marr. diss.), *d* of late Baroness v. Breugel-Douglas, The Hague; one *s*; *m* 2nd, Ida Eleanor, widow of Capt. Lawder B. S. Smith, MC, and *e d* of late William Raymond FitzMaurice Clark, Kilballyskea, Shinrone, Offaly, Eire. *Educ:* Royal Grammar School, Worcester and Birmingham. Joined RE (TA), 1908; Engineering, S America, 1909-14; served European War, 1914-18, RE (despatches twice); CRE 28th Division, 1919; Assistant Railway Adviser, British Military Mission with Denekin, S Russia, 1919-20; Asst Director of Railways, GHQ Constantinople and simultaneously Mil. Director, Anatolian and Baghdad Rly and Pres. Inter-Allied Rly Commission in Turkey, 1920-23; Manager and Dir Anatolian Rly Co., rep. interests of Anglo-Turkish Trust Co., and Dir Port of Haidar Pasha and Mersina, Tarsus, Adana Rly Co. 1923-27; reported on transport conditions in Italy, 1928; organised Indian Roads and Transport Devel. Assoc., 1929-39; Member, Bombay Leg. Council and Indian Central Leg. Assembly (Delhi and Simla); served on various Govt Transport cttees and confs; served with Transportation Directorate, GHQ Middle East, Cairo, 1940-41. Dir-Gen., Iraqi State Railways, Baghdad, 1941-50; temp. Amir Al Liwa' (Maj.-Gen.) Iraq Army. Silver Jubilee Medal, 1935; Coronation Medal, 1937. *Address:* 5 Hickman's Close, Lindfield, Sussex.

SMITH, Harvey; *see* Smith, R. H.

SMITH, Hedworth Cunningham, CBE 1972; Chairman, Medical Appeal Tribunals and Pensions Appeals Tribunals, England; Judge of the Supreme Court of the Bahama Islands 1965-72, retired; *b* 12 May 1912; *s* of James Smith and Elizabeth (*née* Brown); unmarried. *Educ:* George Watson's Coll., Edinburgh; Edinburgh University. MA 1933; LLB 1936. Solicitor, Scotland, 1937-40; Barrister-at-Law, Gray's Inn, London, 1950. Served War of 1939-45: commnd 1940; Staff Officer, GHQ India Command, 1943-46 (Major). District Magistrate, 1946, Senior District Magistrate, 1950, Gold Coast; Judge of Supreme Court of Ghana, 1957; retd from Ghana Govt service, 1961; Legal Adviser, Unilever Ltd Gp of Cos in Ghana, 1962-64. *Recreation:* golf. *Address:* c/o 40 Thorne Road, Doncaster, Yorks. *T:* Doncaster 62819. *Club:* East India, Devonshire, Sports and Public Schools.

SMITH, Lt-Col Henry Owen H.; *see* Hugh Smith.

SMITH, Prof. Henry Sidney; Edwards Professor of Egyptology, University College London, since 1970; *b* 14 June 1928; *s* of Prof. Sidney Smith, FBA,

and of Mary, *d* of H. W. Parker; *m* 1961, Hazel Flory Leeper. *Educ:* Merchant Taylors' Sch., Northwood; Christ's Coll., Cambridge (MA). Lectr in Egyptology, Univ. of Cambridge, 1954-63; Budge Fellow in Egyptology, Christ's Coll., Cambridge, 1955-63; Reader in Egyptian Archaeology, University Coll. London, 1963-70. Field Dir for Egypt Exploration Soc. in Nubia, 1961, 1964-65, and at Saqqara and Memphis, Egypt, 1970-. *Publications:* Preliminary Reports of the Egypt Exploration Society's Nubian Survey, 1962; A Visit to Ancient Egypt, 1974; The Fortress of Buhen: the inscriptions, 1976; The Fortress of Buhen: the archaeological report, 1979; (with W. J. Tait) Saqqara Demotic Papyri I, 1983; articles in Kush, Jl of Egyptian Arch., Orientalia, Rev. 'Egyptologie, Bull. Inst. Français d'Arch. Or., Z für Äg. Sprache und Altertümskunde, etc. *Address:* Ailwyn House, Upwood, Huntingdon, Cambs.

SMITH, Sir Henry (Thompson), KBE 1962; CB 1957; *b* 25 Feb. 1905; *y s* of late Ralph Smith, Gateshead; *m* 1929, Jane Harrison (*d* 1982), *y d* of late Robert Wilson, Seahouses; three *d*. *Educ:* Sunderland Road School, Gateshead; London School of Economics. Post Office: Boy messenger, 1918; Sorting-clerk and telegraphist, 1922; Customs and Excise: Clerical officer, 1928; Officer, 1932; Asst Principal, 1934; Air Ministry: Principal, 1940; Asst Secretary, 1944; Assistant Under-Secretary of State, 1953-58; Deputy Under-Secretary of State, 1958-64; Dep. Under-Sec. of State (Air Force Dept), Min. of Defence, 1964-65, retd. *Recreations:* woodwork, gardening. *Address:* 130 Wantage Road, Wallingford, Oxfordshire. *T:* Wallingford 36330.

SMITH, Dr Herbert Williams, FRS 1980; FRCVS, FRCPath; Head of Department of Microbiology, Houghton Poultry Research Station, Cambridgeshire, since 1971; *b* 3 May 1919; *s* of Herbert Harry Smith and Ida Elizabeth Williams; *m* 1942, Kathleen Margaret Mary Bezant; one *s* two *d*. *Educ:* Pontypridd Grammar Sch.; London Univ. (PhD 1947; DSc 1957; DipBact 1948). FRCVS 1953; FRCPath 1970. Wellcome Res. Fellow, London Sch. of Hygiene and Trop. Medicine, 1945-49; Head, Dept of Pathology and Bacteriology, Livestock Res. Stn of Animal Health Trust, 1949-71. *Recreations:* gardening, work. *Address:* 7 Quaker Close, Kings Ripton, Huntingdon, Cambs PE17 2NP. *T:* Abbots Ripton 294.

SMITH, Sir Howard (Frank Trayton), GCMG 1981 (KCMG 1976; CMG 1966); HM Diplomatic Service, retired; *b* 15 Oct. 1919; *m* 1943, Winifred Mary Cropper; one *d*. *Educ:* Sidney Sussex Coll., Cambridge. Employed in FO, 1939; apptd Foreign Service, 1946. Served Oslo; transf. Washington, 2nd Sec. (Inf.) 1950; 1st Sec., Dec. 1950; 1st Sec. and Consul, Caracas, 1953; FO, 1956; Counsellor: Moscow, 1961-63; Foreign Office, 1964-68; Ambassador to Czechoslovakia, 1968-71; UK Rep. in NI, 1971-72; Dep. Sec., Cabinet Office, on secondment, 1972-75; Ambassador in Moscow, 1976-78. *Address:* Coromandel, Cross in Hand, Heathfield, E Sussex. *T:* Heathfield 4420. *Club:* Travellers'.

SMITH, Captain Hugh D.; *see* Dalrymple-Smith.

SMITH, Captain Humphry Gilbert B.; *see* Boys-Smith.

SMITH, Iain-Mór L.; *see* Lindsay-Smith.

SMITH, Ian Douglas; MP, Zimbabwe; *b* Selukwe, S Rhodesia, 8 April 1919; *m* Janet Watt; two *s* one *d*. *Educ:* Selukwe Sch.; Chaplin Sch., Gwelo, S Rhodesia; Rhodes Univ., Grahamstown, S Africa (B Com.). Served War of 1939-45: 130 Sqdn RAF, and 237 (Rhodesia) Sqdn Western Desert and Europe, 1941-45 (Flight-Lieut). Farmer. MLA (Rhodesia Party), Southern Rhodesia, 1948; Mem. Federal Parliament (United Federal Party) 1953; Chief Govt Whip, 1958; resigned from United Federal Party, 1961; Foundn Mem., Republican Front (formerly Rhodesian Front), President, 1965-; MLA (Rhodesian Front), and appointed Minister of the Treasury, S Rhodesia, Dec. 1962; Minister of Defence, April 1964-May 1965; Minister of External Affairs, April-Aug. 1964; Prime Minister of Rhodesia, 1964-79; Minister Without Portfolio, Zimbabwe-Rhodesia, 1979-80. Independence Decoration, Rhodesia, 1970; Grand Comdr, Order of Legion of Merit of Rhodesia, 1979. *Address:* Gwenoro Farm, Selukwe, Zimbabwe. *Clubs:* Salisbury, Salisbury Sports (Zimbabwe).

SMITH, Ivor Otterbein, CMG 1963; OBE 1952; retired as Chairman of Public Service and Police Service Commissions and Member of Judicial Service Commission, British Guiana (1961-66); *b* Georgetown, British Guiana, 13 Dec. 1907; *s* of Bryce Otterbein Smith and late Florette Maud Smith (*née* Chapman); *m* 1936, Leila Muriel Fowler; one *s* two *d*. *Educ:* Queen's Coll., British Guiana; Pitman's Commercial Coll., London. Joined Brit. Guiana CS, as Clerical Asst, Treas., 1925; Sec. Commissioners of Currency, 1933; Asst Dist. Comr, 1941; Private Sec. to Gov., 1943; Dist Comr, 1945; Comr, Cayman Is, 1946-52; Dep. Comr of Local Govt, Brit. Guiana, 1953; Governor's Sec., and Clerk Exec. Coun., 1956; Dep. Chief Sec., 1960; Acted as Chief Sec. on several occasions and was Officer Administering the Govt, Sept.-Oct. 1960. Served with S Caribbean Force, 1941-43; Major, Staff Officer, Brit. Guiana Garrison. Hon. Col, British Guiana Volunteer Force, 1962-66. Chm., Nat. Sports Coun, 1962-66. *Recreations:* tennis; interested in sports of all kinds; rep. Brit. Guiana at Association and Rugby football, cricket, hockey. *Address:* 401-611 Blackford Street, New Westminster, BC V3M 1R7, Canada.

SMITH, Jack, ARCA 1952; artist; *b* 18 June 1928; *s* of John Edward and Laura Smith; *m* 1956, Susan Craigie Halkett. *Educ:* Sheffield College of Art; St Martin's School of Art; Royal College of Art. Exhibitions: Whitechapel Art Gallery, 1959, 1971; Beaux Arts Gallery, 1952-58; Matthiesen Gallery, 1960, 1963; Catherine Viviano Gallery, New York, 1958, 1961; Pittsburgh International, 1955, 1957, 1964; Grosvenor Gallery, 1965; Marlborough Gallery, 1968; Konsthallen, Gothenburg, Sweden, 1968; Hull Univ., 1969; Bear Lane Gallery, Oxford, 1970; Whitechapel Gall., 1970; Redfern Gall., 1973 and 1976; Serpentine Gall., 1978; Fischer Fine Art, London, 1981. Guggenheim Award (Nat.), 1960. Work in permanent collections: Tate Gallery; Arts Council of Great Britain; Contemporary Art Society; British Council. *Address:* 29 Seafield Road, Hove, Sussex. *T:* Brighton 738312.

SMITH, Jack Stanley, CMG 1970; Professor, and Chairman, Graduate School of Business Administration, University of Melbourne, 1973-77, retired; *b* 13 July 1916; *s* of C. P. T. Smith, Avoca, Victoria; *m* 1940, Nancy, *d* of J. C. Beckley, Melbourne; one *s* two *d. Educ:* Ballarat Grammar Sch.; Melbourne Univ. Construction Engineer, Australasian Petroleum Co., 1938-41. Served in Australian Imperial Forces, 1942-45, Lieut. Project Engineer, Melbourne & Metropolitan Bd of Works, 1946-48. P.A. Management Consultants, UK and Australia, 1949-72, Managing Dir, 1964-72. *Recreations:* golf, tennis. *Address:* 15 Glyndebourne Avenue, Toorak, Victoria 3142, Australia. *T:* 20 4581. *Clubs:* Melbourne (Melbourne); Lawn Tennis Association of Victoria, Metropolitan Golf (Vic.).

SMITH, James Aikman, TD; Sheriff of Lothian and Borders (formerly the Lothians and Peebles) at Edinburgh, 1968-76; Hon. Sheriff, 1976; *b* 13 June 1914; *s* of Rev. W. J. Smith, DD; *m* 1947, Ann, *d* of Norman A. Millar, FRICS, Glasgow; three *d. Educ:* Glasgow Academy; The Queen's Coll., Oxford; Edinburgh Univ. BA (Oxford) 1936; LLB (Edinburgh) 1939; Mem. of Faculty of Advocates, 1939. Served War of 1939-45 (despatches): Royal Artillery, 1939-46; Lt-Col 1944. Sheriff-Substitute: of Renfrew and Argyll, 1948-52; of Roxburgh, Berwick and Selkirk, 1952-57; of Aberdeen, Kincardine and Banff, 1957-68. Pres., Sheriffs-Substitute Assoc., 1969; Pres., Sheriffs' Assoc., 1971-72. Member Departmental Cttee on Probation Service, 1959-62. Chm., Edinburgh and E of Scotland Br., English-Speaking Union, 1971. Bronze Star (US), 1945. *Publications:* occasional articles in legal journals. *Address:* 16 Murrayfield Avenue, Edinburgh EH12 6AX. *Club:* New (Edinburgh).

SMITH, Hon. Sir James (Alfred), Kt 1979; CBE 1964; TD; Member of the Court of Appeal for Bermuda, since 1980, and of the Courts of Appeal for the Bahamas and Belize, since 1981; *b* Llandyssul, Cardiganshire, 11 May 1913; *s* of late Charles Silas and Elizabeth Smith (*née* Williams), Timberdine, Lampeter, Cardiganshire. *Educ:* Christ Coll., Brecon. Solicitor of the Supreme Court, 1937; called to the Bar, Lincoln's Inn, 1949. Served War of 1939-45: various Army Staff appointments; on staff of Supreme Allied Commander, South-East Asia, with rank of Major, 1944-45. Appointed to Colonial Legal Service, as Resident Magistrate, Nigeria, 1946; Chief Magistrate, 1951; Chief Registrar of the Supreme Court, Nigeria, 1953; Puisne Judge, Nigeria, 1955; Judge, High Court, Northern Nigeria, 1955; Senior Puisne Judge, High Court, N Nigeria, 1960-65; Puisne Judge, Supreme Court, Bahamas, 1965-75, Sen. Justice, 1975-78, Chief Justice, 1978-80. *Address:* Court of Appeal for the Bahamas, Nassau, Bahamas. *Clubs:* Naval and Military, Royal Commonwealth Society; Lyford Cay (Nassau).

SMITH, James Andrew Buchan, CBE 1959; DSc; retired as Director of the Hannah Dairy Research Institute, Ayr, Scotland, 1951-70 (Acting Director, 1948-51); *b* 26 May 1906; *yr s* of late Dr James Fleming Smith, JP, MB, CM, Whithorn, Wigtownshire; *m* 1933, Elizabeth Marion, *d* of James Kerr, Wallasey, Cheshire; four *d. Educ:* Leamington College, Warwicks; Univ. of Birmingham. PhD (Birmingham) 1929; DSc (London) 1940. Graduate Research Asst: at UCL, 1929-30; at Imperial College, London, 1930-32; Lectr in Biochemistry, Univ. of Liverpool, 1932-36; Biochemist, Hannah Dairy Research Inst., 1936-46; Lectr in Biochemistry, Univ. of Glasgow, 1946-47. President: Society of Dairy Technology, 1951-52; Nutrition Society, 1968-71; Treasurer, Internat. Union of Nutritional Sciences, 1969-75. FRIC; FRSE. Hon. LLD Glasgow, 1972. *Publications:* scientific papers in Biochemical Jl, Jl of Dairy Research, Proc. Nutrition Soc., etc. *Recreation:* gardening. *Address:* Hazelwood, 9 St Leonard's Road, Ayr. *T:* Ayr 264865. *Club:* Farmers'.

SMITH, James Archibald Bruce, CBE 1981; British Council Representative, Indonesia, since 1978; *b* 12 Sept. 1929; *s* of James Thom Smith and Anna Tyrie; *m* 1957, Anne Elizabeth Whittle; three *d. Educ:* Forfar Acad.; Edinburgh Univ. (MA 1952); Sch. of Econs, Dundee (BScEcon 1953); Jesus Coll., Cambridge. RAF, 1953-55. HMOCS, Dist Officer, Kenya, 1956-62; British Council, 1962-: Asst, Edinburgh, 1962-65; Asst Rep., Tanzania, 1965-66; Reg. Dir, Kumasi, Ghana, 1966-69; Rep., Sierra Leone, 1969-72; seconded to ODM, 1973-75; Dir, Personnel Dept, 1975-77; Controller, Personnel and Staff Recruitment Div., 1977-78. *Recreations:* Angusiana, reading, walking, collecting. *Address:* Jalan Teuku Umar 56, Jakarta, Indonesia; Corodale, Hillside Road, Forfar, Angus. *T:* Forfar 64140; 46 Rutland Court, SE5. *T:* 01-733 4602.

SMITH, James Cadzow, DRC; CEng; FIMechE, FIEE, FIMarE; FRSE 1981; Chairman, East Midlands Electricity Board, since 1977; *b* 28 Nov. 1927; *s* of James Smith and Margaret Ann Cadzow; *m* 1954, Moira Barrie Hogg; one

s one *d. Educ:* Bellvue Secondary Sch.; Heriot-Watt Coll.; Strathclyde Univ. Diploma of Royal Coll. of Science and Technology, Glasgow. CBIM. Engineer Officer, Mercantile Marine, 1948-53; various positions in Fossil and Nuclear Power Generation, 1953-73; Director of Engineering, N Ireland Electricity Service, 1973-74; Deputy Chairman and Chief Executive, 1974-77. *Recreations:* music, drama, mountaineering. *Address:* 398 Coppice Road, Arnold, Nottingham NG5 7HX. *T:* Nottingham 269711.

SMITH, Maj.-Gen. (James) Desmond (Blaise), CBE 1944; DSO 1944; CD 1948; Chairman: Blaise Investments Ltd; Desmond Smith Investments Ltd; Director, Daf Indal Ltd, Canada and numerous other companies; *b* 7 Oct. 1911; *s* of William George Smith, Ottawa, Canada; *m* 1st, 1937, Miriam Irene Blackburn (*d* 1969); two *s;* 2nd, 1979, Mrs Belle Shenkman, Ottawa. *Educ:* Ottawa University, Canada; Royal Military College, Canada. Joined Canadian Army, Royal Canadian Dragoons, 1933; National Defence HQ, Ottawa, as Assistant Field Officer in Bde Waiting to Governor-General of Canada, 1939. Served War of 1939-45, in England, Italy and N W Europe holding following commands and appts: CO Royal Canadian Dragoons; Comdr: 4th Cdn Armoured Bde; 5th Cdn Armoured Bde; 1st Cdn Inf. Bde: 5th Cdn Armoured Div.; 1st Cdn Inf. Div.; Chief of Staff, 1st Cdn Corps. Comdt Canadian Army Staff Coll., 1946; Imp. Defence Coll., 1947; Sec. Chiefs of Staff Cttee, 1948-50; Military Sec. Cdn Cabinet Defence Cttee, 1948-50; QMG, Canadian Army, 1951; Chairman, Canadian Joint Staff, London, 1951-54; Commandant, National Defence College of Canada, 1954-58; Adjutant-General of the Canadian Army, 1958-62. Colonel, HM Regt of Canadian Guards, 1961-66. Freedom, City of London, 1954. Croix de Guerre, 1944, Chevalier, Legion of Honour, 1944 (France); Comdr Military Order of Italy, 1944; Officer Legion of Merit (USA), 1944; Order of Valour (Greece), 1945. KStJ 1961 (CStJ 1952). *Recreations:* shooting, tennis, ski-ing, painting. *Address:* 50 Albert Court, SW7 2HB. *Clubs:* Carlton, Mark's; Queen's Tennis.

SMITH, Sir (James) Eric, Kt 1977; CBE 1972; FRS 1958; ScD; Secretary, Marine Biological Association of the UK, and Director Plymouth Laboratory, 1965-74; *b* 23 Feb. 1909; *er s* of Walter Smith and Elsie Kate Smith (*née* Pickett); *m* 1934, Thelma Audrey Cornish; one *s* one *d. Educ:* Hull Grammar School; King's College, London. Student Probat., Plymouth Marine Biol Lab., 1930-32; Asst Lecturer: Univ. of Manchester, 1932-35; Univ. of Sheffield, 1935-38; Univ. of Cambridge, 1938-50; Prof. of Zoology, Queen Mary Coll., Univ. of London, 1950-65 (Vice-Principal, 1963-65). Trustee, British Museum (Natural History), 1963-74, Chm. Trustees, 1969-74. Formerly Vice-President, Zoological Society; Member: Senate, Univ. of London, 1963-65; Scientific Advisory Committee, British Council; Science Research Council, 1965-67; Nature Conservancy, 1969-71; Royal Commn, Barrier Reef, 1970; Adv. Bd for the Research Councils, 1974-77. Pres., Devonshire Assoc., 1980-81. FKC 1964; Fellow: Queen Mary College, 1967; Plymouth Polytechnic, 1977. Hon. Associate, Natural Hist. Mus., 1981. Hon. DSc Exeter, 1968. Frink Medal for British Zoologists, Zoological Soc., 1981. *Publications:* various on marine biology, embryology, nervous anatomy and behaviour. *Recreations:* walking, gardening. *Address:* Wellesley House, 7 Coombe Road, Saltash, Cornwall PL12 4ER. *Club:* Royal Western Yacht.

SMITH, James Ian, CB 1974; Secretary, Department of Agriculture and Fisheries for Scotland, since 1972; *b* 22 April 1924; *s* of late James Smith, Ballater, Aberdeenshire, and of Agnes Michie; *m* 1947, Pearl Myra Fraser; one *s. Educ:* Alderman Newton's Sch., Leicester; St Andrews Univ. Served War of 1939-45: India and Burma; RA (attached Indian Mountain Artillery), Lieut, 1943-46. Entered Dept of Agriculture for Scotland, 1949; Private Sec. to Parly Under-Sec. of State, Scottish Office, 1953; Dept of Agriculture for Scotland: Principal, 1953; Asst Sec., 1959; Asst Sec., Scottish Development Dept, 1965-67; Under-Sec., Dept of Agriculture and Fisheries for Scotland, 1967-72. Mem. ARC, 1967-72. *Recreation:* golf. *Address:* 7 Hillpark Loan, Edinburgh EH4 7ST. *T:* 031-336 4652. *Club:* Royal Commonwealth Society.

SMITH, James Stewart, CMG 1955; Nigerian Administrative Service, retired; *b* 15 Aug. 1900; 4th *s* of late Charles Stewart Smith, HM Consul-General at Odessa; *m* 1955, Rosemary Stella Middlemore, *er d* of late Dr and Mrs P. T. Hughes, Bromsgrove, Worcs. *Educ:* Marlborough; King's College, Cambridge. Entered Nigerian Administrative Service, 1924; Senior District Officer 1943; Resident 1945; Senior Resident 1951; retired 1955. Papal Order of Knight Commander of Order of St Gregory the Great, 1953. *Recreations:* gardening, watching cricket, chess. *Address:* Davenham, Graham Road, Malvern, Worcs. *T:* Malvern 68667. *Club:* United Oxford & Cambridge University.

SMITH, Janet (B.) A.; *see* Adam Smith.

SMITH, Jeremy Fox Eric; Chairman, Smith St Aubyn (Holdings) plc, since 1973; *b* 17 Nov. 1928; *s* of Captain E. C. E. Smith, MC, and B. H. Smith (*née* Williams); *m* 1953, Julia Mary Rona, *d* of Sir Walter Burrell, Bt, *qv*; two *s* two *d. Educ:* Eton; New College, Oxford. Chairman, Transparent Paper Ltd, 1965-76. Chairman, London Discount Market Assoc., 1978-80. *Recreations:* hunting, shooting, stalking, skiing. *Address:* Balcombe House, Balcombe, Sussex RH17 6PB. *T:* Balcombe 267. *Club:* Leander (Henley on Thames).

SMITH, Dr John, OBE 1945; TD 1950; Deputy Chief Medical Officer, Scottish Home and Health Department, 1963-75, retired; *b* 13 July 1913; *e s* of late John Smith, DL, JP, Glasgow and Symington, and Agnes Smith; *m* 1942, Elizabeth Fleming (*d* 1981), twin *d* of late A. F. Wylie, Giffnock; three *s* one *d* (and one *s* decd). *Educ:* High Sch., Glasgow; Sedbergh Sch.; Christ's Coll., Cambridge; Glasgow Univ. BA 1935; MA 1943; MB, BChir Cantab 1938; MB, ChB Glasgow 1938; MRCPG 1965; FRCPG 1967; FRCPE 1969; FFCM 1972. TA (RA) from 1935 (RAMC from 1940); War Service, 1939-46; ADMS Second Army, DDMS (Ops and Plans) 21 Army Group (despatches); OC 155 (Lowland) Fd Amb., 1950-53; ADMS 52 (Lowland) Div., 1953-56; Hon. Col 52 Div. Medical Service, 1961-67. House appts Glasgow Victoria and Western Infirmaries; joined Dept of Health for Scotland, 1947; Medical Supt, Glasgow Victoria Hosp., 1955-58; rejoined Dept of Health for Scotland, 1958; specialised in hospital planning. QHP 1971-74. Officer, Ordre de Leopold I (Belgium), 1947. *Publications:* articles on medical administration and hospital services in various medical jls. *Recreations:* rifle shooting (shot in Scottish and TA representative teams); hill walking, gardening. *Address:* Murrayfield, Biggar, Lanarkshire. *T:* Biggar 20036. *Clubs:* Naval and Military; Western (Glasgow); New (Edinburgh).

SMITH, Rt. Hon. John, PC 1978; MP (Lab) Lanarkshire North, since 1970; *b* 13 Sept. 1938; *s* of late Archibald Leitch Smith and of Sarah Cameron Smith; *m* 1967, Elizabeth Margaret Bennett; three *d*. *Educ:* Dunoon Grammar Sch.; Glasgow Univ. (MA, LLB). Advocate, Scottish Bar, 1967-. Contested East Fife, 1961 by-election and 1964. PPS to Sec. of State for Scotland, Feb.-Oct. 1974; Parly Under-Sec. of State, 1974-75, Minister of State, 1975-76, Dept of Energy; Minister of State, Privy Council Office, 1976-78; Sec. of State for Trade, 1978-79; principal Opposition Spokesman on Trade, Prices and Consumer Protection, 1979-. Winner, Observer Mace, Nat. Debating Tournament, 1962. *Recreations:* tennis, sailing. *Address:* 21 Cluny Drive, Edinburgh EH10 6DW. *T:* 031-447 3667.

SMITH, Professor John Cyril, FBA 1973; QC 1979; Professor of Law in the University of Nottingham since 1958, and Head of Department of Law 1956-74, and since 1977; *b* 15 Jan. 1922; 2nd *s* of Bernard and Madeline Smith; *m* 1957, Shirley Ann Walters; two *s* one *d*. *Educ:* St Mary's Grammar Sch., Darlington; Downing Coll., Cambridge (Hon. Fellow, 1977). Served Royal Artillery, 1942-47 (Captain). BA 1949, LLB 1950, MA 1954, LLD 1975 Cantab. Called to Bar, Lincoln's Inn, 1950; Hon. Bencher, 1977; Hon. Mem., Midland and Oxford Circuit Bar Mess. Nottingham University: Assistant Lecturer in Law, 1950-52; Lecturer, 1952-56; Reader, 1956-57; Pro-Vice-Chancellor, 1973-77; Hon. Pres. of Convocation, 1978-. Commonwealth Fund Fellow, Harvard Law Sch., 1952-53. Member: Criminal Law Revision Cttee, 1977- (co-opted, 1960-66 (staff reference) and 1970-77); Policy Adv. Cttee, 1975-. Pres., Soc. of Public Teachers of Law, 1979-80. *Publications:* (with Professor J. A. C. Thomas) A Casebook on Contract, 1957; (with Brian Hogan) Criminal Law, 1965; Law of Theft, 1968; Criminal Law, Cases and Materials, 1975; articles in legal periodicals. *Recreations:* walking, gardening. *Address:* 445 Derby Road, Lenton, Nottingham NG7 2EB. *T:* Nottingham 782323.

SMITH, John Derek, MA, PhD; FRS 1976; Member of Scientific Staff, Medical Research Council, Laboratory of Molecular Biology, Cambridge, since 1962; *b* 8 Dec. 1924; *s* of Richard Ernest Smith and Winifred Strickland Smith (*née* Davis); *m* 1955, Ruth Irwin Aney (marr. diss. 1968). *Educ:* King James' Grammar Sch., Knaresborough; Clare Coll., Cambridge. Mem., Scientific Staff, Agricl Research Council Virus Research Unit, Cambridge, 1945-59; Research Fellow, Clare Coll., 1949-52; with Institut Pasteur, Paris, 1952-53; Rockefeller Foundn Fellow, Univ. of California, Berkeley, 1955-57; California Institute of Technology: Sen. Research Fellow, 1959-62; Sherman Fairchild Scholar, 1974-75. *Publications:* numerous papers in scientific jls on biochemistry and molecular biology. *Recreation:* travel. *Address:* MRC Laboratory of Molecular Biology, Hills Road, Cambridge CB2 2QH. *T:* Cambridge 248011; 12 Stansgate Avenue, Cambridge. *T:* Cambridge 247841.

SMITH, Air Vice-Marshal John Edward, CB 1979; CBE 1972; AFC 1967; Air Officer Administration, Headquarters Strike Command, 1977-81; retired; *b* 8 June 1924; *m* 1944, Roseanne Margurite (*née* Eriksson); four *s* two *d* (and one *s* decd). *Educ:* Tonbridge Sch. Served in Far East, ME, USA and Germany as well as UK Stations since joining the Service in Nov. 1941. *Recreations:* sailing, travel. *Address:* c/o Lloyds Bank Ltd, 45 Newport Road, Cardiff CF2 1TW. *Club:* Royal Air Force.

SMITH, Rear-Adm. John Edward D.; *see* Dyer-Smith.

SMITH, (John) Edward (McKenzie) L.; *see* Lucie-Smith.

SMITH, John Herbert, CBE 1977; FCA, IPFA, CIGasE, FBCS; Deputy Chairman, British Gas Corporation, since 1976; *b* 30 April 1918; *s* of Thomas Arthur Smith and Pattie Lord; *m* 1945, Phyllis Mary Baxter; two *s* three *d*. *Educ:* Salt High Sch., Shipley, Yorks. Articled Clerk, Bradford and Otley, 1934-39. Served War: RAMC, 1940-46. Dep. Clerk and Chief Financial Officer, Littleborough, Lancs, 1946-49; West Midlands Gas Bd, 1949-61 (various posts, finishing as Asst Chief Accountant); Chief Accountant, Southern Gas Bd, 1961-65; Director of Finance and Administration, East Midlands Gas Bd, 1965-68; Mem. (full-time), East Midlands Gas Bd, 1968 (Dep. Chm., 1968-72); Mem. for Finance, Gas Council, June-Dec. 1972; Mem.

for Finance, British Gas Corp., 1973-76. Chm., Nationalised Industries Finance Panel, 1978-. Member, Management Committee: Pension Funds Property Unit Trust, 1975-; Lazard American Exempt Fund, 1976-; British American Property Trust, 1982-; Chm., Moracrest Investments Ltd, 1977-. Mem. Council, Inst. of Chartered Accountants, 1977-81. *Recreations:* music, piano playing, choral activities. *Address:* 64A Beaconsfield Road, Blackheath, SE3 7LG.

SMITH, John Hilary, CBE 1970 (OBE 1964); Secretary, Imperial College of Science and Technology, and Clerk to the Governors, since 1979; *b* 20 March 1928; 2nd *s* of late P. R. Smith, OBE and Edith Prince; *m* 1964, Mary Sylvester Head; two *s* one *d*. *Educ:* Cardinal Vaughan Sch., London; University Coll. London; University Coll., Oxford. BA Hons London 1948. Mil. service, 1948-50, commnd Queen's Own Royal W Kent Regt. Cadet, Northern Nigerian Administration, 1951; Supervisor, Admin. Service Trng, 1960; Dep. Sec. to Premier, 1963; Dir Staff, Develt Centre, 1964; Perm. Sec., Min. of Finance, Benue Plateau State, 1968; Vis. Lectr, Duke Univ., 1970; Financial Sec., British Solomon Is, 1970; Governor of Gilbert and Ellice Islands, 1973-76, of Gilbert Islands, 1976-78. Mem. Council, Scout Assoc.; Pres., Pacific Is Soc. of UK and Ireland; Governor: St Mary's Coll., Strawberry Hill; Cardinal Vaughan School. *Publications:* How to Write Letters that get Results, 1965; Colonial Cadet in Nigeria, 1968; articles in S Atlantic Quarterly, Administration, Jl of Overseas Administration, Nigeria. *Recreations:* walking, writing, music. *Address:* 65 Wavendon Avenue, Chiswick, W4. *T:* 01-995 8594. *Club:* Royal Commonwealth Society.

SMITH, Sir John Kenneth N.; *see* Newson-Smith.

SMITH, John (Lindsay Eric), CBE 1975; *b* 3 April 1923; *s* of Captain E. C. E. Smith, MC, LLD; *m* 1952, Christian, *d* of late Col U. E. C. Carnegy of Lour, DSO, MC; two *s* three *d*. *Educ:* Eton (Fellow, 1974-); New Coll., Oxford (MA; Hon. Fellow, 1979). Served Fleet Air Arm 1942-46 (Lieut RNVR). MP (C) Cities of London and Westminster, Nov. 1965-1970; Mem., Public Accounts Cttee, 1968-69. Member: Standing Commission on Museums and Galleries, 1958-66; Inland Waterways Redevelopment Cttee, 1959-62; Historic Buildings Cttee, National Trust, 1952-61; Council and Exec. Cttee, National Trust, 1961-; Dep. Chm., National Trust, 1980-; Member: Historic Buildings Council, 1971-78; Redundant Churches Fund, 1972-74; Nat. Heritage Memorial Fund, 1980-82. Director: Coutts & Co., 1950-; Financial Times Ltd, 1959-68; Rolls Royce Ltd, 1955-75; Dep. Governor, Royal Exchange Assurance, 1961-66. Founder, Manifold and Landmark Charitable Trusts. High Steward of Maidenhead, 1966-75. Freeman of Windsor and Maidenhead, 1976. FSA; Hon. FRIBA, 1973. JP Berks, 1964; DL 1978, Lord-Lieut, 1975-78, Berks. *Address:* Shottesbrooke Park, Maidenhead, Berks; 1 Smith Square, SW1. *Clubs:* Pratt's, Beefsteak, Brooks's.

SMITH, John M.; *see* Maynard Smith, J.

SMITH, John Roger B.; *see* Bickford Smith.

SMITH, Rev. John Sandwith B.; *see* Boys Smith.

SMITH, John Wilson, CBE 1982; JP; Chairman, Liverpool Football Club, since 1973; *b* 6 Nov. 1920; *m* 1946, Doris Mabel Parfitt; one *s*. *Educ:* Oulton High School, Liverpool. Dir, Tetley Walker Ltd, 1966-77; Dep. Chm., First Castle Electronics Ltd, 1978-. Member: Sports Council, 1980-; Football Trust, 1980-; Football League Restructuring Cttee, 1982-; Chairman: Duke of Edinburgh's Merseyside Industrial Award Council, 1977-; Cttee of Inquiry into Lawn Tennis (report, 1980). JP Liverpool, 1971. *Recreation:* golf. *Address:* Pine Close, Mill Lane, Gayton, Wirral, Merseyside. *T:* 051-342 5362. *Club:* Reform.

SMITH, Jonathan A.; *see* Ashley-Smith.

SMITH, Prof. Joseph Victor, FRS 1978; Louis Block Professor of Physical Sciences, University of Chicago, since 1977 (Professor of Mineralogy and Crystallography, 1960-76); *b* 30 July 1928; *s* of Henry Victor Smith and Edith (*née* Robinson); *m* 1951, Brenda Florence Wallis; two *d*. *Educ:* Cambridge Univ. (MA, PhD). Fellow, Carnegie Instn of Washington, 1951-54; Demonstrator in Mineralogy and Petrology, Cambridge Univ., 1954-56; Asst then Associate Prof., Pennsylvania State Univ., 1956-60. Editor, Power Diffraction File, 1959-69. Visiting Prof., California Inst. of Technology, 1965; Consultant, Union Carbide Corp., 1956-. Murchison Medal, 1980; Roebling Medal, 1982. *Publications:* Feldspar Minerals, Vols 1 and 2, 1975; numerous articles on crystallography, mineralogy, petrology and planetology. *Recreations:* music, painting. *Address:* Department of the Geophysical Sciences, University of Chicago, 5801 Ellis Avenue, Chicago, Ill 60637, USA. *T:* 312-962-8110. *Club:* Quadrangle (Chicago).

SMITH, Hon. Kenneth George, OJ 1973; Hon. Mr Justice Smith; Chief Justice of Jamaica since 1973; *b* 25 July 1920; *s* of Franklin C. Smith; *m* 1942, Hyacinth Whitfield Connell; two *d*. *Educ:* Primary schs; Cornwall Coll., Jamaica; Inns of Court Sch. of Law, London. Barrister-at-Law, Lincoln's Inn. Asst Clerk of Courts, 1940-48; Dep. Clerk of Courts, 1948-53; Clerk of Courts, 1953-56; Crown Counsel, 1956-62; Asst Attorney-Gen., 1962-65; Supreme Court Judge, 1965-70; Judge of Appeal, Jamaica, 1970-73. *Recreations:* swimming, gardening. *Address:* 16 Farringdon Drive, Kingston 6, Jamaica; Supreme Court, Kingston, Jamaica, W1. *T:* (office) 922-2933.

SMITH, Kenneth Graeme Stewart, CMG 1958; JP; retired as Civil Secretary, The Gambia, West Africa, 1962; *b* 26 July 1918; 3rd *s* of late Prof. H. A. Smith, DCL; unmarried. *Educ*: Bradfield; Magdalen College, Oxford. Cadet, Colonial Administrative Service, Tanganyika, 1940; appointments in Colonial Service, 1945-62. JP Dorset, 1967. *Address*: The Old House, Newland, Sherborne, Dorset DT9 3AQ. *T*: Sherborne 2754.

SMITH, Kenneth Shirley, MD, BSc London, FRCP; Lieutenant-Colonel RAMC 1942; Hon. Physician and Cardiologist, Charing Cross Hospital and to the London Chest Hospital; Chief Medical Officer Marine and General Mutual Life Assurance Society; formerly Consulting Physician, Samaritan Free Hospital for Women; Staff Examiner in Medicine, University of London; Examiner in Medicine, Conjoint Board; *b* 23 Jan. 1900; *s* of E. Shirley Smith; *m* 1929, Alice Mary Hoogewerf; one *s* two *d*. *Educ*: London University; Middlesex Hospital (Senior Scholar). BSc, 1st Class Hons in Physiology, London, 1923; formerly House Physician, Casualty Medical Officer and Medical Registrar Middlesex Hospital; also Resident Medical Officer, Nat. Hosp. for Diseases of the Heart, 1927; Pres., British Cardiac Soc. Member, Assoc. of Physicians of Great Britain. Editor, British Heart Journal. Organizing Secretary, First European Congress of Cardiology, London, 1952. Served with 1st Army in N Africa, later with CMF in Italy, Greece and Austria. Gold Staff Officer, Coronation of King George VI. *Publications*: Contributor to British Encyclopædia of Medical Practice, 1937; Papers on cardiological and pulmonary subjects in British Heart Journal, American Heart Journal, Quarterly Journal of Medicine, Lancet, British Medical Journal, Practitioner, etc. *Recreation*: water colour. *Address*: 5 Asmun's Hill, Hampstead Garden Suburb, NW11. *T*: 01-455 2706. *Club*: Oriental.

SMITH, Laura; *see* Smith, A. L. A.

SMITH, Sir Laurence Barton G.; *see* Grafftey-Smith.

SMITH, Lawrence Delpré; Senior Puisne Judge of the Supreme Court of Sarawak, North Borneo and Brunei, 1951-64, retired; *b* 29 October 1905; *m* ; one *s* three *d*. *Educ*: Christ's Hospital; Hertford College, Oxford; Gray's Inn. Colonial Administrative Service, 1929; Colonial Legal Service, 1934; Tanganyika, 1929; Palestine, 1946; Gambia, 1948. *Address*: 34 The Avenue, Muswell Hill, N10 2QL. *T*: 01-883 7198.

SMITH, Lawrence Joseph, OBE 1976; Executive Officer with Transport and General Workers Union, since 1979; two *d*. Served in HM Forces, 1941-47; joined London Transport, 1947; District Officer, TGWU, 1961, London District Secretary, 1965, National Officer, 1966, National Secretary, Passenger Services Group, 1971. *Recreations*: gardening, football. *Address*: Transport House, Smith Square, SW1P 3JB. *T*: 01-828 7788.

SMITH, Lawrence Roger Hines, FSA; Keeper of Oriental Antiquities, British Museum, since 1977; *b* 19 Feb. 1941; *s* of Frank Ernest Smith and Eva Lilian Smith (*née* Hines); *m* 1965, Louise Geraldine Gallini; one *s* five *d*. *Educ*: Collyer's Grammar Sch., Horsham; Queens' Coll., Cambridge (BA). British Museum: Asst Keeper, Dept of Manuscripts, 1962; Dept of Oriental Antiquities, 1965; Dep. Keeper, 1976. Academic adviser, Great Japan Exhibn, RA, 1981-82, and contrib. to catalogue. *Publications*: Netsuke: the miniature sculpture of Japan (with R. Barker), 1976; Flowers in Art from East and West (with P. Hulton), 1979; Japanese Prints: 300 years of albums and books (with J. Hillier), 1980; (with V. Harris) Japanese Decorative Arts 1600-1900, 1982; articles and reviews in learned jls. *Recreations*: walking, running, bellringing, music. *Address*: 4 Rudall Crescent, NW3. *T*: 01-435 4107; Orchardlea, High Street, Dormansland, Lingfield, Surrey RH7 6PU. *T*: Lingfield 833539.

SMITH, Sir Leonard (Herbert), Kt 1982; CBE 1977 (MBE 1963); Deputy Treasurer, Liberal Party, since 1972; *b* 28 May 1907; *s* of Herbert Thomas and Harriett Smith; *m* 1943, Ruth Pauline Lees; two *d*. *Educ*: King's Sch., Chester. Active member of Liberal Party, 1922-; Sec. and Agent, Chester Div., 1929-39; Chief Agent, 1949-51; Foundn Officer, Liberal Party Orgn, 1946-49; Sec., Campaign Fund, 1948-50; Mem., Party Council, 1952-67 (Hon. Mem., 1967-); Hon. Treasurer, 1967-68; Vice-Pres., 1968; Dep. Chm., Fund Raising Cttee, 1980-; Pres., Eastern Reg., 1982- (Hon. Treasurer, 1972-80). Social Policy Exec., Booker McConnell Ltd, 1957-72. Member: Exec. and Council, Royal Commonwealth Soc. for the Blind, 1957- (Appeal Dir, 1951-57); British Cttee, World Prevention of Blindness Campaign, 1975-82; Exec. Cttee, West India Cttee, 1959-71; Hon. Sec., British Caribbean Assoc., 1958-; Hon. Secretary and Treasurer: London Cttee, English Harbour Restoration Fund, 1959-67; Sir Frank Worrell Commonwealth Meml Fund, 1968-; Hon. Treasurer, Women Caring Trust, 1972-; Jt Chm., Appeal Cttee, E-SU, 1975-. Mem. Council, Football Assoc., 1970-. JP Middlesex, subseq. City of London, 1963-77; Mem., City of London Adv. Cttee, 1965-77, Inner London Adv. Cttee, 1968-77, for appointment of magistrates. *Address*: Fen Farmhouse, Buxhall, Stowmarket, Suffolk IP14 5DG. *T*: Rattlesden 370. *Clubs*: National Liberal (Chm., 1972-), English-Speaking Union, MCC.

SMITH, Leslie Charles, OBE 1968; Director, Eastway Zinc Alloy Co. Ltd, since 1965; *b* 6 March 1918; *s* of Edward A. Smith and Elizabeth Smith; *m* 1948, Nancy Smith; two *s* one *d*. *Educ*: Enfield Central School. Export Buyer, 1938-40; Lieut, RNVR, 1940-46. Founder, Lesney Products, 1947, Jt Man. Dir 1947-73, Man. Dir 1973-80; Chief Exec. Officer, 1980-81, Vice-Chm., 1981-82. FInstM; FBIM 1976. *Recreations*: ski-ing, sailing, golf. *Address*: White Timbers, 9a Broad Walk, N21 3DA. *T*: 01-886 1656. *Clubs*: Naval;

RNVR Sailing, Royal Thames Yacht, Royal Ocean Racing, Royal Motor Yacht, Parkstone Yacht, Poole Harbour Yacht; North Middlesex Golf, South Hertfordshire Golf.

SMITH, Sir Leslie (Edward George), Kt 1977; Chairman, BOC Group (formerly The British Oxygen Co. Ltd), since 1972; *b* 15 April 1919; *m* 1st, 1943, Lorna Bell Pickworth; two *d* ; 2nd, 1964, Cynthia Barbara Holmes; one *s* one *d*. *Educ*: Christ's Hospital, Horsham, Sussex. Served War, Army (Royal Artillery, Royal Fusiliers), 1940-46. Variety of activities, 1946-55. Joined British Oxygen as Accountant, 1956, Group Man. Dir, 1969-72. Dir, Cadbury Schweppes, 1977-. Member: Foundn Bd, Internat. Management Inst. (Geneva), 1976-; Exec. Cttee, King Edward VII Hospital for Officers, 1978-; British Gas Corp., 1982-. FCA. *Recreations*: unremarkable. *Address*: Cookley House, Cookley Green, Swyncombe, near Henley-on-Thames, Oxon RG9 6EN.

SMITH, Maggie, (Mrs Margaret Natalie Cross), CBE 1970; Actress; *b* 28 Dec. 1934; *d* of Nathaniel Smith and Margaret Little (*née* Hutton); *m* 1st, 1967, Robert Stephens, *qv* (marr. diss. 1975); two *s* ; 2nd, 1975, Beverley Cross, *qv*. *Educ*: Oxford High School for Girls. Studied at Oxford Playhouse School under Isabel van Beers. Hon. DLitt St Andrews, 1971; Hon. DLitt Leicester, 1982. First appearance, June 1952, as Viola in OUDS Twelfth Night; 1st New York appearance, Ethel Barrymore Theatre, June 1956, as comedienne in New Faces. Played in Share My Lettuce, Lyric, Hammersmith, 1957; The Stepmother, St Martin's, 1958. Old Vic Co., 1959-60 season: The Double Dealer; As You Like It; Richard II; The Merry Wives of Windsor; What Every Woman Knows; Rhinoceros, Strand, 1960; Strip the Willow, Cambridge, 1960; The Rehearsal, Globe, 1961; The Private Ear and The Public Eye (Evening Standard Drama Award, best actress of 1962), Globe, 1962; Mary, Mary, Queen's, 1963 (Variety Club of Gt Britain, best actress of the year); The Country Wife, Chichester, 1969; Design for Living, LA, 1971; Private Lives, Queen's, 1972, Globe, 1973, NY, 1975 (Variety Club of GB Stage Actress Award, 1972); Peter Pan, Coliseum, 1973; Snap, Vaudeville, 1974; Night and Day, Phoenix, 1979; Virginia, Haymarket, 1981 (Standard Best Actress Award, 1982); at National Theatre: The Recruiting Officer, 1963; Othello, The Master Builder, Hay Fever, 1964; Much Ado About Nothing, Miss Julie, 1965; A Bond Honoured, 1966; The Beaux' Stratagem, 1970 (also USA); Hedda Gabler, 1970 (Evening Standard Best Actress award); at Festival Theatre, Stratford, Ontario: 1976: Antony and Cleopatra, The Way of the World, Measure for Measure, The Three Sisters; 1977: Midsummer Night's Dream, Richard III, The Guardsman, As You Like It, Hay Fever; 1978: As You Like It, Macbeth, Private Lives; 1980: Virginia; Much Ado About Nothing. *Films*: The VIP's, 1963; The Pumpkin Eater, 1964; Young Cassidy, 1965; Othello, 1966; The Honey Pot, 1967; Hot Millions, 1968 (Variety Club of GB Award); The Prime of Miss Jean Brodie, 1968 (Oscar; SFTA award); Oh! What a Lovely War, 1968; Love and Pain (and the Whole Damned Thing), 1973; Travels with my Aunt, 1973; Murder by Death, 1976; California Suite, 1977 (Oscar); Death on the Nile, 1978; Quartet, 1981; Clash of the Titans, 1981; Evil Under the Sun, 1982; The Missionary, 1982. *Recreation*: reading. *Address*: c/o Fraser and Dunlop, 91 Regent Street, W1R 8RU. *T*: 01-734 7311.

SMITH, Dame Margôt, DBE 1974; *b* 5 Sept. 1918; *d* of Leonard Graham Brown, MC, FRCS, and Margaret Jane Menzies; *m* 1947, Roy Smith; two *s* one *d*. *Educ*: Westonbirt. Chm., Nat. Conservative Women's Adv. Cttee, 1969-72; Chm., Nat. Union of Conservative and Unionist Assocs, 1973-74. Mem., NSPCC Central Exec. Cttee. *Address*: Howden Lodge, Spennithorne, Leyburn, N Yorks DL8 5PR. *T*: Wensleydale 23621.

SMITH, Mark Barnet; His Honour Judge Mark Smith; a Circuit Judge since 1972; *b* 11 Feb. 1917; *s* of David Smith and Sophie Smith (*née* Abrahams); *m* 1943, Edith Winifred Harrison; two *d*. *Educ*: Freehold Council Sch., Oldham; Manchester Grammar Sch.; Sidney Sussex Coll., Cambridge. MA (Hons) (Natural Sci.). Asst Examr in HM Patent Office, 1939 (and promoted Examr in 1944, while on war service). Served War, RA (Staff Sergt), 1940-46. Returned to Patent Office, 1946. Called to Bar, Middle Temple, 1948. Left Patent Office, end of 1948; pupil at the Bar, 1949. Temp. Recorder of Folkestone, 1971; a Recorder of the Crown Court, Jan.-Apr. 1972. *Address*: 28 Avenue Elmers, Surbiton, Surrey KT6 4SL. *T*: 01-399 0634.

SMITH, Maurice George; retired; Under-Secretary, Ministry of Overseas Development, 1968-76; *b* 4 Sept. 1915; *s* of Alfred Graham and Laura Maria Smith; *m* 1940, Eva Margaret Vanstone; two *s*. *Educ*: Sir Walter St John's School, Battersea. Examiner, Estate Duty Office, 1939. Flt Lieut RAF, 1942-46. Asst Principal, Min. of Civil Aviation, 1947; Principal, 1948; transferred to Colonial Office, 1950; seconded Commonwealth Office, 1954-55; Asst Secretary, Colonial Office, 1959; transferred to Dept of Technical Co-operation, 1961; Min. of Overseas Development, 1964; Under-Sec. and Principal Finance Officer, ODM, 1968. Chairman, Knights' Assoc. of Christian Youth Clubs, Lambeth, 1970- (Hon. Sec., 1950-70). *Recreations*: voluntary work in youth service, travel. *Address*: 52 Woodfield Avenue, SW16. *T*: 01-769 5356.

SMITH, Michael Edward C.; *see* Carleton-Smith.

SMITH, Prof. Michael G.; Crosby Professor of Human Environment, Department of Anthropology, Yale University, since 1978; *b* 18 Aug. 1921;

m ; three s. *Educ:* University College London. BA 1948, PhD 1951. Research Fellow, Inst. of Social and Economic Research, University Coll. of the West Indies, 1952-56, Sen. Research Fellow, there, 1956-58; Sen. Research Fellow, Nigerian Inst. of Social and Economic Research, Ibadan, 1958-60; Sen. Lectr (Sociology), Univ. Coll. of the WI, 1960-61; Prof. of Anthropology: Univ. of California, Los Angeles, 1961-69; University Coll. London, 1969-75. Special Advr to Prime Minister of Jamaica, 1975-78. Hon. LLD McGill, 1976. Order of Merit (Jamaica), 1973. *Publications:* The Economy of Hausa Communities of Zaria, 1955; Labour Supply in Rural Jamaica, 1956; (with G. J. Kruijer) A Sociological Manual for Caribbean Extension Workers, 1957; Government in Zazzau, 1800-1950, 1960; Kinship and Community in Carriacou, 1962; West Indian Family Structure, 1962; Dark Puritan, 1963; The Plural Society in the British West Indies, 1965; Stratification in Grenada, 1965; (ed, with Leo Kuper) Pluralism in Africa, 1969; Corporations and Society, 1974; The Affairs of Daura, 1978. *Address:* Department of Anthropology, Yale University, New Haven, Conn 06520, USA.

SMITH, Michael J. B.; *see* Babington Smith.

SMITH, Michael K.; *see* Kinchin Smith.

SMITH, (Newlands) Guy B.; *see* Bassett Smith.

SMITH, Dr Norman Brian, CBE 1980; Director, Imperial Chemical Industries Ltd, since 1978; *b* 10 Sept. 1928; *s* of late Vincent and Louise Smith; *m* 1955, Phyllis Crossley; one *s* one *d* (and one *s* decd). *Educ:* Sir John Deane's Grammar Sch., Northwich; Manchester Univ. (PhD Phys. Chemistry, 1954). Joined ICI Ltd, Terylene Council, 1954; Fibres Division: Textile Develt Dir, 1969; Dep. Chm., 1972; Chm., 1975-78; ICI Main Bd, 1978-; Director: Fiber Industries Inc., 1972-; Canadian Industries Ltd, 1981-; Territorial Dir for the Americas, and Chm., ICI Americas Inc., 1981- (Dir, 1980-); Non-Exec. Dir, Carrington Viyella Ltd, 1979-81. Pres., British Textile Confedn, 1977-79; Chairman: Man-Made Fibres Producers Cttee, 1976-78; EDC for Wool Textile Industry, 1979-81; Mem., BOTB and British Overseas Trade Adv. Cttee, 1980-81. *Recreations:* cricket, sailing, tennis, gardening, watching football. *Address:* Imperial Chemical Industries Ltd, Imperial Chemical House, Millbank, SW1P 3JF. *T:* 01-834 4444.

SMITH, Norman Jack, MA, MPhil; FInstPet; Chairman, British Underwater Engineering Ltd, since 1980; Managing Director, Smith Rea Energy Associates Ltd, since 1981; *b* 14 April 1936; *s* of late Maurice Leslie and Ellen Dorothy Smith; *m* 1967, Valerie Ann, *o d* of late A. E. Frost; one *s* one *d*. *Educ:* Grammar Sch., Henley-on-Thames; Oriel Coll., Oxford (MA); City Univ. (MPhil). Dexion Ltd, 1957; Vickers Ltd, 1960; Baring Brothers & Co. Ltd, 1969; seconded as Industrial Director, 1977, Dir-Gen., 1978-80, Offshore Supplies Office, Dept of Energy. Member: Soc. of Business Economists, 1958-; Offshore Energy Technology Bd, 1978-80. *Publications:* sundry articles in economic and similar jls. *Recreations:* walking, swimming, photography, history. *Address:* c/o Smith Rea Energy Associates Ltd, 3 Beer Cart Lane, Canterbury, Kent CT1 2NJ. *T:* Canterbury 59441.

SMITH, Prof. (Norman John) David; Head of Department of Dental Radiology, King's College Hospital Dental School, since 1972, and Professor of Dental Radiology, University of London, since 1978; *b* 2 Feb. 1931; *s* of late Norman S. Smith; *m* 1954, Regina Eileen Lugg; one *s*. *Educ:* King's Coll. Sch., Wimbledon; King's Coll., London; KCH Dental Sch. (BDS 1963; MPhil 1969); Royal Free Hosp. Sch. of Medicine (MSc 1966). Apprenticed to Pacific Steam Navigation Co., 1948-51; Officer Service, Royal Mail Lines, 1952-58 (Master Mariner, 1957); part-time posts at KCH Dental Sch., Guy's Hosp. Dental Sch. and in gen. dental practice, 1966-69; Sen. Lectr in Dental Surg., KCH Dental Sch., 1969-72; Reader in Dental Radiol., Univ. of London, 1973. Member: Southwark Bor. Council, 1974-78; GLC for Norwood, 1977- (Leader of Opposition, ILEA, 1979-); Thames Water Authority, 1977-; SE Thames RHA, 1978-; Council, Open Univ., 1978-81, 1982-; Court, Univ. of London, 1982-; Governor, Bethlem Royal and Maudsley Hosps, 1980-82; Mem., Bethlem Royal and Maudsley SHA, 1982-. Liveryman, Hon. Co. of Master Mariners. Sir Charlton Briscoe Res. Prize, KCH Med. Sch., 1969. *Publications:* Simple Navigation by the Sun, 1974; Dental Radiography, 1980; articles in dental jls. *Recreations:* sailing, nature photography. *Address:* c/o King's College Hospital Dental School, Denmark Hill, SE5 8RX. *T:* 01-274 6222, ext. 2863.

SMITH, Patrick Wykeham M.; *see* Montague-Smith.

SMITH, Ven. Percival; *see* Smith, Ven. A. M. P.

SMITH, Peter, FSA; Secretary, Royal Commission on Ancient Monuments in Wales, since 1973; *b* 15 June 1926; *s* of L. W. Smith, HMI, and late Mrs H. Smith (*née* Halsted); *m* 1954, Joyce Evelyn, *d* of late J. W. Abbott and of Alice Abbott (*née* Lloyd); two *s* one *d*. *Educ:* Peter Symonds' Sch., Winchester; Oriel Coll. and Lincoln Coll. (Open Scholar), Oxford (BA, Hons Mod. Hist. 1947); Hammersmith Sch. of Building (Inter ARIBA 1950). Royal Commission on Ancient Monuments in Wales: Jun. Investigator, 1949; Sen. Investigator, 1954; Investigator in Charge of Nat. Monuments Record, 1963. Pres., Cambrian Archaeological Assoc., 1979. G. T. Clark Prize, 1969; Alice Davis Hitchcock Medallion, 1978. *Publications:* Houses of the Welsh Countryside, 1975; contribs to Agrarian History of England; periodical literature on historic domestic architecture. *Recreations:* reading, drawing,

learning Welsh. *Address:* Tŷ-coch, Lluest, Llanbadarn Fawr, Aberystwyth, Dyfed SY23 3AU. *T:* Aberystwyth 3556.

SMITH, Peter Alexander Charles, OBE 1981; Chairman and Managing Director, Securicor Group Ltd and Security Services Ltd, since 1974; *b* 18 Aug. 1920; *s* of Alexander Alfred Smith and Gwendoline Mary (*née* Beer); *m* 1945, Marjorie May Humphrey; one *s*. *Educ:* St Paul's Sch., London. Admitted solicitor, 1948. Served RA, 1941-46: Captain; Adjt, 17th Medium Regt. Partner, Hextall, Erskine & Co., 1953-79. Chm., British Security Industry Assoc. Ltd, 1977-81; Dir, Metal Closures Gp Ltd, 1972- (Dep. Chm., 1981-). Mem. Council, Royal Warrant Holders Assoc., 1976-, Vice-Pres., 1981-82, Pres., 1982-83. CBIM. *Recreations:* golf, music, photography. *Address:* Vigilant House, 24 Gillingham Street, SW1V 1HZ. *T:* 01-828 5611. *Club:* British Racing Drivers (Hon. Life Mem.).

SMITH, Peter Claudius G.; *see* Gautier-Smith.

SMITH, Peter John, IPFA; County Treasurer, Tyne and Wear County Council, since 1980; *b* 31 Dec. 1936; *s* of Frank and Sarah Ann Smith; *m* 1959, Marie Louise Smith; one *s* one *d*. *Educ:* Rastrick Grammar Sch., Brighouse, W Yorkshire. Trainee Accountant, Huddersfield CBC, 1953-59; Accountancy Asst, Bradford CBC, 1959-61; Asst Chief Accountant, Chester CBC, 1961-63; Computer Manager, Keighley BC, 1963-66; Asst City Treasurer, Gloucester CBC, 1966-69; Dep. Borough Treasurer, Gateshead CBC, 1969-73; Asst County Treasurer, Tyne and Wear CC, 1973-74, Dep. County Treasurer, 1974-80. Treasurer: NE Regional Airport Jt Cttee, 1980-; Northumbria Police Authority, 1980-; Northumbria Probation and After Care Cttee, 1980-; Mem., Tyne and Wear Passenger Transport Exec. Bd, 1981-. *Recreations:* fell walking, squash. *Address:* 5 Cromarty, Ouston, Chester le Street, Co. Durham DH2 1LA. *T:* Birtley 404303. *Clubs:* Gateshead Squash, Beamish Park Golf.

SMITH, Philip; Deputy Director Warship Design (Electrical), Ministry of Defence (Navy), 1969-73, retired; *b* 19 May 1913; *m* 1940, Joan Mary Harker; one *s* one *d*. *Educ:* Bishop Wordsworth's Sch., Salisbury; Bristol Univ. BSc (First Cl. Hons). Graduate Trainee Apprentice, BTH Co., 1934-37; Outside Construction Engrg, BTH Co., 1937-38; Central Electricity Bd, 1938-39; Admty (Electrical Engrg Dept) (now MoD Navy), 1939-: past service at Chatham Dockyard and Dockyard Dept, HQ; Electrical Engrg Design Divs; Head of Electrical Dept, Admty Engrg Laboratory, West Drayton. CEng, FIEE, FIMechE; RCNC. *Recreations:* horticulture, golf, oil painting. *Address:* Myrfield, Summer Lane, Combe Down, Bath. *T:* Combe Down 833408. *Club:* Bath Golf.

SMITH, Philip George, CBE 1973; Chairman, Metal Market & Exchange Co. Ltd, since 1967 (Director since 1954); Director, Bassett Smith & Co. Ltd, since 1946. *Educ:* St Lawrence Coll., Ramsgate; Royal School of Mines, London. ARSM, BSc (Eng). Director: Bardyke Chemicals Ltd, 1968-; Tennant Trading (Metals) Ltd, 1975-82; (non-exec.), Comfin (Commodity & Finance) Co. Ltd, 1978-82; Hewitt and Hill Communications Ltd, 1979-. Mem. Inst. Exports; Mem. Cttee, London Metal Exchange, 1949-64 (Chm. 1954-64). Adviser to Dept of Trade and Industry; part-time Mem. Sugar Bd, 1967-76. *Address:* c/o Metal Market & Exchange Co. Ltd, Plantation House, Fenchurch Street, EC3M 3AP.

SMITH, Ralph E. K. T.; *see* Taylor-Smith.

SMITH, (Raymond) Gordon (Antony); *see* Etherington-Smith.

SMITH, Sir Raymond (Horace), KBE 1967 (CBE 1960); Chairman of Hawker Siddeley and other British companies in Venezuela; Consultant to: Rolls-Royce Ltd; British Aerospace; Economist; *b* 1917; *s* of Horace P. Smith and Mabelle (*née* Osborne-Couzens); *m* 1943, Dorothy, *d* of Robert Cheney Hart. *Educ:* Salesian College, London; Barcelona University. Served War of 1939-45, with British Security Co-ordination, NY, and with Intelligence Corps, in France, India, Burma, Malaya, Indonesia, USA and S America. Civil Attaché British Embassy, Caracas, 1941; Negotiator, sale of British owned railway cos to Venezuelan Govt and other S American govts, 1946-50; Rep., London Reinsurers in Venezuela, 1958-70; Consultant: Cammell Laird; Mirrlees; Provincial Insurance Co. Ltd; Fairey Engrg Ltd, etc; Director: Británica de Seguros (Insurance), Daily Journal; Anglo-Venezuelan Cultural Inst., 1946-80. Board Director: Caracas Mus. Fine Arts Foundn; Anglo-Venezuelan Trade Assoc.; Pres. British Commonwealth Soc. of Venezuela, 1955-57. Companion of Royal Aeronautical Society. Knight Grand Cross, St Lazarus of Jerusalem; Venezuelan Air Force Cross. *Recreations:* tennis, water ski-ing, winter sports (Cresta Run and ski-ing). *Address:* Edificio Las Américas, Calle Real de Sabana Grande, Caracas 1050, Venezuela; c/o Claridges Hotel, Brook Street, W1A 2JQ. *Clubs:* White's, Naval and Military; Caracas Country, Jockey (Caracas).

SMITH, Reginald Arthur; journalist and author; writer on education, religion, politics and social relations; *b* 23 July 1904; *e* surv. *s* of late Arthur and late Clara Smith, Burton-on-Trent; *m* 1931, Doris Fletcher Lean; one *s* one *d*. *Educ:* Victoria Road and Guild Street elementary schools, Burton-on-Trent. Junior Asst, Burton-on-Trent public library, 1918-21; reporter, Burton Daily Mail, Burton-on-Trent, 1921-30; sub-editor, Sheffield Mail, 1930-31; editor Westmorland Gazette, Kendal, 1931-34; reporter and special correspt Manchester Guardian, 1934-43; editor: Manchester Guardian Weekly, 1943-

47; British Weekly, 1947-50; managing editor, Liberal Party publications, 1951-60; Sec., Friends' Temperance and Moral Welfare Union, 1960-75 (Hon. Sec., 1975-77); Personal Asst to Ernest Bader, Scott-Bader Commonwealth, 1960-62; Sec., Soc. for Democratic Integration in Industry, 1961-63; Chm. of the Religious Weekly Press Group, 1950-51. Mem. of Soc. of Friends. *Publications:* Can Conscience be Measured?, 1940; Towards a Living Encyclopaedia, 1942; King of Little Everywhere, 1942; A Liberal Window on the World, 1946; Industrial Implications of Christian Equality, 1949; (joint editor with A. R. J. Wise) Voices on the Green, 1945. *Address:* Walnut, Albury Heath, Guildford, Surrey GU5 9DG. *Club:* National Liberal.

SMITH, Reginald John, CVO 1954; *b* 21 Aug. 1895; *o s* of late John Smith, Hardwicke, Gloucestershire; *m* 1921, Irene Victoria Hauser; two *d. Educ:* Sir Thomas Rich's School, Gloucester. Joined Metropolitan Police, 1915; served Royal Artillery, France and Flanders, 1917-19; rejoined Met. Police, 1919; Sergt, 1920; Inspector, 1932; Supt 1940; Assistant Chief, British Police Mission to Greece, 1945-46; Deputy Commander, 1946; Commander, 1947-58. King's Police Medal, 1945 for distinguished service during Flying Bomb attack. Chevalier, The Order of Dannebrog, 1951; OStJ. *Recreations:* cricket, bowls.

SMITH, Sir Reginald Verdon; *see* Verdon-Smith.

SMITH, Richard; *see* Smith, W. R.

SMITH, Richard H. S.; *see* Sandford Smith.

SMITH, Richard Maybury H.; *see* Hastie-Smith.

SMITH, Sir Richard P.; *see* Prince-Smith, Sir (William) Richard.

SMITH, Sir Richard Robert L.; *see* Law-Smith.

SMITH, Sir Richard R. V.; *see* Vassar-Smith.

SMITH, Prof. R(ichard) Selby, OBE 1981; MA (Oxon), MA (Harvard); Professor of Education and Head of Department of Education, University of Tasmania, 1973-79, now Professor Emeritus; *b* 1914; *s* of Selby Smith, Hall Place, Barming, Maidstone, Kent, and Annie Rachel Smith (*née* Rawlins); *m* 1940, Rachel Hebe Philippa Pease, Rounton, Northallerton, Yorks; two *s. Educ:* Rugby Sch.; Magdalen Coll., Oxford; Harvard Univ. Asst Master, Milton Acad., Milton, Mass, USA, 1938-39; House Tutor and Sixth Form Master, Sedbergh Sch., 1939-40; War of 1939-45: Royal Navy, 1940-46; final rank of Lt-Comdr, RNVR. Administrative Asst, Kent Education Cttee, 1946-48; Asst Education Officer, Kent, 1948-50; Dep. Chief Education Officer, Warwickshire, 1950-53; Principal, Scotch Coll., Melbourne, 1953-64; Foundation Prof. of Educn, Monash Univ., 1964, Dean of Faculty of Educn, 1965-71; Principal, Tasmanian Coll. of Advanced Education, 1971-73. Chairman: Victorian Univs and Schools Examinations Bd, 1967-71; State Planning and Finance Cttee, Australian Schools Commn, 1974-77, 1980-; Vice-Pres., Australian Council for Educnl Research, 1976-79. *Publications:* Towards an Australian Philosophy of Education, 1965; (ed jtly) Fundamental Issues in Australian Education, 1971; The Education Policy Process in Tasmania, 1980. *Recreations:* fishing, shooting, gardening, sailing and ornithology. *Address:* 297 Nelson Road, Mount Nelson, Tasmania 7007, Australia. *Clubs:* Naval; Melbourne (Melbourne).

SMITH, Robert Courtney, CBE 1980; MA, CA, JP; Chairman: Scottish United Investors Ltd, since 1974; Sidlaw Group, since 1980; Standard Life Assurance, since 1982; *b* 10 Sept. 1927; 4th *s* of late John Smith, DL, JP, and Agnes Smith, Glasgow and Symington; *m* 1954, Moira Rose, *d* of late Wilfred H. Macdougall, CA, Glasgow; one *s* two *d* (and one *s* decd). *Educ:* Kelvinside Academy, Glasgow; Sedbergh Sch.; Trinity Coll., Cambridge. BA 1950, MA 1957. Served, Royal Marines, 1945-47, and RMFVR, 1951-57. Partner, Arthur Young McClelland Moores & Co., Chartered Accountants, 1957-78. Director: Alliance and Second Alliance Trusts; British Aluminium; Wm Collins (Vice-Chm.); Volvo Trucks (GB). Mem., Horserace Betting Levy Bd, 1977-82; Chm., Scottish Industrial Develt Adv. Bd (Mem. 1972-); Pres., Business Archives Council of Scotland; Dir, Nat. Register of Archives (Scotland). Deacon Convener, Trades House of Glasgow, 1976-78. Mem. Council, Inst. of Chartered Accountants of Scotland, 1974-79. Trustee, Carnegie Trust for Univs of Scotland. Mem. Ct, Glasgow Univ., 1978-. Hon. LLD Glasgow, 1978. OStJ. *Recreations:* racing, gardening. *Address:* North Lodge, Dunkeld, Perthshire. *T:* Dunkeld 574; (professional) 37 Renfield Street, Glasgow G2 1JU. *Clubs:* East India; Western (Glasgow); Hawks (Cambridge).

SMITH, (Robert) Harvey; show jumper, farmer; *b* 29 Dec. 1938; *m* Irene Shuttleworth; two *s.* First major win with Farmer's Boy. Leading Show Jumper of the Year; other major wins include: King George V Cup, Royal Internat. Horse Show, 1958; has won the John Player Trophy 7 times, King George V Gold Cup once, and the British Jumping Derby 4 times; Grand Prix and Prix des Nations wins in UK, Ireland, Europe and USA; took part in Olympic Games, 1968 and 1972; best-known mounts: Farmer's Boy, Mattie Brown, Olympic Star, O'Malley, Salvador, Harvester. *Publication:* Show Jumping with Harvey Smith, 1979.

SMITH, Roger Bonham; Chairman and Chief Executive Officer, General Motors, since 1981; *b* Columbus, Ohio, 12 July 1925. *Educ:* Detroit University Sch.; Univ. of Michigan (BBA, MBA). Served US Navy, 1944-46. General Motors: Sen. Clerk, subseq. Director, general accounting, Detroit Central Office, 1949-58; Dir, financial analysis sect., NY Central Office, 1960, later Asst Treas.; transf. to Detroit as Gen. Asst Comptroller, then Gen. Asst Treas., 1968; Treasurer, 1970; Vice-Pres. i/c Financial Staff, 1971, also Mem. Admin Cttee, 1971-; Vice-Pres. and Gp Exec. i/c Nonautomotive and Defense Gp, 1972; Exec. Vice-Pres., Mem. Bd of Dirs and Mem. Finance Cttee, 1974, also Mem. Exec. Cttee, 1974-; Vice-Chm. Finance Cttee, 1975-80, Chm., 1981-. Conceived GM Cancer Res. Awards, 1978 (Chm., administering Foundn); Trustee: Cranbrook Schs and Mich Colls Foundn Inc., 1981-; Chm. Vis. Cttee, Univ. of Michigan Grad. Sch. of Business Admin, 1979-; Member: Bd of Dirs, Associates of Harvard Grad. Sch. of Business Admin, 1978-; Policy Cttee, Business Roundtable, 1981-; Business Council, 1981-; Chairman: Motor Vehicle Manufrs Assoc., 1981-82; United Foundn, Detroit, 1975-; Mem., Soc. of Automotive Engrs, 1978-. Hon. Dr DePauw, 1979; Hon. Dr Albion Coll., 1982. *Address:* General Motors, 3044 West Grand Boulevard, Detroit, Michigan 48202, USA; (home) Bloomfield Hills, Michigan 48013. *Clubs:* Economic, Detroit, Detroit Athletic (Detroit); Links (NY).

SMITH, Roger C.; *see* Castle-Smith.

SMITH, Prof. Roland; Professor of Marketing, University of Manchester Institute of Science and Technology, since 1966; *b* 1 Oct. 1928; *s* of late Joshua Smith and of Mrs Hannah Smith; *m* 1954, Joan (*née* Shaw); no *c. Educ:* Univs of Birmingham and Manchester. BA, MSc, PhD (Econ). Flying Officer, RAF, 1953. Asst Dir, Footwear Manufacturers' Fedn, 1955; Lectr in Econs, Univ. of Liverpool, 1960; Dir, Univ. of Liverpool Business Sch., 1963. Non-Executive Chairman: Senior Engineering Ltd, 1973; Barrow Hepburn Group, 1974; Chairman: Temple Bar Investment Trust Ltd, 1980-; House of Fraser, 1981- (Dep. Chm., 1980-81); Dep. Chm., Möben Gp, 1980-; Dir-Consultant to a number of public companies. *Recreation:* walking. *Address:* Branksome, Enville Road, Bowdon, Cheshire. *T:* 061-928 1119.

SMITH, Ron, CBE 1973; Member, British Steel Corporation, 1967-77 (Managing Director (Personnel and Social Policy), 1967-72); Member (part-time), British Transport Docks Board, since 1978; *b* 15 July 1915; *s* of Henry Sidney Smith and Bertha Clara (*née* Barnwell); *m* 1940, Daisy Hope (*d* 1974), *d* of Herbert Leggatt Nicholson; one *d. Educ:* Workers' Education Association. Post Office Messenger, 1929; Postman, 1934; Postal and Telegraph Officer, 1951; Treasurer, Union of Post Office Workers, 1953; Gen. Sec., Union of Post Office Workers, 1957-66. General Council, TUC, 1957-66; Civil Service National Whitley Council, 1957-66; Exec. Cttee, Postal, Telegraph and Telephone International, 1957-66; Vice-Chairman, Post Office Dept, Whitley Council, 1959-66. Member: Cttee on Grants to Students, 1958-60; Development Areas, Treasury Advisory Cttee, 1959-60; Cttee on Company Law, 1960-62; National Economic Development Council, 1962-66; Court of Enquiry into Ford Motor Co. Dispute, 1963; Cttee of Enquiry into Pay, etc, of London Transport Bus Staff, 1963-64; Organising Cttee for Nat. Steel Corp., 1966; President, Postal, Telegraph and Telephone Internat., 1966; Director, BOAC, 1964-70. *Recreations:* photography, golf. *Address:* 3 Beech Grove, Epsom, Surrey. *Club:* Tyrrells Wood Golf.

SMITH, Ronald A. D.; *see* Dingwall-Smith.

SMITH, Rosemary Ann, (Mrs G. F. Smith); Headmistress, Wimbledon High School, GPDST, since 1982; *b* 10 Feb. 1932; *d* of late Harold Edward Wincott, CBE, editor of the Investors Chronicle, and of Joyce Mary Wincott; *m* 1954, Rev. Canon Graham Francis Smith; two *s. Educ:* Brighton and Hove High School, GPDST; Westfield College, Univ. of London (BA Hons); London Univ. Inst. of Education (post grad. Cert. in Education). Assistant Teacher: Central Foundation Girls' School, 1964-69; Rosa Bassett Girls' School, 1970-77; Furzedown Secondary School, 1977-80; Deputy Head, Rowan High School, 1980-82. *Recreations:* theatre, gardening, dressmaking, reading, camping. *Address:* St Anne's Vicarage, 2 St Ann's Crescent, SW18 2LR. *T:* 01-874 2809.

SMITH, Sir Rowland; *see* Smith, Sir Alexander R.

SMITH, Air Marshal Sir Roy David A.; *see* Austen-Smith.

SMITH, Rupert Alexander A.; *see* Alec-Smith.

SMITH, Rupert R. R.; *see* Rawden-Smith.

SMITH, Sidney William; Regional Administrator, East Anglian Regional Health Authority, since 1975; *b* 17 May 1920; *s* of late Sidney John and Harriet May Smith; *m* 1943, Doreen Kelly; one *s* one *d. Educ:* Wirral Grammar Sch., Cheshire. FHA, ACIS. Dep. Group Sec.: Mansfield Hosp. Management Cttee, 1948-61; Wolverhampton Hosp. Management Cttee, 1961-63; Group Sec., Wakefield Hosp. Management Cttee, 1963-73; Area Administrator, Wakefield Area Health Authority, 1973-75. Mem. Management Side, Ancillary Staff, Whitley Council, 1969-; Chairman: Assoc. of Chief Administrators of Health Authorities, 1974-76; Health Services Panel, Inst. of Chartered Secretaries and Administrators, 1978-; Management Side, Ancillary Staff Whitley Council, 1982-. *Recreations:* gardening, walking. *Address:* 77

Gough Way, Cambridge CB3 9LN. *T:* Cambridge 62307; Dalar Wen, Denbigh, Clwyd, North Wales LL16 3HT.

SMITH, Prof. Stanley Desmond, FRS 1976; FRSE 1972; Professor of Physics and Head of Department of Physics, since 1970, Dean of the Faculty of Science, since 1981, Heriot-Watt University, Edinburgh; *b* 3 March 1931; *s* of Henry George Stanley Smith and Sarah Emily Ruth Smith; *m* 1956, Gillian Anne Parish; one *s* one *d. Educ:* Cotham Grammar Sch., Bristol; Bristol Univ. (BSc, DSc); Reading Univ. (PhD). SSO, RAE, Farnborough, 1956-58; Research Asst, Dept of Meteorology, Imperial Coll., London, 1958-59; Lectr, then Reader, Univ. of Reading, 1960-70. Chm., Edinburgh Instruments Ltd, 1971-. C. V. Boys Prizeman, Inst. of Physics, 1976. *Publications:* Infra-red Physics, 1966; numerous papers on semi-conductor and laser physics and satellite meteorology. *Recreations:* tennis, skiing, mountaineering. *Address:* 4 Cherry Tree View, Balerno, Edinburgh EH14 5AP. *T:* 031-449 4520.

SMITH, Stanley Frank, MA; CEng, FIMechE, FCIT; General Manager, Research Development, Urban Transport Development Company, Kingston, Ontario, since 1981; *b* 15 Dec. 1924; *s* of Frederick and Edith Maria Smith; *m* 1946, Margaret (*née* Garrett); two *s* three *d. Educ:* Purley Sch.; Hertford Coll., Oxford (MA). Served War, RAF Pilot, 1943-46. Oxford Univ., 1946-49. Rolls-Royce Ltd, 1949-65 (Chief Research Engineer, 1963); British Railways, 1965-71 (Dir of Engineering Research, 1965; Dir of Research, 1966); joined London Transport, 1971: Dir-Gen. of Research and Develt, 1971-72; Chief Mech. Engr, 1972-81, retired. *Recreations:* tennis, sailing. *Address:* Bridge House, Cromford, Derbyshire; Rural Road 1, Bath, Ontario K0H 1G0, Canada. *T:* 613-352-7429.

SMITH, Stanley G.; *see* Graham Smith.

SMITH, Stewart Ranson; British Council Representative, Spain, since 1980; *b* 16 Feb. 1931; *s* of John Smith and Elizabeth Smith; *m* 1960, Lee Tjam Mui, Singapore. *Educ:* Bedlington Grammar Sch., Northumberland; Nottingham Univ. (BA, MA); Yale Univ., USA (MA). British Council: Asst Rep., Singapore, 1957-59; Reg. Officer, Overseas A, 1959-61; Dir, Curitiba, Brazil, 1961-65; Asst Rep., Sri Lanka, 1965-69; Planning Officer, London, 1969-70; seconded Min. of Overseas Develt, 1970-73; Rep., Kenya, 1973-76; Controller, Overseas B, British Council, 1976-80. *Recreations:* music, cricket, football, writing, birdwatching. *Address:* c/o British Council, 10 Spring Gardens, SW1A 2BN; 53 Sutherland Avenue, Petts Wood, Kent BR5 1QY.

SMITH, Alderman Sydney Herbert, MA; *s* of late Charles Edward and Emma Hedges, of London, Woodbridge, Suffolk, and Aylesbury, Bucks. *Educ:* Ruskin Coll.; St Catherine's, Oxford Univ. (Hons graduate). Member Hull City Council, 1923-70; Hon. Alderman; Lord Mayor, 1940-41; Hon. Freeman of Hull, 1968. MP (Lab) Hull, South-West, 1945-50. Life Mem., Court of Hull University. Former Chairman, Hull Education Cttee and Hull Housing and Town Planning Cttee. Hon. LLD Hull, 1967. Queen Marie of Roumania's Cross for Services, 1917. *Address:* 16 Southfield, Hessle, North Humberside HU13 0EX. *T:* 648979.

SMITH, Prof. Sir Thomas (Broun), Kt 1981; QC Scotland 1956; DCL Oxon, 1956; LLD Edinburgh, 1963; FRSE 1977; FBA 1958; Professor Emeritus of Edinburgh University, 1980; General Editor, The Laws of Scotland, Stair Memorial Encyclopædia; *b* 3 Dec. 1915; 2nd *s* of late J. Smith, DL, JP, and Agnes Smith, Symington, Lanarkshire; *m* 1940, Ann Dorothea, *d* of late Christian Tindall, CIE, ICS, Exmouth, Devon; one *d* (one *s* one *d* decd). *Educ:* High Sch. of Glasgow; Sedbergh Sch.; Christ Church, Oxford (MA). Boulter Exhibitioner, 1st Class Hons School of Jurisprudence, 1937; Eldon Scholar, 1937; Edinburgh Univ.; 1st Class and Certificate of Honour English Bar Final, Called to English Bar by Grays Inn, 1938. Served TA from 1937; War Service, 1939-46; BEF, Home Forces, Middle East and Central Mediterranean; London Scottish (Gordon Highlanders) and RA (Fd.); variously employed on regimental and intelligence duties and at School of Infantry; Lieut-Colonel (despatches); Lieut-Colonel (TA) Gordon Highlanders, 1950; OC Aberdeen University Contingent, Officers Training Corps, 1950-55; Hon. Colonel, 1964-73. Attached to Foreign Office, 1946-47. Examined by and admitted to Faculty of Advocates in Scotland, 1947. Professor of Scots Law, University of Aberdeen, 1949-58; Dean of Faculty of Law, 1950-53 and 1956-58; Prof. of Civil Law, University of Edinburgh, 1958-68, of Scots Law, 1968-72; Hon. Prof., 1972-80. Hon. Sheriff of Aberdeen, 1950 and of Lothians and Peebles, 1964; Member: Scottish Law Reform Cttee, 1954; Scottish Law Commn, part-time 1965-72, full-time, 1972-80. Director Scottish Universities Law Inst., 1960; Hon. Member Council Louisiana State Law Inst., 1960; Mem., Academic Advisory Cttee, Universities of St Andrews and Dundee, 1964-; Ford Visiting Professor, Tulane Univ. (Louisiana), 1957-58; Visiting Lecturer, Cape Town and Witwatersrand Universities, 1958; Visiting Prof., Harvard Law Sch., 1962-63; Tagore Prof., Calcutta, 1977. Hon. Foreign Mem., Amer. Acad. of Arts and Sciences, 1969. Hon. LLD: Cape Town, 1959; Aberdeen, 1969; Glasgow, 1978. *Publications:* Doctrines of Judicial Precedent in Scots Law, 1952; Scotland: The Development of its Laws and Constitution, 1955; British Justice: The Scottish Contribution, 1961; Studies Critical and Comparative, 1962; A Short Commentary on the Law of Scotland, 1962; Property Problems in Sale, 1978; Basic Rights and their Enforcement, 1979; contribs to legal publications on Scottish, historical and comparative law. *Recreations:* gardening, foreign travel. *Address:* 11 India Street, Edinburgh EH3 6HA. *T:* 031-225 8030;

Kirkton of Morham, Morham, Haddington, East Lothian EH41 4LQ. *Clubs:* Naval and Military; New (Edinburgh).

SMITH, T(homas) Dan; Founder, New Directions, projects to assist ex-offenders, 1978; *b* 11 May 1915; *m* 1939; one *s* two *d.* City Councillor, Newcastle upon Tyne, 1950-65 (Chairman, Finance Cttee); Member: Nat. Sports Council, 1965-69; Royal Commission on Local Government, 1966-69; Shakespeare Theatre Trust, 1968-. Chairman: Northern Economic Planning Council, 1965-70; Peterlee and Aycliffe Develt Corp., 1968-70. Hon. DCL Newcastle University, 1966. *Publications:* Essays in Local Government, 1965; contrib. to Which Way, 1970; Education, Science and Technology (paper to British Assoc. for Advancement of Science), 1970; An Autobiography, 1971. *Recreations:* painting, music, writing, sport. *Address:* Leazes Edge, 13 Belle Grove Terrace, Spital Tongues, Newcastle upon Tyne NE2 4LL.

SMITH, Sir (Thomas) Gilbert, 4th Bt, *cr* 1897; Area Manager; *b* 2 July 1937; *er s* of Sir Thomas Turner Smith, 3rd Bt, and Agnes, *o d* of Bernard Page, Wellington, New Zealand; *S* father, 1961; *m* 1962, Patricia Christine Cooper; two *s* one *d. Educ:* Huntley Sch.; Nelson Coll. *Recreation:* skiing. *Heir:* *s* Andrew Thomas Smith, *b* 17 Oct. 1965. *Address:* PO Box 654, 50 Titoki Street, Masterton, New Zealand.

SMITH, Thomas I.; *see* Irvine Smith.

SMITH, Rt. Rev. Timothy D.; *see* Thetford, Bishop Suffragan of.

SMITH, Timothy John; MP (C) Beaconsfield, since May 1982; *b* 5 Oct. 1947; *s* of late Captain Norman Wesley Smith, CBE and of Nancy Phyllis Smith; *m* 1980, Jennifer Jane Scott-Hopkins, *d* of Sir James Scott-Hopkins, *qv. Educ:* Harrow Sch.; St Peter's Coll., Oxford (MA). FCA. Articled with Gibson, Harris & Turnbull, 1969; Audit Sen., Peat, Marwick, Mitchell & Co., 1971; Company Sec., Coubro & Scrutton (Hldgs) Ltd, 1973. Pres., Oxford Univ. Conservative Assoc., 1968; Chm., Coningsby Club, 1977-78. MP (C) Ashfield, April 1977-1979. Secretary: Cons. Prices and Consumer Protection Cttee, 1977-79; Cons. Health and Social Services Cttee, 1982-; Parly and Law Cttee, ICA, 1979-82. *Recreation:* theatre. *Address:* 27 Rosenau Crescent, SW11. *T:* 01-223 3378.

SMITH, Adm. Sir Victor (Alfred Trumper), AC 1975; KBE 1969 (CBE 1963); CB 1968; DSC 1941; Chairman, Australian Chiefs of Staff Committee, 1970-75; Military Adviser to SEATO, 1970-74; *b* 9 May 1913; *s* of George Smith; *m* 1944, Nanette Suzanne Harrison; three *s. Educ:* Royal Australian Naval College. Sub-Lieut, 1935; Lieut, 1936; Lieut-Commander, 1944; Commander, 1947; Captain, 1953; Rear-Admiral, 1963; Vice-Admiral, 1968; Chief of Naval Staff and First Naval Member, Austr. Commonwealth Naval Bd, 1968-70; Admiral, 1970. *Recreation:* walking. *Address:* Fishburn Street, Red Hill, ACT 2603, Australia. *T:* Canberra 958942.

SMITH, Walter Campbell, CBE 1949; MC; TD; MA, ScD; *b* 30 Nov. 1887; 2nd *s* of late George Hamilton Smith, Solihull, Warwickshire; *m* 1936, Susan, *y d* of late John Finnegan, Belfast; one *s* one *d. Educ:* Solihull; Corpus Christi, Cambridge. Wiltshire Prize, Cambridge Univ., 1909; Assistant, Dept of Minerals, British Museum, 1910; Deputy Keeper, 1931-37; Deputy Chief Scientific Officer, British Museum (Natural History), 1948-52; also Keeper of Minerals, 1937-52; Non-resident Fellow Corpus Christi, Cambridge, 1921-24; Honorary Secretary, Geological Society of London, 1921-33 (Murchison Medallist, 1945), President, 1955-56, Hon. Mem., 1982; General Secretary, Mineralogical Society, 1927-38, President, 1945-48; President, geological section, British Assoc., 1950; Governor, Royal Holloway Coll., 1922-43, representing Cambridge University; served in the Artists' Rifles, 1910-35 and 1939-42; European War, France, 1914-18 (MC, despatches twice, 1914 Star); Acting Lieut-Colonel, 1918; Brevet Lieut-Colonel, 1935; Second-in-Command, 163 OCTU (The Artists' Rifles), 1939-41. *Publications:* numerous papers on minerals, rocks and meteorites. *Address:* Flat 2, Burley Lodge, Rockdale Road, Sevenoaks, Kent.

SMITH, Walter Purvis, CB 1982; OBE 1960 (MBE 1945); Director General, Ordnance Survey, since 1977; *b* 8 March 1920; *s* of John William Smith and Margaret Jane (*née* Purvis); *m* 1946, Bettie Cox; one *s* one *d. Educ:* Wellfield Grammar Sch., Co. Durham; St Edmund Hall, Oxford (MA). FRICS 1951. Commnd RE (Survey), 1940; served War, UK and Europe, 1940-46; CO 135 Survey Engr Regt (TA), 1957-60. Directorate of Colonial (later Overseas) Surveys: served in Ghana, Tanzania, Malaŵi, 1946-50; Gen. Man., Air Survey Co. of Rhodesia Ltd, 1950-54; Fairey Surveys Ltd, 1954-75 (Man. Dir, 1969-75); Adviser, Surveying and Mapping, UN, NY, 1975-77. Mem., Field Mission, Argentine-Chile Frontier Case, 1965. 15th British Commonwealth Lectr, RAeS, 1968. Pres., Photogrammetric Soc., 1972-73; Mem., Gen. Council, RICS, 1967-70 (Chm., Land Survey Cttee, 1963-64). *Publications:* papers and technical jls. *Recreations:* music, walking, golf. *Address:* 15 Forest Gardens, Lyndhurst, Hants. *T:* Lyndhurst 2566; (office) Southampton 775555. *Club:* Oriental.

SMITH, (Walter) Richard; Regional Chairman of Industrial Tribunals, since 1976; *b* 12 Oct. 1926; *s* of Walter Richard and Ivy Millicent Smith; *m* 1959, Jean Monica Law; one *s* one *d. Educ:* Bromsgrove Sch.; Birmingham Univ. (LLB). Called to the Bar, Gray's Inn, 1954. A Chairman of Industrial Tribunals, 1971. *Address:* Punter's Hill, Moorwood, near Cirencester, Glos GL7 7EA. *T:* North Cerney 340.

SMITH, Walter Riddell, CB 1973; FRAgS 1971; FIBiol; Welsh Secretary, Ministry of Agriculture, Fisheries and Food, 1975–78; livestock adviser, West Yorkshire; *b* 18 Sept. 1914; *s* of John Riddell Smith and Ethel Smith (*née* Liddell); *m* 1942, Janet Henderson Mitchell; one *s* one *d*. *Educ*: Durham Univ. NDA 1936; BSc(Agric.) Dunelm, 1936. Record Keeper: Cockle Park, Northumberland, 1936–37; School of Agriculture, Durham, 1937–39; Asst Agricultural Organiser, Northumberland CC, 1939–42; Animal Husbandry Officer, Northumberland War Agric. Exec. Cttee, 1942–47; Nat. Agric. Adv. Service, 1948–52; Livestock Adviser: WR, 1948–52; Eastern Region, 1952–55; Wales, 1955–61; Dep. Regional Director, Yorks and Lancs, 1961–64; Regional Director, Northern Region, 1964–66; Dir, Nat. Agricultural Adv. Service, 1967–71; Dep. Dir-Gen., Agricultural Develt and Adv. Service, 1971–75. President: Univ. of Newcastle upon Tyne Agricultural Soc., 1969; British Grassland Soc., 1971–72; NPK Club, 1971; Nat. Sheep Assoc., 1978–82. *Publications*: contributions to press, popular agric. and technical journals. *Recreations*: gardening, sport, theatre. *Address*: 14 West Point, 49 Putney Hill, SW15. *T*: 01-788 2684.

SMITH, Wilbur Addison; author; *b* 1933; *m*; two *s* one *d*. *Educ*: Michaelhouse, Natal; Rhodes Univ. (BCom). Business executive, 1954–58; factory owner, 1958–64; full-time author, 1964–. *Publications*: When the Lion Feeds, 1964; Dark of the Sun, 1965; Sound of Thunder, 1966; Shout at the Devil, 1968; Gold Mine, 1970; Diamond Hunters, 1971; The Sunbird, 1972; Eagle in the Sky, 1974; Eye of the Tiger, 1975; Cry Wolf, 1976; Sparrow Falls, 1977; Hungry as the Sea, 1978; Wild Justice, 1979; A Falcon Flies, 1980; Men of Men, 1981; The Angels Weep, 1982. *Recreations*: golf, fishing, hunting. *Address*: c/o Heinemann, 10 Upper Grosvenor Street, W1X 9PA.

SMITH, William Austin N.; *see* Nimmo Smith.

SMITH, William Frederick Bottrill, CBE 1964; Accountant and Comptroller General of Inland Revenue, 1958–68; Principal, Uganda Resettlement Board, 1972–74; *b* 29 Oct. 1903; *s* of late Arthur and Harriet Frances Smith; *m* 1926, Edyth Kilbourne (*d* 1970); *m* 1971, M. Jane Smith, Washington DC; three step *c*. *Educ*: Newton's, Leicester. Entered the Inland Revenue Dept, Civil Service, 1934. President, Inland Revenue Staff Federation, 1945–47. Vice-Pres., CS Fedn Drama Socs. *Address*: 11 Preston Avenue, Rustington-on-Sea, Littlehampton, W Sussex.

SMITH, William French; Attorney General of the United States of America, since 1981; *b* Aug. 1917; *s* of William and Margaret Smith; *m* 1964, Jean Webb; three *s* one *d*. *Educ*: Univ. of Calif (AB); Harvard Univ. (LLB). Served USNR, 1942–46 (Lieut). Barrister, 1942; Partner, Gibson, Dunn and Crutcher, LA, 1946–80. Member: US Adv. Commn on Internat. Educnl and Cultural Affairs, 1971–78; Stanton Panel on Internat. Inf., Educn and Cultural Relns, 1974–75. Mem., LA Cttee on For. Relns, 1954–74; Pres., LA World Affairs Council, 1975–76 (Mem., Bd of Dirs, 1970–81). Mem., Bd of Dirs, Legal Aid Foundn, LA, 1963–72; Trustee, Henry E. Huntington Library and Art Gall., 1971–. *Address*: Department of Justice, Constitution Avenue and 10th Street, NW, Washington, DC 20530, USA.

SMITH, Sir (William) Gordon, 2nd Bt *cr* 1945; VRD; Lieut-Commander, RNR, retired; *b* 30 Jan. 1916; *s* of Sir Robert Workman Smith, 1st Bt, and Jessie Hill (*d* 1978), *yr d* of late William Workman, Belfast; *S* father, 1957; *m* 1st, 1941, Diana Gundreda, *d* of late Major C. H. Malden, Aberdeenshire; 2nd, 1958, Diana Goodchild; two *s*. *Educ*: Westminster; Trinity Coll., Cambridge (BA). Called to Bar, Inner Temple, 1939. Served War of 1939–45 as Lieut, RNVR (despatches). *Recreation*: yachting (Winner, International Dragon Gold Cup, 1961). *Heir*: *s* Robert Hill Smith, *b* 15 April 1958. *Address*: 15 Cadogan Court, Draycott Avenue, SW3 3BX; (Seat) Crowmallie, Pitcaple, Aberdeenshire. *Clubs*: Royal Yacht Squadron; New (Edinburgh).

SMITH, William Jeffrey, CB 1976; Under-Secretary, Northern Ireland Office, 1972–76; *b* 14 Oct. 1916; 2nd *s* of Frederick Smith, Sheffield, and Ellen Hickinson, Ringinglow, Derbyshire; *m* 1942, Marie Hughes; one *s* one *d*. *Educ*: King Edward VII Sch., Sheffield; University Coll., Oxford (Schol.) (MA). Employed by Calico Printers' Assoc., Manchester, 1938–40 and in 1946. Served War, Army: enlisted Sept. 1939, embodied, 1940; RA and York and Lancaster Regt (Captain), 1940–46. Dominions Office (subseq. CRO), 1946; Principal, 1948; Office of UK High Commissioner in South Africa, 1953–56; Asst Sec., 1959; sundry internat. confs; Dept of Technical Co-operation, 1961–64; Min. of Overseas Development, 1964–70; Overseas Develt Admin., 1970–72; UK Rep. to UNESCO, 1969–72. Sec. to Widgery Tribunal on loss of life in Londonderry, 1972; Northern Ireland Office, 1972. *Recreations*: theatre, scrambling up mountains, walking, ski-ing. *Address*: Salmons, 121 Salmons Lane, Whyteleafe, Surrey CR3 0HB. *T*: 01-660 5493.

SMITH, William McGregor, OBE 1970; HM Inspector of Constabulary for Scotland, 1970–75, retired; *b* 14 April 1910; *s* of John Smith, Milngavie and Agnes Smith (*née* Haldane); *m* 1939, Alice Mary Ewen, Montrose; one *s* one *d*. *Educ*: Bearsden Academy and Glasgow University (MA 1930). Joined City of Glasgow Police, 1933; Deputy Commandant, Scottish Police College, 1951; Chief Constable of Aberdeen, 1963. *Recreations*: golf, bridge. *Address*: Sherwood, 2 Cherry Tree Park, Balerno, Midlothian. *Clubs*: Luffness Golf, Baberton Golf.

SMITH, Sir William Reardon Reardon-, 3rd Bt, *cr* 1920; Major, RA (TA); *b* 12 March 1911; *e s* of Sir Willie Reardon-Smith, 2nd Bt, and Elizabeth Ann, *d* of John and Mary Wakely; *S* father, 1950; *m* 1st, 1935, Nesta (marr. diss., 1954; she *d* 1959), *d* of late Frederick J. Phillips; three *s* one *d*; 2nd, 1954, Beryl, *d* of William H. Powell; one *s* three *d*. *Educ*: Blundell's Sch., Tiverton. Served War of 1939–45. *Heir*: *s* (William) Antony (John) Reardon-Smith [*b* 20 June 1937; *m* 1962, Susan, *d* of H. W. Gibson, Cardiff; three *s* one *d*. *Educ*: Wycliffe Coll., Glos]. *Address*: Rhode Farm, Romansleigh, South Molton, Devon EX36 4JW. *T*: Bishops Nympton 371. *Club*: Cardiff and County (Cardiff).

SMITH, Sir William Reginald Verdon; *see* Verdon-Smith.

SMITH-DODSWORTH, Sir John (Christopher), 8th Bt, *cr* 1784; *b* 4 March 1935; *s* of Sir Claude Smith-Dodsworth, 7th Bt, and Cyrilla Marie Louise von Sobbe, 3rd *d* of William Ernest Taylor, Linnet Lane, Liverpool; *S* father, 1940; *m* 1961, Margaret Anne (*née* Jones); one *s* one *d*. *Educ*: Ampleforth Coll., Yorks. *Heir*: *s* David John Smith-Dodsworth, *b* 23 Oct. 1963.

SMITH-GORDON, Sir (Lionel) Eldred (Peter), 5th Bt *cr* 1838; *b* 7 May 1935; *s* of Sir Lionel Eldred Pottinger Smith-Gordon, 4th Bt, and Eileen Laura (*d* 1979), *d* of late Captain H. G. Adams-Connor, CVO; *S* father, 1976; *m* 1962, Sandra Rosamund Ann, *d* of late Wing Commander Walter Farley, DFC and of Mrs Dennis Poore; one *s* one *d*. *Educ*: Eton College; Trinity College, Oxford. *Heir*: *s* Lionel George Eldred Smith-Gordon, *b* 1 July 1964. *Address*: 13 Shalcomb Street, SW10. *T*: 01-352 8506.

SMITH-MARRIOTT, Sir Ralph George Cavendish, 10th Bt, *cr* 1774; retired Bank Official; *b* 16 Dec. 1900; *s* of late George Rudolph Wyldbore Smith-Marriott and of Dorothy Magdalene, *d* of Rev. John Parry; *S* uncle, 1944; *m* 1st, Phyllis Elizabeth (*d* 1932), *d* of Richard Kemp (late Governor HM Prison, Bristol); two *s* one *d*; 2nd, 1933, Doris Mary (*d* 1951), *d* of R. L. C. Morrison, Tenby, Pembs; 3rd, 1966, Mrs Barbara Mary Cantlay. *Educ*: Cranleigh Sch., Surrey. Bristol Univ. OTC, 1918. *Recreations*: tennis, golf, cricket. *Heir*: *s* Hugh Cavendish Smith-Marriott [*b* 22 March 1925; *m* 1953, Pauline Anne, *d* of F. F. Holt, Bristol; one *d*]. *Address*: 28a Westover Road, Westbury-on-Trym, Bristol. *T*: Bristol 628827.

SMITH-RYLAND, Charles Mortimer Tollemache; Lord-Lieutenant of Warwickshire since 1968; *b* 24 May 1927; *s* of Charles Ivor Phipson Smith-Ryland and Leila Mary Tollemache; *m* 1952, Hon. Jeryl Marcia Saran Gurdon, *d* of Hon. Robin Gurdon; two *s* three *d*. *Educ*: Eton. Lt, Coldstream Guards, 1945–48; Reserve, Warwickshire Yeomanry. Warwickshire: CC, 1949; DL, 1955; Alderman, 1958; Vice-Chm. CC, 1963; Chm. CC, 1964–67; Vice-Chm. Police Authority, 1966–68; Chm., Warwickshire and Coventry Police Authority, 1969–74; High Sheriff, 1967–68. Chm. Council, RASE, 1976–. KStJ 1968. *Recreations*: hunting, shooting, golf. *Address*: Sherbourne Park, Warwick. *T*: Barford 624255. *Clubs*: White's; Leamington Tennis. *See also Baron Cranworth.*

SMITHERMAN, Frank, MBE 1951; HM Diplomatic Service, retired; *b* 13 Oct. 1913; *s* of Lt-Col H. C. Smitherman and Mildred E. Holten; *m* 1937, Frances Ellen Rivers Calvert; one *s* one *d*. *Educ*: Sir Joseph Williamson's Mathematical Sch., Rochester. Indian Police, Burma, 1933; served in: Yenangyaung; Rangoon; Myitkyina; Sagaing; Thayetmyo; Thaton. Served War of 1939–45 (despatches, 1945), Burma Army Reserve of Officers; Maj. 1945. Joined Civil Affairs Service; Foreign Office, 1949; subseq. served in: Amoy; Cairo; Rome; Khartoum; Miami; Consul-General, Bordeaux, 1967–69; Counsellor, Moscow, 1969–70; Ambassador to Togo and Dahomey, 1970–73. *Recreations*: fishing, gardening. *Address*: Pickwick Cottage, New Buckenham, Norfolk. *T*: Attleborough 860388. *See also Sir T. F. V. Buxton, Bt.*

SMITHERS, Prof. Sir David (Waldron), Kt 1969; MD, FRCP, FRCS, FRCR; Professor of Radiotherapy in the University of London, 1943–73, now Emeritus; Director of the Radiotherapy Department at the Royal Marsden Hospital, 1943–73; *b* 17 Jan. 1908; *s* of late Sir Waldron Smithers, MP; *m* 1933, Gwladys Margaret (Marjorie), *d* of Harry Reeve Angel, Officer (1st class) Order of White Rose of Finland; one *s* one *d*. *Educ*: Boxgrove School, Guildford; Charterhouse; Clare College, Cambridge; St Thomas's Hospital. MRCS, LRCP 1933; MB, BChir (Cantab) 1934; MD (Cantab) 1937; DMR (London) 1937; MRCP 1946; FRCP 1952; FFR 1953, now FRCR; FRCS 1963. Pres. British Inst. of Radiology, 1946–47; President, Faculty of Radiologists, 1959–61; Kt Comdr, Order of St John of Jerusalem, Kts of Malta, 1973. *Publications*: Dickens's Doctors, 1979; Castles in Kent, 1980; Jane Austen in Kent, 1981; papers on cancer and radiotherapy. *Recreations*: growing roses, book collecting. *Address*: Ringfield, Knockholt, Kent. *T*: Knockholt 32122.

SMITHERS, Donald William, CB 1967; retired; *b* 21 Aug. 1905; *s* of William John and Mary Smithers, Portsmouth, Hants; *m* 1929, Kathleen Margery Gibbons; three *s* one *d*. *Educ*: Portsmouth; Royal Naval Coll., Greenwich. Asst Constructor until 1937, then Constructor, Chatham; Principal Ship Overseer, 1939–44; Constructor Captain to C-in-C Mediterranean, 1944–47; Chief Constructor: Admiralty, 1947–52; Portsmouth, 1952–54; Singapore, 1954–56; Asst Dir of Dockyards, 1956–58; Manager HM Dockyard, Chatham, 1958–61; Director of Dockyards, 1961–67; retd 1967.

CEng; FRINA; RCNC. *Address:* Chevithorne, Greenway Lane, Bath. *T:* Bath 311093.

SMITHERS, Professor Geoffrey Victor; Professor of English Language, University of Durham, 1960-74, now Emeritus; *b* 5 May 1909; *s* of William Henry and Agnes Madeline Smithers; *m* 1953, Jean Buglass Hay McDonald; three *s* one *d. Educ:* Durban High School; Natal University College; Hertford College, Oxford. Rhodes Schol. for Natal, 1930; 1st Cl. in Final Hon. School of English, Oxford, 1933. Asst Lecturer: King's Coll., London, 1936; University Coll., London, 1938; Lectr in English Language, 1940, Senior Lecturer in English Language, 1950, Reader in Medieval English, 1954, Univ. of Oxford, and professorial Fellow of Merton Coll., 1954. *Publications:* 2nd edn of C. Brown's Religious Lyrics of the Fourteenth Century, 1952; Kyng Alisaunder, Vol. I 1952, Vol. II 1957; (with J. A. W. Bennett and N. Davis) Early Middle English Verse and Prose, 1966 (rev. edn 1974); contribs to vols in honour of M. Schlauch, G. N. Garmonsway, D. Meritt, and A. McIntosh; papers in Med. Æv., English and Germanic Studies, Archivum Linguisticum, Rev. Eng. Studies, Durham Univ. Jl. *Recreation:* music. *Address:* 6 Manor Close, Shincliffe, Durham. *T:* 61094.

SMITHERS, Sir Peter (Henry Berry Otway), Kt 1970; VRD with clasp; DPhil Oxon; Lt-Comdr RNR, retired; *b* 9 Dec. 1913; *o s* of late Lt-Col H. O. Smithers, JP, Hants, and Ethel Berry; *m* 1943, Dojean, *d* of late T. M. Sayman, St Louis, Mo; two *d. Educ:* Hawtrey's; Harrow Sch.; Magdalen Coll., Oxford. Demyship in History, 1931; 1st cl. Hons Modern History, 1934. Called to Bar, Inner Temple, 1936; joined Lincoln's Inn, 1937. Commn, London Div. RNVR, 1939; British Staff, Paris, 1940; Naval Intelligence Div., Admiralty; Asst Naval Attaché, British Embassy, Washington; Actg Naval Attaché, Mexico, Central Amer. Republics and Panama. RD Councillor, Winchester, 1946-49. MP (C) Winchester Div. of Hampshire, 1950-64; PPS to Minister of State for Colonies, 1952-56 and to Sec. of State for Colonies, 1956-59; Deleg., Consultative Assembly of Council of Europe, 1952-56 and 1960; UK Deleg. to UN Gen. Assembly, 1960-62; Parly Under-Sec. of State, FO, 1962-64; Sec.-Gen., Council of Europe, 1964-69; Senior Research Fellow, UN Inst. for Trng and Research, 1969-72; General Rapporteur, European Conf. of Parliamentarians and Scientists, 1970-77. Chairman: British-Mexican Soc., 1952-55; Conservative Overseas Bureau, 1956-59; Vice-Chm., Conservative Parly Foreign Affairs Cttee, 1958-62; Vice-Pres., European Assembly of Local Authorities, 1959-62. Master, Turners' Co., 1955; Liveryman, Goldsmiths' Co. Dr of Law *hc* Zürich, 1969. RHS Gold Medal, 1981. Chevalier de la Légion d'Honneur. Orden Mexicana del Aguila Azteca. Alexander von Humboldt Gold Medal, 1969. *Publication:* Life of Joseph Addison, 1954, 2nd edn, 1966. *Recreations:* observational astronomy, gardening. *Address:* CH-6911 Vico Morcote, Switzerland. *Clubs:* Carlton; The Everglades.

SMITHERS, Hon. Sir Reginald (Allfree), Kt 1980; **Hon. Mr Justice Smithers;** Judge of Federal Court of Australia, since 1977 (Judge, Australian Industrial Court, 1965-77); Additional Judge, Supreme Court of ACT and Supreme Court of NT, since 1964; *b* Echuca, 3 Feb. 1903; *s* of F. Smithers, Hove, Brighton, England; *m* 1932, Dorothy, *d* of J. Smalley, Bendigo; two *s* one *d. Educ:* Melbourne Grammar School; Melbourne Univ. (LLB 1924). Admitted to Victorian Bar, 1929; QC 1951. Served War, RAAF, 1942-45 (Sqdn Ldr); Censorship Liaison Officer to Gen. MacArthur, 1944-45, New Guinea and Philippines. Judge of Supreme Court of Papua and NG, 1962-64; Dep. Pres., Administrative Appeals Tribunal, 1977-80. Chancellor, La Trobe Univ., 1972-80 (DUniv); Pres., Australian Assoc. of Youth Clubs, 1967-. *Address:* 11 Florence Avenue, Kew, Victoria 3101, Australia.

SMITHIES, Frederick Albert; General Secretary, National Association of Schoolmasters and Union of Women Teachers, since 1983; *b* 12 May 1929; *s* of Frederick Albert and Lilian Smithies; *m* 1960, Olga Margaret Yates. *Educ:* St Mary's Coll., Blackburn, Lancs; St Mary's Coll., Twickenham, Mddx. Schoolteacher: Accrington, Lancs, 1948-60; Northampton, 1960-76. NAS/UWT (before 1975, NAS): Nat. Executive Member, 1966-76; Chm. of Education Cttee, 1972-76; Vice-President, 1976; Asst Gen. Secretary, 1976-81; Dep. Gen. Secretary, 1981-82; Gen. Sec. Designate, 1982-83. *Recreations:* reading, music, theatre, fell-walking. *Address:* 22 Upper Brook Street, Mayfair, W1. *T:* 01-629 3916.

SMITHIES, Kenneth Charles Lester; His Honour Judge Smithies; a Circuit Judge, since 1975; *b* 15 Aug. 1927; *s* of late Harold King Smithies and Kathleen Margaret (*née* Walsh); *m* 1950, Joan Winifred (*née* Ellis); one *s* two *d. Educ:* City of London Sch. (Corporation Schol.); University College London (LLB). Volunteered 60th Rifles, 1945, later commnd in Royal Artillery, in India; demobilised, 1948. Called to Bar, Gray's Inn, 1955. *Recreations:* music, gardening, bridge. *Address:* 1 Russell Place, Southampton SO2 1NU.

SMITHSON, Peter Denham; architect in private practice since 1950; *b* 18 Sept. 1923; *s* of William Blenkiron Smithson and Elizabeth Smithson; *m* 1949, Alison Margaret (*née* Gill); one *s* two *d. Educ:* The Grammar School, Stockton-on-Tees; King's College, Univ. of Durham. Served War of 1939-45: Queen Victoria's Own Madras Sappers and Miners, India and Burma, 1942-45. Asst in Schools Div. LCC, 1949-50; subseq. in private practice with wife. Banister Fletcher Prof. of Architecture, UCL, 1976-77; Prof. of Architecture, Bath Univ., 1978-. *Buildings:* Hunstanton School, 1950-54; Economist Building, St James's, 1959-64; Robin Hood Gardens, Tower Hamlets, 1963-

72; Garden Bldg, St Hilda's Coll., Oxford, 1968-70; Amenity Bldg, Bath Univ., 1979-80; Second Arts Bldg, Bath Univ., 1980-81. *Publications:* (all with A. Smithson) Uppercase 3, 1960; The Heroic Period of Modern Architecture, 1965, rev. edn 1981; Urban Structuring Studies of Alison and Peter Smithson, 1967; Team 10 Primer, 1968; The Euston Arch, 1968; Ordinariness and Light, 1970; Without Rhetoric, 1973; Bath: Walks Within the Walls, 1980; The Shift, 1982; theoretical work on town structuring in Architectural Review, Architectural Design and most foreign periodicals (most with A. Smithson). *Relevant publication:* synopsis of professional life in Arch. Assoc.'s Arena, Feb. 1966. *Address:* 24 Gilston Road, SW10. *T:* 01-373 7423.

SMOUT, David Arthur Lister, QC 1975; a Recorder of the Crown Court, since 1972; *b* 17 Dec. 1923; *s* of Sir Arthur Smout and Hilda Smout (*née* Follows); *m* 1957, Kathleen Sally, *d* of Dr J. L. Potts, Salisbury; two *s* two *d. Educ:* Leys Sch.; Clare Coll., Cambridge (MA, LLB); Birmingham Univ. (LLM). Served War, F/O, RAFVR, 1943-45. Cecil Peace Prize, 1948. Admitted solicitor, 1949; called to Ontario Bar, 1949. Lectr, Osgoode Hall, Toronto, 1949-53, Vis. Prof., 1977. Called to English Bar, Gray's Inn, 1953; Midland and Oxford Circuit. Dir, Murex Ltd and associated cos, 1954-67. Bar Council, 1958-62; prosecuting counsel, DTI, 1967-75; Dep.-Chm., Lincs QS (parts of Holland), 1968-71. *Publications:* Chalmers, Bills of Exchange (13th edn), 1964; (with B. E. Basden) Department of Trade Investigations: Bernard Russell Ltd, 1975; Blanes Ltd, 1975. *Recreations:* fishing, Canadiana. *Address:* 1 King's Bench Walk, Temple, EC4Y 7DB.

SMYTH, Rev. Canon Charles Hugh Egerton, MA, FRHistS; Fellow of Corpus Christi College, Cambridge, 1925-32 and since 1937; *b* Ningpo, China, 31 March 1903; *s* of Richard Smyth, MD; *m* 1934, Violet, *e d* of Rev. Canon Alexander Copland, Forfar. *Educ:* Repton; Corpus Christi College, Cambridge (Scholar); Wells Theological Coll. 1st class, Historical Tripos, Part 1, 1923, and Part 2, 1924; Thirlwall Medal and Gladstone Prize, 1925. Tutor and Lectr in History, Harvard Univ., USA, 1926-27; Deacon, 1929; Priest, 1930; University Lecturer in History, Cambridge, 1929-32 and 1944-46; Curate of St Clement's, Barnsbury, Islington, 1933-34; of St Saviour's, Upper Chelsea, 1934-36; of St Giles', Cambridge, 1936-37. Birkbeck Lecturer in Ecclesiastical History, Trinity College, Cambridge, 1937-38; Dean of Chapel, Corpus Christi College, 1937-46; Hon. Canon of Derby and Chaplain to Bishop of Derby at the University of Cambridge, 1938-46; Select Preacher, Oxford, 1941-43 and 1965; Canon of Westminster and Rector of St Margaret's, Westminster, 1946-56; Hon. Canon and Prebendary of Nassington in Lincoln Cathedral, 1965-79; Canon Emeritus of Derby Cathedral, 1977-, of Lincoln Cathedral, 1979-. Editor of the Cambridge Review, 1925 and 1940-41. *Publications:* Cranmer and the Reformation under Edward VI, 1926; The Art of Preaching (747-1939), 1940; Simeon and Church Order (Birkbeck Lectures), 1940; Religion and Politics, 1943; The Friendship of Christ, 1945; Dean Milman, 1949; Church and Parish (Bishop Paddock Lectures), 1955; Good Friday at St Margaret's, 1957; Cyril Forster Garbett, Archbishop of York, 1959; The Two Families, 1962; The Church and the Nation, 1962. *Address:* 12 Manor Court, Grange Road, Cambridge CB3 9BE. *T:* Cambridge 356390; Corpus Christi College, Cambridge.

SMYTH, (James) Robert Staples; Stipendiary Magistrate, West Midlands, since 1978; *b* 11 July 1926; *s* of Robert Smyth, Gaybrook, Co. Westmeath, and Mabel Anne Georgina (*née* MacGeough-Bond); *m* 1971, Fenella Joan Mowat; one *s. Educ:* St Columba's, Dublin; Merton Coll., Oxford (BA 1948, MA). Served RAF, 1944-46. Called to Bar, Inner Temple, 1949. Resident Magistrate, Northern Rhodesia, 1951-55; a Dep. Circuit Judge, 1974. Dep. Chairman, Agricultural Land Tribunal, 1974. *Recreations:* shooting, fishing, English literature. *Address:* The Leys, Shelsley Beauchamp, Worcs WR6 6RB. *T:* Shelsley Beauchamp 291.

SMYTH, Brig. Rt. Hon. Sir John (George), 1st Bt *cr* 1955; VC 1915; PC 1962; MC 1920; *b* 24 Oct. 1893; *e s* of W. J. Smyth, Indian Civil Service; *m* 1920, Margaret, *d* of late Charles Dundas, ICS, Sialkot; one *s* one *d* (and two *s* decd, of whom *e* s killed in action 1944); *m* 1940, Frances Read, *d* of late Lieut-Colonel R. A. Chambers, OBE, IMS. *Educ:* Repton; Sandhurst. Entered army, 1912; served European War, 1914-15 (despatches, VC, Russian Order of St George); Senussi Campaign, Western Egypt, 1915-16; Mohmand Expedition, India, 1916; Afghan War, 1919; Waziristan Frontier Expedition, 1919-20 (despatches, MC); Mesopotamia Insurrection, 1920-21 (despatches); Operations on NW Frontier, 1930 (despatches); Mohmand Operations, 1935 (despatches); Brevet-Major, 1928; Brevet Lieut-Colonel, 1933; Colonel, 1936; Instructor, Staff College, Camberley, 1931-34; Comdt 45th Rattrays Sikhs, 1936-39; GSO1, 2nd London Division, 1939-40; Commander 127 Inf. Bde in operations with BEF in France and Belgium (despatches); Acting Maj.-Gen. 1941; raised 19th Division in India; Comd 17th Division in Burma at time of Japanese invasion; retired, Nov. 1942; Hon. Brig. 1943. Military Correspondent: Kemsley newspapers, 1943-44; Daily Sketch and Sunday Times, 1945-46; Lawn Tennis Correspondent: Sunday Times, 1946-51; News of the World, 1956-57. Author, Wimbledon Programme articles, 1947-73. Comptroller Royal Alexandra and Albert School, 1948-63; Governor: Gypsy Road and West Norwood Secondary Schs, 1947-49; Strand and West Norwood Secondary Schools, 1949-51; St Martin's High School for Girls, 1950-52; Dragon School, Oxford, 1953-66; Queen Mary's Hosp., Roehampton, 1956-62. Exec., Returned Brit. POW Assoc., 1946-51. First Chm. Victoria Cross Assoc., 1956-71 (Centenary of the Victoria Cross), Life Pres. 1966; Vice-Pres. Not Forgotten Assoc., 1956; Pres. S London Branch

Burma Star Assoc., 1957–; Vice-Pres. Distinguished Conduct Medal League, 1957, Pres. 1958–70; Director Creative Journals Ltd, 1957–63. Govt Apptd Trustee, Far East POW and Internee Fund, 1959–61; Hon. Vice-Pres. Far Eastern POW Federation, 1960; President Old Reptonian Society, 1960 and 1961; Vice-President: Dunkirk Veterans Assoc., 1963–; Internat. Lawn Tennis Club of GB, 1966. Contested (C) Wandsworth Central, 1945. MP (C) Norwood Div. of Lambeth, 1950–66; Parly Sec., Min. of Pensions, 1951–53; Jt Parly Sec., Min. of Pensions and Nat. Insce, 1953–55. Freeman of City of London in Worshipful Co. of Farriers, 1951; Master of Farriers' Co., 1961–62. *Publications:* Defence Is Our Business, 1945; The Western Defences (ed and introd), 1951; Lawn Tennis, 1953; The Game's the Same, 1956; Before the Dawn (story of two historic retreats), 1957; Paradise Island (children's adventure story), 1958; The Only Enemy (autobiography), 1959; Trouble in Paradise, 1959; Ann Goes Hunting (children's book), 1960; Sandhurst (A History of the Military Cadet Colleges), 1961; The Story of the Victoria Cross, 1962; Beloved Cats, 1963; Blue Magnolia, 1964; (with Col Macaulay) Behind the Scenes at Wimbledon, 1965; Ming (the story of a cat family), 1966; The Rebellious Rani (a story of the Indian Mutiny), 1966; Bolo Whistler (biography), 1967; The Story of the George Cross, 1968; In This Sign Conquer (The Story of the Army Chaplains), 1968; The Valiant, 1969; Will to Live: the story of Dame Margot Turner, 1970; Percival and the Tragedy of Singapore, 1971; Jean Borotra: the Bounding Basque, 1974; Leadership in War, 1939–1945, 1974; Leadership in Battle, 1914–1918, 1975; Great Stories of the Victoria Cross, 1977; Milestones: a memoir, 1979; *plays:* Burma Road (with Ian Hay), 1945; Until the Morning (with Ian Hay), 1950. *Heir: g s* Timothy John Smyth, MB BS (NSW) [*b* 16 April 1953; *m* 1981, Bernadette, *d* of Leo Askew; one *s*]. *Address:* 807 Nelson House, Dolphin Square, SW1A 3PA. *Clubs:* All England Lawn Tennis, International Lawn Tennis Clubs of Britain, USA and France.

SMYTH, John Jackson; QC 1979; barrister-at-law; a Recorder of the Crown Court, since 1978; *b* 27 June 1941; *e s* of Col Edward Hugh Jackson Smyth, FRCSEd, and Ursula Helen Lucie (*née* Ross), c/o Cambridge Military Hospital, Aldershot; *m* 1968, Josephine Anne, *er d* of late Walter Leggott and Miriam Moss Leggott, Manor Farm, Burtoft, Lincs; one *s* three *d*. *Educ:* Strathcona Sch., Calgary, Alberta; St Lawrence Coll.; Trinity Hall, Cambridge. MA, LLB (Cantab). Called to Bar, Inner Temple (Major Schol.), 1965. *Recreations:* skiing, sailing, rackets, real tennis. *Address:* 2 Crown Office Row, Temple, EC4. *Clubs:* Army and Navy, Ski Club of GB, Bar Yacht; Hampshire (Winchester).

SMYTH, Margaret Jane, CBE 1959 (OBE 1955); retired; *b* 23 Sept. 1897; *d* of late Colonel John Smyth, IMS. *Educ:* Uplands School (Church Education Corporation); Clifton High School. Trained at Univ. Settlement, Bristol; Health Visitors Certificate. Roy. Sanitary Inst., 1918; Central Midwives Board, SCM, 1920; Maternity and Child Welfare Certificate, RSI, 1921; SRN, 1925, trained in Nightingale Trng School, St Thomas Hosp.; Sister, St Thomas Hosp., 1926–34; Matron, St Thomas Babies' Hostel, 1934–37; Warden, St Christopher's Nursery Trng College, 1937–39; Dep. Matron, St Thomas Hosp., 1939–45, Supt, Nightingale Trng School and Matron, St Thomas Hospital, 1945–55; Chairman of the General Nursing Council for England and Wales, 1955–60; President Royal College of Nursing, 1960–62; Chairman, South West Metropolitan Area, Nurse Training Cttee, 1952–64, Mem., 1964–66; Vice-Chm., Long Grove Hospital Management Cttee, 1964–67; Mem., Kingston and Long Grove Hosp. Management Cttee, 1967–69. *Address:* 9 Stockbridge Gardens, Chichester, West Sussex.

SMYTH, Rev. Martin; *see* Smyth, Rev. W. M.

SMYTH, Robert Staples; *see* Smyth, J. R. S.

SMYTH, Sir Thomas Weyland Bowyer-, 15th Bt *cr* 1661; *b* 25 June 1960; *s* of Captain Sir Philip Weyland Bowyer-Smyth, 14th Bt, RN, and of Veronica Mary, *d* of Captain C. W. Bower, DSC, RN; *S* father, 1978. *Heir:* kinsman John Jeremy Windham [*b* 22 Nov. 1948; *m* 1976, Rachel Mary Finney]. *Address:* 3 Lillian Road, Barnes, SW13.

SMYTH, Rev. (William) Martin; MP (OUP) Belfast South, since March 1982; Member (OUP) Belfast South, Northern Ireland Assembly, since 1982; *b* 15 June 1931; *s* of James Smyth, JP, and Minnie Kane; *m* 1957, Kathleen Jean Johnston, BA; two *d* (and one *d* decd). *Educ:* Methodist Coll., Belfast; Magee University Coll., Londonderry; Trinity Coll., Dublin (BA 1953, BD 1961); Assembly's Coll., Belfast. Assistant Minister, Lowe Memorial, Finaghy, 1953–57; Raffrey Presbyterian Church, Crossgar, 1957–63; Alexandra Presbyterian Church, Belfast, 1963–82. Member, Northern Ireland Convention, 1975; Chm. of Executive 1974–76, Vice-Pres. 1974–, Ulster Unionist Council. Governor, Belfast City Mission. Grand Master, Grand Orange Lodge of Ireland, 1972–; Grand Master of World Orange Council, 1974–82; Hon. Past Grand Master, Canada, and Hon. Deputy Grand Master, USA, NZ, NSW, of Orange Order. *Publications:* (ed) Faith for Today, 1961; pamphlets: Why Presbyterian?, 1963; Till Death Us Do Part, 1965; In Defence of Ulster, 1970; The Battle for Northern Ireland, 1972; occasional papers, and articles in Christian Irishman, Evangelical Quarterly, Biblical Theology. *Recreations:* reading, photography; former Rugby player (capped for Magee University College). *Address:* 117 Cregagh Road, Belfast BT6 0LA. *T:* Belfast 57009. *Club:* Royal Commonwealth Society.

SMYTHE, Clifford Anthony, (Tony); consultant; *b* 2 Aug. 1938; *s* of Clifford John and Florence May Smythe; *m*; four *d*. *Educ:* University College School. Conscientious Objector, 1958; General Secretary, War Resisters' International, 1959–64; Council Member, Internat. Confederation for Disarmament and Peace, 1963–71; Gen. Sec., Nat. Council for Civil Liberties, 1966–72, Mem. Exec., 1981–; Field Dir, American Civil Liberties Union, 1973; Dir, Mind (Nat. Assoc. for Mental Health), 1973–81. Board Member: Volunteer Centre, 1977–81; Retired Execs Clearing Hse (REACH), 1978–; Member: Nat. Adv. Council on Employment of Disabled People, 1975–81; Nat. Develt Council for Mentally Handicapped People, 1981; Chm., Campaign for Homeless Single People, 1982–; Treasurer, War Resisters' Internat., 1982–. *Publications:* Conscription: a World Survey, 1968; (with D. Madgwick) The Invasion of Privacy, 1974. *Address:* 136 Stapleton Hall Road, N4.

SMYTHE, Captain George Quentin Murray, VC 1942; Officer Instructor, Department of Defence, South Africa, 1970–81; *b* 6 Aug. 1916; *s* of Edric Murray Smythe and *g s* of 1st Administrator of Natal (Hon. Charles Smythe, Methven Castle, Perthshire, Scotland); *m* 1945, Dale Griffiths (marr. diss. 1970), Capetown; three *s* one *d*; *m* 1970, Margaret Joan Shatwell (*d* 1980). *Educ:* Estcourt High Sch. Went through Abyssinian Campaign with Regt, Natal Carabineers; Sgt at Alem Hanza, Egypt (VC). *Recreations:* cricket, tennis, fishing. *Address:* 54 Seadoone Road, Amanzimtoti, Natal, Republic of South Africa.

SMYTHE, Henry James Drew-, MC, TD; MS, MD (London); FRCS; MMSA; FRCOG; late Hon. Consulting Gynæcologist United Bristol Hospitals and Southmead General Hospital; late Gynæcologist, Weston-super-Mare and Burnham Hospitals; Colonel RAMCT; *b* 1 June 1891; *s* of Frank Thompson Smythe and Ada Josephine Drew; *m* 1914, Enid Audrey Cloutman (*d* 1971); two *s*. *Educ:* Taunton School; Bristol Medical School; London Hospital. Qualified 1913; House Surgeon and House Physician Bristol Children's Hospital, 1913–14; House Surgeon Bristol General Hospital, 1914; served European War, 1914–19; also served War of 1939–45; House Surgeon Royal Infirmary, 1919; Demonstrator of Anatomy, Royal Free Hospital for Women, 1921; Post-Graduate Course London Hospital, 1921–22; Surgical Registrar, Bristol General Hospital, 1923; Asst Gynæcologist, 1925; Professor of Obstetrics, University of Bristol, 1934–51. Liveryman Society of Apothecaries; Freeman of City of London. *Publications:* various in Practitioner, Bristol Med. Chir. Jl, Jl of Obst. of British Empire, etc; Operative Obstetrics (Butterworth's Modern Trends), 1949. *Recreations:* Rugby football, hockey, tennis. *Address:* 2 Charlton Close, Charlton Kings, Cheltenham, Glos. *T:* Cheltenham 25117.

SMYTHE, Patricia Rosemary; *see* Koechlin, P. R.

SMYTHE, Sir Reginald Harry, KBE 1971; Chairman, NZ Forest Products Ltd, 1973–77; *b* 2 May 1905; *s* of Reginald Harry Smythe; *m* 1930, Colleen Valmar, *d* of George Mobberley; one *s*. *Educ:* Auckland Grammar Sch.; FCIS. Accountant to: Morris Duncan & Gylls, 1922–24; Smith Wylie Co. Ltd, 1924–30; Asst Sec., 1930–32, Sec., 1932–35, NZ Perpetual Forests; NZ Forest Products Ltd: Sec., 1935–60; Dir, 1954–77; Gen. Manager, 1960–63; Man. Dir, 1963–73; Chm., NZ Maritime Holdings Ltd; Deputy Chairman: Tasman Union Co. Ltd; Union Steam Ship Co. Ltd; former Chairman: D. Henry & Co. Ltd; Carter Kumeu Ltd; Fibre Products NZ Ltd; NZ Paper Mills Ltd. Member: Salvation Army Adv. Bd (Auckland); Bd of Mental Health Foundn. JP 1948. *Recreation:* gardening. *Address:* 178 Remuera Road, Auckland 5, New Zealand.

SMYTHE, Tony; *see* Smythe, C. A.

SNAGGE, John Derrick Mordaunt, OBE 1944; *b* 1904; 2nd *s* of late Judge Sir Mordaunt Snagge; *m* 1936, Eileen Mary (*d* 1980), *e d* of H. P. Joscelyne, Alvechurch, Worcestershire. *Educ:* Winchester College; Pembroke College, Oxford. Assistant Station Director BBC, Stoke-on-Trent, 1924; Announcer London (Savoy Hill), 1928; Assistant Outside Broadcast Department 1933; Commentator Oxford and Cambridge Boat Race, 1931–80; Assistant Director Outside Broadcasts, 1939; Presentation Director BBC, 1939–45; Head of Presentation (Home Service), 1945–57; Head of Presentation (Sound) BBC, 1957–63; Special Duties, BBC, 1963–65. Retired from BBC 1965. Chairman of the Lord's Taverners, 1956, 1960, 1961; President, 1952, 1964; Secretary, 1965–67; Trustee, 1970–76. *Publication:* (with Michael Barsley) Those Vintage Years of Radio, 1972. *Recreation:* fishing. *Address:* Delgaty, Village Road, Dorney, near Windsor, Berks SL4 6QJ. *T:* Burnham 61303. *Clubs:* St James's, MCC, Leander, Lord's Taverners, Sportsman's.

SNAGGE, Dame Nancy (Marion), DBE 1955 (OBE 1945); *b* 2 May 1906; *d* of late Henry Thomas Salmon; *m* 1962, Thomas Geoffrey Mordaunt Snagge, DSC, *e s* of late His Hon. Sir Mordaunt Snagge. *Educ:* Notting Hill, High Sch. Joined the WAAF on its inception, March 1939; served as a commnd officer in the WAAF and WRAF from Sept. 1939. ADC to King George VI, 1950–52; ADC to the Queen, 1952–56; Director Women's Royal Air Force, 1950–56, retired as Air Commandant. *Address:* Test Lodge, Longstock, Stockbridge, Hampshire. *T:* Stockbridge 558.

SNAITH, George Robert, FRINA; Director of Research, British Shipbuilders, since 1977; *b* 9 July 1930; *s* of late Robert and Clara Snaith; *m* 1953, Verna Patricia (*née* Codling); one *s* one *d*. *Educ:* University of Durham.

BSc Applied Science (Naval Architecture), 1952. A. Kari & Co., Consulting Naval Architects, Newcastle, 1952-57; Northern Aluminium Co. Ltd, Bambury, 1957-59; Burness, Corlett & Partners, Consulting Naval Architects, Basingstoke, 1959-64; British Ship Research Association, 1964-77, Dir of Research, 1976-77. Vis. Prof., Dept of Naval Architecture and Shipbldg, Univ. of Newcastle upon Tyne, 1980-. Vice-Pres., NE Coast Instn of Engrs and Shipbuilders, 1979; Member: Council, RINA, 1977-; Ship and Marine Technol. Requirements Bd, Dept of Industry, 1978-81; Bd, National Maritime Inst., 1978-. *Recreations:* reading, literature and discussion. *Address:* 10 Fieldhouse Close, Hepscott, Morpeth, Northumberland. *T:* Morpeth 55319. *Club:* Athenæum.

SNAITH, Group Captain Leonard Somerville, CB 1952; AFC 1933; retired; *b* 30 June 1902; *s* of David Somerville Snaith; *m* 1931, Joyce Edith Taylor; two *s. Educ:* Carlisle Cathedral Sch. Commnd, 1927; Comd 83 Sqdn, 1937-40; service in: Iraq, 1934-36; USA (Test flying), 1940-41; Egypt, Italy, Palestine, Aden, 1945-47. Schneider Trophy Team, 1931; Commandant Empire Test Pilot School, 1948-50; Comdg Officer, Experimental Flying, Royal Aircraft Establishment, Farnborough, 1950-52; retired from RAF, 1952. DL Beds, 1961-69. *Address:* Pyghtle Cottage, Wilden, Bedford. *Club:* Royal Air Force.

SNAPE, Peter Charles; MP (Lab) West Bromwich East since Feb. 1974; *b* 12 Feb. 1942; *s* of Thomas and Kathleen Snape; *m* 1963, Winifred Grimshaw (marr. diss. 1980); two *d. Educ:* St Joseph's RC Sch., Stockport; St Winifred's Sch., Stockport. Railway signalman, 1957-61; regular soldier, RE & RCT, 1961-67; goods guard, 1967-70; clerical officer BR, 1970-74. Mem., Council of Europe and WEU, May-Nov. 1975. An Asst Govt Whip, 1975-77; a Lord Comr, HM Treasury, 1977-79; opposition spokesman for Defence, 1979-82, for Home Affairs, 1982-. Mem., Bredbury and Romiley UDC, 1971-74 (Chm., Finance Cttee). *Address:* c/o House of Commons, SW1A 0AA.

SNAPE, Royden Eric; a Recorder of the Crown Court, since 1979; *b* 20 April 1922; *s* of John Robert and Gwladys Constance Snape; *m* 1949, Unity Frances Money; one *s* one *d. Educ:* Bromsgrove Sch. Served War, Royal Regt of Artillery (Field), 1940-46; Adjt, 80th Field Regt, 1945. Admitted Solicitor, 1949; a Deputy Circuit Judge, 1975. Governor, St John's Sch., Porthcawl, 1971-. *Recreations:* golf, Rugby Union football, cricket. *Address:* West Winds, Llanblethian, Cowbridge, South Glamorgan, Wales CF7 7JQ. *T:* Cowbridge 2362. *Clubs:* Royal Porthcawl Golf; Cardiff Athletic; Glamorgan CCC.

SNEDDEN, Rt. Hon. Sir Billy (Mackie), KCMG 1978; PC 1972; QC (Australia); Federal Member of Parliament for Bruce (Victoria), Commonwealth of Australia, since 1955; Speaker, House of Representatives, since 1976; *b* 31 Dec. 1926; *s* of A. Snedden, Scotland; *m* 1950, Joy; two *s* two *d. Educ:* Univ. of Western Australia (LLB). Barrister, admitted Supreme Ct of Western Australia, 1951; admitted Victorian Bar, 1955. Australian Govt: Attorney-General, 1963-66; Minister for Immigration, 1966-69; Leader of the House, 1966-71; Minister for Labour and Nat. Service, 1969-71; Treasurer, 1971-72; Leader of the Opposition, 1972-75; Leader, Parliamentary Liberal Party, 1972-75 (Dep. Leader, 1971-72). Chm., Standing Cttee of Conf. of Commonwealth Speakers and Presiding Officers, 1978-81. National Patron, Young Liberal Movement, 1980-. Pres., Melbourne Football Club, 1981-. *Recreations:* squash, tennis. *Address:* 22 Pine Crescent, Ringwood, Victoria 3134, Australia. *Clubs:* Melbourne, Melbourne Scots, Naval and Military (Melbourne).

SNEDDEN, David King, CA; Chief Executive and Managing Director, Liverpool Daily Post and Echo, since 1982; *b* 23 Feb. 1933; *s* of David King Snedden and Isabella (*née* Martin); *m* 1958, Jean Swan Smith; two *s* one *d. Educ:* Daniel Stewart's College, Edinburgh. CA 1956. Flying Officer, RAF, 1956-57. Investment Adviser, Guinness Mahon, 1958-59; Chief Accountant, Scotsman Publications Ltd, Thomson British Publications Ltd, Thomson Scottish Associates Ltd, 1959-64; Commercial Controller, The Scotsman Publications Ltd, 1964-66; Managing Director: Belfast Telegraph Newspapers Ltd, 1967-70 (Director, 1979-82); The Scotsman Publications Ltd, 1970-78 (Director, 1970-82). Thomson Regional Newspapers Ltd: Dir, 1974-82; Gp Asst Man. Dir, 1979-80; Jt Man. Dir, 1980-82. Member: Regional Council, CBI, N Ireland, 1968-70; Press Council, 1976-80; Organiser, Ulster Innocent Victims Appeal Fund, 1969. Director: Radio Forth Ltd, 1973-77; Scottish Council Research Inst. Ltd, 1975-77; Mem., Edinburgh Chamber of Commerce, 1976-78; Pres., Scottish Daily Newspaper Soc., 1975-78. *Recreations:* golf, shooting, fishing. *Address:* Fairleigh, Hinderton Lane, Neston, Cheshire; 15 Great King Street, Edinburgh. *Clubs:* Caledonian; Bruntsfield Links Golfing Society.

SNEDDON, Hutchison B., OBE 1968; JP; Chairman, Cumbernauld Development Corporation, since 1979; *b* 17 April 1929; *s* of Robert and Catherine Sneddon; *m* 1960, Elizabeth Jardine; one *s* two *d. Educ:* Wishaw High School. Member: Bd, Housing Corp.; Scottish Tourist Bd. JP Motherwell District. *Recreation:* football (watching). *Address:* Cumbernauld Development Corporation, Cumbernauld House, Cumbernauld, Dunbartonshire, Scotland. *T:* Cumbernauld 21155.

SNEDDON, Prof. Ian Naismith, OBE 1969; MA Cantab, DSc Glasgow; FRSE; FIMA; Member of the Polish Academy of Sciences; part-time Professor of Mathematics, University of Glasgow since 1982; *b* 8 Dec. 1919;

o s of Naismith Sneddon and Mary Ann Cameron; *m* 1943, Mary Campbell Macgregor; two *s* one *d. Educ:* Hyndland School, Glasgow; The University of Glasgow; Trinity College, Cambridge (Senior Scholar, 1941). Scientific Officer, Ministry of Supply, 1942-45; Research Worker, H. H. Wills Physical Lab., Univ. of Bristol, 1945-46; Lecturer in Natural Philosophy, Univ. of Glasgow, 1946-50; Professor of Mathematics in University Coll. of N Staffordshire, 1950-56 (Senior Tutor of the College, 1954-56); Simson Prof. of Mathematics, Univ. of Glasgow, 1956-82 (Dean of Faculty of Science, 1970-72, Senate Assessor on Univ. Court, 1973-77); Visiting Professor: Duke Univ., North Carolina, 1959 and 1960; Michigan State Univ., 1967; Univ. of California, Berkeley, 1979; Adjunct Prof., North Carolina State Univ., 1965-72; Visiting Lecturer: Univ. of Palermo, 1953 and 1980; Serbian Acad. of Sciences, 1958; Univ. of Warsaw, 1959, 1973, 1975; Canadian Mathematical Congress, 1961; Polish Acad. of Sciences, 1962; US Midwest Mechanics Research Seminar, 1963 and 1981; Univ. of Zagreb, 1964; Univ. of Calgary, 1968; Indiana Univ., 1970-80; Kuwait Univ., 1972; CISM, Udine, 1972, 1974; Britton Lectr, McMaster Univ., 1979; Huber Lectr, Polish Acad. of Sciences, 1980. NSF Distinguished Vis. Scientist, State Univ., New York, 1969. Member: various govt scientific cttees, 1950-; Adv. Council on Scientific Research and Tech. Development, Min. of Supply, 1953-56, Min. of Defence, 1965-68; Univs Science and Technology Bd (SRC), 1965-69; Adv. Council of Scottish Opera, 1972-; Bd of Scottish Nat. Orch., 1976-; Bd of Citizens Theatre, Glasgow, 1975-; BBC Central Music Adv. Cttee, 1978-; Chm., BBC Scottish Music Adv. Cttee, 1978-; Mem. Council, Scottish Soc. of Composers, 1981-; Vice-Pres., RSE, 1966-69 and 1979-82. Kelvin Medal, Univ. of Glasgow, 1948; Makdougall-Brisbane Prize, RSE, 1956-58; Soc. of Engrg Sci. Medal, 1979. FRSA. Mem., Order of Long-Leaf Pine, USA, 1964; Hon. Fellow, Soc. of Engng Sci., USA, 1977. Hon. DSc: Warsaw, 1973; Heriot-Watt, 1982. Comdr's Cross, Order of Polonia Restituta, 1969; Comdr, Order of Merit (Poland), 1979. *Publications:* (with N. F. Mott) Wave Mechanics and Its Applications, 1948; Fourier Transforms, 1951; Special Functions of Mathematical Physics and Chemistry, 1956; The Elements of Partial Differential Equations, 1956; Introduction to the Mathematics of Biology and Medicine (with J. G. Defares), 1960; Fourier Series, 1961; Zagadnienie Szczelin w Teorii Sprezystasci, 1962; Mixed Boundary Value Problems in Potential Theory, 1966; Crack Problems in the Mathematical Theory of Elasticity (with M. Lowengrub), 1969; An Introduction to the Use of Integral Transforms, 1972; Metoda Transformacji Calkowych w Mieszanych Zogadnieniach Brzegowych, 1974; The Linear Theory of Thermoelasticity, 1974; (ed) Encyclopedic Dictionary of Mathematics for Engineers, 1976; (with G. Eason, W. Nowacki and Z. Olesiak) Integral Transform Methods in Elasticity, 1977; articles in Handbuch der Physik, 1956-58; scientific papers on quantum theory of nuclei, theory of elasticity, and boundary value problems in jls. *Recreations:* music, painting and photography. *Address:* 15 Victoria Park Gardens South, Glasgow G11 7BX. *T:* 041-339 4114. *Club:* Glasgow Art.

SNEDDON, Robert, CMG 1976; MBE 1945; HM Diplomatic Service, retired; *b* 8 June 1920; *m* 1945, Kathleen Margaret Smith; two *d. Educ:* Dalziel High Sch., Motherwell; Kettering Grammar Sch.; University Coll., Nottingham. HM Forces, 1940-46: 8th Army, ME and Italy, 1942-45; 30 Corps, Germany (Major), 1945-46. Joined Foreign (subseq. Diplomatic) Service, 1946; 3rd Sec., Warsaw, 1946; 2nd Sec., Stockholm, 1950; FO, 1954; 1st Sec., Oslo, 1956; 1st Sec., Berlin, 1961; FO, 1963; Counsellor, Bonn, 1969; FCO, 1971, retired 1977. *Recreations:* tennis, golf, music. *Address:* Windrose, Church Road, Horsell, Woking, Surrey. *T:* Woking 4335. *Clubs:* Woking Lawn Tennis and Croquet, Westhill Golf.

SNELGROVE, Rt. Rev. Donald George; *see* Hull, Bishop Suffragan of.

SNELL, Ven. Basil Clark; Archdeacon of St Albans, 1962-73, now Archdeacon Emeritus; *b* 2 Feb. 1907; *s* of Charles Clark Snell, Vicar of Littlehampton; *m* 1933, Isobel Eills Nedeham Browne (*d* 1975); two *d. Educ:* King's School, Canterbury; Queens' College, Cambridge. Curate of Crosthwaite, Keswick, 1933-35; Chaplain of Aldenham School, 1935-40; Chaplain, Loretto Sch. and Army Chaplain, 1940-47; Rector of Tattingstone, Suffolk, 1947-55; Residentiary Canon of St Edmundsbury, 1955-58; Dir of Religious Education: Dio. of St Edmundsbury and Ipswich, 1947-58; Dio. of St Albans, 1958-68. Archdeacon of Bedford, 1958-62. *Recreations:* golf, gardening. *Address:* Glebe House, Melbourn, Royston, Herts.

SNELL, Frederick Rowlandson, MA, BSc; *b* 18 Sept. 1903; *s* of Rev. C. D. Snell; *m* 1928, Margaret Lucy Sidebottom; one *s* three *d. Educ:* Winchester College (Scholar); Oriel College, Oxford (Scholar). BA, 1925; BSc, 1927; Lecturer in Chemistry, St John's College, Agra, UP, India, 1927-32; Senior Science Master, Eastbourne College, 1932-38; Rector of Michaelhouse, Natal, SA, 1939-52; Founder and first Rector of Peterhouse, Rhodesia, 1953-67; Treasurer, Anglican Church in Central Africa, 1968-82. *Recreations:* walking and music. *Address:* 54 1st Street, Marondera, Zimbabwe. *Club:* Royal Commonwealth Society.

SNELL, Rt. Rev. Geoffrey Stuart; *see* Croydon, Bishop Suffragan of.

SNELL, Rt. Rev. George Boyd, DD, PhD; *b* Toronto, Ontario, 17 June 1907; *s* of John George Snell and Minnie Alice Boyd; *m* 1934, Esther Mary. *Educ:* Trinity College, Toronto. BA 1929, MA 1930, PhD 1937, DD 1948. Deacon, Toronto, 1931; Priest, Niagara (for Tor.), 1932; Curate of St Michael and All Angels, Tor., 1931-39; Rector, 1940-48; Private Chaplain to Bp of Tor.,

1945-48; Rector of Pro-Cathedral, Calgary, and Dean of Calgary, 1948-51; Exam. Chaplain to Bp of Calgary, 1948-51; Rector of St Clem. Eglinton, Tor., 1951-56; Archdeacon of Toronto, 1953-56; Exam. Chaplain to Bp of Toronto, 1953-55. Consecrated Bp Suffragan of Toronto, 1956; elected Bp-Coadjutor of Toronto, 1959; Bishop of Toronto, 1966-72. Hon. DD: Wycliffe Coll., Toronto, 1959; Huron Coll., Ontario, 1968. *Address:* 1210 Glen Road, Mississauga, Ont., Canada. *Club:* National (Toronto).

SNELL, Dr George Davis; geneticist; *b* Bradford, Mass, 19 Dec. 1903; *s* of Cullen Bryant and Katharine Davis Snell; *m* 1937, Rhoda Carson; three *s. Educ:* Dartmouth Coll. (BS 1926); Harvard Univ. (MS 1928; ScD 1930). Instr in Zoology, Dartmouth Coll., 1929-30, Brown Univ., 1930-31; Res. Fellow, Texas Univ., 1931-33; Asst Prof., Washington Univ. St Louis, 1933-34; Jackson Laboratory: Res. Associate, 1935-56; Sen. Staff Scientist, 1957-69, now Emeritus. Guggenheim Fellow, Texas Univ., 1953-54. Mem., Allergy and Immunology Study Sect., NIH, 1958-62. Member: Amer. Acad. of Arts and Scis; Nat. Acad. of Scis; French Acad. of Scis (foreign associate); Amer. Philosophical Soc., 1982; Hon. Mem., British Transplantation Soc. Hon. MD Charles Univ., Prague, 1967; Hon. DSc: Dartmouth, 1974; Gustavus Adolphus Coll., 1981; Bates Coll., 1981; Hon. LLD: Univ. of Maine, 1981; Colby Coll., 1981. Bertner Foundn Award, 1962; Gregor Mendel Medal, Czechoslovak Acad. of Scis, 1967; Gairdner Foundn Award, 1976; Prize in Medicine, Wolf Foundn, 1978; (jt) Nobel Prize for Physiology or Medicine, 1980. *Publications:* (ed) The Biology of the Laboratory Mouse, 1941; (jtly) Histocompatibility, 1976; contribs to learned jls. *Address:* The Jackson Laboratory, Bar Harbor, Maine 04609, USA; 21 Atlantic Avenue, Bar Harbor, Maine 04609, USA.

SNELL, John Nicholas B.; *see* Blashford-Snell.

SNELL, Philip D.; Member (Lab), Tyne and Wear County Council, since 1974, Chairman, General Services Committee, 1981; *b* 14 Oct. 1915; *s* of Alfred William Snell and Jane Herdman; *m* 1939, Selina Waite; two *d. Educ:* Causey Road Council Sch., Gateshead. Miner, Marley Hill Colliery, Gateshead, 1929-57; Industrial Relations Advr, NCB, 1957-61; Education and Welfare Officer; Durham CC, 1961-73; Gateshead MDC, 1973. Chm., Tyne and Wear CC, 1980-81. Trustee, Whickham Glebe Sports Club. *Recreation:* enjoying Northern Federation Brewery Beer. *Address:* School House, Marley Hill, Whickham, Gateshead, Tyne and Wear. *T:* Gateshead 887006. *Club:* Sunniside Social (Gateshead).

SNELL, William Edward, MD; FRCP; Consultant Physician Superintendent, Colindale Chest Hospital, 1938-67; Demonstrator in Tuberculosis, St Bartholomew's Hospital Medical College, 1948-67; Consultant Chest Physician, Napsbury and Shenley Hospitals, 1963-67; *b* 16 Aug. 1902; *er s* of late S. H. Snell, MD; *m* 1934, Yvonne Creagh Brown; two *s* one *d. Educ:* Stubbington House; Bradfield College; Corpus Christi College, Cambridge (Exhibitioner and Prizeman); University College Hospital. MA Cambridge; BSc Hons London; MD; FRCP; DPH. Tuberculosis Scholarship Tour, Canada and USA, 1930. Formerly: Pres. Brit. Tuberculosis Assoc., 1955-57; Chairman: NW Metropolitan Thoracic Soc.; Metropolitan Branch, Soc. of Med. Supts; Editorial Cttee TB Index; Member: Management Cttees, Hendon and Chelsea Groups of Hosps; Brit. Tuberculosis Research Cttee; Examiner to Gen. Nursing Council. Mem. Council (twice Vice-Pres.), History of Medicine Section, RSM. *Publications:* articles in medical press relating to tuberculosis and chest disease, accidents to patients and history of medicine. *Recreations:* gardening, sailing, collecting ship models and prints; late part owner 15 ton ketch Craignair. *Address:* Yewden Manor, Hambleden, Henley-on-Thames, Oxon. *T:* Hambleden 351. *Clubs:* Keyhaven Yacht, Cambridge University Cruising, etc.

SNELLGROVE, David Llewellyn, LittD; PhD; FBA 1969; Professor of Tibetan in the University of London, 1974-82, now Emeritus Professor (Reader, 1960-74, Lecturer, 1950-60); Founder Director of Institute of Tibetan Studies, Tring, 1966-82; *b* Portsmouth, 29 June 1920; *s* of Lt-Comdr Clifford Snellgrove, RN, and Eleanor Maud Snellgrove. *Educ:* Christ's Hospital, Horsham; Southampton Univ.; Queens' Coll., Cambridge. Served War of 1939-45: commissioned in Infantry, 1942; Intell. Officer in India until 1946. Then started seriously on oriental studies at Cambridge, 1946, cont. Rome, 1949-50. BA Cantab 1949, MA Cantab 1953; PhD London 1954; LittD Cantab 1969. Made expedns to India and the Himalayas, 1953-54, 1956, 1960, 1964, 1967, 1974-75, 1978-80, 1982; founded with Mr Hugh E. Richardson an Inst. of Tibetan Studies, 1966. Apptd Consultant to Vatican in new Secretariat for non-Christian Religions, 1967. Many professional visits abroad, mainly to W Europe and USA. *Publications:* Buddhist Himalaya, 1957; The Hevajra Tantra, 1959; Himalayan Pilgrimage, 1961, 2nd edn 1981; Four Lamas of Dolpo, 1967; The Nine Ways of Bon, 1967, repr. 1980; (with H. E. Richardson) A Cultural History of Tibet, 1968, 2nd edn 1980; (with T. Skorupski) The Cultural Heritage of Ladakh, vol. I, 1977, vol. II, 1980; (ed) The Image of the Buddha, 1978; articles in Arts Asiatiques (Paris), Bulletin of the Secretariat for non-Christian Religions (Rome), etc. *Address:* Rest-harrow, 113 Cross Oak Road, Berkhamsted, Herts. *T:* Berkhamsted 4782. *Club:* Explorers' (New York).

SNELLGROVE, John Anthony; HM Diplomatic Service, retired; Secretary, British Brush Manufacturers' Association, since 1977; *b* 29 Jan. 1922; *s* of late John Snellgrove and of Anne Mary Priscilla (*née* Brown); *m* 1956, Rose Jeanne Marie Suzanne (*née* Paris); two *d. Educ:* Wimbledon Coll.; Stonyhurst

Coll.; Peterhouse, Cambridge (1940-41 and 1945-48; BA and MA). Served War, Royal Navy, latterly as temp. actg Lieut, RNVR, 1941-45. Asst Principal, Colonial Office, 1948-49; joined Foreign Service, Oct. 1949; 2nd Sec., Prague, 1950-51; FO (Econ. Relations Dept), 1951-53; HM Vice-Consul, Tamsui (Formosa), 1953-56; 1st Sec., 1954; FO (SE Asia Dept and UN (E&S) Dept), 1956-59; 1st Sec., Bangkok, 1959-62; 1st Sec. and Consul, Mogadishu (Somali Republic), 1962-63; FO (Arabian and European Econ. Org. Depts), 1963-66; 1st Sec., Holy See, 1967-71; Counsellor, 1971; Dep. Sec.-Gen. (Economic), CENTO, 1971-73; Counsellor and Head of Chancery, Carácas, 1973-75, retired, 1976. *Recreations:* golf, music, bridge. *Address:* 13 Chantry Hurst, Woodcote, Epsom, Surrey KT18 7BN.

SNELLING, Sir Arthur (Wendell), KCMG 1960 (CMG 1954); KCVO 1962; HM Diplomatic Service, retired; *b* 7 May 1914; *s* of Arthur and Ellen Snelling; *m* 1939, Frieda, *d* of late Lt-Col F. C. Barnes; one *s. Educ:* Ackworth Sch., Yorks; University Coll., London (BSc Econ.). Study Gp Sec., Royal Inst. of Internat. Affairs, 1934-36; Dominions Office, 1936; Private Sec. to Parl. Under-Sec., 1939; Joint Sec. to UK Delegn to Internat. Monetary Conference, Bretton Woods, USA, 1944; accompanied Lord Keynes on missions to USA and Canada, 1943 and 1944; Dep. High Comr for UK in New Zealand, 1947-50, in S Africa, 1953-55; Assistant Under-Secretary of State, Commonwealth Relations Office, 1956-59; British High Comr in Ghana, 1959-61; Dep. Under-Sec. of State, FCO (formerly CRO), 1961-69; Ambassador to South Africa, 1970-72. Dir, Gordon and Gotch Holdings Ltd, 1973-81. Fellow, UCL, 1970; Mem., College Council, UCL, 1976. Vice-Pres., UK-S Africa Trade Assoc., 1974-80; Mem., Ciskei Commn, 1978-80. *Address:* 19 Albany Park Road, Kingston-upon-Thames, Surrey KT2 5SW. *T:* 01-549 4160. *Club:* Reform.

SNELSON, Sir Edward Alec Abbott, KBE 1954 (OBE 1946); Justice, Supreme Restitution Court, Herford, German Federal Republic, since 1962; Judge, Arbitral Tribunal for Agreement on German External Debts and Mixed Commission, Koblenz, 1969-77; *b* 31 Oct. 1904; *er s* of Thomas Edward and Alice Martha Snelson; *m* 1956, Prof. Jean Johnston Mackay, MA, 3rd *d* of Donald and Isabella Mackay; two *s. Educ:* St Olave's; Gonville and Caius Coll., Cambridge. Called to Bar, Gray's Inn, 1929; entered ICS 1929; served in Central Provinces, District and Sessions Judge, 1936; Registrar, High Court, 1941; Legal Secretary, 1946; Joint Secretary, Govt of India, 1947; retired, 1947; Official Draftsman, Govt of Pakistan, 1948; Sec. Min. of Law, 1951-61, also of Parliamentary Affairs, 1952-58. Mem. Exec. Cttee, Arts Council of Pakistan, 1953-61. *Publication:* Father Damien, 1938. *Recreations:* sailing, music, theatre. *Address:* c/o Barclays Bank, Piccadilly Circus, W1A 3BJ. *Clubs:* United Oxford & Cambridge University; Challoner.

SNELUS, Alan Roe, CMG 1960; retired as Deputy Chief Secretary, Sarawak (1955-64); *b* 19 May 1911; *s* of John Ernest Snelus, late of Ennerdale Hall, Cumberland; *m* 1947, Margaret Bird Deacon-Elliott; one *s* one *d. Educ:* Haileybury Coll.; St Catharine's Coll., Cambridge. Barrister, Gray's Inn, 1934. Joined Sarawak Civil Service as an Administrative Officer, 1934; Actg Chief Sec., 1958-59; Officer Administering the Government of Sarawak, March-April 1959. *Recreations:* gardening and contemplation. *Address:* Cleaveside, Morcombelake, Bridport, Dorset.

SNODGRASS, Prof. Anthony McElrea, FSA; FBA 1979; Laurence Professor of Classical Archaeology, University of Cambridge, since 1976; Fellow of Clare College, Cambridge, since 1977; *b* 7 July 1934; *s* of William McElrea Snodgrass, MC (Major, RAMC), and Kathleen Mabel (*née* Owen); *m* 1959, Ann Elizabeth Vaughan (marr. diss.); three *d. Educ:* Marlborough Coll.; Worcester Coll., Oxford (BA 1959, MA, DPhil 1963). FSA 1978. Served with RAF in Iraq, 1953-55 (National Service). Student of the British School, Athens, 1959-60; University of Edinburgh: Lectr in Classical Archaeology, 1961; Reader, 1969; Prof., 1975. Myres Meml Lectr, Oxford, 1981. Corresp. Mem., German Archaeol. Inst., 1977. *Publications:* Early Greek Armour and Weapons, 1964; Arms and Armour of the Greeks, 1967; The Dark Age of Greece, 1971; Archaic Greece, 1980; contrib. Jl of Hellenic Studies, Proc. of Prehistoric Soc., Gnomon, etc. *Recreations:* mountaineering, skiing. *Address:* Museum of Classical Archaeology, Little St Mary's Lane, Cambridge CB2 1RR. *T:* Cambridge 65621 (ext. 204). *Club:* Alpine Ski.
See also J. M. O. Snodgrass.

SNODGRASS, John Michael Owen, CMG 1981; HM Diplomatic Service; Ambassador to the Republic of Zaire, since 1980; also accredited to the Republic of Burundi, the Republic of Rwanda and the People's Republic of Congo; *b* 12 Aug. 1928; *e s* of Major W. M. Snodgrass, MC, RAMC; *m* 1957, Jennifer James; three *s. Educ:* Marlborough Coll.; Trinity Hall, Cambridge (MA, Maths and Moral Scis). Diplomatic Service: 3rd Sec., Rome, 1953-56; FO, 1956-60; 1st Sec., Beirut, 1960-63; S Africa, 1964-67; FCO, 1967-70; Consul-Gen., Jerusalem, 1970-74; Counsellor, South Africa, 1974-77; Hd of Pacific Territories, later South Pacific, Dept, FCO, 1977-80. CStJ 1975. *Recreations:* ski-ing, tennis, travel. *Address:* c/o Foreign and Commonwealth Office, SW1. *Clubs:* Royal Commonwealth Society, Ski Club of Great Britain.
See also A. McE. Snodgrass.

SNOW, Adrian John, MA; Headmaster, The Oratory School, since 1973; *b* 20 March 1939; *e s* of Edward Percy John Snow and Marjory Ellen Nicholls; *m* 1963, Alessina Teresa Kilkelly; one *s* one *d. Educ:* Hurstpierpoint Coll.; Trinity Coll., Dublin (BA, MA, HDipEd); Reading Univ. (MEd). Asst

Master, The New Beacon, Sevenoaks, 1958-59; RAF Pilot Officer, 1963; Assistant Master: King's Sch., Sherborne, 1964; High Sch., Dublin, 1964-65 (part-time); Brighton Coll., 1965-66; The Oratory School: Head of Econ. and Pol Studies, 1966-73; Head of Hist., 1967-73; Housemaster, 1967-73; acting Headmaster, Sept. 1972-Mar. 1973. Governor, Prior Park Coll., 1981- (Mem., Action Cttee, 1980-81). Mem., RYA. *Recreations:* athletics (univ. colour), cricket, farming, hockey (Jun. Internat. trialist), Rugby (Combined Univs-Leinster trial), sailing, squash. *Address:* The Oratory School, Woodcote, near Reading RG8 0PJ. *T:* Checkendon 680207. *Clubs:* Leander (Henley); Emeriti CC, Sussex Martlets CC.

SNOW, Jonathan George; Television Reporter, Independent Television News, since 1976; *b* 28 Sept. 1947; *s* of late Rt Rev. George Snow, sometime Bishop of Whitby, and of Joan Snow. *Educ:* St Edward's School, Oxford; Liverpool Univ. (no degree; sent down following political disturbances, 1970). VSO, Uganda, 1967-68; Co-ordinator, New Horizon Youth Centre, Covent Garden, 1970-73; Journalist, Independent Radio News, LBC, 1973-76. TV Journalist of the Year (Royal Television Soc.), 1981; Valiant for Truth Media Award, 1982. Member, NUJ. *Address:* ITN House, 48 Wells Street, W1. *T:* 01-637 2424.

SNOW, Thomas; Secretary to Oxford University Appointments Committee, since 1970; Fellow, New College, Oxford, since 1973; *b* 16 June 1929; *e s* of Thomas Maitland Snow, *qv*; *m* 1961, Elena Tidmarsh; two *s* one *d*. *Educ:* Winchester Coll.; New Coll., Oxford. Joined Crittall Manufacturing Co. Ltd as Management Trainee, 1952; Dir 1966; Director: Crittall Hope Ltd, Darlington Simpson Rolling Mills, Minex Metals Ltd, 1968. Held various positions in local govt; Marriage Counsellor, 1964-70; Chm., Oxford Marriage Guidance Council, 1974-. JP 1964-69. *Address:* 157 Woodstock Road, Oxford.

SNOW, Thomas Maitland, CMG 1934; *b* 21 May 1890; *s* of Thomas Snow, Cleve, Exeter, and Edith Banbury; *m* 1st, 1927, Phyllis Annette Malcolmson; three *s*; 2nd, 1949, Sylvia, *d* of W. Delmar, Buda-Pest. *Educ:* Winchester; New Coll., Oxford. 1st Secretary, HM Diplomatic Service, 1923; Counsellor, 1930; Minister: to Cuba, 1935-37; to Finland, 1937-40; to Colombia, 1941-44 (Ambassador, 1944-45); to Switzerland, 1946-49. Retired, 1950. *Recreation:* metaphysics. *Address:* 12 Chemin de la Becque, 1814 La Tour-de-Peilz, Switzerland.

See also Thomas Snow.

SNOWDEN, Rt. Rev. John Samuel Philip; *see* Cariboo, Bishop of.

SNOWDON, 1st Earl of, *cr* 1961; **Antony Charles Robert Armstrong-Jones,** GCVO 1969; RDI 1978; FSIAD; Viscount Linley, 1961; an Artistic Adviser to the Sunday Times and Sunday Times Publications Ltd, since 1962; Constable of Caernarvon Castle since 1963; *b* 7 March 1930; *s* of Ronald Owen Lloyd Armstrong-Jones, MBE, QC, DL (*d* 1966), and of Anne, *o d* of Lt-Col Leonard Messel, OBE (later Countess of Rosse); *m* 1st, 1960, HRH The Princess Margaret (marr. diss. 1978); one *s* one *d*; 2nd, 1978, Lucy Lindsay-Hogg, *d* of Donald Davies; one *d*. *Educ:* Eton; Jesus Coll., Cambridge. Joined Staff of Council of Industrial Design, 1961, continuing on a consultative basis, 1962, also an Editorial Adviser of Design Magazine. Designed: Snowdon Aviary, London Zoo, 1965; Chairmobile, 1972. Mem. Council, National Fund for Research for Crippling Diseases; Patron, Circle of Guide Dog Owners; Chm., Working Party on Integrating the Disabled (Report 1976); Pres. for England, Cttee, International Year for Disabled People, 1981. Hon. Fellow: Institute of British Photographers; Royal Photographic Soc.; Manchester College of Art and Design; Hon. Member: North Wales Society of Architects; South Wales Institute of Architects; Royal Welsh Yacht Club; Patron: Welsh Nat. Rowing Club; National Youth Theatre; Metropolitan Union of YMCAs; British Water Ski Federation. President: Contemp. Art Society for Wales; Civic Trust for Wales; British Theatre Museum; Welsh Theatre Company; Greater London Arts Assoc.; Mem. Council, English Stage Co., 1978-. FRSA. *Television films:* Don't Count the Candles, 1968 (2 Hollywood Emmy Awards; St George Prize, Venice; awards at Prague and Barcelona film festivals); Love of a Kind, 1969; Born to be Small, 1971 (Chicago Hugo Award); Happy being Happy, 1973; Mary Kingsley, 1975; Burke and Wills, 1975; Peter, Tina and Steve, 1977; Snowdon on Camera, BBC (presenter), 1981. *Exhibitions:* Photocall, London, 1958; Assignments, Cologne, London, Brussels, USA, 1972, Japan, Canada, Denmark, Holland, 1975, Australia, 1976, France, 1977. *Publications:* London, 1958; Malta (in collaboration), 1958; Private View (in collaboration), 1965; A View of Venice, 1972; Assignments, 1972; Inchcape Review, 1977; (jtly) Pride of the Shires, 1979; Personal View, 1979. *Heir:* s Viscount Linley, *qv*. *Address:* 22 Launceston Place, W8 5RL. *Clubs:* Leander (Henley-on-Thames); Hawks (Cambridge).

See also under Royal Family, and Earl of Rosse.

SNOY ET d'OPPUERS, Baron Jean-Charles, Hon. KBE 1975 (OBE 1948); Grand Officier de l'Ordre de Léopold, Belgium; Grand Officier de l'Ordre de la Couronne, Belgium; Member of Belgian Parliament, 1968-71; Minister of Finance, Belgium, 1968-72; *b* 2 July 1907; *s* of 9th Baron and Claire de Beughem de Houtem; *m* 1935, Nathalie, Countess d'Alcantara; two *s* five *d*. *Educ:* Collège Saint-Pierre, Uccle; University of Louvain; Harvard Univ. Secretary Société Belge de Banque, 1932; Attaché Cabinet Minister of Economic Affairs, 1934; Directeur Ministry Econ. Aff., 1936; Secrétaire Général, Ministère des Affaires Economiques, 1939-60; Président du Conseil

de l'Union Benelux, 1945-60. War Service: Services de Renseignements et d'Action, 1940-44. Chairman, Four Party Supply Cttee, Belgium, 1945; Président du Conseil, Organisation Européenne de Coopération Economique, 1948-50 (OEEC in English); Chm., Steering Board for Trade, OEEC, 1952-61; Chef de la délégation Belge pour la négociation des Traités de Rome, 1957; Président, Comité Intérimaire du Marché Commun et de l'Euratom, 1957-58; Representant Permanant de la Belgique, Communauté Economique Européenne, 1958-59; Administrateur-Délégué de la Compagnie Lambert pour l'Industrie et la Finance, Brussels, 1960-68. Holds several foreign decorations. *Publications:* La Commission des Douanes, 1932; L'Aristocratie de Demain, 1936; La Profession et l'Organisation de la Production, 1942; Revue Générale Belge; La Libre Belgique. *Recreations:* shooting, tennis. *Heir:* s Bernard, Baron Snoy, *b* 27 March 1945. *Address:* Château de Bois-Seigneur-Isaac, 1421 Braine l'Allend, Belgium. *T:* Nivelles 22.22.27. *Club:* Club de la Fondation Universitaire (Brussels).

SNYDER, John Wesley; Director, The Overland Corporation, 500 Security Building, Toledo, Ohio, since 1953 (Chairman Finance Committee and President, 1953-66); *b* 21 June 1895; *s* of Jerre Hartwell Snyder and Ellen Hatcher; *m* 1920, Evlyn Cook (*d* 1956); one *d*. *Educ:* Jonesboro Grade and High Sch.; Vanderbilt Univ. Various offices in Arkansas and Missouri banks, 1920-30; national bank receiver, office of Comptroller of the Currency, Washington, DC, 1930-37; in 1937 selected to head St Louis Loan Agency of RFC; and Exec. VP and Director of Defense Plant Corp., a subsidiary; early in 1943 resigned all Federal posts to become Exec. VP First National Bank of St Louis; Federal Loan Administrator, Washington, 30 April 1945; Dir of Office War Mobilization and Reconversion, July 1945-June 1946; Secretary of the Treasury, United States, 1946-53; US Governor of International Monetary Fund and International Bank for Reconstruction and Development, 1946-53; Advr, US Treasury, 1955-69. Delegate International Financial Conferences: Mexico City, 1945-52; Rio de Janeiro, 1957; London, 1947; Paris, 1950-52; Ottawa, 1951; Rome, 1951; Lisbon, 1952. Served as Captain, Field Artillery, 57th Bde, during War, 1917-18; retired Colonel US Army, 1955. Member: Omicron Delta Kappa; American Legion; Reserve Officers' Association. Trustee, Harry S. Truman Memorial Library. Episcopalian. *Address:* 3110 Seabrook Island Road, Johns Island, SC 29455, USA. *Clubs:* Missouri Athletic (St Louis); Chevy Chase, Alfalfa, National Press (Washington); Toledo (Toledo, Ohio).

SOAME, Sir Charles (John) Buckworth-Herne-, 12th Bt *cr* 1697; *b* 28 May 1932; *s* of Sir Charles Burnett Buckworth-Herne-Soame, 11th Bt, and Elsie May (*d* 1972), *d* of Walter Alfred Lloyd; *S* father, 1977; *m* 1958, Eileen Margaret Mary, *d* of Leonard Minton; one *s*. *Heir:* s Richard John Buckworth-Herne-Soame, *b* 17 Aug. 1970. *Address:* Sheen Cottage, Coalbrookdale, Telford, Salop.

SOAMES, family name of **Baron Soames.**

SOAMES, Baron *cr* 1978 (Life Peer), of Fletching in the County of E Sussex; **Arthur Christopher John Soames,** PC 1958; GCMG 1972; GCVO 1972; CH 1980; CBE 1955; *b* 12 Oct. 1920; *m* 1947, Mary Churchill (*see* Lady Soames); three *s* two *d*. *Educ:* Eton; Royal Military Coll., Sandhurst. 2nd Lieut, Coldstream Guards, 1939; Captain, 1942; served Middle East, Italy and France. Assistant Military Attaché British Embassy, Paris, 1946-47, MP (C) Bedford Division of Bedfordshire, 1950-66. Parliamentary Private Secretary to the Prime Minister, 1952-55; Parliamentary Under-Secretary of State, Air Ministry, Dec. 1955-Jan. 1957; Parliamentary and Financial Secretary, Admiralty, 1957-58; Secretary of State for War, Jan. 1958-July 1960; Minister of Agriculture, Fisheries and Food, 1960-64. Director: Decca Ltd, 1964-68; James Hole & Co. Ltd, 1964-68. Ambassador to France, 1968-72. A Vice-Pres., Commn of the European Communities, 1973-Jan. 1977. Director: N. M. Rothschild & Sons Ltd, 1977-79; Nat. Westminster Bank Ltd, 1978-79. Governor of Southern Rhodesia, 1979-80. Lord President of the Council and Leader of the House of Lords, 1979-81. Pres., RASE, 1973. Hon. LLD St Andrews, 1974; Hon. DCL Oxon, 1981. Croix de Guerre (France), 1942; Grand Officier de la Légion d'honneur, 1972; Grand Cross of St Olav (Norway), 1974. Medal of the City of Paris, 1972. *Address:* House of Lords, SW1A 0PW. *Clubs:* White's, Portland.

SOAMES, Lady; Mary Soames, DBE 1980 (MBE (mil.) 1945); President, National Benevolent Fund for the Aged, since 1978; Member, Winston Churchill Memorial Trust Council, since 1978; Chairman, International Year of the Child Trust, since 1980; *b* 15 Sept. 1922; *y d* of late Rt Hon. Sir Winston Churchill, KG, OM, CH, FRS, and late Baroness Spencer-Churchill, GBE; *m* 1947, Captain Christopher Soames, Coldstream Guards (now Baron Soames, *qv*); three *s* two *d*. *Educ:* privately. Served War: Red Cross and WVS, 1939-41; ATS, 1941-46, with mixed anti-aircraft batteries in UK and Europe (Jun. Comdr). Accompanied father on various journeys; campaigned with husband through six elections whilst he was Conservative MP for Bedford, 1950-66; accompanied husband to Paris where he was Ambassador, 1968-72, and to Brussels where he was first British Vice Pres. of Eur. Commn, 1973-76; accompanied husband when he was appointed last British Governor of Southern Rhodesia, Dec. 1979-April 1980. Associated with Church Army, 1945-77, esp. in connection with scheme for housing old people (Churchill Houses) and with their work for delinquent girls; Chm., UK Assoc. for Internat. Year of the Child, 1979; Mem. Council, Winston Churchill Meml Trust, 1978-. Governor, Harrow Sch., 1980-. JP E Sussex, 1960-74. *Publications:* Clementine Churchill by Her Daughter Mary Soames, 1979 (a

Wolfson Prize for History, and Yorkshire Post Prize for Best First Work, 1979); A Churchill Family Album—A Personal Anthology Selected by Mary Soames, 1982. *Recreations:* reading, sight-seeing, gardening.

SOANE, Leslie James, CEng, MICE, FCIT; General Manager, Scottish Region, British Rail, since 1977; *b* 15 Jan. 1926; *s* of Arthur Edward Soane and Florence May Herring; *m* 1950, Joan Edith Mayo; one *s* one *d. Educ:* Watford Central Sch.; London Univ. Civil Engineer posts: London Midland Region, 1948-55; Eastern Region, 1955-62; LMR, 1962-71; Chief Civil Engr, Western Region, 1971-75; Dep. Gen. Manager, WR, 1975-77. FBIM. *Recreations:* theatre, reading, golf. *Address:* Millers Shaw, Milton Brae, Dumbarton, Scotland G82 2SG. *T:* Dumbarton 61409.

SOBELL, Sir Michael, Kt 1972; Chairman: GEC (Radio & Television) Ltd; Radio & Allied (Holdings) Ltd; President, National Society for Cancer Relief; *b* 1 Nov. 1892; *s* of Lewis and Esther Sobell; *m* 1917, Anne Rakusen; two *d. Educ:* Central London Foundation Sch. Freeman and Liveryman, Carmen Co. Hon. FRCPath, 1981; Hon. Fellow: Bar Ilan Univ.; Jews' Coll.; Hon. Dr Science and Technol., Technion Inst., Haifa, 1980. *Recreations:* racing, charitable work. *Address:* Bakeham House, Englefield Green, Surrey. *Clubs:* Royal Automobile, City Livery; Jockey (Newmarket).
See also Baron Weinstock.

SOBERS, Sir Garfield (St Auburn), (Sir Garry Sobers); Kt 1975; cricketer; *b* Bridgetown, Barbados, 28 July 1936; *m* 1969, Prudence Kirby; two *s* one *d. Educ:* Bay Street Sch., Barbados. First major match, 1953, for Barbados; played in 93 Test Matches for West Indies, 39 as Captain, 1953-74 (made world record Test Match score, Kingston, 1958); captained West Indies and Barbados teams, 1965-74; Captain of Nottinghamshire CCC, 1968-74. On retirement from Test cricket held the following world records in Test Matches: 365 not out; 26 centuries; 235 wickets; 110 catches. *Publications:* Cricket Advance, 1965; Cricket Crusader, 1966; King Cricket, 1967; (with J. S. Barker) Cricket in the Sun, 1967; Bonaventure and the Flashing Blade, 1967; *relevant publication:* Sir Gary: a biography by Trevor Bailey, 1976. *Address:* Melbourne, Victoria, Australia.

SOBHI, Mohamed Ibrahim; Order of Merit, 1st Class, Egypt, 1974; Director General, International Bureau of Universal Postal Union, Berne, since 1975; *b* Alexandria, 28 March 1925; *s* of Gen. Ibrahim Sobhi and Mrs Zenab Afifi; *m* 1950, Laila Ahmed Sobhi; two *s* one *d. Educ:* Cairo Univ. (BE 1949). Construction of roads and airports, Engr Corps, 1950; Technical Sec., Communications Commn, Permanent Council for Develt and National Prodn, Cairo, 1954; Fellow, Vanderbilt Univ., Nashville, Tenn (studying transport and communications services in USA), 1955-56; Tech. Dir, Office of Minister of Communications for Posts, Railways and Coordination between means of transp. and communications, Cairo, 1956-61; Dir-Gen., Sea Transp. Authority (remaining Mem. Tech. Cttees, Postal Org.), 1961-64; Under Sec. of State for Communications and Mem. Bd, Postal Org., Cairo, 1964-68; Chm. Bd, Postal Org., and Sec.-Gen., African Postal Union, Cairo, 1968-74. Universal Postal Union: attended Congress, Ottawa, 1957; attended Cons. Council for Postal Studies session, Brussels, 1958; Head of Egyptian Delegn, Tokyo and Lausanne Congresses, and sessions of CCPS (set up by Tokyo Congress), 1969-74; Dir, Exec. Bureau i/c Egyptian projects in Africa, incl. construction of Hôtel de l'Amitié, Bamako, Mali, and roads, Cairo, 1963-74; as Director-General of UPU, acts as Sec.-Gen. of the Congress, Exec. Council, and Cons. Council for Postal Studies; acts as intermediary between UPU and Restricted Unions, UN and internat. orgns; visits member countries and attends many meetings and congresses, inc. those of Restricted Unions, in all continents. Heinrich von Stephan Medal (Germany), 1979; Order of Postal Merit (Gran Placa) (Spain), 1979. *Recreations:* croquet, philately, music. *Address:* Bureau international de l'Union postale universelle, Weltpoststrasse 4, CH-3000 Berne 15, Switzerland. *T:* Berne 43 22 11.

SODDY, Dr Kenneth; Consulting Physician, University College Hospital, London, 1976 (Physician in charge, Children's and Adolescents' Psychiatric Department and Lecturer in Child Psychiatry, 1948-76); Hon. Lecturer in Child Development, University College, London, 1951-76; Hon. Consultant in Child Psychiatry, Royal Free Hospital, 1973-76; *b* 27 July 1911; *s* of Rev. T. E. Soddy, BA; *m* 1936, Emmeline (*d* 1972), *d* of H. E. Johnson; one *s* two *d*; *m* 1972, Mary, *d* of Canon N. S. Kidson, MC, MA. *Educ:* Taunton Sch.; University College, London; University College Hospital Medical School. MB, BS 1934; DPM 1937; MD 1938; FRCPsych (Foundn Fellow). Commonwealth Fund Fellowship in Child Guidance, 1938; Psychiatrist, London Child Guidance Clinic, 1939. Temp. Commn, RAMC, 1940; Specialist Psychiatrist (Major), 1941; Advisor in Psychiatry (Lieut-Colonel), AG's Dept, India Comd, 1943; Dep. Director, Selection of Personnel, India Comd, (Colonel), 1944; Hon. Lieut-Colonel, RAMC, 1946. Medical Director, National Assoc. for Mental Health, 1946; Psychiatrist, Tavistock Clinic, 1947; Psychiatrist, 1948, Med. Dir, 1953-58, Child Guidance Training Centre. Scientific Adviser, World Federation for Mental Health, 1961-64 (Hon. Secretary, 1948; Assistant Director, 1949; Scientific Director, 1958); Member, Expert Panel on Mental Health, World Health Organisation, 1949-77; Mem., St Lawrence's Hosp., Caterham, Management Cttee, 1962-74; Consultant: to WHO, 1950 and 1957; to UKAEA, 1964-74; to Nat. Suicides Soc., 1965-77; Pres., Inst. of Religion and Medicine, 1975-76 (Chm., 1964-71; Pro-Chm., 1971-74). Mem., Marriage Commn of Gen. Synod of C of E, 1975-78. Organist, St Michael's Church, Chagford. Member various Study Groups, etc; Hon. Mem. American Psychiatric Assoc., 1953-. Fellow, UCL,

1979. *Publications:* Clinical Child Psychiatry, 1960; (with R. F. Tredgold) Mental Retardation, 11th edn, 1970; (with Mary C. Kidson) Men in Middle Life, 1967; Editor: Mental Health and Infant Development, 2 vols, 1955; Identity; Mental Health and Value Systems, 1961; (with R. H. Ahrenfeldt) Mental Health in a Changing World, 1965; Mental Health and Contemporary Thought, 1967; Mental Health in the Service of the Community, 1967; many articles in British, American and internat. medical and sociological jls. *Recreations:* organ playing, moor walking. *Address:* The Manor Cottage, Doccombe, Moretonhampstead, Devon TQ13 8SS. *T:* Moretonhampstead 378.

SODOR AND MAN, Bishop of, 1974-31 May 1983; **Rt. Rev. Vernon Sampson Nicholls,** JP; *b* 3 Sept. 1917; *s* of Ernest C. Nicholls, Truro, Cornwall; *m* 1943, Phyllis, *d* of Edwin Potter, Stratford-on-Avon; one *s* one *d. Educ:* Truro Sch.; Univ. of Durham and Clifton Theological Coll., Bristol. Curate: St Oswald, Bedminster Down, Bristol, 1941-42; Liskeard, Cornwall, 1942-43. CF, 1944-46 (Hon. CF 1946). Vicar of Meopham, 1946-56; Rural Dean of Cobham, 1953-56; Vicar and Rural Dean of Walsall, and Chaplain to Walsall Gen. Hosp., 1956-67; Preb of Curborough, Lichfield Cath., 1964-67; Archdeacon of Birmingham, 1967-74; Diocesan Planning Officer and Co-ordinating Officer for Christian Stewardship, 1967-74. Dean of St German's Cathedral, Peel, 1974-. MLC, Tynwald, IoM; Member: IoM Bd of Educn; IoM Health Services Bd. JP, IoM. *Recreations:* meeting people, gardening, motoring. *Address:* (to May 1983) The Bishop's House, Quarterbridge Road, Douglas, Isle of Man. *T:* Douglas 22108; (from June 1983) 4 Winston Close, Hathaway Park, Shottery, Stratford-upon-Avon, Warwickshire CV37 9ER. *T:* Stratford-upon-Avon 294478.

SOFER, Mrs Anne Hallowell; Member (SDP), GLC/ILEA for St Pancras North, since Oct. 1981 (by-election) (Labour, 1977-81); Director, Channel Four Television Co. Ltd, since 1981; *b* 19 April 1937; *d* of Geoffrey Crowther (later Baron Crowther) and Margaret Worth; *m* 1958, Jonathan Sofer; two *s* one *d. Educ:* St Paul's Sch.; Swarthmore Coll., USA; Somerville Coll., Oxford (MA); DipEd London. Secretary, National Assoc. of Governors and Managers, 1972-75; Additional Member, ILEA Education Cttee, 1974-77; Chairman, ILEA Schools Sub-Cttee, 1978-81. *Publication:* (with Tyrrell Burgess) The School Governors and Managers Handbook and Training Guide, 1978. *Address:* 46 Regent's Park Road, NW1 7SX. *T:* 01-722 8970.

SOLANKI, Ramniklal Chhaganlal; Editor, Garavi Gujarat, London, since 1968; Correspondant, Janmabhoomi Group, Bombay, since 1968; *b* 12 July 1931; *s* of Chhaganlal Kalidas and Mrs Ichchhaben Solanki, Surat, Gujarat, India; *m* 1955, Mrs Parvatiben, *d* of Makanji Dullabhji Chavda, Nani Pethan, India; two *s* two *d. Educ:* Irish Presbyterian Mission Sch., Surat (Matriculation Gold Medal, 1949); MTB Coll., Gujarat Univ. (BA(Econ)); Sarvajanik Law Coll., Surat, Gujarat (LLB). Pres., Rander Student Union, 1950-54; Sec., Surat Dist Students' Assoc., 1954-55. Sub-Editor, Nutan Bharat and Lok Vani, Surat, 1954-56; freelance columnist for several newspapers, while serving State Govt in India, 1956-63; London correspondent, Gujarat Mitra Surat, 1964-68; European Correspondent, Janmabhoomi Gp of Newspapers, 1968-; Man. Dir, Garavi Gujarat Publications Ltd and Garavi Gujarat Property Ltd. Member: Guild of British Newspaper Editors, 1976-; Asian Adv. Cttee, BBC, 1976-80; Nat. Centre for Ind. Language Trng Steering Gp, 1976-; Exec. Cttee, Gujarati Arya Kshtriya Maha Sabha UK, 1979-; Exec. Cttee, Gujarati Arya Assoc. (Vice-Pres., 1980-81); CPU, 1964-; Parly Press Gallery, House of Commons; Sec., Indian Journalists Assoc. of Europe, 1978-79. Best Reporter of the Year in Gujarati, 1970. *Publications:* contrib. many articles. *Recreations:* reading, writing. *Address:* 74 Harrowdene Road, N Wembley, Mddx. *T:* 01-902 2879; *office:* Garavi Gujarat House, 1/2 Silex Street, SE1 0DW. *T:* 01-261 1527; *Telex:* 8955335 Gujrat G.

SOLDATOV, Aleksandr Alekseyevich; Rector, Moscow State Institute of International Relations, since 1970; *b* 27 Aug. 1915; *m* Rufina B.; two *d. Educ:* Moscow Teachers' Training Inst. (grad. Hist. Sciences, 1939). Member Soviet Foreign Service, 1941; Senior Counsellor of Soviet Delegation to the UN and Representative on Trusteeship Council, 1948-53; Head of UN Div., 1953-54, of American Div., 1954-60, Soviet Foreign Ministry; Soviet Ambassador to the Court of St James's, 1960-66; Deputy Foreign Minister, 1966-68; Ambassador in Cuba, 1968-70. Member Soviet Delegation to Geneva Conferences: on Germany, 1959; on Laos, 1961. Mem., CPSU Central Auditing Commn, 1966-71. *Address:* Moscow State Institute of International Relations, Ulitsa Metrostroevskaya 53, Moscow, USSR.

SOLER, Antonio R.; *see* Ruiz Soler, A.

SOLESBY, Tessa Audrey Hilda; HM Diplomatic Service; Head of Central African Department, Foreign and Commonwealth Office, since 1982; *b* 1932; *d* of Charles Solesby and Hilda Solesby (*née* Willis). *Educ:* Clifton High School; St Hugh's College, Oxford. MA. Min. of Labour and Nat. Service, 1954-55; joined Diplomatic Service, 1956; FO, 1956; Manila, 1957-59; Lisbon, 1959-62; FO, 1962-64; First Sec., UK Mission to UN, Geneva, 1964-68; FO, 1968-70; First Sec., UK Mission to UN, NY, 1970-72; FCO, 1972-75, Counsellor, 1975; on secondment to NATO Internat. Staff, Brussels, 1975-78; Counsellor, East Berlin, 1978-81; temp. Minister, UK Mission to UN, NY, 1981-82. *Recreations:* hill-walking, music. *Address:* c/o Foreign and Commonwealth Office, SW1A 2AH.

SOLEY, Clive Stafford; MP (Lab) Hammersmith North, since 1979; *b* 7 May 1939. *Educ:* Downshall Sec. Modern School; Newbattle Abbey Coll.; Strathclyde Univ. (BA Hons); Southampton Univ. (Dip. in Applied Social Studies). Various appointments; Probation Officer, 1970-75; Senior Probation Officer, 1975-79. *Address:* House of Commons, SW1.

SOLLBERGER, Edmond, FBA 1973; Keeper of Western Asiatic Antiquities, The British Museum, since 1974 (Deputy Keeper, 1970-74); *b* 12 Oct. 1920; *s* of W. Sollberger and M.-A. Calavassy; *m* 1949, Ariane Zender; two *d. Educ:* Univ. of Geneva, LicLitt 1945; DLitt 1952. Asst Keeper of Archæology, Musée d'art et d'histoire, Geneva, 1949; Keeper, 1952; Principal Keeper, 1958; Actg-Dir, 1959; Privat-Docent for Sumerian and Akkadian, Faculty of Letters, Univ. of Geneva, 1956-61; Asst Keeper of Western Asiatic Antiquities, The British Museum, 1961. Member: Council and Exec. Cttee, British Sch. of Archæology in Iraq, 1961; Council of Management, British Inst. of Archæology at Ankara, 1961-70, 1976-; British Sch. of Archæology, Jerusalem, 1974; Governing Body, SOAS, 1975-80; Governing Council, British Inst. of Persian Studies, 1977. Corresp. Mem., German Archæological Inst., 1961. Hon. Mem., American Oriental Soc., 1977. Mem., Internat. Cttee for study of the texts from Ebla, Rome Univ., 1978-. *Publications:* Le Système verbal dans les inscriptions royales présargoniques de Lagash, 1952 (Geneva); Corpus des inscriptions royales présargoniques de Lagash, 1956 (Geneva); Ur Excavations Texts VIII: Royal Inscriptions, 1965 (London); The Business and Administrative Correspondence under the Kings of Ur, 1966 (New York); (with J. R. Kupper) Inscriptions royales sumériennes et akkadiennes, 1971 (Paris); Pre-Sargonic and Sargonic Economic Texts, 1972 (London); The Pinches Manuscript, 1978 (Rome); numerous articles on Cuneiform and related studies in learned jls; jt editor: Littératures anciennes du Proche Orient, 1963- (Paris); Texts from Cuneiform Sources, 1965- (New York); Cambridge Ancient History, vols I-III (rev. edn), 1969-; editor-in-chief, Royal Inscriptions of Mesopotamia, Toronto Univ., 1981-. *Address:* 26 Kingfisher Drive, Ham, Richmond, Surrey. *T:* 01-940 4465.

SOLOMON, CBE 1946; pianist; *b* London, 9 Aug. 1902; *m* 1970, Gwendoline Byrne. First public appearance at Queen's Hall at age of eight, June 1910; frequent appearances till 1916 then studied in London and Paris; reappeared in London at Wigmore Hall, Oct. 1921, and has since toured in the British Isles, America, France, Germany, Holland, Italy, Australia, and New Zealand. Hon. LLD St Andrews; Hon. MusD Cantab. *Recreations:* golf, bridge, motoring. *Address:* 16 Blenheim Road, NW8.

SOLOMON, (Alan) Peter; His Honour Judge Solomon; a Circuit Judge, since 1973; *b* 6 July 1923; *s* of late Jacob Ovid Solomon, Manchester; *m* 1st, 1954, Deirdre Anne Punter (marr. diss. 1969); one *d* ; 2nd, 1973, Gloria Sophia Turower (marr. diss. 1979); one *d* ; 3rd, 1981, Susan Jennifer Hunter. *Educ:* Mill Hill Sch.; Lincoln College, Oxford; MA. Served War 1942-46, Fleet Air Arm, Petty Officer Airman. Called to Bar, Inner Temple, 1949; practised South-Eastern circuit. *Publications:* poetry: The Lunatic, Balance, in Keats Prize Poems, 1973. *Recreations:* the turf, travel, poetry, burgundy. *Address:* The Crown Court, Middlesex Guildhall, Parliament Square, Westminster, SW1. *Club:* Garrick.

SOLOMON, Sir David (Arnold), Kt 1973; MBE 1944; *b* 13 Nov. 1907; *s* of Richard Solomon and Sarah Annie Solomon (*née* Simpson); *m* 1935, Marjorie Miles; two *s* one *d. Educ:* Leys Sch., Cambridge; Liverpool Univ. Qualified a Solicitor, 1933; became Mem. Liverpool Stock Exchange, 1935. Served War of 1939-45, RAF (MBE). Practised as a Stockbroker until retirement, March 1969. Chairman: Liverpool RHB, 1968-73; Community Health Council, SE Cumbria, 1973-76. *Recreation:* music. *Address:* Tithe Barn, Cartmel, Grange over Sands, Cumbria LA11 6PP. *T:* Cartmel 558.

SOLOMON, Edwin, CBE 1972; QPM 1967; DL; Chief Constable, West Midlands Constabulary, 1967-74; *b* 20 Sept. 1914; *s* of Richard and Jane Solomon, Co. Durham; *m* 1942, Susan Clarke; two *s. Educ:* The Grammar Sch., Chester-le-Street. Joined Metropolitan Police as Constable, 1934; served through ranks to Supt; Dep. Chief Constable, Newcastle upon Tyne, 1956; Chief Constable, Walsall County Borough, 1964. DL Staffs, 1969. *Recreations:* walking, fishing, gardening. *Address:* Catalan Cottage, Gibraltar Lane, Dunsley Road, Kinver, near Stourbridge, West Midlands. *T:* Kinver 2047.

SOLOMON, Jonathan Hilali Moïse; Under-Secretary, Posts and Telecommunications Division, Department of Industry, since 1980; *b* 3 March 1939; *s* of Samuel and Moselle Solomon; *m* 1966, Hester McFarland; one *s. Educ:* Clifton College; King's College, Cambridge. BA Hons, MA. Research worker, Supervisor and Tutor, Cambridge and London Univs, 1960-63, 1965. Entered Home Civil Service, 1963; Asst Private Sec. to Pres. of Board of Trade, 1966-67; Principal, Companies Div., BoT, transferred to DTI, 1970; to Treasury, 1972; Asst Sec., Dept of Prices and Consumer Protection, 1974; returned to Dept of Industry, Electronics Divs, 1977-80. *Publications:* contribs to journals such as Platon, Contemporary Review, New Outlook, Frontier. *Recreations:* sport, futurology, writing. *Address:* 53 Hollycroft Avenue, NW3. *T:* 01-794 6230. *Club:* English-Speaking Union.

SOLOMON, Dr Patrick Vincent Joseph; High Commissioner for Trinidad and Tobago in London, 1971-76, concurrently Ambassador for Trinidad and Tobago to Switzerland, France, Germany, Austria, Luxembourg, Denmark, Norway, Sweden, Italy, Netherlands and Finland; President of Assembly,

IMCO, 1976-77; *b* 12 April 1910; *s* of late Charles William Solomon and late Euphemia Alexia (*née* Payne); *m* ; two *s* ; *m* 1974, Mrs Leslie Richardson, widow of late William A. Richardson, Trinidad and Tobago. *Educ:* Tranquility Boys' Sch.; St Mary's Coll., Trinidad; Island Science Scholar, 1928; studied Medicine at Belfast and Edinburgh Univs, graduating in 1934. Practised medicine in Scotland, Ireland and Wales, to 1939; Leeward Island Medical Service, 1939-42; practised medicine in Trinidad, 1943-. Entered Politics, 1944. Elected: MLC, 1946-50 and 1956; MP (MHR) 1961; Minister of: Education, 1956-60; Home Affairs, 1960-64; External Affairs, 1964-66; Dep. Prime Minister, 1962-66; Dep. Political Leader of People's Nat. Movement, 1956-66; Permanent Rep. of Trinidad and Tobago to the United Nations, NY, 1966-71; Vice-Pres., UN General Assembly, 21st Session, 1966; Chm., UN Fourth Cttee, 23rd Session, 1968; Trinidad and Tobago Rep., Special Cttee on Apartheid, 1966-71, and Special Cttee of 24 on question of Decolonization; Mem. Preparatory Cttees concerning: celebration of Tenth Anniversary of Declaration on granting of Independence to Colonial Countries and Peoples (Resolution 1514, xv), 1968 and 1969; Commemoration of 25th Anniversary of United Nations. Is a Roman Catholic. *Recreations:* bridge, fishing. *Address:* c/o Ministry of External Affairs, Knowsley, Queen's Park West, Port of Spain, Trinidad.

SOLOMON, Peter; *see* Solomon, A. P.

SOLOMONS, Anthony Nathan, FCA; Chairman since 1976, and Chief Executive since 1973, Singer & Friedlander Ltd; Director, European Ferries Ltd, since 1980; *b* 26 Jan. 1930; *s* of Leslie Emanuel Solomons and Susie Schneiders; *m* 1957, Jean Golding; two *d. Educ:* Qual. as chartered accountant, 1953; FCA 1963. National Service, 1953-54: commnd Dorset Regt. Accountant, Kennedy & Fox Oldfield & Co., 1955; Asst Accountant, then Chief Accountant, Lobitos Oilfields Ltd, 1955-58; Singer & Friedlander Ltd, 1958-: successively Exec. Dir, Man. Dir, and Jt Chief Exec. *Address:* 20 Cannon Street, EC4M 6XE. *T:* 01-248 9646.

SOLOMONS, Prof. David; Professor of Accounting in the University of Pennsylvania (Wharton School), USA, since 1959, Chairman of Accounting Department, 1969-75, designated Arthur Young Professor, 1974; *b* London, 11 Oct. 1912; *e s* of Louis Solomons and Hannah Solomons (*née* Isaacs); *m* 1945, Kate Miriam (*née* Goldschmidt); one *s* one *d. Educ:* Hackney Downs Sch., London, E8; London School of Economics. BCom (London) 1932; DSc (Econ.) (London), 1966. Chartered accountant, 1936; engaged in professional accountancy until Sept. 1939. Enlisted in ranks on outbreak of war; 2nd Lieut, RASC, 1941; Temp. Captain, 1942; Petrol Supply Officer, HQ 88 Area (Tobruk), 1942; prisoner-of-war in Italy and Germany, 1942-45. Lectr in Accounting, LSE, 1946; Reader in Accounting, Univ. of London, 1948-55; Prof. of Accounting, University of Bristol, 1955-59. Visiting Assoc. Prof., University of California, 1954; Prof. at Institut pour l'Etude des Méthodes de Direction de l'Entreprise (IMEDE), Lausanne, 1963-64; Director of Research, Amer. Accounting Assoc., 1968-70, Pres., 1977-78; Vis. Erskine Fellow, Univ. of Canterbury, NZ, 1976. Mem., AICPA Study on Establishment of Accounting Principles, 1971-72; directed (UK) Adv. Bd of Accountancy Educn Long-range Enquiry into Educn and Trg for Accountancy Profession, 1972-74. AICPA Award for Notable Contribution to Accounting Literature, 1969; Jl of Accountancy Literary Award, 1979; AAA Outstanding Accounting Educator Award, 1980. *Publications:* Divisional Performance: Measurement and Control, 1965; ed and contrib. to Studies in Cost Analysis, 1968; Prospectus for a Profession, 1974; articles in Economic Jl, Economica, Jl of Business, Accounting Review, Accountancy, etc. *Address:* 205 Elm Avenue, Swarthmore, Pa 19081, USA. *T:* 215-544-8193.

SOLTI, Sir Georg, KBE 1971 (CBE (Hon.) 1968); Music Director, Chicago Symphony Orchestra, since 1969; Principal Conductor and Artistic Director, London Philharmonic Orchestra, 1979-Sept. 1983, then Conductor Emeritus; *b* Budapest, 21 Oct. 1912; adopted British nationality, 1972; *m* 1st, 1946, Hedwig Oeschli; 2nd, 1967, Anne Valerie Pitts; two *d. Educ:* High School of Music, Budapest. Studied with Kodály, Bartók, and Dobnányi. Conductor and pianist, State Opera, Budapest, 1930-39; first prize, as pianist, Concours Internationale, Geneva, 1942; Musical Director, Munich State Opera, 1946-52; Musical Director, Frankfurt Opera, and Permanent Conductor, Museums Concerts, Frankfurt, 1952-61; Musical Director: Covent Garden Opera Co., 1961-71; Orchestre de Paris, 1971-75. Guest Conductor: Berlin, Salzburg, Vienna, Munich, Paris, London (first conducted London Philharmonic Orchestra, 1947; Covent Garden début, 1959), Glyndebourne Festival, Edinburgh Festival, San Francisco, New York, Los Angeles, Chicago, etc. Has made numerous recordings (many of which have received international awards or prizes, incl. Grand Prix Mondiale du Disque (8 times), and 18 Grammy Awards, Nat. Acad. of Recorded Arts and Scis). Hon. FRCM, 1980. Hon. DMus: Leeds, 1971; Oxon, 1972; Yale Univ., 1974; Harvard, 1979. *Address:* Chalet Haut Pré, Villars s. Ollon, Switzerland. *Club:* Athenæum.

SOLZHENITSYN, Alexander Isayevitch; author; Hon. Fellow, Hoover Institution on War, Revolution and Peace, 1975; *b* 11 Dec. 1918; *m* ; three *s. Educ:* Univ. of Rostov (degree in maths and physics); Moscow Inst. of History, Philosophy and Literature (correspondence course). Joined Army, 1941; grad. from Artillery School, 1942; in comd artillery battery and served at front until 1945 (twice decorated); sentenced to eight years' imprisonment, 1945, released, 1953; exile in Siberia, 1953-56; officially rehabilitated, 1957; taught and wrote in Ryazan and Moscow; expelled from Soviet Union, 1974. Member Union of Soviet writers, 1962, expelled 1969; Member Amer. Acad.

of Arts and Sciences, 1969. Awarded Nobel Prize for Literature, 1970. *Publications:* One Day in the Life of Ivan Denisovich, 1962, new edn 1970, filmed 1971; An Incident at Krechetovka Station, and Matryona's House (publ. US as We Never Make Mistakes, 1969), 1963; For the Good of the Cause, 1964; The First Circle, 1968; Cancer Ward, part 1, 1968, part 2, 1969 (Prix du Meilleur Livre Etranger, Paris); The Love Girl and the Innocent, 1969; Stories and Prose Poems, 1970; August 1914, 1972; One Word of Truth: the Nobel speech on literature, 1972; The Gulag Archipelago: an experiment in literary investigation, vol. 1, 1973, vol. 2, 1974, vol. 3, 1976; The Oak and the Calf, (autobiog.), 1975; Lenin in Zurich, 1975; Prussian Nights (poem), 1977. *Address:* c/o Harper & Row Inc., 10 East 53rd Street, New York, NY 10022, USA.

SOMARE, Rt. Hon. Michael Thomas, CH 1978; PC 1977; MP; first Prime Minister of Papua New Guinea, 1975–80, and again since 1982; *b* 9 April 1936; *m* 1965, Veronica Somare; three *s* two *d. Educ:* Sogeri Secondary Sch.; Admin. Coll. Teaching, 1956–62; Asst Area Educn Officer, Madang, 1962–63; Broadcasts Officer, Dept of Information and Extension Services, Wewack, 1963–66; Journalism, 1966–68. Member for E Sepik Region (Nat. Parl.) House of Assembly, 1968–; Parly Leader, Pangu Pati, 1968–; First Chief Minister, 1972–75; Leader of Opposition in House of Assembly, 1980–82. Dep. Chm., Exec. Council, 1972–73, Chm., 1973-75. Mem., Second Select Cttee on Constitutional Develt, 1968–72; Mem. Adv. Cttee, Australian Broadcasting Commission. *Address:* House of Assembly, Port Moresby, Papua New Guinea; (home) Karan, Murik Lakes, East Sepik, Papua New Guinea.

SOMERFIELD, Stafford William; editorial consultant, since 1970; *b* 9 Jan. 1911; *m* 1st, 1933, Gertrude Camfield (marr. diss. 1951); two *d* ; 2nd, 1951, Elizabeth Montgomery (*d* 1977); 3rd, 1977, Ferelith Hamilton. *Educ:* Ashleigh Road School, Barnstaple. Exeter Express and Echo, Bristol Evening World, Daily Telegraph, 1934–39; News Chronicle, 1939, until outbreak of War. Rifleman, Queen's Westminsters, 1939–40; Major, Gloucestershire Regt. 1945. News of the World: Features Editor, Asst Editor, Northern Editor, Dep. Editor; Editor, 1960–70; Chm., Dog World, 1982; Dir, Scanset, 1979. *Publications:* John George Haigh, 1950; Banner Headlines, 1979. *Recreation:* pedigree dogs. *Address:* Straw Paddock, 1 High Street, Cricklade, Wilts. *T:* Swindon 750246. *Clubs:* Kennel, Press.

SOMERLEYTON, 3rd Baron *cr* 1916; **Savile William Francis Crossley;** Bt 1863; DL; farmer; a Lord in Waiting to the Queen, since 1978; *b* 17 Sept. 1928; *er s* of 2nd Baron Somerleyton, MC; *S* father, 1959; *m* 1963, Belinda Maris Loyd, *d* of late Vivian Loyd and of Mrs Gerald Critchley; one *s* four *d. Educ:* Eton Coll. Captain Coldstream Guards, 1948; retired, 1956. Royal Agricultural Coll., Cirencester, 1958-59; farming, 1959–. DL Suffolk, 1964. *Heir: s* Hon. Hugh Francis Savile Crossley, *b* 27 Sept. 1971. *Address:* Somerleyton Hall, Lowestoft, Suffolk. *T:* Lowestoft 730308. *Clubs:* Turf, White's.

SOMERS, 8th Baron *cr* 1784; **John Patrick Somers Cocks;** Bt 1772; *b* 30 April 1907; *o s* of 7th Baron and Mary Benita (*d* 1950), *d* of late Major Luther M. Sabin, United States Army; *S* father, 1953; *m* 1st, 1935, Barbara Marianne (*d* 1959), *d* of Charles Henry Southall, Norwich; 2nd, 1961, Dora Helen, *d* of late John Mountfort. *Educ:* privately; Royal College of Music, London. 2nd Music Master, Westonbirt School, 1935-38; Director of Music, Epsom Coll., 1949-53; Prof. of Composition and Theory, RCM, 1967-77. BMus, ARCM. *Heir: cousin* Philip Sebastian Somers-Cocks, *b* 4 Jan. 1948. *Address:* 35 Links Road, Epsom, Surrey.

SOMERS, Rt Hon. Edward Jonathan, PC 1981; **Rt. Hon. Mr Justice Somers;** Judge of the Court of Appeal, New Zealand, since 1981; *b* 9 Sept. 1928; *s* of Ewart Somers and Muriel Ann Crossley; 1923, Mollie Louise Morison; one *s* two *d. Educ:* Christ's Coll., Christchurch; Canterbury University Coll., Christchurch, NZ (BA, LLB). Practised as barrister and solicitor, 1952-71; practised as barrister, 1971; QC (NZ) 1973; Judge of Supreme Court of New Zealand, 1974. *Recreation:* gardening. *Address:* Waverley, Kaiapoi, RD2, New Zealand. *T:* Kaiapoi 7094. *Club:* Christchurch (New Zealand).

SOMERSCALES, Thomas Lawrence, CBE 1970; General Secretary, Joint Committee of the Order of St John of Jerusalem and the British Red Cross Society, 1960-78; *b* 1 July 1913; *s* of Wilfred Somerscales; *m* 1941, Ann Teresa, *d* of Robert Victor Kearney; three *s* one *d. Educ:* Riley High Sch., Hull. FCA 1939. KStJ 1978. Finance Sec., Jt Cttee, OStJ and BRCS, 1953-60. Mem., Adv. Council, ITA, 1964-67. *Address:* 17 Hamilton Way, Finchley, N3.

SOMERSET, family name of **Duke of Beaufort** and of **Baron Raglan.**

SOMERSET, 18th Duke of *cr* 1546; **Percy Hamilton Seymour;** Bt 1611; DL; Major, Wilts Regt, retired; *b* 27 Sept. 1910; *e* surv. *s* of 17th Duke of Somerset, DSO, OBE, and Edith Mary (*d* 1962), *d* of W. Parker, JP, Whittington Hall, Derbyshire; *S* father, 1954; *m* 1951, Gwendoline Collette (Jane), 2nd *d* of late Major J. C. C. Thomas and Mrs Thomas; two *s* one *d. Educ:* Blundell's Sch., Tiverton; Clare Coll., Cambridge. BA 1933. DL Wiltshire, 1960. *Heir: s* Lord Seymour, *qv. Address:* Maiden Bradley, Warminster, Wilts. *Clubs:* MCC, Surrey CC, British Automobile Racing.

SOMERSET, David Henry Fitzroy, FIB; Chief of the Banking Department and Chief Cashier of the Bank of England, since 1980; Chairman, EBS Investments, since 1977; Director, Securities Management Trust, since 1980; *b* 19 June 1930; *s* of Brig. Hon. Nigel Somerset, *qv* ; *m* 1955, Ruth Ivy, *d* of late W. R. Wildbur; one *s* one *d. Educ:* Wellington Coll.; Peterhouse, Cambridge (MA). CBIM. Entered Bank of England, 1952; Personal Asst to Managing Director, International Monetary Fund, Washington DC, 1959-62; Private Secretary to Governor of Bank of England, 1962-63; Asst Chief Cashier, 1968-69; Asst Chief of Establishments, 1969-73; Dep. Chief Cashier, 1973-80. Mem. Court of Governors, City of London Polytechnic, 1980-. *Recreations:* gardening, tennis, shooting. *Address:* Bank of England, Threadneedle Street, EC2R 8AH. *T:* 01-601 4444.

SOMERSET, David Robert; Chairman, Marlborough Fine Art Ltd, since 1977; *b* 23 Feb. 1928; *s* of late Captain Henry Robert Somers Fitzroy de Vere Somerset, DSO, and late Bettine Violet Somerset (*née* Malcolm); *m* 1950, Lady Caroline Jane Thynne, *d* of Marquess of Bath, *qv* ; three *s* one *d. Educ:* Eton. Formerly Lieutenant, Coldstream Guards. *Address:* 90 Eaton Terrace, SW1; The Cottage, Badminton, Glos.

SOMERSET, Sir Henry Beaufort, Kt 1966; CBE 1961; *b* 21 May 1906; *s* of Henry St John Somerset; *m* 1930, Patricia Agnes Strickland; two *d. Educ:* St Peter's Coll., Adelaide; Trinity Coll., University of Melbourne; MSc 1928. Former Chairman: Humes Ltd; Goliath Cement Hldgs Ltd; Director: Associated Pulp & Paper Mills Ltd, 1937-81 (Man. Dir, 1948-70; Dep. Chm., 1970-81); Electrolytic Zinc Co. of Australasia Ltd, 1953-78; Perpetual Exors Trustees Ltd, 1971-81 (Chm., 1973-81); Tioxide Australia Pty Ltd; Central Norseman Gold Corp. Ltd. Chancellor, University of Tasmania, 1964-72; Member: Council, Australasian Inst. of Mining and Metallurgy, 1956- (President, 1958 and 1966); Exec., CSIRO, 1965-74; Council, Nat. Museum of Victoria, 1968-77; Pres., Australian Mineral Found, 1972-. FRACI; FTS. Hon. DSc Tasmania, 1973. *Address:* 193 Domain Road, South Yarra, Victoria 3141, Australia. *Clubs:* Melbourne, Australian (Melbourne).

SOMERSET, Brigadier Hon. Nigel FitzRoy, CBE 1945; DSO; MC; *b* Cefntilla Court, Usk, Monmouthshire, 27 July 1893; 3rd *s* of 3rd Baron Raglan, GBE, CB; *m* 1922, Phyllis Marion Offley Irwin (*d* 1979), Western Australia; one *s* one *d. Educ:* King William's Coll., IOM; RMC Sandhurst. Served France with 1st Bn Gloucestershire Regt, 12 Aug. 1914 till wounded at the Battle of the Aisne, 15 Sept. 1914; 3 Dec. 1914, till wounded at Cuinchy, 12 May 1915; Mesopotamia, Oct. 1916-May 1919, comdg 14th Light Armoured Motor Battery (despatches thrice, DSO, MC); Bt Majority on promotion to Subst. Captain, 1918; Afghan War, 1919, with Armoured Motor Brigade (Medal and Clasp); ADC to Governor of South Australia, 1920-22; Assistant Military Secretary, Headquarters, Southern Command, India, 1926-30; Major 1933; Lieut-Colonel Comdg 2nd Bn The Gloucestershire Regt, 1938; served War of 1939-45 comdg 145 Inf. Bde (PoW 1940-45; despatches; CBE); Comdg Kent Sub District, 1946-47; Brig. Special Appt Germany, 1947-48; retired pay, 1949. *Address:* 8 Regency Close, Uckfield, East Sussex TN22 1DS.
See also D. H. F. Somerset.

SOMERSET FRY, Peter George Robin Plantagenet; author and journalist, since 1955; *b* 3 Jan. 1931; *s* of late Comdr Peter K. Ll. Fry, OBE, RN, and Ruth Emily (*née* Marriott), LRAM; *m* 1st, 1958, Daphne Diana Elizabeth Caroline Yorke (*d* 1961); 2nd, 1961, Hon. Mrs Leri Butler (marr. diss. 1973); 3rd, 1974, Pamela Fiona Ileene (author, Horses, 1981), *d* of Col H. M. Whitcombe, MBE. *Educ:* Lancing; St Thomas's Hosp. Med. Sch., London; St Catherine's Coll., Oxford (Sec. Oxford Union, Hilary 1956). Mem. editorial staff: technical jl, 1957-58; magazine, 1958; public relations, 1960-64; Information Officer: Incorp. Assoc. of Architects and Surveyors, 1965-67; MPBW, 1967-70; Head of Inf. Services, COSIRA, 1970-74; Editor of Books, HM Stationery Office, 1975-80. Gen. Editor, Macmillan History in Pictures series, 1977-. Vis. Senior Mem., Wolfson Coll., Cambridge, 1980-. Mem. Council, East Anglian Writers, 1977-. Founder and Hon. Secretary: Little Bardfield Village Community Trust, 1971-74; Daphne Somerset Fry Meml Trust for Kidney Disease Res., 1961-; Burgh Soc., 1978-80. FRSA 1966. *Publications:* Mysteries of History, 1957; The Cankered Rose, 1959; Rulers of Britain, 1967 (3rd edn 1973); They Made History, 1970 (2nd edn 1973); The World of Antiques, 1970 (4th edn 1972); Antique Furniture, 1971 (2nd edn 1972); Constantinople, 1970; The Wonderful Story of the Jews, 1970; Children's History of the World, 1972 (9th edn 1982); Answer Book of History, 1972 (2nd edn 1973); Zebra Book of Famous Men, 1972; Zebra Book of Famous Women, 1972; Collecting Inexpensive Antiques, 1973 (5th edn 1980); Zebra Book of Castles, 1974; Great Caesar, 1974; British Mediaeval Castles, 1974; 1000 Great Lives, 1975 (6th edn 1982); Questions, 1976; 2,000 Years of British Life, 1976; Chequers: the country home of Britain's Prime Ministers, 1977 (official history); 3,000 Questions and Answers, 1977 (9th edn 1982); Boudicca, 1978; David & Charles Book of Castles, 1980; Fountains Abbey (official souvenir guide), 1980; Beautiful Britain, 1981; (with Fiona Somerset Fry) History of Scotland, 1982. *Recreations:* studying 18th Century French furniture, Roman history, visiting British castles, gardening. *Address:* Wood Cottage, Wattisfield, Bury St Edmunds, Suffolk. *T:* Stanton 51324.

SOMERSET JONES, Eric, QC 1978; a Recorder of the Crown Court, since 1975; *b* 21 Nov. 1925; *s* of late Daniel Jones and of Florence Somerset Jones; *m* 1966, Brenda Marion, *yr d* of late Hedley Shimmin and Doris Shimmin (*née* Beacroft); two *d. Educ:* Birkenhead Institute; Lincoln College, Oxford. MA Oxon. Served with RAF, 1944-47; RAF Coll., Cranwell; Link Trainer

Instructor, SEAC. Oxford Univ., 1947-50. Called to Bar, Middle Temple, 1952; Mem., Northern Circuit; Member, Lord Chancellor's County Courts Rule Cttee, 1975-78. *Recreations:* family pursuits; travel; listening to music; photography. *Address:* Southmead, Mill Lane, Willaston, Wirral L64 1RL. *T:* 051-327 5138. *Clubs:* United Oxford & Cambridge University; Royal Chester Rowing (Chester).

SOMERTON, Viscount; James Shaun Christian Welbore Ellis Agar; *b* 7 Sept. 1982; *s* and *heir* of 6th Earl of Normanton, *qv*.

SOMERVILLE, David, CB 1971; Under-Secretary, Department of Health and Social Security, 1968-77; *b* 27 Feb. 1917; *e s* of late Rev. David Somerville and of Euphemia Somerville; *m* 1950, Patricia Amy Johnston; *two s two d. Educ:* George Watson's Coll.; Fettes Coll.; Edinburgh Univ.; Christ Church, Oxford. Served with Army, 1940-45; Major, Royal Artillery. Entered Civil Service as Asst Principal, Ministry of Health, 1946; Under-Secretary, Min. of Health, 1963-67. *Recreations:* golf, gardening, adult education. *Address:* Wyndley, Deepdene Park Road, Dorking, Surrey RH5 4AW. *T:* Dorking 885102. *Club:* Betchworth Park Golf.
See also R. M. Somerville.

SOMERVILLE, Jane, MD; FRCP; Consultant Physician, National Heart Hospital, since 1974; Hon. Consultant Physician, Hospital for Sick Children, Great Ormond Street, since 1968; *b* 24 Jan. 1933; *d* of Joseph Bertram Platnauer and Pearl Ashton; *m* 1957, Dr Walter Somerville, *qv*; *three s one d. Educ:* Queen's Coll., London; Guy's Hosp., London Univ. MB, BS ('Treasurer's Gold Medal for Clin. Surg.) 1955; MD 1966. MRCS 1955; FRCP 1973 (LRCP 1955, MRCP 1957). FACC 1972. Guy's Hospital: Ho. Phys., Dept of Med., 1955; Ho. Surg. under Lord Brock, 1956; Med. Registrar, 1956-58; Registrar, Nat. Heart Hosp., 1958-59; First Asst to Dr Paul Wood, 1959-63, Sen. Lectr 1964-74, Inst. of Cardiol.; Hon. Cons. Phys., Nat. Heart Hosp., 1967-74. 6 months' sabbat. leave, Neonatal Unit, UCH, 1973; Lectr in Cardiovascular Disease, Turin Univ., 1973. Vis. Prof. and Guest Lectr, Europe, ME, USA, Mexico, S America, 1968-; St Cyres Lectr, Imperial Coll., London, 1976; first Mahboubian Lectr, NY, 1981; Vis. Consultant, British Amer. Hosp., Madrid. Sci. Sec., World Congress, Ped. Cardiol., 1980. Member: Assoc. Europ. Pæd. Cardiol.; British Cardiac Soc.; British Ped. Assoc., 1977; Anglo-Argentine Soc.; Hon. Member: Argentine Pæd. Soc.; Chilean Cardiol. Soc.; Argentine Soc. of Cardiol. Mem. R.SocMed. Governor: Queen's Coll., London; Nat. Heart and Chest Hosp. Woman of the Year, 1968. *Publications:* numerous contribs to med. lit. on heart disease in children, congenital heart disease and results of cardiac surgery; chapters in Paul Wood's Diseases of Heart and Circulation (3rd edn). *Recreations:* collecting stone eggs, pictures, porcelain soldiers; chess, orchid culture. *Address:* 30 York House, Upper Montagu Street, W1H 1FR. *T:* 01-262 2144.

SOMERVILLE, John Arthur Fownes, CB 1977; CBE 1964; an Under-Secretary, Government Communications Headquarters, 1969-78; *b* 5 Dec. 1917; *s* of late Admiral of the Fleet Sir James Fownes Somerville, GCB, GBE, DSO; *m* 1945, Julia Elizabeth Payne; *one s two d. Educ:* RNC Dartmouth. Midshipman 1936; Sub-Lieut 1938; Lieut 1940; Lieut-Comdr 1945; retd 1950. Govt Communications Headquarters, 1950-78. *Recreation:* walking. *Address:* The Old Rectory, Dinder, Wells, Som. *T:* Wells 74900. *Club:* Army and Navy.

SOMERVILLE, Mrs (Katherine) Lilian, CMG 1971; OBE 1958; FMA 1962; Director, Fine Arts Department, British Council, 1948-70; *b* 7 Oct. 1905; *d* of Captain Arthur George Tillard and Emily Katherine Close-Brooks; *m* 1928, Horace Somerville (*d* 1959); *one d. Educ:* Abbot's Hill; Slade School of Art, London. Painted until war. Joined British Council, 1941. Fellow, UCL, 1973. Hon. Dr, RCA, 1972. *Address:* The Studio, 16a Hill Road, NW8 9QG. *T:* 01-286 1087.

SOMERVILLE, Sir Robert, KCVO 1961 (CVO 1953); MA; FSA; FRHistS; Clerk of the Council of the Duchy of Lancaster, 1952-70; *b* 5 June 1906; *s* of late Robert Somerville, FRSE, Dunfermline; *m* 1st, 1932, Marie-Louise Cornelia Bergené (*d* 1976); *one d*; 2nd, 1981, Mrs Jessie B. Warburton. *Educ:* Fettes; St John's Coll., Cambridge (1st cl. Class. Tripos, 1929); Edinburgh Univ. Entered Duchy of Lancaster Office, 1930; Ministry of Shipping, 1940; Chief Clerk, Duchy of Lancaster, 1945; Hon. Research Asst, History of Medicine, UCL, 1935-38; Chairman: Council, British Records Assoc., 1957-67 (Hon. Secretary, 1947-56); London Record Soc.; Lewisham Archives Cttee; Member: Advisory Council on Public Records, 1959-64; Royal Commn on Historical MSS, 1966-; Corr. Member, Indian Historical Records Commn. Alexander Medallist, Royal Historical Society, 1940. *Publications:* History of the Duchy of Lancaster, 2 vols, 1953, 1970; The Savoy, 1960; Handlist of Record Publications, 1951; Duchy of Lancaster Office-Holders from 1603, 1972; (joint editor) John of Gaunt's Register, 1937; contribs to Chambers's Encyclopædia, historical journals, etc. *Address:* 3 Hunt's Close, Morden Road, SE3 0AH.

SOMERVILLE, Maj.-Gen. Ronald Macaulay, CB 1974; OBE 1963; General Manager, Scottish Special Housing Association, since 1975; *b* 2 July 1919; 2nd *s* of late Rev. David Somerville and of Euphemia Somerville; *m* 1947, Jean McEwen Balderston; *no c. Educ:* George Watson's Coll., Edinburgh. Joined TA, 1939; commnd RA, 1940; regtl and Staff War Service in UK, NW Europe and Far East, 1939-45 (MBE, despatches, 1945); psc 1944; jssc 1956; comd Maiwand Battery, Cyprus Emergency, 1957-59 (despatches, 1958); Bt

Lt-Col, 1960; CO 4th Light Regt RA, 1963-65; Borneo Emergency, 1965; CRA 51st (H) Div., 1965-66; idc 1967; DQMG, BAOR, 1968-70; GOC Yorks District, 1970-72; Vice-QMG, MoD, 1972-74; Chm., Logistic Reorganisation Cttee, 1974-75; retd 1975. Hon. Col, 3rd Bn Yorkshire Volunteers, 1972-77; Col Comdt, RA, 1974-79. Comr, Royal Hospital, Chelsea, 1972-74; Chm., RA Council for Scotland, 1975-79; Pres., RA Assoc., Scotland, 1978-; Mem., TA&VRA, Scotland, 1978-. Chm., West End Community Council, Edinburgh, 1980-. FBIM 1980; MIH 1980. Kt Officer, Order of Orange Nassau, with Swords, 1946. *Recreations:* golf, gardening, fishing. *Address:* 6 Magdala Mews, Edinburgh EH12 5BX. *T:* 031-346 0371; Bynack Mhor, Boat of Garten, Inverness-shire PH24 3BP. *T:* Boat of Garten 245. *Club:* New (Edinburgh).
See also David Somerville.

SOMERVILLE, Most Rev. Thomas David; Anglican Chaplain, Vancouver School of Theology, since 1981; *b* 11 Nov. 1915; *s* of Thomas Alexander Somerville and Martha Stephenson Scott; unmarried. *Educ:* King George High Sch., Vancouver; Univ. of British Columbia (BA 1937); Anglican Theological Coll. of BC (LTh 1939, BD 1951). Deacon, 1939; priest, 1940; Incumbent of: Princeton, 1940-44; Sardis with Rosedale, 1944-49; Curate of St James, Vancouver, 1949-52, Rector, 1952-60; Chapter Canon, Dio. of New Westminster, 1957; Dean of Residence, Anglican Theological Coll. of BC, 1960-65; Gen. Sec., Gen. Bd of Religious Education, Anglican Church of Canada, 1965-66; Director of Planning and Research, Anglican Church of Canada, 1966-69; Coadjutor Bishop of New Westminster, 1969-71; Bishop of New Westminster, 1971; Archbishop of New Westminster and Metropolitan of Ecclesiastical Province of British Columbia, 1975-80, retd. Hon. DD Anglican Theol. Coll. of BC, 1969. *Recreations:* music, botany. *Address:* 3102 1011 Beach Avenue, Vancouver, BC V6E 1T8, Canada.

SOMERVILLE, Walter, CBE 1979; MD, FRCP; Hon. Physician to Department of Cardiology, Middlesex Hospital, since 1979 (Physician, 1954-79); to Cardiac Surgical Unit, Harefield Hospital, 1952-78; Lecturer in Cardiology, Middlesex Hospital Medical School, 1954-79; Consultant in Cardiology to the Army, 1963-79, Hon. Consultant, since 1980; Hon. Civil Consultant in Cardiology to Royal Air Force, Civil Aviation Authority, and Royal Hospital, Chelsea, since 1963, to Association of Naval Officers, since 1960; to King Edward VII Convalescent Home for Officers, Osborne, since 1970; *b* 2 Oct. 1913; *s* of late Patrick and Catherine Somerville, Dublin; *m* 1957, Jane Platnauer (*see Jane Somerville*); *three s one d. Educ:* Belvedere Coll., Dublin; University College, Dublin. House appts, Mater Hosp., Dublin, 1937; out-patients Assistant, Brompton Hosp. and Chelsea Chest Clinic, 1938-39. Served in War 1939-45; attached: Canadian Dept of Defense, 1942; US Army, 1943; Lt-Col RAMC 1944. Fellow in Med., Mass General Hosp., Boston, 1946; Registrar, British Postgraduate Med. School, Hammersmith, 1947; studied in Paris, Stockholm and Univ. of Michigan, 1948; Fellow in Medicine, Peter Bent Brigham Hosp. Boston and Harvard Med. Sch., 1949; Med. Registrar, Nat. Heart Hosp. and Inst. of Cardiology, 1951; Sen. Med. Registrar, Middlesex Hosp., 1951-54. Lectures: Carey Coombs, Bristol Univ., 1977; St Cyres, Nat. Heart Hosp., 1978. Editor, British Heart Journal, 1973-80; Editorial Board: American Heart Journal, 1975-; Revista Portuguesa de cardiologia, 1982-. Pres., British Cardiac Soc., 1976-80; former Pres., British Acad. of Forensic Sciences; Mem., Assoc. of Physicians of Great Britain and Ireland and other socs; Corr. Member: Colombian Soc. of Cardiology; Chilean Soc. of Cardiology; Fellow, Amer. Coll. of Cardiology. Vis. Prof., Cleveland Clinic, Cleveland, Ohio, 1980. Purkyne Medal, Czechoslovakian Cardiac Soc., 1981. Officer, Legion of Merit, USA, 1945. *Publications:* (ed) Paul Wood's Diseases of the Heart and Circulation (3rd edn), 1968; various articles on cardiovascular subjects in British, continental European and American journals. *Address:* 149 Harley Street, W1. *T:* 01-935 4444; 30 York House, Upper Montagu Street, W1H 1FR. *T:* 01-262 2144.

SOMES, Michael (George), CBE 1959; Principal Repetiteur, Royal Ballet, Covent Garden; *b* 28 Sept. 1917; British; *m* 1956, Deirdre Annette Dixon (*d* 1959). *Educ:* Huish's Grammar Sch., Taunton, Somerset. Started dancing at Sadler's Wells, 1934; first important rôle in Horoscope, 1938; Leading Male Dancer, Royal Ballet, Covent Garden, 1951-68; Asst Director, 1963-70. *Recreation:* music.

SOMMER, André D.; see Dupont-Sommer.

SONDES, 5th Earl *cr* 1880; **Henry George Herbert Milles-Lade;** Baron Sondes, 1760; Viscount Throwley, 1880; *b* 1 May 1940; *o s* of 4th Earl Sondes, and Pamela (*d* 1967), *d* of Col H. McDougall; *S* father, 1970; *m* 1968, Primrose Creswell (marr. diss. 1969), *d* of late Lawrence Stopford Llewellyn Cotter; *m* 1976, Sissy Fürstin zu Salm-Reifferscheidt-Raitz (marr. diss. 1981). *Recreations:* shooting, skiing. *Address:* Stringman's Farm, Faversham, Kent. *T:* Chilham 336.

SONDHEIM, Stephen Joshua; composer-lyricist; *b* 22 March 1930; *s* of Herbert Sondheim and Janet (*née* Fox). *Educ:* Williams Coll. (BA 1950). Lyrics: West Side Story, 1957; Gypsy, 1959; Do I Hear a Waltz?, 1965. Music and Lyrics: A Funny Thing Happened on the Way to the Forum, 1962; Anyone Can Whistle, 1964; Evening Primrose (TV), 1966; Company, 1970; Follies, 1971; A Little Night Music, 1973; Stavisky (film score), 1974; Pacific Overtures, 1976; Sweeney Todd, 1979; Reds (film score), 1981; Merrily We Roll Along, 1981. Pres., Dramatists Guild, 1973-81. Hon. Doctorate, Williams Coll., 1971. *Publications:* (book and vocal score): West Side Story,

1958; Gypsy, 1960; A Funny Thing Happened on the Way to the Forum, 1963; Anyone Can Whistle, 1965; Do I Hear a Waltz?, 1966; Company, 1971; Follies, 1972; A Little Night Music, 1974; Pacific Overtures, 1977; Sweeney Todd, 1979. *Address:* c/o Flora Roberts, 157 West 57th Street, New York, NY 10019, USA.

SONDHEIMER, Professor Ernst Helmut, MA, ScD; Professor of Mathematics, Westfield College, University of London, 1960-82, now Emeritus; *b* 8 Sept. 1923; *er s* of Max and Ida Sondheimer; *m* 1950, Janet Harrington Matthews, PhD; one *s* one *d*. *Educ:* University College School; Trinity Coll., Cambridge. Smith's Prize, 1947; Fellow of Trinity Coll., 1948-52; Research Fellow, H. H. Wills Physical Lab., University of Bristol, 1948-49; Research Associate, Massachusetts Inst. of Technology, 1949-50; Lecturer in Mathematics, Imperial College of Science and Technology, 1951-54; Reader in Applied Mathematics, Queen Mary Coll., Univ. of London, 1954-60. Vis. Research Asst Prof. of Physics, Univ. of Illinois, USA, 1958-59; Vis. Prof. of Theoretical Physics, University of Cologne, 1967. Member of Council, Queen Elizabeth Coll., London. *Publications:* Green's Functions for Solid State Physicists (with S. Doniach), 1974; (with A. Rogerson) Numbers and Infinity, 1981; papers on the electron theory of metals. *Recreations:* mountaineering, photography, books. *Address:* 51 Cholmeley Crescent, Highgate, N6. *T:* 01-340 6607. *Club:* Alpine.

SOPER, family name of **Baron Soper**.

SOPER, Baron, *cr* 1965 (Life Peer); **Rev. Donald Oliver Soper**, MA Cantab; PhD (London); Methodist Minister; President of the Methodist Conference, 1953, Superintendent West London Mission, Kingsway Hall, 1936-78; *b* 31 Jan. 1903; *s* of late Ernest and Caroline Soper; *m* 1929, Marie Dean, *d* of late Arthur Dean, Norbury; four *d*. *Educ:* Aske's School, Hatcham; St Catharine's College, Cambridge University; Wesley House, Cambridge; London School of Economics, London University. Hon. Fellow, St Catharine's Coll., Cambridge, 1966. Minister, South London Mission, 1926-29; Central London Mission, 1929-36. Chm., Shelter, 1974-78. President, League against Cruel Sports. Peace Award, World Methodist Council, 1981. *Publications:* Christianity and its Critics; Popular Fallacies about the Christian Faith; Will Christianity Work?; Practical Christianity To-day; Questions and Answers in Ceylon; All His Grace (Methodist Lent Book for 1957); It is hard to work for God; The Advocacy of the Gospel; Tower Hill 12.30; Aflame with Faith; Christian Politics. *Recreations:* music, golf. *Address:* Kingsway Hall, WC2B 6TA.

SOPER, Dr J. Dewey; naturalist, explorer; Canadian Wildlife Service, Department of Indian Affairs and Northern Development, Ottawa, retired Nov. 1952; *b* Guelph, Ont, 5 May 1893; *m* 1927, C. K. Freeman, Wetaskiwin, Alberta; one *s* one *d*. *Educ:* Alberta Coll. and Univ. of Alberta, Edmonton. Studied music 6 yrs; then took up science, specialising in ornithology and mammalogy, especially the latter; naturalist to the Canadian Arctic Expedition of 1923, visiting Greenland, Ellesmere, North Devon and Baffin Islands; engaged in biological research and exploration on Baffin Island for the Canadian Government, 1924-26; engaged in biological research, exploration and mapping of Foxe Land, Baffin Island, for Dept of the Interior, Canada, 1928-29, resulting among other things in the discovery of the mysterious breeding grounds of the Blue Goose, and for Dept of Interior, Lake Harbour region, Baffin Island, 1930-31, and Wood Buffalo Park, Alta, and NWT 1932-34, then transferred as Chief Federal Migratory Bird Officer for the Prairie Provinces. Bronze Plaque and framed Citation from Federal Govt for explorations in the Canadian Arctic, 1928; Achievements Award of Alberta Govt, 1972; Bronze Award and Citation of Northwest Territories Govt, for explorations, mapping and natural history res. in Canadian Eastern Arctic in the 20s and 30s, chiefly in Baffin Island, 1978. Hon. LLD Univ. Alberta, 1960. *Publications:* 131, including The Weasels of Canada; Bird Life in the Alberta Wilds; Mammalian and Avian Fauna of Islay, Alberta; Mammals of Wellington and Waterloo Counties, Ontario; Birds of Wellington and Waterloo Counties, Ontario; Mammals of the Ridout Region, Northern Ontario; A Biological Reconnaissance of Nipissing and Timiskaming Districts, Northern Ontario; A Faunal Investigation of Southern Baffin Island; Discovery of the Breeding Grounds of the Blue Goose; The Blue Goose; Solitudes of the Arctic; Intimate Glimpses of Eskimo Life in Baffin Island; The Lake Harbour Region, Baffin Island; Notes on the Beavers of Wood Buffalo Park; Local Distribution of Eastern Canadian Arctic Birds; History, Range and Home Life of the Northern Bison; Mammals of Wood Buffalo Park; Birds of Wood Buffalo Park and Vicinity; Life History of the Blue Goose; The Mammals of Southern Baffin Island, NWT; Ornithological Results of the Baffin Island Expeditions of 1928-29 and 1930-31, together with more Recent Records; Mammals of the Northern Great Plains along the International Boundary in Canada; Observations on Mammals and Birds in the Rocky Mountains of Alberta; Field Data on the Mammals of Southern Saskatchewan; The Mammals of Manitoba; The Mammals of Alberta; The Mammals of Jasper National Park, Alberta; The Conquest of Pangnirtung Pass; The Mammals of Waterton Lakes National Park, Alberta; Kingnait Pass, Baffin Island; The mysterious West Coast. *Recreations:* water-colour painting, reading and writing. *Address:* Strathcona Place, 7720-108 Street, Edmonton, Alberta, Canada.

SOPWITH, Sir Charles (Ronald), Kt 1966; Second Counsel to Chairman of Committees, House of Lords, 1974-82; *b* 12 Nov. 1905; *s* of Alfred Sopwith, S Shields, Co. Durham; *m* 1946, Ivy Violet (*d* 1968), *d* of Frederick Leonard

Yeates, Gidea Park, Essex. *Educ:* S Shields High School. Chartered Accountant, 1928; Solicitor, 1938. Assistant Director, Press Censorship, 1943-45; Assistant Solicitor, 1952-56, Principal Asst Solicitor, 1956-61, Solicitor, 1963-70, Board of Inland Revenue; Public Trustee, 1961-63; Deputy Sec., Cabinet Office, 1970-72. *Recreations:* music, reading history, golf. *Address:* 18 Moor Lane, Rickmansworth, Herts. *Club:* Reform.

SOPWITH, Sir Thomas Octave Murdoch, Kt 1953; CBE 1918; Founder President, Hawker Siddeley Group Ltd (Chairman, 1935-63); *s* of Thomas Sopwith, MICE; *b* 1888; *m* 1st, 1914, Hon. Beatrix Mary Leslie Hore-Ruthven (*d* 1930), *d* of 8th Baron Ruthven; no *c*; 2nd, 1932, Phyllis Brodie (*d* 1978), 2nd *d* of late F. P. A. Gordon; one *s*. Founded the Sopwith Aviation Co. Ltd, Kingston-on-Thames, 1912; Chairman, 1925-27, Society of British Aircraft Constructors. *Recreations:* yachting, shooting, fishing. *Address:* Compton Manor, Kings Somborne, Hampshire. *Club:* Royal Yacht Squadron.

SOREF, Harold Benjamin; Chairman, since 1976, and Managing Director, since 1959, Soref Bros Ltd; *b* 18 Dec. 1916; *o s* of late Paul Soref and Zelma Soref (*née* Goodman), Hampstead. *Educ:* Hall Sch., Hampstead; St Paul's Sch.; Queen's Coll., Oxford. Served with Royal Scots and Intell. Corps, 1940-45. Contested (C): Dudley, 1951; Rugby, 1955. MP (C) Lancashire, Ormskirk, 1970-Feb. 1974. Delegate, first all-British Africa Conf. held Bulawayo, 1938, to form Africa Defence Fedn; formerly Vice-Chm., Monday Club and Chm., Africa Cttee, Monday Club; Mem. Council, Anglo-Jewish Assoc.; Founder Mem., Conservative Commonwealth Council. *Publications:* (jtly) The War of 1939, 1940; (with Ian Greig) The Puppeteers, 1965; numerous articles in press and periodicals. *Recreations:* research, reading, writing. *Address:* 69-85 Old Street, EC1. *T:* 01-253 9311. *Clubs:* Carlton, PEN, 1900.

SOREL CAMERON, Brig. John, CBE 1957; DSO 1943; DL; retired as Chief of Staff, Headquarters Scottish Command (Oct. 1958-60); ADC to the Queen, 1957-60; *b* 19 July 1907; *er s* of late Lt-Col G. C. M. Sorel Cameron, CBE and Mrs Sorel Cameron, Gorthleck, Inverness-shire; *m* 1937, Catherine Nancy, *yr d* of late Frank Lee, JP, Halifax, Yorks; one *d*. *Educ:* Wellington; RMC Sandhurst. Gazetted 2nd Lieut Queen's Own Cameron Highlanders, 1927; regimental service, 1927-40; served War of 1939-45 in Middle East, Sicily, NW Europe (wounded thrice, despatches twice); Staff Coll., 1940; Staff, 1940-42; comd: 5/7th Camerons, 1942; 5th Camerons, 1943; Staff, 1944-50; comd: 1st Camerons, 1951-53; 154 Highland Bde, 1953-55; Chief of Staff, British Commonwealth Forces in Korea, 1955-56; BGS, HQ Scottish Comd, 1957. DL Inverness, 1971-. *Recreations:* field sports, history. *Address:* 47 Drummond Road, Inverness, Scotland. *T:* Inverness 30029.

SORINJ, Dr L. T.; *see* Tončić-Sorinj.

SORN, Hon. Lord; James Gordon McIntyre, MC; Senator of College of Justice in Scotland, 1944-63, retired; *b* 21 July 1896; *s* of late T. W. McIntyre, of Sorn; *m* 1923, Madeline (*d* 1954), *d* of late Robert Scott Moncrieff, Downhill; one *s* one *d*. *Educ:* Winchester; Balliol Coll., Oxford (BA); Glasgow Univ. (LLB). Served European War, 1914-18, Ayrshire Yeomanry, Captain 1917 (MC and bar, French Croix de Guerre); called Scottish Bar, 1922; KC 1936; Dean of the Faculty of Advocates, 1939-44. Hon. LLD Glasgow University. *Recreation:* fishing. *Address:* Sorn Castle, Ayrshire. *Club:* New (Edinburgh).

SOROKOS, Lt-Gen. John A., Greek Gold Medal for Gallantry (3 times); Greek Military Cross (twice); Medal for Distinguished Services (3 times); Silver and Gold Cross (with swords) of Order of George I; Comdr, Order of George I and Order of Phoenix; Military Medal of Merit (1st Class); Ambassador of Greece to the United States of America, 1972-74; *b* 1917; *s* of A. and P. Sorokos; *m* 1954, Pia Madaros; one *s*. *Educ:* Mil. Acad. of Greece; Staff and Nat. Defence Colls, Greece; British Staff Coll., Camberley; US Mil. Schools. Company Comdr: in Second World War in Greece, 1940-41; in El Alamein Campaign, N Africa, 1942-43; Div. Staff Officer and Bn Comdr, 1947-49; served as Staff Officer: in Mil. Units in Army HQ and Armed Forces HQ, 1952-63; in NATO Allied Forces Southern Europe, 1957-59; Instructor, Nat. Defence Coll., Greece, 1963-64; Regt Comdr, 1965; Mil. Attaché to Greek Embassies in Washington and Ottawa, 1966-68; Div. Comdr, 1968-69; Dep. Comdr, Greek Armed Forces, 1969; Ambassador to UK, 1969-72. Officer, Legion of Merit (US). *Recreations:* horses, boating, fishing. *Address:* Mimnermou 2, Athens 138, Greece.

SORRELL, Alec Albert; Director of Statistics, Department of the Environment, 1981-82; *b* 20 July 1925; *s* of Albert Edward Sorrell and Jessie (*née* Morris); *m* 1962, Eileen Joan Orchard; one *s*. *Educ:* George Gascoigne Sch., Walthamstow; SW Essex Technical College. BSc (Econ). Statistical Officer, MAP, 1945; Board of Trade: Asst Statistician, 1950; Statistician, 1954; Chief Statistician, 1966; Chief Statistician: Min. of Technology, 1969; Dept of Trade and Industry, 1970; Central Statistical Office, 1971; Asst Dir, Central Statistical Office, Cabinet Office, 1972-78; Principal Dir of Statistics, Depts of the Environment and Transport, 1978-81. *Publications:* various articles in trade, professional and learned jls. *Recreations:* walking, reading, beachcombing. *Address:* 8 Ravensmere, Epping, Essex. *T:* Epping 73961; River Cottage, West Putford, Devon.

SORSBIE, Sir Malin, Kt 1965; CBE 1956 (OBE 1942); *b* 25 May 1906; *s* of late Rev. William Frances Sorsbie and late Blanche Georgina Sorsbie; *m* 1955,

Constantine Eugenie, *d* of late Albert Wheeler Johnston, Greenwich, Connecticut, USA; one step *d. Educ:* Brighton College; Manitoba University. Royal Canadian Mounted Police, 1926-29; RAF, 1930-35; Imperial Airways, 1936-39; BOAC, 1940-47; East African Airways (Gen. Manager), 1947-56. Life Fellow, RGS. KStJ. *Publications:* Dragonfly, 1971; Brandy for Breakfast, 1972. *Address:* PO Box 45337, Nairobi, Kenya. *T:* 65331 and 65343. *Clubs:* Carlton, Royal Air Force; RAF Yacht; Muthaiga Country, Nairobi (Nairobi).

SOTERIADES, Antis Georghios; Ambassador of Cyprus to Yugoslavia, concurrently accredited to Algeria and Sudan, since 1979; *b* 10 Sept. 1924; *m* 1962, Mona, *yr d* of Petros Petrides, Nicosia; one *s* one *d. Educ:* London Univ.; Inns of Court, London. Practising lawyer until 1956; joined patriotic Organization EOKA and fought British Colonialism in Cyprus, 1956-59; President of the first political party formed in Cyprus after independence, 1959; High Commissioner for Cyprus in the UK, 1960-66; Ambassador to Egypt, concurrently to Syrian Arab Republic, Iraq and Lebanon, 1966-78. Kt Order of St Gregory the Great (Vatican), 1963. *Address:* Diplomatska Koloniya No 9, Belgrade, Yugoslavia.

SOUKOP, Wilhelm Josef, RA 1969 (ARA 1963); RBA 1950; FRBS 1956; Master of Sculpture, Royal Academy Schools, 1969-82; freelance sculptor; *b* 5 Jan. 1907; *s* of Karl Soukop and Anna Soukop (*née* Vogel); *m* 1945, Simone (*née* Moser), Paris; one *s* one *d. Educ:* Vienna State School; apprenticed to an engraver; Academy of Fine Art, Vienna. Arrived in England, Dartington Hall, 1934; taught at Dartington Hall, Bryanston and Blundell's Schools, 1935-45; moved to London, 1945, and taught at Bromley Sch. of Art, 1945-46, Guildford Sch. of Art, 1945-47; sculpture teacher, Chelsea Sch. of Art, 1947-72. Examr for Scotland, 1959-62. Sculptures for new schools in Herts, Leics, Derbs, Staffs, LCC. Work for housing estates. Sculptures in museums: USA; Cordova Mus., Boston; Chantry Bequest; Tate Gallery; Cheltenham Mus. and Gall.; Collection of LCC Educn Cttee. Work in many private collections England, America, Canada, Europe. Archibald McIndoe Award, 1964. *Recreation:* gardening. *Address:* 26 Greville Road, NW6. *T:* 01-624 5987.

SOULBURY, 2nd Viscount *cr* 1954, of Soulbury; **James Herwald Ramsbotham;** Baron 1941; *b* 21 March 1915; *s* of 1st Viscount Soulbury, PC, GCMG, GCVO, OBE, MC, and Doris Violet (*d* 1954), *d* of late S. de Stein; *S* father, 1971; *m* 1949, Anthea Margaret (*d* 1950), *d* of late David Wilton. *Educ:* Eton; Magdalen College, Oxford. *Heir: b* Hon. Sir Peter Edward Ramsbotham, *qv.*

SOULSBY, Prof. Ernest Jackson Lawson, MRCVS; Professor of Animal Pathology, University of Cambridge, since 1978; Fellow, Wolfson College, Cambridge, since 1978; *b* 23 June 1926; *s* of William George Lawson Soulsby and Agnes Soulsby; *m* 1962, Georgina Elizabeth Annette Williams; one *s* one *d. Educ:* Queen Elizabeth Grammar Sch., Penrith; Univ. of Edinburgh. MRCVS; DVSM; PhD; MA (Cantab). Veterinary Officer, City of Edinburgh, 1949-52; Lectr in Clinical Parasitology, Univ. of Bristol, 1952-54; Univ. Lectr in Animal Pathology, Univ. of Cambridge, 1954-63; Prof. of Parasitology, Univ. of Pennsylvania, 1964-78. Ford Foundn Visiting Prof., Univ. of Ibadan, 1964; Richard Merton Guest Prof., Justus Liebig Univ., 1974-75. Corres. Mem., German Parasitology Soc.; Hon. Mem., Mexican Parasitology Soc.; Expert Advisor and Consultant, and Member, Scientific Groups: various internat. agencies and govts. Hon. AM, Univ. of Pennsylvania; R. N. Chaudhury Gold Medal, Calcutta Sch. of Tropical Med., Calcutta, 1976; Behring-Bilharz Prize, Cairo, 1977; Ludwig-Schunk Prize, Justus-Liebig Universitat, Giessen, 1979. *Publications:* Textbook of Veterinary Clinical Parasitology, 1965; Biology of Parasites, 1966; Reaction of the Host to Parasitism, 1968; Helminths, Arthropods and Protozoa of Domesticated Animals, 6th edn 1968, 7th edn 1982; Immunity to Animal Parasites, 1972; Parasitic Zoonoses, 1974; Pathophysiology of Parasitic Infections, 1976; Epidemiology and Control of Nematodiasis in Cattle; articles in jls of parasitology, immunology and pathology. *Recreations:* travel, gardening, photography. *Address:* Old Barn House, Swaffham Prior, Cambridge CB5 0LD. *T:* Newmarket 741304. *Clubs:* Farmers', United Oxford & Cambridge University; Explorers' (New York).

SOUROZH, Metropolitan of; see Anthony, Archbishop.

SOUSTELLE, Jacques; Commandeur, Légion d'Honneur, 1981; Hon. CBE; Member, Lyon Municipal Council, 1954-62 and 1971-77; *b* 3 Feb. 1912. *Educ:* Ecole Normale supérieure, Paris; Univ. of Lyon. Agrégé de l'Université 1932, PhD 1937. Asst Dir, Musée de l'Homme, 1937; Nat. Comr for Information in London, 1942; Head of French special services, Algiers, 1943-44; Governor of Bordeaux, 1945; Minister of Information and Colonies, 1945-46. Prof. of Sociology, Ecole des Hautes Etudes, 1951. Mem. Nat. Assembly, 1945-46, 1951-59, 1973-78. Gov.-Gen. of Algeria, 1955-56; Minister of Information, 1958; Minister delegate to the Prime Minister, France, 1959-60. Mem., New York Acad. of Scis. FRAI. Order of Polonia Restituta, 1944; US Medal of Freedom, 1945; Hon. CBE, Great Britain, 1946; Comdr, Aztec Eagle (Mexico), 1978. *Publications:* Mexique, terre indienne, 1935; Envers et contre tout, 1947; La Vie quotidienne des Aztèques, 1955 (Daily Life of the Aztecs, 1962); Aimée et souffrante Algérie, 1956; L'espérance trahie, 1962; Sur une route nouvelle, 1964; L'Art du Mexique ancien, 1966 (Arts of Ancient Mexico, 1967); Archæologia Mundi: Mexique, 1967 (Archæologia Mundi: Mexico, 1967, repr. as The Ancient Civilizations of Mexico, 1969); Les quatre

soleils, 1967 (The Four Suns, 1971); La longue marche d'Israël, 1968 (The Long March of Israel, 1969); Vingt-huit ans de Gaullisme, 1968; Les Aztèques, 1970; Lettre ouverte aux victimes de la décolonisation, 1973; L'Univers des Aztèques, 1979; Les Olmèques, 1979; Les Maya, 1982; papers and memoirs on anthropology and ethnology, in learned jls. *Address:* 85 avenue Henri-Martin, 75016 Paris, France.

SOUTAR, Air Marshal Sir Charles (John Williamson), KBE 1978 (MBE 1958); Director-General, Medical Services (RAF), 1978-81; *b* 12 June 1920; *s* of Charles Alexander Soutar and Mary Helen (*née* Watson); *m* 1944, Joy Dorée Upton; one *s* two *d. Educ:* Brentwood Sch.; London Hosp. MB, BS, LMSSA, FFCM, DPH, DIH. Commissioned RAF, 1946. Various appts, then PMO, Middle East Command, 1967-68; Dep. Dir, Med. Organisation, RAF, 1968-70; OC, PMRAF Hosp., Halton, 1970-73; Comdt, RAF Inst. of Aviation Medicine, 1973-75; PMO, Strike Command, 1975-78. QHS 1974-81. CStJ 1972. *Recreations:* sport, gardening, ornithology, music. *Address:* Oak Cottage, High Street, Aldeburgh, Suffolk IP15 5DT. *T:* Aldeburgh 2201. *Club:* Royal Air Force.

SOUTER, family name of **Baron Audley.**

SOUTH, Sir Arthur, Kt 1974; JP; Managing Director, Arthur South Furs (Wholesale) Ltd, since 1962; Senior Partner, Norwich Fur Company, since 1947; *b* 29 Oct. 1914; *s* of Arthur and Violet South, Norwich; *m* 1st, 1937, May Adamson (marr. diss. 1976); two *s*; 2nd, 1976, Mary June (*d* 1982), widow of Robert Edward Carter, JP, DL. *Educ:* City of Norwich Sch. RAF and MAP, 1941-46. Mem., Norwich, Lowestoft, Gt Yarmouth Hosp. Management Cttee, 1948-74 (Vice-Chm., 1954-66, Chm., 1966-74); Chairman: Norfolk Area Health Authority, 1974-78; E Anglian RHA, 1978-; Mem., E Anglia Regional Hosp. Bd, 1969-74. Member: Assoc. of Educn Cttees, 1963-74; Assoc. of Municipal Corporations, 1965-74; E Anglia Econ. Planning Council, 1966-80; E Anglia Rent Assessment Panel, 1967-74; E Anglia Adv. Cttee to BBC, 1970-74; Univ. of E Anglia Council, 1964-80 (Life Mem., Court, 1964). Norwich: City Councillor, 1935-41 and 1946-61; Alderman, 1961-74; Sheriff, 1953-54; Lord Mayor, 1956-57, Dep. Lord Mayor, 1959-60; JP 1949; Dep. Leader, Norwich City Council, 1959-60; Chm., Labour Party Gp and Leader Norwich City Council, 1960-78. Norwich City Football Club: Vice-Pres., 1957-66; Dir, 1966-73; Chm., 1973-; Member: FA Council, 1981-; Football League Management Cttee, 1981-. *Recreations:* football, bowls, cricket. *Address:* The Lowlands, Drayton, Norfolk NR8 6HA. *T:* Norwich 867 355 ext. 207. *Clubs:* MCC; Mitre Bowls, Norfolk Cricket, Norwich City Football.

SOUTHALL, Kenneth Charles; Under-Secretary, Inland Revenue, 1975-82; *b* 3 Aug. 1922; *s* of Arthur and Margarette Jane Southall; *m* 1947, Audrey Kathleen Skeels; one *s. Educ:* Queen Elizabeth's Grammar Sch., Hartlebury, Worcs. Inland Revenue, 1939; RAF, 1942-46; Administrative Staff College, 1962. *Address:* Field House, Bicester Road, Marsh Gibbon, Bicester, Oxon OX6 0EU.

SOUTHAM, Gordon Ronald, BSc; AInstP; Headmaster, Ashville College, 1958-77; *b* 20 March 1918; *s* of G. H. Southam, Brackley; *m* 1948, Joan, *d* of W. Thompson; one *d. Educ:* Magdalen College School, Brackley; Westminster College, and King's College, London. BSc (Gen. Hons) 1938, BSc (Special Physics) 1st Class Hons 1939. Teacher's diploma, 1947, AInstP 1947. Served Royal Air Force, 1940-46: Bomber Comd, 1940-43; Staff Officer in HQ, ACSEA, 1943-46 (Sqdn Ldr). Senior Physics Master, Culford School, 1947-49; Lecturer, Royal Military Academy, Sandhurst, 1950-52; Head of Department of Science, Royal Military Academy, Sandhurst, 1953-57. *Recreations:* motoring, electronics; formerly Rugby football, athletics. *Address:* Greycott, Hartley, Kirkby Stephen, Cumbria. *T:* Kirkby Stephen 71652.

SOUTHAMPTON, Barony of (*cr* 1780); title disclaimed by 5th Baron; *see under* FitzRoy, Charles.

SOUTHAMPTON, Bishop Suffragan of, since 1972; **Rt. Rev. John Kingsmill Cavell;** Bishop to HM Prisons and Borstals, since 1975; *b* 4 Nov. 1916; *o s* of late William H. G. Cavell and Edith May (*née* Warner), Deal, Kent; *m* 1942, Mary Grossett (*née* Penman), Devizes, Wilts; one *d. Educ:* Sir Roger Manwood's Sch., Sandwich; Queens' Coll., Cambridge; MA; Wycliffe Hall, Oxford. Ryle Reading Prize. Ordained May 1940; Curate: Christ Church, Folkestone, 1940; Addington Parish Church, Croydon, 1940-44; CMS Area Secretary, dio. Oxford and Peterborough, and CMS Training Officer, 1944-52; Vicar: Christ Church, Cheltenham, 1952-62; St Andrew's, Plymouth, 1962-72; Rural Dean of Plymouth, 1967-72; Prebendary of Exeter Cathedral, 1967-72. Hon. Canon, Winchester Cathedral, 1972-. Proctor in Convocation; Member of General Synod (Mem., Bd for Social Responsibility, 1982-); Surrogate. Chm., Home Cttee, CMS London. Chaplain, Greenbank and Freedom Fields Hosps, Plymouth; Member: Plymouth City Educn Cttee, 1967-72; City Youth Cttee; Plymouth Exec. Council, NHS, 1968-72. Fellow, Pilgrim Soc., Massachusetts, 1974. Patron, Southampton RNLI Bd, 1976-. Governor: Cheltenham Colls of Educn; King Alfred's College of Educn, 1973-; Chairman: St Mary's Coll. Building Cttee, 1957-62; Talbot Heath Sch., Bournemouth, 1975-; Queensmount Sch., Bournemouth, 1980-. *Recreations:* historical research, genealogy, philately, cricket. *Address:* Shepherds, Shepherds Lane, Compton, Winchester, Hants. *T:* Twyford 713285.

SOUTHBOROUGH, 4th Baron cr 1917; **Francis Michael Hopwood**; b 3 May 1922; s of 3rd Baron Southborough and of Audrey, Baroness Southborough (Audrey Evelyn Dorothy, d of late Edgar George Money); S father, 1982; m 1945, Moyna Kemp, d of Robert John Kemp Chattey; one d. Educ: Wellington College; Christ Church, Oxford. An Underwriting Member of Lloyd's, 1949–; Dep. Chairman, Glanvill, Enthoven & Co. Ltd, 1977–80 (Director, 1966); Chairman, Robert Woodson Ltd, 1970–72 (Director, 1950). Served War of 1939–45 as Lieut, The Rifle Brigade. Heir: none. Address: 50A Eaton Square, SW1W 9BE. Clubs: Brooks's, City of London.

SOUTHBY, Sir (Archibald) Richard (Charles), 2nd Bt cr 1937; OBE 1945; Lt-Col (retd), Rifle Brigade; b 18 June 1910; s of Sir Archibald Richard James Southby, 1st Bt, and Phyllis Mary (d 1974), er d of late Charles Henry Garton, Banstead Wood, Surrey; S father, 1969; m 1st, 1935, Joan Alice (marr. diss. 1947), o d of Reginald Balston; 2nd, 1947, Olive Marion (marr. diss. 1964), d of late Sir Thomas Bilbe-Robinson; one s ; 3rd, 1964, Hon. Ethel Peggy (d 1978), d of 1st Baron Cunliffe and widow of Brig. Bernard Lorenzo de Robeck, MC, RA; 4th, 1979, Iris Mackay Robertson, d of late Lt-Col G. Mackay Heriot, DSO, RM, and widow of Brig. I. C. A. Robertson. Educ: Eton; Magdalen Coll., Oxford (MA). Medal of Freedom (US). Heir: s John Richard Bilbe Southby [b 2 April 1948; m 1971, Victoria, d of William James Sturrock; one s one d]. Address: 9 Gleneagles Road, Hurlingham, Johannesburg, Transvaal, 2196, Republic of South Africa; Greystone House, Stone, Tenterden, Kent TN30 7JT. T: Appledore 400.

SOUTHEND, Archdeacon of; see Bailey, Ven. J. S.

SOUTHERN, Michael William; Adviser to HE the Minister of Health, Kingdom of Saudi Arabia, 1978, now retired; Regional Administrator, South West Thames Regional Health Authority, 1973–77; b 22 June 1918; s of William Southern and Ida Frances Southern; m 1945, Nancy Russell Golsworthy; three d. Educ: Tiffin Boys' Sch., Kingston-upon-Thames; London Univ. (DPA); Open Univ. (BA Humanities). FHA. Surrey CC Public Health Dept, 1934–39 and 1945–48; served with RAMC (NCO), 1939–45: Technician in No 1 Malaria Field Lab., 1940–41; POW Germany, 1941–44; Planning Officer and later Sec. of SW Metropolitan Regional Hosp. Bd, 1948–73. Publications: various articles in Hospital and Health Services Review, Health and Social Service Jl. Recreations: music, travel, philately. Address: 14 Poole Road, West Ewell, Epsom, Surrey KT19 9RY. T: 01-393 5096.

SOUTHERN, Richard; Theatre Consultant (private) since 1947; b 5 Oct. 1903; o s of Harry Southern and Edith (née Hockney); m 1933, Grace Kathleen Loosemore; two d. Educ: St Dunstan's College; Goldsmiths' Art School; Royal Academy of Art. Designed scenery, 1928–, for over fifty shows (Everyman Theatre, Cambridge Festival Theatre and various London theatres); also acted and stage-managed; specialized in study of stage technique and theatre architecture. Technical Lectr, Goldsmiths' College, 1932, London Theatre Studio, 1937, Royal Academy of Dramatic Art, 1945, Old Vic Theatre Centre, 1947; Theatre planning adviser to Arts Council, 1947; Director, Nuffield Theatre, Univ. of Southampton, 1964–66; Lectr, Drama Dept, Bristol Univ., 1959–60, and Special Lectr in Theatre Architecture, 1961–69, retired. Has planned various modern theatres and stages includ. Bristol Univ., 1951, Royal College of Art, 1952, Glasgow, 1953, Reading University, 1957, Nottingham, 1961, Southampton University, 1961, University Coll., London, 1967, also various reconstructions of historical theatres, Richmond, Yorkshire, 1950, King's Lynn, 1951, Williamsburg, Virginia, 1953. Hon. DLitt (Bristol), 1956. Publications: Stage Setting, 1937; Proscenium and Sightlines, 1939; The Georgian Playhouse, 1948; The Essentials of Stage Planning (with Stanley Bell and Norman Marshall), 1949; Changeable Scenery, 1952; The Open Stage, 1953; The Medieval Theatre in the Round, 1957; The Seven Ages of the Theatre, 1961; The Victorian Theatre, 1970; The Staging of Plays before Shakespeare, 1973; contrib. to specialist journals and encyclopædias. Recreation: figure drawing. Address: 37 Langham Road, Teddington TW11 9HF. T: 01-943 1979.

SOUTHERN, Sir Richard (William), Kt 1974; FBA 1960; President of St John's College, Oxford, 1969–81, Honorary Fellow, 1981; b 8 Feb. 1912; 2nd s of Matthew Henry Southern, Newcastle upon Tyne; m 1944, Sheila (née Cobley), widow of Sqdn Ldr C. Crichton-Miller; two s. Educ: Royal Grammar Sch., Newcastle upon Tyne; Balliol College, Oxford (Domus Exhibr). 1st Class Hons Modern History, 1932. Junior Research Fellow, Exeter College, Oxford, 1933–37; studied in Paris, 1933–34 and Munich, 1935; Fellow and Tutor, Balliol Coll., Oxford, 1937–61 (Hon. Fellow 1966). Served Oxford and Bucks LI, 1940; 2nd Lt Durham LI 1941; 155th Regt RAC, 1942; Captain 1943; Major 1944; Political Intelligence Dept, Foreign Office, 1943–45. Junior Proctor, Oxford Univ., 1948–49; Birkbeck Lectr in Ecclesiastical History, Trinity College, Cambridge, 1959–60; Chichele Prof. of Modern History, Oxford, 1961–69; President Royal Historical Soc., 1968–72; Selden Soc., 1973–76. Lectures: Raleigh, British Academy, 1962; David Murray, Glasgow Univ., 1963; Gifford, Glasgow Univ., 1970–72; G. M. Trevelyan, Cambridge Univ., 1980-81. Corresponding Fellow: Medieval Academy of America, 1965; Monumenta Germaniae Historica, 1982; For. Hon. Mem., Amer. Acad. of Arts and Scis, 1972. Hon. Fellow, Sidney Sussex Coll., Cambridge, 1971; Hon. DLitt: Glasgow, 1964; Durham, 1969; Cantab, 1971; Bristol, 1974; Newcastle, 1977; Warwick, 1978; St Anselm's Coll., 1981; Columbia, 1982; Hon. LLD Harvard, 1977. Publications: The Making of the

Middle Ages, 1953 (numerous foreign translations); (ed) Eadmer's Vita Anselmi, 1963; St Anselm and his Biographer, 1963; Western Views of Islam in the Middle Ages, 1962; (ed with F. S. Schmitt) Memorials of St Anselm, 1969; Medieval Humanism and other studies, 1970 (RSL award 1970); Western Society and the Church in the Middle Ages, 1970; articles in English Historical Review, Medieval and Renaissance Studies, etc. Address: 40 St John Street, Oxford.

SOUTHERN, Sir Robert, Kt 1970; CBE 1953; General Secretary, Co-operative Union Ltd, 1948–72; b 17 March 1907; s of Job Southern and Margaret (née Tonge); m 1933, Lena Chapman; one s one d. Educ: Stand Grammar Sch.; Co-operative Coll.; Manchester University. Co-operative Wholesale Soc., Bank Dept, 1925–29; Co-operative Union Ltd, 1929. Publication: Handbook to the Industrial and Provident Societies' Act, 1938. Recreations: photography, gardening. Address: 22 Glebelands Road, Prestwich, Manchester M25 5NE. T: 061-773 2699.

SOUTHERTON, Thomas Henry, BSc (Eng); CEng, MIEE; Member, Industrial Tribunals, since 1978; b 1 July 1917; s of C. H. Southerton, Birmingham; m 1st, 1945, Marjorie Elizabeth Sheen (d 1979); one s ; 2nd, 1981, Joyce Try. Educ: Bemrose Sch., Derby; Northampton Coll., London (BSc(Eng)). PO Apprentice, Derby, 1933–36; Engineering Workman, Derby and Nottingham, 1936–40; Inspector, Engineer-in-Chief's Office, 1940–45; Engineer, 1945–50; Sen. Exec. Engr, 1950–53; Factory Manager, PO Provinces, 1953–56; Dep. Controller, Factories Dept, 1956–64; Controller, Factories Dept, 1964–67; Dir, Telecommunications Management Services, 1967–73; Sen. Dir Telecommunications Personnel, 1973–75; Sen. Dir Data Processing, 1975–78. Recreations: art, architecture, music. Address: 92 Greenways, Hinchley Wood, Esher, Surrey. T: 01-398 1985.

SOUTHESK, 11th Earl of cr 1633; **Charles Alexander Carnegie**, KCVO, cr 1926; DL; Major late Scots Guards; Baron Carnegie, 1616; Baron Balinhard (UK), 1869; Bt of Nova Scotia, 1663; b 23 Sept. 1893; e s of 10th Earl of Southesk and Ethel (d 1947), o c of Sir Alexander Bannerman, 9th Bt of Elsick; S father, 1941; m 1st, 1923, HH Princess Maud (d 1945), 2nd d of HRH Princess Louise, Princess Royal and late Duke of Fife; one s ; 2nd, 1952, Evelyn, e d of Lieut-Colonel A. P. Williams-Freeman, and widow of Major Ion E. F. Campbell, DCLI. Educ: Eton; Sandhurst. DL Angus. Heir: s Duke of Fife, qv. Address: Kinnaird Castle, Brechin, Angus. T: Bridge of Dun 209.

See also Vice-Admiral Sir E. M. C. Abel Smith.

SOUTHEY, Sir Robert (John), Kt 1976; CMG 1970; Chairman, Wm Haughton & Co. Ltd, 1968–80; Federal President, Liberal Party of Australia, 1970–75; Chairman, Australian Ballet Foundation, since 1980; b 20 March 1922; s of Allen Hope Southey and Ethel Thorpe McComas, MBE; m 1st, 1946, Valerie Janet Cotton (d 1977), y d of late Hon. Sir Francis Grenville Clarke, KBE, MLC; five s ; 2nd, 1982, Marigold Merlyn Baillieu, widow of Ross Shelmerdine, CMG, OBE, y d of Dame Merlyn Myer, qv. Educ: Geelong Grammar Sch.; Magdalen Coll., Oxford (MA). Coldstream Guards, 1941–46 (Captain 1944). BA, 1st cl. PPE Oxon, 1948. Wm Haughton & Co. Ltd: Dir 1953; Man. Dir, 1959–75; Chm. 1968; Director: British Petroleum Co. of Australia Ltd; International Computers (Aust.) Pty Ltd; Kinnears Ltd; Chairman: McArthur Shipping (Vic.) Pty Ltd, 1974–81; Australian Adv. Council, General Accident Assurance Corp. Ltd; Computer Benefits (Aust.) Pty Ltd, 1982-. Mem. Executive, Liberal Party, 1966-82; Victorian State Pres., Liberal Party, 1966–70; Chm. of Council, Geelong Grammar Sch., 1966–72; Chm. Australian Adv. Cttee, Nuffield Foundn, 1970–81; Mem., Rhodes Scholarship Selection Cttee, Victoria, 1973–76. Publication: (with C. J. Puplick) Liberal Thinking, 1980. Recreations: fishing, golf. Address: Denistoun Avenue, Mount Eliza, Victoria 3930, Australia. T: 7871701. Clubs: Cavalry and Guards, MCC; Melbourne, Australian (Melbourne); Union (Sydney); Vincent's (Oxford); Leander.

SOUTHGATE, Air Vice-Marshal Harry Charles, CB 1976; CBE 1973 (MBE 1950); Director General of Engineering and Supply Policy and Planning, Ministry of Defence (Air), 1973–76, retired; b 30 Oct. 1921; s of George Harry Southgate and Lily Maud (née Clarke); m 1945, Violet Louise Davies; one s. Educ: St Saviour's Sch., Walthamstow. Entered RAF, 1941; India, 1942–45; HQ 90 Gp, 1946–50; RAF Stafford, 1950–52; Air Min., 1952–53; transf. to Equipment Br., 1953; RAF Tangmere, 1953–55; Singapore, 1955-57; psc 1957; Air Min., 1958-60; jssc 1961; Dirg Staff, RAF Staff Coll., Bracknell, 1961–64; CO 35 MU RAF Heywood, 1965–66; SESO, RAF Germany, 1967–68; idc 1969; Dir Supply Management, MoD Air, 1970–73. Recreations: travel, golf, painting, bird-watching. Address: The Rushings, Winksley, near Ripon, North Yorkshire HG4 3NR. T: Kirkby Malzeard 582. Club: Royal Air Force.

SOUTHGATE, Ven. John Eliot; Archdeacon of Cleveland since 1974; b 2 Sept. 1926; m 1958, Patricia Mary Plumb; two s one d. Educ: City of Norwich Sch.; Durham Univ. BA 1953, DipTh 1955. Ordained 1955; Vicar of Plumstead, 1962; Rector of Old Charlton, 1966; Dean of Greenwich, 1968; York Diocesan Sec. for Mission and Evangelism, 1972–81, and Vicar of Harome, 1972–77. Recreations: music, sailing, Egyptology. Address: 79 Middleton Road, Pickering, N Yorks YO18 8NQ. T: Pickering 73605.

SOUTHWARD, Dr Nigel Ralph; Apothecary to the Queen, Apothecary to the Household and to the Households of Princess Margaret Countess of

Snowdon, Princess Alice Duchess of Gloucester and the Duke and Duchess of Gloucester, since 1975; *b* 8 Feb. 1941; *s* of Sir Ralph Southward, *qv* ; *m* 1965, Annette, *d* of J. H. Hoffmann; one *s* two *d*. *Educ*: Rugby Sch.; Trinity Hall, Cambridge; Middlesex Hosp. Med. Sch. MA, MB, BChir, 1965; MRCP 1969. Ho. Surg., Mddx Hosp., 1965; Ho. Phys., Royal Berkshire Hosp., Reading, 1966; Ho. Phys., Central Mddx Hosp., 1966; Casualty MO, Mddx Hosp., 1967; Vis. MO, King Edward VII Hosp. for Officers, 1972-. *Recreations*: sailing, golf, ski-ing. *Address*: 9 Devonshire Place, W1N 1PB. *T*: 01-935 8425; 56 Primrose Gardens, NW3 4TP. *Club*: Royal Yacht Squadron.

SOUTHWARD, Sir Ralph, KCVO 1975; Apothecary to the Household of Queen Elizabeth the Queen Mother, since 1966 (Apothecary to Household of HRH the Duke of Gloucester, 1966-75, to HM Household, 1964-74, to HM the Queen, 1972-74); *b* 2 Jan. 1908; *s* of Henry Stalker Southward; *m* 1935, Evelyn, *d* of J. G. Tassell; four *s*. *Educ*: High School of Glasgow; Glasgow Univ. MB, ChB (Glasgow) 1930; MRCP 1939; FRCP 1970. Western Infirmary, and Royal Hospital for Sick Children, Glasgow; Postgraduate Medical School, Hammersmith, London. Served War of 1939-45: Medical Officer, 215 Field Ambulance, North Africa, 1940-41; Medical Specialist, Egypt, India and Ceylon, and Lieut-Colonel in charge Medical Division, 1942-43; Colonel Comdg Combined General Hospital, 1944-45. Hon. Freeman, Worshipful Soc. of Apothecaries of London, 1975. *Recreations*: trout and salmon fishing. *Address*: 9 Devonshire Place, W1. *T*: 01-935 7969; Amerden Priory, Taplow, Bucks. *T*: Maidenhead 23525.
See also N. R. Southward.

SOUTHWARK, Archbishop and Metropolitan of, (RC), since 1977; **Most Rev. Michael George Bowen;** *b* 23 April 1930; *s* of late Major C. L. J. Bowen and of Lady Makins (who *m* 1945, Sir Paul Makins, Bt, *qv*). *Educ*: Downside; Trinity Coll., Cambridge; Gregorian Univ., Rome. Army, 1948-49, 2nd Lieut Irish Guards; Wine Trade, 1951-52; English Coll., Rome, 1952-59; ordained 1958; Curate at Earlsfield and at Walworth, South London, 1959-63; taught theology, Beda Coll., Rome, 1963-66; Chancellor of Diocese of Arundel and Brighton, 1966-70; Coadjutor Bishop with right of succession to See of Arundel and Brighton, 1970-71; Bishop of Arundel and Brighton, 1971-77. *Recreations*: golf, tennis. *Address*: Archbishop's House, St George's Road, Southwark, SE1 6HX. *T*: 01-928 2495/5592.

SOUTHWARK, Bishop of, since 1980; **Rt. Rev. Ronald Oliver Bowlby;** *b* 16 August 1926; *s* of Oliver and Helena Bowlby; *m* 1956, Elizabeth Trevelyan Monro; three *s* two *d*. *Educ*: Eton Coll.; Trinity College, Oxford (MA); Westcott House, Cambridge. Curate of St Luke's, Pallion, Sunderland, 1952-56; Priest-in-charge and Vicar of St Aidan, Billingham, 1956-66; Vicar of Croydon, 1966-72; Bishop of Newcastle, 1973-80. *Publication*: contrib. Church without Walls, ed Lindars, 1969. *Recreations*: hill-walking, music. *Address*: Bishop's House, 38 Tooting Bec Gardens, SW16 1QZ.

SOUTHWARK, Auxiliary Bishops in, (RC); *see* Henderson, Rt Rev. C. J.; Jukes, Rt Rev. J.; Tripp, Rt Rev. H. G.

SOUTHWARK, Provost of; *see* Edwards, Very Rev. D. L.

SOUTHWARK, Archdeacon of; *see* Wood, Ven. W. D.

SOUTHWELL, family name of **Viscount Southwell.**

SOUTHWELL, 7th Viscount, *cr* 1776; **Pyers Anthony Joseph Southwell;** Bt 1662; Baron Southwell, 1717; International Management and Marketing Consultant; *b* 14 Sept. 1930; *s* of Hon. Francis Joseph Southwell (2nd *s* of 5th Viscount) and Agnes Mary Annette Southwell (*née* Clifford); *S* uncle, 1960; *m* 1955, Barbara Jacqueline Raynes; two *s*. *Educ*: Beaumont Coll., Old Windsor, Berks; Royal Military Academy, Sandhurst. Commissioned into 8th King's Royal Irish Hussars, 1951; resigned commission, 1955. *Recreation*: golf. *Heir*: *s* Hon. Richard Andrew Pyers Southwell, *b* 15 June 1956. *Address*: 4 Rosebery Avenue, Harpenden, Herts AL5 2QP. *T*: Harpenden 5831. *Clubs*: Army and Navy, MCC.

SOUTHWELL, Bishop of, since 1970; **Rt. Rev. John Denis Wakeling,** MC 1945; *b* 12 Dec. 1918; *s* of Rev. John Lucas Wakeling and Mary Louise (*née* Glover); *m* 1941, Josephine Margaret, *d* of Dr Benjamin Charles Broomhall and Marion (*née* Aldwinckle); two *s*. *Educ*: Dean Close Sch., Cheltenham; St Catharine's Coll., Cambridge. MA Cantab 1944. Commnd Officer in Royal Marines, 1939-45 (Actg Maj.): Ridley Hall, Cambridge, 1946-47. Deacon, 1947; Priest, 1948. Asst Curate, Barwell, Leics, 1947; Chaplain of Clare Coll., Cambridge, and Chaplain to the Cambridge Pastorate, 1950-52; Vicar of Emmanuel, Plymouth, 1952-59; Prebendary of Exeter Cathedral, 1957, Prebendary Emeritus, 1959; Vicar of Barking, Essex, 1959-65; Archdeacon of West Ham, 1965-70. Entered House of Lords, June 1974. Chairman: Archbishops' Council on Evangelism, 1976-79; Lee Abbey Council, 1976. *Recreations*: cricket; formerly hockey (Cambridge Univ. Hockey Club, 1938, 1939, 1945, 1946, English Trials Caps, 1939, 1946, 1947, 1948, 1949). *Address*: Bishop's Manor, Southwell, Notts. *Clubs*: Army and Navy, National; Hawks (Cambridge).

SOUTHWELL, Provost of; *see* Irvine, Very Rev. J. M.

SOUTHWELL, Richard Charles, QC 1977; *s* of Sir Philip Southwell, CBE, MC and late Mary Burnett, *d* of Thomas Scarratt, Belmont Hall, Ipstones,

Staffs; *m* 1962, Belinda Mary, *d* of Col F. H. Pownall, MC; two *s* one *d*. *Address*: 1 Hare Court, Temple, EC4. *T*: 01-353 3171/6628.

SOUTHWELL, Ven. Roy; Archdeacon of Northolt, 1970-80, Archdeacon Emeritus, since 1980; *b* 3 Dec. 1914; *s* of William Thomas and Lilian Southwell; *m* 1948, Nancy Elizabeth Lindsay Sharp; two *d*. *Educ*: Sudbury Grammar Sch.; King's Coll., London (AKC 1942). Curate: St Michael's, Wigan, 1942-44; St John the Divine, Kennington, 1944-48; Vicar of Ixworth, 1948-51; Vicar of St John's, Bury St Edmunds, 1951-56; Rector of Bucklesham with Brightwell and Foxhall, 1956-59; Asst Director of Religious Education, Diocese of St Edmundsbury and Ipswich, 1956-58, Director, 1959-67. Hon. Canon of St Edmundsbury, 1959-68; Vicar of Hendon, 1968-71. *Recreations*: reading, singing and watching TV. *Address*: 397 Sprowston Road, Norwich NR3 4HY. *T*: Norwich 405977.

SOUTHWOOD, Captain Horace Gerald, CBE 1966; DSC 1941; Royal Navy; Managing Director, Silley, Cox & Co. Ltd, Falmouth Docks, 1974-78; Chairman, Falmouth Group, 1976-78; *b* 19 April 1912; *s* of late Horace George Southwood; *m* 1936, Ruby Edith Hayes; two *s* one *d*. *Educ*: HMS Fisgard, RN Coll., Greenwich. Joined RN, 1927; HMS Resolution, Medit. Stn, 1932-34; HMS Barham, 1934-35; RN Coll., Greenwich, 1935-36; HMS Royal Oak, Home Fleet, 1936-38; specialised in Submarines, 1938; HMS Lucia, 1938-39. HM Submarine, Regent, 1939-41, China and Medit. (despatches, DSC); HMS Medway, Medit., 1941-42; HM Submarine, Amphion (first of Class), 1943-45. HMS Dolphin, 1946-48; HMS Vengeance, 1948-49; Comdr, 1948; HMS Glory, 1949-51; HMS Forth, 1951-52; Admty, Whitehall, 1952-54; HM Dockyard, Portsmouth (Dep. Man.), 1954-58; jssc, 1958-59; Capt., 1958. Chief Engr, Singapore, 1959-62; Sen. Officers' War Course, 1962; Manager, Engrg Dept, HM Dockyard, Portsmouth, 1963-67; Gen. Manager, HM Dockyard, Devonport, 1967-72, retd. Management Consultant, Productivity and Management Services Ltd, 1972-74. CEng, FIMechE. *Recreations*: sailing, fishing, golf, caravanning. *Address*: Dolphin Cottage, Riverside, Newton Ferrers, Devon. *T*: Plymouth 872401. *Clubs*: Royal Western Yacht (Plymouth); Yealm Yacht (Newton Ferrers).

SOUTHWOOD, Prof. (Thomas) Richard (Edmund), FRS 1977; Linacre Professor of Zoology, University of Oxford and Fellow of Merton College, Oxford, since 1979; Chairman, Royal Commission on Environmental Pollution, since 1981 (Member, since 1974); *b* 20 June 1931; *s* of Edmund W. Southwood and late A. Mary, *d* of Archdeacon T. R. Regg, and *g s* of W. E. W. Southwood; *m* 1955, Alison Langley, *d* of A. L. Harden, Harpenden, Herts; two *s*. *Educ*: Gravesend Grammar Sch.; Imperial Coll., London. BSc, ARCS 1952; PhD London, 1955; DSc London, 1963; MA Oxon 1979. FIBiol 1968. ARC Research Schol., Rothamsted Experimental Station, 1952-55; Res. Asst and Lecturer, Zoology Dept, Imperial Coll., London, 1955-64; Vis. Prof., Dept. of Entomology, University of California, Berkeley, 1964-65; Reader in Insect Ecology, University of London, 1964-67; Prof. of Zoology and Applied Entomology, London Univ., Head of Dept of Zoology and Applied Entomol., and Dir of Field Station, Imperial Coll., 1967-79; Dean, Royal Coll. of Science, 1971-72; Chm., Division of Life Sciences, Imperial Coll., 1974-77. Member: ARC Adv. Cttee on Plants and Soils, 1970-72; ARC Res. Grants Bd, 1972-; JCO Arable and Forage Crops Bd, 1972-79; NERC Terrestrial Life Sciences (formerly Nature Conservancy) Grants Cttee, 1971-76 (Chm., 1972-76); Council, St George's House, Windsor, 1974-80; Adv. Bd Research Councils, 1977-80; Trop. Medicine Panel, Wellcome Trust, 1977-79; Nat. Radiological Protection Bd, 1980-; Pres., British Ecological Soc., 1976-78 (Hon. Treas., 1960-64 and 1967-68). Governor, Glasshouse Crops Research Inst., 1969-81; Trustee, British Museum (Natural History), 1974- (Chm., 1980-); Delegate, OUP, 1980-; Mem., Hebdomadal Council, 1981-. Plenary speaker, 15th Internat. Congress on Entomology, Washington, 1976; Spencer Lectr, Univ. of British Columbia, 1978; Bawden Lectr, British Crop Protection Conf., 1979. Foreign Hon. Mem., Amer. Acad. of Arts and Sciences, 1981. Scientific Medal, Zool. Soc., London, 1969. *Publications*: (with D. Leston) Land and Water Bugs of the British Isles, 1959; Life of the Wayside and Woodland, 1963; Ecological Methods, 1966, 2nd edn 1978; many papers in entomological and ecological jls. *Recreations*: natural history, gardening. *Address*: Merton College, Oxford. *Clubs*: Athenæum; Royal Society.
See also W. F. W. Southwood.

SOUTHWOOD, William Frederick Walter, MD; MChir; FRCS; Consultant Surgeon, Bath Health District, since 1966; *b* 8 June 1925; *s* of late Stuart W. Southwood, MC, and of Mildred M. Southwood, and *g s* of W. E. W. Southwood; *m* 1965, Margaret Carleton Holderness, *d* of late Sir Ernest Holderness, Bt, CBE, and Lady Holderness; two *s*. *Educ*: Charterhouse; Trinity Coll., Cambridge (MA 1951, MD 1964, MChir 1956); Guy's Hosp. FRCS 1954. Surg. Registrar, West London Hosp. and St Mark's Hosp. for Diseases of the Rectum, 1954-60; Sen. Surg. Registrar, Royal Infirmary, Bristol, 1960-66. Hunterian Prof., RCS, 1961. Member: Court of Assts, Worshipful Soc. of Apothecaries of London, 1975- (Chm., Exams Cttee, 1981-); Temp. Registration Assessment Bd, GMC, 1976-; Cttee, Non-Univ. Medical Licencing Bodies, 1979-. Examr in Anatomy and Surgery to GNC, 1957-72. *Publications*: articles in surgical jls. *Recreations*: fishing, snooker. *Address*: Upton House, Bathwick Hill, Bath, Avon. *T*: Bath 65152. *Clubs*: East India; Bath and County (Bath).

SOUTHWORTH, Sir Frederick, Kt 1965; QC; Chief Justice, Malawi, 1964-70, retired 1970; *b* Blackburn, Lancashire, 9 May 1910; *s* of late Harper Southworth, Blackburn, Lancs; *m* 1942, Margaret, *d* of James Rice,

Monaghan, Ireland; three d. Educ: Queen Elizabeth's Grammar Sch., Blackburn; Exeter Coll., Oxford. Called to the Bar, Gray's Inn, 1936. War of 1939-45; commissioned 1939; served with South Lancashire Regiment and Lancashire Fusiliers, and with Department of the Judge Advocate General in India, 1939-46; Hon. Colonel, Crown Counsel, Palestine, 1946-47; Crown Counsel, Tanganyika, 1947-51; Attorney-General, Bahamas, 1951-55; QC Bahamas, 1952; Acting Governor, July-Aug. 1952; Acting Chief Justice, July-Oct. 1954; Puisne Judge, Nyasaland, 1955-64; Acting Governor-General, Malawi, 1964 and 1965. Publications: Specimen Charges, in use in the courts of Tanzania, Zanzibar, Kenya and Uganda; The Southworth Commission Report: an inquiry into allegations made by the international press against the Nyasaland Police, 1960. Address: c/o Barclays Bank, Darwen Street, Blackburn, Lancs.

SOUTHWORTH, Jean May, QC 1973; a Recorder of the Crown Court, since 1972; b 20 April 1926; o c of late Edgar and Jane Southworth, Clitheroe. Educ: Queen Ethelburga's Sch., Harrogate; St Anne's Coll., Oxford (MA). Served in WRNS, 1944-45. Called to Bar, Gray's Inn, 1954; Bencher, 1980. Standing Counsel to Dept of Trade and Industry for Central Criminal Court and Inner London Sessions, 1969-73. Fellow, Woodard Corporation (Northern Div.), 1974. Recreations: music, watching cricket. Address: 21 Caroline Place, W2 4AN; Queen Elizabeth Building, Temple, EC4Y 9BS.

SOUYAVE, Sir (Louis) Georges, Kt 1971; His Honour Judge Souyave; District Judge, Hong Kong, since 1980; b 29 May 1926; m 1953, Mona de Chermont; two s four d. Educ: St Louis Coll., Seychelles; Gray's Inn, London. Barrister-at-Law, Gray's Inn, 1949. In private practice, Seychelles, 1949-56; Asst Attorney-Gen., Seychelles, 1956-62; Supreme Court, Seychelles: Additional Judge, 1962-64; Puisne Judge, 1964-70; Chief Justice, 1970-76; New Hebrides: Resident Judge of the High Court (British jurisdiction) and British Judge of the Supreme Ct of the Condominium, 1976-80. Recreations: golf, swimming. Address: District Court, Victoria, Hong Kong.

SOUZAY, Gérard, (né Gérard Marcel Tisserand), Chevalier, Légion d'Honneur; Chevalier de l'Ordre des Arts et Lettres; French baritone; b 8 Dec. 1921. Educ: Paris Conservatoire Musique. World Première, Stravinsky's Canticum Sacrum, Venice Festival, 1956; Bach B Minor Mass at Salzburg Festival; Pelléas et Mélisande, Rome Opera, Opera Comique, 1962, Scala, Milan, 1973; Don Giovanni, Paris Opera, 1963; second tour of Australia and New Zealand, 1964. Also tours in US, South America, Japan, Africa, Europe. Annual Lieder recitals, Salzburg Festival. Has made recordings; Grand Prix du Disque, for Ravel Recital, etc. Recreations: tennis, painting. Address: 26 rue Freycinet, 75116 Paris, France.

SOWDEN, John Percival; Chairman, Costain Group Ltd (formerly Richard Costain Ltd), 1972-80 (Director, 1967-82); Regional Director, Central London Regional Board, Lloyds Bank, since 1980; b 6 Jan. 1917; s of Percy Sowden and Gertrude Sowden (née Moss); m 1st, 1940, Ruth Dorothy Keane (marr. diss. 1969); one s; 2nd, 1969, Joyce Diana Timson. Educ: Silcoates Sch., Wakefield, Yorks; The Grammar Sch., Hebden Bridge, Yorks; City and Guilds Coll., Imperial Coll. of Science (BScEng, ACGI; FCGI 1973). FIStructE. Served War: commnd, RE, with service in UK, ME and Italy, 1939-46. Joined Richard Costain Ltd, 1948; Site Project Manager on various construction projects, incl. Festival of Britain, Apapa Wharf, Nigeria, and Bridgetown Harbour, Barbados, 1948-60; Joint Managing Director: Richard Costain (Associates) Ltd, 1961-62; Costain-Blankevoort Internat. Dredging Co. Ltd, 1963-65; Richard Costain Ltd: Manager, Civil Engrg Div., 1965-69; Board Member, 1967; Chief Executive, Internat. Area, 1969-70; Chief Executive, 1970-75. Member, Governing Body, Imperial Coll. of Science and Technology, 1971-, Fellow, 1980. Recreations: reading, joinery. Address: 22 Wildcroft Manor, SW15 3TS. T: 01-788 5336. Club: Royal Automobile.

SOWREY, Air Marshal Sir Frederick (Beresford), KCB 1978 (CB 1968); CBE 1965; AFC 1954; b 14 Sept. 1922; s of late Group Captain Frederick Sowrey, DSO, MC, AFC; m 1946, Anne Margaret, d of late Captain C. T. A. Bunbury, OBE, RN; one s one d. Educ: Charterhouse. Joined RAF 1940; flying training in Canada, 1941; Fighter-reconnaissance Squadron, European theatre, 1942-44; Flying Instructors Sch., 1944; Airborne Forces, 1945; No 615 (Co. of Surrey) Squadron, RAuxAF, 1946-48; Fighter Gunnery Sch., 1949-50, comdg 615 Sqdn, 1951-54; RAF Staff Coll., Bracknell, 1954; Chiefs of Staff Secretariat, 1955-58; comdg No 46 Sqdn, 1958-60; Personal Staff Officer to CAS, 1960-62; comdg RAF Abingdon, 1962-64; IDC 1965; SASO, Middle East Comd (Aden), 1966-67; Dir Defence Policy, MoD, 1968-70; SASO, RAF Trng Comd, 1970-72; Comdt, Nat. Defence Coll., 1972-75; Dir-Gen. RAF Training, 1975-77; UK Representative, Permanent Military Deputies Group CENTO, 1977-79. Research Fellow, IISS, 1980-81. Vice-Chm., Victory Services Assoc. Publications: contribs and book reviews for defence jls. Recreations: motoring sport (world class records 1956), veteran aircraft and cars, mechanical devices of any kind and age, fishing. Address: 40 Adam and Eve Mews, W8. Club: Royal Air Force.

SOWRY, Dr (George Stephen) Clive, FRCP; Physician, Edgware General Hospital, 1953-82; b 26 Dec. 1917; s of Dr George H. Sowry and Mrs Stella Sowry; m 1943, Jeanne (née Adams); one s one d. Educ: Bilton Grange, near Rugby; Epsom Coll., Surrey; St Mary's Hosp. Med. Sch., London (MB, BS 1940; MD 1947). FRCP 1963 (MRCP 1946). Served War, RNVR, 1941-45 (Surg. Lieut). Med. appts, St Mary's Hosp., Brompton Hosp. and

Hammersmith Hosp., until 1953; med. admin, Edgware Gen. Hosp., 1957-73. Royal College of Physicians: Pro Censor, 1975; Censor, 1976; Sen. Censor and Vice-Pres., 1978-79; Mem. Qualification Cttee, and Examnr, Faculty of Occupational Medicine. FRSM. Silver Jubilee Medal, 1977. Publication: (jtly) article on aetiology of essential hypertension in Clin. Science. Recreations: sailing, singing. Address: 53 Aldenham Avenue, Radlett, Herts. T: Radlett 6046.

SOYSA, Sir Warusahennedige Abraham Bastian, Kt 1954; CBE 1953 (MBE 1950); JP; formerly Mayor of Kandy, Sri Lanka. Address: 32/36 Sangaraja Mawatha, Kandy, Sri Lanka.

SPAFFORD, Very Rev. Christopher Garnett Howsin; Provost and Vicar of Newcastle, since 1976; b 10 Sept. 1924; s of late Rev. Canon Douglas Norman Spafford and Frances Alison Spafford; m 1953, Stephanie Peel; three s. Educ: Marlborough Coll.; St John's Coll., Oxford (MA 2nd Cl. Hons Modern History); Wells Theological Coll. Curate of Brighouse, 1950; Curate of Huddersfield Parish Church, 1953; Vicar of Hebden Bridge, 1955; Rector of Thornhill, Dewsbury, 1961; Vicar of St Chad's, Shrewsbury, 1969. Recreations: reading, gardening, walking. Address: The Cathedral Vicarage, 23 Montagu Avenue, Gosforth, Newcastle upon Tyne NE3 4HY. T: Newcastle upon Tyne 853472.

SPAFFORD, George Christopher Howsin; a Recorder of the Crown Court, since 1975; Chancellor, Manchester Diocese, since 1976; b 1 Sept. 1921; s of Christopher Howsin Spafford and Clara Margaret Spafford; m 1959, Iola Margaret, 3rd d of Bertrand Leslie Hallward, qv ; one s one d. Educ: Rugby; Brasenose Coll., Oxford (MA, BCL Hons). Served RA, 1939-46 (Captain). Called to Bar, Middle Temple, 1948. Recreation: painting pictures. Address: 460 The Royal Exchange, Cross Street, Manchester M2 7EW.

SPAGHT, Monroe E., MA, PhD; retired Director, Royal Dutch/Shell companies; Director: Shell Oil Co., USA, 1953-80 (Chairman, 1965-70); Royal Dutch Petroleum Co., 1965-80; various Royal Dutch/Shell companies, 1965-80; b Eureka, California, 9 Dec. 1909; s of Fred E. and Alpha L. Spaght; m two s one d. Educ: Humboldt State Univ.; Stanford Univ.; University of Leipzig. AB 1929, MA 1930, PhD 1933, Stanford Univ. (Chemistry). Research scientist and technologist, Shell Oil Co., 1933-45; Vice-President, Shell Development Co., 1945-48, President, 1949-52; Exec. Vice-President, Shell Oil Co., 1953-60, President, 1961-65; Man. Dir, Royal Dutch/Shell Group, 1965-70; Director: Stanford Research Inst., 1953-70; Inst. of International Education, 1953- (Chm., 1971-74); American Petroleum Inst., 1953-; American Standard, 1972-; Mem. Adv. Bd, The Boston Co., 1979- (Dir, 1971-79). Chm., Internat. Adv. Bd of Chemical Bank, 1977-80; Mem., Internat. Adv. Cttee, Wells Fargo Bank, 1977-. Trustee, Stanford Univ., 1955-65. President, Economic Club of New York, 1964-65. Hon. DSc: Rensselaer Polytechnic Inst., 1958; Drexel Inst. of Technology, 1962; Hon. LLD: Manchester, 1964; California State Colleges, 1965; Millikin Univ., Illinois, 1967; Wesleyan Univ., Middletown, Conn, 1968; Hon. DEng, Colorado Sch. of Mines, 1971. Order of Francisco de Miranda, Venezuela, 1968; Comdr, Order of Oranje Nassau, 1970. Publications: The Bright Key, 1965; Minding My Own Business, 1971; Here's What I Said, 1977; The Multinational Corporation, its Manners, Methods and Myths, 1977; contribs to scientific journals. Address: 70 Arlington House, SW1A 1RL. Clubs: Athenæum; Sunningdale; Blind Brook Country, Links (New York).

SPALDING, Prof. Dudley Brian, MA, ScD; FIMechE, FInstF; Professor of Heat Transfer in the University of London at the Imperial College of Science and Technology, since 1958; b New Malden, Surrey, 9 Jan. 1923; s of H. A. Spalding; m 1947, Eda Ilse-Lotte (née Goericke); two s two d. Educ: King's College Sch., Wimbledon; The Queen's Coll., Oxford; Pembroke Coll., Cambridge. BA (Oxon) 1944; MA (Cantab) 1948, PhD (Cantab) 1951. Bataafsche Petroleum Matschapij, 1944-45; Ministry of Supply, 1945-47; National Physical Laboratory, 1947-48; ICI Research Fellow at Cambridge Univ., 1948-50; Cambridge University Demonstrator in Engineering, 1950-54; Reader in Applied Heat, Imperial College of Science and Technology, 1954-58. Managing Director: Combustion, Heat and Mass Transfer Ltd, 1970-; Concentration, Heat and Momentum Ltd, 1975-. Publications: Some Fundamentals of Combustion, 1955; (with E. H. Cole) Engineering Thermodynamics, 1958; Convective Mass Transfer, 1963; (with S. V. Patankar) Heat and Mass Transfer in Boundary Layers, 1967, rev. edn 1970; (co-author) Heat and Mass Transfer in Recirculating Flows, 1969; (with B. E. Launder) Mathematical Models of Turbulence, 1972; numerous scientific papers. Recreations: squash, poetry. Address: (home) 2 Vineyard Hill Road, SW19. T: 01-946 2514; (business) Imperial College, Exhibition Road, SW7. T: 01-589 5111.

SPALDING, Rear-Adm. Ian Jaffery L.; see Lees-Spalding.

SPALDING, John Oliver; Director and Chief General Manager, Halifax Building Society, since 1982; b 4 Aug. 1924; s of John and Winifred Ethel Spalding; m 1952, Mary Whitworth Hull; one s one d. Educ: William Hulme's Grammar School, Manchester; Jesus College, Cambridge (MA). Served in HM Forces, India, Burma, Singapore and Java, 1943-47; Captain RA. Admitted a Solicitor, 1952; service with Manchester Corporation and Hampshire CC, latterly as Senior Assistant Solicitor, 1952-62; Assistant Solicitor, Halifax Building Soc., 1962-64; Head Office Solicitor, 1964-74; General Manager, 1970; Director, 1975; Deputy Chief General Manager, 1981.

Recreations: boats and bird-watching. *Address:* Halifax Building Society, Trinity Road, Halifax HX1 2RG.

SPANN, Keith, CB 1980; CVO 1977; Secretary, Premier's Department, Queensland, since 1978; *b* 8 Nov. 1922; *s* of late G. F. A. Spann; *m* 1946, Marjorie, *d* of W. R. Golding, CMG, MBE; three *s. Educ:* State High School, Gympie. Joined Queensland Public Service, 1938; Dept of Auditor-Gen., 1948-61; Sec. to Cabinet, 1961-64; Asst Under Sec., Premier's Dept, 1964-70, Under Sec., 1970-78. *Recreations:* fishing, golf, gemmology. *Address:* 14 Valiant Street, Chermside West, Queensland 4032, Australia.

SPANSWICK, (Ernest) Albert (George), JP; General Secretary, Confederation of Health Service Employees, since 1974; Member, TUC General Council, since 1977; *b* 2 Oct. 1919; *m* Joyce Redmore; one *s* two *d.* SRN, RMN. Regional Sec., Northern Region, Confedn of Health Service Employees, 1959; apptd National Officer, 1962; elected Asst General Secretary, 1969; elected General Secretary, 1973, and took up duties in July 1974. Chm., TUC Health Services Cttee, 1977-. JP Co. Surrey, 1970. *Recreations:* swimming, walking, fishing. *Address:* Confederation of Health Service Employees, Glen House, High Street, Banstead, Surrey SM7 2LH. *T:* Burgh Heath 53322.

SPANTON, Harry Merrik, OBE 1975; CEng, FIMinE; CBIM; Board Member, National Coal Board, since 1980; *b* 27 Nov. 1924; *s* of late Henry Broadley Spanton and Edith Jane Spanton; *m* 1945, Mary Margaret Hawkins; one *s. Educ:* Eastbourne Coll.; Royal Sch. of Mines (BSc (Min) (Eng) 1945; ARSM). CEng, FIMinE 1957; CBIM 1979. Colliery Manager, 1950; Agent, 1954; Gp Man., 1956; Dep. Prodn Man., 1958; Dep. Prodn Dir, 1960; Asst Gen. Man., 1962; Gen. Man., 1964; Area Dir, 1967-80. Chairman: British Mining Consultants Ltd, 1981-; J. H. Sankey & Son, 1982-; Director: Compower, 1981-; NCB (Coal Products), 1981-; Staveley Chemicals, 1981-; Coal Processing Consultants, 1981-. Member: W European Coal Producers Assoc., 1980-; CBI Overseas Cttee, 1981-. Vice-Pres., Coal Trade Benevolent Assoc., 1979- (Chm., 1978). *Publications:* articles in prof. jls. *Recreations:* travel, shooting. *Address:* Hobart House, Grosvenor Place, SW1X 7AE. *T:* 01-235 2020.

SPAREY, John Raymond, MA; Secretary, Institution of Municipal Engineers, since 1977; Secretary-General, International Federation of Municipal Engineers, since 1979; *b* 28 July 1924; *s* of late Henry Sparey and Lilian May (*née* Coles); *m* 1950, Audrie Kathleen, *d* of Col E. J. W. Porter, OBE, TD, Portsmouth; two *s* one *d. Educ:* City of Bath Sch.; King's Coll., London; Trinity Coll., Cambridge (BA 1950, MA 1954). Royal Naval Scientific Service, 1944-47; Asst Secretary, Assoc. of Certified Accountants, 1952-69; Royal Institution of Chartered Surveyors: Dep. Sec., 1969-70; Sec. for Educn and Membership, 1970-74; Sec., Planning and Development Div., 1976. *Recreations:* gardening, sailing. *Address:* Oakdene, 21 Broomfield Ride, Oxshott KT22 0LP. *T:* Oxshott 2587. *Clubs:* Reform; Seaview Yacht (Seaview, IoW).

SPARK, Mrs Muriel Sarah, OBE 1967; writer; *b* Edinburgh; *d* of Bernard Camberg and Sarah Elizabeth Maud (*née* Uezzell); *m* 1937 (marr. diss.); one *s. Educ:* James Gillespie's School for Girls, Edinburgh. General Secretary, The Poetry Society, Editor, The Poetry Review, 1947-49. FRSL 1963. Hon. Mem., Amer. Acad. of Arts and Letters, 1978. Hon. DLitt Strathclyde, 1971. *Publications: critical and biographical:* (ed jtly) Tribute to Wordsworth, 1950; (ed) Selected Poems of Emily Brontë, 1952; Child of Light: a Reassessment of Mary Shelley, 1951; (ed jtly) My Best Mary: the letters of Mary Shelley, 1953; John Masefield, 1953; (joint) Emily Brontë: her Life and Work, 1953; (ed) The Brontë Letters, 1954; (ed jointly) Letters of John Henry Newman, 1957; *poems:* The Fanfarlo and Other Verse, 1952; *fiction:* The Comforters, 1957; Robinson, 1958; The Go-Away Bird, 1958; Memento Mori, 1959 (adapted for stage, 1964); The Ballad of Peckham Rye, 1960 (Italia prize, for dramatic radio, 1962); The Bachelors, 1960; Voices at Play, 1961; The Prime of Miss Jean Brodie, 1961 (adapted for stage, 1966, filmed 1969, and BBC TV, 1978); Doctors of Philosophy (play), 1963; The Girls of Slender Means, 1963 (adapted for radio, 1964, and BBC TV, 1975); The Mandelbaum Gate, 1965 (James Tait Black Memorial Prize); Collected Stories I, 1967; Collected Poems I, 1967; The Public Image, 1968; The Very Fine Clock (for children), 1969; The Driver's Seat, 1970 (filmed 1974); Not to Disturb, 1971; The Hothouse by the East River, 1973; The Abbess of Crewe, 1974 (filmed 1977); The Takeover, 1976; Territorial Rights, 1979; Loitering with Intent, 1981. *Recreations:* poetry, travel. *Address:* c/o Macmillan & Co. Ltd, Little Essex Street, WC2.

SPARKES, Sir Robert Lyndley, Kt 1979; State President, National Party of Australia (formerly Country Party), Queensland, since 1970; Managing Partner, Lyndley Pastoral Co., since 1974; *b* 30 May 1929; *s* of late Sir James Sparkes, Jandowae, Queensland; *m* 1953, June, *d* of M. Morgan; two *s. Educ:* Southport Sch., Queensland. Chairman: National Party (formerly Country Party) Lands Cttee, Queensland, 1966-; NPA Nominees Pty Ltd; Wambo Shire Council, 1967- (Mem., 1952-55 and 1964-). *Recreation:* reading. *Address:* Dundonald, PO Box 117, Jandowae, Queensland 4410, Australia. *T:* (074) 68 5196.

SPARKMAN, John J.; US Senator from Alabama, 1946-78; Chairman, Senate Committee on Foreign Relations, 1975-78; *b* 20 Dec. 1899; *s* of Whitten J. Sparkman and Julia Mitchell (*née* Kent); *m* 1923, Ivo Hall; one *d. Educ:*

University of Alabama. AB 1921, LLB 1923, AM 1924; Phi Beta Kappa. Admitted to Alabama Bar, 1925; practised as Attorney, Huntsville, Ala, 1925-36; US Commissioner, 1930-31; Member of US House of Representatives, 1937-46; Democratic Nomination for Vice-Presidency, 1952. Chm., Senate Banking Cttee, 1967. Hon. degrees: Alabama; Spring Hill Coll., Ala; Athens Coll., Ala; Huntingdon Coll., Ala; Auburn; Seoul, Korea. Methodist. *Address:* 223 East Side Square, Huntsville, Alabama 35801, USA. *Clubs:* 1925 F Street (Washington); Huntsville Country (Alabama).

SPARKS, Arthur Charles, BSc (Econ); Under-Secretary, Ministry of Agriculture, Fisheries and Food, 1959-74; *b* 1914; *s* of late Charles Herbert and Kate Dorothy Sparks; *m* 1939, Betty Joan (*d* 1978), *d* of late Harry Oswald and Lilian Mary Simmons; three *d. Educ:* Selhurst Grammar Sch.; London School of Economics. Clerk, Ministry of Agriculture and Fisheries, 1931; Administrative Grade, 1936; National Fire Service, 1942-44; Principal Private Secretary to Minister of Agriculture and Fisheries, 1946-47; Asst Secretary, Ministry of Agriculture and Fisheries, 1947-49 and 1951-59; Asst Secretary, Treasury, 1949-51. Chm., Internat. Wheat Council, 1968-69. *Recreations:* reading, walking. *Address:* 2 Stratton Close, Merton Park, SW19 3JF. *T:* 01-542 4827.

SPARKS, Rev. Hedley Frederick Davis, DD Oxon, 1949; FBA 1959; ATCL 1927; Oriel Professor of the Interpretation of Holy Scripture, University of Oxford, 1952-76; *b* 14 Nov. 1908; *s* of late Rev. Frederick Sparks and late Blanche Barnes Sparks (formerly Jackson); *m* 1953, Margaret Joan, *d* of late C. H. Davy; two *s* one *d. Educ:* St Edmund's Sch., Canterbury; BNC, Oxford; Ripon Hall, Oxford. Hon. DD (St Andrews), 1963; Hon. Fellow, Oriel Coll., Oxford, 1980. *Publications:* The Old Testament in the Christian Church, 1944; The Formation of the New Testament, 1952; A Synopsis of the Gospels, part I: The Synoptic Gospels with the Johannine Parallels, 1964, 2nd edn 1970; part II: The Gospel according to St John with the Synoptic Parallels, 1974, combined volume edn, 1977; *Joint Editor:* Novum Testamentum Domini Nostri Iesu Christi Latine secundum editionem Sancti Hieronymi, Part ii, fasc. 5, 1937, fasc. 6, 1939, fasc. 7, 1941, Part iii, fasc. 2, 1949, fasc. 3, 1953; Biblia Sacra iuxta Vulgatam versionem, 1969, 2nd edn 1975; *Contributor:* The Bible in its Ancient and English Versions, 1940, 2nd edn 1954; Studies in the Gospels, 1955; The Cambridge History of the Bible, vol. 1, 1970, 2nd edn, 1975. *Recreations:* music and railways. *Address:* 14 Longport, Canterbury, Kent. *T:* Canterbury 66265.

SPARROW, (Albert) Charles, QC 1966; barrister; *b* Kasauli, India, 16 Sept. 1925; *e s* of Captain Charles Thomas Sparrow, sometime Essex Regt, and Antonia Sparrow; *m* 1949, Edith Rosalie Taylor; two *s* one *d. Educ:* Royal Grammar Sch., Colchester. Served Civil Defence, 1939-43; joined Army, 1943; posted as cadet to India, commnd into Royal Signals and served in Far East, 1944-47; OC, GHQ Signals, Simla, 1947. Admitted to Gray's Inn, 1947 (Holker Senior Scholar, Atkin Scholar, Lee Prizeman and Richards Prizeman); called to Bar, 1950, Master of the Bench, 1976; LLB London Univ., 1951; admitted to Lincoln's Inn, 1967; in practice in Chancery and before Parliament, 1950-. Member: General Council of the Bar, 1969-73; Senate of the Four Inns of Court, 1970-73; Incorp. Council of Law Reporting, 1977-. Hon. Legal Adviser to Council for British Archæology (concerned notably with legal protection of antiquities and reform of treasure trove; produced two draft Antiquities Bills), 1966-. Chm., independent Panel of Inquiry for affairs of RSPCA, 1973-74. FSA 1972; Pres., Essex Archæological Soc., 1975-78. Chm., Stock Branch, British Legion, 1970-75. Hon. Counsellor to Freemen of England, 1978; Freeman, City of London. OStJ 1982. *Recreation:* Romano-British archæology. *Address:* 13 Old Square, Lincoln's Inn, WC2A 3UA. *T:* 01-242 6105; Croyde Lodge, Stock, Essex.

SPARROW, Bryan; HM Diplomatic Service; Ambassador to the United Republic of Cameroon, since 1981; also to Republic of Equatorial Guinea and Central African Republic, since 1982; *b* 8 June 1933; *m* 1958, Fiona Mary Mylechreest; one *s* one *d. Educ:* Hemel Hempstead Grammar Sch.; Pembroke Coll., Oxford (BA Hons). Served Army, 1951-53. Belgrade, 1958-61; FO, 1961-64; Moscow, 1964-66; Tunis, 1967-68; Casablanca, 1968-70; FO, 1970-72; Kinshasa, 1972-76; Prague, 1976-78; Counsellor (Commercial), Belgrade, 1978-81. *Recreations:* fishing, gardening, travel. *Address:* c/o Foreign and Commonwealth Office, SW1; 35 Linton Street, N1.

SPARROW, Charles; see Sparrow, A. C.

SPARROW, John, FCA; Head of Central Policy Review Staff, Cabinet Office, since 1982; *b* 4 June 1933; *s* of Richard A. and Winifred R. Sparrow; *m* 1967, Cynthia Whitehouse. *Educ:* Stationers' Company's School; London School of Economics (BSc Econ). FCA 1957. With Rawlinson & Hunter, Chartered Accountants, 1954-59; Ford Motor Co. Ltd, 1960; AEI-Hotpoint Ltd, 1960-63; United Leasing Corporation, 1963-64; Morgan Grenfell & Co., 1964-82. Director: Morgan Grenfell Holdings Ltd, 1971-82; Morgan Grenfell & Co. Ltd, 1970-82; Coalite Group plc, 1974-82; United Gas Industries plc, 1974-82. *Recreations:* cricket, crosswords, horse-racing. *Address:* 70 Whitehall, SW1. *Club:* MCC.

SPARROW, John Hanbury Angus, OBE 1946; Warden of All Souls College, Oxford, 1952-77; *b* New Oxley, near Wolverhampton, 13 Nov. 1906; *e s* of I. S. Sparrow and Margaret Macgregor; unmarried. *Educ:* Winchester (Scholar); New Coll., Oxford (Scholar). 1st Class, Hon. Mods, 1927; 1st Class, Lit Hum, 1929; Fellow of All Souls Coll., 1929 (re-elected

1937, 1946); Chancellor's Prize for Latin Verse, 1929; Eldon Scholar, 1929; called to Bar, Middle Temple, 1931; practised in Chancery Division, 1931-39; enlisted in Oxford and Bucks LI, 1939; Commnd Coldstream Guards, 1940; Military Asst to Lt-Gen. Sir H. C. B. Wemyss in War Office and on Military Mission in Washington, Feb.-Dec. 1941; rejoined regt in England, 1942; DAAG and AAG, War Office, 1942-45; resumed practice at Bar, 1946; ceased to practise on appointment as Warden of All Souls Coll., 1952; Hon. Bencher, Middle Temple, 1952; Fellow of Winchester Coll., 1951-81; Hon. Fellow, New Coll., 1956. Hon. DLitt, Univ. of Warwick, 1967. *Publications:* various; mostly reviews and essays in periodicals, some of which were collected in Independent Essays, 1963, and Controversial Essays, 1966; Half-lines and Repetitions in Virgil, 1931; Sense and Poetry: essays on the place of meaning in contemporary verse, 1934; Mark Pattison and the Idea of a University (Clark Lectures), 1967; After the Assassination, 1968; Visible Words (Sandars Lectures), 1969; (with A. Perosa) Renaissance Latin Verse: an anthology, 1979; Grave Epigrams and Other Verses, 1981; Words on the Air, 1981; (ed jtly) Geoffrey Madan's Notebooks, 1981. *Address:* Beechwood House, Iffley Turn, Oxford. *Clubs:* Garrick, Reform, Beefsteak.

SPAWFORTH, David Meredith, MA; Headmaster, Merchiston Castle School, Edinburgh, since April 1981; *b* 2 Jan. 1938; *s* of Lawrence and Gwen Spawforth, Wakefield, Yorks; *m* 1963, Yvonne Mary Gude; one *s* one *d. Educ:* Silcoates School; Hertford Coll., Oxford (Heath Harrison Travelling Schol.; MA ModLang). Assistant Master: Winchester Coll., 1961-64; Wellington Coll., 1964-80; Housemaster, Wellington Coll., 1968-80. British Petroleum Education Fellow, Keble Coll., Oxford, 1977. *Publications:* articles in Conference and Teaching about Europe. *Recreations:* gardening, France, history, theatre, walking. *Address:* Castle Gates, Merchiston Castle School, Colinton, Edinburgh EH13 0PU. *T:* 031-441 3468.

SPEAKMAN-PITT, William, VC 1951; *b* 21 Sept. 1927; *m* 1st, 1956, Rachel Snitch; one *s*; 2nd, Jill; one *d. Educ:* Wellington Road Senior Boys' Sch., Altrincham. Entered Army as Private. Served Korean War, 1950-53 (VC), King's Own Scottish Borderers. *Recreations:* swimming, and ski-ing.

SPEAR, Harold Cumming, CBE 1976; Member, Central Arbitration Committee, since 1976; *b* 26 Oct. 1909; *yr s* of late Rev. Edwin A. and Elizabeth Spear; *m* 1935, Gwendolen (*née* Richards); one *s* one *d. Educ:* Kingswood Sch., Bath. Asst to Employment Manager, Gramophone Co. Ltd, 1928-33; Labour and Welfare Supervisor, Mitcham Works Ltd, 1933-35; Employment Supervisor, Hoover Ltd, 1935-38; Personnel Manager, Sperry Gyroscope Co. Ltd, 1938-40; appts with British Overseas Airways Corp., finally as Chief Personnel Officer, 1941-59; Dir of Personnel Management, Central Electricity Generating Bd, 1959-72; Mem., Electricity Council, 1972-76. Pres., Inst. of Personnel Management, 1969-71; CIPM. *Recreation:* golf. *Address:* 4 Royal Parade, Bayshill Road, Cheltenham, Glos GL50 3AY. *Clubs:* Roehampton; Cotswold Hills Golf.

SPEAR, Ruskin, CBE 1979; RA 1954 (ARA 1944); artist; *b* 30 June 1911; *s* of Augustus and Jane Spear; *m* 1935, Mary Hill; one *s. Educ:* Brook Green School; Hammersmith School of Art; Royal College of Art, Kensington, under Sir William Rothenstein. Diploma, 1934; first exhibited Royal Academy, 1932; elected London Group, 1942; President London Group, 1949-50; Visiting teacher, Royal College of Art, 1952-77. Pictures purchased by Chantrey Bequest, Contemporary Art Society, Arts Council of Great Britain, and British Council. Exhibited work in Pushkin Museum, Moscow, 1957; has also exhibited in Paris, USA, Belgium, S Africa, Australia, NZ. Commissions include: Altar Piece for RAF Memorial Church, St Clement Danes, 1959; four mural panels for P&O Liner Canberra. Recent portraits include: Lord Adrian; Herbert Butterfield; Sir Stewart Duke-Elder; Sir Laurence Olivier as Macbeth (Stratford Memorial Theatre); Lord Chandos; Sir Ian Jacob; Sir Robin Darwin; Miss Ruth Cohen; Sir Eric Ashby; S. S. Eriks, KBE; Dr Ramsey, Archbishop of Canterbury; Sir Aubrey Lewis; Arthur Armitage; Harold Wilson; 5th Duke of Westminster; Sir Hugh Greene; Lord Goodman; Dr Charles Bosanquet; Sir James Tait; Sir John Mellor; Sir Alan Herbert; Sir Geoffrey Taylor; G. F. Taylor; Sir Peter Allen; Sir Maurice Bridgemen; Lord Butler of Saffron Walden. Visiting teacher, RCA, until 1976. *Address:* 60 British Grove, Hammersmith, W4. *T:* 01-741 2894.

SPEAR, Prof. Walter Eric, PhD, DSc; FRS 1980, FRSE; Harris Professor of Physics, University of Dundee, since 1968; *b* 20 Jan. 1921; *s* of David and Eva Spear; *m* 1952, Hilda Doris King; two *d. Educ:* Musterschule, Frankfurt/Main; Univ. of London (BSc 1947, PhD 1950, DSc 1967). Lecturer, 1953, Reader, 1967, in Physics, Univ. of Leicester; Vis. Professor, Purdue Univ., 1957-58. FRSE 1972; FInstP 1962. Max Born Prize and Medal 1977; Europhysics Prize 1977. *Publications:* numerous research papers on electronic and transport properties in crystalline solids, liquids and amorphous semiconductors. *Recreations:* literature, music (particularly chamber music), languages. *Address:* Carnegie Laboratory of Physics, University of Dundee, Dundee DD1 4HN. *T:* Dundee 23181; 323 Blackness Road, Dundee DD2 1SH. *T:* Dundee 67649.

SPEARING, George David; Regional Director, Eastern Region, Departments of the Environment and Transport, and Chairman, East Anglia Regional Board, since 1978; *b* 16 Dec. 1927; *s* of late George Thomas and of Edith Lydia Anna Spearing; *m* 1951, Josephine Mary Newbould; two *s* one *d. Educ:* Rotherham Grammar Sch.; Sheffield Univ. BEng; MICE, FIHE.

RAF, Airfield Construction Br., 1948. Asst Divl Surveyor, Somerset CC, 1951; Asst Civil Engr, W Riding of Yorks CC, 1953; Asst Engr, MoT, 1957; Supt. Engr, Midland Road Construction Unit, 1967; Asst Chief Engr, MoT, 1969; Regional Controller (Roads and Transportation), West Midlands, 1972; Dep. Chief Engr, DoE, 1973; Under Sec., DoE, 1974; Under Sec., Dept of Transport, and Dir Highways Planning and Management, 1974-78. *Publications:* papers in Proc. Instn CE and Jl Instn HE. *Address:* Wysswood, Dayseys Hill, Outwood, Surrey RH1 5QY. *T:* Smallfield 2715.

SPEARING, Nigel John; MP (Lab) Newham South, since May 1974; *b* 8 Oct. 1930; *s* of Austen and May Spearing; *m* 1956, Wendy, *d* of Percy and Molly Newman, Newport, Mon; one *s* two *d. Educ:* Latymer Upper School, Hammersmith. Ranks and commission, Royal Signals, 1950-52; St Catharine's Coll., Cambridge, 1953-56. Tutor and later Sen. Geography Master, Wandsworth School, 1956-68; Director, Thameside Research and Development Group, Inst. of Community Studies, 1968-69; Housemaster, Elliott School, Putney, 1969-70. Chairman: Barons Court Labour Party, 1961-63; Hammersmith Local Govt Cttee of the Labour Party, 1966-68. Contested (Lab) Warwick and Leamington, 1964. MP (Lab) Acton, 1970-74; Secretary: Parly Lab. Party Educn Gp, 1971-74; Parly Inland Waterways Gp, 1970-74; Member Select Cttee: Overseas Develt, 1973-74, 1977-79; Members' Interests, 1974-75; Procedure, 1975-79; Foreign and Commonwealth Affairs, 1980-. Vice-Pres., River Thames Soc.; Pres., Socialist Envt and Resources Assoc., 1977-; Chm., British Anti-Common Market Campaign, 1977-. Co-opted Mem. GLC Cttees, 1966-73. *Publication:* the Thames Barrier-Barrage Controversy (Inst. of Community Studies), 1969. *Recreations:* rowing, reading. *Address:* House of Commons, SW1. *T:* 01-219 3000.

SPEARMAN, Sir Alexander Young Richard Mainwaring, 5th Bt *cr* 1840; *b* 3 Feb. 1969; *s* of Sir Alexander Bowyer Spearman, 4th Bt, and Martha, *d* of John Green, Naauwpoort, S Africa; *S* father, 1977. *Heir:* uncle Dr Richard Ian Campbell Spearman, FLS, FZS, *b* 14 Aug. 1926. *Address:* Windwards, Klein Constantia Road, Constantia, Cape Town, 7800, S Africa.

SPEARMAN, Clement, CBE 1979; HM Diplomatic Service, retired; Ambassador and Consul-General to the Dominican Republic, 1975-79; *b* 10 Sept. 1919; *y s* of late Edward and Clara Spearman; *m* 1950, Olwen Regina Morgan; one *s* two *d. Educ:* Cardiff High School. RN (Air Arm), 1942-46. Entered Foreign (subseq. Diplomatic) Service, 1947; 3rd Sec., Brussels, 1948-49; 2nd Sec., FO, 1949-51; HM Consul, Skopje, 1951-53; FO, 1953-56; 1st Sec., Buenos Aires, 1956-60; FO, 1960-62; Counsellor, CENTO, Ankara, 1962-65; Reykjavik, 1965-69; FCO, 1969-71; Manila, 1971-74; Toronto, 1974-75. *Recreations:* tennis, swimming. *Address:* 56 Riverview Gardens, SW13 9QZ. *T:* 01-748 9339. *Clubs:* Travellers', Naval, Roehampton.

SPECTOR, Prof. Roy Geoffrey, MD, PhD; FRCP, FRCPath; Professor of Applied Pharmacology, Guy's Hospital Medical School, since 1972; *b* 27 Aug. 1931; *s* of Paul Spector and Esther Cohen; *m* 1960, Evie Joan Freeman (marr. diss. 1979); two *s* one *d. Educ:* Roundhay Sch., Leeds; Sch. of Medicine, Leeds Univ. (MB, ChB, MD); PhD Lond 1964, Dip. in Biochem. 1966. FRCP 1971; FRCPath 1976; FRSM. Lectr in Paediatric Res. Unit, Guy's Hosp., 1961-67; Guy's Hosp. Medical School: Reader in Pharmacology, 1968-71; Sub Dean for Admissions, 1975-. Vice-Chm., British Univs' Film Council, 1976-. *Publications:* (jtly) The Nerve Cell, 1964; (jtly) Clinical Pharmacology in Dentistry, 1975, 3rd edn 1982; (jtly) Mechanisms in Pharmacology and Therapeutics, 1976; (jtly) Aids to Pharmacology, 1980; (jtly) Textbook of Clinical Pharmacology, 1981; contribs to jls on pathology, gen. science, and applied pharmacology. *Recreations:* music, walking. *Address:* Department of Pharmacology, Guy's Hospital Medical School, SE1 9RT. *T:* 01-407 7600, ext. 3651.

SPEED, (Herbert) Keith, RD 1967; MP (C) Ashford, since Oct. 1974; *b* 11 March 1934; *s* of late Herbert Victor Speed and of Dorothy Barbara (*née* Mumford); *m* 1961, Peggy Voss Clarke; two *s* one *d* (and one *s* decd). *Educ:* Greenhill Sch., Evesham; Bedford Modern Sch.; RNC, Dartmouth and Greenwich. Officer, RN, 1947-56; Lt-Comdr RNR, until 1979. Sales Man., Amos (Electronics) Ltd, 1957-60; Marketing Man., Plysu Products Ltd, 1960-65; Officer, Conservative Res. Dept, 1965-68. MP (C) Meriden, March 1968-Feb. 1974; An Asst Govt Whip, 1970-71; a Lord Comr of HM Treasury, 1971-72; Parly Under-Sec. of State, DoE, 1972-74; Opposition spokesman on local govt, 1976-77, on home affairs, 1977-79; Parly Under Sec. of State for Defence for RN, 1979-81. *Publications:* Blue Print for Britain, 1965; contribs to various political and defence jls. *Recreations:* classical music, motor cycling, reading. *Address:* Strood House, Rolvenden, Cranbrook, Kent.

SPEED, Sir Robert (William Arney), Kt 1954; CB 1946; QC 1963; Counsel to the Speaker, 1960-80; *b* 1905; *s* of late Sir Edwin Arney Speed; *m* 1929, Phyllis, *d* of Rev. P. Armitage; one *s* one *d. Educ:* Rugby; Trinity College, Cambridge. Called to Bar, Inner Temple, 1928; Bencher, 1961; Principal Assistant Solicitor, Office of HM Procurator-General and Treasury Solicitor, 1945-48; Solicitor to the Board of Trade, 1948-60. *Address:* Upper Culham, Wargrave, Berks. *T:* Henley-on-Thames 4271. *Club:* United Oxford & Cambridge University.

SPEELMAN, Sir Cornelis Jacob, 8th Bt *cr* 1686; BA; *b* 17 March 1917; *s* of Sir Cornelis Jacob Speelman, 7th Bt and Maria Catharina Helena, Castendijk; *S* father, 1949; *m* 1972, Julia Mona Le Besque (*d* 1978). Education Dept, Royal Dutch Army, 1947-49; with The Shell Company (Marketing

Service Dept), 1950. Student, Univ. of Western Australia, 1952; formerly Master of Modern Languages at Clifton Coll., Geelong Grammar Sch.; Exeter Tutorial Coll. *Address:* 29 Blackall Road, Exeter, Devon. *T:* Exeter 51158.

SPEIDEL, General Hans, Dr phil; Grosskreuz Militärverdienstorden, Württemberg Order of Merit (1914–18); Kt, Iron Cross, 1943; President, Foundation of Science and Politics, 1964–78; Hon. Professor, 1971; *b* Metzingen/Württemberg, 28 Oct. 1897; *m* 1925, Ruth Stahl; one *s* two *d*. *Educ:* Eberhard-Ludwig-Gymnasium of the Humanities, Stuttgart; Univs of Berlin and Tübingen, Technische Hochschule, Stuttgart. Ensign, Grenadier Regt, König Karl (5. Württ.) Nr 123, 1914; Gruppen Zug und Kompaniefuhrer, Battalion and Regimental Adjutant, Western Front, 1915–18; entered Reichswehr (3 years at Military Academy); during War of 1939–45 was successively Chief of Staff of Army Corps and Army (8) (Eastern Front), and of Field Marshal Rommel's Army Group (Western Front); arrested on Himmler's orders, 1944; released from Gestapo imprisonment at end of the War. Lecturer, Tübingen Univ. and Leibniz University Coll.; Military Adviser, Federal Govt, 1951; Military Delegate-in-Chief to EDC (European Defence Community) and NATO negotiations, 1951–55; Commander-in-Chief of Combined German Forces, 1955–57; Commander Allied Land Forces, Central Europe, 1957–63; Special Counsellor to Federal Government, W Germany, 1963–64. Commander, US Legion of Merit, 1961; Grosses Verdienstkreuz BRD mit Stern und Schulterband; Ehrenburger, Stadt Metzingen, 1972. *Publications:* Invasion 1944 (a contribution to the fate of Rommel and the Reich), 1949; Zeitbetrachtungen, 1969; Aus unserer Zeit (memoirs), 1977; Editor and commentator on Vol. of Essays by Gen. Ludwig Beck, 1955; essays on Ernst Jünger, Theodor Heuss, Eugen Bircher, Gneisenau and Beck, etc. *Recreation:* study of history and literature. *Address:* Am Spitzenbach 21, Bad Honnef, Germany.

SPEIGHT, Johnny; writer; *b* 2 June 1920; *s* of John and Johanna Speight; *m* 1956, Constance Beatrice Barrett; two *s* one *d*. *Educ:* St Helen's RC School. Has written for: Arthur Haynes Show; Morecambe and Wise Show; Peter Sellers; Till Death Us Do Part (Screenwriters Guild Award, 1966, 1967, 1968); with Ray Galton: Tea Ladies, 1979; Spooner's Patch, 1979. *Plays:* Compartment (Screenwriters Guild Award, 1962); Playmates; Salesman; Knackers Yard; If There Weren't any Blacks You Would Have to Invent Them (Prague Festival Award, 1969). Evening Standard Drama Award for Best Comedy. *Publications:* It Stands to Reason, 1974; The Thoughts of Chairman Alf, 1974; various scripts. *Recreation:* golf. *Address:* Fouracres, Heronsgate, Chorleywood, Herts. *T:* Chorleywood 2463. *Clubs:* 21; White Elephant; Stage Golf, Variety Golf, Pinner Hill Golf.

SPEIR, Sir Rupert (Malise), Kt 1964; *b* 10 Sept. 1910; *y s* of late Guy Thomas Speir and late Mary Lucy Fletcher, of Saltoun. *Educ:* Eton Coll.; Pembroke Coll., Cambridge (BA). Admitted Solicitor, 1936. Special Mem., Hops Marketing Board, 1958. Served in Army throughout War of 1939–45; commissioned in Intelligence Corps, Sept. 1939; retired with rank of Lt-Col, 1945. Contested (C) Linlithgow, 1945, Leek, 1950; MP (C) Hexham Div. of Northumberland, 1951–66, retired. Sponsor of: Litter Act, 1958; Noise Abatement Act, 1960; Local Government (Financial Provisions) Act, 1963; Parliamentary Private Secretary: to Minister of State for Foreign Affairs and to Parly Sec., CRO, 1956–59; to Parly and Fin. Sec., Admty and to Civil Lord of Admty, 1952–56. Hon. Fellow, Inst. of Public Cleansing; Vice-Pres., Keep Britain Tidy Group. *Recreations:* golf, shooting, fishing. *Address:* Birtley Hall, Hexham, Northumberland. *T:* Bellingham 30275.

SPEIRS, Graham Hamilton; Secretary, Convention of Scottish Local Authorities, since 1975; *b* 9 Jan. 1927; *s* of Graham Mushet Speirs and Jane (*née* McChesney); *m* 1954, Myra Reid (*née* Mills); one *s* one *d*. *Educ:* High Sch. of Glasgow; Glasgow Univ. (MA 1950, LLB 1952). Anderson, Young and Dickson, Writers, Glasgow, 1950–52; Legal Asst, Dunbarton CC, 1952–54; Sen. Legal Asst, Stirling CC, 1954–59; Depute Sec., then Sec., Assoc. of County Councils in Scotland, 1959–75. Sec. Gén., Council of European Municipalities (British Section), 1980–. *Recreation:* golf. *Address:* (home) 3 Dirleton Avenue, North Berwick EH39 4AX. *T:* North Berwick 2801; (office) 16 Moray Place, Edinburgh EH3 6BL. *T:* 031-225 1626. *Clubs:* Royal Scottish Automobile (Glasgow); North Berwick Golf (North Berwick).

SPEIRS, William James McLaren; Group Security Adviser, Gallaher Ltd, since 1979; *b* 22 Nov. 1924; *s* of Alec McLaren Speirs and Olivia (*née* Petersen); *m* 1952, Jane Downing; two *s* one *d* (and one *d* decd). *Educ:* Clifton Coll.; Jesus Coll., Cambridge. Served Royal Signals, 1943–47; ADC to Governor of Singapore, 1946–47. HM Diplomatic Service, 1948–79: Rangoon, 1950; Jakarta, 1953; Berlin, 1957; Munich, 1963; Tel Aviv, 1970; Counsellor, FCO, 1979. *Recreations:* walking, collecting topographical books. *Address:* 24 Kingswood Firs, Grayshott, Hindhead, Surrey GU26 6ET. *T:* Hindhead 4112. *Clubs:* Army and Navy, Special Forces.

SPELLER, Antony; MP (C) North Devon, since 1979; *b* 12 June 1929; *s* of John and Ethel Speller; *m* 1960, Maureen R. McLellan; one *s* one *d*. *Educ:* Univ. of London (BScEcon); Univ. of Exeter (BA Social Studies); MHCIMA; MIRT. Subaltern, Devonshire Regt, 1951. Nigerian Produce Marketing Boards, 1953; Director: Atlas Co., Nigeria, 1956; Copyshops of SW England, 1963. Councillor, Exeter CC, 1963–74, Chm., Education Cttee. Chm., W Country Cons. MPs. Pres., Catering Industry Liaison Cttee.

Address: House of Commons, SW1A 0AA. *T:* 01-219 4589. *Clubs:* Carlton; North Devon (Barnstaple); Lagos Motor Boat (Nigeria).

SPELLER, Maj.-Gen. Norman Henry, CB 1976; Government Relations Adviser, ICL International Division, since 1976; *b* 5 March 1921; *s* of late Col Norman Speller and Emily Florence Speller (*née* Lambert); *m* 1950, Barbara Eleanor (*née* Earle); two *s*. *Educ:* Wallingford Grammar School. Commnd RA, 1940; War Service N Africa; transf. to RAOC, 1945; psc 1952; DAA&QMG 39 Inf. Bde, 1953–55; Dirg Staff, Staff Coll., 1955–58; OC 20 Ordnance Field Park, 1958–60; Admin. Staff Coll., 1961; AA&QMG N Ireland, 1961–63; D/SPO COD Donnington, 1964–65; Col AQ 54 (EA) Div./District, 1965–66; AAG AG9, MoD, 1967; DDOS 1 British Corps, 1968–69; idc 1970; Dir of Systems Coordination, MoD, 1971–73; Dir of Ordnance Services, MoD, 1973–76, retired. Col Comdt, RAOC, 1978–. *Recreations:* sailing, golf. *Address:* 1 Steeple Close, SW6. *Clubs:* Roehampton; Royal Southampton Yacht.

SPENALE, Georges; Officer de la Légion d'Honneur; Palmes Académiques; Grand Officier de l'Ordre National Italien; Grand Officier de l'Ordre National de la Côte d'Ivoire; Commandeur de l'Ordre de l'Aigle du Mexique; Senator from Tarn, French Senate, since 1977; *b* Carcassonne, 29 Nov. 1913; *m* 1935, Carmen Delcayré; one *s* one *d*. *Educ:* Licencié en Droit; Diplômé de l'Ecole Nationale de la France d'outre-Mer. Economic Bureau, French Guinea, 1938–39; served War, with the colours, 1939–40 and 1943–45; Chief of District, Upper Volta, 1941–42; Inspector of Labour, Ivory Coast, 1942–43; Director of Cabinet for Fedn of Equatorial Africa, 1946–48; Chief of Information Service, Ivory Coast, 1949–50; Director of Cabinet, Fr. Cameroons, 1951–53, Sec.-Gen. 1953–54, acting High Comr 1954–55; Ministry of France d'outre-Mer: Adj. Dir, 1955–56; Governor, 1956; Director, Cabinet of M Gaston Defferre (took part in framing Fundamental Law), 1956–57; High Comr in Togo (until Independence), 1957–60. Deputy from Tarn, French Nat. Assembly, 1962–77. European Parliament: Mem., 1964–79; Pres., Commn of Finances, 1966–75; Pres., Socialist Group, 1974–75; Pres., 1975–77; First Vice-Pres., 1977–79. Mayor of Saint-Sulpice, Tarn, 1965–; Vice-Pres., Regional Council, Midi-Pyrénées, 1975. Mem. Directing Cttee, Fr. Socialist Party, 1968–71. Holds decorations from African countries. *Address:* Faubourg Saint-Jean, 81370 Saint-Sulpice, France. *T:* 578003 (63).

SPENCE, Allan William, MA, MD Cantab; FRCP; Hon. Consultant Physician: St Bartholomew's Hospital, since 1965; Luton and Dunstable Hospital, since 1965; King George Hospital, Ilford, since 1967; Governor, St Bartholomew's Hospital Medical College, since 1965; *b* 4 Aug. 1900; *s* of late William Ritchie Spence and Emma (*née* Allan), Bath; *m* 1930, Martha Lena (*d* 1981), *d* of late Hugh Hamilton Hutchinson, JP, Girvan, Ayrshire; two *s*. *Educ:* King Edward's VI School, Bath; Gonville and Caius College, Cambridge; St Bartholomew's Hospital, London. Brackenbury Schol. in Medicine, 1926, Lawrence Research Schol. and Gold Medal, 1929–30, Cattlin Research Fell., 1938, St Bartholomew's Hosp.; Rockefeller Travelling Fellow, USA, 1931–32. House Phys., 1927, Demonstrator of Physiology, 1928–30, of Pathology, 1930–31, First Asst, 1933–36, Asst Dir of Med. Unit, 1936–37, St Bartholomew's Hospital; Physician St Bartholomew's Hosp., London, 1937–65; King George Hospital, Ilford, 1938–67; Luton and Dunstable Hospital, 1946–65; Hon. Consultant in Endocrinology to Army at Home, 1954–65; Med. Referee to Civil Service Commn, 1952–70; Physician on Med. Appeal Tribunal, DHSS, 1965–72; Member Medical Research Coun. Adv. Cttee: on Iodine Deficiency and Thyroid Disease, 1933–39; and on Hormones, 1937–41. Hon. Lt-Col, RAMC; service in North Africa and Greece as OC Med. Div., 97th Gen. Hosp., 1943–45. Mem. Assoc. of Physicians of Gt Brit.; Foundation Mem. Soc. for Endocrinology, to 1965; Fellow RSM, 1926–72 (Vice-Pres., Section of Med., 1949, Pres. Section of Endocrinology, 1951–52, Councillor, 1958–61); Foundn Mem. Internat. Soc. of Internal Medicine; Fellow Medical Soc. of London, 1937–72 (Councillor, 1957–60); Foundn Mem., London Thyroid Club; Mem., Physiological Soc., 1935–52; Emeritus Mem., Endocrine Society, USA, 1966. Examr in Medicine: Univ. of Cambridge, 1946–50; to Society of Apothecaries of London, 1947–52; in Therapeutics to University of London, 1953–57; to the Conjoint Examining Bd in England, 1955–59; to Fellowship of Faculty of Anæsthetists, RCS, 1964–66. Trustee, Peel Med. Res. Trust, 1961–. Mem. of Editorial Bd, Jl of Endocrinology, 1956–63. Freeman of City of London; Member of Livery, Society of Apothecaries of London. *Publications:* Clinical Endocrinology, 1953 (translated into Spanish); articles to medical and scientific journals on endocrinological and general medical subjects. *Recreations:* reading, gardening; formerly rowing (Pres. Caius Boat Club, 1922–23). *Address:* Oak Spinney, 60 Liphook Road, Lindford, Bordon, Hants GU35 0PN. *T:* Bordon 2450. *Club:* Hawks (Cambridge).

See also M. H. Spence.

SPENCE, Captain (Frederick) Michael (Alexander) T.; *see* Torrens-Spence.

SPENCE, Gabriel John; Under Secretary, Department of Education and Science, retired; *b* 5 April 1924; *s* of G. S. and D. A. Spence, Hope, Flints; *m* 1950, Averil Kingston (*née* Beresford); one *s* decd. *Educ:* Arnold House; King's Sch., Chester (King's Schol., Head of School); Wadham Coll., Oxon (Schol.). MA 1949; Stanhope Prize and Proxime, Gibbs Schol., Oxon, 1947; Haldane Essay Prize, Inst. Public Admin, 1959. Civil Service from 1949 (Min. of Works, Science Office, Min. of Housing and Local Govt, DES); Jt Sec., Adv. Council on Scientific Policy, 1959–62; Asst Sec., DES, 1964–73; Sec., Council for Scientific Policy, 1964–67; Under Sec., DES, 1973–81. Admin.

Staff Coll., Henley, 1957. Trustee, The Oates Meml and Gilbert White Library and Museum, 1982. *Recreations:* natural history, photography. *Address:* Old Heath, Hillbrow Road, Liss, Hants. *T:* Liss 3235. *Club:* Athenæum.

SPENCE, John Deane; MP (C) Thirsk and Malton, since 1974 (Sheffield, Heeley, 1970-74); civil engineering and building contractor; director of various companies connected with construction industry; *b* 7 Dec. 1920; *s* of George Spence, Belfast; *m* 1944, Hester Nicholson; one *s* one *d*. *Educ:* Queen's Univ. of Belfast. Mem., Public Relations and Organization Cttee, Building Industry, 1967; Nat. Pres., UK Commercial Travellers' Assoc., 1965-66. PPS to Minister of Local Govt and Develt, 1971-74; Mem., Speaker's Panel of Cttee Chairmen 1974-. Vice-Chm., Yorks Cons. Members Gp, 1979- (Hon. Sec., 1970-79); Hon. Sec., Cons. Back-benchers' Industry Cttee, 1971-72; Jt Hon. Sec., Cons. Back-benchers' Agriculture, Fisheries and Food Cttee, 1974-76, 1981-; Member: Select Cttee, Nationalised Industries, 1974-79; Select Cttee for Agric., 1979-; Jt Chm., All-Party Scotch Whisky Industry Gp, 1979-; Chm., All-Party Management Gp, 1979-. Member: IPU, 1979-; CPA, 1979-. NFU; Country Landowners' Assoc.; Yorkshire Derwent Trust; Anglo-Israel Friendship Soc. *Recreations:* golf, walking, travel. *Address:* House of Commons, SW1A 0AA; Greystones, Maltongate, Thornton Dale, North Yorkshire. *Club:* Carlton.

SPENCE, Malcolm Hugh, QC 1979; barrister-at-law, since 1958; *b* 23 March 1934; *s* of Allan William Spence, *qv; m* 1967, Jennifer Jane, *d* of Lt-Gen. Sir George Cole, KCB, CBE; one *s* one *d*. *Educ:* Summer Fields, Oxford; Stowe Sch.; Gonville and Caius Coll., Cambridge (MA, LLB). James Mould Schol., Holker Sen. Exhibnr, Lee Prizeman, Gray's Inn, called to the Bar, 1958. Worcester Regt, First Lieut, 1954. Marshal to Mr Justice McNair, 1957; Pupil to Mr Nigel Bridge (now Lord Bridge of Harwich), 1958; entered chambers of Mr John Widgery, QC, 1958; practises mainly in Town and Country Planning and Compensation for Compulsory Purchase. Chairman of Panel, Examination-in-Public of Hartlepool and Cleveland Structure Plans, 1979-. *Publication:* (jtly) Rating Law and Valuation, 1961. *Recreations:* golf (Captain: Cambridge University Stymies, 1957; Old Stoic Golfing Soc., 1972; Gray's Inn Golfing Soc., 1979; Semi-finalist, Scandinavian Amateur Championship, 1964), also trout fishing. *Address:* 23 Ennerdale Road, Kew, Surrey TW9 3PE. *T:* 01-940 9884; Scamadale, Arisaig, Inverness-shire. *Clubs:* Royal Mid-Surrey Golf; Hawks (Cambridge).

SPENCER, family name of **Viscount Churchill** and of **Earl Spencer.**

SPENCER, 8th Earl *cr* 1765; **Edward John Spencer,** MVO 1954; DL; Baron and Viscount Spencer, 1761; Viscount Althorp, 1765; Viscount Althorp (UK), 1905; President, Northamptonshire Association of Boys' Clubs; Deputy President, National Association of Boys' Clubs, since 1980 (Chairman, 1962-80); *b* 24 Jan. 1924; *o s* of 7th Earl Spencer, TD, and Lady Cynthia Elinor Beatrix Hamilton, DCVO, OBE (*d* 1972), *d* of 3rd Duke of Abercorn; *S* father, 1975; *m* 1st, 1954, Hon. Frances Ruth Burke Roche (marr. diss. 1969), *yr d* of 4th Baron Fermoy; one *s* three *d* (and one *s* decd); 2nd, 1976, Raine (*see* Countess Spencer). *Educ:* Eton; RMC Sandhurst and RAC, Cirencester. ADC to Gov. of South Australia, 1947-50; Equerry to the Queen, 1952-54 (to King George VI, 1950-52). Formerly Capt RS Greys. Hon. Col The Northamptonshire Regt (Territorials), T&AVR, 1967-71; a Dep. Hon. Col, The Royal Anglian Regt, 1971-79. Chairman: SGBI, 1962-; The Nene Foundn, 1978-. Trustee: King George's Jubilee Trust; Queen's Silver Jubilee Appeal; Mem. UK Council European Architectural Heritage Year, 1975. CC Northants, 1952-81; High Sheriff of Northants, 1959; DL Northants, 1961; JP Norfolk, 1970. *Heir:* s Viscount Althorp, *qv*. *Address:* Althorp, Northampton NN7 4HG. *Clubs:* Turf, Brooks's, MCC, Royal Over-Seas League.
See also under Royal Family, and R. Fellowes.

SPENCER, Countess; Raine Spencer; *b* 9 Sept. 1929; *d* of late Alexander George McCorquodale and of Barbara Cartland, *qv; m* 1st, 1948, Earl of Dartmouth (marr. diss. 1976), *qv*; three *s* one *d*; 2nd, 1976, Earl Spencer, *qv*. Westminster City Councillor, 1954-65 (served on various cttees); Member: for Lewisham West, LCC, 1958-65 (served on Town Planning, Parks, Staff Appeals Cttees); for Richmond upon Thames, GLC, 1967-73; GLC Gen. Purposes Cttee, 1971-73; Chm., GLC Historic Buildings Bd, 1968-71; Mem., Environmental Planning Cttee, 1967-71; Chm., Covent Garden Develt Cttee, 1971-72; Chm., Govt working party on Human Habitat in connection with UN Conf. on Environment, Stockholm (June 1972), 1971-72 (report: How Do You Want to Live?); Chm., UK Exec., European Architectural Heritage Year, 1975; Member: English Tourist Bd, 1971-75; BTA Infrastructure Cttee, 1972-; Adv. Council, V&A Museum, 1980-; Cttee of Honour, Business Sponsorship of the Arts, 1980-; Mem. Bd, British Tourist Authority, 1982-. Formerly LCC Voluntary Care Cttee Worker, Wandsworth and Vauxhall. Hon. Dr Laws, Dartmouth Coll., USA. *Publication:* What Is Our Heritage?, 1975. *Address:* Althorp, Northampton NN7 4HG. *T:* (estate office) East Haddon 209.

SPENCER, Alan Douglas, CBIM; Director: Owen Owen plc, since 1980; Amos Hinton and Sons plc, since 1980; Johnson Wax (UK) Ltd, since 1981; Member, East Midlands Electricity Board, since 1976; *b* 22 Aug. 1920; *s* of Thomas Spencer and late Laura Spencer; *m* 1944, Dorothy Joan Harper; two *d*. *Educ:* Prince Henry's Grammar Sch., Evesham. FBIM 1975. Commnd Gloucester Regt, 1940; served War with Green Howards, 1940-45; Instr, Sch. of Infantry, 1945-47. Joined Boots Co., 1938; rejoined 1947; Dir, 1963-81;

Man. Dir, 1975, Vice-Chm., 1978-80, Boots Co. Ltd; Man. Dir, 1977-79, Chm., 1977-80, Boots The Chemist Ltd. Pres., British Multiple Retailers Assoc., 1981. Governor, Trent Coll. *Recreation:* shooting. *Address:* Oakwood, Grange Road, Edwalton, Nottingham. *T:* Nottingham 231722. *Club:* Naval and Military.

SPENCER, Brian; HM Diplomatic Service, retired; Counsellor and Consul-General, Washington, 1978-82; *b* 20 March 1922; *s* of Alphaeus and Ethel Audrey Palmer Spencer; *m* 1950, Jean Edmunds; one *s*. *Educ:* Holgate Grammar Sch., Barnsley. Entered Civil Service in Mines Dept, BoT, 1939. Army, 1940-46: commnd, S Staffs Regt, 1942, with subseq. service in E Surrey Regt, N Africa, Sicily, Italy, Austria and Greece (Captain, despatches). Joined FO, 1950; Second Sec., Bagdad, 1952, Jakarta, 1955; FO, 1956; First Sec., Singapore, 1959; FO, 1962; First Secretary (Information): Helsinki, 1964; Canberra, 1967; Sydney, 1968; First Sec., Ottawa, 1969; Consul, Chicago, 1971; FCO, 1972; Counsellor and Consul-Gen., Moscow, 1975-77. *Recreations:* tennis, cricket, football, ballet, music. *Address:* 68 Old Shoreham Road, Hove, E Sussex. *Club:* Royal Over-Seas League.

SPENCER, Cyril; Executive Chairman, Burton Group Ltd, 1980-81; *b* 31 Aug. 1924; *s* of Isaac and Lily Spencer; *m* 1971, Wendy Lois Sutton; two *s* one *d* and two step *s* one step *d*. *Educ:* Christ Coll., Finchley; London Univ. (BSc). Joined Evans (Outsizes) Ltd, 1946: Managing Director, 1956; Chairman, 1969; Take Over of Evans by Burton Group Ltd, 1971; Head of Womenswear, 1972; Group Man. Dir and Chief Exec., 1976; Chairman, Burton Menswear, 1977. *Recreations:* tennis, swimming, golf. *Address:* Eliot House, The Bishops Avenue, N2 0BA. *Club:* Royal Automobile.

SPENCER, Cyril Charles, CMG 1951; First Deputy Executive Director, International Coffee Organisation, London, 1964-68; *b* 1 Feb. 1912; *s* of late Albert Edward Spencer, CBE, and Elsie Maud Spencer; *m* 1st, 1938; one *d*; 2nd, 1949, Catherine Dewar Robertson. *Educ:* Royal Grammar Sch., Worcester; St John's Coll., Cambridge (BA 1934). Uganda: Asst Treas., 1935; Asst District Officer, 1937; Asst Financial Sec., 1946; Economic Sec., E Africa High Commission, 1948; Financial Sec., 1948; Acting Chief Sec. at various dates; Acting Governor, July 1951; Chairman: Uganda Lint Marketing Bd; Uganda Coffee Marketing Board; Member: Uganda Electricity Board; Uganda Development Corp.; Comr on Special Duty, Uganda, 1953-61; Sec.-Gen., Inter-African Coffee Organisation, Paris, 1961-64. *Recreations:* golf, fishing. *Address:* Shandon, Coreway, Sidford, Sidmouth, Devon. *Club:* MCC.

SPENCER, Derek Harold, QC 1980; a Recorder of the Crown Court, since 1979; *b* 31 March 1936; *s* of Thomas Harold Spencer and Gladys Spencer (*née* Heslop); *m* 1960, Joan (*née* Nutter); two *s* one *d*. *Educ:* Clitheroe Royal Grammar Sch.; Keble Coll., Oxford (MA, BCL). 2nd/Lieut King's Own Royal Regt, 1954-56. Called to Bar, Gray's Inn, 1961. Councillor, London Borough of Camden, 1978-; Dep. Leader, Conservative Party, London Borough of Camden, 1979-81. *Recreations:* reading, swimming, golf. *Address:* 2D Oakford Road, NW5. *T:* 01-482 1876. *Club:* Highgate Golf.

SPENCER, Prof. Herbert, MD London, PhD; FRCP, FRCS, FRCPath; Professor of Morbid Anatomy, St Thomas's Hospital Medical School, 1965-80, now Emeritus Professor; Visiting Professor of Pathology, St Mary's Hospital Medical School; *b* 8 Feb. 1915; *s* of Hubert and Emma Maude Spencer; *m* 1940, Eileen Mabel Morgan; one *s* three *d*. *Educ:* Highgate Sch.; St Mary's Hosp. Med. Sch. Served War of 1939-45: Specialist Pathologist, RAMC, 1942-47. Reader in Pathology, St Thomas's Hosp. Med. Sch., 1954-65; Visiting Associate Prof. of Pathology, Yale Univ. Sch. of Med., 1961. Examiner: RCS, 1958-70; Univ. of London, 1974-77; Univ. of Liverpool, 1972-76; RCP, 1973-. *Publications:* Pathology of the Lung, 1962, 3rd edn 1977; Tropical Pathology, 1973; contribs to numerous British and foreign med. jls and books. *Recreation:* woodwork. *Address:* Uplands Cottage, Barnet Road, Arkley, Barnet, Herts EN5 3ET. *T:* 01-449 7030.

SPENCER, Prof. Herbert, RDI 1965; DrRCA; FSIAD; Professor of Graphic Arts, Royal College of Art, since 1978; *b* 22 June 1924; *m* 1954, Marianne Möls, Dordrecht; one *d*. DrRCA 1970; FSIA 1947. Sen. Res. Fellow, RCA, 1966-78. Internat. Pres., Alliance Graphique Internat., 1971-74; Mem., PO Stamp Adv. Cttee, 1968-; External advr to Design Cttee, British Telecom, 1981-. Dir, Lund Humphries Publishers Ltd, 1970-. Master, Faculty of Royal Designers for Industry, 1979-81; Vice-Pres., RSA, 1979-81. Governor, Bath Acad. of Art, Corsham, 1982-. Editor: Typographica, 1949-67; Penrose Annual, 1964-73. *Publications:* Design in Business Printing, 1952; London's Canal, 1961, 2nd edn 1976; Traces of Man, 1967; The Visible Word, 1968, 2nd edn 1969; Pioneers of Modern Typography, 1969, 2nd edn 1982, German edn 1970; (with Colin Forbes) New Alphabets A-Z, 1973, French edn 1974; (with Mafalda Spencer) The Book of Numbers, 1975. *Recreation:* photography. *Address:* 30 Acacia Road, St John's Wood, NW8 6BB. *T:* 01-722 3498.

SPENCER, Air Vice-Marshal Ian James, CB 1963; DFC 1941 (Bar 1943); Chairman: I. J. Spencer and Partners; Spencer Partners SA; *b* 6 June 1916; *s* of late Percival James Spencer; *m* 1940, Kathleen Jeune Follis, *d* of late Canon Charles Follis; two *s*. Commissioned 1937. War of 1939-45: bomber sqdns of No 2 Gp (despatches). RAF Staff College, 1948; Air Attaché, Berne, 1950-53; CO, Univ. of London Air Sqdn, 1954-56; Director of Plans Second Allied TAF, 1956-59; commanded RAF Benson, 1959-61; AOA, Transport

Command, 1961-64; Dir of Personnel, MoD, 1964-65; AOA, Far East Air Force, 1965-67; retired 1968. Member: CPRE; Franco-British Soc.; Anglo-Swiss Soc.; Internat. Inst. for Strategic Studies; BIM. Freeman, Guild of Air Pilots and Air Navigators. Croix de Guerre, 1940; Légion d'Honneur 1945. Interests: internat. affairs, the countryside. *Clubs:* MCC; Sussex CCC.

SPENCER, Mrs Joanna Miriam, CB 1971; CBE 1961; CompIGasE; *b* 26 July 1910; *d* of late Rev. R. S. Franks; *m* 1954, Frank Woolley Sim Spencer (*d* 1975). *Educ:* Redland High School for Girls, Bristol; Girton College, Cambridge (MA). Asst, Lancs County Library, 1934-35; Asst Librarian: Hull Univ. Coll., 1936-37; Regent Street Polytechnic, 1938; Librarian, Selly Oak Colls, 1938-42. Temp. Civil Servant, Min. of Aircraft Production, 1942-45. Principal, Min. of Supply, 1946; Assistant Secretary, Min. of Supply, 1949-55, Board of Trade, 1955-56, Min. of Power, 1957-64; Under-Secretary: Min. of Power, 1964-69; Min. of Technology, 1969-70; DTI, 1970-72. *Address:* 4 Rostrevor Road, SW19 7AP. *T:* 01-946 4969.

SPENCER, John Loraine, TD; Headmaster, Berkhamsted School, 1972-Sept. 1983; *b* 19 Jan. 1923; *s* of Arthur Loraine Spencer, OBE, and Emily Maude Spencer, OBE, Woodford Green; *m* 1954, Brenda Elizabeth (*née* Loft); two *s* one *d. Educ:* Bancroft's Sch.; Gonville and Caius Coll., Cambridge (MA). 1st cl. hons Class. Tripos Pts I and II. War Service in Essex Regt, 1942-45 (Captain, despatches). Asst Master, Housemaster and Sixth Form Classics Master, Haileybury Coll., 1947-61; Headmaster, Lancaster Royal Grammar Sch., 1961-72. Mem. Council, Lancaster Univ., 1968-72. *Address:* (until Sept. 1983) Wilson House, Berkhamsted School, Berkhamsted, Herts. *T:* Berkhamsted 4827; (from Sept. 1983) Crofts Close, 7 Aston Road, Haddenham, Bucks HP17 8AF.

SPENCER, Sir Kelvin (Tallent), Kt 1959; CBE 1950; MC 1918; Chief Scientist, Ministry of Power, 1954-59, retired; *b* 7 July 1898; *s* of Charles Tallent and Edith Ælfrida Spencer; *m* 1927, Phœbe Mary Wills; one *s. Educ:* University College School, Hampstead; City and Guilds Engineering Coll., London Univ. Founder Mem., Scientific and Medical Network. FCGI 1959. Formerly MICE, FRAeS. Hon. LLD Exeter, 1981. *Address:* Wootans, Branscombe, Seaton, Devon EX12 3DN. *T:* Branscombe 242. *Club:* Farmers'.

SPENCER, Noël, ARCA (London); retired as Principal, Norwich School of Art (1946-64); *b* 29 Dec. 1900; *s* of late John William Spencer; *m* 1929, Vera K. Wheeler; no *c. Educ:* Ashton-under-Lyne School of Art; Manchester School of Art; Royal College of Art. Art Teacher, Central School of Arts and Crafts, Birmingham, 1926-32; Headmaster, Moseley School of Art, Birmingham, 1929-32; Second Master, Sheffield College of Arts and Crafts, 1932-34; Headmaster, Huddersfield Art School, 1934-46. *Exhibitions:* Royal Academy, New English Art Club, Royal Birmingham Society of Artists, Sheffield Society of Artists, Liverpool, Bradford, Wakefield and Doncaster Art Galleries, Norwich Art Circle and Twenty Group, Chicago Art Institute and Los Angeles Art Museum, USA, etc. Collection of more than 215 drawings and prints donated to Museum of London. *Publications:* A Scrap Book of Huddersfield, Book I, 1944, Book II, 1948; (with Arnold Kent) The Old Churches of Norwich, 1970; Sculptured Monuments in Norfolk Churches, 1977; Norwich Drawings, 1978. *Recreations:* drawing and painting. *Address:* 18 Upton Close, Norwich, Norfolk. *T:* Norwich 51683.

SPENCER, Oscar Alan, CMG 1957; Economic Adviser to Government of Seychelles, since 1976; Deputy Chairman, Seychelles National Investment Corporation, since 1979; *b* Eastleigh, Hants, 12 Dec. 1913; *m* 1952, Diana Mary, *d* of late Edmund Walker, Henley-on-Thames; two *s* one *d. Educ:* Mayfield Coll., Sussex; London Sch. of Economics. BCom (Hons) 1936. Premchand Prize in Banking and Currency, 1936; John Coleman Postgraduate Scholar in Business Administration, 1936-37. Served War of 1939-45, Lt-Col (despatches twice). Economic Adviser and Development Comr, British Guiana, 1945; also Comr, Interior, 1949; Economic Sec., Malaya, 1950; Member, 1951, Minister, 1955, for Economic Affairs, Economic Adviser, and Head of Economic Secretariat, Fedn of Malaya, 1956-60. UN Tech. Assistance Service, 1960-76: Econ. Adviser to Govt of Sudan, 1960-64; Sen. Regl Adviser on Public Finance and Head of Fiscal Sect., UN Econ. Commn for Africa, 1964-66; Financial Adviser to Govt of Ethiopia, 1966-76. Chm., Central Electricity Board, Malaya, 1952-55, 1956-60; British Guiana Delegate, Caribbean Commn, 1948; Malayan Adviser to Sec. of State. Commonwealth Finance Ministers' Conf., 1951; Leader of Malayan Reps, Internat. Rubber Study Gp, London, 1952, Copenhagen, 1953; Malayan Deleg., Internat. Tin Conf., Geneva, 1953; Adviser to Malayan Delegation, London Constitutional and Financial Confs 1956 and 1957. Comdr, Order of St Agatha, San Marino, 1944; Knight of the Order of Defenders of the Realm (PMN), Malaya, 1958. *Publications:* The Finances of British Guiana, 1920-45, 1946; The Development Plan of British Guiana, 1947. *Recreation:* swimming. *Address:* Gatehurst, Pett, near Hastings, East Sussex. *T:* Pett 2197; Ministry of Economic Development, Seychelles. *Club:* East India, Devonshire, Sports and Public Schools.

SPENCER, Rosemary Jane; HM Diplomatic Service; Counsellor (Agriculture and Economic Affairs), Paris, since 1980; *b* 1 April 1941; *d* of Air Vice-Marshal Geoffrey Roger Cole Spencer, CB, CBE, and Juliet Mary Spencer (*née* Warwick). *Educ:* Upper Chine Sch., Shanklin, IoW; St Hilda's Coll., Oxford (BA Hons Modern Langs). Joined Foreign Office, 1962; FO, 1962-65; Third Secretary, Nairobi, 1965-67; Second Sec., FCO, 1967-70;

Second Sec., UK Delegn to EEC, and Private Sec. to Hon. Sir Con O'Neill, Official Leader of UK negotiating team, 1970-71; First Sec., Office of UK Permanent Representative to EEC, Brussels, 1972-73; First Sec. (Economic), Lagos, 1974-77; First Sec., Asst Head of Rhodesia Dept, FCO, 1977-80; RCDS 1980. *Recreations:* country walking, sailing, travel, domestic arts. *Address:* c/o Foreign and Commonwealth Office, SW1. *Club:* Royal Commonwealth Society.

SPENCER, Thomas Newnham Bayley, (Tom Spencer); Member (C) Derbyshire, European Parliament, since 1979; *b* 10 April 1948; *s* of Captain Thomas Henry Newnham Spencer and Anne Hester (*née* Readett-Bayley); *m* 1979, Elizabeth Nan Maltby, *er d* of late Captain Ronald Edgar Bath and of Doreen Lester (*née* Bush); one *d* and one step *d. Educ:* Nautical Coll., Pangbourne; Southampton Univ. (BSc Social Sciences). Peat, Marwick, Mitchell & Co., 1972-75; Asst to Dir, Britain-in-Europe Campaign, 1975; J. Walter Thompson & Co., 1975-79; Dir, Spencer Bayley Ltd, 1975-. European Democratic Gp spokesman on: Social Affairs and Employment, 1979-81; External Econ. Relations, 1982-. Chm., European Union Cons. and Christian-Democratic Students, 1971-73. *Recreations:* gardening, swimming, fencing, opera. *Address:* The Manor House, Doveridge, Derbyshire. *Clubs:* Carlton, Brass Monkey.

SPENCER-CHURCHILL, family name of **Duke of Marlborough.**

SPENCER CHURCHILL, John George; *see* Churchill, J. G. S.

SPENCER-NAIRN, Sir Robert (Arnold), 3rd Bt *cr* 1933; *b* 11 Oct. 1933; *s* of Sir Douglas Spencer-Nairn, 2nd Bt, TD, and Elizabeth Livingston, *d* of late Arnold J. Henderson; *S* father, 1970; *m* 1963, Joanna Elizabeth, *d* of late Lt-Comdr G. S. Salt, RN; two *s* one *d. Educ:* Eton College; Trinity Hall, Cambridge (MA). *Heir: s* James Robert Spencer-Nairn, *b* 7 Dec. 1966. *Address:* Barham, Cupar, Fife KY15 5RG. *Clubs:* New (Edinburgh); Royal and Ancient Golf (St Andrews).

SPENCER PATERSON, Arthur; *see* Paterson, A. S.

SPENCER-SILVER, Prof. Peter Hele; S. A. Courtauld Professor of Anatomy in the University of London, at the Middlesex Hospital Medical School, since 1974; *b* 29 Oct. 1922; *2nd s* of late Lt-Col J. H. Spencer Silver; *m* 1948, Patricia Anne, *e d* of late Col J. A. F. Cuffe, CMG, DSO, Wyke Mark, Winchester; two *s* one *d. Educ:* Harrow School; Middlesex Hosp. Med. School, Univ. of London. MRCS, LRCP; MB, BS London 1945; PhD London 1952. Res., Middlesex Hosp., 1945-46. RAF, 1946-48. Demonstrator in Anatomy, Middlesex Hosp. Med. Sch., 1948-57; Mem. 2nd Internat. Team in Embryology, Hübrecht Laboratory, Utrecht, Netherlands Govt Fellowship, 1956; Reader in Anatomy, Univ. of London, 1957; US Nat. Inst. of Health Post-doctoral Travelling Fellowship, 1961; Carnegie Inst. of Washington, Dept of Embryology, Baltimore, 1961-62; Prof. of Embryology, Mddx Hosp. Medical Sch., 1964-74, Sub-Dean, 1976-81. WHO Vis. Prof., 1976, 1979, 1981. FRSM. *Publications:* An Introduction to Human Anatomy, 1981; contribs to Jl Embryology and Experimental Morphology, Jl Physiol., Jl Anat., Lancet, etc. *Recreation:* music. *Address:* 7 More's Garden, 90 Cheyne Walk, SW3 5BB. *T:* 01-352 2990.

SPENCER SMITH, Prof. David, PhD; Hope Professor of Entomology, University of Oxford, and Fellow of Jesus College, Oxford, since 1980; *b* 10 April 1934; *s* of Rev. Harry Chadwick Smith and Mary Edith (*née* Lupton); *m* 1st, 1964, Una Scully; one *d*; 2nd, 1974, Sylvia Hyder. *Educ:* Kingswood Sch.; Cambridge Univ. (BA, MA, PhD). Research Fellow: Rockefeller Univ., NY, 1958-61; St Catharine's Coll., Cambridge, 1961-63 (Res. Fellow); Asst Prof., Univ. of Virginia, 1963-66; Associate Prof. of Medicine and Biology, Univ. of Miami, Fla, 1966-70; Prof. of Medicine, Pharmacology and Biology, Univ. of Miami, and Sen. Scientist, Papanicolaou Cancer Res. Inst., Miami, 1970-80. Editor, Tissue & Cell, 1969-. *Publications:* Insect Cells: their structure and function, 1968; Muscle: a monograph, 1972; papers and chapters in books and jls. *Recreations:* the ceramics and coinage of China; the coinage of the Indian subcontinent; orchids; the history of entomology; cricket, American football (spectator). *Address:* Jesus College, Oxford.

SPENCER-SMITH, Maj.-Gen. Jeremy Michael, CB 1971; OBE 1959; MC 1945; Director of Manning (Army), Ministry of Defence, 1970-72; retired; *b* 28 July 1917; *s* of Michael Spencer-Smith, DSO, MC, and Penelope, *née* Delmé-Radcliffe (she *m* 2nd, 1934, Elliot Francis Montagu Butler, and *d* 1974). *Educ:* Eton; New Coll., Oxford. Welsh Guards, 1940; Adjutant, 1st Bn, 1944-46; Staff, 1st Guards Brigade, MELF, 1950-51; comd 3 KAR, Kenya, 1959-60; Staff, HQ BAOR, 1960-63; comd 148 Infantry Bde (TA), 1964-67; Dep. Dir of Manning, Ministry of Defence (Army), 1967-68; GOC Wales, 1968-70. *Recreations:* shooting, racing, travel. *Address:* The White Cottages, Cheveley, Newmarket, Suffolk.

SPENCER-SMITH, Sir John Hamilton-, 7th Bt, *cr* 1804; contract gardener; *b* 18 March 1947; *s* of Sir Thomas Cospatric Hamilton-Spencer-Smith, 6th Bt, and Lucy Ashton, *o d* of late Thomas Ashton Ingram, Hopes, Norton-sub-Hamdon, Somerset; *S* father, 1959; *m* 1980, Christine, *d* of late John Theodore Charles Osborne, Durrington, Worthing, Sussex. *Educ:* Milton Abbey; Lackham College of Agriculture, Wilts. *Recreation:* watching polo. *Heir: cousin* Peter Compton Hamilton-Spencer-Smith [*b* 12 Nov. 1912; *m* 1950,

Philippa Mary, *yr d* of late Captain Richard Ford; two *s*]. *Address:* Iping Mill, Iping, Midhurst, West Sussex GU29 0PE.

SPENCER WILLS, Sir John; *see* Wills.

SPENDER, Hon. Sir Percy Claude, KCVO 1957; KBE 1952; QC (NSW), 1935; BA; LLB; President of the International Court of Justice at The Hague, 1964–67 (Judge, 1958–64); Australian lawyer; *b* Sydney, 5 Oct. 1897; *s* of late Frank Henry Spender, Sydney, and Mary Hanson (*née* Murray); *m* 1925, Jean Maude (*d* 1970), *d* of Samuel B. Henderson; two *s. Educ:* Fort Street High Sch., Sydney; Sydney Univ. BA 1918 (distinction in economics); LLB 1922, with 1st class Honours and University Medal; George and Matilda Harris Scholar, 1920; Special Wigram Allen Prize for proficiency in Roman and Constitutional Law, 1918; Morven K. Nolan Memorial Prize for Political Science, 1920; Member of Sydney Univ. Senate, 1939–44; called to NSW Bar, 1923. Member of Menzies Ministry, 1939–41; Vice-President, Fed. Exec. Council, 1940 (Member 1939); Minister without portfolio assisting Treas., and Ministerial Secretary to Cabinet, 1939; Acting Treas. 1939, Treas. 1940; Member of Economic Cabinet, 1939–40; Chairman Australian Loan Council, 1939–40; Chairman of Nat. Debt Commn, 1940; Minister for the Army, Chairman of Mil. Board, and Member War Cabinet, 1940–41; Government, then Opposition Member of Advisory War Council, 1940–45; Minister for External Affairs and of External Territories, Australia, 1949–51; MHR for Warringah, 1937–51; Australian Ambassador to the United States, 1951–58. Chairman: Australian Delegn at Conference of British Commonwealth Foreign Ministers, Colombo, 1950 (at which he put forward a plan for economic aid to S and SE Asia, subseq. known as the Colombo Plan); Conf. of British Commonwealth Consultative Cttee on Economic Aid to S and SE Asia, Sydney, 1950; Australian delegate at British Commonwealth Consultative Cttee Meeting, London, 1950; Vice-Pres., 5th General Assembly, UN, 1950–51, and Chm. and Vice-Chm., Australian Delegn UN General Assembly, 1952–56; Australian Representative at negotiation Canberra and subsequently at signing Regional Security Treaty between USA, NZ, and Australia, San Francisco, 1951; Vice-President Jap. Peace Treaty Conf., San Francisco, 1951 (Chm., Australian Delegn); Australian Governor of Internat. Monetary Fund and Internat. Bank, 1951–53; alternate Governor, Internat. Monetary Fund, 1954; Chm. Australian Delegn to UN Commemorative Session, San Francisco, 1955; Special Envoy on goodwill mission to South and Central America, July–Aug. 1955; Chairman, Australian Delegation Internat. Sugar Conf., May–June 1956 and Conf. to establish Atomic Energy Internat. Agency, Sept.–Oct. 1956; Chairman, Australian Delegation to 2nd Suez Conf., London, Sept. 1956, and to Commonwealth Finance Ministers' meeting, Washington, Oct. 1956. Mem. Gen. Council, Assicurazioni Generali (Italy), 1969–. European War, 1914–18, enlisted AIF, 1918; War of 1939–45, Lieut-Colonel on Active List AMF part-time special duties, 1942–45; now on retired list with hon. rank of Lieut-Colonel. Member: Board of Directors of USA Educational Foundation in Australia, 1950–51; US Cttee of Study and Training in Australia, 1950–51; Member of Council (1949–51) and Life Member Convocation Australian Nat. Univ.; Vice-President, Royal Commonwealth Society (President, NSW Br., 1949–51); President: Sydney Club, 1967–; NSW Br. of Overseas League, 1967–72. Chm., Aust. Museum Bd of Trustees for compilation of National Photographic Index of Australian Birds, 1969–. Hon. LLD: Univ. of British Columbia; Hamilton Coll., NY, 1952; Univ. of Colorado, 1953; Trinity Coll., Hartford, Conn, 1955; Yale, 1957; California, 1965; University of the East (Philippines), 1966; Sydney, 1973; Hon. DCL and Hon. Chancellor, Union Univ., Schenectady, 1955; Hon. LittD Springfield Coll., Mass, 1955. Coronation Medal, 1937 and 1953. KStJ 1958. Grande Ufficiale dell' Ordine al Merito della Repubblica Italiana, 1976. C of E. *Publications:* Company Law and Practice, 1939; Australia's Foreign Policy, the Next Phase, 1944; Exercises in Diplomacy, 1969; Politics and a Man, 1972. *Recreations:* reading, surfing, golf. *Address:* Headingley House, Wellington Street, Woollahra, NSW 2025, Australia. *Clubs:* Elanora Country, Australasian Pioneers (Sydney); Athenæum (Melbourne).

SPENDER, Stephen (Harold), CBE 1962; CLit 1977; FRSL; poet and critic; Professor of English, University College, London University, 1970–77, now Emeritus; *b* 28 Feb. 1909; *s* of Edward Harold Spender and Violet Hilda Schuster; *m* 1st, 1936, Agnes Marie (Inez), *o d* of late William Henry Pearn; 2nd, 1941, Natasha Litvin; one *s* one *d. Educ:* University College Sch.; University College, Oxford (Hon. Fellow, 1973). Co-editor Horizon Magazine, 1939–41; Counsellor, Section of Letters, Unesco, 1947; Co-Editor Encounter, 1953–67. Fireman in NFS, 1941–44. Hon. Mem. Phi Beta Kappa (Harvard Univ.); Elliston Chair of Poetry, Univ. of Cincinnati, 1953; Beckman Prof., Univ. of California, 1959; Visiting Lecturer, Northwestern Univ., Illinois, 1963; Consultant in Poetry in English, Library of Congress, Washington, 1965; Clark Lectures (Cambridge), 1966; Mellon Lectures, Washington, DC, 1968; Northcliffe Lectures (London Univ.), 1969. Pres., English Centre, PEN Internat., 1975–. Fellow, Inst. of Advanced Studies, Wesleyan Univ., 1967. Visiting Professor: Univ. of Connecticut, 1969; Vanderbilt Univ., 1979. Hon. Mem. Amer. Acad. of Arts and Letters and Nat. Inst. of Arts and Letters, 1969. Queen's Gold Medal for Poetry for 1971. Hon. DLitt: Montpellier Univ.; Cornell Coll.; Loyola Univ. *Publications:* 20 Poems; Poems, the Destructive Element, 1934; Vienna, 1934; The Burning Cactus, 1936; Forward from Liberalism, 1937; Trial of a Judge, 1937; Poems for Spain, 1939; The Still Centre, 1939; Ruins and Visions, 1941; Life and the Poet, 1942; Citizens in War and After, 1945; Poems of Dedication, 1946; European Witness, 1946; The Edge of Being, 1949; essay, in The God that Failed, 1949; World Within World (autobiog.), 1951; Learning Laughter

(travels in Israel), 1952; The Creative Element, 1953; Collected Poems, 1954; The Making of a Poem, 1955; Engaged in Writing (stories), 1958; Schiller's Mary Stuart (trans.), 1958; The Struggle of the Modern, 1963; Selected Poems, 1965; The Year of the Young Rebels, 1969; The Generous Days (poems), 1971; (ed) A Choice of Shelley's Verse, 1971; (ed) D. H. Lawrence: novelist, poet, prophet, 1973; Love-Hate Relations, 1974; T. S. Eliot, 1975; (ed) W. H. Auden: a tribute, 1975; The Thirties and After, 1978; (with David Hockney) Chinese Journal, 1982. *Address:* 15 Loudoun Road, NW8.

SPENDLOVE, Peter Roy, CVO 1981; HM Diplomatic Service; Deputy High Commissioner, Sri Lanka, since 1981; *b* 11 Nov. 1925; *s* of H. A. Spendlove and Florence (*née* Jackson); *m* 1952, Wendy Margaret Valentine; two *s* three *d. Educ:* Chichester High Sch.; London Sch. of Economics; Edinburgh and Cambridge Univs. BScEcon Hons 1951. Called to Bar, Middle Temple, 1964. Served HM Forces, 1943–47: commnd, Indian Army/Royal Indian Artillery. LSE, 1947–51; Internat. Law Scholar at The Hague, 1951; Univ. of Cambridge, 1951–52. Apptd District Officer, Kenya, 1952; retired after serving in Provincial Admin and Central Govt, 1964. First Secretary, FCO, 1964; served in E Malaysia, Washington, Manila, FO, Jamaica; Counsellor, Economic, Commercial and Aid, Jakarta, 1977–80. *Recreations:* riding, skiing, hill walking. *Address:* c/o Foreign and Commonwealth Office, SW1.

SPENS, family name of Baron Spens.

SPENS, 2nd Baron *cr* 1959; **William George Michael Spens;** *b* 18 Sept. 1914; *s* of 1st Baron Spens, PC, KBE, QC, and Hilda Mary (*d* 1962), *e d* of Lt-Col Wentworth Grenville Bowyer; *S* father, 1973; *m* 1941, Joan Elizabeth, *d* of late Reginald Goodall; two *s* one *d. Educ:* Rugby; New Coll., Oxford (MA). Barrister, Inner Temple, 1945. Served War of 1939–45 with RA; British Control Commission (later High Commission), Germany, 1945–55. *Heir:* s Hon. Patrick Michael Rex Spens, ACA [*b* 22 July 1942; *m* 1966, Barbara Janet Lindsay, *d* of Rear-Adm. Ralph Lindsay Fisher; one *s* one *d*].

SPENS, Colin Hope, CB 1962; FICE, FIWES, FInstWPC; Deputy Chairman, Sutton and District Water Co. since 1971; *b* 22 May 1906; *er s* of late Archibald Hope Spens, Lathallan, Fifeshire and Hilda Constance Hooper; *m* 1941, Josephine, *d* of late Septimus Simond; two *s* one *d. Educ:* Lancing Coll.; Imperial College of Science and Technology. Consulting engineering experience, 1928–39. Served War of 1939–45 with Royal Signals, 1939–41; PA to Director of Works in Ministry of Works, 1941–44; Engineering Inspectorate of Min. of Health, 1944–51, Min. of Housing and Local Govt, 1951–60; Chief Engineer, Min. of Housing and Local Govt, 1960–67. Senior Consultant, Rofe, Kennard and Lapworth, 1967–76. Pres., IWES, 1974–75. Hon. FInstPHE. *Address:* 10 Ashbourne Court, Burlington Place, Eastbourne BN21 4AX. *T:* Eastbourne 638742.

SPENS, John Alexander, RD 1970; Partner, Maclay, Murray & Spens, Solicitors, Glasgow and Edinburgh, since 1960; *b* 7 June 1933; *s* of Thomas Patrick Spens and Nancy F. Spens (*née* Anderson); *m* 1961, Finella Jane, *d* of Donald Duff Gilroy; two *s* one *d* (and one *s* decd). *Educ:* Cargilfield; Rugby School; Corpus Christi College, Cambridge (BA); Glasgow Univ. (LLB). Director: Scottish Amicable Life Assurance Soc., 1963– (Chairman, 1978–81); Standard Property Investment PLC, 1977–. Carrick Pursuivant, 1974–. *Recreations:* sailing, countryside and opera. *Address:* The Old Manse, Gartocharn, Dunbartonshire G83 8RX. *T:* Gartocharn 329. *Clubs:* Naval; Western (Glasgow).

SPENSLEY, Philip Calvert, DPhil, FRSC; Consultant in Post-Harvest Science and Technology and the Organisation of Research and Development; Director, Tropical Products Institute, Overseas Development Administration, Foreign and Commonwealth Office, 1966–81; *b* 7 May 1920; *s* of late Kent and Mary Spensley, Ealing; *m* 1957, Sheila Ross Fraser, *d* of late Alexander and Annie Fraser, Forres, Scotland; one *s* three *d. Educ:* St Paul's Sch., London; Keble Coll., Oxford (MA, BSc). Technical Officer, Royal Ordnance Factories, Ministry of Supply, 1940–45; Research Chemist, Nat. Inst. for Medical Research, MRC, 1950–54; Scientific Secretary, Colonial Products Council, Colonial Office, 1954–58; Asst Director Tropical Products Inst., DSIR, 1958–61, Dep. Director, 1961–66, Director, 1966. Chairman, Cttee of Visitors, Royal Institution, 1959. Member: FAO/WHO/Unicef Protein Adv. Gp, 1968–71; Cttee on Needs of Developing Countries, Internat. Union of Food Science and Technology, 1970–78; Food Science and Technol. Bd, MAFF/ARC/Dept of Agric. and Fisheries for Scotland Jt Consultative Organisation, 1973–79; UK Rep., CENTO Council for Scientific Educn and Research, 1970–78. Received MRC/NRDC Inventors Awards, 1963 and 1971. Freeman, City of London, 1951. *Publications:* Tropical Products Institute Crop and Product Digests, vol. 1, 1971; various research and review papers, particularly in the fields of chemotherapeutic substances, plant sources of drugs, aflatoxin, food losses, and work of Tropical Products Inst.; patents on extraction of hecogenin from sisal. *Recreations:* gardening, lawn tennis, boating. *Address:* 96 Laurel Way, Totteridge, N20. *T:* 01-445 7895. *Clubs:* Athenæum, Royal Automobile; Island Cruising.

SPERRY, Rt. Rev. John Reginald; *see* Arctic, Bishop of The.

SPERRY, Prof. Roger Wolcott, PhD; Hixon Professor of Psychobiology, California Institute of Technology, since 1954; *b* 20 Aug. 1913; *s* of Francis Bushnell Sperry and Florence Kraemer Sperry; *m* 1949, Norma Gay Deupree;

one s one d. Educ: Oberlin Coll. (Amos C. Miller Schol.; AB English 1935; MA Psych. 1937); Univ. of Chicago (PhD Zoology 1941). Nat. Research Council Fellow, Harvard Univ., 1941-42; Biology Research Fellow, Harvard Univ. at Yerkes Labs of Primate Biology, 1942-46; Asst Prof., Dept of Anatomy, Univ. of Chicago, 1946-52; Section Chief, Neurolog. Diseases and Blindness, NIH, 1952-53; Assoc. Prof. of Psychology, Univ. of Chicago, 1952-53. For. Mem. of Royal Soc., 1976-; Fellow: Amer. Psycholog. Assoc. (Distinguished Scientific Contrib Award, 1971); Amer. Assoc. for Advancement of Sci.; Member: Nat. Acad. of Scis, 1960-; Pontifical Acad. of Scis, 1978-; Amer. Philosophical Soc., 1974- (Karl Lashley Award, 1976); Amer. Acad. of Arts and Scis, 1963-; (Hon.) Amer. Neurolog. Assoc., 1974-; Internat. Neuropsychology Soc.; Amer. Assoc. for Anatomists; Soc. for Developmental Biology; Amer. Physiological Soc.; Psychonomic Soc.; Soc. for Neuroscience (Ralph Gerard Award, 1979); Internat. Brain Res. Org.; Internat. Soc. of Developmental Biologists; Soc. of Sigma XI; Amer. Assoc. of Univ. Profs. Hon. Dr of Science: Cambridge, 1972; Chicago, 1976; Kenyon Coll., 1979; Rockefeller, 1980; Oberlin Coll., 1982; Howard Crosby Warren Medal, Soc. of Exper. Psychologists, 1969; Calif. Scientist of the Year Award, Calif. Mus. of Sci. and Industry, 1972; (jtly) William Thomson Wakeman Res. Award, Nat. Paraplegia Foundn, 1972; Passano Award in Med. Sci., 1973; Claude Bernard Science Journalism Award, 1975; (jtly) Wolf Prize in Medicine, 1979; Internat. Visual Literacy Assoc. Special Award, 1979; Albert Lasker Med. Res. Award, 1979; Golden Plate Award of Amer. Acad. of Achievement, 1980; (jtly) Nobel Prize in Physiology or Medicine, 1981. Publications: Science and Moral Priority, 1982; many contribs to scientific jls, chapters in books, and scattered theoretical, philosophical and humanistic articles. Recreations: paleontology, camping, cameras and sculpture. Address: 3625 Lombardy Road, Pasadena, California 91107, USA. T: (213) 793-0117. Club: Athenæum of Pasadena (Calif.).

SPICER, Clive Colquhoun; Honorary Research Fellow, Exeter University; Director, Medical Research Council Computer Unit, 1967-79; b 5 Nov. 1917; s of John Bishop Spicer and Marion Isobel Spicer; m 1st, 1941, Faith Haughton James, MB (marr. diss. 1979); one s two d; 2nd, 1979, Anne Nolan. Educ: Charterhouse Sch.; Guy's Hospital. Operational research on war casualties, 1941-46; Hon. Sqdn Leader, RAF; Staff, Imperial Cancer Research Fund, 1946-49; Dept of Biometry, University Coll., London, 1946-47; Public Health Laboratory Service, 1949-59; WHO Fellow, Univ. of Wisconsin, 1952-53; Vis. Scientist, US Nat. Insts of Health, 1959-60; Statistician, Imperial Cancer Research Fund, 1960-62; Chief Medical Statistician, General Register Office, 1962-66. Main interest has been in application of mathematical methods to medical problems. Publications: papers in scientific journals on epidemiology and medical statistics. Recreations: sailing, reading. Address: c/o Department of Mathematical Statistics, Streatham Court, Rennes Drive, Exeter EX4 4PU.

SPICER, James Wilton; MP (C) Dorset West since Feb. 1974; Member (C) Wessex, European Parliament, since 1979; company director and farmer; b 4 Oct. 1925; s of James and Florence Clara Spicer; m 1954, Winifred Douglas Shanks; two d. Educ: Latymer. Regular army, 1943-57, retd (Major); commnd Royal Fusiliers, 1944; served with King's African Rifles; Para. Regt. Nat. Chm., CPC, 1968-71; Mem., European Parlt, 1975-; Chief Whip, European Democratic Gp, 1975-79; Dir, Cons. Group for Europe, 1972-74, Chm., 1975-78. Recreations: swimming, tennis, squash. Address: Whatley, Beaminster, Dorset. T: Beaminster 862337. Clubs: Naval and Military, Institute of Directors.

SPICER, Michael; see Spicer, W. M. H.

SPICER, (Sir) Peter James, 4th Bt cr 1906 (but does not use the title); retired; b 20 May 1921; s of Captain Sir Stewart Dykes Spicer, 3rd Bt, RN, and Margaret Grace (née Gillespie) (d 1967); S father, 1968; m 1949, Margaret, e d of Sir Steuart Wilson (d 1966), and Ann Mary Grace, now Lady Boult; one s three d (and one s decd). Educ: Winchester Coll. (Schol.); Trinity Coll., Cambridge (Exhibr); Christ Church, Oxford (MA). Served War of 1939-45 (despatches, 1944); Royal Sussex Regt, then RN (Temp. Lieut, RNVR). Trinity Coll., Cambridge, 1939-40; Christ Church, Oxford, 1945-47. Member of publishing staff, Oxford University Press, 1947-81. Co-opted Member, Educn Cttee of Oxfordshire CC, 1959-74 (Chairman, Libraries Sub-Cttee, 1961-74). Congregational Rep., British Council of Churches, 1963-72; Chm., Educational Publishers' Council, 1976-78. Recreations: theology, gardening, walking, sailing, music, large family gatherings. Heir: s Dr Nicholas Adrian Albert Spicer, b 28 Oct. 1953. Address: Salt Mill House, Fishbourne, Chichester PO19 3JN. T: Chichester 782825.

SPICER, (William) Michael (Hardy); MP (C) South Worcestershire since Feb. 1974; b 22 Jan. 1943; s of late Brig. L. H. Spicer; m 1967, Patricia Ann Hunter; one s two d. Educ: Wellington Coll.; Emmanuel Coll., Cambridge (MA Econs). Asst to Editor, The Statist, 1964-66; Conservative Research Dept, 1966-68; Dir, Conservative Systems Research Centre, 1968-70; Man. Dir, Economic Models Ltd, 1970-80. PPS, Dept of Trade, 1979-81; a Vice-Chm. of Conservative Party, 1981-. Publications: Final Act (political novel), 1981; contrib. Jl Royal Inst. Public Admin. Recreations: painting, tennis, writing, travelling. Address: House of Commons, SW1. T: 01-219 3000.

SPICKERNELL, Rear-Adm. Derek Garland, CB 1974; CEng, FIMechE, FIProdE, MIPM, CBIM, MIMarE; Director General, British Standards Institution, since 1981 (Technical Director, 1976-81); b 1 June 1921; s of late Comdr Sidney Garland Spickernell, RN, and Florence Elizabeth (née March); m 1946, Ursula Rosemary Sheila Money; one s one d (and one s decd). Educ: RNEC, Keyham. Served War, HM Ships Abdiel, Wayland, and Engr Officer HM Submarine Statesman, 1943-45. Engr Officer HM Submarines Telemachus, Tudor and Alcide, 1945-50; Submarine Trials Officer, 1950-51; Engrg Dept, HM Dockyard, Portsmouth, 1951-53; SEO: Portsmouth Frigate Sqdn, 1954-55; 2nd Submarine Sqdn, 1956-57; Supt, ULE, Bournemouth, 1958-59; Dep. Captain Supt, AUWE, Portland, 1959-62; Dep. Manager, Engrg Dept, HM Dockyard, Portsmouth, 1962-64; in command, HMS Fisgard, 1965-66; Dep. Dir, Naval Ship Production, 1967-70; Dep. Chief Exec., Defence Quality Assurance Bd, 1970-71; Dir-Gen., Quality Assurance, MoD (PE), 1972-75; Chm., Nat. Council for Quality and Reliability, 1973-75; A Vice-Pres., Inst. of Quality Assurance, 1974- (Hon. FIQA); Member: Internat. Acad. of Quality Assurance, 1977-; Agrément Bd, 1980-; Council, IMechE; Council, Cranfield Inst. of Technol. Publications: papers on Quality Assurance. Recreation: golf. Address: Ridgefield, Shawford, Hants. T: Twyford 712157. Clubs: Naval and Military, English-Speaking Union; Royal Fowey Yacht.

SPIEGL, Fritz; musician, writer, broadcaster; b 27 Jan. 1926; s of Rudolf Spiegl and Josefine Geiringer; m 1st, 1952, Bridget Katharine Fry (marr. diss. 1970); three d; 2nd, 1976, Ingrid Frances Romnes. Educ: Magdalen College Sch.; Royal Academy of Music (ARAM). Designer/typographer, Colman Prentis & Varley, 1941-46; Principal Flautist, Royal Liverpool Philharmonic, 1948-63; occasional spare flautist: RPO, 1963; CBSO, 1965-70; Hallé, 1965-72; BBC NSO, 1963-; Founder/Conductor, Liverpool Music Group, Liverpool Wind Ensemble, 1949-; Director, The Spieglers, 1975-; Columnist: Liverpool Daily Post, 1970-; Classical Music, 1979-; Reviews: The Listener, 1974-, Guardian, 1959-, Times Lit. Supp., 1980-; broadcaster in various capacities, 1950-: Start the Week, 1972-; Words, 1978; Fritz on Friday, 1978, 1979, 1980; Up to the Hour, 1977-78; A-Z of Musical Curios, 1978-79. Publications: various edns of music, 1950-; (regularly reprinted): What the Papers Didn't Mean to Say, 1964; ed/comp., Lern Yerself Scouse, 1965; ABZ of Scouse, 1967; The Growth of a City, 1967; Liverpool Ballads, 1967; The Liverpool Manchester Railway, 1970; Slavers and Privateers, 1970; A Small Book of Grave Humour, 1971; Dead Funny: more grave humour, 1982; contrib. Grove's Dictionary of Music, 1980. Recreations: printing, cooking, inventing and several deadly sins. Address: 4 Windermere Terrace, Liverpool L8 3SB. T: 051-727 2727.

SPIERS, Donald Maurice, TD 1966; Director General Aircraft 1, Ministry of Defence (Procurement Executive), since 1981; b 27 Jan. 1934; s of Harold Herbert Spiers and Emma (née Foster); m 1958, Sylvia Mary Lowman; two s. Educ: Raynes Park County Grammar Sch.; Trinity Coll., Cambridge (MA). CEng, MRAeS 1966. Commnd RE, 1952-54. de Havilland Engine Co., Hatfield, 1957-60; joined Air Min. as SSO, 1960; operational res. on deterrence, 1960-63; trials and analysis, Aden and Radfan, 1964; Kestrel evaluation trial, 1965; Scientific Adviser to FEAF, Singapore, 1967-70; Asst Chief Scientist (RAF), MoD, 1972-77; Asst Dir, Mil. Aircraft Projs, MoD (PE), 1978; Dir of Aircraft Post Design Services, MoD (PE), 1979-81. Recreations: keeping horses, carting hay, mending fences. Address: 20 Paddock Close, Camberley, Surrey GU15 2BN. T: Camberley 28164.

SPIERS, Prof. Frederick William, CBE 1962; Part-time Director, Bone Dosimetry Research, University of Leeds, 1972-78; Professor of Medical Physics, University of Leeds, 1950-72; b 29 July 1907; er s of Charles Edward and Annie Spiers; m 1936, Kathleen M. Brown; one d. Educ: Prince Henry's Grammar Sch., Evesham; University of Birmingham. 1st Class Hons Physics, 1929; PhD 1932; DSc 1952. Anglo-German Exchange Scholar, Univ. of Munich, 1930. Demonstrator in Physics, University of Leeds, 1931; Senior Physicist, General Infirmary, Leeds, 1935; Vis. Lecturer, Washington Univ., St Louis, USA, 1950. Hon. Director: MRC Environmental Radiation Unit, 1959-72; MRC Regional Radiological Protection Service, Leeds, 1963-70; Chief Regional Scientific Adviser for Civil Defence, NE Region, 1952-77; President, British Inst. of Radiology, 1955-56; Chairman: Hospital Physicists Assoc., 1944-45; British Cttee on Radiation Units and Measurements, 1967-77; Home Defence Scientific Adv. Standing Conference, 1972-77; Hon. Mem., Royal Coll. of Radiologists; Member: MRC Protection Cttee; Radio-active Substances Adv. Cttee, 1960-70; Internat. Commn on Radiation Units and Measurements, 1969-73; Statutory Adv. Cttee to National Radiological Protection Bd; Adv. Council on Calibration and Measurement, 1973-77. Silvanus Thompson Meml Lectr, British Inst. Radiology, 1973; Vis. Scientist, Argonne Nat. Laboratory, Univ. of Chicago, 1979. Röntgen Prize, 1950; Barclay Medal, 1970; Silver Jubilee Medal, 1977. FInstP 1970. Publications: Radioisotopes in the Human Body, 1968; articles on radiation physics and radiobiology in scientific journals; contribs in: British Practice in Radiotherapy, 1955; Radiation Dosimetry, 1956, 1969; Encyclopedia of Medical Radiology, 1968; Manual on Radiation Haematology, 1971. Recreations: photography, music, gardening. Address: Lanesfield House, Old Lane, Bramhope, near Leeds LS16 9AZ. T: Arthington 842680.

SPIERS, Ven. Graeme Hendry Gordon; Archdeacon of Liverpool, since 1979; b 15 Jan. 1925; s of Gordon and Mary Spiers; m 1958, Ann Chadwick; two s. Educ: Mercers Sch.; London College of Divinity. Westminster Bank, 1941-49; served RNVR, 1943-47. Deacon 1952, Priest 1953; Curate of Addiscombe, 1952-56; Succentor of Bradford Cathedral, 1956-58; Vicar of Speke, 1958-66; Vicar of Aigburth, 1966-80 and Rural Dean of Childwall,

1975-79. *Recreation:* gardening. *Address:* 40 Sinclair Drive, Liverpool L18 0HW. *T:* 051-722 6675.

SPIERS, Air Cdre Reginald James, OBE 1972; FRAeS; Commandant, Aeroplane and Armament Experimental Establishment, Boscombe Down, since 1979; *b* 8 Nov. 1928; *s* of Alfred James Oscar and Rose Emma Alice Spiers; *m* 1956, Cynthia Jeanette Williams; two *d. Educ:* Haberdashers' Aske's Sch.; RAF Coll., Cranwell. FRAeS 1975. Commissioned 1949; 247 and 64 Fighter Sqdns, 1950-54; Graduate, Empire Test Pilots' Sch., 1955; Fighter Test Sqdn, A&AEE, 1955-58; CO 4 Fighter Sqdn, 1958-61; PSO to C-in-C RAF Germany, 1961-63; RAF Staff Coll., 1964; FCO, 1965-67; CO RAF Masirah, 1967-68; Chief Test Flying Instructor, ETPS, 1968-71; Air Warfare Course, 1972; Air Secretary's Dept, MoD, 1972-73; MA to Governor of Gibraltar, 1973-75; CO Experimental Flying Dept, RAE Farnborough, 1975-78; Director, Defence Operational Requirements Staff, MoD, 1978-79. *Recreations:* shooting, aviation. *Address:* Old Malt House, Barton Stacey, Winchester, Hants SO21 3RS. *T:* Sutton Scotney 250. *Club:* Royal Air Force.

SPIERS, Ronald Ian; United States Ambassador to Pakistan, since 1981; *b* 9 July 1925; *s* of Tomas H. and Blanca De P. Spiers; *m* 1949, Patience Baker; one *s* three *d. Educ:* Dartmouth Coll., New Hampshire (BA); Princeton Univ. (Master in Public Affairs, PhD). Mem., US Delegn to UN, 1956-60; US Department of State: Dir, Office of Disarmament and Arms Control, 1960-62; Dir, Office of NATO Affairs, 1962-66; Political Counsellor, London, 1966-69; Asst Sec. of State, Politico-Military Affairs, 1969-73; Ambassador to the Bahamas, 1973-74; Minister, London, 1974-77; Ambassador to Turkey, 1977-80; Dir, Bureau of Intelligence and Research, Dept of State, 1980-81. *Recreations:* swimming, music, theatre-going, gardening. *Address:* c/o Department of State, Washington, DC 20520, USA.

SPIKINGS, Barry Peter; Chairman and Chief Executive, EMI Films Group Worldwide, since 1980; Chairman: Elstree Studios Ltd, since 1979; EMI TV Programms Inc., since 1979; Director, EMI Cinemas, since 1979; *b* 23 Nov. 1939; *m* 1st, 1962, Judith Anne Spikings; one *s* one *d;* 2nd, 1978, Dorothy Spikings; two step *d. Educ:* Boston Grammar School. Managing Director, British Lion Films Ltd, 1973-75; Chairman, Shepperton Studios Ltd, 1973-75; Managing Director, EMI Films Ltd, Director, EMI Films Inc., 1975. Oscar award as Producer of Best Picture of the Year, for The Deer Hunter, Acad. of Motion Picture Arts and Sciences, 1979. *Recreation:* making films. *Clubs:* Mark's, White Elephant, Burkes.

SPINELLI, Altiero; a Deputy (Independent), Parliament of Italy, since 1976; Member of the European Parliament, since 1976; *b* 31 Aug. 1907; *s* of Carlo Spinelli and Maria Ricci; *m* 1944, Ursula Hirschmann; three *d. Educ:* Univ. of Rome. Political prisoner in Italy, 1927-43; partisan in Italian Resistance, 1943-45; Leader of European Federalist Movement, 1945-61. Visiting Prof., Johns Hopkins Univ. Center for Advanced Internat. Studies, in Bologna, 1961-64. Founder and Director, Istituto Affari Internationali, Rome, 1965-70; Mem., Commn of the European Communities, 1970-76. *Publications:* Degli Stati Sovrani agli Stati Uniti d'Europa, 1952; L'Europa non cade dal cielo, 1960; Tedeschi al bivio, 1960; The Eurocrats, 1966; The European Adventure, 1973; Il lungo monologo, 1970; PCI: che fare?, 1978; La mia battaglia per un'Europa diversa, 1979. *Address:* Camera dei Deputati, Rome, Italy; Clivo Rutario 5, 00152 Roma, Italy.

SPINK, Prof. John Stephenson; Professor of French Language and Literature in the University of London (Bedford College), 1952-73; *b* 22 Aug. 1909; *s* of William Spink and Rosetta Spink (*née* Williamson); *m* 1940, Dorothy Knowles, MA, DèsL, LRAM. *Educ:* Pickering Grammar Sch.; Universities of Leeds and Paris. BA (Leeds), 1930; MA (Leeds), 1932; Docteur de l'Université de Paris, 1934; Lauréat de l'Académie Française, 1935. Assistant at Lycée Henri IV, Paris, 1930-33; Lecteur at the Sorbonne, 1931; Asst Lectr in Univ. of Leeds, 1933-36; Lectr in Univ. of London, King's Coll., 1937-50; Prof. of French at University College, Southampton, 1950-52. Officier de l'ordre nat. du mérite, 1973. *Publications:* J.-J. Rousseau et Genève, 1934 (Paris); critical edition of J.-J. Rousseau, Les Rêveries du Promeneur solitaire, 1948; Literature and the sciences in the age of Molière, 1953; French Free-Thought from Gassendi to Voltaire, 1960; critical edn of Rousseau's educational writings in Pléiade œuvres complètes, t. IV, 1969; (ed jointly) Diderot, Œuvres complètes, I, II, 1975, IV, 1978; articles in Annales J.-J. Rousseau, Mercure de France, Revue d'Histoire littéraire, Modern Language Review, French Studies, Bulletin des Historiens du théâtre, Horizon, Europe, Revue de Littérature Comparée, Problèmes des Genres Littéraires, Cahiers de l'Association internat. des Études Françaises, Dix-huitième siècle; trans. of Krimov, The Tanker Derbent, 1944 (Penguin). *Address:* 48 Woodside Park Road, N12.

SPIRO, Sidney, MC 1945; *b* 27 July 1914; *m* 1949, Diana Susskind; two *d.* Law degree. RA in Middle East, Italy, 1939-45. Joined Anglo American Corp., 1953, Exec. Dir 1961-77; International Banking Consultant, 1977-; Man. Dir and Dep. Chm., Charter Consolidated, 1969, Chm. 1971-76; Director: Hambros Ltd; Rio Tinto-Zinc Corp. Ltd; De Beers Consolidated Mines Ltd; Minerals & Resources Corp. Ltd. Mem., Internat. Adv. Council, Canadian Imperial Bank of Commerce. *Recreations:* shooting, golf, tennis, music. *Address:* 9 Cedar House, Marloes Road, W8. *Clubs:* White's, MCC; Swinley Forest Golf.

SPITZ, Kathleen Emily, (Mrs Heinz Spitz); *see* Gales, Kathleen Emily.

SPITZ, Prof. Lewis, PhD; FRCS, FRCSE; Nuffield Professor of Paediatric Surgery, Institute of Child Health, London, since 1979; Hon. Consultant Surgeon, Hospital for Sick Children, Great Ormond Street, and Queen Elizabeth Hospital for Children, London, since 1979; *b* 25 Aug. 1939; *s* of Woolf and Selma Spitz; *m* 1972, Louise Ruth Dyzenhaus; one *s* one *d. Educ:* Univ. of Pretoria (MB, ChB); Univ. of the Witwatersrand (PhD). FRCS (*ad eundem*) 1980; FRCSE 1969. Smith and Nephew Fellow, Liverpool and London, 1971; Paediatric Surgeon, Johannesburg, 1971-74; Consultant Paediatric Surgeon, Sheffield Children's Hosp., 1974-79. Member: UK Children's Cancer Study Gp, 1982-; British Assoc. of Paediatric Surgeons; Assoc. of Surgeons of GB and Ireland; British Paediatric Assoc.; British Soc. of Gastroenterology; MRSocMed. Exec. Editor, Progress in Paediatric Surgery, 1982; Mem. Editorial Bd, Jl of Paediatric Surgery, 1980. *Publications:* A Colour Atlas of Paediatric Surgical Diagnosis, 1981; chapters in books on paediatrics and surgery; articles on pyloric stenosis, biliary atresia and choledochal cyst, gastro-oesophageal reflux, and neonatal surgery. *Recreation:* tennis. *Address:* 78 Wood Vale, N10 3DN. *T:* 01-444 9985.

SPITZER, Prof. Lyman, (Jr), BA; PhD; Professor of Astronomy, 1947-82 (Charles A. Young Professor, 1952-82), Princeton University; Chairman of Astrophysical Sciences Department, and Director of Observatory, Princeton University, 1947-79; Chairman, Research Board, 1967-72; *b* 26 June 1914; *s* of Lyman Spitzer and Blanche B. (*née* Brumback); *m* 1940, Doreen D. Canaday; one *s* three *d. Educ:* Phillips Academy, Andover; Yale Univ. (BA); Cambridge Univ., England; Princeton Univ. (PhD). Instructor in Physics and Astronomy, Yale Univ., 1939-42; Scientist, Special Studies Group, Columbia Univ. Div. of War Research, 1942-44; Dir, Sonar Analysis Group, Columbia Univ. Div. of War Research, 1944-46; Assoc. Prof. of Astrophysics, Yale Univ., 1946-47. Dir Project Matterhorn, Princeton Univ., 1953-61; Chm. Exec. Cttee, Plasma Physics Lab., Princeton Univ., 1961-66; Principal Investigator, Princeton telescope on Copernicus satellite. Member: Nat. Acad. of Sciences; American Academy of Arts and Sciences; American Philosophical Society; Internat. Acad. of Astronautics; Corr. Member, Société Royale des Sciences, Liège; Foreign Associate, Royal Astronomical Soc.; Pres., American Astronomical Soc., 1959-61. Hon. Dr of Science: Yale Univ., 1958; Case Inst. of Technology, 1961; Harvard, 1975; Hon. Dr of Laws, Toledo Univ., 1963. Rittenhouse Medal, 1957; NASA Medal, 1972; Bruce Medal, 1973; Draper Medal, 1974; Maxwell Prize, 1975; Dist. Public Service Medal, NASA, 1976; Gold Medal, RAS, 1978; Nat. Medal of Science, 1980; Janssen Medal, Soc. Astron. de France, 1980; Franklin Medal, Franklin Inst., 1980. *Publications:* (ed) Physics of Sound in the Sea, 1946; Physics of Fully Ionized Gases, 1956 (2nd edn 1962); Diffuse Matter in Space, 1968; Physical Processes in the Interstellar Medium, 1978; Searching between the Stars, 1982; papers in Astrophysical Jl, Monthly Notices of Royal Astronomical Soc., Physical Review, Physics of Fluids, on interstellar matter, stellar dynamics, plasma physics, etc. *Recreations:* ski-ing, mountain climbing. *Address:* 659 Lake Drive, Princeton, NJ 08540, USA. *T:* 609-924 3007. *Club:* American Alpine.

SPOCK, Dr Benjamin McLane; Professor of Child Development, Western Reserve University, USA, 1955-67, now writing and working for peace; *b* New Haven, Connecticut, 2 May 1903; *s* of Benjamin Ives Spock and Mildred Louise (née Stoughton); *m* 1st, 1927, Jane Davenport Cheney (marr. diss.); two *s;* 2nd, 1976, Mrs Mary Councille. *Educ:* Yale Univ. (BA); Yale Medical Sch.; Coll. Physicians and Surgeons, Columbia Univ. (MD). In practice (Pediatrics) from 1933; Cornell Med. Coll.; NY Hospital; NYC Health Dept. Served, 1944-46 in US Navy. Subseq. on Staff of: Rochester (Minn) Child Health Inst., Mayo Clinic, University of Minnesota; Prof. of Child Development, University of Pittsburgh, 1951-55. *Publications:* Common Sense Book of Baby and Child Care, 1946 (repr. as Pocket Book, 1946); (with John Reinhart and Wayne Miller) A Baby's First Year, 1955; (with Miriam E. Lowenberg) Feeding Your Baby and Child, 1955; Dr Spock Talks with Mothers, 1961; Problems of Parents, 1962; (with Marion Lerrigo) Caring for Your Disabled Child, 1964; (with Mitchell Zimmerman) Dr Spock on Vietnam, 1968; Decent and Indecent: our personal and political behaviour, 1970; A Young Person's Guide to Life and Love, 1971; Raising Children in a Difficult Time, 1974 (UK as Bringing Up Children in a Difficult Time, 1974). *Relevant publications:* The Trial of Doctor Spock, by Jessica Mitford, 1969; Dr Spock: biography of a conservative radical, by Lynn Z. Bloom, 1972. *Address:* Box N, Rogers, Arkansas 72756, USA.

SPOFFORD, Charles Merville, CBE (Hon.) 1945; DSM and Purple Heart (US), 1945; Lawyer (US); Trustee: Carnegie Corporation of New York; Juillard Musical Foundation; Director Emeritus: Council on Foreign Relations; Metropolitan Opera Association (Chairman Exec. Cttee, 1956-71, Member since 1971, President, 1946-50); Vice-Chairman and Director Emeritus, Lincoln Center for the Performing Arts, Inc.; Member Exec. Cttee, American Branch, International Law Association; former Member Exec. Council, American Society International Law, etc.; Trustee, The Mutual Life Insurance Co. of New York; *b* 17 Nov. 1902; *s* of Charles W. and Beulah Merville Spofford; *m* 1st, 1930, Margaret Mercer Walker (marr. diss. 1969); two *s* two *d;* 2nd, 1960, Carolyn Storrs Andre (*d* 1970); 3rd, 1970, Sydney Brewster Luddy. *Educ:* Northwest Univ.; University of Grenoble; Yale Univ. (AB 1924; Hon. MA 1956); Harvard Law Sch. JD 1928. Instructor, European History, Yale Univ., 1924-25, and sometime Alumni Fellow; practised Law, Chicago, 1929-30, New York (Davis Polk & Wardwell), 1930-40; member of firm, 1940-50 and 1952-. Lieut-Colonel 1942, AFHQ Algiers; adv. on econ. and supply, French N Africa and French W Africa, 1942-43; Chief of Planning

Staff (for AMG Sicily and Italy); Dep. Chief Civil Affairs Officer for Sicily and S Italy, 1943-44; AFHQ, Asst Chief of Staff, (G-5) Med. Theatre, 1944-45; War Dept as Military Adv. to State Dept, 1945; Colonel, 1943; Brig-General, 1944. Asst to President and Special Counsel to American National Red Cross, 1946-50; also other former civic activities. Deputy US Representative, North Atlantic Council, and Chairman, North Atlantic Council Deputies, 1950-52; Member European Co-ordinating Cttee (US); resigned 1952, to rejoin law firm. Formerly Director: American Univ. in Beirut, 1957-63; Nat. Council, English-Speaking Union, 1954-76; The Distillers Co. Ltd, 1952-76; subsid. CIBA Corp., 1957-71; Inst. for Defense Analyses, 1960-70. Carnegie Lectr, Hague Acad. of Internat. Law, 1964. Hon. LLD Northwestern Univ., 1959. Comdr, Order of Nishan Iftikhar, Tunisia, 1943; Croix de Guerre with palm, France, 1945; Commander, Order of SS Maurice and Lazarus, Italy, 1945; Commander, Legion of Honour, France, 1952; Commander with Star, Order of the Falcon, Iceland, 1953; Grand Officer, Order of the Crown, Belgium. *Recreation:* golf. *Publications:* articles in journals. *Address:* (business) 1 Chase Manhattan Plaza, New York, NY 10005, USA; (residence) Windmill Lane, East Hampton, New York, NY 11937. *Clubs:* Century Association, Links (New York); Maidstone (East Hampton).

SPOKES, John Arthur Clayton, QC 1973; a Recorder of the Crown Court, since 1972; *b* 6 Feb. 1931; 2nd *s* of late Peter Spencer Spokes and Lilla Jane Spokes (*née* Clayton), Oxford; *m* 1961, Jean, *yr d* of late Dr Robert McLean, Carluke, and Jean Symington McLean (*née* Barr); one *s* one *d. Educ:* Westminster Sch.; Brasenose Coll., Oxford. BA 1954; MA 1959. Nat. Service, Royal Artillery, 1949-51 (commnd 1950). Called to Bar, Gray's Inn, 1955. *Recreations:* gardening, walking. *Address:* 3 Pump Court, Temple, EC4Y 7AJ. *T:* 01-353 0711. *Club:* Leander (Henley-on-Thames).

SPOONER, Edward Tenney Casswell, CMG 1966; MD, MA, MRCS, LRCP; FRCP; *b* 22 May 1904; *s* of William Casswell Spooner, MB, and Edith Maud Spooner, Blandford, Dorset; *m* 1948, Colin Mary Stewart. *Educ:* Epsom Coll.; Clare Coll., Cambridge; St Bartholomew's Hospital. Foundation Scholar of Clare Coll., 1923; House Physician, St Bartholomew's Hospital, 1927-28; Commonwealth Fellow, Harvard Medical Sch., 1929-31; Fellow of Clare Coll., 1929-47; Tutor of Clare Coll., 1939-47; University Demonstrator and Lecturer, Dept of Pathology, University of Cambridge, 1931-46; Professor of Bacteriology and Immunology, London School of Hygiene and Tropical Medicine, 1947-60, Dean, 1960-70. Temporary Major, RAMC, in No 1 Medical Research Section, 1942-43; Director, Emergency Public Health Laboratory, Cambridge, 1943-44; Editor, Journal of Hygiene, 1949-55; Member Medical Research Council, 1953-57; Member Council Epsom Coll., 1955-65; Chm., Public Health Lab. Service Bd, 1963-72. *Publications:* papers on tetanus, certain virus diseases and wound infection. *Address:* Ellergarth, Dalditch Lane, Knowle, Budleigh Salterton, Devon EX9 7AH. *Club:* Athenæum.

SPOONER, Prof. Frank Clyffurde, MA, PhD; Professor of Economic History, University of Durham, since 1966; *b* 5 March 1924; *s* of Harry Gordon Morrison Spooner. *Educ:* Bromley Grammar Sch.; Christ's Coll., Cambridge. Hist. Tripos, 1st cl., Pt I 1947 and Pt II 1948; MA 1949; PhD 1953. War Service, Sub-Lt (S) RNVR, 1943-46; Bachelor Research Scholar, 1948; Chargé de Recherches, CNRS, Paris, 1949-50; Allen Scholar, 1951; Fellow, Christ's Coll., Cambridge, 1951-57; Commonwealth Fund Fellow, 1955-57 at Chicago, Columbia, New York, and Harvard Univs; Ecole Pratique des Hautes Etudes, VI Section, Sorbonne, 1957-61; Lectr, Univ. of Oxford, 1958-59; Vis. Lectr in Econs, Harvard Univ., 1961-62; Irving Fisher Research Prof. of Econs, Yale Univ., 1962-63; Univ. of Durham: Lectr, 1963; Reader, 1964; Resident Tutor-in-charge, Lumley Castle, 1965-70; Dir, Inst. of European Studies, 1969-76; Leverhulme Fellow, 1976-78. Prix Limantour de l'Académie des Sciences Morales et Politiques, 1957; West European Award, British Academy, 1979. FRHS 1970. *Publications:* L'economie mondiale et les frappes monétaires en France, 1493-1680, 1956, revised edn The International Economy and Monetary Movements in France, 1493-1725, 1972; contrib. Congrès et Colloques, 1965; Mediterraneo e Oceano Indiano, 1970; Annales (ESC); Annales de Normandie; Cambridge Hist. Jl; Revised Cambridge Modern History; Cambridge Econ. History of Europe; essays in honour of Armando Sapori, Amintore Fanfani, Fernand Braudel and Federigo Melis. *Recreations:* music, photography, walking. *Address:* 145 Gilesgate, Durham DH1 1QQ. *Club:* United Oxford & Cambridge University.

SPOONER, Sir James (Douglas), Kt 1981; Chairman: Vantona Group, since 1969; NAAFI, since 1973 (Director, since 1968); Deputy Chairman, Hogg Robinson Group, since 1971; Director, John Swire & Sons, since 1970; *b* 11 July 1932; *s* of late Vice-Adm. E. J. Spooner, DSO, and Megan Spooner (*née* Megan Foster, the singer); *m* 1958, Jane Alyson, *d* of Sir Gerald Glover, *qv*; two *s* one *d. Educ:* Eton Coll.; Christ Church, Oxford. Chartered Accountant 1962; Partner, Dixon Wilson & Co., Chartered Accountants, 1963-72. Director: Morgan Crucible Co., 1978-; J. Sainsbury, 1981-; Barclays Bank UK, 1982-. Chairman, KIDS, a national society for deprived and handicapped children, 1976-. *Recreations:* music, history, tennis, riding, shooting. *Address:* 52 Clarendon Road, W11. *T:* 01-727 6756. *Clubs:* White's, Beefsteak.

SPORBORG, Henry Nathan, CMG 1945; Chairman: SKF (UK) until 1975; Stirling International Civil Engineering (formerly Stirling-Astaldi); Gomme Holdings, until 1980; Berkeley Hambro Property Co. until 1980; Vice-Chairman, Sun Alliance & London Insurance Ltd, 1969-79; Deputy Chairman,

Thorn Electrical Industries, 1973-78; Director of other companies; Commissioner to the Fitzwilliam Estates and Executor of the late Earl Fitzwilliam; *b* 17 Sept. 1905; *e c* of late H. N. and M. A. Sporborg; *m* 1935, Mary Rowlands; one *s* three *d. Educ:* Rugby Sch.; Emmanuel Coll., Cambridge. Admitted Solicitor, 1930; partner in firm of Slaughter & May, 1935; joined Ministry of Economic Warfare, 1939; Director and later Vice-Chief, Special Operations Executive, 1940-46. A Director: Hambros Bank Ltd, 1949-70; Hambros Ltd, 1970-77. Mem., Port of London Authority, 1967-75. Chairman, Board of Governors, St Mary's Hospital, 1964-74. JP Herts, 1957. Chevalier, Legion of Honour, Croix de Guerre, Order of St Olav (Norway), etc. *Recreation:* fox-hunting. *Address:* Upwick Hall, Albury, near Ware, Herts. *T:* Albury 769. *Clubs:* Boodle's, Carlton.

SPOTSWOOD, Marshal of the Royal Air Force Sir Denis (Frank), GCB 1971 (KCB 1966; CB 1961); CBE 1946; DSO 1943; DFC 1942; Chairman, Smiths Industries International Aerospace and Defence Companies, since 1980; Director, Dowty Group, since 1980; *b* 26 Sept. 1916; *s* of late F. H. Spotswood and M. C. Spotswood; *m* 1942, Ann (*née* Child); one *s*. Commissioned in RAF, 1936; UK Service in Squadrons, 1937-41; No 209 Squadron, 1939-41. Served War of 1939-45 (despatches twice, DSO). Chief Instructor, Operation Training Unit, 1941-42; Officer Commanding No 500 (County of Kent) Squadron, RAuxAF, 1942-43; Director of Plans, HQ Supreme Allied Commander, South-East Asia, 1944-46; Directing Staff, RAF Staff Coll., 1946-48; Officer Commanding RAF (Fighter) Stations, Horsham St Faith and Coltishall, 1948-50; Directing Staff, Imperial Defence Coll., 1950-52; Exchange Duties, HQUSAF in USA, 1952-54; Officer Commanding RAF (Fighter) Station, Linton-on-Ouse, 1954-56; Deputy Director of Plans, Air Ministry, 1956-58; AOC and Commandant, RAF Coll., Cranwell, 1958-61; Assistant Chief of Staff (Air Defence), SHAPE, 1961-63; AOC No 3 Group, RAF Bomber Command, 1964-65; C-in-C RAF Germany, 1965-68; Commander, 2nd Allied Tactical Air Force, 1966-68; AOC-in-C, RAF Strike Command, 1968-71; Comdr, UK Air Defence Region, 1968-71; Chief of the Air Staff, 1971-74. Group Captain, 1954; Air Commodore, 1958; Air Vice-Marshal, 1961; Air Marshal, 1965; Air Chief Marshal, 1968; Marshal of the RAF, 1974. ADC to the Queen, 1957-61, Air ADC to the Queen, 1970-74. Vice-Chm. and Dir, Rolls Royce Ltd, 1974-80; Chm., Turbo Union Ltd, 1975-80; Dir, RR/Turbomeca Ltd. Pres., SBAC, 1978-79. Chm. of Governors, Royal Star and Garter Home; Vice-Patron, RAF Museum (Chm. of Trustees, 1974-80). FRAeS 1975. Officer of the Legion of Merit (USA). *Recreations:* golf, sailing, shooting, bridge. *Address:* c/o Williams & Glyn's Bank Ltd, Whitehall, SW1. *Club:* Royal Air Force.

SPRAGG, Cyril Douglas, CBE 1949; Hon. FRIBA 1971 (Hon. ARIBA 1959); Secretary, Royal Institute of British Architects, 1945-59; *b* 22 July 1894; *y s* of late Charles and Emily Spragg; unmarried. *Educ:* Christ's Hospital. Served European War, Queen's Westminster Rifles, 1914-19. Asst Secretary, RIBA, 1926-44. Governor of Christ's Hospital; Thames Conservancy, 1966-70; Hon. Member American Institute of Architects, 1955; Hon. Corresp. Member, Royal Architectural Inst. of Canada, 1956; Hon. Associate Royal Australian Inst. of Architects, 1957; Hon. Fellow, New Zealand Institute of Architects, 1957; Hon. Member Inst. South African Architects; Hon. Member Ghana Society of Architects, 1959; Hon. Fellow Royal Incorporation of Architects in Scotland, 1960; Hon. Member Fedn of Malaya Society Architects, 1961. Hon. MA Durham Univ., 1958. Member: Middlesex CC, 1961; Surrey CC, 1965, Alderman, 1967-70. *Address:* Tower Cottage, Vicarage Road, Egham, Surrey TW20 9JN. *T:* Egham 34224.

SPRAGGS, Rear-Adm. Trevor Owen Keith, CEng, FIEE; Chief of Staff to Commander-in-Chief, Naval Home Command, since 1981; *b* 17 June 1926; *s* of Cecil James Spraggs and Gladys Maude (*née* Morey); *m* 1955, Mary Patricia Light; two *s. Educ:* Portsmouth Grammar Sch.; St John's Coll., Southsea; Imperial College of Science and Technology, London (BScEng, ACGI). Joined Royal Navy, 1945; courses: HM Ships: King Alfred, Leander, Harrier, 1945-47; Admiralty Compass Obs., Slough, 1948; BRNC, Dartmouth, 1948-50; HM Ships: Dryad, Vanguard, Vernon, Collingwood, Ariel, Falcon, 1950-61; AEI, Manchester, 1962; RNEC, 1962-66; HMS Collingwood, 1966-69 and 1972-75; RNEC, 1969-72, and as Dean, 1979-80; Dean, RNC, Greenwich, 1975-77; Dir of Naval Trng Support, Dir of Naval Educn and Trng Support, 1977-79; Chief Naval Instr Officer, 1981-. ADC to the Queen, 1979. Member: Nautical Studies Bd of CNAA, 1975-80; Maritime Studies Adv. Cttee of Plymouth Polytech., 1979-80; Cttee of Management, Royal Hosp. Sch., Holbrook, 1981-; Governor: Fareham Technical Coll., 1972-75; RN Sch. for Officers' Daughters, Haslemere, 1975-77. Pres., Combined Services and RN Amateur Athletic Assocs, 1981-. *Recreations:* golf, sailing, rifle shooting, gardening. *Address:* c/o Lloyds Bank Ltd, 46 Station Road, Hayling Island, Hants. *Club:* Royal Naval Sailing Association.

SPRECKLEY, John Nicholas Teague; HM Diplomatic Service; Head of European Community Department (Internal), Foreign and Commonwealth Office, since 1979; *b* 6 Dec. 1934; *s* of late Air Marshal Sir Herbert Spreckley, KBE, CB, and Winifred Emery Teague; *m* 1958, Margaret Paula Jane, *er d* of Prof. W. McC. Stewart, *qv*; one *s* one *d. Educ:* Winchester Coll.; Magdalene Coll., Cambridge (BA). Tokyo, 1957-62; American Dept, FO, 1962-64; Asst Private Sec. to Lord Carrington and Mr Eadly, 1964; Defence Dept, FO, 1964-66; Head of Chancery, Dakar, 1966-70; Paris, 1970-75; Head of Referendum Unit, FCO, 1975; Counsellor and Head of Chancery, Tokyo, 1976-78; Fellow, Center for Internat. Affairs, Harvard Univ., 1978-79.

Address: c/o Foreign and Commonwealth Office, SW1A 2AL. *Club:* Army and Navy.

SPREULL, Professor James (Spreull Andrew); William Dick Professor of Veterinary Surgery, at the University of Edinburgh, 1959-78, now Emeritus; *b* 2 May 1908; *s* of late Lt-Col Andrew Spreull, DSO, TD, MRCVS, and Effie Andrew Spreull; *m* 1951, Kirsten Brummerstedt-Hansen; three *s. Educ:* Dundee High Sch.; Edinburgh Univ. (PhD); Royal Dick Veterinary Coll. (MRCVS). Royal Dick Veterinary College: Demonstrator of Anatomy, 1930-34, Lecturer in Applied Anatomy, 1931-34. Engaged in general practice in Dundee, 1934-59. FRSE 1965. *Publications:* various contributions to Veterinary Journals. *Recreations:* agriculture, fishing, badminton, antiques. *Address:* Spencerfield House, Hillend, Fife KY11 5LA. *T:* Inverkeithing 414255.

SPRIDDELL, Peter Henry; Director: Marks & Spencer, since 1970; National Freight Consortium, since 1982; *b* 18 Aug. 1928; *s* of Thomas Henry Spriddell and Eva Florence Spriddell; *m* 1952, Joyce Patricia (*née* Haycock); two *s* one *d. Educ:* Plymouth Coll.; Exeter Coll., Oxford (MA); Harvard Business Sch. Marks & Spencer Ltd: Management Trainee, 1951; Asst Store Manager, 1954; Store Man., 1960; Divl Store Exec., 1967; Alternate Dir Store Ops, 1970, full Dir, 1972; Dir of Personnel, 1972-75; Dir Estates, Bldg, Store Ops, Physical Distribution, 1975-. Dir, NFC, 1978-82. Member Council: Oxford Centre for Management Studies, 1978-; Town and Country Planning Assoc.; Vice-Pres., Devon Historic Bldgs Trust, 1970-. FRSA. Freeman, City of London. *Recreations:* music, golf. *Address:* 37 Main Avenue, Moor Park Estate, Northwood, Mddx. *T:* Northwood 29318. *Clubs:* Wellington; Moor Park Golf.

SPRIGGE, Prof. Timothy Lauro Squire, PhD; Professor of Logic and Metaphysics, University of Edinburgh, since 1979; *b* 14 Jan. 1932; *s* of Cecil and Katriona Sprigge; *m* 1959, Giglia Gordon; one *s* twin *d. Educ:* Gonville and Caius Coll., Cambridge (MA, PhD). Lecturer in Philosophy, University Coll. London, 1961-63; Lectr in Philosophy, 1963-70, Reader in Philosophy, 1970-79, Univ. of Sussex. Visiting Associate Professor, Univ. of Cincinnati, 1968-69. Member: Aristotelian Soc., 1960-; Mind Assoc., 1955-; Assoc. for the Advancement of Amer. Philosophy, 1978-; Scots Philosophical Club, 1979-. *Publications:* ed, Correspondence of Jeremy Bentham, vols 1 and 2, 1968; Facts, Words and Beliefs, 1970; Santayana: an examination of his philosophy, 1974; contribs to various vols of philosophical essays and to periodicals, incl. Mind, Philosophy, Inquiry, Nous. *Recreation:* backgammon. *Address:* David Hume Tower, University of Edinburgh, George Square, Edinburgh EH8 9JX. *T:* 031-667 1011.

SPRIGGS, Leslie, JP; MP (Lab) St Helens since June 1958; *b* 22 April 1910; British; *m* 1931, Elfrida Mary Brindle Parkinson. *Educ:* Council Sch.; Trade Union Adult Schools. TU Scholarship to Belgium, 1951. Merchant Service, then Railwayman until 1958. Formerly: President, NW (NUR) District Council, Political Section, 1954; Vice-President, Industrial Section, 1955. Served as Auditor to Lancs and Cheshire Region of the Labour Party. Formerly Lecturer, National Council of Labour Colleges on Industrial Law, Economics, Foreign Affairs, Local Government, Trade Union History. Member Parliamentary Groups: Employment, Environment, Health, Industry, Transport, and Trade, incl. aviation, shipping, textiles, clothing and footwear. JP N Fylde, 1955. *Recreations:* Rugby League, athletics, water polo, soccer, bowls, gardening. *Address:* House of Commons, SW1; 38 Knowle Avenue, Cleveleys, Lancs FY5 3PP. *T:* Cleveleys 852746. *Club:* St Helens Labour (St Helens).

SPRING, Frank Stuart, FRS 1952; DSc (Manchester), PhD (Liverpool), FRSC; Director, Laporte Industries Ltd, London, W1, 1959-71; retired; *b* 5 Sept. 1907; 3rd *s* of John Spring and Isabella Spring, Crosby, Liverpool; *m* 1932, Mary, 2nd *d* of Rev. John Mackintosh, MA, Heswall; one *s* one *d. Educ:* Waterloo Grammar Sch.; University of Liverpool. United Alkali Research Scholar, University of Liverpool, 1928-29; University Fellow, Liverpool, 1929-30. Assistant Lecturer, Lecturer and Senior Lecturer in Chemistry, University of Manchester, 1930-46; Freeland Professor of Chemistry, The Royal College of Science and Technology, Glasgow, 1946-59. Chemical Society, Tilden Lecturer, 1950. Hon. DSc: Salford, 1967; Strathclyde, 1981. *Publications:* papers in chemical journals. *Address:* Flat 26, 1 Hyde Park Square, W2. *T:* 01-262 8174.

SPRING RICE, family name of **Baron Monteagle of Brandon.**

SPRINGALL, Harold Douglas; Professor of Chemistry, University of Keele, 1950-75, now Emeritus (Head of Department, 1950-74); *b* 24 June 1910; *o s* of Harold Springall and Margaret Springall (*née* Wright); *m* 1940, Jean Helen McArthur Gordon, *d* of L. McArthur Gordon and H. Violet Gordon (*née* Holbeche); two *s* one *d. Educ:* Colfe's Grammar School, London; Lincoln College, Oxford (Scholar). BA (Cl) 1934; BSc 1934; Magdalen College, Oxford (Senior Demy), 1934-36; DPhil 1936; MA Oxon 1938. Commonwealth Fund Fellowship, Calif Tech., Pasadena, Calif, Cornell Univ., 1936-38; Rockefeller Research Grant, Oxford, 1938-39. Min. of Supply: Sci. Officer (Armament Res. Dept), Univ. of Bristol, 1939-44; Sen. Sci. Officer, 1944-45. Univ. of Manchester: Lectr in Chemistry, 1945-48, Sen. Lectr, 1948-50; Asst Tutor to Faculty of Science, 1949-50; Tutor in Chemistry, Dalton Hall, 1945-50; Univ. Coll. of North Staffs: Dir of Studies, 1951-52; Vice-Principal, 1957-59; Actg Vice-Principal, 1960-61. Mem. Council Chem.

Soc., 1954-57; Mem. Publication Cttee, Faraday Soc., 1957-71. CChem; FRIC 1948; FRSA 1971. DSc Keele, 1972. *Publications:* The Structural Chemistry of Proteins, 1954; Sidgwick's Organic Chemistry of Nitrogen, 1966; A Shorter Sidgwick's Organic Chemistry of Nitrogen, 1969; articles in Jl Chem. Soc., Jl Amer. Chem. Soc., Trans. Faraday Soc., Nature, etc. *Address:* 21 Springpool, The University, Keele, Staffordshire. *T:* Newcastle (Staffs) 627395. *Club:* Climbers'.

SPRINGER, Axel; Chairman, Axel Springer Publishing Group; *b* 2 May 1912; *s* of late Hinrich and Ottilie Springer; *m* ; one *s* one *d* (and one *s* decd). *Educ:* Altona Realgymnasium. Apprentice, with Wolff Telegrafenbüro, Hamburg, and reporter on several suburban newspapers, 1931; sports editor, 1934, Associate Editor, 1937, Altonaer Nachrichten; established own publishing co., 1945. Magazines and newspapers published by Springer Verlag, 1946-, include: Hörzu, Hamburger Abendblatt, Bild, Bild am Sonntag, Die Welt, Welt am Sonntag, Berliner Morgenpost, BZ, and Funk Uhr; owner of book-publishing houses Propyläen and Ullstein; founder, Ullstein Tele Vido. Hon. Fellow, Weizmann Inst., Israel, 1969. Hon. degrees: Temple Univ., Philadelphia, 1971; Bar-Ilan Univ., Israel, 1974; Hebrew Univ., Israel, 1976; Boston, 1981. Friendship Medal, USA, 1978; Leo Baeck Medal, NY, 1978; Ernst Reuter Medal, Berlin, 1982. Bavarian Order of Merit, 1974; Bundesverdienstkreuz with star and sash (Germany), 1977. *Publications:* Von Berlin aus gesehen, 1971; Aus Sorge um Deutschland, 1980. *Address:* Kochstrasse 50, D-1000 Berlin 61, Germany.

SPRINGER, Sir Hugh (Worrell), KCMG 1971; CBE 1961 (OBE 1954); Secretary-General, Association of Commonwealth Universities, 1970-80; Barrister-at-Law; *b* 1913; 2nd *s* of late Charles W. Springer, Barbados, and late Florence Springer; *m* 1942, Dorothy Drinan, 3rd *d* of late Lionel Gittens, Barbados, and Cora Gittens; three *s* one *d. Educ:* Harrison Coll., Barbados; Hertford Coll., Oxford (Hon. Fellow 1974). BA 1936, MA 1944. Called to Bar, Inner Temple, 1938. Practice at the Bar, Barbados, 1938-47; MCP, 1940-47, MEC 1944-47, Barbados; Gen.-Sec., Barbados Lab. Party, 1940-47; Organiser and first Gen.-Sec., Workers' Union, 1940-47; Mem., West Indies Cttee of the Asquith Commn on Higher Educn, 1944; Mem., Provisional Council, University Coll. of the West Indies, 1947; first Registrar, Univ. Coll. of WI, 1947-63; John Simon Guggenheim Fellow and Fellow of Harvard Center for Internat. Affairs, 1962-63; first Dir, Univ. of WI Inst. of Educn, 1963-66; Commonwealth Asst Sec.-Gen., 1966-70. Past Mem., Public Service and other Commns and Cttees; Sen. Vis. Fellow of All Souls Coll., Oxford, 1962-63; Actg Governor of Barbados, 1964; Mem., Bermuda Civil Disorder Commn, 1968. Chm., Commonwealth Caribbean Med. Res. Council (formerly Brit. Caribbean Med. Research Cttee), 1965-; Vice-Pres., British Caribbean Assoc., 1974-80; Trustee, Bernard Van Leer Foundn, 1967-78; Barbados Trustee, Commonwealth Foundn, 1967-80, and Chm., 1974-77; Member, Court of Governors: LSE, 1970-80; Exeter Univ., 1970-80; Hull Univ., 1970-80; London Sch. of Hygiene and Tropical Medicine, 1974-77; Inst. of Commonwealth Studies, 1974-80. Trustee, Harlow Campus, Meml Univ. of Newfoundland, 1975-79. Jt Sec., UK Commonwealth Scholarships Commn, 1970-80; Exec. Sec., Marshall Scholarships Commn, 1970-80; Sec., Kennedy Memorial Trust, 1970-80; Chm., Commonwealth Human Ecology Council, 1971-; Member: Council, USPG, 1972-79; Adv. Cttee, Sci. Policy Foundn, 1977-; Bd of Dirs, United World Colleges, 1978-; Bd of Trustees, Sir Ernest Cassel Educational Trust, 1978-81; Pres., Educn Section, British Assoc., 1974-75; Chm., Jt Commonwealth Socs Council, 1978-80. Hon. Prof. of Educn, Mauritius, 1981. Hon. DSc Soc Laval, 1958; Hon. LLD: Victoria, BC, 1972; Univ. of WI, 1973; City, 1978; Manchester, 1979; York, Ontario, 1980; Zimbabwe, 1981; Bristol, 1982; Hon. DLitt: Warwick, 1974; Ulster, 1974; Heriot-Watt, 1976; Hong Kong, 1977; St Andrews, 1977; Hon. DCL: New Brunswick, 1980; Oxon, 1980; East Anglia, 1980. *Publications:* Reflections on the Failure of the First West Indian Federation, 1962 (USA); articles and lectures on West Indian and Commonwealth Educn and Development, in: The Round Table, Commonwealth, RSA Jl, Caribbean Quarterly, Internat. Organisation, Jl of Negro History, etc. *Recreations:* walking, talking. *Address:* Gibbes, St Peter, Barbados. *T:* 22743. *Clubs:* Athenæum, Royal Commonwealth Society.

SPRINGER, Tobias; a Metropolitan Stipendiary Magistrate, 1963-82; Barrister-at-law; *b* 3 April 1907; *o c* of late Samuel Springer, MBE; *m* 1937, Stella Rauchwerger. *Educ:* Mill Hill Sch.; Caius Coll., Cambridge. Law Tripos 1928; called to Bar, Gray's Inn, 1929. Practised London and SE Circuit. Served War of 1939-45: 60th Rifles, 1940-45; Lt-Col GSO1, GHQ, H Forces, 1944. Returned to practise at Bar, 1945. Actg Dep. Chm., Co. London Sessions, periods 1962, 1963; sometime Dep. Circuit Judge. Life Governor: Mill Hill School; Metropolitan Hosp. Freedom, City of London, 1982. *Recreations:* travel, golf, reading. *Address:* 82 Cholmley Gardens, Fortune Green Road, NW6 1UN. *T:* 01-435 0817. *Club:* Porters Park Golf.

SPRINGETT, Jack Allan, CBE 1978; MA (Cantab); Education Officer, Association of Metropolitan Authorities, 1980-82; *b* 1 Feb. 1916; *s* of Arthur John and Agnes Springett; *m* 1950, Patricia Winifred Springett; three *s* one *d. Educ:* Windsor Grammar Sch.; Fitzwilliam House, Cambridge. Asst Master, Christ's Hospital, Horsham, 1938-47. Served War, Royal Signals and Gen. Staff, 1940-46. Administrative Asst, North Riding, 1947-52; Asst Educn Officer, Birmingham, 1952-62; Dep. Educn Officer, Essex, 1962-73; County Educn Officer, Essex, 1973-80. *Address:* 3 Roxwell Road, Chelmsford, Essex CM1 2LY. *T:* Chelmsford 58669.

SPRINGFORD, John Frederick Charles, CBE 1980 (OBE 1970); retired British Council Officer; *b* 6 June 1919; *s* of Frederick Charles Springford and Bertha Agnes Springford (*née* Trenery); *m* 1945, Phyllis Wharton; one *s* two *d. Educ:* Latymer Upper Sch.; Christ's College, Cambridge (MA). Served War 1940-46, RAC; seconded Indian Armoured Corps, 1942; Asst Political Agent II in Mekran, 1945. British Council Service, Baghdad and Mosul, Iraq, 1947-51, Isfahan, Iran, 1951-52; British Council Representative: Tanzania, 1952-57; Sudan, 1957-62; Dir, Overseas Students Dept, 1962-66; Representative: Jordan, 1966-69; Iraq, 1969-74; Canada, 1974-79, and Counsellor, Cultural Affairs, British High Commission, Ottawa. Mem. Council, British Sch. of Archaeology in Iraq, 1980-. Hon. Sec., Sussex Heritage Trust, 1980-; Chm., Sussex E Sub-Area, RSCM, 1981-. *Recreations:* archaeology, organ music. *Address:* Precinct, Crowhurst, Battle, East Sussex TN33 9AA. *T:* Crowhurst 200.

SPRINGMAN, Dame Ann (Marcella), DBE 1980 (OBE 1974); Chairman, National Union of Conservative and Unionist Associations, 1980-81 (Vice-Chairman, 1978-80); *b* 5 Jan. 1933; *d* of late Lt-Col Noel Mulloy, The Scinde Horse, and Marcella Mulloy; *m* 1955, Michael Springman; three *s* one *d. Educ:* St George's Sch., Ascot; Harcombe House, Uplyme, Lyme Regis. Founder secretary, Bracknell and District Br., RNLI, 1960-63. Councillor, Easthampstead, subseq. Bracknell District Council, 1968-76 (Chm., Planning Cttee, 1970-72); Council Representative, Bracknell Development Corp. Jt Consultative Cttee, 1968-71. Chairman: Wessex Conservative Women's Adv. Cttee, 1970-73; Wokingham Conservative Assoc., 1972-75; Conservative Women's Nat. Adv. Cttee, 1975-78; District Commissioner, Bracknell West Girl Guides, 1970-72; Governor, Easthampstead Park Sch. and Adult Educn Centre, 1975-77. Member: Women's National Commn, 1978-; SSRC, 1979-. *Recreation:* family life. *Address:* The Old Farmhouse, Horstedpond Farm, Uckfield, Sussex TN22 5TR. *T:* Uckfield 5406.

SPROAT, Iain Mac Donald; MP (C) Aberdeen (South) since 1970; Parliamentary Under Secretary of State, Department of Trade, since 1981; *b* Dollar, Clackmannanshire, 8 Nov. 1938; *s* of late William Sproat and of Lydia Sproat. *Educ:* Melrose; Winchester; Oxford. *Publications:* (ed) Cricketers' Who's Who, annually 1980-; Wodehouse at War, 1981. *Recreations:* collecting books, cricket. *Address:* Dhualt House, by Banchory, Grampian.

SPROT, Lt-Col Aidan Mark, MC 1944; JP; Lord-Lieutenant of Tweeddale, since 1980; landed proprietor and farmer (Haystoun Estate); *b* 17 June 1919; *s* of Major Mark Sprot of Riddell. *Educ:* Stowe. Commissioned Royal Scots Greys, 1940; served: Middle East, 1941-43; Italy, 1943-44; NW Europe, 1944-45, and after the war in Germany, Libya, Egypt, Jordan and UK; Adjt 1945-46; CO, 1959-62, retired. Councillor, Peeblesshire CC, 1963-75; JP 1966, DL 1966-80, Peeblesshire. Member, Royal Company of Archers (Queen's Body Guard for Scotland), 1950-; Vice-Pres., Lowlands of Scotland, TAVRA, 1980-. *Recreations:* country pursuits, motor cycle touring. *Address:* Crookston, Peebles. *T:* Kirkton Manor 209. *Club:* New (Edinburgh).

SPROTT, Rt. Rev. John Chappell, MA; DD St Andrews 1965; *b* 16 Oct. 1903; *s* of Thomas Sprott, Master Mariner, and Catherine Chappell; *m* 1932, Winifred Helen Cameron, *d* of late Sir David W. Bone, CBE, LLD; three *s* one *d. Educ:* Castle Hill Sch., Ealing; Glasgow Univ.; Edinburgh Theological Coll. Deacon, 1927; Priest, 1928; Chaplain and Succentor, St Mary's Cathedral, Edinburgh, 1927-29; Lecturer in Music, Edinburgh Theological College, 1928-29; Curate, All Saints, Glasgow, 1929-33; St George the Martyr, Holborn, 1933-37; Rector, West Hackney, 1937-40; Provost of St Paul's Cathedral, Dundee, 1940-59; Bishop of Brechin, 1959-75; Hon. Curate, St Ninian's, Troon, 1975-81. *Recreation:* music. *Address:* 29 Bruntsfield Gardens, Edinburgh EH10 4DY.

SPRY, Brig. Sir Charles Chambers Fowell, Kt 1964; CBE 1956; DSO 1943; retired as Director-General, Australian Security Intelligence Organization, 1950-70; *b* 26 June 1910; *s* of A. F. Spry, Brisbane; *m* 1939, Kathleen Edith Hull, *d* of Rev. Godfrey Smith; one *s* two *d. Educ:* Brisbane Grammar School. Graduated Royal Military College, Duntroon. Served War of 1939-45 as Col, Australian Imperial Force in SW Pacific (DSO) and Middle East. Director of Military Intelligence, 1946-50. *Recreation:* golf. *Address:* 2 Mandeville Crescent, Toorak, Victoria 3142, Australia. *Clubs:* Melbourne; Royal Melbourne Golf.

SPRY, Maj.-Gen. Daniel Charles, CBE 1945; DSO 1944; CD; *b* Winnipeg, Man, 4 Feb. 1913; *s* of Major-General Daniel William Bigelow Spry and Ethelyn Alma (*née* Rich); *m* 1939, Elisabeth, *d* of Roy Fletcher Forbes, Halifax, NS; one *s* one *d. Educ:* Public Schools, Calgary and Halifax; Ashford School, England; Dalhousie University. Served with Canadian Militia; 2nd Lt, Princess Louise Fusiliers, 1932; Royal Canadian Regt (permanent force), 1934. Served War, 1939-46 (CBE, DSO, CD, despatches twice); Captain 1939, Major 1940, Lt-Col 1943, Brig. 1943, Maj.-Gen. 1944; GOC 3rd Canadian Infantry Div., 1944-45; retired as Vice-Chief of Gen. Staff, 1946. Col, The Royal Canadian Regt, 1965-78. Chief Exec. Comr, The Boy Scouts' Assoc. of Canada, 1946-51; Dep. Dir, Boy Scouts World Bureau, 1951-53, Dir, 1953-65. Commander, Order of the Crown of Belgium, 1945; Croix de Guerre, Belgium, 1945. *Recreations:* sailing, gardening, fishing. *Address:* 4 Rock Avenue, Ottawa, Ontario K1M 1A6, Canada. *Club:* Rideau (Ottawa).

See also Graham Spry.

SPRY, Graham, CC (Canada) 1971; Agent General for Saskatchewan in the United Kingdom and Europe, 1947-67, retired 1968; *b* St Thomas, Ontario, 20 Feb. 1900; *e s* of Maj.-Gen. D. W. B. Spry, OBE, ED, and Ethelyn Alma Rich; *m* 1938, Professor Irene Mary Biss; one *s* one *d* (and one *s* decd). *Educ:* public schools, Toronto, Montreal and Winnipeg; University of Manitoba (BA, Rhodes Scholar); University College, Oxford (MA); Sorbonne, Paris. Served Canadian Army, Gunner, 1918. Editorial Staff, Winnipeg Free Press, 1919-22 (while at University); Internat. Labour Office, Geneva, 1925-26; Nat. Sec., Assoc. of Canadian Clubs, 1926-32. Organized and chm. of Canadian Radio League (voluntary group which advocated and secured, by unanimous vote of House of Commons, establishment of public service broadcasting), 1929-33; Canadian Politics, 1933-37. California Standard Oil Co. Ltd, London, Eng., 1938-39, Dir, and Manager, 1940-46; Director: Associated Ethyl Co., Ceylon Petroleum Co., 1940-47; British Ethyl Corp., 1944-47; Personal Asst to Rt Hon. Sir Stafford Cripps, Lord Privy Seal and Minister of Aircraft Production, 1942-45, Member of Mission to India, 1942; duties in USA for Sir Stafford Cripps, 1942, and for Rt Hon. R. K. Law, 1943. Member Inter-deptl Cttee on Internat. Civil Aviation, War Corresp., Canadian Army, Italy, Aug.-Sept., 1944, and Germany, April-May, 1945. XXth Century Fund Survey of Turkey, 1947. FRGS. Hon. LLD: Brock, 1968; Saskatchewan, 1968; York, 1976. *Publications:* (joint) Social Planning for Canada, 1934; Canada 1941; Canada, 1946; (joint) Turkey: An Economic Appraisal, 1949. *Recreations:* books, history, ski-ing, and Tuscany. *Address:* 446 Cloverdale Road, Ottawa, Ontario K1M 0Y6, Canada. *Clubs:* Brooks's; Travellers'; Leander (Hon. Mem.); Rideau (Ottawa).

See also D. C. Spry.

SPRY, Sir John (Farley), Kt 1975; Justice of Appeal, Gibraltar, since 1980; Chief Justice of the British Indian Ocean Territory, since 1981; *b* 11 March 1910; *s* of Joseph Farley Spry and Fanny Seagrave Treloar Spry; *m* 1st (marr. diss. 1940); one *s* one *d*; 2nd, Stella Marie (*née* Fichat). *Educ:* Perse School and Peterhouse, Cambridge (MA). Solicitor, 1935; Asst Registrar of Titles and Conveyancer, Uganda, 1936-44; Chief Inspector of Land Registration, Palestine, 1944; Asst Director of Land Registration, Palestine, 1944-48; Registrar-General, Tanganyika 1948-50, Kenya 1950-52; Tanganyika: Registrar-Gen., 1952-56; Legal Draftsman, 1956-60; Principal Sec., Public Service Commn 1960-61; Puisne Judge, 1961-64; Justice of Appeal, Court of Appeal for Eastern Africa, 1964-70; Vice-President, 1970-75; Chm., Pensions Appeal Tribunals, 1975-76; Chief Justice of Gibraltar, 1976-80. Comr for Revision of Laws of Gibraltar, 1981-. *Publications:* Sea Shells of Dar es Salaam, Part I, 1961 (3rd edn 1968), Part II, 1964; Civil Procedure in East Africa, 1969; Civil Law of Defamation in East Africa, 1976. *Recreation:* conchology. *Address:* 15 De Vere Gardens, W8 5AN.

SPURGEON, Maj.-Gen. Peter Lester, CB 1980; Secretary, Royal Agricultural Benevolent Institution, since 1982; *b* 27 Aug. 1927; *s* of Harold Sidney Spurgeon and Emily Anne (*née* Bolton); *m* 1959, Susan Ann (*née* Aylward); one *s* one *d. Educ:* Merchant Taylors' Sch., Northwood. Commnd, 1946; 1949-66: HMS Glory; Depot, RM Deal; 40 Commando RM; ADC to Maj.-Gen. Plymouth Gp RM; DS Officers' Sch., RM; RAF Staff Coll. Bracknell; Staff of Comdt Gen. RM; 40 Commando RM; Jt Warfare Estab.; GS02 HQ: ME Comd, Aden, 1967; Army Strategic Comd, 1968-69; Second-in-Comd, 41 Commando RM, 1969-71; DS National Defence Coll., Latimer, 1971-73; CO RM Poole, 1973-75; Dir of Drafting and Records, RM, 1975-76; Comdr, Training Gp, RM, 1977-79 and Training and Reserve Forces, RM, 1979-80; retd 1980. *Recreations:* golf, dinghy sailing, tennis. *Address:* Shaw House, 27 West Way, Oxford OX2 0QH. *T:* Oxford 724931. *Club:* Army and Navy.

SPURLING, Antony Cuthbert, QC (Sierra Leone); *b* 12 Oct. 1906; 3rd *s* of late Cuthbert Spurling; *m* 1935, Elizabeth Frances, *d* of late J. C. Stobart; two *s* one *d. Educ:* Berkhamsted; St Paul's; Hertford College, Oxford. Called to Bar, Inner Temple, 1931; Temp. Legal Asst, Ministry of Health, 1934; Resident Magistrate, Kenya, 1935; Crown Counsel, Kenya, 1939; Solicitor-General, Trinidad, 1946; Attorney-General, Gambia, 1951. Attorney-General, Sierra Leone, 1955-61. Retired, 1961. *Publication:* Digest and Guide to the Criminal Law of Kenya, 1946. *Recreation:* gardening. *Address:* Wheelwright Cottage, Bodle Street Green, near Hailsham, Sussex BN27 4UB. *T:* Herstmonceux 832308.

SPURLING, Hon. Sir (Arthur) Dudley, Kt 1975; CBE 1963; JP; Barrister and Attorney; Senior Partner, Appleby, Spurling & Kempe; Speaker of the House of Assembly, Bermuda, 1972-76; *b* 9 Nov. 1913; *m* 1941, Marian Taylor, *d* of Frank Gurr, St George's, Bermuda; three *s* one *d. Educ:* St George's Grammar Sch.; Saltus Grammar Sch.; Rossall Sch., Lancs; Trinity Coll., Oxford (Rhodes Scholar); Lincoln's Inn. Called to Bar: Lincoln's Inn, 1937; Bermuda 1938. Served War, 1939-45, Bermuda Volunteer Rifle Corps. MHA, 1943-76; MEC, 1957-69; former Chairman: Educn Bd; Bd of Public Works; Bd of Immigration; Bd of Trade. JP Bermuda. *Recreations:* golf, boating, swimming. *Address:* Three Chimneys, St George's, Bermuda. *Clubs:* Royal Bermuda Yacht, Royal Hamilton Amateur Dinghy, Mid Ocean, St George's Dinghy and Sports (all in Bermuda).

SQUIBB, George Drewry, MVO 1982; QC 1956; Norfolk Herald Extraordinary since 1959; Earl Marshal's Lieutenant, Assessor and Surrogate in the Court of Chivalry, since 1976; *b* 1 Dec. 1906; *o s* of Reginald Augustus Hodder Squibb, Chester; *m* 1st 1936, Bessie (*d* 1954), *d* of George Whittaker, Burley, Hants; one *d*; 2nd, 1955, Evelyn May, *d* of Frederick Richard

Higgins, of Overleigh Manor, Chester. *Educ:* King's School, Chester; Queen's College, Oxford (BCL, MA). Barrister-at-Law, Inner Temple, 1930; Bencher, 1951; Reader, 1975; Treasurer, 1976. Army Officers' Emergency Reserve, 1938. Deputy Chairman Dorset Quarter Sessions, 1950-53, Chairman, 1953-71; Junior Counsel to the Crown in Peerage and Baronetcy Cases, 1954-56; Hon. Historical Adviser in Peerage Cases to the Attorney-General, 1965-; Pres., Transport Tribunal, 1962-81; Chief Commons Commissioner, 1971-82. Member: Cttee on Rating of Charities, 1958-59; Adv. Council on Public Records, 1964-81; Council, Selden Soc., 1961- (Vice-Pres., 1969-72). FSA 1946; FSG 1973; FRHistS 1978. Master, Scriveners' Co., 1979-80. JP Dorset, 1943. *Publications:* The Law of Arms in England, 1953; Wiltshire Visitation Pedigrees, 1623, 1955; Reports of Heraldic Cases in the Court of Chivalry, 1956; The High Court of Chivalry, 1959; Visitation Pedigrees and the Genealogist, 1964, 2nd edn 1978; Founders' Kin, 1972; Doctors' Commons, 1977; Visitation of Dorset 1677, 1977; Precedence in England and Wales, 1981; papers in legal and antiquarian journals. *Recreation:* genealogical and heraldic research. *Address:* 5 Paper Buildings, Temple, EC4Y 7HB. *T:* 01-353 3436; The Old House, Cerne Abbas, Dorset DT2 7JQ. *T:* Cerne Abbas 272. *Clubs:* Athenæum, United Oxford & Cambridge University.

SQUIRE, Clifford William, CMG 1978; MVO 1972; HM Diplomatic Service; Assistant Under Secretary of State, Foreign and Commonwealth Office, since 1982; *b* 7 Oct. 1928; *s* of Clifford John Squire and Eleanor Eliza Harpley; *m* 1st, 1959, Marie José Carlier (*d* 1973); one *s* two *d* (and one *s* decd); 2nd, 1976, Sara Laetitia Hutchison; one *s* one *d*. *Educ:* Royal Masonic Sch., Bushey; St John's Coll., Oxford; Coll. of Europe, Bruges. PhD London 1979. British Army, 1947-49. Nigerian Admin. Service, 1953-59; FO, 1959-60; British Legation, Bucharest, 1961-63; FO, 1963-65; UK Mission to UN, New York, 1965-69; Head of Chancery, Bangkok, 1969-72; Head of SE Asian Dept, FCO, 1972-75; Extramural Fellow, Sch. of Oriental and African Studies, London Univ., 1975-76; Counsellor, later Head of Chancery, Washington, 1976-79; Ambassador to Senegal, 1979-82, concurrently to Cape Verde Is, Guinea (Bissau), Guinea (Conakry), Mali and Mauritania. *Address:* c/o Foreign and Commonwealth Office, SW1. *Clubs:* Travellers'; Cosmos (Washington, DC).

SQUIRE, Peter John; Headmaster, Bedford Modern School, since 1977; *b* 15 Feb. 1937; *s* of Leslie Ernest Squire and Doris Eileen Squire; *m* 1965, Susan Elizabeth (*née* Edwards); one *s* one *d*. *Educ:* King Edward's Sch., Birmingham; Jesus Coll., Oxford (BA 1960, MA 1964); Pembroke Coll. and Dept of Educn, Cambridge (Cert. in Educn 1961). Asst Master, Monkton Combe Sch., Bath, 1961-65; Haberdashers' Aske's Sch., Elstree, 1965-77: Sen. Boarding Housemaster, 1968-77; Sen. History Master, 1970-77. *Recreations:* Rugby, squash, gardening, antique collecting. *Address:* Bedford Modern School, Manton Lane, Bedford MK41 7NT. *T:* Bedford 64331.

SQUIRE, Raglan, FRIBA, MSIA; Senior Partner Raglan Squire & Partners, Consultants in Architecture, Engineering, Town Planning, etc; *b* 30 Jan. 1912; *e s* of late Sir John Squire, Kt; *m* 1st, 1938, Rachel, (*d* 1968), *d* of James Atkey, Oxshott, Surrey; two *s* ; 2nd, 1968, Bridget Lawless. *Educ:* Blundell's; St John's Coll., Cambridge. Private practice in London, 1935-. War service with Royal Engineers, 1942-45. Founded firm of Raglan Squire & Partners, 1948. Principal projects: housing, educational and industrial work, 1935-41; pre-fabricated bldgs and industrial design, 1945-48; Eaton Sq. Conversion Scheme, 1945-56; Rangoon Univ. Engineering Coll., 1953-56; Associated Architect, Transport Pavilion, Festival of Britain Exhib., 1951; Town Planning Scheme for Mosul, Iraq, 1955; Bagdad airport report, 1955; factories at Weybridge, Huddersfield, etc; office buildings London, Eastbourne, Bournemouth, etc; gen. practice at home and over-seas incl. major hotels at Teheran, Tunis, Nicosia, Malta and Singapore, Gibraltar, Caribbean and Middle East, 1955-74. Sec. RIBA Reconstruction Cttee, 1941-42; Council of Architectural Assoc., 1951-52; Guest Editor Architects' Journal, 1947. *Publications:* articles in technical press on organisation of Building Industry, Architectural Education, etc. *Recreations:* gardening, chess, ocean racing and designing small yachts. *Address:* 1 Chester Row, SW1. *T:* 01-730 7225. *Clubs:* Royal Thames Yacht, Royal Ocean Racing.

SQUIRE, Robin Clifford; MP (C) Havering, Hornchurch, since 1979; *b* 12 July 1944; *s* of Sidney John Squire and Mabel Alice Squire (*née* Gilmore); *m* 1981, Susan Margaret Fey, *d* of Arthur Frederick Branch and Mahala Branch (*née* Parker); one step *s* one step *d*. *Educ:* Tiffin School, Kingston-upon-Thames. FCA. Qualified as Chartered Accountant, 1966; joined Lombard Banking Ltd (subsequently Lombard North Central Ltd) as Accountant, 1968, becoming Asst Chief Accountant, 1972-79. Councillor, London Borough of Sutton, 1968-82; Chm., Finance Cttee, 1972-76; Leader of Council, 1976-79. Chm., Greater London Young Conservatives, 1973; Vice-Chm., Nat. Young Conservatives, 1974-75. Personal Asst to Rt Hon. Robert Carr, Gen. Election, Feb. 1974; contested (C) Havering, Hornchurch, Oct. 1974. Mem., Commons Select Cttee on Environment, 1979-; Sec., Cons. Parly European Affairs Cttee, 1979-80; Vice-Chm., Cons. Parly Trade Cttee, 1980-. Dep. Chm., Anglo-Asian Con. Soc., 1982-; Mem. Bd, Shelter, 1982-. *Publication:* (jtly) Set the Party Free, 1969. *Recreations:* films, theatre and modern music. *Address:* House of Commons, SW1A 0AA. *T:* 01-219 4526. *Club:* Carlton.

SRAFFA, Piero, FBA 1954; MA; Fellow of Trinity College, Cambridge, since 1939; Emeritus Reader in Economics, University of Cambridge; *b* Turin, Italy, 1898. *Educ:* Univ. of Turin. *Publications:* (ed) The Works and Correspondence of David Ricardo, 11 vols, 1951-73; Production of

---

Commodities by Means of Commodities, 1960. *Address:* Trinity College, Cambridge.

SRISKANDAN, Kanagaretnam, CEng, FICE, FIHE; Chief Highway Engineer, Department of Transport, since 1980; *b* 12 Aug. 1930; *s* of Kanagaretnam Kathiravelu and Kanmanyammal Kumaraswamy; *m* 1956, Dorothy (*née* Harley); two *s* one *d*. *Educ:* Royal College, Colombo; Univ. of Ceylon. BSc Hons London 1952. Junior Asst Engineer, PWD, Ceylon, 1953; Asst Engr, Sir William Halcrowe and Partners, Cons. Engrs, London, 1956; Section Engr, Tarmac Civil Engineering Ltd, 1958; Asst Engr, West Riding of Yorkshire CC, 1959, left as Principal Engr; Dept of Transport: Superintending Engr, Midland Road Construction Unit, 1968; Asst Chief Engr, 1971; Deputy Chief Highway Engr, 1976. *Publications:* papers on various engrg topics. *Recreations:* squash, golf. *Address:* Department of Transport, Room N 12/06, 2 Marsham Street, SW1. *T:* 01-212 4426.

SRIVASTAVA, Chandrika Prasad, Padma Bhushan 1972; Secretary-General, Inter-Governmental Maritime Consultative Organization, since 1974; *b* 8 July 1920; *s* of B. B. Srivastava; *m* 1947, Nirmala Salve; two *d*. *Educ:* Lucknow, India. 1st cl. BA 1940, 1st cl. BA Hons 1941, 1st cl. MA 1942, 1st cl. LLB 1944; gold medals for proficiency in Eng. Lit. and Polit. Science. Under-Sec., Min. of Commerce, India, 1949; City Magistrate, Lucknow, 1950; Addtl Dist. Magistrate, Meerut, 1951-52; Directorate-Gen. of Shipping, 1953; Dep. Dir-Gen. of Shipping, 1954-57; Dep. Sec., Min. of Transport, and Pvte Sec. to Minister of Transport and Communications, 1958; Sen. Dep. Dir-Gen. of Shipping, 1959-60; Man. Dir, Shipping Corp. of India, 1961-64; Jt Sec. to Prime Minister, 1964-66; Chm. and Man. Dir, Shipping Corp. of India, 1966-73; Director: Central Inland Water Transport Corp., 1967; Central Bd, Reserve Bank of India, 1972-73; Chm., Mogul Line Ltd, 1967-73. Vice-Pres., Sea Cadet Council, 1970-73. President: Indian Nat. Shipowners' Assoc., 1971-73; Inst. Mar. Technologists, India, 1972 (Hon. Mem., 1981); UN Conf. on Code of Conduct for Liner Confs, 1973-74; Internat. Maritime Lectrs' Assoc., 1980-; Chm., Cttee of Invisibles, 3rd UN Conf. on Trade and Develt, 1972; Member: Nat. Shipping Bd, 1959-73; Merchant Navy Trng Bd, 1959-73; Nat. Welfare Bd for Seafarers, 1966-73; Amer. Bureau of Shipping, 1969; Governing Body, Indian Inst. of Foreign Trade, 1970; State Bd of Tourism, 1970; Nat. Harbour Bd, 1970-73; Gen. Cttee, Bombay Chamber of Commerce and Ind., 1971; Governing Body Indian Inst. of Management, 1972-73; Adv. Bd, Seatrade Acad., 1978-; Europort Internat. Cttee of Honour, 1980-; Internat. Chamber of Commerce Internat. Maritime Bureau, 1981-. Hon. Mem., Master Mariners' Co., 1978; Hon. Fellow, Plymouth Polytech., 1979. Admiral Padilla Award, Colombia, 1978; Gran Amigo del Mar Award, Colombia, 1978. *Publications:* articles on shipping in newspapers and jls. *Recreation:* music. *Address:* 48 Brompton Square, SW3. *Clubs:* Willingdon (Bombay); Delhi Symphony Society.

STABB, Sir William (Walter), Kt 1981; QC 1968; His Honour Judge Stabb; a Circuit Judge (formerly Official Referee, Supreme Court of Judicature), since 1969; Senior Official Referee, since 1978; *b* 6 Oct. 1913; 2nd *s* of late Sir Newton Stabb, OBE and late Lady E. M. Stabb; *m* 1940, Dorothy Margaret Leckie; four *d*. *Educ:* Rugby; University Coll., Oxford. Called to the Bar, 1936; Master of the Bench, Inner Temple, 1964. Served with RAF, 1940-46, attaining rank of Sqdn Ldr. Junior Counsel to Ministry of Labour, 1960; Prosecuting Counsel to BoT, 1962-68. Chm. 1961-69, Dep. Chm. 1969-71, Bedfordshire QS. *Recreations:* fishing, golf. *Address:* The Pale Farm, Chipperfield, Kings Langley, Herts. *T:* Kings Langley 63124; 8 King's Bench Walk, Temple, EC4. *T:* 01-583 4306; Royal Courts of Justice, Strand, WC2.

STABLE, Maj.-Gen. Hugh Huntington, CB 1947; CIE 1938; Major-General, IA (retired) *b* 1896; *s* of late Alfred Henry Stable, MA and Ada Huntington; *m* 1923, Cyrille Helen Dorothy (*d* 1979), *d* of late Rev. M. A. Bayfield, MA. *Educ:* Malvern. First Commission 2/4th Dorset Regt 1914; served Palestine, 1917-18 (despatches); Central India Horse, 1919; Bt Lt-Col 1935; Staff Coll., Camberley, 1929-30; Army Headquarters, India, Staff Officer to Major-General Cavalry, 1932; Assistant Military Secretary (Personal) to Commander-in-Chief, 1933-36; Military Secretary to the Viceroy of India, 1936-38; Comdt, 8th KGO Cavalry, 1939-40; Bde Comdr, 1941-43; DQMG, GHQ, India, 1943-44; Comdr Lucknow Sub Area, 1945-46; Comdr Bihar and Orissa Area, 1947; QMG India, Dec. 1947; retd 1950. A Governor, Malvern Coll.; Emeritus Comr, Boy Scouts of South Africa. *Address:* 810 Rapallo, Sea Point, Cape Town, SA. *Clubs:* Army and Navy; City and Civil Service (Cape Town).

STABLE, (Rondle) Owen (Charles), QC 1963; His Honour Judge Stable; a Circuit Judge, since 1979; *b* 1923; *yr s* of late Rt Hon. Sir Wintringham Norton Stable, MC, and Lucie Haden (*née* Freeman); *m* 1949, Yvonne Brook, *y d* of late Maj. L. B. Holliday, OBE; two *d*. *Educ:* Winchester. Served with Rifle Bde, 1940-46 (Captain). Barrister, Middle Temple, 1948; Bencher, 1969. Dep. Chm., QS, Herts, 1963-71; a Recorder of the Crown Court, 1972-79. Board of Trade Inspector: Cadco Group of Cos, 1963-64; H. S. Whiteside & Co Ltd, 1965-67; International Learning Systems Corp. Ltd, 1969-71; Pergamon Press, 1969-73. Sec. National Reference Tribunal for the Coal Mining Industry, 1953-64; Chancellor of Diocese of Bangor, 1959-; Member, Governing Body of the Church in Wales, 1960-; Licensed Parochial Lay Reader, Diocese of St Albans, 1961-; Member: General Council of the Bar, 1962-66; Senate of 4 Inns of Court, 1971-74; Senate of the Inns of Court and the Bar, 1974-75. Chm., Horserace Betting Levy Appeal Tribunal, 1969-74.

JP Hertfordshire, 1963-71. *Publication:* (with R. M. Stuttard) A Review of Coursing, 1971. *Recreations:* shooting, listening to music. *Address:* Buckler's Hall, Much Hadham, Hertfordshire. *T:* Much Hadham 2604. *Clubs:* Boodle's, Pratt's.
See also P. L. W. Owen.

STABLER, Arthur Fletcher; District Councillor, Newcastle upon Tyne; Member, Supplementary Benefits Commission, 1976-79; *b* 1919; *s* of Edward and Maggie Stabler; *m* 1948, Margaret Stabler; two *s. Educ:* Cruddas Park Sch. Engineer apprenticeship, Vickers Armstrong, 1935-39. Served War, Royal Northumberland Fusiliers, 1939-46. With Vickers Armstrong, 1946-78. Newcastle upon Tyne: City Councillor, 1963-74; District Councillor, 1973-; Dep. Lord Mayor, 1982-83; Chairman: Housing Renewals, 1975-76; Arts and Recreation, 1976-77; Case Work Sub-Cttee, 1974-77; Tenancy Relations Sub-Cttee, 1975-77; Community Develt Sub-Cttee, 1975-76; Town Moor Sub-Cttee, 1976-77; Personnel Sub-Cttee, 1982; Vice-Chairman: Social Services Cttee, 1974-76; Housing Management Cttee, 1975-76; Tyneside Summer Exhibn Cttee, 1982. Chm., Axwell Park Community Homes, 1978-79; Mem., numerous Tenants' Assocs. Chm., Newcastle upon Tyne Central Labour Party, 1965-78. Pres., No 6 Br., AUEW. Chm., Westerhope Golf Club Jt Sub-Cttee, 1976-77. President: Newcastle-upon-Tyne and District Allotments and Garden Council, 1980-; Elswick Park Bowling Club, 1980-; Cttee, Tyne Wear Polish Solidarity Club, 1981. Hon. Mem., Casino Royal Club, 1980. *Publication:* Gannin Along the Scotswood Road, 1976. *Recreations:* social work, local history. *Address:* 10 Whitebeam Place, Elswick, Newcastle upon Tyne NE4 7EJ. *T:* Newcastle upon Tyne 732362. *Clubs:* Pineapple CIU, Polish White Eagle, Tyneside Irish (Hon.) (Newcastle upon Tyne).

STACEY, Air Vice-Marshal John Nichol, CBE 1971; DSO 1945; DFC 1942; Member, Tunbridge Wells Health Authority, since 1982; *b* 14 Sept. 1920; *s* of Captain Herbert Chambers Stacey and Mrs May Stacey; *m* 1950, Veronica Satterly; two *d. Educ:* Whitgift Middle Sch., Croydon. Merchant Marine Apprentice, 1937-38; joined RAF, 1938; flying throughout War of 1939-45; comd No 160 Sqdn, 1944-45; Asst Air Attaché, Washington, 1947-48; psc 1949; on staff at Staff Coll., 1958-60; Chief of Air Staff, Royal Malayan Air Force, 1960-63 (JMN); comd RAF Laarbruch, Germany, 1963-66; AOC, Air Cadets, 1968-71; Dir, Orgn and Admin. Planning (RAF), MoD, 1971-74; AOA, Support Comd, 1974-75, retired. Dir, Stonham Housing Assoc., 1976-81. Pres., Headcorn Br., RAFA; Vice-Pres., RAF Gliding and Soaring Assoc.; Trustee, Housing Assocs Charitable Trust. *Recreations:* sailing, golf. *Address:* Riseden Cottage, Riseden, Goudhurst, Cranbrook, Kent. *T:* Goudhurst 211239. *Clubs:* Royal Air Force; Dale Hill Golf.

STACEY, Prof. Margaret; Professor of Sociology, University of Warwick, since 1974; *b* 27 March 1922; *d* of Conrad Eugene Petrie and Grace Priscilla Boyce; *m* 1945, Frank Arthur Stacey (*d* 1977); three *s* two *d. Educ:* City of London Sch. for Girls; London Sch. of Econs (BScEcon, 1st Cl. Hons Sociology). Labour Officer, Royal Ordnance Factory, 1943-44; Tutor, Oxford Univ., 1944-51; University Coll. of Swansea: Res. Officer and Fellow, 1961-63; Lectr in Sociol., 1963-70; Sen. Lectr in Sociol., 1970-74; Dir, Medical Sociol. Res. Centre, 1972-74. British Sociol Association: Mem. Exec. Cttee, 1965-70, 1975-79; Hon. Gen. Sec., 1968-70; Chairperson, 1977-79; Pres., 1981-83; Mem. Women's Caucus, 1974-. Pres., Assoc. for Welfare of Children in Hosp. (Wales), 1974-; Member: Assoc. for Welfare of Children in Hosp., 1960-; Welsh Hosp. Bd, 1970-74; Davies Cttee on Hosp. Complaints Procedure, 1971-73; GMC, 1976-; Sociol. Cttee, SSRC, 1969-71; Health and Health Policy Cttee, SSRC, 1976-77. *Publications:* Tradition and Change: a study of Banbury, 1960, paperback 1970; (ed) Comparability in Social Research, 1969; (ed and jt author) Hospitals, Children and their Families: a study of the welfare of children in hospital, 1970; Methods of Social Research, 1970; (jtly) Power, Persistence and Change: a second study of Banbury, 1975; (ed) The Sociology of the NHS, 1976; (ed jtly and contrib.) Beyond Separation: further studies of children in hospital, 1979; (jtly) Women, Politics and Power, 1981 (Fawcett Book Prize, 1982); contrib. to Sociol Rev., Sociol., Brit. Jl of Sociol., Social Science and Med., Jl of Med. Ethics, and Sociol. of Health and Illness. *Recreations:* walking, gardening. *Address:* 8 Lansdowne Circus, Leamington Spa, Warwicks CV32 4SW. *T:* Leamington Spa 312094. *Club:* Royal Commonwealth Society.

STACEY, Prof. Maurice, CBE 1966; FRS 1950; Mason Professor of Chemistry, 1956-74, now Emeritus, and Head of Department, 1956-74, University of Birmingham; Dean of Faculty of Science, 1963-66; Hon. Senior Research Fellow, 1974-76; *b* 8 April 1907; *s* of J. H. Stacey, Bromstead, Newport, Shropshire; *m* 1937, Constance Mary, *d* of Wm Pugh, Birmingham; two *s* two *d. Educ:* Adam's School, Newport, Shropshire; Universities of Birmingham, London and Columbia (New York). BSc (Hons) Birmingham Univ., 1929; Demonstrator, Chemistry, Birmingham Univ., 1929-32; PhD 1932; Meldola Medal, 1933; Beit Memorial Fellow for Medical Research, School of Tropical Medicine, London Univ., 1933-37 (DSc 1939); Travelling Fellow, Columbia Univ., New York, 1937; Lecturer in Chemistry, Univ. of Birmingham, 1937-44, Reader in Biological Chemistry, 1944-46, Prof. of Chemistry, 1946-56. Tilden Lecturer of Chemical Society, 1946; P. F. Frankland Lectr, Roy. Inst. of Chemistry, 1955; Ivan Levinstein Lectr, 1956, Jubilee Meml Lectr, 1973, Soc. Chem. Industry; Vice-Pres. Chemical Society, 1950-53, 1955-58, 1960-63, 1968-71; Associate Editor, Advances in Carbohydrate Chem., 1950-; Editor, Advances in Fluorine Chem., 1960-73;

Editor-in-Chief, European Polymer Jl. Chief Scientific Adviser for Civil Defence, Midland Region, 1957-78; Governor, National Vegetable Research Institute, 1961-73. Former Member, Court of Governors: Univ. of Keele; Univ. of Warwick; Univ. of Loughborough; Gov., Adam's Sch., 1956-74; Mem. Council, Edgbaston High Sch. for Girls, 1963-; Mem., Home Office Science Council, 1966-76. Sugar Research Prize of National Academy of Science, New York, 1950; John Scott Medal and Award, 1969; Haworth Meml Medal, 1970. Captain, 2nd in Command Birmingham Home Guard, Chemical Warfare School, 1942-44. Defence Medal, 1945. Visiting Lecturer, Universities of Oslo, Stockholm, Uppsala and Lund, 1949, Helsinki, 1955. Has foreign Hon. doctorate and medals. John Scott Medal and Award, 1969; Haworth Meml Medal, 1970. Hon. DSc Keele, 1977. *Publications:* (with S. A. Barker) Polysaccharides of Micro-organisms, 1961, and Carbohydrates of Living Tissues; about 400 scientific contribs to Jl of Chem. Soc., Proc. Royal Soc., etc., on organic and biological chemistry subjects. *Recreations:* foreign travel, athletics (Hon. Life Mem. AAA), horticulture, science antiques. *Address:* 12 Bryony Road, Weoley Hill, Birmingham B29 4BU. *T:* 021-475 2065; The University, Birmingham. *T:* 021-472 1301. *Club:* Athenæum.

STACEY, Rear-Adm. Michael Lawrence, CB 1979; Director, Marine Pollution Control Unit, Marine Division, Department of Trade, since 1979; *b* 6 July 1924; *s* of Maurice Stacey and Dorice Evelyn (*née* Bulling); *m* 1955, Penelope Leana (*née* Riddoch); two *s. Educ:* Epsom Coll. Entered RN as Cadet, 1942; Normandy landings, HMS Hawkins, 1944; served on HM Ships Rotherham, Cambrian, Shoreham, Hornet, Vernon, Euryalus, Bermuda, Vigilant; Comdr 1958; staff of RN Staff Coll.; in comd HMS Blackpool, 1960-62; JSSC; Captain 1966; Chief Staff Officer to Admiral Commanding Reserves, 1966-68; in comd HMS Andromeda and Captain (F) Sixth Frigate Sqdn, 1968-70; Dep. Dir of Naval Warfare, 1970-73; in comd HMS Tiger, 1973-75; Asst Chief of Naval Staff (Policy), 1975-76; Flag Officer, Gibraltar, 1976-78. ADC to the Queen, 1975. MNI; FBIM. Younger Brother, Trinity House, 1979. *Recreations:* golf, yachting, gardening. *Address:* Little Hintock, 40 Lynch Road, Farnham, Surrey. *T:* Farnham 713032. *Club:* Army and Navy.

STACEY, Morna Dorothy, (Mrs W. D. Stacey); *see* Hooker, Prof. M. D.

STACEY, Rev. Nicolas David; Director of Social Services for Kent County Council, since 1974; *b* 27 Nov. 1927; *s* of David and Gwen Stacey; *m* 1955, Hon. Anne Bridgeman, *er d* of 2nd Viscount Bridgeman, *qv* ; one *s* two *d. Educ:* RNC, Dartmouth; St Edmund Hall, Oxford (hons degree Mod. Hist.); Cuddesdon Theol Coll., Oxford. Midshipman, HMS Anson, 1945-46; Sub-Lt, 1946-48. Asst Curate, St Mark's, Portsea, 1953-58; Domestic Chap. to Bp of Birmingham, 1958-60; Rector of Woolwich, 1960-68; Dean of London Borough of Greenwich, 1965-68; Dep. Dir of Oxfam, 1968-70; Dir of Social Services, London Borough of Ealing, 1971-74. Chm., Youth Call, 1981-. Sporting career: internat. sprinter, 1948-52, incl. British Empire Games, 1949, and Olympic Games, 1952 (semi-finalist 200 metres and finalist 4×400 metres relay); Pres., OUAC, 1951; winner, Oxf. v Cambridge 220 yds, 1948-51; Captain, Combined Oxf. and Camb. Athletic Team, 1951. *Publication:* Who Cares (autobiog.), 1971. *Address:* The Old Vicarage, Selling, Faversham, Kent ME13 9RD. *T:* Selling 833. *Clubs:* Beefsteak; Royal St George's Golf (Sandwich, Kent).

STACK, (Ann) Prunella, (Mrs Brian St Quentin Power), OBE 1980; President, The Women's League of Health and Beauty; *b* 28 July 1914; *d* of Capt. Hugh Bagot Stack, 8th Ghurka Rifles, and Mary Meta Bagot Stack, Founder of The Women's League of Health and Beauty; *m* 1st, 1938, Lord David Douglas-Hamilton (*d* 1944); two *s* ; 2nd, 1950, Alfred G. Albers, FRCS (*d* 1951), Cape Town, S Africa; 3rd, 1964, Brian St Quentin Power. *Educ:* The Abbey, Malvern Wells. Mem. of the National Fitness Council, 1937-39. Vice-Pres., Outward Bound Trust, 1980-. *Publications:* The Way to Health and Beauty, 1938; Movement is Life, 1973; Island Quest, 1979. *Recreations:* poetry, music, travel. *Address:* 14 Gertrude Street, SW10.

STACK, Air Chief Marshal Sir Neville; *see* Stack, Air Chief Marshal Sir T. N.

STACK, Neville; Editor, Leicester Mercury, since 1974; *b* 2 Sept. 1928; *m* 1953, Molly Rowe; one *s* one *d. Educ:* Arnold School. Reporter: Ashton-under-Lyne Reporter, 1948; Express & Star, 1950; Sheffield Telegraph, and Kemsley National Papers, 1955; Northern News Editor, IPC national papers, 1971; Sub-editor, Daily Express, 1973; Editor, Stockport Advertiser, 1974. *Publication:* The Empty Palace, 1976. *Recreations:* writing, sailing, riding, flying. *Address:* Fydell's Barn, Morcott, Rutland, Leicestershire. *T:* Morcott 330. *Clubs:* The Leicestershire (Leicester); Rutland Sailing, Leicestershire Aero.

STACK, Prunella; *see* Stack, A. P.

STACK, Air Chief Marshal Sir (Thomas) Neville, KCB 1972 (CB 1969); CVO 1963; CBE 1965; AFC 1957; Director-General, Asbestos International Association, since 1978; Gentleman Usher to the Queen, since 1978; *b* 19 Oct. 1919; *s* of late T. Neville Stack, AFC, and Edythe Neville Stack; *m* 1955, Diana Virginia, *d* of late Oliver Stuart Todd, MBE; one *s. Educ:* St Edmund's College, Ware; RAF College, Cranwell. Served on flying boats, 1939-45; Coastal Command, 1945-52; Transport Support flying in Far East and UK, 1954-59; Dep. Captain of The Queen's Flight, 1960-62; Transport Support in Far East, 1963-64; Comdt, RAF Coll., Cranwell, 1967-70; UK Perm. Mil. Deputy, CENTO, Ankara, 1970-72; AOC-in-C, RAF Trng Comd, 1973-75; Air Sec., 1976-78. Air ADC to the Queen, 1976-78. Freeman, City of London; Liveryman, Guild of Air Pilots and Navigators; Governor, Wellington Coll. FRMetS; FBIM. *Recreations:* various outdoor sports; undergardening. *Address:* 4 Perrymead Street, Fulham, SW6. *Clubs:* Royal Air Force, Boodle's.

STACPOOLE, John Wentworth; Deputy Secretary, Department of Health and Social Security, 1979-82; *b* 16 June 1926; *s* of G. W. Stacpoole and Mrs M. G. Butt; *m* 1954, Charmian, *d* of late J. P. Bishop and Mrs E. M. Bishop; one *s* one *d. Educ:* Sedbergh; Magdalen Coll., Oxford (Demy; MA). Army, 1944-47 (Lieut, Assam Regt). Asst Principal, Colonial Office, 1951; Asst Private Sec. to Sec. of State, 1954-56; seconded to Sierra Leone Govt, 1958-60; jt sec. to Uganda Relationships Commn, 1960-61; Principal Private Sec. to Sec. of State, 1964-65; Asst Sec., 1965; transf. to Min. of Social Security, 1968; Under-Sec., 1973. *Recreations:* reading, walking, sketching. *Address:* Fairseat Lodge, Fairseat, near Sevenoaks, Kent. *T:* Fairseat 822201.

STAFFORD, 14th Baron *cr* 1640, *confirmed* 1825; **Basil Francis Nicholas Fitzherbert;** DL; *b* 7 April 1926; *s* of late Capt. Hon. Thomas Charles Fitzherbert, AM 1917, and Beryl (*d* 1959), 2nd *d* of John Waters and *widow* of Major Henry Brougham, RA; *S* uncle, 1941; *m* 1952, Morag Nada, *yr d* of late Lt-Col Alastair Campbell, Altries, Milltimber, Aberdeenshire; three *s* three *d. Educ:* Ampleforth College, York; St John's Coll., Cambridge. Lieut Scots Guards, 1945-48. Local Director, Barclays Bank Ltd (Birmingham), retired 1982; President: Stafford Rugby FC; Staffs Assoc. of Boys' Clubs; Staffs Playing Fields Assoc.; North Staffs Br. Inst. of Marketing, 1955-76; Patron, City of Stoke on Trent Amateur Operatic Soc.; Pres., Staffs CLA; Show Dir, Staffs Agric. Soc.; President: Old Amplefordian Cricket Club; North Staffs Sporting Club; Nat. Assoc. of Young Cricketers; Staffs Gentleman CC. FInstM. DL Stafford, 1981. *Recreations:* cricket, shooting, yachting, fishing, tennis. *Heir: s* Hon. Francis Melfort William Fitzherbert, *b* 13 March 1954. *Address:* Swynnerton Park, Stone, Staffordshire ST15 0QE. *TA* and *T:* Swynnerton 228; Salt Winds, West Wittering, Chichester, West Sussex. *T:* West Wittering 2181. *Clubs:* Army and Navy; IZ; Free Foresters; MCC; Lord's Taverners.

STAFFORD, Bishop Suffragan of, since 1979; **Rt. Rev. John Stevens Waller;** *b* 18 April 1924; *m* 1951, Pamela Peregrine; two *s* three *d. Educ:* St Edward's School, Oxford; Peterhouse, Cambridge (MA); Wells Theol Coll. War service with RNVR, 1942-46. Deacon 1950, priest 1951, London. Leader, Strood Gp of Parishes, 1967-72, Team Rector of Strood 1972-73; Rector of St Nicholas, Harpenden, Herts, 1973-79. *Recreations:* anything to do with the sea. *Address:* Park Lodge, 3 Beech Court, Stone, Staffs ST17 8QG. *T:* Stone 816007.

STAFFORD, Archdeaconry of; *see* Lichfield.

STAFFORD, Frank Edmund, CMG 1951; CBE 1946 (OBE 1931); Malayan CS, retired 1951; *b* 24 Aug. 1895; *s* of late Frank Stafford and Marie Stafford; *m* 1943, Ida Wadham (marr. diss., 1950), *d* of late Conway Burton-Durham; one *s*; *m* 1953, Catherine Rolfe. *Educ:* Royal Gram. School, Guildford. Served World War I, 1914-19, India and Mesopotamia, Queen's Royal West Surrey Regt. Joined staff of Civil Commissioner, Iraq, 1919; appointed to High Commission, Iraq, 1921; Financial Secretary, 1924; Financial Adviser, British Embassy, Baghdad, 1931; Colonial Service, Nigeria, 1936 (Asst Treasurer, Principal Asst Sec., Actg Financial Sec.). War of 1939-45, commissioned in Army (Lt-Col) for service with Occupied Enemy Territory Administration, 1941; Financial Adviser, Ethiopian Govt, 1942; attached LHQ Australia, 1944; Col, Military Administration, British Borneo, 1945; demobilized, 1946 (Brig.); seconded to Foreign Office, 1946; Member UK Delegn Italian Peace Conference and Council of Foreign Ministers; Head UK Delegn Four Power Commission, 1947; Member UK Delegn to UN, 1948, 1949, 1950, 1952; Foreign Office Adviser (Minister) to Chief Administrator, Eritrea, 1951-53; Adviser to Ethiopian Govt, 1953-60. Chm. Council, Royal Soc. of St George, 1978. FRAS, FRGS. Order Star of Ethiopia, 1944; Grand Officer, Star of Honour, 1955. *Publications:* contributions to Encyc. Britannica and to Kipling Jl, and International Affairs. *Recreations:* astronomy, horticulture, hagiology. *Address:* 3 Holbrook Park, Horsham, West Sussex RH12 4PW. *T:* Horsham 52497. *Clubs:* Travellers', National Liberal.

STAFFORD, Godfrey Harry, CBE 1976; PhD; FRS 1979; FInstP; Master of St Cross College, Oxford, since 1979; *b* 15 April 1920; *s* of Henry and Sarah Stafford; *m* 1950, Helen Goldthorp (*née* Clark); one *s* twin *d. Educ:* Rondebosch Boys High Sch., S Africa; Univ. of Cape Town; Gonville and Caius Coll., Cambridge. MSc Cape Town, 1941; South African Naval Forces, 1941-46; Ebden Scholar, PhD Cantab 1950; Harwell, 1949-51; Head of Biophysics Subdiv., CSIR, Pretoria, 1951-54; Cyclotron Gp, AERE, 1954-57; Rutherford Laboratory: Head of Proton Linear Accelerator Gp, 1957; Head of High Energy Physics Div., 1963; Dep. Dir, 1966; Dir, Rutherford Lab., Chilton, 1969-79; Dir Gen., Rutherford and Appleton Laboratories, 1979-81. Fellow, St Cross Coll., Oxford, MA, 1971. CERN appointments: UK deleg. to Council, 1973; Vice-Pres., Council, 1973; Scientific Policy Cttee, 1973, Vice-Chm., 1976, Chm., 1978. Vice-Pres. for meetings, Inst. of Physics, 1976; Vice-Pres., European Physical Soc., 1982. Glazebrook Prize and Medal, Inst.

of Physics, 1981. Hon. DSc Birmingham, 1980. *Publications:* papers and articles in learned jls on: biophysics, nuclear physics, high energy physics. *Address:* Ferry Cottage, North Hinksey Village, Oxford OX2 0NA. *T:* (home) Oxford 47621, (office) Oxford 512411.

STAFFORD, John, OBE 1977; HM Diplomatic Service, retired; *b* 15 June 1920; *s* of late Frank and Gertrude Stafford, Sheffield; *m* 1949, Mary Jocelyn Goodwin, *d* of late Capt. J. G. Budge, RN. *Educ:* High Storrs Grammar Sch. Exchequer and Audit Dept, 1939. RAF, W/O Pilot, 1940. Board of Trade, 1946; Assistant Trade Commissioner, Delhi, Karachi, Bulawayo, 1946-56; Trade Commissioner, Karachi, Lahore, Bombay, Madras, Lahore, 1956-65; Dep. High Comr, Lahore, 1965-69; Consul, Houston, Texas, 1969-71; First Sec. (Commercial), New Delhi, 1974-77; Consul Gen., Brisbane, 1978-80. *Recreations:* cricket, tennis, theatre, music. *Address:* Leacroft, 268 Brooklands Road, Weybridge, Surrey. *Clubs:* East India, Devonshire, Sports and Public Schools; Royal Bombay Yacht; Punjab (Lahore).

STAFFORD-CLARK, David, MD; DPM; FRCP; FRCPsych; Consultant Emeritus, Guy's Hospital; formerly Physician in Charge, Department of Psychological Medicine, and Director of The York Clinic, Guy's Hospital, 1954-73; Chairman, Psychiatric Division, Guy's Group, 1973-74; Consultant Physician, Bethlem Royal and Maudsley Hospitals and the Institute of Psychiatry, 1954-73; retired; *b* 17 March 1916; *s* of Francis and Cordelia Susan Stafford Clark; *m* 1941, Dorothy Stewart (*née* Oldfield); three *s* one *d. Educ:* Felsted; University of London. Guy's Hospital. MRCS, LRCP, 1939; MB, BS, 1939. Served War of 1939-45, RAFVR; trained as Medical Parachutist (despatches twice); demobilised 1945. Guy's Hosp., MRCP, Nuffield Med. Fellow, 1946; 3 years postgrad. trg appts, Inst. of Psychiatry, Maudsley Hosp.; MD London, 1947, DPM London, 1948; Registrar, Nat. Hosp., Queen Sq., 1948. Resident Massachusetts Gen. Hosp., Dept of Psychiatry, and Teaching Clinical Fellow, Harvard Med. School, 1949; First Asst, Professorial Unit, Maudsley Hosp., 1950; Mem. Assoc. for Research in Mental and Nervous Disorders, NY, 1950-53; Consultant Staff, Guy's Hosp., 1950; Lectureship, Psychology (Faculty of Letters), Reading Univ., 1950-54. Gifford Lectr and Vis. Prof., St Andrews Univ., 1938. Member: Archbishop of Canterbury's Commn on Divine Healing; Council, Royal Medico-Psychological Assoc.; Council, Medico-Legal Soc.; Examr, RCP London and Cambridge MD; Editorial Bds, Guy's Hosp. Reports, and Mod. Med. of Gt Britain. Acted as adviser to various motion picture companies (Universal International etc) on medical aspects of their productions; has also acted as adviser and director on a large number of medical programmes on sound radio, and both BBC and Independent Television, including the "Lifeline" series of programmes for the BBC, and documentary programmes for ITV on the emotional and intellectual growth of normal children, and the life and work of Freud; Author of Brain and Behaviour Series in Adult Education Television Programmes on BBC Channel 2; Mind and Motive Series, 1966. FRCP, 1958; Mem., NY Acad. of Sciences; FRSA (Silver Medal), 1959; Hon. RCM, 1966; Foundn Fellow, RCPsych, 1972, Hon. Fellow, 1976. *Publications:* poetry: Autumn Shadow, 1941; Sound in the Sky, 1944; *novels:* Soldier Without a Rifle (part 1 of a trilogy), 1979; Front Row at the Accident; *medical:* Psychiatry Today (Pelican), 1951; Psychiatry for Students, 1964, 5th edn, 1978; What Freud Really Said, 1965; Five Questions in Search of an Answer, 1970, repr. 1972; chapters in: Emergencies in Medical Practice, 1st, 2nd and 3rd edns, 1948, 1950, 1952; Compendium of Emergencies, 1st and 2nd edns; Case Histories in Psychosomatic Medicine, 1952; Taylor's Medical Jurisprudence, 12th edn, 1965; Schizophrenia: Somatic Aspects, 1st edn, 1957; Frontiers in General Hospital Psychiatry, 1961; A Short Textbook of Medicine, 1963; The Pathology and Treatment of Sexual Deviation, 1964; Modern Trends in Psychological Medicine, 1970; Psychiatric Treatment, Concepts of, in Encyclopædia Britannica, 200th anniv. edn, 1973; contributions to various medical textbooks and to medical and scientific jls. *Recreations:* travel, reading, writing, making and watching films, theatre. *Club:* Royal Air Force.

STAFFORD-KING-HARMAN, Sir Cecil William Francis, 2nd Bt, *cr* 1913; *b* 6 Jan. 1895; *s* of late Rt Hon. Sir Thomas Stafford, Bt, CB, and Frances Agnes King-Harman; *S* father, 1935; assumed additional surname of King-Harman, 1932; *m* 1917, Sarah Beatrice (*d* 1979), *y d* of late Col A. D. Acland, CBE, and Hon. Mrs Acland, Feniton Court, Honiton, Devon; one *d* (one *s* killed in action and one *d* decd). *Educ:* RN Colleges, Osborne and Dartmouth; RMC Sandhurst; Christ Church, Oxford. Formerly Midshipman, Royal Navy, retired, 1912; commissioned 2nd Lt, The King's Royal Rifle Corps, 1914; Captain, 1917; served throughout European War in France and Italy (despatches); after war went to Christ Church, Oxford, MA (Hons) Agriculture; Steward, Irish Turf Club, 1938-40, 1943-46, 1948-51, 1952-55, 1959-62; Mem. of Racing Board, 1945-50. Appointed Member, Council of State for Ireland, 1956. War substantive Captain, 1940; Temporary Major, 1941; Temporary Lt-Col 1942. *Recreations:* shooting, racing, fishing. *Address:* St Catherines Park, Leixlip, Co. Kildare, Ireland. *T:* 280421. *Clubs:* Kildare Street and University, Irish Turf (Dublin).

STAGG, Prof. Geoffrey Leonard, MBE 1945; Professor Emeritus, Department of Spanish and Portuguese, University of Toronto; *b* 10 May 1913; *s* of Henry Percy Stagg and Maude Emily Bradbury; *m* 1948, Amy Southwell, Wellesley Hills, Mass, USA; two *s* one *d. Educ:* King Edward's School, Birmingham (Scholar); Trinity Hall, Cambridge (Scholar). BA 1st cl. Hons Modern and Medieval Languages Tripos, 1934; MA 1946; Joseph Hodges Choate Mem. Fellow, Harvard Univ., 1934-36; AM (Harvard), 1935;

Modern Languages Master, King Edward's School, Birmingham, 1938-40, 1946-47; served in Intelligence Corps, 1940-46; Lecturer in Spanish and Italian, Nottingham Univ., 1947-53, and Head of Dept of Spanish, 1954-56; Dept of Italian and Hispanic Studies, Toronto Univ.: Prof., 1956-82; Chm., 1956-66, 1969-78. Vice-Pres., Assoc. of Teachers of Spanish and Portuguese of GB and Ireland, 1948-; Pres., Canadian Assoc. of Hispanists, 1964-66, 1972-74; Vice-Pres., Asociación Internacional de Hispanistas, 1977-. Fellow, New Coll., Univ. of Toronto, 1962; Senior Fellow, Massey Coll., Univ. of Toronto, 1965-70; Canada Council Senior Fellowship, 1967-68. *Publications:* articles on Spanish literature in learned jls. *Address:* c/o Department of Spanish and Portuguese, University of Toronto, Toronto M5S 1A1, Canada.

STAGG, Air Commodore (retired) Walter Allan, CB 1958; CBE 1953 (OBE 1950); *b* 2 April 1903; *s* of late Frederick Edward and late Emma Jane Stagg; *m* 1943, Olive Georgina Legg (*d* 1978); no *c. Educ:* privately. Commnd in RAF, 1926; served India, 1928-33 (India General Service Medal, NW Frontier Clasp, 1930-31). Air Ministry (Directorate of Equipment), 1935-37. Joined HMS Glorious in Mediterranean, 1937-39. On staff of HQ Training, Flying Training and Maintenance Comds, 1940-43; Dep. Director of Equipment (2) in Air Ministry, 1943-45; Senior Equipment Staff Officer, No 214 Group, Italy, 1945; Comd No 25 Maintenance Unit, 1945-46. In Ministry of Civil Aviation, 1946-47; on staffs of HQ Maintenance Comd, 40 Group and Flying Training Comd, 1947-51; Dep. Asst Chief of Staff (Logistics) at SHAPE, 1951-53; Director of Equipment (A) Air Ministry, 1954-55; Director of Movements, Air Ministry, 1955-58; Director, Supply Services Division, NATO. Maintenance Supply Services Agency, 1958-60, retired. *Address:* 3 Ingleside Court, Budleigh Salterton, Devon. *T:* Budleigh Salterton 5282. *Club:* Royal Air Force.

STAHL, Professor Ernest Ludwig, DLitt; Taylor Professor of the German Language and Literature and Fellow of The Queen's College, Oxford, 1959-69, Supernumerary Fellow, since 1969; *b* Senekal, OFS, S Africa, 10 Dec. 1902; *s* of Philip and Theresa Stahl; *m* 1942, Kathleen Mary Hudson; no *c. Educ:* Univ. of Capetown (MA 1925); Heidelberg Univ.; Oxford Univ. (First Class Hons, 1927; DLitt 1980); Berne Univ. (PhD *magna cum laude* 1931). Assistant Lecturer in German, Birmingham, 1932; Lecturer in German, Oxford, 1935; Reader in German Literature, Oxford, 1945; Student of Christ Church, Oxford, 1945, Student Emeritus, 1960. Vis. Professor: Cornell, 1956; Princeton, 1958; Yale, 1964; Kansas, 1968; Calif (Davis), 1969-70. Gold Medal, Goethe Gesellschaft, 1966. *Publications:* Die religiöse und die philosophische Bildungsidee und die Entstehung des Bildungsromans, 1934; Hölderlin's Symbolism, 1944; The Dramas of Heinrich von Kleist, 1948 (revised edn, 1961); (trans. with Louis MacNeice) Goethe's Faust pts I and II (abridged), 1951; Schiller's Drama: Theory and Practice, 1954; Goethe's Iphigenie auf Tauris, 1962. Editions of Goethe's Werther, 1942 (new edn, 1972), Lessing's Emilia Galotti, 1946, Goethe's Torquato Tasso, 1962, and R. M. Rilke's Duino Elegies, 1961; revised edn, Oxford Book of German Verse, 1967; (with W. E. Yuill) Introduction to German Literature, vol. III, 1970; The Faust Translation in Time Was Away: the world of Louis MacNeice, 1975; articles in Modern Language Review, Germanic Review, German Life and Letters, Journal of English and Germanic Philology, Oxford German Studies, Yearbook of Comparative Criticism; contrib. to Festschrift for Ralph Farrell. *Address:* 43 Plantation Road, Oxford OX2 6JE. *T:* Oxford 55896.

STAINE, Albert Llewellyn, CBE 1979; **Hon. Mr Justice Staine;** Chief Justice of Belize, since 1979; Judge of the Court of Appeal, since 1983; *b* 4 July 1928; *s* of Robert George and Beatrice Staine; *m* 1973, Marina Diana (née Andrewin); one *s. Educ:* St Michael's College, Belize; Hull University; LLB (Hons). Clerical Service, 1946; called to the Bar, Middle Temple, 1963; Crown Counsel, 1963; Solicitor General, 1968; Dir of Public Prosecutions, 1969; Acting Puisne Judge, 1971; Puisne Judge, 1973. *Recreations:* reading, photography, tape recording. *Address:* 17 Princess Margaret Drive, Belize. *T:* 44385; (Chambers) 7397.

STAINFORTH, Maj.-Gen. Charles Herbert, CB 1969; OBE 1955; Editor, Army Quarterly and Defence Journal, since 1974; *b* 12 Dec. 1914; *s* of Lt-Col Stainforth, CMG, 4th Cavalry, IA, and Georgina Helen, *d* of Maj.-Gen. H. Pipon, CB; *m* Elizabeth, *d* of late John Tait Easdale; one *s* one *d. Educ:* Wellington Coll.; RMC, Sandhurst. Commnd into 2nd Royal Lancers, IA; transferred British Army, 1947; Chief of Staff, Southern Comd, 1965-66; GOC Aldershot District and SE Dist, 1966-69; Head of UK Future Command Structure, MoD, 1969-72. Col Comdt, RCT, 1970-72. Chm. Combined Cadet Forces, 1970-72. Consultant to Nat. Tourist Bds, 1973-. *Address:* Powderham House, Dippenhall, near Farnham, Surrey. *Clubs:* Army and Navy, MCC.
See also G. H. Stainforth.

STAINFORTH, Graham Henry; *b* 3 Oct. 1906; *s* of Lt-Col H. G. Stainforth, CMG, Indian Cavalry, and Georgina Helen, *d* of Maj.-Gen. H. Pipon, CB; *m* 1943, Ruth Ellen Douglas-Cooper; one *s* two *d. Educ:* Wellington Coll., Berks; Emmanuel Coll., Cambridge. Assistant Master at Merchant Taylors' Sch., 1928-35, and Assistant Housemaster, 1933-35; Assistant Master and Tutor at Wellington Coll., and Head of the English Department, 1935-45; Hon. Secretary of Wellington College Clubs at Walworth, 1935-45; Headmaster of Oundle and Laxton Grammar Schools, 1945-56; Master of Wellington, 1956-66. Mem., Berks Educn Cttee, 1961-74; Fellow of Woodard Corpn., 1966-80; Governor: Ardingly College, 1966-80; Portsmouth Grammar School, 1966-77; Wallingford Comprehensive School, 1976-82. Hon.

Liveryman, Grocers' Co., 1975. *Address:* The Cottage, Winterbrook, Wallingford, Oxon OX10 9EF. *T:* Wallingford 36414.
See also C. H. Stainforth.

STAINTON, Sir Anthony (Nathaniel), KCB 1974 (CB 1967); QC 1975; First Parliamentary Counsel to HM Treasury, 1972-76 (Parliamentary Counsel, 1956-72); *b* 8 Jan. 1913; *s* of Evelyn Stainton, Barham Court, Canterbury; *m* 1st, 1947, Barbara Russell; three *d* ; 2nd, 1966, Rachel Frances, *d* of late Col C. E. Coghill, CMG. *Educ:* Eton; Christ Church, Oxford. Called to the Bar, Lincoln's Inn, 1937.

STAINTON, Sir (John) Ross, Kt 1981; CBE 1971; retired; *b* 27 May 1914; *s* of late George Stainton and Helen Ross; *m* 1939, Doreen Werner; three *d. Educ:* Glengorse, Eastbourne; Malvern Coll., Worcestershire. Joined Imperial Airways as Trainee, 1933; served in Italy, Egypt, Sudan. Served with RAF in England and West Indies, 1940-42. BOAC in USA, 1942; Man. N America, 1949-53; General Sales Man. BOAC, and other Head Office posts, 1954-64; Commercial Director, 1964; Dep. Man. Dir, 1968-71; Man. Dir, 1971-72; Mem., BOAC (AC), 1961-72; Mem., BOAC Bd, 1968, Chm. and Chief Exec., 1972, until merged into British Airways, 1974; Mem., 1971-, Dep. Chm. and Chief Exec., 1977-79, Chairman, 1979-80, British Airways Bd. Director: Private Patients Plan; Giltspur Ltd. FCIT (Pres., 1970-71). FBIM. *Clubs:* Royal Air Force; Royal and Ancient Golf (St Andrews); Sunningdale Golf.

STAINTON, Keith; MP (C) Sudbury and Woodbridge since Dec. 1963; *b* 8 Nov. 1921; *m* 1946, Vanessa Ann Heald; three *s* three *d* ; *m* 1980, Frances Easton. *Educ:* Kendal Sch.; Manchester Univ. (BA (Com.) Dist. in Economics). Insurance clerk, 1936-39. Served War of 1939-45: Lieut, RNVR, Submarines and with French Resistance, 1940-46. Manchester Univ., 1946-49; Leader Writer, Financial Times, 1949-52; Industrial Consultant, 1952-57; joined Burton, Son & Sanders, Ltd, 1957, Man. Dir 1961-69, Chm. 1962-69; Chm. Scotia Investments Ltd, 1969-72. Mem., House of Commons Select Cttees on Expenditure and Science and Technology. Mem. Council of Europe and WEU, 1979-. Légion d'Honneur, Croix de Guerre avec Palmes, Ordre de l'Armée, 1943. *Address:* Little Bealings House, Woodbridge, Suffolk. *T:* Ipswich 624205.

STAINTON, Sir Ross; *see* Stainton, Sir J. R.

STAIR, 13th Earl of, *cr* 1703; **John Aymer Dalrymple,** KCVO 1978 (CVO 1964); MBE 1941; Bt 1664 and (Scot.) 1698; Viscount Stair, Lord Glenluce and Stranraer, 1690; Viscount Dalrymple, Lord Newliston, 1703; Baron Oxenfoord (UK) 1841; Colonel (retired) Scots Guards; Lord-Lieutenant of Wigtown, 1961-81; Captain General of the Queen's Body Guard for Scotland, Royal Company of Archers, since 1973; *b* 9 Oct. 1906; *e s* of 12th Earl of Stair, KT, DSO, and Violet Evelyn (née Harford) (*d* 1968); *S* father, 1961; *m* 1960, Davina, *d* of late Hon. Sir David Bowes-Lyon, KCVO; three *s. Educ:* Eton; Sandhurst. Bde Major, 3rd (London) Infantry Bde and Regimental Adjt Scots Guards, 1935-38; served Middle East, 1941; Bde Major, 16th Inf. Bde (despatches, MBE); Lieut-Colonel 1942; commanded 1st Scots Guards, 1942-43; AMS Headquarters AAI, 1944; Comd Trg Bn Scots Guards, 1945; Comd 2nd Scots Guards, 1946-49; Comd Scots Guards, Temp. Colonel, 1949-52; retired, 1953; retired as Hon. Colonel Scots Guards, 1953. *Heir: s* Viscount Dalrymple, *qv. Address:* Lochinch Castle, Stranraer, Wigtownshire. *Club:* Cavalry and Guards.
See also Lady Marion Philipps, Lady Jean Rankin.

STALKER, Prof. Alexander Logie, TD; DL; Regius Professor of Pathology, University of Aberdeen, since 1972; Consultant Pathologist, North East Regional Hospital Board, since 1955; *b* 15 Feb. 1920; *s* of late J. S. Stalker and Jean Logie; *m* 1945, Mary E. C. MacLean, MB, ChB; one *s* three *d. Educ:* Morrison's Academy, Crieff; Univ. of Aberdeen. MB, ChB 1942; MD 1961; FRCPath 1970. RAMC War Service, 1942-47 and TA Service, 1948-64; ADMS 51 (H) Div., 1958-64; QHS, 1963-65. Univ. of Aberdeen: Sen. Lectr in Pathology, 1948-65; Reader in Pathology, 1965-69; Personal Prof. of Pathology, 1969-72; Dean of Faculty of Medicine, 1979-82. County Comr Scouts, City of Aberdeen, 1965-68. Pres., British Microcirculation Soc., 1968-73; Pres., European Soc. for Microcirculation, 1970-72; Mem., Pathological Soc. of Gt Britain and Ireland. DL Aberdeen, 1967. *Publications:* scientific papers in medical jls, esp. in field of microcirculation. *Recreations:* fishing, hill walking, Norwegian studies. *Address:* Coach End, Banchory, Kincardineshire AB3 3HS. *T:* Banchory 2460.

STALLARD, Albert William; MP (Lab) Camden, St Pancras North, since 1974 (St Pancras North, 1970-74); *b* 5 Nov. 1921; *m* 1944; one *s* one *d. Educ:* Low Waters Public School; Hamilton Academy, Scotland. Engineer, 1937-65; Technical Training Officer, 1965-70. Councillor, St Pancras, 1953-59, Alderman, 1962-65; Councillor, Camden, 1965-70, Alderman, 1971-. PPS to: Minister of State, Agriculture, Fisheries and Food, 1974; Minister of State for Housing and Construction, 1974-76. An Asst Govt Whip, 1976-78; a Lord Comr, HM Treasury, 1978-79. Chairman: Camden Town Disablement Cttee (Mem., 1951-); Camden Assoc. for Mental Health. Mem., Inst. of Training Officers, 1971. AEU Order of Merit, 1968. *Address:* House of Commons, SW1A 0AA. *T:* 01-219 4214.

STALLARD, Sir Peter (Hyla Gawne), KCMG 1961 (CMG 1960); CVO 1956; MBE 1945; President, Devon and Cornwall Rent Assessment Panel, since 1976; *b* 6 March 1915; *y c* of Rev. L. B. Stallard and Eleanor, *e d* of Colonel J. M. Gawne; *m* 1941, Mary Elizabeth Kirke, CStJ; one *s* one *d*. *Educ:* Bromsgrove Sch.; Corpus Christi Coll., Oxford (MA). Cadet, Colonial Administrative Service, Northern Nigeria, 1937. Military Service; Nigeria, Gold Coast, Burma, 1939-45. Secretary to the Prime Minister of the Federation of Nigeria, 1958-61; Governor and Commander-in-Chief of British Honduras, 1961-66; Lt Governor of the Isle of Man, 1966-74. Pres., Somerset Assoc. of Boys Clubs, 1977-; Chm., Dartmoor Steering Gp, 1978-. KStJ 1961; Chapter-Gen., Order of St John, 1976-. *Recreation:* golf. *Address:* 18 Henley Road, Taunton, Somerset. *T:* Taunton 81505. *Club:* Athenæum.

See also R. D. Wilson.

STALLIBRASS, Geoffrey Ward, CB 1972; OBE 1952; FRAeS; Controller, National Air Traffic Services (Civil Aviation Authority/Ministry of Defence), 1969-74 (Joint Field Commander, 1966-69); *b* 17 Dec. 1911; *s* of Thomas and Ivy Stallibrass, Midhurst; *m* 1940, Alison, *e d* of late James and Rita Scott, Norwich; two *s* three *d*. *Educ:* Wellingborough Sch. Air Service Training, Hamble (Commercial Pilot/Instrument Rating Course), 1948. Dep. Director, Civil Aviation Ops, Ministry of Civil Aviation, 1946; attached to BOAC, 1949; Dep. Director of Control and Navigation (Development), 1950; Director of Aerodromes (Tech.), Ministry of Transport and Civil Aviation, 1953; Director of Flight Safety, Min. of Aviation, 1961. *Publications:* articles on aviation subjects. *Recreations:* walking, birdwatching, conservation work, music. *Address:* Turkey Island Corner, East Harting, Petersfield, Hants. *T:* Harting 220.

STALLWORTHY, Sir John (Arthur), Kt 1972; Nuffield Professor of Obstetrics and Gynæcology, University of Oxford, 1967-73, now Emeritus; Fellow Emeritus, Oriel College, Oxford, 1973, Hon. Fellow, 1974; *b* 26 July 1906; *s* of Arthur John Stallworthy; *m* 1934, Margaret Wright Howie (*d* 1980); one *s* twin *d*. *Educ:* Auckland Grammar Sch.; Universities of Auckland and Otago, NZ. Distinction and gold medal in surgery, gynæcology and obstetrics, 1930; travelling med. schol., 1931; obstetrical travelling schol., 1932; postgrad. experience in Melbourne, London and Vienna. MRCOG 1935; FRCS 1936; FRCOG 1951. Joseph Price Orator, US, 1950; McIlrath Guest Prof., Sydney, 1952; Sommer Mem. Lecturer, US, 1958; Hunterian Prof., RCS, 1963; Sims Black Prof. S Africa, 1964. Sometime Examiner in Obstetrics and Gynæcology for RCOG, RCS of S Africa, Universities of Oxford, Birmingham, Leeds, E Africa and Singapore. Hon. Cons., Royal Prince Alfred Hospital, Sydney, 1952; Assoc. Obstetrician, National Maternity Hospital, Dublin, 1959. Vice-Pres., RCOG, 1969; President: RSM, 1974-75, 1980-81 (Hon. Fellow, 1976); Medical Protection Soc.; BMA, 1975. Hon. Fellow, Surgical, Obstetrical and Gynæcological Societies in US, Wales, Canada, S Africa, Spain and Turkey; Hon. FACS 1954; Hon. FCOG (SA) 1964; Hon. FACOG 1974; Hon. FRCSI 1976. Hon. DSc: Otago, 1975; Leeds, 1975. Victor Bonney Prize, RCS, 1970. Member, Honourable Order of Kentucky Colonels, 1968. *Publications:* (jointly) Problems of Fertility in General Practice, 1948; (jointly) Recent Advances in Obstetrics and Gynæcology, 1966-79; (jointly) Bonney's Gynaecological Surgery, 8th edn; joint contrib. to British Obstetric Practice and British Gynæcological Practice, 1959, and 1963. *Recreations:* formerly Rugby football, tennis, swimming, driving fast cars; now gardening, writing, driving fast cars more slowly. *Address:* Shotover Edge, Headington, Oxford. *T:* Oxford 62481. *Club:* Athenæum.

See also J. H. Stallworthy.

STALLWORTHY, Prof. Jon Howie; John Wendell Anderson Professor of English Literature, Cornell University, since 1977; *b* 18 Jan. 1935; *s* of Sir John (Arthur) Stallworthy, *qv*; *m* 1960, Gillian Meredith (*née* Waldock); two *s* one *d*. *Educ:* The Dragon Sch., Oxford; Rugby Sch.; Magdalen Coll., Oxford (MA, BLitt). Served RWAFF (pre-Oxford). At Oxford won Newdigate Prize, 1958 (runner-up, 1957). Joined Oxford Univ. Press, 1959, Dep. Head, Academic Div., 1975-77. Gave Chatterton Lecture on an English Poet to British Academy, 1970; during a sabbatical year, 1971-72, was a Visiting Fellow at All Souls Coll., Oxford. FRSL, 1971. *Publications: poems:* (7 collections) The Astronomy of Love, 1961; Out of Bounds, 1963; Root and Branch, 1969; Positives, 1969; The Apple Barrel: selected poems, 1955-63, 1974; Hand in Hand, 1974; A Familiar Tree, 1978; *criticism:* Between the Lines, W. B. Yeats's Poetry in the Making, 1963; Vision and Revision in Yeats's Last Poems, 1969; *biography:* Wilfred Owen, 1974 (winner of Duff Cooper Meml Prize, W. H. Smith Literary Award and E. M. Forster Award); *translations:* (with Peter France) Alexander Blok: The Twelve and other poems, 1970; (with Jerzy Peterkiewicz) poems for 2nd of Five Centuries of Polish Poetry, 1970; (with Peter France) Boris Pasternak: Selected Poems, 1983; ed, The Penguin Book of Love Poetry, 1973; Wilfred Owen: Complete Poems and Fragments, 1983. *Address:* Department of English, Cornell University, Ithaca, NY 14853, USA; (Christmas and summer) Long Farm, Elsfield Road, Old Marston, Oxford. *Club:* Vincent's (Oxford).

STAMENKOVIĆ, Dragi; Order of National Hero, Yugoslavia, 1952; Yugoslav Star with ribbon, 1981; Yugoslav Ambassador to the Court of St James's, since 1981; *b* 29 Feb. 1920; *s* of Todor Stamenković and Darinka Malešević; *m* 1945, Jelica Purić; two *s* one *d*. *Educ:* Belgrade Univ. Mem., Supreme HQ, Nat. Liberation Army for Serbia, 1939-45. Mem., Liberation Cttee for Belgrade Dist, 1945-48; Minister in Govt of Serbia, 1949-51; Pres., Fedn of Trade Unions of Serbia 1951-62 (now Vice-Pres.); President: Exec. Council of Serbia, 1964-67; Working People of Serbia, 1967-71; Mem.,

Presidency of Yugoslavia, 1971-74; Ambassador to Brazil, 1974-78; Ambassador in Federal Secretariat for Foreign Affairs, 1978-81. Deputy of Fed. Assembly in three convocations, and of Republican Assembly in four; Mem., Presidency of Fed. Conf., Socialist Alliance of Working People of Yugoslavia; sometime head or mem., Yugoslav delegns abroad. Holder of many Yugoslav and foreign decorations. *Publications:* From Travels through China, 1955; contribs to jls and newspapers on economic and political affairs of Yugoslavia, 1945-75. *Recreations:* tennis, football. *Address:* Yugoslav Embassy, 5 Lexham Gardens, W8 5JU. *T:* 01-370 6105. *Club:* Hurlingham.

STAMER, Sir (Lovelace) Anthony, 5th Bt, *cr* 1809; MA; AMIMI; *b* 28 Feb. 1917; *s* of Sir Lovelace Stamer, 4th Bt, and Eva Mary (*d* 1974), *e d* of R. C. Otter; *S* father, 1941; *m* 1st, 1948, Stella Huguette (marr. diss., 1953), *d* of Paul Burnell Binnie, Brussels; one *s* one *d*; 2nd, 1955, Margaret Lucy (marr. diss., 1959), *d* of late Major Belben and Mrs Stewart, Marandellas, S Rhodesia; 3rd, 1960, Marjorie June (marr. diss. 1968), *d* of T. C. Noakes, St James, Cape. *Educ:* Harrow; Trinity Coll., Cambridge; Royal Agricultural Coll., Cirencester. BA 1947; MA 1963; AMIMI 1963. Served RAF 1939-41; Officer in ATA 1941-45. Executive Director: Bentley Drivers Club Ltd, 1969-72; Bugatti & Ferrari Owners Club, 1972-74; Hon. Treasurer, Ferrari Owners' Club, 1977-81. *Heir: s* Peter Tomlinson Stamer, Flight Lieut, RAF, *b* 19 Nov. 1951. *Address:* The Mill House, Chardstock, Axminster, Devon.

STAMLER, Samuel Aaron, QC 1971; a Recorder of the Crown Court, since 1974; *b* 3 Dec. 1925; *s* of late Herman Stamler and Bronia Stamler; *m* 1953, Honor, *d* of A. G. Brotman; two *s* one *d*. *Educ:* Berkhamsted; King's College, Cambridge. Called to Bar, Middle Temple, 1949, Bencher, 1979. *Recreations:* tennis, children. *Address:* 1 Essex Court, Temple, EC4. *T:* 01-353 5362. *Club:* Athenæum.

STAMM, Temple Theodore, FRCS; Orthopædic Surgeon Emeritus, Guy's Hospital; *b* 22 Dec. 1905; *s* of Dr Louis Edward Stamm, Streatham, and Louisa Ethel (*née* Perry), Caterham, Surrey; *m* 1945, Pamela, *d* of Charles Russell, Chislehurst, Kent. *Educ:* Rose Hill Sch., Surrey; Haileybury Coll.; Guy's Hospital Medical School. MB, BS (London), 1930, MRCS, LRCP 1928, FRCS 1934. Fellow Royal Society of Medicine; Fellow British Orthopædic Assoc.; Member British Med. Assoc. Formerly: Orthopædic Surgeon, Bromley Hospital, 1941-66; Asst Orthopædic Surgeon and Orthopædic Registrar, Royal Nat. Orthopædic Hospital; Asst Orthopædic Surgeon, Orthopædic Registrar, Asst Anæsthetist and Demonstrator of Anatomy, Guy's Hospital. Major RAMC. *Publications:* Foot Troubles, 1957; Guide to Orthopædics, 1958; Surgery of the Foot, British Surgical Practice, Vol. 4; contributions to Blackburn and Lawrie's Textbook of Surgery, 1958; articles in: Lancet, Guy's Hospital Reports, Journal of Bone and Joint Surgery, Medical Press, etc. *Recreations:* farming, sailing, music. *Address:* Hambrook Lodge, West Ashling, Chichester, West Sussex PO18 8DQ.

See also Air Vice-Marshal W. P. Stamm.

STAMM, Air Vice-Marshal William Percivale, CBE 1960; *b* 27 Aug. 1909; *s* of Dr L. E. Stamm and L. E. (*née* Perry); *m* 1939, Mary Magdalene Van Zeller; two *s* one *d*; *m* 1974, Mrs J. M. Turner (*née* Erleigh). *Educ:* Haileybury Coll.; Guy's Hospital. MRCS, LRCP, 1932; MB, BS (London) 1933; DCP (London) 1946; DTM&H 1947; MRCP 1951; FRCP 1956; FRCPath 1964. House appointments, anatomy demonstrator, Guy's Hospital. Commissioned RAF, 1934; specialised in pathology and tropical medicine, 1938; comd RAF Hospital, Takoradi, 1942-43; Sen. RAF Consultnt in Pathol. and Trop. Medicine, and OC RAF Inst. of Pathol. and Trop. Medicine, 1951-69, retired. Dir, Amoebiasis Res. Unit, 1970-77; Clinical Res. Manager, May & Baker Ltd, 1977-79. Member Council: Royal Society Trop. Med. and Hygiene, 1951-57, 1959-69, 1971-72 (Vice-President, 1957-59, and 1969-71); Assoc. of Clinical Pathologists, 1958-61 (President, 1966-67); United Services Sect., Royal Society Med., 1952-62 and 1966-69. Pres., British Div., Internat. Acad. Pathology, 1966; Hon. lectr, tropical pathology, Royal Free Med. Sch.; Cons., King's Coll. Hospital. QHS 1959-69. *Publications:* contrib. to Symposium, The Pathology of Parasitic Diseases; chapter on amoebiasis in Clinical Tropical Diseases (ed B. Maegraith); papers in Lancet, BMJ, Journal Clin. Pathology, Trans. Royal Society Tropical Med. and Hygiene, and Proc. Royal Society of Medicine. *Recreations:* building and decorating, opera and theatre. *Address:* 17 Ennismore Gardens, SW7. *T:* 01-589 5351. *Club:* Royal Air Force.

See also T. T. Stamm.

STAMMERS, Professor Francis Alan Roland, CBE 1945; TD (with clasp) 1949; Emeritus Professor of Surgery, University of Birmingham (Professor, 1946-63); Hon. Cons. Surgeon, United Birmingham Hospitals; Cons.-Adviser in Surgery to Birmingham Regional Hospital Board, 1963-68, Hon. Cons.-Adviser, 1968-71; *b* 31 Jan. 1898; *s* of Charles Roland Stammers and Eliza Nellie Pettitt; *m* 1933, Lois Mildred Marris (*d* 1978); one *s* two *d*. *Educ:* Dudley Grammar School; Birmingham Univ.; London Hospital; Mayo Clinic, USA. Served European War, 1914-18, 2nd Lieut, Lieut RGA, 1916-18; BSc (Birmingham) 1920; MB, ChB (Birmingham), MRCS, LRCP 1923; FRCS 1925; ChM (Birmingham), 1936. Late Surgeon: General, Children's and Queen Elizabeth Hospitals, 1929; Rockefeller Fellowship Mayo Clinic, USA, 1928; served War of 1939-45: surgical specialist and OC Surgical Division, RAMC, 1939-42; Cons. Surgeon, Brigadier AMS, W Command and forward areas of and Italy, 1942-45 (despatches); Hon. Colonel, AMS; Late Member Council (late Member Court of Examiners),

Royal College of Surgeons, 1957-65; late External Examiner: University of London; University of Durham. Visiting Surgeon to Harvard University Medical School, Boston, Mass, USA, 1950; President, Surgical Section of Royal Society of Med. (now Hon. Member), 1952-53; British Council and BMA Lecturer in Cyprus, Baghdad and Khartoum, 1952; Australasian Postgrad. Federation in Medicine Lecturer, 1958. President: Assoc. of Surgeons of Great Britain and Ireland, 1960-61; Midland Med. Society, 1960-61; Moynihan Chirurgical Club, 1962-63; W Midlands Surgical Soc., 1955; Mem. Council and Cases Cttee, Medical Protection Society. *Publications:* Partial Gastrectomy Complications with Metabolic Consequences (with J. Alexander Williams), 1963; numerous articles in medical and surgical journals and textbooks. *Recreations:* gardening, bowls, reading. *Address:* 56 Middle Park Road, Weoley Hill, Birmingham B29 4BJ. *T:* 021-475 1022. *Club:* University Staff (Birmingham).

STAMP, family name of **Baron Stamp.**

STAMP, 3rd Baron, *cr* 1938, of Shortlands; **Trevor Charles Stamp,** MA, MD, FRCPath; Emeritus Professor of Bacteriology, Royal Postgraduate Medical School, University of London (Reader, 1937-48, Professor, 1948-70); *b* 13 Feb. 1907; *s* of 1st Baron Stamp, GCB, GBE; *S* brother, 1941; *m* 1932, Frances Dawes, *d* of late Charles Henry Bosworth, Evanston, Illinois, USA; two *s.* *Educ:* The Leys Sch., Cambridge; Gonville and Caius Coll., Cambridge; St Bartholomew's Hospital. MRCS, LRCP, BCh Cambridge, MA Cambridge, 1931; MB Cambridge, 1937. MD 1966. Demonstrator in Bacteriology, 1932-34, Lecturer in Bacteriology, 1934-37, London School of Hygiene and Tropical Medicine; Dir, Emergency Public Health Lab. Service Sect. 9, 1939-41; attached to the Ministry of Supply, 1941-45; Governor: Imperial College of Science and Technology, 1949-79; The Leys School, 1942-77; Pres. of Governors, Queenswood School, 1981- (Governor, 1941-81; Chm., 1971-81). Mem., Exec. and Scientific Adv. Cttees, Animal Health Trust (formerly Vet. Educnl Trust), 1946-79. Mem., Parly Delegn of IPU to Egypt, 1973, to Tokyo, 1974, to Sofia, 1977, to Prague and Caracas, 1979. Founder Fellow, College of Pathologists, 1963 (now RCPath); Fellow, Royal Postgrad. Med. Sch., 1972. US Medal of Freedom with Silver Palm, 1947. Hon. Freeman, Barbers' Company, 1958. *Publications:* Various papers on bacteriological subjects. *Recreation:* gardening. *Heir: s* Dr the Hon. Trevor Charles Bosworth Stamp, MD, FRCP [*b* 18 Sept. 1935; *m* 1st, 1963, Anne Carolynn Churchill (marr. diss. 1971); two *d* ; 2nd, 1975, Carol Anne, *d* of Keith Russell, Lower Bourne, Farnham, Surrey; one *s* one *d*]. *Address:* Middle House, 7 Hyde Park Street, W2. *T:* 01-723 8363; Pennyroyal, Hedgerley, Bucks. *T:* Farnham Common 2737. *Club:* Athenæum.

STAMP, Hon. (Arthur) Maxwell; Member, Civil Aviation Authority, 1976-81; Director: CYTO Ltd (Jersey), since 1982; Olympic Holidays Ltd, since 1981; Pan Electric Corp. (Nevada), since 1978; Economics International Inc., since 1965; Adviser, Sun Banks of Florida (USA), since 1981; *b* 20 Sept. 1915; 3rd *s* of 1st Baron Stamp, GCB, GBE; *m* 1944, Alice Mary Richards; one *s* two *d.* *Educ:* Leys Sch., Cambridge; Clare Coll., Cambridge. Called to the Bar, Inner Temple, 1939; War of 1939-45, 2nd Lieut Intelligence Corps, 1940; Major 1943; Lieut-Colonel 1944. Financial Adviser, John Lewis Partnership Ltd, 1947-49; Acting Adviser, Bank of England, 1950-53. Alternate Executive Director for the UK, International Monetary Fund, Washington, DC, USA, 1951-53; Director, European Dept, IMF, 1953-54. Adviser to the Governors, the Bank of England, 1954-57. Director: Hill Samuel & Co. Ltd, 1958-76; Triplex Hldgs Ltd, 1963-75. Chairman: Maxwell Stamp Associates Ltd, 1962-79; Maxwell Stamp (Africa) Ltd, 1964-78; Bonsacks Baths Ltd, 1978-80. Member: Council of Foreign Bondholders, 1950-53, 1955-57; Council, Internat. Chamber of Commerce, 1961-75; Exec. Cttee, Nat. Inst. of Economic and Social Research, 1962; Exec. Cttee, European League for Economic Co-operation, 1962; Council, Trade Policy Research Centre; Economic Cttee, CBI, 1968-; Chm., Home Office Cttee on London Taxi-Cab Trade, 1967. Mem., Panel of Conciliators, Internat. Centre for Settlement of Investment Disputes, Washington, 1968. Chm., The Rehearsal Orchestra. Governor, British Inst. for Recorded Sound, 1979, Chm., 1980. Chm., Truman and Knightley Educnl Trust, 1982-. Governor, LSE, 1968. *Recreations:* music, photography. *Address:* Mulberry Green Farmhouse, Copford, Essex. *T:* Colchester 210231; 19 Clarence Gate Gardens, Glentworth Street, NW1. *T:* 01-723 9538. *Club:* Athenæum.

STAMP, Prof. Edward, MA (Cantab), CA; FCA (Canada); Research Professor in Accountancy since 1975, Professor of Accounting Theory, since 1971, Director of International Centre for Research in Accounting, since 1971, University of Lancaster; *b* 11 Nov. 1928; *s* of William Stamp and Anne Wilson; *m* 1953, Margaret Douglas Higgins, *d* of Douglas Gordon Higgins, MC, Toronto, Canada; one *s* three *d.* *Educ:* Quarry Bank, Liverpool; Cambridge Univ. Open Exhibnr, Foundation Scholar, Prizeman, First cl. Hons Natural Sciences. Lieut, RCNR. Fulbright Schol., 1950. With Arthur Young, Clarkson, Gordon & Co., Chartered Accountants and Management Consultants, Toronto and Montreal, 1951-62 (Manager, 1957; Partner, 1961); Sen. Lectr in Accountancy, Victoria Univ. of Wellington, NZ, 1962-65; Prof. of Accountancy, 1965-67; Prof. and Head of Dept of Accounting and Finance, Univ. of Edinburgh, 1967-71. Hon. Treas., NZ Inst. of Internat. Affairs, 1963-65; Member: Govt Cttee on Taxation, NZ, 1967; Bd of Research and Pubn, NZ Soc. of Accountants, 1964-67; Jt Standing Cttee on Degree Studies and Accounting Profession (UK), 1967-72 (Exec. Cttee, 1969-72); UK Adv. Bd of Accountancy Educn, 1969-72. Advr, HM Treasury, 1971-76 (resigned). Mem. various editorial bds in UK, USA, Germany and Australia. Chm., Brit.

Accounting and Finance Assoc., 1968-71; Member: Steering Cttee, Long-Range Enquiry into Accounting Educn, 1971-; ASSC Working Party on scope and aims of Financial Accounts, 1974-75; ICA Research Bd, 1982-. Visiting Professor, various univs in Europe, Africa, N America, Japan and Australasia; AAA Distinguished Internat. Vis. Lectr, USA, 1977; ASA Endowed Lectr, Univ. of Sydney, 1966 and 1979; Distinguished Vis. Prof., La Trobe Univ., Melbourne, 1982. Mem. Council, Lancaster Univ., 1981-. *Publications:* The Elements of Consolidation Accounting, 1965; Looking at Balance Sheets, 1967; (with C. I. Marley) Accounting Principles and the City Code: the case for reform, 1970; Corporate Financial Reporting, 1972; (jtly) The Corporate Report, 1975; (with M. Moonitz) International Auditing Standards, 1978; The Future of Accounting and Auditing Standards, 1979; Corporate Reporting: Its Future Evolution, 1980; (with Sir Ronald Leach) British Accountancy Standards: the first ten years, 1981; Notable Financial Causes Célèbres, 1981; articles and papers in professional and academic jls in several countries, also papers to World Congresses of Accountants. *Recreation:* tormenting dinosaurs. *Address:* Roxburghe House, Haverbreaks, Lancaster. *T:* Lancaster 32056; International Centre for Research in Accounting, Gillow House, Bailrigg, Lancaster. *T:* Lancaster 65201. *Clubs:* United Oxford & Cambridge University; Lancaster Golf and Country (Lancaster).

STAMP, Rt. Hon. Sir (Edward) Blanshard, PC 1971; Kt 1964; a Lord Justice of Appeal, 1971-78; *b* 21 March 1905; *s* of late Alfred Edward Stamp, CB, and Edith Florence Guthrie; *m* 1st, 1934, Mildred Evelyn (*d* 1971), *d* of John Marcus Poer O'Shee; no *c* ; 2nd, 1973, Mrs Pamela Joan Peters (separated 1975). *Educ:* Gresham's Sch., Holt; Trinity Coll., Cambridge. Called to Bar, Inner Temple, 1929; Bencher of Lincoln's Inn, 1956. Served War of 1939-45 as civilian attached General Staff, War Office. Junior Counsel to Commissioners of Inland Revenue (Chancery), 1954; Junior Counsel to Treasury (Chancery), 1960-64; a Judge of the High Court of Justice, Chancery Div., 1964-71. Mem., Restrictive Practices Court, 1970-71. *Recreations:* walking, travelling. *Address:* 30 Hanover House, St John's Wood High Street, NW8 7DY. *T:* 01-722 1855. *Clubs:* United Oxford & Cambridge University, Garrick.

STAMP, Hon. Maxwell; see Stamp, Hon. A. M.

STAMPER, John Trevor, MA, FEng, FRAeS; Corporate Technical Director, British Aerospace, since 1977; *b* 12 Oct. 1926; *s* of late Col Horace John Stamper and Clara Jane (née Collin); *m* 1950, Cynthia Joan Parsons; two *s* one *d.* *Educ:* Loughborough Grammar Sch.; Jesus Coll., Cambridge (MA 1951). FRAeS 1965; CEng 1966; Fellow, Fellowship of Engrg, 1977. Blackburn Aircraft Ltd: Post-grad. apprenticeship, 1947; Dep. Head of Aerodynamics, 1955; Head of Structures, 1956; Flight Test Manager, 1960; Chief Designer (Buccaneer), 1961; Dir and Chief Designer, 1963; Hawker Siddeley Aviation Ltd (following merger): Exec. Dir Design (Military), 1966; Exec. Dir and Dep. Chief Engr (Civil), 1968; Tech. Dir, 1968-77. Member: Council, RAeS, 1971-77, 1978- (Pres., 1981-82); Tech. Bd, SBAC, 1966- (Chm., 1972-74); Council, SBAC, 1981-; Council, Aircraft Res. Assoc., 1966- (Chm., 1976-78); Aeronautical Res. Council, 1971-74; Air Warfare Adv. Bd, Defence Scientific Adv. Council, 1973-; Noise Adv. Council, 1975-78; Comité Technique et Industriel, Assoc. Européenne des Constructeurs de Matériel Aerospatial, 1971-81 (Chm., 1974-81); Airworthiness Requirements Bd, CAA, 1976-78. Hodgeson Prize, RAeS, 1975; British Gold Medal for Aeronautics, RAeS, 1976. *Publications:* (contrib.) The Future of Aeronautics, 1970; Air Power in the Next Generation, 1979; papers in Jl RAeS. *Recreations:* sailing, photography. *Address:* 8 Brendon Drive, Esher, Surrey KT10 9EQ. *T:* Esher 66009.

STANAGE, Rt. Rev. Thomas Shaun; see Bloemfontein, Bishop of.

STANBRIDGE, Air Vice-Marshal Sir Brian (Gerald Tivy), KCVO 1979 (MVO 1958); CBE 1974; AFC 1952; Director-General, Air Transport Users' Committee, since 1979; *b* 6 July 1924; *s* of late Gerald Edward and Violet Georgina Stanbridge; *m* 1949, Kathleen Diana Hayes, Cheltenham; two *d.* *Educ:* Thurlestone Coll., Dartmouth. Served War: RAFVR, 1942; commnd, 1944; No 31 Sqdn (SE Asia), 1944-46; No 47 Sqdn, 1947-49; 2FTS/CFS, 1950-52; British Services Mission to Burma, 1952-54; The Queen's Flight (personal pilot and flying instructor to Duke of Edinburgh), 1954-58; Naval Staff Coll., 1958; PSO to AOC-in-C Coastal Comd, 1958-59; W/Cdr, Flying, RAF St Mawgan, 1960-62; jssc, 1962; RAFDS, Army Staff Coll., Camberley, 1962-63; Gp Captain on staff of NATO Standing Gp, Washington, DC, 1963-66; RAF Dir, Jt Anti-Submarine Sch., Londonderry, and Sen. RAF Officer, NI, 1966-68; Gp Captain Ops, HQ Coastal Comd, 1968-70; IDC, 1970; Air Cdre, 1970; Sec., Chiefs of Staff Cttee, MoD, 1971-73; Dep. Comdt, RAF Staff Coll., Bracknell, 1973-75; ADC to the Queen, 1973-75; Air Vice-Marshal, 1975; Defence Services Sec., MoD, 1975-79; retired 1979. Vice Pres., RAF Gliding and Soaring Assoc. *Address:* c/o National Westminster Bank Ltd, 13 Bridge Street, Pinner, Mddx. *Club:* Royal Air Force.

STANBRIDGE, Ven. Leslie Cyril; Archdeacon of York since 1972; *b* 19 May 1920. *Educ:* Bromley County Grammar Sch., Kent; St John's Coll., Durham Univ. (MA, DipTheol). Asst Curate of Erith Parish Church, Kent, 1949-51; Tutor and Chaplain, St John's Coll., Durham, 1951-55; Vicar of St Martin's, Hull, 1955-64; Examining Chaplain to the Archbishop of York, 1962-; Rector of Cottingham, Yorks, 1964-72; Canon of York, 1968-; Rural Dean of

Kingston-upon-Hull, 1970–72. *Recreations:* fell walking, cycling. *Address:* 14 St George's Place, York YO2 2DR. *T:* York 23775.

STANBRIDGE, Air Vice-Marshal (retired) Reginald Horace, CB 1956; OBE 1944; MRCS, LRCP, DPM, DIH; *b* 24 Nov. 1897; *s* of Horace John Stanbridge; *m* 1945, Inez Valerie, *d* of Arthur Holland; one *s. Educ:* Eastbourne; St Mary Coll., London Univ.; London Hospital Medical College. Served War, 1915–18, Lieut RGA, and RFC. Principal Medical Officer in following RAF Commands: Aden, 1938–41; Transport, 1948–49; Bomber, 1950–53; KHP, 1952, QHP, 1952–56; Principal Medical Officer, Middle East Air Force, 1953–56; retired, 1956. BoT later CAA Med. Dept, 1966–78. Mem., Gray's Inn. Liveryman, Soc. of Apothecaries; Freeman, City of London. CStJ 1952. *Publications:* various articles in The Lancet, RAF Quarterly, Wine and Food. *Recreations:* sailing, tennis. *Address:* The Dial House, Birdshill Road, Oxshott, Surrey. *T:* Oxshott 2175. *Club:* Royal Air Force.

STANBROOK, Ivor Robert; MP (C) Bromley, Orpington, since 1974 (Orpington, 1970–74); Barrister-at-Law; *b* 13 Jan. 1924; *y s* of Arthur William and Lilian Stanbrook; *m* 1946, Joan (*née* Clement); two *s. Educ:* state schools and London and Oxford Universities. Served RAF, 1942–46. Colonial Administrative Service, Nigeria, 1950–60: Asst Sec., Council of Ministers, Lagos, 1956; Dist Officer, N Region, 1957–60. Called to the Bar, Inner Temple, 1960; practising barrister, 1960–; Partner, Stanbrook & Hooper, European Law Office, Brussels, 1980–. *Publications:* Extradition—the Law and Practice, 1979; British Nationality—the New Law, 1981. *Address:* 6 Sevenoaks Road, Orpington, Kent. *T:* Orpington 20347; 42 rue du Taciturne, Brussels 1040, Belgium. *T:* 230 5059. *Club:* Carlton.

STANBURY, Richard Vivian Macaulay; HM Diplomatic Service, retired; *b* 5 Feb. 1916; *s* of late Gilbert Vivian Stanbury and Doris Marguerite (*née* Smythe); *m* 1953, Geraldine Anne, *d* of late R. F. W. Grant and of Winifred Helen Grant; one *s* one *d. Educ:* Shrewsbury Sch. (exhibr, 1st cl Hons in Classical Tripos); Magdalene Coll., Cambridge (exhibnr). Sudan Political Service, 1937–50 (District Comr in 12 districts, and Magistrate); HM Foreign (subseq. Diplomatic) Service, 1951–71: 2nd Sec., Cairo, 1951; FO 1954; Bahrain, Persian Gulf, 1956; FO 1959; Counsellor, Buenos Aires, 1968. *Recreations:* tennis, golf, and watching cricket (played for Somerset); trying to avoid playing bridge. *Address:* Shepherds House, Peasmarsh, near Rye, East Sussex. *Clubs:* Naval & Military; Hawks (Cambridge); Rye Golf; Hurlingham (Buenos Aires).

STANBURY, Prof. Sydney William, MD, FRCP; Professor of Medicine, University of Manchester, since 1965; *b* 21 April 1919; *s* of F. A. W. Stanbury and A. B. Stanbury (*née* Rowe); *m* 1943, Helen, *d* of Harry and Patty Jackson; one *s* four *d. Educ:* Hulme Grammar Sch., Oldham; Manchester Univ. MB, ChB (1st Cl. Hons) 1942; MD (Gold Medal) 1948; MRCP 1947, FRCP 1958. Served RAMC, Burma and India, 1944–47. Beit Meml Res. Fellow, 1948–51; Rockefeller Travelling Fellow, 1951–52; Registrar, Lectr and Reader, Dept of Medicine, Manchester Royal Infirmary, 1947–65; Consultant Phys., United Manchester Hosps, 1959–; Dir, Metabolic Ward, Manch. Royal Inf., 1963–. Member: Assoc. of Physicians; Medical Res. Soc.; Bone and Tooth Soc. Visiting Professor: John Howard Means, Massachusetts Gen. Hosp., Boston, 1958; Henry M. Winans, Univ. of Texas, Dallas, 1958; W. T. Connoll, Queen's Univ., Kingston, Ont, 1978; Weild Lectr, RCP and S, Glasgow, 1958; Vis. Lectr: Univ. of Washington, Mayo Clinic, etc. *Publications:* contrib. European and American med. books and jls on: renal function, electrolyte metabolism, metabolic bone disease and vitamin D metabolism. *Recreation:* gardening. *Address:* Department of Medicine, Royal Infirmary, Manchester M13 9WL; Hey Tor, Leicester Road, Hale, Cheshire. *T:* 061-928 5247.

STANCLIFFE, Very Rev. David Staffurth; Provost of Portsmouth, since 1982; *b* 1 Oct. 1942; *s* of Very Rev. Michael Staffurth Stancliffe, *qv*; *m* 1965, Sarah Loveday Smith; one *s* two *d. Educ:* Westminster School; Trinity College, Oxford (MA); Cuddesdon Theological College. Assistant Curate, St Bartholomew's, Armley, Leeds, 1967–70; Chaplain to Clifton Coll., Bristol, 1970–77; Canon Residentiary of Portsmouth Cathedral, Diocesan Director of Ordinands and Lay Ministry Adviser, 1977–82. *Recreations:* old music, Italy. *Address:* Provost's House, Pembroke Road, Portsmouth PO1 2NS. *T:* Portsmouth 824400.

STANCLIFFE, Very Rev. Michael Staffurth, MA; Dean of Winchester, since 1969; *b* 8 April 1916; *s* of late Rev. Canon Harold Emmet Stancliffe, Lincoln; *m* 1940, Barbara Elizabeth, *yr d* of late Rev. Canon Tissington Tatlow; two *s* one *d. Educ:* Haileybury; Trinity Coll., Oxford. Curate of St James, Southbroom, Devizes, 1940–43; priest-in-charge, Ramsbury, 1943–44; curate of Cirencester and priest-in-charge of Holy Trinity, Watermoor, 1944–49; Chaplain and Master, Westminster School, 1949–57; Canon of Westminster and Rector of St Margaret's, Westminster, 1957–69; Speaker's Chaplain, 1961–69; Preacher to Lincoln's Inn, 1954–57. Mem., General Synod 1970–80; Chm., Council for Places of Worship, 1972–75; Mem. Cathedrals Advisory Commn for England, 1981–. Fellow, Winchester Coll., 1973. *Publication:* contrib. to A House of Kings, 1966. *Address:* The Deanery, Winchester, Hants.
See also Very Rev. D. S. Stancliffe.

STANDARD, Prof. Sir Kenneth (Livingstone), Kt 1982; CD 1976; MD; Professor, since 1968, and Head of Department of Social and Preventive Medicine, since 1966, University of the West Indies at Mona; *b* 8 Dec. 1920; *m* 1955, Evelyn Francis; one *d. Educ:* UC of West Indies (MB BS); Univ. of Pittsburgh (MPH); Univ. of London (MD). Headmaster, Lynch's Secondary Sch., Barbados, 1940–48; Med. House Officer, UCH of WI, 1956; MO, Nutrition Res., Jamaica, 1957–58; MOH, Barbados, 1958–61; MO, MRC Epidemiol. Res. Unit, Jamaica, 1961–66; Lectr, 1961–65, Sen. Lectr, 1965–68, Dept of Social and Preventive Medicine, Univ. of WI, Jamaica. *Publications:* Manual for Community Health Workers, 1974; Epidemiology and Community Health in Warm Climate Countries, 1976; Four Decades of Advances in Health in the Commonwealth Caribbean, 1979. *Recreations:* reading, poetry, gardening. *Address:* Department of Social and Preventive Medicine, University of the West Indies, Mona, Jamaica. *T:* 092-70773. *Club:* Royal Commonwealth Society.

STANDING, John; see Leon, Sir J. R.

STANDING, Michael Frederick Cecil, CBE 1959; retired as Controller of Programme Organisation (sound), BBC, 1957–70; *b* 28 Feb. 1910; *s* of late Sir Guy Standing, KBE, and of late Lady Standing; *m* 1947, Helen Jean Dawson, widow of Flying Officer Michael Hope Lumley and *d* of late Lt-Comdr Dawson Miller, CBE, RN, retired; one *s* two *d* (one *s* decd). *Educ:* Charterhouse. Baring Brothers & Co. Ltd, 1927–35; BBC, 1935; Director of Outside Broadcasting, 1940–45; Head of Variety, 1945–52; Controller of Sound Entertainment, BBC, 1952–57. *Recreations:* painting, gardening, cricket. *Address:* Trottiscliffe House, near West Malling, Kent. *T:* Fairseat 822293.

STANFIELD, Hon. Robert Lorne, PC (Canada) 1967; QC; MP (Progressive C) Halifax, NS, since 1968 (Colchester-Hants, NS, 1967); Leader of Opposition and National Leader of Progressive Conservative Party of Canada, 1967–76; *b* Truro, NS, 11 April 1914; *s* of late Frank Stanfield, sometime MLA and Lieutenant-Governor of NS, and Sarah (*née* Thomas); *m* 1st, 1940, N. Joyce (*d* 1954), *d* of C. W. Frazee, Vancouver; one *s* three *d*; 2nd, 1957, Mary Margaret (*d* 1977), *d* of late Hon. W. L. Hall, Judge of Supreme Court and formerly Attorney-Gen. of NS; 3rd, 1978, Anne Margaret Austin, *d* of Dr D. Nelson, Henderson, Toronto. *Educ:* Colchester County Academy, Truro; Ashbury Coll., Ottawa; Dalhousie Univ.; Harvard Law Sch. Southam Cup, Ashbury Coll.; BA Political Science and Economics 1936, Governor-General's Gold Medal, Dalhousie Univ.; LLB Harvard, 1939. War of 1939–45: attached Halifax Office of Wartime Prices and Trade Bd as Regional Rentals Officer, later as Enforcement Counsel. Admitted Bar of NS, 1940. Practised law, McInnes and Stanfield, Halifax, 1945–56; KC 1950. President, Nova Scotia Progressive Cons. Assoc., 1947–; Leader, Nova Scotia Progressive Cons. Party, 1948–67; elected to Legislature of NS, 1949, Mem. for Colchester Co.; re-elected Mem., 1953, 1960, 1963, 1967; Premier and Minister of Education, NS, 1956; resigned as Premier of NS, 1967. Ambassador at Large and special representative of Govt of Canada in Middle East, 1979–80. Hon. LLD: University of New Brunswick, 1958; St Dunstan's Univ., PEI, 1964; McGill Univ., PQ, 1967; St Mary's Univ., NS, 1969. Anglican. *Address:* 136 Acacia Avenue, Rockcliffe Park, Ottawa, Ontario K1M 0R1, Canada.

STANFORD, Bedell; see Stanford, W. B.

STANFORD, Vice-Adm. Peter Maxwell, MVO 1970; Vice Chief of Naval Staff, since 1982; *b* 11 July 1929; *s* of late Brig. Henry Morrant Stanford, CBE, MC, and of Edith Hamilton Stanford; *m* 1957, Helen Ann Lingard; one *s* two *d. Educ:* Britannia Royal Naval College. Midshipman, W Indies Sqdn, 1947–48; HMS Kenya, Korea, 1950–51; HMS Welfare, 1952–54; French Interpreter, 1954; HMS Camberford, 1954–56; Long Signals Course, 1956–57; Staff of C-in-C Mediterranean, 1957–58; Signal Officer, 3rd Destroyer Sqdn, 1958–59; HM Signal Sch., 1960–62; i/c HMS Grafton, 1962–63; Signal Div., Naval Staff, 1963–65; i/c HMS Brighton, 1966–67; HM Signal Sch., 1967–68; HM Yacht Britannia, 1969–70; Asst Dir Naval Plans, 1970–72; RCDS 1973; i/c HMS Hermione and Captain (F) 5, 1974–75; Commodore 1975; Sec., Chiefs of Staff Cttee, 1975–78; Flag Officer, Second Flotilla, 1978–80; Asst Chief of Naval Staff (Op. Reg.), 1980–82. *Publications:* various papers for Naval Review. *Recreations:* field sports, ornithology. *Address:* c/o Lloyd's Bank Ltd, Cox's & King's Branch, 6 Pall Mall, SW1Y 5NH. *Club:* Flyfishers'.

STANFORD, (William) Bedell, MA, LittD; Regius Professor of Greek in University of Dublin, 1940–80, Pro-Chancellor, since 1977; Fellow of Trinity College, Dublin, 1934, Senior Fellow, 1962, Emeritus Fellow, 1980; Tutor, 1938–54; Public Orator, 1970–71 (Deputy Public Orator, 1958–60); Senior Master, Non-regent, 1960–62; *b* 1910; *s* of Rev. Bedell Stanford, then Rector of Trinity Church, Belfast, and Susan Stanford; *m* 1935, Dorothy Isobel Wright; two *s* two *d. Educ:* Bishop Foy Sch., Waterford; Trinity Coll., Dublin (Scholar). Formerly External Examiner in Greek for National Univ., Queen's Univ., University of Wales, University of Leeds and Royal Colleges of Physicians and Surgeons, Ireland. MRIA. Sather Professor of Classical Literature, University of California, Berkeley, 1966; Visiting Prof., McGill Univ., Montreal, 1968, Wayne State Univ., 1971, Princeton Univ., 1974, Texas Univ., 1977, Vassar Coll., 1980. Has lectured on over 40 other campuses in North America. Editor of Hermathena, 1942–62. Rep. of Dublin Univ. in the Irish Senate, 1948–69. Irish Rep., Council of Europe, Strasbourg, 1951, European Parliamentary Conf., Vienna, 1956 and Inter-parliamentary Conf., Warsaw, 1959. Member Irish Radio Advisory Council until 1952. Governor, Erasmus Smith's Sch.; Mem., General Synod and Dublin Diocesan Synod of

Church of Ireland and of Episcopal Electoral Coll. for Southern Province; Sec., Appointments Cttee, TCD, 1936-37, Hon. Sec., TCD Assoc., 1950-55. Mem. Council, Hellenic Soc., 1965-68; Pres., Birmingham Branch, Classical Assoc., 1968; Vice-Pres. RIA, 1969; Chairman: Irish Nat. Cttee for Greek and Latin Studies, 1968-72; Council of Dublin Inst. for Advanced Studies, 1973-80. Higher Comdr, Order of Phoenix, Greece, 1980. *Publications:* Greek Metaphor, 1936; Ambiguity in Greek Literature, 1939; Livy XXIV edited for schools, 1942; Aeschylus in His Style, 1942; Homer's Odyssey, edited, 1947-48 (2nd edn, 1961-62); The Ulysses Theme, 1954 (2nd edn, 1963); Aristophanes' Frogs, edited, 1957 (2nd edn, 1963); Sophocles' Ajax, edited, 1963; The Sound of Greek, 1967; (with R. B. McDowell) Mahaffy, 1971; (with J. V. Luce) The Quest for Ulysses, 1975; (with Robert Fagles) Aeschylus: The Oresteia, 1976; Ireland and the Classical Tradition, 1976; Enemies of Poetry, 1980; various shorter publications on literary, linguistic, ecclesiastical and historical subjects. *Address:* 25 Trinity College, Dublin; 2 Mount Salus, Dalkey, Co. Dublin. *T:* Dublin 859120. *Club:* Royal Irish Yacht (Dun Laoghaire).

STANFORD-TUCK, Wing Commander Robert Roland, DSO 1940; DFC (2 bars); *b* 1 July 1916; *s* of Stanley Lewis Tuck and Ethel Constance Tuck; *m* 1945; two *s. Educ:* St Dunstan's Preparatory School and College, Reading. Left school, 1932, and went to sea as a cadet with Lamport and Holt; joined Royal Air Force, Sept. 1935; posted to No 65 Fighter Sqdn, Aug. 1936, and served with them until outbreak of war; posted to 92 (F) Sqdn, and went through air fighting at Dunkirk, shooting down 8 enemy aircraft (DFC); posted to Comd No 257 Burma Fighter Sqdn, Sept. 1940, till July 1941, when given command of Wing; comd Duxford and Biggin Hill Wings; prisoner 1942, escaped 1945. Record to end July 1941: 27 confirmed victories, 8 probably destroyed, 6 damaged; wounded twice, baled out 4 times. Retired list, 1948. *Relevant publication:* Fly For Your Life (by L. Forrester). *Recreations:* fencing, riding, shooting. *Address:* 2 Whitehall, Sandwich Bay, Kent.

STANHOPE, family name of Earl of Harrington.

STANIER, Brigadier Sir Alexander Beville Gibbons, 2nd Bt, *cr* 1917; DSO 1940 (and Bar, 1945); MC; DL, JP, CStJ; *b* 31 Jan. 1899; *s* of 1st Bt, and Constance (*d* 1948), *d* of late Rev. B. Gibbons; *S* father, 1921; *m* 1927, Dorothy Gladys (*d* 1973), *e d* of late Brig.-Gen. Alfred Douglas Miller, CBE, DSO; one *s* one *d. Educ:* Eton; RMC, Sandhurst. Served European War in France, 1918 (MC); served War of 1939-45, in France 1940 and 1944 (despatches, DSO and Bar, American Silver Star, Comdr Order of Leopold of Belgium with palm, Belgian Croix de Guerre with palm). Adjutant 1st Bn Welsh Guards, 1923-26; Military Secretary, Gibraltar, 1927-30; commanded 2nd Battalion Welsh Guards, 1939-40; temp. Brigadier, 1940-45; Lieut.-Colonel Commanding Welsh Guards, 1945-48. CC Salop, 1950-58. High Sheriff of Shropshire, 1951. County President of the St John Ambulance Bde, 1950-60. *Heir: s* Beville Douglas Stanier [*b* 20 April 1934; *m* 1963, Shelagh, *er d* of late Major and Mrs J. S. Sinnott, Tetbury, Glos; one *s* two *d*]. *Address:* Hill House, Shotover Park, Wheatley, Oxford. *T:* Wheatley 2996; Park Cottage, Ludford, Ludlow. *T:* Ludlow 2675.

STANIER, Gen. Sir John (Wilfred), GCB 1982 (KCB 1978); MBE 1961; Chief of the General Staff, since 1982; Aide-de-Camp General to the Queen, since 1981; *b* 6 Oct. 1925; *s* of late Harold Allan Stanier and Penelope Rose Stanier (*née* Price); *m* 1955, Cicely Constance Lambert; four *d. Educ:* Marlborough Coll.; Merton Coll., Oxford. MBIM, FRGS. Commd in 7th Queen's Own Hussars, 1946; served in N Italy, Germany and Hong Kong; comd Royal Scots Greys, 1966-68; comd 20th Armd Bde, 1969-70; GOC 1st Div., 1973-75; Comdt, Staff Coll., Camberley, 1975-78; Vice Chief of the General Staff, 1978-80; C-in-C, UKLF, 1981-82. Col, The Royal Scots Dragoon Guards, 1979-; Col Comdt, RAC, 1982-. *Recreations:* hunting, fishing, sailing, talking. *Address:* c/o Coutts & Co., 440 Strand, WC2R 0QS. *Club:* Cavalry and Guards.

STANIFORTH, John Arthur Reginald, CBE 1969; Director: John Brown & Co., Ltd; Constructors John Brown Ltd; John Brown Engineering (Clydebank) Ltd; *b* 19 Sept. 1912; *o s* of Captain Staniforth, MC, Anston House, Anston, Yorks; *m* 1936, Penelope Cecile, *y d* of Maj.-Gen. Sir Henry Freeland; one *s* one *d. Educ:* Marlborough Coll. Joined John Brown Group 1929-. Mem., Export Guarantees Adv. Council, 1971-76, Dep. Chm., 1975-76. Founder Chm., British Chemical Engrg Contractors Assoc., 1965-68. Governor, Bryanston Sch. *Recreations:* golf, fishing. *Address:* Spindlewood, Old Bosham, West Sussex. *T:* Bosham 572401. *Clubs:* MCC; Goodwood Golf.

STANISZEWSKI, Stefan; 1st and 2nd Class, Cross of Poland's Rebirth (Polonia Restituta) Order; Ambassador of the Polish People's Republic to the Court of St James's, since 1981; *b* 11 Feb. 1931; *s* of Andrzej and Katarzyna Staniszewski; *m* 1953, Wanda Szuszkiewicz; one *d. Educ:* Warsaw Univ. (BA Philosophy); Jagiellonian Univ. (BA Pol. Sciences). Active in students' and social organizations at university; Chm., Polish Youth Union's Jagiellonian Univ. Bd; official, Warsaw Cttee of Polish United Workers' Party, 1951-58; Head of Editorial Dept, ISKRY state publishing firm, 1958-60; entered foreign service, 1960; Minister's Cabinet, Min. of Foreign Affairs, 1960-63; successively 2nd Sec., 1st Sec. and Counsellor, Polish Embassy, Paris, 1963-69; Head of West European Dept and Mem. of Minister's Council, Min. of Foreign Affairs, 1969-72; Ambassador to Sweden, 1972-77; Head of Press, Cultural and Scientific Co-operation Dept, Min. of Foreign Affairs, 1977-81.

Commander, Légion d'Honneur, 1972; Order of the Star of the North, Sweden, 1977; Commander, Order of the Aztec Eagle, Mexico, 1979. *Recreations:* swimming, modern painting. *Address:* Embassy of the Polish People's Republic, 47 Portland Place, W1N 3AG. *T:* 01-580 4324. *Club:* Hurlingham.

STANLEY, family name of Earl of Derby and Baron Stanley of Alderley.

STANLEY OF ALDERLEY, 8th Baron (UK) *cr* 1839; **Thomas Henry Oliver Stanley;** Bt 1660; Baron Sheffield (Ire), 1783; Baron Eddisbury, 1848; Captain (retired), Coldstream Guards; Tenant Farmer of New College, Oxford, since 1954; *b* 28 Sept. 1927; *s* of Lt-Col The Hon. Oliver Hugh Stanley, DSO, JP (3rd *s* of 4th Baron) (*d* 1952), and Lady Kathleen Stanley (*d* 1977), *e d* of 5th Marquess of Bath; *S* cousin (known as Baron Sheffield), 1971; *m* 1955, Jane Barrett, *d* of Ernest George Hartley; three *s* one *d. Educ:* Wellington College, Berks. Coldstream Guards, 1945-52; Guards Parachute Battalion and Independent Company, 1947-50; Northamptonshire Institute of Agriculture, 1952-53. Director: Thames Valley Cereals, 1976- (Chm., 1979-); Group Cereal Services, 1978-. Cttee of Management, RNLI, 1981-. Governor, St Edward's Sch., Oxford, 1979-. *Recreations:* sailing, skiing, fishing. *Heir: e s* Hon. Richard Oliver Stanley, BSc, *b* 24 April 1956. *Address:* Rectory Farm, Stanton St John, Oxford. *T:* Stanton St John 214; Trysglwyn Fawr, Amlwch, Anglesey. *T:* Amlwch 830364. *Club:* Farmers'.

STANLEY, Brian Taylor, MA; *b* 1907; *s* of T. T. and Ada A. Stanley, Birmingham; *m* 1938, Audrey, *d* of H. and E. C. Topsfield, Sunbury on Thames; one *s* one *d. Educ:* King Edward's Sch., Birmingham; Christ Church, Oxford; London Day Trng Coll., Columbia Univ., New York; Pädagogische Akademie, Hanover. Teacher under the Warwickshire County Council and Resident Tutor, Fircroft Working Men's College, 1931; Lecturer in Education, Manchester University, 1932; Professor of Education, King's College, Newcastle upon Tyne, 1936-48; Director Institute of Education: Univ. of Durham, 1948-63, Univ. of Newcastle upon Tyne, 1963-72; In-Service Trng Adviser, St Mary's Coll. of Educn, Newcastle upon Tyne, 1972-81. Order of St Olav, Norway, 1972. *Publications:* The Education of Junior Citizens, 1945; contributions to various educational jls, at home and abroad. *Address:* 5 Corchester Avenue, Corbridge, Northumberland. *T:* Corbridge 2075.

STANLEY, Charles Orr, CBE 1945 (OBE 1943); Hon. President, Sunbeam Wolsey Ltd; Director: Arts Theatre Trust; Stanley Foundation Ltd; Orr Investments Ltd; *b* 15 April 1899; *s* of John and Louisa A. Stanley; *m* 1st, 1924, Elsie Florence Gibbs; one *s* ; 2nd, 1934, Velma Dardis Price (*d* 1970); 3rd, 1971, Lorna Katherine Sheppard (*d* 1977). *Educ:* Bishop Foy School, Waterford; City and Guilds, Finsbury. Served European War, RFC, 1917-18; Civil Engineer, 1922. Chm., Radio Industry Council, 1962-65; Pres., British Radio Equipment Manufrs Assoc., 1962-64. Hon. Pres., Pye of Cambridge Ltd. Hon. LLD Trinity College, Dublin, 1960. FCGI 1961. *Address:* Sainsfoins, Little Shelford, Cambs CB2 5EU; Lisselan, Clonakilty, County Cork, Ireland. *T:* Bandon 43699. *Clubs:* Royal Automobile; Royal Thames Yacht; Royal Cork Yacht.

STANLEY, Prof. Eric Gerald, MA (Oxford and Yale); PhD (Birmingham); Rawlinson and Bosworth Professor of Anglo-Saxon in the University of Oxford, since Jan. 1977; *b* 19 Oct. 1923; *m* 1959, Mary Bateman, MD, FRCP; one *d. Educ:* Queen Elizabeth's Grammar Sch., Blackburn; University Coll., Oxford. Lectr in Eng. Lang. and Lit., Birmingham Univ., 1951-62; Reader in Eng. Lang. and Lit., 1962-64, Prof. of English, 1964-75, Univ. of London at QMC; Prof. of English, Yale Univ., 1975-76. Co-Editor, Notes and Queries, 1963-. Member: Mediaeval Acad. of America, 1975-; Connecticut Acad. of Arts and Scis, 1976-. *Publications:* academic articles and books. *Recreation:* photography. *Address:* Pembroke College, Oxford.

STANLEY, Henry Sydney Herbert Cloete, CMG 1968; HM Diplomatic Service, retired; British High Commissioner to Trinidad and Tobago and (non-resident) to Grenada, 1977-80; *b* 5 March 1920; *er s* of late Sir Herbert Stanley, GCMG and Reniera (*née* Cloete), DBE; *m* 1941, Margaret, *d* of late Professor H. B. Dixon, CBE, FRS; three *s. Educ:* Eton; Balliol College, Oxford. Served with King's Royal Rifle Corps, 1940-46 (Capt.); N-W Europe, 1944-46, also HQ, CCG. Appointed to Commonwealth Relations Office, 1947. Served in Pakistan, 1950-52; Swaziland and South Africa, 1954-57; USA, 1959-61; Tanganyika, 1961-63; Kenya, 1963-65; Inspector, HM Diplomatic Service, 1966-68; Chief Inspector, 1968-70; High Comr, Ghana, 1970-75; Asst Under Sec. of State, FCO, 1975-77; High Comr for the New Hebrides (non-resident), 1976-77. *Address:* Silver How, 7 Harberton Mead, Oxford OX3 0DB.

STANLEY, Dr Herbert Muggleton, FRS 1966; *b* Stratford-upon-Avon, 20 July 1903; *m* 1930, Marjorie Mary (*née* Johnson); two *s* two *d. Educ:* King Edward VI Grammar School, Stratford-on-Avon; Birmingham University (1919-29). BSc 1923; MSc 1925; PhD 1930, FRIC; Mem. Council, Royal Soc., 1968. *Publications:* articles in numerous journals, including Jl Chem. Soc., Soc. Chem. Ind. *Recreations:* archæology, gardening. *Address:* West Halse, Bow, Crediton, Devon. *T:* Bow 262.

STANLEY, John Paul; MP (C) Tonbridge and Malling since Feb. 1974; Minister of State (Minister for Housing and Construction), Department of the

Environment, since 1979; *b* 19 Jan. 1942; *s* of H. Stanley; *m* 1968, Susan Elizabeth Giles; one *s* one *d*. *Educ:* Repton Sch.; Lincoln Coll., Oxford (MA). Conservative Research Dept with responsibility for Housing, 1967-68; Research Associate, Internat. Inst. for Strategic Studies, 1968-69; Rio Tinto-Zinc Corp. Ltd, 1969-74. Mem. Parly Select Cttee on Nationalised Industries, 1974; PPS to Rt Hon. Margaret Thatcher, 1976-79. *Publication:* (jtly) The International Trade in Arms, 1972. *Recreations:* music and the arts, sailing. *Address:* House of Commons, SW1A 0AA. *Club:* Leander (Henley-on-Thames).

STANLEY, Michael Charles, MBE 1945; Director of The Proprietors of Hay's Wharf Ltd, and various subsidiary companies, 1955-80; *b* 11 Aug. 1921; *s* of late Col Rt Hon. O. F. G. Stanley, PC, MC, MP, and Lady Maureen Stanley (*née* Vane-Tempest-Stewart); *m* 1951, Ailleen Fortune Hugh Smith, *d* of Owen Hugh Smith, Old Hall, Langham, Rutland; two *s*. *Educ:* Eton; Trinity College, Cambridge. Served 1939-46 with Royal Signals (Capt. 1943); N Africa, Sicily and Italy with 78th Infantry Div. Trinity, 1946-49 (Nat. Science and Engineering, MA). Served Engineering Apprenticeship with Metropolitan Vickers Electrical Co. Ltd, 1949-52. CEng 1966; MIEE 1966 (AMIEE 1952). Mem. Court, Lancaster University, 1980-. High Sheriff for Westmorland, 1959; Westmorland County Councillor, 1961-74; Vice-Lieutenant of Westmorland, 1965-74; DL Westmorland, 1964-74, Cumbria, 1974; High Sheriff, Cumbria, 1975. Hon. Col 33rd Signal Regt (V), 1981. *Recreations:* idleness, walking, wine. *Address:* Halecat, Witherslack, Grange-over-Sands, Cumbria LA11 6RU. *T:* Witherslack 229. *Clubs:* White's, Beefsteak, Brooks's; St James's (Manchester); Puffins (Edinburgh).
See also K. E. H. Dugdale.

STANLEY, Hon. Pamela Margaret; *b* 6 Sept. 1909; *d* of 5th Lord Stanley of Alderley and Margaret Evans Gordon; *m* 1941, Sir David Cunynghame, 11th Bt (*d* 1978); three *s*. *Educ:* Switzerland; France. Studied at Webber-Douglas School of Acting and Singing; first appearance Lyric, Hammersmith, 1932, in Derby Day; six months at Oxford Repertory, 1933; with Martin Harvey in The Bells, Savoy, 1933; Sydney Carroll's Open Air Theatre, 1934; Wendy in Peter Pan, 1934; Queen Victoria in Victoria Regina, Gate Theatre, 1935; went to USA with Leslie Howard in Hamlet, 1936; Queen Victoria in Victoria Regina, Lyric, 1937-38; Open Air Theatre, 1938; Queen Victoria in The Queen's Highland Servant, Savoy, 1968. *Address:* 83 Clarendon Street, Leamington Spa, Warwickshire.
See also Sir A. D. F. Cunynghame, Bt.

STANLEY, Hon. Richard Oliver; *b* 29 Jan. 1920; 2nd *s* of Colonel Rt Hon. Lord Stanley, PC, MC (*d* 1938), and Sibyl Louise Beatrix Cadogan (*d* 1969), *e d* of Henry Arthur, late Viscount Chelsea, and Lady Meux; *g s* of 17th Earl of Derby, KG, PC, GCB, GCVO; *b* and *heir-pres* to 18th Earl of Derby, *qv*; *m* 1st, 1965, Susan (*d*'1976), *o d* of Sir John Aubrey-Fletcher, *qv*; 2nd, 1979, Mrs Mary Harrison. *Educ:* Eton. Served War of 1939-45; 2nd Lieutenant, Grenadier Guards, 1940, later Captain. Joined staff of Conservative Central Office after the war. Parliamentary Private Secretary to First Lord of the Admiralty, 1951-55. MP (C) N Fylde Div. of Lancashire, 1950-66, retired. Joint Treasurer, Conservative Party, 1962-66. Mem., Gaming Bd, 1968-73. *Address:* 26a North Audley Street, W.1. *T:* 01-493 0813; New England House, Newmarket, Suffolk. *T:* Cambridge 811394.

STANLEY-CLARKE, Brig. Arthur Christopher Lancelot, CBE 1940; DSO 1918; *b* 1886; *s* of late Ronald Stanley Clarke and late Mabel Octavia Shadwell; *m* 1931, Olive, 3rd *d* of late Thomas Carroll-Leahy of Woodfort, Mallow, Co. Cork; no *c*. *Educ:* Winchester; Oxford. Capt. OUAFC, 1908-9; gazetted The Cameronians (Scottish Rifles), 1909; commanded 1st Royal Scots Fusiliers, 1931-34; Assist Comdt and Chief Instructor, Netheravon Wing, Small Arms School, 1934-37, Comdr 154th (Argyll and Sutherland) Infantry Brigade TA, 1937; Commander Lothian and Border District, 1941-44; retired pay, 1944. Served European War, 1914-18 (despatches, DSO, and bar, Legion of Honour, Croix de Guerre); War of 1939-45 (CBE). *Address:* Shiel, Baily, Co. Dublin, Ireland.

STANLEY PRICE, Peter, QC 1956; **His Honour Judge Stanley Price;** a Circuit Judge (formerly a Judge of the Central Criminal Court), since 1969; President, National Reference Tribunal for the Coal Mining Industry, since 1979; Judge of the Chancery Court of York, since 1967; *b* 27 Nov. 1911; *s* of late Herbert Stanley Price and late Gertrude Rangeley S. P. (*née* Wightman); *m* 1st, 1946, Harriett Ella Theresa (*d* 1948), *o d* of late Rev. R. E. Pownall; two *s*; 2nd, 1950, Margaret Jane, *o d* of late Samuel Milkins (she *m* 1937, William Hebditch, RAF; he *d* 1941); one *d* one step *s*. *Educ:* Cheltenham; Exeter College, Oxford (1st cl. Final Hons Sch. of Jurisprudence, 1933). Barrister, Inner Temple, 1936, Master of the Bench, 1963. Served War of 1939-45, Lieut (S) RNVR. Recorder of Pontefract, 1954, of York, 1955, of Kingston-upon-Hull, 1958, of Sheffield, 1965-69. Dep. Chm., N Riding QS, 1955-58, 1970-71, Chm., 1958-70; Judge of Appeal, Jersey and Guernsey, 1964-69; Solicitor-General, County Palatine of Durham, 1965-69. Pres., Nat. Reference Tribunal, Officials Conciliation Scheme, 1967-79. *Recreations:* birds and trees; gardening, shooting. *Address:* Church Hill, Great Ouseburn, York. *T:* Green Hammerton 30252. *Clubs:* Brooks's; Yorkshire (York).

STANNARD, John Anthony; barrister; a Recorder of the Crown Court, since 1980; *s* of Anthony Stannard and Joan Stannard (*née* Joslin); *m* 1956, Madeline Betty (*née* Limb); two *d*. *Educ:* Quarry Bank High School, Liverpool; Trinity College, Cambridge. Called to the Bar, Lincoln's Inn, 1956.

Address: Robinswood, Glenrose Road, Woolton, Liverpool. *T:* 051-428 1187. *Club:* Athenæum (Liverpool).

STANNARD, Rt. Rev. Robert William, MA; *b* 20 Oct. 1895; *s* of late Robert John and Fanny Rebecca Stannard; *m* 1922, Muriel Rose Sylvia Knight; one *s* (elder son killed in action April 1945). *Educ:* Westminster; Christ Ch., Oxford; Cuddesdon Theological College. Served army, 1915-19, Lieut Middlesex Regiment. Oxford: Distinction in Lit. Hum., First in Theology, Liddon Student; Ordained, 1922; Curate Bermondsey Parish Church, 1922-24; Curate-in-Charge S Mary's, Putney, 1924-27; Vicar of St James, Barrow-in-Furness, 1927-34; Rural Dean of Dalton, 1934; Rector of Bishopwearmouth (Sunderland), 1934-41; Rural Dean of Sunderland, 1937-41; Archdeacon of Doncaster, 1941-47; Chaplain to the King, 1944-47; Bishop Suffragan of Woolwich, 1947-59; Dean of Rochester, 1959-66. Grand Chaplain, United Grand Lodge of England, 1948-50. Master, Worshipful Co. of Gardeners, 1972-73. *Recreations:* gardening and music. *Address:* Dendron, Reading Road North, Fleet, Hants. *T:* Fleet 4059.

STANSBY, John; Chairman, UIE (UK) Ltd, since 1974 (UK parent company of UIE Shipbuilding (Scotland) Ltd and Hersent Offshore Ltd); Deputy Chairman, H. Pickup Structural Engineering Ltd, since 1982 (Chairman, 1978-81); *b* 2 July 1930; *s* of late Dumon Stansby and Vera Margaret Main; *m* 1966, Anna Maria Kruschewsky; one *d* and one step *s* one step *d*. *Educ:* Oundle; Jesus Coll., Cambridge (Schol., MA). FInstPet, FCIT, FRSA, MInstM. Commissioned, Queen's Own Royal Regt, 1949; Service, 1949-50, Somaliland Scouts. Shell Mex & BP Ltd, 1955-62; AIC Ltd, 1962-66; Rank Organisation, 1966-70; P&OSN Co., 1970-74; Dep. Chm., London Transport Exec., 1978-80. Director: Dumon Stansby & Co. Ltd, 1974; Allied Plant Group plc, 1976; Milton Keynes Shopping Management Co. Ltd, 1976; SAFT (UK) Ltd, 1981; Aeronautical and General Instruments plc, 1982; LaJet Exploration (UK) Ltd, 1982. European Bobsleigh Championship, 1952. *Address:* 19 Brook Green, W6 7BL. *T:* 01-603 0886. *Club:* Travellers'.

STANSFIELD, George Norman, OBE 1980; HM Diplomatic Service; High Commissioner to the Solomon Islands, since 1982; *b* 28 Feb. 1926; *s* of George Stansfield and Martha Alice (*née* Leadbetter); *m* 1947, Elizabeth Margaret Williams. *Educ:* Liscard High Sch. Served War, RAF, 1944-47. Ministries of Food and Supply, 1948-58; Private Sec. to Dir-Gen. of Armament Prodn, 1958-61; CRO, 1961; Second Secretary: Calcutta, 1962-66; Port of Spain, 1966-68; First Secretary: FCO, 1968-71; Singapore, 1971-74; Consul, Durban, 1974-78; FCO, 1978; Counsellor, and Head of Overseas Estate Dept, 1980-82. *Recreations:* sailing, cine-photography. *Address:* c/o Foreign and Commonwealth Office, SW1A 2AH.

STANSFIELD, His Honour James Warden; a Circuit Judge (formerly County Court Judge), 1963-78; *b* 7 April 1906; *s* of James Hampson Stansfield, Sunny Lea, Wilmslow, Cheshire; *m* 1937, Florence Evelyn, *d* of Arthur Harry Holdcroft, Congleton, Cheshire; two *s* one *d*. *Educ:* King's School, Macclesfield; Sidney Sussex College, University of Cambridge. BA 1927; LLB 1928; MA 1935. Called to the Bar, Inner Temple, 1929; practised Northern Circuit. Contested (C) Platting Division of Manchester, 1935. Served War of 1939-45: Royal Air Force, Middle East, and Staff of Judge Advocate-General; formerly RAFVR (Squadron Leader). Chairman: Manchester Licensing Planning Cttee, 1955-63; Manchester Mental Health Review Tribunal, 1962; Warrington Licensed Premises Cttee, 1970. *Recreations:* golf, walking. *Address:* Oak Lea, Victoria Road, Wilmslow, Cheshire. *T:* Wilmslow 523915.

STANSFIELD, Sir Walter, Kt 1979; CBE 1974; MC 1945; QPM 1969; CPM 1959; Chief Constable of Derbyshire, 1967-79; Director of Companies; *b* 15 Feb. 1917; *er s* of Frederick and Annie Georgina Stansfield; *m* 1939, Jennie Margery Biggs; one *d*. *Educ:* Chartres, Eure et Loire, France; Heath Grammar Sch., Halifax. West Riding Constabulary, 1939-42, 1950-56, 1959-64 (Asst Chief Constable, 1962-64). Served War, 1942-46: commnd in RA (Field), 1943; Special Ops Exec., 1943-45. Control Commission (Germany), 1945-46; seconded to: Special Police Corps, Germany, 1946-50; Cyprus Police Force, 1956-59. Chief Constable of Denbighshire, 1964-67. CStJ 1979. Croix de Guerre (France), 1947. *Publication:* (Jt Editor) Moriarty's Police Law, 24th edn, 1981. *Recreations:* music, photography, gardening. *Address:* 82 Park Avenue, Wrexham, Clwyd LL12 7AH. *T:* Wrexham 364072. *Clubs:* Army and Navy, Special Forces.
See also R. A. Fitch.

STANSGATE, Viscountcy of (*cr* 1942, of Stansgate); title disclaimed by 2nd Viscount.

STANTON, Maj.-Gen. Anthony Francis, OBE 1955; *b* 6 Aug. 1915; *s* of Brig.-Gen. F. H. G. Stanton and Hilda Margaret (*née* Parkin); *m* 1943, Elizabeth Mary, *d* of John Reginald Blackett-Ord, Whitfield Hall, Hexham; one *s* two *d*. *Educ:* Eton Coll.; RMA Woolwich. Commissioned RA, 1936. Served in: India, 1936-41; ME, 1941-43; NW Europe, 1944-45; subseq. in Germany, Far East and UK; Imp. Def. Coll., 1962; COS, HQ Northern Comd, 1967-70, retired 1970. Col Comdt, RA, 1972-77. *Recreation:* country sporting pursuits. *Address:* Wooperton Hall, Alnwick, Northumberland. *T:* Wooperton 241. *Club:* Army and Navy.

STANTON, Rev. John Maurice, MA; Rector of Chesham Bois, since 1973; *b* 29 Aug. 1918; *s* of Frederick William Stanton, MInstCE and Maude Lozel (née Cole); m 1947, Helen Winifred (née Bowden); one s two d. Educ: King's School, Rochester (King's Scholar); University College, Oxford (Gunsley Scholar in Science). 2nd Class Hons, Final Hon. Sch. of Nat. Science, 1947; MA 1947. Fellow of Chemical Society, 1947. Commissioned Royal Artillery, 1940, 92nd Field Regt, RA, 1940-43. ISLD, CMF, 1943-46. Assistant Master, Tonbridge School, 1947-59; Headmaster, Blundell's School, Tiverton, Devon, 1959-71; Curate, St Matthew's, Exeter, 1972. Ordained Deacon, 1952; Priest, 1953. *Recreations:* water colour painting (Mem. Royal Water Colour Soc.'s Art Club), gardening. *Address:* The Rectory, Chesham Bois, Amersham, Bucks HP6 5NA.

STANWAY, Rt. Rev. Alfred; President, Australian Christian Literature Society, since 1971; b 9 Sept. 1908; s of Alfred Stanway, Millicent, S Australia, and Rosa Dawson; m 1939, Marjory Dixon Harrison. *Educ:* Melbourne High Sch.; Ridley Coll., Melbourne; Australian Coll. of Theology (ThL (Hons), 1934); Melbourne Teachers Coll. MA (Lamb), 1951. Diocese of Melbourne: Curate of St Albans, 1935-36; Mission of St James and St John, 1936-37; Diocese of Mombasa: Missionary, Giriama District, 1937-44; Principal Kaloleni Sch., 1938-44; Acting Gen. Sec., Victorian Branch, Church Missionary Soc., 1941; Hon. CF, 1942-46; Missionary, Maseno District, 1944-45; Rural Dean of Nyanza, 1945-47; Examining Chaplain to Bishop of Mombasa, 1945-51; Sec. African Council and African Education Board, Diocese of Mombasa, 1948-50; Commissary to Bishop of Mombasa, 1949-51; Archdeacon and Canon of Diocese of Mombasa, 1949-51; Bishop of Central Tanganyika, 1951-71; Dep. Principal, Ridley Coll., Melbourne Univ., 1971-75; Pres., Trinity Episcopal Sch. for Ministry, Pittsburgh, 1975-78. *Recreation:* chess. *Address:* 7 Elm Grove, Mt Waverly, Victoria 3149, Australia.

STANYER, Maj.-Gen. John Turner, CBE 1971 (OBE 1967); b 28 July 1920; s of late Charles T. Stanyer and late Mrs R. H. Stanyer; m 1942, Mary Patricia Pattie; three s four d. *Educ:* Latymer Upper Sch., Hammersmith. Served War, 2/Lieut The Middlesex Regt, 1941; Lieut to Captain, The Middlesex Regt, 1941-47: Iceland, France, Germany, Palestine. Captain, Royal Army Ordnance Corps, 1947; Student, Staff Coll., Camberley, 1951; AA&QMG, UN Force in Cyprus, 1966; Dir of Ordnance Services, BAOR, 1968-71; Commandant, Central Ordnance Depot, Bicester, 1971-73; Comdr, Base Orgn, RAOC, 1973-75, retired. Col Comdt, RAOC, 1977-82. Dir Gen., Supply Co-ordination, MoD, 1975-80. CBIM. *Recreation:* sailing. *Address:* 36 Jack Straws Lane, Headington, Oxford. *T:* Oxford 68757. *Club:* Army and Navy.

STAPLES, Rev. Canon Edward Eric, CBE 1977 (OBE 1973); Chaplain to the Queen, 1973-80; Chaplain to the Anglican congregations in Helsinki and throughout Finland, in Moscow, Leningrad and elsewhere in the Soviet Union, and in Outer Mongolia, 1964-80; Hon. Chaplain, British Embassy: Helsinki, 1967-80, Moscow, 1968-80, Ulan Bator since 1970; Hon. Lecturer, English History, University of Helsinki, 1972-80; Hon. Canon of Gibraltar Cathedral, since 1974; b 15 Nov. 1910; yr s of Christopher Walter Staples and Esther Jane Staples; m 1962, Kate Ethel Thusberg (née Rönngren); two step d. *Educ:* Chichester Theol Coll. (earlier opportunities so misused that it is unwise to name the establishments concerned!). MA, PhD. Niger Company, 1932. Served with RNVR, 1939-46. Ordained 1948. Assistant of Court of Russia Company, 1977, Consul 1978. Life Mem., Finnish-British Soc.; Mem., Anglo-Mongolian Soc. Medal of Univ. of Helsinki, 1980. Kt, Order of the Lion (Finland), 1976; Order of St Vladimir (3rd cl.) (Russian Orthodox Church), 1977. *Recreations:* climbing, cricket (no longer actively), fishing, gardening, historical research. *Address:* Coombe Cottage, Templecombe BA8 0HQ. *T:* Templecombe 70340; Suvisaari, Heinävesi as, Finland. *Clubs:* MCC; Helsinki Cricket (Founder Mem.); Moscow Cricket (Founder Mem.); Ulan Bator Golf (Hon. Life Mem.).

STAPLES, (Hubert Anthony) Justin, CMG 1981; HM Diplomatic Service; Ambassador to Thailand, since 1981; b 14 Nov. 1929; s of late Francis Hammond Staples, formerly ICS, and Catherine Margaret Mary Pownall; m 1962, Susan Angela Collingwood Carter; one s one d. *Educ:* Downside; Oriel Coll., Oxford. Served in RAF 1952-54 (Pilot Officer). Entered Foreign (later Diplomatic) Service, 1954; 3rd Sec., Bangkok, 1955; Foreign Office, 1959; 1st Sec., Berlin (Dep. Political Adviser), 1962; Vientiane, 1965 (acted as Chargé d'Affaires in 1966 and 1967); transf. to FO and seconded to Cabinet Office, 1968; Counsellor, UK Delegn to NATO, Brussels, 1971; Counsellor and Consul-General, Bangkok, 1974 (acted as Chargé d'affaires, 1975 and 1977); Counsellor, Dublin, 1978-81. *Address:* c/o Foreign and Commonwealth Office, SW1. *Clubs:* Travellers'; Kildare Street and University (Dublin); Royal Bangkok Sports (Bangkok).

STAPLES, Sir John (Richard), 14th Bt cr 1628; b 5 April 1906; s of John Molesworth Staples (d 1948) and of Helen Lucy Johnstone, yr d of late Richard Williams Barrington; S kinsman, Sir Robert George Alexander Staples, 13th Bt, 1970; m 1933, Sybella, d of late Dr Charles Henry Wade; two d. *Heir: cousin* Thomas Staples [b 9 Feb. 1905; m 1952, Frances Ann Irvine]. *Address:* Butter Hill House, Dorking, Surrey.

STAPLES, Justin; see Staples, H. A. J.

STAPLETON, Sir Alfred; see Stapleton, Sir H. A.

STAPLETON, Air Vice-Marshal Deryck Cameron, CB 1960; CBE 1948; DFC; AFC; psa; Head of British Aerospace Dynamics Group, Peking, China, since 1979; b 1918; s of John Rouse Stapleton, OBE, Sarnia, Natal; m 1942, Ethleen Joan Clifford, d of late Sir Cuthbert William Whiteside. *Educ:* King Edward VI Sch., Totnes. Joined RAF, 1936; served Transjordan and Palestine (AFC), 1937-39; War of 1939-45 (DFC). Middle East, N Africa, Italy. Asst Sec. (Air), War Cabinet Offices, 1945-46; Secretary, Chiefs of Staff Cttee, Ministry of Defence, 1947-49; OC RAF, Odiham, 1949-51; subsequently, Plans, Fighter Comd HQ; OC, RAF, Oldenburg (Germany); Plans, Bomber Comd HQ, 1957-60; Air Ministry, 1960-62; Dir, Defence Plans, Min. of Defence, 1963-64; AOC No 1 Group, RAF Bomber Command, 1964-66; Comdt, RAF Staff Coll., Bracknell, 1966-68. BAC Area Manager, Libya, 1969-70; BAC Rep. CENTO Area, Tehran, later BAe Chief Exec. Iran, and Man. Dir, Irano-British Dynamics Co. Iran, 1970-79. Assoc. Fellow, British Interplanetary Soc., 1960. *Recreations:* most sports. *Address:* c/o National Westminster Bank, Haymarket, SW1. *Club:* White's.

STAPLETON, Guy; Under Secretary, Cabinet Office, since 1982; b 10 Nov. 1935; s of William Algernon Swann Stapleton and Joan Denise Stapleton. *Educ:* Malvern Coll. Clerical Officer, Min. of Transport and Civil Aviation, 1954-58; Exec. Officer, 1958; transf. to Min. of Aviation, 1959; Civil Aviation Asst, British Embassy, Rome, 1960-63; Private Sec. to Controller of National Air Traffic Control Services, 1963-65; Asst Principal, MAFF, 1965; Private Sec. to Jt Parly Sec., 1967-68; Principal, 1968; Asst Sec., 1973; Asst Sec., Dept of Prices and Consumer Protection, 1974-76; returned to MAFF as Head of Agricl Resources Policy Div., 1976-81; Under Sec., European Community and Agricl Support Policy Gp, 1981-82. *Publications:* A Walk of Verse, 1961; (compiled) Poet's England: 2, Gloucestershire, 1977, 2nd edn 1982; 4, Avon and Somerset, 1981; pamphlets; contrib. learned jls; newspaper articles on history of Moreton in Marsh, Glos. *Recreations:* history of North Cotswolds, genealogy, topographical verse. *Address:* Cabinet Office, 70 Whitehall, SW1A 2AS. *T:* 01-233 3000. *Club:* Civil Service.

STAPLETON, Sir (Henry) Alfred, 10th Bt cr 1679; b 2 May 1913; s of Brig. Francis Harry Stapleton, CMG (d 1956) and g g s of 7th Bt, and Maud Ellen (d 1958), d of late Major Alfred Edward Wrottesley; S kinsman, 1977; m 1961, Rosslyne Murray, d of late Captain H. S. Warren, RN. *Educ:* Marlborough; Christ Church, Oxford. Served War of 1939-45, Oxfordshire and Bucks Light Infantry. *Recreations:* cricket umpiring, campanology. *Heir:* none. *Address:* 7 Ridgeway, Horsecastles Lane, Sherborne, Dorset. *Clubs:* Garrick, MCC.

STAPLETON, Prof. Richard Christopher, PhD; National Westminster Bank Professor of Business Finance, Manchester Business School, University of Manchester, since 1977; b 11 Oct. 1942; s of Leonard Stapleton and Rosamund Kathleen May Stapleton; m 1968, Linda Cairns; one s one d. *Educ:* Univ. of Sheffield (BAEcon, PhD Business Studies); Open Univ. (BA Maths). Lectr in Business Finance, Sheffield Univ., 1965-73; Asst Prof. of Finance, New York Univ., 1973-76; Sen. Res. Fellow, Manchester Business Sch., 1976-77. Hon. MBA Manchester, 1980. *Publications:* The Theory of Corporate Finance, 1970; International Tax Systems and Financing Policy, 1978; Capital Markets and Corporate Financial Decisions, 1980; contrib. Econ. Jl, Jl of Finance, Jl of Financial Econs, Qly Jl of Econs. *Recreations:* golf, reading, travel. *Address:* 9 Beechway, Wilmslow, Cheshire SK9 1PX. *T:* Wilmslow 522719.

STAPLETON-COTTON, family name of **Viscount Combermere.**

STAREWICZ, Artur, 2 Orders of Banner of Labour (1st cl.); Polonia Restituta; and other orders; Ambassador of Poland to the Court of St James's, 1971-78; b Warsaw, 20 March 1917; m 1947, Maria Rutkiewicz; two s two d. *Educ:* Warsaw Univ.; Institut Chimique de Rouen, 1938-39; Lvov Technical Univ., 1940-41; Charkov Chem. Inst., 1941-43; Grad. Engr, Soviet Electrochemical Inst., 1943. Chemical engr. Mem., revolutionary youth orgns incl. Communist Union of Polish Youth; arrested 1935 and 1936; Mem., Polish Workers Party (PPR), 1944-48; worked in PPR Voivoidship Cttees: Rzeszow; Cracow; Warsaw; First Sec., Wroclaw, 1947-48; Polish United Workers Party (PZPR): Mem., 1948-; Head of Propaganda, Central Cttee, 1948-53; Sec., Central Council of Trade Unions, 1954-56; Dep. Editor-in-Chief, daily newspaper Trybuna Ludu, 1956; Alternate Mem., Central Cttee, 1954-59, Mem., 1959-71; Head of Press Office, 1957-63; Sec., Central Cttee, 1963-71. Mem., Seym, 1957-72; Chairman: Polish Gp, Interparty Union; Polish Cttee for Security and Cooperation in Europe, 1978-; Editor, Polish Perspectives, 1979-. *Recreation:* aquatic sport. *Address:* Swietoierska 16 m3, Warsaw, Poland.

STARK, Sir Andrew (Alexander Steel), KCMG 1975 (CMG 1964); CVO 1965; DL; HM Diplomatic Service, retired; Chairman, The Maersk Co., since 1978; Director: Scandinavian Bank Ltd, since 1978; Carlsberg Brewery Ltd, since 1980; Adviser on European Affairs, Society of Motor Manufacturers and Traders, since 1977; b 30 Dec. 1916; yr s of late Thomas Bow Stark and of late Barbara Black Stark (née Steel), Fauldhouse, West Lothian; m 1944, Helen Rosemary, er d of late Lt-Col J. Oxley Parker, TD, and Mary Monica (née Hills); two s (one s decd). *Educ:* Bathgate Acad.; Edinburgh Univ. MA (Hons), Eng. Lit, Edinburgh, 1938. Served War of 1939-45, Green Howards and Staff appts. Major 1945. Entered Foreign Service, 1948, and served in Foreign Office until 1950; 1st Secretary, Vienna, 1951-53; Asst Private Sec. to Foreign Secretary, 1953-55; Head of Chancery: Belgrade, 1956-58; Rome,

1958-60; Counsellor: FO, 1960-64; Bonn, 1964-68; attached to Mission to UN with rank of Ambassador, Jan. 1968; British Mem., Seven Nation Cttee on Reorganisation of UN Secretariat; seconded to UN, NY, as Under-Secretary-General, Oct. 1968-1971; HM Ambassador to Denmark, 1971-76; Dep. Under-Sec. of State, FCO, 1976-77. Mem., CBI Europe Cttee, 1980-. Pres., Essex Physically Handicapped Assoc., 1979-. Vice-Chm. Council, Univ. of Essex, 1980- (Mem., 1978-). DL Essex, 1981. Grosses Verdienstkreuz, German Federal Republic, 1965; Grand Cross, Order of the Dannebrog, Denmark, 1974. *Recreations:* ski-ing, tennis, shooting. *Address:* Fambridge Hall, White Notley, Essex. *T:* Silver End 83117. *Clubs:* Travellers' (Chairman 1978-81), MCC.

STARK, Dame Freya (Madeline), DBE 1972 (CBE 1953); *d* of late Robert Stark, sculptor, Ford Park, Chagford, Devon; *m* 1947, Stewart Perowne, *qv. Educ:* privately in Italy; Bedford College, London University; School of Oriental Studies, London. Engaged on Govt service in Middle East and elsewhere, 1939-45. Awarded Back Grant, 1933, for travel in Luristan; Triennial Burton Memorial Medal from Royal Asiatic Society, 1934; Mungo Park Medal from Royal Scottish Geographical Society, 1936; Founder's Medal from Royal Geographical Society, 1942; Percy Sykes Memorial Medal from R Central Asian Soc., 1951. Sister of the Order of St John of Jerusalem, 1949, Sister Comdr, 1981. LLD Glasgow Univ., 1951; DLitt Durham, 1971. *Publications:* Bagdad Sketches, 1933, enlarged edition, 1937; The Valleys of the Assassins, 1934; The Southern Gates of Arabia, 1936; Seen in the Hadhramaut, 1938; A Winter in Arabia, 1940; Letters from Syria, 1942; East is West, 1945; Perseus in the Wind, 1948; Traveller's Prelude, 1950; Beyond Euphrates, 1951; The Coast of Incense, 1953; Ionia: a Quest, 1954; The Lycian Shore, 1956; Alexander's Path, 1958; Riding to the Tigris, 1959; Dust in the Lion's Paw, 1961; The Journey's Echo, 1963; Rome on the Euphrates, 1966; The Zodiac Arch, 1968; Space, Time and Movement in Landscape, 1969; The Minaret of Djam, 1970; Turkey: a sketch of Turkish History, 1971; A Peak in Darien, 1976; Letters (ed Lucy Moorehead): vol. 1, The Furnace and the Cup, 1914-1930, 1974; vol. 2, The Open Road, 1930-1935, 1975; vol. 3, The Growth of Danger, 1935-1939, 1976; vol. 4, The Bridge of the Levant, 1940-1943, 1977; vol. 5, New Worlds for Old, 1943-1946, 1978; vol. 6, The Broken Road, 1947-1952, 1981. *Recreations:* travel, mountaineering and embroidery. *Address:* Via Canova, Asolo (Treviso), Italy; c/o John Murray, 50 Albemarle Street, W1.

STARKE, Hon. Sir John Erskine, Kt 1976; **Hon. Mr Justice Starke;** Judge of Supreme Court of Victoria, Australia, since 1964. Admitted to Victorian Bar, 1939; QC 1955; Judge, 1946. *Address:* Supreme Court, Melbourne, Victoria 3000, Australia; Mount Eliza, Victoria, Australia.

STARKE, Leslie Gordon Knowles, CBE 1953; *b* 23 May 1898; *s* of William and Martha Starke; *m* 1929, Joan Mary Davidson; no *c. Educ:* Andover Grammar School; University College, Southampton; Queen's College, Oxford. Served European War, 1914-18, RE (Signal Service), 1918. Entered Government Actuary's Dept, 1919; Ministry of Food, 1939-46 (Director of Statistics and Intelligence, 1943-46); Principal Actuary and Establishment Officer, Government Actuary's Dept, 1946-58; Deputy Government Actuary, 1958-63. *Recreations:* gardening, walking. *Address:* Brack Mound House, Castle Precincts, Lewes, East Sussex. *T:* Lewes 4139.

STARKER, Janos; concert cellist, recording artist; Distinguished Professor of Music, Indiana University, since 1958; *b* 5 July 1924; *s* of F. Sandor and M. Margit; *m* 1944, Eva Uranyi; one *d* ; *m* 1960, Rae D. Busch; one *d. Educ:* Franz Liszt Academy of Music, Budapest; Zrinyi Gymnasium, Budapest. Solo cellist: Budapest Opera and Philh., 1945-46; Dallas Symphony, 1948-49; Metropolitan Opera, 1949-53; Chicago Symphony, 1953-58; numerous recordings. Grand Prix du Disque, 1948; George Washington Award; Sanford Fellowship Award, Yale, 1974; Herzl Award, 1978. Hon. Mem., Royal Acad., 1981. Hon. DMus, Chicago Conservatory Coll., 1961; Hon. Dr Cornell, 1978. Invented the Starker Bridge. *Publications:* Cello Method: an organised method of string playing, 1963; Bach Suites, 1971; Cadenzas, 1976; many articles in various magazines. *Recreations:* writing, swimming. *Address:* Indiana University Music Department, Bloomington, Ind 47401, USA.

STARKEY, Sir John (Philip), 3rd Bt *cr* 1935; DL; *b* 8 May 1938; *s* of Sir William Randle Starkey, 2nd Bt, and Irene Myrtle Starkey (*née* Francklin) (*d* 1965); *S* father, 1977; *m* 1966, Victoria Henrietta Fleetwood, *y d* of Lt-Col Christopher Fuller, TD; one *s* three *d. Educ:* Eton College; Christ Church, Oxford. Sloan Fellow, London Business School. DL Notts, 1981. *Recreation:* cricket. *Heir:* *s* Henry John Starkey, *b* 13 Oct. 1973. *Address:* Norwood Park, Southwell, Notts. *T:* Southwell 812762. *Club:* MCC.

STARLEY, Hubert Granville, CBE 1946; FIMI; Chairman, Starleys Estates Ltd, since 1974; *b* Skipton, 16 April 1909; *s* of late Hubert Ernest and Fanny Starley, Coventry; great nephew of J. K. Starley, founder of Rover Co.; *g g s* of James Starley of Coventry, inventor of the bicycle and differential gear; *m* 1933, Lilian Amy Heron, Bournemouth; one *s* one *d. Educ:* Ermysteds; Skipton, Yorks. Man. Dir, 1963-72, Vice-Chm., 1972-74, Champion Sparking Plug Co. Ltd; Assistant to Lord Beaverbrook, Minister of Supply, 1941; Advisor to War Office and Air Ministry on Stores Packaging, 1943; Hon. Chairman Anglo-American Packaging Exhibition Committee, 1944; Member Barlow Mission to the USA, 1944; Hon. Chm., Motor Industry Jubilee Committee, 1946; Society of Motor Manufacturers and Traders, Ltd: Chm., Accessory and Component Manufrs' Cttee, 1945-46, 1953-55, 1961-62; Mem.

Council Management Cttees, 1953-73; Mem., General Purposes Cttee, 1968-72; Vice-Pres., 1972-73. Chm., Fellowship of the Motor Industry, 1969-70; Pres., Cycle and Motor Cycle Assoc., 1970 (Mem., 1950-75); Hon. Chm. Inter-Services Packaging Cttee, MoD, 1958-65; Founder, Mem. Council and Dir, Aims of Industry Ltd, 1942-71, Vice-Pres., 1972-80. Vice-Pres., Inst. of Motor Industry, 1973-75; Mem. Council, CBI, 1970-75. Hon. Chm., Home Office Mobile Crime Prevention Cttee, 1968-78. Past Pres. and Patron, Twickenham Conservative Assoc. Master, Livery Company of Coachmakers and Coach Harness Makers, 1966-67; Pres., Pickwick Bicycle Club, 1954. Hon. Pageant Master and Organiser, History of British Motoring Cavalcades, Lord Mayor's Show, 1964; Hon. Organiser, 6 day Cycle Race, Earl's Court, 1967. *Address:* Rothesay House, London Road, Twickenham TW1 1ES. *T:* 01-892 5187. *Clubs:* Carlton, Royal Automobile, Royal Thames Yacht; Royal Motor Yacht (Sandbanks, Poole).

STARLING, Brigadier John Sieveking, CBE 1945; retired; *b* 18 Jan. 1898; *o s* of late Prof. Ernest H. Starling, CMG, MD, FRS, and Florence, *d* of late Sir Edward Sieveking; *m* 1st, 1924, Vivian Barbara, *d* of late Henry J. Wagg, OBE (marriage dissolved 1948); one *s* ; 2nd, 1948, Marion, *d* of late A. G. Pool, and *widow* of C. A. Morell-Miller. *Educ:* University College School; Royal Military Academy; Trinity College, Cambridge. Commissioned 2nd Lt RA, 1916; served European War, France and Flanders, 1916-18 (wounded twice); normal career of a Regimental Officer in UK, Egypt and India. Attached French Army, 1939; served France and Flanders, Middle East and Italy, 1939-46 (despatches, wounded, CBE); retired from Regular Army as Hon. Brig., 1948. *Recreations:* fishing, shooting, sailing. *Address:* Le Hurel, Trinity, Jersey, CI. *T:* 61066. *Club:* Army and Navy.

STASSEN, Harold Edward; lawyer, politician, educator, United States; Partner in law firm Stassen, Kostos and Mason; Chairman, International Law Committee of Philadelphia Bar Association, 1973; *b* W St Paul, Minn, 13 April 1907; *s* of William Andrew Stassen and Elsie Emma Mueller; *m* 1929, Esther G. Glewwe; one *s* one *d. Educ:* Univ. of Minnesota Coll. (BA 1927; LLB 1929); Law School. Has several hon. degrees. Admitted to Minnesota Bar, 1929; practised South St Paul; County Attorney, Dakota County, 1930-38; thrice elected Governor of Minnesota, 1939-43; resigned for service with Navy; Lt Comdr, USN; Comdr on staff of Admiral Halsey in South Pacific, 1943-44; Asst Chief of Staff, 1944; Capt., USN; released to inactive duty, 1945. One of US delegates to San Francisco Conference, drafting and signing UN Charter, 1945. Pres., Minnesota Young Republicans; Delegate to Republican Convention, 1936; Temporary Chairman and Keynoter of Republican National Convention and floor manager for Wendell Wilkie, 1940; twice elected National Chairman National Governors' Conference, and of Council of State Governments, 1940-41. President, University of Pennsylvania, 1948-53. President International Council of Religious Education, 1942, 1950; Vice-Pres. and a Founder, Nat. Council of Churches, 1951-52; President, Div. of Christian Educ. of Nat. Council of Churches, 1953-. Director Foreign Operations Admin., 1953-55; Special Assistant to the President for Disarmament, 1955-58; Dep. US Rep. on Disarmament Commn, UN, 1955-58. Chief Consultant to ME Tech. Univ., Ankara, 1958; Mem., Nat. Security Council, 1953-58. Delivered Godkind Lectures on Human Rights, Harvard Univ., 1946; candidate for Republican nomination for President of US, 1948-. Chm., World Law Day, Geneva, 1968. Bronze Star, 1944; Legion of Merit, Six Battle Stars (Western Pacific campaign), 1945. Baptist. Mason. *Publications:* Where I Stand, 1947; Man was meant to be Free, 1951. *Address:* (office) 2300 Two Girard Plaza, Philadelphia, Pennsylvania 19102, USA.

STATHAM, Sir Norman, KCMG 1977 (CMG 1967); CVO 1968; HM Diplomatic Service, retired; Executive Vice-President, British Chamber of Commerce in Germany, since 1981; Vice-President, Council of British Chambers of Commerce in Continental Europe, since 1982; Member, European Trade Committee, British Overseas Trade Board, since 1981; *b* Stretford, Lancs, 15 Aug. 1922; *s* of Frederick William and Maud Statham; *m* 1948, Hedwig Gerlich; one *s* one *d* (and one *s* decd). *Educ:* Seymour Park Council School, Stretford; Manchester Grammar School; Gonville and Caius College, Cambridge (MA). Intelligence Corps, 1943-47; Manchester Oil Refinery Ltd and Petrochemicals Ltd, 1948-50; Foreign Service, 1951: Foreign Office, 1951; Consul (Commercial), New York, 1954-58; First Secretary (Commercial), Bonn, 1958-63; Administrative Staff College, Henley, 1963; Foreign Office, 1964; Counsellor, Head of European Economic Integration Dept, 1965-68, 1970-71; Consul-General, São Paulo, 1968-70; Minister (Economic), Bonn, 1971-75; Asst Under Sec. of State, FCO, 1975; Dep. Under Sec. of State, FCO, 1975-77; Ambassador to Brazil, 1977-79. *Recreations:* gardening, hill-walking, reading. *Address:* 11 Underhill Park Road, Reigate, Surrey RH2 9LU. *Clubs:* Travellers'; Lancashire County Cricket.

STATON, Air Vice-Marshal William Ernest, CB 1947; DSO and Bar, 1940; MC 1918; DFC and Bar, 1918; *b* 1898; *m* 1st, 1919, Norah Carina Workman (*d* 1969); two *s* ; 2nd, 1973, Jean Patricia Primrose (*née* Richardson). Served European War, 1914-19 (despatches); War of 1939-45 (despatches); Wing Comdr, 1939; Group Capt., 1940; Actg Air Commodore, 1941; Air Vice-Marshal, 1950; SASO Singapore, 1942; prisoner of war, Japan, 1942-45 (despatches); ADC to the King, 1940-46; AOC No 46 Group, 1945-47; Commandant Central Bomber Establishment, 1947-49; Air Officer-in-Charge of Administration, Technical Training Command, 1949-52; retired 1952. Helper, RAF Benevolent Fund, 1952-. Chm. RAF Small Arms Assoc.,

1947-52; Capt. British Shooting Teams, Olympic Games, 1948 and 1952. Ex-Mem. of Councils; Internat. Shooting Union, Stockholm; Nat. Rifle Assoc.; Nat. Small Bore Rifle Assoc.; Brit. Olympic Assoc. (1952-57). *Address:* Wildhern, Creek End, Emsworth, Hants. *Club:* Emsworth Sailing (Flag Officer, 1968; Commodore, 1972-).

STAUGHTON, Hon. Sir Christopher (Stephen Thomas Jonathan Thayer), Kt 1981; **Hon. Mr Justice Staughton;** Judge of the High Court of Justice, Queen's Bench Division, since 1981; *b* 24 May 1933; *yr s* of late Simon Thomas Samuel Staughton and Edith Madeline Jones; *m* 1960, Joanna Susan Elizabeth, *er d* of late George Frederick Arthur Burgess; two *d. Educ:* Eton Coll. (Scholar); Magdalene Coll., Cambridge (Scholar). 2nd Lieut, 11th Hussars PAO, 1952-53; Lieut, Derbyshire Yeomanry TA, 1954-56. George Long Prize for Roman Law, Cambridge, 1955; BA 1956; MA 1961. Called to Bar, Inner Temple, 1957, Bencher, 1978; QC 1970; a Recorder of the Crown Court, 1972-81. Mem., Senate of the Inns of Court and the Bar, 1974-81; Chm., Code of Conduct sub-cttee, 1979-80. Chm., St Peter's Eaton Square Church of England Sch., 1974-. *Publication:* (Jt Editor) The Law of General Average (British Shipping Laws vol. 7), 1964, new edn, 1975. *Recreations:* bridge, growing dahlias. *Address:* Royal Courts of Justice, Strand, WC2. *T:* 01-405 7641. *Club:* Brooks's.

STAVELEY, Sir John (Malfroy), KBE 1980 (OBE 1972); MC 1941; FRCP; FRACPath; Director, Auckland Blood Transfusion Service, 1965-76; Hon. Medical Director, New Zealand Blood Foundation, since 1978; *b* 30 Aug. 1914; *s* of William Staveley and Annie May Staveley (*née* Malfroy); *m* 1940, Elvira Cliafe Wycherley; one *s* one *d. Educ:* Univ. of Dunedin (MB ChB); Univ. of Edinburgh. FRCP 1958; FRACPath 1965. House Surgeon, Auckland Hosp., 1939; war service with 2NZEF, Middle East, 1940-45; post graduate educn, UK, 1946-47; Pathologist, Auckland Hosp., 1948-50; Haematologist, Auckland Hosp. Bd, 1950-64. Landsteiner Award, USA, for medical research, 1980. *Publications:* papers in medical and scientific jls (British, American and NZ). *Recreations:* mountaineering, fishing, music. *Address:* 11 Matanui Street, Northcote, Auckland 9, New Zealand. *Club:* New Zealand Alpine.

STAVELEY, Martin Samuel, CMG 1966; CVO 1966; CBE 1962 (MBE 1955); *b* 3 Oct. 1921; fourth *s* of late Herbert Samuel Staveley and Edith Ellen Staveley (*née* Shepherd); *m* 1942, Edith Eileen Baker; one *s* two *d. Educ:* Stamford School; Trinity College, Oxford. Appointed Cadet, Colonial Administrative Service, Nigeria, 1942; Secretary, Development and Welfare Organisation in the West Indies, 1946-57; Secretary to Governor-General, Federation of the West Indies, 1958-62; Administrator, British Virgin Islands, 1962-67; HM Diplomatic Service, 1967-74; Home Civil Service, 1974-. *Recreations:* golf, music. *Address:* The Cottage Farm House, Great Bentley, Essex.

STAVELEY, Maj.-Gen. Robert; *b* 3 June 1928; *s* of Brig. Robin Staveley, DSO, and Ilys (*née* Sutherland); *m* 1958, Airlie, *d* of Maj.-Gen. W. H. Lambert, CB, CBE; one *s* one *d. Educ:* Wellington. RMA, Sandhurst, 1947; commissioned RA, 1948; served BAOR, 1949-51; ADC to GOC Malta, 1951-53; Air OP pilot, Malaya, 1954-57 (despatches); ADC to GOC-in-C Northern Command, 1957-58; Indian Staff Coll., 1959; Staff Officer and Missile Battery Comdr, BAOR, 1960-65; Instructor, Staff Coll., 1966-68; commanded 47 Lt Regt RA, UK and Hong Kong, 1969-71; CRA 2nd Div., BAOR, 1973-74; RCDS 1975; Director of Operational Requirements, MoD, 1976-79; C of S, Logistic Exec. (Army), 1979-82. Col Comdt, RA, 1982-. *Recreations:* good food, sailing, skiing, music. *Address:* c/o Lloyds Bank Ltd (Cox's & King's Branch), 6 Pall Mall, SW1Y 5NH. *Clubs:* Army and Navy, Royal Ocean Racing; Royal Artillery Yacht (Commodore, 1980-83).

STAVELEY, Adm. Sir William (Doveton Minet), KCB 1981; Commander-in-Chief, Fleet, and Allied Commander-in-Chief, Channel and Eastern Atlantic, since 1982; *b* 10 Nov. 1928; *s* of late Adm. Cecil Minet Staveley, CB, CMG, and Margaret Adela (*née* Sturdee); *m* 1954, Bettina Kirstine Shuter; one *s* one *d. Educ:* West Downs, Winchester; RN Colls, Dartmouth and Greenwich. Entered Royal Navy as Cadet, 1942; Midshipman, HMS Ajax, Mediterranean, 1946-47; Sub-Lieut/Lieut, HM Ships Nigeria and Bermuda, S Atlantic, 1949-51; Flag Lieut to Adm. Sir George Creasy, C-in-C Home Fleet, HM Ships Indomitable and Vanguard, 1952-54; Staff, Britannia, RNC, Dartmouth, 1954-56; HM Yacht Britannia, 1957; First Lieut, HMS Cavalier, Far East, 1958-59; Lt-Comdr, 1958; RN Staff Coll., 1959; Staff, C-in-C Nore and Flag Officer Medway, 1959-61; Comdr 1961; Sen. Officer, 104th and 6th Minesweeping Sqdn, HMS Houghton, Far East, 1962-63; Comdr, Sea Trng, Staff of Flag Officer, Sea Trng, Portland, 1964-66; comd HMS Zulu, ME and Home Station, 1967; Captain 1967; Asst Dir, Naval Plans, Naval Staff, 1967-70; Command: HM Ships Intrepid, Far and ME, 1970-72; Albion, Home Station, 1972; RCDS, 1973; Dir of Naval Plans, Naval Staff, 1974-76; Flag Officer, Second Flotilla, 1976-77; Flag Officer, Carriers and Amphibious Ships, and NATO Commander, Carrier Striking Group Two, 1977-78; Chief of Staff to C-in-C Fleet, 1978-80; Vice-Chief of Naval Staff, 1980-82. Chairman: Combined Services Equitation Assoc., 1980-82; Council, British Horse Soc., 1982-; Member: Royal Naval Sailing Assoc.; Royal Yachting Assoc.; RHS; Royal Nat. Rose Soc. A Younger Brother of Trinity House, 1973. *Recreations:* gardening, shooting, tennis, riding, sailing, restoring antiques. *Address:* Admiralty House, Northwood, Mddx.

STAWELL, Maj.-Gen. William Arthur Macdonald, CB 1945; CBE 1944; MC 1917; *b* 22 Jan. 1895; *s* of G. C. Stawell, ICS; *m* 1926, Amy, *d* of C. W. Bowring, New York; one *s. Educ:* Clifton College; RMA, Woolwich. Served European War, 1914-21, France, Greek Macedonia, Serbia, Bulgaria, Turkey (wounded, MC); 2nd Lieut 1914; Temp. Captain, 1916-17; Acting Major, Mar.-April 1917 and 1918-19; Captain, 1917; Major 1929; Lieut-Col 1937; Col 1940; Brig. 1940. GSO3 War Office, 1931-32; Brigade Maj., Aldershot, 1932-35; DAAG India, 1935-37; CRE 1937-40; AA and QMG Feb.-July 1940; GSO1 July-Nov. 1940; DDMI War Office, 1940-42; Brig., Comdr Home Forces, Feb.-Nov. 1942; Brig. General Staff, Home Forces, 1942-43; MEF and CMF, 1943-45 (CBE, CB); Temp. Maj.-Gen. 1943-45; Deputy Chief of Operations UNRRA, Nov. 1945-Aug. 1946; Deputy Chief Intelligence Division, CCG, 1947-48; retired. *Recreations:* yachting, golf. *Address:* Crobeg, The Common, Southwold, Suffolk. *Clubs:* Army and Navy; Royal Norfolk and Suffolk Yacht.

STEAD, Christina Ellen; Fellow in Creative Arts, Australian National University, Canberra, 1969-80, now Emeritus; *b* 17 July 1902; *d* of Ellen Butters and David George Stead; *m* William J. Blake (*d* 1968). *Educ:* Sydney Univ., NSW. In business: London, 1928-29, Paris, 1930-35. Cinema: Senior Writer, MGM, Hollywood, Calif, 1943. Instructor, Workshop in the Novel, New York Univ., 1943-44. *Publications:* Short Story Collection: Salzburg Tales, London, 1934, NY, 1935, Melbourne, 1966. Novels: Seven Poor Men of Sydney, London and NY, 1935, Sydney and London, 1966 (new edn, 1970); The Beauties and Furies, London and NY, 1936; House of All Nations, London and NY, 1938, NY 1972; The Man who Loved Children, London, 1941, NY, 1940, new edn 1965, London 1966; For Love Alone, NY, 1944, London, 1945, new edn, New York, 1965, new edn, London, 1966, Sydney, 1969; Letty Fox, Her Luck, NY, 1946, London, 1947; A Little Tea, A Little Chat, NY, 1948; The People with the Dogs, Boston, 1951; Dark Places of the Heart, New York, 1966; The Little Hotel, 1974; Miss Herbert, the Suburban Wife, NY, 1976, UK 1979; Seven Poor Men of Sydney, 1978; The Puzzleheaded Girl, novellas, 1967; short stories: in Southerly, 1963; in Kenyon Review, Saturday Evening Post, 1965; in Meanjin, 1968, 1970; in Hemisphere, 1970; in New Yorker, 1970; in Commentary, 1971; in Partisan Review, 1971; in Overland, 1972. *Address:* c/o Laurence Pollinger, Ltd, 18 Maddox Street, W1.

STEAD, Rev. Canon (George) Christopher, LittD, FBA 1980; Fellow, King's College, Cambridge (Professorial Fellow, 1971-80); Emeritus Fellow, Keble College, Oxford, since 1981; *b* 9 April 1913; *s* of Francis Bernard Stead, CBE, and Rachel Elizabeth, *d* of Rev. Canon G. C. Bell; *m* 1958, Doris Elizabeth Odom; two *s* one *d. Educ:* Marlborough Coll.; King's Coll., Cambridge (scholar). 1st cl. Classical Tripos Pt I, 1933; Pitt Scholar, 1934; 1st cl. Moral Science Tripos Pt II, 1935; BA 1935, MA 1938, LittD Cantab 1978; New Coll., Oxford (BA 1935); Cuddesdon Coll., Oxford, 1938. Ordained, 1938; Curate, St John's, Newcastle upon Tyne, 1939; Fellow and Lectr in Divinity, King's Coll., Cambridge, 1938-48; Asst Master, Eton Coll., 1940-44; Fellow and Chaplain, Keble Coll., Oxford, 1949-71 (MA Oxon 1949); Ely Professor of Divinity, Cambridge, and Canon Residentiary of Ely Cathedral, 1971-80, Canon Emeritus, 1981. *Publications:* Divine Substance, 1977; contributor to: Faith and Logic, 1957; New Testament Apocrypha, 1965; articles and reviews in Jl of Theol Studies, Vigiliae Christianae. *Recreations:* walking, sailing, music. *Address:* 13 Station Road, Haddenham, Ely, Cambs.

STEAD, Ralph Edmund, FCA, FCMA; retired; Chairman, Eastern Region, British Gas Corporation, 1977-81; *b* 7 Jan. 1917; *s* of Albert Stead and Mabel Stead; *m* 1946, Evelyn Annie Ness; two *s* two *d. Educ:* Manchester Grammar Sch.; Ilford County High Sch. FCA 1949; FCMA 1952. Served War, RASC, 1940-46. *Recreations:* golf, gardening, reading. *Address:* 28 Church Hill, Edinburgh.

STEAD, Robert, CBE 1965; retired as Controller, BBC North Region, 1958-69; *b* 10 Aug. 1909; *s* of Charles Fearnley Stead and Mary Ellen Taylor; *m* 1932, Constance Ann Sharpley; two *s. Educ:* Morley Gram. Sch. In Journalism, 1926-40; served in RN, 1940-45. Talks Producer, BBC North Region, 1946-48; Head of North Region Programmes, 1948-53; BBC Australian Representative, 1953-57. *Recreations:* golf, gardening, theatre. *Address:* 20 Fulshaw Court, Wilmslow, Cheshire. *T:* Wilmslow 525536.

STEADMAN, Ralph Idris; freelance cartoonist; illustrator; *b* 15 May 1936; *s* of Lionel Raphael Steadman (English), and Gwendoline (Welsh); *m* 1st, 1959, Sheila Thwaite (marr. diss. 1971); two *s* two *d*; 2nd, 1972, Anna Deverson; one *d. Educ:* Abergele Grammar Sch.; London Coll. of Printing and Graphic Arts. Apprentice, de Havilland Aircraft Co., 1952; Cartoonist, Kemsley (Thomson) Newspapers, 1956-59; freelance for Punch, Private Eye, Telegraph, during 1960s; Political Cartoonist, New Statesman, 1978-80; retired to work on book about Leonardo da Vinci. Retrospective exhibition, Nat. Theatre, 1977. Designers and Art Directors Assoc. Gold Award (for outstanding contribution to illustration), 1977, and Silver Award (for outstanding editorial illustration), 1977. *Publications:* (with Frank Dickens) Fly Away Peter, 1961; (with Mischa Damjan) The Big Squirrel and the Little Rhinoceros, 1962; The False Flamingoes, 1963; The Little Prince and the Tiger Cat, 1964; (with Richard Ingrams) The Tale of Driver Grope, 1964; (with Fiona Saint) The Yellow Flowers, 1965; (with Mischa Damjan) Two Cats in America, 1968; (with Tariq Ali) The Thoughts of Chairman Harold, 1968; Jelly Book, 1968; Still Life with Raspberry; collected drawings, 1969; The

Little Red Computer, 1970; Dogs Bodies, 1971; Bumper to Bumper Book, 1973; Two Donkeys and the Bridge, 1974; Flowers for the Moon, 1974; The Watchdog and the Lazy Dog, 1974; America: drawings, 1975; America: collected drawings, 1977; *written and illustrated:* Sigmund Freud, 1979 (as The Penguin Sigmund Freud, 1982); A Leg in the Wind and other Canine Curses, 1982; designed and printed, Steam Press Broadsheets; *illustrated:* Love and Marriage, 1964; Where Love Lies Deepest, 1964; Alice in Wonderland, 1967; Midnight, 1967; Fear and Loathing in Las Vegas, 1972; Contemporary Poets set to Music series, 1972; Through the Looking Glass, 1972; Night Edge: poems, 1973; The Poor Mouth, 1973; John Letts Limericks, 1974; The Hunting of the Snark, 1975; Cherrywood Cannon, 1978; Emergency Mouse, 1978; Ted Hughes, The Threshold (limited edn), 1979; (with Bernard Stone) Inspector Mouse, 1980; For Beauty Douglas, 1982; Flann O'Brien, More of Myles, 1982; Dr Hunter S. Thompson, The Curse of Lono, 1983. *Recreations:* gardening, collecting, writing, goat husbandry, fishing. *Club:* Chelsea Arts.

STEARN, Dr William Thomas; botanical consultant; retired as Senior Principal Scientific Officer, Department of Botany, British Museum (Natural History), 1976; Hon. Botanical Curator, Linnean Society, since 1959; Editor, Annales Musei Goulandris, since 1976; *b* 16 April 1911; *e s* of late Thomas Stearn, Cambridge; *m* 1940, Eldwyth Ruth Alford, *d* of late Roger R. Alford, Tavistock; one *s* two *d. Educ:* Cambridge High Sch. for Boys; part-time research at Botany Sch., Cambridge; apprentice antiquarian bookseller, Bowes & Bowes, Cambridge, 1929-32. Librarian, Royal Horticultural Soc., 1933-41, 1946-52. Served RAF, in Britain, India and Burma, 1941-46. Botanist, British Museum (Natural History), 1952-76. Hon. Sec., Internat. Cttee for Nomenclature of Cultivated Plants, 1950-53; former Council Member: Botanical Soc. of British Isles (Vice-Pres., 1973-77); British Soc. for History of Science (Vice-Pres., 1969-72); British Soc. for History of Medicine; Field Studies Council; Garden History Soc. (Founder Mem., 1965; Pres., 1977-82); Linnean Soc. (Vice-Pres., 1961-62; Pres., 1979-82); Ray Soc. (Vice-Pres., 1964-67, 1970-73, Pres., 1974-77); Richmond Scientific Soc. (Pres., 1969-71); Soc. for Bibliography of Natural History (Founder Mem., 1936, Hon. Mem., 1976); Systematics Assoc. Masters Meml Lectr, 1964; Sandars Reader in Bibliography, Cambridge, 1965; Vis. Prof., Dept of Botany and Agricl Botany, Univ. of Reading, 1977-. Has lectured in Australia, Austria, Canada, Germany, Greece, Holland, Jamaica, Papua New Guinea, Sweden, USA; botanical collections made in Europe, Jamaica, USA, Australia. Royal Horticultural Society: Hon. Fellow, 1946; Veitch Meml Medal, 1964; Victoria Medal of Honour, 1965. FLS 1934; FIBiol 1967 (MIBiol 1965); Hon. Member: Kungl. Vetenskaps-Societeten i Uppsala, 1967; Svenska Linné-Sällskapet, 1971; Corr. Mem., Amer. Soc. of Plant Taxonomists, 1980. Freeman, Gardeners' Co., 1982. Hon. Fellow, Sidney Sussex Coll., Cambridge, 1968. DSc *hc* Leiden, 1960; Hon. ScD Cantab, 1967; FilDr *hc* Uppsala, 1972. Boerhaave Commem. Medal, Leiden, 1969; Linnaeus Medal, Royal Swedish Acad. of Sciences, 1972; Linnaean Gold Medal, Linnean Soc., 1976. Comdr, Order of the Star of the North (Sweden), 1980. *Publications:* (with H. B. D. Woodcock) Lilies of the World, 1950; (with E. Blatter and W. S. Millard) Some Beautiful Indian Trees, 1955; Introduction to the *Species Plantarum* of Carl Linnaeus, 1957; Early Leyden Botany, 1961; Botanical Latin, 1966, 2nd edn 1973; Three Prefaces on Linnaeus and Robert Brown, 1967; Humboldt, Bonpland, Kunth and Tropical American Botany, 1968; (with C. N. Goulimis and N. Goulandris) Wild Flowers of Greece, 1968; (with A. W. Smith) Gardener's Dictionary of Plant Names, 1972; (with W. Blunt) Captain Cook's Florilegium, 1973; (with M. Page) Culinary Herbs, 1974; (with W. Blunt) Australian Flower Paintings of Ferdinand Bauer, 1976; The Wondrous Transformation of Caterpillars: M. S. Merian (Biog.), 1978; (with H. Hara and L. H. J. Williams) Enumeration of Flowering Plants of Nepal, vol. 1, 1978; The Natural History Museum at South Kensington, 1981; numerous bibliographical, biographical, botanical and horticultural contribs to learned jls (listed in Biological Jl of Linnean Soc. vol. 8, 1976), RHS Dictionary of Gardening, Chambers's Encyclopaedia, Dictionary of Scientific Biography, Flora Europaea, etc. *Recreations:* gardening, talking. *Address:* 17 High Park Road, Kew Gardens, Richmond, Surrey.

STEBBINGS, Sir John (Chalmer), Kt 1980; Partner, Payne Hicks Beach & Co., Solicitors, since 1951; *b* 10 Oct. 1924; *s* of late John Morley Stebbings, MC, EM, TD, and of Doris Percy (*née* Chalmer); *m* 1949, Patricia (*née* Strange); two *s* three *d. Educ:* Stone House, Broadstairs, Kent; Harrow (Rendalls); New Coll., Oxford (MA). Admitted solicitor, 1949. Law Society: Mem. Council, 1964; Treasurer, 1969-75; Vice Pres., 1978-79; Pres., 1979. Mem., Lord Chancellor's Cttee on Age of Majority, 1965-66. *Recreations:* swimming, sailing. *Address:* 435 Fulham Road, Chelsea, SW10 9TX. *T:* 01-352 7190. *Clubs:* Hurlingham; Royal Temple Yacht (Ramsgate).

STEDMAN, family name of **Baroness Stedman.**

STEDMAN, Baroness *cr* 1974 (Life Peer), of Longthorpe, Peterborough; **Phyllis Stedman,** OBE 1965; *b* 14 July 1916; *o d* of Percy and Emmie Adams; *m* 1941, Henry William Stedman, OBE 1981. *Educ:* County Grammar Sch., Peterborough. Branch Librarian, Peterborough City Council, 1934-41; Group Officer, National Fire Service, 1942-45. Baroness-in-Waiting (a Govt Whip), 1975-79; Parly Under-Sec. of State, DoE, 1979; Govt spokesman for Transport, the Environment, Educn and Trade, 1975-79; Opposition spokesman on the environment, local govt, new towns and transport, 1979-81; Mem., SDP, 1981-; SDP Whip in House of Lords, 1982-. County Councillor: Soke of Peterborough, 1946-65; Huntingdon and Peterborough, 1965-74; Cambridgeshire, 1974-76; Vice-Chm.,

Cambridgeshire County Council, 1974-76. Member: Board, Peterborough Development Corp., 1972-76; IBA, 1974-75; Board, Hereward Radio, 1979-; Vice-Chm., Nat. PHAB, 1978-; Vice-Pres., Assoc. of District Councils, 1979-. Mem. Exec. Council, Fire Services Nat. Benevolent Fund, 1976-. *Address:* Green Pastures, Grove Lane, Longthorpe, Peterborough PE3 6ND.

STEDMAN, Sir George (Foster), KBE 1957; CB 1948; MC 1919; Civil Service, retired; *b* 1895; *s* of James Mathew and Marguerite Adele Stedman, Leytonstone, Essex; *m* 1925, Olive May Scrivener (*d* 1979); one *d* (one *s* decd). *Educ:* Mercers' School, London; Trinity Coll., Camb. Served European War, 1914-18, with York and Lancaster Regt, France and Macedonia (MC, despatches twice). Entered Civil Service, Ministry of Transport, 1920; Private Secretary to Minister, 1926-30; Under-Sec., 1946. Deputy Secretary, Ministry of Transport and Civil Aviation, 1954-57. *Address:* Longcroft, Honeyknab Lane, Oxton, Southwell, Notts.

STEEDMAN, Air Chief Marshal Sir Alexander McKay Sinclair, (Sir Alasdair Steedman), GCB 1980 (KCB 1976; CB 1973); CBE 1965; DFC 1944; Controller, Royal Air Force Benevolent Fund, since 1981; *b* 29 Jan. 1922; *s* of late James Steedman, Hampton-on-Thames, Mddx, and late Anna McKay Steedman (*née* Sinclair), Fulford, York; *m* 1945, Dorothy Isobel, *d* of Col Walter Todd, Knockbrex, Kirkcudbright; one *s* two *d. Educ:* Hampton Grammar School. Entered RAF, 1941; Flt Comdr, 241 Sqdn, 1942-44, 2 Sqdn, 1945; Air Min., 1945-48; comd 39 Sqdn, Khartoum, 1948-49; comd 8 Sqdn, Aden, 1949-50; CFS Course, 1951; Trng Sqdn Comdr, 201 AFS, 1951-53; Syndicate Ldr, Aircrew Selection Centre, Hornchurch, 1953-54; psa 1955; Chief Instructor, CFS (B), 1955-57; Comdr Royal Ceylon Air Force, Katanyake, 1957-59; jssc 1959-60; Directing Staff, Jt Services Staff Coll., 1960-62; Comdr RAF Lyneham, 1962-65; Gp Capt. (Ops), HQ Transport Comd, 1965; CAS, Royal Malaysian Air Force, 1965-67; Dir of Defence Plans (Air), MoD, 1967-68. Dir, Defence Ops Staff, MoD, 1968-69; ACAS (Policy), MoD, 1969-71; SASO, Strike Comd, 1971-72; Comdt, RAF Staff Coll., 1972-75; Air Member for Supply and Organisation, 1976-77; UK Mil. Rep. to NATO, 1977-80. Governor, Hampton Sch., 1976-. FRAeS 1981; CBIM 1979. Johan Mangku Negara (Malaysia), 1967. *Recreations:* golf, reading, motoring. *Address:* Rutherford, Gatehouse of Fleet, Scotland. *Clubs:* Royal Air Force; Royal Selangor (Kuala Lumpur).

STEEDMAN, Maj.-Gen. John Francis Dawes, CMG 1963; CBE 1945; MC 1918; *b* 30 Nov. 1897; *s* of John Francis Steedman, FRCS, Streatham; *m* 1931, Olive Ursula (Kaisar-i-Hind Medal, Silver Jubilee Medal, 1935), *d* of Earl Oliver Besant, Reading; one *d. Educ:* Bradfield; RMA, Woolwich. 2nd Lt, RE, 1916; Served European War, 1914-18, Salonika (MC, despatches twice); Afghanistan, 1919; Waziristan (MBE, despatches), 1920-21; Khajuri (despatches), 1930-31; Malaya, as CRE 11 Ind. Div. (Despatches), 1941-42; Comdt QVO Madras Sappers and Miners, 1942-43; Burma, as CE 33 Ind. Corps and XII Army (CBE, despatches), 1944-46; Chief Engineer, Southern Command, India, 1946; Engineer-in-Chief, Dominion of India, 1947; Chief Engineer, Southern Command, UK, 1948-51; ADC to HM King George VI, 1949-51; retired as Hon. Maj.-Gen., 1951; Director of Works, Commonwealth War Graves Commission, 1951-63. *Address:* Valley Farm House, East Knoyle, Salisbury, Wiltshire SP3 6BG. *T:* East Knoyle 329.

STEEDMAN, Martha, (Mrs R. R. Steedman); see Hamilton, M.

STEEDMAN, Robert Russell, RSA 1979 (ARSA 1973); RIBA; FRIAS; ALI; Partner, Morris and Steedman, Architects and Landscape Architects, Edinburgh, since 1959; *b* 3 Jan. 1929; *s* of late Robert Smith Steedman and Helen Hope Brazier; *m* 1st, 1956, Susan Elizabeth (marr. diss. 1974), *d* of Sir Robert Scott, GCMG, CBE; one *s* two *d* ; 2nd, 1977, Martha Hamilton, *qv. Educ:* Loretto Sch.; School of Architecture, Edinburgh College of Art (DA); Univ. of Pennsylvania (MLA). RIBA 1955; ALI 1979. Lieut, RWAFF, 1947-48. Worked in office, Alfred Roth, Zürich, 1953. Architectural works include: Principal's House, Univ. of Stirling; Head Offices for Christian Salvesen, Edinburgh; Administration Building for Shell Exploration and Production; Moss Morran Fife; Restoration of Old Waterworks, Perth, to form Tourist Information Centre and Offices. Nine Civic Trust Awards, 1963-78; British Steel Award, 1971; Saltire Award, 1971; RIBA Award for Scotland, 1974; European Architectural Heritage Medal, 1975; Assoc. for Preservation of Rural Scotland Award, 1977. Commissioner, Countryside Commn for Scotland, 1980-; Mem. Council, Royal Scottish Acad., 1981- (Dep. Pres. 1982-83); Governor, Edinburgh College of Art, 1974-; Mem., Edinburgh Festival Soc., 1978-; past Mem. Council, RIAS and Soc. of Scottish Artists. *Recreations:* skiing, tennis, shooting, sketching. *Address:* St Leonards School, St Andrews, Fife; (office) 37 Young Street Lane North, Edinburgh. *T:* 031-226 6563. *Clubs:* New, Scottish Arts (Edinburgh).

STEEGMULLER, Francis; writer; *b* New Haven, Conn, 3 July 1906; *s* of Joseph Francis Steegmuller and Bertha Tierney; *m* 1st, 1935, Beatrice Stein (decd); 2nd, 1963, Shirley Hazzard. *Educ:* Columbia University, New York. Member, Nat. Inst. of Arts and Letters, 1966. Gold Medal for Biography, 1982. Chevalier de la Légion d'Honneur, 1957. *Publications:* O Rare Ben Jonson (under pseudonym Byron Steel), 1928; Flaubert and Madame Bovary, 1939, reprinted 1947, 1958, 1968; States of Grace, 1947; Maupassant, 1950, repr. 1973; Blue Harpsichord (under pseudonym David Keith), 1950; The Two Lives of James Jackson Jarves, 1953; (trans. and ed) The Selected Letters of Gustave Flaubert, 1954; La Grande Mademoiselle, 1955; The Christening Party, 1961; Le Hibou et la Poussiquette, 1961; Apollinaire, 1963, repr. 1973;

Papillot, Clignot et Dodo (with Norbert Guterman), 1965; (trans.) Gustave Flaubert, Intimate Notebook, 1967; Cocteau, 1970 (Nat. Book Award 1971); Stories and True Stories, 1972; (trans. and ed) Flaubert in Egypt, 1972; (ed) Your Isadora, 1975; (trans. and ed) The Letters of Gustave Flaubert, 1830-1857, 1980 (American Book Award 1981), 2nd vol. 1982; works published abroad include a translation of Madame Bovary, 1957, Silence at Salerno (novel), 1979, and many short stories and articles in The New Yorker. *Address:* 200 East 66th Street, New York, NY 10021, USA. *Clubs:* Century, Coffee House (New York).

STEEL, Byron; *see* Steegmuller, Francis.

STEEL, Brig. Charles Deane, CMG 1957; OBE 1941; *b* 29 May 1901; *s* of Dr Gerard Steel, JP, Leominster, Herefs; *m* 1932, Elizabeth Chenevix-Trench (*d* 1973); two *s*. *Educ:* Bedford; Royal Military Academy, Woolwich. Prize Cadetship, Woolwich, 1919. Armstrong Memorial Prize, 1921. Commissioned 2nd Lieut RE, 1921; served in India (Bengal Sappers and Miners), 1924-29; Staff College, Camberley, 1936-37; War of 1939-45; E Africa and Abyssinia, 1941; Western Desert, 1942; POW, 1942; Switzerland, 1943; Dep. Head, British Mil. Mission to Greece, 1945-49; Dep. Mil Sec., 1949-52; retd Feb. 1952; Head of Conference and Supply Dept, Foreign Office, 1952-64; Head of Accommodation Department Diplomatic Service, 1965-67. *Recreations:* golf, and gardening. *Address:* Little Hill, Nettlebed, Oxfordshire. *T:* Nettlebed 641287. *Clubs:* Naval and Military, Shikar.

STEEL, Very Rev. David; Minister of St Michael's, Linlithgow, 1959-76, now Minister Emeritus; Moderator of the General Assembly of the Church of Scotland, 1974-75; *b* 5 Oct. 1910; *s* of John S. G. Steel and Jane Scott, Hamilton; *m* 1937, Sheila Martin, Aberdeen; three *s* two *d*. *Educ:* Peterhead Academy; Robert Gordon's Coll., Aberdeen; Aberdeen Univ. MA 1932, BD 1935. Minister of Church of Scotland: Denbeath, Fife, 1936-41; Bridgend, Dumbarton, 1941-46; Home Organisation Foreign Mission Secretary, 1946-49; Minister of Parish of East Africa and of St Andrew's, Nairobi, 1949-57; Associate Minister, St Cuthbert's, Edinburgh, 1957-59. Vis. Prof., Columbia Theol Seminary, Atlanta, 1979 and 1980. Chm. of Governors Callendar Park Coll. of Educn, 1974-79; Vice-Pres., Boys' Brigade, 1974-79. Hon. DD Aberdeen 1964; Hon. LLD Dundee, 1977. *Publications:* History of St Michael's, Linlithgow, 1961; Preaching Through the Year, 1980; contrib. theological and church jls. *Recreation:* trout fishing. *Address:* 13A Chamberlain Road, Edinburgh. *T:* 031-447 2180. *Clubs:* Scottish Liberal (Edinburgh); Edinburgh Amateur Angling.
See also Rt Hon. D. M. S. Steel.

STEEL, Sir David (Edward Charles), Kt 1977; DSO 1940; MC 1945; TD; Chairman, The Wellcome Trust, since 1982; President, London Chamber of Commerce and Industry, since 1982; *b* 29 Nov. 1916; *s* of late Gerald Arthur Steel, CB; *m* 1956, Ann Wynne, *d* of Maj.-Gen. C. B. Price, CB, DSO, DCM, VD, CD; one *s* two *d*. *Educ:* Rugby School; University Coll., Oxford (BA; Hon. Fellow, 1981). Inns of Court Regt, 1938; Commissioned 9 QR Lancers, 1940; served 1940-45 France, Middle East, North Africa, Italy (DSO, MC, despatches thrice). Admitted a Solicitor, June 1948; Linklaters and Paines, 1948-50; Legal Dept of The British Petroleum Co. Ltd, 1950-56; Pres. BP (N Amer.) Ltd, 1959-61; Man. Dir, Kuwait Oil Co. Ltd, 1962-65; Man. Dir, 1965-75, a Dep. Chm., 1972-75 and Chm., 1975-81, BP. A Dir, Bank of England, 1978-. Trustee, The Economist, 1979-. Dep. Chm. of Governors, Rugby Sch. Order of TAJ III, Iran, 1974; Comdr, Order of Leopold, Belgium, 1980. *Address:* 51 Onslow Square, SW7 3LR. *Club:* Cavalry and Guards.

STEEL, Rt. Hon. David (Martin Scott), PC 1977; MP (L) Roxburgh, Selkirk and Peebles since 1965; Leader of the Liberal Party, since 1976; journalist and broadcaster; *b* Scotland, March 1938; *s* of Very Rev. Dr David Steel, *qv* ; *m* 1962, Judith Mary, *d* of W. D. MacGregor, CBE, Dunblane; two *s* one *d* and two adopted *s*. *Educ:* Prince of Wales School, Nairobi, Kenya; George Watson's College and Edinburgh University. MA 1960; LLB 1962. Rector, Edinburgh Univ., 1982-. President: Edinburgh University Liberals, 1959; Students' Representative Council, 1960. Visited Soviet Union, 1961. Asst Secretary, Scottish Liberal Party, 1962-64; Youngest Member of 1964-66 Parliament, of Privy Council, 1977; Liberal Chief Whip, 1970-75; Mem. Parly Delegn to UN Gen. Assembly, 1967; Sponsor, Private Member's Bill to reform law on abortion, 1966-67; Pres., Anti-Apartheid Movement of GB, 1966-69; Chm., Shelter, Scotland, 1969-73. Member: Acton Trust, 1970-; British Council of Churches, 1971-75; Council of Management, Centre for Studies in Social Policy, 1971-76; Adv. Council, European Discussion Centre, 1971-76. BBC television interviewer in Scotland, 1964-65; Presenter of STV weekly religious programme, 1966-67, and for Granada, 1969, and BBC, 1971-76. *Publications:* Boost for the Borders, 1964; Out of Control, 1968; No Entry, 1969; The Liberal Way Forward, 1975; A New Political Agenda, 1976; Militant for the Reasonable Man, 1977; New Majority for a New Parliament, 1978; High Ground of Politics, 1979; A House Divided, 1980; contrib. to The Times, The Guardian, other newspapers and political weeklies. *Recreations:* angling, riding, motoring. *Address:* House of Commons, SW1A 0AA; Cherry Dene, Ettrick Bridge, Selkirkshire. *T:* Ettrick Bridge 253.

STEEL, David William, QC 1981; *b* 7 May 1943; *s* of Sir Lincoln Steel, *qv* ; *m* 1970, Charlotte Elizabeth Ramsay; two *s*. *Educ:* Eton Coll.; Keble Coll., Oxford (MA Hons Jurisprudence). Called to the Bar, Inner Temple, 1966. With Coudert Bros (Attorneys), New York, 1967-68; commenced practice in England, 1969. *Publications:* Editor: Temperley: Merchant Shipping Acts,

1976-; Forms and Precedents: British Shipping Laws, 1977-; Kennedy: Salvage, 1981-. *Recreations:* shooting, fishing. *Address:* The Bell House, Askett, near Aylesbury, Bucks. *T:* Princes Risborough 3453. *Club:* Turf.

STEEL, Major Sir (Fiennes) William Strang, 2nd Bt, *cr* 1938; DL; JP; Major (retired), 17/21st Lancers; Forestry Commissioner, 1958-73; *b* 24 July 1912; *e s* of Sir Samuel Steel, 1st Bt and of Hon. Vere Mabel (*d* 1964), *d* of 1st Baron Cornwallis; *S* father, 1961; *m* 1941, Joan (*d* 1982), *d* of late Brig.-Gen. Sir Brodie Haldane Henderson, KCMG, CB, Braughing, Ware; two *s* (one *d* decd). *Educ:* Eton; RMC, Sandhurst; joined 17/21st Lancers, 1933; Major, 1941; retired, 1947. Convener, Selkirk CC, 1967-75. DL Selkirkshire, 1955, JP 1965. *Heir: s* Major (Fiennes) Michael Strang Steel, 17/21 Lancers [*b* 22 Feb. 1943; *m* 1977, Sarah Russell; one *s* one *d*]. *Address:* Philiphaugh, Selkirk. *T:* Selkirk 21216. *Club:* Cavalry and Guards.

STEEL, Henry, CMG 1976; OBE 1965; Legal Secretary, Law Officers' Department, since 1983; *b* 13 Jan. 1926; *yr s* of late Raphael Steel; *m* 1960, Jennifer Isobel Margaret, *d* of late Brig. M. M. Simpson, MBE; two *s* two *d*. *Educ:* Christ's Coll., Finchley; New Coll., Oxford. BA Oxon 1950. Military Service, RASC and Intell. Corps, 1944-47. Called to Bar, Lincoln's Inn, 1951; Legal Asst, Colonial Office, 1955; Senior Legal Asst, CO, 1960; Asst Legal Adviser, CRO, 1965; Legal Counsellor, FCO, 1967-73; Legal Adviser, UK Mission to UN, NY, 1973-76; Legal Counsellor, FCO, 1976-79; Asst Under-Sec. of State (on loan to Law Officers' Dept), 1979; Legal Adviser to Governor of Southern Rhodesia, 1979-80; Asst Legal Secretary (Under-Secretary), Law Officers' Dept, 1980-83. *Address:* Law Officers' Department, Royal Courts of Justice, WC2.

STEEL, Sir James, Kt 1967; CBE 1964; Lord-Lieutenant of Tyne and Wear, since 1974; Chairman: Furness Withy & Co. Ltd, 1975-79; North of England Building Society; Director: Rea Brothers Ltd; Aeronautical and General Instruments Ltd; *b* 19 May 1909; *s* of Alfred Steel and Katharine (*née* Meikle); *m* 1935, Margaret Jean MacLauchlan; two *s* two *d*. *Educ:* Trent College. Mem., Commn on the Constitution, 1969-73. Trustee, Sir John Priestman Charity Trust; Vice-Chm. of Council, Durham University (Vice-Chm., 1978-). Chairman: British Productivity Council, 1966-67; Textile Council, 1968-72; Washington Develt Corp., 1964-77. President: Northumbria Assoc. of Youth Clubs; Durham Co. Conservation Trust; TA for N of England; YMCA, Sunderland; Vice-Pres., Wildfowl Trust; Jt Pres., Council of the Order of St John for Northumbria; Governor, Trent College. Liveryman, Worshipful Co. of Founders. CBIM. JP Sunderland, 1964; Durham: DL 1969; Sheriff 1972-73. KStJ 1975. Hon. DCL Dunelm, 1978. *Recreations:* ornithology, photography. *Address:* Fawnlees Hall, Wolsingham, County Durham DL13 3LW. *T:* 7307. *Club:* Carlton.

STEEL, Sir (Joseph) Lincoln (Spedding), Kt 1965; JP; formerly Director: ICI Ltd; Charterhouse Investment Trust; Chairman, Triplex Holdings Ltd, 1961-66; *b* 24 March 1900; *s* of late Comdr Joseph Steel, RD, RNR, and Esther Alice (*née* Spedding); *m* 1st, 1928, Cynthia Smith (*d* 1929); one *s* ; 2nd, 1938, Barbara I. T., *y d* of late Colonel S. G. Goldschmidt; one *s*. *Educ:* Christ's Hospital; St John's College, Oxford (Open Scholar, MA). Served RE, 1918-19. Joined Brunner Mond & Co. Ltd, 1922; Delegate Dir, ICI (Alkali) Ltd, 1932; Man. Dir, Alkali Div. of ICI Ltd, 1942; Chm. Alkali Div. of ICI Ltd, 1943; Dir, Imperial Chemical Industries Ltd, 1945-60, retd. Chm. British Nat. Cttee of International Chamber of Commerce, 1951-63; Pres. Internat. Chamber of Commerce, 1963-65; Vice-Pres. 1951-63; Hon. Pres. 1965-; Chairman Overseas Cttee of FBI, 1950-65; Member: Council of CBI, 1965-68; EFTA Consultative Cttee, 1960-69. Leader, UK Industrial Mission to W Indies, 1952. Member Cheshire County Council, 1937-45; JP Cheshire, 1939; JP Bucks, 1960; Gen. Comr for Income Tax, Burnham District, 1968-75. FRSA 1963. *Recreations:* gardening, walking, travel. *Address:* The Warren, 87 Bois Lane, Chesham Bois, Amersham, Bucks. *T:* Amersham 6406. *Club:* Beefsteak.
See also D. W. Steel.

STEEL, Robert, CBE 1979; Secretary-General, Royal Institution of Chartered Surveyors, since 1968; *b* 7 April 1920; *e s* of late John Thomas Steel, Wooler, Northumberland; *m* 1943, Averal Frances, *d* of Arthur Pettitt; one *s* one *d*. *Educ:* Duke's Sch., Alnwick, Northumb.; Univ. of London (BSc 1945); Gray's Inn (Barrister, 1956). Surveyor, 1937-46; Asst Sec., Under Sec., Royal Instn of Surveyors, 1946-61; Dir of Town Development, Basingstoke, 1962-67. Sec.-Gen., Internat. Fedn of Surveyors, 1967-69, Vice-Pres., 1970-72; Sec., Commonwealth Assoc. of Surveying and Land Economy, 1969-; Sec., Aubrey Barker Trust, 1970-; Member: South East Economic Planning Council, 1974-76; Council, British Consultants Bureau, 1977-. Chm., Geometers Liaison Cttee, EEC, 1972-. Hon. Editor, Commonwealth Surveying and Land Economy. Organised national networks of beacons for Queen's Silver Jubilee celebrations, 1977, and for the Wedding of Prince Charles and Lady Diana Spencer, 1981. Raised £71,210 for RICS Ben. Fund by sponsored walk of 1000 miles, John O'Groats to Land's End, 1979 (world record for largest sum raised by a single walker). FRICS; FRGS. *Publications:* on Property Law; contrib. professional jls. *Recreations:* mountain walking, travel, music. *Address:* 12 Great George Street, SW1. *T:* 01-222 7000.

STEEL, Prof. Robert Walter, BSc, MA Oxon; Principal, University College of Swansea, 1974-82; Vice-Chancellor, 1979-81, Emeritus Professor 1982, University of Wales; *b* 31 July 1915; *er s* of late Frederick Grabham and Winifred Barry Steel; *m* 1940, Eileen Margaret, *er d* of late Arthur Ernest and Evelyn Beatrice Page, Bournemouth; one *s* two *d. Educ:* Great Yarmouth Grammar Sch.; Cambridge and County High School for Boys; Jesus College, Oxford (Open Exhibitioner in Geography; Hon. Fellow 1982). RGS Essay Prize, 1936. Drapers' Co. Research Scholarship for Geography, 1937-39, for work in Sierra Leone; Departmental Lectr in Geography, Univ. of Oxford, 1939-47; Naval Intelligence Div., Admiralty, 1940-45; attached to Sociological Dept of W African Inst. of Arts, Industry and Social Science as geographer to Ashanti Social Survey, Gold Coast, 1945-46; University of Oxford: Univ. Lectr in Commonwealth Geography, 1947-56; Lectr in Geography, St Peter's Hall, 1951-56; Official Fellow and Tutor in Geography, Jesus Coll., 1954-56 (Supernumary Welsh Fellow, 1974-75 and 1979-80; Hon. Fellow 1982); Univ. of Liverpool: John Rankin Prof. of Geography, 1957-74; Dean, Faculty of Arts, 1965-68, Pro-Vice-Chancellor, 1971-73. Murchison Grant (RGS), 1948; Council RGS, 1949-53, 1968-71; Inst. of Brit. Geographers: Council, 1947-60; Actg Sec., 1948, Asst Sec., 1949-50; Hon. Editor of Publications, 1950-60; Vice-Pres., 1966-67, Pres. 1968, Hon. Mem. 1974; President: Section E (Geography), British Association for the Adv. of Science, 1966; African Studies Assoc. of the UK, 1970-71 (Vice-Pres., 1969-70); Geographical Assoc., 1973 (Hon. Mem. 1982). Dir, Commonwealth Geographical Bureau, 1972-81; Member: Inter-Univ. Council for Higher Educn Overseas, 1974-; Cttee for Internat. Co-operation in Higher Educn, British Council (Higher Educn Div.); Chairman: Universities Council for Adult Educn, 1976-80; Governors, Westhill Coll., Birmingham, 1981-; Bd, Welsh Adv. Body on Local Authority Higher Educn, 1982-; Council, National Univ. of Lesotho, 1981-. Vice-Pres., Royal African Soc., 1977-; Council, Nat. Inst. of Adult Educn, 1977-80. Vis. Prof., Univ. of Ghana, 1964; Canadian Commonwealth Vis. Fellow, Carleton Univ., 1970. Hon. DSc Salford, 1977. *Publications:* ed (with A. F. Martin), and contrib. to, The Oxford Region: a Scientific and Historical Survey, 1954; ed (with C. A. Fisher), and contrib. to Geographical Essays on British Tropical Lands, 1956; ed (with R. M. Prothero), and contrib. to Geographers and the Tropics: Liverpool Essays, 1964; ed (with R. Lawton), and contrib. to Liverpool Essays on Geography: a Jubilee Collection, 1967; (with Eileen M. Steel) Africa, 1974, 3rd edn 1982; ed, Human Ecology and Hong Kong: report for the Commonwealth Human Ecology Council, 1975; The Institute of British Geographers, the First Fifty Years, 1983; (ed) British Geography, 1918-1945: Issues and Ideas, 1983; articles, mainly on tropical Africa, in Geographical Jl and other geog. jls. *Recreations:* walking, gardening, music. *Address:* 12 Cambridge Road, Langland, Swansea SA3 4PE. *T:* Swansea 69087. *Club:* Royal Commonwealth Society.

STEEL, Rupert Oliver; Chairman, Everards Brewery Ltd, since 1978; *b* 30 April 1922; *s* of Joseph Steel and Beatrice Elizabeth Courage; *m* 1st, Marigold Katharine, *d* of Percy Lowe; two *s* ; 2nd, Lucinda Evelyn Tennant, *d* of Arthur James; one *s* one *d. Educ:* Eton. Served War of 1939-45, Pilot, RNVR, Fleet Air Arm, 1941-46. Courage & Co. Ltd, 1946-78; Imperial Group Ltd, 1975-78; Director: Lloyds Bank Ltd, 1977-79; Lloyds Bank UK Management, 1979-; Umeco Holdings Ltd, 1979-; South Uist Estates Ltd, 1980-. *Recreation:* country. *Address:* Winterbourne Holt, Newbury, Berks RG16 8AP. *T:* Chieveley 220. *Club:* Brooks's.

STEEL, Major Sir William Strang; *see* Steel, Major Sir F. W. S.

STEELE, Prof. Alan John; Professor of French, University of Edinburgh, 1972-80, retired; *b* Bellshill, Lanark, 11 April 1916; *s* of John Steele, MA, BD, and Anne (*née* Lawson); *m* 1947, Claire Alice Louise Belet; one *s* one *d. Educ:* Royal Grammar School, Newcastle upon Tyne; Blyth Secondary School, Northumberland; Universities of Edinburgh, Grenoble and Paris. MA 1st Cl. Hons in French Language and Literature, Vans Dunlop Schol., Univ. of Edinburgh, 1938. Served War of 1939-45, at sea with 4th Maritime AA Regt, RA, 1941-42; commissioned, 1942, with 64th LAA Regt RA in Algeria, Italy and Greece. Lecturer in French, University of Edinburgh, 1946, Prof. of French Literature, 1961-72. Chairman: Scottish Central Cttee for Modern Languages, 1972-81; Assoc. of Univ. Profs of French, 1974-75; Consultative Cttee, Institut Français d'Ecosse, 1981-; Vice-Pres., Franco-Scottish Soc. 1961-. Mem., Church of Scotland Panel on Doctrine, 1978-. Editor, Modern Language Review (French Section), 1971-79. Chevalier, Légion d'Honneur, 1973. *Publications:* (with R. A. Leigh) Contemporary French Translation Passages, 1956; Three Centuries of French Verse, 1956, new edn, 1961; contrib. to Cahiers de l'Assoc. Internat. des Etudes françaises, Modern Language Review. *Recreation:* golf. *Address:* 17 Polwarth Grove, Edinburgh EH11 1LY. *T:* 031-337 5092.

STEELE, Dr Bernard Robert; Director, Science and Research Policy, Departments of the Environment and of Transport, since 1978; *b* 21 July 1929; *s* of Robert Walter and late Phyllis Mabel Steele; *m* 1953, Dorothy Anne Newman; one *s* two *d. Educ:* Oakham Sch.; Selwyn Coll., Cambridge (MA, PhD). Scientific Officer, Min. of Supply, 1953-55; Section Leader, UKAEA, Springfields, 1955-66; Building Research Station: Head, Materials Div., 1966-69; Asst Dir, 1969-72; Dep. Dir, Building Res. Estabt, 1972-75; Borough Housing Officer, Haringey, 1975-78. Chm., Environment Cttee, SRC, later SERC, 1978-81. Pres., RILEM (Internat. Union of Testing and Res. Labs for Materials and Structures), 1974-75. Chm., Watford Churches Housing Assoc., 1975-78. *Publications:* contrib. numerous scientific publications on chemistry, materials science and building. *Recreations:* travelling, photography. *Address:* 1 Broom Grove, Watford WD1 3RY. *T:* Watford 41271.

STEELE, (Francis) Howard, FCGI, BSc(Eng), CEng, FIEE, FIERE; Managing Director, Sony Broadcast Ltd, since 1978; *b* Gt Bookham, Surrey, 23 Sept. 1929; *s* of late Arnold Francis Steele, MBE, and of Florence Anne Winifred Steele; *m* 1953, Elaine Barnes Steele (*née* Mason); two *s. Educ:* Mill Hill School; Imperial College of Science and Technology. Engineer, Marconi Company, Chelmsford, 1952-57; Asst Engineer in Charge, Alpha Television Services, Birmingham, 1957-58; Head of Planning and Installation Dept, 1958-61, Chief Engineer, 1961-66, ABC Television Ltd; Chief Engineer, ITA, 1966-69; Dir of Engineering, ITA, later IBA, 1969-78. Member: EBU Tech. Cttee, 1964-78; Nat. Electronics Council, 1967-71 and 1974-77; Chm., Montreux Internat. Symposium Awards Cttee, 1977-79. IEE: Mem. Council, 1965-68, 1976-77 and 1979-; Faraday Lectr, 1975-76; Chm., Electronics Div., 1980-81. FRTS 1971 (Mem. Council, 1969-72). Hon. Fellow, British Kinematograph, Sound and Television Soc., 1974. Freeman, City of London, 1955. Montreux Internat. TV Symposium Citation, 1969. *Recreations:* motoring and sailing. *Address:* The White Cottage, Pitt, near Winchester, Hants. *Club:* Royal Southern Yacht.

STEELE, Frank Fenwick, OBE 1969; Chairman, Network Television Ltd, since 1981; joined Kleinwort, Benson as Adviser, 1975; Director: Arab British Chamber of Commerce, since 1978; Cluff Oil Ltd, since 1979; *b* 11 Feb. 1923; *s* of Frank Robert and Mary Fenwick Steele; *m* ; one *s* one *d. Educ:* St Peter's Sch., York; Emmanuel Coll., Cambridge (MA). Army, 1943-47. Joined HM Diplomatic Service, 1951; FO, 1951; Vice-Consul, Basra, 1951; Third, later Second Sec., Tripoli, 1953; Foreign Office, 1956; Second Sec., Beirut, 1958; FO, 1961; First Sec.: Amman, 1965; Nairobi, 1968; Counsellor and Dep. UK Rep., Belfast, 1971; FCO, 1973; retd 1975. Member Council: Anglo-Jordanian Soc., 1980-; Royal Soc. for Asian Affairs, 1981-. *Recreation:* travel. *Address:* 9 Ashley Gardens, SW1. *T:* 01-834 7596. *Clubs:* Travellers', Beefsteak, Shikar.

STEELE, Howard; *see* Steele, F. H.

STEELE, Dr John Hyslop, FRS 1978; FRSE; Director, Woods Hole Oceanographic Institution, Mass, since 1977; *b* 15 Nov. 1926; *s* of Adam Steele and Annie Hyslop Steele; *m* 1956, Margaret Evelyn Travis; one *s. Educ:* George Watson's Boys' Coll., Edinburgh (Higher Cert. of Educn); University Coll., London Univ. (BSc, DSc). FRSE 1968. Marine Lab., Aberdeen, Scotland: Marine Scientist, 1951-66; Sen. Principal Scientific Officer, 1966-73; Dep. Dir, 1973-77. Fellow, Amer. Acad. of Arts and Sciences, 1980. Agassiz Medal, Nat. Acad. of Sciences, USA, 1973. *Publications:* Structure of Marine Ecosystems, 1974; over 70 pubns in oceanographic and ecological jls. *Recreation:* sailing. *Address:* Woods Hole Oceanographic Institution, Woods Hole, Mass 02543, USA. *T:* (617) 548-1400. *Club:* Cosmos (Washington, DC).

STEELE, John Roderic, CB 1979; Director-General for Transport, Commission of the European Communities, since 1981; *b* 22 Feb. 1929; *s* of late Harold Graham Steele and Doris Steele (*née* Hall); *m* 1956, Margaret Marie, *d* of late Joseph and Alice Stevens; two *s* two *d. Educ:* Queen Elizabeth Grammar Sch., Wakefield; Queen's Coll., Oxford (MA). Asst Principal, Min. Civil Aviation, 1951; Private Sec. to Parly Sec., MTCA, 1954; Principal, Road Trans. Div., 1957; Sea Transport, 1960; Shipping Policy, 1962; Asst Sec., Shipping Policy, BoT, 1964; Counsellor (Shipping), British Embassy, Washington, 1967; Asst Sec., Civil Aviation Div., DTI, 1971, Under-Sec., Space Div., 1973, Shipping Policy Div., 1974, Gen. Div., 1975, Dept of Trade; Dep. Sec., Dept of Trade, 1976-80, Dept of Industry, 1980-81. *Recreations:* normal. *Address:* 7 Kemerton Road, Beckenham, Kent; Square Ambiorix 30, Bte 30, 1040 Bruxelles, Belgium. *Club:* Philippics.

STEELE, Sir Kenneth (Charles), Kt 1981; DFC 1944; Group Chairman, Myer Emporium, 1976-78, retired; *b* 2 March 1913; *s* of late K. S. Steele and E. M. Dunbier; *m* 1947, Barbara Harrison; one *s. Educ:* Hawthorn West High Sch. Served War of 1939-45, UK RAF Bomber Comd, 78 Sqdn. Joined Myer Emporium Ltd, 1928; Gp Man. Dir, 1966-76; period of employment unbroken except for war service. Mem., Fed. Govt Economic Consultative Gp Cttee, 1975-78. Inaugural Pres., Australian Retailers' Assoc., 1974-75. Silver Jubilee Medal, 1977. *Recreations:* fresh and saltwater flyfishing, golf, Thoroughbred breeding and racing. *Address:* 212 Doncaster Road, North Balwyn, Melbourne, Vic 3104, Australia. *T:* 03-8579851. *Clubs:* Athenæum (Melbourne); Riversdale Golf, Racing, VRC, VATC, MVRC.

STEELE, Kenneth Walter Lawrence, CBE 1980 (OBE 1967); KPM 1936; Chief Constable, Avon and Somerset Constabulary, 1974-79; *b* 28 July 1914; *s* of Walter and Susan Steele, Godalming, Surrey. *Educ:* Wellington Sch., Wellington, Somerset. Served War: with Somerset LI and Royal Northumberland Fusiliers, 1942-45. Asst Chief Constable, Buckinghamshire, 1953-55; Chief Constable: Somerset, 1955-66; Somerset and Bath, 1966-74. *Recreations:* badminton, tennis. *Address:* Lloyds Bank Ltd, 31 Fore Street, Taunton, Somerset.

STEELE, Sir (Philip John) Rupert, Kt 1980; Member, Racecourses Licensing Board, 1975-81; *b* 3 Nov. 1920; *s* of late C. Steele; *m* 1946, Judith, *d* of Dr Clifford Sharp; one *s* two *d. Educ:* Melbourne C of E Grammar School. Served RAAF and 115 Sqdn (Lancaster), RAF; POW 1944. Director: Steele & Co. Ltd, 1949-59; Carlton Brewery Ltd, 1964-73; Carlton and United Breweries, 1973-. Mem. Council, Royal Agr. Soc. of Victoria, 1961-74. Mem. Cttee, Victoria Racing Club, 1958-, Hon. Treasurer, 1971-73, Vice-Chm.,

1973-77, Chm., 1977-82; Pres., Prahran Football Club, 1980-. *Recreation:* racing thoroughbred horses. *Address:* 2/64 Irving Road, Toorak, Victoria 3142, Australia.

STEELE, Richard Charles, FIBiol, FICFor; Director General, Nature Conservancy Council, since 1980; *b* 26 May 1928; *s* of Richard Orson Steele and Helen Curtis Steele (*née* Robertson); *m* 1966, Anne Freda Nelson; two *s* one *d. Educ:* Univ. of Wales (BSc Forestry and Botany); Univ. of Oxford. National Service, 1946-48. Assistant Conservator of Forests, Colonial Forest Service (later HMOCS), Tanganyika (later Tanzania), 1951-63; Head: Woodland Management Section, Nature Conservancy, Monks Wood, 1963-73; Terrestrial Life Sciences Section, Natural Environment Research Council, London, 1973-78; Division of Scientific Services, NERC Inst. of Terrestrial Ecology, Cambridge, 1978-80. Past Pres., Inst. of Foresters of Gt Britain. *Publications:* Wildlife Conservation in Woodlands, 1972; ed, Monks Wood: a nature reserve record, 1974; numerous papers on nature conservation, ecology and forestry in professional and scientific jls. *Recreations:* hill-walking, gardening, collecting books on natural history and E African travel. *Address:* 150 Girton Road, Cambridge CB3 0PQ. *T:* Cambridge 276347. *Clubs:* Athenæum, Royal Commonwealth Society.

STEELE, Sir Rupert; *see* Steele, Sir P. J. R.

STEELE, Tommy, (Thomas Hicks), OBE 1979; Actor; *b* Bermondsey London, 17 Dec. 1936; *s* of late Thomas Walter Hicks and Elizabeth Ellen (*née* Bennett); *m* 1960, Ann Donoghue; one *d. Educ:* Bacon's Sch. for Boys, Bermondsey. First appearance on stage in variety, Empire Theatre, Sunderland, Nov. 1956; first London appearance, variety, Dominion Theatre, 1957; Buttons in Rodgers and Hammerstein's Cinderella, Coliseum, 1958; Tony Lumpkin in She Stoops to Conquer, Old Vic, 1960; Arthur Kipps in Half a Sixpence, Cambridge Theatre, London, 1963-64 and Broadhurst Theatre (first NY appearance), 1965; Truffaldino in The Servant of Two Masters, Queen's, 1969; Dick Whittington, London Palladium, 1969; Meet Me In London, Adelphi, 1971; Jack Point, in The Yeomen of the Guard, City of London Fest., 1978; London Palladium: The Tommy Steele Show, 1973; Hans Andersen, 1974 and 1977; one-man show, Prince of Wales, 1979; *films:* Kill Me Tomorrow, 1956; The Tommy Steele Story; The Duke Wore Jeans; Tommy the Toreador; Touch It Light; It's All Happening; The Happiest Millionaire; Half a Sixpence; Finian's Rainbow; Where's Jack?; *television:* wrote and acted in Quincy's Quest, 1979. Composed and recorded, My Life, My Song, 1974. *Publication:* Quincy, 1981. *Recreations:* squash, painting. *Address:* c/o Talent Artists Ltd, 13 Bruton Street, W1X 8JY. *T:* 01-493 0343.

STEELE-BODGER, Prof. Alasdair, CBE 1980; FRCVS; Professor of Veterinary Clinical Studies, University of Cambridge, since 1979; *b* 1 Jan. 1924; *s* of late Harry Steele-Bodger, MRCVS, and Mrs K. Steele-Bodger (*née* MacDonald); *m* 1948, Anne, 2nd *d* of late Captain A. W. J. Finlayson, RN, and Mrs Nancy Finlayson; three *d. Educ:* Shrewsbury Sch.; Caius Coll., Cambridge (BA 1945, MA); Royal 'Dick' Veterinary Coll., Edinburgh Univ. (BSc, MRCVS 1948). Hon. FRCVS 1975. Gen. vet. practice, Lichfield, Staffs, 1948-77; consultant practice, Fordingbridge, Hants, 1977-79. Hon. Vet. Consultant to British Agricl Export Council, 1967-. Pres., British Small Animal Vet. Assoc., 1962; Member: Animal Feedingstuffs Industry/BVA/Agricl Develt and Adv. Service HQ Liaison Cttee; Jockey Club's Horserace Anti-Doping Cttee, 1973-; UGC's Agricl and Vet. Sub-Cttee, 1973-82; Council, BVA, 1957- (Pres., 1966); RCVS, 1960- (Pres., 1972); Jt RCVS/BVA Cttee on Eur. Vet. Affairs, 1967-; Eur. Liaison Gp for Agriculture, 1972-; Cttee of Inquiry on Experiments on Animals, 1963-65; Council, Royal Agricl Soc. of England, 1967-. UK Deleg. to Fedn of Veterinarians of EEC, 1967-; EEC Official Vet. Expert, 1974-; Mem., EEC Adv. Cttee on Vet. Trng, 1981-. Hon. Vet. Consultant, Nat. Cattle Breeders' Assoc., 1979-. Gen. Comr to Bd of Inland Revenue, 1969-82. Chm., Editorial Bd, Veterinary Drug, 1978-. Crookes' Prize, 1970; Dalrymple-Champneys Cup and Medal, 1972. Cambridge Triple Blue. *Publications:* Society of Practising Veterinary Surgeons Economics Report, 1961, and papers in vet. jls on clinical subjects and vet. econs. *Recreations:* swimming, fishing, travel. *Address:* Midsummer House, Littlebury, Saffron Walden, Essex. *Clubs:* Farmers' Hawks (Cambridge).
See also M. R. Steele-Bodger.

STEELE-BODGER, Michael Roland; veterinary surgeon in private practice; *b* 4 Sept. 1925; *s* of late Henry William Steele-Bodger and Kathrine Macdonald; *m* 1955, Violet Mary St Clair Murray; two *s* one *d. Educ:* Rugby Sch.; Gonville and Caius Coll., Cambridge. MRCVS. Mem., Sports Council, 1976-. England Rugby Selector, 1954-70; Pres., RFU, 1973-74; Mem., Internat. Rugby Football Bd, 1974-; Chm., Four Home Rugby Unions' Tours Cttee, 1976-. Cambridge Univ. Rugby Blue, Captain 1946; England Rugby Internat., 1947-48. *Recreation:* interest in all sport. *Address:* Laxford Lodge, Bonehill, Tamworth, Staffs. *T:* Tamworth 61010. *Clubs:* East India, Devonshire, Sports and Public Schools; Hawks (Cambridge).
See also A. Steele-Bodger.

STEELE-PERKINS, Surgeon Vice-Admiral Sir Derek (Duncombe), KCB 1966 (CB 1963); KCVO 1964 (CVO 1954); FRCS; FRACS; *b* 19 June 1908; *s* of late Dr Duncombe Steele-Perkins, Honiton, Devon, and Sybil Mary Hill-Jones, Edinburgh; *m* 1937, Joan Boddan, Birkdale, Lancashire; three *d. Educ:* Allhallows School, Rousdon; Edinburgh University and College of

Surgeons (Edin.). Entered RN, 1932; RN Hosp., Haslar, 1932; HMS Mantis, China, 1934-36; HMS Ganges, Shotley, 1936-38; HMS Vindictive, 1938-39; RN Hospitals: Haslar, 1939-40; Chatham, 1940-44; Sydney, Australia, 1944-46; Malta, 1946-50; R Y Gothic, 1951-52; Chatham, 1952-59; Senior Surgical Specialist, RN Hosp., Bighi, Malta, Oct. 1959-61; Medical Officer-in-Charge, Royal Naval Hospital, Haslar, 1961; Command MO to C-in-C, Portsmouth, 1962-63; Medical Director of the Navy, 1963-66. FRSocMed. Royal Commonwealth Tours, 1953-54, 1959. QHS 1961. CStJ. *Recreations:* sailing, fly-fishing, shooting. *Address:* c/o National Westminster Bank, Haven Road, Canford Cliffs, Dorset. *Clubs:* Royal Cruising; Royal Lymington Yacht (Cdre 1969-72).

STEEN, Anthony David; MP (C) Liverpool Wavertree, since Feb. 1974; barrister; youth leader; social worker; underwriter; *b* 22 July 1939; *s* of Stephen Nicholas Steen, *qv*; *m* 1965, Carolyn Padfield, educational psychologist; one *s* one *d. Educ:* Westminster Sch.; occasional student University Coll., London. Called to Bar, Gray's Inn, 1962; practising Barrister, 1962-74, Defence Counsel, MoD (Court Martials). Lectr in Law, Council of Legal Educn, 1964-68; Adv. Tutor, Sch. of Environment, Central London Poly., 1981-. Founder and First Director: Task Force to help London's old and lonely, with Govt support, 1964; Govt Foundn YVFF, tackling urban deprivation, 1968-74; Consultant to Canadian Govt on student and employment matters, 1970-71. Mem., Select Cttee on Race Relations, 1975-79; Chairman: Cons. Mems Parly Gp, 1974; Cons. Party Back Bench Cttee on Cities, Urban and New Town Affairs, 1979-; All Party Friends of Cycling, 1979-; Vice-Chm., Health and Social Services, 1979-80; Sec., Parly Caribbean Gp, 1979-; Co-ordinator, Chm's Unit for Marginal and Critical Seats, Cons. Central Office, 1982-. Vice-Pres., Merseyside Young Conservatives. Member: Exec. Council, NPFA; Board, Community Transport; Council of Reference, Internat. Christian Relief; Chm., Outlandos Charitable Trust; Vice-Chm., Task Force Trust; Vice-President: Ecology Bldg Soc.; Internat. Centre for Child Studies; Bentley Operatic Soc. Patron, Liverpool's Open Circle for Detached Youth Work. *Publications:* New Life for Old Cities, 1981; jt author of booklets on urban problems; regular contributor to The Times and Daily Telegraph. *Recreations:* piano, hill climbing, swimming, cycling. *Address:* House of Commons, SW1; Waverton, Church Road, Liverpool. *T:* 051-733 7402. *Clubs:* Royal Automobile; Old Swan, Churchill and Broadgreen Conservative.

STEEN, Stephen Nicholas; President, Smith & Nephew Associated Companies Ltd, since 1976 (Chairman, 1968-76); Chairman, British Tissues Limited, 1971-77; *b* 19 July 1907; *m* 1934; one *s* one *d.* Arthur Berton & Co. Ltd, 1943; Director, Smith & Nephew Associated Companies Ltd, 1958, Dep. Chm. 1962. Underwriting Member, Matthews Wrightson Pulbrook Ltd; called to the Bar, Gray's Inn, 1949. Mem., Ct of Patrons, RCS, 1973-. *Recreation:* golf. *Address:* (office) 2 Temple Place, WC2R 3BP. *T:* 01-836 7922. *Club:* Carlton.
See also A. D. Steen.

STEER, Prof. John Richardson, FSA 1981; Professor of the History of Art, Birkbeck College, University of London, since 1980; art-historian and director; *b* 14 Oct. 1928; *s* of Walter Wallis Steer and Elsie Gertrude (*née* Colman). *Educ:* Clayesmore Sch., Dorset; Keble Coll., Oxford (MA); Courtauld Inst. of Art, Univ. of London (BA). Gen. Asst, City Art Gall., Birmingham, 1953-56; Asst Lectr, Dept of Fine Art, Univ. of Glasgow, 1956-59; Lectr in Hist. of European Art, Univ. of Bristol, 1959-67; Prof. of Fine Arts, Univ. of St Andrews, 1967-80. Chm., Adv. Cttee on Validation, Heriot-Watt Univ./Edinburgh Coll. of Art, 1978-; Chm., Art Historians Assoc. of GB, 1980-; Vice-Chm., Scottish Theatre Ballet, 1969-71; Mem., Cttee for Art and Design, CNAA, 1977-82 (Chm., Hist. of Art/Design and Complementary Studies Bd, 1977-79). Adjudicator, National Student Drama Festival, 1977. Theatrical prodns include: The Seagull, St Andrews, 1971; And When Love Speaks, Edinburgh, 1975; The Privacy of the Patients, Edinburgh Fringe, 1977, ICA, 1978; Waiting for Godot, St Andrews, 1978. *Publications:* A Concise History of Venetian Painting, 1967; Mr Bacon's Titian (Selwyn Brinton Lecture, RSA), 1977; Alvise Vivarini, 1982; contribs to Burlington Magazine, Art History. *Recreation:* travel. *Address:* 1 Cheriton Square, SW17 8AE.

STEER, Kenneth Arthur, CBE 1978; MA, PhD, FSA, FSAScot; Secretary, Royal Commission on the Ancient and Historical Monuments of Scotland, 1957-78; *b* 12 Nov. 1913; *o s* of Harold Steer and Emily Florence Thompson; *m* 1941, Rona Mary Mitchell; one *d. Educ:* Wath Grammar School; Durham University. Research Fellowship, 1936-38. Joined staff of Royal Commission on Ancient and Historical Monuments of Scotland, 1938. Intelligence Officer in Army, 1941-45 (despatches twice). Monuments, Fine Arts and Archives Officer, North Rhine Region, 1945-46. Corresponding Member, German Archæological Inst.; Horsley Memorial Lecturer, Durham University, 1963; Rhind Lectr, 1968. Pres., Soc. of Antiquaries of Scotland, 1972-75. Arts Council Literary Award, 1978. *Publications:* Late Medieval Monumental Sculpture in the West Highlands (with J. W. M. Bannerman), 1976; numerous articles in archæological journals. *Address:* 1 Silver Hay, Dumbleton, near Evesham, Worcs. *T:* Evesham 881783.

STEER, Rt. Rev. Stanley Charles; Bishop of Saskatoon, 1950-70; *s* of S. E. and E. G. Steer; *m* 1936, Marjorie Slater. *Educ:* Guildford Gram. Sch.; Univ. of Saskatchewan (B), Oxford Univ. (MA). Hon. DD: Wycliffe Coll., Toronto, 1947, Emmanuel Coll., Saskatoon, 1952; St Chad's Coll., Regina,

1964. Missionary at Vanderhoof, BC, 1929; Chaplain, St Mark's Church, Alexandria, 1931; Chaplain, University Coll., Oxford, 1932-33; St John's Hall, Univ. of London: Tutor, 1933; Vice-Principal, 1936. Chaplain, The Mercers' Company, City of London, 1937; Principal, Emmanuel Coll., Saskatoon, 1941; Hon. Canon of St John's Cathedral, Saskatoon, and CF (R of O), 1943. *Recreation:* tennis. *Address:* 2383 Lincoln Road, Victoria, BC V8R 6A3, Canada. *T:* 592 9888.

STEER, Wilfred Reed, QC 1972; *b* 23 Aug. 1926; *s* of George William and Dorothy Steer; *m* 1953, Jill Park; one *s* one *d*, and two step *s. Educ:* Bede Collegiate Sch., Sunderland, Co. Durham; London Sch. of Economics. LLB (Lond.) 1949. Called to the Bar, Gray's Inn, 1950. *Address:* 51 Westgate Road, Newcastle upon Tyne. *T:* Newcastle upon Tyne 20541.

STEER, William Reed Hornby, DL, MA, LLB, Barrister-at-Law; Recorder of South Molton, 1936-51; Deputy Chairman, London County Council, 1948-49; Lt-Col in the Army (released); *b* 5 April 1899; *s* of late Rev. W. H. Hornby Steer, TD MA, JP; unmarried. *Educ:* Eton; Trinity College, Cambridge. Commissioned in Royal Field Artillery; served European War, France and Belgium; called to Bar, Inner Temple, 1922; joined Western Circuit; Standing Counsel to Commons, Open Spaces, and Footpaths Preservation Society; to Council for Preservation of Rural England; to National Smoke Abatement Society and to Pure Rivers Society; an Examiner in Law to Chartered Institute of Secretaries; Legal Member of Town Planning Inst.; Fellow of Royal Soc. of Health; Associate of Royal Institution of Chartered Surveyors; a representative for Hampstead on London County Council, 1931-52; a representative of London County Council on International Union of Local Authorities; Master of Worshipful Company of Turners, 1949-50; a Governor of Haberdashers' Aske's Schools and of Royal Free Hospital; a Governor and an Almoner of Christ's Hospital, Dep. Chm. Council of Almoners, 1970-75; Chairman Children's Hospital, Hampstead; Vice-Chairman London Old Age Pensions Committee; Treasurer, London Soc.; Kt of Justice, Order of St John; Joint Hon. Secretary of League of Mercy; Gold Staff Officer at Coronation of King George VI; Inspector of Metropolitan Special Constabulary; Army Officers Emergency Reserve, 1938; Extra Regimentally Employed, Military Dept, Judge Advocate-General's Office, 1939; Deputy Judge Advocate-General, Malta, 1941-43; graded Assistant Adjutant-General, War Office, 1944; Staff Officer (I), Control Commission for Germany, 1945; Captain, 1939; Major, 1941; Lt-Col 1943; Member of Territorial Army and Air Force Association of the County of London. *Publications:* articles on the law relating to Highways; Assistant Editor of Glen's Public Health Act, 1936; Steer's Law of Smoke Nuisances, 1938, 2nd edn 1948; contributions to Lord Macmillan's Local Government Law and Administration. *Recreation:* sailing. *Address:* 71A Whitehall Court, SW1A 2EL. *T:* 01-930 3160. *Clubs:* United Oxford & Cambridge University, Carlton, Pratt's, MCC; Royal Corinthian Yacht (Burnham-on-Crouch).

STEERE, Sir Ernest H. L.; *see* Lee-Steere, Sir E. H.

STEERS, James Alfred, CBE 1973; MA; Professor Emeritus of Geography and Emeritus Fellow of St Catharine's College, Cambridge; Chairman, National Committee of Geography, 1967-72; Coastal Consultant to Conservation Committee of Council of Europe, 1968; Chairman, Coastal Conferences, 1966-67; *b* 8 Aug. 1899; *s* of J. A. Steers, Bedford; *m* 1942, Harriet, *d* of J. A. Wanklyn, Cambridge; one *s* one *d. Educ:* Elstow (Private) School, Bedford; St Catharine's Coll., Cambridge. Senior Geography Master, Framlingham Coll., 1921-22; elected Fellow of St Catharine's, 1925, subsequently Dean, Tutor and President, Univ. Demonstrator, 1926-27; Univ. Lecturer, 1927-49; Prof. of Geography, 1949-66; Member of the British Expedition to the Great Barrier Reefs, 1928; Leader of Geographical Expedition to the Reefs, 1936; Expedition to the Jamaica Cays, 1939; War Service, 1917-18; Vice-Pres., Royal Geographical Soc., 1959-63, 1967-72, Hon. Vice-Pres., 1972-; Hon. Mem., 1977-; Pres. Norfolk and Norwich Naturalists Soc., 1940-41; Pres., Section E British Association (Oxford), 1954; President, Inst. Brit. Geographers (Reading), 1956; President: Geographical Assoc., 1959; Estuarine and Brackish Water Science Assoc., 1977-80. Corresp. Mem., Royal Dutch Geographical Soc.; Hon. Mem., Ges. für Erdkunde Berlin; Member: Council of Senate, Cambridge, 1941-48; Wild Life Conservation Cttee; Nature Conservancy, 1949-54, 1957-66; Scientific Policy Cttee, 1949-66; Cttee for England, 1949-68, 1970-73; Nat. Parks Commn, 1960-66; Properties Cttee, Nat. Trust, 1969-76; Hon. Adviser on Coastal Preservation to Ministry of Town and Country Planning and to Department of Health, Scotland; Departmental Cttee on Coastal Flooding, 1953; Advisory Committee... to improve Sea Defences, 1954-; Hydraulics Research Board, DSIR, 1957-61; Visiting Prof., Berkeley, Calif, 1959; Visiting Fellow, Aust. Nat. Univ., 1967. Hon. LLD Aberdeen, 1971; Hon. DSc East Anglia, 1978. Victoria Medal, RGS, 1960; Scottish Geographical Medal, 1969. *Publications:* Introduction to the Study of Map Projections, 1927, 15th edn 1970; The Unstable Earth, 1932 (new edn 1950); Editor and contrib. to Scolt Head Island, 1934, 2nd rev. edn, 1960; The Coastline of England and Wales, 1946 (2nd edn 1969); A Picture Book of the Whole Coast of England and Wales, 1948; The Sea Coast, 1953, 4th edn 1969; The Coast of England and Wales in Pictures, 1960; The English Coast and the Coast of Wales, 1966; Coasts and Beaches, 1969; Introduction to Coastline and Development, 1970; The Coastline of Scotland, 1973; Coastal Features of England and Wales, 1980; Editor: new edns of P. Lake's Physical Geography, 1958; Vol. on Field Studies in the British Isles, Internat. Geog. Union. London meeting, 1964; Brit. Assoc. Advancement of Science, The Cambridge Region, 1965; Engl. edn of V. P.

Zenkovitch, Processes of Coastal Development, 1967; papers on Coastal Physiography, Coral Islands, etc., in various scientific publications. *Recreations:* walking, philately, travel. *Address:* 47 Gretton Court, Girton, Cambridge CB3 0QN. *T:* Cambridge 276007. *Clubs:* Travellers', Geographical (Hon. Mem.).

STEIL, John Wellesley, CMG 1951; MBE 1937; *b* 15 Aug. 1899; *s* of late Lt W. J. Steil, RN; *m* Annetta Elise (*d* 1961), 2nd *d* of late S. Fichat, Nairobi, Kenya; one *s* one *d. Educ:* Christ's Hospital, Horsham; Portsmouth Grammar School; Cadet Ship HMS Conway. Served European War, 1917-19, Harwich Force, HMTB 85, HMS Dragon, Malayan American Rubber Co., Malaya and Sumatra, 1920-24; Colonial Administrative Service, Cadet, Uganda, 1925; Asst District Officer, 1927; District Officer, 1936; Provincial Comr, 1947, Senior Provincial Commissioner, 1949; Secretary for African Affairs, Uganda, MEC and MLC, 1950-51. Farming in WA, 1957-62. *Address:* The Weld Club, GPO Box B54, Perth, WA 6001, Australia. *Clubs:* Royal Commonwealth Society; Weld (Perth, WA).

STEIN, John, CBE 1970; Scotland Football Team Manager, since 1978; *b* 5 Oct. 1922; *s* of George Stein and Jane Armstrong; *m* 1946, Jean McAuley; one *s* one *d. Educ:* Greenfield Public Sch., Lanarkshire. Miner, 1937-50; Professional Footballer, 1950-57; Coach, 1957-60; Manager: Dunfermline, 1960-64; Hibernians, 1964-65; Celtic, 1965-78. Under his management, Celtic won: Scottish League Cup, 1965-66, 1966-67, 1967-68, 1968-69, 1969-70, 1974-75; Scottish Cup, 1964-65, 1966-67, 1968-69, 1970-71, 1971-72, 1973-74, 1974-75, 1976-77; European Cup, 1966-67; Scottish League Championship, 1965-74 inclusive, 1976-77. *Recreations:* golf, bowling. *Address:* 9 Southwood Drive, Glasgow G44 5SH.

STEIN, Prof. Peter Gonville, FBA 1974; JP; Regius Professor of Civil Law in the University of Cambridge, and Fellow of Queens' College, since 1968; *b* 29 May 1926; *o s* of late Walter Stein, MA, Solicitor, and Effie Stein (*née* Walker); *m* 1st, 1953, Janet Chamberlain; three *d*; 2nd, 1978, Anne M. Howard; one step *s. Educ:* Liverpool Coll.; Gonville and Caius Coll., Camb. (Classical Exhibitioner); University of Pavia. Served in RN, Sub-lieut (Sp) RNVR, 1944-47. Admitted a Solicitor, 1951; Italian Govt Scholar, 1951-52; Asst Lecturer in Law, Nottingham Univ., 1952-53; Lecturer in Jurisprudence, 1953-56, Prof. of Jurisprudence, 1956-68, Dean of Faculty of Law, 1961-64, Aberdeen Univ.; Chm., Faculty Bd of Law, Cambridge, 1973-76; Vice Pres., Queens' Coll., 1974-81 (Acting Pres., 1976 and 1980-81). Visiting Prof. of Law: Univ. of Virginia, 1965-66, 1978-79; Colorado, 1966; Witwatersrand, 1970; Louisiana State Univ., 1974, 1977; lectures: R. M. Jones, QUB, 1978; Irvine, Cornell, 1979; Sherman, Boston, 1979. Fellow, Winchester Coll., 1976-. Member: Council, Max Planck Inst. for European Legal History, Frankfurt, 1966-; Council, Internat. Assoc. of Legal History, 1970-; Sec. of State for Scotland's Working Party on Hospital Endowments, 1966-69; Bd of Management, Royal Cornhill and Assoc. (Mental) Hospitals, Aberdeen, 1963-68 (Chm. 1967-68); UGC, 1971-76. Pres., Soc. of Public Teachers of Law, 1980-81. For. Fellow, Accad. di Scienze morali e politiche, Naples, 1982. Hon. Dr jur, Göttingen, 1980. JP Cambridge, 1970-. *Publications:* Fault in the formation of Contract in Roman Law and Scots Law, 1958; editor, Buckland's Textbook of Roman Law, 3rd edn, 1963; Regulae Iuris: from juristic rules to legal maxims, 1966; Roman Law in Scotland in Ius Romanum Medii Aevi, 1968; Roman Law and English Jurisprudence, 1969; (with J. Shand) Legal Values in Western Society, 1974, Italian edn 1981; (ed jtly) Adam Smith's Lectures on Jurisprudence, 1978; Legal Evolution, 1980; articles in legal periodicals mainly on Roman Law and legal history. *Recreations:* hill walking, gardening. *Address:* Queens' College, Cambridge. *T:* Cambridge 65511; Wimple Cottage, Wimpole Road, Great Eversden, Cambridge. *T:* Comberton 2349.

STEINBERG, Professor Hannah; Professor of Psychopharmacology in the University of London at University College, since 1970; *d* of late Michael Steinberg, doctor of law, and Marie (*née* Wein). *Educ:* Schwarzwaldschule, Vienna; Putney High School; Queen Anne's School, Caversham; Univ. of Reading (Cert. Comm.); Denton Secretarial Coll., London; University College London (BA 1st cl. Hons Psychology, PhD; Troughton Schol., 1948-50). FBPsS, FZS. Pres., Univ. of London Union, 1947-48; Univ. of London Postgrad. Studentship, 1948-50. Sec. to Man. Dir, Omes Ltd, 1943-44. University College London: Asst Lectr in Pharmacology, 1954-55; Lectr, 1955-62; Reader in Psychopharmacology, 1962-70; Prof. of Psychopharmacology (first in UK), 1970-. Hon. consulting Clinical Psychologist, Dept of Psychological Medicine, Royal Free Hosp., 1970. Member MRC working parties on: Biochemistry and Pharmacology of Drug Dependence, 1968-73; Biological Aspects of Drug Dependence, 1971-75. Vice-President: Collegium Internationale Neuro-Psychopharmacologicum (CINP), 1968-74; Brit. Assoc. of Psychopharmacology, 1973-77; Mem., Biological Council, 1977-80. Distinguished Affiliate of Amer. Psychol Assoc., Psychopharmacology Div., 1978; Member: British Pharmacol Soc.; Experimental Psychol. Soc., etc. *Publications:* (trans. and ed jtly) Animals and Men, 1951; organiser of symposia and editor: Animal Behaviour and Drug Action (jt), 1963; Scientific Basis of Drug Dependence, 1968; Psychopharmacology, Sexual Disorders and Drug Abuse (jt), 1972, etc; articles and reviews on animal and human psychopharmacology in scientific jls and books; past or present editor of learned jls. *Address:* University College London, Gower Street, WC1E 6BT. *T:* 01-387 7050.

STEINBERG, Jack; President, Steinberg Group, since 1982 (Chairman, 1966–81); *b* 23 May 1913; *s* of Alexander and Sophie Steinberg; *m* 1938, Hannah Anne, *d* of late Solomon Wolfson, JP; two *d*. *Educ:* privately, London. Underwriting Member of Lloyd's. Chairman: Horrockses Fashions Ltd; Butte-Knit (London) Ltd; Member, NEDC; Vice-President: British Mantle Manufacturers' Assoc.; Clothing Export Council (Chm., 1970–74); Chm., Voluntary Research Trust, King's Coll. Hosp. Member of Plumbers' Livery Co.; Freeman, City of London. *Recreation:* farming. *Address:* 74 Portland Place, W1. *T:* 01-580 5908; Chartners Farm, Hartfield, Sussex. *T:* Hartfield 248. *Clubs:* Brooks's, Portland, Carlton.

STEINER, Prof. George, MA, DPhil; Extraordinary Fellow, Churchill College, Cambridge, since 1969; Professor of English and Comparative Literature, University of Geneva, since 1974; *b* 23 April 1929; *s* of Dr F. G. and Mrs E. Steiner; *m* 1955, Zara Steiner (*née* Shakow); one *s* one *d*. *Educ:* Paris (BèsL); Univ. of Chicago (BA); Harvard (MA); Oxford (DPhil). Member, staff of the Economist, in London, 1952–56; Inst. for Advanced Study, Princeton, 1956–58; Gauss Lectr, Princeton Univ., 1959–60; Massey Lectr, 1974; Fellow of Churchill Coll., 1961–. Fulbright Professorship, 1958–69; O. Henry Short Story Award, 1958; Guggenheim Fellowship, 1971–72; Zabel Award of Nat. Inst. of Arts and Letters of the US, 1970. Pres., English Assoc., 1975; Corresp. Mem., (Federal) German Acad. of Literature, 1981. FRSL 1964. Hon. DLitt: East Anglia, 1976; Louvain, 1980. *Publications:* Tolstoy or Dostoevsky, 1958; The Death of Tragedy, 1960; Anno Domini, 1964; Language and Silence, 1967; Extraterritorial, 1971; In Bluebeard's Castle, 1971; The Sporting Scene: White Knights in Reykjavik, 1973; After Babel, 1975 (adapted for TV as The Tongues of Men, 1977); Heidegger, 1978; On Difficulty and Other Essays, 1978; The Portage to San Cristobal of A. H., 1981. *Recreations:* music, chess, mountain walking. *Address:* 32 Barrow Road, Cambridge. *T:* Cambridge 61200. *Clubs:* Athenæum, Savile; Harvard (New York).

STEINER, Rear-Adm. Ottokar Harold Mojmir St John, CB 1967; Asst Chief of Defence Staff, 1966–68, retired; *b* 8 July 1916; *e s* of late O. F. Steiner; *m* 1st, 1940, Evelyn Mary Young (marr. diss. 1975); one *s* one *d*; 2nd, 1975, Eleanor, widow of Sqdn Leader W. J. H. Powell, RAF. *Educ:* St Paul's School. Special entry cadet, RN, 1935. Served War of 1939–45 (despatches twice), HMS Ilex, Havelock, Frobisher, Superb. Naval Staff Course, 1947; Staff of C-in-C, Far East Fleet, 1948–50; Comdr 1950; jssc 1953; HMS Ceylon, 1953–54; NATO Defence Coll., 1955; HMS Daedalus, 1955–56; Capt. 1956; Admiralty, 1956–58; in comd HMS Saintes and Capt. (D) 3rd Destroyer Squdn, 1958–60; Naval Adviser to UK High Commission, Canada, 1960–62; Senior Offrs War Course, 1962; in comd HMS Centaur, 1963–65; ADC to HM the Queen, 1965; Rear-Adm., 1966. Chm. Council, Shipwrecked Fishermen and Mariners Royal Benevolent Soc. Freeman, City of London; Liveryman, Coachmakers and Coach Harness Makers. *Recreations:* sailing, golf. *Address:* The Cottage, Moons Hill, Totland, IoW. *T:* Freshwater 753404. *Clubs:* Royal Cruising, Royal Yacht Squadron; Royal Naval Sailing Association; Royal Solent; Union (Malta).

STEINER, Prof. Robert Emil, CBE 1979; Professor of Diagnostic Radiology, University of London, Royal Postgraduate Medical School, since 1961; *b* 1 Feb. 1918; *s* of Rudolf Steiner and Clary (*née* Nordlinger); *m* 1945, Gertrude Margaret Konirsch; two *d*. *Educ:* University of Vienna; University College, Dublin. Dep. Director, Dept of Radiology, Hammersmith Hosp.; Lecturer Diagnostic Radiology, Postgraduate Med. School of London, 1950, Sen. Lecturer, 1955, Director, 1955–. Vice-Chm., Nat. Radiological Protection Bd, 1972–. Consultant Adviser in Radiology to DHSS; Civil Consultant in Radiology to Med. Dir-Gen., Navy. Warden of Fellowship, Faculty of Radiologists. Former Mem. Council, RCS; Past Pres., British Inst. Radiology; Pres., RCR, 1977–80. Hon. Fellow: Amer. Coll. of Radiology; Australian Coll. of Radiology; Faculty of Radiologists, RCSI. Barclay Medal British Inst. of Radiology. Former Editor, British Jl of Radiology. *Publications:* Clinical Disorders of the Pulmonary Circulation, 1960; Recent Advances of Radiology, 1979; contrib. to British Journal of Radiology, Clinical Radiology, British Heart Jl, Lancet, BMJ, etc. *Address:* 12 Stonehill Road, East Sheen, SW14. *T:* 01-876 4038.

STELL, Prof. Philip Michael, FRCS, FRCSE; Professor of Oto-rhino-laryngology, University of Liverpool, since 1979; *b* 14 Aug. 1934; *s* of Frank Law Stell and Ada Stell; *m* 1959, Shirley Kathleen Mills; four *s* one *d*. *Educ:* Archbishop Holgate's Grammar Sch., York; Edinburgh Univ. (MB, ChB 1958). ChM Liverpool, 1976. FRCS 1966; FRCSE 1962. Jun. hosp. appts, Edinburgh and Liverpool, 1958–63; Fellow, Washington Univ., St Louis, USA, 1964–65; Sen. Lectr, Univ. of Liverpool, 1965–78. Hunterian Prof., RCS, 1976. Yearsley Gold Medal, 1980; Harrison Prize, RSM, 1982. *Publications:* approx. 20 books and 80 articles in learned jls on surgery for cancer of head and neck. *Recreations:* squash, rowing, gardening. *Address:* 7 Partridge Road, Blundellsands, Liverpool 23. *T:* 051-924 2725. *Club:* Royal Artillery Association (Crosby).

STEMBRIDGE, David Harry; a Recorder of the Crown Court, since 1977; *b* 23 Dec. 1932; *s* of Percy G. Stembridge and Emily W. Stembridge; *m* 1956, Therese C. Furer; three *s* one *d*. *Educ:* St Chad's Cathedral Choir Sch., Lichfield; Bromsgrove Sch.; Birmingham Univ. (LLB Hons). Called to the Bar, Gray's Inn, 1955; practising barrister, 1956 –. *Recreations:* flute and organ playing, sailing. *Address:* Heath Lodge, Ullenhall, Warwickshire. *Clubs:* Bar Yacht, Royal Dart Yacht.

STENHAM, Anthony William Paul, (Cob), FCA; Financial Director, Unilever Ltd and Unilever NV, since 1970; *b* 28 Jan. 1932; *s* of Bernard Basil Stenham and Annie Josephine (*née* Naylor); *m* 1966, Hon. Sheila Marion Poole (marr. diss.). *Educ:* Eton Coll.; Trinity Coll., Cambridge. MA. Qualified Accountant FCA 1958. Mem., Inner Temple, 1954. Price Waterhouse, 1955–61; Philip Hill Higginson Erlanger, 1962–64; William Baird & Co., 1964–69; Unilever, 1969–. Director: Equity Capital for Industry, 1976–81; Capital Radio, 1982–. Underwriting Mem. of Lloyd's, 1978. Chm., Institute of Contemporary Arts, 1977–; Mem. Council, Architectural Assoc., 1982–; Royal Coll. of Art: Mem. Court, 1978–; Mem. Council, 1978–81; Chm. Council and Pro-Provost, 1979–81; Hon. Fellow, 1980. FRSA. *Recreations:* cinema, theatre, opera, painting. *Address:* 4 The Grove, Highgate, N6 6JU. *T:* 01-340 2266. *Club:* Turf.

STENHOUSE, John Godwyn, TD with bar; FCIB; Director, Stenhouse Holdings plc, since 1957 (Chairman, 1978–80); *b* 16 Nov. 1908; *s* of Alexander Rennie Stenhouse and Hughina Cowan Stenhouse; *m* 1st, 1936, Margaret Constance Thornton (*d* 1965); two *d*; 2nd, 1967, Jean Ann Bennie (*née* Finlayson); one step *s*. *Educ:* Warriston Sch., Moffat; Kelvinside Acad., Glasgow. With an insurance co., 1927; joined A. R. Stenhouse & Partners, Ltd, Insurance Brokers (later Stenhouse Holdings Ltd), 1931. *Recreations:* sailing, mechanical engineering. *Address:* Rossendale, 7 Upper Glenburn Road, Bearsden, Glasgow G61 4BW. *T:* 041-942 0151. *Clubs:* Royal Scottish Automobile (Glasgow); Royal Scottish Motor Yacht, Royal Gourock Yacht.

STENHOUSE, Sir Nicol, Kt 1962; *b* 14 Feb. 1911; 2nd *s* of late John Stenhouse, Shanghai, China, and Tring, Hertfordshire; *m* 1951, Barbara Heath Wilson; two *s* one *d*. *Educ:* Repton. Joined Andrew Yule & Co. Ltd, Calcutta, India, 1937; Managing Director, 1953–59; Chairman and Senior Managing Director, 1959–62; President: Bengal Chamber of Commerce and Industry, Calcutta, 1961–62; Associated Chambers of Commerce of India, Calcutta, 1961–62. *Recreation:* gardening. *Address:* 3 St Mary's Court, Sixpenny Handley, near Salisbury, Wilts SP5 5PH.

STENING, Sir George (Grafton Lees), Kt 1968; ED; Hon. Consultant Gynæcological Surgeon, Royal Prince Alfred Hosp., Sydney; *b* 16 Feb. 1904; *s* of George Smith Stening and Muriel Grafton Lees; *m* 1935, Kathleen Mary Packer; one *s* one *d*. *Educ:* Sydney High Sch.; Univ. of Sydney. MB, BS (Syd.) 1927 (Hons Cl. II); FRCS (Ed.) 1931; FRACS 1935; FRCOG 1947; Fellow, Aust. Coll. Obst. and Gyn., 1980. Carnegie Trav. Fellow, 1948. Served War of 1939–45: Middle East, New Guinea, Australia; OC, 3rd Aust. Surgical Team, Libyan Desert, 1941; CO, 2/11 Aust. Gen. Hosp., 1941–44; CO, 113 Aust. Gen. Hosp. 1945. Hon. Col, RAAMC. GCStJ 1971; Chancellor, Order of St John, in Australia, 1961–82. Past Pres., Sen. Golfers' Soc. of Aust. *Publication:* A Text Book of Gynæcology (co-author), 1948. *Recreations:* golf, yachting. *Address:* 2/22 Wolseley Road, Point Piper, NSW 2027, Australia. *Clubs:* Royal Sydney Golf (Sydney); Australian Jockey.

STEPHEN, Derek Ronald James, CB 1975; Assistant Secretary, Royal Hospital Chelsea, since 1982; *b* 22 June 1922; *s* of late Ronald James Stephen; *m* 1948, Gwendolen Margaret, *d* of late William James Heasman, CBE; two *s* one *d* (and one *s* decd). *Educ:* Bec Sch.; Christ's Coll., Cambridge (Scholar). 1st cl. Class. Tripos, Pt I, 1941; 1st cl. Class. Tripos, Pt II, 1946. Served War, 1941–45; Royal Armoured Corps (Captain), N Africa, Italy, NW Europe. Asst Principal, War Office, 1946; Asst Private Sec. to Sec. of State for War, 1949–50; Principal, 1951; Private Sec. to Sec. of Cabinet, 1958–60; Asst Sec., WO (later Ministry of Defence), 1960; IDC 1966; HM Treasury, 1968; Civil Service Dept (on its formation), 1968; Under-Sec., 1969–71; Asst Under-Sec. of State, MoD, 1972–73; Dep. Under-Sec. of State (Navy), MoD, and Mem. Admiralty Bd, 1973–78; Dep. Under-Sec. of State (Army), MoD, and Mem., Army Bd, 1978–82. *Recreations:* travel, music, tennis. *Address:* Light Horse Court, The Royal Hospital, Chelsea, SW3 4SL.

STEPHEN, Harbourne Mackay, DSO 1941; DFC and bar 1940; Managing Director, Daily Telegraph and Sunday Telegraph, since 1963; *b* 18 April 1916; *s* of Thomas Milne Stephen, JP, and Kathleen Vincent Park; *m* 1947, Sybil Erica Palmer; two *d*. *Educ:* Shrewsbury. Staff of Allied Newspapers, London, 1931; Evening Standard, 1936–39. RAFVR, 1937; served RAF, 1939–45 (destroyed numerous enemy aircraft): 605 and 74 Sqdns, 1939–40; at MAP, 1941, then formed 130 Sqdn and comd 234 Sqdn; served Far East, 1942–45; Wing Comdr (Flying) Dum Dum; RAF Jessore, Bengal; comd 166 Fighter Wing; then to Fighter Ops, 224 Gp Arakan; Ops "A" Air Comd SEA. Was OC 602 City of Glasgow (F) Sqdn RAuxAF, 1950–52. AE. Returned to Beaverbrook Newspapers, Oct. 1945; worked on Scottish Daily Express, Scottish Sunday Express, and Evening Citizen in Glasgow, 1945–55. General Manager, Sunday Express, 1958; General Manager, Sunday Graphic, 1960, and thereafter General Manager, Thomson Papers, London. Dir., International Newspaper Colour Assoc., Darmstadt, 1964–69. Council Mem., RSPB, 1972–73. *Recreations:* normal, occasionally. *Address:* Donnington Fields, Newbury, Berks. *T:* Newbury 40105. *Clubs:* Royal Automobile, Royal Air Force.

STEPHEN, Henrietta Hamilton, (Rita Stephen), MBE 1973; Executive Secretary, Association of Professional, Executive, Clerical and Computer Staff, since 1965; *b* 9 Dec. 1925; *d* of late James Pithie Stephen, engine driver, Montrose and late Mary Hamilton Morton, South Queensferry. *Educ:* Wolseley Street and King's Park Elem. Schs, Glasgow; Queen's Park Sen.

Secondary, Glasgow; Glasgow Univ. (extra-mural); LSE (TUC Schol.). Imperial Relations Trust Schol., McGill Univ. and Canada/US Travel, 1958-59; Duke of Edinburgh's Commonwealth Study Conf., 1968. Law office junior, 1941; Clerk, Labour Exchange (Mem. MLSA), 1941-42; Post Office Telephonist, 1942-60; Mem. Union of Post Office Workers, Glasgow Br., 1942-60 (Br. Cttee Mem., Vice-Chm., Chm., Sec., Deleg. to Trades Council, UPW District Council, Scottish Council, Annual Conf., etc); Mem. UPW Parly Panel, 1957; Glasgow City Labour Party Deleg., 1955; Educn Officer, Cathcart Ward Labour Party, 1955-58; Election Agent (Municipal); London and Home Counties Area Organiser, CAWU, 1960-65; Asst Sec., CAWU, 1965 (Union renamed APEX and post renamed Exec. Sec., 1972). Negotiator in public and private sectors of industry, 1960-; Editor, The Clerk, 1965-71; Union Educn Officer, 1965-; Delegate: TUC; Labour Party Annual Confs; Member: EDC for Distributive Trades, 1966-; WEA Nat. Cttee, 1968-; Food Standards Cttee, 1968-; Industrial Soc. Council and Exec., 1968-; Mary Macarthur Educnl Trust, 1965 (Hon. Sec. 1972-); Distributive Industry Trng Bd, 1968-73; Monopolies and Mergers Commn, 1973-; British Wool Marketing Bd, 1973-; Governor: Ruskin Coll., 1966-78; Duke of Edinburgh's 1974 Commonwealth Study Conf., 1973; LSE, 1976-. *Publications:* (jtly) Training Shop Stewards, 1968; (with Roy Moore) Statistics for Negotiators, 1973; contrib. Clerk, Industrial Soc. Jl, Target, etc. *Recreations:* food, walking, conversation, theatre, reading. *Address:* 3 Pond Road, SE3. *T:* 01-852 7797, 01-947 3131.

STEPHEN, Sir James Alexander, 4th Bt, *cr* 1891; *b* 25 Feb. 1908; *o c* of 3rd Bt and Barbara, *y d* of late W. Shore-Nightingale of Embley, Hants and Lea Hurst, Derbyshire; *S* father, 1945. *Educ:* Eton; Trinity College, Cambridge. Law Student, Inner Temple; embraced Roman Catholic faith, 1936; Resident, Toynbee Hall, 1936-39; Air Raid Warden, 1940; served RA (AA), 1940-41, discharged unfit; worked on the land as a volunteer, 1941-45; certified insane, 1945; name restored to vote, 1960; discharged from hospital, 1972. FRGS. Interested in exploration; has raised money for Outward Bound Trust. *Heir:* none. *Recreation:* contract bridge. *Address:* 48 Princess Road, Branksome, Poole, Dorset BH12 1BH. *T:* Bournemouth 764481.

STEPHEN, John Low, ChM (Aberdeen), FRCSE, FRCS; Surgeon St Mary's Hospital, W2 since 1958; Senior Surgeon, St Mary's Hospital, W9, 1948-77, retired; *b* 13 May 1912; 2nd *s* of late Dr J. H. Stephen, Aberdeen; *m* 1938, Mary Milne, MA, BSc; one *s* one *d*. *Educ:* Aberdeen Grammar School; Aberdeen and Edinburgh Universities. MA 1931, MB 1935, Aberd.; FRCSEd, 1937; ChM Aberd., 1945; FRCS (ad eundem), 1968. Various university and hospital appointments in Scotland and England. Associate Teacher in Surgery, St Mary's Hosp. Med. School, 1950-. FRSocMed. *Publications:* chapters in Operative Surgery (Smith and Rob); various articles on abdominal surgery in Brit. Jl of Surgery. *Recreations:* golf, motoring. *Address:* Luibeg, Groombridge, Tunbridge Wells, East Sussex.

STEPHEN, Lessel Bruce; His Honour Judge Stephen, a Circuit Judge, since 1972; *b* 15 Feb. 1920; *s* of L. P. Stephen, FRCS(E); *m* 1949, Brenda (*née* Tinkler). *Educ:* Marlborough; Sydney Sussex Coll., Cambridge (BA). Called to the Bar, Inner Temple, 1948; subsequently practised NE Circuit; Recorder, 1972. *Recreations:* golf, wine. *Address:* 2 Harcourt Buildings, Temple, EC4Y 9DB. *T:* 01-353 2548.

STEPHEN, Rt. Hon. Sir Ninian (Martin), AK 1982; GCMG 1982; KBE 1972; PC 1979; Governor-General of Australia, since 1982; *b* 15 June 1923; *o s* of late Frederick Stephen and Barbara Stephen (*née* Cruickshank); *m* 1949, Valery Mary, *d* of late A. Q. Sinclair and of Mrs G. M. Sinclair; five *d*. *Educ:* Edinburgh Acad.; St Paul's Sch., London; Scotch Coll., Melbourne; Melbourne Univ. (LLB). Served War, HM Forces (Australian Army), 1941-46. Admitted as Barrister and Solicitor, in State of Victoria, 1949; signed Roll of Victorian Bar, 1951; QC 1966. Appointed Judge of Supreme Court of Victoria, 1970; Justice of High Court of Australia, 1972-82. Hon. Bencher Gray's Inn, 1981. KStJ 1982. *Address:* Government House, Canberra, ACT 2600, Australia.

STEPHEN, Rita; *see* Stephen, H. H.

STEPHEN, Maj.-Gen. Robert Alexander, CB 1965; CBE 1958 (OBE 1954); MD, ChM; FRCS; QHS 1960-67; Director of Army Surgery and Consulting Surgeon to the Army, Royal Army Medical College, 1959-67; Consultant in Surgery, Royal Hospital, Chelsea; *b* 20 June 1907; *s* of late James Alexander Stephen, MB, ChB, DPH; *m* 1st, 1935, Audrey Vivien (*d* 1972), *d* of late George William Royce, Cambridge; one *d* ; 2nd, 1977, Mrs Patricia O'Reilly (*née* Wrixon-Harris). *Educ:* Aberdeen Grammar School; Aberdeen University. MD 1933, ChM 1960, Aberdeen. FRCS 1947. MS Malaya, 1959. Lieut, RAMC, 1934. Served War of 1939-45, in France, Egypt, Libya, Greece, Crete, Belgium, Holland and Germany; Lt-Col 1941. Formerly Asst Prof. of Military Surgery, Royal Army Medical College, London; Consulting Surgeon, FARELF, 1956-59; Hon. Consulting Surgeon, General Hospital, Singapore, 1956; Brigadier, 1958; Major-General, 1961. Hunterian Prof., RCS, 1958. Fellow: Royal Society of Medicine; Assoc. of Surgeons of Great Britain and Ireland. OStJ. *Recreations:* golf and gardening. *Address:* Pinnocks, 44a Shortheath Road, Farnham, Surrey GU9 8SL. *T:* Farnham 723848.

STEPHENS, Air Commandant Dame Anne, DBE 1961 (MBE 1946); Hon. ADC to the Queen, 1960-63; Director, Women's Royal Air Force, 1960-63; *b* 4 Nov. 1912; *d* of late General Sir Reginald Byng Stephens, KCB, CMG

and late Lady Stephens. *Educ:* privately. Joined WAAF, 1939; served in UK, Belgium and Germany, 1939-45. Command WRAF Depot, Hawkinge, 1950-52; promoted Group Officer, 1951; Inspector WRAF, 1952-54; Deputy Director, 1954-57; Staff Officer, HQ 2nd TAF, 1957-59; promoted Air Commandant, 1960. *Address:* The Forge, Sibford Ferris, Banbury, Oxfordshire. *T:* Swalcliffe 452.

STEPHENS, Anthony William, CMG 1976; Assistant Under Secretary of State, Ministry of Defence, since 1979; *b* 9 Jan. 1930; *s* of late Donald Martyn Stephens and Norah Stephens (*née* Smith-Cleburne); *m* 1954, Mytyl Joy, *d* of late William Gay Burdett; four *d*. *Educ:* Bradfield Coll.; Bristol Univ. (LLB); Corpus Christi Coll., Cambridge. RM, 1948-50. Colonial Administrative Service, 1953; District Officer, Kenya, 1954-63; Home Civil Service, 1964; Principal, MoD, 1964-70; Asst Private Sec. to successive Secretaries of State for Defence, 1970-71; Asst Sec., 1971; Chief Officer, Sovereign Base Areas, Cyprus, 1974-76; Under Sec., NI Office, 1976-79. *Recreations:* travel and the outdoor life, music, theatre. *Address:* 55 Arlington Road, NW1 7ES. *Club:* Royal Commonwealth Society.

STEPHENS, Prof. Arthur Veryan, MA Cantab; CEng; FRAeS; Professor of Aeronautical Engineering, The Queen's University, Belfast, 1956-73, now Emeritus Professor; *b* 9 July 1908; *s* of Arthur John Stephens and Mildred, *d* of Robert Fowler Sturge; *m* 1st, 1938, Jane Dows, *d* of F. W. Lester; three *s* one *d* ; 2nd, 1981, Marjorie Phyllis Irene Sprince. *Educ:* Clifton College; St John's College, Cambridge (Mechanical Sciences Tripos, John Bernard Seely Prize). Scientific Officer, Royal Aircraft Establishment, 1930-34; Fellow of St John's College, Cambridge, 1934-39; Lawrence Hargrave Professor of Aeronautics, 1939-56, Dean of the Faculty of Engineering, 1947-56, University of Sydney, NSW. Edward Busk Memorial Prize of RAeS, 1934; Member: Australian Flying Personnel Research Cttee, 1940-45; Australian Council for Aeronautics, 1941-46; Chairman, Aeronautical Research Consultative Cttee, 1947-54; Chairman, Australian Aeronautical Research Committee, 1954-56; Member Australian Defence Research and Development Policy Committee, 1953-56; Chairman, Australian Division of Royal Aeronautical Society, 1947-56. Dean of Faculty of Applied Science and Technology, 1961-64; Vice-President (Buildings), 1964-67. *Publications:* numerous papers on applied aerodynamics published by Aeronautical Research Council, Australian Dept of Supply and in Jl of RAeS. *Recreations:* golf, real tennis. *Address:* 118 Loudoun Road, NW8. *Club:* Athenæum.

STEPHENS, Cedric John; consultant; retired; *b* 13 Feb. 1921; *s* of late Col J. E. Stephens, Truro, Cornwall. *Educ:* London University (BSc (Eng.) Hons); CEng, FRAeS, FIEE. Entered Scientific Civil Service, 1951; Dir, Space Activities, Min. of Aviation, 1961; Mem. Coun., European Launcher Development Organisation, Paris, 1962; Chm. Technical Cttee, European Coun. on Satellite Communications, 1964; Imperial Defence Coll., 1965; Director, Signals Research and Develt Estabt, Min. of Technology, 1966-67; Chief Scientific Adviser, Home Office, 1968; Dir-Gen. of Research and Chief Scientist, Home Office, 1969-73. Called to Bar, Gray's Inn, 1971. Mem., Electronics Div. Bd, IEE, 1972. *Address:* 7 Exeter Court, Wharncliffe Road, Christchurch, Dorset. *Club:* Athenæum.

STEPHENS, Christopher Wilson T.; *see* Stephens, Wilson T.

STEPHENS, Sir David, KCB 1964; CVO 1960; Clerk of the Parliaments, House of Lords, 1963-74; *b* 25 April 1910; *s* of late Berkeley John Byng Stephens, CIE, and Gwendolen Elizabeth (*née* Cripps), Cirencester; *m* 1st, 1941, Mary Clemency, JP (*d* 1966), *er d* of late Colonel Sir Eric Gore Browne, DSO, OBE, TD; three *s* one *d* ; 2nd, 1967, Charlotte Evelyn, widow of Henry Manisty, *d* of late Rev. A. M. Baird-Smith; three step *s*. *Educ:* Winchester College; Christ Church. Oxford (2nd cl. Lit. Hum.). Laming Travelling Fellow, the Queen's College, Oxford, 1932-34; Clerk in the Parliament Office, House of Lords, 1935-38; Member Runciman Mission to Czechoslovakia, 1938; Transf. HM Treasury, 1938; Political Warfare Executive, 1941-43; Prin. Priv. Sec. to the Lord Pres. of the Council (Mr Herbert Morrison), 1947-49; Asst Sec., HM Treasury, 1949; Secretary for Appointments to two Prime Ministers (Sir Anthony Eden and Mr Harold Macmillan), 1955-61; Reading Clerk and Clerk of the Journals, House of Lords, 1961-63. Chm., Redundant Churches Fund, 1976-81. Chm. of Governors, Maidwell Hall Sch., 1964-70. Mem., Cotswold DC, 1976-. Pres., Friends of Cirencester Parish Church, 1976-. *Recreations:* gardening, tennis and country life; preserving the Cotswolds. *Address:* The Old Rectory, Coates, near Cirencester, Glos GL7 6NS. *T:* Kemble 258. *Clubs:* Brooks's, MCC.

See also R. A. Ryder.

STEPHENS, Ian Melville, CIE 1935; MA Cantab; *b* 1903; *e s* of J. A. Melville Stephens, Fleet, Hants; unmarried; hon. adopted son, Dr Arthur Kwok Cheung Li. *Educ:* Winchester; King's Coll., Cambridge (foundn scholar, R. J. Smith research student); 1st class hons, Natural Sciences Tripos, Pt I, 1924, and Historical Tripos, Pt II, 1925. Business appts, 1927-30; Deputy Dir, Bureau of Public Information, Govt of India, 1930-32; wrote the M & MP Reports for 1929-30 and 1930-31; was India corresp., The Round Table; Publicity Officer, Indian Franchise (Lothian) Cttee, 1932; Dir, Bureau of Public Information, 1932-37; Asst Editor, The Statesman newspaper, Calcutta and Delhi, 1937; also on the Board, 1939; Editor, 1942-51 (also aeronautical corresp., and a staff photographer). War Corresp., SEAC and SHAEF, 1943-45. Member: Standing Cttee, All-India Newspaper Editors' Conf.,

1942-51; Indian Delegn to Commonwealth Press Conf., Canada, 1950; Brit. Group, Inst. of Pacific Relations Conf., Lucknow, 1950. Retired from India, 1951. Fellow, King's Coll., Cambridge, 1952-58; also Mem. Council, and Hon. Treasurer Appeals Cttee, New Hall, Cambridge. Chm., Mount Vernon (Ceylon) Tea Co., 1953-57. Historian, Pakistan Govt, GHQ, Rawalpindi, 1957-60. Has travelled in South Asia, Australia, NZ, Canada, USA. Jinnah Medal, 1977; Iqbal Medal, 1979. *Publications:* Horned Moon, illus. with own photographs, 1953 (3rd edn 1966); Pakistan, 1963 (paperback edn 1964, 3rd edn 1967); Monsoon Morning, 1966; (ed) Sir R. Reid's Years of Change, 1966; The Pakistanis, 1968; A Curiosity, 1970; Unmade Journey, 1977; contribs to Chambers's Encyclopaedia (1966 edn); articles, lectures, broadcasts, reviews. *Address:* c/o Lloyds Bank, 3 Sidney Street, Cambridge.

STEPHENS, Maj.-Gen. Keith Fielding, CB 1970; OBE 1957; Medical Officer, Department of Health and Social Security, since 1970; *b* Taplow, Bucks, 28 July 1910; *s* of late Edgar Percy and Mary Louise Stephens; *m* 1937, Margaret Ann, *d* of late Alexander MacGregor; two *s*. *Educ:* Eastbourne College; St Bartholomew's Hospital. MB, BS London 1934; FFARCS 1953; DA 1941. Commissioned into RAMC, 1937; served in India, 1937-43; France and Germany, 1944-46; Cyprus, 1954-56; Adviser in Anæsthetics to the Army, 1949-53 and 1957-66; Commandant and Director of Studies, Royal Army Medical College, 1966-68; DDMS, Southern Command, 1968-70, retired. FRSocMed (Pres., Sect. of Anæsthetics, 1970-71); Hon. Member, Assoc. of Anæsthetists of Gt Brit. and Ireland. Fellow, Med. Soc. of London. Hon. FFARCS (Ireland), 1970; QHS, 1964-70. Hon. Col, 221 (Surrey) Field Ambulance RAMC(V), 1972-76. Mitchiner Medal, 1962. CStJ 1967. *Publications:* numerous articles in medical journals. *Address:* 3 Carnegie Place, Parkside, Wimbledon, SW19. *T:* 01-946 0911. *Club:* Naval and Military.

STEPHENS, Malcolm George; International Finance Director, Barclays Bank International, since 1982; *b* 14 July 1937; *s* of Frank Ernest Stephens and Janet (*née* McQueen); *m* 1975, Lynette Marie Caffery, Brisbane, Australia. *Educ:* St Michael's and All Angels; Shooter's Hill Grammar Sch.; St John's Coll., Oxford (Casberd Scholar; BA 1st Cl. Hons PPE). National Service, RAOC, 1956-58. CRO, 1953; British High Commission: Ghana, 1959-62; Kenya, 1963-65; Export Credits Guarantee Dept, 1965-82: Principal, 1970; seconded to Civil Service Coll., 1971-72; Asst Sec., 1973; Estab. Officer, 1977; Under Sec., 1978; Head of Proj. Gp B, 1978-79; Principal Finance Officer, 1979-82. *Recreations:* gardening, reading. *Address:* 111 Woolwich Road, Bexleyheath, Kent DA7 4LP. *T:* 01-303 6782.

STEPHENS, Martin; see Stephens, S. M.

STEPHENS, Peter Norman Stuart; Director, News Group Newspapers, since 1978, Editorial Director, since 1981; *b* 19 Dec. 1927; *s* of J. G. Stephens; *m* 1950, Constance Mary Ratheram; two *s* one *d*. *Educ:* Mundella Grammar Sch., Nottingham. Newark Advertiser, 1945-48; Northern Echo, 1948-50; Daily Dispatch, 1950-55; Daily Mirror, Manchester, 1955-57; Asst Editor, Newcastle Journal, 1957-60; Asst Editor, Evening Chronicle, Newcastle, 1960-62, Editor 1962-66; Editor, Newcastle Journal, 1966-70; Asst Editor, The Sun, 1970-72, Dep. Editor 1972; Associate Editor, News of the World, 1973, Editor, 1974-75; Associate Editor, The Sun, 1975-81. *Recreation:* supporting Derby County Football Club. *Address:* 30 Bouverie Street, EC4Y 8DE. *T:* 01-353 3030.

STEPHENS, Major Robert, CVO 1964; ERD; Administrative Officer, Hillsborough Castle (formerly Government House), 1973-78; retired; *b* 1909; *s* of late John Samuel Stephens; *m* 1939, Kathleen, *d* of late R. I. Trelford, Helen's Bay, Belfast. *Educ:* Campbell Coll., Belfast. Ulster Bank, 1929-39. Served War of 1939-45: RA, Middle East, 1941-45. Commercial Manager, Newforge Ltd, 1946-55; Private Secretary to the Governor of Northern Ireland, 1955-73; Comptroller to: Lord Wakehurst, 1955-64; Lord Erskine of Rerrick, 1964-68; Lord Grey of Naunton, 1968-73. *Recreation:* golf. *Address:* 13 Ballynahinch Street, Hillsborough, Co. Down, Northern Ireland. *T:* Hillsborough 682550.

STEPHENS, Robert; actor; *b* 14 July 1931; *s* of Rueben Stephens and Gladys (*née* Deverell); *m* Tarn Bassett; one *d*; *m* 1967, Maggie Smith, *qv* (marr. diss. 1975); two *s*. *Educ:* Bradford Civic Theatre School. Started with Caryl Jenner Mobile Theatre Co.; Mem. English Stage Co., Royal Court, 1956. *Stage:* The Crucible, Don Juan, The Death of Satan, Cards of Identity, The Good Woman of Setzuan and The Country Wife (also at Adelphi, 1957); The Apollo de Bellac, Yes-and After, The Making of Moo, How Can We Save Father?, The Waters of Babylon, Royal Court, 1957; The Entertainer, Palace, 1957; Epitaph for George Dillon, Royal Court, Comedy, Golden (NY), 1958 and Henry Miller, 1959; Look After Lulu (also at New) and The Kitchen (also 1961), Royal Court, 1959; The Wrong Side of the Park, Cambridge, 1960; The Sponge Room, Squat Betty, Royal Court, 1962; Chichester and Edinburgh Festival, 1963; Design for Living (Los Angeles), 1971; Private Lives, Queen's, 1972; The Seagull, Chichester, 1973; Ápropos The Falling Sleet (dir.), Open Space, 1973; Ghosts, The Seagull, Hamlet, Greenwich, 1974; Sherlock Holmes, NY and Canada, 1975; Murderer, Garrick, 1975; Zoo Story, 1975, Othello, 1976, Open Air, Regent's Park; Pygmalion, Los Angeles, 1979; Othello, Cape Town, SA, 1982; WCPC, Half Moon, 1982; *National Theatre Company:* Hamlet, St Joan, The Recruiting Officer, 1963; Andorra, Play, The Royal Hunt of the Sun (also Chichester Fest.), Hay Fever, 1964; Much Ado About Nothing, Armstrong's Last Goodnight, Trelawny of the Wells (also Chichester Fest.), 1965; A Bond Honoured, Black Comedy, 1966; The Dance

of Death, The Three Sisters (at Los Angeles, 1968), As You Like It, Tartuffe, 1967; Most Unwarrantable Intrusion (also dir.), Home and Beauty, 1968; Macrune's Guevara (also co-dir), 1969; The Beaux' Stratagem (also Los Angeles), Hedda Gabler, 1970; The Cherry Orchard, Brand, The Double Dealer, Has "Washington" Legs?, 1978. *Films:* A Taste of Honey; Cleopatra; The Small World of Sammy Lee; The Prime of Miss Jean Brodie; The Private Life of Sherlock Holmes; Travels with my Aunt; The Asphyx; Luther; QBVIII; Alexander the Great, etc. TV performances include: Vienna 1900 (6 part series), 1973; Tribute to J. B. Priestley, 1974; Kean, 1978; Voyage of Charles Darwin, 1978; Office Story, 1978; Friends in Space, 1979; Suez, 1979; The Executioner, 1980; Adelaide Bartlett (series), 1980; Winter's Tale, 1980; The Double Dealer, 1980; The Trial of Madame Famay, 1980; Holocaust (USA), 1980; Eden End, 1981; The Year of the French (RTE), 1981, etc. Variety Club Award for stage actor, 1965. *Recreations:* cooking, gymnastics, swimming. *Address:* c/o Film Rights Ltd, 113-117 Wardour Street, W1. *T:* 01-437 7151.

STEPHENS, (Stephen) Martin, QC 1982; barrister-at-law; a Recorder of the Crown Court, since 1979; *b* 26 June 1939; *s* of late Abraham Stephens and of Freda Stephens, Swansea; *m* 1965, Patricia Alison, *d* of Joseph and Anne Morris, Mapperley, Nottingham; two *s* one *d*. *Educ:* Swansea Grammar Sch.; Wadham Coll., Oxford (BA). Called to the Bar, Middle Temple, 1963; Wales and Chester Circuit. *Recreations:* cricket, tennis, theatre. *Address:* The Red House, 87 Cyncoed Road, Cyncoed, Cardiff. *T:* Cardiff 484553. *Club:* Cardiff Lawn Tennis (Cardiff).

STEPHENS, William Henry, CB 1961; DSc, MSc, CEng, FRAeS; Senior Executive Director, General Technology Systems Ltd, since 1974; *b* Kilkenny, Ireland, 18 March 1913; *s* of William Henry Stephens, MBE, and Helena Read Stephens (*née* Cantely); *m* 1938, Elizabeth Margaret Brown, BSc; one *s* one *d*. *Educ:* Methodist College and Queen's University, Belfast. Air Ministry, Royal Aircraft Establishment (Aerodynamic Research), 1935-38; War Office, Woolwich (Rocket Research), 1938-39; Ministry of Aircraft Prod., London (Air Defence Research), 1939-44; Asst Scientific Attaché and Asst Director, UK Scientific Mission, British Commonwealth Scientific Office, Washington, USA, 1944-47; Min. of Supply, RAE, Head of Guided Weapons Dept and later Dep. Director, 1947-58; Dir-Gen. Ballistic Missiles, Ministry of Aviation, 1959-62; Technical Dir, European Space Launcher Develt Organisation, Paris, 1962-69; Minister, Defence R&D, British Embassy, Washington, 1969-72; Special Advr (Internat. Affairs), Controllerate of Res., MoD, 1972-73. Mem., Internat. Acad. of Astronautics; Fellow, British Interplanetary Soc. *Publications:* contrib. to Jl Royal Aeronautical Soc.; Proc. Brit. Assoc.; Proc. Internat. Congress of Aeronautical Sciences. *Recreations:* travel, music, art, theatre. *Address:* Rosebrook House, Oriel Hill, Camberley, Surrey. *Club:* Athenæum.

STEPHENS, Wilson (Treeve); Editor of The Field, 1950-77; *b* 2 June 1912; *s* of Rev. Arthur Treeve Stephens, Shepton Beauchamp, Somerset, and Margaret Wilson; *m* 1st, 1934, Nina, *d* of Arthur Frederick Curzon, Derby; two *d*; 2nd, 1960, Marygold Anne, *o d* of Major-General G. O. Crawford, *qv*; two *d*. *Educ:* Christ's Hosp. Formerly on editorial staffs of several provincial newspapers, and of The Daily Express. Served War of 1939-45, Royal Artillery. *Publications:* The Guinness Guide to Field Sports, 1979; Gundog Sense and Sensibility, 1982; contrib to The Field and other jls. *Recreation:* fly-fishing. *Address:* c/o The Field, Carmelite House, Fleet Street, EC4. *Club:* Kennel.

STEPHENSON, Ashley; see Stephenson, R. A. S.

STEPHENSON, Donald, CBE 1957 (OBE 1943); Controller, Overseas and Foreign Relations, BBC, 1966-71; *b* 18 May 1909; *yr s* of late J. V. G. Stephenson; *m* 1940, Alison (*d* 1965), *yr d* of late Wynn ap H. Thomas, OBE, LLB; three *d* (one *s* decd). *Educ:* Denstone College (Scholar); Paris; Baghdad. Banking business, 1925-31; permanent commission, RAF, 1932; Flt Lt, 1936; served France and Middle East, 1935-37; language specialist (interpreter, French and Arabic); Special Duty List, 1938; Arabic Editor, BBC, 1939; Director, BBC, New Delhi, 1944-45; Director, Eastern Services, 1946-47; Asst Controller in Overseas Div., 1948; Controller, North Region, 1948-56; Controller, Overseas Services, BBC, 1956-58; Chief Executive, Anglia Television Ltd, 1959; Head of Overseas and Foreign Relations, BBC, Dec. 1960. A Governor of Manchester Univ., 1950-58. A delegate to 5th Commonwealth Broadcasting Conf., Canada, 1963, to 7th Conf., NZ, 1968, and 8th Conf., Jamaica, 1970. *Recreation:* family life. *Address:* 21 Boulthurst Way, Oxted, Surrey. *T:* Limpsfield Chart 3151.

STEPHENSON, Ven. Edgar, MM 1918; TD 1950; Archdeacon Emeritus of Rochdale, since 1962, Archdeacon, 1951-62; Director of Religious Education in Diocese of Manchester, 1955-62; *b* 24 Sept. 1894; *y s* of late T. J. Stephenson, Tamworth, Staffs; *m* 1926, Kathleen, *d* of late William Taws, Macclesfield, Cheshire; no *c*. *Educ:* Manchester University. BA 1922; BD 1925; MA 1929. CF(TA), 1933-50. Vicar of St Mary's, Oldham, 1947-55. *Address:* College of St Mark, Audley End, Saffron Walden, Essex CB11 4JD. *T:* Saffron Walden 22895.

STEPHENSON, Prof. Gordon, CBE 1967; FRIBA, FRTPI, LFRAPI, FILA, DisTP; Professor Emeritus of Architecture, University of Western Australia; Member, National Capital Planning Committee, Canberra, 1967-73; *b* 6 June 1908; *s* of Francis E. and Eva E. Stephenson, Liverpool; *m* 1938, Flora Bartlett

Crockett (decd), Boston, USA; three d. Educ: Liverpool Institute; University of Liverpool; University of Paris; Massachusetts Institute of Technology. Elmes Scholar, Univ. of Liverpool, 1925–30; Holt Scholar, 1928; First Cl. Hons in Architecture, 1930; Chadwick Scholar at Brit. Inst. in Paris and Univ. of Paris, 1930–32; BArch; MCP(MIT). Lecturer and Studio Instructor in Architecture, University of Liverpool, 1932–36; Commonwealth Fellow and Medallist, Massachusetts Inst. of Technology, 1936–38; Studio Master, Architectural Assoc., School of Architecture, 1939–40; Lever Professor of Civic Design, School of Architecture, University of Liverpool, 1948–53; Professor of Town and Regional Planning in the University of Toronto, Canada, 1955–60; Prof. of Architecture, Univ. of WA, 1960–72. Architectural and Planning practice: asst to Corbett, Harrison and McMurray, NY City, 1929; asst to Le Corbusier and Pierre Jeanneret, Paris, 1930–32; Div. Architect, with W. G. Holford, on Royal Ordnance Factory work, 1940–42; Research Officer, Sen. Research Officer, and Chief Planning Officer, Min. of Works and Planning, and Min. of Town and Country Planning, 1942–47; seconded to assist Sir Patrick Abercrombie on Greater London Plan, 1943–44; Cnslt Architect, Univ. of WA, 1960–69; in partnership with R. J. Ferguson, as architects and planners for Murdoch Univ., WA, 1972–76; in private practice, houses, militia camp, university bldgs, community centre, housing schemes, town and regional planning studies. Editor, Town Planning Review, 1949–54. Hon. MCIP 1960. Hon. LLD Univ. of WA. Publications: (with Flora Stephenson) Community Centres, 1941; (with F. R. S. Yorke) Planning for Reconstruction, 1944; (with J. A. Hepburn) Plan for the Metropolitan Region of Perth and Fremantle, 1955; a Redevelopment Study of Halifax, Nova Scotia, 1957; (with G. G. Muirhead) A Planning Study of Kingston, Ontario, 1959; The Design of Central Perth, 1975; Joondalup Regional Centre, 1977; articles and papers in British, Australian, Canadian Technical Professional Jls. Recreations: architectural practice, drawing and travel. Address: 3/109 Broadway, Nedlands, WA 6009, Australia. T: (09) 386.6699.

STEPHENSON, Henry Shepherd, CEng, FIMinE; Chairman, Mining Qualifications Board, 1970–75; b 1 Oct. 1905; m 1934, Faith Estelle, 3rd d of Tom Edward Arnold, Bolton Old Hall, Bradford; two d. Educ: Whitehaven Grammar School; Armstrong College, Durham University (BSc). Articled apprentice Mining Engineer, Whitehaven Colliery Co., 1924–28; official posts, Whitehaven Colliery Co., 1928–35; HM Junior Inspector of Mines Northern Div., 1935–39; Mining Agent, Cumberland Coal Co., 1939–41; HM Junior Inspector of Mines and Quarries (Yorkshire), 1941–44; Senior Inspector (Scotland), 1944–47; Senior Dist Inspector (Durham), 1948–52; Senior Dist Inspector (West Midland), 1952–58; Divisional Inspector (East Midland), 1958–62; Deputy Chief Inspector, Jan. 1962; Chief Inspector, 1962–70. Hon. DSc Newcastle upon Tyne, 1971. Recreations: gardening, golf. Address: Flat 13, The Redlands, Manor Road, Sidmouth, Devon.

STEPHENSON, Sir Henry Upton, 3rd Bt cr 1936; TD; Director: Stephenson, Blake (Holdings) Ltd; Thos Turton and Sons Ltd; b 26 Nov. 1926; s of Lt-Col Sir Henry Francis Blake Stephenson, 2nd Bt, OBE, TD, and of Joan, d of Major John Herbert Upton (formerly Upton Cottrell-Dormer); S father, 1982; m 1962, Susan, o d of Major J. E. Clowes, Ashbourne, Derbyshire; four d. Educ: Eton. Formerly Captain, QO Yorkshire Yeomanry. High Sheriff of Derbyshire, 1975. Heir: cousin Timothy Hugh Stephenson [b 5 Jan. 1930; m 1959, Susan Lesley, yr d of late George Arthur Harris; two s]. Address: Tissington Cottage, Rowland, Bakewell, Derbyshire.

STEPHENSON, Hugh; Editor, The New Statesman, since 1982; b 18 July 1938; s of late Sir Hugh Stephenson, GBE, KCMG, CIE, CVO, and of Lady Stephenson; m 1962, Auriol Stevens; two s one d. Educ: Winchester Coll.; New Coll., Oxford (BA); Univ. of Calif, Berkeley. Pres., Oxford Union, 1962. HM Diplomatic Service, 1964–68; joined The Times, 1968; Editor, The Times Business News, 1972–81. Mem., Cttee to Review Functioning of Financial Instns, 1977–80. Councillor, London Bor. of Wandsworth, 1971–78. Publications: The Coming Clash, 1972; Mrs Thatcher's First Year, 1980; Claret and Chips, 1982. Address: 28 Gwendolen Avenue, SW15. T: 01-788 5047.

STEPHENSON, (James) Ian (Love), ARA 1975; painter; Director, Postgraduate Painting, Chelsea School of Art, since 1970; b 11 Jan. 1934; o s of James Stephenson and May (née Emery); m 1959, Kate, o d of James Brown; one s one d. Educ: King Edward VII School of Art, King's Coll., Univ. of Durham, Newcastle upon Tyne (3 prizes; Hatton Schol.; BA Dunelm 1956, 1st Class Hons in Fine Art). Tutorial Student, 1956-57, Studio Demonstrator, 1957-58, King's Coll., Newcastle upon Tyne (pioneered 1st foundn course in UK dedicated to new creativity in art); Boise School. (Italy), Univ. of London, 1958-59; Vis. Lectr, Polytechnic Sch. of Art, London, 1959-62; Vis. Painter, Chelsea Sch. of Art, 1959-66; Dir, Foundn Studies, Dept of Fine Art, Univ. of Newcastle, 1966-70 (introd alternating approach between perceptual and conceptual studies to academic syllabus); Internat. Course Leader, Voss Summer Sch., 1979. Vice-Pres., Sunderland Arts Centre, 1982-; Member: Visual Arts Panel, Northern Arts Assoc., Newcastle, 1967-70; Fine Art Panel, NCDAD, 1972-74; Perm. Cttee, New Contemp. Assoc., 1973-75; Fine Art Board, CNAA, 1974-75; Adv. Cttee, Nat. Exhibn of Children's Art, Manchester, 1975-; Working Party, RA Jubilee Exhbn, 1976-77; Selection Cttee, Arts Council Awards, 1977-78; Painting Faculty, Rome and Abbey Major Scholarships, 1978-82; Recommending Cttee, Chantrey Bequest, 1979-80; RA Steward, Artists' Gen. Benevolent Instn, 1979-80; Specialist Adviser, CNAA, 1980-83. Examiner: Birmingham Poly., 1972-73; Portsmouth Poly., 1973-76; London Univ., 1975-; Leicester Poly.,

1976-78; Ulster Poly., 1979-82; Canterbury Art Coll., 1981-; Newcastle Poly., 1982-. Exhibitions include: British Painting in the Sixties, London, 1963; 5e Biennale, Paris, 1967; Junge Generation Grossbritannien, Berlin, 1968; Retrospective, Newcastle, 1970; La Peinture Anglaise Aujourd'hui, Paris, 1973; Elf Englische Zeichner, Baden Baden and Bremen, 1973; Recente Britse Tekenkunst, Antwerp, 1973; 13a Bienal, São Paulo, 1975; Arte Inglese Oggi, Milan, 1976; Retrospective, London and Bristol, 1977; Englische Kunst der Gegenwart, Bregenz, 1977; British Painting 1952-77, London, 1977; Color en la Pintura Britanica, Rio de Janeiro, 1977; Abstract Paintings from UK, Washington, 1978; Retrospective, Birmingham and Cardiff, 1978; Art Anglais d'Aujourd'hui, Geneva, 1980; British Art 1940-80, London, 1980; Colour in British Painting, Hong Kong and Far East, 1980-81; Contemporary British Drawings, Tel-Aviv and Near East, 1980-82; The Deck of Cards, Athens and Arabia, 1980-82; A Taste of British Art Today, Brussels, 1982; Arteder Muestra Internacional, Bilbao, 1982; La Couleur en la Peinture Britannique, Luxembourg and Bucharest, 1982-83; illustrations include: Cubism and After (BBC film), 1962; Contemporary British Art, 1965; Private View, 1965; Blow Up (film), 1966; Art of Our Time, 1967; Recent British Painting, 1968; Adventure in Art, 1969; In Vogue, 1975; Painting in Britain 1525-1975, 1976; British Painting, 1976; Contemporary Artists, 1977 and 1982; Contemporary British Artists, 1979; work in collections: Arnolfini Trust, Arts Council, Birmingham and Bristol City Art Galls, British Council, BP Chemicals and Co., Bury Art Gall., Contemp. Art Soc., Creasey Lit. Museum, DoE, Economist Newspaper, Granada TV, Gulbenkian Foundn, Hatton Gall., Hunterian Museum, Kettle's Yard, Leeds City Art Gall., Leicestershire Educn Authority, Madison Art Center, Marzotto Roma, Nat. West. Bank, Northern Arts Assoc., Nuffield Foundn, Stuyvesant Foundn, Sunderland Art Gall., Tate Gall., Unilever Ltd, V&A Museum, Victoria Nat. Gall., Welsh Nat. Museum, Whitworth Art Gall. Prizes include: Junior Section, Moores Exhibn, Liverpool, 1957; European Selection, Premio Marzotto, Valdagno, 1964; First, Northern Painters' Exhibn, 1966. Address: Chelsea School of Art, Manresa Road, SW3 6LS. T: 01-351 3844.

STEPHENSON, Jim; a Recorder of the Crown Court, since 1974; barrister-at-law; b 17 July 1932; s of late Alex Stephenson, Heworth, Co. Durham, and of Mrs Stephenson; m 1964, Jill Christine, d of Dr Lindeck, Fairwarp, Sussex; three s. Educ: Royal Grammar Sch. and Dame Allan's Sch., Newcastle; Exeter Coll., Oxford (Exhibnr, BA). Pres., Oxford Univ. Law Society, Michaelmas, 1955. Called to Bar, Gray's Inn, 1957. Mem., General Council of the Bar, 1961-64; Junior, NE Circuit, 1961. Recreations: reading, fell-walking. Address: 51 Westgate Road, Newcastle upon Tyne NE1 1SS. T: Newcastle upon Tyne 20541.

STEPHENSON, Maj.-Gen. John Aubrey, CB 1982; OBE 1971; Managing Director, Weapon Systems Ltd, since 1982; Deputy Master General of the Ordnance, 1980–81; b 15 May 1929; s of Reginald Jack Stephenson and Florence Stephenson; m 1953, Sheila Colbeck; two s one d. Educ: Dorchester Grammar School. Commnd RA, 1948; served Malaya (despatches, 1951), Libya, Canal Zone and Germany, 1949-58 (student pilot, 1953-54); student, RMCS, 1958-60; 39 Missile Regt, 1960-61; student, RMCS and Staff Coll., 1961-62; served UK and Germany, 1962-67; Staff, RMCS, 1967-69; CO 16 Light Air Defence Regt RA, 1969-71; Project Manager, 155mm Systems, Woolwich, 1971-73; student, RCDS, 1974; Comdr, 1st Artillery Bde, Germany, 1975-77; Sen. Mil. Officer, RARDE, 1977-78; Dir Gen. Weapons (Army), 1978-80. Mem., Inst. of Dirs; FBIM. Recreations: fishing, sailing, gardening, bridge, golf, military history. Address: Collingwood, 27 Trafalgar Way, Stockbridge, Hants SO20 6ET. T: Stockbridge 458. Club: Royal Commonwealth Society.

STEPHENSON, Rt. Hon. Sir John (Frederick Eustace), PC 1971; Kt 1962; Rt. Hon. Lord Justice Stephenson; a Lord Justice of Appeal, since 1971; b 28 March 1910; 2nd s of late Sir Guy Stephenson, CB, and of late Gwendolen, d of Rt Hon. J. G. Talbot; m 1951, Frances Rose, yr d of late Lord Asquith of Bishopstone, PC; two s two d. Educ: Winchester College (Schol.); New Coll., Oxford (Schol.); Hon. Fellow, 1979. 1st Cl. Hon. Mods. 1930, 1st Cl. Litt Hum. 1932, BA 1932, MA 1956. Called to Bar, Inner Temple (Entrance Scholarship), 1934; Bencher, 1962. Sapper RE (TA), 1938; War Office, 1940; Intelligence Corps, Captain 1943, Major 1944 and Lieut-Col 1946; Middle East and NW Europe; Regional Intelligence Officer, Hamburg, 1946; Recorder of Bridgwater, 1954-59; Recorder of Winchester, 1959-62; Chancellor of the Diocese: of Peterborough, 1956-62; of Winchester, 1958-62; QC 1960; Dep. Chm., Dorset QS, 1962-71; Judge of Queen's Bench Div., High Court of Justice, 1962-71. Publication: A Royal Correspondence, 1938. Address: Royal Courts of Justice, Strand, WC2; 30 Drayton Gardens, SW10. T: 01-373 8289. Clubs: Hurlingham; MCC.

STEPHENSON, Air Vice-Marshal John Noel Tracy, CB 1956; CBE 1954; Retired; Member Directing Staff, Administrative Staff College, 1960, Director of Studies, 1968-69, retired 1970; b Nov. 1907; m 1959, Jill Sheila Fitzgerald, d of William Fitzgerald Hervey. Educ: Whitgift; RAF College. Served War of 1939-45: in UK, in Burma and on loan to Australian Defence Ministry. Berlin Airlift, 1948. Comdt, RAF Staff Coll., 1949-52; Dir of Organisation (Air Ministry), 1952-54; Sen. Air Staff Officer, Middle East Air Forces, 1954-57; Suez Operations, 1957 (despatches); Asst Chief of Air Staff, 1957-59. Officer, American Legion of Merit. Address: Hill Grove, Dymock, Glos. Club: Royal Air Force.

STEPHENSON, Margaret Maud; see Tyzack, M. M.

STEPHENSON, Prof. Patrick Hay, MA, CEng, FIMechE; consultant Mechanical Engineer; research advisor to Institution of Mechanical Engineers; *b* 31 March 1916; *e s* of late Stanley George Stephenson; *m* 1947, Pauline Coupland; two *s* one *d. Educ:* Wyggeston Sch., Leicester; Cambridge Univ. (MA). Apprenticeship and Research Engr, Brit. United Shoe Machinery Co., 1932-39. War Service as Ordnance Mechanical Engr and REME, India and Far East, 1939-45. Chief Mechanical Engr, Pye Ltd, 1949-67; Prof. of Mech. Engrg, Univ. of Strathclyde, 1967-79; Dir, Inst. of Advanced Machine Tool and Control Technology, Min. of Technology, 1967-70; Dir, Birniehill Inst. and Manufacturing Systems Group, DTI, 1970-72; Head of Research Requirements Branch 2, DoI, 1972-77. Mem. Council, IMechE, 1960-68; Member: Bd, UKAC, 1964-73; Engrg Bd, SRC, 1973-. *Publications:* papers and articles in technical press. *Recreations:* music, vintage motoring. *Address:* Toft Lane, Great Wilbraham, Cambridge. *T:* Cambridge 880854. *Clubs:* Army and Navy; Vintage Sports Car.

STEPHENSON, Paul; Senior Liaison Officer, Commission for Racial Equality, since 1980; *b* 6 May 1937; *s* of Olive Stephenson; *m* 1965, Joyce Annikie; one *s* one *d. Educ:* Westhill Coll. of Educn, Selly Oak, Birmingham. MIPR 1978. Youth Tutor, St Paul's, Bristol, 1962-68; Sen. Community Relations Officer, Coventry, 1968-72; National Youth Trng Officer, Community Relations Commn, 1972-77. Chm., Muhammad Ali Sports Develt Assoc., Brixton and Lambeth, 1974-; Mem., British Sports Council, 1976-82. *Recreations:* travel, cinema, reading, international politics. *Address:* 7 Avenue Park Road, West Norwood, SE17. *T:* 01-670 0070.

STEPHENSON, Philip Robert, CMG 1962; OBE 1951; *b* 29 May 1914; *s* of late Robert Barnard Stephenson and Lilian Stephenson (*née* Sharp); *m* 1947, Marianne Hurst Wraith; two *s. Educ:* Berkhamsted School; Imperial College, London; Downing College, Cambridge; Imperial College of Tropical Agriculture, Trinidad. Colonial Agricultural Service, Entomologist, Uganda, 1938. Military Service, 1940-43. East African Anti-Locust Directorate, 1943-47, Director, Desert Locust Survey, 1948-62, HM Overseas Service. Member, British Advisory Mission on Tropical Agriculture in Bolivia, Dept of Technical Co-operation, 1963-64. *Address:* c/o Lloyds Bank, Berkhamsted, Herts. *Club:* MCC.

STEPHENSON, (Robert) Ashley (Shute), MVO 1979; Bailiff of the Royal Parks, since 1980; *b* 1 Sept. 1927; *s* of late James Stephenson and of Agnes Maud Stephenson; *m* 1955, Isabel Dunn; one *s* one *d. Educ:* Walbottle Secondary Sch. Diploma in Horticulture, RHS, Wisley, 1954. Apprenticeship, Newcastle upon Tyne Parks Dept, 1942; served RASC, Palestine and Cyprus, 1946; Landscape Gardener, Donald Ireland Ltd, 1949; Student, RHS's gardens, Wisley, 1952; Royal Parks, 1954-: Supt, Regent's Park, 1969; Supt, Central Royal Parks, 1972. Member: Cttee, RHS, 1981-; London in Bloom Cttee, English Tourist Bd, 1980-. Contributor to television and radio programmes; gardening correspondent to professional and amateur papers. *Publication:* The Garden Planner, 1981. *Recreations:* sport, judging horticultural shows, natural history, walking. *Address:* Ranger's Lodge, Hyde Park, W2 2UH. *T:* 01-402 7994.

STEPHENSON, Stanley; HM Diplomatic Service; Ambassador to Panama, since 1981; *b* 30 Sept. 1926; *s* of George Stephenson and Margaret Jane (*née* Nicholson); *m* 1957, Grace Claire Lyons; one *s* one *d. Educ:* Bede Sch., Sunderland. Inland Revenue, 1942; Royal Navy, 1944-48; Foreign (later Diplomatic) Service, 1948-: Cairo, Jedda, Damascus, Curaçao, Ciudad Trujillo (now Santo Domingo), San José, Seoul, Santiago de Cuba, Bogotá (twice), Asunción, San Francisco, FCO; Diplomatic Service Inspector, 1978-80. *Recreations:* tennis, cricket, Rugby (non-active!), theatre, gardening. *Address:* c/o Foreign and Commonwealth Office, SW1. *Club:* Civil Service.

STEPHENSON, Air Vice-Marshal Tom Birkett, CB 1982; Assistant Chief of Defence Staff (Signals), 1980-82, retired; *b* 18 Aug. 1926; *s* of Richard and Isabel Stephenson; *m* 1951, Rosemary Patricia (*née* Kaye); one *s* three *d. Educ:* Workington Secondary Sch.; Manchester Univ.; Southampton Univ. (DipEl). Commissioned in RAF Engrg Branch, 1945; Staff Coll., 1962; Wing Comdr, Station and Staff appointments, until 1967; Command Electrical Engr, HQASC, 1967-69; Dep. Director Op. Requirements, 1969-72; AOEng, HQ NEAF, 1972-74; RCDS 1975; Director of Signals (Air), 1976-79. *Recreations:* sport, walking, reading. *Address:* c/o National Westminster Bank, 14 Coney Street, York YO1 1YH. *Club:* Royal Air Force.

STEPHENSON, Sir William Samuel, CC 1980; Kt 1945; MC; DFC; *b* 1896; *s* of Victor Stephenson, Canada; *m* 1924, Mary French (*d* 1978), *d* of William Simmons, of Tennessee. *Educ:* Canada. Served European War, Capt. RFC, 1914-18. Formerly: Personal Representative of Winston Churchill, and Director of British Security Co-ordination in the Western Hemisphere, 1940-46 (Jt Hon. Governor, Camp X, which was BSC training camp in World War II; now permanently memorialized as modern city). Chairman Caribbean Development Corporation. Hon. Life Mem., Royal Military Inst., Canada. Hon. DSc, Univ. of West Indies, 1950; Hon. DScMil, Royal Military Coll.; Hon. LLD Winnipeg; Hon. DSc Manitoba, 1979; Hon. DSc Winnipeg, 1980. Hon Citizen, Cities of Oshawa and Whitby, Ont. Croix de Guerre avec Palmes, 1918; French Légion d'Honneur; US Medal for Merit. CC specially invested, in Bermuda, by Governor-Gen. of Canada, 1980. *Relevant publications:* (biography by H. M. Hyde) The Quiet Canadian, 1962 (as Room 3603, in USA); Heroes of the Sunlit Sky, by Arch Whitehouse, USA, 1968; Canadians at War, vol. II, 1969; A Man called Intrepid, by William

Stevenson, 1977. *Address:* PO Box 445, Devonshire, Bermuda. *TA:* Inter, Bermuda. *Clubs:* Carlton; Royal Yacht (Bermuda).

STEPNEY, Area Bishop of; Rt. Rev. James Lawton Thompson; appointed Bishop Suffragan of Stepney, 1978; *b* 11 Aug. 1936; *s* of Bernard Isaac and Marjorie May Thompson; *m* 1965, Sally Patricia Stallworthy; one *s* one *d. Educ:* Dean Close School, Cheltenham; Emmanuel Coll., Cambridge (MA 1964). FCA 1959. 2nd Lt, 3rd Royal Tank Regt, 1960-61. Deacon, 1966; Curate, East Ham, 1966-68; Chaplain, Cuddesdon Coll., Oxford, 1968-71; Rector of Thamesmead and Ecumenical Team Leader, 1971-78. *Recreations:* painting, a pony, sport. *Address:* 400 Commercial Road, E1 0LB. *T:* 01-790 4382.

STEPTOE, Patrick Christopher, FRCSE 1951, FRCOG 1961; Director of Centre for Human Reproduction, Oldham, 1969-79; Medical Director, Bourn Hall Clinic, Bourn, Cambridgeshire, since 1980; *b* 9 June 1913; *s* of Harry Arthur Steptoe and Grace Maud (*née* Minns); *m* 1943, Sheena Macleod Kennedy; one *s* one *d. Educ:* Grammar Sch., Witney; King's Coll., London Univ.; St George's Hosp. Med. Sch. (qual. 1939). MRCS, LRCP; MRCOG 1948. Served War, RNVR, 1939-46: Surg. Lieut, 1939; POW, Italy, 1941-43; seconded to Admiralty, 1943; Surg. Lt-Comdr; demob. 1946. Chief Asst Obstetrician and Gynaecol., St George's Hosp., 1947; Sen. Registrar, Whittington Hosps, 1949; Sen. Obstetrician and Gynaecologist, Oldham Hosps, 1951-78. President: Internat. Fedn of Fertility Socs, 1977-; Brit. Fertility Soc., 1973- (Founder Chm.). Blair Bell Gold Medal, RSM, 1975. Commandant du Tastevin de Bourgogne, 1969. *Publications:* Laparoscopy in Gynaecology, 1967 (2nd edn 1979); Progress in Fertility, 1976; (contrib.) Recent Advances in Obstetrics and Gynaecology, 1977; A Matter of Life, 1980; contributor, author and jt author of papers in Lancet, Jl of Reprodn, Annals of RSM, and Brit. Med. Bull. (inc. 'In vitro fertilization of human ova'). *Recreations:* music, travel, wine, sailing. *Address:* 38 Caxton End, Bourn, Cambridge.

STERLING, Jeffrey Maurice, CBE 1977; Chairman: Sterling Guarantee Trust Ltd, since 1969; Town & City Properties Ltd, since 1974; Director, P&O Steam Navigation Co., since 1980; Special Adviser to Secretary of State for Industry, since 1982; *b* 27 Dec. 1934; *s* of Harry and Alice Sterling. *Educ:* Reigate Grammar Sch.; Preston Manor County Sch.; Guildhall School of Music. Paul Schweder & Co. (Stock Exchange), 1955-57; Dir, Eberstadt & Co. (Investment Bankers), 1957-63; Fin. Dir, General Guarantee Corp., 1963-64; Man. Dir, Gula Investments Ltd, 1964-69. Mem., British Airways Bd, 1979-82. Mem. Exec., 1966-, Chm. Organisation Cttee, 1969-73, World ORT Union; Chm., ORT Technical Services, 1974-; Vice-Pres., British ORT, 1978-. Dep. Chm. and Hon. Treasurer, London Celebrations Cttee, Queen's Silver Jubilee, 1975-. Chm., Young Vic Co., 1975-; Governor and Dep. Chm., Royal Ballet Sch., 1976-; Vice-Chm. and Chm. of the Exec., Motability, 1977-. *Recreations:* music, swimming, tennis. *Address:* 17 Brompton Square, SW3; Quennells, Plaistow, West Sussex. *Clubs:* Garrick, Carlton, Hurlingham.

STERN, family name of **Baron Michelham.**

STERN, Isaac; violinist; *b* Kreminiecz, Russia, 21 July 1920; *s* of Solomon and Clara Stern; *m* 1948, Nora Kaye; *m* 1951, Vera Lindenblit; three *c.* Studied San Francisco Conservatory, 1930-37. First public concert as guest artist San Francisco Symphony Orchestra, 1934; played with Los Angeles Philharmonic Orchestra and in concerts in Pacific Coast cities; New York début, 1937. Has since played in concerts throughout USA, in Europe, Israel, Australia, South America, Japan, China, India, The Philippines, Soviet Union and Iceland; has played with major American and European orchestras. Took part in Prades Festivals, 1950-52; Edinburgh and other major festivals in Europe and US. Film, Mao to Mozart: Isaac Stern in China (Best Full-length Documentary Acad. Award, 1981). Chm., America-Israel Cultural Foundn, NY; President, Carnegie Hall, NY. Hon. Degrees from Univs of Columbia, Johns Hopkins, Dalhousie, Brown, and San Francisco Conservatory of Music. Albert Schweitzer Music Award. Officer, Légion d'Honneur. *Address:* c/o ICM Artists Ltd, 40 West 57th Street, New York, NY 10019, USA. *Club:* Athenæum.

STERN, Prof. Joseph Peter Maria, PhD, LittD; Professor of German, University of London, and Head of Department, University College, since 1972; *b* 25 Dec. 1920; *s* of Gustav Stern and Louisa (*née* Bondy); *m* 1944, Sheila Frances (*née* McMullan); two *s* two *d. Educ:* Czech schs in Prague and Vienna; Barry County Sch. for Boys, Glam; St John's Coll., Cambridge (MA 1947, PhD 1949, LittD 1975). Wartime service in Czech Army and RAF (VR). Asst Lectr, Bedford Coll., London, 1950-52; Asst Lectr, then Lectr, Cambridge Univ., 1952-72; Fellow, St John's Coll., Cambridge, 1954-72 (Tutor, 1963-70, 1972). Chm. of Bd, Germanic Languages and Literature, Univ. of London, 1978-79; Hon. Dir, Inst. of Germanic Studies, Univ. of London, 1981-. Prof.-at-Large, Cornell Univ., Ithaca, NY, 1976-82. Vis. Professor: City Coll. of New York, 1958; Univ. of Calif at Berkeley, 1964 and 1967; State Univ. of NY at Buffalo, 1969; Univ. of Va, Charlottesville, 1971. Merton Prof., Univ. of Göttingen, 1965. Fellow, Center for Humanities, Wesleyan Univ., 1972. Lewis Fry Meml Lectr, Univ. of Bristol, 1973; British Academy Master Mind Lectr, 1978. Goethe Medal, Goethe Inst., 1980; Alexander von Humboldt Research Prize, 1980. *Publications:* Ernst Jünger: a writer of our time, 1952; (trans.) R. W. Meyer, Leibnitz and the seventeenth-century revolution, 1952; (trans.) H.-E. Holthusen, R. M. Rilke:

a study of his later poetry, 1952; G. C. Lichtenberg: a doctrine of scattered occasions, 1959; Re-Interpretations: seven studies in nineteenth-century German literature, 1964, repr. 1981; (ed) Arthur Schnitzler, Liebelei. Leutnant Gustl. Die letzten Masken, 1966; Idylls and Realities: studies in nineteenth-century German literature, 1971; On Realism, 1973, rev. German version, 1982; Hitler: the Führer and the People, 1975 (4th repr. 1978, rev. German version 1978); Nietzsche (Fontana Modern Masters), 1978; A Study of Nietzsche, 1979, rev. German version, 1982; (with Michael Silk) Nietzsche on Tragedy, 1981; (ed) The World of Franz Kafka, 1981; contribs (incl. 42 Poems from the Czech, trans. with S. F. Stern) and articles in English and foreign jls and newspapers. *Recreations:* hacking, hunting with the Cambridgeshire Foxhounds. *Address:* 83 Barton Road, Cambridge CB3 9LL. *T:* Cambridge 353078.

STERN, Vivien Helen; Director, National Association for the Care and Resettlement of Offenders (NACRO), since 1977; *b* 25 Sept. 1941; *d* of Frederick Stern and Renate Mills. *Educ:* Kent Coll., Pembury, Kent; Bristol Univ. (BA, MLitt, CertEd). Lectr in Further Educn until 1970; Community Relations Commn, 1970-77. Member: Special Programmes Bd, Manpower Services Commn, 1980-; Gen. Adv. Bd, IBA. *Address:* National Association for the Care and Resettlement of Offenders, 169 Clapham Road, SW9.

STERNBERG, Sir Sigmund, Kt 1976; JP; Chairman: Commodities Research Unit Ltd; Martin Slowe Estates Ltd; Director, Forex Research Ltd; Lloyds Underwriter; *b* Budapest, 2 June 1921; *s* of Abraham and Elizabeth Sternberg; *m* 1970, Hazel (*née* Everett Jones); two *s* two *d*. Served War of 1939-45, Civil Defence Corps. Former Ring-Dealing Mem., London Metal Exchange. Co-Chm., Arbitration Cttee, Bureau Internat. de la Récupération, 1966. Instituted Res. Gp for Labour Shadow Cabinet, 1973-74; Econ. and Industry Cttee, Fabian Soc., 1976 (Chm., Appeals Cttee, 1975-77); Treasurer, 1972 Industry Gp., St Charles Gp, HMC, 1974; NW Metrop. RHB, 1974; Member: Camden and Islington AHA, 1974-77; Gen. Purposes Cttee, NAMH, 1972; Vice-Pres., Coll. of Speech Therapists; Chm., Inst. for Archaeo-Metallurgical Studies. Pres., VOCAL (Voluntary Organisation Communications and Language); Hon. Treasurer and Chm. of Friends, CRUSE National Org. for the Widowed and their Children; Hon. Treasurer, Council of Christians and Jews; Chm., Internat. Council of Christians and Jews; Mem., Board of Deputies of British Jews; Governor, Hebrew Univ. of Jerusalem (Hon. Treas., Friends of Hebrew Univ. of Jerusalem); Chm., Friends of Oxford Centre of Post-grad. Hebrew Studies. Speaker Chm., Rotary Club of London, 1980. Mem., Court, Essex Univ. Liveryman, Co. of Horners; Freeman, City of London. JP Middlesex, 1965 (Middlesex Probation (Case) Cttee, 1973). Hon. FRSM 1981. Brotherhood Award, Nat. Conf. of Christians and Jews Inc., 1980. *Recreations:* golf, swimming. *Address:* 31 Mount Pleasant, WC1X 0AD. *T:* 01-278 0414. *Telex* 264008. *Clubs:* Reform, City Livery.

STERNE, Laurence Henry Gordon, MA, CEng, FIMechE; *b* 2 July 1916; *o s* of late Henry Herbert Sterne and late Hilda Davey; *m* 1944, Katharine Clover; two *d*. *Educ:* Culford Sch.; Jesus Coll. (Open Exhibnr and Hon. Schol.), Oxford (MA). Royal Aircraft Establishment: Structures and Mechanical Engrg Depts, 1940; Aerodynamics Dept, 1949; Head of Naval Air Dept, 1954; Chief Supt at Bedford, 1955. Prof. and Dir, von Karman Inst., Rhode Saint Genèse, Belgium, 1958-62; Aviation Mem., Research Policy Staff, MoD, 1962-64; Dir, Royal Naval Aircraft and Helicopters, 1964-68; Dep. Dir, Nat. Engineering Lab., E Kilbride, 1968-77. Vis. Prof., Strathclyde Univ., 1971-76. *Publications:* reports and memoranda of Aeronautical Research Council; ed jtly, early vols of Progress in Aeronautical Sciences. *Recreation:* gardening. *Address:* 10 Trinity Street, Bungay, Suffolk NR35 1EH.

STEVAS, Norman Antony Francis St J.; *see* St John-Stevas.

STEVENS, Air Marshal Sir Alick (Charles), KBE, *cr* 1952; CB 1944; retired; *b* 31 July 1898; *s* of late Charles Edward Russell Stevens, Jersey; *m* 1927, Beryl, *d* of B. J. Gates, Wing, Bucks; one *s*. *Educ:* Victoria College, Jersey. Joined RNAS 1916; transferred to RAF on formation, 1918; Wing Comdr, 1937; Air Commodore, 1942. Dep. Director, 1940-42, and then Director of Operations (Naval Co-operation) at Air Ministry, 1942-43; SASO, No 18 Group, 1943-44 (despatches); AOC, RAF, Gibraltar, 1944-45; AOC No 47 Group, 1945; AOC No 4 Group, Transport Command, 1946; Air Vice-Marshal, 1947; AOC No 22 Group, Technical Training Comd, 1946-48; AOC British Forces, Aden, 1948-50; SASO, Coastal Comd, 1950-51; AOC-in-C, Coastal Comd, 1951-53; Air C-in-C, Eastern Atlantic Area, Atlantic Comd, 1952-53; Allied Maritime Air C-in-C Channel and Southern North Sea, Channel Comd, 1952-53; retd Dec. 1953; Vice-Chairman, Gloucestershire T&AFA, 1955-63. *Address:* Cherry Tree Cottage, Cadmore End, near High Wycombe, Bucks HP14 3PT. *T:* High Wycombe 881569. *Club:* Royal Air Force.

STEVENS, Anthony John; Director, Veterinary Laboratories, Ministry of Agriculture, Fisheries and Food, since 1979; *b* 29 July 1926; *s* of John Walker Stevens and Hilda Stevens; *m* 1954, Patricia Frances, *d* of Robert Gill, Ponteland; one *s* two *d*. *Educ:* Liverpool and Manchester Univs; Magdalene Coll., Cambridge. MA, BVSc, MRCVS, DipBact. Veterinary Investigation Officer, Cambridge, 1956-65; Animal Health Expert for UNO, 1959-63; Suptg Veterinary Investigation Officer, Leeds, 1965-68; Ministry of Agriculture, Fisheries and Food: Dep. Dir, Central Vet. Lab., 1968-71; Asst

Chief Vet. Officer, 1971-73; Dep. Chief Vet. Officer, 1973-78. External Examr, Dublin, Liverpool and Edinburgh Univs., 1964-70. Past Pres., Veterinary Research Club. FRSA. *Publications:* UN/FAO Manual of Diagnostic Techniques; regular contributor to Veterinary Record, etc. *Recreations:* canals, sailing and all forms of livestock. *Address:* Marigold Cottage, Great Halfpenny Farm, Guildford, Surrey. *T:* Guildford 63575.

STEVENS, (Arthur) Edwin, CBE 1979; *b* 17 Oct. 1905; *s* of Arthur Edwin Stevens and Bessie Annie (*née* Dowden); *m* 1933, Kathleen Alberta James; three *s*. *Educ:* West Monmouth Sch.; University Coll., Cardiff (BSc Hons 1927; Hon. Fellow 1981); Jesus Coll., Oxford (MA Hons 1929). FInstP 1937. Founder, Amplivox Ltd: Chm. and Man. Dir, 1935-75; designed world's first wearable electronic hearing aid, 1935; collector of world's most comprehensive exhibn of aids to hearing covering 400 yrs. Hon. Fellow, Jesus Coll., Oxford, 1973; financed building of Stevens Close, Jesus Coll. Hall of Residence opened by the Queen, 1970; founded RSM Edwin Stevens Lectures for Laity, 1970; Hon. FRSM 1981. Patron, English National Opera. *Recreations:* golf, gardening. *Address:* Penates, Littleworth Common Road, Esher, Surrey. *T:* Esher 64829.

See also D. R. Stevens.

STEVENS, David Robert; Chairman: United Newspapers Ltd, since 1981 (Director, since 1974); Drayton Montagu Portfolio Management Ltd, since 1980 (Managing Director, since 1974); Managing Director, Samuel Montagu Ltd, since 1980; *b* 26 May 1936; *s* of (Arthur) Edwin Stevens, *qv*; *m* 1977, Melissa, Countess Andrassy; one *s* one *d*. *Educ:* Stowe Sch.; Sidney Sussex Coll., Cambridge (MA Hons Econ). Management Trainee, Elliott Automation, 1959; Director: Hill Samuel Securities, 1959-68; Drayton Group, 1968-74. Chairman: British Industries & General, 1976-; City & Foreign, 1976-; Drayton Far East, 1976-; English & International, 1976-; Dualvest, 1979-; Montagu Boston, 1979-; Triplevest, 1979-; Drayton Consolidated, 1980-; Drayton Japan, 1980-. *Recreation:* golf. *Address:* 6 West Eaton Place, SW1X 8LS. *Clubs:* White's; Sunningdale Golf.

STEVENS, Prof. Denis William; President and Artistic Director, Accademia Monteverdiana, since 1961; *b* 2 March 1922; *s* of William J. Stevens and Edith Driver; *m* 1st, 1949, Sheila Elizabeth Holloway; two *s* one *d*; 2nd, 1975, Leocadia Elzbieta Kwasny. *Educ:* Royal Grammar Sch., High Wycombe; Jesus College, Oxford. Served War of 1939-45, RAF Intelligence, India and Burma, 1942-46. Producer, BBC Music Div., 1949-54; Assoc. Founder and Conductor, Ambrosian Singers, 1952; Vis. Professor of Musicology, Cornell Univ., 1955, Columbia Univ., 1956; Secretary, Plainsong and Mediaeval Music Soc., 1958-63; Editor, Grove's Dictionary of Music and Musicians, 1959-63. Professor, Royal Acad. of Music, 1960. Vis. Prof. Univ. of California (Berkeley), 1962; Dist. Vis. Prof., Pennsylvania State Univ., 1962-63; Prof. of Musicology, Columbia Univ., 1964-76; Vis. Prof. Univ. of California (Santa Barbara), 1974-75; Brechemin Dist. Vis. Prof., Univ. of Washington, Seattle, 1976; Vis. Prof., Univ. of Michigan, Ann Arbor, 1977, San Diego State Univ., 1978. Lectures on music, especially British, in England, France, Germany, Italy, USA; concerts, conducting own and ancillary ensembles at internat. festivals in GB, Europe and USA; TV and radio programmes in Europe and N America; cons. for films. FSA; Member Worshipful Company of Musicians. Hon. RAM, 1960. Hon.D, Humane Letters, Fairfield Univ., Connecticut, 1967. *Publications:* The Mulliner Book, 1952; Thomas Tomkins, 1957, rev. edn 1966; A History of Song, 1960, rev. edn, 1971; Tudor Church Music, 1966; A Treasury of English Church Music (I), 1965; (ed) First and Second Penguin Book of English Madrigals, 1967, 1971; Early Tudor Organ Music (II), 1969; Music in Honour of St Thomas of Canterbury, 1970; Monteverdi: sacred, secular and occasional music, 1978; Musicology: a practical guide, 1980; The Letters of Monteverdi, 1980; Renaissance Dialogues, 1981; The Worcester Fragments, 1981; many edns of early music, including Monteverdi Vespers and Orfeo; choral works by Gabrieli, Lassus, Machaut, Tallis, Tomkins; articles in English and foreign journals; also many stereo recordings ranging from plainsong to Beethoven. *Recreations:* travel, photography. *Address:* 2203 Las Tunas Road, Santa Barbara, Calif 93103, USA. *Club:* Garrick.

STEVENS, Edwin; *see* Stevens, A. E.

STEVENS, Frank Leonard; formerly Editor, FBI Review and Publicity Officer, Federation of British Industries; *b* Mexborough, 8 Jan. 1898; *s* of late Frederick Thomas Stevens; *m* 1925, Winifred, 2nd *d* of Alexander Bruce, JP; two *s*. *Educ:* Mexborough Grammar School; University College, London. After a year as teacher, three years in the Army (1916-19), entered journalism, South Yorkshire Times, Allied Newspapers, Manchester; Manchester Evening News; assistant editor, John O' London's Weekly; Daily News sub-editorial staff; associate editor, Everyman; joint editor, monthly Clarion. *Publications:* Through Merrie England, 1926; On Going to Press, 1928; Under London, 1939. *Recreations:* reading and sketching. *Address:* Barn Cottage, Singleton, Chichester, West Sussex. *T:* Singleton 653.

STEVENS, Jocelyn Edward Greville; Director, Centaur Communications, since 1982; Chairman, London Sound, since 1982; *b* 14 Feb. 1932; *s* of Major C. G. B. Stewart-Stevens and of Mrs Greville Stevens; *m* 1956, Jane Armyne Sheffield (marr. diss. 1979); two *s* two *d*. *Educ:* Eton; Cambridge. Military service in Rifle Bde, 1950-52; Journalist, Hulton Press Ltd, 1955-56; Chairman and Managing Dir, Stevens Press Ltd, and Editor of Queen Magazine, 1957-68; Personal Asst to Chairman of Beaverbrook Newspapers, May-Dec.

1968; Director, 1971–81; Managing Director: Evening Standard Co. Ltd, 1969–72; Daily Express, 1972–74; Beaverbrook Newspapers, 1974–77; Express Newspapers, 1977–81 (Dep. Chm. and Man. Dir). *Address:* Testbourne, Longparish, near Andover, Hants. *T:* Longparish 232. *Clubs:* Buck's, Beefsteak, White's.

STEVENS, Prof. John Edgar, CBE 1980; PhD; FBA 1975; Fellow of Magdalene College, Cambridge, since 1950; Professor of Medieval and Renaissance English, University of Cambridge, since 1978; *b* 8 Oct. 1921; *s* of William Charles James and Fanny Stevens; *m* 1946, Charlotte Ethel Mary (*née* Somner); two *s* two *d. Educ:* Christ's Hospital, Horsham; Magdalene College, Cambridge (Schol.; MA, PhD). Served Royal Navy; Temp. Lieut RNVR. Cambridge University: Bye-Fellow 1948, Research Fellow 1950, Fellow 1953 and Tutor 1958–74, Magdalene Coll.; Univ. Lectr in English, 1954–74; Reader in English and Musical History, 1974–78. *Publications:* Medieval Carols (Musica Britannica vol. 4), 1952, 2nd edn 1958; Music and Poetry in the Early Tudor Court, 1961; Music at the Court of Henry VIII (Musica Britannica vol. 18), 1962, 2nd edn 1969; (with Richard Axton) Medieval French Plays, 1971; Medieval Romance, 1973; Early Tudor Songs & Carols (Musica Britannica vol. 36), 1975. *Recreations:* viol-playing, sailing, bricklaying. *Address:* 4 & 5 Bell's Court, Cambridge.

STEVENS, Vice-Adm. Sir John (Felgate), KBE 1955 (CBE 1945); CB 1951; *b* 1 June 1900; *o surv. s* of late Henry Marshall Stevens, Droveway Corner, Hove; *m* 1928, Mary, *o d* of J. Harry Gilkes, JP, Wychcote, Patcham, Sussex; one *s* two *d.* Midshipman, 1918; King's Coll., Cambridge, 1922, specialised in Navigation, 1924; Staff College, 1930; Commander, 1933; Captain, 1940. Served War of 1939–45 (despatches, CBE); Director of Plans, Admiralty, 1946–47; commanded HMS Implacable, 1948–49; Rear-Admiral, 1949; Director of Naval Training, 1949–50; Chief of Staff to Head of British Joint Services Mission, Washington, 1950–52; Flag Officer, Home Fleet Training Squadron, 1952–53; Commander-in-Chief, America and West Indies Station, and Deputy Supreme Allied Commander, Atlantic, 1953–55; retired list, 1956. *Address:* Withy Springs, Petworth Road, Haslemere, Surrey. *T:* Haslemere 2970. *Club:* Naval and Military.

STEVENS, Hon. John Paul; Associate Justice, Supreme Court of the United States, since 1975; *b* 20 April 1920; *s* of Ernest James Stevens and Elizabeth Stevens (*née* Street); *m* 1st, 1942, Elizabeth Jane Sheeren; one *s* three *d* ; 2nd, 1979, Maryan Mulholland Simon. *Educ:* Univ. of Chicago (AB 1941); Northwestern Univ. (JD 1947). Served War, USNR, 1942–45 (Bronze Star). Law Clerk to US Supreme Ct Justice Wiley Rutledge, 1947–48; Associate, Poppenhusen, Johnston, Thompson & Raymond, 1948–50; Associate Counsel, sub-cttee on Study Monopoly Power, Cttee on Judiciary, US House of Reps, 1951; Partner, Rothschild, Hart, Stevens & Barry, 1952–70; US Circuit Judge, 1970–75. Lectr, anti-trust law, Northwestern Univ. Sch. of Law, 1953; Univ. of Chicago Law Sch., 1954–55; Mem., Attorney-Gen.'s Nat. Cttee to study Anti-Trust Laws, 1953–55. Mem., Chicago Bar Assoc. (2nd Vice-Pres. 1970). Order of Coif, Phi Beta Kappa, Psi Upsilon, Phi Delta Phi. *Publications:* chap. in book, Mr Justice (ed Dunham and Kurland); contrib. to Antitrust Developments: a supp. to Report of Attorney-Gen.'s Nat. Cttee to Study the Anti-trust Laws, 1955–68; various articles etc, in Ill. Law Rev., Proc. confs, and reports. *Recreations:* flying, tennis, bridge, reading, travel. *Address:* Supreme Court of the United States, Washington, DC 20543, USA.

STEVENS, Kenneth Henry; Chief Executive Commissioner, The Scout Association, since 1970; *b* 8 Oct. 1922; *s* of late Horace J. Stevens, CBE, sometime Senior Principal Inspector of Taxes, and late Nora Stevens (*née* Kauntze); *m* 1947, Yvonne Grace Ruth (*née* Mitchell); one *s* one *d. Educ:* Brighton Coll.; Brighton Technical Coll. South Coast Civil Defence, 1941–44. Alliance Assurance Co., 1944–47; Asst Dir of Adult Leader Training, Internat. Scout Training Centre, Gilwell Park, Chingford, 1947–56; Organising Comr, World Scout Jamboree, Indaba and Rover Moot, Sutton Coldfield, 1956–58; Dep. Dir of Adult Leader Training, Internat. Scout Training Centre, 1958–61; Asst Chief Exec. Comr, The Scout Assoc., 1961–63; Dep. Chief Exec. Comr, 1963–70. FBIM. *Publication:* Ceremonies of The Scout Movement, 1958. *Recreations:* motoring, gardening. *Address:* 69 Ashley Road, Epsom, Surrey. *T:* Epsom 25031. *Club:* MCC.

STEVENS, Prof. Kenneth William Harry; Professor of Theoretical Physics, University of Nottingham since 1958; *b* 17 Sept. 1922; *s* of Harry and Rose Stevens; *m* 1949, Audrey A. Gawthrop; one *s* one *d. Educ:* Magdalen College School, Oxford; Jesus and Merton Colleges, Oxford. MA 1947, DPhil 1949. Pressed Steel Company Ltd Research Fellow, Oxford University, 1949–53; Research Fellow, Harvard University, 1953–54; Reader in Theoretical Physics, University of Nottingham 1953–58. (Jointly) Maxwell Medal and Prize, 1968. *Publications:* contrib. to learned journals. *Recreations:* music, tennis, squash. *Address:* The University, Nottingham.

STEVENS, Martin, JP; MP (C) Fulham, since 1979; marketing consultant; *b* 31 July 1929; *s* of John Rowland Stevens and Muriel Stevens, London; unmarried. *Educ:* Orley Farm Sch., Harrow-on-the-Hill; Bradfield; Trinity Coll., Oxford (BA Law 1952, MA 1962). Rank Org., 1954–67; Man. Dir, Granada Television Internat., 1967–69; management and marketing consultant, 1969–. Member: LCC (Cons. Dulwich), 1955–58; Camberwell Bor. Council, 1959–65; Camberwell Gp Hosps Management Cttee, 1956–66; National Appeals Cttee, Cancer Res. Campaign, 1956– (Chm., 1968). Contested Dulwich, 1964 and 1966, and Fulham, Feb. and Oct. 1974. Mem., Select Cttee

on Industry and Trade, 1982–. JP Inner London, 1972. *Publications:* contrib. to business and prof. pubns. *Recreations:* books, theatre, travel, good fellowship. *Address:* C5 Albany, Piccadilly, W1V 9RF. *T:* 01-439 7980. *Clubs:* Carlton, Garrick, Hurlingham, Special Forces (Hon. Life Mem.).

STEVENS, Philip Theodore; Professor of Greek in the University of London (Bedford College), 1950–74, now Emeritus; *b* 11 Nov. 1906; *s* of late Rev. Herbert Stevens, Vicar of Milwich; *m* 1939, Evelyn Grace, 2nd *d* of late G. L. Crickmay, FRIBA, Oatlands Park, Weybridge, Surrey; one *s. Educ:* Wolverhampton Grammar School; New Coll., Oxford (Scholar). 1st Cl. Hon. Mods, 1927; 2nd Cl. Lit. Hum., 1929; Asst Master, Liverpool Institute, 1929–30; Tutor at Univ. Corresp. Coll., Cambridge, 1930–32; Asst Lecturer in Greek, Univ. of Aberdeen, 1933–38; PhD Aberdeen 1939. Lectr in Classics, Univ. of Cape Town, 1938–41. War Service, S African Mil. Intelligence, 1941–45. Lecturer in Latin and Greek, University of Liverpool, 1945–50. Trustee, Hellenic Soc., 1961–. *Publications:* Euripides, Andromache, 1971; Colloquial Expressions in Euripides, 1976; The Society for the Promotion of Hellenic Studies 1879–1979, 1979; contribs to English and foreign classical periodicals. *Recreation:* music. *Address:* Baywell Cottage, Charlbury, Oxon. *Club:* Reform.

STEVENS, Richard William, RDI 1973; BSc; FSIAD, FCIBS; Design Manager, British Telecom (formerly Post Office Telecommunications), since 1969; *b* 1 Oct. 1924; *s* of William Edward Stevens and Caroline Alice (*née* Mills); *m* 1947, Anne Clara Hammond; one *s* one *d. Educ:* Dorking County Grammar Sch.; Regent St Polytechnic (BSc). FSIAD 1960, FCIBS 1977. Designer, then Chief Designer, Atlas Lighting Ltd, 1954–63; Industrial Design Manager, Standard Telephones and Cables Ltd, 1963–69. Pres., SIAD, 1972–73; Treasurer, ICSID, 1975–77. Gold Medal, Milan Triennale, 1957; three Design Centre Awards, London. *Recreations:* gardening, music, photography, walking. *Address:* Hazel Cottage, Ewood Lane, Newdigate, Dorking, Surrey RH5 5AR. *Club:* Arts.

STEVENS, HE Dr Siaka (Probyn), Hon. GCMG 1980; First Prime Minister and First Executive President, Republic of Sierra Leone, since April 1971; elected Secretary-General of All People's Congress (ruling party), 1979; *b* 24 Aug. 1905; *m* 1940, Rebecca Stevens; seven *s* five *d. Educ:* Albert Academy, Freetown; Ruskin Coll., Oxford. Joined Sierra Leone Police Force, 1923–30, became 1st Cl. Sergt and Musketry Instr; worked for Sierra Leone Development Co., became first Gen. Sec. of United Mine Workers Union (co-founder), 1931–46. Member: Moyamba Dist Council; Freetown City Council (rep. Protectorate Assembly); several Govt Cttees, 1946–48; Sec., Sierra Leone TUC, 1948–50; MLC (elec. by Assembly), 1951, and first Minister of Lands, Mines and Labour; Dep. Leader of (the now dissolved) Peoples' National Party, 1958–60; formed Election before Independence Movement (which later became the All Peoples' Congress), 1960; Leader of the Opposition, All Peoples' Congress, 1962; Mayor of Freetown, 1964; sworn in as Prime Minister of Sierra Leone in 1967, re-appointed 1968. Chm., OAU, 1980–81. Hon. DCL Univ. of Sierra Leone, 1969; Hon. DLitt Lincoln Univ., USA, 1979. *Recreation:* walking. *Address:* State House, Freetown, Sierra Leone.

STEVENS, Prof. Thomas Stevens, FRS 1963; FRSE 1964; Emeritus Professor of Chemistry, University of Sheffield; *b* 8 Oct. 1900; *o c* of John Stevens and Jane E. Stevens (*née* Irving); *m* 1949, Janet Wilson Forsyth; no *c. Educ:* Paisley Grammar Sch.; Glasgow Academy; Universities of Glasgow and Oxford. DPhil 1925. Assistant in Chemistry, Univ. of Glasgow, 1921–23, Lecturer, 1925–47; Ramsay Memorial Fellow, Oxford, 1923–25; Sen. Lectr in Organic Chemistry, Univ. of Sheffield, 1947–49, Reader, 1949–63, Prof., 1963–66; Visiting Prof. of Chemistry, Univ. of Strathclyde, Oct. 1966–Sept. 1967. *Publications:* (with W. E. Watts) Selected Molecular Rearrangements, 1973; contrib. to Elsevier-Rodd, Chemistry of Carbon Compounds, 1957–60. Papers in scientific jls. *Recreation:* unsophisticated bridge. *Address:* 313 Albert Drive, Glasgow G41 5RP.

STEVENS, Thomas Terry Hoar; *see* Terry-Thomas.

STEVENS, Thomas Wilson, CBE 1962; RD 1942; Commodore, Royal Mail Line Fleet, 1961–63, retired; *b* 16 Oct. 1901; *s* of John Wilson Stevens and Susan Eliza Smith; *m* 1939, Mary Doreen Whitington; one *s* one *d. Educ:* Sir Walter St John's, Battersea. Joined Royal Mail Steam Packet Co. as a Cadet, 1917; joined Royal Naval Reserve as Sub-Lieut 1927. Active service, Royal Navy, 1939–47. Younger Brother of Trinity House, 1944. Captain Royal Mail Lines, 1947; Captain Royal Naval Reserve, 1950. *Recreation:* golf. *Address:* 79 Offington Lane, Worthing, West Sussex. *T:* Worthing 61100.

STEVENS, Timothy John; Director, Merseyside County Council Art Galleries, since 1974; *b* 17 Jan. 1940; *s* of Seymour Stevens; *m* 1969, Caroline Sankey; twin *s. Educ:* King's Sch., Canterbury; Hertford Coll., Oxford (MA); Courtauld Inst., Univ. of London (Academic Diploma, History of Art). Walker Art Gallery: Asst Keeper of British Art, 1964–65; Keeper of Foreign Art, 1965–67; Dep. Dir, 1967–70; Dir, 1971–74. *Recreation:* gardening. *Address:* Walker Art Gallery, William Brown Street, Liverpool L3 8EL. *T:* 051-227 5234.

STEVENS, William David; Vice President, Esso Europe, since 1978; *b* USA, 18 Sept. 1934; *s* of Walter Gerald and Amy Grace Stevens; *m* 1954, Barbara Ann Duncan; one *s* three *d. Educ:* Texas A&I Univ. (BScEng). Joined Humble

Oil, 1958: various assignments, US Gulf Coast, 1959–73; Exxon Corporation: Executive Asst to President, 1973–74; various assignments, New York, 1974–77; Vice Pres., Gas, 1977–78. President, UK Offshore Operators Assoc., 1980–. *Recreations:* golf, shooting, hiking. *Address:* 24 Harley House, Marylebone Road, NW1 5HE. *T:* (office) 01-493 7030; (home) 01-935 6003. *Club:* Les Ambassadeurs.

STEVENSON, Dr Alan Carruth; *b* 27 Jan. 1909; *s* of Allan Stevenson, CBE, and Christina Kennedy Lawson; *m* 1937, Annie Gordon Sheila Steven; two *s* one *d. Educ:* Glasgow Academy; Glasgow University. BSc 1930, MB, ChB 1933, MD 1946, Glasgow; MRCP 1935; FRCP 1955. Appointments: Royal Infirmary, Glasgow; Highgate Hospital, London; London Hospital. Served RAMC 1939–45 (despatches); retired with hon. rank of Lieutenant-Colonel, 1946–48. Professor of Social and Preventive Medicine, The Queen's University, Belfast, 1948–58; Reader in Public Health, London University; Dir, MRC Population Genetics Unit, Oxford, and Lectr in Human Genetics, Oxford Univ., 1958–74. *Publications:* Build your own Enlarger, 1943; Recent Advances in Social Medicine, 1948; Genetic Counselling, 1971; articles on Tropical and Preventive Medicine and human genetics in appropriate scientific journals. *Recreation:* fishing. *Address:* Dunera, Dores Road, Inverness.

STEVENSON, Alan Leslie; Metropolitan Magistrate, 1951–73; *b* 1 Apr. 1901; *yr s* of late James Stevenson, London and Calcutta. *Educ:* Bradfield College; Christ Church, Oxford (BA). Called to the Bar, Inner Temple, 1926; South Eastern Circuit, Kent and London Sessions. Part time Ministry of Food, London Divisional Food Office, Licensing (Revocations) Officer, 1942–49; Chairman Milk Marketing Board Disciplinary Committee, 1950–51. *Recreations:* golf and tennis. *Address:* 48 Lincoln House, Basil Street, SW3. *T:* 01-589 9026. *Clubs:* Royal St George's Golf (Sandwich); Royal Cinque Ports Golf (Deal).

STEVENSON, Rt. Hon. Sir (Aubrey) Melford (Steed), PC 1973; Kt 1957; Justice of the High Court, 1957–79 (Queen's Bench Division, 1961–79; Probate, Divorce and Admiralty Division, 1957–61); *b* 17 October 1902; *o s* of late Rev. J. G. Stevenson; one *d* (by 1st marriage); *m* 2nd, Rosalind Monica, *d* of late Orlando H. Wagner; one *s* one *d. Educ:* Dulwich Coll. LLB (London). Called to Bar, Inner Temple, 1925, Treasurer, 1972; Major and Dep. Judge Advocate, 1940–45; KC 1943; Bencher, 1950. Recorder of Rye, 1944–51, of City of Cambridge, 1952–57; Dep. Chairman, West Kent Quarter Sessions, 1949–55; Presiding Judge, South-Eastern Circuit, 1970–75. Mem. Inter-Departmental Committee on Human Artificial Insemination, 1958–60. *Address:* Truncheons, Winchelsea, East Sussex. *T:* Winchelsea 223. *Club:* Garrick.

STEVENSON, Sir David; *see* Stevenson, Sir H. D.

STEVENSON, Dennis; *see* Stevenson, H. D.

STEVENSON, Dr Derek Paul, CBE 1972; MRCS, LRCP; *b* 11 July 1911; *s* of late Frederick Stevenson and Maud Coucher; *m* 1941, Pamela Mary, *d* of late Col C. N. Jervelund, OBE; two *s* one *d. Educ:* Epsom College; Guy's Hospital. Lieut RAMC, 1935 (Montefiore Prize, Royal Army Med. Coll., 1935); Capt. RAMC 1936; Maj. 1942; Lt-Col 1943; service in China and Malaya. Asst Director-General Army Medical Service, War Office, 1942–46; Sec. Army Medical Advisory Bd 1943–46. War Office hon. on Central Med., War Cttee, 1943–46. British Medical Association: Asst Sec., 1946–48; Dep. Sec., 1948–58; Sec., 1958–76. Sec. Jt Consultants Cttee 1948–76; Mem., Health Services Bd, and Scottish Cttee, 1977–80. Vice-Pres. British Medical Students Assoc.; Hon. Sec./Treas., British Commonwealth Med. Conf.; Delegate, Gen. Assembly World Medical Association: Sydney, 1968, Paris, 1969, Oslo, 1970 Ottawa, 1971, Amsterdam, 1972, Munich, 1973, Stockholm, 1974, Chm. Council, 1969, 1970–71 (Mem. Council, 1967-). Medical Sec. to Nat. Ophthalmic Treatment Board Assoc.; Mem. Council of London Hospital Service Plan; Mem. Cttee of Management: Medical Insurance Agency; Medical and Dental Retirement Adv. Service. Adviser: Sterling Winthrop, Mediscope Jl; Mem. Adv. Bd, Allied Investments; Dir, Tavistock Computer Services; Gen. Comr, Inland Revenue. Hon. Sec. and Treas., British Commonwealth Medical Assoc., 1964; Sec. Gen., Permanent Cttee of Doctors, EEC, 1973–76; Hon. Sec., British Life Assurance Trust. Liaison Officer, MoD, 1964. Mem. Bd of Governors, Epsom College; Pres., Old Epsomian Club, 1974–75. Mem., Chichester Dio. Bd; Lay Chm., Rural Deanery. CC West Sussex, 1980-. Fellow, Royal Commonwealth Soc., 1968; Fellow, BMA, 1976 (Gold Medal, 1976). Hon. LLD, Manchester, 1964. *Publications:* contrib. Irish Medical Jl; BMA Lecture delivered to Irish Medical Assoc.; contrib. Canadian Med. Assoc. Jl, and address at Centennial meeting, Montreal; NHS Reorganisation (in RSH Jl), address to RSH Congress 1973; regular contribs to Medical Interface. *Recreations:* golf, sailing, gardening. *Address:* Bodrigy, Holycombe, Liphook, Hants. *T:* Liphook 724205. *Clubs:* Athenæum, Garrick, Royal Commonwealth Society; Hindhead Golf.

STEVENSON, Henry Dennistoun, (Dennis Stevenson), CBE 1981; Partner, Specialist Research Unit, since 1972; Director, London Docklands Development Corporation, since 1981; *b* 19 July 1945; *s* of Alexander James Stevenson and Sylvia Florence Stevenson (*née* Ingleby); *m* 1972, Charlotte Susan, *d* of Hon. Sir Peter Vanneck, *qv* ; three *s. Educ:* Glenalmond; King's Coll., Cambridge (MA). Chm., Newton Aycliffe and Peterlee New Town Develt Corp., 1971–80. Chairman: govt working party on role of voluntary movements and youth in the environment, 1971, '50 Million Volunteers'

(HMSO); Indep. Advisory Cttee on Pop Festivals, 1972–76, 'Pop Festivals, Report and Code of Practice' (HMSO); Adviser on Agricultural Marketing to Minister of Agriculture, 1979–. Chm., Nat. Assoc. of Youth Clubs, 1973–81. Mem. Admin. Council, Royal Jubilee Trusts, 1978–80. Director: Nat. Building Agency, 1977–81. Nat. Enterprise Bd, 1979–. *Recreations:* watching most sports, cooking, reading, writing, talking. *Address:* 20 Surrey Square, SE17 2JX. *T:* 01-703 8316; 320 East 57th Street, New York, NY 10022, USA. *T:* 212-935-9815. *Club:* MCC.

STEVENSON, Dame Hilda (Mabel), DBE 1967 (CBE 1963; OBE 1960); Vice-President, Royal Children's Hospital, Melbourne, Victoria, Australia, 1938–72; *b* 1895; *d* of H. V. McKay, CBE, Sunshine, Vic; *m* 1st, Cleveland Kidd (*d* 1925); one *d* ; 2nd, Col G. I. Stevenson (*d* 1958), CMG, DSO, VD. *Educ:* Presbyterian Ladies' College. Hon. LLD Melbourne, 1973. *Address:* 17 St George's Road, Toorak, Victoria 3142, Australia. *T:* 24-4628. *Clubs:* International Sportsmen's; Sunningdale Golf; Alexandra (Melbourne).

STEVENSON, Vice-Adm. Sir (Hugh) David, KBE 1977 (CBE 1970); AC 1976; Royal Australian Navy, retired; *b* 24 Aug. 1918; *s* of late Rt Rev. William Henry Webster Stevenson, Bishop of Grafton, NSW, and Mrs Katherine Saumarez Stevenson; *m* 1st, 1944, Myra Joyce Clarke (*d* 1978); one *s* one *d* ; 2nd, Margaret Lorraine Wright. *Educ:* Southport Sch., Qld; RAN Coll. psc RN 1956; idc 1966. Commnd, 1938; served War: Mediterranean, East Indies, Pacific; minesweeping post, SW Pacific; specialised in navigation, 1944 (HM Navigation Sch.); Commands: HMAS Tobruk and 10th Destroyer Sqdn, 1959–60; HMNZS Royalist, 1960–61; HMAS Sydney, 1964; HMAS Melbourne, 1965–66; Dir of Plans, 1962–63; Naval Officer i/c W Australian area, 1967; Dep. Chief of Naval Staff, 1968–69; Comdr Aust. Fleet, 1970–71; Chief of: Naval Personnel, 1972–73; Naval Staff, 1973–76; retd 1976. Comdr 1952; Captain 1958; Cdre 1967; Rear-Adm. 1968; Vice-Adm. 1973. Chm. for Territories, Queen Elizabeth Jubilee Fund for Young Australians, 1977. *Publication:* (contrib.) The Use of Radar at Sea, 1952. *Recreations:* golf, fishing, gardening. *Address:* 4 Charlotte Street, Red Hill, ACT 2603, Australia. *T:* Canberra 95-6172. *Clubs:* Royal Commonwealth Society; Canberra Yacht, Federal Golf (Canberra).

STEVENSON, John; Secretary, Association of County Councils, since 1980; *b* 15 June 1927; *s* of John and Harriet Esther Stevenson; *m* 1956, Kathleen Petch; one *s* one *d. Educ:* Durham Univ. (LLB); MA Oxon 1982. Solicitor. Legal Asst, Borough of Hartlepool, 1951; Junior Solicitor, County Borough of Sunderland, 1952; Solicitor, Hertfordshire CC, 1953, Asst Clerk, 1964; Clerk of the Peace and County Solicitor, Gloucestershire CC, 1969; Chief Executive, Buckinghamshire CC, 1974. Hon. Fellow, Inst. Local Govt Studies, Birmingham Univ., 1981; Vis. Fellow, Nuffield Coll., Oxford, 1982. *Address:* (home) Herb of Grace, Nether Winchendon, Aylesbury, Bucks; 405 Keyes House, Dolphin Square, SW1. *T:* 01-834 2149; (office) Eaton House, 66a Eaton Square, SW1W 9BH. *T:* 01-235 1200.

STEVENSON, Air Vice-Marshal Leigh Forbes, CB 1944; *b* 24 May 1895; *s* of John Henry Stevenson and Mary Ann Irving; *m* 1926, Lillian Myrtle Comber; two *d. Educ:* Richibucto Grammar School, Richibucto, NB, Canada. Canadian Expeditionary Force, 1914–17; Commissioned, 1916; RFC 1917–18; RAF 1918–19; RCAF 1920–45. Air Vice-Marshal, 1942; Graduate Royal Naval Staff College, Greenwich, 1930; AOC, RCAF Overseas, 1940–41; retired, Oct. 1945. MLA of BC, 1946–53. US Commander of Legion of Merit, 1945. *Recreations:* shooting, fishing. *Address:* 1163 Balfour Avenue, Vancouver, BC V6H 1X3, Canada. *Club:* Vancouver (BC).

STEVENSON, Rt. Hon. Sir Melford; *see* Stevenson, Rt Hon. Sir A. M. S.

STEVENSON, Prof. Olive; Professor of Social Work Studies, University of Liverpool, since 1983; *b* 13 Dec. 1930; *d* of John and Evelyn Stevenson. *Educ:* Purley County Grammar Sch. for Girls; Lady Margaret Hall, Oxford (BA EngLitt, MA 1955); London Sch. of Economics (Dip. in Social Studies, Dip. in Child Care). Tavistock Clinic; Child Care Officer, Devon CC, 1954–58; Lecturer in Applied Social Studies: Univ. of Bristol, 1959–61; Univ. of Oxford, 1961–68; Social Work Adviser, Supplementary Benefits Commn, 1968–70; Reader in Applied Social Studies, Univ. of Oxford, and Professorial Fellow, St Anne's Coll., Oxford, 1970–76; Prof. of Social Policy and Social Work, Univ. of Keele, 1976–82. Member: Royal Commn on Civil Liability, 1973–78; Social Security Adv. Cttee, 1982–; Chairman: Adv. Cttee, Rent Rebates and Rent Allowances, 1977; Age Concern England, 1980. *Publications:* Someone Else's Child, 1965, rev. edn 1977; Claimant or Client?, 1970; Social Service Teams: the practitioner's view, 1978; Child Abuse: interprofessional communication, 1979; Specialisation in Social Service Teams, 1981; contrib. Brit. Jl Social Work. *Recreations:* music, cookery, conversation. *Address:* c/o Department of Sociology, University of Liverpool, PO Box 147, Liverpool L69 3BX.

STEVENSON, Robert, MA; Writer; formerly Motion Picture Director, Walt Disney Productions Inc., California; *b* 1905; *s* of late Hugh Hunter Stevenson, Buxton; *m* Ursula Henderson, MB, BS (London), FAPA (USA). *Educ:* Shrewsbury School; St John's College, Cambridge (Scholar), 1st Class Mechanical Sciences Tripos and John Bernard Seely Prize for Aeronautics, 1926; Editor of Granta 1927; President of Cambridge Union Society, and research in psychology, 1928. Entered motion picture industry 1929. Motion Picture Producer for US War Dept, 1942, Capt, 1943–46; Maj. US Army Res.,

1946-53. Films directed include Tudor Rose (in America, Nine Days a Queen), King Solomon's Mines, Owd Bob (in America, To the Victor), The Ware Case, Young Man's Fancy, Tom Brown's Schooldays, Back Street, Joan of Paris, Jane Eyre, To the Ends of the Earth, Walk Softly Stranger, The Las Vegas Story, Old Yeller, Darby O'Gill and the Little People, Kidnapped, The Absent-minded Professor, The Castaways, Son of Flubber, Mary Poppins, That Darn Cat, The Gnome-Mobile, Blackbeard's Ghost, The Love Bug, Bedknobs and Broomsticks, Herbie Rides Again, Island on Top of the World, One of Our Dinosaurs is Missing, The Shaggy D. A. Has also written and directed very many television films. Film stories which he has written include Tudor Rose and Young Man's Fancy. *Publication:* Darkness in the Land, 1938. *Address:* 131 La Vereda Road, Santa Barbara, Calif 93108, USA.

STEVENSON, Robert Barron Kerr, CBE 1976; MA; FSA; Keeper, National Museum of Antiquities of Scotland, 1946-78, Trustee, 1975-78; *b* 16 July 1913; *s* of late Professor William B. Stevenson; *m* 1950, Elizabeth M. Begg; twin *s.* Member: Ancient Monuments Board for Scotland, 1961-79; Cttees of Inquiry: Field Monuments, 1966-68; Provincial Museums, 1972-73. Pres., Soc. of Antiquaries of Scotland, 1975-78. Fellow, UCL, 1977. Hon. FRNS 1979; Hon. DLitt Edinburgh, 1981. *Address:* 8 Cobden Crescent, Edinburgh EH9 2BG. *T:* 031-667 3164.

STEVENSON, Robert Bryce; General President, National Union of Footwear Leather and Allied Trades, since 1980; *b* 26 June 1926; *s* of Daniel Liddle Stevenson and Christina Stevenson; *m* 1947, Margaret Eugenia; two *d. Educ:* Caldercruix Advanced Sch., Airdrie, Lanarks. Full-time Officer NUFLAT, Street, Som. Branch, 1961-80. Member, 1980-: Internat. Textile, Garment and Leather Workers Fedn Exec. Council and Cttee (Brussels); Jt Cttee, Footwear Industry in Europe (Brussels); Footwear Econ. Develt Cttee; TUC Textile, Clothing and Footwear Industries Cttee; Footwear Leather and Fur Skin Industry Trng Bd; Council, Shoe and Allied Trades Res. Assoc.; Boot and Shoe Repairing Wages Council for GB; Bd of Management, Boot Trade Benevolent Soc. JP Wells and Glastonbury 1970 (on Supplementary List, Northants, 1981). *Recreations:* listening to and playing music, all sports. *Address:* 27 Wentworth Avenue, Wellingborough, Northants. *T:* Wellingborough 676959. *Club:* Unity (Street, Som.).

STEVENSON, Sir Simpson, Kt 1976; Chairman: Greater Glasgow Health Board, since 1973; Scottish Health Services Common Service Agency, 1973-77; *b* 18 Aug. 1921; *s* of T. H. Stevenson, Greenock; *m* 1945, Jean Holmes Henry, JP, Port Glasgow. *Educ:* Greenock High Sch. Member: Greenock Town Council, 1949-67 and 1971-; Inverclyde DC, 1974-; Provost of Greenock, 1962-65; Vice-Chm., Clyde Port Authority, 1966-69. Member: Western Regional Hosp. Bd (Scotland), 1959-; Scottish Hosp. Administrative Staffs Cttee, 1965-74 (Chm., 1972-74); Chm., W Regional Hosp. Bd (Scotland), Glasgow, 1967-74; Member: Scottish Hosp. Endowments Commn, 1969-70; Scottish Health Services Planning Council; Royal Commn on the NHS, 1976-79. Chm., Consortium of Local Authorities Special Programme (CLASP), 1974. Hon. LLD Glasgow, 1982. *Recreations:* football, reading, choral singing. *Address:* Greater Glasgow Health Board, 351 Sauchiehall Street, Glasgow, G2 3HT. *T:* 041-332 2977; 64A Reservoir Road, Gourock, Renfrewshire PA19 1YQ.

STEVENSON, Sir William Alfred, KBE 1965 (OBE 1954); JP (NZ); civil engineering contractor; Managing Director, W. Stevenson and Sons Ltd. Formerly Mayor of Howick for 9 years. Manager and Coach, rowing section, Empire Games team, Vancouver, BC, 1954; Manager, NZ Olympic team, Tokyo, 1964. Hon. Mem., RACS, Melbourne, 1975; Hon. DSc Auckland, 1978. KStJ 1968. *Recreation:* NZ Champion: single sculls, 1923, 1924, 1926, 1927; double sculls, 1925, 1926. *Address:* W. Stevenson and Sons Ltd, Otahuhu, Auckland, New Zealand; Cockle Bay Road, Howick, Auckland.

STEVENSON, William Trevor; Chairman: Scottish Transport Group, since 1981; Gleneagles Hotels, since 1981; Hodgson Martin Ventures, since 1982; Alexander Wilkie, since 1977; Deputy Chairman, A. H. McIntosh & Co., since 1982; *b* 21 March 1921; *o s* of late William Houston Stevenson and Mabel Rose Stevenson (*née* Hunt); *m* 1948, Alison Wilson (*née* Roy). *Educ:* Edinburgh Acad. Apprentice mechanical engineer, 1937-41; engineer, 1941-45; entered family food manufacturing business, Cottage Rusks, 1945; Man. Dir, 1948-54; Chm., 1954-59; Chief Executive, Cottage Rusks Associates, (following merger with Joseph Rank Ltd), 1959-69; Reg. Dir, Ranks Hovis McDougall, 1969-74; Dir, various cos in food, engrg and aviation industries, 1974-. Master, Co. of Merchants of City of Edinburgh, 1978-80. *Recreations:* flying, sailing, curling. *Address:* 45 Pentland View, Edinburgh EH10 6PY. *T:* 031-445 1512. *Clubs:* Caledonian; New (Edinburgh).

STEWARD, Prof. Frederick Campion, FRS 1957; Charles A. Alexander Professor of Biological Sciences and Director of Laboratory for Cell Physiology and Growth, Cornell University, Ithaca, NY, 1965-72, now Professor Emeritus (Professor of Botany in the University, 1950-65); *b* 16 June 1904; *s* of Fredk Walter and Mary Daglish Steward; *m* 1929, Anne Temple Gordon, Richmond, Va, USA; one *s. Educ:* Heckmondwike Gram. Sch., Yorks; Leeds Univ. BSc 1924 (1st Class Hons); PhD 1926. DSc London 1937. Demonstrator in Botany, Leeds Univ., 1926; Rockefeller Fellow: Cornell Univ., 1927, Univ. of California, 1928; Asst Lecturer, Univ. of Leeds (Botany), 1929; Rockefeller Foundation Fellow, 1933-34; Reader in Botany, Univ. of London (Birkbeck Coll.), 1934; War Service with MAP (Dir of Aircraft Equipment), 1940-45; Prof. of Botany and Chm. of Dept, Univ. of Rochester, Rochester, NY, 1946-50. John Simon Guggenheim Fell., 1963-64; Sir C. V. Raman Vis. Prof., Madras Univ., 1974. Fellow American Academy of Arts and Sciences, 1956. Merit Award, Botanical Society of America, 1961. Hon. DSc Delhi, 1974. *Publications:* Plants at Work, 1964; Growth and Organisation in Plants, 1968; Plants, Chemicals and Growth, 1971; (ed) Treatise on Plant Physiology (6 vols and 11 tomes), 1959-72; papers in scientific journals and proceedings of learned societies. *Recreations:* gardening, swimming. *Address:* 1612 Inglewood Drive, Charlottesville, Va 22901, USA.

STEWARD, George Coton, MA, ScD, DSc; Professor of Mathematics, The University, Hull, 1930-61, Emeritus Professor, since 1961; *b* 6 April 1896; *o c* of Joseph Steward and Minnie, *d* of William Coton, Wolverhampton; unmarried. *Educ:* The Grammar School, Wolverhampton; Gonville and Caius College, Cambridge (Senior Scholar). Wrangler, with distinction in schedule b, Mathematical Tripos, 1920; ScD, 1937; First Class Honours in Mathematics in BSc (Honours), Univ. of London, 1917; DSc, 1926; Smith's Prize, Univ. of Cambridge, 1922, for contributions on Geometrical and Physical Optics; Member of Scientific Staff of Optics Department of National Physical Laboratory, 1918; Assistant Lecturer in Applied Mathematics, University of Leeds, 1920; Fellow of Gonville and Caius College, Cambridge, 1922; Fellow and Mathematical Lecturer, Emmanuel College, Cambridge, 1923. *Publications:* The Symmetrical Optical System, Cambridge Mathematical and Physical Tracts, No 25, 1928, 1958; papers on Geometrical and Physical Optics, and Plane Kinematics, in Transactions of Royal Society, of Cambridge Philosophical Society, etc. *Address:* 42 South Street, Cottingham, North Humberside. *T:* Hull 847654.

STEWARD, Nigel Oliver Willoughby, OBE 1946; MA Oxon, BA Cantab; Consul-General, Haifa, 1955-59, retired; *b* 16 October 1899; *s* of Arthur Bennett Steward, ICS, and Alice Willoughby; *m* 1933, Raquel Wyneken, of Viña del Mar, Chile; three *d. Educ:* Winchester (Scholar); Trinity College, Oxford. Entered Consular Service, 1924. Vice-Consul at San Francisco, Valparaiso, Guatemala (Second Secretary), and Paris; Consul and First Secretary at Montevideo; Minister (local rank) to Paraguay; First Secretary, Bucharest, 1946; Deputy Consul-Gen., New York, 1946-48; Minister to Nicaragua, 1948-52; Consul-General, Nice and Monaco, 1952-55. *Address:* Church Cottage, 13 Gravel Walk, Cullompton, Devon EX15 1DA. *Club:* United Oxford & Cambridge University.

STEWARD, Stanley Feargus, CBE 1947; CEng; FIProdE; Chairman: George Thurlow and Sons Ltd; Thurlow Nunn & Sons Ltd; Thurlow Wright Ltd; Thurlow Nunn International Ltd; Director: ERA Technology Ltd; Bull Motors Ltd; *b* 9 July 1904; *s* of late Arthur Robert and late Minnie Elizabeth Steward, Mundesley, Norfolk; *m* 1929, Phyllis Minard, *d* of late J. Thurlow, Stowmarket, Suffolk; one *s* one *d. Educ:* The Paston Sch., North Walsham, Norfolk. Was apprenticed to East Anglian Engineering Co. (subseq. Bull Motors Ltd) and subseq. held positions of Chief Designer, Sales Manager and Dir. Min. of Supply Electrical Adviser to Machine Tool Control, 1940; Director of Industrial Electrical Equipment, 1941-44; Dir Gen. of Machine Tools, 1944-45; Chm. Machine Tool Advisory Council, 1946-47; Chm. Gauge & Tool Advisory Council, 1946-47. Director: E. R. & F. Turner, Ltd, Ipswich, 1944-48. Chm., South Western Electricity Board, 1948-55; Man. Dir, Lancashire Dynamo Holdings Ltd, 1956-59 (Chm., 1957-58); Former Chm., Lancashire Dynamo and Crypto Ltd, Lancashire Dynamo Electronic Products Ltd and Lancashire Dynamo Group Sales; Chm., William Steward (Holdings) Ltd and William Steward & Co. Ltd, 1970-80. Member: British Electricity Authority, 1952-53; Elect. Engineering EDC, 1962-71; Machine Tool EDC, 1971-80; Chm., British Electrical Development Assoc., 1954; President: Ipswich and District Electrical Assoc., 1964-67, 1972-78; Electrical Industries Club, 1966-67; Assoc. of Supervisory and Exec. Engineers, 1970-74; Electrical and Electronic Industries Benevolent Assoc., 1971-72; Instn of Engineer in charge, 1982-; Man. Dir, BEAMA, 1959-71; Pres., Exec. Cttee, Organisme de Liaison des Industries Metalliques Europeénes, 1963-67. Freeman of City of London; Master, Worshipful Company of Glaziers and Painters of Glass, 1964. *Publications:* Electricity and Food Production, 1953; British Electrical Manufacture in the National Economy, 1961; Twenty Five Years of South Western Electricity, 1973; regular 'Personal View' contribs to Electrical Review and other jls. *Recreations:* books, music, watching cricket. *Address:* 41 Fairacres, Roehampton Lane, SW15 5LX. *T:* 01-876 2457. *Clubs:* Athenæum, MCC.

STEWARD, Sir William Arthur, Kt 1955; Director of food manufacturing companies; *b* 20 Apr. 1901; *s* of late W. A. Steward and of Mrs C. E. Steward, Norwich; *m* 1939. *Educ:* Norwich Model Sch., and privately. Freeman of City of London; Master, Worshipful Co. of Distillers, 1964-65; Liveryman, Worshipful Co. of Fruiterers. Served RAF, 1938-45; Sen. Catering Officer at Air Min., 1943-45; retired with rank of Squadron Leader. MP (C) Woolwich West, 1950-59; Chm. Kitchen Cttee, House of Commons, Nov. 1951-Sept. 1959. Mem. of London County Council for Woolwich West, 1949-52. Chm., London Conservative Union, 1953-55. *Recreations:* composing music for both organ and piano, and writing. *Address:* Palazzo Marnisi, Marsaxlokk, Malta.

STEWART, family name of **Earl of Galloway, Baroness Stewart of Alvechurch** and **Baron Stewart of Fulham.**

STEWART; see Vane-Tempest-Stewart, family name of Marquess of Londonderry.

STEWART, Hon. Lord; Ewan George Francis Stewart, MC 1945; a Senator of the College of Justice in Scotland, since 1975; b 9 May 1923; s of late George Duncan Stewart, CA, Edinburgh, and late Catherine Wilson Stewart; m 1953, Sheila Margaret, er d of late Major K. G. Richman, East Lancs Regt; one s one d. Educ: George Watson's Coll., Edinburgh; Edinburgh Univ. Served War of 1939-45 with 7/9 (Highlanders) Bn, The Royal Scots, in 52 (L) Division. Mem. of Faculty of Advocates, 1949; QC (Scotland) 1960; standing junior counsel to Min. of Civil Aviation in Scotland, 1955-60; Hon. Sheriff-Substitute of the Lothians and Peebles, 1961-64; practised at New Zealand Bar, 1962-64; resumed practice at Scottish Bar, 1964; Home Advocate-Depute, 1965-67; Solicitor-General for Scotland, 1967-70; Scottish Law Commissioner, 1971-75. Member: Cttee on Criminal Procedure in Scotland, 1971-77; Cttee on Preparation of Legislation, 1973-75; Chm., Cttee on Alternatives to Prosecution, 1977-. Governor, St Denis School, Edinburgh, 1967-76; Chm., Court, Univ. of Stirling, 1976-. Address: 5 Munro Drive, Edinburgh EH13 0EG. Club: Caledonian.

STEWART OF ALVECHURCH, Baroness cr 1974 (Life Peer), of Fulham; **Mary Elizabeth Henderson Stewart,** JP; d of Herbert and Isabel Birkinshaw; m 1941, Baron Stewart of Fulham, qv. Educ: King Edward VI High Sch., Birmingham; Bedford Coll., London Univ. (BA Hons Philosophy). Served War with WRAF, 1941-45. Tutor, WEA, 1945-64. Mem., Fabian Soc. Executive, 1950- (Chm. 1963); Chairman: Governors, Charing Cross Hosp., 1966-74; Fulham-Gilliatt Comprehensive School, 1974-79; Mem., Jt Governing Body, Fulham Gilliatt and Mary Boon Schs, 1980-. JP Co. London, 1949; Chm. Juvenile Court, 1956-66. Publications: Fabian Society pamphlets. Recreations: walking, music. Address: 11 Felden Street, SW6. T: 01-736 5194.

STEWART OF FULHAM, Baron cr 1979 (Life Peer), of Fulham in Greater London; **Robert Michael Maitland Stewart;** PC 1964; CH 1969; b 6 Nov. 1906; s of Robert Wallace Stewart, DSc and Eva Stewart; m 1941, Mary Elizabeth (see Baroness Stewart of Alvechurch); no c. Educ: Christ's Hosp.; St John's Coll., Oxford. Pres. Oxford Union, 1929; Asst Master, Merchant Taylors' Sch., 1930-31; Asst Master, Coopers' Company's School, and Lectr for Workers' Educational Assoc., 1931-42. Joined Army Intelligence Corps, 1942. Trans. to Army Educational Corps, 1943; commissioned and promoted to Capt., 1944. Contested (Lab) West Lewisham, 1931 and 1935; MP (Lab) Fulham East, 1945-55, Fulham, 1955-74, Hammersmith, Fulham, 1974-79; Vice-Chamberlain of HM Household, 1946-47; Comptroller of HM Household, 1946-47; Under-Sec. of State for War, 1947-51; Parly Sec., Min. of Supply, May-Oct. 1951; Sec. of State for Education and Science, Oct. 1964-Jan. 1965; Sec. of State for Foreign Affairs, Jan. 1965-Aug. 1966; First Sec. of State, 1966-68; Sec. of State for Economic Affairs, 1966-67; Secretary of State for Foreign and Commonwealth Affairs, 1968-70. Mem., European Parlt, 1975-76. Freeman of Hammersmith, 1967. Hon. Fellow, St John's Coll. Oxford, 1965; Hon. LLD Leeds, 1966; Hon. DSc Benin, 1972. Publications: The Forty Hour Week (Fabian Soc.), 1936; Bias and Education for Democracy, 1937; The British Approach to Politics, 1938; Modern Forms of Government, 1959; Life and Labour (autobiography), 1980; European Security: the case against unilateral nuclear disarmament, 1981. Recreations: chess, painting. Address: 11 Felden Street, SW6. T: 01-736 5194.

STEWART, Sir Alan, KBE 1981 (CBE 1972); Vice-Chancellor of Massey University, 1964-83; b 8 Dec. 1917; s of Kenneth and Vera Mary Stewart; m 1950, Joan Cecily Sisam; one s three d. Educ: Massey Agricultural College; University College, Oxford. Sen. Lectr, Massey Agric. Coll., 1950-54; Chief Consulting Officer, Milk Marketing Board, England and Wales, 1954-58; Principal, Massey Agric. Coll., 1959-63. Address: 10 Waiewe Street, Whakatane, New Zealand.

STEWART, Sir Alan (d'Arcy), 13th Bt cr 1623; Boatyard Owner; b 29 Nov. 1932; s of Sir Jocelyn Harry Stewart, 12th Bt, and Constance Mary (d 1940), d of D'Arcy Shillaber; S father, 1982; m 1952, Patricia, d of Lawrence Turner; two s two d. Educ: All Saints College, Bathurst, NSW. Recreations: yachting, motor racing. Heir: s Nicholas Courtney d'Arcy Stewart, BSc, HDipEd, b 4 Aug. 1953. Address: One Acre House, Ramelton, Co. Donegal. T: Ramelton 82.

STEWART, Alastair Lindsay; Sheriff of Grampian, Highland and Islands, at Aberdeen and Stonehaven, since 1979; b 28 Nov. 1938; s of Alexander Lindsay Stewart and Anna Stewart; m 1968, Annabel Claire Stewart, yr d of Prof. W. McC. Stewart, qv; two s. Educ: Edinburgh Academy; St Edmund Hall, Oxford (BA); Univ. of Edinburgh (LLB). Admitted to Faculty of Advocates, 1963; Tutor, Faculty of Law, Univ. of Edinburgh, 1963-73; Standing Junior Counsel to Registrar of Restrictive Trading Agreements, 1968-70; Advocate Depute, 1970-73; Sheriff of South Strathclyde, Dumfries and Galloway, at Airdrie, 1973-79. Governor, Robert Gordon's Inst. of Technology, 1982-. Publications: various articles in legal jls. Recreations: reading, listening to music. Address: 131 Desswood Place, Aberdeen AB2 4DP. T: Aberdeen 644683.

STEWART, Allan; see Stewart, J. A.

STEWART, Prof. Andrew; b 17 Jan. 1904; s of Andrew Stewart, Edinburgh, Scotland, and Marcia Sabina (née Sprot); m 1931, Jessie Christobel Borland; four s two d. Educ: Daniel Stewart's College, Edinburgh, Scotland; East of Scotland College of Agriculture (CDA); University of Manitoba. BSA 1931, MA 1932 (Univ. of Manitoba). Lecturer in Agricultural Economics, Univ. of Manitoba, 1932-33; Lecturer, 1935, Prof. 1946, of Political Economy, Dean of Business Affairs, 1949, President, 1950-59, Univ. of Alberta; Chm. Bd of Broadcast Governors, Ottawa, 1958-68; Chm. Alberta Univs Commn, 1968-70; Prof. of Education, Univ. of Ibadan, Nigeria, 1970-72. Member of Royal Commissions: Province of Alberta (Natural Gas), 1948; Canada (Economic Prospects), 1955-57; Canada (Price Spreads of Food Products) (Chairman), 1958-59; Pres. Nat. Conf. of Canadian Univs, 1958; Chm. Assoc. of Univs of British Commonwealth, 1958. Hon. LLD Manitoba, New Brunswick, Melbourne, Alberta; Hon. DEcon Laval; FRSC; Fellow, Agricultural Inst. of Canada. Address: 10435 Allbay Road, Sidney, BC, Canada.

STEWART, Andrew, CBE 1954; b 23 June 1907; s of James Stewart; m 1937, Agnes Isabella Burnet, d of James McKechnie, JP. Educ: Glasgow University (MA). Hon LLD Glasgow, 1970. Joined BBC at Glasgow, 1926; Glasgow Representative, 1931-35; Scottish Programme Director, 1935-48; Controller (N Ire.), 1948-52; Controller (Home Service), 1953-57; Controller, Scotland, 1957-68. Min. of Information, 1939-41. Director, Scottish Television, 1968-77. Chm., Scottish Music Archive, 1972-; Chm., Films of Scotland Committee. Governor, National Film School, 1971-76. Hon. Pres., Scottish Radio Industries Club, 1972-. Recreations: reading, the theatre, mountaineering. Address: 36 Sherbrooke Avenue, Glasgow G41 4EP.

STEWART, (Bernard Harold) Ian (Halley), RD 1972; FBA 1981; MP (C) Hitchin since Feb. 1974; Director: Brown, Shipley & Co. Ltd, Merchant Bankers, since 1971; Brown Shipley Holdings Ltd, since 1980; Victory Insurance Co. Ltd, since 1976; b 10 Aug. 1935; s of Prof. H. C. Stewart, qv; m 1966, Deborah Charlotte, d of Hon. William Buchan and late Barbara Howard Ensor, JP; one s two d. Educ: Haileybury; Jesus Coll., Cambridge (MA; LittD 1978). 1st cl. hons Class. Tripos Cantab. Nat. Service, RNVR, 1954-56; subseq. Lt-Cmdr RNR. Seccombe, Marshall & Campion Ltd, bill brokers, 1959-60; joined Brown, Shipley & Co. Ltd, 1960, Asst Man. 1963, Man. 1966, Dir 1971. Jt Sec., Cons. Parly Finance Cttee, 1975-76, 1977-79; Mem. Public Expenditure Cttee, 1977-79. Opposition spokesman on Banking Bill, 1978-79; PPS to Chancellor of the Exchequer, 1979-. Mem. British Academy Cttee for Sylloge of Coins of British Isles, 1967-; Hon. Treas., Westminster Cttee for Protection of Children, 1960-70, Vice-Chm., 1975-. FSA (Mem. Council 1974-76); FSA Scot; Dir, British Numismatic Soc., 1965-75 (Sanford Saltus Gold Medal 1971); FRNS (Parkes Weber Prize). Vice-Pres., Hertfordshire Soc., 1974-; Mem. Council, British Museum Soc., 1975-76. Life Governor, 1977, Mem. Council, 1980-, Haileybury; Trustee, Sir Halley Stewart Trust, 1978-. County Vice-Pres., St John Ambulance for Herts, 1978-; OStJ 1980. Publications: The Scottish Coinage, 1955 (2nd edn 1967); Scottish Mints, 1971; many papers in Proc. Soc. Antiquaries of Scotland, Numismatic Chronicle, British Numismatic Jl, etc. Recreations: history; tennis (Captain CU Tennis Club, 1958-59; 1st string v Oxford, 1958 and 1959; winner Coupe de Bordeaux 1959; led 1st Oxford and Cambridge Tennis and Rackets team to USA, 1958; played squash for Herts); Homer. Address: 2 Baldwin Crescent, SE5. Clubs: MCC; Hawks, Pitt (Cambridge).

STEWART, Brian Thomas Webster, CMG 1969; Special Representative, Rubber Growers Association, Malaysia, since 1979; b 27 April 1922; s of late Redvers Buller Stewart and Mabel Banks Sparks, Broich, Crieff; m 1946, Millicent Peggy Pollock (marr. diss. 1970); two d; m 1972, Sally Nugent; one s one d. Educ: Trinity Coll., Glenalmond; Worcester Coll., Oxford (MA). Commnd The Black Watch (RHR), 1942; served Europe and Far East (Capt.). Joined Malayan Civil Service, 1946; studying Chinese Macau, 1947; Asst Sec., Chinese Affairs, Singapore, 1949; Devonshire Course, Oxford, 1950; Asst Comr for Labour, Kuala Lumpur, 1951; Sec. for Chinese Affairs, Supt of Chinese Schs, Malacca and Penang, 1952-57; joined HM Diplomatic Service, 1957; served Rangoon, Peking, Shanghai, Manila, Kuala Lumpur, Hanoi; Asst Sec., Cabinet Office, 1968-72; Counsellor, Hong Kong, 1972-74; FCO, 1974-78. Publication: All Men's Wisdom (anthology of Chinese Proverbs), 1957. Recreations: climbing, sailing, ski-ing, chamber music, orientalia particularly chinoiserie. Address: c/o Hongkong and Shanghai Banking Corporation, 9 Waterloo Place, SW1. Clubs: Athenæum, Royal Commonwealth Society; Lake (Kuala Lumpur).

STEWART, Charles Cosmo Bruce, CMG 1962; Head of Cultural Relations Department, Foreign and Commonwealth Office (formerly Foreign Office), 1967-72; b 29 July 1912; o s of late Brig.-Gen. Cosmo Gordon Stewart, CB, CMG, DSO, and Mrs Gladys Berry Stewart (née Honeyman). Educ: Eton; King's Coll., Cambridge. Barrister-at-law, Middle Temple, 1938. Served War, 1939-46. Foreign Service Officer, 1946; First Sec., Rome, 1949; First Secretary (Commercial), Cologne, 1951; transf. to Foreign Office, 1954; Head of Information Policy Dept, 1955-58; Counsellor and Consul-General, Saigon, Vietnam, 1958-61; Counsellor and Head of Chancery, Copenhagen, 1961-63; Consul-General at Luanda, 1963-68. Club: Travellers'.

STEWART, Colin MacDonald, FIA, FSS; Directing Actuary, Government Actuary's Department, London, since 1974; b 26 Dec. 1922; s of John Stewart and Lillias Cecilia MacDonald Fraser; m 1948, Gladys Edith Thwaites; three d. Educ: Queen's Park Secondary Sch., Glasgow. Clerical Officer, Rosyth Dockyard, 1939-42. Served War: Fleet Air Arm (Lieut (A) RNVR), 1942-46.

Govt Actuary's Dept, London, 1946-. FIA 1953. *Publications:* numerous articles on actuarial and demographic subjects in British and internat. jls. *Recreations:* golf, genealogical research, reading about (and where possible visiting) other countries, participation in affairs of Inst. of Actuaries. *Address:* 8 The Chase, Coulsdon, Surrey CR3 2EG. *T:* 01-660 3966.

STEWART, Air Vice-Marshal Colin Murray, CB 1962; CBE 1952 (OBE 1945); RAF, retired; *b* 17 June 1910; *s* of Archie Stewart, Sherborne, Dorset; *m* 1940, Anthea, *d* of Maynard Loveless, Stockbridge, Hants; four *s. Educ:* Wycliffe College, Stonehouse, Glos. Joined RAF, 1932; served in 5 Sqdn, NWF, India, and 16 Sqdn at home; specialised in Signals, 1937. Served War of 1939-45 (despatches, OBE): CSO various formations at home and in Europe. Chairman: British Joint Communications Board, 1952-55; Communications Electronics Cttee of Standing Group, Washington, 1955-57; AOC, No 27 Gp, 1957-58; Comd Electronics Officer, Fighter Comd, 1958-61; Dir-Gen. of Signals, Air Ministry, 1961-64; STSO, Fighter Comd, 1964-67; SASO, Technical Training Comd, 1967-68, retired. Controller, Computing Services, Univ. of London, 1968-73. *Recreations:* fishing, gardening, etc. *Address:* Byelanes, Moult Road, Salcombe, S Devon TQ8 8LG. *T:* Salcombe 2042.

STEWART, Sir David (Brodribb), 2nd Bt *cr* 1960, TD 1948; Managing Director, Francis Price (Fabrics) Ltd, Manchester, 1960-81; *b* 20 Dec. 1913; *s* of Sir Kenneth Dugald Stewart, 1st Bt, GBE, and Noel (*d* 1946), *y d* of Kenric Brodribb, Melbourne; *S* father, 1972; *m* 1963, Barbara Dykes, *widow* of Donald Ian Stewart and *d* of late Harry Dykes Lloyd. *Educ:* Marlborough College; Manchester College of Technology (BSc (Tech), Textile Technology). Joined Stewart Thomson & Co. Ltd, Textile Merchant Converters, 1935; continuously employed in this company, except for six years war service, until absorbed into the Haighton & Dewhurst Group, 1958; Francis Price (Fabrics) Ltd is a subsidiary of this Group. Commissioned 8th Bn Lancashire Fusiliers (TA), 1934; war service, 1939-45; joined Duke of Lancaster's Own Yeomanry (TA) on re-formation of TA, 1947; in comd, 1952-56; retd with rank of Bt Col. *Recreation:* gardening. *Heir:* b Robin Alastair Stewart [*b* 26 Sept. 1925; *m* 1953, Patricia Helen, *d* of late J. A. Merrett; *one s three d*]. *Address:* Delamere, Heyes Lane, Alderley Edge, Cheshire SK9 7JY. *T:* Alderley Edge 582312.

STEWART, Sir David James H.; *see* Henderson-Stewart.

STEWART, Rt. Hon. Donald James, PC 1977; MP (SNP) Western Isles, since 1970; *b* 17 Oct. 1920; *m* 1955, Christina Macaulay. *Educ:* Nicolson Institute, Stornoway. Provost of Stornoway, 1958-64 and 1968-70; Hon. Sheriff, 1960. Leader, Parly SNP, 1974-; Pres., SNP, 1982-. *Recreations:* fishing, photography, gardening. *Address:* Hillcrest, 41 Goathill Road, Stornoway, Isle of Lewis. *T:* Stornoway 2672.

STEWART of Appin, Sir Dugald Leslie Lorn, KCVO 1972; CMG 1969; HM Diplomatic Service, retired; British Ambassador to Yugoslavia, 1971-77; *b* 10 Sept. 1921; *m* 1947, Sibyl Anne Sturrock, MBE; three *s. one d. Educ:* Eton; Magdalen College, Oxford. Foreign Office, 1942. Served in Belgrade, Berlin, Iraq, Cairo; Counsellor (Commercial), Moscow, 1962; IDC, 1965; Inspector Diplomatic Service, 1966; Counsellor, Cairo, 1968. *Recreations:* shooting, fishing, golf. *Address:* Salachail, Glen Creran, Appin, Argyll.

STEWART, Duncan Montgomery; Principal of Lady Margaret Hall, Oxford, since 1979; *b* 14 Feb. 1930; *s* of William Montgomery Stewart and Mary Pauline (*née* Checkley); *m* 1961, Valerie Mary Grace, *er d* of Major E. H. T. Boileau, Rampisham, Dorset; *one s one d. Educ:* Greymouth Technical High Sch.; Christ's Coll., NZ; Canterbury University Coll., NZ (MA 1st Cl. French 1951, 1st Cl. Latin 1952); Rhodes Scholar, 1953; Queen's Coll., Oxford (1st Cl. Hons Mod. Langs 1955). Lectr, Wadham Coll., Oxford, 1955, Fellow, 1956-79. Vice-Chm., Oxford Univ. Gen. Bd of Faculties, 1976-78. *Publications:* articles and revs on French Literature, esp. later medieval. *Recreations:* senescent cricket and tennis, opera, wine. *Address:* 6 Fyfield Road, Oxford.

STEWART, Sir Edward (Jackson), Kt 1980; Chairman and Managing Director, Stewarts Hotels Pty Ltd, since 1956; Chairman: Castlemaine Perkins Ltd, since 1977 (Director, 1970); Castlemaine Tooheys Ltd, since 1980; *b* 10 Dec. 1923; *s* of Charles Jackson Stewart and Jessie Stewart (*née* Dobbie); *m* 1956, Shirley Patricia Holmes; four *s. Educ:* St Joseph's College, Brisbane. Fellow Catering Inst. of Australia (FCIA). Served with Australian Army, RAA, 1942-44. Director: Birch Carroll & Coyle Ltd, 1967-; Roadshow (Qld) Pty Ltd, 1970-; Darwin Cinemas Pty Ltd, 1972-; G. R. E. (Australia) Ltd, 1980-; Besser (Qld) Ltd, 1981-. President: Queensland Hotels Assoc., 1963-69; Aust. Hotels Assoc., 1966-69. Mem. Totalisator Administration Bd of Queensland, 1977-81. Chm., Queensland Inst. of Medical Research Trust, 1980. *Recreations:* reading, fishing and thoroughbred breeding. *Address:* 34 Charlton Street, Ascot, Brisbane, Queensland, Australia. *T:* 268 1805. *Clubs:* Brisbane, Tattersall's (Past Pres.); Queensland Turf, Victorian Racing.

STEWART, Ewan George Francis; *see* Stewart, Hon. Lord.

STEWART, Ewen; Sheriff at Wick, Caithness, since 1962 and at Dornoch, Sutherland and Tain, Ross and Cromarty, since 1977; *b* 22 April 1926; *o s* of late Duncan Stewart and Kate Blunt, and *gs* of late Ewen Stewart, Kinlocheil; *m* 1959, Norma Porteous Hollands, *d* of late William Charteris

Hollands, Earlston; *one d. Educ:* Edinburgh University. BSc (Agric.) 1946; MA (Econ.) 1950; LLB 1952. Asst Agricultural Economist, East of Scotland Coll. of Agriculture, 1946-49; practised at Scottish Bar, 1952-62; lectr on Agricultural Law, Univ. of Edinburgh, 1957-62; former standing junior counsel, Min. of Fuel and Power; Parly Cand. (Lab.) Banffshire, 1962; Chm., Caithness Gen. Comrs for Inland Revenue; Chm., Scrabster Harbour Trust. *Address:* Strath of Bylbster, Watten, Wick, Caithness KW1 5UQ. *T:* Watten 210.

STEWART, Prof. Sir Frederick (Henry), Kt 1974; FRS 1964; PhD Cantab; FRSE; FGS; Regius Professor of Geology, 1956-82, now Emeritus, Dean of Science Faculty, 1966-68, and Member, University Court, 1969-70, Edinburgh University; *b* 16 Jan. 1916; *o s* of Frederick Robert Stewart and Hester Alexander, Aberdeen; *m* 1945, Mary Florence Elinor Rainbow (*see* Mary Stewart); no *c. Educ:* Fettes Coll.; Univ. of Aberdeen (BSc); Emmanuel Coll., Cambridge. Mineralogist in Research Dept of ICI Ltd (Billingham Div.), 1941-43; Lectr in Geology, Durham Colls in the Univ. of Durham, 1943-56. Vice-Pres., Geological Soc. of London, 1965-66; Member: Council for Scientific Policy, 1967-71; Adv. Council for Applied R&D, 1976-79; Chairman: NERC, 1971-73 (Mem., Geol. Geophysics Cttee, 1967-70); Adv. Bd for Res. Councils, 1973-79 (Mem., 1972-73); Mem. Council, Royal Soc., 1969-70. Lyell Fund Award, 1951, J. B. Tyrrell Fund, 1952, Geological Soc. of London; Mineralogical Soc. of America Award, 1952; Lyell Medal, 1970; Clough Medal, Edinburgh Geol. Soc., 1971; Sorby Medal, Yorks Geol. Soc., 1975. Hon. DSc: Aberdeen, 1975; Leicester, 1977; Heriot-Watt, 1978. *Publications:* papers in Mineralogical Magazine, Jl of Geol. Soc. of London, etc., dealing with igneous and metamorphic petrology and salt deposits. *Recreation:* fishing. *Address:* 79 Morningside Park, Edinburgh EH10 5EZ. *T:* 031-447 2620. *Club:* New (Edinburgh).

STEWART, George Girdwood, CB 1979; MC 1945; TD 1954; Representative, National Trust for Scotland, Branklyn Garden, Perth, since 1980; *b* 12 Dec. 1919; *o s* of late Herbert A. Stewart, BSc, and of Janetta Dunlop Girdwood; *m* 1950, Shelagh Jean Morven Murray; *one s one d. Educ:* Kelvinside Academy, Glasgow; Glasgow Univ.; Edinburgh Univ. (BSc). Served RA, 1940-46 (MC, despatches); CO 278 (Lowland) Field Regt RA (TA), 1957-60. Dist. Officer, Forestry Commn, 1949; Asst Conservator, 1961; Conservator, West Scotland, 1966; Comr for Forest and Estate Management, 1969-79. Member: BR Bd Envt Panel, 1980-; Countryside Commn for Scotland, 1981-; Chm., Scottish Wildlife Trust, 1981-. FRSA; FICFor; Hon. FLI. Pres., Scottish Ski Club, 1971-75; Vice-Pres., Nat. Ski Fedn of GB; Chm., Alpine Racing Cttee, 1975-78. *Recreations:* ski-ing, gardening. *Address:* Branklyn House, Dundee Road, Perth. *T:* Perth 25535. *Clubs:* Ski Club of Great Britain; Royal Perth Golfing Society.

STEWART, (George Robert) Gordon; Secretary, Institute of Chartered Accountants of Scotland, since 1976; *b* 13 Oct. 1924; *s* of David Gordon Stewart and Mary Grant Thompson or Stewart; *m* 1952, Rachel Jean Morrison; *two s one d. Educ:* George Watson's Coll., Edinburgh; Edinburgh Univ. (MA 1947, LLB 1949). WS and Mem., Law Soc. of Scotland, 1949. Served War, 1943-46: Captain, Royal Signals; Burma and SEAC. In practice as WS, Melville & Lindesay, WS, Edinburgh, 1950-59; Asst Sec., subseq. Sec., and Dir, Ideal-Standard Ltd, Hull, 1959-75. *Recreation:* golf. *Address:* 15 Hillpark Loan, Edinburgh EH4 7BH. *T:* 01-336 7079. *Clubs:* Caledonian; Royal Scots (Edinburgh).

STEWART, Prof. Gordon Thallon, MD; Mechan Professor of Public Health, University of Glasgow, since 1972; Hon. Consultant in Epidemiology and Preventive Medicine, Glasgow Area Health Board; *b* 5 Feb. 1919; *s* of John Stewart and Mary L. Thallon; *m* 1946, Joan Kego; *two s two d ; m* 1975, Neena Walker. *Educ:* Paisley Grammar Sch.; Univs of Glasgow and Liverpool. BSc 1939; MB, ChB 1942; DTM&H 1947; MD (High Commendation) 1949; FRCPath 1964; FFCM 1972; MRCPGlas 1972; FRCPGlas 1975. House Phys. and House Surg., 1942-43; Surg. Lieut RNVR, 1943-46; Res. Fellow (MRC), Univ. of Liverpool, 1946-48; Sen. Registrar and Tutor, Wright-Fleming Inst., St Mary's Hosp., London, 1948-52; Cons. Pathologist, SW Metrop. Regional Hosp. Bd, 1954-63; Res. Worker at MRC Labs Carshalton, 1955-63; Prof. of Epidem. and Path., Univ. of N Carolina, 1964-68; Watkins Prof. of Epidem., Tulane Univ. Med. Center, New Orleans, 1968-72. Vis. Prof., Dow Med. Coll., Karachi, 1952-53 and Cornell Univ. Med. Coll., 1970-71; Cons. to WHO, and to NYC Dept of Health; Vis. Lectr and Examr, various univs in UK and overseas. Sen. Fellow, Nat. Science Foundn, Washington, 1964; Delta omega, 1969. *Publications:* (ed) Trends in Epidemiology, 1972; (ed jtly) Penicillin Allergy, 1970; Penicillin Group of Drugs, 1965; papers on chemotherapy of infectious diseases, drug allergy and epidemiology in various med. and sci. jls. *Recreations:* sailing, drawing, music. *Address:* 23 Hamilton Drive, Glasgow G12 8DN. *T:* 041-946 7120.

STEWART, Gordon William, CVO 1964; Chairman and General Manager, Scottish Region, British Railways, 1967-71; Chairman and Managing Director, British Transport Ship Management (Scotland) Ltd, 1967-71; Director, British Transport Hotels Ltd, 1968-71, retired; *b* 13 April 1906; *s* of James E. Stewart and Margaret Stewart; *m* 1935, Dorothy Swan Taylor, MA. *Educ:* Daniel Stewart's Coll.; George Heriot Sch., Edinburgh. L&NER: Traffic Apprentice, 1929; appts in London, Lincoln and Manchester, 1942-52; Prin. Asst to Gen. Man., Eastern Region, 1952; Asst Gen. Man., Scottish Region, 1956. Member: Stirling CC, 1972-75; Bridge of Allan Town Council, 1972-75. *Recreations:* golf, shooting. *Address:* Creag Mor,

Blairforkie Drive, Bridge of Allan, Stirlingshire. *T:* Bridge of Allan 832266.

STEWART, Prof. Harold Charles, CBE 1975; FRCP; FRSE; DL; Head of Pharmacology Department, St Mary's Hospital Medical School, 1950-74; Professor of Pharmacology in the University of London 1965-74, now Emeritus Professor (Reader, 1949-64); Consultant in Pharmacology to: St Mary's Hospital, 1946; Ministry of Defence (Army), since 1961; *b* 23 Nov. 1906; *s* of Bernard Halley Stewart, MA, MD, FRSE, FKC, Pres. of Sir Halley Stewart Trust, and Mabel Florence Wyatt; *m* 1st, 1929, Dorothy Irene Lowen (*d* 1969); one *s* one *d*; 2nd, 1970, Audrey Patricia Nicolle. *Educ:* Mill Hill Sch.; University Coll. London; Jesus Coll., Cambridge; University Coll. Hospital. Cambridge Univ.: BA 1928, MA 1934; MB, BCh 1931, MD 1935. London Univ.: PhD 1941, MRCP 1949. Gen. practice, Barnet, Herts, 1932-36. Sub-Dean, St Mary's Hospital Med. Sch., 1950-52; Gresham Prof. in Physic, City Univ., 1968-70. Examr now or formerly, Univs of London, Cambridge, Birmingham, Bristol and Wales, RCS, Soc. of Apothecaries. Research work, mainly on fat absorption and transport in the human subject, and on problems of pain and analgesia. Cons. in Pharmacology to Army; Med. Adviser and Mem. Commonwealth Council, Brit. Commonwealth Ex-Services League; Chm., Sir Halley Stewart Trust for Research and Buttle Trust for Children, 1979-; Mem. Asthma Research Council; Dir-Gen., St John Ambulance Assoc., 1976-78 (Dep Dir-Gen., 1973-76; Dist Surg. for London, SJAB, 1950-64); Mem. Chapter-Gen., Order of St John (KStJ); Mem. Council, Stewart Soc.; Vice-Chairman: Med. Council of Alcoholism; St Christopher's Hospice for terminal cases; Sen. Vice-Pres. and British Rep., Assoc. Internat. de Sauvetage et de Premiers Secours en Cas d'Accidents, 1974-. Liveryman, Soc. of Apothecaries of London; Freeman, City of London: Mem. Physiolog., Brit. Pharmacolog., Nutrition and Genealog. Socs. FFA, RCS, 1969. FRSE 1974. RAMC, T, 1935; Mem. LDV, later Major and Med. Adviser, HG; comd and reformed Med. Unit, Univ. of London STC as Major RAMC, 1942-46. Defence Medal; Gen. Serv. Medal, 1939-46; Coronation Medal, 1953; Guthrie Meml Medal, 1974. DL Greater London, 1967-82. *Publications:* Drugs in Anaesthetic Practice (with F. G. Wood-Smith), 1962; (with W. H. Hughes) Concise Antibiotic Treatment, 2nd edn 1973; contribs to jls. *Recreations:* voluntary service; sport (lacrosse: Cambridge Half-Blue 1928; lawn tennis); genealogy and heraldry. *Address:* 41 The Glen, Green Lane, Northwood, Mddx. *T:* Northwood 24893. *Club:* Athenæum.
See also B. H. I. H. Stewart.

STEWART, Sir Hector (Hamilton), KBE 1976; MD; FRCS, FRACS; retired; *b* 4 Nov. 1901; *s* of Hector Joseph Stewart and Maggie Russell Robertson; *m* 1935, Viotti Winifred Wheatley; three *s* one *d*. *Educ:* Modern Sch., Perth; Univ. of WA (MB, BS 1926); Univ. of Vic. (MD). FRCS 1930; FRACS 1933. AMF, 1939-45 (Lt-Col). WA Branch, BMA: Mem. Council, 1933-48; Pres., 1948; Mem. Council, Aust. Coll. of Surgeons, 1958-69; Fellow, Aust. Med. Assoc., 1965. Univ. of WA: Mem. Senate, 1962-74; Pro Chancellor, 1970-74. *Recreations:* sailing, golf, bowls. *Address:* 20 Mounts Bay Road, Crawley, WA 6009, Australia. *T:* 386.2676. *Club:* Weld (Perth).

STEWART, Sir Herbert (Ray), Kt 1946; CIE 1939; FRCScI, DIC, NDA, MSc; *b* 10 July 1890; *s* of Hugh Stewart, Ballyward, Co. Down; *m* 1917, Eva (*d* 1955), *d* of William Rea, JP, Ballygawley, Co. Tyrone; one *d*; *m* 1957, Elsie, *d* of Walter J. Pyne, London. *Educ:* Excelsior Academy, Banbridge; Royal College of Science, Dublin; Imperial College of Science and Technology, London. Military Service, 1915-19; entered the Indian Agricultural Service as Deputy Director of Agriculture, 1920; Professor of Agriculture, Punjab, 1921-27; Assistant Director of Agriculture, 1928-32; Agricultural Expert, Imperial Council of Agricultural Research, Government of India, 1938; Director of Agriculture, Punjab, 1932-43; Member of the Punjab Legislative Council from time to time, 1927-36; Fellow of the University of the Punjab, 1929-43; Dean of the Faculty of Agriculture, 1933-43; Agriculture Commissioner with Government of India, 1943-46; Vice-Chairman, Imperial Council of Agricultural Research, 1944-46; Agricultural Adviser to British Middle East Office, Cairo, 1946-51; Principal Consultant, Agriculture, to UN Economic Survey Mission for Middle East, 1949; Agricultural Adviser to UN Relief and Works Agency for Palestine Refugees, 1950-51; Chief, Agricultural Mission to Colombia of Internat. Bank for Reconstruction and Development, 1955-56; Agricultural Consultant to Bank Missions to Pakistan, 1956, 1958, Italy, 1957, Yugoslavia and Uganda, 1960 and Kenya, 1961-62. *Publications:* various pamphlets and reports on agriculture and farm accounts in India, and on agriculture in Middle East. *Address:* 29 Alyth Road, Bournemouth, Dorset BH3 7DG. *T:* Bournemouth 764782.

STEWART, Sir Houston Mark S.; *see* Shaw-Stewart.

STEWART, Sir Hugh Charlie Godfray, 6th Bt, *cr* 1803, of Athenree; Major; DL; High Sheriff, Co. Tyrone, 1955; *b* 13 April 1897; *s* of Colonel Sir George Powell Stewart, 5th Bt, and Florence Maria Georgina, *d* of Sir James Godfray; *S* father, 1945; *m* 1st, 1929 (marr. diss. 1942); one *s* one *d*; 2nd, 1948, Diana Margaret, *d* of late Capt. J. E. Hibbert, MC, DFC, and late Mrs R. B. Bannon, Jersey; one *s* one *d*. *Educ:* Bradfield Coll., Berkshire; RMC, Sandhurst. Served European War, Royal Inniskilling Fusiliers, 1916; Arras, 1917 (wounded); France, 1939-40. Foreign Service has included India, Iraq, China, Malaya, South Africa and Syria; retired. DL Co. Tyrone, 1971. *Heir: s* David John

Christopher Stewart [*b* 19 June 1935; *m* 1959, Bridget Anne, *er d* of late Patrick W. Sim and of Mrs Leslie Parkhouse; three *d*].

STEWART, Sir Iain (Maxwell), Kt 1968; BSc, FIMechE, FRINA, FIMarE; Chairman: HPL Management Consultants; Caledonian Airways; Director: Dorchester Hotel Ltd (Consultative); Dunbar & Co. Ltd; Eagle Star Insurance Co. Ltd; Heatherset Management and Advisory Services Ltd; Royal Bank of Scotland Ltd; Scottish Television Ltd; *b* 16 June 1916; *s* of William Maxwell Stewart and Jessie Naismith Brown; *m* 1st, 1941, Margaret Jean Walker (marr. diss. 1967); two *s* two *d*; 2nd, 1979, Mrs Anne Griggs. *Educ:* Loretto Sch.; Glasgow Univ. (BSc Mech. Eng.). Apprenticeship at Thermotank Ltd, 1935-39. Served War of 1939-45, Technical Adjutant, Fife and Forfar Yeomanry, 1939-41. Dir, Thermotank Ltd, 1941, Man. Dir, 1946, Chairman, 1950-65; Dir, Lyle Shipping Co. Ltd, 1953-78; Chm., Fairfields (Glasgow) Ltd, 1966-68; Dep. Chm., Upper Clyde Shipbuilders Ltd, 1967-68. Mem. Bd, BEA, 1966-73. Pres., Inst. of Engineers & Shipbuilders in Scotland, 1961-63; Prime Warden, Worshipful Co. of Shipwrights; Mem. Chamber of Commerce, Glasgow. President's Medal, IPR, 1970. Hon. LLD: Strathclyde, 1975; St Andrews, 1978. *Recreation:* golf. *Address:* 148/150 Drymen Road, Bearsden, Glasgow. *T:* 041-942 7952. *Clubs:* Carlton, Garrick, Caledonian; Western (Glasgow).

STEWART, Ian; *see* Stewart, B. H. I. H.

STEWART, Jackie; *see* Stewart, John Young.

STEWART, James Cecil Campbell, CBE 1960; Director, National Nuclear Corporation, since 1980; Deputy Chairman, Nuclear Power Co. Ltd, since 1975; Chairman: British Nuclear Forum, since 1974; Nuclear Power Company Pension Trustee Ltd, since 1979; *b* 1916; *s* of late James Stewart and Mary Campbell Stewart; *m* 1946, Pamela Rouselle, *d* of William King-Smith; one *d*. *Educ:* Armstrong College and King's College, Durham University (BSc Physics). Telecommunications Research Establishment, 1939-46; Atomic Energy Research Establishment, Harwell, 1946-49; Industrial Group, UKAEA, 1949-63; Dep. Chm., British Nuclear Design and Construction, 1969-75; Member: UKAEA, 1963-69; Central Electricity Generating Bd, 1965-69. *Recreation:* gardening. *Address:* Whitethorns, Higher Whitley, Cheshire WA4 4QJ. *T:* Norcott Brook 377. *Club:* East India, Devonshire, Sports and Public Schools.

STEWART, Prof. James Douglas; Principal, Lincoln University College of Agriculture, since 1974; *b* 11 Aug. 1925; *s* of Charles Edward Stewart and Edith May Stewart (*née* Caldwell); *m* 1953, Nancy Elizabeth Dunbar; one *s* three *d*. *Educ:* Lincoln UC (Dip. Valuation and Farm Management); Canterbury Univ. (MA); Reading Univ. (DPhil). Lectr in Farm Management, Lincoln Coll., NZ, 1951-59; Research Fellow, Reading Univ., 1959-61; Sen. Lectr, Lincoln Coll., 1962-64; Prof. of Farm Management, Lincoln Coll., 1964-74. Chm., NZ Vice-Chancellors Cttee, 1981-; Mem., Govt Adv. Cttee on External Aid and Develt, 1975-. Director: China NZ Agricultural Consultants, 1979-; Pyne Gould Guinness Ltd, 1980-. Queen's Jubilee Medal, 1977. *Publications:* contrib. Jl Agricl Econs, Jl Farm Econs, Econ. Record, etc. *Recreations:* Provincial Rugby Union Coach, squash raquets, fishing. *Address:* PO Box 16, Lincoln College, Canterbury, NZ. *T:* Lincoln 796.

STEWART, James Gill, CB 1958; CBE 1952; Hon. FITO; *b* 13 March 1907; *s* of John Stewart (builder) and Isabella Stewart, late of Edinburgh; *m* 1936, Jessie Dodd; one *s* one *d*. *Educ:* George Watson's College, Edinburgh; Edinburgh University. Passed Home Civil Service Administrative Class Competition, 1929; entered Min. of Labour, Asst Principal, 1930; Private Sec. to Permanent Sec., 1934; Principal, 1936; Asst Sec., 1941; on loan to Min. of Works, 1941-43; on loan to UN (Bureau of Personnel), 1946-47; on loan to Cabinet Office, 1947-49; Industrial Relations Dept, 1950-53; Under-Sec., Employment Dept, 1953; Training Dept, 1960, retired, 1967. *Recreations:* choral singing, hill walking. *Address:* 104 Highgate West Hill, N6. *T:* 01-340 2014.

STEWART, James Lablache; *see* Granger, Stewart.

STEWART, James (Maitland), DFC with 2 oak leaf clusters (US); Air Medal with 3 oak leaf clusters; DSM (US); actor, stage and film; *b* Indiana, Pa, 20 May 1908; *s* of Alexander Maitland Stewart and Elizabeth Ruth (*née* Jackson); *m* 1949, Gloria McLean; two *s* twin *d*. *Educ:* Mercersburg Academy, Pa; Princeton University (BS Arch.). War Service, 1942-45: Lt-Col Air Corps; Europe, 1943-45 (Air Medal, DFC); Colonel, 1945. USAF Reserve; Brig.-Gen. 1959. Dir, Air Force Assoc. First New York appearance, Carry Nation, 1932; subseq. played in Goodbye Again, Spring in Autumn, All Good Americans, Yellow Jack, Divided by Three, Page Miss Glory, A Journey by Night. Entered films, 1935; *films include:* Murder Man, Next Time We Love, Seventh Heaven, You Can't Take It With You, Made for Each Other, Vivacious Lady, The Shopworn Angel, Mr Smith Goes to Washington, Destry Rides Again, No Time for Comedy, Philadelphia Story, The Shop around the Corner, Pot o' Gold, Ziegfeld Girl, Come Live with Me, It's a Wonderful Life, Magic Town, On Our Merry Way, You Gotta Stay Happy, Call Northside 777, Rope, The Stratton Story, Malaya, The Jackpot, Harvey, Winchester '73, Broken Arrow, No Highway in the Sky, Bend of the River, Carbine Williams, The Greatest Show on Earth, Thunder Bay, Naked Spur, The Glenn Miller Story, Rear Window, The Man from Laramie, The Far Country, Strategic Air Command, The Man Who Knew Too Much, Night

Passage, Spirit of St Louis, Midnight Story, Vertigo, Bell, Book and Candle, Anatomy of a Murder, The FBI Story, The Mountain Road, The Man Who Shot Liberty Valance, Mr Hobbs Takes a Vacation, Take her, She's Mine, Cheyenne Autumn, Shenandoah, The Rare Breed, Firecreek, Bandalero, The Cheyenne Social Club, Fool's Parade, Dynamite Man from Glory Jail, The Shootist, Airport 77, The Big Sleep, Magic of Lassie. *Play:* Harvey (Broadway), 1970, (Prince of Wales), 1975. Holds many awards including: five Academy Award nominations; Oscar award as best actor of the year; two NY Film Critics best actor awards; Venice Film Festival best actor award; France's Victoire Trophy for best actor; Screen Actors Guild award. Hon. degrees include: DLitt, Pennsylvania; MA, Princeton. *Address:* PO Box 90, Beverly Hills, Calif 90213, USA.

STEWART, James Moray; Assistant Under Secretary of State, Ministry of Defence, since 1980; *b* 21 June 1938; third *s* of James and Evelyn Stewart; *m* 1963, Dorothy May Batey, *o d* of A. C. and M. Batey; three *s. Educ:* Marlborough Coll.; Univ. of Keele (BA First Cl. Hons History and Econs). Sec., Univ. of Keele Union, 1960-61. Breakdown and Information Service Operator, AA, 1956-57; Asst Master, Northcliffe Sch., Bognor Regis, 1957-58; Asst Principal, Air Min., 1962-65; Private Sec. to 2nd Permanent Under Sec. of State (RAF), MoD, 1965-66; Principal, MoD, 1966-70; First Sec. (Defence), UK Delegn to NATO, 1970-73; Asst Sec., MoD, 1974-75; Private Sec. to successive Secs of State for NI, 1975-77; Dir, Naval Manpower Requirements, MoD, 1977; Dir, Defence Policy Staff, MoD, 1978-80. *Recreations:* reading, listening to music, walking. *Address:* Littlehurst, The Warren, Ashtead, Surrey. *T:* Ashtead 73682. *Club:* Royal Commonwealth Society.

STEWART, James Robertson, CBE 1971 (OBE 1964); Principal, University of London, since 1978; *b* 1917; *s* of James and Isabella Stewart; *m* 1941, Grace Margaret Kirsop; two *s* one *d. Educ:* Perth Acad.; Whitley and Monkseaton High Sch.; Armstrong Coll. (later King's Coll.), Newcastle, Univ. of Durham. BA Dunelm (1st cl. hons Mod. History) 1937; DThPT (1st cl.) 1938; research in Canada (Canada Co.), 1938-39; awarded Holland Rose Studentship, Cambridge, and William Black Noble Fellowship, Durham, 1939; MA Dunelm 1941. Served Army, 1939-46: Royal Artillery (BEF); Combined Ops HQ; Directorate of Combined Ops, India and SE Asia; Major (Actg Lt-Col); Certif. of Good Service. Dep. Clerk of Court, Univ. of London, 1946-49, Clerk of Court, 1950-82. Hon. Fellow: Westfield Coll., London, 1981; KCL, 1982; Sch. of Pharmacy, London Univ., 1982. *Recreations:* golf, gardening, watching (now) soccer and cricket. *Address:* University of London, Senate House, WC1E 7HU. *T:* 01-636 8000. *Clubs:* Athenæum; Cuddington (Banstead) Golf.

STEWART, James Simeon Hamilton, QC 1982; barrister; a Recorder of the Crown Court, since 1982; *b* 2 May 1943; *s* of late Henry Hamilton Stewart, MD, FRCS and of Edna Mary Hamilton Stewart; *m* 1972, Helen Margaret Whiteley; two *d. Educ:* Cheltenham Coll.; Univ. of Leeds (LLB Hons). Called to the Bar, Inner Temple, 1966. *Recreations:* cricket, golf, gardening. *Address:* Shaftesbury House, Chellow Dene, Bradford BD9 6BD. *T:* Bradford 493043. *Clubs:* Bradford (Bradford); Leeds Taverners (Leeds).

STEWART, Very Rev. James Stuart, MA, Hon. DD; Professor Emeritus of New Testament Language, Literature and Theology, University of Edinburgh, New College (retired 1966); Extra Chaplain to the Queen in Scotland (Chaplain, 1952-66); *b* 21 July 1896; *s* of William Stewart, Dundee, and Katharine Jane Stuart Duke; *m* 1931, Rosamund Anne Barron, Berkeley Lodge, Blandford, Dorset; two *s. Educ:* High School, Dundee; St Andrews University (MA, BD); New College, Edinburgh; University of Bonn, Germany. Minister of following Church of Scotland Congregations: St Andrews, Auchterarder, 1924-28; Beechgrove, Aberdeen, 1928-35; North Morningside, Edinburgh, 1935-46. Hon. DD, St Andrews Univ., 1945. Held following special lectureships: Cunningham Lectures, New Coll., Edinburgh, 1934; Warrack Lectures, Edinburgh and St Andrews Univs, 1944; Hoyt Lectures, Union Seminary, New York, 1949; Lyman Beecher Lectures, Yale University, USA, 1952; Duff Missionary Lectures, 1953; Turnbull Trust Preacher, Scots Church, Melbourne, 1959; Stone Lectures, Princeton, 1962; Earl Lectures, Berkeley, California, 1967; Moderator of General Assembly of Church of Scotland, May 1963-64. *Publications:* The Life and Teaching of Jesus Christ, 1932; A Man in Christ: St Paul's Theology, 1935; The Gates of New Life, 1937; The Strong Name, 1941; Heralds of God, 1945; A Faith To Proclaim, 1953; Thine Is The Kingdom, 1956; The Wind of the Spirit, 1968; River of Life, 1972; King for Ever, 1975; Joint Editor, English Trans. of Schleiermacher, The Christian Faith, 1928. *Address:* 6 Crawfurd Road, Edinburgh EH16 5PQ. *T:* 031-667 1810.

STEWART, Sir James Watson, 4th Bt, *cr* 1920; *b* 8 Nov. 1922; *s* of Sir James Watson Stewart, 3rd Bt and Janie Steuart Stewart (*née* Sim) (she *m* 2nd, 1961, Neil Charteris Riddell); *S* father 1955; *m* 1st, 1946, Anne Elizabeth Glaister (*d* 1979); no *c*; 2nd, 1980, Avril Veronica Gibb, FRSA, Hon. FBID, *o d* of late Andrew Adamson Gibb. *Educ:* Uppingham; Aberdeen University. Served 1940-47: Royal Artillery; 1st Special Air Service: Parachute Regiment. *Heir:* brother John Keith Watson Stewart [*b* 25 Feb. 1929; *m* 1954, Mary Elizabeth, *d* of John Francis Moxon; two *s* one *d*]. *Address:* Beach House, Skelmorlie, Ayrshire. *T:* Wemyss Bay 520220.

STEWART of Ardvorlich, John Alexander MacLaren, TD; Vice-Lord-Lieutenant, Perth and Kinross (formerly Perthshire), since 1974; *b* 25 March 1904; *s* of late Major William Stewart of Ardvorlich and of Lily, *d* of late Dr A. C. MacLaren, Harley Street, London; *m* 1930, Violet Hermione (*d* 1979), *er d* of late Col Sir Donald Walter Cameron of Lochiel, KT, CMG; one *s* one *d. Educ:* Wellington Coll., Berks. Landowner and farmer. Served War, 1939-45: 6th Bn, The Black Watch (France, 1940; Tunisia, 1943; Italy, 1944). *Publications:* The Stewarts, 1954, 2nd edn 1963; The Grahams, 1958, 2nd edn 1970; The Camerons: A History of Clan Cameron, 1974, 2nd edn 1981. *Recreations:* normal country pursuits in Highlands. *Address:* Ardvorlich, Lochearnhead, Perthshire. *T:* Lochearnhead 218. *Clubs:* Royal Perth Golfing, County and City (Perth).

STEWART, (John) Allan; MP (C) East Renfrewshire, since 1979; Parliamentary Under Secretary of State, Scottish Office, since 1981; *b* 1 June 1942; *s* of Edward MacPherson Stewart and Eadie Barrie Stewart; *m* 1973, Marjorie Sally (Susie); one *s* one *d. Educ:* Bell Baxter High Sch., Cupar; St Andrews Univ. (1st Cl. Hons MA 1964); Harvard Univ. (Rotary Internat. Foundn Fellow, 1964-65). Lectr in Polit. Economy, St Andrews Univ., 1965-70 (Warden, John Burnet Hall, 1968-70); Confederation of British Industry: Head of Regional Develt Dept, 1971-73; Dep. Dir (Econs), 1973-76; Scottish Sec., 1976-78; Scottish Dir, 1978-79. Conservative Parly Candidate, Dundee E, 1970; Councillor, London Bor. of Bromley, 1975-76. PPS to Minister of State for Energy, 1981. Mem., Select Cttee on Scottish Affairs, 1979-81. *Publications:* articles in academic and gen. pubns on econ. and polit. affairs. *Recreations:* golf, bridge. *Address:* 34 Rowan Road, Dumbreck, Glasgow G41 5BZ. *T:* 041-427 2178. *Club:* St Stephen's Constitutional.

STEWART, John Anthony Benedict, CMG 1979; OBE 1973; HM Diplomatic Service; Ambassador to Mozambique, since 1980; *b* 24 May 1927; *e s* of late Edward Vincent Stewart and Emily Veronica (*née* Jones); *m* 1960, Geraldine Margaret, *o d* of late Captain G. C. Clifton; one *s* one *d* (and one *s* decd). *Educ:* St Illtyd's Coll.; Univ. of Wales; Cambridge Univ.; Imperial Coll. of Science and Technology; Cox Gold medal for Geology, 1950. RNVR Ordinary Seaman, later Midshipman, 1944-47. Colonial Geol. Survey Service, Somaliland Protectorate, 1952-56; Dist Officer, 1956-57; seconded to Anglo-Ethiopian Liaison Service, 1957-60 (Sen. Liaison Officer, 1960); transf. N Rhodesia as Dist Officer, 1960, Dist Comr, 1962-64; Resident Local Govt Officer, Barotseland, 1964-67. Entered HM Diplomatic Service, 1968; served FCO, Barbados, Uganda; RCDS, 1974; Ambassador to Democratic Republic of Vietnam, 1975-76; Head of Hong Kong Dept, FCO, 1976-78; Ambassador to Laos, 1978-80. *Publications:* The Geology of the Mait Area, 1955; papers in geological jls. *Recreations:* shooting, fishing, flying light aeroplanes. *Address:* c/o Foreign and Commonwealth Office, SW1. *Clubs:* Travellers'; Three Counties Aero (Blackbushe).

STEWART, John Innes Mackintosh; Reader in English Literature, Oxford University, 1969-73; Student of Christ Church, Oxford, 1949-73, now Emeritus; *b* 30 Sept. 1906; *s* of late John Stewart, Director of Education in the City of Edinburgh, and Eliza Jane, *d* of James Clark, Golford, Nairn; *m* 1932, Margaret Hardwick (*d* 1979); three *s* two *d. Educ:* Edinburgh Academy; Oriel College, Oxford. Bishop Fraser's Scholar, 1930; 1st class Eng. Lang. and Lit. 1928; Matthew Arnold Memorial Prize, 1929; Lectr in English in Univ. of Leeds, 1930-35; Jury Professor of English in Univ. of Adelaide, 1935-45; Lectr in Queen's Univ., Belfast, 1946-48; Walker-Ames Prof., Univ. of Washington, 1961. Hon. DLitt: New Brunswick, 1962; Leicester, 1979; St Andrews, 1980. *Publications:* Montaigne's Essays: John Florio's Translation, 1931; Character and Motive in Shakespeare, 1949; Eight Modern Writers, 1963; Rudyard Kipling, 1966; Joseph Conrad, 1968; Thomas Hardy, 1971; Shakespeare's Lofty Scene (Shakespeare Lectr, British Acad.), 1971. Detective novels and broadcast scripts (under pseudonym of Michael Innes) Death at the President's Lodging, 1936; Hamlet Revenge!, 1937; Lament for a Maker, 1938; Stop Press, 1939; There Came Both Mist and Snow, 1940; The Secret Vanguard, 1940; Appleby on Ararat, 1941; The Daffodil Affair, 1942; The Weight of the Evidence, 1944; Appleby's End, 1945; From London Far, 1946; What Happened at Hazelwood, 1947; A Night of Errors, 1948; The Hawk and the Handsaw, 1948; The Journeying Boy, 1949; Operation Pax, 1951; A Private View, 1952; Christmas at Candleshoe, 1953; Appleby Talking, 1954; The Man From the Sea, 1955; Old Hall, New Hall, 1956; Appleby Talks Again, 1956; Appleby Plays Chicken, 1956; The Long Farewell, 1958; Hare Sitting Up, 1959; The New Sonia Wayward, 1960; Silence Observed, 1961; A Connoisseur's Case, 1962; Money from Holme, 1964; The Bloody Wood, 1966; A Change of Heir, 1966; Appleby at Allington, 1968; A Family Affair, 1969; Death at the Chase, 1970; An Awkward Lie, 1971; The Open House, 1972; Appleby's Answer, 1973; Appleby's Other Story, 1974; The Mysterious Commission, 1974; The Appleby File, 1975; The Gay Phoenix, 1976; Honeybath's Haven, 1977; The Ampersand Papers, 1978; Going It Alone, 1980; Lord Mullion's Secret, 1981; Sheiks and Adders, 1982; (*novels* as J. I. M. Stewart): Mark Lambert's Supper, 1954; The Guardians, 1955; A Use of Riches, 1957; The Man Who Wrote Detective Stories, 1959; The Man Who Won the Pools, 1961; The Last Tresilians, 1963; An Acre of Grass, 1965; The Aylwins, 1966; Vanderlyn's Kingdom, 1967; Cucumber Sandwiches, 1969; Avery's Mission, 1971; A Palace of Art, 1972; Mungo's Dream, 1973; quintet, A Staircase in Surrey, 1974-78 (The Gaudy, 1974; Young Pattullo, 1975; A Memorial Service, 1976; The Madonna of the Astrolabe, 1977; Full Term, 1978); Our England is a Garden and other stories, 1979; Andrew and Tobias, 1981; The Bridge at Arta and other stories, 1981; A Villa in France, 1982. *Recreation:* walking. *Address:* Fawler Copse, Fawler, Wantage, Oxon. *See also* M. J. Stewart.

STEWART, John Philip, MD, FRCSE, FSA Scotland; Hon. Consulting Surgeon, Deaconess Hospital; Hon. Consulting Surgeon, Royal Infirmary, Edinburgh; former Hon. Senior Lecturer and Head of Department of Otorhinolaryngology, member, Faculty of Medicine and Senatus Academicus, University of Edinburgh; *b* 1 Feb. 1900; *s* of late George Stewart, SSC, JP, and Flora Philip, MA; *m* 1928, Elizabeth Josephine Forbes Wedderburn; *m* 1982, Phyllis Mary Cave. *Educ:* Daniel Stewart's College and University, Edinburgh; Paris and Vienna. 2nd Lieut RFA 1918; MB, ChB Edinburgh Univ. 1923; MD 1925; FRCSE 1926; Lt-Col RAMC, Adviser in Oto-Rhino-Laryngology, BLA; served France, 1940; Egypt and Persia, 1942–43; North-West Europe, 1944–45 (despatches). Hon. Mem., Section of Laryngology, RSocMed (Former Pres.). *Publication:* Turner's Diseases of Ear, Nose and Throat. *Recreation:* golf. *Address:* 20 Gallow Hill, Peebles EH45 9BG. *T:* Peebles 20447.

STEWART, John Young, (Jackie Stewart), OBE 1972; racing driver, retired 1973; *b* 11 June 1939; *s* of late Robert Paul Stewart and of Jean Clark Young; *m* 1962, Helen McGregor; two *s*. *Educ:* Dumbarton Academy. First raced, 1961; competed in 4 meetings, 1961–62, driving for Barry Filer, Glasgow; drove for Ecurie Ecosse and Barry Filer, winning 14 out of 23 starts, 1963; 28 wins out of 53 starts, 1964; drove Formula 1 for BRM, 1965–67 and for Ken Tyrrell, 1968–73; has won Australian, New Zealand, Swedish, Mediterranean, Japanese and many other non-championship, major internat. Motor Races; set up new world record by winning his 26th World Championship Grand Prix (Zandvoort), July 1973, and 27th (Nurburgring), Aug. 1973; 3rd in World Championship, 1965; 2nd in 1968 and 1972; World Champion, 1969, 1971, 1973. BARC Gold Medal, 1971, 1973. Daily Express Sportsman of the Year, 1971, 1973; BBC Sports Personality of the Year, 1973; Scottish Sportsman of the Year, 1973; US Sportsman of the Year, 1973; Segrave Trophy, 1973. *Film:* Weekend of a Champion, 1972. *Publication:* Faster!, 1972 (with Peter Manso). *Recreations:* golf, fishing, tennis, shooting (Mem. British Team for Clay Pigeon shooting; former Scottish, English, Irish, Welsh and British Champion; won Coupe des Nations, 1959 and 1960; reserve for two-man team, 1960 Olympics). *Address:* Clayton House, 1268 Begnins, Vaud, Switzerland. *T:* Geneva 61.01.52. *Clubs:* (Hon.) Royal Automobile, British Racing Drivers' (Vice-Pres.); (Hon.) Royal Scottish Automobile; (Pres.) Scottish Motor Racing (Duns); Royal and Ancient (St Andrews).

STEWART, Kenneth Hope, PhD; Director of Research, Meteorological Office, since 1976; *b* 29 March 1922; *s* of Harry Sinclair Stewart and Nora Hassan Parry; *m* 1950, Hilary Guest; four *s* four *d*. *Educ:* Trinity Coll., Cambridge (MA, PhD). Entered Meteorol Office, 1949; Dep. Dir, Physical Res., 1974. *Publications:* Ferromagnetic Domains, 1951; contrib. physical and meteorol jls. *Address:* 33 Ravenswood Avenue, Crowthorne, Berks.

STEWART, Mary (Florence Elinor), (Lady Stewart); *b* 17 Sept. 1916; *d* of Rev. Frederick A. Rainbow, Durham Diocese, and Mary Edith (*née* Matthews), NZ; *m* 1945, Sir Frederick Henry Stewart, *qv*; no *c*. *Educ:* Eden Hall, Penrith, Cumberland; Skellfield School, Ripon, Yorks; St Hild's Coll., Durham Univ. 1938; MA 1941. Asst Lectr in English, Durham Univ., 1941–45; Part-time Lectr in English, St Hild's Training Coll., Durham, and Durham Univ., 1948–56. FRSA 1968. *Publications:* novels: Madam, Will You Talk?, 1954; Wildfire at Midnight, 1956; Thunder on the Right, 1957; Nine Coaches Waiting, 1958; My Brother Michael, 1959; The Ivy Tree, 1961; The Moonspinners, 1962; This Rough Magic, 1964; Airs Above the Ground, 1965; The Gabriel Hounds, 1967; The Wind Off The Small Isles, 1968; The Crystal Cave, 1970 (Frederick Niven Award); The Little Broomstick, 1971; The Hollow Hills, 1973; Ludo and the Star Horse, 1974 (Scottish Arts Council Award); Touch Not the Cat, 1976; The Last Enchantment, 1979; A Walk in Wolf Wood, 1980; also articles, poems, radio plays. *Recreations:* gardening, music, painting. *Address:* 79 Morningside Park, Edinburgh EH10 5EZ. *T:* 031-447 2620.

STEWART, Michael James; Reader in Political Economy, University College, London University, since 1969; *b* 6 Feb. 1933; *s* of John Innes Mackintosh Stewart, *qv*; *m* 1962, Hon. Frances Kaldor, *d* of Baron Kaldor, *qv*; one *s* two *d* (and one *d* decd). *Educ:* Campbell Coll., Belfast; St Edward's Sch., Oxford; Magdalen Coll., Oxford. 1st cl. PPE (Oxon), 1955. Asst Res. Off., Oxford Univ. Inst. of Statistics, 1955–56; Barnett Fellow, Cornell Univ., 1956–57; Econ. Asst, HM Treasury, 1957–60; Sec. to Council on Prices, Productivity and Incomes, 1960–61; Econ. Adviser, HM Treasury, 1961–62, Cabinet Office, 1964–67 (Senior Econ. Advr, 1967), Kenya Treasury, 1967–69; Special Adviser to Sec. of State for Trade, Apr.–Oct. 1974; Economic Adviser to Malta Labour Party, 1970–73; Special Econ. Advr to Foreign Sec., 1977–78. Guest Scholar, Brookings Instn, Washington, DC, 1978–79. Mem., Acad. Adv. Panel, Bank of England, 1977–. Contested (Lab): Folkestone and Hythe, 1964; Croydon North-West, 1966. Asst Editor, Nat. Inst. Econ. Review, 1962–64. Consultant to various UN agencies, 1971–. *Publications:* Keynes and After, 1967; The Jekyll and Hyde Years: politics and economic policy since 1964, 1977. *Recreations:* looking at paintings, eating in restaurants. *Address:* 79 South Hill Park, NW3 2SS. *T:* 01-435 3686. *Club:* United Oxford & Cambridge University.

STEWART, Sir Michael (Norman Francis), KCMG 1966 (CMG 1957); OBE 1948; HM Diplomatic Service, retired; Director, Sotheby's, since 1977; *b* 18 Jan. 1911; *s* of late Sir Francis Stewart, CIE, and of Lady Stewart; *m* 1951, Katharine Damaris Houssemayne du Boulay; one *s* two *d*. *Educ:* Shrewsbury; Trinity College, Cambridge. Assistant Keeper, Victoria and

Albert Museum, 1935–39; Ministry of Information, 1939–41; Press Attaché: HM Embassy, Lisbon, 1941–44; HM Embassy, Rome, 1944–48; employed in Foreign Office, 1948–51; Counsellor, Office of Comr-Gen. for UK in SE Asia, 1951–54; Counsellor, HM Embassy, Ankara, 1954–59; HM Chargé d'Affaires, Peking, 1959–62; Senior Civilian Instructor, IDC, 1962–64; HM Minister, British Embassy, Washington, 1964–67; Ambassador to Greece, 1967–71. Dir, Ditchley Foundn, 1971–76. *Recreation:* country life. *Address:* Combe, near Newbury, Berks.

STEWART, Dame Muriel (Acadia), DBE 1968; Headmistress, Northumberland LEA, 1940–70; *b* 22 Oct. 1905; *d* of late James Edmund Stewart. *Educ:* Gateshead Grammar Sch.; Durham Univ. BA Hons 1926; MA 1929. Teacher: Newcastle upon Tyne, 1927–29; Northumberland, 1929–70 (a headteacher of Secondary Schools, 1940–69); Headmistress, Shiremoor Middle School, 1969–70. Nat. Pres., Nat. Union of Teachers, 1964–65; Chm., Schools Council, 1969–72. Vice-Chm., Bullock Cttee, 1972–74. Hon. MEd, Newcastle Univ., 1965. *Recreation:* music. *Address:* 44 Caldwell Road, Gosforth, Newcastle upon Tyne NE3 2AX. *T:* Newcastle upon Tyne 853400.

STEWART, Potter; retired Justice of the Supreme Court of the United States (Associate Justice, 1958–81); *b* 23 Jan. 1915; *s* of James Garfield Stewart and Harriet Loomis Stewart (*née* Potter); *m* 1943, Mary Ann Bertles; two *s* one *d*. *Educ:* Hotchkiss School, Lakeville, Connecticut; Yale College; Yale Law School. One-year fellowship, Cambridge, Eng. General practice of law as associate with Debevoise, Stevenson, Plimpton and Page, New York City, 1941–42, 1945–47; associate with Dinsmore, Shohl, Sawyer and Dinsmore, Cincinnati, O, 1947; partner of that firm, 1951–54; Judge, US Court of Appeals for 6th Circuit, 1954–58. Member, Cincinnati City Council, 1950–53 (Vice-Mayor, 1952–53). Hon. LLD: Yale Univ., 1959; Kenyon Coll., 1960; Wilmington Coll., 1962; Univ. of Cincinnati, 1963; Ohio Univ., 1964; Univ. of Michigan, 1966; Miami Univ., 1974. *Address:* Supreme Court Building, Washington, DC 20543, USA. *Clubs:* Camargo (Cincinnati, Ohio); Chevy Chase (Chevy Chase, Md).

STEWART, Richard, CBE 1976; JP; Leader of Administration, Strathclyde Regional Council, since 1974; *b* 27 May 1920; *s* of Richard Stewart and Agnes (*née* Cunningham); *m* 1942, Elizabeth Peat; one *d*. *Educ:* Harthill Sch., Harthill. Mem., Lanark CC for 15 years (Chm. several cttees, finally Chm., Social Work Cttee). Full-time Sec./Organiser, Labour Party; Agent for: Rt Hon. Miss Margaret Herbison for 20 years; Mr John Smith, MP, 1970–. Mem., Bd of Dirs, Scottish Transport Group, 1975–. Past Chairman: Scottish Council of Labour Party; Nat. Union of Labour Organisers. JP Lanark County Council 1964. *Recreations:* music, chess. *Address:* 28 Hawthorn Drive, Harthill, Shotts ML7 5SG. *T:* Harthill 303.

STEWART, Lt-Col Robert Christie, TD 1962; Lord Lieutenant of Kinross-shire, 1966–74; *b* 3 Aug. 1926; *m* 1953, Ann Grizel Cochrane; three *s* two *d*. *Educ:* Eton; University College, Oxford. Lt Scots Guards, 1945–49. Oxford Univ., 1949–51 (BA Agric.). TA, 7 Argyll and Sutherland Highlanders, 1948–66; Lt-Col Comdg 7 A & SH, 1963–66. Hon. Col, 1/51 Highland Volunteers, 1972. Chm. and Pres., Bd of Governors, E of Scotland Coll. of Agric., 1970–. DL Kinross 1956, VL 1958; Chairman Kinross County Council, 1963–73. *Address:* Arndean, By Dollar, Kinross-shire. *T:* Dollar 2527. *Club:* New (Edinburgh).

STEWART, Dr Robert William, OC 1979; FRS 1970; FRSC 1967; Deputy Minister, Ministry of Universities, Science and Communications, Province of British Columbia, Canada, since 1979; Hon. Professor of Physics and Oceanography, University of British Columbia; *b* 21 Aug. 1923; *m* 1st, 1948, V. Brande (marr. diss. 1972); two *s* one *d* ; 2nd, 1973, Anne-Marie Robert; one *s*. *Educ:* Queen's Univ., Ontario. BSc 1945, MSc 1947, Queen's; PhD Cantab 1952. Canadian Defence Research Bd, 1950–61; Prof. of Physics and Oceanography, Univ. of British Columbia, 1961–70; Dir, Marine Scis Br., Pacific Reg., Environment Canada, 1970–74; Dir-Gen., Ocean and Aquatic Scis, Pacific Reg., Fisheries and Marine Service, Dept of Fisheries and Oceans, Canada, 1974–79. Vis. Professor: Dalhousie Univ., 1960–61; Harvard Univ., 1964; Pennsylvania State Univ., 1964; Commonwealth Vis. Prof., Cambridge Univ., 1967–68. Vice-Chm., 1968–72, Chm., 1972–76, Jt Organizing Cttee, Global Atmospheric Res. Program; President: Internat. Assoc. of Physical Scis of Ocean, 1975–79; Cttee on Climatic Changes and the Ocean, 1980–; Chm., Liaison Panel with Jt Scientific Cttee for World Climate Res. Program, ICSU/WMO. *Publications:* numerous, on turbulence, oceanography and meteorology. *Address:* Room 109, Ministry of Universities, Science and Communications, Parliament Buildings, Victoria, BC V8V 1X4, Canada.

STEWART, Sir Robertson (Huntly), Kt 1979; CBE 1970; CEng, FIProdE, FPRI, FNZIM, FInstD; Executive Chairman: PDL Holdings Ltd (manufacturers of electrical and plastic products), since 1957; PDL (Asia), since 1975; *b* 21 Sept. 1913; *s* of Robert McGregor Stewart and Ivy Emily (*née* Grigg); *m* 1st, 1937, Ada Gladys Gunter; two *s* one *d* ; 2nd, 1970, Ellen Adrienne Cansdale; two *s*. *Educ:* Christchurch Boys' High Sch.; Christchurch Technical Inst. CEng, FIProdE 1967, FPRI 1960, FNZIM 1962, FInstD 1970. Introd plastics industry to NZ, 1936; commenced manuf. of electrical products in NZ, 1937; estabd PDL Gp of Cos, 1947. Led NZ Trade Missions, 1962, 1964, 1966, 1967, 1970 and 1972. Pres., NZ Manufrs Fedn, 1963–64. Hon. Malaysian Consul. *Recreations:* motor racing, tennis, fishing. *Address:* 10 Coldstream Court, Christchurch 4, New Zealand. *T:* Christchurch 515831. *Club:* Canterbury (Christchurch).

STEWART, Robin Milton, QC 1978; a Recorder of the Crown Court, since 1978; *b* 5 Aug. 1938; *s* of late Brig. Guy Milton Stewart and of Dr Elaine Oenone Stewart, MD, BS; *m* 1962, Lynda Grace Medhurst; three *s. Educ:* Winchester; New Coll., Oxford (MA). Called to the Bar, Middle Temple, 1963; called to the Irish Bar, King's Inns, Dublin, 1975. Prosecuting Counsel to Inland Revenue, NE Circuit, 1976-78. *Recreations:* pictures, gardening, Scottish family history. *Address:* 2 Harcourt Buildings, Temple, EC4Y 9DB. *T:* 01-353 2548; Delwood Croft, Fenwick's Lane, Fulford, York YO1 4PL. *T:* York 39416. *Clubs:* Oriental; Durham County (Durham).

STEWART, Sir Ronald (Compton), 2nd Bt, *cr* 1937; DL; Chairman, London Brick Co. Ltd 1966-79; *b* 14 Aug. 1903; *s* of Sir (Percy) Malcolm Stewart, 1st Bt, OBE, and Cordelia (*d* 1906,) *d* of late Rt Hon. Sir Joseph Compton Rickett, DL, MP; *S* father, 1951; *m* 1936, Cynthia, OBE, JP, *d* of Harold Farmiloe. *Educ:* Rugby; Jesus College, Cambridge. High Sheriff of Bedfordshire, 1954, DL 1974. *Heir:* half-*b* Malcolm Stewart [*b* 20 Dec. 1909; *m* 1935 Mary Stephanie (marr. diss. 1957), *d* of Frederick Ramon de Bertodano, 8th Marquis del Moral (Spain)]. *Address:* Maulden Grange, Maulden, Bedfordshire.

STEWART, Stanley Toft; Company Director; *b* 13 June 1910; *s* of Charles Campbell Stewart and Jeanette Matilda Doral; *m* 1935, Therese Zelie de Souza; seven *d. Educ:* St Xavier's Instn, Penang; Raffles Coll., Singapore. Straits Settlements CS, 1934-46; Overseas Civil Service, 1946-55; District Officer, Butterworth, Province Wellesley, 1947-52; Dep. Chm., Rural Board, Singapore, 1952-54; Chm., Rural Board, Singapore, 1954; Dep. Sec., Ministry of Local Government, Lands and Housing, Singapore, 1955, Actg Permanent Sec., 1955; Actg Chief Sec., Singapore, Oct. 1957-Jan. 1958; Permanent Secretary: Home Affairs, 1959-63; to Prime Minister, 1961-66; Singapore High Comr in Australia, 1966-69; Permanent Sec., Min. of Foreign Affairs, Singapore, 1969-72; Exec. Sec., Nat. Stadium Corp., 1973. *Recreations:* tennis, gardening. *Address:* 49 Jalan Jelita, Singapore 1027, Republic of Singapore. *Clubs:* Singapore Recreation, Club 200 (Singapore).

STEWART, Stephen Malcolm, QC 1979; *b* 22 April 1914; *s* of Dr Siegmund and Helen Strauss; *m* 1946, Marie Josephine (*née* Bere); two *s. Educ:* Univ. of Vienna (LLD 1936); Ecole des Sciences Politiques, Paris (Diploma 1938); Univ. of London. Overseas Service, BBC, 1939; served Army, 1940-47; Captain, Liaison Officer, Free French Forces and Belgian Army, 1944-45; Major JAG's Branch, 21 Army Group, 1945; Chief Prosecuting Officer, War Crimes Trials, 1946-47; UN War Crimes Commn, 1947-48; called to the Bar, Inner Temple, 1948; practice at the Bar, 1948-61; Director General, IFPI, 1961-79. Mem., Gen. Council of the Bar, 1969-71; Vice-Chm., Bar Assoc. for Commerce, Finance and Industry, 1974-76, Chm., 1976-78; Member of Senate of the Inns of Court and Bar, 1976-81. Governor: Polytechnic of the South Bank, 1967-70; Sevenoaks School, 1968-. *Publications:* The Clearinghouse System for Copyright Licences, 1966; 200 Years of English Copyright Law, 1976; International Copyright in the 1980s (Geiringer Meml Lecture, NY), 1980; International Copyright and Neighbouring Rights, 1983; articles in Guardian Gazette, Copyright, Bulletin of Copyright of USA. *Recreations:* music, skiing, tennis, golf, swimming. *Address:* Tanglewood, Kippington Road, Sevenoaks, Kent. *T:* Sevenoaks 453855. *Club:* Reform.

STEWART, Mrs Suzanne Freda; *see* Norwood, S. F.

STEWART, Victor Colvin, FCA; Registrar General for Scotland, 1978-82; *b* 12 April 1921; *s* of Victor Stewart and Jean Cameron; *m* 1949, Aileen Laurie; one *s. Educ:* Selkirk High Sch.; Edinburgh Univ. (BCom). FCA 1954. Served War in RAF, Africa and ME, 1942-46. Joined Dept of Health for Scotland, 1938; Chief Exec. Officer, 1959; Principal, SHHD, 1963, Asst Sec. 1971; Dep. Registrar gen. for Scotland, 1976. *Recreations:* golf, walking, bridge. *Address:* 28 Bryce Road, Currie, Midlothian EH14 5LW. *T:* 031-449 2642. *Club:* Royal Commonwealth Society.

STEWART, Dr William, CB 1977; DSc; Deputy Controller Aircraft, Ministry of Defence (Procurement Executive), 1978-81 (Deputy Controller, Aircraft A, 1973-78); *b* Hamilton, 29 Aug. 1921; *m* 1955, Helen Cairney; two *d. Educ:* St John's Grammar Sch.; Hamilton Acad.; Glasgow Univ. BSc Hons (engin.); DSc 1958. RAE, Farnborough, 1942-53; British Jt Services Mission, Washington, 1953-56; Dep. Head of Naval Air Dept, RAE, Bedford, 1956-63; Imperial Defence College, 1964; Asst Dir, Project Time and Cost Analysis, 1965-66; Dir, Anglo-French Combat Trainer Aircraft Projects, 1966-70; Dir-Gen., Multi-Role combat Aircraft, 1970-73. Silver Medal, RAeS, 1981. *Address:* 25 Brickhill Drive, Bedford.

STEWART, Prof. William Alexander Campbell, MA, PhD; DL; Vice-Chancellor, University of Keele, 1967-79; *b* Glasgow, 17 Dec. 1915; *s* of late Thomas Stewart, Glasgow, and Helen Fraser, Elgin, Morayshire; *m* 1947, Ella Elizabeth Burnett, of Edinburgh; one *s* one *d. Educ:* Colfe's Grammar Sch., London; University Coll., and Inst. of Education, Univ. of London. Exhibitioner, University Coll., London, 1934-37; BA 1937; MA 1941; PhD 1947; Diploma in Education, 1938; Fellow, UCL, 1975. Sen. English Master: (and Housemaster), Friends' School, Saffron Walden, Essex, 1938-43; Abbotsholme School, Derbyshire, 1943-44 (Member of Governing Body, 1960-80; Chm., Council, 1974-80); Asst Lectr and Lectr in Education, University Coll., Nottingham, 1944-47; Lectr in Education, Univ. of Wales (Cardiff), 1947-50; Prof. of Education, Univ. of Keele, 1950-67. Vis. Prof., McGill Univ., 1957, Univ. of Calif., Los Angeles 1959; Simon Vis. Prof.,

Univ. of Manchester, 1962-63; Prestige Fellow, NZ Univs, 1969; Vis. Professorial Fellow, Univ. of Sussex, 1979-. Chairman: YMCA Educn Cttee, 1962-67; Nat. Adv. Council for Child Care, 1968-71; Univs Council for Adult Educn, 1969-73; Council, Roehampton Inst. of Higher Educn, 1979-; Member: Inter-Univ. Council for Higher Education Overseas; Commonwealth Univ. Interchange Council, 1968-80; Council, Univ. of Sierra Leone, 1968-; Adv. Council, Supply and Training of Teachers, 1974-78; US-UK Educnl Commn, 1977-81. Fellow, Internat. Inst. of Art and Letters. DL Stafford, 1973. Hon. DLitt: Ulster, 1973; Keele, 1981. *Publications:* Quakers and Education, 1953; (ed with J. Eros) Systematic Sociology of Karl Mannheim, 1957; (with K. Mannheim) An Introduction to the Sociology of Education, 1962; contrib. to The American College (ed Sanford), 1962; The Educational Innovators (Vol. 1, with W. P. McCann), 1967; The Educational Innovators (Vol. 2), 1968; Progressives and Radicals in English Education 1750-1970, 1972. *Recreations:* formerly most games; travelling, talking, theatre, music. *Address:* 42 Dean Court Road, Rottingdean, Brighton, Sussex. *Clubs:* Athenæum, Oriental; Federation House (Stoke on Trent).

STEWART, Prof. William Duncan Paterson, PhD, DSc; FRS 1977; FRSE; Boyd-Baxter Professor of Biology and Head of Department of Biological Sciences, University of Dundee, since 1968; *b* 7 June 1935; *s* of John Stewart and Margaret (*née* Paterson); *m* 1958, Catherine MacLeod; one *s. Educ:* Bowmore Junior Secondary Sch., Isle-of-Islay; Dunoon Grammar Sch.; Glasgow Univ. (BSc, PhD, DSc). FRSE 1973. Asst Lectr, Univ. of Nottingham, 1961-63; Lectr, Westfield Coll., Univ. of London, 1963-68. Vis. Res. Worker, Univ. of Wisconsin, 1966 and 1968; Vis. Prof., Univ. of Kuwait, 1980. Dir, ARC Res. Gp on Cyanobacteria, 1981-. Chairman: Royal Soc. Biological Educn Cttee, 1977-80; Aquatic Life Sciences Grants Cttee, NERC, 1973-78; Sci. Adv. Cttee, Freshwater Biol. Assoc., 1974-; Royal Soc. Study Group on Nitrogen Cycle, 1979-; Royal Soc. Biotechnology and Educn Wkg Gp, 1980-81; Vice-Pres., 1973-75, Pres., 1975-77, British Phycological Soc.; Trustee, Estuarine and Brackish-Water Sciences Assoc., 1978-; Sec., Internat. Cttee on Microbial Ecology, 1980; Member: Council, RSE, 1976-; Council, Marine Biol. Assoc., 1973-76, 1977-80, 1981-; Plants and Soils Res. Grants Bd, ARC, 1978-; Council, Scottish Marine Biol. Assoc., 1969-74, 1982-; Governing Body, Scottish Hort. Res. Inst., 1971-80; British Nat. Cttee for problems of environment, Royal Soc., 1979-; UNESCO Panel on Microbiology, 1975-; Council, NERC, 1979- (Chm., Marine Life Scis Prep. Gp, 1982-); Internat. Cell Res. Org., 1979-; Governing Body, Scottish Crop Res. Inst., 1980-; Royal Soc. Study Gp on Science Educn, 1981-82. Lectures: Phycological Soc. of America Dist., 1977; Barton-Wright, Inst. Biol., 1977; Sir David Martin Royal Soc.-BAYS, 1979; Plenary Lectr, 2nd Internat. Symp. on Microbial Ecology, 1980. *Publications:* Nitrogen Fixation in Plants, 1966; (jtly) The Blue-Green Algae, 1973; Algal Physiology and Biochemistry, 1974; (ed) Nitrogen Fixation by Free-living Organisms, 1975; (ed jtly) Nitrogen Fixation, 1980; papers in learned jls of repute. *Recreations:* soccer, playing the bagpipes. *Address:* Department of Biological Sciences, University of Dundee, Dundee DD1 4HN. *T:* Dundee 23181, ext. 324; 45 Fairfield Road, West Ferry, Dundee. *T:* Dundee 76702.

STEWART, William Ian; *see* Allanbridge, Hon. Lord.

STEWART, William McCausland; Professor of French, University of Bristol, 1945-66; Emeritus, 1966; *b* 17 Sept. 1900; *yr s* of late Abraham McCausland Stewart, Londonderry, and Alexandrina Catherine Margaret Elsner, Dublin; *m* 1933, Ann Cecilia Selo (*d* 1969); two *d. Educ:* Foyle Coll., Londonderry; Trinity Coll., Dublin (Sizar, Schol. and Sen. Moderator in Mod. Literature-French and German; Prizeman in Old and Mod. English; Vice-Chancellor's Prizeman in English Verse). BA 1922; MA 1926; Lecteur d'Anglais, Univ. of Montpellier, 1922-23 (Certificat de Licence en Phonétique, 1923). Resident Lecteur d'Anglais at Ecole Normale Supérieure, Paris, 1923-26; also studied Sorbonne (Diplôme d'Etudes Supérieures de Lettres: Langues Classiques, 1925) and Ecole des Hautes Etudes, Paris, and taught Collège Sainte-Barbe, Paris; Lectr in French, Univ. of Sheffield, 1927 and 1928; Lectr in French and Joint Head of French Dept, Univ. of St Andrews and University College, Dundee, from 1928 onwards. Seconded for War Service in Foreign Research and Press Service (Chatham House), Balliol College, Oxford, Sept. 1939; Head of French Section of same, 1940-43; Head of French Section, Research Dept of Foreign Office, 1943-45. Chairman, University of Bristol Art Lectures Committee, 1946-66; Dean of Faculty of Arts, 1960-62; Visiting Professor, Univ. of Auckland, 1967. Member Council, RWA; Pres., Clifton Arts Club; Governor, Bath Academy of Art, Corsham Court; Chairman, Bristol-Bordeaux Assoc., 1953-76; Corr. Mem. Acad. des Sciences, Belles Lettres et Arts de Bordeaux and of Acad. Montesquieu. Chevalier de la Légion d'Honneur, 1950. Officier des Palmes Académiques, 1957, Commandeur, 1966. DLitt (*hc*), Nat. Univ. of Ireland, 1963. *Publications:* Les Etudes Françaises en Grand Bretagne, Paris, 1929 (with G. T. Clapton); translation of Paul Valéry's Eupalinos, with Preface, Oxford, 1932, and of his Dialogues, Bollingen Series XLV, New York, 1956 and London, 1958; Les Chœurs d'Athalie (record), 1958; Aspects of the French Classical Ideal, 1967; Tokens in Time (poems), 1968; Alcaics for our Age, 1976; Bristol-Bordeaux: The First Thirty Years, 1977; contribs to literary reviews and learned periodicals, mainly on Classical and Modern France (incl. Descartes, Racine, Montesquieu, Valéry). *Address:* 5 Cotham Park, Bristol BS6 6BZ. *T:* Bristol 48156. *Club:* Europe House.

See also J. N. T. Spreckley, A. L. Stewart.

STEWART-CLARK, Sir John, 3rd Bt *cr* 1918; Member (C) Sussex East, European Parliament, since 1979; *b* 17 Sept. 1929; *e s* of Sir Stewart Stewart-Clark, 2nd Bt, and of Jane Pamela, *d* of late Major Arundell Clarke; *S* father, 1971; *m* 1958, Lydia Frederike, *d* of J. W. Loudon, Holland; one *s* four *d*. *Educ:* Eton; Balliol College, Oxford; Harvard Business School. Commissioned with HM Coldstream Guards, 1948-49. Oxford, 1949-52. With J. & P. Coats Ltd, 1952-69; Managing Director: J. & P. Coats, Pakistan, Ltd, 1961-67; J. A. Carp's Garenfabrieken, Holland, 1967-69; Philips Electrical Ltd, London, 1971-75; Pye of Cambridge Ltd, 1975-79. Member Royal Company of Archers, Queen's Body Guard for Scotland. Contested (U) North Aberdeen, Gen. Election, 1959. *Recreations:* golf, tennis, shooting, photography, vintage cars. *Heir: s* Alexander Dudley Stewart-Clark, *b* 21 Nov. 1960. *Address:* Holmsley House, near Cowden, Kent. *T:* Cowden 541. *Clubs:* White's; Royal Ashdown Golf.

STEWART COX, Maj.-Gen. Arthur George Ernest, DFC 1952; General Officer Commanding Wales, 1978-80; *b* 11 April 1925; *s* of Lt-Col Arthur Stewart Cox and Mrs Dorothea Stewart Cox, *d* of Maj.-Gen. Sir Edward May; *m* 1953, Mary Pamela, *d* of Hon. George Lyttelton; three *s* one *d*. *Educ:* Marlborough Coll.; Aberdeen Univ. Commissioned RA, 1944; parachutist, RA regts, 1945-50; army pilot, Far East and Korea, 1950-52; ADC to Comdt, RMA Sandhurst, 1954-56; Staff Coll., 1956; SO 99 Gurkha Inf. Bde, 1957-58; SO MoD, Malaya, 1963-65; CO 29 Commando Light Regt, RA, 1965-68; SO Sch. of Artillery, 1968-69; Comdr RA 4th Div., 1969-72; RCDS, 1973; Dep. Dir of Manning (Army), MoD, 1974-76. Col Comdt, RA, 1980-; Hon. Col, 3rd Bn RWF, TAVR, 1980-. *Recreations:* shooting, fishing, lepidoptery, gardening. *Address:* The Old Rectory, Bishopstrow, Warminster, Wilts. *T:* Warminster 214584.

STEWART-JONES, Mrs Richard; *see* Smith, Emma.

STEWART-MOORE, Alexander Wyndham Hume; Chairman, Gallaher Ltd, 1975-79 (Managing Director, 1966-75); Director, American Brands Inc., 1975-79; *b* 14 Feb. 1915; 2nd *s* of late James Stewart-Moore, DL, Ballydivity, Dervock, Co. Antrim, and of Katherine Marion (*née* Jackson); *m* 1948, Magdalene Clare, *y d* of Sir David Richard Llewellyn, 1st Bt, LLD, JP; three *s* one *d*. *Educ:* Shrewsbury. Joined Gallaher Ltd, Nov. 1934. Served War, Royal Artillery (Middle East and Italy), 1939-46. *Recreations:* farming, fishing, gardening. *Address:* Seaport, Portballintrae, Bushmills, Co. Antrim, NI. *T:* Bushmills 31361. *Club:* Ulster.

STEWART-RICHARDSON, Sir Simon (Alaisdair), 17th Bt *cr* 1630; *b* 9 June 1947; *er s* of Sir Ian Rorie Hay Stewart-Richardson, 16th Bt, and of Audrey Meryl (who *m* 1975, P. A. P. Robertson, *qv*), *e d* of late Claude Odlum; *S* father, 1969. *Educ:* Trinity College, Glenalmond. *Heir: b* Ninian Rorie Stewart-Richardson, *b* 20 Jan. 1949. *Address:* Lynedale House, Longcross, near Chertsey, Surrey KT16 0DP. *T:* Ottershaw 2329.

STEWART-SMITH, Rev. Canon David Cree, MA; *b* 22 May 1913; 3rd *s* of late Thomas Stewart Stewart-Smith, JP, Heathlands, Kinver, Staffs, and Mabel (*née* McDougall); *m* 1943, Kathleen Georgiana Maule Ffinch, *d* of Rev. K. M. Ffinch, Ifield, Kent. *Educ:* Marlborough; King's Coll., Cambridge; Cuddesdon Theol. College. BA 1939, MA 1943. Vicar-Choral and Sacrist, York Minster, 1944-49; Vicar of Shadwell, Leeds, 1949-52; Warden, Brasted Place Coll., 1952-63; Dean of St George's Cath., Jerusalem, and Administrator of St George's Coll., 1964-67; Commissary for Archbishop in Jerusalem, 1968-76; Archdeacon of Bromley and Hon. Canon of Rochester, 1968-69; Archdeacon of Rochester and Canon Residentiary of Rochester Cathedral, 1969-76; Hon. Canon of Rochester, 1976-78; Canon Emeritus, 1978-; Director of Ordinands, dio. Rochester, 1968-74; Mem., C of E Pensions Bd, 1970-; a Church Commissioner, 1973-78; Home Sec., Jerusalem and Middle East Church Assoc., 1976-78; Fellow of Woodard Corp.: Northern Div., 1949-52; Southern Div., 1959-64. *Recreations:* architecture, music, travel, collecting. *Address:* Flat 3, 7 Fortfield Terrace, Sidmouth, Devon EX10 8NT. *T:* Sidmouth 4440. *Club:* United Oxford & Cambridge University.

STEWART-SMITH, (Dudley) Geoffrey; Director, Foreign Affairs Research Institute, since 1976; *b* 28 Dec. 1933; *s* of Dudley Cautley Stewart-Smith; *m* 1956, Kay Mary; three *s*. *Educ:* Winchester; RMA Sandhurst. Regular Officer, The Black Watch, 1952-60. Director Foreign Affairs Circle; Freedom Communications Internat. News Agency; Editor, East-West Digest; Dir, Foreign Affairs Publishing Co.; Financial Times, 1968. MP (C) Derbyshire, Belper, 1970-Feb 1974. *Publications:* The Defeat of Communism, 1964; No Vision Here: Non-Military Warfare in Britain, 1966; (ed) Brandt and the Destruction of NATO, 1973; The Struggle for Freedom, 1980; contribs to various foreign, defence and communist affairs jls at home and overseas. *Recreations:* walking, swimming, shooting and stalking. *Address:* Church House, Petersham, Surrey. *T:* 01-940 2885.

STEWART-WILSON, Lt-Col Blair Aubyn; Deputy Master of the Household and Equerry to Her Majesty, since 1976; *b* 17 July 1929; *s* of late Aubyn Wilson and late Muriel Stewart; *m* 1962, Helen Mary Fox; three *d*. *Educ:* Eton; Sandhurst. Commnd Scots Guards, 1949; served with Regt in UK, Germany and Far East; Adjutant 2nd Bn, 1955-57; ADC to Viscount Cobham, Governor General and C-in-C, New Zealand, 1957-59; Equerry to late Duke of Gloucester, 1960-62; Regtl Adjutant, 1966-68; GSO1, Foreign Liaison Sect. (Army), MoD, 1970-73; Defence, Military and Air Attaché,

British Embassy, Vienna, 1975-76. *Address:* 3 Browning Close, W9 1BW. *T:* 01-286 9891; Thorn Falcon House, Taunton, Somerset. *T:* Henlade 442248. *Clubs:* Turf, Pratt's.

STEWARTSON, Prof. Keith, FRS 1965; Goldsmid Professor of Mathematics, University College London, since 1964; *b* 20 Sept. 1925; *s* of late G. C. Stewartson and M. Stewartson (*née* Hyde); *m* 1953, Elizabeth Jean Forrester; two *s* one *d*. *Educ:* Stockton Secondary Sch.; St Catharine's Coll., Cambridge. Lectr in Applied Mathematics at Bristol Univ., 1949-53; Research Fellow in Aeronautics, California Inst. of Technology, 1953-54; Reader in Applied Mathematics at Bristol Univ., 1954-58; Prof. of Applied Mathematics, Durham Univ. (late Durham Colls), 1958-64. Hon. DSc East Anglia, 1979. *Publications:* Laminar Compressible Boundary Layers, 1964; papers in mathematical and aeronautical journals. *Address:* 67 Southway, NW11 6SB. *T:* 01-458 3534.

STEYN, Johan Van Zyl, QC 1979; barrister-at-law; *b* 15 Aug. 1932; *s* of Izak Van Zyl Steyn and Janet Lacey Steyn (*née* Blignaut); *m* Susan Leonore (*née* Lewis); two *s* two *d* by previous *m*. *Educ:* Jan van Riebeeck Sch., Cape Town, S Africa; Univ. of Stellenbosch, S Africa (BA, LLB); University Coll., Oxford (MA). Cape Province Rhodes Scholar, 1955; commenced practice at S African Bar, 1958; Sen. Counsel of Supreme Court of SA, 1970; settled in UK, called to the Bar, Lincoln's Inn, and commenced practice at English Bar, 1973. *Address:* 4 Essex Court, Temple, EC4Y 9AJ. *T:* 01-583 9191; Hazelbourne, Hitchen Hatch Lane, Sevenoaks, Kent. *T:* Sevenoaks 450512.

STEYN, Hon. (Stephanus Jacobus) Marais, DMS 1981; South African Ambassador to the Court of St James's, since 1980; *b* 25 Dec. 1914; *m* 1940, Susanne Moolman; two *s* two *d*. *Educ:* Univ. of Cape Town (BA); Univ. of the Witwatersrand (LLB). Journalist, various newspapers and on staff of State Information Office, 1938-42; Sec., United Party, Witwatersrand, 1942-48 (Asst Chief Sec., 1946-48); Opposition MP representing consecutively constituencies of Alberton, Vereeniging and Yeoville, specialising in labour and transport matters, 1948-73; National Party MP for Turffontein, 1974-79; Minister of: Indian Affairs and Tourism, 1975; Community Develt, 1976-79; Community Develt, Coloured Relations and Indian Affairs, 1979. *Recreations:* bowls, chess, grandchildren. *Address:* South African Embassy, Trafalgar Square, WC2N 5DP. *T:* 01-930 4488. *Clubs:* Travellers'; City and Civil Service (Cape Town).

STIBBE, Philip Godfrey, JP; MA; Head Master of Norwich School, since 1975; *b* 20 July 1921; *m* 1956, Mary Joy, *d* of late Canon C. G. Thornton; two *s* one *d*. *Educ:* Mill Hill Sch.; Merton Coll., Oxford (MA). Served War of 1939-45; joined Royal Sussex Regt, 1941; seconded King's (Liverpool) Regt, 1942; 1st Wingate Expedn into Burma (wounded, despatches), 1943; POW, 1943-45. Asst Master, 1948-75, Housemaster, 1953-74, Bradfield Coll. JP Norwich, 1979. *Publication:* Return via Rangoon, 1947. *Recreations:* people, places, books. *Address:* 16 The Close, Norwich NR1 4DZ. *T:* Norwich 25425. *Club:* East India, Devonshire, Sports and Public Schools.

STIBBS, Prof. Douglas Walter Noble, MSc Sydney, DPhil Oxon; FRAS, FRSE; Napier Professor of Astronomy and Director of the University Observatory, University of St Andrews, since 1959; *b* 17 Feb. 1919; 2nd *s* of Edward John Stibbs, Sydney, NSW; *m* 1949, Margaret Lilian Calvert, BSc, DipEd (Sydney), AID, *er d* of Rev. John Calvert, Sydney, NSW; two *d*. *Educ:* Sydney High Sch.; Univ. of Sydney; New College, Oxford. Deas Thomson Scholar, Sch. of Physics, Univ. of Sydney, 1940; BSc (Sydney), 1st Class Hons, Univ. Medal in Physics, 1942; MSc (Sydney), 1943; DPhil (Oxon), 1954. Johnson Memorial Prize and Gold Medal for Advancement of Astronomy and Meteorology, Oxford Univ., 1956. Res. Asst, Commonwealth Solar Observatory, Canberra, ACT, 1940-42; Asst Lectr, Dept of Mathematics and Physics, New England University Coll., Armidale, NSW (now the Univ. of New England), 1942-45; Scientific Officer and Sen. Scientific Officer, Commonwealth Observatory, Canberra, ACT, 1945-51; Radcliffe Travelling Fellow in Astronomy, Radcliffe Observatory, Pretoria, S Africa, and Univ. Observatory, Oxford, 1951-54; PSO, UKAEA, 1955-59; Vis. Prof. of Astrophysics, Yale Univ. Observatory, 1966-67; British Council Vis. Prof., Univ. of Utrecht, 1968; Prof., Collège de France, 1975-76. Member: Internat. Astronomical Union, 1951- (Chm. Finance Cttee, 1964-67, 1973-76, 1976-79); Amer. Astronomical Soc., 1956-73; Adv. Cttee on Meteorology for Scotland, 1960-69, 1972-75, 1978-80; Board of Visitors, Royal Greenwich Observatory, 1963-65; Council RAS, 1964-67, 1970-73 (Vice-Pres., 1972-73), Editorial Board, 1970-73; Council, RSE, 1970-72; National Cttee for Astronomy, 1964-76; SRC Cttees for Royal Greenwich Observatory, 1966-70, and Royal Observatory, Edinburgh, 1966-76, Chm., 1970-76; SRC Astronomy, Space and Radio Bd, 1970-76; SRC, 1972-76; S African Astron. Obs. Adv. Cttee, 1972-76; Chairman: Astronomy Policy and Grants Cttee, 1972-74; Astronomy II Cttee, 1974-75; Centre National de la Recherche Scientifique Cttee, Obs. de Haute Provence, 1973-82. Mem. New Coll. Soc., 1953-. *Publications:* The Outer Layers of a Star (with Sir Richard Woolley), 1953; contrib. Theoretical Astrophysics and Astronomy in Monthly Notices of RAS and other jls. *Recreations:* music, ornithology, photography, golf. *Address:* University Observatory, Buchanan Gardens, St Andrews, Fife KY16 9LZ. *T:* St Andrews 72643. *Club:* Royal and Ancient (St Andrews).

STIFF, Rt. Rev. Hugh Vernon; Rector of St James Cathedral and Dean of Toronto, since 1974; Assistant Bishop, Diocese of Toronto, since 1977; *b* 15

Sept. 1916; unmarried. *Educ:* Univ. of Toronto (BA); Trinity Coll., Toronto (LTh). BD General Synod; Hon. DD, Trinity Coll., Toronto. Bishop of Keewatin, 1969-74. *Address:* 65 Church Street, Toronto, Ontario, Canada.

STIGLITZ, Prof. Joseph Eugene, PhD; Professor of Economics, Princeton University, since 1979; *b* 9 Feb. 1943; *m* M. J. Hannaway; two *s* one *d*. *Educ:* Amherst Coll. (BA 1964); MIT (PhD 1966); Cambridge Univ. (MA 1970). Professor of Economics: Yale Univ. 1970-74; Stanford Univ., 1974-76; Drummond Prof. of Political Economy, Oxford Univ. and All Souls Coll., 1976-79. Fellowships: Nat. Sci. Foundn, 1964-65; Fulbright, 1965-66; SSRC Faculty, 1969-70; Guggenheim, 1969-70; Oskar Morgenstern Distinguished Fellowship, Mathematica and Inst. for Advanced Study, Princeton, 1978-79. Consultant: Nat. Sci. Foundn, 1972-75; Ford Foundn Energy Policy Study, 1973; Dept of Labor (Pensions and Labor Turnover), 1974; Dept of Interior (Offshore Oil Leasing Programs), 1975; Federal Energy Admin (Intertemporal Biases in Market Allocation of Natural Resources), 1975-; World Bank (Cost Benefit Analysis; Urban Rural Migration; Natural Resources), 1975-; Electric Power Res. Inst., 1976-; OECD; Office of Fair Trading; Federal Trade Commn; Inter-American Development Bank; Bell Laboratories. Gen. Editor, Econometric Soc. Reprint Series; Associate Editor: Jl of Economic Theory, 1968-73; American Economic Rev., 1972-75; Co-editor, Jl of Public Economics, 1968-; American Editor, Rev. of Economic Studies, 1968-76. Fellow, Econometric Soc., 1972 (Sec./Treasurer, 1972-75). Hon. MA Yale, 1970; Hon. DHL Amherst, 1974. John Bates Clark Medal, Amer. Econ. Assoc. *Publications:* (ed) Collected Scientific Papers of P. A. Samuelson, 1965; (ed with H. Uzawa) Readings in Modern Theory of Economic Growth, 1969; (with A. B. Atkinson) Lectures in Public Finance, 1980; (with D. Newbery) The Economic Impact of Price Stabilization, 1980; contribs on economics of growth, development, natural resources, information, uncertainty, imperfect competition, corporate finance and public finance in Amer. Econ. Rev., Qly Jl of Econs, Jl of Pol. Econ., Econometrica, Internat. Econ. Rev., Econ. Jl, Rev. of Econ. Studies, Jl of Public Econs, Jl of Econ. Theory, Oxford Econ. Papers. *Address:* 139 Broadmead, Princeton, NJ, USA.

STILES, Walter Stanley, OBE 1946; FRS 1957; PhD, DSc; formerly Deputy Chief Scientific Officer, The National Physical Laboratory, Teddington, retired 1961; *b* 15 June 1901; *s* of Walter Stiles and Elizabeth Catherine (*née* Smith); *m* 1928, Pauline Frida Octavia, *d* of Judge Henrik Brendstrup, Hillerød, Denmark; no *c*. *Educ:* University College, London; St John's College, Cambridge. Andrews Scholar, University Coll., London, 1918. Demonstrator in Physics, 1920-22; PhD London 1929, DSc London 1939; Carpenter Medallist, London Univ., 1944. Technical Officer, RN Signal School, 1923-25; Scientific Officer, Nat. Physical Lab., 1925-61. Gen. Sec. Internat. Commn on Illumination, 1928-31; Vice-President Physical Soc., 1948-49; President, Illuminating Engineering Soc., 1960, Gold Medallist, 1967; Chm. Colour Group of Physical Soc., 1949-51, Newton Lectr, 1967; Thomas Young Orator (Physical Soc.), 1955; Regents' Lectr (UCLA), 1964; Tillyer Medallist (Optical Society of America), 1965; Finsen Medallist (Congr. Internat. de Photobiologie), 1968. *Publications:* Thermionic Emission, 1932; Color Science (with G. Wyszecki), 1967; Mechanisms of Colour Vision, 1978; many papers on illuminating engineering and physiological optics in Proc. Royal Soc., Trans Illum. Eng Soc., etc. *Recreation:* painting. *Address:* 89 Richmond Hill Court, Richmond, Surrey. *T:* 01-940 4334.

STIMSON, Robert Frederick; HM Diplomatic Service; Head of Home Inspectorate, since 1982; *b* 16 May 1939; *s* of Frederick Henry and Gladys Alma Stimson (*née* Joel); *m* 1961, Margaret Faith Kerry; two *s* one *d*. *Educ:* Rendcomb Coll.; Queen Mary Coll., London (BSc First Cl. Hons; MSc (by thesis) mathematical physics). HM Diplomatic Service: FO, 1966-67; Saigon, 1967-68; Singapore, 1968-70; Cabinet Office, 1970-73; Mexico City, 1973-75; FCO, 1975-80; Counsellor, East Berlin, 1980-81; Inspector, 1981-82. Order of Aztec Eagle, Mexico, 1975. *Publications:* contrib. Jl Physics and Chemistry of Solids. *Address:* c/o Foreign and Commonwealth Office, SW1A 2AH.

STINSON, Sir Charles (Alexander), KBE 1979 (OBE 1962); Minister of Finance, Fiji, 1972-79, retired; *b* 22 June 1919; *s* of William John Bolton Stinson and Ella Josephine (*née* Griffiths); *m* 1946, Mollie, *d* of Albert Dean; two *s* one *d*. *Educ:* Levuka Public Sch.; Suva Grammar Sch. Morris Hedstrom Ltd, Fiji, 1935-38; Emperor Gold Mining Co. Ltd, Fiji, 1939-40; Fiji RNVR, 1940-45; Man. Dir, Stinsons Ltd, 1946-66. Elected to Suva City Council, 1952; Mayor of Suva, 1959-66; elected Gen. Mem. for Suva, 1964; Mem. for Communications, Works and Tourism, 1966-70; Minister for Communications, Works and Tourism, 1970-72. *Recreations:* fishing, flying, boating, golf. *Address:* PO Box 798, Suva, Fiji. *T:* Suva 311287. *Clubs:* Defence, Royal Suva Yacht, Fiji Golf, Fiji (Suva); Northern (Lautoka); Royal Naval Sailing Association.

STINSON, David John; His Honour Judge David Stinson; a Circuit Judge (formerly County Court Judge), since 1969; Chancellor, Diocese of Carlisle, since 1971; *b* 22 Feb. 1921; *s* of late Henry John Edwin Stinson, MC, MA, LLB, Beckenham, Kent (sometime Chief Commoner of City of London, solicitor), and late Margaret Stinson (*née* Little); *m* 1950, Eleanor Judith (*née* Chance); two *s* two *d* (and one *s* decd). *Educ:* Eastbourne Coll.; Emmanuel Coll., Cambridge. MA 1946; Jesters Club, 1949 (Rugby Fives). Served War of 1939-45: Essex Yeomanry, Captain, RA, and Air OP, 1941-46 (despatches). Called to Bar, Middle Temple, 1947; Dep. Chm., Herts QS, 1965-71; Suffolk

and Essex County Court Circuit, 1973-. Liveryman, Worshipful Co. of Needlemakers. *Recreations:* bird-watching, sailing. *Address:* The Maltings, Waldringfield, Woodbridge, Suffolk IP12 4QZ. *T:* Waldringfield 280. *Clubs:* Army and Navy; Waldringfield Sailing.

STIRLING, Sir Alexander (John Dickson), KBE 1981; CMG 1976; HM Diplomatic Service; Ambassador to the Tunisian Republic, since 1981; *b* 20 Oct. 1926; *e s* of late Brig. A. Dickson Stirling, DSO, MB, ChB, DPH, and of Isobel Stirling, MA, DipEd, DipPsych, *d* of late Rev. J. C. Matthew (former senior Presidency Chaplain, Bombay); *m* 1955, Alison Mary, *y d* of Gp Capt. A. P. Campbell, CBE; two *s* two *d*. *Educ:* Edinburgh Academy; Lincoln Coll., Oxford (MA). RAFVR, 1945-48 (Egypt, 1945-47). Entered Foreign Office, 1951; Lebanon, 1952; British Embassy, Cairo, 1952-56 (Oriental Sec., 1955-56); FO, 1956-59; First Sec., British Embassy, Baghdad, 1959-62; First Sec. and Consul, Amman, 1962-64; First Sec., British Embassy, Santiago, 1965-67; FO, 1967-69; British Political Agent, Bahrain, 1969-71, Ambassador, 1971-72; Counsellor, Beirut, 1972-75; RCDS 1976; Ambassador to Iraq, 1977-80. *Address:* c/o Williams & Glyn's Bank Ltd, Kirkland House, Whitehall, SW1.

STIRLING, Angus Duncan Æneas; Deputy Director-General, The National Trust, since 1979; *b* 10 Dec. 1933; *s* of Duncan Alexander Stirling, *qv* ; *m* 1959, Armyne Morar Helen Schofield, *e d* of W. G. B. Schofield; one *s* two *d*. *Educ:* Eton Coll.; Trinity Coll., Cambridge; London Univ. (Extra Mural) (Dip. History of Art). Christie, Manson and Woods Ltd, 1954-57; Lazard Bros and Co. Ltd, 1957-66; Asst Dir, Paul Mellon Foundn for British Art, 1966-69 (Jt Dir, 1969-70); Dep. Sec.-General, Arts Council of GB, 1971-79. Dir, Royal Opera House, Covent Garden, 1979-; Chm., Friends of Covent Garden, 1981-; Member: Crafts Council, 1980-; Council of Management, Byam Shaw Sch. of Art, 1965-; Management Cttee, Courtauld Inst. of Art, 1981-; Exec. Cttee, London Symphony Orchestra, 1979-; Bd of Dirs, Old Vic Theatre Co. (Prospect), 1980-81; Bd of Governors, Live Music Now, 1982-. *Recreations:* music, travel, walking. *Address:* 25 Ladbroke Grove, W11. *T:* 01-727 8500. *Clubs:* Garrick, Brooks's.

STIRLING, (Archibald) David, DSO 1942; OBE 1946; Chairman, Television International Enterprises Ltd; *b* 15 Nov. 1915; *s* of late Brigadier-General Archibald Stirling of Keir, and Hon. Mrs Margaret Stirling, OBE, 4th *d* of 13th Baron Lovat. *Educ:* Ampleforth College, Yorks; (for a brief period) Cambridge University. In Sept. 1939 was Mem. SRO, Scots Guards and served with that Regt for first six months of War when he was transferred to No 3 Commando (Brigade of Guards) and went out with this unit to Middle East; subseq. served with First SAS Regt (POW, 1943-45). President, Capricorn Africa Society, 1947-59, living at that time in Africa based on Salisbury and Nairobi. Officer, Légion d'Honneur; Officer, Orange Nassau. *Address:* 22 South Audley Street, W1. *T:* 01-499 9252. *Clubs:* White's, Turf, Pratt's.

STIRLING, Sir Charles (Norman), KCMG 1955 (CMG 1941); KCVO 1957; *b* 19 Nov. 1901; *er s* of late F. H. Stirling, Victoria, British Columbia; *m* 1950, Ann, *o d* of J. H. Moore; one *s* two *d*. *Educ:* Wellington College; Corpus Christi College, Oxford. Third Secretary, Diplomatic Service, 1925; Second Secretary, 1930; First Secretary, 1937; Head of a Department in Ministry of Economic Warfare, 1939-42; Acting Counsellor in the Foreign Office, 1942; Counsellor, British Embassy, Lisbon, 1946; Consul-General, Tangier, 1949-51; Ambassador to Chile, 1951-54; Ambassador to Portugal, 1955-60. *Recreation:* fishing. *Address:* 17 Park Row, Farnham, Surrey. *Club:* Travellers'.

STIRLING, David; *see* Stirling, Archibald D.

STIRLING, Duncan Alexander; *b* 6 Oct. 1899; 4th *s* of late Major William Stirling, JP, DL, of Fairburn, Ross-shire, and Charlotte Eva, *d* of late Æneas Mackintosh, Daviot, Inverness-shire; *m* 1926, Lady Marjorie Murray, *e d* of 8th Earl of Dunmore, VC, DSO, MVO; two *s*. *Educ:* Harrow; New College, Oxford. Coldstream Guards, 1918 and again 1940-43. Partner, H. S. Lefevre & Co., Merchant Bankers, 1929-49; Director: Westminster Bank, and Westminster Foreign Bank, 1935-69 (Chm. 1962-69); National Westminster Bank, 1968-74 (Chm., 1968-69); London Life Association, 1935-80 (Pres., 1951-65). Pres., Inst. of Bankers, 1964-66; Chm., Cttee of London Clearing Bankers and Pres., British Bankers' Assoc., 1966-68. Prime Warden Fishmongers Co., 1954-55. *Address:* 28 St James's Place, SW1; Lake House, Avington, Winchester, Hants. *Club:* Brooks's.
See also A. D. Æ. *Stirling.*

STIRLING of Garden, Lt-Col James, TD; DL; FRICS; *b* 8 Sept. 1930; *s* of Col Archibald Stirling of Garden, OBE; *m* 1958, Fiona Janetta Sophia Wood Parker; two *s* two *d*. *Educ:* Rugby; Trinity Coll., Cambridge. BA; Dip. Estate Management. Partner, K. Ryden and Partners, Chartered Surveyors, 1962-; Director: Local Bd, Scotland and N Ireland, Woolwich Building Soc., 1973-; Scottish Widows and Life Insurance Fund, 1975-. Chm., Highland TAVR Assoc., 1982. Vice-Lieutenant of Stirling, 1979-. Hon. Col, 3/51st Highland Volunteers, TA, 1979. *Address:* Garden, Buchlyvie, Stirlingshire. *T:* Buchlyvie 212. *Club:* New (Edinburgh).

STIRLING, James Frazer, ARIBA 1950; Architect; *b* 1926; *s* of Joseph Stirling and Louisa Frazer; *m* 1966, Mary, *d* of Morton Shand and Sybil Sissons; one *s* two *d*. *Educ:* Quarry Bank High Sch., Liverpool; Liverpool Sch.

of Art, 1942. Served War of 1939-45: Lieut, Black Watch and Paratroops (D-Day Landing). Sch. of Architecture, Liverpool Univ., 1945-50. With Assoc. of Town Planning and Regional Research, London, 1950-52; worked for Lyons, Israel and Ellis, London, 1953-56; entered a series of architectural competitions, and Mem. ICA Indep. Gp, 1952-56. Private practice, 1956- (Partners: James Gowan until 1963 and Michael Wilford, 1971-). Projects include: Flats at Ham Common, 1955-58; Churchill Coll. Comp., 1958 (finalist); Selwyn Coll., Cambridge, 1959; Leicester Univ. Engrg Bldg, 1959-63 (USA Reynolds Award); History Faculty, Cambridge Univ., 1964-67; Andrew Melville Hall, St Andrews Univ., 1964-68; Dorman Long Steel Co. HQ, 1965; Runcorn New Town Housing, 1968-; Florey Bldg at Queen's Coll., Oxford, 1967-71; Olivetti Trng Sch., Surrey, 1969-. Visiting teacher at: Architectural Assoc., London, 1955; Regent Street Polytechnic, London, 1956-57; Cambridge Univ. Sch. of Architecture, 1958; RIBA Lecture (An Architect's Approach to Architecture), 1965; lectures in Europe and USA, 1960-; Charles Davenport Visiting Prof., Yale Univ. Sch. of Architecture, USA, 1970. Re-development plan of West Mid-Town Manhatten, for New York City Planning Commn, USA, 1968-69; invited UK Architect, in internat. limited competitions for Govt/United Nations low cost housing for Peru, 1969, and Siemens AG Computer Centre Munich, 1970; buildings in Iran, Berlin and Stuttgart, 1977; Museum buildings for Univs of Harvard, Columbia and Rice, Houston, 1979. Hon. Mem., Akademie der Kunst, Berlin, 1969; Hon. FAIA, 1976; Hon. Dr RCA, 1979. Exhibitions: "James Stirling—Three Buildings", at Museum of Modern Art, NY, USA, 1969; (drawings) RIBA Heinz Gall., 1974 (associated pubn, James Stirling, 1974); Venice, 1976; Minneapolis and NY, 1977. BBC/Arts Council film, James Stirling's Architecture, 1973. Brunner Award, USA, 1976; Aalto Medal, Finland, 1978; Royal Gold Medal, RIBA, 1980; Pritzker Prize, 1981. *Relevant publication:* James Stirling: Buildings and Projects, 1950-74, 1975. *Address:* 75 Gloucester Place, W1H 3PF.

STIRLING, John Bertram, OC 1970; Chancellor, Queen's University, Kingston, Ontario, 1960-73; *b* 29 Nov. 1888; *s* of Dr James A. Stirling and Jessie Bertram, Picton, Ont; *m* 1928, Emily P., *d* of Col and Mrs E. T. Sturdee, Saint John, NB; one *d. Educ:* Queen's University, Kingston, Canada. BA 1909, BSc 1911, Queen's Univ., Kingston. Resident Engineer, Chipman and Power, Cons. Engineers, Toronto, 1911-15; with E. G. M. Cape and Co. Ltd from 1915; Field Engineer, 1915; Supt 1924; Gen. Supt, 1930; Vice-Pres., 1940; Chm., 1960-65. President: Canadian Construction Assoc., 1942; Montreal Board of Trade, 1950; Engineering Inst. of Canada, 1952 (Chm., Nat. Honours and Awards Cttee to 1981). Hon. LLD: Queen's, Kingston, 1951; Toronto, 1961; Hon. DSc: Royal Mil. Coll., Canada, 1962; McGill, 1963. Hon. Col 3rd Field Regt Royal Can. Engrs. Sir John Kennedy Medal of Eng. Inst. of Canada, 1954; Montreal Medal, Queen's Univ. Alumni Assoc., 1955; Julian Smith Medal, Eng. Inst. of Canada, 1963. *Recreations:* sailing, country life, music. *Address:* 10 Richelieu Place, Montreal, Quebec H3G 1E7, Canada. *Club:* Saint James's (Montreal).

STIRLING, Rear-Adm. Michael Grote; Agent-General for British Columbia in the United Kingdom and Europe, 1968-75; *b* 29 June 1915; *s* of late Hon. Grote Stirling and late Mabel Katherine (*née* Brigstocke), Kelowna, British Columbia; *m* 1942, Sheelagh Kathleen Russell; two *s* one *d. Educ:* Shawnigan Lake School, BC; RNC Greenwich. Cadet, RCN, 1933; HMS Frobisher for training till 1934, then as Midshipman and Sub-Lt in RN, returning Canada Jan. 1938; Ships of RCN until 1941; specialized in Signals at HM Signal School, Portsmouth, then Home Fleet; Deputy Director, Signal Div., Naval Service HQ, Ottawa, 1942-43; SSO to C-in-C, Canadian North-West Atlantic, 1943-44; Commanded destroyers, 1944-46; Director Naval Communications, rank of Commander, 1949-51; promoted Captain and staff of Supreme Allied Commander Atlantic, Norfolk, Va, 1953-55; Commanded HMCS Cornwallis, 1955-57; 2nd Cdn Escort Sqdn, 1957-58; Naval Member of Directing Staff, Nat. Defence College as Commodore, 1958-61; Senior Canadian Officer Afloat, 1961-62; Chief of Naval Personnel, 1962-64; Maritime Comdr, Pacific, 1964-66. Rear-Adm. 1962. Director: Univ. of Victoria Foundation, 1967-68; Schenley Canada Inc., 1980-. *Recreations:* golf, ski-ing. *Address:* 302-1280 Newport Avenue, Victoria, BC V8S 5E7, Canada. *Club:* Victoria Golf (Victoria, BC).

STIRLING, Viola Henrietta Christian, CBE 1947; TD 1951; DL; *b* 3 June 1907; *d* of late Charles Stirling of Gargunnock. *Educ:* Queen Ethelburga's Sch., Harrogate; Lady Margaret Hall, Oxford (BA). Joined Auxiliary Territorial Service, 1939; Deputy Director ATS Scottish Command, 1945; released 1949. Member: Finance Committee, ATS Benevolent Fund, 1948-64; of Stirling and Clackmannan Hospitals Board of Management, 1948-64; selected military member TA & AFA, County of Stirling, 1948-68; Hon. Colonel 317 (Sc. Comd) Bn WRAC/TA, 1959-62. Member of Stirling County Council, 1958-67; DL Co. of Stirling, 1965. *Address:* Gargunnock, Stirlingshire. *T:* Gargunnock 202.

STIRLING-HAMILTON, Sir Bruce, 13th Bt *cr* 1673; Training Manager, Seismograph Service (England) Ltd, since 1979; *b* 5 Aug. 1940; *s* of Captain Sir Robert William Stirling-Hamilton, 12th Bt, JP, DL, RN (retd), and of Eileen, *d* of late Rt Rev. H. K. Southwell, CMG; *S* father, 1982; *m* 1968, Stephanie, *d* of Dr William Campbell, LRCP, LRCS; one *s* one *d. Educ:* Nautical College, Pangbourne; RMA Sandhurst. Commissioned, Queen's Own Highlanders (Seaforth and Camerons), 1961; Lieut 1963; ADC to GOC 51st (Highland) Div., 1964; Captain 1967; resigned commn, 1971. Personnel Officer (Sales and Marketing), Kimberly-Clark Ltd, 1971; Senior Personnel

Officer, Seismograph Service (England) Ltd, 1974. *Heir: s* Malcolm William Bruce Stirling-Hamilton, *b* 6 Aug. 1979. *Address:* c/o Williams & Glyn's Bank Ltd, Holt's Branch, Kirkland House, Whitehall, SW1A 2EB.

STIRRAT, Prof. Gordon Macmillan, MD, FRCOG; Professor of Obstetrics and Gynaecology, University of Bristol, since 1982; *b* 12 March 1940; *s* of Alexander and Caroline Mary Stirrat; *m* 1965, Janeen Mary (*née* Brown); three *d. Educ:* Hutcheson's Boys' Grammar Sch., Glasgow; Glasgow Univ. (MB, ChB). MA Oxon, MD London. FRCOG 1981. Jun. hosp. doctor appts, Glasgow and environs, and London, 1964-71; Lectr, St Mary's Hosp. Med. Sch., London, 1971-75; Clinical Reader, Univ. of Oxford, 1975-81. *Publications:* Legalised Abortion—the Continuing Dilemma, 1979; Obstetrics Pocket Consultant, 1981; (jtly) You and Your Baby—a Mother's Guide to Health, 1982. *Recreations:* fly-fishing, model galleons, family. *Address:* Malpas Lodge, 24 Henbury Road, Westbury-on-Trym, Bristol BS9 3HJ. *T:* Bristol 505310. *Club:* Royal Society of Medicine.

STOATE, Isabel Dorothy; HM Diplomatic Service, retired; Counsellor, Foreign and Commonwealth Office, 1980-82; *b* 31 May 1927; *d* of William Maurice Stoate and Dorothy Evelyn Stoate (*née* French). *Educ:* Talbot Heath Sch., Bournemouth; St Andrews Univ. Athlone Press, London Univ., 1950-52; joined HM Diplomatic Service, 1952; served Cyprus, Vienna, Buenos Aires, Tokyo, Athens, Rio de Janeiro and FCO, 1952-80. *Recreations:* travel, tapestry. *Address:* 177 Gloucester Street, Cirencester, Glos. *Club:* Naval and Military.

STOBART, Patrick Desmond, CBE 1976 (MBE 1950); HM Diplomatic Service, retired; Member of Secretariat, International Primary Aluminium Institute, since 1979; *b* 14 Feb. 1920; *s* of late Reginald and Eva Stobart; *m* 1951, Sheila (marr. diss. 1973), *d* of late A. W. Brown, Belfast; three *s* one *d. Educ:* Cathedral and Cleveland House Schools, Salisbury; St Edmund Hall, Oxford. Served Royal Artillery and Wilts Regiment, 1940-46. Tübingen University, 1946; Political Officer, Trucial Oman, 1947; Chancery, Bonn, 1951-53; FO, 1953-54; Consul, Benghazi, 1954-58; FO, 1958-60; Commercial Counsellor, British Embassy, Helsinki, 1960-64, Copenhagen, 1964-66; Consul-General, Gothenburg, 1966-68; seconded to Aero-Engine Div., Rolls-Royce Ltd, 1968-69; Gwilym Gibbon Research Fellow, Nuffield College, Oxford, 1969-70; Head of Export Promotion Dept, FCO, 1970-71; Consul-Gen., Zürich, 1971-75; seconded to Commercial Relations and Exports Div., DoT, 1976-79. *Recreations:* history, sailing, fishing. *Address:* 44B Manor View, Finchley, N3. *T:* 01-346 7322. *Club:* Travellers'.

STOBY, Sir Kenneth Sievewright, Kt 1961; Chairman, Guyana Match Co. Ltd; Director, Shawinigan Engineering (Guyana) Co. Ltd; *b* 19 Oct. 1903; *s* of late Mr and Mrs W. S. Stoby; *m* 1935, Eunice Badley; one *s* one *d. Educ:* Christ Church Sch., Georgetown; Queen's Coll., Georgetown. Called to Bar, Lincoln's Inn; private practice until 1940; seconded Dep. Controller of Prices, 1944; seconded again, 1947, Controller Supplies and Prices; acted Legal Draftsman; Chairman several Boards and Committees; Magistrate Nigeria, 1948; Registrar of Deeds and Supreme Court, British Guiana, 1950; Puisne Judge, 1953; Chief Justice, Barbados, 1959-65; Chancellor of the Judiciary, Guyana, 1966-68. Pro-Chancellor, Univ. of Guyana, 1966-. *Address:* 7A New Providence, East Bank, Demerara, Guyana.

STOCK, Prof. Francis Edgar, CBE 1977 (OBE 1961); FRCS, FACS; Principal and Vice-Chancellor of the University of Natal, South Africa, 1970-77; now Emeritus Professor; *b* 5 July 1914; *o s* of late Edgar Stephen and Olive Blanche Stock; *m* 1939, Gwendoline Mary Thomas; two *s* one *d. Educ:* Colfe's Grammar Sch., Lewisham; (Sambrooke schol.) King's Coll., London; King's Coll. Hosp., London (Jelf medal, Todd medal and prize in clin. med.; Hygiene and Psychological med. prizes); Univ. of Edinburgh. AKC, MB, BS (Lond), FRCS, FACS, DTMH (Edin.). Ho. Surg., Cancer Research Registrar, Radium Registrar, King's Coll. Hosp., 1938-39; MO, Colonial Med. Service, Nigeria, 1940-45; Lectr and Asst to Prof. of Surg., Univ. of Liverpool, 1946-48; Prof. of Surgery, Univ. of Hong Kong, 1948-63; Cons. in Surg. to Hong Kong Govt, Brit. Mil. Hosps in Hong Kong, and Ruttonjee Sanatorium, 1948-63; Cons. Surg., RN, 1949-70; Dean, Fac. of Med., Univ. of Hong Kong, 1957-62; Med. Coun., Hong Kong, 1957-60; Pro-Vice-Chancellor, Univ. of Hong Kong, 1959-63; McIlrath Guest Prof., Royal Prince Alfred Hosp., Sydney, NSW, 1960 (Hon. Cons. Surg., 1960-); Prof. of Surg., Univ. of Liverpool, 1964-70; Cons. Surg., Liverpool Royal Infirmary and Liverpool Regional Hosp. Bd, 1964-70; Dean, Fac. of Med., Univ. of Liverpool, 1969-70. Visiting Prof. or Lectr: Univs of Alberta, Edinburgh, Qld, Singapore, W Australia, QUB, State Univ. of NY. Brit. Council Lectr: in Thailand, Burma, Fiji, Mauritius; Hunterian Prof., RCS London, 1948 and 1951. Member: BMA (Council 1964-69; Bd of Science and Educn, 1978-80); Bd of Governors, United Liverpool Hosps, 1967-70; Med. Adv. Council and Chm. Techn. Adv. Cttee on Surg., Liverpool Reg. Hosp. Bd, 1964-70; Gen. Med. Council, 1969-70; Med. Appeals Tribunals, Liverpool and N Wales, 1966-70; Council, Edgewood Coll. of Education, 1976-77; Univs Adv. Council, 1976-; Cttee of Univ. Principals, 1970-77 (Chm., 1976-77). Examr in Surgery: to Univs of Edinburgh, Glasgow, Liverpool, Hong Kong, Malaya, Singapore and NUI, at various times, 1949-70; to Soc. of Apothecaries, 1958-60; Mem. Ct of Examrs, RCS, 1965-69. Sen. Fellow, Assoc. of Surgeons of GB and Ire.; Sen. Mem. Pan Pacific Surg. Assoc. (past Mem. Coun. and Bd of Trustees). Mem., Board of Control, Nat. Inst. of Metallurgy, 1975-77. Liveryman, Soc. of Apothecaries. Hon. FACCP. *Publications:* Surgical Principles (with J. Moroney), 1968; chapters in: Surgery of Liver and Bile Ducts (ed Smith and Sherlock); Clinical Surgery (ed Rob and Smith); Scientific Foundations of Surgery (ed Wells and Kyle); Abdominal Operations (ed Maingot), and others; numerous articles in scientific jls. *Recreations:* swimming (Univ. of London colours, 1934, Kent Co. colours, 1935), sailing (Pres., Hong Kong Yacht Racing Assoc., 1961-63, Vice-Pres., Far East Yacht Racing Fedn, 1961-62), gardening, photography, music (Dep. Organist, Grouville Parish Church, Jersey). *Address:* Hebe Haven, 7 Old Forge Lane, Fauvic, Jersey, CI. *T:* Central 53269. *Clubs:* Royal Over-Seas League; Royal Hong Kong Yacht (Cdre, 1957-63).

STOCK, Keith L(ievesley), CB 1957; Under Secretary, Department of Economic Affairs, 1965-68, retired; *b* 24 Oct. 1911; *s* of late Cyril Lievesley Stock and Irene Mary Stock (*née* Tomkins); *m* 1937, Joan Katherine Stock (*née* Milne); two *s* one *d*. *Educ:* Charterhouse; New College, Oxford. Petroleum Department, Board of Trade, 1935; Ministry of Fuel and Power, 1942; Imperial Defence College, 1951; Cabinet Office, 1954; Ministry of Fuel and Power, 1955; Min. of Technology, 1964. *Address:* c/o Barclays Bank, Millbank, SW1.

STOCK, Raymond, QC 1964; **His Honour Judge Stock**; a Circuit Judge (formerly Judge of County Courts), since 1971; *b* 1913; *s* of late A. E. and M. E. Stock; *m* 1969, E. Dorothy Thorpe, JP. *Educ:* West Monmouth School; Balliol College, Oxford. Barrister-at-law, Gray's Inn, 1936, Bencher, 1969. Royal Artillery, 1939-45. Recorder: Penzance, 1962-64; Exeter, 1964-66; Southampton, 1966-71; Dep. Chm., Dorset QS, 1964-71. *Address:* Brambridge House, Bishopstoke, Hants. *Clubs:* Athenæum, Royal Automobile.

STOCKDALE, Sir Edmund (Villiers Minshull), 1st Bt *cr* 1960; Kt 1955; JP; *b* 16 April 1903; 2nd *s* of late Major H. M. Stockdale, JP, and Mrs Stockdale, Mears Ashby Hall, Northants; *m* 1937, Hon. Louise Fermor-Hesketh, *er d* of 1st Lord Hesketh; two *s* one *d*. *Educ:* Wellington College. Entered Bank of England, 1921; Assistant to Governors, Reserve Bank of India, 1935; Asst Principal, Bank of England, 1937, Dep. Principal, 1941; pensioned, 1945. Elected Court of Common Council, City of London, 1946, Alderman, Ward of Cornhill, 1948; one of HM Lieuts, City of London, Comr of Assize, 1948-63; Sheriff, City of London 1953; Lord Mayor of London, 1959-60; Chm., Lord Mayor's Appeal Fund, King George's Jubilee Trust, 1960; Mem., Adv. Bd, etc., Holloway Prison, 1948-60. Chairman 1951-53; Member, Holloway Discharged Prisoners Aid Society Cttee, 1964; Vice-President, The Griffins (formerly Holloway DPAS), 1965; Member, Boards: Bridewell, Christ's, Royal Bethlem and Maudsley Hosps, 1948-63; Mem., Emerg. Bed Service Cttee, King Edward Hosp. Fund, 1963-69; Vice-Pres. King Edward's School, Witley, 1960-63; Governor, United Westminster Schools, 1948-54; Wellington College, 1955-74; Eagle House Preparatory, 1964-74. Director, Embankment Trust Ltd, 1948-74, and other Cos. A Church Comr for England, 1962; Mem. Winchester Dioc. Bd of Finance (Exec. Cttee), 1963. Junior Grand Warden (Acting), Grand Lodge of England, 1960-61. Partner, Read Hurst-Brown and Co.; Member: London Stock Exchange, 1946-60; Court of Assistants, Carpenters' Co. (Master, 1970), Glaziers' Co. (Master 1973). JP London (Inner London Sessions), 1968. Grand Officer, Legion of Honour; Grand Cross, Order of Merit, Peru; Grand Official, Order of Mayo, Argentina; Knight Comdr, Order of Crown, Thailand; Order of Triple Power, Nepal; Comdr, Royal Order of North Star, Sweden; KStJ. Gold Medal, Madrid. *Publications:* The Bank of England in 1934, 1966; "Ptolemy Tortoise", 1979. *Recreations:* shooting, drawing. *Heir:* *er s* Thomas Minshull Stockdale [*b* 7 Jan. 1940; *m* 1965, Jacqueline Ha-Van-Vuong; one *s* one *d*]. *Address:* Hoddington House, Upton Grey, Basingstoke. *T:* Long Sutton 437. *Clubs:* Buck's, City Livery.

STOCKDALE, Eric; His Honour Judge Eric Stockdale; a Circuit Judge since 1972; *b* 8 Feb. 1929; *m* 1952, Joan (*née* Berry); two *s*. *Educ:* Collyers Sch., Horsham; London Sch. of Economics. LLB, BSc(Econ.), LLM, PhD. 2nd Lieut, RA, 1947-49. Called to the Bar, Middle Temple, 1950. Mem., Supreme Court Procedure Cttee, 1982-. Tech. Advr, Central Council of Probation Cttees, 1979-. Mem. Council, Inst. for the Study and Treatment of Delinquency (ISTD), 1966-78; Vice-Pres., NACRO, 1980- (Mem. Council, 1970-80); Pres., British Soc. of Criminology, 1978-81. Governor, Hatfield Polytechnic, 1977-. *Publications:* The Court and the Offender, 1967; A Study of Bedford Prison 1660-1877, 1977; Law and Order in Georgian Bedfordshire, 1982. *Address:* 20 Lyonsdown Road, New Barnet, Herts. *T:* 01-449 7181.

STOCKDALE, His Honour Frank Alleyne, MA; a Circuit Judge (formerly County Court Judge, Ilford and Westminster Courts), 1964-79; *b* 16 Oct. 1910; *er s* of late Sir Frank Stockdale, GCMG, CBE, MA; *m* 1942, Frances Jean, *er d* of late Sir FitzRoy Anstruther-Gough-Calthorpe, Bt; one *s* two *d*. *Educ:* Repton; Magdalene College, Cambridge. Called to Bar, Gray's Inn, 1934; Bencher, 1964. Served War of 1939-45: 5th Royal Inniskilling Dragoon Guards, BEF, 1939-40; North Africa, 1942-43 (despatches); psc; Lt.-Col. Dep. Chm., Hampshire QS, 1954-66; Dep. Chm., Greater London QS, 1966-71. Mem., Inter-Deptl Cttee on Adoption Law, 1969-72, Chm. 1971-72. *Address:* Victoria Place, Monmouth, Gwent NP5 3BR. *T:* Monmouth 5039. *Club:* Garrick.

STOCKER, Prof. Bruce Arnold Dunbar, FRS 1966; MD; Professor of Medical Microbiology in Stanford University, since 1966; *b* 26 May 1917. *Educ:* King's College, London; Westminster Hospital, MB, BS, 1940; MRCS, LRCP, 1940; MD 1947. Guinness Prof. of Microbiology, Univ. of London,

and Dir of Guinness-Lister Microbiological Research Unit, Lister Inst. of Preventive Med., until Dec. 1965. *Publications:* articles in scientific jls. *Address:* Department of Medical Microbiology, Stanford University, Stanford, Calif 94305, USA. *T:* 415-497 2006.

STOCKER, Hon. Sir John (Dexter), Kt 1973; MC, TD; **Hon. Mr Justice Stocker;** a Judge of the High Court, Queen's Bench Division, since 1973; *b* 7 Oct. 1918; *s* of late John Augustus Stocker and Emma Eyre Stocker (*née* Kettle), Hampstead; *m* 1956, Margaret Mary Hegarty; no *c*. *Educ:* Westminster Sch.; London University. 2nd Lt, QO Royal West Kent Regt, 1939; France, 1940; Middle East, 1942-43; Italy, 1943-46; Maj. 1943; Lt-Col 1945. LLB London 1947. Called to Bar, Middle Temple, 1948, Master of the Bench, 1971. QC 1965; a Recorder, 1972-73; Presiding Judge, SE Circuit, 1976-79. *Recreations:* golf, cricket. *Address:* Royal Courts of Justice, Strand, WC2. *Clubs:* Naval and Military; MCC, Royal Wimbledon Golf.

STOCKHAUSEN, Karlheinz; composer and conductor; *b* 22 Aug. 1928; *s* of late Simon and Gertrud Stockhausen; *m* 1st, 1951, Doris Andreae; four *c* ; 2nd, 1967, Mary Bauermeister; two *c*. *Educ:* Hochschule für Musik, and Univ., Cologne, 1947-51; studied with: Messaien, 1952-53; Prof. Werner Meyer-Eppler, Bonn Univ., 1954-56. With Westdeutscher Rundfunk Electronic Music Studio, 1953-, Artistic Dir, 1963-. Lectr, Internat. Summer Sch. for New Music, Darmstadt, 1953-; Dir, Interpretation Group for live electronic music, 1964-; Founder, and Artistic Dir, Kölner Kurse für Neue Musik, 1963-68; Visiting Professor: Univ. of Pa, 1965; Univ. of Calif., 1966-67; Cologne State Conservatory, 1971-. Co-Editor, Die Reihe, 1954-59. First annual tour of 30 concert-lectures, 1958, USA and Canada, since then throughout world. Has composed 71 works and made over 70 records of his own works. *Publications:* Texte, 4 vols, 1963-77; compositions: Chöre für Doris, Drei Lieder, Choral, 1950-51; Sonatine, Kreuzspiel, Formel, 1951; Schlagtrio, Spiel für Orchester, Etude, 1952; Punkte, 1952, rev. 1962, Klavierstücke I-XI, 1952-56, 1961; Kontra-Punkte, 1953; Elektronische Studien I and II, 1953-54; Zeitmasze, Gesang der Jünglinge, 1956; Gruppen, 1957; Zyklus, Refrain, 1959; Carré, Kontakte, 1960; Originale (musical play), 1961; Plus Minus, 1963; Momente, 1962-64; Mixtur (new arr. 1967), Mikrophonie I, 1964; Mikrophonie II, Stop (new arr. 1969), 1965; Telemusik, Solo, Adieu, 1966; Hymnen, Prozession, Ensemble, 1967; Kurzwellen, Stimmung, Aus den sieben Tagen, Spiral, Musik für ein Haus, 1968; Hymnen mit Orchester, Fresco, Dr K-Sextett, 1969; Pole, Expo, Mantra, Für Kommende Zeiten, 1970; Sternklang, Trans, 1971; Alphabet, Am Himmel wandre ich, (Indianerlieder), Ylem, 1972; Vortrag über Hu, Inori, 1973-74; Herbstmusik, Atmen gibt das Leben..., 1974; Musik im Bauch, Tierkreis, Harlekin, Der Kleine Harlekin, 1975; Sirius, 1975-76; Amour, 1976; Jubiläum, In Freundschaft, 1977; Der Jahreslauf, 1977; Donnerstag aus Licht (opera), 1978-80; Donnerstags-Gruss, or Michaels-Gruss, 1978; Michaels Jugend, 1979; Michaels Reise um die Erde, 1978; Michaels Heimkehr, 1980; Donnerstags-Abschied, 1980; Luzifers Traum or Klavierstück XIII, 1981. *Address:* Stockhausen-Verlag, 5067 Kürten, West Germany.

STOCKIL, Sir Raymond (Osborne), KBE 1964 (OBE 1958); Farmer and Director of Companies; *b* 15 April 1907; *s* of Francis Robert Stockil and Ruth (*née* Coventry); *m* 1929, Virginia Fortner (*d* 1972); one *s* three *d* (and one *s* decd); *m* 1973, Margot Susan Lovett Hodgson. *Educ:* Heldeberg College, Cape Province; Washington University, USA (BA). Took up Civil Aviation and Manufacturing in USA, 1929-33 (5 USA Patents); returned to Natal, 1934; commenced farming in Fort Victoria, 1936. Served War of 1939-45 with SR Signal Corps. MP for Victoria, 1946-62; Leader of Opposition, 1948-53 and 1956-59; resigned from Parliament, 1962. Chairman, Hippo Valley Estates Ltd, 1956. *Recreation:* owner and trainer of racehorses. *Address:* PO Box 1108, Harare, Zimbabwe; PO Box 7462, Newton Park, Port Elizabeth, 6055, Republic of South Africa; (home) Cranstoun Lodge, Kragga Kamma Road, PO Box 7462, Port Elizabeth, 6055. *T:* Port Elizabeth 731476. *Club:* Salisbury (Harare, Zimbabwe).

STOCKPORT, Suffragan Bishop of, since 1965; **Rt. Rev. Rupert Gordon Strutt**, BD; *b* 15 Jan. 1912; *s* of Rupert Henry and Maude Mortlock Strutt; *m* 1st, 1936, Eva Gertrude Rabbitts; one *s* one *d* ; 2nd, 1949, Constance Mary Fergusson Foden; one *s* two *d*. *Educ:* University of London; London College of Divinity; Wycliffe Hall, Oxford. Deacon, 1942; Priest, 1943. Curate of Carlton-in-the-Willows, 1942-43; Chaplain to the Forces (Emergency Commission), 1943-45; Rector of Normanton-on-Soar, 1945-48; Vicar of Holy Trinity, Leicester, 1948-52; Curate-in-Charge, St John the Divine, Leicester, 1949-52; Vicar of Addiscombe, Diocese of Canterbury, 1952-59. Chaplain to HM Prison, Leicester, 1948-52. Commissary to the Bishop of Saskatoon, 1958-81. Archdeacon of Maidstone and Canon Residentiary of Canterbury Cathedral, also Prior of St John's Hospital, Canterbury, 1959-65. *Address:* Bishop's Lodge, Macclesfield Road, Alderley Edge, Cheshire SK9 7BH. *T:* Alderley Edge 582074.

STOCKS, Alfred James, CBE 1981; DL; Chief Executive, Liverpool City Council, since 1973; *b* 24 March 1926; *s* of James and Mary Stocks; *m* 1958, Jillian Margery Gedye; one *s* one *d*. *Educ:* Bootham Sch., York; Clare Coll., Cambridge (MA). Admitted solicitor, 1949. Appointed Dep. Town Clerk, Liverpool, 1968. DL Merseyside, 1982. Hon. LLD Liverpool, 1980. *Address:* 38 Glendyke Road, Liverpool L18 6JR. *T:* 051-724 2448. *Club:* Athenæum (Liverpool).

STOCKWELL, Air Cdre Edmund Arthur, CB 1967; MA; Command Education Officer, Training Command, 1968–72 (Flying Training Command, 1964–68); retired 1972; *b* 15 Dec. 1911; *e s* of Arthur Davenport Stockwell, Dewsbury; *m* 1937, Pearl Arber; one *s* two *d*; *m* 1955, Lillian Gertrude Moore (*d* 1965), OBE, MRCP; two *s*; *m* 1970, Mrs Kathleen (Betty) Clarke, Chesham. *Educ:* Wheelwright Grammar School; Balliol Coll., Oxford. Entered RAF Educational Service, Cranwell, 1935; RAF Educn in India, 1936; Punjab and NW Frontier, 1936–38; RAFVR (Admin and Special Duties), 1939; Lahore, Simla, Delhi, 1939–44; Group Educn Officer, No 6 (RCAF) Group, 1944; Air Min., 1944–48; OC, RAF Sch. of Educn, 1948–51; Comd Educn Officer, Coastal Comd, 1951–53; Comd Educn Officer, Far East Air Force, 1953–55; Principal Educn Officer, Halton, 1956–59; Comd Educn Officer, Maintenance Comd, 1959–62; Dep. Dir of Educational Services, Air Min., 1962–64. Group Captain, 1954; Air Commodore, 1964. *Recreations:* golf, gardening. *Address:* Trendles, Ryme Intrinseca, Sherborne, Dorset DT9 6JX. *T:* Yetminster 872085.

STOCKWELL, Gen. Sir Hugh Charles, GCB 1959 (KCB 1954; CB 1946); KBE 1949 (CBE 1945); DSO 1940 and Bar 1957; late Infantry; Chairman: Inland Waterways Amenity Advisory Council, 1971–74; Kennet and Avon Canal Trust, 1966–75; Member: British Waterways Board, 1971–74; Water Space Amenity Commission, 1973–74; *b* 16 June 1903; *s* of late Lt-Col H. C. Stockwell, OBE, late Highland Light Infantry, Chief Constable of Colchester, and Gertrude Forrest; *m* 1931, Joan Rickman Garrard, *d* of Charles and Marion Garrard, Kingston Lisle, Berkshire; two *d*. *Educ:* Cothill House, Abingdon; Marlborough; Royal Military Coll., Sandhurst. Joined 2/Royal Welch Fusiliers, 1923; served West Africa, 1929–35; Instructor, Small Arms School, Netheravon, 1935–38; Brigade-Major, Royal Welch Brigade, 1938–40; served in Norway (DSO); 30 East African Bde, 1942–43; 29th Independent Bde, 1943–45; Burma (DSO); Commander 82 (WA) Division, Jan. 1945–June 1946; Commander, Home Counties District, UK, July 1946–47; Commander Sixth Airborne Division, Palestine, 1947–48; Commandant, RMA, Sandhurst, 1948–50; Comdr, 3rd Inf. Div., and Comdr, East Anglian Dist, 1951–52; General Officer Commanding: Malaya, 1952–54; 1 Corps, BAOR, 1954–56; Ground Forces, Suez Operation, 1956; Military Secretary to the Secretary of State for War, 1957–59; Adjutant-General to the Forces, 1959–60; Deputy Supreme Allied Commander, Europe, 1960–64, retired. Gen., 1957. Col, The Royal Welch Fusiliers, 1952–65; Col, The Royal Malay Regt 1954–59; Col Commandant, Army Air Corps, 1957–63; Col Commandant, Royal Army Educational Corps October 1959–64. ADC General to the Queen, 1959–62. Governor, Felsted School, 1954–65. Grand Officier, Légion d'Honneur (France), 1958. *Recreations:* conservation, painting, travel. *Address:* Horton, near Devizes, Wilts. *T:* Cannings 617; The Clydesdale Bank, 31 St James's Street, SW1. *Clubs:* MCC, Army and Navy.

STOCKWIN, Prof. James Arthur Ainscow; Nissan Professor of Modern Japanese Studies, University of Oxford and Fellow, St Antony's College, Oxford, since 1982; *b* 28 Nov. 1935; *s* of Wilfred Arthur Stockwin and Edith Mary Stockwin; *m* 1960, Audrey Lucretia Hobson Stockwin (*née* Wood); two *s* two *d. Educ:* Exeter Coll., Oxford Univ. (MA); Australian Nat. Univ. (PhD). Australian National University: Lectr, Dept of Political Science, 1964–66; Sen. Lectr, 1966–72; Reader, 1972–82. *Publications:* The Japanese Socialist Party and Neutralism, 1968; (ed) Japan and Australia in the Seventies, 1972; Japan, Divided Politics in a Growth Economy, 1975, 2nd edn 1982; articles, largely on Japanese politics and foreign policy, in Pacific Affairs, Aust. Outlook, Aust. Jl Politics and History, Japan Interpreter, Pacific Community, Asian Survey, etc. *Recreations:* sailing, languages, bushwalking, skiing. *Address:* Nissan Institute of Japanese Studies, Oxford.

STOCKWOOD, Rt. Rev. (Arthur) Mervyn, DD; *b* 27 May 1913; *s* of late Arthur Stockwood, solicitor, and Beatrice Ethel Stockwood; unmarried. *Educ:* Kelly Coll., Tavistock; Christ's Coll., Cambridge (MA). Curate of St Matthew, Moorfields, Bristol, 1936–41; Blundell's Sch., Missioner, 1936–41; Vicar, St Matthew, Moorfields, Bristol, 1941–55; Hon. Canon of Bristol, 1952–55; Vicar of the University Church, Cambridge, 1955–59; Bishop of Southwark, 1959–80. Member: Bristol CC, 1946–55; Cambridge CC, 1956–59; House of Lords, 1963–80. Mem. Council, Bath Univ., 1980–. Freeman of City of London, 1976. DD Lambeth, 1959; Hon. DLitt Sussex, 1963; Hon. DD Bucharest, 1977. *Publications:* There is a Tide, 1946; Whom They Pierced, 1948; Christianity and Marxism, 1949; I Went to Moscow, 1955; The Faith To-day, 1959; Cambridge Sermons, 1959; Bishop's Journal, 1965; The Cross and the Sickle, 1978; From Strength to Strength, 1980; Chanctonbury Ring (autobiog.), 1982. *Address:* 15 Sydney Buildings, Bath, Avon BA2 6BZ. *T:* Bath 63978.

STODART, family name of Baron Stodart of Leaston.

STODART OF LEASTON, Baron *cr* 1981 (Life Peer), of Humbie in the District of East Lothian; **James Anthony Stodart;** PC 1974; *b* 6 June 1916; *yr s* of late Col Thomas Stodart, CIE, IMS, and of Mary Alice Coullie; *m* 1940, Hazel Jean Usher. *Educ:* Wellington. Farming at Kingston, North Berwick, 1934–58, and now at Leaston, Humbie, East Lothian. Hon. Pres., Edinburgh Univ. Agricultural Soc., 1952; Pres. East Lothian Boy Scouts' Assoc., 1960–63. Contested: (L) Berwick and East Lothian, 1950; (C) Midlothian and Peebles, 1951; Midlothian, 1955; MP (C) Edinburgh West, 1959–Oct. 1974; Jt Parly Under-Sec. of State, Scottish Office, Sept. 1963–Oct. 1964; An Opposition spokesman on Agriculture and on Scottish Affairs, 1966–69; Parly Sec., MAFF, 1970–72; Minister of State, MAFF, 1972–74;

Vice-Chm., Conservative Agric. Cttee, House of Commons, 1962–63, 1964–65, 1966–70. Led Parly Delegn to Canada, 1974. Chm., Agricultural Credit Corp. Ltd, 1975–. Dir, FMC, 1980–82. Chm., Cttee of Inquiry into Local Govt in Scotland, 1980. *Publications:* (jt author) Land of Abundance, a study of Scottish Agriculture in the 20th Century, 1962; contrib. on farming topics to agricultural journals and newspapers. *Recreations:* music, playing golf and preserving a sense of humour. *Address:* Lorimers, North Berwick, East Lothian. *T:* North Berwick 2457. *Clubs:* New (Edinburgh); Hon. Company of Edinburgh Golfers.

STODDART, Anne Elizabeth; HM Diplomatic Service; Deputy Permanent UK Representative to Council of Europe, Strasbourg, since 1981; *b* 29 March 1937; *d* of James Stoddart and Ann Jack Stoddart (*née* Inglis). *Educ:* Kirby Grammar School, Middlesbrough; Somerville College, Oxford. MA. Entered Foreign Office, 1960; British Military Govt, Berlin, 1963–67; FCO, 1967–70; First Secretary (Economic), Ankara, 1970–73; Head of Chancery, Colombo, 1974–76; FCO, 1977–81. *Address:* c/o Foreign and Commonwealth Office, SW1A 2AH; 18 rue Gottfried, 67000 Strasbourg, France. *T:* (88)35.00.88.

STODDART, David Leonard; MP (Lab) Swindon, since 1970; *b* 4 May 1926; *s* of Arthur Leonard Stoddart, coal miner, and Queenie Victoria Stoddart (*née* Price); *m* 1961, Jennifer Percival-Alwyn; two *s* (one *d* by previous marr.). *Educ:* elementary; St Clement Danes and Henley Grammar Schools. Youth in training, PO Telephones, 1942–44; business on own account, 1944–46; Railway Clerk, 1947–49; Hospital Clerk, 1949–51; Power Station Clerical Worker, 1951–70. Joined Labour Party, 1947; Member Reading County Borough Council, 1954–72; served at various times as Chairman of Housing, Transport and Finance Cttees; Leader of the Reading Labour Group of Councillors, 1962–70. Contested (Lab) Newbury, 1959 and 1964, Swindon, 1969. PPS to Minister for Housing and Construction, 1974–75; an Asst Govt Whip, 1975; a Lord Comr, HM Treasury, 1976–77. *Recreations:* gardening, music. *Address:* Sintra, 37A Bath Road, Reading, Berks. *T:* Reading 56726.

STODDART, Wing Comdr Kenneth Maxwell, AE 1942; JP; Lord-Lieutenant, Metropolitan County of Merseyside, since 1979; *b* 26 May 1914; *s* of late Wilfrid Bowring Stoddart and Mary Hyslop Stoddart (*née* Maxwell); *m* 1940, Jean Roberta Benson Young; two *d. Educ:* Sedbergh; Clare Coll., Cambridge. Chairman: Cearns and Brown Ltd, 1973–; United Mersey Supply Co. Ltd, 1978–81. Commissioned No 611 (West Lancashire) Sqdn, Auxiliary Air Force, 1936; served War, UK and Europe; comd W Lancashire Wing, Air Trng Corps, 1946–54; Vice-Chm. (Air) W Lancashire T&AFA, 1954–64. Chairman, Liverpool Child Welfare Assoc., 1965–81. DL Lancashire 1958 (transf. to Metropolitan County of Merseyside, 1974); JP Liverpool 1952; High Sheriff of Merseyside, 1974. KStJ 1979. *Recreations:* gardening, walking. *Address:* The Spinney, Overdale Road, Willaston, South Wirral L64 1SY. *T:* 051-327 5183. *Clubs:* Lyceum, Atlantic (Liverpool).

STOESSEL, Walter J., Jr; Deputy Secretary of State, US, 1982; *b* 24 Jan. 1920; *s* of Walter John Stoessel and Katherine Stoessel (*née* Haston); *m* 1946, Mary Ann (*née* Ferrandou); three *d. Educ:* Lausanne Univ.; Stanford Univ. (BA); Russian Inst., Columbia Univ.; Center for Internat. Affairs, Harvard Univ. US Foreign Service, 1942; Polit. Officer, Caracas, 1942–46; Dept of State, 1946–47; Moscow, 1947–49; Bad-Nauheim, 1950–52; Officer i/c Soviet Affairs, Dept of State, 1952–56; White House, 1956; Paris, 1956–59; Dir, Exec. Secretariat, Dept of State, 1960–61; Polit. Adviser to SHAPE, Paris, 1961–63; Moscow, 1963–65; Dep. Asst Sec. for European Affairs, Dept of State, 1965–68; US Ambassador to Poland, 1968–72; Asst Sec. for European Affairs, Dept of State, 1972–74; US Ambassador to: USSR, 1974–76; Fed. Rep. of Germany, 1976–81; Under Sec. of State for Political Affairs, 1981–82. *Recreations:* tennis, ski-ing, swimming, painting. *Address:* 5155 Rockwood Parkway NW, Washington, DC 20016, USA.

STOGDON, Norman Francis; a Recorder of the Crown Court, since 1972; *b* 14 June 1909; *s* of late F. R. Stogdon and late L. Stogdon (*née* Reynolds); *m* 1959, Yvonne (*née* Jaques). *Educ:* Harrow; Brasenose Coll., Oxford (BA, BCL). Called to Bar, Middle Temple, 1932. War Service, Army, 1939–45; served with Royal Fusiliers, King's African Rifles, 1941–45; Staff Officer; sc Middle East 1944. *Publications:* contrib. 2nd and 3rd edns Halsbury's Laws of England. *Recreations:* golf, ski-ing. *Address:* 2 Harcourt Buildings, Temple, EC4Y 9DB. *T:* 01-353 2548. *Club:* Moor Park Golf.

STOICHEFF, Prof. Boris Peter, FRS 1975; FRSC 1965; Centennial Medal of Canada, 1967; Professor of Physics, since 1974 and University Professor, since 1977, University of Toronto; *b* 1 June 1924; *s* of Peter and Vasilka Stoicheff; *m* 1954, Lillian Joan Ambridge; one *s* one *d. Educ:* Univ. of Toronto, Faculty of Applied Science and Engineering (BASc), Dept of Physics (MA, PhD). McKee-Gilchrist Fellowship, Univ. of Toronto, 1950–51; National Research Council of Canada: Fellowship, Ottawa, 1952–53; Res. Officer in Div. of Pure Physics, 1953–64; Member, 1978–. Visiting Scientist, Mass Inst. of Technology, 1963–64. Chm., Engrg Science, Univ. of Toronto, 1972–77. Izaak Walton Killam Meml Scholarship, 1977–79; Senior Fellow, Massey Coll., Univ. of Toronto, 1979. Fellow, Optical Soc. of America, 1965 (Pres. 1976); Fellow, Amer. Phys. Soc., 1969; Geoffrey Frew Fellow, Australian Acad. of Science, 1980; Hon. Fellow, Indian Acad. of Scis, 1971. DSc: York, Canada, 1982; Skopje, Yugoslavia, 1982. Gold Medal for Achievement in Physics of Canadian Assoc. of Physicists, 1974; William F. Meggers Award, Optical Soc. of America, 1981. *Publications:* numerous scientific contribs to phys. and chem. jls. *Address:* Department of Physics, University of Toronto, Toronto, Ontario M5S 1A7, Canada. *T:* (416) 978-2948.

STOKE-UPON-TRENT, Archdeacon of; *see* Delight, Ven. J. D.

STOKER, Sir Michael (George Parke), Kt 1980; CBE 1974; FRCP 1979; FRS 1968, FRSE 1960; President of Clare Hall, Cambridge, since 1980 (Fellow, 1978); *b* 4 July 1918; *e s* of Dr S. P. Stoker, Maypole, Monmouth; *m* 1942, Veronica Mary English; three *s* two *d. Educ:* Oakham Sch.; Sidney Sussex Coll., Cambridge (Hon. Fellow 1981); St Thomas' Hosp., London. MRCS, LRCP 1942; MB, BChir 1943; MD 1947. RAMC, 1942-47; Demonstrator in Pathology, Cambridge Univ., 1947-48; Univ. Lecturer in Pathology, 1948-50; Huddersfield Lecturer in Special Pathology, 1950-58; Asst Tutor and Dir of Medical Studies, Clare Coll., 1949-58; Fellow of Clare College, 1948-58, Hon. Fellow, 1976; Prof. of Virology, Glasgow Univ., and Hon. Dir, MRC Experimental Virus Research Unit, 1959-68; Dir, Imperial Cancer Res. Fund Laboratories, 1968-79. WHO Travel Fellow, 1951; Vis. Prof., UCL, 1968-79. Leeuwenhoek Lecture, Royal Soc., 1971. For. Sec., 1977-81, and a Vice-Pres., 1977-, Royal Soc. Member: European Molecular Biology Organisation; Council for Scientific Policy, DES, 1970-73; Gen. Cttee, Internat. Council of Scientific Unions, 1977-. Foreign Hon. Member: Amer. Acad. of Arts and Scis, 1973; Czech Acad. of Scis, 1980. *Publications:* various articles on cell biology and virology. *Address:* Clare Hall, Cambridge CB3 9AL.

STOKES, family name of **Baron Stokes.**

STOKES, Baron *cr* 1969 (Life Peer), of Leyland; **Donald Gresham Stokes,** Kt 1965; TD; DL; FEng, FIMechE; MSAE; FIMI; FCIT; Chairman: Dutton Forshaw Motor Group Ltd, since 1980; Jack Barclay Ltd, since 1980; Chairman and Managing Director, 1968-75, Chief Executive, 1973-75, British Leyland Motor Corporation Ltd; President, BL Ltd, 1975-79; Consultant to Leyland Vehicles, 1979-81; *b* 22 March 1914; *o s* of Harry Potts Stokes; *m* 1939, Laura Elizabeth Courteney Lamb; one *s. Educ:* Blundell's School; Harris Institute of Technology, Preston. Started Student Apprenticeship, Leyland Motors Ltd, 1930. Served War of 1939-45: REME, 1939-46 (Lt-Col). Re-joined Leyland as Exports Manager, 1946; General Sales and Service Manager, 1950; Director, 1954; Managing Director, and Deputy Chairman, Leyland Motor Corp., 1963, Chm. 1967; Chm. and Man. Dir, British Leyland Ltd, 1973. Director: National Westminster Bank, 1969-81; London Weekend Television Ltd, 1967-71; Opus Public Relations Ltd, 1979-; Scottish & Universal Investments Ltd, 1980-; Dovercourt Motor Co. Ltd, 1982-; Royal Motor Yacht Club Pty Ltd. Vice-President, Empresa Nacional de Autocamiones SA, Spain, 1959-73. Chairman: British Arabian Adv. Co. Ltd, 1977-; Two Counties Radio Ltd, 1978-; British Arabian Technical Co-operation Ltd, 1981-; Riverside Develt Consortium-Preston Ltd, 1981-. Vice-Pres., Engineering Employers Fedn, 1967-75; President: SMMT, 1961-62; Motor Industry Res. Assoc., 1965-66; Manchester Univ. Inst. of Science and Technology, 1972-76 (Vice-Pres., 1968-71); Vice-Pres., IMechE, 1971, Pres., 1972; Chm., EDC for Electronics Industry, 1966-67; Member: NW Economic Planning Council, 1965-70; IRC, 1966-71 (Dep. Chm. 1969); EDC for the Motor Manufacturing Industry, 1967-; Council, Public Transport Assoc.; Cttee of Common Market Constructors, 1972-; Worshipful Co. of Carmen. DL Lancs 1968. Hon. Fellow, Keble Coll., Oxford, 1968. Hon. FIRTE. Hon. LLD Lancaster, 1967; Hon. DTech Loughborough, 1968; Hon. DSc: Southampton, 1969; Salford, 1971. Officier de l'Ordre de la Couronne (Belgium), 1964; Commandeur de l'ordre de Leopold II (Belgium), 1972. *Recreation:* boating. *Address:* Jack Barclay Ltd, 18 Berkeley Square, W1X 6AE. *Clubs:* Beefsteak, Brooks's; Royal Western Yacht, Royal Motor Yacht (Commodore, 1979-).

STOKES, Harry Michael; HM Diplomatic Service, retired; Counsellor, Foreign and Commonwealth Office, 1979-81; *b* 22 July 1926; *s* of late Wing Comdr Henry Alban Stokes, RAF, and Lilian Frances (*née* Ede); *m* 1951, Prudence Mary Watling; two *s* one *d. Educ:* Rossall Sch.; Worcester Coll., Oxford (BA, Dip. Slavonic Studies). Served RAF, 1944-47. Joined Foreign Service, 1951; attached Control Commission, Germany, 1952-55; Foreign Office, 1955; Singapore, 1958; FO, 1959; Washington, 1961; Copenhagen, 1963; FO 1965; New Delhi, 1976; FO, 1977. *Recreations:* walking, racquet games, photography, music. *Clubs:* United Oxford & Cambridge University, Royal Commonwealth Society.

STOKES, John Fisher, MA, MD, FRCP; Physician, University College Hospital, since 1947; *b* 19 Sept. 1912; *e s* of late Dr Kenneth Stokes and Mary (*née* Fisher); *m* 1940, Elizabeth Joan, *d* of Thomas Rooke and Elizabeth Frances (*née* Pearce); one *s* one *d. Educ:* Haileybury (exhibitioner); Gonville and Caius Coll., Cambridge (exhibitioner); University Coll. Hosp. (Fellowes Silver Medal for clinical medicine). MB BChir (Cambridge) 1937; MRCP 1939; MD (Cambridge) 1947 (proxime accessit, Horton Smith prize); FRCP 1947; FRCPE 1975; Thruston Medal, Gonville and Caius Coll., 1948. Appointments on junior staff University Coll. Hosp. and Victoria Hosp. for Children, Tite St, 1937-42; RAMC 1942-46; served in Far East, 1943-46, Lt-Col (despatches). Examiner in Medicine, various Univs, 1949-70. Member of Council, Royal Soc. of Med., 1951-54, 1967-69. Vice-Pres., RCP, 1968-69. Amateur Squash Rackets Champion of Surrey, 1935, of East of England, 1936, Runner-up of British Isles, 1937; English International, 1938; Technical Adviser to Squash Rackets Assoc., 1948-52; Chm. Jesters Club, 1953-59.

Publications: Examinations in Medicine (jtly), 1976; contrib. on liver disease and general medicine in medical journals. *Recreations:* music, tennis, painting. *Address:* Ossicles, Newnham Hill, near Henley-on-Thames, Oxon RG9 5TL. *Clubs:* Athenæum, Savile.

See also Prof. Sir W. D. M. Paton.

STOKES, John Heydon Romaine; MP (C) Halesowen and Stourbridge, since 1974 (Oldbury and Halesowen, 1970-74); *b* 23 July 1917; *o* surv. *s* of late Victor Romaine Stokes, Hitchin; *m* 1939, Barbara Esmée, *y d* of late R. E. Yorke, Wellingborough; one *s* two *d. Educ:* Temple Grove; Haileybury Coll.; Queen's Coll., Oxford. BA 1938; MA 1946. Hon. Agent and Treas., Oxford Univ. Conservative Assoc., 1937; Pres., Monarchist Soc., 1937; Pres., Mermaid Club, 1937. Asst Master, Prep. Sch., 1938-39. Served War, 1939-46: Dakar Expedn, 1940; wounded in N Africa, 1943; Mil. Asst to HM Minister Beirut and Damascus, 1944-46; Major, Royal Fusiliers. Personnel Officer, Imperial Chemical Industries, 1946-51; Personnel Manager, British Celanese, 1951-59; Dep. Personnel Manager, Courtaulds, 1957-59; Dir, Clive & Stokes, Personnel Consultants, 1959-80. Mem., Select Cttee on Parly Commn for Admin (Ombudsman), 1979-. Leader, Parly delegn to Portugal, 1980. Contested (C): Gloucester, 1964, Hitchin, 1966. Mem. Exec. Cttee, Oxford Soc.; Chm., Gen. Purposes Cttee, Primrose League; Vice-Pres., Royal Stuart Soc. *Publications:* articles on political and personnel subjects. *Recreations:* gardening, travel, English history, church affairs. *Address:* Jasmine Cottage, Aston Rowant, Oxford OX9 5ST. *T:* Kingston Blount 51506. *Clubs:* Carlton, Buck's.

STOLLERY, Prof. John Leslie, DScEng; FRAeS; Professor of Aerodynamics since 1973, and Head since 1976, College of Aeronautics, Cranfield Institute of Technology; *b* 21 April 1930; *s* of George and Emma Stollery; *m* 1956, Jane Elizabeth, *d* of Walter and Mildred Reynolds; four *s. Educ:* East Barnet Grammar Sch.; Imperial Coll. of Science and Technol., London Univ. (BScEng 1951, MScEng 1953, DScEng 1973). DIC; CEng; FRAeS 1975. Aerodynamics Dept, De Havilland Aircraft Co., 1952-56; Lectr, 1956, Reader, 1962, Aeronautics Dept, Imperial Coll., London; Dean, Faculty of Engrg, Cranfield Inst. of Technol., 1976-79. Chm., Machines and Power Cttee, SRC later SERC, 1979-82. Visiting Professor: Cornell Aeronautical Labs, Buffalo, USA, 1964; Aeronaut. Res. Lab., Wright Patterson Air Force Base, 1971; Nat. Aeronaut. Lab., Bangalore, India, 1977; Peking Inst. of Aeronautics and Astronautics, 1979. *Publications:* (Chief Editor) Shock Tube Research, 1971; papers in Jl of Fluid Mechanics, and Aeronaut. Qly. *Recreations:* playing tennis, watching football, travelling. *Address:* 28 The Embankment, Bedford. *T:* Bedford 55087.

STONE, family name of **Baron Stone.**

STONE, Baron *cr* 1976 (Life Peer), of Hendon; **Joseph Ellis Stone,** Kt 1970; Medical Practitioner; *b* 27 May 1903; 2nd *s* of late Henry Silverstone and Rebecca Silverstone (*née* Ellis); *m* 1932, Beryl, *y d* of late Alexander and Jane Bernstein; one *s* one *d. Educ:* Llanelli County Intermediate Sch.; Cardiff Univ.; Westminster Hosp., SW1. MB, BS London 1927; MRCS, LRCP 1925. Casualty Officer and Ho. Surg., Westminster Hosp., 1925-26; Sen. Ho. Surg., N Staffs Royal Infirmary, 1926-28; MO, St George in the East Hosp., 1928-32; gen. med. practice, 1932-. Served RAMC, 1940-45, Captain; graded med. specialist. Personal Physician to PM, 1964-70 and 1974-76. Mem. Med. Soc. of London; Mem. Hampstead Med. Soc. Yeoman of Worshipful Soc. of Apothecaries. *Recreation:* golf. *Address:* 615 Finchley Road, Hampstead, NW3. *T:* 01-435 7333.

STONE, Evan David Robert, QC 1979; a Recorder of the Crown Court, since 1979; *b* 26 Aug. 1928; *s* of Laurence George and Lillian Stone; *m* 1959, Gisela Bridget Mann; one *s. Educ:* Berkhamsted; Worcester Coll., Oxford (MA). National Service (commnd, Army), 1947-49; served Middle East and UK. Called to Bar, Inner Temple, 1954; sometime HM Deputy Coroner: Inner West London; West Middlesex; City of London. Formerly Associate Editor, Medico-Legal Journal. Councillor, later Alderman, London Borough of Islington, 1969-74 (Dep. Leader, later Leader of Opposition). Governor: Moorfields Eye Hosp., 1970-79; Highbury Grove Sch., 1971- (Chm. of Governors, 1978-82). *Publications:* contrib. Social Welfare and the Citizen (paperback), 1957; contribs to Medico-Legal Jl and other professional jls. *Recreations:* reading, writing, sport, listening to music. *Address:* 60 Canonbury Park South, N1 2JG. *T:* 01-226 6820; The Mill House, Ridgewell, Halstead, Essex. *T:* Ridgewell 338; (chambers) 2 Dr Johnson's Buildings, Temple, EC4. *T:* 01-353 7291. *Clubs:* Garrick, MCC, St Stephen's Constitutional; Norfolk (Norwich); Colne Yacht (Brightlingsea).

STONE, Prof. Francis Gordon Albert, FRS 1976; Head of Department of Inorganic Chemistry, and Professor since 1963, Bristol University; *b* 19 May 1925; *s* of Sidney Charles and Florence Stone; *m* 1956, Judith M. Hislop, Sydney, Australia; three *s. Educ:* Exeter Sch.; Christ's Coll., Cambridge. BA 1948, MA and PhD 1952, ScD 1963, Cambridge. Fulbright Schol., Univ. of Southern Calif., 1952-54; Instructor and Asst Prof., Harvard Univ., 1954-62; Reader, Queen Mary Coll., London, 1962-63. Vis. Professor: Monash Univ., 1966; Princeton Univ., 1967; Univ. of Arizona, 1970; Carnegie-Mellon Univ., 1972; Texas A&M Univ., 1980; Guggenheim Fellow, 1961; Sen. Vis. Fellow, Australian Acad. of Sciences, 1966; A. R. Gordon Distinguished Lectr, Univ. of Toronto, 1977; Misha Strassberg Vis. Lectr, Univ. of WA, 1982. Lectures: Boomer, Univ. of Alberta, 1965; Firestone, Univ. of Wisconsin, 1970; Tilden, Chem. Soc., 1971; Ludwig Mond, RSC, 1982. Member: Council, Royal Soc. of Chemistry (formerly Chemical Soc.), 1968-70, 1981-83; Dalton Div.

Council, 1971-74, 1981- (Vice-Pres. 1973; Pres., 1981-83); Chemistry Cttee, SERC, 1982- (Mem., Chem. Cttee, SRC, 1971-74). Organometallic Chemistry Medal, 1972, Transition Metal Chemistry Medal, 1979, Chem. Soc.; Chugaev Medal, Inst. of Inorganic Chem., USSR Acad. of Sciences, 1978. *Publications:* (Editor) Inorganic Polymers, 1962; Hydrogen Compounds of the Group IV Elements, 1962; (Editor) Advances in Organometallic Chemistry, vols 1-21, 1964-83; numerous papers in Jl Chem. Soc., Jl Amer. Chem. Soc., etc. *Recreation:* world travel. *Address:* 6 Rylestone Grove, Bristol BS9 3UT. *T:* Bristol 622127.

STONE, Frederick Alistair; solicitor; Clerk and Chief Executive, Surrey County Council, since 1973; *b* 13 Sept. 1927; *s* of Cyril Jackson and Elsie May Stone; *m* 1963, Anne Teresa Connor; one *s* one *d*. *Educ:* William Hulme's Grammar Sch.; Dulwich Coll.; Brasenose Coll., Oxford (BCL, MA). Asst Solicitor: Norwich City Council, 1954-58; Hampshire CC, 1958-60; Sen. Solicitor, CC of Lincoln (Parts of Lindsey), 1960-63; Asst Clerk, Hampshire CC, 1963-65; Dep. Clerk, Cheshire CC, 1965-73. Chm., RIPA, 1979-81; Mem. Council, Industrial Soc. *Recreations:* music, walking, gardening. *Address:* (office) County Hall, Kingston upon Thames, Surrey. *T:* 01-546 1050; (home) North Lodge, Brockham Green, Betchworth RH3 7JS. *T:* Betchworth 2178.

STONE, Gilbert Seymour, FCA; private practice as chartered accountant; *b* 4 Feb. 1915; *s* of J. Stone; *m* 1941, Josephine Tolhurst; one *s*. *Educ:* Clifton College. War service as Air Gunner with RAF, 1939-45 (Sqdn-Ldr); with Industrial & Commercial Finance Corp. Ltd, 1945-59, latterly Asst Gen. Manager; Dir, Gresham Trust Ltd, 1959-61; practised on own account, 1961-72; Dir, Industrial Develt Unit, DTI, 1972-74. Director: Babcock International plc; Industrial and Commercial Finance Corp. plc; Finance for Industry plc; London Amer. International Corp. Ltd; The Frizzell Group Ltd; New Shakespeare Co. Ltd; Manganese Bronze Holdings plc. *Recreations:* golf, travel. *Address:* Deepcut Place, Deepcut, Surrey. *Clubs:* Garrick; Sunningdale Golf.

STONE, Sir (John) Richard (Nicholas), Kt 1978; CBE 1946; MA; FBA 1956; P. D. Leake Professor of Finance and Accounting, University of Cambridge, 1955-80, retired; Fellow of King's College, Cambridge, since 1945; *b* 30 Aug. 1913; *o c* of late Sir Gilbert Stone; *m* 1941, Feodora Leontinoff (*d* 1956); one *d*; *m* 1960, Mrs Giovanna Croft-Murray, *d* of Count Aurelio Saffi. *Educ:* Westminster School; Gonville and Caius College, Cambridge (Hon. Fellow, 1976). With C. E. Heath and Co., Lloyd's Brokers, 1936-39; Ministry of Economic Warfare, 1939-40; Offices of the War Cabinet, Central Statistical Office, 1940-45; Dir Dept of Applied Economics, Cambridge, 1945-55. Mem., Internat. Statistical Inst. President: Econometric Soc., 1955; Royal Econ. Soc., 1978-80; Hon. Member: Soc. of Incorp. Accountants, 1947; Amer. Economic Assoc., 1976; For. Hon. Mem., Amer. Acad. of Arts and Sciences, 1968. ScD 1957. Hon. doctorates, Univs of Oslo and Brussels, 1965, Geneva, 1971, Warwick, 1975, Paris, 1977, Bristol, 1978. *Publications:* National Income and Expenditure, 1st edn (with J. E. Meade), 1944, 10th edn (with G. Stone), 1977; The Role of Measurement in Economics, 1951; (with others) The Measurement of Consumers' Expenditure and Behaviour in the United Kingdom 1920-1938, vol. 1 1954, vol. 2 1966; Quantity and Price Indexes in National Accounts, 1956; Input-Output and National Accounts, 1961; Mathematics in the Social Sciences, and Other Essays, 1966; Mathematical Models of the Economy, and Other Essays, 1970; Demographic Accounting and Model Building, 1971; Aspects of Economic and Social Modelling, 1980; gen. editor and pt author series A Programme for Growth, 1962-74; numerous articles in learned journals, particularly on social accounting and econometrics, 1936-. *Recreation:* staying at home. *Address:* 13 Millington Road, Cambridge.

STONE, Prof. Julius, AO 1981; OBE 1973; Professor of Law, University of New South Wales, since 1973; Distinguished Professor of International Law and Jurisprudence, Hastings College of Law, California University, since 1973; Emeritus Professor, University of Sydney; Member of New Zealand and Victorian Bars; Solicitor, Supreme Court, England; *b* 7 July 1907; *s* of Israel and Ellen Stone, Leeds, Yorkshire; *m* 1934, Reca Lieberman, BSc, LDS; two *s* one *d*. *Educ:* Univs of Oxford, Leeds, Harvard. BA, BCL, DCL (Oxford); LLM (Leeds); SJD (Harvard). Asst Lectr, University Coll., Hull, 1928-30; Rockefeller Fellow in Social Sciences, 1931; Asst Prof. of Law, Harvard Univ., 1933-36; Prof. of Internat. Law and Organisation, Fletcher Sch. of Law and Diplomacy, USA, 1933-36; Lectr in Law, Univ. of Leeds, 1936-38; Prof. and Dean Faculty of Law, Auckland University Coll., NZ, 1938-42; Challis Prof. of Internat. Law and Jurisprudence, Univ. of Sydney, 1942-72. Acting Dean, Sydney Faculty of Law, 1954-55, 1958-59; Visiting Professor: New York Univ. and Fletcher Sch. of Law and Diplomacy, 1949; Columbia Univ., 1956; Harvard Univ., 1956-57; Hague Academy of Internat. Law, 1956; Charles Inglis Thomson Guest Prof., Univ. of Colorado, 1956; Indian Sch. of Internat. Affairs, 1960; Monash Univ., 1972 (and Wilfred Fullagar Lectr); Lectures: Roscoe Pound, Univ. of Nebraska, 1957; John Field Sims Meml, Univ. of New Mexico, 1959; Isaacs Marks Inaugural, Univ. of Arizona, 1980; first Pres., Internat. Law Assoc., Aust. Br., 1959; Council, Internat. Commn of Jurists, Aust. Section, 1959; Fellow, Woodrow Wilson Center for Scholars, 1973. Chm., NSW Research Group, Aust. Inst. of Internat. Affairs, 1942-45; Vice-Chm., Prime Minister's Cttee on National Morale, and with Directorate of Research, LHQ, War of 1939-45 (Lt-Col). Founding and Exec. Mem., Aust. SSRC; Chm. Aust. Unesco Cttee for Social Sciences; Aust. Deleg., 6th Unesco Gen. Conf., Paris, 1951; Aust. rep., Second Corning Conf.

on The Individual in the Modern World, 1961; Official Observer of Internat. Commn of Jurists, Eichmann Trial, 1961; General Editor, Sydney Law Review, 1953-60; Fellow: Aust. Acad. of Social Sciences; Centre for Study of the Behavioral Sciences, 1964; World Acad. of Arts and Sciences, 1964; Mem., Royal Netherlands Acad. of Arts and Sciences, 1978; Mem. Titulaire, Inst. of Internat. Law, 1964-82; Associate, Internat. Acad. of Comparative Law; Hon. Life Member: Amer. Soc. of Internat. Law, 1962; Indian Soc. Internat. Law, 1964. Patron, Amnesty International, 1963. Mem., Advisory Cttee, Internat. League for Rights of Man, 1964; Regular Broadcaster on Internat. Affairs (Australian Broadcasting Commn), 1945-. Hon. LLD: Leeds, 1973; Sydney, 1981. Amer. Soc. Internat. Law Award, 1956; Legatum Visserianum Prize, Leyden Univ., 1956; Joint Swiney Prize, RSA, 1964; Hon. QC 1982. *Publications:* International Guarantees of Minority Rights, 1932; Regional Guarantees of Minority Rights, 1933; The Atlantic Charter—New Worlds for Old, 1943; Stand Up and Be Counted, 1944; The Province and Function of Law, Law as Logic, Justice and Social Control (Aust., Eng. and Amer. edns), 1946, 1947, 1950, 1961, 1968; (with the late S. P. Simpson) Law and Society (3 vols), 1949-50; Legal Controls of International Conflict, A Treatise on the Dynamics of Disputes- and War- Law, 1954 (Aust., Eng. and Amer. edns; revised impression, 1958, repr. 1973); Sociological Inquiries concerning International Law, 1956; Aggression and World Order, 1958 (Aust., Eng. and Amer. edns); Legal Education and Public Responsibility, 1959; Quest for Survival, 1961 (German, Portuguese, Japanese and Arabic trans); The International Court and World Crisis, 1962; Legal System and Lawyers' Reasonings, 1964; Human Law and Human Justice, 1965; Social Dimensions of Law and Justice, 1966, 1972 (German trans. in 3 vols, 1976); Law and the Social Sciences in the 2nd Half-Century, 1966; The Middle East Under Cease-Fire, 1967; No Peace—No War in The Middle East, 1969; Approaches to International Justice, 1970; (with R. K. Woetzel) Towards a Feasible International Criminal Court, 1970; Of Law and Nations, 1974; Conflict Through Consensus, 1977; Palestine and Israel: assault on the law of nations, 1981; contrib. Sketch of a Code for Science to Science and Ethics, ed D. Oldroyd, 1982; numerous articles in Anglo-American legal journals. *Recreations:* gardening, landscape gardening. *Address:* 24 Blake Street, Rose Bay, NSW 2029, Australia. *T:* 371 9714.

STONE, Prof. Lawrence, MA Oxon; Dodge Professor of History, since 1963, and Director, Shelby Cullom Davis Center for Historical Studies, since 1968, Princeton University; *b* 4 Dec. 1919; *s* of Lawrence Frederick Stone and Mabel Julia Annie Stone; *m* 1943, Jeanne Caecilia, *d* of Prof. Robert Fawtier, Membre de l'Institut, Paris; one *s* one *d*. *Educ:* Charterhouse School, 1933-38; Sorbonne, Paris, 1938; Christ Church, Oxford, 1938-40, 1945-46. Lieut RNVR 1940-45. Bryce Research Student, Oxford Univ., 1946-47; Lectr, University Coll. Oxford, 1947-50; Fellow, Wadham Coll., Oxford, 1950-63; Mem. Inst. for Advanced Study, Princeton, 1960-61; Chm., Dept of History, 1967-70. Mem., Amer. Philosophical Soc., 1970. Fellow, Amer. Acad. of Arts and Sciences, 1968. Hon. DHL Chicago, 1979. *Publications:* Sculpture in Britain: The Middle Ages, 1955; An Elizabethan: Sir Horatio Palavicino, 1956; The Crisis of the Aristocracy, 1558-1641, 1965; The Causes of the English Revolution, 1529-1642, 1972; Family and Fortune: Studies in Aristocratic Finance in the 16th and 17th Centuries, 1973; (ed) The University in Society, 1975; (ed) Schooling and Society, 1977; Family, Sex and Marriage in England 1500-1800, 1977; The Past and the Present, 1981; numerous articles in History, Economic History Review, Past and Present, Archæological Jl, English Historical Review, Bulletin of the Inst. for Historical Research, Malone Soc., Comparative Studies in Society and History, History Today, etc. *Address:* 266 Moore Street, Princeton, NJ 08540, USA. *T:* Princeton 921.2717; 231A Woodstock Road, Oxford. *T:* Oxford 59174.

STONE, Marcus; Sheriff of Glasgow and Strathkelvin, since 1976; Advocate; *b* 22 March 1921; *s* of Morris and Reva Stone; *m* 1956, Jacqueline Barnoin; three *s* two *d*. *Educ:* High Sch. of Glasgow; Univ. of Glasgow (MA 1940, LLB 1948). Served War of 1939-45, RASC: overseas service, West Africa, att. RWAFF. Admitted Solicitor, 1949; Post Grad. Dip., Psychology, Univ. of Glasgow, 1953; admitted Faculty of Advocates, 1965; apptd Hon. Sheriff Substitute, 1967, Sheriff, 1971-76, of Stirling, Dunbarton and Clackmannan, later N Strathclyde at Dumbarton. *Recreations:* swimming, golf. *Address:* Sheriff's Chambers, Sheriff Court, County Buildings, Ingram Street, Glasgow. *T:* 041-552 3434.

STONE, Sir Richard; see Stone, Sir J. R. N.

STONE, Richard Frederick, QC 1968; *b* 11 March 1928; *s* of Sir Leonard Stone, OBE, QC, and Madeleine Marie (*née* Scheffler); *m* 1st, 1957, Georgina Maxwell Morris (decd); two *d*; 2nd, 1964, Susan van Heel; two *d*. *Educ:* Lakefield College Sch., Canada; Rugby; Trinity Hall, Cambridge (MA). Lt, Worcs Regt, 1946-48. Called to Bar, Gray's Inn, 1952, Bencher, 1974; Mem., Bar Council, 1957-61; Member: Panel of Lloyd's Arbitrators in Salvage Cases; Panel of Wreck Comrs. *Recreation:* sailing. *Address:* 5 Raymond Buildings, Gray's Inn, WC1. *T:* 01-242 2697; Orchard Gap, Wittering Road, Hayling Island, Hants.

STONE, Riversdale Garland, CMG 1956; OBE 1946; HM Consul-General, Los Angeles, 1957-59; *b* 19 Jan. 1903; *m* 1927, Cassie Gaisford; no *c*. Information Officer, Rio de Janeiro, Brazil, 1946; transf. to Singapore, 1948; First Secretary (Economic), Staff of Commissioner-General for the UK in SE Asia, 1948; transf. to Batavia, 1949; Counsellor (Commercial), Mexico City,

1952; Counsellor, HM Diplomatic Service, retired. *Address:* c/o National Westminster Bank Ltd, Piccadilly Circus Branch, Glasshouse Street, W1.

STONEFROST, Maurice Frank; Comptroller of Financial Services, Greater London Council, since 1973; *b* 1 Sept. 1927; *s* of Arthur and Anne Stonefrost, Bristol; *m* 1953, Audrey Jean Fishlock; one *s* one *d. Educ:* Merrywood Grammar Sch., Bristol (DPA). IPFA, FBCS, FRSS, MBIM. Nat. Service, RAF, 1948-51; local govt finance: Bristol County Borough, 1951-54; Slough Borough, 1954-56; Coventry County Borough, 1956-61; W Sussex CC, 1961-64; Sec., Inst. of Municipal Treasurers and Accountants, 1964-73. Pres., Soc. of County Treasurers, 1982-83. *Recreation:* gardening. *Address:* 33 Birdham Road, Chichester, Sussex. *T:* Chichester 783304.

STONEHOUSE, John Thomson; *b* 28 July 1925; *m* 1st, 1948, Barbara Joan Smith (marr. diss. 1978); one *s* two *d* ; 2nd, 1981, Mrs Sheila Buckley. *Educ:* Elementary Sch. and Tauntons Sch., Southampton; Univ. of London (London Sch. of Econs and Political Science). Asst to Senior Probation Officer, Southampton, 1941-44. Served in RAF as pilot and education officer, 1944-47. Studied at LSE, 1947-51 (Chm., Labour Soc., 1950-51); BSc (Econ.) Hons, 1951. Man. for African Co-op. Socs in Uganda, 1952-54; Sec., Kampala Mutual Co-op Soc. Ltd (Uganda), 1953-54; Dir of London Co-operative Soc. Ltd, 1956-62 (Pres., 1962-64); Mem. until 1962 of Development Cttee of the Co-operative Union; Dir of Society Footwear Ltd until 1963. Contested Norwood, London CC Election, 1949; contested (Lab) Twickenham, General Election, 1950; Burton, General Election, 1951; MP (Lab Co-op): Wednesbury, Feb. 1957-74; Walsall N, 1974-76, (English Nat. Party, April-Aug. 1976); Parly Sec., Min. of Aviation, 1964-66; Parly Under-Sec. of State for the Colonies, 1966-67; Minister of Aviation, 1967; Minister of State, Technology, 1967-68; Postmaster-General, 1968-69; Minister of Posts and Telecommunications, 1969-70. Chm., Parly Cttee of ASTMS, 1974-75; Mem. Exec. Cttee, UK Br. IPU. UK Deleg. to Council of Europe and WEU, 1962-64; Leader, UK Govt Delegns, Independence Ceremonies in Botswana and Lesotho, 1966; attended Independence Ceremonies in Uganda, 1962, Kenya, 1963, Zambia, 1964, and Mauritius, 1968, as special guest of Independence Governments. Granted citizenship of Bangladesh, 1972. Councillor, Islington Borough Council, 1956-59. Member, RIIA, 1955-65. *Publications:* (jtly) Gangrene, 1959; Prohibited Immigrant, 1960; Death of an Idealist, 1975; My Trial, 1976; Ralph, 1982. *Recreations:* music, learning to ski, desmology. *Address:* c/o Jonathan Cape Ltd, 30 Bedford Square, WC1B 3EL. *Club:* Royal Automobile.

STONES, Prof. Edward Lionel Gregory, MA, PhD; FBA 1979; Professor of Mediæval History, University of Glasgow, 1956-78, now Emeritus Professor; *b* Croydon, 4 March 1914; *s* of Edward Edison Stones, Elland, Yorks, and Eleanor Gregory; *m* 1947, Jeanne Marie Beatrice, *d* of A. J. Fradin and Florence B. Timbury; one *s* one *d. Educ:* Glasgow High Sch.; Glasgow Univ.; Balliol Coll., Oxford. 1st Cl. English Lang. and Lit. (Glasgow), 1936; 1st Class Modern History (Oxford), 1939; PhD (Glasgow), 1950; FRHistS, 1950; FSA, 1962. Asst Lectr in History, Glasgow Univ., 1939. War of 1939-45: joined Royal Signals, 1940; Major 1943; GSO2, GHQ, New Delhi (Signals Directorate), 1943-45. Lectr in History, Glasgow, 1945-56. Vis. Res. Fellow, Westfield Coll., London Univ., 1972-73. Lay Mem., Provincial Synod, Episcopal Church of Scotland, 1963-66. Pres., Glasgow Archaeological Soc., 1969-72; Member: Ancient Monuments Board for Scotland, 1964-79 (Chm. 1968-73); Council, Royal Hist. Soc., 1968-72; Council, Soc. Antiquaries, London, 1972-74. Corresp. Fellow, Mediaeval Acad. of America, 1980. *Publications:* Anglo-Scottish Relations, 1174-1328, 1965; Edward I, 1968; (ed) Maitland's Letters to Neilson, 1976; (with G. G. Simpson) Edward I and the Throne of Scotland, 1978; and articles in various historical journals. *Recreations:* books, music, photography. *Address:* 34 Alexandra Road, Parkstone, Poole, Dorset BH14 9EN. *T:* Poole 742803. *Club:* United Oxford & Cambridge University.

STONES, (Elsie) Margaret, MBE 1977; botanical artist; Visiting Artist, Louisiana State University, Baton Rouge, since 1977; *b* 28 Aug. 1920; *d* of Frederick Stones and Agnes Kirkwood (*née* Fleming). *Educ:* Swinburne Technical Coll., Melbourne; Melbourne National Gall. Art Sch. Came to England, 1951; working independently as botanical artist, 1951-: at Royal Botanic Gardens, Kew; Nat. Hist. Museum; Royal Horticultural Soc., and at other botanical instns; Contrib. Artist to Curtis's Botanical Magazine, 1957-. Drawings (water-colour): 20, Aust. plants, National Library, Canberra, 1962-63; 250, Tasmanian endemic plants, 1962-77; Basalt Plains flora, Melbourne Univ., 1975-76; to spend 3-4 months annually for 10 years at Louisiana State Univ. doing 200 water-colour drawings of Louisiana flora, 1977-. Exhibitions: Colnaghi's, London, 1967-; Retrospective Exhibn, Melbourne Univ., 1976; Louisiana Drawings, Smithsonian, USA, 1980. *Publications:* The Endemic Flora of Tasmania (text by W. M. Curtis), 6 Parts, 1967-78; illus. various books. *Recreations:* gardening, reading. *Address:* 1 Bushwood Road, Kew, Richmond, Surrey. *T:* 01-940 6183.

STONEY, Brigadier Ralph Francis Ewart, CBE 1952 (OBE, 1943); Director-General, The Royal Society for the Prevention of Accidents, 1959-68; *b* 28 June 1903; *o s* of late Col R. D. S. Stoney, The Downs, Delgany, Co. Wicklow and of Mrs E. M. M. Stoney; *m* 1st, 1939, Kathleen Nina (*née* Kirkland) (*d* 1973); one *d* ; 2nd, 1979, Bridget Mary St John Browne. *Educ:* Royal Naval Colleges, Osborne and Dartmouth; Royal Military Academy, Woolwich. Commissioned Royal Engineers, 1923; Staff College, Camberley, 1937-38. Served War of 1939-45 as GSO, 1939-43 (OBE) and as CRE, 82

Div., 1943-46, in Burma (despatches twice). CRE 5th Div. and 2nd Div., 1947-48; Col GS (Intelligence), War Office, 1949-51; Brig. GS (Intelligence), Middle East, 1952-54. Retired, 1954. *Recreations:* sailing; workshop practice. *Address:* Kinsale, Hook Heath Avenue, Woking, Surrey.

STONHOUSE, Sir Philip (Allan), 18th Bt, *cr* 1628, and 14th Bt *cr* 1670; Assessor and Land Appraiser, Government of Alberta; *b* 24 Oct. 1916; *s* of Sir Arthur Allan Stonhouse, 17th Bt, and Beatrice C. Féron; *S* father, 1967; *m* 1946, Winnifred Emily Shield; two *s. Educ:* Western Canada Coll.; Queen's Univ., Kingston, Ontario. Gold Mining, 1936-40; General Construction, 1940-42; Ranching, 1942-54; Assessing, 1954-68. Is a Freemason. *Recreations:* water-fowl and upland game hunting, tennis, ski-ing. *Heir: s* Rev. Michael Philip Stonhouse, BA, LTh [*b* 4 Sept. 1948; *m* 1977, Colleen Coucill, Toronto; one *s. Educ:* Wycliffe Coll., Toronto]. *Address:* 521-12 Street SW, Medicine Hat, Alberta, Canada. *T:* 526-5832. *Club:* Medicine Hat Ski.

STONHOUSE-GOSTLING, Maj.-Gen. Philip Le Marchant Stonhouse, CB 1955; CBE 1953; retired; *b* 28 August 1899; *s* of Colonel Charles Henry Stonhouse-Gostling and Alice Seton (*née* Fraser-Tytler); *m* 1946, Helen Rimington Myra (*née* Pereira), Ottawa, Ontario, Canada. *Educ:* Cheltenham College; RMA Woolwich. Entered RA, 1919; served India with RA, 1920-26; Mil. Coll. of Science, 1927-29; i/c Technical Intelligence, WO, 1930; Woolwich Arsenal: Asst Inspector Guns and Carriages, 1931-38; Supt Carriage Design, 1939; Technical Adviser to Canadian Govt and British Purchasing Commn for Armaments, 1939-40; Dep. Dir of Supply, British Supply Mission, Washington, 1941-44; Director of Supply (Armaments), 1944-46; Dep. Dir Technical Services, British Jt Staff Mission, 1942-46; Director, 1946-50; Dep. Chief Engineer, Armaments Design Establishment in UK, 1951; President, Ordnance Board, Feb. 1954-Feb. 1955; Retired from Army, March 1955. Exec. Engineer, Beemer Engineering Co., Philadelphia, 1955-64. Legion of Merit (Officer), USA 1944. *Recreations:* sailing, photography. *Address:* Island House West, 325 Beach Road, Tequesta, Florida 33458, USA; c/o Lloyds Bank, Cox's and King's Branch, 6 Pall Mall, SW1. *Club:* Army and Navy.

STONIER, George Walter, MA; author; critic; journalist; *b* Sydney, Australia, 1903; *m* 1951, Patricia, *d* of James Nelson Dover. *Educ:* Westminster School; Christ Church, Oxford. Assistant Literary Editor of the New Statesman and Nation, 1928-45. Has written plays for BBC: Robert Tasker Deceased, Squeaky Shoes, Chap in a Bowler Hat, etc. *Publications:* Gog Magog, 1933; The Shadow Across the Page, 1937; Shaving Through the Blitz, 1943; My Dear Bunny, 1946; The Memoirs of a Ghost, 1947; Round London with the Unicorn, 1951; Pictures on the Pavement, 1954; English Countryside in Colour, 1956; Off the Rails, 1967; Rhodesian Spring, 1968; (ed) International Film Annual, vols 2 and 3. Contributions to Observer, New Statesman and Nation, Punch, Sunday Telegraph, Sight and Sound. *Address:* Early Mist, PO Juliasdale, Zimbabwe.

STONOR, family name of **Baron Camoys.**

STOODLEY, Peter Ernest William; County Treasurer of Kent, 1972-80; *b* 27 July 1925; *s* of Ernest and Esther Stoodley; *m* 1970, June (*née* Bennett). *Educ:* Weymouth Grammar Sch.; Administrative Staff Coll.; Inst. of Public Finance Accountants. Accountant with County Council of: Dorset, 1947-56; Staffordshire, 1956-61; Kent, 1961-65; Asst Co. Treasurer of Kent, 1965-69; Dep. Co. Treasurer of Kent, 1969-72. *Recreations:* ornithology, cricket. *Address:* Cranby, Horseshoe Lane, Leeds, Maidstone, Kent. *T:* Maidstone 861287.

STOOKE, Sir George Beresford-, KCMG 1948 (CMG 1943); Gentleman Usher of the Blue Rod in the Order of St Michael and St George, 1959-71; *b* 3 Jan. 1897; *m* 1931, Creenagh, *y d* of late Sir Henry Richards; one *s* one *d.* Royal Navy, 1914-19; Colonial Service, 1920-48; Governor and C-in-C, Sierra Leone, 1948-53; Second Crown Agent for Oversea Governments and Administrations, 1953-55. Member, Kenya Camps Inquiry, 1959. Overseas Comr, Boy Scouts Assoc., 1954-61. Vice-Chm., Internat. African Inst., 1954-74. President, Anglo-Sierra Leone Society, 1962-72. 2nd Class Order of Brilliant Star of Zanzibar, 1942. KStJ, 1951. *Address:* Little Rydon, Hillfarrance, Taunton, Somerset.

STOPFORD, family name of **Earl of Courtown.**

STOPFORD, Edward Kennedy, CB 1955; Assistant Under-Secretary of State, Ministry of Defence, 1964-71, retired; *b* 10 Oct. 1911; *yr s* of late Major Heneage Frank Stopford, Royal Field Artillery, and Margaret, *d* of late Edward Briggs Kennedy; *m* 1952, Patricia Iona Mary, widow of Duncan Stewart, CMG, and *d* of late Howard Carrick; one *s. Educ:* Winchester; New College, Oxford. 1st Class, Lit Hum, 1933. Entered War Office, 1936; Under-Secretary, 1954-64. *Address:* The Folly, Fifield, Oxford. *T:* Shipton-under-Wychwood 830484.

STOPPARD, Miriam, MD, MRCP; writer and broadcaster; *b* 12 May 1937; *d* of Sydney and Jenny Stern; *m* 1972, Tom Stoppard, *qv* ; two *s* and two step *s. Educ:* Newcastle upon Tyne Central High Sch. (State Scholar, 1955); Royal Free Hosp. Sch. of Medicine, Univ. of London (Prize for Experimental Physiol., 1958); King's Coll. Med. Sch. (Univ. of Durham), Newcastle upon Tyne (MB, BS Durham, 1961; MD Newcastle, 1966). MRCP 1964. Royal Victoria Infirmary, King's Coll. Hosp., Newcastle upon Tyne: House Surg.,

1961; House Phys., 1962; Sen. House Officer in Medicine, 1962-63; Univ. of Bristol: Res. Fellow, Dept of Chem. Pathol., 1963-65 (MRC Scholar in Chem. Pathol.); Registrar in Dermatol., 1965-66 (MRC Scholar in Dermatol.); Sen. Registrar in Dermatol., 1966-68; Syntex Pharmaceuticals Ltd: Associate Med. Dir, 1968; Dep. Med. Dir, 1971; Med. Dir, 1974; Dep. Man. Dir, 1976; Man. Dir, 1977-81. MRSocMed (Mem. Dermatol. Sect., Endocrinol. Sect.); Member: Heberden Soc.; Brit. Assoc. of Rheumatology and Rehabilitation. *Publications:* Miriam Stoppard's Book of Baby Care, 1977; (contrib.) My Medical School, 1978; Miriam Stoppard's Book of Health Care, 1979; The Face and Body Book, 1980; Everywoman's Lifeguard, 1982; over 40 pubns in med. jls. *Recreations:* my family, gardening. *Address:* Iver Grove, Iver, Bucks.

STOPPARD, Tom, CBE 1978; FRSL; playwright and novelist; *b* 3 July 1937; *yr s* of late Eugene Straussler and of Mrs Martha Stoppard; *m* 1st, 1965, Jose (marr. diss. 1972), *yr d* of John and Alice Ingle; two *s*; 2nd, 1972, Dr Miriam Moore-Robinson (*see* Miriam Stoppard); two *s*. *Educ:* abroad; Dolphin Sch., Notts; Pocklington, Yorks. Journalist: Western Daily Press, Bristol, 1954-58; Bristol Evening World, 1958-60; freelance, 1960-63. Hon. degrees: Bristol, 1976; Brunel, 1979; Leeds, 1980; Sussex, 1980. Shakespeare Prize, 1979. *Plays:* Enter a Free Man, London, 1968 (TV play, A Walk on the Water, 1963); Rosencrantz and Guildenstern are Dead, Nat. Theatre, 1967, subseq. NY, etc (Tony Award, NY, 1968; NY Drama Critics Circle Award, 1968); The Real Inspector Hound, London, 1968; After Magritte, Ambiance Theatre, 1970; Dogg's Our Pet, Ambiance Theatre, 1972; Jumpers, National Theatre, 1972 (Evening Standard Award); Travesties, Aldwych, 1974 (Evening Standard Award; Tony Award, NY, 1976); Dirty Linen, Newfoundland, Ambiance Theatre, 1976; Every Good Boy Deserves Favour (music-theatre), 1977; Night and Day, Phoenix, 1978 (Evening Standard Award); Dogg's Hamlet and Cahoot's Macbeth, Collegiate, 1979; Undiscovered Country (adaptation), NT, 1979; On the Razzle, NT, 1981; *radio:* The Dissolution of Dominic Boot, 1964; M is for Moon Among Other Things, 1964; If You're Glad I'll Be Frank, 1965; Albert's Bridge, 1967 (Prix Italia); Where Are They Now?, 1970; Artist Descending a Staircase, 1972; *television:* A Separate Peace, 1966; Teeth, 1967; Another Moon Called Earth, 1967; Neutral Ground, 1968; (with Clive Exton) Boundaries, 1975; (adapted) Three Men in a Boat, 1976; Professional Foul, 1977; *film scripts:* (with T. Wiseman) The Romantic Englishwoman, 1975; Despair, 1978; The Human Factor, 1979. John Whiting Award, Arts Council, 1967; Evening Standard Award for Most Promising Playwright, 1968. *Publications:* (short stories) Introduction 2, 1964; (novel) Lord Malquist and Mr Moon, 1965; *plays:* Rosencrantz and Guildenstern are Dead, 1967; The Real Inspector Hound, 1968; Albert's Bridge, 1968; Enter a Free Man, 1968; After Magritte, 1971; Jumpers, 1972; Artists Descending a Staircase, and, Where Are They Now?, 1973; Travesties, 1975; Dirty Linen, and New-Found-Land, 1976; Every Good Boy Deserves Favour, 1978; Professional Foul, 1978; Night and Day, 1978; Undiscovered Country, 1980; Dogg's Hamlet, Cahoot's Macbeth, 1980; On the Razzle, 1982. *Address:* Iver Grove, Iver, Bucks.

STORAR, Leonore Elizabeth Therese; retired; *b* 3 May 1920. Served HM Forces, 1942-46. Min. of Labour, 1941; Min. of Works, 1947; joined CRO, 1948; First Sec., Delhi and Calcutta, 1951-53; Salisbury, 1956-58; Colombo, 1960-62; Counsellor, 1963; Head of General and Migration Dept, CRO, 1962; Dep. Consul-Gen., NY, 1967; Consul-Gen., Boston, 1969; Head of Commonwealth Co-ordination Dept, FCO, 1971-75; Dir, Colombo Plan Bureau, Colombo, Sri Lanka, 1976-78. *Address:* Lavender Cottage, Dippenhall Street, Crondall, Hants GU10 5PF.

STORER, David George; Director of Corporate Services, Manpower Services Commission, since 1977; *b* 27 June 1929; *s* of Herbert Edwards Storer; *m* 1960, Jean Mary Isobel Jenkin; one *s* two *d*. *Educ:* Monmouth School; St John's Coll., Cambridge (MA). Assistant Principal, Min. of Labour, 1952; Principal, 1957; Cabinet Office, 1963-66; Asst Secretary, Dept of Employment, 1966-73; Director, Training Opportunities Scheme, 1973-77. *Recreations:* walking, squash, sailing. *Address:* 5a Carlton Road, Redhill, Surrey RH1 2BY.

STORER, James Donald, CEng, MRAeS; Keeper, Department of Technology, Royal Scottish Museum, Edinburgh, since 1978; *b* 11 Jan. 1928; *s* of James Arthur Storer and Elizabeth May Gartshore (*née* Pirie); *m* 1955, Shirley Anne (*née* Kent); one *s* one *d*. *Educ:* Hemsworth Grammar Sch., Yorks; Imperial Coll., London (BSc Hons, ACGI). Design Office, Vickers Armstrongs (Aircraft) Ltd, and British Aircraft Corporation, Weybridge, 1948-66; Dept of Technology, Royal Scottish Museum, 1966-. MRAeS (AFRAeS 1958). *Publications:* Steel and Engineering, 1959; Behind the Scenes in an Aircraft Factory, 1965; It's Made Like This: Cars, 1967; The World We Are Making: Aviation, 1968; A Simple History of the Steam Engine, 1969; How to Run An Airport, 1971; How We Find Out About Flight, 1973; Flying Feats, 1977; Book of the Air, 1979; Great Inventions, 1980. *Recreation:* aircraft preservation. *Address:* 52 Thomson Road, Currie, Edinburgh EH14 5HW. *T:* 031-449 2843. *Club:* University of Edinburgh Staff (Edinburgh).

STORER, Prof. Roy; Professor of Prosthodontics since 1968 and Dean of Dentistry since 1977 (Clinical Sub-Dean, 1970-77) The Dental School, University of Newcastle upon Tyne; *b* 21 Feb. 1928; *s* of late Harry and Jessie Storer; *m* 1953, Kathleen Mary Frances Pitman; one *s* two *d*. *Educ:* Wallasey Grammar Sch.; Univ. of Liverpool. LDS (Liverpool) 1950; FDSRCS 1954; MSc (Liverpool) 1960; DRD RCS Ed, 1978. House Surg., 1950, and

Registrar, 1952-54, United Liverpool Hosps; Lieut (later Captain) Royal Army Dental Corps, 1950-52; Lectr in Dental Prosthetics, Univ. of Liverpool, 1954-61; Visiting Associate Prof., Northwestern Univ., Chicago, 1961-62; Sen. Lectr in Dental Prosthetics, Univ. of Liverpool, 1962-67; Hon. Cons. Dental Surgeon: United Liverpool Hosps, 1962-67; United Newcastle Hosps (now Newcastle Health Authority), 1968-. Mem. Council and Sec., British Soc. for the Study of Prosthetic Dentistry, 1960-69 (Pres., 1968-69); Mem., Bd of Faculty, RCS, 1982-. Pres., Med. Rugby Football Club (Newcastle), 1968-82; Mem., Northern Sports Council, 1973-; Chm., Div. of Dentistry, Newcastle Univ. Hosps, 1972-75. External Examiner in Dental Subjects: Univs of Belfast, Birmingham, Bristol, Dublin, Dundee, Leeds, London, Newcastle upon Tyne, and Royal Coll. of Surgeons of England. *Publications:* A Laboratory Course in Dental Materials for Dental Hygienists (with D. C. Smith), 1963; Immediate and Replacement Dentures (with J. N. Anderson), 3rd edn, 1981; papers on sci. and clin. subjects in dental and med. jls. *Recreations:* Rugby football, cricket, squash, gardening. *Address:* The Dental School, Framlington Place, Newcastle upon Tyne NE2 4BW; 164 Eastern Way, Darras Hall, Ponteland, Newcastle upon Tyne NE20 9RH. *T:* Ponteland 24399. *Clubs:* Athenæum, MCC, East India, Devonshire, Sports and Public Schools.

STOREY, Christopher, MA, PhD; Headmaster, Culford School, Bury St Edmunds, 1951-71; *b* 23 July 1908; *s* of William Storey and Margaret T. B. Cowan, Newcastle upon Tyne; *m* 1937, Gertrude Appleby, Scarborough; four *s*. *Educ:* Rutherford Coll., Newcastle upon Tyne; King's Coll., Univ. of Durham (BA Hons French, cl. I); Univ. of Strasbourg (PhD). Modern Languages Master, Mundella Sch., Nottingham, 1931-34; French Master: Scarborough High Sch. for Boys, 1934-36; City of London Sch., 1936-42. Headmaster, Johnston Grammar Sch., Durham, 1942-51. Officier d'Académie, 1947. *Publications:* Etude critique de la Vie de St Alexis, 1934; Apprenons le mot juste!, 1939; (ed) La Vie de St Alexis, 1946, 2nd rev. edn, 1968; Sprechen und Schreiben (with C. E. Bond), 1950; articles in Modern Language Review, French Studies, and Medium Aevum. *Address:* 36 Lakeside, Oxford OX2 8JH. *T:* Oxford 52328.

STOREY, David Malcolm; writer and dramatist; *b* 13 July 1933; *s* of Frank Richmond Storey and Lily (*née* Cartwright); *m* 1956, Barbara Rudd Hamilton; two *s* two *d*. *Educ:* Queen Elizabeth Grammar Sch., Wakefield, Yorks; Slade School of Fine Art, London; Fellow, UCL, 1974. *Plays:* The Restoration of Arnold Middleton, 1967 (Evening Standard Award); In Celebration, 1969 (Los Angeles Critics' Award); The Contractor, 1969 (Writer of the Year Award, Variety Club of GB, NY Critics' Award); Home, 1970 (Evening Standard Award, Critics' Award, NY); The Changing Room, 1971 (Critics' Award, NY); Cromwell, 1973; The Farm, 1973; Life Class, 1974; Mother's Day, 1976; Sisters, 1978; Early Days, 1980. *Publications:* This Sporting Life, 1960 (Macmillan Fiction Award, US); Flight into Camden, 1960 (John Llewellyn Meml Prize, Somerset Maugham award); Radcliffe, 1963; Pasmore, 1972 (Geoffrey Faber Meml Prize, 1973); A Temporary Life, 1973; Edward, 1973; Saville, 1976 (Booker Prize, 1976); A Prodigal Child, 1982. *Address:* c/o Jonathan Cape Ltd, 30 Bedford Square, WC1B 3EL.

STOREY, Maude; Chief Executive Officer, United Kingdom Central Council for Nursing, Midwifery and Health Visiting, since 1981; *b* 24 March 1930; *d* of late Henry Storey and of Sarah Farrimond Storey. *Educ:* Wigan and District Mining and Techn. Coll.; St Mary's Hosp., Manchester; Lancaster Royal Infirmary; Paddington Gen. Hosp.; Royal Coll. of Nursing, Edinburgh; Queen Elizabeth Coll., London. SRN 1952; SCM 1953; RCI (Edin.) 1962; RNT 1965. Domiciliary Midwife, Wigan County Borough, 1953-56; Midwifery Sister, St Mary's Hosp., Manchester, 1956-57; Charge Nurse, Intensive Therapy, Mayo Clinic, USA, 1957-59; Theatre Sister, Clinical Instructor, 1959-63, subseq. Nurse Tutor, 1965-68, Royal Albert Edward Infirmary, Wigan; Lectr in Community Nursing, Manchester Univ., 1968-71; Asst, subseq. Principal Regional Nursing Officer, Liverpool Regional Hosp. Bd, 1971-73; Regional Nursing Officer, Mersey RHA, 1973-77; Registrar, GNC for England and Wales, 1977-81. Member: Standing Nursing and Midwifery Adv. Cttee, 1977-; West Berks DHA, 1982-. FBIM. *Recreations:* travel, theatre, amateur dramatics. *Address:* 14 Conifer Drive, Long Lane, Tilehurst, Berks. *T:* Reading 412082. *Club:* Royal Commonwealth Society.

STOREY, Hon. Sir Richard, 2nd Bt *cr* 1960; Chairman of Portsmouth and Sunderland Newspapers plc, since 1973; Member, Press Council, since 1980; *b* 23 Jan. 1937; *s* of Baron Buckton (Life Peer) and Elisabeth (*d* 1951), *d* of late Brig.-Gen. W. J. Woodcock, DSO; *S* to baronetcy of father, 1978; *m* 1961, Virginia Anne, 3rd *d* of Sir Kenelm Cayley, 10th Bt; one *s* two *d*. *Educ:* Winchester; Trinity Coll., Cambridge (BA, LLB). National service commission, RNVR, 1956. Called to the Bar, Inner Temple, 1962. Director, Portsmouth and Sunderland Newspapers plc, 1962. Mem. Exec. Cttee, CLA. *Recreations:* sport and silviculture. *Heir:* *s* Kenelm Storey, *b* 4 Jan. 1963. *Address:* Settrington House, Malton, North Yorks. *T:* North Grimston 200; 7 Douro Place, W8 5PH. *T:* 01-937 8823.

STORIE-PUGH, Col Peter David, CBE 1981 (MBE 1945); MC 1940; TD 1945 and 3 clasps; DL; Member, Economic and Social Committee of the European Communities, since 1982; Lecturer, University of Cambridge, 1953-82; Fellow of Wolfson College, Cambridge, since 1967; *b* 1 Nov. 1919; *s* of Prof. Leslie Pugh, *qv*; *m* 1st, 1946, Alison (marr. diss. 1971), *d* of late Sir Oliver Lyle, OBE; one *s* two *d*; 2nd, 1971, Leslie Helen, *d* of Earl Striegel;

three s one d. *Educ:* Malvern; Queens' Coll., Cambridge (Hon. Foundn Scholar); Royal Veterinary Coll., Univ. of London. MA, PhD, FRCVS, CChem, FRSC. Served War of 1939-45, Queen's Own Royal W Kent Regt (escaped from Spangenberg and Colditz); comd 1st Bn, Cambs Regt, comd 1st Bn Suffolk and Cambs Regt; Col, Dep. Comdr, 161 Inf. Bde, ACF County Comdt. Wellcome Res. Fellow, Cambridge, 1950-52. Mem. Council, RCVS, 1956- (Chm. Parly Cttee, 1962-67; Pres., 1977-78); President: Cambridge Soc. for Study of Comparative Medicine, 1966-67; Internat. Pig Vet. Soc., 1967-69 (Life Pres., 1969); British Veterinary Assoc., 1968-69 and 1970-71; Mem. Exec. Cttee, Cambridgeshire Farmers Union, 1960-65; UK delegate, EEC Vet. Liaison Cttee, 1962-75 (Pres., 1973-75); UK Rep., Fedn of Veterinarians of EEC, 1975- (Pres. of Fedn, 1975-79); Chm., Eurovet, 1971-73; Mem. Jt RCVS/BVA Cttee on European Vet. Affairs, 1971-; Observer, European Liaison Gp for Agric., 1972-80; Jt Pres., 1st European Vet. Congress, Wiesbaden, 1972; Permanent Mem. EEC Adv. Vet. Cttee, 1976-82; Mem. Council, Secrétariat Européen des Professions Libérales, Intellectuelles et Sociales, 1976-80; Mem. Permanent Cttee, World Vet. Assoc., 1964-75. Member: Parly and Sci. Cttee, 1962-67; Home Sec.'s Adv. Cttee (Cruelty to Animals Act, 1876), 1963-80; Nat. Agric. Centre Adv. Bd, 1966-69; Production Cttee, Meat and Livestock Commn, 1967-70; Min. of Agriculture's Farm Animal Adv. Cttee, 1970-73. Chm., Nat. Sheep Breeders' Assoc., 1964-68; Vice-Pres., Agric. Section, British Assocn, 1970-71. Corresp. Mem., Bund Deutscher Veterinäroffiziere, 1979-. Robert von Ostertag Medal, German Vet. Assoc., 1972. DL Cambs, 1963. *Publications:* (and ed jtly) Eurovet: an Anatomy of Veterinary Europe, 1972; Eurovet-2, 1975. *Address:* Duxford Grange, Duxford, Cambridge CB2 4QF. *T:* Fowlmere 403. *Club:* United Oxford & Cambridge University.

STORK, Herbert Cecil, CIE 1945; *b* 28 June 1890; *s* of Herbert William and Florence Stork; *m* 1919, Marjorie (*née* Cosens); two *d. Educ:* Merchant Taylors' School; Queen's College, Oxford (BA). Appointed to ICS, Dec. 1913; served Bengal and Assam, various posts, concluding with Legal Remembrancer and Secretary to Government of Assam; retired from ICS, 1947. Served European War, 1914-18; GSO III, 9th (Secunderabad) Division, and Staff Captain, Dunsterforce, MEF. *Address:* 49 Wood Green, Witney, Oxon. *T:* Witney 72880. *Club:* Oxford Union Society.

STORK, Joseph Whiteley, CB 1959; CBE 1949; retired as Director of Studies, Britannia Royal Naval College, Dartmouth (1955-59) (Headmaster, 1942-55); *b* Huddersfield, 9 Aug. 1902; *s* of John Arthur Stork, Huddersfield; *m* 1927, Kathleen, *d* of Alderman J. H. Waddington, JP, Halifax; one *s* three *d. Educ:* Uppingham; Downing Coll., Cambridge (scholar). 1st Class Nat. Sci. Tripos Pt 1, 2nd Class Nat. Sci. Tripos Pt II (Zoology); Senior Biology Master, Cambridge and County School, 1926; Head of Biological Dept, Charterhouse School, 1926-36; Headmaster, Portsmouth Grammar School, 1936-42. *Publications:* Joint Author of: Fundamentals of Biology, 1932, Junior Biology, 1933, Plant and Animal Ecology, 1933. *Address:* Peverell Old School, Peverell Terrace, Portleven, Helston, Cornwall TR13 9DH.

STORMONT, Viscount; Alexander David Mungo Murray; *b* 17 Oct. 1956; *s* and *heir* of 8th Earl of Mansfield and Mansfield, *qv. Address:* Scone Palace, Perthshire.

STORMONTH DARLING, James Carlisle, CBE 1972; MC 1945; TD; Director, The National Trust for Scotland, 1971-July 1983 (Secretary, as Chief Executive, 1949-71); *b* 18 July 1918; *s* of late Robert Stormonth Darling, Writer to the Signet, Rosebank, Kelso, Roxburghshire, and late Beryl Madeleine Sayer, Battle, Sussex; *m* 1948, Mary Finella, BEM 1945, *d* of late Lt.-Gen. Sir James Gammell, KCB, DSO, MC; one *s* two *d. Educ:* Winchester Coll.; Christ Church, Oxford; BA 1939, MA 1972; Edinburgh Univ.; LLB 1949. 2nd Lt KOSB (TA), 1938; War Service, 1939-46, in KOSB and 52nd (L) Reconnaissance Regt, RAC, of which Lt-Col comdg in 1945 (TD). Admitted Writer to the Signet, 1949. Member, Queen's Body Guard for Scotland (Royal Company of Archers), 1958-. *Address:* Chapel Hill House, Dirleton, East Lothian. *T:* Dirleton 296; (until July 1983) National Trust for Scotland, 5 Charlotte Square, Edinburgh EH2 4DU. *Clubs:* New, Puffins (Edinburgh).

STORR, (Charles) Anthony, FRCP, FRCPsych; writer and psychiatrist; Clinical Lecturer in Psychiatry, Faculty of Medicine, University of Oxford, since 1974; Fellow, Green College, Oxford, since 1979; *b* 18 May 1920; *y s* of Vernon Faithfull Storr, Subdean of Westminster and Katherine Cecilia Storr; *m* 1st, 1942, Catherine Cole; three *d*; 2nd, 1970, Catherine Barton (*née* Peters). *Educ:* Winchester Coll.; Christ's Coll., Cambridge; Westminster Hosp. Medical School. MB, BChir Cantab; Qual. in medicine, 1944; postgrad. trng in psychiatry, Maudsley Hosp., 1947-50; held various positions as psychiatrist in different hospitals; Conslt Psychotherapist, Oxford AHA, 1974-. Member: Parole Bd, 1976-77; Cttee on Obscenity and Film Censorship, 1977-79. *Publications:* The Integrity of the Personality, 1960; Sexual Deviation, 1964; Human Aggression, 1968; Human Destructiveness, 1972; The Dynamics of Creation, 1972; Jung, 1973; The Art of Psychotherapy, 1979; contrib. several books and jls. *Recreations:* music, broadcasting, journalism. *Address:* 7 St Margaret's Road, Oxford OX2 6RU. *T:* Oxford 53348. *Club:* Savile.

STORR, Norman, OBE 1947; with Charity Commission, 1967-73; *b* 9 Dec. 1907; *s* of Herbert Storr and Beatrice Emily Storr, Barnsley; *m* 1937, Kathleen Mary Ward; two *s* one *d. Educ:* Holgate's Grammar School, Barnsley; Keble

College, Oxford. Open schol. in Mod. History, Keble Coll., Oxford, 1926; BA Hons Mod. History, 1929. Entered Indian Civil Service, 1930; Session Judge, 1935; Registrar, Allahabad High Court, 1939; Registrar, Federal Court of India, 1943-47. Principal, Home Office, 1947; Principal, 1952, Establishment Officer, 1958, Comr and Sec., 1962, Prison Commission; Asst Sec., Estab. Div. Home Office, 1966-67, retired. *Recreation:* painting. *Address:* Moorlands, Amberley, near Stroud, Glos. *Club:* Royal Over-Seas League.

STORRAR, Sir John, Kt 1953; CBE 1949; MC 1917; Town Clerk of Edinburgh, 1941-56; *b* 8 Dec. 1891; *s* of late Rev. Wm Storrar, Hardgate, Dalbeattie, Kirkcudbrightshire; *m* Agnes Drennan (*d* 1978), *d* of late James Cameron, Hollos, Lenzie; one *d. Educ:* Castle Douglas Academy; Edinburgh Univ. Solicitor, 1914. Served European War, Royal Scots, 1914-19 (despatches, MC). Local Government service, 1923; Depute Town Clerk, Edinburgh, 1934. Member of various government committees. Hon. LLD Edinburgh, 1957. *Address:* 3 Merchiston Park, Edinburgh.

STORRAR, Air Vice-Marshal Ronald Charles, CB 1957; OBE 1945; psc; *b* 4 Sept. 1904; *m* 1932, Vera Winifred Butler; one *s.* Commissioned RAF, 1929; Served in India, 1932-37; Student RAF Staff Coll., 1938; USA, 1942-44; CO No 21 MU, Fauld, 1945-46; Directing Staff, RAF Staff Coll., 1946-49; CO No 16 MU, Stafford, 1952-54; ACC No 42 Group, 1955; SASO No 40 Group, 1956-60, Maintenance Command, 1960-63. *Address:* Apartado 45, Fuengirola, near Malaga, Spain. *Club:* Royal Air Force.

STOTESBURY, Herbert Wentworth; Assistant Under-Secretary of State, Home Office, 1966-75; Probation and Aftercare Department, 1969-75; *b* 22 Jan. 1916; *s* of Charles and Ada Stotesbury; *m* 1944, Berenice Mary Simpson; one *s* two *d. Educ:* Christ's Hospital; Emmanuel College, Cambridge. Home Office, 1939; Army, 1940-45. Lecturer, Military Coll. of Science, 1941-45. Home Office, 1945-75; Asst Secretary, 1953. Chm., Working Party on Marriage Guidance, 1976-78 (consultative document: Marriage Matters). *Recreations:* music, gardening, travel. *Address:* 65 Woodside, Wimbledon, SW19. *T:* 01-946 9523.

STOTT, Rt. Hon. Lord; George Gordon Stott, PC 1964; Senator of College of Justice in Scotland since 1967; *b* 22 Dec. 1909; *s* of Rev. Dr G. Gordon Stott; *m* 1947, Nancy, *d* of A. D. Braggins; one *s* one *d. Educ:* Cramond Sch.; Edinburgh Acad.; Edinburgh Univ. Advocate 1936; QC (Scotland) 1950; Advocate-Depute, 1947-51; Editor, Edinburgh Clarion, 1939-44; Member, Monopolies Commission, 1949-56; Sheriff of Roxburgh, Berwick and Selkirk, 1961-64; Lord Advocate, 1964-67. *Address:* 12 Midmar Gardens, Edinburgh. *T:* 031-447 4251.

STOTT, Sir Adrian (George Ellingham), 4th Bt *cr* 1920; town planning consultant, since 1977; *b* 7 Oct. 1948; *s* of Sir Philip Sidney Stott, 3rd Bt, and of Cicely Florence, *o d* of Bertram Ellingham; *S* father, 1979. *Educ:* Univ. of British Columbia (BSc (Maths) 1968, MSc (Town Planning) 1974); Univ. of Waterloo, Ont (MMaths (Computer Science) 1971). Mem. Cdn Inst. of Planners (MCIP). Dir of Planning for a rural region of BC, 1974; formed own consulting practice in planning, 1977. *Recreations:* music, inland waterways, politics. *Heir: b* Vyvyan Philip Stott, *b* 5 Aug. 1952. *Address:* 45 Knoll Wood, Victoria, BC V9B 1E4, Canada. *T:* (604) 479-8652.

STOTT, Rt. Hon. George Gordon; *see* Stott, Rt Hon. Lord.

STOTT, Rev. John Robert Walmsley, MA Cantab; Director, London Institute for Contemporary Christianity, since 1982; Hon. Chaplain to the Queen, since 1959; *b* 27 April 1921; *s* of late Sir Arnold W. Stott, KBE, physician, and late Emily Caroline Holland. *Educ:* Rugby Sch.; Trinity Coll., Cambridge; Ridley Hall, Cambridge. Curate of All Souls, Langham Place, 1945; Rector of All Souls, 1950-75 (with St Peter's, Vere Street, 1952), now Rector Emeritus. Chm., C of E Evangelical Council, 1967. Hon. DD, Trinity Evangelical Divinity Sch., Deerfield, USA, 1971. *Publications:* Men with a Message, 1954; What Christ Thinks of the Church, 1958; Basic Christianity, 1958; Your Confirmation, 1958; Fundamentalism and Evangelism, 1959; The Preacher's Portrait, 1961; Confess Your Sins, 1964; The Epistles of John, 1964; Canticles and Selected Psalms, 1966; Men Made New, 1966; Our Guilty Silence, 1967; The Message of Galatians, 1968; One People, 1969; Christ The Controversialist, 1970; Understanding the Bible, 1972; Guard the Gospel, 1973; Balanced Christianity, 1975; Christian Mission in the Modern World, 1975; Baptism and Fullness, 1975; The Lausanne Covenant, 1975; Christian Counter-Culture, 1978; Focus on Christ, 1979; God's New Society, 1979; I Believe in Preaching, 1982. *Recreations:* bird watching and photography. *Address:* 13 Bridford Mews, Devonshire Street, W1.

STOTT, Peter Frank, CBE 1978; MA, FEng, FICE, FIHE, FIEAust, FCIT; Director-General, National Water Council, 1973-83; *b* 8 Aug. 1927; *s* of late Clarence Stott and of Mabel Sutcliffe; *m* 1953, Vera Watkins; two *s. Educ:* Bradford Grammar Sch.; Clare Coll., Cambridge. Partner, G. Maunsell & Partners, Consulting Engineers, 1955-63; Deputy Chief Engineer (Roads) and later Chief Engineer, London County Council, 1963-65; Dir of Highways and Transportation, GLC, 1964-67; Traffic Comr and Dir of Transportation, GLC, 1967-69; Controller of Planning and Transportation, GLC, 1969-73. Sec.-Gen., Internat. Water Supply Assoc., 1980-. President: Reinforced Concrete Assoc., 1964; Concrete Soc., 1967; Instn of Highway Engineers,

1971-72; Mem. Council, ICE, 1966-71, 1972-75 and 1976-79. *Address:* 7 Frank Dixon Way, SE21. *T:* 01-693 5121. *Club:* Athenæum.

STOTT, Roger, CBE 1979; MP (Lab) Westhoughton, since May 1973; *b* 7 Aug. 1943; *s* of Richard and Edith Stott; *m* 1969, Irene Mills (marr. diss. 1982); two *s*. *Educ:* Rochdale Tech. Coll. Served in Merchant Navy, 1959-64. Post Office Telephone Engineer, 1964-73. PPS to Sec. of State for Industry, 1975-76; PPS to the Prime Minister, 1976-79, to Leader of the Opposition, 1979; opposition spokesman on transport, 1980-. Mem., Select Cttee on Agriculture, 1980-. Pres., Bass Wingates Band. *Recreations:* football, cricket, gardening. *Address:* House of Commons, SW1A 0AA; 24 Highgate Crescent, Appley Bridge, Wigan.

STOURTON, family name of **Baron Mowbray, Segrave and Stourton.**

STOURTON, Sir Ivo (Herbert Evelyn Joseph), Kt 1961; CMG 1951; OBE 1939; KPM 1949; Inspector General of Colonial Police 1957-66; *b* 18 July 1901; *s* of late Major H. M. Stourton, OBE, and late Hon. Mrs H. Stourton; *m* 1st, 1926, Lilian (*d* 1942), *d* of late G. Dickson; two *s* one *d*; 2nd, 1945, Virginia, *d* of late Sir Horace Seymour, GCMG, CVO, and of Violet (*née* Erskine); one *d*. *Educ:* Stonyhurst College, Lancs. Joined Colonial Police Service, 1921; Asst Supt of Police; served Mauritius, 1921-33; Commissioner of Police: Bermuda, 1933-39; Zanzibar, 1939-40; Aden, 1940-45; Uganda, 1945-50; Nigeria, 1950; Inspector-Gen. of Police, Nigeria, 1951, retd 1953. Re-appointed as Deputy Inspector General of Colonial Police, 1953-57. Kt of Malta. *Address:* The Old Bakery, Kimpton, Andover, Hants. *T:* Weyhill 2446.

STOURTON, Hon. John Joseph, TD; *b* 5 March 1899; *yr s* of 24th Lord Mowbray; *m* 1st, 1923, Kathleen Alice (marr. diss. 1933), *d* of late Robert Louis George Gunther, of 8 Princes Gardens and Park Wood, Englefield Green, Surrey; two *s* two *d*; 2nd, 1934, Gladys Leila (marr. diss. 1947), *d* of late Col Sir W. J. Waldron. *Educ:* Downside School. MP (C) South Salford, 1931-45. Served N Russian Relief Force at Archangel, 1919; and in European War, 1939-43; late Lt 10th Royal Hussars; Major The Royal Norfolk Regiment.
See also Earl of Gainsborough, H. L. C. Greig.

STOUT, Alan Ker, MA, FAHA; FASSA; Professor of Philosophy, University of Sydney, 1939-65, now Emeritus Professor; *b* Oxford, 9 May 1900; *s* of late Professor G. F. Stout and Ella Ker; *m* Evelyn Roberts, BA; one *s* one *d*. *Educ:* Fettes College, Edinburgh; Oriel College, Oxford. First Class Hon. Mods Oxford; Second Class Lit Hum Oxford; Bishop Fraser Research Scholar, Oriel Coll., 1922; Lecturer in Philosophy, Univ. College of North Wales, Bangor, 1924-34, Univ. of Edinburgh, 1934-39. Visiting Prof., Univ. of Wisconsin, 1966. Pres., Council for Civil Liberties, 1964-67; Member: Aust. National Film Board, 1945-47; Aust. Nat. Adv. Cttee for UNESCO, 1949-74; Bd of Dirs, Tasmanian Theatre Co., 1972-77; Governor, Aust. Film Inst., 1960-75. Mem. Council, Aust. Consumers' Assoc., 1963-79. Fellow, Univ. Senate, Univ. of Sydney, 1954-69. Drama Critic, Aust. Quarterly, 1961-65. Editor, Australasian Jl of Philosophy, 1950-67. *Publications:* Articles and Reviews (especially on the Philosophy of Descartes and on Moral Theory) in Mind, Proceedings of Aristotelian Soc., Philosophy, Australasian Journal of Philosophy, Australian Quarterly, etc., from 1926; Editor God and Nature (posthumously published Gifford lectures of G. F. Stout), 1952. *Recreation:* the theatre. *Address:* 12 Lambert Avenue, Sandy Bay, Hobart, Tasmania 7005, Australia.
See also D. K. Stout.

STOUT, Prof. David Ker; Head of Economics, Unilever plc, since 1982; Visiting Professor of Economics, Leicester University, since 1982 (Professor of Economics, 1980-81); *b* Bangor, N Wales, 27 Jan. 1932; *s* of Prof. Alan Ker Stout, *qv*; *m* 1956, Margaret Sugden; two *s* two *d*. *Educ:* Sydney High Sch.; Sydney Univ., NSW (BA 1st Cl. English Lit, Econs, and University Medal in Econs, 1953); NSW Rhodes Scholar 1954; Magdalen Coll., Oxford; George Webb Medley Jun. Scholar 1955, Sen. Scholar 1956; PPE 1st Cl. 1956; Nuffield Coll., Oxford (Studentship 1956); Magdalen Prize Fellow by Examination, 1958-59. Fellow and Lectr in Econs, University Coll., Oxford, 1959-76; Economic Dir, NEDO, 1971-72 and 1976-80. Adviser on tax structure to Syrian Govt, 1965, and New Hebrides Condominium, 1966; Sen. Econ. Adviser to Monopolies Commn, 1969; Consultant on VAT, Nat. Bureau of Econ. Res., NY, 1970; Adviser to Australian Govt on Prices Justification, 1973, and on Wage Indexation, 1975-76. Member: Management Cttee, NIESR, 1974-; EEC Expert Gp on Community Planning, 1976-78, and on Adjustment Policy, 1979-80. *Publications:* papers on taxation policy, VAT, investment, incomes policy, trade performance, indust. policy, de-industrialisation, and European planning. *Recreations:* music, fell-running. *Address:* Unilever Ltd, PO Box 68, EC4P 4BQ. *T:* 01-822 6557. *Club:* United Oxford & Cambridge University.

STOUT, Samuel Coredon; HM Diplomatic Service, retired; *b* 17 Feb. 1913; *m* 1st, Mary Finn (*d* 1965); two *s* one *d*; 2nd, 1966, Jill Emery. Ministry of National Insurance, 1937-40; Admiralty, 1940-46; Board of Trade, 1946-65 (Trade Commissioner, Singapore, Bombay and Melbourne); Counsellor (Commercial), Canberra, 1966-68; Dep. High Comr and Minister (Commercial), Karachi, 1968-70; Consul-Gen, St Louis, USA, 1970-72. *Address:* Richmond House, Alverston Avenue, Woodhall Spa, Lincs.

STOUT, William Ferguson, CB 1964; Security Adviser to Government of Northern Ireland, 1971-72, retired; *b* Holywood, Co. Down, 22 Feb. 1907; *s* of late Robert and Amelia Stout; *m* 1938, Muriel Kilner; one *s* one *d*. *Educ:* Sullivan Upper Sch., Holywood; Queen's Univ., Belfast. Ministry of Home Affairs: Principal, 1943; Asst Sec., 1954; Senior Asst Sec., 1959; Permanent Sec., 1961-64; Permanent Secretary: Min. of Health and Local Govt, 1964; Min. of Development, 1965-71. *Recreation:* golf.

STOW, Archdeacon of; see Scott, Ven. David.

STOW, Sir Christopher P.; see Philipson-Stow.

STOW, Sir John Montague, GCMG 1966 (KCMG 1959; CMG 1950); KCVO 1966; Governor-General of Barbados, 1966-67; retired, 1967; *b* 3 Oct. 1911; *s* of late Sir Alexander Stow, KCIE; *m* 1939, Beatrice Tryhorne; two *s*. *Educ:* Harrow School; Pembroke College, Cambridge. Administrative Officer, Nigeria, 1934; Secretariat, Gambia, 1938; Chief Sec., Windward Islands, 1944; Administrator, St Lucia, BWI, 1947; Dir of Establishments, Kenya, 1952-55; Chief Sec., Jamaica, 1955-59; Governor and C-in-C Barbados, 1959-66. Vice-Chm., Commonwealth Soc. for Deaf, 1969-. KStJ 1959. *Recreations:* cricket, tennis. *Address:* 26a Tregunter Road, SW10. *T:* 01-370 1921. *Clubs:* Caledonian, MCC.

STOW, (Julian) Randolph; writer; *b* Geraldton, W Australia, 28 Nov. 1935; *s* of Cedric Ernest Stow, barrister and Mary Stow (*née* Sewell). *Educ:* Guildford Grammar Sch., W Australia; Univ. of Western Australia. Lecturer in English Literature: Univ. of Leeds, 1962; Univ. of Western Australia, 1963-64; Harkness Fellow, United States, 1964-66; Lectr in English and Commonwealth Lit., Univ. of Leeds, 1968-69. Miles Franklin Award, 1958; Britannica Australia Award, 1966; Patrick White Award, 1979. *Publications: poems:* Outrider, 1962; A Counterfeit Silence, 1969; *novels:* To The Islands, 1958, rev. edn 1981; Tourmaline, 1963; The Merry-go-round in the Sea, 1965; Visitants, 1979; The Girl Green as Elderflower, 1980; *music theatre* (with Peter Maxwell Davies): Eight Songs for a Mad King, 1969; Miss Donnithorne's Maggot, 1974; *for children:* Midnite, 1967. *Address:* c/o Richard Scott Simon Ltd, 32 College Cross, N1 1PR.

STOW, Ralph Conyers, CBE 1981; FCIS, FCBSI; President and Chairman, Cheltenham & Gloucester Building Society, since 1982 (Managing Director, 1973-82); Chairman, Cheltenham District Health Authority, since 1981; *b* 19 Dec. 1916; *s* of Albert Conyers Stow and Mabel Louise Bourlet; *m* 1943, Eleanor Joyce Appleby; one *s* one *d*. *Educ:* Woodhouse Sch., Finchley. FCIS 1959; FBS 1952. Supt of Branches, Temperance Permanent Bldg Soc., 1950, Asst Manager 1958; Gen. Man. and Sec., Cheltenham & Gloucester Bldg Soc., 1962, Dir 1967. Pres., Bldg Socs Inst., 1971-72; Chm., Midland Assoc. of Bldg Socs, 1973-74; Chm., Bldg Socs Assoc., 1977-79. Mem., Glos AHA, 1973-81. Mem. Council, Cheltenham Coll.; Governor, Bournside Sch., Cheltenham. *Recreations:* photography, oil painting. *Address:* Shepherds Fold, Charlton Hill, Charlton Kings, Cheltenham, Glos. *T:* Cheltenham 87305. *Clubs:* Royal Automobile; Rotary, The New (Cheltenham).

STOW, Randolph; see Stow, J. R.

STOWE, Sir Kenneth (Ronald), KCB 1980 (CB 1977); CVO 1979; Permanent Secretary, Department of Health and Social Security, since 1981; *b* 17 July 1927; *er s* of Arthur and Emily Stowe; *m* 1949, Joan Frances Cullen; two *s* one *d*. *Educ:* County High Sch., Dagenham; Exeter Coll., Oxford (MA). Asst Principal, Nat. Assistance Board, 1951; Principal, 1956; seconded UN Secretariat, New York, 1958; Asst Sec., 1964; Asst Under-Sec. of State, DHSS, 1970-73; Under Sec., Cabinet Office, 1973-75; Dep. Sec., 1976; Principal Private Sec. to the Prime Minister, 1975-79; Dep. Sec., 1979, Permanent Under Sec. of State, 1979-81, NI Office. *Recreations:* opera, theatre, hill walking. *Address:* Thistlelark, Church Road, Newton, Sudbury, Suffolk. *Club:* Athenæum.

STOY, Prof. Philip Joseph; Professor of Dentistry, Queen's University of Belfast, 1948-73, now Professor Emeritus; *b* 19 Jan. 1906; *m* 1945, Isabella Mary Beatrice Crispin; two *s*. *Educ:* Wolverhampton School. Queen's Scholar, Birmingham Univ., 1929; LDS, RCS, 1931; BDS (Hons), Birmingham 1932; FDS, RCS, 1947; Fellow of the Faculty of Dentistry, RCSI, 1963 (FFDRCSI). Lectr in Dental Mechanics, Univ. of Bristol, 1934; Lectr in Dental Surgery, Univ. of Bristol, 1940. *Publications:* articles in British Dental Journal, Dental Record. *Recreations:* reading, walking, painting, dental history, chess. *Address:* Westward Ho!, 57 Imperial Road, Exmouth, Devon EX8 1DQ. *T:* Exmouth 5113.

STOYLE, Roger John B.; see Blin-Stoyle.

STRABOLGI, 11th Baron of England, *cr* 1318; **David Montague de Burgh Kenworthy;** Opposition Spokesman on Energy, since 1979, and the Arts, since 1981, House of Lords; *b* 1 Nov. 1914; *e s* of 10th Baron Strabolgi and Doris, *o c* of late Sir Frederick Whitley-Thomson, MP; *S* father, 1953; *m* 1961, Doreen Margaret, *e d* of late Alexander Morgan, Ashton-under-Lyne. *Educ:* Gresham's School; Chelsea Sch. of Art; Paris. Served with HM Forces, BEF, 1939-40; MEF, 1940-45, as Lt-Col RAOC. Mem. Parly Delegations to USSR, 1954, SHAPE, 1955. PPS to Minister of State, Home Office, 1968-69; PPS to Leader of the House of Lords and Lord Privy Seal, 1969-70; Asst Opposition Whip, and spokesman on the Arts, House of Lords, 1970-74;

Captain of the Yeomen of the Guard (Dep. Govt Chief Whip), and Govt spokesman on Energy and Agriculture, 1974-79. Member: Franco-British Parly Relations Cttee; British Sect., Franco-British Council, 1981; Council, Franco-British Soc.; Council, Alliance Française in GB; Labour Party. Dir, Bolton Building Soc., 1958-74, 1979-. Officier de la Légion d'Honneur. *Heir-pres:* b Rev. Hon. Jonathan Malcolm Atholl Kenworthy, MA; retired; Chaplain HM's Forces in World War II [b 16 Sept. 1916; m 1st, 1943, Joan Gaster (d 1963); two d ; 2nd, 1963, Victoria Hewitt; two s one d]. *Address:* House of Lords, SW1A 0PW.

See also Sir Harold Hood, Bt.

STRACEY, Sir John (Simon), 9th Bt cr 1818; b 30 Nov. 1938; s of Captain Algernon Augustus Henry Stracey (2nd s of 6th Bt) (d 1940) and Olive Beryl (d 1972), d of late Major Charles Robert Eustace Radclyffe; S cousin, 1971; m 1968, Martha Maria, d of late Johann Egger; two d. *Heir:* cousin Henry Mounteney Stracey [b 24 April 1920; m 1st, 1943, Susanna, d of Adair Tracey; one d ; 2nd, 1950, Lysbeth, o d of Charles Ashford, NZ; one s one d ; 3rd, 1961, Jeltje, y d of Scholte de Boer]. *Address:* 652 Belmont Avenue, Westmount, Quebec H3Y 2W2, Canada. T: (514) 489-8904. *Club:* Royal St Lawrence Yacht (Montreal).

STRACHAN, Alan Lockhart Thomson; Artistic Director, Greenwich Theatre, since 1978; b 3 Sept. 1946; s of Roualeyn Robert Scott Strachan and Ellen Strachan (née Graham); m 1977, Jennifer Piercey-Thompson. *Educ:* Morgan Acad., Dundee; St Andrews Univ. (MA); Merton Coll., Oxford (B.Litt). Associate Dir, Mermaid Theatre, 1970-75; freelance director, 1975-78. Productions include: Mermaid: The Watched Pot, 1970; John Bull's Other Island, The Old Boys, 1971; (co-deviser) Cowardy Custard, 1972; Misalliance, 1973; Children, (co-deviser and dir) Cole, 1974; Greenwich: An Audience Called Edouard, 1978; The Play's the Thing, I Sent a Letter to my Love, 1979; Private Lives (transf. Duchess), Time and the Conways, 1980; Present Laughter (transf. Vaudeville), The Golden Age, The Doctor's Dilemma, 1981; Design for Living (transf. Globe), 1982; A Family and a Fortune, Apollo, 1975; (deviser and dir) Shakespeare's People, world tours, 1975-78; Confusions, Apollo, 1976; (also jt author) Yahoo, Queen's, 1976; Just Between Ourselves, Queen's, 1977; The Immortal Haydon, Mermaid and Greenwich, Bedroom Farce, Amsterdam, 1978. *Publications:* contribs to periodicals. *Recreations:* music, tennis, travelling. *Address:* 11 Garlies Road, SE23 2RU. T: 01-699 3360.

STRACHAN, Alexander William Bruce, OBE 1971; HM Diplomatic Service, retired; b 2 July 1917; s of William Fyfe and Winifred Orchar Strachan; m 1940, Rebecca Price MacFarlane; one s one d. *Educ:* Daniel Stewart's Coll., Edinburgh; Allen Glen's High Sch., Glasgow. GPO, 1935; Army, 1939-46; Asst Postal Controller, 1949-64; Postal Advisor to Iraq Govt, 1964-66; First Sec., FCO, 1967-68; Jordan, 1968-72; Addis Ababa, 1972-73; Consul General, Lahore, 1973-74; Counsellor (Economic and Commercial) and Consul General, Islamabad, 1975-77. Order of Istiqlal, Hashemite Kingdom of Jordan, 1971. *Address:* c/o Barclays Bank Ltd, 12 Station Parade, Sanderstead, Surrey CR2 0PH.

STRACHAN, Major Benjamin Leckie, CMG 1978; HM Diplomatic Service; Ambassador to Algeria, since 1981; b 4 Jan. 1924; e s of late Dr C. G. Strachan, MC, FRCPE and Annie Primrose (née Leckie); m 1958, Lize Lund; three s and one step s one step d. *Educ:* Rossall Sch. (Scholar); RMCS. Royal Dragoons, 1944; France and Germany Campaign, 1944-45 (despatches); 4th QO Hussars, Malayan Campaign, 1948-51; Middle East Centre for Arab Studies, 1952-53; GSO2, HQ British Troops Egypt, 1954-55; Technical Staff Course, RMCS, 1956-58; 10th Royal Hussars, 1959-61; GSO2, WO, 1961; retd from Army and joined Foreign (subseq. Diplomatic) Service, 1961; 1st Sec., FO, 1961-62; Information Adviser to Governor of Aden, 1962-63; FO, 1964-66; Commercial Sec., Kuwait, 1966-69; Counsellor, Amman, 1969-71; Trade Comr, Toronto, 1971-74; Consul General, Vancouver, 1974-76; Ambassador to Yemen Arab Republic, 1977-78, and to Republic of Jibuti (non-resident), 1978, to the Lebanon, 1978-81. *Recreations:* golf, tennis, squash, fishing. *Address:* c/o Foreign and Commonwealth Office, SW1.

STRACHAN, Graham Robert, CBE 1977; DL; FEng, FIMechE, FIMarE; Group Managing Director, John Brown Engineering Ltd, since 1975 (Director and General Manager 1966, Managing Director 1968); Chairman, John Brown Engineering Gas Turbines Ltd, since 1976 (Director, 1975); Director, John Brown & Co. (Overseas) Ltd, since 1978; b 1 Nov. 1931; o c of George Strachan and Lily Elizabeth (née Ayres); m 1960, Catherine Nicol Liston, o d of John and Eileen Vivian; two s. *Educ:* Trinity Coll., Glenalmond; Trinity Coll., Cambridge (MA, 3rd Cl. Hons Mech. Scis Tripos). Apprentice Engineer: Alexander Stephen and Sons Ltd, 1950-52; John Brown & Co. (Clydebank) Ltd, 1952-55. National Service, RNVR, Actg Sub-Lieut (E), 1955-57. John Brown & Co. (Clydebank) Ltd: Design Engr, 1957; Devolt Engr, 1959; Engrg Dir, 1963; Director: British Smelter Constructions Ltd, 1968-73; CJB Offshore Ltd, 1975-80; Chm., JBE Offshore Ltd, 1976-81 (Dep. Chm., 1974). Member: CBI Oil Steering Gp, 1975-79; Exec. Cttee, Scottish Engrg Employers' Assoc., 1966-82; W of Scotland Cttee, Scottish Council (Develt and Industry), 1977-. Dir, Glasgow Chamber of Commerce, 1978-. Mem. Court, Univ. of Strathclyde, 1979-. DL Dumbarton, 1979. *Recreations:* skiing, golf, jogging, early jazz. *Address:* Arns Brae, 12 Ledcameroch Road, Bearsden, Glasgow G61 4AB. T: 041-942 4862. *Clubs:* Caledonian; Scottish Ski (Glencoe), Buchananan Castle Golf (Drymen).

STRACHAN, Michael Francis, CBE 1980 (MBE 1945); FRSE 1979; Chairman, Ben Line Steamers Ltd and Ben Line Containers Ltd, 1970-82; Director, Bank of Scotland; b 23 Oct. 1919; s of Francis William Strachan and Violet Blackwell (née Palmer); m 1948, Iris Hemingway; two s two d. *Educ:* Rugby Sch. (Scholar); Corpus Christi Coll., Cambridge (Exhibnr, MA). Served in Army, 1939-46; Bde Major 26th Armd Bde, Italy, 1944-45 (MBE, despatches); demobilised 1946 (Lt-Col); subseq. served with Lothians and Border Horse, TA. Joined Wm Thomson & Co., Edinburgh, Managers of Ben Line, 1946; Partner, 1950-64; Jt Man. Dir, Ben Line Steamers Ltd, 1964. Chm., Associated Container Transportation Ltd, 1971-75. Trustee: Nat. Galleries of Scotland, 1972-74; Carnegie Trust for Univs of Scotland, 1976-; Chm. Bd of Trustees, Nat. Library of Scotland, 1974-. Mem. Council, Hakluyt Soc., 1979-. Member of Queen's Body Guard for Scotland. *Publications:* The Life and Adventures of Thomas Coryate, 1962; (ed jtly) The East India Company Journals of Captain William Keeling and Master Thomas Bonner, 1615-1617, 1971; articles in Blackwood's, Hakluyt Society's Hakluyt Handbook, History Today, Jl Soc. for Nautical Research. *Recreations:* country pursuits, silviculture. *Address:* 33 St Mary's Street, Edinburgh EH1 1TN. *Clubs:* Naval and Military; New (Edinburgh).

STRACHAN, Robert Martin; Agent-General for British Columbia in the United Kingdom and Europe, 1975-77; b 1 Dec. 1913; s of Alexander Strachan and Sarah Martin; m 1937, Anne Elsie Paget; two s one d. *Educ:* schools in Glasgow, Scotland. Mem., British Columbia Legislature, 1952-75; Leader of Opposition, 1956-69; Minister: of Highways, 1972-73; of Transport and Communications, 1973-75; resigned seat Oct. 1975, to accept appointment as Agent-General. *Recreations:* swimming, fishing, painting. *Address:* RR2, Cedar Road, Nanaimo, Vancouver Island, British Columbia. *Club:* Royal Over-Seas League.

STRACHAN, Mrs Valerie Patricia Marie; Commissioner of Customs and Excise, since 1980; b 10 Jan. 1940; d of John Jonas Nicholls and Louise Nicholls; m 1965, John Strachan; one s one d. *Educ:* Newland High Sch., Hull; Manchester Univ. (BA). Joined Customs and Excise, 1961; Dept of Economic Affairs, 1964; Home Office, 1966; Principal, Customs and Excise, 1966; Treasury, 1972; Asst Secretary, Customs and Excise, 1974. *Address:* 9 College Gardens, SE21 7BE. T: 01-693 5335.

STRACHAN, Walter, CBE 1967; CEng, FRAeS; Consulting Engineer since 1971; b 14 Oct. 1910; s of William John Strachan, Rothes, Morayshire, and Eva Hitchins, Bristol; m 1937, Elizabeth Dora Bradshaw, Aldershot; two s. *Educ:* Newfoundland Road Sch., Bristol; Merchant Venturers Technical Coll., Bristol. Bristol Aeroplane Co.: Apprentice, 1925; Aircraft Ground Engr, 1932; RAE, Farnborough, 1934; Inspector: Bristol Aeroplane Co., 1937. BAC Service Engr, RAF Martlesham Heath, 1938; BAC: Asst Service Manager, 1940; Asst Works Manager, 1942; Manager, Banwell, building Beaufort and Tempest aircraft, 1943; Gen.-Manager, Banwell and Weston Factories, manufrg Aluminium Houses, 1945; Gen. Manager, Banwell and Weston Factories, building helicopters and aircraft components, 1951; Managing Dir, Bristol Aerojet, Banwell, Rocket Motor Develt and Prod., 1958. *Recreations:* golf, music, ornithology. *Address:* 18 Clarence Road East, Weston-Super-Mare, Somerset. T: Weston-Super-Mare 23878. *Clubs:* Naval and Military; Royal Automobile.

STRACHEY, family name of Baron O'Hagan.

STRACHEY, Charles, (6th Bt cr 1801, but does not use the title); b 20 June 1934; s of Rt Hon. Evelyn John St Loe Strachey (d 1963) and Celia (d 1980), 3rd d of late Rev. Arthur Hume Simpson; S to baronetcy of cousin, 2nd Baron Strachie, 1973; m 1973, Janet Megan, d of Alexander Miller; one d. *Heir:* kinsman John Ralph Severs Strachey [b 22 Oct. 1905; m 1st, 1933, Isobel Bertha (marr. diss. 1942), d of Ronald Leslie; one d ; 2nd, 1945, Rosemary, d of Douglas Mavor; one s]. *Address:* 30 Gibson Square, N1 0RD. T: 01-226 8216.

STRADBROKE, 4th Earl of, cr 1821; **John Anthony Alexander Rous;** Bt 1660; Baron Rous, 1796; Viscount Dunwich, 1821; Lord-Lieutenant and Custos Rotulorum for the County of Suffolk, 1948-78; Commander Royal Navy, retired list; b 1 April 1903 (to whom Queen Alexandra stood sponsor); e s of 3rd Earl of Stradbroke, KCMG, CB, CVO, CBE, and Helena Violet Alice, DBE, cr 1927, Lady of Grace of St John (d 1949), d of Gen. Keith Fraser; S father, 1947; m 1929, Barbara d (d 1977), yr d of late Lord Arthur Grosvenor; two d. *Educ:* RN Colleges, Osborne and Dartmouth; Christ Church (Hon. MA), Oxford. Member E Suffolk CC 1931-45, Alderman 1953-64. Private Sec. to Governor of Victoria and Acting Governor General, Australia, 1946-47. Estate Owner, Agriculturist and Forester. National Vice-Pres., Royal British Legion; Vice-Pres., Assoc. of (Land) Drainage Authorities. Dir, Daejan Holdings Ltd. Served Royal Navy, 1917-28, and on Naval Staff, Admiralty 1939-46. Lately Hon. Colonel 660 HAA Regiment (TA); Lay Canon of St Edmundsbury Cathedral, 1978. FRSA. Scout Movement's Silver Wolf Award, 1978. KStJ. *Heir:* b Hon. (William) Keith Rous [b 10 Mar. 1907; m 1st, 1935, Pamela Catherine Mabell (marr. diss. 1941), d of late Capt. Hon. Edward James Kay-Shuttleworth; two s ; 2nd, 1943, April Mary, d of late Brig.-General Hon. Arthur Melland Asquith, DSO; one s three d]. *Address:* Henham, Wangford, Beccles, Suffolk. T: Wangford 212 and 214. *Clubs:* Travellers'; Jockey Club Rooms; Royal Norfolk and Suffolk Yacht.

STRADLING, Donald George; Group Personnel Director, John Laing plc, since 1978; *b* 7 Sept. 1929; *s* of George Frederic and Olive Emily Stradling; *m* 1955, Mary Anne Hartridge; two *d. Educ:* Clifton Coll.; Magdalen Coll., Oxford (Open Exhibnr; MA). CIPM. School Master, St Albans Sch., 1954-55; Group Trng and Educn Officer, John Laing & Son Ltd, Building and Civil Engrg Contractors, 1955; Group Personnel Director, John Laing & Son Ltd, 1969. Commissioner, Manpower Services Commission, 1980-; Mem. Council, Inst. of Manpower Studies, 1975-81; Member: Employment Policy Cttee, 1978-, Council, 1982-, CBI; FCEC Wages and Industrial Cttee, 1978-; Vice-Pres., Inst. of Personnel Management, 1974-76; Vice-Chm. of Governors, St Albans High Sch., 1977-; Mem. Council, Tyndale House, 1977-. *Publications:* contribs on music and musical instruments, et al. to New Bible Dictionary, 1962. *Recreations:* singing (choral music), listening to music (espec. opera), walking. *Address:* Courts Edge, 12 The Warren, Harpenden, Herts AL5 2NH. *T:* Harpenden 2744. *Clubs:* Institute of Directors, English-Speaking Union.

STRADLING, Rt. Rev. Leslie Edward, MA; *b* 11 Feb. 1908; *er s* of late Rev. W. H. Stradling; unmarried. *Educ:* King Edward VII Sch., Sheffield; The Queen's Coll., Oxford; Westcott House, Cambridge. Curate of St Paul's, Lorrimore Square, 1933-38; Vicar of St Luke's Camberwell, 1938-43; of St Anne's, Wandsworth, 1943-45; Bishop of Masasi, 1945-52; Bishop of South West Tanganyika, 1952-61; Bishop of Johannesburg, 1961-74. Hon. DCL Bishops' Univ., Lennoxville, Canada, 1968. *Publications:* A Bishop on Safari, 1960; The Acts through Modern Eyes, 1963; An Open Door, 1966; A Bishop at Prayer, 1971; Praying Now, 1976; Praying the Psalms, 1977. *Address:* 197 Main Road, Kalk Bay, South Africa 7975. *Clubs:* United Oxford & Cambridge University; City and Civil Service (Cape Town).

STRADLING THOMAS, John; MP (C) Monmouth, since 1970; Treasurer of HM Household, and Deputy Chief Whip, since 1979; farmer; *b* 10 June 1925; *s* of Thomas Roger Thomas and Catherine Thomas (*née* Delahay); *m* 1957, Freda Rhys Evans; one *s* two *d. Educ:* Rugby School. Contested (C) Aberavon, 1964; Cardigan, 1966. Asst Govt Whip, 1971-73; a Lord Comr, HM Treasury, 1973-74; an Opposition Whip, 1974-79; Mem., Select Cttee on the Civil List, 1971. Member Council, NFU, 1963-70. *Address:* House of Commons, SW1A 0AA.

STRAFFORD, 7th Earl of, *cr* 1847; Robert Cecil Byng; Baron Strafford (UK), 1835; Viscount Enfield, 1847; *b* 29 July 1904; *o* surv. *s* of late Hon. Ivo Francis Byng (4th *s* of 5th Earl) and late Agnes Constance, *d* of S. Smith Travers, Hobart, Tasmania; *S* uncle 1951; *m* 1st, 1934, Maria Magdalena Elizabeth (marr. diss. 1947), *d* of late Henry Cloete, CMG, Alphen, S Africa; two *s*; 2nd, 1948, Clara Evelyn, *d* of late Sir Ness Nowrosjee Wadia, KBE, CIE. *Heir: s* Viscount Enfield, *qv. Address:* c/o C. Hoare & Co., 37 Fleet Street, EC4.

STRAKER, Rear-Adm. Bryan John, CB 1980; OBE 1966; Head of Personnel Services, Imperial Cancer Research Fund; *b* 26 May 1929; *s* of late George Straker and Marjorie Straker; *m* 1954, Elizabeth Rosemary, *d* of Maj.-Gen. C. W. Greenway, CB, CBE, and Mrs C. W. Greenway; two *d. Educ:* St Albans Sch. FBIM 1978. Cadet, RNC Dartmouth, 1946; Flag Lieut to Flag Officer, Malayan Area, 1952-53; qual. in communications, 1955; Flag Lieut and Staff Ops Officer to Sen. Naval Officer, WI, 1960-62; CO: HMS Malcolm, 1962-63; HMS Defender, 1966-67; Asst Dir, Naval Operational Requirements, MoD, 1968-70; CO HMS Fearless, 1970-72; Dir of Naval Plans, MoD, 1972-74; Sen. Naval Officer, WI, and Island Comdr, Bermuda, 1974-76; Asst Chief of Naval Staff (Policy), 1976-78; Sen. Naval Mem., DS, RCDS, 1978-80; RN retd, 1981. Freeman, City of London. *Recreations:* tennis, cricket, gardening. *Address:* c/o National Westminster Bank, Petersfield, Hants. *Clubs:* Farmers', Forty, West India.

STRAKER, Michael Ian Bowstead, CBE 1973; JP; farmer, since 1951; Chairman: Aycliffe and Peterlee Development Corporations, since 1980; Northumbrian Water Authority, since 1982; *b* 10 March 1928; *s* of late Edward Charles Straker and of Margaret Alice Bridget Straker. *Educ:* Eton. Served in Coldstream Guards, 1946-50. Dir, Newcastle and Gateshead Water Co., 1975-82 (Chm., 1979-82); Chairman: Newcastle upon Tyne AHA(T), 1973-81; Newcastle Univ. HMC, 1971; Mem. Newcastle Univ. Court and Council, 1972-. Mem. Council, RASE, 1970-. Chm., Northern Area Conservative Assoc., 1969-72. High Sheriff of Northumberland, 1977; JP Northumberland, 1962. *Address:* High Warden, Hexham, Northumberland NE46 4SR. *T:* Hexham 602083. *Clubs:* Brooks's; Northern Counties (Newcastle upon Tyne).

STRAND, Prof. Kenneth T.; Professor, Department of Economics, Simon Fraser University, since 1968; *b* Yakima, Wash, 30 June 1931; Canadian citizen since 1974; *m* 1960, Elna K. Tomaske; no *c. Educ:* Washington State Coll. (BA); Univ. of Wisconsin (PhD, MS). Woodrow Wilson Fellow, 1955-56; Ford Foundn Fellow, 1957-58; Herfurth Award, Univ. of Wisconsin, 1961 (for PhD thesis). Asst Exec. Sec., Hanford Contractors Negotiation Cttee, Richland, Wash, 1953-55; Asst Prof., Washington State Univ., 1959-60; Asst Prof., Oberlin Coll., 1960-65 (on leave, 1963-65); Economist, Manpower and Social Affairs Div., OECD, Paris, 1964-66; Assoc. Prof., Dept of Econs and Commerce, Simon Fraser Univ., 1966-68; Pres., Simon Fraser Univ., 1969-74 (Acting Pres., 1968-69). Member: Industrial Relations Research Assoc.; American Econ. Assoc.; Internat. Industrial Relations Assoc.; Canadian Industrial Relations Assoc.; Canadian Econs Assoc. FRSA 1972. *Publications:*

Jurisdictional Disputes in Construction: The Causes, The Joint Board and the NLRB, 1961; contribs to Review of Econs and Statistics, Amer. Econ. Review, Industrial Relations, Sociaal Mannblad Arbeid. *Recreations:* sailing, ski-ing. *Address:* RR1, Box 9C, Port Moody, BC V3H 3C8, Canada.

STRANG, family name of Baron Strang.

STRANG, 2nd Baron *cr* 1954, of Stonesfield; Colin Strang; Professor of Philosophy, University of Newcastle upon Tyne, 1975-82; Dean of the Faculty of Arts, 1976-79; *b* 12 June 1922; *s* of 1st Baron Strang, GCB, GCMG, MBE, and Elsie Wynne (*d* 1974), *d* of late J. E. Jones; *S* father, 1978; *m* 1st, 1948, Patricia Marie, *d* of Meiert C. Avis, Johannesburg; 2nd, 1955, Barbara Mary Hope Carr (*d* 1982); one *d. Educ:* Merchant Taylors' School; St John's Coll., Oxford (MA, BPhil). *Heir:* none. *Address:* Station House, Angerton, Morpeth, Northumberland NE61 4EY.

STRANG, Gavin Steel; MP (Lab) Edinburgh East since 1970; *b* 10 July 1943; *s* of James Steel Strang and Marie Strang (*née* Finkle); *m. Educ:* Univs of Edinburgh and Cambridge. BSc Hons Edinburgh, 1964; DipAgricSci Cambridge, 1965; PhD Edinburgh, 1968. Mem., Tayside Econ. Planning Consultative Group, 1966-68; Scientist with ARC, 1968-70. Parly Under-Sec. of State, Dept of Energy, March-Oct. 1974; Parly Sec., MAFF, 1974-79. *Publications:* articles in Animal Production. *Recreations:* golf, swimming, films. *Address:* 80 Argyle Crescent, Edinburgh EH15 2QD. *T:* 031-669 5999. *Club:* New Craighall Miners' Welfare (Edinburgh).

STRANG, William John, CBE 1973; PhD; FRS 1977, FEng, FRAeS; Deputy Technical Director, British Aerospace, Aircraft Group, since 1978; *b* 29 June 1921; *s* of late John F. Strang and Violet Strang (*née* Terrell); *m* 1946, Margaret Nicholas Howells; three *s* one *d. Educ:* Torquay Grammar Sch.; King's Coll., London Univ. (BSc). Bristol Aeroplane Co., Ltd, Stress Office, 1939-46; King's Coll., London Univ., 1946-48; Aeronautical Research Lab., Melbourne, Aust., 1948-51; Bristol Aeroplane Co. Ltd: Dep. Head, Guided Weapons Dept, 1951-52; Head of Aerodynamics and Flight Research, 1952-55; Chief Designer, 1955-60; British Aircraft Corporation: Dir and Chief Engr, 1960-67, Technical Dir, 1967-71; Filton Div.; Technical Dir, 1971-77, Commercial Aircraft Div. Mem., Airworthiness Requirements Bd, 1979-. Fellow, Fellowship of Engineering, 1977. *Recreation:* sailing. *Address:* 11 Broom Park, Teddington, Mddx TW11 9RW. *T:* 01-977 3114; April Cottage, Castle Combe, Wilts. *T:* Castle Combe 782220. *Clubs:* Royal Yachting Association; Island Cruising (Salcombe), Salcombe Yacht.

STRANG STEEL, Major Sir (Fiennes) William; *see* Steel, Major Sir F. W. S.

STRANGE, Prof. Susan, (Mrs Clifford Selly); Montague Burton Professor of International Relations, London School of Economics and Political Science, since 1978; *b* 9 June 1923; *d* of Col Louis Strange and Marjorie Beath; *m* 1st, 1942, Dr Denis Merritt (marr. diss. 1955); one *s* one *d*; 2nd, 1955, Clifford Selly; three *s* one *d. Educ:* Royal Sch., Bath; Université de Caen; London Sch. of Econs (BScEcon). The Economist, 1944-46; The Observer, 1946-57 (Washington, UN, and Econ. Corresp.); Lectr in Internat. Relations, University Coll., London, 1949-64; Res. Fellow, RIIA, 1965-76; German Marshall Fund Fellow, 1976-78; Vis. Prof., Univ. of Southern Calif, 1978. *Publications:* Sterling and British Policy, 1971; International Monetary Relations, 1976; (ed with R. Tooze) The International Politics of Surplus Capacity, 1981. *Recreations:* cooking, gardening, tennis, canoeing. *Address:* Weedon Hill House, Aylesbury, Bucks. *T:* Aylesbury 22236.

STRANGER-JONES, Leonard Ivan; Registrar of the Supreme Court Family Division, 1967-82; *b* 8 May 1913; *s* of Walter Stranger-Jones; *m* 1st, 1935, Elizabeth Evelyn Williams (marr. diss., 1942); 2nd, 1943, Iris Christine Truscott; one *s* one *d. Educ:* Lancing; Oriel Coll., Oxford (MA). Called to the Bar, 1938. Served War of 1939-45: RAF, Sept. 1939; Pilot, 1942. Returned to the Bar, Sept. 1945; Bencher, Middle Temple, Nov. 1967. *Publication:* Eversley on Domestic Relations, 1951. *Recreations:* photography, history. *Address:* 18 Chelmsford Square, Brondesbury Park, NW10 3AR. *T:* 01-459 3757.

STRANGWAYS; *see* Fox-Strangways, family name of Earl of Ilchester.

STRANKS, Prof. Donald Richard, PhD; Vice-Chancellor, University of Adelaide, since 1977; *b* 18 July 1929; *s* of R. G. Stranks; *m* 1st, 1954; two *s* one *d*; 2nd, 1978, Caroline Anne-Marie; one step *s. Educ:* Melbourne High Sch.; Univ. of Melb. (MSc 1952, PhD 1954). ICIANZ Res. Fellow, Univ. of Melb., 1952-54. Lectr in Radio Chemistry, Univ. of Leeds, 1954-60; Sen. Lectr, then Reader in Inorganic Chem., Univ. of Melb., 1960-64; Foundn Chair of Inorg. Chem., Univ. of Adelaide, 1964-73; Prof. of Inorg. Chem., Univ. of Melb., 1973-77. Vis. Professor: Univ. of Bristol, 1976; Washington Univ., 1967; Goethe Univ. 1971; Univ. of Calgary, 1972. Consultant and Examr, Univ. of Papua and New Guinea, 1969-73; Examr, Universiti Sains Malaysia, 1976-78. Member: Aust. Adv. Cttee of Nuffield Foundn, 1970-81; Exec., Aust. Vice-Chancellors' Cttee, 1979-; Chm., SA Council for Technological Change, 1980-. Royal Aust. Chemical Institute: Rennie Meml Medal, 1956; COMO Award and Medal for Inorg. Chem. Res., 1977. *Publications:* Modern Coordination Chemistry, 1960; Chemistry: a structural view, 1967, 2nd edn 1972; Chemical Science, 1976; eighty scientific pubns in internat. jls; articles on chemical educn. *Recreations:* music, badminton, tennis.

Address: 2 Bartley Avenue, Netherby, SA 5062, Australia. *T:* 791266; University of Adelaide, North Terrace, Adelaide, SA 5001. *T:* 228-5201.

STRASSER, Sir Paul, Kt 1973; Director: Walden Properties Ltd; Nicron Resources NL; N & K Properties Ltd; Petrocarb Exploration NL; *b* 22 Sept. 1911; *s* of Eugene Strasser and Elizabeth Klein de Ney; *m* 1935, Veronica Gero; one *s*. *Educ:* Univ. of Budapest. Dr of Law, 1933; practised in Hungary for 10 yrs; emigrated to Australia, 1948. Career in fields of construction, mining and oil exploration, hotel and motel chains, meat processing and exporting, merchant banking. Associated with and promoter of several charitable foundns, etc, incl. Jewish Residential Coll. at Univ. of NSW, Children's Surgical Research Fund and Australian Youth Ballet. *Recreations:* playing bridge, swimming, reading. *Address:* Suite 106, Edgecliff Centre, Edgecliff, NSW 2027, Australia. *Clubs:* American, Sydney Turf (Sydney).

STRATFORD, Neil Martin; Keeper of Medieval and Later Antiquities, British Museum, since 1975; *b* 26 April 1938; *s* of Dr Martin Gould Stratford and Dr Mavis Stratford (*née* Beddall); *m* 1966, Anita Jennifer Lewis; two *d*. *Educ:* Marlborough Coll.; Magdalene Coll., Cambridge (BA Hons English 1961, MA); Courtauld Inst., London Univ. (BA Hons History of Art 1966). 2nd Lieut Coldstream Guards, 1956-58; Trainee Kleinwort, Benson, Lonsdale Ltd, 1961-63; Lecturer Westfield Coll., London Univ., 1969-75. Liveryman, Haberdashers' Company 1959-. Hon. Mem., Académie de Dijon, 1975. FSA 1976. *Publications:* articles in French and English periodicals. *Recreations:* opera, food and wine, cricket and football. *Address:* 17 Church Row, NW3. *T:* 01-794 5688. *Clubs:* Beefsteak, MCC, I Zingari; University Pitt, Hawks (Cambridge).

STRATHALLAN, Viscount; John Eric Drummond; *b* 7 July 1935; *e s* of 17th Earl of Perth, *qv*; *m* 1963, Margaret Ann (marr. diss.), *o d* of Robin Gordon; two *s*. Heir: *s* Hon. James David Drummond, *b* 24 Oct. 1965. *Address:* Stobhall, by Perth.

STRATHALMOND, 3rd Baron *cr* 1955; **William Roberton Fraser;** *b* 22 July 1947; *s* of 2nd Baron Strathalmond, CMG, OBE, TD, and of Letitia, *d* of late Walter Krementz, New Jersey, USA; *S* father, 1976; *m* 1973, Amanda Rose, *yr d* of Rev. Gordon Clifford Taylor; two *s*. *Educ:* Loretto. Heir: *s* Hon. William Gordon Fraser, *b* 24 Sept. 1976. *Address:* 8 Stokenchurch Street, SW6 3TR.

STRATHCARRON, 2nd Baron, *cr* 1936, of Banchor; **David William Anthony Blyth Macpherson;** Bt, *cr* 1933; Partner, Strathcarron & Co.; Director: Kirchhoff (London) Ltd; Seabourne Express Ltd; Dorada Holdings Ltd; Forster and Hales Ltd; *b* 23 Jan. 1924; *s* of 1st Baron and Jill (*d* 1956), *o d* of Sir George Rhodes, 1st Bt; *S* father, 1937; *m* 1st, 1947, Valerie Cole (marr. annulled on his petition, 1947); 2nd, 1948, Mrs Diana Hawtrey Curle (*d* 1973), *o d* of Comdr R. H. Deane; two *s*; 3rd 1974, Mrs Eve Samuel, *o d* of late J. C. Higgins, CIE. *Educ:* Eton; Jesus College, Cambridge. Served War of 1939-45, RAFVR, 1942-47. Motoring Correspondent of The Field, 1954-. Member, British Parly Delegn to Austria, 1964. Pres., Inst. of Freight Forwarders, 1974-75. Member Council: Inst. of Advanced Motorists; Order of the Road. President: Guild of Motoring Writers; Company of Veteran Motorists. *Publication:* Motoring for Pleasure, 1963. *Recreations:* motorracing, flying, golf. Heir: *s* Hon. Ian David Patrick Macpherson, *b* 31 March 1949. *Address:* 55 Cumberland Terrace, Regent's Park, NW1. *T:* 01-935 5913; Otterwood, Beaulieu, Hants. *T:* Beaulieu 612334. *Clubs:* Boodle's, Royal Air Force.

STRATHCLYDE, 1st Baron, *cr* 1955, of Barskimming; **Thomas Dunlop Galbraith,** PC 1953; Commander, Royal Navy, retired; *b* 20 March 1891; 2nd *s* of William Brodie Galbraith, JP, CA, Glasgow, and Annie Dunlop; *m* 1915, Ida, *e d* of Thomas Galloway, Auchendrane, Ayrshire; three *s* two *d* (and one *s* killed in action, 1940, and one decd). *Educ:* Glasgow Academy; RN Colleges, Osborne and Dartmouth. Entered Royal Navy, 1903; served throughout European War, 1914-18, in HMS Audacious and HMS Queen Elizabeth; RN Staff College, Greenwich, 1920-22; retired 1922; War of 1939-45, on Staff of C-in-C Coast of Scotland, 1939-40; Deputy British Admiralty Supply Representative in USA, 1940-42. MP (Nat. C) for Pollok Div. of Glasgow, 1940-April 1955; Jt Parly Under-Sec. of State for Scotland, 1945 and 1951-55; Minister of State, Scottish Office, 1955-58, resigned; Chm., North of Scotland Hydro-Electric Board, 1959-67; Mem., South of Scotland Electricity Board, 1965-67. Chartered Accountant, 1925; Partner Galbraith, Dunlop & Co., CA, Glasgow, 1925-70; Member of Corporation of Glasgow, 1933-40; Magistrate, 1938-40. President, Electrical Research Association, 1965-66. Hon. FRCPE; Hon. FRCPSGlas; a Governor of Wellington College, 1948-61; Hon. Governor, Glasgow Academy. Freedom of Dingwall, 1965; Freedom of Aberdeen, 1966. Heir: *g s* Thomas Galloway Dunlop du Roy de Blicquy Galbraith, *b* 22 Feb. 1960. *Address:* Barskimming, Mauchline, Ayrshire. *T:* Mauchline 50202. *Clubs:* Carlton, Naval and Military; Western (Glasgow).

STRATHCONA AND MOUNT ROYAL, 4th Baron, *cr* 1900; **Donald Euan Palmer Howard;** *b* 26 Nov. 1923; *s* of 3rd Baron Strathcona and Mount Royal and Diana Evelyn, twin *d* of Baron Wakehurst; *S* father 1959; *m* 1st, 1954, Lady Jane Mary Waldegrave (marr. diss. 1977), 2nd *d* of Earl Waldegrave, *qv*; two *s* four *d*; 2nd, 1978, Patricia (*née* Thomas), *widow* of John Middleton. *Educ:* King's Mead, Seaford; Eton; Trinity Coll., Cambridge; McGill University, Montreal (1947-50). Served War of 1939-45:

RN, 1942-47: Midshipman, RNVR, 1943; Lieutenant, 1945. With Urwick, Orr and Partners (Industrial Consultants), 1950-56. Lord in Waiting (Govt Whip), 1973-74; Parly Under-Sec. of State for Defence (RAF), MoD, 1974; Jt Dep. Leader of the Opposition, House of Lords, 1976-79; Minister of State, MoD, 1979-81. Director: Dundonian plc; Computing Devices, Hastings; TAN Systems Ltd; Mediterranean Investors Group Ltd. Chairman, Bath Festival Society, 1966-70. Dep. Chm., SS Great Britain Project, 1970-73. *Recreations:* gardening, sailing. Heir: *s* Hon. Donald Alexander Smith Howard, *b* 24 June 1961. *Address:* 1 Highbury Road, Wimbledon, SW19. *T:* 01-947 8157; Kiloran, Isle of Colonsay, Scotland. *T:* Colonsay 301. *Clubs:* Brooks's, Pratt's; Royal Yacht Squadron.

STRATHEDEN, 5th Baron *cr* 1836, **AND CAMPBELL, 5th Baron** *cr* 1841; **Gavin Campbell;** Major (retired) KRRC and Lt-Col 19th (Kenya) Bn, KAR; *b* 28 Aug. 1901; *s* of Hon. John Beresford Campbell, DSO (killed in action, 1915) (*s* of 3rd Baron) and Hon. Alice Susan Hamilton (*d* 1949), *d* of 1st Baron Hamilton of Dalzell; *S* brother, 1981; *m* 1933, Evelyn Mary Austen, *d* of late Col Herbert Austen Smith, CIE; one *s*. *Educ:* Eton; RMC Sandhurst. Served War of 1939-45, Abyssinia and Madagascar. Heir: *s* Hon. Donald Campbell [*b* 4 April 1934; *m* 1957, Hilary Ann Holland, *d* of Lt-Col W. D. Turner; one *s* three *d*]. *Address:* 7 Denway Grove, South Norwood, Launceston, Tasmania 7250, Australia.

STRATHERN, Prof. Andrew Jamieson, PhD; Professor of Anthropology and Head of Department of Anthropology, University College London, since 1976; *b* 19 Jan. 1939; *s* of Robert Strathern and Mary Strathern (*née* Sharp); *m* 1963, Ann Marilyn Evans; two *s* one *d*. *Educ:* Colchester Royal Grammar Sch.; Trinity Coll., Cambridge (BA, PhD). Research Fellow, Trinity Coll., Cambridge, 1965-68; Research Fellow, then Fellow, Australian National Univ., 1969-72; Professor, later Vis. Professor, Dept of Anthropology and Sociology, Univ. of Papua New Guinea, 1973-77; Hon. Research Fellow, Inst. of Papua New Guinea Studies, 1977, Dir (on secondment), 1981-83. Rivers Memorial Medal, RAI, 1976. *Publications:* The Rope of Moka, 1971; One Father, One Blood (ANU), 1972; (with M. Strathern) Self-decoration in Mount Hagen, 1972; Ongka, 1979; (with Malcolm Kirk) Man as Art, 1981; articles in Man, Oceania, Ethnology, Jl Polyn Soc., Amer. Anthropology, Amer. Ethnology. *Address:* 13 Tenison Avenue, Cambridge CB1 2DX. *T:* Cambridge 356073.

STRATHMORE AND KINGHORNE, 17th Earl of, *cr* 1677; Earl (UK), *cr* 1937; **Fergus Michael Claude Bowes Lyon;** Lord Glamis, 1445; Earl of Kinghorne, Lord Lyon and Glamis, 1606; Viscount Lyon, Lord Glamis, Tannadyce, Sydlaw, and Strathdichtie, 1677; Baron Bowes (UK), 1887; Vice Lord-Lieutenant, County of Angus, since 1981; *b* 31 Dec. 1928; *e s* of Hon. Michael Claude Hamilton Bowes Lyon (5th *s* of 14th Earl) (*d* 1953), and Elizabeth Margaret (*d* 1959), *d* of late John Cator; *S* cousin, 1972; *m* 1956, Mary Pamela, *d* of Brig. Norman Duncan McCorquodale, MC; one *s* two *d*. *Educ:* Eton; RMA, Sandhurst. Commissioned Scots Guards, 1949; Captain 1953; transferred to RARO, 1961. Member of Edinburgh Stock Exchange, 1963. Dir, T. Cowie, 1978-. Member of Royal Company of Archers, Queen's Body Guard for Scotland; Hon. Col, Tayforth Univs OTC, 1974-81. DL Angus, 1973. *Recreations:* shooting, fishing. Heir: *s* Lord Glamis, *qv*. *Address:* Glamis Castle, Forfar, Angus. *T:* Glamis 244. *Clubs:* White's, Pratt's; New (Edinburgh).

STRATHNAVER, Lord; Alistair Charles St Clair Sutherland; Master of Sutherland; with Sutherland Estates, since 1979; *b* 7 Jan. 1947; *e s* of Charles Noel Janson, DL, and the Countess of Sutherland, *qv*; heir to mother's titles; *m* 1st, 1968, Eileen Elizabeth, *o d* of Richard Wheeler Baker, Jr, Princeton, NJ; two *d*; 2nd, 1980, Gillian, *er d* of Robert Murray, Gourock, Renfrewshire; one *s*. *Educ:* Eton; Christ Church, Oxford. BA. Metropolitan Police, 1969-74; with IBM UK Ltd, 1976-79. Heir: *s* Hon. Alexander Charles Robert Sutherland, *b* 1 Oct. 1981. *Address:* Sutherland Estates Office, Golspie, Sutherland. *T:* Golspie 3268. *Club:* Pratt's.

STRATHON, Eric Colwill, FRICS; Member of the Lands Tribunal, 1969-80, retired; *b* 20 Feb. 1908; *s* of Daniel Millward Strathon and Ann Colwill; *m* 1932, Margaret Mary Cocks (*d* 1973); one *s* one *d*. *Educ:* Taunton Sch. Chartered Surveyor, election 1929. Served War, 1944-46: Major RA; 14th Army HQ. Articled to chartered surveyors, 1925-28; partner, private practice in London, 1934-69. Crown Estate Comr, 1965-69. Pres., RICS, 1961. *Publication:* Compensation (Defence), 1943. *Recreation:* fishing. *Address:* 106 Rivermead Court, Hurlingham, SW6 3SB. *T:* 01-736 3192. *Clubs:* Naval and Military, Hurlingham.

STRATHSPEY, 5th Baron, *cr* 1884; **Donald Patrick Trevor Grant of Grant,** 17th Bt, of Nova Scotia, *cr* 1625; 32nd Chief of Grant; Lieutenant-Colonel retired; *b* 18 March 1912; *s* of 4th Baron and Alice Louisa (*d* 1945), *d* of T. M. Hardy-Johnston, MICE London, of Christchurch, NZ; *S* father, 1948; *m* 1st, 1938, Alice (marr. diss. 1951), *o c* of late Francis Bowe, Timaru, NZ; one *s* two *d*; 2nd, 1951, Olive, *d* of W. H. Grant, Norwich; one *s* one *d*. *Educ:* Stowe Sch.; South Eastern Agricultural Coll. War Dept Land Agent and Valuer, Portsmouth, 1944-48; Command Land Agent, HQ Scottish Command, 1948-60; Asst Chief Land Agent and Valuer, War Office, 1960-63; Command Land Agent, HQ Cyprus District, 1963-64; Asst Director of Lands, NW Europe, 1964-66; Asst Chief Land Agent, MoD HQ, 1966-72. Associate, Land Agents' Soc. Fellow, Royal Institution of Chartered Surveyors, retd 1972. Member: Standing Council of Scottish Chiefs; Highland Soc. of

London; Clan Grant Socs of NZ and America; West Wittering Horticultural Soc.; Hon. Mem., Los Angeles Saint Andrew's Soc.; Knight, Mark Twain Soc., Missouri; Patron: American Scottish Foundn; Soc. for Protection of Rural Species. Defence Medal; Coronation medal. *Recreations:* yachting, gardening. *Heir:* s Hon. James Patrick Grant of Grant, b 9 Sept. 1943. *Address:* Elms Cottage, Elms Ride, West Wittering, West Sussex. *Clubs:* Lancia Motor, House of Lords Motor, House of Lords Sailing, Civil Service Motoring Association (Pres.), West Wittering Sailing.

STRATTON, Andrew, MSc, FInstP, CEng, FIEE, FInstNav, FIMA; part-time Member, Civil Aviation Authority, since 1980; b 5 Sept. 1918; m 1949, Ruth Deutsch; one s one d. *Educ:* Skinners' Company Sch., Tunbridge Wells; University Coll. of the South West, Exeter; Univ. of London (BSc 1st cl. Hons Physics). RAE Farnborough: Air Defence and Armament Depts, 1939–54; Supt, Instruments and Inertial Navigation Div., 1954–62; Head of Weapon Research and Assessment Group, 1962–66; Prof. and Head of Maths Dept, Coll. of Aeronautics, Cranfield, 1966–68; Dir, Defence Operational Analysis Estabt, 1968–76; Under Sec., MoD, on secondment as Consultant, 1977, Senior Consultant, 1978–81, ICI Ltd. Faraday Lecture, IEE, 1972–73. Former Chm. and Mem. of Cttees, Aeronautical and Electronics Research Councils; Mem., Home Office Scientific Adv. Council. Pres., Inst. of Navigation, 1967–70; Chm. of Convocation, Univ. of Exeter. Hon. DSc Exeter, 1972. Hodgson Prize, RAeS, 1969; Bronze Medal, 1971 and 1975, Gold Medal, 1973, Royal Inst of Navigation. US Medal of Freedom with Bronze Palm, 1947. *Publications:* contrib. to Unless Peace Comes, 1968; to The Future of Aeronautics, 1970; papers on: aircraft instruments, navigation, air traffic, operational analysis in Jl IEE, Jl IMechE, Jl RAeS, Jl Inst. Navigation; energy, and chemical feedstock in Chem. and Ind., Omega, Process Econ. Internat. *Recreations:* painting, rambling. *Address:* Chartley, 39 Salisbury Road, Farnborough, Hants. *T:* Farnborough 542514.

STRATTON, Ven. Basil; Archdeacon of Stafford and Canon Residentiary of Lichfield Cathedral, 1959–April 1974; Archdeacon Emeritus, since 1974; Chaplain to the Queen, 1965–76; b 1906; s of Reverend Samuel Henry Stratton and Kate Mabel Stratton; m 1934, Euphemia Frances Stuart; one s three d. *Educ:* Lincoln School; Hatfield College, Durham University. BA 1929, MA 1932. Deacon 1930; Priest 1931; Curate, St Stephen's, Grimsby, 1930–32; SPG Missionary, India, 1932–34; Indian Ecclesiastical Establishment, 1935–47. Chaplain to the Forces on service in Iraq, India, Burma and Malaya, 1941–46 (despatches); officiated as Chaplain-General in India, 1946. Vicar of Figheldean with Milston, Wilts, 1948–53; Vicar of Market Drayton, Shropshire, 1953–59. *Address:* Woodlands Cottage, Mere, Wilts. *T:* Mere 860235.

STRATTON, Julius Adams, ScD; President Emeritus, Massachusetts Institute of Technology; b Seattle, 18 May 1901; s of Julius A. Stratton and Laura (née Adams); m 1935, Catherine N. Coffman; three d. *Educ:* Univ. of Washington; Mass Inst. of Technology (SB, SM); Eidgenössische Technische Hochschule, Zurich (ScD). Expert Consultant, Sec. of War, 1942–46. MIT: Res. Assoc. in Communications, 1924–26; Asst Prof., Electrical Engrg, 1928–31; Asst Prof., Physics, 1931–35; Assoc. Prof., Physics, 1935–41; Prof., Physics, 1941–51; Mem. Staff, Radiation Lab., 1940–45; Dir, Res. Lab. of Electronics, 1946–49; Provost, 1949–56; Vice-Pres., 1951–56; Chancellor, 1956–59; Actg Pres., 1957–59; Pres., 1959–66; Pres. Emer., 1966–. Trustee, Ford Foundn, 1955–71 (Chm. of Board, 1966–71). Chm., Commn on Marine Science, Engrg and Resources, 1967–69; Member: National Adv. Cttee on Oceans and Atmosphere, 1971–73; National Science Bd, 1956–62 and 1964–67; Naval Res. Adv. Cttee, 1954–59 (Chm., 1956–57). Life Mem. Corp., MIT; Life Trustee, Boston Museum of Science. Hon. Life FIEEE; Fellow: Amer. Acad. of Arts and Scis; Amer. Phys. Soc.; Founding Mem., National Acad. of Engrg (Mem., Council on For. Relations); Member: Amer. Philos. Soc.; Nat. Acad. of Scis (Vice-Pres., 1961–65); Sigma Xi; Tau Beta Pi; Zeta Psi; Eminent Mem., Eta Kappa Nu. Hon. Fellow, Coll. of Science and Technology, Manchester, England, 1963; Hon. Mem. Senate, Technical Univ. of Berlin, 1966. Holds numerous hon. doctorates of Engrg, Humane Letters, Laws and Science incl. DSc: Leeds, 1967; Heriot-Watt, 1971; ScD Cantab 1972. Medal for Merit, 1946; Distinguished Public Service Award, US Navy, 1957; Medal of Honor, Inst. Radio Engrs, 1957; Faraday Medal, IEE (England), 1961; Boston Medal for Distinguished Achievement, 1966. Officer, Legion of Honour, France, 1961; Orden de Boyacá, Colombia, 1964; Kt Comdr, Order of Merit, Germany, 1966. *Publications:* Electromagnetic Theory, 1941; Science and the Educated Man, 1966; numerous papers in scientific and professional jls. *Address:* (home) 100 Memorial Drive, Cambridge, Mass 02142, USA; (office) Massachusetts Institute of Technology, Cambridge, Mass 02139. *Clubs:* Century Association, University (New York); St Botolph (Boston).

STRATTON, Sir Richard (James), KCMG 1982 (CMG 1974); HM Diplomatic Service; High Commissioner to New Zealand, since 1980, and concurrently to Western Samoa (non-resident); Governor of Pitcairn Island, since 1980; b 16 July 1924; s of William Henry and Cicely Muriel Stratton. *Educ:* The King's Sch., Rochester; Merton Coll., Oxford. Served in Coldstream Guards, 1943–46. Joined Foreign Service, Oct. 1947; British Embassy, Rio de Janeiro, 1948–50; FO, 1951–53; British Embassy, Tokyo, March-Aug. 1953; British Legation, Seoul, 1953–55; Private Sec. to Parly Under-Sec. of State, FO, Nov. 1955-Feb. 1958; NATO Defence Coll., Paris, Feb.-Aug. 1958; British Embassy, Bonn, Sept. 1958-July 1960; British Embassy, Abidjan, Ivory Coast, Aug.-1960-Feb. 1962; Private Sec. to Lord Carrington, as Minister without Portfolio, FO, 1963–64; to Minister of State

for Foreign Affairs, 1964–66; Counsellor, British High Commn, Rawalpindi, 1966–69; IDC, 1970; FCO, 1971–72; Political Adviser to Govt of Hong Kong, 1972–74; HM Ambassador: to Republic of Zaire and People's Republic of the Congo, 1974–77; to Republic of Burundi, 1975–77; to Rwandan Republic, 1977; Assistant Under-Sec. of State, FCO, 1977–80. *Recreations:* music, bridge. *Address:* c/o Foreign and Commonwealth Office, SW1. *Clubs:* Travellers', Royal Commonwealth Society.

STRATTON, Mrs Roy Olin; see Dickens, Monica Enid.

STRATTON, Air Vice-Marshal William Hector, CB 1970; CBE 1963; DFC 1939 and Bar 1944; company director; Chief of the Air Staff, RNZAF, 1969–71, retired 1971; b 22 July 1916; s of V. J. Stratton; m 1954, Dorothy M., d of J. D. Whyte; one s two d. *Educ:* Hawera Tech. High School, and privately. RAF, 1937–44. Appointments include: in comd RNZAF, Ohakea; Air Member for Personnel; assistant chief of Air Staff; Head NZ Defence Staff, Canberra; Head NZ Defence Staff, London. *Address:* 62 Paramatta Road, Doubleview, Perth, WA 6018, Australia.

STRATTON, Lt.-Gen. Sir William (Henry), KCB 1957 (CB 1948); CVO 1944; CBE 1943; DSO 1945; b 1903; o s of late Lt-Col H. W. Stratton, OBE; m 1930, Noreen Mabel Brabazon, d of late Dr and Mrs F. H. B. Noble, Sittingbourne, Kent; no c. *Educ:* Dulwich Coll.; RMA, Woolwich. 2nd Lieut RE 1924; psc; Lt-Col (temp.), 1940; Brig. (temp.), 1941; Comdr 169 Inf. Bde, 1944–45; Col 1945; idc 1946; Maj.-Gen. 1947; Chief of Staff, BAOR, 1947–49; Comdt Joint Services Staff Coll., 1949–52; Commander British Army Staff, and Military Member British Joint Services Mission, Washington, 1952–53; Comdr 42 (Lancs) Inf. Div. (TA), 1953–55; Lt-Gen. 1955; Commander, British Forces, Hong Kong, 1955–57; Vice-Chief of the Imperial General Staff, 1957–60, retired. Col Comdt RE, 1960–68; Inspector-General of Civil Defence, Home Office, 1960–62. Chairman: Edwin Danks (Oldbury) Ltd, 1961–71; Penman & Co. Ltd, 1961–71; Babcock-Moxey Ltd, 1965–71.

STRAUB, Marianne, RDI 1972; textile designer; b 23 Sept. 1909; d of Karl Straub and Cécile (née Kappeler). *Educ:* in Switzerland. Dip. Kunstgewerbeschule, Zürich. Textile Designer: Rural Industries Bureau, 1934–37; Helios Ltd, Bolton, 1937–50; Warner & Sons Ltd, Braintree, 1950–69. Teaching posts: Central School of Art and Design, 1958–63; Hornsey College of Art, 1963–68; Royal College of Art, 1968–74. Now retired, but working freelance and teaching by invitation at various colleges. Hon. Fellow, RCA, 1981. *Publication:* Hand Weaving and Cloth Design, 1977. *Address:* 67 Highsett, Hills Road, Cambridge CB2 1NZ. *T:* Cambridge 61947.

STRAUSS, family name of Baron Strauss.

STRAUSS, Baron cr 1979 (Life Peer), of Vauxhall in the London Borough of Lambeth; **George Russell Strauss;** PC 1947; b 18 July 1901; s of Arthur Strauss, formerly MP (C) Camborne Div. of Cornwall and N Paddington; m 1932, Patricia O'Flynn (see Lady Strauss); two s one d. *Educ:* Rugby. MP (Lab) Lambeth North, 1929–31 and 1934–50, Lambeth, Vauxhall, 1950–79; PPS to Minister of Transport, 1929–31, to Lord Privy Seal, and later Minister of Aircraft Production, 1942–45; Parly Sec., Min. of Transport, 1945–47; Minister of Supply, 1947–51 (introd. Iron and Steel Nationalisation Bill, 1949). LCC Representative: N Lambeth, 1925–31; SE Southwark, 1932–46; LCC: Chm. Highways Cttee, 1934–37; Vice-Chm. Finance Cttee, 1934–37; Chm. Supplies Cttee, 1937–39; Mem. London and Home Counties Traffic Advisory Cttee, 1934–39. Introduced Theatres Bill for the abolition of stage censorship, 1968. Father of the House of Commons, 1974. *Recreations:* painting and chess. *Address:* 1 Palace Green, W8. *T:* 01-937 1630; Naylands, Slaugham, West Sussex. *T:* Handcross 400270.

STRAUSS, Lady; Patricia Frances Strauss; Governor: the Old Vic since 1951; Sadler's Wells Theatre since 1951; St Martin's School of Art, since 1952; the Royal Ballet since 1957; Whitechapel Art Gallery since 1957; Ballet Rambert, since 1958; Goldsmith School of Art, since 1969; b 21 Oct. 1909; m 1932, Rt Hon. Lord Strauss, qv; two s one d. Member of London County Council, 1946–58; Chairman: Parks Cttee (LCC), 1947–49; Supplies Cttee (LCC), 1949–52. Contested (Lab) South Kensington, Parliamentary General Election, 1945. Governor: Royal Ballet Sch., 1951–72; London Opera Centre, 1965–79; Sadler's Wells Opera (Coliseum), 1968–78. *Publications:* Bevin and Co., 1941; Cripps, Advocate and Rebel, 1942. *Recreations:* painting, chess, foreign travel. *Address:* 1 Palace Green, W8. *T:* 01-937 1630; Naylands, Slaugham, Sussex. *T:* Handcross 400270.

STRAUSS, Claude L.; see Levi-Strauss.

STRAUSS, Franz Josef; Grand Cross, Order of Merit, Federal Republic of Germany; Prime Minister of Bavaria, since 1978; President, Christian Social Union (CSU), since 1961; b Munich, 6 Sept. 1915; s of Franz Josef Strauss and Walburga (née Schiessl); m 1957, Marianne (née Zwicknagl); two s one d. *Educ:* Gymnasium, Munich; Munich Univ. Served in War of 1939–45, 1st Lieut. In Bavarian State Govt, 1946–49; Pres., Govt Cttee on Youth in Bavaria, 1946–48; Member of Bundestag, Fed. Republic of Germany, 1949–78; Minister for Special Tasks, 1953–55; Minister for Nuclear Issues, 1955–56; Minister of Defence, 1956–62; Minister of Finance, 1966–69. President: Landrat (County Commissioner) of Schongau, 1946–49; Committee on Questions of European Security. Dr hc: Detroit University, USA, 1956; Kalamazoo College, 1962; Case Institute of Technology, Cleveland (Ohio), 1962; De Paul

University, Chicago, 1964; Univ. Santiago de Chile, 1977; Dallas Univ., 1980. Holds decorations from other European countries. *Publications:* The Grand Design, 1965; Herausforderung and Antwort, 1968; Challenge and Response: A programme for Europe, 1969; Finanzpolitik: Theorie und Wirklichkeit, 1969; Deutschland Deine Zukunft, 1975; Bundestagsreden, 1975; Signale, 1978; Gebote der Freiheit, 1980; many articles on political affairs in newspapers and periodicals. *Address:* Nymphenburger Strasse 64, Munich 2, Germany. *T:* 1243-215.

STRAUSS, Hon. Jacobus Gideon Nel, QC (South Africa) 1944; Leader of the South African United Party, 1950-56; MP for Germiston District 1932-57; *b* Calvinia CP, 17 Dec. 1900; *s* of late H. J. Strauss; *m* 1928, Joy Carpenter; two *s* two *d* (and one *s* decd). *Educ:* Calvinia High Sch.; Univ. of Cape Town; Univ. of South Africa. Private Sec. to the Prime Minister (General J. C. Smuts), 1923-24; practice at Johannesburg Bar, 1926-53; Minister of Agriculture and Forestry in Smuts Cabinet, 1944; succeeded Field Marshal J. C. Smuts as Leader of the Opposition, 1950. *Recreations:* riding, mountaineering and golf. *Address:* PO Box 67398, Bryanston, Transvaal 2021, South Africa. *Clubs:* Rand, Royal Johannesburg Golf (Johannesburg).

STRAW, Jack, (John Whitaker Straw); MP (Lab) Blackburn, since 1979; Opposition Treasury spokesman, since 1980; Barrister; *b* 3 Aug. 1946; *s* of Walter Arthur Whitaker Straw and of Joan Sylvia Straw; *m* 1st, 1968, Anthea Lilian Weston (marr. diss. 1978); one *d* (decd); 2nd, 1978, Alice Elizabeth Perkins; one *s* one *d*. *Educ:* Brentwood Sch., Essex; Univ. of Leeds. LLB 1967. Called to Bar, Inner Temple, 1972. Political Advr to Sec. of State for Social Services, 1974-76; Special Advr to Sec. of State for Environment, 1976-77; on staff of Granada TV (World in Action), 1977-79. Pres., Leeds Univ. Union, 1967-68; Pres., Nat. Union of Students, 1969-71; Mem., Islington Borough Council, 1971-78; Dep. Leader, Inner London Educn Authority, 1973-74; Mem., Labour Party's Nat. Exec. Sub-Cttee on Educn and Science, 1970-; Chm., Jt Adv. Cttee on Polytechnics of N London, 1973-75. Contested (Lab) Tonbridge and Malling, Feb. 1974. *Publications:* Granada Guildhall Lecture, 1969; University of Leeds Convocation Lecture, 1978; contrib. pamphlets, articles. *Recreations:* cycling, walking, cooking, music. *Address:* House of Commons, SW1A 0AA; 36 Church Street, Blackburn.

STRAWSON, Maj.-Gen. John Michael, CB 1975; OBE 1964; idc, jssc, psc; Senior Military Adviser, Westland Aircraft Ltd, since 1978 (Head of Cairo Office, 1976-78); *b* 1 Jan. 1921; *s* of late Cyril Walter and Nellie Dora Strawson; *m* 1960, Baroness Wilfried von Schellersheim; two *d. Educ:* Christ's Coll., Finchley. Joined Army, 1940; commnd, 1942; served with 4th QO Hussars in Middle East, Italy, Germany, Malaya, 1942-50, 1953-54, 1956-58; Staff Coll., Camberley, 1950; Bde Major, 1951-53; Instructor, Staff Coll. and Master of Drag Hounds, 1958-60; GSO1 and Col GS in WO and MoD, 1961-62 and 1965-66; comd QR Irish Hussars, Malaysia and BAOR, 1963-65; comd 39 Inf. Bde, 1967-68; idc 1969; COS, Live Oak, SHAPE, 1970-72; COS, HQ UKLF, 1972-76. Col, Queen's Royal Irish Hussars, 1975-. US Bronze Star, 1945. *Publications:* The Battle for North Africa, 1969; Hitler as Military Commander, 1971; The Battle for the Ardennes, 1972; The Battle for Berlin, 1974; (jtly) The Third World War, 1978; El Alamein, 1981; (jtly) The Third World War: the untold story, 1982. *Recreations:* equitation, golf, reading. *Address:* The Old Rectory, Boyton, Warminster, Wilts BA12 0SS. *Club:* Cavalry and Guards.
See also Sir P. F. Strawson.

STRAWSON, Sir Peter (Frederick), Kt 1977; FBA 1960; Fellow of Magdalen College, and Waynflete Professor of Metaphysical Philosophy in the University of Oxford, since 1968 (Reader, 1966-68); Fellow of University College, Oxford, 1948-68, Honorary Fellow since 1979; *b* 23 November 1919; *s* of late Cyril Walter and Nellie Dora Strawson; *m* 1945, Grace Hall Martin; two *s* two *d. Educ:* Christ's College, Finchley; St John's College, Oxford (scholar; Hon. Fellow, 1973). Served War of 1939-45, RA, REME, Capt. Asst Lecturer in Philosophy, University Coll. of N. Wales, 1946; John Locke Schol., Univ. of Oxford, 1946; Lecturer in Philosophy, 1947, Fellow and Praelector, 1948, University Coll., Oxford. Vis. Prof., Duke Univ., N Carolina, 1955-56; Fellow of Humanities Council and Vis. Associate Prof., Princeton Univ., 1960-61, Vis. Prof., 1972. For. Hon. Mem., Amer. Acad. Arts and Scis, 1971. *Publications:* Introduction to Logical Theory, 1952; Individuals, 1959; The Bounds of Sense, 1966; (ed) Philosophical Logic, 1967; (ed) Studies in the Philosophy of Thought and Action, 1968; Logico-Linguistic Papers, 1971; Freedom and Resentment, 1974; Subject and Predicate in Logic and Grammar, 1974; contrib. to Mind, Philosophy, Proc. Aristotelian Soc., Philosophical Review, etc. *Address:* 25 Farndon Road, Oxford. *T:* Oxford 55026. *Club:* Athenæum.
See also J. M. Strawson.

STREAMS, Peter John; HM Diplomatic Service; Consul-General, Karachi, since 1982; *b* 8 March 1935; *s* of Horace Stanley Streams and Isabel Esther (*née* Ellaway); *m* 1956, Margareta Decker; two *s* one *d. Educ:* Wallington County Grammar Sch. Exec. Officer, BoT, 1953; British Trade Commn, Bombay, 1960; 2nd Sec., British Trade Commn, Calcutta, 1962; 2nd Sec., British Embassy, Oslo, 1966; 1st Sec., FCO, 1970; Head of Chancery, Mexico, 1973; 1st Sec., FCO, 1977, Counsellor, 1979. *Recreations:* walking, golf. *Address:* c/o Foreign and Commonwealth Office, SW1.

STREATFEILD, Noel; Novelist; *d* of late William Champion Streatfeild, Bishop of Lewes and late Janet Mary Venn; *b* 24 Dec. 1895; unmarried. *Educ:* Laleham; Eastbourne. *Publications:* Whicharts, 1931; Parson's Nine, 1932; Tops and Bottoms, 1933; Children's Matinee, 1934; Shepherdess of Sheep, 1934; Ballet Shoes, 1936; It Pays to be Good, 1936; Wisdom Teeth: a play, 1936; Tennis Shoes, 1937; Caroline England, 1937; Circus is Coming (Carnegie Gold Medal), 1938; Luke, 1940; Secret of the Lodge, 1940; House in Cornwall, 1940; Children of Primrose Lane, 1941; Winter is Past, 1942; I Ordered a Table for Six, 1942; Myra Carrol, 1944; Curtain Up, 1944; Saplings, 1945; Party Frock, 1946; Grass in Piccadilly, 1947; Painted Garden, 1949; Mothering Sunday, 1950; (ed) Years of Grace, 1950; White Boots, 1951; Aunt Clara, 1952; (ed) By Special Request, 1953; The Fearless Treasure, 1953, new edn, 1963; The First Book of Ballet, 1953 (US), rev. edn, 1963 (UK); The Bell Family, 1954; (ed) Growing Up Gracefully, 1955; The Grey Family, 1956; Judith, 1956; (ed) The Day Before Yesterday, 1956; Wintles Wonders, 1957; Magic and the Magician, 1958; Bertram, 1959; The Royal Ballet School, 1959; The Ballet Annual, 1960; Christmas with the Crystals, 1960; Look at the Circus, 1960; New Town, 1960; Queen Victoria, 1961; The Silent Speaker, 1961; Apple Bough, 1962; Lisa Goes to Russia, 1963; A Vicarage Family (autobiog.), 1963; The Children on the Top Floor, 1964; Away from the Vicarage (autobiog.), 1965; Let's Go Coaching, 1965; Enjoying Opera, 1966; The Growing Summer, 1966; Old Chairs to Mend, 1966; The Thames, 1966; Before Confirmation, 1967; Caldicott Place, 1967; The Barrow Lane Gang, 1968; (ed) Nicholas, 1968; Red Riding Hood, 1970; Thursday's Child, 1970; Beyond the Vicarage (autobiog.), 1971; The First Book of Shoes, 1971; Ballet Shoes for Anna, 1972; The Boy Pharaoh, Tutankhamen, 1972; When the Siren Wailed, 1974; Gran-Nannie, 1976; Far To Go, 1976; Meet the Maitlands, Part 1, 1978; The Maitlands: All Change of Cuckly Place, 1979. *Recreation:* wild flowers. *Address:* 61 St George's Square, SW1V 3QR. *T:* 01-821 1884.

STREATFEILD, Maj.-Gen. Timothy Stuart Champion, CB 1980; MBE 1960; Director, Royal Artillery, 1978-81; *b* 9 Sept. 1926; *s* of Henry Grey Champion and Edythe Streatfeild; *m* 1951, Annette Catherine, *d* of Sir John Clague, CMG, CIE, and Lady Clague; two *s* one *d. Educ:* Eton; Christ Church, Oxford. FBIM. Commnd into RA, 1946; Instructor, Staff Coll., Camberley, 1963-65; Chief Instructor, Sudan Armed Forces Staff Coll., 1965-67; Commander, 7th Parachute Regt, RHA, 1967-69; Col Adjt and QMG, 4 Div., 1969-70; Commander, RA 2 Div., 1971-72; RCDS, 1973; Brigadier Adjt and QMG, 1st Corps, 1974-75; COS, Logistic Exec., MoD, 1976-78. Col. Commandant: RA, 1980-; RHA, 1981-. *Recreations:* fishing, sporting, the countryside, music. *Address:* Toatley Farm, Chawleigh, Chulmleigh, N Devon. *T:* Lapford 363. *Clubs:* Army and Navy, MCC.

STREATFEILD-JAMES, Captain John Jocelyn, ADC 1982; RN; Captain, HMS Excellent, Royal Naval Leadership Centre, since 1981; *b* 14 April 1929; *s* of Comdr Rev. Eric Cardew Streatfeild-James, OBE, and Elizabeth Ann (*née* Kirby); *m* 1962, Sally Madeline (*née* Stewart); three *s* (one *d* decd). *Educ:* RNC, Dartmouth. Specialist in Undersea Warfare. FBIM; MNI 1982. Naval Cadet, 1943-47; Midshipman, 1947-49; Sub-Lt, 1949-51; Lieutenant: Minesweeping, Diving and Anti-Bandit Ops, Far East Stn, 1951; Officer and Rating Trng, Home Stn, 1952-53; specialised in Undersea Warfare, 1954-55; Ship and Staff Duties, Far East Stn, 1955-57; Exchange Service, RAN, 1957-59; Lieutenant-Commander: instructed Officers specialising in Undersea Warfare, 1960-61; Sea Duty, Staff Home Stn, 1962-63; Sen. Instr, Jt Anti-Submarine Sch., HMS Sea Eagle, 1964-65; Commander: Staff of C-in-C Western Fleet and C-in-C Eastern Atlantic Area, 1965-67; Jt Services Staff Coll., 1968; Staff of Comdr Allied Naval Forces, Southern Europe, Malta, 1968-71; HMS Dryad, 1971-73; Captain: Sen. Officers' War Course, RNC, Greenwich, 1974; Dir, OPCON Proj., 1974-77; Head of British Defence Liaison Staff, Ottawa, and Defence Advr to British High Comr in Canada, 1978-80 (as Cdre). *Recreations:* sailing, carpentry, squash, amateur theatricals. *Address:* Captain's Residence, HMS Excellent, Whale Island, Portsmouth PO2 8ER. *T:* Portsmouth 661901; South Lodge, Tower Road, Hindhead, Surrey. *T:* Hindhead 6064. *Clubs:* Royal Commonwealth Society; Rideau (Ottawa).

STREATOR, Edward James; Minister, United States Embassy, London, since 1977; *b* 12 Dec. 1930; *s* of Edward J. and Ella S. Streator; *m* 1957, Priscilla Craig Kenney; one *s* two *d. Educ:* Princeton Univ. (AB). US Naval Reserve, served to Lieut (jg), 1952-56; entered Foreign Service, 1956; Third Sec., US Embassy, Addis Ababa, 1958-60; Second Sec., Lome, 1960-62; Office of Intelligence and Research, Dept of State, 1962-64; Staff Asst to Sec. of State, 1964-66; First Sec., US Mission to NATO, 1966-69; Dep. Director, then Director, Office of NATO Affairs, Dept of State, 1969-75; Dep. US Permanent Representative to NATO, Brussels, 1975-77. *Recreation:* swimming. *Address:* United States Embassy, Grosvenor Square, W1A 1AE. *T:* 01-499 9000, ext. 2225. *Clubs:* Brooks's, Garrick; Metropolitan (Washington); Mill Reef (Antigua).

STREDDER, James Cecil; Headmaster, Wellington School, Somerset, 1957-73; *b* 22 Sept. 1912; 4th *s* of late Rev. J. Clifton Stredder and late Mrs Stredder; *m* 1938, Catherine Jane, er *d* of late Rev. A. R. Price, RN (Retd), Paignton, Devon; one *d. Educ:* King Edward VI School, Stratford-on-Avon; Jesus College, Oxford. Senior Chemistry Master at: Victoria College, Alexandria, Egypt, 1935; St Lawrence Coll., Ramsgate, 1936; Fettes Coll., Edinburgh, 1940; Tonbridge School, 1942-57. BA (Hons) Natural Science (Chemistry) Oxon 1935, MA 1943. *Recreation:* walking. *Address:* 21 Crouch Cross Lane, Boxgrove, near Chichester, Sussex.

STREET, Hon. Anthony Austin; Minister for Foreign Affairs, Australia, since 1980; MP (L) Corangamite, Victoria, since 1966; *b* 8 Feb. 1926; *s* of late Brig. the Hon. G. A. Street, MC, MHR; *m* 1951, Valerie Erica, *d* of J. A. Rickard; three *s. Educ:* Melbourne C of E Grammar Sch. RAN, 1945-46. Mem., various Govt Mems Cttees, 1967-71; Mem., Fed. Exec. Council, 1971-; Asst Minister for Labour and Nat. Service, 1971-72; Mem., Opposition Exec., 1973-75 (Special Asst to Leader of Opposition and Shadow Minister for Labour and Immigration, March-Nov. 1975); Minister for Labour and Immigration, Caretaker Ministry after dissolution of Parliament, Nov. 1975; Minister for Employment and Industrial Relations and Minister Assisting Prime Minister in Public Service Matters, 1975-78; Minister for Industrial Relations, 1978-80. Chm., Fed. Rural Cttee, Liberal Party, 1970-74. *Recreations:* cricket, golf, tennis, flying. *Address:* Eildon, Lismore, Vic 3324, Australia. *Clubs:* MCC; Royal Melbourne Golf, Barwon Heads Golf.

STREET, Prof. Harry, CBE 1978; LLM, PhD; FBA 1968; Professor of English Law, Manchester University, since 1960; *b* 17 June 1919; *s* of Alfred and Lilian Street; *m* 1947, Muriel Helène Swain; two *s* one *d. Educ:* Farnworth Grammar School; Manchester Univ. LLB 1938, LLM 1948; PhD 1951. Qualified as Solicitor, 1940. Flt-Lt, RAF, 1942-46. Lectr in Law, Manchester Univ., 1946-47; Commonwealth Fund Fellow at Columbia Univ., USA, 1947-48; Lectr in Law, 1948-51, Senior Lectr in Law, 1951-52, Manchester Univ.; Prof. of Law, Nottingham Univ., 1952-56; Prof. of Public Law and Common Law, Manchester Univ., 1956-60. Visiting Prof. of Law, Harvard Univ., USA, 1957-58. Chairman: Cttee on Racial Discrimination, 1967; Royal Commn on Fiji electoral system, 1975-76; Member: Commn on the Constitution, 1969-73; Monopolies and Mergers Commn, 1973-80. Hon. LLD Southampton, 1974. *Publications:* Principles of Administrative Law (with J. A. G. Griffith), 1952, 5th edn 1973; A Comparative Study of Governmental Liability, 1953; Law of Torts, 1955, 6th edn 1976; Law of Damages, 1961; Freedom, the Individual and the Law, 1963, 5th edn 1981; Law relating to Nuclear Energy (with F. R. Frame), 1966; Road Accidents (with D. W. Elliott), 1968; Justice in the Welfare State (Hamlyn Lectures), 1968. Articles in numerous English, Canadian and American Jls of law and public administration. *Recreation:* mountain walking. *Address:* Faculty of Law, Manchester University, Manchester M13 9PL; 1 Queen's Gate, Bramhall, Stockport SK7 1JT. *T:* 061-439 4922.

STREET, John Edmund Dudley, CMG 1966; retired; *b* 21 April 1918; *er s* of late Philip Edmund Wells Street and of Elinor Gladys Whittington-Ince; *m* 1940, Noreen Mary (*d* 1981), *o d* of Edward John Griffin Comerford and Mary Elizabeth Winstone; three *s* one *d. Educ:* Tonbridge School; Exeter College, Oxford. Served War of 1939-45, HM Forces, 1940-46. Entered Foreign Service, 1947; First Secretary: British Embassy, Oslo, 1950; British Embassy, Lisbon, 1952; Foreign Office, 1954; First Secretary and Head of Chancery, British Legation, Budapest, 1957-60; HM Ambassador to Malagasy Republic, 1961-62, also Consul-General for the Island of Réunion and the Comoro Islands, 1961-62; Asst Sec., MoD, 1967-76; Asst Under-Sec. of State, MoD, 1976-78. *Recreations:* reading, golf, bridge. *Address:* Cornerways, High Street, Old Woking, Surrey. *T:* Woking 64371.

STREET, Hon. Sir Laurence (Whistler), KCMG 1976; Lieutenant-Governor of New South Wales since 1974; Chief Justice of New South Wales since 1974; *b* Sydney, 3 July 1926; *s* of Hon. Sir Kenneth Street, KCMG; *m* 1952, Susan Gai, *d* of E. A. S. Watt; two *s* two *d. Educ:* Cranbrook Sch.; Univ. of Sydney (LLB Hons). Ord. Seaman, RANR, 1943-44; Midshipman, RANVR, 1944-45; Sub-Lt 1945-47; Comdr, Sen. Officer RANR Legal Br., 1964-65. Admitted to NSW Bar, 1951; QC 1963; Judge, Supreme Court of NSW, 1965; Judge of Appeal, 1972-74; Chief Judge in Equity, 1972-74. Lectr in Procedure, Univ. of Sydney, 1962-63, Lectr in Bankruptcy, 1964-65; Mem., Public Accountants Regn Bd, 1962-65; Mem., Companies Auditors Bd, 1962-65; Pres., Courts-Martial Appeal Tribunal, 1971-74; Pres., Cranbrook Sch. Council, 1966-74. KStJ 1976. Grand Officer of Merit, SMO Malta, 1977. *Address:* Supreme Court, Queen's Square, Sydney, NSW, Australia. *Clubs:* Union (Sydney); Royal Sydney Golf.

STREET, Prof. Robert, DSc; Vice-Chancellor, University of Western Australia, since 1978; *b* 16 Dec. 1920; *s* of late J. Street, Allerton Bywater, Yorkshire, UK; *m* 1943, Joan Marjorie Bere; one *s* one *d. Educ:* Hanley Sch.; King's Coll. London. BSc, MSc, PhD, DSc (London). MIEE, FInstP, FAIP, FAA. Scientific Officer, Dept of Supply, UK, 1942-45; Lectr, Dept of Physics, Univ. of Nottingham, 1945-54; Sen. Lectr, Dept of Physics, Univ. of Sheffield, 1954-60; Foundn Prof. of Physics, Monash Univ., Melbourne, Vic., 1960-74; Dir, Research Sch. of Physical Sciences, Aust. Nat. Univ., 1974-78. Former President: Aust. Inst. of Nuclear Science and Engrg; Aust. Inst. of Physics; Mem. and Chm., Aust. Research Grants Cttee, 1970-76; Chm., Nat. Standards Commn, 1967-78; Member: State Energy Adv. Council, WA, 1981-; Australian Science and Technology Council, 1977-80; Council, Univ. of Technology, Lae, Papua New Guinea, 1982-; Bd of Management, Royal Perth Hosp., 1978-. Fellow, Aust. Acad. of Science, 1973 (Treas., 1976-77). *Publications:* research papers in scientific jls. *Recreations:* fly fishing, golf. *Address:* The University of Western Australia, Nedlands, WA 6009, Australia. *T:* 380-2801; (home) 12 Wattle Avenue, Dalkeith, WA 6009. *Clubs:* Weld (Perth); Cottesloe Golf.

STREETEN, Paul Patrick, DLitt; Director, Center for Asian Development Studies and Professor at Boston University, since 1980; *b* 18 July 1917; *e s* of Wilhelm Hornig, Vienna; changed name to Streeten under Army Council Instruction, 1943; *m* 1951, Ann Hilary Palmer, *d* of Edgar Higgins, Woodstock, Vermont; two *d* (and one step *s*). *Educ:* Vienna; Aberdeen Univ.; Balliol Coll., Oxford (Hon. Schol.); 1st cl. PPE, 1947; Student, Nuffield Coll., Oxford, 1947-48. DLitt Oxon, 1976. Mil. service in Commandos, 1941-43; wounded in Sicily, 1943. Fellow, Balliol Coll., Oxford, 1948-66; Associate, Oxford Univ. Inst. of Econs and Statistics, 1960-64; Dep. Dir-Gen., Econ. Planning Staff, Min. of Overseas Devlt, 1964-66; Prof. of Econs, Fellow and Dep. Dir of Inst. of Devlt Studies, Sussex Univ., 1966-68; Warden of Queen Elizabeth House, Dir, Inst. of Commonwealth Studies, Univ. of Oxford, and Fellow of Balliol Coll., 1968-78; Special Adviser, World Bank, 1976-79. Rockefeller Fellow, USA, 1950-51; Fellow, Johns Hopkins Univ., Baltimore, 1955-56; Fellow, Center for Advanced Studies, Wesleyan Univ., Conn.; Sec., Oxford Econ. Papers, until 1961, Mem. Edit. Bd, 1971-78; Editor, Bulletin of Oxford Univ. Inst. of Econs and Statistics, 1961-64; Chm., Edit. Bd, World Development; Member: UK Nat. Commn of Unesco, 1966; Provisional Council of Univ. of Mauritius, 1966-72; Commonwealth Devlt Corp., 1967-72; Statutory Commn, Royal Univ. of Malta, 1972-; Royal Commn on Environmental Pollution, 1974-76. Mem., Internat. Adv. Panel, Canadian Univ. Service Overseas. Vice-Chm., Social Sciences Adv. Cttee, 1971; Member, Governing Body: Queen Elizabeth House, Oxford, 1966-68; Inst. of Devlt Studies, Univ. of Sussex, 1968-80 (Vice-Chm.); Dominion Students' Hall Trust, London House; Mem. Council, Overseas Devlt Institute, until 1979. Pres., UK Chapter, Soc. for Internat. Devlt until 1976. Hon. Fellow, Inst. of Devlt Studies, Sussex, 1980; Hon. LLD Aberdeen, 1980. Chm. Editorial Bd, World Devlt. *Publications:* (ed) Value in Social Theory, 1958; Economic Integration, 1961; contrib. to Economic Growth in Britain, 1966; The Teaching of Development Economics, 1967; (ed with M. Lipton) Crisis in Indian Planning, 1968; (contrib. to) Gunnar Myrdal, Asian Drama, 1968; (ed) Unfashionable Economics, 1970; (ed, with Hugh Corbet) Commonwealth Policy in a Global Context, 1971; Frontiers of Development Studies, 1972; (ed) Trade Strategies for Development, 1973; The Limits of Development Research, 1975; (with S. Lall) Foreign Investment, Transnationals and Developing Countries, 1977; Development Perspectives, 1981; First Things First, 1981; (ed with Richard Jolly) Recent Issues in World Development, 1981; contribs to learned journals. *Address:* Center for Asian Development Studies, Boston University, 264 Bay State Road, Boston, Mass 02215, USA. *Club:* United Oxford & Cambridge University.

STREETER, John Stuart; His Honour Judge Streeter; a Circuit Judge (formerly Deputy Chairman 1967-71, Chairman 1971, Kent Quarter Sessions); *b* 20 May 1920; *yr s* of late Wilfrid A. Streeter, osteopath, and of Mrs R. L. Streeter; *m* 1956, Margaret Nancy Richardson; one *s* two *d. Educ:* Sherborne. Served War of 1939-45 (despatches): Captain, Royal Scots Fusiliers, 1940-46. Called to Bar, Gray's Inn, Nov. 1947. Post Office Counsel SE Circuit, 1957; Treasury Counsel, London Sessions, 1959; Part-time Dep. Chm., Kent Quarter Sessions, 1963. *Recreation:* gardening. *Address:* Playstole, Sissinghurst, Cranbrook, Kent TN17 2JN. *T:* Cranbrook 712847.

STREETON, Terence George, CMG 1981; MBE 1969; HM Diplomatic Service; Assistant Under-Secretary of State and Principal Finance Officer, Foreign and Commonwealth Office, since 1982; *b* 12 Jan. 1930; *er s* of Alfred Victor Streeton and Edith Streeton (*née* Deiton); *m* 1962, Molly Horsburgh; two *s* two *d. Educ:* Wellingborough Grammar School. Inland Revenue, 1946; Prison Commission, 1947; Government Communications Headquarters, 1952; Foreign Office (Diplomatic Wireless Service), 1953; Diplomatic Service, 1965-: First Secretary, Bonn, 1966; FCO, 1970; First Secretary and Head of Chancery, Bombay, 1972; Counsellor and Head of Joint Admin Office, Brussels, 1975; Head of Finance Dept, FCO, 1979. *Recreations:* private flying, walking. *Address:* c/o Foreign and Commonwealth Office, SW1A 2AH.

STREIT, Clarence Kirshman; President, International Movement for Atlantic Union, since 1958, and Federal Union, Inc., USA, since 1939; author; lecturer since 1939; Editor, Freedom & Union, since 1946; *b* 21 Jan. 1896; *s* of Louis L. Streit and Emma Kirshman, California, Mo, USA; *m* 1921, Jeanne Defrance, of Paris, France; one *s* two *d. Educ:* Missouri and Montana public schs; State Univ. of Montana; Sorbonne; University Coll., Oxford (Rhodes Schol.). Hon. LLD, LittD, DHL. US public land surveyor in Montana and Alaska, 1912-16; served as volunteer in American Expeditionary Force, France, 1917-19, first as private, 18th Engineers Railway, then as sergeant in Intelligence Service, attached to American Delegation, Paris Peace Conference; then Rhodes Scholar, Oxford; correspondent Philadelphia Public Ledger, 1920-24, Greco-Turk War, Rome, Istanbul, Paris; correspondent, New York Times, 1925-39, Carthage excavations, Riff war, Vienna, New York, Latin America, Geneva, 1929-38, Washington, DC, 1938-39. First Recipient, Estes Kefauver Union of the Free Award, 1968. *Publications:* Where Iron is, There is the Fatherland, 1920; Hafiz: The Tongue of the Hidden (rubaiyat), 1928; Report on How to Combat False News, League of Nations, 1932; Union Now, 1939; Union Now with Britain, 1941; Chapter on Briand in Dictators and Democrats, 1941; (joint) The New Federalist, 1950; Freedom Against Itself, 1954; Freedom's Frontier-Atlantic Union Now, 1960. *Address:* (home) 2853 Ontario Road NW, Washington, DC 20009, USA. *T:* 202. 234-3232; (office) 1875 Connecticut Avenue NW, Washington DC 20009, USA.

STRETTON, Eric Hugh Alexander, CB 1972; Deputy Chief Executive in Property Services Agency, Department of the Environment, 1972-76, Deputy Chairman, 1973-76; *b* 22 June 1916; *y s* of Major S. G. Stretton, Wigston,

Leicester; *m* 1946, Sheila Woodroffe Anderson, MB, BS, *d* of Dr A. W. Anderson, Cardiff (formerly of Ogmore Vale); one *s* one *d. Educ:* Wyggeston Sch; Pembroke Coll., Oxford. BA 1939, MA 1942. Leics Regt and 2/4 PWO Gurkha Rifles (Major), 1939-46. Asst Secs., Birmingham Univ. Appointments Board, 1946. Entered Ministry of Works, 1947; Prin. Private Sec. to Minister of Works, 1952-54; Asst Sec., 1954; Under-Secretary: MPBW, 1962-70; DoE, 1970-72; Dep. Sec., 1972. Chm., Structure Plan Examns in Public, Salop, 1979, Lincs, 1980, Central and N Lancs, 1981. *Address:* Dacre Castle, Penrith, Cumbria. *T:* Pooley Bridge 375. *Club:* United Oxford & Cambridge University.

STRICK, Robert Charles Gordon; Clerk to the Drapers' Company, since 1980; *b* 23 March 1931; *s* of Charles Gordon Strick and late Doris Gwendoline Strick; *m* 1960, Jennifer Mary Hathway; one *s* one *d. Educ:* Royal Grammar Sch., Guildford; Sidney Sussex Coll., Cambridge. MA. Served RA, 1949-51; TA, 1951-55. Spicers Ltd, 1954-55; joined HMOCS, 1955; Dist Officer, Fiji, 1955-59; Sec., Burns Commn into Natural Resources and Population Trends, 1959-60; Asst Sec., Suva, 1960-61; Sec. to Govt, Tonga, 1961-63; Develt Officer and Divl Comr, 1963-67, Sec. for Natural Resources, 1967-71, Fiji; retired 1971; Under Sec., ICA, 1971-72; Asst Sec.-Gen., RICS, 1972-80; Clerk, Chartered Surveyors' Co., 1977-80. Clerk to Governors, Howells Sch., Denbigh, 1980-; Governor, QMC, London Univ., 1980-. *Recreations:* the countryside, walking, cycling, gardening. *Address:* 11 Stoatley Rise, Haslemere, Surrey GU27 1AF. *T:* Haslemere 51360.

STRICKLAND, Maj.-Gen. Eugene Vincent Michael, CMG 1960; DSO 1944; OBE 1955; MM 1940; Chief of Joint Services Liaison Organization, British Forces, Germany, 1966-69, retired; *b* 25 Aug. 1913; *s* of Capt. V. N. Strickland (*d* of wounds, 1917) and of Mary Erina Strickland (*née* O'Sullivan); *m* 1939, Barbara Mary Farquharson Meares Lamb; four *s* one *d. Educ:* Mayfield College; RMC Sandhurst. Commissioned, 1934; served in India, 1934-35; resigned commn, 1935; re-joined; War of 1939-45, in France and Belgium, 1940; re-commissioned, 1940, RAC; comd of 145 Regt, RAC, N Africa, 1942-43; Italy, 1943-45, comd of N Irish Horse, 145 Regt, RAC and RAC Sch.; Greece, 1945-46, comd of 40th RTR; Egypt, 1948; WO, (MI), 1948-50; Min. of Defence, 1952-54; Arab Legion, 1955-56; Sen. British Officer, Jordan, 1956-57; Min. of Defence, on staff of Chief of Defence Staff, 1957-58; Mil. Adviser to King Hussein of Jordan, 1958-59; Director of Plans, War Office, 1960-63; psc 1947; jssc 1952; idc 1960; NATO Defence College, 1963; DAQMG 1st Corps, 1963-66. Star of Jordan, 1959. CStJ 1960. *Recreations:* shooting, cricket, etc. *Address:* 46 Olivers Battery Road, Winchester, Hants.

STRICKLAND, Hon. Mabel Edeline, OBE 1944; Leader of the Progressive Constitutional Party in Malta, since 1953; *b* Malta, 8 Jan. 1899; 3rd *d* of 1st and last Baron Strickland, of Sizergh Castle, Kendal (and 6th Count della Catena in the Island of Malta) and of late Lady Edeline Sackville. *Educ:* privately in Australia. Maltese Naval HQ, Malta, 1917-18; War Correspondent, attached 21st Army Group, BAOR, Aug. 1945. Asst Sec., Constitutional Party, 1921-45; Editor: Times of Malta, 1935-50; Sunday Times of Malta, 1935-56; Member: Malta Legislative Assembly, 1950, 1951-53, 1962-66; Malta Chamber of Commerce; Man. Dir, Allied Malta Newspapers Ltd, 1940-55; Chairman: Xara Palace Hotel Co. Ltd, 1949-61, 1966-; Allied Malta Newspapers Ltd, 1950-55, 1966-; Director, Progress Press Co. Ltd, 1957-61, 1966-. Life Member: Commonwealth Parliamentary Assoc.; Air League; RSA; Mem. Royal Horticultural Soc.; Hon. Corresp. Sec. (Malta), Royal Commonwealth Soc. Astor Award, CPU, 1971. CStJ 1969. Coronation medal, 1953. *Publications:* A Collection of Essays on Malta, 1923-54; Maltese Constitutional and Economic Issue, 1955-59. *Recreations:* gardening, reading. *Address:* Villa Parisio, Lija, Malta. *T:* 41286. *Clubs:* Lansdowne; Marsa Sports.

STRICKLAND-CONSTABLE, Sir Robert (Frederick), 11th Bt *cr* 1641; *b* 22 Oct. 1903; 2nd *s* of Lt-Col Frederick Charles Strickland-Constable (*d* 1917) (*g g s* of 7th Bt) and Margaret Elizabeth (*d* 1961), *d* of late Rear-Adm. Hon. Thomas Alexander Pakenham; *S* brother, 1975; *m* 1936, Lettice, *y d* of late Major Frederick Strickland; two *s* two *d. Educ:* Magdalen Coll., Oxford (BA 1925, MA 1936, DPhil 1940). Served War of 1939-45, Lieut Comdr RNVR. Teaching Staff, Chem. Engineering Dept, Imperial Coll., Univ. of London, 1948-71, Readership 1963-71. Mem. Faraday Soc. *Publications:* Kinetics and Mechanism of Crystallization, 1968; contribs to jls. *Recreations:* music, mountains, bird-watching. *Heir: s* Frederick Strickland-Constable, *b* 21 Oct. 1944. *Address:* Combe Wood, Brasted, Westerham, Kent.

STRINGER, Donald Arthur, OBE 1975; Member since 1969, and Deputy Chairman and Joint Managing Director since 1982, British Transport Docks Board (Deputy Managing Director, 1967-71 and 1978-82); Member, National Dock Labour Board, since 1976; *b* 15 June 1922; *s* of late Harry William Stringer and Helen Stringer; *m* 1945, Hazel Handley; one *s* one *d. Educ:* Dorking High Sch.; Borden Grammar Sch. FCIT. Joined Southern Railway Co., 1938; service with RAF, 1941-46; Docks Manager: Fleetwood, 1957-58; East Coast Scottish Ports, 1958-62; Chief Docks Man., Southampton, 1963-67, Port Director, 1970-77. Chairman: BTDB Bds: Southampton, 1972-; Humber, 1978-; Southampton Cargo Handling Co. Ltd, 1968-; Nat. Assoc. of Port Employers, 1982- (Mem. Exec. Cttee, 1964-); Past Pres., Southampton Chamber of Commerce. Col, E and RS Corps, RE(TA). *Recreations:* gardening, sailing. *Address:* Hillcrest, Pinehurst Road, Bassett, Southampton.

T: Southampton 768887. *Clubs:* Army and Navy; (Hon.) Royal Yacht Squadron, (Hon.) Royal Southern Yacht, Royal Southampton Yacht.

STRINGER, Pamela Mary; Headmistress, Clifton High School for Girls, since 1965; *b* 30 Aug. 1928; *e d* of late E. Allen Stringer. *Educ:* Worcester Grammar Sch. for Girls; St Hugh's Coll., Oxford. MA (Hons Lit Hum). Asst Classics Mistress, Sherborne Sch. for Girls, 1950-59; Head of Classics Dept, Pate's Grammar Sch. for Girls, Cheltenham, 1959-64 (Dep. Head, 1963-64). Member: Exec. Cttee, Assoc. of Headmistresses, 1975-; Exec. Cttee, Girls Schools Assoc., 1975 (Pres., 1978-79); Council, Secondary Heads Assoc., 1978-79 (Pres. Area 7, 1978-79). *Recreations:* travel in Tuscany and Umbria, reading, theatre, cooking. *Address:* Glendower House, Clifton Park, Clifton, Bristol BS8 3JX.

STRONACH, Ancell, ARSA 1934; DA (Edin); *b* Dundee, 6 Dec. 1901; *s* of Alexander Stronach and Margaret Ancell; *m* 1941, Joan Cunningham. *Educ:* Hutcheson's Grammar School; privately. GSA (diploma), 1920; Guthrie Award bronze and silver medallist; travelling scholarship; Terrance Memorial Prize given by G. A. Lauder Prize GAC. Exhibited at Paris Salon, RA, WAG, RSA, Canada, New Zealand and America; official purchasers, Ross and Thorburn and Modern Arts Association permanent collections. Professor of Mural Painting, Glasgow School of Art, to 1939. *Recreations:* walking, menagerie and collection of British and foreign fish and reptiles. *Address:* Alma House, 25 Gillingham Road, Gillingham, Kent. *T:* Medway 54077.

STRONACH, David Brian, OBE 1975; FSA; Professor of Near Eastern Studies, University of California, Berkeley, since 1981; *b* 10 June 1931; *s* of Ian David Stronach, MB, FRCSE, and Marjorie Jessie Duncan (*née* Minto); *m* 1966, Ruth Vaadia; two *d. Educ:* Gordonstoun; St John's Coll., Cambridge (MA). Pres., Cambridge Univ. Archaeological Field Club, 1954. British Inst. of Archaeology at Ankara: Scholar, 1955-56; Fellow, 1957-58; Fellow, British Sch. of Archaeology in Iraq, 1957-60; Brit. Acad. Archaeological Attaché in Iran, 1960-61; Dir, British Inst. of Persian Studies, 1961-80, Hon. Vice Pres., 1981-. Asst on excavations at: Istanbul, 1954; Tell Rifa'at, 1956; Beycesultan, 1956-57; Hacilar, 1957-59; Nimrud, 1957-60; Charsada, 1958. Dir, excavations at: Ras al'Amiya, 1960; Yarim Tepe, 1960-62; Pasargadae, 1961-63; Tepe Nush-i Jan, 1967-; Co-dir, excavs at Shahr-i Qumis, 1967-. Mem., Internat. Cttee of Internat. Congresses of Iranian Art and Archaeology, 1968-. Hagop Kevorkian Visiting Lectr in Iranian Art and Archaeology, Univ. of Pennsylvania, 1967; Rhind Lectr, Edin., 1973; Norton Lectr, Amer. Inst. of Archaeology, 1980. Vis. Prof. of Archaeology, Hebrew Univ., Jerusalem, 1977; Vis. Prof. of Archaeology and Iranian Studies, Univ. of Arizona, Tucson, 1980-81. Mem., German Archaeological Inst., 1973 (Corr. Mem., 1966). Ghirshman Prize, Académie des Inscriptions et Belles-Lettres, Paris, 1979; Sir Percy Sykes Meml Medal, Royal Soc. for Asian Affairs, 1980. Adv. Editor: Jl of Mithraic Studies, 1976-; Iran, 1980-. *Publications:* Pasargadae, a Report on the Excavations conducted by the British Institute of Persian Studies, 1978; archaeological articles in: Jl of Near Eastern Studies; Iran; Iraq; Anatolian Studies, etc. *Recreations:* fly fishing, mediaeval architecture, tribal carpets; repr. Cambridge in athletics, 1953. *Address:* Department of Near Eastern Studies, University of California, Berkeley, Calif 94720, USA. *Clubs:* Achilles; Hawks (Cambridge); Explorers' (New York).

STRONG, Sir Charles Love, KCVO 1974 (MVO 1962); chartered physiotherapist in private practice in London, since 1938; *b* 16 April 1908; *o s* of late Alfred Strong; *m* 1st, 1933, Ivy Maud (*d* 1976), *yr d* of late Arthur Stockley; one *d*; 2nd, 1977, Ruth Mary, *d* of late Charles Hermon Smith. *Educ:* privately (Bailey Sch., Durham). Miner and merchant seaman, 1924-26; RN (Sick Berth Br.), qualified MCSP; Physiotherapist, RN Hosps, Haslar and Malta. Devised new apparatus and technique for treatment of injury to humans by faradism; developed manipulative techniques, 1926-38; running parallel with human practice designed special apparatus and technique for treatment of injuries to horses by faradism with outstanding success; under observation of leading equine veterinarian treated 100 cases of lameness in horses which had failed to respond to previous treatment, curing 88 per cent; some hundreds of races have now been won by horses cured of lameness by this method and which had failed to respond to other treatments. Formed firm of 'Transeva' for development, manufacture and marketing of horse apparatus, which is now supplied to many parts of the world. Served War, RAF Marine Section, 1st cl. Coxwain, 1940-44 (invalided). *Publications:* Common-Sense Therapy for Horses' Injuries, 1956; Horses' Injuries, 1967. *Recreation:* racing. *Address:* 73 Portland Place, W1N 3AL. *T:* 01-935 4523.

STRONG, Air Cdre David Malcolm, CB 1964; AFC 1941; *b* 30 Sept. 1913; *s* of Theo Strong; *m* 1941, Daphne Irene Warren-Brown; two *s* one *d. Educ:* Cardiff High School. Pilot, under trng, 1936; Bomber Sqdn, 1937-41; POW, 1941-45. Station Commander, RAF Jurby, RAF Driffield, 1946-48; Staff Coll. (psa), 1949; Staff Officer, Rhodesian Air Trng Grp, 1949-51; Directing Staff, Staff Coll., 1952-55; Air Warfare Coll. (pfc), 1956; Station Comdr, RAF Coningsby, 1957-59; Dir of Personnel, Air Min., 1959-61; Senior Air Staff Officer, RAF Germany, 1962-63; Officer Commanding, RAF Halton, 1964-66. Retired, 1966. Chairman: RAF Rugby Union, 1954-56; RAF Golf Soc., 1964-66. *Recreation:* golf. *Address:* Old Coach House, Wendover, Bucks. *T:* Wendover 624724. *Clubs:* Royal Air Force; Ashridge Golf.

STRONG, Dr John Anderson, CBE 1978 (MBE (mil.) 1942); MD; FRCP; FRCPE; FRSE; President, Royal College of Physicians of Edinburgh, 1979-82; *b* 18 Feb. 1915; *s* of Charles James Strong and Mabel Emma Strong (*née* Anderson); *m* 1939, Anne Frances Moira Heaney; one *s* two *d*. *Educ:* Monkton Combe Sch., Bath; Trinity Coll., Dublin (MB 1937, MA, MD). Served RAMC, UK, India and Burma, 1939–46 (despatches, Burma, 1945); Hon. Lt-Col RAMC, 1946. Senior Lecturer, Dept of Medicine, Univ. of Edinburgh, 1949; Hon. Cons. Phys., Western General Hosp., Edinburgh, 1949; Hon. Physician, MRC Clinical and Population Cytogenetics Unit, 1959–80; Professor of Medicine, Univ. of Edinburgh, 1966–80, Professor Emeritus, 1981. Mem., Medicines Commn, 1976–. Hon. FACP 1980; Hon. FRCPI 1980; Hon. Fellow: Coll. of Physicians of Philadelphia, 1981; TCD, 1982; Coll. of Physicians of S Africa, 1982; Fellow *ad eundem*, RCGP, 1982. *Publications:* chapter on Endocrinology in Principles and Practice of Medicine, ed L. S. P. Davidson, 1952, 12th edn 1977; articles in general medical and endocrinological jls. *Recreations:* fishing, golf, stalking, natural history. *Address:* 6 York Road, Edinburgh EH5 3EH. *T:* 031-552 2865. *Clubs:* New (Edinburgh); Hon. Company of Edinburgh Golfers (Muirfield).

STRONG, John Clifford, CBE 1980; HM Diplomatic Service, retired; Governor, Turks and Caicos Islands, 1978–82; *b* 14 Jan. 1922; *m* 1942, Janet Browning; three *d*. *Educ:* Beckenham Grammar Sch.; London Sch. of Economics and Political Science. LLB 1953. Served RN, 1942–46; HMOCS Tanzania, 1946–63; CRO, 1963; First Sec., Nairobi, 1964–68; FCO, 1968–73; Counsellor and Head of Chancery, Dar es Salaam, 1973–78. *Address:* Oakover, 24 Crescent Road, Beckenham BR3 2NE. *Club:* Royal Over-Seas League.

STRONG, Julia Trevelyan; *see* Oman, J. T.

STRONG, Maurice F.; Chairman: International Energy Development Corporation, since 1980; AZL Resources; Crédit Immobilier, Geneva, Switzerland; Procor Inc.; *b* 29 April 1929; *s* of Frederick Milton Strong and late Mary Fyfe Strong; *m* 1950 (marr. diss. 1980); two *s* two *d* ; *m* 1981, Hanne Marstrand. *Educ:* Public and High Sch., Oak Lake, Manitoba, Canada. Served in UN Secretariat, 1947; Pres. or Dir, various Canadian and internat. corporations, 1954–66; Dir-Gen., External Aid Office (later Canadian Internat. Develt Agency), Canadian Govt, 1966–71; Under-Sec.-Gen. with responsibility for environmental affairs, and Sec.-Gen. of 1972 Conf. on the Human Environment, Stockholm, 1971–72; Exec. Dir, UN Environmental Programme, 1972–75. Chairman: Centre for Internat. Management Studies, Geneva, Switzerland, 1971–78; Bd of Governors, Internat. Develt Res. Centre, 1977–78; Bd of Petro-Canada, 1976–78; Alt. Governor, IBRD, ADB, Caribbean Develt Bank. Chairman: North South Energy Roundtable, Washington, DC; Adv. Cttee, UN Univ., Tokyo, Japan; Vice-Chm., Société Générale pour l'Energie et les Ressources, Geneva; Director: (also Mem. Exec. Cttee) Canada Develt Corp.: Toronto; Lindisfarne Assoc.; Mem., Internat. Asia Soc., New York. Trustee: Rockefeller Foundn, 1971–78; Aspen Inst., 1971–; Internat. Foundn for Develt Alternatives. Holds numerous hon. degrees from univs and colls in Canada, USA and UK. *Publications:* articles in various journals, including Foreign Affairs Magazine, Natural History Magazine. *Recreations:* swimming, skin-diving, farming, reading. *Address:* 32 St James's Street, SW1A 1HD. *Clubs:* Farmers'; Mount Royal (Montreal); Canadian, Yale, Century (New York); Rideau (Ottawa); Ranchmen's (Calgary).

STRONG, Most Rev. Philip Nigel Warrington, KBE 1970; CMG 1958; MA Cantab; ThD ACT; DD Lambeth, 1968; *b* Sutton-on-the-Hill, Etwall, 11 July 1899; *s* of late Rev. John Warrington Strong, Oxford, formerly Vicar of Dodford with Brockhall, and late Rosamond Maria, *d* of late John Digby Wingfield Digby, Sherborne Castle, Dorset. *Educ:* King's School, Worcester; Selwyn Coll., Cambridge; Bishops' College, Cheshunt. Served European War with RE (Signal Service), 1918–19; BA Cambridge, 1921; MA 1924; Deacon, 1922; Priest, 1923; Curate of St Mary's, Tyne Dock, 1922–26; Vicar of Christ Church, Leeds, 1926–31; Vicar of St Ignatius the Martyr, Sunderland, 1931–36; Proctor of Convocation of York and Member of Church Assembly for Archdeaconry of Durham, 1936; Bishop of New Guinea, 1936–62; MLC, Territory of Papua and New Guinea, 1955–63; Archbishop of Brisbane and Metropolitan of Queensland, 1962–70; Primate of Australia, 1966–70. Senior CF (Australian Army), 1943–45. Hon. Fellow, Selwyn College, Cambridge, 1966. Sub-Prelate, Order of St John of Jerusalem, 1967. *Publications:* Out of Great Tribulation, 1947; (ed D. Wetherell) Diaries of Philip Strong, 1981. *Address:* 11 Cathedral Close, Wangaratta, Victoria 3677, Australia. *T:* Wangaratta 21-5603. *Club:* Melbourne.

STRONG, Sir Roy (Colin), Kt 1982; PhD, FSA; Director, Victoria and Albert Museum, since 1974; *b* 23 Aug. 1935; *s* of G. E. C. Strong; *m* 1971, Julia Trevelyan Oman, *qv. Educ:* Edmonton Co. Grammar Sch.; Queen Mary Coll., London (Fellow, 1976); Warburg Inst., London. Asst Keeper, 1959, Director, Keeper and Secretary 1967–73, Nat. Portrait Gallery. Ferens Prof. of Fine Art, Univ. of Hull, 1971. Walls Lectures, Pierpont Morgan Library, 1974. Lecturer, critic, contributor to radio and TV and organiser of exhibitions. Member: Fine Arts Adv. Cttee, British Council, 1974–; Westminster Abbey Architectl Panel, 1975–; Council, Royal Archaeol Inst., 1975–; Council, RCA, 1979–; Trustee: Arundel Castle, 1974–; Chevening, 1974–; Sutton Place, 1982–. Shakespeare Prize, FVS Foundn, Hamburg, 1980. *Publications:* Portraits of Queen Elizabeth I, 1963; (with J. A. van Dorsten) Leicester's Triumph, 1964; Holbein and Henry VIII, 1967; Tudor and Jacobean Portraits, 1969; The English Icon: Elizabethan and Jacobean Portraiture, 1969; (with Julia Trevelyan Oman) Elizabeth R, 1971; Van Dyck: Charles I on Horseback, 1972; (with Julia Trevelyan Oman) Mary Queen of Scots, 1972; (with Stephen Orgel) Inigo Jones: the theatre of the Stuart court, 1973;

contrib. Burke's Guide to the Royal Family, 1973; Splendour at Court: Renaissance Spectacle and Illusion, 1973; (with Colin Ford) An Early Victorian Album: the Hill-Adamson collection, 1973; Nicholas Hilliard, 1975; (contrib.) Spirit of the Age, 1975; The Cult of Elizabeth: Elizabethan Portraiture and Pageantry, 1977; And When Did You Last See Your Father?, 1978; The Renaissance Garden in England, 1979; (contrib.) The Garden, 1979; Britannia Triumphans: Inigo Jones, Rubens and Whitehall Palace, 1980; (introd.) Holbein, 1980; (contrib.) Designing for the Dancer, 1981; (jtly) The English Miniature, 1981; (with Julia Trevelyan Oman) The English Year, 1982; contrib., Inigo Jones, Vitruvius Britannicus, in Pelican Guide to English Literature vol. 3, 1982; contributor to learned jls. *Recreations:* gardening, cooking, country life. *Address:* c/o Victoria and Albert Museum, South Kensington, SW7 2RL. *Clubs:* Beefsteak, Garrick, Grillions.

STRONGE, Sir James Anselan Maxwell, 10th Bt *cr* 1803; *b* 17 July 1946; *s* of Maxwell Du Pré James Stronge (*d* 1973) (*g g s* of 2nd Bt) and Eileen Mary (*d* 1976), *d* of Rt Hon. Maurice Marcus McCausland, PC, Drenagh, Limavady, Co. Londonderry; *S* cousin, 1981. *Heir:* none. *Address:* Shannagh Camphill Community, Kilkeel, Co. Down; c/o 1 Sidmonton Square, Bray, Co. Wicklow.

STROUD, Prof. (Charles) Eric, FRCP; Professor of Child Health, King's College Hospital Medical School, and Director, Department of Child Health, since 1968; *b* 15 May 1924; *s* of Frank Edmund and Lavinia Stroud; *m* 1950, June, *d* of Harold Neep; one *s* two *d*. *Educ:* Cardiff High Sch. for Boys; Welsh National Sch. of Medicine. BSc 1945, MB, BCh 1948 (Wales); MRCP 1955, DCH 1955, FRCP 1968 (London). Sqdn Ldr, RAF, 1950–52. Med. Qual., 1948; Paediatric Registrar, Welsh Nat. Sch. of Med.; Sen. Registrar, Great Ormond Street Children's Hosp., 1957–61; Paediatrician, Uganda Govt, 1958–60; Asst to Dir, Dept of Child Health, Guy's Hosp., 1961–62; Cons. Paediatrician, King's Coll. Hosp., 1962–68. *Publications:* chapters in Textbook of Obstetrics, 1958; Childhealth in the Tropics, 1961; various articles in med. jls. *Recreations:* bad golf, good fishing, cheap antiques. *Address:* 84 Copse Hill, Wimbledon, SW20. *T:* 01-947 1336.

STROUD, Derek H.; *see* Hammond-Stroud.

STROUD, Dorothy Nancy, MBE 1968; Assistant Curator, Sir John Soane's Museum, since 1945; *b* London, 11 Jan. 1910; *o c* of late Nancy and Alfred Stroud, London. *Educ:* Claremont, Eastbourne; Edgbaston High Sch. On staff of: Country Life, 1930–41; National Monuments Record, 1941–45; Sir John Soane's Museum, 1945–. Vice-Pres., Garden History Soc., 1982–; Mem., Historic Buildings Council, 1974–82. FSA 1951; Hon. RIBA, 1975. *Publications:* Capability Brown, 1950, new edn 1975; The Thurloe Estate, 1959; The Architecture of Sir John Soane, 1961; Humphry Repton, 1962; Henry Holland, 1966; George Dance, 1971; The South Kensington Estate of Henry Smith's Charity, 1975. *Address:* 24 Onslow Square, SW7 3NS.

STROUD, Prof. Eric; *see* Stroud, Prof. C. E.

STROWGER, Gaston Jack, CBE 1976; Managing Director, Thorn Electrical Industries, 1970–79; *b* 8 Feb. 1916; *s* of Alfred Henry Strowger, Lowestoft boat-owner, and Lily Ellen Tripp; *m* 1939, Katherine Ellen Gilbert; two *s* one *d*. *Educ:* Lowestoft Grammar School. Joined London Electrical Supply Co., 1934; HM Forces, 1939–43. Joined TEI, as an Accountant, 1943; Group Chief Accountant, 1952; joined Tricity Finance Corp. as Dir, 1959; Exec. Dir, TEI, 1961; full Dir 1966; Financial Dir 1967; Dep. Chm., Tricity Finance Corp., 1968. FBIM 1971. *Recreations:* gardening, bowling. *Address:* Kesslee, 29 Beech Hill Avenue, Hadley Wood, Barnet, Herts EN4 0IN. *T:* 01-449 6289.

STROYAN, Ronald Angus Ropner, QC 1972; His Honour Judge Stroyan; a Circuit Judge, since 1975; *b* 27 Nov. 1924; *e s* of Ronald S. Stroyan of Boreland, Killin; *m* 1st, 1952, Elisabeth Anna Grant (marr. diss. 1965), *y d* of Col J. P. Grant of Rothiemurchus; one *s* two *d* ; 2nd, 1967, Jill Annette Johnston, *d* of late Sir Douglas Marshall; one *s*. *Educ:* Harrow School; Trinity College, Cambridge; BA(Hons). Served 1943–45 with The Black Watch (NW Europe); attd Argyll and Sutherland Highlanders, Palestine, 1945–47 (despatches); Captain; later with Black Watch TA. Barrister-at-Law, 1950, Inner Temple. Dep. Chm., North Riding QS, 1962–70, Chm., 1970–71; a Recorder of the Crown Court, 1972–75. Mem. Gen. Council of the Bar, 1963–67, 1969–73 and 1975. *Recreations:* shooting, stalking, fishing. *Address:* Chapel Cottage, Whashton, near Richmond, Yorks; Duncroisk, Killin, Perthshire. *T:* Killin 309. *Clubs:* Caledonian; Yorkshire (York).

STRUDWICK, Air Cdre Arthur Sidney Ronald, CB 1976; DFC 1945; Defence Liaison Officer, The Singer Co., Link-Miles Division, since 1976; *b* 16 April 1921; *s* of Percival and Mary Strudwick; *m* 1941, Cissily (*née* Stedman); two *s* one *d*. *Educ:* Guildford Tech. Coll.; RAF Colls. Joined RAF 1940; War Service as Fighter Pilot, 941–43; POW Germany, 1944; Test Flying, Canada, 1948–50; CO No 98 Sqdn, 1951–53; Staff Coll., Camberley, 1954; Commanded Jt Services Trials Unit, Woomera, 1956–59; JSSC, 1959–60; MoD Planning Staff, 1960–62; Dir of Plans, Far East, 1962–64; Commanded RAF Leuchars, 1965–67; Air Cdre Plans, Strategic Comd, 1967–69; IDC 1969; Dir of Flying (R&D), MoD PE, 1970–73; AOC Central Tactics and Trials Orgn, 1973–76, retired 1976. *Recreations:* golf and gardening. *Address:* 37 Upper Brighton Road, Worthing, Sussex. *Club:* Royal Air Force.

STRUDWICK, John Philip, CBE 1970; CVO 1973; Assistant Secretary, Board of Inland Revenue, 1950-74, retired; *b* 30 May 1914; *s* of Philip Strudwick, FRICS and Marjorie Strudwick (*née* Clements); *m* 1942, Elizabeth Marion Stemson; two *s* three *d* (and one *d* decd). *Educ:* Eltham Coll.; St John's Coll., Cambridge. BA 1936, MA 1973. Asst Principal, Bd of Inland Revenue, 1937; Principal 1942. Sec., Millard Tucker Cttee on Taxation Treatment of Provisions for Retirement, 1951-53. KSG 1977. *Recreations:* music, gardening, voluntary social work (Chm. of Univ. of Sussex Catholic Chaplaincy Assoc., 1972-76 and Edenbridge Volunteer Bureau, 1978-). *Address:* The Moat, Cowden, Edenbridge, Kent TN8 7DP. *T:* Cowden 441.

STRUTT, family name of **Barons Belper** and **Rayleigh.**

STRUTT, Sir Nigel (Edward), Kt 1972; TD; DL; Chairman, Strutt & Parker (Farms) Ltd; Managing Director, Lord Rayleigh's Farms Inc.; *b* 18 Jan. 1916; *yr s* of late Edward Jolliffe Strutt. *Educ:* Winchester; Wye Agricultural College (Fellow, 1970). Essex Yeomanry (Major), 1937-56. Member: Eastern Electricity Bd, 1964-76; Agricultural Advisory Council, 1963- (Chm. 1969-73; Chm., Adv. Council for Agriculture and Horticulture, 1973-80); NEDC for Agriculture, 1967-. President: Country Landowners' Association, 1967-69; British Friesian Cattle Soc., 1974-75. Master, Farmers' Co., 1976-77. DL Essex 1954; High Sheriff of Essex, 1966. Hon. FRASE, 1971. Hon. DSc Cranfield, 1979; DU Essex, 1981. Massey Ferguson Award, 1976. Von Thünen Gold Medal, Kiel Univ., 1974. *Recreations:* shooting, ski-ing. *Address:* Sparrows, Terling, Essex. *T:* Terling 213. *Clubs:* Brooks's, Farmers'.

STRUTT, Rt. Rev. Rupert Gordon; *see* Stockport, Suffragan Bishop of.

STUART, family name of **Earl Castle Stewart, Earl of Moray** and **Viscount Stuart of Findhorn.**

STUART; *see* Crichton-Stuart, family name of Marquess of Bute.

STUART, Viscount; Andrew Richard Charles Stuart; *b* 7 Oct. 1953; *s* and *heir* of 8th Earl Castle Stewart, *qv*; *m* 1973, Annie Le Poulain, St Malo, France; one *d*. *Educ:* Wynstones, Glos; Millfield, Som. *Recreation:* flying. *Address:* Combe Hayes Farm, Buckerell, near Honiton, Devon.

STUART OF FINDHORN, 2nd Viscount *cr* 1959; **David Randolph Moray Stuart;** *b* 20 June 1924; *s* of 1st Viscount Stuart of Findhorn, PC, CH, MVO, MC, and Lady Rachel Cavendish, OBE (*d* 1977), 4th *d* of 9th Duke of Devonshire; *S* father, 1971; *m* 1st, 1945, Grizel Mary Wilfreda (*d* 1948), *d* of D. T. Fyfe and *widow* of Michael Gillilan; one *s*; 2nd, 1951, Marian Emelia (marr. diss. 1979), *d* of Gerald H. Wilson; one *s*; 3rd, 1979, Margaret Anne, *yr d* of Comdr Peter Du Cane, *qv*. *Educ:* Eton; Cirencester Agricultural College. FRICS. Partner, Bernard Thorpe & Partners. *Heir: s* Hon. James Dominic Stuart, *b* 25 March 1948. *Address:* 63 Winchenden Road, SW6. *T:* 01-736 8760. *Clubs:* White's, Buck's.

STUART, Prof. Alan; Professor Emeritus, University of Exeter, 1959 (Professor, and Head Department of Geology, 1957-59); *b* 25 April 1894; *s* of James Anderson Stuart and Elizabeth (*née* Gladwell); *m* 1921, Ruth May Hugill; one *s* two *d*. *Educ:* Gateshead Secondary Sch.; Armstrong Coll. (now University of Newcastle upon Tyne). BSc Hons Geology, 1921; MSc 1923. Dip. RMS, 1973. Asst Lectr, Lectr and First Lectr, Dept of Geology, University Coll. of Swansea, 1921-47; Indep. Head of Dept of Geology, University Coll., Exeter, 1947-57. War Service: RAMC Dardanelles and Egypt, 1915-16; India, 1916-18; Indian Army, (TC), 2/27 Punjabis (Adjutant), Afghan War, 1919. Civil Defence, 1939-45; at University Coll., Swansea, during War, worked on crystallography of explosives for Ministry of Supply. *Publications:* (with N. H. Hartshorne): Crystals and the Polarising Microscope, 4th edn, 1970; Practical Optical Crystallography, 2nd edn 1969. Contribs to jls mainly concerned with sedimentary petrology and applications of microscopy to chemical problems. *Recreations:* photography, study of landscape, microscopy. *Address:* Bridge House, Neopardy, Crediton, Devon EX17 5EP. *T:* Crediton 2992.

STUART, Alexander John Mackenzie; *see* Mackenzie Stuart, Hon. Lord.

STUART, Andrew Christopher, CMG 1979; CPM 1961; Head, United World College of the Atlantic, since 1983; *b* 30 Nov. 1928; *s* of late Rt Rev. Cyril Edgar Stuart and Mary Summerhayes; *m* 1959, Patricia Kelly; two *s* one *d*. *Educ:* Bryanston; Clare Coll., Cambridge (MA). Royal Navy, 1947-49. Colonial Admin. Service, Uganda, 1953; retd from HMOCS as Judicial Adviser, 1965. Called to Bar, Middle Temple, 1965. Entered HM Diplomatic Service, 1965; 1st Sec. and Head of Chancery, Helsinki, 1968; Asst, S Asian Dept, FCO, 1971; Head of Hong Kong and Indian Ocean Dept, FCO, 1972-75; Counsellor, Jakarta, 1975-78; British Resident Comr, New Hebrides, 1978-80; Ambassador to Finland, 1980-83. *Recreations:* sailing, gliding, squash, diving, mountaineering. *Address:* United World College of the Atlantic, Llantwit Major, South Glamorgan CF6 9WF. *Clubs:* United Oxford & Cambridge University, Alpine; Jesters; Royal Naval Sailing Association.

STUART, Duncan; HM Diplomatic Service; Counsellor, British Embassy, Bonn, since 1980; *b* 1 July 1934; *s* of Ian Cameron Stuart and Patricia Forbes; *m* 1961, Leonore Luise Liederwald; one *s* one *d*. *Educ:* Rugby Sch.; Brasenose Coll., Oxford (MA). Served 1st Bn Oxfordshire and Bucks LI, 1955-57 (2nd

Lieut). Joined Foreign, later Diplomatic, Service, 1959; Office of Political Advr, Berlin, 1960-61; FO, 1961-64; Helsinki, 1964-66; Head of Chancery, Dar-es-Salaam, 1966-69; FCO, 1969-70; Helsinki, 1970-74; FCO, 1974-80. *Address:* c/o Foreign and Commonwealth Office, SW1A 2AH. *Clubs:* United Oxford & Cambridge University, MCC.

STUART, Francis; *b* Queensland, Australia, 1902; *s* of Henry and Elizabeth Stuart, Co. Antrim, Ireland; *m* 1st, 1920, Iseult Gonne; one *s* one *d*; 2nd, 1954, Gertrude Meiszner. *Educ:* Rugby. First book, poems, which received an American prize and also award of the Royal Irish Academy, published at age of twenty-one; first novel published in 1931 at age of 29; contributor to various newspapers and periodicals. *Publications:* novels: Women and God, 1931; Pigeon Irish, 1932; The Coloured Dome, 1933; Try the Sky, 1933; Glory, 1934; The Pillar of Cloud, 1948; Redemption, 1949; The Flowering Cross, 1950; Good Friday's Daughter, 1951; The Chariot, 1953; The Pilgrimage, 1955; Victors and Vanquished, 1958; Angels of Providence, 1959; Black List, Section H, 1971; Memorial, 1973; A Hole in the Head, 1977; The High Consistory, 1980; *poetry:* We Have Kept the Faith; *autobiography:* Things to Live For, 1936. *Recreations:* horse-racing, golf. *Address:* 2 Highfield Park, Dublin 14, Ireland.

STUART, Ven. Herbert James; QHC 1978; Chaplain-in-Chief, Royal Air Force, since 1980; Canon of Lincoln Cathedral, since 1980; *b* 16 Nov. 1926; *s* of Joseph and Jane Stuart; *m* 1955, Adrienne Le Fanu; two *s* one *d*. *Educ:* Mountjoy School, Dublin; Trinity Coll., Dublin (BA Hons, MA). Priest, 1950; served in Church of Ireland, 1950-55; Chaplain, RAF, 1955; Asst Chaplain-in-Chief, RAF, 1973. *Recreations:* gardening, travel, books. *Address:* 1 Abbots Walk, Lechlade Park, Lechlade, Glos GL7 3DB. *T:* Lechlade 52064. *Club:* Royal Air Force.

STUART, James Keith; Chairman, British Transport Docks Board, since 1982; *b* 4 March 1940; *s* of James and Marjorie Stuart; *m* 1966, Kathleen Anne Pinder (*née* Woodman); three *s* one *d*. *Educ:* King George V School, Southport; Gonville and Caius College, Cambridge (MA). FCIT, CBIM. District Manager, South Western Electricity Bd, 1970-72; British Transport Docks Board: Sec., 1972-75; Gen. Manager, 1976-77; Man. Dir, 1977-82; Dep. Chm., 1980-82. Alternate Dir, Internat. Assoc. of Ports and Harbors, 1978- (Chm., Cttee on Internat. Port Develt, 1979-). Mem. Council, CIT, 1979-, a Vice-Pres., 1982-. *Recreation:* music. *Address:* British Transport Docks Board, Melbury House, Melbury Terrace, NW1 6JY. *T:* 01-486 6621. *Clubs:* Brooks's, United Oxford & Cambridge University.

STUART, Prof. John Trevor, FRS 1974; Professor of Theoretical Fluid Mechanics since 1966, Head of Mathematics Department, 1974-79, Imperial College of Science and Technology, University of London; *b* 28 Jan. 1929; *s* of Horace Stuart and Phyllis Emily Stuart (*née* Potter); *m* 1957, Christine Mary (*née* Tracy); two *s* one *d*. *Educ:* Gateway Sch., Leicester; Imperial Coll., London. BSc 1949, PhD 1951. Aerodynamics Div., Nat. Physical Lab., Teddington, 1951-66; Sen. Principal Scientific Officer (Special Merit), 1961. Vis. Lectr, Dept of Maths, MIT, 1956-57; Vis. Prof. of Maths, MIT, 1965-66; Vis. Prof. of Theoretical Fluid Mechanics, Brown Univ., 1978-. *Publications:* (contrib.) Laminar Boundary Layers, ed L. Rosenhead, 1963; articles in Proc. Royal Soc., Phil. Trans Royal Soc., Jl Fluid Mech., Proc. 10th Int. Cong. Appl. Mech., Jl Lub. Tech. (ASME). *Recreations:* theatre, gardening, reading, do-it-yourself, ornithology. *Address:* Mathematics Department, Imperial College, SW7 2AZ. *T:* 01-589 5111; 3 Steeple Close, Wimbledon, SW19 5AD. *T:* 01-946 7019.

STUART, Prof. Sir Kenneth (Lamonte), Kt 1977; MD, FRCP, FRCPE, FACP, DTM&H; Medical Adviser, Commonwealth Secretariat, since 1976; *b* 16 June 1920; *s* of Egbert and Louise Stuart; *m* 1958, Barbara Cecille Ashby; one *s* two *d*. *Educ:* Harrison Coll., Barbados; Queen's Univ., Belfast (MB, BCh, BAO 1948). Consultant Physician, University Coll. Hospital of the West Indies, 1954-76; University of the West Indies: Prof. of Medicine, 1966-76; Dean, Medical Faculty, 1969-71; Head, Dept of Medicine, 1972-76; Mem. Council, 1971-76. Rockefeller Foundation Fellow in Cardiology, Massachusetts Gen. Hosp., Boston, 1956-57; Wellcome Foundation Research Fellow, Harvard Univ., Boston, 1960-61; Consultant to WHO on Cardiovascular Disorders, 1969-. *Publications:* articles on hepatic and cardiovascular disorders in medical journals. *Recreations:* tennis, music. *Address:* Commonwealth Secretariat, Marlborough House, Pall Mall, SW1Y 5HX. *T:* 01-839 3411.

STUART, Malcolm Moncrieff, CIE 1947; OBE 1944; ICS retired; Recorder to Council of Lord High Commissioners to the General Assembly of the Church of Scotland; *b* 21 May 1903; *s* of George Malcolm Stuart and Mary Elizabeth Scott Moncrieff; *m* 1928, Grizel Graham Balfour Paul; one *s* one *d*. *Educ:* Sedbergh; St John's College, Cambridge; Queen's Coll., Oxford. Entered ICS 1927; served as Dist Magistrate of various districts and was on special duty for Govt Estates, 1938; during War of 1939-45 was mostly Dist Magistrate of Chittagong and also Comr there. Served in Pakistan until 1950, as additional Member, Board of Revenue. Hon. MA Edinburgh, 1978. *Publications:* Bob Potts at Murshedabad (Bengal Past and Present), 1933; Handbook to Bengal Records, 1948; and other stories. *Recreations:* golf, shooting, bridge. *Address:* Old Manse, Pilmuir, Haddington, East Lothian. *Clubs:* New (Edinburgh); Muirfield Golf.

STUART, Michael Francis Harvey; Treasury Adviser, UK Mission to the United Nations, 1974-82; *b* 3 Oct. 1926; *s* of late Willoughby Stuart and Ethel Candy; *m* 1961, Ruth Tennyson-d'Eyncourt; one *s* one *d. Educ:* Harrow; Magdalen Coll., Oxford. Air Min., 1950-65; DEA, 1965-69; HM Treasury, 1969-74. Mem., UN Adv. Cttee on Administrative and Budgetary Questions, 1975-80. *Recreations:* music, tennis. *Address:* Bourne House, Chertsey Road, Chobham, Woking, Surrey. *T:* Chobham 7954.

STUART, Nicholas Willoughby; Under Secretary, Department of Education and Science, since 1981; *b* 2 Oct. 1942; *s* of Douglas Willoughby Stuart and Margaret Eileen Stuart; *m* 1st, 1963, Sarah Mustard (marr. diss. 1974); one *d* (one *s* decd); 2nd, 1975, Susan Jane Fletcher. *Educ:* Harrow Sch.; Christ Church Coll., Oxford (MA). Asst Principal, DES, 1964-68; Private Sec. to Minister for the Arts, 1968-69; Principal, DES, 1969-73; Private Secretary to: Head of the Civil Service, 1973; Prime Minister, 1973-76; Asst Sec., DES, 1976-78; Advr, Cabinet of Pres. of EEC, 1978-80. *Recreation:* collecting Tunbridgeware. *Address:* 33 Kensington Park Gardens, W11. *T:* 01-727 6470.

STUART, Sir Phillip (Luttrell), 9th Bt *cr* 1660; late F/O RCAF; President, Agassiz Industries Ltd; *b* 7 September 1937; *s* of late Luttrell Hamilton Stuart and late Irene Ethel Jackman; *S* uncle, Sir Houlton John Stuart, 8th Bt, 1959; *m* 1st, 1962, Marlene Rose Muth (marr. diss. 1968); two *d*; 2nd, 1969, Beverley Clare Pieri; one *s* one *d. Educ:* Vancouver. Enlisted RCAF, Nov. 1955; commnd FO (1957-62). *Heir: s* Geoffrey Phillip Stuart, *b* 5 July 1973. *Address:* 3 Windermere Bay, Winnipeg, Manitoba R3T 1B1, Canada.
[But his name does not, at the time of going to press, appear on the official Roll of Baronets.]

STUART BLACK, Ian Hervey; *see* Black, I. H. S.

STUART-COLE, James; Chairman, Birkenhead Region, Co-operative Retail Services Ltd, since 1974; *b* 6 March 1916; *s* of Charles Albert Stuart-Cole and Gertrude Mary Stuart-Cole; *m* 1937, Margaret Evelyn Robb; one *s* two *d. Educ:* Birley Street Central Sch., Manchester. Engr, 1930-55; Political Organiser, Labour Party, 1955-60; Political Sec., Co-operative Soc., 1960-81. Member: Merseyside CC, 1973- (Leader, 1981-82); Bd, Merseyside Development Corp. *Recreations:* sport, grandchildren. *Address:* 85 Kylemore Drive, Pensby, Wirral, Merseyside L61 6XZ. *T:* 051-342 6180.

STUART-FORBES, Sir Charles Edward; *see* Forbes.

STUART-HARRIS, Sir Charles (Herbert), Kt 1970; CBE 1961; MD; FRCP; Fogarty Scholar-in-Residence, National Institutes of Health, Bethesda, Maryland, USA, 1979-80; Postgraduate Dean of Medicine, University of Sheffield, 1972-77; Professor of Medicine, 1946-72, now Emeritus Professor; Physician United Sheffield Hospitals, 1946-74; *b* 12 July 1909; *s* of late Dr and Mrs Herbert Harris, Birmingham; *m* 1937, Marjorie, *y d* of late Mr and Mrs F. Robinson, Dulwich; two *s* one *d. Educ:* King Edward's School, Birmingham; St Bartholomew's Hospital Medical School. MB, BS London 1931 (Gold Medal); MD 1933 (Gold Medal); FRCP 1944. House-Physician and Demonstrator in Pathology, St Bartholomew's Hosp.; First Asst, Dept of Medicine, Brit. Postgrad. Medical Sch., 1935; Sir Henry Royce Research Fellow. Univ. of London, 1935; Foulerton Research Fellow, Royal Society, 1938. War Service, 1939-46; Specialist Pathologist Comdg Mobile Bacteriological, Command and Field Laboratories; Colonel RAMC, 1945. Goulstonian Lectr, Royal College of Physicians, 1945; Visiting Prof. of Medicine, Albany Medical Coll., New York, 1953; Sir Arthur Sims Commonwealth Travelling Prof., 1962. Vis. Professor of Medicine: Vanderbilt Univ., Tennessee, 1961; Univ. of Southern California, Los Angeles, 1962; Croonian Lectr, Royal Coll. of Physicians, 1962; Henry Cohen Lectr, Hebrew Univ. of Jerusalem, 1966; Waring Prof., Univ. of Colorado and Stanford Univ., Calif., 1967; Harveian Orator, RCP, 1974. Member: MRC, 1957-61; Public Health Lab. Service Bd, 1954-66; UGC 1968-77 (Chm., Med. Sub-Cttee, 1973-77); UPGC, Hong Kong, 1982-. Pres., Assoc. of Physicians of GB and Ireland, 1971. Hon. Member: Assoc. of Amer. Physicians; Infectious Diseases Soc. of Amer. Hon. DSc: Hull, 1973; Sheffield, 1978. *Publications:* (co-author) Chronic bronchitis emphysema and cor pulmonale, 1961; (co-author) Influenza and other virus infections of the respiratory tract, 1965; (co-author) Virus and Rickettsial Diseases, 1967; (co-author) Influenza—the Viruses and the Disease, 1976; papers in med. and scientific jls on influenza, typhus and bronchitis. *Recreation:* music. *Address:* 28 Whitworth Road, Sheffield S10 3HD. *T:* Sheffield 301200.

STUART-MENTETH, Sir James; *see* Menteth.

STUART-SHAW, Max, CBE 1963; Executive Director, Olympic Airways, 1969-71; *b* 20 Dec. 1912; *e s* of Herman and Anne Louise Stuart-Shaw; *m* 1967, Janna Job, *d* of C. W. Howard. *Educ:* Belmont School, Sussex; St Paul's, London. Imperial Airways/BOAC, 1931-46; Aer Lingus Irish Airlines; Traffic Manager, Commercial Manager, Asst Gen. Manager, 1947-57; Chief Exec. and Gen. Manager Central African Airways, Salisbury, Rhodesia, 1958-65; Man. Dir, BUA, 1966-67; Vice-Chairman, British United Airways, 1967-68. FCIT. *Recreation:* air transport. *Address:* c/o Barclays Bank, 160 Piccadilly, W1A 2AB. *Club:* Salisbury (Zimbabwe).

STUART-SMITH, James; Vice Judge Advocate General, since 1979; *b* 13 Sept. 1919; *s* of James Stuart-Smith and Florence Emma (*née* Armfield); *m* 1957, Jean Marie Therese Young Groundsell, *d* of Hubert Young Groundsell, Newport, IoW; one *s* one *d. Educ:* Brighton Coll.; London Hospital. Medical student, 1938. Served War of 1939-45: commnd KRRC, 1940; served ME and Italy, and staff appointments in UK; demobilised 1947. Called to Bar, Middle Temple, 1948; practised in London, 1948-55; Legal Asst, JAG's Office, 1955; Dep. Judge Advocate, 1957; Asst Judge Advocate General, 1968; Dep. Judge Advocate, Middle East Comd (Aden), 1964-65; Dep. Judge Advocate General, British Forces Germany, 1976-79. Vice-Pres., Internat. Soc. for Military Law and the Law of War, 1979. *Publications:* contribs to Internat. Soc. for Military Law and Law of War Rev. and Law Qly Rev., on history and practice of British military law. *Recreations:* composing letters, lawn tennis, mowing lawns. *Address:* The Firs, Copthorne, Sussex RH10 4HH. *T:* Copthorne 712395. *Club:* Royal Air Force.

STUART-SMITH, Hon. Sir Murray, Kt 1981; **Hon. Mr Justice Stuart-Smith;** Judge of the High Court of Justice, Queen's Bench Division, since 1981; Presiding Judge of the Western Circuit, since 1983; *b* 18 Nov. 1927; *s* of Edward Stuart-Smith and Doris Mary Laughland; *m* 1953, Joan Elizabeth Mary Motion, BA, JP; three *s* three *d. Educ:* Radley; Corpus Christi Coll., Cambridge (Foundn Scholar; 1st Cl. Hons Law Tripos, Pts I and II; 1st Cl. Hons LLB; MA). Called to the Bar, Gray's Inn, 1952 (Atkin Scholar), Bencher 1977; QC 1970; a Recorder of the Crown Court, 1972-81. Jt Inspector into Grays Bldg Soc., 1979. Mem., Criminal Injuries Compensation Bd, 1980-81. *Recreations:* playing 'cello, shooting. *Address:* Serge Hill, Abbots Langley, Herts. *T:* Kings Langley 62116.

STUART TAYLOR, Sir Nicholas (Richard), 4th Bt *cr* 1917; *b* 14 Jan. 1952; *s* of Sir Richard Laurence Stuart Taylor, 3rd Bt, and of Iris Mary, *d* of Rev. Edwin John Gargery; *S* father, 1978. *Educ:* Bradfield. Admitted solicitor, 1977. *Recreation:* ski-ing. *Heir:* none. *Address:* White Lodge, Hambrook, Chichester, West Sussex. *Club:* Ski Club of Great Britain.

STUART-WHITE, Christopher Stuart; His Honour Judge Stuart-White; a Circuit Judge, since 1978; *b* 18 Dec. 1933; *s* of Reginald Stuart-White and Catherine Mary Wigmore Stuart-White (*née* Higginson); *m* 1957, Pamela (*née* Grant); one *s* two *d. Educ:* Winchester; Trinity Coll., Oxford (BA). Called to Bar, Inner Temple, 1957. Practising Barrister on the Midland and Oxford Circuit, 1958-78; a Recorder of the Crown Court, 1974-78. *Recreations:* gardening, hill walking. *Address:* Triangle Farm, Far Forest, Rock, near Kidderminster, Worcs DY14 9UB. *T:* Rock 266260.

STUBBLEFIELD, Sir (Cyril) James, Kt 1965; FRS 1944; FGS; FZS; DSc (London); ARCS; formerly Director, Geological Survey of Great Britain and Museum of Practical Geology, 1960-66; Director, Geological Survey of Northern Ireland, 1960-66; *b* 6 Sept. 1901; *s* of late James Stubblefield; *m* 1932, Muriel Elizabeth, *d* of late L. R. Yakchee; two *s. Educ:* The Perse Sch.; Chelsea Polytechnic; Royal College of Science, London (Royal Scholar); London Univ. Geology Scholar, 1921. Demonstrator in Geology, Imperial College of Science and Technology, 1923-28; Warden of pioneer Imperial Coll. Hostel, 1926-28. Apptd Geological Survey as Geologist, 1928; Chief Palæontologist, 1947-53; Asst Director, 1953-60. Mem., Anglo-French Commn of Surveillance, Channel Tunnel, 1964-67. Pres. Geological Soc. of London, 1958-60; Bigsby Medallist, 1941; Murchison Medallist, 1955. Sec. of Palæontographical Soc., 1934-48; Pres., 1966-71, Hon. Mem., 1974. Member Council Brit. Assoc. for Advancement of Science, 1946-52, 1958-63; Pres. Section C (Geology), Oxford, 1954. Pres., Cambrian Subcommn, Internat. Geol. Union's Commn on Stratigraphy, 1964-72; Pres. Internat. Congress Carboniferous Stratigraphy and Geology, 6th Session, Sheffield, 1967, and Editor, 4 vol. Compte rendu, 1968-72. Vice-Pres. International Paleontological Union, 1948-56. Corresp. Paleont. Soc. (USA), 1950-; Corresp. Mem. Geol. Soc. Stockholm, 1952-; Senckenbergische Naturforschende Gesellschaft, 1957-. Mem. Gov. Body, Chelsea Coll. of Science and Technology, 1958-. Mem. Council, Royal Soc., 1960-62. Hon. Fellow Pal. Soc. India, 1961-. Fellow Imperial Coll. of Science and Technology, 1962-; Hon. Member: Geologists' Assoc., 1973-; Liverpool Geol. Soc., 1960-; For. Corr., Geol. Soc., France, 1963-, For. Vice-Pres., 1966. Hon. DSc Southampton, 1965. *Publications:* papers on Palæozoic fossils and rocks; also contributions to: Geological Survey Memoirs; Trilobita, Zoological Record, 1938-51, 1965-77. Joint Editor of the Handbook of the Geology of Great Britain, 1929; Reviser, Introduction to Palæontology (A. Morley Davies), 3rd edn, 1961. *Address:* 35 Kent Avenue, Ealing, W13 8BE. *T:* 01-997 5051.

STUBBS, Sir James (Wilfrid), KCVO 1979; TD 1946; Grand Secretary, United Grand Lodge of England, 1958-80; *b* 13 Aug. 1910; *s* of Rev. Wilfrid Thomas Stubbs and Muriel Elizabeth (*née* Pope); *m* Richenda Katherine Theodora Streatfeild; one *s* (and one *d* decd). *Educ:* Charterhouse (junior and senior scholar); Brasenose Coll., Oxford (Scholar; MA). Assistant Master, St Paul's Sch., London, 1934-46. Served War, Royal Signals, 1941-46: Captain 1941, Major 1945, Lt-Col 1946 (2nd Lieut, SR, 1932, Lieut 1935). Asst Grand Sec., United Grand Lodge of England, 1948-54; Dep. Grand Sec., 1954-58. *Recreations:* family history, travel. *Address:* 5 Pensioners Court, The Charterhouse, EC1. *T:* 01-253 1982. *Club:* Athenæum.

STUBBS, John F. A. H.; *see* Heath-Stubbs.

STUBBS, William Frederick, CMG 1955; CBE 1952 (OBE 1941); HMOCS, retired; *b* 19 June 1902; *e s* of late Lawrence Morley Stubbs, CSI,

CIE, ICS (retd); *m* 1929, Eileen Mary (*d* 1963), *y d* of late Sir W. E. Stanford, KBE, CB, CMG, Rondebosch, S Africa; one *d. Educ:* Winchester, Joined British S Africa Police, S Rhodesia, 1921; N Rhodesia Police on transfer, 1924; Colonial Administrative Service, Northern Rhodesia, 1926; District Officer, 1928; District Comr of various districts; seconded to Labour Department, 1940; Labour Comr, 1944-48; Provincial Comr, 1949; acted as Secretary for Native Affairs, 1951 and 1953; Secretary for Native Affairs, 1954-57; *Ex-officio* member of Executive and Legislative Councils (Speaker, Legislative Council, and Chm. Public Service Commn Somaliland Protectorate, 1960, until Union with Somalia). Associate Commonwealth Parliamentary Association. *Recreation:* fishing. *Address:* Nash Barn, Marnhull, Dorset. *Club:* Royal Commonwealth Society.

STUBBS, William Frederick, QC 1978; *b* 27 Nov. 1934; *s* of William John Stubbs and Winifred Hilda (*née* Johnson); *m* 1961, Anne Katharine (*d* 1966), *d* of late Prof. W. K. C. Guthrie, FBA; one *s* one *d. Educ:* The High Sch., Newcastle-under-Lyme, Staffs; Gonville and Caius Coll., Cambridge; Harvard Law Sch. Open Minor Scholar in Nat. Sci., Gonville and Caius Coll., 1951; Student, Gray's Inn, 1953; 1st Cl. Hons Law Tripos Pt I, and George Long Prize for Roman Law, Cambridge, 1954; Major Scholar, Gonville and Caius Coll., 1954; 1st Cl. Hons with Distinction Law Tripos Pt II, Cambridge, 1955; LLB 1st Cl. Hons with Dist., and Chancellor's Medal for English Law, Cambridge, 1956; Tapp Post-Grad. Law Scholar, Gonville and Caius Coll., 1956 (also awarded Schuldham Plate); Joseph Hodges Choate Meml Fellow, Harvard Coll., 1957; Bar Final Exam., 2nd Cl. Hons Div. 1, 1957; Holker Sen. Scholar and Macaskie Scholar, Gray's Inn, 1957; called to the Bar, Gray's Inn, 1957. *Recreations:* reading, walking, natural history. *Address:* 24 Old Buildings, Lincoln's Inn, WC2A 3UJ. *T:* 01-242 5532; 3 Atherton Drive, SW19 5LB. *T:* 01-947 3986; Pant-y-Beudy, Trefasser, Dyfed. *Club:* MCC.

STUBBS, William Hamilton; Education Officer, Inner London Education Authority, since 1982; *b* 5 Nov. 1937; *s* of Joseph Stubbs and Mary Stubbs (*née* McNicol); *m* 1963, Marie Margaret Pierce; three *d. Educ:* Workington Grammar Sch.; St Aloysius Coll., Glasgow; Glasgow Univ. (BSc, PhD). Res. Associate, Univ. of Arizona, 1963-64; with Shell Oil Co., San Francisco, 1964-67; teaching, 1967-72; Asst Dir of Educn, Carlisle, 1972-74; Asst Dir of Educn, 1974-76, Second Dep. Dir of Educn, 1976-77, Cumbria; Second Dep. Educn Officer, 1977-79, Dir of Educn (Schools), 1979-82, ILEA. *Address:* 18 Foxgrove Avenue, Beckenham, Kent. *T:* 01-650 5669.

STUCHBERY, Arthur Leslie, CBE 1971 (OBE 1968); Chairman, Remploy, 1969-72; *b* 14 Feb. 1903; *s* of Harry and Martha Stuchbery; *m* 1930, Dorothy Blanche Willmott; one *s* one *d. Educ:* Hackney Techn. Coll.; Borough Polytechnic. CEng, FIMechE, FIProdE, FRSA. Metal Box Co.: Plant Manager, 1929; Chief Engr, 1939; Dir of R&D, 1961. Founder Councillor, PERA (Chm. 1962-67); Founder Mem., IProdE, 1924, President 1969-72; Chm., Brunel Univ., 1965-73. Clayton Lectr, 1966. Hon. DTech Brunel, 1970. *Publications:* numerous technical papers. *Recreations:* hand crafts, writing. *Address:* Dyke End House, Littlestone, Kent. *T:* New Romney 2076. *Clubs:* City Livery, St Stephen's Constitutional.

STÜCKLEN, Richard; Grosskreuz des Verdienstordens der Bundesrepublik Deutschland; Bayerischer Verdienstorden; President of the Bundestag, Federal Republic of Germany, since 1979; *b* 20 Aug. 1916; *s* of Georg Stücklen and Mathilde (*née* Bach); *m* 1943, Ruth Stücklen (*née* Geissler); one *s* one *d. Educ:* primary sch.; technical sch.; engineering sch. Industrial Dept Manager and Manager in family business, 1945-49. Mem. of Bundestag, 1949-; Dep. Chm., CDU/Christian Social Union and Parly Leader, Christian Social Union, 1953-57 and 1967-76; Federal Minister of Posts and Telegraphs, 1957-66; Vice-Pres. of Bundestag, 1976-79. *Publications:* Bundestagsreden und Zeitdokumente, 1979; and others. *Recreations:* skating, chess, soccer. *Address:* Bundeshaus, 5300 Bonn, Germany. *T:* Bonn 16 29 00. *Club:* Lions.

STUCLEY, Major Sir Dennis Frederic Bankes, 5th Bt, *cr* 1859; DL; *b* 29 Oct. 1907; *s* of Sir Hugh Nicholas Granville Stucley, 4th Bt, and Gladys (*d* 1950), *d* of W. A. Bankes, Wolfeton House, Dorchester; *S* father, 1956; *m* 1932, Hon. Sheila Bampfylde, *o d* of 4th Baron Poltimore; one *s* four *d* (and one *s* decd). *Educ:* Harrow; RMC Sandhurst. 2nd Lt Grenadier Guards, 1927; retired, 1932. Devon CC, 1934, CA, 1955. Capt. Royal Devon Yeomanry, 1937, Major, 1944. JP Devon, 1934-62; DL Devon, 1956; Mayor of Bideford, 1954-56; High Sheriff of Devon, 1956, County Alderman, Devon, 1956. Joint Master, Dulverton Foxhounds, 1952-54. Chairman: Regional Adv. Cttee, Forestry Commn, SW, 1958-75; Timber Growers Organization, 1966-69; Exmoor Nat. Park (Devon) Cttee, 1968-74. *Recreations:* hunting, shooting and fishing. *Heir: s* Lieut Hugh George Coplestone Bampfylde Stucley, Royal Horse Guards [*b* 8 Jan. 1945; *m* 1969, Angela Caroline, *e d* of Richard Toller, Theale, Berks; two *s* two *d*]. *Address:* Hartland Abbey, Bideford, Devon. *T:* Hartland 234; Court Hall, North Molton, South Molton, Devon. *T:* North Molton 224. *Club:* Cavalry and Guards.
See also *Viscount Boyne, Baron Cobbold, Sir M. H. B. Peto, Bt, J. H. A. Stucley.*

STUCLEY, John Humphrey Albert, DSC 1945; **His Honour Judge Stucley;** a Circuit Judge, since 1974; *b* 12 July 1916; 2nd *s* of Sir Hugh Stucley, 4th Bt, Affeton Castle, Devon; *m* 1941, Natalia, *d* of Don Alberto Jiménez, CBE and Natalia Cossio de Jiménez; no *c. Educ:* RN Colls, Dartmouth and Greenwich. Cadet, RN, 1930; served China, Mediterranean

and Home stns and throughout War of 1939-45; Lt-Comdr 1945. Called to Bar, Middle Temple, 1957. A Recorder of the Crown Court, 1972-74. Dep. Chm., SE England Agricultural Land Tribunal, 1971. *Recreations:* gardening, travel. *Address:* 14 Chester Row, SW1W 9JH.
See also *Major Sir D. F. B. Stucley, Bt.*

STUDD, Sir Edward (Fairfax), 4th Bt *cr* 1929; Director, Inchcape plc and other Inchcape Group Companies, since 1974; *b* 3 May 1929; *s* of Sir Eric Studd, 2nd Bt, OBE, and Stephana (*d* 1976), *o d* of L. J. Langmead; *S* brother, 1977; *m* 1960, Prudence Janet, *o d* of Alastair Douglas Fyfe, OBE, Riding Mill, Northumberland; two *s* one *d. Educ:* Winchester College. Lieutenant Coldstream Guards, London and Malaya, 1947-49; Macneill & Barry Ltd, Calcutta, 1951-62; Inchcape & Co. Ltd, London, 1962-. *Recreations:* walking, shooting, fishing. *Heir: s* Philip Alastair Fairfax Studd, *b* 27 Oct. 1961. *Address:* Danceys, Clavering, near Saffron Walden, Essex. *T:* Clavering 444. *Clubs:* Boodle's, MCC, City of London; Royal Calcutta Turf (Calcutta).

STUDD, Sir Peter Malden, GBE 1971; KCVO 1979; Kt 1969; MA, DSc; Director, Lloyds & Scottish Ltd; *b* 15 Sept. 1916; *s* of late Brig. Malden Augustus Studd, DSO, MC; *m* 1943, Angela Mary Hamilton (*née* Garnier); two *s. Educ:* Harrow; Clare Coll., Cambridge (MA). Served War of 1939-45, ME and European campaigns. Alderman, City of London, 1960-76; Sheriff, 1967-68; Lord Mayor of London, 1970-71; Hon. DSc City Univ., 1970. Trustee, Royal Jubilee Trusts, 1980-. Patron, Lady Eleanor Holles Sch., Hampton. Liveryman, Merchant Taylors' Co. (Asst, 1959-, Master, 1973-74); Hon. Liveryman, Worshipful Cos of Fruiterers and Plaisterers. KStJ. *Recreations:* gardening, fishing, shooting, 'lighting up the Thames'. *Address:* c/o Messrs C. Hoare & Co., 37 Fleet Street, EC4P 4DQ. *Clubs:* City Livery, MCC, I Zingari.

STUDHOLME, Sir Henry (Gray), 1st Bt, *cr* 1956; CVO 1953; DL; *b* 13 June 1899; *s* of late William Paul Studholme, Perridge House, Exeter; *m* 1929, Judith, *d* of Henry William Whitbread, Norton Bavant Manor, Warminster; two *s* one *d. Educ:* Eton; Magdalen Coll., Oxford (MA). Served European War with Scots Guards, 1917-19; Member LCC, 1931-45; rejoined Scots Guards, 1940; Staff appointments, 1941-44. MP (C) Tavistock Division, 1942-66. PPS to late Comdr R. Brabner, Under-Sec. of State for Air, Nov. 1944-March 1945; Conservative Whip, 1945-56; Joint Treas. of the Conservative Party, 1956-62. Vice-Chamberlain of King George VI's Household, 1951-52, of the Queen's Household, 1952-56. DL Devon, 1969. *Heir: s* Paul Henry William Studholme, late Capt. Coldstream Guards [*b* 16 Jan. 1930; *m* 1957, Virginia Katherine, *yr d* of late Sir Richmond Palmer, KCMG; two *s* one *d*]. *Address:* Wembury House, Wembury, Plymouth. *T:* Plymouth 862210. *Club:* MCC.

STURDEE, Rear-Adm. Arthur Rodney Barry, CB 1971; DSC 1945; *b* 6 Dec. 1919; *s* of Comdr Barry V. Sturdee, RN, and Barbara (*née* Sturdee); *m* 1953, Marie-Claire Amstoutz, Mulhouse, France; one *s* one *d. Educ:* Canford Sch. Entered Royal Navy as Special Entry Cadet, 1937. Served War of 1939-45: Midshipman in HMS Exeter at Battle of the River Plate, 1939; Lieut, 1941; specialised in Navigation, 1944; minesweeping in Mediterranean, 1944-45 (DSC). Lt-Comdr, 1949; RN Staff Coll., 1950-51; Staff of Navigation Sch., 1951-52; Comdr, 1952; JSSC, 1953; BJSM, Washington, 1953-55; Fleet Navigating Officer, Medit., 1955-57; Exec. Officer, RNAS, Culdrose, 1958-59; Captain 1960; NATO Defence Coll., 1960-63; Queen's Harbour-Master, Singapore, 1963-65; Staff of Chief of Defence Staff, 1965-67; Chief of Staff to C-in-C, Portsmouth (as Cdre), 1967-69; Rear-Adm. 1969; Flag Officer, Gibraltar, 1969-72; retired 1972. ADC to the Queen, 1969. *Address:* 9 Avenue Road, Malvern, Worcestershire. *T:* Malvern 5402.

STURDY, Henry William, OBE 1975 (MBE 1968); HM Diplomatic Service, retired; Deputy Consul General and Counsellor Commercial, Chicago, 1976-78; *b* 17 Feb. 1919; *s* of Henry William Dawson Sturdy and late Jemima Aixill; *m* 1945, Anne Jamieson Marr; one *s* one *d. Educ:* Woolwich Polytechnic (Mechanical Engineering). Served War in Middle East, 1939-45; Allied Control Commission, Germany, 1946. Executive Branch of Civil Service and Board of Trade, 1951; tour in Trade Commission Service, 1953; appointments: Pakistan, Bangladesh, Sri Lanka, Canada. First Secretary, Diplomatic Service, 1965; Counsellor, Korea, 1976. Defence Medal; 1939-45 Medal; General Service Medal, 1939, with Palestine Clasp, 1945. *Recreations:* squash, bridge, reading, argument, international cuisine. *Address:* Middle Farm House, Village Square, Cramlington, Northumberland. *T:* Cramlington 733125.

STURGE, Arthur Collwyn, MC 1945; *b* 27 Sept. 1912; *yr s* of Arthur Lloyd Sturge and Jessie Katherine Howard; *m* 1938, Beryl Gwenllian, *yr d* of Thomas Arthur, Hong Kong; two *s* two *d. Educ:* Harrow; Brasenose Coll., Oxford (BA). Underwriting Member of Lloyd's, 1933; Joined A. L. Sturge & Co., 1934, Chm., 1970-77. Mem., Cttee of Lloyd's, 1967-75 (Dep. Chm., 1969, 1970); Mem. Gen. Cttee, Lloyd's Register of Shipping, 1969-77. Chm., Lloyd's of London Press Ltd. Commissioned 64 Field Regt RA (TA), 1937; served War of 1939-45, Middle East, Italy. High Sheriff, East Sussex, 1977. *Recreations:* golf, shooting, fishing. *Address:* 12 St Luke's Street, SW3 3RS. *T:* 01-351 1345. *Clubs:* City of London, Flyfishers'.
See also *R. W. Sturge.*

STURGE, Harold Francis Ralph; Metropolitan Magistrate, 1947-68; *b* 15 May 1902; *y s* of Ernest Harold Sturge; *m* 1936, Doreen, *e d* of Sir Percy

Greenaway, 1st Bt; two s (and one s decd). *Educ:* Highgate Sch.; Oriel Coll., Oxford, MA (Lit. Hum.). Called to Bar, Inner Temple, 1925; Midland Circuit. War of 1939-45, served on staff of Judge Advocate-General. Member Departmental Cttee on the Probation Service, 1959; President, Old Cholmelian Society, 1962-63. *Publications:* The Road Haulage Wages Act, 1938; (with T. D. Corpe, OBE) Road Haulage Law and Compensation, 1947; (with C. A. Reston, LLB) The Main Rules of Evidence in Criminal Cases, 1972. *Recreation:* painting. *Address:* 10 Tilney Court, Catherine Road, Surbiton, Surrey KT6 4HA.

STURGE, Maj.-Gen. Henry Arthur John, CB 1978; General Manager, Marconi Space and Defence Systems, Portsmouth, since 1981; *b* 27 April 1925; *s* of Henry George Arthur Sturge and Lilian Beatrice Sturge; *m* 1953, Jean Ailsa Mountain; two *s* one *d. Educ:* Wilson's Sch., (formerly) Camberwell, London; Queen Mary Coll., London. Commissioned, Royal Signals, 1946; UK, 1946-50; Egypt, 1950-53; UK, incl. psc, 1953-59; Far East, 1959-62; jssc, 1962; BAOR, 1963-64; RMA, Sandhurst, 1965-66; BAOR, incl. Command, 1966-69; Min. of Defence, 1970-75; Chief Signal Officer, BAOR, 1975-77; ACDS (Signals), 1977-80. Col Comdt, Royal Corps of Signals, 1977-. Colonel, Queen's Gurkha Signals, 1980-. Vice Chm., Governors, Wilson's Sch., 1979-. *Recreations:* sailing, (formerly) Rugby. *Address:* Border Hill, Dippenhall, Farnham, Surrey. *Club:* Army and Navy.

STURGE, Raymond Wilson; Chairman of Lloyd's, 1964, 1965 and 1966; *b* 10 June 1904; *er s* of late Arthur Lloyd Sturge and late Jessie Katharine (*née* Howard); *m* 1929, Margaret, *y d* of late Walter J. Keep, Sydney, NSW; one *s* four *d. Educ:* Harrow; Brasenose Coll., Oxford (BA). Mem. of Lloyd's, 1926; first elected to Committee, 1953; Dep. Chm., 1963. Served War of 1939-45, Royal Scots Fusiliers, Staff Duties. Pres., Insurance Institute of London, 1967-68 (Dep. Pres., 1966-67). *Address:* Ashmore, near Salisbury, Wilts. *T:* Fontmell Magna 811261. *Club:* City of London.
　　See also Hon. J. D. Eccles, A. C. Sturge.

STUTTAFORD, Dr (Irving) Thomas; medical practitioner; *b* 4 May 1931; 2nd *s* of late Dr W. J. E. Stuttaford, MC, Horning, Norfolk; *m* 1957, Pamela, *d* of late Col Richard Ropner, TD, DL, Tain; three *s. Educ:* Gresham's Sch.; Brasenose Coll., Oxford; West London Hosp. 2nd Lieut, 10th Royal Hussars (PWO), 1953-55; Lieut, Scottish Horse (TA), 1955-59. Qualif. MRCS, LRCP, 1959; junior hosp. appts, 1959 and 1960. Gen. Med. practice, 1960-70. Mem. Blofield and Flegg RDC, 1964-66; Mem., Norwich City Council, 1969-71. MP (C) Norwich S, 1970-Feb. 1974; Mem. Select Cttee Science and Technology, 1970-74. Contested (C) Isle of Ely, Oct. 1974, 1979. Physician, BUPA Medical Centre; Clinical Assistant to: The London Hosp.; Queen Mary's Hosp. for East End; Moorfields Eye Hosp., 1975-79. Member: Council, Research Defence Soc., 1970-79; Birth Control Campaign Cttee, 1970-79; British Cancer Council, 1970-79. *Recreation:* country life. *Address:* Snowre Hall, Hilgay, Downham Market, Norfolk. *Clubs:* Athenæum, Reform, Cavalry and Guards; Norfolk (Norwich).

STYLE, Lt-Comdr Sir Godfrey (William), Kt 1973; CBE 1961; DSC 1941; RN; Governor, Queen Elizabeth's Foundation; Member of Council, Sir Oswald Stoll Foundation; Director, Star Centre for Youth, Cheltenham; also Member of a number of allied advisory bodies and panels; a Member of Lloyd's, since 1945; *b* 3 April 1915; *er s* of Brig.-Gen. R. C. Style (*y s* of Sir William Henry Marsham Style, 9th Bt), and Hélène Pauline, *d* of Herman Greverus Kleinwort; *m* 1st, 1942, Jill Elizabeth Caruth (marr. diss. 1951); one *s* two *d* ; 2nd, 1951, Sigrid Elisabeth Julin (*née* Carlberg); one *s. Educ:* Eton. Joined Royal Navy as a Regular Officer, 1933; served in Royal Yacht Victoria and Albert, 1938. Served War, Flag-Lieut to C-in-C, Home Fleet, 1939-41 (despatches, DSC, 1941; wounded, 1942, in Mediterranean); despatches, 1943; invalided from Royal Navy, due to war wounds and injuries, 1945. Dep. Underwriter at Lloyd's, 1945-55; thereafter concentrated increasingly on work of, and concerned with, the National Advisory Council on Employment of Disabled People (Chm., 1963-74). *Recreations:* the field sports, horticulture, lapidary work. *Address:* Rocklands, Norton-sub-Hamdon, Somerset TA14 6SR. *T:* Chiselborough 279. *Clubs:* Naval and Military; Union (Malta).

STYLE, Sir William Montague, 12th Bt, *cr* 1627; *b* 21 July 1916; *s* of Sir William Frederick Style, 11th Bt, and Florence (*d* 1918), *d* of J. Timm; *S* father, 1943; *m* 1941, La Verne, *d* of T. M. Comstock; two *s. Heir: s* William Frederick Style, *b* 13 May 1945. *Address:* c/o Muehlmeier, Wildwood, 2919 North Mill Road, Oconomowoc, Wisconsin 53066, USA.

STYLES, (Frank) Showell, FRGS; author; *b* 14 March 1908; *s* of Frank Styles and Edith (*née* Showell); *m* 1954, Kathleen Jane Humphreys; one *s* two *d. Educ:* Bishop Vesey's Grammar Sch., Sutton Coldfield. Served Royal Navy, 1939; retd (Comdr), 1946. Professional author, 1946-76, retd. Led two private Arctic expedns, 1952-53; led private Himalayan expedn, 1954. FRGS 1954. *Publications:* 115 books on travel, fiction, children's books, biography, mountain guidebooks, instructional books (including, recently, The Mountains of North Wales, The Baltic Convoy, Backpacking in Alps and Pyrenees); detective works under pen-name Glyn Carr. *Recreations:* mountaineering, gardening, music. *Address:* Trwyn Cae Iago, Borth-y-Gest, Porthmadog, Gwynedd. *T:* Porthmadog 2849. *Club:* Midland Association of Mountaineers (Birmingham).

STYLES, Fredrick William, BEM 1943; Director, Royal Arsenal Co-operative Society, since 1968 (Chairman, 1975-79); *b* 18 Dec. 1914; *s* of Henry Albert Styles and Mabel Louise (*née* Sherwood); *m* 1942, Mary Gwendoline Harrison; one *s* three *d. Educ:* LCC elementary sch.; London Univ. (Dipl. economics); NCLC (Dipls Local and Central Govt). Salesman, Co-op, 1929-39. RAFVR Air Sea Rescue Service, 1939-46. Royal Humane Soc. Silver Medal, 1939; BEM for gallantry, 1943. Trade union official, NUPE (London divisional officer), 1946-52; social worker, hospital, 1952-58; social worker, LCC and GLC, 1958-68. Mem. Exec., 1973, Vice-Chm., 1974-79, Chm., 1979-80, Bexley and Greenwich AHA. Mem. for Greenwich, GLC, 1974-81; Mem., Greenwich Borough Council, 1971-78; Mem., 1971-81, Vice-Chm., 1974-75, Chm., 1975-76, ILEA; Chm. Staff and General Cttee, ILEA, 1977-81; Vice Chm., ILEA schools: Nansen (partially sighted), Hawthorn Cottage (physically handicapped), and Rose Cottage (educationally sub-normal). Chm., Co-operative Metropolitan Industrial Relations Cttee, 1979- (Exec. Mem., 1970; Vice-Chm., 1973). Governor: Averyhill Teachers Trng Coll., 1971-; Woolwich Coll., 1971-; Thameside Inst., 1971-. *Recreations:* problems, people, pensioners, politics. *Address:* 49 Court Farm Road, Mottingham, SE9 4JN. *T:* 01-857 1508.

STYLES, Showell; *see* Styles, F. S.

STYLES, Lt-Col Stephen George, GC 1972; retired; company director, since 1974; *b* 16 March 1928; *s* of Stephen Styles and Grace Lily Styles (*née* Preston); *m* 1952, Mary Rose Styles (*née* Woolgar); one *s* two *d. Educ:* Collyers Sch., Horsham; Royal Military Coll. of Science. Ammunition Technical Officer, commissioned RAOC, Nov. 1947; seconded to 1 Bn KOYLI, 1949-51 (despatches, 1952); RMCS, 1952-56; HQ Ammunition Organisation, 1956-58; OC 28 Commonwealth Bde, Ordnance Field Park, Malaya, 1958-61; 2i/c 16 Bn RAOC, Bicester, 1961-64; OC Eastern Command Ammunition Inspectorate, 1964-67; Sen. Ammo Tech. Officer, 3 BAPD, BAOR, 1967-68; OC 1(BR) Corps Vehicle Company, 1968-69; Sen. Ammo Tech. Officer, Northern Ireland, 1969-72; Chief Ammo Tech. Officer (EOD), HQ DOS (CILSA), 1972-74. Member: Royal Soc. of St George, NRA, NSRA. *Publications:* Bombs Have No Pity, 1975; contrib. Proc. ICE, Jl of Forensic Science Soc. *Recreation:* rifle and game shooting, cartridge collector. *Address:* c/o Barclays Bank Ltd, Wantage.

SUAREZ, Juan L.; *see* Lechin-Suarez.

SUBAK-SHARPE, Prof. John Herbert, FRSE 1970; Professor of Virology, University of Glasgow, since 1968; Hon. Director, Medical Research Council Virology Unit, since 1968; *b* 14 Feb. 1924; *s* of late Robert Subak and late Nelly (*née* Bruell), Vienna, Austria; *m* 1953, Barbara Naomi Morris; two *s* one *d. Educ:* Humanistic Gymnasium, Vienna; Univ. of Birmingham. BSc (Genetics) (1st Cl. Hons) 1952; PhD 1956. Refugee from Nazi oppression, 1939; farm pupil, 1939-44; HM Forces (Parachute Regt), 1944-47. Asst Lectr in Genetics, Glasgow Univ., 1954-56; Mem. scientific staff, ARC Animal Virus Research Inst., Pirbright, 1956-60; Nat. Foundn Fellow, California Inst. of Technology, 1961; Mem. Scientific staff of MRC, in Experimental Virus Research Unit, Glasgow, 1961-68. Vis. Prof., US Nat. Insts of Health, Bethesda, Md, 1967; Sec., Genetical Soc., 1966-72, Vice-Pres. 1972-75, Trustee 1971-. Member: European Molecular Biology Orgn, 1969- (Chm., Course and Workshops Cttee, 1976-78); Genetic Manipulation Adv. Gp, 1976-80; Biomed. Res. Cttee, SHHD Chief Scientist Orgn, 1979-; British Nat. Cttee of Biophysics, 1970-76; Governing Body, W of Scotland Oncological Orgn, 1974-; Scientific Adv. Body, W German Cancer Res. Centre, 1977-. *Publications:* articles in scientific jls on genetic studies with viruses and cells. *Recreations:* mountain walking and bridge. *Address:* 17 Kingsborough Gardens, Glasgow G12 9NH. *T:* 041-334 1863. *Club:* Athenæum.

SUBONO, Adm. Richardus; Ambassador of Indonesia to the Court of St James's, 1974-78; *b* 27 June 1927; *s* of R. S. Suryosumarno and Sukimah Suryosumarno; *m* 1959, Veronica Maria Umboh; one *s* three *d. Educ:* naval sch. and coll.; courses in Indonesia and abroad (Holland and UK). Various appts in fleet and naval HQ, 1950-61; Dep. C-in-C Theatre Comd for liberation of West Irian, 1962; Dir-Gen. Planning, Naval HQ, 1963; Dep. Governor, Nat. Defence Coll., 1964; Dep. Chief of Staff of Navy, 1966; Chief of Gen. Staff, Armed Forces HQ, 1969; Chief of Staff of Navy, 1973. Awarded 22 medals, 1950-74. *Recreation:* golf. *Club:* Highgate Golf.

SUBRAMANIAM, Chidambaram; Chairman, Rajaji International Institute of Public Affairs and Administration, since 1980; *b* 30 Jan. 1910; *s* of Chidambara Gounder and Valliammal; *m* 1945, Sakuntala; one *s* two *d. Educ:* Madras (BA, LLB). Set up legal practice, Coimbatore, 1936; took active part in freedom movt, imprisoned 1932, 1941 and again 1942; Pres., District Congress Committee, Coimbatore; Mem. Working Cttee of State Congress Cttee; Mem. Constituent Assembly; Minister of Finance, Educn and Law, Govt of Madras, 1952; MP 1962; Minister of Steel, 1962-63; Minister of Steel, Mines and Heavy Engrg, 1963-64; Minister of Food and Agric., 1964-66; Minister of Food and Agriculture, CD and Coopn, 1966-67; Chm. Cttee on Aeronautics Industry, 1967-69; Interim Pres., Indian Nat. Congress, July-Dec. 1969; Chm. Nat. Commn on Agric., 1970; Minister of Planning and Dep. Chm., Planning Commn, 1971; also i/c Dept of Science and Technology; Minister of Industrial Develt and Science and Technology, 1972 (also Agric., temp., 1974); Minister of Finance, 1974-77; Minister of Defence, 1979. Hon. DLitt: Wattair; Sri Venkateswara; Madurai; Hon. LLD Andhra. *Publications:* Nan Sendra Sila Nadugal (Travelogues); War on Poverty; Ulagam Sutrinen (in Tamil); India of My Dreams (in English); Strategy Statement for Fighting Protein Hunger in Developing Countries; The New Strategy in Indian Agriculture. *Recreation:* yoga. *Address:* River View, Madras 85, India. *T:* 414298. *Clubs:* Cosmopolitan, Gymkhana (Madras); Cosmopolitan (Coimbatore).

SUCH, Frederick Rudolph Charles; a Recorder of the Crown Court, since 1979; *b* 19 June 1936; *s* of Frederick Sidney Such and Anne Marie Louise (*née* Martin); *m* 1961, Elizabeth, *d* of late Judge Norman and Mrs Harper, Cloughton, Yorkshire; one *s* one *d. Educ:* Mbeya Sch., Tanganyika Territory, E Africa (Tanzania); Taunton Sch.; Keble Coll., Oxford (MA). Called to the Bar, Gray's Inn, 1960; practised: London, 1960–69, then North Eastern Circuit, 1969–; *Recreations:* theatre, opera, hockey, squash, tennis. *Address:* The Rift Barns, Wylam, Northumberland NE41 8BL. *T:* Wylam 2763. *Club:* Northern Counties (Newcastle upon Tyne).

SUCKLING, Dr Charles Walter, FRS 1978; FRSC; Chairman, Bradbury, Suckling and Partners Ltd; Non-Executive Director, Albright and Wilson, since 1982; *b* 24 July 1920; *s* of Edward Ernest and Barbara Suckling (*née* Thomson); *m* 1946, Eleanor Margaret Watterson; two *s* one *d. Educ:* Oldershaw Grammar Sch., Wallasey; Liverpool Univ. (BSc, PhD). ICI: joined Gen. Chemicals Div., 1942; R&D Director, Mond Div., 1967; Dep. Chairman, Mond Div., 1969; Chairman, Paints Div., 1972; Gen. Man., Res. and Technol., 1977–82. Hon. Vis. Professor: Univ. of Stirling; Univ. of E Anglia. Member: BBC Science Consultative Gp, 1980–; Royal Commn on Environmental Pollution, 1982–; Council, RCA, 1981–. Hon. DSc Liverpool, 1980. Liverpool Univ. Chem. Soc. Medal, 1964; John Scott Medal, City of Philadelphia, 1973. *Publications:* (with A. Baines and F. R. Bradbury) Research in the Chemical Industry, 1969; (with C. J. Suckling and K. E. Suckling) Chemistry through Models, 1978; papers on industrial research and strategy in journals. *Recreations:* music, gardening, languages, writing. *Address:* Willowhay, Shoppenhangers Road, Maidenhead, Berks SL6 2QA. *T:* Maidenhead 27502.

SUCKSDORFF, Mrs Åke; *see* Jonzen, Mrs Karin.

SUCRE-TRIAS, Dr Juan Manuel; Ambassador of Venezuela to the Court of St James's, 1977–79; *b* 25 Oct. 1940; *m* 2nd, 1977, Tatiana Perez; three *s* of former marriage. Economist. Economist, Corporación Venezolana de Guayana; as Economist, Ministry of Public Works, Caracas: Head of Studies Unit; Asst Director of Programming and Budgeting. Member of Congress, Venezuela; President, Finance Commission of Congress of the Republic. Holds several military decorations (Venezuelan); Orden del Libertador (1st cl.). *Recreations:* swimming, tennis, golf. *Address:* Apt. No 50164, Sabana Grande, Caracas 105, Venezuela.

SUDBURY, Archdeacon of; *see* Child, Ven. Kenneth.

SUDBURY, Col Frederick Arthur, OBE 1942; ERD 1951; JP; *b* 14 Sept. 1904. *Educ:* Colfe Grammar School, Lewisham; London School of Economics. Tate & Lyle, 1922–69. Served War of 1939–45, Army Officers Emergency Reserve; Col, Dir of Inland Water Transport, Iraq, 1941–43; Col, Movements and Transportation, 14th Army, 1944–45; Lt-Col Supplementary Reserve, 1947–51; Col, Army Emergency Reserve, 1951–62; Hon. Col., RE (AER), 1951–66. Mem. Thames Conservancy, 1958–65 (Vice-Chm., 1960–65). Underwriting Mem. of Lloyd's. Liveryman and Mem. Court Shipwrights' Co.; Freeman and Mem. Court, Co. of Watermen and Lightermen (Master, 1960–61–62). JP Inner London, 1962–. *Recreation:* yachting. *Address:* 1 Abbotsbury Close, W14. *T:* 01-603 2880. *Club:* Royal Thames Yacht.

SUDDABY, Arthur, CBE 1980; PhD, MSc; CChem, FRSC; CEng, MIChemE; scientific consultant on the carriage of goods by sea; Provost, City of London Polytechnic, 1970–81; *b* 26 Feb. 1919; *e s* of George Suddaby, Kingston-upon-Hull, Yorks; *m* 1944, Elizabeth Bullin Vyse (decd), *d* of Charles Vyse; two *s. Educ:* Riley High Sch., Kingston-upon-Hull; Hull Technical Coll.; Chelsea Polytechnic; Queen Mary Coll. London. Chemist and Chemical Engr, in industry, 1937–47; Lectr in Physical Chemistry, and later Sen. Lectr in Chem. Engrg, West Ham Coll. of Technology, 1947–50; Sir John Cass Coll.: Sen. Lectr in Physics, 1950–61; Head of Dept of Physics, 1961–66; Principal, 1966–70. Chm., Cttee of Directors of Polytechnics, 1976–78; Member: Chem. Engrg Cttee, 1948–51; London and Home Counties Regional Adv. Council, 1971–; Bd of Examrs and Educn Cttee, Inst. of Chem. Engrs, 1948–51; CNAA: Chem. Engrg Bd, 1969–75; Nautical Studies Bd, 1972–75; Chm., Standing Conf. of Approved Coll. Res. Deg. Cttees, 1979–81; Court of the City University, 1967–81; Vis. Cttee, Cranfield Inst. of Technology, 1979–; Chm., Assoc. of Navigation Schs, 1972. *Publications:* various original research papers in theoretical physics, in scientific jls; review articles. *Recreation:* hunting. *Address:* Flat 3, 16 Elm Park Gardens, Chelsea, SW10. *T:* 01-352 9164; Bothkerran House, Dengie, Essex. *T:* Tillingham 340. *Club:* Athenæum.

SUDDARDS, His Honour (Henry) Gaunt; a Circuit Judge (formerly Judge of County Courts), 1963–80; *b* 30 July 1910; *s* of Fred Suddards and Agnes Suddards (*née* Gaunt); unmarried. *Educ:* Cheltenham College; Trinity College, Cambridge (MA). Barrister, Inner Temple, 1932; joined NE Circuit, 1933. Served War of 1939–45, RAFVR, 1940–46. Recorder of Pontefract, 1960–61; Recorder of Middlesbrough, 1961–63; Dep. Chm., West Riding QS, 1961–71; Chairman, Agricultural Land Tribunal, Northern Area, 1961–63,

Dep. Chairman 1960. *Recreations:* fishing, shooting, sailing. *Address:* Rockville, Frizinghall, Shipley, West Yorkshire. *Club:* Bradford (Bradford).

SUDELEY, 7th Baron *cr* 1838; **Merlin Charles Sainthill Hanbury-Tracy;** *b* 17 June 1939; *o c* of late Captain Michael David Charles Hanbury-Tracy, Scots Guards, and Colline Ammabel, *d* of late Lt-Col C. G. H. St Hill and widow of Lt-Col Frank King, DSO, OBE; *S* cousin, 1941; *m* 1980, Hon. Mrs Elizabeth Villiers, *d* of late Viscount Bury (*s* of 9th Earl of Albemarle). *Educ:* at Eton and in the ranks of the Scots Guards. Vice-Pres., Prayer Book Soc.; Chairman, Human Rights Soc. Patron: Anglican Assoc.; St Peter's, Petersham, Richmond, Surrey. *Publications:* contribs to Quarterly Review, Contemporary Review, Family History, Trans of Bristol and Gloucestershire Archaeol. Soc., Montgomeryshire Collections, Bull. of Manorial Soc., Die Waage (Zeitschrift der Chemie Grünenthal). *Recreations:* ancestor worship; cultivating his sensibility. *Heir: kinsman* Claud Edward Frederick Hanbury-Tracy-Domvile, TD [*b* 11 Jan. 1904; assumed by deed poll, 1961, additional surname of Domvile; *m* 1st, 1927, Veronica May (marr. diss. 1948), *d* of late Cyril Grant Cunard; two *s* one *d* ; 2nd, 1954, Marcella Elizabeth Willis, *er d* of late Rev. Canon John Willis Price]. *Address:* c/o Williams & Glyn's Bank Ltd, 21 Grosvenor Gardens, SW1. *Clubs:* Brooks's, (as Member of Parliament) House of Lords.

SUDLEY, Viscount; Arthur Desmond Colquhoun Gore; *b* 14 July 1938; *er s* of 8th Earl of Arran, *qv* ; *m* 1974, Eleanor, *er d* of Bernard van Cutsem and Lady Margaret Fortescue; two *d. Educ:* Eton; Balliol College, Oxford. 2nd Lieutenant, 1st Bn Grenadier Guards (National Service). Asst Manager, Daily Mail, 1972–73; Man. Dir, Clark Nelson, 1973–74; Asst Gen. Manager Daily and Sunday Express, June–Nov. 1974. Co-Founder, Gore Publishing Ltd, 1980. Co-Chm., Children's Country Holidays Fund; Mem., Exec. Cttee, C of E Children's Soc. *Recreations:* tennis, shooting, gardening, croquet. *Address:* Crocker End House, Nettlebed, Henley-on-Thames, Oxon. *T:* Nettlebed 641659. *Clubs:* Turf, Beefsteak.

SUENENS, His Eminence Cardinal Leo Joseph, DTheol, DPhil; Cardinal since 1962; Archbishop of Malines–Brussels and Primate of Belgium, 1961–79; *b* Ixelles (Brussels), 16 July 1904. *Educ:* primary sch., Inst. of Marist Brothers, Brussels; secondary sch., St Mary's High Sch., Brussels; Gregorian Univ., Rome (BCL, DPhil, DrTheol). Priest, 1927; Teacher, St Mary's High Sch., Brussels, 1929; Prof. of Philosophy, Diocesan Seminary, Malines, 1930; Vice-Rector, Cath. Univ. of Louvain, 1940; Vicar-Gen., Archdio. of Malines, 1945; Auxiliary Bp to Archbp of Malines, 1945. Moderator of Second Vatican Council, 1962–65; Pres., Belgian Bishops' Conf.; Internat. Pastoral Delegate for Catholic Charismatic Renewal. Templeton Prize for Religion, 1976. *Publications:* Theology of the Apostolate of the Legion of Mary, 1951 (Cork); Edel Quinn, 1952 (Dublin); (ed) The Right View on Moral Rearmament, 1953 (London); (ed) The Gospel to Every Creature, 1955 (London); (ed) Mary the Mother of God, 1957 (New York); (ed) Love and Control, 1959 (London); (ed) Christian Life Day by Day, 1961 (London); (ed) The Nun in the World, 1962 (London); (ed) Co-responsibility in the Church, 1968 (New York), 1969 (London); (ed, with Archbp Ramsey) The Future of the Christian Church, 1971 (New York); A New Pentecost?, 1975 (New York); Open the Frontiers, 1980; Renewal and Powers of Darkness, 1982. *Address:* Boulevard de Smet de Mayer 570, 1020 Bruxelles, Belgium. *T:* 02/4791950.

SUENSON-TAYLOR, family name of **Baron Grantchester.**

SUFFIELD, 11th Baron *cr* 1786; **Anthony Philip Harbord-Hamond,** Bt, *cr* 1745; MC 1950; Major, retired, 1961; *b* 19 June 1922; *o s* of 10th Baron and Nina Annette Mary Crawfuird (*d* 1955), *e d* of John Hutchison of Laurieston and Edingham, Stewartry of Kirkcudbright; *S* father 1951; *m* 1952, Elizabeth Eve, *er d* of late Judge Edgedale; three *s* one *d. Educ:* Eton. Commission, Coldstream Guards, 1942; served War of 1939–45, in North African and Italian campaigns, 1942–45; Malaya, 1948–50. One of HM Hon. Corps of Gentlemen-at-Arms, 1973–. Officer of the Order of Orange Nassau, 1950. *Recreations:* normal. *Heir: s* Hon. Charles Anthony Assheton Harbord-Hamond [*b* 3 Dec. 1953; commissioned Coldstream Guards, 1972, RARO 1979]. *Address:* Wood Norton Grange, Dereham, Norfolk NR20 5BD. *T:* Foulsham 235. *Clubs:* Army and Navy, Pratt's.

SUFFIELD, Sir (Henry John) Lester, Kt 1973; Head of Defence Sales, Ministry of Defence, 1969–76; *b* 28 April 1911; *m* 1940, Elizabeth Mary White; one *s* one *d. Educ:* Camberwell Central, LCC. Served with RASC, 1939–45 (Major). 1926–35; Morris Motors, 1935–38 and 1945–52; Pres., British Motor Corp., Canada and USA, 1952–64; Dep. Man. Dir, British Motor Corp., Birmingham, 1964–68; Sales Dir, British Leyland Motor Corp., 1968–69. Freeman of City of London, 1978; Liveryman, Coachmakers and Coach Harness Makers Co. *Recreation:* golf. *Address:* Vikings, Clifford Manor Road, Guildford. *T:* Guildford 35538. *Clubs:* Royal Automobile; Royal Wimbledon Golf.

SUFFOLK AND BERKSHIRE, 21st Earl of, *cr* 1603; **Michael John James George Robert Howard;** Viscount Andover and Baron Howard, 1622; Earl of Berkshire, 1626; *b* 27 March 1935; *s* of 20th Earl (killed by enemy action, 1941) and Mimi (*d* 1966), *yr d* of late A. G. Forde Pigott; *S* father 1941; *m* 1st, 1960, Mme Simone Paulmier (marr. diss. 1967), *d* of late Georges Litman, Paris; (one *d* decd); 2nd, 1973, Anita (marr. diss. 1980), *d* of R. R. Fuglesang, Haywards Heath, Sussex; one *s* one *d.* Owns 5,000 acres. *Heir: s* Viscount

Andover, qv. *Address:* Charlton Park, Malmesbury, Wilts.
See also Hon. G. R. Howard.

SUFFOLK, Archdeacon of; *see* Smith, Ven. Donald John.

SUGDEN, family name of **Baron St Leonards.**

SUGDEN, Sir Arthur, Kt 1978; Director: Manchester Ship Canal Limited, since 1978; Co-operative Development Agency, since 1978; Chief Executive Officer, Co-operative Wholesale Society Ltd, 1974-80; Chairman: Co-operative Bank Ltd, 1974-80; Co-operative Commercial Bank Ltd, 1974-80; *b* 12 Sept. 1918; *s* of late Arthur and Elizabeth Ann Sugden; *m* 1946, Agnes Grayston; two *s. Educ:* Thomas Street, Manchester. Certified Accountant, Chartered Secretary. FIB 1975. Served War of 1939-45, Royal Artillery; CPO 6th Super Heavy Battery; Adjt 12th Medium Regt; Staff Captain 16th Army Group. CWS Ltd: Accountancy Asst, 1946; Office Man., 1950; Factory Man., 1954; Group Man., Edible Oils and Fats Factories, 1964; Controller, Food Div., 1967; Dep. Chief Exec. Officer, 1971. Chairman, 1974-80: FC Finance Ltd; CWS (Longburn) Ltd; CWS (New Zealand) Ltd; CWS Marketing Ltd; CWS (India) Ltd; Ocean Beach Freezing Co. Ltd; Shaw's Smokers' Products Ltd; Former Director: Co-operative City Investments Ltd; Co-operative Pension Funds Unit Trust Managers' Ltd; Associated Co-operative Creameries Ltd; CWS Svineslagterier A/S Denmark; CWS (Overseas) Ltd; Tukuyu Tea Estates Ltd; Spillers French Holdings Ltd; J. W. French (Milling & Baking Holdings) Ltd; North Eastern Co-operative Soc. Ltd; Manchester Chamber of Commerce. Former Vice-President: Inst. of Bankers; Inst. of Grocery Distribution Ltd. Member: Central Cttee, Internat. Co-operative Alliance; Management Bds, Euro-Coop and Inter-Coop (Pres., 1979-80). Pres., Co-operative Congress, 1978. CBIM; FIGD. *Recreations:* music, reading, walking. *Address:* 56 Old Wool Lane, Cheadle Hulme, Cheadle, Cheshire.

SUGDEN, John Goldthorp, MA; ARCM; Headmaster, Wellingborough School, 1965-73; *b* 22 July 1921; *s* of A. G. Sugden, Brighouse, Yorkshire; *m* 1954, Jane Machin; two *s. Educ:* Radley; Magdalene College, Cambridge. War Service, Royal Signals, 1941-46. Asst Master, Bilton Grange Prep. School, 1948-52; Asst Master, The King's School, Canterbury, 1952-59; Headmaster, Foster's School, Sherborne, 1959-64. *Publication:* Niccolo Paganini, 1980. *Recreations:* music, golf. *Address:* Woodlands, 2 Linksview Avenue, Parkstone, Poole, Dorset BH14 9QT. *T:* Parkstone 707497.

SUGDEN, Theodore Morris, CBE 1975; MA, ScD; FRS 1963; Master of Trinity Hall, Cambridge, since 1976; *b* 31 Dec. 1919; *s* of Frederick Morris Sugden and Florence Sugden (née Chadwick); *m* 1945, Marian Florence Cotton; one *s. Educ:* Sowerby Bridge Grammar School; Jesus College, Cambridge (Hon. Fellow 1977). Stokes Student, Pembroke Coll., Cambridge, 1945-46; H. O. Jones Lecturer in Physical Chemistry, Univ. of Cambridge, 1950-60; Reader in Physical Chemistry, Univ. of Cambridge, 1960-63; Fellow, Queens' Coll., Cambridge, 1957-63 (Hon. Fellow, 1976). Dir, Thornton Research Centre, Chester, 1967-75; Chief Executive, Shell Research Ltd, 1974-75. Associate Prof., Molecular Sciences, Univ. of Warwick, 1965-74; Vis. Prof. Chemical Technology, Imp. Coll., 1974-75. Chm., Adv. Cttee on Safety in Nuclear Installations, Health and Safety Commn, 1977–. Pres., Chem. Soc., 1978-79; Physical Sec., Royal Soc., 1979-. Hon. DTech Bradford, 1967; Hon. DSc: York, Ont, 1973; Liverpool, 1977; Leeds, 1978. Medallist of the Combustion Inst., 1960, 1976; Davy Medal, Royal Soc., 1975. *Publications:* (with C. N. Kenney) Microwave Spectroscopy of Gases, 1965; articles in Proc. Royal Soc., Transactions of Faraday Soc., Nature, etc. *Recreations:* pianoforte, travel. *Address:* The Master's Lodge, Trinity Hall, Cambridge CB2 1TJ. *T:* Cambridge 352396.

SUGG, Aldhelm St John, CMG 1963; retired as Provincial Commissioner, Southern Provinces of Northern Rhodesia, August 1963; *b* 21 Oct. 1909; *s* of H. G. St J. Sugg; *m* 1935, Jessie May Parker; one *s* one *d. Educ:* Colchester Royal Grammar School. Palestine Police, 1930-31; Northern Rhodesia Police, 1932-43; Colonial Administrative Service, in N Rhodesia, 1943-63. Retired to England, 1963. *Recreations:* sailing, field sports. *Address:* Bushbury, Blackboys, Uckfield, East Sussex. *T:* Framfield 282. *Club:* Royal Commonwealth Society.

SUIRDALE, Viscount; John Michael James Hely-Hutchinson; company director since 1981; *b* 7 Aug. 1952; *s* and *heir* of 8th Earl of Donoughmore, qv; *m* 1976, Marie-Claire Carola Etienne van den Driessche; one *s* one *d. Educ:* Harrow. *Recreations:* shooting, ski-ing, fishing, etc. *Heir: s* Hon. Richard Gregory Hely-Hutchinson, *b* 3 July 1980. *Address:* 15 Rue de Luzarches, 60580 Coye-la-Forêt, France. *T:* 4/458 7117.

SULLIVAN, David Douglas Hooper, QC 1975; barrister-at-law; *b* 10 April 1926; *s* of Michael and Maude Sullivan; *m* 1st, 1951, Sheila, *d* of Henry and Georgina Bathurst; three *d*; 2nd, 1981, Ann Munro, *d* of Malcolm and Eva Betten. *Educ:* Haileybury (schol.); Christ Church, Oxford (schol.). MA 1949, BCL 1951. Served War, with RNVR (Sub-Lieut), 1944-46. Called to Bar, Inner Temple, 1951. *Recreations:* painting, walking, geology. *Address:* 9 Gayton Road, NW3 1TX. *T:* 01-431 3433.

SULLIVAN, Prof. (Donovan) Michael; Professor of Oriental Art since 1966, Christensen Professor since 1975, Stanford University, California; Fellow, St Catherine's College, Oxford, since 1979; *b* 29 Oct. 1916; *s* of Alan Sullivan and Elisabeth Hees; *m* 1943, Khoan, *d* of Ngo Eng-lim, Kulangsu, Amoy, China; no *c. Educ:* Rugby School; Corpus Christi College, Cambridge (MA); Univ. of London (BA Hons); Harvard Univ. (PhD); LittD Cambridge, 1966; MA, DLitt Oxon, 1973. Chinese Govt Scholarship, Univ. of London, 1947-50; Rockefeller Foundn Travelling Fellowship in USA, 1950-51; Bollingen Foundn Research Fellowship, 1952-54; Curator of Art Museum and Lectr in the History of Art, Univ. of Malaya (now Univ. of Singapore), Singapore, 1954-60; Lectr in Asian Art, Sch. of Oriental and African Studies, Univ. of London, 1960-66. Vis. Prof. of Far Eastern Art, Univ. of Michigan (Spring Semester), 1964; Slade Prof. of Fine Art, Oxford Univ., 1973-74; Guggenheim Foundn Fellowship, 1974; Vis. Fellow, St Antony's Coll., Oxford, 1976-77; Nat. Endowment for the Humanities Fellowship, 1976-77. FRSA; Fellow, Amer. Acad. of Arts and Sciences, 1977. *Publications:* Chinese Art in the Twentieth Century, 1959; An Introduction to Chinese Art, 1961; The Birth of Landscape Painting in China, 1962; Chinese Ceramics, Bronzes and Jades in the Collection of Sir Alan and Lady Barlow, 1963; Chinese and Japanese Art, 1965; A Short History of Chinese Art, 1967, 3rd edn as The Arts of China, 1973, rev. edns 1977, 1983; The Cave Temples of Maichishan, 1969; The Meeting of Eastern and Western Art, 1973; Chinese Art: recent discoveries, 1973; The Three Perfections, 1975; Chinese Landscape Painting, vol. II, The Sui and T'ang Dynasties, 1979; Symbols of Eternity: the art of landscape painting in China, 1979; contrib. to learned journals, Encyclopedia Britannica, Chambers's Encyclopædia, etc. *Address:* St Catherine's College, Oxford OX1 3UJ; Department of Art, Stanford University, Stanford, Calif 94305, USA. *Club:* Athenæum.

SULLIVAN, Jeremy Mirth; QC 1982; *b* 17 Sept. 1945; *s* of Arthur Brian and Pamela Jean Sullivan; *m* 1970, Ursula Klara Marie Hildenbrock; two *s. Educ:* Framlingham Coll.; King's Coll., London. LLB 1967, LLM 1968; LAMTPI 1970, LMRTPI 1976. 2nd Lieut, Suffolk & Cambs Regt (TA), 1963. Called to the Bar, Inner Temple, 1968; Lectr in Law, City of London Polytechnic, 1968-71; in practice, Planning and Local Govt Bar, 1971–; Mem., Supplemental Panel of Junior Counsel to Crown (Common Law), 1978-82. *Publications:* contribs to Jl of Planning Law. *Recreations:* walking, railways, canals, reading history. *Address:* 4-5 Gray's Inn Square, WC1R 5JA. *T:* 01-404 5252.

SULLIVAN, Prof. Michael; *see* Sullivan, D. M.

SULLIVAN, Richard Arthur, (9th Bt *cr* 1804, but does not use the title); Manager, Geotechnical Services, Woodward-Clyde Consultants, since 1981; *b* 9 Aug. 1931; *s* of Sir Richard Benjamin Magniac Sullivan, 8th Bt, and Muriel Mary Paget, *d* of late Francis Charles Trayler Pineo; *S* father, 1977; *m* 1962, Elenor Mary, *e d* of K. M. Thorpe; one *s* three *d. Educ:* Univ. of Cape Town (BSc); Massachusetts Inst. of Technology (SM). Chartered Engineer, UK; Professional Engineer, Texas and Louisiana. *Publications:* technical papers to international conferences and geotechnical journals. *Recreation:* tennis. *Heir: s* Charles Merson Sullivan, *b* 15 Dec. 1962. *Address:* 11810 Longleaf Lane, Houston, Texas 77024, USA.

SULLIVAN, Tod; National Secretary, Association of Clerical, Technical and Supervisory Staffs, since 1974; *b* 3 Jan. 1934; *s* of Timothy William and Elizabeth Sullivan; *m* 1963, Patricia Norma Roughsedge; one *s* three *d. Educ:* Fanshawe Crescent Sch., Dagenham. Merchant Navy, 1950-52; RAF, 1952-55; Electrician, 1955-60; Children's Journalist, 1960-68; Industrial Relations Officer: ATV, 1968-71; CIR, 1971-72; Gen. Sec., Union of Kodak Workers, 1973-74 (until transfer of engagements to TGWU). *Recreations:* reading, music, golf. *Address:* 267 Luton Road, Harpenden, Herts. *T:* Harpenden 5034.

SULLY, Leonard Thomas George, CBE 1963; Covent Garden Market Authority, since 1967; Member, Industrial Tribunals Panel, since 1976; *b* 25 June 1909; British; *m* 1935, Phyllis Emily Phipps, Bristol; one *d. Educ:* elementary schs; Fairfield Grammar Sch., Bristol. Public Health Dept, Bristol Corp., 1927; Assistance Officer, Unemployment Assistance Board, Bristol District, 1934; subseq. served in Bath, Weston-super-Mare, etc.; Staff Officer, Air Ministry, London, 1943; Principal, and allocated to Air Ministry, 1949; Asst Sec., 1954, Dir of Contracts, 1960; Dir of Contracts (Air) MoD, 1964. *Recreation:* gardening. *Address:* Coppins, 20 Brackendale Close, Camberley, Surrey. *T:* Camberley 63604.

SULTAN, Syed Abdus; *b* 1 Feb. 1917; Bengali Muslim; lawyer, Supreme Court of Bangladesh, Dacca, since 1976; *m* 1938, Begum Kulsum Sultan; two *s* two *d. Educ:* Calcutta and Dacca Univs. Grad. Calcutta 1936, LLB Dacca 1949. Joined Dacca High Court Bar, 1949; Mem. Nat. Assembly of Pakistan, 1962; Delegate Inter-Parly Union Conf., Belgrade, 1963; toured Europe and Middle East; Mem. Pakistan Bar Council, 1967; Mem. Pakistan Nat. Assembly, 1970 with Sheikh Mujibur Rahman (Mem. Constitution Drafting Cttee); joined Bangladesh liberation movt, 1971; visited India, UK, USA and Canada to project cause of Bangladesh; Mem. Unofficial Delegn of Govt of Bangladesh to UN; Ambassador, later High Comr, for Bangladesh in UK, 1972-75. Member: Bangladesh Inst. of Law and Internat. Affairs; Bangla Academy. *Publications:* (in Bengali): Biography of M. A. Jinnah, 1948; Pancha Nadir Palimati, 1953; Ibne Sina, 1955; Man Over the Ages (history), 1969; Manirag (Belles Lettres), 1969; Byati Kramer Ek Adhyaya (One Chapter of Difference), 1981; Ar Rakta Nay (No more Blood), 1982; translations of short stories. *Recreations:* tennis, cricket, literature, literary and cultural activities. *Address:* Supreme Court Bar Association, Dacca, Bangladesh.

SULZBERGER, Arthur Ochs; President and Publisher of The New York Times since 1963; *b* 5 Feb. 1926; *s* of late Arthur Hays Sulzberger; *m* 1st, 1948, Barbara Grant (marr. diss. 1956); one *s* one *d* ; 2nd, 1956, Carol Fox Fuhrman; one *d* (and one adopted *d*). *Educ:* Browning School, New York City; Loomis School, Windsor, Conn; Columbia University, NYC. Reporter, Milwaukee Journal, 1953-54; Foreign Correspondent, New York Times, 1954-55; Asst to the Publisher, New York Times, 1956-57; Asst Treasurer, New York Times, 1957-63. Trustee: Metropolitan Mus. of Art; Columbia Univ. Hon. LLD: Dartmouth, 1964; Bard, 1967; Hon LHD Montclair State Coll. *Recreation:* golf. *Address:* 229 West 43rd Street, New York, NY 10036, USA. *T:* 556-1771. *Clubs:* Overseas Press, Century Country, Explorers (New York); Metropolitan, Federal City (Washington, DC).

SUMMERFIELD, Prof. Arthur, BSc Tech; BSc; FBPsS; Professor of Psychology, University of London, and Head of the Department of Psychology at Birkbeck College since 1961; *b* 31 March 1923; *s* of late Arthur and Dora Gertrude Summerfield; *m* 1st, 1946, Aline Whalley; one *s* one *d* ; 2nd, 1974, Angela Barbara, MA Cantab, PhD London, *d* of late George Frederick Steer and of Estelle Steer. *Educ:* Manchester Grammar Sch.; Manchester Univ.; University Coll. London (1st cl. hons Psychology). Served War of 1939-45, Electrical Officer, RNVR, 1943-46: Naval Air Stations, 1943-46; Dept of Sen. Psychologist to the Admiralty, 1946. Asst Lectr in Psychology, University Coll. London, 1949-51, Lectr, 1951-61, Hon. Research Associate, 1961-70, Hon. Research Fellow, 1970-; first Dean, Fac. of Econs, Birkbeck Coll., 1971-72, Governor, 1982-; Hon. Lectr in Psychology, Westminster Med. Sch., 1974-76. Mem. Council, British Psychological Soc., 1953-65, 1967-75, 1977- (Hon. Gen. Sec., 1954-59; Pres., 1963-64; Vice-Pres., 1964-65; first Chm., Scientific Affairs Bd, 1974-75); Member: Cttee on Internat. Relations in Psychology, Amer. Psychological Assoc., 1977-79; Bd of Dirs, European Coordination Centre for Res. and Documentation in Social Scis (Vienna Centre), 1977-81; Pres., International Union of Psychological Science, 1976-80 (Mem., Exec. Cttee, 1963-, Assembly, 1957-; Vice-Pres., 1972-76); Pres., Section J (Psychology) BAAS, 1976-77; Pres., Internat. Soc. Sci. Council, 1977-81 (Mem. Prog. Cttee, 1973-; Mem. Exec. Cttee, 1977-); Chm., DES Working Party on Psychologists in Educn Services, 1965-68. Member: DSIR Human Sciences Res. Grants Cttee, 1962-65; SSRC, 1979-81; Psychology Cttee, SSRC, 1979-81. Vis. Prof., Univ. of California (at Dept of Psychobiology, Irvine Campus), 1968. Governor, Enfield Coll. of Technology, 1968-72. Asst Editor, Brit. Jl Psychology (Statistical Section), 1950-54; Editor, British Journal of Psychology, 1964-67; Scientific Editor, British Med. Bulletin issues on Experimental Psychology, 1964, Cognitive Psychology, 1971, Psychobiology, 1981. *Publications:* articles on perception, memory, statistical methods and psycho-pharmacology in scientific periodicals. *Address:* Birkbeck College, Malet Street, WC1E 7HX.

SUMMERFIELD, Hon. Sir John (Crampton), Kt 1973; CBE 1966 (OBE 1961); **Hon. Mr Justice Summerfield;** Judge of the Grand Court and Chief Justice of the Cayman Islands, since 1977; Judge of the Supreme Court of the Turks and Caicos Islands, since 1978; Justice of Appeal of the Court of Appeal for Bermuda, since 1979; President, Court of Appeal for Belize, since 1982; *b* 20 Sept. 1920; *s* of late Arthur Fred Summerfield and late Lilian Winifred Summerfield (née Staas); *m* 1945, Patricia Sandra Musgrave; two *s* two *d*. *Educ:* Lucton Sch., Herefordshire. Called to Bar, Gray's Inn, 1949. Served War, 1939-46: East Africa, Abyssinia, Somaliland, Madagascar; Captain, Royal Signals. Crown Counsel, Tanganyika (now Tanzania), 1949; Legal Draftsman, 1953; Dep. Legal Sec., EA High Commission, 1958. Attorney-Gen., Bermuda, 1962; QC (Bermuda) 1963; MEC, 1962-68, and MLC, 1962-68 (Bermuda); Chief Justice of Bermuda, 1972-77. *Publications:* Preparation of Revised Laws of Bermuda, 1963 and 1971 edns. *Recreations:* photography, chess, sailing. *Address:* c/o The Grand Court, Grand Cayman, Cayman Islands, West Indies. *Club:* Naval and Military.

SUMMERHAYES, Sir Christopher (Henry), KBE 1955 (MBE 1929); CMG 1949; *b* 8 March 1896; *s* of late Rev. H. Summerhayes; *m* 1921, Anna (Johnson) (*d* 1972); two *s* two *d*. Served HM Forces, 1914-19 and 1940-45, Gloucestershire Regt (despatches). HM Foreign Service; Consul-General at Alexandria, 1946-51; Ambassador to Nepal, 1951-55. *Address:* Tara, Limpsfield Chart, Oxted, Surrey.
See also D. M. Summerhayes.

SUMMERHAYES, David Michael, CMG 1975; HM Diplomatic Service, retired; Ambassador and Leader, UK Delegation to Committee on Disarmament, Geneva, 1979-82; *b* 29 Sept. 1922; *s* of Sir Christopher Summerhayes, *qv* ; *m* 1959, June van der Hardt Aberson; two *s* one *d*. *Educ:* Marlborough; Emmanuel Coll., Cambridge. Served War of 1939-45 in Royal Artillery (Capt.) N Africa and Italy. 3rd Sec., FO, 1948; Baghdad, 1949; Brussels, 1950-53; 2nd Sec., FO, 1953-56; 1st Sec. (Commercial), The Hague, 1956-59; 1st Sec. and Consul, Reykjavik, 1959-61; FO, 1961-65; Consul-General and Counsellor, Buenos Aires, 1965-70; Head of Arms Control and Disarmament Dept, FCO, 1970-74; Minister, Pretoria/Cape Town, 1974-78. Hon. Officer, Order of Orange Nassau. *Recreations:* sailing, tennis, wildlife. *Address:* 6 Kingsmere Road, Wimbledon, SW19. *Clubs:* United Oxford & Cambridge University; Hurlingham; Itchenor Sailing; Swiss Alpine.

SUMMERHAYES, Gerald Victor, CMG 1979; OBE 1969; HMOCS on leave since June 1981; *b* 28 Jan. 1928; *s* of Victor Samuel and Florence A. V. Summerhayes. *Educ:* King's Sch., Ely; Brasenose Coll., Oxford (BA 1949,

MA 1952). Served Royal Artillery, 1949-51; First Devonshire Course, 1951-52; Provincial Administration, Northern Nigeria, 1952-63; Min. for Local Govt, N Nigeria, 1963-68; Director, Staff Development Centre, Kaduna, 1968-71; Permanent Secretary: North Western State, 1971-76: Cabinet Office, 1971-72; Health, 1972-73; Cabinet Office, 1973-75; Local Govt, 1975-76; Sokoto State, 1976-81: Local Govt, 1976-77; Cabinet Office (Political and Training), 1977-79; Dir of Trng, Cabinet Office, Sokoto, 1979-81. *Recreations:* gardening, bird watching. *Address:* Bridge Cottage, Bridge Street, Sidbury, Devon EX10 0RU. *T:* Sidbury 311; PO Box 172, Sokoto, Nigeria.

SUMMERS, (Sir) Felix Roland Brattan, 2nd Bt *cr* 1952; does not use the title and his name is not on the Official Roll of Baronets.

SUMMERS, Henry Forbes, CB 1961; Under-Secretary, Department of the Environment (formerly Ministry of Housing and Local Government), 1955-71; *b* 18 August 1911; *s* of late Rev. H. H. Summers, Harrogate, Yorks; *m* 1937, Rosemary, *d* of late Robert L. Roberts, CBE; two *s* one *d*. *Educ:* Fettes Coll., Edinburgh; Trinity College, Oxford. *Publications:* Smoke After Flame, 1944; Hinterland, 1947; Tomorrow is my Love, 1978; The Burning Book, 1982. *Address:* Folly Fields, Tunbridge Wells, Kent. *T:* 27671.
See also N. Summers.

SUMMERS, Janet Margaret, (Mrs L. J. Summers); *see* Bately, J. M.

SUMMERS, Nicholas; Under Secretary, Department of Education and Science, since 1981; *b* 11 July 1939; *s* of Henry Forbes Summers, *qv* ; *m* 1964, Marian Elizabeth Ottley; four *s*. *Educ:* Tonbridge Sch.; Corpus Christi Coll., Oxford. Min. of Educn, 1961-64; DES, 1964-74; Private Sec. to Minister for the Arts, 1965-66; Cabinet Office, 1974-76; DES, 1976-. *Recreations:* family, music. *Address:* c/o Department of Education and Science, Elizabeth House, York Road, SE1 7PH.

SUMMERSCALE, David Michael, MA; Master of Haileybury, since 1976; *b* 22 April 1937; *s* of Noel Tynwald Summerscale and Beatrice (*née* Wilson); *m* 1975, Pauline, *d* of Prof. Michel Fleury, Président de l'Ecole des Hautes Etudes, Paris, Directeur des Antiquités Historiques de l'Ile-de-France. *Educ:* Northaw; Sherborne Sch.; Trinity Hall, Cambridge. Lectr in English Literature and Tutor, St Stephen's Coll., Univ. of Delhi, 1959-63; Charterhouse, 1963-75 (Head of English, Housemaster). Oxford and Cambridge Schs Examination Bd Awarder and Reviser in English. Vice-Chm., E-SU Scholarship Cttee; Member: Managing Cttee of Cambridge Mission to Delhi; C. F. Andrews Centenary Appeal Cttee; HMC Academic Policy Sub-Cttee. *Publications:* articles on English and Indian literature; dramatisations of novels and verse. *Recreations:* music, play production, reading, mountaineering, games (squash (Mem. SRA), cricket, tennis, rackets (Mem. Tennis and Rackets Assoc.), golf, football, cross-country, hockey). *Address:* The Master's Lodge, Haileybury, Hertford SG13 7NU. *T:* Hoddesdon 62352. *Clubs:* Athenæum, I Zingari, Free Foresters, Jesters; Club Alpin Suisse.

SUMMERSCALE, Peter Wayne; HM Diplomatic Service; Ambassador to Costa Rica, since 1982; *b* 22 April 1935; *s* of Sir John Summerscale, KBE; *m* 1964, Valerie Turner; one *s* two *d*. *Educ:* Rugby Sch.; New Coll., Oxford Univ. (Exhibnr; 1st Cl. Hons Modern History); Russian Res. Centre, Harvard Univ. FO, 1960-62; Polit. Residency, Bahrain, 1962-65: 1st Sec., Tokyo, 1965-68; FCO, 1968-69; Cabinet Office, 1969-71; 1st Sec. and Head of Chancery, Santiago, Chile, 1971-75; Head of CSCE Unit, FCO, 1976-77; Dep. Leader, UK Delegn, Belgrade Rev. Conf., 1977-78; Counsellor and Head of Chancery, Brussels, 1978-79; Vis. FCO Res. Fellow, RIIA, Chatham House, 1979-81; Head of Civilian Faculty, Nat. Defence Coll., 1981-82. *Publication:* (jtly) Soviet-East European Dilemmas, 1981; The East European Predicament, 1982; articles on E Europe and communism. *Recreations:* sailing, skiing, walking. *Address:* c/o Foreign and Commonwealth Office, SW1; 5 Grove Terrace, NW5. *Club:* Royal Automobile.

SUMMERSKILL, Dr the Hon. Shirley Catherine Wynne; MP (Lab) Halifax since 1964; an Opposition Spokesman on home affairs, since 1979; Member, Labour Party National Executive Committee, since 1981; Medical Practitioner since 1960; *b* London, 9 Sept. 1931; *d* of Dr E. J. Samuel and Baroness Summerskill, CH, PC. *Educ:* St Paul's Girls' Sch.; Somerville Coll., Oxford; St Thomas' Hospital. MA, BM, BCh., 1958. Treas., Oxford Univ. Labour Club, 1952. Resident House Surgeon, later House Physician, St Helier Hosp., Carshalton, 1959. Contested (Lab) Blackpool North by-election, 1962. UK delegate, UN Status of Women Commn, 1968 and 1969; Mem. British delegn, Council of Europe and WEU, 1968, 1969. Vice-Chm., Parly Labour Party Health Group, 1964-69, Chm., 1969-70. Opposition spokesman on health, 1970-74; Parly Under-Sec. of State, Home Office, 1974-79. *Publication:* A Surgical Affair (novel), 1963. *Address:* House of Commons, SW1.

SUMMERSON, Sir John (Newenham), Kt 1958; CBE 1952; FBA 1954; BA(Arch); FSA; ARIBA; Curator of Sir John Soane's Museum since 1945; *b* 25 Nov. 1904; *o s* of late Samuel James Summerson of Darlington and Dorothea Worth Newenham; *m* 1938, Elizabeth Alison, *d* of H. R. Hepworth, CBE, Leeds; three *s*. *Educ:* Harrow; University College, London. From 1926 worked in architects' offices, including those of late W. D. Caröe and Sir Giles Gilbert Scott, OM. Instructor in Sch. of Architecture, Edinburgh

Coll. of Art, 1929-30. Asst Editor, Architect and Building News, 1934-41; Dep. Dir, National Buildings Record, 1941-45. Lectr in History of Architecture: Architectural Assoc., 1949-62; Birkbeck Coll., 1950-67; Slade Prof. of Fine Art, Oxford, 1958-59; Ferens Prof. of Fine Art, Hull, 1960-61 and 1970-71; Slade Prof. of Fine Art, Cambridge, 1966-67; Bampton Lectr, Columbia Univ., 1968; Page-Barbour Lectr, Virginia Univ., 1972; Banister Fletcher Prof., UCL, 1981. Member: Royal Fine Art Commn, 1947-54; Royal Commn on Historical Monuments (England), 1953-74; Historic Buildings Council, 1953-78; Arts Council Art Panel, 1953-56; Historical Manuscripts Commn, 1959-; Listed Buildings Cttee Min. of Housing and Local Govt, 1944-66 (Chm., 1960-62); Adv. Council on Public Records, 1968-74; Council, Architectural Assoc., 1940-45; Trustee, National Portrait Gallery, 1966-73. Hon. Fellow, Trinity Hall, Cambridge, 1968; Fellow, UCL. Foreign Hon. Mem., Amer. Acad. of Arts and Sciences, 1967; Chairman, National Council for Diplomas in Art and Design, 1961-70. Hon. DLitt: Leicester, 1959; Oxford, 1963; Hull, 1971; Newcastle, 1973; Hon. DSc Edinburgh, 1968; Hon. Dr, RCA, 1975. Hon. RSA 1982. RIBA Silver Medal (Essay), 1937; RIBA Royal Gold Medal for Architecture, 1976. Publications: Architecture Here and Now (with C. Williams-Ellis), 1934; John Nash, Architect to George IV, 1935; The Bombed Buildings of Britain (with J. M. Richards), 1942 and 1945; Georgian London, 1946, rev. edn 1970; The Architectural Association (Centenary History), 1947; Ben Nicholson (Penguin Modern Painters), 1948; Heavenly Mansions (essays), 1949; Sir John Soane, 1952; Sir Christopher Wren, 1953; Architecture in Britain, 1530-1830 (Pelican History of Art), 1953, 6th edn 1977; New Description of Sir J. Soane's Museum, 1955; The Classical Language of Architecture, 1964, rev. edn 1980; The Book of John Thorpe (Walpole Soc., vol. 40), 1966; Inigo Jones, 1966; Victorian Architecture (four studies in evaluation), 1969; (ed) Concerning Architecture, 1969; The London Building World of the Eighteen-Sixties, 1974; (jt author) The History of the King's Works (ed H. M. Colvin), vol. 3, 1976, vol. 4, 1982; The Life and Work of John Nash, Architect, 1981. Recreation: music. Address: 1 Eton Villas, NW3. T: 01-722 6247. Clubs: Athenæum, Beefsteak.

SUMMERSON, Thomas Hawksley, OBE 1971; JP; b 22 April 1903; s of late Robert Bradley Summerson, Coatham Mundeville, Co. Durham; m 1943, Joan, d of late Walter Rogers, Ashington, Sussex; three s one d. Educ: Harrow. Dir for Steel Castings, Iron and Steel Control, Ministry of Supply, 1940-43; Chairman and Joint Man. Dir, Summerson Holdings Ltd, 1944-65; Chairman: British Steel Founders' Association, 1951-54; NE Industrial and Development Association, 1952-55; Home Affairs and Transport Division, Assoc. of British Chambers of Commerce, 1952-59 (Vice-President, 1954, Deputy President, 1960-62, President, 1962-64); Darlington and N Yorks Local Employment Cttee, 1953-74; Design Panel, British Transport Commn, 1956-63; St Paul's Jarrow Development Trust, 1971-75; Civic Trust for NE, 1970-76; Trustee, Civic Trust, 1970-76; Dep. Chairman, Peterlee Development Corp., 1954-55. Chairman, North Eastern Area Board, British Transport Commission, 1955, and Part-time Member of the Commission, until 1962; Part-time Member, British Railways Board, Jan. 1963-Oct. 1963, and Chm. North Eastern Railway Bd, Jan.-Oct. 1963. Member: Aycliffe New Town Development Corp., 1947-61; Development Areas Treasury Advisory Cttee, 1951-55; President: Tees-side and S-W Durham Chamber of Commerce, 1948-50; Tees-side Industrial Development Board, 1954-57; Member, Independent Television Authority, 1957-60; Mem., North East Development Council, 1965-73. Mem. Darlington RDC, 1937-74 (Chm. 1949-52); Chm. Sedgefield Div. Conservative and Unionist Assoc., 1965-71. JP Co. Durham, 1946; Chm. Darlington County Bench, 1951-53 and 1955-61; High Sheriff, County Durham, 1953-54; DL County Durham, 1958-76. Chm. South Durham Hunt, 1955-73. Recreation: fishing. Address: The Old Manse, Errogie, Inverness. T: Gorthleck 649; 3 Terrett's Place, Upper Street, Islington, N1. T: 01-359 5316. Club: Brooks's.

SUMNER, Donald; see Sumner, W. D. M.

SUMNER, Victor Emmanuel; High Commissioner for Sierra Leone in the United Kingdom and Ambassador to Sweden, Denmark and Norway, since 1980; b 17 April 1929; s of D. R. Sumner; m 1962, Gladys Victoria Small; two s one d. Educ: Fourah Bay Coll., Sierra Leone; Otterbein Coll., Ohio, USA; Laval Univ., Canada. BA, MA. School teacher, 1949-55; Sierra Leone Commonwealth and Foreign Service: Asst Sec., 1961; Sen. Asst Sec., 1965; Dep. Sec., 1968; Counsellor: Washington, 1969; Bonn, 1970; Permanent Secretary: Min. of For. Affairs, 1971; Min. of Health, 1974-76; Asst to Sec. to Pres., 1976-77; Permanent Sec., Min. of For. Affairs, 1977-80. Recreations: fishing, walking, volleyball, football. Address: 33 Portland Place, W1N 3AG. T: 01-636 6483.

SUMNER, (William) Donald (Massey), OBE 1945; QC 1960; **His Honour Judge Sumner;** a Circuit Judge (formerly Judge of County Courts), since 1961; b 13 Aug. 1913; s of Harold Sumner, OBE, Standish, Lancs. Educ: Charterhouse; Sidney Sussex Coll., Cambridge. Called to the Bar, Lincoln's Inn, 1937. Served War of 1939-45 with Royal Artillery; Lt-Col and Asst Adjutant-General, 21st Army Group. Mem. Orpington UDC, 1950-53. Acted as Asst Recorder of Plymouth frequently, 1954-61. MP (C) Orpington Div. of Kent, Jan. 1955-Oct. 1961; PPS to Solicitor-General, Nov. 1959-Oct. 1961. Officier, Ordre de la Couronne and Croix de Guerre (Belgian); Bronze Star Medal (American). Address: 2 Harcourt Buildings, Temple, EC4; East Brabourne House, near Ashford, Kent.

SUMPTION, Anthony James Chadwick, DSC 1944; a Recorder of the Crown Court, since 1980; b 15 May 1919; s of late John Chadwick Sumption and late Winifred Fanny Sumption; m 1946, Hedy Hedigan (marr. diss. 1979); two s two d. Educ: Cheltenham; London Sch. of Economics. Served RNVR, 1939-46; HM Submarines, 1941-45: comd Varangian, 1944; Upright, 1945. Solicitor, 1946; called to the Bar, Lincoln's Inn, 1971. Member (C): LCC, 1949-52; Westminster City Council, 1953-56. Contested (C): Hayes and Harlington, March 1953; Middlesbrough W, 1964. Publications: Taxation of Overseas Income and Gains, 1973, 4th edn 1982; (with Philip Lawton) Tax Planning, 6th edn 1973—10th edn 1982; Capital Gains Tax, 1981. Recreations: painting, angling. Address: 43 Lowndes Square, SW1X 9JL; 3 Verulam Buildings, Gray's Inn, WC1R 5LQ. T: 01-242 3529. Club: Garrick.

SUMSION, Herbert Whitton, CBE 1961; DMus Lambeth; FRCM, Hon. RAM, FRCO, FRSCM; Organist of Gloucester Cathedral, 1928-67; Director of Music, Ladies' College, Cheltenham, 1935-68; b Gloucester, 19 Jan. 1899; m 1927, Alice Hartley Garlichs, BA; three s. Educ: Durham Univ. (MusBac 1920). DMus Lambeth, 1947. Organist and Choirmaster at Christ Church, Lancaster Gate; Director of Music, Bishop's Stortford College; Asst Instructor in Music at Morley Coll., London; Teacher of Harmony and Counterpoint, Curtis Institute, Philadelphia, 1926-28; Conductor Three Choirs Fest., 1928, 1931, 1934, 1937, 1947, 1950, 1953, 1956, 1959, 1962, 1965. Publications: Introduction and Theme for Organ, 1935; Morning and Evening Service in G, 1935; Two pieces for Cello and Piano, 1939 (No 1 arranged for String Orchestra); Magnificat and Nunc Dimittis in G for Boys' Voices, 1953, for Men's Voices, 1953, for Boys' Voices in D, 1973; Cradle Song for Organ, 1953; Benedicite in B flat, 1955; Four Carol Preludes for Organ, 1956; Festival Benedicite in D, 1971; They That Go Down to the Sea in Ships, 1979; Transposition Exercises, 1980; Piano Technique, a Book of Exercises, 1980; There is a Green Hill Far Away, 1981; Two Anthems for Holy Communion, 1981; In Exile (By the Waters of Babylon), 1981. Address: Hartley, Private Road, Rodborough Common, Stroud, Glos GL5 5BT. T: Amberley 3528.

SUNDARAVADIVELU, Neyyadupakkam Duraiswamy; Vice-Chancellor, University of Madras, 1969-75; b 15 Oct. 1912. Educ: Univ. of Madras (MA, Licentiate in Teaching). Asst Panchayat Officer (organising and directing village panchayats), 1935-40; Madras Educnl Subordinate Service, inspection of primary schs, 1940-42; Madras Educnl Service, inspection of secondary schs and gen. direction of primary schs, 1942-54; Dir of Public Instruction, and Comr for Public Examns, Tamil Nadu, 1954-65; Dir of Higher Educn, Tamil Nadu, 1965-66; Dir of Public Libraries, Tamil Nadu, 1954-69; Jt Educnl Adviser to Govt of India, Min. of Educn, New Delhi, 1966-68; Chief Educnl Adviser and Additional Sec. to Govt of Tamil Nadu, Educn Dept, 1968-69; Dir of Collegiate Educn, Tamil Nadu, 1968-69. Visited: UK, 1951, 1962, 1973; USSR, 1961, 1967, 1971, 1973; USA, 1964, 1970; France, 1951, 1968, 1970, 1971, 1973; Malaysia, 1966, 1975; Philippines, 1971, 1972; Ghana, 1971; Canada, 1970; Singapore, 1966, 1975; Hong Kong, 1970, 1975; German Dem. Republic, 1973; participated in various confs, meetings, etc. Mem., Nat. Council of Educnl Research and Trng, New Delhi; Past Mem., Nat. Commn on UNESCO; Mem., Nat. Council for Rural Higher Educn; Mem., Madras Cttee of World Univ. Service (Vice-Pres., Indian Nat. Cttee); Mem., Nat. Bd of Adult Educn; Chm., Southern Languages Book Trust; Mem., Standing Cttee of Inter-Univ. Bd of India and Ceylon, New Delhi; Vice-Pres., Indian Adult Educn Assoc.; Mem., Central Cttee of Tamil Nadu Tuberculosis Assoc.; Chm., Kendriya Vidyalaya, Gill Nagar, Madras. Originator of schemes, Free Mid-day Meals, School Improvement, and Free Supply of Uniforms to School Children, recommended to all Asian countries for adoption (personally commended by Pres. of India, 1960). Padma Shri (presidential award), 1961. Publications: 30 books in Tamil, incl. 13 for children. Address: 90C Shenoynagar, Madras 600030, India. T: Madras 612516.

SUNDERLAND, His Honour (George Frederick) Irvon; DL; a Circuit Judge (formerly Judge of County Courts), 1963-79; b 8 May 1905; o s of Frederick and Mary Jane Sunderland; m 1929, Mary Katharine, d of Arthur John Bowen; three s (and one s decd). Educ: privately. Called to Bar, Gray's Inn, 1932 (H. C. Richards Prizeman); joined Midland Circuit; Assistant Recorder: Birmingham Quarter Sessions, 1960-63; Coventry Quarter Sessions, 1962-63; County Court Judge, Derbyshire, 1964-66; Chairman: Warwick County QS, 1967-71. Deputy Chairman: East Midlands Agricultural Land Tribunal, 1959-63; Birmingham Mental Health Review Tribunal, 1959-63; Chm., Birmingham Local Bar Cttee, 1959-63. DL Warwicks, 1967. Recreations: gardening, the theatre. Address: 70 Woodbourne, Augustus Road, Edgbaston, Birmingham B15 3PJ. T: 021-454 7236.

SUNDERLAND, (Godfrey) Russell; Under Secretary, Overseas Trade Division, Department of Trade, since 1979; b 28 July 1936; s of Allan and Laura Sunderland; m 1965, Greta Jones; one s one d. Educ: Heath Grammar Sch., Halifax; The Queen's College, Oxford (MA). Ministry of Aviation: Asst Principal, 1962; Asst Private Sec. to Minister, 1964; Principal, 1965; HM Diplomatic Service: First Sec. (Civil Air), Beirut, and other Middle East posts, 1969; Principal, Board of Trade (later DTI), 1971; Asst Sec., DTI (later DoT), 1973. Address: Windrush, Silkmore Lane, West Horsley, Leatherhead, Surrey KT24 6JQ. T: East Horsley 2660.

SUNDERLAND, Irvon; see Sunderland, G. F. I.

SUNDERLAND, Russell; see Sunderland, G. R.

SUNDERLAND, Prof. Sir Sydney, Kt 1971; CMG 1961; FAA 1954; Professor of Experimental Neurology, 1961-75, now Emeritus Professor, and Dean of the Faculty of Medicine 1953-71, University of Melbourne; *b* Brisbane, Aust., 31 Dec. 1910; *s* of Harry and Anne Sunderland; *m* 1939, Nina Gwendoline Johnston, LLB; one *s. Educ:* University of Melbourne. BM, BS 1935, DSc 1945, DMed 1946, Melbourne. FRACP 1941; FRACS 1952. Sen. Lectr in Anatomy, Univ. of Melbourne, 1936-37; Demonstrator in Human Anatomy, Oxford, 1938-39; Prof. of Anatomy, Univ. of Melbourne, 1940-61. Visiting Specialist (Hon. Major) 115 Aust. Gen. Mil. Hosp., 1941-45. Mem. Zool. Bd of Vict., 1944-65 (Chm. Scientific Cttee, 1958-62); Dep. Chm., Adv. Cttee to Mental Hygiene Dept, Vict., 1952-63; Mem. Nat. Health and MRC, 1953-69; Chm., Med. Research Adv. Cttee of Nat. Health and MRC, 1964-69. Visiting Prof. of Anatomy, Johns Hopkins Univ., 1953-54; Sec., Div. of Biol Sciences, Aust. Acad. Sci., 1955-58; Member: Nat. Radiation Adv. Cttee, 1957-64 (Chm. 1958-64); Defence Research and Development Policy Cttee, 1957-75; Med. Services Cttee, Dept of Defence, 1957-78; Council, AMA, Victorian Branch, 1960-68; Safety Review Cttee, Aust. Atomic Energy Commn, 1961-74 (Chm.); Aust. Univs Commn, 1962-76; Cttee of Management, Royal Melbourne Hosp., 1963-71; Protective Chemistry Research Adv. Cttee, Dept of Supply, 1964-73 (Chm.); Victorian Med. Adv. Cttee, 1962-71; Board of Walter and Eliza Hall Inst. of Med. Research, 1968-75. Governor, Ian Potter Foundn, 1964-. Trustee: National Museum, 1954-; Van Cleef Foundn, 1971-. Fogarty Scholar in residence, Nat. Inst. of Health, Bethesda, USA, 1972-73. Foundn Fellow, Aust. Acad. of Science, 1954, and rep. on Pacific Science Council, 1957-69. Hon. MD: Tasmania, 1970; Queensland, 1975; Hon. LLD: Melbourne, 1975; Monash, 1977. *Publications:* Nerves and Nerve Injuries, 1968; about 100 articles in scientific jls in Gt Britain, Europe, US and Australia. *Address:* 11 Scotsburn Grove, Toorak, Victoria 3142, Australia. *T:* 203431. *Club:* Melbourne.

SUPHAMONGKHON, Dr Konthi, Kt Grand Cordon of the White Elephant, Kt Grand Cordon, Order of the Crown of Thailand; Kt Grand Commander, Order of Chula Chom Klao; Hon. GCVO 1972; Ambassador of Thailand to the Court of St James's, 1970-76; *b* 3 Aug. 1916; *m* 1951, Dootsdi Atthakravi; two *s* one *d. Educ:* Univ. of Moral and Political Sciences, Bangkok (LLB); Univ. of Paris (Dr-en-Droit). Joined Min. of Foreign Affairs, 1940; Second Sec., Tokyo, 1942-44; Chief of Polit. Div., 1944-48; Dir-Gen., Western Affairs Dept, 1948-50; UN Affairs Dept, 1950-52; Minister to Australia, 1952-56, Ambassador, June 1956-59, and to New Zealand, Oct. 1956-59; Dir-Gen. of Internat. Organizations, 1959-63; Adviser on Foreign Affairs to the Prime Minister, 1962-64; Sec.-Gen., SEATO, 1964-65; Ambassador to Federal Republic of Germany, 1965-70, and to Finland, 1967-70. Frequent Lecturer, 1944-; notably at Thammasat Univ., 1944-52, at National Defence Coll., 1960-62, and at Army War Coll., Bangkok, 1960-63. Holds foreign decorations. *Publication:* Thailand and her relations with France, 1940 (in French). *Recreations:* tennis, golf, swimming. *Address:* c/o Ministry of Foreign Affairs, Bangkok, Thailand. *Clubs:* Travellers', Hurlingham; Royal Wimbledon Golf, Cuddington Golf.

SUPPLE, Prof. Barry Emanuel, FRHistS; Professor of Economic History, and Professorial Fellow of Christ's College, University of Cambridge, since 1981; *b* 27 Oct. 1930; *s* of Solomon and Rose Supple; *m* 1958, Sonia (*née* Caller); two *s* one *d. Educ:* Hackney Downs Grammar Sch.;London Sch. of Econs and Polit. Science (BScEcon 1952); Christ's Coll., Cambridge (PhD 1955). FRHistS 1972. Asst Prof. of Business History, Grad. Sch. of Business Admin, Harvard Univ., 1955-60; Associate Prof. of Econ. Hist., McGill Univ., 1960-62; University of Sussex: Lectr, Reader, then Prof. of Econ. and Social Hist., 1962-78; Dean, Sch. of Social Sciences, 1965-68; Pro-Vice-Chancellor (Arts and Social Studies), 1968-72; Pro-Vice-Chancellor, 1978; University of Oxford: Reader in Recent Social and Econ. Hist., 1978-81; Professorial Fellow, Nuffield Coll., 1978-81. Chm., Consultative Cttee of Assessment of Performance Unit, DES, 1975-80; Member: Council, SSRC, 1972-77; Social Science Fellowship Cttee, Nuffield Foundn, 1974-. Co-editor, Econ. Hist. Rev., 1973-. *Publications:* Commercial Crisis and Change in England, 1600-42, 1959; (ed) The Experience of Economic Growth, 1963; Boston Capitalists and Western Railroads, 1967; The Royal Exchange Assurance: a history of British insurance, 1720-1970, 1970; (ed) Essays in Business History, 1977; articles and revs in learned jls. *Recreations:* tennis, photography. *Address:* 1A Prospect Row, Cambridge. *T:* Cambridge 314428.

SURREY, Archdeacon of; see Barber, Ven. P. E.

SURRIDGE, Sir (Ernest) Rex (Edward), Kt 1951; CMG 1946; retired; *b* 21 Feb. 1899; *s* of late E. E. Surridge, Coggeshall, Essex; *m* Roy (*d* 1982), *d* of late Major F. E. Bradstock, DSO, MC; two *s. Educ:* Felsted; St John's College, Oxford. European War, 1917-20, Lieut 7th Bn DCLI; St John's College, Oxford, 1920-22, Mod. Hist. (Hons); Colonial Admin. Service, 1924, Tanganyika; Assistant Chief Secretary, Tanganyika, 1936; Deputy Chief Secretary, Kenya, 1940; Chief Secretary to Govt of Tanganyika, 1946-51; Salaries Comr, Cyprus, 1953-54; Financial Comr, Seychelles, 1957-58; Salaries Comr, High Commn Territories (South Africa), 1958-59; Salaries Comr, Gibraltar, 1959-60. *Address:* Flat 4, Wytham Abbey, Oxford. *T:* Oxford 44733.

SURTEES, John, MBE 1961; controls companies in automobile construction and development; garage group; *b* 11 Feb. 1934; *s* of late John Norman and

Dorothy Surtees; *m* 1962, Patricia Phyllis Burke (marr. diss. 1979); no *c. Educ:* Ashburton School, Croydon. 5 year engineering apprenticeship, Vincent Engrs, Stevenage, Herts. Motorcycle racing, 1952-60; British Champion, 1954, 1955; World 500 cc Motorcycle Champion, 1956; World 350 and 500 cc Motorcycle Champion, 1958, 1959, 1960. At end of 1960 he retd from motorcycling; motor racing, 1961-72; with Ferrari Co., won World Motor Racing title, 1964; 5th in World Championship, 1965 (following accident in Canada due to suspension failure); in 1966 left Ferrari in mid-season and joined Cooper, finishing 2nd in World Championship; in 1967 with Honda Motor Co. as first driver and develt engr (1967-68); 3rd in World Championship; with BRM as No 1 driver, 1969; designed and built own Formula 1 car, 1970. *Publications:* Motorcycle Racing and Preparation, 1958; John Surtees Book of Motorcycling, 1960; Speed, 1963; Six Days in August, 1968. *Recreations:* music, architecture; interested in most sports. *Address:* c/o Surtees Developments Ltd, Station Road, Edenbridge, Kent. *T:* Edenbridge 863773.

SUSMAN, Maurice Philip, MB, ChM Sydney; FRCS; FRACS; AAMC; Hon. Consulting Surgeon, Sydney Hospital, 1958; Hon. Consulting Thoracic Surgeon, Royal North Shore Hospital, Sydney, 1958; *b* 4 Aug. 1898; *s* of Philip Tasman Susman and Gertrude Lehane; *m* 1934, Ina May Shanahan; one *d. Educ:* Sydney Church of England Grammar School; University of Sydney. *Publications:* some ephemeral light verse, essays and medical and surgical articles. *Recreations:* chess, flying light aircraft, meditating, reading books enjoyed in the past and an occasional new one. *Address:* 22 Bathurst Street, Woollahra, NSW 2025, Australia. *T:* 389 6053. *Club:* Royal Aero (NSW).

SUTCLIFF, Rosemary, OBE 1975; writer of historical novels for adults and children; *b* 14 Dec. 1920; *d* of George Ernest Sutcliff and Elizabeth Sutcliff (*née* Lawton). *Educ:* privately. Carnegie Medal, 1959; The Other Award, 1978. *Publications:* Chronicles of Robin Hood, 1950; The Queen Elizabeth Story, 1950; The Armourer's House, 1951; Brother Dusty-feet, 1952; Simon, 1953; The Eagle of the Ninth, 1954; Outcast, 1955; Lady in Waiting, 1956; The Shield Ring, 1956; The Silver Branch, 1957; Warrior Scarlet, 1958; Rider of the White Horse, 1959; Lantern Bearers, 1959; Houses and History, 1960; Knights Fee, 1960; Rudyard Kipling, 1960; Beowulf, 1961; Dawn Wind, 1961; Sword at Sunset, 1963; The Hound of Ulster, 1963; The Mark of the Horse Lord, 1965; Heroes and History, 1965; The Chief's Daughter, 1967; The High Deeds of Finn McCool, 1967; A Circlet of Oak Leaves, 1968; The Flowers of Adonis, 1969; The Witches' Brat, 1970; Tristan and Iseult, 1971; The Capricorn Bracelet, 1973; The Changeling, 1974; Blood Feud, 1977; Sun Horse, Moon Horse, 1977; Shifting Sands, 1977; Song for a Dark Queen, 1978; The Light Beyond the Forest, 1979; Frontier Wolf, 1980; The Sword and the Circle: King Arthur and the Knights of the Round Table, 1981; Eagle's Egg, 1981; The Road to Camlann, 1981; Blue Remembered Hills (childhood memoir), 1982. *Recreations:* painting, needlework, dogs, travel. *Address:* Swallowshaw, Walberton, Arundel, West Sussex BN18 0PO. *T:* Yapton 551316.

SUTCLIFFE, Edward Davis, QC 1959; **His Honour Judge Sutcliffe;** a Circuit Judge and Additional Judge of the Central Criminal Court, since 1969; *b* 25 Aug. 1917; 3rd *s* of late Richard Joseph and Anne Sutcliffe; *m* 1939, Elsie Eileen Brooks; two *d. Educ:* University College School, Hampstead; Wadham College, Oxford (MA). Served Royal Artillery, 1939-46 (despatches). Called to Bar, Inner Temple, 1946; Bencher, 1966. Recorder of Canterbury, 1968-69, and Hon. Recorder, 1974-. Mem., Criminal Injuries Compensation Board, 1964-69; Legal Assessor, GMC and GDC, 1967-69. Governor: Bedford Coll., London, 1968-76; St Michael's Sch., Otford. Liveryman, Needlemakers' Co. *Address:* Central Criminal Court, Old Bailey, EC4M 7EH.
  See also A. J. C. Britton.

SUTCLIFFE, Prof. Frank Edmund; Emeritus Professor, University of Manchester, since 1982; *b* 8 Aug. 1918; *er s* of Charles Edmund Taylor Sutcliffe and of Ellen Sutcliffe; *m* 1966, Jane Ceridwen Bevan. *Educ:* Huddersfield College; University of Manchester. BA 1940, MA 1948, PhD 1958. Served War of 1939-45, with Royal Artillery and Hong Kong and Singapore Royal Artillery, 1940-46. Univ. of Manchester: Asst Lectr in French, 1946-49; Lecturer in French, 1949-55; Senior Lecturer in French, 1955-61; Professor of Modern French Literature, 1961-66; Prof. of Classical French Literature, 1966-82; Dean of Faculty of Arts, 1972-74. Visiting Professor: Univ. of Kiel, 1968; Université Laval, Québec, 1968-69. Chevalier de l'Ordre National du Mérite, 1965. *Publications:* La Pensée de Paul Valéry, 1955; Guez de Balzac et son temps; littérature et politique, 1960; Le réalisme de Charles Sorel: problèmes humains du XVIIe siècle, 1965; (ed) Discours politiques et militaires by Fr de la Noue, 1967; (trans.) Descartes, Discours de la Méthode, 1968; Politique et culture 1560-1660, 1973; book reviews; contrib. to French Studies, Le Bayou (Houston, Texas), Jahrbuch (Univ. of Hamburg), Bulletin of the John Rylands Library. *Address:* 61 Daisy Bank Road, Victoria Park, Manchester M14 5QL. *T:* 061-224 1864.

SUTCLIFFE, Geoffrey Scott, OBE 1944; TD 1952; *b* 12 June 1912; *o s* of late John Walton Sutcliffe and late Alice Mary Sutcliffe (*née* Scott); *m* 1946, Mary Sylvia, *d* of late George Herbert Kay; two *s* one *d. Educ:* Repton. TA 2nd Lieut, 1939; Lt-Col, 1943; GSO1, AFHQ, N Africa and Italy; served France and Belgium, 1940; N Africa and Italy, 1943-45 (despatches, OBE). Ferodo Ltd, 1932: Works Dir, 1947; Home Sales Dir, 1952; Man. Dir, 1955; Chm., 1956-67; Turner & Newall Ltd: Dir, 1957-75; Jt Man. Dir, 1963-74;

Dep. Chm., 1967-74. *Recreations:* cricket, gardening, reading. *Address:* Hill Farm House, Inkpen Road, Kintbury, Berks RG15 0TX. *T:* Kintbury 681. *Clubs:* Army and Navy, MCC.

SUTCLIFFE, John Harold Vick; Barrister-at-Law; *b* 30 April 1931; *o s* of late Sir Harold Sutcliffe and Emily Theodora Cochrane; *m* 1959, Cecilia Mary, *e d* of Ralph Meredyth Turton; three *s* one *d. Educ:* Winchester Coll.; New Coll., Oxford (Scholar; MA). 2nd Lieut RA, 1950-51. Called to Bar, Inner Temple, 1956; practised until 1960, Midland Circuit. Company Director. Contested (C): Oldham West, 1959; Chorley, Lancs, 1964; Middlesbrough West, 1966. MP (C) Middlesbrough W, 1970-Feb. 1974. Contested (C) Teesside Thornaby, Oct. 1974. *Recreations:* gardening, travel, reading. *Address:* Chapelgarth, Great Broughton, Middlesbrough, Cleveland. *T:* Stokesley 712228.

SUTCLIFFE, Joseph Richard, ED, BSc; Member, Stock Exchange of Melbourne, 1950-74; *b* 25 Jan. 1897; *s* of late A. H. Sutcliffe and Kate Elizabeth Haybittle; *m* 1923, Aileen, *d* of Henry H. Batchelor, NZ; one *s* one *d. Educ:* Palmerston North Boys' High School; Victoria University College, New Zealand. War Service, 1916-19, with NZ Machine Gun Corps and Royal Air Force; Major retd; Headmaster Scots College, Wellington, NZ, 1930-38; Melbourne Church of England Grammar School, 1938-49. *Publication:* Why be a Headmaster?, 1977. *Address:* c/o The Perpetual Executors and Trustees Association of Australia Ltd, 50 Queen Street, Melbourne, Victoria 3000, Australia. *Club:* Melbourne (Melbourne).

SUTCLIFFE, Kenneth Edward; Headmaster, Latymer Upper School, Hammersmith, W6, 1958-71; *b* 24 March 1911; *s* of late Rev. James Sutcliffe; *m* 1937, Nora, *d* of late Charles Herbert Burcham; two *d. Educ:* Manchester Grammar School; King's College, Cambridge (Scholar). BA Modern and Medieval Languages Tripos 1932; MA 1936. Assistant Master, Stockport Grammar School, 1933-38; Assistant Master, Liverpool Institute High School, 1938-46; Headmaster, Cockburn High School, Leeds, 1946-57. Served with Royal Armoured Corps and Intelligence Corps, 1940-46, Captain (General Staff). Lay Reader, dios of Ripon, Guildford, Bath and Wells, 1953-81. *Publications:* German Translation and Composition, 1948; French Translation and Composition, 1951; Fahrt ins Blaue (a German course for schools), 1960. *Address:* Hatherlow, Springfield Drive, Wedmore, Somerset.

SUTCLIFFE, Prof. Reginald Cockcroft, CB 1961; OBE 1942; FRS 1957; BSc, PhD Leeds; Professor of Meteorology, Reading University, 1965-70, now Emeritus Professor; *b* 16 Nov. 1904; 2nd *s* of late O. G. Sutcliffe and late Jessie Sutcliffe (*née* Cockcroft), Cleckheaton, Yorkshire; *m* 1929, Evelyn, *d* of late Rev. William Williams, Halkyn; two *d. Educ:* Whitcliffe Mount Grammar Sch., Cleckheaton; Leeds Univ.; University Coll., Bangor. Professional Asst, Meteorological Office, 1927; Meteorological Office appointments: Malta, 1928-32, Felixstowe, 1932-35; Air Ministry, 1935-37; Thorney Island, 1937-39. Squadron Leader RAFVR, France, 1939-40; Sen. Meteorological Officer, No. 3 Bomber Group RAF, 1941-44; Group Capt., Chief Meteorological Officer AEAF, later BAFO, Germany, 1944-46. Research in Meteorological Office, 1946-; Director of Research, 1957-65. President, Commission for Aerology of World Meteorological Organization, 1957-61; Mem. Adv. Cttee, World Meteorological Organization, 1964-68; Mem. Council, Royal Soc., 1968-70; Pres., Internat. Assoc. of Meteorology, 1967-71; Pres. Royal Meteorological Soc., 1955-57; Hon. Mem., Amer. Meteorological Soc., 1975-; Editor, Quarterly Jl, 1970-73 (Buchan Prize, 1950, Symons Gold Medal, 1955); Charles Chree Medal, Physical Soc., 1959; Internat. Meteorological Organization Prize, 1963. *Publications:* Meteorology for Aviators, 1938; Weather and Climate, 1966; meteorological papers in jls. *Address:* Little Acre, 11 Winslow Road, Nash, Milton Keynes, Bucks MK17 0EJ. *T:* Whaddon 343.

SUTCLIFFE, Air Cdre Walter Philip, CB 1958; DFC 1940; *b* 15 Aug. 1910; *s* of late W. Sutcliffe, Brampton, Cumberland; *m* 1947, Margery Anne Taylor, *d* of W. L. Taylor, Tulse Hill, SW2; one *s. Educ:* Durham School; Royal Air Force Coll., Cranwell. Fleet Air Arm, 1933-35 and 1937-39; Central Flying Sch., 1936. War of 1939-45: Bomber Command, 1939-42, India and Burma, 1942-45 (despatches). RAF Staff College, 1946; Director of Operational Training, Air Ministry, 1948-50; Standing Group, NATO, 1950-51; RAF Station, Wittering, 1953-55; SHAPE, 1955-56; Atomic Weapon Trials, Australia, 1957; Director of Intelligence, Air Ministry, 1958-61; retd April 1961; Officers' Association, 1961-75. Officer, Legion of Merit (USA) 1945. *Address:* The Pond House, Pluckley, Kent. *T:* Pluckley 209.

SUTHERLAND, family name of Countess of Sutherland.

SUTHERLAND, 6th Duke of, *cr* 1833; **John Sutherland Egerton,** TD; DL; Bt 1620; Baron Gower, 1703; Earl Gower, Viscount Trentham, 1746; Marquis of Stafford (1786); Viscount Brackley and Earl of Ellesmere, 1846; *b* 10 May 1915; *o s* of 4th Earl of Ellesmere and Violet (*d* 1976) *e d* of 4th Earl of Durham; *S* father, 1944; *S* kinsman as Duke of Sutherland, 1963; *m* 1st, 1939, Lady Diana Percy (*d* 1978), *yr d* of 8th Duke of Northumberland; 2nd, 1979, Evelyn, *e d* of late Maj. Robert Moubray. Served War of 1939-45 (prisoner). DL Berwickshire, 1955. *Heir: c* Cyril Reginald Egerton [*b* 7 Sept. 1905; *m* 1st, 1934, Mary (*d* 1949), *d* of late Rt Hon. Sir Ronald Hugh Campbell, PC, GCMG; one *s* three *d* ; 2nd, 1954, Mary, *d* of late Sir Sydney Lea, Dunley Hall, Worcestershire]. *Address:* Mertoun, St Boswell's, Roxburghshire; Lingay Cottage, Hall Farm, Newmarket. *Clubs:* White's,

Turf; Jockey (Newmarket).
See also J. M. E. Askew, Lady M. Colville, Baron Home of the Hirsel, Viscount Rochdale.

SUTHERLAND, Countess of (24th in line) *cr* (*c*) 1235; **Elizabeth Millicent Sutherland;** Lady Strathnaver (*c*) 1235; Chief of Clan Sutherland; *b* 30 March 1921; *o c* of Lord Alastair St Clair Sutherland-Leveson-Gower, MC (*d* 1921; 2nd *s* of 4th Duke), and Baroness Osten Driesen (*d* 1931); *niece* of 5th Duke of Sutherland, KT, PC; *S* (to uncle's Earldom of Sutherland and Lordship of Strathnaver), 1963; *m* 1946, Charles Noel Janson, DL, late Welsh Guards; two *s* one *d* (and one *s* decd). *Educ:* Queen's College, Harley Street, W1, and abroad. Land Army, 1939-41; Laboratory Technician: Raigmore Hospital, Inverness, 1941-43; St Thomas' Hospital, SE1, 1943-45. Chairman: Dunrobin Castle Ltd; The Northern Times Ltd. *Recreations:* reading, swimming. *Heir: e s* Lord Strathnaver, *qv. Address:* Dunrobin Castle, Sutherland; House of Tongue, by Lairg, Sutherland; 39 Edwardes Square, W8. *T:* 01-603 0659.

SUTHERLAND, Anthony (Frederic Arthur); Under-Secretary, Department of Employment, retired; *b* 19 Oct. 1916; *e s* of Bertram and Grace Sutherland; *m* 1940, Betty Josephine Glass; one *s* two *d. Educ:* Christ's Hosp.; Gonville and Caius Coll., Cambridge (Classical Schol.). 1st cl. hons Classics, 1938; MA 1944. HM Forces, 1940-45 (Major, Mddx Regt). Asst Prin., Min. of Labour, 1938; Prin., 1943; Prin. Private Sec. to Ministers of Labour, 1948-53; Counsellor (Labour), British Embassy, Rome, 1953-55; Asst Sec., 1955; Imp. Def. Coll., 1960; Under-Sec., 1967. Coronation Medal, 1953; Silver Jubilee Medal, 1977. *Recreations:* philately, bird watching. *Address:* 53 Wieland Road, Northwood, Mddx. *T:* Northwood 22078. *Club:* Civil Service.

SUTHERLAND, Carol Humphrey Vivian, CBE 1970; FBA 1970; Keeper of the Heberden Coin Room, Ashmolean Museum, Oxford, 1957-75; Student of Christ Church, Oxford, 1945-75, Emeritus Student since 1975; *b* 5 May 1908; *s* of late George Humphreys Vivian and Elsie Sutherland; *m* 1933, Monica La Fontaine Porter (*see* Monica La F. Sutherland); no *c. Educ:* Westminster Sch.; Christ Church, Oxford. Barclay Head Prize for Ancient Numismatics, 1934; Asst Keeper of Coins, Ashmolean Museum, Oxford, 1932-52; Deputy Keeper, 1952-57; University Lecturer in Numismatics, 1939-75; DLitt, 1945. Curator of Pictures, Christ Church, 1947-55, 1970-75; President, Royal Numismatic Society, 1948-53; Winslow Lectr, Hamilton Coll., Clinton, NY, 1949 and 1957; Huntington Medallist of the American Numismatic Soc., 1950; Royal Numismatic Soc. Medallist, 1954; Silver Medallist, Royal Soc. of Arts, 1955; ed Numismatic Chronicle, 1953-66; Pres., Commn Internationale de Numismatique, 1960-73; Pres., Centro Internazionale di Studi Numismatici, Naples, 1966-73; Visiting Mem. Inst. for Advanced Study, Princeton, 1962-63, 1968, 1973; Leverhulme Emeritus Fellow, 1977-79; Mem. Royal Mint Advisory Cttee, 1963-; Hon. Member: Société française de numismatique; Société royale de numismatique de Belgique; Commission Internationale de Numismatique; Corresp. Mem., German Archaeol Inst. Governor, Wallingford Sch., 1960-82. Officier, Palmes Académiques (France), 1965. *Publications:* Coinage and Currency in Roman Britain, 1937; (with H. Mattingly, E. A. Sydenham and R. A. G. Carson) The Roman Imperial Coinage, 1939-; The Romans in Spain, 1939; Anglo-Saxon Gold Coinage in the Light of the Crondall Hoard, 1948; (with J. G. Milne and J. D. A. Thompson) Coin Collecting, 1950; Coinage in Roman Imperial Policy, 1951; Art in Coinage, 1955; Gold, 1959; The Cistophori of Augustus, 1970; English Coinage, 600-1900, 1973; Roman Coins, 1974; (with C. M. Kraay) Catalogue of the Coins of the Roman Empire in the Ashmolean Museum, 1976; The Emperor and the Coinage, 1976; articles in Numismatic Chronicle, Jl Roman Studies, etc. *Recreations:* music, gardening. *Address:* Westfield House, Cumnor, Oxford. *T:* Oxford 862178.

SUTHERLAND, Sir (Frederick) Neil, Kt 1969; CBE 1955; MA; Chairman, The Marconi Co. (formerly Marconi's Wireless Telegraph Co. Ltd), and of Marconi Instruments, 1965-69, retired; Director, English Electric Co. Ltd, 1965; *b* 4 March 1900; *s* of late Neil Hugh Sutherland; *m* 1st, 1931, Naruna d'Amorim Jordan (*d* 1970); one *s*; 2nd, 1973, Gladys Jackman. *Educ:* St Catharine's College, Cambridge. MA 1922. Served apprenticeship with English Electric Co. Ltd; Gen. Manager, English Electric Co. in Brazil, 1928; Man. Dir, English Electric (South Africa) Ltd, 1937; Gen. Manager, Marconi's Wireless Telegraph Co. Ltd, 1948; Man. Dir, Marconi Co. Ltd, 1958-65, Chm., 1962-65. *Recreation:* golf. *Address:* 44 Springfield Green, Chelmsford, Essex. *T:* Chelmsford 353980.

SUTHERLAND, Sir Iain (Johnstone Macbeth), KCMG 1982 (CMG 1974); HM Diplomatic Service; Ambassador to the Soviet Union, since 1982; *b* Edinburgh, 15 June 1925; *s* of late Dr D. M. Sutherland, MC, RSA, and Dorothy Johnstone, ARSA; *m* 1955, Jeanne Edith Nutt; one *s* two *d. Educ:* Aberdeen Grammar School; Aberdeen Univ.; Balliol College, Oxford. Served in HM Forces (Lieut, RA), 1944-47. Entered Foreign (now Diplomatic) Service, 1950; Third Secretary, Moscow, 1951; Foreign Office, 1953; First Secretary, Belgrade, 1956; Head of Chancery, Havana, 1959; transf. Washington, 1962; Asst, Northern Dept, FO, 1965; Counsellor and Consul-Gen., Djakarta, 1967-69; Head of South Asian Dept, FCO, 1969-73; Fellow, Centre for Internat. Affairs, Harvard Univ., 1973-74; Minister, Moscow, 1974-76; Asst Under-Sec. of State, FCO, 1976-78; Ambassador to Greece, 1978-82. *Address:* c/o Foreign and Commonwealth Office, SW1. *Club:* Travellers'.

SUTHERLAND, Ian, MA; Director of Education and Training to Health Education Council, since 1971; *b* 7 July 1926; *m* 1951, Virginia Scovil Bliss (marr. diss. 1978); one *s* one *d. Educ:* Wyggeston Grammar School, Leicester; Sidney Sussex College, Cambridge. Assistant Professor of Classics, Univ. of New Brunswick, NB, Canada, 1949-50; Asst Master: Christ's Hospital, 1951-52; Harrow School, 1952-60; Head Master, St John's School, Leatherhead, 1960-70; Dir of Educn, Health Educn Council, 1970-71. FRSA 1969. *Publications:* From Pericles to Cleophon, 1954; (ed) Health Education: perspectives and choices, 1979. *Recreations:* painting, cricket. *Address:* 57 Burntwood Grange Road, Wandsworth Common, SW18 3JY. *Clubs:* United Oxford & Cambridge University, MCC, Free Foresters'.

SUTHERLAND, Dr Ian Boyd; Community Medicine Specialist, Lothian Health Board, since 1980; *b* 19 Oct. 1926; *s* of William Sutherland and Grace Alexandra Campbell; *m* 1950, Charlotte Winifred Cordin; two *d. Educ:* Bradford Grammar Sch.; Edinburgh Univ. MB, ChB; MRCPE, FFCM, DPH. Medical Officer, RAF, 1950-52; Asst MOH, Counties of Roxburgh and Selkirk, 1953-55; Dep. MOH, County and Borough of Inverness, 1955-59; Dep. County MOH, Oxfordshire CC, 1959-60; Asst Sen. MO, Leeds Regional Hosp. Bd, 1960-63. South Western Regional Hosp. Bd: Dep. Sen. Admin. MO, 1963-70; Sen. Admin. MO, 1970-73; Regional MO, S Western RHA, 1973-80. *Recreations:* golf, reading, archaeology. *Address:* 11 Belford Terrace, Edinburgh EH4 3DQ.

SUTHERLAND, James, CBE 1974; Partner, McClure Naismith Brodie & Co., Solicitors, Glasgow, since 1951; *b* 15 Feb. 1920; *s* of James Sutherland, JP and Agnes Walker; *m* 1948, Elizabeth Kelly Barr; two *s. Educ:* Queens Park Secondary Sch., Glasgow; Glasgow Univ. MA 1940, LLB 1948. Served Royal Signals, 1940-46. Examr in Scots Law, 1951-55 and Mercantile Law and Industrial Law, 1968-69, Glasgow Univ.; Chm., Glasgow South Nat. Insce Tribunal, 1964-66; Member: Bd of Management, Glasgow Maternity and Women's Hosps, 1964-74 (Chm. 1966-74); Council, Law Soc. of Scotland, 1959-77 (Vice-Pres. 1969-70; Pres. 1972-74); Council, Internat. Bar Assoc., 1972- (Chm., Gen. Practice Section, 1978-80; Sec.-Gen., 1980-); GDC, 1975-; Vice-Chm., Glasgow Eastern Health Council, 1975-77; Deacon, Incorporation of Barbers, Glasgow, 1962-63; Sec., Local Dental Cttee, City of Glasgow, 1955-65; Dean, Royal Faculty of Procurators in Glasgow, 1977-80. Mem. Court, Univ. of Strathclyde, 1977-. *Recreation:* golf. *Address:* 75 Glencairn Drive, Glasgow G41 4PS. *T:* 041-423 1436. *Clubs:* Caledonian; Western (Glasgow); Royal and Ancient.

SUTHERLAND, Prof. James Runciman, FBA 1953; MA, BLitt; Emeritus Professor of Modern English Literature, University College, London (Lord Northcliffe Professor, 1951-67); *b* Aberdeen, 26 April 1900; *s* of Henry Edward Sutherland, Stockbroker; *m* 1st, 1931, Helen (*d* 1975) *d* of Will H. Dircks; 2nd, 1977, Eve Betts, *widow* of Ernest Betts. *Educ:* Aberdeen Grammar Sch.; Univ. of Aberdeen; Oxford Univ. Lecturer in English, Univ. of Saskatchewan, 1921-23; Merton Coll., Oxford, 1923-25; Chancellor's English Essay Prize, Oxford, 1925; Lecturer in English, University College, Southampton, 1925; BLitt, Oxford, 1927; Lecturer in English, University of Glasgow, 1925-30; Senior Lecturer in English, University College, London, 1930-36; Professor of English Literature, Birkbeck College, London, 1936-44; Prof. of English Language and Literature, Queen Mary College, London, 1944-51; Warton lecturer on English Poetry to the British Academy, 1944; editor of The Review of English Studies, 1940-47. Visiting Professor: Harvard Univ., 1947; Indiana Univ., 1950-51; Univ. California, Los Angeles, 1967-68; Mellon Prof., Univ. of Pittsburgh, 1965; Berg Prof., NY Univ., 1969-70. Sir Walter Scott Lectures, Edinburgh University, 1952; Clark Lectures, Cambridge University, 1956; Alexander Lectures, Toronto University, 1956; Public Orator, University of London, 1957-62; W. P. Ker Memorial Lecture, Glasgow Univ., 1962; Clark Library Fellow, Univ. of California, Los Angeles, 1962-63. Hon. Mem. Modern Language Assoc. of America, 1960. Hon. LLD Aberdeen, 1955; Hon. DLitt Edinburgh, 1968; Hon. Doctor, Liège, 1979. *Publications:* Leucocholy (Poems), 1926; Jasper Weeple, 1930; The Medium of Poetry, 1934; Defoe, 1937; Background for Queen Anne, 1939; The Dunciad, 1943; English in the Universities, 1945; A Preface to Eighteenth Century Poetry, 1948; The English Critic, 1952; The Oxford Book of English Talk, 1953; On English Prose, 1957; English Satire, 1958; English Literature of the late Seventeenth Century, 1969; Daniel Defoe: a critical study, 1971; editions of plays by Nicholas Rowe, Thomas Dekker, John Dryden, William Shakespeare, and of Lucy Hutchinson's Memoirs of the Life of Colonel Hutchinson, 1973; (ed) The Oxford Book of Literary Anecdotes, 1975; contributions to various literary journals. *Recreations:* fishing, second-hand book catalogues. *Address:* Courtenay Pitts, All Saints Lane, Sutton Courtenay OX14 4AG. *T:* Sutton Courtenay 237.

SUTHERLAND, Dame Joan, AC 1975; DBE 1979 (CBE 1961); soprano; *b* 7 Nov. 1926; *d* of McDonald Sutherland, Sydney, NSW; *m* 1954, Richard Bonynge, *qv*; one *s. Educ:* St Catherine's, Waverley, Sydney. Début as Dido in Purcell's Dido and Aeneas, Sydney, 1947; subsequently concerts, oratorios and broadcasts throughout Australia. Came to London, 1951; joined Covent Garden, 1952, where she remained resident soprano for 7 years; won international fame with début as Lucia di Lammermoor, Covent Garden, 1959, and by early 1960s had sung throughout the Americas and Europe. Has specialised throughout her career in the popular and lesser-known bel canto operatic repertoire of 18th and 19th centuries, and has made many recordings. *Relevant publications:* Joan Sutherland, by R. Braddon, 1962; Joan Sutherland, by E. Greenfield, 1972; La Stupenda, by B. Adams, 1980.

Recreations: reading, gardening, needlepoint. *Address:* c/o Ingpen & Williams, 14 Kensington Court, W8.

SUTHERLAND, John Brewer; (3rd Bt *cr* 1921, but does not use the title); *b* 19 Oct. 1931; *s* of Sir (Benjamin) Ivan Sutherland, 2nd Bt, and Marjorie Constance Daniel (*d* 1980), *yr d* of Frederic William Brewer, OBE; *S* father, 1980; *m* 1958, Alice Muireall, *d* of late W. Stamford Henderson, Kelso; three *s* one *d. Educ:* Sedbergh; St Catharine's Coll., Cambridge. *Heir: s* Peter William Sutherland, *b* 18 May 1963. *Address:* Ross Farm, Belford, Northumberland.

SUTHERLAND, Sir Maurice, Kt 1976; Leader of Cleveland County Council, 1973-77 and since 1981 (Leader of Opposition, 1977-81); *b* 12 July 1915; *s* of Thomas Daniel and Ada Sutherland; *m* 1st, 1941, Beatrice (*née* Skinner); one *s*; *m* 2nd, 1960, Jane Ellen (*née* Bell); one step-*d. Educ:* Stockton Secondary Sch. War service with Green Howards and RCS, N Africa and NW Europe. Solicitor, 1937-. Mem. Stockton Borough Council, 1957-67; Chm., Teesside Steering Cttee, 1966-67; Leader of Labour Party, Teesside County Borough Council, 1967-74; Mayor of Teesside, 1973-74. Chm., Northern Econ. Planning Council, 1977-79. *Recreations:* cricket, walking, chess, politics. *Address:* 15 Valley Drive, Leven Road, Yarm, Cleveland. *T:* Eaglescliffe 782799.

SUTHERLAND, Monica La Fontaine; author; *d* of C. M. McAnally, Hon. Canon of Norwich, and Mabel Adelaide McAnally (*née* La Fontaine); *m* 1st, R. W. Porter, Hon. Canon of Chelmsford, Vicar of East Ham; two *d* (one *s* killed in action); 2nd, C. H. V. Sutherland, *qv*; no *c. Educ:* Eastbourne; Paris. Formerly: served in National Fire Service and Red Cross Prisoner-of-War Books Section, 1941-45. Vice-Chm., Oxford Diocesan Council for Social Work, 1972-77. *Publications:* La Fontaine, 1953; Louis XIV and Marie Mancini, 1956; The San Francisco Disaster, 1959; various newspaper and magazine articles. *Recreations:* travel, languages. *Address:* Westfield House, Cumnor, Oxford. *T:* Cumnor 2178.

SUTHERLAND, Sir Neil; see Sutherland, Sir F. N.

SUTHERLAND, Prof. (Norman) Stuart, MA, DPhil; Professor of Experimental Psychology, University of Sussex, since 1965; *b* 26 March 1927; *s* of Norman McLeod Sutherland; *m* 1966, Jose Louise Fogden; two *d. Educ:* Magdalen Coll., Oxford. BA Hons Lit. Hum. 1949 and PPP 1953; John Locke Scholar 1953. Fellow; Magdalen Coll., 1954-58; Merton Coll., 1962-64; Oxford Univ. Lectr in Exper. Psychol., 1960-64. Vis. Prof., MIT, 1961-62, 1964-65. Dir, William Schlackman Ltd, 1968-81. *Publications:* Shape Discrimination by Animals, 1959; (ed jtly) Animal Discrimination Learning, 1969; (with N. J. Mackintosh) Mechanisms of Animal Discrimination Learning, 1971; Breakdown: a personal crisis and a medical dilemma, 1976; (ed) Tutorial Essays in Psychology, vol. 1, 1977, vol. 2, 1979; Discovering the Mind, 1982; scientific papers mainly on perception and learning. *Address:* Centre for Research on Perception and Cognition, Sussex University, Brighton BN1 9QG. *T:* Brighton 606755.

SUTHERLAND, Ranald Iain, QC (Scot) 1969; *b* 23 Jan. 1932; *s* of J. W. and A. K. Sutherland, Edinburgh; *m* 1964, Janice Mary, *d* of W. S. Miller, Edinburgh; two *s. Educ:* Edinburgh Academy; Edinburgh University. MA 1951, LLB 1953. Admitted to Faculty of Advocates, 1956; Advocate Depute, 1962-64, 1971-77; Standing Junior Counsel to Min. of Defence (Army Dept), 1964-69. Mem., Criminal Injuries Compensation Bd, 1977-. *Recreations:* sailing, shooting. *Address:* 38 Lauder Road, Edinburgh. *T:* 031-667 5280. *Clubs:* New (Edinburgh); Royal Forth Yacht.

SUTHERLAND, Scott, RSA 1970; Head of Sculpture Department, Duncan of Jordanstone College of Art, Dundee, 1947-75, retired; *b* 15 May 1910; *s* of Major David Sutherland, MC, TD; *m* 1942; one *s* two *d. Educ:* Wick Academy; Wick High Sch.; Edinburgh Coll. of Art; Ecole des Beaux Arts, Paris. Works include: Commando Memorial, Spean Bridge, 1952; Black Watch Memorial, 1959; Hercules Linton 'Cutty Sark' Meml, Inverbervie, 1969; Leaping Salmon fountain gp for Norie-Miller Walk, Perth, 1971; The Beacon Lighter, silver statuette presented to HM the Queen by ROC, 1977. *Address:* 17 Norwood, Newport-on-Tay, Fife. *T:* Newport-on-Tay 3336.

SUTHERLAND, Prof. Stuart; see Sutherland, Prof. N. S.

SUTHERLAND, Veronica Evelyn; see Beckett, V. E.

SUTHERLAND-HARRIS, Sir Jack (Alexander), KCVO 1968; CB 1959; Second Crown Estate Commissioner, 1960-68; *b* 8 May 1908; *s* of late Lieut-Colonel A. S. Sutherland-Harris, DL, JP, Burwash, Sussex; *m* 1934, Rachel Owen Jones, *yr d* of late Capt. Owen Jones, CBE, Worplesdon, Surrey; two *s* two *d. Educ:* Winchester Coll.; New Coll., Oxford. Entered Min. of Agriculture and Fisheries as Asst Principal, 1932; Principal Private Secretary to Minister of Agriculture and Fisheries, 1941-43; Asst Sec., 1943-50; Under-Sec., 1950-60. *Address:* Old Well Cottage, Bury, Pulborough, West Sussex. *T:* Bury 465. *Club:* Royal Commonwealth Society.

SUTTIE, Sir (George) Philip Grant-, 8th Bt, *cr* 1702; *b* 20 Dec. 1938; *o s* of late Maj. George Donald Grant-Suttie and Marjorie Neville, *d* of Capt. C. E. Carter, RN, of Newfoundland; *S* cousin, 1947; *m* 1962, Elspeth Mary (marr. diss. 1969), *e d* of Maj.-Gen. R. E. Urquhart, *qv* ; one *s. Educ:* Sussex

Composite High School, NB, Canada; Macdonald College, McGill University, Montreal. *Recreations:* flying, fishing, farming, forestry. *Heir:* s James Edward Grant-Suttie, b 29 May 1965. *Address:* (seat) Balgone, North Berwick; Sheriff Hall, North Berwick, East Lothian. *T:* 2569. *Club:* Puffin's (Edinburgh).

SUTTILL, Dr Margaret Joan, (Mrs G. A. Rink); d of Ernest Montrose and Caroline Hyde; m 1st, 1935, F. A. Suttill, DSO, LLB (d 1945); two s; 2nd, 1949, G. A. Rink, QC, qv. *Educ:* Royal Free Hospital Medical School. MB, BS 1935; MRCP (London) 1972. Director, Medical Dept, and Chief Medical Advr, British Council, retired. *Recreations:* music (especially opera), reading, walking, bird watching, consumer problems. *Address:* 173 Oakwood Court, W14. *T:* 01-602 2143.

SUTTON, Alan John; Executive Director (Industry and Investment), Welsh Development Agency, since 1979; b 16 March 1936; s of William Clifford Sutton and Emily Sutton (née Batten); m 1957, Glenis (née Henry); one s one d. *Educ:* Bristol Univ. BSc (Hons) Elec. Engrg; MIEE. Design, Production and Trials Evaluation of Guided Missiles, English Electric Aviation Ltd, 1957-63; Design, Production, Sales and General Management of Scientific Digital, Analogue and Hybrid Computers, Solartron Electronic Group Ltd, 1963-69; International Sales Manager, Sales Director, of A. B. Electronic Components Ltd, 1969-73; Managing Director, A. B. Connectors, 1973-76; Industrial Dir, Welsh Office, 1976-79. *Recreations:* squash, golf. *Address:* 56 Heol-y-Delyn, Lisvane, Cardiff CF4 5SR. *T:* (office) Treforest 2666; (home) Cardiff 753194.

SUTTON, Denys; Editor of Apollo since 1962; b 10 Aug. 1917; s of Edmund Sutton and Dulcie Laura Wheeler; m 1940, Sonja Kilbansky (marr. diss.); 1952, Gertrud Kœbke-Knudson (marr. diss.); 1960, Cynthia Sassoon; one s one d. *Educ:* Uppingham School; Exeter Coll., Oxford (BA, BLitt). Foreign Office Research Dept, 1940-46; Sec., Internat. Commn for Restitution of Cultural Material, 1946; Fine Arts Specialist at UNESCO 1948; Visiting lectr at Yale Univ., 1949. Organiser of exhibitions: Bonnard Exhibition, RA, 1966; France in the 18th Century, RA, 1968; British Art, Columbus, Ohio, 1971; Venice Rediscovered, Wildenstein, London, 1972; Irish Art, Columbus, Ohio, 1974; Fragonard, Tokyo, 1980; Boucher, Tokyo, 1982. Formerly: Art Critic to Country Life and to Financial Times; Saleroom Correspondent of Daily Telegraph. Mem. Exec. Cttee, Nat. Art Collections Fund. Corresp. Membre de l'Institut. Chevalier, Légion d'Honneur. *Publications:* Watteau's Les Charmes de la Vie, 1946; Matisse, 1946; Picasso, Blue and Pink Periods, 1948; French Drawings of the 18th Century, 1949; American Painting, 1949; Flemish Painting, 1950; Bonnard, 1957; Christie's since the War, 1959; André Derain, 1959; Nicholas de Staël, 1960; Gaspard Dughet, 1962; Toulouse-Lautrec, 1962; Titian, 1963; Nocturne; The Art of Whistler, 1964; Sergio de Castro, 1965; Triumphant Satyr, 1966; Whistler: Paintings, Drawings, Etchings and Water-colours, 1966; Vélazquez, 1967; An Italian Sketchbook by Richard Wilson RA, 1968; Van Dongen, 1971; (ed and introd) Letters of Roger Fry, 1973; Manguin, 1974; Walter Sickert: a biography, 1976; Fads and Fancies, 1980; Delights of a Dilettante, 1980; R. L. Douglas, Connoisseur of Art and Life, 1980; The World of Sacheverell Sitwell, 1981; *introductions:* Vlaminck, Dangerous Corner, 1961; R. A. M. Stevenson, Velasquez, 1962; *jointly:* Artists in 17th Century Rome (with Denis Mahon), 1955; Catalogue of French, Spanish and German schools in Fitzwilliam Museum, Cambridge (with J. W. Goodison), 1960; Painting in Florence and Siena (with St John Gore), 1965; Richard Ford in Spain (with Brinsley Ford), 1974; contribs to magazines, etc. *Recreation:* theatre. *Address:* 22 Chelsea Park Gardens, SW3. *T:* 01-352 5141; Westwood Manor, Bradford-on-Avon, Wilts. *Club:* Travellers'.

SUTTON, Sir Frederick (Walter), Kt 1974; OBE 1971; Founder and Chairman of Directors of the Sutton Group of Companies; b 1 Feb. 1915; s of late William W. Sutton and Daisy Sutton; m 1934; three s; m 1977, Morna Patricia Smyth. *Educ:* Sydney Technical College. Motor Engineer, founder and Chief Executive of the Sutton group of Companies; Mem. Bd of Directors, and life Governor, Royal New South Wales Inst. for Deaf and Blind Children. *Recreations:* flying, going fishing, boating. *Address:* 114 Bourke Street, East Sydney, NSW, Australia. *T:* Sydney 357-1777. *Clubs:* Royal Aero of NSW (Life Member); Royal Automobile of Australia; Royal Automobile of Victoria; American (Sydney).

SUTTON, Janet Vida; see Watson, J. V.

SUTTON, Prof. John, FRS 1966; FGS; DSc, PhD; ARCS; Professor of Geology, since 1958 and Pro-Rector, since 1980 (Pro-Rector, External Development, 1979-80), Imperial College of Science and Technology, London; b 8 July 1919; s of Gerald John Sutton; m 1949, Janet Vida Watson, qv. *Educ:* King's School, Worcester; Royal College of Science, London. Service with RAOC and REME, 1941-46. Imperial College: Research, 1946-48; Lecturer in Geology, 1948; Reader in Geology, 1956; Head of Geol. Dept, 1964-74; Dean, Royal Sch. of Mines, 1965-68, 1974-77. A Trustee, BM (Nat. Hist.), 1976-81. Mem., NERC, 1977-79. Mem. Council, Univ. of Zimbabwe, 1980-. President, Geologists' Association, 1966-68. A Vice-Pres., Royal Society, 1975-77; Pres., Remote Sensing Soc., 1977-. For. Mem., Royal Netherlands Acad., 1978; Hon. For. Fellow, Geol Soc. of Amer. Bigsby Medal, Geological Society of London, 1965 (jointly with Mrs Sutton); Murchison Medal, 1975. *Publications:* papers dealing with the Geology of the Scottish Highlands. *Recreation:* gardening. *Address:* Imperial College of

Science and Technology, SW7; Hartfield, Sandy Drive, Cobham, Surrey. *T:* Oxshott 3129.

SUTTON, Air Vice-Marshal John Matthias Dobson, CB 1981; Assistant Chief of Defence Staff (Operations), since 1982; b 9 July 1932; s of Harry Rowston Sutton and late Gertrude Sutton; m 1954 (marr. diss. 1968); one s one d; m 1969, Angela Faith Gray; two s. *Educ:* Queen Elizabeth's Grammar Sch., Alford, Lincs. Joined RAF, 1950; pilot trng, commnd, 1951; served on Fighter Sqdns, UK and Germany; Staff Coll., 1963; OC 249 Sqdn, 1964-66; Asst Sec., Chiefs of Staff Cttee, 1966-69; OC 14 Sqdn, 1970-71; Asst Chief of Staff (Policy and Plans), HQ 2 ATAF, 1971-73; Staff, Chief of Def. Staff, 1973-74; RCDS, 1975; Comdt Central Flying Sch., 1976-77; Asst Chief of Air Staff (Policy), 1977-79; Dep. Comdr, RAF Germany, 1980-82. *Recreations:* golf, sailing. *Address:* c/o National Westminster Bank Ltd, 58 Broadway, Leigh-on-Sea, Essex. *Clubs:* Royal Air Force; Liphook Golf.

SUTTON, Rt. Rev. Keith Norman; see Kingston-upon-Thames, Bishop Suffragan of.

SUTTON, Leslie Ernest, MA, DPhil Oxon; FRS 1950; Fellow and Lecturer in Chemistry, Magdalen College, Oxford, 1936-73, Fellow Emeritus, 1973; Reader in Physical Chemistry, 1962-73 (University Demonstrator and Lecturer in Chemistry, 1945-62); b 22 June 1906; o c of Edgar William Sutton; m 1st, 1932, Catharine Virginia Stock (d 1962), er d of Wallace Teall Stock, Maplewood, NY, USA; two s one d; 2nd, 1963, Rachel Ann Long, er d of Lt-Col J. F. Batten, Swyncombe, Henley-on-Thames; two s. *Educ:* Watford Gram. Sch.; Lincoln Coll., Oxford (Scholar). 1st Class Hon. School Chemistry, 1928; research at Leipzig Univ., 1928-29, and at Oxford University; Fellow by Examination, Magdalen College, 1932-36; Rockefeller Fellow, California Inst. of Technology, 1933-34; Tilden Lectr, Chemical Soc., 1940; Visiting Prof., Heidelberg Univ., 1960, 1964, 1967. Vice-Pres., Magdalen College, 1947-48. Hon. Sec., Chemical Soc., 1951-57, Vice-Pres., 1957-60. Chm., Lawes Agricl Trust Cttee, Rothamsted Experimental Stn, 1982- (Treas., 1978-82). Hon. DSc Salford, 1973. Meldola Medal, RIC, 1932; Harrison Prize, Chemical Soc., 1935. *Publications:* papers in scientific jls; (as scientific Editor) Tables of Interatomic Distances and Configuration in Molecules and Ions, 1958, 1964; Chemische Bindung und Molekülstruktur, 1961. *Address:* 62 Osler Road, Headington, Oxford OX3 9BN. *T:* Oxford 66456.

SUTTON, Rt. Rev. Peter (Eves); see Nelson, NZ, Bishop of.

SUTTON, Dr Peter Morgan; Director, Public Health Laboratory Service Centre for Applied Microbiology and Research, Porton Down, since 1979; b 21 June 1932; s of Sir Graham Sutton, CBE, FRS and Lady Sutton (née Doris Morgan); m 1959, Helen Ersy Economides; two s two d. *Educ:* Bishop Wordsworth Sch., Salisbury; Wrekin Coll., Wellington; University Coll. and University Coll. Hosp. Med. Sch., London. House Surgeon and House Physician, UCH, 1956-57; Graham Scholar in Pathology, Univ. of London, 1958-59; on academic staff of UCH Med. Sch., 1960-65; Vis. Asst Prof. of Pathology, Univ. of Pittsburg, USA, 1966-67; Hon. Consultant Pathologist, UCH, 1967-79; Reader in Pathology, Univ. of London, 1971-79; Vice-Dean, UCH Med. Sch., 1973-78. Sometime Examr in Pathology, Univ. of London and RCS. *Publications:* The Nature of Cancer, 1962; various papers on cancer and liver pathology. *Recreations:* English literature, history of science. *Address:* Idmiston Manor, 28 Church Road, Idmiston, Salisbury, Wilts SP4 0AZ. *T:* Idmiston 610298.

SUTTON, Philip John, ARA 1977; b 20 Oct. 1928; m 1954; one s three d. *Educ:* Slade Sch. of Fine Art, UCL. One-man exhibitions: Roland Browse and Delbanco (now Browse and Darby) Gallery, London, annually 1953-56, biennially 1958-82; Geffrye Museum, London, 1959; Leeds City Art Gallery, 1960; Newcastle-on-Tyne, 1962; Bradford, 1962; Edinburgh, 1962; Sydney, 1963, 1966, 1970, 1973; Perth, 1963; Battersea, 1963, 1972; Detroit, 1967; Bristol, 1970; Folkestone, 1970, 1974; Cape Town, 1976; Johannesburg, 1976; Falmouth Sch. of Art, 1977; Royal Acad. (Diploma Gall.), London, 1977; Annexe Gall., London, 1979; Holsworthy Gall., London, 1980; David Jones Gall., Sydney, 1980; Annexe Art Gall., 1980; Minden Gall., CI, 1981; Bonython Art Gall., Adelaide, 1981. *Recreations:* swimming, running. *Address:* 10 Soudan Road, Battersea, SW11 4HH. *T:* 01-622 2647.

SUTTON, Dr Richard, MB, MRCP, FACC; Consultant Cardiologist: Westminster and St Stephen's Hospitals, London, since 1976; to British Airways, since 1976; b 1 Sept. 1940; s of late Dick Brasnett Sutton and Greta Mary (née Leadbeter); m 1964, Anna Gunilla (née Cassö); one s. *Educ:* Gresham's Sch.; King's Coll., London; King's Coll. Hosp. (MB, BS 1964). MRCP 1967; FACC 1975. Gen. medical trng followed graduation; career in cardiology began at St George's Hosp., London, 1967; Fellow in Cardiol., Univ. of NC, 1968-69; Registrar, Sen. Registrar, then Temp. Consultant, National Heart Hosp., London, 1970-76. Hon. Cons. Cardiologist: Italian Hosp., London, 1977-; SW Thames RHA, 1979-; St Luke's Hosp., London, 1980-. Member: British Medical Assoc.; British Cardiac Soc.; British Pacing Group (Co-Founder, Mem. Council and Past Hon. Sec.). Governors' Award, Amer. Coll. of Cardiol., 1979 (Scientific Exhibit, Physiol Cardiac Pacing), and 1982 (1st Prize; Scientific Exhibit, 5 yrs of Physiol Cardiac Pacing). *Publications:* articles on many aspects of cardiology incl. cardiac pacing, coronary artery disease, left ventricular function, and assessment of pharm. agents, in Circulation, Amer. Jl of Cardiol., Amer. Heart Jl, Brit. Heart Jl,

Lancet, and BMJ, 1967-. *Recreations:* opera, foreign travel, swimming. *Address:* 149 Harley Street, W1N 1HG. *T:* 01-935 4444.

SUTTON, Richard Lewis; Regional Director, Northern Region, Department of Industry, 1974-81; *b* 3 Feb. 1923; *s* of William Richard Sutton and Marina Susan Sutton (*née* Chudleigh); *m* 1944, Jean Muriel (*née* Turner). *Educ:* Ealing County Grammar Sch. Board of Trade, 1939. Served War: HM Forces (Lieut RA), 1942-47. Asst Trade Comr, Port of Spain, 1950-52; BoT, 1953-62; Trade Comr, Kuala Lumpur, 1962-66; Monopolies Commn, 1966; BoT, 1967-68; Dir, British Industrial Develt Office, New York, 1968-71; Regional Dir, West Midland Region, Dept of Trade and Industry, 1971-74. *Recreations:* music, walking, bridge. *Address:* Barton Toft, Dowlish Wake, Ilminster, Somerset. *T:* Ilminster 5127.

SUTTON, Sir Richard (Lexington), 9th Bt *cr* 1772; farmer; *b* 27 April 1937; *s* of Sir Robert Lexington Sutton, 8th Bt, and of Gwynneth Gwladys, *o d* of Major Arnold Charles Gover, MC; *S* father, 1981; *m* 1959, Fiamma, *o d* of G. M. Ferrari, Rome; one *s* one *d. Educ:* Stowe. *Recreations:* skiing, sailing, swimming, tennis. *Heir: s* David Robert Sutton, *b* 26 Feb. 1960. *Address:* Moorhill, Langham, Gillingham, Dorset. *T:* Gillingham 2665.

SUTTON, Robert William, CB 1962; OBE 1946; retired as Superintendent and Chief Scientific Officer, Services Electronics Research Laboratories, Baldock, Herts, 1946-70; *b* 13 Nov. 1905; *s* of late William Sutton; *m* 1951, Elizabeth Mary, *d* of George Maurice Wright, CBE, Chelmsford; one *s* two *d. Educ:* Brighton College; Royal College of Science, London University. Formerly with Ferranti Ltd, and then with E. K. Cole Ltd until 1938. Admiralty from 1939. *Address:* 33 Hitchin Street, Baldock, Herts. *T:* Baldock 3373.

SUTTON, Shaun Alfred Graham, OBE 1979; television producer and writer; Head of Drama Group, BBC Television, 1969-81; *b* 14 Oct. 1919; *s* of Eric Graham Sutton and Beryl Astley-Marsden; *m* 1948, Barbara Leslie; one *s* three *d. Educ:* Latymer Upper Sch.; Embassy Sch. of Acting, London. Actor and Stage Manager, Q, Embassy, Aldwych, Adelphi, Arts, Criterion Theatres, 1938-40. Royal Navy, 1940-46, Lieut RNVR. Stage Dir, Embassy and provincial theatres, 1946-48; Producer, Embassy, Buxton, Croydon Theatres, 1948-50; toured S Africa as Producer, 1950; Producer, Embassy, Ipswich, Buxton, 1951-52; entered BBC TV Service, 1952; produced and wrote many children's TV plays and serials; directed many series incl. Z Cars, Softly Softly, Sherlock Holmes, Kipling, etc; Head of BBC Drama Serials Dept, 1966-69; dramatised Rogue Herries and Judith Paris for BBC Radio, 1971; Producer, BBC TV Shakespeare series, 1982-. Fellow, Royal TV Soc.; Mem., BAFTA. *Publications:* A Christmas Carol (stage adaptation), 1949; Queen's Champion (children's novel), 1961; The Largest Theatre in the World, 1982. *Recreations:* gardening, walking. *Address:* The Firs, Marsh Lane, Mill Hill, NW7. *T:* 01-959 2613; The Cottage, Brewery Road, Trunch, Norfolk. *Club:* Lord's Taverners.

SUTTON, Sir Stafford William Powell F.; *see* Foster-Sutton.

SUTTON, Thomas Francis; Director and Executive Vice-President, J. Walter Thompson Co., New York, since 1965; Executive Vice-President, JWT Group Inc., New York, responsible for Euro Advertising, since 1982; *b* 9 Feb. 1923; *m* 1950, Anne Fleming (marr. diss. 1974); one *s* two *d*; *m* 1982, Maki Watanabe. *Educ:* King's School, Worcester; St Peter's College, Oxford. Research Officer, British Market Research Bureau Ltd, 1949-51; Advertising Manager, Pasolds Ltd, 1951-52; Managing Director, J. Walter Thompson GmbH, Frankfurt, Germany, 1952-59; Dir, J. Walter Thompson Co. Ltd, 1960-73, Man. Dir, 1960-66; Dir, internat. operations, J. Walter Thompson, NY, 1966-72; Man. Dir, J. Walter Thompson Co. Japan, Tokyo, 1972-80; Exec. Vice-Pres./Dir, J. Walter Thompson Asia/Pacific, 1980-81. FIPA; FIS; Fellow, Royal Statistical Soc. Internat. Advertising Man of the Year Award, 1970. *Recreations:* chess, riding. *Address:* 18 rue de Berri, 75008 Paris, France.

SUTTON, William Godfrey; Principal and Vice-Chancellor, University of the Witwatersrand, Johannesburg, 1954-62; *b* 28 March 1894; *s* of late William Godfrey Sutton, and late Mary Sutton (*née* Bennett); *m* 1st, 1954, Aletta McMenamin (*née* Wilson) (*d* 1967); 2nd, 1970, Olive Henwood (*née* Hiles) (*d* 1973). *Educ:* King Edward VII School, Johannesburg; University of Cape Town. Served European War, 1916-18, in German East African Campaign; Asst Engineer, Union Irrigation Dept, 1918-26; attached to US Reclamation Service, 1921-22; Professor of Civil Engineering, Univ. of the Witwatersrand, Johannesburg, 1926-54; War of 1939-45 Gen. Manager Central Organisation for Tech. Trg, Dept of Defence, 1941-44; Chief Technical Advisor, Dept of Commerce and Industries, 1944-45. Former Mem., Exec. Council, Univs of British Commonwealth. President: South African Institute of Engineers, 1936; SA Instn of Civil Engrs, 1945; Associated Scientific and Tech. Socs of SA, 1951; former Mem. Council, ICE, London. Hon. LLD Witwatersrand, 1963. KStJ 1972. *Recreation:* bowls. *Address:* 48 Eastwood Road, Dunkeld, Johannesburg, South Africa. *T:* 788-3053. *Clubs:* Rand, Country (Johannesburg).

SUTTON CURTIS, John, CBE 1974; Chairman, Workington Saw Mills Ltd, 1966-76; *b* 2 July 1913; *s* of Harold Ernest Curtis; *m* 1936, Muriel Rose Hastwell; one *s. Educ:* Watford Grammar School. Served War of 1939-45, Royal Artillery. Thames Board Mills Ltd: Director, 1958; Vice-Chm., 1965;

Dep. Chm. and Man. Dir, 1966-69; Chm., 1969-76. Chm., Assoc. of Board Makers, 1965-70; Pres., British Paper and Board Makers' Assoc., 1971-73 (Dep. Pres., 1973-75); Pres., Confederation of European Pulp, Paper and Board Industries (CEPAC), 1974-75 (Vice-Pres., 1973). Paper Industry Gold Medal, 1973. *Recreation:* motoring. *Address:* Covertside, 115a Langley Road, Watford, Herts WD1 3RP. *T:* Watford 26375.

SUVA, Archbishop of, (RC), since 1976; **Most Rev. Petero Mataca;** *b* 28 April 1933; *s* of Gabriele Daunivucu and Akeneta Taina. *Educ:* Holy Name Seminary, Dunedin, NZ; Propaganda Fidei, Rome. Priest, Rome, 1959; Vicar-Gen. of Archdiocese of Suva, 1966; Rector of Pacific Regional Seminary, 1973; Auxiliary Bishop of Suva, 1974. Pres., Episcopal Conf. of South Pacific, 1981. *Address:* Archbishop's House, Box 393, Suva, Fiji. *T:* 22851.

SUYIN; *see* Han Suyin.

SUZMAN, Mrs Helen; MP (Progressive Federal Party), Houghton, Republic of South Africa; *b* 7 Nov. 1917; *d* of late Samuel Gavronsky; *m* Dr M. M. Suzman, FRCP; two *d. Educ:* Parktown Convent, Johannesburg; Univ. of Witwatersrand (BCom). Lectr in Economic History, Univ. of Witwatersrand, 1944-52. Elected MP 1953; United Party 1953-61; Progressive Party (later Progressive Reform Party and Progressive Federal Party), 1961-. Hon. Fellow: St Hugh's Coll., Oxford, 1973; London Sch. of Economics, 1975. Hon. DCL Oxford, 1973; Hon. LLD: Harvard, 1976; Witwatersrand, 1976; Columbia, 1977; Smith Coll., 1977; Brandeis, 1981; Hon. DHL Denison, 1982. *Recreations:* golf, swimming, fishing, bridge. *Address:* 49 Melville Road, Hyde Park, Sandton, 2146 Transvaal, South Africa. *T:* 788-2833. *Clubs:* Lansdowne; River, Wanderers, Wanderers Golf, Houghton Golf, Glendower (Johannesburg).

SUZMAN, Janet; actress; *b* 9 Feb. 1939; *d* of Saul Suzman; *m* 1969, Trevor Nunn, *qv*; one *s. Educ:* Kingsmead Coll., Johannesburg; Univ. of the Witwatersrand (BA); London Acad. of Music and Dramatic Art. Roles played for Royal Shakespeare Co. incl.: Joan La Pucelle in The Wars of the Roses, 1963-64; Lulu in The Birthday Party, Rosaline, Portia, 1965; Ophelia, 1965-66; Katharina, Celia, and Berinthia in The Relapse, 1967; Beatrice, Rosalind, 1968-69; Cleopatra and Lavinia, 1972-73; Clytemnestra and Helen of Troy in The Greeks, 1980. Kate Hardcastle, and Carmen in The Balcony, Oxford Playhouse, 1966; Hester in Hello and Goodbye, King's Head Theatre, 1973; Masha in Three Sisters, Cambridge, 1976; Good Woman of Setzuan, Newcastle, 1976, Royal Court, 1977; Hedda Gabler, Duke of York's, 1977; Boo-hoo, Open Space, 1978; The Duchess of Malfi, Birmingham, 1979. *Films:* A Day in the Death of Joe Egg, 1970; Nicholas and Alexandra, 1971; The Priest of Love, 1980; The Draughtsman's Contract, 1981; Plays for BBC and ITV incl.: St Joan, 1968; Three Sisters, 1969; Macbeth, 1970; Hedda Gabler, 1972; Twelfth Night, 1973; Antony and Cleopatra, 1974; Miss Nightingale, 1974; Clayhanger, serial, 1975-76. Acad. Award Nomination, Best Actress, 1971; Evening Standard Drama Awards, Best Actress, 1973, 1976; Plays and Players Award, Best Actress, 1976. Member: Theatres Trust, 1977; LAMDA Council. *Address:* William Morris (UK) Ltd, 147/149 Wardour Street, W1V 3TB. *T:* 01-734 9361..

SVENNINGSEN, Nils Thomas; Grand Cross, Order of Dannebrog, Denmark; *b* 28 March 1894; *s* of Anders Svenningsen (Norwegian), Average Adjuster, and Anna Svenningsen (*née* Bennet, Swede); *m* 1922, Eva (*née* Larsen) (*d* 1960); one *d. Educ:* University of Copenhagen. Candidatus juris, 1917; practised as Assistant to a Danish Advocate in Copenhagen; entered Min. of Justice, Copenhagen, 1918. Joined Danish Foreign Service, 1920; Secretary to Danish Legation in Berlin, 1924-30; then different posts in Danish Foreign Ministry. Permanent Under-Secretary of State for Foreign Affairs, 1941-45; and 1951-61; Danish Ambassador to: Stockholm, 1945-50; Paris, 1950-51; the Court of St James's, 1961-64; retd. Chm., Swedish-Norwegian Commn on reindeer grazing, 1964. Hon. GBE 1957. *Recreation:* riding. *Address:* Overgaden oven Vandet 50, Copenhagen K, Denmark. *T:* 541566.

SVENSON, Mrs Sven G.; *see* Grey, Beryl.

SVOBODA, Prof. Josef; Chief Scenographer, National Theatre, Prague, CSSR, since 1948; Professor at Academy of Applied Arts, since 1968; *b* Čáslav, 10 May 1920; *m* 1948, Libuše Svobodová; one *d. Educ:* Gymnasium; special sch. for interior architecture; Academy of Applied Arts (architecture). EXPO 58, Brussels: success with Laterna Magica; EXPO 67, Montreal: polyvision, polydiaekran. He co-operates with many theatres all over the world (Metropolitan Opera, New York; Covent Garden; Geneva; Bayreuth; Frankfurt, etc.); Chief of Laterna Magica, experimental scene of National Theatre, Prague, 1973-. Laureate of State Prize, 1954; merited Artist of CSSR, 1966; National Artist of CSSR, 1968; Hon. RA, London, 1969. *Publications:* relevant monographs: Josef Svoboda (by Theatre Inst.) 1967 (Prague); Josef Svoboda (by Denis Bablet) 1970 (France); The Scenography of J. Svoboda (by Jarka Burian) 1971, 1974 (USA); Teatr Josefa Svobody (by V. Berjozkin) 1973 (USSR). *Recreations:* theatre, photography, creative arts, music, literature. *Address:* Filmařská 53517, 150 00 Prague 5, CSSR.

SWAFFIELD, Sir James (Chesebrough), Kt 1976; CBE 1971; RD 1967; DL; Director-General and Clerk to the Greater London Council, Clerk to Inner London Education Authority and Clerk of Lieutenancy for Greater London, since 1973; solicitor; *b* 16 Feb. 1924; *s* of Frederick and Kate Elizabeth

Swaffield, Cheltenham; *m* 1950, Elizabeth Margaret Ellen, 2nd *d* of A. V. and K. E. Maunder, Belfast; two *s* two *d*. *Educ:* Cheltenham Grammar Sch.; Haberdashers' Aske's Hampstead Sch.; London Univ. (LLB); MA Oxon 1974. RNVR, 1942-46. Articled Town Clerk, Lincoln, 1946-49; Asst Solicitor: Norwich Corp., 1949-52; Cheltenham Corp., 1952-53; Southend-on-Sea Corp., 1953-56; Dep. Town Clerk, subseq. Town Clerk and Clerk of Peace, Blackpool, 1956-62; Sec., Assoc. of Municipal Corpns, 1962-72. Past Pres., Soc. of Local Authority Chief Executives; Vice-Pres., RIPA; Member: Council, Law Soc.; Internat. City Management Assoc.; Standing Technological Conf., EEC. Hon. Fellow, Inst. Local Govt Studies, Birmingham Univ. Member: Ct of Governors, Admin. Staff Coll.; Bd of Governors, Nat. Inst. for Social Work; Council, St Paul's Cathedral Trust. DL Greater London, 1978. OStJ. *Address:* 10 Kelsey Way, Beckenham, Kent. *Clubs:* Reform, Naval.

SWAIN, Air Commodore (Francis) Ronald Downs, CB 1954; CBE 1946 (OBE 1941); AFC 1937; psa; retired; *b* 31 Aug. 1903; *s* of late Major Charles Sanchez de Pina Swain, TD, Southsea, Hants; *m* 1938, Sarah Mitchell, *d* of Charles H. Le Fèvre, Washington, DC; three *d*. *Educ:* Stonyhurst Coll. Joined Royal Air Force, 1922; Wing Comdr, 1939; Air Commodore, 1949. Commanded Cairo-Rhodesia Flight, 1933; gained World High Altitude Record, 1936 (AFC); served War of 1939-45 (despatches, OBE, CBE); Air Officer Commanding No 28 Group, RAF, 1949-50; Senior Air Staff Officer and Deputy Head of Air Force Staff, British Joint Services Mission, Washington, 1950-54, retired 1954.

SWAIN, Freda Mary, FRCM; composer and pianist; *b* Portsmouth, Hants; *d* of Thomas Swain and Gertrude Mary (Allen) Swain; *m* Arthur Alexander (pianist, composer, Prof. at RCM) (*d* 1969). *Educ:* St John's Southsea (private sch.); Matthay Pianoforte Sch. (under Dora Matthay); RCM. Won Associated Board Exhibition for piano, Ada Lewis Scholarship for piano (RAM) and Portsmouth-Whitcombe Scholarship for Composition (RCM), all at an early age; chose latter and studied under Sir Charles Villiers Stanford at RCM and (during last year) under Arthur Alexander (piano); Sullivan Prize for composition and Ellen Shaw Williams Prize for piano; Prof. of piano, RCM, for 14 years; founded British Music Movement, later NEMO concerts, with which former is now incorporated; founded NEMO Music Teaching Centre (Oxon & Bucks), Matthay Method, 1971. Extensive tours of S Africa and Australia (lecturing and piano), mainly on behalf of British music. FRCM 1963. *Works in manuscript* include: orchestral; concertos (two piano, one clarinet); chamber music (two string quartets, one pianoforte quartet, violin and piano sonata, Poems for violin and piano, 'The River' for violin and piano, Sonata for violin solo, Summer Rhapsody for viola and piano, Rhapsody No 2 for viola and piano, piano Sonata for right hand, Three Movements for violin and piano, 'Quiddities' for piano); anthems and wedding anthems; hymns, various; Second Chance, one-act opera; Perceptions, Whirling Wheels and Flourish (for 2 pianos); two piano pieces for left hand alone; over 109 songs; arrangements of works for two pianos, various folk songs, pieces for recorder and piano. *Published and reproduced works:* Carol of the Seasons; Te Deum, Jubilate (both for choir and organ); Cantata in Memoriam; Bird of the Wilderness (Song Cycle); Hymns; Ballet-Scherzo for three pianos; Setting of Psalms 150 and 121 (voice and organ); Two Sonatas, Prelude and Toccata (piano); Unseen Heralds (choral with piano); Sing to Heaven (choir and piano, negro spiritual style); 2 piano sonatas. *Works for occasions:* Fanfare and Anthem for 70th anniv. Tormead Sch., 1976, Guildford Cath.; A Queen's Prayer, to words by Elizabeth I, Fanfare for a Queen, and Royal Fanfare, first performance Royal Jubilee Concert, Guildford Cath., 1977. *Publications* include: *Piano:* Humoresque; Mountain Ash; An English Idyll; Two S African Impressions; Autumn Landscape; Wayward Waltz; Marionette on Holiday; Croon of the Sea; Musical Box; Windmill; *Clarinet:* The Willow Tree; Two Contrasts; Waving Grass; Laburnum Tree; Three Whimsies (solo); *Oboe and Piano:* Paspy; Fantasy-Suite; *Piano and Flute or Violin:* Tambourin Gai; *Organ:* English Pastoral; *Hymn:* Breathe on me; *Songs:* The Lark on Portsdown Hill; The Green Lad from Donegal; settings of poems by Coppard, Strong, de la Mare, Housman, Shelley, Burns, Bridges and many others; 5 Shakespeare sonnets; part songs and numerous teaching pieces; *Choral:* A Chinnor Carol (unaccomp. voices); Sweet Content (SATB and piano); Two Christmas Carols; A Gaelic Prayer (choir and organ). *Recreations:* reading, the English countryside. *Address:* High Woods, Chinnor Hill, Chinnor, Oxfordshire. *T:* Kingston Blount 51285.

SWAIN, Henry Thornhill, CBE 1971; RIBA; County Architect, Nottinghamshire County Council, since 1964; *b* 14 Feb. 1924; *s* of Thornhill Madge Swain and Bessie Marion Swain; *m*; three *d*. *Educ:* Bryanston Sch.; Architectural Assoc. (Hons Dipl.). Served with RN, 1943-46. Herts County Architect's Dept, 1949; worked in primary school group; Notts CC, 1955; Group Leader i/c initial develt of CLASP construction; Dep. County Architect, 1958. *Publications:* many articles in architectural jls. *Recreation:* sailing. *Address:* 50 Loughborough Road, West Bridgford, Nottingham. *T:* Nottingham 818059.

SWAINE, Edward Thomas William, CMG 1968; MBE 1952; Director, Exhibitions Division, Central Office of Information, 1961-71, retired; *b* 17 July 1907; *s* of Edward James Swaine; *m* 1942, Ruby Louise (*née* Tickehurst) (*d* 1974). Entered Govt Service, Min. of Information, 1940; Festival of Britain, 1948-52; Dir of Exhibns, British Pavilion, Montreal World Exhibn, 1967; UK Dep. Comr-Gen. and Dir of Exhbns, Japan World Exhbn, 1970.

Recreation: photography. *Address:* 6/12 Northwood Hall, Highgate, N6. *T:* 01-340 4392.

SWAINSON, Eric, CBE 1981; Managing Director, IMI plc, since 1974; *b* 5 Dec. 1926; *m* 1953, Betty Heywood; two *d*. *Educ:* Sheffield Univ. (BMet 1st cl. Hons; W. H. A. Robertson medal, 1959). Joined Imperial Chemical Industries Metals Div. (now IMI), 1946; Technical Officer, Res. Dept, 1946-53; Manager, Titanium Melting Plant, 1953-56; Asst Manager, Technical Dept, 1956-59; Gen. Manager and Man. Dir, Lightning Fasteners, 1961-69; Dir, IMI, 1969-; Asst Man. Dir, 1972-74. Dir, Birmingham Broadcasting, 1973-; Reg. Dir, Birmingham and West Midlands, Lloyds Bank, 1979-. Member: Review Bd for Govt Contracts, 1978-; NEDC Cttee on Finance for Industry, 1978-; Council, CBI, 1975-; W Midlands Reg. Council, CBI, 1973- (Chm. 1976-78). Pro-Chancellor, Aston Univ., 1981-. *Address:* 268 Station Road, Knowle, Solihull, W Midlands B93 0ES. *T:* Knowle 3102.

SWALLOW, Comdt Daphne Patricia; Director, Women's Royal Naval Service, since 1982; Hon. ADC to the Queen, since 1982; *b* 25 Sept. 1932; *d* of Captain Ralph Geoffrey Swallow, RN retd and Daphne Lucy Regina Swallow (*née* Parry). *Educ:* St George's Sch., Ascot; Portsmouth Polytechnic. Joined WRNS as Signal Wren, 1950; qualified as WRNS Communications Officer, 1955; served in HMS Drake and Malta, 1956-58; Oslo, Portsmouth, HMS Mercury, Northwood and Gibraltar, 1958-67; HMS Pembroke and HMS Heron, 1968-71; passed Naval Staff Course, 1972; HMS Dauntless, 1973-74; C-in-C Naval Home Comd and MoD, 1974-76; National Defence College Latimer Course, 1976-77; Staff of Naval Secretary, 1977; Command Personnel Officer to C-in-C Naval Home Comd, 1977-79; Dep. Dir, WRNS, 1979-81; Staff Officer Training Coordination and Comd WRNS Officer to C-in-C Naval Home Comd, 1981-82. *Recreations:* tennis, dressmaking and needlework, reading, theatre, opera, music. *Address:* Archway Block South, Old Admiralty Building, Spring Gardens, SW1A 2BE.

SWALLOW, John Crossley, PhD; FRS 1968; physical oceanographer, Institute of Oceanographic Sciences (formerly National Institute of Oceanography), since 1954; *b* 11 Oct. 1923; *s* of Alfred Swallow and Elizabeth (*née* Crossley); *m* 1958, Mary Morgan (*née* McKenzie); one *step d*. *Educ:* Holme Valley Gram. Sch.; St John's Coll., Cambridge. Admty Signal Estabt, 1943-47; research in marine geophysics, at Cambridge and in HMS Challenger, 1948-54; work on ocean circulation, in RRS Discovery II, and in RRS Discovery, and other vessels, 1954-. Rossby Fellow, Woods Hole Oceanographic Inst., 1973-74. Murchison Grant of RGS, 1965. Foreign Hon. Mem., Amer. Acad. of Arts and Sciences, 1975. Holds American awards in oceanography. *Publications:* papers on physical oceanography. *Address:* Institute of Oceanographic Sciences, Brook Road, Wormley, Godalming, Surrey GU8 5UB. *T:* Wormley 4141.

SWALLOW, Sydney; Chief Procurement Officer, and Chief Executive, Consumer Products, British Telecom, since 1981; *b* 29 June 1919; *s* of William and Charlotte Lucy Swallow; *m* 1950, Monica Williams; one *s*. *Educ:* Woking County Sch.; St Catharine's Coll., Cambridge (MA). Mines Dept, Board of Trade, 1940-42. Served War: Royal Engineers (Survey), 1942-46. Nat. Coal Bd, 1946-59; Central Electricity Generating Bd, 1959-65; Associated Electrical Industries Ltd, 1965-68; General Electric Co. Ltd, 1968; Dir of Supplies, GLC, 1968-77; Senior Dir, Procurement, Post Office, 1977-81. Chm., Educn Cttee, Inst. of Purchasing and Supply, 1967-77; Visiting Prof., Univ. of Bradford Management Centre, 1972-75; Vis. Fellow, ASC, 1976-80. FInstPS. *Publications:* various articles on purchasing and supply in professional jls. *Recreations:* narrowboats, cricket. *Address:* 101 Muswell Hill Road, N10. *T:* 01-444 8775.

SWALLOW, Sir William, Kt 1967; FIMechE; *b* 2 Jan. 1905; *s* of William Turner Swallow, Gomersal, Yorks; *m* 1929, Kathleen Lucy Smith; no *c*. *Educ:* Batley and Huddersfield Technical Colleges. Draughtsman, Karrier Motors Ltd, 1923; senior draughtsman, chief body designer, Short Bros, 1926; Gilford Motors Ltd, 1930; development engineer, Pressed Steel Co., 1932; chief production engineer, Short Bros, 1943; development engineer, General Motors Overseas Operations, New York, 1947; i/c manufacturing staff, General Motors Ltd, 1948; gen. man., A. C. Sphinx Spark Plug Div. of Gen. Motors Ltd, 1950; Managing Director, General Motors Ltd, 1953, Chairman, 1958; Chm., Vauxhall Motors Ltd, Luton, Beds, 1961-66 (Man. Dir, 1961-65). Mem., Advisory Council on Technology, 1968-70; Chairman: NPL Adv. Bd, 1969-; Shipbuilding and Shiprepairing Council, 1967-71; EDC for Hotel and Catering Industry, 1966-72; Shipbuilding Industry Bd, 1966-71. Governor, Ashridge Coll., 1965-72. ARAeS; MSAE. President: SMMT, 1964-65 (Dep. Pres. 1966-67); Inst. Road Tspt Engrs, 1966-68. *Address:* Alderton Lodge, Ashridge Park, Berkhamsted, Herts. *T:* Little Gaddesden 2284.

SWAMINATHAN, Dr Monkombu Sambasivan, FRS 1973; Director-General, International Rice Research Institute, Manila, since 1982; *b* 7 Aug. 1925; *m* Mina Swaminathan; three *d*. *Educ:* Univs of Kerala, Madras and Cambridge. BSc Kerala, 1944; BSc (Agric.) Madras, 1947; Assoc. IARI 1949; PhD Cantab, 1952. Responsible for developing Nat. Demonstration Project, 1964, and for evolving Seed Village concept; actively involved in develt of High Yielding Varieties, Dryland Farming and Multiple Cropping Programmes. Vice-Pres., Internat. Congress of Genetics, The Hague, 1963; Gen. Pres., Indian Science Congress, 1976; Mem. (Agriculture), Planning Commn, 1980-82 (formerly Dir-Gen., Indian Council of Agricultural Research). First Zakir Hussain Meml Lectr, 1970; UGC Nat. Lectr, 1971;

lectures at many internat. scientific symposia. Foreign Associate, US Nat. Acad. of Scis; For. Mem., All Union Acad. of Agricl Scis, USSR; Hon. Mem., Swedish Seed Assoc.; Hon. Fellow, Indian Nat. Acad. of Sciences. FNA. Shanti Swarup Bhatnagar Award for contribs in Biological Scis, 1961; Mendel Centenary Award, Czechoslovak Acad. of Scis, 1965; Birbal Sahni Award, Indian Bot. Soc., 1965; Ramon Magsaysay Award for Community Leadership, 1971; Silver Jubilee Award, 1973, Meghnath Saha Medal, 1981, Indian Nat. Science Acad. Padma Shri, 1967; Padma Bhushan, 1972. Hon. DSc from sixteen universities. *Publications:* numerous scientific papers. *Address:* International Rice Research Institute, PO Box 933, Manila, The Philippines.

SWAN, Conrad Marshall John Fisher, MVO 1978; PhD; York Herald of Arms, since 1968; Registrar, College of Arms, since 1982; Genealogist: of Order of the Bath, since 1972; of Grand Priory, OStJ, since 1976; *b* 13 May 1924; *yr s* of late Dr Henry Peter Swan, Major RAMC and RCAMC, of BC, Canada and Colchester, Essex, and of Edna Hanson Magdalen (*née* Green), Cross of Honour Pro Ecclesia et Pontifice; *m* 1957, Lady Hilda Susan Mary Northcote, Dame of Honour and Devotion, SMO Malta, 1979, and of Justice of SMO of Constantine St George, 1975, *yr d* of 3rd Earl of Iddesleigh; one *s* four *d*. *Educ:* St George's Coll., Weybridge; Sch. of Oriental and African Studies, Univ. of London; Univ. of Western Ontario; Peterhouse, Cambridge. BA 1949, MA 1951, Univ. of W Ont; PhD 1955, Cambridge. Served Europe and India (Capt. Madras Regt, IA), 1942-47. Assumption Univ. of Windsor, Ont.: Lectr in History, 1955-57; Asst Prof. of Hist., 1957-60; Univ. Beadle, 1957-60. Rouge Dragon Pursuivant of Arms, 1962-68. On Earl Marshal's staff for State Funeral of Sir Winston Churchill and Investiture of HRH Prince of Wales, 1969. In attendance: upon HM The Queen at Installation of HRH Prince of Wales as Great Master of Order of the Bath, 1975; during Silver Jubilee Thanksgiving Service, 1977; on Australasian Tour, 1977; Gentleman Usher-in-Waiting to HH the Pope, GB visit, 1982. Woodward Lectr, Yale, 1964; Centennial Lectr, St Thomas More Coll., Univ. of Saskatchewan, 1967; Inaugural Sir William Scott Meml Lectr, Ulster-Scot Hist. Foundn, 1968; first Herald to execute duties in Tabard across Atlantic (Bermuda, 1969) and in S Hemisphere (Brisbane, Qld, 1977); to visit Australia, 1970, S America, 1972, Thailand, Japan, 1973, NZ, 1976. World lecture tours, 1970, 1973, 1976. Adviser to PM of Canada on establishment of Nat. Flag of Canada and Order of Canada, 1964-67. Hon. Citizen, State of Texas; Freemanships in USA; Freeman: St George's, Bermuda, 1969; City of London, 1974. Fellow, 1976, Hon. Vice-Pres. and a Founder, Heraldry Soc. of Canada; Fellow, Geneal. Soc. of Victoria (Australia), 1970; FSA 1971. Liveryman and Freeman, Gunmakers' Co., 1974. KStJ 1976. Kt of Honour and Devotion, SMO of Malta, 1979 (Kt of Grace and Devotion, 1964) (Genealogist Br. Assoc., 1974-). *Publications:* Heraldry: Ulster and North American Connections, 1972; Canada: Symbols of Sovereignty, 1977; many articles in learned jls on heraldic, sigillographic and related subjects. *Recreations:* hunting, driving (horse drawn vehicles), rearing ornamental pheasants and waterfowl, marine biology. *Address:* College of Arms, Queen Victoria Street, EC4V 4BT. *T:* 01-248 1850; Boxford House, Boxford, near Colchester. *T:* Boxford (Suffolk) 210208.

SWAN, Maj.-Gen. Dennis Charles Tarrant, CB 1953; CBE 1948; *b* 2 Sept. 1900; *s* of late Lt-Col C. T. Swan, IA; *m* 1930, Patricia Ethel Mary Thorne (*d* 1960); one *s* one *d*. *Educ:* Wellington Coll., Berks; Royal Military Academy, Woolwich. Commissioned as 2nd Lt RE, 1919; served War of 1939-45 (despatches twice): with BEF France, Feb.-May 1940; CRE 1 Burma Div., 1941; Comdt No 6 Mech. Eqpt Group, IE, 1944; Chief Engineer, 15 Ind. Corps, 1945; District Chief Engineer, BAOR, 1946, Chief Engineer, 1948; Director of Fortification and Works, War Office, 1952-55, retired. Captain 1930; Adjutant, 36 (Mx) AA Bn, 1935; Major, 1938; Lt-Col, 1945; Colonel 1947; Brig. 1948; Maj.-Gen., 1952. Pres., Instn of Royal Engineers, 1961-65. *Address:* 15 Lancastrian Grange, Tower Street, Chichester, West Sussex. *T:* Chichester 786899.

SWAN, Dermot Joseph, MVO 1972; HM Diplomatic Service, retired; HM Consul-General, Marseilles, 1971-77; *b* 24 Oct. 1917; *s* of Dr William Swan and Anne Cosgrave; *m* 1947, Jeanne Labat; one *d*. *Educ:* St George's, Weybridge; University Coll., London Univ. BA (Hons) French and German. Served War, HM Forces, 1939-46. HM Foreign (later Diplomatic) Service: Vice-Consul, Marseilles, 1947; Saigon, 1949; Foreign Office, 1951; Brazzaville, 1951; Budapest, 1953; FO 1955; First Sec., 1958; Head of Chancery, Phnom Penh, 1959, and Budapest, 1961; UK Mission, New York, 1963; FO (later FCO), 1967; Counsellor, Special Asst to Sec.-Gen. of CENTO, Ankara, 1969. *Recreations:* concerts and opera; tennis, ice-skating, skiing, swimming. *Address:* Résidence du Golf, 66120 Font Romeu, France. *Club:* Roehampton.

SWAN, Hon. John (William David), JP; MP (United Bermuda Party) Paget East, since 1972; Premier of Bermuda, since 1982; *b* 3 July 1935; *s* of late John N. Swan and of Margaret E. Swan; *m* 1965, Jacqueline A. D. Roberts; one *s* two *d*. *Educ:* West Virginia Wesleyan Coll. (BA). Mem., Lloyd's of London. Salesman, Real Estate, Rego Ltd, 1960-62; Founder, Chairman and Chief Exec., John W. Swan Ltd, 1962-. Minister for: Marine and Air Services; Labour and Immigration, 1977-78; Home Affairs, 1978-82; formerly: Parly Sec. for Finance; Chairman: Bermuda Hosps Bd; Dept of Civil Aviation. Mem., Young Presidents Organization Inc. *Recreations:* sailing, tennis. *Address:* Grape Bay, Paget, Bermuda. *T:* (809) 292-1301. *Clubs:* Hamilton Rotary, Royal Bermuda Yacht (Bermuda).

SWAN, Sheriton Clements; *b* 15 Jan. 1909; *s* of late Sir Charles Sheriton Swan, Stocksfield-on-Tyne; *m* 1936, Rosalind Maitland, *d* of late D. S. Waterlow; two *s* one *d*. *Educ:* Cambridge Univ. Went to Architectural Assoc. in London to complete architectural training; joined firm of Swan, Hunter and Wigham Richardson, Ltd, in 1935; retired 1971. *Address:* Milestone Cottage, Wall, Hexham, Northumberland NE46 4ED. *T:* Humshaugh 319.

SWAN, Lt-Col William Bertram, CBE 1968; TD 1955; JP; farmer since 1933; Lord-Lieutenant of Berwickshire since 1969; *b* 19 Sept. 1914; *er s* of late N. A. Swan, Duns, Berwickshire; *m* 1948, Ann Gilroy, *d* of late G. G. Hogarth, Ayton, Berwickshire; four *s*. *Educ:* St Mary's Sch., Melrose; Edinburgh Academy. Served 1939-42 with 4 Bn KOSB (UK and France) and 1942-45 with IA. Pres., Nat. Farmers Union of Scotland, 1961-62; Pres., Scottish Agric. Organisation Society Ltd, 1966-68; Mem., Development Commn, 1964-76. Pres., Scottish Cricket Union, 1972-73. JP 1964. *Recreation:* sport. *Address:* Blackhouse, Reston, Eyemouth, Berwickshire. *T:* Cumleage 242.

SWANN, Baron *cr* 1981 (Life Peer); **Michael Meredith Swann;** Kt 1972; MA, PhD; FRS 1962; FRSE 1952; Principal and Vice-Chancellor, University of Edinburgh, 1965-73; Chairman, BBC, 1973-80; Chancellor, University of York, since 1979; *b* 1 March 1920; *er s* of late M. B. R. Swann, MD, Fellow of Gonville and Caius Coll., Cambridge, and late Marjorie (*née* Dykes) (she *m* 2nd, Sir Sydney Roberts, he *d* 1966); *m* 1942, Tess, ARCM, ARCO, *d* of late Prof. R. M. Y. Gleadowe, CVO, Winchester and late Cecil (*née* Rotton); two *s* two *d*. *Educ:* Winchester (Fellow, 1979); Gonville and Caius College, Cambridge (Hon. Fellow, 1977). Served War, 1940-46, in various capacities, mainly scientific (despatches, 1944). Fellow of Gonville and Caius College, Cambridge, 1946-52; University Demonstrator in Zoology, Cambridge, 1946-52; Professor of Natural History, University of Edinburgh, 1952-65 (Dean, Faculty of Science, 1963-65). Member: Adv. Council on Educn in Scotland, 1957-61; Fisheries Adv. Cttee, Scottish Commn, 1957-65. Council St George's School for Girls, 1959-75; Edinburgh Univ. Court, 1959-62; MRC, 1962-65; Cttee on Manpower Resources, 1963-68; Council for Scientific Policy, 1965-69; SRC, 1969-73; Adv. Council, Civil Service Coll., 1970-76; Council, St George's House, Windsor, 1975-; Scientific Foundn Bd, RCGP, 1978-; House of Lords Select Cttee on Sci. and Technology, Sci. and Govt Sub-Cttee, 1981-82. Chairman: Nuffield Foundation Biology Project, 1962-65; Jt Cttee on Use of Antibiotics in Animal Husbandry and Veterinary Medicine, 1967-68; Scottish Health Services Scientific Council, 1971-72; Jt Cttee of Inquiry into the Veterinary Profession, 1971-75; Council for Science and Society, 1974-78; Council for Applied Science in Scotland, 1978-80; Technical Change Centre, 1980- (Chm. Board); Cttee of Inquiry into Educn of Children from Ethnic Minority Gps, 1981-. Author of Swann reports on Scientific Manpower, 300 GEV Accelerator, Antibiotics, Veterinary Profession. Director: Inveresk Res. Internat., Midlothian, 1969-72; New Court Natural Resources Ltd, 1973-; Roy. Acad. of Music, 1980-; Charities Investment Managers Ltd, 1981-; M & G Group plc, 1981. Mem. Bd of Trustees, Wellcome Trust, 1973-; Trustee, BM (Nat. Hist.), 1982-. Pres., Aslib, 1982-. Governor, Ditchley Foundn, 1975-. Provost, Oriel Coll., Oxford, 1980-81. FIBiol; Hon. FRCSE 1967; Hon. FRCPE 1972; Hon. ARCVS 1976. Hon. LLD Aberdeen, 1967; DUniv York, 1968; Hon. DSc Leicester, 1968; Hon. DLitt Heriot Watt, 1971. *Publications:* papers in scientific journals. *Recreations:* gardening, sailing. *Address:* 23 Sheffield Terrace, W8; Tallat Steps, Coln St Denys, near Cheltenham. *T:* Fossebridge 533. *Clubs:* Athenæum; New (Edinburgh).

See also Bishop of London.

SWANN, Sir Anthony (Charles Christopher), 3rd Bt *cr* 1906; CMG 1958; OBE 1950; Minister for Defence and Internal Security, Kenya, 1959-63; *b* 29 June 1913; *s* of Sir (Charles) Duncan Swann, 2nd Bt,; *m* 1940, Jean Margaret Niblock-Stuart; one *s*. *Educ:* Eton College; New College, Oxford. Joined Colonial Service, Kenya, 1936. Served, 1940-43, with King's African Rifles (Major). District Commissioner, Kenya, 1954-56; Provincial Commissioner, Kenya, 1955-59. Chairman East African Land Forces Organisation, 1959-60. *Recreations:* music, reading, fishing, shooting. *Heir: s* Michael Christopher Swann [*b* 23 Sept. 1941; *m* 1965, Hon. Lydia Mary Hewitt, *e d* of Viscount Lifford, *qv*; two *s* one *d*]. *Address:* 23 Montpelier Square, SW7. *Clubs:* Army and Navy, Pratt's.

SWANN, Benjamin Colin Lewis; Controller, Finance, British Council, 1975-79, retired; *b* 9 May 1922; *s* of Henry Basil Swann and Olivia Ophelia Lewis; *m* 1946, Phyllis Julia Sybil Lewis; three *s* one *d*. *Educ:* Bridgend County School. CA. RAFVR, 1941; Transatlantic Ferry, 1942; Flt Lieut, Transport Command, 1944; Flt Supervisor, BOAC, 1946. Apprentice Chartered Accountant, 1950; Audit Asst, George A. Touche & Co., 1953; Treasury Acct, Malaya, 1954; Financial Adviser, Petaling Jaya, 1956; Partner, Milligan Swann & Co., Chartered Accountants, Exeter, 1957; British Council, 1960; Regional Acct, SE Asia, 1961; Dep. Dir Audit, 1965; Asst Representative, Delhi, 1970; Director, Budget, 1972; Dep. Controller, Finance, 1972. *Recreations:* cuisine, lepidoptery. *Address:* Les Malardeaux, St Sernin de Duras 47120, France.

SWANN, Donald Ibrahim, MA; composer and performer, free-lance since 1948; *b* 30 Sept. 1923; *s* of late Dr Herbert William Swann, Richmond, Surrey and Naguimé Sultan; *m* 1955, Janet Mary (*née* Oxborrow), Ipswich, Suffolk; two *d*. *Educ:* Westminster School; Christ Church, Oxford. Hons Degree

Mod. Lang. (Russian and Mod. Greek). Contributed music to London revues, including Airs on a Shoestring, 1953-54, as joint leader writer with Michael Flanders; Wild Thyme, musical play, with Philip Guard, 1955; in At the Drop of a Hat, 1957, appeared for first time (with Michael Flanders) as singer and accompanist of own songs (this show ran over 2 yrs in London, was part of Edinburgh Festival, 1959; Broadway, 1959-60; American and Canadian tour, 1960-61; tour of Great Britain and Ireland, 1962-63); At the Drop of Another Hat (with Michael Flanders), Haymarket, 1963-64, Globe, 1965; Aust. and NZ tour, 1964; US Tour, 1966-67. Arranged concerts of own settings: Set by Swann, An Evening in Crete; Soundings by Swann; Between the Bars: an autobiography in music; A Crack in Time, a concert in search of peace. Musician in Residence, Quaker Study Center, Pendle Hill, USA, Jan.-June 1983; works in song-writers' trio with Jeremy Taylor and Sydney Carter; solo entertainment in theatres and concert halls. Founded Albert House Press for special publications, 1974. *Compositions and Publications include:* satirical music to Third Programme series by Henry Reed, ghosting for Hilda Tablet. London Sketches with Sebastian Shaw, 1958; Festival Matins, 1962; Perelandra, music drama with David Marsh based on the novel of C. S. Lewis, 1961-62; Settings of John Betjeman Poems, 1964; Sing Round the Year (Book of New Carols for Children), 1965; The Road Goes Ever On, book of songs with J. R. R. Tolkien, 1968, rev. edn 1978; The Space Between the Bars: a book of reflections, 1968; Requiem for the Living, to words of C. Day Lewis, 1969; The Rope of Love: around the earth in song, 1973; Swann's Way Out: a posthumous adventure, 1974; (with Albert Friedlander) The Five Scrolls, 1975; Omnibus Flanders and Swann Songbook, 1977; Round the Piano with Donald Swann, 1979; (with Alec Davidson) The Yeast Factory, 1979; Alphabetaphon: 26 essays A-Z (illus. by Natasha Swann); *songs and operas* with Arthur Scholey: The Song of Caedmon, 1971; Singalive, 1978; Wacky and his Fuddlejig (children's musical play), 1978; Candle Tree, 1980; Baboushka (a Christmas cantata), 1980. *Recreation:* going to the launderette. *Address:* 13 Albert Bridge Road, SW11 4PX. *T:* 01-622 4281.

SWANN, Frederick Ralph Holland, CBE 1974 (OBE (mil.) 1944); Life Vice President, Royal National Lifeboat Institution (Chairman, 1972-75); *b* 4 Oct. 1904; *s* of F. Holland Swann, JP, Steeple, Dorset; *m* 1940, Philippa Jocelyn Braithwaite (*d* 1968); no *c. Educ:* Eton; Trinity Coll., Cambridge (MA). Mem. London Stock Exchange, 1932-64. Joined RNVSR, 1937; served in HMS Northern Gift, 1939-40 (despatches); comd HMS Sapphire, 1940-41; Senior fighter Direction Officer, HMS Formidable, 1941-43; Comdr RNVR 1944; Exec. Officer, HMS Biter, 1944 and HMS Hunter, 1944-45 (in comd, 1945). Mem. Cttee of Management, RNLI, 1953, Dep. Chm. 1964-72. A Vice-Pres., Royal Humane Soc., 1973; Hon. Life Mem., Norwegian Soc. for Sea Rescue, 1975. A Comr of Income Tax, City of London, 1964-76. *Recreations:* making miniature ship models, fishing, gardening. *Address:* Stratford Mill, Stratford-sub-Castle, Salisbury, Wilts SP1 3LJ. *T:* Salisbury 6563. *Clubs:* United Oxford & Cambridge University, Royal Cruising (Cdre 1966-72); Royal Corinthian Yacht.

SWANN, Julian Dana Nimmo H.; *see* Hartland-Swann.

SWANN, Peter Geoffrey, CBE 1981 (OBE 1973); MD, FRCP, FFOM; FInstPet; Director of Medical Services, Esso Europe Inc., since 1975; Dean, Faculty of Occupational Medicine, Royal College of Physicians of London, 1978-81 (Fellow of Faculty, 1978); Civil Consultant in Occupational Medicine to the Royal Air Force and the Royal Navy, since 1979; *b* 18 Feb. 1921; *s* of Arthur Swann and Annette (*née* Watkins); *m* 1954, Ruth Audrey Stapleton; one *s* one *d. Educ:* Chigwell Sch.; London Hosp. Med. Coll. (MB, BS 1943; MD 1949). LRCP 1942, MRCP 1949, FRCP 1969; MRCS 1942. FInstPet. Served War, RAFVR Med. Br., 1943-46, Flt Lieut. House physician appts, London Hosp., 1942; jt appt in pathology, Univ. of Oxford and Emergency Public Health Lab. Service, Oxford, 1943; Med. Registrar, subseq. Sen. Registrar, London Hosp. and Oldchurch Hosp., 1946-54; SMO, Esso Petroleum Co., 1954-61, CMO, 1961-75. FRSM (Pres., Occup. Med. Sect., 1975). Chairman: Working Party on Occup. Med., RCP, 1976; Standing Cttee on Occup. Med., RCP, 1971-78; Health Adv. Cttee, Oil Cos Internat. Study Gp for Conservation of Clean Air and Water, Europe, 1972-. Member: Specialist Adv. Cttee on Occup. Med., 1971-76 (Chm., 1973-76); Jt Cttee on Higher Med. Trng, 1973-76; Bd, Offshore Medical Support Ltd, Aberdeen, 1977-; Working Party of MOs in Chemical Industry, EEC, Luxembourg, 1976-; Standing Med. Adv. Cttee, DHSS, 1980-; BMA; Council, RCP; Soc. of Occup. Med. (Hon. Sec., 1966-70); Exec. Cttee and Advisory Bd, Inst. of Occupational Health, Univ. of Birmingham, 1980-. Mem., Conf. on Med. Royal Colls and their Faculties, UK, 1978-81. Dep. Pres., RoSPA, 1980-. Clinical Prof., Univ. of Miami, 1979. *Publications:* contrib. med. jls. *Recreations:* sailing, golf, squash. *Address:* 43 Upper Berkeley Street, W1H 7PL. *T:* 01-723 8333; Robinswood, Second Avenue, Frinton-on-Sea, Essex. *T:* Frinton-on-Sea 3678. *Clubs:* Royal Air Force; Royal Harwich Yacht; Frinton Golf.

SWANN, Robert Swinney, MBE 1947; HM Diplomatic Service, retired; *b* 17 Nov. 1915; *s* of R. N. and F. Swann. *Educ:* George Watson's Boys' College, Edinburgh; Edinburgh University. Indian Civil Service, 1938-47; joined Diplomatic Service, 1947; Counsellor Addis Ababa, 1965-69; Diplomatic Service Inspector, 1969-72; Counsellor, Bonn, 1972-74. Now engaged in legal-historical research. *Recreations:* music, theatre. *Address:* 6 Collingham Gardens, SW5. *T:* 01-373 0445.

SWANSEA, 4th Baron *cr* 1893; **John Hussey Hamilton Vivian,** Bt 1882; DL; *b* 1 Jan. 1925; *s* of 3rd Baron and Hon. Winifred Hamilton (*d* 1944), 4th *d* of 1st Baron Holm Patrick; *S* father, 1934; *m* 1956, Miriam Antoinette (marr. diss. 1973; she *d* 1975), 2nd *d* of A. W. F. Caccia-Birch, MC, of Guernsey Lodge, Marton, NZ; one *s* two *d. Educ:* Eton; Trinity Coll., Cambridge. DL Powys (formerly Brecknock), 1962. OStJ 1980. *Recreations:* shooting, fishing, rifle shooting. *Heir: s* Hon. Richard Anthony Hussey Vivian, *b* 24 Jan. 1957. *Address:* Glanyrafon, Erwood, Powys. *T:* Erwood 662. *Clubs:* Carlton; Cardiff and County (Cardiff).

SWANSEA and BRECON, Bishop of, since 1976; **Rt. Rev. Benjamin Noel Young Vaughan;** *b* 25 Dec. 1917; *s* of late Alderman and Mrs J. O. Vaughan, Newport, Pembs; *m* 1945, Nesta Lewis (*d* 1980). *Educ:* St David's Coll., Lampeter (BA); St Edmund Hall, Oxford (MA); Westcott House, Cambridge. Deacon, 1943; Priest, 1944. Curate of: Llannon, 1943-45; St David's, Carmarthen, 1945-48; Tutor, Codrington Coll., Barbados, 1948-52; Lecturer in Theology, St David's Coll., Lampeter, and Public Preacher, Diocese of St David's, 1952-55; Rector, Holy Trinity Cathedral, Port of Spain, and Dean of Trinidad, 1955-61; Bishop Suffragan of Mandeville, 1961-67; Bishop of British Honduras, 1967-71; Assistant Bishop and Dean of Bangor, 1971-76. Examining Chaplain to Bishop of Barbados, 1951-52, to Bishop of Trinidad, 1955-61; Commissary for Barbados, 1952-55. Formerly Chairman: Nat. Council for Educn in British Honduras; Govt Junior Secondary Sch.; Provincial Commn on Theological Educn in WI; Provincial Cttee on Reunion of Churches, Christian Social Council of British Honduras; Ecumenical Commn of British Honduras; Agric. Commn of Churches of British Honduras. Chairman: Provincial Cttee on Missions, Church in Wales; Church and Society Dept, Council of Churches for Wales; Adv. Cttee on Church and Society, Church in Wales, 1977; Judge of Provincial Court, Church in Wales. Pres., Council of Churches for Wales, 1980-. Member: Council, St David's Univ. Coll., Lampeter, 1976; Council and Ct, Swansea Univ. Coll., 1976. Sub-Prelate, OStJ, 1977; Order of Druids, Gorsedd y Beirdd. *Publications:* Structures for Renewal, 1967; Wealth, Peace and Godliness, 1968; The Expectation of the Poor, 1972. *Address:* Ely Tower, Brecon, Powys.

SWANSON, Gloria, (Gloria May Josephine Swanson); American film actress; *b* Chicago, 27 March 1899; *d* of Joseph and Adelaide Swanson; *m* 1st, Wallace Beery (marr. diss.); 2nd, Herbert K. Somborn (marr. diss.); one *d*; 3rd, Marquis de la Falaise de la Coudraye (marr. diss.); 4th, Michael Farmer (marr. diss.); one *d*; 5th, William N. Davey (marr. diss.); 6th, William Dufty. Began career at Essanay in Chicago, then Keystone Comedies, Hollywood; starred in Triangle Films, for Cecil B. DeMille (six consec. films) and 20 for Famous Players-Lasky in Hollywood and NY; later formed Gloria Swanson Productions; and became owner-member of United Artists which released Loves of Sunya (which opened NY Roxy Theatre), Sadie Thompson, Queen Kelly (unreleased), The Trespasser (the first all-talking picture), What a Widow, and Perfect Understanding (with Laurence Olivier, made in England); among many other films starred in Music in the Air, Father Takes a Wife, Sunset Boulevard, 1950, and Airport, 1975. Has also appeared in various theatrical rôles: 20th Century, with José Ferrer, Broadway, 1951; The Inkwell, 1962-63, and Reprise, 1967; Butterflies are Free, toured and on Broadway, 1970-72. Own television show, The Gloria Swanson Hour, 1948. Exhibn of paintings and sculpture, Hamiltons Gall., London, 1978. Palms and Officer, Académie des Beaux Arts; Cross of Honour and Merit, SMO Malta; OStJ 1963; Award from City of Paris and, among others, Foreign Critics Award; Neiman-Marcus Award for style; Hon. Comr of Youth and Fitness of NY, 1976. *Publication:* Swanson on Swanson, 1981. *Recreations:* sculpture, painting. *Address:* Gloria Swanson Archives, 920 5th Avenue, New York, NY 10021, USA.

SWANSON, Prof. Sydney Alan Vasey; Professor of Biomechanics, Imperial College, University of London, since 1974; *b* 31 Oct. 1931; *s* of Charles Henry William Swanson and Hannah Elizabeth Swanson (*née* Vasey); *m* 1956, Mary Howarth; one *s* one *d. Educ:* Scarborough Boys' High Sch.; Imperial Coll., London. DSc (Eng), PhD, DIC, ACGI, MIMechE. Engineering Laboratories, Bristol Aircraft Ltd, 1955-58; Lectr, Mechanical Engineering, Imperial Coll., London, 1958-69; Reader in Biomechanics, 1969-74; Dean, City and Guilds Coll., 1976-79; Head of Mechanical Engineering Dept, 1978-. *Publications:* Engineering Dynamics, 1963; Engineering in Medicine (with B. M. Sayers and B. Watson), 1975; (with M. A. R. Freeman) The Scientific Basis of Joint Replacement, 1977; papers on bone, cartilage and joints in learned jls. *Recreations:* photography, fell-walking. *Address:* Mechanical Engineering Department, Imperial College, SW7 2BX. *T:* 01-589 5111, ext. 2400. *Club:* Lyke Wake (Northallerton).

SWANSTON, Commander David, DSO 1945; DSC 1941, and Bar, 1942; RN; Deputy Serjeant at Arms, House of Commons, 1976-81; *b* 13 Feb. 1919; *s* of late Capt. D. S. Swanston, OBE RN; *m* 1st, 1942, Sheila Ann Lang (marr. diss.); one *s* (and one *s* decd); 2nd, 1953, Joan Margaret Nest Stockwood, *d* of late I. H. Stockwood and Mrs Stockwood; one *s* one *d. Educ:* Royal Naval College, Dartmouth. Joined Royal Navy, 1932; served in submarines at Home, Mediterranean, and East Indies Stations, from 1939. Comd Shakespeare, 1944-45; Alaric, 1948; Tudor, 1949; Naval Liaison Officer, RMA Sandhurst, 1951-53; passed RN Staff course, 1953; Commander, 1953; invalided from Royal Navy, 1955. Asst Serjeant at Arms, House of Commons, 1957-76. Industrial employment, 1955-56. *Recreations:* golf, rifle shooting. *Address:* High Meadow, Linchmere, Haslemere, Surrey GU27 3NF.

SWANTON, Ernest William, OBE 1965; formerly Cricket and Rugby football Correspondent to the Daily Telegraph, retired 1975; BBC Commentator, 1934–75; *b* 11 Feb. 1907; *s* of late William Swanton; *m* 1958, Ann, *d* of late R. H. de Montmorency and *widow* of G. H. Carbutt. *Educ:* Cranleigh. Evening Standard, 1927–39. Played Cricket for Middlesex, 1937–38. Served 1939–46; captured at Singapore, 1942; POW Siam, 1942–45; Actg Maj. Bedfordshire Yeomanry (RA). Joined Daily Telegraph staff, 1946. Covered 20 Test tours to Australia, W Indies, S Africa, New Zealand and India; managed own XI to West Indies, 1956 and 1961 and to Malaya and Far East, 1964. Editorial Director, The Cricketer. Mem. Cttee, MCC and Kent CCC (Pres. 1981–82); Pres., Cricket Soc., 1976–. *Publications:* (with H. S. Altham) A History of Cricket, 1938, 4th edn 1962; Denis Compton, A Cricket Sketch, 1948; Elusive Victory, 1951; Cricket and The Clock, 1952; Best Cricket Stories, 1953; West Indian Adventure, 1954; Victory in Australia, 1954/5, 1955; Report from South Africa, 1957; West Indies Revisited, 1960; The Ashes in Suspense, 1963; Cricket from all Angles, 1968; Sort of a Cricket Person (memoirs), 1972; Swanton in Australia, 1975; Follow On (memoirs), 1977; General Editor, The World of Cricket, 1966, revised as Barclay's World of Cricket, 1980, 2nd edn 1981. *Recreations:* cricket, golf. *Address:* Delf House, Sandwich, Kent. *Clubs:* Naval and Military, MCC; Royal and Ancient.

SWANWICK, Betty, RA 1979 (ARA 1972); RWS 1976; artist; book illustrator and mural painter; now painting in watercolours; *b* 22 May 1915; *d* of Henry Gerad Swanwick. *Educ:* Lewisham Prendergast Sch.; Goldsmiths' Coll. Sch. of Art; Royal Coll. of Art. Has designed posters and press advertisements for LPTB, Shell-Mex, etc; murals for various organizations. *Publications:* The Cross Purposes, 1945; Hoodwinked, 1957; Beauty and the Burglar, 1958. *Recreation:* gardening. *Address:* Caxton Cottage, Frog Lane, Tunbridge Wells, Kent.

SWANWICK, Sir Graham Russell, Kt 1966; MBE 1944; Judge of the High Court of Justice (Queen's Bench Division), 1966–80; Presiding Judge, Midland and Oxford Circuit, 1975–78; *b* 24 August 1906; *s* of Eric Drayton Swanwick and Margery Eleanor (*née* Norton), Whittington House, Chesterfield; *m* 1st, 1933, Helen Barbara Reid (marr. diss., 1945; she *d* 1970); two *s* ; 2nd, 1952, Audrey Celia Parkinson. *Educ:* Winchester Coll.; University Coll., Oxford (BA). Called to Bar, Inner Temple, 1930, Master of the Bench, 1962; QC 1956; Leader Midland Circuit, 1961–65. Wing Comdr RAFVR, 1940–45 (MBE, despatches). Recorder: City of Lincoln, 1957–59; City of Leicester, 1959–66; Judge of Appeal, Channel Islands, 1964–66; Derbyshire QS: Chm., 1963–66; Dep. Chm., 1966–71. *Recreation:* shooting. *Address:* Burnett's Ashurst, Steyning, West Sussex. *T:* Partridge Green 710241. *Club:* Royal Air Force.

SWARBRICK, Prof. James, PhD, DSc; FRSC, CChem; Professor of Pharmaceutics and Chairman, Division of Pharmaceutics, University of North Carolina, since 1982; *b* 8 May 1934; *s* of George Winston Swarbrick and Edith M. C. Cooper; *m* 1960, Pamela Margaret Oliver. *Educ:* Sloane Grammar Sch.; Chelsea Coll., Univ. of London (BPharm Hons 1960; PhD 1964; DSc 1972). MPS 1961; FRIC 1970; FPS 1978. Asst Lectr, 1962, Lectr, 1964, Chelsea Coll.; Vis. Asst Prof., Purdue Univ., 1964; Associate Prof., 1966, Prof. and Chm. of Dept of Pharmaceutics, 1969, Asst Dean, 1970, Univ. of Conn; Dir of Product Develt, Sterling-Winthrop Res. Inst., NY, 1972; first Prof. of Pharmaceutics, Univ. of Sydney, 1975–76; Dean, Sch. of Pharmacy, Univ. of London, 1976–78; Prof. of Pharmacy and Chm., Res. Council, Univ. of S California, Los Angeles, 1978–82. Vis. Scientist, Astra Labs, Sweden, 1971; Indust. Cons., 1965–72, 1975–; Cons., Aust. Dept. of Health, 1975–76; Mem., Cttee on Specifications, National Formulary, 1970–75; Chm., Jt US Pharmacopoeia-Nat. Formulary Panel on Disintegration and Dissolution Testing, 1971–75. Member: Cttee on Grad. Programs, Amer. Assoc. of Colls of Pharmacy, 1969–71; Practice Trng Cttee, Pharm. Soc. of NSW, 1975–76; Academic Bd, Univ. of Sydney, 1975–76; Collegiate Council, 1976–78; Educn Cttee, Pharmaceutical Soc. of GB, 1976–78; Working Party on Pre-Registration Training, 1977–78. FAAAS 1966; Fellow, Acad. of Pharm. Sciences, 1973. Mem. Editorial Board: Jl of Biopharmaceutics and Pharmacokinetics, 1973–79; Drug Development Communications, 1974–; series Editor, Current Concepts in the Pharmaceutical Sciences, and, Drugs and the Pharmaceutical Sciences. *Publications:* (with A. N. Martin and A. Cammarata) Physical Pharmacy, 2nd edn 1969; contributed: American Pharmacy, 6th edn 1966 and 7th edn 1974; Remington's Pharmaceutical Sciences, 14th edn 1970, 15th edn 1975, 16th edn 1980; contrib. Current Concepts in the Pharmaceutical Sciences: Biopharmaceutics, 1970; res. contribs to internat. sci. jls. *Recreation:* chasing golf and tennis balls. *Address:* School of Pharmacy, University of North Carolina at Chapel Hill, Beard Hall 200H, Chapel Hill, NC 27514, USA. *T:* (919) 962-0092.

SWARTZ, Rt. Rev. George Alfred; a Bishop Suffragan of Cape Town, since 1972; Canon of St George's Cathedral, Cape Town, since 1969; *b* 8 Sept. 1928; *s* of Philip and Julia Swartz; *m* 1957, Sylvia Agatha (*née* George); one *s* one *d*. *Educ:* Umbilo Road High Sch., Durban; Univ. of the Witwatersrand, Johannesburg; Coll. of the Resurrection, Mirfield, Yorks; St Augustine's Coll., Canterbury. BA, Primary Lower Teacher's Cert., Central Coll. Dip. (Canterbury). Asst Teacher, Sydenham Primary Sch., 1951–52; Deacon, 1954; Priest, 1955; Asst Curate, St Paul's Church, Cape Town, 1955–56; Priest in Charge, Parochial Dist of St Helena Bay, Cape, 1957–60; St Augustine's Coll., Canterbury, 1960–61; Dir, Cape Town Dio. Mission to Muslims, 1962–63; Dir, Mission to Muslims and Rector St Philip's Church, Cape Town, 1963–70;

Regional Dean of Woodstock Deanery, 1966–70; Priest in Charge, Church of the Resurrection, Bonteheuwel, Cape, 1971–72. *Recreations:* cinema, music (traditional jazz; instruments played are guitar and saxophone). *Address:* Bishopsholme, 18 Rue Ursula, Glenhaven, Bellville 7530, Republic of South Africa. *T:* 94-0184.

SWARTZ, Col Hon. Sir Reginald (William Colin), KBE 1972 (MBE (mil.) 1948); ED; FAIM, FBIM; company director; *b* 14 April 1911; *s* of late J. Swartz, Toowoomba, Qld; *m* 1936, Hilda, *d* of late G. C. Robinson; two *s* one *d*. *Educ:* Toowoomba and Brisbane Grammar Schs. Commonwealth Military Forces, 1928–40, Lieut, 1934. Served War of 1939–45: Captain 2-26 Bn, 8 Div., AIF, 1940; Malaya (PoW): Singapore, Malaya, Thailand (Burma-Thailand Rly); CMF, in Darling Downs Regt, Lt-Col, AQMG, CMF, N Comd, Col (RL), 1961. Hon. Col Australian Army Aviation Corps, 1969–75. MHR (L) Darling Downs, Qld, 1949–72; Parly Under-Sec. for Commerce and Agric., 1952–56; Parly Sec. for Trade, 1956–61; Minister: (of State) for Repatriation, Dec. 1961–Dec. 1964; for Health, 1964–66; for Social Services, 1965; for Civil Aviation, 1966–69; for Nat. Develt, 1969–72; Leader, House of Representatives, Canberra, 1971–72. Leader of many delegns overseas incl. Aust. Delegn to India, 1967, and Trade Mission to SE Asia, 1958; Parly Delegn to S and SE Asia, 1966. Patron and/or Vice-Pres. or Mem. of numerous public organizations. Life Chm. of Trustees, Australian Army Aviation Corps. Past Chm., Inst. of Dirs (Queensland). Member, RSL. JP Queensland, 1947–81. *Recreations:* bowls, boating. *Address:* 32 Leawarra Crescent, Doncaster East, Melbourne, Victoria 3109, Australia. *Clubs:* United Service (Brisbane); Royal Automobile Club of Victoria; Australian (Melbourne); Twin Towns Services (Tweed Head); Darling Downs Aero; Probus (Doncaster) (Pres.); Templestowe Bowling (Melbourne).

SWASH, Stanley Victor, MC 1917 and Bar 1918; *b* 29 February 1896; British; *s* of A. W. Swash, JP and Sylvia Swash; *m* 1924; *m* 1955, Jane Henderson. *Educ:* Llandovery College; St John's College, Oxford; Lincoln's Inn. Served European War, 1915–19, RFA. MA (Mathematics); short period in Ministry of Pensions; served Royal Navy as Lieut Inst., 1921–24; worked in Woolworth Company, 1924–55; Director, 1939, Chairman, 1951–55; retired 1955. Called to Bar, Lincoln's Inn, 1938. OC 57 County of London Home Guard Battalion, Lieut-Colonel, 1940–45. Chairman, Horticultural Marketing Advisory Council, 1958; Member Milk Marketing Board, 1957–63; Chm. BOAC/MEA Cttee of Enquiry, 1963–64. *Recreations:* swimming, bridge. *Address:* Park Avenue, St Andrews, Malta. *Club:* United Oxford & Cambridge University.

SWAYNE, Sir Ronald (Oliver Carless), Kt 1979; MC 1945; Director: National Freight Co., since 1973, Consortium since 1982; Banque Nationale de Paris Ltd, since 1981; Member, Monopolies and Mergers Commission, since 1982; *b* 11 May 1918; *s* of Col. O. R. Swayne, DSO, and Brenda (*née* Butler); *m* 1941, Charmian, *d* of Major W. E. P. Cairnes, Bollingham, Herefordshire; one *s* one *d*. *Educ:* Bromsgrove Sch., Worcester; University Coll., Oxford, 1936–39 and 1945–46 (MA). Served with Herefordshire Regt, 1939–40, No 1 Commando, 1940–45 (MC). Joined Ocean Steam Ship Co., 1946; became partner of Alfred Holt & Co. and Man. Dir of Ocean Steam Ship Co., 1955. Dir, 1965, Dep. Chm., 1969, Chm., 1973–82, Man. Dir, 1978–82, Overseas Containers Ltd. Vice-Chm., British Shipping Fedn, 1967; Pres., Cttee des Assocs d'Armateurs of EEC, 1974–75; President: Gen. Council of British Shipping, 1978–79; Inst. of Freight Forwarders, 1980. Industrial Adviser, Churchill Coll., Cambridge, 1974; Member: Design Council, 1975–78; Careers Res. Adv. Council, 1975; New Philharmonia Trust, 1968; Vice-Pres., British Maritime League, 1982–. *Recreations:* fishing, shooting, music, bull terriers. *Address:* Puddle House, Chicksgrove, Tisbury, Salisbury SP3 6NA. *T:* Teffont 454. *Clubs:* Travellers', Flyfishers'; Houghton (Stockbridge).

SWAYTHLING, 3rd Baron, *cr* 1907; Stuart Albert Samuel Montagu, Bt, *cr* 1894; OBE 1947; late Grenadier Guards; formerly director, Messrs Samuel Montagu and Co. Ltd; *b* 19 Dec. 1898; *e s* of 2nd Baron and Gladys Helen Rachel, OBE, (*d* 1965), *d* of late Col A. E. Goldsmid; *S* father, 1927; *m* 1925, Mary Violet (from whom he obtained a divorce, 1942), *e d* of late Major Levy, DSO, and late Hon. Mrs Ionides; two *s* one *d* ; *m* 1945, Mrs Jean Knox, Director ATS (*see* Lady Swaythling). *Educ:* Clifton; Westminster; Trinity College, Cambridge. JP: Co. Southampton, 1928–48; Surrey, 1948–80. Pres., English Guernsey Cattle Society, 1950–51, 1971–72; Dep. Pres., Royal Assoc. of British Dairy Farmers, 1970–72, 1973–74 (Pres., 1972–73). Master of The Company of Farmers, 1962–63. *Heir: s* Hon. David Charles Samuel Montagu, *qv*. *Address:* La Haye Du Puits, Castel, Guernsey, Channel Islands. *T:* Guernsey 53637.

See also Hon. E. E. S. Montagu, Ivor Montagu.

SWAYTHLING, Lady, (Jean M.), CBE 1943; Chief Controller and Director, Auxilliary Territorial Service, 1941–43 (as Mrs Jean Knox); *b* 14 Aug. 1908; *m* Squadron Leader G. R. M. Knox; one *d* ; *m* 1945, 3rd Baron Swaythling, *qv*. *Address:* La Haye Du Puits, Castel, Guernsey, Channel Islands. *T:* Guernsey 53637.

SWEANEY, William Douglas, CMG 1965; retired 1972, as Establishment Officer, Overseas Development Administration, Foreign and Commonwealth Office; *b* 12 Nov. 1912; *s* of late Lt-Comdr William Sweaney, MBE, RN, and late Elizabeth Bridson; *m* 1939, Dorothy Beatrice Parsons; one *s*. *Educ:* Gillingham County Sch.; London Sch. of Economics. BSc(Econ). Clerical Officer, Inland Revenue (Special Comrs of Income Tax), 1929; Officer of

Customs and Excise, 1932; seconded to Colonial Office, 1943 (promoted Surveyor of Customs and Excise *in absentia*); transferred to Colonial Office, 1948; Principal, 1948; Private Sec. to Minister of State for Colonial Affairs, 1953; Asst Sec., 1955; Dept of Technical Co-operation, 1961; ODM, later ODA, FCO, 1964–72, Establishment Officer, 1965. *Recreations:* travel, ornithology. *Address:* 1 Beech Hurst Close, Haywards Heath, West Sussex. *T:* Haywards Heath 450341.

SWEENEY, Thomas Kevin; Senior Principal Medical Officer, Department of Health and Social Security, since 1979; *b* 10 Aug. 1923; *s* of John Francis and Mildred Sweeney; *m* 1950, Eveleen Moira Ryan; two *s* two *d*. *Educ:* O'Connell Sch., Dublin; University Coll., Dublin (MB, BCh, BAO NUI; DTM&H London; TDD Wales). MFCM. Principal Med. Officer, Colonial Medical Service, 1950–65, retd; Asst Sen. Med. Officer, Welsh Hosp. Bd, 1965–68; Department of Health and Social Security: Med. Officer, 1968–72; Sen. Med. Officer, 1972–79. *Publication:* contrib. BMJ. *Recreations:* gardening, golf, cathedrals. *Address:* The White House, Sheerwater Avenue, Woodham, Weybridge, Surrey. *T:* Byfleet 43559.

SWEET, Prof. Peter Alan, MA, PhD; Regius Professor of Astronomy in the University of Glasgow, 1959–82; *b* 15 May 1921; *s* of David Frank Sweet; *m* 1947, Myrtle Vera Parnell; two *s*. *Educ:* Kingsbury County Grammar School, London; Sidney Sussex College, Cambridge. Open Maj. Schol. in Maths, Sidney Sussex Coll., 1940–42, Wrangler, 1942, BA Cantab 1943. Junior Scientific Officer, Min. of Aircraft Prod., 1942–45; BA Scholar, at Sidney Sussex Coll., 1945–47; MA Cantab 1946; Mayhew Prizeman, 1946, PhD Cantab 1950. Lectr in Astronomy, Univ. of Glasgow, 1947–52; Lectr in Astronomy and Asst Director of the Observatory, Univ. of London, 1952–59; Dean, Faculty of Science, Univ. of Glasgow, 1973–75. Visiting Asst Professor of Astronomy, Univ. of California, Berkeley, 1957–58; Vis. Sen. Res. Fellow, NASA Inst. for Space Studies, NY, 1965–66. *Publications:* papers on Stellar Evolution, Cosmic Magnetism, and Solar Flares in Monthly Notices of Royal Astronomical Soc., etc. *Recreations:* music, gardening. *Address:* 17 Westbourne Crescent, Glasgow G61 4HB. *T:* 041-942 4425.

SWEETING, William Hart, CMG 1969; CBE 1961; Chairman, Board of Directors, Bank of London and Montreal, 1970–79; *b* 18 Dec. 1909; *s* of late Charles Cecil Sweeting, Nassau, Bahamas; *m* 1950, Isabel Jean (*née* Woodall). *Educ:* Queen's Coll., Nassau; London Univ. Entered Bahamas Public Service as Cadet, 1927; served in Colonial Secretary's Office, 1927–37; acted as Asst Colonial Sec. for short periods in 1928 and 1936; transferred to Treasury, 1937; Cashier, Public Treasury, 1941; Asst Treasurer and Receiver of Crown Dues, 1946; seconded as Financial Sec., Dominica, 1950–52; Receiver-Gen. and Treasurer, Bahamas, 1955; MLC, Bahamas, 1960–64; Chairman: Bahamas Currency Comrs, 1955–63; Bahamas Broadcasting and Television Commn, 1957–62; Bahamas Public Disclosure Commn, 1978–. Acted as Governor various periods 1959, 1964, 1965, 1966, 1968, 1969; acted as Colonial Secretary various periods, 1962–63; Chief Secretary, Bahamas 1964; Dep. Governor, Bahamas, 1969, retired 1970. Mem., Bahamas Music Soc.; Elder, St Andrew's Presbyterian Church; Chairman: Trinity Coll. of Music Local Exams Cttee; Hon. Treasurer, United World Colleges Local Cttee. *Recreations:* swimming, painting, music, bird watching. *Address:* PO Box N 573, Nassau, Bahamas. *T:* 3-1518. *Club:* Corona.

SWEETMAN, Mrs Ronald Andrew; see Dickson, Jennifer J.

SWEETMAN, Seamus George, MBE 1945; *b* 7 Nov. 1914; *s* of late James Michael Sweetman, KC and Agnes (*née* Fottrell); *m* 1939, Mary Alberta Giblett; one *s*. *Educ:* Beaumont Coll.; St John's Coll., Cambridge (BA). Pte Suffolk Regt, 1939; commnd The Buffs, 1940; Italian campaign (despatches); Lt-Col, GSO1, Sec. to Supreme Allied Comdr, Mediterranean, 1944–45. Various Unilever subsids, 1936–39; D. & W. Gibbs, 1950–55; Unilever NV, Rotterdam, 1955–57; Margarine Union, Germany, 1957–61; Dir, Unilever Ltd and Unilever NV, 1961–78; Vice-Chm., Unilever Ltd, 1974–78; Director: Commonwealth Development Finance Co., 1975–; Mercedes-Benz (UK) Ltd, 1980–. A Dep. Chm., Price Commn, 1977–79. Trustee, Leverhulme Trust, 1973–. CBIM. Officer, US Legion of Merit. *Recreations:* history, gardening, mountain walking. *Address:* Greenloaning, West Common Close, Harpenden, Herts. *T:* Harpenden 3221.

SWEETNAM, (David) Rodney, MA; FRCS; Orthopaedic Surgeon to the Queen, since 1982; Consultant Surgeon to: The Middlesex Hospital and Ealing Hospital, since 1960; King Edward VII Hospital for Officers, London, since 1964; *b* 5 Feb. 1927; second *s* of late Dr William Sweetnam and Irene (*née* Black); *m* 1959, Patricia Ann, er *d* of A. Staveley Gough, OBE, FRCS; one *s* one *d*. *Educ:* Clayesmore; Peterhouse, Cambridge (Titular Scholar; BA 1947, MA 1951); Middlesex Hosp. Med. Sch. (MB, BChir 1950). FRCS 1955. Surg. Lieut RNVR, 1950–52. Jun. appts, Mddx Hosp., London Hosp. and Royal National Orthopaedic Hosp. Hon. Consultant, King Edward VII's Convalescent Home for Officers, IW, 1980–; Hon. Civil Consultant in Orth. Surgery to the Army, 1974–; Consultant Advisor in Orth. Surgery to DHSS, 1981–. Chm., MRC's Working Party on Bone Sarcoma, 1980–. Royal College of Surgeons: Jacksonian Prize, 1966; Hunterian Prof., 1967; Gordon Taylor Meml Lectr, 1982. *Publications:* (ed jtly) The Basis and Practice of Orthopaedics, 1980; contrib. med. books and jls in field of gen. orth. surgery, trauma and bone tumours. *Recreation:* gardening. *Address:* 33 Harley Street, W1N 1DA. *T:* 01-580 5409.

SWEETT, Cyril, CEng, AIStructE, FRICS; Consultant, Cyril Sweett & Partners, Chartered Quantity Surveyors (Founder Partner, 1928); *b* 7 April 1903; *s* of William Thomas Sweett; *m* 1931, Barbara Mary, *d* of late Henry Thomas Loft, Canterbury and London; one *d*. *Educ:* Whitgift Sch.; Coll. of Estate Management. Artists Rifles, TA, 1923–27. Army Service: RE, 1939–43, France, N Africa and Italy; demob. as Lt-Col. Member: Council, RICS; Cttee, London Library; Chm., Nat. Jt Consultative Cttee of Architects, Quantity Surveyors and Builders, 1962–63. Master, Worshipful Co. of Painter Stainers, 1964–65, 1966–67; Sheriff of City of London, 1965–66. Jordanian Star, 1966; Silver Star of Honour, Austria, 1966. *Address:* 5 Oak Lodge, 47/49 Palmeira Avenue, Hove, East Sussex BN3 3GE. *T:* Brighton 777292. *Clubs:* Garrick, MCC; Royal Burnham Yacht (Cdre, 1963–65).

SWIFT, John Anthony; QC 1981; *b* 11 July 1940; *s* of late Jack Swift and of Mrs Clare Medcalf; *m* 1972, Jane Carol Sharples; one *s* one *d*. *Educ:* Birkenhead Sch.; University Coll., Oxford (MA); Johns Hopkins Univ.; Bologna. Called to the Bar, Inner Temple, 1965. *Address:* 6 Lord Napier Place, W6; The Old School House, Coryates, Portesham, Dorset. *Clubs:* Reform, Hurlingham.

SWIFT, Lionel, QC 1975; JD; Practising Barrister, since 1961; a Recorder of the Crown Court, since 1979; *b* Bristol, 3 Oct. 1931; *s* of late Harris and of Bessie Swift, Hampstead; *m* 1966, Elizabeth (*née* Herzig); one *d*. *Educ:* Whittingehame Coll., Brighton; University Coll., London (LLB 1951); Brasenose Coll., Oxford (BCL 1959); Univ. of Chicago (Juris Doc, 1960). Solicitor, Natal, S Africa, 1954; called to the Bar, Inner Temple, 1959. British Commonwealth Fellow, Univ. of Chicago Law Sch., 1960; Amer. Social Science Res. Council Grant for work on admin of criminal justice, 1960. Jun. Counsel to Treasury in Probate Matters, 1974. A Governor, Royal Nat. Throat Nose and Ear Hosp. *Publication:* The South African Law of Criminal Procedure (Gen. Editor, A. B. Harcourt, QC), 1957. *Address:* (chambers) 4 Paper Buildings, Temple, EC4Y 7EX.

SWIFT, Michael Charles, MC 1943; Secretary-General, British Bankers' Association, 1978–82, retired; Chairman, European Communities Banking Federation Central Committee, 1980–82 (UK representative, 1978–82); *b* 29 Aug. 1921; *s* of late Comdr C. C. Swift, OBE, RN; *m* 1957, Dorothy Jill, *d* of late R. G. Bundey; one *s* one *d*. *Educ:* Radley College. Served War, Royal Artillery (Captain), 1940–45. Bank of England, 1946–58; Committee of London Clearing Bankers, 1958–75; Dep. Sec., British Bankers' Assoc., 1975–78. Gen. Comr for City of London, 1982–. *Recreations:* golf, birdwatching. *Address:* c/o 10 Lombard Street, EC3V 9EL. *T:* 01-623 4001. *Club:* Royal West Norfolk Golf.

SWIFT, Reginald Stanley, CB 1969; Under-Secretary, Department of Health and Social Security, 1968–76, retired; *b* 2 Nov. 1914; *e s* of Stanley John and Annie Swift; *m* 1940, Mildred Joan Easter; no *c*. *Educ:* Watford Grammar School; Christ's College, Cambridge. BA Cantab (1st Cl. Hons in Classics) 1936; MA Cantab 1940; BSc (Econ.) London 1944. Entered Civil Service as Asst Comr, National Savings Cttee, 1938; transferred to Min. of National Insurance as Principal, 1947; Principal Private Secretary to Minister, 1953–54; Assistant Secretary, 1954; Under-Secretary, 1962. *Recreations:* gardening, golf. *Address:* 16 Beechfield, Banstead, Surrey. *T:* Burgh Heath 61773. *Club:* Kingswood Golf.

SWINBURNE, Ivan Archie, CMG 1973; Member of Legislative Council of Victoria, Australia, 1946–76, retired; *b* 6 March 1908; *s* of George Arthur and Hilda Maud Swinburne; *m* 1950, Isabella Mary, *d* of James Alexander Moore; one *d*. *Educ:* Hurdle Creek West and Milawa State Schs; Wangaratta and Essendon High Schs. MLC, for NE Prov., 1946–76; Dep. Leader of Country Party, 1954–69; Leader of Country Party in Legislative Council, 1969–76; Minister of Housing and Materials, 1950–52; Mem., Subordinate Legislation Cttee, 1961–67 and 1973. Councillor, Shire of Bright, 1940–47 (Pres., 1943–44). Mem., Bush Nursing Council of Victoria, 1948–; Chm. Cttee of Management, Mount Buffalo National Park, 1963–. *Recreation:* football administration. *Address:* PO Box 340, Myrtle Street, Myrtleford, Victoria 3737, Australia. *T:* Myrtleford 521167. *Clubs:* RACV (Melbourne); Wangaratta (Wangaratta).

SWINBURNE, Nora; actress; *b* Bath, 24 July 1902; *d* of H. Swinburne Johnson; *m* 1st, Francis Lister (marr. diss.); one *s*; 2nd, Edward Ashley-Cooper (marr. diss.); 3rd, 1946, Esmond Knight, *qv*. *Educ:* Rossholme College, Weston-super-Mare; Royal Academy of Dramatic Art. First West End appearance, 1916; went to America, 1923; returned to London stage, 1924; New York, again, 1930; continuous successes in London, from 1931; went into management, 1938, in addition to acting. Played as Diana Wentworth in The Years Between (which ran for more than a year), Wyndhams, 1945; Red Letter Day, Garrick; A Woman of No Importance, Savoy, 1953; The Lost Generation, Garrick, 1955; Fool's Paradise, Apollo, 1959; Music at Midnight, Westminster, 1962; All Good Children, Hampstead, 1964; Family Reunion, 1973, The Cocktail Party, 1975, Royal Exchange, Manchester. *Films include:* Jassy, Good Time Girl, The Blind Goddess, Fanny by Gaslight, They Knew Mr Knight, Quartet, Christopher Columbus, My Daughter Joy, The River (made in India), Quo Vadis, also Helen of Troy (made in Italy), Third Man on the Mountain, Conspiracy of Hearts, Music at Midnight, Interlude, Anne of the Thousand Days. Has appeared on television (incl. Forsyte Saga, Post Mortem, Kate serial, Fall of Eagles). *Address:* 52 Cranmer Court, SW3.

SWINDELLS, Maj.-Gen. George Michael Geoffrey; Chief of Joint Services Liaison Organisation, Bonn, since 1980; *b* 15 Jan. 1930; *s* of George Martyn Swindells and Marjorie Swindells; *m* 1955, Prudence Bridget Barbara Tully; one *s* one *d. Educ:* Rugby School. Nat. Service Commission, 5th Royal Inniskilling Dragoon Guards, 1949; served in Germany, Korea and Canal Zone; Regular Commission, 1953; Adjutant, Cheshire Yeomanry, 1955-56; Staff Coll., 1960; Brigade Major, 7th Armd Brigade, 1967-69; transfer to 9th/12th Royal Lancers, to command, 1969-71; GSO1 Directing Staff and Col GS, Staff Coll., 1972-74; Comdr 11th Armd Brigade, 1975-76; RCDS course, 1977; Dir of Op. Requirements (3), MoD, 1978-79. *Recreations:* skiing and country life. *Address:* Headquarters, Joint Services Liaison Organisation, Bonn, BFPO 19. *T:* Bonn (0228) 218051 ext 21. *Club:* Army and Navy.

SWINDEN, (Thomas) Alan, CBE 1971; Chairman, since 1974, Director, since 1980, Kingston Regional Management Centre; *b* 27 Aug. 1915; *s* of Thomas and Ethel Swinden; *m* 1941, Brenda Elise Roe; one *d. Educ:* Rydal Sch.; Sheffield Univ. (BEng). With Rolls-Royce, 1937-55; seconded to AFV Div., Min. of Supply, 1941-45; with Engrg Employers Fedn, 1955-65, Dir, 1964-65; Dir, Engrg Industry Trng Bd, 1965-70; Confederation of British Industry: Dep. Dir Gen. (Industrial Relations), 1970-74; Chief Advr, Social Affairs, 1974-78; Consultant, 1978-81. Chm., Derby No 1 HMC, 1953-55. Council Member: British Employers Confedn, 1955-65; ACAS, 1974-; Mem., BBC Consultative Gp on Industrial and Business Affairs, 1977-. Chm., Exec. Cttee, Inst. of Manpower Studies, 1978-. *Address:* 85 College Road, Epsom, Surrey KT17 4HH. *T:* Epsom 20848. *Club:* Royal Automobile.

SWINDLEHURST, Rt. Rev. Owen Francis; Bishop Auxiliary of Hexham and Newcastle, (RC), since 1977; Titular Bishop of Chester-le-Street; *b* 10 May 1928; *s* of Francis and Ellen Swindlehurst. *Educ:* Ushaw College, Durham; English College, Rome. PhL, STL, LCL (Gregorian Univ., Rome). Assistant Priest: St Matthew's, Ponteland, 1959-67; St Bede's, Denton Burn, Newcastle, 1967-72; Parish Priest at Holy Name, Jesmond, Newcastle, 1967-77. *Recreations:* walking, gardening, reading. *Address:* Oaklea, Tunstall Road, Sunderland SR2 7JR. *T:* Sunderland 41158.

SWINDON, Archdeacon of; *see* Clark, Ven. K. J.

SWINFEN, 3rd Baron *cr* 1919; **Roger Mynors Swinfen Eady;** *b* 14 Dec. 1938; *s* of 2nd Baron Swinfen and of Mary Aline, *d* of late Col H. Mynors Farmar, CMG, DSO; *S* father, 1977; *m* 1962, Patricia Anne, *o d* of late F. D. Blackmore, Dundrum, Dublin; one *s* three *d. Educ:* Westminster; RMA, Sandhurst. ARICS 1970. *Heir: s* Hon. Charles Roger Peregrine Swinfen Eady, *b* 8 March 1971. *Address:* House of Lords, SW1.

SWINGLAND, Owen Merlin Webb, QC 1974; Barrister-at-Law; *b* 26 Sept. 1919; *er s* of Charles and Maggie Eveline Swingland; *m* 1941, Kathleen Joan Eason (*née* Parry), Newport, Mon; one *s* two *d. Educ:* Haberdashers' Aske's Hatcham Sch.; King's Coll., London. LLB 1941, AKC. Called to Bar, Gray's Inn, 1946; practice at Chancery Bar, 1948-; Barrister of Lincoln's Inn, 1977. Assistant Comr, Boundary Commn for England; a Church Comr, 1982-. Past Pres., British Insurance Law Assoc. Mem., Court of Assts, Haberdashers' Co.; Freeman of the City of London. Foundation Governor, Haberdashers' Aske's Hatcham Schools. *Recreations:* music, theatre, fishing, sailing, reading; interested in most competitive sports. *Address:* Ightham Warren, Kent. *T:* Borough Green 884157.

SWINGLER, Bryan Edwin, CBE 1979; British Council Representative in France, since 1980; *b* 20 Sept. 1924; *s* of late George Edwin Swingler, Birmingham, and Mary Eliza Frayne; *m* 1954, Herta, *er d* of late Edwin Jaeger, Schoenlinde; one *d. Educ:* King Edward's Sch., Birmingham; Peterhouse, Cambridge (Sen. Schol.); Charles Univ., Prague. BA 1948, MA 1953. Served War, Royal Navy (Leading Signalman), 1943-46. Apptd to British Council, 1949; Vienna, 1949-52; Lahore, 1952-55; Karachi, 1955-56; Oslo, 1956-59; Berlin, 1959-61; Cologne, 1961-63; Dir, Scholarships, 1963-67; Dep. Controller, Commonwealth Div., 1967-68; Rep. Indonesia, Djakarta, 1968-71; Controller Finance, 1972-73; Controller, Home, 1973-75; Asst Dir-Gen., 1975-77; Head of British Council Div., India, and Minister (Educn), British High Commn, New Delhi, 1977-80. Vice-Chm., British Council Staff Assoc., 1965-67; Member: British-Austrian Mixed Commn, 1973-77; British-French Mixed Commn, 1976-77. *Recreations:* music, painting, oriental ceramics, recollections of sailing in warm waters. *Address:* c/o Foreign and Commonwealth Office, SW1; Beverley, Porthpean, St Austell, Cornwall. *T:* St Austell 3347. *Club:* Travellers'.

SWINGLER, Raymond John Peter; Secretary, Press Council, and conciliator, since 1980; *b* 8 Oct. 1933; *s* of Raymond Joseph and Mary Swingler; *m* 1960, Shirley (*d* 1980), *e d* of Frederick and Dorothy Wilkinson, Plymouth; two *d. Educ:* St Bede's Coll., Christchurch, NZ; Canterbury Univ. Journalist, The Press, Christchurch, NZ, 1956-57; Marlborough Express, 1957-59; Nelson Mail, 1959-61; freelance Middle East, 1961-62; Cambridge Evening News, 1962-79. Member: Press Council, 1975-78, Press Council Complaints Cttee, 1976-78; Nat. Exec. Council, Nat. Union of Journalists, 1973-75, 1978-79; Provincial Newspapers Industrial Council, 1976-79; Chm., General Purposes Cttee (when journalists' Code of Professional Conduct (revised) introduced), 1974-75. *Recreations:* horses, and horsewomen. *Address:* Wicken Hall, Wicken, Cambs CB7 5XT. *T:* Ely 720745.

SWINLEY, Captain Casper Silas Balfour, DSO 1941; DSC 1940; Royal Navy; *b* 28 Oct. 1898; *y s* of late Gordon Herbert Swinley, Assam, India, and Margaret Eliza, *d* of late Prof. J. H. Balfour, Edin.; *m* 1928, Sylvia Jocosa, 4th *d* of late Canon W. H. Carnegie, Rector of St Margaret's, Westminster, and Sub-Dean of Westminster Abbey; two *s* twin *d. Educ:* Epsom College. Entered Royal Navy with Special Entry Cadetship, 1916; served European War, 1916-18, as Midshipman and Sub-Lieut in HMS New Zealand; HMS Ceres, evacuation of Odessa, 1919-20; Queens' Coll., Cambridge, 1920; ADC and Private Sec. to Sir Charles O'Brien, Governor of Barbados, 1921-22; HMS Curacoa, evacuation of Smyrna, 1922-23; HMS Calcutta, Flagship West Indies Station, 1924-26; HMS Ganges, Boys' Training Establishment, Shotley, 1926-28; Flag-Lieut to Adm. Sir E. Alexander-Sinclair, C-in-C the Nore, 1928-30; HMS Repulse, 1930-32; HMS Carlisle, Africa Station, under Adm. Sir Edward Evans, 1932-34; Comdr 1934; commanded HMS Express, 5th Destroyer Flotilla, Abyssinian crisis, Spanish War, Jubilee Review, 1935-37; NID, Admiralty Naval Staff, 1937-39; commanded HMS Impregnable, Boys' Training Establishment, Devonport, 1939; commanded HMS Codrington and Dover Patrol Destroyers, taking King George VI to France and back; also Mr Winston Churchill to Boulogne, 1939-40; French Destroyer Brestois for Liaison duties; evacuation of Namsos, Norway; commanded demolition party at Calais (DSC), 1940; commanded HMS Isis, North Sea, Genoa, Greece, Crete (DSO); Syrian campaign, 1940-41; commanded HMS Miranda and Minesweepers, Great Yarmouth; Capt. 1942; Chief Staff Officer to Vice-Adm. Sir Ralph Leatham, Malta, 1942; Director of Service Conditions, Admiralty, 1943-45; Commanded HMS Arethusa, 1945; Chief Staff Officer to Vice-Adm. Sir F. Dalrymple Hamilton, Malta, 1946; commanded HMS Flamingo and Senior Officer Reserve Fleet, Devonport, 1946-47; Chief of Naval Information, Admiralty, 1947-48; Captain in Charge, Captain Superintendent and King's Harbour Master, Portland, 1949-51. Naval ADC to King George VI, 1951; Commodore and Chief of Staff, Royal Pakistan Navy, 1953-54. Senior Whale Fishery Inspector, South Georgia, 1959-60. Appeals Organiser, BRCS, Gloucestershire, 1963-67. *Recreation:* scrap-book collecting. *Address:* Broughtons, near Newnham, Glos. *T:* Westbury-on-Severn 328.

SWINNERTON, Frank Arthur; novelist and critic; President, Royal Literary Fund, 1962-66; *b* Wood Green, 12 Aug. 1884; *y s* of Charles Swinnerton and Rose Cottam; *m* 1924, Mary Dorothy Bennett; one *d. Publications:* The Merry Heart, 1909; The Young Idea, 1910; The Casement, 1911; The Happy Family, 1912; George Gissing: a Critical Study, 1912; On the Staircase, 1914; R. L. Stevenson: a Critical Study, 1914; The Chaste Wife, 1916; Nocturne, 1917; Shops and Houses, 1918; September, 1919; Coquette, 1921; The Three Lovers, 1922; Young Felix, 1923; The Elder Sister, 1925; Summer Storm, 1926; Tokefield Papers, 1927; A London Bookman, 1928; A Brood of Ducklings, 1928; Sketch of a Sinner, 1929; Authors and the Book Trade, 1932; The Georgian House, 1932; Elizabeth, 1934; The Georgian Literary Scene, 1935; Swinnerton: an Autobiography, 1937; Harvest Comedy, 1937; The Two Wives, 1939; The Reviewing and Criticism of Books, 1939; The Fortunate Lady, 1941; Thankless Child, 1942; A Woman in Sunshine, 1944; English Maiden, 1946; The Cats and Rosemary, (US) 1948, (England) 1950; Faithful Company, 1948; The Doctor's Wife Comes to Stay, 1949; A Flower for Catherine, 1950; The Bookman's London, 1951; Master Jim Probity, 1952; Londoner's Post, 1952; A Month in Gordon Square, 1953; The Sumner Intrigue, 1955; Authors I Never Met, 1956; Background with Chorus, 1956; The Woman from Sicily, 1957; A Tigress in Prothero, 1959; The Grace Divorce, 1960; Death of a Highbrow, 1961; Figures in the Foreground, 1963; Quadrille, 1965; A Galaxy of Fathers, 1966; Sanctuary, 1966; The Bright Lights, 1968; Reflections from a Village, 1969; On the Shady Side, 1970; Nor all thy Tears, 1972; Rosalind Passes, 1973; Some Achieve Greatness, 1976; Arnold Bennett: a last word, 1978. *Address:* Old Tokefield, Cranleigh, Surrey. *Club:* Reform (Hon. Life Mem.).

SWINNERTON-DYER, Prof. Sir (Henry) Peter (Francis), 16th Bt *cr* 1678; FRS 1967; Professor of Mathematics, University of Cambridge, since 1971 (Lecturer 1960-71); Master of St Catharine's College, Cambridge, since 1973; *b* 2 Aug. 1927; *s* of Sir Leonard Schroeder Swinnerton Dyer, 15th Bt, and of Barbara, *d* of Hereward Brackenbury, CBE; *S* father, 1975. *Educ:* Eton; Trinity College, Cambridge (Hon. Fellow 1981). Trinity College, Cambridge: Research Fellow, 1950-54; Fellow, 1955-73; Dean, 1963-73; Univ. Lectr, Mathematical Laboratory, Cambridge, 1960-67; Vice-Chancellor, Univ. of Cambridge, 1979-81. Commonwealth Fund Fellow, Univ. of Chicago, 1954-55. Vis. Prof., Harvard Univ., 1971. Hon. Fellow, Worcester Coll., Oxford, 1980. Chairman: Cttee on Academic Organisation, Univ. of London, 1980-82; Meteorological Cttee, 1983-. Hon. DSc Bath, 1981. *Publications:* numerous papers in mathematical journals. *Recreations:* tennis, squash. *Heir: kinsman* Richard Stewart Dyer-Bennet [*b* 6 Oct. 1886; *m* 1912, Miriam Wolcott (*d* 1973), *d* of late Prof. Edward B. Clapp; four *s* one *d*]. *Address:* St Catharine's College, Cambridge.

SWINTON, 2nd Earl of, *cr* 1955; **David Yarburgh Cunliffe-Lister,** JP; DL; Viscount Swinton, 1935; Baron Masham, 1955; Captain of the Yeomen of the Guard (Deputy Government Chief Whip), since 1982; *b* 21 March 1937; *s* of Major Hon. John Yarburgh Cunliffe-Lister (*d* of wounds received in action, 1943) and Anne Irvine (*d* 1961), *yr d* of late Rev. Canon R. S. Medlicott (she *m* 2nd, 1944, Donald Chapple-Gill); *S* grandfather, 1972; *m* 1959, Susan Lilian Primrose Sinclair (*see* Baroness Masham of Ilton); one *s* one *d* (both adopted). *Educ:* Winchester; Royal Agricultural College. Member: N Riding Yorks CC, 1961-74; N Yorks CC, 1973-77. JP North (formerly NR) Yorks,

1971; DL North Yorks, 1978. *Heir: b* Hon. Nicholas John Cunliffe-Lister [*b* 4 Sept. 1939; *m* 1966, Elizabeth Susan, *e d of* Rt Hon. William Whitelaw, *qv* ; two *s* one *d*]. *Address:* Dykes Hill House, Masham, N Yorks. *T:* Masham 241; c/o Midland Bank Ltd, 1 Sydney Place, Onslow Square, SW7.

SWINTON, Countess of; *see* Masham of Ilton, Baroness.

SWINTON, Maj.-Gen. Sir John, KCVO 1979; OBE 1969; DL; *b* 21 April 1925; *s* of late Brig. A. H. C. Swinton, MC, Scots Guards; *m* 1954, Judith, *d* of late Harold Killen, Merribee, NSW; three *s* one *d. Educ:* Harrow. Enlisted, Scots Guards, 1943, commissioned, 1944; served NW Europe, 1945 (twice wounded); Malaya, 1948-51 (despatches); ADC to Field Marshal Sir William Slim, Governor-General of Australia, 1953-54; Staff College, 1957; DAA&QMG 1st Guards Brigade, 1958-59; Regimental Adjutant Scots Guards, 1960-62; Adjutant, RMA Sandhurst, 1962-64; comd 2nd Bn Scots Guards, 1966-68; AAG PS12 MoD, 1968-70; Lt Col Comdg Scots Guards, 1970-71; Comdr, 4th Guards Armoured Brigade, BAOR, 1972-73; RCDS 1974; Brigadier Lowlands and Comdr Edinburgh and Glasgow Garrisons, 1975-76; GOC London Dist and Maj.-Gen. Comdg Household Divn, 1976-79. Brig., Queen's Body Guard for Scotland (Royal Co. of Archers), 1977-. Trustee, Army Museums Ogilby Trust, 1978-. Co-ordinator, Scotland, Duke of Edinburgh's Award 25th Anniversary Appeal, 1980-82. DL Berwickshire, 1980. *Address:* Kimmerghame, Duns, Berwickshire. *T:* Duns 3277.

SWIRE, Sir Adrian (Christopher), Kt 1982; Deputy Chairman, John Swire and Sons Ltd, since 1966 (Director, 1961); Deputy Chairman: Overseas Containers Pacific Ltd; NAAFI; Director: Swire Pacific Ltd, Cathay Pacific Airways and other Swire Group companies; Brooke Bond Liebig; *b* 15 Feb. 1932; *yr s* of John Kidston Swire, *qv* ; *m* 1970, Lady Judith Compton, *e d* of 6th Marquess of Northampton, DSO; two *s* one *d. Educ:* Eton; University Coll., Oxford (MA). Coldstream Guards, 1950-52; pilot, RAFVR and Royal Hong Kong AAF (AE 1961). Joined Butterfield & Swire in Far East, 1956. Chm., China Navigation Co. Ltd, 1968. Mem., Gen. Cttee, Lloyd's Register. Pres., General Council of British Shipping, 1980-81. Vis. Fellow, Nuffield Coll., Oxford, 1981-. *Address:* Regis House, 43 King William Street, EC4. *Clubs:* White's, Brooks's, City of London.

SWIRE, John Anthony, CBE 1977; Chairman, John Swire & Sons Ltd, since 1966; Director: James Finlay plc, since 1976; (non-executive), Ocean Transport & Trading Ltd, since 1977; *b* 28 Feb. 1927; *s* of John Kidston Swire, *qv* ; *m* 1961, Moira Cecilia Ducharne; two *s* one *d. Educ:* Eton; University Coll., Oxford (MA). Served Irish Guards, UK and Palestine, 1945-48. Joined Butterfield & Swire, Hong Kong, 1950; Dir, John Swire & Sons Ltd, 1955. Chm., Hong Kong Assoc., 1975. Member: London Adv. Cttee, Hongkong and Shanghai Banking Corp., 1969-; Euro-Asia Centre Adv. Bd, 1980-; Stanford Univ. Adv. Council, 1981-. *Address:* Luton House, Selling, near Faversham, Kent ME13 9RQ. *T:* Selling 234. *Clubs:* Brooks's, Pratt's, Cavalry and Guards, City, Flyfishers'; Union (Sydney).
See also Sir A. C. Swire.

SWIRE, John Kidston; Director, John Swire & Sons, Ltd, 1920-68 (Chairman, 1946-66); Hon. President, Cathay Pacific Airways Ltd; Member, General Committee, Lloyd's Register of Shipping, 1940-68; *b* 19 Feb. 1893; *er s* of late John Swire, Hillingdon House, Harlow, Essex; *m* 1923, Juliet Richenda (*d* 1981), *d* of Theodore Barclay, Fanshaws, Hertford; two *s* two *d. Educ:* Eton Coll.; University Coll., Oxford. Major Essex Yeomanry, with whom he served in European War 1914-19. DL Essex, 1928-68; High Sheriff, Essex, 1941-42. Min. of Shipping Rep. at Min. of Economic Warfare and on the Contraband Cttee, 1939-40; Chm. Port Employers in London and Port Labour Exec. Cttee, 1941-45. Chm. China Association, 1951-55. *Address:* Hubbards Hall, Harlow, Essex. *TA* and *T:* Harlow 29470. *Clubs:* Turf, Cavalry and Guards (Hon. Life Mem.), City of London (Hon. Life Mem.).
See also Sir A. C. Swire, J. A. Swire.

SWISS, Sir Rodney (Geoffrey), Kt 1975; OBE 1964; JP; FDSRCS; President, General Dental Council, 1974-79 (Member, 1957-79); *b* 4 Aug. 1904; *e s* of Henry H. Swiss, Devonport, Devon, and Emma Jane Swiss (*nee* Williams); *m* 1928, Muriel Alberta Gledhill. *Educ:* Plymouth Coll.; Dean Close Sch., Cheltenham; Guy's Hosp. LDSRCS 1926, FDSRCS 1978. General dental practice, Harrow, Mddx, 1930-69 (Hon. dental surgeon, Harrow Hosp., 1935-67). NHS Mddx Exec. Council, 1947-74 (Chm., 1970-71); Chm., Central Health Services Council, 1964-74; Chairman: Standing Dental Advisory Cttee, 1964-74; Hendon Juvenile Court, 1959-64; Gore Petty Sessional Div., 1965-67 and 1970-74; Management Cttee, Sch. for Dental Auxiliaries, 1972-74. JP Mddx area, 1949. *Publications:* contribs to dental press. *Recreation:* philately. *Address:* Shrublands, 23 West Way, Pinner, Mddx HA5 3NX.

SWORD, John Howe; Director, Oral History Project, University of Toronto, since 1981; *b* Saskatoon, Saskatchewan, 22 Jan. 1915; *m* 1947, Constance A. Offen; one *s* one *d. Educ:* public and high schs, Winnipeg; Univ. of Manitoba (BA); Univ. of Toronto (MA). Served War, RCAF, Aircrew navigation trg and instr in Western Canada. Taught for six years, before War, in Roland, Teulon and Winnipeg, Manitoba. Secretary, Manitoba Royal Commn on Adult Educn, 1945-46. Univ. of Toronto: Asst Sec. and Sec., Sch. of Grad. Studies, 1947-60; Exec. Asst to the President, 1960-65; Vice-Provost, 1965-67;

Actg Pres., 1967-68; Exec. Vice-Pres. (Academic), and Provost, 1968-71; Actg Pres., 1971-72; Vice-Pres., Institutional Relations and Planning, 1972-74; Special Asst to the President, Institutional Relations, 1974-80; Acting Dir, Sch. of Continuing Studies, 1980-81. Chm., Art Cttee, Hart House, Univ. of Toronto, 1979-; Member: Bd, Addiction Res. Foundn of Ont, 1981-; Council, Royal Canadian Inst., Toronto, 1981-; Management Bd, Geneva Park YMCA. Mem., United Church. Hon. LLD, Univ. of Manitoba, 1970. *Recreations:* tennis, swimming. *Address:* 8 Wychwood Park, Toronto, Ontario M6G 2V5, Canada. *T:* 6565876. *Clubs:* Faculty (Univ. of Toronto); Arts and Letters, Queen's.

SWYER, Dr Gerald Isaac Macdonald, FRCP; Consultant Endocrinologist, Department of Obstetrics and Gynæcology, University College Hospital, London, 1951-78, retired; Councillor, London Borough of Camden; *b* 17 Nov. 1917; *s* of Nathan Swyer; *m* 1945, Lynda Irene (*née* Nash); one *s* one *d. Educ:* St Paul's School; Magdalen College and St John's College, Oxford; University of California; Middlesex Hospital Medical School. Foundation Schol. and Leaving Exhib., St Paul's School, 1931-36; Open Exhib. and Casberd Schol., St John's Coll., Oxford, 1936-39; Welsh Memorial Prize, 1937; Theodore Williams Schol. in Anatomy, 1938; 1st Cl. Final Honour School of Animal Physiology, 1939; Senior Demy, Magdalen Coll., 1940; Rockefeller Medical Student, Univ. of Calif, 1941. MA, DPhil, BM Oxon 1943; MD Calif, 1943; DM Oxon 1948; MRCP 1945; FRCP 1964; Hon FRCOG 1975. Mem. of Scientific Staff, Nat. Inst. for Med. Res., 1946-47; Endocrinologist, UCH Med. Sch., 1947. 1st Sec., formerly Chm., Soc. for the Study of Fertility; formerly Mem. Council, Soc. for Endocrinology; formerly Pres., Sect. of Endocrinology, Roy. Soc. Med.; formerly Sec.-Gen., Internat. Fedn of Fertility Societies and Mem. Exec. Sub-Cttee Internat. Endocrine Soc. *Publications:* Reproduction and Sex, 1954; papers in medical and scientific journals. *Recreations:* music, gardening. *Address:* 2 Prince Arthur Road, NW3 6AU. *T:* 01-435 4723.

SWYNNERTON, Sir Roger (John Massy), Kt 1976; CMG 1959; OBE 1951; MC 1941; consultant in tropical agriculture and development; Director, Booker Agriculture International Ltd; *b* S Rhodesia, 16 Jan. 1911; *s* of late C. F. M. Swynnerton, CMG, formerly Dir Tsetse Research, Tanganyika, and Mrs N. A. G. Swynnerton (*née* Watt Smyth); *m* Grizel Beryl Miller, *d* of late R. W. R. Miller, CMG, formerly Member for Agriculture and Natural Resources, Tanganyika; two *s. Educ:* Lancing Coll.; Gonville and Caius Coll., Cambridge (BA Hons 1932; DipAgric 1933); Imperial Coll. of Tropical Agriculture, Trinidad. AICTA 1934. O/c CUOTC Artillery Bty, 1932-33; TARO, 1933-60. Entered Colonial Agricultural Service as Agric. Officer and Sen. Agric. Officer, 1934-50, in Tanganyika Territory. Served War, 1939-42, with 1/6 Bn KAR (Temp. Capt.), Abyssinian Campaign. Seconded to Malta on Agric. duty, 1942-43. Transferred to Kenya on promotion, Asst Director of Agric., 1951, Dep. Dir, 1954, Director, 1956. Nominated Member of Kenya Legislative Council, 1956-61; Permanent Sec., Min. of Agriculture, 1960-62; Temp. Minister for Agriculture, Animal Husbandry and Water Resources, 1961, retd 1963. Mem. Advisory Cttee on Development of Economic Resources of S Rhodesia, 1961-62; Agric. Adviser and Mem. Exec. Management Bd, Commonwealth Develt Corp., 1962-76. Mem. Adv. Bd, Inst. of Irrigation Studies, Southampton Univ., 1980-. *Publications:* All About KNCU Coffee, 1948; A Plan to Intensify the Development of African Agriculture in Kenya, 1954; various agricultural and scientific papers. *Address:* 35 Lower Road, Fetcham, Leatherhead, Surrey KT22 9EL. *Clubs:* Royal Commonwealth Society, Royal Over-Seas League; Nairobi (Kenya).

SYCAMORE, Thomas Andrew Harding, CBE 1949; retired; a Managing Director, Liebig's Extract of Meat Co. Ltd, 1963-66; Chairman, Chipmunk Ltd, 1962-66; Director: Beefex Products Ltd, 1954-66; Bellamy's Wharf & Dock Ltd, 1958-66; Oxo Ltd, 1954-66 (Managing Director 1954-63); Oxo (Canada) Ltd, 1954-66; Oxo (Ireland) Ltd, 1954-66; Oxo (USA) Ltd, 1954-66; Thames Side Properties Ltd, 1955-66; Produits Liebig SA, Basle, 1965-66; Euro-Liebig SC, Antwerp, 1964-66; Compagnie Française des Produits Liebig SA, Paris, 1963-66; Compagnie Liebig SA, Antwerp, 1963-66; Compagnia Italiana Liebig SpA, Milan, 1963-66; Nederlandse Oxo Maatschappij NV, Rotterdam, 1963-66; Liebig GmbH, Cologne, 1963-66; Beefco Corp., New York, 1963-66 (Chairman, 1964-66); London Philharmonic Society Ltd, 1960-66; *b* 31 Aug. 1907; *s* of late Henry Andrew and Caroline Helen Sycamore; *m* 1932, Winifred Clara Pellett; one *s* two *d. Educ:* privately. At Oxford Univ. Press, 1924-35; Manufacturing Confectioners' Alliance, 1936-40 (Asst Sec. 1940); Food Manufacturers' Federation Inc., 1936-54; Asst Sec., 1940; Sec., 1945; Director and Gen. Sec., 1947. Secretary, Bacon Marketing Bd, and many other food manufacturers' associations, etc; Mem., Food Research Adv. Cttee, 1960-66; Vice-Pres., Assoc. Internat. de l'Industrie des Bouillons et Potages (Paris), 1963-65. Member Council: British Food Manufacturing Industries Research Association (formerly Sec.); Food Manufacturers' Federation, Inc.; Grocers' Institute (a Vice-Pres. 1958-66, Hon. Treas. 1961-66); English Stage Soc.; Mem. Grand Council, FBI (member many committees); Deputy Leader and Sec. of two productivity teams which went to the US; helped to create Food Industries Council (Sec. for many years); helped in formation of National College of Food Technology, and to establish British Food Fair at Olympia (Sec. for many years). Served on Councils or Committees of various other bodies; a Governor of several schools. President of Appeal, Royal Commercial Travellers' Schools, 1960-61; Life Hon. Vice-President, Huddersfield Branch, United Commercial Travellers' Assoc., 1962; Chm., Nat. Music Council of Gt Brit., 1963-64. Freeman, City of London. Liveryman, Worshipful

Company of Loriners; Life Mem., Guild of Freemen of City of London; FREconS; Hon. Fellow, Grocers' Institute; Officier de l'Ordre de la Couronne (Belgium), 1965. *Recreations:* music, theatre, reading, tennis, cricket. *Address:* 36 Meadow Way, Fairlight, near Hastings, E Sussex TN35 4BN. *T:* Pett 2364.

SYDNEY, Archbishop of, and Metropolitan of New South Wales, since 1982; **Most Rev. Donald William Bradley Robinson;** *b* 9 Nov. 1922; *s* of Rev. Richard Bradley Robinson and Gertrude Marston Robinson (*née* Ross); *m* 1949, Marie Elizabeth Taubman; three *s* one *d. Educ:* Sydney Church of England Gram. Sch.; Univ. of Sydney (BA); Queens' Coll., Cambridge (MA). Australian Army, 1941–45, Lieut Intell. Corps, 1944. Deacon 1950, Sydney; priest 1951; Curate, Manly, NSW, 1950–52; St Philip's, Sydney, 1952–53; Lecturer: Moore Coll., 1952–81 (Vice-Principal, 1959–72); Sydney Univ., 1964–81; Asst Bishop, Diocese of Sydney (Bishop in Parramatta), 1973–82. Hon. ThD Aust. Coll. of Theology, 1979. *Address:* St Andrew's House, Sydney Square, NSW 2000, Australia. *T:* (02) 269 0642.

SYDNEY, Archbishop of, (RC), since 1971; **His Eminence Sir James Darcy Cardinal Freeman,** KBE 1977; Knight of the Holy Sepulchre; *b* 19 Nov. 1907; *s* of Robert Freeman and Margaret Smith. *Educ:* Christian Brothers' High School, St Mary's Cathedral, Sydney; St Columba's Coll., Springwood, NSW; St Patrick's Coll., Manly, NSW. Priest, 1930; Private Secretary to HE Cardinal Gilroy, Archbishop of Sydney, 1941–46; Auxiliary Bishop to HE Cardinal Gilroy, 1957; Bishop of Armidale, 1968. Cardinal, 1973. Hon. DD 1957. *Address:* St Mary's Cathedral, Sydney, NSW 2000, Australia. *T:* 232-3788.

SYDNEY, Assistant Bishops of; *see* Cameron, Rt Rev. E. D.; Dain, Rt Rev. A. J.; Reid, Rt Rev. J. R.; Short, Rt Rev. K. H.

SYER, William George, CVO 1961; CBE 1957; *b* 22 June 1913; *s* of late William Robert Syer and late Beatrice Alice Theresa Syer, Alton, Hants; *m* 1948, Marjorie Leila, *d* of late S. G. Pike, Essex; no *c. Educ:* Kent College, Canterbury. Joined Colonial Police Service, 1933; Gibraltar, 1933–35; Jamaica, 1935–40; Nigeria, 1940–51; Comr of Police, Sierra Leone, 1951; retired, 1962; Comr of Police, Swaziland, 1964–68. Sec., West Africa Cttee, 1970–78. Formerly Comr St John Ambulance Brigade, Sierra Leone. CStJ 1969. *Recreations:* travelling, birdwatching, walking. *Address:* 2 Lansdowne Court, Lansdowne Road, Budleigh Salterton, Devon. *T:* Budleigh Salterton 3016.

SYKES, Lt-Col Arthur Patrick, MBE 1945; JP; DL; *b* 1 Sept. 1906; *e s* of late Herbert R. Sykes, JP; *m* 1949, Prudence Margaret, *d* of late Maj.-Gen. D. E. Robertson, CB, DSO, Indian Army; one *s* one *d. Educ:* Eton; Magdalene College, Cambridge. 2nd Lt 60th Rifles, 1929; served India, Burma, Palestine; ADC to Governor of Bengal, 1933–35; War of 1939–45, Middle East (wounded); Lt-Col 1944. JP 1950, DL 1951, High Sheriff, 1961, Shropshire. *Address:* Lydham Manor, Bishops Castle, Shropshire. *T:* Bishops Castle 486.

SYKES, Bonar Hugh Charles; farmer; formerly Counsellor in HM Diplomatic Service; *b* 20 Dec. 1922; *s* of late Sir Frederick Sykes and of Isabel, *d* of Andrew Bonar Law; *m* 1949, Mary, *d* of late Sir Eric Phipps and of Frances Phipps; four *s. Educ:* Eton; The Queen's Coll., Oxford. War service in Navy (Lieut RNVR), 1942–46. Trainee with Ford Motor Co. (Tractor Div.), 1948–49. Joined Foreign Service, 1949: served in Prague, Bonn, Tehran, Ottawa, FCO; retired 1970. Pres., Wiltshire Archaeological and Natural History Soc., 1975–. Member: Bd of Visitors of Erlestoke Prison, 1977; Council, Museums Assoc., 1981–. *Address:* Conock Manor, Devizes, Wiltshire. *T:* Chirton 227.

SYKES, Christopher Hugh, FRSL; author; Member, London Library Committee, 1965–74; *b* 17 Nov. 1907; 2nd *s* of late Sir Mark Sykes, Bt, Sledmere; *m* 1936, Camilla Georgiana, *d* of El Lewa Sir Thomas Russell Pasha, CMG; one *s. Educ:* Downside; Christ Church, Oxford. Hon. Attaché to HM Embassy, Berlin, 1928–29, and to HM Legation, Tehran, 1930–31. Served War of 1939–45: 7 Battalion The Green Howards; GHQ, Cairo; HM Legation, Tehran; SAS Bde (despatches, Croix de Guerre). Special correspondent of the Daily Mail for the Persian Azerbaijan Campaign, 1946; Deputy Controller, Third Programme, BBC, 1948; Features Dept, BBC, 1949–68. *Publications:* Wassmuss, 1936; (with late R. Byron), Innocence and Design, 1936; Stranger Wonders, 1937; High Minded Murder, 1943; Four Studies in Loyalty, 1946; The Answer to Question 33, 1948; Character and Situation, 1949; Two Studies in Virtue, 1953; A Song of A Shirt, 1953; Dates and Parties, 1955; Orde Wingate, 1959; Cross Roads to Israel, 1965; Troubled Loyalty: a Biography of Adam von Trott, 1968; Nancy, the life of Lady Astor, 1972; Evelyn Waugh, 1975. *Recreation:* music. *Address:* Swyre House, Swyre, Dorchester, Dorset.

SYKES, Dr Donald Armstrong; Principal of Mansfield College, Oxford, since 1977; *b* 13 Feb. 1930; *s* of Rev. Leonard Sykes and late Edith Mary Sykes (*née* Armstrong); *m* 1962, Marta Sproul Whitehouse; two *s. Educ:* The High Sch. of Dundee; Univ. of St Andrews (MA 2nd cl. Classics 1952; Guthrie Scholar); Mansfield Coll., Oxford (BA 1st cl. Theol. 1958; MA 1961; DPhil 1967); Univ. of Glasgow (DipEd). Fellow in Theology, 1959–77, and Senior Tutor, 1970–77, Mansfield Coll., Oxford. Vis. Prof. in Religion, St Olaf Coll., Northfield, Minn, 1969–70 (Hon. DD 1979). *Publications:* articles and reviews in Jl Theological Studies, Studia Patristica, Byzantinische Zeitschrift.

Recreations: gramophone records, gardening, walking. *Address:* The Principal's Lodgings, Mansfield College, Oxford OX1 3TF. *T:* Oxford 42340 and 43507. *Club:* United Oxford & Cambridge University.

SYKES, Edwin Leonard, CMG 1966; *b* 1 May 1914; *m* 1st, 1946, Margaret Elizabeth McCulloch (*d* 1973); 2nd, 1976, Dorothy Soderberg. *Educ:* Leys School, Cambridge (Schol.); Trinity Coll., Cambridge (Senior Schol.). Entered Dominions Office, 1937; Asst Priv. Sec. to Secretary of State, 1939. Served War, 1939–45 (despatches). Served in British High Commissions, Canada, 1945–47, India, 1952–54; idc 1955; Dep. UK High Commissioner in Federation of Rhodesia and Nyasaland, 1956–59; Asst Under-Sec. of State, CRO, 1964–65; Dep. UK High Commissioner in Pakistan, 1965–66; Sec., Office of the Parly Comr for Administration, 1967–74. *Address:* 7 Upper Rose Hill, Dorking, Surrey.

SYKES, Sir Francis (Godfrey), 9th Bt, *cr* 1781, of Basildon; *b* 27 Aug. 1907; *s* of Francis William Sykes (*d* 1945) (*g g s* of 2nd Bt) and Beatrice Agnes Sykes (*née* Webb) (*d* 1953); *S* cousin, Rev. Sir Frederic John Sykes, 8th Bt, 1956; *m* 1st, 1934, Eira Betty (*d* 1970), *d* of G. W. Badcock; one *s* one *d*; 2nd, 1972, Nesta Mabel (*d* 1982), *d* of late Col and Mrs Harold Platt Sykes. *Educ:* Blundell's School, Devon; Nelson College, New Zealand. Tea planting, 1930; Air Ministry, 1939; fruit farming and estate management, 1945–57; Regional Sec., Country Landowners' Assoc., 1957–72. FCIS. *Heir: s* Francis John Badcock Sykes [*b* 7 June 1942; *m* 1966, Susan Alexandra, *er d* of Adm. of the Fleet Sir E. B. Ashmore, *qv*; three *s*]. *Address:* 7 Linney, Ludlow, Salop SY8 1EF. *T:* Ludlow 4336. *Club:* Salop (Shrewsbury).

SYKES, James Richard, QC 1981; *b* 28 May 1934; *s* of Philip James and Lucy Barbara Sykes; *m* 1959, Susan Ethne Patricia Allen; one *s* three *d. Educ:* Charterhouse; Pembroke Coll., Cambridge. BA 1957, MA 1971. Nat. Service, 2nd Lieut RASC, 1952–54. Called to the Bar, Lincoln's Inn, 1958. Member: City Company Law Cttee, 1974–79; City Capital Markets Cttee, 1980–. *Publications:* (Consultant Editor) Gore-Browne on Companies, 42nd edn 1972, 43rd edn 1977; (ed jtly) The Conduct of Meetings, 20th edn 1966, 21st edn 1975. *Recreations:* woodwork, photography. *Address:* Vassars, Langley, Hitchin, Herts SG4 7PH. *T:* Stevenage 52271.

SYKES, Dr John Bradbury; Head of German Dictionaries, Oxford University Press, since 1981; *b* Folkestone, Kent, 26 Jan. 1929; *s* of late Stanley William Sykes and late Eleanor Sykes (*née* Bradbury); *m* 1955, Avril Barbara Hart; one *s. Educ:* Wallasey Grammar Sch.; Rochdale High Sch.; St Lawrence Coll.; Wadham Coll., Oxford (BA Maths 1950); Balliol Coll., Oxford (Skynner Sen. Student); Merton Coll., Oxford (Harmsworth Sen. Schol., MA and DPhil Astrophysics 1953). AERE, Harwell, 1953–71 (Head of Translations Office 1958, Principal Scientific Officer 1960); Member, Internat. Astronomical Union, 1958 (Pres., Commn for Documentation, 1967–73). Editor, Concise and Pocket Oxford Dictionaries, 1971–81. Mem. Bd, Translators' Guild Ltd, 1980–. Fellow, Inst. of Linguists, 1960 (Mem. Council, 1977–; Editor, Incorporated Linguist, 1980–). *Publications:* (with B Davison) Neutron Transport Theory, 1957; (ed) Technical Translator's Manual, 1971; (ed) Concise Oxford Dictionary, 6th edn, 1976, 7th edn, 1982; (ed) Pocket Oxford Dictionary, 6th edn, 1978; translations of many Russian textbooks in physics and astronomy; contribs to Incorporated Linguist. *Recreation:* crossword-solving (National Champion 1958, 1972–75, 1977, 1980). *Address:* 19 Walton Manor Court, Adelaide Street, Oxford OX2 6EL. *T:* Oxford 57532. *Club:* PEN.

SYKES, Sir John (Charles Anthony le Gallais), 3rd Bt *cr* 1921; *b* 19 April 1928; *s* of Stanley Edgar Sykes (*d* 1963) (2nd *s* of 1st Bt) and Florence Anaise le Gallais (*d* 1955); *S* uncle, 1974; *m* (marr. diss.). *Educ:* Churchers College. Export merchant. Mem., British Epicure Soc. *Recreations:* golf, wine, food, travel. *Heir: nephew* David Michael Sykes [*b* 10 June 1954; *m* 1974, Susan Elizabeth, 3rd *d* of G. W. Hall; one *s*]. *Address:* 58 Alders View Drive, East Grinstead, Sussex RH19 2DN. *T:* East Grinstead 22027.

SYKES, Joseph Walter, CMG 1962; CVO 1953; Chairman, Fiji Public Service Commission, 1971–80; *b* 10 July 1915; *s* of Samuel Sykes and Lucy M. Womack; *m* 1940, Elima Petrie, *d* of late Sir Hugh Hall Ragg; three *s* two *d. Educ:* De La Salle Coll., Sheffield; Rotherham Gram. Sch.; Jesus Coll., Oxford. Colonial Administrative Service, Fiji; Cadet, 1938; Dist Officer, 1940; District Commissioner, 1950; Deputy Secretary for Fijian Affairs, 1952; Assistant Colonial Secretary, 1953; transferred to Cyprus as Dep. Colonial Sec., Nov. 1954; Admin. Sec., Cyprus. 1955–56; Colonial Sec., Bermuda, 1956–68; Chief Sec., Bermuda, 1968–71; retired. *Publication:* The Royal Visit to Fiji 1953, 1954. *Recreations:* photography, tennis. *Address:* 8 Dorking Road, City Beach, Perth, WA, Australia. *Club:* United Oxford & Cambridge University.

SYKES, Prof. Keble Watson; Vice-Principal, since 1978, Professor of Physical Chemistry, since 1956, Queen Mary College, University of London; *b* 7 Jan. 1921; *s* of Watson and Victoria May Sykes; *m* 1950, Elizabeth Margaret Ewing Forsyth; three *d* (and one *s* decd). *Educ:* Seascale Preparatory Sch.; St Bees Sch.; The Queen's Coll., Oxford, MA, BSc, DPhil (Oxon.). ICI Research Fellow, Physical Chemistry Lab., Oxford, 1945–48; Lecturer, 1948–51, and Senior Lecturer in Chemistry, 1951–56, University Coll. of Swansea, Univ. of Wales; Head of Chemistry Dept, 1959–78, and Dean, Fac. of Science, 1970–73, QMC, London. Hon. Sec. Chemical Soc. of London, 1960–66, Vice-Pres., 1966–69, Mem. Council, 1977–80. Member Council, Westfield

College, University of London, 1962-77. *Publications:* scientific papers in journals of Royal Society, Faraday Soc. and Chem. Soc. *Address:* 58 Wood Vale, Muswell Hill, N10 3DN. *T:* 01-883 1502.

SYKES, Prof. Malcolm Keith; Nuffield Professor of Anaesthetics, University of Oxford, since 1980; *b* 13 Sept. 1925; *s* of Joseph and Phyllis Mary Sykes; *m* 1956, Michelle June (*née* Ratcliffe); one *s* three *d. Educ:* Magdalene Coll., Cambridge (MA, MB, BChir); University Coll. Hosp., London (DA; FFARCS). RAMC, 1950-52. House appointments, University Coll. and Norfolk and Norwich Hosps, 1949-50; Sen. House Officer, Registrar and Sen. Registrar in anaesthetics, UCH, 1952-54 and 1955-58; Rickman Godlee Travelling Scholar and Fellow in Anesthesia, Mass. General Hosp., Boston, USA, 1954-55; RPMS and Hammersmith Hosp., 1958-80: Lectr and Sen. Lectr, 1958-67; Reader, 1967-70; Prof. of Clinical Anaesthesia, 1970-80. Vis. Prof., univs in Canada, USA, Australia, NZ, Malaysia, Europe. Eponymous lectures: Holme, 1970; Clover, 1976; Weinbren, 1976; Rowbottom, 1978; Gillespie, 1979. Member: Council, Assoc. of Anaesthetists, 1967-70; Bd, Fac. of Anaesthetists, 1969-; Senator and Chm., Scientific Cttee, European Acad. of Anaesthesiology, 1978-. Hon. FFARACS 1979. Dudley Buxton Prize, Fac. of Anaesthetists, 1980. *Publications:* Respiratory Failure, 1969, 2nd edn 1976; Principles of Measurement for Anaesthetists, 1970; Principles of Clinical Measurement, 1980; chapters and papers on respiratory failure, intensive care, respiratory and cardiovascular physiology applied to anaesthesia, etc. *Recreations:* sailing, walking, birdwatching, gardening, music. *Address:* 10 Fitzherbert Close, Iffley, Oxford. *T:* Oxford 771152.

SYKES, Rev. Prof. Stephen Whitefield, MA; Van Mildert Canon Professor of Divinity, Durham University, since 1974; *b* 1939; *m* 1962; one *s* two *d. Educ:* St John's Coll., Cambridge. BA (Cantab) 1961 (1st cl. Theol), Pt iii Theol Tripos 1962 (1st cl. with dist.); MA (Cantab) 1964. Univ. Asst Lectr in Divinity, Cambridge Univ., 1964-68, Lectr, 1968-74; Fellow and Dean, St John's Coll., Cambridge, 1964-74. Mem., Archbishop's Cttee on Religious Educn, 1967. Examining Chaplain to Bishop of Chelmsford, 1970-. Edward Cadbury Lectr, Univ. of Birmingham, 1978. Chm., North of England Inst. for Christian Educn, 1980-. *Publications:* Friedrich Schleiermacher, 1971; Christian Theology Today, 1971; (ed) Christ, Faith and History, 1972; The Integrity of Anglicanism, 1978; (ed) Karl Barth: studies in his theological method, 1980; (ed) New Studies in Theology, 1980. *Recreation:* walking. *Address:* 14 The College, Durham DH1 3EQ.

SYKES, Sir Tatton (Christopher Mark), 8th Bt *cr* 1783; landowner; *b* 24 Dec. 1943; *s* of Sir (Mark Tatton) Richard Tatton-Sykes, 7th Bt and Virginia (*d* 1970), *d* of late John Francis Grey Gilliat; *S* father, 1978; granted use of additional arms of Tatton, 1980. *Educ:* Eton; Univ. d'Aix-Marseille; Royal Agric. Coll., Cirencester. *Heir: b* Jeremy John Sykes, *b* 8 March 1946. *Address:* Sledmere, Driffield, East Yorkshire.

SYKES, Air Vice-Marshal William, OBE; CEng, FRAeS; FIIM; FBIM; RAF retired, 1975; Resident Executive, British Aerospace (Oman); *b* 14 March 1920; *s* of Edmund and Margaret Sykes, Appleby, Westmorland; *m* 1946, Jean Begg, *d* of Alexander and Wilemena Harrold, Watten, Caithness; one *s* one *d. Educ:* Raley Sch. and Technical Coll., Barnsley, Yorks. HNC Mech. and Aero Eng. 1942; CEng, AFRAeS 1968, FRAeS 1974, FBIM (MBIM 1975), FIIM 1979. Joined RAF as Aircraft Apprentice, 1936. Served War: No 51 (Bomber) Sqdn, 1939-41; various engrg specialist courses; commissioned, 1942; Coastal Command: Invergordon, Pembroke Dock, Gibraltar, Hamworthy, Reykjavik (Iceland) and Tain. After 1945: appts at Marine Aircraft Exptl Estabt, Felixstowe; HQ No 23 Gp; Central Servicing Develt Estabt (CSDE); RAE; 2nd TAF, Germany; Dept of ACAS(OR); Electrical Specialist Course, 1948; Staff Coll., 1953-54; jssc 1959-60. During period 1960-72: served a further tour with CSDE as OC Projects Wing; was OC Engrg Wing, Wyton; Station Comdr, No 8 of TT, Weeton; Comd Engrg Officer, FEAF; Dir of Mechanical Engrg (RAF), MoD (AFD); Air Officer Engrg, NEAF; Vice-Pres., Ordnance Board, 1972-74, Pres., 1974-75. Attended IDC, 1967. *Recreations:* travel, motor sports. *Address:* PO Box 3074, Seeb Airport, Muscat, Sultanate of Oman; 5 Clifton Court, Clifton Drive South, St Anne's-on-Sea, Lancs. *T:* St Anne's 727689. *Club:* Royal Air Force.

SYLVESTER, Albert James, CBE 1920; JP; *b* Harlaston, Staffs, 24 Nov. 1889; *s* of late Albert and Edith Sylvester; *m* Evelyn (*d* 1962), *d* of late Rev. W. Welman, Reading; one *d. Educ:* Guild Street School, Burton-on-Trent; privately (champion typist). Private Secretary to Sec. of Cttee of Imperial Defence, 1914-21; Private Sec. to Sec. of War Cabinet and of Cabinet, 1916-21; Private Secretary to Secretary, Imperial War Cabinet, 1917; Private Secretary to British Secretary, Peace Conference, 1919; Private Secretary to successive Prime Ministers, 1921-23; Principal Secretary to Earl Lloyd George of Dwyfor, 1923-45. Film, The Very Private Secretary, BBC TV, 1974; portrayed in BBC TV Series The Life and Times of Lloyd George, 1981; work in progress, 1982, for BBC radio programme on life story. JP Wilts. 1953. Commander of the Order of the Crown of Italy, and Sacred Treasure of Japan. Supreme Award (with Honours), Ballroom and Latin American Dancing, Imperial Soc. of Teachers of Dancing, 1977; Alex Moore Award, 1977; Guinness Book of Records states is the oldest competitive ballroom dancer. *Publications:* The Real Lloyd George, 1947; Life with Lloyd George (diaries, ed Colin Cross), 1975. *Recreations:* riding and golf. *Address:* Rudloe Cottage, Corsham, Wilts. *T:* Hawthorn 810375. *Club:* National Liberal.
See also A. Sylvester-Evans.

SYLVESTER, (Anthony) David (Bernard); writer on art, etc; editing catalogue raisonné of Rene Magritte; *b* 21 Sept. 1924; *s* of Philip Silvester and Sybil Rosen; *m* Pamela Briddon; three *d.* Arts Council of Great Britain: Mem., 1980-82; Mem., Art Panel, 1962-70, 1972-77, Chm., 1980-82. Mem., BFI Prodn Bd, 1966-69; Trustee, Tate Gall., 1967-69. Vis. Lecturer: Slade Sch. of Fine Art, 1953-57; RCA, 1960-70; Swarthmore Coll., Pa, 1967-68. *Exhibitions:* Henry Moore, Tate, 1951; Alberto Giacometti, Arts Council, 1955; Chaim Soutine, Tate, 1963; Giacometti, Tate, 1965; Moore, Tate, 1968; René Magritte, Tate, 1969; Robert Morris, Tate, 1971; Henri Laurens, Hayward, 1971; Joan Miró bronzes, Hayward, 1972; Islamic carpets, Hayward, 1972; Willem de Kooning, Serpentine, 1977; Dada and Surrealism Reviewed (Chm. of Cttee), Hayward, 1978; Moore, Serpentine, 1978; Magritte, Palais des Beaux-Arts, Brussels, and Musée National d'Art Moderne, Paris, 1978-79, etc; *films and TV:* Ten Modern Artists (writer/presenter of series), 1964; Giacometti (writer/producer), 1967; Matisse and His Model (writer), 1968; Magritte: The False Mirror (dir), 1970, etc; *radio:* many interviews, talks and discussions for BBC. *Publications:* Henry Moore, 1968; Magritte, 1969; Interviews with Francis Bacon, 1975, enlarged edn 1980; exhibn catalogues; articles, incl. some on films or sport, 1942-, in Tribune, New Statesman, Burlington Mag., Listener, Encounter, The Times, Observer, Sunday Times Mag., etc. *Address:* 35 Walpole Street, SW3 4QS. *T:* 01-730 2284.

SYLVESTER, George Harold, CBE 1967; retired 1967 as Chief Education Officer for Bristol; *b* 26 May 1907; *s* of late George Henry and Martha Sylvester; *m* 1936, Elsie Emmett; one *s. Educ:* Stretford Grammar School; Manchester University. BA Manchester 1928; MA Bristol 1944. Teaching, Manchester, 1929-32; Administrative posts (Education) in Wolverhampton and Bradford, 1932-39; Assistant Education Officer, Bristol, 1939-42; Chief Education Officer, Bristol, 1942-67. Hon. MEd Bristol, 1967. *Recreations:* golf, music. *Address:* 43 Hill View, Henleaze, Bristol BS9 4QE. *T:* Bristol 629287.

SYLVESTER-EVANS, Alun, CB 1975; Deputy Chief Executive, Property Services Agency, Department of the Environment, 1973-78, retired; Member, Chairman's Panel of Assessors, Civil Service Selection Boards, since 1980; *b* 21 April 1918; *o c* of Daniel Elias Evans and Esther Evans, Rhymney, Mon.; *m* 1945, Joan Maureen, *o c* of A. J. Sylvester, *qv* ; two *s. Educ:* Lewis' School, Pengam; University of Wales, Aberystwyth. Armed services, 1940-46. Asst Research Officer, Min. of Town and Country Planning, 1946-47; Asst Principal, 1947-48; Principal Private Sec. to Minister of Housing and Local Govt, 1954-57; Asst Secretary, 1957-66, Under-Sec., 1966-73, Min. of Housing and Local Govt, later DoE. *Recreation:* golf. *Address:* 2 Enmore Road, Putney, SW15. *T:* 01-788 3043. *Club:* Hurlingham.

SYME, Sir Colin (York), AK 1977; Kt 1963; LLB; retired solicitor and company director; Chairman, Broken Hill Pty Co. Ltd, 1952-71 (Director, since 1937); *b* 22 April 1903; *s* of Francis Mark Syme; *m* 1933, Patricia Baird (*d* 1981); three *s* one *d. Educ:* Scotch College, Claremont, WA; Universities of Perth and Melbourne, Australia. Partner, Hedderwick, Fookes & Alston, Solicitors, 1928-66. Pres., The Walter & Eliza Hall Inst. of Medical Research, 1961-78; Chairman: Cttee of Inquiry into Victorian (Aust.) Health Services, 1973-75; Victorian Health Planning Cttee, 1975-78; Hon. Mem., Aust. Inst. of Mining and Metallurgy. Hon. DSc Univ. of NSW, 1960; Hon. LLD Monash, 1981. Storey Medal, Aust. Inst. Management, 1971. *Recreation:* fishing. *Address:* 22 Stonnington Place, Toorak, Victoria 3142, Australia. *Clubs:* Melbourne, Australian (Melbourne); Adelaide (Adelaide); Links (New York).

SYME, Sir Ronald, OM 1976; Kt 1959; FBA 1944; retired as Camden Professor of Ancient History, Oxford, 1949-70; *b* 11 March 1903; *e s* of David and Florence Syme, Eltham, New Zealand. *Educ:* NZ; Oriel College, Oxford (Classical Prizes and First Class Hons, Lit Hum, 1927). Fellow of Trinity College, 1929-49; Conington Prize, 1939. Press Attaché with rank of First Secretary, HM Legation, Belgrade, 1940-41; HM Embassy, Ankara, 1941-42; Professor of Classical Philology, University of Istanbul, 1942-45; President, Society for the Promotion of Roman Studies, 1948-52; President, International Federation of Classical Societies, 1951-54; Secretary-General, Internat. Council for Philosophy and Humanistic Studies, 1952-71, Pres., 1971-75; Vice-President: Prize Cttee of Balzan Foundation, 1963; Assoc. Internat. pour l'Etude du Sud-Est Européen, 1967. Prof. of Ancient History, Royal Acad. of Arts, 1976-. Hon. Fellow: Oriel College, Oxford, 1958; Trinity College, Oxford, 1972; Emeritus Fellow, Brasenose College, 1970; Fellow, Wolfson Coll., 1970. Hon. LittD NZ, 1949; Hon. DLitt: Durham, 1952; Liège, 1952; Belfast, 1961; Graz, 1963; Emory, US, 1963; D ès L: Paris, 1963; Lyon, 1967; Ohio, 1970; Boston Coll., 1974; Tel-Aviv, 1975; Louvain, 1976. Membre Associé de l'Institut de France (Académie des Inscriptions et Belles-Lettres), 1967; Corresp. Member, German Archæological Institute, 1931, Member, 1953; Member, Royal Danish Acad. of Letters and Sciences, 1951; For. Mem. Lund Society of Letters, 1948. Corresponding Member Bavarian Academy, 1955; For. Member: American Philosophical Soc., 1959; Amer. Acad. of Arts and Sciences, 1959; Massachusetts Historical Society, 1960; Istituto di Studi Romani, 1960; Amer. Historical Soc., 1963; Real Academia de la Historia, 1963; Istituto Lombardo, 1964; Acc. Torino, 1972. Corresponding Member Austrian Academy, 1960. Kenyon Medal, British Acad., 1975. Commandeur de l'Ordre des Arts et des Lettres, 1975; Member, Orden Pour le Mérite für Wissenschaften und Künste, 1975. *Publications:* The Roman Revolution, 1939; Tacitus (2 vols), 1958; Colonial Elites, 1958; Sallust, 1964; Ammianus and the Historia Augusta, 1968; Ten Studies in

Tacitus, 1970; Emperors and Biography, 1971; The Historia Augusta: a call for clarity, 1971; Danubian Papers, 1971; History in Ovid, 1978; Roman Papers, 2 vols, 1979; Some Arval Brethren, 1980. *Address:* Wolfson College, Oxford. *Clubs:* Athenæum; Odd Volumes (Boston).

SYMES, (Lilian) Mary; Clerk to Justices, 6 Divisions in Suffolk, 1943–74; Chairman, Norfolk and Suffolk Rent Tribunal, since 1974; *b* 18 Oct. 1912; *d* of Walter Ernest and Lilian May Hollowell; *m* 1953, Thomas Alban Symes; one *s. Educ:* St Mary's Convent, Lowestoft; Great Yarmouth High School. Articled in Solicitor's Office; qualified as Solicitor, 1936. Became first woman Clerk to Justices (Stowmarket), 1942; first woman Deputy Coroner, 1945; Clerk to the Justices, Woodbridge, 1946, Bosmere and Claydon, 1951; first woman Coroner, 1951; Deputy Coroner, Northern District, Suffolk, 1956–. *Recreations:* Worcester porcelain, gardening. *Address:* Gusford Lodge, California, Woodbridge, Suffolk. *T:* Woodbridge 3682.

SYMINGTON, David, CSI 1947; CIE 1943; *b* 4 July 1904; 2nd *s* of James Halliday Symington, merchant, Bombay, India, and Maud McGrigor (*née* Aitken); *m* 1929, Anne Ellen Harker; one *s* one *d. Educ:* Cheltenham College; Oriel College, Oxford (Scholar). Entered Indian Civil Service, 1926; held various appointments including Backward Classes Officer, Bombay Province, 1934–37; Municipal Commissioner, City of Bombay, 1938; ARP Controller, Bombay, 1941; Secretary to Government of Bombay, Home Dept, 1942, Secretary to Governor, 1943–47; retired from ICS, 1948; Member, John Lewis Partnership, 1948–52; Director, N Rhodesia Chamber of Mines, 1953–60; Chairman Copperbelt Technical Foundation, 1955–60. Councillor, Royal Borough of Kensington, 1950. Member of Council, Cheltenham College, 1961–76. *Publications:* Report on Aboriginal Tribes of the Bombay Province, 1938; (as James Halliday): I Speak of Africa, 1965; A Special India, 1968 (repub. in Marathi, Poona, India, 1977); also short stories; (TV play) The Brahmin Widow, 1968. *Recreations:* writing, bridge. *Address:* 5 Paragon Terrace, Cheltenham, Glos.

SYMINGTON, Stuart; United States Senator from Missouri, 1952–76; Director and Vice-Chairman, Financial General Bankshares Inc., Washington DC; *b* Amherst, Massachusetts, 26 June 1901; *s* of William Stuart and Emily Haxall Symington; *m* 1924, Evelyn Wadsworth (decd); two *s; m* 1978, Ann Hemingway Watson. *Educ:* Yale University; International Correspondence School. Joined Symington Companies, Rochester, New York, 1923; President Colonial Radio Co., Rochester, 1930–35; President, Rustless Iron & Steel Co., Baltimore, 1935–37; President and Chairman, Emerson Electric Manufacturing Co., St Louis, 1938–45; Surplus Property Administrator, Washington, 1945–46; Assistant Secretary of War for Air, 1946–47; Secretary of Air Force, National Defense, 1947–50; Chairman, National Security Resources Board, 1950–51; Administrator, Reconstruction Finance Corporation, 1951–52. Is a Democrat. *Address:* Box 1087, New Canaan, Conn 06840, USA.

SYMINGTON, Prof. Sir Thomas, Kt 1978; MD; FRSE; Director, 1970–77, and Professor of Pathology, 1970–77, Institute of Cancer Research, Royal Cancer Hospital; *b* 1 April 1915; *m* 1943, Esther Margaret Forsyth, MB, ChB; two *s* one *d. Educ:* Cumnock Academy. BSc 1936; MB ChB, 1941; MD 1950. St Mungo (Notman) Prof. of Pathology, Univ. of Glasgow, 1954–70. Visiting Prof. of Pathology, Stanford Univ., Calif., 1965–66. Member, Medical Research Council, 1968–72. FRSE, 1956; FRIC, 1958 (ARIC, 1951); FRCP (G), 1963; FRFPS (G), 1958; FRCPath, 1964; Hon. MD Szeged Univ., 1971. *Publications:* Functional Pathology of the Human Adrenal Gland, 1969; Scientific Foundations of Oncology, 1976; numerous papers on problems of adrenal glands in Journals of Endocrinology and Pathology. *Recreation:* golf. *Address:* Greenbriar, 2 Lady Margaret Drive, Troon KA10 7AL. *T:* Troon 315707. *Club:* Royal Automobile.

SYMMERS, William St Clair, senior; MD, DSc, PhD; FRCP, FRCPI, FRCPE, FRCS, FRCPA, FRCPath; retired; Hon. Consultant Pathologist, Charing Cross Hospital, 1953–82; *b* 16 Aug. 1917; *s* of William St Clair Symmers, Columbia, S Carolina (Musgrave Professor of Pathology and Bacteriology, QUB) and Marion Latimer (*née* Macredie), Sydney, NSW; *m* 1941, Jean Noble Wright, Paisley, Renfrewshire; one *s. Educ:* Royal Belfast Academical Instn; Queen's Univ. of Belfast (MB, BCh, BAO 1939; Johnson Symington Medal in Anatomy, 1936; Sinclair Medal in Surgery, 1939; MD 1946); Univ. of Freiburg, Breisgau, Germany. PhD Birmingham, 1953; DSc London, 1979. Surg.-Lieut, RNVR, 1940–46. Demonstrator in Pathology and pupil of Prof. G. Payling Wright, Guy's Hosp. Med. Sch., 1946–47; Registrar in Clinical Pathology, Guy's Hosp., 1946–47; Deptl Demonstrator of Pathology, Univ. of Oxford, 1947; Sen. Asst Pathologist, 1947–48, Consultant, 1948, Radcliffe Infirmary, Oxford; Sen. Lectr in Pathology, Univ. of Birmingham, England, 1948–53; Hon. Consultant Pathologist: United Birmingham Hosps, 1948–53; Birmingham Regional Hosp. Bd, 1949–53; Prof. of Morbid Anatomy, later of Histopathology, Univ. of London at Charing Cross Hosp. Med. Sch., 1953–82. Pres., Section of Pathology, RSM, 1969–70. Hon. FRCPA 1980; Hon. FACP 1982. Dr Dhayagude Meml Prize, Seth GS Med. Sch., Univ. of Bombay, 1967; Yamagiwa Medal, Univ. of Tokyo, 1969; Scott-Heron Medal, Royal Victoria Hosp., Belfast, 1975; Morgagni Medal, Univ. of Padua, 1979. *Publications:* (ed) Systemic Pathology, (with late Prof. G. Payling Wright) 1966, 2nd edn, 6 vols, 1976–80; Curiosa, 1974; Exotica, 1983. *Address:* 30 Sandy Lodge Way, Northwood, Middlesex HA6 2AS.

SYMMONDS, Algernon Washington, GCM 1980; High Commissioner for Barbados in the UK, since 1979 and non-resident Ambassador to Denmark, Finland, Iceland, Norway and Sweden, since 1981, to the Holy See, since 1982; *b* 19 Nov. 1926; *s* of late Algernon F. Symmonds and Olga Ianthe (*née* Harper); *m* 1954, Gladwyn Ward; one *s* one *d. Educ:* Combermere Sch.; Harrison Coll.; Codrington Coll., Barbados. Solicitor, Barbados, 1953, enrolled in UK, 1958; in practice as Solicitor, Barbados, 1953–55; Dep. Registrar, Barbados, 1955–59; Crown Solicitor, Barbados, 1959–66; Permanent Secretary: Min. of Home Affairs, 1966–72; Min. of Educn, 1972–76; Min. of External Affairs and Head of Foreign Service, 1976–79; appointed to rank of Ambassador, 1977. President: Barbados CS Assoc., 1958–65; Fedn of British CS Assocs in Caribbean, 1960–64; Dep. Mem. Exec., Public Services Internat., 1964–66. Dep. Chm., Caribbean Examinations Council, 1973–76. Past Pres., Barbados Lawn Tennis Assoc. *Recreations:* tennis, cricket broadcasting (represented Barbados in football, lawn tennis, basketball). *Address:* Barbados High Commission, 6 Upper Belgrave Street, SW1X 8AZ. *T:* 01-235 8686. *Clubs:* Empire (Cricket and Football) (Life Mem. and Past Vice-Pres.), Summerhayes Tennis (Past Pres.) (Barbados).

SYMONDS, Jane Ursula; see Kellock, J. U.

SYMONDS, (John) Richard (Charters); Senior Research Officer (Honorary), Oxford University Institute of Commonwealth Studies, and Senior Associate Member, St Antony's College, Oxford, since 1979; *b* 2 Oct. 1918; *s* of Sir Charles Putnam Symonds, KBE, CB, DM, FRCP, and Janet (*née* Poulton); *m* 1st, 1948, Juanita Ellington (*d* 1979); two *s*; 2nd, 1980, Ann Hazel, *d* of late Peter Spencer Spokes. *Educ:* Rugby Sch.; Corpus Christi Coll., Oxford (Scholar in Mod. History, MA); Secretary Elect, Oxford Union, 1939. Friends Amb. Unit, 1939–44; Dep. Dir Relief and Rehab., Govt of Bengal, 1944–45; UNRRA, Austria, 1946–47; Friends Service Unit, Punjab and Kashmir, 1947–48; UN Commn for India and Pakistan (Kashmir), 1948–49; UN Technical Assistance Board: New York, 1950–51; Liaison Officer in Europe, 1952–53; Resident Rep., Ceylon, 1953–55, Yugoslavia, 1955–58; Rep. in Europe, 1959–62; Reg. Rep., E Africa, 1961. Sen. Res. Officer, Oxford Univ. Inst. of Commonwealth Studies, 1962–65; Reg. Rep. in Southern Africa, UNTAB, 1964–65; Professorial Fellow, IDS, Univ. of Sussex, 1966–69, later Vis. Prof.; Consultant, UN Population Div., 1968–69; Rep. in Europe, UNITAR, 1969–71; UNDP Resident Rep. in Greece, 1972–75, and in Tunisia, 1975–78; Sen. Adviser, UNDP and UN Fund for Population Activities, NY, 1978–79; Consultant: Commonwealth Foundn, 1980; WHO, 1981. *Publications:* The Making of Pakistan, 1950; The British and their Successors, 1966; (ed) International Targets for Development, 1970; (with M. Carder) The United Nations and the Population Question, 1973. *Recreation:* walking. *Address:* 43 Davenant Road, Oxford OX2 8BU. *T:* Oxford 55661. *Clubs:* Royal Commonwealth Society, United Oxford & Cambridge University.
See also R. C. Symonds.

SYMONDS, Joseph Bede, OBE 1957; *b* 17 Jan. 1900; *m* 1921; four *s* six *d* (three *s* decd). *Educ:* St Bede's Secondary School, Jarrow. Councillor, Jarrow, 1929; Alderman 1935; Mayor 1945; County Councillor, Durham, 1946; Freeman, Borough of Jarrow, 1955. Past Chairman National Housing and Town Planning Council, 1948–50 (Exec. Member, 1938–65); Chairman Jarrow Housing Cttee, 1935. MP (Lab) Whitehaven, June 1959–70. *Recreations:* cricket; welfare work (old people); Air Training Corps. *Address:* 11 Hedworth View, Jarrow, Tyne and Wear NE32 4EW. *T:* Jarrow 897246.

SYMONDS, Richard; see Symonds, J. R. C.

SYMONDS, Ronald Charters, CB 1975; *b* 25 June 1916; *e s* of late Sir Charles Symonds, KBE, CB, and late Janet Palmer Poulton; *m* 1939, Pamela Painton; two *s* one *d. Educ:* Rugby Sch.; New Coll., Oxford. British Council, 1938–39 and 1946–51. Military Service, 1939–45. War Office, later MoD, 1951–76, retired. Advr, Royal Commn on Gambling, 1976–78. Consultant, ICI Ltd, 1978–81. United States Bronze Star, 1948. *Recreations:* walking, ornithology. *Address:* 10 Bisham Gardens, N6 6DD.
See also J. R. C. Symonds.

SYMONS, Ernest Vize, CB 1975; Director General, Board of Inland Revenue, 1975–77; *b* 19 June 1913; *s* of Ernest William Symons and Edith Florence Elphick; *m* 1938, Elizabeth Megan Jenkins; one *s* two *d. Educ:* Stationers' Company's Sch.; University Coll., London (Fellow, 1979). Asst Inspector, 1934; Admin. Staff Coll., Henley, 1956; Dep. Chief Inspector of Taxes, 1964–73; Chief Inspector of Taxes, 1973–75. Mem., Keith Cttee on Enforcement Powers of the Revenue Depts, 1980. Governor, E-SU, 1978; Hon. Treas., Nat Assoc. for Care of Offenders and Prevention of Crime, 1979. Mem. College Council, UCL, 1975; Vice-Chm., London Welsh Trust, 1981– (Mem. Council, 1978–). Hon. Treasurer, Hon. Soc. of Cymmrodorion, 1980–. *Recreations:* chess, bridge. *Address:* 1 Terrace House, 128 Richmond Hill, Richmond, Surrey. *T:* 01-940 4967. *Club:* Athenæum.

SYMONS, Julian Gustave, FRSL; author; *b* 30 May 1912; *y s* of M. A. Symons; *m* 1941, Kathleen Clark; one *s* (one *d* decd). Editor, Twentieth Century Verse, 1937–39. Chairman: Crime Writers Association, 1958–59; Cttee of Management, Soc. of Authors, 1970–71; Sunday Times Reviewer, 1958–. Pres., Detection Club, 1976–. Mem. Council, Westfield Coll., Univ. of London, 1972–75. Grand Master: Swedish Acad. of Detection, 1977;

Mystery Writers of America, 1982. FRSL 1975. *Publications:* Confusions About X, 1938; (ed) Anthology of War Poetry, 1942; The Second Man, 1944; A. J. A. Symons, 1950; Charles Dickens, 1951; Thomas Carlyle, 1952; Horatio Bottomley, 1955; The General Strike, 1957; A Reasonable Doubt, 1960; The Thirties, 1960; The Detective Story in Britain, 1962; Buller's Campaign, 1963; England's Pride, 1965; Critical Occasions, 1966; A Picture History of Crime and Detection, 1966; (ed) Essays and Biographies by A. J. A. Symons, 1969; Bloody Murder: from the detective story to the crime novel, a history, 1972 (MWA Edgar Allan Poe Award); Notes from Another Country, 1972; Between the Wars, 1972; A Three Pipe Problem, 1975; The Hungry Thirties, 1976; The Tell-Tale Heart, 1978; Conan Doyle, 1979; The Great Detectives, 1981; Critical Observations, 1981; author of 22 crime novels, including: The 31st of February, 1950; The Broken Penny, 1952; The Colour of Murder, 1957 (CWA Critics Award); The Progress of a Crime, 1960 (MWA Edgar Allan Poe Award); The End of Solomon Grundy, 1964; The Man Who Killed Himself, 1967; The Man Whose Dreams Came True, 1968; The Man Who Lost His Wife, 1970; The Players and the Game, 1972; The Blackheath Poisonings, 1978; Sweet Adelaide, 1980; The Detling Murders, 1982; The Tigers of Subtopia (short stories), 1982; several plays for television. *Recreations:* watching cricket and Association football, wandering in cities. *Address:* Groton House, 330 Dover Road, Walmer, Deal, Kent. *T:* Deal 65209.

SYMONS, Noel Victor Housman, CIE 1941; MC 1916; JP; Major, Army in India Reserve of Officers, 1934; *b* 27 Nov. 1894; *s* of late Edward William Symons, MA (Oxon.), Headmaster King Edward VI's School, Bath, and Katharine Elizabeth, *sister* of A. E. and Laurence Housman; *m* 1924, Cicely Dorothea Richards; no *c. Educ:* King Edward VI's School, Bath. British Army, 1914-19, Lt Worcestershire Regt; Indian Civil Service, 1920; District work till 1931; Secretary, Board of Revenue, 1931-34; Private Secretary to Governor of Bengal, 1934-35; Revenue Secretary, Govt of Bengal, 1938-40; Commissioner, Presidency Division, and ARP Controller, Bengal, 1940; Commissioner, Rajshahi Division, and Additional Secretary, Civil Defence, Bengal, 1941; Joint Secretary, Civil Defence Dept, Govt of India, 1942; Director-General, Civil Defence, and Additional Secretary, Defence Dept, Govt of India, 1943; retired from ICS Aug. 1946. JP Hampshire, 1951. Appointed to Appeal Cttee, Quarter Sessions, 1959; Dep. Chm., Lymington Petty Sessions and Mem. Council, Magistrates' Assoc., 1964; Chm., Lymington Petty Sessions, 1966; supplemental list, 1969. *Publication:* The Story of Government House (Calcutta), 1935. *Recreations:* yachting, beagling, fell walking. *Address:* Bucklands, Lymington, Hants SO4 9DS. *T:* Lymington 72719. *Club:* Royal Lymington Yacht.

SYMONS, Rear-Adm. Patrick Jeremy; Naval Attaché, Washington, since 1982; *b* 9 June 1933; *s* of Ronald and Joanne Symons; *m* 1961, Elizabeth Lawrence; one *s* one *d. Educ:* Dartmouth Royal Naval College. Commissioned 1951; in command, HMS Torquay, 1968-70, HMS Birmingham, 1976-77, HMS Bulwark, 1980-81. *Recreations:* sailing, skiing, swimming. *Address:* c/o Lloyds Bank, Cox's and King's, 6 Pall Mall, SW1. *Clubs:* Royal Commonwealth Society; Royal Naval Sailing Association (Portsmouth).

SYMS, John Grenville St George, OBE 1981; QC 1962; Barrister-at-Law; a Recorder of the Crown Court, 1972-80; *b* 6 Jan. 1913; *s* of late Harold St George Syms and Margaret (*née* Wordley); *m* 1951, Yvonne Yolande (*née* Rigby) (marr. diss. 1971); one *s. Educ:* Harrow; Magdalen College, Oxford (BA). Called to the Bar, 1936. Dep. Chm., Huntingdon and Peterborough QS, 1965-71. Chm., SE Agricultural Land Tribunal, 1972. Served in RAFVR, 1940-45 (despatches); Wing Commander, 1944. *Recreations:* shooting and fishing. *Address:* Willinghurst, Shamley Green, Surrey. *T:* Cranleigh 272828. *Club:* Flyfishers'.

SYNGE, Henry Millington; Chairman, Union International Co. Ltd, since 1969 (Director since 1955); Partner in Tilney & Co. (Stockbrokers), Liverpool and Shrewsbury; *b* 3 April 1921; *s* of Richard Millington Synge, MC, Liverpool and Eileen Hall; *m* 1947, Joyce Helen, *d* of Alexander Ross Topping and Mrs Topping (*née* Stileman); two *s* one *d. Educ:* Shrewsbury School. Mercantile Marine: Radio Officer, 1941; Purser, Bibby Line, 1943; demobilised, 1946. Partner, Sing White & Co. (Stockbrokers), 1947. Manager, Liverpool Trustee Savings Bank, 1957, Chm. 1968-69; Trustee and Mem. Bd of Mgt, Trustee Savings Bank of Wales and Border Counties, 1977-. *Recreations:* private flying, fishing, amateur radio. *Address:* Wilcot House, Nesscliffe, Shrewsbury, Salop SY4 1BJ. *T:* Nesscliffe 392. *Club:* Salop (Shrewsbury).

SYNGE, John Lighton, FRS 1943; MA, ScD Dublin; MRIA, FRSC (Tory Medal, 1943); Senior Professor, School of Theoretical Physics, Dublin Institute for Advanced Studies, 1948-72, now Emeritus; *b* Dublin, 1897; *y s* of Edward Synge; *m* 1918, Elizabeth Allen; three *d. Educ:* St Andrew's Coll., Dublin; Trinity Coll., Dublin. Senior Moderator and Gold Medallist in Mathematics and Experimental Science, 1919; Lecturer in Mathematics, Trinity College, Dublin, 1920; Assistant Professor of Mathematics, University of Toronto, 1920-25; Secretary to the International Mathematical Congress, Toronto, 1924; Fellow of Trinity College, Dublin, and University Professor of Natural Philosophy, 1925-30; Treas., Royal Irish Academy, 1929-30. Sec., 1949-52. Pres., 1961-64; Professor of Applied Mathematics, Univ. of Toronto, 1930-43; Professor of Mathematics and Chm. of Dept, Ohio State Univ., 1943-46; Prof. of Mathematics and Head of Dept, Carnegie Inst. of

Technology, 1946-48; Visiting Lecturer, Princeton Univ., 1939; Vis. Prof.: Brown Univ., 1941-42; Inst. for Fluid Dynamics and Applied Maths, University of Maryland, 1951. Ballistics Mathematician, United States Army Air Force, 1944-45. Hon. FTCD. Hon. LLD St Andrews, 1966; Hon. ScD: QUB, 1969; NUI, 1970. Boyle Medal, RDS, 1972. *Publications:* Geometrical Optics, 1937; (with B. A. Griffith) Principles of Mechanics, 1942; (with A. E. Schild) Tensor Calculus, 1949; Science: Sense and Nonsense, 1951; Geometrical Mechanics and de Broglie Waves, 1954; Relativity: the Special Theory, 1956; The Hypercircle in Mathematical Physics, 1957; The Relativistic Gas, 1957; Kandelman's Krim, 1957; Relativity: the General Theory, 1960; Talking about Relativity, 1970; papers on geometry and applied mathematics; Ed. Sir W. R. Hamilton's Mathematical Papers, Vol. I. *Address:* Torfan, 8 Stillorgan Park, Blackrock, Co. Dublin. *T:* 881251.

SYNGE, Richard Laurence Millington, FRS 1950; Hon. Professor of Biology, University of East Anglia, Norwich, since 1968; *b* 28 Oct. 1914; *s* of late Laurence M. Synge and Katharine C. Synge (*née* Swan), Great Barrow, Chester; *m* 1943, Ann, *d* of late Adrian L. Stephen and Karin Stephen (*née* Costelloe), both of London; three *s* four *d. Educ:* Winchester College; Trinity College, Cambridge (Hon. Fellow, 1972). International Wool Secretariat Research Student, University of Cambridge, 1938; Biochemist: Wool Industries Research Assoc., Leeds, 1941; Lister Institute of Preventive Medicine, London, 1943; Rowett Research Inst., Bucksburn, Aberdeen, 1948; Food Research Inst., Norwich, 1967-76. Editorial Board, Biochemical Journal, 1949-55. Hon. MRIA 1972; Hon. DSc East Anglia, 1977; Hon. PhD Uppsala, 1980. (Jtly) Nobel Prize for Chemistry, 1952. *Publications:* papers in biochemical and chemical journals, etc, 1937-. *Address:* School of Chemical Sciences, University of East Anglia, Norwich NR4 7TJ; 19 Meadow Rise Road, Norwich NR2 3QE. *T:* Norwich 53503.

SYNGE, Sir Robert Carson, 8th Bt, *cr* 1801; Manager and Owner, Rob's Furniture; *b* 4 May 1922; *s* of late Neale Hutchinson Synge (2nd *s* of 6th Bt) and Edith Elizabeth Thurlow (*d* 1933), Great Parndon, Essex; *m* 1944, Dorothy Jean Johnson, *d* of T. Johnson, Cloverdale; two *d. S* uncle, 1942. *Heir: cousin* Neale Francis Synge [*b* 28 Feb. 1917; *m* 1939, Kathleen Caroline Bowes; one *s* one *d*]. *Address:* 19364 Fraser Highway, RR4, Langley, British Columbia, Canada.

SYNNOT, Adm. Sir Anthony (Monckton), KBE 1979 (CBE 1972); AO 1976; Hon. JMN 1965; Hon. PSM 1982; Chairman, Australian War Memorial Council, since 1982; *b* 5 Jan. 1922; *m* 1st, 1959, M. Virginia (*d* 1965), *d* of late Dr W. K. Davenport; two *d*; 2nd, 1968, E. Anne, *d* of late E. W. Manifold, MC. *Educ:* Geelong Grammar School. Joined RAN, 1939; served War of 1939-45 in HMA Ships Canberra, Stuart, Quiberon; HM Ships Barham, Punjabi; CO HMAS Warramunga, 1956-57; HMAS Vampire, 1961-62; OC Royal Malaysian Navy, 1962-65; CO HMAS Sydney, 1966, HMAS Melbourne, 1967; IDC 1968; Chief of Naval Personnel, 1970; Dep. Chief of Naval Staff, 1971-72; Commanding HM Australian Fleet, 1973; Director Joint Staff, 1974-76; Chief of Naval Staff, 1976-79; Chief of Defence Force Staff, 1979-82, retired. *Recreations:* tennis, golf, sailing. *Address:* Wanna Wanna, Box 33, Queanbeyan, NSW 2620, Australia. *T:* 062-971161. *Clubs:* Commonwealth (Canberra); Melbourne (Melbourne).

SYSONBY, 3rd Baron, *cr* 1935, of Wonersh; **John Frederick Ponsonby;** *b* 5 Aug. 1945; *s* of 2nd Baron Sysonby, DSO and Sallie Monkland, *d* of Dr Leonard Sanford, New York; *S* father 1956. *Address:* Newby Hall, Ripon, North Yorks.

SYTHES, Percy Arthur, CB 1980; retired 1980; Comptroller and Auditor General for Northern Ireland, 1974-80; *b* 21 Dec. 1915; *s* of William Sythes and Alice Maud Grice; *m* 1941, Doreen Smyth Fitzsimmons; three *d. Educ:* Campbell Coll., Belfast; Trinity Coll., Dublin. Scholar; BA (Mod. Lit.), 1st cl. hons Gold Medal 1938; Vice-Chancellor's Prizeman 1939. Asst Master: Royal Sch., Dungannon, 1939; Portadown Coll., 1940. Royal Artillery, 1940-46 (Major); GSO2, 1946. Asst Principal, NI Civil Service, 1946; Private Sec. to Dame Dehra Parker, 1950; Principal 1958; Asst Sec. 1963; Sen. Asst Sec., NI Min. of Develt, 1970, Dep. Sec. 1971; Dep. Sec., NI Executive, 1974. Chm., Bd of Governors, Strathearn Sch., 1982 (Mem., 1966-). *Recreations:* gardens, family. *Address:* Malory, 37 Tweskard Park, Belfast BT4 2JZ. *T:* Belfast 63310.

SZEMERÉNYI, Prof. Oswald John Louis, DrPhil (Budapest); FBA 1982; Professor of Indo-European and General Linguistics, University of Freiburg-im-Breisgau, 1965-81, now Emeritus Professor; *b* London, 7 Sept. 1913; *m* 1940, Elizabeth Kövér; one *s. Educ:* Madách Imre Gimnazium; University of Budapest. Classics Master in Beregszász and Mátyásföld, 1939-41; Lecturer in Greek, 1942-45, Reader, 1946, Professor of Comparative Indo-European Philology in University of Budapest, 1947-48. Came to England, Oct. 1948; employed in industry, 1949-52; Research Fellow, Bedford Coll., London, 1952-53; Asst Lecturer, 1953-54, Lecturer, 1954-58, Reader, 1958-60, in Greek at Bedford College; Professor of Comparative Philology, University College, London, 1960-65. Collitz Prof., Linguistic Inst., USA, 1963; Vis. Prof., Seattle, 1964. *Publications:* The Indo-European liquid sonants in Latin, 1941; Studies in the Indo-European System of Numerals, 1960; Syncope in Greek and Indo-European, 1964; Einführung in die vergleichende Sprachwissenschaft, 1970; Richtungen der modernen Sprachwissenschaft, part I, 1971, part II 1-2, 1982; (contrib.) Comparative Linguistics in Current Trends in Linguistics 9, 1972; The Kinship Terminology of the Indo-European Languages, 1978; Four

Old Iranian Ethnic Names, 1980; contrib. to British and foreign learned journals. *Recreations:* motoring, chess. *Address:* Albert-Ludwigs-Universität, 78 Freiburg-im-Breisgau, W Germany.

SZENT-GYORGYI, Albert, MD, PhD Cantab, Dhc; Scientific Director, National Foundation for Cancer Research, Massachusetts, USA, since 1975; *b* Budapest, 16 Sept. 1893; *s* of Nicholas Szent-Györgyi and Josephine, *d* of Joseph Lenhossék, Professor of Anatomy; *m* 1st, 1941; one *d*; 2nd, Marcia Houston. *Educ:* Budapest University; Cambridge University. Matriculated Medical Faculty, Budapest, 1911; war service, 1914-18 (wounded); Assistant, University Pozsony, 1918; working at Prague and Berlin, 1919; in Hamburg in scientific research, 1919-20; Assistant at Univ. Leiden, Holland, 1920-22; privaat dozent at Groningen, 1922-26; working at Cambridge, England, with the interrruption of one year spent in USA, 1926-30; Prof. of Medical Chemistry, Szeged Univ., 1931-45; Professor of Biochemistry Univ. of Budapest, Hungary, 1945-47; Dir of Research, Inst. of Muscle Research, Mass, 1947-75. Formerly: Pres. Acad. of Sciences, Budapest; Vice-Pres. Nat. Acad., Budapest. Prix Nobel of Medicine, 1937; Visiting Prof., Harvard Univ., 1936; Franchi Prof., Univ. of Liége, Belgium, 1938. Cameron Prize (Edinburgh), 1946. Lasker Award, 1954. Hon. ScD Cantab, 1963. Hon. Fellow, Fitzwilliam Coll., Cambridge, 1967. *Publications:* Oxidation, Fermentation, Vitamins, Health and Disease, 1939; Muscular Contraction, 1947; The Nature of Life, 1947; Contraction in Body and Heart Muscle, 1953; Bioenergetics, 1957; Submolecular Biology, 1960; Science, Ethics and Politics, 1962; Bioelectronics, 1968; The Living State, 1972; Electronic Biology and Cancer, 1976; many scientific papers. *Recreations:* sport of all kinds, chiefly sailing, swimming and fishing. *Address:* Marine Biological Laboratory, Woods Hole, Mass 02543, USA; Penzance, Woods Hole, Mass, USA.

SZERYNG, Henryk; Hon. Professor, Faculty of Music, Mexican National University, Mexico City; Concert Violinist, since 1933; *b* Warsaw, 22 Sept. 1918; Mexican Citizen since 1946. *Educ:* Warsaw, Berlin, Paris. Graduated violin class of Carl Flesch, Berlin, 1933; 1st Prize special mention, Paris Conservatoire, 1937; Composition study with Nadia Boulanger, 1934-39. War of 1939-45: played over 300 concerts for Allied Armed Forces, Red Cross and other welfare institutions in Scotland, England, Canada, USA, Caribbean area, Middle East, North Africa, Brazil and Mexico. Has covered the five continents in recitals, also soloist with major orchestras, 1953-. Mexican Cultural Ambassador, 1960-; Cultural Adviser to Mexican delegn, UNESCO, Paris, and to Mexican Foreign Ministry, 1970-. Numerous recordings; Grand Prix du Disque, 1955, 1957, 1960, 1961, 1967, 1969. Hon. Mem., RAM, 1969. Hon. Pres., Musical Youth of Mexico, 1974. Officer of Cultural Merit, Roumania, 1935; Kt Comdr, Order of Polonia Restituta (Poland), 1956; Silver Medal of City of Paris, 1963; Officer, Order of Arts and Letters (France), 1964; Comdr, Order of the Lion (Finland), 1966; Chevalier, Légion d'Honneur, 1972; Mozart Medal, Salzburg, 1972; Comdr Al Merito (Italy), 1974; Comdr, Order of Flag with Golden Star (Yugoslavia), 1976; Gran Premio Nacional, Mexico, 1979; Golden Medal, City of Paris, 1981; Hon. Citizen, Poznan, Poland, 1981. *Publications:* several chamber music works, also for piano and violin. Revised violin concertos by Nardini, Vivaldi and others, sonatas and partitas by Bach; re-discovered Paganini Concerto No 3 (World Première, London, 1971). *Recreations:* golf, reading. *Address:* c/o Mexican Embassy, 9 rue Longchamp, 75116 Paris, France.

SZWARC, Michael M., FRS 1966; formerly Distinguished Professor of Chemistry of the State University of New York, now Professor Emeritus; *b* 9 June 1909; Polish; *m* 1933, Marja Frenkel; one *s* two *d*. *Educ:* Warsaw Inst. of Technology (Chem. Eng. 1933); Hebrew Univ., Jerusalem (PhD 1942). University of Manchester (Lecturer), 1945-52; PhD (Phys. Chem.) 1947; DSc 1949; State University Coll. of Environmental Scis at Syracuse, NY,, 1952-82: Prof. of Physical and Polymer Chemistry; Research Prof.; Distinguished Prof. of Chemistry; Dir, Polymer Research Inst. Baker Lectr, Cornell Univ., 1972. Nobel Guest Prof., Univ. of Uppsala, 1969; Vis. Prof., Univ. of Leuven, 1974. Hon. Dr: Leuven, Belgium, 1974; Uppsala, Sweden, 1975; Louis Pasteur Univ., France, 1978. Amer. Chem. Soc. Award for Outstanding Achievements in Polymer Chemistry, 1969; Gold Medal, Soc. of Plastic Engrs, 1972; Gold Medal, Benjamin Franklin Inst., 1978. *Publications:* Carbanions, Living Polymers and Electron Transfer Processes, 1968; Ions and Ion-pairs in Organic Chemistry, Vol. I, 1972, Vol. II, 1974; numerous contribs to Jl Chem. Soc., Trans Faraday Soc., Proc. Royal Soc., Jl Am. Chem. Soc., Jl Chem. Phys., Jl Phys. Chem., Jl Polymer Sci., Nature, Chem. Rev., Quarterly Reviews, etc. *Address:* 1176 Santa Luisa Drive, Solana Beach, Calif 92075, USA. *T:* (714) 481-1863.

T

TABACHNIK, Eldred, QC 1982; *b* 5 Nov. 1943; *s* of Solomon Joseph Tabachnik and Esther Tabachnik; *m* 1966, Jennifer Kay Lawson; two *s* one *d*. *Educ:* Univ. of Cape Town (BA, LLB); Univ. of London (LLM). Called to the Bar, Inner Temple, 1970. Lectr, UCL, 1969-72. *Recreation:* reading. *Address:* 3 Drax Avenue, SW20 0EG. *T:* 01-947 0699. *Club:* Reform.

TABOR, Prof. David, PhD, ScD; FRS 1963; Professor of Physics in the University of Cambridge, 1973-81, now Emeritus, and Head of Physics and Chemistry of Solids, Cavendish Laboratory, 1969-81; Fellow of Gonville and Caius College, Cambridge, since 1957; *b* 23 Oct. 1913; *s* of Charles Tabor and Rebecca Weinstein; *m* 1943, Hannalene Stillschweig; two *s*. *Educ:* Regent St Polytechnic; Universities of London and Cambridge. BSc London 1934; PhD Cambridge 1939; ScD Cambridge 1956. Reader in Physics, Cambridge Univ., 1964-73. Inaugural Gold Medal of Tribology, Inst. of Engrs, 1972; Guthrie Medal, Inst. Physics, 1975. *Publications:* The Hardness of Metals, 1951; Gases, Liquids and Solids, 1969, 2nd edn 1979; (with F. P. Bowden) Friction and Lubrication of Solids, Part I, 1950 (rev. edn, 1954); Part II, 1964; contributions to learned jls on friction, adhesion, lubrication and hardness. *Recreation:* Judaica. *Address:* Cavendish Laboratory, Madingley Road, Cambridge CB3 0HE; Gonville and Caius College, Cambridge; 8 Rutherford Road, Cambridge. *T:* Cambridge 841336.

TABOR, Maj.-Gen. David John St Maur, CB 1977; MC 1944; late Royal Horse Guards; GOC Eastern District, 1975-77, retired; *b* 5 Oct. 1922; *y s* of late Harry Tabor, Hitchin, Herts; *m* 1955, Hon. Pamela Roxane, 2nd *d* of 2nd Baron Glendyne; two *s*. *Educ:* Eton; RMA, Sandhurst. Served War: 2nd Lieut, RHG, 1942; NW Europe, 1944-45 (wounded, 1944); Major, 1946. Lt-Col Comdg RHG, 1960; Lt-Col Comdg Household Cavalry, and Silver Stick in Waiting, 1964; Col, 1964; Brig., 1966; Comdr Berlin Infty Bde, 1966; Comdr, British Army Staff and Mil. Attaché, Washington, 1968; RCDS, 1971; Maj.-Gen., 1972; Defence Attaché, Paris, 1972-74. Vice-Chm., ACFA, 1979. *Recreations:* shooting, fishing, sailing, golf, gardening. *Address:* Shipton Sollars Manor, Andoversford, Glos. *T:* Andoversford 207. *Clubs:* Turf, Royal Automobile, MCC; Royal Yacht Squadron.
See also Baron Glendyne.

TABOUIS, Geneviève; Officier de la Légion d'Honneur, 1959; Commandeur de l'Ordre National du Mérite; Rédacteur Diplomatique quotidien à Paris Jour, à Radio-Luxembourg, La Dépêche du Midi, Juvenal; *b* 23 Feb. 1892; *fille* du peintre Le Quesne; nièce de l'Ambassadeur Jules Cambon et du Général Tabouis; *m* 1916, Robert Tabouis (*d* 1973), Président-Directeur Général de la Cie Générale de Télégraphie sans Fil; one *s* one *d*. *Educ:* Couvent de l'Assomption; Faculté des fettres, Paris, Ecole archéologique du Louvre. Journaliste diplomatique; débuta en 1924 à la SDN comme correspondante de La Petite Gironde, du Petit Marseillais; chargée de 1924 à 1932 de toutes les grandes enquêtes diplomatiques, de tous les grands reportages politiques et de nombreuses conférences diplomatiques; diplomatic Leader a La Petite Gironde et Le Petit Marseillais, 1932-37, à l'Œuvre 1932-40; fonda et dirigea l'hebdomadaire français, Pour La Victoire, New York, 1939-45; retour à Paris, 1946-56; diplomatic leader à La France Libre, L'Information, L'Espoir. Correspondant diplomatique du Sunday Dispatch de Londres, de La Critica de Buenos-Ayres; collaboratrice à de nombreux journaux et revues; déployé une grande activité dans les meetings politiques et les conférences politiques et diplomatiques; nombreuses hautes décorations étrangères. Hon. Vice-Présidente de l'Association de la Presse Diplomatique française. *Publications:* 4 livres historiques couronnés par l'Académie Française: Tout Ank Amon, Nabuchodonosor, Salomon, Sybaris; une biographie: Jules Cambon par l'un des siens (couronné par l'Académie Française): un livre de politique: Le Chantage a la Guerre; Albion Perfide ou Loyale; tous ces ouvrages ont paru également en Angleterre; Ils l'ont appelée Cassandre (New York); Grandeurs et Servitudes américaines (Paris); Quand Paris Résiste; 20 Ans de Suspense Diplomatique; Les princes de la paix, 1980. *Recreations:* Aucune récréation; travaille tout le temps, même le dimanche, ne connait pas le week-end; comme seule distraction aime recevoir diplomates, hommes politiques et amis; sa table est célèbre par ses surtouts extraordinaires; objets d'art, ou céramiques commandées à L. E. Chevallier, et décors originaux adaptés aux événements diplomatiques d'actualité. *Address:* 3 square Claude-Debussy, 75017 Paris, France. *Club:* Soroptimist Interallié.

TACKABERRY, John Antony, QC 1982; FCIArb, FFB; *b* 13 Nov. 1939; *s* of Thomas Raphael Tackaberry and Mary Catherine (*née* Geoghegan); *m* 1966, Penelope Holt; two *s*. *Educ:* Downside; Trinity Coll., Dublin; Downing Coll., Cambridge (MA, LLB). Called to the Bar, Gray's Inn, 1967. FFB 1979. Teacher in China, 1963-64 and in London, 1965-66. *Recreations:* good food, good wine, good company; and if there's any time left, wind-surfing and photography. *Address:* 22 Willes Road, NW5 3DS. *T:* 01-267 2137.

TACON, Air Cdre Ernest William, CBE 1958; DSO 1944; MVO 1950; DFC 1940 (Bar 1944); AFC 1942 (Bar 1953); *b* 6 Dec. 1917; *s* of Ernest Richard Tacon, Hastings, New Zealand; *m* 1st, 1949, Clare Keating (*d* 1956), *d* of late Michael Keating, Greymouth, NZ; one *s* two *d*; 2nd, 1960, Bernardine, *d* of Cecil Leamy, Wellington, NZ; three *s*. *Educ:* St Patrick's College, Silverstream, New Zealand. Joined RNZAF, 1938. Served with RAF, 1939-46. Transferred to RAF, 1946. CO, King's Flight, Benson, 1946-49. Overseas Services since War: Canal Zone, 1951-53; Cyprus, 1956-58; Persian Gulf, 1961-63; Commandant, Central Fighter Establishment, 1963-65; Air Cdre, Tactics, HQ Fighter Comd, 1966-67; AOC Military Air Traffic Ops, 1968-71, retired. MBIM. *Address:* 69 McLeans Road, Bucklands Beach, Auckland, NZ. *Club:* United Services Officers (Wellington).

TAFT, Charles Phelps; Attorney at Law; Mayor of Cincinnati, USA, 1955-57; Hon. Chairman, US Advisory Committee on Voluntary Foreign Aid (Agency for International Development) (formerly Chairman); General Counsel, Committee for a National Trade Policy; *b* 20 Sept. 1897; *s* of William H. Taft

(27th President of the US and Chief Justice) and Helen Herron; *m* 1917, Eleanor Kellogg (*d* 1961), *d* of Irving H. Chase of Ingersoll-Waterbury Co.; two *s* three *d* (and two *d* decd). *Educ*: The Taft School, Watertown, Connecticut; Yale University. BA 1918, LLB 1921; Hon. LLD (Yale), 1952, etc.; Doctor of Hebrew Letters, Hebrew Union College, 1948. Enlisted 12 FA 2nd Div., AEF, 1917 (Fr., Jan.-Dec. 1918), discharged as 1st Lt 1919. Prosecuting Attorney Hamilton County, 1927-28; Partner: Taft, Stettinius & Hollister, 1924-37; Headley, Sibbald & Taft, 1946-59; Taft & Lavercombe, 1959-66; Taft & Luken, 1967-74; Chm. Fed. Steel Mediation Bd, 1937; Dir, Community War Services, Fed. Security Agency, 1941-43; Dir, Wartime Economic Affairs. Department of State, 1944-45; City Councilman of Cincinnati, 1938-42, 1948-51, 1955-77. Trustee, Twentieth Century Fund, Carnegie Institution of Washington, Committee for Economic Development; Senior Warden, Christ Episcopal Church, Cincinnati; Pres. Fed. Council of Churches of Christ in America, 1947-48. Medal for Merit, 1946. *Publications:* City Management: The Cincinnati Experiment, 1933; You and I-and Roosevelt, 1936; Why I am for the Church, 1947; Democracy in Politics and Economics, 1950. *Recreations:* fishing, local politics, topical daily broadcasting. *Address:* 3550 Shaw Avenue, Cincinnati, Ohio 45208, USA.

TAFTI, Rt. Rev. Hassan Barnaba D.; *see* Dehqani-Tafti.

TAHOURDIN, John Gabriel, CMG 1961; HM Diplomatic Service, retired; *b* 15 Nov. 1913; *s* of late John St Clair Tahourdin; *m* 1957, Margaret Michie; one *s* one *d. Educ:* Merchant Taylors' School; St John's College, Oxford. Served HM Embassy, Peking, 1936-37; Private Secretary to HM Ambassador at Shanghai, 1937-40; BoT, 1940-41; Vice-Consul, Baltimore, 1941; Foreign Office, 1942; Private Secretary to Parliamentary Under-Secretary of State, 1943, and to Minister of State, 1945; Athens, 1946; returned to Foreign Office, 1949; Counsellor, British Embassy, The Hague, 1955; Foreign Office, 1957; Minister, UK Delegn to 18 Nation Disarmament Conf., Geneva, 1963-66; HM Ambassador to: Senegal, 1966-71, and concurrently to Mauritania, 1968-71, to Mali, 1969-71, and to Guinea, 1970-71; Bolivia, 1971-73. Mem., Internat. Inst. for Strategic Studies. Price Commission, 1975-77; Kleinwort Benson, 1977-79. *Recreations:* music cinematography, foreign languages, travel. *Address:* Swafield Hall, North Walsham, Norfolk NR28 0RP. *Clubs:* Athenæum, Travellers', Beefsteak; Norfolk.
  See also P. A. I. Tahourdin.

TAHOURDIN, Dr Peter Anthony Ivan, CBE 1970 (OBE 1956); British Council Service, retired; *b* 12 Oct. 1920; *yr s* of John St Clair Tahourdin and Suzanne Perscheid; *m* 1945, Betty Yeo, Court Colman, Glam; one *s* two *d. Educ:* Merchant Taylors' Sch.; University Coll., Oxford (Open Scholar, Edmund Spenser Exhibr, MA, BSc, DPhil). Research scientist, UK Atomic Energy Project, 1942-46; joined British Council, 1946: Science Officer, Italy, 1946-54; Asst Rep., Yugoslavia, 1954-58; Rep., Israel, 1958-61; Asst Controller, Books, Arts and Science Div., 1961-67; Rep., Yugoslavia, 1967-69; Dep. Controller, Books, Arts and Science Div., 1969-70; Controller, Educn and Science Div., 1970-73; Asst Dir-Gen., 1973-77; Dep. Dir-Gen., 1977-81. Research Associate, Airey Neave Meml Trust Project, 1981-. *Publications:* contrib. professional jls on sci. subjects and the cinema. *Recreations:* talking, the cinema, industrial archaeology, photography. *Address:* 2 Twyford Avenue, W3 9QA. *T:* 01-992 5758.
  See also J. G. Tahourdin.

TAIT, Prof. Alan Anderson; Deputy Director, Fiscal Affairs Department, International Monetary Fund, Washington, since 1982; *b* 1 July 1934; *s* of Stanley Tait and Margaret Ruth (*née* Anderson); *m* 1963, Susan Valerie Somers; one *s. Educ:* Heriot's Sch., Edinburgh; Univ. of Edinburgh (MA); Trinity Coll., Dublin (PhD). Lectr, Trinity Coll., Dublin, 1959-71 (Fellow, 1968, Sen. Tutor, 1970); Visiting Prof., Univ. of Illinois, 1965-66. Economic adviser to Irish Govt on industrial develt and taxation and chief economic adviser to Confedn of Irish Industry, 1967-71; economic consultant to Sec. of State for Scotland, 1972-77; International Monetary Fund: Visiting Scholar, 1972; Consultant, 1973 and 1974; Chief, Fiscal Analysis Div., 1976-79; Asst Dir, 1979-82. Prof. of Money and Finance, Univ. of Strathclyde, 1971-77. *Publications:* The Taxation of Personal Wealth, 1967; (with J. Bristow) Economic Policy in Ireland, 1968; (with J. Bristow) Ireland: some problems of a developing economy, 1971; The Value Added Tax, 1972; articles on public finance in Rev. of Economic Studies, Finanzarchiv, Public Finance, Staff Papers, etc. *Recreations:* sailing, painting. *Address:* 4284 Vacation Lane, Arlington, Va 22207, USA. *T:* 202-477 4415. *Clubs:* Cosmos (Washington DC); Royal Irish Yacht (Dun Laoghaire).

TAIT, Adm. Sir (Allan) Gordon, KCB 1977; DSC 1943; Chief of Naval Personnel and Second Sea Lord, 1977-79; *b* 30 Oct. 1921; *s* of Allan G. Tait and Ann Gordon, Timaru, NZ; *m* 1952, Philippa, *d* of Sir Bryan Todd, *qv*; two *s* two *d. Educ:* Timaru Boys' High Sch.; RNC Dartmouth; War Service, Atlantic and N Russia Convoys, 1939-42; Submarines, Mediterranean and Far East, 1942-45 (despatches); Commanded HM Submarines: Teredo, 1947; Solent, 1948; ADC to Governor-General of New Zealand, 1949-51; commanded HM Submarines: Ambush, 1951; Aurochs, 1951-53; Tally Ho, 1955; Sanguine, 1955-56; Asst Naval Adviser, UK High Commn, Canada, 1957-59; commanded HM Ships: Caprice, 1960-62; Ajax, 1965-66; Maidstone, 1967; commanded: 2nd Destroyer Squadron (Far East), 1965-66; 3rd Submarine Sqdn, 1967-69; Britannia RNC, 1970-72; Rear-Adm., 1972; Naval Secretary, MoD, 1972-74; Vice-Adm., 1974; Flag Officer, Plymouth, Port Admiral, Devonport, NATO Comdr, Central Sub Area, Eastern Atlantic,

1975-77; Adm., 1978. Naval ADC to the Queen, 1972. NZ Dir, Bank of NSW; Director: Mount Cook Group Ltd; Todd Bros Ltd; Todd Motors Corp. Ltd. Pres. and Chm. of Trustees, NZ Sports Foundn; Mem., Spirit of Adventure Trust Board. *Address:* 22 Orakei Road, Auckland 5, New Zealand. *Club:* Royal Yacht Squadron.

TAIT, Andrew Wilson, OBE 1967; Director-General, National House-Building Council, since 1967; *b* 25 Sept. 1922; *s* of late Dr Adam and Jenny Tait; *m* 1954, Elizabeth Isobel Maclennan; three *d. Educ:* George Watson's Coll., Edinburgh; Edinburgh Univ. MA Hons History. Served Army, 1942-45. Leader writer, The Scotsman, 1947-48; Scottish Information Office, 1948-59; Principal, SHHD, 1959; Jt Sec., Cohen Cttee on Health Educn in UK, 1962-63; Dir, NHBC, 1964. Dir, Housing Res. Foundn, 1969-. Consultant: Nat. Assoc. of Home Builders of US, 1973-74; Home Owners Warranty Corp. of US, 1974-76; New Home Warranty Prog., Ontario, 1976-80. Founder, Internat. Housing and Home Warranty Assoc., 1979; Chm., Jt Land Requirements Cttee, 1981. *Recreations:* golf, tennis, chess. *Address:* Orchard Croft, Grimmshill, Great Missenden, Bucks. *T:* Great Missenden 2061. *Club:* Caledonian.

TAIT, Sir James (Blair), Kt 1963; QC (Australia); Barrister; *b* 15 October 1890; *s* of John Tait; *m* 1st, 1922, Annie Frances (decd), *d* of Dr George Howard; one *s* one *d*; 2nd, 1964, Sophie, *widow* of Dr J. Thomson-Tait. *Educ:* Geelong College; Melbourne University. War, 1914-18: Lt Aust. Flying Corps; Pilot Officer in France. Called to Bar in Victoria, 1919; KC 1945. Hon. Treas., Victorian Bar Council, 1939-74 (Chm., 1952-53); Past Pres., Graduate Union, Melbourne Univ.; Chairman: Equity Trustees Co, Ltd; Barristers' Chambers Ltd; Dir, Group Holdings Ltd. Chairman, Cttee of Inquiry into Stevedoring Industry in Australia, 1955-57. *Recreations:* golf and bowls. *Address:* Owen Dixon Chambers, 205 William Street, Melbourne, Victoria 3000, Australia. *T:* Melbourne 60.0791. *Clubs:* Australian, RACV (Melbourne).

TAIT, Prof. James Francis, PhD; FRS 1959; Emeritus Professor, University of London, since 1982; Co-Director, Biophysical Endocrinology Unit, Physics Department, Middlesex Hospital Medical School; *b* 1 December 1925; *s* of Herbert Tait and Constance Levinia Brotherton; *m* 1956, Sylvia Agnes Simpson (*née* Wardropper) (*see* S. A. Tait). *Educ:* Darlington Grammar Sch.; Leeds Univ. Lectr in Medical Physics, Middlesex Hospital Medical School, 1948-55; External Scientific Staff, Medical Research Council, Middlesex Hospital Medical School, 1955-58; Senior Scientist, Worcester Foundation for Experimental Biology, Shrewsbury, Mass, 1958-70; Joel Prof. of Physics as Applied to Medicine, Univ. of London, 1970-82. Hon. DSc Hull, 1979. Society for Endocrinology: Medal, 1969 and Sir Henry Dale Medal, 1979; Tadens Reichstein Award, Internat. Soc. of Endocrinology, 1976; CIBA Award, Amer. Heart Assoc. for Hypertension Research, 1977. *Publications:* papers on medical physics, biophysics and endocrinology. *Recreation:* gardening. *Address:* Biophysical Endocrinology Unit, Department of Physics as Applied to Medicine, Middlesex Hospital Medical School, Cleveland Street, W1P 6DB. *T:* 01-636 8333 (ext. 7612).

TAIT, Sir James (Sharp), Kt 1969; DSc, LLD, PhD, BSc(Eng), CEng, FIEE, FIMechE; Vice-Chancellor and Principal, The City University, 1966-74, retired (formerly Northampton College of Advanced Technology, London, of which he was Principal, 1957-66); *b* 13 June 1912; *s* of William Blyth Tait and Helen Sharp; *m* 1939, Mary C. Linton; two *s* one *d. Educ:* Royal Technical College, Glasgow; Glasgow Univ. (BSc (Eng.), PhD). Lecturer, Royal Technical Coll., Glasgow, 1935-46; Head of Electrical Engineering Department: Portsmouth Municipal Coll., 1946-47; Northampton Polytechnic, EC1, 1947-51; Principal, Woolwich Polytechnic, SE18, 1951-56. Member: Adv. Council on Scientific Policy, 1959-62; National Electronics Council, 1964-76, Hon. Mem., 1976. Pres., Inst. of Information Scientists, 1970-72. Hon. Fellow: Inst. of Measurement and Control, 1970; Inst. of Inf. Scientists, 1973. Hon. LLD Strathclyde, 1967; Hon. DSc City, 1974. *Recreation:* open-air pursuits. *Address:* 23 Trowlock Avenue, Teddington, Mddx. *T:* 01-977 6541.

TAIT, Sir Peter, KBE 1975 (OBE 1967); JP; financial consultant, New Zealand; Chairman: Bowring Burgess Finance Co. Ltd, since 1976; Tait Associates Ltd, since 1972; South Pacific Orchards Ltd, since 1974; Director: J. Herries & Co. Ltd; Financial Enterprises Ltd; *b* Wellington, NZ, 5 Sept. 1915; *s* of John Oliver Tait and Barbara Ann Isbister; *m* 1946, Lilian Jean Dunn; one *s* one *d. Educ:* Wellington Coll., NZ. MP, New Zealand National Party, 1951-54; Mayor, City of Napier, 1956-74; Pres., NZ Municipal Assoc., 1968-69. Chairman: Napier Fire Bd, 1956-75; Hawke's Bay Airport Authority, 1962-74; Napier Marineland Trust Bd, 1963-; Princess Alexandra Hosp. Bd, 1972-. Exec., Hawke's Bay Med. Res. Foundn; Patron, Napier Develt Assoc.; Freeman, City of Napier. JP 1956-. *Recreations:* bowls, gardening. *Address:* 1 Avon Terrace, Taradale, Napier, New Zealand. *T:* (private) 445266, (business) 55555. *Clubs:* Royal Over-Seas League; Lions, (Hon.) Cosmopolitan (both Napier).

TAIT, Mrs Sylvia Agnes Sophia, (Mrs James F. Tait), FRS 1959; Honorary Research Associate and Co-Director, Biophysical Endocrinology Unit, Physics Department, Middlesex Hospital Medical School, since 1982; biochemist; distinguished for her work on the hormones controlling the distribution of salts in the body; *m* 1956, James Francis Tait, *qv*. Research Asst, Courtauld Inst. of Biochemistry, Middlesex Hosp. Med. Sch., 1944-45;

External Scientific Staff, MRC, Middlesex Hosp. Med. Sch., 1955-58; Senior Scientist, Worcester Foundn for Experimental Biology, USA, 1958-70; Research Associate and Co-Director, Biophysical Endocrinology Unit, Dept of Physics as Applied to Medicine, Middlesex Hosp. Med. School. Hon. DSc Hull, 1979. Tadeus Reichstein Award, Internat. Endocrine Society, 1976; Gregory Pincus Meml Medal, 1977; CIBA Award, American Heart Assoc. for Hypertension Research, 1977; Sir Henry Dale Medal of Soc. for Endocrinology, 1979. *Address:* Biophysical Endocrinology Unit, Department of Physics as Applied to Medicine, Middlesex Hospital Medical School, Cleveland Street, W1P 6DB. *T:* 01-636 8333 (ext. 7162).

TAIT, Air Vice-Marshal Sir Victor Hubert, KBE 1944 (OBE 1938); CB 1943; *b* 8 July 1892; *s* of Samuel Tait, Winnipeg; *m* 1st, 1917; one *d* ; 2nd, 1929; one *s* ; 3rd, 1957, Nancy Margaret, *d* of late Andrew Muecke, Adelaide, Australia. *Educ:* University of Manitoba (BSc). Canadian Army, 1914-17; RFC and RAF, 1917-45. Director of Radar and Director-General of Signals, Air Ministry, 1942-45; Operations Director, BOAC, 1945-56. Chairman: International Aeradio Ltd, 1946-63; Lindley Thompson Transformer Co., 1959-66; Ultra Electronics (Holdings) Ltd, 1963-67 (Dir, 1955-72); Dir, Ultra Electronics Ltd, 1956-72. Air Transport Electronic Council, UK, 1958. Governor, Flight Safety Foundn of America, 1959-69. President, British Ice Hockey Assoc., 1958-71. Mem. Council, RGS, 1965-70. Order of the Nile (Egypt), 1936; Order of Merit (USA), 1945. *Address:* 81 Swan Court, SW3. *T:* 01-352 6864. *Clubs:* Hurlingham, Royal Air Force.

TALBOT, family name of **Baron Talbot of Malahide.**

TALBOT OF MALAHIDE, 9th Baron *cr* 1831 (Ire.); **Joseph Hubert George Talbot;** Baron Malahide of Malahide (Ire.), 1831; Hereditary Lord Admiral of Malahide and adjacent seas (15 Edward IV); retired; *b* 22 April 1899; *s* of John Reginald Charles Talbot (*d* 1909) and Maria Josephine (*d* 1939), *d* of 3rd Duc de Stacpoole; *S* brother, 1975; *m* 1st, 1924, Hélene (*d* 1961), *o d* of M. Gouley; 2nd, 1962, Beatrice Bros (marr. diss. 1970). *Educ:* Beaumont College. *Heir:* cousin Reginald John Richard Arundell [*b* 9 Jan. 1931; *m* 1955, Laura Duff, *yr d* of late Group Captain Edward John Tennant, DSO, MC; one *s* four *d*].

TALBOT, Vice-Adm. Sir (Arthur Allison) FitzRoy, KBE 1964; CB 1961; DSO 1940 and Bar 1942; DL; Commander-in-Chief, Plymouth, 1965-67; retired; *b* 22 October 1909; *s* of late Henry FitzRoy George Talbot, Captain Royal Navy, and of Susan Blair Athol Allison; *m* 1940, Joyce Gertrude Linley (*d* 1981); two *d. Educ:* RN College, Dartmouth. Served War of 1939-45: Comd 10th A/S Striking Force, North Sea, 1939, and 3rd MGB Flotilla, Channel, 1940-41 (DSO); Comd HMS Whitshed, East Coast, 1942 (Bar to DSO); Comd HMS Teazer, Mediterranean, 1943-44. Comdr 1945; Chief Staff Officer, Commodore Western Isles, 1945; Staff Officer Ops to C-in-C Brit. Pacific Fleet and Far East Station, 1947-48; Comd HMS Alert, 1949. Capt. 1950; Naval Attaché, Moscow and Helsinki, 1951-53. Imperial Defence College, 1954. Capt. (D) 3rd Destroyer Squadron, 1955-57; Commodore RN Barracks Portsmouth, 1957-59; Rear-Adm. 1960; Flag Officer: Arabian Seas and Persian Gulf, 1960-61; Middle East, 1961-62; Vice-Adm. 1962; Commander-in-Chief, S Atlantic and S America, 1963-65. DL Somerset, 1973. *Recreations:* riding, shooting. *Address:* Folly Farm, Ashill, Ilminster, Somerset. *T:* Hatch Beauchamp 480058. *Club:* Naval and Military.

TALBOT, Maj.-Gen. Dennis Edmund Blacquière, CB 1960; CBE 1955; DSO 1945; MC 1944; DL; *b* 23 Sept. 1908; *s* of late Walter Blacquière Talbot, St John, Jersey and The White House, Hadlow, Kent; *m* 1939, Barbara Anne, *o d* of late Rev. R. B. Pyper, Rector of Pluckley, Kent; three *s* two *d. Educ:* Tonbridge; RMC Sandhurst. 2nd Lieut Roy. West Kent Regt, 1928. Served War of 1939-45 (despatches, DSO, MC); Brigade Major, 30th Infantry, Bde, BEF; GSO 2, HQ 1st Corps; GSO 2 and 1, Combined Ops; 2nd i/c 5th Bn Dorset Regt; in command, 1st Bn Hampshire Regt, NW Europe, 1944-45. 1/c 2nd Bn Royal W Kent Regt, 1945-46; GSO 1, HQ, Far ELF, 1947-48; Senior UK Army Liaison Officer, NZ, 1948-51; Lt-Col 1949; Col 1952; i/c 18th Inf. Bde and 99th Gurkha Inf. Bde, Malaya, 1953-55; Brig. 1956; BGS, HQ, BAOR, 1957-58; Maj.-Gen. 1958; GOC, E Anglian Dist and 54th Inf. Div. (TA), 1958-61; Dep. Comdr, BAOR, and Comdr British Army Group Troops, 1961-63; Chief of Staff, BAOR, and GOC Rhine Army Troops, 1963-64, retired; Civil Service, 1964-73. Chm., Kent Cttee, Army Benev. Fund. Graduate of: Staff Coll., Camberley; RN Staff Coll., Greenwich; Joint Services Staff Coll., Latimer; Imperial Defence College, London; Civil Defence Staff Coll., Sunningdale. Col, The Queen's Own Royal West Kent Regt, 1959-61; Dep. Colonel, The Queen's Own Buffs, The Royal Kent Regt, 1961-65; Hon. Col, 8 Queen's Cadre (formerly 8 Bn The Queen's Regt (West Kent)), 1968-71. DL Kent, 1964. Knight Commander 1962, Grand Cross 1965, Order of the Dannebrog (Denmark). *Recreation:* gardening. *Address:* Oast Court, Barham, near Canterbury, Kent.

TALBOT, Vice-Adm. Sir FitzRoy, *see* Talbot, Vice-Adm. Sir A. A. F.

TALBOT, Frank Heyworth, QC 1949; LLB (London) 1929; Barrister; *b* 4 June 1895; *s* of Edward John Talbot and Susan (*née* Heyworth); *m* 1st, 1922, Mabel (*d* 1956), *d* of John Williams, Brecon; two *s* ; 2nd, 1969, Heather, *d* of J. F. Williams, Great Missenden, Bucks. *Educ:* Tottenham Grammar School; London Univ. Civil Service, 1912-31. Inns of Court Regt, 1918. Called to the Bar, Middle Temple, 1931; practice at the Bar, 1931-. Bencher, Middle Temple, 1958. *Recreation:* music. *Address:* Flat no 11, 24 Old

Buildings, Lincoln's Inn, WC2; *T:* 01-242 0494; 11 New Square, Lincoln's Inn, WC2. *T:* 01-242 4017.

TALBOT, Godfrey Walker, MVO 1960; OBE 1946; author, broadcaster, lecturer, journalist; Senior News Reporter and Commentator on staff of British Broadcasting Corporation, 1946-69; official BBC observer accredited to Buckingham Palace, 1948-69; *b* 8 Oct. 1908; *s* of Frank Talbot and Kate Bertha Talbot (*née* Walker); *m* 1933, Bess, *d* of Robert and Clara Owen, Bradford House, Wigan; one *s* (and one *s* decd). *Educ:* Leeds Grammar School. Joined editorial staff on The Yorkshire Post, 1928; Editor of The Manchester City News, 1932-34; Editorial Staff, Daily Dispatch, 1934-37. Joined BBC, 1937; War of 1939-45: BBC war correspondent overseas, 1941-45 (despatches, OBE); organised BBC Home Reporting Unit, as Chief Reporter, after the war. BBC Commentator, Royal Commonwealth Tour, 1953-54, and other overseas visits by HM the Queen. Pres., Queen's English Soc., 1982-. *Publications:* Speaking from the Desert, 1944; Ten Seconds from Now, 1973; Queen Elizabeth the Queen Mother, 1973; Permission to Speak, 1976; Royal Heritage, 1977; Royalty Annual, 1952, 1953, 1954, 1955, 1956; The Country Life Book of Queen Elizabeth The Queen Mother, 1978, new edn 1983; The Country Life Book of the Royal Family, 1980. *Recreation:* keeping quiet. *Address:* Holmwell, Hook Hill, Sanderstead, Surrey. *T:* 01-657 3476. *Club:* Royal Over-Seas League.

TALBOT, Hon. Sir Hilary Gwynne, Kt 1968; Hon. Mr Justice Talbot; a Judge of the High Court of Justice, Queen's Bench Division, since 1968; Judge of the Employment Appeals Tribunal, since 1978; *b* 22 Jan. 1912; *s* of late Rev. Prebendary A. T. S. Talbot, RD, and Mrs Talbot; *m* 1963, Jean Whitworth (JP Wilts), *o d* of late Mr and Mrs Kenneth Fisher. *Educ:* Haileybury Coll.; Worcester Coll., Oxford. MA Oxon. Served War of 1939-45; Captain, RA. Called to Bar by Middle Temple Jan. 1935. Dep. Chm., Northants QS, 1948-62; Chm., Derbyshire QS, 1958-63; Dep. Chm. Hants QS, 1964-71; Judge of County Courts, 1962-68; a Presiding Judge, Wales and Chester Circuit, 1970-74. Mem., Parole Bd, 1980-82. Dep. Chm., Boundary Commn for Wales, 1980-. Formerly Dep. Chm., Agricultural Land Tribunals. *Recreations:* fishing, walking, bird-watching. *Address:* Royal Courts of Justice, WC2.

TALBOT, Commandant Mary (Irene), CB; Director, Women's Royal Naval Service, 1973-76; *b* 17 Feb. 1922. *Educ:* Bristol Univ. BA Hons, Philosophy and Economics. Joined WRNS as a Naval recruiting asst, Nov. 1943; Officer training course, 1944, and apptd to HMS Eagle, in Liverpool, as an Educn and Resettlement Officer; served on staffs of C-in-Cs: Mediterranean; the Nore; Portsmouth, 1945-61; First Officer, and apptd to staff of Dir Naval Educn Service, 1952; subseq. served HMS Condor, Dauntless and Raleigh; Chief Officer, and apptd Sen. WRNS Officer, the Nore, 1960; on staff of Dir Naval Manning, 1963-66, and then became Asst Dir, WRNS; Superintendent, and served on staff of C-in-C Naval Home Command, 1969; Supt in charge, WRNS training estabt, HMS Dauntless, near Reading, 1972-73. Hon. ADC, 1973-76. *Recreations:* usual spinster ones: bridge, gardening, racing. *Address:* Sonning Cottage, Pound Lane, Sonning-on-Thames. *T:* Sonning 3323; Flat 2, 35 Buckingham Gate, SW1. *T:* 01-834 2579.

TALBOT, Very Rev. Maurice John; Dean Emeritus of Limerick; Rector of Drumcliffe, since 1980; *b* 29 March 1912; 2nd *s* of late Very Rev. Joseph Talbot, sometime Dean of Cashel; *m* 1942, Elisabeth Enid Westropp (*d* 1975); four *s* ; 2nd, 1980, Reta Soames. *Educ:* St Columba's College; Trinity College, Dublin (MA). Curate of Nantenan, 1935; Rector of Rathkeale, 1942; Rector of Killarney, 1952; Dean of Limerick, 1954-71; Prebendary of Taney, St Patrick's Nat. Cathedral, Dublin; Bishop's Curate, Kilmallock Union of Parishes, 1971-73. *Publications:* Pictorial Guide to St Mary's Cathedral, Limerick, 1969; contrib. to North Munster Studies, 1967; The Monuments of St Mary's Cathedral, 1976. *Recreations:* tennis, shooting, fishing. *Address:* 4 Meadow Close, Caherdavin, Limerick, Ireland; The Rectory, Ennis, Co. Clare, Ireland.

TALBOT, Richard Michael Arthur Chetwynd; His Honour Judge Chetwynd-Talbot; a Circuit Judge, since 1972; *b* 28 Sept. 1911; 3rd *s* of late Reverend Prebendary A. H. Talbot and late Mrs E. M. Talbot; unmarried. *Educ:* Harrow; Magdalene College, Cambridge (MA). Called to Bar by Middle Temple, 1936, Bencher, 1962. Mem. Bar Council, 1957-61. Dep. Chm., 1950-67, Chm., 1967-71, Shropshire QS; Recorder of Banbury, 1955-71, Hon. Recorder, 1972-. Served War of 1939-45, in Army; Major, King's Shropshire Light Infantry. *Address:* 7 St Leonard's Close, Bridgnorth, Salop WV16 4EJ. *T:* Bridgnorth 3619.

TALBOT, Thomas George, CB 1960; QC 1954; Counsel to the Chairman of Committees, House of Lords, 1953-77; *b* 21 Dec. 1904; *s* of late Rt Hon. Sir George John Talbot and late Gertrude Harriet, *d* of late Albemarle Cator, Woodbastwick Hall, Norfolk; *m* 1933, Hon. Cynthia Edith Guest; one *s* three *d. Educ:* Winchester; New Coll., Oxford. Called to Bar, Inner Temple, 1929; Bencher, 1960. RE (TA), 1938; Scots Guards, 1940-44 (Hon. Captain). Assistant, subsequently Deputy, Parliamentary Counsel to Treasury, 1944-53; Counsel to Chm. of Cttees, H of L, 1977-82. *Address:* Falconhurst, Edenbridge, Kent. *T:* Cowden 641. *Club:* Brooks's.

TALBOYS, Rt. Hon. Brian Edward, Hon. AC 1982; CH 1981; PC 1977; Deputy Prime Minister and Minister of Foreign Affairs and Overseas Trade,

New Zealand, 1975-81; Chairman, Board, Indosuez New Zealand Ltd, since 1982; *b* Wanganui, 1921; *m* ; two *s*. *Educ:* Wanganui Collegiate Sch.; Univ. of Manitoba; Victoria Univ., Wellington (BA). Served war of 1939-45, RNZAF. MP for Wallace, NZ, 1957-81; Dep. Leader, National Party, 1974-81; Parly Under-Sec. to Minister of Trade and Industry, 1960; Minister of Agriculture, 1962-69; Minister of Science, 1964-72; Minister of Education, 1969-72; Minister of Overseas Trade and Trade and Industry, 1972; Minister of Nat. Develt, 1975-77. Leader of a number of NZ delegns to overseas confs. Owns 500 acre sheep farm, Heddon Bush. Hon. DSc Massey Univ., 1981. *Address:* 1 Hamilton Avenue, Winton, New Zealand.

TALINTYRE, Douglas George; Head of Health and Safety Liaison, Department of Employment, since 1980; *b* 26 July 1932; *o s* of late Henry Matthew Talintyre and of Gladys Talintyre; *m* 1956, Maureen Dana Lyons; one *s* one *d*. *Educ:* Harrow County Grammar School; London School of Economics. BSc (Econ.) 1956. Joined National Coal Board, 1956: Administrative Assistant, 1956-59; Marketing Officer, Durham Div., 1959-61; Head of Manpower Planning and Intelligence, HQ, 1961-62; Dep. Head of Manpower, HQ, 1962-64; Head of Wages and Control, NW Div., 1964-66. Entered Civil Service, 1966; Principal, Naval Personnel (Pay) Div., MoD, 1966-69; Senior Industrial Relations Officer, CIR, 1969-71; Director of Industrial Relations, CIR, 1971-74; Asst Secretary, Training Services Agency, 1974-75; Counsellor (Labour), HM Embassy, Washington DC, 1975-77; Head of Policy and Planning, Manpower Services Commn, 1977-80. Freeman, Co. of Cordwainers, Newcastle-upon-Tyne, 1952. *Recreations:* squash, chess, gardening. *Address:* Woodwards, School Lane, Cookham Dean, Berks SL6 9PQ.

TALLACK, Sir Hugh M.; *see* Mackay-Tallack.

TALLBOYS, Richard Gilbert, CMG 1981; OBE 1974; FCA; FCIS; HM Diplomatic Service; Consul-General, Houston, since 1980; *b* 25 April 1931; *s* of late Harry Tallboys; *m* 1954, Margaret Evelyn, *d* of Brig. H. W. Strutt, DSO, ED, Hobart; two *s* two *d*. *Educ:* Palmer's School. LLB (London), BCom (Tasmania). Lt-Comdr RANR. Accounting profession in Australia, 1955-62; Alderman, Hobart City Council, 1958-62; Australian Govt Trade Commissioner, Johannesburg, Singapore, Jakarta, 1962-68. HM Diplomatic Service, 1968; First Secretary i/c Brasilia, 1969; Head of Chancery, Phnom Penh, 1972 (Chargé d'Affaires *ai* 1972, 1973); FO, 1973; Counsellor Commercial, Seoul, 1976-80 (Chargé d'Affaires *ai* 1977, 1978, 1979). *Address:* c/o Foreign and Commonwealth Office, SW1. *Clubs:* Travellers'; Naval; Tasmanian.

TALLING, John Francis, DSc; FRS 1978; Senior Principal Scientific Officer, Freshwater Biological Association, since 1958; *b* 23 March 1929; *s* of Frank and Miriam Talling; *m* 1959, Ida Björnsson; one *s* one *d*. *Educ:* Sir William Turner's Sch., Coatham; Univ. of Leeds. BSc, PhD, DSc. Lecturer in Botany, Univ. of Khartoum, 1953-56; Visiting Research Fellow, Univ. of California, 1957; Plant Physiologist, Freshwater Biological Assoc., 1958–; Hon. Reader, Univ. of Lancaster, 1979-. *Publications:* co-author, Water Analysis: some revised methods for limnologists, 1978; papers in various learned jls. *Recreation:* country walking. *Address:* Buhuka, Brow Crescent, Windermere, Cumbria LA23 2EZ. *T:* Windermere 2836.

TALLIS, Gillian Helen, (Mrs Walter Tallis); *see* Mackay, G. H.

TAMBLIN, Air Cdre Pamela Joy, CB 1980; retired; Director, Women's Royal Air Force, 1976-80; *b* 11 Jan. 1926; *d* of late Albert Laing and of Olga Victoria Laing; *m* 1970, Douglas Victor Tamblin; one step *s* one step *d*. *Educ:* James Gillespie's High Sch., Edinburgh; Heaton High Sch., Newcastle upon Tyne; Durham Univ. (BA Hons). ATS, 1943-45. Essex County Council Planning Officer, 1949-51. Joined Royal Air Force, 1951; served Education Branch, 1951-55; RAF Locking; RAF Stanmore Park; RAF Wahn, Germany; Secretarial (now Administrative) Branch, 1955-76; Schools Liaison Recruiting, 1955-59; Accountant Officer, RAF St Mawgan and RAF Steamer Point, Aden, 1959-61; Staff College, 1962-63; MoD, Air Secretary's Dept, 1963-66; Sen. Trng Officer, RAF Spitalgate, 1966-68; Admin. Plans Officer, HQ Maintenance Comd, 1968-69; Command WRAF Admin. Officer, HQ Strike Comd, 1969-71; Station Comdr, RAF Spitalgate, 1971-74; Command Accountant, HQ Strike Comd, 1974-76. Chm., Cttee on Women in Nato Forces, 1977-79. FBIM 1977, CBIM 1979; FRSA 1979. *Recreations:* fell-walking, gardening, cookery, tapestry, woodworking. *Address:* 2 Carlton Court, Eastbury Road, Watford, Herts. *Club:* Royal Air Force.

TAME, William Charles, CB 1963; Deputy Secretary, Ministry of Agriculture, Fisheries and Food, 1967-71; *b* 25 June 1909; *s* of late Charles Henry Tame, Wimbledon, Surrey; *m* 1935, Alice Margaret, *o d* of late G. B. Forrest, Witherslack, Cumbria; one *s* one *d*. *Educ:* King's College School, Wimbledon; Hertford College, Oxford. Entered Ministry of Agriculture as Assistant Principal, 1933. Chairman: International Whaling Commission, 1966-68; Fisheries R&D Bd, 1972-78. Member: Council, Royal Veterinary Coll., Univ. of London, 1972-80 (Vice-Chm., 1973-80); Governing Body, Animal Virus Res. Inst., 1972-76. *Recreation:* music. *Address:* Windrush, Walton Lane, Bosham, Chichester. *T:* Bosham 573217.

TAMMADGE, Alan Richard; Headmaster, Sevenoaks School, 1971-81; *b* 9 July 1921; *m* 1950, Rosemary Anne Broadribb; two *s* one *d*. *Educ:* Bromley County Sch.; Dulwich Coll.; Emmanuel Coll., Cambridge. BA (Maths) 1950;

MA 1957. Royal Navy Special Entry, 1940; resigned, 1947 (Lt); Cambridge, 1947-50; Lectr, RMA Sandhurst, 1950-55; Asst Master, Dulwich College, 1956-58; Head of Mathematics Dept, Abingdon School, 1958-67; Master, Magdalen College School, Oxford, 1967-71. Pres., Mathematical Assoc., 1978-79. FIMA 1965. *Publications:* Complex Numbers, 1965; (jtly) School Mathematics Project Books 1-5, 1965-69; (jtly) General Education, 1969; Parents' Guide to School Mathematics, 1976; articles in Mathemat. Gazette, Mathematics Teacher (USA), Aspects of Education (Hull Univ.). *Recreations:* music, gardens. *Address:* 20 Claverham Way, Battle, East Sussex.

TAMUNO, Prof. Tekena Nitonye, PhD; Research Professor in History, Institute of African Studies, University of Ibadan, since 1979; Pro-Chancellor and Chairman of Council, Rivers State University of Science and Technology, Port-Harcourt, since 1981; *b* 28 Jan. 1932; *s* of Chief Mark Tamuno Igbiri and late Mrs Ransoline I. Tamuno; *m* 1963, Olu Grace Tamuno (*née* Esho); two *s* two *d*. *Educ:* University Coll., Ibadan; Birkbeck Coll., Univ. of London; Columbia Univ., New York City. BA (Hons) History, PhD History (London). Univ. of Ibadan: Professor of History, 1971; Head, Dept of History, 1972-75; Dean of Arts, 1973-75; Chairman, Cttee of Deans, 1974-75; Vice-Chancellor, 1975-79. Principal, University Coll., Ilorin, Oct.-Nov. 1975. Nat. Vice-Pres., Historical Soc. of Nigeria, 1974–. JP Ibadan, 1976. *Publications:* Nigeria and Elective Representation, 1923-1947, 1966; The Police in Modern Nigeria, 1861-1965, 1970; The Evolution of the Nigerian State: The Southern Phase, 1898-1914, 1972; (ed, with Prof. J. F. A. Ajayi) The University of Ibadan, 1948-1973: A History of the First Twenty-Five Years, 1973; History and History-makers in Modern Nigeria, 1973; Herbert Macaulay, Nigerian Patriot, 1975; (ed with E. J. Alagoa) Eminent Nigerians of the Rivers State, 1980; (ed) Ibadan Voices: Ibadan University in Transition, 1981. *Recreations:* music, photography, swimming, horse-riding. *Address:* University of Ibadan, Ibadan, Nigeria. *T:* (office) 400550, (home) 410540. *Club:* (Hon.) Senior Staff (University of Ibadan).

TAMWORTH, Viscount; Robert William Saswalo Shirley; Group Auditor with BICC plc; *b* 29 Dec. 1952; *s* and *heir* of 13th Earl Ferrers, *qv* ; *m* 1980, Susannah, *y d* of C. E. W. Sheepshanks, Arthington Hall, Yorks. *Educ:* Ampleforth. Teaching in Kenya, under Youth Service Abroad Scheme, 1971-72. Articled to Whinney Murray & Co, CA, 1972-76, employed at Ernst & Whinney, 1976-82. Admitted to Inst. of Chartered Accountants of England and Wales, 1976. *Recreations:* the countryside and related activities. *Address:* Shirley Common Farm, Shirley, Derby DE6 3AZ.

TANBURN, Jennifer Jephcott; Head of Research and Consumer Affairs, since 1975, a Director, since 1976, Booker McConnell Food Distribution Division; Member: Marketing Policy Committee, since 1977, and of Potato Product Group, since 1980, of the Central Council for Agricultural and Horticultural Co-operation; Packaging Council, since 1978; *b* 6 Oct. 1929; *d* of late Harold Jephcott Tanburn and of Elise Noel Tanburn (*née* Armour). *Educ:* St Joseph's Priory, Dorking; Settrington Sch., Hampstead; University Coll. of the South West, Exeter (BSc(Econ)). Market Research Dept, Unilever Ltd, 1951-52; Research and Information, Lintas Ltd, 1952-66, Head of Div., 1962-66, Head of Special Projects, 1966-74; British Airways Board, 1974-76. Member: Market Research Soc.; Marketing Gp of GB. *Publications:* Food, Women and Shops, 1968; People, Shops and the '70s, 1970; Superstores in the '70s, 1972; Retailing and the Competitive Challenge: a study of retail trends in the Common Market, Sweden and the USA, 1974; Food Distribution: its impact on marketing in the '80s, 1981; articles on retailing and marketing subjects. *Recreations:* travel, golf, gardening, dressmaking, television viewing, reading. *Address:* 8 Ellwood Rise, Vache Lane, Chalfont St Giles, Bucks HP8 4SU. *T:* Chalfont St Giles 5205. *Club:* Beaconsfield Golf.

TANCRED, Sir H. L.; *see* Lawson-Tancred.

TANDY, Jessica; actress, stage and screen; *b* London, 7 June 1909; *d* of Harry Tandy and Jessie Helen (*née* Horspool); *m* 1st, 1932, Jack Hawkins (marr. diss.); one *d* ; 2nd, 1942, Hume Cronyn (Young); one *s* one *d*. *Educ:* Dame Owen's Girls' Sch.; Ben Greet Acad. of Acting. Birmingham Repertory Theatre, 1928; first London appearance, 1929; first New York appearance, 1930; subsequently alternated between London and New York. *New York plays include:* The Matriarch, 1930; The Last Enemy, 1930; Time and the Conways, 1937; The White Steed, 1939; Geneva, 1940; Jupiter Laughs, 1940; Anne of England, 1941; Yesterday's Magic, 1942; A Streetcar Named Desire, 1947-49 (Antoinette Perry Award, 1948); Hilda Crane, 1950; The Fourposter, 1951-53 (Comœdia Matinee Club Bronze Medallion, 1952); Madame Will You Walk?, 1953; Face to Face, 1954; the Honeys, 1955; A Day by the Sea, 1955; The Man in the Dog Suit, 1957-58; Triple Play, 1959; Five Finger Exercise, 1959 (New York League's Delia Austria Medal, 1960); The Physicists, 1964; A Delicate Balance, 1966-67; Camino Real, 1970; Home, 1971; All Over, 1971; Promenade All (tour), 1972; Happy Days, Not I (Samuel Beckett Festival), 1972 (Drama Desk Award, 1973); Tours: Not I, 1973; Many Faces of Love, 1974, 1975 and 1976; Noel Coward in Two Keys, 1974, 1975; The Gin Game, 1977 (US and USSR Tour, 1978-79; Sarah Siddons Award, Chicago and Los Angeles Critics' Award). *London plays include:* The Rumour, 1929; Autumn Crocus, Lyric, 1931; Children in Uniform, Duchess, 1932; Hamlet, New, 1934; French without Tears, Criterion, 1936; Anthony and Anna, Whitehall, 1935; The Gin Game, Lyric, 1979. Open-Air Theatre, London, 1933 and 1939; Old Vic, 1937 and 1940, leading Shakespearian rôles, etc. Toured Canada, 1939; tour of US with husband, (poetry and prose readings), 1954; they also toured Summer Theatres (in plays), 1957. Opening Season of the Tyrone Guthrie Theatre Minneapolis, USA: 1963: Hamlet; Three Sisters; Death of A Salesman; 1965: The Way of the World, The Cherry Orchard and The Caucasian Chalk Circle. The Miser, Los Angeles, 1968; Heartbreak House, Shaw Festival, Niagara-on-the-Lake, Ontario, 1968; Tchin-Tchin, Chicago, 1969; Eve, The Way of the World and A Midsummer Night's Dream, Stratford, Ontario Festival, 1976; Long Day's Journey Into Night, London, Ontario, 1977; The Gin Game, Long Wharf Theatre, New Haven, Conn, 1977 (Drama Desk Award, 1977-78; Antoinette Perry Award, 1978); Long Day's Journey, Foxfire, Stratford, Ont., 1980; Rose, NYC, 1981. *Films include*: The Indiscretions of Eve, The Seventh Cross, The Valley of Decision, Dragonwyck, The Green Years, A Woman's Vengeance, Forever Amber, September Affair, Rommel-Desert Fox, A Light in the Forest, Adventures of a Young Man, The Birds, Butley; Honky Tonk Freeway, 1980; Stab, 1981; Garp, 1981; Best Friends, 1982. *Television*: all major American dramatic programs. Obie Award, 1972-73; Brandeis Theatre Arts Medal, 1978; Elected to Theatre Hall of Fame, 1979. Hon. LLD, Univ. of Western Ontario, 1974.

TANG, Sir Shiu-kin, Kt 1964; CBE 1957 (OBE 1949; MBE 1934); JP; Chairman and Managing Director of Kowloon Motor Bus Co. (1933) Ltd since its inception; *b* 21 Mar. 1901; *s* of late Tang Chi-Ngong, JP; *m* May Fung. *Educ*: Queen's Coll., Hong Kong; St Stephen's Coll., Hong Kong. Dir, Tung Wah Hosp., 1924 (Chm. Bd of Dirs, 1928); Life Mem., Court of Univ. of Hong Kong; Member: Urban Coun., 1938-41; St John Coun. for Hong Kong, St John Ambulance Assoc. and Bde; Grantham Scholarships Fund Cttee; Cttee of Aberdeen Tech. Sch.; Chinese Temples Cttee, 1934-64; Bd of Chinese Perm. Cemetery; Tung Wah Gp of Hosps Adv. Bd; Po Leung Kuk Perm. Bd of Dirs (Chm. 1932); Exec. Cttee, Nethersole, Alice and Ho Miu Ling Hosp.; Trustee, Street Sleepers' Shelter Soc.; Vice-Pres. and Trustee of Hong Kong Br., Brit. Red Cross Soc.; Vice-President: The Boy Scouts' Assoc.; S China Athletic Assoc.; Adviser: Hongkong Juvenile Care Centre; Chinese Chamber of Commerce. Hon. LLD, Hong Kong, 1961. JP Hong Kong, 1929. Certificate of Honour Class I, and Life Mem., British Red Cross Soc., 1967. KStJ 1962. *Address*: 5 Broom Road, Hong Kong.

TANGANYIKA, WESTERN, Bishop of; *see* Tanzania, Archbishop of.

TANGE, Sir Arthur (Harold), AC 1977; Kt 1959; CBE 1955 (OBE 1953); retired civil servant; *b* 18 August 1914; 2nd *s* of late Charles L. Tange, Solicitor, Gosford, New South Wales; *m* 1940, Marjorie Florence, 2nd *d* of late Professor Edward O. G. Shann; one *s* one *d*. *Educ*: Gosford High School; Western Australia University (BA; 1st Cl. Hons Economics). Joined Bank of NSW, 1931; Economist, Bank of NSW, 1938; Economic Research in Commonwealth Depts, Canberra, 1942-46. Entered Australian Diplomatic Service, 1946; First Secretary, Australian Mission to United Nations, 1946-48; Counsellor, United Nations Division, Canberra, 1948-50; Assistant Secretary, Department of External Affairs, Canberra, 1950-53; Minister at Australian Embassy, Washington, 1953-54; Secretary of Dept of External Affairs, Canberra, 1954-65; High Comr in India and Ambassador to Nepal, 1965-70; Sec., Dept of Defence, 1970-79. Represented Australia at many international economic and trade conferences, 1944-63. *Publication*: (jointly) Australia Foots the Bill, 1942. *Recreation*: fishing. *Address*: 32 La Perouse Street, Canberra, ACT 2603, Australia. *Club*: Commonwealth (Canberra).

TANGNEY, Dame Dorothy Margaret, DBE 1968; Senator for West Australia, 1943-68; *b* 13 March 1911; *d* of E. Tangney, Claremont, West Australia. *Educ*: St Joseph's Convent, Fremantle, University of West Australia. Teaching staff, Education Department, West Australia. First woman to be elected to Commonwealth Senate. Mem., Standing Cttee, Convocation, University of West Australia. *Recreations*: tennis, motoring, badminton, reading. *Address*: 12 Mary Street, Claremont, WA 6010, Australia. *T*: 31 2631.

TANKERVILLE, 10th Earl of, *cr* 1714; **Peter Grey Bennet**; Baron Ossulston, 1682; *b* 18 Oct. 1956; *s* of 9th Earl of Tankerville, and of Georgiana Lilian Maude, *d* of late Gilbert Wilson, MA, DD, PhD; *S* father, 1980. *Educ*: Oberlin Conservatory, Ohio (Bachelor of Music). Working as musician, San Francisco. *Heir*: *uncle* Rev. the Hon. George Arthur Grey Bennet [*b* 12 March 1925; *m* 1957, Hazel Glyddon, *d* of late E. W. G. Judson; two *s* one *d*]. *Address*: 139 Olympia Way, San Francisco, California 94131, USA. *T*: 415-826-6639.

TANLAW, Baron *cr* 1971 (Life Peer), of Tanlawhill, Dumfries; **Simon Brooke Mackay**; Chairman and Managing Director, Fandstan Ltd, since 1973; *b* 30 March 1934; *s* of 2nd Earl of Inchcape; *m* 1st, 1959, Joanna Susan, *d* of Major J. S. Hirsch; one *s* two *d* (and one *s* decd); 2nd, 1976, Rina Siew Yong Tan, *d* of late Tiong Cha Tan and Mrs Tan; one *s* one *d*. *Educ*: Eton College; Trinity College, Cambridge (MA 1966). Served as 2nd Lt XII Royal Lancers, Malaya. Inchcape Group of Companies, India and Far East, 1960-66; Managing Director, Inchcape & Co., 1967-71, Dir 1971-; Chm., Thwaites & Reed Ltd, 1971-74; Chm. and Man. Dir, Fandstan Group of private cos, 1973-. Chm., Building Cttee, UC at Buckingham, 1973-78, Mem. Council of Management 1973-, Hon. Fellow, 1981; Mem. Ct of Governors and External Relations Cttee, LSE, 1980-. Mem., Lord Chancellor's Inner London Adv. Cttee on Justices of the Peace, 1972-. Contested (L) Galloway, by-election and gen. election, 1959, and gen. election, 1964; Liberal energy and transport spokesman, House of Lords, 1979-. Mem., EC Cttee Sub-Cttee F (Energy,

Transport Technology and Research), 1980-. Joint Treasurer, 1971-72, Dep. Chm., 1972, Scottish Liberal Party. Pres., Sarawak Assoc., 1973-75. Inventor, Chronolog system of time measurement. *Recreations*: normal. *Address*: Tanlawhill, Eskdalemuir, By Langholm, Dumfriesshire. *T*: Eskdalemuir 273; The Manor House, Little Venice, W9. *Clubs*: White's, Oriental, Buck's.

TANNER, Dr Bernice Alture; FRCGP; General Practitioner in London W11 area, since 1948; *b* 23 Sept. 1917; *m* 1942, Prof. James M. Tanner, MD, FRCP, FRCPsych; one *d* (one *s* decd). *Educ*: Cornell Univ., USA; New York Univ.; McGill Univ., Canada; Medical Coll. of Pennsylvania, USA. BA 1939; MD 1943 (Med. Coll., Pa); FRCGP 1980. Convenor, Educational Cttee, London NW Faculty RCGP; Course organizer, St Charles Hosp. Vocational Trng Scheme for Gen. Practice; Mem., AHA Cttee paediatric care, London NW Area. Mem., Supplementary Benefits Commn, 1976-79. *Publication*: (ed) Language and Communication in General Practice, 1976. *Recreations*: music, postgraduate medical education. *Address*: 127 Oakwood Court, W14. *T*: 01-603 7881.

TANNER, David Williamson, DPhil; Under Secretary, Head of Science Branch, Department of Education and Science, since 1981; *b* 28 Dec. 1930; *s* of late Arthur Bertram Tanner, MBE and of Susan (*née* Williamson); *m* 1960, Glenis Mary (*née* Stringer); one *s* two *d*. *Educ*: Raynes Park County Grammar Sch.; University Coll., Oxford. MA, DPhil (Oxon). Univ. of Minnesota (post-doctoral research), USA, 1954-56; Dept of Scientific and Industrial Research (Fuel Research Station and Warren Spring Lab.), 1957-64; Dept of Educn and Science, 1964-. *Publications*: papers on physical chem. in Trans. Faraday Soc., Jl Applied Chem., Jl Heat and Mass Transfer, etc. *Recreations*: family, yoga, PUTTing. *Address*: 17 Rocks Lane, Barnes, SW13. *T*: 01-878 6179.

TANNER, Dr John Ian, CBE 1979; Founding Director: Royal Air Force Museum, since 1963; Battle of Britain Museum, since 1978; Cosford Aero-Space Museum, since 1978; *b* London, 2 Jan. 1927; *o s* of R. A. and I. D. M. Tanner; *m* 1953, April Rothery; one *d*. *Educ*: City of London Library Sch.; Universities of London, Nottingham and Oxford. MA, PhD Nottingham. Reading Public Library, 1950; Archivist-Librarian, Kensington Library, 1950-51; Leighton House Art Gall. and Museum, 1951-53; Curator, Librarian and Tutor, RAF Coll., 1953-63; Hon. Sec., Old Cranwellian Assoc., 1956-64; Extra-mural Lectr in History of Art, Univ. of Nottingham, 1959-63. Hon. Archivist, Pembroke College, Oxford. Walmsley Lectr, City Univ., 1980. Mem., Adv. Council, Inst. of Heraldic and Genealogical Studies. Chm., Internat. Air Museum Cttee; Vice-President: Guild of Aviation Artists; Croydon Airport Museum Soc.; Trustee, Manchester Air and Space Museum; Mem. Founding Cttee, All England Lawn Tennis Museum; Pres., Anglo-American Ecumenical Assoc. FLA, FMA, FRHistS, FRAeS, FSA. Hon. DLitt City, 1982. Freeman, City of London, 1966; Liveryman: Worshipful Co. of Gold and Silver Wyre Drawers, 1966; Scriveners' Co., 1978. Freeman, Guild of Air Pilots and Air Navigators, 1979. Hon. Mem. Collegio Araldico of Rome, 1963; Tissandier Award, Fedn Aeronautique Internat., 1977. KStJ 1978 (OStJ 1964); KSG 1977; Cross of Merit, Order of Malta, 1978. Grand Comdr, OM Holy Sepulchre (Vatican). *Publications*: (ed) List of Cranwell Graduates, 2nd edn, 1963; (jtly) Encyclopedic Dictionary of Heraldry, 1968; How to trace your Ancestors, 1971; Man in Flight (limited edn), 1973; The Royal Air Force Museum: one hundred years of aviation history, 1973; (with W. E. May and W. Y. Carman) Badges and Insignia of the British Armed Services, 1974; Charles I, 1974; Who's Famous in Your Family: a Reader's Digest guide to genealogy, 1975, 2nd edn 1979; Wings of the Eagle (exhibition catalogue), 1976; (ed) They Fell in the Battle, 1980 (limited edn, to commemorate 40th anniv. of Battle of Britain); Editor, RAF Museum Air Publication series, 10 vols; General Editor: Museums and Libraries (Internat. Series); Studies in Air History; reviews and articles in professional and other jls. *Recreations*: cricket, opera, reading. *Address*: Flat One, 57 Drayton Gardens, SW10 9RU. *Clubs*: Athenæum, Buck's, Reform, MCC, Royal Air Force.

TANNER, John W., FRIBA, FRTPI; Director, United Nations Relief and Works Agency for Palestine Refugees, Jordan, since 1971 (accorded rank of Ambassador to Hashemite Kingdom of Jordan, 1973); *b* 15 Nov. 1923; *s* of Walter George Tanner and Elizabeth Wilkes Tanner (*née* Humphreys); *m* 1948, Hazel Harford Harford-Jones; one *s* two *d*. *Educ*: Clifton Coll.; Liverpool Univ. Sch. of Architecture and Dept of Civic Design. MCD, BArch (Hons). Sen. Planning Officer, Nairobi, 1951; Architect, Nairobi, 1953; Hon. Sec., Kenya Chapter of Architects, 1954; UN Relief and Works Agency: Architect and Planning Officer, Beirut, 1955; Chief Techn. Div., 1957. Past Mem. Cttee, Fedn of Internat. Civil Servants Assoc., 1968-70. *Buildings*: vocational and teacher training centres, schools; low cost housing and health centres; E African Rugby Union HQ, Nairobi; training centres: Damascus Vocational, Syria; Siblin, Lebanon; Ramallah Women's; Wadi Seer; Amman, Jordan. *Publications*: The Colour Problem in Liverpool: accommodation or assimilation, 1951; Building for the UNRWA/UNESCO Education and Training Programme, 1968. *Recreations*: formerly: Rugby football (Waterloo, Lancs, 1950; Kenya Harlequins (Captain 1955), Kenya and E Africa); skiing. *Address*: UNRWA, Jordan; 10 Yeomans Drive, Aston, Herts. *Clubs*: Ski Club of GB; Kandahar Ski.

TANSLEY, Sir Eric (Crawford), Kt 1953; CMG 1946; Chairman, Pacol, 1962-72; formerly Director: Bank of West Africa; Standard Bank Ltd; Standard & Chartered Banking Group Ltd; Gill & Duffus Ltd; *b* 25 May 1901; *o s* of William and Margaret Tansley; *m* 1931, Iris, *yr d* of Thomas Richards;

one s one d. *Educ:* Mercers' Sch. Formerly: Mem., Colonial, now Commonwealth, Development Corporation, 1948-51, 1961-68; Chairman: London Cocoa Terminal Market Assoc., 1932; Cocoa Assoc. of London, 1936-37; Marketing Director, West African Produce Control Board (Colonial Office), 1940-47. Retired, 1961 as Managing Director, Ghana Cocoa Marketing Co. and Adviser, Nigerian Produce Marketing Co. *Address:* 11 Cadogan Square, SW1. *T:* 01-235 2752.

TANZANIA, Archbishop of, since 1979; **Most Rev. Musa Kahurananga;** Bishop of Western Tanganyika, since 1966; *b* 1921; *s* of Samweli and Mariamu Kahurananga; *m* 1941, Raheli Lutozi; three *s* four *d* (and one *s* decd). *Educ:* Teachers' Training College, Katoke Bukoba. Teacher; Deacon 1952, Priest 1953; Asst Bishop in Diocese of Central Tanganyika, 1962. *Recreation:* farming. *Address:* Diocese of Western Tanganyika, PO Box 13, Kasulu, Tanzania.

TAPLIN, Walter; author and journalist; *b* Southampton, 4 Aug. 1910; *m* ; three *s* two *d*. *Educ:* University College, Southampton (Foundation Scholar); The Queen's Coll., Oxford (Southampton Exhibitioner). Tutor-Organiser for Adult Education, W Hants and E Dorset, 1936-38; Editorial Staff of The Economist, 1938-40; Ministry of Food, 1940-42; Offices of the War Cabinet (Central Statistical Office), 1942-45; joined the Spectator as Asst Editor, 1946; Editor, 1953-54; Senior Economist, Iron and Steel Board, 1955-56; Research Fellow in Advertising and Promotional Activity, London School of Economics and Political Science, 1957-61. Editor: Accountancy, 1961-71; Accounting and Business Research, 1971-75. *Publications:* Advertising: A New Approach, 1960; Origin of Television Advertising, 1961; History of the British Steel Industry (with J. C. Carr), 1962. *Recreation:* reading. *Address:* Parson's Field, Long Bredy, Dorchester, Dorset. *T:* Long Bredy 360. *Club:* Reform.

TAPP, Maj.-Gen. Sir Nigel (Prior Hanson), KBE 1960 (CBE 1954); CB 1956; DSO 1945; DL; *b* 12 June 1904; *y s* of late Lt-Col J. Hanson Tapp, DSO, and of late Mrs Hanson Tapp (*née* Molesworth), Duns, Berwickshire; *m* 1948, Dorothy (*d* 1978), *y d* of late Alexander Harvey. *Educ:* Cheltenham College; Royal Military Academy, Woolwich. 2nd Lieutenant RA, 1924; Sudan Defence Force, 1932-38; ADC to Governor-General, Sudan, 1935-36; Staff College, Camberley, 1939; GSO 3, 1 Corps BEF, 1940; GSO 2, War Office, 1940-41; GSO 1 Staff College, Camberley, 1941-42; CO, 7 Field Regt, RA, UK, Normandy, Belgium, and Holland, 1942-45; Comd RA 25 Div., SEAC, 1945; District Commander, Eritrea, 1946-47; Dep. Dir Land/Air Warfare, 1948; Dep. Dir RA, 1949; idc, 1950; Commander 1 Corps Royal Artillery, BAOR, 1951-53; General Officer Commanding 2 AA Group, 1954; Director of Military Training, War Office, 1955-57; GOC East Africa Command, 1957-60; retd 1961; Lieut-Governor and Sec., Royal Hosp., Chelsea, 1967-73. Pres., Assoc. of Service Newspapers, 1974-. Col Comdt, Royal Regt of Artillery, 1963-68. Hon. Freeman, City of London, 1978. DL Greater London, 1973-82. *Recreations:* reading, fishing. *Address:* 9 Cadogan Square, SW1. *Club:* Army and Navy.

TAPPER-JONES, Sydney, LLB (London); Town Clerk and Clerk of the Peace, Cardiff, 1942-70; *b* 12 March 1904; *s* of David and Frances Caroline Mary Jones; *m* 1947, Florence Mary (Joan) Hellyer; one *d*. *Educ:* Pentre (Rhondda) Secondary School. Articled Cousins, Botsford & Co., Solicitors, Cardiff. LLB Lond. (External) (Hons), 1924. Solicitors' Final Exam. (Hons), 1925; Admitted Solicitor, 1925. Managing Clerk with Allen Pratt & Geldard (with whom were amalgamated Vachell & Co.), Solicitors, Cardiff, 1925-27; Cardiff Corporation: Conveyancing Solicitor, 1927-29, Prosecuting Solicitor, 1929-33; Deputy Town Clerk and Deputy Clerk of the Peace, 1933-42; Commissioner for Oaths. Member of Convocation, 1925. Member: Finance and Gen. Purposes Cttee, Nat. Museum of Wales; S Wales Cancer Res. Council; Exec. Cttee, Cancer Inf. Centre, Cardiff; a Drapers' Co. Rep. on Bd of Governors, Howell's Sch., Llandaff. Member, Order of St John, 1966. *Address:* Maes-y-Coed, 59 Heath Park Avenue, Cardiff. *T:* Cardiff 751306.

TAPPS-GERVIS-MEYRICK, Lt-Col Sir George David Eliott; see Meyrick.

TAPSELL, Peter Hannay Bailey; MP (C) Horncastle (Lincs) since 1966 (Nottingham West, 1959-64); *b* 1 Feb. 1930; *s* of late Eustace Tapsell; *m* 1st, 1963, Hon. Cecilia Hawke (marr. diss. 1971), 3rd *d* of 9th Baron Hawke; one *s* ; 2nd, 1974, Mlle Gabrielle Jocelyne Mahieu, *e d* of late Jean Mahieu, Normandy, France. *Educ:* Tonbridge; Merton Coll., Oxford (MA). Nat. Service Commn, Royal Sussex Regt, 1948-50 (Middle East). 1st Cl. Hons Mod. Hist., 1953; Hon. Postmaster of Merton Coll., 1953; Librarian of Oxford Union, 1953; Rep. Oxford Union on debating tour of United States, 1954. Personal Asst to Prime Minister (Anthony Eden) during 1955 General Election Campaign. Conservative Research Department, 1954-57 (Social Services and Agriculture). Contested (C) Wednesbury, bye-election, 1957. Opposition front bench spokesman on Foreign and Commonwealth affairs, 1976-77, on Treasury and economic affairs, 1977-78. Member of London Stock Exchange; Member: James Capel & Co. (Stockbrokers); Trilateral Commn; Chairman, Coningsby Club, 1957-58; Jt Chm., British-Caribbean Assoc., 1963-64. Court Mem., Univs of Nottingham and Hull. Vice Pres., Tennyson Soc. Hon. Mem., Brunei Govt Investment Adv. Bd, 1976-. Mem. Organising Cttee, Zaire River Expedn, 1974-75. Hon. Life Mem., 6th Sqdn RAF, 1971. Brunei Dato, 1971. *Recreations:* overseas travel, walking, reading.

Address: Albany, Piccadilly, W1. *T:* 01-734 6641; Roughton Hall, near Woodhall Spa, Lincolnshire. *T:* Horncastle 2572. *Clubs:* Carlton, Hurlingham; Skegness Working Men's.

TARBAT, Viscount; John Ruaridh Grant MacKenzie; MIExpE; explosives engineer; *b* 12 June 1948; *s* and *heir* of 4th Earl of Cromartie, *qv* ; *m* 1973, Helen, *d* of John Murray; (one *s* decd). *Educ:* Rannoch School, Perthshire; Strathclyde University. Mem., Mountaineering Council of Scotland Cttee. *Publications:* Selected Climbs in Skye, 1982; articles in Classic Rock Climbs and Cold Climbs. *Recreations:* mountaineering, art, astronomy, geology. *Address:* Castle Leod, Strathpeffer, Ross-shire. *Clubs:* Army and Navy; Scottish Mountaineering.

TARN, Prof. John Nelson; Roscoe Professor of Architecture, University of Liverpool, since 1974; *b* 23 Nov. 1934; *s* of Percival Nelson Tarn and Mary I. Tarn (*née* Purvis); unmarried. *Educ:* Royal Grammar Sch., Newcastle upon Tyne; Univ. of Durham (BArch); Univ. of Cambridge (PhD). 1st cl. hons Dunelm; FRIBA, FRSA, FRHistS. Lectr in Architecture, Univ. of Sheffield, 1963-70; Prof. of Architecture, Univ. of Nottingham, 1970-73. Member: Professional Literature Cttee, RIBA, 1968-77; RIBA Educn Cttee, 1978- (Chm., Moderators and Examiners Cttee, 1975-); Council, ARCUK, 1980- (Vice-Chm., Bd of Educn, 1981-); Technology Sub-Cttee, UGC, 1974-; Ministerial nominee, Peak Park Jt Planning Bd, 1973-82, a rep. of Greater Manchester Council, PPJPB, 1982-; Chm., Planning Control Cttee, 1979- (Vice-Chm., 1981-); Mem., Design and Planning Cttee, Central Council for Care of Churches, 1981-; Mem., Diocesan Adv. Cttee for Derby, 1979-. *Publications:* Working Class Housing in Nineteenth Century Britain, 1971; The Peak District National Park: its architecture, 1971; Five Per Cent Philanthropy, 1974. *Recreation:* music. *Address:* 2 Ashmore Close, Barton Hey Drive, Caldy, Wirral, Merseyside L48 2JX. *T:* 051-625 9557. *Club:* Athenæum.

TASKER, Antony Greaves, CBE 1966 (OBE 1945; MBE 1943); Assistant Secretary-General and Managing Director Commonwealth Fund for Technical Co-operation, Commonwealth Secretariat, 1974-78; *b* 27 March 1916; *o s* of late Captain R. G. Tasker, Worcestershire Regt, and of Vera, *d* of Rev. T. M. Everett (she *m* 2nd, Harold Raymond, OBE, MC, who *d* 1975); *m* 1940, Elizabeth Gilmor, *e d* of late Maj. Harold Carter, TD. *Educ:* Bradfield Coll.; Christ Church, Oxford. Served War of 1939-45 (despatches twice); Western Desert, Sicily, Italy, NW Europe, SE Asia; Col GS(I). Org. Dir, Internat. Tea Market Expansion Bd, 1948-52; Dir Public Rel., Booker Gp of Cos in Guyana, 1954-62 (Chm., 1962-67); Dir, Overseas Develt Inst., 1968-74. Member, Br. Guiana Senate, 1961-64 (MLC, 1957-61); Governor: Inst. of Develt Studies, Sussex, 1968-78; Oversea Service Coll., 1968-78; Mem. Council, Overseas Develt Inst., 1975-78. Member: Econ. and Social Cttee, EEC, 1973-74; Exec. Cttee, British Council, 1970-74; Voluntary Cttee on Overseas Aid and Develt, 1968-74; British Volunteer Programme, 1968-74. US Bronze Star, 1944; Officer, US Legion of Merit, 1945. *Address:* 104 Ashley Gardens, SW1P 1HJ. *T:* 01-828 0184.

TASMANIA, Bishop of, since 1982; **Rt. Rev. Phillip Keith Newell;** *b* 30 Jan. 1930; *s* of Frank James and Ada Miriam Newell; *m* 1959, Merle Edith Callaghan; three *s*. *Educ:* Univ. of Melbourne; Trinity Coll., Melbourne. BSc 1953; DiplEd(Hons) 1954; ThL(Hons) 1959; BEd 1960; MEd 1969; MACE. Mathematics Master: Melbourne High School, 1954-56; University High School, 1957-58; Tutor in Physics, Secondary Teachers' Coll., 1957; Assistant Curate: All Saints, East St Kilda, Melbourne, 1960-61; S Andrew's, Brighton, Melbourne, 1962-63; Asst Priest, S James, King Street, Sydney, 1963-67; Chaplain, Sydney Hosp., 1963-67; Rector, Christ Church, St Lucia, Brisbane, 1967-82; Residentiary Canon, S John's Cathedral, Brisbane, 1973-82; Archdeacon of Lilley, Brisbane, 1976-82. KStJ 1981. *Recreations:* education; music (classical and light opera); singing; choral conducting; wine making; travel; cricket (spectator); tennis (occasional game). *Address:* GPO Box 748H, Hobart, Tasmania 7001. *T:* 236128. *Club:* University of Queensland (Brisbane).

TATA, Dr Jamshed Rustom, FRS 1973; Head, Laboratory of Developmental Biochemistry, National Institute for Medical Research, since 1973; *b* 13 April 1930; *s* of Rustom and Gool Tata; *m* 1954, Renée Suzanne Zanetto; two *s* one *d*. *Educ:* Univ. of Bombay (BSc); Univ. of Paris, Sorbonne (D-ès-Sc). Post-doctoral Fellow, Sloan-Kettering Inst., New York, 1954-56; Beit Memorial Fellow, Nat. Inst. for Med. Research, 1956-60; Vis. Scientist, Wenner-Gren Inst., Stockholm, 1960-62; Mem., Scientific Staff, MRC, Nat. Inst. for Med. Research, 1962-. Visiting Prof.: King's Coll., London, 1968-69, and 1970-77; Univ. of California, Berkeley, 1969-70; Vis. Senior Scientist, Nat. Institutes of Health, USA, 1977; Fogarty Scholar, NIH, USA, 1977. Fellow, Indian Nat. Science Acad., 1978. Van Meter Award, 1954; Colworth Medal, 1966; Medal of Soc. for Endocrinology, 1973. *Publications:* (jtly): The Thyroid Hormones, 1959; The Chemistry of Thyroid Diseases, 1960; papers in jls of: Biochemistry; Developmental Biology. *Address:* 15 Bittacy Park Avenue, Mill Hill, NW7 2HA. *T:* 01-346 6291.

TATE, Ellalice; see Hibbert, Eleanor.

TATE, Francis Herbert; Vice-Chairman, Tate & Lyle Ltd, 1962-78; *b* 3 April 1913; 2nd *s* of late Alfred Herbert Tate and late Elsie Tate (*née* Jelf Petit); *g g s* of Sir Henry Tate, Bt, founder of Henry Tate & Sons (now Tate & Lyle, Ltd) and donor of the Tate Gallery; *m* 1937, Esther, *d* of late Sir John

Bromhead-Matthews, KC, JP, and late Lady Matthews, JP; one s two d. *Educ:* Private Tutor; Christ Church Oxford (BA 1934, MA 1963). Called to the Bar, Inner Temple, 1937. War Service, 1940-46, Royal Corps of Military Police (Lt-Col). Joined Tate & Lyle Ltd, 1946; Man. Dir, 1949. Chairman: British Sugar Bureau, 1966-78; Council, London Chamber of Commerce, 1962-64 (Vice-Pres., 1964-); Federation of Commonwealth Chambers of Commerce, 1964-69. Chm. Central Council, Royal Commonwealth Society, 1969-72; Mem. Council, Australia Soc., 1974-78. Governor, Commonwealth Inst., 1975-. Dir, Lloyds Bank Ltd, Southern Region, 1977-; a Managing Trustee, Bustamente Foundn, 1979-. General Comr for Income Tax, Woking Div., 1980-. Master of Mercers' Company, 1967-68. *Recreations:* golf (played for Oxford, 1934-35); motoring. *Address:* Little Wissett, Hook Heath, Woking, Surrey. *T:* Woking 60532.

TATE, Lt-Col Sir Henry, 4th Bt, *cr* 1898; TD; DL; late Royal Welch Fusiliers TA; *b* 29 June 1902; *s* of Sir Ernest Tate, 3rd Bt and Mildred Mary, 2nd *d* of F. H. Gossage of Camp Hill, Woolton, Liverpool; *S* father, 1939; *m* 1927, Nairne, *d* of late Saxon Gregson-Ellis, JP; two *s*. Sometime Lt Grenadier Guards. Joint Master Cottesmore Hounds, 1946-58. Councillor Rutland CC, 1958-69, 1970-74; High Sheriff of Rutland, 1949-50. Commanding 1st Bn Rutland Home Guard, 1954-57. DL, Co. of Rutland, 1964. *Heir: s* Henry Saxon Tate, *qv. Address:* Preston Lodge, Withcote, Oakham, Rutland, Leics LE15 8DP. *Club:* Buck's.

TATE, (Henry) Saxon; Chief Executive, Industrial Development Board of Northern Ireland, since 1982; Director, Tate & Lyle Ltd; *b* 28 Nov. 1931; *s* and *heir* of Lt-Col Sir Henry Tate, Bt, *qv*; *m* 1st, 1953, Sheila Ann (marr. diss. 1975), *e d* of Duncan Robertson; four *s* (incl. twin *s*); 2nd, 1975, Virginia Sturm. *Educ:* Eton; Christ Church, Oxford. FBIM 1975. National Service, Life Guards (Lieut), 1949-50. Joined Tate & Lyle Ltd, 1952, Director, 1956; Pres. and Chief Executive Officer, Redpath Industries Ltd, Canada, 1965-72; Tate & Lyle Ltd: Chm., Executive Cttee, 1973-78; Man. Dir, 1978-80; Vice Chm., 1980-82. Fellow, Amer. Management Assoc., 1972. *Recreations:* various. *Address:* c/o Industrial Development Board, IDB House, 64 Chichester Street, Belfast BT1 4JX. *Club:* Buck's.

TATE, Phyllis (Margaret Duncan), (Mrs Alan Frank); composer (freelance); *b* 6 April 1911; *d* of Duncan Tate, FRIBA, and Annie S. Holl; *m* 1935, Alan Frank; one *s* one *d. Educ:* Royal Academy of Music, London. FRAM 1964. *Works:* (some commissioned by the BBC, and for festivals, etc, and several commercially recorded): Saxophone Concerto, 1944; Nocturne for four voices, 1945; Sonata for clarinet and cello, 1947; Choral Scene from The Bacchae, 1953; The Lady of Shalott, for tenor and instruments, 1956; Air and Variations for violin, clarinet and piano, 1958; London Fields, 1958; Opera: The Lodger, 1960; Television Opera: Dark Pilgrimage, 1963; A Victorian Garland, for two voices and instruments, 1965; Gravestones, for Cleo Laine, 1966; Seven Lincolnshire Folk Songs, for chorus and instruments, 1966; A Secular Requiem, for chorus and orchestra, 1967; Christmas Ale, for soloist, chorus and orchestra, 1967; Apparitions, for tenor and instruments, 1968; Coastal Ballads, for baritone and instruments, 1969; Illustrations, for brass band, 1969; To Words by Joseph Beaumont, for women's chorus, 1970; Variegations, for solo viola, 1970; Serenade to Christmas, for mezzo-soprano, chorus and orchestra, 1972; Lyric Suite, for piano duet, Explorations around a Troubadour Song, for piano solo, 1973; The Rainbow and the Cuckoo, for oboe, violin, viola and cello, 1974; Sonatina Pastorale for harmonica and harpsichord, 1974; Songs of Sundrie Kindes, for tenor and lute, 1975; St Martha and the Dragon, for narrator, soloists, chorus and orchestra, 1976; Scenes from Kipling, for baritone and piano, 1976; A Seasonal Sequence, for viola and piano, 1977; Panorama, for strings, 1977; All the World's a Stage, 1977, Compassion, 1978, for chorus and organ (or orchestra); Three Pieces for Solo Clarinet, 1979; The Ballad of Reading Gaol, for baritone, organ and cello, 1980; Movements, for string quartet, 1980; Prelude Aria Interlude Finale, for clarinet and piano, 1981; and many small choral pieces, songs and works for young people, including: Street Sounds, The Story of Lieutenant Cockatoo; Twice in a Blue Moon; A Pride of Lions; Scarecrow. *Address:* 12 Heath Hurst Road, NW3. *T:* 01-435 0607.

TATE, Prof. Robert Brian, FBA 1980; Professor and Head of Department of Hispanic Studies, Nottingham University, since 1958; *b* 27 Dec. 1921; *s* of Robert and Jane Grantie Tate; *m* 1951, Beth Ida Lewis; one *s* one *d. Educ:* Royal Belfast Academical Instn; Queen's Univ. Belfast (MA, PhD). Asst Lectr, Manchester Univ., 1949-52; Lectr, QUB, 1952-56; Reader in Hispanic Studies, Nottingham Univ., 1956-58. Corresponding Fellow: Institut d'Estudis Catalans, Barcelona, 1964; Real Academia de Historia, Madrid, 1974; Real Academia de Buenas Letras de Barcelona, 1980. *Publications:* Joan Margarit i Pau, Cardinal Bishop of Gerona: a biographical study, 1954; Ensayos sobre la historiografía peninsular del siglo XV, 1970; The Medieval Kingdoms of the Iberian Peninsula, in P. E. Russell, Spain: a companion to Spanish studies, 1973; El Cardenal Joan Margarit, vida i obra, 1976; (ed with A. Yates) Actes del Colloqui internacional de llengua i literatura catalanes, 1976; (ed) Essays on Narrative Fiction in the Iberian Peninsula, 1982; *edited with introduction and notes:* Fernán Pérez de Guzmán, Generaciones y Semblanzas, 1966; Fernando del Pulgar, Claros varones de Castilla, 1971; (with I. R. Macpherson) Don Juan Manuel, Libro de los estados, 1974; Anon, Directorio de príncipes, 1977; contrib. articles in numerous learned jls. *Recreations:* architecture and the history of art, jazz. *Address:* 42 Main Street, Sutton Bonington, Loughborough, Leics. *T:* Kegworth 2559.

TATE, Saxon; *see* Tate, H. S.

TATHAM, David Everard; HM Diplomatic Service; Counsellor, Dublin, since 1981; *b* 28 June 1939; *s* of Lt-Col Francis Everard Tatham and Eileen Mary Wilson; *m* 1963, Valerie Ann Mylechreest; three *s. Educ:* St Lawrence Coll., Ramsgate; Wadham Coll., Oxford (BA History). Entered HM Diplomatic Service, 1960; 3rd Sec., UK Mission to the UN, New York, 1962-63; Vice-Consul (Commercial), Milan, 1963-67; ME Centre for Arabic Studies, 1967-69; Jeddah, 1969-70; FCO, 1971-74; Muscat, 1974-77; Asst Head of ME Dept, FCO, 1977-80. *Recreation:* walking uphill. *Address:* c/o Foreign and Commonwealth Office, SW1.

TATHAM, Francis Hugh Currer; Editor of Whitaker's Almanack, 1950-81; *b* 29 May 1916; *s* of late Harold Lewis Tatham, Gravesend, Kent, and late Frances Eva (née Crook); *m* 1945, Nancy Margaret, *d* of John Robins, Newton Abbot; two *s. Educ:* Charterhouse; Christ Church, Oxford. Missioner, Shrewsbury School Mission, Liverpool, 1939-42; Sub-Warden, Mary Ward Settlement, 1942-45; Army Cadet Force, 1943-45; Editor, Church of England Newspaper, 1945-47. Vice-Pres., Harrow RFC. *Recreations:* cricket, travel. *Address:* Two Trees, Fee Farm Road, Claygate, Surrey. *T:* Esher 62493. *Clubs:* Lansdowne, MCC.

TATI, Jacques, (Jacques Tatischeff); French film actor and Director; *b* Pecq, Seine et Oise, 9 Oct. 1908. Stage début as Music Hall artist; subsequently, 1933-, Actor, Director and Script-writer, Gérant de Cady Films. *Films* (many of which have received international awards or prizes) include: Gai Dimanche, 1935; Soigne ton gauche, 1936; L'Ecole des Facteurs, 1947; Jour de Fête, 1947; Les Vacances de Monsieur Hulot, 1951; Mon Oncle, 1958; Playtime, 1968; Trafic (originally titled Yes Monsieur Hulot), 1971; Parade, 1974. Has won several awards for films. *Address:* 12 rue du Château, 92 La Garenne-Colombes, France.

TATISCHEFF, Jacques; *see* Tati, Jacques.

TATLOW, John Colin, PhD, DSc (Birmingham); CChem; FRSC; Professor of Organic Chemistry, University of Birmingham, since 1959; *b* 19 Jan. 1923; *s* of Thomas George and Florence Annie Tatlow, Cannock, Staffs; *m* 1946, Clarice Evelyn Mabel, *d* of Eric Millward and Mabel Evelyn Joiner, Sutton Coldfield; two *d. Educ:* Rugeley Grammar School, Staffs; University of Birmingham. Scientific Officer, Min. of Supply, 1946-48; University of Birmingham: Lectr in Chemistry, 1948-56; Sen. Lectr, 1956-57; Reader in Organic Chemistry, 1957-59; Head of Dept of Chemistry, 1974-81. Council of Chemical Society, 1957-60. Examiner, Royal Inst. of Chemistry, 1963-67. *Publications:* scientific papers mainly in Jl of Chem. Soc., Tetrahedron, Nature, and Jl of Fluorine Chem.; Editor: Advances in Fluorine Chemistry; Jl of Fluorine Chemistry. *Address:* 30 Grassmoor Road, King's Norton, Birmingham B38 8BP. *T:* 021-458 1260.

TATTON BROWN, William Eden, CB 1965; ARIBA; retired architect; *b* 13 Oct. 1910; *m* 1936, Aileen Hope Johnston Sparrow; two *s* one *d* (and one *d* decd). *Educ:* Wellington Coll.; King's Coll., Cambridge (MA); Architectural Association School, London; School of Planning, London. Special Final Examination of Town Planning Institute. Chief Design Asst, Messrs Tecton, Architects, 1934-38; private practice, 1938-40; Finsbury Borough Council, 1940-41. Served in HM Forces, Major, Royal Engineers, 1941-46. Asst Regional Planning Officer, Min. of Town and Country Planning, 1946-48; Dep. County Architect, Herts CC, 1948-59; Chief Architect, Min. of Health, later Dept of Health and Social Security, 1959-71. Steuben-Corning Research Fellowship, Travelling Scholarship to USA, 1957. Guest Lectr, Internat. Hosp. Confs: Finland, 1966; Holland, 1967; Australia, 1967; Düsseldorf, 1969; Tunisia, 1969; Sweden, 1970; Canada, 1970; S Africa, 1971; WHO Commn to Madrid, 1968. Lecturer and broadcaster. *Publications:* contributor to technical and national press. *Recreations:* building, water-skiing, oil painting. *Address:* 47 Lansdowne Road, W11. *T:* 01-727 4529.

TAUNTON, Suffragan Bishop of, since 1977; **Rt. Rev. Peter John Nott;** *b* 30 Dec. 1933; *s* of Cecil Frederick Wilder Nott and Rosina Mabel Bailey; *m* 1961, Elizabeth May Maingot; one *s* three *d. Educ:* Bristol Grammar School; Dulwich Coll.; RMA Sandhurst; Fitzwilliam House, Cambridge; Westcott House, Cambridge (MA). Curate of Harpenden, 1961-64; Chaplain of Fitzwilliam Coll., Cambridge, 1964-69; Fellow of Fitzwilliam Coll., 1967-69; Chaplain of New Hall, Cambridge, 1966-69; Rector of Beaconsfield, 1969-77. Archbishop's Adviser to HMC, 1980-; President: SW Region, Mencap, 1978-; Somerset Rural Music Sch., 1981-. *Address:* Sherford Farm House, Sherford, Taunton, Somerset TA1 3RF. *T:* Taunton 88759.

TAUNTON, Archdeacon of; *see* Olyott, Ven. L. E.

TAUNTON, Doidge Estcourt, CB 1951; DSO and bar 1945; DL; Secretary, Northamptonshire TA and AFA, 1952-68; *b* 9 Nov. 1902; *s* of late J. G. C. Taunton, Launceston, Cornwall; *m* 1930, Rhona Caroline Wetherall (*d* 1951); one *s* (and one *s* decd). *Educ:* Cheltenham College; RMC Sandhurst; 2nd Lt Northamptonshire Regt, 1923; Lt 1925; Capt. 1935, and Adjt TA, 1932-36; Major 1940; Lt-Col 1941; Col 1948; Temp. Brig. 1944-45 and 1948-52. Served NWF India, 1936-38 (Medal and 2 clasps); War of 1939-45, India and Burma, 1936-45; French Indo-China and Netherlands East Indies, 1945-46 (Medal and clasp); Comd Somaliland Area, 1948-50; Comd 2nd Inf. Brigade, 1950-51;

retired pay, 1951. DL Northants, 1969. *Address:* Great Hayne, Duston, Northampton.

TAUSKY, Vilem, CBE 1981; FGSM 1968; Director of Opera, Guildhall School of Music, since 1966; Artistic Director, Phoenix Opera Co., since 1967; BBC Conductor since 1950; *b* 20 July 1910; *s* of Emil Tausky, MD, Prerov, Czechoslovakia, and Josefine Ascher, opera singer; *m* 1948, Margaret Helen Powell (*d* 1982). *Educ:* Univ. of Brno; Janáček Conservatoire, Brno; Meisterschule, Prague. Military Service in France and England, 1939-45. National Opera House, Brno, Czechoslovakia, 1929-39; Musical Director, Carl Rosa Opera, 1945-49. Guest Conductor: Royal Opera House, Covent Garden, 1951-; Sadler's Wells Opera, 1953-. Freeman, City of London, 1979. Czechoslovak Military Cross, 1944; Czechoslovak Order of Merit, 1945. *Publications:* Czechoslovak Christmas Carols, 1942; Oboe Concerto, 1957; Concertino for harmonica and orchestra, 1963; Divertimento for strings, 1966; Soho: Scherzo for orchestra, 1966; Concert Overture for Brass Band, 1969; Cakes and Ale: Overture for Brass Band, 1971; Ballad for Cello and Piano; From Our Village: orchestral suite, 1972; Sonata for Cello and Piano, 1976; Suite for Violin and Piano, 1979; String Quartet, 1981; (book) Vilem Tausky Tells his Story, 1979; Leoš Janáček, Leaves from his Life, 1982; contribs to: Tension in the Performance of Music, 1979; The Spectator, 1979. *Recreation:* country life. *Address:* 44 Haven Green Court, W5. *T:* 01-997 6512; Rose Cottage, Towersey, near Thame, Oxon. *T:* Thame 2192.

TAVARÉ, Andrew Kenneth; Special Commissioner of Income Tax, since 1976; *b* 10 Jan. 1918; *s* of late L. A. Tavaré, Bromley, Kent; *m* 1950, June Elinor Attwood, Beckenham, Kent; three *s. Educ:* Chatham House School, Ramsgate; King's College, London University. LLB (London). Solicitor of the Supreme Court. Served War with 79th HAA Regt (Hertfordshire Yeomanry), RA, 1940-45; N Africa and Italy, rank of Captain. Admitted Solicitor, 1948; Solicitor's Office, Inland Revenue, 1953-; Assistant Solicitor, 1965-75. Consultant Editor of Sergeant on Stamp Duties, 4th edition 1963, to 8th edition 1982. *Publications:* (contrib.) Simon's Taxes, 2nd edn, 1965, and 3rd edn, 1970. *Address:* 32 Marlborough Crescent, Sevenoaks, Kent.

TAVENER, John; composer; Professor of Music at Trinity College of Music since 1969; *b* 28 Jan. 1944; *m* 1974, Victoria Marangopoulou. *Educ:* Highgate Sch.; Royal Academy of Music (LRAM). Hon. ARAM, Hon. FTCL. Russian Orthodox religion. *Publications:* compositions: Piano Concerto; Three Holy Sonnets (Donne); Cain and Abel (1st Prize, Monaco); Chamber Concerto; The Cappe-makers; Three Songs of T. S. Eliot; Grandma's Footsteps; In Memoriam Igor Stravinsky; Responsorium in memory of Annon Lee; The Whale; Introit for March 27th; Three Surrealist Songs; In Alium; Celtic Requiem; Ultimos Ritos; Thérèse (opera); A Gentle Spirit (opera); Kyklike Kinesis; Palin; Palintropos: Canticle of the Mother of God; Divine Liturgy of St John Chrysostom; The Immurement of Antigone; Lamentation, Last Prayer and Exaltation; Six Abbasid Songs; Greek Interlude; Akhmatova: Rékviem; Sappho: Lyrical Fragments; Prayer for the World; The Great Canon of St Andrew of Crete; Trisagion; Risen! *Address:* c/o Chester Music, 7 Eagle Court, EC1M 5QD.

TAVERNE, Dick, QC 1965; Chairman, Institute for Fiscal Studies, since 1981 (Director-General, 1970-81); *b* 18 Oct. 1928; *s* of N. J. M. and Mrs L. V. Taverne; *m* 1955, Janice Hennessey; two *d. Educ:* Charterhouse School; Balliol College, Oxford (First in Greats). Oxford Union Debating tour of USA, 1951. Called to Bar, 1954. MP (Lab) Lincoln, March 1962-Oct. 1972, resigned; MP (Democratic Lab) Lincoln, March 1973-Sept. 1974; Parliamentary Under-Secretary of State, Home Office, 1966-68; Minister of State, Treasury, 1968-69; Financial Secretary to the Treasury, 1969-70. Chm., Public Expenditure (General) Sub-Cttee, 1971-72. Director: Equity and Law Life Assurance Co. Ltd; BOC Group; Mem., Internat. Ind. Review Body to review workings of European Commn, 1979. Mem. Steering Cttee, SDP, 1981-; contested (SDP) Southwark, Peckham, Oct. 1982. *Publication:* The Future of the Left: Lincoln and after, 1973. *Recreations:* running, sailing. *Address:* 60 Cambridge Street, SW1V 4QQ.

TAVISTOCK, Marquess of; Henry Robin Ian Russell; a Director, Trafalgar House Ltd, since 1977; *b* 21 Jan. 1940; *s* and *heir* of 13th Duke of Bedford, *qv*; *m* 1961, Henrietta Joan, *d* of Henry F. Tiarks, *qv*; three *s. Educ:* Le Rosey, Switzerland; Harvard University. Partner, De Zoete and Bevan, 1970-82; Chairman: Cedar Investment Trust, 1977-; TR Property Investment Trust, 1982-; Director: Touche, Remnant and Co., 1977-; United Racecourses, 1977-. Pres., Woburn Golf and Country Club. *Heir: s* Lord Howland, *qv. Address:* Woburn Abbey, Woburn, Bedfordshire MK43 0TP. *T:* Woburn 666. *Clubs:* White's; Jockey Club Rooms; The Brook (New York).

TAYLER, Harold Clive, QC 1979; a Recorder of the Crown Court, since 1974; *b* 4 Nov. 1932; *m* 1959, Catherine Jane (*née* Thomas); two *s* one *d. Educ:* Solihull Sch.; Balliol Coll., Oxford. BCL and BA (Jurisprudence). Called to the Bar, Inner Temple, 1956; in practice, Birmingham, from 1958, and London, from 1979; Midland and Oxford Circuit. *Address:* c/o Midland and Oxford Circuit Administrators' Office, 2 Newton Street, Birmingham B4 7LU.

TAYLOR; *see* Suenson-Taylor, family name of Baron Grantchester.

TAYLOR, family name of Barons Taylor, Taylor of Blackburn, Taylor of Gryfe and Taylor of Mansfield.

TAYLOR, Baron *cr* 1958 (Life Peer), of Harlow; **Stephen James Lake Taylor,** MD, BSc, FRCP; FRCGP; Visiting Professor of Medicine, Memorial University of Newfoundland, since 1973; *b* 30 Dec. 1910; *s* of John Reginald Taylor, MInstCE, and Beatrice Violet Lake Taylor; *m* 1939, Dr May Doris Charity Clifford (*see* Lady Taylor); two *s* one *d. Educ:* Stowe Sch.; St Thomas's Hosp. Med. Sch., Univ. of London. BSc 1st cl. Hons; MB, BS (Hons Hygiene and Forensic Medicine); MD. FRCP 1960; FFOM RCP, 1979. Served War of 1939-45: Surg. Lt-Comdr (Neuro-psychiatric Specialist), RNVR; Dir of Home Intelligence and Wartime Social Survey, MOI, 1941-45. Formerly: Casualty Officer and HP, St Thomas' Hosp.; Grocers' Co. Research Scholar, Med. Unit, St Thomas' Hosp.; Sen. Resident Med. Officer, Royal Free Hosp.; HP, Bethlem Royal Hosp.; Asst Med. Officer, Maudsley Hosp. MP (Lab) Barnet Div. of Herts, 1945-50; PPS to Dep. Prime Minister and Lord President of Council, 1947-50; Under-Sec. of State for Commonwealth Relations and Colonies, 1964-65; resigned from Labour Party, 1981, to sit as a cross-bencher. Consultant in Occupational Health, Richard Costain Ltd, 1951-64 and 1966-67; Med. Dir, Harlow Industrial Health Service, 1955-64 and 1965-67; Pres. and Vice-Chancellor, Meml Univ. of Newfoundland, 1967-73. Visiting Research Fellow, Nuffield Provincial Hospitals Trust, 1953-55; Mem., Harlow New Town Develt Corp., 1950-64 and 1966-67. Former Chm., Labour Party Study Group on Higher Educn; Vice-Chm., British Film Inst.; former Member: N-W Metropolitan Regional Hosp. Bd; Health Adv. Cttee of Labour Party; Cohen Cttee on Gen. Practice, Beveridge Cttee on BBC; Mem., Bd of Governors, UCH. Lectures: Chadwick, RSH, 1963; Clarke, Univ. of Surrey, 1975; Lloyd Hughes, Liverpool, 1981. Hon. LLD St Thomas Univ., NB, 1972. *Publications:* Scurvy and Carditis, 1937; The Suburban Neurosis, 1938; Mental Illness as a Clue to Normality, 1940; The Psychopathic Tenth, 1941; The Study of Public Opinion, 1943; Battle for Health, 1944; The Psychopath in our Midst, 1949; Shadows in the Sun, 1949; Good General Practice, 1954; The Health Centres of Harlow, 1955; The Survey of Sickness, 1958; First Aid in the Factory, 1960; Mental Health and Environment, 1964; articles in Lancet, BMJ, World Medicine, etc. *Address:* Plas y Garth, Glyn Ceiriog, near Llangollen, Clwyd. *T:* Glyn Ceiriog 216.
See also M. J. L. Ellis.

TAYLOR, Lady, (Charity), MB, BS, MRCS, LRCP; retired as Assistant Director and Inspector of Prisons (Women), (1959-66); Member, BBC General Advisory Council, 1964-67; President, Newfoundland and Labrador Social Welfare Council, 1968-71; *b* Sept. 1914; *d* of W. George and Emma Clifford; *m* 1939, Stephen J. L. Taylor (*see* Lord Taylor); two *s* one *d. Educ:* The Grammar School, Huntingdon; London (Royal Free Hospital) School of Medicine for Women. HS Royal Free Hospital; HS Elizabeth Garrett Anderson Hospital; Assistant Medical Officer HM Prison, Holloway; Medical Officer, HM Prison Holloway; Governor, HM Prison, Holloway, 1945-59. *Recreations:* reading, conversation. *Address:* Plas y Garth, Glyn Ceiriog, near Llangollen, Clwyd.

TAYLOR OF BLACKBURN, Baron *cr* 1978 (Life Peer), of Blackburn in the County of Lancashire; **Thomas Taylor,** CBE 1974 (OBE 1969); JP; Consultant, Shorrock Security Systems Ltd, and other companies, since 1976; *b* 10 June 1929; *s* of James and Edith Gladys Taylor; *m* 1950, Kathleen Nurton; one *s. Educ:* Mill Hill Primary Sch.; Blakey Moor Elementary Sch. Mem., Blackburn Town Council, 1954-76 (Leader, chm. of cttees and rep. on various bodies); Treas., Blackburn Labour Party, 1964-76; former Chm., Blackburn Br., USDAW. Chm., Electricity Cons. Council for NW and Mem. Norweb Bd, 1977-80; Member: NW Econ. Planning Council; NW AHA (Chm. Brockhall HMC, 1972-74, Vice-Chm. Blackburn HMC, 1964-74); Council for Educational Technology in UK; Nat. Foundn for Educn Research in Eng. and Wales; Schools Council; Regional Rent Tribunal. Chairman: Govt Cttee of Enquiry into Management and Govt of Schools; Nat. Foundn for Visual Aids. Former Mem., Public Schools Commn; past Pres., Assoc. of Educn Cttees. Dir, Councils and Education Press. Univ. of Lancaster: Founder Mem. and Mem. Council; Rep. on Lancs CC Educn Cttee; author of Taylor Report on problems; Dep. Pro-Chancellor. Former Dep. Dir, Central Lancs Family and Community Project. JP Blackburn; JP 1960; former Chm., Juvenile Bench. Elder, URC; Pres., Free Church Council, 1962-63. Chm., Mill Hill Operatic Soc., 1953-63. *Address:* 34 Tower Road, Feniscliffe, Blackburn. *T:* Blackburn 21754. *Club:* Institute of Directors.

TAYLOR OF GRYFE, Baron *cr* 1968 (Life Peer), of Bridge of Weir; **Thomas Johnston Taylor;** DL; FRSE 1977; Chairman, Morgan Grenfell (Scotland) Ltd, since 1973; *b* 27 April 1912; *m* 1943, Isobel Wands; two *d. Educ:* Bellahouston Acad., Glasgow. Member: British Railways Bd, 1968-80 (Chm., Scottish Railways Board, 1971-80); Board of Scottish Television Ltd, 1968; Forestry Commn, 1963-76 (Chm., 1970-76). President, Scottish CWS, 1965-70; Mem., Scottish Economic Council, 1971-74. Director: Whiteaway Laidlaw & Co. Ltd, 1971-; Friends' Provident Life Office, 1972-; Scottish Metropolitan Property Co. Ltd, 1972-; BR Property Bd, 1972-; Mem., Internat. Adv. Council, Morgan Grenfell. Chm., Economic Forestry Group, 1976-81. Trustee, Dulverton Trust, 1980-; Chm., Isaac and Edith Wolfson Trust, 1972-. DL Renfrewshire, 1970. Hon. LLD Strathclyde, 1974. *Recreations:* theatre, golf, walking. *Address:* The Cottage, Auchenames, Kilbarchan, Renfrewshire PA10 2PM. *T:* Kilbarchan 2648. *Clubs:* Caledonian; New (Edinburgh); Royal and Ancient (St Andrews).

TAYLOR OF MANSFIELD, Baron *cr* 1966 (Life Peer), of Mansfield; **Harry Bernard Taylor**, CBE 1966; *b* 18 Sept. 1895; *s* of Henry Taylor, Mansfield Woodhouse; *m* 1921, Clara, *d* of John Ashley; one *s. Educ:* Council Schools. A Coal Miner. MP (Lab.) Mansfield Div. of Nottinghamshire, 1941-66; Parliamentary Private Secretary to Parliamentary Secretary, Ministry of Aircraft Production, 1942; to Minister of National Insurance, 1945; Parliamentary Secretary, Ministry of National Insurance, 1950-51. *Publication:* Uphill all the Way (autobiog.), 1973. *Address:* 47 Shakespeare Avenue, Mansfield Woodhouse, Nottinghamshire.

TAYLOR, Alan Broughton; barrister-at-law; a Recorder of the Crown Court (Midland and Oxford Circuit), since 1979; *b* 23 Jan. 1939; *yr s* of Valentine James Broughton Taylor and Gladys Maud Taylor; *m* 1964, Diana Hindmarsh; two *s. Educ:* Malvern Coll.; Geneva Univ.; Birmingham Univ. (LLB); Brasenose Coll., Oxford (BLitt, re-designated MLitt 1979). Called to the Bar, Gray's Inn, 1961; barrister on Oxford Circuit, subseq. Midland and Oxford Circuit, 1963-. *Publication:* (contrib.) A Practical Guide to the Care of the Injured, ed P. S. London, 1967. *Recreations:* Christian youth work, philately, walking. *Address:* 94 Augustus Road, Edgbaston, Birmingham B15 3LT. *T:* 021-454 8600.

TAYLOR, Alan John Percivale; historian and journalist; Hon. Fellow of Magdalen College, Oxford, 1976 and of Oriel College, Oxford, 1980; *b* Birkdale, Lancs, 25 March 1906; *o s* of Percy Lees and Constance Sumner Taylor; four *s* two *d. Educ:* Bootham School, York; Oriel Coll., Oxford. Formerly Lectr in Modern History, University of Manchester. Lecturer in International History, Oxford University, 1953-63; Tutor in Modern History, Magdalen College, 1938-63, Fellow, 1938-76. Lectures: Ford's, in English History, Oxford Univ., 1955-56; Leslie Stephen, Cambridge Univ., 1960-61; Creighton, London Univ., 1973; Andrew Lang, St Andrews Univ., 1974; Romanes, Oxford, 1981; Benjamin Meaker Vis. Prof. of History, Bristol Univ., 1976-78. Pres., City Music Soc. (London). FBA 1956-80. Hon. DCL, New Brunswick, 1961; DUniv York, 1970; Hon. DLitt: Bristol, 1978; Warwick, 1981; Manchester, 1982. *Publications:* (many of them translated into other languages): The Italian Problem in European Diplomacy 1847-49, 1934; Germany's First Bid for Colonies 1884-85, 1938; The Habsburg Monarchy 1815-1918, 1941, rewritten 1948; The Course of German History, 1945; From Napoleon to Stalin, 1950; Rumours of Wars, 1952; The Struggle for Mastery in Europe, 1848-1918, 1954; Bismarck, 1955; Englishmen and Others, 1956; The Trouble Makers: Dissent over Foreign Policy, 1792-1939, 1957; The Russian Revolution of 1917, 1958 (script of first lectures ever given on television); The Origins of the Second World War, 1961; The First World War: an Illustrated History, 1963; Politics in Wartime and Other Essays, 1964; English History, 1914-1945, 1965; From Sarajevo to Potsdam, 1966; Europe: Grandeur and Decline, 1967; War by Timetable, 1969; Beaverbrook, 1972; The Second World War: an illustrated history, 1975; Essays in English History, 1976; The Last of Old Europe, 1976; The War Lords, 1977; The Russian War, 1978; How Wars Begin, 1979; Revolutions and Revolutionaries, 1980; Politicians, Socialism and Historians, 1980; (ed) Lloyd George: twelve essays, 1971; (ed) Lloyd George, a Diary by Frances Stevenson, 1971; (ed) Off the Record: political interviews 1933-43 by W. P. Crozier, 1973; (ed) My Darling Pussy: the letters of Lloyd George and Frances Stevenson, 1975. *Address:* 32 Twisden Road, NW5 1DN. *T:* 01-485 1507.

TAYLOR, Alec C.; *see* Clifton-Taylor, A.

TAYLOR, Lt-Gen. Sir Allan (Macnab), KBE 1972; MC 1944; Deputy Commander-in-Chief, United Kingdom Land Forces, 1973-76, retired; *b* 26 March 1919; *s* of Alexander Lawrence Taylor and Winifred Ethel (*née* Nisbet); *m* 1945, Madeleine Turpin (marr. diss. 1963); two *d. Educ:* Fyling Hall School, Robin Hood's Bay. Joined TA, 1938; Troop Leader, 10th R Tank Regt, 1940; Squadron Leader, 7th R Tank Regt, 1942; 6th R Tank Regt, 1946; Staff College, 1948; GSO, 2, 56 London Armoured Div., 1949; Bde Major 20 Armoured Bde, 1952; Instructor, Staff College, 1954; Squadron Leader, 1st R Tank Regt, 1957; Second in Comd 5th RTR, 1959; Comdg Officer: 5th RTR, 1960 and 3rd, 1961; AA & QMG, 1st Div., 1962; Commandant, RAC Gunnery School, 1963; Comd Berlin Brigade, 1964; Imperial Defence College, 1967; Comdr, 1st Div., 1968; Commandant, Staff College, Camberley, 1969-72; GOC South East District, April-Dec. 1972. Chm., Cttee on Regular Officer Training, 1972-. Col Comdt, RTR, 1973-. *Recreation:* golf. *Address:* 4 Mill Close, Middle Assendon, Henley-on-Thames, Oxon.

TAYLOR, Sir Alvin B.; *see* Burton-Taylor.

TAYLOR, Andrew James, CBE 1965; Chairman, British Manufacturing and Research Co., Grantham, Lincs, 1968-73; *b* 1902; *s* of late Alfred George Ralph Meston Taylor, Broughty Ferry, Dundee; *m* 1925, Mary Ann Symmers, *d* of George Cowie, Aberdeen; three *s* one *d. Educ:* Robert Gordon's Coll., Aberdeen. Dir of Manufacture and Exec. Dir, Ford Motor Co. Ltd, 1962-65; Deputy Managing Director, 1965-67. *Recreations:* photography, fishing. *Address:* Flat 107, Queen's Court, Queen's Promenade, Ramsey, Isle of Man. *Club:* Royal Automobile.

TAYLOR, Mrs Ann; *see* Taylor, Mrs W. A.

TAYLOR, Arnold Joseph, CBE 1971; DLitt, MA; Docteur *hc* Caen; FBA 1972; FSA; Hon. Vice-President, Society of Antiquaries, since 1978 (Vice-President, 1963-64; Secretary, 1964-70; Director, 1970-75; President, 1975-78); *b* 24 July 1911; *y s* of late John George Taylor, Headmaster of Sir Walter St John's School, Battersea; *m* 1940, Patricia Katharine, *d* of late S. A. Guilbride, Victoria, BC; one *s* one *d. Educ:* Merchant Taylors' School; St John's College, Oxford (MA). Assistant master, Chard School, Somerset, 1934; Assistant Inspector of Ancient Monuments, HM Office of Works, 1935. Served War of 1939-45, Intelligence Officer, RAF, 1942-46. Inspector of Ancient Monuments for Wales, Min. of Works, 1946-54, Asst Chief Inspector, 1954-61; Chief Inspector of Ancient Monuments and Historic Buildings, MPBW, later DoE, 1961-72. Commissioner: Royal Commissions on Ancient and Historical Monuments (Wales and Monmouthshire), 1956-; Historical Monuments (England), 1963-78; Mem., Ancient Monuments Board: for England, 1973-82; for Scotland, 1974-79; for Wales, 1974-. Member: Cathedrals Advisory Cttee, 1964-80; Adv. Bd for Redundant Churches, 1973-82 (Chm., 1975-77); Westminster Abbey Architectural Adv. Panel, 1979; Council, English Place-Name Soc., 1980; Vice-Pres., Royal Archaeol. Inst., 1968; President: Cambrian Archaeolog. Assoc., 1969; London and Mddx Archaeolog. Soc., 1971-74; Soc. for Medieval Archaeology, 1972-75. Mem., Sir Walter St John's Schools Trust, 1970. Reckitt Lectr, British Acad., 1977. Hon. DLitt Wales, 1970. Docteur *hc* Caen, 1980. Silver Jubilee Medal, 1977. *Publications:* Records of the Barony and Honour of the Rape of Lewes, 1940; official guides to various historical monuments in care Ministry of Works (now DoE), 1939-80; chapter on Military Architecture, in vol. Medieval England, 1958; (part author) History of the King's Works, 1963; contribs to medieval architectural history in Eng. Hist. Rev., Antiquaries Jl, Archaeologia Cambrensis, etc. *Address:* Rose Cottage, Lincoln's Hill, Chiddingfold, Surrey. *T:* Wormley 2069. *Club:* Athenæum.

TAYLOR, Sir (Arthur) Godfrey, Kt 1980; Managing Trustee, Municipal Mutual Insurance Ltd, since 1979; Chairman, Southern Water Authority, since 1981; *b* 3 Aug. 1925; *s* of Fred and Lucy Taylor; *m* 1945, Eileen Dorothy Daniel; one *s* three *d. Educ:* Stockport Secondary Sch. Sutton and Cheam Borough Council: Councillor, 1951-62; Alderman, 1962-65; London Bor. of Sutton: Alderman, 1964-78; Councillor, 1978-82; Hon. Freeman, 1978. Chm., Assoc. of Metropolitan Authorities, 1978-80. Chm., London Bor. Assoc., 1968-71. *Recreation:* golf. *Address:* 23 Somerhill Lodge, Somerhill Road, Hove, E Sussex BN3 1RU. *T:* Brighton 776161.

TAYLOR, Prof. Arthur John; Professor of Modern History, Leeds University, since 1961; *b* 29 Aug. 1919; *s* of Victor Henry and Mary Lydia Taylor, Manchester; *m* 1955, Elizabeth Ann Jeffries; one *s* two *d. Educ:* Manchester Grammar School; Manchester University. Assistant Lecturer in History, University Coll., London, 1948; Lecturer, 1950. Pro-Vice Chancellor, Leeds Univ., 1971-73. Chm., Jt Matriculation Bd, 1970-73. *Publications:* Laissez-faire and State Intervention in Nineteenth Century Britain, 1973; The Standard of Living in Britain in the Industrial Revolution, 1975; (with P. H. J. H. Gosden) Studies in the History of a University: Leeds 1874-1974, 1975; contrib. to books and learned journals. *Address:* Redgarth, Leeds Road, Collingham, Wetherby, West Yorks. *T:* Collingham Bridge 72930.

TAYLOR, Arthur Robert; Chairman, Arthur Taylor & Co., Inc., since 1977; Chairman, President and Chief Executive Officer, RCTV Inc., since 1981; *b* 6 July 1935; *s* of Arthur Earl Taylor and Marian Hilda Scott; *m* 1959, Marion McFarland Taylor; three *d. Educ:* Brown Univ., USA (AB, MA). Asst Dir Admissions, Brown Univ., June 1957-Dec. 1960; Vice-Pres./Dir, The First Boston Co., Jan. 1961-May 1970; Exec. Vice-Pres./Director, Internat. Paper Co., 1970-72; Pres., CBS Inc., 1972-76. Hon. degrees: Dr Humane Letters: Simmons Coll., 1975; Rensselaer Polytechnic Inst., 1975; Dr of Humanities, Bucknell Univ., 1975. *Publication:* contrib. chapter to The Other Side of Profit, 1975. *Recreations:* sailing, tennis. *Address:* (office) 30 Rockefeller Plaza Suite 4300, New York, NY 10112, USA. *Clubs:* The Brook, Century, Larchmont Yacht, Links Golf (all NY); California (Los Angeles); Lyford Cay (Nassau, The Bahamas).

TAYLOR, Arthur Ronald, MBE (mil.) 1945; Chairman, Willis Faber Ltd, 1978-81; Director, Legal and General Group, since 1982; *b* 13 June 1921; *yr s* of late Arthur Taylor and Kathleen Frances (*née* Constable Curtis); *m* 1949, Elizabeth Josephine Kiek; three *s. Educ:* Winchester Coll.; Trinity Coll., Oxford (MA). Served Grenadier Guards, 1940-53 (despatches); sc; Bde Major 32nd Guards Bde. Laurence Philipps & Co. (Insurance) Ltd, 1953-58; Member of Lloyd's, 1955; Director, Willis, Faber and Dumas Ltd, 1959; Dep. Chm., Willis Faber Ltd, 1974. Vice-President: Corporation of Insurance Brokers, 1967-78; British Insurance Brokers Assoc., 1978-81. *Recreations:* golf, shooting. *Address:* Brighton Wood, Alresford, Hants. *Club:* City of London.

TAYLOR, Arthur William Charles, CBE 1981; PhD; CChem, FRSC; Chairman: Tees and Hartlepool Port Authority, 1976-82 (Member, 1974-83); Tees Pilotage Authority, since 1978; *b* 4 Jan. 1913; *s* of Edward Charles Taylor and Alice (*née* Lucas); *m* 1936, Rosina Peggy (*née* Gardner); one *s* one *d. Educ:* Brighton Hove and Sussex Grammar Sch.; University Coll. London (BSc, PhD). FInstPet. Imperial Chemical Industries Ltd: Billingham Division: Research Chemist, 1935-45; Jt Research Manager, 1945-57; Plastics Division: Technical and Research Director, 1958-64; Heavy Organics (Petrochemical Division): Technical Dir, 1964-66; Dep. Chm., 1966-72; Chm., 1972-75. Chm., British Ports Assoc., 1978-80; Mem., Nat. Ports Council, 1978-80;

Chm., NE Industrial Develt Bd, 1979-81. Chm. of Governors, Teesside Polytechnic, 1975-78. Fellow, University Coll. London, 1977; FRSA 1976. *Publications:* papers in Chemistry and Industry, particularly the Holroyd Meml Lecture, 1976. *Address:* 35 The Grove, Marton, Middlesbrough, Cleveland TS7 8AF. *T:* Middlesbrough 315639.

TAYLOR, Arthur Wood, CB 1953; *b* 23 June 1909; *s* of late Richard Wood and Ann Taylor; *m* 1936, Mary Beatrice Forster; one *d. Educ:* Royal School, Wolverhampton; Wolverhampton Grammar School; Sidney Sussex College, Cambridge. Wrangler (Tyson Medal), 1930; joined HM Customs and Excise, 1931; Principal, 1936; Asst Secretary, 1943. Comr of Customs and Excise, 1949; Under-Secretary, HM Treasury, 1957-63; Comr of Customs and Excise, 1964-65, Dep. Chm., 1965-70. Chm., Horserace Totalisator Bd, 1970-72 (Dep. Chm., 1972-73). *Publications:* Amusements with Prizes: social implications, 1974 (report for Churches Council on Gambling); History of Beaconsfield, 1976. *Address:* 72 Wattleton Road, Beaconsfield, Bucks. *T:* 2285. *Club:* Reform.

TAYLOR, Dr Charity; *see* Taylor, Lady.

TAYLOR, Prof. Charles Margrave, DPhil; FBA 1979; Professor of Political Science, McGill University, since 1982; *b* 5 Nov. 1931; *s* of Walter Margrave Taylor and Simone Beaubien; *m* 1956, Alba Romer; five *d. Educ:* McGill Univ. (BA History); Oxford Univ. (BA PPE, MA, DPhil). Fellow, All Souls Coll., Oxford, 1956-61; McGill University: Asst Prof., later Associate Prof., later Prof. of Polit. Science, Dept of Polit. Science, 1961-76; Prof. of Philosophy, Dept. of Philos., 1973-76; Chichele Prof. of Social and Political Theory, and Fellow of All Souls Coll., Oxford Univ., 1976-81; Mem., Sch. of Social Science, Inst. for Advanced Study, Princeton, 1981-82. Prof. asst, later Prof. agrégé, later Prof. titulaire, Ecole Normale Supérieure, 1962-64, Dept de Philos., 1971-77, Univ. de Montréal. Vis. Prof. in Philos., Princeton Univ., 1965; Mills Vis. Prof. in Philos., Univ. of Calif, Berkeley, 1974. *Publications:* The Explanation of Behavior, 1964; Pattern of Politics, 1970; Hegel, 1975; Erklarung und Interpretation in den Wissenschaften vom Menschen, 1975. *Recreations:* skiing, swimming. *Address:* 344 Metcalfe Avenue, Montréal, Canada.

TAYLOR, Sir Charles (Stuart), Kt 1954; TD; MA Cantab; DL; *b* 10 April 1910; *s* of Alfred George and Mary Taylor; *m* 1936, Constance Ada Shotter; three *s* one *d. Educ:* Epsom College; Trinity College, Cambridge (BA 1932); Hons Degree Law Tripos. Chm., Onyx Country Estates Co. Ltd, and other cos; formerly: Man. Dir, Unigate & Cow & Gate Ltd; Dir, Trust Houses Ltd; Chm., later Pres., Grosvenor House (Park Lane) Ltd. President, Residential Hotels Association of Great Britain, until 1948 and Vice-Chairman of Council of British Hotels and Restaurants Association until 1951; Mem. of Honour, Internat. Hotels Assoc.; Vice-President Building Societies Association. MP (C) Eastbourne, March 1935-Feb. 1974; Leader of Parly Delegns to Germany, Ethiopia, Mauritius; Mem., Parly Delegn to Romania. Joined TA 1937 (Royal Artillery), Capt., August 1939; DAAG and Temp. Major, Jan. 1941; attended Staff College, June 1941 (war course), graduated sc. Hon. Colonel. DL Sussex, 1948. Serving Brother, Order of St John. Master, Worshipful Co. of Bakers, 1980-81. Hon. Freeman, Co. Borough of Eastbourne, 1971. Paduka Seri Laila Jasa (Dato), Brunei, 1971. *Recreations:* yachting (rep. Gt Britain *v* USA and Old World *v* New World in six-metre yacht races, 1955), shooting, fishing. *Address:* 4 Reeves House, Reeves Mews, W1. *T:* 01-499 3730. *Clubs:* 1900, Buck's, MCC; Royal Thames Yacht; Ski Club of Great Britain (Hon. Life Mem.).

TAYLOR, Dr Daniel Brumhall Cochrane; Vice-Chancellor, Victoria University of Wellington, New Zealand, 1968-82; *b* 13 May 1921; *s* of Daniel Brumhall Taylor, Coleraine, NI and Anna Martha Taylor (*née* Rice); *m* 1955, Elizabeth Page, Christchurch, NZ; one *s* one *d. Educ:* Coleraine Academical Instn, NI; Queen's Univ., Belfast. BSc (Mech. Engrg) 1942, BSc (Elec. Engrg) 1943, MSc 1946, PhD 1948, QUB; MA Cantab 1956; FIMechE 1968. Lecturer in Engineering: Liverpool Univ., 1948-50; Nottingham Univ., 1950-53; ICI Fellow, Cambridge Univ., 1953-56; Lectr in Mechanical Sciences, Cambridge Univ., 1956-68; Fellow of Peterhouse, 1958-68, Fellow Emeritus, 1968; Tutor of Peterhouse, 1958-65, Senior Tutor, 1965-68. Member: NZ/USA Educnl Foundn, 1970-; Council, Assoc. of Commonwealth Univs, 1974-77 (Chm., 1975-76); Chm., NZ Vice-Chancellors' Cttee, 1975-77. *Publications:* numerous engrg and metallurgical papers. *Recreation:* golf. *Address:* PO Box 40895, Upper Hutt, New Zealand. *T:* Wellington 267904. *Clubs:* Athenæum; Leander (Henley-on-Thames); Wellington (NZ).

TAYLOR, Desmond S.; *see* Shawe-Taylor.

TAYLOR, Dorothy Mary, CBE 1960; MD, DPH; late Senior Medical Officer, for Maternity and Child Welfare, Ministry of Health; *b* 17 August 1902; *d* of late Thomas Taylor, Highfield, Dreghorn Loan, Colinton, Edinburgh 13; unmarried. *Educ:* George Watson's Ladies' Coll., Edinburgh; Edinburgh Univ. House Surgeon Female VD Department, Edinburgh Royal Infirmary, 1925-26; Clinical Assistant, Maternity and Child Welfare Department, Edinburgh, Apr.-Oct. 1926; House Physician, Royal Hospital for Sick Children, Edinburgh, 1926-27; Resident Medical Officer, Sick Children's Hospital, Newcastle on Tyne, 1927-28; Senior Clinical Assistant, Female VD Department, Royal Infirmary, Edinburgh, 1928-30; Medical Officer, Maternity and Child Welfare Department, Edinburgh, 1930-31; Assistant MOH, Maternity and Child Welfare Department, Sunderland,

1932-35. *Address:* 4 Clerk's Acre, Keymer, Hassocks, West Sussex BN6 8QY. *T:* Hassocks 2143. *Club:* University Women's.

TAYLOR, Edward Macmillan; MP (C) Southend East, since 1980; journalist, consultant and company director; *b* 18 April 1937; *s* of late Edward Taylor and of Minnie Hamilton Taylor; *m* 1970, Sheila Duncan; two *s* one *d. Educ:* Glasgow High School and University (MA (Hons) Econ. and Politics). Commercial Editorial Staff of Glasgow Herald, 1958-59; Industrial Relations Officer on Staff of Clyde Shipbuilders' Assoc., 1959-64. MP (C) Glasgow, Cathcart, 1964-79; Parly Under-Sec. of State, Scottish Office, 1970-71, resigned; Parly Under-Sec. of State, Scottish Office, 1974; Opposition spokesman on Trade, 1977, on Scotland affairs, 1977-79. *Publications:* (novel) Hearts of Stone, 1968; contributions to the press. *Address:* 4 Ladram Road, Southend-on-Sea, Essex.

TAYLOR, Edward Plunket, CMG 1946; President: Lyford Cay Co. Ltd; Windfields Farm Ltd; Chairman: New Providence Development Co., Nassau; International Housing Ltd, Bermuda; Director, several companies; *b* Ottawa, Ontario, 29 January 1901; *s* of late Lieut-Colonel Plunket Bourchier Taylor and Florence Gertrude Magee; *m* 1927, Winifred Thornton, *d* of late Charles F. M. Duguid, Ottawa, Ontario; one *s* two *d. Educ:* Ashbury College; Ottawa Collegiate Institute, Ottawa; McGill University, Montreal (BSc in Mechanical Engineering, 1922). Director Brading Breweries Limited, 1923, also entered the investment house of McLeod, Young, Weir & Co., Limited, Ottawa, 1923, a Director 1929, resigned to become Pres. Canadian Breweries Ltd, 1930 (Chm. of Board, 1944). Mem. Bd of Governors: Trinity Coll. Sch.; Ashbury College. Wartime appointments held: Member, Executive Committee, Dept of Munitions and Supply, Ottawa, April 1940; Joint Director-General of Munitions Production, Nov. 1940; Executive Assistant to the Minister of Munitions and Supply, Feb. 1941; President War Supplies Limited, Washington, DC, April 1941; by Prime Minister Churchill appointed President and Vice-Chairman, British Supply Council in North America, Sept. 1941; Director-General British Ministry of Supply Mission, Feb. 1942; Canadian Deputy Member on the Combined Production and Resources Board, Nov. 1942; also Canadian Chairman, Joint War Aid Committee, US-Canada, Sept. 1943. Hon. Chairman: Jockey Club of Canada; Ontario Jockey Club; Mem., Jockey Club, NY. Member, Delta Upsilon Fraternity. Anglican. Hon. LLD McGill, 1977. *Recreation:* riding. *Address:* Lyford Cay, New Providence, Bahamas. *Clubs:* Buck's, Turf; Royal Yacht Squadron (Cowes); Toronto, York (Toronto); Rideau (Ottawa); Metropolitan (New York); Lyford Cay, East Hill (Nassau).

TAYLOR, Prof. Edwin William, FRS 1978; Professor, Department of Biophysics, since 1975, Associate Dean, Division of Biological Science and Medicine, 1977-79, Professor and Chairman, Department of Biology, since 1979, University of Chicago; *b* Toronto, 8 June 1929; *s* of William Taylor and Jean Taylor (*née* Christie); *m* 1956, Jean Heather Logan; two *s* one *d. Educ:* Univ. of Toronto (BA 1952); McMaster Univ. (MSc 1955); Univ. of Chicago (PhD 1957). Asst Prof., 1959-63, Associate Prof., 1963-67, Prof., 1967-72, Univ. of Chicago; Prof. of Biology, King's College and MRC Unit, London, 1972-74. Rockefeller Foundn Fellow, 1957-58; Nat. Insts of Health Fellow, 1958-59, cons. to NIH, 1970-72, 1976-80. Member: Amer. Biochem. Soc.; Biophysical Soc. *Address:* Department of Biophysics, University of Chicago, 920 East 58th Street, Chicago, Ill 60637, USA.

TAYLOR, Elizabeth; film actress; *b* London, 27 Feb. 1932; *d* of Francis Taylor and Sara (*née* Sothern); *m* 1st, 1950, Conrad Nicholas Hilton, Jr (marr. diss.; he *d* 1969); 2nd, 1952, Michael Wilding, *qv* (marr. diss.; two *s*; 3rd, 1957, Mike Todd (*d* 1958); one *d*; 4th, 1959, Eddie Fisher (marr. diss.); 5th, 1964, Richard Burton, *qv* (marr. diss.; remarried 1975; marr. diss. 1976); 7th, 1976, Senator John Warner. *Educ:* Byron House, Hampstead; Hawthorne School, Beverly Hills; Metro-Goldwyn-Mayer School; University High School, Hollywood. *Films include:* Lassie Come Home, 1942; National Velvet, 1944; Courage of Lassie, 1946; Little Women, 1948; The Conspirator, 1949; Father of the Bride, 1950; A Place in the Sun, 1950; Ivanhoe, 1951; Beau Brummel, 1954; Giant, 1956; Raintree County, 1957; Suddenly Last Summer, 1959; Butterfield 8 (Academy Award for Best Actress), 1960; Cleopatra, 1963; the VIPs, 1963; The Sandpiper, 1965; Who's Afraid of Virginia Woolf?, 1966; The Taming of the Shrew, 1967; Boom, 1968; The Comedians, 1968; Reflections in a Golden Eye, 1968; Secret Ceremony, 1968; The Only Game in Town, 1970; Under Milk Wood, 1972; Zee and Co., 1972; Hammersmith is Out, 1972; Night Watch, 1973; Blue Bird, 1975; A Little Night Music, 1976; The Mirror Cracked, 1980. Stage debut as Regina in The Little Foxes, NY, 1981, London stage debut, Victoria Palace, 1982. *Publication:* Elizabeth Taylor, 1966. *Address:* c/o Major D. Neville-Willing, 85 Kinnerton Street, Belgravia, SW1. *T:* 01-235 4640.

TAYLOR, Eric; *a* Recorder of the Crown Court, since 1978; *b* 22 Jan. 1931; *s* of Sydney Taylor and Sarah Helen (*née* Lea); *m* 1958, Margaret Jessie Taylor, *qv. Educ:* Wigan Grammar Sch.; Manchester Univ. (LLB 1952; Dauntesey Sen. Legal Scholar; LLM 1954). Admitted solicitor, 1955. Partner, Temperley Taylor & Wilkinson, Middleton, Manchester, 1957-. Part-time Lectr in Law, Manchester Univ., 1958-80, Hon. Special Lectr in Law, 1980-. Examr (Old) Law Soc. Final Exams, 1968-81, Chief Examr (New) Law Soc. Final Exams, 1978-83. Pres., Oldham Law Assoc., 1970-72. Chairman: Manchester Young Solicitors' Gp, 1966; Manchester Nat. Insurance Appeal Tribunal, 1967-73. Member: Council, Law Soc., 1972- (Chm., Educn and Trng Cttee, 1980-83); CNAA Legal Studies Bd, 1975-; Lord Chancellor's Adv. Cttee on Trng of

Magistrates, 1974-79. *Publications:* Modern Conveyancing Precedents, 1964; Modern Wills Precedents, 1969; contrib. legal jls. *Recreations:* riding, squash, chess. *Address:* 10 Mercers Road, Heywood, Lancs OL10 2NP. *T:* Heywood 66630. *Clubs:* Carlton, Farmers'.

TAYLOR, Eric Scollick, PhD; Clerk of Committee Records, House of Commons, since 1975; *b* 16 April 1918; *s* of late Percy Scollick Taylor and Jessie Devlin. *Educ:* Durham Univ. (MA); Edinburgh Univ. (PhD 1942). Asst Clerk, House of Commons, 1942; Dep. Principal Clerk, 1962; Principal Clerk, 1972. Clerk to: Cttee of Privileges, 1949-57; Estimates Cttee, 1957-64; Cttee of Public Accounts, 1964-68; Clerk of the Journals, 1972-75. *Publications:* The House of Commons at Work, 1951, 9th rev. edn 1979; The Liberal Catholic Church-what is it?, 1966, 2nd edn 1979 (also foreign trans); The Houses of Parliament, 1976; contribs to Times Lit. Supp., etc. *Recreations:* walking, listening to music, preaching to the converted, worship. *Address:* 113 Beaufort Street, SW3 6BA. *T:* 01-351 1765; 71 Woodbine Road, Gosforth, Newcastle upon Tyne NE3 1DE. *T:* Newcastle upon Tyne 857040.

TAYLOR, Eric W., RE 1948 (ARE 1935); ARCA 1934; ASIA (Ed) 1965; printmaker, painter and sculptor; *b* 6 Aug. 1909; *s* of Thomas John and Ethel Annie Taylor; *m* 1939, Alfreda Marjorie Hurren; one *s* one *d*. *Educ:* William Ellis School, Hampstead; Royal College of Art, South Kensington. Worked for 3 years in London Studio; then as a free-lance illustrator; won British Inst. Scholarship, 1932; runner-up in Prix de Rome, 1934, while at Royal College of Art. Exhibited: Royal Academy; Royal Scottish Academy; Doncaster Art Gallery; New York; Brooklyn; Chicago; London Group; New English Art Club. Pictures in permanent Collections of Stockholm Art Gallery, Art Inst. of Chicago, Washington Art Gallery, War Museum, London. Logan Prize for best Etching in International Exhibition of Etching and Engraving at Art Institute of Chicago, 1937. Selected by British Council to exhibit in Scandinavian Exhibition, 1940, S America, 1942-44, Spain and Portugal, 1942-44, Turkey, 1943-45, Iceland, 1943, Mexico, 1943-45, China, 1945, Czechoslovakia, 1948, and Rotterdam, 1948. Associate Chicago Society of Etchers, 1937. War pictures bought by National Gallery Advisory Committee for Imperial War Museum, 1945. Volunteered for RA, Nov. 1939. Instructor at Northern Command Camouflage School, 1941-43; Royal Engineers, France and Germany, 1943-45; Normandy Landing, Battle of Caen, crossings of Rhine and Maas. instructing for Educational Corps Germany, 1946; Art Instructor Camberwell School of Art, 1936-39; Willesden School of Art, 1936-49; Central School of Art, 1948-49; Examiner: Bristol Univ., 1948-51; Durham Univ., 1971-74; Min. of Education NDD Pictorial Subjects, 1957-59. Designer and Supervisor of Lubeck School of Art for the Services, 1946. Head of the Design School, Leeds Coll. of Art, 1949-56, Principal, 1956-69, Organiser and Administrator of revolutionary Leeds Basic Course which played considerable part in changing whole direction of British art education; Asst Dir, Leeds Polytechnic, 1969-71. Leverhulme Research Awards, 1958-59, visiting Colleges of Art in Austria, Germany, Holland, Denmark and Italy. Study of Mosaics, Italy, 1965. Representative Exhibitions: Wakefield Art Gall., 1960; Goosewell Gall., Menston, 1972, 1973, 1976; Middlesbrough Art Gall., 1972; Northern Artists Gall., Harrogate, 1977. British Representative Speaker, International Design Conference, Karachi, 1962. Print selected by Royal Soc. of Painter Etchers for Presentation to Print Collections Club, 1947. Mem. of Senefelder Club, 1947. Picture purchased by British Council, 1948. *Publications:* etching published in Fine Prints of the Year, 1935, 1936, 1937, and in 1939 and 1940 issues of Print Collectors Quarterly. *Address:* Gordale, 13 Tregold Avenue, Bramhope, near Leeds, W Yorks.

TAYLOR, Ernest Richard; Headmaster of Wolverhampton Grammar School, 1956-April 1973; *b* Oldham, 9 Aug. 1910; *e s* of late Louis Whitfield and Annie Taylor; *m* 1936, Muriel Hardill; twin *s*. *Educ:* Hulme Grammar School, Oldham; Trinity College, Cambridge. Hist. Tripos, Class I, 1931; Sen. Schol. and Earl of Derby Research Student (Trinity), 1931-32; Thirlwall and Gladstone Prizes, 1933; MA 1935. Asst Master, Culford School, 1932-36; Moseley Gram. Sch., Birmingham, 1936-39; Manchester Gram. Sch., 1939-47. War Service in RA and AEC, 1940-46. Headmaster of Quarry Bank High School, Liverpool, 1947-56; Member, Schools Council for Curriculum and Examinations (formerly Secondary Schools Examinations Council), 1962-. Walter Hines Page Scholar, HMC, 1964. Pres. Incorporated Assoc. of Head Masters, 1965; Chm. Central Exec., Jt Four Secondary Assocs, 1970-72. Member: President's Council of Methodist Church, 1976-79; Churches' Council for Covenanting, 1978-. *Publications:* Methodism and Politics, (1791-1851), 1935; Padre Brown of Gibraltar, 1955; Religious Education of pupils from 16 to 19 years, 1962. *Recreation:* golf. *Address:* Highcliff, Whitcliffe, Ludlow, Salop. *T:* Ludlow 2093.

TAYLOR, Sir Francis, (Sir Frank Taylor), Kt 1974; Founder, 1921, and President and Executive Director, since 1979, Taylor Woodrow Group (Managing Director, 1935-79; Chairman, 1937-74); Director: Taylor Woodrow of Canada Ltd since 1953; Monarch Investments Ltd, Canada, since 1954; Blitman Construction Corp., since 1964; *b* 7 Jan. 1905; *s* of late Francis Taylor and late Sarah Ann Earnshaw; *m* 1st, 1929 (marr. diss.); two *d*; 2nd, 1956, Christine Enid Hughes; one *d*. Founded, 1921, Taylor Woodrow, Building, Civil & Mechanical Engineering Contractors, which became Public Company, in 1935. Member of Advisory Council to Minister of State, 1954-55; Chm. Export Group for Constructional Industries, 1954-55; President Provident Institution of Builders' Foremen and Clerks of Works, 1950; Dir, Freedom Federal Savings and Loan Assoc., Worcester, Mass, 1972-82. Dir, BOAC, 1958-60. Vice-Pres., Aims, 1978-. Governor,

Queenswood School for Girls, 1948-77. Hon. DSc Salford, 1973. Fellow, Chartered Inst. of Building, Hon. Fellow 1979. *Recreations:* tennis, swimming, riding. *Address:* (office) 10 Park Street, W1Y 4DD; (home) Long Common, Wanborough, near Guildford, Surrey GU3 2JL. *Clubs:* Royal Automobile, Queen's, Hurlingham, All England.

TAYLOR, Sir Frank; *see* Taylor, Sir Francis.

TAYLOR, Frank, CBE 1969; QFSM 1965; fire consultant; Chief Fire Officer, Merseyside County Fire Brigade, 1974-76, retired (Liverpool Fire Brigade, 1962-74); *b* 6 April 1915; *s* of Percy and Beatrice Taylor; *m* 1940, Nancy (*née* Hefford); two *s* two *d*; *m* 1976, Florence Mary Latham. *Educ:* Council Sch., Sheffield. Fireman, Sheffield Fire Bde, 1935-41; Instr, NFS West Riding, 1941-42; Company Officer up to Station Officer (ops), NFS in Yorkshire, 1942-49; Chief Officer, Western Fire Authority, N Ire., 1949-51; Divl Officer N Ire. Fire Authority, 1951-57; Belfast: Dep. Chief Officer, 1958-60; Chief Officer, 1960-62. *Recreations:* football, gardening. *Address:* Onchan, Hall Lane, Wrightington, near Wigan, Lancs.

TAYLOR, Dr Frank; Deputy Director and Principal Keeper, The John Rylands University Library of Manchester, 1972-77; Hon. Lecturer in Manuscript Studies, University of Manchester, since 1967. *Educ:* Univ. of Manchester (MA, PhD). FSA. Served with RN, 1942-46: Lieut, RNVR, 1943-46. Research for Cttee on History of Parlt, 1934-35; Keeper of Western Manuscripts, 1935-49, Keeper of Manuscripts, 1949-72, Librarian, 1970-72, John Rylands Library. Jt. Hon. Sec., Lancs Parish Record Soc., 1937-56, Hon. Sec., 1956-82; Registrar of Research, Soc. of Architectural Historians, 1978-82. Editor, Bulletin of the John Rylands Univ. Lib. of Manchester. *Publications:* various Calendars of Western Manuscripts and Charter Room collections in the Rylands Library, 1937-77; The Chronicle of John Strecche for the Reign of Henry 5, 1932; An Early Seventeenth Century Calendar of Records Preserved in Westminster Palace Treasury, 1939; The Parish Registers of Aughton, 1541-1764, 1942; contrib. to Some Twentieth Century Interpretations of Boswell's Life of Johnson (ed J. L. Clifford), 1970; The Oriental Manuscript Collections in the John Rylands Library, 1972; (ed with J. S. Roskell) Gesta Henrici Quinti, 1975; (with G. A. Matheson) Hand-List of Personal Papers from the Muniments of the Earl of Crawford and Balcarres, 1976; revised edn of M. R. James's Descriptive Catalogue of Latin Manuscripts in the John Rylands Library (1921), 1980; (ed) Society of Architectural Historians, Research Register No 5, 1981; The John Rylands University Library of Manchester, 1982; articles in Bulletin of John Rylands Library, Indian Archives. *Recreations:* cricket, walking. *Address:* The John Rylands University Library of Manchester, Deansgate, Manchester M3 3EH. *T:* 061-834 5343.

TAYLOR, Frank Henry; Principal, Frank H. Taylor & Co., City of London, Chartered Accountants; *b* 10 Oct. 1907; 2nd *s* of George Henry Taylor, Cambridgeshire; *m* 1936, Margaret Dora Mackay (*d* 1944), Invernesshire; one *d*; *m* 1948, Mabel Hills (*d* 1974), Hertfordshire; two *s*; *m* 1978, Glenys Mary Edwards, MBE, Bethesda, N Wales. *Educ:* Rutlish School, Merton, Surrey, FCIS 1929; FCA 1930. Commenced in practice as Chartered Accountant, 1930; Ministry of Food Finance Director of Tea, Coffee, Cocoa and Yeast, 1942; Min. of War Transport Finance Rep. overseas, 1944; visited over 40 countries on financial and political missions. Lt-Colonel comdg 1st Caernarvonshire Bn Home Guard, 1943. Contested (C) Newcastle under Lyme, 1955, Chorley, 1959; MP (C) Manchester, Moss Side, Nov. 1961-Feb. 1974. Governor of Rutlish School, 1946-. Liveryman, City of London. Master, Bakers' Co.; Mem., Guild of Air Pilots. *Recreations:* numerous including Rugby (for Surrey County), Sculling (Thames Championship), punting (several Thames championships), golf (Captain RAC 1962). *Address:* 4 Barrie House, Lancaster Gate, W2; Tinker Taylor, Sennen Cove, Cornwall. *T:* Sennen 220. *Clubs:* City Livery, Arts, Royal Automobile, British Sportsman's.

TAYLOR, Prof. Frederick William, MA Cantab, LLM Wales; Professor of Law, University of Hull, 1956-74, now Emeritus (Dean of Faculty of Arts, 1954-57); *b* 8 March 1909; *e s* of late James Edward Taylor, Solicitor, and of Emily Price; *m* 1938, Muriel Vera Markreed, *d* of Onek Vosguerchian; two *d*. *Educ:* Twynyrodyn Elementary and Cyfarthfa Secondary Schools, Merthyr Tydfil; University College of Wales, Aberystwyth; St John's College, Cambridge. Solicitor, 1931; LLB Wales, Sir Samuel Evans Prize 1933, BA Cantab, Scholar of St John's Coll., 1935; Asst Lectr in Law, University Coll., Hull, 1935; Acting Head, Dept of Law: University Coll., Southampton, 1940; Hull, 1941; called to Bar, Cert. of Honour, Middle Temple Prize, 1943; Head of Dept of Law, University Coll., Hull, 1949; LLM Wales 1954. Formerly Mem. of Bd of Studies in Laws of Univ. of London. Equity draftsman and conveyancer, 1944-, formerly at Leeds and later at Hull. *Publications:* articles in Law Journal, The Conveyancer, Jl of Soc. of Public Teachers of Law, Solicitors' Journal, The Solicitor, Secretaries Chronicle. *Recreations:* natural history, etc. *Address:* 40 Porthill Road, Shrewsbury, Shropshire.

TAYLOR, Geoffrey H.; *see* Handley-Taylor.

TAYLOR, Geoffrey William, FIB; Director and Group Chief Executive, Midland Bank plc, since 1982; *b* 4 Feb. 1927; *s* of late Joseph William Taylor and Doris Taylor (*née* Parr); *m* 1951, Joyce (*née* Walker); three *s* one *d*. *Educ:* Heckmondwike Grammar School; Univ. of London. BComm. Joined Midland Bank Ltd, 1943; Gen. Man. and Man. Dir, Midland Bank Finance

Corp. Ltd, 1967-76; Asst Chief General Manager, 1974-80, Dep. Group Chief Exec., 1980-82, Midland Bank Ltd. Gilbart Banking Lectr, 1973. *Recreations:* golf, reading, music. *Address:* Midland Bank plc, 27-32 Poultry, EC2P 2BX. *T:* 01-606 9911. *Club:* Overseas Bankers'.

TAYLOR, Sir George, Kt 1962; DSc; FRS 1968, FRSE, FLS; Director, Stanley Smith Horticultural Trust, since 1970; Visiting Professor, Reading University, since 1969; *b* 15 February 1904; *o s* of George William Taylor and Jane Sloan; *m* 1st, 1929, Alice Helen Pendrich (*d* 1977); two *s*; 2nd, Norah English (*d* 1967); 3rd, Beryl, Lady Colwyn. *Educ:* George Heriot's Sch., Edinburgh; Edinburgh Univ. BSc (1st class hons Botany), 1926; Vans Dunlop Scholar. Member of Botanical Expedition to South Africa and Rhodesia, 1927-28; Joint Leader of British Museum Expedition to Ruwenzori and mountains of East Africa, 1934-35; Expedition to SE Tibet and Bhutan, 1938. Principal in Air Ministry, 1940-45. Deputy Keeper of Botany, British Museum (Natural History), 1945-50; Keeper of Botany, 1950-56; Dir, Royal Botanic Gardens, Kew, 1956-71. Botanical Soc. Linnean Soc., 1950-56; Vice-Pres. 1956. Percy Sladen Trustee, 1951-81. Royal Horticultural Soc.: Mem. Council, 1951-73, Vice-Pres., and Prof. of Botany, 1974-; Council Member: National Trust (Chm. Gardens Cttee), 1961-72; RGS 1957-61 (Vice-Pres. 1964); Mem. Min. of Transport Adv. Cttee on Landscaping Treatment of Trunk Roads, 1956-81 (Chm. 1969-81). Editor, Curtis's Botanical Magazine, 1962-71. Gen. Sec., Brit. Assoc. for the Advancement of Science, 1951-58. Hon. Botanical Adviser, Commonwealth War Graves Commn, 1956-77. President: Botanical Society of British Isles, 1955; Division of Botany, Internat. Union Biol Sci., 1964-69; Internat. Assoc. for Plant Taxonomy, 1972. Member Royal Society Science, Uppsala, 1956; Corr. Member Royal Botanical Soc. Netherlands; Hon. Mem., Botanical Soc. of S Africa; Hon. Mem., American Orchid Soc. Hon. FRHS 1948. Hon. Freeman, Worshipful Co. of Gardeners, 1967. Hon. LLD Dundee, 1972. VMH 1956; Veitch Gold Medal, Royal Horticultural Soc., 1963; Bradford Washburn Award, Museum of Science, Boston, USA, 1969. Hon. DrPhil Gothenburg, 1958. *Publications:* An Account of the Genus Meconopsis, 1934; contributions on flowering plants to various periodicals. *Recreations:* angling, gardening, music. *Address:* Belhaven House, Dunbar, East Lothian EH42 1NS. *T:* Dunbar 62392, 63546; 26 Harley Place, W1. *T:* 01-580 1736. *Clubs:* Athenæum; New (Edinburgh).

TAYLOR, Prof. Gerard William, MS, FRCS; Hon. FACS; Professor of Surgery, University of London, since 1960; Surgeon and Director Surgical Professorial Unit, St Bartholomew's Hospital, London; Honorary Consultant in Vascular Surgery to the Army since 1962; *b* 23 September 1920; *s* of William Ivan Taylor; *m* 1951, Olivia Gay; one *s* one *d*. *Educ:* Bemrose School, Derby; St Bartholomew's Hospital Medical College. Served War of 1939-45, Capt. RAMC, 1944-47. Fellow in Surgery, Asst Resident, Fulbright Schol., Stanford Univ. Hosp., San Francisco, Calif., 1950-51; Surgeon, St Bartholomew's Hosp., London, Reader in Surgery, Univ. of London, 1955; Hunterian Prof., RCS, 1962; Vis. Prof. of Surgery: Univ. of Calif., Los Angeles, 1965; Univ. of Melbourne, 1969; Sir James Wattie Prof., NZ, 1972. Examiner in Surgery: Univ. of London, 1960; NUI, 1966; Univ. of Cambridge, 1966; Trinity Coll., Dublin, 1969; Univ. of Liverpool, 1974; Univ. of Birmingham, 1978. Governor, St Bartholomew's Hosp., 1971; Mem. Council, Epsom Coll., 1972. President: Vascular Surgical Soc. of GB and Ireland, 1975; Surgical Res. Soc., 1976; Assoc. of Surgeons of GB and Ireland, 1979. *Publications:* articles on general and arterial surgery in scientific journals. *Recreation:* motoring. *Address:* Maple Farm, Shantock Lane, Bovingdon, Herts. *T:* Hemel Hempstead 833170.

TAYLOR, Sir Godfrey; *see* Taylor, Sir A. G.

TAYLOR, Dr Gordon William; Managing Director, Robson Refractories Ltd, 1970; *b* 26 June 1928; *s* of William and Elizabeth Taylor; *m* 1954, Audrey Catherine Bull; three *s* two *d*. *Educ:* J. H. Burrows Sch., Grays, Essex; Army Apprentice Sch.; London Univ. (BScEng Hons, PhDEng). MICE, MIMechE, AMIEE. Kellogg Internat. Corp., 1954-59; W. R. Grace, 1960-62; Gen. Man., Nalco Ltd, 1962-66; BTR Industries, 1966-68; Managing Director: Kestrel Chemicals, 1968-69; Astral Marketing, 1969-70. Greater London Council: Alderman, 1972-77; Mem. for Croydon Central, 1973; Chairman: Public Services Cttee, 1977-78; London Transp. Cttee, 1978-79. *Recreations:* theatre, reading, tennis. *Address:* 7 Ilchester Place, Kensington, W14 8AA. *Club:* Holland Park Lawn Tennis.

TAYLOR, Greville Laughton; company director; *b* 23 Oct. 1902; *s* of Rowland Henry and Edith Louise Taylor; *m* 1947, Mary Eileen Reece Mahon; one *s* one *d*. *Educ:* Lodge School, Barbados; St John's College, Oxford. Called to the Bar, Lincoln's Inn, 1927. Clerk to the House of Assembly, Barbados, 1930-36. Police Magistrate, Barbados, 1936-44; Army 1940-44 (UK, N Africa, Italy); Registrar, Barbados, 1944-46; Judge of the Assistant Court of Appeal, Barbados, 1947-57; Puisne Judge, Windward Islands and Leeward Islands, 1957-64. *Recreations:* reading, shooting, fishing. *Address:* Cole's House, Cole's, St Philip, Barbados, West Indies. *T:* 207. *Clubs:* Royal Barbados Yacht; Bridgetown (Bridgetown).

TAYLOR, Harold Joseph, CBE 1966; Chief Director, Prison Department, Home Office, 1965-68, retired; *b* 7 May 1904; *s* of Herbert Taylor and Gertrude Mary Taylor; *m* 1940, Olive Alice Slade, *d* of Harry Slade, Honor Oak Park, SE; one *s* (adopted). *Educ:* Blandford Sec. Gram. Sch.; Southampton University. Teacher, Brighton Education Authority, 1924-28;

Asst Housemaster, Prison Commission, HM Borstal, Portland, 1928; Housemaster, Portland Borstal, 1930; Superintendent, Borstal Training School, Thayetmyo, Burma, 1933-37; Governor, HM Borstal: Feltham, Middx, 1938-41; Lowdham Grange, 1941-46; Governor, HM Prison: Camp Hill, IoW, 1946-49; Sudbury, Derby, 1949-51; Asst Comr, HM Prison Commission, 1951-57; Comr and Director of Borstal Administration, 1958-65. *Recreations:* fishing, country lore, tinkering. *Address:* 45 Church Way, Pagham, Bognor Regis, West Sussex. *T:* Pagham 3750.

TAYLOR, Harold McCarter, CBE 1955; TD 1945; retired, 1967; *b* Dunedin, New Zealand, 13 May 1907; *s* of late James Taylor, and late Louisa Urquhart Taylor; *m* 1st, 1933, Joan (*d* 1965), *d* of late George Reginald Sills, Lincoln; two *s* two *d*; 2nd, 1966, Dorothy Judith, *d* of late Charles Samuel, Liverpool. *Educ:* Otago Boys' High School and Univ. of Otago, NZ; Clare Coll., Cambridge. MSc New Zealand, 1928; MA, PhD Cambridge, 1933. Allen Scholar and Smith's Prizeman, 1932. Fellow of Clare College, Cambridge, 1933-61; Hon. Fellow, 1961-; Lecturer in Mathematics, University of Cambridge, 1934-45; Treasurer of the University, 1945-53; Secretary General of the Faculties, 1953-61; Vice-Chancellor, University of Keele, 1962-67 (Principal, University College of North Staffordshire, 1961-62); Rede Lecturer, Cambridge University, 1966. Mem., Royal Commn on Historical Monuments (England), 1972-78. Pres., Royal Archaeol Inst., 1972-75; Vice-Pres., Soc. of Antiquaries of London, 1974-77. Hon. LLD Cambridge, 1967; Hon. DLitt Keele, 1968. Commissioned in TA, NZ, 1925; served War of 1939-45 as Major and Lieut-Col RA; Instructor and Senior Instructor in Gunnery at School of Artillery, Larkhill. *Publications:* Anglo-Saxon Architecture, vols I and II (with Joan Taylor), 1965, vol. III, 1978; many articles in nat. and county archaeological jls. *Recreations:* mountaineering and ski-ing; Anglo-Saxon art and architecture; photography. *Address:* 192 Huntingdon Road, Cambridge CB3 0LB. *T:* 276324.

TAYLOR, Henry George, DSc(Eng); Director of Electrical Research Association, 1957-69, retired; *b* 4 Nov. 1904; *m* 1931, Gwendolyn Hilda Adams; one *s* two *d*. *Educ:* Taunton School; Battersea Polytechnic Inst., City and Guilds Engineering College. Metropolitan Vickers, 1929-30; Electrical Research Assoc., 1930-38; Copper Development Assoc., 1938-42; Philips Lamps Ltd, 1942-47; British Welding Research Assoc., 1947-57. *Publications:* contribs to: Instn of Electrical Engineers Jl, Jl of Inst. of Physics, etc. *Recreation:* walking. *Address:* The Island, Ford Street, Wellington TA21 9PE.

TAYLOR, Sir Henry Milton, Kt 1980; Editor of Hansard, Bahamas House of Assembly, since 1979; *b* 4 Nov. 1903; adopted *s* of Joseph and Evelyn Taylor; *m* 1962, Eula Mae Sisco; three step *c*; four *d* by previous marriage. *Educ:* Govt Grade Sch.; privately. Teacher; Headmaster, Public Sch. at Pompey Bay, Acklins Island, 1925-26. Elected Mem., House of Assembly, 1949; Co-founded and organized estabt of Progressive Liberal Party of Bahamas (first political party of Bahamas), 1953-64; Nat. Party Chm., 1953-64, Hon. Chm. for life, 1963; MP for 10 yrs; Leader of delegns to Westminster: to upgrade antiquated Acts of Parliament, 1956; in interest of Women's Suffrage, 1960. Temp. Dep. Governor-General of The Bahamas, July-Aug. and Nov. 1981. Mem., Develt Bd (Tourist), 1960-62; successfully toured Britain, Eire, W Germany and Sweden in interests of tourism and financial investments; officially visited Nassau/Lahn. (First) Dir, Princess Margaret Hosp. Blood Bank, 1954-55. Letters Patent for Armorial Bearing approved by Duke of Norfolk, 1981. *Publication:* (compiled and ed) United Bahamian Party Annual Handbook, 1967, 1968. *Address:* PO Box N10846, Nassau, Bahamas; Lucaya at Brentwood, 221 NE 44 Street, Miami, Fla 33137, USA. *Club:* British Floridian (Miami).

TAYLOR, Hermon, MA, MD, MChir, FRCS; retired; formerly Consulting Surgeon: London Hospital, E1; King George Hospital, Ilford; *b* 14 March, 1904; *s* of Enoch Oliver Taylor and A. M. Taylor (née Harrison); *m* 1932, Méarie Amélie Pearson (*d* 1981); three *s* two *d*. *Educ:* Latymer School, Edmonton; St John's Coll., Cambridge (scholar); St Bartholomew's Hospital (Entrance Scholar). BA 1926; MRCS, LRCP 1929; MB, ChB Cantab. 1930; FRCS Eng. 1930. House Surgeon, Demonstr of Pathology, St Bart's Hosp.; Res. Surgical Officer: Hertford Co. Hosp., Lincoln Co. Hosp.; Surgical Registrar, Prince of Wales' Hosp., Tottenham. MChir Cantab 1932; MD Cantab 1934; Horton Smith Prize, Univ. Cantab; Luther Holden Research Scholar, St Bartholomew's Hospital; BMA Research Scholar, Surgical First Assistant London Hospital. Moynihan Fellow, Assoc. of Surgeons of GB and Ireland; Hunterian Professor, RCS. Past President, British Society of Gastro-enterology; Hon. Member Amer. Gastro-enterological Assoc. *Publications:* Carcinoma of the Stomach, in Modern Trends in Gastro-Enterology, 1952; contrib. to BMJ, Lancet, etc, 1942-. *Address:* Coppice Field, Bosham Hoe, Chichester, West Sussex PO18 8ET. *T:* Chichester 573385. *Club:* Athenæum.

TAYLOR, Prof. Ian Galbraith; Ellis Llwyd Jones Professor of Audiology and Education of the Deaf, University of Manchester, since 1964; *b* 24 Apr. 1924; *s* of David Oswald Taylor, MD, and Margaret Ballantine Taylor; *m* 1954, Audrey Wolstenholme; two *d*. *Educ:* Manchester Grammar Sch.; Univ. of Manchester. MB, ChB, DPH Manchester; MD (Gold Medal) Manchester 1963; MRCP 1973; FRCP 1977. Ho. Surg., Manchester Royal Infirm., 1948; DAD, Army Health of N Regional Canal Zone, and OC Army Sch. of Hygiene, ME, 1949-51; Asst MO, City of Manchester, 1951-54. Univ. of Manchester: Hon. Special Lectr and Ewing Foundn Fellow, Dept of

Education of the Deaf, 1956-60; Lectr in Clinical Audiology, 1963-64. Consultant in Audiological Medicine, United Manchester Hosps, 1968. FCST (Hon.) 1966. *Publication:* Neurological Mechanisms of Hearing and Speech in Children, 1964. *Recreations:* gardening, fishing. *Address:* 7 Hall Moss Lane, Bramhall, Cheshire SK7 1RB. *T:* 061-440 8410.

TAYLOR, Ivor Ralph, QC 1973; **His Honour Judge Taylor;** a Circuit Judge, since 1976; *b* 26 Oct. 1927; *s* of Abraham Taylor and late Ruth Taylor; *m* 1st, 1954, Ruth Cassel (marr. diss. 1974); one *s* one *d* (and one *d* decd); 2nd, 1974, Jane Elizabeth Ann Gibson (marr. diss. 1978). *Educ:* Stand Grammar Sch., Whitefield; Manchester Univ. Served War of 1939-45, AC2 in RAF, 1945. Called to Bar, Gray's Inn, 1951. Standing Counsel to Inland Revenue, N Circuit, 1969-73; a Recorder of the Crown Court, 1972-76. Pres., Manchester and District Medico Legal Soc., 1974, 1975. *Recreations:* walking, indifferent golfing. *Address:* 7 Moorside House, Oakleigh Court, Stockport Road, Timperley, Cheshire WA15 6UG. *Club:* Dunham Forest Golf and Country.

TAYLOR, Sir James, Kt 1966; MBE 1945; DSc, FRSC, Hon. FInstP, Hon. MIMinE; Deputy Chairman: Royal Ordnance Factories Board, 1959-72 (Member, 1952-72); Chairman, Chloride Silent Power Ltd, 1974-81; *b* 16 Aug. 1902; *s* of James and Alice Taylor; *m* 1929, Margaret Lennox Stewart; two *s* one *d*. *Educ:* Bede College, Sunderland; Rutherford College, Newcastle upon Tyne; Universities of Durham, Sorbonne, Utrecht, Cambridge. BSc (1st cl. Hons Physics) 1923; PhD 1925; Dr of Physics and Maths (*cum laude*) Utrecht, 1927; DSc Dunelm, 1931. ICI Ltd: joined Nobel Div. 1928; Research Dir, 1946; Jt Man. Dir, 1951; Director, 1952-64. Chairman: Yorkshire Imperial Metals Ltd, 1958-64; Imperial Aluminium Co. Ltd, 1959-64; Imperial Metal Industries Ltd, 1962-64; Fulmer Res. Institute, 1976-78. Director: Nuclear Developments Ltd, 1961-64; European Plumbing Materials Ltd, 1962-64; BDH Group Ltd, 1965-67; Oldham & Son Ltd, 1965-69; Oldham (International) Ltd, 1969-72; Surrey Independent Hospital Ltd, 1981-. Member: Adv. Coun. on Scientific Research and Tech. Develt, MoD, 1965-68; NPL Steering Committee, 1966; Adv. Coun. on Calibration and Measurement, 1966; Chm., Glazebrook Cttee, NPL, 1966. Member: Court, Brunel Univ., 1967-82; Council, British Non-Ferrous Metals Research Assoc., 1954-67 (Vice-Chm. 1961-67); Council, City and Guilds of London, 1969-71; Court, RCA, 1969-71; Pres. Section B British Assoc. 1960, Council 1965; Pres. Inst. of Physics and Physical Society, 1966-68 (Hon. Treas. 1957-66); FRIC 1945; MIMinE 1947 (Hon. Member, 1960); FInstP 1948 (Hon. FInstP 1972); FRSA 1962 (Member Council 1964-, Vice-Pres., 1969, Chm., 1969-71, Silver Medal, 1969); Hon. Pres., Research and Development Soc., 1970; Hon. Mem., Newcomen Soc. in N America, 1970. Mem., Inst. of Dirs, 1964-. Hon. DSc Bradford, 1968; Hon. DCL Newcastle, 1969. Medal, Society Chemical Industry, 1965; Silver Medal, Chem. Soc., 1972. *Publications:* On the Sparking Potentials of Electric Discharge Tubes, 1927; Detonation in Condensed Explosives, 1952; British Coal Mining Explosives, 1958; Solid Propellant and Exothermic Compositions, 1959; The Modern Chemical Industry in Great Britain (Cantor Lectures, Jl of Roy. Soc. Arts), 1961; Restrictive Practices (Soc. of Chem. Ind. Lecture), 1965; Monopolies and Restrictive Practices (RSA), 1967; The Scientist and The Technologist in Britain today (Pres. Address, IPPS), 1967; Britain's Technological Future (IOP Jubilee Address), 1968; Arts, Crafts and Technology (RSA), 1969; Cobalt, Madder and Computers (RSA), 1969; The Seventies and the Society (RSA), 1970; The American Dream and the RSA, 1971; New Horizons in Research and Development (RSA), 1971; The Scientific Community, 1973; numerous contribs to Proc. Roy. Soc., Phil. Mag., Trans Inst. Min. Eng., Advancement of Science, ICI Magazine. *Recreations:* gardening, cooking and writing. *Address:* Culvers, Seale, near Farnham, Surrey GU10 1JN. *T:* Runfold 2210. *Club:* RNVR Carrick (Hon.) (Glasgow).

TAYLOR, Dame Jean (Elizabeth); DCVO 1978 (CVO 1976; MVO 4th Cl. 1971, 5th Cl. 1964); retired; *b* 7 Nov. 1916; *d* of late Captain William Taylor (killed in action, 1917). *Educ:* Tunbridge Wells High School (GPDST). Entered Office of Private Secretary to the Queen, 1958; Chief Clerk, 1961-78. *Recreations:* music, walking, looking at old buildings. *Address:* Balcombe Farm, Frittenden, Cranbrook, Kent TN17 2EL.

TAYLOR, Jessie; *see* Taylor, M. J.

TAYLOR, Dr Joe; JP; Councillor, Greater Manchester County Council, since 1973 (Chairman, 1981-82); *b* 6 Sept. 1906; *s* of Sam Taylor and Anne Taylor; *m* 1935, Edith Dante; two *s*. *Educ:* Leeds Central High School; Leeds University and Leeds Med. Sch. MB ChB 1932. Medical Practitioner in Manchester, 1935-; Mem., Crossley Hosp. Board, 1955-. Councillor, Manchester City, 1954-70, Alderman, 1970-73. Appeals Advisory Cttees, BBC and ITA: Chm., N Regional, 1961-67; Chm., Northern, 1967-76; Central, 1961-79. Member: Salvation Army Adv. Council, Manchester Region, 1965-; Gtr Manchester Police Authority, 1973-; NW Water Authority, 1977-; Court, Univ. of Manchester, 1981-; Court, Univ. of Salford, 1981-; Royal Exchange Theatre Trust, 1981-; Palace Theatre Trust, 1981-; NW Arts Executive, 1981-; Gtr Manchester County Disaster Relief Trust, 1980-; Hallé Concerts Soc., 1973-; President: Gtr Manchester Council for Voluntary Service, 1981-; Gtr Manchester Schools Football Assoc., 1981-; Gtr Manchester Council Olympic Wrestling Team, 1981-; Vice-Pres., Gtr Manchester Youth Assoc., 1981; Mem., Manchester Lit. and Phil. Soc. JP Manchester City, 1961. *Recreations:* fishing, gardening, reading. *Address:* 32

Old Hall Road, Broughton Park, Salford M7 0JH. *T:* 061-740 4433. *Club:* Manchester Luncheon.

TAYLOR, Sir John (Aked), Kt 1972; OBE 1960; TD 1951; DL; JP; Chairman and Managing Director, Timothy Taylor & Co. Ltd; Vice Lord-Lieutenant of West Yorkshire, since 1976; *b* 15 Aug. 1917; *s* of Percy Taylor, Knowle Spring House, Keighley, and Gladys Broster (who *m* 2nd, 1953, Sir (John) Donald Horsfall, 2nd Bt); *m* 1949, Barbara Mary, *d* of Percy Wright Stirk, Keighley; two *d*. *Educ:* Shrewsbury Sch. Served War of 1939-45: Duke of Wellington's Regt and Royal Signals, Major; Norway, Middle East, Sicily, NW Europe and Far East. Mem., Keighley Town Council, 1946-67 (Mayor, 1956; Chm., Educn Cttee, 1949-61; Chm., Finance Cttee, 1961-67); Mem. Council, Magistrates' Assoc., 1957- (Vice-Chm., Exec. Cttee, 1975-76; Chm., Licensing Cttee, 1969-76; Hon. Treasurer, 1976-; Past Pres. and Chm., WR Br.); Chm., Keighley Conservative Assoc., 1952-56 and 1957-67 (Jt Hon. Treas., 1947-52, and Chm., Young Conservatives, 1946-47); Chm., Yorkshire Area, Nat. Union of Conservative and Unionist Assocs, 1966-71 (Vice-Chm., 1965-66); Chm., Exec. Cttee of Nat. Union of Conservative and Unionist Assocs, 1971-76 (Mem., 1964-; Pres., 1982). Gen. Comr of Income Tax, 1965. JP Borough of Keighley 1949; DL West (formerly WR) Yorks, 1971. *Recreation:* cricket. *Address:* Fieldhead, Keighley, West Yorkshire. *T:* Keighley 603895. *Club:* Carlton.

TAYLOR, John Barrington, MBE 1945; TD 1957; JP; **His Honour Judge John Taylor;** a Circuit Judge, since 1977; *b* 3 Aug. 1914; *y s* of Robert Edward Taylor, Bath; *m* 1941, Constance Aleen, *y d* of J. Barkly Macadam, Edinburgh and Suffolk; two *s* three *d* (and one *s* decd). *Educ:* King Edward's Sch., Bath. LLB (London). Admitted a Solicitor, 1936, and practised at Bath until 1960. Enlisted Somerset LI, 1939; overseas service 1942-46: DAAG, HQ 5 Corps, 1943; AAG, Allied Commn for Austria, 1945; AAG, No 1 Dist. (Milan), 1946. HM Coroner, City of Bath, 1958-72; Registrar, Bath Gp of County Courts, 1960-77; a Recorder of the Crown Court, 1972-77. Mem., County Court Rule Cttee, 1980-. JP Somerset, 1962, Essex, 1978. *Recreation:* gardening. *Address:* Lascelles Lodge, Matching Green, near Harlow, Essex. *T:* Matching 256.

TAYLOR, Rt. Rev. John Bernard; *see* St Albans, Bishop of.

TAYLOR, Dr John Bryan, FRS 1970; Chief Physicist, Culham Laboratory, since 1981; *b* 26 Dec. 1928; *s* of Frank and Ada Taylor, Birmingham; *m* 1951, Joan M. Hargest; one *s* one *d*. *Educ:* Oldbury Grammar Sch.; Birmingham Univ., 1947-50 and 1952-55. RAF, 1950-52. Atomic Weapons Research Establishment, Aldermaston, 1955-59 and 1960-62; Harkness Fellow, Commonwealth Fund, Univ. of California (Berkeley), 1959-60; Culham Laboratory (UKAEA), 1962-69 and 1970- (Head of Theoretical Physics Div., 1963-81); Inst. for Advanced Study, Princeton, 1969. FInstP 1969. Maxwell Medal, IPPS, 1971; Max Born Medal, German Phys. Soc., 1979. *Publications:* contribs to scientific learned jls. *Recreation:* gliding. *Address:* Culham Laboratory, Abingdon, Oxon. *T:* Abingdon 463344, Abingdon 21840 ext. 3344.

TAYLOR, Prof. John Clayton, PhD; FRS 1981; Professor of Mathematical Physics, Cambridge University, and Fellow of Robinson College, since 1980; *b* 4 Aug. 1930; *s* of Leonard Taylor and Edith (*née* Tytherleigh); *m* 1959, Gillian Mary (*née* Schofield); two *s*. *Educ:* Selhurst Grammar Sch., Croydon; Cambridge Univ. (MA). Lectr, Imperial Coll., London, 1956-60; Lectr, Cambridge Univ., and Fellow of Peterhouse, 1960-64; Reader in Theoretical Physics, Oxford Univ., and Fellow of University Coll., Oxford, 1964-80. *Publication:* Gauge Theories of Weak Interactions, 1976. *Recreation:* pottering about. *Address:* 9 Bowers Croft, Cambridge CB1 4RP.

TAYLOR, Rt. Hon. John David, PC (N Ire.) 1970; Member (UU) Northern Ireland, European Parliament, since 1979; Member (OUP) North Down, Northern Ireland Assembly, since 1982; *b* 24 Dec. 1937; *er s* of George D. Taylor and Georgina Baird; *m* 1970, Mary Frances Todd; one *s* four *d*. *Educ:* Royal Sch., Armagh; Queen's Univ. of Belfast (BSc). CEng; AMInstHE, AMICEl. MP (UU) S Tyrone, NI Parlt, 1965-73; Mem. (UU), Fermanagh and S Tyrone, NI Assembly, 1973-75; Mem. (UU), North Down, NI Constitutional Convention, 1975-76; Parly Sec. to Min. of Home Affairs, 1969-70; Minister of State, Min. of Home Affairs, 1970-72. Partner, G. D. Taylor and Associates, Architects and Civil Engineers, 1966-74; Director: Bramley Apple Restaurant Ltd, 1974-; West Ulster Estates Ltd, 1968-; West Ulster Hotels Co. Ltd, 1976-; Gosford Housing Assoc. Ltd, 1977-; Tontine Rooms Ltd, 1978-. *Publication:* (jtly) Ulster—the facts, 1982. *Address:* Mullinure, Portadown Road, Armagh, Northern Ireland BT61 9EL. *T:* Armagh 522409. *Club:* Armagh County (Armagh).

TAYLOR, John D.; *see* Debenham Taylor.

TAYLOR, Prof. John Gerald; Professor of Mathematics, King's College, University of London, since 1971; *b* 18 Aug. 1931; *s* of William and Elsie Taylor; *m* Pamela Nancy (*née* Cutmore); two *s* three *d*. *Educ:* King Edward VI Grammar Sch., Chelmsford; Mid-Essex Polytechnic, Chelmsford; Christ's Coll., Cambridge. Fellow, Inst. for Advanced Study, Princeton, NJ, USA, 1956-58 (Mem., 1961-63); Fellow, Christ's Coll., Cambridge, 1958-60; Asst Lectr, Faculty of Mathematics, Univ. of Cambridge, 1959-60. Member: Inst. des Hautes Etudes Scient., Paris, 1960; Res. Inst. Advanced Study, Baltimore, Md, USA, 1960. Sen. Res. Fellow, Churchill Coll., Cambridge, 1963-64; Prof.

of Physics, Rutgers Univ., New Brunswick, NJ, 1964-66; Fellow, Hertford Coll., Oxford, and Lectr, Math. Inst., Oxford, 1966-67; Reader in Particles and Fields, Queen Mary Coll., London, 1967-69; Prof. of Physics, Univ. of Southampton, 1969-71. *Publications:* Quantum Mechanics, an Introduction, 1969; The Shape of Minds to Come, 1970; The New Physics, 1972; Black Holes: the end of the Universe?, 1973; Superminds, 1975; Special Relativity, 1975; Science and the Supernatural, 1980; The Horizons of Knowledge, 1982; also scientific papers in Proc. Royal Soc., Phys. Rev., Proc. Camb. Phil. Soc., Jl Math. Phys. etc. *Recreations:* listening to music, walking. *Address:* 42 Fairmead Road, N19. *T:* 01-272 1558.

TAYLOR, John Hugh, MA; Member, Civil Service Appeal Board, since 1978; *b* 1 Dec. 1916; *yr s* of late Arthur and Etna Taylor, Steeton, Yorks; *m* 1954, Romayne F. E. Good, *d* of late I. E. Good, Fulmer; two *s. Educ:* Boys' Grammar Sch., Keighley; Peterhouse, Cambridge (Scholar). 1st Cl. Historical Tripos Part I, 1938, 1st Cl. Part II, 1939. Administrative Class, Civil Service, 1939, Asst Principal, Admiralty; Private Secretary to Civil Lord, 1941-42; Private Secretary to Civil Lord and also to Parliamentary Secretary, 1942-43; Principal Private Secretary to First Lord, 1950-51; Assistant Secretary, 1951-61; Under-Secretary, Admiralty, 1961-64; Asst Under-Sec. of State, MoD, 1964-69; Under-Sec., Civil Service Dept, 1969-70; Dep. Principal, Civil Service Coll., 1970-72; Asst Under Sec. of State, MoD, 1972-76. *Recreations:* ornithology and photography. *Address:* 14 Duke's Wood Drive, Gerrards Cross, Bucks. *T:* Gerrards Cross 84241.

TAYLOR, Sir John Lang, (Sir Jock Taylor), KCMG 1979 (CMG 1974); HM Diplomatic Service; Ambassador to the Federal Republic of Germany, since 1981; *b* 3 Aug. 1924; *y s* of Sir John William Taylor, KBE, CMG; *m* 1952, Molly, *o d* of James Rushworth; five *s* three *d. Educ:* Prague; Vienna; Imperial Services Coll., Windsor; Baltimore Polytechnic Inst., Md; Cornell Univ.; Trinity Coll., Cambridge. RAFVR, 1944-47 (Flt-Lt 1946). Joined HM Foreign (now Diplomatic) Service, 1949; served in: FO, 1949-50 and 1957-60; Saigon, 1950-52; Hanoi, 1951; Beirut, 1952-55; Prague, 1955-57; Montevideo, 1960-64; Bonn, 1964-69; Minister (Commercial), Buenos Aires, 1969-71; RCDS, 1972; Head of Industry, Science and Energy Dept, FCO, 1972-73; Asst Under-Sec. of State, FCO, 1973-74; Under-Sec., Dept of Energy, 1974-75; Ambassador to Venezuela, 1975-79; to the Netherlands, 1979-81. *Address:* c/o Foreign and Commonwealth Office, SW1. *Club:* Travellers'.

TAYLOR, John Mark; Member (C) Midlands East, European Parliament, since 1979; *b* 19 Aug. 1941; *s* of Wilfred and Eileen Martha Taylor; *m* 1979, Catherine Ann Hall. *Educ:* Eversfield Prep. School; Bromsgrove School and College of Law. Admitted Solicitor, 1966; Partner in Reynolds & Co., 1968-78; Senior Partner, Taylor, Allsopp & Co., 1978-. Member: Solihull County Borough Council, 1971-74; W Midlands Metropolitan County Council, 1973- (Opposition (Conservative) Leader, 1975-77; Leader, 1977-79). Vice-Pres., AMA, 1979- (Dep. Chm., 1978-79). Mem., W Midlands Economic Planning Council, 1978-79; Governor, Univ. of Birmingham, 1977-81. Contested (C) Dudley East, Feb. and Oct. 1974. European Democratic Group spokesman on Community Budget, 1979-81, Group Dep. Chm., 1981-82. *Recreations:* fellowship, cricket, reading. *Address:* 211 St Bernards Road, Solihull, West Midlands B92 7DL. *T:* 021-707 1076; (office) 021-704 3071. *Clubs:* Carlton, MCC; Birmingham (Birmingham).

TAYLOR, John Ralph Carlisle, CIE 1943; Past Director, Davy-Ashmore International Co. Ltd; *b* Sydney, NSW, Australia, 18 Aug. 1902; *o s* of Charles Carlisle Taylor and Jean Sawers; *m* 1933, Nancy (Ann) Marguerite Sorel-Cameron (*d* 1972); one *s* decd. *Educ:* Winchester. Shaw Wallace & Co., London, Calcutta, Karachi, 1921-28; Burmah-Shell, 1928-39 and 1945-54; General Manager in India, 1951-54. Service in RIASC (Lt-Col) 1941-42, GHQ India (Lt-Col) 1942; Petroleum Officer; *ex-officio* Mem., Defence Dept, Govt of India, 1942-45. Chairman, Shell Group of Companies in Australia, 1955-60; retired from Shell, 1960. *Recreations:* walking, reading, racing. *Address:* 166 Oakwood Court, W14. *Clubs:* Hurlingham, Oriental.

TAYLOR, John Russell; Art Critic, The Times, since 1978; *b* 19 June 1935; *s* of Arthur Russell and Kathleen Mary Taylor (*née* Picker). *Educ:* Dover Grammar Sch.; Jesus Coll., Cambridge (MA); Courtauld Inst. of Art, London. Sub-Editor, Times Educational Supplement, 1959; Editorial Asst, Times Literary Supplement, 1960; Film Critic, The Times, 1962-73. Lectr on Film, Tufts Univ., in London, 1970-71; Prof., Div. of Cinema, Univ. of Southern California, 1972-78. *Publications:* Anger and After, 1962; Anatomy of a Television Play, 1962; Cinema Eye, Cinema Ear, 1964; Penguin Dictionary of the Theatre, 1966; The Art Nouveau Book in Britain, 1966; The Rise and Fall of the Well-Made Play, 1967; The Art Dealers, 1969; Harold Pinter, 1969; The Hollywood Musical, 1971; The Second Wave, 1971; David Storey, 1974; Directors and Directions, 1975; Peter Shaffer, 1975; Hitch, 1978; The Revels History of Drama in English, vol. VII, 1978; Impressionism, 1981. *Address:* c/o The Times, Gray's Inn Road, WC1X 8EZ.

TAYLOR, Rt. Rev. John Vernon; *see* Winchester, Bishop of.

TAYLOR, John William Ransom; Editor and Compiler, Jane's All the World's Aircraft, since 1959; *b* 8 June 1922; *s* of late Victor Charles Taylor and late Florence Hilda Taylor (*née* Ransom); *m* 1946, Doris Alice Haddrick; one *s* one *d. Educ:* Ely Cathedral Choir Sch., Soham Grammar Sch., Cambs. FRAeS, FRHistS, FSLAET. Design Dept, Hawker Aircraft Ltd, 1941-47; Editorial Publicity Officer, Fairey Aviation Gp, 1947-55; Author/Editor,

1955-; Air Corresp., Meccano Magazine, 1943-72; Editor, Air BP Magazine, British Petroleum, 1956-72; Jt Editor, Guinness Book of Air Facts and Feats, 1974-; Contributing Editor: Air Force Magazine (USA), 1971-; Jane's Defence Review, 1980-. Pres., Chiltern Aviation Soc.; Vice-President: Horse Rangers Assoc.; Guild of Aviation Artists. Warden, Christ Church, Surbiton Hill, 1976-80. C. P. Robertson Memorial Trophy, 1959. *Publications:* Spitfire, 1946; Aircraft Annual, 1949-75; Civil Aircraft Markings, 1950-78; Wings for Tomorrow, 1951; Military Aircraft Recognition, 1952-79; Civil Airliner Recognition, 1953-79; Picture History of Flight, 1955; Science in the Atomic Age, 1956; Rockets and Space Travel, 1956; Best Flying Stories, 1956; Jane's All the World's Aircraft, 1956-; Helicopters Work Like This, 1957; Royal Air Force, 1957; Fleet Air Arm, 1957; Jet Planes Work Like This, 1957; Russian Aircraft, 1957; Rockets and Missiles, 1958; CFS, Birthplace of Air Power, 1958; Rockets and Spacecraft Work Like This; British Airports, 1959; US Military Aircraft, 1959; Warplanes of the World, 1959, rev. as Military Aircraft of the World; BP Book of Flight Today, 1960; Combat Aircraft of the World, 1969; Westland 50, 1965; Pictorial History of the Royal Air Force, 3 vols 1968-71, rev. 1980; Aircraft Aircraft, 1967, 4th edn 1974; Encyclopaedia of World Aircraft, 1966; The Lore of Flight, 1971; Rockets and Missiles, 1971; Light Plane Recognition, 1970; Civil Aircraft of the World, 1970-79; British Civil Aircraft Register, 1971; (with M. J. H. Taylor) Missiles of the World, 1972-79; (with D. Mondey) Spies in the Sky, 1972; (with K. Munson) History of Aviation, 1973, 2nd edn, 1978; Jane's Aircraft Pocket Books, 1973-; History of Aerial Warfare, 1974; (with S. H. H. Young) Passenger Aircraft and Airlines, 1975; Jets, 1976; (with M. J. H. Taylor) Helicopters of the World, 1976-79. *Recreations:* historical studies, travel, ski-ing. *Address:* 36 Alexandra Drive, Surbiton, Surrey KT5 9AF. *T:* 01-399 5435. *Clubs:* Royal Aero, Royal Air Force (Hon.); Fenland Motor.

TAYLOR, Judy, (Julia Marie), (Judy Hough), MBE 1971; Director, The Bodley Head Ltd, since 1967 (Deputy Managing Director, 1971-80); *b* 12 Aug. 1932; adopted *d* of Gladys Spicer Taylor; *m* 1980, Richard Hough, *qv. Educ:* St Paul's Girls' Sch. Joined The Bodley Head, 1951, specialising in children's books; Director: Chatto, Bodley Head & Jonathan Cape Ltd, 1973-80; Chatto, Bodley Head & Jonathan Cape Australia Pty Ltd, 1977-80. Publishers Association: Chm., Children's Book Gp, 1969-72; Mem. Council, 1972-78; Member: Book Develt Council, 1973-76; Unicef Internat. Art Cttee, 1968-70, 1976, 1982; UK Unicef Greeting Card Cttee, 1982-. Consultant to Frederick Warne plc on Beatrix Potter, 1981-. *Publications:* Sophie and Jack; numerous professional articles. *Recreations:* collecting early children's books, gardening. *Address:* Denfurlong, Lower Chedworth, near Cheltenham, Glos GL54 4AP. *T:* Fossebridge 422; Flat 7, 217 Sussex Gardens, W2 2RJ.

TAYLOR, Keith Breden, MA, DM; FRCP; George de Forest Barnett Professor of Medicine, Stanford University, 1966-81 and since 1982; *b* 16 April 1924; *yr s* of Francis Henry Taylor and Florence (*née* Latham); *m* 1st, 1949, Ann Gaynor Hughes Jones (*d* 1971); three *s* one *d* (and one *s* decd); 2nd, 1972, Kym Williams, Adelaide, Aust. *Educ:* King's College Sch., Wimbledon; Magdalen Coll., Oxford (Exhibnr; BA Hons Physiology 1946, BM BCh 1949). Member, SHAEF Nutrition Survey Team, 1945; RAMC (Major), 1951-53; Dir Gen., Health Educn Council, 1981-82. Late Hon. Consultant, Central Middlesex Hosp.; Mem., MRC Gastroenterology Research Unit; Asst in Nuffield Dept Clin. Med., Oxford. Radcliffe Travelling Fellow, 1953; Rockefeller Foundn Fellow, 1959; Guggenheim Fellow, 1971; Fogarty Sen. Fellow, USPHS, 1978-79. Consts., US National Insts of Health; Mem., USPHS Trng Grants Cttee in Gastroenterology and Nutrition, 1965-70; Chm., Stanford Univ. Cttee on Human Nutrition, 1974-81; Vis. Professorships include: Rochester, NY, 1966; Columbia-Presbyterian, NY, 1969; Univ. of Adelaide, 1971; Academic Medical Unit, Royal Free Hosp., 1978-79. *Publications:* contribs to scientific jls, also texts, espec. in biochemistry and physiology of vitamin B12, immunological and other aspects of gastrointestinal disease and nutrition. *Recreations:* theatre, tennis, walking, sailing, gardening. *Address:* School of Medicine, Stanford University, Stanford, Calif 94305, USA.

TAYLOR, Kenneth, CB 1975; Secretary, Export Credits Guarantee Department, since 1975; *b* 10 Oct. 1923; *s* of William and May Taylor; *m* 1952, Mary Matilda Jacobs; one *s* one *d. Educ:* Merchant Taylors' Sch., Crosby; University Coll., Oxford (MA). Commnd RAF, 1943; Flt-Lt 212 Sqdn, 1944-45. Entered Min. of Civil Aviation as Asst Principal, 1947; BoT, later DTI, 1948-56, 1959-74; Treasury, 1957-59; Asst Sec. 1963; idc 1967; Under-Sec., 1969-73; Dep. Sec., 1973; Secretary, Price Commn, 1973-74. Mem., BOTB, 1975-. *Recreations:* tennis, chess. *Address:* High Trees, West Hill Way, Totteridge, N20. *T:* 01-445 7173. *Club:* Overseas Bankers.

TAYLOR, Kenneth, OBE 1981; FEng, FIMechE, FIEE; FCIT; Director of Mechanical and Electrical Engineering, British Railways Board, 1977-83; *b* 29 Sept. 1921; *s* of Charles Taylor and Amy (*née* Booth); *m* 1945, Elsie Armitt; one *d. Educ:* Manchester Coll. of Technol. FIMechE, FIEE 1971; FCIT 1977; FEng 1981. Principal appts with British Railways: Electric Traction Engr, Manchester, 1956; Electrical Engr, LMR, 1963; Chief Mech. and Elec. Engr, LMR, 1970; Traction Engr, BR Bd HQ, 1971. *Recreation:* golf. *Address:* 137 Burley Lane, Quarndon, Derby DE6 4JS. *T:* Derby 550123.

TAYLOR, Kenneth John; His Honour Judge Kenneth Taylor; a Circuit Judge, since 1977; *b* 29 March 1929; *s* of Hereford Phillips Taylor and Florence Gertrude Taylor; *m* 1953, Joan Cattermole; one *s* one *d. Educ:* William

Hulme's Grammar Sch., Manchester; Manchester Univ. (LLB). Called to Bar, Middle Temple, 1951. A Recorder of the Crown Court, 1972-77. *Recreations:* reading, music. *Address:* 25 Mill Lane, off The Bank, Scholar Green, Stoke-on-Trent. *T:* Stoke-on-Trent 512102.

TAYLOR, Kenneth Roy E.; *see* Eldin-Taylor.

TAYLOR, Prof. Laurie, (Laurence John); Professor of Sociology and Head of Department of Sociology, University of York, since 1974; *b* 1 Aug. 1935; *s* of Stanley Douglas Taylor and Winifred Agnes (*née* Cooper); *m* 1975, Anna Coote; one *s* by former marriage. *Educ:* St Mary's Coll., Liverpool; Rose Bruford College of Drama, Kent; Birkbeck Coll., Univ. of London (BA); Univ. of Leicester (MA). Librarian, 1952-54; Sales Asst, 1954-56; Professional Actor, 1960-61; English Teacher, 1961-64; Lectr in Sociology, 1965-73, Reader in Sociology, 1973-74, Univ. of York. *Publications:* Deviance and Society, 1971; (jtly) Psychological Survival, 1972; (jtly) Crime, Deviance and Socio-Legal Control, 1972; (ed jtly) Politics and Deviance, 1973; Man's Experience of the World, 1976; (jtly) Escape Attempts, 1976; (jtly) Prison Secrets, 1978; (jtly) In Whose Best Interests?, 1980; articles, reviews, broadcasts, TV series. *Recreation:* restless socializing. *Address:* c/o Department of Sociology, University of York, Heslington, York YO1 5DD. *T:* York 59861, ext. 5925.

TAYLOR, Len Clive; Director, Calouste Gulbenkian Foundation (UK and Commonwealth Branch), since 1982; *b* 4 Aug. 1922; *s* of late S. R. Taylor, Calcutta, India; *m* 1951, Suzanne Dufault, Spencer, Massachusetts, USA; one *s* two *d. Educ:* Sevenoaks School; New College, Oxford; Chicago University. New College, Oxford; 1st Cl. Hons Mod. Hist.; Commonwealth Fund Fellowship. Assistant Master, St Paul's School, Darjeeling, India, 1940-42 and 1945-46; Indian Army Intelligence Corps, 1942-45; New College, Oxford, 1946-49; Chicago University, 1949-50; Senior History Master, Repton School, 1950-54; Headmaster, Sevenoaks School, 1954-68; Dir, Nuffield Foundn 'Resources for Learning' Project, 1966-72; Principal Administrator, Centre for Educnl Res. and Innovation, OECD, Paris, 1972-77; Head of Educnl Prog. Services, IBA, 1977-82. *Publications:* Experiments in Education at Sevenoaks, 1965; Resources for Learning, 1971. *Address:* 43 The Drive, Sevenoaks, Kent. *T:* Sevenoaks 51448.

TAYLOR, Leon Eric Manners; Research Analyst; *b* 28 Oct. 1917; *s* of late Leon Eric Taylor and Veronica Dalmahoy (*née* Rogers); *m* 1963, Margaret Betty Thompson; no *c. Educ:* Fettes Coll., Edinburgh; Oriel Coll., Oxford. Captain RA (Service, 1939-46). Asst Principal, 1945, Principal, 1948, in Bd of Trade until 1963. First Sec., UK Delegn to the European Communities, 1963-66; Econ. Counsellor, British High Commn, Kuala Lumpur, 1966-70. Called to Bar, Inner Temple, 1951. Attended Joint Services Staff College, 1952. Hon. Visiting Fellow, Centre for Contemporary European Studies, University of Sussex, 1970-71; Counsellor (Commercial), The Hague, 1971-72; Research Fellow, Univ. of Sussex, 1973-75. *Recreations:* walking, amateur theatre, golf. *Address:* Sam's Hill Cottage, 47 North Street, Middle Barton, Oxford OX5 4BH. *T:* Steeple Aston 47256.

TAYLOR, (Margaret) Jessie; Headmistress, Whalley Range High School for Girls, since 1976; *b* 30 Nov. 1924; *d* of Thomas Brown Gowland and Ann Goldie Gowland; *m* 1958, Eric Taylor, *qv. Educ:* Queen Elizabeth's Grammar Sch., Middleton; Manchester Univ. (BA Hons, DipEd). Jun. Classics Teacher, Cheadle Hulme Sch., 1946-49; North Manchester Grammar School for Girls: Sen. Classics Teacher, 1950; Sen. Mistress, 1963; Actg Headmistress, Jan.-July 1967; Dep. Head Teacher, Wright Robinson Comprehensive High Sch., 1967-75. Member: Council and Exams Cttee, Associated Lancs Schs Examining Bd, 1976- (Mem. Classics Panel, 1968-72); Nursing Educn Cttee, S Manchester Area, 1976-; Home Office Cttee on Obscenity and Film Censorship, 1977-79; Consultant Course Tutor, NW Educnl Management Centre, Padgate, 1980-82. FRSA 1980. *Recreations:* music, drama, riding. *Address:* 10 Mercers Road, Hopwood, Heywood, Lancs OL10 2NP. *T:* Heywood 66630.

TAYLOR, Rt. Rev. Maurice; *see* Galloway, Bishop of, (RC).

TAYLOR, General Maxwell Davenport, DSC (US) 1944; DSM (US) 1945 (3 Oak Leaf Clusters, 1954, 1959, 1964); Silver Star 1943 (Oak Leaf Cluster, 1944); Legion of Merit; Bronze Star; Purple Heart; Consultant to President of US; President, Institute of Defense Analyses; Member, Foreign Intelligence Advisory Board, since 1965; *b* 26 Aug. 1901; *s* of John Earle Maxwell Taylor and Pearle Davenport; *m* 1925, Lydia Gardner (*née* Happer); two *s. Educ:* US Milit. Academy (BS). Became artillery commander of 82nd Airborne Division by Dec. 1942; served in Sicilian and Italian Campaigns; in 1944 became Commanding Gen. of 101st Airborne Div., which he led in the airborne invasion of Normandy, the airborne invasion of Holland, and in the Ardennes and Central Europe Campaigns; supt US Mil. Acad., 1945; Chief of Staff, European Comd HQ, Heidelberg, Jan. 1949; first US Comdr, Berlin, Sept. 1949; Asst Chief of Staff for Ops, G3, Dept of Army, Feb. 1951; Dep. Chief of Staff for Ops and Admin. of Army, Aug. 1951; Comdg Gen., 8th US Army in Korea, 1953; Comdr of all ground forces in Japan, Okinawa and Korea, at Camp Zama, Japan, Nov. 1954; C-in-C of Far East Comd and UN Comd, 1955; Chief of Staff, US Army, 1955-59; Mil. Representative of the President of the USA, 1961-62; Chairman, Joint Chiefs of Staff, US, Oct. 1962-June 1964; American Ambassador to South Vietnam, 1964-65; Special Consultant to President, 1965-69. Formerly Director of companies (including Chairman

Board, Mexican Light & Power Co.); was also President, Lincoln Center for the Performing Arts. Holds fifteen Honorary doctorates. Many foreign decorations. *Publications:* The Uncertain Trumpet, 1960; Responsibility and Response, 1967; Swords and Plowshares, 1972; Precarious Security, 1976. *Recreations:* tennis, handball and squash. *Address:* 2500 Massachusetts Avenue NW, Washington, DC 20008, USA. *Clubs:* University (NYC); Army and Navy, International, Chevy Chase, Alibi (Washington).

TAYLOR, Neville; Chief of Public Relations, Ministry of Defence, since 1982; *b* 17 Nov. 1930; *y s* of late Frederick Taylor and of Lottie Taylor; *m* 1954, Margaret Ann, *y d* of late Thomas Bainbridge Vickers and Gladys Vickers; two *s. Educ:* Sir Joseph Williamson's Mathematical Sch., Rochester; Coll. of Commerce, Gillingham, Kent. Junior Reporter, Chatham News Group, 1947; Royal Signals, 1948-50; Journalism, 1950-58; Asst Information Officer, Admiralty, 1958; Information Officer (Press), Admiralty, 1960; Fleet Information Officer, Singapore, 1963; Chief Press Officer, MoD, 1966; Information Adviser to Nat. Economic Develt Office, 1968; Dep. Dir, Public Relns (Royal Navy), 1970; Head of Information, Min. of Agriculture, Fisheries and Food, 1971; Dep. Dir of Information, DoE, 1973-74, Dir of Information, 1974-79; Dir of Information, DHSS, 1979-82. *Recreation:* fishing. *Address:* Crow Lane House, Crow Lane, Rochester, Kent ME1 1RF. *T:* Medway 42990.

TAYLOR, Nicholas George Frederick, CMG 1970; FIPR 1973; Development Director, East Caribbean; Higgs & Hill (UK) Ltd, 1973-80; Higgs & Hill (St Kitts) Ltd (Chairman), 1973-80; Director, Cariblue Hotels Ltd, St Lucia, since 1968; Local Adviser, Barclays Bank International, St Lucia, since 1974; *b* 14 Feb. 1917; 3rd *s* of Louis Joseph Taylor and Philipsie (*née* Phillip); *m* 1952, Morella Agnes, *e d* of George Duncan Pitcairn and Florence (*née* La Guerre); two *s* two *d. Educ:* St Mary's Coll., St Lucia; LSE, London; Gonville and Caius Coll., Cambridge. Clerk, various Depts, St Lucia, 1937-46; Asst Social Welfare Officer, 1948-49; Public Relations and Social Welfare Officer, 1949-54; District Officer, and Authorised Officer, Ordnance Area, St Lucia, 1954-57; Dep. Dir St Lucia Br., Red Cross Soc., 1956-57; Perm. Sec., Min. of Trade and Production, 1957-58 (acted Harbour Master in conjunction with substantive duties); Commn for W Indies in UK: Administrative Asst, 1959; Asst Sec.-Chief Community Development Officer, Migrants Services Div., 1961; Commn in UK for Eastern Caribbean Govts: Officer-in-Charge, 1962-63; Actg Comr, 1964-66; Comr for E Caribbean Govts in UK, 1967-73. Dir, St Lucia (Co-operative) Bank Ltd, 1973-74. Mem., Civil Service Appeals Bd, 1973-77. Vice-Chm. Commonwealth Assoc., Bexley, Crayford and Erith, 1965-67; a Patron, British-Caribbean Assoc., 1962-73. Member: West India Committee Executive, 1968-; Bd of Governors, Commonwealth Inst., 1968-73. Assoc. Mem. 1951, Mem. 1962, Fellow, 1973, (British) Inst. of Public Relations. Chairman: Central Library Bd, 1973-81, Nat. Insurance Scheme, 1979-81, St Lucia; Central Housing Authority, St Lucia, 1975-77; Income Tax Comrs Appeals Bd, 1980-; St Lucia Boy Scouts Assoc., 1977-79. Vice-Chm., Nat. Develt Corp., 1979-. Founder Life Mem., Cambridge Soc., 1976. JP 1948. Coronation Medal, 1953; British Red Cross Medal, 1949-59. *Recreations:* cricket, lawn tennis, reading. *Address:* PO Box 816, Castries, St Lucia, West Indies. *T:* 8513. *Clubs:* Royal Commonwealth Society (West Indian), Travellers'.

TAYLOR, Sir Nicholas Richard S.; *see* Stuart Taylor.

TAYLOR, Peter, BScEcon, FCIS; Clerk of the Senate, University of London, since 1977; *b* 5 Jan. 1924; *s* of late Frederick and Doris Taylor; *m* 1948, Jeannette (*née* Evans); two *d. Educ:* Salt Boys' High Sch., Saltaire, Yorks; Bradford Technical Coll. (BScEcon London, 1949). FCIS 1959. Served War, FAA, 1942-46. WR Treasurer's Dept, 1940-50; Registrar, Lincoln Technical Coll., 1950-58; Secretary: Wolverhampton and Staffs Coll. of Technol., 1959-60; Chelsea Coll., Univ. of London, 1961-70. Pres., Assoc. of Coll. Registrars, 1970-72. *Recreations:* walking, painting, sailing. *Address:* 26 Grove Farm Park, Batchworth Lane, Northwood, Mddx. *T:* Northwood 21281.

TAYLOR, Hon. Sir Peter (Murray), Kt 1980; **Hon. Mr Justice Taylor;** a Judge of the High Court of Justice, Queen's Bench Division, since 1980; *b* 1 May 1930; *s* of Herman Louis Taylor, medical practitioner and Raie Helena Taylor (*née* Shockett); *m* 1956, Irene Shirley, *d* of Lionel and Mary Harris; one *s* three *d. Educ:* Newcastle upon Tyne Royal Gram. Sch.; Pembroke Coll., Cambridge (Exhibr). Called to Bar, Inner Temple, 1954, Bencher, 1975; QC 1967; Vice-Chm. of the Bar, 1978-79, Chm., 1979-80. Recorder of: Huddersfield, 1969-70; Teesside, 1970-71; Dep. Chm., Northumberland QS, 1970-71; a Recorder of the Crown Court, 1972-80. Leader of NE Circuit, 1975-80. *Recreation:* music. *Address:* Royal Courts of Justice, Strand, WC2A 2LL. *Club:* Garrick.

TAYLOR, Peter William Edward, QC 1981; *b* 27 July 1917; *s* of the late Peter and Julia A. Taylor; *m* 1948, Julia Mary Brown, *d* of Air Cdre Sir Vernon Brown, *qv* ; two *s. Educ:* Peter Symonds' Sch., Winchester; Christ's Coll., Cambridge (MA; Wrangler, Math. Tripos, Part II; 1st Class, Law Tripos, Part II). Served RA, 1939-46: France and Belgium, 1939-40; N Africa, 1942-43; NW Europe, 1944-45 (mentioned in dispatches); Actg Lt-Col 1945; transferred to TARO as Hon. Major, 1946. Called to the Bar, Inner Temple, 1946; Lincoln's Inn, *ad eundem,* 1953 (Bencher, 1976); practice at the Bar, 1947-; Occasional Lectr, LSE, 1946-56; Lectr in Construction of Documents, Council of Legal Educn, 1952-70; Conveyancing Counsel of the Court,

1974-81. Member: General Council of the Bar, 1971-74; Senate of Inns of Court and the Bar, 1974-75; Inter-Professional Cttee on Retirement Provision, 1974-; Land Registration Rule Cttee, 1976-81; Incorporated Council of Law Reporting, 1977-; Council, Selden Soc., 1977-. *Recreations:* sailing, shooting, music. *Address:* 46 Onslow Square, SW7 3NX. *T:* 01-589 1301; Carey Sconce, Yarmouth, Isle of Wight.

TAYLOR, Philippe Arthur; Director, Birmingham Convention and Visitor Bureau Ltd; Managing Director, Taylor and Partners Ltd, since 1980; *b* 9 Feb. 1937; *s* of Arthur Peach Taylor and Simone Vacquin; *m* 1973, Margaret Nancy Wilkins; two *s. Educ:* Trinity College, Glenalmond; St Andrews University. Procter & Gamble, 1963; Masius International, 1967; British Tourist Authority, 1970; Chief Executive, Scottish Tourist Board, 1975-80. *Publications:* childrens' books; various papers and articles on tourism. *Recreations:* sailing, making things, tourism, reading. *Address:* Cadogan House, Beauchamp Avenue, Leamington Spa, Warwickshire. *Clubs:* Royal Yachting Association; Royal Northumberland Yacht (Blyth).

TAYLOR, Phyllis Mary Constance, MA; Headmistress, Wanstead High School, London Borough of Redbridge, since 1976; *b* 29 Sept. 1926; *d* of Cecil and Constance Tedder; *m* 1949, Peter Royston Taylor; one *s. Educ:* Woodford High Sch.; Sudbury High Sch., Suffolk; Girton Coll., Cambridge (State Scholar; BA Hons History, 1948; MA 1951). Asst Hist. Mistress, Loughton High Sch., 1948-51, Head of Hist., 1951-58; Teacher of Hist. and Religious Educn, Lancaster Royal Grammar Sch. for Boys, 1959; Head of Hist., Casterton Sch. (private boarding), Kirby Lonsdale, 1960; Teacher of Gen. Subjects, Lancaster Girls' Grammar Sch., 1960-61, Head of Hist., 1961-62; Dep. Headmistress, Carlisle Sch., Chelsea, 1962-64; Headmistress, Walthamstow High Sch. for Girls, 1964-68, and Walthamstow Sen. High Sch., 1968-75. Consultant Head to NE London Polytechnic (Counselling/Careers sect.), 1974-78; Moderator, Part-time Diploma, Pastoral Care and Counselling, 1979-. Pres., Essex Sector, Secondary Heads' Assoc., 1978-79. Mem., UGC, 1978-; Mem., Teacher Trng Sub-Cttee, Adv. Cttee on Supply and Educn of Teachers; former Mem., Nat. Exec., Assoc. of Head Mistresses. *Recreations:* music, theatre, horse riding, driving, country life, ecology. *Address:* White Horses, High Roding, Great Dunmow, Essex. *T:* Great Dunmow 3161.

TAYLOR, Robert Carruthers; a Recorder of the Crown Court, since 1976; *b* 6 Jan. 1939; *o s* of John Houston Taylor, CBE, TD, MA, DL and Barbara Mary Taylor; *m* 1968, Jacqueline Marjorie, *er d* of Nigel and Marjorie Chambers; one *s* one *d. Educ:* Moorlands School, Leeds; Wycliffe Coll.; St John's Coll., Oxford (Exhibnr). MA 1967. Called to Bar, Middle Temple, 1961; Member, NE Circuit, 1962- (Junior, 1964); Prosecuting Counsel to Inland Revenue, NE Circuit, 1978-. Chm., Agricl Land Tribunal, Yorks and Lancs Area, 1979-82, Yorks and Humberside Area, 1982-; Asst Parly Boundary Comr, Rotherham, 1981, Sheffield, Bolton, 1982. *Recreations:* reading, music, spectating, gardening, domestic life. *Address:* 37 Park Square, Leeds LS1 2PB. *T:* Leeds 452702; 2 Harcourt Buildings, Temple, EC47 7BE. *T:* 01-353 2548. *Club:* Leeds (Leeds).

TAYLOR, Sir Robert (Mackinlay), Kt 1963; CBE 1956; Chairman, Thomas Tilling Ltd, since 1976; Senior Deputy Chairman: Standard Chartered Bank plc, since 1974; Standard Bank, since 1974; Chartered Bank, since 1974; Director: Standard Bank Investment Corporation, Johannesburg; Standard Bank of South Africa; *b* 29 Sept. 1912; *s* of late Commander R. M. Taylor, DSC, Royal Navy, and late Mrs Taylor; *m* 1944, Alda Cecilia Ignesti; one *d. Educ:* Plymouth College; Hele's School, Exeter; University Coll. of the SW, Exeter (MSc(Econ.) London). Entered Home CS, 1937; transf. Colonial Service, 1948. Dep. Comr, Nat. Savings Cttee, 1939. War Service, 1939-46; Commnd 2 Lieut, RA, 1940; Occupied Enemy Territory Admin., Eritrea, 1941-43, Finance Officer (Major); Dep. Controller Finance and Accounts (Lt-Col), Brit. Somaliland, Reserved Areas of Ethiopia, Italian Somaliland, 1943-45; Controller, Finance and Accounts (Col) E Africa Comd, 1945, Middle East Comd, 1945-46. Economic Adviser, Govt of Fiji, 1947; Fin. Sec., Fiji, 1948-52; Fin. Sec., N Rhodesia, 1952-58; seconded to Govt of Fedn of Rhodesia and Nyasaland, 1953; Sec. for Transport until end 1954; thereafter Sec. to Federal Treasury; retd from HMOCS, Dec. 1958. Chm., Richard Costain Ltd, 1969-73. Mem. Adv. Commn on Review of Constitution of Rhodesia and Nyasaland (Monckton Commn), 1960. *Publication:* A Social Survey of Plymouth, 1937. *Recreation:* golf. *Address:* Flat 8, 24 Park Road, NW1. *Clubs:* Athenæum, Naval and Military; MCC; Salisbury (Zimbabwe).

TAYLOR, Robert Martin, OBE 1976; Editorial Director, The Croydon Advertiser Ltd, 1967-76; *b* 25 Nov. 1914; *s* of Ernest H. and Charlotte Taylor; *m* 1947, Ray Turney; one *s* one *d. Educ:* Simon Langton, Canterbury. Croydon Advertiser: Editor, 1950-58; Managing Editor, 1958-74; Dir, 1967-76. Mem., Nat. Council for the Training of Journalists, 1967-71; Pres., Guild of British Newspaper Editors, 1971-72, Hon. Vice-Pres., 1976; Mem., Press Council, 1974-76. *Publication:* Editor and co-author, Essential Law for Journalists, 1954, 6th edn 1975. *Address:* Glengarry, Milton, Drumnadrochit, Inverness-shire. *T:* Drumnadrochit 291.

TAYLOR, Robert Richardson, QC (Scotland) 1959; MA, LLB, PhD; Sheriff-Principal of Tayside Central and Fife, since 1975; *b* 16 Sept. 1919; *m* 1949, Märtha Birgitta Björkling; two *s* one *d. Educ:* Glasgow High School; Glasgow University. Called to Bar, Scotland, 1944; called to Bar, Middle

Temple, 1948. Lectr in Internat. Private Law, Edinburgh Univ., 1947-69; Sheriff-Principal, Stirling, Dunbarton and Clackmannan, 1971-75. Contested (U and NL): Dundee East, 1955; Dundee West, 1959 and Nov. 1963. Chm., Central and Southern Region, Scottish Cons. Assoc., 1969-71. *Recreations:* fishing, ski-ing. *Address:* 51 Northumberland Street, Edinburgh. *T:* 031-556 1722.

TAYLOR, (Robert) Ronald, CBE 1971; Chairman: Robert Taylor Ironfounders (Holdings) Ltd; Tayforth Foundry Ltd; *b* 25 Aug. 1916; *e s* of late Robert Taylor, ironfounder, Larbert; *m* 1941, Margaret, *d* of late William Purdie, Coatbridge; two *s* two *d. Educ:* High Sch., Stirling. Chm., Glenrothes Develt Corp., 1964-78. *Recreations:* fishing, shooting, golf. *Address:* Beoraid, Caledonian Crescent, Auchterarder, Perthshire. *Club:* Army and Navy.

TAYLOR, Rt. Rev. Robert Selby; see Zambia, Central, Bishop of.

TAYLOR, Ronald; see Taylor, R. R.

TAYLOR, Rupert Sutton, OBE 1945; TD (three bars) 1943; FDSRCS; MRCS, LRCP; Hon. Consulting Dental Surgeon, Westminster Hospital Teaching Group and Seamen's Hospital Group, 1970; Consultant Dental Surgeon, Westminster Hospital, 1937-70, Seamen's Hospital, 1930-70; Recognised Teacher, University of London, since 1948; *b* 18 July 1905; *s* of G. W. and M. F. Taylor; *m* 1951, Mary Angela Tebbs. *Educ:* Newtown School, Waterford; Middlesex Hospital; Royal Dental Hospital. LDS 1928; commissioned RAMC, TA (Hygiene Coys), 1928; Dental Ho. Surg., Middlesex Hosp., 1928; Clin. Asst, Dental Dept, Westminster Hosp., 1929-31; Sen. Clin. Asst. to Dental Surgeon, Nose, Ear, and Throat Hosp., Golden Square, 1931-32; Hon. Dental Surgeon, Nat. Hosp., Queen's Square, 1933-37. External Examr Dental Surgery and Materia Medica, Queen's Univ., Belfast, 1938-39 and 1945-48. Dental Member, London Exec. Council (National Health Service), 1948-62; Chm. London Executive Council, 1953 and 1954-Mar. 1956 (Vice-Chm., 1951-53); FDS, RCS (by election), 1948. Served with RAMC War of 1939-45; Major, 1938-42, Lt-Col, 1942-45; commanded 127 Light Field Amb. and 146 Field Amb.; 161 Field Ambulance, TA, 1957-58; Hon. Col Medical Units 54 (EA) Infantry division, 1959-66. OStJ 1959; CStJ 1961. *Publications:* various articles on oral surgery. *Recreations:* sailing, fishing. *Address:* Thie-ny-Chibbyr, Lezayre Road, Ramsey, Isle of Man. *T:* Ramsey, IoM 812585. *Club:* Savage.

TAYLOR, Selwyn Francis, DM, MCh, FRCS; Dean Emeritus and Fellow, Royal Postgraduate Medical School, London; Senior Lecturer in Surgery, and Surgeon, Hammersmith Hospital; Emeritus Consultant to Royal Navy; Member, Armed Forces Medical Advisory Board; Examiner in Surgery, Universities of Oxford, London, Manchester, Leeds, National University of Ireland, West Indies, Makerere and Society of Apothecaries; *b* Sale, Cheshire, 16 Sept. 1913; *s* of late Alfred Petre Taylor and Emily Taylor, Salcombe, Devon; *m* 1939, Ruth Margaret, 2nd *d* of late Sir Alfred Howitt, CVO; one *s* one *d. Educ:* Peter Symonds, Winchester; Keble College, Oxford; King's College Hospital. BA (Hons) Oxford, 1936; Burney Yeo Schol., King's Coll. Hosp., 1936; MA Oxon; MRCS, LRCP, 1939; FRCS 1940; MCh, 1946; DM 1959. Surgical Registrar, King's Coll. Hosp., 1946-47; Oxford Univ. George Herbert Hunt Travelling Schol., Stockholm, 1947; Rockefeller Travelling Fellow in Surgery, 1948-49; Research Fellow, Harvard Univ., and Fellow in Clin. Surgery, Massachusetts Gen. Hosp., Boston, Mass, USA, 1948-49. RNVR, 1940-46; Surgeon Lt-Comdr; Surgeon Specialist, Kintyre, East Indies, Australia; Surgeon: Belgrave Hosp. for Children, 1946-65; King's Coll. Hospital, 1951-65. Bradshaw Lectr, RCS, 1977. President: Harveian Soc., 1969; Internat. Assoc. Endocrine Surgeons, 1979-81; Member: Council, RCS, 1966- (Senior Vice-Pres., 1976-77 and 1977-78; Joll Prize, 1976); GMC, 1974-; Surgical Research Soc.; Internat. Soc. for Surgery; Fellow Assoc. Surgeons of GB; FRSM; Hon. FRCSE 1976; Hon. FCS (S Africa) 1978; Corresp. Fellow Amer. Thyroid Assoc.; Pres., London Thyroid Club and Sec., Fourth Internat. Goitre Conference. Mem., Senate of London Univ., 1970-75. Chm., Heinemann Medical Books. *Publications:* books and papers on surgical subjects and thyroid physiology. *Recreations:* sailing, tennis, wine. *Address:* Trippets, Bosham, West Sussex. *T:* Bosham 573387. *Clubs:* Garrick, Hurlingham; Bosham Sailing (Trustee).

TAYLOR, Maj.-Gen. Walter Reynell, CB 1981; Chief of Staff, HQ British Army of the Rhine, since 1980; *b* 5 April 1928; *s* of Col Richard Reynell Taylor and Margaret Catherine Taylor (*née* Holme); *m* 1st, 1954, Doreen Myrtle Dodge; one *s* one *d* ; 2nd, 1982, Mrs Rosemary Gardner (*née* Breed). *Educ:* Wellington; RMC, Sandhurst. Commissioned 4th/7th Royal Dragoon Guards, Dec. 1948; Directing Staff, Staff Coll., 1963-66; GSO1 Jt Planning Staff, Far East Comd, 1967-69; Commanded: 4th/7th Royal Dragoon Guards, 1969-71; 12 Mechanised Bde, 1972-74; rcds 1975; Brig., Mil. Operations, MoD, 1976-78; Administrator, Sovereign Base Areas of Cyprus, Comdr British Forces and Land Forces, Cyprus, 1978-80. *Recreations:* sailing, riding, golf, polo. *Address:* 3 Blenheim Road, Chiswick, W4. *Club:* Special Forces.

TAYLOR, Walter Ross; see Ross Taylor.

TAYLOR, Wendy Ann; sculptor; Member: Fine Art Board, Council of National Academic Awards, since 1980; Royal Fine Art Commission, since 1981; *b* 29 July 1945; *d* of Edward Philip Taylor and Lilian Maude Wright. *Educ:* St Martin's School of Art. LDAD (Hons). One-man exhibitions: Axiom

Gall., London, 1970; Angela Flowers Gall., London, 1972; 24th King's Lynn Fest., Norfolk, and World Trade Centre, London, 1974; Annely Juda Fine Art, London, 1975; Oxford Gall., Oxford, 1976; Oliver Dowling Gall., Dublin, 1976 and 1979. Shown in over 100 group exhibitions, 1964-82. Represented in collections in GB, USA, Eire, NZ, Germany, Sweden, Qatar, Switzerland, Seychelles. Major commissions: The Travellers 1969, London; Gazebo (edn of 4) 1970-72, London, New York, Suffolk, Oxford; Triad 1971, Oxford; Timepiece 1973, London; Calthae 1977, Leicestershire; Octo 1979, Milton Keynes; Counterpoise 1980, Birmingham; Compass Bowl 1980, Basildon; Sentinel 1981, Reigate; Bronze Relief 1981, Canterbury; Equatorial Sundial 1982, Bletchley; Essence 1982, Milton Keynes. Examiner, Univ. of London, 1982. Awards: Walter Neurath, 1964; Pratt, 1965; Sainsbury, 1966; Arts Council, 1977; Duais Na Riochta (Kingdom Prize) Gold Medal, Eire, 1977; 1st Prize Silk Screen, Barcham Green Print Comp., 1978. *Recreation:* gardening. *Address:* 96 Nightingale House, St Katherine-by-the-Tower, E1 9UB. *T:* 01-488 0955.

TAYLOR, Dr William, CBE 1982; Director, University of London Institute of Education, 1973-July 1983; Principal, University of London, from Aug. 1983; *b* 31 May 1930; *s* of Herbert and Maud E. Taylor, Crayford, Kent; *m* 1954, Rita, *d* of Ronald and Marjorie Hague, Sheffield; one *s* two *d. Educ:* Erith Grammar Sch.; London Sch. of Economics; Westminster Coll.; Univ. of London Inst. of Educn. BSc Econ 1952, PhD 1960. Teaching in Kent, 1953-56; Deputy Head, Slade Green Secondary Sch., 1956-59; Sen. Lectr, St Luke's Coll., Exeter, 1959-61; Head of Educn Dept, Bede Coll., Durham, 1961-64; Tutor and Lectr in Educn, Univ. of Oxford, 1964-66; Prof. of Educn and Dir of Sch. of Educn, Univ. of Bristol, 1966-73. Research Consultant, Dept of Educn and Science (part-time), 1968-73; Chm., European Cttee for Educnl Research, 1969-71. UK Rep., Permanent Educn Steering Cttee, Council of Europe, 1971-73; Chairman: UK Nat. Commn for UNESCO, 1975- (Mem., 1973-); Educnl Adv. Council, IBA, 1974-82; UCET, 1976-79. Member: UGC Educn Cttee, 1971-80; British Library Res. and Develt Cttee, 1975-79; Open Univ. Academic Adv. Cttee, 1975-; SSRC Educnl Research Board, 1976-80 (Vice-Chm., 1978-80); Adv. Cttee on Supply and Training of Teachers, 1976-79; Teacher Educn Adv. Cttee, 1977-; Working Gp on Management of Higher Educn, 1977-78; Steering Cttee on Future of Examinations at 16+, 1977-78; Cttee of Vice-Chancellors and Principals, 1980-; Adv. Cttee on Supply and Educn of Teachers (Sec. of State's nominee), 1980-. Mem. Senate, Univ. of London, 1977-, Cttee on Management, Inst. of Advanced Legal Studies, 1980-. Commonwealth Vis. Fellow, Australian States, 1975; NZ UGC Prestige Fellowship, 1977. President: Council for Educn in World Citizenship, 1979-; English New Educn Fellowship, 1979-; Comparative Educn Soc. of GB, 1981-. Governor, Wye Coll., 1981-. Hon. DSc Aston (Birmingham), 1977; Hon. LittD Leeds, 1979; Hon. DCL Kent, 1981. Hon. FCP 1977. Hon. FCCEA 1980. *Publications:* The Secondary Modern School, 1963; Society and the Education of Teachers, 1969; (ed with G. Baron) Educational Administration and the Social Sciences, 1969; Heading for Change, 1969; Planning and Policy in Post Secondary Education, 1972; Theory into Practice, 1972; Research Perspectives in Education, 1973; (ed with R. Farquhar and R. Thomas) Educational Administration in Australia and Abroad, 1975; Research and Reform in Teacher Education, 1978; (ed with B. Simon) Education in the Eighties: the central issues, 1981; (ed) The Metaphors of Education, 1983. *Recreations:* writing, walking. *Address:* (until July 1983) Institute of Education, Bedford Way, WC1H 0AL. *T:* 01-636 1500; (from Aug. 1983) Senate House, Malet Street, WC1E 7HU.

TAYLOR, William Bernard; Treasurer, Kent County Council, since 1980; *b* 13 Dec. 1930; *s* of Frank and Elizabeth Taylor; *m* 1956, Rachel May Davies; one *s* two *d. Educ:* Dynevor Sch., Swansea; Univ. of Kent. MA; IPFA, FBIM. Nat. Service, RN, 1949-51; commnd RNVR; served in coastal forces. District Audit Service, 1951-61; Llwchwr UDC, 1961-70; Asst Educn Officer, Manchester Corp., 1970-72; Asst County Treasurer, 1972-73, Dep. County Treasurer, 1973-80, Kent. Mem., Rotary Club. *Publications:* The Management of Assets: terotechnology in the pursuit of economic life cycle costs, 1980; contribs to local govt and other learned journals. *Recreations:* cricket, Rugby, public speaking. *Address:* Little Dossit, Workhouse Lane, East Farleigh, near Maidstone, Kent ME15 0PZ. *T:* Maidstone 45022.

TAYLOR, Lt-Comdr William Horace, GC 1941; MBE 1973; Commissioner of the Scout Association, since 1946; *b* 23 Oct. 1908; *s* of William Arthur Taylor; *m* 1946, Joan Isabel Skaife d'Ingerthorpe; one *s* three *d. Educ:* Manchester Grammar Sch. Junior Partner, 1929; Managing Dir, 1937. Served War: Dept of Torpedoes and Mines, Admiralty, 1940 (despatches, 1941); Founder Mem., Naval Clearance Divers, HMS Vernon (D), 1944. Travelling Commissioner for Sea Scouts of UK, 1946; Field Commissioner for SW England, Scout Association, 1952-74, Estate Manager, 1975-. *Recreations:* scouting, boating, music. *Address:* The Bungalow, Carbeth, Blanefield, near Glasgow. *T:* Blanefield 70847. *Clubs:* Naval; Manchester Cruising Association.

TAYLOR, William Leonard, CBE 1982; JP; DL; solicitor in private practice; *b* 21 Dec. 1916; *s* of Joseph and May Taylor; *m* 1943, Gladys Carling; one *s. Educ:* Whitehill School; Glasgow Univ. (BL). Chairman: Livingston Develt Corp., 1965-72; Scottish Water Adv. Cttee, 1969-72; Mem., Scottish Adv. Cttee on Civil Aviation, 1965-72; Chm., Panel of Assessors, River Clyde Planning Study, 1972-74. Chairman: Planning Exchange, 1972-; Scottish Adv. Council on Social Work, 1974-81; Vice-Chm., Commn for Local Authority Accounts in Scotland, 1974-; Mem., Housing Corp., 1974-80; Chm. Scottish

Special Housing Assoc., 1978-81; Member: Scottish Economic Council, 1975-81; Extra-Parly Panel under Private Legislation Procedure (Scotland) Act 1936, 1971-. Councillor, City of Glasgow, 1952-69; Magistrate, City of Glasgow, 1956-60; Sen. Magistrate, 1960-61; Leader, Labour Gp in Glasgow Corp., 1962-69; Leader of Council, 1962-68; Convener of Cttees: Planning, Glasgow Airport, Sports Centre, Parly Bills. Governor, Centre for Environmental Studies, 1966-79; Trustee, Scottish Civic Trust, 1967-; Chm., Glasgow Citizens' Theatre Ltd, 1970-; Mem., Nat. Executive (and Chm. Scottish Exec.), Town & Country Planning Assoc. Hon. Vice-Pres., Scotland-USSR Friendship Soc. Hon. FRTPI. JP 1953; DL Glasgow, 1971. Knight, Order of Polonia Restituta (Poland), 1969. *Recreations:* fishing, theatre, reading. *Address:* Cruachan, 18 Bruce Road, Glasgow G41 5EF. *T:* 041-429 1776. *Clubs:* Arts, Carrick (Glasgow).

TAYLOR, Mrs (Winifred) Ann; MP (Lab) Bolton West, since Oct. 1974; *b* Motherwell, 2 July 1947. *Educ:* Bolton Sch.; Bradford Univ.; Sheffield Univ. Formerly teaching. Past part-time Tutor, Open Univ.; interested in housing, regional policy, and education. Member: Association of Univ. Teachers; APEX; Holmfirth Urban District Council, 1972-74. Contested (Lab) Bolton West, Feb. 1974. PPS to Sec. of State for Educn and Science, 1975-76; PPS to Sec. of State for Defence, 1976-77; an Asst Govt Whip, 1977-79; Opposition spokesman on Education, 1979, on Housing, 1980-. *Address:* Glyn Garth, Stoney Bank Road, Thongsbridge, Huddersfield, Yorks; c/o House of Commons, SW1. *Club:* Labour (Bolton).

TAYLOR-SMITH, Prof. Ralph Emeric Kasope; Professor of Chemistry, Fourah Bay College, University of Sierra Leone, since 1980 (formerly Associate Professor, on leave, as Ambassador of Sierra Leone to Peking, 1971-74, High Commissioner in London for Sierra Leone, and Ambassador to Norway, Sweden and Denmark, 1974-78); *b* 24 Sept. 1924; *m* 1953, Sarian Dorothea; five *s. Educ:* CMS Grammar Sch., Sierra Leone; Univ. of London (BSc (2nd Cl. Hons Upper Div.); PhD (Org. Chem.)). CChem, FRSC. Analytical chemist, 1954; Demonstrator, Woolwich Polytechnic, 1956-59; Lectr, Fourah Bay Coll., Sierra Leone, 1959-62 and 1963; post-doctoral Fellow, Weizmann Inst. of Sci., 1962-63; Research Associate, Princeton Univ., 1965-69; Fourah Bay College: Sen. Lectr, 1965; Dean, Faculty of Pure and Applied Sci., 1967; Associate Prof., 1968 and 1969; Visiting Prof., Kalamazoo Coll., Mich, 1969. Service in academic and public cttees, including: Mem. Council, Fourah Bay Coll., 1963-65 and 1967-69; Member: Senate, 1967-69, Court, 1967-69, Univ. of Sierra Leone; Mem., Student Welfare Cttee, 1967-69; Univ. Rep., Sierra Leone Govt Schol. Cttee, 1965-68; Mem., Bd of Educn, 1970. Pres., Teaching Staff Assoc., Fourah Bay Coll., 1971. Chm., Sierra Leone Petroleum Refining Co., 1970. Delegate or observer to academic confs, 1958-69, incl. those of W African Science Assoc., and Commonwealth Univ. Conf., Sydney, Aust., 1968. Fellow, Thames Polytechnic, 1975; FRSA 1979. *Publications:* papers to learned jls, especially on Investigations on Plants of West Africa. *Recreations:* tennis, swimming. *Address:* Department of Chemistry, Fourah Bay College, University of Sierra Leone, Private Mail Bag, Freetown, Sierra Leone.

TAYLOR THOMPSON, John Derek; Commissioner of Inland Revenue, since 1973; *b* 6 Aug. 1927; *o s* of John Taylor Thompson and Marjorie (*née* Westcott); *m* 1954, Helen Laurie Walker; two *d. Educ:* St Peter's Sch., York; Balliol Coll., Oxford. MA. Asst Principal, Inland Revenue, 1951; Private Sec. to Chm., 1954; Private Sec. to Minister without Portfolio, 1962; Asst Sec., Inland Revenue, 1965. *Recreations:* rural pursuits, reading. *Address:* Jessops, Nutley, Sussex. *Club:* United Oxford & Cambridge University.

TAYLORSON, John Brown; Head of Catering Services, British Airways, since 1981; *b* 5 March 1931; *s* of John Brown Taylorson and Edith Maria Taylorson; *m* 1960, Barbara June (*née* Hagg) (marr. diss.); one *s* one *d. Educ:* Forest School, Snaresbrook; Hotel School, Westminster. Sales Director, Gardner Merchant Food Services Ltd, 1970-73; Managing Director: International Division, Gardner Merchant Food Services, 1973-77; Fedics Food Services, 1977-80; Chief Executive, Civil Service Catering Organisation, 1980-81. *Recreations:* squash, tennis, theatre, crossword puzzles. *Address:* 14 Park Road, Esher, Surrey KT10 8NP. *T:* Esher 62802. *Clubs:* Old Foresters; Lingfield Park Squash; Wanderers (RSA).

TAYLOUR, family name of Marquess of Headfort.

TEAGUE, Colonel John, CMG 1958; CBE 1946 (OBE 1925); MC 1916; Retired; *b* 16 Nov. 1896; *y s* of William and Helen Teague; *m* 1st, 1926, Heather Fairley (*d* 1966), *d* of late Captain James William Fairley, Tunbridge Wells; two *s* one *d*; 2nd, 1973, Mrs Nora Ballard. *Educ:* Portsmouth Grammar School. Studied music under Dr A. K. Blackall, FRAM, and was his Assistant Organist at St Mary's, Warwick, 1913. Commissioned Royal Warwickshire Regt, 1914; served in France, 1915-17 (wounded twice, despatches, MC). Transf. Indian Army (Baluch Regt). With Sykes' Mission in South Persia and Staff Capt., Shiraz Brigade, 1918. Attached Indian Political Service as Vice-Consul Shiraz, 1919. Iraq Insurrection (despatches) 1920. General Staff (intelligence), GHQ Baghdad, 1920, later with RAF, Iraq, Kurdistan Operations (severely wounded), 1922. NW Frontier, India, 1930. Language student in Persia (Interpreter), 1933. Liaison Officer, RAF Palestine during Arab Revolt, 1936-39. GHQ, Middle East, 1942. Transferred to Foreign Office, 1945. Director, Passport Control, 1953-58. Polonia Restituta, 1945; Legion of Merit (USA), 1946; White Lion (Czechoslovakia), 1947. *Publications:* occasional articles for press about Middle East. *Recreations:*

music, reading and walking. *Address:* 5 Hungershall Park, Tunbridge Wells, Kent. *T:* Tunbridge Wells 26959. *Club:* Royal Air Force.

TEAR, Robert; concert and operatic tenor; *b* 8 March 1939; *s* of Thomas Arthur and Edith Tear; *m* 1961, Hilary Thomas; two *d. Educ:* Barry Grammar Sch.; King's Coll., Cambridge (MA). Hon. RCM, RAM. FRSA. Mem., King's Coll. Choir, 1957-60; subseq. St Paul's Cathedral and solo career; joined English Opera Group, 1964. By 1968 worked with world's leading conductors, notably Karajan, Giulini, Bernstein and Solti; during this period created many rôles in operas by Benjamin Britten. Has appeared in all major festivals; close association with Sir Michael Tippett, 1970-; Covent Garden: début, The Knot Garden, 1970, closely followed by Lensky in Eugène Onégin; Fledermaus, 1977; Peter Grimes, 1978; Rake's Progress, 1979; Thérèse, 1979; Loge in Rheingold, 1980; Admetus in Alceste, 1981; David in Die Meistersinger, 1982; Captain Vere in Billy Budd, 1982; appears regularly with Royal Opera. Started relationship with Scottish Opera (singing in La Traviata, Alceste, Don Giovanni), 1974. Paris Opera: début, 1976; Lulu 1979. Début as conductor with Thames Chamber Orchestra, QEH, 1980. Has worked with every major recording co. and made numerous recordings (incl. solo recital discs). *Publication:* Victorian Songs and Duets, 1980. *Recreations:* any sport; interested in 18th and 19th century English water colours. *Address:* 11 Ravenscourt Square, W6. *T:* 01-748 6130. *Club:* Garrick.

TEARE, Dr (Hugo) Douglas, CVO 1973; MHK 1981; Physician Superintendent, King Edward VII Hospital, Midhurst, Sussex, 1971-77; *b* 20 April 1917; *s* of A. H. Teare, JP, and Margaret Green; *m* 1945, Evelyn Bertha Hider; three *s. Educ:* King William's Coll., Isle of Man; Gonville and Caius Coll., Cambridge; St George's Hospital, London. BA 1938; MRCS, LRCP 1941; MB, BChir 1942. House Physician and Casualty Officer, St George's Hospital, 1941; Resident Surgical Officer and Med. Registrar, Brompton Hospital, 1943; Dep. Med. Superintendent, King Edward VII Hospital (Sanatorium), Midhurst, 1946-70. OStJ. *Recreation:* golf. *Address:* Lismore, 6 St Olave's Close, Ramsey, Isle of Man. *T:* Ramsey 812065.

TE ATAIRANGIKAAHU, Arikinui, DBE 1970; Arikinui and Head of Maori Kingship, since 1966; *b* 23 July 1931; *o d* of King Koroki V; *m* 1952, Whatumoana; two *s* five *d. Educ:* Waikato Diocesan School, Hamilton, NZ. Elected by the Maori people as Head of the Maori Kingship on the death of King Koroki, the fifth Maori King, with title of Arikinui (Queen), in 1966. *Recreation:* the fostering of all aspects of Maori culture and traditions. Hon. Dr Waikato, 1979. *Heir: s* Tuheitia, *b* 21 April 1955. *Address:* Turongo House, Turangawaewae Marae, Ngaruawahia, New Zealand.

TEBALDI, Renata; Italian Soprano; *b* Pesaro, Italy, 1 Feb. 1922; *o c* of Teobaldo and Giuseppina (Barbieri) Tebaldi. Studied at Arrigo Boito Conservatory, Parma; Gioacchino Rossini Conservatory, Pesaro; subsequently a pupil of Carmen Melis and later of Giuseppe Pais. Made professional début as Elena in Mefistofele, Rovigo, 1944. First sang at La Scala, Milan, at post-war reopening concert (conductor Toscanini), 1946. Has sung at Covent Garden and in opera houses of Naples, Rome, Venice, Pompeii, Turin, Cesana, Modena, Bologna and Florence; toured England, France, Spain and South America. American début in title rôle Aida, San Francisco, 1950; Metropolitan Opera House Season, New York, 1955. Recordings of complete operas include: Otello; Adriana Lecouvreur; Il Trittico; Don Carlo; La Gioconda; Un Ballo in Maschera; Madame Butterfly; Mefistofele; La Fanciulla Del West; La Forza Del Destino; Andrea Chenier; Manon Lescaut; La Tosca; Il Trovatore; Aida, La Bohème. *Address:* c/o S. A. Gorlinsky Ltd, 35 Dover Street, W1; 1 Piazza della Guastella, Milan, Italy.

TEBBIT, Sir Donald (Claude), GCMG 1980 (KCMG 1975; CMG 1965); HM Diplomatic Service, retired; Director General, British Property Federation, since 1980; *b* 4 May 1920; *m* 1947, Barbara Margaret Olson Matheson; one *s* three *d. Educ:* Perse School; Trinity Hall, Cambridge (MA). Served War of 1939-45, RNVR. Joined Foreign (now Diplomatic) Service, 1946; Second Secretary, Washington, 1948; transferred to Foreign Office, 1951; First Secretary, 1952; transferred to Bonn, 1954; Private Secretary to Minister of State, Foreign Office, 1958; Counsellor, 1962; transferred to Copenhagen, 1964; Commonwealth Office, 1967; Asst Under-Sec. of State, FCO, 1968-70; Minister, British Embassy, Washington, 1970-72; Chief Clerk, FCO, 1972-76; High Comr in Australia, 1976-80. Chm., Diplomatic Service Appeals Bd, 1980-; Mem., Appeals Bd, Council of Europe, 1981-. Dir, Rio Tinto Zinc Corp., 1980-. Pres. (UK), Australian-British Trade Assoc., 1980-; Governor, Nuffield Nursing Homes Trust, 1980-; Pres., Old Persean Soc., 1981-82. *Address:* Priory Cottage, Toft, Cambridge CB3 7RH; 35 Buckingham Gate, SW1E 6PA.

TEBBIT, Rt. Hon. Norman (Beresford), PC 1981; MP (C) Waltham Forest, Chingford, since 1974 (Epping, 1970-74); Secretary of State for Employment, since 1981; journalist; *b* 29 March 1931; 2nd *s* of Leonard and Edith Tebbit, Enfield; *m* 1956, Margaret Elizabeth Daines; two *s* one *d. Educ:* Edmonton County Grammar Sch. Embarked on career in journalism, 1947. Served RAF: commissioned GD Branch; qualif. Pilot, 1949-51; Reserve service R.AuxAF, No 604 City of Mddx Sqdn, 1952-55. Entered and left publishing and advertising, 1951-53. Civil Airline Pilot, 1953-70 (Mem. BALPA; former holder various offices in that Assoc.). Active mem. and former holder various offices, Conservative Party, 1946-. PPS to Minister of State, Dept of Employment, 1972-73; Parly Under Sec. of State, Dept of Trade, 1979-81; Minister of State, Dept of Industry, 1981. Former Chm., Cons. Members

Aviation Cttee; former Vice-Chm. and Sec., Cons. Members Housing and Construction Cttee; Sec. House of Commons New Town Members Cttee. *Address:* House of Commons, SW1.

TEBBLE, Norman, DSc; FRSE; FIBiol; Director, Royal Scottish Museum, since 1971; *b* 17 Aug. 1924; 3rd *s* of late Robert Soulsby Tebble and Jane Anne (*née* Graham); *m* 1954, Mary Olivia Archer, *o d* of H. B. and J. I. Archer, Kenilworth; two *s* one *d. Educ:* Bedlington Grammar School; St Andrews Univ.; BSc 1950, DSc 1968; MA, Merton Coll., Oxford, 1971; FIBiol 1971, FRSE 1976. St Andrews Univ. Air Squadron, 1942-43; Pilot, RAFVR, Canada, India and Burma, 1943-46. Scientific Officer, British Museum (Natural History), 1950, Curator of Annelida; John Murray Travelling Student in Oceanography, Royal Soc., 1958; Vis. Curator, Univ. of California, Scripps Inst. of Oceanography, 1959; Curator of Molluscs, British Museum, 1961; Univ. Lecturer in Zoology and Curator, zoological collection, Univ. of Oxford, 1968; Curator, Oxford Univ. Museum, 1969. Member Council: Marine Biological Assoc., UK, 1963-66; Scottish Marine Biological Assoc., 1973-78; Museums Assoc., 1972- (Vice-Pres., 1976-77; Pres., 1977-78). *Publications:* (ed jtly) Speciation in the Sea, 1963; British Bivalve Seashells, 1966, 2nd edn 1976; (ed jtly) Bibliography British Fauna and Flora, 1967; scientific papers in Systematics of Annelida and Distribution in the World Oceans. *Recreations:* Tebbel-Tebble genealogy, gardening, walking. *Address:* 4 Bright's Crescent, Edinburgh EH9 2DB. *T:* 031-667 5260.

TEBBUTT, Dame Grace, DBE 1966 (CBE 1960); JP; Member of Sheffield City Council, 1929-67, Alderman, 1934-67; *b* 5 January 1893; *d* of Alfred and Ann Elizabeth Mellar; *m* 1913, Frank Tebbutt; two *d. Educ:* Coleridge Road School, Sheffield 9. Chairman: Parks Cttee, Sheffield, 1934-47 and 1950-55; Health Cttee, 1947-49; Children's Committee, 1956-67. Formerly: Vice-Chm., Nat. Bureau for Co-operation in Child Care; Mem., Home Office Central Adv. Council in Child Care and Central Training Council in Child Care. Lord Mayor of Sheffield, 1949-50; JP 1950; Hon. Freeman of Sheffield, 1959. Hon. LLD Sheffield Univ., 1965. *Address:* Edgelow, 501 Lowedges Crescent, Sheffield S8 7LN. *T:* Sheffield 746783.

TEDDER, family name of Baron Tedder.

TEDDER, 2nd Baron, *cr* 1946, of Glenguin; **John Michael Tedder,** MA, ScD, PhD, DSc; Purdie Professor of Chemistry, St Salvator's College, University of St Andrews, since 1969; *b* 4 July 1926; 2nd and *er surv. s* of 1st Baron Tedder, GCB, and Rosalinde (*née* Maclardy); *S* father, 1967; *m* 1952, Peggy Eileen Growcott; two *s* one *d. Educ:* Dauntsey's School, Wilts; Magdalene College, Cambridge (MA 1951; ScD 1965); University of Birmingham (PhD 1951; DSc 1961). Roscoe Professor of Chemistry, University of Dundee, 1964-69. Mem., Ct of Univ. of St Andrews, 1971-76. Vice-Pres., Perkin Div., RSC, 1980-. FRSE; FRSC. *Publications:* Valence Theory, 1966; Basic Organic Chemistry, 1966; The Chemical Bond, 1978; Radicals, 1979; papers in Jl of RSC and other scientific jls. *Heir: s* Hon. Robin John Tedder, *b* 6 April 1955. *Address:* Little Rathmore, Kennedy Gardens, St Andrews, Fife. *T:* St Andrews 73546; Department of Chemistry, St Salvator's College, St Andrews, Fife, Scotland. *T:* St Andrews 75771.

TEESDALE, Edmund Brinsley, CMG 1964; MC 1945; *b* 30 Sept. 1915; *s* of late John Herman Teesdale and late Winifred Mary (*née* Gull); *m* 1947, Joyce, *d* of late Walter Mills and of Mrs J. T. Murray; three *d. Educ:* Lancing; Trinity College, Oxford. Entered Colonial Administrative Service, Hong Kong, 1938. Active Service in Hong Kong, China, India, 1941-45. Subsequently various administrative posts in Hong Kong; Colonial Secretary, Hong Kong, 1963-65. Dir, Assoc. of British Pharmaceutical Industry, 1965-76. *Recreations:* gardening, swimming, reading. *Address:* The Hogge House, Buxted, Sussex.

TE HEUHEU, Sir Hepi (Hoani), KBE 1979; New Zealand sheep and cattle farmer; Paramount Chief of Ngati-Tuwharetoa tribe of Maoris; *b* 1919; *m* ; six *c.* Chairman: Tuwharetoa Maori Trust Board; Puketapu 3A Block (near Taupo); Rotoaira Lake Trust; Rotoaira Forest Trust; Tauranga-Taupo Trust; Motutere Point Trust; Turamakina Tribal Cttee; Lake Taupo Forest Trust; Oraukura 3 Block; Hauhungaroa 1C Block; Tuaropaki D2 Block; Member: Waitangi Trust Board; Maori Land Board; Waihi Pukawa Block; Tongariro National Park Board (great grandson of original donor). OStJ. *Address:* Taumarunui, New Zealand.

TEI ABAL, Sir, Kt 1976; CBE 1974; MHA, PNG; *b* 1932; *m* ; six *c.* Became a tea-planter and trader in Papua New Guinea; a Leader of the Engi Clan in Western Highlands. Member for Wabag, open electorate, PNG; Former Member (Ministerial) in 1st, 2nd and 3rd Houses of Assembly; Leader of the Opposition, UP, and later Minister of Public Utilities, 1979-80, in Somare Govt. *Address:* c/o PO Box 3534, Port Moresby, Papua New Guinea; Wabag, Papua New Guinea.

TEJAN-SIE, Sir Banja, GCMG 1970 (CMG 1967); Governor-General of Sierra Leone, 1971-72 (Acting Governor-General, 1968-70); international business and legal consultant; *b* 7 Aug. 1917; *s* of late Alpha Ahmed Tejan-Sie; *m* 1946, Admira Stapleton; three *s* one *d. Educ:* Bo Sch., Freetown; Prince of Wales Sch., Freetown; LSE, London University. Called to Bar, Lincoln's Inn, 1951. Station Clerk, Sierra Leone Railway,1938-39; Nurse, Medical Dept, 1940-46; Ed., West African Students' Union, 1948-51; Nat. Vice-Pres., Sierra Leone People's Party, 1953-56; Police Magistrate: Eastern Province, 1955;

Northern Province, 1958; Sen. Police Magistrate Provinces, 1961; Speaker, Sierra Leone House of Representatives, 1962-67; Chief Justice of Sierra Leone, 1967-70. Mem. Keith Lucas Commn on Electoral Reform, 1954. Hon. Sec. Sierra Leone Bar Assoc., 1957-58. Chm. Bd of Management, Cheshire Foundn, Sierra Leone, 1966. Has led delegations and paid official visits to many countries throughout the world. Hon. Treasurer, Internat. African Inst., London, 1978-. Pres., Freetown Golf Club, 1970-. GCFR (Nigeria), 1970; Grand Band, Order of Star of Africa (Liberia), 1969; Special Grand Cordon, Order of propitious clouds (Taiwan), 1970; Grand Cordon, Order of Knighthood of Pioneers (Liberia), 1970; Order of Cedar (Lebanon), 1970. *Recreations:* music, reading. *Address:* 3 Tracy Avenue, NW2. *T:* 01-452 2324. *Club:* Royal Commonwealth Society.

TE KANAWA, Dame Kiri, DBE 1982 (OBE 1973); opera singer; *b* Gisborne, New Zealand, 6 March 1944; *m* 1967, Desmond Stephen Park; one *s* one *d*. *Educ:* St Mary's Coll., Auckland, NZ; London Opera Centre. Major rôles at Royal Opera House, Covent Garden, include: the Countess, in Marriage of Figaro; Elvira, in Don Giovanni; Mimi, in La Bohème; Desdemona, in Otello; Marguerite, in Faust; Amelia, in Simon Boccanegra; Fiordiligi, in Cosi Fan Tutti; Tatiana, in Eugene Onegin; title rôle in Arabella; Rosalinde, in Die Fledermaus; Violetta, in La Traviata. Has sung leading rôles at Metropolitan Opera, New York, notably, Desdemona, Elvira, and Countess; also at the Paris Opera, Elvira, Fiordiligi and Pamina in Magic Flute, title rôle in Tosca; at San Francisco Opera, Amelia and Pamina; at Sydney Opera House, Mimi, Amelia, and Violetta in La Traviata; Elvira, with Cologne Opera; Amelia at la Scala, Milan; Countess in Le Nozze di Figaro at Salzburg fest. *Recreations:* golf, swimming. *Address:* c/o Basil Horsfield, L'Estoril (B), Avenue Princess Grace 31, Monte Carlo, Monaco.

TELFORD, Sir Robert, Kt 1978; CBE 1967; DL; FEng, FIProdE, CBIM, FRSA; Chairman: The Marconi Company Ltd, since 1981 (Managing Director, 1965-81); Marconi Avionics Ltd, since 1982; Managing Director, GEC-Marconi Electronics Ltd, since Dec. 1968; Director: The General Electric Co., since 1973; A. B. Dick Co., Chicago, since 1978; Canadian Marconi Co., Montreal, since 1968; Fisher Controls International Inc., Clayton, Missouri, since 1979; SRA Communications, AB, Stockholm, since 1969; *b* 1 Oct. 1915; *s* of Robert and Sarah Annie Telford; *m* 1st, 1941 (marr. diss. 1950); one *s* ; 2nd, 1958, Elizabeth Mary (*née* Shelley); three *d*. *Educ:* Quarry Bank Sch., Liverpool; Queen Elizabeth's Grammar Sch., Tamworth; Christ's Coll., Cambridge (MA). Manager, Hackbridge Works, The Marconi Co. Ltd, 1940-46; Man. Dir, Companhia Marconi Brasileira, 1946-50; The Marconi Company Ltd: Asst to Gen. Manager, 1950-53; Gen. Works Manager, 1953-61; Gen. Manager, 1961-65. Pres., IProdE, 1982-83; Member: Engrg Industry Trng Bd, 1968-; Court, Univ. of Essex, 1981-. DL Essex, 1981. Hon. DSc Salford, 1981; Hon. DSc Cranfield, 1982. *Address:* Rettendon House, Rettendon, Chelmsford, Essex CM3 5DW. *T:* Wickford 3131. *Club:* Royal Air Force.

TELLER, Prof. Edward; Senior Research Fellow, Hoover Institution, since 1975; University Professor, University of California, Berkeley, 1971-75, now Emeritus (Professor of Physics, 1960-71); Chairman, Department of Applied Science, University of California, 1963-66; Associate Director, Lawrence Radiation Laboratory, University of California, 1954-75, now Emeritus; *b* Budapest, Hungary, 15 January 1908; *s* of a lawyer; became US citizen, 1941; *m* 1934, Augusta Harkanyi; one *s* one *d*. *Educ:* Karlsruhe Technical Inst., Germany; Univ. of Munich; Leipzig (PhD). Research Associate, Leipzig, 1929-31; Research Associate, Göttingen, 1931-33; Rockefeller Fellow, Copenhagen, 1934; Lectr, Univ. of London, 1934-35; Prof. of Physics, George Washington Univ., Washington, DC, 1935-41; Prof. of Physics, Columbia Univ., 1941-42; Physicist, Manhattan, Engineer District, 1942-46, Univ. of Chicago, 1942-43; Los Alamos Scientific Laboratory, 1943-46; Prof. of Physics, Univ. of Chicago, 1946-52; Asst Dir, Los Alamos (on leave, Chicago), 1949-52; Consultant, Livermore Br., Univ. of Calif, Radiation Laboratory, 1952-53; Prof. of Physics, Univ. of Calif, Dir, Livermore Br., Lawrence Livermore Lab., Univ. of Calif, 1958-60. Mem. Nat. Acad. of Sciences, etc. Holds several hon. degrees, 1954-. Has gained awards, 1957-, incl. Harvey Prize, Israel, 1975, Herzl Prize, 1978; Gold Medal, Amer. Coll. of Nuclear Med., 1980; Man of the Year, Achievement Rewards for College Scientists, 1980. *Publications:* The Structure of Matter, 1949; Our Nuclear Future, 1958; The Legacy of Hiroshima, 1962; The Reluctant Revolutionary, 1964; The Constructive Uses of Nuclear Explosives, 1968; Great Men of Physics, 1969; Nuclear Energy in a Developing World, 1977; Energy from Heaven and Earth, 1979; Pursuit of Simplicity, 1980. *Address:* Stanford, Ca 94305, USA.

TELLO, Manuel, CMG (Hon.) 1975; Under Secretary, Department of Foreign Affairs, Mexico, since 1979; *b* 15 March 1935; *s* of late Manuel Tello and Guadalupe M. de Tello; *m* 1959, Sonia D. de Tello. *Educ:* schools in Mexico City; Georgetown Univ.; Sch. for Foreign Service, Washington, DC; Escuela Libre de Derecho; Institut de Hautes Etudes Internationales, Geneva. Equivalent of BA in Foreign Service Studies and post-grad. studies in Internat. Law. Joined Mexican Foreign Service, 1957; Asst Dir Gen. for Internat. Organizations, 1967-70, Dir Gen., 1970-72; Dir for Multilateral Affairs, 1972-74; Dir for Political Affairs, 1975-76. Alternate Rep. of Mexico to: OAS, 1959-63; Internat. Orgs, Geneva, 1963-66; Conf. of Cttee on Disarmament, Geneva, 1963-66; Rep. of Mexico to: Org. for Proscription of Nuclear Weapons in Latin America, 1970-73; 3rd UN Conf. on Law of the Sea, 1971-76; Ambassador to UK, 1977-79. Has attended 14 Sessions of UN

Gen. Assembly. Holds decorations from Chile, Ecuador, Egypt, France, Italy, Jordan, Panama, Senegal, Venezuela, Yugoslavia, Sweden. *Publications:* contribs to learned jls in the field of international relations. *Recreations:* tennis, theatre, music. *Address:* Secretaria de Relaciones Exteriores, Flores Magon 1, 06995 Mexico DF, Mexico.

TEMIN, Prof. Howard M(artin), PhD; Professor of Oncology, since 1969, Harry Steenbock Professor of Biological Science, since 1982, Harold P. Rusch Professor of Cancer Research, since 1980 and American Cancer Society Professor of Viral Oncology and Cell Biology, since 1974, University of Wisconsin-Madison; *b* 10 Dec. 1934; *s* of Henry Temin and Annette Lehman Temin; *m* 1962, Rayla Greenberg; two *d*. *Educ:* Swarthmore Coll., Swarthmore, Pa (BA 1955); Calif Inst. of Technol., Pasadena (PhD 1959). Postdoctoral Fellow, Calif Inst. of Technol., Pasadena, 1959-60; Asst Prof. of Oncology, Univ. of Wis-Madison, 1960-64, Associate Prof. of Oncol., 1964-69, Wisconsin Alumni Res. Foundn Prof. of Cancer Res, 1971-80. US Public Health Service Res. Career Develt Award, National Cancer Inst., 1964-74; (jtly) Nobel Prize for Physiology or Medicine, 1975. Hon. DSc: Swarthmore Coll., 1972; NY Med. Coll., 1972; Univ. of Pa, 1976; Hahnemann Med. Coll., 1976; Lawrence Univ., 1976; Temple Univ., 1979; Medical Coll., Wisconsin, 1981. *Publications:* articles on viruses and cancer, on RNA-directed DNA synthesis and on evolution of viruses from cellular movable genetic elements. *Address:* McArdle Laboratory, University of Wisconsin-Madison, Madison, Wis 53706, USA. *T:* 608-262-1209.

TEMPEST, Prof. Norton Robert; William Roscoe Professor of Education, Liverpool University, 1954-72, now Emeritus; *b* 29 Dec. 1904; *s* of James Henry and Veronica Tempest (*née* Fletcher); *m* 1st, 1932, Mary MacDermott (*d* 1962), Danvers, Mass, USA; one *s* ; 2nd, 1970, Maureen Kennedy, Litherland, Liverpool. *Educ:* Liverpool Univ.; Harvard Univ. William Noble Fellow, Liverpool Univ., 1927-28; Commonwealth Fund Fellow, 1930-32. Taught in Grammar Schools; asst lecturer, later lecturer, Manchester and Sheffield Univs, 1932-45; senior lecturer in Education, Liverpool Univ., 1945-49; Director, Sheffield Univ. Inst. of Education, 1949-54. *Publications:* The Rhythm of English Prose, 1930; Teaching Clever Children 7-11, 1974; articles and reviews in various journals. *Address:* 5 Parson's Walk, Pembridge, Leominster, Herefordshire HR6 9EP.

TEMPLE OF STOWE, 7th Earl, *cr* 1822; **Ronald Stephen Brydges Temple-Gore-Langton;** *b* 5 November 1910; *s* of Captain Hon. Chandos Graham Temple-Gore-Langton (*d* 1921); granted rank, title and precedence as an Earl's son, which would have been his had his father survived to succeed to the title; nephew of 5th Earl; *S* brother, 1966. Company representative. *Recreations:* sailing, swimming, bird watching, conservation, radio. Resident in Victoria, Australia.

TEMPLE, Ernest Sanderson, MBE; MA; QC 1969; **His Honour Judge Temple;** a Circuit Judge, since 1977; Honorary Recorder of Kendal, since 1972, and of Liverpool, since 1978; *b* 23 May 1921; *o s* of Ernest Temple, Oxenholme House, Kendal; *m* 1946, June Debonnaire, *o d* of W. M. Saunders, JP, Wennington Hall, Lancaster; one *s* two *d*. *Educ:* Kendal School; Queen's Coll., Oxford. Served in Border Regt in India and Burma, attaining temp. rank of Lt-Col (despatches, 1945). Barrister-at-Law, 1943. Joined Northern Circuit, 1946; Chm., Westmorland QS, 1969-71 (Dep. Chm., 1967); a Recorder of the Crown Court, 1972-77. Hon. FICW. *Recreations:* farming and horses. *Address:* Yealand Hall, Yealand Redmayne, near Carnforth, Lancs. *T:* Burton (Cumbria) 781200. *Club:* Racquet (Liverpool).

TEMPLE, Frances Gertrude Acland, (Mrs William Temple); *b* 23 Dec. 1890; *yr d* of late Frederick Henry Anson, 72 St George's Square, SW1; *m* 1916, William Temple, later Archbishop of Canterbury (*d* 1944). *Educ:* Francis Holland School for Girls, SW1; Queen's College, Harley Street, W1. JP for City of Manchester, 1926-29. Member of Care of Children Cttee (The Curtis Cttee), 1945-47. Church Commissioner, 1949-59; Mem. of Board of Visitors of Rochester Borstal Institution, 1943-60. A Vice-Pres., YHA. MA (*hc*) Manchester Univ., 1954. *Address:* Brackenlea, Shawford, Winchester, Hants.

TEMPLE, Rt. Rev. Frederick Stephen; *see* Malmesbury, Bishop Suffragan of.

TEMPLE, George, CBE 1955; PhD, DSc, MA; FRS 1943; Sedleian Professor of Natural Philosophy, University of Oxford, 1953-68, now Professor Emeritus; Honorary Fellow of Queen's College, Oxford; *b* 2 Sept. 1901; *o s* of late James Temple, London; *m* 1930, Dorothy Lydia (*d* 1979), *e d* of late Thomas Ellis Carson, Liverpool. *Educ:* Ealing County School; Birkbeck College, University of London; Trinity College, Cambridge. Research Assistant and Demonstrator, Physics Dept, Birkbeck College, 1922-24; Assistant Lecturer, Maths Dept, City and Guilds (Eng.) College, 1924-28; Keddey Fletcher Warr Studentship, 1928; 1851 Exhibition Research Student, 1928-30; Assistant Professor in Maths Dept, Royal College of Science, 1930-32; Professor of Mathematics, University of London, King's College, 1932-53. Seconded to Royal Aircraft Establishment, Farnborough, 1939-45. Chairman, Aeronautical Research Council, 1961-64. Professed as Benedictine monk, 1982. Leverhulme Emeritus Fellowship, 1973. Hon. DSc: Dublin, 1961; Louvain, 1966; Reading, 1980; Hon. LLD W Ontario, 1969. Sylvester Medal (Royal Soc.), 1970. *Publications:* An Introduction to Quantum Theory, 1931; Rayleigh's Principle, 1933; General Principles of Quantum

Theory, 1934; An Introduction to Fluid Dynamics, 1958; Cartesian Tensors, 1960; The Structure of Lebesgue Integration Theory, 1971; papers on Mathematical Physics, Relativity, Quantum Theory, Aerodynamics, Distribution Theory, History of Mathematics. *Address:* Quarr Abbey, Ryde, Isle of Wight.

TEMPLE, Ven. George Frederick; Archdeacon of Bodmin, since 1981; Vicar of Saltash, since 1982; *b* 16 March 1933; *s* of George Frederick and Lilian Rose Temple; *m* 1961, Jacqueline Rose Urwin; one *s* one *d. Educ:* St Paul's, Jersey; Wells Theological College. Deacon 1968, priest 1969, Guildford; Curate: St Nicholas, Great Bookham, 1968-70; St Mary the Virgin, Penzance, 1970-72; Vicar of St Just in Penwith with Sancreed, 1972-74; Vicar of St Gluvias, Penryn, 1974-81. *Recreations:* poetry, history, walking. *Address:* The Vicarage, 11 Higher Port View, Saltash, Cornwall PL12 4BZ.

TEMPLE, John Meredith, JP; DL; *b* 1910; *m* 1942, Nancy Violet, *d* of late Brig.-Gen. Robert Wm Hare, CMG, DSO, DL, Cobh, Eire, and Norwich; one *s* one *d. Educ:* Charterhouse; Clare College, Cambridge (BA). Served War of 1939-45 (despatches). ADC to Governor of S Australia, 1941. MP (C) City of Chester, Nov. 1956-Feb. 1974. Vice-Pres., Chester Conservative Club; Vice-Pres., Army Benevolent Fund (Chester Branch); Vice-Chairman: British Group, IPU, 1973-74; Cons. Finance Cttee, 1966-68; Vice-President: Anglo-Colombian Society; Cerro Galan Expedn, Argentina, 1981; Salmon and Trout Assoc. JP Cheshire 1949, DL 1975; High Sheriff of Cheshire, 1980-81. Great Officer: Order of San Carlos, Colombia, 1973; Order of Boyacà, Colombia, 1974; Order of the Liberator, Venezuela, 1974. *Address:* Picton Gorse, near Chester CH2 4JU. *T:* Mickle Trafford 300239. *Clubs:* Carlton, Army and Navy; Racquet (Liverpool); City (Chester).

TEMPLE, Sir Rawden (John Afamado), Kt 1980; CBE 1964; QC 1951; Chief Social Security (formerly National Insurance) Commissioner, 1975-81 (a National Insurance Commissioner, 1969); a Referee under Child Benefit Act, 1975, since 1976; *b* 1908; *m* 1936, Margaret Jessie Wiseman (*d* 1980), *d* of late Sir James Gunson, CMG, CBE; two *s. Educ:* King Edward's School, Birmingham; The Queen's College, Oxford. BA 1930; BCL, 1931; called to Bar, 1931; Master of the Bench, Inner Temple, 1960 (Reader, 1982); Vice-Chairman, General Council of the Bar, 1960-64. Mem., Industrial Injuries Adv. Council, 1981. War Service, 1941-45. Liveryman Worshipful Company of Pattenmakers, 1948. *Recreations:* fishing; collecting portraits and oriental rugs. *Address:* 3 North King's Bench Walk, Temple, EC4.

TEMPLE, Reginald Robert, CMG 1979; HM Diplomatic Service, retired; Oman Government Service, since 1979; *b* 12 Feb. 1922; *s* of Lt-Gen. R. C. Temple, CB, OBE, RM, and Z. E. Temple (*née* Hunt); *m* 1st, 1952, Julia Jasmine Anthony (marr. diss. 1979); one *s* one *d*; 2nd, 1979, Susan McCorquodale (*née* Pick); one *d* (one step *s* one step *d). Educ:* Wellington College; Peterhouse, Cambridge. HM Forces, 1940-46, RE and Para Regt; Stockbroking, 1947-51; entered Foreign Service, 1951; Office of HM Comr Gen. for SE Asia, 1952-56; 2nd Sec., Beirut, 1958-62; 1st Sec., Algiers, 1964-66, Paris, 1967-69; FCO, 1969-79; Counsellor 1975. American Silver Star, 1944. *Recreation:* sailing. *Address:* c/o Lloyds Bank Ltd, 6 Pall Mall, SW1; PO Box 5227, Ruwi, Sultanate of Oman. *Clubs:* Army and Navy; Royal Cruising, Royal Ocean Racing, Hurlingham.

TEMPLE, Sir Richard Anthony Purbeck, 4th Bt, *cr* 1876; MC 1941; *b* 19 Jan. 1913; *s* of Sir Richard Durand Temple, 3rd Bt, DSO; *S* father, 1962; *m* 1st, 1936, Lucy Geils (marr. diss., 1946), 2nd *d* of late Alain Joly de Lotbinière, Montreal; two *s*; 2nd, 1950, Jean, *d* of late James T. Finnie, and *widow* of Oliver P. Croom-Johnson; one *d. Educ:* Stowe; Trinity Hall, Cambridge; Lausanne University. Served War of 1939-45 (wounded, MC). Sometime Major, KRRC. *Recreation:* sailing. *Heir: s* Richard Temple [*b* 17 Aug. 1937; *m* 1964, Emma Rose, 2nd *d* of late Maj.-Gen. Sir Robert Laycock, KCMG, CB, DSO; three *d*]. *Address:* c/o Westminster Bank Ltd, 94 Kensington High Street, W8.

TEMPLE, Mrs William; *see* Temple, F. G. A.

TEMPLE-BLACKWOOD; *see* Blackwood, Hamilton-Temple-.

TEMPLE-GORE-LANGTON, family name of **Earl Temple of Stowe.**

TEMPLE-MORRIS, His Honour Sir Owen, Kt 1967; QC 1937; Judge of Cardiff County Court Circuit No 27, 1968-69; Monmouthshire Quarter Sessions, 1950-69; Chancellor of Diocese of Llandaff, 1935-79; *s* of late Dr Frederick Temple Morris, Cardiff, and Florence, *e d* of Col Charles Lanyon Owen, CB, Portsmouth; *m* 1927, Vera, *er d* of D. Hamilton Thompson; one *s*. Solicitor for five years in practice; Deputy Magistrate's Clerk, Dinas Powis Div., Glamorgan; called to Bar, Gray's Inn, 1925; Wales and Chester Circuits; Judge of County Court Circuit No 24, Cardiff, etc, 1955-68 (Circuit No 31, 1942-48; No 30, 1948-55). Comr of Assize, Oxford Autumn Assize, 1946; Comr of Assize, Welsh Circuit Summer Assize, 1960, 1961, Autumn Assize, 1963, Winter Assize and Summer Assize, 1965, 1966, 1967, 1968, 1969. Mem. Royal Commn on the Police, 1960-62. Prosecuting Counsel to the Post Office, South Wales Circuit, 1931-37; Recorder of Merthyr Tydfil, 1936-42; Acting Recorder of Swansea, 1940-42; Dep. Recorder of Cardiff, 1969-71; Chm. of Quarter Sessions: Town and Co. Haverfordwest, 1942-48; Co. Carmarthenshire, 1942-50; Brecknockshire, 1948-55; Dep.-Chm. of Quarter Sessions: Glamorgan, 1938-48; Pembrokeshire, 1942-48; formerly Chm.,

County Court Rule Cttee. MP (Nat C) Cardiff East, 1931-42; contested Caerphilly Division of Glamorgan, General Election, 1929; Vice-Pres. Wales and Mon Conservative and Unionist Association, 1931-42; Chm. Wales and Mon Conservative Education Cttee, 1938-42; Mem. Governing Body, Association of Conservative Clubs, 1929-42; Chm. Wales and Mon Conservative Clubs Advisory Cttee, 1929-42; Mem. of Governing Body and Vice-Chm., Representative Body of the Church in Wales; President, Provincial Court of Church in Wales; Chm. of Legal Cttee and Pensions Cttee of Representative Body, 1945-55; Hon. Lay Sec. Llandaff Diocesan Conf., 1927-35; Mem. of Cymmrodorion Soc.; Chief Comdt Cardiff Volunteer Special Constabulary, 1938-45; Chm. and Sec. Commandants of Special Constabularies Conf., No 8 Region, 1942-45. CStJ. *Address:* 8 Raglan House, Westgate Street, Cardiff. *Club:* Cardiff and County (Cardiff).

See also P. Temple-Morris.

TEMPLE-MORRIS, Peter; MP (C) Leominster since Feb. 1974; *b* 12 Feb. 1938; *o s* of His Honour Sir Owen Temple-Morris, *qv* ; *m* 1964, Taheré, *e d* of HE Senator Khozeimé Alam, Teheran; two *s* two *d. Educ:* Hillstone Sch., Malvern; Malvern Coll.; St Catharine's Coll., Cambridge (MA). Chm., Cambridge Univ. Conservative Assoc., 1961; Mem. Cambridge Afro-Asian Expedn, 1961. Called to Bar, Inner Temple, 1962. Judge's Marshal, Midland Circuit, 1958; Mem., Young Barristers' Cttee, Bar Council, 1962-63; in practice on Wales and Chester Circuit, 1963-66; London and SE Circuit, 1966-76; 2nd Prosecuting Counsel to Inland Revenue, SE Circuit, 1971-74. Contested (C): Newport (Mon), 1964 and 1966; Norwood (Lambeth), 1970. PPS to Minister of Transport, 1979. Mem. Exec. Cttee, Soc. of Conservative Lawyers, 1971; Chm., Hampstead Conservative Political Centre, 1971-73; Mem. Council, Iran Soc., 1968-80; Secretary: Anglo-Iranian Parly Gp; Anglo-Lebanese Parly Gp; Mem. Royal Inst. Internat. Affairs; Chm., Bow Group Standing Cttee on Home Affairs, 1975-79; Vice-Chm., Soc. of Cons. Lawyers' Standing Cttee on Criminal Law, 1976-79; Secretary: Conservative Parly Transport Cttee, 1976-79; Cons. Parly Legal Cttee, 1977-78; Cons. Parly Foreign and Commonwealth Affairs Cttee, 1979-; Mem. Exec. British Branch, IPU, 1977-82, Chm., 1982-; British delegate, IPU fact-finding mission on Namibia, 1977; Mem., Parly Delegation to UN Gen. Assembly, 1980. Chm., Afghanistan Support Cttee, 1981-. Consultant to Manganese Bronze Holdings; Dir, BSA Sintered Components Ltd. Freeman, City of London; Liveryman, Basketmakers' Co. Governor, Malvern Coll., 1975- (Council Mem., 1978-). Hon. Associate, BVA, 1976. *Recreations:* shooting; wine and food; family relaxation. *Address:* House of Commons, SW1A 0AA; Huntington Court, Three Elms, Hereford HR4 7RA. *T:* Hereford 272684. *Club:* Carlton.

TEMPLEMAN, family name of **Baron Templeman.**

TEMPLEMAN, Baron *cr* 1982 (Life Peer), of White Lackington in the County of Somerset; **Sydney William Templeman;** Kt 1972; MBE 1946; PC 1978; a Lord of Appeal in Ordinary, since 1982; *b* 3 March 1920; *s* of late Herbert William and Lilian Templeman; *m* 1946, Margaret Joan (*née* Rowles); two *s. Educ:* Southall Grammar School; St John's College, Cambridge (Schol.; MA 1944; Hon. Fellow 1982). Served War of 1939-45: commnd 4/1st Gurkha Rifles, 1941; NW Frontier, 1942; Arakan 1943; Imphal, 1944; Burma with 7 Ind. and 17 Ind. Divisions, 1945 (despatches; Hon. Major). Called to the Bar, 1947; Harmsworth and MacMahon schols; Mem., Middle Temple and Lincoln's Inn; Mem., Bar Council, 1961-65, 1970-72; QC 1964; Bencher, Middle Temple, 1969. Attorney Gen. of the Duchy of Lancaster, 1970-72; a Judge of the High Court of Justice, Chancery Div., 1972-78; a Lord Justice of Appeal, 1978-82. Member: Tribunal to inquire into matters relating to the Vehicle and General Insurance Co., 1971; Adv. Cttee on Legal Education, 1972-74; Royal Commn on Legal Services, 1976-79. Treasurer, Senate of the Four Inns, 1972-74; Pres., Senate of the Inns of Court and the Bar, 1974-76. Hon. Member: Canadian Bar Assoc., 1976; Amer. Bar Assoc., 1976. Hon. DLitt Reading, 1980. *Address:* Manor Heath, Knowl Hill, Woking, Surrey. *T:* Woking 61930.

TEMPLEMAN, Geoffrey, CBE 1980; MA London; PhD Birmingham; FSA; DL; Vice-Chancellor, University of Kent at Canterbury, 1963-80; *b* 15 February 1914; *s* of R. C. Templeman; *m* 1939, Dorothy May Heathcote; two *s* one *d. Educ:* Handsworth Grammar School; Universities of Birmingham, London and Paris. University of Birmingham: teaching history from 1938, Registrar, 1955-62. Chairman: Northern Univs Jt Matric. Bd, 1961-64; Universities Central Council on Admissions, 1964-75; Schs Cttee, Bd of Educn, General Synod of C of E, 1971-76 (Mem., 1971-); Univ. Authorities Panel, 1972-80. Mem., SE Metropolitan Reg. Hosp. Bd, 1972-74; Mem., SE Thames RHA, 1974-. Mem. Review Body on Doctors' and Dentists' Remuneration, 1965-70. DL Kent 1979. Hon. DTech Brunel, 1974; Hon. DCL Kent, 1980. Hon. Fellow, Inst. of Germanic Studies, Univ. of London, 1982. *Publications:* Dugdale Soc. Pubs vol. XI together with articles in learned jls, incl. Trans Royal Hist. Soc. and Cambridge Hist. Jl. *Address:* 2a St Augustine's Road, Canterbury, Kent. *Club:* Athenæum.

TEMPLETON, Darwin Herbert, CBE 1975; Senior Partner, Price Waterhouse, Northern Ireland (formerly Ashworth Rowan Craig Gardner & Co.), since 1967; *b* 14 July 1922; *s* of Malcolm and Mary Templeton; *m* 1950, Hazel Gregg; two *s* one *d. Educ:* Rocavan Sch.; Ballymena Academy. FICAI. Qualified as Chartered Accountant, 1945. Partner, Ashworth Rowan, 1947. Chm., Ulster Soc. of Chartered Accountants, 1961-62; Pres., ICAI, 1970-71. Mem., Royal Commn on Legal Services, 1976-79. Chairman: Lear Fan Ltd;

William W. Cleland Holdings Ltd; W. W. Cleland Ltd; Cleland (Belfast) Ltd; Cullingtree Trust Ltd; Northern Publishing Office (UK) Ltd; Bally Cassidy Sawmills Ltd; Director: British Enkalon Ltd; Ulsterbus Ltd; Citybus Ltd; Byturn Developments Ltd; Nationwide Building Soc. (Chm., NI Region); NI Telecommunications Bd. *Recreations:* music, golf, motor racing. *Address:* Braes, 169 Malone Road, Belfast, Northern Ireland BT9 6TA. *T:* (home) Belfast 660033; (office) 44001. *Clubs:* Royal Scottish Automobile; Ulster (Belfast).

TEMPLETON, Mrs Edith; author, since 1950; *b* 7 April 1916; *m* Edmund Ronald, MD; one *s. Educ:* Prague and Paris; Prague Medical University. During War of 1939-45 worked in American War Office, in office of Surgeon General. Conference (1945-46) and Law Court Interpreter for British Forces in Germany, rank of Capt. *Publications:* Summer in the Country, 1950 (USA 1951); Living on Yesterday, 1951; The Island of Desire, 1952; The Surprise of Cremona, 1954 (USA 1957); This Charming Pastime, 1955; Three (USA 1971). Contributor to The New Yorker, Holiday, Atlantic Monthly, Vogue, Harper's Magazine. *Recreation:* travel, with the greatest comfort possible.

TEMPLETON-COTILL, Rear-Adm. John Atrill, CB 1972; RN retired; Director: Sotheby Parke-Bernet (France), since 1974; Sotheby Parke-Bernet (Monaco), since 1975; *b* 4 June 1920; *s* of late Captain Jack Lionel Cottle, Tank Corps. *Educ:* Canford Sch.; New Coll., Oxford. Joined RNVR, 1939; served war 1939-45; HMS Crocus, 1940-41; British Naval Liason Officer, French warship Chevreuil, 1941-42; staff, GOC New Caledonia (US), 1942; US Embassy, London, 1943; Flag Lieutenant to Vice-Adm., Malta, 1943-44; 1st Lieut, MTB 421, 1944-45; ADC to Governor of Victoria, 1945-46; served in HMS London, Loch Quoich, Whirlwind, Jutland, Barrosa and Sparrow, 1946-55; Comdr 1955; comd HMS Sefton and 108th Minesweeping Sqdn, 1955-56; jssc 1956; Comdr-in-Charge, RN School of Work Study, 1957-59; HMS Tiger, 1959-61; Captain 1961; British Naval Attaché, Moscow, 1962-64; comd HMS Rhyl and Captain (D), 23rd Escort Sqdn, 1964-66; Senior Naval Mem., Defence Operational Analysis Estabt, 1966-68; comd HMS Bulwark, 1968-69; Rear-Adm. Jan. 1970; Chief of Staff to Comdr Far East Fleet, 1970-71; Flag Officer, Malta, and NATO Comdr, SE Area Mediterranean, 1971-73; Comdr, British Forces Malta, 1972-73. *Recreations:* riding, shooting, skiing, walking, travel. *Address:* 85 rue du Faubourg St Honoré, 75008 Paris, France; Château de Roaix, 84110 Vaison-la-Romaine, France. *Club:* Automobile Club de France (Paris).

TENBY, 2nd Viscount, *cr* 1957, of Bulford; **David Lloyd George;** *b* 4 Nov. 1922; *s* of 1st Viscount Tenby and Edna, Viscountess Tenby (*d* 1971); *S* father, 1967. *Educ:* Eastbourne Coll.; Jesus Coll. (Scholar), Cambridge (MA). Served War 1942-47: as Captain, Royal Artillery, NW Europe, 1944-45. Called to the Bar, Inner Temple, 1953. *Heir: b* hon. William Lloyd George [*b* 7 Nov. 1927; *m* 1955, Ursula Diana Ethel Medlicott; one *s* two *d*]. *Address:* Flat 2, 40 Preston Park Avenue, Brighton, East Sussex. *Club:* Reform.

TENCH, David Edward; Legal Adviser, Consumers' Association (publishers of Which?), since 1969; *b* 14 June 1929; *s* of late Henry George Tench and Emma Rose (*née* Orsborn); *m* 1957, Judith April Seaton Gurney; two *s* one *d. Educ:* Merchant Taylors' Sch., Northwood, Mddx. Solicitor, 1952. Private practice, 1954-58; Office of Solicitor of Inland Revenue, 1958-69. Chm., Domestic Coal Consumers' Council, 1976-; Energy Comr, 1977-79. Broadcaster on consumer affairs, 1964-. *Publications:* The Law for Consumers, 1962; The Legal Side of Buying a House, 1965 (2nd edn 1974); Wills and Probate, 1967 (6th edn 1977); How to Sue in the County Court, 1973; Towards a Middle System of Law, 1981. *Recreations:* music, amateur re-upholstery, avoiding gardening. *Address:* Pleasant View, The Platt, Amersham, Bucks. *T:* Amersham 4974.
See also W. H. Tench.

TENCH, William Henry, CBE 1980; Chief Inspector of Accidents, Department of Trade, 1974-81; *b* 2 Aug. 1921; *s* of Henry George Tench and Emma Rose Tench (*née* Orsborn); *m* 1944, Margaret Ireland; one *d. Educ:* Portsmouth Grammar School. CEng, FRaeS. Learned to fly in Fleet Air Arm, 1940; pilot with oil co. in S America, 1947 and 1948; joined KLM Royal Dutch Airlines, W Indies Div., 1948; transf. to Holland, 1951, flying N and S Atlantic, S African, ME and European routes; joined Min. of Transport and Civil Aviation as Inspector of Accidents, 1955. *Recreations:* music, sailing. *Address:* Seaways, Restronguet Point, Feock, Cornwall TR3 6RB.
See also D. E. Tench.

TENISON; *see* Hanbury Tenison and Hanbury-Tenison.

TENISON; *see* King-Tenison.

TENISON, Lt-Col William Percival Cosnahan, DSO 1917; late Royal Artillery; *b* 25 June 1884; *e s* of Col William Tenison, DL, JP, of Loughbawn, Ballybay, Ireland; *m* 1915, Olive Leonora (*d* 1979), *d* of late C. L. Mackenzie and Baroness Wesselenyi of Hadad, Hungary; two *d. Educ:* Marlborough; RMA, Woolwich. First commn, 1903; served European War, 1914-17 (DSO); retired pay, 1922. Guildford Borough Council, 1925-31; Hon. Associate British Museum (Natural History); FLS, FZS (Mem. Council, 1943-47), MBOU; Compiler Zoological Record (Aves, 1944-63); zoological artist; Field Studies Council; Worshipful Company of Farriers; Mem., Old Contemptibles Association; a Governor of Archbishop Tenison's Grammar

School. Raised and commanded 54th Surrey (Wimbledon) Bn Home Guard, 1940-45. *Address:* The Manor Farm, Stanton-by-Dale, near Ilkeston, Derby DE7 4QF.

TENNANT, family name of **Baron Glenconner.**

TENNANT, Hon. Colin (Christopher Paget); Governing Director, Tennants Estate Ltd, since 1967; Chairman, Mustique Co. Ltd, since 1969; *b* 1 Dec. 1926; *s* and *heir* of 2nd Baron Glenconner, *qv* ; *m* 1956, Lady Anne Coke, *e d* of 5th Earl of Leicester, MVO; three *s* twin *d. Educ:* Eton; New College, Oxford. Director, C. Tennant Sons & Co. Ltd, 1953; Deputy Chairman, 1960-67, resigned 1967. *Address:* 50 Victoria Road, W8. *T:* 01-937 0556.

TENNANT, Harry; Member, Civil Service Appeal Board; *b* 10 Dec. 1917; *s* of late Robert and Mary Tennant; *m* 1944, Bernice Baker; one *s. Educ:* Oldham High School. Appointed Officer of Customs and Excise, 1938; Inspector, 1960; Principal Inspector, 1970; Asst Sec., 1971; Dep. Chief Inspector, 1973; Commissioner of Customs and Excise, 1975-78. *Publications:* Moses My Servant, 1966, repr. 1975; The Man David, 1968, repr. 1973. *Recreations:* walking, travel. *Address:* Strathtay, Alexandra Road, Watford, Herts WD1 3QY. *T:* Watford 22079.

TENNANT, Captain Iain Mark, JP; Lord-Lieutenant of Morayshire, since 1963; Crown Estate Commissioner, since 1970; *b* 11 March 1919; *s* of late Col Edward Tennant, Innes, Elgin and Mrs Georgina Tennant; *m* 1946, Lady Margaret Helen Isla Marion Ogilvy, 2nd *d* of 12th Earl of Airlie, Kt, GCVO, MC; two *s* one *d. Educ:* Eton College; Magdalene College, Cambridge. Scots Guards, 1939-46. Caledonian Cinemas, 1947; Chm., Grampian Television Ltd, 1968-; Director: Times Publishing Co. Ltd, 1962-66; Clydesdale Bank Ltd, 1968-; The Seagram Co. Ltd, Montreal, 1978-; Chairman: The Glenlivet Distillers Ltd, 1964-; Seagram Distillers, 1979-. Mem. Newspaper Panel, Monopolies and Mergers Commn, 1981-. Chm. Bd of Governors, Gordonstoun School, 1954-71. Ensign, Queen's Body Guard for Scotland (Royal Company of Archers), 1981-. FRSA 1971. DL Moray, 1954; JP Moray, 1961. *Recreations:* shooting, fishing; formerly rowing (rowed for Eton, 1937). *Address:* (home) Lochnabo, Lhanbryde, Moray. *T:* Lhanbryde 2228; (office) Innes House, Elgin, Moray. *T:* Lhanbryde 2410.

TENNANT, Sir Mark (Dalcour), KCMG 1964 (CMG 1951); CB 1961; Deputy Secretary, Department of the Environment, 1970-71; *b* 26 Dec. 1911; *o surv. s* of late N. R. D. Tennant, Haileybury, Hertford; *m* 1936, Clare Elisabeth Ross, *o d* of late Sir Ross Barker, KCIE, CB. *Educ:* Marlborough; New College, Oxford (Open Classical Schol.). Entered Min. of Labour as Asst Principal, 1935; Private Secretary to Parliamentary Secretary, Ministry of Labour, 1938-39; and to Parliamentary Secretary, Ministry of Food, 1939-40. Served War of 1939-45, Royal Artillery, 1942-44. Assistant Secretary, 1945; Member of UK Delegation to International Labour Conference, 1949-53; Student Imperial Defence College, 1956; Under-Secretary, 1957; Secretary-General Monckton Commission on the Review of the Constitution of the Federation of Rhodesia and Nyasaland, 1960; Dir Organisation and Establishments, Min. of Labour, 1960; Secretary, Central African Office, 1962-64. Third Secretary, HM Treasury, 1964-65; Dep. Sec., Min. of Public Building and Works, 1965-70. *Address:* c/o Barclays Bank Ltd, 1 Pall Mall East, SW1. *Club:* Travellers'.

TENNANT, Sir Peter (Frank Dalrymple), Kt 1972; CMG 1958; OBE 1945; Director-General, British National Export Council, 1965-71; Industrial Adviser, Barclays Bank International Ltd, 1972-81; Director: Prudential Assurance Company Ltd, 1973-81; Prudential Corporation plc, since 1979; C. Tennant Sons & Company Ltd, 1972-80; Anglo-Rumanian Bank, 1973-81; Northern Engineering Industries (International) Ltd, since 1979; International Energy Bank, since 1981; *b* 29 Nov. 1910; *s* of G. F. D. Tennant and Barbara Tennant (*née* Beck); *m* 1st, 1934 (marr. diss. 1952), Hellis, *d* of Professor Fellenius, Stockholm; one *s* two *d* ; 2nd, 1953, Galina Bosley, *d* of K. Grunberg, Helsinki; one *step s. Educ:* Marlborough; Trinity College, Cambridge. Sen. Mod. Languages Scholar, Trinity College, Cambridge, 1929; Cholmondely Studentship, Lincoln's Inn; 1st Cl. Hons Mod. Langs Tripos, 1932; BA 1932, MA 1936, Cambridge. Cambridge Scandinavian Studentship, Oslo, Copenhagen, Stockholm, 1932-33; Fellow Queens' College, Cambridge, and University Lecturer, Scandinavian Languages, 1933; Press Attaché, British Legation, Stockholm, 1939-45; Information Counsellor, British Embassy, Paris, 1945-50; Deputy Commandant, British Sector, Berlin, 1950-52; resigned Foreign Service to become Overseas Director, FBI, 1952-63. Deputy Director-General, FBI, 1963-65. Special Advr, CBI, 1964-65. Former Mem., Council of Industrial Design; Dep. Chm., Wilton Park Academic Council; former Mem. Bd, Centre for Internat. Briefing, Farnham Castle; past Chm., Gabbitas Thring Educational Trust; Pres., London Chamber of Commerce and Industry, 1978-79 (Chm., 1976-78); Chm., British Cttee, European Cultural Foundn. *Publications:* Ibsen's Dramatic Technique, 1947; The Scandinavian Book, 1952. *Recreations:* writing, talking, painting, travel, languages, sailing, country life. *Address:* Blue Anchor House, Linchmere Road, Haslemere, Surrey GU27 3QF. *T:* Haslemere 3124. *Club:* Travellers'.

TENNEKOON, Victor; Chairman, Law Commission of Sri Lanka, since 1978; Chancellor, University of Peradeniya, since 1979; *b* 9 Sept. 1914; *s* of Loku Banda Tennekoon and Nandu Menike Tennekoon (*née* Rambukwella); *m*

1946, Semitha Muriel Wijeyewardene; one *s* two *d*. *Educ*: St Anthony's Coll., Kandy; University Coll., Colombo. BA London Univ. (External) 1935. Called to Sri Lanka Bar, 1942. QC 1965. Practised at Kegalle, 1943-46; Crown Counsel, 1946; Solicitor-General, 1964; Attorney-General, 1970; Judge of Court of Appeal, Sri Lanka, 1973; Chief Justice of Sri Lanka, 1974-77. *Recreations*: tennis, golf, billiards, bridge, chess. *Address*: 40/1 Ananda Coomaraswamy Nawata, Green Path, Colombo 3, Sri Lanka. *T*: 20853. *Clubs*: Orient, Sinhalese Sports, Royal Colombo Golf (Colombo).

TENNYSON, family name of **Baron Tennyson**.

TENNYSON, 4th Baron *cr* 1884; **Harold Christopher Tennyson;** *b* 25 March 1919; *e s* of 3rd Baron and Hon. Clarissa Tennant (*d* 1960), *o d* of 1st Baron Glenconner; *S* father 1951. *Educ*: Eton; Trinity Coll., Cambridge. BA 1940. Employed War Office, 1939-46. Hon. Freeman, City of Lincoln, 1964. *Heir*: *b* Hon. Mark Aubrey Tennyson, DSC 1943; RN ret. [*b* 28 March 1920; *m* 1944, Deline Celeste Budler. *Educ*: RN College, Dartmouth. Served War of 1939-45 (despatches, DSC); Comdr RN, 1954]. *Address*: 18 Rue Galilée, 75016 Paris, France. *Clubs*: White's, Royal Automobile; Royal and Ancient.

TENNYSON-d'EYNCOURT, Sir (John) Jeremy (Eustace), 3rd Bt *cr* 1930; *b* 8 July 1927; *s* of Sir Eustace Gervais Tennyson-d'Eyncourt, 2nd Bt, and Pamela (*d* 1962), *d* of late W. B. Gladstone; *S* father, 1971; *m* 1st, 1964, Mrs Sally Fyfe-Jamieson (marr. diss.), *e d* of Robin Stratford, QC; 2nd, 1972, Brenda Mary Veronica (marr. diss. 1976), *d* of Dr Austin Stafford; 3rd, 1977, Norah, *d* of late Thomas Gill. *Educ*: Eton; Glasgow University. Served as Sub Lieut, RNVR, 1945-48. *Recreations*: fishing and wild-life; cooking and gardening. *Address*: c/o Hyde Mahon & Pascall, 33 Ely Place, EC1N 6TS.

TENZING NORGAY, GM 1953; Sherpa Climber; Director of Field Training, Himalayan Mountaineering Institute, Darjeeling (established by Indian Government, 1954); *b* Tami, Nepal, 1914; *m* Anglahmu; two *c*; *m* 1962, Dawa Phuti; four *c*. Migrated to Bengal, 1932. High altitude Sherpa in British mountaineering expeditions, 1935, 1936 and 1938; took part in expeditions to Karakoram, 1950, and Nanda Devi, 1951, climbing to east peak; Sirdar and full Member to 2 Swiss expedns (climbing record 28,215 ft), 1952; Sirdar and Full Member to Sir John Hunt's expedition, 1953; with Sir Edmund Hilary reached summit of Mount Everest, May 1953; accompanied him on jet boat expedition up the Ganges, 1977. President of Sherpa Buddhist and Climber's association. Coronation Medal, 1953; Hon. Citizen of Chamonix, 1954. Star of Nepal, 1953. Holds numerous foreign medals and awards. *Publication*: After Everest (autobiog.), 1977; *relevant publication*: Man of Everest by James Ramsay Ullman, 1955 (Amer. edn Tiger of the Snows). *Address*: Himalayan Mountaineering Institute, Birch Hill, Darjeeling, W Bengal; 1 Tonga Road, Ghang-La, Darjeeling, W Bengal.

TEŌ, Sir (Fiatau) Penitala, GCMG 1979; ISO 1970; MBE 1956; Governor-General of Tuvalu, since 1978; *b* 23 July 1911; *s* of Teō Veli, Niutao, and Tilesa Samuelu, Funafuti; *m* 1st, 1931, Muniara Apelu, Vaitupu; one *d* (one *s* decd); 2nd, 1949, Uimai Tofiga, Nanumaga; eight *s* three *d* (and one *d* decd). *Educ*: Elisefou, Vaitupu, Tuvalu. Asst Sch. Master, Elisefou, 1930-32; Clerk and Ellice Interpreter: Dist Admin, Funafuti, 1932-37; Resident Comr's Office, Ocean Is., 1937-42; under Japanese Occupation (Ocean Is. and Tarawa), 1942-43 (1939-45 Star, Pacific Star and War Medal); re-joined Res. Comr's Office, 1943 (i/c Labour Force), Special Clerk 1944; Asst Admin. Officer and Mem., Gilbert and Ellice Is Defence Force (2nd Lieut), 1944; Asst and Actg Dist Officer for Ellice Is, 1944-50; transf. to Tarawa to re-organise Information Office, 1953; Dep. Comr for Western Pacific, 1960; Lands Officer for Gilbert and Ellice Is, 1960-62; Dist Commissioner: Ocean Is., 1963; Ellice Is, 1967-69; Asst and Actg Supt of Labour, British Phosphate Comrs, Ocean Is., 1971-78. ADC to High Comr of Western Pacific during tours, 1954 and 1957; Dist Officer for visit of Prince Philip to Vaitupu Is., Ellice Is, 1959. Represented Gilbert and Ellice Is at confs. Coronation Medal, 1953. *Recreations*: formerly fishing, cricket, football, Rugby, local games. *Address*: Alapi, Funafuti, Tuvalu.

TERESA, Mother, (Agnes Gonxha Bojaxhiu); Roman Catholic missionary; *b* 27 Aug. 1910; *d* of Albanian parents. *Educ*: Government school in Yugoslavia. Joined Sisters of Loretto, 1928; worked at Loretto insts in Ireland and India; Principal, St Mary's High School, Calcutta; founded the Missionaries of Charity, 1950, and through them set up over fifty schools, orphanages and houses for the poor in India and other countries; opened Nirmal Hriday (Pure Heart) Home for Dying Destitutes, 1952; started a leper colony in West Bengal, 1964. Pope John XXIII Peace Prize, 1971; Templeton Foundation Prize, 1973; Nobel Peace Prize, 1979. Hon. DD Cambridge, 1977. *Publication*: Gift for God, 1975. *Address*: Missionaries of Charity, Nirmal Hriday Home for Dying Destitutes, 5A Lower Circular Road, Calcutta, India.

TERESHKOVA, Valentina N.; *see* Nikolayeva-Tereshkova.

TERRAINE, John Alfred; author; *b* 15 Jan. 1921; *s* of Charles William Terraine and Eveline Holmes; *m* 1945, Joyce Eileen Waite; one *d*. *Educ*: Stamford Sch.; Keble Coll., Oxford. Joined BBC, 1944; Pacific and S African Programme Organiser, 1953-63; resigned from BBC, 1964. Associate producer and chief scriptwriter of The Great War, BBC TV, 1963-64; part-scriptwriter

The Lost Peace, BBC TV, 1965; scriptwriter, The Life and Times of Lord Mountbatten, Rediffusion/Thames TV, 1966-68; scriptwriter, The Mighty Continent, BBC TV, 1974-75. Pres., Western Front Assoc.; Mem. Council, RUSI. Chesney Gold Medal, RUSI, 1982. *Publications*: Mons: The Retreat to Victory, 1960; Douglas Haig: The Educated Soldier, 1963; The Western Front, 1964; General Jack's Diary, 1964; The Great War: An Illustrated History, 1965 (NY); The Life and Times of Lord Mountbatten, 1968; Impacts of War 1914 and 1918, 1970; The Mighty Continent, 1974; Trafalgar, 1976; The Road to Passchendaele, 1977; To Win a War: 1918 The Year of Victory, 1978; The Smoke and the Fire, 1980; White Heat: the new warfare 1914-1918, 1982. *Recreation*: convivial and congenial conversation. *Address*: 74 Kensington Park Road, W11. *T*: 01-229 8152; Vittoria, Church Street, Amberley, Arundel, West Sussex. *T*: Bury 638.

TERRELL, Colonel Stephen, OBE 1952; TD; QC 1965; DL. Called to the Bar, Gray's Inn, 1946; Bencher, Gray's Inn, 1970. South Eastern Circuit. Pres., Liberal Party, 1972. Contested (L) Eastbourne, Feb. 1974. DL Middlesex, 1961.

TERRINGTON, 4th Baron, *cr* 1918, of Huddersfield; **James Allen David Woodhouse;** former Member, Stock Exchange; Partner in Sheppards and Chase, 1952-80; *b* 30 December 1915; *er s* of 3rd Baron Terrington, KBE, and Valerie (*née* Phillips) (*d* 1958), Leyden's House, Edenbridge, Kent; *S* father, 1961; *m* 1942, Suzanne, *y d* of Colonel T. S. Irwin, DL, JP, late Royal Dragoons, Justicetown, Carlisle, and Mill House, Holton, Suffolk; three *d*. *Educ*: Winchester; Royal Military College, Sandhurst. Joined Royal Norfolk Regiment, 1937. Served War of 1939-45 in India, North Africa and Middle East (wounded); ADC to GOC Madras, 1940; Staff Coll., Haifa, 1944; psc 1944; GSOII, Allied Force HQ Algiers, Ninth Army, Middle East and War Office, Military Operations; retired as Major, 1948; joined Queen's Westminster Rifles (KRRC), TA. Joined Messrs Chase Henderson and Tennant, 1949 (now Sheppards and Chase). Deputy Chairman of Cttees, House of Lords, 1961-63. Member: Ecclesiastical Cttee, 1979-; Exec. Cttee, Wider Shareownership Council, 1981- (former Dep. Chm. of Council). *Recreations*: shooting, racing. *Heir*: *b* Hon. Christopher Montague Woodhouse, qv. *Address*: The Manor House, Barford St Martin, Salisbury, Wilts. *Clubs*: Boodle's, Pratt's.

See also Earl Alexander of Tunis.

TERRY, Sir Andrew Henry Bouhier I.; *see* Imbert-Terry.

TERRY, Sir George (Walter Roberts), Kt 1982; CBE 1976; QPM 1967; Chief Constable of Sussex, since 1973; *b* 29 May 1921; *s* of late Walter George Tygh Terry and Constance Elizabeth Terry; *m* 1942, Charlotte Elizabeth Kresina; one *s*. *Educ*: Peterborough, Northants. Served War, Northamptonshire Regt, in Italy, 1942-46 (Staff Captain). Chief Constable: Pembrokeshire, 1958-65; East Sussex, 1965-67; Dep. Chief Constable, Sussex, 1968-69; Chief Constable, Lincolnshire, 1970-73. Chm., Traffic Cttee, 1976-79, Pres., 1980-81, Assoc. of Chief Police Officers; Dir, Police Extended Interviews, 1977. Mem. Council, Inst. of Advanced Motorists, 1974. CStJ. *Recreations*: horticulture, motoring. *Address*: Police Headquarters, Malling House, Lewes, Sussex BN7 2DZ. *T*: Lewes 5432.

TERRY, Sir John Elliott, Kt 1976; Consultant with Denton Hall & Burgin; Managing Director, National Film Finance Corporation, 1958-78; *b* 11 June 1913; *s* of Ernest Fairchild Terry, OBE, FRICS, and Zabelle Terry (*née* Costikyan), Pulborough, Sussex; *m* 1940, Joan Christine, *d* of Frank Alfred Ernest Howard Fell and Ethel Christine Fell (*née* Nilson), Stoke D'Abernon, Surrey; one *s* one *d*. *Educ*: Mill Hill School; Univ. of London (LLB). Articled with Denton Hall & Burgin, London; admitted solicitor, 1938. London Fire Service, 1939-40; Friends' Ambulance Unit, 1941-44; Mem. Nat. Council of Social Service, 1944-46; Film Producers' Guild, 1946-47; The Rank Organisation's Legal Dept, 1947-49; joined Nat. Film Finance Corp. as Solicitor, 1949, also Sec., 1956. Governor: Nat. Film Sch., 1970-81; London Internat. Film Sch., 1982-; Royal Nat. Coll. for the Blind, 1980-; Pres., Copinger Soc., 1981-83. *Address*: Still Point, Fairmile Lane, Cobham, Surrey.

TERRY, Michael, FRGS; FRGSA; explorer and author; *b* Newcastle upon Tyne, 3 May 1899; *s* of late Major A. M. and late Catherine Terry; *m* 1940, Ursula (marr. diss. 1945), *yr d* of Captain Noel Livingstone-Learmonth. *Educ*: Preston House School, East Grinstead; King Edward School, Birmingham; Durham University. Served in Russia; invalided out; went to Australia upon discharge; took first motor across Northern Australia from Winton, Queensland, to Broome on the North-West Coast, in 1923; Cuthbert-Peek Grant in support of expedition undertaken, 1925, from Darwin to Broome; authorised to name Dummer Range and Mount Rosamund; third expedition started Port Hedland, 1928; proceeded Broome, Halls Creek, Tanami, Alice Springs, Melbourne. Made gold and potassium nitrate discoveries. Explored extensively in N Territory, also in S and W Australia, 1929-33; found Hidden Basin, a 40x20 mile subsided area, covered 1200 miles on camels and collected data for Waite Research Inst., Met. Bureau, and Lands Dept; Sept.-Nov. 1933, Tennants Creek Goldfield; 1934-36, prospecting NE of Laverton, WA; farming, Terrigal, NSW, 1946-60. Received by Prince of Wales, 1926; presented to King George, 1939. Has completed 14 Australian inland expeditions. Life Member: Aust. Soc. Authors; Life Associate, Path Finders Assoc. of NSW; Mem., Nat. Geographic Soc., Washington, USA. *Publications*: Across Unknown Australia, 1925; Through a Land of Promise, 1927; Untold Miles, 1928; Hidden Wealth and Hiding People, 1931; Sand and

Sun, 1937; Bulldozer, 1945; War of the Warramullas, 1974; My Historical Years, 1980; and in numerous journals. *Recreation:* riding. *Address:* c/o GPO Box 5089, Sydney, NSW 2001, Australia.

TERRY, Air Chief Marshal Sir Peter (David George), KCB 1978 (CB 1975); AFC 1968; QCVSA 1959 and 1962; Deputy Supreme Allied Commander, Europe, since 1981; *b* 18 Oct. 1926; *s* of James George Terry and Laura Chilton Terry (*née* Powell); *m* 1946, Betty Martha Louisa Thompson; one *s* one *d* (and one *s* decd). *Educ:* Chatham House Sch., Ramsgate. Joined RAF, 1945; commnd in RAF Regt, 1946; Pilot, 1953. Staff Coll., 1962; OC, No 51 Sqdn, 1966–68; OC, RAF El Adem, 1968–70; Dir, Air Staff Briefing, MoD, 1970–71; Dir of Forward Policy for RAF, 1971–74; ACOS (Policy and Plans), SHAPE, 1975–77; VCAS, 1977–79; C-in-C RAF Germany and Comdr Second Allied Tactical Air Force, 1979–81; Dep. C-in-C, Allied Forces Central Europe, Feb.–April 1981. *Recreation:* golf. *Address:* DSACEUR, SHAPE, BFPO 26. *Club:* Royal Air Force.

TERRY, Walter Frederick; Political Editor, The Sun, since 1978 (Member of Political Staff, since 1976); *b* 18 Aug. 1924; *s* of Frederick George Terry and Helen MacKenzie Bruce; *m* 1950, Mavis Landen; one *s* one *d* (and one *s* decd). *Educ:* at school and later by experience. Entered journalism, Glossop Chronicle, 1943; Derby Evening Telegraph, 1947; Nottingham Journal, 1948; Daily Mail, Manchester, 1949; Daily Mail: Parliamentary Staff, 1955; Political Correspondent, 1959; Political Editor, 1965; Washington Correspondent, 1969; Dep.-Editor, 1970–71; Political Editor, 1971–73; Political Editor, Daily Express, 1973–75. Journalist of the Year (first awards), 1963. *Address:* St Germans House, Eliot Place, SE3 0QL. *T:* 01-852 2526; 8 Fort Rise, Newhaven Harbour, Sussex BN9 9DW. *T:* Newhaven 4347. *Club:* Reform.

TERRY-THOMAS, (Thomas Terry Hoar Stevens); Actor; *b* 14 July 1911; *s* of Ernest Frederick Stevens and Ellen Elizabeth (*née* Hoar); *m* 1938, Ida Patlanskey; *m* 1963, Belinda Cunningham; two *s. Educ:* Ardingly Coll., Sussex. Served War of 1939–45: in army, Royal Corps of Signals, 1941–46. Piccadilly Hayride, Prince of Wales Theatre, 1946–47; Radio Series: To Town With Terry, 1948–49; Top Of The Town, 1951–52; TV Series: How Do You View, 1951–52. *Films:* Private's Progress, Green Man, 1956; Brothers-in-Law, Blue Murder at St Trinians, Lucky Jim, Naked Truth, 1957; Tom Thumb, Happy is the Bride, 1958; Carlton Browne of the FO, I'm All Right Jack, Too Many Crooks, 1959; Make Mine Mink, School for Scoundrels, His and Hers, 1960; A Matter of Who, Bachelor Flat, Operation Snatch, The Wonderful World of the Brothers Grimm, 1961; Kill or Cure, Its a Mad, Mad, Mad, Mad World, 1962; Wild Affair, 1963; How to Murder Your Wife, 1964; Those Magnificent Men in their Flying Machines, 1965; Jules Verne's Rocket to the Moon, 1967; Don't Look Now, 1968; Where Were You When the Lights Went Out?, 1968; Monte Carlo or Bust!, 1969; Thirteen, 1970; Seven Times Seven, 1970; Arthur, Arthur, 1970; Atlantic Wall, 1970; Dr Phibes, 1970; Lei, Lui, Loro, la Legge, 1971; Dr Phibes rises again, 1972; The Heros, 1972; Tom Jones, 1975; Side by Side, 1975; Spanish Fly, 1975; The Last Remake of Beau Geste, 1976; The Hound of the Baskervilles, 1978. *Publication:* (as Terry-Thomas) Filling the Gap, 1959. *Recreations:* horse-riding and water ski-ing. *Address:* Suite Eleven, 15 Berkeley Street, W1. *T:* 01-499 3034. *Club:* Savage.

TESH, Robert Mathieson, CMG 1968; HM Diplomatic Service; Ambassador to Ethiopia, 1979–82; *b* 15 Sept. 1922; *s* of late E. Tesh, Hurst Green, Surrey; *m* 1950, Jean Bowker; two *s* one *d. Educ:* Queen Elizabeth's, Wakefield; Queen's College, Oxford (MA). Oxford, 1940–42 and 1945–47; Rifle Brigade, 1942–45; HM Foreign Service, 1947: New Delhi, 1948–50; FO, 1950–53 and 1957–60; Delegation to NATO, Paris, 1953–55; Beirut, 1955–57; Bangkok, 1960–64; Dep. High Comr, Ghana, 1965–66; Lusaka, 1966; Consul-General British Interests Section, Canadian Embassy, Cairo, 1966–67; Counsellor, British Embassy, Cairo, 1968; IDC, 1969; Head of Defence Dept, FCO, 1970–72; Ambassador to Bahrain, 1972–75; Ambassador to: the Democratic Republic of Vietnam, 1976; the Socialist Republic of Vietnam, 1976–78; FCO, 1978–79. *Recreations:* riding, sea fishing, water ski-ing. *Address:* c/o National Westminster Bank, Caxton House, 6 Tothill Street, SW1. *Club:* Travellers'.

TESLER, Brian; Managing Director, since 1976, Deputy Chairman, since 1982, London Weekend Television Ltd; *b* 19 Feb. 1929; *s* of late David Tesler and of Stella Tesler; *m* 1959, Audrey Mary Maclean; one *s. Educ:* Chiswick County School for Boys; Exeter Coll., Oxford (State Schol.; MA). Theatre Editor, The Isis, 1950–51; Pres., Oxford Univ. Experimental Theatre Club, 1951–52. British Forces Broadcasting Service, 1947–49; Producer/Director: BBC Television, 1952; ATV, 1957; ABC Television: Head of Features and Light Entertainment, 1960; Programme Controller, 1961; Dir of Programmes, 1962; Dir of Programmes, Thames Television, 1968; Dep. Chief Exec., London Weekend Television, 1974; Director: ITN, 1979–; Channel Four Television Ltd, 1980–; Oracle Teletext Ltd, 1980–; LWT International Ltd, 1982–; Services Kinema Corp., 1981–82; Services Sound and Vision Corp., 1982–. Member: Working Party on future of British film industry, 1975–77; Interim Action Cttee on film industry, 1977–; Governor, Nat. Film Sch.; Pres., Radio Industries Club, 1979–80; Chm., Indep. TV Cos Assoc., 1980–82. Daily Mail Nat. Television Award, 1954; Guild of Television Producers and Directors Award, 1957. *Recreations:* books, theatre, cinema, music, dog walking. *Address:* London Weekend Television Ltd, South Bank Television Centre, Kent House, Upper Ground, SE1 9LT. *T:* 01-261 3434.

TESTAFERRATA, Marquis; *see* San Vincenzo Ferreri, Marquis of.

TETLEY, Glen; choreographer, since 1948; *b* 3 Feb. 1926; *s* of Glenford Andrew Tetley and Mary Eleanor (*née* Byrne). *Educ:* Franklyn and Marshal Coll., Lancaster, USA (pre-med); New York Univ. (BSc). Studied medicine, then dance with Hanya Holm, Antony Tudor, Martha Graham. Danced with Holm's Co., 1946–51; New York City Opera, 1952–54; John Butler Dance Theatre, 1955; Joffrey Ballet, 1956–57; Martha Graham Co., 1958; American Ballet Theatre, 1960; Robbins Ballets USA, 1961. Joined Netherlands Dance Theatre as dancer and choreographer, 1962, eventually becoming artistic co-director; directed own company, 1969; Dir, Stuttgart Ballet, 1974–76. *Choreography:* Pierrot Lunaire, own company, 1962; The Anatomy Lesson, Netherlands Dance Theatre, 1964; Mythical Hunters, Batsheva Dance Co., 1965; Ricercare, American Ballet Theatre, 1966; Freefall, Ballet Rambert, 1967; Ziggurat, Ballet Rambert, 1967; Circles, NDT, 1968; Embrace Tiger and Return to Mountain, Ballet Rambert, 1968; Field Figures, Royal Ballet, 1970; Imaginary Film, NDT, 1970; Mutations, NDT, 1970; Rag Dances, Ballet Rambert, 1971; Laborintus, Royal Ballet, 1972; Voluntaries, Stuttgart Ballet, 1973; Le Sacre du Printemps, Munich State Opera Ballet, 1974; Tristan, Paris Opera, 1974; Daphnis and Chloe, Stuttgart Ballet, 1975; Greening, Stuttgart Ballet, 1975; Nocturne, ABT, 1977; Sphinx, ABT, 1977; Praeludium, Ballet Rambert, 1978; Contredances, ABT, 1979; The Tempest, first full-length work, Ballet Rambert, 1979; Summer's End, NDT, 1980; Dances of Albion, Royal Ballet, 1980; Firebird, Royal Danish Ballet, 1981. Queen Elizabeth Coronation Award, Royal Acad. of Dancing, 1980. *Address:* 15 West Ninth Street, New York, NY 10011, USA. *T:* (212) 4754604.

TETLEY, Sir Herbert, KBE 1965; CB 1958; Government Actuary, 1958–73; *b* 23 April 1908; *s* of Albert Tetley, Leeds; *m* 1941, Agnes Maclean Macfarlane Macphee; one *s. Educ:* Leeds Grammar School; The Queen's College, Oxford. Hastings Scholar, Queen's College, 1927–30; 1st Cl. Hons Mods (Mathematics), 1928; 1st Cl. Final Hons School of Mathematics, 1930. Fellow of Institute of Actuaries, 1934; Fellow of Royal Statistical Society; served with London Life Assoc., 1930–36; Scottish Provident Instn, 1936–38; National Provident Instn, 1938–51 (Joint Actuary). Joined Government Actuary's Dept as Principal Actuary, 1951; Deputy Government Actuary, 1953; Chairman: Civil Service Insurance Soc., 1961–73; Cttee on Economics Road Research Board, 1962–65; Cttee on Road Traffic Research, 1966–73. Pres., Inst. of Actuaries, 1964–66. *Publications:* Actuarial Statistics, Vol. I, 1946; (jointly) Statistics, An Intermediate Text Book, Vol. I, 1949, Vol. II, 1950. *Recreations:* gardening, music, fell-walking. *Address:* 8-b Langley Avenue, Surbiton, Surrey KT6 6QL. *T:* 01-399 3001.

TETLEY, Kenneth James; a Recorder of the Crown Court, since 1972; *b* Ashton-under-Lyne, Lancs, 17 Oct. 1921; *o s* of William Tetley, Dukinfield, Cheshire, and Annie Lees, Oldham; *m* 1945, Edna Rita, *e d* of Peter Charles Spurrin Gray and Annie Gray, Audenshaw, Manchester; one *s* three *d. Educ:* Ashton-under-Lyne Grammar Sch.; Manchester Univ. Served War of 1939–45: joined RN, 1941; Lieut RNVR (attached Combined Ops); discharged, 1945. Admitted Solicitor, 1947; Councillor, Ashton-under-Lyne Borough Council, 1955; Alderman, 1967. *Recreations:* Rugby Union football, golf, photography. *Address:* Green Meadows, Ley Hey Park, Marple, Cheshire. *T:* 061-427 3755. *Clubs:* Rugby, Golf (Ashton-under-Lyne); Romiley Golf; Lancashire County RFU.

TETT, Sir Hugh (Charles), Kt 1966; ARCS, BSc, DIC; *b* Exeter, Devon, 28 Oct. 1906; *e s* of late James Charles Tett and late Florence Tett (*née* Lihou); *m* 1st, 1931, Katie Sargent (*d* 1948); one *d*; 2nd, 1949, Joyce Lilian (*née* Mansell) (*d* 1979); one *d*; 3rd, 1980, Barbara Mary (*née* Mackenzie). *Educ:* Hele's School, Exeter; University College, Exeter; Royal College of Science (Kitchener's Scholar). Joined Esso Petroleum Co. Ltd, 1928; Technical Advisory Committee, Petroleum Board, 1940–45; Lieut-Colonel, Combined Intelligence Objectives Sub-Cttee, 1944–45; Chairman of Council, Institute of Petroleum, 1947–48; Managing Director, Esso Research Ltd, 1947–49; Director, Esso Petroleum Co. Ltd, 1951, Chairman, 1959–67. Member: Council for Scientific and Industrial Research, 1961–64; Advisory Council, Ministry of Technology, 1964–67. Chairman, Economic Development Cttee for Motor Manufacturing Industry, 1967–69. Pro-Chancellor, Univ. of Southampton, 1967–79. Fellow, Imperial Coll. of Science and Technology, 1964. Hon. DSc: Southampton, 1965; Exeter, 1970. *Address:* Primrose Cottage, Bosham, Chichester, West Sussex PO18 8HZ. *T:* Bosham 572705. *Club:* Athenæum.

TEUSNER, Hon. Berthold Herbert, CMG 1972; JP; Solicitor since 1931; Speaker, South Australian Parliament, 1956–62; *b* 16 May 1907; *s* of Carl Theodor Teusner and Agnes Sophie Elisabeth Teusner (*née* Christian); *m* 1934, Viola Hilda Kleeman; two *s. Educ:* Immanuel Coll., Adelaide; Univ. of Adelaide (LLB). Legal Practice at Tanunda, SA, 1932–. MP for Angas, S Australian Parlt, 1944–70; Govt Whip, 1954–55; Dep. Speaker and Chm. of Cttees: 1955–56, 1962–65 and 1968–70. Councillor, Dist. Council of Tanunda, 1936–56 (Chm. for 17 years); JP, 1939–. Member: Bd of Governors, Adelaide Botanical Gdns, 1956–70; SA Nat. Fitness Council, 1953–70; Royal Adelaide Hosp. and Queen Elizabeth Hosp. Advisory Cttees (Chm., 1962–65); Immanuel Coll. Council, 1933–71; Hon. Assoc. Life Mem., SA Br. of Commonwealth Parly Assoc.; Mem., Transport Control Bd of SA, 1971–74. *Recreations:* bowls, gardening. *Address:* 18 Elizabeth Street, Tanunda, South Australia. *T:* 632422.

TEVIOT, 2nd Baron, *cr* 1940, of Burghclere; **Charles John Kerr;** *b* 16 Dec. 1934; *s* of 1st Baron Teviot, DSO, MC, and Florence Angela (*d* 1979), *d* of late Lt-Col Charles Walter Villiers, CBE, DSO; *S* father, 1968; *m* 1965, Patricia Mary Harris; one *s* one *d*. *Educ:* Eton. Sales Representative; Bus Conductor and Driver; Salesman; genealogical and historical record agent. Dir, Debrett's Peerage Ltd, 1977-. Mem., Adv. Council on Public Records, 1974-. Fellow, Soc. of Genealogists, 1975. *Recreations:* reading, walking. *Heir: s* Hon. Charles Robert Kerr, *b* 19 Sept. 1971. *Address:* 12 Grand Avenue, Hassocks, West Sussex. *T:* Hassocks 4471.

TEW, Prof. John Hedley Brian, PhD; External Professor, Economics Department, University of Loughborough, since 1982; Midland Bank Professor of Money and Banking, University of Nottingham, 1967-82; *b* 1 Feb. 1917; *s* of Herbert and Catherine Mary Tew; *m* 1944, Marjorie Hoey Craigie; one *s* one *d*. *Educ:* Mill Hill School, Leicester; University College, Leicester; Peterhouse, Cambridge. BSc (Econ.) London; PhD Cantab. Iron and Steel Control, 1940-42; Ministry of Aircraft Production, 1942-45; Industrial and Commercial Finance Corp., 1946; Professor of Economics, Univ. of Adelaide (Australia), 1947-49; Professor of Economics, University of Nottingham, 1950-67. Part-time Member: Iron and Steel Board, 1964-67; East Midlands Electricity Board, 1965-76; Tubes Div., BSC, 1969-73; Mem., Cttee of Enquiry on Small Firms, Dept of Trade and Industry, 1969-71. *Publications:* Wealth and Income, 1950; International Monetary Co-operation 1952; (jt editor) Studies in Company Finance, 1959; Monetary Theory, 1969; The Evolution of the International Monetary System, 1977. *Address:* 121 Bramcote Lane, Wollaton, Notts.

TEWKESBURY, Bishop Suffragan of, since 1973; **Rt. Rev. Thomas Carlyle Joseph Robert Hamish Deakin;** *b* 16 Feb. 1917; *s* of Rev. Thomas Carlyle Deakin (Rector of Uley, Glos, 1943-57), and Harriet Herries Deakin; *m* 1942, Marion, *d* of E. J. and Mrs E. Anson Dyer, Stratford Abbey, Stroud; one *s* (and one *s* decd). *Educ:* Wadham Coll., Oxford (MA); Wells Theological Coll. Deacon 1940, priest 1941, Diocese of Gloucester. Curate of St Lawrence, Stroud, 1940-44; Vicar of Holy Trinity, Forest of Dean, 1944-49; Vicar of Charlton Kings, 1949-73; Rural Dean of Cheltenham, 1963-73; Hon. Canon of Gloucester, 1966-73. *Address:* Green Acre, 166 Hempsted Lane, Gloucester GL2 6LG. *T:* Gloucester 21824.

TEYNHAM, 20th Baron *cr* 1616; **John Christopher Ingham Roper-Curzon;** *b* 25 Dec. 1928; *s* of 19th Baron Teynham, DSO, DSC, and Elspeth Grace (who *m* 2nd, 1958, 6th Marquess of Northampton, DSO, and *d* 1976), *e d* of late William Ingham Whitaker; *S* father, 1972; *m* 1964, Elizabeth, *yr d* of Lt-Col the Hon. David Scrymgeour-Wedderburn, DSO, Scots Guards (killed on active service 1944), and of the Countess of Dundee; five *s* four *d* (of whom one *s* one *d* are twins). *Educ:* Eton. A Land Agent. Late Captain, The Buffs (TA), formerly Coldstream Guards; active service in Palestine, 1948. ADC to Governor of Bermuda, 1953 and 1955; ADC to Governor of Leeward Islands, 1955; Private Secretary and ADC, 1956; ADC to Governor of Jamaica, 1962. Pres., Inst. of Commerce, 1972-. Member of Council, Sail Training Association, 1964-. OStJ. *Recreations:* shooting and fishing. *Heir: s* Hon. David John Henry Ingham Roper-Curzon, *b* 5 Oct. 1965. *Address:* The Walton Canonry, The Close, Salisbury, Wilts. *T:* Salisbury 6896. *Clubs:* Turf; House of Lords Yacht; Ocean Cruising; Puffins (Edinburgh).

THACKER, Prof. Thomas William, MA Oxon; Director of School of Oriental Studies, and Professor of Semitic Philology, University of Durham, 1951-77, now Emeritus; *b* 6 Nov. 1911; *s* of late Thomas William and of Edith Maud Thacker; *m* 1939, Katharine E. Hawthorn; one *s*. *Educ:* City of Oxford School; St Catherine's, Oxford; Berlin University. Clothworkers' Exhibitioner, 1931-33; BA 1933; Goldsmiths' Research Scholar, 1933-35; University Senior Student, Oxford, 1935-37; Mark Quested Exhibitioner, Oxford, 1937-39; studied in Berlin, 1933-36. Member of Egypt Exploration Society's expedition to Tell-el-Amarna, 1935; Asst Lecturer in Semitic Languages, University Coll. of N Wales, Bangor, 1937; Reader in Hebrew, Univ. of Durham, 1938-45; Prof. of Hebrew and Oriental Languages, Univ. of Durham, 1945-51; Foreign Office, 1940-45. Examiner at Univs of Wales (Hebrew and Old Testament), Manchester, Liverpool and Leeds (Semitic Languages), Oxford (Egyptology and Hebrew). Foreign Mem., Royal Flemish Acad. *Publications:* The Relationship of the Semitic and Egyptian Verbal Systems, 1954; articles and reviews in various periodicals. *Address:* 28 Church Street, Durham. *T:* Durham 64385.

THAIN, Eric Malcolm, PhD; FRSC; Director, Tropical Products Institute, Overseas Development Administration, since 1981; *b* 29 Nov. 1925; *s* of late Arthur Robert Thain and Olive Grace (*née* Parsons); *m* 1954, Nancy Garbutt Key, *d* of late Mr and Mrs T. G. Key; one *s* one *d*. *Educ:* St Dunstan's Coll., Catford; Univ. of London (BSc, PhD). Lister Institute of Preventive Medicine, 1949; ICI Research Fellow, 1953-54; Royal Society/National Academy of Science Research Fellow, Univ. of California, Berkeley, 1954-55; ICI Research Fellow, University Coll. London, 1955-57; Tropical Products Institute: Member, Scientific Staff, 1957; Asst Director, 1963; Dep. Director, 1969. Member: WHO and FAO Expert Committees on Pesticides, 1961-; Executive Cttee, Essex Bird Watching and Preservation Soc., 1950- (Chm. 1970-73). *Publications:* research papers on organic chemistry and pesticides in jls of various learned societies. *Recreations:* natural history, visiting museums. *Address:* 2 Middleton Road, Shenfield, Essex CM15 8DL. *T:* Brentwood 212920. *Clubs:* Athenæum, Queckett Microscopical (President, 1980-).

THALBEN-BALL, Sir George (Thomas), Kt 1982; CBE 1967; DMus Cantuar 1935; ARCM; FRCM 1951; FRCO; FRSCM 1956 (diploma 1963); FRSA; Bard Ylewyth Mur; Freeman of City of London; Civic and University Organist, Birmingham, 1949; Organist, the Temple Church, 1923-81, Organist Emeritus, since 1982; Curator-Organist, The Royal Albert Hall, London; Professor and Examiner, the Royal College of Music; Examiner to the Associated Board of the Royal Academy of Music and the Royal College of Music; Member of the Council and Examiner of Royal College of Organists; Examiner on behalf of the Cape University, 1925; Adviser and Consultant to BBC, 1941; *b* Sydney, NSW; *s* of George Charles Thalben-Ball and Mary Hannah Spear, Newquay, Cornwall; *m* Evelyn (*d* 1961), *d* of Francis Chapman, NZ; one *s* one *d*. *Educ:* private tuition. Exhbnr and Grove Scholar, RCM, Chappell and Hopkinson Gold Medallist; Lafontaine Prize, RCO; Organist: Whitefield's Tabernacle; Holy Trinity Church, Castlenau; Paddington Parish Church; acting Organist, the Hon. Socs of Temple, 1919, Organist, 1923-; studied pianoforte with Fritz Hartvigson, Franklin Taylor, and Fanny Davies; harmony and composition with Sir Frederick Bridge, Sir Charles Stanford, and Dr Charles Wood; musical history with Sir Hubert Parry; organ with Sir Walter Parratt and F. A. Sewell. President: London Soc. of Organists, 1936; RCO, 1948; Incorporated Assoc. of Organists, 1944-46; Mem. Bd of Governors, Royal Nat. Coll. of the Blind. FRSA 1961; Fellow, Royal Canadian Coll. of Organists. Hon. RAM 1973. Hon. Bencher, Inner Temple, 1959. Guest Organist, Les Amis de l'Orgue, Paris, 1937; Toured Australia as guest organist in connection with Jubilee of the formation of the Commonwealth, 1951, toured: South Africa, 1954, New Zealand, 1971; Guest of honour, Amer. Guild of Organists Convention, NY, 1956; Guest, Philadelphia, 1973; toured USA and Canada, 1975 (opening organ recital, Carnegie Hall, NY). Mem. Jury, Concours international d'orgue, Grand Prix de Chartres, 1973. EMI Gold Disc, 1963. Has played the organ on the Continent and in America and was a regular broadcaster and performer at the Sir Henry Wood Promenade Concerts. Composer of Organ and Choral music including Sursum Corda for chorus, orchestra and trumpet fanfares (commissioned by BBC). Hon. DMus and Gold Medal, Birmingham, 1972. *Recreations:* golf and riding. *Address:* 3 Paper Buildings, Inner Temple, EC4. *Club:* Athenæum.

THALMANN, Dr Ernesto; retired Swiss Ambassador; President, National Swiss Unesco Commission; *b* 14 Jan. 1914; *s* of Friedrich Thalmann and Clara (*née* Good); *m* 1943, Paula Degen; two *s* one *d*. *Educ:* Gymnasien, Berne and Zürich; Univ. of Zürich (LLD). Entered Federal Dept of Public Economy, 1941; Federal Political Dept (Swiss Foreign Office), 1945; Minister/Counsellor and Dep. Head of Mission, Swiss Embassy, Washington, 1957-61; Permanent Observer to UN, New York (Ambassador Extraordinary and Plenipotentiary), 1961-66; Head of Internat. Organizations Div., Fed. Political Dept, Berne, 1966-71; Special Mission in Jerusalem, after 6-day war, as Personal Rep. of UN Secretary-General, U Thant, 1967; Secretary-General, Fed. Political Dept and Director of Political Affairs, 1971-75; Swiss Ambassador to the Court of St James's, 1976-79. *Address:* 8 Anselmstrasse, 3005 Berne, Switzerland.

THAPAR, Prem Nath, CIE 1944; lately Vice-Chancellor, Punjab Agricultural University, Lydhiana, 1962-68; Indian Civil Service; *b* 13 April 1903; *s* of Diwan Bahadur Kunj Behari Thapar, CBE; *m* 1932, Leela Dutta; one *s* two *d*. *Educ:* Govt Coll., Lahore; New Coll., Oxford. Joined ICS 1926. Dep. Commissioner, Kangra, Attock; Deputy Commissioner and Colonisation Officer, Montgomery, 1934-37; Settlement Officer, Jhelum, 1937-41; Joint Secretary, Information and Broadcasting Department, Government of India, 1941-46; Secretary, Food and Civil Supplies Department, Punjab, 1946-47; Commissioner, Lahore Division, 1947; Financial Commissioner, East Punjab, 1947-53; Chief Administrator, Chandigarh Capital Project, 1950-53; Adviser, Planning Commission, Government of India, 1953-54; Sec., Min. of Food and Agric., Govt of India, 1954-58; Member, Atomic Energy Commission and *ex officio* Secretary to Government of India, Dept of Atomic Energy, Bombay, 1958-62. Mem. Punjab Admin. Reforms Commn, 1964-65; Consultant, Review Team, FAO, UN, Rome, 1966-67. Trustee, Internat. Rice Research Inst., Manila, Philippines. *Publications:* Settlement Report, Jhelum District, 1945; Customary Law, Jhelum District, 1946. *Address:* Ashok Farm, PO Maidan Garhi, New Delhi-30, India. *T:* 72382.

THATCHER, Arthur Roger, CB 1974; Director, Office of Population Censuses and Surveys, and Registrar General for England and Wales, since 1978; *b* 22 Oct. 1926; *s* of Arthur Thatcher; *m* 1950, Mary Audrey Betty (*née* Street); two *d*. *Educ:* The Leys Sch.; St John's Coll., Cambridge (MA). Royal Navy, 1947-49. North Western Gas Board, 1949-52; Admiralty, 1952-61; Cabinet Office, 1961-63; Ministry of Labour, 1963-68; Director of Statistics, Dept of Employment, 1968-78, Dep. Sec., 1972-78. *Publications:* official publications; articles in statistical jls. *Address:* Office of Population Censuses and Surveys, St Catherine's House, 10 Kingsway, WC2B 6JP. *Club:* Army and Navy.

THATCHER, Rt. Hon. Mrs Margaret (Hilda), PC 1970; MP (C) Barnet, Finchley, since 1974 (Finchley, 1959-74); Prime Minister and First Lord of the Treasury, since 1979; *b* 13 Oct. 1925; *d* of late Alfred Roberts, Grantham, Lincs; *m* 1951, Denis Thatcher; one *s* one *d* (twins). *Educ:* Kesteven and Grantham Girls' School; Somerville College, Oxford (MA, BSc). Research Chemist, 1947-51; called to the Bar, Lincoln's Inn, 1953, Hon. Bencher, 1975. Joint Parly Sec., Min. of Pensions and National Insurance, Oct. 1961-64; Sec. of State for Educn and Sci., 1970-74; Leader of the Opposition, 1975-79.

Co-Chm., Women's Nat. Commn, 1970-74. Hon. Fellow, Somerville Coll., Oxford, 1970. Freedom of Borough of Barnet, 1980. Donovan Award, USA, 1981. *Recreations:* music, reading. *Address:* House of Commons, SW1. *Clubs:* Carlton, St Stephen's Constitutional.

THAW, Mrs John; *see* Hancock, Sheila.

THAYRE, Albert Jesse, CBE 1980 (MBE 1945); Director, N. C. Bailey Organisation Ltd, since 1982; Chief General Manager and Director, Halifax Building Society, 1974-82; *b* 30 May 1917; *s* of Alfred and Louisa Thayre; *m* 1940, Margaret Elizabeth Wheeler; one *d. Educ:* Bromley County Sch. for Boys; City of London Coll. BCom (London) 1948. Stockbrokers' Clerk, 1933-39. Served War: Rifleman/NCO with 2/London Irish Rifles, 1939-41; Lieut to Captain 51 (H) Bn Reconnaissance Corps, 1941-42; Captain, then Major and Lt-Col 14 Highland LI, 1942-46 (incl. appts as DAQMG and AA&QMG). Investment Analyst, 1946-50. Halifax Building Soc.: Clerk, then Inspector and Br. Manager, 1951-55; Staff Manager, 1955-56; Asst Gen. Man., 1956-60; Gen. Man., 1960; Dir, 1968; Asst Chief Gen. Man., 1970. Bradford Univ.: Mem. Council, 1966-; Chm. Finance Cttee, 1966-; Pro-Chancellor, 1969-. Mem., Univs Authorities Panel, 1970-79; Dir and Dep. Chm., Univs Superannuation Scheme Ltd, 1974-79. FSS, FCBSI, CBIM. Hon. DLitt Bradford, 1982. *Address:* Stonedale, 42 Northowram Green, Halifax, West Yorkshire HX3 7SL. *T:* Halifax 202581.

THELLUSSON, family name of **Baron Rendlesham.**

THELWELL, Norman; freelance artist-cartoonist since 1957; *b* Birkenhead, 3 May 1923; *s* of Christopher Thelwell and Emily (*née* Vick); *m* 1949, Rhona Evelyn Ladbury; one *s* one *d. Educ:* Rock Ferry High Sch., Birkenhead; Liverpool Coll. of Art. Nat. Diploma of Art; ATD. Teacher of Art, Wolverhampton Coll. of Art, 1950-57. Regular contributor to Punch, 1952-; cartoonist for: News Chronicle, 1956-60; Sunday Dispatch, 1960-61; Sunday Express, 1962-. Drawings for general publications, advertising, book jackets, illustrations, etc. *Publications:* Angels on Horseback, 1957; Thelwell Country, 1959; A Place of Your Own, 1960; Thelwell in Orbit, 1961; A Leg at Each Corner, 1962; The Penguin Thelwell, 1963; Top Dog, 1964; Thelwell's Riding Academy, 1965; Drawing Ponies, 1966; Up the Garden Path, 1967; Thelwell's Compleat Tangler, 1967; Thelwell's Book of Leisure, 1968; This Desirable Plot, 1970; The Effluent Society, 1971; Penelope, 1972; Three Sheets in the Wind, 1973; Belt Up, 1974; Thelwell Goes West, 1975; Thelwell's Brat Race, 1977; A Plank Bridge by a Pool, 1978; Thelwell's Gymkhana, 1979; Thelwell Annual, 1980; A Millstone Round My Neck, 1981; Thelwell Annual, 1981; Pony Cavalcade, 1981; How to Draw Ponies, 1982; Some Damn Fool's Signed the Rubens Again, 1982. *Recreations:* trout and salmon angling, painting. *Address:* Herons Mead, Timsbury, Romsey, Hants SO5 0NE. *T:* Braishfield 68238. *Club:* Savage.

THEOBALD, George Peter, JP; company director, since 1958; *b* 5 Aug. 1931; *s* of late George Oswald Theobald and Helen (*née* Moore); *m* 1955, Josephine Mary (*née* Boodle); two *s* three *d. Educ:* Betteshanger Sch.; Harrow. National Service commission, 5 Regt RHA, 1950-52; 290 (City of London) RA (TA), 1953-59. Robert Warner Ltd, 1953-74: Director, 1958; Man. Dir, Chm. Gp subsidiaries, 1965; Director of four private companies, 1974-; Tea Clearing House, 1959-72 (Chm., 1970-72); Moran Tea Holdings plc, 1980-; Moran Tea (India) plc, 1981-. City of London (Queenhithe Ward): Chm., Ward Club, 1966-68; Common Councilman, 1968-74; Alderman, 1974-79. Member, Transport Users' Consultative Cttee for London, 1969 (Dep. Chm. 1978); Governor: Bridewell Royal Hosp., 1974-; King Edward's Sch., Witley, 1974- (Dep. Chm., Bursary Appeal, 1978-; Trustee, Educational Trust, 1977-); Donation Governor, Christ's Hosp., 1976-; Governor, St Leonards-Mayfield Sch., 1982-; Mem. Cttee, Langford Cross Children's Home, 1976-; Trustee: National Flood and Tempest Distress Fund, 1977-; Harrow Club W10, 1978-. Church Commissioner for England, 1978-79. JP City of London, 1974. *Recreations:* skiing, squash, swimming, tennis, walking. *Address:* Towerhill Manor, Gomshall, Guildford, Surrey GU5 9LP. *T:* Shere 2381. *Clubs:* Oriental, City Livery, Guildhall.

THEROUX, Paul Edward; FRSL; FRGS; writer; *b* 10 April 1941; *s* of Albert Eugene Theroux and Anne Dittami Theroux; *m* 1967, Anne Castle; two *s. Educ:* Univ. of Massachusetts (BA). Lecturer: Univ. of Urbino, 1963; Soche Hill Coll., Malawi, 1963-65; Makerere Univ., Kampala, Uganda, 1965-68; Univ. of Singapore, 1968-71; Writer-in-Residence, Univ. of Virginia, 1972. Hon. DLitt: Trinity Coll., Washington DC, 1980; Tufts Univ., Mass, 1980. *Publications:* novels: Waldo, 1967; Fong and the Indians, 1968; Girls at Play, 1969; Murder in Mount Holly, 1969; Jungle Lovers, 1971; Sinning with Annie, 1972; Saint Jack, 1973 (filmed, 1979); The Black House, 1974; The Family Arsenal, 1976; The Consul's File, 1977; Picture Palace, 1978 (Whitbread Award, 1978); A Christmas Card, 1978; London Snow, 1980; World's End, 1980; The Mosquito Coast, 1981; The London Embassy, 1982; *criticism:* V. S. Naipaul, 1972; *travel:* The Great Railway Bazaar, 1975; The Old Patagonian Express, 1979; *screenplay:* Saint Jack, 1979; reviews in The Sunday Times, New York Times, etc. *Recreation:* rowing. *Address:* 35 Elsynge Road, SW18 2HR.

THESIGER, family name of **Viscount Chelmsford.**

THESIGER, Roderic Miles Doughty; Director, P. & D. Colnaghi and Co. Ltd, 1955-71; *b* 8 Nov. 1915; *y s* of late Hon. Wilfred Thesiger, DSO, and

Mrs Reginald Astley, CBE; *m* 1st, 1940, Mary Rose (marr. diss. 1946; she *d* 1962), *d* of Hon. Guy Charteris; 2nd, 1946, Ursula, *d* of A. W. Whitworth, Woollas Hall, Pershore; one *s* one *d. Educ:* Eton; Christ Church, Oxford; Courtauld Institute. Served War of 1939-45, Welsh Guards, 1939-41; 1st Parachute Bde, 1941-44 (twice wounded, POW). Assistant, Tate Gallery, 1945-46; afterwards worked with Messrs Sotheby and privately until 1954. *Recreations:* visiting Italy and France. *Address:* The Paddocks, Lucton, Leominster, Herefordshire. *T:* Yarpole 327.

See also W. P. *Thesiger.*

THESIGER, Wilfred Patrick, CBE 1968; DSO 1941; MA Oxon; *b* 3 June 1910; *e s* of late Hon. Wilfred Thesiger, DSO, and Mrs Reginald Astley, CBE. *Educ:* Eton; Magdalen College, Oxford (MA). Repres. Oxford at boxing, 1930-33; Captain Oxford Boxing Team, 1933; Hon. Attaché Duke of Gloucester's Mission to Abyssinia, 1930; served Middle East, 1941 (DSO); explored Danakil country of Abyssinia and the Aussa Sultanate, 1933-34 (awarded Back Grant by RGS, 1935); Sudan Political Service, Darfur-Upper Nile, 1935-40; served in Ethiopian, Syrian and Western Desert campaigns with SDF and SAS regiment with rank of Major; explored in Southern Arabia, 1945-49; twice crossed the Empty Quarter. Founder's Medal, RGS, 1948; Lawrence of Arabia Medal, RCAS, 1955; Livingstone Medal, RSGS, 1962; W. H. Heinemann Award (for 1964), RSL, 1965; Burton Memorial Medal, Roy. Asiatic Soc., 1966. FRSL; Hon. FBA 1982; Hon. DLitt Leicester. 3rd Class Star of Ethiopia. *Publications:* Arabian Sands, 1959; The Marsh Arabs, 1964; Desert, Marsh and Mountain: the world of a nomad, 1979. *Recreations:* travelling, photography. *Address:* 15 Shelley Court, Tite Street, SW3. *T:* 01-352 7213. *Clubs:* Travellers', Beefsteak.

See also R. M. D. *Thesiger.*

THETFORD, Bishop Suffragan of, since 1981; **Rt. Rev. Timothy Dudley-Smith;** *b* 26 Dec. 1926; *o s* of Arthur and Phyllis Dudley Smith, Buxton, Derbyshire; *m* 1959, June Arlette MacDonald; one *s* two *d. Educ:* Tonbridge Sch.; Pembroke Coll., and Ridley Hall, Cambridge. BA 1947, MA 1951; Certif. in Educn 1948. Deacon, 1950; priest, 1951; Asst Curate, St Paul, Northumberland Heath, 1950-53; Head of Cambridge Univ. Mission in Bermondsey, 1953-55; Hon. Chaplain to Bp of Rochester, 1953-60; Editor, Crusade, and Editorial Sec. of Evangelical Alliance, 1955-59; Asst Sec. of Church Pastoral-Aid Soc., 1959-65, Sec., 1965-73; Archdeacon of Norwich, 1973-81; Commissary to Archbp of Sydney, 1971-81; Exam. Chap. to Bp of Norwich, 1971-. *Publications:* Christian Literature and the Church Bookstall, 1963; What Makes a Man a Christian?, 1966; A Man Named Jesus, 1971; Someone who Beckons, 1978; contributor to various hymn books. *Recreations:* reading, verse, woodwork, family and friends. *Address:* Rectory Meadow, Bramerton, Norwich NR14 7DW. *T:* Surlingham 251. *Club:* Norfolk (Norwich).

THEUNISSEN, Most Rev. John Baptist Hubert, DD; Titular Archbishop of Skálholt, since 1968; *b* Schimmert, Holland, 3 Oct. 1905; *Educ:* Schimmert and Oirschot, Holland; Rome University. DD 1929. Professor, Major Seminary, Oirschot, Holland, 1930; Professor, Major Seminary, Portugal, 1935; Superior Regional of the Missions in Portuguese East Africa, 1937; Superior Provincial of Dutch Province of Montfort Fathers, 1947; consecrated Bishop of Blantyre, 1950; Archbishop of Blantyre, Malawi, 1959; Apostolic Administrator of Iceland, 1967; retd, 1968. Knight, Order of the Lion (Netherlands), 1960. *Recreation:* music. *Address:* Bishop's House, Langstraat 84, Schimmert (L.), The Netherlands.

THIESS, Sir Leslie Charles, Kt 1971; CBE 1968; President, Thiess Holdings Ltd, 1980-82; Chairman of Directors, Thiess Consortium Ltd; Chairman: Thiess Toyota Pty Ltd; Daihatsu Distributors Pty Ltd; Director, Thiess Dampier Mitsui Pty Ltd; Governing Dir, Drayton Investments Pty Ltd; *b* 8 April 1909; *m* 1929, Christina Mary (*née* Erbacher); two *s* three *d. Educ:* Drayton, Queensland. Founded Thiess Bros as a private company, 1933; Managing Dir, Thiess Holdings Ltd when it was formed in 1950; also when firm became a public company, 1958; Chm., Thiess Group of Cos, 1968-80. FCIT (London), 1971. Order of the Sacred Treasure (third class), Japan, 1972. *Recreation:* deep sea fishing. *Address:* 121 King Arthur Terrace, Tennyson, Qld 4105, Australia. *T:* 48 1147. *Clubs:* Brisbane, Tattersalls, Royal Queensland Yacht (all of Brisbane); Huntington, NSW Sports (NSW).

THIMANN, Prof. Kenneth Vivian; Professor of Biology, 1965-72, and Provost of Crown College, 1966-72, Emeritus Professor, recalled to duty since 1972, University of California, Santa Cruz, Calif, USA; *b* 5 Aug. 1904; *s* of Phoebus Thimann and Muriel Kate Thimann (*née* Harding); *m* 1931, Ann Mary Bateman, Sutton Bridge, Lincs; three *d. Educ:* Caterham Sch., Surrey; Imperial Coll., London. BSc, ARCS 1924; DIC 1925; PhD 1928. Beit Memorial Res. Fellow, 1927-29; Demonstr in Bacteriology, King's Coll. for Women, 1926-28; Instr in Biochem., Calif Inst. of Techn., 1930-35; Harvard University: Lectr on Botany, 1935; (Biology): Asst Prof., 1936, Associate Prof., 1939, Prof., 1946, and Higgins Prof., 1962-65, now Prof. Emeritus. Vis. Professor: Sorbonne, 1954; Univ. of Massachusetts, 1974; Univ. of Texas, 1976. Scientific Consultant, US Navy, 1942-45. Dir, Amer. Assoc. for Adv. of Science, 1968-71. Pres., XIth Internat. Botanical Congress, Seattle, USA, 1969; 2nd Nat. Biol Congress, Miami, 1971. Hon. AM Harvard, 1940; PhD (Hon.) Univ. of Basle, 1959; Doctor (Hon.) Univ. of Clermont-Ferrand, 1961. Fellow: Nat. Acad. of Scis (Councillor, 1967-71); Amer. Acad. of Arts and Scis; Amer. Philosophical Soc. (Councillor, 1973-76); and professional biological socs in USA and England; Foreign Member: Royal Society

(London); Institut de France (Acad. des Sciences, Paris); Accademia Nazionale dei Lincei (Rome); Leopoldina Akademie (Halle); Roumanian Academy (Bucharest); Botanical Societies of Japan and Netherlands. Silver Medal, Internat. Plant Growth Substance Assoc. *Publications:* (in USA) Phytohormones (with F. W. Went), 1937; The Action of Hormones in Plants and Invertebrates, 1948; The Life of Bacteria, 1955, 2nd edn 1963 (German edn 1964); L'Origine et les Fonctions des Auxines, 1956; The Natural Plant Hormones, 1972; Hormones in the Whole Life of Plants, 1977; (ed) Senescence in Plants, 1980; (with J. Langenheim) Botany: Plant Biology in relation to Human Affairs, 1981; about 280 papers in biological and biochemical jls. *Recreations:* music (piano), gardening. *Address:* 36 Pasatiempo Drive, Santa Cruz, California 95060, USA. *T:* (408) 423-0437. *Clubs:* Harvard Faculty (Cambridge, Mass); Harvard (San Francisco).

THIMONT, Bernard Maurice, CB 1979; Secretary, Churches' Main Committee, since 1981; *b* 1 July 1920; *s* of Georges André Thimont; *m* 1949, Joy Rowe; one *s* one *d. Educ:* St Ignatius Coll., London. Served War of 1939-45, in Army (Major), 1939-48. Foreign Office, 1948-50; HM Treasury, 1950-65; IDC, 1966; Cabinet Office, 1967; HM Treasury, 1967-68; Civil Service Dept, 1968-77; Controller, HM Stationery Office and Queen's Printer of Acts of Parlt, 1977-80. *Recreations:* music, building. *Address:* 10 Oakhill Court, Edge Hill, Wimbledon, SW19. *T:* 01-946 0918.

THIRD, Rt. Rev. Richard Henry McPhail; *see* Dover, Bishop Suffragan of.

THIRKELL, Lancelot George, (Lance Thirkell); Secretary and Administrator, New Bridge Association for befriending ex-offenders, since 1980; *b* 9 Jan. 1921; *s* of George Lancelot Thirkell, engineer, and Angela Margaret Mackail (Angela Thirkell, novelist); *m* 1946, Katherine Mary Lowinsky, *d* of Thomas Esmond Lowinsky, artist, and Ruth Jeanette Hirsch; two *s* two *d. Educ:* Saint Paul's School (Schol.); Magdalen Coll. Oxford (Demy). HM Forces, 1942-46; active service D-day to the Rhine with Essex Yeo. and in SE Asia with RA. HM Foreign Service, 1946-50; granted Civil Service Certificate, 1946; Third Sec., Western Dept, 1946; Third Sec., Budapest, 1947; Second Sec., Eastern Dept, 1948. Joined BBC as Report Writer, Monitoring Service, 1950; Assistant, Appointments Dept, 1953; Assistant Staff Administration, 1956; Head of Secretariat, 1961; Controller, Staff Trng and Appointments, 1964; Chief Asst to Man. Dir, External Broadcasting, 1972-75; Controller, Administration, External Broadcasting, 1975-80. Dir, Caribbean Relay Co., 1976. Governor, Thomson Foundn Television Coll., 1964-72. Councillor, Royal Borough of Kensington, 1959-62; Chm. Notting Hill Adventure Playground, 1964-76; Appeals Sec., Portobello Project for unattached youth; Mem., European Adv. Council, Salzburg Seminar in American Studies. Pres., Angela Thirkell Soc., 1980-. *Publications:* A Garden Full of Weeds, 1962; (with Ruth Lowinsky) Russian Food for Pleasure, 1953. *Recreations:* ski-ing, sailing. *Address:* 31 Lansdowne Road, W11. *T:* 01-727 6046; Oxbow, Harkstead, Suffolk. *Clubs:* Leander (Henley-on-Thames); Royal Harwich Yacht.

THIRKETTLE, William Ellis, CBE 1959; Principal, London College of Printing, 1939-67; *b* 26 July 1904; *s* of William Edward Thirkettle; *m* 1930, Alva, *d* of Thomas Tough Watson; two *s. Educ:* Tiffin School. Principal, Stow College of Printing, Glasgow, 1936-39. *Address:* Little White Horse, Pewsey, Wilts.

THIRLWALL, Air Vice-Marshal George Edwin, CB 1976; Director, Ceramics, Glass and Mineral Products Industry Training Board, since 1979; *b* 24 Dec. 1924; *s* of Albert and Clarice Editha Thirlwall; *m* 1st, 1949, Daphne Patricia Wynn Giles (*d* 1975); 2nd, 1977, Louisa Buck Russell (*née* Cranston). *Educ:* Sheffield Univ.; Cranfield Inst. of Technology. BEng, MSc, CEng, FRAeS, FBIM. Joined RAF, 1950; OC RAF Sealand, 1969; Dir Air Guided Weapons, MoD, 1972; AO Ground Trng, RAF Trng Comd, 1974-76; AO Engineering, Strike Command, 1976-79, retired. *Recreations:* gardening, golf. *Address:* Che Sara Sara, Gosmore Road, Hitchin, Herts. *T:* Hitchin 4182. *Club:* Royal Air Force.

THIRSK, Dr (Irene) Joan, FBA 1974; Reader in Economic History in the University of Oxford, since 1965; Fellow of St Hilda's College, Oxford, since 1965; *b* 19 June 1922; *d* of William Henry Watkins and Daisy (*née* Frayer); *m* 1945, James Wood Thirsk; one *s* one *d. Educ:* Camden School for Girls, NW5; Westfield Coll., Univ. of London. BA, PhD London; MA Oxford. Subaltern, ATS, Intelligence Corps, 1942-45. Asst Lectr in Sociology, LSE, 1950-51; Sen. Res. Fellow in Agrarian History, Dept of English Local History, Leicester Univ., 1951-65. Ford Lectr in English History, Oxford, 1975. Member: Royal Commn on Historical Monuments (England), 1977-; Econ. and Social Hist. Cttee, SSRC, 1978-82. Vice-Chm., Standing Conf. for Local Hist., 1965-82; Member: Exec. Cttee, British Agricl Hist. Soc., 1953- (Chm. Cttee, 1974-77); Council, Economic Hist. Soc., 1955-; President: Edmonton Hundred Historical Soc., 1978-; Oxfordshire Local Hist. Assoc., 1981- (Vice-Pres., 1980-81); Conf. of Teachers of Regional and Local Hist. in Tertiary Educn, 1981-82; Vice-Pres., Soc. for Lincs Hist. and Archaeol., 1979-; Foreign Mem., Amer. Philos. Soc., 1982-. Editor, Agricultural History Review, 1964-72; Gen. Editor, The Agrarian History of England and Wales, 1974- (Dep. Gen. Ed., 1966-74); Mem. Editorial Bd, Past and Present, 1956-. *Publications:* English Peasant Farming, 1957; Suffolk Farming in the Nineteenth Century, 1958; Tudor Enclosures, 1959; The Agrarian History of England and Wales vol. IV, 1500-1640, 1967; (with J. P. Cooper)

Seventeenth-Century Economic Documents, 1972; The Restoration, 1976; Economic Policy and Projects, 1978; articles in Economic History Rev., Agric. History Rev., Past and Present, History, Jl Modern History, etc. *Recreations:* gardening, sewing. *Address:* The Kilns, Lewis Close, Headington, Oxford.

THISTLETHWAITE, Prof. Frank, CBE 1979; Emeritus Professor, University of East Anglia; first Vice-Chancellor, 1961-80; *b* 24 July 1915; *s* of late Lee Thistlethwaite and of Florence Nightingale Thistlethwaite; *m* 1940, Jane, *d* of H. Lindley Hosford, Lyme, Connecticut, USA; one *s* three *d* (and one *s* decd). *Educ:* Bootham School; St John's College, Cambridge (Exhibitioner and Scholar). BA 1938, MA 1941. Editor, The Cambridge Review, 1937. Commonwealth Fund Fellow, University of Minnesota, 1938-40; British Press Service, New York, 1940-41. RAF, 1941-45; seconded to Office of War Cabinet, 1942-45. Fellow, St John's College, Cambridge, 1945-61; at various times, Tutor, Praelector, Steward; University Lecturer in Faculty of Economics and Politics, 1949-61; Visiting Prof. of American Civilization, Univ. of Pennsylvania, 1956; Vis. Fellow, Henry E. Huntington Library, Calif. 1973. Member: Inst. for Advanced Study, Princeton, 1954; Academic Adv. Committee: Chelsea Coll. of Science and Technology, 1964-66; Open Univ., 1969-74; Provisional Council, Univ. of Zambia, 1965-69; Univ. of Malawi, 1971-75; Univ. of Mauritius, 1974-; Marshall Aid Commemoration Commn, 1964-80; US-UK Educnl Commn, 1964-79; European Adv. Council, Salzburg Seminar in Amer. Studies, 1969-74; Bd, British Council, 1971-82; British Cttee of Award, Harkness Fellowships, 1974-80; Chairman: British Assoc. for American Studies, 1955-59; Cttee of Management, Inst. of US Studies, Univ. of London, 1966-80; Inter-Univ. Council for Higher Educn Overseas, 1977-81 (Mem., 1962-81); Adviser to Nat. Council of Higher Educn, Ceylon, 1967. Governor, Sedbergh Sch., 1958-73. Hon. Fellow, St John's Coll., Cambridge, 1974. Hon. Prof. of History, Univ. of Mauritius, 1981. Hon. LHD Colorado, 1972; Hon. DCL East Anglia, 1980. FRHistS. *Publications:* The Great Experiment: An Introduction to the History of the American People, 1955; The Anglo-American Connection in the Early Nineteenth Century, 1958; contrib. New Cambridge Modern History and other historical works and journals; New Universities in the Modern World (ed M. G. Ross). *Recreation:* music. *Address:* 15 Park Parade, Cambridge CB5 8AL; Island Cottage, Winson, Glos. *Club:* Athenæum.

THISTLETON-SMITH, Vice-Admiral Sir Geoffrey, KBE 1959; CB 1956; GM 1941; DL; *b* 10 May 1905; *m* 1st, 1931, Mary Katherine Harvey (*d* 1976); one *s* one *d*; 2nd, 1982, Joyce, Lady Fairhaven. Captain, 1944; HMS Pembroke, Royal Naval Barracks, Chatham (in Command), 1952; Chief of Staff to C-in-C Home Fleet and Eastern Atlantic, Dec. 1953; Rear-Admiral, 1954; Admiral Commanding Reserves, 1956-58; Vice-Admiral, 1957; Admiral, British Joint Services Mission, Washington, 1958-60, retd. CC West Sussex, 1964-77. DL Sussex, 1972. *Address:* Down Place, Harting, Petersfield, Hants.

THODAY, Prof. John Marion, FRS 1965; BSc Wales, PhD Cantab; Arthur Balfour Professor of Genetics, Cambridge University, 1959-Sept. 1983; Fellow of Emmanuel College, 1959; *b* 30 Aug. 1916; *s* of Professor D. Thoday, FRS; *m* 1950, Doris Joan Rich, PhD (Vice-Pres., Lucy Cavendish College); one *s* one *d. Educ:* Bootham School, York; University Coll. of N Wales, Bangor; Trinity College, Cambridge. Photographic Intelligence, Royal Air Force, 1941-46; Cytologist, Mount Vernon Hospital, 1946-47; Asst Lectr, then Lectr for Cytogenetics, Departments of Botany and Zoology, University of Sheffield, 1947-54; Head of Department of Genetics, Sheffield, 1954-59. Director, OECD Project for reform of secondary school Biology teaching 1962, 1963. Chm., UK Nat. Cttee for Biology, 1982. Pres., Genetical Soc., 1975-78. *Publications:* (with J. N. Thompson) Quantitive Genetics, 1979; articles on radiation cytology, experimental evolution, the genetics of continuous variables, biological progress and on genetics and society. *Address:* 7 Clarkson Road, Cambridge CB3 0EH.

THODE, Dr Henry George, CC (Canada) 1967; MBE 1946; FRS 1954; FRSC 1943; FCIC 1948; Professor Emeritus, McMaster University, Canada, since 1979; *b* 10 September 1910; Canadian; *m* 1935, Sadie Alicia Patrick; three *s. Educ:* University of Saskatchewan (BSc 1930, MSc 1932); University of Chicago (PhD 1934). Research Asst, Columbia Univ., 1936-38; Research Chemist, US Rubber Co., 1938; McMaster University: Asst Prof. of Chem., 1939-42; Assoc. Prof. of Chem., 1942-44; Prof. of Chem., 1944-79; Head, Department of Chemistry, 1948-52; Dir of Res., 1947-61; Principal of Hamilton Coll., 1944-63; Vice-Pres., 1957-61; Pres. and Vice-Chancellor, 1961-72. California Inst. of Technology, Pasadena, Calif: Nat. Science Foundn Sen. Foreign Res. Fellow, 1970; Sherman Fairchild Distinguished Scholar, 1977. National Research Council, War Research-Atomic Energy, 1943-45. Member: Nat. Research Council, 1955-61; Defence Research Bd, 1955-61; Commn on Atomic Weights (SAIC), IUPAC; Board of Governors, Ontario Research Foundn, 1955-82; Director: Atomic Energy of Canada Ltd, 1966-81; Stelco Inc. Hon. Fellow, Chemical Inst. of Canada, 1972; Shell Canada Merit Fellowship, 1974. Hon. DSc: Universities: Toronto, 1955; BC, Acadia, 1960; Laval, 1963; RMC, 1964; McGill, 1966; Queen's, 1967; York, 1972; McMaster, 1973. Hon. LLD Sask., 1958. Medal of Chemical Inst. of Canada, 1957; Tory Medal, Royal Soc. of Canada, 1959; Arthur L. Day Medal, Geological Soc. of America, 1980; Centenary Medal, Royal Soc. of Canada, 1982. *Publications:* 147 publications on nuclear chemistry, isotope chemistry, isotope abundances in terrestrial and extraterrestrial material, separation of isotopes, magnetic susceptibilities, electrical discharges in gases, sulphur concentrations and isotope ratios in lunar materials. *Recreations:* swimming, farming. *Address:* Department of Chemistry, Nuclear Research Building, McMaster University, 1280 Main Street West, Hamilton, Ontario L8S 4K1, Canada. *T:* (416) 525-9140. *Club:* Rotary (Hamilton, Ont.).

THODY, Prof. Philip Malcolm Waller; Professor of French Literature, University of Leeds, since 1965; *b* Lincoln, 21 March 1928; *s* of Thomas Edwin Thody and Florence Ethel (*née* Hart); *m* 1954, Joyce Elizabeth Woodin; two *s* two *d. Educ:* Lincoln Sch.; King's Coll., Univ. of London. FIL 1981. Temp. Asst Lectr, Univ. of Birmingham, 1954-55; Asst Lectr, subseq. Lectr, QUB, 1956-65; Chairman: Dept of French, Univ. of Leeds, 1968-72, 1975-; Bd of Faculties of Arts, Social Studies and Law, Univ. of Leeds, 1972-74. Vis. Professor: Univ. of Western Ontario, Canada, 1963-64; Berkeley Summer Sch., 1964; Harvard Summer Sch., 1968; Centenary Vis. Prof., Adelaide Univ., 1974; Canterbury Vis. Fellow, Univ. of Canterbury, NZ, 1977. Pres., Modern Languages Assoc., 1980, 1981. Officer dans l'Ordre des Palmes Académiques, 1981. *Publications:* Albert Camus, a study of his work, 1957; Jean-Paul Sartre, a literary and political study, 1960; Albert Camus, 1913-1960, 1961; Jean Genet, a study of his novels and plays, 1968; Jean Anouilh, 1968; Choderlos de Laclos, 1970; Jean-Paul Sartre, a biographical introduction, 1971; Aldous Huxley, a biographical introduction, 1973; Roland Barthes: a conservative estimate, 1977; A True Life Reader for Children and Parents, 1977; Dog Days in Babel (novel), 1979; contribs to French Studies, Times Literary Supplement, Times Higher Educational Supplement, Modern Languages Review, London Magazine, Twentieth Century, Encounter, Yorkshire Post. *Recreations:* talking; Wodehouse inter-war first editions. *Address:* 6 The Nook, Primley Park, Alwoodley, Leeds LS17 7JU. *T:* Leeds 687350.

THOM, Alexander; Professor of Engineering Science, Oxford University, 1945-61; *b* 26 March 1894; Scottish parents; *m* 1917, Jeanie Boyd Kirkwood (*d* 1975); one *s* one *d* (one *s* killed 1945). *Educ:* Glasgow University. BSc 1915, PhD 1926, DSc 1929, Glasgow; MA (Oxford) 1945; Emeritus Fellow, Brasenose College, 1961. Employed by various engineering and aeronautical firms, 1913-21; Lectr, Glasgow University, 1922-39; Royal Aircraft Establishment, Farnborough, on aeronautical research, 1939-45. Hon. LLD Glasgow, 1960; Hon. DSc Strathclyde, 1976. *Publications:* Standard Tables and Formulae for Setting out Road Spirals, 1935; (with C. J. Apelt) Field Computations in Engineering and Physics, 1960; Megalithic Sites in Britain, 1967; Megalithic Lunar Observatories, 1971; (with A. S. Thom) Megalithic Remains in Britain and Brittany, 1978; Megalithic Rings, 1980; papers to various scientific institutions. *Recreation:* sailing. *Address:* The Hill, Dunlop, Ayrshire.

THOM, Kenneth Cadwallader; HM Diplomatic Service, retired; re-employed in Foreign and Commonwealth Office, since 1981; *b* 4 Dec. 1922; *m* 1948, Patience Myra (*née* Collingridge); three *s* one *d. Educ:* University College School, London; St Andrews Univ.; MA(Hons). Army Service, 1942-47; Assistant District Officer, then District Officer, Northern Nigerian Administration, 1950-59; 1st Secretary: FO, 1959; UK Mission to UN, NY, 1960-63; FO, 1963-66; Budapest, 1966-68; FCO, 1968-72; Counsellor, Dublin, 1972-74; Head of Accommodation and Services Dept, FCO, 1974-78; Consul-General: Hanover, 1978-79; Hamburg, 1979-81. *Address:* c/o Foreign and Commonwealth Office, 4 Central Buildings, Matthew Parker Street, SW1.

THOMAS OF SWYNNERTON, Baron *cr* 1981 (Life Peer), of Notting Hill in Greater London; **Hugh Swynnerton Thomas;** historian; Chairman, Centre for Policy Studies, since 1979; *b* 21 Oct. 1931; *s* of Hugh Whitelegge Thomas, CMG, Colonial Service, Gold Coast (later) and Margery Swynnerton; *m* 1962, Vanessa Jebb, *d* of 1st Baron Gladwyn, *qv* ; two *s* one *d. Educ:* Sherborne; Queens' Coll., Cambridge (Scholar); Sorbonne, Paris. Pres. Cambridge Union, 1953. Foreign Office, 1954-57; Sec. to UK delegn to UN Disarmament Sub-Cttee, 1955-56; Lectr at RMA Sandhurst, 1957; Prof. of History, 1966-76, and Chm., Grad. Sch. of Contemp. European Studies, 1973-76, Univ. of Reading. Mem., academic adv. bd, Cons. Research Dept, 1982-. Governor, Univ. of the Negev, 1976. Somerset Maugham Prize, 1962; Arts Council prize for History (1st Nat. Book Awards), 1980. *Publications:* The World's Game, 1957; The Spanish Civil War, 1961, rev. edn 1977, newly rev. illustrated edn, Spain, 1979; The Story of Sandhurst, 1961; The Suez Affair, 1967; Cuba, or the Pursuit of Freedom, 1971; (ed) The selected writings of José Antonio Primo de Rivera, 1972; Goya and The Third of May 1808, 1972; Europe, the Radical Challenge, 1973; John Strachey, 1973; The Cuban Revolution, 1977; An Unfinished History of the World, 1979, rev. edn 1982 (US 1979, A History of the World). *Address:* Centre for Policy Studies, 8 Wilfred Street, SW1. *T:* 01-828 1177; 29 Ladbroke Grove, W11. *T:* 01-727 2288. *Clubs:* Beefsteak, Garrick.

THOMAS, Rt. Rev. Albert; *see* Bathurst (NSW), Bishop of, (RC).

THOMAS, Alston Havard Rees; Diary Editor, Bristol Evening Post, since 1970; Member, Press Council, since 1979; *b* Dinas, Pembrokeshire, 8 July 1925. Trainee and reporter, West Wales Guardian, 1939-44; Dist Reporter, Wilts Times, 1944-46; Bristol Evening Post, 1946-: successively Industrial, Speedway, Municipal, Ecclesiastical, Crime and Med. correspondent. Chm., Nat. Exec., Inst. of Journalists, 1981- (Mem., 1974-; Chm., SW Region, 1975-). Mem., St John Council (Avon Co., 1974-). *Recreations:* rugby union,

music, travel, gardening. *Address:* Havene, Maysmead Lane, Langford, Avon BS18 7HX. *T:* Weston-super-Mare 862515. *Club:* Savages (Bristol).

THOMAS, Ambler Reginald, CMG 1951; Under-Secretary, Ministry of Overseas Development, retired 1975; *b* 12 Feb. 1913; *s* of late John Frederick Ivor Thomas, OBE, MICE, MIME and Elizabeth Thomas; *m* 1943, Diana Beresford Gresham; two *s* three *d. Educ:* Gresham's School, Holt; Corpus Christi College, Cambridge. Entered Home Civil Service as Asst Principal and apptd to Ministry of Agriculture and Fisheries, 1935; transferred to Colonial Office, 1936. Asst Private Sec. to Sec. of State for Colonies, 1938-39; Principal, Colonial Office, 1939; Asst Sec., 1946; Chief Sec. to Govt of Aden, 1947-49; Establishment and Organization Officer, Colonial Office, 1950-52; Assistant Under-Sec. of State, Colonial Office, 1952-64; Under-Sec., Min. of Overseas Develt, and Overseas Develt Administration, 1964-73. Member, Exec. Cttee, British Council, 1965-68. Chairman: Commn of Inquiry into Gilbert Is Develt Authority, 1976; Corona Club. *Address:* Champsland, North Chideock, Bridport, Dorset. *Club:* United Oxford & Cambridge University.

THOMAS, Aneurin Morgan; Director, Welsh Arts Council, since 1967; *b* 3 April 1921; *s* of Philip Thomas and Olwen Amy Thomas (*née* Davies); *m* 1947, Mary Dineen; two *s* three *d. Educ:* Ystalyfera Intermediate Sch., Glamorgan; Swansea School of Art and Crafts. British and Indian Armies, 1941-46 (Major). Lecturer, Vice-Principal, Somerset College of Art, 1947-60; Vice-Principal, Hornsey College of Art, 1960-67. Chairman, Assoc. of Art Instns, 1977-78. *Publications:* periodic contribs to books and professional jls. *Recreations:* reading, music, painting, gardening. *Address:* Netherwood, 8 Lower Cwrt-y-vil Road, Penarth, South Glamorgan CF6 2HQ. *T:* Penarth 702239.

THOMAS, Prof. (Antony) Charles, FSA; Professor of Cornish Studies, University of Exeter, and Director, Institute of Cornish Studies, since 1971; *b* 24 April 1928; *s* of late Donald Woodroffe Thomas and Viva Warrington Thomas; *m* 1959, Jessica Dorothea Esther Mann; two *s* two *d. Educ:* Winchester; Corpus Christi Coll., Oxon (BA Hons Jurisp.); Univ. of London (Dipl. Prehist. Archaeol.). Lectr in Archaeology, Univ. of Edinburgh, 1957-67; Prof. of Archaeology, Univ. of Leicester, 1967-71. Leverhulme Fellowship, 1965-67; Lectures: Hunter Marshall, Univ. of Glasgow, 1968; O'Donnell, Univ. of Edinburgh, 1970; Jarrow, 1973; Willans, UC, Aberystwyth, 1975; Henry Lewis, UC, Swansea, 1977; O'Donnell, Univ. of Wales, 1978. President: Council for British Archaeology, 1970-73; Royal Instn of Cornwall, 1970-72; Sect. H, BAAS, Bath, 1978; Chairman: BBC SW Reg. Adv. Council, 1975-80; DoE Area Archaeol Cttee, Cornwall and Devon, 1975-79; Cornwall Cttee Rescue Archaeol., 1976-; Hon. Archaeol Consultant, National Trust, 1970-. Hon. Mem., Royal Irish Acad., 1973; Hon. Fellow, RSAI, 1975. William Frend Medal, Soc. of Antiquaries, 1982. *Publications:* Christian Antiquities of Camborne, 1967; The Early Christian Archaeology of North Britain, 1971; Britain and Ireland in Early Christian Times, 1971; (with A. Small and D. Wilson) St Ninian's Isle and its Treasure, 1973; (with D. Ivall) Military Insignia of Cornwall, 1974; Christianity in Roman Britain to AD 500, 1981. *Recreations:* military history, archaeological fieldwork. *Address:* Lambessow, St Clement, Truro, Cornwall; Pencobben, Gwithian, Cornwall.

THOMAS, Brig. Arthur Frank Friend, CIE 1942; *b* 8 Aug. 1897; *s* of Arthur Ernest Thomas, Parkhurst, South Norwood; *m* 1928, Elizabeth Stephenson Walker, MB, BCh, DPH, *d* of Rev. S. Walker, MA, Donaghadee, Co. Down; one *s* one *d. Educ:* Melbourne College. ADC, EEF, 1920-21; DADOS Waziristan District, 1928-31; Staff Capt. AHQ 1931-33; DADOS, AHQ, 1933-36; AD of C, AHQ, 1936-39; DD of C 1939-40; D of C 1940; CCPM 1940-41; Deputy Controller-General of Inspection, GHQ, India, 1941-45; Director of Civil Personnel, 1945-47; retired, 1947. Served European War, 1914-21, Egypt, 1914-16, France, 1916-17, EEF 1918 (wounded, despatches); NW Frontier, India, 1930; War of 1939-45. *Recreations:* gardening, cine-photography. *Address:* Drayton House, Loxley Road, Stratford-on-Avon, Warwicks CV37 7DU.

THOMAS, Brian (Dick Lauder), OBE 1961; Mural Painter and Stained Glass Designer; *b* 19 Sept. 1912; *s* of Frank Leslie Thomas, MB, BS, and Margaret Mary (*née* Lauder). *Educ:* Bradfield College. Rome Scholarship in Mural Painting, 1934; Camouflage Directorate, Min. of Home Security, 1939-45; Principal, Byam Shaw Sch. of Art, 1946-54; Master, Art Workers Guild, 1957, Editor, Artifex, 1968-71; Fellow, Brit. Soc. of Master Glass Painters, 1958; Chm. of Governors, Hurstpierpoint Coll., 1958-67; Mem. Council, Artists' Gen. Benevolent Instn, 1964; Chm. Council, Fedn of British Craft Socs, 1971-73; Mem., Crafts Adv. Cttee, 1971-73. Vice-Pres., SPCK, 1976. Master, Glaziers Co., 1976. *Principal works:* St Paul's Cathedral (stained glass in American and OBE Chapels); Westminster Abbey (stained glass); Winchester Cathedral (shrine of St Swithun); Wellington Cathedral, NZ (War Memorial windows); St George's Chapel, Windsor (panels in altar rails); St George's Church, Stevenage New Town (stained glass); Livery Co. Windows: London Guildhall, Pewterers' Hall, Innholders' Hall, Watermen's Hall; Biographical Window in Harpur Trust Court-Room, Bedford; memorials to Dame Nellie Melba, John Ireland, Russell Colman, Sir Harold Graham-Hodgson, Lord Webb-Johnson and others; painted ceiling at Templewood, Norfolk; murals and mosaics in many religious and secular buildings of London and the provinces. *Publications:* Vision and Technique in European Painting, 1952; Geometry in Pictorial Composition, 1971; (ed) Directory of Master Glass-

Painters, 1972. *Address:* The Studio, 3 Hill Road, NW8. *T:* 01-286 0804. *Clubs:* Arts, Athenæum.

THOMAS, Brinley, CBE 1971 (OBE 1955); MA, PhD; FBA 1973; Professor of Economics, University College, Cardiff, 1946-73, Director, Manpower Research Unit, 1974-76; *b* 6 Jan. 1906; *e s* of late Thomas Thomas and Anne Walters; *m* 1943, Cynthia, *d* of late Dr Charles T. Loram, New Haven, Connecticut; one *d. Educ:* Port Talbot County School; University College of Wales, Aberystwyth; London School of Economics. MA (Wales) (with distinction), 1928; Fellow of the University of Wales, 1929-31; Social Science Research Training Scholar, 1929-31; PhD (London), 1931; Hutchinson Silver Medal, London School of Economics, 1931; Acland Travelling Scholar in Germany and Sweden, 1932-34; Lecturer in Economics, London School of Economics, 1931-39; War Trade Department, British Embassy, Washington, 1941-42; Dir, Northern Section, Political Intelligence Dept of Foreign Office, 1942-45. Member: National Assistance Bd, 1948-53; Anderson Cttee on Grants to Students, 1958-60; Dept of Employment Retail Prices Index Advisory Cttee; Prince of Wales Cttee, 1969-76. Chairman: Welsh Advisory Cttee of British Council, 1966-74; Welsh Council, 1968-71; Assoc. of Univ. Teachers of Econs, 1965-68; Mem. Exec. Cttee, British Council, 1966-74; Pres., Atlantic Economic Soc. Nat. Science Foundn Fellow, 1971. University of California, Berkeley: Ford Vis. Res. Prof., 1976-77; Vis. Prof., 1978-79 and 1979-83; Vis. Prof., Queen's Univ., Canada, 1977-78. Governor, Centre for Environmental Studies, 1972-74. *Publications:* Monetary Policy and Crises, A Study of Swedish Experience, 1936; Migration and Economic Growth, A Study of Great Britain and the Atlantic Economy, 1954, 2nd edn 1973; International Migration and Economic Development: A Trend Report and Bibliography, 1961; Migration and Urban Development, 1972; (ed) Economics of International Migration, 1958; (ed) The Welsh Economy: Studies in Expansion, 1962; articles in various journals. *Address:* 44a Church Road, Whitchurch, Cardiff. *T:* Cardiff 62835. *Club:* Reform.

THOMAS, Charles; see Thomas, A. C.

THOMAS, Ven. Charles Edward; Archdeacon of Wells, since 1983; *b* 1927. *Educ:* St David's College, Lampeter (BA 1951); College of the Resurrection, Mirfield. Deacon 1953, priest 1954; Curate of Ilminster, 1953-56; Chaplain and Asst Master, St Michael's Coll., Tenbury, 1956-57; Curate of St Stephen's, St Albans, 1957-58; Vicar, St Michael and All Angels, Boreham Wood, 1958-66; Rector, Monksilver with Elworthy, 1966-74, with Brompton Ralph and Nettlecombe, 1969-74 (Curate-in-charge of Nettlecombe, 1968-69); Vicar of South Petherton with the Seavingtons, 1974-83. RD of Crewkerne, 1977-82. *Address:* 6 The Liberty, Wells, Som BA5 2SU. *T:* Wells 72224.

THOMAS, Dr Claudius Cornelius, CMG 1979; Commissioner for the Eastern Caribbean Governments in the United Kingdom, since 1975; High Commissioner for St Lucia, and for St Vincent and the Grenadines, in the United Kingdom, since 1979; for Antigua-Barbuda, since 1981; *b* 1 Oct. 1928; *s* of Charles Malin Thomas and Ada Thomas (*née* Dyer). *Educ:* Castries Intermed. Sch., St Lucia; London Univ. (LLB); Univ. de Strasbourg (Dr en droit). Called to Bar, Gray's Inn, 1957. Cadet Officer, Commn for the West Indies in UK, 1961; Translator, EEC, Brussels, 1962; Attaché, L'Institut Internat. des Sciences Administratives, Brussels, 1962-63; Free University of (West) Berlin: Wissenschaftlicher Asst, 1963-72, Asst Prof., 1972. *Publications:* contrib. to and assisted in, Multitudo Legum Ius Unum, 1973; contrib. Deutches Jahrbuch des Öffentlichen Rechts, 1966, and other legal jls. *Recreations:* cricket, table tennis, sailing. *Address:* Paddock Cottage, Hampton Court Road, Hampton Court, Surrey. *T:* 01-977 5686.

THOMAS, Colin Agnew; chartered accountant; *b* 14 Feb. 1921; *s* of Harold Alfred Thomas and Nora (*née* Williams); *m* 1947, Jane Jardine Barnish, *d* of Leonard Barnish, FRIBA; one *s* one *d. Educ:* Oundle School. Lieut, RNVR, 1941-46. Finance Comptroller, Lloyd's, 1964-75, Sec.-Gen., 1976-79. HM Lieut for City of London. *Recreations:* golf, sailing, gardening. *Address:* 33 Cobham Road, Leatherhead, Surrey KT22 9AY. *T:* Leatherhead 374335; 15 Ravenspoint, Trearddur Bay, Anglesey. *Clubs:* Effingham Golf, Holyhead Golf, Trearddur Bay Sailing.

THOMAS, Dafydd Elis; MP (Plaid Cymru) Merioneth, since Feb. 1974; *b* 18 Oct. 1946; *m* 1970, Elen M. Williams; three *s. Educ:* Ysgol Dyffryn Conwy; UC North Wales. Research worker, Bd of Celtic Studies, 1970; Tutor in Welsh Studies, Coleg Harlech, 1970; Lectr, Dept of English, UC North Wales, 1974. Part-time freelance broadcaster, BBC Wales, HTV, 1970-73. *Recreations:* hill walking, camping. *Address:* 7 Fron Wnion, Dolgellau, Gwynedd LL40 1SL. *T:* (home) Dolgellau 422303; (constituency office) Dolgellau 422661; (London) 01-219 4172/5021. *Club:* Sport and Social (Trawsfynydd).

THOMAS, Rev. David; Principal, St Stephen's House, Oxford, since 1982; *b* 22 July 1942; *s* of Rt Rev. John James Absalom Thomas, *qv*; *m* 1967, Rosemary Christine Calton; one *s* one *d. Educ:* Christ College, Brecon; Keble College, Oxford; St Stephen's House, Oxford. MA Oxon. Curate of Hawarden, 1967-69; Tutor, St Michael's College, Llandaff, Cardiff, 1969-70; Chaplain 1970-75; Secretary, Church in Wales Liturgical Commn, 1970-75; Vice-Principal, St Stephen's House, Oxford, 1975-79; Vicar of Chepstow, 1979-82. *Publication:* (contrib.) The Ministry of the Word (ed G. J. Cuming), 1979. *Recreations:* music, walking. *Address:* St Stephen's House, 16 Marston Street, Oxford OX4 1JX. *T:* Oxford 47874.

THOMAS, David Bowen, PhD; Keeper, Department of Physics, Science Museum, since 1978; *b* 28 Dec. 1931; *s* of Evan Thomas and Florence Annie Bowen. *Educ:* Tredegar Grammar Sch.; Manchester Univ. (BSc). Research Fellow, Wayne Univ., Detroit, USA, 1955-57; Research Scientist, Min. of Agriculture, Fisheries and Food, Aberdeen, 1957-61; Asst Keeper, Science Museum, Dept of Chemistry, 1961-73; Keeper, Dept of Museum Services, 1973-78. *Publications:* The First Negatives, 1964; The Science Museum Photography Collection, 1969; The First Colour Motion Pictures, 1969. *Recreation:* country walking. *Address:* 81 Lambton Road, SW20.

THOMAS, David Churchill, CMG 1982; HM Diplomatic Service; Ambassador to Cuba, since 1981; *b* 21 Oct. 1933; *o s* of late David Bernard Thomas and Violet Churchill Thomas (*née* Quicke); *m* 1958, Susan Petronella Arrow; one *s* two *d. Educ:* Eton Coll.; New Coll., Oxford (Exhibnr). Mod. Hist. 1st Cl., 1957. Army, 2nd Lieut, Rifle Brigade, 1952-54. Foreign Office, 1958; 3rd Sec., Moscow, 1959-61; 2nd Sec., Lisbon, 1961-64; FCO, 1964-68; 1st Sec. (Commercial), Lima, 1968-70; FCO, 1970-73; Head of South West European Dept, 1974; Asst Sec., Cabinet Office, 1973-78; Counsellor (Internal Affairs), Washington, 1978-81. *Recreations:* photography, listening to music. *Address:* c/o Foreign and Commonwealth Office, SW1. *Club:* London Welsh RFC.

THOMAS, David Hamilton Pryce, CBE 1977; solicitor; Chairman, Land Authority for Wales, since 1980 (Deputy Chairman, 1975-80); President, Rent Assessment Panel for Wales, since 1971; *b* 3 July 1922; *s* of Trevor John Thomas and Eleanor Maud Thomas; *m* 1948, Eluned Mair Morgan; two *s* one *d. Educ:* Barry County Sch.; University College, Cardiff. Served War of 1939-45; British and Indian Armies, terminal rank T/Captain (GSO III), 1941-46. Qualified as Solicitor, 1948, with hons; Partner in J. A. Hughes & Co., Solicitors, Barry, 1950-75; Notary Public, 1953. Director 1962, Vice-Chm. 1967, Chm. 1971-78, Barry Mutual Building Society; Vice Chm., 1978, Chm., 1982, Glam. Building Soc. Member: Rent Assessment Panel for Wales, 1966; Adv. Cttee on Fair Rents, 1973; Chm., E Glam. Rent Tribunal, 1967-71; District Comr of Scouts, Barry and District, 1963-70; Chm., Barry District Scout Assoc. 1971-81; Vice-Chm., S Glam. Scout Council, 1975-81. *Recreations:* books, music. *Address:* 27 Romilly Park, Barry, South Glamorgan. *T:* Barry 732229.

See also R. L. Thomas.

THOMAS, David Monro; retired; *b* 31 July 1915; *s* of late Henry Monro and Winifred Thomas, East Hagbourne, Berks; *m* 1948, Ursula Mary, *d* of late H. W. Liversidge; two *s* one *d. Educ:* St Edward's School, Oxford; St Edmund Hall, Oxford. Oxford House, 1937; Army, 1939, Major, Royal Welch Fusiliers; Head of Oxford House, 1946-48; Secretary of Greek House, 1948-51; Legal & General Assurance Soc. Ltd, 1951-75; YWCA, 1975-80; Co. Sec., YWCA, 1977-80. *Address:* Watcombe Corner, Watlington, Oxon. *T:* Watlington 2403.

THOMAS, David Owen, QC 1972; a Recorder of the Crown Court, since 1972; *b* 22 Aug. 1926; *s* of Emrys Aeron Thomas and Dorothy May Thomas; *m* 1967, Mary Susan Atkinson; four *d. Educ:* Queen Elizabeth's, Barnet; John Bright Sch., Llandudno; Queen's Univ., Belfast. Served War, HM Forces, 1943-45 and to 1948. Called to the Bar, Middle Temple, 1952; Dep. Chairman, Devon QS, 1971. *Recreations:* acting, cricket, Rugby football. *Address:* 2 King's Bench Walk, Temple, EC4Y 7DE. *T:* 01-353 1746; 8 Chesil Street, Winchester, Hants. *T:* Winchester 65142. *Clubs:* MCC; Hampshire (Winchester).

THOMAS, Derek John, IPFA; County Treasurer, Surrey County Council, since 1979; *b* 3 Dec. 1934; *s* of late James Llewellyn Thomas and Winifred Mary Thomas; *m* 1st (marr. diss.); three *d* ; 2nd, 1978, Christine (*née* Brewer). *Educ:* Hele's Sch., Exeter. Formerly: Treasurer's Depts: Devon CC; Corby Development Corporation; Bath CC; Taunton Bor. Council; Sen. Asst Bor. Treasurer, Poole Bor. Council; Asst County Treasurer, Gloucestershire CC; Principal Asst County Treasurer, Avon CC. CIPFA: Mem. Council, 1977-78; Sec., S Wales and W of England Region, 1977-78; Chm., Higher Educn Finance Panel, 1980-. *Recreations:* sport (both playing and watching), wine. *Address:* County Hall, Penrhyn Road, Kingston upon Thames, Surrey. *T:* 01-546 1050.

THOMAS, Derek Morison David, CMG 1977; HM Diplomatic Service; Minister, British Embassy, Washington, since 1981; *b* 31 Oct. 1929; *s* of K. P. D. Thomas and Mali McL. Thomas; *m* 1956, Carolina Jacoba van der Mast; two *c. Educ:* Radley Coll., Abingdon; Trinity Hall, Cambridge (MA). Mod. Langs Tripos. Articled apprentice, Dolphin Industrial Developments Ltd, 1947. Entered HM Foreign Service, 1953; Midshipman 1953, Sub-Lt 1955, RNVR; FO, 1955; 3rd, later 2nd, Sec., Moscow, 1956-59; 2nd Sec., Manila, 1959-61; UK Delegn to Brussels Conf., 1961-62; 1st Sec., FO, 1962; Sofia, 1964-67; Ottawa, 1967-69; seconded to Treasury, 1969-70; Financial Counsellor, Paris, 1971-75; Head of N American Dept, FCO, 1975-76; Asst Under Sec. of State, FCO, 1976-79; Minister Commercial, Washington, 1979-82. *Recreations:* listening to people and music; being in, or on water. *Address:* c/o Foreign and Commonwealth Office, SW1. *Clubs:* United Oxford & Cambridge University; Leander.

THOMAS, Dewi Alun, MBE; **His Honour Judge Thomas;** a Circuit Judge since 1972; *b* 3 Dec. 1917; *e s* of late Joshua and Martha Ann Thomas; *m* 1952, Doris Maureen Smith, Barrister; one *s* one *d. Educ:* Christ Coll., Brecon; Jesus

Coll., Oxford (MA). Served War of 1939-45 (MBE, despatches): mobilised with TA (RA), 1939; served Sicily, Italy, the Balkans; Major, 2nd in Comd, No 2 Commando; demobilised 1946. Called to Bar, Inner Temple, 1951, Bencher 1969. *Recreations:* golf, watching Rugby football. *Address:* 16 Westhall Park, Warlingham, Surrey. *T:* Upper Warlingham 4127. *Club:* Cardiff and County.

THOMAS, Prof. Dewi-Prys, BArch, DipCD; FRIBA, MRTPI; Head of Welsh School of Architecture, 1960-81, and first Professor of Architecture in University of Wales, 1964-81 (Institute of Science and Technology), Cardiff; *b* Liverpool, 5 Aug. 1916; *o s* of A. Dan Thomas, Martin's Bank, and Elysabeth Watkin Thomas; *m* 1965, Joyce Ffoulkes Davies, *e d* of Rev. Robert Ff. Parry, Ballarat and Geelong, Australia; two step *s* two step *d*. *Educ:* Liverpool Inst.; Univ. of Liverpool Sch. of Architecture. Ravenhead Schol. and John Lewis Partnership Prizeman, 1935; John Rankin Prizeman, 1935 and 1936; Holland, Hannen and Cubitts Prizeman and Holt Travelling Schol., 1936; RIBA Archibald Dawnay Schol., 1936-38; Honan Trav. Schol., 1938; BArch (1st Cl. Hons) 1938; DipCD (Distinction) Liverpool, 1942. Architect in office of T. Alwyn Lloyd, FRIBA, PPTPI, Cardiff (S Wales Outline Plan), 1942-47; Lectr and Sen. Lectr, Univ. of Liverpool, 1947-60. Dean of Environmental Design, UWIST, 1967-69 and 1971-73; Vice-Principal, UWIST, 1969-71; Mem. Bd, Univ. of Wales Press, 1969-75; Mem. Court, Univ. of Wales,1972-75. Comr, Royal Commn on Ancient Monuments in Wales, 1970-; Member Board: Civic Trust for Wales, 1964-; Member: Court of Governors, Nat. Theatre for Wales, 1967-; Founder Mem., Cardiff 2000 (Cardiff Civic Soc.), 1964- (Chm., 1973-75). Frequent lectr and broadcaster (Welsh and English) radio and TV, 1942-; Sir Sydney Jones Meml Lectures (The British Underground), Univ. of Liverpool, 1975; BBC Wales TV Heritage Year Lecture (Arthur Lives!), 1975. *Publications:* Treftadaeth: the heritage, 1975; (memoir in) Artists in Wales, 3, 1976; contrib. to jls. *Recreations:* Celtic affairs, Welsh poetry and history, art. *Address:* Tower House, 1A Cefn Coed Road, Cardiff CF2 6AN. *T:* Cardiff 754217; Taldir, Dolgellau. *T:* Dolgellau 422201.

THOMAS, Donald Martin; *see* Thomas, Martin.

THOMAS, Elizabeth Marjorie; Secretary General, The Authors' Lending and Copyright Society, since 1979; *b* 10 Aug. 1919; *d* of Frank Porter and Marjorie Porter (*née* Pascall); *m* 1941, George Thomas; one *s* one *d*. *Educ:* St George's Sch., Harpenden; Girton Coll., Cambridge (BA 1st Cl.). Journalist, 1951-59 and Literary Editor, 1959-71, Tribune; Asst Literary Editor, New Statesman, 1971-76; Political Adviser to Rt Hon. Michael Foot, MP, Lord Pres. of the Council and Leader of the House of Commons, 1976-79. Mem., Arts Council, 1974-77 (Mem., Literature Panel, 1971-77); Chm., Literature Panel, Eastern Arts Assoc., 1978-; Member: Ethnic Minority Arts Cttee, Commission for Racial Equality, 1979-82; British Council Bd, 1982-. *Publication:* (ed) Tribune 21, 1959. *Address:* c/o ALCS, 430 Edgware Road, W2 1EH. *T:* 01-724 1386.

THOMAS, Emyr, CBE 1980; LLB, LMTPI; DL; General Manager, Telford New Town Development Corporation, 1969-80; Chairman, Telford Community Council, since 1980; *b* 25 April 1920; *s* of late Brinley Thomas, MA, Aldershot; *m* 1947, Barbara J. May; one *d*. *Educ:* Aldershot County High School. Served War of 1939-45, RASC. Admitted Solicitor, 1947. Asst Solicitor, Exeter City Council, 1947-50; Sen. Asst Solicitor, Reading County Borough Council, 1950-53; Dep. Town Clerk, West Bromwich County Borough Council, 1953-64; Sec. and Solicitor, Dawley (later Telford) Development Corp., 1964-69. First Hon. Sec., Ironbridge Gorge Museum Trust, 1968-. DL Salop, 1979. *Recreation:* gardening. *Address:* 8 Kynnersley Lane, Leighton, near Shrewsbury, Salop. *T:* (business) Telford 595307.

THOMAS, Rt. Rev. Eryl Stephen; *b* 20 Oct. 1910; *s* of Edward Stephen and Margaret Susannah Thomas; *m* 1939, Jean Mary Alice Wilson; three *s* one *d*. *Educ:* Rossall Sch.; St John's Coll., Oxford; Wells Theological Coll. BA 2nd Class Hon. Theology, Oxford, 1932; MA 1935. Curate of Colwyn Bay, 1933-38, of Hawarden, 1938-43; Vicar of Risca, Mon, 1943-48; Warden of St Michael's Theological Coll., Llandaff, 1948-54; Dean of Llandaff, 1954-68; Bishop of Monmouth, 1968-71, of Llandaff, 1971-75. Chaplain and Sub-Prelate, Order of St John of Jerusalem, 1969. *Address:* 17 Orchard Close, Gilwern, Abergavenny, Gwent NP7 0EN. *T:* Gilwern 831050.

THOMAS, Rt. Rev. Francis Gerard; *see* Northampton, Bishop of, (RC).

THOMAS, Frank; *see* Thomas, J. F. P.

THOMAS, Franklin Augustine; President, Ford Foundation, since 1979; *b* 27 May 1934; *s* of James Thomas and Viola Thomas (*née* Atherley); *m* (marr. diss.); two *s* two *d*. *Educ:* Columbia College, New York (BA 1956); Columbia Univ. (LLB 1963). Admitted to NY State Bar, 1964; Attorney, Fed. Housing and Home Finance Agency, NYC, 1963-64; Asst US Attorney for Southern District, NY, 1964-65; Dep. Police Comr, charge legal matters, NYC, 1965-67; Pres., Chief Exec. Officer, Bedford Stuyvesant Restoration Corp., Brooklyn, 1967-77. Hon. LLD: Yale, 1970; Fordham, 1972; Pratt Institute, 1974; Pace, 1977; Columbia, 1979. *Address:* The Ford Foundation, 320 East 43rd Street, New York, NY 10017, USA. *T:* (212) 573-5383.

THOMAS, Frederick Maginley, CMG 1962; retired Civil Servant; *b* 1 July 1908; 3rd *s* of Rev. Canon F. Thomas; *m* 1941, Dorothea Mary (*d* 1969), *o*

d of Edward North; two *d*. *Educ:* Truro Cathedral School; Exeter College, Oxford. Cadet, Colonial Administrative Service, 1931; District Officer, Northern Rhodesia, 1933; Asst Secretary, 1949; Provincial Commissioner, 1954; Minister of Native Affairs, Northern Rhodesia Government, 1960-63; Deputy Governor, Northern Rhodesia, 1964-65. Served 1940-47; 3rd Battalion KAR; 3 Bn NRR; GSO1 Civil Affairs, Lt-Col. *Publication:* Historical Notes on the Bisa, 1953. *Recreations:* most outdoor pursuits and water colours. *Address:* Rock House, Halse, Taunton, Somerset. *T:* Bishops Lydeard 432293.

THOMAS, Sir Frederick William, Kt 1959; Councillor, City of Melbourne, 1953-65 (Lord Mayor, 1957-59); *b* 27 June 1906; *s* of F. J. Thomas; *m* 1968, Dorothy Alexa Gordon; three *s* by former marr. *Educ:* Melbourne Grammar School. Served War of 1939-45, RAAF (Air Efficiency Award, two bars); Group Captain. Comdr Order of Orange Nassau with swords (Holland), 1943. *Recreation:* golf. *Address:* 35 Hitchcock Avenue, Barwon Heads, Victoria 3227, Australia. *Clubs:* Naval and Military, Australian (Melbourne); Barwon Heads Golf.

THOMAS, Air Vice-Marshal Geoffrey Percy Sansom, CB 1970; OBE 1945; retired; *b* 24 April 1915; *s* of Reginald Ernest Sansom Thomas, New Malden; *m* 1940, Sally, *d* of Horace Biddle, Gainsborough; one *s* one *d*. *Educ:* King's College School, Wimbledon. Commissioned RAF, 1939; served India and Ceylon, 1942-45; lent to Turkish Air Force, 1950-52; Group Captain, 1958; served with RAAF, 1960-62; Air Commodore, 1965; Director of Movements, 1965; Air Vice-Marshal, 1969; SASO, Maintenance Comd, 1969-71. *Address:* Elms Wood House, Elms Vale, Dover, Kent. *T:* Dover 206375.

THOMAS, Rt. Hon. George; *see* Thomas, Rt Hon. T. G.

THOMAS, Maj.-Gen. George Arthur, CB 1960; CBE 1957; retired; *b* 2 May 1906; *s* of Colonel F. H. S. Thomas, CB, and Diana Thomas; *m* 1936, Diana Zaidee Browne; one *s* one *d*. *Educ:* Cheltenham College; Royal Military Academy, Woolwich. Commissioned, Royal Artillery, 1926; served in UK and Egypt; Staff College, 1940; CO 17 Field Regt, 1st Army, 1942-43; GSO1, 4 Division, 1943-44; BGS 8th Army, 1944-45; CRA 16 Airborne Div., 1947-48; Imperial Defence Coll., 1952; BGS, MELF, 1955-57; Chief of Staff, HQ Northern Command, 1958-60; Chief of Staff, GHQ Far ELF, 1960-62. Retired, 1962. *Recreations:* games and sports of all kinds. *Address:* Fishing Cottage, Upper Clatford, Andover, Hants. *T:* Andover 52120. *Club:* Army and Navy.

THOMAS, Sir (Godfrey) Michael (David), 11th Bt, *cr* 1694; Member of Stock Exchange, London, since 1959; *b* 10 Oct. 1925; *o s* of Rt Hon. Sir Godfrey Thomas, PC, GCVO, KCB, CSI, 10th Bt, and Diana, *d* of late Ven. B. G. Hoskyns; *S* father 1968; *m* 1956, Margaret Greta Cleland, *yr d* of John Cleland, Stormont Court, Godden Green, Kent; one *s* two *d*, of whom one *s* one *d* are twins. *Educ:* Harrow. The Rifle Brigade, 1944-56. *Heir:* *s* David John Godfrey Thomas, *b* 11 June 1961. *Address:* 2 Napier Avenue, SW6. *T:* 01-736 6896. *Clubs:* MCC, Hurlingham.

THOMAS, Gwyn Edward Ward; *see* Ward Thomas.

THOMAS, Howard, CBE 1967; Chairman: Thames Television Ltd, 1974-79; Thames Television International Ltd, 1974-81; Independent Television News, 1974-76 (Director, since 1956); broadcasting consultant: to EMI Ltd and Rediffusion Television Ltd, 1979-81; to Thames Television International Ltd, since 1982; Managing Director of ABC Television, 1955-68, of Thames Television, 1968-74; *b* 5 March 1909; *s* of W. G. Thomas and A. M. Thomas; *m* 1934, Hilda, *d* of Harrison Fogg; two *d*. Trained in advertising, journalism and broadcasting. Started Commercial Radio Department, London Press Exchange Ltd, 1938. Writer and Producer for BBC Sound Radio and during 3 years directed and produced 500 programmes. Entered film industry as Producer-in-Chief, Associated British Pathé Ltd, 1944. Divnl Dir, EMI Ltd; Director: EMI Film and Theatre Corp. Ltd; EMI Film Distributors Ltd; Euston Films Ltd; Independent Television Companies Association; Literators Ltd; Argus Press Ltd, 1973-; BAFTA Management Ltd, 1975-80; Logospheres Ltd, 1979-; Thames Valley Broadcasting Ltd, 1975-80; Tempo Video Ltd, 1981-. A Governor, BFI, 1974- (Chm., BFI Funding and Develt Cttee). Member: Advertising Standards Authority, 1962-73; Govt Adv. Cttee on Advertising, 1973-. Vice-Chm., Advertising Assoc., 1973-77. Dir, Internat. Council, Nat. Acad. of TV Arts & Scis (USA), 1971-78. Mem., 'London Looks Forward' Silver Jubilee 1977 Conf. Hon. Fellow, British Kinematograph Sound & Television Soc., 1967; FRSA 1975 (Mem. Council, 1978-); Vice-Pres., Royal Television Soc., 1976-; Hon. Life Mem., Gtr London Arts Assoc., 1977-; Mem., Internat. Inst. of Communications; Former President: Radio Industries Club; Cinema & Television Veterans. Radio Programmes: Showmen of England, Beauty Queen, The Brains Trust, Shipmates Ashore, etc. Films: Elizabeth is Queen (Coronation) and many documentaries. *Publications:* The Brighter Blackout Book, 1939; How to Write for Broadcasting, 1940; Britain's Brains Trust, 1944; The Truth About Television, 1962; With an Independent Air, 1977. *Address:* Beechwood, Lambridge Lane, Henley-on-Thames, Oxon.

THOMAS, Ivor B.; *see* Bulmer-Thomas.

THOMAS, Jeffrey, QC 1974; MP Abertillery since 1970 (Lab 1970–81, SDP since 1981); a Recorder of the Crown Court, since 1975; *b* 12 Nov. 1933; *s* of John James Thomas and Phyllis Thomas (*née* Hile). *Educ:* Abertillery Grammar Sch.; King's Coll. London; Gray's Inn. Called to the Bar, Gray's Inn, 1957. Pres., Univ. of London Union, 1955–56. Served Army (National Service): commnd in Royal Corps of Transport, 1959 (Senior Under Officer); later served in Directorate of Army Legal Services: Major, Dep. Asst Dir, HQ BAOR, 1961. Contested (Lab) Barry, 1966. PPS to Sec. of State for Wales, 1977–79; opposition spokesman on legal affairs, 1979–81; SDP spokesman on legal affairs, 1981–. Chm., Brit. Caribbean Assoc.; Mem. Council, Justice; Vice Chm., British Gp, IPU. Mem. Court, Univ. of London, 1981–; Member Court of Governors: University Coll. of Wales, Aberystwyth; Nat. Museum of Wales (ex officio); Nat. Library of Wales; Vice Pres., North Monmouthshire Youth Rugby Union. *Recreations:* watching Rugby football, travelling. *Address:* (home) 26 Ellington Street, N7. *T:* 01-629 2440; 1 Gladstone Street, Abertillery, Gwent. *T:* Abertillery 2937; (chambers) 3 Temple Gardens, Temple, EC4. *T:* 01-583 8333. *Clubs:* Reform; Abertillery Rugby Football.

THOMAS, Jenkin; HM Diplomatic Service; Counsellor (Economic and Commercial), Athens, since 1983; *b* 2 Jan. 1938; *s* of late William John Thomas and of Annie Muriel (*née* Thomas). *Educ:* Maesydderwen Sch.; University Coll. London (BA Hons); Univ. of Michigan, Ann Arbor (MA). Joined HM Foreign (subseq. Diplomatic) Service, 1960; Foreign Office, 1960–63; Pretoria/Cape Town, 1963–66; Saigon, 1966–68; FCO, 1968–73; Washington, 1973–77; FCO, 1977–79; Cabinet Office, 1979–80; Tokyo, 1980–82. *Recreations:* reading, music. *Address:* c/o Foreign and Commonwealth Office, SW1.

THOMAS, Jeremy Cashel, CMG 1980; HM Diplomatic Service; Assistant Under-Secretary of State, Foreign and Commonwealth Office, since 1982; *b* 1 June 1931; *s* of Rev. H. C. Thomas and Margaret Betty (*née* Humby); *m* 1957, Diana Mary Summerhayes; three *s*. *Educ:* Eton; Merton Coll., Oxford. HM Forces, 1949–51; entered FO, 1954; served Singapore, Rome and Belgrade; Dep. Head, Personnel Ops Dept, FCO, 1970–74; Counsellor and Head of Chancery, UK Mission to UN, NY, 1974–76; Head of Perm. Under-Sec.'s Dept, FCO, 1977–79; Ambassador to Luxembourg, 1979–82. *Recreations:* sailing, fishing. *Address:* c/o Foreign and Commonwealth Office, SW1. *Clubs:* United Oxford & Cambridge University; Leander, Oxford and Cambridge Sailing Society, Itchenor Sailing.

THOMAS, (John) Frank (Phillips); Telecommunications Consultant to British Telecom and industry; *b* 11 April 1920; *s* of late John and of Catherine Myfanwy Phillips Thomas; *m* 1942, Edith V. Milne; one *s* one *d*. *Educ:* Christ's Coll., Finchley; Univ. of London (BSc). CEng, MIEE. Joined Post Office Research Dept, 1937; trans-oceanic telephone cable system devclt, 1947–63; planning UK inland telephone network, 1963–69; Dep. Dir London Telephone Region, 1969–71; Dep. Dir Engrg, Network Planning Dept, 1971; Dir, Network Planning Dept, 1972–79; Dir, Overseas Liaison and Consultancy Dept, Post Office, 1979–81. *Publications:* contrib. scientific and technical jls on telecommunications subjects. *Recreation:* fly fishing. *Address:* 24 Shepherds Way, Rickmansworth, Herts. *T:* Rickmansworth 72992. *Club:* Rickmansworth Lawn Tennis (Vice-Pres.).

THOMAS, Rt. Rev. John James Absalom, DD Lambeth 1958; *b* 17 May 1908; *s* of William David and Martha Thomas; *m* 1941, Elizabeth Louise, *d* of Very Rev. H. L. James, DD, former Dean of Bangor; one *s*. *Educ:* University College of Wales, Aberystwyth; Keble College, Oxford. Curate of Llanguicke, 1931–34; Curate of Sketty, 1934–36; Bishop's Messenger and Examining Chaplain, 1936–40; Warden of Church Hostel, Bangor, and Lecturer in University Coll. of N Wales, 1940–44; Vicar of Swansea, 1945–58, also Chaplain to Bishop of Swansea and Brecon; Canon of Brecon Cathedral, 1946; Precentor, 1952; Rural Dean of Swansea, 1952–54; Archdeacon of Gower, 1954–58; Bishop of Swansea and Brecon, 1958–76. Chm. of Governors, Christ Coll., Brecon, 1961–. Chaplain and Sub-Prelate, Order of St John of Jerusalem, 1965. *Address:* Woodbine Cottage, St Mary Street, Tenby, Dyfed.

See also Rev. David Thomas.

THOMAS, John Maldwyn; Director, International Military Services Ltd, since 1978; Member Board, Thomas Cook Inc., USA, since 1980; *b* 17 June 1918; *m* 1975, Maureen Elizabeth. *Educ:* Porth Rhondda Grammar Sch. FCIS. Called to Bar, Gray's Inn, 1953; Solicitor, 1965. Lewis & Tylor Ltd, Cardiff, 1940–56; Signode Ltd, Swansea, 1956–59; Commercial Agreements Manager, UKAEA, 1959–63; Rank Xerox Ltd: Sec. 1964–70, Man. Dir 1970–72, Chm., 1972–79. Vice-Pres., London Welsh Rugby Football Club. *Address:* 4 Abbey Orchard Street, SW1P 2JJ.

THOMAS, Prof. John Meurig, MA, PhD, DSc; FRS 1977; Professor and Head of Department of Physical Chemistry, and Fellow of King's College, University of Cambridge, since 1978; *b* Llanelli, Wales, 15 Dec. 1932; *s* of David John and Edyth Thomas; *m* 1959, Margaret (*née* Edwards); two *d*. *Educ:* Gwendraeth Grammar Sch.; University College of Swansea; Queen Mary Coll., London. Scientific Officer, UKAEA, 1957–58; Asst Lectr 1958–59, Lectr 1959–65, Reader 1965–69, in Chemistry, UCNW, Bangor; Prof. and Head of Dept of Chemistry, UCW, Aberystwyth, 1969–78. Visiting appointments: Holland, 1962; USA, 1963, 1975; Germany, 1966; Israel, 1969; Italy, 1972; Egypt, 1973. Ind. Mem., Radioactive Waste Management Cttee,

1978–80; Member: Chem. Cttee, SRC, 1976–78; Adv. Cttee, Davy-Faraday Labs, Royal Instn, 1978–80; Scientific Adv. Cttee, Sci. Center, Alexandria, 1979–; ACARD (Cabinet Office), 1982–; Bd of Governors, Weizmann Inst., 1982–. Corday Morgan Silver Medal, Chem. Soc., 1967; first Pettinos Prize, American Carbon Soc., 1969; Tilden Medal and Lectr, Chem. Soc., 1973; Chem. Soc. Prizewinner in Solid State Chem., 1978. BBC Welsh Radio Annual Lectr, 1978; Gerhardt Schmidt Meml Lectr, Weizmann Inst., 1979; Distinguished Vis. Lectr, London Univ., 1980; Royal Soc.-British Assoc. Lectr, 1980; Baker Lectr, Cornell Univ., 1982–83. Hon. Fellow, Indian Acad. of Science, 1980. *Publications:* (with W. J. Thomas) Introduction to the Principles of Heterogeneous Catalysis, 1967; Pan edrychwyf ar y nefoedd, 1978; numerous articles on solid state and surface chemistry, and influence of crystalline imperfections, in Proc. Royal Soc., Jl Chem. Soc., etc. *Recreations:* ancient civilizations, bird watching, hill walking, Welsh literature. *Address:* 37 Sedley Taylor Road, Cambridge CB2 2PN. *T:* Cambridge 211362; Cambridge 66499.

THOMAS, Gen. Sir (John) Noel, KCB 1969 (CB 1967); DSO 1945; MC 1945; BEng; Member, 1971–81, Vice-Chairman, 1974–81, Commonwealth War Graves Commission; *b* 28 Feb. 1915; *s* of John Ernest Thomas; *m* 1946, Jill, *d* of Edward Gordon Cuthbert Quilter; two *s*. *Educ:* Royal Grammar School, Newcastle upon Tyne; Liverpool University. 2nd Lieut, Royal Engineers, 1936. Served War of 1939–45 (MC, DSO). Imperial Defence College, 1963; General Officer Commanding 42 (Lancashire and Cheshire) Div. (TA), North West District, 1964; Director, Combat Development (Army), MoD, 1965–68; Dep. Chief of Defence Staff (Operational Requirements), MoD, 1968–70; Master-Gen. of the Ordnance, 1971–74. Lt-Gen. 1968; Gen. 1971. Hon. Col, Liverpool Univ. Contingent, OTC, 1965–80. Colonel Commandant: Royal Pioneer Corps, 1968–75; Royal Engineers, 1968–73. Pres. Sussex Council, Royal British Legion, 1981–. FRSA 1971. Hon. DEng Liverpool, 1972. *Address:* Chandlers House, The Trippet, Old Bosham, Sussex. *Club:* Royal Ocean Racing.

THOMAS, Rev. John Roland Lloyd; Principal of St David's College, Lampeter, 1953–75; Canon of St David's, 1956–75, Chancellor, 1963–75; *b* 22 Feb. 1908; 2nd *s* of late John Thomas, ME, and Mrs Ann Thomas; *m* 1949, Mrs Elizabeth Swaffield (*née* Rees); three *d*. *Educ:* King's, Taunton; St David's Coll., Lampeter; Jesus College, Oxford. Welsh Church Scholar, St David's College, Lampeter, BA (1st Class Hons History), 1930, Senior Scholar, 1929–30; Meyricke Graduate Scholar, 1930–32, Jesus Coll., Oxford, BA (2nd Class Th. Hons), 1932; MA 1936. Deacon, 1932; priest, 1933; Curate of St John Baptist, Cardiff, 1932–40. CF (EC) 1940–44. Rector of Canton, Cardiff, 1944–49; Vicar of St Mark's, Newport, 1949–52; Dean of Monmouth and Vicar of St Woolos Parish, Newport, 1952–53. CF(TA), 1949–52; SCF (TA), 1950–52; Hon. CF 1952. Hon. LLD Wales, 1976. *Publication:* Moth or Phoenix, 1980. *Address:* 1 Rock House, St Julian Street, Tenby, Dyfed. *T:* Tenby 2679.

THOMAS, John S.; *see* Stradling Thomas.

THOMAS, Keith Henry Westcott, CB 1982; OBE 1962; FEng, FRINA, FIIM; RCNC; Chief Executive, Royal Dockyards, since 1979; *b* 30 May 1923; *s* of Henry and Norah Thomas; *m* 1946, Brenda Jeanette Crofton; two *s*. *Educ:* Portsmouth Southern Secondary Sch.; HM Dockyard Sch., Portsmouth; RNC, Greenwich. Asst Constructor, Admiralty Experiment Works, Haslar, 1947–49; Constructor: Admty, London, 1949–56; Large Carrier Design Section, Admty, Bath, 1956–60; Submarines and New Construction, HM Dockyard, Portsmouth, 1960–63; Project Leader, Special Refit HMS Hermes, Devonport, 1963–66; Dep. Planning Manager, HM Dockyard, Devonport, 1966–68; Project Man., Ikara Leanders, MoD(N), 1968–70; Dir-Gen. of Naval Design, Dept of Navy, Canberra, Aust. (on secondment), 1970–73; Planning Man., 1973–75, Gen. Man., 1975–77, HM Dockyard, Rosyth; Gen. Manager, HM Dockyard, Devonport, 1977–79. FBIM. *Recreations:* music, fencing, lapidary. *Address:* 11 Englishcombe Way, Bath, Avon.

THOMAS, Keith Vivian, FBA 1979; Fellow and Tutor, St John's College, Oxford, since 1957; Reader in Modern History, University of Oxford, since 1978; *b* 2 Jan. 1933; *s* of Vivian Jones Thomas and late Hilda Janet Eirene (*née* Davies); *m* 1961, Valerie Little; one *s* one *d*. *Educ:* Barry County Grammar Sch.; Balliol Coll., Oxford (Brackenbury Schol.; 1st Cl. Hons Mod. History, 1955). Senior Scholar, St Antony's Coll., Oxford, 1955; Fellow of All Souls Coll., Oxford, 1955–57; Vis. Professor, Louisiana State Univ., 1970; Vis. Fellow, Princeton Univ., 1978. Joint Literary Director, Royal Historical Soc., 1970–74, Mem. Council, 1975–78, Vice-Pres., 1980–. Delegate, OUP, 1980–. Lectures: Stenton, Univ. of Reading, 1975; Raleigh, British Acad., 1976; Neale, University Coll. London, 1976; G. M. Trevelyan, Univ. of Cambridge, 1978–79; Sir D. Owen Evans, University Coll. of Wales, Aberystwyth, 1980. *Publications:* Religion and the Decline of Magic, 1971 (Wolfson Lit. Award for History, 1972); Rule and Misrule in the Schools of Early Modern England, 1976; Age and Authority in Early Modern England, 1977; ed (with Donald Pennington), Puritans and Revolutionaries, 1978; contribs to historical books and jls. *Recreation:* visiting secondhand bookshops. *Address:* St John's College, Oxford. *T:* Oxford 47671; 17 St Giles, Oxford. *T:* Oxford 52357.

THOMAS, Kenneth Rowland; General Secretary, Civil and Public Services Association, 1976–82; *b* 7 Feb. 1927; *s* of William Rowland Thomas and Anne

Thomas; *m* 1955, Nora (*née* Hughes); four *s. Educ:* St Joseph's Elementary Sch., Penarth; Penarth Grammar Sch. Trainee Reporter, South Wales Echo and Western Mail, 1943-44; Civil Servant, 1944-54; Asst Sec., Civil and Public Services Assoc., 1955, Dep. Gen. Sec., 1967. Mem., TUC Gen. Council, 1977-82. Mem., Occupational Pensions Bd, 1981-; Trustee, PO Superannuation Fund; Dir, W Midlands Enterprise Bd. *Recreations:* building harpsichords, music, anything Welsh. *Address:* 66 Canonbie Road, SE23 3AG. *T:* 01-699 9762.

THOMAS, Leslie John; author; *b* 22 March 1931; *s* of late David James Thomas and late Dorothy Hilda Court Thomas, Newport (Mon); *m* 1st, 1956, Maureen Crane (marr. diss.); two *s* one *d* ; 2nd, 1970, Diana Miles; one *s. Educ:* Dr Barnardo's, Kingston-upon-Thames; Kingston Technical Sch.; SW Essex Technical Coll., Walthamstow. Local Newspapers, London area, 1948-49 and 1951-53; Army, 1949-51 (rose to Lance-Corporal); Exchange Telegraph News Agency, 1953-55; Special Writer, London Evening News, 1955-66; subseq. author. *Publications: autobiography:* This Time Next Week, 1964; *novels:* The Virgin Soldiers, 1966; Orange Wednesday, 1967; The Love Beach, 1968; Come to the War, 1969; His Lordship, 1970; Onward Virgin Soldiers, 1971; Arthur McCann and All His Women, 1972; The Man with Power, 1973; Tropic of Ruislip, 1974; Stand up Virgin Soldiers, 1975; Dangerous Davies, 1976; Bare Nell, 1977; Ormerod's Landing, 1978; That Old Gang of Mine, 1979; The Magic Army, 1981; *non-fiction:* Some Lovely Islands, 1968; The Hidden Places of Britain, 1981; TV Plays and Documentaries, etc. *Recreations:* golf, islands, antiques, cricket. *Address:* The Vale House, Somerton, Somerset. *Clubs:* Wig and Pen, Lord's Taverners; Press.

THOMAS, (Lewis John) Wynford V.; *see* Vaughan-Thomas.

THOMAS, Maldwyn; *see* Thomas, J. M.

THOMAS, Margaret, RBA 1947; RWA 1971; NEAC 1950; Women's International Art Club, 1940; Contemporary Portrait Society, 1970; Practising Artist (Painter); *b* 26 Sept. 1916; *d* of late Francis Stewart Thomas and of Grace Wetherly. *Educ:* privately; Slade Sch.; RA Schools. Slade Scholar, 1936. Hon. Sec. Artists International Assoc., 1944-45; FRSA 1971. Group exhibitions, Wildensteins, 1946, 1949 and 1962; First one-man show at Leicester Galls, 1949, and subsequently at same gallery, 1950; one-man shows in Edinburgh (Aitken Dotts), 1952, 1955, 1966, and at Outlook Tower, Edinburgh, during Internat. Fest., 1961; RBA Galleries, London, 1953; at Canaletto Gall. (a barge, at Little Venice), 1961; Exhibition of Women Artists, Wakefield Art Gall., 1961; Howard Roberts Gallery Cardiff, 1963, The Minories, Colchester, 1964, QUB, 1967, Mall Galls, London, 1972; Octagon Gall., Belfast, 1973; Court Lodge Gallery, Kent, 1974; Gallery Paton, Edinburgh, 1977; Regular exhibitor Royal Academy and Royal Scottish Academy. Official purchases: Prince Philip, Duke of Edinburgh; Chantrey Bequest; Arts Council; Exeter College, Oxford; Min. of Education; Min. of Works; Wakefield, Hull, Paisley and Carlisle Art Galleries; Edinburgh City Corporation; Nuffield Foundation Trust; Steel Co. of Wales; Financial Times; Mitsukoshi Ltd, Tokyo; Scottish Nat. Orchestra; GLC and county education authorities in Yorks, Bucks, Monmouth, Derbyshire, Hampshire and Wales. Coronation painting purchased by Min. of Works for British Embassy in Santiago. Winner, Hunting Gp Award for best oil painting of the year, 1981. *Publications:* work reproduced in: Daily Telegraph, News Chronicle, Listener, Studio, Scottish Field, Music and Musicians, The Lady, Arts Review, Western Mail; Illustrated London News, The Artist. *Recreations:* antique collecting, gardening, vintage cars. *Address:* Halfway Cottage, 11a North Road, Highgate Village, N6 4BD. *T:* 01-340 2527; 8 North Bank Street, Edinburgh EH1 2LP. *T:* 031-225 3343.

THOMAS, Martin, OBE 1982; QC 1979; a Recorder of the Crown Court, since 1976; *b* 13 March 1937; *s* of Hywel and Olwen Thomas; *m* 1961, Nan Thomas (*née* Kerr); three *s* one *d. Educ:* Grove Park Grammar Sch., Wrexham; Peterhouse, Cambridge. MA, LLB (Cantab). Solicitor at Wrexham, 1961-66; Lectr in Law, 1966-68; called to the Bar, Gray's Inn, 1967; Barrister, Wales and Chester Circuit, 1968-; Dep. Circuit Judge, 1974-76. Contested (L): W Flints, 1964, 1966, 1970; Wrexham, Feb. and Oct. 1974, 1979; Vice Chm., Welsh Liberal Party, 1967-69, Chm. 1969-74; President: Wrexham Liberal Assoc., 1975-; Welsh Liberal Party, 1977, 1978, 1979. *Recreations:* Rugby football, golf, music-making, amateur theatre. *Address:* Glasfryn, Gresford, Wrexham, Clwyd. *T:* Gresford 2205. *Clubs:* Reform; Wrexham Rugby Football, Wrexham Golf.

THOMAS, Rt. Rev. Maxwell McNee; *see* Wangaratta, Bishop of.

THOMAS, Melbourne, QPM 1953; Chairman, St John Council, Mid Glamorgan, 1972-80; *b* 1 May 1906; *s* of David and Charlotte Frances Thomas; *m* 1930, Marjorie Elizabeth Phillips; one *d. Educ:* Newport (St Julian's) High School. Metropolitan Police, 1928-29; Newport Borough Police, 1929-45 (Dep. Chief Constable, 1941-45); Chief Constable: Merthyr Borough Police, 1945-63; Glamorgan Constabulary, 1963-69; 1st Chief Constable, South Wales Police, 1969-71. Chm., Bd of Governors, Coleg-y-Fro, 1971; Almoner, St John Priory, Wales, 1978. KStJ 1974. *Recreations:* Rugby, cricket, athletics. *Address:* The Lower Flat, Stafford Coach House, Westgate, Cowbridge, South Glamorgan. *T:* Cowbridge 4245.

THOMAS, Air Vice-Marshal Meredith, CSI 1946; CBE 1941; DFC 1922; AFC; Royal Air Force, retired; *b* 6 July 1892. Served European War, 1914-19;

Flying Officer, RFC, 1917; Group Captain, 1938; SASO, No 5 Grp, 1938; Dir of Techn. Trg, Air Min., 1940; Air Cdre, 1943; AOC, India, 1944-46; retired, 1946. *Address:* c/o Ministry of Defence (Air), Whitehall, SW1.

THOMAS, Sir Michael, 3rd Bt; *see* Thomas, Sir W. M. M.

THOMAS, Sir Michael, 11th Bt; *see* Thomas, Sir G. M. D.

THOMAS, Michael David, QC 1973; *b* 8 Sept. 1933; *s* of late D. Cardigan Thomas and Kathleen Thomas; *m* 1st, 1958, Jane Lena Mary (marr. diss. 1978), *e d* of Francis Neate; two *s* two *d* ; 2nd, 1981, Mrs Gabrielle Blakemore. *Educ:* Chigwell Sch., Essex; London Sch. of Economics. LLB 1954. Called to Bar, Middle Temple, 1955 (Blackstone Entrance Schol., 1952; Harmsworth Schol., 1957); Bencher, 1981. Nat. Service with RN, Sub-Lt RNVR, 1955-57. In practice at Bar from 1958. Junior Counsel to Minister of Defence (RN) and to Treasury in Admty matters, 1966-73. Wreck Commissioner under Merchant Shipping Act 1970; one of Lloyd's salvage arbitrators. Governor, Chigwell Sch., 1971-. *Publications:* (ed jtly) Temperley: Merchant Shipping Acts, 6th edn 1963 and 7th edn 1974. *Recreations:* music, travel. *Address:* 2 Essex Court, Temple, EC4Y 9AP. *T:* 01-353 4559; Tynllidiart, Brithdir, Gwynedd. *Club:* Garrick.

THOMAS, Lt-Col Michael John Glyn, RAMC; Exchange Pathologist, Walter Reed Army Institute of Research, since 1982; *b* 14 Feb. 1938; *s* of Glyn Pritchard Thomas and Mary Thomas (*née* Moseley); *m* 1969, Sheelagh Thorpe; one *d. Educ:* Haileybury and ISC; Trinity College, Cambridge; St Bartholomew's Hosp. MA, MB, BChir, LMSSA, DTM&H. Qualified 1962; House Surgeon, Essex County Hosp. and House Physician, St James, Balham, 1963; Regtl MO, 2nd Bn The Parachute Regt, 1965; Trainee Pathologist, BMH Singapore, 1968; Specialist in Pathology, Colchester Mil. Hosp., 1971; Senior Specialist in Pathology, Army Blood Supply Depot, 1977. Mem. Council, BMA, 1974- (Chm., Junior Mems Forum, 1974-75; Chm., Central Ethical Cttee, 1978-). *Publications:* contribs to ref. books and jls on Medical Ethics, Haematology and Blood Banking and Malariology. *Recreations:* sailing, travel, photography, philately. *Address:* British Army Staff, Washington, BFPO 2. *Club:* Tanglin (Singapore).

THOMAS, Michael Stuart, (Mike Thomas); MP Newcastle upon Tyne East, since Oct. 1974 (Lab and Co-op, 1974-81, SDP, since 1981); *b* 24 May 1944; *s* of Arthur Edward Thomas. *Educ:* Latymer Upper Sch.; King's Sch., Macclesfield; Liverpool Univ. (BA). Pres., Liverpool Univ. Guild of Undergraduates, 1965-66; Past Mem. Nat. Exec., NUS. Head of Research Dept, Co-operative Party, 1966-68; Sen. Res. Officer, Political and Economic Planning, 1968-73; Dir, Volunteer Centre, 1973-74. Mem., Select Cttee on Nationalised Industries, 1975-79; Chm., PLP Trade Gp, 1979-81; SDP spokesman on health and social services, 1981-; Mem., SDP Nat. Steering Cttee, 1981-; Chm., Organisation Cttee of SDP, 1981-. Mem., USDAW; founder of parly jl The House Magazine. *Publications:* Participation and the Redcliffe Maud Report, 1970; (ed) The BBC Guide to Parliament, 1979; various PEP pamphlets, contribs, etc, 1971-; various articles, reviews, etc. *Recreations:* theatre, music, cooking, collecting political and historical objects (particularly pottery). *Address:* House of Commons, SW1A 1AA. *T:* 01-219 4083. *Club:* Walker Social (Newcastle upon Tyne).

THOMAS, Neville; *see* Thomas, R. N.

THOMAS, Sir Noel; *see* Thomas, Sir J. N.

THOMAS, Norman, CBE 1980; HM Chief Inspector of Schools 1973-81; *b* 1 June 1921; *s* of Bowen Thomas and Ada Thomas (*née* Redding); *m* 1942, Rose Henshaw; one *s* one *d. Educ:* Latymer's Sch., Edmonton; Camden Coll. Qual. Teacher. Commerce and Industry, then primary schs in London and Herts, 1948-56; Head, Longmeadow Sch., Stevenage, 1956-61; HM Inspector of Schools, Lincs and SE England, 1962-68; HMI, Staff Inspector for Primary (Junior and Middle) Schs, 1969-73. *Publications:* articles in professional jls. *Recreations:* photography, reading. *Address:* 19 Langley Way, Watford, Herts WD1 3EJ.

THOMAS, Sir Patrick (Muirhead), Kt 1974; DSO 1945; TD 1945; DL; *b* 31 Jan. 1914; *s* of Herbert James Thomas, Barrister-at-Law and Charis Thomas (*née* Muirhead); *m* 1939, Ethel Mary Lawrence; one *s* three *d. Educ:* Clifton Coll.; Corpus Christi Coll., Cambridge (MA). FInstT. Served War of 1939-45, France, N Africa, Italy, Greece, Middle East, Austria; Lt-Col comdg 71st Field Regt RA, 1944-45. Steel Industry, United Steel Cos and Arthur Balfour & Co. Ltd, Sheffield, 1935-39; Wm Beardmore & Co. Ltd, Parkhead Steelworks, Glasgow, 1946: Man. Dir, 1954; Dir, 1967-76. Hon. Vice-Pres., Iron and Steel Inst., 1968. Col Comdt, City of Glasgow Army Cadet Force, 1956 (Hon. Col 1963-70, 1977-). Pres., FBI Scottish Council, 1961-62; Pres., Scottish Engrg Employers' Assoc., 1967-68; Chm., Scottish Transport Gp, 1968-77; Part-time Mem., Scottish Gas Board, 1966-72; Director: Brightside Engrg Holdings Ltd, 1967-71; Midland Caledonian Investment Trust Ltd, 1972-75. Chm., Scottish Opera, 1976-81 (Dir, 1965-81); Member: Court, Univ. of Strathclyde, 1970- (Chm., 1970-75); Lloyd's Register of Shipping Scottish Cttee, 1967-81; Panel Mem., Industrial Tribunals, 1967-80; Deacon Convener, Trades of Glasgow, 1970-71; Member: Exec. Cttee, Officers Assoc. (Scotland), 1964-75, 1978-; Exec. Cttee, Earl Haig Fund (Scotland), 1964-75, 1978- (Chm., 1981-); Artillery Council for Scotland, 1978-; Chairman: Lady Haig's Poppy Factory, 1967-72; Royal Artillery Assoc. (Scottish Region),

1978-. Governor, Clifton Coll., 1979-. DL Renfrewshire, 1980. Hon. LLD Strathclyde, 1973. US Bronze Star, 1945. OStJ 1970. *Recreations:* golf, gardening. *Address:* Bemersyde, Kilmacolm, Renfrewshire PA13 4EA. *T:* Kilmacolm 2710.

THOMAS, Rt. Hon. Peter John Mitchell, PC 1964; QC 1965; MP (C) Barnet, Hendon South, since 1974 (Hendon South, 1970-74); a Recorder of the Crown Court, since 1974; *b* 31 July 1920; *o s* of late David Thomas, Solicitor, Llanrwst, Denbighshire, and Anne Gwendoline Mitchell; *m* 1947, Frances Elizabeth Tessa, *o d* of late Basil Dean, CBE and Lady Mercy Greville; *two s two d. Educ:* Epworth College, Rhyl; Jesus College, Oxford (MA). Served War of 1939-45, in RAF; Prisoner of War (Germany), 1941-45. Called to Bar, 1947, Middle Temple, Bencher, 1971, Member of Wales and Chester Circuit. MP (C) Conway Div. of Caernarvonshire, 1951-66; PPS to the Solicitor-General, 1954-59; Parly Secretary, Min. of Labour, 1959-61; Parly Under-Sec. of State, Foreign Office, 1961-63; Minister of State for Foreign Affairs, 1963-64; Opp. Front Bench Spokesman on Foreign Affairs and Law, 1964-66; Sec. of State for Wales, 1970-74. Chm., Cons. Party Organisation, 1970-72. Pres., Nat. Union of Conservative and Unionist Assocs, 1974 and 1975. Dep. Chairman: Cheshire QS, 1966-70; Denbighshire QS, 1968-70. Member, Historic Buildings Council for Wales, 1965-67. *Address:* 37 Chester Way, SE11. *T:* 01-735 6047; Millicent Cottage, Elstead, Surrey. *Clubs:* Carlton; Cardiff and County (Cardiff).

THOMAS, Ralph Philip, MC 1942; Film Director; *b* Hull, Yorks, 10 Aug.; *m* 1944, Joy Spanjer; one *s* one *d. Educ:* Tellisford School, Clifton. Entered film industry, 1932, and worked in all production depts, particularly editing, until 1939. Served War of 1939-45, as Regimental Officer 9th Lancers until 1944; thereafter Instructor Royal Military College. Returned to Film Industry, in Rank Organisation Trailer Dept, 1946; Joined Gainsborough Pictures, 1948, and directed Once Upon a Dream, Traveller's Joy. Films directed at Pinewood Studios: The Clouded Yellow, Appointment with Venus, The Venetian Bird, A Day to Remember, Doctor in the House, Mad About Men, Above Us The Waves, Doctor at Sea, The Iron Petticoat, Checkpoint, Doctor at Large, Campbell's Kingdom, A Tale of Two Cities, The Wind Cannot Read, The 39 Steps, Upstairs and Downstairs, Conspiracy of Hearts, Doctor in Love, No My Darling Daughter, No Love for Johnnie, The Wild and the Willing, Doctor in Distress, Hot enough for June, The High Bright Sun, Doctor in Clover, Deadlier than the Male, Nobody Runs Forever, Some Girls Do, Doctor in Trouble, Quest, Percy, It's a 2 foot 6 inch Above the Ground World, Percy's Progress, A Nightingale Sang in Berkeley Square, Doctors' Daughters. *Address:* 20 Hyde Park Gardens Mews, W2. *Clubs:* Garrick, Cavalry and Guards.

THOMAS, Dr Reginald; Austrian Ambassador to the Court of St James's, since 1982; *b* 28 Feb. 1928; *s* of Dr Leopold Thomas and Irma Thomas (*née* von Smekal); *m* 1960, Ingrid Renate Leitner; three *s* one *d. Educ:* Univ. of Vienna (Dr jur 1950). Entered Austrian Foreign Service, 1951; Austrian Legation, Bern, 1952-56; Dep. Legal Adviser on Internat. Law, Min. of Foreign Affairs, Vienna, 1956-59; Austrian Embassy, Tokyo, 1959-62; Head of Office of Sec. Gen. for Foreign Affairs, Vienna, 1962-68; Ambassador to Pakistan and concurrently accredited to Union of Burma, 1968-71; Ambassador to Japan and concurrently accredited to Republic of Korea, 1971-75; Head of Dept of Administration, Min. of Foreign Affairs, Vienna, 1975-82; concurrently Dep. Sec. Gen. for Foreign Affairs, Vienna, 1978-82. Mem., Austrian Assoc. for Foreign Policy and Internat. Relations, Vienna, 1978-82. Foreign orders include: Grand Cross: Order of the Rising Sun (Japan); Order of Diplomatic Service (Korea); Independence Order (Jordan); Order of F. de Miranda (Venezuela); Hilal-i-Qaid-i-Azam (Pakistan). *Recreations:* sports, photography. *Address:* 18 Belgrave Square, SW1. *T:* 01-235 7268. *Clubs:* Travellers', Hurlingham.

THOMAS, Lt-Col Reginald Silvers W.; *see* Williams-Thomas.

THOMAS, Richard; HM Diplomatic Service; Counsellor and Head of Chancery, HM Embassy, Prague, since 1979; *b* 1938; *s* of Anthony Hugh Thomas and Molly Thomas, MBE; *m* 1966, Catherine Jane Hayes, Sydney, NSW; one *s* two *d. Educ:* Leighton Park; Merton Coll., Oxford (MA). Nat. Service, 2nd Lt, RASC, 1959-61. Asst Principal, CRO, 1961; Private Sec. to Parly Under Sec., 1962-63; Second Secretary: Accra, 1963-65; Lomé, 1965-66; (later First Sec.) UK Delegn NATO, Paris and Brussels, 1966-69; First Secretary: FCO, 1969-72; (Economic), New Delhi, 1972-75; and Asst Head of Dept, FCO, 1976-78; FCO Visiting Res. Fellow, RIIA, 1978-79. *Publication:* India's Emergence as an Industrial Power: Middle Eastern Contracts, 1982. *Recreations:* music, mountains, gardening, sailing. *Address:* c/o Foreign and Commonwealth Office, SW1A 2AH. *Club:* Royal Commonwealth Society.

THOMAS, Sir Robert (Evan), Kt 1967; DL; JP; Leader, Greater Manchester Metropolitan County Council, 1973-77; Deputy Chairman, Manchester Ship Canal, 1971-74; *b* 8 Oct. 1901; *s* of Jesse and Anne Thomas; *m* 1924, Edna Isherwood; one *s* one *d. Educ:* St Peter's, Leigh, Lancs. Miner, 1914; served Army, 1919-21; Bus Driver, 1924-37; Trade Union Official, 1937-66; Member, Manchester City Council, 1944-74; Lord Mayor of Manchester, 1962-63. Chairman: Assoc. of Municipal Corps, 1973-74; Assoc. of Metropolitan Authorities, 1974-77; British Sector, Internat. Union of Local Authorities, 1974-77. JP Manchester, 1948; DL: County Palatine of Lancaster, 1967-73, County Palatine of Greater Manchester, 1974. Hon. MA Manchester

1974. *Recreations:* dancing, gardening, golf. *Address:* 29 Milwain Road, Manchester M19 2PX. *T:* 061-224 5778.

THOMAS, (Robert) Neville, QC 1975; barrister-at-law; a Recorder of the Crown Court, 1975-82; *b* 31 March 1936; *s* of Robert Derfel Thomas and Enid Anne Thomas; *m* 1970, Jennifer Anne Brownrigg; one *s* one *d. Educ:* Ruthin Sch.; University Coll., Oxford (MA, BCL). Called to Bar, Inner Temple, 1962. *Recreations:* fishing, walking, reading. *Address:* Eithinog Hall, Cyfronydd, Welshpool, Powys SY21 9ED. *Club:* Garrick.

THOMAS, Dr Roger Gareth; MP (Lab) Carmarthen, since 1979; Family Medical Practitioner, since 1952; *b* 14 Nov. 1925; *m* 1958, Indeg Thomas; one *s* one *d. Educ:* Amman Valley Grammar Sch.; London Hosp. Med. Coll. Captain, RAMC, 1949-52. *Recreation:* music. *Address:* Ffynnon Wên, Capel Hendre, Ammanford, Dyfed SA18 3SD. *T:* Cross Hands 843093.

THOMAS, Roger Lloyd; Senior Clerk (Acting), Committee Office, House of Commons, since 1979; *b* 7 Feb. 1919; *s* of Trevor John Thomas and Eleanor Maud (*née* Jones), Abercarn, Mon; *m* 1945, Stella Mary, *d* of Reginald Ernest Willmett, Newport, Mon; three *s* one *d. Educ:* Barry County Sch.; Magdalen Coll., Oxford (Doncaster Schol.; Heath Harrison Trav. Schol.). BA 2nd Mod. Langs, 1939; MA 1946. Served 1939-46, RA and Gen. Staff (Major GSO2) in India, Middle East, N Africa, Italy and Germany. Civil Servant, 1948-70: Min. of Fuel and Power, Home Office, Treasury, Welsh Office and Min. of Housing and Local Govt; Private Sec. to Perm. Under-Sec. of State, Home Office, 1950 and to successive Parly Under-Secs of State, 1951-53; Sec., Interdeptl Cttee on powers of Subpoena, 1960; Asst Sec., 1963; Sec., Aberfan Inquiry Tribunal, 1966-67; Chm., Working Party on Building by Direct Labour Organisations, 1968-69; Gen. Manager, The Housing Corporation, 1970-73; Asst Sec., DoE, 1974-79. *Publications:* sundry reports. *Recreation:* growing flowers. *Address:* 5 Park Avenue, Caterham, Surrey. *T:* Caterham 42080. *Club:* Union (Oxford).
See also D. H. P. *Thomas.*

THOMAS, Ronald Richard; *b* March 1929. *Educ:* Ruskin Coll. and Balliol Coll., Oxford (MA). Sen. Lectr, Econ. and Indust. Studies, Univ. of Bristol. Contested (Lab) Bristol North-West, Feb. 1974; MP (Lab) Bristol NW, Oct. 1974-1979. Former Mem., Bristol DC. Mem. ASTMS. *Address:* 64 Morris Road, Lockleaze, Bristol BS7 9TA.

THOMAS, Rev. Ronald Stuart; poet; Vicar of St Hywyn, Aberdaron, with St Mary, Bodferin, since 1967; Rector of Rhiw with Llanfaelrhys, since 1973; *b* 1915; *m* Mildred E. Eldridge; one *s. Educ:* University of Wales (BA); St Michael's College, Llandaff. Ordained deacon, 1936; priest, 1937. Curate of Chirk, 1936-40; Curate of Hanmer, in charge of Talarn Green, 1940-42; Rector of Manafon, 1942-54; Vicar of Eglwysfach, 1954-67. First record, reading his own poems, 1977. Queen's Gold Medal for Poetry, 1964; Cholmondeley Award, 1978. *Publications:* poems: Stones of the Field (privately printed), 1947; Song at the Year's Turning, 1955 (Heinemann Award of the Royal Society of Literature, 1956); Poetry for Supper, 1958; Tares, 1961; Bread of Truth, 1963; Pieta, 1966; Not That He Brought Flowers, 1968; H'm, 1972; Selected Poems 1946-1968, 1974; Laboratories of the Spirit, 1976; Frequencies, 1978; Between Here and Now, 1981; edited: A Book of Country Verse, 1961; George Herbert, A Choice of Verse, 1967; A Choice of Wordsworth's Verse, 1971. *Address:* Sarn-y-Plas, Y Rhiw, Pwllheli, Gwynedd.

THOMAS, Ryland Lowell Degwel, CB 1974; Deputy Director of Public Prosecutions, 1971-74; *b* 24 April 1914; *er s* of Rev. William Degwel Thomas and Sarah Maud Thomas (*née* Richards), Neath, Glam; *m* 1942, Mair Eluned, *d* of Rev. J. L. Williams, Swansea, Glam; one *s* one *d. Educ:* University Coll. of Wales, Aberystwyth (LLB); Trinity Hall, Cambridge (MA). Barrister-at-Law, Inner Temple. Ministry of Supply, 1941; Dept of Dir of Public Prosecutions, 1942; Asst Dir, 1965. *Recreations:* walking, motoring, travel. *Address:* 58 Strathearn Avenue, Whitton, Twickenham, Mddx. *Club:* London Welsh RFC (Vice-Pres.).

THOMAS, Swinton Barclay, QC 1975; a Recorder of the Crown Court, since 1975; *b* 12 Jan. 1931; *s* of Brig. William Bain Thomas, CBE, DSO, and Mary Georgina Thomas; *m* 1967, Angela, Lady Cope; one *s* one *d. Educ:* Ampleforth Coll.; Lincoln Coll., Oxford (Scholar) (MA). Called to Bar, Inner Temple, 1955. *Recreations:* reading, travel. *Address:* 36 Sheffield Terrace, W8. *T:* 01-727 2923. *Club:* Garrick.

THOMAS, Terry; *see* Terry-Thomas.

THOMAS, Rt. Hon. (Thomas) George, PC 1968; MP Cardiff West; Speaker of the House of Commons, since 1976. *Educ:* University Coll., Southampton. PPS, Min. of Civil Aviation, 1951. Chm., Welsh Parly Labour Party, 1950-51. Member, Chairman's Panel, House of Commons, 1951-64; Pres., National Brotherhood Movement, 1955. Schoolmaster. Vice-Pres. the Methodist Conference, 1960-61. MP (Lab): Cardiff Central, 1945-50; Cardiff W, 1950-76 (when elected Speaker); First Chm. of the Welsh Parliamentary Grand Committee; Jt Parly Under-Sec. of State, Home Office, 1964-66; Minister of State: Welsh Office, 1966-67; Commonwealth Office, 1967-68; Secretary of State for Wales, 1968-70; Dep. Speaker and Chm. of Ways and Means, House of Commons, 1974-76. Hon. Fellow: UC Cardiff, 1972; College of Preceptors, 1977; Polytechnic of Wales, 1982; Hon. LLD: Asbury

Coll., Kentucky, 1976; Southampton, 1977; Wales, 1977; Birmingham, 1978; Oklahoma, 1981; Liverpool, 1982. Freeman: Borough of Rhondda, 1970; City of Cardiff, 1975; City of London, 1980; Hon. Mem., Court of Assistants, Worshipful Company of Blacksmiths, 1980. Dato Setia Negara, Brunei, 1971; Grand Cross of the Peruvian Congress, 1982. *Publication:* The Christian Heritage in Politics. *Address:* Tilbury, 173 King George V Drive East, Cardiff; Speaker's House, House of Commons, SW1A 0AA. *Clubs:* Athenæum, Reform, English-Speaking Union; County (Cardiff).

THOMAS, Trevor, BA; artist, author; retired; *b* 8 June 1907; 2nd *s* of William Thomas and Mary Richards; *m* 1947; two *s. Educ:* Sir Alfred Jones Scholar, University Coll. of Wales, Aberystwyth. Demonstrator, Dept of Geography and Anthropology, University Coll. of Wales, Aberystwyth, 1929–30; Secretary and Lecturer-Assistant, Department of Geography, Victoria University, Manchester, 1930–31; Cartographer to Geographical Association, Manchester, 1930–31; Keeper, Departments of Ethnology and Shipping, Liverpool Public Museums, 1931–40; Rockefeller Foundation Museums Fellow, USA, 1938–39; Director, Museum and Art Gallery, Leicester, 1940–46; Surveyor, Regional Guide to Works of Art, Arts Council of Great Britain, 1946–48; Designer of Exhibitions for the British Institute of Adult Education, 1946–48; Director, Crafts Centre of Great Britain, 1947–48; Programme Specialist for Education through the Arts, UNESCO, Paris, 1949–56; Visiting Prof. of Art Education, Teachers' Coll., Columbia Univ., NY, USA, 1956; Prof. of Art, State Univ. of New York, College for Teachers, Buffalo, 1957–58; Prof. of Art Hist., University of Buffalo, and Art Critic, Buffalo Evening News, 1959–60; Art Editor, Gordon Fraser Gall. Ltd, 1960–72. Mem. Exec. Cttee, Campaign for Homosexual Equality, 1976–78, 1979–; Hon. Sec., Gaydaid, help for gay disabled people, 1980–; Mem., Exec. Cttee, Gay Humanist Group, 1980–; Hon. Mem., United Soc. of Artists, 1980. *Publications:* Penny Plain Twopence Coloured: the Aesthetics of Museum Display (Museums Jl, April 1939); Education and Art: a Symposium (jt Editor with Edwin Ziegfeld), Unesco, 1953; Creating with Paper: basic forms and variations (Foreword and associate writer with Pauline Johnson), 1958; contribs to: Museums Journal, Dec. 1933, April 1935, April 1939, Oct. 1941; Parnassus, Jan. and April 1940; Unesco Educn Abstracts, Feb. 1953. *Recreations:* art, music, theatre, lecturing. Research: Art. *Address:* 36 Pembroke Street, Bedford MK40 3RH. *T:* Bedford 58879.

THOMAS, Trevor Cawdor, MA, LLB Cantab, LLB Wales; Vice-Chancellor, University of Liverpool, 1970–76; Emeritus Professor, 1976; *b* 19 April 1914; *o s* of James Elwyn Thomas and Charlotte Thomas (*née* Ivatt); *m* 1943, Mrs Marjory Molony, widow of John Bernard Molony, and *y d* of Samuel Harry Guteridge Higgs and Fanny Higgs, Reading. *Educ:* University College of Wales, Aberystwyth; Trinity Hall, Cambridge. LLB Wales 1936 (first class (at Aberystwyth) and Sir Samuel Evans prizeman); Fountain Schol., Trinity Hall, 1937; Trinity Hall Law Studentship, 1938; Joseph Hodges Choate Memorial Fellowship, 1938; BA; LLB Cantab 1938. Entrance Schol., Gray's Inn, 1936; Bar Final Examinations, 1940 (first class with certif. of honour); called to Bar, Gray's Inn, 1941, Hon. Bencher, 1975. Lecturer in Law, Univ. of Leeds, 1939–41. RAF, Intell. Br., 1941–45. Fellow of Trinity Hall, Cambridge, 1945–60, Hon. Fellow, 1970; Univ. Lectr in Law, Univ. of Cambridge, 1945–60; Fellow and Sen. Bursar, St John's Coll., Cambridge, 1960–69; Hon. Fellow, Darwin Coll., Cambridge, 1972. Mem. Statutory Commn for Royal Univ. of Malta, 1960–69. Chm., Nuffield Foundn Cttee of Inquiry into Dental Educn, 1978. JP, City of Cambridge, 1966–69. Hon. LLD: Liverpool, 1972; Wales, 1978. Hon. FDSRCS Eng., 1982. *Publications:* co-editor, Jenks' Digest of English Civil Law, 4th edn 1947; articles in Cambridge Law Jl. *Recreations:* gardening, travel, fishing. *Address:* Dolphins, Roncombe Lane, Sidbury, near Sidmouth, Devon EX10 0QL. *Club:* Farmers'.

THOMAS, Maj.-Gen. Vivian Davenport, CB 1949; CBE 1946 (OBE 1942); Royal Marines, retired; *b* 31 Oct. 1897; *s* of Arnold Frederick Davenport Thomas, London; *m* 1929, Theresa, *d* of Colonel E. J. Previte, VD, TD, Burstow, Surrey; one *s. Educ:* St Paul's. Served European War, 1914–18: with Royal Marines, 1914–19; HMS Princess Royal, 1st Battle Cruiser Squadron, 1915–18. War of 1939–45, North Africa; Lieutenant-Colonel, 1942; acting Colonel Commandant (temp. Brig.) 1943; Comdr 1st RM AA Bde, India, 1943; COS to Chief of Combined Ops, 1944–46; Maj.-Gen. 1946; COS to Comdt Gen., RM, 1946–50; Chief of Amphibious Warfare, 1950–54; retired, 1954. Cdre, 1951–55, Life Vice-Cdre, 1974, Royal Naval Sailing Assoc. Hon. Col Comdt, Plymouth Group Royal Marines, 1957–61. Vice Patron, Sail Training Assoc., 1969; Vice-Pres., London Fedn of Boy's Clubs, 1978. Master, 1962–63, Father, 1982, Armourers' and Brasiers' Company. *Address:* Coppinghall, 46 Church Street, Uckfield, East Sussex TN22 1BT. *Clubs:* Caledonian; Royal Yacht Squadron.

THOMAS, Maj.-Gen. Walter Babington, CB 1971; DSO 1943; MC and Bar, 1942; Commander, HQ Far East Land Forces, Nov. 1970–Nov. 1971 (Chief of Staff, April–Oct. 1970); retired Jan. 1972; *b* Nelson, NZ, 29 June 1919; *s* of Walter Harington Thomas, Farmer; *m* 1947, Iredale Edith Lauchlan (*née* Trent); three *d. Educ:* Motueka Dist High Sch., Nelson, NZ. Clerk, Bank of New Zealand, 1936–39. Served War of 1939–45 (despatches, MC and Bar, DSO): 2nd NZEF, 1940–46, in Greece, Crete, Western Desert, Tunis and Italy; Comd 23 (NZ) Bn, 1944–45; Comd 22 (NZ) Bn, in Japan, 1946; transf. to Brit. Army, Royal Hampshire Regt, 1947; Bde Major, 39 Inf. Bde Gp, 1953–55 (despatches); GSO2, UK JSLS, Aust., 1958–60; AA&QMG, HQ 1 Div. BAOR, 1962–64; Comd 12 Inf. Bde Gp, 1964–66; IDC, 1967; GOC 5th

Div., 1968–70. Silver Star, Medal, 1945 (USA). *Publications:* Dare to be Free, 1951; Touch of Pitch, 1956. *Recreation:* riding. *Address:* PO Box 2161, Darwin, NT 5794, Australia.

THOMAS, Sir William James Cooper, 2nd Bt, *cr* 1919; TD; JP; DL; Captain RA; *b* 7 May 1919; *er s* of Sir William James Thomas, 1st Bt, and Maud Mary Cooper, Bexhill-on-Sea; *S* father 1945; *m* 1947, Freida Dunbar, *yr d* of late F. A. Whyte; two *s* one *d. Educ:* Harrow; Downing Coll., Cambridge. Barrister, Inner Temple, 1948. Member TA, 1938. Served War of 1939–45. Monmouthshire: JP 1958; DL 1973; High Sheriff, 1973. *Heir: s* William Michael Thomas, *b* 5 Dec. 1948. *Address:* Tump House, Llanrothal, Monmouth, Gwent. *T:* Monmouth 2757. *Club:* Army and Navy.

THOMAS, Ven. William Jordison; Archdeacon of Northumberland, since 1983; *b* 16 Dec. 1927; *s* of Henry William and Dorothy Newton Thomas; *m* 1954, Kathleen Jeffrey Robson, *d* of William Robson, Reaveley, Powburn, Alnwick. *Educ:* Holmwood Prep. School, Middlesbrough; Acklam Hall Grammar School, Middlesbrough; Giggleswick School; King's Coll., Cambridge (BA 1951, MA 1955); Cuddesdon College. National Service, RN, 1946–48. Assistant Curate: St Anthony of Egypt, Newcastle upon Tyne, 1953–56; Berwick Parish Church, 1956–59; Vicar: Alwinton with Holystone and Alnham and the Lordship of Kidland, 1959–70; Alston with Garrigill, Nenthead and Kirkhaugh, 1970–80, i/c Knaresdale, 1973–80; Team Rector of Glendale, 1980–82; RD of Bamburgh and Glendale, 1980–82. *Recreations:* sailing own dinghy and other people's yachts, making pictures, travelling and making magic. *Address:* 80 Moorside North, Fenham, Newcastle upon Tyne NE4 9DU. *T:* Newcastle upon Tyne 738245. *Club:* Victory Ex-Services.

THOMAS, Sir (William) Michael (Marsh), 3rd Bt *cr* 1918; *b* 4 Dec. 1930; *s* of Sir William Eustace Rhyddlad Thomas, 2nd Bt, and Enid Helena Marsh; *S* father 1957; *m* 1953, Geraldine Mary, *d* of Robert Drysdale, Anglesey; three *d. Educ:* Oundle School, Northants. Formerly Man. Dir, Gors Nurseries Ltd. *Heir: u* Robert Freeman Thomas [*b* 8 Jan. 1911; *m* 1947, Marcia, *d* of Walter Lucas]. *Address:* Belan, Rhosneigr, Gwynedd LL64 5JE.

THOMAS, Wyndham, CBE 1982; General Manager, Peterborough New Town Development Corporation, since 1968; *b* 1 Feb. 1924; *s* of Robert John Thomas and Hannah Mary; *m* 1947, Elizabeth Tarry Hopkin; one *s* three *d. Educ:* Maesteg Grammar School. Served Army (Lieut, Royal Welch Fusiliers), 1943–47. Schoolmaster, 1950–53; Director, Town and Country Planning Association, 1955–67; Member: Land Commission, 1967–68; Commission for the New Towns, 1964–68; London Docklands Develt Corp., 1981–. Mayor of Hemel Hempstead, 1958–59. Hon. MRTPI 1979. *Publications:* many articles on town planning, housing, etc, in learned jls. *Recreations:* collecting old furniture, work, golf. *Address:* 20 High Street, Castor, Peterborough. *T:* Castor 409.

THOMAS, Wynford V.; *see* Vaughan-Thomas.

THOMASON, Prof. George Frederick; Montague Burton Professor of Industrial Relations, University College, Cardiff, since 1969; *b* 27 Nov. 1927; *s* of George Frederick Thomason and Eva Elizabeth (*née* Walker); *m* 1953, Jean Elizabeth Horsley; one *s* one *d. Educ:* Kelsick Grammar Sch.; Univ. of Sheffield (BA); Univ. of Toronto (MA); PhD (Wales). CIPM,MBIM. University College, Cardiff: Research Asst, 1953; Asst Lectr, 1954; Research Associate, 1956; Lectr, 1959; Asst Man. Dir, Flex Fasteners Ltd, Rhondda, 1960; University College, Cardiff: Lectr, 1962; Sen. Lectr, 1963; Reader, 1969; Dean, Faculty of Economics, 1971–73; Dep. Principal (Humanities), 1974–77. Mem., Doctors' and Dentists' Pay Review Body, 1979–. *Publications:* Welsh Society in Transition, 1963; Personnel Manager's Guide to Job Evaluation, 1968; Professional Approach to Community Work, 1969; The Management of Research and Development, 1970; Improving the Quality of Organization, 1973; Textbook of Personnel Management, 1975, 4th edn 1981; Job Evaluation: Objectives and Methods, 1980. *Recreation:* gardening. *Address:* The Red House, 12 Mill Road, Llanishen, Cardiff CF4 5XB. *T:* Cardiff 754236. *Clubs:* Athenæum; Cardiff and County (Cardiff).

THOMPSON, Alan, CB 1978; Chairman, Review Group on the Youth Service; *b* 16 July 1920; *s* of Herbert and Esther Thompson; *m* 1944, Joyce Nora Banks; two *s* one *d. Educ:* Carlisle Grammar Sch.; Queen's Coll., Oxford. Joined Min. of Education, 1946; Private Sec. to Minister of Education, 1954–56; Asst Sec., Further Education Br., 1956–64; Under Sec., UGC, 1964–71; Under Sec., Science Br., DES, 1971–75; Dep. Sec., DES, 1975–80. *Address:* 1 Drax Avenue, Wimbledon, SW20. *T:* 01-946 1837.

THOMPSON, Prof. Alan Eric; Professor of the Economics of Government, Heriot-Watt University, since 1972; *b* 16 Sept. 1924; *o c* of late Eric Joseph Thompson and of Florence Thompson; *m* 1960, Mary Heather Long; three *s* one *d. Educ:* University of Edinburgh (MA 1949, MA (Hons Class I, Economic Science), 1951, PhD 1953, Carnegie Research Scholar, 1951–52). Served army (including service with Central Mediterranean Forces), 1943–47. Asst in Political Economy, 1952–53, Lectr in Economics (formerly Political Economy), 1953–59, and 1964–71, Univ. of Edinburgh. Parly Adviser to Scottish Television, 1964–76; Scottish Governor, BBC, 1976–79. Visiting Professor, Graduate School of Business, Stanford Univ., USA, 1966, 1968. MP (Lab) Dunfermline, 1959–64. Chm., Adv. Bd on Economics Educn (Esmée Fairbairn Research Project), 1970–76; Member: Scottish Cttee, Public Schools Commn, 1969–70; Cttee enquiring into conditions of service life for young servicemen, 1969; Scottish Council for Adult Educn in HM Forces, 1973-; Jt Mil. Educn Cttee, Edinburgh and Heriot-Watt Univs, 1975-; Local Govt Boundary Commn for Scotland, 1975-; Royal Fine Art Commn for Scotland, 1975-80; Chm., Northern Offshore (Maritime) Resources Study, 1974-. Hon. Vice-Pres., Assoc. of Nazi War Camp Survivors, 1960-; Pres., Edinburgh Amenity and Transport Assoc., 1970-75. Mem. Court, Heriot-Watt Univ., 1980-; Chm. of Governors, Newbattle Abbey Coll., 1980- (Governor, 1975-); Governor, Leith Nautical Coll., 1981-; Trustee, Bell's Nautical Trust, 1981-. Has broadcast and appeared on TV (economic and political talks and discussions) in Britain and USA. FRSA 1972. *Publications:* Development of Economic Doctrine (jtly), 1980; contribs to learned journals. *Recreation:* writing children's stories and plays. *Address:* 11 Upper Gray Street, Edinburgh EH9 1SN. *T:* 031-667 2140; Ardtrostan Cottage, St Fillans, Perthshire. *T:* St Fillans 275. *Clubs:* New, Edinburgh University Staff (Edinburgh); Loch Earn Sailing.

THOMPSON, Anthony Arthur Richard, QC 1980; *b* 4 July 1932; *s* of late William Frank McGregor Thompson and of Doris Louise Thompson (*née* Hill); *m* 1958, Françoise Alix Marie Reynier; two *s* one *d* (and one *s* decd). *Educ:* Latymer; University Coll., Oxford; La Sorbonne. Called to the Bar, Inner Temple, 1957. Contested (Lab) Arundel and Shoreham, Oct. 1964. *Recreations:* food and wine, lawn tennis, squash. *Address:* 1 Essex Court, Temple, EC4. *T:* 01-353 5362. *Club:* Roehampton.

THOMPSON, Aubrey Gordon D.; *see* Denton-Thompson.

THOMPSON, Brenda, (Mrs Gordon Thompson); writer on education; *b* 27 Jan. 1935; *d* of Thomas Barnes Houghton and Marjorie Houghton; *m* 1956, Gordon Thompson; one *s. Educ:* Leeds Univ. BSc Hons in Biochemistry. Food chemist with J. Lyons & Co., 1957; Hosp. Biochemist, Chelsea Women's Hosp., 1958-60. Entered primary school teaching, 1964; Head Teacher, Northwold I (Primary) Sch., 1971-78, Stamford Hill Sch., 1978-81. Mem., Press Council, 1973-76. Indep. Councillor for London Borough of Islington, 1968-71. *Publications:* Learning to Read, 1970; Learning to Teach, 1973; The Pre-School Book, 1976; Reading Success, 1979; Editor various children's books. *Address:* Nantddu, Rhandirmwyn, Llandovery, Dyfed SA20 0NG. *T:* Llandovery 20159.

THOMPSON, Charles Allister; HM Diplomatic Service, retired; *b* 21 July 1922; *yr s* of late Herbert Ivie and Margaret (*née* Browne-Webber) Thompson, Managua, Nicaragua; *m* 1950, Jean Margaret, *er d* of late Alexander Bruce Dickson; two *s* two *d. Educ:* Haileybury; Hertford Coll., Oxford (MA, BLitt). War Service, 1942-46, 1st King's Dragoon Guards. Joined Foreign Service (now Diplomatic Service), 1947, and served in FO until 1949; 3rd Sec., Prague, 1949-50; 2nd Sec. (Commercial), Mexico City, 1950-53; FO 1953-56; 1st Sec., Karachi, 1956-59; Head of Chancery, Luxembourg, 1959-62; FO, 1962-65; Counsellor, 1965; Dep. Consul-Gen., New York, 1965-67; Dep. High Comr, Port of Spain, 1967-70; HM Consul-Gen., Philadelphia, 1970-74; Vis. Fellow, Centre for Internat. Studies, LSE, 1974-75; Head of Training Dept, FCO, and Dir, Diplomatic Service Language Centre, 1975-76. *Recreations:* gardening, golf, gerontology.

THOMPSON, Charles Norman, CBE 1978; FInstPet; CChem; FRSC; Head of Research and Development Liaison, and Health, Safety and Environment Administration, Shell UK Ltd, since 1978; *b* 23 Oct. 1922; *s* of Robert Norman Thompson and Evelyn Tivendale Thompson (*née* Wood); *m* 1946, Pamela Margaret Wicks; one *d. Educ:* Birkenhead Institute; Liverpool Univ. (BSc). Research Chemist, Thornton Research Centre (Shell Refining & Marketing Co. Ltd), 1943; Lectr, Petroleum Chemistry and Technology, Liverpool Coll. of Technology, 1947-51; Personnel Supt and Dep. Associate Manager, Thornton Research Centre, Shell Research Ltd, 1959-61; Dir (Res. Admin), Shell Research Ltd, 1961-78. Mem. Council, 1976-, Vice Pres., 1977-80, 1981-82, Inst. of Petroleum (Chm., Res. Adv. Cttee, 1973-). Pres., RIC, 1976-78. Chairman: Professional Affairs Bd, RSC, 1980-; Council of Science and Technology Insts, 1981-; Member: Thames Water Authority, 1980-; Technician Educn Council, 1980-; Ct, Univ. of Surrey, 1980-. *Publications:* Reviews of Petroleum Technology, vol. 13: insulating and hydraulic oils, 1953; numerous papers in Jl Inst. Petroleum, Chem. and Ind., Chem. in Brit., on hydrocarbon dielectrics, insulating oils, diffusion as rate-limiting factor in oxidation, antioxidants in the oil industry, mechanism of copper catalysis in insulating oil oxidation, scientific manpower, etc. *Recreation:* golf. *Address:* Delamere, Horsell Park, Woking, Surrey GU21 4LW. *T:* Woking 4939.

THOMPSON, Charles Paxton, CMG 1961; OBE 1956; Bursar, University of Birmingham, 1961-73; *b* 31 May 1911; *s* of W. P. Thompson; *m* 1938, Gweneth Barbara Toby (*d* 1981); one *s* one *d. Educ:* Merchant Taylors' School, London; University College, London; Trinity Hall, Cambridge. Cadet, Colonial Administrative Service (Nigeria), 1933; Economic Secretary to Prime Minister of Federation of Nigeria, 1958; Permanent Secretary, Ministry of Economic Development, Lagos, 1960. *Address:* 31 Warnham Court, Grand Avenue, Hove, Sussex BN3 2NJ. *Club:* Oriental.

THOMPSON, Colin Edward, FRSE 1978; Director, National Galleries of Scotland, since 1977; *b* 2 Nov. 1919; *s* of late Edward Vincent Thompson, CB, and Jessie Forbes Cameron; *m* 1950, Jean Agnes Jardine O'Connell; one *s* one *d. Educ:* Sedbergh Sch.; King's College, Cambridge; Chelsea Polytechnic Sch. of Art. MA (Cantab). FS Wing CMP, 1940-41; Foreign Office, 1941-45.

Lectr, Bath Acad. of Art, Corsham, 1948-54; Asst Keeper, 1954, Keeper, 1967, National Gall. of Scotland. Sen. Adviser, Res. Centre in Art Educn, Bath Acad. of Art, 1962-65; Member: Scottish Arts Council, 1976-; Edinburgh Fest. Council, 1979-82 (Chm., Art Adv. Panel, 1979-). *Publications:* (with Lorne Campbell) Hugo van der Goes and the Trinity Panels in Edinburgh, 1974; guide books, catalogues and a history of the National Gallery of Scotland; articles in Burlington Magazine, Museums Jl, etc. *Address:* Edenkerry, Lasswade, Midlothian. *T:* 031-663 7927. *Clubs:* New, Scottish Arts (Edinburgh).
See also D. C. Thompson.

THOMPSON, David Richard, CB 1974; QC 1980; Master of the Crown Office and Queen's Coroner and Attorney, Registrar of Criminal Appeals and of the Courts Martial Appeal Court since 1965; *b* 11 Feb. 1916; *s* of William George Thompson; *m* 1952, Sally Jennifer Rowntree Thompson (*née* Stockton); two *s* four *d. Educ:* Alleyn's Sch., Dulwich; Jesus Coll., Oxford. BA Physics 1938. Royal Corps of Signals, 1939-46 (despatches). Called to Bar, Lincoln's Inn, 1946, Bencher, 1982; Office of Director of Public Prosecutions, 1948-54; Dep. Asst Registrar, then Asst Registrar, Court of Criminal Appeal, 1954-65. Mem., Judicial Studies Bd, 1979-. *Publications:* (with H. W. Wollaston) Court of Appeal Criminal Division, 1969; (with Morrish and McLean) Proceedings in the Criminal Division of the Court of Appeal, 1979. *Recreations:* family, rough gardening, work. *Address:* 54 Highbury Grove, N5. *T:* 01-226 6514.

THOMPSON, Dennis Cameron, FCIArb; Consultant to UNCTAD on Restrictive Business Practices and Transfer of Technology, since 1977; Founder, 1967, and Editor since 1977, Journal of World Trade Law; Director, Restrictive Practices and Dominant Positions, Commission of the European Communities, 1973-76; *b* 25 Oct. 1914; *s* of late Edward Vincent Thompson, CB, and late Jessie Forbes; *m* 1959, Maria von Skramlik; one *d. Educ:* Oundle; King's Coll., Cambridge. Nat. Sci. Tripos Pt I, Law Pt II; MA 1949. RAF, 1940-45: Sqdn-Ldr, personnel staff, Desert Air Force, and Germany. Called to Bar, Inner Temple, 1939; practised London and Midland Circuit, 1946-63; Asst Dir (European Law), British Inst. of Internat. and Comparative Law, 1963-66; Legal Adviser, Secretariat of EFTA, Geneva, 1967-73; participated in negotiations for European Patent Convention, 1969-73. Vis. Prof., Athens Univ. Sch. of Law, Georgia, 1978. Trustee, Federal Trust, 1962-71. Member: Assoc. Suisse de L'Arbitrage; Panel of Arbitrators, Amer. Arbitration Assoc. *Publications:* (ed) Kennedy, CIF Contracts, 3rd edn 1959; (with Alan Campbell) Common Market Law, 1962; The Proposal for a European Company, 1969; articles in Internat. and Compar. Law Quarterly; (ed jtly) Common Market Law Review, 1963-67. *Recreations:* walking, ski-ing, sailing. *Address:* 8 rue des Belles Filles, 1299 Crans, Switzerland. *T:* (22) 76 16 87. *Club:* United Oxford & Cambridge University.
See also C. E. Thompson.

THOMPSON, Donald; MP (C) Sowerby, since 1979; an Assistant Government Whip, since 1981; *b* 13 Nov. 1931; *s* of Geoffrey and Rachel Thompson; *m* 1957, Patricia Ann Hopkins; two *s. Educ:* Hipperholme Grammar School. National Service, 1950-52. Farmer/butcher, 1952-74. Formerly Dir, Halifax Farmers' Trading Assoc.; Man. Dir, Armadillo Plastics (Glass Fibre Manufacturers), 1974-79, Dir, 1979-. Member: WR CC, 1967-74; W Yorks CC, 1974-75; Calderdale Dist Council, 1975-79 (Chm. Educn Cttee, 1975-76). Contested (C): Batley and Morley, 1970; Sowerby, Feb. and Oct. 1974. Chm., Cons. Candidates' Assoc., 1972-74. *Recreations:* Rugby football, poor golf, conversation. *Address:* Moravian House, Lightcliffe, near Halifax, West Yorks. *T:* Halifax 202920. *Clubs:* St Stephen's Constitutional; Brodleians (Hipperholme).

THOMPSON, Donald Henry, MA Oxon; JP; Headmaster, Chigwell School, Essex, 1947-71; *b* 29 Aug. 1911; *s* of H. R. Thompson, solicitor, Swansea; *m* 1942, Helen Mary Wray; four *s. Educ:* Shrewsbury School; Merton College, Oxford. Postmaster in Classics, Merton Coll., Oxford, 1930; 1st Class Hon. Mod., 1932; 1st Class Literae Humaniores, 1934; Asst Master Haileybury Coll., Hertford, 1934-46. Served War of 1939-45, RA, 1940-45. JP Essex, 1955. *Recreations:* cricket, bird-watching, walking. *Address:* Glasses Farm, Holcombe Bath, Somerset. *T:* Stratton-on-Fosse 232322.

THOMPSON, Prof. Edward Arthur, FBA 1964; Professor of Classics, University of Nottingham, 1948-79; *b* 22 May 1914; *s* of late Robert J. Thompson and late Margaret Thompson, Rathmines, Dublin. *Educ:* Trinity Coll., Dublin. Lecturer in Classics: Swansea, 1942-45; King's College, London, 1945-48. Vis. Bentley Prof. of History, Univ. of Michigan, 1969-71; H. F. Johnson Res. Prof., Univ. of Wisconsin (Madison), 1979-80. *Publications:* The Historical Work of Ammianus Marcellinus, 1947; A History of Attila and The Huns, 1948; A Roman Reformer and Inventor, 1952; The Early Germans, 1965; The Visigoths in the Time of Ulfila, 1966; The Goths in Spain, 1969; Romans and Barbarians, 1982. *Address:* 21A Westgate, Southwell, Notts.

THOMPSON, Sir Edward (Hugh Dudley), Kt 1967; MBE 1945; TD; DL; Director: Allied Breweries Ltd, 1961-78; P-E Consulting Group Ltd, 1968-73 (Chm., 1971-73); *b* 12 May 1907; *s* of Neale Dudley Thompson and Mary Gwendoline Scutt; *m* 1st, 1931, Ruth Monica, 3rd *d* of Charles Henry Wainwright, JP; two *s*; 2nd, 1947, Doreen Maud, *d* of George Tibbitt; one *s* one *d. Educ:* Uppingham; Lincoln Coll., Oxford. Served War of 1939-45 (despatches twice, MBE); 1st Derbyshire Yeomanry, 1939-43, in N Africa;

General Staff, 1943–45, in Italy and Germany. Solicitor, 1931-36. Asst Man. Dir, Ind Coope & Allsopp Ltd, 1936-39, Managing Director, 1939; Chairman: Ind Coope Ltd, Burton on Trent, 1955-62; Allied Breweries Ltd (formerly Ind Coope Tetley Ansell Ltd), 1961-68. Director: Sun Insurance Ltd, 1946-59; Sun Alliance & London Insurance Ltd, 1959-77. Chm., Brewers' Soc., 1959-61; Trustee, Civic Trust; Mem. Northumberland Foot and Mouth Cttee. Mem. Council, Nottingham Univ., 1969-. Mem. Council, RASE, 1972-. High Sheriff of Derbyshire, 1964; DL Derbyshire, 1978. *Recreations:* farming, sailing, ski-ing. *Address:* Culland Hall, Brailsford, Derby. *T:* Brailsford 247. *Club:* Boodle's.

THOMPSON, Sir Edward (Walter), Kt 1957; JP; Chairman, John Thompson Ltd, Wolverhampton, 1947-67; Director, Barclays Bank, 1958-73; Local Director, Barclays Bank (Birmingham), 1952-73; *b* 11 June 1902; *s* of late Albert E. Thompson and late Mary Thompson; *m* 1930, Ann E., *d* of Rev. George L. Amphlett, Four Ashes Hall, Stourbridge, Worcs; one *s* three *d*. *Educ:* Oundle; Trinity Hall, Cambridge. MA (Engineering) Cambridge. Joined family firm of John Thompson's, 1924; Dir John Thompson Watertube Boilers, 1930; Joint Man. Dir John Thompson Ltd, 1936-62. Chm. Watertube Boilermakers Assoc., 1951-54; Pres. Brit. Engineers Assoc., 1957-59 (Vice-Pres. 1956). Mem. Midland Chapter Woodard Schools. Chairman: Birmingham Regional Hosp. Bd, 1957-61; Redditch Development Corp., 1964-74; Leader SE Asia Trade Delegation, 1961. JP Co. Salop, 1953; Dep. Chm. Bridgnorth Bench, 1956-66; High Sheriff, Staffordshire, 1955-56. *Recreations:* shooting, fishing, gardening. *Address:* Gatacre Park, Bridgnorth, Salop. *T:* Bobbington 211.

See also Viscount Bledisloe.

THOMPSON, Eric John; Principal Director of Statistics, Departments of the Environment and Transport, since 1981; *b* Beverley, E Yorks, 26 Sept. 1934; *o s* of Herbert William Thompson and late Florence Thompson (*née* Brewer). *Educ:* Beverley Grammar Sch.; London School of Economics (BScEcon). National Service: Pilot Officer in Dept of Scientific Adviser to Air Ministry, 1956-58. Operations Planning Dept, International Computers and Tabulators Ltd, 1958-60; Supply and Planning Dept, Shell International Petroleum Co. Ltd, 1960-65; Head of Regional Demography Unit, General Register Office, 1965-67; Head of Population Studies Section, 1967-72, Asst Dir of Intelligence, 1972-74, GLC Research and Intelligence Unit; Head of Social Monitoring Branch, Central Statistical Office, 1975-80; Under Sec., Directorate of Economics and Statistics B, Depts of Environment and Transport, 1980-81. Royal Statistical Society: Fellow, 1956, Mem. Council, 1981-, Vice-Pres., 1982-; SSRC: Assessor, Statistics Cttee, 1979-80, Mem., Adv. Cttee, Centre for Population Studies, 1981-, Mem., Research Resources and Methods Cttee, 1982-; Mem., British Computer Soc., 1959-76 (MBCS 1968). Member: East Yorkshire Local History Soc., 1974-; Housman Soc., 1976-; Richard III Soc., 1979-; Friends of Nat. Libraries, 1981-. *Publications:* ed, Social Trends, Nos 6-10, 1975-80; contrib. chapters in three books on regional and urban planning; articles and reviews in GLC Intelligence Unit's quarterly bulletin and various statistical jls; article on historical bibliography in The Ricardian. *Recreations:* reading and collecting books, British mediæval history, English literature. *Address:* 90 Uplands Road, N8 9NJ. *T:* 01-348 5726.

THOMPSON, Prof. Francis Michael Longstreth, FBA 1979; Director, Institute of Historical Research, and Professor of History in the University of London, since 1977; *b* 13 Aug. 1925; *s* of late Francis Longstreth-Thompson, OBE; *m* 1951, Anne Challoner; two *s* one *d*. *Educ:* Bootham Sch., York; Queen's Coll., Oxford (Hastings Schol.; MA, DPhil). ARICS 1968. War service, with Indian Artillery, 1943-47; James Bryce Sen. Schol., Oxford, 1949-50; Harmsworth Sen. Schol., Merton Coll., Oxford, 1949-51; Lectr in History, UCL, 1951-63; Reader in Economic History, UCL, 1963-68; Prof. of Modern Hist., Univ. of London, and Head of Dept of Hist., Bedford Coll., London, 1968-77. Joint Editor, Economic History Review, 1968-80. Sec., British Nat. Cttee of Historical Scis, 1978-. Member: Senate and Academic Council, Univ. of London, 1970-78; Senate and Collegiate Council, 1981-. FRHistS 1964. *Publications:* English Landed Society in the Nineteenth Century, 1963; Chartered Surveyors: the growth of a profession, 1968; Victorian England: the horse-drawn society, 1970 (Countrysides, in The Nineteenth Century, ed Asa Briggs, 1970; Hampstead: building a borough, 1650-1964, 1974; introd. to General Report on Gosford Estates in County Armagh 1821, by William Greig, 1976; Britain, in European Landed Elites in the Nineteenth Century, ed David Spring, 1977; Landowners and Farmers, in The Faces of Europe (ed Alan Bullock), 1980; 2 chapters in The Victorian Countryside (ed G. E. Mingay), 1981; (ed) The Rise of Suburbia, 1982; numerous articles in Economic History Review, History, English Historical Review, etc. *Recreations:* gardening, walking, carpentry, tennis. *Address:* Holly Cottage, Sheepcote Lane, Wheathampstead, Herts. *T:* Wheathampstead 3129.

THOMPSON, Air Commodore Frederick William, CBE 1957; DSO 1944; DFC 1942; AFC 1944; Director, Air Weapons, British Aerospace Dynamics Group, 1977-80; *b* 9 July 1914; *s* of William Edward Thompson, Winster, Poulton-le-Fylde, Lancs; *m* 1941, Marian, *d* of Wm Bootyman, Hessle, E Yorks; two *d*. *Educ:* Baines's Grammar School; Liverpool University. BSc 2nd Cl. Hons Maths; Advanced Diploma in General Hygiene (Hons). Joined RAF, 1935, invalided 1936. S Rhodesian Education Dept, 1936-39. Served War of 1939-45 (despatches, DFC, AFC, DSO): S Rhodesian Air Force, 1940, Pilot Officer; seconded to RAFVR, 4 Gp Bomber Command, 1940; Flight Comdr

10 Sqdn Bombers, 1941; 1658 HCU, 1942; CO 44 Bomber Sqdn, 1944; Bomber Command Instructor's School, 1944; Station Commander, RAF Heany, 1945; HQ Mid Med., 1946-47; Min. of Defence, 1947-50; HQ CC, 1950-53; OC Aswdu, 1953; Group Capt., CO Luqa, 1954; Deputy Director Operational Requirements (1), Air Ministry, 1957-60. Air Cdre Imperial Defence Coll., 1960; Director of Guided Weapons (Trials), Ministry of Aviation, 1961. Retired from RAF at own request to join de Havilland Aircraft Co. Ltd as Representative of the Company on the West Coast of America; Engrg Manager, Hawker Siddeley Dynamics Co. Ltd, 1964, Divisional Manager, Air Weapons Div., 1972-77. idc, jssc, psc, cfs. *Recreations:* tennis, swimming. *Address:* Westwick, Lye Green Road, Chesham, Bucks. *T:* Chesham 785413. *Club:* Royal Air Force.

THOMPSON, Rt. Rev. Geoffrey Hewlett; see Willesden, Area Bishop of.

THOMPSON, Lt.-Gen. Sir Geoffrey (Stuart), KBE 1960 (MBE 1941); CB 1954; DSO 1944; late Royal Artillery; *b* 6 Jan. 1905; 3rd *s* of late Brig.-Gen. W. A. M. Thompson, CB, CMG; *m* 1934, Agnes Mary Colville (*d* 1974), *e d* of late Captain H. D. Wakeman-Colville, RN retd; one *d*. *Educ:* Sherborne Sch.; RN Colls, Osborne and Dartmouth. Commissioned, 1925; served War of 1939-45 (North Africa and Italy); Commander 1st Field Regiment RA, Italy, 1944-45; Commander No. 2 Army Group, Royal Artillery, Egypt, 1950-52; Director Land/Air Warfare and Dir for NATO Standardisation, War Office, 1952-54; Senior Army Instructor, Imperial Defence College, 1955-57; Director of Staff Duties, War Office, 1957-59; Military Secretary to the Secretary of State for War, 1959-61. Col Comdt, RA, 1961-69. Asst Man. Dir, Arthur Guinness Son & Co., Dublin, 1961-70. Officer of Legion of Merit, USA, 1945; Commander of Order of Leopold, Belgium, 1950; Croix de Guerre, Belgium, 1950. *Recreations:* fishing, hunting. *Address:* Swainstown, Dunsany, Co. Meath. *T:* (046) 25312. *Club:* Army and Navy.

THOMPSON, George H.; Principal Teacher of French, Annan Academy, Dumfriesshire, since 1979; *b* Sept. 1928. *Educ:* Dalry Sch.; Kirkcudbright Acad.; Edinburgh Univ. Teacher, modern languages, Kirkcudbright Academy. Contested (SNP) Galloway, Feb. 1974. Former SNP Asst Nat. Sec.; MP (SNP) Galloway, Oct. 1974-1979; SNP Spokesman: on health, Oct. 1974-79; on forestry, 1975. *Address:* 53 Kirkland Street, St John's Town of Dalry, Castle Douglas, Kircudbrightshire. *T:* Dalry 254.

THOMPSON, Gerald Francis Michael Perronet; Chairman, Kleinwort Benson Ltd, 1971-75, retired (Director 1961, Vice-Chairman 1970); Member, Accepting Houses Committee, 1971-75; *b* 10 Oct. 1910; *s* of late Sir John Perronet Thompson, KCSI, KCIE, and Ada Lucia Tyrrell; *m* 1944, Margaret Mary Bodenham Smith; two *s* one *d*. *Educ:* Repton; King's Coll., Cambridge (Scholar, MA); London Sch. of Economics (post graduate). Kleinwort Sons & Co., 1933. Served War, RAFVR, 1939-46 (despatches): in France, UK, and Middle East, Wing Comdr. Director: Kleinwort Sons & Co., 1960; Kleinwort Benson Lonsdale Ltd, 1970-82. Governor, New Hall Sch., 1977-. *Recreations:* travel, garden. *Address:* Whitewebs, Margaretting, Essex. *T:* Ingatestone 2002. *Club:* United Oxford & Cambridge University.

See also Rear-Adm. J. Y. Thompson, L. P. Thompson-McCausland, Sir E. H. T. Wakefield, Bt.

THOMPSON, Gertrude C.; see Caton-Thompson.

THOMPSON, Godfrey; see Thompson, W. G.

THOMPSON, Mrs Gordon; see Thompson, B.

THOMPSON, Sir Harold (Warris), Kt 1968; CBE 1959; FRS 1946; MA, DSc (Oxon); PhilD (Berlin); Professor of Chemistry, Oxford University, 1964-75, now Emeritus; *b* 15 Feb. 1908; *m* 1938, Grace Penelope Stradling; one *s* one *d*. *Educ:* King Edward VII Sch., Sheffield; Trinity College, Oxford (Open Millard Scholar), Hon. Fellow, 1978; Berlin University. 1st Class Hons Chemistry, Oxford, 1929; Junior Research Fellow, St John's College, Oxford; Official Fellow and Tutor, St John's College, 1930-64, Professorial Fellow, 1964-75, Hon. Fellow, 1975; University Reader in Infra red spectroscopy, 1954-64; Leverhulme Research Fellow (Pasadena), 1937; Tilden Lecturer, 1943; Gnehm Lecturer, Zürich, 1948; Reilly Lecturer, 1961; Cherwell Memorial Fellow, 1961. Chemical Research for Ministry of Supply and Ministry of Aircraft Production, 1939-45; Member, Chemical Research Board, DSIR, 1949-54 and Committees of Scientific Advisory Council and MRC, 1947-55; Scientific Adviser, Home Office Civil Defence, Southern Region, 1952-63; Member General Board, Oxford University, 1949-55; Hebdomadal Council, 1957-61; President: Internat. Council of Scientific Unions, 1963-66; Inst. Information Scientists, 1967-70; Aslib, 1973-74; Chm., Commn on Molecular Spectroscopy of Internat. Union of Pure and Applied Chem., 1955-61, and of IUPAC Publications Cttee, 1957-; Pres., IUPAC, 1973-75 (Mem. Bureau, 1963-71; Exec. Cttee, 1967-71, Vice-Pres., 1971-73); Member: UK Unesco Commn, 1966-; Exec. Cttee, British Council, 1966-80; Chm., GB/China Cttee, 1972-74, GB/China Centre, 1974-80 (a Vice-Pres., 1980-); Member, Council, Royal Soc., 1959-64, Vice-Pres., 1963-64, 1965-71, For. Sec., 1965-71; Vice-Pres., Chem. Soc., 1970-73. Hon. Corresp. Mem., Inst. Nat. Sci., Ecuador, 1971; Hon. Member: Leopoldina Acad.; Japan Chemical Soc.; Spanish Royal Soc. Phys. Chem. Ciamician Medal, Bologna, 1959; Davy Medal of Royal Society, 1965; John Torrance Tate Gold Medal

(Am. Inst. Physics), 1966. Hon. Treasurer OUAFC, 1931-; Founder and Chairman of Pegasus FC, Secretary, 1948-54; Member, FA Council, 1941-, Vice-Chm., 1967-76, Chm., 1976-81, a Life Vice-Pres., 1980-; Life Vice-Pres., AFA (Pres. 1969-71); Mem., Exec. Cttee UEFA, 1974-82 (a Vice Pres., 1978-82). Editor, Spectrochimica Acta, 1957-. Hon. Counsellor, Spanish SRC, 1971-. Hon. DSc: Newcastle upon Tyne, 1970; Strasbourg, 1972; Hon. ScD Cambridge, 1974. Order of Aztec Eagle, Mexico, 1970; Chevalier, Légion d'Honneur, 1971; Grand Service Cross, German Federal Republic, 1971. *Publications:* A Course in Chemical Spectroscopy, 1938; (ed) Advances in Spectroscopy, Vol. I 1959, II 1961; Papers in Proc. of scientific socs and journals. *Recreation:* Association football (Oxford v Cambridge, 1928-29). *Address:* 33 Linton Road, Oxford. *T:* Oxford 58925.

THOMPSON, Sir Herbert; *see* Thompson, Sir (Joseph) Herbert.

THOMPSON, Rt. Rev. Hewlett; *see* Thompson, Rt Rev. G. H.

THOMPSON, Sir (Humphrey) Simon M.; *see* Meysey-Thompson.

THOMPSON, Dr Ian McKim; Senior Under Secretary, British Medical Association, since 1969; *b* 19 Aug. 1938; *s* of late J. W. Thompson and of Dr E. M. Thompson; *m* 1962, Dr Veronica Jane Richards; two *s* one *d. Educ:* Epsom Coll.; Birmingham Univ. (MB, ChB 1961). Lectr in Pathology, Univ. of Birmingham, 1964-67; Sen. Registrar, Birmingham RHB, 1967-69. Consulting Forensic Pathologist to HM Coroner, City of Birmingham, 1966-. Member: GMC, 1979-; Birmingham Med. Inst. Hon. Collegian, Med. Colls of Spain, 1975. *Publications:* (ed) The Hospital Gazeteer, 1972; (ed) BMA Handbook for Hospital Junior Doctors, 1977, 2nd edn 1980; various medical scientific papers. *Recreations:* inland waterways, rambling. *Address:* 9 Old Rectory Green, Fladbury, Pershore, Worcs WR10 2QX. *T:* Evesham 860668.

THOMPSON, James Craig; Managing Director, since 1973, Chairman, since 1979, Adverkit International Ltd; *b* 27 Oct. 1933; *s* of Alfred Thompson and Eleanor (*née* Craig); *m* 1957, Catherine (*née* Warburton); one *s* one *d. Educ:* Heaton Grammar Sch., Newcastle upon Tyne; Rutherford Coll., Newcastle upon Tyne. Director: Ad Builder Ltd, 1971-; Commercial Union Assurance Co. Ltd, 1977- (Chm., SE Reg. Bd, 1978-). Mem. Bd of Governors, St Simon Stock Sch., 1972-. Life Governor, Kent County Agricl Soc., 1976. Hon. Life Mem., Kent CCC, 1978; Member: MCC; Catenian Assoc. (Pres., Maidstone Circle, 1974-75); Dir, Weekly Newspaper Advtsg Bureau, 1977. Chairman: Southern Football League, 1977-79; Alliance Premier Football League, 1979-; Pres., Eastern Professional Floodlight League, 1976-; Chm., Maidstone United FC, 1970-. Member: Internat. Advertising Assoc.; Internat. Newspaper Advertising Execs Assoc.; Council, Netherlands British Chamber of Commerce; Council, FA, 1982. Fellow, Inst. of Dirs; MInstM; MBIM. Liveryman, Worshipful Co. of Stationers and Newspaper Makers; Freeman, City of London. Distinguished Service Award, Internat. Classified Advertising Assoc., Baltimore, 1968. *Publications:* numerous articles on commercial aspects of newspaper publishing and Association football. *Recreations:* squash, Northumbrian history. *Address:* Prescott House, Otham, Kent ME15 8RL. *T:* Maidstone 861606. *Clubs:* Eccentric; Press; Elwick (Ashford); Maidstone (Maidstone); Fairchild Wine Society (Oklahoma).

THOMPSON, Rt. Rev. James Lawton; *see* Stepney, Area Bishop of.

THOMPSON, Sir John, Kt 1961; Judge of the High Court of Justice, Queen's Bench Division, 1961-82; *b* Glasgow, 16 Dec. 1907; *e s* of Donald Cameron Thompson and Jeanie Dunn Thompson (*née* Nisbet); *m* 1934, Agnes Baird, (Nancy), *o d* of John and Jeanie Drummond, Glasgow; two *s. Educ:* Bellahouston Academy; Glasgow University; Oriel College, Oxford. Glasgow University: MA and Arthur Jones Memorial Prize, 1928; Ewing Gold Medal, 1929; Oxford University: BA, 1930; MA 1943. Barrister-at-Law, Powell Prize, Middle Temple, 1933. QC 1954; Bencher, Middle Temple, 1961; Lent Reader, 1977; Dep. Treasurer, 1977; Treasurer, 1978. Vice-Chm., Gen. Council of the Bar, 1960-61 (Mem. 1958-61). Commissioner of Assize (Birmingham) 1961. *Publications:* (edited with H. R. Rogers) Redgrave's Factories, Truck and Shops Acts. *Recreation:* golf. *Address:* 73 Sevenoaks Road, Orpington, Kent. *T:* Orpington 22339.

THOMPSON, John Alan, CMG 1974; HM Diplomatic Service, retired; *b* 21 June 1926; *m* 1956, Maureen Sayers. *Educ:* Bromsgrove Sch.; Brasenose Coll., Oxford. Control Commission for Germany, 1952; Vice-Consul, Hanoi, 1954; Second Sec., Saigon, 1956; Warsaw, 1959; Foreign Office, 1961; First Sec. (Commercial), Havana, 1964; First Sec., FO (later FCO), 1966-75; Counsellor, 1973. *Recreations:* music, mountains. *Address:* Sun House, Hall Street, Long Melford, Suffolk CO10 9HZ. *T:* Sudbury 78252. *Club:* United Oxford & Cambridge University.

THOMPSON, John Brian, CBE 1980; Director of Radio, Independent Broadcasting Authority, since 1973; *b* 8 June 1928; *y s* of John and late Lilian Thompson; *m* 1957, Sylvia, *d* of late Thomas Waterhouse, CBE, and of Doris Waterhouse (*née* Gough); two *s* one *d. Educ:* St Paul's; Pembroke College, Oxford (BA; MA). Eileen Power Studentship, LSE, 1950; Glaxo Laboratories Ltd, 1950-54; Masius & Fergusson Ltd, 1955; Asst Editor, Truth, 1956-57; Daily Express, 1957-59 (New York Correspondent; Drama Critic); ITN, 1959-60 (Newscaster/Reporter); Editor, Time and Tide, 1960-62; News Editor, The Observer, 1962-66; Editor, Observer Colour Magazine, 1966-70;

Publisher and Editorial Dir, BPC Publishing Ltd, 1971. Sen. Advr on Radio to Minister of Posts and Telecommunications, 1972. *Address:* 4 Edith Grove, SW10. *T:* 01-352 5414.

THOMPSON, John Derek T.; *see* Taylor Thompson.

THOMPSON, Prof. John Griggs, PhD; FRS 1979; Rouse Ball Professor of Mathematics, University of Cambridge, since 1971; Fellow of Churchill College, since 1968; *b* Kansas, 13 Oct. 1932; *s* of John and Eleanor Thompson; *m* 1960, Diane Oenning; one *d. Educ:* Yale (BA 1955); Chicago (PhD 1959); MA Cantab 1972. Prof. of Mathematics, Chicago Univ., 1962-68; Vis. Prof. of Mathematics, Cambridge Univ., 1968-70. Cole Prize, 1966; Field Medal, 1970. *Address:* Churchill College, Cambridge.

THOMPSON, John Handby; Under Secretary, Department of Education and Science, since 1978; *b* 21 Feb. 1929; *s* of late Rev. John Thomas Thompson and Clara Handby; *m* 1957, Catherine Rose, *d* of Charles Bowman Heald; two *s* one *d. Educ:* Silcoates Sch., Wakefield; St John's Coll., Oxford (MA). Served Intell. Corps, 1947-49. HM Inspector of Taxes, 1953-63; Dept of Educn and Science, 1964-: Schs Council, 1971-73; Mem., Prep. Cttee of European Univ. Inst., 1973-75; Head of Schs Br. 1, 1978-80; Head of Further and Higher Educn Br. 1, 1980-. *Recreations:* fell walking, reading about Albania. *Club:* National Liberal.

THOMPSON, John Keith Lumley, CMG 1982; MBE (mil.) 1965; TD 1961; Counsellor (Science and Technology), British Embassy, Washington, DC, since 1978; *b* 31 March 1923; *s* of late John V. V. and Gertrude Thompson; *m* 1950, Audrey Olley; one *s. Educ:* Wallsend Grammar Sch.; King's Coll., Durham Univ. (BSc). FBIM (MBIM 1975). Served War of 1939-45: Officer in REME, 1942-47, NW Europe; BEME 44 Para Bde (v), 1948-70. Dep. Inspector, REME (v) Southern Comd, 1970-72 (Lt-Col); Dep. Comdr, 44 Para Bde (v), 1972-75 (Col). Road Research Lab., DSIR, 1948-55; AWRE, Aldermaston, 1955-64; Staff of Chief Scientific Adviser, MoD, 1964-65; Head of E Midlands Regional Office, Min. Tech., 1965-70; Head, Internat. Affairs, Atomic Energy Div., Dep of Energy, 1972-74; Regional Dir, W Midlands and Northern Regional Offices, DoI, 1970-72 and 1974-78. ADC to the Queen (TAVR), 1974-78. *Publications:* papers on vehicle behaviour, crash helmets and implosion systems; numerous articles on American science and technology. *Recreations:* outdoor activities, reading. *Address:* British Embassy, 3100 Massachusetts Avenue NW, Washington, DC 20008, USA. *T:* (202) 462-1340. *Clubs:* Civil Service; Cosmos (Washington).

THOMPSON, John Kenneth, CMG 1963; Director of the Commonwealth Institute, 1969-77; *b* Halstead, Essex, 12 May 1913; *e s* of late W. Stanton Thompson, MBE; *m* 1937, Jenny More; two *s. Educ:* Dover County School; King's College, London; Lausanne Univ. BA, AKC, DipEd Mod. Lang. Master, Queen's Royal Coll., Trinidad, 1935-39; Censor, Trinidad, 1939-41; Chief Censor, 1941-42; Asst Sec., Postal and Tel. Censorship, London, 1943-45; Principal, Colonial Office, 1945-49; Colonial Attaché, Brit. Embassy, Washington, 1950-53; Asst Sec., Colonial Office, 1953-59; Director, Colombo Plan Bureau, SE Asia, 1959-62; Asst Sec., Dept of Technical Co-operation, 1962-64; Dir of Overseas Appointments, ODM, 1964-69. Consultant to Commonwealth Secretariat, 1981-82. Governor: Hartwell House, Aylesbury; Centre for Internat. Briefing, Farnham Castle. Chm. Exec. Cttee, Royal Commonwealth Soc. for the Blind. Council Member: Royal Commonwealth Soc.; Royal Over-Seas League; British Exec. Service Overseas. *Address:* 9 Grove Way, Esher, Surrey. *T:* 01-398 4461. *Club:* Royal Commonwealth Society.

THOMPSON, John Leonard C.; *see* Cloudsley-Thompson.

THOMPSON, Air Commodore John Marlow, CBE 1954; DSO 1943; DFC 1940 (and Bar 1942); RAF retired; Director, Monte Carlo Golf Club, Monaco, since 1973; *b* 16 Aug. 1914; *s* of late John Thompson and Florence Thompson (*née* Marlow); *m* 1938, Margaret Sylvia Rowlands; one *s* one *d* (and one *s* decd). *Educ:* Bristol Grammar School. Joined RAF 1934; comd 111 Sqdn, Battle of Britain; Spitfire Wing, Malta, 1942-43; SASO 11 Group, 1952-54; comd RAF Leeming, 1956-57; Dir of Air Defence, Air Ministry, 1958-60; AOC, Military Air Traffic Ops, 1962-65; Gen. Manager, Airwork Services, Saudi Arabia, 1966-68. Graduate Imperial Defence College, 1961. Belgian MC 1st Class, 1942; Danish Order of Dannebrog, 1951. *Recreation:* golf. *Address:* Le Bahia, Avenue Princesse Grace, Monte-Carlo, Principauté de Monaco. *T:* Monte-Carlo (93) 304137. *Clubs:* Royal Air Force; Monte-Carlo; Moor Park Golf.

THOMPSON, John William McWean; Editor, Sunday Telegraph, since 1976; *b* 12 June 1920; *s* of Charles and Charlotte Thompson; *m* 1947, Cynthia Ledsham; one *s* one *d. Educ:* Roundhay Sch., Leeds. Previously on staffs of Yorkshire Evening News, Evening Standard, London, and The Spectator (Dep. Editor); joined Sunday Telegraph, 1970; Asst Editor, 1975. *Publication:* (as Peter Quince) Country Life, 1975. *Address:* St Andrew's Cottage, Much Hadham, Herts SG10 6DH. *T:* Much Hadham 2309. *Club:* Travellers'.

THOMPSON, Rear-Adm. John Yelverton, CB 1960; DL; retired 1961; *b* 25 May 1909; *s* of late Sir John Perronet Thompson, KCSI, KCIE, and Ada Lucia, Lady Thompson (*née* Tyrrell); *m* 1934, Barbara Helen Mary Aston Key; two *s. Educ:* Mourne Grange, Kilkeel, Co. Down; RN College, Dartmouth. Midshipman: HMS Repulse and Berwick, 1926-29; Sub-

Lieutenant: HMS Warspite, 1931; Lieutenant: HMS Queen Elizabeth, 1931-32, Restless 1933, Excellent 1933-34, Queen Elizabeth 1935, Glasgow 1936-39; Lieut-Commander: HMS Excellent 1939-41, Anson 1941-43; Commander: Admiralty, Naval Ordnance Dept, 1943-45; US Fifth Fleet, 1946; HMS Liverpool, 1947; HMS Newcastle, 1948; Captain: Ordnance Board, 1948-50; HMS Unicorn, 1951-52; Director, Gunnery Division, Naval Staff, 1952-54; Imperial Defence College, 1955; Commodore: Royal Naval Barracks, Portsmouth, 1956-57; Rear-Admiral: Admiralty Interview Boards, 1958; Adm. Superintendent, HM Dockyard, Chatham, 1958-61. ADC to the Queen, 1957. Governor, Aldenham Sch., 1967-73. DL: Hertfordshire, 1966-73; Cornwall, 1973. American Legion of Merit, 1953. *Address:* Flushing Meadow, Manaccan, near Helston, Cornwall.

See also G. F. M. P. Thompson, L. P. Thompson-McCausland.

THOMPSON, Sir (Joseph) Herbert, Kt 1947; CIE 1945; *b* 9 March 1898; *o s* of J. Arnold Thompson, JP, and Ellen Stewart Fraser, Wilmslow, Cheshire; *m* 1925, Kathleen (Kaiser-i-Hind Silver medal, 1948), *d* of J. H. Rodier; three *d. Educ:* Manchester Grammar School; Brasenose College, Oxford (MA). Royal Naval Air Service (Sub-Lt) 1916, RAF (Capt.) 1918 and served principally as a fighter pilot (despatches). Assistant Master, Oundle School, 1921-22; ICS 1922; served in Madras Presidency; appointed to Foreign and Political Department, Govt of India (later Indian Political Service), 1926; served NWF Province, Hyderabad and Rajputana, 1926-41; Dep. Sec., Political Department, 1941-43; Revenue and Divisional Commissioner NWF Province, 1943; Resident for Kolhapur and Deccan States, 1944-45; Resident for the Punjab States, 1945-47; on special duty in connection with lapse of Paramountcy, 1947, retd 1949. General Secretary, London Council of Social Service, 1949-50; Diocesan Secretary, Worcester, 1951-53; Rowing Corresp., Sunday Times, 1954-68; BBC (Appointments Dept), 1956-59. Member: Bd of Governors, St Thomas' Hosp., 1950-70; SW Metropolitan Regional Hospitals Board, 1959-63. *Recreations:* walking, gardening, being a great-grandfather. *Address:* Fair Acre, Haddenham, Bucks HP17 8HB. *T:* Haddenham 291212. *Clubs:* Leander; Vincent's (Oxford).

THOMPSON, Julian; *see* Thompson, R. J. de la M.

THOMPSON, Sir Kenneth (Pugh), 1st Bt *cr* 1963; Chairman, Merseyside County Council, 1977-81, Leader, Conservative Group, 1974-80; *b* 24 Dec. 1909; *s* of Ernest S. and Annie Thompson; *m* 1936, Nanne Broome, Walton; one *s* one *d. Educ:* Bootle Grammar School. Formerly newspaper reporter, and subsequently entered commercial life; lectured for the Economic League. Worked for Ministry of Information as Regional Officer during War of 1939-45. Member of Liverpool City Council, 1938-58. Director of several Liverpool companies. MP (C) Walton Div. Liverpool, 1950-64; Chairman Conservative Nat. Advisory Cttee on Local Govt, 1956-57; Assistant Postmaster-General, 1957-Oct. 1959; Parliamentary Secretary, Ministry of Education, October 1959-July 1962. Sec., 1922 Cttee, 1951-57. Dep. Chm., Merseyside Develt Corp., 1980-. Hon. LLD Liverpool, 1982. *Publications:* Member's Lobby, 1966; Pattern of Conquest, 1967. *Heir: s* Paul Anthony Thompson [*b* 6 Oct. 1939; *m* 1971, Pauline Dorothy Spencer, *d* of Robert Spencer, Bolton, Lancs]. *Address:* Atherton Cottage, Formby, Merseyside L37 2DD.

THOMPSON, Hon. Lindsay Hamilton Simpson, CMG 1975; MLA (Lib) Malvern, Victoria, since 1970; Leader of the Opposition, Victoria, since 1982; *b* 15 Oct. 1923; *s* of Arthur K. Thompson and Ethel M. Thompson; *m* 1950, Joan Margaret Poynder; two *s* one *d. Educ:* Caulfield Grammar Sch., Victoria (Captain and Dux 1941); Melbourne Univ. (BA Hons, BEd). MACE. MP (Lib.) in Victorian Legislative Council: Higinbotham Prov., 1955-67; Monash Prov., 1967-70; Member of Cabinet, 1956-82; Parly Sec. of Cabinet, 1956-58; Asst Chief Sec. and Asst Attorney-Gen., 1958-61; Asst Minister of Transport, 1960-61; Minister of Housing and Forests, 1961-67; Dep. Leader of Govt in Legislative Council, 1962-70; Minister in charge of Aboriginal Welfare, 1965-67; Minister of Educn, 1967-79 (longest term ever in this portfolio); Leader of Legislative Assembly, 1972-79; Dep. Premier of Victoria, 1972-81; Minister for Police and Emergency Services, 1979-81; Treasurer, 1979-82; Premier, 1981-82. State Govt Rep., Melbourne Univ. Council, 1955-59. Pres., Royal Life Saving Soc., 1970-. Bronze Medal, Royal Humane Soc., 1974. Trustee, Melb. Cricket Ground, 1967-; Patron, Victorian Cricket Assoc. *Publications:* Australian Housing Today and Tomorrow, 1965; Looking Ahead in Education, 1969. *Recreations:* cricket, golf, tennis. *Address:* 19 Allenby Avenue, Glen Iris, Victoria, Australia. *T:* 25 6191. *Clubs:* Melbourne (Melbourne), Kingston Heath Golf (Victoria).

THOMPSON, Sir Lionel; *see* Thompson, Sir L. L. H. *and* Thompson, Sir T. L. T., Bt.

THOMPSON, Major Lloyd H.; *see* Hall-Thompson, Major R. L.

THOMPSON, Sir (Louis) Lionel (Harry), Kt 1953; CBE 1946; Deputy Master and Comptroller of the Royal Mint and ex-officio Engraver of HM's Seals, 1950-57; retired 1957; *b* 10 March 1893; *o s* of William Thompson, Eaton, Retford; *m* Mary (*d* 1979), *d* of William White, MD, Hadfield, Derbyshire; two *s. Educ:* King Edward VI School, Retford; Sheffield Univ.; Exeter Coll., Oxford (scholar). First Cl. Classical Mods, 1913. Served European War, 1914-18, Cheshire Regt (Territorial), Temp. Major. Asst Principal Treasury, 1919; Asst Secretary to Commissioner for Special Areas, 1937-39; Under-Secretary, Treasury, 1947-50. *Recreations:* walking,

gardening. *Address:* Pendean Convalescent Home, Midhurst, Sussex. *T:* Midhurst 4586. *Club:* United Oxford & Cambridge University.

THOMPSON, Michael Jacques, OBE 1977; HM Diplomatic Service; seconded to Commander, British Land Forces, Hong Kong, since 1982; *b* 31 Jan. 1936; *s* of late Christopher Thompson and of Colette Jeanne-Marie Thompson; *m* 1968, Mary Susan (*née* Everard); one *s* one *d. Educ:* Uppingham; Christ's Coll., Cambridge (Law Tripos, 1956-60; MA). National Service, Aden and Cyprus, 1954-56. HMOCS, Kenya, 1960-63; FCO, 1964; served Kuala Lumpur, Saigon, Lusaka and FCO, 1965-79; Counsellor, Kuala Lumpur, 1979-82. *Recreations:* squash, tennis, golf, gardening. *Address:* c/o Foreign and Commonwealth Office, SW1. *Clubs:* United Oxford & Cambridge University; Selangor, Lake (Kuala Lumpur).

THOMPSON, Prof. Michael Warwick, DSc; FInstP; Vice-Chancellor, University of East Anglia, since 1980; *b* 1 June 1931; *s* of Kelvin Warwick Thompson and Madeleine Thompson; *m* 1954, Sybil (*née* Spooner); two *s. Educ:* Rydal Sch.; Univ. of Liverpool (BSc, DSc). Research scientist, AERE, Harwell, 1953-65. Pro-Vice-Chancellor, Univ. of Sussex, 1973-77 (actg Vice-Chancellor, 1976). Prof. of Experimental Physics, Univ. of Sussex, 1965-80. Member: E Sussex AHA, 1974-79; E Sussex Educn Cttee, 1973-78. Director, Alliance Building Soc., 1979-. Oliver Lodge Prizewinner, Univ. of Liverpool, 1953; Prizewinner, Materials Science Club, 1970; C. V Boys Prizewinner, Inst. of Physics, 1972. *Publications:* Defects and Radiation Damage in Metals, 1969; (jtly) Channelling, 1973; over 80 papers in sci. jls, incl. Philosophical Magazine, Radiation Effects, Proc. Royal Society. *Recreations:* the arts, sailing. *Address:* Wood Hall, Hethersett, Norwich.

THOMPSON, Dr Noel Brentnall Watson; Under Secretary, Department of Education and Science (Head of Higher and Further Education III Branch), since 1980; *b* 11 Dec. 1932; *s* of George Watson Thompson and Mary Henrietta Gibson; *m* 1957, Margaret Angela Elizabeth Baston; one *s. Educ:* Manchester Grammar School; Cambridge Univ. (MA); Imperial College, London (MSc Eng, PhD). National Service, RN (Sub-Lieut), 1951-53. Research, Imperial Coll., 1958-61; Lectr in Physical Metallurgy, Univ. of Birmingham, 1961-65; Dept of Education and Science, 1966-67, 1969-77 and 1979-; Secretary, National Libraries Cttee, 1967-69; Cabinet Office, 1977-79. *Publications:* papers in scientific journals. *Recreations:* railways of all sizes, mechanics, music, modern history, photography, walking. *Address:* c/o Department of Education and Science, Elizabeth House, York Road, SE1 7PH. *T:* 01-928 9222. *Clubs:* other people's.

THOMPSON, Norman Sinclair, CBE 1980; industrial and financial consultant; *b* 7 July 1920; *s* of Norman Whitfield Thompson and Jane Thompson (*née* Robinson); *m* 1945, Peggy Sivil; two *s* (one *d* decd). *Educ:* Middlesbrough High Sch. Qual. Chartered Accountant, 1947 (FCA); Cost and Management Accountant (ACMA). Served War, Merchant Seaman, 1940-45. Asst Sec., Paton's and Baldwin's Ltd, 1947; Commercial Manager, Cowan's Sheldon & Co. Ltd, 1955; Group Secretary, Richardson's Westgarth & Co. Ltd, 1957; Financial Dir, David Brown & Sons (Huddersfield) Ltd, 1961; Gen. Manager, Malta Drydocks, Swan Hunter Group Ltd, 1963; apptd Swan Hunter Bd, 1964; Overseas Dir, 1967; Dep. Managing Dir, 1969; The Cunard Steam-Ship Co. Ltd: Man. Dir, Cargo Shipping, 1970; Man. Dir, 1971-74; Chm., Mass Transit Railway Corp., Hong Kong, 1975-83; Dir, Hongkong and Shanghai Banking Corp., 1978-83. *Recreations:* sailing, music. *Address:* Shadrach House, Burton Bradstock, Dorset. *T:* Burton Bradstock 897670. *Clubs:* Oriental, Royal Automobile; Hong Kong; Royal Hong Kong Yacht.

THOMPSON, Oliver Frederic, OBE 1945; Pro-Chancellor of The City University, 1966-72; *b* 26 Jan. 1905; 3rd *s* of late W. Graham Thompson and late Oliveria C. Prescott; *m* 1939, Frances Phyllida, *d* of late F. H. Bryant; one *s* three *d. Educ:* Tonbridge. Mem. Shell Gp of Cos, 1924-46: managerial posts in USA, Caribbean, London. Head of Oil Sect., Min. of Econ. Warfare, and Mem. War Cabinet Sub-Cttee on Oil, 1942-46; rep. UK, Suez Canal Users Assoc.; rep. UK on various UN and OECD Cttees; Mem. Parly and Sci. Cttee, 1955-65. Past Master and Mem. Ct, Worshipful Co. of Skinners. Chm. Governing Body, Northampton Coll. of Advanced Technology, 1956-66 (now City University); Governor, Tonbridge Sch. FInstP (Past Mem. Council); Chm. Qualifications Cttee, British Computer Society, 1968 (Hon. Fellow, 1972). County Councillor, Surrey, 1965-77 (Majority Leader, 1970-73). Hon. DSc, City Univ., 1967. *Publications:* various papers on economics of energy and petroleum. *Recreation:* country pursuits. *Address:* 32 Park Road, Aldeburgh, Suffolk IP15 5EU. *T:* Aldeburgh 2424.

THOMPSON, Paul Richard, DPhil; social historian; Reader in Sociology, University of Essex, since 1971; *b* 1935; *m* 1st, Thea Vigne; one *s* one *d* ; 2nd, Natasha Burchardt; one *d. Educ:* Bishop's Stortford Coll., Corpus Christi Coll., Oxford; The Queen's Coll., Oxford (Junior Research Fellow, 1961-64). MA, DPhil 1964. Lectr in Sociology, Univ. of Essex, 1964-69, Sen. Lectr, 1969-71; Sen. Res. Fellow, Nuffield Coll., Oxford, 1968-69; Vis. Prof. of Art History, Johns Hopkins Univ., 1972; Hoffman Wood Prof. of Architecture, Univ. of Leeds, 1977-78. Editor: Victorian Soc. Conf. Reports, 1965-67; Oral History, 1970-. *Publications:* History of English Architecture (with Peter Kidson and Peter Murray), 1965, 2nd edn 1979; The Work of William Morris, 1967, new edn 1977; Socialists, Liberals and Labour: the struggle for London 1880-1914, 1967; The Edwardians: the remaking of British Society, 1975; The

Voice of the Past: Oral History, 1978. *Address:* Department of Sociology, University of Essex, Wivenhoe Park, Colchester CO4 3SQ.

THOMPSON, Sir Peile, 5th Bt *cr* 1890; OBE 1959 (MBE 1950); Lieutenant-Colonel (retired), The Manchester Regiment and King's African Rifles; *b* 28 Feb. 1911; *s* of Sir Peile Beaumont Thompson, 4th Bt, and Stella Mary (*d* 1972), *d* of late Arthur Harris; *S* father, 1972; *m* 1937, Barbara Johnson, *d* of late H. J. Rampling, Old Manor House, Harston; one *s* one *d*. *Educ:* Canford School; St Catharine's College, Cambridge (BA 1933, MA 1950). 2nd Lieutenant, Manchester Regt, 1932; served War of 1939-45; commanded 26 Bn, KAR, Kenya Emergency, 1954-56 (despatches). *Recreation:* gardening. *Heir: s* Christopher Peile Thompson [*b* 21 Dec. 1944; *m* 1969, Anna, *d* of Major Arthur Callander; one *s* one *d*]. *Address:* Old Farm, Augres, Trinity, Jersey, CI. *T:* Jersey 62289.

THOMPSON, Peter Anthony, FCIT; Chairman and Chief Executive, National Freight Consortium, since 1982; *b* 14 April 1928; *s* of late Herbert Thompson and of Sarah Jane Thompson; *m* 1958, Patricia Anne Norcott; one *s* two *d*. *Educ:* Royal Drapers Sch.; Bradford Grammar Sch.; Leeds Univ. BA. Unilever, 1952-62; GKN, 1962-64; Transport Controller, Rank Organisation, 1964-66; Head of Transport, BSC, 1968-72; Group Co-ordinator, BRS Ltd, 1972-75; Exec. Vice-Chm. (Operations), NFC, 1976-77; Dep. Chm. and Chief Exec., Nat. Freight Corp., later Nat. Freight Co., 1977-82. Chm., Community Hospitals Ltd. Pres., Inst. of Freight Forwarders, 1982-83; Vice-Pres., Inst. of Transport, 1982-. CBIM. *Recreations:* golf, tennis, squash, Rugby (at one time). *Address:* 37 Newlands Avenue, Radlett, Herts. *T:* Radlett 5996; (office) National Freight Consortium, Merton Centre, 45 St Peters Street, Bedford MK40 2UB. *T:* Bedford 67444. *Club:* Royal Automobile.

THOMPSON, Peter Kenneth James; Under Secretary, Lord Chancellor's Department, since 1981; *b* 30 July 1937; *s* of Kenneth George Thompson and Doreen May Thompson; *m* 1970, Sandy Lynne Harper; two *d*. *Educ:* Worksop Coll.; Christ's Coll., Cambridge (MA, LLB). Called to the Bar, Lincoln's Inn, 1961; practised at Common Law Bar, 1961-73; Lawyer in Govt Service: Law Commission, 1973-78; Lord Chancellor's Dept, 1978-. *Publications:* The Unfair Contract Terms Act 1977, 1978; *radio plays:* A Matter of Form, 1977; Dormer and Grand-Daughter, 1978. *Recreation:* writing. *Address:* 9 Hillfield Park, Muswell Hill, N10 3QT.

THOMPSON, Pratt; *see* Thompson, W. P.

THOMPSON, Sir Ralph (Patrick), Kt 1980; Barrister and Solicitor of the Supreme Court of New Zealand, since 1938; chairman and director of companies; *b* 19 June 1916; *m* 1940, Dorothy Maud Simes; one *s* two *d*. *Educ:* Napier Boys High Sch.; Dannevirke High Sch.; Canterbury Univ. (LLB 1937). Admitted barrister and solicitor, 1938; in practice in Christchurch. Chairman: United Building Soc., 1956-; Burkes Caterers Ltd, 1974-; Waitaki NZ Refrigerating Ltd, 1975-; Lion Breweries Ltd, 1978-; Canterbury (NZ) Malting Co. Ltd, 1978-; Canterbury (NZ) Seed Co. Ltd, 1978-. Director: McWilliams Wines Ltd, 1961-; Phoenix Assurance Co. Ltd, 1962-; Provident Life Assurance Co. Ltd, 1962-; Leopard Brewery Ltd, 1966-; New Zealand Refining Co. Ltd, 1967-; New Zealand Wines & Spirits Ltd, 1976-; New Zealand United Corp. Ltd, 1976-; Cadbury Schweppes Hudson Ltd, 1976-. *Recreations:* reading, racing, walking. *Address:* 115 Heaton Street, Christchurch 5, New Zealand. *T:* 557.490. *Clubs:* Canterbury, Canterbury University (Hon. Life Mem.).

THOMPSON, Prof. Raymond, PhD; FRSC; CEng, FIMM; Research Director, Borax Holdings Ltd, since 1969; Managing Director, Borax Research Ltd, since 1980; *b* 4 April 1925; *s* of late William Edward Thompson and of Hilda Thompson (*née* Rowley). *Educ:* Longton High Sch.; Univ. of Nottingham (MSc 1950, PhD 1952); Imperial Coll., Univ. of London (DIC 1953). Research Manager, Borax Consolidated, 1961. Special Professor of Inorganic Chemistry, Univ. of Nottingham, 1975-; Hon. Prof., Molecular Sciences, Univ. of Warwick, 1975-. Member Council: Royal Inst. of Chemistry, 1969-72; Chemical Soc., 1977-80 (Chm., Inorganic Chemicals Gp, 1972-); Vice-Pres., Industrial Div., RSC, 1981-. Governor, Kingston-upon-Thames Polytechnic, 1978-. Industrial Chemistry Award, Chemical Soc., 1976. *Publications:* ed, The Modern Inorganic Chemicals Industry, 1977; ed, Mellors Comprehensive Treatise, Boron Supplement, Part A, 1979, Part B1, 1981; ed, Speciality Inorganic Chemicals, 1981; (ed) Energy and Chemistry, 1981; various papers on inorganic boron and nitrogen chemistry. *Recreation:* gardening. *Address:* The Garth, Winchester Close, Esher, Surrey KT10 8QH. *T:* Esher 64428.

THOMPSON, Reginald Aubrey, CMG 1964; *b* 22 Nov. 1905; *s* of John Thompson, Mansfield; *m* 1932, Gwendoline Marian Jackson (*d* 1978); one *s*. *Educ:* Brunts Sch., Mansfield; University Coll., Nottingham. BSc London (1st Cl. Hons Chemistry), 1927. Research, Organic Chemistry, 1927-29; Science Master, various grammar schools, 1929-41; Scientific Civil Service, Min. of Supply, 1941-46; transf. to Admin. Class (Principal), 1946; Asst Sec., 1953; Assistant Secretary, Department of Education and Science (formerly Office of Minister of Science), 1956-64; Ministry of Technology, 1964; retd, 1966. Led UK Delegn at Confs on: liability of operators of nuclear ships, Brussels Convention, 1962; liability for nuclear damage, Vienna Convention, 1963. *Recreations:* golf, gardening, music. *Address:* Qualicum, Bentsbrook Park, North Holmwood, Dorking, Surrey. *T:* Dorking 882289.

THOMPSON, Reginald Stanley; Headmaster of Bloxham School, 1952-65, retired; *b* 23 Sept. 1899; *s* of late Reverend Canon C. H. Thompson, formerly Vicar of Eastleigh, Hants, and of Newport, Isle of Wight; *m* 1938, Phyllis Barbara, *y d* of Henry White, Solicitor, Winchester, Hants; one *s* two *d*. *Educ:* Hereford Cathedral School; Lancing College; Oriel College, Oxford. Assistant Master at Sherborne School, 1922-52 (Housemaster, 1936-52). *Recreations:* music, gardening, books, cricket. *Address:* Westcott Close, Clifton-upon-Teme, Worcestershire. *T:* Shelsley Beauchamp 234.

THOMPSON, Sir Richard (Hilton Marler), 1st Bt *cr* 1963; *b* Calcutta, India, 5 Oct. 1912; *m* 1939, Anne Christabel de Vere, *d* of late Philip de Vere Annesley, MA, and of Mrs Annesley, BEM; one *s*. *Educ:* Malvern College. In business in India, Burma and Ceylon, 1930-40; travelled in Tibet, Persia, Iraq, Turkey, etc. Served in RNVR, 1940-46, volunteering as ordinary seaman; commissioned, 1941 (despatches, 1942); Lieut-Comdr 1944. MP (C) Croydon West, 1950-55; Assistant-Government Whip, 1952; Lord Commissioner of the Treasury, 1954; MP (C) Croydon South, 1955-66 and 1970-Feb. 1974; Vice-Chamberlain of HM Household, 1956; Parly Sec., Ministry of Health, 1957-59; Under-Secretary of State, CRO, 1959-60; Parly Sec., Ministry of Works, Oct. 1960-July 1962. Mem., Public Accounts Cttee, 1973-74. A Cottonian family Trustee of the British Museum, 1951-63; re-apptd as a Prime Minister's Trustee, 1963, 1971, 1976, 1981; Trustees' representative on Council of Nat. Trust, 1978. Chm., Overseas Migration Bd, 1959; led UK delegation to ECAFE in Bangkok, 1960; signed Indus Waters Agreement with India, Pakistan and World Bank for UK, Sept. 1960; led UK Parly Delegn to Tanganyika, to present Speaker's chair, Jan. 1963. Chm., Capital and Counties Property Co., 1971-77, retired; Pres., British Property Fedn, 1976-77; Director: Rediffusion Television Ltd; Rediffusion Holdings Ltd; British Museum Publications Ltd. Chm., British Museum Society, 1970-74. *Recreations:* gardening, collecting, study of history. *Heir: s* Nicholas Annesley Marler Thompson, *b* 19 March 1947. *Address:* Rhodes House, Sellindge, Kent. *Club:* Carlton.

THOMPSON, Richard Paul Hepworth, DM; FRCP; Physician to the Royal Household, since 1982; Consultant Physician, St Thomas' Hospital, since 1972; Physician, King Edward VII Hospital for Officers, since 1982; *b* 14 April 1940; *s* of Stanley Henry and Winifred Lilian Thompson; *m* 1974, Eleanor Mary Hughes. *Educ:* Epsom Coll.; Worcester Coll., Oxford (MA, DM); St Thomas's Hosp. Med. Sch. MRC Clinical Res. Fellow, Liver Unit, KCH, 1967-69; Fellow, Gastroenterology Unit, Mayo Clinic, USA, 1969-71; Lectr, Liver Unit, KCH, 1971-72. Mem., Lambeth, Southwark and Lewisham AHA, 1979-82. Examiner in Medicine: Soc. of Apothecaries, 1976-80; Faculty of Dental Surgery, RCS, 1980-. Governor, Guy's Hosp. Med. Sch., 1980-82; Mem. Cttee of Management, Inst. of Psychiatry, 1981-. *Publications:* Physical Signs in Medicine, 1980; papers and reviews in med. jls. *Address:* 36 Dealtry Road, SW15. *T:* 01-789 3839.

THOMPSON, Sir Robert Grainger Ker, KBE 1965; CMG 1961; DSO 1945; MC 1943; *b* 12 April 1916; *s* of late Canon W. G. Thompson; *m* 1950, Merryn Newboult; one *s* one *d*. *Educ:* Marlborough; Sidney Sussex College, Cambridge (MA). Cadet, Malayan Civil Service, 1938. Served War of 1939-45 (MC, DSO), RAF, 1941-46. Asst Commissioner of Labour, Perak, 1946; jssc 1948-49; Staff Officer (Civil) to Director of Operations, 1950; Co-ordinating Officer, Security, 1955; Dep. Sec. for Def., Fedn of Malaya, 1957; Perm. Sec. for Def., 1959-61; Head, British Advisory Mission to Vietnam, 1961-65. Author and consultant. Johan Mangku Negara (JMN), Malaya, 1958. *Publications:* Defeating Communist Insurgency, 1966; The Royal Flying Corps, 1968; No Exit from Vietnam, 1969; Revolutionary War in World Strategy, 1945-1969, 1970; Peace Is Not At Hand, 1974; (ed) War in Peace: an analysis of warfare since 1945, 1981. *Recreations:* all country pursuits. *Address:* Pitcott House, Winsford, Minehead, Som. *Club:* Special Forces.

THOMPSON, Robert Henry Stewart, CBE 1973; MA, DSc, DM, BCh; FRS 1974; FRCP; FRCPath; Courtauld Professor of Biochemistry, Middlesex Hospital Medical School, University of London, 1965-76; now Emeritus Professor; Trustee, Wellcome Trust, 1963-82; *b* 2 Feb. 1912; *s* of Dr Joseph Henry Thompson and Mary Eleanor Rutherford; *m* 1938, Inge Vilma Anita Gebert; one *s* two *d*. *Educ:* Epsom College; Trinity College, Oxford; Guy's Hospital Medical School. Millard Scholar, Trinity College, Oxford, 1930; Theodore Williams Scholar in Physiology, Oxford, 1932; 1st Class Animal Physiology, Oxford, 1933; Senior Demy, Magdalen College, Oxford, 1933; Univ. Scholar, Guy's Hosp. Med. School, 1933; Adrian Stokes Travelling Fellowship to Hosp. of Rockefeller Inst., New York, 1937-38; Gillson Research Scholar in Pathology, Soc. of Apothecaries of London, 1938; Fellow of University Coll., Oxford, 1938-47; Demonstrator in Biochemistry, Oxford, 1938-47; Dean of Medical School, Oxford, 1946-47; Prof. of Chemical Pathology, Guy's Hosp. Medical School, Univ. of London, 1947-65; Secretary-General International Union of Biochemistry, 1955-64; Hon. Sec. Royal Society of Medicine, 1958-64; Mem. of Medical Research Council, 1958-62; Mem., Bd of Governors, Middlesex Hosp., 1972-74. Governor, Epsom Coll., 1982. Radcliffe Prize for Medical Research, Oxford, 1943. Served War of 1939-45, Major, RAMC, 1944-46. *Publications:* (with C. W. Carter) Biochemistry in relation to Medicine, 1949; Joint Editor (with E. J. King) Biochemical Disorders in Human Disease, 1957; numerous papers on biochemical and pathological subjects in various scientific journals. *Recreation:* gardening. *Address:* 1 Church Way, Hurst Green, Oxted, Surrey

RH8 9EA. *T:* Oxted 3526; Orchard's Almshouses, Launcells, N Cornwall. *T:* Bude 3817. *Club:* Athenæum.

THOMPSON, Major Robert Lloyd H.; *see* Hall-Thompson.

THOMPSON, (Rupert) Julian (de la Mare); Chairman: Sotheby Parke Bernet & Co., since 1982; Sotheby Parke Bernet International, since 1982; *b* 23 July 1941; *s* of Rupert Spens Thompson and Florence Elizabeth (*née* de la Mare); *m* 1965, Jacqueline Julie Ivimy; three *d*. *Educ:* Eton Coll.; King's Coll., Cambridge (MA). Joined Sotheby's, 1963; appointed a Director, 1969. *Address:* 43 Clarendon Road, W11 4JD. *T:* 01-727 6039.

THOMPSON, Sir (Thomas) Lionel Tennyson, 5th Bt, *cr* 1806; Barrister-at-Law; *b* 19 June 1921; *s* of Lt-Col Sir Thomas Thompson, 4th Bt, MC, and of Milicent Ellen Jean, *d* of late Edmund Charles Tennyson-d'Eyncourt, Bayons Manor, Lincolnshire; *S* father, 1964; *m* 1955, Mrs Margaret van Beers (marr. diss. 1962), *d* of late Walter Herbert Browne; one *s* one *d*. *Educ:* Eton. Served War of 1939-45: Royal Air Force Volunteer Reserve, 1940; Flying Officer, 1942 (invalided, 1944); Able Seaman, Royal Fleet Auxiliary, 1944-46. Awarded 1939-45 Star, Aircrew (Europe) Star, Defence and Victory Medals. Called to the Bar, Lincoln's Inn, 1952. *Recreations:* shooting, sailing, flying and photography. *Heir: s* Thomas d'Eyncourt John Thompson, *b* 22 Dec. 1956. *Address:* 81 Chancery Lane, WC2A 1DD. *T:* 01-242 8844; 16 Old Buildings, Lincoln's Inn, WC2. *T:* 01-405 7929.

THOMPSON, Vernon Cecil, MB, BS London; FRCS; retired 1970 as Surgeon to Department of Thoracic Surgery, The London Hospital; Surgeon, London Chest Hospital; Hon. Consulting Thoracic Surgeon to: West London Hospital, Hammersmith; King Edward VII Hospital, Windsor; Harefield Hospital, Middlesex; Broomfield and Black Notley Hospitals, Essex; *b* 17 Sept. 1905; 2nd *s* of Dr C. C. B. Thompson, Tidenham, Glos; *m* 1942, Jean, *d* of late H. J. Hilary; one *s* one *d*. *Educ:* Monmouth School; St Bartholomew's Hospital. Resident House appointments followed by First Assistant to a Surgical Unit, St Bartholomew's Hospital, 1929-37. Dorothy Temple Cross Travelling Fellowship, Vienna, and University Hosp., Ann Arbor, Michigan, USA, 1937. President, Soc. of Thoracic Surgeons of Great Britain and Ireland, 1966; Hon. Mem. Amer. Soc. for Thoracic Surgery, 1967. *Publications:* contrib. on surgical diseases of the chest to jls and text books. *Recreations:* fishing, shooting, gardening. *Address:* Vicarage House, Llowes, Hereford. *T:* Glasbury 323.

THOMPSON, William Bell, MA, PhD; Professor of Physics, University of California, since 1965; Chairman, Department of Physics, University of California at San Diego, 1969-72; *b* N Ireland, 27 Feb. 1922; *m* 1953, Gertrud Helene Goldschmidt, PhD (marr. diss. 1972); one *s* one *d*; *m* 1972, Johanna Elzelina Ladestein Korevaar. *Educ:* Universities of British Columbia and Toronto, Canada. BA 1945, MA 1947, Univ. of BC; PhD Toronto, 1950. AERE Harwell: Senior Research Fellow, 1950; Deputy Chief Scientist, 1959. Visiting Prof., Univ. of California, 1961; Head, Theoretical Physics Division, Culham Laboratory, UKAEA, 1961-63; Prof. of Theoretical Plasma Physics, Oxford Univ., 1963-65. *Publications:* Introduction to Plasma Physics, 1962; numerous papers in learned journals, on controlled thermonuclear research, plasma physics, kinetic theory, etc. *Recreations:* music, literature. *Address:* Physics Department, University of California at San Diego, La Jolla, California 92037, USA.

THOMPSON, (William) Godfrey, MA; FSA, FLA, FRSA; Guildhall Librarian and Director of Art Galleries, City of London, since 1966; *b* 28 June 1921; *s* of late A. and E. M. Thompson, Coventry; *m* 1946, Doreen Mary Cattell; one *s*. *Educ:* King Henry VIII Sch., Coventry. MA Loughborough, 1977. Served with Royal Signals, 1941-46. Entered Library Service, Coventry, 1937; Dep. Borough Librarian, Chatham, 1946; Dep. City Librarian: Kingston-upon-Hull, 1952; Manchester, 1958; City Librarian, Leeds, 1963. Hon. Librarian to Clockmakers' Co., Gardeners' Co., Charles Lamb Soc.; Pres., Assoc. of Assistant Librarians, 1962. Member: Council, Library Assoc., 1968- (Hon. Treasurer, 1974-; Pres., 1978); Council, Aslib, 1968-71; Hon. Sec. Internat. Assoc. Metropolitan Libraries, 1968-70; Adv. Bd, New Library World. Member: Adv. Panel to Sec. of State on allocation of books received under Capital Transfer Tax; Adv. Panel to Sec. of State on Export of Works of Art. Mem. Exec. Cttee, Friends of the Nat. Libraries. Governor, St Bride Foundn. Consultant on libraries to several overseas governments, including the planning of five nat. libraries. *Publications:* London's Statues, 1971; Planning and Design of Libraries, 1972, 2nd edn 1977; (ed) London for Everyman, 1969; (ed) Encyclopædia of London, 1969. *Address:* Guildhall Library, EC2. *T:* 01-606 3030.

THOMPSON, (William) Pratt; Vice-Chairman, Colbert Group, Geneva, since 1981; *b* 9 Feb. 1933; *s* of Philip Amos Thompson and Regina Beatrice (*née* Kirby); *m* 1963, Jenny Frances Styles; two *d*. *Educ:* Princeton Univ.; Columbia Univ. (BA Econ *Magna cum Laude*, Phi Beta Kappa); Centre d'Etudes Industrielles, Geneva (MBA). AMF Incorporated, 1959-73: Research Analyst, New York, 1959-62; Executive Asst, Tobacco Machinery Gp, Geneva, 1962-63; Director, Marketing and Planning, AMF-C. Itoh Co. Ltd, Tokyo, 1963-66; Vice-Pres. and Gen. Manager, AMF Overseas Corp., Hong Kong, 1966-67; Vice-Pres., AMF Incorporated, London, 1968-73; Dep. Managing Director, Bowthorpe Holdings Ltd, 1973-78; BL Limited, 1978-81: Man. Dir, Jaguar Rover Triumph Ltd, 1978-79; Chm., BL Internat. Ltd, 1979-81. Dir, Metalurgica de Santa Ana SA (Madrid), 1978-81. Member:

Council, SMM&T, 1978-; Council on Foreign Relations (US), 1980-. *Recreations:* flying, cooking, photography. *Address:* 17 Argyll Road, W8 7DA. *Clubs:* Hurlingham; Knickerbocker (New York); Hong Kong (Hong Kong).

THOMPSON, Willoughby Harry, CMG 1974; CBE 1968 (MBE 1954); *b* 3 Dec. 1919; *m* 1963, Sheelah O'Grady; no *c*. Served War: RA, and E African Artillery, 1939-47. Kenya Govt Service, 1947-48; Colonial Administrative Service, Kenya, 1948-63; Colonial Sec., Falkland Islands, 1963-69 (Actg Governor, 1964 and 1967); Actg Judge, Falkland Islands and Dependencies Supreme Court, 1965-69; Actg Administrator, British Virgin Islands, May-July 1969; HM Commissioner in Anguilla, July 1969-71; Governor of Montserrat, 1971-74. *Address:* 38 Holland Park, Clacton on Sea, Essex.

THOMPSON HANCOCK, P(ercy) E(llis); *see* Hancock.

THOMPSON-McCAUSLAND, Lucius Perronet, CMG 1966; *b* 12 Dec. 1904; *e s* of late Sir John Perronet Thompson, KCSI, KCIE and Ada Lucia Tyrrell; *m* Helen Laura, *d* of late Rt Hon. M. M. McCausland, sometime Lieut of Co. Londonderry; two *s* three *d* (and one *s* decd). *Educ:* Repton; King's Coll., Cambridge (Scholar). Helbert Wagg & Co., 1928; Financial News, 1929-34; Moody's Economist Service, 1929-39; Bank of England, 1939-65, Adviser to Governor, 1949-65 (accompanied Lord Keynes to pre-Bretton Woods Conf., 1943), Havana Conf., 1948; Consultant to HM Treasury on internat. monetary problems, 1965-68. Director: Dun & Bradstreet Ltd, 1965-75; Tricentrol Ltd, 1967-76 (Chm., 1970-76); Moodies Services Ltd, 1968-75 (Chm., 1970-75). Governor of Repton, 1952-77 (Chm., 1959-71); Chm., Corp. of Working Men's Coll., 1964-69, Principal, 1969-80. High Sheriff of Hertfordshire, 1965-66. *Recreations:* garden, travel. *Address:* Epcombs, Hertingfordbury, Hertford. *T:* Hertford 52580. *Clubs:* Athenæum; Leander (Henley).

See also G. F. M. P. Thompson, *Rear-Adm. J. Y. Thompson.*

THOMSON, family name of **Barons Thomson of Fleet** and **Thomson of Monifieth.**

THOMSON OF FLEET, 2nd Baron *cr* 1964; **Kenneth Roy Thomson;** newspaper proprietor; Chairman of the Board, President, Chief Executive Officer and Director, Thomson Newspapers Ltd (owners of 40 daily newspapers in Canada); Chairman of the Board and Director: International Thomson Organisation PLC; International Thomson Holdings Inc.; The Thomson Corporation Ltd; Thomson International Corporation Ltd; The Thomson Organisation PLC; The Woodbridge Co. Ltd; Thomson Equitable Corp. Ltd; Thomson Investments Ltd; Ontario Newspapers Ltd; Thomson Newspapers Inc. (owners of 78 daily newspapers in the USA); Standard St Lawrence Co. Ltd; TECL Holdings Ltd; *b* Toronto, Ont., 1 Sept. 1923; *s* of 1st Baron Thomson of Fleet, GBE, founder of Thomson Newspapers, and Edna Alice (*d* 1951), *d* of John Irvine, Drayton, Ont.; *S* father, 1976; *m* 1956, Nora Marilyn, *d* of A. V. Lavis; two *s* one *d*. *Educ:* Upper Canada Coll.; Univ. of Cambridge, England (MA). Served War of 1939-45 with RCAF. Began in editorial dept of Timmins Daily Press., Timmins, Ont., 1947; Advertising Dept, Galt Reporter, Galt, 1948-50, General Manager, 1950-53; returned to Toronto Head Office of Thomson Newspapers to take over direction of Company's Canadian and American operations. President and Director: Dominion-Consolidated Holdings Ltd; Fleet Street Publishers Ltd; Kenthom Holdings Ltd; Thomfleet Holdings Ltd; Thomson Mississauga Properties Ltd; Thomson Works of Art Ltd; Vice President and Director: Cablevue (Quinte) Ltd; Veribest Products Ltd; Director: Abitibi-Price Inc.; The Advocate Company Ltd; Caribbean Trust Ltd; Central Canada Insurance Service Ltd; Hudson's Bay Co.; IBM (Canada) Ltd; Load & Go Transport Inc.; McCallum Transport Inc.; Nipa Lodge Co. Ltd; Orchid Lodge Co. Ltd; Scottish & York Holdings Ltd; Scottish & York Insurance Co. Ltd; Simpsons, Ltd; Thomson Scottish Associates Ltd; Thomson Television Ltd; The Toronto-Dominion Bank; Victoria Insurance Co. of Canada. Dep. Chm., 1966-67, Chm., 1968-70, Co-Pres., 1971-81, Times Newspapers Ltd. Member, Baptist Church. *Recreations:* collecting paintings and works of art, walking. *Heir: s* Hon. David Kenneth Roy Thomson, *b* 12 June 1957. *Address:* (home) 8 Kensington Palace Gardens, W8; 8 Castle Frank Road, Toronto, Ont. M4W 2Z4, Canada; (office) The Thomson Organisation PLC, 4 Stratford Place, W1A 4YG; Thomson Newspapers Ltd, 65 Queen Street West, Toronto, Ont. M5H 2M8, Canada. *Clubs:* York Downs, National, Toronto, Granite, York, Toronto Hunt (Toronto).

THOMSON OF MONIFIETH, Baron *cr* 1977 (Life Peer), of Monifieth, Dundee; **George Morgan Thomson,** KT 1981; PC 1966; Chairman, Independent Broadcasting Authority, since 1981 (Deputy Chairman, 1980); Chancellor, Heriot Watt University, since 1977; *b* 16 Jan. 1921; *s* of late James Thomson, Monifieth; *m* 1948, Grace Jenkins; two *d*. *Educ:* Grove Academy, Dundee. Served War of 1939-45, in Royal Air Force, 1940-45. Assistant Editor, Forward, 1946, Editor, 1948-53. Contested (Lab) Glasgow, Hillhead, 1950; MP (Lab) Dundee East, July 1952-72. Joint Chm., Council for Education in the Commonwealth, 1959-64; Adviser to Educational Institute of Scotland, 1960-64. Minister of State, Foreign Office, 1964-66; Chancellor of the Duchy of Lancaster, 1966-67; Joint Minister of State, Foreign Office, 1967; Secretary of State for Commonwealth Affairs, Aug. 1967-Oct. 1968; Minister Without Portfolio, 1968-69; Chancellor of the Duchy of Lancaster, 1969-70; Shadow Defence Minister, 1970-72. Chm., Labour Cttee for Europe, 1972-73; Commissioner, EEC, 1973-Jan. 1977. Chairman: European

Movement in Britain, 1977-80; Advertising Standards Authority, 1977-80; First Crown Estate Comr, 1978-80. Director: Royal Bank of Scotland Gp, 1982-; ICI plc; Woolwich Equitable Building Soc. Hon. LLD Dundee, 1967; Hon. DLitt Heriot-Watt, 1973; Hon. DSc Aston, 1976. *Address:* IBA, 70 Brompton Road, SW3 1EY. *T:* 01-584 7011. *Club:* Brooks's.

THOMSON, Adam, CBE 1976; Chairman and Chief Executive, The Caledonian Aviation Group plc, since 1970 (formerly Airways Interests (Thomson) Ltd, Chairman and Managing Director, 1964-70); Chairman, British Caledonian Airways Ltd; *b* 7 July 1926; *s* of Frank Thomson and Jemina Rodgers; *m* 1948, Dawn Elizabeth Burt; two *s*. *Educ:* Rutherglen Acad.; Coatbridge Coll.; Royal Technical Coll., Glasgow. Pilot; Fleet Air Arm, 1944-47; Flying Instructor 1947-50; BEA, West African Airways, Britavia, 1951-59. Chairman: Blue Sky Holidays Ltd; Caledonian Airmotive Ltd; British Caledonian Helicopters Ltd; Caledonian Hotel Management. Director: Williams & Glyn's Bank Ltd, 1978-82; Royal Bank of Scotland Gp, 1982-; Otis Elevators Ltd, 1978-; MEPC plc, 1982-. Mem., Airworthiness Requirements Bd, 1972-82. Chm., Assoc. of European Airlines, 1977-78. FRAeS; FCIT; FBIM. Hon. LLD Glasgow, 1979. Businessman of the Year, Hambro Award, 1970; first Scottish Free Enterprise Award, Aims for Freedom and Enterprise, 1976. *Recreations:* golf, sailing, skin-diving. *Address:* 154 Buckswood Drive, Crawley, West Sussex. *Clubs:* Caledonian, Institute of Directors.

THOMSON, Brian Harold, TD 1947; Chairman, since 1974, Joint Managing Director, since 1948, D. C. Thomson & Co. Ltd; *b* 21 Nov. 1918; *e s* of late William Harold Thomson of Kemback and Helen Irene, *d* of Sir Charles Ballance; *m* 1947, Agnes Jane Patricia Cunninghame; one *s* four *d*. *Educ:* Charterhouse. Served War of 1939-45: 1st Fife and Forfar Yeomanry, and on Staff, DAQMG 1st Armoured Div., N Africa and Italy, 1943-44. GS02 Instructor, Staff Coll., Haifa, 1944-46; Lt-Col Comdg Fife and Forfar Yeomanry TA, 1953-56. Entered D. C. Thomson & Co. Ltd, 1937. Director: John Leng & Co. Ltd, 1948-; Southern Television, 1959-; Alliance Trust and Second Alliance Trust, 1961-. *Recreations:* golf, shooting. *Address:* Brooksby, St Andrews, Fife, Scotland. *T:* St Andrews 72900. *Club:* Royal and Ancient Golf (St Andrews).

THOMSON, Bryden; Orchestral Conductor; Artistic Director and Principal Conductor, Ulster Orchestra, since 1977; Artistic Director, Northern Ireland Opera Trust, since 1980; Principal Conductor: BBC Welsh Symphony Orchestra, since 1978; RTE Symphony Orchestra, from Jan. 1984; *b* Ayr, Scotland. *Educ:* Ayr Academy; Royal Scottish Academy of Music; Staatliche Hochschule für Musik, Hamburg. BMus Dunelm; DipMusEd (Hons); RSAM; LRAM; ARCM; FRSAMD. Asst Conductor, BBC Scottish Orchestra, 1958; Conductor: Royal Ballet, 1962; Den Norske Opera, Oslo, 1964; Stora Teatern, Göteborg, Sweden, 1965; Royal Opera, Stockholm, 1966; Associate Conductor, Scottish National Orch., 1966; Principal Conductor, BBC Northern Symphony Orch., 1968-73. Guest Conducting: Norway; Sweden; Denmark; Canada; Germany; S Africa; Principal Guest Conductor, Trondheim Symphony Orch., 1977. *Recreations:* golf, learning about music. *Address:* 2 Leeson Village, Dublin 4.

THOMSON, Sir David; *see* Thomson, Sir F. D. D.

THOMSON, David Kinnear, CBE 1972 (MBE 1945); JP, DL; Chairman, Peter Thomson (Perth) Ltd, whisky blenders and exporters; Chairman, Tayside Health Board, 1973-77; *b* Perth, 26 March 1910; *s* of Peter Thomson, whisky blender, and Jessie Kinnear; unmarried. *Educ:* Perth Academy; Strathallan School. Mem., Perth Local Authority, 1949-72; Chm. Bd of Management, Perth Technical Coll., 1972-75; Mem., ITA (Scottish Br.), 1968-73; Mem., Scottish Economic Council, 1968-75; Director: Scottish Transport Gp, 1972-76; Scottish Opera, 1973-81; Chm., Perth Festival of the Arts, 1973-. Mem. Court, Dundee Univ., 1975-79. Chm., Scottish Licensed Trade, 1981-82. Lord Provost of Perth, 1966-72, and Hon. Sheriff of Perth; DL 1966-72, 1980-, JP 1955, Perth and Kinross; Freedom, Perth and Kinross District, 1982. OStJ. *Recreations:* golf, walking, listening to music. *Address:* Fairhill, Oakbank Road, Perth. *T:* Perth 26593. *Club:* Royal Perth Golfing Society.

THOMSON, Rt. Hon. David Spence, MC 1942; ED; PC 1981; MP (National) for Stratford/Taranaki, New Zealand, since 1963; Minister of State Services and Leader, House of Representatives, since 1978, Minister of Defence, War Pensions and Rehabilitation, since 1980; *b* Stratford, 14 Nov. 1915; *s* of Percy Thomson, MBE; *m* 1942, June Grace Adams; one *s* three *d*. *Educ:* Stratford Primary and High Sch. Territorial Army, 1931-; served Middle East, 19th Inf. Bat. 1st Echelon, 1939-42; 2nd NZED, 1939-45; POW 1942; Hon. Col, 5 RNZIR, 1955-81; Brigadier (Reserve of Officers), 2nd Inf. Brig., 1959-60. Dairy farmer; Pres., NZ Federated Farmers Central Taranaki Exec., 1959-63. Minister of Defence, War Pensions and Rehabilitation, 1966-72; Minister of Tourism, 1966-69; Minister of Police, 1969-72; Minister of Labour and Immigration, 1972; Minister of Justice, 1975-78. *Recreations:* golf, gardening, classical music. *Address:* Parliament Buildings, Wellington, New Zealand; (home) 22 Bird Road, Stratford, New Zealand.

THOMSON, Sir Evan (Rees Whitaker), Kt 1977; FRCS, FRACS, FACS; Hon. Consultant Surgeon, Princess Alexandra Hospital, Brisbane; *b* 14 July 1919; *s* of Frederick Thorpe Thomson and Ann Margaret Thomson (*née* Evans); *m* 1955, Mary Kennedy. *Educ:* Brisbane Boys' Coll.; Univ. of Queensland (MB BS). Full time staff, Brisbane General Hospital, 1942-48; RAAF Reserve, 1942-45; Visiting Surgeon: Brisbane General Hospital, 1950-56; Princess Alexandra Hospital, 1956-71; Clinical Lectr in Surgery, Univ. of Queensland, 1951-71. Qld Branch, Australian Medical Association: Councillor, 1966-78; Pres., 1967-68; a Vice-Pres., 1980-; Chm. of Council; Chm. of Ethics Cttee. Pres., 4th Aust. Med. Congress, 1971. Member: Med. Bd of Queensland; Wesley Hospital Bd, etc.; Pres., Qld Council of Professions, 1970-72; Vice-Patron, Medico-Legal Soc. of Qld; Governor, Univ. of Qld Foundn; Life Governor, Aust. Postgrad. Fedn in Medicine. Silver Jubilee Medal, 1977. *Publications:* Future Needs for Medical Education in Queensland (ed), 1981; papers in medical and allied jls. *Recreations:* golf, swimming. *Address:* Alexandra, 201 Wickham Terrace, Brisbane, Queensland 4000, Australia. *T:* 221 4688. *Clubs:* Queensland; Headland Golf; Mooloolaba Yacht.

THOMSON, Ewen Cameron, CMG 1964; nutrition consultant; *b* 12 April 1915; *s* of Francis Murphy Thomson, Woodhill, Forfar, Angus; *m* 1948, Betty, *d* of Lt-Col J. H. Preston, MBE, Far Horizons, Trearddur Bay, Anglesey; one *s* three *d*. *Educ:* Forfar Academy; St Andrews University. Cadet, Northern Rhodesia Provincial Admin., 1938. War Service, 1st Bn Northern Rhodesia Regt, 1939-46. District Commissioner, 1946; Dep. Prov. Comr, 1956; Prov. Comr, 1957; Senior Provincial Commissioner, 1961; Permanent Sec. for Native Affairs, 1962; Minister for Native Affairs, 1962; Permanent Secretary, Ministry of Transport and Works, Zambia, 1964; Director of Communications, Contingency Planning Organisation, Zambia, 1966; Exec. Sec., Nat. Food and Nutrition Commn, Zambia, 1967; Temp. Project Manager, UNDP/FAO, Nat. Food and Nutrition Programme, Zambia, 1970. Consultant: SIDA Nat. Food and Nutrition Programme, Tanzania, 1972; World Bank, 1974-80; Nat. Food and Nutrition Projects, Indonesia and Brazil, 1974-82; Urban Projects, Kenya, Botswana and Lesotho; Nutrition Component, Philippines, 1977-78; State Nutrition Project, Tamil Nadu, India, 1978-82; Food and Nutrition Project, Egypt, 1980-81; Leader FFHC UK Reconnaissance Mission, Malaŵi, 1972; Co-Dir, Preparatory Team, Tanzania Food and Nutrition Centre, 1973. Leader, Planning Team, Nat. Food and Nutrition Programme, Malaŵi, 1973. Gave keynote address, Rockefeller Conf. on Nutrition and Govt Policy in Developing Countries, 1975. *Publication:* Symbiosis of Scientist, Planner and Administrator in Nutrition Programme Intervention, 1978. *Recreations:* walking, cooking, winemaking. *Address:* Manleys, Beacon Hill Park, Hindhead, Surrey. *T:* Hindhead 6972. *Club:* Royal Commonwealth Society.

THOMSON, Rt. Rev. Francis; *see* Motherwell, Bishop of, (RC).

THOMSON, Francis Paul, OBE 1975; CEng, MIERE; Consultant on Post Office and Bank Giro Systems, since 1968; *b* Corstorphine, Edinburgh, 17 Dec. 1914; *y s* of late William George and Elizabeth Hannah Thomson, Goring-by-Sea; *m* 1954, E. Sylvia, *e d* of late Lokförare J. Erik Nilsson, Bollnäs, Sweden. *Educ:* Friends' Sch., Sibford Ferris; Sch. of Engrg, Polytechnic, London; in Denmark and Sweden. TV and radar research, 1935-42; Special Ops Exec., 1942-44; Sen. Planning Engr, Postwar research and reconstruction, communications industry; founded British Post Giro Campaign, 1946 and conducted Campaign to victory in Parlt, 1965; Lectr, Stockholm Univ. Extension, 1947-49; Founder, and Man. Editor, English Illustrated, 1950-61; techn. exports promotion with various firms, esp. electronic equipment, 1950-60; pioneered electronic language laboratory equipment and methods, 1930, subseq. joined consultancy-production groups; Bank Computerisation Consultant, 1967-. Governor, Watford Coll. of Technology, 1965-70 (Engrg Dept Adv. Cttee, 1972-); Mem., Communication of Technical Information Adv. Cttee, CGLI; Advr to PO Users' Nat. Council's Giro Sub Cttee, 1975; Founder and first Hon. Sec., SW Herts Post Office Adv. Cttee, 1976; Cttee Mem., Writers Guild of GB; First British Cttee Mem., Internat. Centre for Ancient and Modern Tapestry (CITAM), Lausanne, 1974-. Founder and Hon. Sec., St Andrews Residents' Assoc. (Watford). AMBIM; FIQA 1978. Hon. Fellow, Inst. of Scientific and Technical Communicators, 1975. Life Member: Corstorphine Trust; Anglo-Swedish Soc. *Publications:* Giro Credit Transfer Systems, 1964; Money in the Computer Age, 1968; (ed jtly) Banking Automation, 1971; (ed with E. S. Thomson) rev. repr. of A History of Tapestry (2nd edn), by W. G. Thomson, 1973; Tapestry: mirror of history, 1979; Engineer Extraordinary: a biography of Alan Dower Blumlein, 1983; originated jtly Household Directory, Personal Record books, Home and Car Emergency Card series; numerous papers in European and other learned jls. *Recreations:* gardening, archaeology. *Address:* The Cottage, 39 Church Road, Watford, Herts WD1 3PY.

THOMSON, Sir (Frederick Douglas) David, 3rd Bt *cr* 1929; Managing Director, Ben Line Steamers Ltd, since 1964; Chairman, Ben Line Ship Management, since 1972; *b* 14 Feb. 1940; *s* of Sir James Douglas Wishart Thomson, 2nd Bt, and of Evelyn Margaret Isabel, (Bettina), *d* of Lt-Comdr D. W. S. Douglas, RN; *S* father, 1977; *m* 1967, Caroline Anne, *d* of Major Timothy Stuart Lewis; two *s* one *d*. *Educ:* Eton; University College, Oxford (BA Agric). Joined family business, Ben Line, 1961; Partner, Wm Thomson & Co., 1963-64. Member: Queen's Body Guard for Scotland, Royal Company of Archers. *Recreation:* shooting. *Heir: s* Simon Douglas Charles Thomson, *b* 16 June 1969. *Address:* Glenbrook House, Balerno, Midlothian. *T:* 031-449 4116.

THOMSON, Garry; Scientific Adviser to the Trustees and Head of the Scientific Department, National Gallery, London, since 1960; *b* 13 Sept. 1925;

s of Robert Thomson and Mona Spence; m 1954, M. R. Saisvasdi Svasti; four s. Educ: Charterhouse; Magdalene College, Cambridge (MA). Editorial Staff of A History of Technology, 1951; Research Chemist, National Gallery, 1955; Hon. Editor, Studies in Conservation, 1959-67, Vice-Pres., Internat. Inst. for Conservation of Historic and Artistic Works, 1978. Vice-Pres., Buddhist Soc., London. Publications: Recent Advances in Conservation (ed), 1963; Museum Climatology (ed), 1967; The Museum Environment, 1978; Reflections on the Life of the Buddha, 1982; reviews and articles in Nature, Museums Journal, Studies in Conservation, etc. Recreation: underwater swimming. Address: Squire's Hill, Tilford, Surrey. T: Runfold 2206. Club: Athenæum.

THOMSON, Prof. George Derwent; Professor of Greek, University of Birmingham, 1937-70; b 19 Aug. 1903; s of William Henry and Minnie Thomson; m 1934, Katharine Fraser Stewart; two d. Educ: Dulwich College; King's College, Cambridge. Craven Student, University of Cambridge, 1926-27; Fellow of King's College, Cambridge, 1927-33 and 1934-36. Member, Czechoslovak Academy of Sciences, 1960-. Hon. Dr Univ. of Thessaloniki, 1979. Publications: Greek Lyric Metre, 1929 (new edn, 1960); Aeschylus, Prometheus Bound, 1932; M. O'Sullivan, Twenty Years A-Growing (trans. from the Irish), 1933 (World's Classics edition, 1953); Aeschylus, Oresteia, 2 vols, 1938 (new edn, 1966); Aeschylus and Athens, 1941 (new edn 1973); Marxism and Poetry, 1946 (new edn, 1954); Studies in Ancient Greek Society, Vol. I, The Prehistoric Aegean, 1949 (new edn 1973); Vol. II, The First Philosophers, 1955 (new edn, 1973); The Greek Language, 1960 (new edn, 1966); Geras: Studies Presented to G. T. on his Sixtieth Birthday, 1963; A Manual of Modern Greek, 1966; Palamas, Twelve Lays of the Gipsy, 1969; From Marx to Mao Tse-tung, 1971; Capitalism and After, 1973; The Human Essence, 1975; The Blasket That Was, 1982; books in Irish and Greek and articles in learned and other journals; foreign editions of his books in 22 languages. Address: 58 Billesley Lane, Birmingham B13 9QS. T: 021-449 2656.

THOMSON, Rev. George Ian Falconer; Chaplain of All Souls College, Oxford, since 1981; b 2 Sept. 1912; s of Rev. G. D. Thomson, DD; m 1st, 1938, Hon. Bridget de Courcy (marr. diss. 1951), e d of 34th Baron Kingsale, DSO; one d; 2nd, 1952, Mary Josephine Lambart Dixon, OBE, d of Archdeacon H. T. Dixon, DD, Hereford; one s. Educ: Shrewsbury Sch.; Balliol Coll., Oxford (MA); Westcott House, Cambridge. Ellerton Theol Essay Prize, Oxford, 1936. Pilot, RAFO, 1932-37; Chaplain, RAFVR, 1942-46. Curate, St Luke's, Chelsea, 1936-37; Chaplain, Hertford Coll., Oxford, 1937-46, Junior Dean and Dean of Degrees, 1939-42; Rector of Hilgay, Norfolk, 1946-51; Sec. of Gen. Ordination Examn, 1946-52; Master, Maidstone Grammar Sch., 1951-62; Chaplain and Sen. Lectr, St Paul's Coll., Cheltenham, 1962-66; Exam. Chaplain to Bp of Gloucester, 1964-76; Vis. Lectr, McMaster Univ., Ont, 1964; Dir, research project, Conf. of British Missionary Socs, 1966-68; re-visited China during Cultural Revolution, 1967. Director, Bible Reading Fellowship, 1968-77. Rowing Corresp., The Observer, 1938-65. NADFAS Lectr on James Tissot, 1980-. Press Officer, Oxford Diocese, 1979-. Freeman, City of London. Publications: History of the Oxford Pastorate, 1946; Experiment in Worship, 1951; The Rise of Modern Asia, 1957; Changing Patterns in South Asia, 1961; Two Hundred School Assemblies, 1966; Mowbray's Mini-Commentary No 4, 1970. Recreations: rowing (Oxford Blue, 1934), travel, writing. Address: Jackson's Farm, Yarnton, Oxford OX5 1QD. Clubs: Royal Air Force; Leander.

THOMSON, George Malcolm; Author and Journalist; b Leith, Scotland, 2 Aug. 1899; e s of Charles Thomson, journalist, and Mary Arthur, d of John Eason; m 1926, Else (d 1957), d of Harald Ellefsen, Tœnsberg, Norway; one s one d; m 1963, Diana Van Cortland Robertson. Educ: Daniel Stewart's College, Edinburgh; Edinburgh University. Journalist. Publications: Caledonia, or the Future of the Scots, 1927; A Short History of Scotland, 1930; Crisis in Zanat, 1942; The Twelve Days, 1964; The Robbers Passing By, 1966; The Crime of Mary Stuart, 1967; Vote of Censure, 1968; A Kind of Justice, 1970; Sir Francis Drake, 1972; Lord Castlerosse, 1973; The North-West Passage, 1975; Warrior Prince: Prince Rupert of the Rhine, 1976; The First Churchill: the life of John, 1st Duke of Marlborough, 1979; The Prime Ministers, 1980; The Ball at Glenkerran, 1982. Address: 5 The Mount Square, NW3. T: 01-435 8775. Club: Garrick.

THOMSON, Very Rev. Ian; see White-Thomson.

THOMSON, Sir Ivo Wilfrid Home, 2nd Bt, cr 1925; b 14 Oct. 1902; s of Sir Wilfrid Thomson, 1st Bt, and Ethel Henrietta, 2nd d of late Hon. Reginald Parker; S father 1939; m 1st, 1933, Sybil Marguerite (from whom he obt. a divorce), yr d of C. W. Thompson, The Red House, Escrick; one s (and one d decd); 2nd, 1954, Viola Mabel (who m 1937, Keith Home Thomson, from whom she obt. a divorce), d of Roland Dudley, Linkenholt Manor, Andover. Educ: Eton. Heir: s Mark Wilfrid Home Thomson [b 29 Dec. 1939; m 1976, Lady Jacqueline Rufus Isaacs, d of 3rd Marquess of Reading, MBE, MC; one s one d].

THOMSON, Tun Sir James (Beveridge), KBE 1966; Kt 1959; b 24 March 1902, e s of late Rev. William Archibald Thomson, Dalmellington, Ayrshire; m 1931, Dr Florence Adam; one s. Educ: Dalmellington Village School; George Watson's College, Edinburgh; Edinburgh University. MA, 1st Cl. Hons History, Edin. Called to English Bar, Middle Temple, 1929; admitted Advocate in Scotland, 1955. District Officer, 1926 and Resident Magistrate, 1932, N Rhodesia; Judge, Fiji, Chief Justice of Tonga and a Judicial

Commissioner for Western Pacific, 1945-48; Judge, Federation of Malaya, 1948; Chief Justice 1956; (first) Lord President of the Federal Court of Malaysia, 1963-66; (last) President of the High Court of S Arabia, 1967; Chm., Delimitation Commn, Republic of Botswana, 1968. Hon. Sheriff, Inverness, 1972. Meritorious Service Medal (Perak), 1957; Panglima Mangku Negara (Federation of Malaya), 1958; Seri Maharajah Mangku Negara (Malaysia), 1966. Publications: The Laws of the British Solomon Islands, 1948; The Law of Tonga, 1951. Address: Craig Gowan, Carr Bridge, Inverness-shire. T: Carr Bridge 257.
   See also W. A. R. Thomson.

THOMSON, James Frederick Gordon; see Migdale, Hon. Lord.

THOMSON, Prof. James Leonard, CBE 1955; Professor Emeritus in Civil Engineering, Royal Military College of Science, Shrivenham, since 1970; b 9 Aug. 1905; s of James Thomson, Liverpool. Educ: University of Manchester; St John's College, Cambridge. Mather & Platt, Ltd, Manchester, 1923-26; Univ. of Manchester, 1926-30 (BSc (Tech.) 1st Cl. Hons and Stoney Prizeman); Lecturer, Technical College, Horwich, 1930-32; Whitworth Senior Scholar, 1931; St John's Coll., Cambridge, 1932-34 (BA 1934, MA 1938); Research Engineer, ICI, Billingham-on-Tees, 1934-38; Lecturer, Dept of Civil and Mechanical Engineering, Univ. of London, King's College, 1938. Seconded for War-time Service: Managing Engineer, HM Royal Ordnance Factory, Pembrey, Carms, 1940-42; Principal Technical Officer, School of Tank Technology, 1942-46. Royal Military College of Science, Shrivenham: Prof. of Mechanical Engrg and Head of Dept of Civil and Mechanical Engrg, 1946-61; Prof. of Civil Engrg and Head of Dept of Civil Engrg, 1965-70; seconded to ME Technical Univ., Ankara, Turkey, 1961-65 : Consultant Dean and Mechanical Engrg Specialist; later Chief Technical Adviser for UNESCO project in Turkey. Publications: various scientific papers dealing with High Pressure Techniques. Recreations: mountaineering, sailing. Address: Astral House, Netherbury, Bridport, Dorset DT6 5LU.

THOMSON, Sir John, KBE 1972; TD 1944; MA; Chairman, Morland and Co. Ltd, since 1979; Director: Barclays Bank Ltd, 1947-78 (Chairman, 1962-73); Union Discount Company of London Ltd, 1960-74; b 1908; s of late Guy Thomson, JP, Woodperry, Oxford; m 1st, 1935, Elizabeth, JP (d 1977), d of late Stanley Brotherhood, JP, Thornhaugh Hall, Peterborough; no c ; 2nd, 1979, Eva Elizabeth, d of Marcus Ralph Russell, and widow of Tom Dreaper. Educ: Winchester; Magdalen College, Oxford. Commanded Oxfordshire Yeomanry Regt, RATA, 1942-44 and 1947-50. Deputy High Steward of Oxford University; a Curator of Oxford University Chest, 1949-74; Chairman: Nuffield Medical Benefactors, 1951- (Trustee, 1947-82); Nuffield Orthopædic Centre Trust, 1949-81. President, British Bankers' Association, 1964-66 (Vice-President, 1963-64); FIB. Mem. Royal Commn on Trade Unions and Employers' Assocs, 1965-68; Mem. BNEC, 1968-71. Hon. Fellow St Catherine's Coll., Oxford. Hon. Colonel: 299 Fd Regt RA (TA), 1964-67; Oxfordshire Territorials, 1967-75; Bt Col, 1950. DL Oxfordshire 1947-57; High Sheriff of Oxfordshire, 1957; Vice-Lieut, 1957-63; Lord-Lieut, 1963-79. A Steward, Jockey Club, 1974-77. Hon. DCL Oxford, 1957. KStJ 1973. Address: Manor Farm House, Spelsbury, Oxford. T: Charlbury 810266. Club: Cavalry and Guards.

THOMSON, Sir John (Adam), KCMG 1978 (CMG 1972); MA; HM Diplomatic Service; United Kingdom Permanent Representative to the United Nations, since 1982; b 27 April 1927; s of late Sir George Thomson, FRS, Master of Corpus Christi Coll., Cambridge, 1952-62 (s of Sir J. J. Thomson, OM, FRS, Master of Trinity Coll., Cambridge, 1919-40), and late Kathleen, d of Very Rev. Sir George Adam Smith, DD, LLD, Principal of Aberdeen Univ., 1909-35; m 1953, Elizabeth Anne McClure, d of late Norman McClure, Pres. of Ursinus Coll., Penn, USA; three s one d. Educ: Phillips Exeter Acad., USA; Univ. of Aberdeen; Trinity Coll., Cambridge. Foreign Office, 1950; Third Sec., Jedda, 1951; Damascus, 1954; FO, 1955; Private Sec. to Permanent Under-Secretary, 1958-60; First Sec., Washington, 1960-64; FO, 1964; Acting Head of Planning Staff, 1966; Counsellor, 1967; Head of Planning Staff, FO, 1967; seconded to Cabinet Office as Chief of Assessments Staff, 1968-71; Minister and Dep. Permanent Rep. to N Atlantic Council, 1972-73; Head of UK Delegn to MBFR Exploratory Talks, Vienna, 1973; Asst Under-Sec. of State, FCO, 1973-76; High Comr to India, 1977-82. Publication: Crusader Castles (with R. Fedden), 1956. Recreations: carpets, castles, walking. Address: c/o Foreign and Commonwealth Office, SW1. Club: Athenæum.
   See also Janet Adam Smith (Mrs John Carleton), Baron Balerno.

THOMSON, John (Ian) Sutherland, CMG 1968; MBE 1944; Independent Chairman, Fiji Sugar Industry, since 1971; Chairman: Fiji Coconut Board, since 1973; Economic Development Board, since 1980; b 8 Jan. 1920; s of late William Sutherland Thomson and of Jessie McCaig Malloch; m 1945, Nancy Marguerite Kearsley, Suva, Fiji; seven s one d. Educ: High Sch. of Glasgow; Univ. of Glasgow (MA Hons). Served War of 1939-45: Black Watch, 1940; Fiji Military Forces, 1941-45 (Captain). Appointed Cadet, Colonial Administrative Service, Fiji and Western Pacific, 1941; District Administration and Secretariat, Fiji, 1946-54; Seconded to Colonial Office, 1954-56; Dep. Comr, Native Lands and Fisheries, Fiji, 1957-58; Comr of Native Reserves and Chairman, Native Lands and Fisheries Commission, Fiji, 1958-62; Divisional Commissioner, Fiji, 1963-66; Administrator, British Virgin Islands, 1967-71; Acting Governor-Gen., Fiji, 1980, 1981. Recreations:

golf, gardening. *Address:* GPO Box 644, Honson Building, Thomson Street, Suva, Fiji. *T:* 23142.

THOMSON, Nigel Ernest Drummond; Sheriff of Lothian and Borders, at Edinburgh, since 1976; *b* 19 June 1926; *y s* of late Rev. James Kyd Thomson, and late Joan Drummond; *m* 1964, Snjólaug Magnússon, *yr d* of Consul-General Sigursteinn Magnússon; one *s* one *d*. *Educ:* George Watson's College, Edinburgh; Univs of St Andrews and Edinburgh. Served with Scots Guards and Indian Grenadiers, 1944-47. MA (St Andrews) 1950; LLB (Edin.) 1953. Called to Scottish Bar, 1953. Standing Counsel to Scottish Educn Dept, 1961-66; Sheriff of Lanarkshire, later S Strathclyde, Dumfries and Galloway, at Hamilton, 1966-76. Chm., Music Cttee, Scottish Arts Council, 1978-. Pres., Speculative Soc., Edinburgh, 1960. Chm., Tenovus, Edinburgh. *Recreations:* music, woodwork, golf. *Address:* 5 Abinger Gardens, Edinburgh. *T:* 031-337 2066. *Clubs:* Arts (Strathaven); Bruntsfield Golf (Edinburgh).

THOMSON, Peter; *b* 1914; *s* of John Thomson, SSC, and Martha Lindsay Miller; *m* 1939, Jean Laird Nicoll; two *s* one *d*. *Educ:* Royal High School, Edinburgh; Edinburgh University. Gordon Highlanders, 1941-46; Capt. 1944. Called to Scottish Bar, 1946. Founded Scottish Plebiscite Society, 1947. Sheriff Substitute of Caithness, Sutherland, Orkney and Zetland, 1955; Sheriff of South Strathclyde, Dumfries and Galloway (formerly Lanarkshire) at Hamilton, 1962-77. Dir, Inst. of Scotland, 1979-. *Recreations:* walking, golf. *Address:* Haughhead Farm House, Uddingston, Lanarkshire.

THOMSON, Robert Howard Garry; *see* Thomson, Garry.

THOMSON, Robert John Stewart, CMG 1969; MBE 1955; Ministry of Defence, 1969-81; *b* 5 May 1922; *s* of late John Stewart Thomson, FRIBA, and late Nellie Thomson (*née* Morris). *Educ:* Bromsgrove Sch.; Worcester Coll., Oxford. Service with Sudan Defence Force, 1943-45. Sudan Political Service, 1943-54 (District Commissioner, 1950-54). Attached Ministry of Defence, 1955-56; First Sec., British High Commission, Accra, 1956-60, 1962-64, Counsellor, 1966-69. *Recreations:* gardening, singing. *Address:* Ardgowan, Lenthay Road, Sherborne, Dorset DT9 6AQ. *Clubs:* Royal Over-Seas League; Polo (Accra).

THOMSON, Air Vice-Marshal Ronald Bain, CB 1959; DSO 1943; DFC 1943; *b* 15 April 1912; *s* of George Thomson, Aberdeen, and Christina Ann (*née* Reid); *m* 1940, Elizabeth Napier (*née* Ayling); two *d*. *Educ:* Robert Gordon's College, Aberdeen. Joined Royal Auxiliary Air Force (612 County of Aberdeen Squadron), 1937. Senior Lecturer Physical Educ. and Hygiene, Pretoria Technical College, S Africa, 1939. War of 1939-45, Coastal Command. AOC, RAF, Gibraltar, 1958-60; AOC, RAF, Scotland and Northern Ireland, 1960-63; AOA, Flying Training Command, 1963-66; retired. Member of the Queen's Body Guard for Scotland, The Royal Company of Archers. Commander Order of St Olav, 1963. *Recreations:* shooting, golf. *Club:* Royal Air Force.

THOMSON, Thomas Davidson, CMG 1962; OBE 1959; *b* 1 April 1911; *s* of J. A. Thomson, FFA, FRSE, and Barbara M. Davidson, Edinburgh; *m* 1st, 1947, Marjorie Constance (*d* 1980), *d* of T. R. Aldred, Limbe, Nyasaland; one *s*; 2nd, 1981, Kathleen Ramsay, *d* of D. Craig, Morebattle, Roxburghshire and *widow* of Nicholas Pestereff. *Educ:* George Watson's Coll., Edinburgh; Edinburgh Univ. (MA, LLB); Magdalene Coll., Cambridge. Editor, The Student, 1932; Travel Secretary, Scottish National Union of Students, 1932; Cadet, Nyasaland Administration, 1934; Civil Demobilisation Officer, 1945; Assistant Secretary, Nyasaland, 1947; Officer in charge, Domasi Community Development Scheme, 1949; Officer in charge, School of Local Government, 1955, Social Development, 1958; retired as Commissioner for Social Development, Nyasaland, 1963. Carried out survey of Adult Education in Nyasaland, 1956-57; organised Nyasaland Council of Social Service, 1959. Served War of 1939-45, E Africa (Major). Sec., Eastern Border Development Assoc., 1962-67. Chairman: Scottish Community Development Cttee, 1968-75; Berwicks Council of Social Service, 1971-75; Hon. Vice-Pres., Scottish Council of Social Service, 1976-. Pres., Berwickshire Naturalists' Club, 1969-70. Vice-Pres., Soc. of Antiquaries of Scotland, 1971-74. Brain of Britain, BBC Radio, 1969. *Publications:* A Practical Approach to Chinyanja, 1947; Coldingham Priory, 1973; sundry reports and papers on Nyasaland affairs; papers in Hist. Berwickshire Naturalists' Club; sundry papers in philatelic jls. *Recreations:* gardening, philately, contemplative archaeology, Scouting (Chief Commissioner, Nyasaland, 1958; County Commissioner, Berwickshire, 1966-75). *Address:* The Hill, Coldingham, Berwickshire. *T:* Coldingham 209.

THOMSON, William Archibald Robson, MD; FRCPEd; Editor of The Practitioner, 1944-73; Medical Correspondent, The Times, 1956-71; Medical Consultant, The Daily Telegraph; Chairman: The Leprosy Study Centre, 1953-80; Council, Sesame; *b* 6 Nov. 1906; 2nd *s* of late Rev. W. A. Thomson; *m* 1934, Marion Lucy Nannette, *d* of late Sir Leonard Hill, FRS; two *s*. *Educ:* Dalmellington Higher Grade Public Sch.; Wigan Grammar Sch.; University of Edinburgh. MB, ChB 1929, MD (Hons), 1933, University of Edinburgh; FRCPEd 1976. Clin. Asst, Ho. Phys. and Clin. Tutor, Royal Infirmary, Edinburgh; Asst, Dept of Medicine, also Davidson Research Fellow in Applied Bacteriology, Univ. of Edinburgh; Surg. Lieut, RN, seconded for res. work on deep diving; Paterson Research Scholar and Chief Asst, Cardiac Dept, London Hospital; First Assistant, Medical Unit, St Thomas' Hospital. FRSocMed; FRIPHH; Founder Member, The British Academy of Forensic Sciences (Dep. Chm. Exec. Council, 1972-77, 1980-81; Pres., 1981-82); Foundation Mem. and Vice-Chm. of Council, British Institute for the Study of the Arts in Therapy. Patron, Action Cttee for Bath Spa Preservation. Bengué Meml Award Lectr, RIPH&H; Cavendish Lectr, W London Medico-Chirurgical Soc., 1975. Abercrombie Award, RCGP, 1973. *Publications:* Black's Medical Dictionary, 19th edn 1948 to 33rd edn 1981; Thomson's Concise Medical Dictionary, 1973; The Searching Mind in Medicine, 1960; (ed) The Practitioner's Handbook, 1960; (ed) Practical Dietetics, 1960; (ed) Calling the Laboratory, 3rd edn, 1971; (ed) The Doctor's Surgery, 1964; (ed) Sex and Its Problems, 1968; Herbs That Heal, 1976; (Exec. Editor) Practice, 1976; A Dictionary of Medical Ethics and Practice, 1977; Spas that Heal, 1978; (ed) Medicines from the Earth, 1978; (ed) Healing Plants, 1978; Healing Herbs, 1978; A Change of Air, 1979; Faiths that Heal, 1980; Medical Consultant, Fishbein's Illustrated Medical and Health Encyclopedia, 1977; contribs to: Gradwohl's Legal Medicine, 3rd edn 1976; Encyclopaedia Britannica, 14th and 15th edns; various articles on medical and cardiological subjects in Quarterly Journal of Medicine, British Heart Jl, Lancet, etc. *Address:* 4 Rutland Court, Queens Drive, W3 0HL. *T:* 01-992 8685. *Club:* Athenæum.

See also Tun Sir James Thomson.

THOMSON, William Oliver, MD, DPH, DIH; Chief Administrative Medical Officer, Lanarkshire Health Board, since 1973; *b* 23 March 1925; *s* of William Crosbie Thomson and Mary Jolie Johnston; *m* 1956, Isobel Lauder Glendinning Brady; two *s*. *Educ:* Allan Glen's Sch., Glasgow; Univ. of Glasgow (MB ChB, MD). DPA; FFCM. Chronic student of Gray's Inn, London. Captain, RAMC, 1948-50. Hospital appointments, 1951-53; appointments in Public Health, Glasgow, 1953-60; Admin. MO, Western Regional Hospital Bd, 1960-70; Group Medical Superintendent, Glasgow Maternity and Women's Hospitals, 1970-73; Mem., Health Services Ind. Adv. Cttee, 1980-. Visiting Lecturer: Univ. of Michigan, Ann Arbor; Ministry of Health, Ontario; Hon. Lectr, Univ. of Glasgow. Diploma of Scottish Council for Health Educn (for services to health educn), 1979. *Publications:* articles on clinical medicine, community medicine, general practice, occupational health and health education, in various medical jls; humorous pieces in The Lancet, BMJ, etc. *Recreations:* walking, talking, writing. *Address:* 14 Stewarton Drive, Cambuslang, Glasgow G72 8DF. *T:* 041-641 2300.

THONEMANN, Peter Clive, MSc, DPhil; Professor and Head of Department of Physics, University College, Swansea, since 1968; *b* 3 June 1917. *Educ:* Melbourne Grammar Sch.; Melbourne; Sydney and Oxford Univs. BSc Melbourne, 1940; MSc Sydney, 1945; DPhil Oxford, 1949. Munition Supply Laboratories, Victoria, Australia, 1940; Amalgamated Wireless, Australia, 1942; University of Sydney, Commonwealth Research Fellow, 1944; Clarendon Laboratory, Oxford, ICI Research Fellow, 1946; United Kingdom Atomic Energy Authority, 1949; Chief Scientist, 1964; Dep. Dir, Culham Laboratory, 1967-68. *Address:* Department of Physics, University College, Swansea, Singleton Park, Swansea, Wales; 33 Cumnor Hill, Oxford.

THORLEY, Charles Graham; *b* 4 Jan. 1914; *s* of Charles Loof Thorley; *m* 1958, Peggy Percival Ellis (*née* Boor); one step *s* one step *d*. *Educ:* Manchester Grammar Sch.; King's Coll., Cambridge (Mod. Lang. Scholar). Served War of 1939-45, Eritrea and Cyrenaica (Lt-Col). Entered Civil Service as Economist, Bd of Trade, 1936; attached to British Embassy, China, 1936-38; Mem. British Economic Mission to Belgian Congo, 1940-41; HM Treasury, 1940-57; served on UK financial delegns and missions in Japan, US, Egypt, France, Switzerland, W Germany, etc; Min. of Power, 1957; Under-Secretary and Head of Coal Div., 1965-69; Acct-Gen. and Dir of Finance, 1969. Chm., NATO Petroleum Planning Cttee, 1962-65; Under-Sec., Min. of Technology and DTI, 1969-74. Specialist Advr, House of Lords, 1975-79. *Recreation:* travel. *Address:* Preston House, Corton Denham, Sherborne, Dorset DT9 4LS. *T:* Corton Denham 269.

THORLEY, Sir Gerald (Bowers), Kt 1973; TD; Chairman, MEPC plc, since 1976; Vice-Chairman, Rockware Group plc, since 1976; Director, Fitch Lovell plc; *b* 26 Aug. 1913; *s* of Clement Thorley and Ethel May Davy; *m* 1947, Beryl Preston, *d* of G. Preston Rhodes; one *s* one *d*. *Educ:* Ratcliffe College. FRICS. FRSA. Served War of 1939-45, RA; BEF, 1939-40; Malaya, 1941; POW, 1942-45. Ind Coope & Allsopp Ltd, 1936. Underwriting Member of Lloyd's, 1952. Chairman: Allied Breweries Ltd, 1970-75; British Sugar plc, 1968-82. *Recreations:* gardening, golf. *Address:* Church House, Bale, Fakenham, Norfolk. *T:* Thursford 314. *Club:* Naval and Military.

THORN, Gaston; Politician, Luxembourg; President of the Commission of the European Economic Community, since 1981; *b* 3 Sept. 1928; *s* of Edouard Thorn and Suzanne Weber; *m* 1957, Liliane Petit; one *s*. *Educ:* Univs of Montpellier, Lausanne, and Paris. DenD. Admitted to Luxembourg Bar; Pres., Nat. Union of Students, Luxembourg, 1959; Member, European Parlt, 1959-69; Vice-Pres., Liberal Group, Pres., Democratic Party, Luxembourg, 1961; Minister of Foreign Affairs and of Foreign Trade, 1969, also Minister of Physical Educn and Sport, 1969-77; Prime Minister and Minister of State, 1974-79; Minister of Nat. Econ. and Middle Classes, 1977; of Justice, 1979; Dep. Prime Minister, and Minister of Foreign Affairs, July 1979-1980. Pres., 30th Session of UN Gen. Assembly, 1975-76. President: Liberal International, 1970; Fedn of Liberal and Democratic Parties of European Community, 1976-80. Decorations include Grand Cross of Orders of Adolphe de Nassau, Couronne de Chêne, and Mérite (Luxembourg), Grand Cross of Légion d'Honneur (France), GCVO and GCMG (GB) and several other Grand

Crosses. *Recreations:* golf, tennis, reading. *Address:* 200 rue de la Loi, 1049 Brussels, Belgium. *T:* 735.00.40.

THORN, John Leonard, MA; Headmaster of Winchester College since 1968; *b* 28 April 1925; *s* of late Stanley L. Thorn and Winifred M. Thorn (*née* King); *m* 1955, Veronica Laura, *d* of late Sir Robert Maconochie, OBE, QC; one *s* one *d. Educ:* St Paul's School; Corpus Christi College, Cambridge. Served War of 1939-45, Sub-Lieutenant, RNVR, 1943-46. 1st Class Historical Tripos, Parts I and II, 1948-49; Assistant Master, Clifton College, 1949-61 (Head of History Dept, 1951-58, Housemaster, 1958-61); Headmaster, Repton School, 1961-68. Dir, Royal Opera House, Covent Garden, 1971-76. Chm., Headmasters' Conference, 1981. Trustee of the British Museum, 1980-. *Publication:* (joint) A History of England, 1961. *Address:* Headmaster's House, Winchester College, Winchester. *T:* 4328. *Club:* Garrick.

THORNE, Benjamin, CMG 1969; MBE 1966; consultant on Far East trade; *b* 19 June 1922; *m* 1949, Sylvia Una (*née* Graves); one *s* two *d. Educ:* St Marylebone Grammar Sch.; Regent Street Polytechnic. Served War, RAF, 1940-46. Joined Civil Service, 1946; British Trade Commission: India, 1950-54; Ghana, 1954-58; Nigeria, 1958-61; Hong Kong, 1964-68; Dir, British Week in Tokyo, 1968-69; Commercial Counsellor, Tokyo, 1973-79, retd. Japanese Order of the Sacred Treasure, 3rd cl., 1975. *Recreations:* cricket, travel, gardening, reading. *Address:* Hill Brow, 34 Quarry Hill Road, Borough Green, Sevenoaks, Kent. *T:* Borough Green 882547. *Clubs:* Civil Service; Hong Kong (Hong Kong); Foreign Correspondents' (Tokyo); Yokohama Country and Athletic.

THORNE, Prof. Christopher Guy, DLitt; FBA 1982; FRHistS; Professor of International Relations, University of Sussex, since 1977; *b* 17 May 1934; *s* of Reginald Harry Thorne and late Alice Thorne (*née* Pickard); *m* 1958, Beryl Lloyd Jones; two *d. Educ:* King Edward VI Royal Grammar Sch., Guildford; St Edmund Hall, Oxford. BA 1958; MA 1962; DLitt 1980. Nat. Service, RN, 1953-55. Teacher, St Paul's Sch., London, 1958-61; Sen. Hist. Master, Charterhouse, 1961-66; Head of Further Educn, BBC Radio, 1966-68; Lectr in Internat. Relations, 1968, Reader, 1972, Univ. of Sussex. Resident Fellow, Netherlands Inst. for Advanced Study, 1979-80. Lees-Knowles Lectr, Cambridge, 1977; Raleigh Lectr, British Acad., 1980. *Publications:* Ideology and Power, 1965; Chartism, 1966; The Approach of War 1938-39, 1967; The Limits of Foreign Policy: the West, the League, and the Far Eastern Crisis of 1931-33, 1972; Allies of a Kind: the United States, Britain, and the war against Japan 1941-1945, 1978 (Bancroft Prize, 1979); Racial Aspects of the Far Eastern War of 1941-45, 1982. *Recreations:* making music (lieder) and country wines. *Address:* School of European Studies, University of Sussex, Brighton, Sussex BN1 9QN. *T:* Brighton 606755.

THORNE, Maj.-Gen. David Calthrop, CBE 1979 (OBE 1975); Commander, British Forces Falkland Islands, since July 1982; *b* 13 Dec. 1933; *s* of Richard Everard Thorne and Audrey Ursula (*née* Bone); *m* 1962, Susan Anne Goldsmith; one *s* two *d. Educ:* St Edward's Sch., Oxford; RMA, Sandhurst. Staff Coll., Camberley, 1963; jssc 1967; Defence Intelligence Staff, MoD, 1968-70; Instructor, RAF Staff Coll., 1970-72; CO 1 Royal Anglian, 1972-74; Col, General Staff, MoD, 1975-77; Comdr, 3rd Inf. Bde, 1978-79; RCDS 1980; VQMG, 1981-82. Dep. Col, Royal Anglian Regt, 1981-. *Recreations:* cricket, squash, butterfly collecting. *Address:* c/o Barclays Bank Ltd, 52 Abbeygate Street, Bury St Edmunds, Suffolk IP33 1LL. *Clubs:* Army and Navy, MCC, Jesters'; I Zingari; Free Foresters.

THORNE, Rear-Adm. (retd) Edward Courtney, CB 1975; CBE 1971; FNZIM; Chairman, New Zealand Fire Service Commission, since 1977; Chief of Naval Staff, New Zealand, 1972-75; *b* 29 Oct. 1923; *s* of Ernest Alexander Thorne and Ethel Violet Thorne; *m* 1949, Fay Bradburn (*née* Kerr); three *s. Educ:* Nelson Coll., NZ. Chm., Nat. Council, United World Colls, 1982-; Mem., Nat. Council, Duke of Edinburgh Award Scheme; Pres., NZ Navy League Council, 1982-. FNZIM 1980. *Recreations:* golf, gardening. *Address:* 75 Hatton Street, Karori, Wellington 5, New Zealand. *Club:* Wellington (New Zealand).

THORNE, Neil Gordon, OBE 1980; TD 1969; MP (C) Redbridge, Ilford South, since 1979; *b* 8 Aug. 1932; *s* of late Henry Frederick Thorne and Ivy Gladys Thorne. *Educ:* City of London Sch.; London Univ. BSc. FRICS. Asst Adjt, 58 Med. Regt, RA, BAOR, 1957-59. Sen. Partner, Hull & Co., Chartered Surveyors, 1962-76. Councillor, London Borough of Redbridge, 1965-68, Alderman, 1975-78; Mem., GLC and Chm., Central Area Bd, 1967-73. Mem., TA, 1952-82; CO, London Univ. OTC, 1976-80. Fellow, Industry and Parliament Trust, 1980. Silver Jubilee Medal, 1977. *Publication:* Pedestrianised Streets: a study of Europe and America, 1973. *Address:* House of Commons, SW1A 0AA. *T:* 01-219 4123. *Clubs:* Carlton, Ilford Conservative.

THORNE, Sir Peter (Francis), KCVO 1981; CBE 1966; Serjeant at Arms, House of Commons, 1976-82; *b* 1914; *y s* of late Gen. Sir Andrew Thorne, KCB, CMG, DSO; *m* 1959, Lady Anne Pery, MA, DPhil, Senior Lecturer, Imperial College of Science and Technology, *d* of 5th Earl of Limerick, GBE, CH, KCB, DSO, TD; one *s* three *d. Educ:* Eton; Trinity Coll., Oxford. Served War of 1939-45: with 3rd Bn Grenadier Guards (wounded), 1939-41; HQ 2nd Div., 1941-42; Staff College, Quetta, 1942; on staff of India Command and HQ, SACSEA, 1943-45; demobilised with rank of Hon. Lieut-Col, 1946. With Imperial Chemical Industries Ltd, 1946-48. Assistant

Serjeant at Arms, House of Commons, 1948-57, Dep. Serjeant at Arms, 1957-76. *Address:* Chiddinglye Farmhouse, West Hoathly, East Grinstead, West Sussex RH19 4QS. *T:* East Grinstead 810338. *Clubs:* Cavalry and Guards; Royal Yacht Squadron.

THORNE, Robin Horton John, CMG 1966; OBE 1963; HM Overseas Service, retired; *b* 13 July 1917; *s* of late Sir John Anderson Thorne; *m* 1946, Joan Helen Wadman; one *s. Educ:* Dragon Sch., Oxford; Rugby (open scholar); Exeter College, Oxford (open scholar). War Service, Devonshire Regiment and King's African Rifles, 1939-46. Colonial Administrative Service (now HM Overseas Civil Service), 1946-67; Tanganyika Administration, 1946-58; Aden, 1958-67; Asst Chief Sec. (Colony), MLC and Mem. of Governor's Exec. Coun., 1959-63; Ministerial Sec. to Chief Minister, 1963-65; Assistant High Commissioner, 1966-67. With Vice-Chancellors' Cttee, 1967-77; part-time admin. work, Univ. of Sussex, 1978-81. Trustee of Aden Port Trust, 1959-66; Chm., Staines Trust, 1979-. *Recreations:* various. *Address:* The Old Vicarage, Old Heathfield, East Sussex. *T:* Heathfield 3160. *Club:* Royal Commonwealth Society.

THORNE, Stanley George; MP (Lab) Preston South since Feb. 1974; *b* 22 July 1918; *s* of postman and dressmaker; *m* Catherine Mary Rand; two *s* three *d. Educ:* Ruskin Coll., Oxford; Univ. of Liverpool. Dip. Social Studies Oxon 1968; BA Hons Liverpool 1970. 30 yrs in industry and commerce: coal-miner, semi-skilled fitter, chartered accountant's clerk, rly signalman, office manager, auditor, commercial manager, etc; lectr in govt and industrial sociology. *Recreations:* chess, bridge, golf. *Address:* 26 Station Road, Gateacre, Liverpool L25 3PZ. *T:* (office) 01-219 4183.

THORNELY, Gervase Michael Cobham; Headmaster of Sedbergh School, 1954-75; *b* 21 Oct. 1918; *er s* of late Major J. E. B. Thornely, OBE, and late Hon. Mrs M. H. Thornely; *m* 1954, Jennifer Margery, *d* of Sir Hilary Scott, *qv*, Knowle House, Addington, Surrey; two *s* two *d. Educ:* Rugby Sch.; Trinity Hall, Cambridge. Organ Scholar; 2nd Cl. Hons, Modern and Mediæval Languages Tripos, BA, 1940; MA, 1944. FRSA 1968. Assistant Master, Sedbergh School, 1940. *Recreations:* music, fly-fishing. *Address:* High Stangerthwaite, Killington, Cumbria. *T:* Sedbergh 20444. *Club:* East India, Devonshire, Sports and Public Schools.

THORNEYCROFT, family name of **Baron Thorneycroft.**

THORNEYCROFT, Baron *cr* 1967 (Life Peer), of Dunston; **(George Edward) Peter Thorneycroft,** CH 1980; PC 1951; Barrister-at-law; late RA; Chairman of the Conservative Party, 1975-81; Chairman: Pirelli General Cable Works Ltd; Pirelli Ltd; President, Trusthouse Forte Ltd, since 1982 (Chairman, 1969-81); Director, Securicor; *b* 26 July 1909; *s* of late Major George Edward Mervyn Thorneycroft, DSO, and Dorothy Hope, *d* of Sir W. Franklyn, KCB; *m* 1st, 1938, Sheila Wells Page (who obtained a divorce, 1949); one *s*; 2nd, 1949, Countess Carla Roberti; one *d. Educ:* Eton; Roy. Mil. Acad., Woolwich. Commissioned in Royal Artillery, 1930; resigned Commission, 1933; called to Bar, Inner Temple, 1935; practised Birmingham (Oxford Circuit); MP (C) Stafford, 1938-45, Monmouth, 1945-66. Parliamentary Secretary, Ministry of War Transport, 1945. President of the Board of Trade, October 1951-January 1957; Chancellor of the Exchequer, Jan. 1957-Jan. 1958, resigned; Minister of Aviation, July 1960-July 1962; Minister of Defence, 1962-64; Secretary of State for Defence, Apr.-Oct. 1964. Chairman: SITPRO, 1968-75; BOTB, 1972-75; Pye of Cambridge Ltd, 1967-79; British Reserve Insurance Co. Ltd, 1980-; Gil, Carvajal & Partners Ltd, 1981-; Cinzano UK Ltd, 1982-; Dir, Riunione Adriatica di Sicurta, 1981-. Exhibitions of paintings, Trafford Gallery, 1961, 1970. Mem., Royal Soc. of British Artists, 1978. *Address:* House of Lords, SW1. *T:* 01-219 4093. *Club:* Army and Navy.

THORNHILL, Lt-Col Edmund Basil, MC 1918; *b* 27 Feb. 1898; *e s* of late E. H. Thornhill, Manor House, Boxworth, Cambridge; *m* 1934, Diana Pearl Day, *d* of late Hubert G. D. Beales, Hambleden and Cambridge; two *s* one *d. Educ:* St Bees School; Royal Military Academy. 2nd Lieut Royal Artillery, 1916; served European War, 1914-18, France and Belgium (wounded, MC); served War of 1939-45, France, Western Desert (Eighth Army) and Italy (despatches); psc 1934; Lt-Col 1945; retd 1948. Chm., Cambs and I of Ely TA & AFA, 1957-62. DL Cambs and Isle of Ely, 1956, Vice-Lieut, 1965-75. *Address:* Manor House, Boxworth, Cambridge. *T:* Elsworth 209. *Club:* Army and Navy.

THORNLEY, Sir Colin (Hardwick), KCMG 1957 (CMG 1953); CVO 1954; *b* 1907; *s* of late Dr and Mrs J. H. Thornley; *m* 1940, Muriel Betty Hobson; one *s* two *d. Educ:* Bramcote School, Scarborough; Uppingham; Brasenose College, Oxford. MA (hons jurisp.). Colonial Administrative Service, The Tanganyika Territory, 1930-39, seconded to Colonial Office, 1939-45; Principal Private Secretary to Secretary of State for the Colonies, 1941-45; Admin. Secretary, Kenya, 1945-47; Dep. Chief Secretary, Kenya, 1947-52; Chief Secretary, Govt of Protectorate of Uganda, 1952-55; Governor and Commander-in-Chief, British Honduras, 1955-61; retired, 1962. Dir-Gen., Save the Children Fund, 1965-74 (Dep. Dir, 1963-65). Mem., Regional Boundaries Commn, Kenya, 1962; Trustee, Imp. War Museum, 1968-77. *Recreations:* lawn tennis, golf, cricket. *Address:* Spinaway Cottage, Church Lane, Slindon, near Arundel, West Sussex. *T:* Slindon 308. *Clubs:* East India, Devonshire, Sports and Public Schools, Royal Commonwealth Society.

THORNTON, Dr (Clara) Grace, CBE 1964 (OBE 1959); MVO 1957; *b* 27 June 1913; *d* of late Arthur Augustus Thornton and Clara Maud Hines; unmarried. *Educ:* Kettering High School; Newnham Coll., Cambridge (MA, PhD; Hon. Fellow, 1982). Research: Iceland, Cambridge, 1935-39. Min. of Information, 1940-45. Press Attaché, Copenhagen, 1945-48; Vice-Consul, Reykjavik, 1948-51 (Chargé d'Affaires during 1949 and 1950); Foreign Office, 1951-54; 1st Sec. and Consul, Copenhagen, 1954-60; 1st Sec. and Information Officer, Brussels, 1960-62; 1st Sec. and Consul, Djakarta, 1962-64 (Consul-General, 1963-64); Consul-General, Lisbon, 1965-70; Head of Consular Dept, FCO, 1970-73; Sec., Women's Nat. Commn, Cabinet Office, 1973-78. Alternate UK Deleg., UN Status of Women Commn, 1978. Associate Fellow, Newnham Coll., Cambridge, 1972-81. President: London Assoc. of University Women, 1974-78; Associates of Newnham Coll., 1975-78; Vice-Pres., Newnham Roll, 1980-. FRSA 1969. Danish Freedom Medal, 1945; Order of Dannebrog, 1957. *Publications:* (trans. and ed) A Visit to Portugal, by Hans Christian Andersen, 1972; (trans. and ed) A Visit to Spain, by Hans Christian Andersen, 1975; Conversation Piece (University Women's Club), 1979; Notes on No 2 Audley Square, 1980; (ed) Take Your Hare When it is Cased, 1980 (recipes). *Recreations:* music, embroidery, Scandinavica, cats. *Address:* 17 Onslow Court, Drayton Gardens, SW10. *T:* 01-373 2965. *Club:* University Women's (Chm. 1976-79).

THORNTON, Clive Edward Ian, LLB (Lond); FInstLEx, FCBSI; Chief General Manager, since 1979, Director, since 1980, Abbey National Building Society; *b* 12 Dec. 1929; *s* of Albert and Margaret Thornton; *m* 1956, Maureen Carmine (*née* Crane); one *s* one *d*. *Educ:* St Anthony's Sch., Newcastle upon Tyne; Coll. of Commerce, Newcastle upon Tyne; College of Law, London; LLB London. Solicitor. FInstLEx 1958; FCBSI 1970. Associate, Pensions Management Inst. Articled to Kenneth Hudson, solicitor, London, 1959; admitted solicitor of Supreme Court, 1963. Asst Solicitor, Nationwide Building Soc., 1963; Solicitor, Cassel Arenz Ltd, Merchant Bankers, 1964-67; Chief Solicitor, Abbey National Bldg Soc., 1967, Dep. Chief Gen. Man., 1978. Chm., Metropolitan Assoc. of Building Socs, 1981-82. Member: Law Soc. (Chm., Commerce and Industry Gp, 1974); Council, Chartered Bldg Socs Inst., 1973-81; Council, Building Socs Assoc., 1979-; Bd, Housing Corp., 1980-. Freeman, City of London; Liveryman, Worshipful Co. of Bakers. *Publication:* Building Society Law, Cases and Materials, 1969 (2nd edn 1975). *Recreations:* antique collecting, music, reading. *Address:* The Old Rectory, Creeton, Grantham, Lincs. *Club:* City Livery.

THORNTON, Ernest, MBE 1951; JP; DL; *b* Burnley, Lancs, 18 May 1905; *s* of Charles Thornton and Margaret (*née* Whittaker); *m* 1930, Evelyn, *d* of Fred Ingham, Blacko, Nelson; one *s* (and one *s* decd). *Educ:* Walverden Council Sch., Nelson, Lancs. Cotton weaver, 1918-26; costing clerk, 1926-29. Rochdale Weavers and Winders' Assoc.; Asst Secretary, 1929-40, Secretary, 1940-70. President, Amalgamated Weavers' Assoc., 1960-65. Secretary, United Textile Factory Workers' Assoc., 1943-53. Member: Lord President's Advisory Council for Scientific and Industrial Research, 1943-48; Council of British Cotton Industry Research Assoc., 1948-53. MP (Lab) Farnworth, 1952-70; Joint Parliamentary Secretary, Min. of Labour, 1964-66. Member: UK Trade Mission to China, 1946; Anglo-American Cotton Textile Mission to Japan, 1950; Cotton Board's Mission to India, 1950. Mayor of County Borough of Rochdale, 1942-43. Comp. TI 1966. JP 1944, DL Manchester Metropolitan County (formerly Lancaster), 1970. *Address:* 33 Lynnwood Drive, Rochdale, Lancs. *T:* Rochdale 31954.

THORNTON, George Edwin, CMG 1948; MBE 1932; *b* 1899; *m* 1926, Charlotte, *d* of Edward Brian Coulson. Served European War 1914-18, in E Africa, 1916-17; Colonial Service, Northern Rhodesia, 1918; Financial Secretary, Northern Rhodesia, 1945-51. *Address:* 79 Kew Drive, Highlands, Harare, Zimbabwe.

THORNTON, (George) Malcolm; MP (C) Liverpool, Garston, since 1979; *b* 3 April 1939; *s* of George Edmund and Ethel Thornton; *m* 1st, 1962; 2nd, 1972, Shirley Ann, (Sue) (*née* Banton); one step *s* one step *d*. *Educ:* Wallasey Grammar Sch.; Liverpool Nautical Coll. Liverpool Pilot Service, 1955-79 (Sen. 1st cl. Licence holder). Member: Wallasey County Borough Council, 1965-74 (Chm., Transport Cttee, 1968-69); Wirral Metropolitan Council, 1973-79 (Council Leader, 1974-77); Chairman: Merseyside Metropolitan Districts Liaison Cttee, 1975-77; Educn Cttee, AMA, 1978-79 (Mem., 1974-79); Council of Local Educn Authorities, 1978. Mem., Burnham (Primary and Secondary) Cttee, 1975-79. PPS to Sec. of State for Industry, 1981-. *Recreations:* fishing, sailing, squash, cooking. *Address:* House of Commons, SW1A 0AA. *T:* 01-219 4489. *Clubs:* Carlton, Europe House; Birkenhead Squash Raquets, Heswall Squash Raquets (Wirral).

THORNTON, Dr Grace; see Thornton, Dr C. G.

THORNTON, Jack Edward Clive, CB 1978; OBE 1964 (MBE 1945); *b* 22 Nov. 1915; *s* of late Stanley Henry Thornton and Elizabeth (*née* Baxter); *m* 1st, Margaret, JP, *d* of John David and Emily Copeland, Crewe, Cheshire; 2nd, Helen Ann Elizabeth, *d* of Henry Gerard and Valerie Meixner, Ravenshoe, N Qld, Australia. *Educ:* Solihull Sch.; Christ's Coll. Cambridge (Open Exhibnr 1936). Cert. Educn 1939; MA 1942. Served in RASC, 1939-46 (despatches, 1946); Lt-Col 1944. Teaching in UK, 1946-47; Asst, then Dep. Educn Officer, City of York, 1947-51; Asst Educn Officer, WR Yorks, 1951-54; Dep. Dir of Educn, Cumberland, 1954-62; Sec., Bureau for External Aid for Educn, Fed. Govt of Nigeria, 1962-64; Educn Consultant, IBRD,

1964-65; Adviser on Educn in W Africa and Controller Appts Div., British Council, 1965-68; Dep. Educn Adviser, 1968-70, Chief Educn Adviser and Under Sec., 1970-77, Ministry of Overseas Develt (now Overseas Develt Admin in FCO). Lectr, Dept of Educn in Developing Countries, Inst. of Educn, Univ. of London, 1978-79. Exec. Chm., Council for Educn in the Commonwealth; Chm., Council of Parents' Nat. Educational Union; Mem., Educational Panel, Independent Schs Tribunal. *Recreations:* books, mountains, music, railways, travel. *Address:* 131 Dalling Road, W6 0ET. *T:* 01-748 7692.

THORNTON, Lt-Gen. Sir Leonard (Whitmore), KCB 1967 (CB 1962); CBE 1957 (OBE 1944); Chairman, Alcoholic Liquor Advisory Council, since 1977; *b* Christchurch, 15 Oct. 1916; *s* of late Cuthbert John Thornton and Frances Caverhill Thornton; *m* 1942, Gladys Janet Sloman, Wellington; three *s*; *m* 1971, Ruth Leicester, Wellington. *Educ:* Christchurch Boys' High Sch.; Royal Military Coll., Duntroon, Australia. Commissioned in New Zealand Army, 1937. Served War of 1939-45 (despatches twice, OBE), Middle East and Italy in 2nd New Zealand Expeditionary Force; Commander, Royal Artillery, 2 New Zealand Division. Commander, Tokyo Sub-area, 1946; Deputy Chief of General Staff, 1949; idc 1952; Head, New Zealand Joint Service Liaison Staff, 1953 and 1954; QMG, New Zealand, 1955; AG, 1956-58; Chief, SEATO Planning Office, Thailand, 1958-59; Chief of General Staff, NZ, 1960-65; Chief of Defence Staff, NZ, 1965-71; Ambassador for New Zealand in S Vietnam and Khmer Republic, 1972-74. *Recreation:* fishing. *Address:* 67 Bedford Street, Wellington 5, New Zealand. *Club:* Wellington (Wellington).

THORNTON, Malcolm; see Thornton, G. M.

THORNTON, Michael James, CBE 1978; MC 1942; *b* 6 Dec. 1919; *s* of late Arthur Bruce Thornton and Dorothy Kidston Thornton (*née* Allsop); *m* 1949, Pauline Elizabeth Heppell; one *s* two *d*. *Educ:* Christ's Hospital; London Sch. of Economics (BSc(Econ)). Entered Bank of England, 1938; Deputy Chief Cashier, 1962-67; Chief of Economic Intelligence Dept, 1967-78. *Recreation:* sailing. *Address:* The Priory, St Mawes, Cornwall.

THORNTON, Sir Peter (Eustace), KCB 1974 (CB 1971); Director: Hill Samuel Group, Courtaulds, Rolls Royce, since 1977; Laird Group, since 1978; Superior Oil (UK), since 1980; Pro-Chancellor, Open University, since 1979; Permanent Secretary, Department of Trade, 1974-77; *b* 28 Aug. 1917; *s* of Douglas Oscar Thornton and Dorothy (*née* Shepherd); *m* 1946, Rosamond Hobart Myers, US Medal of Freedom, Sewanee, Tennessee; two *s* one *d*. *Educ:* Charterhouse; Gonville and Caius Coll., Cambridge. Served with RA, mainly in Middle East and Italy, 1940-46. Joined Board of Trade, 1946. Secretary, Company Law Cttee (Jenkins Cttee), 1959-62; Assistant Under-Secretary of State, Department of Economic Affairs, 1964-67; Under-Sec., 1967-70, Dep. Sec., 1970-72, Cabinet Office, with central co-ordinating role during British negotiations for membership of EEC; Dep. Sec., DTI, March-July 1972; Sec. (Aerospace and Shipping), DTI, 1972-74; Second Permanent Sec., Dept of Trade, 1974. Mem., Megaw Cttee of Inquiry into Civil Service Pay, 1981-82. Governor, Sutton's Hosp., Charterhouse, 1980-. *Address:* 22 East Street, Alresford, Hants SO24 9EE.

THORNTON, Peter Kai, FSA 1976; Keeper, Department of Furniture and Woodwork, Victoria and Albert Museum, London, since 1966; *b* 8 April 1925; *s* of Sir Gerard Thornton, FRS, and of Gerda, *d* of Kai Nørregaard, Copenhagen; *m* 1950, Mary Ann Rosamund, *d* of E. A. P. Helps, Cregane, Rosscarbery, Co. Cork; three *d*. *Educ:* Bryanston Sch.; De Havilland Aeronautical Technical Sch.; Trinity Hall, Cambridge. Served with Army, Intelligence Corps, Austria, 1945-48; Cambridge, 1948-50; Voluntary Asst Keeper, Fitzwilliam Museum, Cambridge, 1950-52; Joint Secretary, National Art-Collections Fund, London, 1952-54; entered Victoria and Albert Museum as Asst Keeper, Dept of Textiles, 1954; transf. to Dept of Woodwork, 1962. *Publications:* Baroque and Rococo Silks, 1965; Seventeenth Century Interior Decoration in England, France and Holland, 1978; (jtly) The Furnishing and Decoration of Ham House, 1981; contribs to several joint works including World Furniture, 1965; articles on textiles and furniture in Burlington Magazine, Gazette des Beaux Arts and other journals. *Address:* 15 Cheniston Gardens, W8. *T:* 01-937 8868; Carrigillihy, Union Hall, Co. Cork; Phillips Farm Cottage, Eaton Hastings, Faringdon, Oxon.

THORNTON, Richard Eustace, OBE 1980; DL, JP; *b* 10 Oct. 1922; *m* 1954, Gabrielle Elizabeth Sharpe; four *d*. *Educ:* Eton Coll.; Trinity Coll., Cambridge (MA). Member: Royal Commission on Environmental Pollution, 1977-; Governing Body, Charterhouse Sch. (Chm., 1981). Surrey: DL; High Sheriff 1978-79; JP. *Address:* Hampton, Seale, near Farnham, Surrey. *T:* Guildford 810208.

THORNTON, Robert John, CB 1980; Assistant Under Secretary of State and Director General of Supplies and Transport (Naval), Ministry of Defence, 1977-81; *b* 23 Dec. 1919; *s* of Herbert John Thornton and Ethel Mary Thornton (*née* Dunning); *m* 1944, Joan Elizabeth Roberts; three *s*. *Educ:* Queen Elizabeth Grammar School, Atherstone. MBIM 1970. Joined Naval Store Dept, Admiralty, as Asst Naval Store Officer, 1938; Singapore, 1941; Dep. Naval Store Officer, Colombo, 1942; Support Ship Hong Siang, 1943; Naval Store Officer, Admiralty, 1945; Gibraltar, 1951; Asst Dir of Stores, 1955; Superintending Naval Store Officer, Portsmouth, 1960; Dep. Dir of

Stores, 1964; Dir of Victualling, 1971; Dir of Supplies and Transport (General Stores and Victualling), 1971. *Recreations:* squash, fly fishing, gardening.

THORNTON, Robert Ribblesdale, CBE 1973; DL; solicitor; Deputy Chairman, Local Government Boundary Commission for England, since 1982 (Member, 1976-82); *b* 2 April 1913; *s* of Thomas Thornton and Florence Thornton (*née* Gatenby); *m* 1940, Ruth Eleonore Tuckson; one *s* one *d. Educ:* Leeds Grammar Sch.; St John's Coll., Cambridge (MA, LLB). Asst Solicitor, Leeds, 1938-40 and 1946-47. Served War, 1940-46. Asst Solicitor, Bristol, 1947-53; Dep. Town Clerk, Southampton, 1953-54; Town Clerk: Salford, 1954-66; Leicester, 1966-73; Chief Exec., Leicestershire CC, 1973-76. Pres., Soc. of Town Clerks, 1971. Treasurer, Leicester Univ., 1980-. DL Leicestershire 1974. French Croix de Guerre, 1946. *Recreations:* music, sport. *Address:* Brackenfell, 6 Mill Road, Woodhouse Eaves, Leics LE12 8RD. *T:* Woodhouse Eaves 890646. *Club:* National Liberal.

THORNTON-DUESBERY, Rev. Canon Julian Percy, MA; Canon Emeritus of Liverpool Cathedral (Canon Theologian, 1968-77); *b* 7 Sept. 1902; *s* of late Rt Rev. Charles Leonard Thornton-Duesbery (formerly Bishop of Sodor and Man) and late Ethel Nixon Baumgartner. *Educ:* Forest Sch., Snaresbrook; Rossall Sch.; Balliol Coll., Oxford (Domus Exhbn); Wycliffe Hall, Oxford. Goldsmiths' Exhibition, 1922; *prox acc* Craven Scholarship, 1922; 1st Class Hon. Moderations (Classics), 1923; 1st Class Lit Hum 1925; 1st Class Theology, 1926; Junior Canon Hall Greek Testament Prize, 1926; Senior Denyer and Johnson Scholarship, 1928; Deacon, 1926; Priest, 1927; Chaplain of Wycliffe Hall, Oxford, 1926-27; Vice-Principal, 1927-33; Chaplain, Fellow, and Librarian of Corpus Christi Coll., Oxford, 1928-33; Headmaster of St George's Sch., Jerusalem, 1933-40; Master of St Peter's Hall, 1940-45; Rector of St Peter-le-Bailey, Oxford, 1940-45, 1955-61; Acting Principal, Wycliffe Hall, 1943-44; Principal of Wycliffe Hall, Oxford, 1944-55; Master, St Peter's Coll. (formerly St Peter's Hall), Oxford, 1955-68, Hon. Fellow, 1968. Commissary to Bishop in Jerusalem, 1943-63; Member of Council: St Lawrence Coll., Ramsgate, 1941-79; Headington Sch., 1943-74; Forest Sch., Snaresbrook, 1958-68; St Stephen's Coll., Broadstairs, 1970-77. Examining Chaplain to: Bishop of Blackburn, 1927-33; Bishop in Jerusalem, 1933-40; Bishop of Worcester, 1941-70; Bishop of Oxford, 1955-68; Bishop of Sodor and Man, 1967-. Select Preacher, University of Oxford, 1943-45. *Publication:* The Open Secret of MRA, 1964. *Address:* College of St Barnabas, Lingfield, Surrey RH7 6NJ. *T:* Dormans Park 508.

THORNYCROFT, John Ward, CBE 1957; CEng; FIMechE; beef farmer; Hon. President, John I. Thornycroft & Co. Ltd, since 1966 (Chairman, 1960-66; Managing Director, 1942-66); Director, Southampton, Isle of Wight and South of England Royal Mail Steam Packet Co. Ltd, 1960-77, retired; *b* 14 Oct. 1899; *s* of late Sir John E. Thornycroft; *m* 1930, Esther Katherine, *d* of J. E. Pritchard; one *s* one *d. Educ:* Royal Naval Colleges, Osborne, Dartmouth and Keyham; Trinity Coll., Cambridge. Served War, 1914-18, HMS Canada, HMS Opal, HM Submarine G10, HMS Spenser (1914-15 War Service Star). Hon. Vice-Pres., RINA; FRSA. *Recreations:* golf, sailing and gardening. *Address:* Steyne House, Bembridge, Isle of Wight. *T:* Bembridge 2502. *Clubs:* Naval and Military; Bembridge Sailing (IOW).
See also Baron Inverforth.

THOROGOOD, Alfreda, (Mrs D. R. Wall), ARAD (PDTC); teacher; Principal Dancer, Royal Ballet Company, since 1968; *b* 17 Aug. 1942; *d* of Alfreda and Edward Thorogood; *m* 1967, David Wall, *qv*; one *s* one *d. Educ:* Lady Eden's Sch.; Royal Ballet Sch. Joined Royal Ballet Co., Feb. 1960; Soloist, Aug. 1965. *Recreations:* listening to music, cooking, interior design, art, painting. *Address:* 70 Elmbourne Road, Tooting, SW17. *T:* 01-672 0178; 2 Alma Cottages, Cheriton, Hants. *T:* Bramdean 492.

THOROGOOD, Rev. Bernard George; General Secretary, United Reformed Church, since 1980; *b* 21 July 1927; *s* of Frederick and Winifred Thorogood; *m* 1952, Jannett Lindsay Paton (*née* Cameron); two *s. Educ:* Glasgow Univ. (MA); Scottish Congregational College. Ordained in Congregational church, 1952; missionary appointment under London Missionary Society in South Pacific Islands, 1953-70; Gen. Sec., Council for World Mission, 1971-80. *Publications:* Not Quite Paradise, 1960; Guide to the Book of Amos, 1971. *Recreation:* sketching. *Address:* Church House, 86 Tavistock Place, WC1H 9RT. *T:* 01-837 7661.

THOROGOOD, Kenneth Alfred Charles; Chairman, Tozer Kemsley & Millbourn (Holdings) plc, international finance and investment group, since 1972; *b* 1924; *s* of Albert Jesse and Alice Lucy Thorogood; *m* 1st, 1947, José Patricia Smith; two *d* ; 2nd, 1979, Mrs Gaye Lambourne. *Educ:* Highbury County Grammar School. Pres., Deepsoyal Services Ltd; Director: Alexanders Discount Co. Ltd; Royal Insurance Co. Ltd; Welbeck Finance Ltd, 1980-; Abelson Plant (Holdings) Ltd; Spicer-Firgos Ltd. Chairman, Brit. Export Houses Assoc., 1968-70; Mem., Cttee of Invisibles, 1968-70. *Recreations:* aviation, music. *Address:* 71 Chester Square, SW1W 9DU. *Clubs:* Travellers', City of London, Royal Air Force; Wanderers (Johannesburg).

THOROLD, Captain Sir Anthony (Henry), 15th Bt, *cr* 1642; OBE 1942; DSC 1942, and Bar 1945; DL; JP; RN Retired; *b* 7 Sept. 1903; *s* of Sir James (Ernest) Thorold, 14th Bt; *S* father, 1965; *m* 1939, Jocelyn Elaine Laura, *er d* of late Sir Clifford Heathcote-Smith, KBE, CMG; one *s* two *d. Educ:* Royal Naval Colleges Osborne and Dartmouth. Entered RN 1917; qualified as Navigating Officer, 1928; *psc* 1935; Commander, 1940; served in

Mediterranean and Home Fleets, 1939-40; Staff Officer Operations to Flag Officer Commanding Force 'H', 1941-43; in command of Escort Groups in Western Approaches Comd, 1944-45; Captain, 1946; Naval Assistant Secretary in Cabinet Office and Ministry of Defence, 1945-48; Sen. Officer, Fishery Protection Flotilla, 1949-50; Captain of HMS Dryad (Navigation and Direction Sch.), 1951-52; Commodore in Charge, Hong Kong, 1953-55; ADC to the Queen, 1955-56; retired, 1956. DL Lincs, 1959; JP Lincolnshire (Parts of Kesteven), 1961; High Sheriff of Lincolnshire, 1968. Chairman: Grantham Hospital Management Cttee, 1963-74; Lincoln Diocesan Trust and Board of Finance, 1966-71; Community Council of Lincs, 1974-81; CC Kesteven, 1958-74; Leader, Lincs County Council, 1973-81. *Recreation:* shooting. *Heir: s* (Anthony) Oliver Thorold [*b* 15 April 1945; *m* 1977, Genevra M., *y d* of John Richardson, Midlothian; one *s*]. *Address:* Syston Old Hall, Grantham, Lincs. *T:* Honington 270. *Club:* Army and Navy.

THORPE, Bernard; Founder and Senior Partner, Bernard Thorpe & Partners, 1922-82; Land Agent, Surveyor, Farmer; *b* 27 June 1895; *m* 1st, 1916, Hilda Mary (*d* 1971), *d* of Edwin Wilkinson, Coventry; one *s* one *d* (and one *s* killed as Pilot Officer Royal Air Force); 2nd, 1972, Mary Philomena, *d* of George Cregan, Limerick, Eire. *Educ:* private tutor; Nottingham Univ. Member Godstone (Surrey) RDC and of its Board of Guardians, 1926-36; Past President, (1939) and Past Chairman, Surrey and Sussex Br. Incorp. Society of Auctioneers and Landed Property Agents; sometime Member Council, Home Grown Timber Marketing Assoc.; Director (Tile Section), Redland Holdings Ltd; Chairman, Park Investments Ltd, 1958-63; Chairman, Assoc. of Land and Property Owners, 1962-64. Past Master, Worshipful Company of Gold and Silver Wyre Drawers, 1966 (Member 1938, and Past Warden); Member Court of Assistants, Worshipful Company of Paviors 1938 (past Warden; Master, 1975); Freeman, City of London. Freemason. *Recreations:* hunting and shooting; formerly Rugby football. *Address:* Malin House, The Close, Aldwick Bay, Bognor Regis, Sussex. *T:* Pagham 604. *Club:* City Livery.

THORPE, Rt. Hon. (John) Jeremy, PC 1967; Chairman, Political Committee, United Nations Association, since 1977 (Chairman of Executive, 1976-80); *b* 29 April 1929; *s* of late J. H. Thorpe, OBE, KC, MP (C) Rusholme, and Ursula, *d* of late Sir John Norton-Griffiths, Bt, KCB, DSO, sometime MP (C); *m* 1st, 1968, Caroline (*d* 1970), *d* of Warwick Allpass, Kingswood, Surrey; one *s* ; 2nd, 1973, Marion, *d* of late Erwin Stein. *Educ:* Rectory Sch., Connecticut, USA; Eton Coll.; Trinity Coll., Oxford. Hon. Fellow, 1972. President, Oxford Union Society, Hilary, 1951; Barrister, Inner Temple, 1954. Member Devon Sessions. Contested (L) N Devon, 1955; MP (L) Devon N, 1959-79. Hon. Treasurer, Liberal Party Organisation, 1965-67; Leader, Liberal Party, 1967-76. A Vice-Pres., Anti-Apartheid Movement, 1969-. FRSA. Hon. LLD Exeter, 1974. *Publications:* (jtly) To all who are interested in Democracy, 1951; (jtly) Europe: the case for going in, 1971; contrib. to newspapers and periodicals. *Recreations:* music; collecting Chinese ceramics. *Address:* 2 Orme Square, W2. *Club:* National Liberal.

THORPE, Mathew Alexander, QC 1980; a Recorder of the Crown Court, since 1982; *b* 1938; *s* of late Michael Alexander Thorpe and of Dorothea Margaret Lambert; *m* 1966, Lavinia Hermione Buxton; three *s. Educ:* Stowe; Balliol Coll., Oxford. Called to the Bar, Inner Temple, 1961. *Address:* Seend Green House, Melksham, Wilts. *T:* Seend 493.

THORPE, Sir Ronald Laurence G.; *see* Gardner-Thorpe.

THORPE, Prof. William Homan, FRS 1951; MA, ScD (Cantab); Fellow since 1932, President, 1969-72; Jesus College, Cambridge; Professor of Animal Ethology, Cambridge University, 1966-69, now Emeritus; Joint Editor of "Behaviour: an International Journal of Comparative Ethology"; Chairman: Arthur Stanley Eddington Memorial Trust, 1946-75; International Council for Bird Preservation (British Section), since 1965; *b* 1 April 1902; *o s* of Francis Homan and Mary Amelia Thorpe (*née* Slade), Hastings and Weston-super-Mare; *m* 1936, Winifred Mary (*d* 1978), *o d* of Preb. G. H. Vincent; one *d. Educ:* Mill Hill Sch.; Jesus Coll., Cambridge. Research Fellow of International Education Board (Rockefeller Foundation) at University of California, 1927-29; Research Entomologist at Farnham Royal Parasite Laboratory of Imperial Bureau of Entomology, 1929-32; Tutor Jesus Coll., Cambridge, 1932-45; Lecturer in Entomology in the University, 1932-59; Leverhulme Research Fellow in East Africa, 1939; Senior Tutor, Jesus Coll., Cambridge, 1945-47. President, Association for Study of Animal Behaviour, 1948-52; President, Society British Entomology, 1951-53; Prather Lecturer in Biology, Harvard Univ., 1951-52; President of British Ornithologists Union, 1955-60; President Sect. D (Zoology) British Association (Sheffield), 1956; Visiting Prof., University of California, 1958; Eddington Lecturer, 1960; Riddell Lecturer, Durham Univ., 1961; Fremantle Lecturer, Balliol Coll., Oxford, 1962-63; Gifford Lectr, St Andrews Univ., 1969-71. Leverhulme Emeritus Fellowship, 1971-72. Godman-Salvin Gold Medal, British Ornithologists' Union, 1968; Frink Medal, Zool Soc. of London, 1980; International Prize, Fondation Fyssen, Paris, 1981. *Publications:* Learning and Instinct in Animals, 1956; (ed with O. L. Zangwill) Current Problems in Animal Behaviour, 1961; Bird Song: The Biology of Vocal Communication and Expression in Birds, 1961; Biology and the Nature of Man, 1962; Science, Man and Morals, 1965; Quakers and Humanists, 1968; (ed with A. M. Pantin) The Relations Between the Sciences, by late C. F. A. Pantin, 1968; Duetting and Antiphonal Song in Birds, 1972; Animal Nature and Human Nature, 1974; Purpose in a World of Chance, 1978; The Origins and Rise of Ethology,

1979; articles in Encyclopædia Britannica, 15th edn, 1974; numerous papers on Entomology, Ornithology, Comparative Physiology and Animal Behaviour (Ethology): in Journal Society Exp. Biology, Biol. Reviews, Ibis, Behaviour, etc. *Recreations:* music, swimming. *Address:* Jesus College, Cambridge. *T:* 68611.

THORPE DAVIE, Cedric; *see* Davie, C. T.

THOULESS, Prof. David James, FRS 1979; Professor of Physics, University of Washington, since 1980; *b* 21 Sept. 1934; *s* of Robert Henry Thouless, *qv*; *m* 1958, Margaret Elizabeth Scrase; twos *one d. Educ:* Winchester Coll.; Trinity Hall, Cambridge (BA); Cornell Univ. (PhD). Physicist, Lawrence Radiation Laboratory, Berkeley, Calif, 1958–59; ICI Research Fellow, Birmingham Univ., 1959–61; Lecturer, Cambridge Univ., and Fellow of Churchill Coll., 1961–65; Prof. of Mathematical Physics, Birmingham Univ., 1965–78; Prof. of Applied Science, Yale Univ., 1979–80. *Publication:* Quantum Mechanics of Many-Body Systems, 1961, 2nd edn 1972. *Address:* Department of Physics, FM-15, University of Washington, Seattle, Washington 98195, USA. *T:* (206) 545-2393.

THOULESS, Robert Henry; Reader Emeritus in the University of Cambridge since 1961; Fellow of Corpus Christi College, Cambridge, since 1945; *b* 15 July 1894; *s* of Henry James Thouless; *m* 1924, Priscilla Gorton; one *s* one *d. Educ:* City of Norwich Sch.; Corpus Christi Coll., Cambridge. BA (Nat. Sci.), 1915. Served European War, 2nd Lieut, RE, British Salonika Force, 1917. PhD (Cambridge) 1922; Lecturer in Psychology, Manchester Univ., 1921, Glasgow Univ., 1926, Cambridge Univ., 1938; Reader in Educational Psychology, 1945–61; Consultant NFER, 1964. President, Section J British Association, 1937; Riddell Memorial Lecturer, 1940; President, Society for Psychical Research, 1942; President, British Psychological Society, 1949 (Hon. Fellow 1962); Hulsean Lecturer, 1951. Lecturing in Australia, 1962, 1966; Eddington Memorial Lecturer, 1963, T. B. Davie Memorial Lecturer (Cape Town), 1964. ScD (Cambridge), 1953. *Publications:* An Introduction to the Psychology of Religion, 1923 (rev. edn 1971); The Lady Julian, 1924; Social Psychology, 1925; The Control of the Mind, 1927; Straight and Crooked Thinking, 1930, rev. edn, 1974; General and Social Psychology, 1937, 1951 and 1957; Straight Thinking in War Time, 1942; Authority and Freedom, 1954; Experimental Psychical Research, 1963; Map of Educational Research, 1969; Missing the Message, 1971; From Anecdote to Experiment in Psychical Research, 1972; Articles in British Journal of Psychology, Proc. of Society of Psychical Research, Journal of Parapsychology, etc. *Recreations:* chess, painting. *Address:* 2 Leys Road, Cambridge.

See also D. J. Thouless.

THOURON, Sir John (Rupert Hunt), KBE 1976 (CBE 1967); *b* 10 May 1908; *m* 1st, 1930, Lorna Ellett (marr. diss. 1939); one *s*; 2nd, 1953, Esther duPont. *Educ:* Sherborne School, Dorset. Served War of 1939–45; Major, Black Watch. With Lady Thouron, Founder of the Thouron University of Pennsylvania Fund for British-American Student Exchange, 1960. *Recreations:* shooting, fishing, golf, gardening. *Address:* Glencoe Farm, Unionville, Chester County, Pa 19375, USA. *T:* (215) 384-5542. *Clubs:* White's; Brook (NY); Sunningdale Golf; Royal St George Golf; Wilmington, Wilmington Country, Vicmead (all Delaware); Pine Valley, British Officers Club of Philadelphia (Pennsylvania); Seminole Golf (Florida).

THOYTS, Robert Francis Newman; solicitor in private practice; *b* 13 March 1913; *o s* of late Lt-Comdr Robert Elmhirst Thoyts, RN, and late Kathleen Olive Thoyts (*née* Hobbs); *m* 1938, Joyce Eliza Gillingham, *er d* of late Rev. William Samuel Probert and late Evangeline Eliza Probert; one *s* four *d. Educ:* Bradfield Coll. Admitted Solicitor, 1936. Entered Solicitor's Dept, Min. of Labour, 1936. Served War, RAF, 1941–45; Flt Lieut. Transf. to Min. of Nat. Insurance, 1945; Asst Solicitor, Min. of Pensions and Nat. Insurance, 1962; Principal Asst Solicitor, DHSS, 1971–78. Civil Service Legal Soc.: Gen. Sec. 1945–50, Vice-Chm. 1963–65, Chm. 1965–67. Mem. Salaried Solicitors' Cttee of Law Soc., 1948–78. Hon. Gen. Sec., River Thames Soc., 1978–83. *Recreations:* sailing (Civil Service Rep. Sailing Badge, 1966); amenity interests. *Address:* 37 Queen's Drive, Thames Ditton, Surrey KT7 0TJ. *T:* 01-398 0469. *Clubs:* Law Society; Civil Service Sailing Assoc. (Hon. Life Mem., Chm., 1959–74; Rear-Cdre, 1977–80); River Thames Soc. (Vice-Chm. 1971); Littleton Sailing (Vice-Cdre, 1959–61, Cdre, 1961–65; Hon. Life Mem.); Frostbite Yacht Club of America (Hon. Cdre); Island Sailing, etc.

THRELFALL, Richard Ian, QC 1965; *b* 14 Jan. 1920; *s* of William Bernhard and Evelyn Alice Threlfall; *m* 1948, Annette, *d* of George C. H. Matthey; two *s* three *d* (and one *s* decd). *Educ:* Oundle; Gonville and Caius Coll., Cambridge. War service, 1940–45 (despatches twice); Indian Armoured Corps (Probyn's Horse) and Staff appointments. Barrister, Lincoln's Inn, 1947, Bencher 1973. FSA, 1949. Member: Court of Assistants, Worshipful Co. of Goldsmiths (Prime Warden, 1978–79); British Hallmarking Council; East Surrey HA. *Address:* Pebble Hill House, Limpsfield, Surrey. *T:* Oxted 2452.

THRING, Rear-Adm. George Arthur, CB 1958; DSO 1940 and Bar 1952; DL; *b* 13 Sept. 1903; *s* of late Sir Arthur Thring, KCB; *m* 1929, Betty Mary, *er d* of Colonel Stewart William Ward Blacker, DSO; two *s* two *d. Educ:* Royal Naval Colleges, Osborne and Dartmouth. Commander, 1941; Captain,

1946; Rear-Admiral, 1956; retired, 1958. Commanded: HMS Deptford, 1940–41; 42nd and 20th Escort Groups, Atlantic, 1943–45; HMS Ceylon, 1951–52; Flag Officer, Malayan Area, 1956–58. Officer, Legion of Merit (USA), 1945. DL Somerset, 1968. *Recreations:* golf, shooting and fishing. *Address:* Alford House, Castle Cary, Somerset. *T:* Wheathill 329.

THRING, Prof. Meredith Wooldridge; Professor of Mechanical Engineering, Queen Mary College, London University, 1964–81; *b* 17 Dec. 1915; *s* of Captain W. H. C. S. Thring, CBE, RN, and Dorothy (*née* Wooldridge); *m* 1940, Alice Margaret Hooley; two *s* one *d. Educ:* Malvern Coll., Worcs; Trinity Coll., Cambridge (Senior Scholar, 1937). Hons Degree Maths and Physics, 1937; ScD, 1964. Student's Medal, Inst. of Fuel, for work on producer gas mains, 1938; British Coal Utilisation Research Assoc.: Asst Scientific Officer, 1937; Senior Scientific Officer and Head of Combustion Research Laboratory, 1944; British Iron and Steel Research Assoc.: Head of Physics Dept, 1946; Superintendent, 1950; Assistant Director, 1953; Prof. of Fuel Technology and Chemical Engineering, Sheffield Univ., 1953–64. Sir Robert Hadfield medal of Iron and Steel Inst. for studies on open hearth furnaces, 1949; Parsons Memorial Lecture on Magnetohydrodynamics, 1961; General Superintendent International Flame Radiation Research Foundn, 1951–76. Visitor: Production Engineering Research Assoc., 1967; Machine Tool Industry Research Assoc., 1967. Member Clean Air Council, 1957–62; Fuel Research Board, 1957–58; Fire Research Board, 1961–64; BISRA Council, 1958–60; President, Inst. of Fuel, 1962–63 (Vice-President, 1959–62); Member: Adv. Council on Research and Development, Ministry of Power, 1960–66; Acad. Adv. Council, University of Strathclyde, 1962–67; Education Cttee, RAF, 1968–76; Unesco Commn to Bangladesh, 1979. FInstP 1944; FInstF 1951; FIChemE 1972 (MIChemE 1956); FIMechE 1968 (MIMechE 1964); FIEE 1968 (MIEE 1964); FEng 1976; FRSA 1964; MRI 1965; FRAeS 1969. Elected Mem., Royal Norwegian Scientific Soc., 1974; Corresp. Mem., Nat. Acad. of Engineering of Mexico, 1977. DUniv Open, 1982. *Publications:* The Science of Flames and Furnaces, 1952, 2nd edn, 1960; (with J. H. Chesters) The Influence of Port Design on Open Hearth Furnace Flames (Iron and Steel Institute Special Report 37), 1946; (with R. Edgeworth Johnstone) Pilot Plants, Models and Scale-up Methods in Chemical Engineering, 1957; (ed.) Air Pollution, 1957; Nuclear Propulsion, 1961; Man, Machines and Tomorrow, 1973; Machines—Masters or Slaves of Man?, 1973; (ed with R. J. Crookes) Energy and Humanity, 1974; (with E. R. Laithwaite) How to Invent, 1977; The Engineer's Conscience, 1980. *Recreations:* carpentry, wood-carving. *Address:* Bell Farm, Brundish, Suffolk. *Club:* Athenæum.

THROCKMORTON, Sir Robert George Maxwell, 11th Bt, *cr* 1642; *b* 15 Feb. 1908; *s* of Lt-Col Courtenay Throckmorton (killed in action, 1916), and Lilian (*d* 1955), *o d* of Colonel Langford Brooke, Mere Hall, Cheshire; *S* grandfather, 1927; *m* 1st, 1942, Jean (marr. diss. 1948), (former wife of Arthur Smith-Bingham, *d* of late Charles Garland; she *m* 1959, 3rd Baron Ashcombe, and *d* 1973); 2nd, 1953, Lady Isabel Guinness, *d* of 9th Duke of Rutland. *Educ:* Downside; RMC, Sandhurst. 2nd Lieut, Grenadier Guards, 1928–30; Lieut (A) RNVR, 1940–44. *Heir: cousin* Anthony John Benedict Throckmorton [*b* 9 Feb. 1916; *m* 1972, Violet Virginia, *d* of late Anders William Anderson]. *Address:* Coughton Court, Alcester, Warwickshire. *T:* Alcester 763370; Molland Bottreaux, South Molton, N Devon. *Clubs:* Army and Navy, White's.

THROWER, Frank, FSIAD 1975; glass and ceramic designer; *b* 11 April 1932; *m* G. Inga-Lill (marr. diss.); one *s* two *d* and three adopted *s* (and one *s* decd). *Educ:* flunked out of Stationers' Company's Sch. due to enjoying both fine summer and Denis Compton's batting at Lord's Cricket Ground, 1947; no further trng or educn. Worked in shipbroker's office as general dogsbody, 1947–50; four other people in office: 1 Plymouth Brother, 1 Baptist, 1 Methodist, 1 Quaker; decided against organised religion—and shipbroking; various office jobs carried out with no interest or competence, 1950–51; bought a hat and tried to sell carbon paper, failed, 1951; sold hat and tried to sell pottery and glass, 1953–60; succeeded; saw where there was scope for new ideas and improved design; joined Portmeirion as Sales Director, 1960; sold year's prodn in four weeks; designed some glass to set up as importer under Portmeirion banner; glass sold successfully and ... first talks with Dartington about building glass factory in UK, 1963; Dartington Glass factory opened, 1967. Observer Award for design, 1969; Duke of Edinburgh Award for design, 1972; Design Council Award for design, 1972. *Recreation:* maintaining the level of essential bodily fluids whilst waiting for something to turn up. *Address:* 4 Portland Road, W11 4LD. *Clubs:* MCC, Queen's.

THROWER, Percy John; with garden centre and nursery business (Murrells of Shrewsbury, Portland Nurseries, Shrewsbury); Parks Superintendent, Shrewsbury, 1946–74; *b* 30 Jan. 1913; British; *m* 1939, Constance Margaret (*née* Cook); three *d. Educ:* Church of England Sch., Little Horwood. NDH 1945. Improver, Horwood House Gdns, Winslow, 1927–31; Journeyman Gardener, Royal Gdns, Windsor, 1931–35; Journeyman Gardener, City of Leeds Parks Dept, 1935–37; Asst Parks Supt, Borough of Derby Parks Dept, 1937–46. Frequent broadcaster, radio and TV, 1947–. RHS: Associate of Honour, 1963; VMH 1974. *Publications:* In Your Garden Week by Week, 1959, rev. edn 1973; Encyclopædia of Gardening, 1962; In Your Greenhouse, 1963, rev. edn 1972; Colour in Your Garden, 1966, rev. 1976; Everyday Gardening, 1969; Vegetables and Fruit, 1977; My Lifetime of Gardening, 1977; contrib. Amateur Gardening, Daily Mail. *Recreation:* shooting. *Address:* The Magnolias, Bomere Heath, Shrewsbury, Salop SY4 3QJ. *T:* Bomere Heath 290225.

THRUSH, Prof. Brian Arthur, FRS 1976; Professor of Physical Chemistry, University of Cambridge, since 1978; Fellow of Emmanuel College, Cambridge, since 1960; *b* Hampstead Garden Suburb, 23 July 1928; *s* of late Arthur Albert Thrush and of Dorothy Charlotte Thrush (*née* Money); *m* 1958, Rosemary Catherine Terry, *d* of late George and Gertrude Terry, Ottawa; one *s* one *d. Educ:* Haberdashers' Aske's Sch.; Emmanuel Coll., Cambridge (Schol. 1946-50). BA 1949, MA, PhD 1953, ScD 1965. University of Cambridge: Demonstrator in Physical Chemistry, 1953; Asst Dir of Research, 1959; Lectr in Physical Chemistry, 1964, Reader, 1969; Tutor, 1963-67, and Dir of Studies in Chemistry, 1963-78, Emmanuel Coll. Consultant Physicist, US Nat. Bureau of Standards, Washington, 1957-58; Sen. Vis. Scientist, Nat. Res. Council, Ottawa, 1961, 1971, 1980. Tilden Lectr, Chem. Soc., 1965; Vis. Prof., Chinese Acad. of Science, 1980-; Member: Faraday Council, Chem. Soc., 1976-79; US Nat. Acad. of Scis Panel on Atmospheric Chemistry, 1975-80; Lawes Agric. Trust Cttee, 1979-. M. Polanyi Medal, RSC, 1980. *Publications:* papers on gas kinetics and spectroscopy in Proc. Royal Soc., Trans Faraday Soc., etc. *Recreations:* wine, fell-walking. *Address:* Brook Cottage, Pemberton Terrace, Cambridge CB2 1JA. *T:* Cambridge 357637.

THUILLIER, Maj.-Gen. Leslie de Malapert, CB 1958; CVO 1966; OBE 1944; Consultant, Airwork Services Ltd, since 1969; *b* 26 Sept. 1905; *s* of late Lt-Col L. C. Thuillier, Indian Army; *m* 1936, Barbara Leonard Rawlins; one *s* two *d. Educ:* Berkhamsted Sch.; Royal Military Academy, Woolwich. Commissioned as 2nd Lieut, Royal Corps of Signals, 1926; Lieut, 1929; Captain, 1937; Staff Coll., Camberley, 1939; Temp. Major, 1940; Temp. Lt-Col, 1941; Temp. Colonel, 1945; Colonel, 1949, Brigadier, 1951; Maj.-Gen., 1955. War Office, 1940-41; Middle East and Italy, 1941-45; Chief Signal Officer, Northern Ireland District, 1945-46; British Troops in Egypt, 1951-53; Northern Command, 1954-55; Director of Telecommunications, War Office, 1955-58; Asst Sec., Cabinet Office, 1958-67. CEng; MIEE 1968 (AMIEE 1958). *Recreation:* gardening. *Address:* The Red Barn, Patney, Devizes, Wilts SN10 3RA. *T:* Chirton 669. *Club:* Naval and Military.

THURBURN, Gwynneth Loveday, OBE 1956; Hon. FCST; Principal, Central School of Speech and Drama, 1942-67; *b* 17 July 1899; *d* of Robert Augustus Thurburn and Bertha Loveday. *Educ:* Birklands, St Albans; Central School of Speech and Drama. Vice-Pres., Central Sch. of Speech and Drama. *Publication:* Voice and Speech. *Address:* Church Cottage, Darsham, Saxmundham, Suffolk.

THURBURN, Brigadier Roy Gilbert, CB 1950; CBE 1945 (OBE 1941); Secretary, Army Museums Ogilby Trust, 1957-72; *b* 6 July 1901; *y s* of late Reginald Phibbs Thurburn; *m* 1936, Rhona Moneen Hignett; one *s. Educ:* St Paul's Sch.; Royal Military Coll., Sandhurst. Commissioned in the Cameronians (Scottish Rifles), 1921; took part in operations in Southern Kurdistan, 1923; attended Staff Coll., Camberley, 1933-34. Served War of 1939-45, in Middle East, North Africa and Italy (despatches twice). ADC to the Queen, 1952-53; retired, 1953. Gold Medallist, United Services Institution of India, 1932. Legion of Merit (USA), 1947. *Publications:* (ed) Index to British Military Costume Prints, 1972; various in journals. *Recreations:* many. *Address:* 2 Eversleigh, Buckingham Close, Guildford, Surrey.

THURLOW, 8th Baron *cr* 1792; **Francis Edward Hovell-Thurlow-Cumming-Bruce,** KCMG 1961 (CMG 1957); Governor and C-in-C of the Bahamas, 1968-72; *b* 9 March 1912; *s* of 6th Baron Thurlow and Grace Catherine, *d* of Rev. Henry Trotter; *S* brother, 1971; *m* 1949, Yvonne Diana Aubyn Wilson, CStJ 1969; two *s* two *d. Educ:* Shrewsbury Sch.; Trinity Coll., Cambridge. Asst Principal, Dept of Agriculture for Scotland, 1935; transferred to Dominions Office, 1937; Asst Private Sec. to Sec. of State, 1939; Asst Sec., Office of UK High Comr in NZ, 1939; Asst Sec., Office of UK High Comr in Canada, 1944; Secretariat, Meeting of Commonwealth Prime Ministers in London, 1946; served with UK Delegn at Paris Peace Conf., 1946, and at UN Gen. Assemblies, 1946 and 1948; Principal Private Sec. to Sec. of State, 1946; Asst Sec., CRO, 1948; Head of Political Div., Office of UK High Comr in New Delhi, 1949; Establishment Officer, CRO, 1952; Head of Commodities Dept, CRO, 1954; Adviser on External Affairs to Governor of Gold Coast, 1955; Deputy High Comr for the UK in Ghana, 1957; Asst Under-Sec. of State, CRO, April 1958; Deputy High Comr for the UK in Canada, 1958; High Comr for UK: in New Zealand, 1959-63; in Nigeria, 1964-67; Dep. Under-Sec. of State, FCO, 1964. Chm., Inst. for Comparative Study of History, Philosophy and the Sciences. KStJ 1969. *Recreations:* fishing, golf. *Heir: s* Hon. Roualeyn Robert Hovell-Thurlow-Cumming-Bruce [*b* 13 April 1952; *m* 1980, Bridget Anne, *o d* of H. B. Ismay Cheape, Fossoway Lodge, Kinross]. *Address:* 16 Warwick Avenue, W2. *T:* 01-723 7525. *Club:* Travellers'.

See also Rt Hon. Sir J. R. H.-T.-Cumming-Bruce.

THURLOW, Very Rev. Alfred Gilbert Goddard, MA; Dean of Gloucester, 1972-82; *b* 6 April 1911; *s* of Rev. A. R. Thurlow; *m* 1955, Thelda Mary Hook; two *s. Educ:* Selwyn Coll., Cambridge; Cuddesdon Coll., Oxford. MA Cantab, 1936. Curate, All Saints, Wokingham, 1934-39; Precentor of Norwich Cathedral, 1939-55; Rector of St Clement, St George Colegate and St Edmund Norwich, 1943-52; Vicar of: St Andrew and St Michael at Plea, Norwich, 1952-55; St Nicholas, Great Yarmouth, 1955-64; Canon Residentiary of Norwich, 1964-72, Vice-Dean, 1969-72. FSA 1948; FRHistS 1962. *Publications:* Church Bells and Ringers of Norwich, 1947; St George Colegate Norwich, a Redundant Church, 1950; The Mediæval Painted Panels

of Norwich Cathedral, 1959; Norwich Cathedral, 1962; Great Yarmouth Priory and Parish Church, 1963; Cathedrals at Work, 1966; City of Norwich, 1970; Cathedrals in Colour, 1971; Norwich Cathedral, 1972; Biblical Myths and Mysteries, 1974; Gloucester and Berkeley: Edward II, Martyr King, 1976; City of Gloucester, 1981. *Recreations:* change ringing, travel, interpreting historic buildings. *Address:* 2 East Pallant, Chichester, West Sussex PO19 1TR. *T:* Chichester 783977. *Clubs:* Cambridge Union; Rotary.

THURSO, 2nd Viscount *cr* 1952, of Ulbster; **Robin Macdonald Sinclair;** Bt 1786; Baron of Thurso; JP; Lord-Lieutenant of Caithness, since 1973; Chairman: Sinclair Family Trust Ltd; Lochdhu Hotels Ltd; Thurso Fisheries Ltd; Director: Caithness Glass Ltd; Stephens (Plastics) Ltd; *b* 24 Dec. 1922; *s* of 1st Viscount Thurso, KT, PC, CMG, and Marigold (*d* 1975), *d* of late Col J. S. Forbes, DSO; *S* father, 1970; *m* 1952, Margaret Beaumont Brokensha, *widow* of Lieut G. W. Brokensha, DSC, RN, and *d* of Col J. J. Robertson, DSO, DL, TD; two *s* one *d. Educ:* Eton; New College, Oxford; Edinburgh Univ. Served RAF, 1941-46; Flight Lieut 684 Sqdn, 540 Sqdn, commanded Edinburgh Univ. Air Sqdn, 1946; Captain of Boats, Edinburgh Univ. Boat Club, 1946-47, Green 1946, Blue, 1947. Caithness CC, 1949, 1952, 1955, 1958; Thurso Town Council, 1957, 1960, resigned 1961, re-elected 1965, 1968, 1971, Dean of Guild 1968, Baillie 1960, 1969, Police Judge 1971. Pres. North Country Cheviot Sheep Soc., 1951-54; Chm. Caithness and Sutherland Youth Employment Cttee, 1957-75; Mem., Red Deer Commn, 1965-74. Pres., Highland Soc. of London, 1980-82. DL 1952, JP 1959, Vice-Lieutenant, 1964-73, Caithness. *Recreations:* fishing, shooting, amateur drama. *Heir: s* Hon. John Archibald Sinclair [*b* 10 Sept. 1953; *m* 1976, Marion Ticknor, *d* of Louis D. Sage, Connecticut, USA, and of Mrs A. R. Ward; one *d*]. *Address:* Thurso East Mains, Thurso, Caithness, Scotland. *T:* Thurso 62600. *Clubs:* Royal Air Force; New (Edinburgh).

THURSTON, Thea; *see* King, T.

THWAITE, Anthony Simon, FRSL 1978; poet; co-editor of Encounter since 1973; *b* 23 June 1930; *s* of late Hartley Thwaite, JP, FSA, and of Alice Evelyn Mallinson; *m* 1955, Ann Barbara Harrop; four *d. Educ:* Kingswood Sch.; Christ Church, Oxford (MA). Vis. Lectr in English, Tokyo Univ., 1955-57; Producer, BBC, 1957-62; Literary Editor, The Listener, 1962-65; Asst Prof. of English, Univ. of Libya, 1965-67; Literary Editor, New Statesman, 1968-72; Henfield Writing Fellow, Univ. of East Anglia, 1972; Vis. Prof., Kuwait Univ., 1974. *Publications: poetry:* Home Truths, 1957; The Owl in the Tree, 1963; The Stones of Emptiness, 1967 (Richard Hillary Memorial Prize, 1968); Inscriptions, 1973; New Confessions, 1974; A Portion for Foxes, 1977; Victorian Voices, 1980; *criticism:* Contemporary English Poetry, 1959; Poetry Today, 1973; Twentieth Century English Poetry, 1978; *travel:* (with Roloff Beny) Japan, 1968; The Deserts of Hesperides, 1969; (with Roloff Beny and Peter Porter) In Italy, 1974; (with Roloff Beny) Odyssey: Mirror of the Mediterranean, 1981; *editor:* (with Geoffrey Bownas) Penguin Book of Japanese Verse, 1964; (with Peter Porter) The English Poets, 1974; (with Fleur Adcock) New Poetry 4, 1978; Larkin at Sixty, 1982; *for children:* Beyond the Inhabited World, 1976. *Recreations:* archaeology, travel. *Address:* The Mill House, Low Tharston, Norfolk NR15 2YN. *T:* Fundenhall 569.

THWAITES, Brian St George, CMG 1958; *b* 22 April 1912; *s* of late Henry Thwaites and Ada B. Thwaites (*née* Macnutt); *m* 1938, Madeleine Elizabeth Abell; one *s* two *d. Educ:* Canford School; Clare Coll., Cambridge. Entered Colonial Service (later HM Overseas Civil Service), 1935; served as Administrative Officer in Eastern Nigeria, 1935-47 and 1948-57; Palestine, 1947-48; retired, 1957. Planning Inspector, DoE, 1966-76. *Recreations:* occasional golf, walking uphill. *Address:* Painshill, Donhead St Andrew, Shaftesbury, Dorset SP7 9EA. *T:* Donhead 248.

THWAITES, Dr Bryan, MA, PhD; FIMA; Principal of Westfield College since 1966; Chairman, Wessex Regional Health Authority, since 1982; *b* London, 6 December 1923; *e s* of late Ernest James and Dorothy Marguerite Thwaites; *m* 1948, Katharine Mary, 4th *c* of late H. R. Harries and late Mrs L. Harries, Longhope, Glos; four *s* two *d. Educ:* Dulwich College; Winchester College; Clare College, Cambridge. Scientific Officer, National Physical Laboratory, 1944-47; Lecturer, Imperial College, London, 1947-51; Assistant Master, Winchester College, 1951-59; Professor of Theoretical Mechanics, Southampton Univ., 1959-66. Co-founder and Co-Chm., Education 2000, 1982-; Chm. of Collegiate Council, London Univ., 1973-76. Chm. and Mem. ARC Cttees, 1948-69. Special Lecturer, Imperial College, 1951-58. Director of the School Mathematics Project, 1961-75, Chm. of Trustees, 1967-; Chm., Internat. Mathematical Olympiad, first in UK, 1979; Chm., Adv. Council, ICL/CES, 1968-; Member: United States Educational Commn, 1966-76; Ct of London Univ., 1975-81; Chm. of Delegacy, Goldsmiths' Coll., 1975-80; Mem. Acad. Advisory Committee: Univ. of Bath, 1963-72; Open Univ., 1969-75; Chairman: Council of C of E Colleges of Education, 1969-71; Church of England Higher Educn Cttee, 1974-76; Northwick Park Hosp. Management Cttee, 1970-74; Brent and Harrow AHA, 1973-82; King's Fund Enquiry into Sen. Management Trng in NHS, 1975-76; Heythrop Coll., 1978-82. Trustee, Westfield Coll. Develt Trust, 1979-. Gresham Prof. in Geometry, City Univ., 1969-72; Mercier Lectr, Whitelands Coll., 1973. Shadow Vice-Chancellor, Independent Univ., July-Nov. 1971; Hon. Sec. and Treasurer, Dulwich College Mission, 1946-57; Member of Approved School Committee, Hampshire CC, 1954-58, 1961-66; JP, Winchester City Bench, 1963-66; Governor of various schools; a Vice-Pres., Friends of Girls' Public Day School Trust. Mem. Council, 1964-, Pres., 1966-67, Institute of

Mathematics and its Applications. FRSA. *Publications:* (ed) Incompressible Aerodynamics, 1960; (ed) On Teaching Mathematics, 1961; The SMP: the first ten years, 1973; numerous contributions to Proc. Royal Soc., Reports and Memoranda of Aeronautical Research Council, Quart. Jl of Applied Mech., Jl of Royal Aeronautical Soc., etc. *Recreations:* music, sailing. *Address:* Milnthorpe, Winchester, Hants. *T:* Winchester 2394; The Old House, Westfield College, NW3 7ST. *T:* 01-794 2090. *Club:* Athenæum.

THWAITES, Jacqueline Ann, JP; Principal of Inchbald Schools of Design and Fine Arts since 1960; *b* 16 Dec. 1931; *d* of Mrs Donald Whitaker; *m* 1st, 1955, Michael Inchbald, *qv* (marr. diss. 1964); one *s* one *d*; 2nd, 1974, Brig. Peter Trevenen Thwaites, *qv. Educ:* Convent of the Sacred Heart, Brighton; House of Citizenship, London. Founded: Inchbald Sch. of Design, 1960; Inchbald Sch. of Fine Arts, 1970; Inchbald Sch. of Garden Design, 1972. Member: Monopolies Commn, 1972-75; Whitford Cttee on Copyright and Design, 1974-76; London Electricity Cons. Council, 1973-76; Westminster City Council (Warwick Ward), 1974-78. JP South Westminster, 1976. *Publications:* Directory of Interior Designers, 1966; Bedrooms, 1968; Design and Decoration, 1971. *Recreations:* fishing, travel. *Address:* 24 Clarendon Street, SW1; The Manor, Ayot St Lawrence, Herts; (office) 7 Eaton Gate, SW1W 9BA.

THWAITES, Brig. Peter Trevenen; Chairman: Individual School Direction Ltd, since 1981; Hurlingham Polo Association, since 1982; *b* 30 July 1926; *yr surv. s* of late Lt-Col Norman Graham Thwaites, CBE, MVO, MC, and Eleanor Lucia Thwaites, Barley End, Tring, Herts; *m* 1st, 1950, Ellen Theresa King (marr. diss.; she *d* 1976); one *s* two *d* (and one *s* decd); 2nd, 1974, Jacqueline Ann Inchbald (*see* Jacqueline Ann Thwaites). *Educ:* Rugby. Commnd Grenadier Guards, 1944; served 1st, 2nd and 4th Bns in Germany, Egypt, British Cameroons, British Guiana; Mem., Sir William Penney's Scientific Party to UK Atomic Trials in S Australia, 1956; Staff Coll., Malaya, JSSC, MoD, 1958-67; Aden, 1967; comd Muscat Regt, Sultan of Muscat's Armed Forces, 1967-70; AQMG London Dist, 1970-71; Comdr, British Army Staff, Singapore (Col), and Governor, Singapore Internat. Sch., 1971-73; Dep. Dir, Defence Operational Plans (Army), 1973-74; Brig. 1975; Head of MoD Logistics Survey Team to Saudi Arabia, 1976, retired 1977. Chm., Jt Staff, Sultan of Oman's Armed Forces, 1977-81. Sultan's Commendation, 1967; Sultan's Dist. Service Medal, 1969; Sultan's Bravery Medal, 1970. *Publications:* plays: (with Charles Ross) Love or Money, 1958; (with Charles Ross) Master of None, 1960; Roger's Last Stand, 1976; Caught in the Act, 1981. *Recreations:* polo, shooting. *Address:* 24 Clarendon Street, SW1; The Manor House, Ayot St Lawrence, Herts. *Clubs:* White's, Beefsteak, Cavalry and Guards.

THWAITES, Roy; Leader of South Yorkshire County Council, since 1979; *b* 13 Aug. 1931; *s* of Walter and Emily Alice Thwaites; *m* 1954, Margaret Anne (*née* Noble); one *s. Educ:* Southey Green Secondary Sch.; Sheffield Central Technical Sch. City Councillor, Sheffield, 1965, Chief Whip and Chm. of Transport Cttee, 1969-74; South Yorkshire County Council: Councillor, 1973; Chief Whip and Chm. Passenger Transport Authority, 1973-78; Dep. Leader, 1978-79; Leader, and Chm. of Policy Cttee, 1979-. Dep. Chm., Assoc. of Metropolitan Authorities, 1979-; Mem., Local Authorities' Conditions of Service Adv. Bd, 1979-; Chm., NJC Local Govt Manual Workers Employers, 1980-. Comr, Manpower Services Commn, 1980-. *Recreation:* reading. *Address:* 14 Foxhill Drive, Sheffield S6 1GD. *T:* Sheffield 311222.

THYNE, Malcolm Tod, MA; Headmaster of St Bees School, since 1980; *b* 6 Nov. 1942; *s* of Andrew Tod and Margaret Melrose Thyne; *m* 1969, Eleanor Christine Scott; two *s. Educ:* The Leys Sch., Cambridge; Clare Coll., Cambridge (MA Nat. Scis with Pt II in Chem.; Cert. of Educn). Asst Master, Edinburgh Acad., 1965-69; Asst Master, Oundle Sch., 1969-72, Housemaster, 1972-80. *Publications:* Periodicity, Atomic Structure and Bonding (Revised Nuffield Chemistry), 1976; (chapters in) Revised Nuffield Chemistry Handbook for Pupils, 1978; (contrib.) Revised Nuffield Chemistry Teachers' Guides, Vols II and III, 1978. *Recreation:* mountaineering. *Address:* The School House, St Bees, Cumbria CA27 0DU. *T:* St Bees 822263.

THYNN, Alexander; *see* Weymouth, Viscount.

THYNNE, family name of Marquess of Bath.

THYNNE, John Corelli James, PhD, DSc; Assistant Secretary, Information Technology Division, Department of Industry, since 1978; *b* 27 Nov. 1931; *s* of Corelli James Thynne and Isabel Ann (*née* Griffiths). *Educ:* Milford Haven Grammar Sch.; Nottingham Univ. (BSc, PhD); Edinburgh Univ. (DSc). Res. Chemist, English Electric Co. (Guided Missile Div.), 1956-58; Fellow: Nat. Res. Council, Ottawa, 1958-59; UCLA, 1959-60; Univ. of Leeds, 1960-63; Lectr in Chemistry and Dir of Studies, Univ. of Edinburgh, 1963-70; Principal, DTI, 1970-73; Counsellor (Scientific), British Embassy, Moscow, 1974-78. *Publications:* contribs on physical chemistry to scientific journals. *Recreations:* skiing, sailing, cricket. *Address:* 5 Eldon Grove, NW3. *T:* 01-794 1356. *Clubs:* Athenæum, MCC.

TIARKS, Rt. Rev. Geoffrey Lewis, MA Cantab; Chaplain to Retired Clergy and Widows in the Archdeaconry of Sherborne, since 1976; *b* 8 Oct 1909; *s* of Lewis Herman Tiarks, Clerk in Holy Orders, and Edith Margaret Tiarks; *m* 1934, Betty Lyne, *d* of Henry Stock; one *s* (one *d* decd). *Educ:*

Marlborough; S John's College, Cambridge. Ordained at Southwark, 1932; Curate of St Saviour's with St Peter, Southwark, 1932-33; Chaplain, RN, 1934-47; Chaplain, Diocesan College, Rondebosch, CP, 1948-50; Rector of S Paul's, Rondebosch, 1950-54; Vicar of Lyme Regis, Dorset, 1954-61; Archdeacon of the Isle of Wight, 1961-65; Archdeacon of Portsmouth, 1965-69; Bishop Suffragan of Maidstone, 1969-76; Senior Chaplain to Archbishop of Canterbury, 1969-74. *Address:* Primrose Cottage, Netherbury, Bridport, Dorset. *T:* Netherbury 277.

TIARKS, Henry Frederic, FRAS; *b* 8 Sept. 1900; *e s* of late Frank Cyril Tiarks, OBE; *m* 1st, 1930, Lady Millicent Olivia Taylour (marr. diss. 1936), *d* of 4th Marquess of Headfort; (one *s* decd); 2nd, 1936, Joan, *d* of Francis Marshman-Bell; one *d* (one *s* decd). *Educ:* Eton College. Served European War 1914-19. Midshipman RNVR 1918; Sqdn Ldr AAF, 1940; Wing Commander, 1942-43, Retd (invalided). Former directorships: J. Henry Schroder & Co., Partner 1926-57, J. Henry Schroder & Co. Ltd, 1957-62, J. Henry Schroder Wagg & Co. Ltd, 1962 (May to Sept.), Schroders Ltd, 1962-65; J. Henry Schroder Banking Corpn, NY, 1945-62; Antofagasta (Chili) and Bolivia Railway Co. Ltd, 1926-67 (Chairman 1966-67); Securicor Ltd (founder) 1939-68; Pressed Steel Co. Ltd, 1936-66; Joseph Lucas Ltd, 1946-68; Bank of London & South America Ltd, 1958-68; Bank of London & Montreal Ltd, Nassau, 1959-69; Anglo-Scottish Amalgamated Corpn Ltd, 1935-68. Member: Dollar Exports Council, 1952-60; Western Hemisphere Exports Council, 1960-64; European League for Economic Co-operation (European Central Council); Internat. EFTA Action Cttee, 1967-75; Vice-Pres., European-Atlantic Gp. Mem., The Wildfowl Trust; Trustee, World Wildlife Fund (International), Morges, Switzerland, 1966-76. Mem. Cttee of Managers, RI, 1960-62. Gran Oficial, Order of Merit, Chile. *Recreations:* golf, shooting, observational astronomy, photography. *Address:* Casa Ina, Marbella Club, Marbella, (Malaga) Spain; 120 Cheapside, EC2. *Clubs:* Overseas Member: White's, Royal Thames Yacht; Royal and Ancient Golf (St Andrews), Swinley Forest Golf (Ascot), Royal St George's Golf (Sandwich), Berkshire Golf (Bagshot), The Brook (New York), Lyford Cay (Nassau, Bahamas); Royal Bermuda Yacht.

See also Marquess of Tavistock.

TIBBER, Anthony Harris; His Honour Judge Tibber; a Circuit Judge, since 1977; *b* 23 June 1926; *s* of Maurice and Priscilla Tibber; *m* 1954, Rhona Ann Salter; three *s. Educ:* University College School, London; Magdelen College School, Brackley. Served in Royal Signals, 1945-48; called to the Bar, Gray's Inn, 1950; a Recorder of the Crown Court, 1976. Mem., Matrimonial Causes Rule Cttee, 1980-. *Recreations:* cultivating, idling, pottering. *Address:* c/o Edmonton County Court, 59 Fore Street, N18 2TM. *T:* (home) 01-348 3605.

TIBBITS, Captain Sir David (Stanley), Kt 1976; DSC 1942; FNI; RN retired; Deputy Master and Chairman of Board, Trinity House, 1972-76; *b* 11 April 1911; *s* of late Hubert Tibbits, MB, BCh, Warwick, and Edith Lucy (*née* Harman) Tibbits; *m* 1938, Mary Florence Butterfield, Hamilton, Bermuda; two *d. Educ:* Wells House Sch., Malvern Wells; RNC, Dartmouth. RN Cadet 1925; navigation specialist, 1934; served War, 1939-45, HMS York, Devonshire and Anson; Comdr 1946; Captain 1953; Dir, Radio Equipment Dept, Admty, 1953-56; in comd, HM Ships Manxman, Dryad and Hermes, 1956-61; retd. Trinity House: Elder Brother, 1961; Warden, 1969. Hon. Sec., King George's Fund for Sailors, 1974-80; Lay Vice-Pres., Missions to Seamen. Mem. Court, Worshipful Co. of Shipwrights, 1976. Trustee, National Maritime Museum, 1974-77. Governor, Pangbourne Coll., 1973-78. Founder Mem., 1972, Fellow 1979, Nautical Inst. *Recreations:* sailing, colour photography, classical music. *Address:* Harting Hill, PO Box 1419, Hamilton 5, Bermuda; c/o Trinity House, Tower Hill, EC3N 4DH. *Clubs:* Army and Navy; Royal Yacht Squadron (Naval Mem.); Royal Bermuda Yacht (Bermuda).

TIBBS, Craigie John; Head of Estates and Planning Department, BBC, since 1980; *b* 17 Feb. 1935; *s* of Arthur and Gladys Tibbs; *m* 1959, Carol Ann (*née* Linsell); two *d. Educ:* King George V School, Southport; Heaton Grammar School, Newcastle upon Tyne; RMA Sandhurst; London University. BSc; FRICS. Trainee Estates Officer, London Transport, 1959-62; Valuer and Senior Valuer, Luton Corp., 1962-67; Chief Valuer and Surveyor, London Borough of Newham, 1967-71; Development Officer, City of Birmingham, 1971-73; County Estates Officer, Hants County Council, 1973-76; Under Sec. (Dir of Land Economy), Depts of Environment and Transport, 1976-80. *Recreations:* music, reading, writing, walking, swimming, golf, the Well Game. *Address:* Estates and Planning Department, BBC, Portland Place, W1A 1AA.

TIBBS, (Geoffrey) Michael (Graydon); Secretary of the Royal College of Physicians, since 1968; *b* 21 Nov. 1921; *s* of Rev. Geoffrey Wilberforce Tibbs, sometime Chaplain RN and Vicar of Lynchmere, Sussex, and Margaret Florence Tibbs (*née* Skinner); *m* 1951, Anne Rosemary Wortley; two *s. Educ:* Berkhamsted Sch.; St Peter's Hall, Oxford. BA Hons Geography, 1948; MA 1952. FInstAM; MIPM. Served RNVR, Ordinary Seaman/Lieut, 1940-46 (despatches), HMS Cottesmore, HMS Sheffield, HM S/M Tantalus, HM S/M Varne. Sudan Political Service, 1949-55, retired on independence as Dist Comr, Dar Messeria District. Various appointments in personnel, organisation and overseas touring depts, Automobile Assoc., 1955-68. *Recreations:* producing pantomimes, parish affairs, making bonfires. *Address:* Welkin,

Lynchmere Ridge, Haslemere, Surrey GU27 3PP. *T:* Haslemere 3120, 2176. *Club:* Naval.

TICKELL, Crispin Charles Cervantes, MVO 1958; HM Diplomatic Service; Ambassador to Mexico, since 1981; *b* 25 Aug. 1930; *s* of late Jerrard Tickell and Renée (*née* Haynes); *m* 1st, 1954, Chloë (*marr. diss.* 1976), *d* of late Sir James Gunn, RA, PRP; two *s* one *d* ; 2nd, 1977, Penelope, *d* of late Dr Vernon Thorne Thorne. *Educ:* Westminster (King's Schol.); Christ Church, Oxford (Hinchliffe and Hon. Schol.). 1st Cl. Hons Mod. Hist. 1952. Served with Coldstream Guards, 1952-54; entered HM Diplomatic Service, 1954. Served at: Foreign Office, 1954-55; The Hague, 1955-58; Mexico, 1958-61; FO (Planning Staff), 1961-64; Paris, 1964-70; Private Sec. responsible for negotiations for British entry into EEC, to successive Chancellors of the Duchy of Lancaster, 1970-72; Head of Western Organisations Dept, FCO, 1972-75; Fellow, Center for Internat. Affairs, Harvard Univ., 1975-76; Chef de Cabinet to Rt Hon. Roy Jenkins, Pres. of Commn of European Communities, 1977-81; Vis. Fellow, All Souls Coll., Oxford, 1981. Officer, Order of Orange Nassau (Holland), 1958. *Publications:* (contrib.) The Evacuees, 1968; (contrib.) Life After Death, 1976; Climatic Change and World Affairs, 1977. *Recreations:* climatology, palæohistory, art, especially pre-Columbiana. *Address:* c/o Foreign and Commonwealth Office, SW1. *Club:* Brooks's.

TICKELL, Maj.-Gen. Marston Eustace, CBE 1973 (MBE 1955); MC 1945; CEng, FICE; Commandant Royal Military College of Science, 1975-78, retired; *er s* of late Maj.-Gen. Sir Eustace Tickell, KBE, CB, MC; *m* 1961, Pamela Vere, *d* of Vice-Adm. A. D. Read, CB; no *c. Educ:* Wellington Coll.; Peterhouse, Cambridge (MA). Commnd in RE, 1944; NW Europe Campaign and Middle East, 1944-45; psc 1954; Mil. Ops, MoD, 1955-57; served in Libya, Cyprus and Jordan, 1958-59; US Armed Forces Staff Coll. and Instructor RMCS and Staff Coll., 1959-62; Defence Planning Staff, MoD, 1962-64; CRE 4th Div., 1964-66; comd 12 Engr Bde, 1967-69; Indian Nat. Defence Coll., 1970; COS Northern Ireland, 1971-72; E-in-C, MoD, 1972-75. Col Comdt, RE, 1978-. Pres., Instn of Royal Engrs, 1979-82. FICE 1974. *Recreation:* sailing. *Address:* The Old Vicarage, Branscombe, Seaton, Devon EX12 3DW. *Clubs:* Army and Navy; Royal Ocean Racing.

TICKLE, Brian Percival; Senior Registrar of the Family Division, High Court of Justice, since 1982 (Registrar, since 1970); *b* 31 Oct. 1921; *m* 1945, Margaret Alice Pendrey; one *s* one *d. Educ:* The Judd Sch., Tonbridge. Entered Civil Service, 1938. Served War, Royal Signals, 1939-45. Civil Service, 1946-70. *Publications:* Rees Divorce Handbook, 1963; Atkins Court Forms and Precedents (Probate), 1974. *Recreation:* golf. *Address:* 1A Royal Chase, Tunbridge Wells, Kent. *Club:* Royal Automobile.

TICKLE, Rt. Rev. Gerard William; Titular Bishop of Bela; *b* 2 Nov. 1909; 2nd *s* of William Joseph Tickle and Rosanna Kelly. *Educ:* Douai School; Venerable English College, Rome. Priest, 1934. Curate at St Joseph's Church, Sale, 1935-41; Army Chaplain, 1941-46; Vice-Rector, 1946, Rector, 1952, Venerable English College, Rome. Bishop-in-Ordinary to HM Forces, 1963-78; Apostolic Administrator, 1978-79. Privy Chamberlain to Pope Pius XII, 1949; Domestic Prelate to Pope Pius XII, 1953. *Address:* Beechwood, School Lane, Little Neston, South Wirral L64 4DG.

TIDBURY, Charles Henderson; Chairman, Whitbread & Co. plc, since 1978; *b* 26 Jan. 1926; *s* of late Brig. O. H. Tidbury, MC, and Beryl (*née* Pearce); *m* Anne, *d* of late Brig. H. E. Russell, DSO, and of Lady O'Connor; two *s* three *d. Educ:* Eton Coll. Served KRRC, 1943-52: Palestine, 1946-48 (despatches); Queen's Westminsters TA, 1952-60. Joined Whitbread & Co. Ltd, 1952; a Man. Dir, 1959; Chief Exec., 1974; Dep. Chm., 1977. Chm., Brickwoods Brewery Ltd, 1966-71. Director: Barclays Bank; Barclays UK; Boddington's Breweries Ltd; Marston, Thompson & Evershed Ltd; Whitbread Investment Co., and other cos. Pres., Inst. of Brewing, 1976-78; Vice-Chm., Brewers' Soc., 1980-. Chm., Mary Rose Development Trust, 1980-. *Recreations:* sailing, shooting, countryside. *Address:* Flat 3, 45 Bramham Gardens, SW5. *T:* 01-370 7550. *Clubs:* Brooks's; Royal Yacht Squadron, Island Sailing, Bembridge Sailing.

TIERNEY, Dom Francis Alphonsus, OSB, MA; Parish Priest since 1977; *b* 7 March 1910; *s* of James Francis Tierney and Alice Mary Claypoole. *Educ:* Douai; St Benet's Hall, Oxford. Headmaster of: Douai Junior School, Ditcham Park, 1948-52; Douai Sch., 1952-73. Prior of Douai Abbey, 1973-77. *Address:* Douai Abbey, Woolhampton, Berkshire. *T:* Woolhampton 3163.

TIERNEY, Sydney; JP; President, 1977-81, and National Officer, since 1979, Union of Shop, Distributive and Allied Workers; Member, Labour Party National Executive Committee; *b* Sept. 1923. *Educ:* Secondary Modern Sch., Dearne; Plater Coll., Oxford. Mem., Co-operative Party; an Official and Member, USDAW. Vice-Chm., W Midlands Labour Gp of MPs, 1974-79. MP (Lab) Birmingham, Yardley, Feb. 1974-1979; PPS to Min. of State for Agriculture, 1976-79. JP Leicester, 1966. *Address:* 14 Low Meadow, Whaley Bridge, Stockport, Cheshire SK12 7AY.

TIGHE, Maj.-Gen. Patrick Anthony Macartan, CB 1977; MBE 1958; FBIM; with The Hongkong Land Company Ltd, since 1977; *b* 26 Feb. 1923; *s* of late Macartan H. Tighe, BA, RUI, Barrister-at-Law, Dublin and Dorothy Isabel (*née* Vine); *m* 1st, 1950, Elizabeth Frazer Stewart (*d* 1971); two *s* ; 2nd, 1972, Princine Merendino Calitri, authoress, W Virginia, USA. *Educ:* Christ's

Hospital. Served RAF, 1940-41; commnd Royal Signals, 1943; served NW Europe, 1944-45, Palestine, 1945-47; psc 1955; DAAQMG Gurkha Bde Malaya, 1956 (MBE); Mil. Asst Comd British Forces Hong Kong, 1963; Force Signals Officer Borneo, 1964-66 (despatches); Asst Mil. Sec., 1966; Col Asst Adjt Gen., 1968; Brig. Comd Trng Bde Royal Signals, 1970; Inspector of Intell. Corps, 1973; Signal Officer-in-Chief (Army), 1974-77. Col Comdt, Royal Signals, 1977. *Publications:* radio plays (BBC), film and book reviews for press and radio in Far East. *Recreations:* cinema (Mem. British Film Inst. 1947), golf. *Address:* c/o Lloyds Bank, 6 Pall Mall, SW1Y 5NH; The Hongkong Land Company Ltd, Alexandra House, Hong Kong. *Club:* Army and Navy.

TIKARAM, Sir Moti, KBE 1980; **Hon. Justice Sir Moti Tikaram;** Ombudsman, Fiji, since 1972; *b* 18 March 1925; *s* of Tikaram and Singari; *m* 1944, Satyawati (*d* 1981); two *s* one *d. Educ:* Marist Brothers High Sch., Suva; Victoria Univ., Wellington, NZ (LLB 1954). Started law practice, 1954; Stipendiary Magistrate, 1960; Puisne Judge, 1968; acted as Chief Justice, 1971. Patron, Fiji Lawn Tennis Assoc. *Publications:* articles in The Pacific Way and in Recent Law 131. *Recreation:* tennis. *Address:* (home) PO Box 514, 45 Domain Road, Suva, Fiji. *T:* 22135; (office) PO Box 982, Suva. *T:* 211652. *Clubs:* Fiji, Union (Suva).

TILBE, Douglas Sidney, OBE 1973; JP; Housing Campaign Director, Help the Aged, since 1978; *b* 27 May 1931; *s* of late Norrie Ethelbert Sidney George Tilbe and of Ethel Tilbe (*née* Scott); *m* 1957, Janet Ann Ainger; three *s* one *d. Educ:* LSE; Avery Hill Coll. of Educn; Univ. of Essex (MA Soc. Service Planning). Gen. Sec., Soc. of Friends Race Relations Cttee, 1965-71; Dir, British Council of Churches Community and Race Relations Unit, 1971-73; Chm., Priority Area Children, 1971-73; Mem., Uganda Resettlement Bd, 1972-74; Chm., Co-ordinating Cttee for Welfare of Evacuees from Uganda, 1972-73; Dir, Shelter, 1974-77. Dir, St Albans Co-operative Soc. Vice-Pres., Nat. Children's Centre. Chm., Welwyn Garden City UDC, 1972-73; Mem., Welwyn Hatfield DC (Dep. Chm.), 1979-80; Chm., Environmental Health Cttee). Contested (Lab) Rye, 1959 and 1964. Member: NW Metrop. Mental Health Review Tribunal, 1971-78; Oxford Region Mental Health Review Tribunal, 1974-78. Chm. Governors, Heronswood Sch. JP Herts 1967. Hon. MA Open University. *Publications:* East African Asians, 1968; The Ugandan Asian Crisis, 1972. *Recreations:* soccer referee; watching football, cricket, golf and tennis. *Address:* 15 Beehive Green, Welwyn Garden City, Herts AL7 4BE. *T:* Welwyn Garden 27373.

TILEY, Arthur, CBE 1972; JP; Insurance Broker and Marine Underwriter; Director, Clarkson Puckle & Tiley Ltd, Incorporated Insurance Brokers, Bradford and the North East; *b* 17 January 1910; *m* 1936, Mary, *d* of late Craven and Mary Tankard, Great Horton; one *s* one *d. Educ:* Grange High School, Bradford. Treasurer, Young Women's Christian Association, Bradford, 1934-50. Contested (C and Nat. L) Bradford Central, 1951. MP (C and Nat. L) Bradford West, 1955-66. Served War of 1939-45 as Senior Company Officer, National Fire Service. Mem. Council, Churchill Memorial Trust, 1965-76. Hon. MA Bradford, 1981. JP Bradford, 1967. *Address:* 10 Silverwood Close, Lytham Hall Park, Lytham St Annes, Lancs FY8 4RH.

TILL, Barry Dorn; Principal of Morley College, London, since 1965; *b* 1 June 1923; *s* of John Johnson and Hilda Lucy Till; *m* 1st, 1954, Shirley Philipson (*marr. diss.* 1965); two *s* ; 2nd, 1966, Antonia, *d* of Sir Michael Clapham, *qv* ; two *d. Educ:* Harrow; Jesus College and Westcott House, Cambridge (Lightfoot Schol., 1949). Served War, Coldstream Guards, 1942-46; Italian campaign. Deacon, 1950; Priest, 1951; Asst Curate, Bury Parish Church, Lancs, 1950-53; Fellow of Jesus Coll., Cambridge, 1953-60, Chaplain, 1953-56, Dean, 1956-60, Tutor, 1957-60; Univ. Preacher, Cambridge, 1955; Examining Chaplain to Bishop of Lichfield, 1957-60; Dean of Hong Kong, 1960-64. Chm., Asia Christian Colleges Assoc., 1968-76, Vice-Pres., 1976-. Governor, British Inst. of Recorded Sound, 1967-72; Mem. Board, Youth and Music, 1965-; Adviser to Baring Foundn, 1967-; Mem., Adv. Council, V&A Museum, 1977-. Chm., Greater London AACE, 1976-82. Governor, St Olaf's Grammar Sch., 1973-; Mem., Cultural Cttee, European Culture Foundn, 1976-78. Trustee, Thomas Cubitt Trust, 1978-. *Publications:* contrib. to The Historic Episcopate, 1954; Change and Exchange, 1964; Changing Frontiers in the Mission of the Church, 1965; contrib. to A Holy Week Manual, 1967; The Churches Search for Unity, 1972. *Recreations:* travel, gardening, opera. *Address:* 44 Canonbury Square, N1 2AW. *T:* 01-359 0708.

TILLARD, Maj.-Gen. Philip Blencowe, CBE 1973; Assistant Director, Resort Services, Borough of Brighton, since 1977; *b* 2 Jan. 1923; *s* of late Brig. John Arthur Stuart Tillard, OBE, MC and of Margaret Penelope (*née* Blencowe); *m* 1953, Patricia Susan (*née* Robertson); three *s* one *d. Educ:* Winchester College. Commnd into 60th Rifles, 1942; served Syria, Italy and Greece, 1943-46; transf. to 13th/18th Royal Hussars (QMO), 1947; served in Libya, Malaya and Germany, comd Regt, 1964-66; psc 1956; jssc 1962; Comdr RAC 3rd Div., 1967-69; BGS (Army Trng), MoD, 1970-73; ADC to the Queen, 1970-73; COS, BAOR, 1973-76. *Recreations:* normal family pursuits; shooting. *Address:* Church House, Chailey Green, Lewes, East Sussex. *T:* Newick 2759. *Clubs:* Farmers'; Sussex.

TILLER, Rev. Canon John; Chief Secretary, Advisory Council for the Church's Ministry, since 1978; *b* 22 June 1938; *s* of Harry Maurice Tiller and Lucille Maisie Tiller; *m* 1961, Ruth Alison (*née* Watson); two *s* one *d. Educ:* St Albans Sch.; Christ Church, Oxford (MA, 2nd Cl. Mod. Hist.); Bristol

Univ. (MLitt). Ordained deacon 1962, priest 1963, St Albans. Asst Curate: St Cuthbert, Bedford, 1962-65; Widcombe, Bath, 1965-67; Chaplain and Tutor, Tyndale Hall, Bristol, 1967-71; Lectr in Church History and Worship, Trinity Coll., Bristol, 1971-73; Priest-in-Charge, Christ Church, Bedford, 1973-78. Hon. Canon of St Albans Cathedral, 1979-. *Publications:* The Service of Holy Communion and its Revision (with R. T. Beckwith), 1972; A Modern Liturgical Bibliography, 1974; The Great Acquittal, 1980; (contrib.) Anglican Worship Today, 1980. *Recreations:* caravanning, walking, bird-watching. *Address:* 31 Birch Close, Broom, Beds SG18 9NR. *T:* Biggleswade 313940; Church House, Dean's Yard, Westminster, SW1P 3NZ. *T:* 01-222 9011.

TILLEY, John Vincent; MP (Lab) Lambeth Central, since April 1978; journalist; *b* June 1941. Mem., St John Ward, Wandsworth Borough Council, 1971-78. Member: NUJ; Fabian Soc.; Co-operative Party. Contested (Lab) Kensington Div. of Kensington and Chelsea, Feb. and Oct. 1974. *Address:* House of Commons, SW1A 0AA.

TILLING, George Henry Garfield; Chairman, Scottish Postal Board, since 1977; *b* 24 Jan. 1924; *s* of late Thomas and of Anne Tilling; *m* 1956, Margaret Meriel, *d* of late Rear-Adm. Sir Alexander McGlashan, KBE, CB, DSO; two *s* two *d. Educ:* Hardye's Sch., Dorchester; University Coll., Oxford (Open Exhibnr, Kitchener Schol., Farquharson Prizeman, MA). Served War of 1939-45, NW Europe: Captain, Dorset Regt, 1943-46. Post Office: Asst Principal, 1948; Principal, 1953; Private Sec. to Postmaster General, 1964; Dep. Dir of Finance, 1965; Dir, Eastern Postal Region, 1967; Sec. of the Post Office, 1973-75; Dir of Postal Ops, 1975-77. Mem. Council, Lord Kitchener Nat. Meml Fund, 1979-. Mem. Council, Order of St John for London, 1975-77, Mem. Cttee of the Order for Edinburgh, 1978-. Hon. Mem., St Andrew's Ambulance Assoc., 1980. OStJ. FSAScot. *Recreations:* orders and medals, heraldry, uniforms. *Address:* 4 Glenorchy Terrace, Edinburgh EH9 2DQ. *T:* 031-668 2460. *Club:* Royal Over-Seas League.

TILLINGHAST, Charles Carpenter, Jr; Vice-President, Merrill Lynch Pierce Fenner & Smith Inc., since 1978; *b* 30 Jan. 1911; *s* of Charles Carpenter Tillinghast and Adelaide Barrows Shaw; *m* 1935, Elizabeth (Lisette) Judd Micoleau; one *s* three *d. Educ:* Horace Mann Sch.; Brown Univ. (PhB); Columbia Univ. (JD). Associate, Hughes, Schurman & Dwight, 1935-37; Dep. Asst Dist Attorney, NY County, 1938-40; Associate, Hughes, Richards, Hubbard & Ewing, 1940-42; Partner, Hughes, Hubbard and Ewing (and successor firm, Hughes, Hubbard, Blair & Reed), 1942-57; Vice-Pres. and Dir, The Bendix Corp., 1957-61; Pres. and Chief Exec. Officer, Trans World Airlines Inc., 1961-69 (Director, 1961-81; Chm. and Chief Exec. Officer, 1969-76); Vice-Chm., White, Weld & Co. Inc., 1977-78; Man. Dir, Merrill Lynch White Weld Capital Markets Gp, 1978-; Director: Amstar Corp., 1964-; Merck & Co., 1962-; Trustee: Mutual Life Ins. Co. of NY, 1966-; Brown Univ., 1954-61, 1965-79 (Chancellor, 1968-79; Fellow, 1979-); Mem. IATA Executive Cttee, 1969-76. Hon. Degrees: LHD, South Dakota Sch. of Mines and Tech., 1959; LLD: Franklin Coll., 1963; Univ. of Redlands, 1964; Brown Univ., 1967; Drury Coll., 1967; William Jewell Coll., 1973. *Recreations:* golf, shooting, gardening, woodworking, reading, Philharmonic and opera. *Address:* (business) 165 Broadway, One Liberty Plaza, New York, NY 10080, USA. *T:* (212) 285-2012; (home) 56 Oakledge Road, Bronxville, NY 10708, USA. *T:* (914) 337-6941. *Clubs:* Blind Brook, Brown Univ. (New York); Economic (NY); Hope (RI); Sky; Sakonnet Golf; Siwanoy Country (all in USA).

TILLOTSON, Maj.-Gen. Henry Michael, CBE 1976 (OBE 1970, MBE 1956); *b* 12 May 1928; *er s* of Henry Tillotson, Keighley, Yorks; *m* 1956, Angela, *d* of Bertram Wadsworth Shaw, E Yorks; two *s* one *d. Educ:* Chesterfield Sch.; RMA Sandhurst. Commnd E Yorks Regt, 1948; served: Austria, 1948-50; Germany, 1951-52; Indo-China (attached French Union Forces), 1953; Malaya, 1953-55; Staff Coll., Camberley, 1958; Malaysia, 1964-65; S Arabia, 1965-67 (Queen's Commendation); CO 1st Bn Prince of Wales's Own Regt of Yorks, Cyprus, 1969-71; Col GS, Hong Kong, 1974-76; Chief of Staff UN Force, Cyprus, and Comdr British Contingent, 1976-78; Dep. Dir, Army Staff Duties, MoD, 1978-79; Chief of Staff to C-in-C UKLF, 1980-83. Col, Prince of Wales's Own Regt of Yorks, 1979-. *Recreations:* travel, birds, listening to music. *Address:* c/o Lloyds Bank Ltd, 6 Pall Mall, SW1Y 5NH. *Club:* Army and Navy.

TILLOTSON, Prof. Kathleen Mary, FBA 1965; MA, BLitt; Hildred Carlile Professor of English in the University of London, at Bedford College, 1958-71, now Emeritus; *b* 3 April 1906; *e d* of late Eric A. Constable, BLitt (Durham), journalist, and Catherine H. Constable, Berwick-on-Tweed and Birmingham; *m* 1933, Geoffrey Tillotson, FBA (*d* 1969); two adopted *s. Educ:* Ackworth School; Mount School, York; Somerville College, Oxford (Exhibitioner and Shaw Lefevre Scholar). Charles Oldham Shakespeare Scholarship, 1926; BA 1927; temporary tutor, Somerville College, 1928-29; BLitt 1929; teaching at Somerville and St Hilda's Colleges, 1929-39; part-time Assistant, later Junior Lecturer, 1929, Lecturer, 1939, Fellow, 1971, Bedford College; Reader in the University of London at Bedford College, 1947-58. Vice-Pres., Dickens Fellowship; Trustee: Dove Cottage; Bosanquet Trust. Warton Lecture, British Academy, 1956; Dickens Meml Lecture, 1970; Annual Tennyson Lecture, 1974; Robert Spence Watson Lecture, 1978. James Bryce Memorial Lecture, Somerville College, Oxford, 1963, Hon. Fellow, 1965. Hon. DLit Belfast, 1972; Hon. DLitt: Oxon, 1982; London, 1982. Rose Mary Crawshay prize, British Academy, 1943. *Publications:* (with J. W. Hebel and B. H. Newdigate) Works of Michael Drayton, Vol. V, 1941; Novels of

the Eighteen-Forties, 1954; Matthew Arnold and Carlyle (Warton Lecture), 1957; (with John Butt) Dickens at Work, 1957; Introductions to Trollope's Barsetshire novels, 1958-75; The Tale and the Teller (inaug. lect.), 1959; Vanity Fair (ed with G. Tillotson), 1963; Mid-Victorian Studies (with G. Tillotson), 1965; Letters of Charles Dickens, vol. 1, 1965, vol. 2, 1969, vol. 3, 1974 (Associate Editor); vol. 4, 1977 (Editor) (General Editor, 1978-); Oliver Twist, 1966; (General Editor, Clarendon Dickens, 1957-); (ed with A. Trodd) The Woman in White, 1969; (ed) Oliver Twist (World's Classics), 1982; contributions to periodicals. *Address:* 23 Tanza Road, NW3. *T:* 01-435 5639. *Club:* University Women's.

TILMOUTH, Prof. Michael; first Tovey Professor of Music, University of Edinburgh, since 1971; *b* 30 Nov. 1930; *s* of Herbert George Tilmouth and Amy Tilmouth (*née* Hall); *m* 1966, Mary Jelliman; two *s* one *d. Educ:* Wintringham Grammar Sch., Grimsby; Christ's Coll., Cambridge (MA, PhD). Lectr, Glasgow Univ., 1959-71; Dean, Faculty of Music, Edinburgh Univ., 1973-76, 1980-. Dir, Scottish Opera, 1975-. Mem., BBC Archives Adv. Cttee, 1975-. Mem. Council, Royal Musical Assoc., 1970-76 (Editor, Research Chronicle, 1968-77); Member, Editorial Committee: Musica Britannica, 1972-; Purcell Soc., 1976-. *Publications:* (ed) Matthew Locke: Chamber Music (Musica Britannica, vols xxxi and xxxii), 1971 and 1972; (ed) Purcell: Collected Works, vol. v, 1976, vol. vii, 1981, vol. xxxi, 1982; contribs to: Galpin Soc. Jl, Music & Letters, Proc. of Royal Musical Assoc., Musical Times, Musical Quarterly, Royal Mus. Assoc. Res. Chronicle, Encyc. de la Pléiade, Die Musik in Geschichte und Gegenwart, Grove's Dictionary, Monthly Mus. Record, The Consort, Brio, Early Music. *Recreations:* gardening, hill walking. *Address:* 62 Northumberland Street, Edinburgh EH3 6JE. *T:* 031-556 3293.

TILNEY, Charles Edward, CMG 1956; Minister for Finance and Economics, Tanganyika, 1957-60; *b* 13 April 1909; *yr s* of late Lt-Col N. E. Tilney, CBE, DSO, and late Mrs Tilney; *m* 1952, Rosalind Hull, *e d* of late Lt-Col E. C. de Renzy-Martin, CMG, DSO, MC, and Mrs de Renzy-Martin; two *s. Educ:* Rugby School; Oriel College, Oxford. Ceylon Civil Service, 1932; Tanganyika: Asst Chief Secretary (Finance), 1948; Dep. Financial Secretary, 1948; Secretary for Finance, 1950; Member for Finance and Economics, 1953. Retd from E Africa, 1960. *Address:* 8 Butts Close, Biddestone, Chippenham, Wilts. *T:* Corsham 714770.

TILNEY, Guinevere, (Lady Tilney); UK Representative on United Nations Commission on Status of Women, 1970-73; *b* 8 Sept. 1916; *y d* of late Sir Hamilton Grant, 12th Bt, KCSI, KCIE, and late Lady Grant; *m* 1st, 1944, Captain Lionel Hunter (*d* 1947), Princess Louise Dragoon Guards; one *s* ; 2nd, 1954, Sir John Tilney, *qv. Educ:* Westonbirt. WRNS, 1941-45; Private Sec. to Earl of Selborne, 1945-54; Vice-Chm., SE Lancs Br., British Empire Cancer Campaign, 1957-64; Founder Mem., 1st Chm., 1st Pres., Merseyside Conservative Ladies Luncheon Club, 1957-75, now 1st Hon. Life Mem.; Nat. Council of Women of Great Britain: Vice-Pres., 1958-61, Pres., 1961-68, Liverpool and Birkenhead Br.; Sen. Nat. Vice-Pres., 1966-68; Nat. Pres., 1968-70; Co-Chm., Women's Nat. Commn, 1969-71; Mem., North Thames Gas Consultative Council, 1967-69; Mem., BBC Gen. Adv. Council, 1967-76. Co-Chm., Women Caring Trust, 1972-75. DL: Co. Palatine of Lancaster, 1971-74; Co. Merseyside, 1974-76. *Recreations:* reading, music, theatre. *Address:* 3 Victoria Square, SW1. *T:* 01-828 8674.

TILNEY, Sir John (Dudley Robert Tarleton), Kt 1973; TD; JP; *b* 19 Dec. 1907; *yr s* of late Col R. H. Tilney, DSO; *m* 1954, Guinevere Tilney, *qv* ; one step *s. Educ:* Eton; Magdalen College, Oxford. Served during War of 1939-45 (despatches), with 59th (4th West Lancs) Medium Regt, RA, and 11th Medium Regt, RA; commanded 47/49 359 (4th West Lancs), Medium Regt RATA; Hon. Col 470 (3 W Lancs), LAA Regt, 1957-61. MP (C) Wavertree, Liverpool, 1950-Feb. 1974; Parliamentary Private Sec. to: Sec. of State for War, 1951-55; Postmaster-General, 1957-59; Chm. Inter-Parly Union, Brit. Gp, 1959-62; Chm. Conservative Commonwealth Council W Africa Cttee, 1954-62; PPS to Minister of Transport, 1959-62; Parly Under-Sec. of State for Commonwealth Relations, 1962-64 and for the Colonies, 1963-64; Member: Select Cttee on Expenditure; Exec. Cttee, Nat. Union of Conservative and Unionist Assocs, 1965-73; Chm. Merseyside Conservative MPs, 1964-74 (Vice-Chm., NW Area Cttee); Treasurer, UK Branch, Commonwealth Parly Assoc., 1968-70; Mem., Exec. Cttee, Cons. Political Centre, 1972-81. Chairman: Liverpool Luncheon Club, 1948-49; Liverpool Branch, Royal Commonwealth Soc., 1955-60 (Pres., 1965); Victoria Square Assoc., 1959-; Winston Churchill Meml Statue Cttee; Airey Neave Meml Trust, 1979-. Member: Liverpool Cathedral Gen. Council; Exec. Cttee, Westminster Soc., 1975-; Council, Imperial Soc. of Knights Bachelor, 1978-. Pres., Assoc. of Lancastrians in London, 1980-81. Trustee, Bluecoat Sch.; Governor, Liverpool Coll. JP Liverpool, 1946. Croix de Guerre with Gilt Star, 1945; Legion of Honour, 1960. *Recreations:* gardening, travel. *Address:* 3 Victoria Square, SW1W 0QZ. *T:* 01-828 8674. *Clubs:* Pratt's, MCC, Carlton; Jesters; Liverpool Cricket, Liverpool Racquet.

TILSTON, Col Frederick Albert, VC 1945; CD; *b* Toronto, Ontario, 11 June 1906; *s* of late Fred Tilston, English birth, and late Agnes Estelle Le May, Cdn birth; *m* 1946; one *s. Educ:* De La Salle Collegiate, Toronto; Ontario College of Pharmacy (graduated 1929). Salesman for Sterling Products Ltd, Windsor, Ont., manufacturers of nationally advertised drug products, 1930-36; Canadian Sales Manager for Sterling Products Ltd, 1937-40; Vice-Pres. in charge of sales, Sterling Products Ltd, Windsor, Ontario, 1946-57; Pres.,

Sterling Drug Ltd, 1957-70; retired 1971. Canadian Army, 1941-46. Hon. Col, Essex and Kent Scottish Regt. CStJ. Hon. Dr Laws Windsor, 1977. *Recreations:* swimming, ice hockey, golf; amateur pianist. *Address:* RR No 1, Kettleby, Ont L0G 1J0, Canada. *T:* 416-727 5945. *Clubs:* New Windsor, Press, Essex County Golf and Country (Windsor, Ont); Royal Canadian Military Institute (Toronto); Summitt Golf and Country (Oak Ridges).

TIMBERLAKE, Herman Leslie Patterson, (Tim); Director, Abbey National Building Society, since 1972 (Chief General Manager, 1971-79; Deputy Chairman, 1976-79); *b* 3 Feb. 1914; *s* of William Walter and Mabel Timberlake; *m* 1940, Betty (*née* Curtis); two *s*. *Educ:* Watford Grammar Sch. FCIS; FCBSI; CBIM. Served War of 1939-45. Joined Abbey Road Building Soc., 1930; Asst Branch Manager, Watford, 1936; became Abbey National Building Soc., 1944; Branch Manager appts, 1946-59; Manager: Branches Admin. Dept, 1959; Investments Admin. Dept, 1964; Branches and Agencies, 1966; Jt General Manager, 1968. Mem. Council, Building Societies Assoc.; Pres., Building Societies Institute, 1977-78. *Address:* 1 Rochester Drive, Pinner, Mddx HA5 1DA. *T:* 01-866 1554.

TIMBURY, Prof. Gerald Charles, FRCPE; FRCPGlas; FRCPsych; Dean of Postgraduate Medicine and Professor of Postgraduate Medical Education, University of Glasgow, since 1980; *b* 15 Aug. 1929; *s* of Montague Charles and Marjorie Lilian Timbury, Glasgow; *m* 1954, Morag Crichton McCulloch; one *d*. *Educ:* Glasgow Acad.; Glasgow Univ. MB, ChB; DPM. Captain, RAMC, 1953-55. Usual resident appointments, 1952-53; Hosp. appointments in medicine and psychiatry, Glasgow, 1955-60; Lectr in Psychological Medicine, Univ. of Glasgow, 1960-65; Physician Superintendent, Gartnavel Royal Hosp., 1965-80. *Publications:* papers on psychiatric diagnosis, mental health legislation, and psychiatry of old age. *Recreation:* golf. *Address:* 8/2 Whistlefield, 2 Canniesburn Road, Bearsden, Glasgow G61 1PX. *T:* 041-943 0430. *Clubs:* Caledonian, Royal Scottish Automobile (Glasgow).

TIMMS, Dr Cecil, DEng, CEng, FIMechE, FIProdE; Engineering Consultant, Department of Trade and Industry, later Department of Industry, since 1974; *b* 13 Dec. 1911; *m* ; no *c*. *Educ:* Liverpool Univ. Head of Metrology, Mechanisms and Noise Control Div., 1950-61, Supt of Machinery Group, 1961-65, National Engrg Laboratory; Head of Machine Tools Branch, Min. of Technology, later DTI, 1965-73. *Publications:* contribs to Proc. IMechE, Metalworking Prod. and Prod. Engr. *Address:* Broom House, Ballsdown, Chiddingfold, Surrey. *T:* Wormley 2014.

TIMMS, Ven. George Boorne; Archdeacon of Hackney, 1971-81, now Emeritus; Vicar of St Andrew, Holborn, 1965-81; *b* 4 Oct. 1910; *s* of late George Timms and Annie Elizabeth Timms (*née* Boorne); unmarried. *Educ:* Derby Sch.; St Edmund Hall, Oxford; Coll. of the Resurrection, Mirfield. MA Oxon. Deacon, 1935; Priest, 1936; Curate: St Mary Magdalen, Coventry, 1935-38; St Bartholomew, Reading, 1938-49; Oxford Diocesan Inspector of Schools, 1944-49; Sacrist of Southwark Cath., 1949-52; Vicar of St Mary, Primrose Hill, NW3, 1952-65; Rural Dean of Hampstead, 1959-65; Prebendary of St Paul's Cathedral, 1964-71. Proctor in Conv., 1955-59, 1965-70, 1974-80; Member: Standing Cttee Church Assembly, 1968-70; Anglican-Methodist Unity Commn, 1965-69. Dir of Ordination Trg, and Exam. Chap. to Bp of London, 1965-81; Chm., Alcuin Club, 1968-. Pres., Sion Coll., 1980-81. Papal Medallion for services to Christian Unity, 1976. *Publications:* Dixit Cranmer, 1946; The Liturgical Seasons, 1965; (jtly) The Cloud of Witnesses, 1982; contributor to A Manual for Holy Week, 1967; (ed) English Praise, 1975. *Address:* Cleve Lodge, Minster-in-Thanet, Ramsgate, Kent CT12 4BA. *T:* Thanet 821777.

TIMSON, Penelope Anne Constance; see Keith, P. A. C.

TINBERGEN, Dr Jan; Officer, Order of The Lion; Commander, Order of Orange Nassau; Professor, Netherlands School of Economics, since 1933; *b* 12 April 1903; *s* of Dirk Cornelis Tinbergen and Jeannette Van Eek; *m* 1929, Tine Johanna De Wit; three *d* (and one *d* decd). *Educ:* Leiden University. On Staff, Central Bureau of Statistics, 1929-45; Staff, League of Nations, 1936-38; Director, Central Planning Bureau (Dutch Government), 1945-55; Advisor to various governments and international organisations, 1955-; Chm., UN Develt Planning Cttee, 1965-72. Hon. Degrees from 20 Universities, 1954-. (Jointly) Prize in Economics to the memory of Alfred Nobel, 1969. *Publications:* Economic Policy, Principles and Design, 1956; Selected Papers, 1959; Shaping the World Economy, 1962; Income Distribution, 1975; articles. *Recreations:* languages, drawing. *Address:* Haviklaan 31, 2566XD The Hague, Netherlands. *T:* 070-644630.

See also N. Tinbergen.

TINBERGEN, Prof. Nikolaas, DPhil, MA; FRS 1962; Professor in Animal Behaviour, Oxford University, 1966-74, Emeritus Professor, 1974 (Lecturer, 1949-60, Reader, 1960-66); Fellow of Wolfson College, 1966-74, now Emeritus; *b* 15 April 1907; *s* of Dirk C. Tinbergen and Jeannette Van Eek; *m* 1932, Elisabeth A. Rutten; two *s* three *d*. *Educ:* Leiden; Vienna; Yale. Lecturer, 1936, Prof. of Experimental Zoology, 1947, Leiden University; Fellow, Merton Coll., Oxford Univ., 1950-66. Hon. Mem. of many learned socs. Hon. DSc: Edinburgh, 1973; Leicester, 1974; Santiago de Compostela, 1982. Godman-Salvin Medal, British Ornithol. Union, 1969. Italia Prize (documentaries), 1969; Swammerdam Medal, 1973; Nobel Prize for Physiology or Medicine (jt), 1973. *Publications:* Eskimoland, 1935; The Study of Instinct, 1951; The Herring Gull's World, 1953; Social Behaviour in

Animals, 1953; Curious Naturalists, 1959; Animal Behaviour, 1965; Signals for Survival, 1970; The Animal in its World, vol. 1, 1972, vol. 2, 1973; (with E. A. Tinbergen) 'Autistic' Children: the possibility of a cure, 1982; contribs to German, Dutch, British and American journals. *Address:* 88 Lonsdale Road, Oxford OX2 7ER. *T:* Oxford 58662.

See also Dr J. Tinbergen.

TINDAL-CARILL-WORSLEY, Air Commodore Geoffrey Nicolas Ernest, CB 1954; CBE 1943; Royal Air Force, retired; *b* 8 June 1908; *s* of late Philip Tindal-Carill-Worsley; *m* 1st, 1937, Berys Elizabeth Gilmour (marr. diss., 1951; she *d* 1962); one *s* ; 2nd, 1951, Dorothy Mabel Murray Stanley-Turner. *Educ:* Eton; RAF Coll., Cranwell. Commanding Officer, RAF Station, Halton, Bucks, 1954-56; Sen. Technical Staff Officer, Far East Air Force, 1956-59; Director of Technical Training, Air Ministry, 1959; retired 1960. *Recreation:* country life.

TINDALE, Lawrence Victor Dolman, CBE 1971; Deputy Chairman: Finance For Industry, Industrial & Commercial Finance Corporation, Technical Development Capital, all since 1974; Chairman, Finance For Shipping; *b* 24 April 1921; *s* of late John Stephen and Alice Lilian Tindale; *m* 1946, Beatrice Mabel (Betty) Barton; one *s* one *d*. *Educ:* Upper Latymer Sch., Hammersmith; Inst. of Chartered Accountants of Scotland. Apprenticed McClelland Ker, 1938. Served War, Army, in E Africa and Burma, 1941-45. Returned to McClelland Ker, and qualified, 1946; Partner, 1951. Invited to join ICFC Ltd as Asst Gen. Manager, 1959; Dir and Gen. Manager, 1966-72. On secondment, DTI, as Dir of Industrial Development, 1972-74. Member: DTI Cttee of Inquiry on Small Firms, 1969-71; Adv. Council on Energy Conservation, 1977-80; BNOC, 1980-; British Technology Gp (NRDC, 1974-; NEB, 1981-); Chm., EDC for Mechanical Engrg Industry, 1968-72. Director: Commodore Shipping Co. Ltd, 1969-; Guernsey Gas Light Co. Ltd, 1970-; Investment Trust of Guernsey Ltd, 1970-; General Funds Investment Trust, 1974-; Edbro Holdings Ltd (Chm.), 1974-; Northern Engineering Industries Ltd, 1974-; London American Internat. Corp. Ltd (Dep. Chm.), 1975-82; Trind Ltd (Chm.), 1975-; Flextech Oil Pipe (Holdings) Ltd, 1975-; London Atlantic Investment Trust Ltd (Chm.), 1977-; N British and Canadian Investment Trust Ltd (Chm.), 1979-; Scottish Ontario Investment Trust Ltd, 1979-; Transpec Holdings Ltd, 1980-; Dewrance MacNeil Ltd, 1980-; Caledonian Airways plc, 1980-; London American Marketing Corp. (Dep. Chm.), 1982-. Mem. Council: Consumer Assoc., 1970- (Vice Chm., 1981-); BIM, 1974- (Chm. 1982-); Soc. for Preservation of Ancient Buildings (Hon. Treasurer), 1974-. CA; CBIM. *Recreation:* opera. *Address:* 3 Amyand Park Gardens, Twickenham, TW1 3HS. *T:* 01-892 9457; Le Bouillon House, St George's Esplanade, St Peter Port, Guernsey. *T:* Guernsey 21688. *Clubs:* Reform; St James's (Manchester).

TINDALE, Patricia Randall; Chief Architect, Department of the Environment, since 1982; *b* 11 March 1926; *d* of Thomas John Tindale and May Tindale (*née* Uttin). *Educ:* Blatchington Court, Seaford, Sussex; Architectural Assoc. Sch. of Architecture (AADip.). ARIBA. Architect, Welsh Dept, Min. of Educn, 1949-50; Min. of Educn Develt Gp, 1951-60; Min. of Housing and Local Govt R&D Gp, 1960-70; DoE Housing Develt Gp, 1970-72; Head, Building Regulations Professional Div., DoE, 1972-74; Dir, Housing Develt Directorate, DoE, 1974-81; Dir, Central Unit of Built Environment, DoE, 1981-82. Mem., AA Council, 1965-68. *Publication:* Housebuilding in the USA, 1966. *Recreations:* weaving, travel. *Address:* 34 Crescent Grove, SW4 7AH.

TINDALL, Rev. Canon Frederick Cryer, BD 1923; AKC 1922; Principal Emeritus of Salisbury Theological College since 1965; Canon and Prebendary Emeritus of Salisbury Cathedral since 1981; *b* 2 July 1900; *s* of late Frederick and Frances Tindall, Hove, Sussex; *m* 1942, Rosemary Phyllis, *d* of late Frank and Katharine Alice Newman, Woking; one *s* (one *d* decd). *Educ:* Brighton Grammar Sch.; King's Coll., London (Fellow, 1951-); Ely Theological College. Curate of S Cyprian, S Marylebone, 1924-28; Lecturer and Bursar, Chichester Theological College, 1928-30, Vice-Principal, 1930-36; Warden of Connaught Hall and Lecturer in Theology, University College, Southampton, 1936-39; Vicar of St Augustine, Brighton, 1939-50; Principal, Salisbury Theological Coll., 1950-65 (Sabbatical Year 1945-46). Proctor in Convocation for Diocese of Chichester, 1936-45, 1949-50; Examining Chaplain to Bishop of Chichester, 1941-50, Canon and Prebendary of Chichester Cathedral, 1948-50; Canon and Prebendary of Salisbury Cathedral, 1950-81; Proctor in Convocation for Diocese of Salisbury, 1950-75; Vice-Pres. and Chm. House of Clergy, Salisbury Diocesan Synod, 1970-76; Chm., Salisbury Diocesan Liturgical Cttee, 1973-81; Member: Commn for Revision of the Catechism, 1958; Church Assembly Standing Orders Cttee, 1963; Archbishop's Commn on London and SE England, 1965; Greater London Area Liaison Cttee, 1968; Pastoral Measure Appeal Tribunal, 1969-75; General Synod Standing Orders Cttee, 1970-75. Clerical Judge, Court of Arches, Canterbury, 1969-80. Pro-Prolocutor, Lower House of Convocation of Canterbury, 1959-75. *Publications:* England Expects, 1946; a History of S Augustine's Brighton, 1946; Christian Initiation, Anglican Principles and Practice, 1951; contributor to: History of Christian Thought, 1937; Encyclopædia Britannica Year Book, 1939; Baptism To-Day, 1949; Theology, Church Quarterly Review, Guardian, etc. *Recreations:* music, travelling, golf, gardening. *Address:* 16 The Close, Salisbury, Wilts SP1 2EB. *T:* Salisbury 22373. *Clubs:* Athenæum, Royal Commonwealth Society, Ski Club of Great Britain.

TINDALL, Gillian Elizabeth; novelist, biographer, historian; *b* 4 May 1938; *d* of D. H. Tindall and U. M. D. Orange; *m* 1963, Richard G. Lansdown; one *s. Educ:* Univ. of Oxford (BA 1st cl., MA). Freelance journalism: for Observer; subseq. Guardian and New Statesman, 1960-; for Evening Standard, 1973-. *Publications:* novels: No Name in the Street, 1959; The Water and the Sound, 1961; The Edge of the Paper, 1963; The Youngest, 1967; Someone Else, 1969, 2nd edn 1975; Fly Away Home, 1971 (Somerset Maugham Award, 1972); The Traveller and His Child, 1975; The Intruder, 1979, etc; *short stories:* Dances of Death, 1973; The China Egg and Other Stories, 1981; *biography:* The Born Exile (George Gissing), 1974; *other non-fiction:* A Handbook on Witchcraft, 1965; The Fields Beneath, 1977; City of Gold: the biography of Bombay, 1981; contribs to Encounter. *Recreations:* keeping house, foreign travel. *Address:* c/o Curtis Brown Ltd, 1 Craven Hill, W2.

TINDEMANS, Leo; President, European People's Party; Visiting Professor in the Faculty of Social Sciences, Catholic University, Louvain; *b* Zwijndrecht, 16 April 1922; *m* 1960, Rosa Naesens; two *s* two *d. Educ:* State Univ., Ghent; Catholic Univ., Louvain. Mem., Chamber of Deputies (Christian Social Party), 1961; Mayor of Edegem, 1965-76; Minister of: Community Affairs, 1968-71; Agriculture and Middle Class Affairs, 1972-73; Dep. Prime Minister and Minister for the Budget and Institutional Problems, 1973-74; Prime Minister of Belgium, 1974-78; Minister of For. Relations, 1981-. Pres., Christian People's Party, 1979. Awarded Charlemagne Prize, 1976; St Liborius Medaille für Einheit und Frieden, 1977; Stresemann Medaille, 1979; Schuman Prize, 1980. Hon. DLitt: City Univ., 1976; Heriot-Watt Univ., 1978. *Publications:* Ontwikkeling van de Benelux, 1958; L'autonomie culturelle, 1971; Regionalized Belgium, Transition from the Nation State to the Multinational State, 1972; Een handvest voor woelig België, 1972; Dagboek van de werkgroep Eyskens, 1973; European Union, 1975; Europe, Ideal of our Generation, 1976; Atlantisch Europa, 1980. *Recreations:* reading, writing, walking. *Address:* rue Quatre Bras 2, Brussels, Belgium.

TINDLE, David, RA 1979 (ARA 1973); painter; *b* 29 April 1932; *m* 1969, Janet Trollope; one *s* two *d. Educ:* Coventry Sch. of Art. Worked as scene painter and commercial artist, 1946-51; subseq. taught at Hornsey Coll. of Art; Vis. Tutor, Royal Coll. of Art, 1972-, Fellow, 1981. First showed work, Archer Gall., 1952 and 1953; regular one-man exhibns, Piccadilly Gall., from 1954; one-man exhibns at many public and private galleries in Gt Britain; Galerie du Tours, San Francisco and Los Angeles, 1964; Gallerie Vinciana, Milan, 1968; Galleria Carbonesi, Bologna, 1968; Gallery XX, Hamburg, 1974, 1977, 1980; rep. in exhibns at: Piccadilly Gall., 1954-; Royal Acad.; Internat. Biennale of Realist Art, Bruges, 1958 and Bologna, 1967; British Exhibn Art, Basel, 1958; John Moores, 1959 and 1961; Arts Council Shows: British Self-Portraits; Painters in East Anglia; Thames in Art; The British Art Show, 1979-80; Salon de la Jeune Peinture, Paris, 1967; Mostra Mercato d'Arte Contemporanea, Florence, 1967; British Painting 1974, Hayward Gall.; British Painting 1952-77, RA. Set of 3 Mural decorations for Open Univ., Milton Keynes, 1977-78. Work rep. in numerous public and private collections; Chantrey Bequest purchases, 1974 and 1975, now in Tate Gall. Critic Prize, 1962; Europe Prize for Painting, 1969; Critics' Choice, Tooths, 1974; Waddington Prize, Chichester Nat. Art Exhibn, 1975. *Address:* Clipston House, The Green, Clipston, near Market Harborough, Leics.

TING, Prof. Samuel Chao Chung; Thomas D. Cabot Institute Professor, Massachusetts Institute of Technology, since 1977; *b* 27 Jan. 1936; *s* of K. H. Ting and late T. S. Wang; *m* 1960, Kay Louise Kuhne; two *d. Educ:* Univ. of Michigan (PhD). Ford Fellow, CERN, Geneva, 1963; Asst Prof. of Physics, Columbia Univ., 1965; Prof. of Physics, MIT, 1969. Assoc. Editor, Nuclear Physics B, 1970; Mem. Editorial Bd, Nuclear Instruments and Methods, 1977. Member: US Nat. Acad. of Science, 1976; European Physical Soc.; Italian Physical Soc. Fellow, Amer. Acad. of Arts and Science, 1975. Nobel Prize for Physics (jt), 1976; Ernest Orlando Lawrence Award, US Govt, 1976; A. E. Eringen Medal, Soc. of Engineering Science, USA, 1977. Hon. ScD Michigan, 1978. *Publications:* articles in Physical Review and Physical Review Letters. *Address:* 15 Moon Hill Road, Lexington, Mass 02173, USA. *Club:* Explorers' (NY).

TINKER, Prof. Hugh Russell; Professor of Politics, University of Lancaster, since 1977; *b* 20 July 1921; *s* of late Clement Hugh Tinker and Gertrude Marian Tinker; *m* 1947, Elisabeth McKenzie (*née* Willis); three *s. Educ:* Taunton Sch.; Sidney Sussex Coll., Cambridge (BA Scholar). Indian Army, 1941-45; Indian civil admin, 1945-46. Lectr, Reader and Prof., SOAS, 1948-69; Dir, Inst. of Race Relations 1970-72; Sen. Fellow, Inst. of Commonwealth Studies, Univ. of London, 1972-77. Prof., Univ. of Rangoon, 1954-55; Prof., Cornell Univ., USA, 1959. Mem. Council, Minority Rights Gp; Trustee, Noel Buxton Trust. Contested (L): Barnet, gen. elecs 1964 and 1966; Morecambe and Lonsdale, 1979. *Publications:* The Foundations of Local Self-Government in India, Pakistan and Burma, 1954; The Union of Burma, a Study of the First Years of Independence, 1957 (4th edn 1967); India and Pakistan, a Political Analysis, 1962; Ballot Box and Bayonet, People and Government in Emergent Asian Countries, 1964; Reorientations, Studies on Asia in Transition, 1965; South Asia, a Short History, 1966; Experiment with Freedom, India and Pakistan 1947, 1967; (ed and wrote introduction) Henry Yule: Narrative of the Mission to the Court of Ava in 1855, 1969; A New System of Slavery: the export of Indian labour overseas 1830-1920, 1974; Separate and Unequal: India and the Indians in the British Commonwealth 1920-1950, 1976; The Banyan Tree: overseas emigrants from India, Pakistan and Bangladesh, 1977; Race, Conflict and the International Order: from

Empire to United Nations, 1977; The Ordeal of Love: C. F. Andrews and India, 1979. *Recreations:* writing, walking. *Address:* Montbegon, Hornby, near Lancaster; Aspen Lea, Little Hampden, Bucks.

TINN, James; MP (Lab) Teesside, Redcar, since 1974 (Cleveland, 1964-74); *b* 23 Aug. 1922; *s* of James Tinn and Nora (*née* Davie). *Educ:* Consett Elementary School; Ruskin College; Jesus College, Oxford. Cokeworker until 1953; Branch official, Nat. Union of Blastfurnacemen. Full-time study for BA (PPE Oxon). Teacher, secondary modern school, 1958-64. PPS to Sec. of State for Commonwealth (formerly Commonwealth Relations), 1965-66, to Minister for Overseas Development, 1966-67; an Asst Govt Whip, 1976-79; an Opposition Whip, 1979-82. Mem. Exec. Cttee, CPA. *Address:* 1 Norfolk Road, Moorside, Consett, Co. Durham. *T:* Consett 509313; 8 Woodlands Gate, Putney, SW15. *Club:* United Oxford & Cambridge University.

TINNISWOOD, Maurice Owen; *b* 26 March 1919; *y s* of late Robert Tinniswood, OBE; *m* 1946, Anne Katharine, *yr d* of late Rev. J. Trevor Matchett; one *s* one *d. Educ:* Merchant Taylors' School. Served with Royal Hampshire Regt, 1939-46 (Major). Joined PO, 1938 as Executive Officer, Principal, 1949; Asst Secretary, 1958; Imperial Defence College, 1963; Director of Establishments and Organisation, 1965; Director of Reorganization, 1966; Secretary to the Post Office, 1969-70; Dir of Personnel, BBC, 1970-77. Chm., Kingston, Richmond and Esher Community Health Council, 1980-81; Mem., Kingston and Esher HA, 1982-. CBIM. *Address:* Little Croft, Weston Green Road, Thames Ditton, Surrey. *T:* 01-398 4561. *Club:* Chichester Yacht.

TINSLEY, Charles Henry, FRICS; FRVA; Deputy Chief Valuer, Inland Revenue Valuation Office, 1974-78; *b* 3 March 1914; *s* of Arthur William and Teresa Tinsley; *m* 1938, Solway Lees; two *s* one *d. Educ:* Ratcliffe Coll., Leicester. Served War: joined TA, 1939; commn in Royal Artillery, 1941; with Lanarkshire Yeomanry, RA, in ME, Sicily and Italy; GSOII, in ME Supply Centre, Tehran, 1945-46. Nottinghamshire and W Riding of Yorkshire County Valuation Depts, 1929-39; Co. Valuer, N Riding of Yorkshire, 1948. Re-joined TA, 1948, and retd as Lt-Col, 1955. Joined Valuation Office, 1949; Suptg Valuer (Rating) Northern Region, 1949-68; Asst Chief Valuer, 1968. *Recreations:* coarse travel, reading. *Address:* 44 Belgrave Manor, Brooklyn Road, Woking, Surrey GU22 7TW. *T:* Woking 67444.

TINSLEY, Rt. Rev. Ernest John; *see* Bristol, Bishop of.

TIPPET, Rear-Adm. Anthony Sanders; Flag Officer and Port Admiral, Portsmouth, and Chief Naval Supply and Secretariat Officer, since 1981; *b* 2 Oct. 1928; *s* of W. K. R. Tippet and H. W. P. Kitley (*née* Sanders); *m* 1950, Lola Bassett; two *s* one *d* (and one *s* decd). *Educ:* West Buckland Sch., Devon. Called to the Bar, Gray's Inn, 1959. Entered RN, 1946; Lieut 1950; HM Ships Ceres, Superb, Staff C-in-C Mediterranean; Lt Comdr 1958; HMS Trafalgar, Britannia RNC; Comdr 1963; Secretary: to Director of Naval Intelligence; to Flag Officer Middle East; CO HMS Jufair, Supply Officer, HMS Eagle; Captain 1970: Asst Director Naval Plans (Warfare), 1970-72; CSO (Administration) to Flag Officer Plymouth, 1972-74; Director of Naval Officers' Appointments (Supply and WRNS Officers), 1974-76; Captain HMS Pembroke and Flag Captain to Flag Officer Medway, 1976-79; Rear-Adm. 1979; Asst Chief of Fleet Support, MoD, 1979-81. *Recreations:* sailing, hill walking. *Address:* c/o Lloyds Bank, 260 Union Street, Torquay, Devon TQ2 5QU. *Club:* Royal Naval Sailing Association (Portsmouth).

TIPPETT, Sir Michael (Kemp), CH 1979; Kt 1966; CBE 1959; Composer; *b* 2 Jan. 1905; *s* of Henry William Tippett and Isabel Kemp. *Educ:* Stamford Grammar Sch.; Royal College of Music (Foley Scholar; FRCM 1961). Ran Choral and Orchestral Society, Oxted, Surrey, and taught French at Hazelwood School, till 1931. Entered Adult Education work in music (LCC and Royal Arsenal Co-operative Soc. Educn Depts), 1932. Director of Music at Morley College, London, 1940-51. Sent to prison for 3 months as a conscientious objector, June 1943. A Child of Our Time first performed March 1944, broadcast Jan. 1945. 1st Symphony performed Nov. 1945 by Liverpool Philharmonic Society. Artistic Dir, Bath Festival, 1969-74. Pres., Kent Opera Company, 1979-. Hon. Mem., Amer. Acad. of Arts and Letters, 1976; Extraordinary Mem., Akad. der Künste, Berlin, 1976. Cobbett Medal for Chamber Music, 1948; Gold Medal, Royal Philharmonic Society, 1976. Honorary degrees include: MusD Cambridge, 1964; DMus: Trinity Coll., Dublin, 1964; Leeds, 1965; Oxford, 1967; London, 1975; DUniv York, 1966; DLitt Warwick, 1974. *Works include:* String Quartet No 1, 1935; Piano Sonata, 1937; Concerto for Double String Orchestra, 1939; A Child of Our Time, Oratorio, 1941; Fantasia on a theme of Handel for Piano and Orchestra, 1942; String Quartet, No 2, 1943; Symphony No 1, 1945; String Quartet No 3, 1946; Little Music for Strings, 1946; Suite in D, 1948; Song Cycle, The Heart's Assurance, 1951; Opera, The Midsummer Marriage, 1952 (first performed 1955); Ritual Dances, excerpts from the Opera for Orchestra, 1952; Fantasia Concertante on a Theme of Corelli for String Orchestra, 1953 (commnd for Edinburgh Festival); Divertimento, 1955; Concerto for piano and orchestra, 1956 (commnd by City of Birmingham Symphony Orch.); Symphony No 2, 1957 (commnd by BBC); Crown of the Year (commnd by Badminton School), 1958; Opera, King Priam (commnd by Koussevitzky Foundation of America), 1961; Magnificat and Nunc Dimittis (commnd by St John's Coll., Cambridge), 1961; Piano Sonata No 2, 1962; Incidental music to The Tempest, 1962; Praeludium for Brass etc (commnd by BBC), 1962; Cantata, The Vision of St Augustine, 1966; The Shires Suite, 1970; Opera, The Knot Garden, 1970; Songs for Dov, 1970; Symphony No 3, 1972; Piano Sonata no 3, 1973; Opera, The Ice Break, 1977; Symphony No 4, 1977 (commnd by Chicago SO); String Quartet No 4, 1979; Triple Concerto, 1979 (commnd by LSO with Ralph Vaughan Williams Trust). *Publications:* Moving into Aquarius, 1959, rev. edn 1974; Music of the Angels, 1980. *Recreation:* walking. *Address:* c/o Schott & Co., 48 Great Marlborough Street, W1. *TA:* Shotanco, London. *T:* 01-437 1246.

TIPPETTS, Rutherford Berriman; *b* 8 Feb. 1913; *s* of late Percy William Berriman Tippetts and Katherine Brown Rutherford; *m* 1948, Audrey Helen Wilson Cameron; one *s* one d. *Educ:* Rugby; Trinity Coll., Oxford (MA). Asst Principal, BoT, 1936; Principal Private Sec. to Ministers of Supply and Presidents of BoT, 1941-45; idc 1954; Chief Exec., Dollar Exports Council, 1959-61; served in Commercial Relations and Exports, Industry and Tourism Divs of BoT; Under-Sec., Export Services Div., DTI, 1970-73. Mem., Exec. Cttee and Council, CGLI. Master, Worshipful Co. of Armourers and Brasiers, 1975-76. *Address:* 74 Ebury Mews East, SW1W 9QA. *T:* 01-730 6464. *Clubs:* Carlton, Royal Wimbledon, Roehampton.

TITCHENER, Alan Ronald; Under Secretary, Overseas Trade Division, Department of Trade, since 1982; *b* 18 June 1934; *s* of Edmund Hickman Ronald Titchener and Minnie Ellen Titchener; *m* 1959, Joyce Blakesley; two s. *Educ:* Harrow County Grammar Sch.; London School of Economics. BSc(Econ) 1962. RAF, 1952-54. Colonial Office, 1954-62; Min. of Transport, 1962-64; Board of Trade, 1964-68; HM Diplomatic Service, Consul Commercial, New York, 1969-73; Dept of Trade, Dir for Coordination of Export Services, 1973-78; Consul-Gen. and Dir of Trade Promotion, Johannesburg, 1978-82. *Address:* c/o Department of Trade, 1 Victoria Street, SW1. *Club:* Travellers'.

TITCHENER, John Lanham Bradbury, CMG 1955; OBE 1947; *b* 28 Nov. 1912; *s* of late Alfred Titchener and late Alicia Marion Leonora Bradbury; *m* 1937, Catherine Law Clark (*decd*) (marr. diss. 1958); no *c*; *m* 1958, Rikke Marian Lehmann (*née* Bendixsen), *e d* of late Frederik Carl Bendixsen and Kammerherreinde Nina Grandjean of Vennerslund, Falster, Denmark; two step s. *Educ:* City of London Sch.; Royal College of Music. Nat. Council of Education of Canada, 1934; BBC 1938-43; War of 1939-45: served HM Forces, Jan.-Aug. 1943; Psychological Warfare Branch, Allied Force HQ, Algiers, 1943; 15th Army Group HQ, Italy, 1944-45; Asst Dep. Director, Political Warfare Div., SACSEA, 1945; Political Warfare Adviser to C-in-C, Netherlands East Indies, 1945-46; First Secretary, HM Foreign Service, 1947; served in FO until 1950, when transferred to HM Embassy, Moscow; then at HM Embassy, Ankara, 1953-54; Economic Counsellor, HM Embassy, Tehran, 1954-56, Chargé d'Affaires, 1955. Resigned HM Foreign Service, 1957. *Recreations:* music, gardening, fishing. *Address:* 3 Impasse du Château, 06190 Roquebrune Village, France. *T:* (93) 350785. *Club:* Travellers'.

TITCHENER-BARRETT, Sir Dennis (Charles), Kt 1981; TD 1953, 2 bars; Chairman, Woodstock (London) Ltd (industrial minerals), since 1962; *m* 1940, Joan Wilson; one *s* three d. Served War, RA, 1939-46; commanded 415 Coast Regt RA (TA), 1950-56; Mem., Kent T&AFA, 1950-56. An Underwriting Member of Lloyd's, 1977-. ILEA School Governor, 1956-73; Member: Gtr London Central Valuation Panel, 1964-75; Cons. Bd of Finance, 1968-75; Cons. Policy Gp for Gtr London, 1975-78; National Union of Conservative Associations: Mem., Central Council and Exec. Cttee, 1968-81; Treasurer, 1968-75, Chm., 1975-78, Gtr London Area; Vice-Pres., Nat. Soc. of Cons. Agents, Gtr London Area, 1975-; Chm., S Kensington Cons. Assoc., 1954-57; Pres., Kensington Cons. Assoc., 1975-. Mem., RUSI, 1947-. Fellow, Inst. of Dirs, 1952. High Sheriff of Greater London, 1977-78. *Address:* 8 Launceston Place, W8 5RL. *T:* 01-937 0613. *Club:* Carlton.

TITE, Dr Michael Stanley, FSA; Keeper, Department of Scientific Research and Conservation (formerly Research Laboratory), British Museum, since 1975; *b* 9 Nov. 1938; *s* of Arthur Robert Tite and late Evelyn Frances Violet Tite (*née* Endersby); *m* 1967, Virginia Byng Noel; two d. *Educ:* Trinity Sch. of John Whitgift, Croydon; Christ Church, Oxford (MA, DPhil). FSA 1977. Research Fellow in Ceramics, Univ. of Leeds, 1964-67; Lectr in Physics, Univ. of Essex, 1967-75. *Publications:* Methods of Physical Examination in Archaeology, 1972; papers on scientific methods applied to archaeology in various jls. *Recreation:* travelling with "The Buildings of England". *Address:* Crossing Cottage, Boley Road, White Colne, Colchester, Essex. *T:* Earls Colne 2161.

TITFORD, Rear-Adm. Donald George, CEng, FRAeS; retired 1978; Deputy Controller of Aircraft, Ministry of Defence, 1976-78; *b* 15 June 1925; *s* of late Percy Maurice Titford and Emily Hannah Titford (*née* McLaren). *Educ:* Highgate Sch.; Royal Naval Engineering Coll.; Coll. of Aeronautics, Cranfield. MSc. Entered RN as Cadet, 1943; Comdr 1959; Air Engr Officer, HMS Victorious, 1965; Captain 1967; comd, RN Air Station, Lee-on-Solent, 1972-74; Comd Engr Officer, Naval Air Comd, 1974-76. *Recreations:* modern pentathlon, old English watercolours. *Address:* Merry Hill, North Road, Bath BA2 6HD. *T:* Bath 62132. *Club:* Army and Navy.

TITHERIDGE, Roger Noel, QC 1973; a Recorder of the Crown Court since 1972; Barrister-at-Law; *b* 21 Dec. 1928; *s* of Jack George Ralph Titheridge and Mabel Titheridge (*née* Steains); *m* 1963, Annabel Maureen (*née* Scott-

Fisher); two d. *Educ:* Midhurst Grammar Sch.; Merton Coll., Oxford (Exhibnr). MA (History and Jurisprudence). Called to the Bar, Gray's Inn, 1954; Holker Sen. Scholar, Gray's Inn, 1954. *Recreations:* tennis, sailing. *Address:* 1 Paper Buildings, Temple, EC4. *T:* 01-353 3728; 13 The Moat, Traps Lane, New Malden, Surrey. *T:* 01-942 2747.

TITTERTON, Prof. Sir Ernest (William), Kt 1970; CMG 1957; FRSA; FAA; Professor of Nuclear Physics, Australian National University, since 1950; Dean of the Research School of Physical Sciences, Australian National University, 1966-68, Director of Research School of Physical Sciences, 1968-73; *b* 4 March 1916; *e s* of W. A. Titterton, Tamworth, Staffs; *m* 1942, Peggy Eileen, *o d* of Captain A. Johnson, Hagley, Worcs; one *s* two d. *Educ:* Queen Elizabeth's Grammar Sch., Tamworth; University of Birmingham (BSc, MSc, PhD). Research Officer, Admiralty, 1939-43; Member British Scientific Mission to USA on Atomic Bomb development, 1943-47; Sen. Member of Timing Group at 1st Atomic Bomb Test, Alamagordo, 1945; Adviser on Instrumentation, Bikini Atomic Weapon Tests, 1946; Head of Electronics Div., Los Alamos Lab., USA, 1946-47; Group Leader in charge of Research team at AERE, Harwell, 1947-50. Member Australian Atomic Energy Commn Scientific Advisory Cttee, 1955-64; Dep. Chairman Australian Atomic Weapons Safety Cttee, 1954-56; Chm., Atomic Weapons Safety Cttee, 1957-73 (in this capacity attended all British Atom Bomb tests in Australia, 1952-57); Member, Defence Research and Development Policy Cttee, 1958-75; Member National Radiation Advisory Cttee, 1957-73. Vice-Pres., Aust. Inst. of Nuclear Science and Engineering, 1968-72, Pres., 1973-75. *Publications:* Progress in Nuclear Physics, 4, 1955; Facing the Atomic Future (London, New York, Melbourne), 1955; Selected Lectures in Modern Physics for School Science Teachers, 1958; Uranium: energy source of the future?, 1979; some 212 papers mainly on nuclear physics, atomic energy and electronics in technical journals. *Recreations:* music and tennis. *Address:* 8 Somers Crescent, Forrest, Canberra, ACT 2603, Australia. *T:* Canberra 95-1495.

TIVERTON, Viscount; *see* Giffard, A. E.

TIZARD, Sir (John) Peter (Mills), Kt 1982; Professor of Pædiatrics, University of Oxford, and Fellow of Jesus College, Oxford, since May 1972; Hon. Consultant Children's Physician, Oxfordshire Health Authority, since 1972; *b* London, 1 April 1916; *e s* of late Sir Henry Thomas Tizard, GCB, AFC, FRS, and late Lady (Kathleen Eleanor) Tizard; *m* 1945, Elisabeth Joy, *yr d* of late Clifford John Taylor, FRCSE; two *s* one d. *Educ:* Rugby Sch.; Oriel Coll., Oxford; Middlesex Hospital. BA Oxon 1938 (3rd cl. Hons Honour Sch. of Natural Science); Oxford and Cambridge Schol. (Biochemistry and Physiology), Middlesex Hospital, 1938; MA, BM, BCh Oxon 1941; MRCP 1944; FRCP 1958; DCH England 1947. Served War of 1939-45 with RAMC, 1942-46 (Temp. Major). Med. Registrar and Pathologist, Hospital for Sick Children, Great Ormond Street, 1947; Asst Director, Pædiatric Unit, St Mary's Hospital Medical Sch., 1949; Physician, Paddington Green Children's Hospital, 1949; Nuffield Foundation Medical Fellow, 1951; Research Fellow in Pediatrics, Harvard Univ., 1951; Reader in Child Health, 1954-64, Prof. of Pædiatrics, Inst. of Child Health, Royal Postgraduate Med. Sch., Univ. of London, 1964-72; Hon. Cons. Children's Physician, Hammersmith Hosp., 1954-72; Chm., Med. Cttee, Hammersmith Hosp., 1970-71; Mem., Oxford AHA, 1979-82. Lectures: Blackfan Meml, Harvard Univ., 1963; Samuel Gee, RCP, 1972; Carl Fridericksen, Danish Paediatric Soc., 1972; Perlstein, Louisville Univ., 1973; Clausen Meml, Rochester Univ., NY, 1975; Choremis Meml, Hellenic Paediatric Soc., 1975; Croonian, RCP 1978; Orator, Reading Pathological Soc., 1973. Mem. Ct of Assistants, 1971-, Sen. Warden, 1982-83, Soc. of Apothecaries of London. FRSocMed 1941 (Pres., Sect. of Paediatrics, 1980-81); Second Vice-Pres., RCP, 1977-78; Member: British Pædiatric Assoc., 1953 (Pres. 1982-); European Pædiatric Research Soc., 1959 (Pres., 1970-71); Neonatal Society, 1959- (Hon. Sec. 1964-66; Pres., 1975-78); Assoc. Physicians of Great Britain and Ireland, 1965; Assoc. British Neurologists, 1969; German Acad. of Scientists, Leopoldina, 1972; Harveian Soc., 1974- (Pres., 1977); British Pædiatric Neurol. Assoc., 1975- (Chm. 1979-82); Corresp. Member: Société française de Pédiatrie, 1969; Pædiatric Soc. of Chile, 1968; Austrian Paediatric Soc., 1972; Swiss Paediatric Soc., 1973; Hon. Member: Pædiatric Soc. of Concepcion, 1968; Czechoslovak Med. Assoc. J. E. Purkyněi, 1971; Dutch Pædiatric Soc., 1971; Amer. Pediatric Soc., 1976; Hellenic Soc. Perinatal Medicine, 1979. *Publications:* Medical Care of Newborn Babies (jtly), 1972; papers in scientific and medical journals. *Address:* Ickenham Manor, Ickenham, Uxbridge, Mddx UB10 8QT. *T:* Ruislip 32262; Jesus College, Oxford OX1 3DW. *Club:* Athenæum.

TIZARD, Hon. Robert James; MP for Otahuhu (Pakuranga), New Zealand; *b* 7 June 1924; *s* of Henry James and Jessie May Tizard; *m* 1951, Catherine Anne Maclean; one *s* three d. *Educ:* Auckland Grammar Sch.; Auckland Univ. MA, Hons Hist., 1949. Served War: RNZAF, 1943-46, incl. service in Canada and Britain; (commnd as a Navigator, 1944). Pres., Students' Assoc. Auckland Univ., 1948; Lectr in History, Auckland Univ., 1949-53; teaching, 1954-57 and 1961-62. MP 1957-60 and 1963-; Minister of Health and State Services, 1972-74; Dep. Prime Minister and Minister of Finance, 1974-75; Dep. Leader of the Opposition, 1975-. *Recreation:* golf. *Address:* Flat 3, 69 Alfred Street, Onehunga, Auckland 6, New Zealand.

TOBIAS, Prof. Stephen Albert, DSc, PhD Edinburgh, MA Cantab, DiplIng Budapest; FIMechE; FIProdE; M.ASME; M.CIRP; Chance Professor of

Mechanical Engineering and Head of Department, University of Birmingham, since 1959; *b* Vienna, 10 July 1920; *s* of Bela and Zelma; *m* 1945, Stephanie Paula Garzo; two *s*. *Educ:* Josef Eotvos Gymnasium, Budapest; Technological Univ., Budapest; Edinburgh Univ. DiplIng Technological Univ., Budapest, 1943. Machine Tool Design Engineer, 1943-47; British Council Scholarship, 1947; ICI Research Fellow, 1951-54; Assistant Director of Research, Department of Engineering, Cambridge Univ., 1956. Visiting Professor: Univ. of Cairo, 1963; Univ. of Denver, 1969; Univ. of California, 1969; Nat. Univ. of Mexico, 1970; Russell Severance Springer Prof. of Mech. Engrg, Univ. of Calif, Berkeley, 1979. UNESCO Consultant to Brazil, 1971. Dir, Engineering DRD Ltd. Member: Engineering Industry Trng Bd, 1967- (Chm. Technologist Trng Panel); SRC Manufacturing Technology Cttee, 1972-75. T. Bernard Hall Prize, 1957, and Whitworth Prize, 1959, of Instn of Mechanical Engineers; Blackall Machine Tool Award, 1958, of American Society of Mech. Engineers. Co-editor in chief, Procs Internat. Conf. for Machine Tool Design and Res., 1963-; Editor in Chief, Internat. Jl for Machine Tool Design and Res., 1977- (co-editor in chief, 1959-76). *Publications:* Schwingungen an Werkzeugmaschinen, 1961; Machine-Tool Vibration, 1965 (Japanese edn, 1969, Spanish edn, 1971, Chinese edn, 1979); over 120 contributions to engineering journals and proceedings of learned societies dealing with linear and non-linear vibrations, dynamic stability of metal cutting process, high energy rate forming, design, impact noise and robotics. *Recreations:* colour photography, music, cultivation of cactus plants, petroforging. *Address:* Department of Mechanical Engineering, PO Box 363, University of Birmingham, Birmingham B15 2TT. *T:* 021-472 1301. *Club:* Athenæum.

TOBIN, Prof. James, PhD; Sterling Professor of Economics, Yale University, since 1957; *b* 5 March 1918; *s* of Louis Michael and Margaret Edgerton Tobin; *m* 1946, Elizabeth Fay Ringo; three *s* one *d*. *Educ:* Harvard Univ. AB 1939 (*summa cum laude*); MA 1940; PhD 1947. Economist, Office of Price Admin, and Civilian Supply and War Production Bd, Washington, 1941-42; line officer, destroyer, USN, 1942-46. Teaching Fellow in Econs, 1946-47, Jun. Fellow, Soc. of Fellows, 1947-50, Harvard Univ.; Yale University: Associate Prof. of Econs, 1950-55; Prof. of Econs, 1955-; Dir, Cowles Foundn for Res. in Econs, 1955-61; Chm., Dept of Econs, 1968-69, 1974-78. Vis. Prof., Univ. of Nairobi, 1972-73. Mem., Pres.'s Council of Econ. Advrs, 1961-62. Nobel Prize in Economics, 1981. *Publications:* (jtly) The American Business Creed, 1956; National Economic Policy, 1966; Essays in Economics: vol. 1, Macroeconomics, 1971; vol. 2, Consumption and Econometrics, 1975; vol. 3, Theory and Policy, 1982; The New Economics One Decade Older, 1974; contribs to professional jls. *Recreations:* tennis, ski-ing, sailing, canoeing, fishing, chess. *Address:* Yale University, Box 2125 Yale Station, New Haven, Conn 06520, USA. *T:* 203-436-2330. *Clubs:* Yale (New York); Mory's Association, The Club (New Haven).

TOD, Sir John Hunter H.; *see* Hunter-Tod.

TODD, family name of **Baron Todd.**

TODD, Baron, *cr* 1962, of Trumpington (Life Peer); **Alexander Robertus Todd,** OM 1977; Kt 1954; FRS 1942; DSc Glasgow; Dr Phil nat Frankfurt; DPhil Oxon; MA Cantab; FRSC; Master of Christ's College, Cambridge, 1963-78 (Fellow, 1944); Professor of Organic Chemistry, University of Cambridge, 1944-71; (first) Chancellor, University of Strathclyde, Glasgow; Visitor, Hatfield Polytechnic, since 1978; Director, Fisons Ltd, 1963-78; *b* Glasgow, 2 Oct. 1907; *e s* of Alexander Todd, JP, Glasgow; *m* 1937, Alison Sarah, *e d* of Sir H. H. Dale, OM, GBE, FRS; one *s* two *d*. *Educ:* Allan Glen's Sch.; University of Glasgow. Carnegie Research Scholar, University of Glasgow, 1928-29; Univ. of Frankfurt a M, 1929-31; 1851 Exhibition Senior Student, Univ. of Oxford, 1931-34; Assistant in Medical Chemistry, 1934-35, and Beit Memorial Research Fellow, 1935-36, University of Edinburgh; Member of Staff, Lister Institute of Preventive Medicine, London, 1936-38; Reader in Biochemistry, University of London, 1937-38; Visiting Lecturer, California Institute of Technology, USA, 1938; Sir Samuel Hall Professor of Chemistry and Director of Chemical Laboratories, University of Manchester, 1938-44. Chairman, Advisory Council on Scientific Policy, 1952-64. Visiting Professor: University of Chicago, 1948; University of Sydney, 1950; Mass. Inst. Tech., 1954. Chemical Society, Tilden Lecturer, 1941, Pedler Lecturer, 1946; Meldola Medal, 1936; Leverhulme Lecturer, Society of Chemical Industry, 1948; President: Chemical Soc., 1960-62; Internat. Union of Pure and Applied Chemistry, 1963-65; BAAS, 1969-70; Royal Soc., 1975-80; Soc. of Chem. Industry, 1981-82. Chairman: Royal Commn on Medical Education, 1965-68; Board of Governors, United Cambridge Hospitals, 1969-74. Member Council, Royal Society, 1947-50; Mem., NRDC, 1968-76. Hon. Member French, German, Spanish, Belgian, Swiss, Japanese Chemical Societies; Foreign Member: Nat. Acad. Sciences, USA; American Acad. of Arts and Sciences; Akad. Naturf. Halle; American Phil. Soc.; Australian, Austrian, Indian, Iranian, Japanese, New York and Polish Academies of Science. Hon. Fellow: Australian Chem. Institute; Manchester College Technology; Royal Society Edinburgh. Chairman, Managing Trustees, Nuffield Foundation, 1973-79 (Trustee, 1950-79); Chm., Trustees, Croucher Foundn (Hong Kong), 1980- (Trustee, 1979-); Lavoisier Medallist, French Chemical Society, 1948; Davy Medal of Royal Society, 1949; Bakerian Lecturer, 1954; Royal Medal of Royal Society, 1955; Nobel Prize for Chemistry, 1957; Cannizzaro Medal, Italian Chemical Society, 1958; Paul Karrer Medal, Univ. Zürich, 1962; Stas Medal, Belgian Chemical Society, 1962; Longstaff Medal, Chemical Society, 1963; Copley Medal, Royal Society, 1970; Lomonosov Medal, USSR Acad.

Sci., 1979; Copernicus Medal, Polish Acad. Sci., 1979. Hon. FRCP 1975; Hon. FRCPS (Glas) 1980. Hon. Fellow: Oriel Coll., Oxford, 1955; Churchill Coll., Cambridge, 1971; Darwin Coll., Cambridge, 1981. Hon. LLD: Glasgow, Melbourne, Edinburgh, Manchester, California, Hokkaido; Hon. Dr rer nat Kiel; Hon. DSc: London, Madrid, Exeter, Leicester, Aligarh, Sheffield, Wales, Yale, Strasbourg, Harvard, Liverpool, Adelaide, Strathclyde, Oxford, ANU, Paris, Warwick, Durham, Michigan, Cambridge, Philippines, Tufts, Chinese Univ. of Hong Kong; Hon. DLitt Sydney. Pour le Merite, German Federal Republic, 1966; Order of Rising Sun (Japan), 1978. Master, Salters' Company, 1961. *Publications:* numerous scientific papers in chemical and biochemical journals. *Recreations:* fishing, golf. *Address:* 9 Parker Street, Cambridge. *T:* Cambridge 356688. *Club:* Athenæum.

TODD, Rev. Alastair, CMG 1971; Vicar, St Augustine's, Brighton; *b* 21 Dec. 1920; *s* of late Prof. James Eadie Todd, MA, FRHistS (formerly Prof. of History, Queen's University, Belfast) and Margaret Simpson Johnstone Maybin; *m* 1952, Nancy Hazel Buyers; two *s* two *d*. *Educ:* Royal Belfast Academical Institution; Fettes Coll., Edinburgh; Corpus Christi Coll., Oxford; London Univ. (External); Salisbury and Wells Theological Coll. BA (Oxon), DipTheol (London). Served War, Army, 1940-46, Capt. RHA. Apptd Colonial Administrative Service, Hong Kong, 1946; Joint Services Staff Coll., 1950; Defence Sec., Hong Kong, 1957-60; Dep. Colonial Sec., Hong Kong, 1963-64; Dir of Social Welfare, also MLC, 1966-68; and, again, Defence Sec., 1968-71, retd. Ordained Deacon by Bishop of Chichester, 1973 and Priest, 1974; Asst Curate, Willingdon, 1973-77. *Recreations:* reading, walking, embroidery, gardening. *Address:* St Augustine's Vicarage, 32 Florence Road, Brighton. *T:* Brighton 561755.

TODD, (Alfred) Norman, FCA; CompIEE; Chairman, National Bus Company, 1969-71; retired; *b* 18 Oct. 1904; *s* of late Alfred and Rachel Todd; *m* 1935, Mary Watson; one *s* one *d*. *Educ:* Bishops Stortford College. With Deloitte Plender Griffiths & Co., 1929-48; Assistant, then Deputy Chief Accountant, Merseyside and North Wales Electricity Board, 1948-51; Assistant Chief Accountant, British Electricity Authority, 1951-54; Chief Accountant, London Electricity Board, 1954-56; Dep. Chairman, London Electricity Board, 1956-61; Chairman, East Midlands Electricity Board, 1962-64. Member, Central Electricity Generating Board, 1965-68. Hon. Treasurer, IEE, 1972-75. *Recreation:* golf. *Address:* Allendale, 139 Cooden Drive, Bexhill-on-Sea, East Sussex. *T:* Cooden 4147.

TODD, Ann; Actress; *m* 1933, Victor Malcolm; one *s* ; *m* 1939, Nigel Tangye; one *d* ; *m* 1949, David Lean, *qv* (marr. diss.). Stage plays and films include: *Plays:* Peter, in Peter Pan, Winter Garden, 1942-43; Lottie, in Lottie Dundass, Vaudeville, 1943; Madeleine Smith, in The Rest is Silence, Prince of Wales, 1944; Francesca Cunningham in The Seventh Veil, Princes, 1951; Foreign Field, 1953; Old Vic Season, 1954-55; Macbeth; Love's Labour's Lost; Taming of the Shrew; Henry IV, Parts I and II; Jennifer Dubedat in The Doctor's Dilemma, Saville, 1956; Four Winds, New York, 1957; Duel of Angels, London, 1958. *Films:* The Seventh Veil, 1945; Daybreak, 1948; The Paradine Case, 1948; So Evil My Love, 1948; The Passionate Friends, 1949; Madeleine, 1950; The Sound Barrier, 1952; The Green Scarf, 1954; Time Without Pity, 1956; Taste of Fear, 1960; Son of Captain Blood, 1961; 90 Degrees in the Shade, 1964; The Vortex, 1965; Beware my Brethren, 1970; The Fiend, 1971; The Human Factor, 1979; Persian Fairy Tale; produced, wrote and appeared in Diary Documentaries, 1964-76: Thunder in Heaven (Kathmandu); Thunder of the Gods (Delphi); Thunder of the Kings (Egypt); Free in the Sun (Australia); Thunder of Silence (Jordan); Thunder of Light (Scotland); Hebrides (Scotland). Appears frequently on radio and television both in US and Great Britain, incl. The Last Tangent, BBC, 1972. *Publications:* two novels; The Eighth Veil (autobiog.), 1980. *Address:* 57 Melbury Road, Kensington, W14; Sea Green Cottage, Walberswick, Suffolk.

TODD, Sir Bryan (James), Kt 1976; Chairman: Todd Petroleum Mining Co. Ltd, since 1955; Viking Mining Co. Ltd, since 1970; Director: Todd Motors Ltd, since 1924; Shell, BP & Todd Oil Services Ltd, since 1955; Waipipi Iron Sands Ltd, since 1970; Maui Development Ltd, since 1973; *b* 8 Sept. 1902; *s* of Charles Todd and Mary (*née* Hegarty); *m* 1928, Helen Ann Buddo; three *d*. *Educ:* Christian Bros, Dunedin, NZ; Riverview Coll., Sydney, NSW, Australia. Automotive industry, 1922-; prominent in petroleum industry of NZ, 1930-; Founder and formerly Managing Director: Europa Oil (NZ) Ltd (marketing and refining); Todd Petroleum Mining Co. Ltd (exploration and production of oil and gas in NZ); Viking Mining Co. Ltd (ironsand prodn, refining and export). Chairman: Ruapehu Alpine Lifts Ltd, 1953-; Todd Foundn, 1972-. *Recreations:* skiing, sailing, golf, shooting. *Address:* 38 Wesley Road, Wellington, New Zealand. *T:* (home) 727 040, (office) 722 970. *Clubs:* Wellington, Wellesley (Wellington, NZ); Wellington Golf (Heretaunga, NZ); Ruapehu Ski (NZ).

See also Adm. Sir Gordon Tait.

TODD, Hon. Garfield; *see* Todd, Hon. R. S. G.

TODD, Sir Geoffrey Sydney, KCVO 1951 (CVO 1947); OBE 1946; DL; MB, ChM, FRCP; FRACP; Medical Superintendent, King Edward VII Hospital, Midhurst, 1934-70; *b* 2 Nov. 1900; *s* of late George William Todd, and Amy Louisa Webb; *m* 1955, Margaret Alan Sheen, *o d* of late F. A. Sheen, MC, and of Mrs Sheen, Tudor Cottage, Midhurst. *Educ:* King's Sch., Parramatta, Australia; Sydney Univ., Australia. Resident MO, 1925-26, Medical Superintendent, 1926-27, Wagga District Hospital; House Physician

1929, House Surgeon 1930, Resident MO 1930–34, Brompton Hospital for Chest Diseases, London. DL Sussex, 1968, West Sussex, 1974. Guthrie Meml Medal, 1971. CStJ. *Publications:* various, in medical journals, 1936–56. *Recreations:* sailing, golf, photography. *Address:* Friars Gate, Priory Road, Chichester, West Sussex. *T:* Chichester 82798. *Club:* Naval and Military.

TODD, Sir Herbert John, Kt 1947; CIE 1944; retired as Chief Representative, Iraq Petroleum Company and Associate Companies, Baghdad (1952–59); *b* 15 Oct. 1893; *m* 1919, Nancy (*d* 1981), 2nd *d* of Colonel A. F. Pullen, RA; two *d.* Imperial Police, Burma, 1913; 11th Bengal Lancers (Probyns Horse), 1917; Civil Administration, Mesopotamia, 1919; Indian Political Service, 1921; Asst Political Agent, Sibi, 1921; Kalat, 1922; Political Agent, Gilgit, 1927; Quetta-Pishin, 1932; Political Agent, E Rajputana States, 1935; Prime Minister and Vice-President, Council of State, Jaipur, 1939; Political Agent, Mewar, 1940; Secretary, Baluchistan, 1941; Resident for the Madras States, 1943; Resident for the Eastern States, 1944–47. *Address:* The Pound House, Sandy Lane, Old Oxted, Surrey RH8 9LU. *T:* Oxted 3926.

TODD, James Maclean, MA; Secretary to the Oxford University Delegacy for the Inspection and Examination of Schools and Oxford Secretary to the Oxford and Cambridge Schools Examination Board, 1964–74; Founder Fellow of St Cross College, Oxford; *b* 1907; *s* of late John Todd, Oxford, and Mary, *d* of late Robert Spottiswoode, Gattonside; *m* 1944, Janet, *d* of late Andrew Holmes, Glasgow; one *s* one *d. Educ:* City of Oxford School; The Queen's Coll., Oxford (Open Mathematical Scholar). First Class Mathematical Mods, 1928; 2nd Class Lit. Hum., 1930; 2nd Class Hon. School of Theology, 1931. Awarded Holwell Studentship in Theology. Assistant Master, Radley, Bryanston, Bromsgrove and Stowe. Headmaster, The High School, Newcastle, Staffs, 1948–63. *Publications:* The Ancient World, 1938; Hymns and Psalms for use in Newcastle High School (New Edn), 1951; Voices from the Past: a Classical Anthology (with Janet Maclean Todd), 1955 (Grey Arrow edn, 1960); Peoples of the Past (with Janet Maclean Todd), 1963. *Address:* Foxton Lodge, Foxton Close, Oxford OX2 8LB. *T:* Oxford 58840.

TODD, John Arthur, FRS 1948; PhD; Emeritus Reader in Geometry in the University of Cambridge; Fellow of Downing College, 1958–73, Hon. Fellow 1973; *b* 23 Aug. 1908; *s* of John Arthur and Agnes Todd. *Educ:* Liverpool Collegiate School; Trinity Coll., Cambridge. Assistant Lecturer in Mathematics, University of Manchester, 1931–37; Lecturer in Mathematics in the University of Cambridge, 1937–60, Reader in Geometry 1960–73. *Publications:* Projective and Analytical Geometry, 1947; various mathematical papers. *Address:* 10 Reddington Close, Sanderstead, South Croydon, Surrey CR2 0QZ. *T:* 01-657 4994.

TODD, John Francis James, PhD, CChem, FRSC; Master of Rutherford College, University of Kent at Canterbury, since 1975 (re-elected 1980); Senior Lecturer in Chemistry, Faculty of Natural Sciences, University of Kent at Canterbury, since 1973; Chairman, Canterbury and Thanet Health Authority, since 1982; *b* 20 May 1937; *o s* of late Eric Todd and Annie Lewin Todd (*née* Tinkler); *m* 1963, Mavis Georgina Lee; three *s. Educ:* Leeds Grammar Sch.; Leeds Univ. (BSc, Cl. I Hons Chem.). MInstMC; MIEnvSci. Research Fellow: Leeds Univ., 1962–63; Yale Univ., 1963–65; Univ. of Kent at Canterbury: Asst Lectr in Chemistry, 1965–66; Lectr in Chemistry, 1966–73. J. B. Cohen Prizeman, Leeds Univ., 1963; Fulbright Research Scholar, 1963–65. Chairman: Kent Section of Chem. Soc., 1975; British Mass Spectroscopy Soc., 1980–81. Governor, S Kent Coll. of Technology, 1977–. Titular Mem., IUPAC Commn on Molecular Structures and Spectroscopy, 1979–. Mem., Amer. Soc. of Sigma Xi, Yale Chapter. *Publications:* (jt ed) Dynamic Mass Spectrometry, vol. 4, 1975, vol. 5, 1978, vol. 6, 1981; reviews and papers, mainly on mass spectrometry, in Jl of Chem. Soc. and Jl of Physics, etc. *Recreations:* music, travel. *Address:* Rutherford College, University of Kent at Canterbury, CT2 7NX. *T:* Canterbury 66822 (ext. 470); West Bank, 122 Whitstable Road, Canterbury, Kent CT2 8EG. *T:* Canterbury 69552.

TODD, Mary Williamson Spottiswoode, MA; Headmistress of Harrogate College, 1952–73; *b* 11 June 1909; *d* of John and Mary Todd, Oxford. *Educ:* Oxford High School; Lady Margaret Hall, Oxford. MA Hons Oxon. Final Hon. Sch.: Mathematics, 1932, Nat. Science, 1933; London Diploma in Theology, 1941. Various teaching posts: St Felix School, Southwold, 1933–37; Clifton High School, Bristol, 1937–39; Westonbirt School, Glos, 1939–45; Headmistress of Durham, 1946–52. *Address:* 93 Oakdale, Harrogate, North Yorks. *T:* Harrogate 66411.

TODD, Norman; *see* Todd, A. N.

TODD, Hon. R(eginald) S(tephen) Garfield; *b* 13 July 1908; *s* of late Thomas and Edith C. Todd; *m* 1932, Jean Grace Wilson; three *d. Educ:* Otago Univ.; Glen Leith Coll.; University of Witwatersrand. Minister Oamaru Church of Christ, NZ, 1932–34; Superintendent Dadaya Mission, 1934–53, Chm. Governing Bd 1963–. Man. Dir, Hokonui Ranching Co. MP for Shabani, 1946–58; elected leader, United Rhodesia Party and Prime Minister of S Rhodesia, 1953–58; Federal President, Central Africa Party, 1959–60; President, New Africa Party, 1961. First Vice-President World Convention of Churches of Christ (Disciples), 1955–60; awarded Citation for Christian Leadership in Politics and Race Relations; Member Executive: United Coll. of Educn, Bulawayo, 1965–; Rhodesian Christian Council, 1967–. Has lectured widely, USA, Canada, UK, Australia, NZ, S Africa. Holds hon. doctorates. Arrested by Smith regime in 1965 and confined to ranch for one year; arrested by Smith regime in 1972 and imprisoned without charge or trial for five weeks, then detained at home on Hokonui Ranch, the area being gazetted as a 'protected area' and closed to public under police guard; detention order lifted June 1976; a Political Adviser to Mr Joshua Nkomo at Geneva Conf. on Future of Rhodesia, 1976. *Address:* PO Dadaya, Zimbabwe. *Club:* Bulawayo.

See also Baron Acton.

TODD, Richard, (Richard Andrew Palethorpe-Todd); actor; *b* 11 June 1919; *s* of Major A. W. Palethorpe-Todd, Castlederg, Co. Tyrone, and Marvil Agar-Daly, Ballymalis Castle, Kerry; *m* 1st, 1949, Catherine Stewart Crawford Grant-Bogle (marr. diss. 1970); one *s* one *d* ; 2nd, 1970, Virginia Anne Rollo Mailer; two *s. Educ:* Shrewsbury; privately. Entered the theatre in 1937. Served in King's Own Yorkshire Light Infantry and The Parachute Regt, 1940–46; GSO iii (Ops), 6 Airborne Div., 1944–45. Films since War of 1939–45 include: The Hasty Heart, 1949; Stage Fright, 1950; Robin Hood, 1952; Rob Roy, 1953; A Man Called Peter, 1954; The Dambusters, 1954; The Virgin Queen, 1955; Yangtse Incident, 1957; Chase a Crooked Shadow, 1957; The Long and the Short and the Tall, 1960; The Hellions, 1961; The Longest Day, 1962; Operation Crossbow, 1964; Coast of Skeletons, 1964; The Love-Ins (USA), 1967; Subterfuge, 1968; Dorian Grey, 1969; Asylum, 1972; Secret Agent 008, 1976. Stage appearances include: An Ideal Husband, Strand, 1965–66; Dear Octopus, Haymarket, 1967; USA tour, The Marquise, 1972; Australia tour, Sleuth, 1973; led RSC N American tour, 1974; Equus, Australian Nat. Theatre Co., 1975; On Approval (S Africa), 1976; nat. tour of Quadrille, and The Heat of the Moment, 1977; Nightfall (S Africa), 1979; This Happy Breed (nat. tour), 1980; The Business of Murder, Duchess, 1981, Mayfair, 1982. Formed Triumph Theatre Productions, 1970. Past Grand Steward, Past Master, Lodge of Emulation No 21. *Recreations:* shooting and farming. *Address:* Chinham Farm, Faringdon, Oxon; Little Ponton House, near Grantham, Lincs. *Club:* Army and Navy.

TODD, Ronald; National Organiser, Transport and General Workers' Union, since 1978; *b* 11 March 1927; *s* of George Thomas Todd and Emily Todd; *m* 1945, Josephine Tarrant; one *s* two *d. Educ:* St Patrick's Sch., Walthamstow, E17. Served with Royal Marine Commandos; spent considerable time in China. Joined TGWU; worked at Ford Motor Co., 1954–62, latterly Dep. Convener; full-time officer of TGWU, 1962; Regional Officer, 1969; Reg. Sec., 1976. Chm. (TU side), Ford Nat. Jt Council; Jt Sec., Nat. Jt Council for Stable Staff (Workpeople's side). Hon. Vice-Pres., CND. *Recreations:* collecting Victorian music covers, archaeology. *Address:* Transport and General Workers' Union, Transport House, Smith Square, SW1P 3JB. *T:* 01-828 7788.

TOGANIVALU, Ratu Josua Brown, CBE 1980; JP; High Commissioner for Fiji in London, since 1981; *b* Fiji, 2 May 1930; *m* ; two *s* one *d. Educ:* Levuka Public Sch.; Marist Brothers Sch., Suva; Queensland Agricultural Coll.; Royal Agricultural Coll., Cirencester. With Native Lands Trust Board, 1953–71; MP Fiji, 1966–77: Minister for Lands, Mines and Mineral Resources, 1972–73; Minister for Agriculture, Fisheries and Forests, 1974–77; High Commissioner for Fiji to New Zealand, 1978–81. Represented Fiji at ACP Meeting, Guyana, 1975, ACP Meeting, Malawi, 1976, ACP/EEC Sugar Meetings, Brussels, 1976. JP (Fiji) 1968. *Recreations:* cricket, Rugby, boxing. *Address:* 34 Hyde Park Gate, SW7 5BN. *T:* 01-584 3661; 97 Platts Lane, NW3. *Clubs:* United, Defence (Fiji).

TOH CHIN CHYE, BSc, PhD, DipSc; Member of Parliament, Singapore, since 1959; *b* 10 Dec. 1921; *m. Educ:* Raffles Coll., Singapore; University College, London; Nat. Inst. for Medical Research, London. Reader in Physiology, 1958–64, Research Associate 1964, Vice-Chancellor, 1968–75, Univ. of Singapore. Chm., People's Action Party, 1954–81 (a Founder Mem.); Dep. Prime Minister of Singapore, 1959–68; Minister for Science and Technology, 1968–75; Minister for Health, 1975–81. Chm. Board of Governors: Singapore Polytechnic, 1959–75; Regional Inst. of Higher Educn and Develt, 1970–74; Mem. Admin. Bd, Assoc. of SE Asian Insts of Higher Learning, 1968–75. DLitt (*hc*) Singapore, 1976. *Publications:* papers in Jl of Physiology and other relevant jls. *Address:* 23 Greenview Crescent, Singapore 11.

TOKATY, Prof. Grigori Alexandrovich; Consultant Professor, Jordan, Nigeria and Turkey, since 1979; *b* North Caucasus, Russia; Ossetian by mother tongue; naturalized British. *Educ:* Leningrad Rabfak, 1929–30; Rykov Rabfak, Moscow Higher Technical Coll. MVTU, 1930–32; Zhukovsky Air Force Academy of Aeronautics, Moscow, 1932–37. DEng, PhD, DAeSc, CEng, CanTechSc. Lt Col, Air Force. Zhukovsky Academy: Aeronautical Research Engineer, 1937–38; Head of Aeronautics Laboratory, 1938–41; Dep. Head of Res. Dept, 1941; Lectr in Aerodynamics and Aircraft Design, 1941–45; Acting Prof. of Aviation, Moscow Engrg Inst, 1939–45; Rocket research and development, 1944–45; Rocket scientist, Berlin, 1945–47. Varied work for HM Govt, London, 1948–52; Imperial Coll., and Coll. of Aeronautics, Cranfield, 1953–56; work on theoretical rocket dynamics and orbital flight mechanics associated with Apollo programme, 1956–68; Reader in Aeronautics and Astronautics, Northampton Coll. of Advanced Technology, 1960–61; Head, 1961–74, and Prof., 1967–75, Dept of Aeronautics and Space Technology, Northampton Coll. of Advanced Technology and City Univ., now Emeritus. Chief Scientific Adviser, WTI, 1976–78. Visiting Professor: Univs of the US, Jordan, Nigeria, Iran, Turkey, Holland. FRAeS,

FAIAA, FIMA. *Publications:* numerous, including seven books: Rocketdynamics, 1961; The History of Rocket Technology (jt), 1964; A History and Philosophy of Fluid Mechanics, 1971; Cosmonautics-Astronautics, 1976; articles and booklets (alone or jointly) in the fields of fluid mechanics, gasdynamics, rocketdynamics, theory and philosophy of educn, and non-scientific subjects. *Recreations:* writing, broadcasting, travelling. *Address:* Department of Aeronautics, The City University, St John Street, EC1V 4PB. *Club:* National Liberal.

TOLER; see Graham-Toler, family name of Earl of Norbury.

TOLER, Maj.-Gen. David Arthur Hodges, OBE 1963; MC 1945; DL; *b* 13 Sept. 1920; *s* of Major Thomas Clayton Toler, DL, JP, Swettenham Hall, Congleton; *m* 1951, Judith Mary, *d* of James William Garden, DSO, Aberdeen; one *s* one *d*. *Educ:* Stowe; Christ Church, Oxford (MA). 2nd Lieut Coldstream Guards, 1940; served War of 1939-45, N Africa and Italy; Regimental Adjt, Coldstream Guards, 1952-54; Bde Major, 4th Gds Bde, 1956-57; Adjt, RMA Sandhurst, 1958-60; Bt Lt-Col 1959; comd 2nd Bn Coldstream Guards, 1962-64; comd Coldstream Guards, 1964-65; comd 4th Guards Bde, 1965-68; Dep. Comdt, Staff Coll., Camberley, 1968-69; Dep. Comdr, Army, N Ireland, 1969-70; GOC E Midland Dist, 1970-73; retired 1973. Dep. Hon. Col, Royal Anglian Regt (Lincolnshire) TAVR, 1979-. Emergency Planning Officer, Lincolnshire CC, 1974-77. Chm., Lincoln Dio. Adv. Cttee, 1981-. Pres., SSAFA, Lincs, 1978-. DL Lincs, 1982. *Recreations:* shooting, fishing, gardening. *Address:* Grove House, Fulbeck, Lincs. *Club:* Army and Navy.

TOLLEMACHE, family name of **Baron Tollemache.**

TOLLEMACHE, 5th Baron *cr* 1876; **Timothy John Edward Tollemache;** Director: Tollemache & Cobbold Breweries Ltd, since 1973; NRG London Re-insurance Co. Ltd, since 1976; AMEV Ltd, since 1980, and other companies; Kanga Collections Ltd, since 1982; farmer and landowner; *b* 13 Dec. 1939; *s* of 4th Baron Tollemache, MC, DL, and of Dinah Susan, *d* of late Sir Archibald Auldjo Jamieson, KBE, MC; *S* father, 1975; *m* 1970, Alexandra Dorothy Jean, *d* of late Col Hugo Meynell, MC; two *s* one *d*. *Educ:* Eton. Commissioned into Coldstream Guards, 1959; served Kenya and Persian Gulf, 1960-62; Course of Estate Management at Sandringham, Norfolk, 1962-64; Trainee, Barings Bank Ltd, 1964-65; joined Tollemache & Cobbold Breweries Ltd, 1965. Mem., BTA Marketing Cttee, 1976-79; Pres., Suffolk Assoc. of Local Councils, 1978-; Chm., Historic Houses Assoc. (East Anglia Region), 1979-. Vice Pres., Cheshire Red Cross, 1980-; Chm., St John's Council for Suffolk, 1982-. Pres., Friends of Ipswich Museums, 1980-. *Recreations:* shooting, fishing, natural history. *Heir:* s Hon. Edward John Hugo Tollemache, *b* 12 May 1976. *Address:* Helmingham Hall, Stowmarket, Suffolk IP14 6EF. *T:* Helmingham 217. *Clubs:* White's, Pratt's.

TOLLEMACHE, Maj.-Gen. Sir Humphry (Thomas), 6th Bt *cr* 1793; CB 1952; CBE 1950; DL; *b* 10 Aug. 1897; *s* of Sir Lyonel Tollemache, 4th Bt (*d* 1952), and Hersilia Henrietta Diana (*d* 1953), *d* of late H. R. Oliphant; *S* brother, 1969; *m* 1926, Nora Priscilla, *d* of John Taylor, Broomhill, Eastbourne; two *s* two *d*. *Educ:* Eastbourne Coll. 2nd Lieut, Royal Marines, 1915; served European War, Grand Fleet, 1916-18; War of 1939-45 in Middle East and Far East; Bt Major, 1934; Bt Lt-Col, 1942; Actg Colonel Comdt, temp. Brigadier, 1943; Colonel, 1946; Maj.-Gen., 1949; comd 3rd Mobile Naval Base Bde, 1943-44; comd Small Ops Gp, 1944-45; comd Depot, 1946-47; Director of Pay and Records, 1947-49; commanded Portsmouth Group, Royal Marines, 1949-52 and Hon. Colonel Comdt, 1958-60; Colonel Comdt, Royal Marines, 1961-62; Rep. Colonel Comdt, 1961. Member Hampshire CC, 1957-74; Alderman, 1969-74. Chm., C of E Soldiers, Sailors and Airmen Clubs, 1955-65, Pres., 1974. DL Hampshire, 1965. *Heir:* s Lyonel Humphry John Tollemache [*b* 10 July 1931; *m* 1960, Mary Joscelyne, *e d* of William Henry Whitbread, *qv*; two *s* two *d*]. *Address:* Sheet House, Petersfield, Hants.

TOLLERFIELD, Albert Edward, CB 1963; Assistant Comptroller, Patent Office, 1959-66; retired from Civil Service; *b* 8 Dec. 1906; *s* of late Frank Tollerfield; *m* 1st, 1930, Lilian May (*d* 1972); three *d*; 2nd, 1974, Adelaide Mary. *Educ:* Royal Dockyard School, Portsmouth. Fitter Apprentice, 1922-27; Design Draughtsman, 1929; Examiner, Patent Office, 1930; Intelligence Department, Min. of Shipping, 1939-43; Superintending Examiner and Hearing Officer, Patent Office, 1955-59. Chairman, Patents Appointments Boards, Civil Service Commn, 1966-69. *Recreation:* do-it-yourself. *Address:* 17 Hill Road, Southend-on-Sea, Essex.

TOLLEY, Rev. Canon George; Director, Open Tech Unit, Manpower Services Commission, since 1983; Curate, St Andrew's, Sharrow; Hon. Canon of Sheffield Cathedral, since 1976; *b* 24 May 1925; *s* of George and Elsie Tolley, Old Hill, Staffordshire; *m* 1947, Joan Amelia Grosvenor; two *s* one *d*. *Educ:* Halesowen Grammar Sch.; Birmingham Central Tech. Coll. Coll (part-time); Princeton Univ., USA. BSc, MSc, PhD (London); FRSC; CBIM. Rotary Foundation Fellow, Princeton Univ., 1949-50. Head, Department of Chemistry, College of Advanced Technology, Birmingham, 1954-58; Head of Research and Experimental Dept, Allied Ironfounders Ltd, 1958-61; Principal, Worcester Tech. College, 1961-65; Senior Director of Studies, Royal Air Force Coll., Cranwell, 1965-66; Principal, Sheffield Coll. of Technology, 1966-69, Sheffield City Polytechnic, 1969-82. Chairman: Council, Plastics Inst., 1959-61; Further Educn Adv. Cttee, Food, Drink and

Tobacco Ind. Trng Bd, 1974-78; Bd, Further Educn Curriculum Unit, 1978-; Hon. Sec., Assoc. of Colleges of Further and Higher Educn; Member: CNAA (Chm., Cttee for Business and Management Studies); Yorks and Humberside Economic Planning Council, 1976-79; RAF Trng and Educn Cttee, 1975-80; Editorial Bd, Univs Qly. Sheffield Church Burgess. *Publications:* Meaning and Purpose in Higher Education, 1976; many papers relating to plastics and education in British and foreign journals. *Recreations:* music, hill walking, bird watching. *Address:* 74 Furniss Avenue, Dore, Sheffield S17 3QP. *Clubs:* Athenæum, Royal Commonwealth Society.

TOLLEY, Leslie John, CBE 1973; Chairman, Renold Ltd, 1972-82; *b* Oxford, 11 Nov. 1913; *s* of late Henry Edward Charles and Gertrude Eleanor Tolley; *m* 1939, Margaret Butterfield, *d* of late Walter Bishop and Nellie May Butterfield; one *s* one *d*. *Educ:* Oxford Sch. of Technology. FEng; FIProdE; CBIM. Gen. Manager, Nuffield Metal Products, 1941-52; Gen. Works Manager, 1952, Works Dir, 1954, Renold Chains Ltd; Gp Man. Dir, Renold Ltd, 1962; Chairman: Fodens Ltd, 1975-80; Francis Shaw & Co. Ltd, 1977-81; Dir, NW Regional Bd, Lloyds Bank Ltd, 1975-. A Vice-Chm., 1973-78, Chm., 1978-80, BIM. *Recreation:* golf. *Address:* Silver Birches, Dale Brow, Prestbury, Macclesfield SK10 4BN. *T:* Prestbury 829073.

TOLSTOY, Dimitry, (Dimitry Tolstoy-Miloslavsky), QC 1959; Barrister-at-Law; *b* 8 Nov. 1912; *s* of late Michael Tolstoy-Miloslavsky and Eileen May Hamshaw; *m* 1st, 1934, Frieda Mary Wicksteed (marr. diss.); one *s* one *d*; 2nd, 1943, Natalie Deytrikh; one *s* one *d*. *Educ:* Wellington; Trinity Coll., Cambridge. President of Cambridge Union, 1935. Called to Bar, Gray's Inn, 1937. Lecturer in Divorce to Inns of Court, 1952-68. *Publications:* Tolstoy on Divorce, 1946-7th edn 1971; articles in legal periodicals. *Address:* c/o Barclays Bank, High Street, Guernsey, CI.

TOMALIN, Claire; writer; *b* 20 June 1933; *d* of Emile Delavenay and Muriel Herbert; *m* 1955, Nicholas Osborne Tomalin (*d* 1973); one *s* two *d* (and one *d* decd). *Educ:* Hitchin Girls' Grammar Sch.; Dartington Hall Sch.; Newnham Coll., Cambridge (MA). Publishers' reader and editor, Messrs Heinemann, Hutchinson, Cape, 1955-67; Evening Standard, 1967-68; New Statesman: Asst Literary Editor, 1968-70; Literary Editor, 1974-77; Literary Editor, Sunday Times, 1979-. FRSL. *Publications:* The Life and Death of Mary Wollstonecraft, 1974, paperback 1977; Shelley and his World, 1980; Parents and Children, 1981; Literary journalism. *Address:* 57 Gloucester Crescent, NW1 7EG. *T:* 01-485 6481.

TOMBS, Sir Francis (Leonard), Kt 1978; Chairman, The Weir Group, since 1981; Director: N. M. Rothschild & Sons, since 1981; Rolls-Royce, since 1982; *b* 17 May 1924; *s* of Joseph and Jane Tombs; *m* 1949, Marjorie Evans; three *d*. *Educ:* Elmore Green Sch., Walsall; Birmingham Coll. of Technology. BSc (Econ), FEng, FIMechE, FIEE; FBIM. GEC, 1939-45; Birmingham Corp., 1946-47; British Electricity Authority, Midlands, then Central Electricity Authority, Merseyside and N Wales, 1947-57; GEC, Erith, 1957-65; C. A. Parsons, Erith, 1965-68; James Howden & Godfrey Ltd, 1968-69; successively Dir of Engrg, Dep. Chm., Chm., South of Scotland Electricity Bd, 1969-77; Chm., Electricity Council, 1977-80. Member: Nature Conservancy Council, 1978-; Standing Commn on Energy and the Environment, 1978-; SERC, 1982-. Pres., IEE, 1981-. Vice-Pres., YHA, 1981-; Chm., Assoc. of British Orchestras, 1982-. Hon. LLD Strathclyde, 1976; Hon. D(Tech) Loughborough, 1979; Hon. DSc, Aston, 1979; Lodz, Poland, 1980. *Recreations:* music, golf, sailing. *Address:* 15 Highgate Close, N6 4SD. *Club:* Athenæum.

TOMKINS, Sir Edward Emile, GCMG 1975 (KCMG 1969; CMG 1960); CVO 1957; Commandeur, Légion d'Honneur, 1976; HM Diplomatic Service, retired; HM Ambassador to France, 1972-75; *b* 16 Nov. 1915; *s* of late Lt-Col E. L. Tomkins; *m* 1955, Gillian Benson; one *s* one *d*. *Educ:* Ampleforth Coll.; Trinity Coll., Cambridge. Foreign Office, 1939. Military service, 1940-43. HM Embassy, Moscow, 1944-46; Foreign Office, 1946-51; HM Embassy, Washington, 1951-54; HM Embassy, Paris, 1954-59; Foreign Office, 1959-63; HM Embassy, Bonn, 1963-67; HM Embassy, Washington, 1967-69; Ambassador to the Netherlands, 1970-72. Mem., Bucks CC, 1977-. *Address:* Winslow Hall, Winslow, Bucks. *T:* Winslow 2323; 17 Thurloe Place Mews, SW7. *T:* 01-589 9623. *Club:* Garrick.

TOMKINS, Rt. Rev. Oliver Stratford, MA, DD, LLD; *b* 9 June 1908; *s* of Rev. Leopold Charles Fellows Tomkins and Mary Katie (*née* Stratford); *m* 1939, Ursula Mary Dunn; one *s* three *d*. *Educ:* Trent Coll; Christ's Coll, Cambridge; Westcott House, Cambridge. Asst Gen. Sec., Student Christian Movement, 1933-40, and Editor, Student Movement Magazine, 1937-40. Deacon, 1935; Priest, 1936; Vicar of Holy Trinity, Millhouses, Sheffield, 1940-45; an Associate Gen. Sec. World Council of Churches and Sec. of its Commission on Faith and Order, 1945-52; Warden of Lincoln Theological College (Scholae Cancellarii) and Canon and Prebend, Lincoln Cathedral, 1953-59; Bishop of Bristol, 1959-75. Mem. Central Cttee, World Council of Churches, 1968-75. DD (*hon. causa*) Edinburgh University, 1953; Hon LLD Bristol, 1975. *Publications:* The Wholeness of the Church, 1949; The Church in the Purpose of God, 1950. Editor and contributor The Universal Church in God's Design, 1948; Intercommunion, 1951; (ed) Faith and Order (Lund Conference Report), 1953; Life of E. S. Woods, Bishop of Lichfield, 1957;

A Time for Unity, 1964; Guarded by Faith, 1971. *Recreation:* gardening. *Address:* 14 St George's Square, Worcester WR1 1XH. *T:* Worcester 25330.

See also Very Rev. T. W. I. Cleasby.

TOMKINSON, John Stanley, CBE 1981; FRCS; Secretary General, International Federation of Obstetrics and Gynaecology; Obstetric Surgeon, Queen Charlotte's Maternity Hospital, 1953-79; Obstetric and Gynæcological Surgeon, Guy's Hospital, 1953-79; Gynæcological Surgeon, Chelsea Hospital for Women, 1971-79; *b* 8 March 1916; *o s* of Harry Stanley and Katie Mills Tomkinson, Stafford; *m* 1954, Barbara Marie Pilkington; two *s* one *d. Educ:* Rydal Sch.; Birmingham University Medical Sch.; St Thomas' Hospital. MRCS, LRCP 1941; MB, ChB Birmingham 1941; FRCS 1949; MRCOG 1952; FRCOG 1967. Medal in Surgery and Priestley-Smith Prize, Birmingham. Demonstrator of Anatomy, Birmingham Medical School, 1946; appointments in General Surgery, Obst. and Gynæcol., at Birmingham and Midland Hosp. for Women, Birmingham Maternity Hospital, and Queen Elizabeth Hospital, Birmingham, 1941-42 and 1947-52; Registrar, Professorial Unit in General Surgery and Professorial Unit in Obst. and Gynæcol., Birmingham; Chief Asst, Chelsea Hospital for Women, 1952-53; Resident Obstetrician and Tutor in Obstetrics (Postgrad. Inst. of Obst. and Gynæcol. of University of London), Queen Charlotte's Maternity Hospital, 1952-53. Travelling Fellow (Guy's Hospital), USA and Canada, 1954. Vis. Prof., Spanish Hospital, Mexico City, 1972. Consultant Advr in Obstetrics and Gynæcol., Min. of Health, later DHSS, 1966-81; Consultant, WHO, 1981-. William Hawksworth Meml Lectr, 1969; Sir Winston Churchill Meml Lectr, Canterbury, 1970; Edward Sharp Meml Lectr, 1977; Foundn Lectr, Amer. Assoc. of Gynaecol. and Obstetrics, 1978; Charter Day Lectr, Nat. Maternity Hosp. Dublin, 1979. Examiner for: Univs of Oxford, Cambridge, London, Birmingham, QUB; Univs of Haile Selassie I in Ethiopia, East Africa in Uganda, El Fateh in Tripoli, Singapore; RCOG; Conjoint Examining Bd, Central Midwives Bd. FRSM. Member: Gynæcological Club of Great Britain; Birmingham and Midland Obst. and Gynæcol. Society; Central Midwives Board; Member Council: RCOG; RCS; section of Obstetrics and Gynæcology, RSM; Mem. Exec. Council, Internat. Fedn of Obstetrics and Gynaecology; Past Chm., Jt Study Working Gp of Internat. Confedn of Midwives and Internat. Fedn of Gynaecology and Obstetrics. Jt Editor, Report on Confidential Enquiries into Maternal Deaths in England and Wales, 1964-66, 1967-69, 1970-72, 1973-75, 1976-78. Foreign Member, Continental Gynæcol. Society (of America). Hon. Fellow: Nigerian Soc. Obst. and Gynaecol., 1977; Italian Soc. Obst. and Gynaecol., 1978; Romanian Soc. Obst. and Gynaecol., 1978; South African Soc. Obst. and Gynaecol., 1980; Spanish Soc. Obst. and Gynaecol., 1981. Surgeon Lieut, RNVR, 1942-46. *Publications:* (ed) Queen Charlotte's Textbook of Midwifery; papers of general surgical, obstetric and gynæcological interest. *Recreations:* fly-fishing, painting, and the arts generally. *Address:* 109 Harley Street, W1. *T:* 01-935 5855; 140 Priory Lane, SW15. *T:* 01-876 2006. *Clubs:* Athenæum; MCC.

TOMKYS, William Roger; HM Diplomatic Service; Ambassador to Bahrain, since 1981; *b* 15 March 1937; *s* of William Arthur and Edith Tomkys; *m* 1963, Margaret Jean Abbey; one *s* one *d. Educ:* Bradford Grammar Sch.; Balliol Coll., Oxford (Domus Scholar; 1st cl. Hons Lit. Hum.). Entered Foreign Service, 1960; MECAS, 1960; 3rd Sec., Amman, 1962; 2nd Sec., FCO, 1964; 1st Sec., Head of Chancery, Benghazi, 1967; Planning Staff, FCO, 1969; Head of Chancery, Athens, 1972; Counsellor, seconded to Cabinet Office, 1975; Head of Near East and North Africa Dept, FCO, 1977-80; Counsellor, Rome, 1980-81. *Address:* c/o Foreign and Commonwealth Office, SW1A 2AH. *Clubs:* United Oxford & Cambridge University; Royal Blackheath Golf.

TOMLIN, Eric Walter Frederick, CBE 1965 (OBE 1959); FRSL; author; *b* 30 Jan. 1913; *s* of Edgar Herbert Tomlin and Mary (*née* Dexter); *m* 1st, 1945, Margaret Stuart (marr. diss. 1952); one *s*; 2nd, 1974, Judith, *yr d* of Lt-Gen. Sir Euan Miller, *qv. Educ:* Whitgift; Brasenose Coll., Oxford (BA degrees in PPE and Mod. Hist.); MA (Oxon), 1958; MA (Cantab), 1972. Asst Master: Sloane Sch., Chelsea, 1936-38; Marlborough, 1939; Resident Tutor, Wilts, Bristol Univ. Bd of Extra-Mural Studies, 1939-40; joined Local Defence Volunteers, 1940; British Council Lecturer, Staff Coll. Baghdad and RMC, 1940-41; worked in Information Dept, British Embassy, Baghdad, 1941; British Council: Ankara, 1941-42; Regional Dir, S Turkey, 1942-45; Headquarters London, 1945-47 and 1952-56; Paris, 1947-51; Rep. in Turkey and Cultural Attaché British Embassy, Ankara, 1956-61; Rep. in Japan and Cultural Counsellor British Embassy, Tokyo, 1961-67; Leverhulme Foundn Fellow, 1967-69; British Council Rep. in France, and Cultural Attaché, British Embassy, Paris, 1969-71. Bollingen Foundn Fellow and Vis. Prof., Univ. of Southern California, 1961; Vis. Fellow, Univ. Coll., Cambridge, 1971-72; Vis. Prof., Nice, 1972-74. Mem., Editorial Panel, New Universities Quarterly, 1979-. Fellow: Royal Asiatic Soc.; Inst. of Cultural Research; Life Mem., Royal Inst. of Cornwall; Associate Mem., Magic Circle; Pres., Royal Soc. of St George, Tokyo, 1965. *Publications:* Turkey, the Modern Miracle, 1939; Life in Modern Turkey, 1946; The Approach to Metaphysics, 1947; The Western Philosophers, 1950; The Eastern Philosophers, 1952; Simone Weil, 1954; R. G. Collingwood, 1954; Wyndham Lewis, 1955; Living and Knowing, 1955; La Vie et l'Oeuvre de Bertrand Russell, 1963; (ed) T. S. Eliot: a Tribute from Japan, 1965; Tokyo Essays, 1967; Wyndham Lewis: an Anthology of his Prose, 1969; (ed) Charles Dickens, a Centenary Volume, 1969; Japan, 1973; Man, Time and the New Science, 1973; The Last Country, 1974; (ed) Arnold Toynbee: a selection from his works, 1978; The World of St Boniface, 1980; In Search of St Piran, 1982; The Church of St Morwenna and St John the Baptist, Morwenstow: a guide and history, 1982; contribs to Criterion, Scrutiny, Times Literary Supplement, Economist, Arts Review, and many foreign reviews, etc. *Recreations:* travel, reading, music. *Address:* Tall Trees, Morwenstow, Cornwall. *T:* Morwenstow 206; 31 Redan Street, W14. *T:* 01-602 6414. *Clubs:* Athenæum; Union Society (Oxford).

TOMLINSON, Prof. (Alfred) Charles, FRSL; Professor of English, University of Bristol, since 1982; *b* 8 Jan. 1927; *s* of Alfred Tomlinson and May Lucas; *m* 1948, Brenda Raybould; two *d. Educ:* Longton High School; Queens' Coll., Cambridge (MA); Royal Holloway and Bedford Colls, Univ. of London (MA). Lecturer, 1957-68, Reader in English poetry, 1968-82, Bristol Univ. Visiting Prof., Univ. of New Mexico, 1962-63; O'Connor Prof., Colgate Univ., NY, 1967-68. Arts Council Poetry Panel, 1964-66; Witter Bynner Lectr, Univ. of New Mexico, 1976. Exhibition of Graphics: Ely House, OUP, London, 1972; Clare Coll., Cambridge, 1975; Arts Council touring exhibn, 1978-80. Hon. Fellow, Queens' Coll., Cambridge, 1975. FRSL 1975. Hon. DLitt: Keele, 1981; Colgate, 1981. Cholmondeley Award, 1979. *Publications: poetry:* Relations and Contraries, 1951; The Necklace, 1955, repr. 1966; Seeing is Believing, 1960 (US 1958); A Peopled Landscape, 1963; Poems, 1964; American Scenes, 1966; The Poem as Initiation, (US) 1968; The Way of a World, 1969; Poems, in Penguin Modern Poets, 1969; Renga (France) 1970, (US) 1972, (England) 1979; Written on Water, 1972; The Way In, 1974; Selected Poems, 1978; The Shaft, 1978; (with Octavio Paz) Air Born, 1981 (Mexico 1979); Some Americans: a personal record, (US), 1980; The Flood, 1981; *graphics:* Words and Images, 1972; In Black and White, 1975; *translations:* (with Henry Gifford): Versions from Fyodor Tyutchev, 1960; Castilian Ilexes: Versions from Antonio Machado, 1963; Ten Versions from Trilce by Cesar Vallejo, (US) 1970; *edited:* Marianne Moore: A Collection of Critical Essays, (US) 1969; William Carlos Williams: A Collection of Critical Essays, 1972; William Carlos Williams: Selected Poems, 1976; Octavio Paz: Selected Poems, 1979; The Oxford Book of Verse in English Translation, 1980; contribs to: Essays in Criticism, Hudson Review, Poetry (Chicago), Poetry Nation Review, Sewanee Review, Times Lit. Supp. *Recreations:* music, walking. *Address:* c/o English Department, University of Bristol, Bristol BS8 1TH.

TOMLINSON, Prof. Bernard Evans, CBE 1981; MD, FRCP, FRCPath; Hon. Professor of Pathology, University of Newcastle upon Tyne, since 1973; Consultant Neuropathologist, Newcastle Health Authority (formerly Area Health Authority), since 1976; Chairman, Northern Regional Health Authority, since 1982; *b* 13 July 1920; *s* of James Arthur Tomlinson and Doris Mary (*née* Evans); *m* 1944, Betty Oxley; one *s* one *d. Educ:* Brunts Sch., Mansfield; University Coll. and University Coll. Hosp., London (BS 1943, MD 1962). FRCP 1965; FRCPath 1964. Trainee Pathologist, EMS, 1943-47; served RAMC as Specialist Pathologist, 1947-49 (Major). Newcastle upon Tyne General Hospital: Sen. Registrar, Pathology, 1949-50; Consultant Pathologist, 1950-53; Sen. Consultant Pathologist, 1953-82; Hon. Lectr in Path., Univ. of Newcastle upon Tyne, 1960-71. *Publications:* articles and book chapters on gen. neuropath., partic. on path. of brain injury, brain changes in old age and on dementia. *Recreations:* gardening, golf, music, walking. *Address:* Greyholme, Wynbury Road, Low Fell, Gateshead, Tyne and Wear NE9 6TS.

TOMLINSON, David (Cecil MacAlister); Actor; *b* 7 May 1917; *s* of C. S. Tomlinson, Solicitor, Folkestone, Kent, and F. E. Tomlinson (*née* Sinclair-Thomson); *m* Audrey Freeman, actress; four *s. Educ:* Tonbridge Sch. Served War of 1939-45: Flight Lieut, Pilot, RAF; demobilised, 1946. Chief roles include: Henry, in The Little Hut, Lyric, Aug. 1950-Sept. 1953; Clive, in All for Mary, Duke of York's, June 1954-May 1955; David, in Dear Delinquent, Westminster and Aldwych, June 1957-July 1958; Tom, in The Ring of Truth, Savoy, July 1959; Robert in Boeing Boeing, Apollo, 1962; acted and directed: Mother's Boy (Nero), Globe, 1964; A Friend Indeed, Cambridge, 1966; The Impossible Years, Cambridge, 1966; On the Rocks (Prime Minister), Dublin Festival, 1969; A Friend Indeed, and A Song at Twilight, South Africa, 1973-74; The Turning Point, Duke of York's, 1974. First appeared in films, 1939; since then has appeared, in leading roles, in over 50 films. *Recreation:* antique collecting. *Address:* Brook Cottage, Mursley, Bucks. *T:* Mursley 213. *Club:* Travellers'.

TOMLINSON, Sir (Frank) Stanley, KCMG 1966 (CMG 1954); HM Diplomatic Service, retired; *b* 21 March 1912; *m* 1959, Nancy, *d* of late E. Gleeson-White and Mrs Gleeson-White, Sydney, Australia. *Educ:* High Pavement Sch., Nottingham; University College, Nottingham. Served in various consular posts in Japan, 1935-41; Saigon, 1941-42; United States, 1943; Washington, 1945; Acting Consul-General, Manila, 1945, Chargé d'Affaires, 1946; Foreign Office, 1947; Washington, 1951; Imperial Defence Coll., 1954; Counsellor and Head, SE Asia Dept, 1955; Dep. Commandant, Berlin, 1958; Minister, UK Permanent Delegation to NATO, 1961-64; Consul General, New York, 1964-66; British High Comr, Ceylon, 1966-69; Dep. Under-Sec. of State, FCO, 1969-72. Hon. LLD Nottingham, 1970. *Recreations:* trout fishing, oenophily, reading. *Address:* 32 Long Street, Devizes, Wilts.

TOMLINSON, Rt. Rev. Mgr George Arthur; Hon. Canon of Westminster Cathedral; *b* Hampstead, NW, 21 May 1906; *s* of late George Henry and Frances Tomlinson. *Educ:* Hastings Grammar Sch.; Keble Coll., Oxford. BA 1929; MA 1942. Ordained in Church of England, 1930; Curate of South Kirby, Yorkshire, 1930-32; received into Catholic Church, 1932; Pontifical Beda Coll., Rome, 1933-37; Priest, 1937; Chaplain to the Oratory Sch., 1937-41; Curate at Kentish Town, 1941; Brentford, 1942; Headmaster, The

Oratory Sch., South Oxon, 1943-53; re-established Oratory Preparatory Sch., Branksome Park, Dorset, 1946; Senior Catholic Chaplain to University of London, 1953-64; Administrator Westminster Cathedral, 1964-67; Rector, St James's, Spanish Place, 1967-77, retired. Hon. Chaplain to High Sheriff of Glos, 1982. Prelate of Honour to HH Pope John Paul II. Painter of Frescoes in chapel of Our Lady and the English Martyrs, Little Crosby, Lancs, and various smaller works. *Publications:* regular contributor to theological reviews. *Recreations:* music, painting, swimming. *Address:* Stable Flat, Spetchley Park, Worcester.

TOMLINSON, John Edward; Senior Lecturer in Industrial Relations and Management, Solihull College of Technology, since 1979; *b* 1 Aug. 1939; *s* of Frederick Edwin Tomlinson, headmaster, and Doris Mary Tomlinson; *m* 1963, Marianne Solveig Sommar, Stockholm; three *s* one *d*. *Educ:* Westminster City Sch.; Co-operative Coll., Loughborough; Nottingham Univ. (Dip. Polit. Econ. Social Studies); MA (Industrial Relations) Warwick, 1982. Sec., Sheffield Co-operative Party, 1961-68; Head of Research Dept, AUEW, 1968-70; Lectr in Industrial Relations, 1970-74. MP (Lab) Meriden, Feb. 1974-1979; PPS to Prime Minister, 1975-76; Parly Under-Sec. of State, FCO, 1976-79, and ODM, 1977-79. *Publication:* Left, Right: the march of political extremism in Britain, 1981. *Address:* 23 Meriden Road, Hampton-in-Arden, near Solihull, W Midlands. *Club:* Kingshurst Labour.

TOMLINSON, John Race Godfrey, MA; Director of Education, Cheshire County Council, since 1972; *b* 24 April 1932; *s* of John Angell Tomlinson and Beatrice Elizabeth Race Godfrey; *m* 1954, Audrey Mavis Barrett; two *s* two *d*. *Educ:* Stretford Grammar Sch.; Manchester Univ. (MA); London Inst. of Historical Research. Flt Lt, RAF, 1955-58. Teaching, 1958-60; Admin. Asst, Salop LEA, 1960-63; Asst Educn Officer, Lancs LEA, 1963-67; Dep. Dir of Educn, Cheshire LEA, 1967-72. Chm., Schools Council, 1978-81. Member: Court Cttee on Child Health Services, 1973-76; Gulbenkian enquiries into Drama, Music and Dance, 1974-78; Founder Chm., Further Educn Curriculum Review and Develt Unit, 1976; Member: Special Programmes Bd, Manpower Services Commn, 1977; Delegacy for Continuing Educn, Open Univ., 1978-81; Study Commn on the Family, 1978; Adv. Cttee on Supply and Trng of Teachers, 1979-82. Pres., Soc. of Educn Officers, 1982; Trustee, Community Service Volunteers, 1981-. Hon. Prof., Dept of Educn, Keele Univ., 1981. Lectures: Wilfred Fish Meml, GDC, 1978; Charles Gittens Meml, Univ. of Wales, 1980; Lockyer, RCP, 1980; Schools Council, BAAS, 1981. FRSA 1976 (Mem. Council, 1982-); FBIM (MBIM 1978); FCP 1980. Hon. RNCM 1980. *Publications:* Additional Grenville Papers 1763-65, 1962; articles in various jls. *Recreations:* family and garden, music and walking, a relentless search for good butter. *Address:* Dormy, Brookhurst Road, Bromborough, Wirral L63 0ET. *T:* 051-334 1672. *Club:* Army and Navy.

TOMLINSON, Maj.-Gen. Michael John, CB 1981; OBE 1973 (MBE 1964); Director Royal Artillery, since 1981; *b* 20 May 1929; *s* of Sidney Tomlinson and Rose Hodges; *m* 1955, Patricia, *d* of late Lt-Col A. Rowland; one *s* one *d*. *Educ:* Skinners' Sch.; Royal Military Academy. Commissioned, RA, 1949; served in Brunei (despatches, 1962); GSO2 to Dir of Ops Borneo, 1962-64; DAMS, MoD, 1966-68; GSO1, Staff Coll. Camberley, 1968-70; CO, 2 Field Regt RA, 1970-72; Col GS, Staff Coll. Camberley, 1972-73; CRA 3rd Div., 1973-75; Student, RCDS, 1976; Dep. Mil. Sec. (B), MoD, 1976-78; Dir of Manning, Army, 1978-79; Vice-Adjt Gen., 1979-81. Col Comdt, RA, 1982-. *Recreations:* music, gardening, wine-making. *Address:* Director Royal Artillery, Royal Artillery Barracks, Woolwich, SE18 4BB. *Club:* Army and Navy.

TOMLINSON, Sir Stanley; *see* Tomlinson, Sir F. S.

TOMNEY, Frank; sales and marketing analyst; *s* of Arthur Tomney, Bolton, Lancs; *m* 1936, *d* of Andrew Isham, Watford; one *s* one *d*. Branch Secretary, General and Municipal Workers Union, 1940-50. MP (Lab) Hammersmith N, 1950-79; Mem., House of Commons Select Cttees, 1954-60; Deleg., Council of Europe and WEU, 1963-64, 1971-73, 1974-79; Leader, UK Delegn to UN, 1968; Mem., European Parlt, 1976-79. Member: Watford Town Council, 1946-50; Herts CC, 1950-54. *Recreation:* collecting English and continental water colours. *Address:* 27 Shepherds Way, Rickmansworth, Herts.

TOMPKINS, Prof. Frederick Clifford, FRS 1955; Professor in Physical Chemistry, Imperial College of Science and Technology, SW7, 1959-77, now Emeritus; Editor and Secretary of Faraday Division of The Chemical Society (formerly The Faraday Society), 1950-77, President, 1978; *b* 29 Aug. 1910; *m* 1936, Catherine Livingstone Macdougal; one *d*. *Educ:* Yeovil Sch.; Bristol Univ. Asst Lectr, King's Coll., Strand, 1934-37; Lectr and Senior Lectr, Natal Univ., Natal, S Africa, 1937-46; ICI Fellow, King's College, Strand, 1946-47; Reader in Physical Chemistry, Imperial College of Science and Technology, 1947; Hon. ARCS 1964. Hon. DSc Bradford, 1975. *Publications:* Chemisorption of Gases on Metals, 1978; contributions to Proc. Royal Society, Journal Chem. Soc., Trans Faraday Soc., Jl Chem. Physics, Zeitung Elektrochem. *Address:* 9 St Helens Close, Southsea, Portsmouth, Hants. *T:* Portsmouth 731901.

TOMPKINS, (Granville) Richard (Francis); Founder, Chairman and Managing Director: Green Shield Trading Stamp Co. Ltd, since 1958; Argos Distributors Ltd, 1973-79, President, since 1979; *b* 15 May 1918; *s* of late Richard and Ethel May Tompkins; *m* 1970, Elizabeth Nancy Duke; one *d* (and two *d* of a former marriage). *Educ:* Pakeman St LCC Sch., London, N7.

Laundry delivery man and filling station attendant, 1932; van salesman, 1934; engineering draughtsman, 1938. Founded several companies in printing and advertising, 1945; also Green Shield Trading Stamp Co., 1958. *Recreations:* travel, theatre, golf. *Address:* 7 Belgrave Square, SW1.

TOMS, Carl, OBE 1969; First Head of Design, and Associate Director, for the Young Vic at the National Theatre, since 1970; *b* 29 May 1927. *Educ:* High Oakham Sch., Mansfield, Nottingham; Mansfield College of Art; Royal Coll. of Art; Old Vic Sch. Designing for theatre, films, opera, ballet, etc, on the London stage, 1957-; also for productions at Glyndebourne, Edinburgh Festival, Chichester Festival, and Aldeburgh (world première of Midsummer Night's Dream, 1960). Theatre designs include: Vivat! Vivat Regina!, Chichester and London, 1970, NY 1972; Sherlock Holmes, London, 1974, NY 1974 (Tony Award and Drama Desk Award for Theatre Design); Travesties, London, 1974, NY 1975; Vienna Burgtheater, 1976; Long Day's Journey into Night, LA 1977; Man and Superman, Malvern Festival and London, 1977; The Devil's Disciple, LA 1977, NY 1978; Look After Lulu, Chichester, 1978, Haymarket, 1978; Night and Day, Phoenix, 1978, NY, 1979; Stage Struck, Vaudeville, 1979; Windy City, Victoria Palace, 1982. Designs for the Royal Opera House, Covent Garden, include: Gala perf. for State Visit of King and Queen of Nepal, 1960; Iphigénie en Tauride, 1961; Ballet Imperial, 1963; Die Frau ohne Schatten (costumes), 1967; Fanfare for Europe, 1973; Queen's Silver Jubilee Gala, 1977; for London Festival Ballet: Swan Lake, 1982; for Sadler's Wells: Cenerentola, 1959; The Barber of Seville, 1960; Our Man in Havana, 1963; for Nat. Theatre: Edward II, 1968; Love's Labour's Lost, 1968; Cyrano de Bergerac, 1970; For Services Rendered, 1979; Playbill, 1980; The Provok'd Wife, 1980 (SWET Designer of the Year award); The Second Mrs Tanqueray, 1981; On the Razzle, 1981; for Vienna Nat. Theatre: Travesties, 1977; She Stoops to Conquer, 1978; Betrayal, 1978; The Guardsman, 1979; Night and Day, 1980; for Vienna State Opera: Macbeth, 1982; for NY City Opera: Die Meistersinger von Nürnberg, 1975; The Marriage of Figaro, 1977; The Voice of Ariadne, 1977; Der Freischutz, 1981; for NY Metropolitan Opera: Thais, 1978; for San Diego Opera Co.: Norma, 1976; La Traviata, 1976; The Merry Widow, 1977; Hamlet, 1978; Romeo and Juliet, 1982; for San Francisco Opera: Peter Grimes, 1973; Thais, 1976. Other companies and theatres designed for include Royal Shakespeare Company, Old Vic, Young Vic, Welsh Nat. Opera, NY State Opera. Completed re-designing of Theatre Royal, Windsor, 1965; re-designing of Theatre Royal, Bath, 1982; design consultant for Investiture of Prince of Wales, Caernarvon Castle, 1969. Has designed sets and costumes for numerous films; work has incl. decoration of restaurants, hotels, houses, etc; has also designed exhibns, programmes, cards, etc. *Publications:* Winter's Tale (designs for stage prod.), 1975; Scapino (designs for stage prod.), 1975. *Recreations:* gardening, travel, parrots. *Address:* The White House, Beaumont, near Wormley, Broxbourne, Herts EN10 7QJ. *T:* Hoddesdon 63961.

TOMS, Edward Ernest; Overseas Labour Adviser, Foreign and Commonwealth Office, since 1981; *b* 10 Dec. 1920; *s* of Alfred William and Julia Harrington Toms; *m* 1946, Veronica Rose, Dovercourt, Essex; three *s* one *d*. *Educ:* St Boniface's Coll.; Staff Coll., Camberley (psc), Nat. Defence Coll. (jssc). War service 1939-45; Captain Seaforth Highlanders; Special Forces, W Desert, Italy, Balkans, NW Europe; Regular Army, 1946, Seaforth Highlanders and QO Highlanders; Brigade Major, Berlin, 1959-61; Col GS, 1967-69. Principal, Home Civil Service, 1969; Asst Sec., Dept of Employment, 1973; seconded to Diplomatic Service as Counsellor, Bonn and Vienna, 1977-81. *Publications:* infrequent contribs to Punch and Pick of Punch. *Recreations:* hill-walking (founder Mem., Aberdeen Mountain Rescue Assoc., 1964), squash. *Address:* c/o Clydesdale Bank, 5 Castle Street, Aberdeen. *Club:* Army and Navy.

TOMSETT, Alan Jeffrey, OBE 1974; Finance Director and Member British Transport Docks Board, since 1974; chartered accountant; *b* 3 May 1922; *s* of Maurice Jeffrey Tomsett and Edith Sarah (*née* Mackelworth); *m* 1948, Joyce May Hill; one *s* one *d*. *Educ:* Trinity School of John Whitgift, Croydon; Univ. of London (BCom). JDipMA. Joined Hodgson Harris & Co., Chartered Accountants, London, 1938. Served War, with RAF, 1941-46 (Middle East, 1942-45). Smallfield Rawlins & Co., Chartered Accountants, London, 1951; Accountant and Asst Sec. (later Sec.), Northern Mercantile & Investment Corp. Ltd, 1955; William Baird & Co. Ltd, 1962-63. British Transport Docks Board: Dep. Chief Accountant, 1963; Chief Accountant, 1964; Financial Controller, 1970. Director: BTDB (Pension Trustees) Ltd; Kenny (Stevedores) Ltd, 1975. FCA, FCMA, IPFA, FCIS, FCIT (Vice-Pres. 1981-). *Address:* 102 Ballards Way, Croydon, Surrey CR0 5RG. *T:* 01-657 5069.

TONBRIDGE, Bishop Suffragan of, since 1982; Rt. Rev. David Henry Bartleet; *b* 11 April 1929; *s* of Edmund Arthur Bartleet and Helen Bartleet (*née* Holford); *m* 1956, Jean Mary (*née* Rees); one *s* two *d*. *Educ:* St Edward's School, Oxford; AA School of Architecture, London; St Peter's Hall, Oxford; Westcott House, Cambridge. Curate: St Mary-le-Tower, Ipswich, 1957-60; St George's, Doncaster (in charge of St Edmund's), 1960-64; Vicar: Edenbridge, Kent, 1964-73; Bromley, Kent, 1973-82. *Recreations:* music, woodturning, beekeeping; architecture; icons. *Address:* Bishop's Lodge, 48 St Botolph's Road, Sevenoaks, Kent. *T:* Sevenoaks 456070.

TONBRIDGE, Archdeacon of; *see* Mason, Ven. R. J.

TONČIĆ-SORINJ, Dr Lujo; Secretary-General, Council of Europe, 1969-74; *b* Vienna, 12 April 1915; *s* of Dušan Tončić-Sorinj (formerly Consul-Gen. in service of Imperial Ministry for Foreign Affairs), and Mabel (*née* Plason de la Woesthyne); *m* 1956, Renate Trenker; one *s* four *d*. *Educ:* Secondary sch. (Gymnasium), Salzburg. Studied law and philosophy at Univs of Vienna and Agram (Zagreb), 1934–41, also medicine and psychology (LLD Vienna); political science, Institut d'Etudes Politiques, Paris. Head of Polit. Dept of Austrian Research Inst. for Economics and Politics in Salzburg and Editor of Berichte und Informationen (political periodical published by Austrian Research Inst. for Economics and Politics), 1946–49. MP for Land Salzburg, 1949–66; Chairman: Legal Cttee of Austrian Parl., 1953–56; For. Affairs Cttee, 1956–59; in charge of For. Affairs questions, Austrian People's Party, 1959–66. Austrian Parly Observer to Consultative Assembly of Council of Europe, 1953–56; Austrian Mem., Consultative Assembly, 1956–66; Vice-Pres., Council of Europe; Vice-Pres., Political Commn, 1961–62; Minister for Foreign Affairs, Austria, 1966–68. Permanent Rep. of Austrian People's Party to Christian-Democratic Gp, European Parlt, 1980–. Chm., Austrian Assoc. of UN, 1978–. Grand Cross of several orders including Order of St Michael and St George, Great Britain (Hon. GCMG). *Publications:* Erfüllte Träume (autobiog.), 1982; over 350 articles and essays on politics, economics, internat. law and history. *Recreations:* swimming, diving, history, geography. *Address:* 5020 Salzburg, Schloss Fürberg, Pausingerstrasse 11, Austria. *T:* 06222/73437.

TONGA, HM the King of; **King Taufa'ahau Tupou IV,** Hon. GCMG 1977 (Hon. KCMG 1968); Hon. GCVO 1970; Hon. KBE 1958 (Hon. CBE 1951); *b* 4 July 1918; *s* of Prince Uiliami Tupoulahi Tungi and Queen Salote Tupou of Tonga; *S* mother, 1966; *m* 1947, Halaevalu Mata'aho 'Ahome'e; three *s* one *d*. *Educ:* Tupou College, Tonga; Newington College, Sydney; Wesley College, Sydney University. Minister for Health and Education, Tonga, 1943–50; Prime Minister, 1950–65. *Heir: s* HRH Prince Tupouto'a, *b* 4 May 1948. *Address:* The Palace, Nukualofa, Tonga. *T:* Nukualofa 1.

TONGE, Brian Lawrence, PhD; FRSC; Director, Oxford Polytechnic, since 1981; *b* 19 April 1933; *s* of Lawrence and Louisa Tonge; *m* 1955, Anne Billcliff; one *d*. *Educ:* Bury High Sch.; London Univ. (BSc 1st Cl. Chemistry); Manchester Univ. (PhD). FRIC 1964. Scientific Officer, Hirst Research Centre, GEC Ltd, 1956–59; Chemist, Medical Research Council Carcinogenic Substances Research Unit, Exeter Univ., 1959; Lectr in Chemistry, Plymouth Coll. of Technology, 1960–63; Research Manager, Pure Chemicals Ltd, 1963–65; Principal Lectr in Chemistry, West Ham Coll. of Technology, 1965–67; Head of Dept of Applied Science and Dean of Faculty of Science, Wolverhampton Polytechnic, 1967–71; Dep. Director, Oxford Polytechnic, 1971–81. Member, Wolfson Coll., Oxford, 1975; MA (Status) Oxford, 1981. FRSA 1978. *Publications:* numerous contribs to learned jls and articles in scientific and educnl press. *Recreations:* gardening, reading, music. *Address:* 2 Pullens Field, Oxford OX3 0BU. *T:* Oxford 69666.

TONGE, Prof. Cecil Howard, TD; DDSc; FDSRCS; Professor of Oral Anatomy, 1964–81, Professor Emeritus 1981, and Dental Postgraduate Sub-Dean, 1968–82, University of Newcastle upon Tyne; *b* 16 Dec. 1915; *s* of Norman Cecil Tonge and Gladys Marian (*née* Avison); *m* 1946, Helen Wilson Currie. *Educ:* Univ. of Durham. DDSc, MB, BS, BDS (Dunelm); FDSRCS. House Surg., later Asst Resident MO, Royal Victoria Inf., 1939; Demonstrator in Anatomy, Medical Sch., Newcastle upon Tyne, 1940; Lectr in Anatomy, 1944, Sen. Lectr, 1952, Reader in Oral Anatomy, 1956, Univ. of Durham. Lieut RAMC (TA), 1941; Lt-Col RAMC (TA) Comdg 151 (N) Field Ambulance, 1954–58; Hon. Col, Northumbrian Univ. OTC, 1974–82. Chairman, Council of Military Educn Cttees of Univs of UK, 1968–82; Pres., British Div. Internat. Assoc. for Dental Research, 1968–71; Northern Regional Adviser in Postgrad. Dental Educn of RCS, 1970–; Chm., Dental Cttee, Council for Postgrad. Medical Educn, 1978–; British Dental Association: Pres., 1981–82; Member: Representative Bd, 1970–; Council, 1970–; Chm., Central Cttee for Univ. Teachers and Res. Workers, 1976–81. Member, Sunderland AHA, 1973–82; Vice-Chm., Sunderland DHA, 1982–. *Publications:* chapter in Scientific Foundations of Dentistry, 1976; papers in Dental Anatomy and Embryology; contribs to Brit. Jl of Nutrition, Jl of Anatomy, Jl of Dental Res., Jl of RCSE, Brit. Dental Jl, Dental Update, Nature, Internat. Dental Jl. *Recreation:* history. *Address:* 32 Eslington Terrace, Newcastle upon Tyne NE2 4RN. *T:* Newcastle upon Tyne 811816.

TONKIN, Hon. David Oliver, FRACO; Liberal Member for Bragg, Parliament of South Australia, since 1970; Premier, Treasurer, Minister of State Development and Minister of Ethnic Affairs, Government of South Australia, since 1979; *b* 20 July 1929; *s* of Oliver Athelstone Prisk Tonkin and Bertha Ida Louise (*née* Kennett); *m* 1954, Prudence Anne Juttner; three *s* three *d*. *Educ:* St Peter's Coll., Adelaide; Univ. of Adelaide (MB, BS 1953); Inst. of Ophthalmology, London (DO 1958). FRACO 1974. Private ophthalmic practice, 1958–; vis. staff, Royal Adelaide Hosp., 1958–68. Mem., Social Adv. Council, SA Govt, 1968–70; Leader of Opposition, 1975–79. *Recreations:* the family, music and theatre, sailing. *Address:* 18 Dimora Court, Adelaide, SA 5000, Australia. *Clubs:* Adelaide, Royal Adelaide Golf; Sturt Football.

TONKIN, Derek, CMG 1982; HM Ambassador to Vietnam, 1980–82; *b* 30 Dec. 1929; *s* of Henry James Tonkin and Norah Wearing; *m* 1953, Doreen Rooke; two *s* two *d*. *Educ:* High Pavement Grammar Sch., Nottingham; St Catherine's Society, Oxford (MA). HM Forces, 1948–49; FO, 1952; Warsaw, 1955; Bangkok, 1957; Phnom Penh, 1961; FO, 1963; Warsaw, 1966; Wellington, 1968; FCO, 1972; East Berlin, 1976. *Publication:* Modern Cambodian Writing, 1962. *Recreations:* tennis, music, running. *Address:* c/o

Foreign and Commonwealth Office, SW1. *Club:* United Oxford & Cambridge University.

TONKS, Rt. Rev. Basil; a Suffragan Bishop of Toronto (Credit Valley), since 1981; *b* York, England, 28 April 1930; *s* of Vincent and Alice Tonks; *m* 1955, Ida Catherine Mary (*née* Daunt); two *s* two *d*. *Educ:* Corchester Prep. School; St John's, Leatherhead; Codrington Coll., Barbados (DipTh). Deacon 1954, priest 1955, Port-of-Spain, Trinidad; Asst Curate, Trinity Cathedral, Port-of-Spain, 1954; Rector, St Christopher, Siparia, 1956; Chaplain, Mission to Seamen, Port-of-Spain, 1960; Rector, St Andrew's, Scarborough, Tobago, 1964; Canon of Trinity Cathedral, Port-of-Spain, 1968; Asst Chaplain, Mission to Seamen, Toronto and Asst Curate, St Aidan's, Toronto, 1969; Rector of St Giles', Barrie and St Thomas', Shanty Bay, 1970; Archdeacon of Simcoe, 1972–80; Rector of St Martin-in-the-Fields, Toronto, 1980. Hon. DD, Wycliffe Coll., 1981. Mem. Old Johnians (Leatherhead). *Recreations:* Rugby football (represented Trinidad), boxing, rock climbing, archaeology, camping. *Address:* 123 Prince George Drive, Islington, Ontario M9B 2Y3, Canada. *T:* 416-233-3610.

TOOHEY, Mrs Joyce, CB 1977; Under-Secretary, Department of the Environment, 1970–76; *b* 20 Sept. 1917; *o d* of Louis Zinkin and Lena Zinkin (*née* Daiches); *m* 1947, Monty I. Toohey, MD, MRCP, DCH (*d* 1960); two *d*. *Educ:* Brondesbury and Kilburn High Sch.; Girton Coll., Cambridge; London Sch. of Economics. BA 1938, MA 1945, Cambridge. Asst Principal, Min. of Supply, 1941; transferred to Min. of Works (later Min. of Public Building and Works, now Dept of the Environment), 1946; Principal, 1948; Asst Secretary, 1956; Under-Secretary, 1964. Harvard Business Sch., 1970. *Recreations:* reading, walking. *Address:* 11 Kensington Court Gardens, W8 5QE. *T:* 01-937 1559. *Club:* United Oxford & Cambridge University.

TOOK, John Michael Exton, MBE 1964; British Council Representative, Greece, since 1980; *b* 15 Sept. 1926; *s* of George Took, Dover, and Ailsa Clowes (*née* Turner); *m* 1965, Judith Margaret, *d* of Brig. and Mrs W. J. Birkle; two *d*. *Educ:* Dover Coll.; Jesus Coll., Cambridge (MA, Mod. and Med. Langs Tripos). Served Indian Army, 1944–47, Captain. HM Colonial Admin. Service (later HMOCS), N Rhodesia, 1950–57; Min. of External Affairs, Fedn of Rhodesia & Nyasaland, 1957–63; Min. of External Affairs, Republic of Zambia, 1964–65; joined British Council, 1965; Asst Reg. Dir, Frankfurt, 1965–67; Reg. Dir, Cape Coast, 1967–69; Rep., Cyprus, 1971–74; Cultural Attaché, British Embassy, Budapest, 1974–77; Dep. Controller, European Div., 1977–80. *Publications:* Common Birds of Cyprus, 1973, 3rd edn 1983; contribs to ornithological jls. *Recreations:* ornithology, fishing, natural history. *Address:* The British Council, PO Box 488, Athens, Greece. *T:* 363-3211. *Club:* Royal Commonwealth Society.

TOOKER, H. C. W.; *see* Whalley-Tooker.

TOOLEY, Sir John, Kt 1979; General Director, Royal Opera House, Covent Garden, since 1980; *b* 1 June 1924; *yr s* of late H. R. Tooley; *m* 1st, 1951, Judith Craig Morris (marr. diss., 1965); three *d*; 2nd, 1968, Patricia Janet Norah Bagshawe, 2nd *d* of G. W. S. Bagshawe; one *s*. *Educ:* Repton; Magdalene Coll., Cambridge. Served The Rifle Brigade, 1943–47. Sec., Guildhall School of Music and Drama, 1952–55; Royal Opera House, Covent Garden: Asst to Gen. Administrator, 1955–60; Asst Gen. Administrator, 1960–70; Gen. Administrator, 1970–80. Chm., Nat. Music Council Executive, 1970–72. Hon. FRAM; Hon. GSM. Commendatore, Italian Republic, 1975. *Recreations:* walking, theatre. *Address:* 2 Mart Street, WC2; Winslow Coombe, Ashbury, Swindon, Wilts. *Club:* Garrick.

TOOMEY, Ralph; Under-Secretary, Department of Education and Science, 1969–78; *b* 26 Dec. 1918; *s* of late James and Theresa Toomey; *m* 1951, Patricia Tizard; two *d*. *Educ:* Cyfarthfa Grammar Sch., Merthyr Tydfil; University Coll., London; Univ. of Caen. Served British and Indian Army, 1944–46. Teacher, Enfield Grammar Sch., 1947; Lecturer, Univ. of London, at Sch. of Oriental and African Studies, 1948. Min. of Education, 1948–60 and 1963–78 (seconded to Govt of Mauritius, 1960–63, Principal Asst Sec. in Colonial Secretary's Office and Min. of Local Govt and Co-operative Develt). A UK Rep., High Council, European Univ. Inst., Florence, 1974–78. DUniv Open, 1979. *Address:* 8 The Close, Montreal Park, Sevenoaks, Kent. *T:* Sevenoaks 452553. *Clubs:* Chelsea Arts; Knole Park Golf (Sevenoaks).

TOOTH, Hon. Sir Douglas; *see* Tooth, Hon. Sir S. D.

TOOTH, Geoffrey Cuthbert, MD, MRCP, DPM; Visiting Scientist, National Institute of Mental Health, USA, 1968–71; *b* 1 Sept. 1908; *s* of late Howard Henry Tooth, CB, CMG, MD, FRCP, and late Helen Katherine Tooth, OBE (*née* Chilver); *m* 1st, 1934, Princess Olga Galitzine (*d* 1955), *d* of Prince Alexander Galitzine, MD; 2nd, 1958, HSH Princess Xenia of Russia, *d* of Prince Andrew of Russia. *Educ:* Rugby Sch.; St John's Coll., Cambridge; St Bartholomew's Hosp.; Johns Hopkins Hosp., Baltimore, Md, USA. MRCS, LRCP 1934, MA Cantab 1935, MD Cantab 1946, DPM 1944; MRCP 1965. Asst Psychiatrist, Maudsley Hosp., 1937–39. Surg. Lt-Comdr, RNVR, Neuropsychiatric Specialist, 1939–45. Colonial Social Science Research Fellow, 1946–53; Comr, Bd of Control, 1954–60; transf. to Min. of Health, and retd as Sen. PMO, Head of Mental Health Section, Med. Div., 1960. Mem. Expert Advisory Panel (Mental Health), WHO. *Publications:* Studies in Mental Illness in the Gold Coast, 1950; various reports to learned societies;

articles and papers in med. jls. *Recreations:* sailing, gardening, metal work, photography. *Address:* Grand Prouillac, Plazac, 24580 Rouffignac, France.

TOOTH, Sir Hugh; see Munro-Lucas-Tooth.

TOOTH, Hon. Sir (Seymour) Douglas, Kt 1975; retired from Government of Queensland; *b* 28 Jan. 1904; *s* of Percy Nash Tooth and Laura Tooth; *m* 1937, Eileen Mary O'Connor; one *d. Educ:* Univ. of Queensland (Teacher's Trng). Cl. 1 Teacher's Certif. Certificated Teacher, Qld Dept of Educn, 1922. Entered Qld Parlt as MP: Kelvin Grove, 1957; Ashgrove, 1960-74; apptd Minister for Health in Govt of Qld, 1964; retd from Parlt and Cabinet, 1974. Chairman: Duke of Edinburgh Award Cttee, Qld, 1977-; Brisbane Forest Park Adv. Bd. *Address:* Parmelia Close, 2/61 Bellevue Terrace, Clayfield, Queensland 4011, Australia. *T:* 262-4621.

TOOTHILL, Sir John (Norman), Kt 1964; CBE 1955; FRSE; retired 1975 as Director, Ferranti Ltd, Edinburgh; *b* 11 Nov. 1908; *s* of John Harold and Helena Toothill; *m* 1935, Ethel Amelia Stannard. *Educ:* Beaminster Grammar School. Apprenticed Tilling Stevens Ltd, Hoffman Manufacturing Co. Ltd, Harris Lebus Ltd. Joined Ferranti Ltd, Hollinwood, 1935, as Chief Cost Accountant; Gen. Manager, Ferranti Ltd, Edinburgh, 1943. Chairman: AI Welders Ltd, Inverness; Highland Hydrocarbons, 1979-; Director: R. W. Toothill Ltd, 1972-; W. A. Baxter & Sons Limited, Fochabers, Moray, 1971-. CompIEE, Comp. British IRE, Hon. Comp. Royal Aeronautical Soc. Hon. LLD Aberdeen, 1966; Hon. DSc Heriot-Watt, 1968; Cranfield, 1970. *Publication:* Toothill Report on the Scottish Economy, 1961. *Recreations:* fishing, golf. *Address:* New Lodge, Ordiequish, Fochabers, Morayshire. *Club:* Caledonian.

TOPE, Graham Norman; Deputy General Secretary, Camden Council of Social Service, since 1975; *b* 30 Nov. 1943; *s* of Leslie Tope, Plymouth and late Winifred Tope (*née* Merrick), Bermuda; *m* 1972, Margaret East; two *s. Educ:* Whitgift Sch., S Croydon. Company Sec., 1965-72; Insce Manager, 1970-72. Pres., Nat. League of Young Liberals, 1973- (Vice-Chm., 1971-73); Mem., Liberal Party Nat. Council, 1970-; Councillor and Leader, Liberal Group, Sutton Council, 1974-; Exec. Cttee, London Liberal Party, 1981-. MP (L) Sutton and Cheam, 1972-Feb. 1974; Liberal Party spokesman on environment, Dec. 1972-1974; contested (L) Sutton and Cheam, Oct. 1974. *Publication:* (jtly) Liberals and the Community, 1974. *Address:* 88 The Gallop, Sutton, Surrey. *T:* 01-642 1459.

TOPHAM, Surgeon Captain Lawrence Garth, RN (Retd); Consultant Physician in Geriatric Medicine, Central Hampshire District Winchester and Andover Hospitals, since 1974; *b* 14 Nov. 1914; *s* of late J. Topham and late Mrs Topham; *m* 1943, Olive Barbara Marshall (VAD), *yr d* of late J. Marshall and late Mrs Marshall; one *s* one *d. Educ:* Bradford Grammar Sch.; Univ. of Leeds. MB, ChB 1937; MD 1946; MRCPE 1957; FRCPE 1967; MRCP 1969. Joined RN 1938. Served War: HMS Newcastle and HMS Milford, 1939-41; USN Flight Surgeon's Wings, 1943; RN Fleet Air Arm Pilot's Wings, 1944. Pres., Central Air Med. Bd, 1949; HMS Sheffield, 1951; Med. Specialist and Consultant in Medicine, at RN Hosps, Trincomalee, Haslar and Plymouth, 1952-66; Prof. of Med., RN, and RCP, 1966-71; QHP 1970; retd at own request, from RN, 1971. House Governor and Medical Superintendent, King Edward VII Convalescent Home for Officers, Osborne, IoW, 1971-74. Member: British Nat. Cttee, Internat. Soc. of Internal Medicine; British Geriatric Soc.; Wessex Physicians Club. OStJ (Officer Brother) 1970. *Publications:* several articles in med. jls, especially on subject of diseases of the chest. *Recreations:* Rugby football refereeing, rowing, photography, Oriental cookery. *Address:* Tilings, Holt Close, Wickham, Hants PO17 5EY. *T:* Wickham 832072.

TOPLEY, William Keith, MA; Master of Supreme Court (Queen's Bench Division), since 1980; *b* 19 Jan. 1936; *s* of Bryan Topley and Grizel Hester (*née* Stirling); *m* 1980, Clare Mary Pennington; one *s* by former marriage. *Educ:* Bryanston School; Trinity Coll., Oxford (MA). Called to Bar, Inner Temple, 1959. *Recreations:* golf, sailing. *Address:* Basset Shaw, Checkendon, near Reading, Berks RG8 0TD. *T:* Checkendon 680244. *Clubs:* Garrick; Royal London Yacht (Cowes).

TOPOLSKI, Feliks; Painter; *b* 14 Aug. 1907; *s* of Edward Topolski (actor) and Stanislawa Drutowska; *m* 1st, 1944, Marion Everall (marr. diss. 1975); one *s* one *d* ; 2nd, 1975, Caryl J. Stanley. *Educ:* Mikolaj Rey Sch.; Acad. of Art, Warsaw; Officers' Sch. of Artillery Reserve, Wlodzimierz Wolynski; self-tutoring in Italy, Paris. Settled in England, 1935. Exhibited in London and provincial galleries, in Poland, USA, Canada, Eire, France, India, Australia, Italy, Argentine, Switzerland, Denmark, Norway, Israel, Germany, Brazil and Portugal; has contributed to numerous publications; to BBC television programmes; and designed theatrical settings and costumes; as War Artist (1940-45) pictured Battle of Britain, sea and air war, Russia, Middle East, India, Burma, China, Africa, Italy, Germany. British subject since 1947. Painted the Cavalcade of Commonwealth (60′ × 20′) for Festival of Britain, 1951 (later in Victoria Memorial Hall, Singapore, removed on Independence and returned to artist); four murals for Finsbury Borough Council, 1952 (since erased); Coronation of Elizabeth II (100′ × 4′) for Buckingham Palace, 1958-60; murals for Carlton Tower Hotel, London, 1960; St Regis Hotel, New York, 1965; twenty portraits of English writers for University of Texas, 1961-62. At present engaged on mural-environment, Memoir of the Century (600′ × 12′ to 20′), aided by GLC, 1975-. Films: Topolski's Moscow (for

CBS TV), 1969; Topolski (Polish TV), 1976; Paris Lost, 1980; (with Daniel Topolski) South American Sketchbook (BBC TV), 1982. Works at British Museum, Victoria and Albert Museum, Imperial War Museum, Theatre Museum; Galleries: the Tate, Edinburgh, Glasgow, Aberdeen, Nottingham, Brooklyn, Toronto, Tel Aviv, New Delhi, Melbourne, Lisbon, Warsaw. Dr *hc,* Jagiellonian Univ. of Cracow, 1974. *Publications:* The London Spectacle, 1935; Illustrator of Bernard Shaw's Geneva, 1939, In Good King Charles's Golden Days, 1939, and Pygmalion, 1941; Penguin Prints, 1941; Britain in Peace and War, 1941; Russia in War, 1942; Three Continents, 1944-45; Portrait of GBS, 1946; Confessions of a Congress Delegate, 1949; 88 Pictures, 1951; Coronation, 1953; Sketches of Gandhi, 1954; The Blue Conventions, 1956; Topolski's Chronicle for Students of World Affairs, 1958; Topolski's Legal London, 1961; Face to Face, 1964; Holy China, 1968; (with Conor Cruise O'Brien) The United Nations: Sacred Drama, 1968; Shem Ham & Japheth Inc., 1971; Paris Lost, 1973 (trans. as Paris Disparu, 1974); Topolski's Buckingham Palace Panoramas, 1977; Sua Sanctitas Johannes Paulus Papa II, 1979; The London Symphony Orchestra 75th Anniversary Prints, 1979; Topolski's Panoramas, 1981; prints for Christie's Contemporary Art, 1974, 1975; Topolski's Chronicle, 1953-79, 1982-. *Address:* Bridge Arch 158, opposite Artists' Entrance, Royal Festival Hall, SE1. *T:* 01-928 3405.

TOPP, Air Commodore Roger Leslie, AFC 1950 (Bar 1955, 2nd Bar 1957); Consultant to Ferranti Ltd, Scotland (Aviation and Defence, Federal Republic of Germany), since 1978; *b* 14 May 1923; *s* of William Horace Topp and Kathleen (*née* Peters); *m* 1945, Audrey Jane Jeffery; one *s* one *d. Educ:* North Mundham Sch.; RAF, Cranwell. Served War: Pilot trg, Canada, 1943-44, commissioned 1944; 'E' Sqdn Glider Pilot Regt, Rhine Crossing, 1945. Nos 107 and 98 Mosquito Sqdns, Germany, 1947-50; Empire Test Pilots' Sch. and RAE Farnborough, 1951-54; Commanded No 111 Fighter Sqdn (Black Arrows) Aerobatic Team, 1955-58; Allied Air Forces Central Europe, Fontainbleau, 1959; Sector Operational Centre, Brockzetel, Germany, 1959-61; jssc, Latimer, 1961-62; commanded Fighter Test Sqdn, Boscombe Down, 1962-64; Station Cmdr, RAF Coltishall, 1964-66; Nat. Def. Coll., Canada, 1966-67; Opl Requirements, MoD (Air), London, 1967-69; Multi-role Combat Aircraft Project, Munich, 1969-70; HQ No 38 Gp, Odiham, 1970; Commandant, Aeroplane and Armament Experimental Estabt, Boscombe Down, 1970-72; Dep. Gen. Man., Multi-role Combat Aircraft Develt and Production Agency, Munich, 1972-78; retd from RAF, 1978. *Recreations:* golf, sailing. *Address:* c/o Midland Bank, 22 Market Place, North Walsham, Norfolk. *Clubs:* Royal Air Force; American Embassy (Bonn).

TOPPING, Prof. James, CBE 1977; MSc, PhD, DIC, FInstP; FIMA; Vice-Chancellor, Brunel University, 1966-71; Emeritus Professor, 1971; *b* 9 Dec. 1904; 3rd *s* of James and Mary A. Topping, Ince, Lancashire; *m* 1934, Muriel Phyllis Hall (*d* 1963); one *s* ; *m* 1965, Phyllis Iles. *Educ:* Univ. of Manchester; Imperial Coll. of Science and Technology. BSc (Manchester), 1924; PhD (London), 1926; Beit Scientific Research Fellow, 1926-28. Asst Lectr, Imperial Coll., 1928-30; Lectr Chelsea Polytechnic, 1930-32; Lectr, Coll. of Technology, Manchester, 1932-37; Head, Dept of Maths and Physics, Polytechnic, Regent St, 1937-53; Principal, Technical Coll., Guildford, 1953-54; Principal, Brunel College, W3, 1955-66. Vice-Pres., Inst. of Physics, 1951-54, 1960-63; Chairman: Nuffield Secondary Science Consultative Cttee, 1965-71; Hillingdon Gp Hosp. Management Cttee, 1971-74; London Conf. on Overseas Students, 1971-81; Council, Roehampton Inst. of Higher Educn, 1975-78; Council, Polytechnic of the S Bank, 1975-81; Vis. Cttee, Cranfield Inst. of Technol., 1970-78; Member: Anderson Cttee on Student Grants, 1958-60; Nat. Council for Technological Awards, 1955-64; CNAA, 1964-70. Hon. DTech Brunel, 1967; Hon. DSc CNAA, 1969. *Publications:* Shorter Intermediate Mechanics (with D. Humphrey), 1949; Errors of Observation, 1955; The Beginnings of Brunel University, 1981; papers in scientific jls. *Address:* Forge Cottage, Forest Green, near Dorking, Surrey. *T:* Forest Green 358. *Club:* Athenæum.

TORDOFF, family name of **Baron Tordoff.**

TORDOFF, Baron *cr* 1981 (Life Peer), of Knutsford in the County of Cheshire; **Geoffrey Johnson Tordoff;** Manager, Public Affairs (Chemicals), Shell UK Ltd; *b* 11 Oct. 1928; *s* of Stanley Acomb Tordoff and Annie Tordoff (*née* Johnson); *m* 1953, Mary Patricia (*née* Swarbrick); two *s* three *d. Educ:* North Manchester Grammar School; Manchester Grammar School; Univ. of Manchester. Contested (L), Northwich 1964, Knutsford 1966, 1970. Chairman: Liberal Party Assembly Cttee, 1974-76; Liberal Party, 1976-79 (and its Campaigns and Elections Cttee, 1980, 1981); Member, Liberal Party Nat. Executive, 1975-81. *Address:* House of Lords, SW1.

TORLESSE, Rear-Adm. Arthur David, CB 1953; DSO 1946; retired; Regional Director of Civil Defence, North Midlands Region, 1955-Jan. 1967; *b* 24 Jan. 1902; *e s* of Captain A. W. Torlesse, Royal Navy, and H. M. Torlesse (*née* Jeans); *m* 1933, Sheila Mary Susan, *d* of Lt-Col Duncan Darroch of Gourock; two *s* one *d. Educ:* Stanmore Park; Royal Naval Colleges, Osborne and Dartmouth. Served as midshipman, Grand Fleet, 1918; specialised as observer, Fleet Air Arm, 1926; Commander, 1935; staff appointments in HMS Hood and at Singapore and Bangkok (Naval Attaché), 1936-39; Executive officer, HMS Suffolk, 1939-40; aviation staff appointments at Lee on Solent and Admiralty, 1940-44; Captain, 1942; commanded HMS Hunter, 1944-45; Director of Air Equipment, Admiralty, 1946-48; Imperial Defence College, 1949; commanded HMS Triumph, Far East, 1950, taking part in first 3 months of Korean War (despatches); Rear-Admiral, 1951; Flag Officer, Special

Squadron and in command of Monte Bello atomic trial expedition, 1952; Flag Officer, Ground Training, 1953-54, retired Dec. 1954. Officer, US Legion of Merit, 1954. *Recreations:* fishing, entomology. *Address:* 1 Sway Lodge, Sway, near Lymington, Hants. *T:* Lymington 682550. *Club:* Naval and Military.

TORNARITIS, Criton George, QC (Cyprus); LLB (Hons, Athens); Attorney-General of the Republic of Cyprus, 1960 (Attorney-General, Cyprus, 1952); seconded as Commissioner for Consolidation of the Cyprus Legislation, 1956; *b* 27 May 1902; *m* 1934, Mary (*née* Pitta) (*d* 1973); one *s. Educ:* Gymnasium of Limassol; Athens University; Gray's Inn. Advocate of the Supreme Court of Cyprus, 1924; District Judge, Cyprus, 1940; President District Court, Cyprus, 1942; Solicitor-General, Cyprus, 1944; Attorney-General, Cyprus, 1952. Attached to Legal Div. of the Colonial Office, 1955. Legal Adviser to Greek-Cypriot Delegation on the Mixed Constitutional Commission, 1959; Greek-Cypriot delegate to Ankara for initialling of Constitution of Republic of Cyprus, 1960. *Publications:* The individual as a subject of international law, 1972; The Turkish invasion of Cyprus and legal problems arising therefrom, 1975; The European Convention of Human Rights in the Legal Order of the Republic of Cyprus, 1975; The Ecclesiastical Courts especially in Cyprus, 1976; Cyprus and its Constitutional and other Legal Problems, 1977, 2nd edn 1980; The Public Law of the Republic of Cyprus, 1979, 1982; Federalism and Regionalism in the Contemporary World; contributions to legal journals and periodicals; The Laws of Cyprus, rev. edn, 1959. *Recreations:* walking, reading. *Address:* Penelope Delta Street, Nicosia, Cyprus. *T:* 77242.

TORNEY, Thomas William; JP; MP (Lab) Bradford South since 1970; *b* London, 2 July 1915. *Educ:* elementary school. Joined Labour Party, 1930; Election Agent: Wembley North, 1945; Derbyshire West, 1964. Derby and Dist Area Organizer, USDAW, 1946-70. Member: (Past Chm.) North Midland Regional Joint Apprenticeship Council for catering industry, 1946-68; Local Appeals Tribunal, Min. of Social Security, 1946-68; Parly Select Cttee on Race Relations and Immigration, 1970-; Parly Select Cttee on Agriculture, 1979-; Chm., PLP Gp on Agriculture, Fish and Food, 1981-. Especially interested in education, social security, industrial relations, agriculture and food. JP Derby, 1969. Chevalier, Commanderie of GB, Confrérie des Chevaliers du Sacavan d'Anjou, 1976. *Address:* House of Commons, SW1; 76 The Hollow, Littleover, Derby. *T:* Derby 760705.

ToROBERT, Sir Henry Thomas, KBE 1981; Governor of the Bank of Papua New Guinea since its formation in 1973; Chairman: Management Board, PNG Bankers' College, since 1973; Council, PNG Institute of Applied Social and Economic Research, since 1975; President, PNG Amateur Sports Federation, and PNG Olympic and Commonwealth Games Committees, since 1980; *b* Kokopo, 1942. *Educ:* primary educn in East New Britain; Univ. of Sydney, Aust. (BA Econ. 1965). Asst Research Officer, Bank of Australia, Port Moresby, 1965 (one of first local officers to join the bank); Dep. Manager, Port Moresby Branch, 1971; Manager of the Reserve Bank, 1972 (the first Papua New Guinean to hold such a position at a time when all banks were branches of the Aust. commercial banks). Member of the cttee responsible for working out a PNG banking system which came into effect by an act of parliament in 1973; Chairman: currency working groups advising the Govt on arrangements leading to the introduction of the kina and toea; ToRobert Cttee to look into problems of administration in PNG Public Service, 1979 (ToRobert Report). *Address:* PO Box 898, Port Moresby, Papua New Guinea.

TORONTO, Archbishop of, since 1979; **Most Rev. Lewis Samuel Garnsworthy,** DD; Metropolitan of Ontario; *b* 18 July 1922; *m* 1954, Jean Valance Allen; one *s* one *d. Educ:* Univ. of Alberta (BA); Wycliffe Coll., Toronto (LTh). Asst Curate: St Paul's, Halifax, 1945; St John, Norway, Toronto, 1945-48; Rector: St Nicholas, Birchcliff, Toronto, 1948-56; Transfiguration, Toronto, 1956-59; St John's Church, York Mills, Toronto, 1960-68; Suffragan Bishop, Diocese of Toronto, 1968-72; Bishop of Toronto, 1972. Fellow, Coll. of Preachers, Washington, DC. DD *hc* : Wycliffe Coll., Toronto, 1969; Trinity Coll., Toronto, 1973; Huron Coll., 1976. *Address:* 135 Adelaide Street E, Toronto M5C 1L8, Canada. *T:* 363-6021. *Clubs:* Albany, York (Toronto).

TORONTO, Archbishop of, (RC), since 1978; **His Eminence Cardinal (Gerald) Emmett Carter;** *b* Montreal, Quebec, 1 March 1912; *s* of Thomas Carter and Mary Kelty. *Educ:* Univ. of Montreal (BA, MA, PhD); Grand Seminary of Montreal (STL). Founder, Director and Teacher at St Joseph's Teachers' Coll., Montreal, 1939-61; Auxiliary Bishop of London, Ont., 1961; Bishop of London, 1964. Cardinal, 1979. Chairman, Internat. Cttee for English in the Liturgy, 1971; President, Canadian Catholic Conf. of Bishops, 1975-77. Elected Member, Permanent Council of the Synod of Bishops in Rome, 1977. Hon. LLD: Univ. of W Ontario, 1964; Concordia Univ., 1976; Univ. of Windsor, 1977; McGill Univ., Montreal, 1980; Notre Dame Univ., 1981; Hon. DD, Huron Coll., Univ. of W Ont., 1978; Hon. DHL, Duquesne Univ., Pittsburg, 1965; Hon. DLitt, St Mary's Univ., Halifax, 1980. *Publications:* The Catholic Public Schools of Quebec, 1957; Psychology and the Cross, 1959; The Modern Challenge, 1961. *Recreations:* tennis, skiing. *Address:* Chancery Office, 355 Church Street, Toronto, Ontario M5B 1Z8, Canada. *T:* 416/977-1500.

TORONTO, Bishops Suffragan of; *see* Brown, Rt Rev. A. D.; Hunt, Rt Rev. D. C.; Tonks, Rt Rev. B.

TORPHICHEN, 15th Lord *cr* 1564; **James Andrew Douglas Sandilands;** *b* 27 Aug. 1946; *s* of 14th Lord Torphichen, and Mary Thurstan, *d* of late Randle Henry Neville Vaudrey; *S* father, 1975; *m* 1976, Margaret Elizabeth, *o d* of late William A. Beale and of Mrs Margaret Patten Beale, Peterborough, New Hampshire, USA; two *d. Heir: cousin* Douglas Robert Alexander Sandilands [*b* 31 Aug. 1926; *m* 1949, Ethel Louise Burkitt; one *s* ; *m* Suzette Véva (*née* Pernet); two *s*]. *Address:* Calder House, Mid-Calder, Midlothian.

TORRANCE, Rev. Professor James Bruce; Professor of Systematic Theology, King's College, University of Aberdeen, and Christ's College, Aberdeen, since 1977, Dean of the Faculty of Divinity, since 1978; *b* 3 Feb. 1923; *s* of late Rev. Thomas Torrance and Annie Elizabeth Sharp; *m* 1955, Mary Heather Aitken, medical practitioner; one *s* two *d. Educ:* Royal High School, Edinburgh; Edinburgh Univ. (MA Hons Philosophy, 1st Cl.); New Coll., Edinburgh (BD Systematic Theol., Distinction); Univs of Marburg, Basle and Oxford. Licensed Minister of Church of Scotland, 1950; parish of Invergowrie, Dundee, 1954; Lectr in Divinity and Dogmatics in History of Christian Thought, New Coll., Univ. of Edinburgh, 1961; Sen. Lectr in Christian Dogmatics, New Coll., 1972. Visiting Prof.: of New Testament, Union Theol. Seminary, Richmond, Va., 1960; of Theology, Columbia Theol. Seminary, Decatur, Ga., 1965, and Vancouver Sch. of Theology, BC, 1974-75. *Publications:* (trans. jtly) Oscar Cullmann's Early Christian Worship, 1953; contribs: Essays in Christology for Karl Barth (Karl Barth's Festschrift), 1956; Where Faith and Science Meet, 1954; Calvinus Ecclesiae Doctor, 1978; Incarnation (on Nicene-Constantinopolitan Creed, 381 AD), 1981; articles to Biblical and Biographical Dictionaries, Scottish Jl of Theology, Interpretation, Church Service Society Annual, and other symposia. *Recreations:* beekeeping, fishing, gardening, swimming. *Address:* Don House, 46 Don Street, Old Aberdeen AB2 1UU. *T:* Aberdeen 41526. *See also* Very Rev. Prof. T. F. Torrance.

TORRANCE, Very Rev. Prof. Thomas Forsyth, MBE 1945; DLitt, DTh, DThéol, Dr Teol, DD; FRSE 1979; Professor of Christian Dogmatics, University of Edinburgh, and New College, Edinburgh, 1952-79; Moderator of General Assembly of Church of Scotland, May 1976-77; *b* 30 Aug. 1913; *e s* of late Rev. T. Torrance, then of Chengtu, Szechwan, China; *m* 1946, Margaret Edith, *y d* of late Mr and Mrs G. F. Spear, The Brow, Combe Down, Bath; two *s* one *d. Educ:* Chengtu Canadian School; Bellshill Academy; Univs of Edinburgh, Oxford, Basel. MA Edinburgh 1934; studies in Jerusalem and Athens, 1936; BD Edinburgh 1937; post-grad. studies, Basel, 1937-38; DLitt Edinburgh 1971. Prof. of Theology, Auburn, NY, USA, 1938-39; post-grad. studies, Oriel Coll., Oxford, 1939-40; ordained minister of Alyth Barony Parish, 1940; Church of Scotland chaplain (with Huts and Canteens) in MEF and CMF, 1943-45; returned to Alyth; DTh Univ. of Basel, 1946; minister of Beechgrove Church, Aberdeen, 1947; Professor of Church History, Univ. of Edinburgh, and New Coll., Edinburgh, 1950-52. Participant, World Conf. on Faith and Order, Lund, 1952; Evanston Assembly of WCC, 1954; Faith and Order Commn of WCC, 1952-62; Participant in Conversations between: Church of Scotland and Church of England, 1950-58; World Alliance of Reformed Churches and Greek Orthodox Church, 1979-. Lectures: Hewett, 1959 (NY, Newton Center and Cambridge, Mass); Harris, Dundee, 1970; Anderson, Presbyterian Coll., Montreal, 1971; Taylor, Yale, 1971; Keese, Univ. of Mississippi, Chattanooga, 1971; Cummings, McGill Univ., Montreal, 1978; Richards, Univ. of Virginia at Charlottesville, 1978; Staley, Davidson Coll., NC, 1978; Cosgrove, Glasgow, 1981; Warfield, Princeton, 1981; Payton, Pasadena, 1981; Didsbury, Manchester, 1982. Mem., Académie Internationale des Sciences Religieuses, 1965 (Pres., 1972-); For. Mem., Société de l'Histoire du Protestantisme Français, 1968; Mem. Soc. Internat. pour l'Etude de la Philosophie Médiévale, 1969; Hon. President: Soc. for Study of Theology, 1966-68; Church Service Soc. of the Church of Scotland, 1970-71; New Coll. Union, 1972-73. Vice-Pres., Inst. of Religion and Theology of GB and Ireland, 1973-76 (Pres., 1976-78); Protopresbyter of Greek Orthodox Church (Patriarchate of Alexandria), 1973. Curator, Deutsches Institut für Bildung und Wissen, 1982-. Membre d'honneur, Acad. Internat. de Philosophie des Scis, 1976. DD (*hc*) Presbyterian Coll., Montreal, 1950; DThéol (*hc*) Geneva, 1959; DThéol (*hc*) Paris, 1959; DD (*hc*) St Andrews, 1960; Dr Teol (*hc*) Oslo, 1961; DLitt Edinburgh. Templeton Foundn Prize, 1978. Cross of St Mark (first class), 1970. *Publications:* The Modern Theological Debate, 1942; The Doctrine of Grace in the Apostolic Fathers, 1949; Calvin's Doctrine of Man, 1949; Royal Priesthood, 1955; Kingdom and Church, 1956; When Christ Comes and Comes Again, 1957; The Mystery of the Lord's Supper (Sermons on the Sacrament by Robert Bruce), 1958; ed Calvin's Tracts and Treatises, Vols I-III, 1959; The School of Faith, 1959; Conflict and Agreement in the Church, Vol. I, Order and Disorder, 1959; The Apocalypse Today, 1959; Conflict and Agreement in the Church, Vol. II, The Ministry and the Sacraments of the Gospel, 1960; Karl Barth: an Introduction to his Early Theology, 1910-1930, 1962; ed (with D. W. Torrance) Calvin's NT Commentaries, 1959-73; Theology in Reconstruction, 1965; Theological Science, 1969 (Collins Religious Book Award); Space, Time and Incarnation, 1969; God and Rationality, 1971; Theology in Reconciliation: Essays towards Evangelical and Catholic Unity in East and West, 1975; The Centrality of Christ, 1976; Space, Time and Resurrection, 1976; The Ground and Grammar of Theology, 1980; Christian Theology and Scientific Culture, 1980; (ed) Belief in Science and in Christian Life, 1980; (ed) The Incarnation: ecumenical studies in the Nicene. Constantinopolitan Creed, 1981; Divine and Contingent Order, 1981; Reality and Evangelical Theology, 1982; Juridical Law and Physical Law, 1982; (ed) James Clerk Maxwell: A Dynamical Theory

of the Electromagnetic Field, 1982; Transformation and Convergence in the Frame of Knowledge, 1982; Jt Editor, Church Dogmatics, Vols 1, 2, 3 and 4, by Karl Barth, 1956-69; Jt Editor: Scottish Jl Theology; SJT Monographs. *Recreations:* golf, fishing. *Address:* 37 Braid Farm Road, Edinburgh EH10 6LE. *T:* 031-447 3050. *Clubs:* New, Edinburgh University (Edinburgh).
See also Rev. Prof. J. B. Torrance.

TORRENS-SPENCE, Captain (Frederick) Michael (Alexander), DSO 1941; DSC 1941; AFC 1944; Royal Navy retired; Lord Lieutenant of County Armagh, since 1981; *b* 10 March 1914; *s* of Lt-Col Herbert Frederick Torrens-Spence and Mrs Eileen Torrens-Spence; *m* 1944, Rachel Nora Clarke; three *s* one *d*. *Educ:* RNC, Dartmouth. Commnd Sub Lieut, 1934; specialised as pilot, 1936; Battle of Taranto, 1940; commanded 815 Naval Air Sqdn, 1941; Battle of Matapan, 1941; Chief Instructor, Empire Test Pilots Schs., 1947-48; Dep. Dir, Air Warfare Div., Naval Staff, 1952-54; commanded HMS Delight, 1955-56, HMS Albion, 1959-61; ADC to the Queen, 1960. Comdr 1946, Captain 1952. Co. Comdt, Ulster Special Constabulary, 1961-70; commanded 2nd (Co. Armagh) Bn, Ulster Defence Regt, 1970-71. High Sheriff, Co. Armagh, 1979. DFC, Greece, 1941. *Address:* Mill House, Laurelvale, Tandragee, Co. Armagh BT62 2LN. *T:* Tandragee 840246. *Club:* MCC.

TORRIE, Malcolm; *see* Mitchell, G. M. W.

TORRINGTON, 11th Viscount, *cr* 1721; **Timothy Howard St George Byng;** Bt 1715; Baron Byng of Southill, 1721; Managing Director, Anvil Petroleum Ltd (formerly Attock Petroleum Ltd), since 1976; *b* 13 July 1943; *o s* of Hon. George Byng, RN (*d* on active service, 1944; *o s* of 10th Viscount) and Anne Yvonne Wood (she *m* 2nd, 1951, Howard Henry Masterton Carpenter); *S* grandfather, 1961; *m* 1973, Susan, *d* of M. G. T. Webster, *qv*; three *d*. *Educ:* Harrow; St Edmund Hall, Oxford. *Recreation:* travel. *Heir:* kinsman, John Launcelot Byng, MC [*b* 18 March 1919; *m* 1955, Margaret Ellen Hardy; one *s* two *d*]. *Address:* 60 Cumberland Street, SW1. *Clubs:* White's; Muthaiga (Nairobi).

TORTELIER, Paul; cellist, composer, conductor; *b* 21 March 1914; *s* of Joseph Tortelier, cabinet maker; *m* 1946, Maud Martin; one *s* three *d*. *Educ:* Conservatoire National de Musique, Paris; gen. educn privately. Leading Cellist, Monte Carlo, 1935-37; Cellist, Boston Symphony Orch., 1937-40; Leading Cellist, Société des Concerts du Conservatoire de Paris, 1945-47; Internat. solo career began in Concertgebouw, Amsterdam, 1946, and London, 1947 (under Sir Thomas Beecham's baton). Concert tours: Europe, N America, North Africa, Israel, S America, USSR, Japan, etc. As a conductor: debut with Israel Philharmonic, 1956; Prof. of Violoncello: Conservatoire Nat. Supérieur de Musique, Paris, 1956-69; Folkwang Hochschule, Essen; conducts in Paris and in England. Master classes, for BBC TV, 1970. Hon. Prof., Central Conservatory, Peking, 1980-. Hon. Mem., Royal Acad. of Music (England). Hon. DMus: Leicester, 1972; Oxford, 1975; Birmingham (Aston), 1980. Comdr, Order of the Lion (Finland), 1981. *Publications:* Cello Sonata, Trois p'tits tours; Spirales for cello and piano; Suite for unaccompanied cello; Elegie, Saxe, Toccata for cello and piano; Pièces en trio for oboe and 2 cellos; Edition of Sammartini Sonata; Cadenzas for classical concertos; Offrande, for string quartet or string orch.; Double concerto for 2 cellos (or 2 violins); (book) How I Play, How I Teach, 1973. *Recreations:* no time for these! *Address:* Ibbs & Tillett, 450-452 Edgware Road, W2 1EG.

TORY, Sir Geofroy (William), KCMG 1958 (CMG 1956); HM Diplomatic Service, retired; *b* 31 July 1912; *s* of William Frank Tory and Edith Wreghitt; *m* 1st, 1938, Emilia Strickland; two *s* one *d*; 2nd, 1950, Hazel Winfield. *Educ:* King Edward VII Sch., Sheffield; Queens' Coll., Cambridge. Apptd Dominions Office, 1935; Private Sec. to Perm. Under-Sec. of State, 1938-39; served War, 1939-43, in Royal Artillery; Prin. Private Sec. to Sec. of State, 1945-46; Senior Sec., Office of UK High Comr, Ottawa, 1946-49; Prin. Sec., Office of UK Rep. to Republic of Ireland, 1949-50; Counsellor, UK Embassy, Dublin, 1950-51; idc 1952; Dep. High Comr for UK in Pakistan (Peshawar), 1953-54, in Australia, 1954-57; Asst Under-Sec. of State, CRO, 1957; High Comr for UK in Fedn of Malaya, 1957-63; Ambassador to Ireland, 1964-66; High Commissioner to Malta, 1967-70. PMN (Malaysia) 1963. *Recreations:* fishing, painting, golf. *Address:* Rathclaren House, Kilbrittain, Co. Cork, Ireland.

TOTMAN, Grenfell William, CMG 1973; OBE 1963; FCA; Controller of Finance, Commonwealth Development Corporation, 1955-76; *b* 24 July 1911; *s* of William and Lilian Oldrieve Totman; *m* 1st, 1938, Eileen Joan Gidley (marr. diss. 1962); one *s*; 2nd, 1963, Barbara Florence Cannon. *Educ:* Selhurst Grammar Sch.; London Univ. (BCom). Served War, Royal Air Force, 1942-46. With Edward Moore & Sons, Chartered Accountants, 1931-50; Commonwealth Development Corp., 1950-76. *Recreations:* music, gardening, philately. *Address:* Gayfere, East Hill, Otford, Kent. *T:* Otford 3256.

TOTNES, Archdeacon of; *see* Hawkins, Ven. R. S.

TOTTENHAM, family name of **Marquess of Ely.**

TÖTTERMAN, Richard Evert Björnson, Kt Comdr, Order of the White Rose of Finland; Hon. GCVO 1976 (Hon. KCVO 1969); Hon. OBE 1961; DPhil; Finnish Ambassador to Switzerland, since 1983; *b* 10 Oct. 1926; *s* of Björn B. Tötterman and Katharine C. (*née* Wimpenny); *m* 1953, Camilla

Susanna Veronica Huber; one *s* one *d*. *Educ:* Univ. of Helsinki (LLM); Brasenose Coll., Oxford (DPhil). Entered Finnish Foreign Service, 1952: served Stockholm, 1954-56; Moscow, 1956-58; Ministry for Foreign Affairs, Finland, 1958-62; Berne, 1962-63; Paris, 1963-66; Dep. Dir, Min. for For. Affairs, Helsinki, 1966; Sec.-Gen., Office of the President of Finland, 1966-70; Sec. of State, Min. for For. Aff., 1970-75; Ambassador, UK, 1975-83. Chm. or Mem. of a number of Finnish Govt Cttees, 1959-75, and participated as Finnish rep. in various internat. negotiations; Chm., Multilateral Consultations preparing Conf. on Security and Co-operation in Europe, 1972-73. Holds numerous foreign orders (Grand Cross, Kt Comdr, etc). *Recreations:* music, out-door life. *Address:* Weltpoststrasse 4, Berne, Switzerland.

TOTTLE, Prof. Charles Ronald; Professor of Medical Engineering, University of Bath, 1975-78, now Emeritus, a Pro Vice-Chancellor, 1973-77; Director, Bath Institute of Medical Engineering, 1975-78; Editor, Materials Science, Research Studies Press, since 1977; *b* 2 Sept. 1920; *m* 1944, Eileen P. Geoghegan; one *s* one *d*. *Educ:* Nether Edge Grammar School; University of Sheffield (MMet). English Electric Co. Ltd, 1941-45; Lecturer in Metallurgy, University of Durham, King's College, 1945-50; Ministry of Supply, Atomic Energy Division, Springfields Works, 1950-51; Culcheth Laboratories, 1951-56 (UKAEA); Head of Laboratories, Dounreay, 1956-57; Deputy Director, Dounreay, 1958-59; Prof. of Metallurgy, 1959-67, Dean of Science, 1966, Univ. of Manchester; Prof. and Head of School of Materials Science, Univ. of Bath, 1967-75; Man. Dir, South Western Industrial Research Ltd, 1970-75. Resident Research Associate, Argonne Nat. Laboratory, Illinois, USA, 1964-65. Vice-Pres., Instn of Metallurgists, 1968-70; Jt Editor, Institution of Metallurgists Series of Textbooks, 1962-70. Governor, Dauntsey's Sch., 1979-. CEng 1978; FIM; FInstP, 1958. Hon. MSc Manchester. *Publications:* The Science of Engineering Materials, 1965; various contribs to metallurgical and engineering jls. *Recreations:* music, model making, gardening. *Address:* Thirdacre, Hilperton, Trowbridge, Wilts BA14 7RL.

TOUCH, Dr Arthur Gerald, CMG 1967; Chief Scientist, Government Communications Headquarters, 1961-71; *b* 5 July 1911; *s* of A. H. Touch, Northampton; *m* 1938, Phyllis Wallbank, Birmingham; one *s*. *Educ:* Oundle; Jesus College, Oxford. MA, DPhil 1937. Bawdsey Research Station, Air Ministry, 1936; Radio Dept, RAE, Farnborough, 1940; British Air Commn, Washington, DC, 1941; Supt, Blind Landing Experimental Unit, RAE, 1947; Director: Electronic R and D (Air), Min. of Supply, 1953; Electronic R and D (Ground), Min. of Supply, 1956-59; Imperial Defence College, 1957; Head, Radio Dept, RAE, 1959; Min. of Defence, 1960. *Recreations:* fly fishing, horticulture (orchids). *Address:* Yonder, Ideford, Newton Abbot, Devon TQ13 0BG. *T:* Chudleigh 852258.

TOUCHE, Sir Anthony (George), 3rd Bt *cr* 1920; Director, Touche, Remnant & Co., since 1965 (Chairman, 1971-81); Deputy Chairman, National Westminster Bank Ltd, since 1977; *b* 31 Jan. 1927; *s* of Donovan Meredith Touche (*d* 1952) (2nd *s* of 1st Bt) and of Muriel Amy Frances, *e d* of Rev. Charles R. Thorold Winckley; *S* uncle, 1977; *m* 1961, Hester Christina, *er d* of Dr Werner Pleuger; three *s* one *d*. *Educ:* Eton College. FCA. Partner in George A. Touche & Co. (now Touche Ross & Co.), 1951; Director of investment trust companies, 1952-; retired from Touche Ross & Co., 1968; Director: Westminster Bank Ltd, 1968; Yorkshire Bank, 1979; International Westminster Bank Ltd, 1980; Chairman, Assoc. of Investment Trust Companies, 1971-73. *Recreations:* music, reading, walking. *Heir:* s William George Touche, *b* 26 June 1962. *Address:* Stane House, Ockley, Dorking, Surrey RH5 5TQ. *T:* Oakwood Hill 397.

TOUCHE, Sir Rodney (Gordon), 2nd Bt *cr* 1962; President, Village Lake Louise Ltd, Alberta, Canada, since 1973; *b* 5 Dec. 1928; *s* of Rt Hon. Sir Gordon Touche, 1st Bt, and of Ruby, Lady Touche (formerly Ruby Ann Macpherson); *S* father 1972; *m* 1955, Ouida Ann, *d* of F. G. MacLellan, Moncton, NB, Canada; one *s* three *d*. *Educ:* Marlborough; University Coll., Oxford. Reporter for: Portsmouth Evening News, 1951-53; London Evening Standard, 1953-55; Toronto Financial Post, 1956-59. Subseq. career in oil industry, in a private investment company, and since 1966 as an investment consultant. *Heir:* s Eric MacLellan Touche, *b* 22 Feb. 1960. *Address:* 707 Prospect Avenue, Calgary, Alberta, Canada. *T:* 403-244-6097.

TOULMIN, John Kelvin, QC 1980; barrister-at-law; *b* 14 Feb. 1941; *s* of Arthur Heaton Toulmin and B. Toulmin (*née* Fraser); *m* 1967, Carolyn Merton (*née* Gullick); one *s* two *d*. *Educ:* Winchester Coll.; Trinity Hall, Cambridge (Patterson Law Scholar, 1959; BA 1963, MA 1966); Univ. of Michigan (Ford Foundn Fellow and Fulbright Scholar, 1964; LLM 1965). Middle Temple: Harmsworth Exhibnr, 1960; Astbury Scholar, 1965; called to the Bar, 1965; Western Circuit. Cambridge Univ. Debating Tour, USA, 1963. Chm., Young Barristers, 1973-75; Member: Bar Council, 1971-77, 1978-81; Supreme Court Rules Cttee, 1976-80; Council of Legal Educn, 1981-. Governor, Maudsley and Bethlem Royal Hosps, 1979-; Mem. Cttee of Management, Inst. of Psychiatry, 1982-. *Publication:* (contrib.) The Influence of Litigation in Medical Practice, 1977. *Recreations:* cricket, theatre. *Address:* 4 Paper Buildings, Temple, EC4Y 7EX. *T:* 01-353 3366. *Clubs:* MCC; Surrey County Cricket.

TOULMIN, Stephen Edelston, MA, PhD; Professor in the Committee on Social Thought, University of Chicago, since 1973; *b* 25 March 1922; *s* of late G. E. Toulmin and Mrs E. D. Toulmin. *Educ:* Oundle School; King's College,

Cambridge. BA 1943; MA 1946; PhD 1948; MA (Oxon) 1948. Junior Scientific Officer, Ministry of Aircraft Production, 1942–45; Fellow of King's College, Cambridge, 1947–51; University Lecturer in the Philosophy of Science, Oxford, 1949–55; Acting Head of Department of History and Methods of Science, University of Melbourne, Australia, 1954–55; Professor of Philosophy, University of Leeds, 1955–59; Visiting Prof. of Philosophy, NY Univ. and Stanford Univ. (California) and Columbia Univ. (NY), 1959–60; Director, Nuffield Foundation Unit for History of Ideas, 1960–64; Prof. of Philosophy, Brandeis Univ., 1965–69, Michigan State Univ., 1969–72; Provost, Crown College, Univ. of California, Santa Cruz, 1972–73; Counsellor, Smithsonian Institution, 1966–75. *Publications*: The Place of Reason in Ethics, 1950; The Philosophy of Science: an Introduction, 1953; Metaphysical Beliefs (3 essays: author of one of them), 1957; The Uses of Argument, 1958; Foresight and Understanding, 1961; The Ancestry of Science, Vol. I (The Fabric of the Heavens) 1961, Vol. II (The Architecture of Matter), 1962, Vol. III (The Discovery of Time), 1965; Night Sky at Rhodes, 1963; Human Understanding, vol. 1, 1972; Wittgenstein's Vienna, 1973; Knowing and Acting, 1976; An Introduction to Reasoning, 1979; The Return to Cosmology, 1982; also films, broadcast talks and contribs to learned jls and weeklies. *Address*: Committee on Social Thought, University of Chicago, Chicago, Ill 60637, USA.

TOURS, Kenneth Cecil, CMG 1955; *b* 16 Feb. 1908; *y s* of late Berthold George Tours, CMG, HM Consul-General in China; *m* 1934, Ruth Grace, *y d* of late Hugh Lewis; two *s. Educ*: Aldenham School; Corpus Christi College, Cambridge (MA). Administrative Service, Gold Coast, 1931; Gambia, 1935; Palestine, 1938; Malaya, 1945; Col (Food Control) and (Supplies), Brit. Mil. Administration, Malaya, 1945–46; Chm., Jt Supply Board, 1946; Establishment Office, Singapore, 1947; Permanent Sec., Min. of Finance, Gold Coast, 1950; Financial Sec. and Minister of Finance, 1954; Economic Adviser, Ghana, 1954; retd from Colonial Service, 1957. *Recreation*: reading. *Address*: 19 Freshfields, Comberbach, near Northwich, Cheshire CW9 6BQ. *T*: Northwich 891986.

TOUT, Herbert, CMG 1946; MA; Reader in Political Economy, University College, London, 1947–68, retired; *b* Manchester, 20 April 1904; *e s* of Professor T. F. Tout, Manchester University, and Mary Johnstone; unmarried. *Educ*: Sherborne School; Hertford College, Oxford. Instructor in Economics, University of Minnesota, USA, 1929–35; Assistant Lecturer, University College, London, 1936; Colston Research Fellow and Director of University of Bristol Social Survey, 1936–38; Lecturer, University of Bristol, 1938–47; Temp. Principal, Board of Trade, 1940–41; Assistant Secretary, 1941–45. *Recreations*: walking, farming, gardening. *Address*: Little Greeting, West Hoathly, East Grinstead, West Sussex RH19 4PW. *T*: Sharpthorne 810400.

TOVELL, Laurence, FCA, IPFA; Chief Inspector of Audit, Department of the Environment, 1977–79; *b* 6 March 1919; *s* of William Henry Tovell and Margaret Tovell (*née* Mahoney); *m* 1945, Iris Joan (*née* Lee); two *s* one *d. Educ*: Devonport High School. Entered Civil Service as Audit Assistant, District Audit Service, 1938. Served War, 1940–46; Lieut RNVR, 1942–46. District Auditor, No 4 Audit District, Birmingham, 1962. *Recreation*: do-it-yourself. *Address*: White Lions, Links Road, Bramley, Guildford, Surrey. *T*: Guildford 892702.

TOVEY, Sir Brian (John Maynard), KCMG 1980; Director, Government Communications Headquarters, since 1978; *b* 15 April 1926; *s* of Rev. Collett John Tovey (Canon, Bermuda Cathedral, 1935–38) and Kathleen Edith Maud Tovey (*née* Maynard); *m* 1971, Eliza Gwendoline Herbert. *Educ*: St Edward's Sch., Oxford; St Edmund Hall, Oxford, 1944–45; School of Oriental and African Studies, London, 1948–50. BA Hons London. Service with Royal Navy and subseq. Army (Intelligence Corps and RAEC), 1945–48. Joined Government Communications Headquarters as Jun. Asst, 1950; Principal, 1957; Asst Sec., 1967; Under Sec., 1975; Dep. Sec., 1978. *Recreations*: music, walking, history of art (espec. 16th Century Italian). *Club*: Naval and Military.

TOWER, Maj.-Gen. Philip Thomas, CB 1968; DSO 1944; MBE 1942; National Trust Administrator, Blickling Hall, 1973–82; *b* 1 March 1917; *s* of late Vice-Admiral Sir Thomas Tower, KBE, CB and late Mrs E. H. Tower; *m* 1941, Elizabeth, *y d* of late Thomas Ralph Sneyd-Kynnersley, OBE, MC and late Alice Sneyd-Kynnersley. *Educ*: Harrow; Royal Military Acad., Woolwich. 2nd Lt Royal Artillery, 1937; served in India, 1937–40; served War of 1939–45 (despatches); Middle East, 1940–42; POW Italy, 1942–43; escaped, 1943; Arnhem, 1944; Norway, 1945; Staff Coll., 1948; Instructor at RMA Sandhurst, 1951–53; comd J (Sidi Rezegh) Bty RHA in Middle East, 1954–55; Joint Services Staff Coll., 1955–56; GSO1 Plans, BJSM Washington, DC, 1956–57; comd 3rd Regt RHA, 1957–60; Imperial Defence Coll., 1961; Comd 51 Inf. Bde Gp, 1961–62; Comd 12 Inf. Bde Gp, BAOR, 1962–64; Director of Public Relations (Army), 1965–67; GOC Middle East Land Forces, 1967 (despatches); Comdt, RMA Sandhurst, 1968–72, retd 1972. Col Comdt, Royal Regt of Artillery, 1970–80. County Comr (Norfolk), SJAB, 1975–78. OStJ 1977. *Recreations*: sailing, shooting, gardening. *Address*: Hall Farm, East Raynham, Fakenham, Norfolk. *T*: Fakenham 4904; Studio A, 414 Fulham Road, SW6 1BB. *T*: 01-385 8538. *Clubs*: Army and Navy, Pratt's; Royal Yacht Squadron.

TOWLER, Eric William, CBE 1971; farmer; farms 2,000 acres; *b* 28 April 1900; *s* of William Towler and Laura Mary (*née* Trew); *m* 1st, 1921, Isabel Edith Ina Hemsworth; two *s* (one *d* decd), 2nd, 1964, Stella Prideaux-Brune; two *s. Educ*: Morley Grammar Sch. Founder, Cawoods Holdings Ltd and Cawood Wharton & Co. Ltd, 1931; Managing Dir, Cawood Wharton & Co. Ltd, 1931–42, Chm., 1942–71; Chm., Cawoods Holdings Ltd, 1961–72, Dir, 1972–82, Hon. Pres., 1977–82; Mining Director: Dorman Long & Co. Ltd, 1937–65; Pearson Dorman Long Ltd, 1937–65; Richard Thomas & Co. Ltd, 1929–31. MFH: Badsworth Hunt, 1938–43; South Shropshire Hunt, 1951–56. Chm., Nuffield Orthopaedic Centre, 1960–66; Chm., Bd of Governors, Oxford United Hosp., 1964–72. Hon. MA (Oxon) 1964. *Recreations*: hunting, gardening. *Address*: Glympton Park, near Woodstock, Oxon. *T*: Woodstock 811300; Willett House, Lydeard St Lawrence, Somerset. *T*: Lydeard St Lawrence 234. *Club*: Carlton.

TOWNDROW, Ven. Frank Noel; Archdeacon of Oakham, 1967–77, now Archdeacon Emeritus; Residentiary Canon of Peterborough, 1966–77, now Canon Emeritus; a Chaplain to the Queen, 1975–81; *b* 25 Dec. 1911; *e s* of F. R. and H. A. Towndrow, London; *m* 1947, Olive Helen Weinberger (*d* 1978); one *d* (one *s* decd). *Educ*: St Olave's Grammar Sch.; King's Coll., Cambridge; Coll. of Resurrection, Mirfield. Curate, Chingford, E4, 1937–40; Chaplain, RAFVR, 1940–47; Rector of Grangemouth, Stirlingshire, 1947–51; Vicar of Kirton Lindsey, Lincs, 1951–53; Rector of Greenford, Middx, 1953–62; Vicar of Ravensthorpe, E Haddon and Rector of Holdenby, 1962–66. *Recreation*: modern history. *Address*: 2 Bourne Road, Swinstead, Grantham, Lincs. *T*: Corby Glen 422.

TOWNELEY, Simon Peter Edmund Cosmo William; Lord-Lieutenant and Custos Rotulorum of Lancashire, since 1976; *b* 14 Dec. 1921; *s* of Col A. Koch de Gooreynd, OBE and of Baroness Norman, *qv*; assumed surname and arms of Towneley by royal licence, 1955, by reason of descent from *e d* and senior co-heiress of Col Charles Towneley of Towneley; *m* 1955, Mary, 2nd *d* of Cuthbert Fitzherbert, *qv*; one *s* six *d. Educ*: Stowe; Worcester Coll., Oxford (MA, DPhil). Served War of 1939–45, KRRC. Lectr in History of Music, Worcester Coll., Oxford, 1949–55. Dir, Granada Television, 1981–. CC Lancs, 1961–64; JP 1956; DL 1970; High Sheriff of Lancashire, 1971. Patron, Nat. Assoc. for Mental Health (North-West). President: Community Council of Lancashire; Mid-Pennine Assoc. for the Arts; Lancashire Playing Field Assoc.; Chm., Northern Ballet Theatre; Member: Court and Council, Univ. of Manchester; Court and Council, Royal Northern Coll. of Music; Vice-Pres., NW Arts. Hon. Col, Duke of Lancaster's Own Yeomanry, 1979–. Hon. FRNCM. KStJ; KCSG. *Publications*: Venetian Opera in the Seventeenth Century, 1954 (repr. 1968); contribs to New Oxford History of Music. *Recreation*: playing chamber music. *Address*: Dyneley, Burnley, Lancs. *T*: Burnley 23322. *Clubs*: Boodle's, Pratt's, Beefsteak.
See also P. G. Worsthorne.

TOWNEND, Donald Thomas Alfred, CBE 1952; DSc London, PhD, DIC; FRSC; MIMinE; Fellow, Imperial College of Science and Technology; *b* Hackney, London, 15 July 1897; *s* of Charles Henry Townend; *m* 1924, Lilian (*d* 1974), *er d* of Samuel William Lewis, Bexley, Kent; one *s* one *d. Educ*: Bancroft's School, Woodford Green, Essex. East London (now Queen Mary) College, 1919–20; Imperial College of Science and Technology, 1920–38; Salters' Research Fellow, 1923–24; Rockefeller International Research Fellow, 1924–26; Livesey Prof. of Coal Gas and Fuel Industries, University of Leeds, 1938–46; Dir-Gen., British Coal Utilisation Research Assoc., 1946–62; formerly Research Fell. and Hon. Lectr in Roy. Coll. of Science. Jubilee Memorial Lectr, 1945, Brotherton Memorial Lecturer, 1946 and Hodsman Memorial Lectr, 1954, Soc. of Chemical Industry; Dalton Lecturer, Inst. of Chemistry, 1947; William Young Memorial Lectr, N Brit. Assoc. of Gas Managers, 1947; Des Vœux Memorial Lectr, Nat. Soc. for Clean Air, 1950; Melchett Lectr, Inst. of Energy (formerly Fuel), 1952. Vice-Pres. 1957–61, Vice-Chm. 1961–64, Parly and Sci. Cttee. Gold Medallist, Institut Français des Combustibles et de l'Energie, 1958; BCURA Coal Science Medallist, 1963; Hon. FIGasE (Birmingham Medallist, IGasE); Hon. MInstE (Past Pres. and Melchett Medallist, InstE). Hon. DSc Tech Sheffield. *Publications*: (with late Professor W. A. Bone) Flame and Combustion in Gases, 1927; Gaseous Combustion at High Pressures, 1929; Papers in Proceedings of Royal Society, etc. *Recreations*: cricket, horticulture. *Address*: Uplands, Yarm Way, Leatherhead, Surrey. *T*: Leatherhead 373520. *Club*: Athenæum.

TOWNEND, James Barrie Stanley; QC 1978; a Recorder of the Crown Court, since 1979; *b* 21 Feb. 1938; *s* of late Frederick Stanley Townend and Marjorie Elizabeth Townend (*née* Arnold); *m* 1970, Airelle Claire (*née* Nies); one step *d. Educ*: Tonbridge Sch.; Lincoln Coll., Oxford (MA). National Service in BAOR and UK, 1955–57: 2nd Lieut, 18th Medium Regt, RA. Called to Bar, Middle Temple, 1962. *Recreations*: sailing, fishing. *Address*: 1 King's Bench Walk, Temple, EC4Y 2DB. *T*: 01-353 4423. *Club*: Bar Yacht.

TOWNEND, John Ernest; MP (C) Bridlington, since 1979; *b* 12 June 1934; *s* of Charles Hope Townend and Dorothy Townend; *m* 1963, Jennifer Ann; two *s* two *d. Educ*: Hymers Coll., Hull. FCA (Plender Prize). Articled Clerk, Chartered Accountants, 1951–56; National Service: Pilot Officer, RAF, 1957–59; J. Townend & Sons Ltd (Hull) Ltd: Co. Sec./Dir, 1959–67; Man. Dir, 1967–77; Chm., 1977–. Mem., Hull City Council, 1966–74 (Chm., Finance Cttee, 1968–70); Chm., Humber Bridge Bd, 1969–71; Member, Humberside County Council, 1973–79: Cons. Leader of Opposition, 1973–77; Leader,

1977-79; Chm., Policy Cttee, 1977-79. Mem., Policy Cttee, Assoc. of County Councils, 1977-79. PPS to Minister of State for Social Security, 1981-. *Recreations:* squash, tennis. *Address:* Sigglesthorne Hall, Sigglesthorne, Hull, North Humberside. *Club:* Carlton.

TOWNES, Charles Hard; University Professor, University of California, USA; *b* Greenville, South Carolina, 28 July 1915; *s* of Henry Keith Townes and Ellen Sumter (*née* Hard); *m* 1941, Frances H. Brown; four *d. Educ:* Furman Univ. (BA, BS); Duke Univ. (MA); California Institute of Technology (PhD). Assistant in Physics, California Inst. of Technology, 1937-39; Member Techn Staff, Bell Telephone Labs, 1939-47; Associate Prof. of Physics, Columbia Univ., 1948-50; Prof. of Physics, Columbia Univ., 1950-61; Exec. Director, Columbia Radiation Lab., 1950-52; Chairman, Dept of Physics, Columbia Univ., 1952-55; Vice-President and Director of Research, Inst. for Defense Analyses, 1959-61; Provost and Professor of Physics, MIT, 1961-66; Institute Professor, MIT, 1966-67. Guggenheim Fellow, 1955-56; Fulbright Lecturer, University of Paris, 1955-56, University of Tokyo, 1956; Lecturer, 1955, 1960, Dir, 1963, Enrico Fermi Internat. Sch. of Physics; Scott Lecturer, University of Cambridge, 1963. Centennial Lecturer, University of Toronto, 1967. Director: Perkin-Elmer Corp.; Bulletin of Atomic Scientists, 1964-69. Board of Editors: Review of Scientific Instruments, 1950-52; Physical Review, 1951-53; Journal of Molecular Spectroscopy, 1957-60; Columbia University Forum, 1957-59. Fellow: American Phys. Society (Richtmyer Lecturer, 1959; Member Council, 1959-62, 1965-71; President, 1967); Inst. of Electrical and Electronics Engrs; Chairman, Sci. and Technology Adv. Commn for Manned Space Flight, NASA, 1964-69; Member: President's Science Adv. Cttee, 1966-69 (Vice-Chm., 1967-69); Scientific Adv. Bd, US Air Force, 1958-61; Soc. Française de Physique (Member Council, 1956-58); Nat. Acad. Scis (Mem. Council, 1969-72); American Acad. Arts and Sciences; American Philos. Society; American Astron. Society; American Assoc. of Physics Teachers; Société Royale des Sciences de Liège; Foreign Mem., Royal Society, 1976; Hon. Mem., Optical Soc. of America. Trustee: Salk Inst. for Biological Studies, 1963-68; Rand Corp., 1965-70; Carnegie Instn of Washington, 1965-; Calif Inst. of Technol., 1979-. Chairman: Space Science Bd, Nat. Acad. of Sciences, 1970-73; Science Adv. Cttee, General Motors Corp., 1971-73; Bd of Dirs, General Motors, 1973-; Perkin-Elmer Corp., 1966-. Holds numerous honorary degrees. Nobel Prize for Physics (jointly), 1964. Research Corp. Annual Award, 1958; Comstock Prize, Nat. Acad. of Sciences, 1959; Stuart Ballantine Medal, Franklin Inst., 1959, 1962; Rumford Premium, Amer. Acad. of Arts and Sciences, 1961; Thomas Young Medal and Prize, Inst. of Physics and Physical Soc., England, 1963; Medal of Honor, Inst. of Electrical and Electronics Engineers, 1967; C. E. K. Mees Medal, Optical Soc. of America, 1968; Churchman of the Year Award, Southern Baptist Theological Seminary, 1967; Distinguished Public Service Medal, NASA, 1969; Michelson-Morley Award, 1970; Wilhelm-Exner Award (Austria), 1970; Medal of Honor, Univ. of Liège, 1971; Earle K. Plyler Prize, 1977; Niels Bohr Internat. Gold Medal, 1979. National Inventors Hall of Fame, 1976; S Carolina Hall of Fame, 1977. *Publications:* (with A. L. Schawlow) Microwave Spectroscopy, 1955; (ed) Quantum Electronics, 1960; (ed with P. A. Miles) Quantum Electronics and Coherent Light, 1964; many scientific articles on microwave spectroscopy, molecular and nuclear structure, quantum electronics, radio and infra-red astrophysics; fundamental patents on masers and (with A. L. Schawlow) lasers. *Address:* Department of Physics, University of California, Berkeley, California 94720, USA. *T:* 642-1128. *Clubs:* Cosmos (Washington, DC); University (New York); Bohemian (San Francisco).

TOWNLEY, Sir John (Barton), Kt 1960; *b* 14 June 1914; *s* of Barton Townley and Margaret Alice, *d* of Richard Gorst; *m* 1939, Gwendoline May Ann, *d* of Arthur Simmonds; one *s* three *d. Educ:* Rydal Sch.; Downing Coll., Cambridge; Sorbonne. MA Cambridge, 1939. Man. Dir and Vice-Chm., Northern Commercial Vehicles and associated cos, 1936-72. President: Preston Conservative Assoc., N and S Divisions, 1954-72 (Chairman: Preston S Conserv. Assoc., 1949-54; Preston N Cons. Assoc., 1958, first Life Pres., 1961); Preston Sea Cadet Corps, 1954-72; Preston Circle King George's Fund for Sailors, 1949-72; Preston Charities Assoc., 1949-; Life Vice-Pres., Preston, Chorley, Leyland Conservative Clubs Council (Pres. 1949-; Cons. Clubs Council of GB Medal, 1959). Life Mem., North Western Industrial Assoc. Adv. Bd. Vice-Pres., RNLI. Chairman: Preston YMCA Special Appeals Cttee; British Police Athletic Assoc., 1949-60; Pres., Lancs Police Clubs, 1959-63; Founder, and Pres., Police Hathersall Hall Youth Camp (now Lancs Boys Club), 1949-70; Founder Mem., Nat. Playing Fields Assoc.; Chm., Spastics Appeal, 1950-53; Founder Mem. 1948, and former Pres., OAP's Assoc. Founder many youth clubs (known as Rydal Clubs), inc. Liverpool, Manchester and Bermondsey, from 1934. Chm., Preston Arts Cttee, 1951-59. *Recreations:* talking about rugby, cricket and boxing. *Address:* 24 Agnew Street, Lytham, Lancs FY8 5NJ. *Clubs:* Hawks, Union, Pitt (Cambridge).

TOWNSEND, Albert Alan, FRS 1960; PhD; Reader (Experimental Fluid Mechanics), Cavendish Laboratory, University of Cambridge, since 1961 (Assistant Director of Research, 1950-61); Fellow of Emmanuel College, Cambridge, since 1947; *b* 22 Jan. 1917; *s* of A. R. Townsend and D. Gay; *m* 1950, V. Dees; one *s* two *d. Educ:* Telopea Park IHS; Melbourne and Cambridge Universities. PhD 1947. *Publications:* The Structure of Turbulent Shear Flow, 1956; papers in technical journals. *Address:* Emmanuel College, Cambridge.

TOWNSEND, Cyril David; MP (C) Bexley Bexleyheath since Feb. 1974; *b* 21 Dec. 1937; *s* of Lt-Col Cyril M. Townsend and Lois (*née* Henderson); *m* 1976, Anita, MA, *d* of late Lt-Col F. G. W. Walshe and of Mrs Walshe; two *s. Educ:* Bradfield Coll.; RMA Sandhurst. Commnd into Durham LI; served in Berlin and Hong Kong; active service in Cyprus, 1958 and Borneo, 1966; ADC to Governor and C-in-C Hong Kong, 1964-66; Adjt 1DLI, 1966-68. A Personal Asst to Edward Heath, 1968-70; Mem. Conservative Research Dept, 1970-74. PPS to Minister of State, DHSS, 1979; Member: Select Cttee on Violence in the Family, 1975; SE London Industrial Consultative Gp; Jt Sec., Cons. Parly Defence Cttee; Chairman: Select Cttee on Armed Forces Bill, 1981; British-Cyprus Parly Gp; All-Party Freedom for Rudolf Hess Campaign; Bow Gp Standing Cttee on Foreign Affairs; Jt Chm., Council for Advancement of Arab-British Understanding; Vice-Chairman: Friends of Cyprus; Political Cttee, UNA. Introduced Protection of Children Act, 1979. *Recreations:* books, music, exercise. *Address:* House of Commons, SW1A 0AA.

TOWNSEND, Mrs Joan, MA, MSc; Headmistress, Oxford High School, GPDST, since 1981; *b* 7 Dec. 1936; *d* of Emlyn Davies and Amelia Mary Davies (*née* Tyrer); *m* 1960, Prof. William Godfrey Townsend, RMCS, Shrivenham; two *d. Educ:* Somerville Coll., Oxford (Beilby Schol.); BA (Cl.I), MA); University College of Swansea, Univ. of Wales (MSc). School teaching and lecturing of various kinds, including: Tutor, Open University, 1971-75; Lectr, Oxford Polytechnic, 1975-76; Head of Mathematics, School of S Helen and S Katharine, Abingdon, 1976-81. *Publication:* paper in Qly Jl Maths and Applied Mech., 1965. *Address:* Silver Howe, 62 Iffley Turn, Oxford OX4 4HN. *T:* Oxford 715807.

TOWNSEND, Sir Lance; see Townsend, Sir S. L.

TOWNSEND, Mrs Lena Moncrieff, CBE 1974; Member, Race Relations Board, 1967-72; *b* 3 Nov. 1911; twin *d* of late Captain R. G. Westropp, Cairo, Egypt; *m* (twice); two *s* one *d. Educ:* Downe House, Newbury; Somerville Coll., Oxford; Heidelberg Univ., Germany. During War of 1939-45 was an Organiser in WVS and in Women's Land Army, and then taught at Downe House. Mem. for Hampstead, LCC, 1955-65; Alderman, London Borough of Camden, 1964-65; Mem. for Camden, GLC, 1967-70; Alderman, GLC, 1970-77, and Dep. Chm., 1976-77; Inner London Education Authority: Dep. Leader, later Leader, 1969-70; Leader of the Opposition, 1970-71; Chm., Management Panel, Burnham Cttee, 1967-70; Mem., Women's European Cttee, 1972-75. Pres., Anglo-Egyptian Assoc., 1961-; Exec. Member: British Section, European Union of Women, 1970-; British Council, European Movement, 1970- (Mem., Speaker's Panel); Cons. Gp for Europe, 1967- (Founder Mem.); British Section, Internat. Union of Local Authorities and Council of European Municipalities, 1975- (rep. on Jt Twinning Cttee); London Europe Soc., 1977-; Arkwright Arts Trust, 1971- (Chm., 1971-73); Chairman: London Coll. of Fashion, 1967-; Students' Accommodation Cttee, Univ. of London, 1977- (and Mem., Intercollegiate Halls Management Cttee); Member: Council, Westfield Coll., London Univ., 1965-; Cons Nat. Adv. Cttee on Education, 1976-; Governor: Old Vic Trust, 1976-; Hampstead Parochial Primary Sch., 1979-. Former Patron, Lewis Carroll Soc. *Recreations:* foreign languages, travel, the arts, gardening. *Address:* 16 Holly Mount, NW3 6SG. *T:* 01-435 8555.

TOWNSEND, Rear-Adm. Sir Leslie (William), KCVO 1981; CBE 1973; *b* 22 Feb. 1924; *s* of Ellen (*née* Alford) and William Bligh Townsend; *m* 1947, Marjorie Bennett; one *s* three *d. Educ:* Regent's Park School, Southampton. Joined RN, 1942; served in HMS Durban, 1942-43; Commissioned, 1943; HM Ships Spurwing, Astraea, Liverpool, Duke of York, Ceres, 1944-53; Staff of C-in-C Plymouth, 1954; HMS Ceylon, 1956-58; Secretary to ACNS, 1959, to VCNS, 1967, to First Sea Lord, 1970; MA to CDS, 1971-73, to Chm. NATO Mil. Cttee, 1974; Dir, Naval and WRNS Officers' Appointments, 1977; Rear-Adm. 1979; Defence Services Sec., 1979-82. *Recreations:* sailing, sea fishing, cooking. *Address:* 21 Osborne View Road, Hill Head, near Fareham, Hants. *T:* Stubbington 3446. *Clubs:* Army and Navy; Hill Head Sailing.

TOWNSEND, Rear-Adm. Michael Southcote, CB 1959; DSO 1942; OBE 1940; DSC 1940 (Bar, 1941); *b* 18 June 1908; *s* of Colonel Edward Coplestone Townsend and Gladys Hatt-Cook; *m* 1932, Joan Pendrill Charles; one *s* two *d. Educ:* Royal Naval Coll., Dartmouth. Rear-Admiral, 1956; Flag Officer, Admiralty Interview Boards and President, First Admiralty Interview Board, 1956-58; Commander Allied Naval Forces, Northern Area, Central Europe, 1958-61, retired; Admiralty Officer, Wales, 1962-68. *Address:* The Mythe, 2 College Road, Great Malvern, Worcs WR14 3DD.

TOWNSEND, Prof. Peter Brereton; Professor of Social Policy, University of Bristol, since 1982; *b* 6 April 1928; *s* of Philip Brereton Townsend and Alice Mary Townsend (*née* Southcote); *m* 1st, 1949, Ruth (*née* Pearce); four *s* ; 2nd, 1977, Joy (*née* Skegg); one *d. Educ:* Fleet Road Elementary Sch., London; University Coll. London; St John's Coll., Cambridge Univ.; Free Univ., Berlin. Research Sec., Political and Economic Planning, 1952-54; Research Officer, Inst. of Community Studies, 1954-57; Research Fellow and then Lectr in Social Administration, London Sch. of Economics, 1957-63; Prof. of Sociology, 1963-81, Pro-Vice-Chancellor (Social Policy), 1975-78, Univ. of Essex. Chm., the Fabian Society, 1965-66 (Chm., Social Policy Cttee, 1970-); Pres., Psychiatric Rehabilitation Assoc., 1968-; Chairman: Child Poverty Action Gp, 1969-; Disability Alliance, 1974-; Member: Chief Scientist's Cttee,

DHSS, 1976-78; Govt Working Gp on Inequalities and Health, 1977-80. UNESCO consultant on poverty and development, 1978-80. *Publications:* The Family Life of Old People, 1957; National Superannuation (co-author), 1957; Nursing Homes in England and Wales (co-author), 1961; The Last Refuge: a survey of residential institutions and homes for the aged in England and Wales, 1962; The Aged in the Welfare State (co-author), 1965; The Poor and the Poorest (co-author), 1965; Old People in Three Industrial Societies (co-author), 1968; (ed) The Concept of Poverty, 1970; (ed) Labour and Inequality, 1972; The Social Minority, 1973; Sociology and Social Policy, 1975; Poverty in the United Kingdom: a survey of household resources and standards of living, 1979; (ed) Labour and Equality, 1980; Inequalities in Health (co-author), 1980; Manifesto (co-author), 1981; (ed jtly) Disability in Britain, 1981; The Family and Later Life, 1981; (ed jtly) Responses to Poverty, 1983. *Recreation:* athletics. *Address:* 19 Ashley Road, Bristol.

TOWNSEND, Group Captain Peter Wooldridge, CVO 1947; DSO 1941; DFC and Bar, 1940; *b* 22 Nov. 1914; *s* of late Lt-Col E. C. Townsend; *m* 1959, Marie Luce, *d* of Franz Jamagne, Brussels, Belgium; one *s* two *d* (two *s* by former marriage). *Educ:* Haileybury; Royal Air Force Coll., Cranwell. Royal Air Force, 1933; served War of 1939-45, Wing Commander, 1941 (despatches, DFC and Bar, DSO). Equerry to King George VI, 1944-52; Deputy Master of HM Household, 1950; Equerry to the Queen, 1952-53; Air Attaché, Brussels, 1953-56. *Publications:* Earth, My Friend, 1959; Duel of Eagles, 1970; The Last Emperor, 1975; Time and Chance (autobiog.), 1978; The Smallest Pawns in the Game, 1979; The Girl in the White Ship, 1981. *Address:* La Mare aux Oiseaux, 78116 Saint-Leger-en-Yvelines, France.

TOWNSEND, Sir (Sydney) Lance, Kt 1971; VRD 1955; Chairman, Victorian Health Advisory Committee, since 1979; Professor of Obstetrics and Gynaecology, 1951-79, Dean, Faculty of Medicine, 1971-78, Assistant Vice-Chancellor, 1979-80, University of Melbourne; *b* 17 Dec. 1912; *s* of Edward Henry and Muriel Constance Townsend; *m* 1943, Jean Campbell Smyth; one *s* three *d* (and one *s* decd). *Educ:* Bairnsdale High Sch.; Trinity Coll., Univ. of Melbourne. MD, BS, MGO, DTM&H; FRCSE, FACS, FRACS, FRCOG, FRACP, FRACMA, FRACOG; Hon. FRCS(C), Hon. FACOG, Hon. FCOG (SA), Hon. FRACGP. Residential med. posts at Bendigo, Royal Women's Hosp. and Tenant Creek Hosp., 1936-38; Med. Off., W Middx Hosp., 1939; Med. Off., RN, 1940-46 (Surg. Comdr); Surg. Captain, RANVR, 1965; Hon. Obstetrician and Gynaecologist to Austin, Royal Women's, Royal Melbourne, Queen Victoria and Prince Henry's Hosps, 1948-78; Consultant Obstetrician, WHO Eastern Mediterranean Sector, 1981-. Mem., Hon. Sec., Pres., Australian Council, RCOG, 1951-69; Chm., Cons. Council on Maternal and Perinatal Mortality, 1955-; Mem. Bd of Management, Royal Women's Hosp., 1951-78; Mem., Cttee of Enquiry into Victorian (Aust.) Health Services, 1973-75; Sec., Victorian Bush Nursing Assoc., 1961-73; Chm., Victorian Cytology Service (Gynae.), 1965-; Vice Chm., Australian Medical Examining Council, 1977-. Mem., 1966-, Vice-Pres., 1977-79, Pres., 1979-, Austin Hosp. Chm. of Dirs, Australian and NZ Jl of Obstetrics and Gynaecology, 1961-76. Hon. LLD: Monash, 1979; Melbourne, 1982. *Publications:* High Blood Pressure and Pregnancy, 1959; Gynaecology for Students, 1964, 3rd edn 1979; Obstetrics for Students, 1964, 3rd edn 1978. *Recreations:* sailing, philately. *Address:* 28 Ryeburne Avenue, Hawthorn East, Victoria 3123, Australia. *T:* 823434. *Clubs:* Melbourne, Naval and Military, Royal Melbourne Golf (Melbourne).

TOWNSEND, Air Vice-Marshal William Edwin, CB 1971; CBE 1965 (OBE 1957); RAAF retired; Director-General, Australia-Britain Society, since 1981; *b* 25 April 1916; *s* of William Edwin Townsend (Senior) and Jessie May Lewry; *m* 1939, Linda Ruth Deakins; two *s* two *d*. *Educ:* Longerenong Coll., Vic, Australia. Grad. Pt Cook, 1937; Chief Flying Instr and 2nd i/c No 8 EFTS, 1940; Sen. Trg Staff Officer, 1941; Comdg Officer 67 and 22 Sqdns, 1942-43; shot down over enemy territory, escaped and returned to Aust., 1944; Comdg Officer, 5 Operational Trg Unit, 1944; SASO, NE Area, 1946; OC, Port Moresby, 1947-48; Sec., Australian Jt Staff, Washington, 1949-50; OC, East Sale, 1951-52; CO and Sen. Officer i/c Admin, Home Command, 1953-54; OC 78 Fighter Wing, 1955-56; Dir of Ops, 1957-60; OC, RAAF Williamtown, 1960-62; Dir Gen. Personnel, 1962-64; OC, RAAF, Butterworth, 1964-67; Dep. CAS, 1967-69; AOC Operational Comd, RAAF, 1969-72; Dir, State Emergency Services and Civil Defence, and Chm., Bush Fire Council of NSW, 1973-80. Pres., Aust. Branch, RAF Escaping Soc.; Nat. Pres., Air Force Assoc. of Australia; Vice-Pres., St John Ambulance Assoc., NSW Centre. Councillor, Royal Humane Soc. of NSW. FAIM; Mem., Aust. Inst. of Emergency Services. *Address:* 8 Tutus Street, Balgowlah Heights, NSW 2093, Australia. *Clubs:* Royal Automobile; Imperial Service (Sydney); Manly Golf.

TOWNSHEND, family name of **Marquess Townshend.**

TOWNSHEND, 7th Marquess *cr* 1787; **George John Patrick Dominic Townshend;** Bt 1617; Baron Townshend, 1661; Viscount Townshend, 1682; Chairman: Anglia Television Group plc, since 1976; Anglia Television Ltd, since 1958; Survival Anglia Ltd, since 1971; Anchor Enterprises Ltd, since 1967; AP Bank Ltd, since 1975; Guaranty Trust Bank Ltd, since 1981; Raynham Farm Co. Ltd, since 1957; Norfolk Agricultural Station, since 1974; Vice-Chairman: Norwich Union Life Insurance Society Ltd, since 1973; Norwich Union Fire Insurance Society Ltd, since 1975; Director: Scottish Union & National Insurance Co., since 1968; Maritime Insurance Co. Ltd, since 1968; East Coast Grain Ltd, since 1962; London Merchant Securities plc,

since 1964; D. E. Longe & Co. Ltd, since 1962; Norwich Union (Holdings) plc, since 1981; Trustee, East Anglian Trustee Savings Bank; Chairman, Royal Norfolk Agricultural Association; *b* 13 May 1916; *s* of 6th Marquess and Gladys Ethel Gwendolen Eugenie (*d* 1959), *e d* of late Thomas Sutherst, barrister; *S* father, 1921; *m* 1st, 1939, Elizabeth (marr. diss. 1960: she *m* 1960, Brig. Sir James Gault, KCMG, MVO, OBE), *o d* of Thomas Luby, Indian CS; one *s* two *d*; 2nd, 1960, Ann Frances, *d* of Arthur Pellew Darlow; one *s* one *d*. Norfolk Yeomanry TA, 1936-40; Scots Guards, 1940-45. DL Norfolk, 1951-61. *Heir: s* Viscount Raynham, *qv. Address:* Raynham Hall, Fakenham, Norfolk. *T:* Fakenham 2133. *Clubs:* White's, Pratt's, MCC; Norfolk (Norwich); Royal Yacht Squadron; House of Lords Yacht.

TOWNSING, Sir Kenneth (Joseph), Kt 1982; CMG 1971; ISO 1966; Chairman, Salaries and Allowances Tribunal, since 1975; Director: Western Mining Corporation Ltd, since 1975; Central Norseman Gold Corporation, since 1982; *b* 25 July 1914; *s* of J. W. and L. A. Townsing; *m* 1942, Frances Olive Daniel; two *s* one *d. Educ:* Perth Boys' Sch.; Univ. of Western Australia. Treasury Officer, 1933-39. Served War, AIF (Middle East), 1940-46. Major. Public Service Inspector, 1946-49; Sec., Public Service Commissioner's Office, 1949-52; Dep. Under Treasurer, 1952-57; Public Service Comr, 1958-59; Under Treasurer (Permanent Head), 1959-75. Mem. Senate, Univ. of Western Australia, 1954-70 (Chm. Finance Cttee, 1956-70; Pro-Chancellor, 1968-70); Comr, Rural and Industries Bank, 1959-65; Member: Jackson Cttee on Tertiary Educn, 1967; Tertiary Educn Commn, 1971-74; Past Mem. numerous other Bds and Cttees. Fellow, W Australian Museum, 1975; Hon. Zoo Associate, 1979. FASA. Hon. LLD Univ. of W Australia, 1971; DUniv Murdoch, 1982. *Recreation:* gardening. *Address:* 22 Robin Street, Mount Lawley, WA 6050, Australia. *T:* 272 1393. *Club:* University House (Perth).

TOWNSVILLE, Bishop of, (RC), since 1967; **Most Rev. Leonard Anthony Faulkner;** *b* Booleroo Centre, South Australia, 5 Dec. 1926. *Educ:* Sacred Heart Coll., Glenelg; Corpus Christi Coll., Werribee; Pontifical Urban University, Rome. Ordained Propaganda Fide Coll., Rome, 1 Jan. 1950. Asst Priest, Woodville, SA, 1950-57; Administrator, St Francis Xavier Cathedral, Adelaide, 1957-67; Diocesan Chaplain, Young Christian Workers, 1955-67; Mem., Nat. Fitness Council of SA, 1958-67. Chm., Aust. Episcopal Conference Cttee for Laity, 1982- (Sec., 1968-82); Sec., Aust. Episcopal Conference Cttee for Aborigines, 1975-. *Address:* Bishop's House, Stanley Street, Townsville, Queensland 4810, Australia.

TOWRY, Peter; *see* Piper, D. T.

TOY, Francis Carter, CBE 1947; DSc, FInstP; *b* 5 May 1892; 2nd *s* of late Sir Henry Toy, CA, JP, Helston, Cornwall; *m* 1921, Gladys Marguerite, *d* of late James Thomas, CA, JP, Tregays, Lostwithiel, Cornwall; one *d. Educ:* Launceston Coll., Cornwall; University College, London. Fellow of University College, London. Served European War, 1914-18; Lieut, Cornwall Fortress Engineers, 1914-16; Lieut, First Army Field Survey Co. (Sound Ranging, Y section), BEF France, 1917-18. Physicist, British Photographic Research Association, 1919-29; Deputy Director of the Shirley Institute, Research Station of British Cotton Industry Research Association, 1930-43, Director, 1944-55. President: Manchester Fedn of Scientific Societies, 1953-55; Inst of Physics, 1948-50; Manchester Statistical Society, 1951-53; Manchester Literary and Philosophical Society, 1956-58; Past Chairman Cttee of Directors of Research Associations; Fellow of the Textile Institute; Past Member Court and Council, UMIST. *Publications:* numerous scientific. *Recreations:* travel, music and sport (cricket and golf). *Address:* 8 Fulshaw Court, Wilmslow, Cheshire. *T:* Wilmslow 525141. *Club:* Athenæum.

TOY, Sam, (Samuel Edward Glenwood); Chairman and Managing Director, Ford Motor Co. Ltd, since 1980; *b* 21 Aug. 1923; *s* of Edward and Lillian Toy; *m* 1st, 1944, Jean Balls; one *s*; 2nd, 1950, Joan Franklin Rook; two *s* one *d. Educ:* Falmouth Grammar Sch.; Cambridge Univ. (MA). Pilot (Flt Lieut), RAF, 1942-48. Graduate trainee, Ford Motor Co. Ltd, 1948; thereafter, all business career with Ford Motor Co. Ltd. Vice-Pres., SMMT, 1982-. *Recreations:* trout and salmon fishing, golf. *Address:* c/o Ford Motor Co. Ltd, Eagle Way, Brentwood, Essex CM13 3BW. *T:* Brentwood 253000. *Clubs:* Lord's Taverners', Eccentric.

TOYE, Wendy; theatrical producer; film director; choreographer, actress, dancer. First professional appearance as Mustard-seed in A Midsummer Night's Dream, Old Vic, 1929; principal dancer in Hiawatha, Royal Albert Hall, 1931; Marigold, Phœbe in Toad of Toad Hall and produced dances, Royalty, Christmas, 1931-32; danced in C. B. Cochran's The Miracle, Lyceum, 1932; masked dancer in Ballerina, Gaiety, 1933; member of Ninette de Valois' original Vic Wells Ballet, principal dancer for Ninette de Valois in The Golden Toy, Coliseum, 1934; toured with Anton Dolin's ballet (choreog. for divertissements and ballets), 1934-35; in Tulip Time, Alhambra, then Markova-Dolin Ballet as principal dancer and choreog., 1935; in Love and How to Cure It, Globe, 1937. Arranged dances and ballets for many shows and films including most of George Black's productions for next 7 years, notably Black Velvet in which also principal dancer, 1939. Shakespearean season, Open Air Theatre, 1939. *Theatre productions:* Big Ben, Bless the Bride, Tough at the Top (for C. B. Cochran), Adelphi; The Shepherd Show, Prince's; Co-Director and Choreographer, Peter Pan, New York; And So To Bed, New Theatre; Co-Director and Choreographer, Feu d'Artifice, Paris; Night of Masquerade, Q; Second Threshold, Vaudeville; Choreography for

Three's Company in Joyce Grenfell Requests the Pleasure, Fortune; Wild Thyme, Duke of York's; Lady at the Wheel, Lyric, Hammersmith; Majority of One, Phœnix; Magic Lantern, Saville; As You Like It, Old Vic; Virtue in Danger, Mermaid and Strand; Robert and Elizabeth, Lyric; On the Level, Saville; Midsummer Night's Dream, Shakespeare quatercentenary Latin American tour, 1964; Soldier's Tale, Edinburgh Festival, 1967; Boots and Strawberry Jam, Nottingham Playhouse, 1968; The Great Waltz, Drury Lane, 1970; Showboat, Adelphi, 1971; She Stoops to Conquer, Young Vic, 1972; Cowardy Custard, Mermaid, 1972; Stand and Deliver, Roundhouse, 1972; R loves J, Chichester, 1973; The Confederacy, Chichester, 1974; The Englishman Amused, Young Vic, 1974; Follow The Star, Chichester, 1974, Westminster Theatre, 1976; Made in Heaven, Chichester, 1975; Make Me a World, Chichester, 1976; Once More with Music (with Cicely Courtneidge and Jack Hulbert), 1976; Oh, Mr Porter, Mermaid, 1977; Dance for Gods, Conversations, 1979; Colette, Comedy, 1980; Gingerbread Man, Water Mill, 1981. *Opera Productions:* Bluebeard's Castle (Bartok), Sadler's Wells and Brussels; The Telephone (Menotti), Sadler's Wells; Russalka (Dvořák), Sadler's Wells; Fledermaus, Coliseum and Sadler's Wells; Orpheus in the Underworld, Sadler's Wells and Australia; La Vie Parisienne, Sadler's Wells; Seraglio, Bath Festival, 1967; The Impresario, Don Pasquale (for Phoenix Opera Group), 1968; The Italian Girl in Algiers, Coliseum, 1968; La Cenerentola; Merry Widow, 1979, Orpheus in the Underworld, 1981, ENO North; The Mikado, Nat. Opera Co., Ankara, 1982; Italian Girl in Algiers, ENO, 1982. *Films directed:* The Stranger Left No Card; The Teckman Mystery; Raising a Riot; The Twelfth Day of Christmas; Three Cases of Murder; All for Mary; True as a Turtle; We Joined the Navy; The King's Breakfast; Cliff in Scotland; A Goodly Manor for a Song; Girls Wanted—Istanbul; Trial by Jury (TV). Productions for TV, etc, inc. Golden Gala, ATV, 1978; Follow the Star, BBC2, 1979; Stranger in Town, Anglia, 1981. Appeared with and was choreographer for Camargo Society; guest artist with Sadler's Wells Ballet and Mme Rambert's Ballet Club; went to Denmark as principal dancer with British Ballet, organised by Adeline Geneé, 1932. Trained with Euphen MacLaren, Karsavina, Dolin, Morosoff, Legat, Rambert. *Address:* c/o London Management, 235 Regent Street, W1.

TOYN, Richard John; His Honour Judge Toyn; a Circuit Judge since 1972; *b* 24 Jan. 1927; *s* of Richard Thomas Millington Toyn and Ethel Toyn; *m* 1955, Joyce Evelyn Goodwin; two *s* two *d*. *Educ:* Solihull Sch.; Bristol Grammar Sch.; Bristol Univ. (LLB). Royal Army Service Corps, 1948-50. Called to the Bar, Gray's Inn, 1952. *Recreations:* music, drama, photography. *Address:* c/o Victoria Law Courts, Birmingham.

TOYNBEE, Prof. Jocelyn Mary Catherine, MA, DPhil; FSA; FBA; Laurence Professor Emerita of Classical Archæology, Cambridge University (Professor, 1951-62); Hon. Fellow of Newnham College; *b* 3 March 1897; *d* of late Harry Valpy Toynbee and late Sarah Edith (*née* Marshall). *Educ:* Winchester High School for Girls; Newnham Coll., Cambridge. Classical Tutor, St Hugh's Coll., Oxford, 1921-24; Lecturer in Classics, Reading University, 1924-27; Fellow and Director of Studies in Classics, Newnham Coll., Cambridge, and Lecturer in the Faculty of Classics, Cambridge Univ., 1927-51. Hon. Dlitt: University of Newcastle upon Tyne; University of Liverpool. *Publications:* The Hadrianic School: a Chapter in the History of Greek Art, 1934; Roman Medallions (American Numismatic Society, New York), 1944; Some Notes on Artists in the Roman World, (Brussels) 1951; The Shrine of St Peter and the Vatican Excavation (with John Ward Perkins), 1956; The Flavian Reliefs from the Palazzo della Cancelleria in Rome, 1957; Art in Roman Britain, 1962; Art in Britain under the Romans, 1964; The Art of the Romans, 1965; Death and Burial in the Roman World, 1971; Animals in Roman Life and Art, 1973; Roman Historical Portraits, 1978; contribs to Journal of Roman Studies, Papers of British School, Rome, Numismatic Chronicle, Classical Review, Classical Quarterly, Antiquaries Journal, Archæologia, Antiquity, Gnomon, etc. *Recreation:* travelling. *Address:* 22 Park Town, Oxford. *T:* 57886.

TOYNBEE, Polly; Columnist, The Guardian, since 1977; writer; *b* 27 Dec. 1946; *d* of late Philip Toynbee, and of Anne Powell; *m* 1970, Peter Jenkins, *qv*; two *d* and one step-*d*. *Educ:* Badminton Sch.; Holland Park Comprehensive; St Anne's Coll., Oxford. Reporter, The Observer, 1968-71; Editor, The Washington Monthly, USA, 1972-73; Feature Writer, The Observer, 1974-76. Catherine Pakenham Award for Journalism, 1975; British Press Award, 1977. *Publications:* Leftovers, 1966; A Working Life, 1970 (paperback 1972); Hospital, 1977 (paperback 1979); The Way We Live Now, 1981. *Address:* 1 Crescent Grove, SW4. *T:* 01-622 6492.

TRACY; *see* Hanbury-Tracy, family name of Baron Sudeley.

TRACY, Rear-Adm. Hugh Gordon Henry, CB 1965; DSC 1945; CEng; *b* 15 Nov. 1912; *e s* of Comdr A. F. G. Tracy, RN; *m* 1938, Muriel, *d* of Maj.-Gen. Sir R. B. Ainsworth, CB, DSO, OBE; two *s* one *d*. *Educ:* Nautical Coll., Pangbourne. Joined RN, 1929; Lieut, 1934; served in HMS Shropshire, Hawkins and Furious, in Admiralty and attended Advanced Engineering course before promotion to Lt-Comdr, 1942; Sen. Engineer, HMS Illustrious, 1942-44; Asst to Manager, Engineering Dept, HM Dockyard Chatham, 1944-46; Comdr 1946; served in HMS Manxman, Admiralty, RN Engineering Coll. and HM Dockyard Malta; Captain, 1955; Asst Director of Marine Engineering, Admiralty, 1956-58; CO HMS Sultan, 1959-60; Imperial Defence Coll., 1961; CSO (Tech.) to Flag Officer, Sea Training, 1962-63; Rear-Admiral, 1963; Director of Marine Engineering, Ministry of Defence

(Navy), 1963-66; retired, 1966. *Recreations:* gardening, plant ecology. *Address:* Orchard House, Claverton, Bath BA2 7BG. *T:* Bath 65650. *Club:* Army and Navy.

TRACY, Walter Valentine, RDI; Typographical Consultant to Times Newspapers; *b* 14 Feb. 1914; *s* of Walter Tracy and Anne Nunn; *m* 1942, Muriel Frances Campbell. *Educ:* Central Sch. of Arts and Crafts. Apprentice compositor, Wm Clowes Ltd, 1930-35; typographic studio, Baynard Press, 1935-38; Notley Advertising, 1938-46; freelance, 1946-47; on staff of (British) Linotype Co., editor Linotype Matrix, i/c typographic design, 1947-73; Linotype-Paul, 1973-78. In 1965, assisted Editor of The Times in re-designing the paper for news on front page, May 1966; designed newspaper types: Jubilee, 1953; Adsans, 1959; Maximus, 1967; Telegraph Modern, 1969; Times-Europa, 1972; also designed: Hebrew types Gold, Silver, 1975 (under pseudonym David Silver) for Linotype-Paul; Arabic types Kufic Light, Med., Bold, 1979 for Letraset. RDI 1973. *Publications:* contribs to Penrose Annual, Alphabet, Motif, Typographica, Bulletin of British Society for Middle Eastern Studies. *Address:* 9 Highgate Spinney, Crescent Road, N8 8AR. *T:* 01-348 2605. *Club:* Double Crown (Hon. Mem.).

TRAFFORD; *see* de Trafford.

TRAFFORD, Ian Colton, OBE 1967; Publisher, The Times Supplements, since 1981; Deputy Chairman, Times Books Ltd, since 1981; *s* of Dr Harold Trafford and late Laura Dorothy Trafford; *m* 1st, 1949, Nella Georgara (marr. diss. 1964); one *d* ; 2nd, 1972, Jacqueline Carole Trenque. *Educ:* Charterhouse; St John's Coll., Oxford. Feature writer and industrial correspondent, The Financial Times, 1951-58; UK Correspondent, Barrons Weekly, New York, 1954-60; Director, Industrial and Trade Fairs Holdings Ltd, 1961-71; Managing Director, 1966-71; Director-General British Trade Fairs in: Peking, 1964; Moscow, 1966; Bucharest, 1968; Sao Paulo, 1969; Buenos Aires, 1970; Man. Dir, Economist Newspaper, 1971-81; Chm., Economist Intelligence Unit, 1971-79. Local Dir, W London Board, Commercial Union Assce, 1974-. OBE awarded for services to exports. *Address:* Grafton House, Westhall Road, Warlingham, Surrey CR3 9NA. *T:* Upper Warlingham 2048.

See also *J. A. P. Trafford.*

TRAFFORD, Dr (Joseph) Anthony (Porteous); Consultant Physician, Brighton and Lewes Group of Hospitals, since 1965; *b* 20 July 1932; *s* of Dr Harold Trafford, Warlingham, Surrey, and late Laura Trafford; *m* 1960, Helen Chalk; one *s* one *d*. *Educ:* St Edmund's, Hindhead; Charterhouse; Guy's Hosp., Univ. of London. MB, BS Hons 1957; MRCP 1961. Various medical appts, 1957-63; Sen. Registrar, Guy's Hosp., 1963-66; Fulbright Scholar, Johns Hopkins Univ., 1963; Dir, Artificial Kidney Unit, Brighton, 1967. MP (C) The Wrekin, 1970-Feb. 1974. *Publications:* contribs to BMJ and Lancet. *Recreations:* golf, tennis, squash. *Address:* 103 The Drive, Hove, East Sussex. *T:* Brighton 731567.

See also *I. C. Trafford.*

TRAHAIR, John Rosewarne; Chairman, Plymouth District Health Authority, since 1981; *b* 29 March 1921; *s* of late Percy Edward Trahair and Edith Irene Trahair; *m* 1948, Patricia Elizabeth (*née* Godrich); one *s* one *d*. *Educ:* Leys Sch.; Christ's Coll., Cambridge (MA). FCIS. Served with Royal Artillery, 1941-46 (Captain). Finance Dir, Farleys Infant Food Ltd, 1948-73; Dir 1950-74, Dep. Chm. 1956-74, Western Credit Holdings Ltd. Chairman: Moorhaven HMC, 1959-66; Plymouth and District HMC, 1966-74; Member: SW Regional Hosp. Bd, 1965-74 (Vice-Chm. 1971-73, Chm. 1973-74); South Western RHA, 1974-81. Mem., Devon CC, 1977-81. *Recreations:* sailing, walking. *Address:* West Park, Ivybridge, South Devon. *T:* Ivybridge 2466. *Club:* Royal Western Yacht.

TRAHERNE, Sir Cennydd (George), KG 1970; Kt 1964; TD 1950; MA; HM Lord-Lieutenant of Mid, South and West Glamorgan, since 1974 (HM Lieutenant for Glamorgan, 1952-74); *b* 14 Dec. 1910; *er s* of late Comdr L. E. Traherne, RN, of Coedarhydyglyn, near Cardiff, and Dorothy, *d* of G. F. S. Sinclair; *m* 1934, Olivera Rowena, OBE, BA, JP, DStJ, *d* of late James Binney, and late Lady Marjory Binney, Pampisford Hall, Cambridgeshire. *Educ:* Wellington; Brasenose Coll., Oxford. Barrister, Inner Temple, 1938. 81st Field Regt RA (TA), 1934-43; 102 Provost Coy, Corps of Military Police, 1943-45 (despatches); Dep. Asst Provost Marshal, Second British Army, 1945; 53rd Div. Provost Company, Royal Military Police, 1947-49, TA; Hon. Colonel, 53 Div. Signal Regt, 1953-58; Hon. Colonel 282 (Glamorgan Yeomanry) Field Regt RA (TA), 1958-61; Hon. Colonel: 282 (Glam and Mon) Regt RA (TA), 1962-67; 37 (Wessex and Welsh) Signal Regt, T&AVR, 1971-75. DL 1946, JP 1946, Glamorgan. Deputy Chairman Glamorgan Quarter Sessions, 1949-52; President, Welsh College of Advanced Technology, 1957-65. Chairman, Rep. Body of the Church in Wales, 1965-77; Pres., Welsh Nat. Sch. of Medicine, 1970. Director: Cardiff Building Society, 1953; Wales Gas Board, 1958-71; Commercial Bank of Wales, 1972-; Chm., Wales Gas Consultative Council, 1958-71. Member, Gorsedd of the Bards of Wales. Hon. Freeman, Borough of Cowbridge, 1971. Hon. LLD University of Wales. KStJ (Sub Prior, Priory of Wales, 1978). *Address:* Coedarhydyglyn, near Cardiff, S Wales CF5 6SF. *T:* Peterston-super-Ely 760321. *Clubs:* Athenæum; Cardiff and County (Cardiff).

TRAILL, Alan Towers; Chairman, Traill Attenborough Ltd, since 1980; Underwriting Member of Lloyd's, since 1963; *b* 7 May 1935; *s* of George Traill and Margaret Eleanor (*née* Matthews); *m* 1964, Sarah Jane (*née* Hutt);

one s. *Educ:* St Andrew's Sch., Eastbourne; Charterhouse; Jesus Coll., Cambridge (MA). Founder Director, Traill Attenborough Ltd, Lloyd's Brokers, 1973. Mem. Council, British Insurance Brokers Assoc., 1978-79; Chm., Reinsurance Brokers Cttee of the Assoc., 1978-. Member, Court of Common Council, City of London, 1970; Alderman for Langbourn Ward, 1975-; Sheriff, 1982-83. Master, Worshipful Co. of Cutlers, 1979-; Director and Mem., City Arts Trust, 1980-; Governor, King Edward's Sch., Witley, 1980-; Almoner, Christ's Hosp. Foundn, 1980-. *Recreations:* shooting, skiing, DIY, travel, opera, assisting education. *Address:* 95/97 Fenchurch Street, EC3M 5JB. *T:* 01-480 7447. *Club:* City Livery.

TRAIN, Christopher John; Assistant Under Secretary of State, Home Office, since 1980; Principal Finance Officer, since 1981; *b* 12 March 1932; *s* of Keith Sydney Sayer Train and Edna Ashby Train; *m* 1957, Sheila Mary Watson; one *s* one *d*. *Educ:* Nottingham High Sch.; Christ Church Oxford (BA Lit. Hum., MA). Served Royal Navy, 1955-57; Assistant Master, St Paul's Sch., W Kensington, 1957-67; Principal, Home Office, 1968; Asst Sec., Home Office, 1972; Secretary, Royal Commn on Criminal Procedure, 1978-80. *Recreations:* cricket, refereeing Rugby, gardening. *Address:* 4 Grange Road, Barnes, SW13 9RE. *T:* 01-748 3796. *Clubs:* Reform; Vincent's (Oxford).

TRAIN, David, MC 1945; PhD; FPS, FRSC; CEng, FIChemE; Senior Partner, Cremer and Warner, Consulting Engineers and Scientists, since 1980; *b* 27 Feb. 1919; *s* of Charles and Elsie Louisa Train; *m* 1943, Jeanne Catherine, *d* of late William R. and M. M. Edmunds; two *s*. *Educ:* Lady Hawkins' Grammar Sch., Kington; School of Pharmacy, Univ. of London; Northampton Coll. of Advanced Technology; Imperial Coll., Univ. of London. Fairchild Schol. 1940, MPS 1941, Hewlett Exhibn 1941; BPharm 1942, PhC 1942; BScChemEng 1949, ACGI 1949, PhD 1956, DIC 1956. ARIC 1949, MConsE; MAIChE. Apprenticed to F. T. Roper and Daughter, Kington, 1935-38. War service: St John's Hosp. Reserve, 1939; RAMC (non-med.), NW Europe, 1942-45; 212 Fd Amb. 53rd Welsh (Lieut). Lectr in Pharmaceutical Engrg Science, 1949-59, Reader, 1959-61, Sch. of Pharmacy, London; Vis. Prof., Univ. of Wisconsin, 1959. Partner, Cremer and Warner, 1961. Examiner: for Pharm. Soc. of Gt Brit., 1949-56; IChemE, 1956-66; Mem. Bd of Studies in Chem. Engrg, Univ. of London, 1958-; External Examr, PhD Theses, 1956-75; Jt Hon. Secretary: Brit. Pharm. Conf., 1958-64; IChemE, 1972-77; Mem. Council: Science and Technology Insts, 1972-; Engrg Instns Technical Cttee, 1980-; Member: Adv. Cttee on Oil Pollution of the Sea, 1973-; Air Pollution Control Assoc., USA, 1971-; Fédn Internat. Pharmaceutique, 1970. FRSH 1972. Governor, Wandsworth Sch., 1950-. Liveryman, Worshipful Soc. of Apothecaries, 1975-. *Publications:* various, on compression of powders, protection of the environment, hazards in medicaments, preventative toxicology. *Recreations:* gardening, travelling. *Address:* 140 Buckingham Palace Road, SW1W 9SQ. *T:* 01-730 0777. *Clubs:* Athenæum, Savage.

TRAINOR, James P.; Hon. Mr Justice Trainor; a Judge of the High Court of Kenya, since 1980; *b* Belfast, 14 Oct. 1914; *s* of Owen Trainor and Mary Rose (*née* McArdle); *m* 1954, Angela (*née* O'Connor); one *s* two *d*. *Educ:* Mount St Joseph's, Monaghan, Ireland; University Coll., Dublin (BA). Admitted solicitor, Dublin, 1936; called to Irish Bar, King's Inn, 1950. Colonial Service: Magistrate, Singapore, 1954-55; Justice, Special Court, Cyprus, 1955-60; Called to English Bar, Gray's Inn, 1957; Comr, High Commissioner's Court, W Pacific High Commn, 1960-61; Co-Pres., Jt Court, Anglo-French Condominium of the New Hebrides, 1960-72; Judge, Fiji Court of Appeal, 1960-70; Judge, High Court of the Western Pacific, 1961-72; Judge of Supreme Court, Hong Kong, 1972-79, retired from HM Overseas Judiciary, 1980. Commandeur de l'Ordre Nationale du Mérite (France), 1967. *Recreations:* golf, reading, music. *Address:* Judges' Chambers, High Court, PO Box 30041, Nairobi, Kenya. *T:* Nairobi 722469; Mount Rule, Braden, Isle of Man. *Clubs:* Nairobi, Karen Country (Kenya); Hong Kong, Royal Hong Kong Golf, Royal Hong Kong Jockey (Hong Kong); United Services, Milltown Golf (Dublin).

TRANMIRE, Baron *cr* 1974 (Life Peer), of Upsall, North Yorkshire; **Robert Hugh Turton,** PC 1955; KBE 1971; MC 1942; JP; DL; *b* 8 Aug. 1903; *s* of late Major R. B. Turton, Kildale Hall, Kildale, York; *m* 1928, Ruby Christian, *d* of late Robert T. Scott, Beechmont, Sevenoaks; three *s* one *d*. *Educ:* Eton; Balliol Coll., Oxford. Called to Bar, Inner Temple, 1926; joined 4th Bn of Green Howards at outbreak of war, 1939; served as DAAG 50th (N) Division, AAG GHQ MEF. MP (C) Thirsk and Malton, 1929-Feb. 1974. Parly Sec., Min. of Nat. Insurance, 1951-53. Min. of Pensions and Nat. Insce, 1953-54; Joint Parly Under-Sec. of State for Foreign Affairs, Oct. 1954-Dec. 1955; Minister of Health, Dec. 1955-Jan. 1957; Chm., Select Cttee on Procedure, 1970-74. Chm., Commonwealth Industries Assoc., 1963-74. JP 1936, DL 1962, N Riding, Co. York. Hon. Colonel, 4/5th Bn The Green Howards (TA), 1963-67. *Address:* Upsall Castle, Thirsk, N Yorks YO7 2QJ. *T:* Thirsk 537202; 15 Grey Coat Gardens, SW1P 2QA. *T:* 01-834 1535.

TRANT, Lt-Gen. Sir Richard (Brooking), KCB 1982 (CB 1979); GOC South East District, since 1982; *b* 30 March 1928; *s* of Richard Brooking Trant and Dora Rodney Trant (*née* Lancaster); *m* 1957, Diana Clare, 2nd *d* of Rev. Stephen Zachary and Ruth Beatrice Edwards, Llystanwg, Harlech, N Wales; one *s* two *d*. Commissioned RA 1947; Defence Services Staff Coll., India, 1962-63; Jt Services Staff Coll., 1965; commanded 3rd Regt RHA, 1968-71, 5th Airportable Brigade, 1972-74; Dep. Mil. Sec., MoD (Army), 1975-76; Comdr Land Forces, NI, 1977-79; Dir, Army Staff Duties, 1979-82. Col

Comdt: RAEC, 1979-; RA, 1982-. Order of South Arabia, 3rd Class, 1965. *Recreations:* golf, field sports, natural history. *Address:* c/o Lloyds Bank Ltd, Newquay, Cornwall. *Club:* Army and Navy.

TRANTER, Professor Clement John, CBE 1967 (OBE 1953); Bashforth Professor of Mathematical Physics, Royal Military College of Science, Shrivenham, 1953-74, now Emeritus; *b* 16 Aug. 1909; *s* of late Archibald Tranter, and Mrs Tranter, Cirencester, Glos.; *m* 1937, Joan Louise Hatton, *d* of late J. Hatton, MBE, and Mrs Hatton, Plumstead, SE18. *Educ:* Cirencester Grammar Sch.; Queen's Coll., Oxford (Open Math. Scholar; 1st Class Hons Mathematical Mods, 1929; 1st Class Hons Final Sch. of Maths, 1931; MA (Oxon) 1940; DSc (Oxon) 1953). Commissioned RA, TA, 1932; Captain, 1938. Junior Assistant Research Dept, Woolwich, 1931-34; Senior Lecturer, Gunnery and Mathematics Branch, Military College of Science, Woolwich, 1935-40; Asst Professor 1940-46; Assoc. Professor of Mathematics, Royal Military College of Science, Shrivenham, 1946-53. *Publications:* Integral Transforms in Mathematical Physics, 1951; Advanced Level Pure Mathematics, 1953; Techniques of Mathematical Analysis, 1957; (with C. G. Lambe) Differential Equations for Engineers and Scientists, 1961; Mathematics for Sixth Form Scientists, 1964; (with C. G. Lambe) Advanced Level Mathematics, 1966; Bessel Functions with some Physical Applications, 1968; mathematical papers in various journals. *Recreations:* painting, golf, fly-fishing. *Address:* Flagstones, Stanton Fitzwarren, near Swindon, Wilts SN6 7RZ. *T:* Swindon 762913.

TRANTER, Nigel; novelist and author since 1936; *b* Glasgow, 23 Nov. 1909; *yr s* of Gilbert T. Tranter and Eleanor A. Cass; *m* 1933, May Jean Campbell Grieve (*d* 1979); one *d* (one *s* decd). *Educ:* St James Episcopal Sch., Edinburgh; George Heriot's Sch., Edinburgh. Served War of 1939-45, RASC and RA. Accountancy trng, then in small family insce co., until could live on writing, after war service; much and actively interested in Scottish public affairs; Chm., Scottish Convention, Edinburgh Br., 1948-51; Vice-Convener, Scottish Covenant Assoc., 1951-55; Pres., E Lothian Liberal Assoc., 1960-76; Chm., Nat. Forth Road Bridge Cttee, 1953-57; Pres., Scottish PEN, 1962-66, Hon. Pres., 1973-; Chm., Soc. of Authors, 1966-72; Pres., E Lothian Wildfowlers' Assoc., 1952-73; Chm., St Andrew Soc. of E Lothian, 1966-; Chm., Nat. Book League, Scotland, 1972-77; Mem., Cttee of Aberlady Bay Nature Reserve, 1953-76, etc. Hon. Mem., Mark Twain Soc. of Amer., 1976. Hon. Freeman, Blackstone, Va, 1980. Hon. MA Edinburgh, 1971. Chevalier, Order of St Lazarus of Jerusalem, 1961 (Vice-Chancellor of the Order, Scotland, 1980). *Publications:* fiction: 62 novels, from Trespass, 1937, including: Bridal Path, 1952; Macgregor's Gathering, 1957; the Master of Gray trilogy: The Master of Gray, 1961; The Courtesan, 1963; Past Master, 1965; Chain of Destiny, 1964; the Robert the Bruce trilogy: The Steps to the Empty Throne, 1969; The Path of the Hero King, 1970; The Price of the King's Peace, 1971; The Young Montrose, 1972; Montrose: the Captain General, 1973; The Wisest Fool, 1974; The Wallace, 1975; Lords of Misrule, 1976; A Folly of Princes, 1977; The Captive Crown, 1977; Macbeth the King, 1978; Margaret the Queen, 1979; David the Prince, 1980; True Thomas, 1981; The Patriot, 1982; 12 children's novels; *non-fiction:* The Fortalices and Early Mansions of Southern Scotland, 1935; The Fortified House in Scotland (5 vols), 1962-71; Pegasus Book of Scotland, 1964; Outlaw of the Highlands: Rob Roy, 1965; Land of the Scots, 1968; Portrait of the Border Country, 1972; Portrait of the Lothians, 1979; The Queen's Scotland Series: The Heartland: Clackmannan, Perth and Stirlingshire, 1971; The Eastern Counties: Aberdeen, Angus and Kincardineshire, 1972; The North East: Banff, Moray, Nairn, East Inverness and Easter Ross, 1974; Argyll and Bute, 1977; Nigel Tranter's Scotland, 1981; Scottish Castles: tales and traditions, 1982; contribs to many jls, on Scots history, genealogy, topography, castellated architecture, knighthood, etc. *Recreations:* walking, wildfowling, historical research. *Address:* Quarry House, Aberlady, East Lothian. *T:* Aberlady 258. *Club:* PEN.

TRAPNELL, Alan Stewart; His Honour Judge Trapnell; a Circuit Judge, since 1972; *b* 12 Jan. 1913; *s* of Francis C. Trapnell, MD and Ann Trapnell (*née* Stewart), Beckenham, Kent. *Educ:* The Leys Sch., Cambridge; Jesus Coll., Cambridge. Served War of 1939-45, Queen Victoria's Rifles. Barrister-at-Law. Called to Bar, Inner Temple, 1936. Western Circuit, Hampshire Sessions. Member of Bar Council, 1958-62. Recorder of Barnstaple, 1962-64. Judge of: Bow County Court, 1964-66; Shoreditch County Court, 1966-67; Bromley County Court, 1968-69; Chm., Middlesex QS, 1969-71. *Address:* Francis Taylor Building, Temple, EC4. *Clubs:* Athenæum, United Oxford & Cambridge University.

TRAPNELL, Barry Maurice Waller, CBE 1982; DL; MA, PhD Cantab; Headmaster of Oundle School, since 1968; *b* 18 May 1924; *s* of Waller Bertram and late Rachel Trapnell; *m* 1951, Dorothy Joan, *d* of late P. J. Kerr, ICS; two *d*. *Educ:* University College Sch., Hampstead; St John's Coll., Cambridge (Scholar). Research in physical chemistry in Department of Colloid Science, Cambridge, 1945-46, and Royal Institution, London, 1946-50; Commonwealth Fund Fellow, Northwestern Univ., Ill., 1950-51; Lecturer in chemistry: Worcester Coll., Oxford, 1951-54; Liverpool Univ., 1954-57; Headmaster, Denstone Coll., 1957-68. Visiting Lecturer, American Association for Advancement of Science, 1961. Member: Adv. Cttee on Supply and Training of Teachers; C of E Commn on Religious Education. Mem. Governing Body, UCS. FRSA. DL: Staffs, 1967; Northants, 1974. *Publications:* Chemisorption, 1955 (Russian edition, 1958; 2nd English edition, 1964); Learning and Discerning, 1966; papers in British and American scientific journals. *Recreations:* several games (represented Cambridge v

Oxford at cricket and squash rackets, and Gentlemen v Players at cricket; won Amateur Championships at Rugby Fives); English furniture and silver. *Address:* Cobthorne, Oundle, Northants. *T:* Oundle 3536. *Club:* East India, Devonshire, Sports and Public Schools.

TRAPNELL, John Arthur; Under-Secretary, Departments of Trade and Industry, 1975–77; *b* 7 Sept. 1913; *s* of Arthur Westicote Trapnell and Helen Trapnell (née Alles); *m* 1939, Winifred Chadwick Rushton; two *d. Educ:* privately; Law Soc.'s Sch. of Law. Admitted Solicitor 1938; private practice until 1940; served HM Army, 1940–46: commnd Som. LI, 1943; served with 82nd W African Div. (Major). Civil Service from 1946: Board of Trade, Solicitors Dept. Mem. Law Soc. *Recreations:* golf, bridge. *Address:* 29 Connaught Road, New Malden, Surrey. *T:* 01-942 3183.

TRAPP, Rt. Rev. Eric Joseph; Hon. Assistant Bishop, Diocese of St Albans, since 1976; *b* 17 July 1910; *s* of late Archibald Edward Trapp and Agnes Trapp, Leicester and Coventry; *m* 1937, Edna Noreen Thornton, SRN; two *d. Educ:* Alderman Newton's Sch., Leicester; Leeds Univ.; College of the Resurrection, Mirfield. BA 1st Class, philosophy. Asst Curate, St Olave's, Mitcham, Surrey, 1934–37; Director, Masite Mission, Basutoland, 1937–40; Rector, St Augustine's Bethlehem, Orange Free State, 1940–43; Rector, St John's, Maseru and Director of Maseru Mission, Basutoland, 1943–47; Canon of Bloemfontein Cathedral, 1944–47; Bishop of Zululand, 1947–57; Sec., Soc. for the Propagation of the Gospel, 1957–64; United Soc. for the Propagation of the Gospel, 1965–70; Bishop of Bermuda, 1970–75; Hon. Asst Bishop, Dio. St Albans, 1976–final retirement in 1980. Hon. DD Trinity College, Toronto, 1967. *Address:* 18 Sorrel Garth, Hitchin, Herts SG4 9PS. *T:* Hitchin 4097.

TRAPP, Prof. Joseph Burney, FSA; FBA 1980; Director, Warburg Institute (University of London) and Professor of the History of the Classical Tradition, since 1976; *b* 16 July 1925; *s* of H.M.B. and Frances M. Trapp; *m* 1953, Elayne M. Falla; two *s. Educ:* Dannevirke High Sch. and Victoria University Coll., Wellington, NZ (MA). FSA 1978. Alexander Turnbull Library, Wellington, 1946–50; Jun. Lectr, Victoria University Coll., 1950–51; Asst Lectr, Reading Univ., 1951–53; Asst Librarian, Warburg Inst., 1953–66, Librarian, 1966–76. Visiting Professor: Univ. of Toronto, 1969; Univ. of Melbourne, 1980. Member Advisory Council: V&A Museum, 1977–; British Library, 1980–. *Publications:* (ed) The Apology of Sir Thomas More, 1979; articles in learned jls. *Address:* Warburg Institute, Woburn Square, WC1H 0AB. *T:* 01-580 9663.

TRASENSTER, Michael Augustus Tulk, CVO 1954; Photographer, ARPS 1979; *b* 26 Jan. 1923; *er s* of late Major William Augustus Trasenster, MC, and Brenda de Courcy Trasenster; *m* 1950, Fay Norrie Darley, *d* of late Thomas Bladworth Darley, Cantley Hall, Yorkshire; two *d. Educ:* Winchester. Served with 4th/7th Royal Dragoon Guards, 1942–; NW Europe, 1944; Middle East, 1946; ADC to Governor of South Australia, 1947–49; School of Tank Technology, 1951; Military Secretary and Comptroller to the Governor General of New Zealand, 1952–55. Chevalier of Order of Leopold II of Belgium, 1944; Belgian Croix de Guerre, 1944. *Recreations:* painting, tennis. *Address:* c/o Williams & Glyn's Bank Ltd, High Street, Winchester, Hants.

TRAVANCORE, Rajpramukh of; Maj.-Gen. H. H. Sri Padmanabha Dasa Bala Rama Varma; GCSI 1946; GCIE 1935; *b* 1912. Founder of Travancore University and sometime Chancellor. Formerly: Colonel-in-Chief of Travancore State Forces; Hon. Major-General in British Army. Has introduced many reforms. Holds Hon. Doctorates. *Address:* Kaudiar Palace, Trivandrum 3, Kerala State, S India.

TRAVERS, Basil Holmes, OBE 1943; BA (Sydney); MA (Oxon); BLitt (Oxon); FACE; FRSA; FAIM; Headmaster of Sydney Church of England Grammar School, North Sydney, NSW, since 1959; *b* 7 July 1919; *m* 1942, Margaret Emily Marr; three *d. Educ:* Sydney Church of England Grammar Sch.; Sydney Univ.; New Coll., Oxford Univ. Rhodes Scholar for NSW, 1940. Served War of 1939–45 (despatches, OBE), AIF, 2/2 Australian Infantry Battalion; ADC to Maj.-Gen. Sir I. G. Mackay, 1940; Brigade Major, 15 Aust. Inf. Bde, 1943–44; psc 1944; GSO 2, HQ, 2 Aust. Corps, 1944–45. Assistant Master, Wellington Coll., Berks, England, 1948–49; Assistant Master, Cranbrook Sch., Sydney, 1950–52; Headmaster, Launceston Church Grammar Sch., Launceston, Tasmania, 1953–58. Chm., Headmasters' Conf. of Australia, 1971–73. Lt-Col commanding 12 Inf. Bn (CMF), 1955–58. Member: Soldiers' Children Education Board, 1959–; NSW Cttee, Duke of Edinburgh's Award Scheme in Australia, 1959– (Chm., 1979–). *Publications:* Let's Talk Rugger, 1949; The Captain General, 1952. *Recreations:* cricket (Oxford Blue, 1946, 1948), swimming, rugby (Oxford Blue, 1946, 1947), athletics (Half Blue, 1947); also Sydney Blue, football, cricket; Rugby Union International for England, 1947, 1948, 1949; represented NSW, 1950. *Address:* Sydney Church of England Grammar School, North Sydney, NSW 2060, Australia. *T:* 929 2263. *Clubs:* Union, Rugby Union (Sydney); Elanora Country.

TRAVERS, Rt. Rev. Mgr. Brendan; *b* 21 March 1931; *s* of Dr Charles Travers and Eileen Travers (née Gordon). *Educ:* Belmont Abbey Sch.; Venerable English College, Rome; Gregorian Univ., Rome. STL, JCL, PhL). Ordained priest, 1955; Curate, Salford diocese, 1957–72; Bishop's Secretary, 1961–64; Chm., Manchester Catholic Marriage Adv. Council, 1966–71; Rector, Pontifical Beda College, Rome, 1972–78; Parish Priest, All Souls,

Salford, 1978–. *Recreation:* golf. *Address:* All Souls Presbytery, Liverpool Street, Weaste, Salford M5 2HQ. *Club:* Worsley Golf (Manchester).

TRAVERS, Lt.-Gen. Sir Paul (Anthony), KCB 1981; FCIT; Quarter Master General, since 1982; *b* 5 Aug. 1927; *s* of Michael and Edith Travers; *m* 1956, Therese Sara Keeley; one *s* two *d. Educ:* Clapham Coll. psc; OCDS (Canada). In the ranks, Parachute Regt, 1945–47; Emergency Commn, S Lancs Regt, 1947–49; Reg. Commn, RASC, 1949–65; Staff Coll., Camberley, 1958; RCT, 1965; CO 1 Div. Regt, RCT, 1967; GSO 1 (DS) Staff Coll., 1970; Col AQ 2 Div., 1970–73; Dir of Admin. Planning (Army), 1973–75; Canadian Nat. Def. Coll., 1975–76; DQMG BAOR, 1976–78; Chief of Staff, Logistic Exec. (Army), 1978–79; Vice Quarter Master General, 1979–81; GOC SE District, 1981–82. Col Comdt, RCT, 1981–, Army Legal Corps, 1982–. FBIM. *Recreations:* many—none serious. *Address:* c/o Lloyds Bank, 19 Horseferry Road, SW1P 2AD. *Club:* Naval and Military.

TRAVERS, Sir Thomas (à Beckett), Kt 1972; Consulting Ophthalmologist, Royal Melbourne Hospital, since 1962; *b* 16 Aug. 1902; *s* of late Walter Travers, Warragul, Vic and late Isabelle Travers; *m* Tone, widow of late R. S. Burnard; no *c. Educ:* Melbourne Grammar School. MB, BS 1925, DSc 1941, Melbourne; MRCP 1928; DOMS London 1928; FRACS. *Publications:* various on strabismus. *Recreation:* gardening. *Address:* 55 Victoria Parade, Fitzroy, Vic 3065, Australia. *Club:* Melbourne (Melbourne).

TRAVERSE-HEALY, Tim, FIPR, FPA; Senior Partner, Traverse-Healy Ltd, Corporate Affairs Counsel, since 1947; *b* 25 March 1923; *s* of John Healy, MBE, and Gladys Traverse; *m* 1946, Joan Thompson; two *s* three *d. Educ:* Stonyhurst Coll.; St Mary's Hosp., London Univ. DipCAM. Served War, Royal Marines Commandos and Special Forces, 1941–46. Public Affairs Adviser to: inter alia, National Westminster Bank plc, Hong Kong Bank Group, Royal Bank of Canada, Vickers Ltd. Inst. of Public Relations: Mem. 1948, Fellow 1956, Pres. 1967–68; European PR Federation: Vice-Pres. 1965–69; Internat. PR Assoc.: Sec. 1950–61, Pres. 1968–73, Mem. Emeritus 1982; FRSA 1953; FIPA 1957. Member, US Public Affairs Council, 1975; Board Mem., Centre for Public Affairs Studies, 1969; Pres., World PR Congress: Tel Aviv, 1970; Geneva, 1973. Congress Foundn Lecture: Boston, 1976; Bombay, 1982. *Publications:* numerous published lectures and articles in professional jls. *Recreations:* French politics, Irish Society. *Address:* Knights' Court, St John's Square, EC1. *T:* 01-251 6414. *Clubs:* Athenæum, Norwegian.

TREACHER, Adm. Sir John (Devereux), KCB 1975; Director, since 1978, Group Marketing Director, since 1982, Westland plc; Director, National Car Parks, since 1977; *b* Chile, 23 Sept. 1924; *s* of late Frank Charles Treacher, Bentley, Suffolk; *m* 1st, 1953, Patcie Jane (marr. diss. 1968), *d* of late Dr F. L. McGrath, Evanston, Ill; one *s* one *d*; 2nd, 1969, Kirsteen Forbes, *d* of late D. F. Landale; one *s* one *d. Educ:* St Paul's School. Served in HM Ships Nelson, Glasgow, Keppel and Mermaid in Mediterranean, Russian convoys; qual. Fleet Air Arm pilot, 1947; CO: 778 Sqdn 1951, 849 Sqdn 1952-53; CO, HMS Lowestoft, 1964–66; CO, HMS Eagle, 1968–70; Flag Officer Carriers and Amphibious Ships and Comdr Carrier Striking Gp 2, 1970-72; Flag Officer, Naval Air Comd, 1972–73; Vice-Chief of Naval Staff, 1973–75; C-in-C Fleet, and Allied C-in-C Channel and Eastern Atlantic, 1975-77. Chief Exec., Nat. Car Parks, 1977–81. Non-press Mem., Press Council, 1978–81. FRAeS 1973. *Recreations:* shooting, photography. *Address:* 4 Carlton Gardens, SW1. *Club:* Institute of Directors.

TREADGOLD, Rev. Canon John David; Canon of Windsor and Chaplain to Windsor Great Park, since 1981; *b* 30 Dec. 1931; *s* of Oscar and Sybil Treadgold; *m* 1959, Hazel Rhona (née Bailey); two *s* one *d. Educ:* Nottingham Univ. (BA); Wells Theological College. Deacon 1959, priest 1960; Vicar Choral, Southwell Minster, 1959–64; Rector of Wollaton, Nottingham, 1964–74; Vicar of Darlington, 1974–81. Chaplain, TA, 1962–67; TAVR, 1974–78; Chaplain to High Sheriff: of Nottinghamshire, 1963–64 and 1975–76; of Durham, 1978–79. *Recreations:* musical appreciation; church architecture. *Address:* Chaplain's Lodge, Windsor Great Park, Windsor, Berks SL4 2HP. *T:* Egham 32434.

TREADGOLD, Sydney William, FCA; Under Secretary, Finance and Economic Appraisal Division, Departments of Industry and Trade, since 1979; *b* 10 May 1933; *s* of Harold Bryan Treadgold and Violet Gladys (née Watson); *m* 1961, Elizabeth Ann White; two *s. Educ:* Larkmead Sch., Abingdon. Chartered accountant (ACA 1960, FCA 1970). Served RAF, 1951-53 (Navigator). Wenn Townsend & Co., Chartered Accountants, 1954-62; Asst Finance Officer, Univ. of Liverpool, 1963–65; Principal: Min. of Aviation, 1965–67; Min. of Technol., 1967–71; Asst Sec., DTI, 1972-78; Under Sec., Price Commn, 1978-79. *Address:* 23 Sturges Road, Wokingham, Berks RG11 2HG.

TREADWELL, Charles James, CMG 1972; CVO 1979; HM Diplomatic Service, retired; Adviser on Middle East affairs to: Hill Samuel & Co. Ltd, since 1979; Hill Samuel Investment Management Ltd, since 1981; *b* 10 Feb. 1920; *s* of late C. A. L. Treadwell, OBE, Barrister and Solicitor, Wellington, NZ; *m* 1946, Philippa, *d* of late W. J. Perkins, CBE, MC; three *s. Educ:* Wellington Coll., NZ; University of New Zealand (LLB). Served with HM Forces, 1939–45. Sudan Political Service and Sudan Judiciary, 1945–55; FO, 1955–57; British High Commn, Lahore, 1957–60; HM Embassy, Ankara, 1960–62; HM Embassy, Jedda, 1963–64; British Dep. High Comr for Eastern

Nigeria, 1965-66; Head of Joint Information Services Department, Foreign Office/Commonwealth Office, 1966-68; British Political Agent, Abu Dhabi, 1968-71; Ambassador, United Arab Emirates, 1971-73; High Comr to Bahamas, 1973-75; Ambassador to Oman, 1975-79. *Recreation:* fishing. *Address:* 83 Lexham Gardens, W8 6JN. *Club:* Army and Navy.

TREASE, Geoffrey; *see* Trease, R. G.

TREASE, Prof. George Edward, BPharm, Dr *hc* Strasbourg; Dr *hc* Clermont; FPS, FRSC; Professor of Pharmacognosy, Nottingham University, 1957-67, now Emeritus Professor; Head of Department of Pharmacy, University of Nottingham, 1944-67; *b* 8 July 1902; *e s* of George and Florence Trease; *m* 1928, Phyllis Thornton Wilkinson; two *d* (one *s* decd). *Educ:* Nottingham High Sch.; London College of Pharmacy. Lecturer in Pharmacognosy, University College, Nottingham, 1926. Served in Min. of Economic Warfare, 1939-40. Reader in Pharmacognosy, 1945; Examiner in Pharmacognosy to: Pharmaceutical Society, 1934-; University of London, 1937-; QUB, 1949, 1963-65; University of Glasgow, 1950-; University of Wales, 1945-; University of Nottingham, 1950-; University of Singapore, 1962; University of Bradford, 1966-; Pharmaceutical Society of Eire, 1959-. Vice-Pres., British Soc. for History of Pharmacy, 1967-70. Worshipful Society of Apothecaries of London, 1959. Dr *hc* Strasbourg University, 1954; Dr *hc* Clermont University, 1962. *Publications:* Chemistry of Crude Drugs, 1928 (with Prof. J. E. Driver); Textbook of Pharmacognosy, 1934, 12th edn 1983; Pharmacy in History, 1964; many papers and articles on pharmacognosy, pharmaceutical history and pharmaceutical education. *Recreation:* local history. *Address:* George Hill, Crediton, Devon. *T:* Crediton 2983.
    See also R. G. Trease.

TREASE, (Robert) Geoffrey, FRSL 1979; *b* 11 Aug. 1909; *s* of George Albert Trease and Florence (*née* Dale); *m* 1933, Marian Haselden Granger Boyer; one *d*. *Educ:* Nottingham High Sch.; Queen's Coll., Oxford (schol.). Chm., 1972-73, Mem. Council, 1974-, Society of Authors. *Publications:* Walking in England, 1935; Such Divinity, 1939; Only Natural, 1940; Tales Out of School, 1949; Snared Nightingale, 1957; So Wild the Heart, 1959; The Italian Story, 1963; The Grand Tour, 1967; (ed) Matthew Todd's Journal, 1968; Nottingham, a biography, 1970; The Condottieri, 1970; A Whiff of Burnt Boats, an early autobiography, 1971; Samuel Pepys and his World, 1972; Laughter at the Door, a continued autobiography, 1974; London, a concise history, 1975; Portrait of a Cavalier: William Cavendish, first Duke of Newcastle, 1979; *for young readers:* Bows Against the Barons, 1934; Cue for Treason, 1940; The Hills of Varna, 1948; No Boats on Bannermere, 1949; The Seven Queens of England, 1953; This Is Your Century, 1965; The Red Towers of Granada, 1966; Byron, A Poet Dangerous to Know, 1969; A Masque for the Queen, 1970; Horsemen on the Hills, 1971; D. H. Lawrence: the Phoenix and the Flame, 1973; Popinjay Stairs, 1973; Days to Remember, 1973; The Iron Tsar, 1975; The Chocolate Boy, 1975; When the Drums Beat, 1976; Violet for Bonaparte, 1976; The Field of the Forty Footsteps, 1977; Mandeville, 1980; A Wood by Moonlight and Other Stories, 1981; Saraband for Shadows, 1982, and many others; *plays:* After the Tempest, 1938 (Welwyn Fest. award); Colony, 1939. *Recreations:* walking, the theatre. *Address:* The Croft, Colwall, Malvern, Worcs WR13 6EZ. *T:* Colwall 40366.
    See also Prof. G. E. Trease.

TREASURE, Prof. John Albert Penberthy, PhD; Chairman, Freeman Mathews Treasure, since 1982; *b* 20 June 1924; *s* of Harold Paul Treasure and Constance Frances Treasure; *m* 1954, Valerie Ellen Bell; three *s*. *Educ:* Cardiff High Sch.; University Coll., Cardiff (BA 1946); Univ. of Cambridge (PhD 1956). Joined British Market Research Bureau Ltd, 1952, Man. Dir 1957; Marketing Dir, J. Walter Thompson Co. Ltd, 1960, Chm. 1967; Dir, J. Walter Thompson Co. USA, 1967, Vice Chm. 1974. Dean and Prof. of Marketing, City Univ. Business Sch., 1978-82. President: Inst. of Practitioners in Advertising, 1975-77; Market Res. Soc., 1975-78; Nat. Advertising Benevolent Soc., 1977-78. *Publications:* articles on marketing, market research and economics in Financial Times, Times, New Soc., Econ. Jl, Commentary, Advertising Qly and Three Banks Rev. *Recreations:* golf, tennis. *Address:* Cholmondeley Lodge, Friars Lane, Richmond, Surrey TW9 1NS. *T:* (office) 01-235 6050. *Clubs:* Reform, Queen's, Hurlingham; Royal Mid-Surrey Golf (Richmond).

TREASURE, Col Kenneth David, CB 1972; CBE 1965; TD; DL; Solicitor; HM Coroner, County of Gwent (formerly Monmouth), since 1957; *b* 20 Sept. 1913; *s* of late David John Treasure, Maesycwmmer, and of Olive Treasure; *m* 1941, Jean Mitchell, Heathfield, Sussex; one *s* and one *d*. *Educ:* Cranbrook; Univ. of Wales. Admitted Solicitor, 1937. Served War of 1939-45: Lt-Col, Monmouthshire Regt; (TA) in India and Burma. Legal Adviser, CCG, 1946-49; Col, Army Cadet Force, 1958; Chm., Monmouthshire T&AFA, 1960-68; a Rep. Chm. (Wales), Council of T&AF Assocs; Chm., Wales and Monmouthshire TA&VR Assoc., 1968-71; Mem. Council, TA&VR Assocs and TA Advisory Cttee, MoD. DL Monmouthshire, 1957. *Recreations:* judging show jumping, motoring and work. *Address:* The Court, Lower Machen, Newport, Gwent. *T:* Machen 440258. *Club:* Army and Navy.

TREATT, Hon. Sir Vernon (Haddon), KBE 1970; MM 1918; QC (Austr.) 1940; MA, BCL; private interests; *b* 15 May 1897; *s* of Frank Burford Treatt and Kate Ellen Treatt; *m* 1st, 1930, Dorothy Isobelle Henderson; one *s* one *d*; 2nd, 1960, Franki Embleton Wilson. *Educ:* Sydney C of E Grammar Sch.; St Paul's Coll., Sydney Univ.; New Coll., Oxford. Sydney Univ., 1915-16,

1919-20 (BA); AIF, 1916-18 (Gunner, MM); Rhodes Scholar, 1920; Oxford Univ., 1921-23. Called to Bar, Lincoln's Inn, 1923; Bar of NSW, 1924. NSW Legislative Assembly, 1938-62: Minister of Justice, 1939-41; Leader of Opposition, 1946-54; title of Honourable for life, 1955. Chm., Local Govt Boundaries Commn NSW, 1964-69. Chief Comr (in loco Lord Mayor), City of Sydney, 1967-69. *Publication:* Workers Compensation Law NSW. *Recreations:* swimming, reading, rural property. *Address:* 27 Waruda Street, Kirribilli, NSW 2061, Australia. *T:* 9292668; Riverview, O'Connell, NSW 2795. *T:* O'Connell 375762. *Clubs:* University, Royal Sydney Golf, Australasian Pioneers' (Sydney).

TREDGOLD, Joan Alison, MA Cantab; Principal, Cheltenham Ladies' College, Sept. 1953-July 1964; *b* 6 Sept. 1903; *d* of Alfred Frank Tredgold, MD, FRCP, and Zoë B. T. Tredgold. *Educ:* Cheltenham Ladies' College; Newnham College, Cambridge. Mathematical Tripos part II, Class I, 1924; Fourth Year Scholarship, Newnham, 1924-25. Assistant Mistress, Sherborne School for Girls, 1925-29; Assistant Mistress, Cheltenham Ladies' College, 1929-35. Senior Mathematical Mistress, 1935-53, Assistant House Mistress, 1938-39, Second Mistress, 1939-53, Roedean School. *Recreation:* foreign travel. *Address:* 12 Newcourt Park, Charlton Kings, Cheltenham, Glos. *T:* Cheltenham 519242. *Club:* University Women's.

TREFGARNE; family name of **Baron Trefgarne.**

TREFGARNE, 2nd Baron, *cr* 1947, of Cleddau; **David Garro Trefgarne;** Parliamentary Under Secretary of State, Department of Health and Social Security, since 1982; *b* 31 March 1941; *s* of 1st Baron Trefgarne and of Elizabeth (who *m* 1962, Comdr A. T. Courtney (from whom she obt. a divorce, 1966); *m* 1971, H. C. H. Ker, Dundee), *d* of C. E. Churchill; *S* father, 1960; *m* 1968, Rosalie, *d* of Peter Lane; two *s* one *d*. *Educ:* Haileybury; Princeton University, USA. Opposition Whip, House of Lords, 1977-79; a Lord in Waiting (Govt Whip), 1979-81; Parly Under Sec. of State, DoT, 1981, FCO, 1981-82. Awarded Royal Aero Club Bronze Medal (jointly) for flight from England to Australia and back in light aircraft, 1963. *Recreation:* photography. *Heir: s* Hon. George Garro Trefgarne, *b* 4 Jan. 1970. *Address:* House of Lords, SW1.

TREFUSIS; *see* Fane Trefusis, family name of Baron Clinton.

TREGLOWN, Jeremy Dickinson; Editor, Times Literary Supplement, since 1982; *b* 24 May 1946; *s* of Rev. Geoffrey and of Beryl Treglown; *m* 1970, Rona Bower; one *s* two *d*. *Educ:* Bristol Grammar Sch.; St Peter's Coll., Oxford. MA, BLitt Oxon; PhD London. Lecturer: Lincoln Coll., Oxford, 1974-77; University College London, 1977-80; Asst Editor, Times Literary Supplement, 1980-82. Regular contributor to The New Statesman, Sunday Times, etc. General Editor, the Plays in Performance series, 1981-. *Publications:* (ed) The Letters of John Wilmot, Earl of Rochester, 1980; Spirit of Wit, 1982; articles on poetry and drama in various learned jls. *Address:* Halton House, Charlton-on-Otmoor, Oxon.

TREHANE, Sir (Walter) Richard, Kt 1967; Chairman of the Milk Marketing Board, 1958-77; *b* 14 July 1913; *s* of James Trehane and Muriel Yeoman Cowl; *m* 1948, Elizabeth Mitchell; two *s*. *Educ:* Monkton Combe School, Somerset; University of Reading (BSc (Agric.)). On staff of School of Agriculture, Cambridge, 1933-36; Manager of Hampreston Manor Farm, Dorset, 1936-. Member Dorset War Agric. Exec. Cttee, 1942-47; Mem. Milk Marketing Board, 1947-77 (Vice-Chm., 1952-58); Dep. Chm. Dorset Agric. Exec. Cttee, 1947-52; Mem. (later Vice-Chm.) Avon and Stour Catchment Bd, subseq. Avon & Dorset Rivers Bd, 1944-53; Mem. Dorset County Council and Chm. Secondary Education Cttee, 1946-49; Chm. Dorset National Farmers' Union, 1947-48; Member, Nat. Milk Publicity Council, 1954-77 (1st Pres. 1954-56); Chm. English Country Cheese Council, 1955-77; Pres. British Farm Produce Council, 1963-78 (Chm. 1960-63). Chm. Govg Body, Grassland Research Institute, Hurley, Berks, 1959-78 (Hon. Fellow, 1981); Chm. and Pres. European Cttee on Milk/Butterfat Recording, 1957-60; Director of British Semen Exports Ltd, 1960-77; Vice-President: World Assoc. Animal Production, 1965-68; President: European Assoc. Animal Prodn, 1961-67; British Soc. Animal Prodn, 1954, 1961; British Friesian Cattle Soc., 1969-70; Royal Assoc. British Dairy Farmers, 1968, 1977; Internat. Dairy Fedn, 1968-72, Hon. Pres., 1972-76. Chm., UK Dairy Assoc., 1963-69. Director: Southern Television, 1969-81; The Rank Organisation Ltd, 1970-; Alfa-Laval Co. Ltd, 1977-; Beaumont UK, 1980-. Trustee, UK Farming Scholarship Trust, 1970. Governor: Monkton Combe School, 1957- British Nutrition Foundn, 1975-77. FRAgSs 1970. Hon. DSc Reading, 1976. Justus-von-Liebig Prize, Kiel Univ., 1968; Gold Medal, Soc. of Dairy Technology, 1969; Massey-Fergusson Award, 1971. Comdr du Mérite Agricole, 1964. *Address:* Hampreston Manor Farm, Wimborne, Dorset. *Clubs:* Farmers'; Royal Motor Yacht (Poole).

TREHERNE, John Edwin, ScD, PhD; Hon. Director of ARC Unit of Invertebrate Chemistry and Physiology, Department of Zoology, University of Cambridge, since 1969; University Reader in Invertebrate Physiology, since 1971; Fellow of Downing College, Cambridge, since 1966; *b* 15 May 1929; *s* of Arnold Edwin Wilson Treherne and Marion Grace Spiller; *m* 1955, June Vivienne Freeman; one *s* one *d*. *Educ:* Headlands Sch., Swindon, Wilts; Univ. of Bristol (BSc, PhD); Univ. of Cambridge (MA, ScD). Nat. Service, Lieut RAMC, 1953-55. Principal Sci. Officer, ARC Unit of Insect Physiology, Cambridge, 1955-67; Univ. Lectr in Zoology, Cambridge, 1968-71. Visiting

Prof., Univ. of Virginia, 1963-64. Vice-Pres., Royal Entomological Soc., 1967-68. Scientific Medal of Zoological Soc., 1968. Dir, Company of Biologists Ltd, 1969-74; Editor: Advances in Insect Physiology, 1964-; Jl of Experimental Biology, 1974-; Key Environments series, 1980-; Chm. of Editl Boards of Insect Biochemistry and Jl of Insect Physiology, 1977-. *Publications:* Neurochemistry of Arthropods, 1966; Insect Neurobiology, 1974; research papers in: Jl of Experimental Biology; Tissue and Cell; Nature; Animal Behaviour. *Recreations:* domestic; military and naval Staffordshire figures; postcards of Edwardian actresses; marine insects; writing. *Address:* The Manor House, Soham, Cambs CB7 5HA. *T:* Ely 720688.

TREITEL, Prof. Guenter Heinz, DCL; FBA 1977; Vinerian Professor of English Law, Oxford University, since 1979; Fellow of All Souls College, Oxford, since 1979; *b* 26 Oct. 1928; *s* of Theodor Treitel and Hanna Lilly Treitel (*née* Levy); *m* 1957, Phyllis Margaret Cook; two *s. Educ:* Kilburn Grammar School; Magdalen College, Oxford. BA 1949, BCL 1951, MA 1953, DCL 1976. Called to the Bar, Gray's Inn, 1952. Asst Lectr, LSE, 1951-53; Lectr, University Coll., Oxford, 1953-54; Fellow, Magdalen Coll., Oxford, 1954-79, Fellow Emeritus, 1979; All Souls Reader in English Law, Univ. of Oxford, 1964-79. Vis. Lectr, Univ. of Chicago, 1963-64; Visiting Professor: Chicago, 1968-69 and 1971-72; W Australia, 1976; Houston, 1977; Southern Methodist, 1978; Virginia, 1978-79; Santa Clara, 1981. *Publications:* The Law of Contract, 1962, 5th edn 1979; An Outline of the Law of Contract, 1975, 2nd edn 1979; International Encyclopedia of Comparative Law, Vol. VII Ch. 16, on Remedies for Breach of Contract, 1976; edited jointly: Chitty on Contracts, 23rd edn, 1968 to 25th edn, 1982; Benjamin's Sale of Goods, 1974, 2nd edn 1981; Dicey's Conflict of Laws, 7th edn, 1958; Dicey and Morris, Conflict of Laws, 8th edn, 1967. *Recreations:* music, reading. *Address:* All Souls College, Oxford OX1 4AL. *T:* Oxford 722251.

TRELAWNY, Sir John Barry Salusbury-, 13th Bt *cr* 1628; Joint Deputy Managing Director, Korn/Ferry International Inc., since 1981 (Director, since 1978); *b* 4 Sept. 1934; *s* of Sir John William Robin Maurice Salusbury-Trelawny, 12th Bt and of his 1st wife, Glenys Mary, *d* of John Cameron Kynoch; *S* father, 1956; *m* 1958, Carol Knox, *yr d* of late C. F. K. Watson, The Field, Saltwood, Kent; one *s* three *d. Educ:* HMS Worcester. Subseq. Sub-Lt RNVR (National Service). Dir, The Martin Walter Group Ltd, 1971-74; various directorships, 1974-. FInstM 1974. JP 1973-78. *Heir: s* John William Richard Salusbury-Trelawny, *b* 30 March 1960. *Address:* Beavers Hill, Saltwood, Kent. *T:* Hythe 66476. *Clubs:* Army and Navy, Buck's.

TRELFORD, Donald Gilchrist; Editor of The Observer, since 1975; Director, The Observer Ltd, since 1975; *b* 9 Nov. 1937; *s* of Thomas Trelford and Doris Trelford (*née* Gilchrist); *m* 1st, 1963, Janice Ingram; two *s* one *d* ; 2nd, 1978, Katherine Louise, *d* of Mr and Mrs John Mark, Guernsey, and *g d* of late John Mark and Louisa (*née* Hobson); one *d. Educ:* Bablake Sch., Coventry; Selwyn Coll., Cambridge; MA; University rugby and cricket. Pilot Officer, RAF, 1956-58. Reporter and Sub-Editor, Coventry Standard and Sheffield Telegraph, 1960-63; Editor, Nyasaland Times, 1963-66; Correspondent in Africa for The Observer, The Times, and BBC, 1963-66; Dep. News Editor, The Observer, 1966, Asst Man. Editor, 1968, Dep. Editor, 1969. Mem., British Executive Cttee, IPI, 1976-; Patron, Milton Keynes Civic Forum, 1977-; Mem., British Cttee, Journalists in Europe, 1980-; Mem. Council, Media Soc., 1981-. Frequent broadcasts, TV and radio. *Publications:* Siege, 1980; Sunday Best, 1981, 1982; County Champions, 1982. *Recreations:* golf, squash. *Address:* c/o The Observer, 8 St Andrew's Hill, EC4V 5JA. *T:* 01-236 0202. *Clubs:* Garrick, Royal Air Force, MCC.
See also J. Mark, Sir R. Mark.

TREMLETT, Rt. Rev. Anthony Paul; *b* 14 May 1914; *s* of late Laurence and Nyda Tremlett; unmarried. *Educ:* King's Sch., Bruton; King's Coll., Cambridge; Cuddesdon Theological Coll. Ordained, 1938; Curate of St Barnabas, Northolt Park, Middx. Chaplain to the Forces (Emergency Commission), 1941-46 (despatches). Domestic Chaplain to the Bishop of Trinidad, BWI, 1946-49; Chaplain of Trinity Hall, Cambridge, 1949-58; Vicar of St Stephen with St John, Westminster, 1958-64; Bishop Suffragan of Dover, 1964-80. *Address:* Doctors Commons, The Square, Northleach, Gloucestershire. *T:* Northleach 426.

TREMLETT, Maj.-Gen. Erroll Arthur Edwin, CB 1944; TD 1948; *b* 22 Dec. 1893; *s* of late Col E. J. Tremlett, RA, Bt Lt-Col (despatches), Medal and Clasp Zulu War 1879, Deputy Governor and OC Troops, St Helena, 1884; *m* Dorothy Mary, *d* of late H. W. Capper, 24 Suffolk St, Pall Mall; one *s* one *d.* Served in European War, 1914-19, with RA, (despatches) (awarded Regular Commn in the "Field," Sept. 1916) and in France and Belgium 1940 (despatches); Comdr 44 AA Brigade, Nov. 1940; Major-General, Commander 10 AA Division, Feb. 1942; Commander AA Defences of London, 1942-44; Comdr Flying Bomb Deployment, 1945. Commander 2 AA Group, 1945-46; RARO 1946. Hon. Colonel 656 Light AA Regt RA (RB), 1947-57. Mem., City of London RA Assoc., 1944; Chm., London Region RA Assoc., 1945-46; Pres., RA Assoc. for Co. Devon, 1957-67. Gold Staff Officer, Coronation of HM Queen Elizabeth II. *Address:* Bickham Cottage, Kenn, near Exeter, Devon. *T:* Kennford 832586. *Clubs:* Naval and Military, MCC.

TREMLETT, George William, OBE 1981; author and journalist; Member for Twickenham, Greater London Council, since 1973 (for Hillingdon, 1970-73); Consultant, National Association of Voluntary Hostels, since 1980

(Director, 1977-80); *b* 5 Sept. 1939; *s* of Wilfred George and Elizabeth Tremlett; *m* 1971, Jane, *o c* of late Benjamin James Mitchell and of Mrs P. A. Mitchell; two *s. Educ:* Taunton School; King Edward VI School, Stratford upon Avon. Member of Richmond upon Thames Borough Council, 1963-74; Chairman: Further Education Cttee, 1966-68; Barnes School Governors, 1967-73; Schools Cttee, 1972-73; Shene VIth Form Coll. Governors, 1973-74; Housing Cttee, 1972-74; Thames Water Authority, 1973-74. Greater London Council: Opposition Housing Spokesman, 1974-77; Leader of Housing Policy Cttee, 1977-81. Member: Housing Minister's Adv. Cttee on Co-operatives, 1977-79; Housing Consultative Council for England, 1977-81; Northampton Develt Corp., 1979-. Member: Stonham Housing Assoc., 1978-; Chiswick Family Rescue Appeal Fund, 1979-. Governor, Kingston Polytechnic and Twickenham Coll. of Technology, 1967-70; Court of City Univ., 1968-74. *Publications:* 17 biographies of rock musicians, 1974-77—on John Lennon, David Bowie, 10cc, Paul McCartney, The Osmonds, Alvin Stardust, Cat Stevens, Cliff Richard, Slade, The Who, David Essex, Slik, Gary Glitter, Marc Bolan, Rod Stewart, Queen and the Rolling Stones (published in many different countries); Living Cities, 1979. *Recreations:* ornithology, exploring old churches, local history, rock 'n' roll music. *Address:* 32 Fitzwilliam House, The Little Green, Richmond, Surrey. *Clubs:* Carlton, Wig and Pen.

TRENAMAN, Nancy Kathleen, (Mrs M. S. Trenaman); Principal of St Anne's College, Oxford, since 1966; *b* 1919; *d* of Frederick Broughton Fisher and Edith Fisher; *m* 1967, M. S. Trenaman. *Educ:* Bradford Girls' Grammar School; Somerville College, Oxford (Hon. Fellow, 1977). Board of Trade, 1941-51; Assistant Secretary, Ministry of Materials, 1951-54; Counsellor, British Embassy, Washington, 1951-53; Board of Trade, 1954-66, Under-Sec. 1962-66. Mem., Commn on the Constitution, 1969-73. *Address:* St Anne's College, Oxford; 4 Fairlawn End, Oxford OX2 8AR. *T:* Oxford 57723.

TRENCH, family name of **Baron Ashtown.**

TRENCH, see Le Poer Trench, family name of Earl of Clancarty.

TRENCH, Sir David (Clive Crosbie), GCMG 1969 (KCMG 1962; CMG 1960); MC 1944; DL; Vice-Chairman, Advisory Committee on Distinction Awards, Department of Health and Social Security, 1972-79; Chairman, Dorset Area Health Authority, 1973-82; *b* 2 June 1915; *s* of late William Launcelot Crosbie Trench, CIE, and Margaret Zephanie (*née* Huddleston); *m* 1944, Margaret Gould; one *d. Educ:* Tonbridge School; Jesus College, Cambridge (MA). Cadet, British Solomon Islands Protectorate, 1938; seconded to W Pacific High Commission, 1941. Served War of 1939-45 (MC, US Legion of Merit); British Solomon Islands Defence Force, 1942-46, Lt-Col. Secretary to the Government, British Solomon Islands Protectorate, 1947; attended Joint Services Staff Coll., 1949; Asst Sec., Deputy Defence Sec., Hong Kong, 1950; Deputy Financial Sec., 1956; Commissioner of Labour and Mines, 1957; attended Imperial Defence College, 1958; Deputy Colonial Secretary, Hong Kong, 1959; High Commissioner for The Western Pacific, 1961-63; Governor and C-in-C, Hong Kong, 1964-71. Mem., new Dorset CC, 1973-81. DL Dorset, 1977. Hon. LLD: Univ. of Hong Kong, 1968; Chinese Univ. of Hong Kong, 1968. Legion of Merit (US), 1944. *Recreation:* golf. *Address:* Church House, Church Road, Shillingstone, Blandford, Dorset DT11 0SL.

TRENCH, Sir Nigel (Clive Cosby), KCMG 1976 (CMG 1966); HM Diplomatic Service, retired; *b* 27 Oct. 1916; *s* of Clive Newcome Trench and Kathleen, 2nd *d* of Major Ivar MacIvor, CSI; *m* 1939, Marcelle Catherine Clotterbooke Patyn; one *s. Educ:* Eton; Univ. of Cambridge. Served in KRRC, 1940-46 (despatches). Appointed a Member of the Foreign (subseq. Diplomatic) Service, 1946; Lisbon, 1946; First Secretary, 1948; returned Foreign Office, 1949; First Secretary (Commercial) Lima, 1952; transf. Foreign Office, 1955; Counsellor, Tokyo, 1961; Counsellor, Washington, 1963; Cabinet Office, 1967; HM Ambassador to Korea, 1969-71; CS Selection Board, 1971-73; Ambassador to Portugal, 1974-76. Mem., Police and Prison Service Selection Bds, 1977-. *Address:* 4 Kensington Court Gardens, Kensington Court Place, W8 5QE. *Club:* Naval and Military.

TRENCH, Sir Peter (Edward), Kt 1979; CBE 1964 (OBE 1945); TD 1949; Chairman, Y. J. Lovell (Holdings) plc; *b* 16 June 1918; *s* of James Knights Trench and Grace Sim; *m* 1940, Mary St Clair Morford; one *s* one *d. Educ:* privately; London Sch. of Economics, London Univ.; St John's Coll., Cambridge Univ. BSc (Econ.) Hons. Served in The Queen's Royal Regt, 1939-46: Staff Coll., 1942; AAG, HQ 21 Army Gp, 1944-45 (OBE). Man. Dir, Bovis Ltd, 1954-59; Dir, Nat. Fedn of Bldg Trades Employers, 1959-64; Dir, Nat. Bldg Agency, 1964-66; Part-time Mem., Nat. Bd for Prices and Incomes, 1965-68; Chm., Building Centre, 1970-73. Director: Capital & Counties Property Co. plc; The LEP Group plc; Nationwide Building Society; Crendon Concrete Ltd; The Builder Ltd; Haden plc; Middle East Building Service Ltd. Vis. Prof. in Construction Management, Reading Univ., 1981-. Chm., Construction and Housing Res. Adv. Council, 1973-79; Pres., Construction Health Safety Gp, 1974-80; Mem., Review of Housing Finance Adv. Gp, 1975-76; Chm., Nat. House-Building Council, 1978-; Vice-Pres., Building Centre; Hon. Mem., Architectural Assoc.; Member: Council, CBI; Council, RSA; Court of Governors, LSE; Hon. Treasurer, St Mary's Hosp. Med. Sch. JP Inner London, 1963-71. FCIOB; FCIArb; FRSA; CBIM; Hon. FRIBA. *Recreations:* ski-ing, swimming, travelling. *Address:* 4 Napier Close, Napier Road, W14 8LG. *T:* 01-602 3936. *Club:* MCC.

TRENCHARD, family name of Viscount Trenchard.

TRENCHARD, 2nd Viscount, *cr* 1936, of Wolfeton; **Thomas Trenchard,** MC 1944; Baron, *cr* 1930; Bt, *cr* 1919; Minister of State, Ministry of Defence, since 1981; *b* 15 Dec. 1923; *o* surv. *s* of 1st Viscount Trenchard, GCB, OM, GCVO, DSO, first Marshal of the RAF, and of Katherine Viscountess Trenchard (*d* 1960); *S* father 1956; *m* 1948, Patricia, *d* of late Admiral Sir Sidney Bailey, KBE, CB, DSO and of Lady Bailey; three *s. Educ:* Eton. Served War of 1939-45, Captain, King's Royal Rifle Corps (MC). Director: T. Wall & Sons Ltd, 1953-66; Unilever Ltd and Unilever NV, 1967-77; Carpets International Ltd, 1977-79; Chm., Wall's Meat Co. Ltd, 1960-66. Chm., Sausage and Meat Pie Manufrs Assoc., 1959-73. Minister of State, DoI, 1979-81. President: RIPH&H, 1970-79; Inst. of Grocery Distribution, 1974-77; Bacon and Meat Manufrs Assoc., 1974-79. Mem., ARC, 1970-79. *Heir: s* Hon. Hugh Trenchard, Captain 4th Royal Green Jackets, TA [*b* 12 March 1951; *m* 1975, Fiona, *d* of Hon. James Morrison, *qv* ; one *s* one *d*]. *Address:* House of Lords, SW1. *Club:* Brooks's.

TREND, family name of Baron Trend.

TREND, Baron *cr* 1974 (Life Peer), of Greenwich; **Burke St John Trend,** PC 1972; GCB 1968 (KCB 1962; CB 1955); CVO 1953; Rector, Lincoln College, Oxford since 1973; Pro-Vice-Chancellor, Oxford University, since 1975; *b* 2 Jan. 1914; *o s* of late Walter St John Trend and Marion Tyers; *m* 1949, Patricia Charlotte, *o d* of Rev. Gilbert Shaw; two *s* one *d. Educ:* Whitgift; Merton College, Oxford (Postmaster). 1st Cl. Honour Mods, 1934; 1st Cl. Lit. Hum., 1936; Hon. Fellow, Merton College, 1964. Home Civil Service Administrative Class, 1936; Min. of Education, 1936; transferred to HM Treasury, 1937; Asst Private Sec. to Chancellor of Exchequer, 1939-41; Principal Private Sec. to Chancellor of Exchequer, 1945-49; Under Secretary, HM Treasury, 1949-55; Office of the Lord Privy Seal, 1955-56; Deputy Secretary of the Cabinet, 1956-59; Third Secretary, HM Treasury, 1959-60, Second Secretary, 1960-62; Secretary of the Cabinet, 1963-73. Chm. Trustees, British Museum, 1979- (Trustee, 1973-); Chm., Managing Trustees, Nuffield Foundn, 1980- (Trustee, 1973-); Mem., Adv. Council on Public Records, 1974-. Pres., Royal Commonwealth Soc., 1982-. Member: Governing Body, Westminster Sch.; Council, Cheltenham Coll. Hon. DCL Oxford, 1969; Hon. LLD St Andrews, 1974. *Address:* Lincoln College, Oxford. *Club:* Athenæum.

TRENDALL, Prof. Arthur Dale, AC 1976; CMG 1961; MA, LittD; FSA; FBA; FAHA; Resident Fellow, Menzies College, La Trobe University; Emeritus Professor, University of Sydney, 1954; *b* Auckland, NZ, 28 March 1909; *s* of late Arthur D. Trendall and late Iza W. Uttley-Todd; unmarried. *Educ:* King's College, Auckland; Univs of Otago (MA 1929, LittD 1936) and Cambridge (MA 1937, LittD 1968). NZ Post-Graduate Scholar in Arts, 1931; Rome Scholar in Archæology, 1934-35; Fellow of Trinity Coll., Cambridge, 1936-40; Librarian British School at Rome, 1936-38; FSA 1939; Professor of Greek, Univ. of Sydney, 1939-54; Dean, Faculty of Arts, 1947-50; Chairman Professorial Board, 1949-50, 1952; Acting Vice-Chancellor, 1953; Master of Univ. House, ANU, 1954-69, retd; Hon. Fellow, 1969. Hon. Curator, Greek and Roman Section, Nicholson Museum, 1954, and Hon. Consultant, National Gallery of Victoria, 1957; Deputy Vice-Chancellor, ANU, 1958-64; Mem. Royal Commn on Univ. of Tas., 1955. Geddes-Harrower Professor of Greek Art and Archæology, Aberdeen Univ., 1966-67. Chm. Aust. Humanities Research Council, 1957-59. Mem., Nat. Capital Planning Cttee, 1958-67; Mem. Australian Universities Commission, 1959-70. Member: Accademia dei Lincei, Rome, 1971; Athens Acad., 1973; Corresp. Mem., Pontifical Acad. of Archaeology, Rome, 1973; Life Mem., Nat. Gall. of Victoria, 1976; For. Mem., Royal Netherlands Acad., 1977. Hon. Fellow, Athens Archaeological Soc., 1975; Hon. Mem., Hellenic Soc., 1982. FBA 1968. Hon. LittD: Melbourne, 1956; ANU 1970; Hon. DLitt: Adelaide, 1960; Sydney, 1972; Tasmania, 1979; Hon. Dott. in Lettere Lecce, 1981. For. Galileo Galilei Prize for Archaeology, 1971; Cassano Gold Medal for Magna Graecia Studies, 1971; Britannica Award (Australia), 1973. KCSG, 1956; Commendatore, Ordine al Merito, Republic of Italy, 1965 (Cav. Uff. 1961). *Publications:* Paestan Pottery, 1936; Frühitaliotische Vasen, 1938; Guide to the Cast Collection of the Nicholson Museum, Sydney, 1941; The Shellal Mosaic, 1942, 4th edn 1973; Handbook to the Nicholson Museum (editor), 2nd edn 1948; Paestan Pottery, Supplement, 1952; Vasi Italioti del Vaticano, vol. i, 1953; vol. ii, 1955; The Felton Greek Vases, 1958; Phlyax Vases, 1959, 2nd edn 1967; Paestan Addenda, 1960; Apulian Vase Painters of the Plain Style (with A. Cambitoglou), 1962; South Italian Vase Painting (British Museum Guide), 1966, 2nd edn 1976; The Red-figured Vases of Lucania, Campania and Sicily, 1967, Supplement I, 1970, Supplement II, 1973; Greek Vases in the Felton Collection, 1968, 2nd edn 1978; Greek Vases in the Logie Collection, Christchurch, NZ, 1971; Illustrations of Greek Drama (with T. B. L. Webster), 1971; Early South Italian Vase-painting, 1974; Eine Gruppe Apulischer Grabvasen in Basel (with M. Schmidt and A. Cambitoglou), 1976; Vasi antichi dipinti del Vaticano—Collezione Astarita: (iii) Vasi italioti, 1976; (with A. Cambitoglou) The Red-figured Vases of Apulia, 2 vols, 1978, 1982; several articles in learned periodicals. *Recreations:* travel, walking. *Address:* Menzies College, La Trobe University, Bundoora, Vic 3083, Australia.

TRENT, Group Captain Leonard Henry, VC 1946; DFC 1940; *b* 14 April 1915; *s* of Leonard Noel Trent, Nelson, New Zealand; British; *m* 1940, Ursula Elizabeth Woolhouse; one *s* two *d. Educ:* Nelson Coll., NZ. Entered firm of W. & R. Fletcher (New Zealand) Ltd 1935; joined RNZAF, 1937; joined RAF 1938. Arrived in England, 1938; served War, 1939-43, France and England (POW 1943); transferred to RNZAF, 1944; transferred back to RAF, 1947, Permanent Commission. Formerly: OC 214 Valiant Sqdn, RAF Marham; Trg HQ No. 3 Gp, Mildenhall, 1948-59; Comdg RAF Wittering, 1959-62; Asst Air Attaché, Washington, also SASO and Chief Intell. Officer (RAF), 1962-65. ADC to the Queen, 1962-65. *Recreations:* golf, carpentry, gardening, painting, oils and watercolours. *Address:* c/o Post Office, Leigh, Auckland, New Zealand.

TRENTHAM, Prof. David Rostron, FRS 1982; Edwin M. Chance Professor, Department of Biochemistry and Biophysics, University of Pennsylvania School of Medicine, Philadelphia, USA, since 1977; *b* 22 Sept. 1938; *s* of John Austin and Julia Agnes Mary Trentham; *m* 1966, Kamalini; two *s. Educ:* Univ. of Cambridge (BA Chemistry, PhD Organic Chemistry). Biochemistry Dept, University of Bristol: Jun. Research Fellow (Medical Research Council), 1966-69; Research Associate, 1969-72; Lectr in Biochemistry, 1972-75; Reader in Biochemistry, 1975-77. Colworth Medal (an annual award), Biochemical Soc., UK, 1974. *Publications:* numerous research papers in scientific jls. *Address:* Department of Biochemistry and Biophysics, 302 Anatomy-Chemistry Building/G3, University of Pennsylvania School of Medicine, Philadelphia, Pennsylvania, USA. *T:* (215) 898-4639.

TRESCOWTHICK, Sir Donald (Henry), KBE 1979; Chairman: Charles Davis Ltd and subsidiaries, since 1971; Investment & Merchant Finance Corporation Ltd and subsidiaries, since 1976; Perpetual Insurance and Securities (Aust.) Ltd, since 1979; HSD Property Trust, since 1979; Swann Insurance Ltd and subsidiaries, since 1959; Signet Group Pty Ltd, since 1968; *b* 4 Dec. 1930; *s* of Thomas Patrick Trescowthick; *m* 1952, Norma Margaret Callaghan; two *s* two *d.* FASA. Member, Lloyd's of London. Director: DOXA Youth Welfare Foundn; Minus Children's Fund; Aust. Ballet Develt Fund Appeal; Melbourne to Hobart Yacht Race Cttee; Tasmanian Fiesta; Chm., Sir Donald and Lady Trescowthick Foundn. *Recreations:* tennis, swimming, reading. *Address:* 22-32 William Street, Melbourne, Vic. 3000, Australia. *T:* (03) 614 1233; 38A Lansell Road, Toorak, Vic. 3142, Australia. *T:* (03) 241 5099. *Clubs:* Athenæum, Victoria Racing, Victorian Amateur Turf, Royal Brighton Yacht (Melbourne); Tasmanian Racing (Hobart); Geelong Football.

TRESIDDER, Gerald Charles, FRCS; Lecturer, Department of Anatomy, University of Leicester; *b* Rawalpindi, 5 Dec. 1912; *s* of late Lt-Col A. G. Tresidder, CIE, MD, MS, FRCS; *m* 1940, Marguerite Bell; one *s* two *d. Educ:* Haileybury College; University of London, Queen Mary College and The London Hospital Medical College. LRCP, MRCS 1937; MB, BS London 1938; FRCS 1946. Surgical Specialist, Major, Indian Medical Service, 1940-46. Surgeon, 1951-64, Urologist, 1964-76, at The London Hospital; Lectr in Surgery and part-time Sen. Lectr in Anatomy, The London Hosp. Med. Sch., 1951-76; Senior Lectr, Human Morphology, Univ. of Southampton, 1976-80. FRSM (Past Pres., Section of Urology); Senior Mem., British Assoc. of Urological Surgeons; Sen. Fellow, British Assoc. of Clinical Anatomists; Examr in Anatomy for Primary FRCSEng and Ed. *Publications:* contributions to: Rob and Smith's Operative Surgery; British Jl of Surgery; British Jl of Urology; Lancet; BMJ. *Recreations:* walking and talking. *Address:* Woodspring, 3 Penny Long Lane, Derby DE3 1AW. *T:* Derby 558026.

TRESS, Ronald Charles, CBE 1968; BSc (Econ.) London, DSc Bristol; Director, The Leverhulme Trust, since 1977; *b* Upchurch, Sittingbourne, Kent, 11 Jan. 1915; *er s* of S. C. Tress; *m* 1942, Josephine Kelly, *d* of H. J. Medland; one *s* two *d. Educ:* Gillingham (Kent) County School; Univ. College, Southampton. Gladstone Student, St Deiniol's Library, Hawarden, 1936-37; Drummond Fraser Research Fellow, Univ. of Manchester, 1937-38; Asst Lecturer in Economics, Univ. Coll. of the S West, Exeter, 1938-41; Economic Asst, War Cabinet Offices, 1941-45; Economic Adviser, Cabinet Secretariat, 1945-47; Reader in Public Finance, Univ. of London, 1947-51; Prof. of Political Economy, Univ. of Bristol, 1951-68; Master of Birkbeck Coll., 1968-77, Fellow, 1977-; Mem., Univ. of London Senate, 1968-77, and Court, 1976-77. Managing Editor, London and Cambridge Economic Service, 1949-51; Member: Reorganisation Commn for Pigs and Bacon, 1955-56; Nigeria Fiscal Commn, 1957-58; Departmental Cttee on Rating of Charities, 1958; Financial Enquiry, Aden Colony, 1959; East Africa Economic and Fiscal Commn, 1960, Uganda Fiscal Commn, 1962; Kenya Fiscal Commn (Chm.), 1962-63; National Incomes Commn, 1963-65; Develt Commn, 1959-81; Chm., SW Economic Planning Council, 1965-68; Mem., Cttee of Inquiry into Teachers' Pay, 1974; Chm., Cttee for Univ. Assistance to Adult Educn in HM Forces, 1974-79; Chm., Army Educn Adv. Bd, 1979; Lay Mem., Solicitors' Disciplinary Tribunal, 1975-79; Chm., Lord Chancellor's Adv. Cttee on Legal Aid, 1979-. Trustee, City Parochial Foundn, 1974-77, 1979-. Governor: LSE, 1975-; Christ Church Coll., Canterbury, 1975-; Courtauld Inst. of Art, 1976-79, 1981-; British Inst. in Paris, 1977-; Mem. Council, Kent Univ., 1977-. Royal Economic Society: Council, 1960-70, Sec.-Gen., 1975-79, Vice-Pres., 1979-. Hon. LLD: Furman Univ., S Carolina, 1973; Exeter, 1974; DUniv. Open Univ., 1974; Hon. DSc (SocSc) Southampton, 1978. *Publications:* articles and reviews in Economic Journal, Economica, LCES Bulletin, etc. *Address:* The Leverhulme Trust, 15-19 New Fetter Lane, EC4A 1NR. *T:* 01-822 6938; 22 The Beach, Walmer, Deal, Kent CT14 7HJ. *T:* Deal 3254; 12 Stonehills Court, College Road, Dulwich, SE21 7LZ. *T:* 01-693 6938. *Club:* Athenæum.

TRETHOWAN, Sir (James) Ian (Raley), Kt 1980; Chairman, Horserace Betting Levy Board, since 1982; Director, Barclays Bank (UK), since 1982; Consultant, Thorn EMI; an Independent Director, Times Newspapers Holdings Ltd, since 1982; *b* 20 Oct. 1922; *s* of late Major J. J. R. Trethowan, MBE and Mrs R. Trethowan; *m* 1st, 1951, Patricia Nelson (marr. diss.); 2nd, 1963, Carolyn Reynolds; three *d. Educ:* Christ's Hospital. Entered Journalism, 1939. Fleet Air Arm, 1941-46. Political Corresp., Yorkshire Post, 1947-55; News Chronicle, 1955-57; Dep. Editor/Political Editor, Independent Television News, 1958-63; joined BBC, 1963, as Commentator on Politics and Current Affairs; Man. Dir, Radio, BBC, 1969-75; Man. Dir, Television, BBC, 1976-77; Dir-Gen. of the BBC, 1977-82. Political Commentator: The Economist, 1953-58, 1965-67; The Times, 1967-68. Member: Cttee on Official Secrets Act, 1971; Board, British Council, 1980-. Chm., BM Soc., 1982-; Trustee, Glyndebourne Arts Trust, 1982-. Hon. DCL East Anglia, 1979. *Recreations:* racing, opera, sailing. *Address:* Horserace Betting Levy Board, 17/23 Southampton Row, WC1B 5HH. *T:* 01-405 5346. *Clubs:* Travellers', Beefsteak, MCC.

TRETHOWAN, Prof. Sir William (Henry), Kt 1980; CBE 1975; FRCP, FRACP, FRCPsych; Professor of Psychiatry, University of Birmingham, 1962-82; Hon. Consultant Psychiatrist: Queen Elizabeth Hospital, Birmingham, 1962-82; Hollymoor Hospital, 1964-82; Midland Centre for Neurosurgery, 1975-82; *b* 3 June 1917; *s* of William Henry Trethowan and Joan Durham Trethowan (*née* Hickson); *m* 1941, Pamela (*née* Waters); one *s* two *d. Educ:* Oundle Sch.; Clare Coll., Cambridge; Guy's Hosp. Med. Sch. MA, MB, BChir (Cantab) 1943; MRCP 1948; FRACP 1961; FRCP 1963; FRCPsych 1971. Served War, RAMC: Major, Med. Specialist, 1944-47. Psychiatric Registrar, Maudsley Hosp., 1948-50; Psychiatric Resident, Mass Gen. Hosp., and Hon. Teaching Fellow, Harvard, 1951; Lectr and Sen. Lectr in Psychiatry, Univ. of Manchester, 1951-56; Prof. of Psychiatry, Univ. of Sydney, and Hon. Consultant Psychiatrist, Royal Prince Alfred and Royal North Shore Hosps, Sydney, 1956-62. Mem. GMC, 1969-81 (Treasurer, 1978-81); Cons. Adviser in Psychiatry, DHSS, 1964-78; Dean, Univ. of Birmingham Med. Sch., 1968-74; Chm., Standing Mental Health Adv. Cttee, 1968-74; Mem., UGC Med. Subcttee, 1974-81. Member: Birmingham Reg. Hosp. Bd, 1964-74; Standing Med. Adv. Cttee, 1966-82 (Chm., 1976); Central Health Services Council, 1966-80 (Vice-Chm., 1976-80); W Midlands Regional Health Authority, 1974-76. Chm., Med. Acad. Adv. Cttee, Chinese Univ. of Hong Kong, 1976-. FRSocMed; Hon. Fellow, Royal Aust. and NZ Coll. of Psychiatry (FRANZCP 1962); Corresp. Fellow, Amer. Psychiatric Assoc. Hon. DSc Chinese Univ. of Hong Kong, 1979. *Publications:* Psychiatry, 4th edn 1979; (with M. D. Enoch) Uncommon Psychiatric Syndromes, 2nd edn 1979; numerous scientific and other articles in various jls; book reviews, etc. *Recreation:* music. *Address:* 99 Bristol Road, Edgbaston, Birmingham B5 7TX. *T:* 021-440 3485.

TREVASKIS, Sir (Gerald) Kennedy (Nicholas), KCMG 1963 (CMG 1959); OBE 1948; *b* 1 Jan. 1915; *s* of late Rev. Hugh Kennedy Trevaskis; *m* 1945, Sheila James Harrington, *d* of Col F. T. Harrington; two *s* one *d. Educ:* Summer Fields; Marlborough; King's College, Cambridge. Entered Colonial Service, 1938, as Administrative Cadet, N Rhodesia. Enlisted N Rhodesia Regt 1939; captured by Italian Forces Tug Aqan, Br. Somaliland, 1940 and POW until 1941. Seconded British Military Administration, Eritrea, 1941-48 (Lt-Col) and British Administration, 1948-50; Senior Divisional Officer, Assab, 1943; Serae, 1944; Western Province, 1946; Political Secretary, 1950. Member British delegation four Power Commission ex-Italian Colonies, 1947-48 and Liaison Officer, United Nations Commission, Eritrea, 1950. N Rhodesia, 1950-51; District Commissioner, Ndola. Political Officer, Western Aden Protectorate, 1951; Deputy British Agent, 1952, Adviser and British Agent, 1954; High Commissioner for Aden and the Protectorate of South Arabia, 1963-65 (Deputy High Commissioner, Jan.-Aug. 1963). Member British Delegation, Anglo-Yemeni meeting in London, 1957. *Publications:* A Colony in transition: the British occupation of Eritrea, 1941-52, 1960; Shades of Amber: A South Arabian Episode, 1968. *Recreations:* travel, writing. *Address:* 9th Floor, Berkeley Square House, Berkeley Square, W1. *Clubs:* Carlton, MCC, RAC.

TREVELYAN, family name of **Baron Trevelyan.**

TREVELYAN, Baron *cr* 1968 (Life Peer); **Humphrey Trevelyan,** KG 1974; GCMG 1965 (KCMG 1955; CMG 1951); CIE 1947; OBE 1941; *b* 27 Nov. 1905; 2nd *s* of late Rev. George Philip Trevelyan; *m* 1937, Violet Margaret, *d* of late Gen. Sir William H. Bartholomew, GCB, CMG, DSO; two *d. Educ:* Lancing; Jesus College, Cambridge Univ. (Hon. Fellow, 1968). Entered Indian Civil Service, 1929; Indian Political Service, 1932-47. Served as Political Agent in the Indian States; Washington, 1944; Joint Sec. to Govt of India in External Affairs Dept, 1946; retired from Indian Political Service and entered Foreign (later Diplomatic) Service, 1947; Counsellor in Baghdad, 1948; Economic and Financial Adviser, UK High Commission for Germany, 1951-53; HM Chargé d'Affaires in Peking, 1953-55; Ambassador to Egypt, 1955-56; Under-Sec. at UN, 1958; Ambassador to Iraq, 1958-61; Deputy Under-Secretary of State, Foreign Office, 1962; Ambassador to the USSR, 1962-65, retd. High Commissioner in South Arabia, 1967. Director: British Petroleum Company Ltd, 1965-75; British Bank of the Middle East, 1965-77; General Electric Co. Ltd, 1967-76; President, Council of Foreign Bondholders. Chm. of Trustees, British Museum, 1970-79; Chm., RIIA, 1970-77. Hon. LLD, Cambridge, 1970; Hon. DCL Durham, 1973; Hon. DLitt Leeds, 1975. *Publications:* The Middle East in Revolution, 1970; Worlds

Apart, 1971; The India We Left, 1972; Diplomatic Channels, 1973; Public and Private, 1980. *Address:* 24 Duchess of Bedford House, W8 7QN. *T:* 01-937 3125. *Club:* Beefsteak.

TREVELYAN, Dennis John, CB 1981; Deputy Under-Secretary of State, Home Office, and Director-General, Prison Service, since 1978; *b* 21 July 1929; *s* of John Henry Trevelyan; *m* 1959, Carol Coombes; one *s* one *d. Educ:* Enfield Grammar Sch.; University Coll., Oxford. Entered Home Office, 1950; Treasury, 1953-54; Sec. to Parly Under-Sec. of State, Home Office, 1954-55; Principal Private Sec. to Lord President of Council and Leader of House, 1964-67; Asst Sec., 1966; Asst Under-Sec. of State, NI Office, 1972-76; Asst Under-Sec. of State, Broadcasting Dept, Home Office, 1976-77. Sec., Lord Radcliffe's Cttee of Privy Counsellors to inquire into D Notice Matters, 1967. *Recreations:* sailing, music. *Address:* c/o Home Office, 50 Queen Anne's Gate, SW1H 9AT. *Clubs:* Athenæum; MCC.

TREVELYAN, Sir George (Lowthian), 4th Bt, *cr* 1874; retired; Founder and Director, Wrekin Trust, since 1971; *b* 5 Nov. 1906; *e s* of Rt Hon. Sir C. P. Trevelyan, 3rd Bt; *d* of late John Lindsay-Smith; one adopted *d. Educ:* Sidcot School; Trinity College, Cambridge. Worked as artist-craftsman with Peter Waals workshops, fine furniture, 1930-31. Trained and worked in F. M. Alexander re-education method, 1932-36. Taught at Gordonstoun School and Abinger Hill School, 1936-41. Served War, 1941-45, Home Guard Training (Captain). Taught No 1 Army Coll., Newbattle Abbey, 1945-47. Warden, Shropshire Adult College, Attingham Park, Shrewsbury, 1947-71. *Publications:* A Vision of the Aquarian Age, 1977; The Active Eye in Architecture, 1977; Magic Casements, 1980; Operation Redemption, 1981. *Heir: b* Geoffrey Washington Trevelyan [*b* 4 July 1920; *m* 1947, Gillian Isabel, *d* of late Alexander Wood; one *s* one *d*]. *Address:* The Grove, Taynton, Glos GL19 3AN. *T:* Tibberton 559.

TREVELYAN, Julian Otto; painter and etcher; *b* 20 Feb. 1910; *s* of late R. C. Trevelyan; *m* 1934, Ursula Darwin (divorced, 1950); one *s*; *m* 1951, Mary Fedden. *Educ:* Bedales; Trinity College, Cambridge. Studied art in Paris, Atelier 17, 1930-33; has since lived and worked in Hammersmith. One man exhibns at Lefevre Gall., 1935, 1938, 1942, 1943, 1944, 1946, 1948 and at Gimpel Fils, 1950, Redfern Gall., 1952, Zwemmer Gall., 1955, 1958, 1960, 1963, 1966, 1967, Galerie de France, Paris, 1947, St George's Gall., 1959; Alex Postan Gall., 1974, New Grafton Gall., 1977, Tate Gall., 1977; Holsworthy Gall., 1981. Pictures in public and private collections in England, America, Sweden, France, Eire and the USSR. Served War of 1939-45, as Camouflage Officer in Roy. Engineers, 1940-43. Engraving tutor at the Royal College of Art, 1955-63. *Publications:* Indigo Days, 1957; The Artist and His World, 1960; Etching (Studio Books), 1963; A Place, a State, 1975. *Recreation:* listening to music. *Address:* Durham Wharf, Hammersmith Terrace, W6. *T:* 01-748 2749.

TREVELYAN, Mary, CBE 1968 (OBE 1956); ARCM, ARCO; Founder and Governor, International Students' House, London; *e d* of late Rev. G. P. Trevelyan. *Educ:* Grovely College, Boscombe; Royal College of Music, London (Exhibitioner and George Carter Scholar). Musical posts included: organist and choirtrainer, St Barnabas, Oxford, music staff of Radley College and Marlborough College; conductor Chelsea Madrigal Society and Kensington Choral Society. Travelled from Ceylon to Kashmir, 1930-31; Warden of Student Movement House (international house for University students) London, 1932-46. Travelled to Far East, 1936-37, to study problems concerning migration of students from east to west for study and the effects on their return home; also visited USA to study work of the International Houses. Served on Programme Staff of YMCA with BLA in Belgium and France, Oct. 1944-June 1945; Head of Field Survey Bureau, Reconstruction Section, Paris, and made surveys on post-war priority needs in educn in Greece, the East and Far East, 1946-48; first Adviser to Overseas Students, Univ. of London, 1949-65; British Council Lecture Tour in W and E Africa, 1954; first Dir, Internat. Students House, London, 1965-67. Survey Tours on Ford Foundn award, to univs and internat. centres in USA, Canada, Australia, NZ, the East, Far East and Middle East, 1967-69. *Publications:* From the Ends of the Earth, 1942; I'll Walk Beside You, 1946. *Recreation:* music.

TREVELYAN, Sir Norman Irving, 10th Bt *cr* 1662; *b* 29 Jan. 1915; *s* of Edward Walter Trevelyan (*d* 1947), and of Kathleen E. H., *d* of William Irving; *S* kinsman, Sir Willoughby John Trevelyan, 9th Bt, 1976; *m* 1951, Jennifer Mary, *d* of Arthur E. Riddett, Burgh Heath, Surrey; two *s* one *d. Educ:* The Cate School, Carpinteria, California (grad. 1932); Harvard Univ., Cambridge, Mass (grad. 1936). *Heir: s* Edward Norman Trevelyan, *b* 14 Aug. 1955. *Address:* 1041 Adella Avenue, Coronado, California 92118, USA. [But his name does not at the time of going to press, appear on the Roll of the Baronetage.]

TREVELYAN OMAN, Julia; see Oman.

TREVETHIN, 4th Baron AND OAKSEY, 2nd Baron; see under Oaksey, 2nd Baron.

TREVOR, 4th Baron *cr* 1880; **Charles Edwin Hill-Trevor,** JP; *b* 13 Aug. 1928; *e s* of 3rd Baron and Phyllis May, 2nd *d* of J. A. Sims, Ings House, Kirton-in-Lindsey, Lincolnshire; *S* father, 1950; *m* 1967, Susan Janet Elizabeth, *o d* of Dr Ronald Bence; two *s. Educ:* Shrewsbury. Mem. Council, and Chm., Finance Cttee, Royal Forestry Soc. JP Clwyd (formerly Denbighshire) 1959;

Chm., Berwyn PSD. CStJ. *Recreations:* shooting, fishing. *Heir: s* Hon. Marke Charles Hill-Trevor, *b* 8 Jan. 1970. *Address:* Brynkinalt, Chirk, Wrexham, Clwyd. *T:* Chirk 3425; Auch, Bridge of Orchy, Argyllshire. *T:* Tyndrum 282. *Clubs:* East India, Flyfishers'.

TREVOR, David; Hon. Consulting Orthopædic Surgeon: Charing Cross Hospital; St Bartholomew's Hospital; Hon. Consulting Surgeon Royal National Orthopædic Hospital; *b* 24 July 1906; *m* 1935, Kathleen Fairfax Blyth; two *d. Educ:* Tregaron County School; St Bartholomew's Hospital Medical College; Charing Cross Hospital (Post Graduate). MRCS, LRCP 1931; MB, BS London 1931; FRCS 1932; MS London, University Medal, 1934. Past Mem., Internat. Soc. Orthop. and Traumatology, 1951. Past Pres., Orthopædic Section, RSocMed; late Examr in Surgery, Univ. of London; late Mem. Council, RCS (Hunterian Prof., 1968; late Mem. Court of Examrs); Past Vice-Pres., British Orthopædic Assoc. Robert Jones Lectr, RCS, 1971. *Publications:* contributor to BMJ, Journal of Bone and Joint Surgery, Proc. RSM, Annals RCS. *Recreations:* golf, gardening. *Address:* Tetherdown, 18 Kimpton Road, Blackmore End, Wheathampstead, Herts. *T:* Kimpton 832417.

TREVOR, Elleston; author; *b* Bromley, Kent, 17 Feb. 1920; *m* 1947, Iris May Burgess (known as Jonquil); one *s. Educ:* Sevenoaks. Apprenticed as a racing driver upon leaving school, 1938. Served in Royal Air Force, War of 1939-45. Began writing professionally in 1945. Member: Writers' Guild of GB; Authors' Guild of America. Amer. Mystery Writers' award, 1965; French Grand Prix de Littérature Policière, 1965. *Plays:* Touch of Purple, Globe, London, 1972; Just Before Dawn, Murder by All Means, 1972. *Publications:* Chorus of Echoes, 1950 (filmed); Tiger Street, 1951; Redfern's Miracle, 1951; A Blaze of Roses, 1952; The Passion and the Pity, 1953; The Big Pick-up, 1955 (filmed); Squadron Airborne, 1955; The Killing-Ground, 1956; Gale Force, 1956 (filmed); The Pillars of Midnight, 1957 (filmed); The VIP, 1959 (filmed); The Billboard Madonna, 1961; Flight of the Phœnix, 1964 (filmed); The Shoot, 1966; The Freebooters, 1967 (filmed); A Place for the Wicked, 1968; Bury Him Among Kings, 1970; The Theta Syndrome, 1977; Blue Jay Summer, 1977. Under pseudonym Warwick Scott: Image in the Dust, 1951; The Domesday Story, 1951; Naked Canvas, 1952. Under pseudonym Simon Rattray: Knight Sinister, Queen in Danger, Bishop in Check, Dead Silence, Dead Circuit (all 1951-53). Under pseudonym Adam Hall: Volcanoes of San Domingo, 1964; The Berlin Memorandum, 1964 (filmed as The Quiller Memorandum); The 9th Directive, 1966; The Striker Portfolio, 1969; The Warsaw Document, 1971; The Tango Briefing, 1973; The Mandarin Cypher, 1975; The Kobra Manifesto, 1976; The Sinkiang Executive, 1978; The Scorpion Signal, 1979; The Pekin Target, 1981. Under pseudonym Caesar Smith: Heatwave, 1957 (filmed). Under pseudonym Roger Fitzalan: A Blaze of Arms, 1967. Under pseudonym Howard North: Expressway, 1973; The Paragon (Night Stop, USA), 1974; The Sibling, 1979; The Damocles Sword, 1981; The Penthouse, 1982. *Recreations:* chess, reading, travelling, astronomy. *Address:* 16122 Ocotillo Drive, Fountain Hills, Arizona 85268, USA. *T:* (602)837-1484.

TREVOR, Brig. Kenneth Rowland Swetenham, CBE 1964 (OBE 1952); DSO 1945; Brigadier (retired 1966); *b* 15 April 1914; 2nd *s* of late Mr and Mrs E. S. R. Trevor, formerly of The Acres, Upton Heath, Chester; *m* 1941, Margaret Baynham, *er d* of late Reverend J. H. Baynham, ACG; two *s. Educ:* Rossall; RMC, Camberley. Joined 22nd (Cheshire) Regt, 1934; served in India and with RWAFF in Nigeria. War of 1939-45 (despatches and DSO): No. 1 Commando, N Africa and Burma, 1941-45, as CO, 1943-45; Staff College, Camberley, 1945-46; Bde Major, 29 Infantry Brigade Group, 1949-51; served Korea, 1950-51 (despatches, OBE); GSO1 and Chief Instructor, RMA, Sandhurst, 1954-56; Commanded 1st Bn Cheshire Regt, 1956-58; Malaya, 1957-58 (despatches); Deputy Commander, 50 Infantry Brigade Group/Central Area, Cyprus, 1959; Brigade Col Mercian Brigade, 1960-61; Commander, 2 Infantry Brigade Group and Devon/Cornwall Sub District, 1961-64; Commander, British Guiana Garrison, 1963; Inspector of Boys' Training (Army), 1964-66. With Runcorn Develt Corp., 1966-78. Vice-Pres., The Commando Assoc. *Recreation:* golf. *Address:* Barrelwell Hill, Chester. *Club:* Army and Navy.

TREVOR, Meriol; Author; *b* 15 April 1919; *d* of Lt-Col Arthur Prescott Trevor and Lucy M. E. Trevor (*née* Dimmock). *Educ:* Perse Girls' Sch., Cambridge; St Hugh's Coll., Oxford. FRSL. *Publications:* novels: The Last of Britain, 1956; The New People, 1957; A Narrow Place, 1958; Shadows and Images, 1960; The City and the World, 1970; The Holy Images, 1971; The Fugitives, 1973; The Two Kingdoms, 1973; The Marked Man, 1974; The Enemy at Home, 1974; The Forgotten Country, 1975; The Fortunate Marriage, 1976; The Treacherous Paths, 1976; The Civil Prisoners, 1977; The Fortunes of Peace, 1978; The Wanton Fires, 1979; *poems:* Midsummer, Midwinter, 1957; *biography:* Newman: The Pillar of the Cloud, 1962; Newman: Light in Winter, 1962 (James Tait Black Meml Prize); Apostle of Rome, 1966; Pope John, 1967; Prophets and Guardians, 1969; The Arnolds, 1973; also books for children. *Address:* 70 Pulteney Street, Bath, Avon BA2 4DL.

TREVOR, William, (William Trevor Cox), CBE (Hon.) 1977; writer; *b* 24 May 1928; *er s* of J. W. Cox; *m* 1952, Jane, *yr d* of C. N. Ryan; two *s. Educ:* St Columba's College, Co. Dublin; Trinity College, Dublin. Mem., Irish Acad. Letters. Television plays include: The Mark-2 Wife; O Fat White Woman; The Grass Widows; The General's Day; Love Affair; Last Wishes;

Matilda's England; Secret Orchards; Autumn Sunshine. Allied Irish Banks Award for Literature, 1976. *Publications:* A Standard of Behaviour, 1956; The Old Boys, 1964 (Hawthornden Prize; as play, produced Mermaid, 1971); The Boarding-House, 1965; The Love Department, 1966; The Day We Got Drunk on Cake, 1967; Mrs Eckdorf in O'Neill's Hotel, 1969; Miss Gomez and the Brethren, 1971; The Ballroom of Romance, 1972; Going Home (play), 1972; A Night with Mrs da Tanka (play), 1972; Marriages (play), 1973; Elizabeth Alone, 1973; Angels at the Ritz, 1975 (RSL award); The Children of Dynmouth, 1976 (Whitbread Award); Lovers of Their Time, 1978; Other People's Worlds, 1980; Beyond the Pale, 1981; Scenes from an Album (play), 1981. *Address:* Shobrooke Mill, near Crediton, Devon.

TREVOR COX, Major Horace Brimson, *o s* of late C. Horace Cox, Roche Old Court, Winterslow, Wilts and formerly of Whitby Hall, nr Chester; *m* 1957, Gwenda Mary, *d* of Alfred Ellis, Woodford, Essex; one *d. Educ:* Eton; Germany and USA. Major late Welsh Guards (SR); served in France with BEF, 1939-40, and on General Staff, 1940-44; Major AA Comd. HQ, 1944-46, RARO, 1946-61. Studied commercial and political conditions in Germany, 1927-29, in America and Canada, 1929-30, and in Near East (Egypt and Palestine), 1934; contested (C) NE Derbyshire, 1935, Stalybridge and Hyde, 1937; MP (C) County of Chester, Stalybridge and Hyde, 1937-45; Parliamentary Private Secretary to: Rt Hon. Sir Ronald Cross when Under-Secretary Board of Trade, 1938-39, and when Minister of Economic Warfare, 1939-40; Minister of Health Rt Hon. H. U. Willink, 1945. Hon. Treasr, Russian Relief Assoc., 1944-47. Contested (C) Stalybridge and Hyde, 1945, Birkenhead, 1950; Parly Candidate (C) for Romford and Brentwood, Essex, 1953-55; contested (Ind) Salisbury by-election, 1965; later joined Labour Party; contested (Lab): RDC, Wilts, 1970; Wilts CC, 1973. Mem. Fabian Soc. Member of Exec. County Committee, British Legion, Wilts, 1946-62; Chm., Salisbury and S Wilts Branch, English-Speaking Union, 1957-63; Mem. Exec. Cttee, CLA, for Wilts, Hants, IoW and Berks. Farmer and landowner. Lord of Manor of East Winterslow. *Address:* Roche Old Court, Winterslow, Wilts. *Club:* Brooks's.

TREVOR-ROPER, family name of **Baron Dacre of Glanton.**

TREVOR-ROPER, Patrick Dacre, MA, MD, BChir Cantab; FRCS, DOMS England; FZS; FRGS; Consultant Ophthalmic Surgeon: Westminster Hospital, since 1947; Moorfields Eye Hospital; King Edward VII Hospital for Officers; Teacher of Ophthalmology, University of London; *b* 1916; *yr s* of Dr B. W. E. Trevor-Roper, Alnwick, Northumberland; unmarried. *Educ:* Charterhouse (senior classical schol.); Clare Coll., Cambridge (exhibitioner); Westminster Hospital Medical Sch. (scholar). Served as Captain, NZ Medical Corps, 1943-46, in Central Mediterranean Forces. Held resident appointments, Westminster Hospital and Moorfields Eye Hospital. Formerly Examiner for diploma of Ophthalmology, RCS. Vice-Pres., Ophthalmol Soc. of UK; Member: Ophth. Group Cttee, BMA; Ophth. Services Cttee, London Exec. Council; London Med. Cttee; Chm., Ophth. Qualifications Cttee, 1974-; Founder Mem., Internat. Acad. of Ophthalmology, 1976; FRSocMed (Pres., Ophthalmol Sect., June 1978-80). Hon. Member: Brazilian Society of Ophthalmology, 1958; Ophthalmological Soc. of NZ, 1975; Hon. dipl., Peruvian and Columbian Societies of Otolaryngology and Ophthalmology, 1958; President, etc., of various clubs in connection with sports, music and drama, both hospital and county. Freeman, City of London; Liveryman, Soc. of Spectaclemakers. Doyne medal, 1980; (first) de Lancey medal, RSocMed. *Publications:* (ed) Music at Court (four 18th century studies by A. Yorke-Long), 1954; Ophthalmology, a Textbook for Diploma Students, 1955, new edn 1962; Lecture-notes in Ophthalmology, 1959, 6th rev. edn 1980 (trans. French, Spanish, Portuguese, Malay); (ed) International Ophthalmology Clinics VIII, 1962; The World Through Blunted Sight: an inquiry into the effects of disordered vision on character and art, 1971, new edn 1972; The Eye and Its Disorders, 1973, new edn 1983; (ed) Recent Advances in Ophthalmology, 1975; (ed) The Bowman Lectures, 1980; (ed) Procs 6th Congress of European Ophth. Soc., 1980; Ophthalmology (pocket consultant series), 1981; miscellaneous articles in medical and other journals; Editor, Trans Ophthalmological Society UK, 1949-; Mem. Editorial Board, Modern Medicine, Annals of Ophth., The Broadway. *Recreations:* music, travel. *Address:* 3 Park Square West, Regent's Park, NW1. *T:* 01-935 5052; Long Crichel House, near Wimborne, Dorset. *Clubs:* Athenæum, Beefsteak.

See also Baron Dacre of Glanton.

TREW, Francis Sidney Edward; HM Diplomatic Service; High Commissioner at Belmopan, Belize, since 1981; *b* 22 Feb. 1931; *s* of Harry Francis and Alice Mary Trew; *m* 1958, Marlene Laurette Regnery; three *d. Educ:* Taunton's Sch., Southampton. Served Army, 1949-51; 2nd Lieut, Royal Hampshire Regt. FO, 1951; Lebanon, 1952; Amman, 1953; Bahrain, 1953-54; Jedda, 1954-56; Vice-Consul, Philadelphia, 1956-59; Second Sec., Kuwait, 1959-62; FO, 1962; seconded as Sec., European Conf. on Satellite Communications, 1963-65; Consul, Guatemala City, 1965-70; First Sec., Mexico City, 1971-74; FCO, 1974-77; Consul, Algeciras, 1977-79; FCO, 1980-81. Order of Aztec Eagle (Mexico), 1975. *Recreations:* carpentry, fishing. *Address:* c/o Lloyds Bank Ltd, 6 Pall Mall, SW1.

TREW, Peter John Edward, FCIS, MICE; Director, Rush & Tompkins Group plc, since 1973; *b* 30 April 1932; *s* of Antony Trew, DSC; *m* 1955, Angela, *d* of Kenneth Rush, CBE; two *s* one *d. Educ:* Diocesan Coll., Rondebosch, Cape. Royal Navy, 1950-54; served HMS Devonshire, Unicorn and Charity. Awarded Chartered Inst. of Secretaries Sir Ernest Clarke Prize,

1955. Contested (C) Dartford, 1966; MP (C) Dartford, 1970–Feb. 1974; Jt Sec., Cons. Parly Finance Cttee, 1972–74; Mem., Select Cttee on Tax Credits, 1972–73. Chm., Kent West Cons. European Constituency Council, 1978–80. Mem. Council, CBI, 1975– (Mem., Econ. and Fin. Policy Cttee, 1980–). Foundn Fellow, Assoc. of Corporate Treasurers, 1979. *Address:* Great Oaks, Shipbourne, Kent. *T:* Plaxtol 810739. *Club:* Naval and Military.

TREWBY, Vice-Adm. Sir (George Francis) Allan, KCB 1974; consultant; Director, Fairey Technology Ltd, *b* Simonstown, S Africa, 8 July 1917; *s* of late Vice-Admiral G. Trewby, CMG, DSO, and of Dorothea Trewby (*née* Allan); *m* 1942, Sandra Coleridge Stedham; two *s. Educ:* RNC, Dartmouth; RNEC, Keyham; RNC, Greenwich. Naval Cadet, Dartmouth, 1931 (King's Dirk, 1934). Served in HMS: Frobisher, Barham, Nelson, Duke of York, Dido, Cadiz, Albion. Comdg Officer, HMS Sultan, 1963–64; IDC, 1965; Captain of Naval Base, Portland, 1966–68; Asst Controller (Polaris), MoD, 1968–71; Chief of Fleet Support and Member of Board of Admiralty, 1971–74. Commander, 1950; Captain, 1959; Rear-Adm., 1968; Vice-Adm., 1971. Naval ADC to HM the Queen, 1968. FEng 1978; FIMechE; FIMarE; CBIM. Akroyd Stuart Award of InstMarE for 1954–55. *Publications:* papers on naval marine engineering, in UK, USA, Sweden and Italy. *Recreations:* swimming; Past Captain Navy Athletics Team. *Address:* 2 Radnor Close, Henley-on-Thames RG9 2DA. *T:* Henley 77260. *Clubs:* MCC, Ebury Court; Phyllis Court (Henley).

TREWIN, John Courtenay, OBE 1981; FRSL; dramatic critic and author; *b* 4 Dec. 1908; *o s* of Captain John Trewin, The Lizard, Cornwall, and Annie (*née* James); *m* 1938, Wendy Monk; two *s. Educ:* Plymouth Coll. Editorial Staff: Western Independent, 1926–32; The Morning Post, London, 1932–37; second dramatic critic, 1934–37. Contributor to The Observer, 1937–; editorial staff, 1942–53; Literary Editor, 1943–48; second dramatic critic, 1943–53. Dramatic critic: Punch, 1944–45; John o' London's, 1945–54; The Illustrated London News, 1946–; The Sketch, 1947–59; The Lady, 1949–; The Birmingham Post, 1955–; Radio-drama critic of The Listener, 1951–57; Editor: The West Country Magazine, 1946–52; Plays of the Year series (50 vols), 1948–; The Year's Work in the Theatre (for the British Council), 1949–51. President, The Critics' Circle, 1964–65; Chairman, W Country Writers' Assoc., 1964–73. Hon. MA Birmingham, 1978. Devised (with David Toguri) Farjeon Reviewed, Mermaid Theatre, 1975. *Publications:* Shakespeare Memorial Theatre, 1932; The English Theatre, 1948; Up From The Lizard, 1948; We'll Hear a Play, 1949; (with H. J. Willmott) London-Bodmin, 1950; Stratford-upon-Avon, 1950; The Theatre Since 1900, 1951; The Story of Bath, 1951; Drama 1945-50, 1951; Down To The Lion, 1952; (with E. M. King) Printer to the House, 1952; A Play To-night, 1952; (with T. C. Kemp) The Stratford Festival, 1953; Dramatists of Today, 1953; Edith Evans, 1954; (ed) Theatre Programme, 1954; Mr Macready, 1955; Sybil Thorndike, 1955; Verse Drama Since 1800, 1956; Paul Scofield, 1956; The Night Has Been Unruly, 1957; Alec Clunes, 1958; The Gay Twenties: A Decade of the Theatre, 1958; Benson and the Bensonians, 1960; The Turbulent Thirties, 1960; A Sword for A Prince, 1960; John Neville, 1961; The Birmingham Repertory Theatre, 1963; Shakespeare on the English Stage, 1900-1964, 1964; completion of Lamb's Tales, 1964; Drama in Britain, 1951-64, 1965; (with H. F. Rubinstein) The Drama Bedside Book, 1966; (ed) Macready's Journals, 1967; Robert Donat, 1968; The Pomping Folk, 1968; Shakespeare Country, 1970; (with Arthur Colby Sprague) Shakespeare's Plays Today, 1970; Peter Brook, 1971; (ed) Sean: memoirs of Mrs Eileen O'Casey, 1971; I Call My Name (verse pamphlet), 1971; Portrait of Plymouth, 1973; Long Ago (verse pamphlet), 1973; Theatre Bedside Book, 1974; Tutor to the Tsarevich, 1975; (ed) Eileen, 1976; The Edwardian Theatre, 1976; Going to Shakespeare, 1978; (ed and revd) Nicoll, British Drama, 1978; The West Country Book, 1981; Companion to Shakespeare, 1981; (ed with Lord Miles) Curtain Calls, 1981; ed several other books. *Recreation:* all things Cornish: a Bard of the Cornish Gorsedd (Den an Lesard). *Address:* 15 Eldon Grove, Hampstead, NW3. *T:* 01-435 0207. *Club:* Garrick.

TRIAS, Dr Juan Manuel S.; *see* Sucre-Trias.

TRIBE, Geoffrey Reuben, OBE 1968; Controller, Higher Education Division, British Council, since 1981; *b* 20 Feb. 1924; *s* of late Harry and Olive Tribe; *m* 1st, 1946, Sheila Mackenzie (marr. diss. 1977); 2nd, 1978, Malvina Anne Butt. *Educ:* Southern Grammar Sch., Portsmouth; University Coll. London (BA). Served War, Royal Hampshire Regt (Lieut), 1942-45. Teaching, 1948-58. Appointed to British Council, 1958; Asst Regional Rep., Madras, 1958-63; Regional Dir, Mwanza, 1963-65; Regional Rep., E Nigeria, 1965-67; Asst Controller, Personnel and Staff Recruitment, 1968-73; Controller, Arts Div., 1973-79; Representative, Nigeria, 1979-81. *Recreation:* sailing. *Address:* The British Council, 10 Spring Gardens, SW1A 2BN. *T:* 01-930 8466.

TRIBE, Rear-Admiral Raymond Haydn, CB 1964; MBE 1944; DL; *b* 9 April 1908; *s* of Thomas and Gillian Ada Tribe; *m* 1938, Alice Mary (*née* Golby); no *c.* Served War of 1939-45 (MBE, despatches twice). Commander, 1947; Captain, 1955; Rear-Admiral, 1962. Inspector-General, Fleet Maintenance, and Chief Staff Officer (Technical) to C-in-C Home Fleet, 1962-65; retired from Royal Navy, Sept. 1965. Distinguished Battle Service Medal of Soviet Union, 1943. CC Berks, 1970-77. DL Berks, 1975. *Recreations:* gardening, painting. *Address:* Oak Cottage, Compton, near Newbury, Berks. *T:* Compton, Berks, 253.

TRICKER, Robert Ian, FCA; FCMA; Director, Corporate Policy Group, Oxford, since 1979; Research Fellow, Nuffield College, Oxford, since 1979 (Visiting Fellow, 1971-79); *b* 14 Dec. 1933; *s* of Ralph Edward Tricker, Coventry; *m* 1958, Doreen Murray; two *d. Educ:* King Henry VIII Sch., Coventry; Harvard Business Sch., USA. MA, JDipMA. Articled Clerk, Daffern & Co., 1950-55; Sub-Lt, RNVR, 1956-58; Controller, Unbrako Ltd, 1959-64; Directing Staff, Iron & Steel Fedn Management Coll., 1965; Barclays Bank Prof. of Management Information Systems, Univ. of Warwick, 1968-70. Director, Oxford Centre for Management Studies, 1970-79, Professorial Fellow, 1979- (P. D. Leake Res. Fellow, 1966-67). Institute of Chartered Accountants in England and Wales: Mem. Council, 1979-; Mem. Educn and Trng Directorate, 1979-82; Chairman: Examination Cttee, 1980-82; Tech. and Res. Cttee, 1982-. Member: Council, ICMA, 1969-72; Management and Industrial Relations Cttee, SSRC, 1973-75; Chm., Independent Inquiry into Prescription Pricing Authority for Minister for Health, 1976. Member: Nuffield Hosp. Management Cttee, 1972-74; Adv. Panel on Company Law, Dept of Trade, 1980-; Company Affairs Cttee, Inst. of Directors, 1980-. *Publications:* The Accountant in Management, 1967; Strategy for Accounting Research, 1975; Management Information and Control Systems, 1976, 2nd edn 1982; The Independent Director, 1978; Effective Information Management, 1982. *Address:* Nuffield College, Oxford. *T:* Oxford 48014. *Club:* Naval.

TRICKETT, (Mabel) Rachel; Principal, St Hugh's College, Oxford, since Aug. 1973; *b* 20 Dec. 1923. *Educ:* Lady Margaret Hall, Oxford, 1942-45. BA Hons 1st Cl. in English; MA 1947; Hon. Fellow, 1978. Asst to Curator, Manchester City Art Galleries, 1945-46; Asst Lectr in English, Univ. of Hull, 1946-49; Commonwealth Fund Fellow, Yale Univ., 1949-50; Lectr in English, Hull Univ., 1950-54; Fellow and Tutor in English, St Hugh's Coll., Oxford, 1954-73. *Publications:* The Honest Muse (a study in Augustan verse), 1967; *novels:* The Return Home, 1952; The Course of Love, 1954; Point of Honour, 1958; A Changing Place, 1962; The Elders, 1966; A Visit to Timon, 1970. *Address:* St Hugh's College, Oxford. *T:* Oxford 57341.

TRICKEY, Edward Lorden, FRCS; Dean, Institute of Orthopaedics, London University, since 1981; Consultant Orthopaedic Surgeon, Royal National Orthopaedic Hospital, London, and Edgware General Hospital, since 1960; *b* 22 July 1920; *s* of E. G. W. Trickey and M. C. Trickey; *m* 1944, Ivy Doreen Harold; two *s* one *d. Educ:* Dulwich College; King's College, London Univ. (MB BS). Consultant Orthopaedic Surgeon, Ashton under Lyne, 1957-60. *Publications:* various articles on orthopaedic trauma and knee joint surgery. *Recreations:* cricket, bridge. *Address:* 5 Hive Road, Bushey Heath, Herts. *T:* 01-950 3137. *Clubs:* MCC, Middlesex CC.

TRIER, Peter Eugene, CBE 1980; MA; FEng, FIEE, FInstP, FIMA; Consultant; Director, Philips Industries UK (Director of Research and Development, 1969-81); *b* 12 Sept. 1919; *s* of Ernst and Nellie Trier; *m* 1946, Margaret Nora Holloway; three *s. Educ:* Mill Hill Sch.; Trinity Hall, Cambridge (Wrangler 1941). Royal Naval Scientific Service, 1941-50; Mullard Research Labs, 1950-69, Dir, 1953-69. Dir, Mullard Ltd and other Philips operating cos, 1957-. Chm., Defence Scientific Adv. Council, 1981-; Specialist Advr, House of Lords Select Cttee on Sci and Technol., 1982-; Member: Electronics Res. Council, MoD, 1963-80 (Chm., 1976-80); Electronics and Avionics Requirements Bd, DoI, 1979-; Parly and Scientific Cttee, 1978-; Design Council, 1981-. IEE: Vice-Pres., 1974-77; Faraday Lectr, 1968-69; Chm., Electronics Div. Bd, 1971-72; IMA: Pres., 1980-82 (Vice-Pres., 1980-81). FEng 1978 (Member: Exec. Cttee, 1980-82; Council, 1982-); Member: Electronic Engrg Assoc. (Pres. 1980-81); Management Cttee, Royal Instn, 1978-81; Adv. Cttee, RCDS, 1980-. Pro-Chancellor, Brunel Univ., 1980- (Chm., Council, 1973-78). Mem. Editorial Bds, Interdisciplinary Science Reviews, 1975-; International Jl of Electronics, 1979-. Mem., Management Cttee, Wine Soc., 1977-. Liveryman, Co. of Scientific Instrument Makers, 1967-. Hon. DTech Brunel, 1975. *Publications:* papers in scientific and technical jls. *Recreations:* travel, sailing, railway history. *Address:* Yew Tree House, Bredon, Tewkesbury, Glos. *T:* Bredon 72200. *Club:* Savile.

TRILLO, Rt. Rev. Albert John; *see* Chelmsford, Bishop of.

TRIMBLE, Brigadier (retired) Arthur Philip, CBE 1961; Deputy Surgeon, The Royal Hospital, Chelsea, 1964-76; Consultant Physician, Army Medical Services; *b* 21 Aug. 1909; *s* of Melville and Florence Trimble, Holywood, Co. Down, N Ireland; *m* 1952, Felicia, *d* of W. H. Friend, Bures, Suffolk; two *s. Educ:* St Columba's Coll., Co. Dublin; Queen's Univ., Belfast. MB 1931; MD; FRCPE. Joined RAMC, 1931. Served in Syrian, Western Desert, and Italian Campaigns, 1939-45; SMO 2nd Armoured Brigade. Consultant Physician: FarELF, 1953-56; BAOR, 1957-62; Near ELF, 1963. *Publications:* various articles on tropical diseases and diseases of children in Proc. Royal Society Med., Trans Royal Society of Tropical Med., Archives of Disease in Childhood and Journal of RAMC. *Recreation:* golf. *Address:* Sherbourne Cottage, Edwardstone, Suffolk.

TRIMLESTOWN, 19th Baron *cr* 1461; **Charles Aloysius Barnewall;** *b* 2 June 1899; *o* surv. *s* of 18th Baron and Margaret (*d* 1901), *d* of R. J. Stephens, Brisbane, Queensland; *S* father, 1937; *m* 1st, 1926, Muriel (*d* 1937), *o c* of Edward Oskar Schneider, Mansfield Lodge, Whalley Range, Manchester; two *s* one *d;* 2nd, 1952, Freda Kathleen Watkins, *d* of late Alfred Watkins, Ross-on-Wye. *Educ:* Ampleforth. Lieut, Irish Guards, 1918; served European

War. *Heir: s* Hon. Anthony Edward Barnewall [*b* 2 Feb. 1928; *m* 1977, Mary W., *er d* of late Judge Thomas F. McAllister]. *Address:* Tigley, Dartington, Totnes, Devon.

TRINDER, Sir (Arnold) Charles, GBE 1969; Kt 1966; *b* 12 May 1906; *s* of Arnold Anderson Trinder, Oxshott; *m* 1st, 1929, Elizabeth Cairns; one *d*; 2nd, 1937, Elaine Chaytor; two *d. Educ:* Wellington Coll.; Clare Coll., Cambridge (MA (Hons)). Entered Trinder Anderson & Co., 1927; Sen. Partner, 1940-53; Chm., 1953-72; Consultant, 1972-76. Member, Baltic Exchange, 1928, Hon. Member, 1973. Common Councilman, 1951; Alderman of Aldgate, 1959-76; Sheriff, City of London, 1964; Lord Mayor of London for 1968-69. Chm., London Broadcasting Co. Ltd, 1972-74. Chairman: Family Welfare Assoc., 1967-73; Missions to Seamen (London Reg.), 1972-76. Chm., City of London Archaeol Trust, 1978-79. Chancellor, City University, 1968-69; Trustee, Morden Coll., Blackheath, 1972. Prime Warden, Worshipful Company of Shipwrights, 1973; Master, Worshipful Company of Fletchers, 1966. FICS 1963. Hon. DSc, City Univ., 1968. KStJ 1969. Order of Merit, Chile, 1965; Nat. Order of Niger, 1969; Order of Merit, Italy, 1969; Order of Lion of Finland, 1969. *Publication:* O Men of Athens, 1946. *Recreations:* gardening, astronomy, ancient history, logodaedaly. *Address:* Hoo End Farm, Whitwell, Herts. *Clubs:* Royal Automobile, City Livery, Guildhall.

TRINDER, Air Vice-Marshal Frank Noel, CB 1949; CBE 1944; psa; *b* 24 Dec. 1895; *s* of Alfred Probus Trinder, MRCS, LRCP, Parkstone, Dorset; *m* 1925, Marjorie Agnes Scott, *d* of Archie Scott Blake, Melrose, Scotland; one *s. Educ:* Epsom College. Served European War, 1914-18, with North Staffordshire Regt, 1915-17; France, 1915 (wounded); Lieut, 1916; transferred to RFC, 1917. Egypt, 1917-20; Iraq, 1920; Air Ministry, 1921-28; Staff College, 1929; Headquarters, India, 1930-35; Wing Commander, 1937; War of 1939-45 (despatches, CBE); Group Captain, 1940; Headquarters, Far East, 1938-40; USA, 1940-43; Air Commodore, 1943; Cossac Staff, 1943-44; SHAEF, 1944-45; Air Div. CCG, 1945-46; Senior Air Staff Officer, Headquarters Maintenance Command, 1947-49; Director-General of Equipment, Air Ministry, 1949-52; retired, 1952. *Address:* Broom Lodge, Teddington, Mddx. *Club:* Royal Air Force Yacht.

TRINDER, Thomas Edward, (Tommy Trinder), CBE 1975; comedian; Chairman, Fulham Football Club Ltd, 1955-76, Life President, since 1976; *b* 24 March 1909; *s* of Thomas Henry Trinder and Jean Mills. *Educ:* St Andrew's, Holborn. First London appearance, Collins's Music-hall, 1922; continued in variety, pantomimes and revues, including Band Waggon, Top of the World, Gangway, Best Bib and Tucker, Happy and Glorious, Here, There and Everywhere, Fancy Free; tours in Canada, NZ, South Africa, USA; numerous Royal Variety and Command performances; radio and TV shows. Films include: The Foreman Went to France; The Bells Go Down; Champagne Charlie. *Recreation:* Fulham Football Club.

TRING, A. Stephen; *see* Meynell, L. W.

TRIPP, Rt. Rev. Howard George; an Auxiliary Bishop in Southwark, (RC), since 1980; Titular Bishop of Newport, since 1980; *b* 3 July 1927; *s* of Basil Howard Tripp and Alice Emily Tripp (*née* Haslett). *Educ:* John Fisher School, Purley; St John's Seminary, Wonersh. Priest, 1953; Assistant Priest: Blackheath SE3, 1953-56; East Sheen, 1956-62; Asst Diocesan Financial Sec., 1962-68; Parish Priest, East Sheen, 1965-71; Director, Southwark Catholic Children's Soc., 1971-80. *Recreation:* vegetable gardening. *Address:* 8 Arterberry Road, SW20 8AJ. *T:* 01-946 4609.

TRIPP, (John) Peter, CMG 1971; Political Adviser, Inchcape Group, since 1981; Chairman, Private Investment Co. for Asia (UK), since 1981; *b* 27 March 1921; *s* of Charles Howard and Constance Tripp; *m* 1948, Rosemary Rees Jones; one *s* one *d. Educ:* Bedford Sch.; Sutton Valence Sch.; L'Institut de Touraine. Served War of 1939-45: Royal Marines, 1941-46. Sudan Political Service, 1946-54. Foreign (subsequently Diplomatic) Service, 1954-81; Political Agent, Trucial States, 1955-58; Head of Chancery, Vienna, 1958-61; Economic Secretary, Residency Bahrain, 1961-63; Counsellor 1963; Political Agent, Bahrain, 1963-65; sabbatical year at Durham Univ., 1965; Amman, 1966-68; Head of Near Eastern Dept, FCO, 1969-70; Ambassador to Libya, 1970-74; High Comr in Singapore, 1974-78; Ambassador to Thailand, 1978-81. *Recreations:* theatre, gardening. *Address:* 30 Ormonde Gate, SW3. *Club:* Travellers'.

TRIPPIER, David Austin; JP; MP (C) Rossendale, since 1979; *b* 15 May 1946; *s* of Austin Wilkinson Trippier and late Mary Trippier; *m* 1975, Ruth Worthington, Barrister; one *s. Educ:* Bury Grammar School. Commnd Officer, Royal Marines Reserve, 1968. Member of Stock Exchange, 1968-. Mem., Rochdale Council, 1969-78, Leader Cons. Gp, 1974-76. Secretary: All Party Parly Footwear Cttee, 1979-; Cons. Parly Defence Cttee, 1980-; PPS to Minister for Health, 1982-. Nat. Vice Chm., Assoc. of Cons. Clubs, 1980. JP Rochdale, 1975. *Publication:* Defending the Peace, 1982. *Recreation:* gardening. *Address:* Bethany Farm, Newhey, Rochdale OL16 3TB. *T:* Shaw 842361. *Club:* Army and Navy.

TRISTRAM, William John, CBE 1965; JP; Pharmaceutical Chemist; Liverpool City Council, 1934-55 (Alderman, 1944-55); appointed Hon. Alderman, 1964; *b* 6 Oct. 1896; *s* of late Rev. W. J. Tristram and Elizabeth Critchlow; *m* 1966, Philomena Mary Moylan, Drogheda. *Educ:* Scarborough High Sch.; Leeds Central High Sch.; Liverpool College of Pharmacy. Member

Council Pharmaceutical Society of Great Britain, 1944-67 (President, 1952-53, FPS, 1966, Gold Medal, 1968); Hon. Treasurer and Member Executive National Pharmaceutical Union, 1936-68 (Chairman, 1943-44); Chairman, Joint Cttee for the Pharmaceutical Service, 1946-52; Member Central Health Services Council (Min. of Health), 1948-64. Vice-Chairman, Standing Pharmaceutical Advisory Cttee (Min. of Health), 1946-48 (Chairman, 1948-59); Chairman, Liverpool Licensing Cttee, 1965-70; Dep. Chairman, South Liverpool Hospitals Management Cttee, 1965-70; Liverpool Exec. Council (Min. of Health), 1948- (Chairman, 1960-64); Chairman, Liverpool Homœopathic Hospital, 1960-70. JP, Liverpool, 1938-; Lord Mayor of Liverpool, 1953-54; Dep. Lord Mayor, 1954-55. *Recreations:* cricket-watching, walking. *Address:* Childwall, 6 Westway, Heswall, Wirral, Merseyside L60 8PL. *T:* 051-342 1678. *Clubs:* National Liberal; Lyceum (Liverpool).

TRITTON, Alan George; Director: Barclays Bank Ltd, since 1974; Mercantile Credit Co. Ltd, since 1973; Equitable Life Assurance Society, since 1976; *b* 2 Oct. 1931; *s* of George Henton Tritton, Lyons Hall, Essex, and Iris Mary Baillie, Lochloy; *m* 1st, 1958, Elizabeth Clare d'Abreu (marr. diss.); two *s* one *d*; 2nd, 1972, Diana Marion Spencer. *Educ:* Eton. Member of British Schools Exploring Soc. Expedn, N Norway, 1949. Served with 1st Batt. Seaforth Highlanders, Malaya, 1950-52 (wounded in action, Pahang). Falkland Islands Dependencies Survey, 1952-54; entered Barclays Bank Ltd, 1954; local Dir, 54 Lombard Street, 1966; Dir, Barclays Bank UK Management Ltd, 1972. Member: Cttee, British Trans-Arctic Expedn, 1966-69; Cttee, British Everest SW Face Expedn, 1974-75; Council, Royal Geographical Soc., 1975-79; Cttee of Management, Mount Everest Foundn, 1976-; Friends' Cttee, Scott Polar Research Inst., 1976-. Commissioner, Public Works Loan Bd, 1970-74; Member: Governing Body, British Nat. Cttee, Internat. Chamber of Commerce, 1975-; Council, Essex Agricl Soc., 1973-76; Treasurer, Assoc. of Agriculture, 1979-. *Recreations:* travelling, shooting. *Address:* 54 Lombard Street, EC3. *T:* 01-626 1567. *Clubs:* Boodle's, Pratt's, Antarctic, Geographical, Essex.

TRITTON, Major Sir Anthony (John Ernest), 4th Bt *cr* 1905; *b* 4 March 1927; *s* of Sir Geoffrey Ernest Tritton, 3rd Bt, CBE, and Mary Patience Winifred (*d* 1960), *d* of John Kenneth Foster; *S* father, 1976; *m* 1957, Diana, *d* of Rear-Adm. St J. A. Micklethwait, CB, DSO, and of Clemence Penelope Olga Welby-Everard; one *s* one *d. Educ:* Eton. Commissioned 3rd Hussars, Oct. 1945; retired as Major, 1962, The Queen's Own Hussars. *Recreations:* shooting, fishing. *Heir: s* Jeremy Ernest Tritton, *b* 6 Oct. 1961. *Address:* Stanton House, Highworth, Wilts. *T:* Highworth 762923. *Club:* Cavalry and Guards.

TROLLOPE, Sir Anthony Owen Clavering, 16th Bt, *cr* 1642; *b* 15 Jan. 1917; *s* of Sir Gordon Clavering Trollope, 15th Bt; *S* father, 1958; *m* 1942, Joan Mary Alexis, *d* of Alexis Robert Gibbs, Manly, New South Wales; two *s*. Served War of 1939-45: 2nd/5th Australian Field Regt, Royal Australian Artillery, Middle East and New Guinea. Director, Thomas C. Denton and Co. Pty Ltd. JP for State of NSW. *Heir: s* Anthony Simon Trollope, *b* 1945. *Address:* Clavering, 77 Roseville Avenue, Roseville, NSW 2069, Australia.

TROTMAN-DICKENSON, Dr Aubrey Fiennes; Principal, University of Wales Institute of Science and Technology, Cardiff, since 1968; *b* 12 Feb. 1926; *s* of Edward Newton Trotman-Dickenson and Violet Murray Nicoll; *m* 1953, Danusia Irena Hewell; two *s* one *d. Educ:* Winchester Coll.; Balliol Coll., Oxford. MA Oxon, BSc Oxon; PhD Manchester; DSc Edinburgh. Fellow, National Research Council, Ottawa, 1948-50; Asst Lecturer, ICI Fellow, Manchester Univ., 1950-53; E. I. du Pont de Nemours, Wilmington, USA, 1953-54; Lecturer, Edinburgh Univ., 1954-60; Professor, University College of Wales, Aberystwyth, 1960-68; Vice-Chancellor, Univ. of Wales, 1975-77. Chm., Job Creation Programme, Wales, 1975-78. Member: Welsh Council, 1971-79; Planning and Transport Res. Adv. Council, DoE, 1975-79. Tilden Lectr, Chem. Soc., 1963. *Publications:* Gas Kinetics, 1955; Free Radicals, 1959; Tables of Bimolecular Gas Reactions, 1967; (ed) Comprehensive Inorganic Chemistry, 1973; contrib. to learned journals. *Address:* Radyr Chain, Llantrisant Road, Cardiff CF5 2PW. *T:* Cardiff 563263.

TROTT, Charles Edmund, MBE 1946; FIB, FCIS; Vice-Chairman, Banque Belge, 1974-81; Director: Belgian and General Investments Ltd, 1974-81; Midland Bank Ltd, 1971-81; *b* 3 Dec. 1911; *s* of late Charles Edmund and Florence Katherine Trott; *m* 1938, Edith Maria Willson; two *d. Educ:* County Sch., Tottenham. BCom(London). Served War, RAF, 1941-46. Entered Midland Bank, 1929; Jt Gen. Manager, 1960; Asst Chief Gen. Manager, 1967; Dep. Chief Gen. Manager, 1969; Chief Gen. Manager, 1972-74. Hon. Treas., British Drama League, 1950-58; Governor, Ashridge Management Coll., 1965-74; Member: Nat. Savings Cttee, 1968-74; Council, CBI, 1975-79. *Recreations:* theatre, music, walking. *Address:* 61 Fairacres, Roehampton Lane, SW15 5LY. *T:* 01-876 1791. *Clubs:* Roehampton, Royal Air Force.

TROTTER, Neville Guthrie, FCA; JP; MP (C) Tynemouth, since Feb. 1974; *b* 27 Jan. 1932; *s* of Captain Alexander Trotter and Elizabeth Winifred Trotter (*née* Guthrie). *Educ:* Shrewsbury; King's Coll., Durham (BCom). Short service commn in RAF, 1955-58. Partner, Thornton Baker & Co., Chartered Accountants, 1962-74, now Consultant. Mem., Newcastle City Council, 1963-74 (Alderman, 1970-74; Chm., Finance Cttee, Traffic Highways and

Transport Cttee, Theatre Cttee). Mem., CAA Airline Users Cttee, 1973-79. Mem., Tyne and Wear Metropolitan Council, 1973-74; Vice-Chm., Northumberland Police Authority, 1970-74. Chm., Cons. Parly Shipping and Shipbuilding Cttee, 1979- (Vice-Chm., 1976-79); Sec., Cons. Parly Industry Cttee, 1981; Mil. Sec., Cons. Parly Aviation Cttee, 1976-79; Mem., Industry Sub-Cttee, Select Cttee on Expenditure, 1976-79. Private Member's Bills: Consumer Safety, 1978; Licensing Amendment, 1980. Former Mem.: Northern Economic Planning Council; Tyne Improvement Commn; Tyneside Passenger Transport Authority; Industrial Relations Tribunal. Member: Council, RUSI; US Naval Inst. JP Newcastle upon Tyne, 1973. *Recreation:* travel to outlandish places. *Address:* (office) Higham House, Higham Place, Newcastle upon Tyne NE1 6LB. *T:* 612631. *Clubs:* Carlton, Royal Air Force; Tynemouth and Whitley Bay Conservative.

TROUBRIDGE, Sir Peter, 6th Bt, *cr* 1799; RN retired; *b* 6 June 1927; *s* of late Vice-Admiral Sir T. H. Troubridge, KCB, DSO, and Lily Emily Kleinwort; *S* cousin, 1963; *m* 1954, Hon. Venetia Daphne Weeks; *one s two d. Educ:* Eton; Cambridge. Served Korean War, 1952-53, HMS Ocean; retired from RN (Lt-Comdr), 1967. Chm., Standing Council of the Baronetage, 1981- (Vice-Chm., 1979-81). OStJ 1973. *Recreations:* shooting, gardening, birdwatching. *Heir: s* Thomas Richard Troubridge, *b* 23 Jan. 1955. *Address:* The Manor House, Elsted, Midhurst, West Sussex. *T:* Harting 286. *Clubs:* White's, City of London, MCC.

TROUGHTON, Sir Charles (Hugh Willis), Kt 1977; CBE 1966; MC 1940; TD 1959; Chairman, British Council, since 1977; Director: Electric & General Investment Co., since 1967 (Chairman, 1977-80); Wm Collins and Sons, since 1977; Whitbread & Co. Ltd, since 1978; Whitbread Investment Co. Ltd, since 1981; *b* 27 Aug. 1916; *o s* of late Charles Vivian and Constance Scylla Troughton; *m* 1947, Constance Gillean Mitford, *d* of Colonel Philip Mitford, Berryfield House, Lentran, Inverness-shire; *three s one d. Educ:* Haileybury Coll.; Trinity Coll., Cambridge. BA 1938. Joined TA, 1938; served War of 1939-45, Oxford and Bucks Light Infantry; Prisoner of War, 1940-45. Called to the Bar, 1945. Dir, 1949-77 and Chm., 1972-77, W. H. Smith & Son (Holdings) Ltd; former Dir, Equity & Law Life Assce Soc. Ltd; Director: Thomas Tilling Ltd, 1973-79; Barclays Bank UK Management Ltd, 1973-81; Barclays Bank Internat., 1977-82. Member: Board of Management of NAAFI, 1953-73; Design Council, 1959-78; Council, RCA, 1977-79; Governor, LSE, 1975-. *Address:* Woolleys, Hambleden, Henley-on-Thames, Oxfordshire. *Clubs:* MCC, Boodles.

TROUGHTON, Henry Lionel, BSc(Eng), CEng, FIMechE, MIEE; Deputy Director, Projects and Research, Military Vehicles and Engineering Establishment, Ministry of Defence, 1970-74; *b* 30 March 1914; *o s* of late Henry James Troughton; *m* 1940, Dorothy Janet Louie (*née* Webb); *one d. Educ:* Mill Hill Sch.; University Coll., London. War of 1939-45: commissioned REME (Major), 1940-47; Fighting Vehicles Research and Development Estabt, 1947 (now Mil. Vehicles and Engineering Estabt); Asst Dir (Electrical), later Asst Dir (Power Plant), and Dep. Dir (Vehicles), 1960, retired 1974. *Recreations:* gardening, travel. *Address:* White Gable, Kingsley Avenue, Camberley, Surrey. *T:* Camberley 22422.

TROUNSON, Rev. Ronald Charles, MA; Principal of S Chad's College, and Lecturer in Classics, University of Durham, since 1978; *b* 7 Dec. 1926; *s* of Edwin Trounson and Elsie Mary Trounson (*née* Bolitho); *m* 1952, Leonora Anne Keate; *two s three d. Educ:* Plymouth Coll.; Emmanuel Coll., Cambridge (Schol.); Ripon Hall, Oxford (MA). Deacon, 1956; Priest, 1957. National Service, RAF, 1948-50. Asst Master, Scaitcliffe Sch., Englefield Green, Surrey, 1950-52; Sixth Form Classics Master, Plymouth Coll., 1953-58; Asst Curate, St Gabriel's, Plymouth, 1956-58; Chaplain, Denstone Coll., 1958-76; Second Master, 1968-76, Bursar, 1976-78. *Address:* 25 North Bailey, Durham DH1 3EW. *T:* Durham 47852.

TROUP, Alistair Mewburn; His Honour Judge Troup; a Circuit Judge, since 1980; *b* 23 Nov. 1927; *y s* of late William Annandale Troup, MC, MD, and Margaret Loïs Troup (*née* Mewburn); *m* 1969, Marjorie Cynthia (*née* Hutchinson); *one s three d* by previous marriages. *Educ:* Merchant Taylor's School; New College, Oxford (BA). Served Army, 1946-48. Called to the Bar, Lincoln's Inn, 1952; Crown Counsel, Tanganyika, 1955-62, Sen. Crown Counsel, 1962-64; returned to practice at English bar, 1964; Dep. Circuit Judge, 1975-77; a Recorder of the Crown Court, 1977-80. Member Panel of Counsel: for Courts Martial Appeals Court, 1970-80; for Comrs of Customs and Excise at VAT Tribunals, 1973-80; Inspector for Dept of Trade, Hartley-Baird Ltd Inquiry, 1974-76. *Recreations:* golf, gardening. *Address:* 2 Woodfield Avenue, Hildenborough, Kent TN11 9ES. *T:* Hildenborough 833406. *Club:* Sloane.

TROUP, Sir Anthony; *see* Troup, Sir J. A. R.

TROUP, Vice-Adm. Sir (John) Anthony (Rose), KCB 1975; DSC and Bar; Defence Adviser, Scicon (UK), since 1979; *b* 18 July 1921; *s* of late Captain H. R. Troup, RN and N. M. Troup (*née* Milne-Thompson); *m* 1st, 1943, B. M. J. Gordon-Smith (marr. diss. 1952); *two s one d*; 2nd, 1953, C. M. Hope; *two s one d. Educ:* Naut. Trng Coll., HMS Worcester, 1934; RNC Dartmouth, 1936; service includes: Submarines Turbulent and Strongbow, 1941-45; HMS Victorious, 1956-59; Comd 3rd Submarine Sqdn, 1961-63; HMS Intrepid, 1966-68; Flag Officer Sea Training, 1969-71; Comdr Far East Fleet, 1971; Flag Officer Submarines and NATO Comdr Submarines, Eastern Atlantic, 1972-74; Flag Officer, Scotland and NI, and NATO Comdr Norlant, 1974-77. *Recreations:* sailing, shooting, painting. *Address:* Bridge Gardens, Hungerford, Berks. *T:* Hungerford 2742. *Clubs:* Army and Navy; Royal Yacht Squadron.

TROWBRIDGE, George William Job, CBE 1969; CEng; Deputy Managing Director, Wickman Ltd, Coventry, since 1966; *b* 21 July 1911; *s* of George Clarke Trowbridge and Thirza Lampier Trowbridge (*née* Dingle); *m* 1938, Doris Isobel Morrison (decd); *one s. Educ:* Southall Technical Coll. Works Manager, Gays (Hampton) Ltd, 1938-45; Works Dir, Kingston Instrument Co. Ltd, 1945-52; Wickman Ltd, Coventry, 1952-: London Area Manager, 1952-57; General Sales Manager, 1957-62; General Sales Dir, 1962-64; Man. Dir, Machine Tool Sales Ltd, 1964-79; Dep. Chm., Wickman Machine Tools (Overseas) Ltd, 1966-; Director: Wickman Machine Tool Mfg Co. Ltd, 1962-; Wickman Lang Ltd, Johnstone, 1964-; John Brown & Co. Ltd, 1969-79; Machine Tools (India) Ltd, Calcutta, 1976-; W. Billinton & Co. Ltd, Calcutta, 1976-; Drury Wickman Ltd, Johannesburg, 1976-; Wickman (Australia) Ltd, Melbourne, 1976-; Chairman: Wickman Scrivener Ltd, Birmingham, 1966-; John Stirk & Sons Ltd, Halifax, 1966-; Kitchen & Walker Ltd, Halifax, 1966-; Coventry Machine Tool Works Ltd, Halifax, 1966-; Taylor & Challen Ltd, Birmingham, 1967-; Webster & Bennett Ltd, Coventry; Addison Tool Co., 1982-; Wickman Machine Tools Inc., USA; Wickman Machine Tools SA, France. President: Machine Tool Trades Assoc., 1975-77; Comité Européen de Coopération des Industries de la Machine-Outil, 1975-77; Mem., Economic Develt Cttee for Machine Tools, 1968-. MIProdE. *Publications:* A Handbook for Marketing Machinery, 1970; A Financial Study of British Machine Tool Companies, 1974. *Recreations:* walking, fishing. *Address:* 100 Kenilworth Road, Coventry CV4 7AH. *T:* Coventry 62775. *Club:* Institute of Directors.

TROWBRIDGE, Martin Edward O'Keeffe, CEng; FIChemE; Director General, Chemical Industries Association, since 1973; *b* 9 May 1925; *s* of late Edward Stanley Trowbridge and Ida Trowbridge (*née* O'Keeffe); *m* 1946, Valerie Ann Glazebrook; *one s. Educ:* Royal College of Science; Imperial Coll. of Science and Technology, London Univ. (BSc Eng (Chem. Eng); ACGI); Amer. Management Assoc. Coll., NYC (Dip. Bus. Studies). Hinchley Medallist, IChemE, 1946. FRSA. Technical Officer, ICI (Billingham Div.) Ltd, 1946-48; Division Manager, HWP/Fluor, 1948-53; Technical Dir, Sharples Co., 1953-57; Man. Dir, Sharples Co., 1957-59; Group Managing Director: Sharples International Corp., 1959-63; Pennwalt International Corp., 1963-72; Pegler-Hattersley Ltd, 1972-73. Member: Process Plant Working Party, NEDO, 1970-77; Chemicals EDC, NEDO, 1973-; Process Plant EDC, NEDO, 1977-80; Conseil d'Administration/CEFIC, Brussels, 1973-. *Publications:* Purification of Oils for Marine Service, 1960; Scaling Up Centrifugal Separation Equipment, 1962; Collected Poems, 1963; Centrifugation, 1966; Exhibiting for Profit, 1969; Market Research and Forecasting, 1969; The Financial Performance of Process and Plant Companies, 1970; contribs to Chemical Engineer, Chemistry in Britain, Gems, Engineering and Process Economics, etc. *Recreation:* shooting. *Address:* Alembic House, Albert Embankment, SE1 7TU. *Clubs:* East India, Devonshire, Sports and Public Schools; Frensham Gun (Surrey).

TROWBRIDGE, Rear-Adm. Sir Richard (John), KCVO 1975; Governor of Western Australia, since 1980; *b* 21 Jan. 1920; *s* of A. G. Trowbridge, Andover, Hants; *m* 1955, Anne Mildred Perceval; *two s. Educ:* Andover Grammar Sch.; Royal Navy. Joined RN as Boy Seaman, 1935. War of 1939-45: commissioned as Sub Lieut, Dec. 1940 (despatches Aug. 1945). Comdr, 1953; commanded Destroyer Carysfort, 1956-58; Exec. Officer, HMS Bermuda, 1958-59, and HMS Excellent, 1959-60; Captain, 1960; commanded Fishery Protection Sqdn, 1962-64; completed course IDC, 1966; commanded HMS Hampshire, 1967-69; Rear-Adm., 1970; Flag Officer Royal Yachts, 1970-75. An Extra Equerry to the Queen, 1970-. Younger Brother of Trinity Hse, 1972. KStJ 1980. *Recreations:* fishing, sailing, golf; most outdoor pursuits. *Address:* Government House, Perth, WA 6000, Australia; Old Idsworth Garden, Finchdean, Portsmouth. *T:* Rowlands Castle 2714. *Club:* Army and Navy.

TROWELL, Prof. Brian Lewis, PhD; King Edward Professor of Music, University of London at King's College, since 1974; *b* 21 Feb. 1931; *s* of Richard Lewis and Edith J. R. Trowell; *m* 1958, Rhianon James; *two d. Educ:* Christ's Hospital; Gonville and Caius Coll., Cambridge. MA 1959; PhD 1960. Asst Lectr, later Lectr, in Music, Birmingham Univ., 1957-62; freelance scholar, conductor, opera producer, lecturer and editor, 1962-67; Head of BBC Radio opera, 1967-70; Reader in Music, 1970, Professor of Music, 1973, KCL. Regents' Prof., Univ. of California at Berkeley, 1970; Vis. Gresham Prof. of Music, City Univ., 1971-74. Hon. RAM, 1972; Hon. FGSM, 1972; FRCM 1977; FTCL 1978. *Publications:* The Early Renaissance, Pelican History of Music vol. ii, 1963; Four Motets by John Plummer, 1968; (ed jtly) John Dunstable: Complete Works, ed M. F. Bukofzer, 2nd edn, 1970; (ed) Invitation to Medieval Music, vol. 3 1976, vol. 4 1978; opera translations; contrib. dictionaries of music and articles in learned journals. *Recreations:* theatre, reading, gardening. *Address:* 15 Crescent East, Hadley Wood, near Barnet, Herts EN4 0EY.

TROYAT, Henri; Légion d'Honneur; writer; Member of the French Academy, 1959; *b* Moscow, 1 Nov. 1911; *m* 1948, Marguerite Saintagne; *one s one d. Educ:* Paris. *Publications:* novels: l'Araigne (Prix Goncourt, 1938); Les Semailles et les Moissons (5 vols); Tant que la Terre dura (3 vols); La

Lumière des Justes (5 vols); Viou; biographies: Pushkin, Dostoievsky, Tolstoi, Gogol, Catherine la Grande, Pierre le Grand, Alexandre Ier. *Address:* Académie Française, Quai de Conti, Paris.

TRUBSHAW, (Ernest) Brian, CBE 1970 (OBE 1964); MVO 1948; FRAeS; Divisional Director and General Manager (Bristol), and Director of Flight Test, Weybridge/Bristol Division, British Aerospace plc; *b* 29 Jan. 1924; *s* of late Major H. E. Trubshaw, DL, and Lumly Victoria (*née* Carter); *m* 1973, Mrs Yvonne Edmondson, *widow* of Richard Edmondson, and *d* of late J. A. Clapham, Harrogate, Yorks. *Educ:* Winchester College. Royal Air Force, 1942-50: Bomber Command, 1944; Transport Command, 1945-46; The King's Flight, 1946-48; Empire Flying School, 1949; RAF Flying Coll., 1949-50. Joined Vickers-Armstrongs (Aircraft) Ltd as Experimental Test Pilot, 1950; Dep. Chief Test Pilot, 1953; Chief Test Pilot, 1960; Company renamed British Aircraft Corp. (Operating) Ltd, Weybridge Division, 1964; became part of British Aerospace, 1977. Warden, Guild of Air Pilots, 1958-61; Fellow, Society Experimental Test Pilots, USA. FIWM. Derry and Richards Memorial Medal, 1961 and 1964; Richard Hansford Burroughs Memorial Trophy (USA), 1964; R. P. Alston Memorial Medal, 1964; Segrave Trophy, 1970; Air League Founders' Medal, 1971; Iven C. Kinchloe Award, USA, 1971; Harmon Aviation Trophy, 1971; Bluebird Trophy, 1973; French Aeronautical Medal, 1976. *Recreations:* cricket, golf. *Address:* (office) British Aerospace, Filton, Bristol. *T:* Bristol 693831; Northland Cottage, Tetbury, Glos. *T:* Tetbury 52410. *Club:* Royal Air Force.

TRUDEAU, Rt. Hon. Pierre Elliott; PC (Can.); QC (Can.) 1969; FRSC; MP (L) Mount Royal, Montreal, since 1965; Prime Minister of Canada, 1968-79 and since 1980; Leader of Liberal Party of Canada, since 1968; *b* Montreal, 18 Oct. 1919; *s* of Charles-Emile Trudeau and late Grace Elliott; *m* 1971, Margaret, *d* of James Sinclair and Kathleen Bernard; three *s. Educ:* Jean-de-Brébeuf College, Montreal; University of Montreal; Harvard University; Ecole des Sciences Politiques, Paris; London School of Economics. Called to Bar, Quebec, 1943; practised law, Quebec; co-founder of review Cité Libre; Associate Professor of Law, University of Montreal, 1961-65. Parliamentary Secretary to Prime Minister, Jan. 1966-April 1967; Minister of Justice and Attorney General, April 1967-July 1968; Leader of the Opposition, 1979. Mem., Bars of Provinces of Quebec and Ontario. Founding Member, Montreal Civil Liberties Union. Hon. LLD, Univ. of Alberta, 1968; Dr *hc* Duke Univ., 1974. Hon. Fellow, LSE, 1969; Freeman of City of London, 1975. *Publications:* La Grève de l'Amiante, 1956; (with Jacques Hébert) Deux Innocents en Chine Rouge, 1961 (Two Innocents in Red China, 1969); Le Fédéralisme et la Société canadienne-française, 1968 (Federalism and the French Canadians, 1968); Réponses, 1968. *Recreations:* swimming, ski-ing, flying, scuba diving, canoeing. *Address:* House of Commons, Ottawa, Canada.

TRUEMAN, Prof. Edwin Royden; Beyer Professor of Zoology, University of Manchester, 1974-82, now Emeritus; *b* 7 Jan. 1922; *s* of late Sir Arthur Trueman, KBE, FRS, and late Lady (Florence Kate) Trueman (*née* Offler); *m* 1945, Doreen Burt; two *d. Educ:* Bristol Grammar Sch.; Univ. of Glasgow. DSc Glasgow, MSc Manchester. Technical Officer (Radar), RAF, 1942-46. Asst Lectr and Lectr, Univ. of Hull, 1946-58, Sen. Lectr and Reader, 1958-68; Dean, Faculty of Science, Univ. of Hull, 1954-57; Prof. of Zoology, Univ. of Manchester, 1969-74. R. T. French Vis. Prof., Univ. of Rochester, NY, 1960-61; Nuffield Travelling Fellowship in Tropical Marine Biology, Univ. of West Indies, Jamaica, 1968-69. *Publications:* Locomotion of Soft-bodied Animals, 1975; (ed) Aspects of Animal Movement, 1980; articles on animal locomotion, littoral physiology and Mollusca. *Address:* Heron's Creek, Yealm View Road, Newton Ferrers, Plymouth, Devon. *T:* Plymouth 872775.

TRUEMAN, Frederick Sewards; writer and broadcaster; *b* Stainton, Yorks, 6 Feb. 1931; *s* of late Alan Thomas Trueman; *m* 1st, 1955, Enid (marr. diss.); one *s* two *d* (incl. twin *s* and *d*); 2nd, Veronica. *Educ:* Maltby Secondary Sch. Apprentice bricklayer, 1946; worked in tally office of Maltby Main pit, 1948-51; Nat. service, RAF, 1951-53. Played club cricket, 1945-48; Yorks Fedn cricket tour, 1948; played for Yorks CCC, 1949-69 (took 2304 wickets in first class games, incl. 100 wickets in a season twelve times; also made 3 centuries); county cap, 1951; captained Yorkshire 31 times, 1962-69; played 6 one day matches for Derby CCC, 1972; first Test series, against India, 1952; MCC tours to WI, 1953-54, 1959-60, and to Australia, 1958-59, 1962-63 (took a total of 307 Test wickets, 1952-65, incl. 10 in a match and 7 in an innings three times, and was first bowler to take 300 Test wickets, 1963). Journalist, Sunday People, 1957-; anchorman, Indoor League series, Yorks TV; cricket commentator for BBC. *Publications:* Fast Fury, 1961; Cricket, 1963; Book of Cricket, 1964; The Freddie Trueman Story, 1966; Ball of Fire (autobiog.), 1976; (with John Arlott) On Cricket, 1977; Thoughts of Trueman Now, 1978; (with Frank Hardy) You Nearly Had Him That Time, 1978; My Most Memorable Matches, 1982. *Recreations:* ornithology, working for children's charities. *Address:* c/o BBC, Broadcasting House, W1A 1AA. *Club:* Yorkshire County Cricket (Hon. Life Mem.).

TRUFFAUT, François; Director of films; *b* Paris 17ème, France, 6 Feb. 1932; *s* of Roland Truffaut and Janine Truffaut (*née* de Monferrand); *m* 1957, Madeleine Morgenstern; two *d.* Reporter, film critic, 1954-58; Director of films, 1957, Producer, 1961; *productions include:* Les Mistons, 1958; Les Quatre Cents Coups, 1959 (prize, Cannes Film Festival); Tirez sur le Pianiste, 1960; L'Amour à 20 ans, 1962; Jules et Jim, 1961; La Peau Douce, 1963; Fahrenheit 451, 1966; La Mariée etait en Noir, 1967; Baisers Volés, 1968; La

Sirène du Mississipi, 1969; L'Enfant Sauvage, 1969; Domicile Conjugal, 1970; Les Deux Anglaises et le Continent, 1971; Une Belle Fille comme Moi, 1972; La Nuit Américaine, 1973; L'Histoire d'Adèle H., 1975; L'Argent de Poche, 1976; L'Homme qui aimait les femmes, 1977; La Chambre Verte, 1978; L'amour en fuite, 1979; Le Dernier Métro, 1980; La femme d'à côté, 1981. *Publications:* Hitchcock, 1966; Les Aventures d'Antoine Doinel, 1970; Les Films de ma Vie, 1975 (The Films in My Life, 1980); L'Histoire d'Adèle H., 1975; L'Argent de Poche, 1975; L'Homme qui aimait les femmes, 1977. *Address:* 5 rue Robert-Estienne, Paris 8ème, France.

TRUMPINGTON, Baroness *cr* 1980 (Life Peer), of Sandwich in the County of Kent; **Jean Alys Barker;** JP; UK Delegate to United Nations Status of Women Commission, since 1979; *d* of late Arthur Edward Campbell-Harris, MC and late Doris Marie Robson; *m* 1954, William Alan Barker, *qv* ; one *s. Educ:* privately in England and France. Land Girl to Rt Hon. David Lloyd George, MP, 1940-41; Foreign Office, Bletchley Park, 1941-45; European Central Inland Transport Orgn, 1945-49; Sec. to Viscount Hinchingbrooke, MP, 1950-52. Conservative Councillor, Cambridge City Council, Trumpington Ward, 1963-73; Mayor of Cambridge, 1971-72; Deputy Mayor, 1972-73; Conservative County Councillor, Cambridgeshire, Trumpington Ward, 1973-75; Hon. Councillor of the City of Cambridge, 1975-. Member: Air Transport Users' Cttee, 1972-80 (Dep. Chairman 1978-79, Chm. 1979-80); Bd of Visitors to HM Prison, Pentonville, 1975-81; Mental Health Review Tribunal, 1975-81. Gen. Commissioner of Taxes, 1976-. Pres., Assoc. of Heads of Independent Schs, 1980-. Steward, Folkestone Racecourse, 1980-. Hon. Fellow, Lucy Cavendish Coll., Cambridge, 1980. JP Cambridge, 1972-75, South Westminster, 1976-. *Recreations:* bridge, racing, collecting antiques, needlepoint. *Address:* Luckboat House, King Street, Sandwich, Kent. *T:* Sandwich 613007; 25 Laxford House, Cundy Street, SW1. *T:* 01-730 4016.

TRURO, Bishop of, since 1981; **Rt. Rev. Peter Mumford;** *b* 14 Oct. 1922; *s* of late Peter Walter Mumford, miller, and of Kathleen Eva Mumford (*née* Walshe); *m* 1950, Lilian Jane, *d* of Captain George Henry Glover; two *s* one *d. Educ:* Sherborne School, Dorset; University Coll., Oxford; Cuddesdon Theological Coll. BA 1950, MA 1954 (Hons Theology). War Service, 1942-47, Captain, RA. Deacon, 1951; priest, 1952; Assistant Curate: St Mark, Salisbury, 1951-55; St Alban's Abbey, 1955-57; Vicar: Leagrave, Luton, 1957-63; St Andrew, Bedford, 1963-69; Rector of Crawley, Sussex, 1969-73; Canon and Prebendary of Ferring in Chichester Cathedral, 1972-73; Archdeacon of St Albans, 1973-74; Bishop Suffragan of Hertford, 1974-81. Chm. Central Bd of Finance Christian Stewardship Cttee, 1981-; Chm. Adv. Council, Foundation for Christian Communication, 1981-. *Address:* Lis Escop, Truro, Cornwall TR3 6QQ. *T:* Devoran 862657. *Club:* United Oxford & Cambridge University.

TRURO, Dean of; *see* Shearlock, Very Rev. D. J.

TRUSCOTT, Sir Denis (Henry), GBE 1958; Kt 1953; TD 1950; President of Brown Knight and Truscott Ltd; *b* 9 July 1908; *s* of Henry Dexter Truscott, JP, and Evelyn Metcalf Truscott (*née* Gibbes); *m* 1932, Ethel Margaret, *d* of late Alexander Lyell, of Gardyne Castle, Guthrie, Angus, and Mrs Lyell; four *d. Educ:* Bilton Grange; Rugby Sch.; Magdalene Coll., Cambridge. Joined family firm of Jas. Truscott & Son Ltd, printers, 1929; Director, 1935; Chairman, 1951-66, of Brown, Knight & Truscott Ltd (amalgamation of Jas. Truscott & Son Ltd with Wm Brown & Chas. Knight Ltd, 1936). Director: Bedford General Insurance Co. Ltd (Chm., 1974-78); Zurich Life Assurance Society Ltd (Chm., 1974-78). Elected to Court of Common Council, City of London, 1938, for Ward of Dowgate; Deputy, 1943; Alderman: Dowgate Ward, 1947-73; Bridge Without Ward, 1973-78; Sheriff of City of London, 1951-52; Lord Mayor of London, 1957-58; one of HM Lieutenants, City of London, 1943-78. Master Worshipful Company of Vintners, 1955-56; Master Worshipful Company of Musicians, 1956-57, 1970-71; Master, Guild of Freemen of the City of London, 1957; Master of Worshipful Company of Stationers and Newspaper Makers, 1959-60. Treasurer, St Bartholomew's Hospital Voluntary Bd; Vice-Pres., Royal Hospital and Home for Incurables, Putney; Chairman Trustees Rowland Hill Benevolent Fund; Member Exec. Cttee, Automobile Assoc., 1952-78; President: Printing and Allied Trades Research Assoc., 1956-64; Inst. of Printing, 1961-63; London Cornish Assoc., 1977-; Mem. Council, Soc. for Protection of Animals in N Africa; Chairman, Squash Racquets Assoc. of England, 1961-74. FGSM 1978. Grand Officer of Order of Merit, Italian Republic; Grand Cross of Merit of Order of Merit, Republic of Germany. *Recreations:* lawn tennis, golf. *Address:* Invermark, 30 Drax Avenue, Wimbledon, SW20. *T:* 01-946 6111. *Clubs:* United Oxford & Cambridge University, Royal Automobile, City Livery, All England Lawn Tennis, MCC.

TRUSCOTT, Sir George (James Irving), 3rd Bt *cr* 1909; Company Director; *b* 24 Oct. 1929; *s* of Sir Eric Homewood Stanham Truscott, 2nd Bt, and Lady (Mary Dorcas) Truscott (*née* Irving) (*d* 1948); *S* father, 1973; *m* 1962, Yvonne Dora (*née* Nicholson); one *s* one *d. Educ:* Sherborne School. *Heir: s* Ralph Eric Nicholson Truscott, *b* 21 Feb. 1966. *Address:* BM QUILL, London WC1N 3XX.

TRUSS, Leslie S.; *see* Seldon-Truss.

TRUSTED, Sir Harry Herbert, Kt 1938; QC; *b* 27 June 1888; *s* of the Rev. Wilson Trusted; *m* 1911, Mary, *d* of Sir Marshall Warmington, KC, 1st Bt;

two s three d. Educ: Ellesmere Coll.; Trinity Hall, Cambridge. Called to Bar, Inner Temple, 1913; served overseas (Duke of Cornwall's Light Infantry and Staff), 1914–19; Puisne Judge, Supreme Court, Leeward Islands, 1925–27; Attorney-General, Leeward Islands, 1927–29; Attorney-General, Cyprus, 1929–32; Attorney-General, Palestine, 1932–37; Chief Justice, Palestine, 1937–41; Chief Justice, FMS, 1941–45; Chairman, Malayan Union and Singapore Salaries Commission, 1947; Commissioner to inquire into disturbances at Aden, 1948; special duty with Foreign Office (FOAAT), 1951–53; sat as Divorce Commissioner, 1953–63. Address: Broomhill Court, Esher Close, Esher, Surrey. T: Esher 66606.

TRUSTRAM EVE; see Eve, family name of Baron Silsoe.

TRUSWELL, Prof. (Arthur) Stewart, MD, FRCP, FFCM, FRACP; Boden Professor of Human Nutrition, University of Sydney, since 1978; b 18 Aug. 1928; s of George Truswell and Molly Truswell (née Stewart-Hess); m 1956, Sheila Elspeth (née McGregor); four s. Educ: Ruthin Sch., Clwyd; Liverpool and Cape Town Univs. MB, ChB 1952, MD 1959; FRCP 1975; FFCM 1979; FRACP 1980. Registrar in Pathology, Cape Town Univ., 1954; Registrar in Med., Groote Schuur Hosp., 1955–57; Research Bursar, Clin. Nutrition Unit, Dept. of Med., Cape Town Univ., 1958 and 1959; Adams Meml Trav. Fellowship to London, 1960; Sen. Fellow, Clin. Nutrition, Tulane Univ., USA, 1961; Res. Officer, Clin. Nutrition Unit, Cape Town Univ., 1962; Sen. Mem., Scientific Staff, MRC Atheroma Research Unit, Western Infirmary, Glasgow, 1963 and 1964; full-time Lectr, then Sen. Lectr in Med. and Consultant Gen. Physician, Cape Town Univ. and Groote Schuur Hosp., 1965–71; Warden of Med. Students' Residence, Cape Town Univ., 1967–69; Prof. of Nutrition and Dietetics, Queen Elizabeth Coll., London Univ., 1971–78. Member, numerous cttees, working parties, editorial bds and socs related to nutrition. Publications: Human Nutrition and Dietetics, 7th edn (with S. Davidson, R. Passmore, J. F. Brock), 1979; numerous research papers in sci. jls on various topics in human nutrition and medicine. Recreations: gardening, walking (esp. on mountains), running. Address: 30 Morella Road, Mosman, NSW 2088, Australia. T: 960-1923.

TRYON, family name of **Baron Tryon.**

TRYON, 3rd Baron cr 1940, of Durnford; **Anthony George Merrik Tryon;** Director of Lazard Bros & Co. Ltd and other companies; b 26 May 1940; s of 2nd Baron Tryon, PC, GCVO, KCB, DSO, and of Etheldreda Josephine, d of Sir Merrik Burrell, 7th Bt, CBE; S father, 1976; m 1973, Dale Elizabeth, d of Barry Harper; two s two d (of whom one s one d are twins). Educ: Eton. Page of Honour to the Queen, 1954–56. Captain Wessex Yeomanry, 1972. Dir, Lazard Bros & Co. Ltd, 1976; Chairman, English & Scottish Investors Ltd, 1977. Recreations: fishing and shooting. Heir: s Hon. Charles George Barrington Tryon, b 15 May 1976. Address: 21 Moorfields, EC2P 2HT. T: 01-588 2721. Clubs: Boodle's, Pratt's.

TRYON-WILSON, Brig. Charles Edward, CBE 1945 (MBE 1943); DSO 1944; Vice Lord-Lieutenant for Cumbria, since 1980; b 20 Sept. 1909; 2nd s of late Charles Robert Tryon; m 1st, 1937, Cicely Joan (d 1969), y d of Captain Henry Whitworth; one d (and one d decd); 2nd, 1975, Rosemary Lucas. Educ: Shawnigan Lake School, BC; Trinity Coll., Glenalmond. Served 60th Rifles, 1927–30, Royal Fusiliers, 1930–36 and 1938–45 (N Africa, Italy, Austria; despatches twice). DL Westmorland, 1971. Recreations: shooting, fishing. Address: Dallam Tower, Milnthorpe, Cumbria LA7 7AG. T: Milnthorpe 3368. Clubs: Army and Navy; Flyfishers' (Buck's).

TRYPANIS, Constantine Athanasius, MA (Oxon); DLitt (Oxon) 1970; DPhil (Athens); FRSL; Secretary General, Academy of Athens, since 1981; Minister of Culture and Science, Government of Greece, 1974–77; b Chios, 22 Jan. 1909; s of Athanasius G. Trypanis and Maria Zolota; m 1942, Alice Macri; one d. Educ: Chios Gymnasium; Universities of Athens, Berlin and Munich. Classical Lecturer, Athens Univ., 1939–47; Bywater and Sotheby Professor of Byzantine and Modern Greek Language and Literature, and Fellow of Exeter Coll., Oxford, 1947–68; Emeritus Fellow, 1968–; Univ. Prof. of Classics, Chicago Univ., 1968–74, Emeritus Prof., 1974–. Gray Lectr, Cambridge Univ., 1947. Mem. Poetry Panel, Arts Council of GB, 1962–65. FRSL, 1958; Hon. FBA 1978; Life Fellow, International Institute of Arts and Letters, 1958; Member Institute for Advanced Study, Princeton, USA, 1959–60; Visiting Professor: Hunter Coll., New York, 1963; Harvard Univ., 1963, 1964; Univ. of Chicago, 1965–66; Univ. of Cape Town, 1969; Univ. of Vienna, 1971. Corresp. Mem., Inst. for Balkan Studies (Greece); Member: Athens Academy, 1974 (Corres. Mem., 1971); Medieval Acad. of America; Accademia Tiburina, Rome, 1982. Hon. Fellow, Internat. Poetry Soc., 1977. Dr of Humane Letters hc : MacMurray Coll., USA, 1974; Assumption Coll., 1977. Ordre des Arts et des Lettres; Ordre National du Mérite. Archon Megas Hieromnemon of the Oekumenical Patriarchate. Publications: Influence of Hesiod upon Homeric Hymn of Hermes, 1939; Influence of Hesiod upon Homeric Hymn on Apollo, 1940; Alexandrian Poetry, 1943; Tartessos, 1945; Medieval and Modern Greek Poetry, 1951; Pedasus, 1955; Callimachus, 1956; The Stones of Troy, 1956; The Cocks of Hades, 1958; (with P. Maas) Sancti Romani Melodi Cantica, 1963, vol. II, 1970; Pompeian Dog, 1964; The Elegies of a Glass Adonis, 1967; Fourteen Early Byzantine Cantica, 1968; (ed) The Penguin Book of Greek Verse, 1971; The Glass Adonis, 1973; The Homeric Epics, 1975; Greek Poetry: from Homer to Seferis, 1981; articles in classical and literary periodicals. Recreations: walking, tennis, painting.

Address: 3 Georgiou Nikolaou Kefisia, Athens, Greece. Clubs: Athenæum; Athens.

TRYTHALL, Maj.-Gen. Anthony John; Director of Army Education, since 1980; b 30 March 1927; s of Eric Stewart Trythall and Irene (née Hollingham); m 1952, Celia Haddon; two s one d. Educ: Lawrence Sheriff Sch., Rugby; St Edmund Hall, Oxford (BA Hons Mod. Hist., 1947, DipEd 1951); Institute of Education, London Univ. (Academic DipEd 1962); King's College, London (MA in War Studies, 1969). National Service as RAEC Officer, UK, Egypt and Akaba, 1947–49; teaching, 1951–53; Regular RAEC Officer, 1953; seconded to Malay Regt for service at Fedn Mil. Coll., Port Dickson, 1953–56; WO, 1957–62; BAOR, 1962–66; Inspector, 1967–68; Educn Adviser, Regular Commns Bd, 1969–71; Head of Officer Educn Br., 1971–73; Chief Inspector of Army Educn, and Col Res., 1973–74; MoD, 1974–76; Chief Educn Officer, UKLF, 1976–80. Mem. Council, Royal United Services Instn for Def. Studies, 1978–. 1st Prize, Trench-Gascoigne Essay Competition, 1969. Publications: Boney Fuller: the intellectual general, 1977 (USA, as Boney Fuller: soldier, strategist and writer); (contrib.) The Downfall of Leslie Hore-Belisha in the Second World War, 1982; articles in Army Qly, Jl of RUSI, British Army Rev., and Jl of Contemp. Hist. Address: c/o Williams & Glyn's Bank Ltd, Holt's Farnborough Branch, 31-37 Victoria Road, Farnborough, Hants GU14 7PA. Club: Naval and Military.

TRYTHALL, Rear-Adm. John Douglas, CB 1970; OBE 1953; b 21 June 1914; er s of Alfonso Charles Trythall, Camborne, and Hilda Elizabeth (née Monson); m 1943, Elizabeth Loveday (née Donald); two s two d. Educ: Stretford Grammar Sch. Cadet, 1931; appointments in Home Fleet, America and West Indies, East Indies. Lent to RNZN, 1939; Battle of River Plate; Western Approaches; BJSM, Washington; Pacific; Hong Kong; Mediterranean. Secretary to: Second Sea Lord, C-in-C The Nore, and C-in-C Plymouth; Asst Director of Plans, 1960–62; Captain of the Fleet, Medit., 1964–65; Head of Personnel Panel, MoD, 1966–67; subseq. on MoD Cttee; Asst Chief, Personnel and Logistics, MoD, 1969–72. JSSC, 1953; IDC, 1963. Commander, 1949; Captain, 1959; Rear-Admiral, 1968; retired 1972. FCIS 1956. Comr, St John Ambulance in Somerset, 1975. KStJ 1982 (CStJ 1977). Address: The Old Vicarage, Corfe, Taunton, Som. T: Blagdon Hill 463. Club: MCC.

TS'ONG, Fou; see Fou Ts'ong.

TUAM, Archbishop of, (RC), since 1969; **Most Rev. Joseph Cunnane;** b 5 Oct. 1913; s of William and Margaret Cunnane, Knock, Co. Mayo. Educ: St Jarlath's Coll., Tuam; St Patrick's Coll., Maynooth. BA 1st Hons, Ancient Classics, 1935; DD 1941; Higher Dip. Educn 1941. Priest, 1939. Prof. of Irish, St Jarlath's Coll., 1941–57; Curate, Balla, Co. Mayo, 1957–67; Curate, Clifden, Co. Galway, 1967–69. Cross of Chaplain Conventual, SMO Malta, 1970. Publications: Vatican II on Priests, 1967; contribs to Irish Ecclesiastical Record, Furrow, Doctrine and Life, Studies in Pastoral Liturgy, etc. Address: Archbishop's House, Tuam, Co. Galway, Ireland. T: Tuam 24166.

TUAM, KILLALA AND ACHONRY, Bishop of, since 1970; **Rt. Rev. John Coote Duggan;** b 7 April 1918; s of Rev. Charles Coote Whittaker Duggan, BD and Ella Thackeray Duggan (née Stritch); m 1948, Mary Elizabeth Davin; one s one d (and one d decd). Educ: High School, Dublin; Trinity Coll., Dublin (Schol.). Moderator (1st cl.) Men. and Moral Sci., 1940; Bernard Prize, Div. Test. (2nd cl.); BA 1940; BD 1946. Deacon 1941; Priest 1942. Curate Asst: St Luke, Cork, 1941–43; Taney, Dublin, 1943–48; Hon. Clerical Vicar, Christ Church Cath., 1944–48; Incumbent: Portarlington Union, Kildare, 1948–55; St Paul, Glenageary, Dublin, 1955–69; Westport and Achill Union, Tuam, 1969–70; Archdeacon of Tuam, 1969–70. Exam. Chaplain to Archbp of Dublin, 1958–69; Examiner in BD Degree, Univ. of Dublin, 1960–69. Editor, Irish Churchman's Almanack, 1958–69. Publication: A Short History of Glenageary Parish, 1968. Recreation: fishing. Address: Bishop's House, Knockglass, Crossmolina, Co. Mayo. T: (096)-31317. Club: Kildare Street and University (Dublin).

TUBBS, Oswald Sydney, FRCS; Consulting Surgeon: in Cardiothoracic Surgery, St Bartholomew's Hospital; to Brompton Hospital; b 21 March 1908; s of late Sydney Walter Tubbs, The Glebe, Hadley Common, Hertfordshire; m 1934, Marjorie Betty Wilkins (d 1976); one s one d. Educ: Shrewsbury School; Caius College, Cambridge; St Bartholomew's Hospital. MA, MB, BCh, FRCS. Surgical training at St Bartholomew's Hosp. and Brompton Hosp. Dorothy Temple Cross Fellowship, spent as Surgical Fellow at Lahey Clinic, Boston, USA. Served War of 1939–45, in EMS. Consulting Chest Surgeon to Royal Navy, Papworth Village Settlement and to various Local Authorities. President: Soc. of Thoracic and Cardiovascular Surgeons of GB and Ireland, 1971–72; Thoracic Soc., 1973. Publications: papers on surgical subjects. Recreations: fishing and gardening. Address: The White Cottage, 136 Coast Road, West Mersea, Colchester, Essex CO5 8PA. T: Colchester 382355.

TUBBS, Ralph, OBE 1952; FRIBA; architect; b 9 Jan. 1912; s of late Sydney W. Tubbs and Mabel Frost; m 1946, Mary Taberner; two s one d. Educ: Mill Hill School; Architectural Assoc. School (Hons Dip.). Sec. MARS Group (Modern Architectural Research), 1939; Member: Council and Executive Committee of RIBA, 1944–50, re-elected Council, 1951; Vice-Pres. Architectural Assoc., 1945–47; Associate Institute of Landscape Architects, 1942–. Member Presentation Panel and Design Group for 1951 Festival of

Britain, and architect of Dome of Discovery in London Exhibn (then the largest dome in world, 365 ft diam.). Other works include: Baden-Powell House for Boy Scouts' Assoc., London; Indian Students' Union building, Fitzroy Sq., London; Granada TV Centre and Studios, Manchester; Cambridge Inst. Educn; Halls of residence for University Coll., London, Residential Areas at Harlow and Basildon New Towns; Industrial Buildings. Architect for new Charing Cross Hospital and Med. Sch., London; Consultant for Hospital Develt, Jersey, CI. Pres., British Entomological and Natural Hist. Soc., 1977; Mem. Council, Royal Entomol Soc. of London, 1981–. *Publications:* Living in Cities, 1942; The Englishman Builds (Penguin), 1945. *Recreation:* study of the natural world. *Address:* 46 Queen Anne Street, W1. *T:* 01-935 0694.

TUCK, Anthony; *see* Tuck, J. A.

TUCK, Sir Bruce (Adolph Reginald), 3rd Bt, *cr* 1910; *b* 29 June 1926; *o s* of Major Sir (William) Reginald Tuck, 2nd Bt, and Gladys Emily Kettle (*d* 1966), *d* of late N. Alfred Nathan, Wickford, Auckland, New Zealand, and *widow* of Desmond Fosberry Kettle, Auckland Mounted Rifles; *S* father 1954; *m* 1st, 1949, Luise (marr. diss., in Jamaica, 1964), *d* of John C. Renfro, San Angelo, Texas, USA; two *s* ; 2nd, 1968, Pamela Dorothy Nicholson, *d* of Alfred Nicholson, London; one *d. Educ:* Canford School, Dorset. Lieutenant, Scots Guards, 1945–47. *Heir: s* Richard Bruce Tuck, *b* 7 Oct. 1952. *Club:* Lansdowne.

TUCK, Clarence Edward Henry; Civil Service Commissioner, since 1977; *b* 18 April 1925; *s* of Frederick and May Tuck; *m* 1950, Daphne Robinson; one *s* one *d. Educ:* Rendcomb Coll., Cirencester; Merton Coll., Oxford. BA 1949. Served in Royal Signals, 1943–47. Inland Revenue, 1950; Min. of Supply, 1950–55; seconded to Nigerian Federal Govt, Lagos, 1955–57; Ministry of: Supply, 1957–59; Aviation, 1959–60; Defence, 1960–62; Aviation, 1962–66; IDC, 1967; Min. of Technology, 1968–70; Trade and Industry, 1970; CSD, 1971; Trade and Industry, 1973; Dept of Energy, 1974; Civil Service Dept, 1976; Dir, Civil Service Selection Board, 1977–81. Asst Principal, 1950; Principal, 1953; Asst Sec., 1962; Under-Sec., 1970. *Address:* Civil Service Commission, Alencon Link, Basingstoke, Hants RG21 1JB. *T:* Basingstoke 29222.

TUCK, (John) Anthony, MA, PhD; Master of Collingwood College and Honorary Lecturer in History, University of Durham, since 1978; *b* 14 Nov. 1940; *s* of Prof. John Philip Tuck, *qv; m* 1976, Amanda, *d* of Dr L. J. Cawley, Brotton, Cleveland; two *s. Educ:* Newcastle upon Tyne Royal Grammar Sch.; Jesus Coll., Cambridge (BA, MA, PhD). Lecturer in History, 1965–75, Sen. Lectr, 1975–78, Univ. of Lancaster. *Publications:* Richard II and the English Nobility, 1973; contribs to English Historical Rev., Northern History, etc. *Recreations:* walking, gardening, amateur dramatics. *Address:* The Master's House, Collingwood College, Durham DH1 3LT. *T:* Durham 66465; 25 Castle Street, Warkworth, Northumberland NE65 0UL. *T:* Alnwick 711493.

TUCK, Prof. John Philip; Professor of Education, University of Newcastle upon Tyne (formerly King's College, University of Durham) 1948–76, now Emeritus; *b* 16 April 1911; *s* of late William John and Annie Tuck, Uplyme, Lyme Regis; *m* 1936, Jane Adelaide (*née* Wall); two *s. Educ:* Strand School; Jesus College, Cambridge. BA Hons English and History, Class I, 1933; Cambridge certificate in Education, 1934; Adelaide Stoll Bachelor Research Scholar, Christ's College, 1935; MA 1937. English Master: Gateshead Grammar School, 1936; Manchester Central High School, 1938; Wilson's Grammar School, 1939 and 1946. Served War of 1939–45, East Surrey Regt, and Army Education Corps, N Africa, Sicily, Italy, Austria. Lecturer in Education, King's College, Newcastle upon Tyne, 1946–48. Mem. Council, GPDST, 1976–. FRSA 1970. Hon. Fellow, Coll. of Speech Therapists, 1966. *Address:* Chillingham House, Church Street, Great Gransden, Sandy, Beds. *T:* Great Gransden 512.

See also J. A. Tuck.

TUCK, Wing Comdr Robert Roland S.; *see* Stanford-Tuck.

TUCK, Prof. Ronald Humphrey; Professor of Agricultural Economics, University of Reading, since 1965 (part-time, since 1982); *b* 28 June 1921; *s* of Francis Tuck and Edith Ann Tuck (*née* Bridgewater); *m* Margaret Sylvia Everley; one *s* two *d. Educ:* Harrow County Sch.; Corpus Christi Coll., Oxford. War Service, RAOC and REME, mainly N Africa and Italy, 1941–45 (despatches). Univ. of Reading, Dept of Agric. Economics: Research Economist, 1947–49; Lecturer, 1949–62; Reader, 1962–65; Head of Dept of Agricultural Economics and Management, Univ. of Reading, and Provincial Agricultural Economist (Reading Province), 1965–81; Dean, Faculty of Agriculture and Food, Univ. of Reading, 1971–74. *Publications:* An Essay on the Economic Theory of Rank, 1954; An Introduction to the Principles of Agricultural Economics, 1961 (Italian trans., 1970); reviews etc in Jl of Agric. Economics and Economic Jl. *Recreations:* reading, music, drawing, travelling, walking. *Address:* 211 Kidmore Road, Caversham, Reading, Berks. *T:* Reading 473426.

TUCKER, Brian George, CB 1976; OBE 1963; Deputy Secretary, Department of Energy, 1974–81; Member, UKAEA, 1976–81; *b* 6 May 1922; *s* of late Frank Ernest Tucker and of May Tucker; *m* 1948, Marion Pollitt; three *d. Educ:* Christ's Hospital. Entered Home Civil Service, 1939, as Clerical

Officer, Admty; successive postings at home, in Africa, the Middle East, Ceylon and Hong Kong till 1953; promoted Executive Officer, 1945; Higher Executive Officer, 1949. Min. of Power, Asst Principal, 1954, Principal, 1957; seconded to HMOCS, 1957–62, Asst Sec., Govt of Northern Rhodesia; returned to MOP, 1962, Principal Private Sec. to Minister, 1965–66, Asst Sec., 1966, Under-Sec., Ministry of Technology, 1969–70, Cabinet Office, 1970–72, DTI, 1972–73; Dep. Sec., 1973. *Recreations:* gardening, music. *Address:* 1 Sondes Place Drive, Dorking, Surrey. *T:* Dorking 884720.

TUCKER, Rt. Rev. Cyril James, CBE 1975; *b* 17 Nov. 1911; British; *s* of Henry Castledine and Lilian Beatrice Tucker; *m* 1936, Kathleen Mabel, *d* of Major Merry; one *s* two *d. Educ:* Highgate Sch.; St Catharine's Coll., Cambridge (MA); Ridley Hall, Cambridge. MA Oxford (by Incorporation), 1951. Deacon, 1935; Priest, 1936; Curate, St Mark's, Dalston (in charge Highgate Sch. Mission), 1935; Curate, St Barnabas, Cambridge, 1937; Youth Sec., British and Foreign Bible Soc., 1938. Chaplain, RAFVR, 1939–46. Warden of Monmouth Sch., 1946; Chaplain, Wadham Coll., Oxford, and Chaplain of the Oxford Pastorate, 1949; Vicar of Holy Trinity, Cambridge, 1957–63; Rural Dean of Cambridge, 1959–63; Chaplain of the Cambridge Pastorate, 1957–63; Bishop in Argentina and Eastern S America, 1963–75; Bishop of the Falkland Islands, 1963–76. Hon. Exec. Dir, Argentine Dio. Assoc., 1976–. *Recreations:* sailing, fishing. *Address:* 202 Gilbert Road, Cambridge CB4 3PB. *T:* Cambridge 358345. *Clubs:* Hawks (Cambridge); Hurlingham (Buenos Aires).

TUCKER, Prof. David Gordon; Hon. Senior Research Fellow, Department of Economic History, since 1981, and Professor Emeritus, University of Birmingham; *b* 17 June 1914; *s* of John Ferry and Frances Tucker; *m* 1945, Florence Mary Barton; three *s* one *d. Educ:* Sir George Monoux Grammar School, London; University of London. BSc 1936; PhD 1943; DSc 1948. On research staff of GPO, at the PO Research Station, Dollis Hill, 1934–50; Royal Naval Scientific Service (Senior Principal Scientific Officer), 1950–55; Birmingham University: Prof. and Head of Dept of Electronic and Electrical Engrg, 1955–73; Sen. Fellow in Hist. of Technology, 1974–81. Member: Gen. Council of IERE, 1958–62 and 1965–66, Educn Cttee, 1958–65, Research Cttee, 1962–; Council of British Acoustical Soc. 1965–73 (Vice-Pres., 1967–70; Pres., 1970–73); Council, Soc. for Underwater Technology, 1967–70; National Electronics Research Council, 1963–66; Treasury Cttee on Scientific Civil Service, 1964–65; Oceanography and Fisheries Cttee, NERC, 1965–70; Cttee on History of Technology, IEE, 1970–76, 1978– (Chm., 1973–75); Adv. Cttee for Nat. Archive in Electrical Sci. and Technol. (Chm., 1973–79); Council, Newcomen Soc., 1977– (Vice-Pres., 1981–); Royal Commn on Ancient and Historical Monuments in Wales, 1979–; and of various other Univ., Government, professional and educational committees. FIERE, 1953; FIEE, 1954. Clerk Maxwell Premium of IERE, 1961. *Publications:* Modulators and Frequency-Changers, 1953; Electrical Network Theory, 1964; Circuits with Periodically-Varying Parameters, 1964; Applied Underwater Acoustics (with B. K. Gazey) 1966; Underwater Observation Using Sonar, 1966; Sonar in Fisheries: A Forward Look, 1967; papers in professional, scientific and historical journals. *Recreation:* history of technology. *Address:* 26 Twatling Road, Barnt Green, Birmingham B45 8HT. *T:* 021-445 1820.

TUCKER, Edward William, CB 1969; Head of Royal Naval Engineering Service, 1966–70; Director of Dockyards, Ministry of Defence, at Bath, 1967–70, retired; *b* 3 Nov. 1908; *s* of Henry Tucker, Plymouth; *m* 1935, Eva, *d* of Arthur Banks, Plymouth. *Educ:* Imperial Coll. of Science and Technology, London Univ.; Royal Naval Coll., Greenwich. BSc (Eng). Electrical Engineer in Admiralty service, at Plymouth, London, Hong Kong and Bath, 1935–64; General Manager of HM Dockyard, Chatham, 1964–66. *Recreations:* gardening, golf. *Address:* Gulls Cry, Thurlestone, Kingsbridge, Devon. *T:* Thurlestone 265.

TUCKER, Hon. Sir Henry (James), KBE 1972 (CBE 1946); Kt 1961; Government Leader, Executive Council, Bermuda, 1968–71; General Manager, Bank of Bermuda Ltd, Hamilton, Bermuda, since 1938; *b* 14 March 1903; *s* of Henry James and Nella Louise Tucker; *m* 1925, Catherine Newbold Barstow; two *s* one *d. Educ:* Saltus Grammar School, Bermuda; Sherborne School, Dorset, England. New York Trust Co., 1924–26; Kelley, Drayton and Converse (Brokers), 1926–30; Milne Munro & Tucker (Brokers), 1930–34; joined Bank of Bermuda Ltd, 1934. Pres., Anglo Norness Shipping, 1968–. *Recreation:* golf. *Address:* The Lagoon, Paget, Bermuda. *T:* 2-1657. *Clubs:* Mid-Ocean Golf, Royal Bermuda Yacht, Royal Hamilton Dinghy, Riddells Bay Golf (all in Bermuda).

TUCKER, (Henry John) Martin, QC 1975; His Honour Judge Tucker; a Circuit Judge, since 1981; *b* 8 April 1930; *s* of late P. A. Tucker, LDS, RCS and Mrs Dorothy Tucker (*née* Hobbs); *m* 1957, Sheila Helen Wateridge, LRAM; one *s* four *d. Educ:* St Peter's Sch., Southbourne; Downside Sch.; Christ Church, Oxford (MA). Called to Bar, Inner Temple, 1954; Dep. Chm., Somerset QS, 1971; a Recorder of the Crown Court, 1972–81. *Recreations:* walking occasionally; gardening gently; listening to music. *Address:* Chingri Khal, Sleepers Hill, Winchester, Hants. *T:* Winchester 3927. *Club:* Hampshire (Winchester).

TUCKER, Herbert Harold, OBE 1965; Consul General, Vancouver, since 1979; *b* 4 Dec. 1925; *o s* of late Francis Tucker and late Mary Ann Tucker; *m* 1948, Mary Stewart Dunlop; three *s. Educ:* Queen Elizabeth's, Lincs; Rossington Main, Yorks. Western Morning News, Sheffield Telegraph,

Nottingham Journal, Daily Telegraph, 1944-51; Economic Information Unit, Treasury, 1948-49; FO, later FCO, 1951; Counsellor (Information) and Dir, British Information Services, Canberra, 1974-78. *Recreations:* gardening, reading. *Address:* c/o British Consulate-General, 602 W Hastings Street, Vancouver, BC V6B 1P6, Canada. *Club:* Vancouver (Vancouver).

TUCKER, Martin; *see* Tucker, H. J. M.

TUCKER, Peter Louis; barrister; Chief Executive, Commission for Racial Equality, 1977-82; *b* 11 Dec. 1927; *s* of Peter Louis Tucker and Marion Tucker; *m* 1st, 1955, Clarissa Mary Harleston; three *s* one *d* (and one *d* decd); 2nd, 1972, Teresa Josephine Ganda; one *s*. *Educ:* Fourah Bay Coll., Sierra Leone (MA Latin, Dunelm); Jesus Coll., Oxford (MA Jurisp.); DipEd. Called to Bar, Gray's Inn, 1970. Teacher, 1952-57; Education Officer, 1957-61; Secretary, Training and Recruitment, Sierra Leone Civil Service, 1961-63; Establishment Sec., 1963-66; Sec. to the Prime Minister and Head of Sierra Leone Civil Service, 1966-67; Asst Director, UK Immigrants Advisory Service, 1970-72; Principal Admin. Officer, Community Relations Commn, 1972-74, Dir of Fieldwork and Admin., 1974-77; Dir of Legal and Gen. Services, and Sec., Commn for Racial Equality, 1977. Papal Medal Pro Ecclesia et Pontifice, 1966. *Publications:* miscellaneous booklets and articles for Community Relations Commission. *Recreations:* tennis, photography, listening to music. *Address:* 10 Dene Road, Northwood, Middlesex HA6 2AA. *T:* Northwood 23319.

TUCKER, Richard Howard, QC 1972; a Recorder of the Crown Court, since 1972; *b* 9 July 1930; *s* of Howard Archibald Tucker, later His Honour Judge Tucker, and Margaret Minton Tucker; *m* 1st, 1958, Paula Mary Bennett Frost (marr. diss. 1974); one *s* two *d*; 2nd, 1975, Wendy Kate Standbrook. *Educ:* Shrewsbury Sch.; The Queen's Coll., Oxford (MA). Called to Bar, Lincoln's Inn, 1954; Bencher, 1979. *Recreations:* sailing, shooting, gardening. *Address:* Warren Farmhouse, Stanton, Broadway, Worcs. *T:* Stanton 233; 2 Hale Court, Lincoln's Inn, WC2. *Club:* Garrick.

TUCKER, Robert St John P.; *see* Pitts-Tucker.

TUCKER, William Eldon, CVO 1954; MBE 1944; TD 1951; FRCS; formerly Honorary Orthopædic Surgeon, Royal London Homœopathic Hospital; Director and Surgeon, The Clinic, Park Street, 1936-82; *b* 6 Aug. 1903; *s* of late Dr W. E. Tucker, Hamilton, Bermuda; *m* 1931, Jean Stella (marr. diss. 1953), *d* of James Ferguson, Rudgwick, Sussex; two *s*; *m* 1956, Mary Beatrice Castle. *Educ:* Sherborne; Gonville and Caius Coll., Cambridge. MA 1931; FRCS 1930; MB, BCh 1946. St George's Hospital, 1925-34; Lt RAMC, TA, 1930-34; Major RAMC, Orthopædic Specialist, 1939-45; Lt-Col, RAMC, TA, 1946-51; Col and Hon. Col 17th General Hospital, TA, 1951-63. Surgeon St John's Hosp., Lewisham, 1931-37; Registrar, Royal Nat. Orthop. Hosp. 1933-34; Orthopædic Consultant, Horsham Hosp., 1945, Dorking Hosp., 1956. Hunterian Prof., RCS, Oct. 1958. Fellow, British Orthopædic Assoc. Corresp. Mem., Amer. Orthopædic Assoc.; Emeritus Mem., Société Internationale de Chirugie Orthopædique et Traumatologie. Vice-Pres., Amateur Dancing Assoc.; Pres. and Patron, Blackheath Football Club. Past Master, Co. of Makers of Playing Cards. *Publications:* Active Alerted Posture, 1960; Home Treatment in Injury and Osteoarthritis, 1961, new edn, Home Treatment and Posture in Injury, Rheumatism and Osteoarthritis, 1969; (with J. R. Armstrong) Injury in Sport, 1964; (with Molly Castle) Sportsmen and their Injuries, 1978. *Recreations:* tennis, Rugby football (formerly Cambridge XV, Captain 1925; England XV, 1926-30, 3 caps); ball-room dancing. *Address:* West Dunes, Paget 604, Bermuda. *T:* Bermuda 2-4637. *Clubs:* Pilgrims, MCC (Hon. Life Mem.); Middlesex CCC (Life Vice-Pres.), Surrey CCC (Life Vice-Pres.); Royal Bermuda Yacht, Royal Hamilton Amateur Dinghy.

TUCKEY, Simon Lane, QC 1981; *b* 17 Oct. 1941; *s* of late Henry Lane Tuckey and of Aileen Rosemary Newsom Tuckey; *m* 1964, Jennifer Rosemary (née Hardie); one *s* two *d*. *Educ:* Plumtree School, Zimbabwe. Called to Bar, Lincoln's Inn, 1964. *Recreations:* sailing, tennis. *Address:* 6 Regent's Park Terrace, NW1. *T:* 01-485 8952.

TUCKMAN, Frederick Augustus, FCIS, FIPM; Member (C) Leicester, European Parliament, since 1979; Management Consultant and Partner, Hay Group, since 1965; Partner, Hay Associates, since 1975; *b* 9 June 1922; *s* of Otto and Amy Tina Tuchmann (née Adler); *m* 1966, Patricia Caroline Myers; two *s* one *d*. *Educ:* English and German schools; London School of Economics, 1946-49 (BScEcon). Served RAF, 1942-46. Commercial posts, 1950-65; Managing Director, HAY GmbH, Frankfurt, 1970-80; Chm., Suomen HAY, OY, Helsinki, 1973-81; consultant assignments in Europe, Africa and N America. Hon. Sec., Bow Gp, 1958-59; Councillor, London Borough of Camden, 1965-71 (Chm., Library and Arts, 1968-71). Mem. Council, Inst. of Personnel Management, 1963-70. Chm., Greater London Area, CPC, 1968-70. *Recreations:* reading, arguing, travel, swimming; priority—family. *Address:* 6 Cumberland Road, Barnes, SW13 9LY. *T:* 01-748 2392. *Club:* Carlton.

TUCKWELL, Barry Emmanuel, OBE 1965; horn soloist; Conductor, Tasmanian Symphony Orchestra; *b* 5 March 1931; *s* of Charles Tuckwell, Australia; *m* Hilary Jane, *d* of James Warburton, Australia; two *s* one *d*. *Educ:* various schs, Australia; Sydney Conservatorium. Melbourne Symph. Orch., 1947; Sydney Symph. Orch., 1947-50; Hallé Orch., 1951-53; Scottish Nat.

Orch., 1953-54; Bournemouth Symphony Orch., 1954-55; London Symph. Orch., 1955-68; founded Tuckwell Wind Quintet, 1968; Mem. Chamber Music Soc. of Lincoln Center, 1974-81; Horn Prof., Royal Academy of Music, 1963-74; Pres., Internat. Horn Soc., 1969-77. Plays and conducts annually throughout Europe, Gt Britain, USA and Canada; has appeared at many internat. festivals, incl. Salzburg and Edinburgh; took part in 1st Anglo-Soviet Music Exchange, Leningrad and Moscow, 1963; toured: Far East, 1964 and 1975; Australia, 1970-; S America, 1976; USSR, 1977. Many works dedicated to him; has made numerous recordings. Editor, complete horn literature for G. Schirmer Inc. Hon. RAM, 1966; Hon. GSM, 1967. Harriet Cohen Internat. Award for Solo Instruments, 1968; Grammy Award Nominations. *Publications:* Playing the Horn, 1978; The Horn, 1981. *Recreations:* photography, sailing. *Club:* Athenæum.

TUCKWELL, Sir Edward (George), KCVO 1975; MCh, FRCS; Serjeant-Surgeon to the Queen, 1973-75 (Surgeon to the Queen, 1969-73, to HM Household, 1964-73); Surgeon, St Bartholomew's Hospital, London, 1947-75; Surgeon, Royal Masonic Hospital, 1958-75; Consultant Surgeon, King Edward VII Convalescent Home, Osborne, 1965-78; *b* 12 May 1910; *e s* of Edward Henry Tuckwell and Annie Clarice (née Sansom); *m* 1st, 1934, Phyllis Courthope Regester (*d* 1970); two *s* one *d*; 2nd, 1971, Barbara Gordon, widow of Major A. J. Gordon. *Educ:* Charterhouse; Magdalen College, Oxford; St Bartholomew's Hospital. BM, BCh Oxon 1936; MCh 1948; FRCS 1939. War Service in EMS and RAMC, Surgical Specialist, North-West Europe and South-East Asia, Lt-Col. Examiner in Surgery to Univs of London, Manchester, Oxford, and in Pathology to Conjoint Board and Royal College of Surgeons; Dean of Medical School, St Bartholomew's Hospital, 1952-57; Surgeon, King Edward VII Hospital for Officers, 1961-75. Member: Medical Appeal Tribunal, 1975-82; Vaccine Damage Appeal Tribunal, 1978-82. Pres., Phyllis Tuckwell Meml Hospice, Farnham; Member: Council, Metrop. Hosp. Sunday Fund, 1981-; Governing Body of Charterhouse School, 1966-82 (Chm., 1973-81) (London University representative); Council, Epsom Coll., 1981-; Governor: St Bartholomew's Hosp., 1954-74; Sutton's Hosp. in Charterhouse, 1980-. Mem. Ct of Assts, 1973-, Warden 1978, Master 1981-82, and Freeman, Barbers' Co. *Publications:* articles in medical journals. *Recreations:* gardening, shooting, travelling. *Address:* Berthorpe, Puttenham Heath Road, Guildford, Surrey GU3 1DU. *T:* Guildford 810217.

TUDOR, James Cameron, CMG 1970; Permanent Representative of Barbados to the United Nations, 1976-79; *b* St Michael, Barbados, 18 Oct. 1919; *e s* of James A. Tudor, JP, St Michael, Barbados; unmarried. *Educ:* Roebuck Boys' Sch.; Combermere Sch.; Harrison Coll., Barbados; Lodge Sch.; (again) Harrison Coll.; Keble Coll., Oxford, 1939-43. BA Hons (Mod. Greats), 1943, MA 1948; Pres., Oxford Union, 1942. Broadcaster, BBC: Lobby Correspondent (Parliament); Overseas Service, 1942-44; Lectr, Extra-Mural Dept, Reading Univ., 1944-45; History Master, Combermere Sch., Barbados, 1946-48; Civics and History Master, Queen's Coll., British Guiana, 1948-51; Sixth Form Master, Modern High Sch., Barbados, 1952-61, also free-lance Journalist, Lectr, Broadcaster, over the same period. Mem., Barbados Lab. Party, 1951-52; MLC, Barbados, 1954-72; Foundn Mem., Democratic Lab. Party, 1955 (Gen. Sec., 1955-63; Third Vice-Chm., 1964-65 and 1965-66). Minister: of Educn, 1961-67; of State for Caribbean and Latin American Affairs, 1967-71 (Leader of the House, 1965-71); of External Affairs, 1971-72 (Leader of the Senate, 1971-72); High Comr for Barbados in UK, 1972-75. Mem. Council, Univ. of the West Indies, 1962-65; awarded US State Dept Foreign Leader Grant, to study US Educn Instns, 1962. Silver Star, Order of Christopher Columbus (Dominican Republic), 1969. *Recreations:* reading, lecturing; keen on Masonic and other fraternities. *Address:* Lemon Grove, Westbury New Road, St Michael, Barbados.

TUDOR, Rev. Dr (Richard) John, BA; Superintendent Minister, Westminster Central Hall, London, since 1981; *b* 8 Feb. 1930; *s* of Charles Leonard and Ellen Tudor; *m* 1956, Cynthia Campbell Anderson; one *s* one *d*. *Educ:* Clee Grammar Sch., Grimsby; Queen Elizabeth's, Barnet; Univ. of Manchester, 1951-54 (BA Theology). Served RAF, 1948-51. Junior Methodist Minister, East Ham, London, 1954-57; Ordained, Newark, 1957; Minister, Thornton Cleveleys, Blackpool, 1957-60; Superintendent Minister: Derby Methodist Mission, 1960-71: Chaplain to Mayor of Derby, Factories and Association with Derby Football Club; Coventry Methodist Mission, 1971-75: Chaplain to Lord Mayor; Brighton Dome Mission, 1975-81. Hon. DD, Texas Wesleyan Coll., Forth Worth, USA, 1981; Hon. Texan, 1965; Freeman of Forth Worth, 1970. *Recreations:* motoring, cooking, photography, the delights of family life. *Address:* The Methodist Church, Central Hall, Westminster, SW1. *T:* 01-222 8754/01-222 8553.

TUDOR EVANS, Hon. Sir Haydn, Kt 1974; **Hon. Mr Justice Tudor Evans;** a Judge of the High Court of Justice, Queen's Bench Division, since 1978 (Family Division, 1974-78); a Judge of the Employment Appeal Tribunal, since 1982; *b* 20 June 1920; 4th *s* of Edgar Evans and Ellen Stringer; *m* 1947, Sheilagh Isabella Pilkington; one *s*. *Educ:* West Monmouth School; Lincoln College, Oxford. RNVR, 1940-41. Open Scholar, Lincoln Coll., Oxford (Mod. History), 1940; Stewart Exhibitioner, 1942; Final Hons Sch., Mod. History, 1944; Final Hons Sch., Jurisprudence, 1945. Scholar, Lincoln's Inn, 1946; called to the Bar, Lincoln's Inn, 1947, Bencher 1970. QC 1962; Recorder of Crown Court, 1972-74. *Address:* c/o Royal Courts of Justice, Strand, WC2A 2LL. *Clubs:* Garrick, MCC.

TUDOR PRICE, David William; His Honour Judge Tudor Price; Common Serjeant in the City of London, since 1981; *b* 29 Jan. 1931; *s* of late Tudor Howell Price, OBE, and Mary Tudor Price; *m* 1956, Elspeth Patricia Longwell, JP; two *s* one *d. Educ:* Rugby Sch.; Magdalene Coll., Cambridge (MA). Called to Bar, Inner Temple, 1955, Bencher 1981. Prosecuting Counsel to the Post Office, 1965-69; Junior Treasury Counsel, 1971; First Junior, 1974; Sen. Prosecuting Counsel to the Crown at Central Criminal Ct, 1975-81; a Recorder of the Crown Court, 1979-81. Mem., Royal Commn on Gambling, 1976-78. Appeal Steward, British Bd of Boxing Control, 1978-81. HM Lieut, City of London, 1981; Liveryman, Merchant Taylors' Co. *Recreation:* golf. *Address:* c/o Central Criminal Court, EC4M 7EH. *T:* 01-248 3277. *Clubs:* Moor Park, and Woking Golf, Woburn Golf and Country.

TUDSBERY, Marmaduke Tudsbery, CBE 1941; FCGI 1950; FICE 1932; Fellow, Imperial College of Science and Technology, London University, 1953; Hon. Member Institution of Royal Engineers, 1937; President Smeatonian Society of Civil Engineers, 1956; *b* 4 Oct. 1892; 3rd *s* of late J. H. T. Tudsbery, DSc; unmarried. *Educ:* Westminster; Imperial College, London Univ.; engineering training under John J. Webster, FICE, and at works of Yarrow & Co. Ltd, Glasgow. Commissioned, Special Reserve of Officers, RE: France, 1915 (9th Field Company); subsequently Army of the Rhine, Mesopotamia Expeditionary Force; staff of RE Board, War Office, 1920-25; Member, later Chairman, War Office Cttee on Army Building, 1940-44; Member: Home Office Committee on Structural Precautions against Air-Attack, 1936-39; Science Museum Adv. Council, 1959-69. Governor, Imperial Coll., London Univ., 1942-71. The Civil Engineer to BBC, 1926-52; Consulting Civil Engineer to BBC, 1952-60. *Address:* Littlebourne Nursing Home, Littlebourne, Canterbury, Kent CT3 1UN. *Clubs:* Athenæum, MCC, Royal Cruising, Royal Thames Yacht.

TUDWAY QUILTER, David C.; *see* Quilter.

TUFFIN, Alan David; General Secretary, Union of Communication Workers, since 1982; *b* 4 Aug. 1933; *s* of Oliver Francis and Gertrude Elizabeth Tuffin; *m* 1957, Jean Elizabeth Tuffin; one *s* one d. *Educ:* Eltham Secondary Sch., SE9. Post Office employment, London, 1949-69; London Union Regional Official for UCW, 1957-69; National Official, 1969; Deputy General Secretary, 1979. Mem., TUC Gen. Council, 1982-. *Recreations:* reading, squash. *Address:* 3a Lansdowne Road, Bromley, Kent BR1 3LZ.

TUFTON, family name of **Baron Hothfield.**

TUGENDHAT, Christopher Samuel; Vice President, Commission of the European Communities, since 1981 (Member, since 1977); *b* 23 Feb. 1937; *er s* of late Dr Georg Tugendhat; *m* 1967, Julia Lissant Dobson; two *s. Educ:* Ampleforth Coll.; Gonville and Caius Coll., Cambridge (Pres. of Union). Financial Times leader and feature writer, 1960-70. MP (C) City of London and Westminster South, 1974-76 (Cities of London and Westminster, 1970-74); Opposition spokesman: for Employment, 1974-75; on Foreign and Commonwealth Affairs, 1975-76. Director: Sunningdale Oils, 1971-76; Phillips Petroleum International (UK) Ltd, 1972-76; former Consultant to Wood Mackenzie & Co., Stockbrokers. *Publications:* Oil: the biggest business, 1968; The Multinationals, 1971 (McKinsey Foundn Book Award, 1971); various pamphlets and numerous articles. *Recreations:* being with my family, reading, following football, conversation. *Address:* 200 Rue de la Loi, 1049 Brussels, Belgium. *Club:* Carlton.

TUITE, Sir Christopher (Hugh), 14th Bt *cr* 1622; Higher Scientific Officer, since 1978; *b* 3 Nov. 1949; *s* of Sir Dennis George Harmsworth Tuite, 13th Bt, MBE, and of Margaret Essie, *d* of late Col Walter Leslie Dundas, DSO; *S* father, 1981; *m* 1976, Deborah Anne, *d* of A. E. Martz, Pittsburgh, Pa; two *s. Educ:* Univ. of Liverpool (BSc Hons); Univ. of Bristol (PhD). Research Officer, The Wildfowl Trust, 1978-81. *Publications:* contribs to Jl of Animal Ecology, Jl o Applied Ecology, Freshwater Biology, Wildfowl. *Heir: s* Thomas Livingstone Tuite, *b* 24 July 1977. *Address:* c/o The Midland Bank, 33 The Borough, Farnham, Surrey.

TUIVAGA, Hon. Sir Timoci (Uluiburotu), Kt 1981; Hon. Mr Justice Tuivaga; Chief Justice of Fiji, since 1980; *b* 21 Oct. 1931; *s* of Isimeli Siga Tuivaga and Jessie Hill; *m* 1958, Vilimaina Leba Parrott Tuivaga; three *s* one *d. Educ:* Univ. of Auckland (BA). Called to Bar, Gray's Inn, 1964, and NSW, 1968. Native Magistrate, 1958-61; Crown Counsel, 1965-68; Principal Legal Officer, 1968-70; Acting Director of Public Prosecutions, 1970; Crown Solicitor, 1971; Puisne Judge, 1972; Acting Chief Justice, 1974. *Recreations:* golf, gardening. *Address:* 228 Ratu Sukuna Road, Suva, Fiji. *T:* 313-782. *Club:* Fiji Golf (Suva).

TUKE, Sir Anthony (Favill), Kt 1979; Chairman, Rio Tinto Zinc Corporation, since 1981 (Director, since 1980); Director: Barclays Bank Ltd, since 1965 (Vice-Chairman, 1972-73; Chairman, 1973-81); Barclays Bank International, since 1966 (Chairman, 1972-79; Vice-Chairman, 1968-72); *b* 22 Aug. 1920; *s* of late Anthony William Tuke; *m* 1946, Emilia Mila; one *s* one *d. Educ:* Winchester; Magdalene Coll., Cambridge. Scots Guards, 1940-46. Barclays Bank Ltd, 1946-; Dir, Barclays Bank UK, 1971-81. Director: Merchants Trust, 1969-; Royal Insurance, 1978-; Savoy Hotel, 1982-. Vice-President: Inst. of Bankers, 1973-81; British Bankers' Assoc., 1977-81; Chm., Cttee of London Clearing Bankers, 1976-78 (Dep. Chm., 1974-76); Pres., Internat. Monetary Conference, 1977-78. Mem., Trilateral Commn, 1977-.

Chm., 1980 British Olympic Appeal. Mem., Stevenage Develt Corp., 1959-64. Governor, Motability, 1978-. Mem. Council, Warwick Univ., 1966-73; Treas., English-Speaking Union, 1969-73. *Recreations:* gardening, lawn tennis. *Address:* Freelands, Wherwell, near Andover, Hants. *Club:* MCC.

TUKE, Comdr Seymour Charles, DSO 1940; Royal Navy; *b* 20 May 1903; 3rd *s* of late Rear-Adm. J. A. Tuke; *m* 1928, Marjorie Alice Moller; one *s* one *d. Educ:* Stonyhurst; RNC, Osborne and Dartmouth. Midshipman, 1921; Lieutenant, 1926; Acting Commander, 1945; FAA, 1927-29; Local Fishery Naval Officer, English Channel, 1935-37; served War of 1939-45 (DSO, 1939-45 Medal, Atlantic Star, Italy Star, War Medal); in command of SS Hannah Boge (first prize of the war), 1939; Senior Officer Res. Fleet, Harwich, 1946; Maintenance Comdr to Senior Officer Res. Fleet, 1947-48; retired, 1948. *Address:* Henstridge House, Crudwell, Malmesbury, Wiltshire. *T:* Crudwell 283.

TULLIS, Major Ramsey; Vice Lord-Lieutenant of Clackmannanshire, since 1974; farmer; *b* 16 June 1916; *s* of late Major J. Kennedy Tullis, Tullibody, Clackmannanshire; *m* 1943, Daphne Mabon, *d* of late Lt-Col H. L. Warden, CBE, DSO, Edinburgh; three *s. Educ:* Trinity Coll., Glenalmond; Worcester Coll., Oxford (BA). 2nd Lieut, Cameronians, 1936. Served War, 1939-45: Cameronians, Parachute Regt; Major 1943; psc 1949; retired, 1958. County Comr for Scouts, Clackmannanshire, 1958-73; Income Tax Comr, 1964-; Activities Comr, Scottish HQ, Scout Assoc., 1974; Chm. Visiting Cttee, Glenochil Young Offenders Instn and Detention Centre, 1974-. Clackmannanshire: JP 1960, DL 1962. *Recreations:* golf and gardening. *Address:* Woodacre, Pool of Muckhart, by Dollar, Clackmannanshire FK14 7JW.

TUMIM, Stephen; His Honour Judge Tumim; a Circuit Judge, since 1978; a Judge of the Willesden County Court, since 1980; Chairman, National Deaf Children's Society, 1974-79 (Vice-Chairman, 1966-74); *b* 15 Aug. 1930; *yr s* of late Joseph Tumim, CBE (late Clerk of Assize, Oxford Circuit) and late Renée Tumim; *m* 1962, Winifred, *er d* of late Col A. M. Borthwick; three *d. Educ:* St Edward's Sch., Oxford; Worcester Coll., Oxford (Scholar). Called to Bar, Middle Temple, 1955; practice on Oxford Circuit. A Recorder of the Crown Court, 1977-78. *Recreation:* second-hand book-shops. *Address:* River House, Upper Mall, Hammersmith W6 9TA. *T:* 01-748 5238. *Clubs:* Garrick, Beefsteak.

TUNBRIDGE, Sir Ronald (Ernest), Kt 1967; OBE 1944; JP; Professor of Medicine, University of Leeds, 1946-71, now Emeritus Professor; Chairman, Standing Medical Advisory Committee, Department of Health and Social Security, 1963-72; *b* 2 June 1906; *s* of Rev. W. J. Tunbridge and Norah (*née* Young); *m* 1935, Dorothy Gregg; two *s. Educ:* Kingswood School, Bath; University of Leeds. Research Fellowship in Physiology, 1928; Hons degree in Physiology, BSc, 1928, MSc, 1929; MB, ChB, Hons 1931; MD 1933; MRCP 1933; FRCP 1944; numerous resident appointments in Leeds. Clinical asst for one year at St Bartholomew's Hosp., under Sir Francis Fraser; Reader in Medicine, Univ. of Leeds; Consultant to Hosps in Leeds Region. Military Service, 1941-44; Adviser in Medicine, Malta Command; Cons. in Med., BLA and BAOR, 1945-46 (despatches). FRSocMed. Member: Assoc. of Physicians of GB and Ire. (Pres., 1977-78); Heberden Soc. (serving on Council of latter, Pres., 1954 and 1955); The Diabetic Assoc. (Banting Memorial Lectr, 1953); Vice-Pres., British Diabetic Assoc.; Chairman: Governing Body of 1st and 2nd International Gerontological Congresses (Member, Governing Body of Third Internat. Congress; Chm. Brit. Organizing Cttee of Third Congress); Leeds Regional Hosp. Bd, 1947-51; Mem. Bd of United Leeds Hosps, 1952-71; Chm., Educn Cttee, 1967-72. Mem. Management Cttee, 1967-, King Edward's Hospital Fund for London; Central Health Services Council: Mem., 1959-; Vice-Chm., 1963-72; Chm., Hosp. Records Cttee, 1964; Chm., Health of Hosp. Staff Cttee, 1968; Chm., Rehabilitation Cttee, 1972. Mem. Exec. Cttee, Nat. Old People's Welfare Council (Vice-Chm. Yorkshire Council); Pres., BMA 1974 (Chm. Bd of Science, 1968-72); Vice-President: Med. Defence Union; Age Concern; Chm., Leeds Local Broadcasting Council, 1968-72; Hon. Pres., British Dietetic Assoc.; Past Pres., Brit. Spas Fedn, 1955-63; Fellow, Coll. of Physicians of Ceylon, 1973. Heberden Orator, 1956; Lectures: Proctor Meml, 1958; Frederick Price, TCD, 1969; Founder, British Council for Rehabilitation of Disabled, 1972; Fernando, (and Prize), Ceylon Coll. of Physicians, 1973; Convocation, Univ. of Leeds, 1981. Asst Editor, Gerontologia. JP City of Leeds, 1958. Hon. DSc: Hull, 1974; Leeds, 1975; Warwick, 1979. Bobst Award, Internat. Association of Gerontology, 1957; Osler Award, Canadian Med. Assoc., 1973. *Publications:* articles in Quarterly Jl of Medicine, Lancet, BMJ, etc. *Recreation:* walking. *Address:* 9 Ancaster Road, Leeds LS16 5HH. *Club:* Athenæum.

TUNC, Prof. André Robert; Croix de Guerre 1940; Chevalier de la Légion d'Honneur 1964; Professor, University of Paris, since 1958; *b* 3 May 1917; *s* of Gaston Tunc and Gervaise Letourneur; *m* 1941, Suzanne Fortin. *Educ:* Law Sch., Paris. LLB 1937, LLM 1941. Agrégé des Facultés de Droit, 1943. Prof., Univ. of Grenoble, 1943-47; Counsellor, Internat. Monetary Fund, 1947-50; Prof., Univ. of Grenoble, 1950-58; Legal Adviser, UN Economic Commn for Europe, 1957-58. Hon. Doctorates: Free Univ. of Brussels, 1958; Cath. Univ. of Louvain, 1968; DCL: Oxford, 1970; Stockholm, 1978; MA Cantab, 1972; Corr. FBA (London), 1974; Corresp. Fellow, Royal Acad. of Belgium, 1978; Foreign Member: Royal Acad. of the Netherlands, 1980; Amer. Acad. of Arts and Scis. Officer de l'Ordre d'Orange-Nassau, 1965. *Publications:* Le contrat de garde, 1941; Le particulier au service de l'ordre public, 1942; (with Suzanne

Tunc) Le Système constitutionnel des Etats-Unis d'Amérique, 2 vols, 1953, 1954; (with Suzanne Tunc) Le droit des Etats-Unis d'Amérique, 1955; (with François Givord) (tome 8) Le louage: Contrats civils, du Traité pratique de droit civil français de Planiol et Ripert, 2nd edn 1956; Traité théorique et pratique de la responsabilité civile de Henri et Léon Mazeaud, 3 vols, 1957, 1958, 1960, 5th edn, and 6th edn (Vol. I) 1965; Les Etats-Unis—comment ils sont gouvernés, 1958, 3rd edn 1974; Dans un monde qui souffre, 1962, 4th edn 1968; Le droit des Etats-Unis (Que sais-je?), 1964, 4th edn 1982; La sécurité routière, 1965; Le droit anglais des sociétes anonymes, 1971, 2nd edn 1979; Traffic Accident Compensation: Law and Proposals (Internat. Encycl. of Comparative Law, Vol. XI: Torts, chap. 14), 1971; Le droit américain des sociétes anonymes (roneo.), 1972, 3rd edn 1979; Introd. to Vol. XI: Torts (Internat. Encycl. of Comparative Law), 1974; La cour judiciaire suprême: une enquête comparative, 1978; La responsabilité civile, 1981; Pour une loi sur les accidents de la circulation, 1981; articles in various legal periodicals. *Address:* 112 rue de Vaugirard, 75006 Paris, France.

TUOHY, John Francis, (Frank Tuohy); novelist; short story writer; *b* 2 May 1925; *s* of late Patrick Gerald Tuohy and Dorothy Marion (*née* Annandale). *Educ:* Stowe Sch.; King's College, Cambridge. Prof. of English Language and Literature, Univ. of São Paulo, 1950-56; Contract Prof., Jagiellonian Univ., Cracow, Poland, 1958-60; Vis. Prof., Waseda Univ., Tokyo, 1964-67; Writer-in-Residence, Purdue Univ., Indiana, 1970-71, 1976, 1980. FRSL 1965. *Publications:* The Animal Game, 1957; The Warm Nights of January, 1960; The Admiral and the Nuns, short stories (Katherine Mansfield Memorial Prize), 1962; The Ice Saints (James Tait Black and Geoffrey Faber Memorial Prizes), 1964; Portugal, 1970; Fingers in the Door, short stories (E. M. Forster Meml Award, 1972), 1970; Yeats: a biographical study, 1976; Live Bait, short stories (Heinemann Award, 1979), 1978. *Recreation:* travel. *Address:* c/o Macmillan and Co. Ltd, Little Essex Street, WC2.

TUOHY, Thomas, CBE 1969; Managing Director, British Nuclear Fuels Ltd, 1971-73; *b* 7 Nov. 1917; *s* of late Michael Tuohy and Isabella Tuohy, Cobh, Eire; *m* 1949, Lilian May Barnes (*d* 1971); one *s* one d. *Educ:* St Cuthberts Grammar Sch., Newcastle; Reading Univ. (BSc). Chemist in various Royal Ordnance Factories, 1939-46. Manager: Health Physics, Springfields Nuclear Fuel Plant, Dept Atomic Energy, 1946; Health Physics, Windscale Plutonium Plant, 1949; Plutonium Piles and Metal Plant, Windscale, 1950; Works Manager: Springfields, 1952; Windscale, UKAEA, 1954; Windscale and Calder Hall: Dep. Gen. Manager, 1957; Gen. Manager, 1958; Man. Dir, Production Gp, UKAEA, 1964-71. Managing Director: Urenco, 1973-74; Vorsitzender der Geschäftsführung Centec GmbH, 1973-74; Dep. Chm., Centec, 1973-74; former Dir, Centec-Algermann Co. Mem. Council, Internat. Inst. for Management of Technology, 1971-73. *Publications:* various technical papers on reactor operation and plutonium manufacture. *Recreations:* golf, gardening, travel. *Address:* Ingleberg, Beckermet, Cumbria. *T:* Beckermet 226.

TUPMAN, William Ivan, DPhil; Director General of Internal Audit, Ministry of Defence, 1974-81; *b* 22 July 1921; *s* of Leonard and Elsie Tupman; *m* 1945, Barbara (*née* Capel); two *s* one d. *Educ:* Queen Elizabeth's Hosp., Bristol; New Coll., Oxford (Exhibnr; MA, DPhil). Served War, 1942-45, RN (Lieut RNVR). Entered Admiralty as Asst Principal, 1948; Private Sec. to Parly Sec., 1950-52; Principal, 1952; Civil Affairs Adviser to C-in-C, Far East Station, 1958-61; Private Sec. to First Lord of the Admiralty, 1963; Asst Sec., 1964; IDC, 1967. *Address:* 109 Seal Hollow Road, Sevenoaks, Kent TN13 3SE. *T:* Sevenoaks 455699.

TUPPER, Sir Charles Hibbert, 5th Bt *cr* 1888, of Armdale, Halifax, Nova Scotia; *b* 4 July 1930; *o s* of Sir James Macdonald Tupper, 4th Bt, formerly Assistant Commissioner, Royal Canadian Mounted Police, and of Mary Agnes Jean Collins; *S* father, 1967; *m* (marr. diss. 1976); one *s*. *Heir: s* Charles Hibbert Tupper, *b* 10 July 1964. *Address:* 955 Marine Drive, Apt 1101, West Vancouver, BC V7T 1A9, Canada.

TURBERVILLE, Geoffrey, MA; Principal, Leulumoega High School, Samoa, 1959-62, (retired); *b* 31 Mar. 1899; *o s* of A. E. Turberville, FCA, Stroud Green, London; *m* Jane Campbell Lawson. *Educ:* Westminster Sch. (King's Scholar); Trinity College, Cambridge (Exhibitioner). 2nd Lieut, Queen's Royal West Surrey Regt, 1917-19; Senior Classical Master, Liverpool Collegiate School, 1921-25; Senior Classical Master, Epsom College, 1925-30; Headmaster of Eltham College, 1930-59. Chm. Dorset Congregational Assoc., 1970-71. *Publications:* Cicero and Antony; Arva Latina II; Translation into Latin. *Address:* 4 Spiller's House, Shaftesbury, Dorset.

TURBOTT, Sir Ian (Graham), Kt 1968; CMG 1962; CVO 1966; *b* Whangarei, New Zealand, 9 March 1922; *s* of late Thomas Turbott and late E. A. Turbott, both of New Zealand; *m* 1952, Nancy Hall Lantz, California, USA; three d. *Educ:* Takapuna Grammar School, Auckland, NZ; Auckland University; Jesus College, Cambridge; London University. NZ Forces (Army), 1940-46: Solomon Is area and 2 NZEF, Italy. Colonial Service (Overseas Civil Service): Western Pacific, Gilbert and Ellice Is, 1948-56; Colonial Office, 1956-58; Administrator of Antigua, The West Indies, 1958-64; also Queen's Representative under new constitution, 1960-64; Administrator of Grenada and Queen's Representative, 1964-67; Governor of Associated State of Grenada, 1967-68. Partner, Spencer Stuart and Associates Worldwide, 1973-82; Chairman: Spencer Stuart and Associates Pty Ltd;

Chloride Batteries Australia Ltd, 1978; Hoyts Theatres Ltd; TNT Group 4 Total Security Pty Ltd; Stuart Brooke Consultants Pty Ltd, Sydney, 1974; Stereo FM Pty Ltd; Penrith Lakes Develt Corp.; Amer. Internat. Underwriting (Aust.) Ltd; Director: Suncoast Group of Cos; City Mutual Life Assurance Soc. Ltd; Standard Chartered Finance Ltd. Chairman: Sydney Dance Co.; Internat. Piano Competition Ltd, Sydney. Governor, NSW Conservatorium of Music. FRSA, JP. Silver Jubilee Medal, 1977. Holds 1939-45 Star, Pacific Star, Italy Star, Defence Medal, War Medal, New Zealand Service Medal. CStJ 1964. *Publications:* various technical and scientific, 1948-51, in Jl of Polynesian Society (on Pacific area). *Recreations:* boating, farming, golf, fishing. *Address:* 27 Amiens Road, Clontarf, NSW 2093, Australia; Lazy B Ranch, Mangrove Creek Road, NSW 2255, Australia. *Clubs:* Australian (Sydney); Royal Sydney Yacht.

TURECK, Rosalyn; concert artist (Bach specialist); conductor; writer; *b* Chicago, 14 Dec. 1914; *d* of Samuel Tureck and Monya (*née* Lipson); *m* 1964, George Wallingford Downs (*d* 1964). *Educ:* Juilliard Sch. of Music, NY. Member Faculty: Philadelphia Conservatory of Music, 1935-42; Mannes School, NYC, 1940-44; Juilliard School of Music, 1943-53; Lecturer in Music: Columbia University, NY, 1953-55; London Univ., 1955-56. Visiting Professor, Washington University, St Louis, 1963-64; Regents Professorship, University of California, San Diego, 1966; Prof. of Music, 4th Step, Univ. of California, San Diego, 1966-72; Vis. Fellow, St Hilda's Coll., Oxford, 1974 and 1976-, Hon. Life Fellow, 1974; Vis. Fellow, Wolfson Coll., Oxford, 1975. Has appeared as soloist and conductor of leading orchestras in US, Europe and Israel, and toured US, Canada, South Africa, South America; since 1947 has toured extensively in Europe, and played at festivals in Edinburgh, Venice, Holland, Wexford, Schaffhausen, Bath, Brussels World Fair, Glyndebourne, etc, and in major Amer. festivals including Mostly Mozart Festival, NY, Caramoor, Detroit, etc; extensive tours: India, Australia and Far East, 1971. Formed: Composers of Today, 1951-55; Tureck Bach Players, 1959; Internat. Bach Soc., Inc., 1966; Inst. for Bach Studies, 1968. Hon. Member, Guildhall School of Music and Drama, London, 1961; Member: Royal Musical Assoc., London; Inc. Soc. of Musicians, London; Amer. Musicological Soc. Numerous recordings. Hon. Dr of Music, Colby Coll., USA, 1964; Hon. DMus: Roosevelt Univ., 1968; Wilson Coll., 1968; Oxon, 1977. Has won several awards. *Publications:* An Introduction to the Performance of Bach, 1960; (ed) Bach: Sarabande, C minor, 1950; (transcribed) Paganini: Moto Perpetuo, 1950; (urtext and performance edn) Bach: Italian Concerto, 1979; many articles. *Address:* c/o Ibbs and Tillett Ltd, 450-452 Edgware Road, W2 1EG.

TURING, Sir John Leslie, 11th Bt *cr* 1638; MC; *b* 13 Sept. 1895; *s* of Sir James Walter Turing, 9th Bt and Mabel Rose, *d* of Andrew Caldecott; *S* twin brother, 1970; *m* 1975, Irene Nina, *d* of Trevor John Tatham and widow of Captain W. W. P. Shirley-Rollison, RN. *Educ:* Wellington College. Formerly Lieut, Seaforth Highlanders; served European War, 1914-18 (wounded, MC). *Heir: kinsman* John Ferrier Turing [*b* 1 Sept. 1908; *m* 1st, 1934, Joan (marr. diss. 1960), *d* of Robert Humphreys; three d (one s decd); 2nd, 1960, Beryl Mary Ada, *d* of late Herbert Vaughan Hann; one s]. *Address:* Green's Barn, 67 Mid Lavant, Chichester, W Sussex.

TURNBULL, Prof. Alexander Cuthbert, CBE 1982; MD, FRCOG; Nuffield Professor of Obstetrics and Gynaecology, University of Oxford, since 1973; Fellow of Oriel College, Oxford, since 1973; *b* 18 Jan. 1925; *s* of George Harley and Anne White Turnbull, Aberdeen, Scotland; *m* 1953, Elizabeth Paterson Nicol Bell; one *s* one d. *Educ:* Merchant Taylors' Sch., Crosby; Aberdeen Grammar Sch. (Modern Dux, 1942); Aberdeen Univ. MB, ChB 1947; MD (with Hons and Thursfield Prize) 1966; MRCOG 1954; FRCOG 1966. Sen. Lectr and Hon. Cons. Obstetrician and Gynaecologist (with Prof. J. Walker), Univ. of Dundee, 1957-61; Sen. Lectr and Hon. Cons. Obstetrician and Gynaecologist (with Sir Dugald Baird), Univ. of Aberdeen, 1961-66; Prof. of Obst. and Gynaecol., Welsh Nat. Sch. of Med., Cardiff, and Hon. Cons. Gynaecologist, also Adviser in Obst. and Gynaecol., Welsh Hosp. Bd, 1966-73. Member: Med. Educn Sub-cttee of UGC, 1973-; Lane Commn, 1971-; Clinical Research Bd of MRC, 1969-72. Hon. MA Oxford, 1973. *Publications:* (co-ed) The Oxygen Supply to the Human Fetus, 1960; (chap. in) The Scientific Basis of Obstetrics and Gynaecology (ed R. R. Macdonald), 1969; contribs to: Brit. Jl Obstetrics and Gynaecol., Lancet, BMJ, Jl of Endocrinology and various others. *Recreations:* reading, travelling, occasionally playing golf. *Address:* Nuffield Department of Obstetrics and Gynaecology, University of Oxford, Oxford OX3 9DU; John Radcliffe Hospital, Headington, Oxford.

TURNBULL, Rev. (Anthony) Michael (Arnold); Chief Secretary, Church Army, since 1976; *b* 27 Dec. 1935; *s* of George Ernest Turnbull and Adeline Turnbull (*née* Awty); *m* 1963, Brenda Susan Merchant; one *s* two d. *Educ:* Ilkley Grammar Sch.; Keble Coll., Oxford (MA); St John's Coll., Durham (DipTh). Deacon, 1960; priest, 1961; Curate: Middleton, 1960-61; Luton, 1961-65; Domestic Chaplain to Archbishop of York, 1965-69; Rector of Heslington and Chaplain, York Univ., 1969-76. Mem., General Synod, 1970-75. *Publications:* (contrib.) Unity: the next step?, 1972; God's Front Line, 1979; Parish Evangelism, 1980; Learning to Pray, 1981. *Recreations:* early morning jogging, cricket, family life. *Address:* Church Army, Independents Road, Blackheath, SE3 9LF. *T:* 01-318 1226.

TURNBULL, Sir Frank (Fearon), KBE 1964; CB 1954; CIE 1946; HM Civil Service, retired; *b* 30 April 1905; *m* 1947, Gwynnedd Celia Marian Lewis; three s. *Educ:* Marlborough Coll.; Trinity Hall, Cambridge. Entered

India Office, 1930; Principal Private Secretary to Secretary of State, 1941–46; Secretary to Cabinet Mission to India, 1946; Under-Secretary, HM Treasury, 1949–59; Secretary, Office of the Minister for Science, 1959–64; Deputy Under-Secretary of State, Dept of Education and Science, 1964–66. Member, Board of Governors, Imperial College, 1967–73. Hon. DSc Edinburgh, 1967. *Address:* 26 Green Lane, Amersham, Bucks HP6 6AS. *T:* Amersham 7647.

TURNBULL, George Henry, BSc (Hons), CEng, FIMechE, FIProdE; Chairman, Talbot UK, since 1979; Industrial Adviser, E. F. Hutton & Co. Inc., New York, since 1977; *b* 17 Oct. 1926; *m* 1950, Marion Wing; one *s* two *d. Educ:* King Henry VIII Sch., Coventry; Birmingham Univ. (BSc (Hons)). PA to Techn. Dir, Standard Motors, 1950–51; Liaison Officer between Standard Motors and Rolls Royce, 1951–53; Exec., i/c Experimental, 1954–55; Works Manager, Petters Ltd, 1955–56; Standard Motors: Divl Manager Cars, 1956–59; Gen. Man., 1959–62; Standard Triumph International: Dir and Gen. Man., 1962; Dep. Chm., 1969; British Leyland Motor Corporation Ltd: Dir, 1967; Dep. Man. Dir, 1968–73; Man. Dir, 1973; Man. Dir, BL Austin Morris Ltd, 1968–73; Chm., Truck & Bus Div., BL, 1972–73; Vice-Pres. and Dir, Hyundai Motors, Seoul, South Korea, 1974–77; Consultant Advr to Chm. and Man. Dir, Iran Nat. Motor Co., Tehran, 1977–78, Dep. Man. Dir, 1978–79. Pres., SMMT, 1982–. Mem. Council, Birmingham Chamber of Commerce and Industry, 1972 (Vice-Pres., 1973); past Member: Careers Adv. Bd, Univ. of Warwick; Management Bd, Engineering Employers' Assoc.; Engineering Employers' Fedn; Engrg Industry Trng Bd. Governor, Bablake Sch., Coventry. FIMI; Fellow, Inst. of Directors. *Recreations:* golf, tennis, fishing. *Address:* Talbot Motor Co. Ltd, Administrative Offices, Whitley, Coventry CV3 4GB.

TURNBULL, Rev. Michael; *see* Turnbull, Rev. A. M. A.

TURNBULL, Reginald March; *b* 10 Jan. 1907; *s* of late Sir March and Lady (Gertrude) Turnbull; *m* twice; one *s. Educ:* Horton Sch.; Eton; Cambridge Univ. (MA). Family shipping firm, Turnbull, Scott & Co., 1928–77. *Recreations:* teaching golf, motoring, water mills. *Address:* Sarum, Church Lane, Worplesdon, Surrey.

TURNBULL, Sir Richard (Gordon), GCMG 1962 (KCMG 1958, CMG 1953); *b* 7 July 1909; *s* of Richard Francis Turnbull; *m* 1939, Beatrice, *d* of John Wilson, Glasgow; two *s* one *d. Educ:* University College School, London; University College, London; Magdalene Coll., Cambridge. Colonial Administrative Service, Kenya: District Officer, 1931–48; Provincial Comr, 1948–53; Minister for Internal Security and Defence, 1954; Chief Secretary, Kenya, 1955–58; Governor and C-in-C, Tanganyika, 1958–61; Governor-General and Commander-in-Chief, 1961–62; Chairman, Central Land Board, Kenya, 1963–64; High Commissioner for Aden and the Protectorate of South Arabia, 1965–67. Fellow of University College, London; Hon. Fellow, Magdalene College, Cambridge, 1970–. KStJ 1958. *Address:* Bergamot House, Jedburgh, Roxburghshire. *T:* Jedburgh 2430.

TURNER, family name of **Baron Netherthorpe.**

TURNER, Alan B.; *see* Brooke Turner.

TURNER, Rt. Hon. Sir Alexander (Kingcome), PC 1968; KBE 1973; Kt 1963; *b* Auckland, New Zealand, 18 Nov. 1901; *s* of J. H. Turner; *m* 1934, Dorothea F., *d* of Alan Mulgan; two *s* one *d. Educ:* Auckland Grammar Sch.; Auckland Univ. (Scholar). BA 1921; MA 1922; LLB 1923. Served War of 1939–45, National Military Reserve, New Zealand. Barrister and Solicitor, 1923; QC (NZ) 1952. Carnegie Travelling Fellowship, 1949. Judge of the Supreme Court of New Zealand, 1953–62; Senior Resident Judge at Auckland, 1958–62; Judge of Court of Appeal, 1962–71, Pres., 1972–73. President, Auckland University Students' Assoc., 1928; President, Auckland District Court of Convocation, 1933; Member, Auckland Univ. Council, 1935–51; Vice-President, Auckland Univ., 1950–51; a Governor, Massey Agricultural Coll., 1944–53. Hon. LLD Auckland, 1965. *Publications:* (with George Spencer Bower) The Law of Estoppel by Representation, 1966; Res Judicata, 1969; The Law of Actionable Misrepresentation, 1974. *Recreations:* gardening, golf, Bush conservation, agriculture. *Address:* 14 St Michael's Crescent, Kelburn, Wellington 5, New Zealand. *T:* 757768. *Clubs:* Wellington; Auckland.

TURNER, Amédée Edward, QC 1976; Member (C) Suffolk, European Parliament, since 1979; *b* 26 March 1929; *s* of Frederick William Turner and Ruth Hempson; *m* 1960, Deborah Dudley Owen; one *s* one *d. Educ:* Temple Grove, Heron's Ghyll, Sussex; Dauntsey Sch., Wilts; Christ Church, Oxford (MA). Called to Bar, Inner Temple, 1954; practised patent bar, 1954–57; Associate, Kenyon & Kenyon, patent attorneys, NY, 1957–60; returned to London practice, 1960. Contested (C) Norwich N, gen. elections, 1964, 1966, 1970. Vice Chm., Legal Cttee, European Parlt, 1979. *Publications:* The Law of Trade Secrets, 1962, supplement, 1968; The Law of the New European Patent, 1979; many Conservative Party study papers on defence, oil and Middle East. *Recreations:* garden design, art deco collection, fish keeping, Box M at Albery Theatre, oil painting. *Address:* 3 Montrose Place, SW1. *T:* 01-235 2894, 01-235 3191; 1 Essex Court, Temple, EC4. *T:* 01-353 8507; Widenmayerstrasse 46, D8000 Munich 22, Germany. *T:* 29 51 25; The Barn, Westleton, Saxmundham, Suffolk. *T:* Westleton 235. *Clubs:* Carlton, Coningsby, United & Cecil.

TURNER, Adm. Sir (Arthur) Francis, KCB 1970 (CB 1966); DSC 1945; Chief of Fleet Support, Ministry of Defence, 1967–71; *b* 23 June 1912; *s* of Rear-Admiral A. W. J. Turner and Mrs A. M. Turner (*née* Lochrane); *m* 1963, Elizabeth Clare de Trafford; two *s. Educ:* Stonyhurst Coll. Entered RN, 1931; Commander, 1947; Captain, 1956; Rear-Admiral, 1964; Vice-Admiral, 1968; Admiral, 1970. Dir.-Gen. Aircraft (Navy), MoD, 1966–67. *Recreations:* cricket, golf. *Address:* Plantation House, East Horsley, Surrey. *Clubs:* Army and Navy; Union (Malta).

TURNER, Comdr Bradwell Talbot, CVO 1955; DSO 1940; OBE 1951; JP; RN, retired 1957; *b* 7 April 1907; *s* of late A. F. and A. I. Turner; *m* 1937, Mary G. B., *d* of Professor W. Nixon; three *d. Educ:* Christ's Hospital; RN Colleges Osborne and Dartmouth. Joined Royal Navy, 1921; Barrister-at-Law, 1956; Naval Attaché, Oslo, Norway, 1954–57. With The Marconi Co., 1957–72. MIEE 1946. JP Chelmsford 1962 (Chm. Bench, 1974–77). Officer, Legion of Merit (USA), 1945. *Recreation:* riding. *Address:* 44 St Johns Road, Writtle, Essex CM1 3EB.

TURNER, Air Vice-Marshal Cameron Archer, CB 1968; CBE 1960 (OBE 1947); Royal New Zealand Air Force, retired; *b* Wanganui, NZ, 29 Aug. 1915; *s* of James Oswald Turner and Vida Cathrine Turner; *m* 1941, Josephine Mary, *d* of George Richardson; two *s. Educ:* New Plymouth Boys' High Sch.; Victoria University of Wellington. CEng, FIEE, FRAeS. Commn RAF, 1936–39; commn RNZ Air Force, 1940; served War of 1939–45, UK, NZ, and Pacific; comd RNZAF Station Nausori, Fiji, 1944; comd RNZAF Station, Guadalcanal, Solomon Islands, 1944; Director of Signals, 1945–47; psa 1947; RNZAF Liaison Officer, Melbourne, Australia, 1948–50; comd RNZAF Station, Taieri, NZ, 1950–52; Director of Organization, HQ, RNZAF, 1953–56; comd RNZAF Station Ohakea, NZ, 1956–58; Asst Chief of Air Staff, HQ, RNZAF, 1958; Air Member for Personnel, HQ, RNZAF, 1959; idc 1960; AOC HQ, RNZAF, London, 1961–63; Air Member for Supply, HQ, RNZAF, 1964–65; Chief of Air Staff, HQ RNZAF, 1966–69. Dir, NZ Inventions Develt Authority, 1969–76. Pres., RNZAF Assoc., 1972–81. *Recreations:* fishing, golf. *Address:* 37a Parkvale Road, Wellington 5, New Zealand. *T:* 766063. *Clubs:* Wellington, United Services Officers' (Wellington); Taranaki (New Plymouth).

TURNER, Sir Cedric Oban, Kt 1967; CBE 1958; Chief Executive and General Manager, Qantas Empire Airways Ltd, 1955–67; *b* 13 Feb. 1907; *s* of S. Turner, Gulgong, NSW; *m* 1935, Shirley (*d* 1972), *d* of late Sir Joseph Totterdell, sometime Lord Mayor of Perth, Western Australia; one *s* three *d. Educ:* Sydney High Sch. Chartered Accountant: Robert W. Nelson, 1924–29, UK and Europe, 1929–34. Joined Qantas Empire Airways, 1934; Chief Accountant; Assistant General Manager, 1949–51; General Manager, 1951–55. *Recreation:* golf. *Address:* 16 Livingstone Avenue, Pymble, NSW 2073, Australia.

TURNER, Brig. Charles Edward Francis, CBE 1944 (OBE 1941); DSO 1943; late RE; *b* 23 April 1899; *s* of late Lieut A. E. Turner, RE, and E. B., *d* of Maj.-Gen. Sir C. H. Scott, KCB; *m* 1930, Mary Victoria, *d* of H. Leeds Swift, York; one *s* two *d. Educ:* Twyford Sch., Winchester; Wellington Coll., Berks; Royal Military Academy, Woolwich. Regular Officer, Royal Engineers, Sept. 1917; BEF France, June-Nov. 1918; NREF Russia, July-Sept. 1919; India, 1920–23, including two years on North-West Frontier on service (despatches); Christ's Coll., Cambridge, 1923–24; Ordnance Survey, York and Edinburgh, 1925–30; Staff Coll., Camberley, 1931–32; Singapore, Egypt, Palestine, 1934–37, including service in Palestine (Bt Major, despatches); War Office, 1937–39; MEF 1940–43 (OBE, DSO, CBE, despatches twice); Malaya, 1948–50; retired pay, 1950. National Council of Social Service, 1950–58; Secretary, Iona Appeal Trust, 1958–61. *Address:* The Colleens, Cousley Wood, Wadhurst, East Sussex TN5 6HF. *T:* Wadhurst 2387.

TURNER, Christopher Gilbert; Headmaster, Stowe School, since 1979; *b* 23 Dec. 1929; *s* of Theodore F. Turner, *qv*; *m* 1961, Lucia, *d* of late Prof. S. R. K. Glanville (Provost of King's Coll., Cambridge); one *s* two *d. Educ:* Winchester Coll. (Schol.); New Coll., Oxford (Exhibnr), MA. Asst Master, Radley Coll., 1952–61; Senior Classics Master, Charterhouse, 1961–68; Headmaster, Dean Close Sch., 1968–79. Schoolmaster Student at Christ Church, Oxford, 1968. Foundation Member of Council, Cheltenham Colleges of Educn, 1968. Mem., HMC Cttee, 1974–75; Chm., Common Entrance Cttee, 1976–80; Governor: Oakdene Sch., Elstree; Lambrook Sch.; Chm. of Governors, Beachborough Sch. Lay Reader. FRSA. Rotarian. *Publication:* chapter on History, in Comparative Study of Greek and Latin Literature, 1969. *Recreations:* music (violin-playing), reading, walking, different forms of manual labour; OUBC 1951. *Address:* Stowe School, Buckingham. *T:* Buckingham 3165; Meadow House, Rhossili, near Swansea, Glam. *T:* Gower 582. *Club:* Vincent's (Oxford).
See also W. H. Hughes, M. J. Turner.

TURNER, Christopher John, OBE 1977; Governor, Turks and Caicos Islands, since 1982; *b* 17 Aug. 1933; *s* of Arthur Basil Turner and Joan Meddows (*née* Taylor); *m* 1941, Irene Philomena de Souza; one *s* two *d. Educ:* Truro Cathedral Sch.; Jesus Coll., Cambridge (MA). Served RAF, Pilot Officer (Navigator), 1951–53. Tanganyika/Tanzania: Dist Officer, 1958–61; Dist Comr, 1961–62; Magistrate and Regional Local Courts Officer, 1962–64; Sec., Sch. Admin, 1964–69; Anglo-French Condominium of New Hebrides: Dist Agent, 1970–73; Develt Sec., 1973; Financial Sec., 1975; Chief Sec., 1977–80; Admin. Officer, Hong Kong, 1980–82. Vanuatu Independence

Medal, 1981. *Recreations:* ornithology, photography, diving. *Address:* c/o Foreign and Commonwealth Office, SW1; 98 Christchurch Road, Winchester SO23 9TE. *T:* Winchester 61318.

TURNER, Air Cdre Clifford John, CB 1973; MBE 1953; *b* 21 Dec. 1918; *s* of J. E. Turner; *m* 1942, Isabel Emily Cormack; two *s. Educ:* Parkstone Grammar Sch.; RAF Techn. College. Engrg Apprentice, 1935–38; various RAF engrg appts, 1938–64; Group Dir, RAF Staff Coll., 1965–67; Stn Comdr, RAF Colerne, 1968–69; AO Engineering, Training Comd, 1969–73.

TURNER, Colin Francis; Registrar, Family Division of High Court, since 1971; *b* 11 April 1930; *s* of Sidney F. and Charlotte C. Turner; *m* 1951, Josephine Alma Jones; two *s* one *d. Educ:* Beckenham Grammar Sch.; King's Coll., London. LLB 1955. Entered Principal Probate Registry, 1949; District Probate Registrar, York, 1965–68. *Publications:* (ed jtly) Rayden on Divorce, 9th, 11th, 12th and 13th edns; an editor of Supreme Court Practice, 1972–. *Recreations:* birding, fishing. *Address:* 18 South Eden Park Road, Beckenham, Kent BR3 3BG. *T:* 01-777 0344.

TURNER, Colin William Carstairs, DFC 1944; Managing Director, The Colin Turner Group, International Media Representatives and Marketing Consultants; *b* 4 Jan. 1922; *s* of late Colin C. W. Turner, Enfield; *m* 1949, Evelyn Mary, *d* of late Claude H. Buckard, Enfield; three *s* one *d. Educ:* Highgate Sch. Served War of 1939–45 with RAF, 1940–45, Air observer; S. Africa and E Africa, 223 Squadron; Desert Air Force, N. Africa, 1942–44; commissioned, 1943; invalided out as Flying Officer, 1945, after air crash; Chm., 223 Squadron Assoc., 1975–78. Member Enfield Borough Council, 1956–58. President, Overseas Press and Media Association, 1965–67 (Hon. Secretary, 1967; Hon. Treasurer, 1974–82; Editor, Overseas Media Guide, 1968, 1969, 1970, 1971, 1972, 1973, 1974); Chm., PR Cttee, Commonwealth Press Union, 1970–81; Chm., Cons. Commonwealth and Overseas Council, 1976–82 (Dep. Chm. 1975). Mem., Nat. Exec., Cons. Party, 1946–53, 1968–73, 1976–82; Chm., Enfield North Cons. Assoc., 1979–. Contested (C) Enfield (East), 1950 and 1951; MP (C) Woolwich West, 1959–64. Editor, The Cholmeleian, 1982. *Recreations:* gardening, do-it-yourself, sailing, fishing. *Address:* 55 Rowantree Road, Enfield, Mddx. *T:* 01-363 2403.

TURNER, Dr David Warren, FRS 1973; Fellow of Balliol College, Oxford, since 1967; Reader in Physical Chemistry, Oxford, since 1978; *b* 16 July 1927; *s* of Robert Cecil Turner and Constance Margaret (*née* Bonner); *m* 1954, Barbara Marion Fisher; one *s* one *d. Educ:* Westcliff High Sch.; Univ. of Exeter. MA, BSc, PhD, DIC. Lectr, Imperial Coll., 1958; Reader in Organic Chemistry, Imperial Coll., 1965; Lectr in Physical Chem., Oxford Univ., 1968. Lectures: Kahlbaum, Univ. of Basle, 1971; Van Geuns, Univ. of Amsterdam, 1974; Harkins, Chicago Univ., 1974; Kistiakowski, Harvard, 1979; Liversidge, RSC, 1981–82. Tilden Medal, Chemical Soc., 1967; Harrison Howe Award, Amer. Chem. Soc., 1973. Hon. DTech, Royal Inst., Stockholm, 1971; Hon. DPhil Basle, 1980. *Publications:* Molecular Photoelectron Spectroscopy, 1970; contrib. Phil. Trans Royal Soc., Proc. Royal Soc., Jl Chem. Soc., etc. *Recreations:* music, gardening, tinkering with gadgets. *Address:* Balliol College, Oxford.

TURNER, Donald William, CEng, FICE; Planning Director, British Airports Authority, since 1973; Full-time Member, British Airports Authority Board, since 1975; *b* 17 Aug. 1925; *s* of William John Turner and Agnes Elizabeth Jane (*née* Bristow); *m* 1947, Patricia (*née* Stuteley); one *s* one *d. Educ:* Wanstead County High Sch.; Birmingham Univ. Served War, Army, 1943–45. Subseq. completed engrg trng in Britain; then took up post in Australia with Qld Railways, 1949. Left Qld, 1954; joined firm of UK consulting engrs and then worked in W Africa on rly and highway construction until 1960. Returned to UK, but remained with consultants until 1966, when joined British Airports Authority as a Civil Engr; became Chief Engr of Heathrow Airport, 1970; Dep. Dir of Planning, 1972. *Recreations:* gardening, reading, sketching. *Address:* Peter's Cottage, New England Road, Haywards Heath, Sussex.

TURNER, Dudley Russell Flower, CB 1977; Secretary, Advisory, Conciliation and Arbitration Service, 1974–77; *b* 15 Nov. 1916; *s* of Gerald Flower Turner and Dorothy May Turner (*née* Gillard), Penang; *m* 1941, Sheila Isobel Stewart; one *s* one *d. Educ:* Whitgift Sch.; London Univ. (BA Hons). Served RA (Captain), 1940–46. Entered Ministry of Labour, 1935; HM Treasury, 1953–56; Principal Private Secretary to Minister of Labour, 1956–59; Assistant Secretary: Cabinet Office, 1959–62; Ministry of Labour, 1962–64, 1966; Under-Sec., Ministry of Labour, 1967; Asst Under-Sec. of State, Dept of Employment and Productivity, 1968–70; Under-Sec., Trng Div., 1970–72, Manpower Gen. Div., 1972–73, Dept of Employment; Sec., Commn on Industrial Relations, 1973–74. Imperial Defence Coll., 1965. Chm., East Surrey Decorative and Fine Arts Soc., 1980–. *Recreations:* music, gardening. *Address:* 9 Witherby Close, Croydon, Surrey CR0 5SU. *Club:* Civil Service.

TURNER, Elston Grey; *see* Grey-Turner.

TURNER, Sir Eric (Gardner), Kt 1981; CBE 1975; FBA; Professor of Papyrology, University College, London, 1950–78, now Emeritus; Leverhulme Emeritus Research Fellow, 1982; *b* 26 Feb. 1911; *s* of late William Ernest Stephen Turner; *m* 1940, Louise B. Taylor; one *s* one *d. Educ:* King Edward VII Sch., Sheffield; Magdalen Coll., Oxford (Demy). First Class

Hons Classical Mods, 1932, and Lit Hum, 1934; Goldsmiths' Senior Scholar, 1935; Assistant in Humanity, University of Aberdeen, 1936; Lecturer in Classics, Aberdeen Univ., 1938–48; Reader in Papyrology, University of London, 1948–50; first Dir, Univ. of London Inst. of Classical Studies, 1953–63. Pres., Internat. Assoc. of Papyrologists, 1965–74; Vice-President: Hellenic Soc. (Pres., 1968–71); Roman Soc.; Egypt Exploration Soc., 1978– (Chm. Cttee, 1956–78); Chairman: Organising Cttee, Third Internat. Congress of Classical Studies, London, 1959; Organising Cttee, XIVth Internat. Congress of Papyrologists, Oxford, 1974; Jt Editor, Graeco-Roman publications. Visiting Member, Inst. for Advanced Study, Princeton, NJ, 1961, 1964, 1968, 1978. Hon. Fellow: Warburg Inst., 1978; University Coll., London, 1979. Pres., Union Académique Internationale, 1974–77 (Vice-Pres., 1970–73). Hon. Mem., Socîetâs Scientiarum Fennica (Humanities Section), 1969; For. Member: Accademia di Archeologia, Lettere e Belle Arti (Letters Section) of the Società Nazionale di Scienze, Lettere ed Arti, Naples, 1973; Det Kongelige Danske Videnskabernes Selskab (historisk-filosofiske klasse); Amer. Philosophical Soc., 1977; Corresp. Mem., Österreichische Akademie der Wissenschaften, 1975; Sachsische Akademie der Wissenschaften, 1976; Deutsche Archäologisches Institut, 1976; Associate, Académie royale des Sciences, des Lettres et des Beaux-Arts de Belgique, 1974. Patron of Honour, Fundación Pastor, Madrid, 1981. Hon. Dr Phil et Lettres Brussels, 1956; Hon. DèsL Geneva, 1976; Hon. DLitt Liverpool, 1978. *Publications:* Catalogue of Greek Papyri in University of Aberdeen, 1939; (with C. H. Roberts) Catalogue of Greek Papyri in John Rylands Library, Vol. IV, 1951; The Hibeh Papyri, Part II, 1955; (with others) The Oxyrhynchus Papyri Part XXIV, 1957, Part XXV, 1959, Part XXVII, 1962, Part XXXI, 1966, Part XXXIII, 1968, Part XXXVIII, 1971, Part XLI, 1972, Part XLVIII, 1981, Part L, 1983; (with H. I. Bell, V. Martin, D. van Berchem) The Abinnæus Papyri, 1962; New Fragments of the Misoumenos of Menander, 1965; Greek Papyri, an Introduction, 1968, 2nd edn 1980; Greek Manuscripts of the Ancient World, 1970; Menander: The Girl from Samos, 1972; The Papyrologist at Work, 1973; The Typology of the Early Codex, 1977; Recto and Verso, 1978; various papers in learned journals (bibliography to 1980 in Papyri Edited in Honour of E. G. T., 1981). *Recreations:* chamber music, playing the gramophone, walking, sailing. *Address:* Thornheath, Cathedral Square, Fortrose, Ross-shire. *Club:* United Oxford & Cambridge University.

TURNER, Dame Eva, DBE 1962; FRAM; prima donna; *b* Oldham, Lancashire, 10 March 1892; unmarried. Began to sing at an early age and, whilst in her teens, spent some years at the Royal Academy of Music; joined Royal Carl Rosa Opera Company in 1915, and became the Prima donna of the Company, remaining with it until 1924, when Toscanini engaged her for La Scala, Milan. Appeared all over Europe, USA, and S America; London, at Covent Garden in 1928 when she sang in Puccini's opera Turandot, Aida, and many others; for the Celebrations in connection with the commemoration of the Centenary of Bolivar, was specially chosen by President Gomez to be the Prima Donna. Visiting Professor of Voice to Music Faculty of University of Oklahoma, USA, 1949–59 (resigned); Professor of Voice Royal Academy of Music, London, 1959–66 (resigned). Pres., Wagner Soc., 1971–. Hon. Internat. Member Sigma Alpha Iota, 1951–; Hon. Internat. Soroptomist, 1955–. Member National Assoc. of Teachers of Singing (USA). Hon. GSM 1968; FRCM 1974; FRNCM 1978; Hon. FTCL. Hon. DMus Manchester, 1979. *Recreations:* swimming, riding, motoring. *Address:* 26 Palace Court, W2; Junesca, Brusino-Arsizio, Lake of Lugano, Switzerland. *Club:* Royal Overseas League.

TURNER, Brig. Dame Evelyn Marguerite; *see* Turner, Brig. Dame Margot.

TURNER, Sir Francis; *see* Turner, Sir Arthur Francis.

TURNER, Prof. Grenville, FRS 1980; Professor of Physics, Sheffield University, since 1980; *b* 1 Nov. 1936; *s* of Arnold and Florence Turner, Todmorden, Yorks; *m* 1961, Kathleen, *d* of William and Joan Morris, Rochdale, Lancs; one *s* one *d. Educ:* Todmorden Grammar Sch.; St John's Coll., Cambridge (MA); Balliol Coll., Oxford (DPhil). Asst Prof., Univ. of Calif at Berkeley, 1962–64; Lectr, Sheffield Univ., 1964–74, Sen. Lectr, 1974–79, Reader, 1979–80. Vis. Associate in Nuclear Geophysics, Calif Inst. of Technol., 1970–71. *Publications:* scientific papers. *Recreation:* photography. *Address:* 9 Canterbury Crescent, Sheffield S10 3RW. *T:* Sheffield 305904.

TURNER, Sir Harvey, Kt 1967; CBE 1953; Chairman of Directors of a number of Companies; *b* 11 Sept. 1889; *s* of Edward and Maude Turner; *m* 1914, Margaret Ethel Penman (*d* 1978); three *s* two *d. Educ:* Huia Sch.; Giles Business College; Auckland Technical College. Served War of 1914–18, New Zealand; War of 1939–45 (Middle East, 1941–42; Major; despatches). Past President, Auckland Chamber of Commerce; Past Chairman, Auckland Harbour Board. *Publication:* (with Allan Kirk) Turners of Huia, 1966. *Recreations:* tennis, swimming, gardening. *Address:* PO Box 56, Auckland 1, New Zealand; Summit Drive, Auckland 3, New Zealand. *T:* Auckland 867-572.

TURNER, Rev. Professor Henry Ernest William, DD; Canon Residentiary, Durham Cathedral, 1950–73; Treasurer, 1956–73; Sub-Dean, 1959–73; Acting Dean, 1973; Van Mildert Professor of Divinity, Durham University, 1958–73, now Emeritus; *b* 14 Jan. 1907; *o s* of Henry Frederick Richard and Ethel Turner, Sheffield; *m* 1936, Constance Parker, *d* of Dr E. P. Haythornthwaite, Rowrah, Cumberland; two *s. Educ:* King Edward VII

Sch., Sheffield; St John's Coll., Oxford; Wycliffe Hall, Oxford. MA 1933; BD 1940; DD 1955. Curate, Christ Church, Cockermouth, 1931-34; Curate, Holy Trinity, Wavertree, 1934-35; Fellow, Chaplain and Tutor, Lincoln Coll., Oxford, 1935-50; Chaplain, RAFVR, 1940-45; Librarian, Lincoln Coll., 1945-48; Senior Tutor, Lincoln Coll., 1948-50; Lightfoot Prof. of Divinity, Durham Univ., 1950-58. Select Preacher, Oxford Univ., 1950-51; Member: Anglican delegation to Third Conference of World Council of Churches, Lund, 1952; Anglican-Presbyterian Conversations, 1953-; Doctrine Commn of the Church of England, 1967-; Bampton Lecturer (Oxford), 1954. Theological Consultant to Anglican Roman Catholic Conversations, 1970. *Publications:* The Life and Person of Jesus Christ, 1951; The Patristic Doctrine of Redemption, 1952; Jesus Master and Lord, 1953; The Pattern of Christian Truth (Bampton Lectures), 1955; Why Bishops?, 1955; The Meaning of the Cross, 1959; (jt author with H. Montefiore) Thomas and the Evangelists, 1962; Historicity and the Gospels, 1963; Jesus the Christ, 1976; contributions to the Guardian, Theology and Church Quarterly Review. *Address:* Realands, Eskdale, near Holmrook, Cumbria CA19 1TW. *T:* Eskdale 321.

TURNER, Prof. Herbert Arthur (Frederick), BSc Econ London, PhD Manchester, MA Cantab; Montague Burton Professor of Industrial Relations, University of Cambridge, since 1963; Fellow of Churchill College, Cambridge; *b* 11 Dec. 1919; *s* of Frederick and May Turner. *Educ:* Henry Thornton Sch., Clapham; University of London. BSc (Econ) London, 1939; PhD Manchester, 1960. Member, Trades Union Congress Research and Economic Department, 1944; Assistant Education Secretary, TUC, 1947; Lecturer, 1950, Senior Lecturer, 1959, University of Manchester; Montague Burton Professor of Industrial Relations, University of Leeds, 1961-63. Mem., NBPI, 1967-71. Visiting Professor: Harvard and MIT, 1971-72; Sydney Univ., 1976-77; Hong Kong Univ., 1978-79. Sometime Adviser to Govts of Congo, Zaire, Tanzania, Fiji, Papua New Guinea, Zambia and other developing countries; Chm., Incomes Policies Commn of E African Community, 1973; ILO Adviser, Iran, 1975; Labour Adviser, UNECA, 1980. *Publications:* Trade Union Growth, Structure and Policy, 1962; Wages: the Problems for Underdeveloped Countries, 1965; Prices, Wages and Incomes Policies, 1966; Labour Relations in the Motor Industry, 1967; Is Britain Really Strike-Prone?, 1969; Do Trade Unions Cause Inflation?, 1972, 3rd edn 1978; Management Characteristics and Labour Conflict, 1978; The Last Colony: labour in Hong Kong, 1980; various reports of ILO, monographs, papers and articles on labour economics and statistics, industrial relations. *Recreations:* minimal but mostly excusable. *Address:* Churchill College, Cambridge. *Club:* United Oxford & Cambridge University.

TURNER, Hugh Wason, CMG 1980; Director, National Gas Turbine Establishment, since 1980; *b* 2 April 1923; *s* of Thomas W. Turner and Elizabeth P. Turner (*née* Pooley); *m* 1950, Rosemary Borley; two *s* two *d*. *Educ:* Dollar Academy; Glasgow University. BSc Hons (Mech. Eng); CEng; FRAeS. Aeroplane and Armament Experimental Establishment, 1943-52; Chief Tech. Instructor, Empire Test Pilots School, 1953; A&AEE (Prin. Scientific Officer), 1954-64; Asst Director, RAF Aircraft, Min. of Technology, 1965-68; Superintendent, Trials Management, A&AEE, 1968-69; Division Leader, Systems Engineering, NATO MRCA Management Agency (NAMMA), Munich, 1969-74; Chief Superintendent, A&AEE, 1974-75; DGA1 (Dir Gen., Tornado), MoD (PE), 1976-80. *Recreations:* ski-ing, model building, photography, DIY. *Address:* Lavender Cottage, 1 Highcliff Road, Lyme Regis, Dorset DT7 3EW. *T:* Lyme Regis 2310.

TURNER, James Grant Smith, CMG 1949; *b* 7 Aug. 1897; *s* of Hector and Mary Turner; *m* 1st, 1930, Jemima Cunningham (*d* 1937); one *s* one *d*; 2nd, 1947, Freda Gurling (*d* 1970); one *s*; 3rd, 1981, Margaret Spear. *Educ:* Allan Glen's Sch., Glasgow; Glasgow Univ.; Liverpool Univ. MB, ChB, Glasgow, 1924; BSc, DPH, Glasgow, 1926; DTM, Liverpool, 1927. MO, Nigeria, 1927; Senior Health Officer, 1938; transferred to Sierra Leone, 1941; DDMS, Gold Coast, 1945, DMS, 1946-50; retired Jan. 1950. Military service: European War, 1915-18; War of 1939-45, 1940-41. *Recreations:* walking, fishing. *Address:* Belvedere, Legion Lane, Tywardreath, Par, Cornwall PL24 2QR.

TURNER, James Neil Frederick, MA, FCIOB, FCIArb; Managing Director, E. Turner & Sons Ltd, Cardiff, since 1970; *b* 23 June 1932; *s* of Thomas Henry Huxley Turner and Phoebe Elvira (*née* Evans); *m* 1974, Elizabeth Jillian Wells; one *d*. *Educ:* Shrewsbury Sch.; Christ Church, Oxford (MA). Called to the Bar, Inner Temple, 1957. Holloway Brothers, London, 1957-62; H. R. H. Construction, New York, 1962-63; E. Turner & Sons Ltd, Cardiff, 1963-. *Recreation:* sailing. *Address:* 2 Kymin Terrace, Penarth, South Glamorgan, Wales. *T:* Penarth 701732. *Club:* Cardiff and County (Cardiff).

TURNER, Hon. Joanna Elizabeth, (Hon. Mrs Turner), MA; Classics Teacher, Ellesmere College, Salop, 1975-80; *b* 10 Jan. 1923; 2nd *d* of 1st Baron Piercy, CBE, and Mary Louisa, *d* of Hon. Thomas Pelham; *m* 1968, James Francis Turner, *er s* of late Rev. P. R. Turner. *Educ:* St Paul's Girls' Sch.; Somerville Coll., Oxford (Sen. Classics Schol.). Asst Classics Mistress: Downe House, Newbury, 1944-46; Gordonstoun Sch., 1947-48; Badminton Sch., Bristol, 1948-65, Headmistress, Badminton Sch., Bristol, 1966-69. JP Inner London (Juvenile Courts), 1970-76. *Recreations:* painting, foreign travel, reading. *Address:* The Old Coach House, Burford, Oxon. *T:* Burford 2368.

TURNER, Hon. John Napier, PC (Can.) 1965; QC (Can.); lawyer with McMillan Binch, Toronto, since 1976; *b* 7 June 1929; *s* of Leonard Turner

and Phyllis Turner (*née* Gregory); *m* 1963, Geills McCrae Kilgour; three *s* one *d*. *Educ:* Norman Model Public Sch., Ottawa, Ont.; Ashbury Coll., 1939-42; St Patrick's Coll., 1942-45; Univ. of BC; Oxford Univ. BA (PolSci, Hons) BC, 1949; Rhodes Scholar, Oxford Univ., BA (Juris.) 1951; BCL 1952; MA 1957. Joined Stikeman, Elliott, Tamaki, Mercier & Turner, Montreal, Quebec; practised with them after being called to English Bar, 1953, Bar of Quebec, 1954 and Bar of Ont., 1968; QC (Can.) 1968. MP for St Lawrence-St George, Montreal, 1962-68, Ottawa-Carleton, 1968-75; Parly Sec. to Minister of Northern Affairs and Nat. Resources, 1963-65; Minister without Portfolio, Dec. 1965-April 1967; Registrar-Gen. of Canada April 1967-Jan. 1968; Minister of Consumer and Corporate Affairs, Jan.-July 1968; Solicitor-Gen., April-July 1968; Minister of Justice and Attorney-Gen. of Canada, July 1968-Jan. 1972; Minister of Finance, 1972-75. Joined law firm of McMillan, Binch, Toronto, 1976. Barbados Bar, 1969; Yukon and Northwest Territories, 1969; Trinidad Bar, 1969; British Columbia, 1969. Hon. Dr of Laws: Univ. of New Brunswick, 1968; York Univ., Toronto, 1969; Hon. Dr of Civil Law, Mt Allison Univ., NB, 1980. *Publications:* Senate of Canada, 1961; Politics of Purpose, 1968. *Recreations:* tennis, squash, canoeing; Canadian Track Field Champion 1950-51, Mem. English Track and Field Team. *Address:* (home) 435 Russell Hill Road, Toronto, Ont M5P 2S4, Canada. *T:* (416) 482-4330; (office) PO Box 38, 38th Floor, Royal Bank Plaza, Toronto, Ont M5J 2J7. *T:* (416) 865-7101.

TURNER, Prof. John Stewart, FAA 1979; FRS 1982; Professor of Geophysical Fluid Dynamics, Australian National University, since 1975; *b* Sydney, Aust., 11 Jan. 1930; *s* of Ivan Stewart Turner and Enid Florence (*née* Payne); *m* 1959, Sheila Lloyd Jones; two *s* one *d*. *Educ:* North Sydney Boys' High Sch.; Wesley Coll., Univ. of Sydney (BSc, MSc); Trinity Coll., Univ. of Cambridge (PhD). FInstP 1969. Research Officer, CSIRO cloud physics group, 1953-54 and 1960-61; 1851 Exhibition Overseas Schol., 1954-57; postdoctoral research post, Univ. of Manchester, 1958-59; Rossby Fellow, then Associate Scientist, Woods Hole Oceanographic Instn, 1962-66; Asst Director of Research, then Reader, Dept of Applied Mathematics and Theoretical Physics, Univ. of Cambridge, 1966-75; Fellow of Darwin Coll., Cambridge, 1974; Foundation Prof. of Geophysical Fluid Dynamics in the Research Sch. of Earth Sciences, ANU, 1975-. Member, Australian Marine Sciences and Technologies Adv. Cttee (AMSTAC), 1979-. Associate Editor, Journal of Fluid Mechanics, 1975-; Mem. Editorial Adv. Board, Deep-Sea Research, 1974-. *Publications:* Buoyancy Effects in Fluids, 1973, paperback 1979; papers in various scientific jls. *Recreations:* bushwalking, photography, home handyman. *Address:* (home) 16 Juwin Street, Aranda, ACT 2614, Australia. *T:* (062) 51 1972; (office) Research School of Earth Sciences, Australian National University, PO Box 4, Canberra, ACT 2600. *T:* (062) 49 4530.

TURNER, John Turnage; His Honour Judge Turner; a Circuit Judge, since 1976; *b* 12 Nov. 1929; *s* of Wilfrid Edward and May Martha Turner; *m* 1956, Gillian Mary Rayner; two *d*. *Educ:* Earls Colne Grammar School. Called to the Bar, Inner Temple, 1952. *Recreations:* tennis, music appreciation, gardening, watching cricket. *Address:* Bolberry House, Bures, Suffolk CO8 5JG. *T:* Bures 227207. *Clubs:* MCC; Colchester Garrison Officers'.

TURNER, Brig. Dame Margot, (E. M. Turner), DBE 1965 (MBE 1946); RRC 1956; Matron-in-Chief and Director Army Nursing Service, 1964-68; *b* 10 May 1910; *d* of late Thomas Frederick Turner and late Molly Cecilia (*née* Bryan). *Educ:* Finchley County Sch., Middlesex. Trained at St Bartholomew's Hospital, London, 1931-35. Joined QAIMNS, 1937 (became QARANC, 1949). Served in UK, India, Malaya, Hong Kong, Bermuda, Germany and Near East. POW Sumatra, Feb. 1942-Aug. 1945. Col Comdt, QARANC, 1969-74. CStJ 1966. *Relevant Publication:* Sir John Smyth, Will to Live: the story of Dame Margot Turner, 1970. *Recreations:* reading, photography, golf, tennis. *Address:* 2 Chantry Court, Frimley, Surrey. *T:* Camberley 22030. *Club:* United Nursing Services.

TURNER, Michael John; QC 1973; a Recorder of the Crown Court, since 1972; *b* 3 May 1931; *s* of Theodore F. Turner, *qv* ; *m* 1st, 1956, Hon. Susan Money-Coutts (marr. diss. 1965); one *s* one *d*; 2nd, 1965, Frances Deborah Croom-Johnson; two *s*. *Educ:* Winchester; Magdalene Coll., Cambridge (BA). Called to Bar, Inner Temple, 1954 (Bencher 1981). Chm., E Mids Agricultural Tribunal, 1979-82. *Recreations:* hunting, sailing, music. *Address:* Orchard House, Maidford, Towcester, Northants. *T:* Blakesley 391; 30 Shrewsbury House, Cheyne Walk, SW3. *T:* 01-352 2832.
See also His Honour Judge W. H. Hughes, C. G. Turner.

TURNER, Michael Ralph; Group Managing Director since 1976, and Chief Executive since 1982, Associated Book Publishers PLC; Chairman, Associated Book Publishers (UK) Ltd, since 1977; *b* 26 Jan. 1929; *s* of Ralph Victor Turner and May Turner; *m* 1955, Ruth Baylis; two *s* two *d*. *Educ:* Newport Sch., Essex; Trinity Coll., Cambridge (BA Hons). Served RAF, Transport Comd, 1947-49. Jun. Editor, J. M. Dent & Sons, 1949-50; Methuen & Co.: Jun. Editor, 1953; subseq. Publicity and Promotion Manager, and Dir; Associated Publishers Ltd: Marketing Dir, 1973; Asst Gp Man. Dir, 1975; Gp Man. Dir, 1976. Chm., Methuen Inc., New York, 1981-; Pres., Carswell Co. Ltd, Toronto, 1982-; Dir, ABP Investments (Aust.) Pty Ltd, 1976-. Chm., Book Marketing Council, 1981-; Member: Book Trade Working Party, 1973-74; Council, Publishers Assoc., 1981-; National Council and Exec., NBL, 1980-. *Publications:* The Bluffer's Guide to the Theatre, 1967; Parlour Poetry, 1967; (with Antony Miall) The Parlour Song Book, 1972; (with Antony

Miall) Just a Song at Twilight, 1975; (with Antony Miall) The Edwardian Song Book, 1982; (with Leslie Lonsdale-Cooper) translations of Hergé's Tintin books, 1958-. *Recreations:* reading, music, theatre — the more frivolous arts generally. *Address:* Cobdens, Binsted, Alton, Hants GU34 4PE. *T:* Bentley (Hants) 22273. *Club:* Garrick.

TURNER, Norman Henry, CBE 1977; Official Solicitor to the Supreme Court of Judicature, 1970-80; *b* 11 May 1916; *s* of late Henry James Turner, MA and Hilda Gertrude Turner; *m* 1939, Dora Ardella (*née* Cooper); three *s* two *d. Educ:* Nottingham High School. Articled, Nottingham, 1933; admitted Solicitor (Hons), 1938; joined Official Solicitor's Dept, 1948; Asst Official Solicitor, 1958. *Recreation:* caravanning. *Address:* 48 Rushington Avenue, Maidenhead, Berks. *T:* Maidenhead 22918.

TURNER, Patricia, OBE 1981; Head of National Equal Rights Department, and National Industrial Officer, General and Municipal Workers' Union, since 1971; *b* 14 May 1927; *d* of John Richard and Maire Collins; *m* 1954, Donald Turner, BSc (Econ). *Educ:* London School of Economics (BSc (Econ), MSc (Econ)). Industrial Sociology Lectr, 1965-69; Consultant, Manpower and Productivity Service (Dept of Employment and Productivity), 1969-70; Sen. Industrial Relations Officer, Commn on Industrial Relations, 1970-71. Member: Confedn of Shipbuilding and Engineering Unions Exec. Council, 1971-; Engineering Industry Training Bd, 1971-; Food, Drink and Tobacco Industry Training Bd, 1971-; Women's Nat. Commn, 1971-; Occupational Pensions Bd, 1973-. *Recreations:* reading, theatre. *Address:* (office) G&MWU, Thorne House, Ruxley Ridge, Claygate, Esher, Surrey KT10 0TL. *T:* Esher 62081.

TURNER, Peter; *see* Turner, T. P.

TURNER, Air Vice-Marshal Peter, CB 1979; MA; Bursar, Wolfson College, Cambridge, since 1979; *b* 29 Dec. 1924; *s* of late George Allen and of Emma Turner; *m* 1949, Doreen Newbon; one *s. Educ:* Tapton House Sch., Chesterfield. Served War of 1939-45; 640 Sqdn, 1943-45; Nos 51, 242 and 246 Sqdns, 1945-48; psa 1961; NATO staff, 1963-67; jssc 1967; Chief Equipment and Secretarial Instructor, RAF Coll., Cranwell, 1967-68; Comd Accountant, HQ Air Support Comd, 1968-69; Station Comdr, RAF Uxbridge, 1969-71; RCDS, 1972; Dir of Personnel (Ground) (RAF), MoD, 1973-75; AOA, HQ RAF Support Command, 1975-79, and Head of RAF Admin. Branch, 1976-79. MA Cantab 1979. *Recreations:* walking, gardening, reading. *Address:* Hedge End, Potton Road, Hilton, Cambs PE18 9NG. *Club:* Royal Air Force.

TURNER, Peter William; District Secretary, Transport and General Workers' Union; *m* Maureen Ann Turner (*née* Hill), Councillor, JP. *Educ:* Bordesley Green Infant and Junior Sch.; Saltley Grammar Sch. (until 1940); various Trade Union weekend courses. Appointed District Officer, TGWU, 1969; District Sec., CSEU, 1974-76; seconded as Industrial Advr to DoI, 1976-78. Member of various cttees including: Chemical Industry Area Productivity Cttee, 1969-76 (Vice-Chm., 1970-72, Chm., 1972-74); TUC Regional Educn Adv. Cttee, 1970-76; Birmingham Crime Prevention Panel, 1973-76; W Midlands Consultative Cttee on Race Relations, 1974-76; DoE Working Party on Race Relations, 1974-76; Teaching Co. Management Cttee, 1977-82. Member: Birmingham Trades Council, 1956-76; Local Appeals Tribunal, 1969-74. *Recreations:* motoring, motor cycling, caravanning, do-it-yourself, reading, electronics. *Address:* Transport and General Workers' Union, 8 Severn Street, Worcester WR1 2ND. *T:* Worcester 24894.

TURNER, Phil; Deputy Director of Staff Pay and Conditions, National Coal Board, since 1980; Leader of Camden Borough Council, since 1982; *b* 7 June 1939; *s* of William Morris Turner and Eileen Lascelles Turner; *m* 1963, Gillian Sharp; two *s* two *d. Educ:* Beckenham and Penge Grammar School for Boys; University Coll. London (BScEcon). Joined Labour Party, 1963; Chairman, Hampstead Labour Party, 1968-70; Councillor, Camden Bor. Council, 1971-: Chm., Building Works and Services Cttee, 1978-80. Parly Candidate (Lab) Cities of London and Westminster South, 1974. *Recreations:* family, playing football, conversation at the Blenheim Arms, collecting books. *Address:* 33 Minster Road, NW2 3SH. *T:* 01-794 8805. *Clubs:* Camden Labour, National Coal Board Sports and Social.

TURNER, Philip, CBE 1975; LLB (London); in private practice with Infields, Hampton Wick, Surrey; *b* 1 June 1913; *er s* of late George Francis and late Daisy Louise Turner (*née* Frayn), Alverstoke, Hants; *m* 1938, Hazel Edith, *d* of late Douglas Anton and late Edith Ada Benda; one *d* (one *d* decd). *Educ:* Peter Symonds, Winchester. Admitted Solicitor, 1935. Entered General Post Office Engineering Dept, 1935. Served in Royal Navy, 1940-46 (Lt-Comdr). Asst Solicitor to General Post Office, 1953; Principal Asst Solicitor, 1962-72, Solicitor to the Post Office, 1972-75; temp. mem. of legal staff, DoE, 1976-77. Chm., Civil Service Legal Soc., 1957-58; Chm., Internat. Bar Assoc.'s Cttee on Public Utility Law, 1972-77. FRSA 1955. *Recreations:* piano, golf. *Address:* 27 Westfield, The Marld, Ashtead, Surrey. *T:* Ashtead 73656. *Clubs:* Naval, Royal Automobile, Law Society; Hampshire County Cricket, Surrey County Cricket.

See also Rt Hon. John Adams.

TURNER, Surgeon Rear-Admiral (D) Philip Stanley, CB 1963; QHDS 1960-64; Director of Dental Services, RN, Admiralty, Nov. 1961-64; *b* 31

Oct. 1905; *s* of Frank Overy Turner and Ellen Mary Turner, Langton Green, Tunbridge Wells; *m* 1934, Marguerite Donnelly; one *d* (and one *s* decd). *Educ:* Cranbrook Coll.; Guy's Hospital. LDS, RCS 1927. Surgeon Lieut (D) Royal Navy, 1928; Surgeon Captain (D) 1955; Surgeon Rear-Admiral (D), 1961; Senior Specialist in Dental Surgery, 1946-61. Served in: HMS Ramillies, Vanguard, Implacable, Indomitable; HMHS Maine, Tjitjalengka; RN Hospitals Haslar, Plymouth; RN Barracks Portsmouth, etc; Naval HQ, Malta. Foundation Fellow, British Assoc. of Oral Surgeons, 1962. *Address:* Woodhurst, Warren Lane, Cross-in-Hand, Heathfield, East Sussex. *T:* Heathfield 3532.

TURNER, Sir Ralph Lilley, Kt 1950; MC; FBA 1942; MA, LittD, Hon. DLitt, Benares, 1951; Hon. DLit: Ceylon, 1958; London, 1967; Santiniketan, 1972; Kathmandu, 1977; Director of the School of Oriental and African Studies, 1937-57 (Hon. Fellow, 1957); Professor of Sanskrit, University of London, 1922-54, Emeritus Professor since 1954; *b* 5 Oct. 1888; *s* of George Turner, MA, JP, OBE, Cambridge; *m* 1920, Dorothy Rivers (*d* 1972), *d* of William Howard Goulty, Hale, Cheshire; one *s* three *d. Educ:* Perse Grammar Sch. and Christ's Coll., Cambridge (Senior Scholar). Classical Tripos Part I Class I, Div. 3; Oriental Languages Trip. Class I; Class. Trip. Part II Sect. E, Class I with distinction; Brotherton Memorial Sanskrit Prize; Fellow of Christ's Coll., 1912 (Hon. Fellow, 1950); Indian Educational Service, Lectr in Sanskrit at Queen's Coll., Benares, 1913; Wilson Philological Lectr, Bombay Univ., 1914; Indian Army R of O, attached 2/3rd QAO Gurkha Rifles, 1915-19 (despatches twice); Examiner Or. Lang. Trip. and Class. Trip. Part II Cambridge; Prof. of Indian Linguistics, Benares Hindu Univ., 1920; Wilson Philological Lectr, Bombay Univ., 1922; Hon. Treasurer (Pres., 1939-43) Philological Soc.; Pres., 1952-55, Royal Asiatic Soc. (Gold Medallist, 1953, Hon. Vice-Pres., 1963); 7th International Congress of Linguists, 1952; 23rd International Congress of Orientalists, 1954; Hon. Fellow, Deccan Coll., Poona. Formerly Member: Inter-Services Cttee on Language Training; Linguists' Cttee of Min. of Labour and National Service; Colonial Social Science Research Council; Adv. Cttee on the Humanities of the British Council; Adv. Cttee on Education in the Colonies; Treasury sub-cttee for studentships in foreign languages and cultures; sub-cttee University Grants Cttee on Oriental and African Studies; Corr. Member: Czecho-Slovakian Oriental Institute of Prag, Institut de France, Acad. des Inscriptions et Belles Lettres; Hon. Member: Norwegian Acad. of Science and Letters, Ceylon Acad. of Letters, Soc. Asiatique, Paris, American Oriental Soc., Deutsche Morgenländische Gesellschaft, Bihar Research Soc., Bhandarkar Oriental Research Inst., Ceylon Branch of Royal Asiatic Soc., Nagaripracarini Sabha, Banaras, Sanskrit Vishva Parishad, Vishveshvaranand Vedic Research Inst., Ganganatha Jha Research Inst., Linguistic Soc. of America, Linguistic Soc. of India, Ceylon Linguistic Soc., Linguistic Soc. of Nepal, Mark Twain Soc. Campbell Gold Medallist, Asiatic Soc. of Bombay, 1967; Rabindranath Tagore Centenary Plaque, Asiatic Soc. of Bengal, 1971. Nepalese Order of Gorkha Dakshina Bahu, 2nd Class, 1951, 1st Class, 1960. *Publications:* Gujarati Phonology; The Position of Romani in Indo-Aryan; A Comparative and Etymological Dictionary of the Nepali Language; The Gavimath and Palkigundu Inscriptions of Asoka; ed, Indian Studies presented to Professor E. J. Rapson, Indian and Iranian Studies presented to Sir G. A. Grierson; Report to the Nuffield Foundation on a visit to Nigeria; Problems of Sound-change in Indo-Aryan; A Comparative Dictionary of the Indo-aryan Languages; Collected Papers, 1912-73; articles in Encyclopædia Britannica, etc. *Address:* Haverbrack, Barrells Down Road, Bishop's Stortford, Herts CM23 2SU. *T:* 54135.

TURNER, Raymond C.; *see* Clifford-Turner.

TURNER, Richard, CMG 1956; LRIBA; consultant architect; *b* 2 May 1909; *m* 1933, Annie Elizabeth, *d* of late Rev. R. W. Gair; one *d. Educ:* Dame Alice Owen's School. Entered Office of Works, 1929; in charge of ME Office, 1938-47, centred in Istanbul and, later, Cairo; Asst Chief Architect, Min. of Works, 1951; Dir of Works (Overseas), 1960-65; Dir, Overseas Svcs, MPBW, 1965-69, retired. Mem., Esher UDC, 1969-72. *Address:* Chestnuts, Knowle Drive, Sidmouth, Devon EX10 8HP. *T:* Sidmouth 3805. *Club:* Travellers'.

TURNER, Dr Richard Wainwright Duke, OBE 1945; Senior Research Fellow in Preventive Cardiology, University of Edinburgh, since 1974 (Reader in Medicine, 1960-74); Senior Physician and Physician in Charge of the Cardiac Department, Western General Hospital, Edinburgh, 1946-74; *b* Purley, Surrey, 30 May 1909; *s* of Sydney Duke Turner, MD (General Practitioner), and Lilian Maude, *d* of Sir James Wainwright; *m* Paula, *d* of Henry Meulen, Wimbledon; three *s* one *d. Educ:* Epsom Coll.; Clare Coll., Cambridge; St Thomas' Hosp., London. 1st Class Hons Nat. Sci. Tripos, Cambridge, 1934. MA, MB, BChir Cantab 1934; MRCS, LRCP 1935; MRCP 1936; MD Cantab 1940; FRCP 1950; FRCPE 1952. Served in RAMC, 1939-45: UK, Egypt and Italy (Lt-Col); officer i/c Med. Div. 31st and 92nd British General Hospitals. Examiner in Medicine: Univs of Edinburgh and Leeds; RCP; RCPE. Chm., Coronary Prevention Group, 1978-. Member: Assoc. Physicians of GB; British Cardiac Soc.; Hon. Member, Cardiol Socs of India and Pakistan. *Publications:* Diseases of Cardiovascular System in Davidson's Principles and Practice of Medicine, 1952-65; Electrocardiography, 1963; Auscultation of the Heart, 1963; contribs to British Heart Jl, Lancet, BMJ, Quarterly Jl of Med., American Heart Jl, etc. *Recreations:* travel, climbing, gardening, photography. *Address:* Cotterlings, Ditchling, Sussex BN6 8TS. *T:* Hassocks 3392; Department of Preventive

Cardiology, 21 Buccleuch Place, Edinburgh EH8 9LN. *T:* 031-667 1011. *Clubs:* Royal Over-Seas League; University Staff (Edinburgh).

TURNER, Robert Lockley; barrister; a Recorder of the Crown Court, since 1981; *b* 2 Sept. 1935; *s* of James Lockley Turner and Maud Beatrice Turner; *m* 1963, Jennifer Mary Leather; one *s* one *d. Educ:* Clifton Coll.; St Catharine's Coll., Cambridge (BA 1957, MA 1973). Called to the Bar, Gray's Inn, 1958. Commnd Gloucestershire Regt (28th/61st), 1959 (2nd Lieut); transf. to Army Legal Services, 1960 (Captain); Major 1962; retd from Army, 1966 (GSM with clasp South Arabia, 1966). In practice at the Bar, 1967–. Governor, Twickenham Prep. Sch. *Recreations:* parish churches, music, messing about in boats. *Address:* 2 Dr Johnson's Buildings, Temple EC4Y 7AY; Polruan, by Fowey, Cornwall. *Clubs:* Hurlingham; Royal Fowey Yacht (Fowey).

TURNER, Robert Noel, CMG 1955; retired; *b* 28 Dec. 1912; *s* of late Engr Rear-Adm. A. Turner and late Mrs V. E. Turner; *m* 1946, Evelyn Heynes Dupree (*d* 1976); two *s. Educ:* Dover Coll.; Wadham Coll., Oxford (MA). First Class Hons Modern History. Cadet, Malayan Civil Service, 1935; Third Asst Sec. to Govt, FMS, 1936; Asst District Officer, Lower Perak, FMS, 1938; Supernumerary Duty (Lower Perak), 1939; Asst Resident, Brunei, 1940 (interned by Japanese, Borneo, Dec. 1941–Sept. 1945); Asst Sec. to Governor-General, Malaya, May 1946; Prin. Asst Sec., Sarawak, Aug. 1946; First Asst Malayan Establishment Officer, 1948; Acting Dep. Malayan Establishment Officer, April 1950; Chief Sec., Barbados, 1950-56 (title changed from Colonial Sec., 1954); Acting Governor, Barbados, Nov. 1952–May 1953 and 1955, North Borneo, 1957-62 (commended by Sec. of State 'Hurricane Janet', 1955); Chief Sec., North Borneo, 1956-63 (Mem. Exec. Council and Legislative Council, 1950-63); State Sec., Sabah, Fedn of Malaysia, 1963-64 (Mem. State Cabinet, 1963-64). Hon. Mem., First Grade, Order of Kinabalu, Sabah (title: Datuk; lettering: SPDK), 1963. *Recreations:* reading history, watching cricket. *Address:* Kinabalu, The Rise, Brockenhurst, Hants SO4 7SJ. *T:* Lymington 23197.

TURNER, Theodora, OBE 1961; ARRC 1944; retired as Matron of St Thomas' Hospital and Superintendent Nightingale Training School (1955-65); *b* 5 Aug. 1907; *er d* of H. E. M. Turner. *Educ:* Godolphin School, Salisbury; Edinburgh School of Domestic Economy. Ward Sister, St Thomas' Hosp., 1935-38; Administrative Course, Florence Nightingale Internat. Foundn, 1938-39. QAIMNS Reserve, 1939-45. Administrative Sister, St Thomas' Hosp., 1946-47; Matron Royal Infirmary, Liverpool, 1948-53; Education Officer, Educn Centre, Royal College of Nursing, Birmingham, 1953-55. President: Florence Nightingale Internat. Nurses Assoc., 1971-74; Royal Coll. of Nursing and Nat. Council of Nurses of UK, 1966-68. Mem., Argyll and Clyde Health Bd, 1974-75. *Recreations:* gardening and painting. *Address:* 63 Larkdown, Wantage, Oxon.

TURNER, Theodore Francis, QC 1943; Barrister-at-law; *b* 19 Nov. 1900; *s* of George Lewis and Mabel Mary Turner; *m* 1st, 1925, Elizabeth Alice, *o d* of 1st Baron Schuster, GCB, CVO, QC; two *s* one *d*; 2nd, 1949, Ruth, 2nd *d* of late L. C. Ledyard, Jr, and late Mrs W. E. S. Griswold, NY. *Educ:* Downside; Balliol Coll., Oxford (Exhibitioner). Called to Bar, 1924; joined South Eastern Circuit. Regional Controller, Ministry of Fuel and Power, North Midland Region, 1944-45; Recorder of Rochester, 1946-50; Chairman Mining Subsidence Cttee, 1947-48. Admitted New York Bar, 1962. *Address:* PO Box 303, East Norwich, Long Island, NY 11732, USA; 570 Park Avenue, New York City, NY 10021, USA. *Club:* The Brook (NY).
See also W. H. Hughes, C. G. Turner, M. J. Turner.

TURNER, (Thomas) Peter; Head of Operational Research, HM Treasury, since 1981 (Civil Service Department, 1977-81); *b* 8 May 1928; *s* of Thomas Turner and Laura Crawley; *m* 1952, Jean Rosalie Weston; one *s* one *d. Educ:* Ilford County High Sch.; London University. BSc (1st Class Hons), Maths and Physics. GEC, North Wembley, 1947-50; Armament Design Establishment, 1950-54; Air Ministry (Science 3), 1954-58 and 1962-63; Chief Research Officer, RAF Maintenance Command, 1958-62; Police Research and Development Branch, Home Office, 1963-68; Civil Service Dept (OR), 1968-73; Head of Treasury/CSD Joint Operational Research Unit, 1973-76. *Address:* 8 Waring Drive, Green St Green, Orpington, Kent BR6 6DW. *T:* Farnborough (Kent) 51189.

TURNER, Wilfred, CMG 1977; CVO 1979; HM Diplomatic Service, retired; *b* 10 Oct. 1921; *s* of late Allen Turner and Eliza (*née* Leach); *m* 1947, June Gladys Tite; two *s* one *d. Educ:* Heywood Grammar Sch., Lancs; London Univ. BSc 1942 (external degree by private study). Min. of Labour, 1938-42. Served War, REME, 1942-47. Min. of Labour: Brit. High Commn, New Delhi (Asst Lab. Adviser), 1955-59; Min. of Labour, 1959-60; Min. of Health (Sec., Cttee on Safety of Drugs, 1963-66), 1960-66. Joined HM Diplomatic Service, 1966; Commonwealth Office, 1966; First Sec.: Kaduna, Nigeria, 1966-69; Kuala Lumpur, 1969-73; Dep. High Comr, and Commercial/Economic Counsellor, Accra, 1973-77; High Comr to Botswana, 1977-81. *Recreation:* hill walking. *Address:* 44 Tower Road, Twickenham TW1 4PE. *T:* 01-892 1593. *Club:* Royal Commonwealth Society.

TURNER, Dr William; Regional Medical Officer, Yorkshire Regional Health Authority, since 1976; *b* 23 Feb. 1927; *s* of Clarence and Mabel Turner; *m* 1950, Patricia Bramham Wilkinson; one *s* two *d. Educ:* Prince Henry's Grammar Sch., Otley, Yorks; Leeds Univ. MB, ChB; DPH, FFCM; LLB.

House Officer, Leeds Gen. Infirmary, 1950-51; RAMC, 1951-53; Gen. Practitioner, 1953-55; Public Health Trng, 1955-60; Medical Officer of Health: Hyde, 1960-63; Huddersfield, 1963-67; Bradford, 1967-74; Area MO, Bradford, 1974-76. Member: Standing Med. Adv. Cttee, 1978-82; Health Service Inf. Steering Gp. *Publications:* contrib. BMJ, Medical Officer. *Address:* (home) The Hollies, Parish Ghyll Lane, Ilkley, West Yorks LS29 9QP. *T:* Ilkley 608335; (business) Yorkshire RHA, Park Parade, Harrogate. *T:* Harrogate 65061.

TURNER, Lt-Gen. Sir William (Francis Robert), KBE 1962; CB 1959; DSO 1945; Lord-Lieutenant of Dumfries, 1972-82; *b* 12 Dec. 1907; *er s* of late Mr and Mrs F. R. Turner, Kelso, Roxburghshire; *m* 1938, Nancy Maude Stilwell, *er d* of late Lt-Col and Mrs J. B. L. Stilwell, Yateley, Hants; one *s. Educ:* Winchester College; RMC Sandhurst. 2nd Lieut, KOSB, 1928; served in Great Britain and India, 1928-39; Capt. 1938; BEF, 1939-40; Staff College, 1941; OC, 5 KOSB, 1942-45 (despatches), NW Europe; OC, 1 KOSB, 1945-46, NW Europe and Middle East; GSO1, Middle East and Great Britain, 1947-50. Colonel Brit. Military Mission to Greece, 1950-52; Comd 128 Inf. Bde (TA), 1952-54; BGS HQ Western Comd, 1954-56; GOC 44 (Home Counties) Infantry Div. (TA) and Home Counties District, and Deputy Constable of Dover Castle, 1956-59; President, Regular Commissions Board, 1959-61; GOC-in-C, Scottish Comd, and Governor of Edinburgh Castle, 1961-64; retd 1964; Colonel, King's Own Scottish Borderers, 1961-70; Ensign, Queen's Body Guard for Scotland (Royal Company of Archers). HM Comr, Queen Victoria School, Dunblane. DL, Dumfriesshire, 1970-72. Comdr with Star, Order of Saint Olav, Class II (Norway), 1962; Order of the Two Niles, Class II (Republic of the Sudan), 1963. *Address:* Milnhead, Kirkton, Dumfries. *T:* Dumfries 710319. *Clubs:* Naval and Military; New (Edinburgh).

TURNER CAIN, Maj.-Gen. George Robert, CB 1967; CBE 1963; DSO 1945; Chairman: Anglia Maltings (Holdings) Ltd; Anglia Maltings Ltd; F. & G. Smith Ltd; Walpole & Wright Ltd; Director: Crisp Maltings Ltd; Crisp Malt Products Ltd; Edme Ltd; *b* 16 Feb. 1912; *s* of late Wing Comdr G. Turner Cain; *m* 1938, Lamorna Maturin, *d* of late Col G. B. Hingston; one *s* one *d. Educ:* Norwich Sch.; RMC Sandhurst. 2nd Lt Norfolk Regt, 1932; 1st Bn Royal Norfolk Regt, India, 1933-38; Waziristan Campaign, 1937. Served War of 1939-45 with 1st Royal Norfolk and 1st Hereford Regt, BLA, 1944-45. Comd 1st Royal Norfolk Regt, Berlin, 1947-48; Hong Kong and UK, 1953-55; Comd Tactical Wing, School of Infantry, 1955-57; Comd 1st Fed. Inf. Bde, Malaya, in operations in Malaya, 1957-59; BGS, HQ, BAOR, 1961; Maj.-Gen. Administration, GHQ FARELF, 1964-67, retired; ADC, 1961-64. Dep. Col, Royal Anglian Regt, 1971-74. Croix de Guerre avec Palm, 1945; Star of Kedah (Malaya), 1959. *Recreation:* shooting. *Address:* Holbreck, Hollow Lane, Stiffkey, near Wells-next-the-Sea, Norfolk.

TURNER-SAMUELS, David Jessel, QC 1972; Barrister-at-Law; *b* 5 April 1918; *s* of late Moss Turner-Samuels, QC, MP, and Gladys Deborah Turner-Samuels (*née* Belcher); *m* 1939, Norma Florence Turner-Samuels (marr. diss. 1975); one *s* one *d*; *m* 1976, Norma Florence Negus (*née* Shellabear). *Educ:* Westminster Sch. Called to Bar, Middle Temple, 1939 (Bencher 1980); admitted to Trinidad bar, 1976. Served War of 1939-45, in Army, 1939-46. *Publication:* (jointly) Industrial Negotiation and Arbitration, 1951. *Recreation:* getting away from it all. *Address:* Oak Cottage, The Lane, Thursley, Surrey. *T:* Elstead 702238; New Court, Temple, EC4Y 9BE. *T:* 01-353 7613.

TURNER-WARWICK, Prof. Margaret Elizabeth Harvey, MA, DM, PhD, FRCP; Professor of Medicine (Thoracic Medicine), Cardiothoracic Institute, Brompton Hospital, since 1972; *b* 19 Nov. 1924; *d* of William Harvey Moore, QC, and Maud Baden-Powell; *m* 1950, Richard Trevor Turner-Warwick, *qv*; two *d. Educ:* St Paul's Sch.; Lady Margaret Hall (Open Schol. 1943), Oxford. University Coll. Hosp., 1947-50: Tuke silver medal, Filliter exhibn in Pathology, Magrath Schol. in Medicine, Atchison Schol.; Postgrad. trng at UCH and Brompton Hosp., 1950-61; Cons. Physician: (Gen. Med.), Elizabeth Garrett Anderson Hosp., 1961-67; Brompton and London Chest Hosps, 1967-72. Sen. Lectr, Inst. of Diseases of the Chest, 1961-72. *Publications:* Immunology of the Lung, 1978; (jtly) Occupational Lung Diseases: research approaches and methods, 1981; chapters in various textbooks on immunology and thoracic medicine, particularly fibrosing lung disorders and asthma; contrib. original articles: Lancet, BMJ, Quarterly Jl Med., Thorax, Tubercle, Jl Clin. Experimental Immunology, etc. *Recreations:* her family and their hobbies, gardening, country life, music. *Address:* 55 Fitzroy Park, Highgate, N6 6JA. *T:* 01-340 6339.

TURNER-WARWICK, Richard Trevor, MA, BSc, DM Oxon, MCh, FRCP, FRCS, FACS; specialist in reconstruction and functional restoration of the urinary tract; Surgeon and Senior Urologist to the Middlesex Hospital, W1, since 1961; Urologist to: King Edward VII Hospital for Officers, since 1970; St Peter's Hospital Group and Royal National Orthopædic Hospital, since 1971; Senior Lecturer, London University Institute of Urology, since 1962; Hon. Consultant Urologist, Royal Prince Alfred Hospital, Sydney, since 1980; *b* 21 Feb. 1925; *s* of W. Turner Warwick, FRCS; *m* 1950, Prof. Margaret Elizabeth Turner-Warwick, *qv*; two *d. Educ:* Bedales School; Oriel Coll., Oxford; Middlesex Hosp. Medical School. Pres. OUBC, 1946; Mem. Univ. Boat Race Crew, Isis Head of River crew and Univ. fours, 1946; Winner OU Silver Sculls, 1946; BSc thesis in neuroanatomy, 1946. Sen. Broderip Schol., Lyell Gold Medallist and Freeman Schol., Middx Hosp., 1949; surgical trng at Middx Hosp. and St Paul's Hosp., London, and

Columbia Presbyterian Med. Centre, NY, 1959. Hunterian Prof. of RCS, 1957, 1976; Moynihan Prize of Assoc. of Surgeons, 1957; Comyns Berkeley Travelling Fellowship to USA, 1959; St Peter's Medal, British Assoc. of Urological Assocs, 1978. Fellow: Assoc. of Surgeons of GB and Ireland, 1960; British Assoc. of Urological Surgeons, 1961; Member: Council, RCS, 1980–; Internat. Soc. of Urology; European Soc. of Urology; Soc. of Pelvic Surgeons, 1963; Corresp. Member: Amer. Assoc. of Genito Urinary Surgeons, 1972; American, Australasian and Belgian Urological Assocs. Hon. FRACS, 1981. *Publications:* various articles on surgery, urodynamics, functional and reconstructive urology in scientific journals. *Recreation:* water. *Address:* 61 Harley House, NW1. *T:* 01-935 2550; Tirnanog, 55 Fitzroy Park, Highgate, N6. *T:* 01-340 6339. *Clubs:* Vincent's (Oxford); Leander (Henley); Royal Motor Yacht (Poole).

TURNOUR, family name of **Earl Winterton.**

TURPIN, James Alexander, CMG 1966; HM Diplomatic Service, retired; *b* 7 Jan. 1917; *s* of late Samuel Alexander Turpin; *m* 1942, Kathleen Iris Eadie; one *d. Educ:* King's Hosp., Dublin; Trinity Coll., Dublin (schol., 1st cl. Hons, Gold Medal, MA). Asst Lectr, Trinity College, Dublin, 1940. Served Army (Royal Irish Fusiliers), 1942–46. Joined Foreign Service, 1947; Mem., UK Delegn to OEEC, Paris, 1948; 1st Sec., 1949; FO, 1950; Warsaw, 1953; Tokyo, 1955; Counsellor, 1960; seconded to BoT, 1960–63; Counsellor (Commercial), The Hague, 1963–67; Minister (Economic and Commercial), New Delhi, 1967–70; Asst Under-Sec. of State, FCO, 1971–72; Ambassador to the Philippines, 1972–76; retired, 1977. *Recreations:* tennis, music, swimming. *Address:* 12 Grimwood Road, Twickenham, Middlesex. *Clubs:* Travellers', Roehampton.

TURPIN, Kenneth Charlton; Provost of Oriel College, Oxford, 1957–80, and Hon. Fellow since 1980; Vice-Chancellor, Oxford University, 1966–69 (Pro-Vice Chancellor, 1964–66, 1969–79); Member, Hebdomadal Council, 1959–77; *b* 13 Jan. 1915; *e s* of late Henry John Turpin, Ludlow. *Educ:* Manchester Grammar Sch.; Oriel College, Oxford. Treasury, 1940–43; Asst Private Sec. to C. R. Attlee, Lord President and Dep. Prime Minister, 1943–45; 2nd Asst Registrar, University Registry, Oxford, 1945–47; Sec. of Faculties, Univ. of Oxford, 1947–57; professorial fellow, Oriel Coll., 1948; Hon. Fellow Trinity Coll., Dublin, 1968. *Recreations:* gardening, walking. *Address:* Copthorne, Knighton, Powys. *Clubs:* Athenæum; Vincent's (Oxford).

TURPIN, Maj.-Gen. Patrick George, CB 1962; OBE 1943; FCIT; *b* 27 April 1911; 3rd *s* of late Rev. J. J. Turpin, MA, BD, late Vicar of Misterton, Somerset; *m* 1947, Cherry Leslie Joy, *d* of late Major K. S. Grove, York and Lancaster Regiment; one *s* one *d. Educ:* Haileybury Coll., Hertford; Exeter College, Oxford (Sen. Classical Schol.). BA (Hons) Oxford (Lit. Hum.), 1933; MA 1943. Commd RASC, 2nd Lt, 1933; Lt 1936; Capt. 1941; Major 1946; Lt-Col 1949; Col 1953; Brig. 1959; Maj.-Gen. 1960. Served War of 1939–45 (despatches twice, OBE): Adjt, 1939–40; AQMG, 30 Corps, W Desert, 1943; AA&QMG, 5th Div., Italy, 1943–44; DA&QMG (Brig.), 1 Corps, BLA, 1945; Brig. A, 21 Army Gp, 1945–46; Comd 6 Training Bn, RASC, 1947; ADS&T, WO, 1948; AA&QMG (Plans), HQ, BTE (Egypt), 1950; GSO1 (instructor), Jt Services Staff Coll., 1951–53; ADS&T (Col), WO, 1953–54; DAG, HQ, BAOR, 1956–59; Brig. i/c Adm., 17 Gurkha Div., Malaya, 1959–60; DST, 1960–63; Dir of Movements, MoD (Army), 1963–66; psc 1941; jssc 1949; idc 1955; Col Comdt, Royal Corps of Transport, 1965–71; Col Gurkha Army Service Corps, 1960–65; Col Gurkha Transport Regt, 1965–73. Sec.-Gen., Assoc. of British Travel Agents, 1966–69. Pres., Army Lawn Tennis Assoc., 1968–73. Governor, Royal Sch. for Daughters of Officers of the Army, Bath, 1963–83. FCIT (MInstT 1961). *Recreations:* lawn tennis (Somerset County Champion, 1948, Army Colours, 1952); squash rackets (Bucks County Colours, 1952); golf. *Address:* c/o National Westminster Bank, 121 High Street, Oxford OX1 4DD. *Clubs:* Oxford Union Society; All England Lawn Tennis; International Lawn Tennis; Escorts Squash Rackets.

TURTON, family name of **Baron Tranmire.**

TURTON, Victor Ernest; Managing Director: V. E. Turton (Tools) Ltd; V. E. Turton (Motor Spares) Ltd; V. E. Turton (Wholesalers) Ltd; *b* 29 June 1924; *s* of H. E. Turton; *m* 1951, Jean Edith Murray; two *d. Educ:* Paget Secondary Modern Sch.; Aston Techn. Coll.; Birmingham Central Techn. Coll. Birmingham City Councillor (Lab) Duddeston Ward, 1945–63; Saltley Ward, 1970–71; Alderman, Birmingham, 1963–70 and 1971–74, Hon. Alderman, 1974–; Lord Mayor of Birmingham, 1971–72; Mem., W Midlands CC, 1974–77. Mem., Transportation Cttee, W Midlands CC; Chairman: Smallholdings and Agric. Cttee, 1954–58; Birmingham Airport, 1959–66; Airport Cttee, W Midlands CC, 1974–77; Hall Green Div. Labour Party, 1957–59; West Midlands Regional Adv. Cttee for Civil Aviation, 1966–72; Jt Airports Cttee of Local Authorities, 1975–77; Vice Pres., Heart of England Tourist Bd, 1977– (Chm., 1975–77). Former Governor, Coll. of Technology (now Univ. of Aston in Birmingham). Mem., Inst. of Directors. *Recreations:* football, cricket, table tennis, philately. *Address:* 32 Tenbury Road, King's Heath, Birmingham B14 6AD.

TURTON-HART, Sir Francis (Edmund), KBE 1963 (MBE 1942); *b* 29 May 1908; *s* of David Edwin Hart and Zoe Evelyn Turton; *m* 1947, Margaret Greaves; one *d. Educ:* Uppingham. Served with Royal Engineers, 1939–46 (Hon. Major, 1946). East Africa, 1924–38; Portugal, 1939; West Africa,

1946–65; Federal House of Representatives, Nigeria, 1956–60; President, Lagos Chamber of Commerce, 1960–63. *Recreations:* shooting, fishing, golf. *Address:* 39 Hunters Moon, Dartington, Totnes, South Devon TQ9 6JT. *T:* Totnes 863126. *Clubs:* Sloane; Thurlestone Golf.

TURVEY, Ralph, DSc (Econ); economist; Chief, Bureau of Statistics, International Labour Office, since 1980; *b* 1 May 1927; *s* of John and Margaret Turvey; *m* 1957, Sheila Bucher, *d* of Otto and Doris Bucher; one *s* one *d. Educ:* Sidcot School; London School of Economics; Uppsala University. Lectr, then Reader in Economics, at London School of Economics, 1948–64, with interruptions. Vis. Lectr, Johns Hopkins Univ., 1953; Ford Foundation Vis. Res. Prof., Univ. of Chicago, 1958–59; Economic Section, HM Treasury, 1960–62; Center of Economic Research, Athens, 1963. Chief Economist, The Electricity Council, 1964–67. Member, NBPI, 1967–71; Jt Dep. Chm. 1968–71; Economic Adviser: Scientific Control Systems Ltd, 1971–75; ILO, 1975–80. Mem., Nat. Water Council, 1974–75. Vis. Prof. of Econs, LSE, 1973–75. Governor, Kingston Polytechnic, 1972–75. Mem., Inflation Accounting Cttee, 1974–75. *Publications:* The Economics of Real Property, 1957; Interest Rates and Asset Prices, 1960; Studies in Greek Taxation (joint author), 1964; Optimal Pricing and Investment in Electricity Supply, 1968; Economic Analysis and Public Enterprises, 1971; Demand and Supply, 1971; (jtly) Electricity Economics, 1977; papers on applied welfare economics in Economic Jl, Amer. Economic Review, etc. *Recreations:* computing, alpine walking. *Address:* Case Postale 500, 1211 Geneva 22, Switzerland. *Club:* Reform.

TUSA, John; Presenter, BBC2 Newsnight, since 1979; *b* 2 March 1936; *s* of John Tusa and Lydia Sklenarova; *m* 1960, Ann Hilary Dowson; two *s. Educ:* Trinity Coll., Cambridge (BA 1st Cl. Hons History). BBC general trainee, 1960; Producer, BBC External Services, 1962; freelance radio journalist, 1965; Presenter, BBC Radio 4 The World Tonight, 1968. Mem., Editorial Board, Political Quarterly, 1978–. *Recreations:* squash, opera, talking. *Address:* 21 Christchurch Hill, NW3 1TY. *T:* 01-435 9495. *Club:* United Oxford & Cambridge University.

TUSHINGHAM, Rita; actress; *b* 14 March 1942; *d* of John Tushingham; *m* 1962, Terence William Bicknell (marr. diss. 1976); two *d*; *m* 1981, Ousama Rawi. *Educ:* La Sagesse Convent, Liverpool. Student, Liverpool Playhouse, 1958–60. *Stage appearances:* Royal Court Theatre: The Changeling, 1960; The Kitchen, 1961; A Midsummer Night's Dream, 1962; Twelfth Night, 1962; The Knack, 1962; other London theatres: The Giveaway, 1969; Lorna and Ted, 1970; Mistress of Novices, 1973; My Fat Friend, 1981. *Films:* A Taste of Honey, 1961 (Brit. Film Acad. and Variety Club awards for Most Promising Newcomer, 1961; NY Critics, Cannes Film Festival and Hollywood Foreign Press Assoc. awards); The Leather Boys, 1962; A Place to Go, 1963; Girl with Green Eyes, 1963 (Variety Club award); The Knack, 1964 (Silver Goddess award, Mexican Assoc. of Film Corresps); Dr Zhivago, 1965; The Trap, 1966; Smashing Time, 1967; Diamonds For Breakfast, 1967; The Guru, 1968; The Bed-Sitting Room, 1970; Straight on till Morning, 1972; Situation, 1972; Instant Coffee, 1973; Rachel's Man, 1974; The Human Factor, 1976; Pot Luck, 1977; State of Shock, 1977; Mysteries, 1978; Incredible Mrs Chadwick, 1979; The Spaghetti House Siege, 1982. *TV appearances include:* Red Riding Hood (play), 1973; No Strings (own series), 1974; Don't Let Them Kill Me on Wednesday, 1980; Confessions of Felix Krull, 1980. *Recreation:* cooking. *Address:* c/o Jean Diamond, London Management, 235 Regent Street, W1.

TUSTIN, Arnold; Professor Emeritus, MSc, FIEE, retired; *b* 1899; *m* 1948; no *c. Educ:* King's Coll., Univ. of Durham. Subsequently Chief Asst Engineer, Metropolitan-Vickers Electrical Co., until 1945. Visiting Webster Prof., Massachusetts Inst. of Technology, 1953–54; Prof. of Electrical Engineering, Univ. of Birmingham, 1947–55; Prof. of Heavy Electrical Engineering, Imperial Coll., Univ. of London, 1955–64. Chm. Measurement and Control Section, IEE, 1959–60; Chm. Research Adv. Council, Transport Commn, 1960. Hon. DTech Bradford, 1968. *Publications:* Direct Current Machines for Control Systems, 1952; The Mechanism of Economic Systems, 1953; (ed) Automatic and Manual Control, 1951. *Address:* 17 Orchard Lane, Amersham-on-the-Hill, Bucks HP6 5AA.

TUSTIN, Rt. Rev. David; *see* Grimsby, Bishop Suffragan of.

TUTE, Warren Stanley; author; *b* 22 Feb. 1914; *s* of Stanley Harries Tute and Laura Edith Thompson; *m* 1st, 1944, Annette Elizabeth Neil (marr. diss. 1955); 2nd, 1958, Evelyn Mary Dalley; two *d. Educ:* Dragon Sch., Wrekin Coll. Entered RN 1932, served in HM Ships Nelson and Ajax; took part in N African, Sicilian and Normandy landings (despatches 1944), retired as Lt Comdr, 1946. Wrote for BBC, 1946–47; Dir, Random Film Productions Ltd, 1947–52; made films and trained scriptwriters for US Govt, 1952–54; Argentina, 1955; Dir, Theatrework (London) Ltd, 1960–; produced (jtly) Little Mary Sunshine, Comedy, 1962; Head of Scripts, London Weekend TV, 1968–69; Liaison Officer, Capital Radio—Operation Drake, 1978–. Archivist, Worshipful Co. of Cordwainers, 1976–. *Publications:* novels: The Felthams, 1950; Lady in Thin Armour, 1951; Gentleman in Pink Uniform, 1952; The Younger Felthams, 1953; Girl in the Limelight, 1954; The Cruiser, 1955; The Rock, 1957; Leviathan, 1959; The Golden Greek, 1960; The Admiral, 1963; A Matter of Diplomacy, 1969; The Powder Train, 1970; The Tarnham Connection, 1971; The Resident, 1973; Next Saturday in Milan, 1975; Honours of War and Peace, 1976; The Cairo Sleeper, 1977; *history:* The Grey

Top Hat, 1961; Atlantic Conquest, 1962; Cochrane, 1965; The Deadly Stroke, 1973; Hitler—The Last Ten Days, 1973; D Day, 1974; The North African War, 1976; The True Glory: the story of the Royal Navy over a thousand years, 1982; *plays:* Jessica, 1956; A Time to be Born, 1956; Frost at Midnight (trans.), 1957; Quartet for Five, 1958; A Few Days in Greece, 1959; *other works:* Chico, 1950; Life of a Circus Bear, 1952; Cockney Cats, 1953; Le Petomane (trans.), 1967; (contrib.) The Commanding Sea, 1981 (originator of BBC TV series). *Recreations:* people, cats, wine, France. *Address:* 54 Rosemont Road, Richmond, Surrey. *T:* 01-940 3780. *Clubs:* Garrick, Whitefriars (Chm.).

TUTIN, Dorothy, CBE 1967; actress (stage and films); *b* 8 April 1931; *d* of late John Tutin, DSc, and of Adie Evelyn Tutin; *m* 1963, Derek Barton-Chapple (stage name Derek Waring); one *s* one *d*. *Educ:* St Catherine's, Bramley, Surrey; RADA. Began career, 1950; Stratford Festival, 1958, 1960. *Parts include:* Rose, in The Living Room; Katherine, in Henry V; Sally Bowles, in I am a Camera; St Joan, in The Lark; Catherine, in The Gates of Summer; Hedwig, in The Wild Duck; Viola, in Twelfth Night; Juliet, in Romeo and Juliet; Ophelia, in Hamlet; during Shakespeare Memorial Theatre tour of Russia, 1958, played parts of Ophelia, Viola and Juliet; Dolly, in Once More, With Feeling (New), 1959; Portia, Viola, Cressida (S-on-A), 1960; Sister Jeanne, in The Devils (Aldwych), 1961, 1962; Juliet, Desdemona (S-on-A), 1961; Varya, in The Cherry Orchard (S-on-A, and Aldwych), 1961; Cressida, Prioress, in The Devils (Edinburgh), 1962; Polly Peachum, in The Beggar's Opera (Aldwych), 1963; The Hollow Crown (New York), 1963; Queen Victoria, in Portrait of a Queen, Vaudeville, 1965; Rosalind, As You Like It, Stratford, 1967, Los Angeles, 1968; Portrait of a Queen, NY, 1968; Play on Love, St Martin's, 1970; Old Times, Aldwych, 1971; Peter Pan, Coliseum, 1971, 1972; What Every Woman Knows, 1973, Albery, 1974; Natalya Petrovna, in A Month in the Country, Chichester, 1974, Albery, 1975; Cleopatra, in Antony and Cleopatra, Edinburgh, 1977; Madame Ranevsky, The Cherry Orchard, Lady Macbeth, in Macbeth, Lady Plyant, in The Double Dealer (Soc. of W End Theatre Award, 1978), Nat. Theatre, 1978; Undiscovered Country, Nat. Theatre, 1979; Reflections, Theatre Royal, Haymarket, 1980; The Provok'd Wife, Nat. Theatre, 1980; Hester, in The Deep Blue Sea, Greenwich, 1981. *Films:* Polly Peachum, in The Beggar's Opera; Cecily, in The Importance of Being Earnest; Lucie Manette, in A Tale of Two Cities; Henrietta Maria in Cromwell; Sophie Breska in Savage Messiah (Variety Club of GB Film Actress Award, 1972). Has appeared on television. *Recreations:* music; Isle of Arran. *Address:* c/o Peter Browne Management, 13 St Martin's Road, SW9.

TUTIN, Prof. Thomas Gaskell, FRS 1982; Professor of Taxonomy, University of Leicester, 1967-73, now Emeritus; University Fellow, University of Leicester, 1974; *b* 21 April 1908; *o s* of Frank and Jane Tutin; *m* 1942, Winifred Anne Pennington (see W. A. Tutin); one *s* three *d*. *Educ:* Cotham Sch., Bristol; Downing Coll., Cambridge (schol.). Expedition to British Guiana, 1933; Marine Laboratory, Plymouth, 1934-37; expedition to Lake Titicaca, 1937; part-time Demonstrator, KCL, 1938-39; Asst Lectr, Univ. of Manchester, 1939-42; Geographer, Naval Intelligence Div., 1942-44; Lectr, Univ. College of Leicester, 1944-47; Prof. of Botany, Univ. of Leicester, 1947-67. Pres., Botanical Soc. of British Isles, 1957-61. Foreign Member, Societas Scientiarum Fennica (Section for Natural Science), 1960. Linnean Medal, Linnean Soc., 1977. Hon. ScD Dublin, 1979. *Publications:* (with Clapham and Warburg) Flora of the British Isles, 1952, 2nd edn 1962; (with Clapham and Warburg) Excursion Flora of the British Isles, 1959, 3rd edn 1980; (with V. H. Heywood *et al*) Flora Europaea, Vol. I 1964, Vol. II 1968, Vol. III 1972, Vol. IV 1976, Vol. V 1979; (with A. C. Jermy) British Sedges, 1968; Umbellifers of the British Isles, 1980; papers in Annals of Botany, New Phytologist, Jl of Ecology, Watsonia, etc. *Recreations:* botany, music. *Address:* Home Farm, Knighton, Leicester LE2 3WG. *T:* Leicester 707356.

TUTIN, Mrs Winifred Anne, (Winifred Pennington), PhD; FRS 1979; Principal Scientific Officer, Freshwater Biological Association, 1967-81, retired; *b* 8 Oct. 1915; *d* of Albert R. Pennington and Margaret S. Pennington; *m* 1942, Thomas Gaskell Tutin, *qv*; one *s* three *d*. *Educ:* Barrow-in-Furness Grammar Sch.; Reading Univ. (BSc, PhD). Research posts with Freshwater Biological Assoc., 1940-45; Demonstrator and Special Lectr, Univ. of Leicester, 1947-67; Hon. Reader in Botany, Univ. of Leicester, 1971-79, Hon. Professor, 1980-. Foreign Member, Royal Danish Academy, 1974. *Publications:* (as Winifred Pennington): The History of British Vegetation, 1969, 2nd edn 1974; (with W. H. Pearsall) The Lake District, 1973; papers in New Phytologist, Jl of Ecology, Phil. Trans of Royal Society, and others. *Recreations:* gardening, plain cooking. *Address:* Home Farm, Knighton, Leicester LE2 3WG. *T:* Leicester 707356.

TUTTLE, Sir Geoffrey (William), KBE 1957 (OBE 1940); CB 1945; DFC 1937; FRAeS 1960; Air Marshal retired; *b* 2 Oct. 1906; *s* of late Maj. E. W. Tuttle, Lowestoft. *Educ:* St Paul's School. Joined RAF, 1925; served war, 1939-45: France, Photo Reconnaissance Units, UK, Tunisia, Corsica, Sardinia, Italy, Greece; AOC RAF, Greece, 1944-46; Air Cdre 1948; Dir of Operational Requirements, Air Min., 1948-49; AOA, HQ Coastal Comd, 1950-51; Air Vice-Marshal 1952; ACAS (Operational Requirements), 1951-54; AOC No 19 Gp, RAF, 1954-56; Air Marshal 1957; DCAS, 1956-59, retd. British Aircraft Corp. Ltd, 1959-77; Aerospace Consultant, 1977-81. Order of Patriotic War, 2nd Class (Soviet), 1944; Grand Officer Royal Order of the Phœnix (Greece), 1945; Commandeur Légion d'Honneur (France); Croix de

Guerre (France). *Recreation:* sailing. *Address:* 73 Numa Court, Justin Close, Brentford TW8 8QF. *T:* 01-568 1084. *Club:* Royal Air Force.

TUTU, Rt. Rev. Desmond Mpilo; General Secretary, South African Council of Churches, since 1978; Assistant Bishop of Johannesburg, since 1978; Rector, St Augustine's Parish, Soweto, since 1981; *b* 7 Oct. 1931; *s* of Zachariah and Aletta Tutu; *m* 1955, Leah Nomalizo Shenxane; one *s* three *d*. *Educ:* Western High, Johannesburg; Bantu Normal Coll., Pretoria (Higher Teachers' Dip.); Univ. of S Africa (BA); St Peter's Theol Coll., Johannesburg (LTh); King's Coll. London (BD, MTh). Schoolmaster: Madibane High Sch., Johannesburg, 1954; Munsieville High Sch., Krugersdorp, 1955-57. Theological coll. student, 1958-60; deacon 1960, priest 1961, St Mary's Cathedral, Johannesburg. Curate: St Alban's Church, Benoni, 1960-61; St Philip's Church, Alberton, 1961-62; St Alban's, Golder's Green, London, 1962-65; St Mary's, Bletchingley, Surrey, 1965-66. Lecturer: Federal Theol Seminary, Alice, CP, 1967-69; Univ. of Botswana, Lesotho and Swaziland, Roma, Lesotho, 1970-72; Associate Dir, Theol Education Fund (WCC) based in Bromley, Kent, and Curate, St Augustine's, Grove Park, 1972-75; Dean of Johannesburg, 1975-76; Bishop of Lesotho, 1976-78. Trustee, Phelps Stoke Fund, New York. Athena Prize, Onassis Foundation, 1980. Hon. degrees: DD Gen. Theol Sem., New York, 1978; DCL Kent, 1978; LLD Harvard, 1979; ThD Ruhr, 1981; STD Columbia, NY, 1982. FKC 1978. *Publications:* articles and reviews. *Recreations:* music, reading, jogging. *Address:* 6981 Orlando West, Johannesburg, South Africa. *T:* 940 1460.

TUZO, Gen. Sir Harry (Craufurd), GCB 1973 (KCB 1971); OBE 1961; MC 1945; Chairman, Marconi Space and Defence Systems, since 1979; Master Gunner, St James's Park, since 1977; *b* 26 Aug. 1917; *s* of John Atkinson Tuzo and Annie Katherine (*née* Craufurd); *m* 1943, Monica Patience Salter; one *d*. *Educ:* Wellington Coll.; Oriel Coll., Oxford (Hon. Fellow 1977). BA Oxon 1939, MA 1970. Regimental Service, Royal Artillery, 1939-45; Staff appts, Far East, 1946-49; Royal Horse Artillery, 1950-51 and 1954-58; Staff at Sch. of infantry, 1951-53; GSO1, War Office, 1958-60; CO, 3rd Regt, RHA, 1960-62; Asst Comdt, Sandhurst, 1962-63; Comdr, 51 Gurkha Infantry Bde, 1963-65; Imp. Def. Coll., 1966; Maj.-Gen. 1966; Chief of Staff, BAOR, 1967-69; Director, RA, 1969-71; Lt-Gen. 1971; GOC and Dir of Operations, NI, 1971-73; Gen. 1973; Comdr Northern Army Gp and C-in-C BAOR, 1973-76; Dep. Supreme Allied Comdr, Europe, 1976-78. ADC (Gen.) to the Queen, 1974-77. Colonel Commandant: RA, 1971-; RHA, 1976-. Chm., RUSI, 1980-; Member: Council, IISS; Council, Inst. for Study of Conflict; Governor, Wellington Coll. Dato Setia Negeri Brunei, 1965. *Recreations:* shooting, gardening, music, theatre. *Address:* Heath Farmhouse, Fakenham, Norfolk NR21 8LZ. *Clubs:* Army and Navy; Norfolk County (Norwich).

See also Sir William Garthwaite, Bt.

TWEEDDALE, 13th Marquis of, *cr* 1694; **Edward Douglas John Hay;** Lord Hay of Yester, 1488; Earl of Tweeddale, 1646; Viscount Walden, Earl of Gifford, 1694; Baron Tweeddale (UK), 1881; Hereditary Chamberlain of Dunfermline; *b* 6 Aug. 1947; *s* of 12th Marquis of Tweeddale, GC, and of Sonia Mary, *d* of 1st Viscount Ingleby; *S* father, 1979. *Educ:* Milton Abbey, Blandford, Dorset; Trinity Coll., Oxford (BA Hons PPE). *Heir: yr twin b* Lord Charles David Montagu Hay, *b* 6 Aug. 1947. *Address:* House of Lords, SW1.

TWEEDIE, Jill Sheila; Columnist with the Guardian newspaper, since 1969; *b* 1936; *d* of Patrick Graeme Tweedie, CBE and Sheila (*née* Whittall); *m* 1954, Count Bela Cziraky; one *s* one *d*; 1963, Robert d'Ancona; one *s*; *m* 1973, Alan Brien, *qv*. *Educ:* eight girls' schools, ranging from PNEU to GPDST; education unfinished at Swiss finishing school. Freelance journalist, Press, radio and television. Woman Journalist of the Year, IPC Nat. Press Awards, 1971; Granada TV Award, 1972. *Publications:* In The Name Of Love, 1979; It's Only Me, 1980; Letters from a Faint-hearted Feminist, 1982; contribs to various European and American anthologies. *Recreation:* changing mind. *Address:* 14 Falkland Road, NW5.

TWEEDIE, Brig. John William, CBE 1958; DSO 1944; DL; *b* 5 June 1907; *e s* of late Col William Tweedie, CMG, CBE; *m* 1937, Sheila Mary, *d* of Brig.-Gen. Thomas Hudson, CB; one *s* one *d*. *Educ:* Ampleforth; Royal Military College, Sandhurst. 2/Lt Argyll and Sutherland Highldrs, 1926; Adjutant, 1935-39; OC 2nd Bn, 1942-44; Brigade Commander, 39 Inf. Bde, 1951-54; ADC to the Queen, 1959-61; retired 1961. DL Dumfries, 1975. Croix de Guerre, 1944. *Address:* Woodslee House, Canonbie, Dumfriesshire. *T:* 206. *Club:* Army and Navy.

TWEEDSMUIR, 2nd Baron, *cr* 1935, of Elsfield; **John Norman Stuart Buchan,** CBE 1964 (OBE (mil.) 1945); CD 1964; FRSE; Lt-Col Canadian Infantry Corps, retired; LLD (Hon.), Aberdeen, 1949, Queen's (Canada), 1955; *b* 25 November 1911; *e s* of 1st Baron and Susan Charlotte (*d* 1977), *d* of Hon. Norman Grosvenor; *S* father, 1940; *m* 1st, 1948, Priscilla Jean Fortescue, later Baroness Tweedsmuir of Belhelvie, PC (*d* 1978); one *d*; 2nd, 1980, Jean Margherita, widow of Sir Francis Grant, 12th Bt. *Educ:* Eton; Brasenose Coll., Oxford (BA). Asst District Comr, Uganda Protectorate, 1934-36; joined Hudson's Bay Company, 1937; wintered in their service at Cape Dorset, Baffin Land, Canadian Arctic, 1938-39; served war of 1939-45 in Canadian Army (wounded, despatches twice, OBE (mil.) 1945, Order of Orange-Nassau, with swords); comd Hastings and Prince Edward Regt in Sicily and Italy, 1943; Hon. Col, 1955-60. Rector of Aberdeen Univ.,

1948-51; Chm., Joint East and Central African Board, 1950-52; UK Delegate: UN Assembly, 1951-52; Council of Europe, 1952; Pres., Commonwealth and British Empire Chambers of Commerce, 1955-57; a Governor: Commonwealth Inst., 1958-77, Trustee, 1977-; Ditchley Foundn; Pres., Inst. of Export, 1964-67; Mem. Board, BOAC, 1955-64; Chairman: Advertising Standards Authority, 1971-74; Council on Tribunals, 1973-80. Mem., Scottish Cttee, Nature Conservancy, 1971-73. President: Institute of Rural Life at Home and Overseas, 1951-; British Schools Exploring Society, 1964-; Chm., British Rheumatism and Arthritis Assoc., 1971-78, Pres., 1978-. Chancellor, Primrose League, 1969-75. FRSA. *Publications:* (part author) St Kilda papers, 1931; Hudson's Bay Trader, 1951; Always a Countryman, 1953; One Man's Happiness, 1968. *Recreations:* fishing, shooting, falconry. *Heir:* b Hon. William de l'Aigle Buchan, RAFVR [b 10 Jan. 1916; m 1st, Nesta (marr. diss. 1946), o d of Lt-Col C. D. Crozier; one d; 2nd, 1946, Barbara (marr. diss. 1960), 2nd d of E. N. Ensor, late of Hong Kong; three s three d; 3rd, 1960, Sauré Cynthia Mary, y d of late Major G. E. Tatchell, Royal Lincolnshire Regt; one s. *Educ:* Eton; New College, Oxford]. *Address:* Potterton House, Balmedie, Aberdeenshire. *T:* Balmedie 2230; Kingston House, Kingston Bagpuize, Oxon OX13 5AX. *T:* Oxford 820259. *Clubs:* Carlton, Travellers', Pratt's, Flyfishers'.
See also Lord James Douglas-Hamilton.

TWELVETREE, Eric Alan; County Treasurer, Essex County Council, since 1974; b 26 Dec. 1928; m 1953, Patricia Mary Starkings; two d. *Educ:* Stamford Sch., Lincs; qualif. IPFA and ACCA. Served with Borough Councils: Gt Yarmouth, Ipswich, Stockport, Southampton; County Councils: Gloucestershire, Kent. *Address:* County Hall, Chelmsford, Essex CM1 1JZ. *T:* Chelmsford 67222.

TWINN, John Ernest; consulting engineer; company director; Director General Guided Weapons and Electronics, Ministry of Defence, 1978-81, retired; b 11 July 1921; s of late Col Frank Charles George Twinn, CMG and Lilian May Twinn (née Tomlinson); m 1950, Mary Constance Smallwood; three d. *Educ:* Manchester Grammar Sch.; Christ's Coll., Cambridge (MA). MIEE. Air Min., 1941; Telecommunications Research Estabt (later Royal Radar Estabt), 1943; Head of Guided Weapons Gp, RRE, 1965; Head of Space Dept, RAE, 1968; Head of Weapons Dept, RAE, 1972; Asst Chief Scientific Advr (Projects), MoD, 1973; Dir Underwater Weapons Projects (Naval), 1976. *Recreations:* sailing, music, genealogy. *Address:* Timbers, 9 Woodway, Merrow, Guildford, Surrey. *T:* Guildford 68993.

TWISK, Russell Godfrey; Editor, The Listener, since 1981; b 24 Aug. 1941; s of K. Y. Twisk of Twisk, Holland, and Joyce Brunning; m 1965, Ellen Elizabeth Banbury; two d. *Educ:* Salesian Coll., Farnborough. Harmsworth Press, Dep. Editor, Golf Illustrated, 1960; Sub Editor, Sphere; freelance journalist, 1962; joined BBC, editorial staff Radio Times, 1966; Deputy Editor, Radio Times, 1971; Development Manager, BBC, 1975. Has edited numerous BBC publications; Publisher, BBC Adult Literacy Project; devised Radio Times Drama Awards. Governor, London College of Printing, 1967- (Chm., 1974, 1978). *Recreations:* marathon running, map reading. *Address:* 20 Elm Grove Road, W5 3JJ. *T:* 01-567 5125.

TWISLETON-WYKEHAM-FIENNES; *see* Fiennes.

TWISLETON-WYKEHAM-FIENNES, Gerard Francis Gisborne, OBE 1957; MA; b 7 June 1906; s of Gerard Yorke Twisleton-Wykeham-Fiennes, CBE, and Gwendolen; m 1st, 1934, Norah Davies (d 1960), Penymaes, Llangollen; three s two d; 2nd, 1962, Jean Kerridge. *Educ:* Horris Hill, Newbury; Winchester Coll.; Hertford Coll., Oxford. LNER 1928. Asst Yardmaster, Whitemoor, 1932; Chief Controller, Cambridge, 1934; appts at York, Liverpool Street, Edinburgh and Shenfield; District Supt; Nottingham, 1943; Stratford, 1944; Operating Supt, Eastern Region, 1956; Line Traffic Manager, King's Cross, 1957; Chief Operating Officer, BR, 1961; Chm., Western Railway Board, 1963; Lt-Col Railway Staff and Engrg Corps, 1963; Chm., Eastern Railway Board, and Gen. Manager, Eastern Region, British Railways, 1965-67. Dir, Hargreaves Gp, 1968-76. Broadcasts on radio and TV. FRSA 1966; FCIT (MInstT 1955). ÖStJ 1967. Mayor of Aldeburgh, 1976. *Publications:* I Tried to Run a Railway, 1967; various chapters and articles in railway technical press. *Recreations:* golf, sailing, fishing, railways. *Address:* Dartmouth, Crabbe Street, Aldeburgh, Suffolk IP15 5BN. *T:* 2457. *Club:* MCC.

TWISLETON-WYKEHAM-FIENNES, Sir John (Saye Wingfield), KCB 1970 (CB 1953); QC 1972; First Parliamentary Counsel, 1968-72, retired; b 14 April 1911; s of Gerard Yorke Twisleton-Wykeham-Fiennes and Gwendolen (née Gisborne); m 1937, Sylvia Beatrice, d of Rev. C. R. L. McDowall; two s one d. *Educ:* Winchester; Balliol College, Oxford. Called to Bar, Middle Temple, 1936; Bencher, 1969. Joined parliamentary counsel office, 1939; Second Parly Coun., Treasury, 1956-68. Parliamentary Counsel, Malaya, 1962-63 (Colombo Plan). With Law Commission, 1965-66. Hon. JMN (Malaysia). *Address:* Mill House, Preston, Sudbury, Suffolk.

TWISS, Adm. Sir Frank (Roddam), KCB 1965 (CB 1962); KCVO 1978; DSC 1945; Gentleman Usher of the Black Rod, House of Lords, 1970-78; Serjeant-at-Arms, House of Lords, and Secretary to the Lord Great Chamberlain, 1971-78; b 7 July 1910; s of Col E. K. Twiss, DSO; m 1st, 1936, Prudence Dorothy Hutchison (d 1974); two s one d; 2nd, 1978, Rosemary Maitland (née Howe), widow of Captain Denis Chilton, RN. *Educ:* RNC

Dartmouth. Cadet 1924; Midshipman 1928; Lieut 1931; Comdr 1945; Captain 1950; Rear-Adm. 1960; Vice-Adm. 1963; Adm. 1967. Naval Sec., Admty, 1960-62; Flag Officer, Flotillas, Home Fleet, 1962-64; Comdr Far East Fleet, 1965-67; Second Sea Lord and Chief of Naval Personnel, 1967-70. Mem., Commonwealth War Graves Commn, 1970-79. *Recreations:* fishing, walking. *Address:* East Marsh Farm, Bratton, near Westbury, Wilts. *Club:* Army and Navy.

TWISS, (Lionel) Peter; OBE 1957; DSC 1942 and Bar 1943; General Manager, Hamble Point Marina Ltd, since 1978; formerly Chief Test Pilot of Fairey Aviation Ltd; b 23 July 1921; m 1950, Mrs Vera Maguire (marr. diss.); one d (and one d decd), one step s one step d; m 1960, Cherry (marr. diss.), d of late Sir John Huggins, GCMG, MC; one d; m 1964, Mrs Heather Danby, Titchfield. *Educ:* Sherborne Sch. Joined Fleet Air Arm, 1939; served on catapult ships, aircraft-carriers, 1941-43; night fighter development, 1943-44; served in British Air Commn, America, 1944. Empire Test Pilots School, Boscombe Down, 1945; Test Pilot, Fairey Aviation Co. Ltd, 1946, Chief Test Pilot, 1957-60. Dir, Fairey Marine Ltd, 1968-78. Holder of World's Absolute Speed Record, 10 March 1956. *Publication:* Faster than the Sun, 1963. *Address:* Nettleworth, 33 South Street, Titchfield, Hants. *T:* 43146. *Clubs:* Royal Southern Yacht, Island Sailing.

TWIST, Henry Aloysius, CMG 1966; OBE 1947; company director; Director of Studies, Royal Institute of Public Administration, since 1974; b 18 June 1914; s of John Twist, Preston; m 1941, Mary Monica, yr d of Nicholas Mulhall, Manchester; one s one d. *Educ:* Liverpool Univ. (BA). Senior Classics Master, St Chad's Coll., Wolverhampton, 1936-40; Lecturer in English, South Staffordshire High School of Commerce, 1939-40. Served War of 1939-45 with RASC and RAEC, 1940-46; released with rank of Lt-Col, 1946. Principal, Dominions Office, 1946; Offical Secretary, Office of the British High Commissioner in Ceylon, 1948-49; Office of the British High Commissioner in Australia, 1949-52; Commonwealth Relations Office, 1952-54; Secretariat, Commonwealth Economic Conference, London, 1952; Deputy High Commissioner for the United Kingdom in Bombay, 1954-57; Assistant Secretary, Commonwealth Relations Office, 1957-60; British Deputy High Commissioner, Kaduna, Northern Region, Federation of Nigeria, 1960-62; Commonwealth Service representative on the 1963 Course at Imperial Defence College; Commonwealth Office, 1964; Asst Under-Sec., 1966; Dep High Comr, 1966-70, Minister (Commercial), 1968-70, Rawalpindi; retired 1970. *Recreation:* gardening. *Address:* Pine Lodge, Woodham Lane, Woking, Surrey. *Clubs:* Royal Commonwealth Society; Lighthouse.

TWITCHETT, Prof. Denis Crispin, FBA 1967; Gordon Wu Professor of Chinese Studies, Princeton University, since 1980; b 23 Sept. 1925; m 1956, Umeko (née Ichikawa); two s. *Educ:* St Catharine's Coll., Cambridge. Lectr in Far-Eastern History, Univ. of London, 1954-56; Univ. Lectr in Classical Chinese, Univ. of Cambridge, 1956-60; Prof. of Chinese, SOAS, London Univ., 1960-68; Prof. of Chinese, Univ. of Cambridge, 1968-80. Vis. Prof., Princeton Univ., 1973-74, 1978-79. Principal Editor, Cambridge History of China, 1977-. *Publications:* (ed with A. F. Wright) Confucian Personalities, 1962; The Financial Administration under the T'ang dynasty, 1963, 2nd edn 1971; (ed with A. F. Wright) Perspectives on the T'ang, 1973; (ed with P. J. M. Geelan) The Times Atlas of China, 1975; (ed) Cambridge History of China, Vol. 10 1978, Vol. 3 1979, Vol. 11 1980, Vol. 12 1983; Printing and Publishing in Medieval China, 1982. *Address:* 24 Arbury Road, Cambridge; 14 College Road, Princeton, NJ 08540, USA.

TWYFORD, Donald Henry; Under Secretary, Export Credits Guarantee Department, since 1981; b 4 Feb. 1931; s of Henry John Twyford and Lily Hilda (née Ridler). *Educ:* Wembley County School. Joined Export Credits Guarantee Dept, 1949; Principal, 1965; seconded to Dept of Trade: Principal (Commercial Relations with East Europe), 1972-75; Asst Secretary (Country Policy), 1976; Establishment Officer, 1979-81; Under Secretary, Head of Services Group, ECGD, 1981-; Chairman, European Policy Coordination Group, 1981. *Recreations:* gardening (especially growing exhibition daffodils), music, travel. *Address:* 29 Heath Royal, Putney Heath Lane, SW15. *T:* 01-788 2934.

TYACKE, Maj.-Gen. David Noel Hugh, CB 1970; OBE 1957; Controller, Army Benevolent Fund, 1971-80; b 18 Nov. 1915; s of Capt. Charles Noel Walker Tyacke (killed in action, March 1918) and late Phoebe Mary Cicely (née Coulthard), Cornwall; m 1940, Diana, d of Aubrey Hare Duke; one s. *Educ:* Malvern Coll.; RMC Sandhurst. Commissioned DCLI, 1935; India, 1936-39; France and Belgium, 1939-40; India and Burma, 1943-46; Instructor, Staff Coll., Camberley, 1950-52; CO 1st Bn DCLI, 1957-59; Comdr 130 Inf. Bde (TA), 1961-63; Dir of Administrative Planning (Army), 1963-64; Brig. Gen. Staff (Ops), Min. of Defence, 1965-66; GOC Singapore Dist., 1966-70, retired. Col, The Light Infantry, 1972-77. Mem., Malvern Coll. Council, 1978-. *Recreations:* walking, motoring, bird-watching. *Address:* c/o Lloyds Bank Ltd, Cox's & King's Branch, 6 Pall Mall, SW1. *Club:* Naval and Military.

TYDEMAN, Col Frank William Edward, CMG 1966; CIE 1945; Port Consultant; b 20 January 1901; s of Harvey James and Kate Mary Anne Tydeman; m 1924, Jessie Sarah Mann (d 1947); two s. *Educ:* London University. BSc (Eng) London 1920. Chartered Civil Engineer. FICE, FIMechE, FIStructE, FIEAust, FCIT. Served Palestine; Haifa Harbour, 1930;

Jaffa Port, 1934; Singapore Harbour Board, 1937; Colonel, Deputy Director Transportation, India, Burma and Malaya, 1947; Port Consultant, Australia, to Commonwealth and WA govts and port authorities, on develt of ports of Fremantle, Bunbury, Townsville, Davenport, Mackay, Lae, Tjilatjap; retired 1965. *Recreation:* golf. *Address:* c/o ANZ Banking Group Ltd, Perth, WA 6000, Australia. *Clubs:* Naval and Military, West Australian Golf (Perth).

TYE, James; Director-General, British Safety Council, since 1968; *b* 21 Dec. 1921; *s* of late Benjamin Tye and Rose Tye; *m* 1950, Mrs Rosalie Hooker; one *s* one *d. Educ:* Upper Hornsey LCC Sch. Served War of 1939-45; RAF, 1940-46. Advertising Agent and Contractor, 1946-50; Managing Dir, 1950-62: Sky Press Ltd; Safety Publications Ltd. Joined British Safety Council as Exec. Dir, 1962. Chm., Bd of Governors, Internat. Inst. of Safety Management, 1975-. FBIM; Associate, Inst. of Occupational Safety and Health; Member: Amer. Soc. of Safety Engineers; Amer. Safety Management Soc.; Vice-Pres., Jamaica Safety Council; Fellow, Inst. of Accident Prevention, Zambia. FRSA. Freeman, City of London, 1976; Liveryman, Worshipful Co. of Basketmakers; Mem., Guild of Freemen of City of London. *Publications:* Communicating the Safety Message, 1968; Management Introduction to Total Loss Control, 1971; Safety-Uncensored (with K. Ullyett, JP), 1971; (with Bowes Egan) The Management Guide to Product Liability, 1979; *handbooks:* Industrial Safety Digest, 1953; Skilful Driving, 1952; Advanced Driving, 1954; International Nautical Safety Code (with Uffa Fox), 1961; Why Imprison Untrained Drivers?, 1980; Papers and Reports to Parly Groups and British Safety Council Members on: product liability, training safety officers, vehicle seat belts, anti-jack knife devices for articulated vehicles, lifejackets and buoyancy aids, motorway safety barriers, Britain's filthy beaches, dangers of: mini fire extinguishers, safety in fairgrounds, drip feed oil heaters, children's flammable nightwear, vehicle recall procedures, need for a nat. vehicle defects hotline, brain injuries caused by boxing and recommendations to improve the rules, pollution caused by diesel engines, safe toys, introduction of defensive driving techniques, risk management — stress at work, incr. risk of accidents thereof, use of colour in envt to promote safety and productivity, dangers of smoke masks, fire prevention — recommendations to industry. *Recreations:* squash, photography, sailing. *Address:* 55 Hartington Road, Chiswick, W4 3TS. *T:* 01-995 3206. *Clubs:* London Press, City Livery, Royal Automobile; New Grampians Squash.

TYE, Dr Walter, CBE 1966; CEng; *b* 12 Dec. 1912; *s* of Walter and Alice Tye; *m* 1939, Eileen Mary Whitmore; one *s* one *d. Educ:* Woodbridge Sch.; London Univ. (BScEng). Fairey Aviation Co., 1934; RAE, 1935-38; Air Registration Bd, 1938-39; RAE, 1939-44; Air Registration Bd, 1944-72 (Chief Techn. Officer, 1946, Chief Exec., 1969); Mem., CAA (Controller Safety), 1972-74. Hon. FRAeS; Hon. DSc Cranfield Inst. of Technology, 1972. *Publications:* articles, lectures and contrib. Jl RAeS. *Address:* The Spinney, Fairmile Park Road, Cobham, Surrey. *T:* Cobham 3692.

TYLECOTE, Dame Mabel, DBE 1966; Hon. Life Member of National Federation of Community Associations since 1979 (President, 1958-61; Vice-President, 1961-79); *b* 4 Feb. 1896; *d* of late John Emest Phythian and Ada Prichard Phythian (*née* Crompton); *m* 1932, Frank Edward Tylecote (*d* 1965); one *s* (and one step *s* one step *d*). *Educ:* Univ. of Manchester; Univ. of Wisconsin (USA). BA, PhD (Manchester). Lectr in History, Huddersfield Techn. Coll., 1920-24; Asst Lectr in History, Univ. of Manchester, 1926-30; Warden of Elvington Settlement, 1930-32; part-time Lectr, Univ. of Manchester Joint Cttee for Adult Educn, 1935-51; Vice-Pres., WEA, 1960-68. Member: Pensions Appeal Tribunal, 1944-50; Manchester City Council, 1940-51; (co-opted) Manchester Educn Cttee, 1951-77; Stockport Borough Council, 1956-63; Chm. of Council, Assoc. of Art Instns, 1960-61. Mem. Court, 1945-80. Mem. Council, 1960-75, Univ. of Manchester; Mem. Court, UMIST, 1960-77; Governor, Manchester Polytechnic, 1969-77 (Hon. Fellow, 1973); Vice-President: Manchester and Salford Council of Social Service, 1968-; Union of Lancashire and Cheshire Institutes, 1969-75; Hon. Life Mem. Nat. Inst. of Adult Educn, 1974- (Chm., 1960-63). Contested (Lab): Fylde, 1938; Middleton and Prestwich, 1945; Norwich South, 1950, 1951, 1955. Hon. LLD Manchester, 1978. *Publications:* The Education of Women at Manchester University 1883-1933, 1941; The Mechanics' Institutes of Lancashire and Yorkshire before 1851, 1957; The Future of Adult Education (Fabian pamphlet), 1960; contrib., Artisan to Graduate, ed D. S. L. Cardwell, 1974; The Work of Lady Simon of Wythenshawe for Education in Manchester (address), 1974; articles in various social and educnl jls. *Address:* 1 Rusholme Gardens, Wilmslow Road, Manchester M14 5LG. *T:* 061-224 9366.

TYLER, Brig. Arthur Catchmay, CBE 1960; MC 1945; DL; a Military Knight of Windsor, since 1978; *b* 20 Aug. 1913; 4th *s* of Hugh Griffin Tyler and Muriel Tyler (*née* Barnes); *m* 1938, Sheila, *d* of James Kinloch, Meigle, Perthshire; three *s* one *d. Educ:* Allhallows Sch.; RMC, Sandhurst. Commissioned, The Welch Regt, 1933. Served War of 1939-45: Africa, India and Burma (despatches). Staff Coll., 1946; JSSC, 1951; Sec., BJSM, Washington, 1952-54; Bt Lt-Col, 1953; Comd 4th (Carms) Bn The Welch Regt, 1954-57; Col, 1957; AAG, War Office, 1957-60; Brig. 1960; Senior UK Liaison Officer and Military Adviser to High Commissioner, Canada, 1960; Asst Chief of Staff (Ops and Plans), Allied Forces Central Europe, 1963. Sec., Council, TA&VR Assocs, 1967-72. Hon. Col., 7th(V) Bn, The Queen's Regt, T&AVR, 1971-75. Chm. Governors, Allhallows Sch. DL Surrey, 1968. *Address:* 19 Lower Ward, Windsor Castle, Berks.

TYLER, Cyril, DSc, PhD, FRSC; Professor of Physiology and Biochemistry, University of Reading, 1958-76, now Emeritus; Deputy Vice-Chancellor, 1968-76; *b* 26 Jan. 1911; *er s* of John and Annie Tyler; *m* 1st, 1939, Myra Eileen (*d* 1971), *d* of George and Rosa Batten; two *s* one *d* ; 2nd, 1971, Rita Patricia, *d* of Sidney and Lilian Jones. *Educ:* Ossett Grammar Sch.; Univ. of Leeds. BSc 1st Class Hons 1933, PhD 1935, DSc 1959, Leeds. Lectr in Agricultural Chemistry. RAC, Cirencester, 1935-39; Univ. of Reading: Lecturer in Agricultural Chemistry, 1939-47; Professor, 1947-58; Dean of the Faculty of Agriculture, 1959-62. Playing Mem., Glos CCC, 1936-39. *Publications:* Organic Chemistry for Students of Agriculture, 1946; Animal Nutrition (2nd edn), 1964; Wilhelm von Nathusius 1821-1899 on Avian Eggshells, 1964; numerous papers on poultry metabolism and egg shells in scientific journals. *Recreations:* gardening, history of animal nutrition. *Address:* 22 Belle Avenue, Reading, Berks.

TYLER, Froom, OBE 1969; *b* 30 Jan. 1904; *o s* of John Frederick Tyler, Bristol; *m* 1st, 1928, Doris May (*née* Chubb) (*d* 1963); one *d* ; 2nd, Diana Griffiths (*née* Kirby) (*d* 1971). Editor of the Evening World, Bristol, 1936-40; Foreign Editor, Daily Mail, 1940-43; Staff Officer (Press) to Admiral (Submarines), 1943-45. Editor of Overseas Daily Mail, 1946-50; Editor of Leicester Evening Mail, 1950-57; Editor of South Wales Evening Post, 1957-69; Chm., Swansea Festival of Music and the Arts, 1970-. Hon. MA Wales, 1980. *Publications:* Cripps: A Portrait and a Prospect, 1942; His Majesty's Submarines (the Admiralty Account), 1945; News in Our Time (Daily Mail Jubilee Book), 1946; The Man Who Made Music, 1947. *Address:* 50 Harford Court, The Bryn, Sketty Green, Swansea.

TYLER, Ven. Leonard George; Rector of Easthampstead, since 1973; *b* 15 April 1920; *s* of Hugh Horstead Tyler and Mabel Adam Stewart Tyler; *m* 1946, Sylvia May Wilson; one *s* two *d. Educ:* Darwen Grammar School; Liverpool University; Christ's College, Cambridge; Westcott House. Chaplain, Trinity College, Kandy, Ceylon, 1946-48; Principal, Diocesan Divinity School, Colombo, Ceylon, 1948-50; Rector, Christ Church, Bradford, Manchester, 1950-55; Vicar of Leigh, Lancs, 1955-66 (Rural Dean, 1955-62); Chaplain, Leigh Infirmary, 1955-66; Archdeacon of Rochdale, 1962-66; Principal, William Temple College, Manchester, 1966-73. Anglican Adviser to ABC Television, 1958-68. *Publications:* contributor to Theology. *Address:* The Rectory, Easthampstead, Bracknell, Berks RG12 4ER. *T:* Bracknell 25205.

TYLER, Maj.-Gen. Sir Leslie (Norman), KBE 1961 (OBE 1942); CB 1955; BScEng; CEng; FIMechE; *b* 26 April 1904; *s* of late Major Norman Tyler, Addiscombe, Surrey; *m* 1st, 1930, Louie Teresa Franklin (*d* 1950); one *s* one *d* ; 2nd, 1953, Sheila, *widow* of Maj.-Gen. L. H. Cox, CB, CBE, MC; two *s* two step *d. Educ:* RN Colleges Osborne and Dartmouth; King's College, Univ. of London. Commissioned Lieut, RAOC, 1927; served War of 1939-45, Malta and NW Europe; transferred to REME, 1942; DDME, Second Army, 1945; Comdt REME Training Centre, 1945-47; AAG, War Office, 1948-49; DME, MELF, 1949-50; DDME, War Office, 1950-53; DME, MELF, 1953-55; Commandant, Headquarters Base Workshop Group, REME, 1956-57; Director of Electrical and Mechanical Engineering, War Office, 1957-60; retd 1960. Regional Dir, MPBW, Central Mediterranean Region, 1963-69. Chm., Royal Hosp. and Home for Incurables, Putney, 1971-76. Colonel Commandant, REME, 1962-67. Freeman, City of London; Liveryman, 1961, Master, 1982, Worshipful Company of Turners. Fellow, King's Coll., London, 1969. *Address:* 51 Chiltley Way, Liphook, Hants GU30 7HE. *T:* Liphook 722335. *Club:* Army and Navy.

TYLER, Paul Archer; politician and public affairs consultant; Executive Director, Public Affairs Division, Good Relations plc, since 1982; *b* 29 Oct. 1941; *s* of Oliver Walter Tyler and Ursula Grace Gibbons Tyler (*née* May); *m* 1970, Nicola Mary Ingram; one *s* one *d. Educ:* Mount House Sch., Tavistock; Sherborne Sch.; Exeter Coll., Oxford (MA). Pres., Oxford Univ. Liberal Club, 1962. Royal Inst. of British Architects: Admin. Asst, 1966; Asst Sec., 1967; Dep. Dir Public Affairs, 1971; Dir Public Affairs, 1972. Man. Dir, Cornwall Courier newspaper gp, 1976-81. County Councillor, Devon, 1964-70; Mem., Devon and Cornwall Police Authority, 1965-70; Vice-Chm., Dartmoor Nat. Park Cttee, 1965-70; Chm., CPRE Working Party on the Future of the Village, 1974-81; Mem. Bd of Shelter (Nat. Campaign for the Homeless), and rep. in Devon and Cornwall, 1975-76. Sec., L/SDP Jt Commn on Employment and Industrial Recovery, 1981-82. Chm., Devon and Cornwall Region Liberal Party, 1981-82. Contested (L): Totnes, 1966; Bodmin, 1970, 1979; Beaconsfield, 1982; MP (L) Bodmin, Feb.-Sept. 1974; Parly Liberal Spokesman on Housing and Transport, 1974; Parly Adviser to RIBA, 1974. *Publication:* A New Deal for Rural Britain (jtly), 1978. *Recreations:* sailing, gardening, walking. *Address:* Tregrove House, Rilla Mill, Callington, Cornwall. *Clubs:* National Liberal; Liskeard Liberal (Cornwall); Saltash Sailing.

TYMMS, Sir Frederick, KCIE 1947 (CIE 1935); Kt 1941; MC; FRAeS; *b* 4 Aug. 1889; *s* of William Henry Tymms. *Educ:* Tenby; King's College, London. War Service: 4th Bn South Lancs Regt and Royal Flying Corps, France; British Aviation Mission to the USA, 1915-18 (MC, Chevalier de l'Ordre de la Couronne, Croix de Guerre, Belgium). Civil Aviation Dept, Air Min., 1920-27; Oxford Univ. Arctic Expedition to Spitsbergen, 1924; Air Min. Supt of Egypt-India air route, 1927; seconded to Govts of the Sudan, Kenya, Uganda and Tanganyika, 1928; Chief Technical Asst to Dir of Civil Aviation, Air Min., 1928-31; Air Min. Representative on the Commn to

Africa, to organise the Cape to Cairo air route, 1929-30; Dir of Civil Aviation in India, 1931-42 and 1943-45; Man. Dir, Tata Aircraft Ltd, Bombay, 1942-43; Dir-Gen. of Civil Aviation in India, Sept. 1945-March 1947; UK Representative on Council of Internat. Civil Aviation Organisation, Montreal, 1947-54; retd from Civil Service, 1955. Govt of India delegate to Internat. Civil Aviation Conf., Chicago, 1944; Leader of UK Civil Aviation Mission to New Zealand, 1948. Master of Guild of Air Pilots and Air Navigators, 1957-58. Chm., Commn of Enquiry on Civil Aviation in West Indies, 1960. *Address:* Clare Park, Crondall, near Farnham, Surrey; c/o Lloyds Bank, Pall Mall, SW1. *Club:* Naval and Military.

TYMMS, Prof. Ralph Vincent, MA; Professor of German Language and Literature in the University of London (Royal Holloway College), 1956-80, now Emeritus; Head of German Department 1948-80, Vice-Principal 1969-75, Royal Holloway College; *b* 9 Jan. 1913; *s* of Arthur Hugh Tymms and Janet Scott Coventon; *m* 1980, Dr Marion Gibbs. *Educ:* Bradford Grammar Sch., Yorkshire; Magdalen Coll., Oxford; Univs of Vienna and Giessen. John Doncaster Scholar in German, Magdalen Coll., Oxford, 1931-34; 1st Class Hons, Oxford, 1934. Asst Lectr in German, Univ. of Manchester, 1936. Intelligence Corps, 1941-45; Major, 1945. Lecturer in German, Manchester Univ., 1945; Reader in German Language and Literature in Univ. of London, 1948. *Publications:* Doubles in Literary Psychology, 1949; German Romantic Literature, 1955. *Address:* Merrow Down, Northcroft Road, Englefield Green, Egham, Surrey TW20 0DU. *T:* Egham 32125.

TYNDALE-BISCOE, Rear-Adm. Alec Julian, CB 1959; OBE 1946; lately Chairman of Blaw Knox Ltd; *b* 10 Aug. 1906; *s* of late Lt-Col A. A. T. Tyndale-Biscoe, Aubrey House, Keyhaven, Lymington, Hants; *m* 1st, 1939, Emma Winifred Haselden (*d* 1974); four *d* ; 2nd, 1974, Hugolyne Cotton Cooke, *widow* of Captain Geoffrey Cotton Cooke. *Educ:* RN Colleges Osborne and Dartmouth. Entered RN, 1920. Served War, 1939-46; HMS Vanguard, 1947-49; Captain, 1949; Asst Engineer-in-Chief, Fleet, 1950-53; Comdg RN Air Station, Anthorn, 1953-55; Fleet Engr Officer, Mediterranean, 1955-57; Rear-Adm. 1957; Flag-Officer Reserve Aircraft, 1957-59, retired. *Address:* Bunces Farm Gardens, Birch Grove, Haywards Heath, West Sussex.

TYREE, Sir (Alfred) William, Kt 1975; OBE 1971; engineer and pastoralist; Chairman and Founder A. W. Tyree Foundation (incorporating Medicheck Referral Centre and Tyree Chair of Electrical Engineering, University of New South Wales); *b* 4 Nov. 1921; *m* 1946, Joyce, *d* of F. Lyndon; two *s* one *d.* *Educ:* Auckland Grammar Sch.; Sydney Technical Coll. Founder: Tyree Industries Ltd; Westralian Transformers and subsids; Chairman: Tycan Australia Pty Ltd; Tyree Hldgs Pty Ltd; C. P. R. Constructions Pty Ltd; Reinhausen (Aust.) Pty Ltd. *Recreations:* ski-ing, private flying, water ski-ing; yachting, tennis, music, golf. *Address:* 3 Lindsay Avenue, Darling Point, NSW 2027, Australia. *Clubs:* Royal Aero, American National, Royal Automobile (NSW); Royal Prince Alfred Yacht, Royal Motor Yacht, Cruising Yacht, Kosciusko Alpine, Australian Alpine, RAC, Australian Golf.

TYRELL-KENYON; *see* Kenyon.

TYRONE, Earl of; Henry Nicholas de la Poer Beresford; *b* 23 March 1958; *s* and *heir* of 8th Marquess of Waterford, *qv*. *Educ:* Harrow School.

TYRRELL, Alan Rupert, QC 1976; a Recorder of the Crown Court, since 1972; Barrister-at-Law; Member (C) London East, European Parliament, since 1979; *b* 27 June 1933; *s* of Rev. T. G. R. Tyrrell, and Mrs W. A. Tyrrell, MSc; *m* 1960, Elaine Eleanor Ware, LLB; one *s* one *d.* *Educ:* Bridport Grammar Sch.; London Univ. (LLB). Called to the Bar, Gray's Inn, 1956. Chm. London Reg., and Mem. Nat. Exec., Nat. Fedn of Self-Employed, 1978-79. *Publications:* (ed) Moore's Practical Agreements, 10th edn 1965. *Recreation:* bridge. *Address:* 15 Willifield Way, Hampstead Garden Suburb, NW11. *T:* 01-455 5798; 32 rue Ortelius, 1040 Brussels, Belgium. *Clubs:* Europe House; Hampshire (Winchester), Exeter and County (Exeter).

TYRRELL, Dr David Arthur John, CBE 1980; FRS 1970; FRCP; Deputy Director of Clinical Research Centre, Northwick Park, Harrow, and Head of Division of Communicable Diseases, since 1970; *b* 19 June 1925; *s* of Sidney Charles Tyrrell and Agnes Kate (*née* Blewett); *m* 1950, Betty Moyra Wylie; two *d* (one *s* decd). *Educ:* Sheffield University. Junior hosp. appts, Sheffield, 1948-51; Asst, Rockefeller Inst., New York, 1951-54; Virus Research Lab., Sheffield, 1954-57; Common Cold Research Unit, Salisbury, 1957-70. First Chm., Adv. Cttee on Dangerous Pathogens, 1981-. Managing Trustee, Nuffield Foundn, 1977-. Hon. DSc Sheffield, 1979. Stewart Prize, BMA, 1977. *Publications:* Common Colds and Related Diseases, 1965; Interferon and its Clinical Potential, 1976; (jtly) Microbial Diseases, 1979; numerous papers on infectious diseases and viruses. *Recreations:* music-making, gardening, sailing, walking; various Christian organizations. *Address:* c/o Common Cold Unit, Coombe Road, Salisbury, Wilts; Ash Lodge, Dean Lane, Whiteparish, Salisbury, Wilts SP5 2RN.

TYRRELL, Gerald Fraser; former Buyer, Stewart Dry Goods Co., Louisville, USA, and London; retired 1974; *b* London, 7 March 1907; *s* of late Lt-Col G. E. Tyrrell, DSO, RA, and C. R. Tyrrell (*née* Fraser); *m* 1937, Virginia Lee Gettys, Louisville, Kentucky; three *s* one *d.* *Educ:* Eton; Magdalene Coll., Cambridge. Student Interpreter, China Consular Service, 1930; served in

Tientsin, Chungking, Shanghai, Foochow, Canton; Vice-Consul at San Francisco, 1941; Vice-Consul, Boston, 1942, Acting Consul-General, 1944; 1st Secretary, Washington, 1945; Consul at Cincinnati, 1946; Acting Consul-General, New Orleans, 1947; Consul-General, Canton, 1948; Foreign Office, 1949, resigned, 1950. *Address:* 2333 Glenmary Avenue, Louisville, Kentucky 40204, USA.

TYRRELL, Prof. Henry John Valentine, FRSC; Vice-Principal and Head of Chemistry Department, Chelsea College; Secretary and Vice-President, Royal Institution of Great Britain, since 1978; *b* 14 Feb. 1920; *s* of John Rice Tyrrell and Josephine (*née* McGuinness); *m* 1947, Sheila Mabel (*née* Straw); three *s* three *d.* *Educ:* state schools; Jesus Coll., Oxford. DSc. Chemical Industry, 1942-47; Sheffield Univ., 1947-65; Chelsea College: Professor of Physical and Inorganic Chemistry, 1965; Head of Dept, 1972; Vice-Principal, 1976. *Publications:* Diffusion and Heat Flow in Liquids, 1961; Thermometric Titrimetry, 1968; papers in chemical and physical jls. *Recreations:* foreign travel, gardening. *Address:* 49 Flood Street, SW3 5SU. *Club:* Royal Institution.

TYRRELL, Sir Murray (Louis), KCVO 1968 (CVO 1954); CBE 1959; JP; Official Secretary to Governor-General of Australia, 1947-73; *b* 1 Dec. 1913; *s* of late Thomas Michael and Florence Evelyn Tyrrell; *m* 1939, Ellen St Clair, *d* of late E. W. St Clair Greig; one *s* two *d.* *Educ:* Orbost and Melbourne Boys' High Schools, Victoria. Central Office, Postmaster General's Department, Melbourne, 1929-39; Asst Private Secretary to Minister for Air and Civil Aviation, 1940; Private Secretary to Minister for Air, 1940, to Minister for Munitions, 1940; Personal Asst to Secretary, Min. of Munitions, 1942; Private Secretary: Commonwealth Treas. and Min. for Post-War Reconstruction, 1943, to Prime Minister and Treasurer, 1945; Official Secretary and Comptroller to Governor-General, 1947; resigned Comptrollership, 1953. Attached Royal Household, Buckingham Palace, May-Aug. 1962. Director: Nat. Heart Foundn of Australia, 1970-; Canberra C of E Girls' Grammar Sch., 1952-65; Canberra Grammar Sch., 1954-65; Registrar, Order of St John of Jerusalem in Australia, 1976-; Mem., Buildings and Grounds Cttee, ANU, 1974-. Alderman, Queanbeyan CC, 1974; Mem., Southern Tablelands CC, 1974. CStJ 1969. Australian of the Year, 1977. *Recreation:* fishing. *Address:* 11 Blundell Street, Queanbeyan, NSW 2620, Australia.

TYRWHITT, Brig. Dame Mary (Joan Caroline), DBE 1949 (OBE 1946); TD; *b* 27 Dec. 1903; *d* of Admiral of the Fleet Sir Reginald Tyrwhitt, 1st Bt, GCB, DSO; unmarried. Senior Controller, 1946 (rank altered to Brigadier, 1950); Director, ATS, 1946-49, Women's Royal Army Corps, 1949-50, retired Dec. 1950; Hon. ADC to the King, 1949-50. *Address:* 14 Manor Court, Pewsey, Wilts.

TYRWHITT, Sir Reginald (Thomas Newman), 3rd Bt, *cr* 1919; *b* 21 Feb. 1947; *er s* of Admiral Sir St John Tyrwhitt, 2nd Bt, KCB, DSO, DSC and Bar (*d* 1961), and of Nancy (Veronica) Gilbey (who *m* 1965, Sir Godfrey Agnew, *qv*); *S* father, 1961; *m* 1972, Sheila Gail (marr. diss. 1980), *d* of William Alistair Crawford Nicoll, Liphook, Hants. *Educ:* Downside. 2nd Lieut, RA, 1966, Lieut 1969; RARO 1969. *Recreations:* shooting, fishing. *Heir:* *b* John (Edward Charles) Tyrwhitt [*b* 27 July 1953; *m* 1978, Melinda Ngaire, *o d* of Anthony Philip Towell, MC, Long Island, NY, USA; two *s*]. *Address:* c/o Lloyds Bank Ltd, Ascot, Berks SL5 7JE.
See also Dame Mary Tyrwhitt.

TYSON, Dr Alan Walker, FBA 1978; musicologist and psychoanalyst; Fellow of All Souls College, Oxford, since 1952, Senior Research Fellow, since 1971; *b* 27 Oct. 1926; *e s* of Henry Alan Maurice Tyson and Dorothy (*née* Walker). *Educ:* Rugby School; Magdalen College, Oxford; University College Hospital Medical School, London. BA 1951, MA 1952; MB, BS 1965; MRCPsych 1972. Vis. Lectr in Psychiatry, Montefiore Hosp., NY, 1967-68; Lectr in Psychopathology and Developmental Psychology, Oxford Univ., 1968-70; Vis. Prof. of Music, Columbia Univ., 1969; James P. R. Lyell Reader in Bibliography, Oxford Univ., 1973-74; Ernest Bloch Prof. of Music, Univ. of California at Berkeley, 1977-78. Assoc. Mem., British Psychoanalytical Soc., 1957-. On editorial staff, Standard Edition of Freud's works, 1952-74. *Publications:* The Authentic English Editions of Beethoven, 1963; (with O. W. Neighbour) English Music Publishers' Plate Numbers, 1965; (ed) Selected letters of Beethoven, 1967; Thematic Catalogue of the Works of Muzio Clementi, 1967; (ed) Beethoven Studies, Vol. 1, 1973, Vol. 2, 1977, Vol. 3, 1982. *Address:* 7 Southcote Road, N19 5BJ. *T:* 01-609 2981.

TYSON, Monica Elizabeth; Editor, Special Assignments, IPC Magazines, since 1982; *b* 7 June 1927; *d* of F. S. Hill and E. Hill; *m* R. E. D. Tyson; one *d.* *Educ:* George Watson's Ladies Coll.; Edinburgh Coll. of Domestic Science (Dip. in Dom. Sci.). Asst Home Editor, Modern Woman, 1958-60; Ideal Home: Domestic Planning Editor, 1960-64; Asst Editor, 1964-68; Editor, 1968-77; Editor, Woman's Realm, 1977-82. *Recreations:* walking, reading, cooking. *Address:* 12 Warwick Square, SW1V 2AA.

TYTLER, Christian Helen F.; *see* Fraser-Tytler.

TYTLER, Rt. Rev. Donald Alexander; *see* Middleton, Bishop Suffragan of.

TYZACK, Margaret Maud, OBE 1970; *b* 9 Sept. 1931; *d* of Thomas Edward Tyzack and Doris Moseley; *m* 1958, Alan Stephenson; one *s. Educ:* St Angela's Ursuline Convent; Royal Academy of Dramatic Art. Trained at RADA (Gilbert Prize for Comedy). First engagement, Civic Theatre, Chesterfield. Vassilissa in The Lower Depths, Royal Shakespeare Co., Arts Theatre, 1962; Lady MacBeth, Nottingham, 1962; Miss Frost in The Ginger Man, Royal Court Theatre, London, 1964; Madame Ranevsky in The Cherry Orchard, Exeter and Tour, 1969; Jacqui in Find Your Way Home, Open Space Theatre, London, 1970; Queen Elizabeth in Vivat! Vivat Regina!, Piccadilly, 1971; Tamora in Titus Andronicus, Portia in Julius Caesar and Volumnia in Coriolanus, Royal Shakespeare Co., Stratford-on-Avon, 1972; Portia in Julius Caesar, and Volumnia in Coriolanus, RSC, Aldwych, 1973; Maria Lvovna in Summerfolk, RSC, Aldwych, and NY, 1974–75; Richard III, All's Well That Ends Well, Ghosts, Stratford, Ont., 1977; People Are Living There, Manchester Royal Exchange, 1979; Martha, in Who's Afraid of Virginia Woolf?, Nat. Theatre, 1981. *Films:* Ring of Spies, 2001: A Space Odyssey, The Whisperers, A Clockwork Orange, The Legacy. *Television series include:* The Forsyte Saga; The First Churchills; Cousin Bette, 1970–71; I, Claudius, 1976; Quatermass, 1979; A Winter's Tale. Actress of the Year Award (BAFTA) for Queen Anne in The First Churchills, 1969. *Address:* c/o Representation Joyce Edwards, 8 Theed Street, SE1 8ST. *T:* 01-261 1488.

U

UATIOA, Dame Mere, DBE 1978; *b* 19 Jan. 1924; *d* of Aberam Takenibeia and Bereti Bamatang; *m* 1950, Reuben K. Uatioa, MBE (*d* 1977); three *s* one *d. Educ:* Hiram Bingham High School, Beru Island. Widow of Reuben K. Uatioa, MBE, a leading Gilbertese nationalist and former Speaker, House of Assembly, Gilbert Islands; supported her husband throughout his long public service, demonstrating those qualities of wife and mother which are most admired in the Pacific. After his death, she devoted herself to her family. *Recreations:* social and voluntary work for Churches. *Address:* Erik House, Antebuka, Tarawa, Gilbert Islands.

UBBELOHDE, Prof. Alfred R. J. P., CBE 1963; MA, DSc Oxon; FRS 1951; FRSC; FInstP; FEng; MIChemE; Hon. Laureate, Padua University, 1963; Senior Research Fellow, since 1975, Fellow, since 1981, Imperial College of Science and Technology; Professor of Thermodynamics, University of London (Imperial College), 1954–75, now Emeritus, and Head of Department of Chemical Engineering and Chemical Technology, 1961–75; *b* 14 Dec. 1907; 3rd *s* of F. C. Ubbelohde and Angele Verspreeuwen; unmarried. *Educ:* St Paul's Sch.; Christ Church, Oxford (Hon. Student, 1979). Dewar Fellow of Royal Instn, 1935–40; research on explosives; Min. of Supply, 1940–45; Prof. of Chemistry, Queen's Univ., Belfast, 1945–54, Dean of the Faculty of Science, 1947–51. Chairman Fire Research Board, 1956–61; President of Council Institut Solvay, 1957–64, 1965–; Director of Salters' Institute, 1959–75; Past President, Faraday Society, 1963–; Past Vice-President, Society of Chemical Industry; Chairman, Science and Engineering Panel, British Council, 1964; Member: Agricl Research Council, 1966–76; Pontifical Academy of Sciences, 1968. Hon. FCGI. Dr *hc* Faculty of Science, Univ. Libre, Brussels, 1962; Hon. DSc QUB, 1972. Messel Medal, 1972; George Skakel Award, 1975; Paul Lebeau Medal, 1975. *Publications:* Modern Thermodynamical Principles, 1937 (2nd edn 1952); Time and Thermodynamics, 1947; Man and Energy, 1954, 2nd edn 1963; Graphite and its crystal compounds, 1960; Melting and Crystal Structure, 1965; The Molten State of Matter, 1978; papers in Proceedings and Journals of scientific societies. *Address:* Imperial College, South Kensington, SW7; Platts Farm, Burwash, Sussex. *Clubs:* Athenæum, Royal Automobile.

UBEE, Air Vice-Marshal Sydney Richard, CB 1952; AFC 1939; Royal Air Force; retired as Air Officer Commanding, No 2 Group, 2nd Tactical Air Force, Germany (1955–58); *b* 5 March 1903; *s* of late Edward Joseph Ubee, London; *m* 1942, Marjorie Doris (*d* 1954), *d* of George Clement-Parker, Newport, Mon; two step *s. Educ:* Beaufoy Technical Institute. Joined RAF, 1927, with short service commission; permanent commission, 1932; test pilot, Royal Aircraft Establishment, Farnborough, 1933–37; served in India, Iraq, Iran, Burma, and Ceylon, 1937–43; Airborne Forces Experimental Establishment, 1943–47; Comdg Officer, Experimental Flying, RAE Farnborough, 1946–47; Commandant Empire Test Pilots' Sch., Cranfield, Bucks, and Farnborough, 1947–48; Deputy Director Operational Requirements, Air Min., 1948–51; Commandant RAF Flying Coll., Manby, 1951–54; Director-General of Personnel (II), Air Ministry, 1954–55. *Address:* Harwood House, Lower Bourne, Farnham, Surrey. *Club:* Royal Air Force.

UDOMA, Hon. Sir (Egbert) Udo, CFR 1978; Kt 1964; Justice, Supreme Court of Nigeria, Lagos, since 1969; *b* 21 June 1917; *s* of Chief Udoma Inam of Ibekwe Ntanaran Akama of Opobo, Nigeria; *m* 1950, Grace Bassey; six *s* one *d. Educ:* Methodist Coll., Uzuakoli, Nigeria; Trinity Coll., Dublin; St Catherine's Coll., Oxford. BA 1942; LLB 1942; PhD 1944; MA 1945. President, Dublin Univ. Philosophical Society, 1942–43. Called to Bar, Gray's Inn, 1945; practised as Barrister-at-Law in Nigeria, 1946–61; Member, House of Representatives, Nigeria, 1952–59; Judge of High Court of Federal Territory of Lagos, Nigeria, 1961–63. Member Nigeria Marketing Board and Director Nigeria Marketing Co. Board, 1952–54; Member Managing Cttee, West African Inst. for Oil Palm Research, 1953–63; Nat. President, Ibibio State Union, 1947–63; Vice-President, Nigeria Bar Assoc., 1957–61; Member: Internat. Commn of Jurists; World Assoc. of Judges; Chief Justice, High Court, Uganda, 1963–69; Acting Gov.-Gen., Uganda, 1963; Vice-President, Uganda Sports Union, 1964; Chairman, Board of Trustees, King George V Memorial Fund, 1964–69; Chancellor, Ahmadu Bello Univ., Zaria, 1972–75. Chm., Constituent Assembly for Nigerian Constitution, 1977–78; Dir, Seminar for Judges, 1980–. Patron, Nigerian Soc. of Internat. Law, 1968–; Mem., Nigerian Inst. of Internat. Affairs, 1979–. LLD (*hc*): Ibadan, 1967; Zaria, 1972; TCD, 1973. Awarded title of Obong Ikpa Isong Ibibio, 1961. *Publication:* The Lion and the Oil Palm and other essays, 1943. *Recreations:* billiards, tennis, gardening. *Address:* Mfut Itiat Enin, 8 Dr Udoma Street, Ikot Abasi, Cross River State, Nigeria, West Africa. *Clubs:* Island, Metropolitan, Yoruba Tennis (Lagos, Nigeria).

UFFEN, Kenneth James, CMG 1977; HM Diplomatic Service; Ambassador and UK Permanent Representative to OECD, Paris, since 1982; *b* 29 Sept. 1925; *s* of late Percival James Uffen, MBE, former Civil Servant, and late Gladys Ethel James; *m* 1954, Nancy Elizabeth Winbolt; one *s* two *d. Educ:* Latymer Upper Sch.; St Catharine's Coll., Cambridge. HM Forces (Flt-Lt, RAFVR), 1943–48; St Catharine's Coll., 1948–50; 3rd Sec., FO, 1950–52; Paris, 1952–55; 2nd Sec., Buenos Aires, 1955–58; 1st Sec., FO, 1958–61; 1st Sec. (Commercial), Moscow, 1961–63; seconded to HM Treasury, 1963–65; FCO, 1965–68; Counsellor, Mexico City, 1968–70; Economic Counsellor, Washington, 1970–72; Commercial Counsellor, Moscow, 1972–76; Res. Associate, IISS, 1976–77; Ambassador to Colombia, 1977–82. *Recreation:* music. *Address:* c/o Foreign and Commonwealth Office, SW1A 2AH.

UGANDA, Archbishop of, since 1977; **Most Rev. Silvanus Wani;** Bishop of Kampala; *b* July 1916; *s* of late Mana Ada Wani and late Daa Miriam; *m* 1936, Penina Yopa Wani; six *s* two *d* (and two *s* decd). *Educ:* Kampala Normal School, Makerere (Teacher's Cert.). Teaching, Arua Primary School, 1936–39; student, Buwalasi Theol. Coll., 1940–42; ordained as one of first two priests in West Nile District, 1943; Chaplain, King's African Rifles, 1944–46; Parish Priest: Arua, 1947–50; Koboko, 1951–60; Canon and Rural Dean, Koboko, 1953–60; attended Oak Hill Theological Coll., 1955–56; Diocesan Secretary/Treasurer, N Uganda Diocese, 1961–64; Asst Bishop, later full Bishop, N Uganda, 1964; Bishop of Madi/West Nile Diocese, 1969; Dean, Province of Church of Uganda, Rwanda, Burundi and Boga Zaire, 1974. Chaplain General to Uganda Armed Forces, 1964–. *Recreations:* reading, walking, gardening. *Address:* Provincial Secretariat, Church of Uganda, PO Box 14123, Kampala, Uganda. *T:* Kampala (residence) 70177, (office) 70218.

ULANOVA, Galina Sergeyevna; Order of Lenin, 1953, 1970; Hero of Socialist Labour, 1974, 1980; People's Artist of the USSR, 1951; Order of Red Banner of Labour, 1939, 1951; Badge of Honour, 1940; Prima Ballerina, Bolshoi Theatre, Moscow, 1944–60, retired; ballet-mistress at the Bolshoi Theatre since 1963; *b* 8 Jan. 1910; *d* of Sergei Nikolaevich Ulanov and Maria Feodorovna Romanova (dancers at Mariinsky Theatre, Petersburg). *Educ:* State School of Choreography, Leningrad. Début Kirov Theatre of Opera and Ballet, Leningrad, 1928; danced Odette-Odile in Swan Lake, 1929; Raimonda, 1931; Solweig in The Ice Maiden, 1931; danced Diane Mirelle in first performance of Flames of Paris, 1932; Giselle, 1933; Masha in The Nutcracker Suite, 1933; The Fountain of Bakhchisarai, as Maria, 1934; Lost Illusions, as Coralie, 1936; Romeo and Juliet, as Juliet, 1940; Cinderella, as Cinderella, 1945; Parasha in The Bronze Horseman, 1949; Tao Hua in The Red Poppy, 1950; Katerina in The Stone Flower, 1954. Visited London with the Bolshoi Theatre Ballet, 1956. Awarded State Prize, 1941; for Cinderella, 1945; for Romeo and Juliet, 1947; for Red Poppy, 1950. Awarded Lenin prize for outstanding achievement in ballet, 1957. FRAD, 1963. *Address:* Bolshoi Theatre, Moscow. *Clubs:* All-Russian Theatrical Society, Central House of Workers in the Arts.

ULLENDORFF, Prof. Edward, MA Jerusalem, DPhil Oxford; FBA 1965; Professor of Semitic Languages, School of Oriental and African Studies, University of London, since 1979 (Professor of Ethiopian Studies, 1964–79; Head of Africa Department, 1972–77); *b* 25 Jan. 1920; *s* of late Frederic and Cilli Ullendorff; *m* 1943, Dina Noack. *Educ:* Gymnasium Graues Kloster; Universities of Jerusalem and Oxford. Chief Examiner, British Censorship, Eritrea, 1942–43; Editor, African Publ., British Ministry of Information, Eritrea-Ethiopia, 1943–45; Assistant Political Secretary, British Military Admin., Eritrea, 1945–46; Asst Secretary, Palestine Government, 1947–48; Research Officer and Librarian, Oxford Univ. Inst. of Colonial Studies, 1948–49; Scarbrough Senior Research Studentship in Oriental Languages, 1949–50; Reader (Lectr, 1950–56) in Semitic Languages, St Andrews Univ., 1956–59; Professor of Semitic Languages and Literatures, University of Manchester, 1959–64. Carnegie Travelling Fellow to Ethiopia, 1958; Research Journeys to Ethiopia, 1964, 1966, 1969. Catalogued Ethiopian Manuscripts in Royal Library, Windsor Castle. Chairman: Assoc. of British Orientalists, 1963–64; Anglo-Ethiopian Soc., 1965–68 (Vice-Pres. 1969–77); Pres., Soc. for Old Testament Study, 1971; Vice-Pres., RAS, 1975–79, 1981–. Joint Organizer, 2nd Internat. Congress of Ethiopian Studies, Manchester, 1963. Chm., Editorial Bd, Bulletin of SOAS, 1968–78; Mem., Adv. Bd, British Library, 1975–. Vice-Pres., British Acad., 1980–82; Schweich Lectr, British

Acad., 1967. FRAS. Imperial Ethiopian Gold Medallion, 1960; Haile Sellassie Internat. Prize for Ethiopian studies, 1972. MA Manchester, 1962; Hon. DLitt St Andrews, 1972. *Publications:* The definite article in the Semitic languages, 1941; Exploration and Study of Abyssinia, 1945; Catalogue of Ethiopian Manuscripts in the Bodleian Library, Oxford, 1951; The Semitic Languages of Ethiopia, 1955; The Ethiopians, 1959, 3rd edn 1973; (with Stephen Wright) Catalogue of Ethiopian MSS in Cambridge University Library, 1961; Comparative Semitics in Linguistica Semitica, 1961; (with S. Moscati and others) Introduction to Comparative Grammar of Semitic Languages, 1964; An Amharic Chrestomathy, 1965, 2nd edn 1978; The Challenge of Amharic, 1965; Ethiopia and the Bible, 1968; (with J. B. Pritchard and others) Solomon and Sheba, 1974; annotated and trans., Emperor Haile Sellassie, My Life and Ethiopia's Progress (autobiog.), 1976; Studies in Semitic Languages and Civilizations, 1977; (with M. A. Knibb) Book of Enoch, 1978; The Bawdy Bible, 1979; (jtly) The Amharic Letters of Emperor Theodore of Ethiopia to Queen Victoria, 1979; (with C. F. Beckingham) The Hebrew Letters of Prester John, 1982; Joint Editor of Studies in honour of G. R. Driver, 1962; Joint Editor of Ethiopian Studies, 1964; articles and reviews in journals of learned societies; contribs to Encyclopaedia Britannica, Encyclopaedia of Islam, etc; Joint Editor, Journal of Semitic Studies, 1961-64. *Recreations:* music, motoring in Scotland. *Address:* 4 Bladon Close, Oxford OX2 8AD.

ULLMANN, Liv (Johanne); actress; *b* Tokyo, 16 Dec. 1938; *d* of late Viggo Ullmann and of Janna (*née* Lund), Norway; *m* 1960, Dr Gappe Stang (marr. diss. 1965). *Educ:* Norway; London (dramatic trng). Stage début, The Diary of Anne Frank (title role), Stavanger, 1956; major roles, National Theatre and Norwegian State Theatre, Oslo; Amer. stage début, A Doll's House, New York Shakespeare Festival, 1974-75; Anna Christie, USA, 1977; The Bear, La Voix humaine, Australia, 1978; I Remember Mama, USA, and other plays on Broadway, 1979. Wrote and dir. short film, Parting, 1981. *Films:* Pan, 1965; The Night Visitor, 1971; Pope Joan, 1972; The Emigrants, 1972 (Golden Globe Award); The New Land, 1973 (Best Actress, Nat. Soc. of Film Critics, USA); Lost Horizon, 1973; 40 Carats, 1973; Zandy's Bride, 1973; The Abdication, 1974; (dir. by Ingmar Bergman): Persona, 1966; The Hour of the Wolf, 1968 (Best Actress, Nat. Soc. of Film Critics, USA); Shame, 1968 (Best Actress, Nat. Soc. of Film Critics, USA); The Passion of Anna, 1969; Cries and Whispers, 1972; Scenes from a Marriage, 1974; Face to Face, 1976; The Serpent's Egg, 1977; The Autumn Sonata, 1978. Peer Gynt Award, Norway (1st female recipient). Order of St Olav (Norway), 1979. *Publication:* (autobiog.) Changing, 1977. *Address:* Drammensviens 91, Oslo, Norway.

ULLMANN, Walter, MA, LittD; FBA 1968; Professor of Medieval History, University of Cambridge, 1972-78, now Emeritus Professor; Fellow of Trinity College, Cambridge, since 1959; *b* 29 Nov. 1910; *m* 1940, Mary Elizabeth Finnemore Knapp; two *s*. *Educ:* Universities of Vienna, Innsbruck (JUD), and Munich. Research at Cambridge University; Assistant Lecturer, University of Vienna, 1935-38. War service, 1940-43. History and Modern Languages Master, Ratcliffe Coll., Leicester, 1943-47; part-time Lecturer, Pol. Int. Dept, Foreign Office, 1944-46; Lecturer in Medieval History, University of Leeds, 1947-49; Maitland Mem. Lectr, Univ. of Cambridge, 1947-48; Univ. Lectr in Medieval History, Cambridge, 1949-57, Reader, 1957-65, Prof. of Medieval Ecclesiastical Hist., 1965-72. Co-Editor Ephemerides Juris Canonici, 1951-64, Päpste & Papsttum, 1970-; Editor, Cambridge Studies in Medieval Life and Thought, 1968-. Prof. of Humanities, Johns Hopkins Univ., 1964-65; Vis. Prof., Univs of Tübingen and Munich, 1973. Birkbeck Lectr, Cambridge, 1968-69. Hon. Fellow, St Edmund's House, Cambridge, 1976. Hon. Dr *rerum politicarum* and Jubilee Medal for distinguished services, Univ. of Innsbruck, 1970. Corresponding Member: Bayerische Akad. d. Wissenschaften; Osterreichische Akad. d. Wissenschaften. *Publications:* The Medieval Idea of Law, 1946, repr. 1969, 1972; The Origins of the Great Schism, 1948, repr. 1972 with new introd.; Medieval Papalism, 1949; The Growth of Papal Government in the Middle Ages, 1955 (rev. edn German: Die Machtstellung d. Papsttums im Mittelalter, 1960), 4th edn 1970; The Medieval Papacy, St Thomas and beyond (Aquinas lecture, 1958), 1960; Liber regie capelle, 1961; Principles of Government and Politics in the Middle Ages, 1961, 4th edn 1978 (trans. into Spanish and Italian); Hist. Introd. to Lea's Inquisition, 1963; A History of Political Thought in The Middle Ages, 1965, rev. edn 1970; The Relevance of Medieval Ecclesiastical History (inaug. lecture, 1966) (trans. into Japanese); Papst und König, 1966; The Individual and Society in the Middle Ages, 1967 (trans. into Japanese, German and Italian); The Carolingian Renaissance and the Idea of Kingship, 1969; A Short History of the Papacy in the Middle Ages, 1972, 2nd edn 1974, repr. 1977 (trans. into Italian and German); The Future of Medieval History, 1973; Law and Politics in the Middle Ages, 1975; The Church and the Law in the Earlier Middle Ages (Collected Studies I), 1975; The Papacy and Political Ideas in the Middle Ages (Collected Studies II), 1976; Medieval Foundations of Renaissance Humanism, 1977 (Italian edn 1980); Scholarship and Politics in the Middle Ages (Collected Studies III), 1978; Jurisprudence in the Middle Ages (Collected Studies IV), 1980; Gelasius I: das Papsttum an der Wende der Spätantike zum Mittelalter, 1981; Medieval Monarchy (Sewanee Lectures), 1982; contributed to English Historical Review, Jl of Ecclesiastical History, Jl of Theol Studies, Cambridge Hist. Jl, Law Quarterly Review, Trans. Royal Hist. Society, Studi Gregoriani, Studia Gratiana, Studi Federiciani, Studi Accursio, Misc. Hist. Pont., Rev. Bénédictine, Rev. hist. droit, Europa e il Diritto Romano, Arch. storico Pugliese, Savigny Z., Studia Patristica, Bartolo da Sassoferrato: studi e documenti, Acta Iuridica, Settimana studio Spoleto, Annali storia amministrativa, Recueils Soc. Bodin, Speculum Historiale,

Historische Zeitschrift, Studies in Church History, Virginia Jl of Internat. Law, Hist. Jahrbuch, Annali di storia del diritto, Römische Hist. Mitteil, Wege der Forschung. *Recreations:* music and travelling. *Address:* Trinity College, Cambridge CB2 1TQ.

ULLSWATER, 2nd Viscount *cr* 1921, of Campsea Ashe, Suffolk; **Nicholas James Christopher Lowther;** *b* 9 Jan. 1942; *s* of Lieut John Arthur Lowther, MVO, RNVR (*d* 1942), and Priscilla Violet (*d* 1945), *yr d* of Reginald Everitt Lambert; *S* great-grandfather, 1949; *m* 1967, Susan, *d* of James Howard Weatherby; two *s* two *d*. *Educ:* Eton; Trinity Coll., Cambridge. Captain, Royal Wessex Yeomanry, T&AVR, 1973-78. *Heir:* s Hon. Benjamin James Lowther, *b* 26 Nov. 1975. *Address:* Barrow Street House, near Mere, Warminster, Wilts. *T:* Mere 860621.

ULRICH, Walter Otto; Deputy Secretary, Department of Education and Science, since 1977; *b* 1 April 1927. Ministry of Works: Asst Principal, 1951; Principal, 1955; Treasury 1958-60; Principal Private Sec. to Minister of Public Building and Works, 1963-65; Asst Sec., 1965; Min. of Housing and Local Govt, 1966; DoE, 1970; Under-Sec., 1972; Cabinet Office, 1974-76. *Address:* 208 Shakespeare Crescent, E12 6NB. *T:* 01-471 5318.

ULSTER, Earl of; Alexander Patrick Gregers Richard Windsor; *b* 24 Oct. 1974; *s* of HRH the Duke of Gloucester and HRH the Duchess of Gloucester.
See under Royal Family.

UMFREVILLE, William Henry, CBE 1959; ISO 1951; retired as Accountant and Comptroller-General, Board of Inland Revenue (1954-58); *b* 7 June 1893; *e s* of William Henry Umfreville; *m* 1916, Daisy Catherine Colson; two *d*. *Educ:* Palmer's School. Post Office, 1909-12; Ministry of Agriculture and Fisheries, 1913-23; Inland Revenue, 1924-58, retired. *Address:* 28 Frobisher Way, Worthing, West Sussex.

UNDERHILL, family name of **Baron Underhill.**

UNDERHILL, Baron *cr* 1979 (Life Peer), of Leyton in Greater London; **Henry Reginall Underhill,** CBE 1976; Opposition spokesman on transport in House of Lords, since 1980; an adviser to the Home Secretary, since 1980; *b* 8 May 1914; *s* of Henry James and Alice Maud Underhill; *m* 1937, Flora Janet Philbrick; two *s* one *d*. *Educ:* Norlington Road Elementary School; Tom Hood Central School, Leyton. Junior Clerk, C. A. Hardman & Sons Ltd, Lloyd's Underwriters, 1929; joined Labour Party Head Office as Junior Accounts Clerk, 1933. National Fire Service, 1939-45. Assistant to Mr Morgan Phillips, Labour Party Gen. Sec., 1945; Admin. Assistant to National Agent, 1945; Propaganda Officer, 1947; Regional Organiser, W Midlands, 1948; Assistant National Agent, 1960; National Agent, 1972-79. Joined Labour Party, 1930; Vice-Chm. 1933, Hon. Sec. 1937-48, Leyton West Constituency Labour Party. Member: HO Electoral Adv. Cttee, 1970-79; Houghton Cttee on Financial Aid to Political Parties, 1975-76; Parly deleg. to Zimbabwe, 1980. Hon. Sec., British Workers' Sports Assoc., 1935-37. *Recreations:* golf; life-long support of Leyton Orient FC; formerly cycling (club captain) and track and cross-country athletics. *Address:* 94 Loughton Way, Buckhurst Hill, Essex IG9 6AH. *T:* 01-504 1910.

UNDERHILL, Herbert Stuart; President, Victoria (BC) Press, 1978-79; Publisher, Victoria Times, 1971-78, retired; *b* 20 May 1914; *s* of Canon H. J. Underhill and Helena (*née* Ross); *m* 1937, Emma Gwendolyn MacGregor; one *s* one *d*. *Educ:* University Sch., Victoria, BC. Correspondent and Editor, The Canadian Press, Vancouver, BC, Toronto, New York and London, 1936-50; Reuters North American Editor, 1950; Asst General Manager, Reuters, 1958; Managing Editor, 1965-68; Dep. Gen. Manager, with special responsibility for North and South America and Caribbean, 1963-70. Director: Canadian Daily Newspaper Publishers' Assoc., 1972-76; The Canadian Press, 1972-78. *Recreations:* travel, reading. *Address:* 308 Beach Drive, Victoria, BC, Canada.

UNDERHILL, Michael Thomas Ben, QC 1972; **His Honour Judge Underhill;** a Circuit Judge, since 1978; *b* 10 Feb. 1918; *s* of late Rev. P. C. Underhill and Viola Underhill; *m* 1950, Rosalie Jean Kinloch; three *s*. *Educ:* Radley Coll.; Brasenose Coll., Oxford (MA). Served Glos Regt, 1939-42; 2nd KEO Goorkha Rifles, 1942-46 (Major). Called to the Bar, Gray's Inn, 1947; Master of the Bench, Gray's Inn, 1978; Oxford Circuit; Dep. Chm., Salop QS, 1967-71; Recorder of Reading, later a Recorder of the Crown Court, 1970-78. *Address:* 6 Ormond Road, Richmond, Surrey TW10 6TH; 3 Pump Court, Temple, EC4. *Club:* Leander (Henley-on-Thames).

UNDERWOOD, Michael; see Evelyn, J. M.

UNGER, Michael Ronald; Editor, Daily Post, Liverpool, since 1979; *b* 8 Dec. 1943; *s* of Ronald and Joan Maureen Unger; *m* 1966, Eunice Dickens; one *s* one *d*. *Educ:* Wirral Grammar School. Trainee journalist, Thomson Regional Newspapers, 1963; Reading Evening Post, 1965-67; Perth Daily News, 1967-71; Daily Post, Liverpool, 1971-. *Publication:* ed, The Memoirs of Bridget Hitler, 1979. *Recreation:* reading. *Address:* The Moorings, Lees Lane, Little Neston, South Wirral, Cheshire L64 4DB. *T:* 051-336 5186. *Club:* Press (Liverpool).

UNSTEAD, Robert John; author; *b* 21 Nov. 1915; *s* of Charles and Elizabeth Unstead; *m* 1939, Florence Margaret Thomas; three *d. Educ:* Dover Grammar Sch.; Goldsmiths' Coll., London. Schoolmaster, 1936-40. Served in RAF, 1940-46; Sector Controller, Comb. Ops, Normandy, Greece, Italy. Headmaster, Norton Road CP Sch., Letchworth, 1947-51, Grange Sch., Letchworth, 1951-57. Member, Herts Education Cttee, 1951-57; Chairman, Letchworth Primary Schools' Cttee of Management, 1960-64; Governor, Leiston Middle School, 1973-. Chm., Educational Writers' Group, Soc. of Authors, 1965-68; Mem. Council, East Anglian Writers, 1976-. *Publications:* Looking at History, 1953; People in History, 1955; Teaching History, 1956; Travel by Road, 1958; Houses, 1958; Looking at Ancient History, 1959; Monasteries, 1961; Black's Children's Encyclopædia (co-author), 1961; Some Kings and Queens, 1962; A History of Britain, 1963; Royal Adventurers, 1964; Early Times, 1964; Men and Women in History, 1965; Britain in the Twentieth Century, 1966; The Story of Britain, 1969; Homes in Australia, 1969; Castles, 1970; Transport in Australia, 1970; Pioneer Homelife in Australia, 1971; History of the English-speaking World, 1972; Look and Find Out, 1972; The Twenties, 1973; The Thirties, 1974; Living in Aztec Times, 1974; Living in Samuel Pepys' London, 1975; A Dictionary of History, 1976; Living in Ancient Egypt, 1977; Living in Pompeii, 1977; See Inside a Castle, 1977; See Inside an Egyptian Town, 1977; R. J. Unstead's Book of Kings and Queens, 1978; Greece and Rome, 1978; Egypt and Mesopotamia, 1978; The Assyrians, 1980; The Egyptians, 1980; How They Lived in Cities Long Ago, 1980; general editor, Black's Junior Reference series, Looking at Geography, See Inside series. *Recreations:* golf, gardening, watching cricket. *Address:* Reedlands, Thorpeness, Suffolk. *T:* Aldeburgh 2665. *Club:* MCC.

UNSWORTH, Sir Edgar (Ignatius Godfrey), Kt 1963; CMG 1954; QC (N Rhodesia) 1951; *b* 18 April 1906; *yr s* of John William and Minnie Unsworth; *m* 1964, Eileen, *widow* of Raymond Ritzema. *Educ:* Stonyhurst Coll.; Manchester Univ. (LLB Hons). Barrister-at-Law, Gray's Inn, 1930; private practice, 1930-37. Parly Cand. (C) for Farnworth, General Election, 1935. Crown Counsel: Nigeria, 1937; N Rhodesia, 1942; Solicitor-General: N Rhodesia, 1946; Fedn of Malaya, 1949; Chm. of Cttees, N Rhodesia, 1950; Attorney-General, N Rhodesia, 1951-56. Acting Chief Sec. and Dep. to Governor of N Rhodesia for periods during 1953, 1954 and 1955; Attorney-General, Fedn of Nigeria, 1956-60; Federal Justice of Federal Supreme Court of Nigeria, 1960-62; Chief Justice, Nyasaland, 1962-64; Director of a Course for Government Officers from Overseas, 1964-65; Chief Justice of Gibraltar, 1965-76; Justice of Appeal, Gibraltar, 1976-81. Member Rhodesia Railways Arbitration Tribunal, 1946; Chm., Commn of Enquiry into Central African Airways Corp., 1947; Mem., British Observers' Group, Independence Elections, Rhodesia, 1980. *Publication:* Laws of Northern Rhodesia (rev. edn), 1949. *Recreations:* gardening, bridge. *Address:* The Little House, Charters Road, Sunningdale, Ascot, Berks SL5 9QF. *Club:* Royal Gibraltar Yacht.

UNWIN, Ven. Christopher Philip, TD 1963; MA; Archdeacon of Northumberland, 1963-82; *b* 27 Sept. 1917; *e s* of Rev. Philip Henry and Decima Unwin. *Educ:* Repton Sch.; Magdalene Coll., Cambridge; Queen's Theological Coll., Birmingham. Deacon, 1940, Priest, 1941. Asst Curate of: Benwell, 1940-43; Sugley, 1944-47; Vicar of: Horton, Northumberland, 1947-55; Benwell, 1955-63. *Recreations:* reading, walking. *Address:* 60 Sandringham Avenue, Benton, Newcastle upon Tyne NE12 8JX. *T:* Newcastle upon Tyne 700418.

UNWIN, David Storr; author; *b* 3 Dec. 1918; *e s* of late Sir Stanley Unwin, KCMG; *m* 1945, Periwinkle, *yr d* of late Captain Sidney Herbert, RN; twin *s* and *d. Educ:* Abbotsholme. League of Nations Secretariat, Geneva, 1938-39; George Allen & Unwin Ltd, Publishers, 1940-44. *Publications:* The Governor's Wife, 1954 (Authors' Club First Novel Award, 1955); A View of the Heath, 1956; Fifty Years with Father: a Relationship (autobiog.), 1982; *for children:* (under pen name David Severn) Rick Afire!, 1942; A Cabin for Crusoe, 1943; Waggon for Five, 1944; Hermit in the Hills, 1945; Forest Holiday, 1946; Ponies and Poachers, 1947; Dream Gold, 1948; The Cruise of the Maiden Castle, 1948; Treasure for Three, 1949; My Foreign Correspondent through Africa, 1950; Crazy Castle, 1951; Burglars and Bandicoots, 1952; Drumbeats!, 1953; The Future Took Us, 1958; The Green-eyed Gryphon, 1959; Foxy-boy, 1959; Three at the Sea, 1959; Clouds over the Alberhorn, 1963; Jeff Dickson, Cowhand, 1963; The Girl in the Grove, 1974; The Wishing Bone, 1977. *Recreations:* travel, gardening. *Address:* 31A Belsize Park, NW3. *Club:* PEN.
See also R. S. Unwin.

UNWIN, James Brian; Under Secretary, seconded to Cabinet Office, since 1981; *b* 21 Sept. 1935; *s* of Reginald Unwin and Winifred Annie Walthall; *m* 1964, Diana Susan, *d* of Sir D. A. Scott, *qv* ; three *s. Educ:* Chesterfield School; New College, Oxford (1st class Mods; 2nd class Greats; MA); Yale University (MA). Asst Principal, CRO, 1960; Private Sec. to British High Commissioner, Salisbury, 1961-64; 1st Secretary, British High Commission, Accra, 1964-65; FCO, 1965-68; transferred to HM Treasury, 1968; Private Sec. to Chief Secretary to Treasury, 1970-72; Asst Secretary, 1972; Under Sec., 1976. *Recreations:* bird watching, Wellingtoniana, cricket. *Address:* 25 Links Road, Epsom, Surrey. *T:* Epsom 2418. *Clubs:* Reform; Kingswood Village (Surrey).

UNWIN, Sir Keith, KBE 1964 (OBE 1937); CMG 1954; MA; *b* 3 Aug. 1909; *er s* of late Edwin Ernest Unwin and Jessie Magdalen Black; *m* 1935, Linda

Giersé; one *s* two *d. Educ:* Merchant Taylors' Sch.; Lycée Condorcet, Paris; St John's Coll., Oxford; BA 1931. Department of Overseas Trade, 1932; Mem., Commercial Diplomatic Service, later HM Diplomatic Service, 1934-69; Madrid, 1934; Istanbul, 1937; San Sebastian (later Madrid), 1939; Mexico City, 1944; Paris, 1946; Prague, 1949; Buenos Aires, 1950; Rome, 1955-59; Foreign Service Inspector, 1959-62; UK Representative on Economic and Social Council of the United Nations, 1962-66; HM Ambassador to Uruguay, 1966-69. UK Mem., UN Commn on Human Rights, 1970-78. *Recreations:* gardening, reading. *Address:* Great Kingley, Dodington Lane, Chipping Sodbury, Bristol. *T:* Chipping Sodbury 310913. *Club:* Canning.

UNWIN, Ven. Kenneth; Archdeacon of Pontefract, since 1981; *b* 16 Sept. 1926; *s* of Percy and Elsie Unwin; *m* 1958, Beryl Riley; one *s* four *d. Educ:* Chesterfield Grammar School; St Edmund Hall, Oxford (MA Hons); Ely Theological Coll. Assistant Curate: All Saints, Leeds, 1951-55; St Margaret, Durham City (in charge, St John's, Neville's Cross), 1955-59; Vicar: St John Baptist, Dodworth, Barnsley, 1959-69; St John Baptist, Royston, Barnsley, 1969-73; St John's, Wakefield, 1973-82. Hon. Canon, Wakefield Cathedral, 1980-; RD of Wakefield, 1980-81. *Address:* Pontefract House, 19a Tithe Barn Street, Horbury, Wakefield WF4 6LJ. *T:* Wakefield 263777.

UNWIN, Peter William, CMG 1981; HM Diplomatic Service; Minister (Economic), Bonn, since 1980; *b* 20 May 1932; *s* of Arnold and Norah Unwin; *m* 1955, Monica Steven; two *s* two *d. Educ:* Ampleforth; Christ Church, Oxford (MA). Army, 1954-56; FO, 1956-58; British Legation, Budapest, 1958-61; British Embassy, Tokyo, 1961-63; FCO, 1963-67; British Information Services, NY, 1967-70; FCO, 1970-72; Bank of England, 1973; British Embassy, Bonn, 1973-76; Head of Personnel Policy Dept, FCO, 1976-79; Fellow, Center for Internat. Affairs, Harvard, 1979-80. *Address:* c/o Foreign and Commonwealth Office, SW1; British Embassy, Bonn, BFPO 19. *T:* 23.40.61; 274 East Grafton, near Marlborough, Wilts. *T:* Marlborough 810031.

UNWIN, Rayner Stephens, CBE 1977; Chairman, George Allen & Unwin Ltd, since 1968; *b* 23 Dec. 1925; *s* of late Sir Stanley Unwin and Mary Storr; *m* 1952, Carol Margaret, *d* of Harold Curwen; one *s* three *d. Educ:* Abbotsholme Sch.; Trinity Coll., Oxford (MA); Harvard, USA (MA). Sub-Lt, RNVR, 1944-47. Entered George Allen & Unwin Ltd, 1951. Mem. Council, Publishers' Assoc., 1965- (Treasurer, 1969; Pres., 1971; Vice-Pres., 1973); Chm., British Council Publishers' Adv. Cttee. Chm., Little Missenden Festival. *Publications:* The Rural Muse, 1954; The Defeat of John Hawkins, 1960. *Recreations:* skiing downhill, walking up-hill, birds and gardens. *Address:* (home) Limes Cottage, Little Missenden, near Amersham, Bucks. *T:* Great Missenden 2900. *Club:* Garrick.
See also D. S. Unwin.

UPDIKE, John Hoyer; freelance writer; *b* 18 March 1932; *s* of Wesley R. and Linda G. Updike; *m* 1st, 1953, Mary E. Pennington (marr. diss.); two *s* two *d* ; 2nd, 1977, Martha Bernhard. *Educ:* Harvard Coll. Worked as journalist for The New Yorker magazine, 1955-57. *Publications: poems:* Hoping for a Hoopoe (in America, The Carpentered Hen), 1958; Telephone Poles, 1968; Midpoint and other poems, 1969; Tossing and Turning, 1977; *novels:* The Poorhouse Fair, 1959; Rabbit, Run, 1960; The Centaur, 1963; Of the Farm, 1966; Couples, 1968; Rabbit Redux, 1972; A Month of Sundays, 1975; Marry Me, 1976; The Coup, 1979; Rabbit is Rich (Pulitzer Prize), 1982; *short stories:* The Same Door, 1959; Pigeon Feathers, 1962; The Music School, 1966; Bech: A Book, 1970; Museums and Women, 1973; Problems, 1980; *miscellanies:* Assorted Prose, 1965; Picked-Up Pieces, 1976; *play:* Buchanan Dying, 1974. *Address:* Beverly Farms, Mass 01915, USA.

UPHAM, Captain Charles Hazlitt, VC 1941 and Bar, 1943; JP; sheep-farmer; *b* Christchurch, New Zealand, 21 Sept. 1908; *s* of John Hazlitt Upham, barrister, and Agatha Mary Upham, Christchurch, NZ; *m* 1945, Mary Eileen, *d* of James and Mary McTamney, Dunedin, New Zealand; three *d* (incl. twins). *Educ:* Waihi Prep. School, Winchester; Christ's Coll., Christchurch, NZ; Canterbury Agric. Coll., Lincoln, NZ (Diploma). Post-grad. course in valuation and farm management. Farm manager and musterer, 1930-36; govt valuer, 1937-39; farmer, 1945-. Served War of 1939-45 (VC and Bar, despatches): volunteered, Sept. 1939; 2nd NZEF (Sgt 1st echelon advance party); 2nd Lt; served Greece, Crete, W Desert (VC, Crete; Bar, Ruweisat); Captain; POW, released 1945. *Relevant Publication:* Mark of the Lion: The Story of Captain Charles Upham, VC and Bar (by Kenneth Sandford), 1962. *Recreations:* rowing, Rugby (1st XV Lincoln Coll., NZ). *Address:* Lansdowne, Hundalee, North Canterbury, NZ. *Clubs:* Canterbury, Christchurch, RSA (all NZ).

UPJOHN, Maj.-Gen. Gordon Farleigh, CB 1966; CBE 1959 (OBE 1955); *b* 9 May 1912; *e s* of late Dudley Francis Upjohn; *m* 1946, Rita Joan, *d* of late Major Clarence Walters; three *d. Educ:* Felsted School; RMC Sandhurst. 2nd Lieut, The Duke of Wellington's Regt; RWAFF, 1937; Adjt 3rd Bn The Nigeria Regt, 1940; Staff Coll., 1941; GSO2 Ops GHQ Middle East, 1941; Bde Maj. 3 WA Inf. Bde, 1942 (despatches); Lt-Col Comd 6 Bn The Nigeria Regt, 1944 (despatches); DAA&QMG Southern Comd India, 1946; GSO2 Mil. Ops Directorate WO, 1948; Lt-Col Chief Instructor RMA Sandhurst, 1951; Lt-Col Comd WA Inf. Bn, 1954; Bde Comdr 2 Inf. Bde Malaya, 1957 (despatches); Provost Marshal WO, 1960; GOC Yorkshire District, 1962-65. Automobile Assoc., 1965-76. *Recreations:* golf, cricket, field sports. *Address:*

c/o Lloyds Bank Ltd, 62 Brook Street, W1. *Clubs:* Army and Navy, MCC.

UPWARD, Mrs Janet; consultant on consumer affairs; Deputy Chairman, Domestic Coal Consumers Council, since 1978. *Educ:* Newnham College, Cambridge. BA (Geog. Hons) 1961, MA 1966. Formerly Sec., National Fedn of Consumer Gps. *Address:* 61 Valentine Road, Birmingham B14 7AJ. *T:* 021-444 2837.

URE, James Mathie, OBE 1969; British Council Representative, India, and Minister (Education), British High Commission, New Delhi, since 1980; *b* 5 May 1925; *s* of late William Alexander Ure, and of Helen Jones; *m* 1950, Martha Walker Paterson; one *s* one *d.* *Educ:* Shawlands Acad., Glasgow; Glasgow Univ. (MA); Trinity Coll., Oxford (BLitt). Army Service, 1944-47. Lectr, Edinburgh Univ., 1953-59; British Council: Istanbul, 1956-57; India, 1959-68; Dep. Controller, Arts Div., 1968-71; Rep., Indonesia, 1971-75; Controller, Home Div., 1975-80. *Publications:* Old English Benedictine Office, 1952; (with L. A. Hill) English Sounds and Spellings, 1962; (with L. A. Hill) English Sounds and Spellings—Tests, 1963; (with J. S. Bhandari and C. S. Bhandari) Read and Act, 1965; (with C. S. Bhandari) Short Stories, 1966. *Address:* c/o Foreign and Commonwealth Office, SW1; Southlands, Downs Side, Belmont, Surrey. *T:* 01-642 7241. *Club:* Royal Commonwealth Society.

URE, John Burns, CMG 1980; MVO 1968; HM Diplomatic Service; Assistant Under-Secretary of State, Foreign and Commonwealth Office, since 1981; *b* 5 July 1931; *s* of late Tam Ure; *m* 1972, Caroline, *d* of Charles Allan, Roxburghshire; one *s* one *d.* *Educ:* Uppingham Sch.; Magdalene Coll., Cambridge (MA); Harvard Business Sch. (AMP). Active Service as 2nd Lieut with Cameronians (Scottish Rifles), Malaya, 1950-51; Lieut, London Scottish (Gordon Highlanders) TA, 1952-55. Book publishing with Ernest Benn Ltd, 1951-53; joined Foreign (subseq. Diplomatic) Service, 1956; 3rd Sec. and Private Sec. to Ambassador, Moscow, 1957-59; Resident Clerk, FO, 1960-61; 2nd Sec., Leopoldville, 1962-63; FO, 1964-66; 1st Sec. (Commercial), Santiago, 1967-70; FCO, 1971-72; Counsellor, and intermittently Chargé d'Affaires, Lisbon, 1972-77; Head of South America Dept, FCO, 1977-79; Ambassador to Cuba, 1979-81. Life Fellow and Mem. Council, RGS, 1982-. Comdr, Mil. Order of Christ, Portugal, 1973. *Publications:* Cucumber Sandwiches in the Andes, 1973 (Travel Book Club Choice); Prince Henry the Navigator, 1977 (History Guild Choice); The Trail of Tamerlane, 1980 (Ancient History Club Choice). *Recreation:* travelling uncomfortably in remote places and writing about it comfortably afterwards. *Address:* c/o Foreign and Commonwealth Office, SW1. *Clubs:* White's, Beefsteak.

UREN, Reginald Harold, FRIBA; private practice of architecture, 1933-68; *b* New Zealand, 5 March 1906; *s* of Richard Ellis and Christina Uren; *m* 1930, Dorothy Marion Morgan; one *d.* *Educ:* Hutt Valley High School, New Zealand; London University. Qualified as Architect in New Zealand, 1929; ARIBA, London, 1931; won open architectural competition for Hornsey Town Hall (281 entries), 1933; joined in partnership with J. Alan Slater and A. H. Moberly, 1936; architectural practice includes public buildings, department stores, domestic, commercial and school buildings. Works include: John Lewis Store, Oxford Street; Arthur Sanderson & Sons Building, Berners Street; Norfolk County Hall. Freeman of City of London, 1938; Master, Tylers and Bricklayers Company, 1966. War service, 1942-46, Capt. Royal Engineers. Council, RIBA, 1946-65; London Architecture Bronze Medal, 1935; Tylers and Bricklayers Company Gold Medal, 1936; Min. of Housing and Local Govt Medal for London Region, 1954; New Zealand Inst. of Architects Award of Merit, 1965. *Recreation:* debate. *Address:* PO Box 102, Thames, New Zealand. *Club:* Reform.

URIE, Wing Comdr John Dunlop, AE 1942; bar 1945; Vice Lord-Lieutenant, Strathclyde Region (Dunbartonshire), since 1976; *b* 12 Oct. 1915; *s* of late John Urie, OBE, Glasgow; *m* 1939, Mary Taylor, *d* of Peter Bonnar, Dunfermline; one *s* two *d.* *Educ:* Sedbergh; Glasgow Univ. Served War of 1939-45: with RAuxAF, in Fighter Command and Middle East Command; Wing Comdr, 1942. DL Co. of Glasgow, 1963. OStJ. *Address:* 55 West Regent Street, Glasgow G2 2BL; Ardlarich, Rhu, Dunbartonshire. *Clubs:* Western (Glasgow); Royal Northern and Clyde Yacht.

URMSON, James Opie, MC 1943; Emeritus Professor of Philosophy, Stanford University; Emeritus Fellow of Corpus Christi College, Oxford; *b* 4 March 1915; *s* of Rev. J. O. Urmson; *m* 1940, Marion Joyce Drage; one *d.* *Educ:* Kingswood School, Bath; Corpus Christi College, Oxford. Senior Demy, Magdalen College, 1938; Fellow by examination, Magdalen College, 1939-45. Served Army (Duke of Wellington's Regt), 1939-45. Lecturer in Christ Church, 1945-46; Student of Christ Church, 1946-55; Professor of Philosophy, Queen's College, Dundee, University of St Andrews, 1955-59; Fellow and Tutor in Philosophy, CCC, Oxford, 1959-78. Visiting Associate Prof., Princeton Univ., 1950-51. Visiting Lectr, Univ. of Michigan, 1961-62, 1965-66, and 1969; Stuart Prof. of Philosophy, Stanford, 1975-80. *Publications:* Philosophical Analysis, 1956; The Emotive Theory of Ethics, 1968; Berkeley, 1982; edited: Encyclopedia of Western Philosophy, 1960; J. L. Austin: How to Do Things with Words, 1962; (with G. J. Warnock) J. L. Austin: Philosophical Papers, 2nd edn, 1970; articles in philosophical jls. *Recreations:* gardening, music. *Address:* Standfast, Tumbledown Dick, Cumnor, Oxford. *T:* Oxford 862769.

URQUHART, Sir Andrew, KCMG 1963 (CMG 1960); MBE 1950; Principal, St Godric's College, since 1975 (Vice-Principal, 1970-75); *b* 6 Jan. 1918; *s* of late Rev. Andrew Urquhart and of J. B. Urquhart; *m* 1956, Jessie Stanley Allison; two *s.* *Educ:* Greenock Academy; Glasgow University. Served War of 1939-45, Royal Marines, 1940-46. Cadet, Colonial Administrative Service, 1946; Senior District Officer, 1954; Admin. Officer, Class I, 1957; Permanent Sec., 1958; Deputy Governor, Eastern Region, Nigeria, 1958-63; Gen. Manager, The Housing Corp., 1964-70. *Address:* BM/JNTC, WC1N 3XX.

URQUHART, Brian Edward, MBE 1945; an Under-Secretary-General, United Nations, since 1974; *b* 28 Feb. 1919; *s* of Murray and Bertha Urquhart; *m* 1st, 1944, Alfreda Huntington (marr. diss. 1963); two *s* one *d*; 2nd, 1963, Sidney Damrosch Howard; one *s* one *d.* *Educ:* Westminster; Christ Church, Oxford. British Army: Dorset Regt and Airborne Forces, N Africa, Sicily and Europe, 1939-45; Personal Asst to Gladwyn Jebb, Exec. Sec. of Preparatory Commn of UN, London, 1945-46; Personal Asst to Trygve Lie, 1st Sec.-Gen. of UN, 1946-49; Sec., Collective Measures Cttee, 1951-53; Mem., Office of Under-Sec.-Gen. for Special Political Affairs, 1954-71; Asst Sec.-Gen., UN, 1972-74; Exec. Sec., 1st and 2nd UN Conf. on Peaceful Uses of Atomic Energy, 1955 and 1958; active in organization and direction of UN Emergency Force in Middle East, 1956; Dep. Exec. Sec., Preparatory Commn of Internat. Atomic Energy Agency, 1957; Asst to Sec.-Gen.'s Special Rep. in Congo, July-Oct. 1960; UN Rep. in Katanga, Congo, 1961-62; currently involved in organization and direction of UN peace-keeping ops and special political assignments. Hon. LLD Yale, 1981; DUniv Essex, 1981. *Publications:* Hammarskjold, 1972; various articles and reviews on internat. affairs. *Address:* 131 East 66th Street, New York, NY 10021, USA; Howard Farm, Tyringham, Mass 01264. *T:* LE 5-0805. *Club:* Century (New York).

URQUHART, Donald John, CBE 1970; Director General, British Library Lending Services, 1973-74; *b* 27 Nov. 1909; *s* of late Roderick and Rose Catherine Urquhart, Whitley Bay; *m* 1939, Beatrice Winefride, *d* of late W. G. Parker, Sheffield; two *s.* *Educ:* Barnard Castle School; Sheffield University (BSc, PhD). Research Dept, English Steel Corp., 1934-37; Science Museum Library, 1938-39; Admiralty, 1939-40; Min. of Supply, 1940-45; Science Museum Library, 1945-48; DSIR Headquarters, 1948-61; Dir, Nat. Lending Library for Science and Technology, 1961-73. Hon. Lectr, Postgrad. Sch. of Librarianship and Information Science, Sheffield Univ., 1970-; Vis. Prof., Loughborough Univ. Dept of Library and Information Studies, 1973-80. Chm., Standing Conf. of Nat. and Univ. Libraries, 1969-71. FLA (Pres., Library Assoc., 1972). Hon. DSc: Heriot-Watt, 1974; Sheffield, 1974; Salford, 1974. Hon. Citation, Amer. Library Assoc., 1978. *Publications:* The Principles of Librarianship, 1981; papers on library and scientific information questions. *Recreation:* gardening. *Address:* Wood Garth, First Avenue, Bardsey, near Leeds. *T:* Collingham Bridge 73228. *Club:* Athenæum.

URQUHART, James Graham, FCIT, FIMH; Executive Member, Operations and Productivity, British Railways Board, since 1977; Chairman: British Transport Police, since 1977; BRE-Metro, since 1979; British Rail Engineering, since 1979; *b* 23 April 1925; *s* of James Graham Urquhart and Mary Clark; *m* 1949, Margaret Hutchinson; two *d.* *Educ:* Berwickshire High Sch. Served War, RAF, 1941-44. Management Trainee, Eastern Region, BR, 1949-52; Chief Controller, Fenchurch Street, 1956-59; Dist Traffic Supt, Perth, 1960-62; Divl Operating Supt, Glasgow, 1962-64; Divl Manager, Glasgow and SW Scotland, 1964-67; Asst Gen. Man., Eastern Reg., 1967-69; BR Bd HQ: Chief Ops Man., 1969-72; Exec. Dir, Personnel, 1972-75; Gen. Manager, London Midland Reg., BR, 1975-76. MIPM, MInstM, CBIM, MBMHB. *Recreations:* golf, travel, gardening. *Address:* Rail House, Euston Square, NW1 2DZ. *T:* 01-262 3232.

URQUHART, Maj.-Gen. Robert Elliott, CB 1944; DSO and Bar 1943; *b* 28 Nov. 1901; *e s* of Alexander Urquhart, MD; *m* 1939, Pamela Condon; one *s* three *d.* *Educ:* St Paul's, West Kensington; RMC Sandhurst. 2nd Lt HLI 1920; Staff Coll., Camberley, 1936-37; Staff Capt., India, 1938; DAQMG, AHQ, India, 1939-40; DAAG, 3 Div., 1940; AA&QMG, 3 Div., 1940-41; commanded 2nd DCLI, 1941-42; GSO1, 51st Highland Div. N Africa, 1942-43; commanded 231 Malta Brigade, Sicily, 1943, and in landings Italy, 1943 (DSO and Bar); BGS 12 Corps, 1943; GOC 1st Airborne Div., 1944-45 (CB); Col 1945; Maj.-Gen. 1946; Director Territorial Army and Army Cadet Force, War Office, 1945-46; GOC 16th Airborne Division, TA, 1947-48; Commander, Lowland District, 1948-50; Commander Malaya District and 17th Gurkha Division, Mar.-Aug. 1950; GOC Malaya, 1950-52; GOC-in-C British Troops in Austria, 1952-55; retired, Dec. 1955. Col Highland Light Infantry, 1954-58. Dir, Davy and United Engineering Co. Ltd, 1957-70. Netherlands Bronze Lion, 1944; Norwegian Order of St Olaf, 1945. *Publication:* Arnhem, 1958. *Recreation:* golf. *Address:* Bigram, Port of Menteith, Stirling. *T:* Port of Menteith 267. *Club:* Naval and Military.
See also Sir G. P. Grant-Suttie, Bt, Sir John Kinloch, Bt.

URQUHART, Sir Robert William, KBE 1950 (OBE 1923); CMG 1944; *b* 14 August 1896; *s* of late Robert Urquhart and Margaret Stewart; *m* 1st, 1925, Brenda Gertrude Phillips (*d* 1975); four *d*; 2nd, 1977, Jane Gibson. *Educ:* Aberdeen; Cambridge. Entered Levant Consular Service, 1920; Consul at Tabriz, 1934; transferred to Foreign Office, 1938; Inspector-General of Consulates, 1939; seconded to the Home Office, 1940-41; Consul-General, Tabriz, 1942, transferred to New Orleans, La, USA, 1943; reappointed Inspector-General of HM Consular Establishment, 1945; HM Minister at

Washington, 1947; HM Consul-General at Shanghai, 1948–50; British Ambassador to Venezuela, 1951–55; retired from Foreign Service, 1955. Chairman of the Crofters' Commission, 1955–63. Hon. LLD Aberdeen, 1954. *Address:* 7A Blacket Place, Edinburgh EH9 1RN.

URS, Devaraj Vijayadevaraj; Vice-Chancellor, University of Mysore, India, since 1976; *b* 19 Dec. 1927; *s* of late Devaraj Urs and of Laxammanni Urs; *m* Srimati A. R. Jayalakshammanni. *Educ:* Maharaja's Coll., Univ. of Mysore (BA Hons Social Philosophy). Lectr in Logic, Univ. of Mysore, 1949 (resigned to go abroad for higher studies, 1949); Harvard Univ. and New Sch. for Social Res., USA, 1949–54; Univ. of Mysore: Lectr in Internat. Relations and Polit. Theory, Maharaja's Coll., 1959–65; Sec. to Vice-Chancellor, 1965, full-time Sec., 1969; Sec., Students' Information Bureau, 1965–69; Dep. Dir. Inst. of Correspondence Course and Continuing Educn, Oct. 1969, Dir 1973 (also part-time Sec. to Vice-Chancellor); Registrar, Univ. of Mysore, 1973–76; Actg Vice-Chancellor, 1973–75 (three times). Life Mem., Mysore Music Assoc. Editor: Kautilya (bi-annual of internat. affairs), 1962–74; Report on University Examinations, 1966–74. *Publications:* (ed) University, Society and State, 1973; (ed) Regional Planning and National Development and Strategies for Regional Development, 1977; papers on law and polit. devel. *Address:* Vice-Chancellor, University of Mysore, Crawford Hall, Mysore 570005, S India. *T:* (office) 23555, (home) 20150 or 23658. *Clubs:* Century (Bangalore); Sri Kanteerava Narasimharaja Sports, Films (Mysore).

URSELL, Prof. Fritz Joseph, FRS 1972; Beyer Professor of Applied Mathematics, Manchester University, since 1961; *b* 28 April 1923; *m* 1959, Katharina Renate (*née* Zander); two *d. Educ:* Clifton; Marlborough; Trinity College, Cambridge. BA 1943, MA 1947, ScD 1957, Cambridge. Admiralty Service, 1943–47; ICI Fellow in Applied Mathematics, Manchester Univ., 1947–50. Fellow (Title A), Trinity Coll., Cambridge, 1947–51; Univ. Lecturer in Mathematics, Cambridge, 1950–61; Stringer Fellow in Natural Sciences, King's Coll., Cambridge, 1954–60. FIMA 1964. MSc (Manchester), 1965. *Address:* 28 Old Broadway, Withington, Manchester M20 9DF. *T:* 061-445 5791.

URSELL, Rev. Philip Elliott; Principal of Pusey House, Oxford, since 1982; *b* 3 Dec. 1942; *o s* of Clifford Edwin Ursell and Hilda Jane Ursell (*née* Tucker). *Educ:* Cathays High Sch.; University Coll. Cardiff (Craddock Wells Exhibnr; BA); St Stephen's House, Oxford. MA Oxon. Curate of Newton Nottage, Porthcawl, 1968–71; Asst Chaplain of University Coll. Cardiff, 1971–77; Chaplain of Polytechnic of Wales, 1974–77; Chaplain, Fellow and Dir of Studies in Music, Emmanuel Coll., Cambridge, 1977–82; Fellow, St Cross Coll., Oxford, 1982–. *Publications:* contribs to theological, musical and other journals. *Recreations:* jet travel, wine-making and brewing, electronic and other gadgetry. *Address:* Pusey House, Oxford OX1 3LZ. *T:* Oxford 511014, 59519.

URWICK, Alan Bedford, CMG 1978; HM Diplomatic Service; Ambassador to Jordan, since 1979; *b* 2 May 1930; *s* of Col Lyndall Fownes Urwick, *qv* ; *m* 1960, Marta, *o d* of Adhemar Montagne; three *s. Educ:* Dragon Sch.; Rugby (Schol.); New Coll., Oxford (Exhibr). 1st cl. hons Mod. History 1952. Joined HM Foreign (subseq. Diplomatic) Service, 1952; served in: Brussels, 1954–56; Moscow, 1958–59; Baghdad, 1960–61; Amman, 1965–67; Washington, 1967–70; Cairo, 1971–73; seconded to Cabinet Office as Asst Sec., Central Policy Review Staff, 1973–75; Head of Near East and N Africa Dept, FCO, 1975–76; Minister, Madrid, 1977–79. *Address:* c/o Foreign and Commonwealth Office, SW1. *Club:* Garrick.

URWICK, Lyndall Fownes, OBE, MC; MA; Hon. DSc; CIMechE, MASME, MIPE, FBIM, FRSA; Hon. Associate Manchester College of Technology and College of Technology, Birmingham; President Urwick, Orr & Partners Ltd, since 1963; *b* 3 March 1891; *o c* of late Sir Henry Urwick; *m* 1923, Joan Wilhelmina Bedford; one *s* one *d* ; *m* 1941, Betty, *o d* of late Major H. M. Warrand; one *s* one *d. Educ:* Boxgrove School, Guildford; Repton School; New College, Oxford (Hist. Exhibitioner). Duke of Devonshire Prize, 1910; BA 1913; MA 1919. War Service, 1914–18 (despatches thrice); Employers' Sec., Joint Industrial Council of Glove-making Industry, 1919–20; employed by Rowntree & Co. Ltd, York, 1922–28; Hon. Sec., Management Research Groups, 1926–28; Dir Internat. Management Inst., Geneva, 1928–33; Gen. Sec., Internat. Cttee of Scientific Management, 1932–35; Consultant to HM Treasury, 1940–42; Mem., Manchester Cttee on Min. of Pensions, 1940–41; Lt-Col Petroleum Warfare Dept, 1942–44. Chm., Cttee on Educn for Management, 1946; Vice-Chm. Coun., BIM, 1947–52; Chm., Anglo-Amer. Productivity Team on Educn for Management in USA, 1951; Dir, American Management Assoc. Study of Management Education, 1952–53; Pres., Institutional Management Assoc., 1956–59; Colombo Plan Adviser to Indian Govt, 1956; Pres., European Fedn of Management Consultants' Assocs., 1960–61; Hon. Vis. Prof., Univ. of York, Toronto, 1967. Life Member: American Management Assoc., 1957; American Soc. Mechanical Engineers, 1952. Past Master, Company of Glovers. Hon. DSc Aston Univ., 1969; Hon. LLD York Univ., Toronto, 1972. Kt, 1st Cl. Order of St Olaf (Norway); Silver Medal, RSA, 1948; Gold Medal, Internat. Cttee for Scientific Management, 1951; Wallace Clark Internat. Management Award, 1955; Henry Laurence Gantt Gold Medal, 1961; Taylor Key, 1963; Bowie Medal, 1968. *Publications:* Factory Organisation, 1928; Organising a Sales Office, 1928, 2nd edn 1937; The Meaning of Rationalisation, 1929; Problems of Distribution in Europe and the United States, 1931; Management of To-Morrow, 1933; Committees in Organisation, 1937; Papers on the Science

of Administration, 1937; The Development of Scientific Management in Great Britain, 1938; Dynamic Administration, 1941; The Elements of Administration, 1943; The Making of Scientific Management, vol. i, Thirteen Pioneers, 1945, vol. ii, British Industry, 1946, vol. iii, The Hawthorne Experiments, 1948; Freedom and Coordination, 1949; Management Education in American Business, 1955; The Pattern of Management, 1956; Leadership in the XXth Century, 1957; Organisation, 1964; articles on rationalisation, and scientific management. *Address:* Poyntington, 83 Kenneth Street, Longueville, NSW 2066, Australia. *T:* Sydney 4272102; 134 Buckingham Palace Road, SW1W 9SA. *Clubs:* Savile, Reform.
See also A. B. Urwick.

URWIN, Harry, (Charles Henry); Associate Fellow, Industrial Relations Research Unit, Warwick University, since 1981; Member, TUC General Council, 1969–80; Deputy General-Secretary, Transport and General Workers Union, 1969–80; Chairman, TUC Employment Policy and Organisation Committee, 1973–80; *b* 24 Feb. 1915; *s* of Thomas and Lydia Urwin; *m* 1941, Hilda Pinfold; one *d. Educ:* Durham County Council Sch. Convenor, Machine Tool Industry, until 1947; Coventry Dist Officer, TGWU, 1947–59; Coventry Dist Sec., Confedn of Shipbuilding and Engineering Unions, 1954–59; Regional Officer, TGWU, 1959–69; Member: Industrial Develt Adv. Bd, Industry Act, 1972–79; Sir Don Ryder Inquiry, British Leyland Motor Corp., 1974–75; Manpower Services Commn, 1974–79; Nat. Enterprise Bd, 1975–79; Energy Commn, 1977–79; Council, ACAS, 1978–80; Standing Cttee on Pay Comparability, 1979–80. *Recreation:* swimming. *Address:* 4 Leacliffe Way, Aldridge, Walsall WS9 0PW.

URWIN, Rt. Hon. Thomas (William) PC 1979; MP (Lab) Houghton-le-Spring since 1964; *b* 9 June 1912; *s* of a miner; *m* 1934, Edith Scott, *d* of a miner; three *s* one *d. Educ:* Brandon Colliery and Easington Lane Elementary Schools and NCLC. Bricklayer, 1926–54; full-time Organiser, Amalgamated Union of Building Trade Workers, 1954–64. Minister of State, DEA, 1968–69; Minister of State, with responsibilities for regional policy, and special delegn to Council of Europe and WEU, 1976–79, Leader Lab delegn, 1976–. Chm., Socialist Group, Council of Europe, 1976–. Member Houghton-le-Spring Urban District Council, 1949–65, Chm. 1954–55, Chm. Planning and Housing, 1950–65. *Recreations:* football (local soccer), cricket. *Address:* 28 Stanhope Close, Houghton-le-Spring, Tyne and Wear. *T:* Houghton-le-Spring 3139.

USBORNE, Henry Charles, MA; Chairman, UA Engineering Ltd, Sheffield; Joint President, Parliamentary Group for World Government; *b* 16 Jan. 1909; *s* of Charles Frederick Usborne and Janet Lefroy; *m* 1936; two *s* two *d. Educ:* Bradfield; Corpus Christi, Cambridge. MP (Lab) Yardley Div. of Birmingham, 1950–59 (Acock's Green Div. of Birmingham, 1945–50). JP Worcs, 1964–79. *Address:* Totterdown, The Parks, Evesham, Worcs.
See also R. A. Usborne.

USBORNE, Richard Alexander; Custodian, National Trust, 1974–81; *b* 16 May 1910; *s* of Charles Frederick Usborne, ICS, and Janet Muriel (*née* Lefroy); *m* 1938, Monica, *d* of Archibald Stuart MacArthur, Wagon Mound, New Mexico, USA; one *s* one *d. Educ:* Summer Fields Preparatory Sch.; Charterhouse; Balliol Coll., Oxford. BA Mods and Greats; MA 1981. Served War, 1941–45: Army, SOE and PWE, Middle East, Major, Gen. List. Advertising agencies, 1933–36; part-owner and Editor of What's On, 1936–37; London Press Exchange, 1937–39; BBC Monitoring Service, 1939–41; Asst Editor, Strand Magazine, 1946–50; Dir, Graham & Gillies Ltd, Advertising, retd, 1970. *Publications:* Clubland Heroes, 1953 (rev. 1975); (ed) A Century of Summer Fields, 1964; Wodehouse at Work, 1961, rev. edn, as Wodehouse at Work to the End, 1977; (ed) Sunset at Blandings, 1977; (ed) Vintage Wodehouse, 1977; A Wodehouse Companion, 1981; adaptations of Wodehouse novels for BBC radio serials. *Recreations:* reading, writing light verse. *Address:* Flat 8, Crofton House, 1 New Cavendish Street, W1. *T:* 01-486 9869.
See also H. C. Usborne.

USHER, Sir Peter Lionel, 5th Bt *cr* 1899, of Norton, Midlothian, and of Wells, Co. Roxburgh; *b* 31 Oct. 1931; *er s* of Sir (Robert) Stuart Usher, 4th Bt, and Gertrude Martha, 2nd *d* of Lionel Barnard Sampson, Tresmontes, Villa Valeria, Prov. Cordoba, Argentina; *S* father, 1962. *Educ:* privately. *Heir: b* Robert Edward Usher, *b* 18 April 1934. *Address:* (Seat) Hallrule, Hawick, Roxburghshire. *T:* Bonchester Bridge 216.

USHER, Brig. Thomas Clive, CBE 1945; DSO and Bar 1943; RA, retired 1958; now farming; *b* 21 June 1907; *s* of Sir Robert Usher, 2nd Bt, of Norton and Wells; *m* 1939, Valentine Sears Stockwell; one *d. Educ:* Uppingham; RMA. Served War of 1939–45: North Africa, Sicily and Italy (DSO and Bar, CBE); Temp. Brig. 1944. Lt-Col 1950; Col 1951; Temp. Brig. 1953; ADC, 1957–58. Formerly Military Adviser to UK High Comr in India; OC 18 Trg Bde, RA, 1955–57; Brig. RA, Scottish Comd, 1958. *Recreations:* riding, fishing. *Address:* Wells Stables, Hawick, Roxburghshire. *T:* Denholm 235.

USHER-WILSON, Rt. Rev. Lucian Charles, CBE 1961; MA; Honorary Assistant Bishop of Bristol, since 1972; Hon. Canon of Guildford Cathedral, 1965; *b* 10 Jan. 1903; *s* of Rev. C. Usher-Wilson; *m* 1929, Muriel Constance Wood; one *s* three *d. Educ:* Christ's Hospital; Lincoln College, Oxford; St Augustine's College, Canterbury. Asst Master, King William's College, Isle of Man; Asst Master, King's College, Budo, Kampala, Uganda; CMS Missionary at Jinja, Busoga, Uganda; Rural Dean, Busoga District, Uganda; Bishop on Upper Nile, 1936–61 (when diocese split up); Bishop of Mbale (southern area of former diocese of Upper Nile), 1961–64; an Asst Bishop of Guildford and Vicar of Churt, 1964–72. Mem., Royal African Soc. *Recreation:* gardening. *Address:* 58 The Dell, Westbury-on-Trym, Bristol BS9 3UG. *Clubs:* Old Blues, Royal Commonwealth Society.

USHERWOOD, Kenneth Ascough, CBE 1964; President, Prudential Assurance Co. Ltd, 1979–82; *b* 19 Aug. 1904; *s* of late H. T. Usherwood and late Lettie Ascough; *m* 1st, Molly Tidbeck (marr. diss. 1945), Johannesburg; one *d*; 2nd, 1946, Mary Louise, *d* of T. L. Reepmaker d'Orville; one *s*. *Educ:* City of London School; St John's College, Cambridge (MA). Prudential Assurance Co. Ltd, 1925–82: South Africa, 1932–34; Near East, 1934–37; Dep. Gen. Man. 1947–60; Chief Gen. Man., 1961–67; Dir, 1968–79; Chm., 1970–75; Dir, Prudential Corp., 1978–79. Director of Statistics, Ministry of Supply, 1941–45. Chm., Industrial Life Offices Assoc., 1966–67. Institute of Actuaries: Fellow (FIA) 1925; Pres. 1962–64. Mem. Gaming Board, 1968–72; Treasurer, Field Studies Council, 1969–77. *Address:* 24 Litchfield Way, NW11. *T:* 01-455 7915; Laurel Cottage, Walberswick, Suffolk. *T:* Southwold 723265. *Club:* Oriental.

USTINOV, Peter Alexander, CBE 1975; FRSA, FRSL; actor, dramatist, film director; Rector of the University of Dundee, 1968–74; Goodwill Ambassador for UNICEF, 1969; *b* London, 16 April 1921; *s* of late Iona Ustinov and Nadia Benois, painter; *m* 1st, 1940, Isolde Denham (marr. diss. 1950); one *d*; 2nd, 1954, Suzanne Cloutier (marr. diss. 1971); one *s* two *d*; 3rd, 1972, Hélène du Lau d'Allemans. *Educ:* Westminster School. Served in Army, Royal Sussex Regt and RAOC, 1942–46. Author of plays: House of Regrets, 1940 (prod Arts Theatre 1942); Blow Your Own Trumpet, 1941 (prod Playhouse [Old Vic] 1943); Beyond, 1942 (prod Arts Theatre, 1943); The Banbury Nose, 1943 (prod Wyndham's 1944); The Tragedy of Good Intentions, 1944 (prod Old Vic, Liverpool, 1945); The Indifferent Shepherd (prod Criterion, 1948); Frenzy (adapted from Swedish of Ingmar Bergman, (prod and acted in St Martin's, 1948); The Man in the Raincoat (Edinburgh Festival, 1949); The Love of Four Colonels (and acted in, Wyndham's, 1951); The Moment of Truth (Adelphi, 1951); High Balcony, 1952 (written 1946); No Sign of the Dove (Savoy, 1953); The Empty Chair (Bristol Old Vic, 1956); Romanoff and Juliet (Piccadilly, 1956, film, 1961; musical, R loves J, Chichester, 1973); Photo Finish (prod and acted in it, Saville, 1962); The Life in My Hands, 1963; The Unknown Soldier and his Wife, 1967 (prod and acted in it, Chichester, 1968, New London, 1973); Halfway up the Tree (Queen's), 1967. Co-Author of film: The Way Ahead, 1943–44. Author and Director of films: School for Secrets, 1946; Vice-Versa, 1947. Author, director, producer and main actor in film Private Angelo, 1949; acted in films: Odette, Quo Vadis, Hotel Sahara, 1950; Beau Brummell, The Egyptian, We're No Angels, 1954; An Angel Flew Over Brooklyn, 1957; Spartacus, 1960; The Sundowners, 1961; Topkapi, 1964; John Goldfarb, Please Come Home; Blackbeard's Ghost; The Comedians, 1968; Hot Millions, 1968; Viva Max, 1969; Treasure of Matecumbe, 1977; Un Taxi Mauve, 1977; The Last Remake of Beau Geste, 1977; Death on the Nile, 1978 (Best Film Actor, Variety Club of GB); Ashanti, The Thief of Baghdad, 1979; Charlie Chan and the Curse of the Dragon Queen, 1981; Evil under the Sun, 1981; director, producer and actor in film Billy Budd, 1961; director and actor in film Hammersmith is Out, 1971. Produced operas at Covent Garden, 1962, and Hamburg Opera, 1968; Berlin Opera, 1978. Acted in: revues: Swinging the Gate, 1940, Diversion, 1941; plays: Crime and Punishment, New Theatre, 1946; Love in Albania, St James's, 1949; King Lear, Stratford, Ont, 1979; directed Lady I, 1965; *television:* The Mighty Continent (series), 1974. Member, British Film Academy. Mem., British USA Bicentennial Liaison Cttee, 1973–. Benjamin Franklin Medal, Royal Society of Arts, 1957; Order of the Smile (for dedication to idea of internat. assistance to children), Warsaw, 1974. *Publications:* House of Regrets, 1943; Beyond, 1944; The Banbury Nose, 1945; Plays About People, 1950; The Love of Four Colonels, 1951; The Moment of Truth, 1953; Romanoff and Juliet (Stage and Film); Add a Dash of Pity (short stories), 1959; Ustinov's Diplomats (a book of photographs), 1960; The Loser (novel), 1961; The Frontiers of the Sea, 1966; Krumnagel, 1971; Dear Me (autobiog.), 1977; Overheard (play), 1981; contributor short stories to Atlantic Monthly. *Recreations:* lawn tennis, squash, collecting old masters' drawings, music. *Address:* 11 rue de Silly, 92100 Boulogne, France. *Clubs:* Garrick, Savage, Royal Automobile, Arts Theatre, Queen's.

UTIGER, Ronald Ernest, CBE 1977; Chairman, The British Aluminium Co. Ltd, since 1979; Deputy Chairman and Group Managing Director, TI Group (formerly Tube Investments Ltd) (Director, since 1979); *b* 5 May 1926; *s* of Ernest Frederick Utiger and Kathleen Utiger (*née* Cram); *m* 1953, Barbara Anna von Mohl; one *s* one *d*. *Educ:* Shrewsbury Sch.; Worcester Coll., Oxford (2nd cl. Hons PPE 1950; MA). Economist, Courtaulds Ltd, 1950–61; British Aluminium Ltd: Financial Controller, 1961–64; Commercial Dir, 1965–68; Man. Dir, 1968–79. Dir, 1976–80, Chm., 1979–80, BNOC. Mem., NEDC, 1981–. Chm., Internat. Primary Aluminium Inst., 1976–78; Pres. European Primary Aluminium Assoc., 1976–77. FRSA; FBIM 1975. *Recreations:* music, gardening. *Address:* 9 Ailsa Road, St Margaret's-on-Thames, Twickenham, Mddx. *T:* 01-892 5810.

UTLEY, (Clifton) Garrick; journalist and broadcaster, since 1964; *b* 19 Nov. 1939; *s* of late Clifton Maxwell Utley and of Frayn Garrick Utley; *m* 1973, Gertje Rommeswinkel. *Educ:* Carleton Coll., Northfield, Minn, USA (BA

1961); Free Univ., Berlin. Correspondent, NBC News: Saigon, Vietnam, 1964–65; Berlin, Germany, 1966–68; Paris, France, 1969–71; NY, 1971–72; London (Senior European Correspondent), 1973–79; New York, 1980–. Numerous documentary films on foreign affairs. Hon. LLD, Carleton Coll., 1979. *Recreations:* music, conversation. *Address:* c/o NBC News, 30 Rockefeller Plaza, New York, NY 10020, USA. *T:* 664-4444.

UTLEY, Peter; see Utley, T. E.

UTLEY, Thomas Edwin, (Peter), CBE 1980; Chief Assistant Editor, The Daily Telegraph, since 1980; *b* 1 Feb. 1921; adopted *s* of late Miss Anne Utley; *m* 1951, Brigid Viola Mary, *yr d* of late D. M. M. Morrah, and of Ruth Morrah, *qv*; two *s* two *d*. *Educ:* privately; Corpus Christi Coll., Cambridge (1st cl. Hons Hist. Tripos; Foundn Schol.; MA). Sec., Anglo-French Relations post-War Reconstruction Gp, RIIA, 1942–44; temp. Foreign Leader writer, the Times, 1944–45; Leader writer, Sunday Times, 1945–47; Editorial staff, The Observer, 1947–48; Leader writer, The Times, 1948–54; Associate Editor, Spectator, 1954–55; freelance journalist and broadcasting, 1955–64; Leader writer, The Daily Telegraph, 1964–80. A Governor, House of Citizenship, Hartwell House, Aylesbury, 1957–76. Contested (U) North Antrim, Feb. 1974. Pres., Paddington Cons. Assoc., 1979–80 (Chm., 1977–79); a Consultant Dir, Cons. Res. Dept, 1980–. *Publications:* Essays in Conservatism, 1949; Modern Political Thought, 1952; The Conservatives and the Critics, 1956; (ed jtly) Documents of Modern Political Thought, 1957; Not Guilty, 1957; Edmund Burke, 1957; Occasion for Ombudsmen, 1963; Your Money and Your Life, 1964; Enoch Powell: the Man and his Thinking, 1968; What Laws May Cure, 1968; Lessons of Ulster, 1975. *Address:* 60 St Mary's Mansions, St Mary's Terrace, W2. *T:* 01-723 1149.

UTTING, William Benjamin; Chief Social Work Officer, Department of Health and Social Security, since 1976; *b* 13 May 1931; *s* of John William Utting and Florence Ada Utting; *m* 1954, Mildred Jackson; two *s* one *d*. *Educ:* Great Yarmouth Grammar Sch.; New Coll., Oxford; Barnett House, Oxford. MA Oxon. Probation Officer: Co. Durham, 1956–58; Norfolk, 1958–61; Sen. Probation Officer, Co. Durham, 1961–64; Principal Probation Officer, Newcastle upon Tyne, 1964–68; Lectr in Social Studies, Univ. of Newcastle upon Tyne, 1968–70; Dir of Social Services, Kensington and Chelsea, 1970–76. Member: Chief Scientist's Res. Cttee, DHSS, 1973–76; SSRC, 1979–. *Publications:* contribs to professional jls. *Recreations:* literature, music, art. *Address:* 76 Great Brownings, College Road, SE21 7HR. *T:* 01-670 1201.

UTTLEY, Prof. Albert Maurel, PhD; Research Professor of Experimental Psychology, University of Sussex, 1966–73, now Emeritus; *b* 14 Aug. 1906; *s* of George Uttley and Ethel Uttley (*née* Player), London; *m* 1941, Gwendoline Lucy Richens; two *d*. *Educ:* King's College, London University. BSc Mathematics; PhD Psychology. Dep. Chief Scientific Officer (Individual Merit Post), Royal Radar Establishment, 1940–56; Superintendent of Autonomics Div., NPL, 1956–66. Fellow, Center for Advanced Studies in Behavioral Sciences, Univ. of Stanford, Calif, 1962–63. Pres., Biological Engineering Soc., 1964–66. Kelvin Premium, IEE, 1948; Simms Gold Medal, RAeS, 1950. *Publications:* Information Transmission in the Nervous System, 1978; Brain, Mind and Spirit, 1982; papers in various scientific journals on theory of control and of computers and on theoretical neurophysiology of brain function. *Recreations:* formerly mountaineering, now painting, travel. *Address:* Dunnocks, Lewes Road, Ditchling, East Sussex BN6 8TY.

UVAROV, Olga, CBE 1978; DSc, FRCVS; Hon. Secretary, Research Defence Society, since 1978; *d* of Nikolas and Elena Uvarov. *Educ:* Royal Vet. Coll. (Bronze Medals for Physiol. and Histol.). MRCVS 1934; FRCVS 1973. Asst in gen. mixed practice, 1934–43; own small animal practice, 1944–53; licence to practice and work at greyhound stadium, 1945–68; clinical res., Pharmaceutical industry, 1953–70; Head of Vet. Adv. Dept, Glaxo Laboratories, 1967–70; BVA Technical Inf. Service, 1970–76; Advr on Tech. Inf., BVA, 1976–78; Mem. MAFF Cttees under Medicines Act (1968), 1971–78. RCVS: Mem. Council, 1968–; Chm. Parly Cttee, 1971–74; Jun. Vice-Pres., 1975; Pres., 1976–77; President: Soc. Women Vet. Surgeons, 1947–49 (Sec., 1946); Central Vet. Soc., 1951–52; Assoc. Vet. Teachers and Res. Workers, 1967–68 (Pres. S Reg., 1967–68); Section of Comparative Medicine, RSocMed, 1967–68 (Sec., 1965–67; Sec. for Internat. Affairs, 1971–); Member Council: BVA, 1944–67; RSocMed, 1968–70 (Hon. Fellow, 1982); Res. Defence Soc., 1968–; Member: Medicines Commn, 1978–82; Vet. Res. Club, 1967–; British Small Animal Vet. Assoc.; British Codex Sub-Cttee, Pharmaceutical Soc., 1970–71; Senior Vice-Pres., RCVS, 1977–. FRVC 1979; Hon. DSc Guelph, 1976. Victory Gold Medal, Central Vet. Soc., 1965. *Publications:* contribs to: The Veterinary Annual; International Encyclopaedia of Veterinary Medicine, 1966; also papers in many learned jls. *Recreations:* work, travel, literature, flowers. *Address:* 39 Rodney Gardens, Eastcote, Pinner, Mddx HA5 2RT. *Club:* Royal Society of Medicine.

UXBRIDGE, Earl of; Charles Alexander Vaughan Paget; *b* 13 Nov 1950; *s* and *heir* of 7th Marquess of Anglesey, *qv*. *Educ:* Dragon School, Oxford; Eton; Exeter Coll., Oxford. *Address:* Plâs-Newydd, Llanfairpwll, Gwynedd.

V

VACHON, Most Rev. Louis-Albert; *see* Quebec, Archbishop of, (R.C.).

VAEA, Baron of Houma; Minister for Labour, Commerce and Industries, Tonga, since 1973; *b* 15 May 1921; *s* of Viliami Vilai Tupou and Tupou Seini Vaea; *m* 1952, Tuputupu Ma'afu; three *s* three *d*. *Educ*: Wesley College, Auckland, NZ. RNZAF, 1942-45; Tonga Civil Service, 1945-53; ADC to HM Queen Salote, 1954-59; Governor of Haapai, 1959-68; Commissioner and Consul in UK, 1969; High Comr in UK, 1970-72. Given the title Baron Vaea of Houma by HM The King of Tonga, 1970. *Recreations*: Rugby, cricket, fishing. *Heir: e s* Albert Tuivanuavou Vaea, *b* 19 Sept. 1957. *Address*: PO Box 262, Nuku'alofa, Tonga.

VAES, Robert, Hon. KCMG 1966; LLD; Grand Officer, Order of Leopold; Grand Officer, Order of the Crown, Belgium; Belgian Ambassador to the Court of St James's, since 1976; *b* Antwerp, 9 Jan. 1919; *m* 1947, Anne Albers; one *d*. *Educ*: Brussels Univ. (LLD; special degree in Commercial and Maritime Law). Joined Diplomatic Service, 1946: postings to Washington, Paris, Hong Kong, London and Rome; Personal Private Sec. to Minister of Foreign Trade, 1958-60; Dir-Gen. of Polit. Affairs, 1964-66; Permanent Under-Sec., Min. of For. Affairs, For. Trade and Develt Cooperation, 1966-72; Ambassador to Spain, 1972-76. Formerly, Chairman: Council, Benelux Union; Belgian-Luxemburg Admin. Commn. Foreign decorations from The Netherlands, Italy, Norway, Niger, Luxemburg, Tunisia, Cameroon, Denmark, Austria, Senegal, France, Japan, Peru, and Spain. *Recreations*: tennis, golf, bridge. *Address*: 36 Belgrave Square, SW1X 8QB. *T*: 01-235 1752. *Clubs*: Travellers', White's, Royal Automobile, Anglo-Belgian, Hurlingham; Swinley Forest (Berks); Royal Yacht of Belgium.

VAIZEY, family name of **Baron Vaizey.**

VAIZEY, Baron *cr* 1976 (Life Peer), of Greenwich; **John Ernest Vaizey;** Director of several companies; *b* 1 Oct. 1929; *s* of late Ernest and Lucy Butler Vaizey; *m* 1961, Marina (*see* Lady Vaizey); two *s* one *d*. *Educ*: Queen Mary's Hosp. Sch.; Queens' Coll., Cambridge (Schol.; Econs Tripos, Cambridge, 1951; Gladstone Prizeman, 1954; MA). DSc Brunel; DLitt *aeg* Adelaide. UN, Geneva, 1952-53; Fellow of St Catharine's Coll., Cambridge, 1953-56; Univ. Lectr, Oxford, 1956-60; Dir, Research Unit, Univ. of London, 1960-62; Fellow and Tutor, Worcester Coll., Oxford, 1962-66; Prof. of Econs, Brunel Univ., 1966-82 (Hd, Sch. of Soc. Scis, 1973-81). Prof., Univ. of California, 1965-66; Eleanor Rathbone Lectr, Univs of Liverpool and Durham, 1966; O'Brien Lectr, UCD, 1968; Centenary Prof., Univ. of Adelaide, 1974-75; Hoover Prof., Univ. of NSW, 1977. Principal, St Catharine's, Cumberland Lodge, 1982- (Trustee, 1972-82). Member: Nat. Adv. Council on Trng and Supply of Teachers, 1962-66; UNESCO Nat. Commn, 1965-72, 1978-; Exec., Fabian Soc., 1959-66; Public Schools Commn, 1966-68; Nat. Council on Educn Technology, 1967-73; Inner London Educn Authority, 1970-72; Commn on Educn, Spain, 1968-72; Adv. Council, Radio London, 1970-73; Governing Body, Internat. Inst. for Educnl Planning, 1971-80; Adv. Cttee, Gulbenkian Foundn, 1971-77; Chairman: Cttee on Trng for the Drama, 1974-75; Cttee on Dance, 1974-82; Cttee on Music Training, 1975-77; British-Irish Assoc., 1976-82; Greenwich Festival, 1979-; Vice-Pres., Greater London Arts Assoc., 1974-78; Pres., Blackheath Soc., 1975-. Trustee: Acton Soc. Trust, 1968-78 (Dir 1960-68); Riverside Studios, 1976-81. Governor, Ditchley Foundn, 1973-. Consultant, UN, etc. Order of El Sabio (Spain), 1969. *Publications*: The Costs of Education, 1958; Scenes from Institutional Life, 1959; (with P. Lynch) Guinness's Brewery in the Irish Economy, 1961; The Economics of Education, 1962; Education for Tomorrow, 1962, 5th edn 1970; The Control of Education, 1963; (ed) The Residual Factor and Economic Growth, 1965; (ed with E. A. G. Robinson) The Economics of Education, 1965; Barometer Man, 1967; Education in the Modern World, 1967, 2nd edn, 1975; (with John Sheehan) Resources for Education, 1968; The Sleepless Lunch, 1968; (with colleagues) The Economics of Educational Costing, 4 vols, 1969-71; The Type to Succeed, 1970; Capitalism, 1971; Social Democracy, 1971; The Political Economy of Education, 1972; (with Keith Norris) The Economics of Research and Technology, 1973; History of British Steel, 1974; (ed) Economic Sovereignty and Regional Policy; (ed) Whatever Happened to Equality, 1975; (with C. F. O. Clarke) Education: the state of the debate, 1976; (with Keith Norris) Teach Yourself Economics, 1977; Capitalism and Socialism, 1980; The Squandered Peace, 1983. *Recreations*: arts, travel. *Address*: 24 Heathfield Terrace, W4 4JE. *T*: 01-994 7994. *Clubs*: Garrick, Beefsteak; Kildare Street and University (Dublin).

VAIZEY, Lady; Marina Vaizey; Art Critic of the Sunday Times, since 1974; *b* 16 Jan. 1938; *o d* of Lyman Stansky and late Ruth Stansky; *m* 1961, Lord Vaizey, *qv*; two *s* one *d*. *Educ*: Brearley Sch., New York; Putney Sch., Putney, Vermont; Radcliffe Coll., Harvard Univ. (BA Medieval History and Lit.); Girton Coll., Cambridge (BA, MA). Art Critic, Financial Times, 1970-74; Dance Critic, Now!, 1979-81; Mem. Arts Council, 1976-78 (Mem. Art Panel, 1973-78, Dep. Chm., 1976-78); Member: Advisory Cttee, DoE, 1975-81; Paintings for Hospitals, 1974-; Cttee, Contemporary Art Soc., 1975-79, 1980-; Hist. of Art and Complementary Studies Bd, CNAA, 1978-; Photography Bd, CNAA, 1979-81; Fine Art Bd, CNAA, 1980-; Passenger Services Sub-Cttee, Heathrow Airport, 1979-; Exec. Dir, Mitchell Prize for the Hist. of Art, 1976-. Governor: Camberwell Coll. of Arts and Crafts, 1971-; Bath Acad. of Art, Corsham, 1978-81. Broadcaster, occasional exhibition

organiser and lecturer; organised Critic's Choice, Tooth's, 1974. Co-Sec., Radcliffe Club of London, 1968-74. *Publications*: 100 Masterpieces of Art, 1979; Andrew Wyeth, 1980; The Artist as Photographer, 1982; articles in various periodicals, anthologies, exhibition catalogues. *Recreations*: arts, travel. *Address*: 24 Heathfield Terrace, W4 4JE. *T*: 01-994 7994.

VAJPAYEE, Atal Bihari; MP (Lok Sabha); President, Bharatiya Janata Party, since 1980; *b* Gwalior, Madhya Pradesh, 25 Dec. 1926; *s* of Krishna Bihari; unmarried. *Educ*: Victoria Coll., Gwalior; D.A.V. Coll., Kanpur (MA). Joined Arya Samaj, 1939, RSS, 1940; arrested in freedom movement, 1942; full-time social worker, 1948; joined Bharatiya Jana Sangh from its inception, 1951, Pres., 1968-73; Mem., Lok Sabha 1957-62 and 1967- (elected from UP, 1957 and 1967, from MP, 1971); Rajya Sabha, 1962-67; Leader, Jana Sangh Parly party, 1957-75; detained 26 June 1975; elected to Lok Sabha from New Delhi, 1977 and 1980; Minister of External Affairs, 1977-79. Member: Nat. Integration Council, 1962; Parly delegn to Commonwealth Parly Assoc. meeting, Canada, 1966 and Zambia, 1980; IPU Conf., Tokyo, 1974; Railway Convention Cttee, 1971-72; Hindi Salahkar Samiti. Chairman: Public Accounts Cttee, Lok Sabha, 1969-70; Assurances Cttee, 1967-68. Formerly Editor: Rashtradharma; Panchajanya; Veer Arjun. *Publications*: Amar Balidani; Mrityu Ya Hatya; Jana Sangh aur Mussalman; Kaidi Kavirai ki Kundaliya; New Dimensions of India's Foreign Policy; some periodicals. *Address*: 6 Raisina Road, New Delhi 110001, India. *T*: 385166.

VALDAR, Colin Gordon; Consultant Editor and Chairman, Bouverie Publishing Co. Ltd, since 1964; *b* 18 Dec. 1918; 3rd *s* of Lionel and Mary Valdar; *m* 1st, 1940, Evelyn Margaret Barriff (marr. diss.); two *s*; 2nd, Jill, (*née* Davis). *Educ*: Haberdashers' Aske's Hampstead School. Free-lance journalist, 1936-39. Served War of 1939-45, Royal Engineers, 1939-42. Successively Production Editor, Features Editor, Asst Editor Sunday Pictorial, 1942-46; Features Editor, Daily Express, 1946-51; Asst Editor, Daily Express, 1951-53; Editor, Sunday Pictorial, 1953-59; Editor, Daily Sketch, 1959-62. Director, Sunday Pictorial Newspapers Ltd, 1957-59; Director, Daily Sketch and Daily Graphic Ltd, 1959-62. Founded UK Press Gazette, 1965. *Address*: 94 Clifford's Inn, Fleet Street, EC4. *T*: 01-242 0935.

VALENTIA, 14th Viscount (Ireland) *cr* 1621 (Dormant 1844-1959); Francis Dighton Annesley, Baron Mountmorris (Ireland) 1628; Bt 1620; MC 1918; MRCS, LRCP; Brigadier retired, late RAMC; *b* 12 Aug. 1888; *o s* of late George Dighton Annesley (uncle of *de jure* 13th Viscount); *S* cousin, 1951, established his succession, 1959; *m* 1925, Joan Elizabeth, 2nd *d* of late John Joseph Curtis; one *s* three *d*. *Educ*: St Lawrence Coll.; Guy's Hospital. Lieut, RAMC, 1914; served European War, France, Belgium, Aug. 1914-March 1919; Afghanistan, 1919; Waziristan, 1922-23; War of 1939-45, India, Iraq, Persia, Egypt, France, Germany, Lt-Col 1936; Col 1941; Brig. 1942; retd 1948. Croix de Guerre (Belge), 1918. *Heir: s* Hon. Richard John Dighton Annesley, Captain, RA, retd [*b* 15 Aug. 1929; *m* 1957, Anita Phyllis, *o d* of W. A. Joy; three *s* one *d*]. *Address*: St Michael's, Lea, Malmesbury, Wilts. *T*: Malmesbury 2312.

VALENTINE, Rt. Rev. Barry; *see* Rupert's Land, Bishop of.

VALENTINE, Prof. David Henriques; George Harrison Professor of Botany, University of Manchester, 1966-79, now Emeritus; *b* 16 Feb. 1912; *s* of Emmanuel and Dora Valentine; *m* 1938, Joan Winifred Todd; two *s* three *d*. *Educ*: Manchester Grammar Sch.; St John's Coll., Cambridge. MA 1936, PhD 1937. Curator of the Herbarium and Demonstrator in Botany, Cambridge, 1936; Research Fellow of St John's Coll., Cambridge, 1938; Ministry of Food (Dehydration Division), 1941; Reader in Botany, Durham, 1945, Prof., 1950-66. Trustee, BM (Natural History), 1975-. Foreign Mem., Societas Scientiarum Fennica (Section for Natural Sciences), 1964. *Publications*: Flora Europaea, Vol. 1, 1964, Vol. 2, 1968, Vol. 3, 1972, Vol. 4, 1976; Vol. 5, 1980; Taxonomy, Phytogeography and Evolution, 1972; papers on experimental taxonomy in botanical journals. *Recreation*: reading novels. *Address*: 4 Pine Road, Didsbury, Manchester M20 0UY. *T*: 061-445 7224.

VALLANCE, Iain David Thomas; Board Member for Organisation and Business Systems, British Telecom, since 1981; *b* 20 May 1943; *s* of Edmund Thomas Vallance and Janet Wright Bell Ross Davidson; *m* 1967, Elizabeth Mary McGonnigill; one *s* one *d*. *Educ*: Edinburgh Acad.; Dulwich Coll.; Glasgow Acad.; Brasenose Coll., Oxford; London Graduate School of Business Studies (MSc). Assistant Postal Controller, Post Office, 1966; Personal Asst to Chairman, 1973-75; Head of Finance Planning Division, 1975-76; Director: Central Finance, 1976-78; Telecommunications Finance, 1978-79; Materials Dept, 1979-81. Trustee, Post Office Staff Superannuation Fund, 1980-. *Address*: 22 Dulwich Wood Avenue, SE19 1HD. *T*: 01-670 3433.

VALLANCE, Michael Wilson; Headmaster of Bloxham School since 1982; *b* 9 Sept. 1933; *er s* of late Vivian Victor Wilson Vallance and of Kate Vallance, Wandsworth and Helston; *m* 1970, Mary Winifred Ann, *d* of John Steele Garnett; one *s* two *d*. *Educ*: Brighton Coll.; St John's Coll., Cambridge (MA). On staff of United Steel Companies Ltd, 1952-53; awarded United Steel Companies Scholarship (held at Cambridge), 1953; Asst Master, Abingdon School, 1957-61; Asst Master, Harrow School, 1961-72; Headmaster, Durham Sch., 1972-82. Chairman: Cttee of Northern Isis, 1976-77; NE Div., HMC, 1981-82. *Recreations*: reading, cricket, gardening, the sea. *Address:* Bloxham School, Banbury, Oxon OX15 4PE. *T:* Banbury 720206. *Clubs:* MCC, Jesters; County (Durham).

VALLANCE-OWEN, Prof. John, MA, MD, FRCP, FRCPI, FRCPath; Foundation Professor and Chairman, Department of Medicine, Chinese University of Hong Kong, since 1983; *b* 31 Oct. 1920; *s* of late Prof. E. A. Owen; *m* 1950, Renee Thornton; two *s* two *d. Educ:* Friar's Sch., Bangor; Epsom Coll.; St John's Coll., Cambridge (de Havilland Schol. from Epsom); London Hosp. (Schol.). BA 1943; MA, MB, BChir Cantab, 1946; MD Cantab 1951; FRCP 1962; Hon. FRCPI 1970; FRCPath 1971; FRCPI 1973. Various appts incl. Pathology Asst and Med. 1st Asst, London Hosp., 1946-51; Med. Tutor, Royal Postgrad. Med. Sch., Hammersmith Hosp., 1952-55 and 1956-58; Rockefeller Trav. Fellowship, at George S. Cox Med. Research Inst., Univ. of Pennsylvania, 1955-56; Cons. Phys. and Lectr in Medicine, Univ. of Durham, 1958-64; Cons. Phys., Royal Victoria Infirmary and Reader in Medicine, Univ. of Newcastle upon Tyne, 1964-66; Prof. of Medicine, QUB; Consultant Physician: Royal Victoria Hosp., Belfast, 1966-82 (Chm., Med. Div., 1979-81); Belfast City Hosp., 1966-82; Forster Green Hosp., Belfast, 1975-82 (Chm., Med. Staff Cttee, 1979-82). Member: Standing Med. Adv. Cttee, Min. of Health and Social Services, NI, 1970-73; Specialist Adv. Cttee (General Internal Medicine) to the Govt; Northern Health and Social Services Bd, Dept of Health and Soc. Services, NI; Mem., Exec. Cttee, Assoc. of Physicians of GB and Ireland, 1976-79; Regional Adviser for N Ire, to RCP, 1970-75 and Councillor, RCP, 1976-79 (Oliver-Sharpey Prize, RCP, 1976); Councillor, RCPI, 1978-82; Mem. Research Cttee, Brit. Diabetic Assoc.; Brit. Council Lectr, Dept Medicine, Zürich Univ., 1963; 1st Helen Martin Lectr, Diabetic Assoc. of S Calif, Wm H. Mulberg Lectr, Cincinnati Diabetes Assoc., and Lectr, Brookhaven Nat. Labs, NY, 1965; Brit. Council Lectr, Haile Selassie Univ., Makerere UC and S African Univs, 1966; Guest Lectr: Japan Endocrinological Soc., 1968; Madrid Univ., 1969; Endocrine Soc. of Australia, 1970, Bologna Univ., 1976. *Publications:* Essentials of Cardiology, 1961 (2nd edn 1968); Diabetes: its physiological and biochemical basis, 1976; papers in biochem., med., and scientific jls on carbohydrate and fat metabolism and aetiology of diabetes mellitus and related conditions, with special reference to insulin antagonism. *Recreations:* tennis, golf, music. *Address:* Faculty of Medicine, The Chinese University of Hong Kong, Shatin, New Territories, Hong Kong. *T:* Hong Kong 0-633111. *Club:* East India, Devonshire, Sports and Public Schools.

VALLAT, Prof. Sir Francis Aimé, GBE 1982; KCMG 1962 (CMG 1955); QC 1961; Barrister-at-Law; Emeritus Professor of International Law, University of London; *b* 25 May 1912; *s* of Col Frederick W. Vallat, OBE; *m* 1939, Mary Alison Cockell (marr. diss. 1973); one *s* one *d. Educ:* University College, Toronto (BA Hons); Gonville and Caius Coll., Cambridge (LLB). Called to Bar, Gray's Inn, 1935, Bencher, 1971; Assistant Lecturer, Bristol Univ., 1935-36; practice at Bar, London, 1936-39; RAFVR (Flt Lieut), 1941-45; Asst Legal Adviser, Foreign Office, 1945-50; Legal Adviser, UK Permanent Deleg. to UN, 1950-54; Deputy Legal Adviser, FO, 1954-60, Legal Adviser, 1960-68. (On leave of absence) Actg Director, Inst. of Air and Space Law, and Vis. Prof. of Law, McGill Univ., 1965-66. Dir of International Law Studies, King's Coll. London, 1968-76 (Reader, 1969-70, Prof., 1970-76). Dir of Studies, Internat. Law Assoc., 1969-73. UK Mem., UN Fact Finding Panel, 1969-. Associate Mem., Institut de Droit International, 1965, elected Mem. 1977; Member: Internat. Law Commn, 1973-81 (Chm. 1977-78); Permanent Court of Arbitration, 1980-; Curatorium, Hague Acad., 1982-. Expert Consultant, UN Conf. on Succession of States in respect of Treaties, 1977-78. Dr en dr. *hc*, Lausanne Univ., 1979. *Publications:* International Law and the Practitioner, 1966; Introduction to the Study of Human Rights, 1972; articles in British Year Book of International Law and other journals. *Recreation:* restoration of antiques. *Address:* 17 Ranelagh Grove, SW1. *T:* 01-730 6656; 3 Essex Court, Temple, EC4. *T:* 01-583 9294. *Club:* Hurlingham.

VALOIS, Dame Ninette de; *see* de Valois.

VAN ALLAN, Richard; principal bass; *b* 28 May 1935; *s* of Joseph Arthur and Irene Hannah Van Allan; *m* 1976, Elisabeth Rosemary; two *s. Educ:* Worcester College of Education (DipEd Science); Birmingham School of Music. Glyndebourne, 1964; Welsh National Opera, 1968; English National Opera, 1969; Royal Opera House, Covent Garden, 1971; performances also: l'Opéra de Paris, Bordeaux, Nice, Toulouse; USA: Boston, San Diego, Phoenix; Argentina: Buenos Aires; Spain: Madrid and Barcelona. *Recreations:* shooting, tennis, golf. *Address:* 343 Essex Road, N1 3PT. *T:* 01-226 3448.

VAN ALLEN, Prof. James Alfred; Professor of Physics and Head of Department of Physics (of Physics and Astronomy since 1959), since 1951, Carver Professor of Physics, since 1972, University of Iowa, USA; *b* Iowa, 7 Sept. 1914; *s* of Alfred Morris and Alma Olney Van Allen; *m* 1945, Abigail Fithian Halsey II; two *s* three *d. Educ:* Public High School, and Iowa Wesleyan Coll., Mount Pleasant, Iowa (BSc); University of Iowa, Iowa City (MSc, PhD). Research Fellow, then Physicist, Carnegie Instn of Washington, 1939-42; Physicist, Applied Physics Lab., Johns Hopkins Univ., Md, 1942. Ordnance and Gunnery Officer and Combat Observer, USN, 1942-46, Lt-Comdr 1946. Supervisor of High-Altitude Research Group and of Proximity Fuze Unit, Johns Hopkins Univ., 1946-50. Leader, various scientific expeditions to Central and S Pacific, Arctic and Antarctic, for study of cosmic rays and earth's magnetic field, using Aerobee and balloon-launched rockets, 1949-57. Took part in promotion and planning of International Geophysical Year, 1957-58; developed radiation measuring equipment on first American satellite, Explorer I, and subseq. satellites (discoverer of Van Allen Radiation Belts of the earth, 1958); has continued study of earth's radiation belts, aurorae, cosmic rays, energetic particles in interplanetary space, planetary magnetospheres. Research Fellow, Guggenheim Memorial Foundation, 1951; Research Associate (controlled thermonuclear reactions), Princeton Univ., Project Matterhorn, 1953-54; Regents' Fellow, Smithsonian Inst., 1981. Mem., Space Science Bd of Nat. Acad. of Sciences, 1958-70, 1980-; Fellow: American Phys. Society; Amer. Geophysical Union (Pres., 1982-), etc; Member: Nat. Acad. of Sciences; Royal Swedish Acad. of Sciences; Founder Member, International Acad. of Astronautics, etc. Holds many awards and hon. doctorates; Gold Medal, RAS, 1978. *Publications:* numerous articles in learned journals and contribs to scientific works. *Address:* Department of Physics and Astronomy, University of Iowa, Iowa City, Iowa 52242, USA; 5 Woodland Mounds Road, RFD 6, Iowa City, Iowa 52240, USA.

VANCE, Charles Ivan; actor, director and theatrical producer; *b* 6 Dec. 1929; *s* of Eric Goldblatt and Sarah (*née* Freeman); *m* 1959, Hon. Imogen Moynihan; one *d. Educ:* Royal Sch., Dungannon; Queen's Univ., Belfast. FInstD 1972; FRSA 1975. Early career as broadcaster; acting debut with Anew MacMaster Co., Gaiety, Dublin, 1949; dir, first prodn, The Glass Menagerie, Arts, Cambridge, 1960; founded Civic Theatre, Chelmsford, 1962; i/c rep. cos, Tunbridge Wells, Torquay, Whitby and Hastings, 1962-; as Dir of Charles Vance Prodns, created Eastbourne Theatre Co., 1969; dir. own adaptation of Wuthering Heights, 1972; wrote and staged four pantomimes, 1972-75; devised and dir. The Jolson Revue, 1974 (staged revival, Australia, 1978; world tour, 1981); played Sir Thomas More in A Man for All Seasons, and dir, Oh! What a Lovely War, Greenwood, 1975; prod and dir. world tour of Paddington Bear, 1978; produced: Cinderella, Stafford, 1981; Aladdin, Bognor, 1981. Purchased Leas Pavilion Theatre, Folkestone, 1976 (HQ of own theatre organisation). Produced (London and national tours): Stop the World—I Want to Get Off (revival), 1976; Salad Days (revival), 1977; (also dir.) In Praise of Love, 1977; Witness for the Prosecution, (revival), 1979; Hallo Paris, 1980; This Happy Breed (revival), 1980; Starlite Spectacular, 1981; The Kingfisher (revival), 1981; The Hollow (revival), 1982 (also dir.); The Little Hut, Australia (also dir.); Cinderella, Aladdin, 1982 (also wrote). Theatrical Management Association: Mem. Council, 1969; Pres., 1971-73 and 1973-76; Exec. Vice-Pres., 1976- (also of Council of Reg. Theatre). Advisor to Govt of Ghana on bldg Nat. Theatre, 1969. Director: Theatres Investment Fund, 1975-; Entertainment Investments Ltd, 1980-82; International Holiday Investments, 1980-; Southern Counties Television, 1980-; Channel Radio, 1981-; Gateway Broadcasting Ltd, 1982; Trustee Dir, Folkestone Theatre Co., 1979-. Chairman: Provincial Theatre Council, 1971-; Standing Adv. Cttee on Local Authority and the Theatre, 1977- (Vice-Chm., 1975-77). Vice-Chairman: Theatres Adv. Council, resp. for theatres threatened by develt, 1974-; (also Dir) Festival of Brit. Theatre, 1975-. Member: Theatres Nat. Cttee, 1971-; Drama Adv. Panel, SE Arts Assoc., 1974-; Prince of Wales' Jubilee Entertainments Cttee, 1977; Entertainment Exec. Cttee, Artists' Benev. Fund, 1980-; Rotary Internat., 1971-; Vice-Pres., E Sussex Br., RSPCA, 1975-. Founded Vance Offord (Publications) Ltd, publishers of British Theatre Directory, British Theatre Review, and Municipal Entertainment, 1971. *Publication:* British Theatre Directory, 1972, 1973, 1974, 1975. *Recreations:* sailing (crossed Atlantic single-handed, 1956), cooking (Cordon Bleu, 1957), travelling, animals. *Address:* Quince Cottage, Bilsington, near Ashford, Kent. *T:* Aldington 311. *Clubs:* Hurlingham, Royal Automobile, Directors', Macready's; Royal Eastbourne Golf.

VANCE, Cyrus Robert; Secretary of State, USA, 1977-80; barrister-at-law; *b* Clarksburg, W Va, 27 March 1917; *m* 1947, Grace Elsie Sloane; one *s* four *d. Educ:* Kent Sch.; Yale Univ. (BA 1939); Yale Univ. Law Sch. (LLB 1942). Served War, USNR, to Lieut (s.g.), 1942-46. Asst to Pres., The Mead Corp., 1946-47; admitted to New York Bar, 1947; Associate and Partner of Simpson Thacher & Bartlett, New York, 1947-60, Partner, Jan. 1956-60, 1967-77 and 1980-. Special Counsel, Preparedness Investigation Sub-cttee of Senate Armed Services Cttee, 1957-60; Consulting Counsel, Special Cttee on Space and Astronautics, US Senate, 1958; Gen. Counsel, Dept of Defense, 1961-62; Sec. of the Army, 1962-64; Dep. Sec. of Defense, 1964-67; Special Rep. of the President: in Civil Disturbances in Detroit, July-Aug. 1967 and in Washington, DC, April 1968; in Cyprus, Nov.-Dec. 1967; in Korea, Feb. 1968; one of two US Negotiators, Paris Peace Conf. on Vietnam, May 1968-Feb. 1969; Mem., Commn to Investigate Alleged Police Corruption in NYC, 1970-72; Pres., Assoc. of Bar of City of New York, 1974-76. Mem. Bd of Trustees: Rockefeller Foundn, 1970-77, 1980-82 (Chm., 1975-77); Yale Univ., 1968-78, 1980-; Amer. Ditchley Foundn, 1980- (Chm., 1981-); Mayo Foundn, 1980-. Hon. degrees: Marshall, 1963; Trinity Coll., 1966; Yale, 1968; West Virginia, Bowling Green, 1969; Salem Coll., 1970; Brandeis, 1971; Amherst, W Virginia Wesleyan, 1974; Harvard, Colgate, Gen. Theol Seminary, Williams Coll., 1981. Medal of Freedom (US), 1969. *Address:* Simpson Thacher & Bartlett, One Battery Park Plaza, New York, NY 10004, USA. *T:* 212/483-9000.

VANCOUVER, Archbishop of, (RC), since 1969; **Most Rev. James F. Carney,** DD; *b* Vancouver, BC, 28 June 1915. *Educ:* Vancouver College; St Joseph's Seminary, Edmonton, Alta. Ordained, 1942; Vicar-General and Domestic Prelate, 1964; Auxiliary Bishop of Vancouver, 1966. *Address:* 150 Robson Street, Vancouver, BC V6B 2A7, Canada. *T:* 683-0281.

VANDEN-BEMPDE-JOHNSTONE; *see* Johnstone.

VAN DEN BERGH, James Philip, CBE 1946; Director of Unilever Ltd, 1937-65, retired; Vice-Chairman of Lindustries, 1965-75; Deputy Chairman, William Baird & Co., 1965-75; Chairman, National Cold Stores (Management Ltd), 1965-70; *b* 26 April 1905; *s* of Albert Van den Bergh; *m* 1929, Betty D'Arcy Hart; one *s* one *d. Educ:* Harrow; Trinity Coll., Cambridge. Entered Van den Berghs Ltd, 1927; subseq. Man. Dir; Chm., 1942. Min. of Food: Dir of Margarine and Cooking Fats, 1939; Dir of Dehydration, 1940; Dir of Fish Supplies, 1945. Government Director, British Sugar Corp., 1956-58, retired. Member Exec. Council, Food Manufacturers' Federation, 1957 (President, 1958-61); Member Food Research Advisory Cttee, 1960-65 (Chairman, 1963); Member Council, Queen Elizabeth Coll., London Univ., 1961-73; Hon. Fellow, 1968. *Address:* Field House, Cranleigh, Surrey. *Club:* Leander (Henley).

VAN DEN BOGAERDE, Derek Niven, (Dirk Bogarde); actor; *b* 28 March 1921. *Educ:* University College School; Allan Glen's (Scotland). Served War of 1939-45: Queen's Royal Regt, 1940-46, Europe and Far East, and Air Photographic Intelligence. *Films* include (since 1947): Hunted, Appointment in London, They Who Dare, The Sleeping Tiger, Doctor in the House, Doctor at Sea, Doctor at Large, Simba, The Spanish Gardener, Cast a Dark Shadow, Ill Met by Moonlight, The Blue Lamp, So Long at the Fair, Quartet, A Tale of Two Cities (Sidney Carton), The Wind Cannot Read, The Doctor's Dilemma, Libel, Song Without End, The Angel Wore Red, The Singer Not The Song, Victim, HMS Defiant, The Password is Courage, The Lonely Stage, The Mindbenders, The Servant, Doctor in Distress, Hot Enough for June, The High Bright Sun, King and Country, Darling . . ., Modesty Blaise, Accident, Our Mother's House, Mister Sebastian, The Fixer, Oh What A Lovely War, Götterdämmerung, Justine, Death in Venice, Upon This Rock, Le Serpent, The Night Porter, Permission To Kill, Providence, A Bridge Too Far, Despair; *film for TV:* The Patricia Neal Story (USA), 1981. *Theatre:* Cliff, in Power Without Glory, 1947; Orpheus, in Point of Departure, 1950; Nicky, in The Vortex, 1953; Alberto, in Summertime, 1955-56; Jezebel, Oxford Playhouse, 1958, etc. *Publications:* A Postillion Struck by Lightning (autobiog.), 1977; Snakes and Ladders (autobiog.), 1978; A Gentle Occupation (novel), 1980; Voices in the Garden (novel), 1981; An Orderly Man (autobiog.), 1983. *Recreations:* gardening, painting, motoring. *Address:* London Management, 235-241 Regent Street, W1.

VAN DEN HOVEN, Helmert Frans; *see* Hoven.

VANDERFELT, Sir Robin (Victor), KBE 1973 (OBE 1954); Secretary-General, Commonwealth Parliamentary Association, since 1961; *b* 24 July 1921; *y s* of late Sydney Gorton Vanderfelt, OBE, and Ethel Maude Vanderfelt (*née* Tremayne); *m* 1962, Jean Margaret Becker, *d* of John and Eve Steward; two *s* (and one step *s* one step *d*). *Educ:* Haileybury; Peterhouse, Cambridge. Served War in India and Burma, 1941-45. Asst Secretary, UK Branch, CPA, 1949-59; Secretary, 1960-61. Secretary, UK Delegn, Commonwealth Parly Conf., India, 1957; as Sec.-Gen., CPA, has served as Secretary to Parliamentary Conferences throughout Commonwealth, 1961-; also attended many area and regional confs; Conf. of Commonwealth Speakers and Clerks. Governor, Queen Elizabeth House, Oxford, 1980-. *Recreation:* gardening. *Address:* Commonwealth Parliamentary Association, Headquarters Secretariat, 7 Old Palace Yard, SW1. *T:* 01-219 4281; Penridge House, Penselwood, Wincanton, Som.

VAN DER KISTE, Wing Commander Robert Edgar Guy, DSO 1941; OBE 1957; Royal Auxiliary Air Force, retired; Director, Plymouth Incorporated Chamber of Trade and Commerce, 1974-80 (Secretary, 1964-74); *b* 20 July 1912; *y s* of late Lt-Col F. W. Van der Kiste, DSO; *m* 1939, Nancy Kathleen, *er d* of Alec George Holman, MRCS, LRCP, and Grace Kathleen Brown; one *s* two *d* (and one *s* decd). *Educ:* Cheltenham College. Commissioned Royal Air Force, Nov. 1936. Served War of 1939-45 (despatches, DSO); retired, 1959. Commanded No 3 MHQ Unit, Royal Auxiliary Air Force. *Recreations:* sailing, caravanning. *Address:* Yonder Cross, South Brent, Devon TQ10 9DR.

van der LOON, Prof. Piet; Professor of Chinese, University of Oxford, since 1972; Fellow of University College, Oxford, since 1972; *b* 7 April 1920; *m* 1947, Minnie G. Snellen; two *d. Educ:* Univ. of Leiden. Litt. Drs Leiden, MA Cantab. Univ. Asst Lectr, Cambridge, 1948; Univ. Lectr, Cambridge, 1949. *Publications:* articles in Asia Major, T'oung Pao, Jl Asiatique. *Recreation:* travel. *Address:* University College, Oxford.

VANDERMEER, (Arnold) Roy; QC 1978; a Recorder of the Crown Court, since 1972; *b* London, 26 June 1931; *o s* of late William Arnold Vandermeer and Katherine Nora Vandermeer; *m* 1964, Caroline Veronica (*née* Christopher); one *s* two *d. Educ:* Dame Alice Owen's Sch., Islington; King's Coll., London (LLB). Called to Bar, Gray's Inn, 1955. Flt-Lt, RAF, 1955-58. *Recreations:* reading, cricket. *Address:* The Field House, Barnet Lane, Elstree, Herts. *T:* 01-953 2244.

van der MEULEN, Daniel; Netherlands Indies civil servant and diplomat; Arabist author and traveller; *b* 4 Sept. 1894; *m* 1st, 1917, A. C. E. Kelling; three *s* (and one *s* murdered in Germany) two *d*; 2nd, 1959, Dr H. M. Duhm; one *s. Educ:* Leyden Univ. Netherlands Indies Civil Service, North of Sumatra in Toba-lake district of Toba Batak country, 1915-23; studied Arabic and Islam under Prof. Dr C. Snouck Hurgronje, Leyden Univ.; consular and diplomatic service, Jeddah, Sa'oudi-Arabia, 1926-31; first exploration in South Arabia, 1931; Netherlands Indies Civil Service, Pajakumbuh, Central Sumatra, Palembang, South Sumatra, 1932-38; second exploration in South Arabia, 1939; Netherlands Indies Civil Service, Makassar, South Celebes, 1939-41; Minister in Jeddah, Sa'oudi-Arabia, 1941-45; Resident Adviser to Netherlands East India Government at Batavia, 1945-48; Chief of the Arabic Section of Radio Netherland World-broadcast at Hilversum, 1949-51. Hon. Mem., Royal Netherlands Geographical Soc., 1956. Officer, Oranje Nassau; Patron's Medal, Royal Geographical Society, London, 1947. *Publications:* Hadhramaut, some of its mysteries unveiled (with map by Prof. Dr H. von Wissmann), 1932; Aden to the Hadhramaut, 1947 (numerous trans.); Onbekend Arabië, 1947; Ontwakend Arabië, 1954; Mÿn weg naar Arabië en de Islaam, 1954; The Wells of Ibn Sa'ud, 1954; Verdwijnend Arabië, 1959; Faces in Shem, 1961; Ik Stond Erbÿ, het einde van ons koloniale rÿk, 1965; Hoort Ge de donder niet? (autobiog.), 1977, trans. as Don't You Hear the Thunder?: a Dutchman's story, 1981. *Address:* 9 Flierder Weg, 7213LT Gorssel, Holland. *T:* 05759-1684.

van der POST, Jan Laurens, FEng, FIMechE, FIGasE; Chief Executive, Water Research Centre, since 1978; *b* 26 Dec. 1928; *s* of Lt-Col Sir Laurens van der Post, *qv* ; *m* 1959, Tessa Broom; three *s* one *d. Educ:* Michaelhouse; Univ. of Natal, S Africa (BScEng). FEng 1978; FIMechE 1977; FIGasE 1977. Rolls-Royce Ltd: Trainee, 1952-54; Designer, 1954-57; Atomic Power Constructions Ltd: Technical Engr, 1957-59; Head of Engrg Div., 1959-64; British Gas Corp. (Gas Council): Res. Engr, 1964-66; Dir of Engrg Res. Stn, 1966-78. Member: Computers, Systems and Electronics Requirements Bd, 1976-79; Adv. Council for Applied Res. and Develt, 1980-. Hon. FIWPC 1978. Gold Medal, IGasE, 1978. *Publications:* articles and papers on pipelines and engrg. *Recreation:* gliding. *Address:* 1 Belbroughton Road, Oxford OX2 6UZ. *T:* Oxford 58364. *Club:* Athenæum.

van der POST, Sir Laurens (Jan), Kt 1981; CBE 1947; writer, farmer, soldier, explorer; *b* Philippolis, S Africa, 13 Dec. 1906; *s* of late C. W. H. Van Der Post, Chairman of Orange Free State Republic Volksraad, and late M. M. Lubbe, Boesmansfontein, Wolwekop, and Stilton; *m* 1928, Marjorie Wendt; one *s* one *d*; *m* 1949, Ingaret Giffard. Served War of 1939-45: Ethiopia; North Africa; Syria; Dutch East Indies; Java; commanded 43 Special Military Mission, Prisoner of War 1943-45, thereafter Lord Mountbatten's Military-Political Officer, attached to 15 Indian Army Corps, Java, and subseq. to British Minister, Batavia, until 1947. Since then has undertaken several missions for British Government and Colonial Development Corp. in Africa, including Government Mission to Kalahari, 1952. FRSL. Hon. DLitt: Univ. of Natal, 1964; Univ. of Liverpool, 1976; Rhodes Univ., 1978; St Andrews, 1980; DUniv Surrey, 1971. *Films:* Lost World of Kalahari, 1956; A Region of Shadow, 1971; The Story of Carl Gustav Jung, 1971; All Africa Within Us, 1975; Zulu Wilderness: Black Umfolozi Re-discovered, 1979. *Publications:* In a Province, 1934; Venture to the Interior, 1952 (Book Society choice and Amy Woolf Memorial Prize); A Bar of Shadow, 1952 (repr., 1972); The Face Beside the Fire, 1953; Flamingo Feather, 1955 (German Book Society choice); The Dark Eye in Africa, 1955; Creative Pattern in Primitive Man, 1956; The Lost World of the Kalahari, 1958 (American Literary Guild Choice); The Heart of the Hunter, 1961; The Seed and the Sower, 1963 (South African CNA Award for best work published in 1963); Journey into Russia, 1964; A Portrait of all The Russias, 1967; The Hunter and the Whale, 1967 (CNA and Yorkshire Post Fiction Awards); A Portrait of Japan, 1968; The Night of the New Moon, 1970; A Story like the Wind, 1972; A Far Off Place, 1974; A Mantis Carol, 1975; Jung and the Story of Our Time, 1976; First Catch Your Eland: a taste of Africa, 1977; Yet Being Someone Other, 1982. *Recreations:* walking, climbing, ski-ing, tennis, studying grasses and cooking in winter. *Address:* lives, London, Aldeburgh, Suffolk, and Wolwekop, Philippolis, South Africa.
See also J. L. van der Post.

VANDYK, Neville David, PhD; Editor, Solicitors' Journal, since 1968; *b* 6 Sept. 1923; *yr s* of late Arthur Vandyk, solicitor, and Constance Vandyk (*née* Berton); *m* 1956, Paula (*née* Bochert); one *d. Educ:* St Paul's Sch.; London School of Economics, Univ. of London (BCom 1947, PhD 1950). Admitted Solicitor, 1957. HM Forces, incl. service in India, Burma and Japan, 1942-46; research asst, LSE, 1951-52; with Herbert Oppenheimer, Nathan & Vandyk, Solicitors, 1953-58; Asst Editor, 1958, Managing Editor, 1963, Solicitors' Journal; Member for its duration, Law Society's Constitution Cttee prior to the adoption in 1969 of their mainly current Bye-Laws, 1966-68. Founder Mem., W London Law Soc. (Pres., 1970-71); Mem. Council, Medico-Legal Soc., 1963-66, Vice-Pres. 1966-67, Hon. Treas. 1967-; Founder Mem., Assoc. of Disabled Professionals, Vice-Chm. 1972-80; Mem. for its duration, Royal Bor. of Kensington and Chelsea's Working Gp on the Disabled and their Families, 1980-81. Governor (nominated by Univ. of London) William Blake County Secondary Sch., 1957-70. Freeman 1962, Liveryman 1963, Worshipful Co. of Solicitors of City of London. Founder's Meml Lecture, Brit. Council for Rehabilitation of the Disabled, 1971; Hon. Prof. of Legal Ethics, Univ. of Birmingham, 1981-83. *Publications:* Tribunals and Inquiries, 1965; Accidents and the Law, 1975, 2nd edn 1979; (title) National Health Service, in Halsbury's Laws of England, 3rd edn 1959, 4th edn 1982. *Address:* 7 Addisland Court, Holland Villas Road, W14 8DA. *T:* 01-603 8521.

VANE; *see* Fletcher-Vane, family name of Baron Inglewood.

VANE, family name of **Baron Barnard.**

VANE, Dr John Robert, FRS 1974; Group Research and Development Director, The Wellcome Foundation, since 1973; *b* 29 March 1927; *s* of Maurice Vane and Frances Florence Vane (*née* Fisher); *m* 1948, Elizabeth Daphne Page; two *d*. *Educ:* Univs of Birmingham and Oxford. BSc Chemistry Birmingham, 1946; BSc Pharmacology Oxon, 1949; DPhil 1953; DSc 1970. Stothert Research Fellow of Royal Soc., 1951-53; Asst Prof. of Pharmacology, Yale Univ., 1953-55; Sen. Lectr in Pharmacology, Inst. of Basic Medical Sciences, RCS, 1955-61; Reader in Pharmacology, RCS, Univ. of London, 1961-65; Prof. of Experimental Pharmacology, RCS, Univ. of London, 1966-73. Visiting Professor: King's Coll., London, 1976; Charing Cross Hosp. Med. Sch., 1979; Harvard Univ., 1979. British Pharmacological Soc.: Meetings Sec., 1967-70; Gen. Sec., 1970-73; For. Sec., 1979-. Mem., Royal Acad. of Medicine, Belgium, 1978. Foreign Member: Royal Netherlands Acad. of Arts and Scis, 1979; Polish Acad. of Scis, 1980; For. Hon. Mem., Amer. Acad. of Arts and Scis, 1982; Hon. Mem., Polish Pharmacological Soc., 1973; Hon. FACP, 1978. Hon. DM Krakow, 1977; Hon. Dr René Descartes Univ., Paris, 1978; Hon. DSc Mount Sinai Med. Sch., NY, 1980. (Jtly) Albert Lasker Basic Med. Res. Award, 1977; Baly Medal, RCP, 1977; (jtly) Peter Debye Prize, Univ. of Maastricht, 1980; Feldberg Foundn Prize, 1980; Ciba Geigy Drew Award, Drew Univ., 1980; Dale Medal, Soc. for Endocrinol., 1981; Nobel Prize for Medicine (jtly), 1982. *Publications:* (ed jtly) Adrenergic Mechanisms, 1960; (ed jtly) Prostaglandin Synthetase Inhibitors, 1974; (ed jtly) Metabolic Functions of the Lung, Vol. 4, 1977; (ed jtly) Handbook of Experimental Pharmacology, 1978; (ed jtly) Prostacyclin, 1979; (ed jtly) Interactions Between Platelets and Vessel Walls, 1981; numerous papers in learned jls. *Recreations:* photography, travel, underwater swimming. *Address:* White Angles, 7 Beech Dell, Keston Park, Kent BR2 6EP. *T:* Farnborough 53128. *Club:* Athenæum.

VANE-TEMPEST-STEWART, family name of **Marquess of Londonderry**.

VANGEKE, Most Rev. Sir Louis, MSC, KBE 1980 (OBE 1974); Member, Legion of Honour of French Republic, 1980; Bishop of Bereina, Papua New Guinea, 1976-80, and Auxiliary to Archbishop V. P. Copas (RC), 1974; Member, Society of Missionaries of the Sacred Heart of Jesus, French Province, 1941; *b* 25 June 1904; *s* of Vagu'u Kaoka, Veifa'a; *Educ:* CM Yule Island, 1909-19; Minor and Major Jesuit Seminary of Madagascar; Little Brother Oblate of St Joseph, 1922-28; in training for 12 years for his ordination as first Papuan Priest in the Roman Catholic Church, in Madagascar, 1928-37, and worked for many years among Kuni people in Papua, 1941-70; Auxiliary Bishop of Port Moresby, 1970-73 (RC Bp of Culusi); ordained first indigenous Papuan Bishop of RC Church by Pope Paul VI, in Sydney, 1970, and acclaimed Chief (*hc*) of Mekeo Village of Veifa'a, Papua, 1970. Hon. LLD Univ. of Papua New Guinea, 1974. *Publications:* Liturgical Texts in the Kuni language, 1969-70; composed music for jubilee mass, 1962; hymns; songs. *Address:* Catholic Parish, Kubana CP, PO Box 177, Port Moresby, Papua New Guinea.

van HASSELT, Marc; Headmaster, Cranleigh School, since 1970; *b* 24 April 1924; *s* of Marc and Helen van Hasselt; *m* 1949, Geraldine Frances Sinclair; three *s* one *d*. *Educ:* Sherborne; Selwyn Coll., Cambridge (MA). Served War of 1939-45 (despatches): commissioned in Essex Yeomanry, RHA, 1944; served North-West Europe. Lecturer in Commonwealth Studies, RMA, Sandhurst, 1950-58; Asst Master, Oundle School, 1959-70 (Housemaster, Sanderson House, 1963-70). *Publications:* occasional articles in Yachting World. *Recreation:* cruising under sail. *Address:* Headmaster's House, Cranleigh School, Cranleigh, Surrey. *T:* Cranleigh 274640; Winton Close, Lymington, Hants. *Clubs:* East India, Devonshire, Sports and Public Schools, Royal Cruising.

van HEYNINGEN, William Edward, MA Oxon, ScD Cantab; Master of St Cross College, Oxford, 1965-79, Hon. Fellow, 1979; Reader in Bacterial Chemistry, University of Oxford, 1966-79, now Emeritus; *b* 24 Dec. 1911; *s* of late George Philipus Stephanus van Heyningen and late Mabel Constance (*née* Higgs); *m* 1940, Ruth Eleanor Treverton; one *s* one *d*. *Educ:* village schools in S Africa; Univs of Stellenbosch and Cambridge. Commonwealth Fund Fellow, Harvard Univ., and College of Physicians and Surgeons, Columbia Univ., 1936-38; Senior Student of Royal Commn for Exhibn of 1851, 1938-40. Staff Member, Wellcome Physiological Research Laboratories, 1943-46; Sen. Res. Officer, Sir William Dunn School of Pathology, Oxford Univ., 1947-66; Sec., Soc. for Gen. Microbiology, 1946-52; Curator of the Bodleian Library, 1961-; Mem. Hebdomadal Council, Oxford Univ., 1963-69. Vis. Prof., State Univ. of New York, 1967. Visitor of the Ashmolean Museum, 1969-. Trustee, Ruskin Sch. of Drawing, 1975-77. Consultant, Cholera Adv. Cttee, Nat. Insts of Health, USA, 1968-73. Chevalier de l'Ordre National du Mérite, 1980. *Publications:* Bacterial Toxins, 1950; Cholera: the American scientific experience 1947-1980, 1982; papers mainly concerned with bacterial toxins in various books and journals. *Address:* College Farm, North Hinksey Village, Oxford OX2 0NA. *Club:* Reform.

van LENNEP, Jonkheer Emile; Commander, Order of Orange Nassau; Knight, Order of the Netherlands Lion; Secretary-General, OECD, since Oct. 1969; *b* 20 Jan. 1915; *s* of Louis Henri van Lennep and Catharina Hillegonda Enschede; *m* 1941, Alexa Alison Labberton; two *s* two *d*. *Educ:* Univ. of Amsterdam. Foreign Exchange Inst., 1940-45; Netherlands Bank, 1945-48; Financial Counsellor, High Representative of the Crown, Indonesia, 1948-50; Netherlands Bank, 1950-51. Treasurer-General, Ministry of Finance, The

Netherlands, 1951-69. Chairman: Monetary Cttee, EEC, 1958; Working Party No 3, OECD, 1962; Mem., Board Directors, KLM (Airline), 1951. KStJ. Grand Officer or Comdr in various foreign orders. *Address:* (office) OECD, 2 rue André Pascal, 75775 Paris Cedex 16, France; (private) 92 avenue Henri Martin, 75116 Paris, France. *Club:* Haagsche (The Hague).

van MAURIK, Ernest Henry, OBE 1944; HM Diplomatic Service, retired; *b* 24 Aug. 1916; *s* of late Justus van Maurik and Sybil van Maurik (*née* Ebert); *m* 1945, Winifred Emery Ritchie Hay; one *s* one *d*. *Educ:* Lancing Coll.; Ecole Sup. de Commerce, Neuchatel, Switzerland. Worked in Tea Export, Mincing Lane, 1936-39. Commnd as 2nd Lt, in Wiltshire Regt, 1939; seconded to Special Ops Exec., 1941-46; demob. with hon. rank of Lt-Col (subst. Major), 1946. Joined Foreign Office, 1946; Moscow, 1948-50; West Germany and West Berlin, 1952-56; Buenos Aires, 1958-62; Copenhagen, 1965-67; Rio de Janeiro, 1968-71; FCO, 1971-75. Officier de la Couronne (Belgium), 1944. *Recreations:* golf, gardening, languages. *Address:* Parkside, The Common, Sevenoaks, Kent. *T:* Sevenoaks 452173. *Club:* Special Forces.

van MEERBEKE, René Louis Joseph Marie; Grand Officier, Orders of the Crown and of Léopold II (Belgium); Commander, Order of Leopold II (with swords); Officer, Orders of Léopold and of the Crown (with swords); Croix de Guerre (Belgium), 1914-18 (with palms); Croix de Feu; Civil Cross (1st Class); *b* 15 Nov. 1895; *m* 1926, Léonor Restrepo del Corral; two *s* one *d*. *Educ:* University of Ghent (Licentiate of Faculty of Law in Commercial and Consular Sciences). Entered Diplomatic Service, 1920; Secretary, Legation, Lima, 1921; Chargé d'Affaires a.i. Bogota, 1924; Chargé d'Affaires, 1936; Minister, Bogota, 1945; Ambassador, Rio de Janeiro, 1954; Ambassador to the Court of St James's, 1957-61, and concurrently Belgian Perm. Rep. to Council of WEU. Entrusted with special missions as Representative of the Belgian Government at the investitures of new Presidents of the Republic: in Colombia, in 1946, 1950 and 1958; in Ecuador in 1948 and 1952, and in Brazil in 1956. Grand Cross Orders of Merit (Ecuador), Southern Cross (Brazil), Boyaca and San Carlos (Colombia); Grand Officer of Aztec Eagle (Mexico); Commander, Legion of Honour; Commander, Order of the Liberator (Venezuela); Officer, Order of the Sun (Peru); Golden Medal of the French Reconnaissance, etc. *Recreation:* horse riding. *Address:* Carrera 10, 8450 (Apt 701), Bogotá, Colombia. *Clubs:* Cercle Royal Gaulois (Vice-Pres.) (Brussels); Royal Golf Club de Belgique.

VANN, William Stanley, DMus(Cantuar); *b* 15 Feb. 1910; *s* of Frederick and Bertha Vann; *m* 1934, Frances Wilson; one *s* one *d*. *Educ:* privately. BMus London; FRCO; ARCM. Asst Organist, Leicester Cath., 1931-33; Chorus Master, Leicester Phil. Soc., 1931-36; Organist and Choirmaster, Gainsborough Parish Ch., Dir of Music, Queen Elizabeth Grammar Sch. and High Sch., Gainsborough, Conductor, Gainsborough Mus. and Orch. Socs, also Breckin Choir, Doncaster, 1933-39; Organist and Choirmaster, Holy Trinity PC, Leamington Spa, Founder-Conductor, Leamington Bach Choir and Warwicks Symph. Orch., and Dir of Music, Emscote Lawn Sch., Warwick, 1939-45. Served War of 1939-45, RA, final rank Captain. Master of Music, Chelmsford Cath., Conductor, Chelmsford Singers and Essex Symph Orch., Prof., Trinity Coll. of Music, London, 1949-53; Master of Music, Peterborough Cath., Conductor, Peterborough Phil. Choir and Orch., 1953-77, retired. Examiner, TCL; Mem. Council and Examr RCO, 1972-; Mem., ISM; Adjudicator: Brit. Fed. of Festivals, 1950-; Canadian Fed. Fest.; Hong Kong Fest.; Chairman: Peterborough Music Fest., 1953-; Eastern Area Council, British Fedn of Music Festivals, 1982-. Hon. DMus Cantuar 1971 (for eminent services to church music); Hon. FTCL 1953. *Publications:* Evening Services in E minor and C major; anthems and choral arrangements of folk-songs and of Handel; also various chants. *Recreations:* railway modelling, painting, gardening. *Address:* Holly Tree Cottage, Wansford, Peterborough PE8 6PL. *T:* Stamford 782192.

VANNECK, family name of **Baron Huntingfield**.

VANNECK, Air Commodore Hon. Sir Peter Beckford Rutgers, GBE 1977 (OBE (mil.) 1963); CB 1973; AFC 1955; AE 1954; MA, DSc, JP; DL; Member (C) Cleveland, European Parliament, since 1979; *b* 7 Jan. 1922; *y s* of 5th Baron Huntingfield, KCMG and Margaret Eleanor, *d* of Judge Ernest Crosby, NY; *m* 1943, Cordelia, *y d* of Captain R. H. Errington, RN (retd); one *d* (and one *d* decd). *Educ:* Geelong Grammar Sch.; Stowe Sch. (Scholar); Trinity Coll., Cambridge (MA); Harvard. MIAgrE; TEng (CEI). Cadet, RN, 1939; served in Nelson, King George V, Eskimo, 55th LCA Flot., Wren, MTB 696 (in comd), 771 Sqdn and 807 Sqdn FAA, resigned 1949; Leamington 1949; Cambridge Univ. Air Sqdn, 1949; 601 (Co. of London) Sqdn RAuxAF, 1950-57 (101 Sqdn Mass. Air Nat. Guard, 1953); 3619 (Co. of Suffolk) Fighter Control Unit, 1958-61 (in comd 1959-61); No 1 Maritime HQ Unit, 1961-63; Group Captain, 1963; Inspector RAuxAF, 1963-73, Hon. Inspector-General 1974-; ADC to the Queen, 1963-73; Hon. Air Cdre, No 1 (Co. Hertford) Maritime HQ Unit, RAuxAF, 1973-. Gentleman Usher to the Queen, 1967-79. Mem., Stock Exchange Council, 1968-79 (Dep. Chm., 1973-75). Prime Warden, Fishmongers' Co., 1981-82; Past Master: Gunmakers' Co., 1977; Guild of Air Pilots and Air Navigators, 1976-77; Alderman of Cordwainer Ward, City of London, 1969-79. Member: Ipswich Gp Hosps Bd, 1956-62; Gov. Body Brit. Post Graduate Medical Fedn, Univ. of London, 1963-71; St Bartholomew's Hosp. Bd of Governors, 1971-73; Special Trustee, St Bartholomew's Hosp., 1974-; Trustee: RAF Museum, 1976-; Royal Academy Trust, 1981-; Governor, Royal Shakespeare Theatre, 1974-. Mem., City and E London

AHA, 1973-77. KStJ (Mem. Chapter General). Hon. DSc City Univ. DL Greater London, 1970; Sheriff, City of London, 1974-75; Lord Mayor of London, 1977-78; High Sheriff, Suffolk, 1979. Churchwarden of St Mary-le-Bow. Supernumerary JP, City of London. Commander, Legion of Honour (France), 1981. *Recreations:* sailing, shooting, ski-ing, bad bridge. *Address:* White Lodge, Waldringfield, Suffolk. *T:* Waldringfield 244. *Clubs:* White's, Pratt's; Royal Yacht Squadron, Royal London Yacht (Commodore, 1977-78); Seawanhaka Corinthian Yacht (US).

See also Baron Huntingfield, H. D. Stevenson.

VAN OSS, (Adam) Oliver, MA; FSA; Master of the London Charterhouse, since 1973; *b* 28 March 1909; *s* of S. F. Van Oss, The Hague, newspaper proprietor; *m* 1945, Audrey (*d* 1960), *widow of Capt. J. R. Allsopp; two d. Educ:* Dragon Sch., Oxford; Clifton; Magdalen Coll., Oxford. Housemaster and Head of Modern Language Dept, Eton Coll.; Lower Master, Eton Coll., 1959-64, Acting Headmaster, 1964; Headmaster of Charterhouse, 1965-73. Mem. Council, City Univ.; Governor, Sherborne. Chevalier de la Légion d'Honneur. *Publications:* (ed jtly) Cassell's French Dictionary, 8th edn; articles on ceramics, travel and education. *Recreations:* all forms of art and sport except racing. *Address:* Master's Lodge, The Charterhouse, Charterhouse Square, EC1. *T:* 01-253 0272. *Clubs:* Athenæum, Beefsteak.

VAN PRAAGH, Dame Peggy, DBE 1970 (OBE 1966); Dance Consultant to Victorian Ministry for the Arts, since 1975; Member of Council and Guest Teacher, Australian Ballet School, since 1975; director and producer of ballet in UK and many other countries; *b* London, 1 Sept. 1910; *d* of Harold John Van Praagh, MD, and Ethel Louise Shanks. *Educ:* King Alfred Sch., Hampstead. Studied and trained in the Cecchetti Method of classical ballet with Margaret Craske; passed Advanced Cecchetti Exam., 1932; danced in Tudor's Adam and Eve, Camargo Society, 1932. Joined Ballet Rambert and danced at Ballet Club, 1933-38; created rôles in Tudor's Ballets: Jardin aux Lilas, Dark Elegies, Gala Performance, Soirée Musicale, etc; joined Tudor's Co., the London Ballet, as a Principal Dancer, 1938. Examiner and Cttee member, Cecchetti Society, 1937-. Joined Sadler's Wells Ballet as dancer and teacher, 1941; danced Swanhilda in Coppelia, Blue Girl in Patineurs, etc. Producer and Asst Director to Ninette De Valois, Sadler's Wells Theatre Ballet, and worked with that company, 1946-56. Produced many TV ballets for BBC. Guest Teacher and Producer for National Ballet of Canada, 1956; Guest Producer: Munich, Bavarian Opera House, 1956; Theatre Royal, Stockholm, 1957; Director: Norsk Ballet, 1957-58; Edinburgh International Festival Ballet, 1958; Borovansky Ballet in Australia, 1960; Guest Teacher: Jacob's Pillow, USA, 1959; Ballet of Marquis de Cuevas, 1961; Artistic Dir, Australian Ballet, 1962-74 and 1978. Brought Australian Ballet to Commonwealth Festival, London, 1965; to Expo '67 Montreal, followed by tour of S America, 1967. Hon. DLitt, Univ. of New England, NSW, 1974; Hon. LLD Melbourne, 1981. Queen Elizabeth II Coronation Award, Royal Academy of Dancing, 1965; Distinguished Artist Award, Australia Council, 1975. *Publications:* How I Became a Ballet Dancer, 1954; The Choreographic Art (with Peter Brinson), 1963. *Recreations:* motoring, swimming. *Address:* 5/248 The Avenue, Parkville, Victoria 3052, Australia.

van RIEMSDIJK, John Theodore, CIMechE; Keeper of Mechanical and Civil Engineering, Science Museum, since 1976; author and broadcaster; *b* 13 Nov. 1924; *s* of Adrianus K. van Riemsdijk and Nora P. van Riemsdijk (*née* James); *m* 1957, Jocelyn Kilma Arfon-Price. *Educ:* University College Sch.; Birkbeck Coll. (BA). Served SOE, 1943-46. Manufacturer of gearing, 1946-54; Science Museum: Asst, 1954; Lectr, 1961; Educn Officer, 1969. Engaged in setting up Nat. Railway Mus., York, 1973-75. *Publications:* Pregrouping Railways, 1972; Pictorial History of Steam Power, 1980; Compound Locomotives, 1982; Science Museum Books; contribs to: BBC Publications; Newcomen Soc. Trans. *Recreations:* oil painting, making models. *Address:* 2 Farquhar Street, Hertford. *T:* Hertford 52750.

VANSITTART, Guy Nicholas; *b* 8 Sept. 1893; *y s* of late Capt. Robert Arnold Vansittart and late Alice (*née* Blane). *Educ:* Eton; Trinity Coll., Oxford. BA (Oxon), Honour School of History. Captain, Indian Army, Central India Horse, 1913-22. *Address:* Flat 7, 20 Charles Street, W1X 7HD.

van STRAUBENZEE, Sir William (Radcliffe), Kt 1981; MBE 1954; MP (C) Wokingham since 1959; Second Church Estates Commissioner, since 1979; *b* 27 Jan. 1924; *o s* of late Brig. A. B. van Straubenzee, DSO, MC and late Margaret Joan, 3rd *d* of A. N. Radcliffe, Kensington Square, W8, and Bag Park, Widecombe-in-the-Moor, Newton Abbot, S Devon. *Educ:* Westminster. Served War of 1939-45: five years with Royal Artillery (Major); Regimental and Staff Appointments, including two years in Far East. Admitted a Solicitor, 1952. Chairman, Young Conservative Nat. Advisory Cttee, 1951-53; contested Wandsworth (Clapham), 1955; PPS to Minister of Educn (Sir David Eccles), 1960-62; Jt Parly Under-Sec. of State, Dept of Educn and Science, 1970-72; Minister of State, NI Office, 1972-74; Chm., Select Cttee on Assistance to Private Members, 1975-77; Chm., Cons. Parly Educn Cttee, 1979-. Mem. Exec. Cttee, 1922 Cttee, 1979-. Member of Richmond (Surrey) Borough Council, 1955-58. Chairman: United and Cecil Club, 1965-68 (Hon. Sec., 1952-59); Westminster House Boys' Club, Camberwell, 1965-68 (Hon. Sec., 1952-65); Nat. Council for Drama Training, 1976-81; Mem., Court of Reading Univ. Hon. Sec., Fedn of Conservative Students, 1965-71, Vice-Pres., 1974. A Church Comr; Mem. House of Laity, Church Assembly, 1965-70, Mem. General Synod, 1975-; Chm., Dioceses

Commn, 1978-; Patron of Living of Rockbourne, Hants. Trustee, Lambeth Palace Library. Hon. Vice-Pres., National Union of Students. *Recreations:* walking, swimming, reading. *Address:* 199 Westminster Bridge Road, SE1. *T:* 01-928 6855; 30 Rose Street, Wokingham, Berkshire. *T:* Wokingham 784464. *Clubs:* Carlton; Leander.

van WACHEM, Lodewijk Christiaan; Knight in the Order of the Netherlands Lion, 1981; CBE (Hon.) 1977; mechanical engineer, Netherlands; President, Royal Dutch Petroleum Co., The Hague, since 1982 (Managing Director, 1976-82); Member, Presidium of Board of Directors of Shell Petroleum NV; Managing Director, The Shell Petroleum Co. Ltd; Director, Shell Canada Ltd, since 1982; Chairman, Shell Oil Co., USA, since 1982; *b* Pangkalan Brandan, Indonesia, 31 July 1931; *m* 1958, Elisabeth G. Cristofoli; two *s* one *d. Educ:* Technological Univ., Delft (mech. engr). Joined BPM, The Hague, 1953; Mech. Engr, Compania Shell de Venezuela, 1954-63; Shell-BP Petr. Develt Co. of Nigeria: Chief Engr, 1963-66; Engrg Manager, 1966-67; Brunei Shell Petr. Co. Ltd: Head of Techn. Admin., 1967-69; Techn. Dir, 1969-71; Head of Prod. Div., SIPM, The Hague, 1971-72; Chm. and Managing Dir, Shell-BP Petr. Develt Co. of Nigeria, 1972-76; Co-ordinator, Exploration and Prod., SIPM, The Hague, 1976-79. *Address:* Carel van Bylandtlaan 30, The Hague, Holland. *T:* 070-77.21.18.

VARAH, (Doris) Susan, OBE 1976; Chairman, Mothers' Union Overseas, since 1977; *b* 29 Oct. 1916; *d* of Harry W. and Matilda H. Whanslaw; *m* 1940, Rev. (Edward) Chad Varah, *qv* ; four *s* (three of them triplets) one *d. Educ:* Trinity Coll. of Music. Mothers' Union: Diocesan Pres., Southwark, 1956-64; Vice-Chm., Central Young Members' Cttee, 1962-64; Central Vice-Pres., 1962-70; Vice-Chm., Central Social Problems Cttee, 1965-67, Chm., 1970-76; Chm., Central Overseas Cttee, 1968-70; Central Pres., 1970-76. *Recreations:* music, gardening, motoring. *Address:* 42 Hillersdon Avenue, SW13 0EF. *T:* 01-876 5720.

VARAH, Rev. Dr (Edward) Chad, OBE 1969; Founder, The Samaritans (to befriend the suicidal and despairing), 1953, President of London Branch, since 1974 (Director, 1953-74), Chairman, Befrienders International (Samaritans Worldwide), since 1974; Rector, Lord Mayor's Parish Church of St Stephen Walbrook, in the City of London, since 1953; a Prebendary of St Paul's Cathedral, since 1975; *b* 12 Nov. 1911; *e s* of Canon William Edward Varah, Vicar of Barton-on-Humber, and Mary (*née* Atkinson); *m* 1940, Doris Susan Whanslaw (*see* D. S. Varah); four *s* (three of them triplets) one *d. Educ:* Worksop Coll., Notts; Keble Coll., Oxford (Hon. Fellow 1981); Lincoln Theol. Coll. Exhibnr in Nat. Sci. (Keble); BA Oxon (Hons in PPE), 1933, MA 1943. Secretary: OU Russian Club, 1931; OU Slavonic Club, 1932; Founder Pres., OU Scandinavian Club, 1931-33. Deacon, 1935, Priest, 1936. Curate of: St Giles, Lincoln, 1935-38; Putney, 1938-40; Barrow-in-Furness, 1940-42; Vicar of: Holy Trinity, Blackburn, 1942-49; St Paul, Clapham Junction, 1949-53. Staff Scriptwriter-Visualiser for Eagle and Girl, 1950-61; Sec., Orthodox Churches Aid Fund, 1952-69; Pres., Cttee for Publishing Russian Orthodox Church Music, 1960-76; Chm., The Samaritans (Inc.), 1963-66; Pres., Internat. Fedn for Services of Emergency Telephonic Help, 1964-67. Hon. Liveryman, Worshipful Co. of Carmen, 1977. Hon. LLD Leicester, 1979. Roumanian Patriarchal Cross, 1968. Albert Schweitzer Gold Medal, 1972; Louis Dublin Award, Amer. Assoc. Suicidology, 1974; with Befrienders International, Prix de l'Institut de la Vie, 1978; Honra ao Mérito Medal, São Paulo TV, Brazil, 1982. *Publications:* Notny Sbornik Russkogo Pravoslavnogo Tserkovnogo Peniya, vol. 1 Bozhestveniya Liturgia, 1962, vol. 2 Pt 1 Vsenoshchnaya, 1975; (ed) The Samaritans, 1965; Samariter: Hilfe durchs Telefon, 1966; Vänskap sum hjälp, 1971; (ed) The Samaritans in the 70s, 1973, rev. edn 1977; Telephone Masturbators, 1976; (ed) The Samaritans in the 80s, 1980. *Recreations:* philology, travelling off the beaten track, opposing censorship. *Address:* St Stephen's Church, Walbrook, EC4N 8BN; 39 Walbrook, EC4N 8BP. *T:* 01-283 3400 and 01-283 4444. *Clubs:* Sion College (EC4); Oxford Union.

VARAH, Susan; *see* Varah, Doris S.

VARCOE, Jeremy Richard Lovering Grosvenor; HM Diplomatic Service; Head, Southern African Department, Foreign and Commonwealth Office, since 1982; *b* 20 Sept. 1937; *s* of Ronald Arthur Grosvenor Varcoe and late Zoe Elizabeth Varcoe (*née* Lovering); *m* 1961, Wendy Anne Moss; two *d. Educ:* Charterhouse; Lincoln Coll., Oxford (MA). National Service, Royal Tank Regt, 2nd Lieut, 1956-58. HMOCS: District Officer, Swaziland, 1962-65. Called to the Bar, Gray's Inn, 1966; Lectr in Law, Univ. of Birmingham, 1967-70; resigned to enter HM Diplomatic Service, 1970; FCO, 1970-72; Dep. Secretary General, Pearce Commn on Rhodesian Opinion, 1972; First Sec. (Information), Ankara, 1972-74; First Sec. and Head of Chancery, Lusaka, 1974-78; FCO, 1978-79; Commerical Counsellor, Kuala Lumpur, 1979-82. *Publication:* Legal Aid in Criminal Proceedings—a Regional Survey (Birmingham Univ.), 1970. *Recreations:* sailing, golf. *Address:* 133 Queens Road, Richmond, Surrey. *Club:* Royal Commonwealth Society.

VARLEY, Rt. Hon. Eric Graham, PC 1974; MP (Lab) Chesterfield, since 1964; Treasurer, Labour Party, since 1981; *b* 11 Aug. 1932; *s* of Frank Varley, retired miner, and Eva Varley; *m* 1955, Marjorie Turner; one *s. Educ:* Secondary Modern and Technical Schools; Ruskin Coll., Oxford. Apprentice Engineer's Turner, 1947-52; Engineer's Turner, 1952-55; Mining Industry (Coal) Craftsman, 1955-64. National Union of Mineworkers: Branch Sec.,

1955–64; Mem. Area Exec. Cttee, Derbyshire, 1956–64. Asst Govt Whip, 1967–68; PPS to the Prime Minister, 1968–69; Minister of State, Min. of Technology, 1969–70; Chm., Trade Union Gp of Labour MPs, 1971–74; Secretary of State: for Energy, 1974–75; for Industry, 1975–79; Principal Opposition Spokesman on employment, 1979–. *Recreations:* reading, gardening, music, sport. *Address:* House of Commons, SW1. *T:* 01-219 3000.

VARLEY, George Copley, MA, PhD Cantab, MA Oxon; Hope Professor of Zoology (Entomology), Oxford, 1948–78; *b* 19 Nov. 1910; *s* of late George Percy Varley and Elsie Mary Varley (*née* Sanderson); *m* 1955, Dr Margaret Elizabeth Brown; one *s* one *d*. *Educ:* Manchester Grammar Sch.; Sidney Sussex Coll., Cambridge. Scholar of Sidney Sussex Coll., 1929–33; First Class in both parts of Nat. Sci. Tripos, Frank Smart Prizeman in Zoology, 1933; Research Student, 1933–35; Research Fellow, Sidney Sussex Coll., 1935–38; Hon. Research Fellow, University of California, 1937–38. Supt of Entomological Field Station, Cambridge, 1933–37; University Demonstrator in Zoology, Cambridge, and Curator of Insects in the University Museum of Zoology, 1938–45. Experimental Officer, and later Senior Experimental Officer in Army Operational Research Gp, Min. of Supply, studying centimetric radar on South Coast, 1941–45. Reader in Entomology, King's Coll., Newcastle upon Tyne, 1945–48; Fellow of Jesus Coll., Oxford, 1948–78, Emeritus Fellow, 1978. *Publications:* (with G. R. Gradwell and M. P. Hassell) Insect Population Ecology, 1973; various papers on insects and population dynamics in scientific periodicals. *Recreations:* games included squash racquets, tennis, etc; sedentary pastimes included sailing, gliding, ski-ing; now reduced to gardening. *Address:* 18 Apsley Road, Oxford OX2 7QY. *T:* Oxford 56988.

VARNAM, Ivor, CEng, FIEE; Deputy Director, Royal Armament Research and Development Establishment, 1974–82, retired; *b* 12 Aug. 1922; *s* of Walter Varnam and Gertrude Susan Varnam (*née* Vincent); *m* 1942, Doris May Thomas; two *s*. *Educ:* Alleyn's Coll., Dulwich; University Coll., Cardiff; Birkbeck Coll., London. BSc Wales 1944; BSc (Hons) London 1952; CEng, FIEE 1973. Served War, RAF, 1940–46 (commnd 1944). Joined Tannoy Products, 1946; Atomic Energy Research Estabt, 1947; Siemens Bros., 1948; Royal Armament Research and Development Estabt, 1953–60 and 1962–82 (Defence Research Staff, Washington, USA, 1960–62), as: Supt Mil. ADP Br., 1964; Supt GW Br., 1967; Prin. Supt Systems Div., 1969; Head, Applied Physics Dept, 1972. *Publications:* official reports. *Recreations:* gardening, photography, bridge, music. *Address:* Fort Halstead, Sevenoaks, Kent TN14 7BP. *T:* Sevenoaks 55211.

VARVILL, Michael Hugh, CMG 1959; *b* 29 Sept. 1909; *s* of Dr Bernard and Maud Varvill; unmarried. *Educ:* Marlborough; New Coll., Oxford (Scholar, BA). Appointed to Colonial Service, Nigeria, 1932; seconded to Colonial Office, 1943–47; Senior District Officer, 1951; Nigeria, Permanent Secretary: Ministry of Transport, 1952; Ministry of Works, 1953–54; and again (Federal) Ministry of Transport, 1955, retired 1960. With G. Bell & Sons, publishers, 1960–73 (Dir, 1963–73). *Recreations:* tennis, hockey, chess. *Address:* 125 Marsham Court, Marsham Street, SW1. *Club:* Travellers'.

VASARY, Tamàs; pianist and conductor; Joint Musical Director, Northern Sinfonia Orchestra, since 1979; *b* 8 Nov. 1933; *s* of Jozsef Vàsary and Elizabeth (*née* Baltazàr); *m* 1967, Ildiko (*née* Kovàcs). *Educ:* Franz Liszt Music Academy, Budapest. First concert at age of 8 in Debrecen, Hungary; First Prize, Franz Liszt Competition, Budapest, 1947; prizes at internat. competitions in Warsaw, Paris, Brussels, Rio de Janeiro; Bach and Paderewski medals, London, 1961; début in London, 1961, in Carnegie Hall, NY, 1961; plays with major orchestras and at festivals in Europe, USA, Australasia and Far East; 3 world tours. Conducting debut, 1970; conducts in Europe and USA. Records Chopin, Debussy, Liszt, Rachmaninov (in Germany). *Recreations:* yoga, writing, sports. *Address:* 9 Village Road, N3. *T:* 01-346 2381.

VASCONCELLOS, Josephina de, Hon. DLitt; FRBS; Founder Member, Society of Portrait Sculptors; Founder, Outpost Emmaus; current projects: Adventure Base for Deprived Youngsters; The Harriet Trust, Beached Trawler adapted for Nature-observation Base for Young Disabled; *d* of late H. H. de Vasconcellos, Brazilian Consul-General in England, and Freda Coleman; *m* 1930, Delmar Banner, painter. *Educ:* sculpture: London, Paris, Florence; Royal Academy Schools. Works: High Altar and Statue, Varengeville, Normandy, 1925; Bronze St Hubert, Nat. Gall. of Brazil, 1926; Music in Trees, in stone, Southampton Gall., 1933; Ducks, in marble, Glasgow Art Gall., 1946; Refugees, in stone, Sheffield Art Gall., 1949; Episcopal Crozier in Perspex, for Bristol Cathedral, 1948. Exhibits RA, Leicester Galls. Exhibn with husband, of 46 sculptures in 20 materials at RWS Gall., 1947; Last Chimera, Canongate Kirk, Edinburgh; 8ft Christ (in Portland Stone), Nat. War Meml to Battle of Britain, Aldershot, 1950. Two works, Festival of Britain, Lambeth Palace, 1951; Sculpture Exhibn, with husband, RWS Galls, 1955; War Memorial, St Bees Wood, 1955; two figures, St Bees Priory, 1955; life-size Mary and Child and design group of 11 sculptures by 11 collaborators, for Nativity, St Paul's Cathedral, Christmas 1955; Mary and Child bought for St Paul's, 1956; life-size Resurrection for St Mary, Westfield, Workington, 1956–57; Madonna and Child, St James's, Piccadilly, 1957; Rising Christ in St Bartholomew the Great, Smithfield; Winter, carving in Perspex, Oldham Gallery, 1958; Nativity (for ruins of Coventry Cathedral), 1958; Flight into Egypt, for St Martin-in-the-Fields, 1958 (now

in Cartmel Priory); War Memorial, Reredos of carved oak, Rossall School Chapel, 1959; Nativity Set, life-size figures, St Martin-in-the-Fields, annually in Trafalgar Sq.; Winged Victory Crucifix, Clewer Church, 1964, and Canongate Kirk, Edinburgh; life-size Holy Family, Liverpool Cathedral and Gloucester Cathedral, 1965; life-size Virgin and Child, Blackburn Cathedral, 1974; Reunion, Bradford Univ., 1977; Return of the Carpenter, group of 10 life-size children, Samlesbury Hall, 1978; sculptures at Dallas, Tulsa, Chicago, USA; Portraits: bronze of Lord Denning, 1969; Bishop Fleming; Rev. Austen Williams and Mario Borelli. Documentary film Out of Nature (on her work), 1949; BBC programme, Viewpoint TV, 1968. Pres., Guild of Lakeland Craftsmen, 1971–73. Hon. Member, Glider Pilots Regimental Assoc. Hon. DLitt Bradford, 1977. *Publications:* Woodcut illustrations for The Cup (Poems by F. Johnson), 1938; contrib. to They Became Christians (ed Dewi Morgan), 1966. *Recreation:* working on Jeu Libre (new methods of movements for blind and handicapped children); musical composition. *Address:* The Bield, Little Langdale, Ambleside, Cumbria LA22 9PD. *T:* Langdale 254. *Club:* Royal Over-Seas League.

VASEY, Sir Ernest (Albert), KBE 1959; CMG 1945; Financial and Economic Adviser, World Bank Development Service, 1962–66; Resident Representative, IBRD, Pakistan, 1963–66; *b* 27 Aug. 1901; *m* 1st, 1923, Norah May Mitchell; one *s*; 2nd, 1944, Hannah Strauss (*d* 1981); one *s*. Member Shrewsbury Town Council, England. Mayor of Nairobi, 1941–42, 1944–46; Member Kenya Legislative Council for Nairobi North, 1945–50; Member for Education, Health and Local Government for Kenya, 1950; Minister for Finance and Development, Kenya, 1952–59; Minister for Finance and Economics, Tanganyika, 1959–60; Minister for Finance, Tanganyika, 1960–62. Brilliant Star of Zanzibar, 2nd Class, 1955; Hilal-i-Quaid-i-Azam (Pakistan), 1966. *Address:* Box 14235, Nairobi, Kenya.

VASSAR-SMITH, Major Sir Richard Rathborne, 3rd Bt, *cr* 1917; TD; RA; Partner at St Ronan's Preparatory School, since 1957; *b* 24 Nov. 1909; *s* of late Major Charles Martin Vassar-Smith (2nd *s* of 1st Bt); *s* uncle, 1942; *m* 1932, Mary Dawn, *d* of late Sir Raymond Woods, CBE; one *s* one *d*. *Educ:* Lancing; Pembroke College, Cambridge. Employed by Lloyds Bank Ltd, 1932–37; Schoolmaster, 1938–39. War of 1939–45, Major, RA. *Recreation:* Association football (Cambridge, 1928–31). *Heir: s* John Rathborne Vassar-Smith [*b* 23 July 1936; *m* 1971, Roberta Elaine, *y d* of Wing Comdr N. Williamson; two *s*]. *Address:* Orchard House, Hawkhurst, Kent. *T:* Hawkhurst 2300. *Clubs:* Hawks (Cambridge); Rye Golf.

VAUGHAN, family name of **Earl of Lisburne.**

VAUGHAN, Viscount; David John Francis Malet Vaughan; artist; *b* 15 June 1945; *e s* of 8th Earl of Lisburne, *qv*; *m* 1973, Jennifer Jane Sheila Fraser Campbell, artist, *d* of James and Dorothy Campbell, Invergarry; one *s* one *d*. *Educ:* Ampleforth Coll. *Address:* The Glebe, Cross, Ness, Isle of Lewis.

VAUGHAN, Rt. Rev. Benjamin Noel Young; see Swansea and Brecon, Bishop of.

VAUGHAN, David Arthur John, QC 1981; QC (NI) 1981; *b* 24 Aug. 1938; *s* of late Captain F. H. M. Vaughan, OBE, RN, and of J. M. Vaughan; *m* 1967, Philippa Mary Maclure. *Educ:* Eton Coll.; Trinity Coll., Cambridge (MA). 2nd Lieut, 14th/20th King's Hussars, 1958–59. Called to the Bar, Inner Temple, 1962; Member: Bar Council, 1968–72; International Relations Committee of Bar Council, 1968–; UK Delegation to Consultative Committee of the Bars and Law Societies of the European Communities, 1978–81. *Recreations:* fishing, tennis. *Address:* B3 Albany, Piccadilly, W1; 1 Brick Court, Temple, EC4. *T:* 01-583 0777. *Club:* Brooks's.

VAUGHAN, Sir Edgar; see Vaughan, Sir G. E.

VAUGHAN, Elizabeth, (Mrs Ray Brown), FRAM; international operatic soprano; *b* Llanfyllin, Montgomeryshire; *m* 1968, Ray Brown (Principal Trombone, New Philharmonia, City of Birmingham SO); one *s* one *d*. *Educ:* Llanfyllin Grammar Sch.; RAM; Kathleen Ferrier Prize. Has sung leading roles in: Benvenuto Cellini; La Bohème; Midsummer Night's Dream; Madame Butterfly; Otello; Rigoletto; Simon Boccanegra; La Traviata; Il Trovatore; Turandot; Don Giovanni; Un Ballo in Maschera; Ernani; Nabucco; Aida; Cassandra; La Forza del Destino; Tosca; Idomeneo; Macbeth. Has appeared with: Royal Opera; ENO; WNO; Opera North; Vienna State Opera; Berlin State Opera; Hamburg State Opera; Metropolitan Opera, NY; Paris Opera. Has toured in: Europe; S Africa; USA; Australia; Canada and Japan. *Recreations:* tennis, driving, cookery. *Address:* c/o Music International, 13 Ardilaun Road, Highbury, N5; Oak Hill, Uphampton, Ombersley, Worcs WR9 0JR.

VAUGHAN, Ernest James, CBE 1961; retired as Director of Materials Research, Royal Naval Scientific Service; *b* 19 Oct. 1901; 3rd *s* of late James and Helena Vaughan; *m* 1927, Marjorie Solly; one *s* decd. *Educ:* Brockley; London University. BSc, MSc London; ARCS; DIC. Jun. Chemist, War Dept; Chemist, 1925–27; Chemist, Chemical Dept, Portsmouth Dockyard, 1927–36; Dep. Supt, then Supt, Bragg Laboratory, 1936–49; Dep. Dir, then Dir of Materials Research, Royal Naval Scientific Service, 1949–66. Hon. Treas., Royal Inst. of Chemistry, 1963–72. *Publications:* Protective Coatings for Metals, 1946; (monograph) Metallurgical Analysis; papers in learned jls.

Address: Flat 2, Ashmede, 56 West Cliff Road, Bournemouth, Dorset BH4 8BE. *T:* Bournemouth 764232.

VAUGHAN, Sir (George) Edgar, KBE 1963 (CBE 1956; OBE 1937); *b* 24 Feb. 1907; *s* of late William John Vaughan, BSc, of Cardiff, and Emma Kate Caudle; *m* 1933, Elsie Winifred Deubert (*d* 1982); one *s* two *d. Educ:* Cheltenham Grammar Sch.; Jesus Coll., Oxford (Exhibitioner and later Hon. Scholar; Hon. Fellow, 1966). 1st Cl. Honour School of Mod. Hist., 1928; 1st Cl. Honour School of Philosophy, Politics and Economics, 1929; Laming Travelling Fellow of the Queen's College, Oxford, 1929-31. Entered Consular Service, 1930; Vice-Consul at: Hamburg, 1931; La Paz, 1932-35; Barcelona, 1935-38; Buenos Aires, 1938-44; Chargé d'Affaires, Monrovia, 1945-46; Consul at Seattle, Washington, 1946-49; Consul-General at Lourenço Marques, 1949-53, Amsterdam, 1953-56; Minister and Consul-General at Buenos Aires, 1956-60; Ambassador, 1960-63 and Consul-General, 1963, at Panama; Ambassador to Colombia, 1964-66. Retired from Diplomatic Service, 1966. Univ. of Saskatchewan, Regina Campus: Special Lectr, 1966-67; Prof. of History, 1967-74; Dean of Arts and Science, 1969-73. FRHistS 1965. *Recreation:* golf. *Address:* 27 Birch Grove, W3 9SP. *Club:* Travellers'.

VAUGHAN, Gerard Folliott, FRCP; MP (C) Reading South, since 1974 (Reading, 1970-74); Minister of State (Consumer Affairs), Department of Trade, since 1982; *b* Xinavane, Portuguese E Africa, 11 June 1923; *s* of late Leonard Vaughan, DSO, DFC, and Joan Vaughan (*née* Folliott); *m* 1955, Joyce Thurle (*née* Laver); one *s* one *d. Educ:* privately in E Africa; London Univ.; Guy's Hosp. MB, BS 1947; MRCP 1949; Academic DPM London 1952; FRCP 1966; FRCPsych 1972. Consultant Staff, Guy's Hosp., 1958-79. Minister for Health, DHSS, 1979-82. Parly Mem., MRC, 1973-76; Alderman: LCC, 1955-61; LCC Streatham, 1961-64; GLC Lambeth, 1966-70; Alderman, GLC, 1970-72; Chm., Strategic Planning Cttee GLC, 1968-71; Mem., SE Economic Planning Council, 1968-71. Governor, UCL, 1959-68. Liveryman, Worshipful Co. of Barbers. Contested (C) Poplar, 1955. Hon. FFAS, 1978. *Publications:* various professional and general literary publications. *Recreation:* painting. *Address:* House of Commons, SW1. *Club:* Carlton.

VAUGHAN, Henry William Campbell, JP; DL; Lord Provost and Lord Lieutenant of the City of Dundee, 1977-80; *b* 15 March 1919; *s* of Harry Skene Vaughan and Flora Lamont Campbell Blair; *m* 1947, Margaret Cowie Flett; one *s* one *d. Educ:* Dundee Training Coll.; Logie and Stobswell Secondary Schools. Apprentice Stationer, Burns & Harris, 1934-39; RAF (Volunteer Reserve), 1939-46; Chief Buyer, Messrs Valentine & Son, Fine Art Publishers, Dundee, 1946-64; Group Purchasing Officer, Scott & Robertson (Tay Textiles Ltd), 1964-75; Stationery Manager, Burns & Harris Ltd, Dundee, 1975-78; Paper Sales Rep., James McNaughton Paper Gp Ltd, London, 1978-79. Mem., Inst. of Purchasing and Supply. JP Dundee, 1969; DL Dundee, 1980. Silver Jubilee Medal, 1977. *Recreations:* cine photography, fishing, water colour painting, sketching. *Address:* 15 Fraser Street, Dundee. *T:* Dundee 826175.

VAUGHAN, Hilda, (Mrs Charles Morgan); novelist; *b* Builth, Breconshire, 1892; *d* of late Hugh Vaughan Vaughan; *m* 1923, Charles Morgan, LLD, FRSL (*d* 1958); one *s* one *d. Educ:* privately. FRSL 1963. *Publications:* The Battle to the Weak; Here Are Lovers; The Invader; Her Father's House; The Soldier and the Gentlewoman; A Thing of Nought; The Curtain Rises; Harvest Home; Pardon and Peace; Iron and Gold; The Candle and the Light. *Plays:* She, too, was Young; Forsaking All Other (both with Laurier Lister); Introduction to Thomas Traherne's Centuries. *Address:* c/o Roger Morgan, 30 St Peter's Square, W6 9UH.
See also Marchioness of Anglesey, Roger H. V. C. Morgan.

VAUGHAN, Dame Janet (Maria), DBE 1957 (OBE 1944); DM, FRCP; FRS 1979; Principal of Somerville College, Oxford, 1945-67, Hon. Fellow since 1967; *b* 18 October 1899; *d* of William Wyamar Vaughan and Margaret Symonds; *m* 1930, David Gourlay (*d* 1963); two *d. Educ:* North Foreland Lodge; Somerville College, Oxford; University College Hospital (Goldsmid Entrance Scholar). Asst Clinical Pathologist, Univ. Coll. Hosp.; Rockefeller Fellowship, 1929-30; Beit Memorial Fellowship, 1930-33; Leverhulme Fellow, RCP, 1933-34; Asst in Clinical Pathology, British Post-Graduate Medical School, 1934-39; Mem. Inter-Departmental Cttee on Medical Schools, 1942; Nuffield Trustee, 1943; late Medical Officer in charge North-West London Blood Supply Depot for Medical Research Council. Mem., Royal Commn on Equal Pay, 1944; Chm., Oxford Regional Hosp. Board, 1950-51 (Vice-Chm. 1948); Member: Cttee on Economic and Financial Problems of Provision for Old Age, 1953-54; Medical Adv. Cttee of University Grants Cttee; University Grants Cttee on Libraries; Commonwealth Scholarship Commn in the UK. Fogarty Scholar, NIH, 1973. Hon. FRSM, 1980. Osler Meml Medal, Univ. of Oxford. Hon. Fellow, Wolfson Coll., Oxford, 1981. Hon. DSc: Wales, 1960; Leeds, 1973; Hon. DCL: Oxford, 1967; London, 1968; Bristol, 1971. *Publications:* The Anæmias, 1st edn 1934, 2nd edn 1936; The Physiology of Bone, 1969, 3rd edn 1981; The Effects of Irradiation on the Skeleton, 1973; numerous papers in scientific jls on blood diseases, blood transfusion and metabolism of strontium and plutonium isotopes; section on leukæmias, Brit. Ency. Med. Pract.; section on blood transfusion in British Surgical Practice, 1945. *Recreations:* travel, gardening. *Address:* 1 Fairlawn End, First Turn, Wolvercote, Oxford. *T:* Oxford 514069.

VAUGHAN, John Godfrey, FCA; Director, Brown Boveri Kent Ltd, since 1974 (Chairman, 1974-79); *b* 2 May 1916; *s* of Charles Godfrey Vaughan and Mabel Rose Hart; *m* 1st, 1948, Barbara Josephine Knowles (*d* 1967); one *d* ; 2nd, 1969, Lucia Maria Boer. *Educ:* Bedford Sch. Served War: with 4th Queens Own Hussars in Greece, N Africa, Italy and Austria, 1939-45 (2nd i/comd, 1944). Joined The Charterhouse Group Ltd, 1946; Dir, 1953; Dep. Chm., 1968-71; Chm., 1971-77; Dir, George Kent Ltd, 1961, Dep. Chm., 1963, Chm., 1970-74; Dir, Slough Estates, 1968-. *Recreations:* racing, reading, theatre. *Address:* 82 Hamilton Terrace, NW8 9UL. *T:* 01-286 1338. *Club:* City of London.

VAUGHAN, Roger Davison; General Manager, Fast Reactor Projects, National Nuclear Corporation Ltd, since 1977; *b* 2 Oct. 1923; *s* of David William and late Olive Marion Vaughan; *m* 1951, Doreen Stewart; four *s. Educ:* University High Sch., Melbourne; Univ. of Melbourne, Aust. BMechE. FEng, FIMechE. Engineer Officer, RAAF, 1945-46. Chemical Engr, Commonwealth Serum Laboratories, 1946-47; Works apprenticeship, C. A. Parsons & Co., 1948-49; Chief Engr, C. A. Parsons Calcutta, 1950-53; AERE, Harwell, 1954; Chief Engineer: Nuclear Power Plant Co., 1955-59 (Director, 1958); The Nuclear Power Group, 1960-75; Manager, Technology Div., Nuclear Power Co., 1976-77. Chairman: Gas-cooled Breeder Reactor Assoc., Brussels, 1970-; BSI Nuclear Standards Cttee, 1976-; Mem. Council, IMechE, 1977-81 (Chm., Energy Cttee, 1979). *Publications:* papers in jls of IMechE, Brit. Nuc. Energy Soc., World Energy Conf. *Recreations:* skiing, mountain walking; questionable performer on piano and clarinet. *Address:* Otterburn House, Manor Park South, Knutsford, Cheshire WA16 8AG. *T:* Knutsford 2514. *Clubs:* Ski of Great Britain; Himalayan (Bombay).

VAUGHAN, William Randal; Founder and Proprietor, W. R. Vaughan Ltd, since 1945; *b* 11 March 1912; *m* 1945, K. A. Headland; three *s* one *d. Educ:* Centaur Trade School, Coventry. FIProdE. Apprenticed, Alfred Herbert Ltd, 1926; Coventry Gauge & Tool Co. Ltd, 1933; A. C. Wickman Ltd, 1934; A. Pattison Ltd, 1942; C. G. Wade Ltd, London, 1943. Chairman, Machine Tool Industry Research Assoc., 1974; President, Machine Tool Trades Assoc., 1977-79. Member of Lloyd's. *Recreations:* squash, skiing, sailing, flying. *Address:* Rowley Bank, Rowley Lane, Arkley, Barnet, Herts EN5 3HS. *T:* 01-441 4800. *Clubs:* Lansdowne, Royal Automobile.

VAUGHAN-HUGHES, Brig. Gerald Birdwood, MC 1918; DL; JP; retired 1948; *b* 14 April 1896; *s* of Gerald Mainwaring Vaughan-Hughes and Isabel Bridget Crawford (*née* Birdwood); *m* 1927, Violet Mary Jessie (*d* 1968), *d* of Maj.-Gen. W. H. Kay, CB, DSO; two *s. Educ:* Wellington College; RMA Woolwich. Served European War, 1914-18 (wounded thrice, despatches, MC); RHA and RFA, 2nd Lt, 1914; RHA, 1916; India, RFA, 1919-28; Capt. 1926; ADC to C-in-C India, 1927-28; RHA, 1930; Staff Coll., 1931-32; Maj. 1934; SO: RA Southern Comd, 1934-35; Aldershot, 1936-37; GSO2, Palestine, 1939. War of 1939-45, AAG, Palestine, Greece and Crete, 1941; GSO1 RA, ME, 1941; Comdg Northumberland Hussars and II RHA, 1941-42; CRA (Brig.) 7th Armoured Div., 1942 (despatches twice), retired. DL 1958, JP 1956, High Sheriff, 1960, Monmouthshire. *Address:* Wyelands, Chepstow, Gwent. *T:* Chepstow 2127.

VAUGHAN-JACKSON, Oliver James, VRD 1951; FRCS; Consulting Orthopaedic Surgeon to London Hospital, since 1971; *b* 6 July 1907; *e s* of Surgeon Captain P. Vaughan-Jackson, RN, Carramore, Ballina, County Mayo; *m* 1939, Joan Madeline, *er d* of E. A. Bowring, CBE, St Johns, Newfoundland; two *s. Educ:* Berkhamsted School; Balliol Coll., Oxford; The London Hospital. Kitchener Scholar; BA, BM, BCh Oxon, 1932; MRCS, LRCP, 1932; FRCS 1936. House Physician, Demonstrator of Pathology, House Surgeon, Resident Accoucheur, and Surgical Registrar at The London Hosp. Surgeon Lieut-Comdr RNVR, Retd, Surgical specialist, Roy. Naval Hosp., Sydney, Australia. Sen. Registrar (Orthopædic), The London Hosp.; Orthopaedic Surgeon to: The London Hosp., 1946-71; St Bartholomew's Hosp., Rochester, 1947-70; Medway Hosp., 1970-71; Claybury Mental Hosp., 1946-64; Halliwick Cripples Sch., 1946-71; Cons. In Orthopaedics to Royal Navy, 1956-71; Vis. Prof. of Orthopaedics, Memorial Univ. of Newfoundland, 1971-73; Senior Consultant in Orthopaedics at St John's Gen. Hosp., St Clare Mercy Hosp. and Janeway Child Health Centre, St John's, Newfoundland, 1971-73. Fellow: British Orthopædic Assoc.; RSM (Pres., Section of Orthopædics, 1968-69); Med. Soc. London; Member: Soc. Internat. de Chirurgie Orthopédique et de Traumatologie; British Soc. for Surgery of the Hand. Former Mem., Editorial Board of Jl of Bone and Joint Surgery. Hon. DSc Memorial Univ. of Newfoundland, 1973. *Publications:* Sections on: Arthrodesis (Maingot's Techniques in British Surgery), 1950; Arthrodesis of the Hip, and Osteotomy of the Upper End of Femur (Operative Surgery, ed Rob and Smith), 1958; Surgery of the Hand; Orthopædic Surgery in Spastic conditions; Peripheral Nerve Injuries (Textbook of British Surgery, ed Sir Henry Souttar and Prof. J. C. Goligher), 1959; The Rheumatoid Hand; Carpal Tunnel Compression of the Median Nerve (Clinical Surgery, ed Rob and Smith), 1966; Surgery in Arthritis of the Hand, in Textbook of Rheumatic Diseases, 1968; The Rheumatoid Hand, in Operative Surgery, 2nd edn 1971; contribs to Jl of Bone and Joint Surgery, etc. *Recreations:* gardening, photography. *Address:* The White Cottage, Bowesden Lane, Shorne, near Gravesend, Kent DA12 3LA. *T:* Shorne 2321. *Club:* Naval and Military.

VAUGHAN-LEE, Charles Guy, DSC 1945; Chairman, Messrs J. & A. Scrimgeour Ltd, 1975-78; *b* 9 May 1913; *s* of Adm. Sir Charles Lionel Vaughan-Lee, KCB, and Lady (Rose Cecilia) Vaughan-Lee; *m* 1st, 1940,

Agnes Celestria (*née* King; *d* 1946); one *s* one *d* ; 2nd, 1949, Barbara Cecily Bryce (*née* Bateman; marr. diss. 1968); one *s* two *d* (and one adopted *s*); 3rd, 1978, Avril Barbara Curling (*née* Reed). *Educ:* Eton Coll.; Christ Church, Oxford. Served War, 1939-45: Lieut RNVR (mentioned in despatches, 1944). Joined J. & A. Scrimgeour Ltd, 1933; Partner, 1946; Sen. Partner, 1969. Comr, Public Works Loan Bd, 1973-. Chairman: Mental After-Care Assoc., 1965- (Mem., 1956); Bd, Royal Hosp. Home for Incurables, Putney, 1979- (Mem., 1956-; Hon. Treasurer, 1962-78). Member: Council, White Ensign Assoc., 1978-; RIIA, 1936-; Council, Missions to Seamen, 1981-; Advr, Royal Sailors Rests, 1981. *Recreation:* tennis. *Address:* Somerton Randle, Somerton, Somerset. *T:* Somerton 72205. *Clubs:* Travellers', MCC.

VAUGHAN-MORGAN, family name of **Baron Reigate**.

VAUGHAN-THOMAS, (Lewis John) Wynford, OBE 1974; MA Oxon; radio and television commentator since 1937; author, journalist; Director, Harlech Television Ltd; *b* 15 Aug. 1908; *s* of Dr David Vaughan-Thomas and Morfydd Vaughan-Thomas; *m* 1946, Charlotte Rowlands, MBE; one *s*. *Educ:* Swansea Grammar Sch.; Exeter College, Oxford. Keeper of MSS and Records, National Library of Wales, 1933; Area Officer, S Wales Council of Social Service, 1934-37; joined BBC, 1937. Dir of Programmes, Harlech Television Ltd, 1968-71. Commentator, Royal Commonwealth Tours, BBC War Correspondent, 1942-45; Governor, BFI, 1977-80. FRSA 1980. Hon. MA Open Univ., 1982. Croix de Guerre, 1945. *Publications: Royal Tour*, 1953-54, 1954; *Anzio*, 1961; *Madly in all Directions*, 1967; (with Alun Llewellyn) *The Shell Guide to Wales*, 1969; *The Splendour Falls*, 1973; *Gower*, 1975; *The Countryside Companion*, 1979; *Trust to Talk* (autobiog.), 1980; *Wynford Vaughan-Thomas's Wales*, 1981; *The Princes of Wales*, 1982. *Recreations:* mountaineering, sailing. *Address:* Pentower, Tower Hill, Fishguard, Dyfed. *T:* Fishguard 873424. *Clubs:* Climbers', Savile; Cardiff and County (Cardiff).

VAUX OF HARROWDEN, 10th Baron *cr* 1523; **John Hugh Philip Gilbey**; *b* 4 Aug. 1915; 2nd *s* of William Gordon Gilbey (*d* 1965) and Grace Mary Eleanor, 8th Baroness Vaux of Harrowden (*d* 1958); *S* brother, 1977; *m* 1939, Maureen Pamela, *e d* of Hugh Gilbey; three *s* one *d*. *Educ:* Ampleforth College; Christ Church, Oxford (BA 1937). Formerly Major, Duke of Wellington's Regt; served War of 1939-45. *Heir:* *s* Hon. Anthony William Gilbey [*b* 25 May 1940; *m* 1964, Beverley Anne, *o d* of Charles Alexander Walton; two *s* one *d*]. *Address:* Cholmondeley Cottage, 2 Cholmondeley Walk, Richmond, Surrey.

VAVASOUR, Comdr Sir Geoffrey William, 5th Bt *cr* 1828; DSC 1943; RN (retired); a Director of W. M. Still & Sons; *b* 5 Sept. 1914; *s* of Captain Sir Leonard Vavasour, 4th Bt, RN, and Ellice Margaret Nelson; *S* father, 1961; *m* 1st, 1940, Joan Robb (marr. diss. 1947); two *d* ; 2nd, 1971, Marcia Christine, *d* of late Marshall Lodge, Batley, Yorks. *Educ:* RNC Dartmouth. *Heir:* kinsman Hugh Bernard Moore Vavasour [*b* 4 July 1918; *m* 1950, Monique Pauline Marie Madeleine, *d* of Maurice Erick Beck; one *s* one *d*]. *Address:* 8 Bede House, Manor Fields, Putney, SW15. *Clubs:* Hurlingham; MCC, Royal Wimbledon Golf, All England Lawn Tennis.

VEAL, Group Captain John Bartholomew, CBE 1956; AFC 1940; Civil Aviation Safety Adviser, Department of Trade and Industry, 1972-74, retired; *b* 28 September 1909; *er s* of John Henry and Sarah Grace Veal; *m* 1933, Enid Marjorie Hill; two *s*. *Educ:* Christ's Hosp. Special trainee, Metropolitan-Vickers, 1926-27; commissioned in RAF as pilot officer, 1927; served in Nos 4 and 501 Squadrons and as flying Instructor at Central Flying School, transferring to RAFO, 1932; Flying-Instructor, Chief Flying Instructor, and Test Pilot, Air Service Training Ltd, 1932-39; recalled to regular RAF service, 1939; commanded navigation and flying training schools, 1939-43; Air Staff No. 46 Transport Group, 1944 and Transport Command, 1945-46 (despatches); released from RAF, 1946, to become Deputy Director of Training, Ministry of Civil Aviation; Director of Air Safety and Training, 1947; Director of Operations, Safety and Licensing, 1952; Deputy Director-General of Navigational Services, Ministry of Transport and Civil Aviation, 1958; Director-General of Navigational Services, Ministry of Aviation, 1959-62; Chief Inspector of Accidents, Civil Aviation Department, Board of Trade (formerly Min. of Aviation), 1964-68; Dir Gen. of Safety and Operations, DTI (formerly BOT), 1968-72. FRAeS 1967 (AFRAeS 1958). *Recreation:* trout fishing. *Address:* Woodacre, Horsham Road, Cranleigh, Surrey GU6 8DZ. *T:* Cranleigh 274490. *Club:* Royal Air Force.

VEALL, Harry Truman, CB 1963; Controller of Death Duties, Board of Inland Revenue, 1960-64, retired; *b* 19 Feb. 1901; 2nd *s* of late Wright Veall, Ewyas Harold, Herefs, and late Bertha Veall; *m* 1926, Lily Kershaw, *yr d* of Joshua E. Ryder, Alverthorpe, Wakefield, Yorks; two *d*. *Educ:* Wakefield Grammar Sch. LLB (external) London, 1926. Entered Civil Service, 1916; Asst Controller of Death Duties, 1953, Dep. Controller, 1957. *Address:* 20 Wincombe Drive, Ferndown, Dorset BH22 8HX. *T:* Ferndown 874726.

VEASEY, Josephine, CBE 1970; opera singer (mezzo soprano), retired; Teacher of voice production and interpretation, Royal Academy of Music and privately; *b* London, 10 July 1930; *m* (marr. diss.); one *s* one *d*. *Educ:* coached by Audrey Langford, ARCM. Joined chorus of Royal Opera House, Covent Garden, 1949; a Principal there, 1955- (interval on tour, in opera, for Arts Council). Sings at Royal Opera House, Glyndebourne, Metropolitan (NY), La Scala, and in France, Germany, Spain, Switzerland, South America;

operatic Roles include: Octavian in Der Rosenkavalier, 1966; Cherubino in Figaro; name role in Iphigenie; Dorabella in Cosi fan Tutte; Amneris in Aida, Fricka in Die Walküre; Fricka in Das Rheingold; name role in Carmen; Dido and Cassandra in the Trojans; Marguerite in The Damnation of Faust; Charlotte in The Sorrows of Werther; Eboli, Don Carlos; name role, Orfeo; Adalgesa and name role in Norma; Rosina in The Barber of Seville; Kundry in Parsifal; Gertrude in Hamlet, 1980. Concerts, 1960-70 (Conductors included Giulini, Bernstein, Solti, Mehta, Sargent). Verdi's Requiem; Monteverdi's Combattimento di Tancredi e Clorinda, Aix Festival, 1967; various works of Mahler; two tours of Israel (Solti); subseq. sang in Los Angeles (Mehta); then Berlioz: Death of Cleopatra, Royal Festival Hall, and L'enfance du Christ, London and Paris; Rossini's Petite Messe Solennelle, London and Huddersfield (with late Sir Malcolm Sargent); Handel's Messiah, England, Munich, Oporto, Lisbon; Berlioz' Romeo and Juliette, London, and Bergen Festival; Rossini's Stabat Mater, Festival d'Angers and London, 1971; Berlioz' Beatrice and Benedict, NY, and London; Emperor in 1st perf. Henze's We Come to the River, Covent Garden, 1976. Has sung Elgar's Dream of Gerontius all over England. Frequently makes recordings. Hon. RAM, 1972. *Recreations:* reading, gardening. *Address:* 13 Ballards Farm Road, South Croydon, Surrey CR2 7JB. *T:* 01-657 8158.

VEIL, Simone Annie, Chevalier de l'Ordre national du Mérite; Magistrate; *b* Nice, 13 July 1927; *d* of André Jacob and Yvonne (*née* Steinmetz); *m* 1946, Antoine Veil, Inspecteur des Finances, President of Manurhin and of International Aeroplane Co.; three *s*. *Educ:* Lycée de Nice; Lic. en droit, dipl. de l'Institut d'Etudes Politiques, Paris; qualified as Magistrate, 1956. Deported to Auschwitz and Bergen-Belsen, March 1944-May 1945. Ministry of Justice, 1957-69; Technical Advr to Office of Minister of Justice, 1969; Gen.-Sec., Conseil Supérieur de la magistrature, 1970-74; Minister of Health, France, 1974-79; Mem., European Parliament, 1979- (Pres. 1979-82). Monismanie Prize, 1978; Athens Prize, 1980; Charlemagne Prize, Prix Louise Weiss, 1981. *Dhc* : Princeton, 1975; Institut Weizmann, 1976; Yale, Cambridge, 1980; Edinburgh, Jerusalem, Georgetown, Urbino, 1981; Yeshiva, Sussex, 1982. *Publication:* (with Prof. Launay and Dr Soulé) L'Adoption, données médicales, psychologiques et sociales, 1969. *Address:* 11 place Vauban, 75007 Paris, France.

VENABLES, Harold David Spenser; Official Solicitor to the Supreme Court, since 1980; *b* 14 Oct. 1932; *s* of late Cedric Venables and Gladys Venables (*née* Hall); *m* 1964, Teresa Grace, *d* of late J. C. Watts; one *s* one *d*. *Educ:* Denstone College. Admitted Solicitor, 1956. Pilot Officer, Royal Air Force, 1957-58. Legal Assistant, Official Solicitor's Office, 1960; Secretary, Lord Chancellor's Cttee on the Age of Majority, 1965-67; Asst Official Solicitor, 1977-80. *Publications:* A Guide to the Law Affecting Mental Patients, 1975; contributor, Halsbury's Laws of England, 4th edn. *Recreations:* vintage cars, motoring and military history. *Address:* Penderel House, 287 High Holborn, WC1. *T:* 01-405 7641.

VENABLES, Richard William Ogilvie; Chairman, Apple and Pear Development Council, since 1980; *b* 23 Feb. 1928; *s* of late Canon and Mrs E. M. Venables; *m* 1952, Ann Richards; three *s* two *d*. *Educ:* Marlborough Coll.; Christ Church, Oxford (BA, MA). Joined former Mather and Crowther Ltd, as trainee, 1952; Account Group Director, 1965; Board Member, 1966; Mem. Executive Cttee, 1972; Managing Director, 1974; joined Board of Ogilvy and Mather International, 1975; Chm., Ogilvy Benson and Mather Ltd, 1978-81; retired early, 1981, to pursue new career in the making of musical instruments. *Recreations:* fly fishing, making violins/violas/lutes/harpsichords. *Address:* First Field, Combe Hay, Bath, Avon BA2 8RD. *T:* Bath 833694.

VENABLES-LLEWELYN, Sir John (Michael) Dillwyn-, 4th Bt *cr* 1890; farmer, since 1975; *b* 12 Aug. 1938; *s* of Sir Charles Michael Dillwyn-Venables-Llewelyn, 3rd Bt, MVO, and of Lady Delia Mary Dillwyn-Venables-Llewelyn, *g d* of 1st Earl St Aldwyn; *S* father, 1976; *m* 1st, 1963, Nina (marr. diss. 1972), *d* of late Lt J. S. Hallam; two *d* ; 2nd, 1975, Nina Gay Richardson Oliver; one *d* decd. *Recreation:* racing vintage cars. *Address:* Talwen Uchaf Farm, Garthbrengy, Brecon, Powys LD3 9TE. *T:* Brecon 4263.

VENEZUELA, Bishop of, since 1976; **Rt. Rev. Haydn Harold Jones**; Dean of St Mary's Cathedral, Caracas; *b* 22 Aug. 1920; *s* of Charles Samuel and Blodwen Jones (*née* Williams), Penarth, Glam. *Educ:* Brotherhood of Saint Paul, Barton. RAF, 1941-44. Deacon 1947, priest 1948, Diocese of Bradford. Curate of St Barnabas, Heaton, Bradford, 1947-49; Tor Mohun, Torquay, 1949-51; Chaplain RN, 1951-53; Licence to Officiate, Diocese of London, 1954-62, Diocese of Coventry, 1962-63; Curate of St Peter's, Coventry, 1963-64; Rector of Clutton, Diocese of Bath and Wells, 1964-76, with Cameley, 1975-76; Surrogate, 1972-76. *Recreations:* formerly tennis (rep. RN 1952), badminton, squash, bridge, films, theatre. *Address:* Bishop's House, Apartado 61, 116 del Este, Caracas, Venezuela. *T:* Caracas 91.47.27.

VENKATARAMAN, Ramaswamy; Member, Lok Sabha, 1952-57 and (for Madras South) since 1977; Minister of Finance and Industry, Government of India, since 1980; *b* 4 Dec. 1910; *s* of Ramaswami Iyer; *m* Janata; three *d*. *Educ:* Madras Univ. (MA, LLB). Formerly in practice as a lawyer, Madras High Court and Supreme Court; prominent trade union leader, also political and social worker. Mem., Provisional Parlt, 1950; Leader of the House, Madras Legislative Council, and Minister of Industries, 1957-67; Mem., Planning

Commn, Madras, 1967-71. Chm., Nat. Research and Develt Corp. Leader, Indian delegation to Internat. Labour Organisation, 1958, and delegate, UN Gen. Assembly, 1953-61. Managing Editor, Labour Law Jl, 1971-. *Address:* Ministry of Finance, New Delhi, India.

VENN, Edward James; Director-General, Royal National Institute for the Blind, since 1980; *b* 25 Nov. 1919; *s* of Sidney and Jennie Venn; *m* 1944, Anne Minter; one *s* one *d*. Qualified as Chartered Secretary and Administrator, 1949. Local Government Officer, 1937-51; General Secretary, Royal Leicester, Leicestershire and Rutland Instn for the Blind, 1952-58; Head, Services to the Blind Dept, RNIB, 1959-71; Dep. Director-General, RNIB, 1972-79. Chairman, Rehabilitation Commn, European Regional Cttee, World Council for the Welfare of the Blind, 1977-; Member: British National Cttee for Prevention of Blindness, 1980-; Cttee on Cultural Affairs, World Council for the Welfare of the Blind, 1980-; Council, Royal Commonwealth Soc. for the Blind, 1980-; Gen. Council, Southern and Western Reg. Assoc. for the Blind, 1980-. Director: Greater London Fund for the Blind Trustee Co. Ltd, 1980-; Greater London Fund for the Blind Charitable Purposes Trading Co. Ltd, 1980-; Sunshine Christmas Cards Ltd, 1980-; Sunshine Sales Ltd, 1980-. Hon. Sec., British Wireless for the Blind Fund, 1982-; Trustee, The Gift of Thomas Pocklington. *Publications:* various articles on blind welfare. *Recreations:* gardening, reading. *Address:* 3 Silverdale Avenue, Oxshott, Surrey. *T:* Oxshott 3130. *Club:* Rugby.

VENN, Air Commodore George Oswald, CBE 1945; *b* 15 Sept. 1892; *er s* of George Venn, Warrington; *m* 1st, 1923, Betty (*d* 1953), *d* of Alderman T. Stopher, Winchester; two *s* one *d*; 2nd, 1960, Monica, *d* of Rev. J. B. Cholmeley. *Educ:* Boteler Grammar Sch., Warrington. Architecture, 1909-14 (Student RIBA); served European War, 1914-16, Royal Fusiliers (University Public Sch. Bn), 1916-45, RFC and RAF (despatches twice). War of 1939-45, Iraq, Abyssinia, Western Desert, Fighter Command; Director of Personal Services, Air Ministry, 1943-45; retired, 1945. Executive Director Remploy Ltd, 1945-61. *Address:* Great Glemham, Saxmundham, Suffolk. *Club:* Royal Air Force.

VENTRY, 7th Baron, *cr* 1800; **Arthur Frederick Daubeney Olav Eveleigh-de-Moleyns;** *b* Norton Malreward, Som, 28 July 1898; *er s* of 6th Baron and Evelyn Muriel Stuart (*d* 1966), *y d* of Lansdowne Daubeney, Norton Malreward, Somerset; *S* father, 1936. *Educ:* Old Malthouse, Swanage; Wellington Coll., Berks. Served Irish Guards, 1917-18 (wounded); afterwards in RAF; served RAF, 1939-45. Certificated Aeronaut. King Håkon of Norway Freedom Medal, 1945. *Publications:* on aerostation and scouting. *Recreations:* music, travelling, airship piloting. *Heir:* nephew Andrew (Harold) Wesley Daubeny de Moleyns [*b* 28 May 1943; *m* 1963, Nelly Edouard Renée, *d* of Abel Chaumillon, Torremolinos, Spain; one *s* two *d*]. *Address:* Lindsay Hall, Lindsay Road, Branksome Park, Poole, Dorset. *Clubs:* Naval and Military, Norwegian, Balloon and Airship.

VERCO, Sir Walter (John George), KCVO 1981 (CVO 1970; MVO 1952); OStJ 1954; Secretary of the Order of the Garter, since 1974; Secretary to the Earl Marshal, since 1961; Surrey Herald of Arms Extraordinary, since 1980; *b* 18 January 1907; *s* of late John Walter Verco, Chelsea; *m* 1929, Ada Rose, *d* of late Bertram Leonard Bennett, Lymington, Hants; one *s* one *d*. Served War, 1940-45, with RAFVR, Flight Lt. Secretary to Garter King of Arms, 1949-60; Rouge Croix Pursuivant of Arms, 1954-60; Chester Herald, 1960-71; Norroy and Ulster King of Arms, 1971-80. Hon. Genealogist to Order of the British Empire, 1959-, to Royal Victorian Order, 1968-; Inspector, RAF Badges, 1970-, RAAF Badges, 1971-; Adviser on Naval Heraldry, 1970-. *Address:* College of Arms, Queen Victoria Street, EC4. *T:* 01-248 6185; 8 Park Court, Linkfield Lane, Redhill, Surrey. *T:* Redhill 71794.

VERCOE, Rt. Rev. Whakahuihui; *see* Aotearoa, Bishop of.

VERCORS; (pen-name of Jean Bruller); writer; designer-engraver (as Jean Bruller); Légion d'honneur; médaille de la Résistance; *b* Paris, 26 February 1902; *s* of Louis Bruller and E. Bourbon; *m* 1931, Jeanne Barusseaud (marr. diss.); three *s*; *m* Rita Barisse. *Educ:* Ecole Alsacienne, Paris. Dessinateur-graveur, 1926-; retrospective exhibitions: Vienne, 1970; Budapest, Cologne, 1971. Designed set and costumes for Voltaire's L'Orphelin de la Chine, Comédie Française, 1965. *Plays produced include:* Zoo, Carcassonne, 1963, Paris, 1964, and other European countries and USA; Oedipe-Roi (adaptation), La Rochelle, 1967, Paris, 1970; Le Fer et le Velours, Nîmes, 1969; Hamlet (adaptation), Lyons, 1977; Macbeth (adaptation), Anjou, Paris and Martinique, 1977. Founded Editions de Minuit clandestines, 1941, and began to publish under the name of Vercors. *Publications:* as Jean Bruller: albums: 21 Recettes de Mort Violente, 1926, repr. 1977; Hypothèses sur les Amateurs de Peinture, 1927; Un Homme Coupé en tranches, 1929; Nouvelle Clé des Songes, 1934; L'enfer, 1935; Visions intimes et rassurantes de la guerre, 1936; Silences, 1937; Les Relevés Trimestriels, planches dont l'ensemble (160 planches) forme La Danse des Vivants, 1932-38; nombreuses illustrations pour livres de luxe; as *Vercors:* Le Silence de la Mer, 1942; La Marche à l'Etoile, 1943; Le Songe, 1944; Le Sable du Temps, 1945; Les Armes de la Nuit, 1946; Les Yeux et la Lumière, 1948; Plus ou Moins Homme, 1950; La Puissance du jour, 1951; Les Animaux dénaturés (Borderline), 1952; Les Pas dans le Sable, 1954; Portrait d'une Amitié, 1954; Divagations d'un Français en Chine, 1956; Colères, 1956 (The Insurgents); PPC, 1957; Sur ce rivage (I Le Périple, 1958, II Monsieur Prousthe, 1958, III Liberté de Décembre, 1959); Sylva, 1961; Hamlet (trans. and illus.), 1965; (with P. Misraki) Les Chemins de L'Etre,

1965; (with M. Coronel) Quota ou les Pléthoriens, 1966; La Bataille du Silence, 1967; Le Radeau de la Méduse, 1969; Oedipe et Hamlet, 1970; Contes des Cataplasmes, 1971; Sillages, 1972; Sept Sentiers du Désert (short stories), 1972; Questions sur la vie à Messieurs les Biologistes (essay), 1973; Comme un Frère, 1973; Tendre Naufrage, 1974; Ce que je crois (essay), 1976; Je cuisine comme un chef (cook book), 1976; Les Chevaux du Temps, 1977; Collected Plays, vol. 1 (Zoo, Le Fer et le Velours, Le Silence de la Mer), 1978, Vol. 2, Pour Shakespeare (Hamlet, Macbeth), 1978; Sens et Non-sens de l'Histoire (essay), 1978; Camille ou l'Enfant double (children's story), 1978; Le Piège à Loup (novel), 1979; Assez Mentir! (essay, collab. O. Wormser-Migot), 1980; Moi Aristide Briand (biog.), 1981; Les Occasions Perdues (history), 1982; numerous articles in periodicals. *Address:* Moulin des Iles, 77120 St Augustin, France. *Clubs:* PEN, section française; Comité National des Ecrivains (Hon. Pres.).

VERDON-SMITH, Sir (William) Reginald, Kt 1953; Pro-Chancellor, Bristol University, since 1965; Vice Lord-Lieutenant, Avon, since 1980; *b* 5 Nov. 1912; *s* of late Sir William G. Verdon Smith, CBE, JP; *m* 1946, Jane Margaret, *d* of late V. W. J. Hobbs; one *s* one *d*. *Educ:* Repton School; Brasenose College, Oxford (Scholar), 1st class School of Jurisprudence, 1935; BCL 1936 and Vinerian Law Scholar; Barrister-at-law, Inner Temple. Bristol Aeroplane Co., 1938-68: Dir., 1942; Jt Asst Man. Dir., 1947; Jt Man. Dir., 1952; Chm. 1955. Vice-Chm., Rolls Royce Ltd, 1966-68; Chm., British Aircraft Corp. (Hldgs) Ltd, 1969-72; Dir, Lloyds Bank Ltd, 1951-83; Chairman: Lloyds Bank Internat., 1973-79; Lloyds Bank Bristol Region, 1976-83. Pres. SBAC, 1946-48; Chm., Fatstock and Meat Marketing Committee of Enquiry, 1962-64; Mem. of Council, Univ. of Bristol (Chm., 1949-56). Mem. Cttee on the Working of the Monetary System (Radcliffe Cttee), 1957-59. Mem., Review Body on Remuneration of Doctors and Dentists, 1964-68. Master, Worshipful Co. of Coachmakers and Coach Harness Makers, 1960-61; Master, Soc. of Merchant Venturers, 1968-69. FRSA. DL Avon, 1974. Hon. LLD Bristol, 1959; Hon. DSc, Cranfield Inst. of Technology, 1971; Hon. Fellow, Brasenose Coll., Oxford, 1965. *Recreations:* golf and sailing. *Address:* 13 Redcliffe Parade West, Bristol BS1 6SP. *Clubs:* United Oxford & Cambridge University; Royal Yacht Squadron, Royal Cruising.

VERE OF HANWORTH, Lord; Charles Francis Topham de Vere Beauclerk; *b* 22 Feb. 1965; *s* and *heir* to Earl of Burford, *qv*.

VEREKER, family name of **Viscount Gort.**

VEREY, David Cecil Wynter; DL; retired as Senior Investigator, Historic Buildings, Ministry of Housing and Local Government (1946-65); architectural historian and writer; *b* 9 Sept. 1913; *o s* of Rev. Cecil Henry Verey and Constance Lindaraja Dearman Birchall; *m* 1939, Rosemary Isabel Baird, *d* of Lt-Col Prescott Sandilands, DSO; two *s* two *d*. *Educ:* Eton; Trinity Coll., Cambridge (MA). ARIBA 1940. Capt., Royal Fusiliers, 1940; seconded SOE 1943, N Africa and Italy. Chm., Alan Sutton Publishing Ltd. Chm., Gloucester Diocesan Adv. Cttee on Churches; Vice-Chm., Gloucestershire Historic Churches Preservation Trust; President: Bristol and Gloucestershire Archæological Soc., 1972; Cirencester Arch. and Hist Soc.; Glos and Cheltenham Centre, Nat. Trust; Wotton-under-Edge Civic Soc.; Member: Severn Regional Cttee of Nat. Trust; Gen. Cttee, Inc. Church Building Soc. High Sheriff of County of Gloucester, 1966; DL Glos, 1981. FSA. *Publications:* Shell Guides to six counties, England and Wales; The Buildings of England (Gloucestershire Vols), 1970; Cotswold Churches, 1976; Seven Victorian Architects, 1976; Diary of a Cotswold Parson, 1978; Gloucester Cathedral, 1979; Gloucestershire Churches, 1981; articles on architectural history. *Recreations:* private museum, Arlington Mill, Bibury; gardening. *Address:* Barnsley House, Cirencester, Glos. *T:* Bibury 281.

VEREY, Michael John, TD 1945; Chairman of Trustees, Charities Official Investment Fund, since 1974; *b* 12 Oct. 1912; *yr s* of late Henry Edward and late Lucy Alice Verey; *m* 1947, Sylvia Mary, *widow* of Charles Bartlet and *d* of late Lt-Col Denis Wilson and late Mrs Mary Henrietta Wilson; two *s* one *d*. *Educ:* Eton; Trinity College, Cambridge (MA). Joined Helbert, Wagg & Co. Ltd, 1934. Served War of 1939-45, Middle East, Italy, Warwickshire Yeomanry (Lt-Col). Chairman: J. Henry Schroder Wagg & Co. Ltd, 1972-73 (Dep. Chm., 1966-72); Schroders Ltd, 1973-77; Accepting Houses Cttee, 1974-77; Broadstone Investment Trust Ltd; Brixton Estate Ltd; London American Energy Investments Ltd; Director: British Petroleum Co. Ltd, to 1982; The Boots Co. (Vice-Chm., 1978-); Commercial Union Assurance Co. Ltd (Vice-Chm., 1975-78; Dep. Chm., 1978-); Sviluppo e Gestione Investimenti Mobiliari, SpA, and other cos; Mem., Covent Garden Market Authority, 1961-66. High Sheriff of Berkshire, 1968. Pres., Royal Worcestershire and Warwickshire Yeomanry Regtl Assoc., 1976. *Recreations:* gardening, travel. *Address:* Little Bowden, Pangbourne, Berks. *T:* Pangbourne 2210. *Club:* Boodle's.

VERITY, Group Captain Conrad Edward Howe, OBE (mil.) 1943; CEng, FICE; JP; Engineering Consultant; *b* 18 February 1901; *s* of Edward Storr Verity and Annie Amelia Verity (*née* Howe); *m* 1931, Doreen Louise Bishop; one *s* one *d*. *Educ:* Wellingborough Sch. Engrg Trg, W. H. Allen Sons & Co. Ltd, Bedford, and Bedford Tech. Coll., 1917-22; Contracts Engr, W. H. Allen Sons & Co. Ltd, Bedford, 1922-24; Tech. Engr, Contraflo Engrg Co. Ltd, 1924-27; Tech. Engr (Mech.), London Power Co., 1927-40. Served War, 1940-45: RAF, finishing as Gp Capt.; service in England, USA, NW Africa,

Pacific, India, China, etc. Chief Development and Testing Engineer, London Power Co., 1945-48; Generation Constr Engr, Brit. Elec. Authority, 1948-50; Dep. Chief Engr, Brit. Elec. Authority, and later Central Elec. Authority, 1950-55; Dir, Foster Wheeler Ltd and Manager Steam Div., 1955-59, Managing Dir, 1960-62, Chm., 1962-66; Dep. Chm., Foster Wheeler John Brown Boilers Ltd, 1966-67; Dir, Rolls-Royce and Associates, Derby, 1959-67. Gen. Comr for Income Tax, 1969-75. JP Surrey, 1960. American Legion of Merit (Officer), 1945. *Publications:* technical papers to: Institution Civil Engrs; Electrical Power Engrs Assoc.; Instn of Mech. Engrs, etc. *Recreations:* rowing, and sport generally. *Address:* Farthings, Earleydene, Sunninghill, Berks. *T:* Ascot 22033. *Clubs:* Naval and Military; Remenham; Sunninghill Comrades (Ex-Pres.); Twickenham Rowing (Hon. Life Mem.); Burway Rowing (Vice-Pres.).

VERMEULE, Prof. Emily Dickinson Townsend, FSA; Zemurray-Stone-Radcliffe Professor, Harvard University, since 1970; Fellow for Research, Museum of Fine Arts, Boston, since 1963; *b* 11 Aug. 1928; *d* of Clinton Blake Townsend and Eleanor Mary Meneely; *m* 1957, Cornelius Clarkson Vermeule III; one *s* one *d. Educ:* The Brearley Sch.; Bryn Mawr Coll. (BA, PhD); Radcliffe Coll. (MA). Instructor in Greek: Bryn Mawr, 1956-57; Wellesley Coll., 1957-58; Asst Prof. of Classics, 1958-61, Associate Prof. of Classics, 1961-64, Boston Univ.; Prof. of Greek and Fine Arts, Wellesley, 1965-70. James Loeb Vis. Prof. of Classical Philology, Harvard Univ., 1969; Sather Prof. of Classical Literature, Univ. of California, Berkeley, 1975; Geddes-Harrower Prof. of Greek Art and Archaeology, Univ. of Aberdeen, 1980-81. Corresp. Member: British Academy; German Archaeological Inst. Hon. degrees: DLitt: Douglass Coll., Rutgers, 1968; Smith Coll., 1971; Wheaton Coll., 1973; Tufts, 1980; DFA: Amherst Coll., Mass, 1970; LLD: Regis Coll., 1970; LHD: Trinity Coll., Boston, 1974; Emmanuel Coll., Hartford, Conn, 1980. *Publications:* Euripides' Electra, 1959; Greece in the Bronze Age, 1964, 7th edn 1980; The Trojan War in Greek Art, 1964; Götterkult, Archaeologia Homerica V, 1974; The Art of the Shaft Graves, 1975; Death in Early Greek Art and Poetry, 1979; (with V. Karageorghis) Mycenaean Pictorial Vase-Painting, 1982; contribs to Jl of Hellenic Studies, American Jl of Archaeology, Jahrbuch des d.Arch. Insts, Classical Philology, etc. *Recreations:* dogs, gardening. *Address:* 47 Coolidge Hill Road, Cambridge, Mass 02138, USA. *T:* (617) UN 4-1879. *Club:* Cosmopolitan (New York City).

VERNEY, family name of **Baron Willoughby de Broke.**

VERNEY, Sir John, 2nd Bt, *cr* 1946; MC 1944; TD 1970; painter, illustrator, author; *b* 30 Sept. 1913; *s* of Sir Ralph Verney, 1st Bt (Speaker's Secretary, 1921-55); *S* father, 1959; *m* 1939, Lucinda, *d* of late Major Herbert Musgrave, DSO; one *s* five *d* (and one *s* decd). *Educ:* Eton; Christ Church, Oxford. Served War of 1939-45 with N. Somerset Yeomanry, RAC and SAS Regt in Palestine, Syria, Egypt, Italy, France and Germany (despatches twice, MC). Exhibitor: RBA; London Group; Leicester, Redfern, New Grafton Gall., etc. Légion d'Honneur, 1945. *Publications:* Verney Abroad, 1954; Going to the Wars, 1955; Friday's Tunnel, 1959; Look at Houses, 1959; February's Road, 1961; Every Advantage, 1961; The Mad King of Chichiboo, 1963; ismo, 1964; A Dinner of Herbs, 1966; Fine Day for a Picnic, 1968; Seven Sunflower Seeds, 1968; Samson's Hoard, 1973; periodic contributor to Cornhill etc; annually, The Dodo Pad (the amusing telephone diary). *Heir: s* John Sebastian Verney, *b* 30 Aug. 1945. *Address:* The White House, Clare, Suffolk. *T:* Clare 277494.

VERNEY, Lawrence John, TD 1955; DL; **His Honour Judge Verney;** a Circuit Judge (formerly Deputy Chairman, Middlesex Sessions) since 1971; *b* 19 July 1924; *y s* of Sir Harry Verney, 4th Bt, DSO; *m* 1972, Zoë Auriel, *d* of Lt-Col P. G. Goodeve-Docker. *Educ:* Harrow; Oriel Coll., Oxford. Called to Bar, Inner Temple, 1952. Dep. Chm., Bucks QS, 1962-71. Editor, Harrow School Register, 1948-; Governor, Harrow Sch., 1972-. DL Bucks 1967. *Address:* Windmill House, Oving, Aylesbury, Bucks HP22 4HL.
See also Bishop Suffragan of Repton, Sir R. B. Verney, Bt.

VERNEY, Sir Ralph (Bruce), 5th Bt *cr* 1818; KBE 1974; JP; Landowner; Vice-Lord-Lieutenant (formerly Vice-Lieutenant) of Buckinghamshire since 1965; Chairman, Nature Conservancy Council, since 1980 (Member, 1966-71); *b* 18 Jan. 1915; *e s* of Sir Harry Calvert Williams Verney, 4th Bt, DSO, and Lady Rachel Bruce (*d* 1964), *d* of 9th Earl of Elgin; *S* father, 1974; *m* 1948, Mary Vestey; one *s* three *d. Educ:* Canford; Balliol Coll., Oxford. 2nd Lieut Bucks Yeomanry, 1940; Major, Berks Yeomanry, 1945 and Bucks Yeomanry, 1946. Pres., Country Landowners' Assoc., 1961-63; Vice-President for Great Britain, Confédération Européenne de L'Agriculture, 1965-71, Counsellor, 1971-; Chairman, Forestry Commn Cttee for England, 1967-80; Member: Forestry Commn, 1968-80; Milton Keynes New Town Corporation, 1967-74; BBC Adv. Cttee on Agriculture, 1970-78; Royal Commn on Environmental Pollution, 1973-79; Chm., Sec. of State for the Environment's Adv. Cttee on Aggregates for Construction Industry, 1972-77. Trustee: Radcliffe Trust; Ernest Cook Trust; Chequers Trust; Sch. of Water Sciences, High Wycombe, 1982-. Buckinghamshire County Council: Member, 1951; Chairman, Finance Cttee, 1957; Planning Cttee, 1967; CA 1961; JP Bucks, 1954; High Sheriff of Buckinghamshire, 1957-58; DL Bucks, 1960; High Steward of Buckingham, 1966. Prime Warden, Worshipful Co. of Dyers, 1969-70. Hon. Fellow: RIBA, 1977; Green Coll., Oxford, 1980. Chevalier de Tastevin, Clos Vougeot, 1978. *Recreation:* shooting. *Heir: s* Edmund Ralph Verney [*b* 28 June 1950; *m* 1982, Daphne Fausset-Farquhar]. *Address:* Claydon House, Middle Claydon, Buckingham MK18 2EX. *T:* Steeple Claydon 297;

Plas Rhôscolyn, Holyhead LL65 2NZ. *T:* Trearddur Bay 860288. *Clubs:* Brooks's, Cavalry and Guards.
See also Bishop Suffragan of Repton, L. J. Verney.

VERNEY, Rt. Rev. Stephen Edmund; *see* Repton, Bishop Suffragan of.

VERNEY-CAVE, family name of **Baron Braye.**

VERNIER-PALLIEZ, Bernard Maurice Alexandre; Commandeur de la Légion d'Honneur; Croix de Guerre; Médaille de la Résistance; French Ambassador to Washington, since 1982; *b* 2 March 1918; *s* of Maurice Vernier and Marie-Thérèse Palliez; *m* 1952, Denise Silet-Pathe; one *s* three *d. Educ:* Ecole des Hautes Etudes Commerciales; Ecole Libre des Sciences Politiques. Licencié en Droit. Joined Régie Nationale des Usines, Renault, 1945 (dealing with personnel and trade unions); Sécretaire Général, RNUR, 1948-67; Directeur Général Adjoint, RNUR, 1967-71; Président Directeur Général, SAVIEM, 1967-74; Délégué Général aux Vehicules Industriels, Cars et Bus à la RNUR, Président du Directoire de Berliet, and Vice-Président du Conseil de Surveillance de SAVIEM, Jan.-Dec. 1975; Président Directeur Général, RNUR, Dec. 1975-1981. *Address:* French Embassy, 2535 Belmont Road NW, Washington, DC 20008, USA. *T:* (202) 328 2600.

VERNON, family name of **Barons Lyveden** and **Vernon.**

VERNON, 10th Baron, *cr* 1762; **John Lawrance Vernon;** *b* 1 Feb. 1923; *s* of 9th Baron, and Violet (*d* 1978), *d* of Colonel Clay; *S* father, 1963; *m* 1955, Sheila Jean (marr. diss. 1982), *d* of W. Marshall Clark, Johannesburg; two *d* ; *m* 1982, Sally, *d* of Robin Stratford, QC. *Educ:* Eton; Magdalen Coll., Oxford. Served in Scots Guards, 1942-46, retiring with rank of Captain. Called to Bar, Lincoln's Inn, 1949. Served in various Government Departments, 1950-61; attached to Colonial Office (for service in Kenya), 1957-58. JP Derbyshire, 1965-77. *Heir: kinsman* Robert Vernon-Harcourt [*b* 26 Dec. 1918; *m* 1948, Sylvia Jeanette, *d* of late Lt-Col Charles Henry Kitching, DSO]. *Address:* Sudbury House, Sudbury, Derbyshire DE6 5HT.

VERNON, David Bowater; Under Secretary, Inland Revenue, since 1975; *b* 14 Nov. 1926; *s* of Lt-Col Herbert Bowater Vernon, MC, and Ivy Margaret Vernon; *m* 1954, Anne de Montmorency Fleming; three *s* three *d. Educ:* Marlborough Coll.; Oriel Coll., Oxford (MA). RA, 1945-48 (Lieut). Inland Revenue, 1951-. *Recreation:* gardening. *Address:* The Oast, Gedges Farm, Matfield, Tonbridge, Kent. *T:* Brenchley 2400.

VERNON, Sir James, AC 1980; Kt 1965; CBE 1962 (OBE 1960); Director: MLC Ltd; Westham Dredging Co. Pty Ltd; Chairman: Volvo Australia Pty Ltd; Martin Corporation Group Ltd; *b* 1910; *s* of Donald Vernon, Tamworth, New South Wales; *m* 1935, Mavis, *d* of C. Lonsdale Smith; two *d. Educ:* Sydney Univ. (BSc); University College, London (PhD). Colonial Sugar Refining Co. Ltd: Chief Chemist, 1938-51; Senior Exec. Officer, 1951-56; Asst General Manager, 1956-57; Gen. Manager, 1958-72; Dir, 1958-82; Chm., 1978-80. Chairman: Commonwealth Cttee of Economic Enquiry, 1963-65; Australian Post Office Commn of Inquiry, 1973; Internat. Pres., Pacific Basin Econ. Council; Member: Internat. Adv. Cttee, Chase Manhattan Bank; Internat. Adv. Council, Well Fargo Bank. Leighton Medal, Royal Australian Chemical Inst., 1965; John Storey Medal, Aust. Inst. of Management, 1971. Hon. DSc: Sydney, 1965; Newcastle, 1969. FRACI. *Address:* 27 Manning Road, Double Bay, NSW 2028, Australia. *Clubs:* Australian, Union, Royal Sydney Golf (Sydney).

VERNON, James William, CMG 1964; barrister-at-law; *b* 1915; *s* of late John Alfred Vernon; *m* 1941, Betty Désirée, *d* of Gordon E. Nathan; one *s* one *d. Educ:* Wallasey Grammar Sch.; Emmanuel Coll., Cambridge (Scholar). BA 1937, MA 1940. Entered Civil Service, Ministry of Food, 1939; Flt Lieut, RAF, 1943; Wing Comdr (despatches), 1945; Principal Scientific Officer, Ministry of Works, 1945; Assistant Secretary, Colonial Office, 1954-64; Economic Adviser, British High Commission, Lusaka, 1966; Asst Under-Sec. of State, DEA, 1966-69; Under-Sec., Min. of Housing and Local Govt, later DoE, 1969-72. Called to Bar, Inner Temple, 1975. Queen's Commendation for Brave Conduct, 1955. *Recreations:* gardening, photography, reading. *Address:* 43 The Crescent, Belmont, Sutton, Surrey.

VERNON, Kenneth Robert, CBE 1978; Deputy Chairman and Chief Executive, North of Scotland Hydro-Electric Board, since 1973; *b* 15 March 1923; *s* of late Cecil W. Vernon and Jessie McGaw, Dumfries; *m* 1946, Pamela Hands, Harrow; one *s* three *d* (and one *d* decd). *Educ:* Dumfries Academy; Glasgow University. BSc, FEng, FIEE, FIMechE. BTH Co., Edinburgh Corp., British Electricity Authority, 1948-55; South of Scotland Electricity Bd, 1955-56; North of Scotland Hydro-Electric Bd, 1956: Chief Electrical and Mech. Engr, then Gen. Man., 1966; Bd Mem., 1970. Dir, British Electricity International Ltd, 1976-; Mem. Bd, Northern Ireland Electricity Service, 1979-. *Publications:* various papers to technical instns. *Recreation:* fishing. *Address:* 10 Keith Crescent, Edinburgh EH4 3NH. *T:* 031-332 4610. *Club:* Royal Commonwealth Society.

VERNON, Prof. Magdalen Dorothea, MA (Cantab) 1926; ScD (Cantab) 1953; Professor of Psychology in the University of Reading, 1956-67; *b* 25 June 1901; *d* of Dr Horace Middleton Vernon and Katharine Dorothea Ewart. *Educ:* Oxford High Sch.; Newnham Coll., Cambridge. Asst Investigator to the Industrial Health Research Board, 1924–27; Research Investigator to the Medical Research Council, in the Psychological Laboratory, Cambridge, 1927–46; Lecturer in Psychology, 1946–51, Senior Lecturer in Psychology, 1951–55, Reader in Psychology, 1955–66, University of Reading. President, British Psychological Soc., 1958 (Hon. Fellow, 1970); President, Psychology Section, British Assoc., 1959. *Publications:* The Experimental Study of Reading, 1931; Visual Perception, 1937; A Further Study of Visual Perception, 1952; Backwardness in Reading, 1957; The Psychology of Perception, 1962; Experiments in Visual Perception, 1966; Human Motivation, 1969; Perception through Experience, 1970; Reading and its Difficulties, 1971; numerous papers on Perception, etc. in British Journal of Psychology and British Journal of Educational Psychology. *Recreations:* walking, gardening. *Address:* 50 Cressingham Road, Reading, Berks. *T:* Reading 81088. *Club:* University Women's.

VERNON, Michael; *see* Vernon, William M.

VERNON, Sir Nigel (John Douglas), 4th Bt, *cr* 1914; Director: Robert Barrow (Insurance Services) Ltd, since 1977; Travel Finance Ltd, since 1971; *b* 2 May 1924; *s* of Sir (William) Norman Vernon, 3rd Bt, and Janet Lady Vernon (*d* 1973); *S* father, 1967; *m* 1947, Margaret Ellen (*née* Dobell); two *s* one *d. Educ:* Charterhouse. Royal Naval Volunteer Reserve (Lieutenant), 1942–45. Spillers Ltd, 1945–65; Director: Castle Brick Co Ltd, 1965–71; Deeside Merchants Ltd, 1971–74. *Recreations:* golf, gardening. *Heir: s* James William Vernon, FCA [*b* 2 April 1949; *m* 1981, Davinia, *er d* of Christopher David Howard, Ryton, Shrewsbury]. *Address:* Top-y-Fron Hall, Kelsterton, near Flint, N Wales. *T:* Deeside 812129. *Club:* Naval.

VERNON, Prof. Philip Ewart, MA, PhD, DSc; Professor Emeritus, University of Calgary, 1979; Emeritus Professor, University of London; *b* 6 June 1905; *e s* of late Horace Middleton Vernon; *m* 1st, 1938, Annie C. Gray; 2nd, 1947, Dorothy Anne Fairley Lawson, MA, MEd; one *s. Educ:* Oundle Sch.; St John's Coll., Cambridge; Yale and Harvard Universities. First Class Hons in Nat. Sci. Tripos, Part I, 1926, and Moral Sci. Tripos, Part II, 1927; John Stewart of Rannoch Scholarship in Sacred Music, 1925; Strathcona Research Studentship, 1927–29; Laura Spelman Rockefeller Fellowship in Social Sciences, 1929–31; Fellowship of St John's Coll., Cambridge, 1930–33; Pinsent-Darwin Studentship in Mental Pathology, 1933–35. Psychologist to LCC at Maudsley Hospital Child Guidance Clinic, 1933–35; Head of Psychology Dept, Jordanhill Training Centre, Glasgow, 1935–38; Head of Psychology Dept, University of Glasgow, 1938–47; Psychological Research Adviser to Admiralty and War Office, 1942–45; Prof. of Educational Psychology, Inst. of Education, University of London, 1949–64; Prof. of Psychology, 1964–68; Prof. of Educational Psychology, Univ. of Calgary, 1968–78. Fellow, Centre for Advanced Studies in Behavioural Scis, Stanford, Calif, 1961–62, Vis. Canada Council Fellow, 1975. Visiting Professor: Princeton Univ. and Educnl Testing Service, 1957; Teachers' Coll., Sydney, 1977; numerous internat. educnl consultancies and lect. tours for British Council, 1953–68. President: Psych. Sect., British Assoc. Advancement of Science, 1952; BPsS, 1954–55. Govt of Alberta Achievement Award, 1972. Hon. LLD Univ. of Calgary. *Publications:* (with G. W. Allport) Studies in Expressive Movement, 1933; The Measurement of Abilities, 1940, 2nd edn, 1956; (with J. B. Parry) Personnel Selection in the British Forces, 1949; The Structure of Human Abilities, 1950, 2nd edn, 1961; Personality Tests and Assessments, 1953; Secondary School Selection, 1957; Intelligence and Attainment Tests, 1960; Personality Assessment: A Critical Survey, 1963; Intelligence and Cultural Environment, 1969; Readings in Creativity, 1971; (with G. Adamson and Dorothy F. Vernon) Psychology and Education of Gifted Children, 1977; Intelligence: Heredity and Environment, 1979; Abilities and Achievements of Orientals in North America, 1982; numerous papers in British and American psychological journals. *Recreations:* music, snowshoeing, cross-country ski-ing. *Address:* No 402B 3719 49th Street NW, Calgary, Alberta, Canada.

VERNON, (William) Michael; Chairman: Famous Names Ltd, since 1981; Granville Meat Co. Ltd, since 1981; Director, Strong & Fisher (Holdings) plc, since 1980; *b* 17 April 1926; *o surv. s* of late Sir Wilfred Vernon; *m* 1st, 1952, Rosheen O'Meara; one *s* ; 2nd, 1977, Mrs Jane Colston (*née* Kilham-Roberts). *Educ:* Marlborough Coll.; Trinity Coll., Cambridge. MA 1948. Lieut, Royal Marines, 1944–46. Joined Spillers Ltd, 1948: Dir 1960; Jt Man. Dir 1962; Chm. and Chief Exec., 1968–80; Dir, EMI Ltd, 1973–80. Pres., Nat. Assoc. of British and Irish Millers, 1965; Vice-Chm., Millers' Mutual Assoc., 1968–80; Pres., British Food Export Council, 1977–80; Vice-Pres. and Dep. Chm., Management Cttee, RNLI. CBIM. *Recreations:* sailing, shooting, ski-ing. *Address:* Fyfield Manor, Andover, Hants. *Clubs:* Royal Ocean Racing (Cdre 1964–68); Royal Yacht Squadron.

VERNON-HUNT, Ralph Holmes, DFC; Deputy Chairman, Pan Books Ltd, 1980–82, retired (Managing Director, 1970); *b* 23 May 1923; *m* 1946, Elizabeth Mary Harris; four *s* two *d* (and one *s* decd). *Educ:* Malvern College. Flt-Lt RAF, 1941–46; Bookseller, 1946–47; Sales Dir, Pan Books Ltd, 1947–62; Sales Dir, Paul Hamlyn Ltd, 1963–69. *Recreation:* hydroponics. *Address:* 45 Rosemont Road, Richmond, Surrey TW10 6QN.

VERONESE, Dr Vittorino; Cavaliere di Gran Croce della Repubblica Italiana; Gold Medal Awarded for Culture (Italian Republic); Doctor of Law (Padua, 1930); lawyer, banker, administrator; Chairman, Board of Directors, Banco di Roma, 1961–76 (Auditor, 1945–53; Director, 1953–57); *b* Vicenza,

1 March 1910; *m* 1939, Maria Petrarca; four *s* three *d.* General Secretary: Catholic Movement Graduates, 1939; Italian Catholic Action, 1944–46 (President, 1946–52); Vice-President, Internat. Movement of Catholic Intellectuals of Pax Romana, 1947–55. Vice-President, Banca Cattolica del Veneto, 1952–57; President, Consorzio di Credito per le Opere Pubbliche and Istituto di Credito per le Imprese di Pubblica Utilitá, 1957–58; Italian Deleg. to General Conf. of UNESCO, Beirut, 1950, Paris, 1952–53; Member Italian Nat. Commn, 1953–58; Vice-President, Exec. Board, 1954–56; President, 1956–58. Director-General of UNESCO, 1958–61, resigned; Member, Comité Consultatif International pour l'Alphabétisation, UNESCO, 1967; Vice-President: Comité Consultatif International pour Venise, UNESCO; Societa Italiano per l'Organizzazione Internationale (SIOI); Pres., Italian Consultative Cttee for Human Rights, 1965. Pres., Circolo di Roma, 1968. Lay Observer in Concilio Ecumenico Vaticano II; Member, Pontificia Commissione Justitia et Pax, 1967. Cav. di Gran Groce dell' Ordine di S Silvestro Papa; Commendatore dell' Ordine Piano. Holds several foreign orders. *Address:* c/o Banco di Roma, Via del Corso 307, Rome, Italy; 21 Via Cadlolo, Rome, Italy.

VERSEY, Henry Cherry; Emeritus Professor of Geology, University of Leeds, since 1959; *b* 22 Jan. 1894; *s* of Charles Versey, Welton, East Yorkshire; *m* 1923, Hypatia Ingersoll, *d* of Greevz Fysher, Leeds; two *s* two *d. Educ:* Hymers Coll., Hull; University of Leeds. Service with RAOC, European War, 1916–19. Lecturer in Geology, University of Leeds, 1919–49; Reader in Applied Geology, 1949–56, Professor of Geology, 1956–59, University of Leeds. Hon. LLD (Leeds), 1967. Phillips Medal, Yorkshire Geological Society, 1964. *Publications:* Geology of the Appleby District, 1941; Geology and Scenery of the Countryside round Leeds and Bradford, 1948. Many papers on Yorkshire geology. *Recreation:* philately. *Address:* 1 Stainburn Terrace, Leeds LS17 6NJ. *T:* Leeds 682244.

VERULAM, 7th Earl of, *cr* 1815; **John Duncan Grimston;** Bt 1629; Baron Forrester (Scot.), 1633; Baron Dunboyne and Viscount Grimston (Ire.), 1719; Baron Verulam (Gt. Brit.), 1790; Viscount Grimston (UK), 1815; *b* 21 April 1951; *s* of 6th Earl of Verulam, and of Marjorie Ray, *d* of late Walter Atholl Duncan; *S* father, 1973; *m* 1976, Dione Angela, *e d* of Jeremy Smith, Balcombe House, Sussex; two *s* one *d. Educ:* Eton; Christ Church, Oxford (MA 1976). *Heir: s* Viscount Grimston, *qv. Address:* Gorhambury, St Albans, Herts AL3 6AH. *T:* St Albans 55000. *Clubs:* White's, Beefsteak, Turf.

VERYKIOS, Dr Panaghiotis Andrew; Kt Commander of Order of George I, of Greece, and of Order of the Phoenix; MM (Greece); Greek Ambassador, retired; *b* Athens, 1910; *m* 1939, Mary (*née* Dracoulis); three *s. Educ:* Athens and Paris. Law (Dr) and Political Sciences. Greek Diplomatic Service, 1935. Served in the Army, 1939–40. Various diplomatic posts until 1946; Secretary of Embassy, London, 1947–51; Counsellor, Dep. Representative of NATO, Paris, 1952–54; Counsellor of Embassy, Paris, 1954–56; Head of NATO Div., Min. of Foreign Affairs, Athens, 1956–60; Ambassador to: The Netherlands, 1960–64; Norway, 1961–67; Denmark, 1964–67; Iceland, 1967; Court of St James's, 1967–69; Spain, 1969–70. Holds foreign decorations. *Publication:* La Prescription en Droit International, 1934 (Paris). *Recreation:* music. *Address:* 6 Iras Street, Ekali, Athens. *T:* 8131216; 23 Avenue Juste Olivier, 1006 Lausanne, Switzerland. *T:* (021) 224697. *Club:* Athenian (Athens).

VESEY, family name of **Viscount de Vesci.**

VESEY, Sir Henry; *see* Vesey, Sir N. H. P.

VESEY, Sir (Nathaniel) Henry (Peniston), Kt 1965; CBE 1953; Chairman, H. A. & E. Smith Ltd, since 1939; Chairman, Bank of N. T. Butterfield & Son Ltd, since 1970; Member of House of Assembly, Bermuda, 1938–72; *b* 1 June 1901; *s* of late Hon. Nathaniel Vesey, Devonshire, Bermuda; *m* 1920, Louise Marie, *d* of late Captain J. A. Stubbs, Shelly Bay, Bermuda; two *s. Educ:* Saltus Grammar Sch. Chairman: Food and Supplies Control Board, 1941–42; Board of Trade, 1943; Finance Cttee of House of Assembly, 1943–44; Bermuda Trade Development Board, 1945–56, 1960–69; Board of Civil Aviation, 1957–59; Board of Agriculture, 1957–59. MEC, 1948–57, Mem. Executive Council for Tourism and Trade, 1968–69. *Recreations:* fishing, golf. *Address:* Windward, Shelly Bay, Bermuda. *T:* 3-0186. *Clubs:* Naval and Military; Royal Bermuda Yacht, Mid Ocean (Bermuda).

VESSEY, Prof. Martin Paterson; Professor of Social and Community Medicine, University of Oxford, since 1974; Fellow of St Cross College, Oxford; *b* 22 July 1936; *s* of Sidney J. Vessey and Catherine P. Vessey (*née* Thomson); *m* 1959, Anne Platt; two *s* one *d. Educ:* University College Sch., Hampstead; University Coll. London; University Coll. Hosp. Med. Sch., London. MB, BS London 1959; MD London 1971; FFCM RCP 1972; MA Oxon 1974; MRCPE 1978; FRCPE 1979. Scientific Officer, Dept of Statistics, Rothamsted Exper. Stn, 1960–65; House Surg. and House Phys., Barnet Gen. Hosp., 1965–66; Mem. Sci. Staff, MRC Statistical Research Unit, 1966–69; Lectr in Epidemiology, Univ. of Oxford, 1969–74. *Publications:* many sci. articles in learned jls, notably on med. aspects of fertility control, safety of drugs, and epidemiology of cancer. *Recreations:* motoring, singing, conservation. *Address:* 8 Warnborough Road, Oxford OX2 6HZ. *T:* Oxford 52698.

VESTEY, family name of **Baron Vestey.**

VESTEY, 3rd Baron, *cr* 1922, of Kingswood; **Samuel George Armstrong Vestey**; Bt, *cr* 1913; DL; *b* 19 March 1941; *s* of late Captain the Hon. William Howarth Vestey (killed in action in Italy, 1944; *o s* of 2nd Baron Vestey and Frances Sarah Howarth) and of Pamela Helen Fullerton, *d* of George Nesbitt Armstrong; *S* grandfather, 1954; *m* 1st, 1970, Kathryn Mary (marr. diss. 1981), *er d* of John Eccles, Moor Park, Herts; two *d* ; 2nd, 1981, Celia Elizabeth, *d* of Major Guy Knight, MC, Lockinge Manor, Wantage, Oxon. *Educ:* Eton. Lieut, Scots Guards. Director, Union International plc and associated companies. President: London Meat Trade and Drovers Benevolent Assoc., 1973; Three Counties Agricl Soc., 1978; Inst. of Meat, 1978–. Pres., Glos Assoc. of Boys' Clubs; County Pres., St John Ambulance Brigade (Glos). Liveryman, Butchers' Co. DL Glos, 1982. OStJ. *Recreations:* polo, shooting. *Heir:* *b* Hon. Mark William Vestey [*b* 16 April 1943; *m* 1975, Rose Amelia, *d* of Lt-Col Peter Thomas Clifton, *qv* ; one *s* two *d*. *Educ:* Eton]. *Address:* Stowell Park, Northleach, Glos. *Clubs:* White's; Jockey (Newmarket); Melbourne (Melbourne).

VESTEY, Edmund Hoyle, DL; Chairman: Blue Star Line; Lamport & Holt Line; Albion Insurance Co.; Director: Associated Container Transportation (Australia); Union International Co. and associated companies; *b* 1932; *o s* of Ronald Arthur Vestey, *qv* ; *m* 1960, Anne Moubray, *yr d* of Gen. Sir Geoffry Scoones, KCB, KBE, CSI, DSO, MC; four *s*. *Educ:* Eton. 2nd Lieut Queen's Bays, 1951; Lieut, City of London Yeomanry. Pres., Gen. Council of British Shipping, 1981-82. Joint Master, Puckeridge and Thurlow Foxhounds. High Sheriff, Essex, 1977; DL Essex, 1978. *Address:* Waltons, Ashdon, Saffron Walden, Essex; Glencanisp Lodge, Lochinver, Sutherland; Sunnyside Farmhouse, Hawick, Roxburghshire. *Clubs:* Cavalry and Guards, Carlton; Highland (Inverness).

VESTEY, Sir (John) Derek, 2nd Bt, *cr* 1921; *b* 4 June 1914; *s* of John Joseph Vestey (*d* 1932) and Dorothy Mary (*d* 1918), *d* of John Henry Beaver, Gawthorpe Hall, Bingley, Yorkshire; *g s* of Sir Edmund Vestey, 1st Bt; *S* grandfather 1953; *m* 1938, Phyllis Irene, *o d* of H. Brewer, Banstead, Surrey; one *s* one *d*. *Educ:* Leys Sch., Cambridge. Served War of 1939-45: Flt-Lieut, RAFVR, 1940-45. *Heir:* *s* Paul Edmund Vestey [*b* 15 Feb. 1944; *m* 1971, Victoria Anne Scudamore, *d* of John Salter, Tiverton, Devon; three *d*. *Educ:* Radley]. *Address:* 5 Carlton Gardens, SW1. *T:* 01-930 1610; Harcombe House, Ropley, Hants. *T:* Ropley 2394. *Clubs:* MCC, Farmers', Royal Automobile.

See also R. A. Vestey.

VESTEY, Ronald Arthur; DL; Director: Blue Star Line; Lamport & Holt Line; Albion Insurance Co.; Union International Co. and Associated Companies, and other Companies; *b* 10 May 1898; 4th but *e* surv. *s* of Sir Edmund Hoyle Vestey, 1st Bt; *m* 1923, Florence Ellen McLean (*d* 1966), *e d* of Colonel T. G. Luis, VD, Broughty Ferry, Angus; one *s* three *d*. *Educ:* Malvern Coll. Travelled extensively throughout world, with interests in many countries. High Sheriff of Suffolk, 1961; DL Suffolk, 1970. *Recreations:* shooting, fishing. *Address:* Great Thurlow Hall, Suffolk. *T:* Thurlow 240. *Clubs:* Carlton, MCC.

See also E. H. Vestey.

VEYSEY, Geoffrey Charles, CB 1948; *b* 20 Dec. 1895; *e s* of late Charles Veysey, Exeter; *m* 1925, Eileen Agnes (*d* 1981), *d* of late Charles Henry Byers, Gunnersbury. *Educ:* Latymer Upper Sch., Hammersmith. Served European War, 1914-18. Lieut, RGA. Entered Ministry of Labour, 1919; Private Secretary to Parliamentary Secretaries and Permanent Secretaries of Ministry, 1929-32; Assistant Secretary, 1938; Principal Assistant Secretary, 1944; Under-Secretary, Ministry of Labour and National Service, 1946-60. *Address:* 8 Stokes House, Sutherland Avenue, Bexhill-on-Sea, East Sussex TN39 3QT. *T:* Bexhill-on-Sea 214320. *Club:* Athenæum.

VIAL, Sir Kenneth Harold, Kt 1978; CBE 1969; chartered accountant; retired; *b* 11 Aug. 1912; *s* of G. O. Vial, Melbourne; *m* 1937, Adele, *d* of R. G. R. Ball; one *s* two *d*. *Educ:* Scotch Coll., Melbourne. Served RAAF, 1941-46 (Flight Lieut). Partner, Arthur Andersen & Co. (formerly Fuller King & Co.), 1946-67; Chairman: Yarra Falls Ltd, 1967-74; Rocke Tompsitt & Co. Ltd, 1975-79; Director: Michaelis Bayley Ltd, 1967-81 (Chm., 1975-81); Mono Pumps (Aust.) Pty Ltd; F. H. Faulding & Co. Ltd, 1978–; Hortico Ltd, 1981- (Chm., 1981-). Member: Aust. Nat. Airlines Commn, 1956-79 (Chm., 1975-79); Aviation Industry Adv. Council, 1978-79; Council, Aust. Services Canteens Organisation, 1959-76 (Chm., Bd of Management, 1971-76); Council, La Trobe Univ., 1966-74 (Dep. Chancellor, 1970-72); Melbourne Underground Rail Loop Authority, 1971-81. *Address:* 6-393 Barkers Road, Kew, Vic 3101, Australia. *Clubs:* Athenæum, Naval and Military (Melbourne).

VIBERT, McInroy Este; Consular Service, retired; *b* Chiswick, 6 June 1894; *o s* of late Arthur Reginald Vibert and Margaret Eleanor Fraser; *m* 1st, Joyce Havell; one *s* one *d* ; 2nd, Ellen Fiebiger-Guermanova (*d* 1982). *Educ:* Taunton Sch.; France and Germany. Served European War, 1914-18, 10th Royal Fusiliers; Vice-Consul at Brussels, 1919, and subsequently at Philadelphia, Stettin, Koenigsberg, Memel, Frankfort-on-Main, Punta Arenas, Cologne, and Tunis; Consul at Sarajevo, 1936-39, and Split, 1939-41, Lisbon, 1941-44, Barcelona, 1944, Curacao, 1944-45; Consul-General (local rank) and Counsellor of Legation at Havana, 1945-47; Chargé d'Affaires, July 1946; Foreign Office, 1947-48; Consul at Vigo; retired, 1950, on pension.

Recreations: water-colour painting, philately. *Address:* Hogar del Sol, Santa Maria, Mallorca, Spain. *T:* 62-02-32.

VICARS-HARRIS, Noël Hedley, CMG 1953; *b* 22 Nov. 1901; *o s* of late C. F. Harris and Evelyn C. Vicars, The Gate House, Rugby; *m* 1st, 1926, Maria Guimarães of Sao Paulo, Brazil (marr. dissolved, 1939); two *s* ; 2nd, 1940, Joan Marguerite Francis; one *s*. *Educ:* Charterhouse; St John's Coll., Cambridge. BA Agric., 1924. Employed in Brazil by Brazil Plantations Syndicate Ltd, 1924-27; HM Colonial Service, Tanganyika, 1927-55; Official Member of Legislative and Executive Councils, Tanganyika, 1950-Nov. 1953; Member for Lands and Mines, Tanganyika, 1950-55. *Recreation:* gardening. *Address:* Bampfylde Cottage, Sparkford, Somerset. *T:* North Cadbury 40454.

VICARY, Rev. Canon Douglas Reginald; Canon Residentiary and Precentor of Wells Cathedral, since 1975; Chaplain to HM the Queen, since 1977; *b* 24 Sept. 1916; *e s* of R. W. Vicary, Walthamstow; *m* 1947, Ruth, *y d* of late F. J. L. Hickinbotham, JP, and of Mrs Hickinbotham, Edgbaston; two *s* two *d*. *Educ:* Sir George Monoux Grammar Sch., Walthamstow; Trinity Coll., Oxford (Open Scholar), Wycliffe Hall, Oxford. 1st Class Nat. Sci. 1939; BSc 1939, MA 1942; Diploma in Theology with distinction, 1940; deacon, 1940; priest, 1941. Curate of St Peter and St Paul, Courteenhall, and Asst Chaplain and House Master, St Lawrence Coll., Ramsgate, while evacuated at Courteenhall, Northampton, 1940-44; Chaplain, Hertford Coll., Oxford, 1945-48; Tutor at Wycliffe Hall, 1945-47, Chaplain 1947-48; Dir of Religious Education, Rochester Diocese, 1948-57; Sec., CACTM Exams Cttee and GOE, 1952-57; Dir, Post-Ordination Training, 1952-57, Headmaster of King's School, Rochester, 1957-75. Minor Canon, Rochester Cathedral, 1949-52; Canon Residentiary and Precentor, 1952-57; Hon. Canon, 1957-75. Exam. Chaplain to Bishop of Rochester, 1950-, to Bishop of Bath and Wells, 1975-. Mem. Court, Kent Univ., 1965-75. FRSA 1970. *Publication:* contrib. Canterbury Chapters, 1976. *Recreations:* music, architecture, hill-walking, reading. *Address:* 4 The Liberty, Wells, Somerset BA5 2SU. *T:* Wells 73188.

VICK, Arnold Oughtred Russell; QC 1980; **His Honour Judge Russell Vick**; a Circuit Judge, since 1982; *b* 14 Sept. 1933; *yr s* of late His Honour Judge Sir Godfrey Russell Vick, QC; *m* 1959, Zinnia Mary, *e d* of Thomas Brown Yates, Godalming; two *s* one *d*. *Educ:* The Leys Sch., Cambridge; Jesus Coll., Cambridge (MA). Pilot, RAF, 1952-54. Called to Bar, Inner Temple, 1958; Mem. Gen. Council of the Bar, 1964-68; Prosecuting Counsel to the Post Office, 1964-69; Dep. Recorder, Rochester City QS, 1971; a Recorder of the Crown Court, 1972-82. Mem., Lord Chancellor's County Court Rules Cttee, 1972-80; Recorder, SE Circuit Bar Mess, 1978-80. Master, Curriers' Co., 1976-77. *Recreations:* golf, cricket. *Address:* 2 Harcourt Buildings, Temple, EC4. *T:* 01-583 9020. *Clubs:* MCC; Hawks (Cambridge); Wildernesse (Captain 1978) (Sevenoaks); Royal Worlington and Newmarket Golf.

VICK, Sir (Francis) Arthur, Kt 1973; OBE 1945; PhD; FIEE, FInstP; MRIA; President and Vice-Chancellor, Queen's University of Belfast, 1966-76; Pro-Chancellor and Chairman of Council, University of Warwick, since 1977; *b* 5 June 1911; *s* of late Wallace Devenport Vick and late Clara (*née* Taylor); *m* 1943, Elizabeth Dorothy Story; one *d*. *Educ:* Waverley Grammar School, Birmingham; Birmingham Univ. Asst Lectr in Physics, University Coll., London, 1936-39, Lectr, 1939-44; Asst Dir of Scientific Research, Min. of Supply, 1939-44; Lectr in Physics, Manchester Univ., 1944-47, Sen. Lectr, 1947-50; Prof. of Physics, University Coll. of N Staffs, 1950-59 (Vice-Principal, 1950-54, Actg Principal, 1952-53); Dep. Dir, AERE, Harwell, 1959-60, Dir, 1960-64; Dir of Research Group, UKAEA, 1961-64; Mem. for Research, 1964-66. Institute of Physics: Mem. Bd, 1946-51; Chm., Manchester and District Branch, 1948-51; Vice-Pres., 1953-56; Hon. Sec., 1956-60. Chairman: Manchester Fedn of Scientific Societies, 1949-51; Naval Educn Adv. Cttee, 1964-70; Academic Adv. Council, MoD, 1969-76; Standing Conf. on Univ. Entrance, 1968-75. Pres., Assoc. of Teachers in Colls and Depts of Educn, 1964-72, Hon. Mem., 1972; Vice-Pres., Arts Council of NI, 1966-76. Member: Adv. Council on Bldg Research, Min. of Works, 1955-59; Scientific Adv. Council, Min. of Supply, 1956-59; UGC, 1959-66; Colonial Univ. Grants Adv. Cttee, 1960-65; Adv. Council on Research and Develt, Min. of Power, 1960-63; Nuclear Safety Adv. Cttee, Min. of Power, 1960-66; Governing Body, Nat. Inst. for Research in Nuclear Science, 1964-65. MRIA 1973. Hon. DSc: Keele, 1972; NUI, 1976; Hon. LLD: Dublin, 1973; Belfast, 1977; Hon. DCL Kent, 1977. Kt Comdr, Liberian Humane Order of African Redemption, 1962. *Publications:* various scientific papers and contributions to books. *Recreations:* music, gardening, using tools. *Address:* Fieldhead Cottage, Fieldhead Lane, Myton Road, Warwick CV34 6QF. *T:* Warwick 491822. *Clubs:* Athenæum, Savile.

VICK, Richard (William); **His Honour Judge Vick**; a Circuit Judge (formerly County Court Judge, since 1969, and Deputy Chairman of Quarter Sessions for Middlesex Area of Greater London, since 1965); Resident Judge, Kingston Group of Courts, since 1978; Honorary Recorder of Guildford, since 1973; *b* 9 Dec. 1917; *s* of late Richard William Vick, JP, and Hilda Josephine (*née* Carlton), Mortlake; *m* 1st, 1947, Judith Jean (*d* 1974), *d* of Denis Franklin Warren; one *s* two *d* ; 2nd, 1975, Mrs Joan Chesney Frost, BA, *d* of Arthur Blaney Powe, MA, Sydney, Australia. *Educ:* Stowe; Jesus Coll., Cambridge (BA). Served in RNVR, 1939-46. Called to Bar, Inner Temple, 1940. Dep. Chairman, W Kent QS, 1960-62; Dep. Chairman, Kent

QS, 1962-65. Vice-Chm., Surrey Magistrates Soc., 1972; Member: Magistrates' Courts Cttee; Probation Cttee; Circuit Adviser, Judicial Studies Bd, 1981-. Mem. Court, Surrey Univ. *Publication:* The Administration of Civil Justice in England and Wales, 1967. *Recreations:* sailing, shooting, swimming, bridge. *Address:* The Town House, Godalming, Surrey. *Clubs:* United Oxford & Cambridge University; Hawks (Cambridge).

VICKERS, family name of **Baroness Vickers.**

VICKERS, Baroness *cr* 1974 (Life Peer), of Devonport; **Joan Helen Vickers,** DBE 1964 (MBE 1946); *e d* of late Horace Cecil Vickers and late Lilian Monro Lambert Grose. *Educ:* St Monica's Coll., Burgh Heath, Surrey. Member, LCC, Norwood Division of Lambeth, 1937-45. Contested (C) South Poplar, 1945. Served with British Red Cross in SE Asia (MBE); Colonial Service in Malaya, 1946-50. MP (C) Plymouth, Devonport, 1955-Feb. 1974; UK Delegate (C), Council of Europe and WEU, 1967-74. Chairman: Anglo-Indonesian Society; UK Delegate, UK Status of Women Commn, 1960-64; President: Status of Women Cttee; Internat. Friendship League; Inst. of Qualified Private Secretaries; Europe China Assoc. Chm., National Centre for Cued Speech. Netherlands Red Cross Medal. *Address:* The Manor House, East Chisenbury, Pewsey, Wilts.

VICKERS, Eric, CB 1979; Director of Defence Services, Department of the Environment, 1972-81; *b* 25 April 1921; *s* of late Charles Vickers and late Ida Vickers; *m* 1945, Barbara Mary Jones; one *s* one *d. Educ:* King's School, Grantham. Joined India Office, 1938; RAF (Fl/Lt Coastal Command), 1941-46; Ministry of Works, 1948; Principal, 1950; Assistant Secretary, 1962; Imperial Defence College, 1969; Dir of Home Estate Management, DoE, 1970-72. *Recreation:* photography. *Address:* 16 Place House Lane, Old Coulsdon, Surrey. *T:* Downland 54303.

VICKERS, James Oswald Noel, OBE 1977; General Secretary, Civil Service Union, 1963-77 (Deputy General Secretary, 1960-62); *b* 6 April 1916; *s* of Noel Muschamp and Linda Vickers; *m* 1940, Winifred Mary Lambert; one *s* one *d. Educ:* Stowe Sch.; Queens' Coll., Cambridge. Exhibnr, BA Hons Hist., MA. Served War, HM Forces, 1939-45. Warden, Wedgwood Memorial Coll., 1946-49; Educn Officer, ETU, and Head of Esher Coll., 1949-56. Member: Civil Service Nat. Whitley Council, 1962-77 (Chm. Staff Side, 1975-77); TUC Inter-Union Disputes Panel, 1970-77; TUC Non-Manual Workers Adv. Cttee, 1973-75; Fabian Soc. Trade Union and Industrial Relations Cttee, 1964- (Chm. 1973-78; Vice-Chm., 1978-79); UCL Coll. Cttee, 1974-79; Council, Tavistock Inst., 1976-80; Employment Appeal Tribunal, 1978-; CS Appeal Bd, 1978-. *Publications:* contrib. to Fabian pamphlets. *Recreations:* bird-watching, gardening, travel. *Address:* 5 The Butts, Brentford, Mddx TW8 8BJ. *T:* 01-560 3482; Heber Vale Cottage, Timberscombe, near Minehead, Som.

VICKERS, Jon, CC (Canada) 1968; dramatic tenor; *b* Prince Albert, Saskatchewan, 1926; *m* 1953, Henrietta Outerbridge; three *s* two *d.* Studied under George Lambert, Royal Conservatory of Music, Toronto. Made debut with Toronto Opera Company, 1952; Stratford (Ontario) Festival, 1956. Joined Royal Opera House, Covent Garden, 1957. First sang at: Bayreuth Festival, 1958; Vienna State Opera, San Francisco Opera, and Chicago Lyric, 1959; Metropolitan, New York, and La Scala, Milan, 1960; Buenos Aires, 1962; Salzburg Festival, 1966. *Films:* Carmen; Pagliacci; Otello; Fidelio. Has made many recordings. Presbyterian. Hon. Dr: University of Saskatchewan, 1963; Bishop's Univ., 1965; Univ. West Ontario, 1970; Brandon Univ., 1976; Laval Univ., 1977; Univ. of Guelph, 1978. RAM 1977. Canada Centennial Medal, 1967. *Address:* c/o John Coast, 1 Park Close, SW1.

VICKERS, Prof. Michael Douglas Allen; Professor of Anaesthetics, Welsh National School of Medicine, since 1976; *b* 11 May 1929; *s* of George and Freda Vickers; *m* 1959, Ann Hazel Courtney; two *s* one *d. Educ:* Abingdon Sch.; Guy's Hosp. Med. Sch. MB, BS; FFARCS; FRSM. Lectr, RPMS, 1965-68; Consultant Anaesthetist, Birmingham AHA, 1968-76. Mem. Bd, Faculty of Anaesthetists, 1971-; Vice-Pres. and Sec., European Acad. of Anaesthesiology; Pres., Assoc. of Anaesthetists of GB and Ireland, 1982- (Hon. Sec., 1974-76). Hon. FFARACS. *Publications:* (jtly) Principles of Measurement for Anaesthetists, 1970 (2nd edn, as Principles of Measurement, 1981); (jtly) Drugs in Anaesthetic Practice, 6th edn 1983; Medicine for Anaesthetists, 1977, 2nd edn 1982. *Recreations:* music, theatre. *Address:* Department of Anaesthetics, Welsh National School of Medicine, Heath Park, Cardiff CF4 4XN. *T:* Cardiff 755944.

VICKERS, Ven. Michael Edwin; Archdeacon of the East Riding, since 1981; *b* 13 Jan. 1929; *s* of William Edwin and Florence Alice Vickers; *m* 1960, Janet Cynthia Croasdale; three *d. Educ:* St Lawrence Coll., Ramsgate; Worcester Coll., Oxford (BA Mod. History, 1952, MA 1956); Cranmer Hall, Durham (DipTheol with distinction, 1959). Company Secretary, Hoares (Ceylon) Ltd, 1952-56; Refugee Administrator for British Council for Aid to Refugees, 1956-57; Lay Worker, Diocese of Oklahoma, 1959; Curate of Christ Church, Bexleyheath, 1959-62; Sen. Chaplain, Lee Abbey Community, 1962-67; Vicar of St John's, Newland, Hull, 1967-81; Area Dean, Central and North Hull, 1972-81; Proctor in Convocation, 1975-; Chm., York Diocesan House of Clergy, 1975-; Canon and Prebendary of York, 1981-. *Recreations:* squash, fell-walking, travel, drama. *Address:* Brimley Lodge, 27 Molescroft Road, Beverley, North Humberside HU17 7DX. *T:* Hull 881659.

VICKERS, Lt-Gen. Richard Maurice Hilton, OBE 1970 (MBE 1964); MVO 1959; Director General of Army Training, since 1982; *b* 21 Aug. 1928; *s* of Lt-Gen. W. G. H. Vickers, *qv; m* 1957, Gaie, *d* of Maj.-Gen. G. P. B. Roberts, *qv;* three *d. Educ:* Haileybury and Imperial Service Coll.; RMA. Commissioned Royal Tank Regt, 1948; 1st RTR, BAOR, Korea, Middle East, 1948-54; Equerry to HM The Queen, 1956-59; Brigade Major, 7 Armd Bde, 1962-64; 4th RTR, Borneo and Malaysia, 1964-66; CO The Royal Dragoons, 1967-68, The Blues and Royals, 1968-69; Comdr, 11th Armd Brigade, 1972-74; Dep. Dir of Army Training, 1975-77; GOC 4th Armoured Div., 1977-79; Comdt, RMA, 1979-82. *Recreations:* squash, flyfishing. *Address:* Ministry of Defence (Army), Whitehall, SW1A 2EU. *Club:* Cavalry and Guards.

VICKERS, Thomas Douglas, CMG 1956; *b* 25 Sept. 1916; 2nd *s* of late Ronald Vickers, Scaitcliffe, Englefield Green, Surrey; *m* 1951, Margaret Awdry, *o c* of late E. A. Headley, Wagga, NSW; one *s* one *d. Educ:* Eton; King's Coll., Cambridge (MA Hons). Cadet, Colonial Administrative Service, 1938. Served War of 1939-45; Coldstream Guards, 1940-45. Colonial Office, 1938-40 and 1945-50; Gold Coast, 1950-53; Colonial Secretary, British Honduras, 1953-60; Chief Secretary, Mauritius, 1960-67, Dep. Governor, 1967-68; retired from HMOCS, Oct. 1968. Head of Personnel Services, Imperial Cancer Research Fund, 1969-81. *Address:* Wood End, Worplesdon, Surrey GU3 3RJ. *T:* Worplesdon 233468. *Club:* Army and Navy.

VICKERS, Lt-Gen. Wilmot Gordon Hilton, CB 1942; OBE 1919; DL; *b* 8 June 1890; *s* of late Lt-Col Hilton Vickers, IA; *m* Mary Catherine (*decd*), *d* of Dr A. E. Nuttall; two *s. Educ:* United Services Coll., Westward Ho!, and Windsor (now Haileybury and Imperial Service Coll.). Commissioned Indian Army (Unattached List), 1910; 2nd Lieut, Indian Army, 1911; Captain, 1915; Major, 1926; Bt Lt-Col, 1931; Col, 1935; Maj.-Gen., 1940; Lt-Gen., 1943; Comdt and Chief Instructor, Equitation Sch., India, 1934-35; Dep. Dir of Staff Duties, India, 1935-37; Brigade Comdr, India, 1939-40; Dir of Supplies and Transport, India, 1940-41; Maj.-Gen. i/c Administration, Iraq-Persia, 1941-42; Quarter-master-General, India, 1942-44; retired, 1944. DL County of Gloucestershire, 1946. County Cadet Commandant, Gloucestershire, Army Cadet Force, 1946-55. County Chief Warden, Civil Defence, Gloucestershire, 1949-60. *Address:* 4 Oakhurst Court, Parabola Road, Cheltenham, Glos. *Clubs:* Cavalry and Guards; New (Cheltenham). *See also R. M. H. Vickers.*

VICKERY, Prof. Brian Campbell, FLA, FIInfSc; Professor of Library Studies and Director, School of Library Archive and Information Studies, University College London, since 1973; *b* 11 Sept. 1918; *s* of Adam Cairns McCay and Violet Mary Watson; *m* 1st, 1945, Manuletta McMenamin; one *s* one *d;* 2nd, 1970, Alina Gralewska. *Educ:* King's Sch., Canterbury; Brasenose Coll., Oxford. MA. Chemist, Royal Ordnance Factory, Somerset, 1941-45; Librarian, ICI Ltd, Welwyn, 1946-60; Principal Scientific Officer, Nat. Lending Library for Sci. and Technology, 1960-64; Librarian, UMIST, 1964-66; Head of R&D, Aslib, 1966-73. *Publications:* Classification and Indexing in Science, 1958, 3rd edn 1975; On Retrieval System Theory, 1961, 2nd edn 1965; Techniques of Information Retrieval, 1970; Information Systems, 1973; articles in professional jls. *Recreations:* reading history, poetry, philosophy; music and theatre; personal computing. *Address:* 138 Midhurst Road, W13 9TP. *T:* 01-567 6544.

VICKERY, Sir Philip Crawford, Kt 1948; CIE 1939; OBE 1923; *b* 23 Feb. 1890; *s* of late John Evans Vickery and Alice Maud Mary Vickery; *m* 1920, Phyllis Field Fairweather (*d* 1982); one *s* (*yr s,* Coldstream Guards, died of wounds in Italy, April 1945). *Educ:* Portora Royal Sch., Enniskillen; Dean Close Sch., Cheltenham; Trinity Coll., Dublin. Joined Indian Police, 1909; Coronation Durbar, Delhi, 1911; served European War, 1915-21 and War of 1939-45; Acting Lieut-Colonel, Sept. 1939, and Colonel, 1942. Commonwealth Relations Office, 1952-65. *Club:* East India, Devonshire, Sports and Public Schools.

VIDAL, Gore; author; *b* 3 Oct. 1925; *s* of Eugene and Nina Gore Vidal. *Educ:* Phillips Exeter Academy, New Hampshire, USA (grad. 1943). Army of the US, 1943-46: Private to Warrant Officer (jg) and First Mate, Army FS-35, Pacific Theatre Ops. Democratic-Liberal candidate for US Congress, 1960; candidate for Democratic nomination for election to US Senate from California, 1982. Apptd to President Kennedy's Adv. Council of the Arts, 1961-63. *Publications: novels:* Williwaw, 1946; In a Yellow Wood, 1947; The City and the Pillar, 1948; The Season of Comfort, 1949; A Search for the King, 1950; Dark Green, Bright Red, 1950; The Judgment of Paris, 1952; Messiah, 1954; Julian, 1964; Washington, DC, 1967; Myra Breckinridge, 1968 (filmed 1969); Two Sisters, 1970; Burr, 1973; Myron, 1975; 1876, 1976; Kalki, 1978; Creation, 1981; *essays:* Rocking the Boat, 1962; Reflections upon a Sinking Ship, 1969; Homage to Daniel Shays (collected essays 1952-72), 1972; Matters of Fact and of Fiction, 1977; The Second American Revolution, 1982; Pink Triangle and Yellow Star and other essays (1976-1982), 1982; *short stories:* A Thirsty Evil, 1956; *plays:* Visit to a Small Planet (NY prod.), 1957; The Best Man (NY prod.), 1960; Romulus (adapted from F. Dürrenmatt) (NY prod.), 1962; Weekend (NY prod.), 1968; On the March to the Sea (German prod.), 1962; An Evening with Richard Nixon, 1972; *screenplays,* from 1955: Wedding Breakfast, 1957; Suddenly Last Summer, 1958; The Best Man, 1964, etc; *television plays:* 1954-56: The Death of Billy the Kid (translated to screen as The Lefthanded Gun, 1959), etc; *literary and political* *criticism for:* NY Review of Books, Esquire, Partisan Review, TLS, etc. *Recreations:* as noted above. *Address:* Ravello, (Salerno), Italy.

VIDIC, Dobrivoje, Order of Yugoslav Flag 1st class; Order of Service to the People; Order of Brotherhood and Unity 1st class; Order for Bravery; Partisan Remembrance Medal 1941; Member of Presidium, Central Committee of League of Communists of Yugoslavia, since 1982; *b* 24 Dec. 1918; *m* 1941, Mrs Vukica; one *s*. *Educ:* Skoplje University. Joined Diplomatic Service, 1951; served as: Minister Counsellor, London; Ambassador to Burma; Ambassador to USSR; Under-Sec. of State for Foreign Affairs; Perm. Rep. to UN, New York; Chm., Commn for Internat. Relations of Socialist Alliance of Yugoslavia; Ambassador to USSR; Ambassador of Yugoslavia to the Court of St James's, 1970-73; Mem. Exec. Cttee of Presidium, Central Cttee of League of Communists of Yugoslavia, 1974-79; Pres. of Presidium, Socialist Republic of Serbia, 1978-82. *Address:* Central Committee of League of Communists of Yugoslavia, Bulaver Lengina 6, Belgrade, Yugoslavia.

VIDLER, Rev. Alexander Roper, LittD; Dean of King's College, Cambridge, 1956-66; Fellow of King's College, 1956-67, Hon. Fellow since 1972; *b* 1899; *s* of late Leopold Amon Vidler, JP, Rye, Sussex; unmarried. *Educ:* Sutton Valence Sch.; Selwyn Coll., Cambridge. BA 2nd Class Theol. Tripos, 1921; MA 1925; Norrisian Prize, 1933; BD 1938; LittD 1957; University of Edinburgh, DD, 1946; Hon. DD: University of Toronto, 1961; College of Emmanuel and St Chad, Saskatoon, 1966. Wells Theological Coll.; Deacon, 1922; Priest, 1923; Curate of St Philip's, Newcastle upon Tyne, 1922-24; of St Aidan's, Birmingham, 1925-31; on staff of the Oratory House, Cambridge, 1931-38; Warden of St Deiniol's Library, Hawarden, 1939-48; Hon. Canon of Derby Cathedral, 1946-48; Canon of St George's Chapel, Windsor, 1948-56; licensed by Cambridge Univ. to preach throughout England, 1957; University Lecturer in Divinity, 1959-67; Commissary for Bishop of New Guinea, 1936-62; Hale Lecturer (USA), 1947; Birkbeck Lecturer (Trinity Coll., Cambridge), 1953; Firth Lecturer (Nottingham Univ.), 1955; Robertson Lecturer (Glasgow Univ.), 1964; Sarum Lecturer (Oxford Univ.), 1968-69. Sec., Christian Frontier Council, 1949-56. Mayor of Rye, 1972-74. Acting Principal, Chichester Theological Coll., 1981. Editor, Theology, 1939-64; Co-editor of The Frontier, 1950-52. *Publications:* Magic and Religion, 1930; Sex, Marriage and Religion, 1932; The Modernist Movement in the Roman Church, 1934; A Plain Man's Guide to Christianity, 1936; God's Demand and Man's Response, 1938; God's Judgement on Europe, 1940; Secular Despair and Christian Faith, 1941; Christ's Strange Work, 1944; The Orb and the Cross, 1945; Good News for Mankind, 1947; The Theology of F. D. Maurice, 1949; Christian Belief, 1950; Prophecy and Papacy, 1954; Christian Belief and This World, 1956; Essays in Liberality, 1957; Windsor Sermons, 1958; The Church in an Age of Revolution, 1961; A Century of Social Catholicism, 1964; 20th Century Defenders of the Faith, 1965; F. D. Maurice and Company, 1966; A Variety of Catholic Modernists, 1970; Scenes from a Clerical Life, 1977; Read, Mark, Learn, 1980; (jointly): The Development of Modern Catholicism, 1933; The Gospel of God and the Authority of the Church, 1937; Natural Law, 1946; Editor, Soundings: Essays concerning Christian Understanding, 1962; Objections to Christian Belief, 1963; (with Malcolm Muggeridge) Paul: envoy extraordinary, 1972. *Recreations:* gardening, golf, beekeeping. *Address:* Friars of the Sack, Rye, East Sussex TN31 7HE.

VIELER, Geoffrey Herbert, FCA; Member of Board, Post Office Corporation, 1969-71; *b* 21 Aug. 1910; *s* of late Herbert Charles Stuart Vieler, Huddersfield, and Emily Mary; *m* 1934, Phyllis Violet; one *d*. *Educ:* Fairway Sch., Bexhill-on-Sea. With Vale & West, Chartered Accountants, Reading, 1927-41 (qual. 1932); War Service, 1941-46: commnd RAOC, 1943, Major 1945; joined Binder Hamlyn, Chartered Accountants, 1946, Partner 1959-69; Managing Dir, Posts and National Giro, 1969-71. Mem. Techn. Adv. Cttee, Inst. of Chartered Accountants in England and Wales, 1967-74. Chm., London Chartered Accountants, 1976-77. *Address:* Robins Wood, Monks Drive, South Ascot, Berks SL5 9BB; Riversmeet, Mill Lane, Lower Shiplake RG9 3LY.

VIERTEL, Deborah Kerr; *see* Kerr, D. J.

VIGARS, Robert Lewis; Member for Kensington, Greater London Council; Conservative Opposition Leader, GLC Housing Committee, since 1981; *b* 26 May 1923; *s* of late Francis Henry Vigars and Susan Laurina May Vigars (*née* Lewis); *m* 1962, Margaret Ann Christine, *y d* of late Sir John Walton, KCIE, CB, MC, and Lady Walton; two *d*. *Educ:* Truro Cathedral Sch.; London Univ. (LLB (Hons)). Served War of 1939-45: RA and Royal Corps of Signals, 1942-47; attached Indian Army (Captain), 1944-47; Captain, Princess Louise's Kensington Regt, TA, 1951-54. Qualified as solicitor (Hons), 1948. Partner, Simmons & Simmons, London, EC2, 1951-75. Member: Kensington Borough Council, 1953-59; London and Home Counties Traffic Adv. Cttee, 1956-58; London Roads (Nugent) Cttee, 1958-59; LCC and GLC Kensington (formerly South Kensington), 1955-; Environmental Planning Cttee, GLC, 1967-71 (Chm.); Strategic Planning Cttee, GLC, 1971-73 (Chm.); Leader of Opposition, ILEA, 1974-79; Chm. of the GLC, 1979-80; Mem., Standing Conf. on London and SE Regional Planning and SE Economic Planning Council, 1968-75. Mem. Court, London Univ., 1977-82. FRSA. *Publication:* Let Our Cities Live (Bow Gp, jointly). *Recreation:* mountain walking. *Address:* 24 Cope Place, Kensington, W8 6AA. *Club:* Hurlingham.

VIGGERS, Peter John; MP (C) Gosport, since Feb. 1974; *b* 13 March 1938; *s* of late J. S. Viggers and E. F. Viggers, Gosport; *m* 1968, Jennifer Mary McMillan, MB, BS, LRCP, MRCS, DA, *d* of late Dr R. B. McMillan, MD, FRCP, Guildford, and late Mrs J. T. C. McMillan, MA, MIB; two *s* one *d*. *Educ:* Portsmouth Grammar Sch.; Trinity Hall, Cambridge (MA). Solicitor 1967. Trained as RAF Pilot with Royal Canadian Air Force, awarded Wings 1958. Cambridge, 1958-61; Chm. Cambridge Univ. Conservative Assoc., 1960. Commnd in 457 (Wessex) Regt Royal Artillery (TA), 1963. PPS to Solicitor-General, 1979-; Deleg. to North Atlantic Assembly, 1981-; Vice-Chm., Cons. Energy Cttee, 1977-79 (a Sec., 1975-76). Director: Premier Consolidated Oilfields Ltd; Sweetheart International Ltd. Underwriting Member of Lloyd's. Mem., Management Cttee, RNLI, 1979-. *Recreations:* beagling, walking and messing about in boats. *Address:* House of Commons, SW1.

VIGNOLES, Roger Hutton, ARCM; pianoforte accompanist; *b* 12 July 1945; *s* of Keith Hutton Vignoles and Phyllis Mary (*née* Pearson); *m* 1972, Teresa Ann Elizabeth Henderson (marr. diss. 1982). *Educ:* Canterbury Cathedral Choir Sch.; Sedbergh Sch.; Magdalene Coll., Cambridge (BA, BMus); Royal College of Music, London (ARCM). Accompanist of national and internat. reputation, regularly appearing with distinguished internat. singers and instrumentalists (eg Elisabeth Soederstroem, Pierre Fournier, Rita Streich, Edith Mathis. Elisabeth Connell. Ruggiero Ricci, Kiri te Kanawa, John Shirley-Quirk, Sarah Walker, *inter alios*) both in London and provinces and at major music festivals (eg Aldeburgh, Cheltenham, Edinburgh, Brighton, Bath, etc) and broadcasting for BBC Radio 3 and television. International tours incl. USA, Canada, Australia-New Zealand, Hong Kong, Scandinavia, and recitals at Opera Houses of Cologne, 1982, Frankfurt, 1983, Brussels, 1983. Repetiteur: Royal Opera House, Covent Garden, 1969-71; English Opera Group, 1968-74; Australian Opera Company, 1976. Professor of Accompaniment, RCM, 1974-81. Gramophone records include: English song, various, with Graham Trew, baritone; Lieder by Schumann, and Brahms/Dvorak, with Sarah Walker, mezzo; première recording of The Voice of Love (Nicholas Maw); Franck and Grieg cello sonatas, with Robert Cohen, cello. *Recreations:* drawing, painting, looking at pictures, swimming, sailing. *Address:* 30 Leverton Street, Kentish Town, NW5 2PJ. *T:* 01-267 3187.

VILE, Prof. Maurice John Crawley; Professor of Political Science since 1968, and Deputy Vice-Chancellor since 1981, University of Kent at Canterbury; *b* 23 July 1927; *s* of Edward M. and Elsie M. Vile; two *s*. *Educ:* London Sch. of Economics. BSc (Econ) 1951; PhD London, 1954; MA Oxford, 1962. Lectr in Politics, Univ. of Exeter, 1954-62; Fellow of Nuffield Coll., Oxford, 1962-65; University of Kent: Reader in Politics and Govt, 1965-68; Dean of Faculty of Social Scis, 1969-75; Pro-Vice-Chancellor, 1975-81. Visiting Professor: Univ. of Massachusetts, 1960; Smith College, Mass., 1961. Royer Lectr, Univ. of Calif., Berkeley, 1974. *Publications:* The Structure of American Federalism, 1961; Constitutionalism and the Separation of Powers, 1967; Politics in the USA, 1970, rev. edn 1976; Federalism in the United States, Canada and Australia (Res. Paper No 2, Commn on the Constitution), 1973; The Presidency (Amer. Hist. Documents Vol. IV), 1974. *Address:* Keynes College, The University, Canterbury, Kent. *T:* Canterbury 66822.

VILJOEN, Marais, DMS 1976; State President of the Republic of South Africa, since June 1979; *b* 2 Dec. 1915; *s* of Gabriel François Viljoen and Magdalena Debora (*née* de Villiers); *m* 1940, Dorothea Maria Brink; one *d*. *Educ:* Jan van Riebeeck High Sch., Cape Town; Univ. of Cape Town. After leaving school, employed in Dept of Posts and Telegraphs, 1932-37; on editorial staff, Die Transvaler newspaper, 1937-40; manager, Transvaler book trade business, Potchefstroom, 1940; co-founder and provincial leader of Nat. Youth League, 1940-45; organiser of Transvaal National Party, 1945-49; Member, Provincial Council, Transvaal, 1949-53; Information Officer, Transvaal National Party, several years from 1951; Chairman, Inf. Service of Federal Council, National Party of S Africa, 1969-74; Dep. Chm., Nat. Party, Transvaal, 1966-75. MP Alberton, 1953-76; Dep. Minister of Labour and of Mines, 1958-61; various other ministerial offices, incl. Interior and Immigration, until 1966; Cabinet appointments, 1966-: Minister of Labour and of Coloured Affairs, 1966-69, also of Rehoboth Affairs, 1969-70; Minister of Labour and of Posts and Telecommunications, 1970-76. President of the Senate, 1976-79. Special Cl., Grand Collar, Order of Good Hope, Republic of S Africa, 1981. *Recreations:* golf, bowls, reading. *Address:* Presidensie, Bryntirion, Pretoria, Republic of South Africa. *Clubs:* (Hon. Member) various South African, including: Pretoria, City and Civil Service, Cape Town.

VILLIERS; *see* Child-Villiers, family name of Earl of Jersey.

VILLIERS; *see* de Villiers.

VILLIERS, family name of **Earl of Clarendon.**

VILLIERS, Viscount; George Henry Child Villiers; *b* 29 Aug. 1948; *s* and heir of 9th Earl of Jersey, *qv*; *m* 1st, 1969, Verna (marr. diss. 1973), 2nd *d* of K. A. Stott, St Mary, Jersey; one *d*; 2nd, 1974, Sandra, step *d* of H. Briginshaw, Feremina, St Martin, Guernsey; one *s* two *d*. *Educ:* Eton; Millfield. Late The Royal Hussars (PWO). *Heir:* *s* Hon. George Francis William Child Villiers, *b* 5 Feb. 1976. *Address:* Bel Respiro, Mont au Prêtre, St Helier, Jersey, CI. *Club:* Brooks's.

VILLIERS, Sir Charles (Hyde), Kt 1975; MC 1945; Chairman, BSC (Industry), since 1976 (Chairman, British Steel Corporation, 1976-80); *b* 14 Aug. 1912; *s* of Algernon Hyde Villiers (killed in action, 1917) and Beatrix Paul (later Lady Aldenham) (*d* 1978); *m* 1st, 1938, Pamela Constance Flower (*d* 1943); one *s*; 2nd, 1946, Marie José, *d* of Count Henri de la Barre d'Erquelinnes, Jurbise, Belgium; two *d. Educ:* Eton; New Coll., Oxford. Asst to Rev. P. B. Clayton, of Toc H, 1931; Glyn Mills, Bankers, 1932. Grenadier Guards (SRO), 1936; served at Dunkirk, 1940 (wounded, 1942); Special Ops Exec., London and Italy, 1943-45; parachuted into Yugoslavia and Austria, 1944; Lt-Col and Comd 6 Special Force Staff Section, 1945 (MC). A Man. Dir, Helbert Wagg, 1948, and J. Henry Schroder Wagg, 1960-68; Managing Director, Industrial Reorganisation Corporation, 1968-71; Chm., Guinness Mahon & Co. Ltd, 1971-76; Exec. Dep. Chm., Guinness Peat Gp, 1973-76. Director: Bass Charrington; Courtaulds; Sun Life Assurance; Banque Belge; Financor SA; Darling & Co. (Pty); Formerly Chm., Ashdown Trans-Europe and Trans-Australian Investment Trusts. Chairman: Federal Trust Gp on European Monetary Integration, 1972; Northern Ireland Finance Corp., 1972-73. Co-Chm., Europalia Festival, 1973; Chm., Theatre Royal, Windsor; Trustee, Royal Opera House Trust, 1974-79. Member: Inst. Internat. d'Etudes Bancaires, 1959-76 (Pres. 1964); Minister of Labour's Resettlement Cttee for London and SE, 1958 (Chm. 1961-68); Review Body for N Ireland Economic Develt, 1971; NEDC, 1976-80. Lubbock Meml Lectr, Oxford, 1971. Mem., Chelsea Borough Council, 1950-53. Order of the People, Yugoslavia, 1970; Grand Officier de l'Ordre de Léopold II (Belgium), 1974; Gold Medal of IRI, Italy, 1975. *Recreation:* gardening. *Address:* 65 Eaton Square, SW1. *T:* 01-235 7634; Blacknest House, Sunninghill, Berks. *T:* Ascot 22137. *Club:* Anglo-Belgian.

See also Baron Aldenham.

VILLIERS, Vice-Adm. Sir (John) Michael, KCB 1962 (CB 1960); OBE 1943; *b* 22 June 1907; 3rd *s* of late Rear-Adm. E. C. Villiers, CMG and of Mrs Villiers; *m* 1936, Rosemary, CStJ, 2nd *d* of late Lt-Col B. S. Grissell, DSO, and late Lady Astley-Cubitt; two *d. Educ:* Oundle School; Royal Navy. Served War of 1939-45 (despatches, OBE). Comd HMS Ursa, 1945, and HMS Snipe, 1946-47; directing staff of Joint Services Staff College, 1948-49; Assistant Director of Plans Admiralty, 1950-51; Queen's Harbour Master, Malta, 1952-54; comd HMS Bulwark, 1954-57; Chief of Naval Staff, New Zealand, 1958-60; a Lord Commissioner of the Admiralty, Fourth Sea Lord and Vice-Controller, 1960-63; Lt-Governor and C-in-C Jersey, 1964-69. KStJ 1964. *Address:* Decoy House, Melton, Woodbridge, Suffolk IP13 6DH. *Club:* Army and Navy.

VINCENT, Maj.-Gen. Douglas, CB 1969; OBE 1954; Director, Standard Telephones & Cables Pty Ltd, since 1973; *b* Australia, 10 March 1916; *s* of William Frederick Vincent, civil engineer, and Sarah Jane Vincent; *m* 1947, Margaret Ector, *d* of N. W. Persse, Melbourne; two *s* one *d. Educ:* Brisbane State High School; Royal Military Coll., Duntroon. Commissioned, Dec. 1938; Middle East (7 Div.), 1940-42; BLA, 1944; NW Europe (30 Corps); Borneo Campaign, 1945; Brit. Commonwealth Forces, Korea, 1954; Dir of Signals, 1954-58; Dir of Staff Duties, 1958-60; Chief of Staff, Eastern Command, 1960-62; Commander, Aust. Army Force, 1962-63 (Singapore, Malaya); idc 1964; Commander: 1 Task Force, 1965; 1st Div., 1966; Aust. Force, Vietnam, 1967-68; Head, Aust. Jt Services Staff, Washington, DC, USA, 1968-70; Adjutant General, Australian Army, 1970-73. Mem. Nat. Exec., RSL (Defence Adviser, 1975-). SMIREE(Aust). *Recreations:* golf, swimming. *Address:* 41 Hampton Circuit, Yarralumla, Canberra, ACT 2600, Australia. *Club:* National Press (Canberra).

VINCENT, Prof. Ewart Albert; Professor of Geology, and Fellow of University College, Oxford, since 1967; *b* 23 Aug. 1919; *o s* of Albert and Winifred Vincent, Aylesbury; *m* 1944, Myrtle Ablett; two *d. Educ:* Reading Sch.; Univ. of Reading. BSc (Reading) 1940; PhD 1951; MA (Oxon) 1952; MSc (Manch.) 1966. FRIC, FGS. Chemist, Min. of Supply, 1940-45; Geologist, Anglo-Iranian Oil Co., 1945-46; Lectr in Mineralogy and Crystallography, Univ. of Durham, 1946-51; Lectr in Geology, Oxford Univ., 1951-56; Reader in Mineralogy, Oxford Univ., 1956-62; Prof. of Geology, Manchester Univ., 1962-66. Mem. NERC, 1975-78. Vice-Pres. Internat. Assoc. of Volcanology, 1968-71; Pres., Mineralogical Soc. of GB, 1974-76; Mem. Council, Geol Soc., 1973-76. Fellow, Mineralogical Soc. of Amer. Hon. Corresp. Mem., Soc. Géol. de Belgique. Awarded Wollaston Fund, Geol Soc. London, 1961. *Publications:* scientific papers in learned jls. *Recreations:* music, photography. *Address:* 2 Linch Farm, Wytham, Oxford; Department of Geology and Mineralogy, Parks Road, Oxford. *T:* Oxford 54511.

VINCENT, Ivor Francis Sutherland, CMG 1966; MBE 1945; HM Diplomatic Service, retired; Director, Fairbridge Society (Inc.), since 1978; *b* 14 Oct. 1916; *s* of late Lt-Col Frank Lloyd Vincent and Gladys Clarke; *m* 1949, Patricia Mayne; three *d* (and one *d* decd). *Educ:* St Peter's Coll., Radley; Christ Church, Oxford. Served Indian Army, Royal Garhwal Rifles, 1941-46. Entered HM Foreign Service, 1946; Second Secretary, Foreign Office, 1946-48; First Sec., Buenos Aires, 1948-51; UK Delegn, NATO, Paris, 1951-53; FO, 1954-57; Rabat, 1957-59; Geneva (Disarmt Delegn), 1960; Paris (UK Delegn to OECD), 1960-62; Counsellor, FO, 1962-66; Baghdad, Jan.-June, 1967; Caracas, Oct. 1967-70; Ambassador to Nicaragua, 1970-73; Consul-Gen., Melbourne, 1973-76, retired. *Recreations:* music, walking. *Address:* 101 Barkston Gardens, SW5. *T:* 01-373 5273. *Club:* Travellers'.

VINCENT, Prof. John Joseph, MSc, MSc Tech., CText, FTI; Professor of Textile Technology, University of Manchester Institute of Science and Technology, 1957-74, now Emeritus; *b* 29 June 1907; 2nd *s* of J. H. Vincent, MA, DSc; *m* 1935, M. Monica Watson, MSc, PhD, of Sheffield; one *s* one *d. Educ:* County Grammar Sch., Harrow; University Coll., London. Mathematics Dept, University Coll., London, 1927-29; Shirley Inst., Manchester, 1929-42 and 1945-57. Ministry of Aircraft Production, 1942-45. Hon. Life Mem., Textile Institute, 1976 (Mem. Council, 1959-74; Vice-Pres., 1971-74); Pres., British Assoc. of Managers of Textile Works, 1963-64; Mem., Cotton and Allied Textiles Industry Training Bd, 1966-74. Textile Inst. Medal, 1968; Leverhulme Emeritus Fellowship, 1975-76. *Publications:* Shuttleless Looms, 1980; papers on textile technology. *Recreations:* gardening, reading, listening to music. *Address:* The White House, Perranarworthal, Truro, Cornwall TR3 7QE. *T:* Devoran 863504.

VINCENT, Leonard Grange, CBE 1960; FRIBA, FRTPI, Distinction Town Planning (RIBA); formerly architect and town planner, and Principal Partner, Vincent and Gorbing, Architects and Planning Consultants; *b* 13 April 1916; *s* of late Godfrey Grange Vincent; *m* 1942, Evelyn (*née* Gretton); twin *s* one *d. Educ:* Forest House School. Trained as architect in London, 1933, and subsequently as a town planner; experience in private practice and local government. Served War of 1939-45: Royal Engineers (Major); mostly overseas, in Western Desert, and Italian campaigns with 8th Army, 1940-45. Formerly Chief Architect and Planner, Stevenage Development Corporation. *Publications:* various technical and planning articles in technical press. *Recreations:* archaeology, painting. *Address:* Medbury, Rectory Lane, Stevenage, Hertfordshire. *T:* Stevenage 51175.

VINCENT, Maj.-Gen. Richard Frederick, DSO 1972; Commandant, Royal Military College of Science, since 1980; *b* 23 Aug. 1931; *s* of Frederick Vincent and Frances Elizabeth (*née* Coleshill); *m* 1955, Jean Paterson, *d* of Kenneth Stewart and Jane (*née* Banks); one *s* one *d* (and one *s* decd). *Educ:* Aldenham Sch. Commnd RA, National Service, 1951; Germany, 1951-55; Gunnery Staff, 1959; Technical Staff, 1964; Staff Coll., 1965; Commonwealth Bde, Malaysia, 1966-68; MoD, 1968-70; Comd 12th Light Air Def. Regt, Germany, UK and NI, 1970-72; Instr, Staff Coll., 1972-73; Mil. Dir of Studies, RMCS, 1974-75; Comd 19 Airportable Bde, 1975-77; RCDS, 1978; Dep. Mil. Sec., 1979-80. Col Comdt REME, 1981-. Mem. Court, Cranfield Inst. of Technol., 1981-. *Publications:* contrib. mil. jls and pubns. *Recreations:* travel, reading, film making, pottering around the family cottage. *Address:* c/o Midland Bank, Shaftesbury, Dorset SP7 8JX. *T:* (office) Swindon 782551. *Club:* Army and Navy.

VINCENT, Sir William (Percy Maxwell), 3rd Bt, *cr* 1936; Director, Save & Prosper Investment Management, since 1980; *b* 1 February 1945; *o s* of Sir Lacey Vincent, 2nd Bt, and of Helen Millicent, *d* of Field Marshal Sir William Robert Robertson, 1st Bt, GCB, GCMG, GCVO, DSO; *S* father, 1963; *m* 1976, Christine Margaret, *d* of Rev. E. G. Walton; three *s. Educ:* Eton College. 2nd Lieutenant, Irish Guards, 1964-67. *Recreations:* water ski-ing, sailing. *Heir: s* Edward Mark William Vincent, *b* 6 March 1978. *Address:* Whistlers, Buriton, Petersfield, Hampshire. *T:* Petersfield 3532.

VINCENT BROWN, Kenneth; *see* Brown.

VINCENT-JONES, Captain Desmond, DSC; Royal Navy; retired 1964; *b* 13 Feb. 1912; *s* of late Sir Vincent Jones, KBE; *m* 1944, Jacqueline, *e d* of Col Sloggett, DSO; two *d. Educ:* Beacon School, Crowborough; Royal Naval College, Dartmouth. Served in Royal Navy, 1929-64. War of 1939-45, in aircraft carrier operations in Atlantic and Mediterranean (DSC and Bar); Served in Air Staff appointments and in Command of HM Ships, 1946-64. Graduate of US Armed Forces and British Services Staff Colleges. Naval and Military Attaché to Buenos Aires and Montevideo, 1958-60. On retirement from RN joined Marine Consortiums as consultant. *Recreations:* golf, tennis, fishing, cruising. *Address:* 8 High Street, Chobham, Surrey. *T:* Chobham 7274. *Clubs:* Free Foresters; Sunningdale Golf.

VINCZE, Paul, FRBS, FRNS; *b* Hungary, 15 August 1907; *s* of Lajos Vincze; British subject, 1948; *m* 1958, Emilienne Chauzeix. *Educ:* High School of Arts and Crafts, Budapest, later under E. Telcs. Won a travelling scholarship to Rome, 1935-37; came to England, 1938. *Exhibited:* Royal Academy, Rome, Budapest, Paris, etc; *works represented in:* British Museum, London; Museum of Fine Arts, Budapest; Ashmolean Museum, Oxford; Swedish Historical Museum; Danish Nat. Museum; Museum of Amer. Numismatic Soc.; Smithsonian Instn, Washington; Cabinet des Medailles, Paris, etc. *Works include:* Aga Khan Platinum Jubilee Portrait; Sir Bernard Pares Memorial Tablet, Senate House, London Univ.; President Truman, portrait medallion; Pope Paul VI, portrait medallion; official medal to commemorate 400th Anniversary of birth of William Shakespeare; medal to commemorate Independence of Ghana; official seal of Ghana Govt; (designed) Smithsonian Instn Award Medal (1965); Nat. Commemorative Society (USA) Winston Churchill Medal; Florence Nightingale Medal for Société Commemorative de Femmes Célèbres; E. and J. De Rothschild Medal for inauguration of Knesset, 1966; Yehudi Menuhin 50th Birthday Medal, 1966; Prince Karim Aga Khan 10th Anniversary Medal, 1968; Cassandra Memorial Tablet for Internat. Publishing Corp. Bldg, 1968; Shakespeare-Garrick Medal, 1969; Medal to commemorate 100th Anniversary of birth of Sir Henry J. Wood, 1969; Dickens 100th Anniversary Medal for Dickens Fellowship, 1970; Medal to commemorate J. B. Priestley's 80th birthday, 1974; Internat. Shakespeare

Assoc. Congress Medal, USA, 1976; Self-portrait Medal to commemorate 70th birthday, 1978; Wall Panel illustrating all Shakespeare's plays for new Shakespeare Centre, Stratford-upon-Avon, 1981; Archie F. Carr award medal for Conservation for Florida State Museum, USA. *Coin designs:* obverse and reverses, Libya, 1951; obverses, Guatemala, 1954; reverses, threepence, sixpence and shilling, Cen. African Fedn, 1955; obverses, Ghana, 1958; reverses, Guernsey, 1957; threepence and florin, Nigeria, 1960; Guinea, obverse and reverses, Malawi, 1964; reverse, Uganda crown, 1968; Bustamante Portrait for obverse of Jamaican Dollar, 1969; reverses for decimal coins, Guernsey, 1970, etc. Awarded Premio Especial, Internat. Exhib., Madrid, 1951; Silver Medal, Paris Salon, 1964; first gold Medal of Amer. Numismatic Assoc., 1966 (90th Anniversary Convention Medal, 1981). *Address:* 5 Rossetti Studios, Flood Street, Chelsea, SW3. *T:* 01-352 3975; Villa La Meridienne, Domaine Bastide, avenue La Bastide, 06520 Magagnosc, France. *T:* 36.47.54.

VINE, Prof. Frederick John, FRS 1974; Professor of Environmental Sciences, University of East Anglia, since 1974; *b* 17 June 1939; *s* of Frederick Royston Vine and Ivy Grace Vine (*née* Bryant); *m* 1964, Susan Alice McCall; one *s* one *d. Educ:* Latymer Upper Sch., Hammersmith; St John's Coll., Cambridge (BA, PhD). Instructor, 1965-67, and Asst Professor, 1967-70, Dept of Geological and Geophysical Sciences, Princeton Univ., NJ, USA; Reader, School of Environmental Sciences, Univ. of E Anglia, 1970-74. *Publications:* articles in Nature, Science, Phil. Trans Roy. Soc. London, etc. *Recreations:* walking, camping. *Address:* 144 Christchurch Road, Norwich NR2 3PG. *T:* Norwich 53875.

VINE, Philip Mesban, CBE 1981; DL; Chairman, New Towns Staff Commission, since 1977 (Member, since 1976); Member, New Towns Commission, since 1978; Chairman, London Housing Staff Commission, since 1979; *b* 26 Oct. 1919; *s* of late Major George H. M. Vine and Elsie Mary (*née* Shephard), London; *m* 1944, Paulina, JP, *d* of late Arthur Oyler, Great Hormead Hall, Herts; one *s* one *d. Educ:* Sherborne Sch.; Taft Sch., USA; Sidney Sussex Coll., Cambridge (MA, LLB); Nottingham Univ. (MPhil 1981). Served in Royal Artillery, 1939-45; Adjutant 90th Field Regt, RA. Articled to W. H. Bentley, Town Clerk of Paddington; admitted Solicitor, 1948; Asst Solicitor, Paddington, 1948-50; Chief Asst Solicitor, Birkenhead, 1950-53; Deputy Town Clerk: Wallasey, 1953-59; Southend-on-Sea, 1959-62; Town Clerk, Cambridge, 1963-66; Town Clerk and Chief Exec. Officer, Nottingham, 1966-74. Mem. Court, Nottingham Univ., 1966-74; Chm., Notts Local Valuation Panel, 1974-; Mem., Local Radio Council for BBC Radio Nottingham, 1970-76; Indep. Chm., Home Sec.'s Adv. Cttee, Wireless and Telegraphy Act 1949, 1975-; Member: Panel of Asst Comrs of Local Govt Boundary Commn, 1974-; Panel of Indep. Inspectors, DoE, 1974-; Bd Telford (New Town) Develt Corp., 1975-; Police Complaints Bd, 1977-80; Ind. Review of the Radio Spectrum (30-960 MHz), 1982-. Gen. Comr of Income Tax, 1975-. Liveryman, Clockmakers' Co. (Mem. Court, 1981-). DL Notts, 1974. *Recreations:* fishing, archaeology, enjoyment of music. *Address:* 42 Magdala Road, Mapperley Park, Nottingham NG3 5DF. *T:* Nottingham 621269. *Clubs:* Army and Navy; United Services (Nottingham).

VINE, Col (Roland) Stephen, FRCPath, FZS; Chief Inspector, Cruelty to Animals Act (1876), Home Office, 1962-75; *b* 26 Dec. 1910; *s* of late Joseph Soutter Vine and of Josephine Vine (*née* Moylan); *m* 1935, Flora Betty, *d* of Charles Strutton Brookes, MBE, Dovercourt; three *d. Educ:* Southend-on-Sea High Sch.; Guy's Hosp. BSc; MRCS, LRCP, FRCPath, FZS(Scientific). Royal Army Medical Corps, 1934-60 (incl. War of 1939-45). Home Office, 1960-75. Member: Council, Res. Defence Soc.; Toxicological Cttee, Fund for Replacement of Animals in Med. Experiments. *Publications:* articles in RAMC Jl; chapter in Biomedical Technology in Hospital Diagnosis. *Recreations:* gardening, swimming. *Address:* Shola, Fielden Road, Crowborough, Sussex TN6 1TR. *T:* Crowborough 61381. *Club:* Civil Service.

VINE, Roy; Vice-Chairman, Barclays Bank UK Ltd, since 1982; Director, Barclays Bank PLC, since 1979 (General Manager, 1972; Senior General Manager, 1979-81); *b* 1923; *m* ; one *s* one *d. Educ:* Taunton's Sch., Southampton. Served RAF, 1942-46 and 1951-53 (Flt Lieut). *Recreations:* golf, football, music. *Address:* Barclays Bank PLC, 54 Lombard Street, EC3P 3AH.

VINELOTT, Hon. Sir John (Evelyn), Kt 1978; **Hon. Mr Justice Vinelott;** Judge of the High Court of Justice, Chancery Division, since 1978; *b* 15 Oct. 1923; *s* of George Frederick Vine-Lott and Vera Lilian Vine-Lott (*née* Mockford); *m* 1956, Sally Elizabeth, *d* of His Honour Sir Walker Kelly Carter, *qv* ; two *s* one *d. Educ:* Queen Elizabeth's Gram. Sch., Faversham, Kent; Queens' Coll., Cambridge (MA). War Service, Sub-Lieut RNVR, 1942-46. Called to Bar, Gray's Inn, 1953 (Atkin Scholar); QC 1968; Bencher, 1974; practised at the Chancery Bar. *Publications:* articles on Revenue Law, in specialist periodicals. *Address:* 5 Clarendon Road, W11. *T:* 01-727 4778; The Old Rectory, Campsea Ashe, Woodbridge, Suffolk. *T:* Wickham Market 746524.

VINEN, William Frank, FRS 1973; Poynting Professor of Physics, University of Birmingham, since 1974 (Professor of Physics, 1969-74); *b* 15 Feb. 1930; *o s* of Gilbert Vinen and Olive Maud Vinen (*née* Roach); *m* 1960, Susan-Mary Audrey Master; one *s* one *d. Educ:* Watford Grammar Sch.; Clare College, Cambridge. Research Fellow, Clare College, 1955-58. Royal Air Force, 1948-49. Demonstrator in Physics, Univ. of Cambridge and Fellow of

Pembroke Coll., 1958-62. Simon Meml Prize, Inst. of Physics, 1963; Holweck Medal and Prize, Inst. of Physics and French Physical Soc., 1978; Rumford Medal, Royal Soc., 1980. *Recreation:* good food. *Address:* 52 Middle Park Road, Birmingham B29 4BJ.

VINER, Monique Sylvaine, (Mrs M. S. Gray), QC 1979; MA; barrister-at-law; *b* 3 Oct. 1926; *d* of Hugh Viner and Eliane Viner; *m* 1958, Dr Pieter Francis Gray; one *s* three *d. Educ:* Convent of the Sacred Heart, Roehampton; St Hugh's Coll., Oxford (MA). Called to the Bar, Gray's Inn, 1950. In teaching, publishing, factory and shop work, 1947-50. Chm. or Ind. Mem. of Wages Councils (various), 1952-; Mem., Industrial Court, 1976. *Recreations:* talking, reading, tennis, golf, sailing, walking, gardening, cooking, bird watching, history. *Address:* Old Glebe, Waldron, Heathfield, East Sussex. *T:* Heathfield 3865; 2 Mitre Court Buildings, Temple, EC4Y 7BX. *T:* 01-353 2246.

VINES, Eric Victor, OBE 1971; HM Diplomatic Service; Consul-General, Barcelona, since 1980; *b* 28 May 1929; *s* of late Henry E. Vines; *m* 1953, Ellen-Grethe Ella Küppers; one *s. Educ:* St Dunstan's Coll., London; St Catharine's Coll., Cambridge (MA). Army service, 1947-49. Joined Commonwealth Relations Office, 1952; Colombo, 1954-55; 1st Sec., Singapore, 1958-61; Canberra, 1961-65; Diplomatic Service Administration Office, 1965-68; 1st Sec., Information, Mexico City, 1968-70; Counsellor, Exec. Sec.-Gen., SEATO Conf., London, 1971; Head, Cultural Exchange Dept, FCO, 1971-74; Counsellor (Commercial), Tel Aviv, 1974-77, Stockholm, 1977-80. *Recreations:* opera, archaeology, walking. *Address:* c/o Foreign and Commonwealth Office, King Charles Street, SW1. *Club:* Royal Commonwealth Society.

VINES, Sir William (Joshua), Kt 1977; CMG 1969; FASA, ACIS; psc; Chairman: ANZ Banking Group, since 1982; Associated Pulp & Paper Mills Ltd; Deputy Chairman, Tubemakers of Australia Ltd; Director: Conzinc Rio Tinto of Australia Ltd; Port Phillip Mills Pty Ltd; Dalgety Australia Ltd; grazier at Cliffdale, Currabubula, NSW, since 1982; *b* 27 May 1916; *s* of P. V. Vines, Canterbury, Victoria, Australia; *m* 1939, Thelma J., *d* of late F. J. Ogden; one *s* two *d. Educ:* Haileybury College, Brighton Beach, Victoria. Managing Director: Internat. Wool Secretariat, 1961-69 (Board Mem., 1969-79); Berger, Jenson & Nicholson Ltd, 1960 (Dir, 1961-69); Dalgety Australia Ltd, 1971-76 (Chm., 1970-80); Group Managing Director, Lewis Berger & Sons Ltd, 1955; Director: Lewis Berger & Sons (Aust.) Pty Ltd & Sherwin Williams Co. (Aust.) Pty Ltd, 1952-55; Goodlass Wall & Co. Pty Ltd, 1947-49; Dalgety Ltd; Dalgety New Zealand Ltd, 1969-80; Vice-President Melbourne Legacy, 1949-51; Pres. Building Industry Congress, Vic., 1954-55. Mem. Exec., CSIRO, 1973-78; Chm. Council, Hawkesbury Agric. Coll., 1975-. Mem., Australia New Zealand Foundn, 1979-. Chm., The Sir Robert Menzies Meml Trust. Served War of 1939-45 (despatches), 2nd AIF, 2/23 Aust. Inf. Bn, Middle East, New Guinea and Borneo, Capt. *Address:* 73 Yarranabbe Road, Darling Point, Sydney, NSW 2027, Australia. *T:* 328.7970. *Clubs:* Union, Royal Sydney Golf (Sydney); Australian, Melbourne (Melbourne).

VINEY, Hon. Anne Margaret, (Hon. Mrs Viney), JP; barrister; *b* 14 June 1926; *d* of late Baron Morton of Henryton, PC, MC, and of Lady Morton of Henryton; *m* 1947, Peter Andrew Hopwood Viney; one *s* two *d. Educ:* Priorsfield, Godalming, Surrey. Left school after matriculation, 1943; worked in publicity dept of Internat. Wool Secretariat, 1945-47. Called to the Bar, Lincoln's Inn, 1979. Councillor, Kensington and Chelsea BC, 1960-62. JP, 1961; apptd to Inner London Juvenile Court panel, 1961 (Chm. 1970); currently Jt Co-Chm., Hackney Juvenile Court. Helped to found London Adventure Playground Assoc., 1962 (Sec. 1962-69); Chm., Consumer Protection Adv. Cttee, 1973-82. *Recreations:* conversation, playing poetry game. *Address:* 4 Lansdowne Road, W11 3LW. *T:* 01-727 4884; Worth House, Worth Matravers, near Swanage, Dorset.

VINEY, Elliott (Merriam), DSO 1945; MBE 1946; TD; JP; DL; FSA; Director: British Printing Corporation Ltd, 1964-75; Hazell, Watson & Viney Ltd, 1947-78; *b* 21 Aug. 1913; *s* of late Col. Oscar Viney, TD, DL, and Edith Merriam; *m* 1950, Rosamund Ann Pelly; two *d. Educ:* Oundle; Univ. Coll., Oxford. Bucks Bn, Oxford and Bucks Light Infantry (TA), 1932-46. Governor and Trustee, Museum of London, 1972-. Pres., British Fedn of Master Printers, 1972-73. Master, Grocers' Company, 1970-71. County Dir, Bucks St John Amb. Assoc., 1953-55; Pres., Bucks Archaeol. Soc., 1979 (Hon. Sec., 1954-79). JP 1950, DL 1952, High Sheriff, 1964, Buckinghamshire. OStJ 1953. Editor: Oxford Mountaineering, 1935; Climbers' Club Jl, 1936-39; (jt) Records of Bucks, 1947-74. *Publications:* The Sheriffs of Buckinghamshire, 1965; (jtly) Old Aylesbury, 1976. *Recreations:* conservation, music, walking. *Address:* Cross Farmhouse, Quainton, Aylesbury, Bucks HP22 4AR. *Clubs:* Alpine; County Hall (Aylesbury).

VINING, Rowena Adelaide, OBE 1979 (MBE 1964); HM Diplomatic Service, retired; *b* 25 Sept. 1921; *er d* of late Col Percival Llewellyn Vining and Phyllis Servante Vining. *Educ:* privately, and at Chiddingstone Castle, Edenbridge, Kent. Foreign Office, 1941-52 (war service in Italy, Indonesia, 1943-45). Commonwealth Relations Office, 1952-55; Second Secretary: Karachi, 1955-58; Sydney, 1958-62; First Sec.: CRO, 1962-65; Canberra, 1965-67; Commonwealth Office (later Foreign and Commonwealth Office), 1967-71; Vienna, 1972-74; Consul, Florence and Consul-General, San Marino, 1974-78; Dep. UK Permanent Rep. to the Council of Europe, 1978-81;

Consul-General, Strasbourg, 1979–80. *Recreations:* gardening, music. *Address:* Dorchester Cottage, Greywell, near Basingstoke RG25 1BT. *Club:* Royal Commonwealth Society.

VINSON, Nigel, MVO 1979; Inventor; Chairman, Development Commission, since 1980 (Member, since 1978); President, Industrial Participation Association, since 1979 (Chairman, 1971–78); *b* Nettlestead Place, Kent, 27 Jan. 1931; *s* of late Ronald Vinson and Bettina Vinson (*née* Southwell-Sander); *m* 1972, Yvonne Ann Collin; three *d. Educ:* Pangbourne Naval Coll. Lieut, Queen's Royal Regt, 1949–51. Chm., 1951–72, and Founder, Plastic Coatings Ltd (started in a Nissen hut, 1952, flotation, 1969; Queen's Award to Industry, 1971). Member: Crafts Adv. Cttee, 1971–77; Design Council, 1973–80 (Chm., Finance and Gen. Purposes Cttee); Dep. Chm., CBI Smaller Firms Council, 1979–; Chm., CoSIRA, 1980–82. Director: British Airports Authority, 1973–80; Centre for Policy Studies, 1974–80; Mem. Council: Inst. of Directors, 1971–81; King George V Jubilee Trust, 1974–78; Hon. Dir, Queen's Silver Jubilee Appeal, 1976–78; Director: Sugar Bd, 1968–75; Techn. Investment Trust, 1972–; Electra Investment Trust, 1975–; Barclays Bank UK, 1982–. Member: Northumbrian Nat. Parks Countryside Cttee, 1977–; Regional Cttee, Nat. Trust, 1977–. FRSA, CBIM. *Publications:* financial articles in Spectator, Director, Daily Telegraph, etc. *Recreations:* fine art and craftmanship, horses, conservation (foundation donor Martin Mere Wildfowl Trust), farming. *Address:* 34 Kynance Mews, SW7. *T:* Wooperton 230. *Club:* Boodle's.

VINTER, (Frederick Robert) Peter, CB 1965; *b* 27 March 1914; *e s* of P. J. Vinter (Headmaster, Archbishop Holgate's Grammar Sch., York, 1915–37) and Harriet Mary (*née* Cammack); *m* 1938, Margaret, *d* of S. I. Rake, Pembroke; two *s. Educ:* Haileybury Coll.; King's Coll., Cambridge (2nd cl. hons English Tripos Pt I, 1st cl. hons Hist. Tripos Pt II); MA. Min. of Economic Warfare, 1939; Cabinet Office, 1943; HM Treasury, 1945–69, Third Sec., 1965–69; Dep. Sec., Min. of Technology and DTI, 1969–73. Overseas Adviser to CEGB, 1973–79; Dir (non-Exec.), Vickers Ltd, 1974–80. Nuffield Travelling Fellowship (in India), 1950–51. *Address:* 3 Sunnyside, Wimbledon, SW19 4SL. *T:* 01-946 4137. *Club:* United Oxford & Cambridge University.

VINTER, Peter; *see* Vinter, F. R. P.

VIRTUE, Hon. Sir John (Evenden), KBE 1975; Judge of Supreme Court of Western Australia, 1951–75 (retd); Senior Puisne Judge, 1969–75; *b* 25 April 1905; *s* of Ernest Evenden Virtue and Mary Hamilton Virtue; *m* 1938, Mary Joan, *d* of Reginald and Mary Lloyd. *Educ:* Hale Sch., Perth, WA; Univs of Melbourne and Western Australia. LLM (Melb), BA (WA). Barrister and solicitor, admitted to practise in Supreme Courts of Western Australia and Victoria; in practice as barrister and solicitor, Supreme Court of W Australia, 1928–50. Lectured (part-time) in Torts and Criminal Law, Univ. of WA, 1930–49. Served War, AIF (Major), 1940–43. Pres., Law Soc. of WA, 1950. *Recreations:* lawn bowls, contract bridge. *Address:* 74 Kingsway, Nedlands, Western Australia. *T:* 86-1856. *Clubs:* Weld, Royal Perth Yacht (Perth, WA).

VISHNEVSKAYA, Galina; soprano; *b* 25 Oct. 1926; *m* 1955, Mstislav Rostropovich, *qv*; two *d. Educ:* studied with Vera Garina. Toured with Leningrad Light Opera Co., 1944–48, with Leningrad Philharmonic Soc., 1948–52; joined Bolshoi Theatre, 1952. Concert appearances in Europe and USA, 1950–; first appeared at Metropolitan Opera, NY, 1961. Rôles include: Leonora in Fidelio and Tatiana in Eugene Onegin. Has sung in Britain at Festival Hall, Aldeburgh Festival, Edinburgh Festival, Covent Garden. Makes concert tours with her husband. Has made many recordings. *Address:* c/o Victor Hochhauser, 4 Holland Park Avenue, W11 3QU.

VISSER, John Bancroft; Director of Administration, Science and Engineering Research Council (formerly Science Research Council), since 1974; *b* 29 Jan. 1928; *o s* of late Gilbert and Ethel Visser; *m* 1955, Astrid Margareta Olson; two *s* one *d. Educ:* Mill Hill Sch.; New Coll., Oxford (Exhibnr). Entered Civil Service, Asst Principal, Min. of Supply, 1951; Principal, 1956; Min. of Aviation, 1959; Admin. Staff Coll., 1965; Asst Sec., 1965; Min. of Technology, 1967; Royal Coll. of Defence Studies, 1970; Civil Service Dept, 1971; Procurement Exec., MoD, 1971; Under-Sec., 1974; Sec. of Nat. Defence Industries Council, 1971–74. Dir, Construction Holdings Ltd, 1976–. *Recreations:* sport, music, gardening, walking. *Address:* Rosslyn, 3 Berkeley Road, Cirencester, Glos GL7 1TY. *T:* Cirencester 2626. *Club:* Old Millhillians.

VISSER 't HOOFT, Dr Willem Adolf; General Secretary of World Council of Churches, 1938–66, Hon. President, 1968; *b* 20 Sept. 1900; *m* 1924, Henriette Philippine Jacoba Boddaert (*d* 1968); two *s* one *d. Educ:* Leyden University (DD). Secretary, World Committee of YMCA, 1924–31; General Secretary, World Student Christian Federation, 1931–38. Hon. Professor: Theolog. Faculty, Budapest, 1947; Theolog. Acad., Moscow, 1964. Hon. Fellow, Hebrew Univ. of Jerusalem, 1972. Hon. DD: Aberdeen, 1939; Princetown, USA; Trinity Coll., Toronto, 1950; Geneva, 1951; Yale, 1954; Oberlin Coll., 1954; Oxford, 1955; Harvard, 1958; St Paul's, Tokyo, 1959; Faculté Libre de Théologie, Paris, 1963; Kirchliche Hochschule, Berlin, 1964; Brown Univ., Providence, RI, 1965; Theol Faculty, Zürich, 1966; Univ. Catholique, Louvain, 1967; Open Univ., 1974. Cardinal Bea Prize, 1975; Louise Weiss Foundn Prize, 1976; Hanseatic Goethe Prize, 1977; Wateler

Prize; Peace Prize of German Book Trade; Grotius Medal. Hon. CStJ. Commander, Order of the Lion (Netherlands); Officer, Legion of Honour (France); Grand Cross, Order of Merit, with ribbon and star (Federal Republic of Germany); Cross of Great Comdr of Holy Sepulchre; Order of Vladimir (Orthodox Church of Russia); Comdr, Order of St Andrew (Ecumenical Patriarchate). *Publications:* The Background of the Social Gospel in America, 1928; Anglo-Catholicism and Orthodoxy, 1933; None other Gods, 1937; The Church and its Function in Society (with J. H. Oldham), 1937; Wretchedness and Greatness of the Church, 1943; The Struggle of the Dutch Church, 1946; Kingship of Christ, 1948; Rembrandt et la Bible, 1947; The Meaning of Ecumenical, 1953; The Ecumenical Movement and the Racial Problem, 1954; The Renewal of the Church (Eng. edn 1956); Rembrandt and the Gospel, 1957; The Pressure of our Common Calling, 1959; No Other Name, 1963; Hauptschriften, Bd 1 and 2, 1967; (with Cardinal Bea) Peace Among Christians, 1967; Memoirs, 1973; Has the Ecumenical Movement a Future?, 1974; The Fatherhood of God in an Age of Emancipation, 1982. *Address:* 150, route de Ferney, 1211 Geneva 20, Switzerland. *T:* 98.94.00.

VIVENOT, Baroness de, (Hermine Hallam-Hipwell), OBE 1967; free lance writer; *b* Buenos Aires, 23 April 1907; *d* of late Humphrey Hallam-Hipwell and Gertrude Hermine Isebrée-Moens tot Bloois; *m* 1931, Baron Raoul de Vivenot (*d* 1973), *e s* of Baron de Vivenot and Countess Kuenburg, Vienna; one *s. Educ:* Northlands, Buenos Aires. Joined Min. of Information, 1941; transferred Foreign Office, 1946; appointed to Foreign (subseq. Diplomatic) Service, Jan. 1947; Vice-Consul, Bordeaux, 1949–52, Nantes, 1952–53; Foreign Office, 1953–55; First Secretary (Information), HM Embassy, Brussels, 1955–59; Foreign Office, 1959–62; First Secretary (Information), HM Embassy, The Hague, 1962–66; retired 1967. External Examiner in Spanish, Univ. of London. *Publications:* The Niñas of Balcarce, a novel, 1935; Younger Argentine Painters; Argentine Art Notes; Buenos Aires Vignettes; Poems, etc. *Recreations:* Whippet racing and coursing, gardening, grandchildren. *Address:* The Flat, Aughton House, Collingbourne Kingston, Marlborough, Wilts SN8 3RY. *T:* Collingbourne Ducis 682.

VIVIAN, family name of **Barons Swansea** and **Vivian.**

VIVIAN, 5th Baron, *cr* 1841; **Anthony Crespigny Claude Vivian;** Bt *cr* 1828; *b* 4 March 1906; *e s* of 4th Baron and Barbara, *d* of William A. Fanning; *S* father 1940; *m* 1930, Victoria, *er d* of late Captain H. G. L. Oliphant, DSO, MVO; two *s* one *d. Educ:* Eton. Served RA. *Heir: s* Lt-Col Nicholas Crespigny Laurence Vivian, 16/5 Lancers [*b* 11 Dec. 1935; *m* 1st, 1960, Catherine Joyce (marr. diss. 1972), *y d* of James Kenneth Hope, *qv* ; one *s* one *d* ; 2nd, 1972, Carol, *d* of F. Alan Martineau; two *d*]. *Address:* 154 Coleherne Court, SW5; Boskenna Ros, St Buryan, near Penzance, Cornwall.
See also Marquess of Bath, Earl of Glasgow, Earl Haig.

VIVIAN, Arthur Henry Seymour; Clerk of the Skinners' Company, 1941–59; Hon. Freeman and Member of Court of the Company, 1959–80; *b* 30 June 1899; *o s* of late Henry Chester Vivian, Cardiff; *m* 1927, Elizabeth, *yr d* of late Maj. R. H. Hood-Haggie; one *d. Educ:* Harrow and Magdalen Coll., Oxford (MA). RFA, 1918; called to the Bar, Inner Temple, 1923. Commissioned London Welsh AA Regiment, 1939–43. Hon. Secretary Governing Bodies' Association, 1953–67, Hon. Member, Committee, 1967. *Recreation:* golf (played for Oxford, 1921 and 1922). *Address:* 24 Sandy Lodge Road, Moor Park, Rickmansworth, Herts. *T:* Rickmansworth 74055. *Clubs:* Royal Automobile, MCC; Royal Porthcawl Golf; Moor Park Golf (Pres., 1971-).

VIVIAN, Michael Hugh; Director, CSE Aviation Ltd, since 1980; *b* 15 Dec. 1919; *s* of Hugh Vivian and Mary (*née* Gilbertson); *m* 1st, 1951, June Stiven; one *s* one *d* ; 2nd, Joy D. Maude. *Educ:* Uppingham; Oxford. Served War: RAF (139 Sqdn), Flying Instructor, Test Pilot, 1940–44. Min. of Civil Aviation, 1945; Private Sec. to Parly Sec. for Civil Aviation, 1945–46; various operational appts, 1947–61; Dep. Dir of Flight Safety, 1961–66; Dir of Flight Safety, 1966–67; Dir of Advanced Aircraft Ops, 1967–71; Civil Aviation Authority, 1972: Dir-Gen. Safety Ops, 1972–74; Gp Dir, Safety Services, 1974–78; Full-time Member, 1974–80; Dep. Chm., 1978–80. *Recreations:* golf, vintage cars. *Address:* Willow Cottage, The Dickredge, Steeple Aston, Oxfordshire. *T:* Steeple Aston 47171. *Club:* Royal Air Force.

VOCKLER, Rt. Rev. John Charles, (Rt. Rev. Brother John Charles, SSF); engaged in writing and research; Acting Warden, Poor Clares of Reparation, Mt Sinai, NY, 1982; *b* 22 July 1924; *e s* of John Thomas Vockler and Mary Catherine Vockler (*née* Widerberg), Dee Why, New South Wales. *Educ:* Sydney Boys' High Sch.; after studying accountancy, matriculated by private study and correspondence (Metropolitan Business Coll. and Internat. Correspondence Schs, Sydney) to the University of Sydney; University of Queensland; Moore Theological Coll.; St John's Theological College, Morpeth, NSW; General Theological Seminary, New York. LTheol, Australian College of Theology, 1948; received Hey Sharp Prize for NT Greek. Junior Clerk, W. R. Carpenter & Co. Ltd, Sydney, NSW, 1939–43. Deacon, 1948; priest, 1948; Asst Deacon, Christ Church Cathedral, Newcastle, 1948; Asst Priest, 1948–50; Vice-Warden of S John's Coll., within University of Queensland, 1950–53; Acting Chaplain, C of E Grammar School for Boys, Brisbane, 1953. BA (1st Class Hons History) University of Queensland, 1953; University Gold Medal for outstanding achievement, 1953; BA University of Adelaide, aegr, 1961; Walter and Eliza Hall Foundation Travelling

Scholarship, University of Queensland, 1953; Fulbright Scholar, 1953. Acting Vice-Warden, S John's Coll., Morpeth and Lecturer in Old Testament, 1953; Graduate Student, General Theological Seminary, New York, 1954. MDiv (General Seminary), 1954. Asst Priest, Cathedral of S John the Divine, NY and Chaplain, St Luke's Home for Aged Women and the Home for Old Men and Aged Couples, 1954; Australian Delegate to Anglican Congress, 1954; Fellow and Tutor Gen. Theol. Seminary, 1954-56; STM Gen. Theol. Seminary, 1956. Asst Priest, St Stephen's Church, West 69th Street, NY, 1955; Priest-in-charge, St Stephen's, New York, 1956; Asst Priest, parish of Singleton, NSW, 1956-59; Lecturer in Theology, St John's Theological College, Morpeth, NSW, 1956-59; Secretary, Newcastle Diocesan Board of Education, 1958-59. Titular Bishop of Mount Gambier and Assistant Bishop of Adelaide (Coadjutor, 1959; title changed to Assistant, 1961), until 1962; also Archdeacon of Eyre Peninsula, 1959-62; Vicar-General, Examining Chaplain to Bishop of Adelaide, 1960-62; Bishop of Polynesia, 1962-68. Warden: Community of St Clare, Newcastle, NSW, 1975-80; Soc. of Sacred Advent, 1976-80. President, Harry Charman's All Races Sports and Social Club, Suva, Fiji, 1962-68, Hon. Life Vice-Pres., 1968; Chairman: S Pacific Anglican Council, 1963-68; Council of Pacific Theological Coll., 1963-68; President: Fiji Council of Social Services, 1964-68; Fiji Branch, Royal Commonwealth Soc., 1966-68. Writing Grant, Literature Bd of Australia Council, 1979. Member: Soc. of Authors; Australian Soc. of Authors; PEN (International), Sydney Br. and New York Br.; Guild of Writers Inc., NY; Christian Writers' Fellowship (USA); Aust. Professional Writers' Services; Penman Club (UK); Federated Clerks Union of Aust., 1978-81; Internat. Ecumenical Fellowship; Guild of All Souls; Confraternity of the Blessed Sacrament; Soc. of Mary; Catholic and Evangelical Mission; Anglican Pacifist Fellowship; Fellowship of Reconciliation; Integrity USA; Gay Christian Movement; Fellowship of S Alban and S Sergius; Anglican Fellowship of Prayer, USA; Amnesty Internat., USA. Priest Associate, Shrine of Our Lady, Walsingham and Priory of Our Lady of Pew, Westminster Abbey; Priest Member, Oratory of the Good Shepherd, 1952-75. Entered Soc. of St Francis, 1969, to test vocation to religious life; professed, 1972; Chaplain to Third Order, Soc. of St Francis (European Province), 1972-74; made life profession in Soc. of St Francis, 1975; Guardian, Friary of St Francis, Brisbane, 1975-77, Islington, NSW, 1978-79; Minister Provincial, Pacific Province, Soc. of St Francis, 1976-81; Sec., Adv. Council for Religious Communities in Aust. and Pacific, 1976-80. Permission to officiate: dio. Salisbury, 1969-70; dio. Fulham and Gibraltar, with Episcopal Commn, 1971-73; dio. Newcastle, NSW, 1975-81; dio. Auckland, NZ, 1976-81; Vice-Pres. and Mem. Council, USPG, 1973-74; Vice-Pres., Missions to Seamen, 1963-69; Hon. Asst Bp of Worcester, 1972-73; Assistant Bishop: Chelmsford, 1973-74; Southwark, 1974-75; Hon. Canon of Southwark, 1975, Canon Emeritus 1975; Hon. Mission Chaplain, dio. Brisbane, 1975-79, permission to officiate, 1979-81. Examnr for Aust. Coll. of Theology, 1975-76 and 1979. Permission to officiate, dio. Long Island, 1981-. ThD (*jure dig.*) ACT, 1961; STD (*hc*) Gen. Theological Seminary, NY, 1961; BD (*ad eund.*) Melbourne College of Divinity, 1960. *Publications:* Can Anglicans Believe Anything—The Nature and Spirit of Anglicanism, 1961 (NSW); Forward Day by Day, 1962; (ed) Believing in God (by M. L. Yates), 1962 (Australian edn); One Man's Journey, 1972; St Francis: Franciscanism and the Society of St Francis, 1980; contributions to: Preparatory Volume for Anglican Congress, Toronto, 1963; Mutual Responsibility: Questions and Answers, 1964; All One Body (ed T. Wilson), 1968; Australian Dictionary of Biography (4 articles); St Mark's Review, Australian Church Quarterly, The Anglican, The Young Anglican, Pacific Journal of Theology, New Zealand Theological Review, weekly feature, Newcastle Morning Herald, NSW; Aust. corresp. to New Fire, 1980-81. *Recreations:* classical music, detective stories, theatre, films, prints and engravings. *Address:* Little Portion Friary, PO Box 399, Mount Sinai, New York 11766, USA. *T:* (516) 473-0553. *Clubs:* Tonga (Nukualofa); St John's Coll. (Brisbane) (Hon Mem., 1976-).

VOELCKER, Christopher David, TD 1967; Metropolitan Stipendiary Magistrate, since 1982; *b* 10 May 1933; *s* of Eric Voelcker and Carmen Muriel Lyon Voelcker (*née* Henstock); *m* 1964, Sybil Russell Stoneham; two *d. Educ:* Wellington Coll., Berks. Called to Bar, Middle Temple, 1955. National Service, 8th King's Royal Irish Hussars, 1952-53. 3/4 County of London Yeomanry (Sharpshooters) TA, 1953-60; Kent and County of London Yeomanry (Sharpshooters) TA, 1960-67. *Recreations:* military history, gardening. *Address:* 6 Pump Court, Temple, EC4Y 7AR. *T:* 01-353 7242. *Club:* Cavalry and Guards.

VOGELPOEL, Pauline, MBE 1962; Director, Contemporary Art Society, since 1976; *d* of late Pieter Vogelpoel and Yvonne Vogelpoel, Mozambique; *m* 1975, Richard David Mann. *Educ:* Herschel School, Cape Town; University of Cape Town (BA). Joined Contemporary Art Society, 1954, as Organising Secretary responsible for expansion of exhibitions, events and art travel programme. Mem., Adv. Council, Victoria and Albert Museum, 1977-. *Publications:* occasional journalism. *Recreations:* cooking, music, junkshops, pugs. *Address:* Flat 8, 56 Manchester Street, W1.

VOGT, Dr Marthe Louise, FRS 1952; Dr med Berlin, Dr phil Berlin; PhD Cantab; *b* 1903; *d* of Oskar Vogt and Cécile Vogt (*née* Mugnier). *Educ:* Auguste Viktoria-Schule, Berlin; University of Berlin. Research Assistant, Department of Pharmacology, Berlin Univ., 1930; Research Assistant and head of chemical division, Kaiser Wilhelm Institut für Hirnforschung, Berlin, 1931-35; Rockefeller Travelling Fellow, 1935-36; Research Worker, Dept of Pharmacology, Cambridge Univ., 1935-40; Alfred Yarrow Research Fellow, of Girton Coll., 1937-40; Member Staff of College of Pharmaceutical Society,

London, 1941-46; Lecturer, later Reader, in Pharmacology, University of Edinburgh, 1947-60; Head of Pharmacology Unit, Agricultural Research Council, Institute of Animal Physiology, 1960-68. Vis. Associate Prof. in Pharmacology, Columbia Univ., New York, 1949; Vis. Prof., Sydney 1965, Montreal 1968. Life Fellow, Girton Coll., Cambridge, 1970. For. Hon. Mem., Amer. Acad. of Arts and Scis, 1977. Hon. Fellow RSM 1980. Hon. Mem., Hungarian Acad. of Scis, 1981. Hon. DSc Edinburgh, 1974. Royal Medal, Royal Soc., 1981. *Publications:* papers in neurological, physiological and pharmacological journals. *Address:* Agricultural Research Council Institute of Animal Physiology, Babraham, Cambridge CB2 4AT.

VOKES, Maj.-Gen. Christopher, CB 1945; CBE 1944; DSO 1943; retired from the Canadian Army in 1960; *b* 13 April 1904; *e s* of late Major F. P. Vokes, Kingston, Ontario, and Elizabeth Briens; *m* 1932, Constance Mary Waugh (*d* 1969), Winnipeg; two *s. Educ:* RMC, Kingston; McGill Univ., Montreal. 1st Commission Royal Canadian Engineers, 1925; Staff Coll., Camberley, 1934-35; Brigadier Comd 2 Cdn Inf. Bde, 1942-43; Maj.-Gen. GOC 1 Cdn Div., 1943-44; GOC 4 Cdn Armd Div., 1944-45. Campaigns: Sicily, Italy, NW Europe (despatches twice, DSO, CBE, CB); GOC Cdn Occupation Force, Germany, 1945; Officer of Legion of Honour (France); Croix de Guerre avec Palme (France); Order of Golden Ariston Andrias (Greece); Commander Mil. Order of Italy. *Address:* 105 Allan Street, Apt 702, Oakville, Ontario L6J 3N2, Canada.

VOLCKER, Paul A.; Chairman, American Federal Reserve Board, since 1979; *b* Cape May, New Jersey, 5 Sept, 1927; *s* of Paul A. Volcker and Alma Louise Klippel; *m* 1954, Barbara Marie Bahnson; one *s* one *d. Educ:* Princeton Univ. (AB *summa cum laude*); Harvard Univ. (MA); LSE. Special Asst, Securities Dept, Fed. Reserve Bank, NY, 1953-57; Financial Economist, Chase Manhattan Bank, NYC, 1957-62; Vice-Pres. and Dir of Forward Planning, 1965-69; Dir, Office of Financial Analysis, US Treasury Dept, 1962-63; Dep. Under-Sec. for Monetary Affairs, 1963-65; Under-Sec. for Monetary Affairs, 1969-74; Senior Fellow, Woodrow Wilson Sch. of Public and Internat. Affairs, Princeton Univ., 1974-75; Pres. NY Federal Reserve Bank, 1975-79. *Address:* Federal Reserve, Washington, DC 20551, USA.

VOLLRATH, Prof. Lutz Ernst Wolf; Professor of Histology and Embryology, University of Mainz, Germany, since 1974; *b* 2 Sept. 1936; *s* of Pastor Richard Hermann Vollrath and Rita (*née* Brügmann); *m* 1963, Gisela (*née* Dialer); three *d. Educ:* Ulrich von Hutten-Schule, Berlin; Univs of Berlin, Kiel and Tübingen. Dr med Kiel, 1961. Wissenschaftlicher Assistent, Dept of Anatomy, Würzburg, Germany, 1963; Res. Fellow, Dept of Anatomy, Birmingham, 1964; Wissenschaftlicher Assistent, Dept of Anatomy, Würzburg, 1965-71 (Privatdozent, 1968; Oberassistent, 1969; Universitätsdozent, 1970); King's College London: Reader in Anatomy, 1971; Prof. of Anatomy, 1973-74. *Publications:* (co-editor) Neurosecretion: the final neuroendocrine pathway, 1974; The Pineal Organ, 1981; (editor) Cell & Tissue Research; Handbuch der mikr. Anat. des Menschen; research publications on histochemistry and ultrastructure of organogenesis and various aspects of neuroendocrinology, in Z Zellforsch., Histochemie, Phil. Trans Royal Society B, Erg. Anat. Entw.gesch. *Recreations:* gardening, tennis. *Address:* c/o Anatomisches Institut, 65 Mainz, Saarstr. 19/21, Germany.

von BITTENFELD; *see* Herwarth von Bittenfeld.

von EULER, Prof. Ulf Svante; Comdr North Star of Sweden (1st cl.) 1970; Professor of Physiology, Karolinska Institute, 1939-71; *b* 7 Feb. 1905; *s* of Hans von Euler and Astrid von Euler (*née* Cleve); *m* 1st, 1930, Jane Sodenstierna; two *s* two *d* ; 2nd, 1958, Dagmar Cronstedt. *Educ:* Karolinska Institute, Stockholm. MD 1930. For. Mem., Royal Soc., 1973. Nobel Prize in Physiology or Medicine (jt), 1970. Hon. degrees, Univs of: Umea, 1958; Dijon, 1962; Ghent, 1963; Tübingen, 1964; Buenos Aires, 1971; Edinburgh, 1971; Manchester, 1973; Madrid, 1973; Lodz, 1979. Cross of the Sun (Brazil), 1952; Grand Cross of Merito Civil (Spain), 1979. Comdr, Palmes académiques (France), 1968. *Publications:* Nonadrenaline, 1956; Prostaglandins (with R. Eliasson), 1967; articles in jls of physiology and pharmacology. *Address:* Sturegatan 14, Stockholm S-11436, Sweden. *T:* S-08-636559.

VON HAGEN, Victor Wolfgang, FZS; FRGS; Organiser-Leader, Persian Royal Road Expedition, 1972, American Geographical Society Expedition, 1973-75, explorations in Iran, Iraq and Turkey; Leader, Roman Road Expeditions, 1962; Director: Inca High Expedition; American Geographical Society; History of Science Society; Latin American Adviser, Encyclopedia Americana; Contributor: Encyclopædia Britannica; Geographical Magazine, London; Illustrated London News, since 1935; Research Associate Museum of the American Indian, New York; Consultant UN Guggenheim Fellowship for creative writing, 1949, renewed 1950-51; American Philosophical Society (Research Fellow); *b* Saint Louis, Mo., 29 Feb. 1908; *s* of Henry von Hagen and Eleanor Josephine Stippe-Hornbach; *m* 1933, Christine Inez Brown (marr. diss.); one *d; m* 1951, Silvia Hofmann-Edzard (marr. diss. 1962); two *d. Educ:* Morgan Park Military Acad.; New York Univ.; Univ. de Quito, S America. Served US Army, War of 1941-45, 13th Inf. Regt, Texas. Explorer, naturalist, ethnographer. Expedition Mexico, 1931-33; Ecuador, Amazon, Peru, Galapagos Islands, 1934-36; Honduras, Mosquito Coast, Guatemala, 1937-38, to study quetzal bird for Zoo, Regent's Park; Panama, Costa Rica, 1940; Colombia, Peru, 1947-48; resided BWI, 1949-50; expedition to Peru, 1952-54; studied Roman Roads, Lubeck to Africa, 1955; expedition to Mexico, 1957; Yucatan, 1958-59; Study of Roman Roads in Italy, 1961; exploration of

Roman Roads: throughout Tunisia, Libya, Egypt, Arabia, Petra, 1963; Spain and Yugoslavia, 1965; Egyptian Eastern Desert, Sinai, Turkey, Bulgaria and Greece, 1966; exploration and excavation of Roman Alpine roads in Austria, Italy, France and Germany, 1968-70; physically traversed and mapped the Persian Road from Troy and Istanbul, through Turkey, Iraq and Iran to river Indus, 1973-75; topographical survey of Trajan's Aqueduct, Lago Bracciano to Rome, XXXI miles, 1979-81 (survey text with maps published, 1982). Founder, Charles Darwin Res. Station, Galápagos Is (conceived 1936, permission 1959, in operation 1960). Professor (*hc*) Universidad Catolica del Peru. Member, Academia de Historia de Bogota (Columbia), Centro de historia de Pasto (Columbia), Instituto Investigaciones Historicas (Peru). Discovered "extinct" tribe of Jicaque Indians in Honduras. Orden al Merito, Ecuador; Comdr, Orden al Merito, Peru. *Publications:* Off With their Heads, 1937; Ecuador the Unknown, 1939; Quetzal Quest (with Hawkins), 1940 (repr. 1968); Tsátchela Indians of Western Ecuador, 1939; The Encantadas of Herman Melville, 1940; Treasure of Tortoise Islands, 1940; Riches of South America, 1941; Riches of Central America, 1942; The Jicaque Indians of Honduras, 1943; Natural History of Termites, 1943; Paper and Civilisation, 1943; The Aztec and Maya Papermakers, 1943, 2nd edn, 1944; Jungle in the Clouds, 1945 (American edition, 1940); La Fabricación del Papel entre los aztecas y los Mayas, Mexico, 1945; South America Called Them, a biography, 1945; Maya Explorer, the life of John Lloyd Stephens, 1947; The Green World of the Naturalists (Anthology), 1948; Ecuador and the Galapagos Islands, 1949; Regional Guides to Peru, 1949; Frederick Catherwood, Architect (with Introduction by Aldous Huxley), 1950; El Dorado, The Golden Kingdoms of Colombia, 1951; The Four Seasons of Manuela (biography), 1952, repr. 1973; Highway of the Sun, 1956; The High Voyage, 1956; (Trans.) The Journals of J. B. Boussingault, 1957; Realm of the Incas, 1957; The Aztec: Man and Tribe, 1958; The Sun Kingdom of the Aztecs, 1958; The World of the Maya, 1960; The Ancient Sun Kingdom of The Americas, 1961, repr. 1973; The Desert Kingdoms of Peru, 1965; The Story of the Roman Roads, 1966 (for children; two book awards); F. Catherwood: Architect-Explorer of Two Worlds, 1967; The Roads that Led to Rome (in 6 languages), 1967; Roma nel Mundo, le grande stradi, 1969; The Road Runner (autobiog.), 1970; The German Peoples in the History of the Americas, German edn 1970, Amer. edn 1976; Il Sistema Stradale dell'Impero Romano, 1971; Search for the Mayas, the story of Stephens and Catherwood, 1973; The Golden Man, 1974; The Royal Road of the Incas, 1976; Ecuador: a history, 1976; The Gateways to Persia, 1978; The Gold of El Dorado, 1978; Galápagos: my return to Las Encantadas, 1982; (ed) The Incas (Chronicles) of Pedro de Cieza de Leon, 1959; (ed) Stephens' Incidents of Travel in Yucatan, 1961; (ed) Stephens' Incidents of Travel in Arabia Petraea, 1970; (ed) E. George Squier's Peru (1877), 1981. *Recreation:* watching moods of Lago Bracciano. *Address:* Trevignano Romano, Rome 00069, Italy.

von HASE, Karl-Günther, Hon. GCVO 1972; Hon. KCMG 1965; Chairman, Deutsch-Englische Gesellschaft, Düsseldorf, since 1982; *b* 15 Dec. 1917; *m* 1945, Renate Stumpff; five *d. Educ:* German schools. Professional Soldier, 1936-45; War Academy, 1943-44; Training College for Diplomats, 1950-51; Georgetown Univ., Washington DC, 1952. German Foreign Service: German Embassy, Ottawa, 1953-56; Spokesman, Foreign Office Bonn, 1958-61; Head, West European Dept, 1961-62; Spokesman of German Federal Government, 1962-67; State Secretary, Min. of Defence, German Federal Govt, 1968-69; German Ambassador to the Court of St James's, 1970-77; Dir-Gen., Zweites Deutsches Fernsehen, 1977-82. Holds German and other foreign decorations. *Recreations:* shooting, music. *Address:* Am Stadtwald 60, 53 Bonn 2, West Germany.

VON KARAJAN, Herbert; Conductor; Director: Salzburg Festival, since 1964; Vienna State Opera, since 1976 (Artistic Manager, 1956-64); Life Director Gesellschaft der Musikfreunde, Vienna; Artistic Director, Berlin Philharmonic Orchestra; *b* Salzburg, 5 April 1908; *s* of Ernest van Karajan and Martha v. Karajan Cosmâc. *Educ:* Salzburg Hochschule and Mozarteum; Vienna Univ. Conductor: Ulm Opernhaus, 1927-33; Aachen Opernhaus, 1933-40; Berlin Staatsoper, 1938-42; Festivals: Salzburg; Bayreuth; Edinburgh, 1953-54; Lucerne, 1947-56; Conductor and régisseur, La Scala, Milan, 1948-55; Musical Director, Berlin Philharmonic Orchestra, 1955-56. First European Tour with Philharmonia Orchestra, 1952; Director, Salzburg Festival, 1957. Films directed and conducted include: Bajazzo, Carmen, Beethoven's 9th Symphony. Hon. DMus Oxon, 1978. *Recreations:* ski-ing, mountaineering, flying, yachting, motoring, theatre, acoustical research. *Address:* Festspielhaus, Salzburg, Austria.

VONNEGUT, Kurt, Jr; writer; *b* Indianapolis, 11 Nov. 1922; *m* 1st, 1945, Jane Marie Cox (marr. diss. 1979); one *s* two *d*; 2nd, 1979, Jill Krementz. *Educ:* Cornell Univ.; Carnegie Inst. of Technol.; Univ. of Chicago. Served War, US Army, 1942-45 (POW). Reporter, Chicago City News Bureau, 1945-47; PRO, GEC, Schenectady, 1947-50; freelance writer, 1950-65; Lectr, Writers' Workshop, Univ. of Iowa, 1965-67; Guggenheim Fellow, 1967-68; Lectr in English, Harvard, 1970; Dist. Prof., City Coll., New York, 1973-74. Mem., National Inst. of Arts and Letters. *Publications:* Player Piano, 1951; The Sirens of Titan, 1959; Mother Night, 1961; Cat's Cradle, 1963; God Bless You, Mr Rosewater, 1964; Welcome to the Monkey House (short stories), 1968; Slaughterhouse-Five, 1969; Happy Birthday, Wanda June (play), 1970; Between Time and Timbuktu or Prometheus-5 (TV script), 1972; Breakfast of Champions, 1973; Wampeters, Foma and Granfalloons (essays), 1974; Slapstick, or Lonesome No More, 1976; Jailbird, 1979; (with Ivan Chermayeff) Sun Moon Star, 1980; Palm Sunday (autobiog.), 1981; Deadeye Dick, 1982. *Address:* c/o Donald C. Farber Conboy Hewitt O'Brien & Broadman, 600 Madison Avenue, New York, NY 10022, USA.

von REITZENSTEIN, Hans-Joachim Freiherr; *see* Leech, John.

von SCHRAMEK, Sir Eric (Emil), Kt 1982; FRIBA; Chairman, von Schramek and Dawes Pty Ltd, Architects and Planners, since 1963; *b* 4 April 1921; *s* of Emil and Annie von Schramek; *m* 1948, Edith, *d* of Dipl. Ing. W. Popper; one *s* two *d. Educ:* Stefans Gymnasium, Prague; Technical Univ., Prague. DiplIngArch; LFRAIA, FIArbA, RAPI. Town Planner, Bavaria, 1946-48; Sen. Supervising Architect, Dept of Works and Housing, Darwin, NT, 1948-51; Evans, Bruer & Partners (now von Schramek and Dawes), 1951-. National Pres., Building Science Forum of Aust., 1970-72; President: RAIA (SA Chapter), 1974-76; Inst. of Arbitrators, Aust. (SA Chapter), 1977-80. Past Vis. Lectr, Univ. of Adelaide; past National Dep. Chm., Austcare; past Councillor, Council of Professions; Chm., Commn on Worship and other Depts, Lutheran Church of Australia, 1976-. *Publications:* contribs and articles in architectural pubns. *Recreations:* music, reading, golf. *Address:* 4 Burlington Street, Walkerville, South Australia 5081, Australia. *T:* (08) 44 2125; The Olives, Yankalilla, South Australia 5203. *T:* (085) 58 2205.

von WEIZSÄCKER, Freiherr Carl-Friedrich, Dr Phil; University Professor; Director, Max-Planck-Institut on the preconditions of human life in the modern world, 1970-80; *b* Kiel, 28 June 1912; *m* 1937, Gundalena (*née* Wille); three *s* one *d. Educ:* Universities of Leipzig, Göttingen, Copenhagen, 1929-33. Dr.phil 1933, Dr.phil.habil, 1936, Univ. Leipzig; Asst., Inst. of Theor. Physik, Univ. of Leipzig, 1934-36; Wissenschaftl. Mitarb., Kaiser Wilhelm Inst., Berlin, 1936-42; Dozent, Univ. of Berlin, 1937-42; pl. ao. Prof. Theor. Physik, Univ. of Strassburg, 1942-44; Kaiser-Wilhelm-Inst., Berlin and Hechingen, 1944-45; Hon. Prof., Univ. Göttingen and Abt. Leiter, Max Planck Inst. für Physik, Göttingen, 1946-57; Hon. Prof. of Theor. Physik, Univ. of Göttingen, 1946-57; Ord. Prof. of Philosophy, Univ. of Hamburg, 1957-69. Hon. Prof., Univ. of Munich, 1970-. Gifford Lecturer, Glasgow Univ., 1959-61. Member: Deutsche Akademie der Naturforscher Leopoldina, Halle (DDR); Akademie der Wissenschaften, Göttingen; Joachim-Jungius-Gesellschaft der Wissenschaften, Hamburg; Bayerische Akademie der Wissenschaften, München; Deutsche Akademie für Sprache und Dichtung, Darmstadt; Osterreichische Akademie der Wissenschaften, Wien; Sächsische Akademie der Wissenschaften zu Leipzig. Verdienstorden der Bundesrepublik Deutschland, 1959-73; Orden Pour le Mérite für Wissenschaften und Künste, 1961; Wiss. Mitglied der Max-Planck-Gesellschaft, Göttingen. Max Planck Medal, 1957; Goethe Prize (Frankfurt) 1958; Friedenspreis des deutschen Buchhandels, 1963; Erasmus Prize (with Gabriel Marcel), 1969. Hon. Dr theol, Univ. Tübingen, 1977; Hon. Dr iur, Free Univ., Amsterdam, 1977. *Publications:* Die Atomkerne, 1937; Zum Weltbild der Physik, 11th edn, 1970 (English, London, 1952); Die Geschichte der Natur, 7th edn, 1970 (English, Chicago, 1949); Physik der Gegenwart (with J. Juilfs), 2nd edn, 1958 (Engl., 1957); Die Verantwortung der Wissenschaft im Atomzeitalter, 5th edn, 1969; Atomenergie und Atomzeitalter, 3rd edn, 1958; Bedingungen des Friedens, 1963, 5th edn, 1970; Die Tragweite der Wissenschaft, 1964; Der ungesicherte Friede, 1969; Die Einheit der Natur, 1971, 3rd edn, 1972; (ed) Kriegsfolgen und Kriegsverhütung, 1970, 3rd edn, 1971; Voraussetzungen der naturwissenschaftlichen Denkens, 1972, 2nd edn, 1972; Fragen zur Weltpolitik, 1975; Wege in der Gefahr, 1976; Der Garten des Menschlichen, Beiträge zur geschichtlichen Anthropologie, 1977; Deutlichkeit, Beiträge zu politischen und religiösen Gegenwartsfragen, 1978; Der bedrohte Friede, 1981. *Relevant Publication:* bibliography in Einheit und Vielheit, Festschrift...ed Scheibe and Süssmann, 1973. *Recreations:* hiking, chess. *Address:* 813 Starnberg, Mathildenstrasse 16, Germany.

von WINTERFELDT, (Hans) Dominik; Managing Director and Chief Executive, Hoechst UK Ltd, since 1975; *b* 3 July 1937; *s* of late Curt von Winterfeldt and Anna Franziska Margaretha Luise (*née* Petersen); *m* 1966, Cornelia Waldthausen; one *s* one *d. Educ:* German schools; Stanford-INSEAD, Fontainebleau (Industriekaufmann). DipICC. Joined Hoechst AG, Frankfurt/Main, 1957; Asst Manager, Hoechst Colombiana Ltda, 1960; Commercial Manager, Pharmaceuticals, Hoechst Peruana SA, 1963; General Manager, Hoechst Dyechemie W. L. L., Iraq, 1965; Man. Dir, Hoechst Pakistan Ltd and Hoechst Pharmaceuticals Ltd, 1967; Dep. Man. Dir, Hoechst UK Ltd, 1972. Director: Messer Griesheim Ltd, 1975-; Hoechst Finance Ltd, 1975-; Berger, Jenson & Nicholson Ltd, 1979-; Rochas Perfumes Ltd, 1979-; Balenciaga Ltd, 1980-. Member: British Inst. of Directors, 1975-; Deutsches Industriegespraech/German Chamber of Industry & Commerce in London, 1976-. Chevalier du Tastevin, 1981. *Recreations:* music, deer stalking, golf. *Address:* Hoechst UK Ltd, Hoechst House, Salisbury Road, Hounslow, Mddx TW4 6JH. *T:* 01-570 7712. *Clubs:* Royal Automobile, Anglo-German Association, Les Ambassadeurs; British Deer Society (Warminster); Sind (Karachi).

VORSTER, Hon. Balthazar Johannes, BA, LLB; State President of the Republic of South Africa, 1978-79; *b* 13 Dec. 1915; *s* of late William Carel Vorster; *m* 1941, Martini, *d* of P. A. Malan; two *s* one *d. Educ:* Sterkstroom High Sch.; Stellenbosch Univ. LLB 1938. Attorney, Port Elizabeth and Brakpan, until 1953; Member, Johannesburg Bar, practising 1953-58. Contested Brakpan, 1948; MP Nigel, 1953-78; Deputy Minister of Education, Arts, Science, Social Welfare and Pensions, 1958-61; Minister of Justice, 1961-66; Minister of Justice, of Police and of Prisons, 1966; Prime Minister, Republic of South Africa and Leader, National Party, 1966-78. DPhil (*hc*)

Stellenbosch Univ., 1966; LLD (*hc*); University of Pretoria; Univ. of OFS, 1967; Univ. of Potchefstroom. *Recreations:* golf, chess. *Address:* Oubostrand, c/o PO Humansdorp, Cape, 6300, Republic of South Africa. *Clubs:* Zwartkops Golf; Rondebosch Golf.

VOS, Geoffrey Michael; His Honour Judge Vos; a Circuit Judge, since 1978; *b* 18 Feb. 1927; *s* of Louis and Rachel Eva Vos; *m* 1955, Marcia Joan Goldstone (marr. diss. 1977); two *s* two *d* ; *m* 1981, Mrs Anne Wilson. *Educ:* St Joseph's College, Blackpool; Gonville and Caius College, Cambridge. MA, LLB. Called to the Bar, Gray's Inn, 1950. A Recorder of the Crown Court, 1976-78. *Recreations:* swimming, Regency buildings, walking. *Address:* 7 Winton Court, Winton Road, Bowdon, Cheshire.

VOUEL, Raymond; Member, Commission of the European Communities, responsible for Competition Policy, since 1977; *b* 1923; *m* ; three *c*. Journalist on Socialist daily newspaper, Tageblatt; Admin. Dir, Esch Hosp., 1954-64; Mem. Town Council, Esch (Chm. Bldgs Cttee), 1973. Member, Chamber of Deputies, 1964-76; Sec. of State: for Public Health; for Employment; for Social Security; for Mining Industry, 1964-69. Chm., Parly Socialist Group, 1970-74; Gen. Sec., Parti Ouvrier Socialiste Luxembourgeois (Socialists), 1970; Dep. Prime Minister, Minister for Finance and Land Develt, 1974-76; Mem., Commission of European Communities with responsibility for Competition, July-Dec. 1976. *Address:* Commission of the European Communities, 200 rue de la Loi, 1049 Brussels, Belgium.

VOWDEN, Desmond Harvey Weight, QC 1969; His Honour Judge Vowden; a Circuit Judge, since 1975; *b* 6 Jan. 1921; *s* of late Rev. A. W. J. Vowden, MBE, TD; *m* 1964, Iris, *d* of L. A. Stafford-Northcote. *Educ:* Clifton Coll. Served in RN and RM, 1938-50; Captain RM, retired 1950. Called to the Bar, 1950; Dep. Chm., Wiltshire Quarter Sessions, 1968-71; Recorder of Devizes, later a Recorder of Crown Court, 1971-75. Comr, CCC, 1969-72. Steward of Appeal, BBB of C, 1967-81. *Recreations:* music, gardening. *Address:* Orchard Cottage, Worton, Devizes, Wilts. *T:* Devizes 2877. *Club:* Garrick.

VOWLES, Paul Foster; Academic Registrar, University of London, 1973-82; *b* 12 June 1919; *s* of late E. F. Vowles and G. M. Vowles, Bristol; *m* 1948, Valerie Eleanor Hickman; one *s* two *d*. *Educ:* Bristol Grammar Sch.; Corpus Christi Coll., Oxford (schol.; MA). Served Gloucestershire Regt and King's African Rifles, 1939-46 (despatches, Major). Asst Secretary: Appts Bd, Univ. of Birmingham, 1947-48; Inter-University Council for Higher Educn Overseas, 1948-51; Registrar, Makerere University Coll., E Africa, 1951-63; Sen. Asst to Principal, Univ. of London, 1964-68; Warden, Lillian Penson Hall, 1965-69; External Registrar, 1968-73. *Address:* 13 Dale Close, Oxford OX1 1TU. *T:* Oxford 44042. *Club:* Athenæum.

VOYSEY, Reginald George, FIMechE; Consultant; Deputy Director, National Physical Laboratory, 1970-77; *s* of Richard Voysey and Anne Paul; *m* 1943, Laidley Mary Elizabeth Barley; one *s* three *d* (and one *s* decd). *Educ:* Royal Dockyard Sch., Portsmouth; Imperial Coll. of Science. ACGI, DIC, WhSch. Dep. Develt Manager, Power Jets Ltd, 1944-45; Gas Turbine Dept Manager, C. A. Parsons & Co., 1945-48; Engineering Asst to Chief Scientist, Min. of Fuel and Power, 1948-66; IDC 1963; Scientific Counsellor, British Embassy, and Dir, UK Sci. Mission to Washington, 1966-69. *Publications:* patents and articles in jls. *Recreations:* swimming, sailing, painting. *Address:* 16 Beauchamp Road, East Molesey, Surrey. *T:* 01-979 3762. *Club:* Athenæum.

VREDELING, Hendrikus, (Henk); Member of the Dutch Emancipation Council, since 1981; *b* 20 Nov. 1924. *Educ:* Agricultural Univ., Wageningen. Member: Second Chamber of States-General, Netherlands, 1956-73; European Parliament, 1958-73; Socio-Economic Adviser to Agricultural Workers' Union, Netherlands, 1950-73; Minister of Defence, 1973-76; Mem. and Vice-Pres. of Commn of European Communities (for Employment and Social Affairs), 1977-80. *Address:* Rembrandtlaan 13A, 3712 AJ Huis ter Heide, Netherlands.

VYNER, Clare George; *b* 1894; 2nd *s* of late Lord Alwyne Frederick Compton and Mary Evelyn, *e d* of Robert Charles de Grey Vyner, of Newby Hall, Yorks, and Gautby, Lincs; *m* 1923, Lady Doris Gordon-Lennox (*d* 1980), 2nd *d* of 8th Duke of Richmond and Gordon; one *s* (and one *s* one *d* decd). Formerly Lieut, RN, serving war of 1939-45, Commander. Assumed surname of Vyner, 1912. Formerly DL, W Riding of Yorkshire and City and Co. of York. *Address:* 41a Hays Mews, W1. *T:* 01-499 1431; Keanchulish, Ullapool, Ross-shire. *T:* Ullapool 2100.
See also Marquess of Northampton.

VYSE, Lt-Gen. Sir Edward D. H.; *see* Howard-Vyse.

VYVYAN, Sir John (Stanley), 12th Bt *cr* 1645; Owner and Manager of Trelowarren Estate, since 1950 (property acquired by marriage in 1427); *b* 20 Jan. 1916; *s* of Major-General Ralph Ernest Vyvyan, CBE, MC (*d* 1971) and Vera Grace (*d* 1956), *d* of Robert Arthur Alexander; *S* cousin, 1978; *m* 1958, Jonet Noël, *d* of Lt-Col Alexander Hubert Barclay, DSO, MC; one *s* one *d* (and one *d* of former marriage). *Educ:* Charterhouse; and British-American Tobacco Co. Ltd, who sent him to London School of Oriental Studies. With British-American Tobacco Co. Ltd in England and China until War. Commissioned RCS in India, 1940 and served, 1940-46, in Arakan, Bangalore,

etc; Temp. Major; GSO II Signals, Southern Army, 1944. *Recreations:* gardening, photography and books; travel when possible. *Heir: s* Ralph Ferrers Alexander Vyvyan, *b* 21 Aug. 1960. *Address:* Trelowarren, Mawgan, Helston, Cornwall. *T:* Mawgan 224. *Clubs:* Army and Navy; Royal Cornwall Yacht (Falmouth).

W

WACHER, David Mure; Metropolitan Stipendiary Magistrate, 1962-74, retired; *b* 9 Oct. 1909; *s* of late Dr Harold Wacher, FSA, and Violet Amy Wacher (*née* Peebles); *m* 1935, Kathleen Margaret Roche, *yr d* of late Rev. George Ralph Melvyrn Roche; one *s* one *d*. *Educ:* Charterhouse. Called to Bar, Middle Temple, 1935. Served in Royal Artillery, 1939-43. Acting Attorney-General, Gibraltar, 1943; Stipendiary Magistrate, Gibraltar, 1943-49; Acting Chief Justice, Gibraltar, 1948. Vice-Chairman, Mental Health Review Tribunal for SW Metropolitan RHB Area, 1960-62. *Recreations:* music and the theatre. *Address:* Strapp Farm House, Chiselborough, Stoke-Sub-Hamdon, Somerset TA14 6TW. *T:* Chiselborough 689. *Club:* New (Edinburgh).

WACKETT, Air Vice-Marshal Ellis Charles, CB 1957; CBE 1951 (OBE 1941); CEng; FRAeS; psa; Royal Australian Air Force; *b* 13 Aug. 1901; *yr s* of James Wackett, Townsville, Queensland; *m* 1928, Doreen I. (*d* 1975), *d* of Thomas S. Dove, Mildura, Victoria; two *s* one *d*. *Educ:* Jervis Bay Royal Australian Naval Coll.; Keyham Engineering College, England; Imperial College of Science and Technology, London. Joined Australian Navy, 1914; commissioned, 1921. Transferred to Royal Australian Air Force, 1923; graduated RAF Staff Coll., 1933. Air Vice-Marshal, 1948. Air Member for Engineering and Maintenance, 1942; Air Member for Technical Service, RAAF, 1948; retired 1959. Member, Australian Nat. Airlines Commn (TAA), 1960-68. *Recreation:* angling. *Address:* 13/32 Berkeley Street, Hawthorn, Victoria 3122, Australia. *Club:* Naval and Military (Victoria).

WADDELL, Sir Alexander (Nicol Anton), KCMG 1959 (CMG 1955); DSC 1944; HM Overseas Civil Service, retired; *b* 8 Nov. 1913; *yr s* of late Rev. Alexander Waddell, Eassie, Angus, Scotland, and late Effie Thompson Anton Waddell; *m* 1949, Jean Margot Lesbia, *d* of late W. E. Masters. *Educ:* Fettes Coll., Edinburgh; Edinburgh Univ. (MA); Gonville and Caius Coll., Cambridge. Colonial Administrative Service, 1937; British Solomon Islands Protectorate: Cadet, 1937; District Officer, 1938; District Commissioner, 1945; Acting Resident Commissioner, 1945; Malayan Civil Service, 1946; Principal Asst Secretary, North Borneo, 1947-52 (Acting Dep. Chief Secretary, periods, 1947-51). Colonial Secretary, Gambia, 1952-56; Colonial Secretary, Sierra Leone, 1956-58; Dep. Governor, Sierra Leone, 1958-60; Governor and Commander-in-Chief of Sarawak, 1960-63; UK Comr, British Phosphate Commissioners, 1965-77. Mem., Panel of Independent Inspectors, Dept of the Environment, 1979-. On Naval Service, 1942-44. Lieut, RANVR; on Military Service, 1945-47, Lt-Col, Gen. List [British Mil. Administration]. *Recreations:* golf, gardening. *Address:* Pilgrim Cottage, Ashton Keynes, Wilts. *Clubs:* Naval, Royal Commonwealth Society, East India, Devonshire, Sports and Public Schools.

WADDELL, Gordon Herbert; Director, E. Oppenheimer & Son Ltd, since 1965; Chairman: Johannesburg Consolidated Investment Co. Ltd, since 1981; Rustenburg Platinum Mines Ltd, since 1981; Executive Director, Anglo American Corporation of South Africa Ltd, since 1971; *b* Glasgow, 12 April 1937; *s* of Herbert Waddell; *m* 1st, 1965, Mary (marr. diss. 1971), *d* of H. F. Oppenheimer, *qv* ; 2nd, 1973, Kathy May, *d* of W. S. Gallagher. *Educ:* St Mary's Sch., Melrose; Fettes Coll., Edinburgh; Cambridge Univ. (BA); Stanford Univ. (MBA). Rugby Blue, Cambridge Univ., 1958, 1960, 1961; Member, British Isles Rugby Touring Team: to Australia and NZ, 1955; to South Africa, 1962; fourteen rugby caps for Scotland. *Recreation:* golf. *Address:* Cloud End, West Road South, Morningside, Sandton, Transvaal, SA. *Clubs:* Rand, Hawks, Muirfield, Kimberley, River, Royal and Ancient (St Andrews).

WADDELL, Sir James (Henderson), Kt 1974; CB 1960; Deputy Chairman, Police Complaints Board, 1977-81; *b* 5 Oct. 1914; *s* of D. M. Waddell and J. C. Fleming; *m* 1940, Dorothy Abbie Wright; one *s* one *d*. *Educ:* George Heriot's Sch.; Edinburgh Univ. Assistance Board, 1936; Ministry of Information, 1940; Reconnaissance Corps, 1942; Ministry of Housing and Local Government, 1946; Under-Secretary, 1955; Under-Secretary, Cabinet Office, 1961-63; Dep.-Secretary, Min. of Housing and Local Government, 1963-66; Dep. Under-Sec., Home Office, 1966-75. *Recreation:* sailing. *Address:* Oakwood, East Lavant, Chichester, Sussex. *T:* Chichester 527129.

WADDELL, Rear-Adm. William Angus, CB 1981; OBE 1966; Chief Executive, Royal Institute of Public Health and Hygiene, since 1982; *b* 5 Nov. 1924; *s* of late James Whitefield Waddell and late Christina Maclean; *m* 1950, Thelma Evelyn Tomlins; one *s* one *d*. *Educ:* Glasgow University. BSc (Hons) Maths and Nat. Phil. FIEE. Midshipman, Sub Lieut RNVR (Special Branch), HMS Ranee, HMS Collingwood, 1945-47; Instr Lieut, HMS Collingwood, HMS Glasgow, HMS Siskin, HMS Gambia, 1947-59 (RMCS 1954); Instr

Comdr, HMS Albion, 1959-61; Staff of Dir, Naval Educn Service, 1961-63; Sen. British Naval Officer, Dam Neck, Virginia, 1963-66; Officer i/c RN Polaris Sch., 1966-68; Instr Captain, Staff of SACLANT (Dir, Inf. Systems Gp), 1969-72; Dean, RN Coll., Greenwich, 1973-75; Dir Naval Officer Appointments (Instr), 1975-78; Rear-Adm. 1979; Chief Naval Instructor Officer, 1978-81 and Flag Officer, Admiralty Interview Bd, 1979-81. *Publication*: An Introduction to Servomechanisms (with F. L. Westwater), 1961, repr. 1968. *Address*: c/o National Westminster Bank Ltd, 1 Lee Road, Blackheath, SE3 9RM.

WADDILOVE, Lewis Edgar, CBE 1978 (OBE 1965); JP; Deputy Chairman, Housing Corporation, since 1978 (Member since 1968); Director, Joseph Rowntree Memorial Trust, 1961-79 (Executive Officer of the Trust, 1946-61); *b* 5 Sept. 1914; *s* of Alfred and Edith Waddilove; *m* 1st, 1940, Louise Power (*d* 1967); one *s* one *d* ; 2nd, 1969, Maureen Piper. *Educ*: Westcliff High Sch.; Univ. of London (DPA). Admin. Officer, LCC Educn Dept, 1936-38; Govt Evacuation Scheme, Min. of Health, 1938-43; Friends Ambulance Unit, Middle East, 1943-45 (Exec. Chm. 1946); Chairman, Friends Service Council, 1961-67. Member: Cttee on Housing in Greater London (Milner Holland), 1963-65; Nat. Fedn of Housing Societies, 1965-73, 1977-79 (Chm.); Nat. Cttee for Commonwealth Immigrants, 1966-68; Social Science Research Council, 1967-71; Public Schools Commn, 1968-70; Central Housing Advisory Cttee, 1960-75; Standing Cttee, Centre for Socio-Legal Studies at Oxford, 1972-75; Legal Aid Advisory Cttee, 1972-78; Adv. Cttee on Rent Rebates and Rent Allowances, 1975-81; Cttee on Voluntary Organisations, 1974-78; Working Party on Housing Cooperatives, 1974-76; Central Appeals Adv. Cttee (BBC and IBA), 1974- (Chm., 1978-); Chairman: Advisory Cttee on Fair Rents, 1973-74; Advisory Cttee on Housing Cooperatives, 1976-79; York City Charities, 1957-65 and 1972-; York Univ. Council, 1977-; Personal Social Services Council, 1977-80; Trustee, Shelter, 1966-74 (Chm. 1970-72). Presiding Clerk, 4th World Conf. of Friends, in N Carolina, 1967. Governor, Co. of Merchant Adventurers, City of York, 1978-79. Governor: Leighton Park Sch., 1951-71; Bootham and The Mount Schs., 1972-81 (Chm. 1974-81). JP York, 1968. DUniv Brunel, 1978. *Publications*: One Man's Vision, 1954; Housing Associations (PEP), 1962; Private Philanthropy and Public Welfare, 1983; various articles in technical jls. *Address*: Red Oaks, Hawthorn Terrace, New Earswick, York YO3 8AJ. *T*: York 768696. *Club*: Reform.

WADDINGTON, David Charles, QC 1971; MP (C) Clitheroe, since March 1979; Parliamentary Under-Secretary of State, Department of Employment, since 1981; a Recorder of the Crown Court, since 1972; *b* 2 Aug. 1929; *o s* of late Charles Waddington and of Mrs Minnie Hughan Waddington; *m* 1958, Gillian Rosemary, *d* of Alan Green, *qv* ; three *s* two *d*. *Educ*: Sedbergh; Hertford Coll., Oxford. President, Oxford Univ. Conservative Assoc., 1950. 2nd Lieut, XII Royal Lancers, 1951-53. Called to Bar, Gray's Inn, 1951. Contested (C): Farnworth Div., 1955; Nelson and Colne Div., 1964; Heywood and Royton Div., 1966; MP (C) Nelson and Colne, 1968-Sept. 1974; a Lord Comr, HM Treasury, 1979-81. *Address*: Whins House, Sabden, near Blackburn, Lancs. *T*: Padiham 71070. *Club*: Cavalry and Guards.

WADDINGTON, Gerald Eugene, CBE 1975; QC (Cayman Islands) 1971; Attorney General of the Cayman Islands, 1970-April 1977; *b* 31 Jan. 1909; *o s* of Walter George Waddington and Una Blanche Waddington (*née* Hammond); *m* 1935, Hylda Kathleen (*née* Allen); one *s* one *d*. *Educ*: Jamaica Coll.; Wolmer's Sch., Jamaica. Solicitor, Supreme Court, Jamaica, 1932; LLB (London) 1949; Solicitor, Supreme Court, England, 1950; called to the Bar, Gray's Inn, 1957. Deputy Clerk of Courts, Jamaica, 1939; Asst Crown Solicitor, Jamaica, 1943-48; Resident Magistrate, 1948-58; Puisne Judge, 1959-64; Judge of the Court of Appeal, Jamaica, 1964-70, retired. Joint ed. West Indian Law Reports. Vice-Pres. Nat. Rifle Assoc. Chm. St John Council for Jamaica. CStJ 1962, KStJ 1970. *Recreation*: shooting (Member of Jamaica Rifle Team to Bisley, 1937, 1950, 1953, 1956, 1957, 1960, 1963, 1965, 1967, 1968; Captain, 1950, 1953, 1957, 1967; Captain, WI Rifle Team, 1960). *Address*: PO Box 864, Stittsville, Ontario K0A 3G0, Canada.

WADDINGTON, Very Rev. John Albert Henry, MBE 1945; TD 1951; MA (Lambeth) 1959; Provost of Bury St Edmunds, 1958-76, now Provost Emeritus; a Church Commissioner, 1972-76; *b* 10 Feb. 1910; *s* of H. Waddington, Tooting Graveney, Surrey; *m* 1938, Marguerite Elisabeth, *d* of F. Day, Wallington, Surrey; two *d*. *Educ*: Wandsworth Sch.; London Univ.; London College of Divinity. BCom London Univ.; 1929. Deacon, 1933; priest, 1934; Curate of St Andrew's, Streatham, 1933-35; Curate of St Paul's, Furzedown, 1935-38; Rector of Great Bircham, 1938-45; Vicar of St Peter Mancroft, Norwich, 1945; Chaplain to High Sheriff of Norfolk, 1950; Proctor in Convocation of Canterbury, 1950; Hon. Canon of Norwich, 1951. Chaplain to Forces (TA) 1935-58; Staff Chaplain, Eighth Army, 1943 (despatches twice); DACG XIII Corps, 1945, Eastern Command TA, 1951. *Recreations*: travel, theatre and cinema, religious journalism. *Address*: The Chantry, 67 Churchgate Street, Bury St Edmunds, Suffolk IP33 1RH. *T*: Bury St Edmunds 4494.

WADDINGTON, Leslie; Managing Director, Waddington Galleries, since 1966; *b* Dublin, 9 Feb. 1934; *s* of late Victor and Zelda Waddington; *m* 1967, Ferriel Lyle; two *d*. *Educ*: Portora Royal School; Sorbonne; Ecole du Louvre (Diplôme). Formed Waddington Galleries with father, 1957. *Recreations*: chess, backgammon, ping pong, reading. *Address*: 2 Cork Street, W1. *T*: 01-439 1866.

WADDINGTON, Rev. Canon Robert Murray; General Secretary of Church of England Board of Education and National Society for Promoting Religious Education, since 1977; *b* 24 Oct. 1927; *s* of Percy Nevill and Dorothy Waddington. *Educ*: Dulwich Coll.; Selwyn Coll., Cambridge; Ely Theological Coll. MA (2nd cl. Theol.). Asst Curate St John's, Bethnal Green, 1953-55; Chaplain, Slade Sch., Warwick, Qld, Aust., 1955-59; Curate, St Luke's, Cambridge, 1959-61; Headmaster, St Barnabas Sch., Ravenshoe, N Qld, Aust., 1961-70; Oxford Univ. Dept of Education, 1971-72; Residentiary Canon, Carlisle Cathedral, and Bishop's Adviser for Education, 1972-77. *Recreations*: cooking, films, sociology. *Address*: 22 Wincott Street, SE11; Church House, Westminster, SW1P 3NZ. *T*: 01-222 9011. *Club*: United Oxford & Cambridge University.

WADDS, Mrs Jean Casselman, OC 1982; Canadian High Commissioner to the United Kingdom, since 1980; *b* 16 Sept. 1920; *d* of Hon. Earl Rowe and Treva Lennox Rowe; *m* 1st, 1946, Clair Casselman; one *s* one *d* ; 2nd, 1964, Robert Wadds (marr. diss. 1977). *Educ*: Univ. of Toronto (BA); Weller Business Coll. First elected to Canadian House of Commons (Riding Grenville-Dundas), 1958; re-elected: 1962, 1963, 1965; defeated (Riding Grenville-Carlton), 1968. Member, Canada's Delegn to United Nations, 1961; Parliamentary Sec. to Minister of Health and Welfare, 1962. National Sec., Progressive Conservative Party, 1971-75; Member, Ontario Municipal Bd, 1975-79. Freeman, City of London, 1981. Hon. DCL Acadia Univ., NS, 1981. Hon. Fellowship Award, Bretton Hall Coll., W Yorks, 1982. *Recreations*: golf, skiing, swimming. *Address*: 1 Grosvenor Square, W1. *T*: 01-629 9492.

WADDY, Rev. Lawrence Heber; retired; Lecturer, University of California, San Diego, 1970-80; Hon. Assistant, St James', La Jolla, since 1974; *b* 5 Oct. 1914; *s* of late Archdeacon Stacy Waddy, Secretary of SPG, and Etheldred (*née* Spittal). *Educ*: Marlborough Coll.; Balliol Coll., Oxford. Domus Exhibitioner in Classics, Balliol, 1933; 1st Class Hon. Mods., Oxford, 1935; de Paravicini Scholar, 1935; Craven Scholar, 1935; 2nd Class Lit. Hum., 1937; BA 1937; MA 1945; Asst Master: Marlborough Coll., 1937-38; Winchester Coll., 1938-42 and 1946-49 (Chaplain, 1946). Headmaster, Tonbridge Sch., 1949-62. Select Preacher, Cambridge Univ., 1951; Oxford Univ., 1954-56. Examining Chaplain to the Bishop of Rochester, 1959-63; Hon. Canon of Rochester, 1961-63; Hon. Chaplain to the Bishop of Rochester, 1963. Deacon, 1940; Priest, 1941; Chaplain, RNVR, 1942-46. Lecturer in Classics, University of California, 1961. Education Officer, School Broadcasting Council, 1962-63; Chaplain to The Bishop's School, La Jolla, California, 1963-67; Headmaster, Santa Maria Internat. Acad., Chula Vista, Calif, 1967-70; Vicar, Church of the Good Samaritan, University City, 1970-74. *Publications*: Pax Romana and World Peace, 1950; The Prodigal Son (musical play), 1963; The Bible as Drama, 1974; Faith of Our Fathers, 1975; Symphony, 1977; Drama in Worship, 1978; Mayor's Race, 1980. *Recreations*: cricket and other games. *Address*: 5910 Camino de la Costa, La Jolla, California 92037, USA.

WADE, family name of **Baron Wade**.

WADE, Baron, *cr* 1964 (Life Peer); **Donald William Wade**, DL; MA, LLB; *b* 16 June 1904; *s* of William Mercer and Beatrice Hemington Wade; *m* 1932, Ellenora Beatrice (*née* Bentham); two *s* two *d*. *Educ*: Mill Hill; Trinity Hall, Cambridge. Admitted Solicitor, 1929. MP (L) Huddersfield West, 1950-64; Liberal Whip, 1956-62; Deputy Leader, Liberal Parliamentary Party, 1962-64; Deputy Liberal Whip, House of Lords, 1965-67; President, Liberal Party, 1967-68. DL, W Riding, Yorks, 1967, N Yorks, 1974. *Publications*: Democracy, 1944; Way of the West, 1945; Our Aim and Purpose, 1961; Yorkshire Survey: a report on community relations in Yorkshire, 1972; Europe and the British Health Service, 1974; (with Lord Banks) The Political Insight of Elliott Dodds, 1977; Behind the Speaker's Chair, 1978. *Address*: Meadowbank, Wath Road, Pately Bridge, Harrogate, N Yorks HG3 5PG. *Clubs*: National Liberal, Reform.

WADE, Maj.-Gen. (Douglas) Ashton (Lofft), CB 1946; OBE 1941; MC 1918; BA; CEng; MIEE; *b* 13 March 1898; 2nd *s* of C. S. D. Wade, Solicitor, Saffron Walden, Essex; *m* 1st, 1926, Heather Mary Patricia Bulmer (*d* 1968). Sowerby, Thirsk, Yorkshire; one *d* ; 2nd, 1972, Cynthia Halliday (*née* Allen). *Educ*: St Lawrence Coll., Ramsgate; Royal Military Acad., Woolwich; Clare Coll., Cambridge. Commnd into Royal Artillery, 1916; served European War, France, Italy and S Russia; seconded RE 1918-21; transferred to Royal Signals, 1921; Staff Coll., Camberley, 1933-34; DAQMG India, 1937-40; GSO 1, GHQ, BEF and GHQ Home Forces, 1940-41; AA and QMG 2nd Division, 1941-42; Dep. Ajt.-General, India, 1942-44; Comdr, Madras Area, India, 1944-47; GOC Malaya District, 1947-48; Mem., Indian Armed Forces Nationalisation Cttee, 1947; Special Appointment War Office, 1948-49; retired, 1950; Telecommunications Attaché, British Embassy, Washington, 1951-54; Sen. Planning Engineer, Independent Television Authority, 1954-60; Regional Officer, East Anglia, Independent Television Authority, 1960-64. Technical Consultant: Inter-University Research Unit, Cambridge, 1965-69; WRVS Headquarters, 1970-75. Chm., South East Forum for closed circuit TV in educn, 1967-73. Chm., Royal Signals Institute, 1957-63; National Vice-Chairman Dunkirk Veterans' Association, 1962-67, National Chairman, 1967-74. *Publications*: contributed to various Services publications, including RUSI Journal, United Services Journal (India), and Brassey's Annual. *Recreation*: gardening. *Address*: Phoenix Cottage, 6 Church Street, Old Catton, Norwich NR6 7DS. *T*: Norwich 45755.

WADE, Col Sir George Albert, Kt 1955; MC; JP; Director: Wade Potteries Ltd; Wade (Ireland) Ltd; George Wade & Son Ltd; A. J. Wade Ltd; Wade Heath & Co. Ltd; *b* 1891; *s* of George Wade, JP, Burslem; *m* 1915, Florence (*d* 1971), *d* of Samuel Johnson, JP, Burslem; one *s* two *d. Educ:* Newcastle-under-Lyme High Sch., Staffordshire. Served European War, 1914-18, with S Staffs Regt (MC and Bar); served War of 1939-45, with his Regiment and on General Staff; Colonel (retired) late S Staffs Regiment. Contested (C) Newcastle-under-Lyme, General Election, 1945. Past President: North Staffordshire Political Union; North Staffs Chamber of Commerce. Chairman: Pottery and Glass Trades Benevolent Institution, 1949-54; Machine Gun Corps Old Comrades Association. Pres. N Staffs Medical Inst. Fellow Corporation of Secretaries. JP Stoke-on-Trent. *Publications:* Minor Tactics Training Manual (issued to Home Guard) and a series of 12 books on Military Training, during War of 1939-45. *Recreations:* painting, photography, ornithology. *Address:* Brand Hall, Norton-in-Hales, Market Drayton, Salop. *T:* Market Drayton 3006.

WADE, Prof. Henry William Rawson, QC 1968; FBA 1969; MA; LLD (Cantab); DCL (Oxon); Master of Gonville and Caius College, Cambridge, since 1976; Barrister-at-Law; *b* 16 Jan. 1918; *s* of late Colonel H. O. Wade and of E. L. Rawson-Ackroyd; *m* 1st, 1943, Marie (*d* 1980), *d* of late G. E. Osland-Hill; two *s*; 2nd, 1982, Marjorie, widow of B. C. Browne. *Educ:* Shrewsbury Sch. (Governor, 1977); Gonville and Caius Coll., Cambridge. Henry Fellow, Harvard Univ., 1939; temp. officer, Treasury, 1940-46. Called to the Bar, Lincoln's Inn, 1946; Hon. Bencher, 1964. Fellow of Trinity Coll., Cambridge, 1946-61; University Lecturer, 1947; Reader, 1959; Prof. of English Law, Oxford Univ., 1961-76; Fellow, St John's College, Oxford, 1961-76, Hon. Fellow, 1976; Rouse Ball Prof. of English Law, Cambridge Univ., 1978-82. Lectr, Council of Legal Education, 1957; British Council Lectr in Scandinavia, 1958, and Turkey, 1959; Cooley Lectr, Michigan Univ., 1961; Vithalbai Patel Lectr, New Delhi, 1971; Chettyar Lectr, Madras, 1974. Vice-Pres., British Acad., 1981. Member: Council on Tribunals, 1958-71; Relationships Commn, Uganda, 1961; Royal Commn on Tribunals of Inquiry, 1966. *Publications:* The Law of Real Property, 1957 (with Hon. Mr Justice Megarry), 4th edn, 1975; Administrative Law, 1961, 5th edn, 1982; Towards Administrative Justice, 1963; (with Prof. B. Schwartz) Legal Control of Government, 1972; Constitutional Fundamentals (Hamlyn Lectures), 1980; articles in legal journals; broadcast talks. *Recreations:* climbing, gardening. *Address:* Master's Lodge, Caius College, Cambridge. *T:* Cambridge 312211. *Club:* Alpine.

WADE, John Charles, OBE 1959; JP; Lord-Lieutenant of Cumbria, since 1974 (of the County of Cumberland, 1968-74); *b* 15 Feb. 1908; unmarried. *Educ:* St Bees School. Midland Bank Ltd, 1925-27. West Cumberland Farmers Ltd, 1927, Gen. Manager, 1931-64, Man. Dir, 1964-68, Pres., 1970-. President: Cumbria Assoc. of Boys Clubs; Cumbria Scouts; Whitehaven Rugby Club; Whitehaven Cricket Club; Cumbria Cricket Club; Chm., Whitehaven Harbour Comrs. Governor, St Bees Sch.; Dir, Eskdale Outward Bound Mountain Sch. JP Cumberland, 1956, Cumbria, 1974. Freeman, Borough of Whitehaven. KStJ 1974 (Pres. Cumbria Council of St John). *Recreations:* shooting, fishing. *Address:* Hillcrest, Whitehaven, Cumbria. *T:* Whitehaven 2844. *Club:* Border and County (Carlisle).

WADE, John Roland, CB 1942; retired as Director of Remploy Ltd (1960-63); *b* 11 Oct. 1890; *e s* of late George Alfred Wade; *m* 1928, Penelope Dorothy Haig, *y d* of late Dr Haig Ferguson, Edinburgh; two *s. Educ:* Westminster School (King's Scholar); Queens' Coll., Cambridge (Scholar). Entered War Office, 1914; Director of Establishments, War Office, 1939-53; retired Dec. 1953. Financial Director (part-time), Remploy Ltd, 1954-Oct. 1960. *Address:* 15 St Catherine's Court, Bedford Road, W4.

WADE, Joseph Frederick; General Secretary, National Graphical Association, since 1976; *b* 18 Dec. 1919; *s* of James and Ellen Wade; *m*; two *s. Educ:* elementary sch., Blackburn, Lancs. Trained as compositor, The Blackburn Times, 1934-40; served UK and overseas, East Lancs Regt and RAOC, 1940-46; newspaper compositor, 1946-56. Full-time Trade Union official, Typographical Assoc., 1956; Nat. Officer, NGA, 1964; Asst Gen. Sec., NGA, 1968. Member: Exec. Cttee, Printing and Kindred Trades Fedn, 1971-74; Exec. Cttee, Internat. Graphical Fedn, 1976- (Vice-Pres.); TUC Printing Industries Cttee, 1976-; Printing and Publishing Industry Training Bd, 1977-; Printing Industries Sector Working Party, 1979-. Mem., Blackburn County Borough Council, 1952-56. *Recreations:* walking, Scrabble, swimming. *Address:* National Graphical Association, 63-67 Bromham Road, Bedford MK40 2AG. *T:* Bedford 51521.

WADE, Sir Oulton; see Wade, Sir W. O.

WADE, Prof. Owen Lyndon, MD, FRCP; Professor of Therapeutics and Clinical Pharmacology, since 1971, and Dean of the Faculty of Medicine and Dentistry, since 1978, University of Birmingham; *s* of J. O. D. Wade, MS, FRCS, and Kate Wade, Cardiff; *m* 1948, Margaret Burton, LDS; three *d. Educ:* Repton; Cambridge; University College Hospital, London. Senior Scholar, Emmanuel Coll., Cambridge, 1941; Achison and Atkinson Morley Schol., UCH, 1945; Resident Medical Officer, UCH, 1946; Clinical Assistant, Pneumoconiosis Research Unit of the Medical Research Council, 1948-51; Lecturer and Sen. Lecturer in Medicine, Dept of Medicine, University of Birmingham, 1951-57; Whitla Prof. of Therapeutics and Pharmacology, Queen's Univ., Belfast, 1957-71. Rockefeller Travelling Fellowship in Medicine, 1954-55; Research Fellow, Columbia Univ. at Department of Medicine, Presbyterian Hospital, New York, 1954-55; Consultant, WHO. Chm., Cttee on the Review of Medicines, 1978-; Chm., Jt Formulary Cttee for British Nat. Formulary. *Publications:* (with J. M. Bishop) The Cardiac Output and Regional Blood Flow, 1962; Adverse Reactions to Drugs, 1970, 2nd edn with L. Beeley, 1976; papers on cardiorespiratory research, adverse reactions to drugs and drug use in the community, in Jl Physiology, Clinical Science, Brit. Med. Bull., Jl Clin. Invest. *Recreations:* books, travel and sailing. *Address:* The Office of the Dean, The Medical School, University of Birmingham, Birmingham B15 2TJ. *T:* 021-472 1301.

WADE, R(obert) Hunter; New Zealand diplomat, retired; *b* 14 June 1916; *s* of R. H. Wade, Balclutha, NZ; *m* 1941, Avelda Grace Petersen; two *s* two *d. Educ:* Waitaki; Otago Univ. NZ Treasury and Marketing Depts, 1939; NZ Govt diplomatic appts, Delhi, Simla, Sydney, Canberra, 1941-49; Head of Eastern Political Div., Dept of External Affairs, Wellington, NZ, 1949; NZ Embassy, Washington, 1951; NZ High Commn, Ottawa, 1956; Director of Colombo Plan Bureau, Colombo, 1957; Dir, External Aid, Wellington, 1959; Comr for NZ in Singapore and British Borneo, 1962; High Comr in Malaya/Malaysia, 1963-67; Dep. High Comr in London, 1967-69; NZ Ambassador to Japan and Korea, 1969-71; Dep. Sec.-Gen. of the Commonwealth, 1972-75; NZ Ambassador to Federal Republic of Germany and to Switzerland, 1975-78. Represented New Zealand at Independence of: Uganda, 1962; Botswana, 1966; Lesotho, 1966. Pres., Asiatic Soc. of Japan, 1971. *Address:* 12 Pleasant Place, Howick, Auckland, New Zealand. *Club:* Northern (Auckland, NZ).

WADE, Major-General Ronald Eustace, CB 1961; CBE 1956; retired; *b* 28 Oct. 1905; *s* of late Rev. E. V. Wade and Marcia Wade; *m* 1933, Doris, *d* of late C. K. Ross, Kojonup, WA; one *s* one *d. Educ:* Melbourne Church of England Grammar Sch.; RMC, Duntroon. ACT. Commissioned, 1927; attached 4/7 DG (India), 1928-29; Adjutant 10 LH and 9 LH, 1930-38; Captain, 1935; Major, 1940; served War of 1939-45, Lieut-Colonel (CO 2/10 Aust. Armd Regt), 1942; Colonel (Colonel A, Adv. LHQ, Morotai), 1945; Colonel Q, AHQ, Melbourne, 1946; idc 1948; Director of Cadets, 1949; Director of Quartering, 1950-51; Director of Personal Services, 1951-52; Military Secretary, 1952-53; Comd 11 Inf. Bde (Brig.), 1953-55; Maj.-General (Head Aust. Joint Service Staff, Washington), 1956-57; Adjutant-General, 1957-60; GOC Northern Command, 1961-62, retired, 1962. *Address:* 1A Glyde Street, South Perth, WA 6151, Australia.

WADE, Rosalind (Herschel), (Mrs R. H. Seymour); novelist; Editor, Contemporary Review, since 1970; *d* of Lieut-Colonel H. A. L. H. Wade and Kathleen Adelaide Wade; *m* William Kean Seymour, FRSL (*d* 1975); two *s. Educ:* Glendower Sch., London; privately, abroad and Bedford Coll., London. Member: Society of Women Writers and Journalists (Chairman, 1962-64, Vice President, 1965-); Committee West Country Writers Assoc., 1953-65 (Vice-Pres., 1975-); General and Exec. Councils, The Poetry Society Inc., 1962-64, 1965-66; Guildford Centre of Poetry Soc. (Chm. 1969-71); Alresford Historical and Literary Soc. (Chm. 1968-70, 1972-73); Literature Panel, Southern Arts Assoc., 1973-75; conducting Writing and Literary Courses at Moor Park College, Farnham (jointly with William Kean Seymour, 1962-74), Writers' Workshop, 1976-. Editor, PEN Broadsheet, 1975-77. *Publications: novels:* As the Narcissus, 1946; The Widows, 1948; The Raft, 1950; The Falling Leaves, 1951; Alys at Endon, 1953; The Silly Dove, 1953; Cassandra Calls, 1954; Come Fill The Cup, 1955; Morning Break, 1956; Mrs Jamison's Daughter, 1957; The Grain Will Grow, 1959; The Will of Heaven, 1960; A Small Shower, 1961; The Ramerson Case, 1962; New Pasture, 1964; The Vanished Days, 1966; Ladders, 1968; The Umbrella, 1970; The Golden Bowl, 1970; Mrs Medlend's Private World, 1973; Red Letter Day: Twelve Stories of Cornwall, 1980; *contributor to:* The Fourth Ghost Book, 1965; The Unlikely Ghosts, 1967; Happy Christmas, 1968; Haunted Cornwall, 1973; People Within, 1974; Cornish Harvest, 1974; Tales from the Macabre, 1976; My Favourite Story, 1977; More Tales from the Macabre, 1979; Women Writing, 1979; Contemporary Review, Poetry Review, Books and Bookmen, Cornish Review, etc. *Recreations:* walking and historical research. *Address:* 4 Dollis Drive, Guildford Road, Farnham, Surrey. *T:* Farnham 713883. *Clubs:* Royal Commonwealth Society, PEN.

WADE, Air Chief Marshal Sir Ruthven (Lowry), KCB 1974 (CB 1970); DFC 1944; Chief of Personnel and Logistics, Ministry of Defence, 1976-78, retired 1978; Director, Acatos and Hutcheson, since 1979; *b* 1920. *Educ:* Cheltenham Coll.; RAF Coll., Cranwell. RAF, 1939; served War of 1939-45, UK and Mediterranean (DFC); psa, 1953; HQ 2nd Tactical Air Force, Germany; RAF Flying Coll.; Gp Captain 1960; Staff Officer, Air HQ, Malta; Comdr, Bomber Comd station, RAF Gaydon, 1962-65; Air Cdre, 1964; idc 1965; Air Exec. to Deputy for Nuclear Affairs, SHAPE, 1967-68; AOC No 1 (Bomber) Gp, Strike Comd, 1968-71; Air Vice-Marshal, 1968; Dep. Comdr, RAF Germany, 1971-72; ACAS (Ops), 1973; Vice Chief of Air Staff, 1973-76; Air Marshal, 1974; Air Chief Marshal, 1976. *Address:* White Gables, Westlington, Dinton, Aylesbury, Bucks HP17 8UR. *T:* Stone 8884.

WADE, Sir (William) Oulton, Kt 1982; JP; farmer and company director; Chairman and Managing Director: William Wild & Son (Mollington) Ltd; Wilds Farm (Cheese Exports) Ltd; Chairman, Kendal Stuart Ltd (Grain Merchants); Joint Treasurer, Conservative Party, since 1982; *b* 24 Dec. 1932; *s* of Samuel Norman Wade and Joan Ferris Wade (*née* Wild); *m* 1959, Gillian

Margaret Leete, Buxton, Derbys; one *s* one *d. Educ:* Birkenhead Sch.; Queen's Univ., Belfast. Chm., English Cheese Exporters Consortium. JP Cheshire 1967. Freeman, City of London, 1980; Liveryman, Farmers' Co. 1980–. *Publications:* contribs to Dairy Industries Internat., Jl of Soc. of Dairy Technol. *Recreations:* politics, reading, shooting, food. *Address:* Chorlton Lodge, Chorlton-by-Backford, Chester CH2 4DB. *T:* Chester 381451. *Clubs:* Farmers'; Chester City (Chester); St James's (Manchester).

WADE-GERY, Robert Lucian, CMG 1979; HM Diplomatic Service; High Commissioner to India, since 1982; *b* 22 April 1929; *o s* of late Prof. H. T. Wade-Gery; *m* 1962, Sarah, *er d* of A. D. Marris, *qv* ; one *s* one *d. Educ:* Winchester; New Coll., Oxford. 1st cl. Hon. Mods 1949 and Lit. Hum. 1951. Fellow, All Souls Coll., Oxford, 1951–73. Joined HM Foreign (now Diplomatic) Service, 1951; FO (Economic Relations Dept), 1951–54; Bonn, 1954–57; FO (Private Sec. to Perm. Under-Sec., later Southern Dept), 1957–60; Tel Aviv, 1961–64; FO (Planning Staff), 1964–67; Saigon, 1967–68; Cabinet Office (Sec. to Duncan Cttee), 1968–69; Counsellor 1969; on loan to Bank of England, 1969; Head of Financial Policy and Aid Dept, FCO, 1969–70; Under-Sec., Central Policy Review Staff, Cabinet Office, 1971–73; Minister, Madrid, 1973–77; Minister, Moscow, 1977–79; Dep. Sec. of the Cabinet, 1979–82. *Recreations:* walking, sailing, travel. *Address:* c/o Foreign and Commonwealth Office, SW1; Church Cottage, Cold Aston, Cheltenham. *T:* Bourton-on-the-Water 21115. *Club:* Athenæum.

WADLEY, Sir Douglas, Kt 1969; solicitor; Consultant to O'Shea, Corser & Wadley; *b* 9 Nov. 1904; *s* of John and Honora Wadley; *m* 1928, Vera Joyce Bodman; two *s* two *d. Educ:* various state schools in Qld; Central Technical Coll. High Sch., Brisbane. Admitted Solicitor, Supreme Court of Queensland, 1926. Chm. of Dirs, Queensland Television Ltd. Hon. Councillor, Royal National Agricultural and Industrial Assoc. of Queensland. *Recreation:* racing. *Address:* 18 Nindethana Street, Indooroopilly, Brisbane, Queensland 4068, Australia. *T:* 70-2737. *Clubs:* Brisbane, Tattersalls, Johnsonian, Queensland Turf (Chm.) (Brisbane).

WADSWORTH, James Patrick, QC 1981; barrister; a Recorder of the Crown Court, since 1980; *b* 7 Sept. 1940; *s* of Francis Thomas Bernard Wadsworth, Newcastle, and Geraldine Rosa (*née* Brannan); *m* 1963, Judith Stuart Morrison, *e d* of Morrison Scott, Newport-on-Tay; one *s* one *d. Educ:* Stonyhurst; University Coll., Oxford (MA). Called to the Bar, Inner Temple, 1963 (Scholar, Forster Boulton Prize). *Recreations:* eating, idling. *Address:* 4 Paper Buildings, Temple, EC4. *T:* 01-353 3366.

WADSWORTH, Vivian Michael, DSc; Chairman, Harland and Wolff Ltd, Belfast, since 1981; *b* 12 April 1921; *s* of Frank Wadsworth and Tillie Wadsworth (*née* Widdop); *m* 1943, Ethel Mary Rigby; three *s* four *d. Educ:* Univs of Reading (BScAgric), Bristol, Leeds, and Natal, S Africa (MA, DSc). Economics Lectr, Bristol, Leeds and Natal Univs, 1942–49; Economic Adviser to Govt of S Rhodesia, 1949–55; Under Secretary for Agriculture, Fedn of Rhodesia and Nyasaland, 1955–61; Asst Sec. to Industrial Division, and Principal Economic Adviser, Distillers Co., 1961–63; Man. Dir, Fabrica Nacional de Margerina (SARL), Lisbon, Portugal (food company and former Distillers subsidiary), 1963–68; Tanganyika Concessions: Dir, Chief Exec. and Chm. of all UK subsidiaries, of which Elbar Group Industrial Holding Co. is the principal, 1968–. *Recreations:* gardening, travel, walking. *Address:* The Old Orchard, Rectory, Ightham, Kent TN15 9AJ. *T:* Sevenoaks 882068. *Club:* Buck's.

WAECHTER, Sir (Harry Leonard) d'Arcy, 2nd Bt, *cr* 1911; Lieut, RASC; *b* 22 May 1912; *s* of 1st Bt and Josephine (*d* 1955), *o d* of late John d'Arcy, of Corbetstown, Westmeath; *S* father, 1929; *m* 1939, Philippa Margaret (marr. diss. 1957), *y d* of late James Frederick Twinberrow, Suckley, Worcestershire. *Educ:* Pangbourne Nautical School. Lieut, East Yorkshire Regt (SR), 1931–35; Lieut, RASC, 1942–47; Captain, Worcestershire Regt, GSO 3 159 Inf. Bde (TA), 1947–48; Captain, TARO, 1949. Joint MFH North Ledbury. *Heir:* none. *Recreation:* hunting.

WAGNER, Sir Anthony (Richard), KCB 1978; KCVO 1961 (CVO 1953); DLitt, MA, Oxon; FSA; Clarenceux King of Arms, and Director, Heralds' Museum, Tower of London, since 1978; Kt Principal, Imperial Society of Knights Bachelor, since 1962; Secretary of Order of the Garter, 1952–61; Joint Register of Court of Chivalry, since 1954; Editor, Society of Antiquaries' Dictionary of British Arms, since 1940; *b* 6 Sept. 1908; *o s* of late Orlando Henry Wagner, 90 Queen's Gate, SW7, and late Monica, *d* of late Rev. G. E. Bell, Henley in Arden; *m* 1953, Gillian Mary Millicent (*see* G. M. M. Wagner); two *s* one *d. Educ:* Eton (King's Scholar); Balliol Coll., Oxford (Robin Hollway Scholar; Hon. Fellow, 1979). Portcullis Pursuivant, 1931–43. Richmond Herald, 1943–61; Garter King of Arms, 1961–78; served in WO, 1939–43; Ministry of Town and Country Planning, 1943–46; Private Secretary to Minister, 1944–45; Secretary (1945–46), member, 1947–66, Advisory Cttee on Buildings of special architectural or historic interest. Registrar of College of Arms, 1953–60; Genealogist: the Order of the Bath, 1961–72; the Order of St John, 1961–75. Inspector of Regtl Colours, 1961–77. President: Chelsea Soc., 1967–73; Aldeburgh Soc., 1970–. Mem. Council, Nat. Trust, 1953–74; Trustee, Nat. Portrait Gallery, 1973–80; Chm. of Trustees, Marc Fitch Fund, 1971–77. Master, Vintners' Co., 1973–74. Hon. Fellow, Heraldry Soc. of Canada, 1976. KStJ. *Publications:* Catalogue of the Heralds' Commemorative Exhibition, 1934 (compiler); Historic Heraldry of Britain, 1939, repr. 1972;

Heralds and Heraldry in the Middle Ages, 1939; Heraldry in England, 1946; Catalogue of English Mediæval Rolls of Arms, 1950; The Records and Collections of the College of Arms, 1952; English Genealogy, 1960; English Ancestry, 1961; Heralds of England, 1967; Pedigree and Progress, 1975; Heralds and Ancestors, 1978; Stephen Martin Leake's Heraldo-Memoriale (Roxburghe Club), 1982; genealogical and heraldic articles, incl. in Chambers's Encyclopædia. *Address:* College of Arms, Queen Victoria Street, EC4. *T:* 01-248 4300; 68 Chelsea Square, SW3. *T:* 01-352 0934; Wyndham Cottage, Aldeburgh, Suffolk. *T:* Aldeburgh 2596. *Clubs:* Athenæum, Garrick, Beefsteak.

WAGNER, Prof. Franz William; Professor of Education, and Director of Institute of Education, University of Southampton, 1950–71, now Emeritus; *b* 26 Oct. 1905; *s* of Franz Henry and Adelaide Wagner; *m* 1934, Maria Schiller; one *s* one *d. Educ:* University of Adelaide, (Rhodes Scholar for S. Austr., 1928) Christ Church, Oxford. Asst Master, Christ's Hospital, 1931–39; Tutor and Lecturer, Oxford Univ., Department of Education, 1939–50. *Recreation:* gardening. *Address:* Avonmore, Southdown Road, Shawford, Winchester, Hants SO21 2BY.

WAGNER, Gerrit Abram, KBE (Hon.) 1977 (CBE (Hon.) 1964); Kt, Order of Netherlands Lion, 1969; Commander, Order of Oranje Nassau, 1977; Chairman Supervisory Board, Royal Dutch Petroleum Co., since 1977 (President, 1971–77); *b* 21 Oct. 1916; *m* 1946, M. van der Heul; one *s* three *d. Educ:* Leyden Univ. LLM 1939. After a period in a bank in Rotterdam and in Civil Service in Rotterdam and The Hague, joined Royal Dutch Shell Group, 1946; assignments in The Hague, Curaçao, Venezuela, London and Indonesia; apptd Man. Dir, Royal Dutch Petroleum Co. and Shell Petroleum Co. Ltd; Mem. Presidium of Bd of Directors of Shell Petroleum NV, 1964; Dir, Shell Canada Ltd, 1971–77; Chm., Cttee of Man. Dirs, Royal Dutch/Shell Group, 1972–77; Chm., Shell Oil USA, 1972–77. Chairman: De Nederlandsche Bank NV; Gist-Brocades NV; Board Member: KLM; Estel/Hoogovens; Member, International Advisory Committee: Chase Manhattan Bank, NY; Robert Bosch, Stuttgart. Order of Francisco de Miranda, 2nd class (Venezuela), 1965; Officier Légion d'Honneur (France), 1974. *Address:* c/o Royal Dutch Petroleum Company, 30 Carel van Bylandtlaan, The Hague, The Netherlands.

WAGNER, Gillian Mary Millicent, OBE 1977, **(Lady Wagner);** Chairman of Council, Dr Barnardo's, since 1978 (Member since 1969; Chairman, Executive/Finance Committee, 1973–78); *b* 25 Oct. 1927; *e d* of late Major Henry Archibald Roger Graham, and of Hon. Margaret Beatrix, *d* of 1st Baron Roborough; *m* 1953, Sir Anthony Wagner, *qv* ; two *s* one *d. Educ:* Cheltenham Ladies' Coll.; Geneva Univ. (Licence ès Sciences Morales); London Sch. of Economics (Dip. Social Admin). PhD London 1977. Governor, Thomas Coram Foundation for Children; Mem. Exec. Cttee, Georgian Group, 1970–78; Pres., Nat. Bureau Handicapped Students, 1978. Chm. of Governors, Felixstowe Coll., 1980. *Publications:* Barnardo, 1979; Children of the Empire, 1982. *Recreations:* sailing, gardening, travelling. *Address:* 68 Chelsea Square, SW3. *T:* 01-352 0934; Wyndham Cottage, Crespigny Road, Aldeburgh, Suffolk. *T:* Aldeburgh 2596. *Club:* Aldeburgh Yacht.

WAGSTAFF, Ven. Christopher John Harold; Archdeacon of Gloucester, since 1982; Vicar of Coleford with Staunton, since 1973; *b* 25 June 1936; *s* of Harold Maurice Wagstaff and Kathleen Mary Wagstaff (*née* Bean); *m* 1964, Margaret Louise (*née* Macdonald); two *s* one *d. Educ:* Bishop's Stortford College, Herts; Essex Inst. of Agriculture, Chelmsford (Dipl. in Horticulture 1959); St David's Coll., Lampeter (BA 1962, Dipl. in Theol. 1963). Deacon 1963, priest 1964; Curate, All Saints, Queensbury, 1963–68; Vicar, St Michael's, Tokyngton, Wembley, 1968–73; RD, South Forest, 1975–82. Freeman, City of London; Liveryman, Worshipful Co. of Armourers and Brasiers. *Recreations:* gardening, walking, travel. *Address:* The Vicarage, 40 Boxbush Road, Coleford, Glos GL16 8DN. *T:* Dean 33379.

WAGSTAFF, David St John Rivers; a Recorder of the Crown Court, since 1974; barrister; *b* 22 June 1930; *s* of late Prof. John Edward Pretty Wagstaff and Dorothy Margaret (*née* McRobie); *m* 1970, Dorothy Elizabeth Starkie; two *d. Educ:* Winchester Coll. (Schol.); Trinity Coll., Cambridge (Schol., MA, LLB). Called to Bar, Lincoln's Inn, 1954. *Recreations:* mountaineering, fencing. *Address:* 37 Park Square, Leeds LS1 2PD. *T:* Leeds 452702. *Clubs:* Alpine; Fell and Rock Climbing (Lake District), Leeds (Leeds).

WAGSTAFF, Colonel Henry Wynter, CSI 1945; MC 1917; FCIT; RE (retired); *b* 19 July 1890; *s* of Edward Wynter Wagstaff and Flora de Smidt; *m* 1st, 1918, Jean, MB, BS, *d* of George Frederick Mathieson; two *s* ; 2nd, 1967, Margaret, *o d* of late Sir John Hubert Marshall, CIE. *Educ:* Woodbridge; RMA, Woolwich. Commissioned RE 1910; served in India and Mesopotamia in European War, 1914-18 (despatches, MC); Captain, 1916; seconded Indian State Railways, 1921; Major, 1927; Lieut-Colonel, 1934; Colonel, 1940. 1929–46, employed on problems connected with Labour in general and Railway Labour in particular. Member, Railway Board, Government of India, New Delhi, 1942–46; retired, 1948. *Publication:* Operation of Indian Railways in Recent Years, 1931. *Recreations:* reading and writing. *Address:* c/o Lloyds Bank Ltd, 6 Pall Mall, SW1.

WAHLSTRÖM, General Jarl Holger; International Leader of The Salvation Army, since 1981; *b* 9 July 1918; *s* of Rafael Alexander Wahlström and Aina

Maria Wahlström (*née* Dahlberg); *m* 1944, Maire Helfrid Nyberg; two *s* one *d*. *Educ*: Salvation Army International Training Coll. Salvation Army, Finland: Corps Officer, 1939–45; Scout Organizer, 1945–52; Private Sec. to Territorial Commander, 1952–54; Youth Sec., 1954–60; Divisional Comdr, 1960–63; Principal, Training Coll., 1963–68; Chief Secretary, 1968–72; Territorial Comdr, 1976–80; Salvation Army, Canada and Bermuda: Chief Secretary, 1972–76; Salvation Army, Sweden: Territorial Comdr, 1981. Cross of Liberty, IV cl., Finland, 1941; Knight, Order of Lion of Finland, 1964. *Publications*: contribs to Salvation Army papers and magazines, English, Finnish, Swedish. *Recreation*: music. *Address*: 101 Queen Victoria Street, EC4P 4EP. *T*: 01-236 5222; 2 Park Road, Beckenham, Kent. *Club*: Rotary.

WAIAPU, Bishop of, since 1979; **Rt. Rev. Ralph Vernon Matthews;** *b* 3 April 1928; *s* of Vernon Arthur F. Matthews and Thelma O. Matthews; *m* 1957, Pauline Cecily Glover; two *s*. *Educ*: Napier Boys' High School; Univ. of Auckland and S John's Theological Coll. LTh, 1st Cl. Hons. Assistant Agricultural Master and Scinde Housemaster, Napier Boys' High School, 1949. Deacon 1955, priest 1956, Waiapu; Asst Curate, Hastings, 1955–60; Vicar of Waipukurau, 1960–70; Vicar of Taupo, 1970–76; Hon. Canon, Waiapu, 1969, Canon 1970–76; Vicar of Gisborne and Archdeacon of Waiapu, 1976–79; Chairman, Diocesan Council of Christian Education, 1970–76. Territorial Chaplain, 4th Armoured Regt, RNZAC, 1957–63. *Recreations*: tennis, trout-fishing. *Address*: Bishop's House, 8 Cameron Terrace, Napier, NZ. *T*: Napier 57846.

WAIGHTS, Rev. Kenneth (Laws); Ex-President of the Methodist Conference, 1971–72; *b* 15 May 1909; *s* of Rev. William Waights and Selina Waights; *m* 1935, Dorothy Margaret Rowe. *Educ*: Stationers' Company Sch.; George Watson's Coll., Edinburgh; Handsworth Theological Coll., Birmingham. Served in the following Methodist Churches: Ilfracombe, Exeter, Birmingham Mission, Winson Green Prison (as Chaplain), Hastings, Liverpool, Scarborough, Nottingham (Chm. of District), Bristol, Sunderland, Newcastle upon Tyne; Chairman, Newcastle District of Methodist Church. Mayor of Shaftesbury, 1982–83. *Recreations*: golf, walking, travel; formerly: played Rugby football for Devon County, Moseley and Exeter Rugby Clubs. *Address*: 40 St James, Shaftesbury, Dorset.

WAIKATO, Bishop of, since 1980; **Rt. Rev. Brian Newton Davis;** *b* 28 Oct. 1934; *s* of Leonard Lancelot and Ethel May Davis; *m* 1961, Marie Lynette Waters; four *d*. *Educ*: Stratford Primary and Technical High School; Ardmore Teachers' Training Coll., Auckland; Victoria Univ. of Wellington (MA 1st class Hons Geog.); Christchurch Theol Coll. (LTh). Teacher, Stratford Primary School, 1954; Laboratory Asst, Victoria Univ., 1958. Deacon 1960, priest 1961; Assistant Curate: St Mark's, Wellington, 1960–62; Parish of Karori and Makara, 1962–64; Vicar: Makara and Karori West, 1964–67; Dannevirke, 1967–73; Cathedral Parish of St John the Evangelist and Dean of Waiapu, 1973; Vicar General of Waiapu, 1979–80. Regular columnist for Church Scene (Aust. Anglican newspaper), 1966. *Publication*: (contrib.) An Encyclopaedia of New Zealand, 1966. *Recreations*: squash, wood carving and turning, water colour painting. *Address*: PO Box 21, Hamilton, New Zealand. *T*: 82309.

WAIN, John Barrington; author; Professor of Poetry, University of Oxford, 1973–78; *b* 14 March 1925; *e* surv. *s* of Arnold A. Wain and Anne Wain, Stoke-on-Trent; *m* 1960, Eirian, *o* *d* of late T. E. James; three *s*. *Educ*: The High Sch., Newcastle-under-Lyme; St John's Coll., Oxford. Fereday Fellow, St John's Coll., Oxford, 1946–49; Lecturer in English Literature, University of Reading, 1947–55; resigned to become freelance author and critic. Churchill Visiting Prof., University of Bristol, 1967; Vis. Prof., Centre Universitaire Expérimentale de Vincennes, Paris, 1969. First Fellow in creative arts, Brasenose College, Oxford, 1971–72, Supernumerary Fellow, 1973–. Pres., Johnson Soc. of Lichfield, 1976–77. FRSL 1960, resigned 1961. *Publications* include: *fiction*: Hurry On Down, 1953, repr. 1978; Living in the Present, 1955; The Contenders, 1958; A Travelling Woman, 1959; Nuncle and other stories, 1960; Strike the Father Dead, 1962; The Young Visitors, 1965; Death of the Hind Legs and other stories, 1966; The Smaller Sky, 1967; A Winter in the Hills, 1970; The Life Guard and Other Stories, 1971; The Pardoner's Tale, 1978; Lizzie's Floating Shop, 1981; *play*: Harry in the Night, 1975; *poetry*: A Word Carved on a Sill, 1956; Weep Before God, 1961; Wildtrack, 1965; Letters to Five Artists, 1969; Feng, 1975; Poems 1949-79, 1981; *criticism*: Preliminary Essays, 1957; Essays on Literature and Ideas, 1963; The Living World of Shakespeare, 1964, new edn 1979; A House for the Truth, 1972; Professing Poetry, 1977; *biography*: Samuel Johnson, 1974, new edn 1980 (James Tait Black Meml Prize; Heinemann Award, 1975); *autobiography*: Sprightly Running, 1962; much work as editor, anthologist, reviewer, broadcaster, etc. *Recreations*: canoeing, walking. *Address*: c/o Macmillan & Co. Ltd, Little Essex Street, WC2.

WAIN, Prof. Ralph Louis, CBE 1968; DSc, PhD; FRS 1960, FRSC; Hon. Professor of Chemistry, University of Kent, since 1977 and Emeritus Professor, University of London, since 1978; Professor of Agricultural Chemistry, University of London, 1950–78, and Head of Department of Physical Sciences at Wye College (University of London), 1945–78; Hon. Director, Agricultural Research Council Unit on Plant Growth Substances and Systemic Fungicides, 1953–78; Fellow of Wye College, 1981; *b* 29 May 1911; 2nd *s* of late G. Wain, Hyde, Cheshire; *m* 1940, Joan Bowker; one *s* one *d*. *Educ*: County Grammar Sch., Hyde, Cheshire; University of Sheffield (First Class Hons Chemistry, 1932; MSc 1933; PhD 1935; Hon. DSc 1977);

DSc London, 1949; Town Trustees Fellow, University of Sheffield, 1934; Research Assistant, University of Manchester, 1935–37; Lecturer in Chemistry, Wye Coll., 1937–39; Research Chemist, Long Ashton Research Station (University of Bristol), 1939–45; Rockefeller Fellow, 1950 and 1962. Vice-President, Royal Institute of Chemistry, 1961–64, 1975–78; Member: Governing Body, Glasshouse Crops Res. Inst., 1953–71; E African Natural Resources Res. Council, 1963–; Manager, Royal Instn, 1971–74. Chm., ARC Wain Fellowships Cttee, 1976–. Nuffield Vis. Prof., Ibadan Univ., 1959; Vis. Prof., Cornell Univ., 1966; NZ Prestige Fellowship, 1973; Leverhulme Emeritus Fellowship, 1978–. Elected to Académie Internationale de Lutèce, 1980. Lectures: Sir Thomas Middleton Meml, London, 1955; Frankland Meml, Birmingham, 1965; Benjamin Minge Duggar Meml, Alabama, 1966; Amos Meml, E Malling, 1969; Masters Meml, London, 1973; Sir Jesse Boot Foundn, Nottingham, 1974; Ronald Slack Meml, London, 1975; Extramural Centenary, London Univ., 1976; Vis. Lectr, Pontifical Acad. Scis, 1976; Douglas Wills, Bristol, 1977; Gooding Meml, London, 1978; Drummond Meml, London, 1979; John Dalton, Manchester, 1979. Royal Soc. Vis. Prof. to Czechoslovakia, 1968, Mexico, 1971, China, 1973, Romania, 1974, Poland, 1976, Israel, 1979, Hungary, 1980, West Indies and Philippines, 1981. Pruthivi Gold Medal, 1957; RASE Research Medal, 1960; John Scott Award, 1963; Flintoff Medal, Chem. Soc., 1969; Internat. Award, Amer. Chem. Soc., 1972; Internat. Medal for Research on Plant Growth Substances, 1973; John Jeyes Gold Medal and Award, Chem. Soc., 1976; Royal Instn Actonian Award, 1977. Hon. DAgricSci, Ghent, 1963; Hon. DSc: Kent, 1976; Lausanne, 1977. *Publications*: numerous research publications in Annals of Applied Biology, Journal of Agric. Science, Journal of Chemical Society, Berichte der Deutschen Chemischen Gesellschaft, Proc. Royal Society, etc. *Recreations*: painting, travel. *Address*: Staple Farm, Hastingleigh, near Ashford, Kent. *T*: Elmsted 248.

WAINE, Rt. Rev. John; *see* St Edmundsbury and Ipswich, Bishop of.

WAINWRIGHT, Edwin, BEM 1957; MP (Lab) Dearne Valley Division of West Yorkshire, since Oct. 1959; *b* 12 Aug. 1908; *s* of John Wainwright and Ellen (*née* Hodgson); *m* 1938, Dorothy Metcalfe; two *s* two *d*. *Educ*: Darfield Council School; Wombwell and Barnsley Technical Colleges. WEA student for 20 years. Started work at 14, at Darfield Main Colliery; Nat. Union of Mineworkers: Member Branch Cttee, 1933–39; Delegate, 1939–48; Branch Sec., 1948–59; Member, Nat. Exec. Cttee, 1952–59. Member, Wombwell UDC, 1939–59. Sec./Agent, Dearne Valley Labour Party, 1951–59. Sec. Parly Lab. Party Trade Union Gp, 1966–; Sec. Yorkshire Gp of Parly Lab. Party, 1966–. Mem., Select Cttee on Energy, 1979–. *Recreations*: gardening, reading. *Address*: 20 Dovecliffe Road, Wombwell, near Barnsley, South Yorks. *T*: Barnsley 752153.

WAINWRIGHT, Richard Scurrah; MP (L) Colne Valley, 1966–70 and since Feb. 1974; Liberal Spokesman on the Economy; *b* 11 April 1918; *o* *s* of late Henry Scurrah and Emily Wainwright; *m* 1948, Joyce Mary Hollis; one *s* two *d* (and one *s* decd). *Educ*: Shrewsbury Sch.; Clare Coll., Cambridge (Open Scholar). BA Hons (History), 1939. Friends Ambulance Unit, NW Europe, 1939–46. Retired Partner, Peat Marwick Mitchell & Co., Chartered Accountants. Pres., Leeds/Bradford Society of Chartered Accountants, 1965–66. Chm., Liberal Party Research Dept, 1968–70; Chm., Liberal Party, 1970–72; Mem., Select Cttee on Treasury, 1979–. Dir, Rowntree Social Service Trust. *Recreations*: gardening, swimming. *Address*: The Heath, Adel, Leeds LS16 8EG. *T*: Leeds 673938. *Clubs*: Reform; Golcar Liberal, Honley Liberal, Linthwaite Liberal.

WAINWRIGHT, Robert Everard, CMG 1959; *b* 24 June 1913; *s* of Dr G. B. Wainwright, OBE, MB; *m* 1939, Bridget Alan-Williams; two *s*. *Educ*: Marlborough; Trinity College, Cambridge (BA). District Officer, Kenya, 1935; Provincial Commissioner, Rift Valley Province, 1953–59. Imperial Defence College, 1959. Chief Commissioner, Kenya, 1960–63; Administrator, Turks and Caicos Is, WI, 1967–71. Member: Gp of British observers, Zimbabwe elections, 1980; Gp of Commonwealth observers, Ugandan elections, 1980. *Recreations*: sailing, tennis, shooting, cabinet-making. *Address*: 20 St Peter's Road, Cirencester, Glos. *Club*: Mombasa (Mombasa).

WAINWRIGHT, Rear-Adm. Rupert Charles Purchas, CB 1966; DSC 1943; Vice Naval Deputy to Supreme Allied Commander Europe, 1965–67; retired 1967; with Redditch Development Corporation, 1968–77; *b* 16 Oct. 1913; *s* of late Lieut Comdr O. J. Wainwright and late Mrs S. Wainwright; *m* 1937, Patricia Mary Helen, *d* of late Col F. H. Blackwood, DSO and late Mrs Blackwood; two *s* two *d*. *Educ*: Royal Naval College, Dartmouth. Commanded HM Ships Actaeon, Tintagel Castle, Zephyr, 1952–54; Captain HMS Cambridge, 1955–57; Chief of Staff, S Atlantic and S America Station, 1958–60; Director Naval Recruiting, 1960–62; Commodore Naval Drafting, 1962–64. Comdr 1949; Capt. 1955; Rear-Adm. 1965. ADC to the Queen, 1964. Mem. Council, Missions to Seamen. Vice-President: Stratford-upon-Avon Soc. DC, Stratford-on-Avon, 1973–; Assoc. District Councils, 1976–; Keep Britain Tidy Group, 1976–. Mem., Waste Management Adv. Council, 1978–81. *Publications*: two Prize Essays, RUSI Jl. *Recreations*: hockey (Combined Services; a Vice-Pres., England Hockey Assoc.), swimming (Royal Navy), tennis. *Address*: Regency Cottage, Maidenhead Road, Stratford-upon-Avon, Warwicks CV37 6XS. *Clubs*: Royal Navy, Naval and Military.

WAINWRIGHT, Sam, CBE 1982; Deputy Chairman, Post Office Corporation, since 1981 (Member of Board since 1977); Managing Director, National Girobank, since 1977; *b* 2 Oct. 1924; *m* Ruth Strom; three *s* one *d*. *Educ:* Regent Street Polytechnic; LSE (MSc Econ). Financial journalist, Glasgow Herald, 1950; Deputy City Editor, 1952-55; Director: Rea Brothers Ltd (Merchant Bankers), 1960-77 (Managing Dir, 1965-77); Furness Withy & Co. Ltd, 1971-77; Stothert & Pitt Ltd, 1970-77 (Chm., 1975-77); Aeronautical & General Instruments Ltd, 1968-77; Manders (Holdings) Ltd, 1972-; Lancashire & London Investment Trust Ltd, 1961-77; Scottish Cities Investment Trust Ltd, 1961-77; Scottish & Mercantile Investment Co. Ltd, 1964-77. Mem. Council, Soc. of Investment Analysts, 1961-75, Fellow, 1980. Hon. Editor, The Investment Analyst, 1961-74. CBIM. *Publications:* articles in various Bank Reviews. *Recreations:* reading, bridge. *Address:* 6 Heath Close, NW11 7DX. *T:* 01-455 4448. *Clubs:* Reform, Overseas Bankers'.

WAITE, Hon. Sir John (Douglas), Kt 1982; **Hon. Mr Justice Waite;** a Judge of the High Court of Justice, Family Division, since 1982; *b* 3 July 1932; *s* of late Archibald Harvey Waite, Coleshill, Bucks, and Betty, *d* of late Ernest Bates; *m* 1966, Julia Mary, *er d* of late Joseph Tangye, Bellington, Kidderminster, Worcs; three *s* two step *s*. *Educ:* Sherborne Sch.; Corpus Christi Coll., Cambridge (MA). President of Cambridge Union, 1955. Nat. Service, 2nd Lieut, RA, 1951-52. Called to Bar, Gray's Inn, 1956, Bencher, 1981; QC 1975. Mem., General Council of the Bar, 1968-69; Junior Counsel to Registrar of Trade Unions, 1972-74. *Recreations:* keeping weeds down, boats afloat, and children happy. *Address:* 54 Church Street, Orford, Woodbridge, Suffolk IP12 2NT; 56 Campden Hill Court W8 7HU; Royal Courts of Justice, Strand, WC2A 2LL.
See also Maj.-Gen. Sir (E.) J. (H.) Bates.

WAITE, Terence Hardy, MBE 1982; Adviser to Archbishop of Canterbury on Anglican Communion Affairs, since 1980; *b* 31 May 1939; *s* of Thomas William Waite and Lena (*née* Hardy); *m* 1964, Helen Frances Watters; one *s* three *d*. *Educ:* Wilmslow and Stockton Heath, Cheshire; Church Army Coll., London; privately in USA and Europe. Lay training adviser to Bishop and Diocese of Bristol, 1964-68; Adviser to Archbishop of Uganda, Rwanda and Burundi, 1968-71; Internat. Consultant working with Roman Catholic Church, 1972-79. Member, National Assembly, Church of England, 1966-68 (resigned on moving to Africa); Co-ordinator, Southern Sudan Relief Project, 1969-71. Mem., Royal Inst. of International Affairs, 1980-. *Recreations:* music, walking, travel (esp. in remote parts of the world), Jungian studies, international affairs and politics, Left-Handed Society, preservation of old Blackheath. *Address:* Lambeth Palace, SE1 7JU. *T:* 01-928 8282. *Club:* Travellers'.

WAKE, Sir Hereward, 14th Bt *cr* 1621; MC 1942; DL; Major (retired) King's Royal Rifle Corps; *b* 7 Oct. 1916; *e s* of Sir Hereward Wake, 13th Bt, CB, CMG, DSO, and Margaret W. (*d* 1976), *er d* of R. H. Benson; *S* father, 1963; *m* 1952, Julia Rosemary, JP, *yr d* of late Capt. G. W. M. Lees, Falcutt House, Nr Brackley, Northants; one *s* three *d*. *Educ:* Eton; RMC, Sandhurst. Served War of 1939-45 (wounded, MC). Retired from 60th Rifles, 1947, and studied Estate Management and Agriculture. High Sheriff, 1955, DL 1969, Northants. *Heir: s* Hereward Charles Wake [*b* 22 Nov. 1952; *m* 1977, Lady Doune Ogilvy, *e d* of Earl of Airlie, *qv*; one *s*]. *Address:* Courteenhall, Northampton. *Club:* Brooks's.

WAKE, Hereward Baldwin Lawrence; Headmaster of St John's School, Leatherhead, Surrey, 1948-60, retired; *b* Aug. 1900; *s* late Rev. Preb. Hereward Eyre Wake and Mary Frances, *d* of late James Sealy Lawrence; *m* 1926, Sheila, *d* of late Captain Henry Harris; two *s*. *Educ:* Marlborough (Classical Exhibnr); Keble College, Oxford (Classical Scholar). Oxford Rugby XV (blue 1922); Somerset Rugby XV, 1923-29 (Captain 1927). Asst Housemaster, 1923, Housemaster, 1934-39, 1945-48, Cheltenham College. 7th Bn Gloucester Regt (TA), 1939; War Office, 1941-45 (Lt-Col, GSO1). *Recreations:* ornithology, reading, attempting The Times crossword. *Address:* High Ridge, Knoll Wood, Knoll Road, Godalming, Surrey. *T:* Godalming 22622. *Club:* Vincent's (Oxford).

WAKEFIELD, family name of Baron Wakefield of Kendal.

WAKEFIELD OF KENDAL, 1st Baron, *cr* 1963, of Kendal; William Wavell Wakefield, Kt 1944; Company Director; *b* Beckenham, Kent, 10 March 1898; *s* of late Roger William Wakefield, MB, JP, and Ethel May Knott; *m* 1919, Rowena Doris (*d* 1981), *d* of late Llewellyn Lewis, MD, OBE, JP; three *d*. *Educ:* The Craig Preparatory School; Sedbergh School; Pembroke College, Cambridge. In the RNAS then RAF European War (rose to rank of Captain, despatches); retired from the RAF as Flight-Lieutenant, 1923; transferred to Reserve; rejoined RAF at outbreak of war for flying duty; Director of the Air Training Corps, 1942-44; MP (Nat C) Swindon division of Wiltshire, 1935-45; (C) St Marylebone, 1945-63. Parliamentary Private Sec. to the Marquess of Hartington, 1936-38; to Rt Hon. R. H. Hudson, 1939-40; to Capt. Rt Hon. Harold Balfour, 1940-42; Chm. Parliamentary and Scientific Cttee, 1952-55; Director: Lake District Estates Co. Ltd; Shapland & Petter, Ltd, and other companies; Member of Executive Committee, YMCA; Member Executive Committee and Council, the National Playing Fields Assoc.; formerly Mem. Nature Conservancy; Member, Council of Royal National Mission to Deep Sea Fishermen; President, Metropolitan Assoc. of Building Societies, 1967-78; former Pres., Industrial Transport Assoc.; Vice-Pres., Council of The Roy. Albert Hall. Captained England,

Cambridge Univ., Middlesex, Royal Air Force, Harlequins, at Rugby football; Past President: Rugby Football Union; Ski Club of Great Britain; British Sub-Aqua Club; British Water Ski Fedn. *Publication:* Rugger. *Recreation:* ski-ing. *Heir:* none. *Address:* 71 Park Street, W1; The Old House, Kendal, Cumbria. *T:* Kendal 20861. *Clubs:* Carlton, MCC.
See also R. C. Wakefield.

WAKEFIELD, Bishop of, since 1977; **Rt. Rev. Colin Clement Walter James;** *b* 20 Sept. 1926; *yr s* of late Canon Charles Clement Hancock James and Gwenyth Mary James; *m* 1962, Margaret Joan Henshaw; one *s* two *d*. *Educ:* Aldenham School; King's College, Cambridge (MA, Hons History); Cuddesdon Theological College. Assistant Curate, Stepney Parish Church, 1952-55; Chaplain, Stowe School, 1955-59; BBC Religious Broadcasting Dept, 1959-67; Religious Broadcasting Organizer, BBC South and West, 1960-67; Vicar of St Peter with St Swithin, Bournemouth, 1967-73; Bishop Suffragan of Basingstoke, 1973-77; Canon Residentiary of Winchester Cathedral, 1973-77. Member of General Synod, 1970-; Chm., Church Information Cttee, 1976-79. Chm., BBC and IBA Central Religious Adv. Cttee, 1979-. President: Woodard Corp., 1978-; RADIUS, 1980-. *Recreations:* theatre, travelling. *Address:* Bishop's Lodge, Woodthorpe Lane, Wakefield, W Yorks WF2 6JJ.

WAKEFIELD, Provost of; *see* Allen, Very Rev. J. E.

WAKEFIELD, Derek John, CB 1982; Under Secretary, Government Communications Headquarters, 1978-82; *b* 21 Jan. 1922; *s* of Archibald John Thomas and Evelyn Bessie Wakefield; *m* 1951, Audrey Ellen Smith, FRHS; one *d*. *Educ:* The Commonweal School. Air Ministry, 1939-42 and 1947-52. Served War, Lieut, Royal Pioneer Corps, 1942-47. Government Communications Headquarters, 1952-82. Member: British Balloon and Airship Club; Airship Assoc. Governor, Barrwood House Trust, Gloucester, 1973-. *Recreations:* airships, car building. *Club:* Naval and Military.

WAKEFIELD, Sir (Edward) Humphry (Tyrrell), 2nd Bt *cr* 1962; *b* 11 July 1936; *s* of Sir Edward Birkbeck Wakefield, 1st Bt, CIE, and of Constance Lalage, *e d* of late Sir John Perronet Thompson, KCSI, KCIE; *S* father, 1969; *m* 1st, 1960, Priscilla (marr. diss. 1964), *e d* of O. R. Bagot; 2nd, 1966, Hon. Elizabeth Sophia (from whom he obt. a divorce, 1971), *e d* of Viscount De L'Isle, VC, KG, PC, GCMG, GCVO, and former wife of G. S. O. A. Colthurst; one *s* ; 3rd, 1974, Hon. Katharine Mary Alice Baring, *d* of 1st Baron Howick of Glendale, KG, GCMG, KCVO, and of Lady Mary Howick; one *s* one *d* (and one *s* decd). *Educ:* Gordonstoun; Trinity Coll., Cambridge (MA Hons). Formerly Captain, 10th Royal Hussars. Exec. Vice-Pres., Mallett, America Ltd, 1970-75; Chairman: Tyrrell & Moore Ltd, 1978-; Nicolai Patricia Co. Ltd, 1978-; Director: Mallett & Son (Antiques) Ltd, 1971-78; F. William Free Advertising (UK); International Finance Co., Madrid; Save Piccadilly Foundn. Dir, Spoleto Fest. of Two Worlds, USA and Italy. Appeals Consultant, London Br., British Red Cross Soc. Mem., Standing Council of Baronetage. Fellow, Pierrepont Morgan Library. *Recreations:* riding, writing, music, shooting. *Heir: s* Maximilian Edward Vereker Wakefield, *b* 22 Feb. 1967. *Address: c/o* Barclays Bank, St James' Street, Derby DE1 1QU. *Clubs:* Cavalry and Guards, Turf.

WAKEFIELD, Rev. Gordon Stevens; Principal of the Queen's College, Birmingham, since 1979; *b* 15 Jan. 1921; *s* of Ernest and Lucy Wakefield; *m* 1949, Beryl Dimes; one *s* three *d*. *Educ:* Crewe County Sec. School; Univ. of Manchester; Fitzwilliam Coll. and Wesley House, Cambridge; St Catherine's Coll., Oxford. MA (Cantab); MLitt (Oxon). Methodist Circuit Minister in Edgware, Woodstock, Stockport, Newcastle upon Tyne, Bristol, 1944-63; Methodist Connexional Editor, 1963-72; Chairman, Manchester and Stockport Methodist District, 1971-79. Fernley-Hartley Lectr, 1957; Select Preacher, Univ. of Oxford, 1971 and 1982. Recognized Lectr, Univ. of Birmingham, 1979. Member, Joint Liturgical Group (Chairman, 1978). *Publications:* Puritan Devotion, 1957; (with Hetley Price) Unity at the Local Level, 1965; Methodist Devotion, 1966; The Life of the Spirit in the World of Today, 1969; On the Edge of the Mystery, 1969; Robert Newton Flew, 1971; Fire of Love, 1976; (ed, with biographical introdns of E. C. Hoskyns and F. N. Davey) Crucifixion—Resurrection, 1981; contribs to theological jls. *Recreations:* watching and talking cricket; churches and cathedrals. *Address:* The Queen's College, Birmingham B15 2QH. *T:* 021-454 1527.

WAKEFIELD, Hubert George; *see* Wakefield, Hugh.

WAKEFIELD, Hugh, (Hubert George); MA Cantab; Hon. FMA; FRSA; Keeper of the Department of Circulation, Victoria and Albert Museum, 1960-75; *b* 6 March 1915; *o s* of late George Wakefield; *m* 1939, Nora Hilary Inglis; one *s* one *d*. *Educ:* King Edward's Sch., Birmingham; Trinity Coll., Cambridge. Joined staff of Royal Commission on Historical Monuments (England), 1938. Served War of 1939-45, Temp. Captain (Instructor in Gunnery), RA, 1942-46. Asst Keeper, Victoria and Albert Museum, 1948. Governor of the National Museum of Wales, 1960-75; Mem. Council, Museums' Assoc., 1960-63; Mem., DES Crafts Advisory Cttee, 1971-75; Chm., Cttee for Museums of Applied Art, Internat. Council of Museums, 1974-75; Corresp. Mem., Finnish Soc. of Crafts and Design, 1965-. *Publications:* (ed) Victorian Collector (series); Nineteenth Century British Glass, 1961, 1982; Victorian Pottery, 1962; Contributor to: Connoisseur Early Victorian Period Guide, 1958; World Ceramics (ed R. J. Charleston), 1968;

Das Pompöse Zeitalter, 1970; Encyc. Brit. *Recreation:* travel. *Address:* 32 Strand-on-the-Green, W4. *T:* 01-994 6355; Frigiliana, Malaga, Spain.

WAKEFIELD, Sir Humphry; *see* Wakefield, Sir E. H. T.

WAKEFIELD, Sir Peter (George Arthur), KBE 1977; CMG 1973; HM Diplomatic Service, retired; Director, National Art-Collections Fund, since 1982; *b* 13 May 1922; *s* of John Bunting Wakefield and Dorothy Ina Stace; *m* 1951, Felicity Maurice-Jones; four *s* one *d. Educ:* Cranleigh Sch.; Corpus Christi Coll., Oxford. Army Service, 1942–47; Military Govt, Eritrea, 1946–47; Hulton Press, 1947–49; entered Diplomatic Service, 1949; Middle East Centre for Arab Studies, 1950; 2nd Sec., Amman, 1950–52; Foreign Office, 1953–55; 1st Sec., British Middle East Office, Nicosia, 1955–56; 1st Sec. (Commercial), Cairo, 1956; Administrative Staff Coll., Henley, 1957; 1st Sec. (Commercial), Vienna, 1957–60; 1st Sec. (Commercial), Tokyo, 1960–63; Foreign Office, 1964–66; Consul-General and Counsellor, Benghazi, 1966–69; Econ. and Commercial Counsellor, Tokyo, 1970–72; Econ. and Commercial Minister, Tokyo, 1973; seconded as Special Adviser on the Japanese Market, BOTB, 1973–75; Ambassador to the Lebanon, 1975–78, to Belgium, 1979–82. *Recreations:* ceramics and restoring ruins; tennis, swimming. *Address:* 28 Lincoln House, Montpelier Row, Twickenham, Mddx. *T:* 01-892 6390; La Molineta, Frigiliana, near Malaga, Spain. *Club:* Travellers'.

WAKEFIELD, Roger Cuthbert, CMG 1953; OBE 1950; DL; retired; *b* Cark-in-Cartmel, Lancs, 27 June 1906; 4th and *y s* of late Roger William Wakefield, MB, BCh, Kendal, and Ethel May Knott; *m* 1936, Elizabeth Rhoda, *yr d* of late Sidney R. Davie and Margaret Preston Lawson, West Byfleet, Surrey; one *d. Educ:* Sedbergh School; Trinity College, Cambridge (BA 1928). Joined Sudan Civil Service, 1929; Survey of the Arc of the Thirtieth Meridian, 1935–40. War of 1939–45; Civil Defence Duties and desert navigation, 1940–43; Director of Surveys, Sudan, 1946–54; Survey Consultant to Sudan Government, 1954–55. Director, Equatoria Projects Board, 1949; Chairman, Unclassified Staff Wages Commn, 1951; Councillor without Portfolio on Governor-Gen.'s Exec. Council and Member Legislative Assembly, 1952. Member: British-Argentine Rugby football touring team, 1927; Cambridge East Greenland Exped., 1929; Lake Rudolf Rift Valley Exped., 1934. Chm., Highland Div., Scottish Community Drama Assoc., 1975–78. FRICS, 1949. DL Ross and Cromarty, 1976. *Publication:* (with D. F. Munsey) The Arc of the Thirtieth Meridian between the Egyptian Frontier and Latitude 13° 45', 1950. *Recreations:* mountaineering, sailing, fishing. *Address:* Glendrynoch Lodge, Carbost, Isle of Skye. *Club:* Alpine.
See also Baron Wakefield of Kendal.

WAKEFIELD, William Barry; Director of Statistics, Department of Education and Science, since 1979; *b* 6 June 1930; *s* of Stanley Arthur and Evelyn Grace Wakefield; *m* 1953, Elizabeth Violet (*née* Alexander); three *s* one *d. Educ:* Harrow County Grammar Sch.; University Coll., London. BSc; FSS. Statistician, NCB, 1953–62; DES, 1962–67; Chief Statistician, MoD, 1967–72, CSO, 1972; Asst Dir, CSO, Cabinet Office, 1975–79. Member, United Reformed Church. *Recreations:* horse racing, gardening. *Address:* 7 The Spinneys, Hockley, Essex. *T:* Southend 203514.

WAKEFORD, Geoffrey Michael Montgomery; Clerk to the Worshipful Company of Mercers, since 1974; Barrister-at-Law; *b* 10 Dec. 1937; *o s* of Geoffrey and late Helen Wakeford; *m* 1966, Diana Margaret Loy Cooper; two *s* two *d. Educ:* Downside; Clare Coll., Cambridge (Classical Schol., MA, LLB). Called to Bar, Gray's Inn and South Eastern Circuit, 1961; practised at Common Law Bar until 1971. Apptd Dep. Clerk to the Mercers Co., 1971. Clerk to: Governors St Paul's Schs; Joint Grand Gresham Cttee; City & Metropolitan Welfare Trustees; Collyers Foundn Trustees; Council of Gresham Coll. Vice Chm., Islington Soc. for the Mentally Handicapped. Governor, London Internat. Film Sch. *Address:* Mercers Hall, Ironmonger Lane, EC2V 8HE. *T:* 01-726 4991.

WAKEFORD, John Chrysostom Barnabas, CMG 1948; *b* 23 Aug. 1898; *o s* of Rev. John Wakeford, Anfield, Liverpool; *m* 1st, 1921, Grace (*d* 1965), *d* of Charles Cooke, Church Coppenhall; one *d*; 2nd, 1970, Dorothy May, *d* of Frederick Ward, Aldeburgh, Suffolk. *Educ:* Malvern College; RMA, Woolwich; Clare College, Cambridge. Commissioned Royal Engineers, 1917; served European War, France and Belgium, 1917–18; N Russia Campaign (despatches). Dep. Dir Transportn, W Africa, 1941–43; Ceylon, 1943–44 (Col); Dir of Transportn, SE Asia, 1944–45 (Brig.). Chief Railway Commissioner, Burma; General Manager, Burma Railways and Technical Adviser to Government of Burma, 1945–48; Chief Engineer, Cameroons Development Corporation, W Africa, 1948–50; with Rendel Palmer & Tritton, 1950–63; FICE, FIMechE, FCIT, FRSA. *Address:* 41 South Road, Saffron Walden, Essex. *T:* Saffron Walden 22010.

WAKEFORD, Air Marshal Sir Richard (Gordon), KCB 1976; MVO 1961; OBE 1958; AFC 1952; Secretary, RAF Benevolent Fund, Scotland, since 1978; *b* 20 April 1922; *s* of Charles Edward Augustus Wakeford; *m* 1948, Anne Butler; two *s* two *d. Educ:* Montpelier Sch., Paignton; Kelly Coll., Tavistock. Joined RAF, 1941; flying Catalina flying boats, Coastal Comd, operating out of India, Scotland, N Ireland, 1942–45; flying Liberator and York transport aircraft on overseas routes, 1945–47; CFS 1947; Flying Instructor, RAF Coll. Cranwell; CFS Examining Wing; ground appts incl. 2½ years on staff of Dir of Emergency Ops in Malaya, 1952–58; comdg Queen's Flight, 1958–61; Directing Staff, RAF Staff Coll., 1961–64; subseq.:

comdg RAF Scampton; SASO, HQ 3 Group Bomber Comd; Asst Comdt (Cadets), RAF Coll. Cranwell; idc 1969; Comdr N Maritime Air Region, and Air Officer Scotland and N Ireland, 1970–72; Dir of Service Intelligence, MoD, 1972–73; ANZUK Force Comdr, Singapore, 1974–75; Dep. Chief of Defence Staff (Intell.), 1975–78; HM Comr, Queen Victoria Sch., Dunblane; Vice-Chm. (Air), Lowland T&AVR. Trustee, McRobert Trusts (Chm., 1982–); Director: Thistle Foundn; Cromar Nominees. OStJ 1981. *Recreations:* golf, fishing. *Address:* Earlston House, Forgandenny, Perth. *T:* Bridge of Earn 2392. *Clubs:* Flyfishers', Royal Air Force.

WAKEHAM, John, JP; FCA; MP (C) Maldon since Feb. 1974; Minister of State, HM Treasury, since 1982; *b* 22 June 1932; *s* of late Major W. J. Wakeham and late Mrs E. R. Wakeham; *m* 1965, Anne Roberta Bailey; two *s. Educ:* Charterhouse. Chartered Accountant in practice from 1960; Company Director. Asst Govt Whip, 1979–81; a Lord Comr of HM Treasury (Govt Whip), 1981; Parly Under-Sec. of State, DoI, 1981–82. JP Inner London 1972. *Publications:* The Case against Wealth Tax, 1968; A Personal View, 1969. *Recreations:* farming, sailing, racing, reading. *Address:* House of Commons, SW1. *Clubs:* Carlton, St Stephen's Constitutional.

WAKEHURST, 3rd Baron *cr* 1934, of Ardingly; **(John) Christopher Loder;** Chairman: Continental Illinois Ltd, since 1973; Anglo-American Securities Corporation PLC, since 1980 (Director, since 1968); North Atlantic Securities Corporation PLC, since 1980; Oil & Gas Enterprises (NS) Ltd, since 1971; Hampton Gold Mining Areas PLC, since 1981; Deputy Chairman, London and Manchester Group PLC (Director, since 1966); *b* 23 Sept. 1925; *s* of 2nd Baron Wakehurst, KG, KCMG, and of Dowager Lady Wakehurst, *qv* ; *S* father, 1970; *m* 1956, Ingeborg Krumbholz-Hess (*d* 1977); one *s* one *d. Educ:* Eton; King's School, nr Sydney, NSW; Trinity College, Cambridge (BA 1948, LLB 1949, MA 1953). Served War as Sub Lieut RNVR and RNVR; West Pacific, 1943–45. Barrister, Inner Temple, 1950. Trustee: The Photographers' Gallery, 1979–; The Shakespeare Globe Trust Ltd, 1981–; Governor, Contemporary Dance Trust, 1981–. CStJ. *Heir:* s Hon. Timothy Walter Loder, *b* 28 March 1958. *Address:* c/o Continental Bank House, 162 Queen Victoria Street, EC4V 4BS. *T:* 01-236 5292. *Clubs:* City of London, Chelsea Arts.

WAKEHURST, Dowager Lady; Dame Margaret Wakehurst, DBE 1965; *b* 4 Nov. 1899; *d* of Sir Charles Tennant, Bt and of Marguerite (*née* Miles); *m* 1920, John de Vere Loder (later 2nd Baron Wakehurst, KG, KCMG) (*d* 1970); three *s* one *d.* Founder, Northern Ireland Assoc. for Mental Health; Vice-President: Nat. Assoc. for Mental Health; National Schizophrenia Fellowship; Royal College of Nursing, 1958–78. Hon. LLD Queen's Univ., Belfast; Hon. DLitt New Univ. of Ulster, 1973. DStJ 1959; GCStJ 1970. *Address:* 31 Lennox Gardens, SW1. *T:* 01-589 0956.

WAKELEY, Sir John (Cecil Nicholson), 2nd Bt *cr* 1952; FRCS; Consultant Surgeon, West Cheshire Group of Hospitals, since 1961; *b* 27 Aug. 1926; *s* of Sir Cecil Pembrey Grey Wakeley, 1st Bt, KBE, CB, MCh, FRCS, and of Elizabeth Muriel, *d* of James Nicholson-Smith; *S* father, 1979; *m* 1954, June Leney; two *s* one *d. Educ:* Canford School. MB, BS London 1950; LRCP 1950, FRCS 1955 (MRCS 1950), FACS 1973. Lectr in Anatomy, Univ. of London, 1951–52. Sqdn Ldr, RAF, 1953–54. Councillor, RCS, 1971; Member: Mersey Regional Health Authority, 1974–78; Editorial Bd, Health Trends, DHSS, 1968–71; Examiner for Gen. Nursing Council for England and Wales, 1954–59; Consultant Adviser in Surgery to RAF, 1981–. Liveryman: Worshipful Soc. of Apothecaries; Worshipful Co. of Barbers; Freeman of City of London. FACS 1973. CStJ 1959. *Publications:* papers on leading med. jls, incl. British Empire Cancer Campaign Scientific Report, Vol. II: Zinc 65 and the prostate, 1958; report on distribution and radiation dosimetry of Zinc 65 in the rat, 1959. *Recreations:* music, photography, bird-watching. *Heir:* s Nicholas Jeremy Wakeley, *b* 17 Oct. 1957. *Address:* Mickle Lodge, Mickle Trafford, Chester CH2 4EB. *T:* Mickle Trafford 300316. *Club:* Council Club of Royal College of Surgeons.

WAKELING, Rt. Rev. John Denis; *see* Southwell, Bishop of.

WAKELY, Leonard John Dean, CMG 1965; OBE 1945; *b* 18 June 1909; *s* of Sir Leonard Wakely, KCIE, CB; *m* 1938, Margaret Houssemayne Tinson; two *s. Educ:* Westminster School; Christ Church, Oxford; School of Oriental Studies, London. Indian Civil Service, 1932–47. Served in the Punjab and in the Defence Co-ordination, Defence and Legislative Departments of the Government of India. Appointed to Commonwealth Relations Office, 1947; Office of UK High Commissioner in the Union of South Africa, 1950–52; Dep. UK High Comr in India (Madras), 1953–57; Asst Sec., 1955; Dep. UK High Comr in Ghana, 1957–60; Dep. British High Comr in Canada, 1962–65; British Ambassador in Burma, 1965–67. *Address:* Long Meadow, Forest Road, East Horsley, Surrey.

WAKEMAN, Sir (Offley) David, 5th Bt *cr* 1828; *b* 6 March 1922; *s* of Sir Offley Wakeman, 4th Bt, CBE, and Winifred (*d* 1924), 2nd *d* of late Col C. R. Prideaux-Brune; *S* father, 1975; *m* 1946, Pamela Rose Arabella, *d* of late Lt-Col C. Hunter Little, DSO, MBE. *Educ:* Canford School. *Heir:* half-brother Edward Offley Bertram Wakeman, *b* 31 July 1934. *Address:* Peverey House, Bomere Heath, Shrewsbury, Salop. *T:* Shrewsbury 850561. *Clubs:* Lansdowne; Salop (Shrewsbury).

WAKERLEY, Richard MacLennon; QC 1982; a Recorder of the Crown Court, since 1982; b 7 June 1942; s of late Charles William Wakerley and of Gladys MacLennon Wakerley; m Marian Heather Dawson; two s two d. Educ: De Aston Sch., Market Rasen; Emmanuel Coll., Cambridge (MA), Called to the Bar, Gray's Inn, 1965. Recreations: theatre, bridge, gardening. Address: Croft House, Grendon, Atherstone, Warwicks CV9 3DP. T: Atherstone 2329.

WAKLEY, Bertram Joseph, MBE 1945; **His Honour Judge Wakley;** a Circuit Judge, since 1973; b 7 July 1917; s of Major Bertram Joseph Wakley and Hon. Mrs Dorothy Wakley (née Hamilton); m 1953, Alice Margaret Lorimer. Educ: Wellington Coll.; Christ Church, Oxford. BA 1939, MA 1943. Commnd S Lancs Regt, 1940; Captain 1941; Major 1943; served N Africa, Italy, Greece (despatches). Called to Bar, Gray's Inn, 1948. A Recorder of the Crown Court, 1972–73. Publications: History of the Wimbledon Cricket Club, 1954; Bradman the Great, 1959; Classic Centuries, 1964. Recreations: cricket, golf. Address: Hamilton House, Kingston Hill, Surrey. T: 01-546 9961. Clubs: Carlton, MCC, Roehampton.

WALBANK, Frank William, FBA 1953; MA; Rathbone Professor of Ancient History and Classical Archæology in the University of Liverpool, 1951–77, now Professor Emeritus; Dean, Faculty of Arts, 1974–77; b 10 Dec. 1909; s of A. J. D. Walbank, Bingley, Yorks; m 1935, Mary Woodward, e d of O. C. A. Fox, Shipley, Yorks; one s two d. Educ: Bradford Grammar School; Peterhouse, Cambridge. Scholar of Peterhouse, 1928–31; First Class, Parts I and II Classical Tripos, 1930–31; Hugo de Balsham Research Student, Peterhouse, 1931–32; Senior Classics Master at North Manchester High School, 1932–33; Thirlwall Prize, 1933; Asst Lecturer, 1934–36; Lecturer, 1936–46, in Latin, Professor of Latin, 1946–51, University of Liverpool; Public Orator, 1956–60; Hare Prize, 1939. J. H. Gray Lectr, Univ. of Cambridge, 1957; Andrew Mellon Vis. Prof., Univ. Pittsburgh, 1964; Myres Memorial Lectr, Univ. of Oxford, 1964–65; Sather Prof., Univ. of Calif (Berkeley), 1971. Pres., Cambridge Phil Soc., 1982–83; Member Council: Classical Assoc., 1944–48, 1958–61 (Pres. 1969–70); Roman Soc., 1948–51 (Vice-Pres., 1953–; Pres., 1961–64); Hellenic Soc., 1951–54, 1955–56; Classical Journals Bd, 1948–66; British Acad., 1960–63; British Sch. at Rome, 1979–. Mem., Inst. for Advanced Study Princeton, 1970–71; Foreign Mem., Royal Netherlands Acad. of Arts and Sciences, 1981–. Publications: Aratos of Sicyon, 1933; Philip V of Macedon, 1940; Latin Prose Versions contributed to Key to Bradley's Arnold, Latin Prose Composition, ed J. F. Mountford, 1940; The Decline of the Roman Empire in the West, 1946; contributions to the Oxford Classical Dictionary, 1949, to Chambers's Encyclopædia, 1950 and to Encyclopædia Britannica, 1960 and 1974; Chapters in The Cambridge Economic History of Europe, Vol. II, 1952, and A Scientific Survey of Merseyside, 1953; A Historical Commentary on Polybius, Vol. i, 1957, Vol. ii, 1967, Vol. iii, 1979; The Awful Revolution, 1969; Polybius, 1972; The Hellenistic World, 1981; contributor to English and foreign classical books and periodicals. Address: 64 Grantchester Meadows, Cambridge CB3 9JL. T: Cambridge 64350.

WALD, Prof. George; Higgins Professor of Biology, Harvard University, 1968–77, now Emeritus Professor; b 18 Nov. 1906; s of Isaac Wald and Ernestine (née Rosenmann); m 1st, 1931, Frances Kingsley (marr. diss.); two s; 2nd, 1958, Ruth Hubbard; one s one d. Educ: Washington Square Coll. of New York Univ. (BS); Columbia Univ. (PhD). Nat. Research Coun. Fellowship, 1932–34. Harvard University: Instr and Tutor in Biology, 1934–39; Faculty Instr, 1939–44; Associate Prof., 1944–48; Prof. of Biology, 1948–68. Nobel Prize in Physiology and Medicine (jointly), 1967. Has many hon. doctorates from univs in USA and abroad; Guest, China Assoc. for Friendship with Foreign Peoples, Jan.–Feb. 1972; US/Japan Distinguished Scientist Exchange, 1973. Publications: (co-author) General Education in a Free Society; (co-author) Twenty-six Afternoons of Biology. Many sci. papers (on the biochemistry and physiology of vision and on biochem. evolution) in: Jl of Gen. Physiology, Nature, Science, Jl of Opt. Soc. of Amer., etc. Recreations: art, archæology, ski-ing, horseback riding. Address: 21 Lakeview Avenue, Cambridge, Mass 02138, USA. T: (617) 495-2311.

WALDEGRAVE, family name of **Earl Waldegrave.**

WALDEGRAVE, 12th Earl, cr 1729, **Geoffrey Noel Waldegrave,** KG 1971; GCVO 1976; TD; DL; Bt 1643; Baron Waldegrave, 1685; Viscount Chewton, 1729; Member of the Prince's Council of the Duchy of Cornwall, 1951–58 and 1965–76, Lord Warden of the Stannaries, 1965–76; b 21 Nov. 1905; o s of 11th Earl and Anne Katharine (d 1962), d of late Rev. W. P. Bastard, Ashburton and Kitley, Devon; S father, 1936; m 1930, Mary Hermione, d of Lt-Col A. M. Grenfell, DSO; two s five d. Educ: Winchester; Trinity Coll., Cambridge (BA). Served War of 1939-45, Major RA (TA). Chm., Som AEC, 1948-51; Liaison Officer to Min. of Agriculture, Fisheries and Food (formerly Min. of Agriculture and Fisheries), for Som, Wilts and Glos, 1952-57; Jt Parly Sec., Min. of Agriculture, Fisheries and Food, 1958-62; Chairman: Forestry Commn, 1963-65; Adv. Cttee on Meat Research, 1969-73. Director: Lloyds Bank Ltd, 1964-76 (Chm., Bristol Regional Bd, 1966-76); Bristol Waterworks Co., 1938-58 and 1963-78. Pres., Somerset Trust for Nature Conservation, 1964-80. Member: BBC Gen. Adv. Council, 1963-66; Bristol Univ. Court and Council (former Chm., Agricultural Cttee). Mem. Council and Trustee, Bath and W Southern Counties Soc. (Pres., 1974); Trustee, Partis Coll., Bath; Chm., Friends of Wells Cathedral. Hon. LLD Bristol, 1976. Former Governor: Wells Cathedral Sch.; Nat. Fruit and Cider Inst., Long Ashton. Mem. Som CC, 1937-58; CA, 1949-58; DL Somerset, 1951; Vice-Lieutenant Somerset, 1955-60. Officer, Legion of Merit, USA. Heir: s Viscount Chewton, qv. Address: Chewton House, Chewton Mendip, Bath BA3 4LQ. T: Chewton Mendip 264. Clubs: Travellers', Farmers'.
See also J. D. Boles, Baron Forteviot, M. J. Hussey, Lady Susan Hussey, Baron Strathcona and Mount Royal, Hon. William Waldegrave.

WALDEGRAVE, Hon. William Arthur; MP (C) Bristol West, since 1979; Parliamentary Under-Secretary of State, Department of Education and Science, since 1981; Fellow of All Souls College, Oxford, since 1979 (also from 1971-78); b 15 Aug. 1946; yr s of Earl Waldegrave, qv; m 1977, Caroline, y d of Major and Mrs Richard Burrows, Kemsing, Kent; one d. Educ: Eton (Newcastle Schol.); Corpus Christi Coll., Oxford (Open Schol.; 1st Cl. Lit. Hum. 1969) (President, Oxford Union and Oxford Univ. Conservative Assoc.); Harvard Univ. (Kennedy Fellow). Central Policy Review Staff, Cabinet Office, 1971-73; Political Staff, 10 Downing Street, 1973-74; Head of Leader of Opposition's Office, 1974-75; Vice Chm., Conservative Backbench Finance Cttee, 1980-81. GEC Ltd (Group HQ and GEC Gas Turbines Ltd, Leicester), 1975-81. JP Inner London Juvenile Court, 1975-79. Mem., IBA Adv. Council, 1980-81. Publication: The Binding of Leviathan, 1977. Address: 18 Wellington Terrace, Bristol BS8 4LE. T: Bristol 734817. Clubs: Brooks's, Beefsteak, Pratt's.

WALDEN, (Alastair) Brian; Presenter, Weekend World, London Weekend Television, since 1977; Member, West Midland Board, Central Independent Television; b 8 July 1932; s of W. F. Walden; m Hazel Downes, d of William A. Downes; three s of former marriages. Educ: West Bromwich Grammar School; Queen's College and Nuffield College, Oxford; Pres., Oxford Union, 1957. University Lecturer. MP (Lab): Birmingham, All Saints, 1964-74; Birmingham, Ladywood, 1974-77. TV presenter and journalist. Recreations: chess, gardening. Address: 29 Warwick Avenue, W9.

WALDEN, George Gordon Harvey, CMG 1981; HM Diplomatic Service; Head of Planning Staff, Foreign and Commonwealth Office, since 1982; b 15 Sept. 1939; s of G. G. Walden; m 1970, Sarah Nicolette Hunt; two s one d. Educ: Latymer Upper Sch.; Jesus Coll., Cambridge; Moscow Univ. (postgraduate). Research Dept, Foreign Office, 1962-65; Chinese Language Student, Hong Kong Univ., 1965-67; Second Secretary, Office of HM Chargé d'Affaires, Peking, 1967-70; First Sec., FCO (Soviet Desk), 1970-73; Ecole Nationale d'Administration, Paris, 1973-74; First Sec., HM Embassy, Paris, 1974-78; Principal Private Sec. to Foreign and Commonwealth Sec., 1978-81; sabbatical year, Harvard, 1981. Address: 14 Ashchurch Terrace, W12 9SL.

WALDER, Edwin James, CMG 1971; management consultant and company director, since 1981; b 5 Aug. 1921; s of Edwin James Walder and Dulcie Muriel Walder (née Griffiths); m 1944, Norma Cheslin; two d. Educ: North Newtown High Sch.; Univ. of Sydney (BEc). Apptd NSW Civil Service, 1938; NSW State Treasury: 1945; Asst Under-Sec. (Finance), 1959-61; Dep. Under-Sec., 1961-63; Under-Sec. and Comptroller of Accounts, 1963-65; Pres., Metrop. Water, Sewerage and Drainage Bd, Sydney, 1965-81. Member: State Pollution Control Commn, 1971-81; Metropolitan Waste Disposal Authority (Sydney), 1971-81. Recreations: lawn bowls, fishing, swimming. Address: Unit 9, 12 Alma Road, Padstow Heights, NSW 2211, Australia. Clubs: City Tattersall's, Roselands Bowling, St George Leagues (all in Sydney).

WALDER, Ruth Christabel, (Mrs Wesierska), OBE 1956; b 15 Jan. 1906; d of Rev. Ernest Walder; m 1955, Maj.-Gen. George Wesierski (d 1967), formerly Judge Advocate General of the Polish Forces. Educ: Cheltenham Ladies' College. General Organiser, National Federation of Women's Institutes, 1934-40; Admiralty, 1940-41; Relief Department, Foreign Office, 1942-44; UNRRA, Sec. Food Cttee of Council for Europe, 1944-47; Secretary United Nations Appeal for Children (in the UK), 1948; National General Secretary, YWCA of Great Britain, 1949-67. Lectr for the European Community, 1970-. Defence Medal, 1946. Polish Gold Cross of Merit, 1969. Address: Westhope, Langton Herring, Weymouth, Dorset. T: Abbotsbury 233. Clubs: Naval and Military; Royal Dorset Yacht.

WALDHEIM, Dr Kurt; Secretary-General of the United Nations, 1972-81; Guest Professor of Diplomacy, Georgetown University, Washington, DC; b 21 Dec. 1918; m 1944, Elisabeth Ritschel Waldheim; one s two d. Educ: Consular Academy, Vienna; Univ. of Vienna (Dr Jr 1944). Entered Austrian foreign service, 1945; served in Min. of Foreign Affairs; Mem., Austrian Delegn to Paris, London and Moscow for negotiations on Austrian State Treaty, 1945-47; 1st Sec., Embassy, Paris, 1948-51; apptd Counsellor and Head of Personnel Div., Min. of Foreign Affairs, 1951-55; Permanent Austrian Observer to UN, 1955-56; Minister Plenipotentiary to Canada, 1956-58; Ambassador to Canada, 1958-60; Dir-Gen. for Political Affairs, Min. of Foreign Affairs, 1960-64; Permanent Rep. of Austria to UN, 1964-68 (Chm., Outer Space Cttee of UN 1965-68 and 1970-71); Federal Minister for Foreign Affairs, 1968-70; Candidate for the Presidency of Republic of Austria, 1971; Permanent Rep. of Austria to UN, 1970-Dec. 1971. Hon. LLD: Chile, Carleton, Rutgers, Fordham, 1972; Jawaharlal Nehru, Bucharest, 1973; Wagner Coll., NY, Catholic Univ. of America, Wilfrid Laurier, 1974; Catholic Univ. of Leuven, Charles Univ., Hamilton Coll., Clinton, NY, 1975; Denver, Philippines, Nice, 1976; American Univ., Kent State, Warsaw, Moscow State Univ., Mongolian State Univ., 1977; Atlanta Univ., Humboldt Univ., Univ. of S Carolina, 1979; Keele, Notre Dame, USA, 1980. George Marshall Peace Award, USA, 1977; Dr Karl Renner Prize, City of Vienna,

1978. *Publications:* The Austrian Example, 1971, English edn 1973; The Challenge of Peace, 1977, English edn 1980; Building the Future Order, 1980. *Recreations:* sailing, swimming, skiing, horseback riding. *Address:* Ballhausplatz 2, 1010 Vienna, Austria.

WALDMAN, Stanley John; Master of the Supreme Court, Queen's Bench Division, since 1971; *b* 18 Sept. 1923; *s* of late Michael Ernest Waldman, OBE, JP; *m* 1951, Naomi Sorsky; one *s* two *d. Educ:* Owen's School, London; Pembroke College, Oxford. BA; MA 1948. RAF, 1942-46; called to the Bar, Gray's Inn, 1949; practised in London and on SE Circuit. *Address:* 80 South Hill Park, NW3.

WALDRON, Brig. John Graham Claverhouse, CBE 1958 (OBE 1944); DSO 1945; *b* 15 Nov. 1909; *s* of William Slade Olver (*d* 1909), Falmouth; *m* 1933, Marjorie, *d* of Arthur Waldron (*d* 1953), Newbury; one *s* one *d. Educ:* Marlborough; RMC, Sandhurst. jssc, psc. 2nd Lieut, Gloucestershire Regt, 1929. Served War of 1939-45 (OBE, DSO): 5 British Division and 1st Bn Green Howards, in India, Middle East, Italy, NW Europe. Lt-Col, 10th Gurkha Rifles, 1951; Brigadier, 1958; ADC to the Queen, 1960-61; retired, 1961. *Address:* c/o Banco Hispano Americano, Avenida Ramón y Cajal 12, Marbella, Spain. *Clubs:* Army and Navy, Royal Cruising.

WALDRON-RAMSEY, Waldo Emerson; Barrister and Attorney-at-Law; Ambassador and Permanent Representative for Barbados to the United Nations, 1971-76; *b* 1 Jan. 1930; *s* of Wyatt and Delcina Waldron-Ramsey; *m* 1954, Shiela Pamela Beresford, Georgetown, Guyana; one *s* two *d. Educ:* Barbados; Hague Academy; London Sch. of Economics; Yugoslavia. LLB Hons; BSc (Econ) Hons; PhD. Called to Bar, Middle Temple; practised London Bar and SW Circuit, 1957-60; Marketing Economist, Shell International, 1960-61; Tanzanian Foreign Service, 1961-70; High Comr for Barbados in UK, and Ambassador to France, Netherlands and Germany, 1970-71. UN Legal Expert: in field of human rights, 1967-71; on Israel, 1968-71. Member: Amer. Acad. of Political and Social Sciences; Amer. Soc. of Internat. Law; Amer. Inst. of Petroleum (Marketing Div.). Hon. Fellow, Hebrew Univ. of Jerusalem, 1972. DSc (Pol. Econ) Univ. of Phnom-Penh, 1973; Hon. LLD Chung-Ang Univ., Republic of Korea, 1975. Grand Officer (1st Class), Nat. Order of Human et Mérite, Republic of Haiti, 1968; Grand Officier, Ordre Nat. de l'Amitié et Mérite, Khymèr, 1973; Order of Distinguished Diplomatic Service Merit, Gwangwha (1st Class), Republic of Korea, 1974. *Recreations:* cricket, tennis, bridge, travel. *Address:* (chambers) 22 James Street, Bridgetown, Barbados; (chambers) 26 Court Street, Brooklyn, New York 11225, USA; The Monticello, 30 Park Avenue, Mount Vernon, New York 10550. *Clubs:* Royal Automobile; Lincoln Lodge (Connecticut).

WALES, Geoffrey, RE 1961 (ARE 1948); ARCA 1936; wood engraver; Lecturer, Norwich School of Art, 1953-77; *b* 26 May 1912; *s* of Ernest and Kathleen Wales; *m* 1940, Marjorie Skeeles, painter; two *d. Educ:* Chatham House School, Ramsgate; Thanet School of Art; Royal College of Art. Served War of 1939-45, in Royal Air Force, 1940-46. Prints and drawings in Victoria and Albert Museum; Whitworth Gallery, Manchester; Kunsthaus, Graz; and private collections. Exhibits with Royal Society of Painter Etchers and Engravers. Illustrated books for Golden Cockerel Press, Kynoch Press, Folio Soc. and general graphic work. Engravings included in publications and articles on wood-engraving. *Address:* 15 Heigham Grove, Norwich, Norfolk NR2 3DQ. *T:* Norwich 29066.

WALES, Horace Geoffrey Quaritch, MA, PhD, LittD; Orientalist and Archæologist; *b* 17 Oct. 1900; *s* of late E. Horace Wales; *g s* of late Bernard Quaritch; *m* 1931, Dorothy Clementina Johnson, LLB. *Educ:* Charterhouse; Queens' College, Cambridge. Siamese Government Service, 1924-28; travelled widely in India, Burma, Indochina and Indonesia in connection with Oriental research; during 1934-36, as Field Director of the Greater-India Research Committee, carried out archæological investigations in Siam, and during 1937-40 in Malaya, excavating ancient sites and exploring early trade routes; conducted excavations at early Buddhist sites in Siam, 1955-56, 1964, 1968. Chairman, Bernard Quaritch Ltd, 1951-75 (Director, 1939-75); served IA (Gen. Staff), 1940-41; in USA writing and speaking on Pacific affairs and publicising India's war effort, 1942-45. Member Council, Royal Asiatic Society, 1947-58, 1964-68 (Vice-President, 1958-62); Hon. Member Royal Asiatic Soc., Malayan Branch. *Publications:* Siamese State Ceremonies, 1931; Ancient Siamese Government and Administration, 1934; Towards Angkor, 1937; Archæological Researches on Ancient Indian Colonization in Malaya, 1940; The Making of Greater India, 1951; Ancient South-East Asian Warfare, 1952; The Mountain of God, 1953; Prehistory and Religion in South-east Asia, 1957; Angkor and Rome, 1965; The Indianization of China, 1967; Dvāravati, the Earliest Kingdom of Siam, 1969; Early Burma—Old Siam, 1973; The Malay Peninsula in Hindu Times, 1976; The Universe around Them, 1977; contrib. to The Cambridge History of India, many articles in various learned journals. *Club:* East India, Devonshire, Sports and Public Schools.

WALEY, (Andrew) Felix, VRD 1960 and Clasp 1970; QC 1973; a Recorder of the Crown Court, since 1974; *b* 14 April 1926; *s* of Guy Felix Waley and Anne Elizabeth (*née* Dickson); *m* 1955, Petica Mary, *d* of Sir Philip Rose, 3rd Bt; one *s* three *d.* (and one *d* decd). *Educ:* Charterhouse; Worcester Coll., Oxford (MA). RN, 1944-48; RNR, 1951-70, retd as Comdr. Oxford, 1948-51; called to the Bar, Middle Temple, 1953, Bencher, 1981. Conservative

Councillor, Paddington, 1956-59. Contested (C) Dagenham, 1959. *Recreations:* gardens, boats, birds. *Address:* Pleasure House, East Sutton, Kent ME17 3NW. *T:* Maidstone 842282. *Clubs:* Garrick; Island Sailing (IoW).

WALEY, Daniel Philip, PhD; Keeper of Manuscripts, British Library, since 1973 (Keeper of Manuscripts, British Museum, 1972-73); *b* 20 March 1921; *er s* of late Hubert David Waley and of Margaret Hendelah Waley; *m* 1945, Pamela Joan Griffiths; one *s* two *d. Educ:* Dauntsey's Sch.; King's Coll., Cambridge (MA, PhD). Historical Tripos, Cambridge, 1939-40 and 1945-46 (cl. 1). Served War, 1940-45. Fellow of King's Coll., Cambridge, 1950-54. Asst Lectr in Medieval History, London School of Economics and Political Science, Univ. of London, 1949-51, Lectr, 1951-61, Reader in History, 1961-70, Prof. of History, 1970-72. British Acad. Italian Lectr, 1975. *Publications:* Mediaeval Orvieto, 1952; The Papal State in the 13th Century, 1961; Later Medieval Europe, 1964 (2nd edn 1975); The Italian City Republics, 1969 (2nd edn, 1978); British Public Opinion and the Abyssinian War, 1935-36, 1975; (ed) George Eliot's Blotter: A Commonplace-Book, 1980; contributor to: Dizionario Biografico degli Italiani, English Hist. Review, Trans Royal Hist. Soc., Papers of British Sch. at Rome, Jl of Ecclesiastical Hist., Jl of the History of Ideas, Rivista Storica Italiana, Rivista di Storia della Chiesa in Italia, Procs Brit. Acad., British Library Jl, etc. *Recreations:* walking, tennis. *Address:* Flat 5, 24 Park Road, NW1 4SH.

WALEY, Felix; *see* Waley, A. F.

WALEY-COHEN, Sir Bernard (Nathaniel), 1st Bt *cr* 1961; Kt 1957; Director: Matthews Wrightson Pulbrook Ltd; Lloyds Bank Ltd Central London Region; Kleeman Industrial Holdings Ltd, and other companies; *b* 29 May 1914; *er s* of late Sir Robert Waley Cohen, KBE and Alice Violet, *d* of Henry Edward Beddington, London and Newmarket; *m* 1943, Hon. Joyce Constance Ina Nathan (*see* Lady Waley-Cohen); two *s* two *d. Educ:* HMS Britannia (RNC Dartmouth); Clifton College; Magdalene Coll., Cambridge (MA). Mem. of staff, Duke of York's Camp, Southwold, 1932-36; Mem. of Public School Empire Tour, New Zealand, 1932-33; Liveryman, Clothworkers' Company, 1936, Court 1966, Chm., Finance Cttee, 1971-79, Master, 1975. Gunner, HAC, 1937-38; Underwriting Member of Lloyd's 1939; Principal Ministry of Fuel and Power 1940-47. Alderman, City of London Portsoken Ward, 1949; Sheriff, City of London, 1955-56; Lord Mayor of London, 1960-61; one of HM Lieutenants, City of London, 1949-. Mem. Council and Board of Governors, Clifton Coll., 1952-81; Mem., College Cttee, University College London, 1953-80, Treasurer 1962-70; Vice-Chm. 1970; Chm., 1971-80; Mem. Senate, 1962-78; Court, 1966-78, London Univ.; Governor, Wellesley House Prep. Sch., 1965, Chm., 1965-77. Hon. Sec. and Treasurer, Devon and Somerset Staghounds, 1940, Chm. 1953; Mem. Finance and General Purposes Cttee, British Field Sports Soc., 1957, Treasurer 1965-78, Trustee, 1979, Dep. Pres., 1980; President: Bath and West and Southern Counties Show, 1963; Devon Cattle Breeders' Soc., 1963; W of England Hound Show, Honiton, 1974. Mem., Marshall Aid Commemoration Commn, 1957-60; Member: Jewish Cttee, HM Forces, 1947, Vice-Pres., 1980; Jewish Meml Council, 1947; Treasurer, Jewish Welfare Board, 1948-53; Vice-President: United Synagogue, 1952-61; Anglo-Jewish Assoc., 1962; Trades Adv. Council, 1963, Pres., 1981; Pres., Jewish Museum, 1964; Vice-Chairman: Palestine Corp., 1947-53; Union Bank of Israel Ltd, 1950-53; Chm., Simo Securities Trust Ltd, 1955-70; Mem., Nat. Corporation for Care of Old People, 1965-78; Mem., Executive Cttee and Central Council, Probation and After Care Cttees, 1965-69; Mem., Club Facilities Cttee, MCC, 1965-77; Trustee, Coll. of Arms Trust, 1970; Mem., Exec. Cttee, St Paul's Cathedral Appeal, 1970-72. Comr and Dep. Chm., Public Works Loan Board, 1971-72, Chm. 1972-79. Governor, Hon. Irish Soc., 1973-76. Mem. Foundn Cttee, Cambridge Soc., 1975, Exec. Cttee and Council 1976, Vice-Pres., 1980. Hon. Liveryman of Farmers' Company, 1961. Assoc. KStJ 1961. Hon. LLD London, 1961. *Recreations:* hunting, racing, shooting. *Heir: s* Stephen Harry Waley-Cohen [*b* 22 June 1946; *m* 1972, Pamela Elizabeth Doniger; two *s* one *d. Educ:* Eton (Oppidan Scholar); Magdalene Coll., Cambridge (BA 1968). Financial Journalist, Daily Mail, 1968-73; Exec. Dir. Euromoney, 1973-]. *Address:* 11 Little St James's Street, SW1A 1DP. *T:* 01-629 1615; Honeymead, Simonsbath, Minehead, Somerset. *TA:* 247JX; *T:* Exford 242. *Clubs:* Boodle's, Pratts, MCC, Harlequins RFC, City Livery; Jockey Club Rooms (Newmarket); University Pitt (Cambridge).

WALEY-COHEN, Hon. Joyce Constance Ina, JP; MA; **(Hon. Lady Waley-Cohen);** President, Independent Schools Information Service Council and Management Committee, since 1981 (Member, 1972-80); *b* 20 Jan. 1920; *o d* of 1st Baron Nathan, PC, TD, and Eleanor Joan Clara, *d* of C. Stettauer; *m* 1943, Sir Bernard Nathaniel Waley-Cohen, Bt, *qv* ; two *s* two *d. Educ:* St Felix Sch., Southwold; Girton Coll., Cambridge (MA). Member: Governing Body, St Felix Sch., 1945- (Chm., 1970-); Westminster Hosp. Bd of Governors, 1952-68; Chairman: Westminster Children's Hosp., 1952-68; Gordon Hosp., 1961-68; Governing Bodies of Girls' Schools' Assoc., 1974-79 (Mem., 1963); Ind. Schs Jt Council, 1977-80 (Vice-Chm., 1974-77). Governor: Taunton Sch., 1978-; Wellington Coll., 1979-. JP Mddx 1949-59, Somerset 1959-. *Recreations:* hunting, spinning, family life. *Address:* 11 Little St James's Street, SW1A 1DP. *T:* 01-629 1615; Honeymead, Simonsbath, Minehead, Somerset. *T:* Exford 242.

WALFORD, Major-General Alfred Ernest, CB 1946; CBE 1944; MM 1916; ED; Legion of Merit (USA); CA; FCIS; *b* Montreal, 20 Aug. 1896; *s* of Alfred G. S. and Phoebe Anne Walford, Montreal; *m* 1922, Olive Marjorie, *d* of

James A. Dyke, Westmount Province of Quebec; one *s. Educ:* Westmount Acad. Served European War, 1914-19, with Royal Canadian Artillery, and War of 1939-45, HQ 1st Canadian Div., 1st Canadian Corps and as DA&QMG 1st Canadian Army in NW Europe; Adjutant-General Canadian Forces, and mem., Army Council, Nat. Defence Headquarters, Ottawa, 1944-46. Partner, Alfred Walford & Sons, Chartered Accountants, 1923-29; Dir, Sec. and Treasurer, of James A. Ogilvy Ltd, 1929-39, of Henry Morgan & Co. Ltd, 1946-61; Pres., Morgan Trust Co., 1946-65; Chairman: E. G. M. Cape & Co. Ltd, 1965-68; Canadian Vickers Ltd, 1959-67; Dir and Chm., Montreal Adv. Bd of Canada Trust Co., 1961-72; Dir, Excelsior Life Insurance Co., 1951-70; Dir and Vice-Pres., Mercantile Bank of Canada, 1961-70; Hon. Dir, Canada Trust, 1972-. Member: Metropolitan Adv. Bd, YMCA; Nat Adv. Bd, Salvation Army; Past President: Fedn Commonwealth Chambers of Commerce; National Cttee, English-Speaking Union; Montreal Board of Trade; Past Chairman, Exec. Development Institute. Fellow, Royal Commonwealth Society; FCIS; Life Mem., Order of Chartered Accountants of Quebec. *Address:* (office) Suite 1400, 635 Dorchester Boulevard West, Montreal PQ H3B 1S3, Canada; (home) E90, The Chateau Apartments, 1321 Sherbrooke West, Montreal, PQ H3G 1J4. *Clubs:* St James's, Forest and Stream (Montreal).

WALFORD, John Howard; President, Solicitors' Disciplinary Tribunal, since 1979; *b* 16 May 1927; *s* of Henry Howard Walford and Marjorie Josephine Solomon; *m* 1953, Peggy Ann Jessel; two *s* two *d. Educ:* Cheltenham College; Gonville and Caius College, Cambridge; MA (Hons). Solicitor, 1950; Senior Partner, Bischoff & Co., 1979-. Mem. Council, Law Society, 1961-69; Governor, College of Law, 1967-; Senior Warden, City of London Solicitors' Co., 1980-81, Master, 1981-82. Governor, St John's Hosp. for Diseases of the Skin, 1960-82; Chm., Appeal Cttee, Skin Disease Research Fund. Commander, Order of Bernardo O'Higgins, Chile, 1972. *Address:* 8 Essex Villas, W8; Webb's Farm, Midgham, Berks. *Clubs:* Garrick, City Law.

WALKER, Rev. Sir Alan, Kt 1981; OBE 1955; Director of World Evangelism, World Methodist Council, since 1978; *b* 1911; *s* of Rev. Alfred Edgar Walker, former Pres., NSW Methodist Conf., and Violet Louise Walker; *m* 1938, Winifred Garrard Walker (*née* Channon); three *s* one *d. Educ:* Leigh Theological Coll., Sydney; Univ. of Sydney (BA, MA); Bethany Biblical Seminary, Chicago. Minister, Cessnock, NSW, 1939-44; Supt, Waverley Methodist Mission, 1944-54; Dir, Australian Mission to the Nation, 1953-56; Vis. Professor of: Evangelism, Boston Sch. of Theology, 1957-58; of Evangelism and Preaching, Claremont Sch. of Theol., USA, 1973; Supt, Central Methodist Mission, Sydney, 1958-78. Deleg. to First Assembly of WCC, Amsterdam, 1948; Adviser to: Aust. Delegn at UN, 1949; Third Ass. of WCC, New Delhi, 1962; Fourth Ass., WCC, Uppsala, 1968; Missions to: Fiji, S Africa, S America, Singapore and Malaysia, Sri Lanka, 1962-75; Founder, Sydney Life Line Tel. Counselling Centre, 1963 (Pres., Life Line Internat., 1966-); Sec., NSW Methodist Conf., 1970, Pres., 1971; lectures, various times, USA. Hon. DD Bethany Biblical Sem., 1954; Inst. de la Vie award, Paris, for services to humanity, 1978. *Publications include:* There is Always God, 1938; Everybody's Calvary, 1943; Coal Town, 1944; Heritage Without End, 1953; The Whole Gospel for the Whole World, 1957; The Many Sided Cross of Jesus, 1962; How Jesus Helped People, 1964; A Ringing Call to Mission, 1966; The Life Line Story, 1967 (USA, As Close as the Telephone); Breakthrough, 1969; God, the Disturber, 1973 (USA); Jesus, the Liberator, 1973 (USA); The New Evangelism, 1974 (USA); Love in Action, 1977; Life Grows with Christ, 1981. *Recreations:* swimming, tennis. *Address:* 14 Owen Stanley Avenue, Beacon Hill, NSW 2100, Australia. *T:* 451 3923.

WALKER, Alexander; Film Critic, The Standard (formerly London Evening Standard), since 1960; *b* Portadown, N Ireland, 22 March 1930; *s* of Alfred and Ethel Walker. *Educ:* Portadown Grammar Sch.; The Queen's Univ., Belfast (BA); Collège d'Europe, Bruges; Univ. of Michigan, Ann Arbor. Lecturer in political philosophy and comparative govt, Univ. of Michigan, 1952-54. Features editor, Birmingham Gazette, 1954-56; leader writer and film critic, The Birmingham Post, 1956-59; columnist, Vogue magazine, 1974-. Frequent broadcaster on the arts on radio and television; author of TV series 'Moviemen; author and co-producer of TV programmes on History of Hollywood, Garbo and Chaplin. Member, Wilson Interim Action Cttee on the Film Industry, 1977-. Chevalier de l'Ordre des Arts et des Lettres, 1981. Twice named Critic of the Year, in annual British Press awards, 1970, 1974; Award of Golden Eagle, Philippines, for services to internat. cinema, 1982. *Publications:* The Celluloid Sacrifice: aspects of sex in the movies, 1966; Stardom: the Hollywood phenomenon, 1970; Stanley Kubrick Directs, 1971; Hollywood, England: the British film industry in the sixties, 1974; Rudolph Valentino, 1976; Double Takes: notes and afterthoughts on the movies 1956-76, 1977; Superstars, 1978; The Shattered Silents: how the talkies came to stay, 1978; Garbo, 1980; Peter Sellers: the authorized biography, 1981; Joan Crawford, 1983; contributor to Encounter and other British and for. publications. *Recreations:* ski-ing, persecuting smokers. *Address:* 1 Marlborough, 38-40 Maida Vale, W9 1RW. *T:* 01-289 0985.

WALKER, Sir Allan (Grierson), Kt 1968; QC (Scotland); Sheriff Principal of Lanarkshire, 1963-74; *b* 1 May 1907; *er s* of late Joseph Walker, merchant, London, and Mary Grierson; *m* 1935, Audrey Margaret, *o d* of late Dr T. A. Glover, Doncaster; two *s. Educ:* Whitgift Sch., Croydon; Edinburgh Univ. Practised at Scottish Bar, 1931-39; Sheriff-Substitute of Roxburgh, Berwick, and Selkirk at Selkirk and of the County of Peebles, 1942-45; Sheriff-

Substitute of Stirling, Dumbarton and Clackmannan at Dumbarton, 1945-50; Sheriff-Substitute of Lanarkshire at Glasgow, 1950-63; Member, Law Reform Cttee for Scotland, 1964-70; Chm., Sheriff Court Rules Council, 1972-74. Hon. LLD Glasgow, 1967. *Publications:* The Law of Evidence in Scotland (joint author); Purves' Scottish Licensing Laws (7th, 8th edns). *Recreations:* walking, gardening. *Address:* 24 Moffat Road, Dumfries. *T:* Dumfries 3583.

WALKER, Angus Henry; British Petroleum Co. PLC, since 1979; *b* 30 Aug. 1935; *s* of late Frederick William Walker and of Esther Victoria Nicholas; *m* 1st, 1968, Beverly Phillpotts (marr. diss. 1976); 2nd, 1979, Ann Snow (*née* Griffiths); one *d* and two step-*d. Educ:* Erith Grammar Sch., Kent; Balliol Coll., Oxford (Domus Scholar; BA Mod. Hist.; Stanhope Prize, 1958; MA). Nat. Service, 1954-56 (2nd Lieut RA). Senior Scholar, St Antony's Coll., Oxford, 1959-63; HM Diplomatic Service, 1963-68: FO, 1963-65; First Sec., Washington, 1965-68. Lectr, SSEES, London Univ., 1968-70; Univ. Lectr in Russian Social and Political Thought, Oxford, and Lectr, Balliol Coll., 1971-76; Fellow, Wolfson Coll., Oxford, 1972-76; Dir, SSEES, London Univ., 1976-79. *Publications:* trans. from Polish: Political Economy, by Oskar Lange, vol. 1, 1963; Marx: his theory in its context, 1978. *Address:* 5 North Square, NW11 7AA. *T:* 01-455 2726.

WALKER, Arthur Geoffrey, FRS 1955; Professor of Pure Mathematics, Liverpool University, 1952-74, now Emeritus; *b* 17 July 1909; 2nd *s* of late A. J. Walker, Watford, Herts; *m* 1939, Phyllis Ashcroft, *d* of late Sterry B. Freeman, CBE. *Educ:* Watford Grammar Sch.; Balliol Coll., Oxford. MA (Oxon); PhD, DSc (Edinburgh); FRSE; Lectr at Imperial Coll. Science and Technology, 1935-36; at Liverpool Univ., 1936-47; Prof. of Mathematics in the Univ. of Sheffield, 1947-52. Mem. of Council, Royal Soc., 1962-63. Pres., London Mathematical Soc., 1963-65. Junior Berwick Prize of London Mathematical Soc., 1947; Keith Medal of Royal Society of Edinburgh, 1950. *Publication:* Harmonic Spaces (with H. S. Ruse and T. J. Willmore), 1962. *Address:* Beechcroft, Roundabout Lane, West Chiltington, Pulborough, W Sussex RH20 2RL. *T:* West Chiltington 2412.

WALKER, Air Chief Marshal Sir Augustus; *see* Walker, Air Chief Marshal Sir G. A.

WALKER, Sir Baldwin Patrick, 4th Bt, *cr* 1856; *b* 10 Sept. 1924; *s* of late Comdr Baldwin Charles Walker, *o s* of 3rd Bt and Mary, *d* of F. P. Barnett of Whalton, Northumberland; *S* grandfather, 1928; *m* 1948, Joy Yvonfe (marr. diss., 1954); *m* 1954, Sandra Stewart; *m* 1966, Rosemary Ann, *d* of late Henry Hollingdrake; one *s* one *d.; m* 1980, Vanessa Hilton. *Educ:* Gordonstoun. Served Royal Navy, Fleet Air Arm, 1943-58. Lieut, RN, retired. Mem. Cttee, S African Solar Energy Soc. *Heir:* s Christopher Robert Baldwin Walker, *b* 25 Oct. 1969. *Address:* 27 Rose Avenue, Tokai, 7945, South Africa.

WALKER, Bill; *see* Walker, W. C.

WALKER, Bobby; *see* Walker, W. B. S.

WALKER, Brian Wilson; Director General of Oxfam since 1974; *b* 31 Oct. 1930; *s* of Arthur Walker and Eleanor (*née* Wilson); *m* 1954, Nancy Margaret Gawith; one *s* five *d. Educ:* Heversham Sch., Westmorland; Leicester Coll. of Technology; Faculty Technology, Manchester Univ. Management Trainee, Sommerville Bros, Kendal, 1952-55; Personnel Man., Pye Radio, Larne, 1956-61; Bridgeport Brass Ltd, Lisburn: Personnel Man., 1961-66; Gen. Man. (Develt), 1966-69; Gen. Man. (Manufrg), 1969-74. Founder Chm., New Ulster Movt, 1969-74; Founder Pres., New Ulster Movt Ltd, 1974. Mem., Standing Adv. Commn on Human Rights for NI, 1975-77. Kt, Sov. Order of St Thomas of Acre; Kentucky Colonel, 1966. *Publications:* various political/religious papers on Northern Ireland problem and Third World subjects. *Recreations:* gardening, Irish politics, classical music, active Quaker. *Address:* 14 Upland Park Road, Oxford.

WALKER, Inspector Carl, GC 1972; Police Inspector, since 1976; *b* 31 March 1934; English; *m* 1955, Kathleen Barker; one *s. Educ:* Kendal Grammar Sch., Westmorland. RAF Police, 1952-54 (Corporal). Lancashire Police, Dec. 1954-March 1956, resigned; Blackpool Police, 1959- (amalgamated with Lancashire Constabulary, April 1968); Sergeant, 1971. *Recreations:* Rugby; Cumberland and Westmorland wrestling.

WALKER, Sir (Charles) Michael, GCMG 1976 (KCMG 1963; CMG 1960); HM Diplomatic Service, retired; Chairman: Commonwealth Scholarship Commission in the UK, since 1977; Festival of India Trust, since 1980; *b* 22 Nov. 1916; *s* of late Col C. W. G. Walker, CMG, DSO; *m* 1945, Enid Dorothy, *d* of late W. A. McAdam, CMG; one *s* one *d. Educ:* Charterhouse; New Coll., Oxford. Clerk of House of Lords, June 1939. Enlisted in Army, Oct. 1939, and served in RA until 1946 when released with rank of Lt-Col. Dominions Office, 1947; First Sec., British Embasssy, Washington, 1949-51; Office of United Kingdom High Comr in Calcutta and New Delhi, 1952-55; Establishment Officer, Commonwealth Relations Office, 1955-58. Imperial Defence Coll., 1958; Asst Under-Sec. of State and Dir of Establishment and Organisation, CRO, 1959-62; British High Commissioner in: Ceylon, 1962-65 (concurrently Ambassador to Maldive Islands, July-Nov. 1965), Malaysia, 1966-71; Sec., ODA, FCO, 1971-73; High Comr, India, 1974-76. Hon. DCL City, 1980. *Recreations:* fishing, gardening, golf. *Address:* Herongate House,

West Chiltington Common, Pulborough, Sussex. *T:* West Chiltington 3473. *Club:* Oriental.

WALKER, Vice-Adm. Sir (Charles) Peter (Graham), KBE 1967; CB 1964; DSC 1944; *b* 23 Feb. 1911; *s* of Charles Graham Walker and Lilla Geraldine (*née* Gandy); *m* 1938, Pamela Marcia Hawley, *d* of late George W. Hawley, Cape, SA; one *s* one *d. Educ:* Worksop College. Entered Royal Navy, 1929; Royal Naval Engineering Coll., 1930-34; Advanced Engineering Course at RN Coll., Greenwich, 1935-37. War service in HM Ships Cornwall, Georgetown, Duke of York and Berwick and at the Admiralty; Vice-Admiral, 1965; Dir.-Gen., Dockyards and Maintenance, MoD (Navy), 1962-67; Chief Naval Engr Officer, 1963-67; retired 1967. *Address:* Brookfield Coach House, Weston Lane, Bath BA1 4AG. *T:* Bath 23863.

WALKER, Charls E., PhD; Consultant, Washington, DC, since 1973; *b* Graham, Texas, 24 Dec. 1923; *s* of Pinkney Clay and Sammye McCombs Walker; *m* 1949, Harmolyn Hart, Laurens, S Carolina; one *s* one *d. Educ:* Univ. of Texas (MBA); Wharton Sch. of Finance, Univ. of Pennsylvania (PhD). Instructor in Finance, 1947-48, and later Asst and Associate Prof., 1950-54, at Univ. of Texas, in the interim teaching at Wharton Sch. of Finance, Univ. of Pennsylvania; Associate Economist, Fed. Reserve Bank: of Philadelphia, 1953, of Dallas, 1954 (Vice-Pres. and Economic Advr, 1958-61); Economist and Special Asst to Pres. of Republic Nat. Bank of Dallas, 1955-56 (took leave to serve as Asst to Treasury Sec., Robert B. Anderson, April 1959-Jan. 1961); Exec. Vice-Pres., Amer. Bankers Assoc., 1961-69. Under-Sec. of the Treasury, 1969-72, Dep. Sec., 1972-73. Chm., American Council for Capital Formation; Mem. Bd of Trustees, Jt Council on Economic Educn; Mem. Council on Foreign Relations; Chm. Exec. Cttee and Treasurer, Cttee on the Present Danger. Hon. LLD Ashland Coll., 1970. *Publications:* Co-editor of The Banker's Handbook; contribs to learned jls, periodicals. *Recreations:* golf, fishing, music. *Address:* 10120 Chapel Road, Potomac, Md 20854, USA. *T:* 301/299-5414. *Clubs:* Union League (NYC); Burning Tree Golf (Bethesda, Md); Federal City (Washington, DC).

WALKER, (Christopher) Roy; Under Secretary, Further and Higher Education, Department of Education and Science, since 1980; *b* 5 Dec. 1934; *s* of Christopher Harry Walker and late Dorothy Jessica Walker; *m* 1961, Hilary Mary Biddiscombe; two *s. Educ:* Sir George Monoux Grammar Sch., E17; Sidney Sussex Coll., Cambridge (BA); Université Libre de Bruxelles. National Service, Essex Regt, 1952-54. BoT, 1958; CSD, 1968; Private Sec. to Lord Privy Seal, 1968-71; Treasury, 1973; DTI, 1973; Dept of Energy, 1974; Cabinet Office, 1974; Dept of Energy, 1975; DES, 1977. *Recreations:* hill walking, sailing. *Address:* 54 The Drive, Sevenoaks, Kent. *T:* Sevenoaks 55168. *Club:* Medway Yacht (Rochester).

WALKER, Sir Clive Radzivill Forestier-, 5th Bt *cr* 1835; *b* 30 April 1922; *s* of Radzivill Clive Forestier-Walker (*g s* of 2nd Bt) (*d* 1973) and Kathleen Rose (*d* 1975), *d* of late William George Tinkler, King's Lynn; *S* cousin, Sir George Ferdinand Forestier-Walker, 4th Bt, 1976; *m* 1948, Pamela Mercy (marr. diss., 1976), *d* of late Clifford Leach; three *d. Heir cousin* Michael Leolin Forestier-Walker, *b* 24 April 1949. *Address:* 42 Old Vicarage Park, Narborough, King's Lynn, Norfolk PE32 1TQ. *T:* Narborough 516.

WALKER, Prof. Daniel Pickering, FBA 1974; Professor of the History of the Classical Tradition, in the University of London at the Warburg Institute, 1975-81, retired; *b* 30 June 1914; *s* of Frederick Pickering Walker and Miriam Laura Walker (*née* Crittall). *Educ:* Westminster Sch.; Christ Church, Oxford. BA 1935 (1st cl. French), MA, DPhil 1940, Oxon. Corporal, Infantry and Intell. Corps, 1940-43; Foreign Office, 1943-45. Lectr, then Reader, French Dept, UCL, 1945-61; Reader in Renaissance Studies, Warburg Inst., Univ. of London, 1961-75, Sen. Fellow, 1953-56. Sen. Fellow, Cornell Univ. (Soc. for Humanities), 1971. *Publications:* Musikalischer Humanismus, 1947; Spiritual and Demonic Magic, 1958; The Decline of Hell, 1964; The Ancient Theology, 1972; Studies in Musical Science in the late Renaissance, 1978; Unclean Spirits, 1981; articles in Jl of Warburg and Courtauld Insts, etc. *Recreations:* chamber music, gardening. *Address:* 2 Regent's Park Terrace, NW1. *T:* 01-485 1699.

WALKER, Prof. David Alan, PhD, DSc; FRS 1979; FIBiol; Professor of Biology, University of Sheffield, since 1970; *b* 18 Aug. 1928; *s* of Cyril Walker and Dorothy Walker (*née* Dobson); *m* 1956, Shirley Wynne Walker (*née* Mason); one *s* one *d. Educ:* King's Coll., Univ. of Durham (BSc, PhD, DSc). Royal Naval Air Service, 1946-48. Lecturer, 1958-63, Reader, 1963-65, Queen Mary Coll., Univ. of London; Reader, Imperial Coll., Univ. of London, 1965-70. FIBiol 1971; Corres. Mem., Amer. Soc. Plant Physiol., 1979. *Publications:* Energy Plants and Man, 1979; (with G. E. Edwards) C3, C4—Mechanisms, Cellular and Environmental Regulation of Photosynthesis, 1982; papers, mostly in field of photosynthesis. *Recreation:* singing the Sheffield Carols. *Address:* Department of Botany, The University, Sheffield S10 2TN. *T:* Sheffield 78555.

WALKER, David Alan; Executive Director, Bank of England, since 1982; *b* 31 Dec. 1939; *s* of Thomas Harold and Marian Walker; *m* 1963, Isobel Cooper; one *s* two *d. Educ:* Chesterfield Sch.; Queens' Coll., Cambridge (MA). Joined HM Treasury, 1961; Private Sec. to Sir William Armstrong, Joint Permanent Secretary, 1964-66; seconded to Staff of International Monetary Fund, Washington, 1970-73; Asst Secretary, HM Treasury, 1973-77; joined Bank as Chief Adviser, then Chief of Economic Intelligence Dept,

1977; Asst Director, 1980. *Recreations:* music, long-distance walking. *Address:* Bank of England, Threadneedle Street, EC2R 8AH. *Club:* Reform.

WALKER, David Critchlow, MVO 1976; HM Diplomatic Service; Inspector, Foreign and Commonwealth Office, since 1980; *b* 9 Jan. 1940; *s* of John Walker and Mary Walker (*née* Cross); *m* 1965, Tineke van der Leek; three *s. Educ:* Manchester Grammar Sch.; St Catharine's Coll., Cambridge (BA,MA,DipEd). Assistant Lecturer, Dept of Geography, Manchester Univ., 1962; Commonwealth Relations Office, 1963; Third Secretary, British Embassy, Mexico City, 1965; Second Secretary, Brussels, 1968; First Secretary: FCO, 1970; Washington, 1973; First Sec., later Counsellor, FCO, 1978. *Recreations:* walking, gardening, crabbing. *Address:* c/o Foreign and Commonwealth Office, SW1.

WALKER, Major David Harry, MBE 1946; Author; *b* 9 Feb. 1911; *s* of Harry Giles Walker and Elizabeth Bewley (*née* Newsom); *m* 1939, Willa Magee, Montreal; four *s. Educ:* Shrewsbury; Sandhurst. The Black Watch, 1931-47 (retired); ADC to Gov.-Gen. of Canada, 1938-39; Comptroller to Viceroy of India, 1946-47. Member: Royal Company of Archers; Canada Council, 1957-61; Chm., Roosevelt-Campobello Internat. Park Commn, 1970-72 (Canadian Comr, 1965). Hon. DLitt, Univ. of New Brunswick, 1955. FRSL. *Publications:* novels: The Storm and the Silence, 1950 (USA 1949); Geordie, 1950 (filmed 1955); The Pillar, 1952; Digby, 1953; Harry Black, 1956 (filmed, 1957); Sandy was a Soldier's Boy, 1957; Where the High Winds Blow, 1960; Storms of Our Journey and Other Stories, 1962; Dragon Hill (for children), 1962; Winter of Madness, 1964; Mallabec, 1965; Come Back, Geordie, 1966; Devil's Plunge (USA, Cab-Intersec), 1968; Pirate Rock, 1969; Big Ben (for children), 1970; The Lord's Pink Ocean, 1972; Black Dougal, 1973 (USA 1974); Ash, 1976; Pot of Gold, 1977. *Address:* Strathcroix, St Andrews, New Brunswick, Canada. *Club:* Royal and Ancient.

WALKER, Prof. David Maxwell, QC; FBA 1976; FRSE 1980; Regius Professor of Law, Glasgow University, since 1958; Dean of the Faculty of Law, 1956-59; Senate Assessor on University Court, 1962-66; *b* 9 April 1920; *o s* of James Mitchell Walker, Branch Manager, Union Bank of Scotland, and Mary Paton Colquhoun Irvine; *m* 1954, Margaret Knox, MA, *yr d* of Robert Knox, yarn merchant, Brookfield, Renfrewshire. *Educ:* High School of Glasgow (Mackinlay Prizeman in Classics); Glasgow, Edinburgh and London Universities. MA (Glasgow) 1946; LLB (Distinction), Robertson Schol., 1948; Faulds Fellow in Law, 1949-52; PhD (Edinburgh), 1952; Blackwell Prize, Aberdeen Univ., 1955; LLB (London), 1957; LLD (Edinburgh), 1960; LLD (London), 1968. Served War of 1939-45, NCO Cameronians; commissioned HLI, 1940; seconded to RIASC, 1941; served with Indian Forces in India, 1942, Middle East, 1942-43, and Italy, 1943-46, in MT companies and as Brigade Supply and Transport Officer (Captain). HQ 21 Ind. Inf. Bde, 8 Ind. Div. Advocate of Scottish Bar, 1948; Barrister, Middle Temple, 1957; QC (Scotland) 1958; practised at Scottish Bar, 1948-53; studied at Inst. of Advanced Legal Studies, Univ. of London, 1953-54; Prof. of Jurisprudence, Glasgow Univ., 1954-58. Dir, Scottish Univs' Law Inst., 1974-80. Trustee, Hamlyn Trust, 1954-. Governor Scottish College of Commerce, 1957-64. Hon. Sheriff of Lanarkshire at Glasgow, 1966-. FSA Scotland. Hon. LLD Edinburgh, 1974. *Publications:* (ed) Faculty Digest of Decisions, 1940-50, Supplements, 1951 and 1952; Law of Damages in Scotland, 1955; The Scottish Legal System, 1959, 5th edn, 1981; Law of Delict in Scotland, 1966, 2nd edn, 1981; Scottish Courts and Tribunals, 1969, 4th edn, 1978; Principles of Scottish Private Law (2 vols), 1970, 3rd edn (4 vols), 1982-83; Law of Prescription and Limitation in Scotland, 1973, 3rd edn, 1981; Law of Civil Remedies in Scotland, 1974; Law of Contracts in Scotland, 1979; Oxford Companion to Law, 1980; (ed) Stair's Institutions (6th edn), 1981; (ed) Stair Tercentary Studies, 1981; Scottish Part of Topham and Ivamy's Company Law, 12th edn, 1955, to 16th edn, 1978; contribs to collaborative works; articles in legal periodicals. *Recreations:* motoring, book collecting, Scottish history. *Address:* 1 Beaumont Gate, Glasgow G12 9EE. *T:* 041-339 2802.

WALKER, Maj.-Gen. Derek William Rothwell, CEng, FIMechE, FIEE; Manager, CBI Overseas Scholarships, since 1980; *b* 12 Dec. 1924; *s* of Frederick and Eileen Walker; *m* 1950, Florence Margaret Panting; two *s* (and one *s* decd). *Educ:* Mitcham County Grammar Sch.; Battersea Polytechnic. Commissioned REME, 1946; served: Middle East, 1947-50 (despatches 1949); BAOR, 1951-53; Far East, 1954-56 (despatches 1957); Near East, 1960-62; Far East, 1964-67; psc 1957. Lt-Col 1964, Col 1970, Brig. 1973. Appts include: Comdr, REME Support Group, 1976-77; Dir, Equipment Engineering, 1977-79. Mem. Council, IEE, 1975-79; Pres., SEE, 1979-81. *Recreations:* fishing, caravanning, wine-making. *Address:* 26 Cranford Drive, Holybourne, Alton, Hants GU34 4HJ. *T:* Alton 84737.

WALKER, Sir E(dward) Ronald, Kt 1963; CBE 1956; Australian economist and diplomat; *b* 26 Jan. 1907; *s* of Rev. Frederick Thomas Walker; *m* 1933, Louise Donckers; one *s* one *d. Educ:* Sydney Univ. (MA, DSc Econ); Cambridge Univ. (PhD, LittD). Lecturer in Economics, Sydney Univ., 1927-30, 1933-39; Fellow of Rockefeller Foundation, 1931-33; Economic Adviser: NSW Treasury, 1938-39; Govt of Tasmania, 1939-41; Prof. of Economics, Univ. of Tasmania, 1939-46; Chief Economic Adviser and Dep. Dir-Gen., Australian Dept of War Organisation of Industry, 1941-45; UNRRA HQ, Washington, 1945; Counsellor, Australian Embassy, Paris, 1945-50; Exec. Member, Nat. Security Resources Board, Prime Minister's Dept, Canberra, 1950-52; Australian Ambassador to Japan, 1952-55;

Ambassador and Permanent Representative of Australia at United Nations, 1956-59 (Aust. Rep., Security Council, 1956-57); Ambassador: to France, 1959-68; to the Federal Republic of Germany, 1968-71; to OECD, Paris, 1971-73. Delegate to many confs and cttees connected with UN, ILO, Unesco, etc; Pres., UN Economic and Social Council, 1964. *Publications:* An Outline of Australian Economics, 1931; Australia in the World Depression, 1933; Money, 1935; Unemployment Policy, 1936; Wartime Economics, 1939; From Economic Theory to Policy, 1943; The Australian Economy in War and Reconstruction, 1947. *Address:* 1 rue de Longchamp, 75116 Paris, France. *T:* 553.0300.

WALKER, Frank Stockdale, MC 1919; Chairman, Lever Brothers, Port Sunlight Limited, 1954-60, retired; Director, Thames Board Mills Limited (until 1960); Director, Glycerine Limited; *b* 24 June 1895; *s* of Frank and Mary Elizabeth Walker; *m* 1921, Elsie May Nicholas (*d* 1974); one *s. Address:* 10 Knowle Grange, Knowle Drive, Sidmouth EX10 8HN. *T:* Sidmouth 5470.

WALKER, Geoffrey Basil W.; *see* Woodd Walker.

WALKER, Air Chief Marshal Sir (George) Augustus, GCB 1969 (KCB 1962; CB 1959); CBE 1945; DSO 1941; DFC 1941; AFC 1956; Director, Philips Electronic & Associated Industries Ltd, 1970-82; *b* 24 Aug. 1912; *s* of G. H. Walker, Garforth, Leeds; *m* 1942, Brenda Brewis; one *s* one *d. Educ:* St Bees' Sch.; St Catharine's, Cambridge. Entered RAF Univ. Commission, 1934; Air Min. (R&D), 1938-39; commanded Bomber Sqdn, Stations and Base, 1940-45; SASO No 4 Group, 1945-46; Air Min., Dep. Dir, Operational Training, 1946-48; SASO Rhodesian Air Training Group, 1948-50; JSSC 1950; IDC 1953; Commandant, Royal Air Force Flying Coll., 1954-56; AOC No 1 Group, 1956-59; Chief Information Officer, Air Min., 1959-61; AOC-in-C, Flying Training Command, 1961-64; Inspector-General, RAF, 1964-67; Dep. C-in-C Allied Forces, Central Europe, 1967-70, retd. ADC to the Queen, 1952-56, to King George VI, 1943-52; Air ADC to the Queen, 1968-70. Hon. Col, 33rd (Lancashire and Cheshire) Signal Regt, Royal Corps of Signals, T&AVR, 1970-75. Pres., RFU, 1965-66; Chm., Royal Air Forces Assoc., 1973-78, Pres., 1978-81; Chm., Nat. Sporting Club, 1974-; Chm., Exec. Cttee, Lord Kitchener Nat. Meml Fund, 1977-82 (Chm., Scholarship Cttee, 1974-77). Governor and Commandant, Church Lads Brigade, 1970-78, Church Lads and Church Girls Brigade, 1978-79. *Recreations:* Rugby (played for England, 1939, Barbarians, RAF, Blackheath, Yorkshire; Captained RAF, 1936-39), golf, sailing. *Address:* c/o Barclays Bank, 28/30 Park Row, Leeds LS1 1PA. *Club:* Royal Air Force.

WALKER, Dr George Patrick Leonard, FRS 1975; G. A. Macdonald Professor of Volcanology, University of Hawaii, since 1981; *b* 2 March 1926; *s* of Leonard Richard Thomas Walker and Evelyn Frances Walker; *m* 1958, Hazel Margaret (*née* Smith); one *s* one *d. Educ:* Wallace High Sch., Lisburn, N Ire.; Queen's Univ., Belfast (BSc, MSc); Univ. of Leeds (PhD); Univ. of London (DSc 1982). Research, Univ. of Leeds, 1948-51; Asst Lectr and Lectr, Imperial Coll., 1951-64; Reader in Geology, Imperial Coll., 1964-79; Captain J. Cook Res. Fellow, Royal Soc. of NZ, 1978-80. Awarded moiety of Lyell Fund of Geological Soc. of London, 1963, Lyell Medal, 1982. Hon. Mem., Víisindafjelag Íslendinga, (Iceland), 1968. Icelandic Order of the Falcon, Knight's Class, 1980. *Publications:* scientific papers on mineralogy, the geology of Iceland, and volcanology. *Recreation:* visiting volcanoes. *Address:* Department of Geology and Geophysics, University of Hawaii at Manoa, 2525 Correa Road, Honolulu, Hawaii 96822, USA. *T:* (808) 948-7826.

WALKER, Sir Gervas (George), Kt 1979; JP; DL; Chairman and Leader, Avon County Council, 1973-81; *b* 12 Sept. 1920; *yr s* of late Harry James Walker and Susanna Mary Walker; *m* 1944, Jessie Eileen (*née* Maxwell); two *s. Educ:* Monmouth Sch. Bristol City Council: Councillor, 1956-74; Alderman, 1970-74; Leader of Council, 1966-72; Leader of Opposition Party, 1972-74; Chm., Planning and Transportation Cttee, 1960-63 and 1966-72; Chm., Bristol Avon River Authority, 1963-66. Member: SW Regional Economic Planning Council, 1972-79; Local Authorities' Conditions of Service Adv. Bd, 1974-81; Severn Barrage Cttee, 1978-81; British Rail (Western) Bd, 1979-. Chm., Assoc. of County Councils, 1979-81 (Vice-Chm., 1978-79). Chairman Bristol Conservative Assoc., 1975-79. JP Bristol, 1969; DL Avon, 1982. *Recreation:* fly-fishing. *Address:* The Lodge, Cobblestone Mews, Clifton Park, Bristol BS8 3DQ. *T:* Bristol 737063; Bulverton Well Farm, Sidmouth, Devon EX10 9DW. *T:* Sidmouth 6902. *Club:* Constitutional (Bristol).

WALKER, Rt. Hon. Harold, PC 1979; MP (Lab) Doncaster, since 1964; *b* 12 July 1927; *s* of Harold and Phyllis Walker; widower; one *d. Educ:* Manchester College of Technology. An Assistant Government Whip, 1967-68; Jt Parly Under-Sec. of State, Dept of Employment and Productivity, 1968-70; Opposition Front-Bench spokesman on Industrial Relations, 1970-74, on Employment, 1980-; Parly Under-Sec. of State, Dept of Employment, 1974-76; Minister of State, Dept of Employment, 1976-79. *Recreations:* reading, gardening. *Address:* House of Commons, SW1. *Clubs:* Westminster, Clay Lane, Doncaster Trades, RN, Catholic (all Doncaster).

WALKER, Harold Berners, CMG 1979; HM Diplomatic Service; Ambassador to United Arab Emirates, since 1981; *b* 19 Oct. 1932; *s* of late Admiral Sir Harold Walker, KCB, RN, and of Lady Walker (*née* Berners); *m* 1960, Jane Bittleston; one *s* two *d. Educ:* Winchester (Exhibition 1946);

Worcester Coll., Oxford (Exhibition 1952). BA 1955. 2nd Lieut RE, 1951-52. Foreign Office, 1955; MECAS, 1957; Asst Political Agent, Dubai, 1958; Foreign Office, 1960; Principal Instructor, MECAS, 1963; First Sec., Cairo, 1964; Head of Chancery and Consul, Damascus, 1966; Foreign Office (later FCO), 1967; First Sec. (Commercial), Washington, 1970; Counsellor, Jedda, 1973; Dep. Head, Personnel Operations Dept, FCO, 1975-76, Head of Dept, 1976-78; Corpus Christi Coll., Cambridge, 1978; Ambassador to Bahrein, 1979-81. *Recreation:* tennis. *Address:* c/o Foreign and Commonwealth Office, SW1. *Club:* United Oxford & Cambridge University.

WALKER, His Honour Judge Harry; *see* Walker, P. H. C.

WALKER, Major Sir Hugh (Ronald), 4th Bt, *cr* 1906; *b* 13 Dec. 1925; *s* of Major Sir Cecil Edward Walker, 3rd Bt, DSO, MC, and Violet (*née* McMaster); *S* father, 1964; *m* 1971, Norna, er *d* of Lt-Cdr R. D. Baird, RNR; two *s. Educ:* Wellington Coll., Berks. Joined Royal Artillery, 1943; commissioned Sept. 1945; 2 iC, RA Range, Benbecula, Outer Hebrides, 1964-66; Commanding No 1 Army Information Team, in Aden and Hong Kong, 1966-68; Larkhill, 1969-73, retired. Mem., Assoc. of Supervisory and Executive Engineers. *Recreation:* horses. *Heir:* s Robert Cecil Walker, *b* 26 Sept. 1974. *Address:* Ballinamona, Hospital, Kilmallock, Co. Limerick, Ireland.

WALKER, Sir Hugh Selby N.; *see* Norman-Walker.

WALKER, Ian Royaards; Chief Executive and Managing Director, BP Oil Ltd, since 1981; Chairman: BP Detergents Ltd, since 1979; Alexander Duckham & Co. Ltd, since 1981; BP Ireland Ltd, since 1978; Robert McBride (Middleton) Ltd, since 1978; Young's Paraffin Light and Mineral Oil Co. (Ltd), since 1979; *b* 22 April 1927; *s* of Alexander Walker and Louise Reiniera Jeanne Antoinette; *m* 1956, Margaret Elizabeth Bardsley; three *s. Educ:* Bryanston Sch.; Christ's Coll., Cambridge (MA); Bristol Univ. (CertEd). Shell-Mex and B.P. Ltd, 1952; British Petroleum Co. Ltd, 1954; Managing Director, Companhia Portuguesa dos Petroleos BP, Lisbon, 1963; European Regional Co-ordinator, 1967; General Manager, Corporate Planning Dept, 1972; Dep. Managing Director, BP Oil Ltd, 1976. *Recreation:* music. *Address:* The Old Vicarage, Elsenham, near Bishop's Stortford, Herts. *T:* Bishop's Stortford 813222.

WALKER, Prof. James, CBE 1971; BSc, MD, FRCPGlas, FRCOG; Professor of Obstetrics and Gynæcology, University of Dundee, 1967-81 (University of St Andrews, 1956-67); Professor of Obstetrics and Gynaecology, University Kebangsaan Malaysia, since 1982; *b* 8 March 1916; *s* of James Walker, FEIS; *m* 1940, Catherine Clark Johnston, *d* of George R. A. Johnston; one *s* two *d. Educ:* High Schs of Falkirk and Stirling; Univ. of Glasgow. BSc 1935; MB, ChB (Hons) 1938; Brunton Memorial Prize; MRCOG 1947; MD (Hons) 1954; FRCOG 1957; MRCPGlas 1963, FRCPGlas 1968. Blair Bell Memorial Lectr, Royal Coll. Obstetrics and Gynæcology, 1953. Served War of 1939-45, RAFVR, UK and India, 1941-46. Hon. Surgeon to Out Patients, Royal Infirmary, Glasgow, Hall Tutor in Midwifery, Univ. Glasgow, 1946; Sen. Lectr in Midwifery and Gynæcology, Univ. of Aberdeen, Consultant NE Regional Hospital Board (Scotland), 1948; Reader in Obst. and Gynæcology, Univ. of London, Consultant, Hammersmith Hospital, 1955. Consultant, Eastern Regional Hosp. Bd, Scotland, 1956-81; Chm., Nat. Medical Consultative Cttee, Scotland, 1979-81; Chm., Cttee on Annual Reports and Definition of Terms in Human Reproduction of the Internat. Fedn of Gynæcology and Obstetrics, 1976-. Visiting Professor: New York State, 1957, 1970; Florida, 1965, 1970; McGill, 1967; Alexandria, 1979; Malaysia, 1981; Duke (USA), 1981. *Publications:* senior editor, Combined Textbook of Obstetrics and Gynæcology, 9th edn, 1976; contrib. on Obstetrics and Gynæcology to textbooks and learned jls. *Address:* Beechlea, 1 Ellieslea Road, Dundee DD5 1JG. *T:* Dundee 79238. *Club:* Royal Air Force.

WALKER, James Findlay, QPM 1964; Commandant, National Police College, 1973-76; *b* 20 May 1916; *m* 1941, Gertrude Eleanor Bell; one *s. Educ:* Arbroath High Sch., Angus, Scotland. Joined Metropolitan Police, 1936. Served War, 1943-46: commissioned Black Watch; demobilised rank Captain. Served in Metropolitan Police through ranks to Chief Supt, 1963; Staff of Police Coll., 1963-65; Asst Chief Constable: W Riding Constabulary, 1965-68; W Yorks Constabulary, 1968-70; Dep. Chief Constable, W Yorks Constabulary, 1970-73. *Recreations:* gardening, golf. *Address:* Mayfield, Quarry Hill, Horbury, Wakefield, W Yorks.

WALKER, Sir James (Graham), Kt 1972; MBE 1963; Part Owner of Cumberland Santa Gertrudis Stud and Wakefield Merino Sheep Property; Chairman, Capricornia Electricity Board, since 1977; *b* Bellingen, NSW, 7 May 1913; *s* of late Albert Edward Walker and Adelaide Walker, Sydney, NSW; *m* 1939, Mary Vivienne Maude Poole; two *s* three *d. Educ:* New England Grammar Sch., Glen Innes, NSW. Councillor, Longreach Shire Council, 1953- (Chm., 1957-82); Vice-Pres., Local Authorities of Qld, 1966, Sen. Vice-Chm., 1972. Dep. Chm., Longreach Pastoral Coll., since inception, 1966-78, Chm. 1978-82. Exec. Mem., Central Western Queensland Local Authorities' Assoc. and Queensland Local Authorities' Assoc., 1964-79. Chm., Central Western Electricity Bd, 1966-76; Dir, Longreach Printing Co. Chm., Santa Gertrudis Assoc., Australia, 1976. Past Asst Grand Master, United Grand Lodge of Qld, 1970. Session Clerk, St Andrews Church, Longreach, 1948-.

Fellow, Internat. Inst. of Community Service, 1975. *Recreations:* bowls, clay bird shooting, surfing, oil painting. *Address:* Camden Park, Longreach, Queensland 4730, Australia. *T:* Longreach 331. *Clubs:* Queensland, Tattersall's (Brisbane); Longreach, Longreach Rotary (Longreach).

WALKER, Sir James Heron, 5th Bt, *cr* 1868; *b* 7 April 1914; *s* of 4th Bt and Synolda, *y d* of late James Thursby-Pelham; *S* father, 1930; *m* 1st, 1939, Angela Margaret, *o d* of Victor Alexandre Beaufort; one *s* (one *d* decd); 2nd, 1972, Sharrone, *er d* of David Read; one *s*. *Educ:* Eton Coll.; Magdalene Coll., Cambridge. *Recreations:* long haired Dachshunds and music. *Heir: s* Victor Stewart Heron Walker [*b* 8 Oct. 1942; *m* 1st, 1969, Caroline Louise, *d* of late Lt-Col F. E. B. Wignall; two *s* one *d*; 2nd, 1982, Svea, *o d* of late Captain Hugo Borg and of Mrs Mary Borg]. *Address:* Ringdale Manor, Faringdon, Oxon.
See also Baron Cornwallis.

WALKER, Sir John, KCMG 1959 (CMG 1951); OBE 1947; *b* 27 June 1906; *s* of late Rupert Walker; *m* 1934, Muriel Winifred (*d* 1976) *d* of Henry John Hill; one *s* (and one *s* decd). *Educ:* Ashby Grammar Sch.; London Univ.; Sorbonne. Passed examination and entered Dept of Overseas Trade, 1929; Asst Commercial Sec., Santiago, 1931; transf. to Buenos Aires, 1933; Commercial Sec., Bagdad, 1938, 1943; transf. to Madrid, 1944, Counsellor, (Commercial), 1947; transf. to Tehran, 1948; HM Inspector of Foreign Service Establishments, Foreign Office, 1953-55; Ambassador to Venezuela, 1955-60; Ambassador to Norway, 1961-62. Dir-Gen., Hispanic and Luso-Brazilian Councils, 1963-69. Knight Grand Cross, Order of St Olav (Norway), 1962. Fellow, University College, London, 1968-. *Publications:* Economic Survey of Iraq, 1944; Economic Survey of Spain, 1948. *Recreations:* golf, shooting, fishing. *Address:* Primrose Cottage, Lodsworth, Petworth, West Sussex GU28 9DA. *T:* Lodsworth 350.

WALKER, John; Director, National Gallery of Art, Washington, DC, 1956-69, now Director Emeritus; *b* 24 Dec. 1906; *s* of Hay Walker and Rebekah Jane Friend; *m* 1937, Lady Margaret Gwendolen Mary Drummond; one *s* one *d*. *Educ:* Harvard Univ. (AB). Associate in charge Dept Fine Arts American Acad., Rome, 1935-39 (now Trustee); Chief Curator, National Gall., Washington DC, 1939-56. Connected with protection and preservation of artistic and historic monuments; John Harvard Fellow, Harvard Univ., 1930-31; American Federation of Arts; Board of Advisers, Dumbarton Oaks; Trustee: Andrew W. Mellon Educational and Charitable Trust; American Federation of Arts; Wallace Foundation, NY; National Trust for Historic Preservation; Mem., Art Adv. Panel, National Trust (UK); Member Advisory Council: Univ. of Notre Dame; New York Univ.; Hon. Dr Fine Arts: Tufts Univ., 1958; Brown Univ., 1959; La Salle Coll., 1962; LittD: Notre Dame, 1959, Washington and Jefferson Univs, 1960; LHD: Catholic Univ. of America, 1964; Univ. of New York, 1965; Maryland Inst.; Georgetown Univ., 1966; William and Mary Univ., 1967. Holds foreign decorations. *Publications:* (with Macgill James) Great American Paintings from Smibert to Bellows, 1943; (with Huntington Cairns) Masterpieces of Painting from National Gallery of Art, 1944; (with Huntington Cairns) Paintings from America, 1951; (with Huntington Cairns) Great Paintings from the National Gallery of Art, 1952; National Gallery of Art, Washington, 1956; Bellini and Titian at Ferrara, 1957; Treasures from the National Gallery of Art, 1963; The National Gallery of Art, Washington, DC, 1964; (with H. Cairns) Pageant of Painting, 1966; Self-Portrait with Donors, 1974; National Gallery of Art, 1976; Turner, 1976, Constable, 1978. *Address:* 1729 H Street, NW, Washington, DC 20006, USA. *T:* 965-2253. *Clubs:* Turf, Dilettanti, Pilgrims'; Century Association (New York City); Chevy Chase, Metropolitan (Washington, DC).

WALKER, John; Under Secretary, Scottish Home and Health Department, since 1978; *b* 16 Dec. 1929; *s* of John Walker and Elizabeth Whyte Fish; *m* 1952, Rena Robertson McEwan; two *d*. *Educ:* Falkirk High School. Entered Civil Service, Min. of Labour, as clerical officer, 1946. National Service, RAF, 1948-50. Asst Principal, Dept of Health for Scotland, 1958; Scottish Home and Health Dept: Principal, 1960; Secretary, Ctte on General Medical Services in the Highlands and Islands, 1964-67; Asst Sec., 1969; Scottish Development Dept, 1975-78. *Recreations:* grandparenthood, viticulture, walking. *Address:* Rosyth House, Grahamsdyke Road, Bo'ness, West Lothian EH51 9ED. *T:* Bo'ness 822426. *Club:* Royal Commonwealth Society.

WALKER, John David; His Honour Judge Walker; a Circuit Judge, since 1972; *b* 13 March 1924; *y s* of late L. C. Walker, MA, MB (Cantab), BCh, and late Mrs J. Walker, Malton; *m* 1953, Elizabeth Mary Emma (*née* Owbridge); one *s* two *d*. *Educ:* Oundle (1937-42); Christ's Coll., Cambridge (1947-50); BA 1950, MA 1953. War of 1939-45: commissioned Frontier Force Rifles, Indian Army, 1943; demob., Captain, 1947. Called to the Bar, Middle Temple, 1951; a Recorder, 1972. *Recreations:* shooting, fishing. *Address:* Molescroft Close, Beverley, North Humberside. *T:* Beverley 881359. *Clubs:* Lansdowne; Pacific (Hull).

WALKER, John Riddell Bromhead, CVO 1978 (MVO 1953); MC 1944; Lieutenant-Colonel (retired), late 14th Sikhs; *b* 21 June 1913; *s* of late Col P. G. Walker, IA, and Judith Dorothy Gonville, *d* of late Col Sir Benjamin Bromhead, Bt, CB, Thurlby Hall, Lincoln; *m* 1939, Marjorie, *d* of late Col Frank Fleming, DSO, TD; two *s* (one *d* decd). *Educ:* Dover; Royal Military Coll., Sandhurst. Attached 2nd Bn York and Lancaster Regt, 1933; 1/11th Sikh Regt (14th Sikhs) and 7/11th Sikh Regt, 1934-47; adjutant, 1938-41; various staff appointments in India, 1942-47; Instructor Staff Coll., Haifa,

1944-45; NWF (India), Waziristan, 1937; Ahmedzai, 1940; Datta Khel Relief, 1942; Arakan and Imphal, 1944; Rouge Croix Pursuivant of Arms, 1947-53; Lancaster Herald, 1953-68; Registrar of College of Arms, 1960-67; Clarenceux King of Arms, 1968-78. Dep. Inspector of Regimental Colours, 1958-77, Inspector, 1977-78. *Address:* c/o Grindlays Bank Ltd, 13 St James's Square, SW1Y 4LF. *Club:* Flyfishers'.

WALKER, Julian Fortay, CMG 1981; MBE 1960; HM Diplomatic Service; Ambassador to Yemen Arab Republic, since 1979, and to Republic of Jibuti (non-resident); *b* 7 May 1929; *s* of Kenneth Macfarlane Walker, FRCS, and Eileen Marjorie Walker (*née* Wilson); unmarried. *Educ:* Harvey Sch., Hawthorne, New York; Stowe; Bryanston; Cambridge Univ. (MA). National Service, RN, 1947-49; Cambridge, 1949-52; London Univ. Sch. of African and Oriental Studies, 1952. Foreign Service: MECAS, 1953; Asst Political Agent, Trucial States, 1953-55; 3rd and 2nd Sec., Bahrain Residency, 1955-57; FCO and Frontier Settlement, Oman, 1957-60; 2nd and 1st Sec., Oslo, 1960-63; FCO News Dept Spokesman, 1963-67; 1st Sec., Baghdad, 1967; 1st Sec., Morocco (Rabat), 1967-69; FCO, 1969-71; Political Agent, Dubai, Trucial States, 1971, Consul-Gen. and Counsellor, British Embassy, Dubai, United Arab Emirates, 1971-72; Cambridge Univ. on sabbatical leave, 1972-73; Political Advr and Head of Chancery, British Mil. Govt, Berlin, 1973-76; NI Office, Stormont Castle, 1976-77; Dir, MECAS, 1977-78. *Recreations:* skiing, sailing, tennis, music, cooking. *Address:* c/o Foreign and Commonwealth Office, SW1. *Club:* Royal Automobile.

WALKER, Prof. Kenneth Richard, DPhil; Professor of Economics with Reference to Asia, University of London, School of Oriental and African Studies, since Oct. 1978 (Professor of Economics with Special Reference to China, 1972-78); Head of Department of Economic and Political Studies at School of Oriental and African Studies, since 1972; *b* 17 Oct. 1931; *s* of Arthur Bedford Walker and Olive Walker; *m* 1959, June Abercrombie Collie; one *s* one *d*. *Educ:* Prince Henry's Grammar Sch., Otley, Yorks; Univ. of Leeds (BA); Lincoln Coll., Oxford. DPhil Oxon. Asst in Political Economy, Univ. of Aberdeen, 1956-59; Research Fellow, 1959-61, Lectr, 1961-66, Reader, 1966-72, in Economics at School of Oriental Studies, Univ. of London. *Publications:* Planning in Chinese Agriculture, Socialisation and the Private Sector 1956-1962, 1965; contribs to Scottish Jl of Political Economy, Economic Development and Cultural Change, China Qly. *Recreations:* golf, hill-walking, bird-watching, choral singing. *Address:* 4 Harpenden Road, St Albans, Herts AL3 5AB. *T:* St Albans 50970.

WALKER, Sir Michael; *see* Walker, Sir C. M.

WALKER, Michael; His Honour Judge Michael Walker; a Circuit Judge, since 1978; *b* 13 April 1931; *m* 1959, Elizabeth Mary Currie; two *s*. *Educ:* Chadderton Grammar Sch.; Sheffield Univ. (LLM). Called to the Bar, Gray's Inn, 1956. Joined North Eastern Circuit, 1958. A Recorder of the Crown Court, 1972-78.

WALKER, Prof. Nigel David, CBE 1979; MA Oxon, PhD Edinburgh, DLitt Oxon; Wolfson Professor of Criminology and Fellow of King's College, Cambridge University, since 1973 (Director, Institute of Criminology, 1973-80); *b* 6 Aug. 1917; *s* of David B. Walker and Violet Walker (*née* Johnson); *m* 1939, Sheila Margaret Johnston; one *d*. *Educ:* Tientsin Grammar Sch.; Edinburgh Academy; Christ Church, Oxford (Hon. Scholar). Served War, Infantry officer (Camerons and Lovat Scouts), 1940-46. Scottish Office, 1946-61; Gwilym Gibbon Fellow, Nuffield Coll., 1958-59; University Reader in Criminology and Fellow of Nuffield Coll., Oxford, 1961-73. Visiting Professor: Berkeley, 1965; Yale, 1973; Stockholm, 1978. Chairman: Home Secretary's Adv. Council on Probation and After-care, 1972-76; Study Gp on Legal Training of Social Workers, 1972-73; Pres., Nat. Assoc. of Probation Officers, 1980-; Member: Home Sec.'s TV Research Cttee, 1963-69; Adv. Council on Penal System, 1969-; Cttee on Mentally Abnormal Offenders, 1972-75; Working Party on Judicial Training and Information, 1975-78. Hon. LLD Leicester, 1976. *Publications:* Delphi, 1936; A Short History of Psychotherapy, 1957 (various trans); Morale in the Civil Service, 1961; Crime and Punishment in Britain, 1965; Crime and Insanity in England, 2 vols, 1968 and 1972; Sentencing in a Rational Society, 1969 (various trans.); Crimes, Courts and Figures, 1971; Explaining Misbehaviour (inaug. lecture), 1974; Treatment and Justice (Sandoz lecture), 1976; Behaviour and Misbehaviour, 1977; Punishment, Danger and Stigma, 1980; reports, articles, etc. *Recreations:* chess, hill-climbing. *Address:* Institute of Criminology, 7 West Road, Cambridge. *Club:* Royal Society of Medicine.

WALKER, Dr Paul Crawford, JP; Regional Medical Officer, North East Thames Regional Health Authority, since 1978; *b* 9 Dec. 1940; *s* of Joseph Viccars Walker and Mary Tilley (*née* Crawford); *m* 1962, Barbara Georgina Bliss; three *d*. *Educ:* Queen Elizabeth Grammar Sch., Darlington; Downing Coll., Cambridge (BA); University College Hospital (MB, BChir); Edinburgh Univ. (DipSocMed). FFCM; FRSM 1981. Assistant Senior Medical Officer, Birmingham Regional Hosp. Bd, 1969-72; Dep. Medical Officer of Health and Dep. Principal Sch. MO, 1972-74, Actg Medical Officer of Health and Principal Sch. MO, 1974, Wolverhampton County Borough Council; District Community Physician, N Staffs Health District, Staffordshire AHA, 1974-76; Area MO, Wakefield AHA, 1976-78. Governor, Moorfields Eye Hosp., 1981-. JP Epping and Ongar, 1980-. *Publications:* contribs to medical and health service jls. *Recreations:* music, railway history, languages, anthropology. *Address:* 5 Hartland Road, Epping, Essex CM16 4PH. *T:* Epping 73299.

WALKER, Sir Peter; see Walker, Sir C. P. G.

WALKER, Rt. Hon. Peter Edward, PC 1970; MBE 1960; MP (C) Worcester since March 1961; Minister of Agriculture, Fisheries and Food, since 1979; *b* 25 March 1932; *s* of Sydney and Rose Walker; *m* 1969, Tessa, *d* of G. I. Pout; three *s* one *d. Educ:* Latymer Upper Sch. Member, National Executive of Conservative Party, 1956–; Nat. Chairman, Young Conservatives, 1958–60; Parliamentary Candidate (C) for Dartford, 1955 and 1959. PPS to Leader of House of Commons, 1963–64; Opposition Front Bench Spokesman: on Finance and Economics, 1964–66; on Transport, 1966–68; on Local Government, Housing, and Land, 1968–70; Minister of Housing and Local Govt, June–Oct. 1970; Secretary of State for: the Environment, 1970–72; Trade and Industry, 1972–74; Opposition Spokesman on Trade, Industry and Consumer Affairs, Feb.–June 1974; on Defence, June 1974–Feb. 1975. *Publication:* The Ascent of Britain, 1977. *Address:* Deer Park, Droitwich, Worcs. *Clubs:* Buck's, City of London, Turf; Worcestershire County Cricket, Union and County (Worcester).

WALKER, Rt. Rev. Peter Knight; see Ely, Bishop of.

WALKER, Prof. Peter Martin Brabazon, CBE 1976; FRSE; Honorary Professor and Director, MRC Mammalian Genome Unit, 1973–80; *b* 1 May 1922; *e s* of Major Ernest Walker and Mildred Walker (*née* Heaton-Ellis), Kenya; *m* 1943, Violet Norah Wright; one *s* three *d. Educ:* Haileybury Coll.; Trinity Coll., Cambridge, 1945. BA, PhD. Tool and instrument maker, 1939 (during War); Scientific Staff, MRC Biophysics Research Unit, King's Coll., London, 1948; Royal Society Research Fellow, Edinburgh, 1958; Univ. of Edinburgh: Lectr in Zoology, 1962; Reader in Zoology, 1963; Professor of Natural History, 1966–73. Member: Biological Research Bd, MRC, 1967 (Chm., 1970–72); MRC, 1970–72; Ext. Scientific Staff, MRC; Chief Scientist Cttee, Scottish Home and Health Dept, 1973–; Chm., Equipment Res. Cttee, Scottish Home and Health Dept, 1973–79; Mem. Council, Imp. Cancer Res. Fund, 1971–; Chm., Imp. Cancer Res. Fund Scientific Adv. Cttee, 1975–; Mem., Scientific Adv. Cttee of European Molecular Biology Lab., 1976–81. *Publications:* contribs to the molecular biology of the genetic material of mammals in: Nature; Jl of Molecular Biology, etc. *Recreations:* gardening, design of scientific instruments, railway history. *Address:* House of Ross, Comrie, Perthshire. *T:* Comrie 303; 5 Grange Terrace, Edinburgh EH9 2LD. *T:* 031-667 3060.

WALKER, Philip Gordon, FCA; Chairman: Chapman Industries PLC; Chapman & Co. Engineers (Balham) Ltd; Chapman Envelopes Ltd; Chapman Cartons Ltd; Weir Waste Paper Co. Ltd; The New Waterside Paper Mills Ltd; *b* 9 June 1912; *s* of late William and Kate Blanche Walker; *m* 1st, 1938, Anne May (marr. diss.); one *s* two *d*; 2nd, 1962, Elizabeth Oliver. *Educ:* Epworth Coll., Rhyl, North Wales. Bourner, Bullock & Co., Chartered Accountants, 1929–35; Walkers (Century Oils) Ltd, 1935–40; Layton Bennett, Billingham & Co., Chartered Accountants, 1940, Partner, 1944–51 (now Josolyne Layton-Bennett & Co.); Albert E. Reed & Co Ltd (now Reed International), Man. Dir, 1951–63; Chairman, Sun Life Assurance Soc. Ltd, 1971–82 (Exec. Chm. 1976–82); concurrently Chm. Sun Life Pensions Management Ltd, Sun Life Management Services Ltd, Sun Life Unit Assce Ltd, Sun Life Unit Services Ltd, Sun Life Properties Ltd, Pinner Properties Ltd, Artagen Estates Ltd, Sun Life Management Ltd, Artagen Investments Ltd. Part-time Mem. Monopolies Commn, 1963–65; Member: Performing Right Tribunal, 1971–; Restrictive Practices Court, 1973–. *Recreation:* golf. *Address:* Park Cottage, Penton Mewsey, near Andover, Hants SP11 0RW. *T:* Weyhill 2527. *Clubs:* Brooks's; Wildernesse (Sevenoaks); Rye; Berkshire.

WALKER, Philip Henry Conyers; His Honour Judge Harry Walker; a Circuit Judge, since 1979; *b* 22 Dec. 1926; *o c* of Philip Howard and Kathleen Walker; *m* 1953, Mary Elizabeth Ross; two *s* two *d. Educ:* Marlborough; Oriel Coll., Oxford. MA, BCL (Oxon); DipTh (London). Army (6 AB Sigs), 1944–48 (despatches, 1948). Solicitor in private practice, 1954–79; a Recorder of the Crown Court, 1972–79. Mem., Church Assembly, Nat. Synod of C of E, 1960–80. Chm. Agricultural Land Tribunal (Yorks & Lancs), 1977–79; Mem., Criminal Law Revision Cttee, 1981–. *Recreations:* fishing, shooting, sailing, walking. *Address:* Pond House, Askwith, Otley, West Yorks. *T:* Otley 463196.

WALKER, Richard Alwyne F.; see Fyjis-Walker.

WALKER, Richard John Boileau, MA; FSA; National Portrait Gallery Cataloguer, since 1976; *b* 4 June 1916; *s* of Comdr Kenneth Walker and Caroline Livingstone-Learmonth; *m* 1946, Margaret, *d* of Brig. Roy Firebrace, CBE; one *s* two *d. Educ:* Harrow; Magdalene Coll., Cambridge (MA); Courtauld Institute of Art. Active service, RNVR, 1939–45. British Council, 1946; Tate Gallery, 1947–48; Min. of Works Picture Adviser, 1949–76; Curator of the Palace of Westminster, 1950–76. Trustee: Nat. Maritime Museum, 1977–; Army Museums Ogilby Trust, 1979–. *Publications:* Catalogue of Pictures at Audley End, 1950 and 1973; Old Westminster Bridge, 1979. *Recreations:* looking at pictures and finding quotations. *Address:* 31 Cadogan Place, SW1X 9RX. *T:* 01-235 1801; Ashbrook House, Blewbury, Oxfordshire OX11 9QA. *Clubs:* Athenæum, United Oxford & Cambridge University.

WALKER, Robert; HM Diplomatic Service, retired; *b* 1 May 1924; *s* of Young and Gladys Walker, Luddendenfoot, Yorks; *m* 1949, Rita Thomas; one *s* one *d. Educ:* Sowerby Bridge Grammar Sch.; Peterhouse, Cambridge. Commissioned RNVR 1944; served in minesweepers in home waters. Cambridge, 1942–43 and 1946–48; BA Hons History, 1948; MA 1963. Joined CRO, 1948; served Peshawar and Karachi, 1949–51; New Delhi, 1955–59; Sen. First Sec., Accra, 1962–64; Dep. British High Comr, in Ghana, 1964–65; FCO, 1965–68. IDC, 1969; Commercial Counsellor, Ankara, 1970–71; Dep. High Comr, Nairobi, 1971–72. Dep. Registrar, Hull Univ., 1972–79. Contested (L): Haltemprice, Feb. and Oct. 1974, 1979; Humberside, European election, 1979; Prospective Parly Cand., Liberal/SDP Alliance, South Ribble. Mem., Liberal Party Council; Chm., Yorkshire Liberal Fedn, 1977–81. *Recreations:* coarse golf, country wine making, interior decorating. *Address:* Manor Farm, Langcliffe, North Yorks BD24 9NQ. *T:* Settle 3205.

WALKER, Robert, QC 1982; *b* 17 March 1938; *s* of Ronald Robert Anthony Walker and Mary Helen Walker (*née* Welsh); *m* 1962, Suzanne Diana Leggi; one *s* three *d. Educ:* Downside Sch.; Trinity Coll., Cambridge (BA). Called to Bar, Lincoln's Inn, 1960; in practice at Chancery Bar, 1961–. *Recreations:* riding, running, skiing. *Address:* Freeman's Farm, Thaxted, Essex CM6 3PY. *T:* Thaxted 830577.

WALKER, Robert Milnes, CBE 1964; Director of Surgical Studies, Royal College of Surgeons, 1968–71; Director, Cancer Records Bureau, SW Regional Hospital Board, 1965–71; Professor of Surgery, University of Bristol, 1946–64, Emeritus since 1964; Hon. Surgeon, Bristol Royal Hospital; Member of the Medical Research Council, 1959–63; *b* 2 Aug. 1903; *s* of J. W. Walker, FSA, FRCS, Wakefield, Yorks; *m* 1931, Grace Anna McCormick; two *s* four *d. Educ:* Oundle Sch.; University College Hospital, London. Hon. Surgeon, Royal Hospital, Wolverhampton, 1931–46; Rock Carling Fellow, Nuffield Hospital Trust, 1965. Editor, Medical Annual, 1954–74. Member Council, RCS, 1953–69; Vice-Pres., 1966–68; President: Assoc. Surgeons of GB, 1961; Surgical Research Soc., 1962–64. Fellow of University Coll., London, 1953. Mem., Medical Sub-Cttee, UGC, 1959–67. Master, Worshipful Co. of Barbers, 1974 (Upper Warden, 1973). Hon. FACS; Hon. FRCSE. Hon. Gold Medal, RCS, 1972. *Publications:* Portal Hypertension, 1959; Medical Education in Britain, 1965; Cancer in South West England, 1973; Barbers and Barber Surgeons of London, 1978. *Recreations:* gardening, bird watching, travel. *Address:* Wergs Copse, Kintbury, Newbury, Berks.

WALKER, Robert Scott, FRICS; City Surveyor, City of London Corporation, 1955–75; *b* 13 June 1913; *s* of Harold and Mary Walker; *m* 1946, Anne Armstrong; no *c. Educ:* West Buckland Sch., North Devon. War Service, 1939–45, Major RA. Assistant City Surveyor, Manchester, 1946–55. *Address:* 10 Woodcote Close, Epsom, Surrey. *T:* Epsom 21220.

WALKER, Sir Ronald; see Walker, Sir E. R.

WALKER, Col Ronald Draycott S.; see Sherbrooke-Walker.

WALKER, Ronald Leslie, CSI 1946; CIE 1942; *b* 9 April 1896; *m* 1948, Joyce Edwina Collins, OBE, 1946, Kaisar-i-Hind Gold Medal, 1939, *e d* of late G. Turville Brown. *Educ:* Bedford Sch.; Hertford Coll., Oxford. European War, 1914–18, Northamptonshire Regt, 1915; Machine-Gun Corps, 1916–18. Entered Indian Civil Service, 1920; Finance Secretary, Bengal, 1939–45; Adviser to Governor of Bengal, 1945; Chief Secretary, Bengal, 1946. *Address:* Little Coombe, Coombe Hill Road, East Grinstead, West Sussex. *T:* East Grinstead 25616. *Club:* East India, Devonshire, Sports and Public Schools.

WALKER, Roy; see Walker, C. R.

WALKER, Samuel Richard, CBE 1955; DL; Founder and Hon. President, Walker & Rice (Walric 1975–80); *b* 11 Jan. 1892; *s* of Samuel Reuben and Elizabeth Louise Walker; *m* 1923, Marjorie Jackson Clark (*d* 1977), *d* of A. J. Clark, Hove, Sussex; one *s* two *d. Educ:* William Ellis's. Queen Victoria Rifles, 1909–14; served European War, 1914–19, in France: 1st King Edward's Horse and RFA; Home Guard, 1939–45. City of London: DL 1951; Member Common Council (Bread Street Ward, 1937–76; Deputy, 1951–76), Chief Commoner, 1953–54; Chairman: Officers and Clerks Cttee, 1952; Privileges Cttee, 1957–73; Comr of Income Tax, 1960–66. Sheriff of City of London, 1957–58; one of HM Lieutenants, City of London. Master, Worshipful Company of Farriers, 1954–55; Master, Worshipful Company of Founders, 1962–63; Liveryman of Worshipful Company of Weavers, 1964–; Chairman: Cattle Markets Cttee, 1945–46; Central Criminal Court Extension Cttee, 1964–75; Benevolent Assoc. of Corporation of London, 1970–76; Reconstruction of Guildhall Cttee, 1953–76; various Cttees, City of London, 1950–54. Vice-Pres., Mid Sussex Assoc. for Mentally Handicapped Children, 1970–. Governor, Bridewell Royal Hosp., 1942–; Life Governor and Vice-Chm., City of London Sheriffs' and Recorders' Fund Soc., 1957–; Chm., Thomas Carpenter and John Lane Trust, 1951–; Governor and Almoner, Christ's Hosp., 1966–; Trustee, Seaforth Hall, Warninglid. Commendatore of Order Al Merito della Repubblica (Italy), 1957. *Recreations:* golf, riding. *Address:* Copyhold Rise, Copyhold Lane, Cuckfield, Sussex. *Clubs:* City Livery (President, 1955–56), Guildhall, Oriental; West Hove Golf (Life Pres.), West Sussex Golf, Haywards Heath Golf.

WALKER, Sheila Mosley, (Mrs Owen Walker), CBE 1981; JP; Chief Commissioner, Girl Guides Association, 1975-80; *b* 11 Dec. 1917; *yr d* of late Charles Eric Mosley Mayne, Indian Cavalry, and Evelyn Mary, *d* of Sir Thomas Skewes-Cox, MP; *m* 1st, 1940, Major Bruce Dawson, MC, Royal Berkshire Regt (killed, Arnhem, 1944); one *s* one *d*; 2nd, 1955, Henry William Owen, *s* of late Sir Henry Walker, CBE; one step *s* one step *d*. *Educ*: St Mary's Hall, Brighton; St James' Secretarial Coll., London. Midlands Regional Chief Comr, Girl Guides Assoc., 1970-75. JP Nottingham City, 1970. *Recreations*: children, animals, all country and nature preservation. *Address*: Dingley Hall, near Market Harborough, Leics. *T*: Dingley 388.

WALKER, Stanley Kenneth; Director and Chief General Manager, Leeds Permanent Building Society, 1978-82; *b* 18 Feb. 1916; *s* of Robert and Gertrude Walker; *m* 1956, Diana, *d* of Fred Broadhead; one *s*. *Educ*: Cockburn Sch., Leeds. FCIS, FCBSI. Served War of 1939-45, Middle East (despatches, 1944). Leeds Permanent Building Society: Branch Manager, Newcastle upon Tyne, 1960-62; Asst Sec., 1962-66; Asst Gen. Manager, 1967-77; Gen. Manager, 1977-78. Member: Council, Building Societies Assoc., 1978-81; Council, Leeds Chamber of Commerce and Industry, 1980-. *Recreations*: tennis, walking, theatre. *Club*: Royal Automobile.

WALKER, Dame Susan (Armour), DBE 1972 (CBE 1963); Vice-Chairman, Women's Royal Voluntary Service, 1969-75; *d* of James Walker, Bowmont, Dunbar; unmarried. *Educ*: Grammar School, Dunbar. Conservative Central Office Agent, Yorkshire, 1950-56; Deputy Chief Organisation Officer, Conservative Central Office, 1956-64; Vice-Chm., Cons. Party Organisation, 1964-68, retired 1968. *Recreations*: golf, walking. *Address*: The Glebe House, Hownam, Kelso, Roxburghshire. *T*: Morebattle 277.

WALKER, Terence William, (Terry Walker); *b* 26 Oct. 1935; *s* of William Edwin and Lilian Grace Walker; *m* 1959, Priscilla Dart; two *s* one *d*. *Educ*: Grammar Sch. and Coll. of Further Educn, Bristol. Employed by Courage (Western) Ltd at Bristol for 23 yrs, Mem. Chief Accountant's Dept. MP (Lab) Kingswood, Feb. 1974-1979; Second Church Estates Comr, 1974-79. Mem., Avon CC, 1981-; Chm., Avon Public Protection Cttee, 1981-. *Recreations*: cricket, football. *Address*: 19 Forest Edge, Hanham, Bristol BS15 3PP. *T*: Bristol 672301.

WALKER, Prof. Thomas William, ARCS; DSc; DIC; Professor of Soil Science, Lincoln College, New Zealand, 1961-79; *b* 22 July 1916; *m* 1940, Edith Edna Bott; four *d*. *Educ*: Loughborough Grammar School; Royal College of Science. Royal Scholar and Kitchener Scholar, 1935-39; Salter's Fellow, 1939-41; Lecturer and Adviser in Agricultural Chemistry, Univ. of Manchester, 1941-46. Provincial Advisory Soil Chemist, NAAS, 1946-51; Prof. of Soil Science, Canterbury Agric. Coll., New Zealand, 1952-58; Prof. of Agric., King's Coll., Newcastle upon Tyne, 1958-61. *Publications*: numerous research. *Recreations*: fishing, gardening. *Address*: 843 Cashmere Road, Christchurch 3, New Zealand.

WALKER, Walter Basil Scarlett, (Bobby Walker), MA; FCA; Deputy UK Senior Partner, Peat, Marwick, Mitchell & Co., 1979-82; *b* 19 Dec. 1915; *s* of James and Hilda Walker, Southport; *m* 1945, Teresa Mary Louise John; one *d* (and one *s* decd). *Educ*: Rugby Sch.; Clare Coll., Cambridge (MA). Joined Peat, Marwick, Mitchell & Co., 1937, leaving temporarily, 1939, to join RNVR; service in Home Fleet, incl. convoys to Russia and Malta, 1940-42; finally, Asst Sec. to British Naval C-in-C in Germany; Lt-Comdr. Returned to Peat, Marwick, Mitchell & Co., 1946, becoming a partner, 1956. Mem. (part-time), UKAEA, 1972-81. Governor, Royal Ballet, Covent Garden, 1980-. *Recreations*: ballet, gardening, golf. *Address*: 11 Sloane Avenue, SW3 3JD. *T*: 01-589 4133; Coles, Privett, near Alton, Hants GU34 3PH. *T*: Privett 223. *Club*: Royal Automobile.

WALKER, Gen. Sir Walter (Colyear), KCB 1968 (CB 1964); CBE 1959 (OBE 1949); DSO 1946 and Bars, 1953 and 1965; Commander-in-Chief, Allied Forces Northern Europe, 1969-72, retired; *b* 11 Nov. 1912; *s* of late Arthur Colyear Walker; *m* 1938, Beryl, *d* of late E.N.W. Johnston; two *s* one *d*. *Educ*: Blundell's; RMC, Sandhurst. Waziristan, 1939-41 (despatches twice); Burma, 1942, 1944-46 (despatches, DSO); Malaya, 1949-59 (despatches twice, OBE, Bar to DSO, CBE); Atomic Trials, Maralinga, SA, 1956; Dir of Operations, Borneo, 1962-65 (CB, Bar to DSO); Deputy Chief of Staff, HQ ALFCE, 1965; Acting Chief of Staff, 1966-67; GOC-in-C, Northern Command, 1967-69. psc† 1942; jssc 1950; idc 1960. Dato Seri Setia, Order of Paduka Stia Negara, Brunei, 1964; Hon. Panglima Mangku Negara, Malaysia, 1965. *Publications*: The Bear at the Back Door, 1978; The Next Domino, 1980; Red Alert, 1983. *Recreations*: normal. *Address*: Charlton House, Charlton All Saints, Salisbury, Wilts SP5 4HQ. *Club*: Army and Navy.

WALKER, Prof. William; FRCP, FRCPE; Regius Professor of Materia Medica, University of Aberdeen, 1973-82; retired; *b* 1 Jan. 1920; *s* of William Sharp Walker and Joan Strachan Gloak; *m* 1948, Mary Cathleen Kenny; one adopted *s* one adopted *d*. *Educ*: Harris Academy, Dundee; Univ. of St Andrews. MA, MB, ChB; FRCP, FRCPE. Served War: commissioned Royal Scots, 1939; wounded, 1940; invalided, 1941. Lecturer in Pathology, Univ. of St Andrews, 1947; Medical Registrar, Newcastle, 1948. Research Fellow, Haematology, Boston Univ. Mass, 1954-55; Lectr in Therapeutics, St Andrews, 1952, Sen. Lectr, 1955; Consultant Physician, Aberdeen, 1964; Clinical Reader in Medicine, 1971. Pres., Anglo-German Medical Soc.,

1976-81; Vice Chm., Cttee on the Review of Medicines, 1981- (Mem., 1975-). *Publications*: various medical, chiefly in thrombotic and haemorrhagic disease, and drug therapy. *Recreations*: gardening, philosophy, social and political controversy. *Address*: Woodhill, Kinellar, Aberdeenshire AB5 0RZ. *T*: Aberdeen 79314.

WALKER, William Connoll, (Bill Walker), FIPM; MP (C) Perth and East Perthshire, since 1979; *b* 20 Feb. 1929; *s* of Charles and Williamina Walker; *m* 1956, Mavis Evelyn Lambert; three *d*. *Educ*: Logie Sch., Dundee; Trades Coll., Dundee; College for Distributive Trades. FIPM 1968; FBIM. Message boy, 1943-44; office boy, 1944-46. Commissioned RAF, 1946-49; Flt Lieut RAFVR, 1949-. Salesman, public service vehicle driver, general manager, 1949-59; civil servant, 1959-65; training and education officer, furnishing industry, 1965-67; company director, 1967-79. FRSA 1970. *Recreations*: RAFVR, gliding, caravanning, walking, youth work. *Address*: Candletrees, Golf Course Road, Rosemount, Blairgowrie, Perthshire PH10 6LQ. *T*: Blairgowrie 2660. *Clubs*: Naval, Royal Air Force.

WALKER, Sir William (Giles Newsom), Kt 1959; TD 1942; DL; *b* 20 Nov. 1905; *e s* of late H. Giles Walker, Over Rankeillour, Cupar, Fife and of late Mrs Elizabeth Bewley Newsom (Walker), Cork, Eire; *m* 1930, Mildred Brenda, 3rd *d* of Sir Michael Nairn, 2nd Bt, Elie House, Fife, and Pitcarmick, Blairgowrie; one *s* two *d*. *Educ*: Shrewsbury Sch.; Jesus Coll., Cambridge (BA). War of 1939-45: Lt-Col comdg 1st Fife and Forfar Yeomanry, 1943-45 (mobilised Aug. 1939; despatches, TD). Jute Industries Ltd, Dundee: entered 1927; rejoined after War, 1945; Director, 1946-71; Managing Director, 1947-69; Chairman, 1948-70; Hon. Pres., 1971. Director: Nairn & Williamson (Holdings) Ltd, 1954-75; Clydesdale Bank Ltd; Scottish Television Ltd, 1964-74; Alliance Trust Co. Ltd, 1963-76; Second Alliance Trust Co. Ltd, 1963-76. Formerly: Jute Working Party (Employer Mem.); Dundee Chamber of Commerce (Dir); Scottish Industrial Estates Ltd. (Dir); Member, Scottish Railway Bd. Hon. Colonel: Fife and Forfar Yeomanry/Scottish Horse, 1967-69; Highland Yeomanry, 1969-71. DL Fife, 1958. USA Bronze Star, 1945. *Recreations*: shooting and golf. *Address*: Pitlair, Cupar, Fife. *T*: Ladybank 30413. *Clubs*: Royal and Ancient Golf (Capt. 1962-63) (St Andrews); The Honourable Company of Edinburgh Golfers (Muirfield).

WALKER, William MacLelland, QC (Scot.) 1971; *b* 19 May 1933; *s* of late Hon. Lord Walker; *m* 1957, Joan Margaret, *d* of late Charles Hutchison Wood, headmaster, Dundee; one *d*. *Educ*: Edinburgh Academy; Edinburgh Univ. (MA, LLB). Advocate, 1957; Flying Officer, RAF, 1957-59; Standing Junior Counsel: Min. of Aviation, 1963-68; BoT (Aviation), 1968-71; Min. of Technology, 1968-70; Dept of Trade and Industry (Power), 1971; Min. of Aviation Supply, 1971. Chm. Industrial Tribunals in Scotland, 1972-. *Recreations*: shooting, travel. *Address*: 17 India Street, Edinburgh EH3 6HE. *T*: 031-225 3846; Edenside, Gordon, Berwickshire TD3 6LB. *T*: Gordon 271. *Clubs*: Royal Air Force; New (Edinburgh).

WALKER-OKEOVER, Sir Peter (Ralph Leopold), 4th Bt *cr* 1886; *b* 22 July 1947; *s* of Colonel Sir Ian Peter Andrew Monro Walker-Okeover, 3rd Bt, DSO, TD, and of Dorothy Elizabeth, *yr d* of Captain Josceline Heber-Percy; *S* father, 1982; *m* 1972, Catherine Mary Maule, *d* of Colonel George Maule Ramsay; two *s* one *d*. *Educ*: Eton; RMA Sandhurst. Captain, Blues and Royals, retired. *Heir*: *s* Andrew Peter Monro Walker-Okeover, *b* 22 May 1978. *Address*: Okeover Hall, Osmaston, Ashbourne, Derbyshire; House of Glenmuick, Ballater, Aberdeenshire.

WALKER-SMITH, Rt. Hon. Sir Derek Colclough, 1st Bt, *cr* 1960; PC 1957; QC 1955; TD; MP (C) East Division of Hertfordshire since 1955 (Hertford Division, 1945-55); *b* April 1910; *y s* of late Sir John Walker-Smith; *m* 1938, Dorothy, *d* of late L. J. W. Etherton, Rowlands Castle, Hants; one *s* two *d*. *Educ*: Rossall; Christ Church, Oxford. 1st Class Hons Modern History, Oxford Univ., 1931. Called to Bar, Middle Temple, 1934, Bencher 1963. Chm. Conservative Advisory Cttee on Local Govt, 1954-55; Chm. Conservative Members (1922) Cttee, 1951-55. Parly Sec. to the Board of Trade, 1955-Nov. 1956; Economic Secretary to the Treasury, Nov. 1956-Jan. 1957; Minister of State, Board of Trade, 1957; Minister of Health, 1957-60. Mem., European Parlt, 1973-79. Chm., Soc. of Conservative Lawyers, 1969-75; Chm., Nat. House Building Council, 1973-78. Associate of Royal Institution of Chartered Surveyors. *Heir*: *s* John Jonah Walker-Smith, *qv*. *Address*: 20 Albany Court, Palmer Street, Westminster, SW1.

WALKER-SMITH, John Jonah; a Recorder of the Crown Court, since 1980; *b* 6 Sept. 1939; *s* of Rt Hon. Sir Derek Colclough Walker-Smith, Bt, *qv*; *m* 1974, Aileen Marie Smith; one *s* one *d*. *Educ*: Westminster School; Christ Church, Oxford. Called to Bar, Middle Temple, 1963. *Address*: 1 Dr Johnson's Buildings, Temple, EC4.

WALKEY, Maj.-Gen. John Christopher, CB 1953; CBE 1943; *b* 18 Oct. 1903; *s* of late S. Walkey, Dawlish, Devon; *m* 1947, Beatrice Record Brown; one *d* decd. *Educ*: Newton College, Devon. Commissioned into Royal Engineers from RMA Woolwich, 1923; Chief Engineer, 13 Corps, 1943-47; Asst Comdt, RMA Sandhurst, 1949-51; Chief Engineer, Middle East Land Forces, 1951-54; Engineer-in-Chief, War Office, 1954-57; retired, 1957. Col Comdt RE, 1958-68. Hon. Col RE Resources Units (AER), 1959-64. Officer Legion of Merit (USA), 1945. *Recreations*: usual country pursuits. *Address*: Linden Spinney, Chagford, Devon. *Club*: Naval and Military.

WALKLING, Maj.-Gen. Alec Ernest, CB 1973; OBE 1954; *b* 12 April 1918; *s* of late Ernest George Walkling; *m* 1940, Marian Harris; one *s* one *d. Educ:* Weymouth Grammar School; Keble College, Oxford. MA (Oxon); BA Mod. Langs, 1939; BA Hons Nat. Science, 1949. Commissioned 2nd Lieut RA, 1940; served War of 1939-45, N Africa and Burma (despatches); Staff Coll., Quetta, 1944; Min. of Supply, 1949-53; British Joint Services Mission, Washington, 1956-58; Comd Regt in BAOR, 1961-63; Comd Brigade (TA), 1963-64; Imperial Defence Coll., 1965; Dep. Commandant, RMCS, 1966-68; Dir-Gen. of Artillery, 1969-70; Dep. Master-Gen. of the Ordnance, 1970-73, retired; Col Comdt, RA, 1974-. *Recreations:* golf, oil and water colour painting. *Address:* Brackenhurst, Brackendale Road, Camberley, Surrey. *T:* Camberley 21016. *Club:* Army and Navy.

WALL, Alfreda, (Mrs D. R. Wall); *see* Thorogood, A.

WALL, (Alice) Anne, (Mrs Michael Wall), DCVO 1982 (CVO 1972; MVO 1964); Extra Woman of the Bedchamber to HM the Queen, since 1981; *b* 1928; *d* of late Admiral Sir Geoffrey Hawkins, KBE, CB, MVO, DSC and late Lady Margaret, *d* of 7th Duke of Buccleuch; *m* 1975, Commander Michael E. St Q. Wall, Royal Navy. *Educ:* Miss Faunce's PNEU School. Asst Press Sec. to the Queen, 1958-81. *Address:* 2 Chester House, 231 Kennington Road, SE11 6BY; Ivy House, Lambourn, Berks RG16 7PB. *T:* Lambourn 72348.

WALL, Prof. Charles Terence Clegg, FRS 1969; Professor of Pure Mathematics, Liverpool University, since 1965; *b* 14 Dec. 1936; *s* of Charles Wall, schoolteacher, Woodfield, Dursley, Glos; *m* 1959, Alexandra Joy, *d* of Prof. Leslie Spencer Hearnshaw, *qv* ; two *s* two *d. Educ:* Marlborough Coll.; Trinity Coll., Cambridge. PhD Cantab 1960. Fellow, Trinity Coll., 1959-64; Harkness Fellow, Princeton, 1960-61; Univ. Lectr, Cambridge, 1961-64; Reader in Mathematics, and Fellow of St Catherine's Coll., Oxford, 1964-65. Royal Soc. Leverhulme Vis. Prof., CIEA, Mexico, 1967. Pres., London Mathematical Soc., 1978-80 (Mem. Council, 1973-80). *Publications:* Surgery on Compact Manifolds, 1970; A Geometric Introduction to Topology, 1972; papers on various problems in geometric topology, and related algebra. *Recreations:* gardening, home winemaking. *Address:* 5 Kirby Park, West Kirby, Wirral, Merseyside L48 2HA. *T:* 051-625 5063.

WALL, David (Richard); Principal Dancer, Royal Ballet Company; *b* 15 March 1946; *s* of Charles and Dorothy Wall; *m* 1967, Alfreda Thorogood, *qv* ; one *s* one *d. Educ:* Royal Ballet Sch. Joined Royal Ballet Co., Aug. 1964. Promotion to: Soloist, Aug. 1966; Junior Principal Dancer, Aug. 1967; Senior Principal Dancer, Aug. 1968. During period of employment has danced all major roles and has had many ballets created for him. Evening Standard Award for Ballet, 1977. *Recreations:* music, theatre. *Address:* 70 Elmbourne Road, SW17 8JJ.

WALL, Rt. Rev. Eric St Quintin; *b* 19 April 1915; *s* of Rev. Sydney Herbert Wall, MA, and Ethel Marion Wall (*née* Wilkins); *m* 1942, Doreen Clare (*née* Lovely); one *s* one *d. Educ:* Clifton; Brasenose Coll., Oxford (MA); Wells Theol. College. Deacon, 1938; Priest, 1939; Curate of Boston, 1938-41; Chaplain, RAFVR, 1941-45; Vicar of Sherston Magna, 1944-53; Rural Dean of Malmesbury, 1951-53; Vicar of Cricklade with Latton, 1953-60; Hon. Chaplain to Bp of Bristol, 1960-66; Hon. Canon, Bristol, 1960-72; Diocesan Adviser on Christian Stewardship, Dio. Bristol, 1960-66; Proc. Conv., 1964-69; Vicar, St Alban's, Westbury Park, Bristol, 1966-72; Rural Dean of Clifton, 1967-72; Canon Residentiary of Ely, 1972-80; Bishop Suffragan of Huntingdon, 1972-80. *Recreation:* golf. *Address:* 7 Peregrine Close, Diss, Norfolk. *T:* Diss 4331.

WALL, John William, CMG 1953; HM Diplomatic Service, retired 1966; *b* 6 Nov. 1910; *m* 1950, Eleanor Rosemary Riesle (*d* 1978); one *d. Educ:* Grammar Sch., Mexborough; Jesus Coll., Cambridge. Probationer Vice-Consul, Levant Consular Service, 1933; Vice-Consul, Cairo, 1936; in charge of Vice-Consulate, Suez, 1937; transferred to Jedda as 2nd Sec. in Diplomatic Service, 1939; acting Consul, Jedda, 1942, 1943; transferred to Tabriz, 1944, Isfahan, 1946, Casablanca, 1947; Brit. Middle East Office, Cairo: Head of Polit. Div., 1948, in charge 1949, 1950; Oriental Counsellor, Cairo, 1951; Political Agent, Bahrein, 1952-54; Consul-General at Salonika, 1955-57; HM Ambassador and Consul-General to Paraguay, 1957-59; Counsellor, Foreign Office, 1959-63; Consul-General at Alexandria, 1963-66. *Address:* Beech Cottage, Pen-y-Fan, Monmouth, Gwent. *Club:* United Oxford & Cambridge University.

WALL, Mrs Michael; *see* Wall, A. A.

WALL, Prof. Patrick David, MA, DM; Professor of Anatomy and Director, Cerebral Functions Research Group, University College, London, since 1967; *b* 5 April 1925; *s* of T. Wall, MC, and R. Wall (*née* Cresswell). *Educ:* St Paul's; Christ Church, Oxford. MA 1947; BM, BCh 1948; DM 1960. Instructor, Yale School of Medicine, 1948-50; Asst Prof., Univ. of Chicago, 1950-53; Instructor, Harvard Univ., 1953-55; Assoc. Prof., 1957-60, Professor 1960-67, MIT. Vis. Prof., Hebrew Univ., Jerusalem, 1973-. Founding Chm., Brain Research Assoc. First Editor in Chief, Pain. *Publications:* Trio, The Revolting Intellectuals' Organizations (novel), 1966 (US 1965); (with R. Melzack) The Challenge of Pain, 1982; many papers on anat. and physiol. of nervous system. *Recreation:* kibbitzing. *Address:* Cerebral Functions Research Group, Department of Anatomy, University College, Gower Street, WC1.

WALL, Major Sir Patrick (Henry Bligh), Kt 1981; MC 1945; VRD 1957; RM (retd); MP (C) Haltemprice Division of East Yorkshire, since 1955 (Haltemprice Division of Hull, Feb. 1954-55); *b* 19 Oct. 1916; *s* of Henry Benedict Wall and Gladys Eleanor Finney; *m* 1953, Sheila Elizabeth Putnam; one *d. Educ:* Downside. Commissioned in RM 1935 (specialised in naval gunnery). Served in HM Ships, support craft, with RM Commandos and US Navy. Actg Major, 1943; RN Staff Coll., 1945; Joint Services Staff Coll., 1947; Major, 1949. Contested Cleveland Division (Yorks), 1951 and 1952. Parliamentary Private Secretary to: Minister of Agriculture, Fisheries and Food, 1955-57; Chancellor of the Exchequer, 1958-59. Westminster City Council, 1953-62; CO 47 Commando RMFVR, 1951-57; Comr for Sea Scouts for London, 1950-66; Pres. Yorks Area Young Conservatives, 1955-60; Chm. Mediterranean Group of Conservative Commonwealth Council, 1954-67; Chm. Cons. Parly East and Central Africa Cttee, 1956-59; Vice-Chairman: Conservative Commonwealth Affairs Cttee, 1960-68; Cons. Overseas Bureau, 1963-73; Cons. Defence Cttee, 1965-77; Vice-Chm. or Treasurer, IPU, 1974-82 (Chairman: British-Maltese, Anglo-Bahrain, Anglo-South African, Anglo-Taiwan Groups; Vice-Chm., Anglo-Portuguese, Treasurer, Anglo-Korean Groups). Vice Pres., Mil. Cttee, N Atlantic Assembly, 1981- (Chm., 1978-81; Chm., Cons./Christian Democrat Gp); Chm., Pro Fide Movement, 1970-; Mem. Defence Cttee, WEU and Council of Europe, 1972-75. Chairman: Cons. Fisheries Sub-Cttee, 1962-; Africa Centre, 1961-65; Joint East and Central Africa Board, 1965-75; Cons. Southern Africa Group, 1970-78; Cons. Africa Sub-Cttee, 1979-; RM Parly Group, 1956-; British Rep. at 17th General Assembly of UN, 1962. Mem., Select Cttee on Defence, 1980-. Vice-Pres., British Sub-Aqua Club. Kt, SMO Malta; USA Legion of Merit, 1945. *Publications:* Royal Marine Pocket Book, 1944; Student Power, 1968; Defence Policy, 1969; Overseas Aid, 1969; The Soviet Maritime Threat, 1973; The Indian Ocean and the Threat to the West, 1975; Prelude to Detente, 1975; Southern Oceans and the Security of the Free World, 1977; co-author of a number of political pamphlets. *Recreation:* ship and aircraft models. *Address:* 8 Westminster Gardens, Marsham Street, SW1. *T:* 01-828 1803; Brantinghamthorp, Brantingham, near Brough, North Humberside. *T:* Brough 667248. *Clubs:* Royal Yacht Squadron; Royal Naval Sailing Association.

WALL, Maj.-Gen. Robert Percival Walter, CB 1978; Director, Land Decade Educational Council, since 1982; *b* 23 Aug. 1927; *s* of Frank Ernest and Ethel Elizabeth Wall; *m* 1953, Patricia Kathleen O'Brien (separated 1979); two *s* one *d.* Joined Royal Marines, 1945; regimental soldiering in Commandos, and Commando trng, followed by service at sea and on staff of HQ 3 Commando Bde RM, 1945-54; psc(M) 1959; jssc 1961; Asst Sec., Chiefs of Staff Secretariat, 1962-65; 43 Commando RM, 1965-66; Naval Staff, 1966-68; Directing Staff, JSS Coll., 1969-71; Col GS Commando Forces and Dept of Commandant General RM, 1971-74; course at RCDS, 1975; Chief of Staff to Commandant RM, 1976-79. Chm., River Thames Soc., 1978-; Member: Council, Thames Heritage Trust, 1980-; Cttee, Blackheath Football Club (RFU), 1980-; Council, Officers' Pension Soc., 1980-. Freeman of City of London, 1977; Freeman, Co. of Watermen and Lightermen of River Thames, 1979. FBIM. *Recreations:* cricket, rugby, walking, reading. *Address:* c/o Barclays Bank Ltd, 116 Goodmayes Road, Goodmayes, Ilford, Essex. *Clubs:* Army and Navy, MCC.

WALL, Ronald George Robert, CB 1961; *b* 25 Jan. 1910; *s* of George Thomas and Sophia Jane Wall; *m* 1st, 1936, Winifred Evans (marr. diss., 1950); one *s* ; 2nd, 1960, Mrs Muriel Sorrell (*née* Page). *Educ:* Alleyn's School, Dulwich; St John's College, Oxford (MA). Administrative Civil Service; entered Ministry of Agriculture and Fisheries, 1933; Fisheries Sec., 1952-59. Gwilym Gibbon Research Fellow, Nuffield College, Oxford, 1951-52. President of Permanent Commission under Internat. Fisheries Convention of 1946, 1953-56; Chairman of the International Whaling Commission, 1958-60; Dep. Sec., Min. of Agriculture, Fisheries and Food, 1961-70. Chm., Sugar Bd, 1970-77. *Recreations:* theatre, music, gardening. *Address:* 201 London Road, Twickenham, Mddx. *T:* 01-892 7086. *Clubs:* United Oxford & Cambridge University, Arts Theatre.

WALL, Prof. William Douglas, PhD, DLit; Professor of Educational Psychology, Institute of Education, University of London, 1972-78, now Professor Emeritus; Scientific Adviser, Bernard van Leer Foundation, since 1978; *b* 22 Aug. 1913; *s* of late John Henry Wall and Ann McCulloch Wall, Wallington, Surrey; *m* 1st, 1936, Doris Margaret (*née* Satchel) (marr. diss. 1960); two *s* one *d* ; 2nd, 1960, Ursula Maria (*née* Gallusser); one *s. Educ:* Univ. Coll. London, 1931-34 (BA Hons); Univ. Coll. London/Univ. of Birmingham, 1944-48 (PhD (Psychol.)); DLit (London) 1979. FBPsS. Mem. Cttee of Prof. Psychologists, Social Psych. Sect., Child and Educnl Psych. Sect. Univ. of Birmingham Educn Dept, 1945-51; Reader, 1948-53; Head, Educn and Child Develt Unit, UNESCO, Paris, 1951-56; Dir, Nat. Foundn for Educnl Res. in England and Wales, 1956-68; Dean, Inst. of Educn, Univ. of London, 1968-73. Visiting Professor: Univ. of Michigan, 1957; Univ. of Jerusalem, 1962; Univ. of Tel Aviv, 1967. Chm., Internat. Project Evaluation of Educnl Attainment, 1958-62; Mem., Police Trng Council, 1970-78; Co-Dir, 1955-78, and Chm., Nat. Child Develt Study, 1958-78; Mem. Council, Internat. Children's Centre, Paris, 1970-78. *Publications:* (many trans. various langs): Adolescent Child, 1948 (2nd edn, 1952); Education and Mental Health, 1955; Psychological Services for Schools, 1956; Child of our

Times, 1959; Failure in School, 1962; Adolescents in School and Society, 1968; Longitudinal Studies and the Social Sciences, 1970; Constructive Education for Children, 1975; Constructive Education for Adolescents, 1977; Constructive Education for Handicapped, 1979; contrib: British Jl Educnl Psych.; British Jl Psych., Educnl Res. (Editor, 1958-68), Educnl Rev., Enfance, Human Develt, Internat. Rev. Educn. *Recreations:* painting, gardening. *Address:* La Geneste, Rose Hill, Burnham, Bucks SL1 8LW.

WALLACE, family name of **Barons Wallace of Campsle** and **Wallace of Coslany.**

WALLACE OF CAMPSIE, Baron *cr* 1974 (Life Peer), of Newlands, Glasgow; **George Wallace,** JP; DL; Life President, Wallace, Cameron (Holdings) Ltd, since 1981 (President, 1977-81); Director, Smith & Nephew Associated Companies Ltd, 1973-77; *b* 13 Feb. 1915; *s* of John Wallace and Mary Pollock; *m* 1977, Irene Alice Langdon Phipps, *er d* of Ernest Phipps, Glasgow. *Educ:* Queen's Park Secondary Sch., Glasgow; Glasgow Univ. Estd Wallace, Cameron & Co. Ltd, 1948, Chm., 1950-77. Solicitor before the Supreme Courts, 1950-; Hon. Sheriff at Hamilton, 1971-. Chm., E Kilbride and Stonehouse Develt Corp., 1969-75. Pres., Glasgow Chamber of Commerce, 1974-76; Vice-Pres., Scottish Assoc. of Youth Clubs, 1971-; Chm., Adv. Bd (Strathclyde) Salvation Army, 1972-; Mem. Court, Univ. of Strathclyde, 1973-74; Hon. Pres., Town and Country Planning Assoc. (Scottish Sect.), 1969-; Chm., Scottish Exec. Cttee, Brit. Heart Foundn, 1973-76; Chm., Britannia Cttee, British Sailors' Soc., 1967-77; Vice-Chm., Scottish Retirement Council, 1975-. FRSA 1970; FInstM 1968; MBIM 1969. JP 1968, DL 1971, Glasgow. KStJ 1976. *Recreation:* reading. *Address:* 14 Fernleigh Road, Newlands, Glasgow G43 2UE. *T:* 041-637 3337. *Clubs:* Caledonian; Royal Scottish Automobile (Glasgow).

WALLACE OF COSLANY, Baron *cr* 1974 (Life Peer), of Coslany in the City of Norwich; **George Douglas Wallace;** Opposition Spokesman and Whip, House of Lords, since 1979; *b* 18 April 1906; *e s* of late George Wallace, Cheltenham Spa, Gloucestershire; *m* 1932, Vera Randall, Guildford, Surrey; one *s* one *d. Educ:* Central School, Cheltenham Spa. Mem. of Management Cttee, in early years, of YMCA at East Bristol and Guildford; Mem. Chislehurst-Sidcup UDC, 1937-46; has been Divisional Sec. and also Chm., Chislehurst Labour Party; also Chm. of Parks and Cemeteries Cttee of UDC, Schools Manager and Member of Chislehurst, Sidcup and Orpington Divisional Education Executive; Mem., Cray Valley and Sevenoaks Hosp. Management Cttee; Chm., House Cttee, Queen Mary's Hosp.; Vice-Chm., Greenwich and Bexley AHA, 1974-77. Joined Royal Air Force, reaching rank of Sergeant. Served in No 11 Group Fighter Command, 1941-45. MP (Lab) Chislehurst Div. of Kent, 1945-50; Junior Govt Whip, 1947-50; MP (Lab) Norwich North, Oct. 1964-Feb. 1974; PPS: to Lord President of the Council, Nov. 1964-65; to Sec. of State for Commonwealth Affairs, 1965; to Minister of State, Min. of Housing and Local Govt, 1967-68; Mem. Speaker's Panel of Chairmen, 1970-74; a Lord in Waiting (Govt Whip), 1977-79. Delegate to Council of Europe and WEU, 1975-77. Member: Commonwealth Parly Assoc.; Commonwealth War Graves Commn, 1970-; Kent CC, 1952-57. *Recreations:* interested in Youth Movements and social welfare schemes. *Address:* 44 Shuttle Close, Sidcup, Kent. *T:* 01-300 3634.

WALLACE, Albert Frederick, CBE 1963 (OBE 1955); DFC 1943; Controller of Manpower, Greater London Council, 1978-82; *b* 22 Aug. 1921; *s* of Major Frederick Wallace and Ada Wallace; *m* 1940, Evelyn M. White; one *s* one *d. Educ:* Roan School, Blackheath, SE3. MIPM, MBIM, MILGA. Regular Officer, Royal Air Force, 1939-69; retired in rank of Group Captain. Regional Advisory Officer, Local Authorities Management Services and Computer Cttee, 1969-71; Asst Clerk of the Council, Warwickshire CC, 1971-73; County Personnel Officer, W Midlands CC, 1973-78. *Recreations:* golf, bridge. *Address:* Earleydene, Chesterfield Road, Eastbourne BN20 7NT. *Club:* Royal Air Force.

WALLACE, Charles William, CVO 1975; HM Diplomatic Service; Ambassador to Peru, since 1979; *b* 19 Jan. 1926; *s* of Percival Francis and Julia Wallace; *m* 1957, Gloria Regina de Ros Ribas (*née* Sanz-Agero); two step *s. Educ:* privately and abroad. HM Foreign (later Diplomatic) Service, 1949; served: Asuncion; Barcelona; Bari; Bahrain; Tegucigalpa; Guatemala; Panama; Foreign Office; Baghdad; Buenos Aires; Montevideo; FO, later FCO, Asst Head of American Dept; Counsellor 1969; Rome and Milan; Mexico City; Ambassador, Paraguay, 1976-79. Order of Aztec Eagle, 1975. *Recreations:* sailing, fishing. *Address:* c/o Foreign and Commonwealth Office, SW1A 2AH. *Club:* Travellers'.

WALLACE, Col the Hon. Clarence, CBE 1946; CD; LLD; Lieutenant-Governor of British Columbia, Canada, 1950-55; *b* 22 June 1894; *s* of Alfred Wallace and Eliza E. Wallace (*née* Underhill), both of Vancouver, BC; *m* 1916, Charlotte Hazel (*d* 1974), *d* of Edward Chapman, Vancouver, BC; two *s* (and one *s* killed on active service, RCAF, 1942; one *s* died 1956); *m* 1975, Hilda Ernestine McLennan. *Educ:* St Andrews Coll., Toronto, Ontario. Served overseas as Private, 5th Bn, 1914-16; Hon. Col BC Regt (Duke of Connaught's Own Rifles), 13th Armd Regt. Director of companies. KStJ 1951. *Recreations:* shooting, fishing. *Address:* Plaza del Mar, 1575 Beach Avenue, Vancouver, BC V6G 1Y5, Canada. *T:* 682-2300. *Clubs:* Vancouver, Royal Vancouver Yacht, Capilano Golf (Vancouver); Union (Victoria).

WALLACE, David Mitchell, CBE 1978 (OBE 1942); MS, FRCS; Professor of Urology, Riyadh Medical College, Saudi Arabia, 1974-78; *b* 8 May 1913; *s* of F. David Wallace and M. I. F. Wallace; *m* 1940, Noel Wilson; one *s* three *d. Educ:* Mill Hill; University Coll., London, BSc 1934; MB, BS 1938; FRCS 1939; MS 1948. Served War of 1939-45, Wing Comdr, RAF (despatches). Hunterian Prof., Royal Coll. of Surgeons, London, 1956, 1978. Formerly: Surgeon, St Peter's Hospital; Urologist, Royal Marsden Hospital, Chelsea Hospital for Women, and Manor House Hospitals; Lecturer, Institute of Urology; Adviser on Cancer to WHO. Mem., Amer. Radium Soc., 1968. *Publications:* Tumours of the Bladder, 1957; contrib. to Cancer, British Jl of Urology, Proc. Royal Soc. Med. *Recreations:* cine photography, pistol shooting. *Address:* 45 Fort Picklecombe, Tor Point, Cornwall PL10 1JB.

WALLACE, Doreen, (Mrs D. E. A. Rash), MA; novelist; *b* 18 June 1897; *d* of R. B. Agnew Wallace and Mary Elizabeth Peebles; *m* 1922, Rowland H. Rash (*d* 1977), Wortham, Suffolk; one *s* two *d. Educ:* Malvern Girls' College; Somerville College, Oxford. Honours in English 1919; taught English in a grammar school for three years, then married; first novel published, 1931. *Publications:* -Esques (with E. F. A. Geach), 1918; A Little Learning; The Gentle Heart; The Portion of the Levites; Creatures of an Hour; Even Such is Time; Barnham Rectory, 1934; Latter Howe, 1935; So Long to Learn 1936; Going to the Sea, 1936; Old Father Antic, 1937; The Faithful Compass, 1937; The Time of Wild Roses, 1938; A Handful of Silver, 1939; East Anglia, 1939; The Spring Returns, 1940; English Lakeland, 1941; Green Acres, 1941; Land from the Waters, 1944; Carlotta Green, 1944; The Noble Savage, 1945; Billy Potter, 1946; Willow Farm, 1948; How Little We Know, 1949; Only One Life, 1950; (non-fiction) In a Green Shade, 1950; Norfolk (with R. Bagnall-Oakeley), 1951; Root of Evil, 1952; Sons of Gentlemen, 1953; The Younger Son, 1954; Daughters, 1955; The Interloper, 1956; The Money Field, 1957; Forty Years on, 1958; Richard and Lucy, 1959; Mayland Hall, 1960; Lindsay Langton and Wives, 1961; Woman with a Mirror, 1963; The Mill Pond, 1966; Ashbury People, 1968; The Turtle, 1969; Elegy, 1970; An Earthly Paradise, 1971; A Thinking Reed, 1973; Changes and Chances, 1975; Landscape with Figures, 1976. *Recreations:* painting, gardening. *Address:* 2 Manor Gardens, Diss, Norfolk.

WALLACE, (Dorothy) Jacqueline H.; *see* Hope-Wallace.

WALLACE, Sir Gordon, Kt 1968; President, Court of Appeal, New South Wales, 1966-70; Acting Chief Justice of New South Wales, Oct. 1964-Feb. 1969; *b* 22 Jan. 1900; *s* of A. C. Isaacs, Sydney; *m* 1927, Marjorie (*d* 1980), *d* of A. E. Mullins, Chepstow, Mon.; one *s* one *d. Educ:* Sydney High School; RMC Duntroon; Sydney University. Lt, Australian Staff Corps; AMF and AIF, 1939-44 (Col). KC 1940. Judge of Supreme Court, NSW, 1960-70. Pres., NSW Bar Assoc., 1957-58; Vice-Pres., Australian Law Council, 1957; Pres., Internat. Law Assoc., Aust. Br., 1959-65. Mem., Commonwealth Commn of Enquiry into Income Tax, 1952-53. Chm., Royal Commn on Great Barrier Reef Petroleum Drilling, 1970-74. *Publications:* (jtly with Sir Percy Spender) Company Law, 1937; (jtly with J. McI. Young, QC) Australian Company Law, 1965. *Recreations:* bowls, music. *Address:* 6 Lynwood Avenue, Killara, NSW 2071, Australia. *T:* 498 1818. *Clubs:* University, Pioneers (Sydney); Elanora Country.

WALLACE, Ian Alexander; JP; Headmaster, Canford School, 1961-76; *b* 5 Oct. 1917; *s* of late Very Rev. A. R. Wallace and Winifred, *d* of late Rev. H. C. Sturges; *m* 1947, Janet Glossop; two *s* two *d. Educ:* Clifton; Corpus Christi College, Cambridge (open scholar). Classical Tripos, Part I, 1st Cl.; Theological Tripos Part I, 2nd Cl. Div. One. Served War of 1939-45, Mountain Artillery, NW Frontier, India, 1941; School of Artillery, India, 1942-43; Arakan, 1944; Mandalay, 1945 (despatches). Rossall School: Assistant Master, 1946; Housemaster, 1951-61. SW Regional Sec., Independent Schools Careers Organisation, 1976-. Governor: Portsmouth Grammar Sch., 1977-; King's Sch., Bruton, 1977-. JP Poole Borough, 1966. *Address:* Steeple Close, Hindon, Salisbury, Wilts.

WALLACE, Ian Bryce; Hon. RAM; Hon. RCM; singer, actor and broadcaster; *b* London, 10 July 1919; *o s* of late Sir John Wallace, Kirkcaldy, Fife (one-time MP for Dunfermline), and of Mary Bryce Wallace (*née* Temple), Glasgow; *m* 1948, Patricia Gordon Black, Edenwood, Cupar, Fife; one *s* one *d. Educ:* Charterhouse; Trinity Hall, Cambridge (MA). Served War of 1939-45, (invalided from) RA, 1944. London stage debut in The Forrigan Reel, Sadler's Wells, 1945. Opera debut, as Schaunard, in La Bohème, with New London Opera Co., Cambridge Theatre, London, 1946. Sang principal roles for NLOC, 1946-49, incl. Dr Bartolo in Il Barbiere di Siviglia. Glyndebourne debut, Masetto, Don Giovanni, Edin. Fest., 1948. Regular appearances as principal *buffo* for Glyndebourne, both in Sussex and at Edin. Fest., 1948-61, incl. perfs as Don Magnifico in La Cenerentola, at Berlin Festwoche, 1954. Italian debut: Masetto, Don Giovanni, at Parma, 1950; also Don Magnifico, La Cenerentola, Rome, 1955, Dr Bartolo, Il Barbiere di Siviglia, Venice, 1956, and Bregenz Fest., 1964-65. Regular appearances for Scottish Opera, 1965-, incl. Leporello in Don Giovanni, Pistola in Falstaff, Duke of Plaza Toro in The Gondoliers. Don Pasquale, Welsh Nat. Opera, 1967, Dr Dulcamara, L'Elisir d'Amore, Glyndebourne Touring Opera, 1968. Devised, wrote and presented three series of adult education programmes on opera, entitled Singing For Your Supper, for Scottish Television (ITV), 1967-70. Recordings include: Gilbert and Sullivan Operas with Sir Malcolm Sargent, and humorous songs by Flanders and Swann. Theatrical career includes: a Royal Command Variety Perf., London Palladium, 1952; Cesar in Fanny, Theatre Royal, Drury Lane, 1956; 4 to the Bar, Criterion, 1960; Toad in Toad of Toad Hall, Queen's, 1964. Regular broadcaster, 1944-: radio and TV, as singer, actor and compere: a regular panellist on radio musical quiz game, My Music. Principal concert activity, An Evening With Ian Wallace. Pres., Inc. Soc. of Musicians, 1979-80. *Publications:* Promise Me You'll Sing Mud (autobiog.), 1975; Nothing Quite Like It (autobiog.), 1982. *Recreations:* golf, elementary sailing, photography; singing a song about a hippopotamus to children of all ages. *Address:* 18 Denewood Road, Highgate, N6 4AJ. *T:* 01-340 5802. *Clubs:* Garrick, MCC; Stage Golfing Society.

WALLACE, Sir Ian (James), Kt 1982; CBE 1971 (OBE 1942); Chairman, SNR (Bearings) UK Ltd; *b* 25 Feb. 1916; *s* of John Madder Wallace, CBE; *m* 1942, Catherine Frost Mitchell, *e d* of Cleveland S. Mitchell; one *s* one *d*. *Educ:* Uppingham Sch.; Jesus Coll., Cambridge (BA). Underwriting at Lloyd's, 1935-39. War Service, Fleet Air Arm: Cmdr (A) RNVR, 1939-46. Harry Ferguson Ltd from 1947: Dir 1950; later Massey Ferguson Ltd, Dir Holdings Board until 1970. Chm., Coventry Cons. Assoc., 1968- (Treas., 1956-68); Chm., W Midlands Cons. Council, 1967-70 (Treas., 1962-67); Pres., W Midlands Area Cons. Council. Member: Severn-Trent Water Authy; W Midlands Econ. Planning Council, 1965-75; Vice-Chm., Midland Regional Council, CBI, 1964, Chm., 1967-69; Pres., Coventry Chamber of Commerce, 1972-74. *Recreations:* flying, golf, shooting (rifle and game). *Address:* Little House, 156 High Street, Broadway, Worcs WR12 7AJ. *T:* Broadway 852414. *Clubs:* Carlton, North London Rifle.

WALLACE, Ian Norman Duncan, QC 1973; *b* 21 April 1922; *s* of late Duncan Gardner Wallace, HBM Crown Advocate in Egypt, Paymaster-Comdr RNR and Eileen Agnes Wallace. *Educ:* Loretto; Oriel Coll., Oxford (MA). Served War of 1939-45: Ordinary Seaman RN, 1940; Lieut RNVR, 1941-46. Called to Bar, Middle Temple, 1948; Western Circuit, 1949. Vis. Scholar, Berkeley Univ., Calif, 1977-82. *Publications:* (ed) Hudson on Building and Civil Engineering Contracts, 8th edn 1959, 9th edn 1965 and 10th edn 1970; Building and Civil Engineering Standard Forms, 1969; Further Building and Engineering Standard Forms, 1973; The International Civil Engineering Contract, 1974; The ICE Conditions (5th edn), 1978; contrib. Law Qly Review, Jl of Internat. Law and Commerce. *Recreations:* keeping fit, foreign travel. *Address:* 53 Holland Park, W11 3RS. *T:* 01-727 7640. *Clubs:* Lansdowne, Hurlingham.

WALLACE, Irving; free-lance author; *b* 19 March 1916; *s* of Alexander Wallace and Bessie (*née* Liss); *m* 1941, Sylvia Kahn Wallace; one *s* one *d*. *Educ:* Kenosha (Wisc.) Central High Sch.; Williams Inst., Berkeley, Calif.; Los Angeles City College. Served USAAF and US Army Signal Corps, 1942-46. Magazine writer, Saturday Evening Post, Reader's Digest, Collier's, etc., 1931-54; film scenarist, 1955-58. Exploration: Honduras jungles, Wisconsin Collegiate Expedn, 1934-35. Member: PEN; Soc. of Authors; Authors League of America. Supreme Award of Merit, George Washington Carver Memorial Inst., Washington, DC, 1964; Commonwealth Club of Calif. Lit. Award for 1964; Nat. Bestsellers Inst. Paperback of the Year Award, 1965; Popular Culture Assoc. Award, 1974. *Publications:* The Fabulous Originals, 1955; The Square Pegs, 1957; The Fabulous Showman, 1959; The Sins of Philip Fleming, 1959; The Chapman Report, 1960; The Twenty-Seventh Wife, 1961; The Prize, 1962; The Three Sirens, 1963; The Man, 1964; The Sunday Gentleman, 1965; The Plot, 1967; The Writing of One Novel, 1968; The Seven Minutes, 1969; The Nympho and Other Maniacs, 1971; The Word, 1972; The Fan Club, 1974; The People's Almanac, 1975; The R Document, 1976; The Book of Lists, 1977; The Two, 1978; The People's Almanac 2, 1978; The Pigeon Project, 1979; The Book of Lists 2, 1980; The Second Lady, 1980; The Book of Predictions, 1981; The Intimate Sex Lives of Famous People, 1981; The People's Almanac 3, 1981; The Almighty, 1982; contribs to Collier's Encyclopædia, American Oxford Encyclopædia, Encyclopædia Britannica. *Relevant publication:* Irving Wallace: a writer's profile, by John Leverance, 1974. *Recreations:* tennis and table tennis, hiking, billiards, travel abroad, collecting autographs, French Impressionist art, canes. *Address:* PO Box 49328, Los Angeles, Calif 90049, USA.

WALLACE, Lawrence James, OC 1972; Deputy Minister to the Premier of British Columbia, since 1980; *b* Victoria, BC, Canada, 24 April 1913; *s* of John Wallace and Mary Wallace (*née* Parker); *m* 1942, Lois Leeming; three *d*. *Educ:* Univ. of British Columbia (BA); Univ. of Washington, USA (MEd). Served War, Lt-Comdr, Royal Canadian Navy Voluntary Reserve, 1941-45. Joined British Columbia Govt, as Dir of Community Programmes and Adult Educn, 1953; Dep. Provincial Sec., 1959-77, Dep. to Premier, 1969-72; Agent-General for British Columbia in UK and Europe, 1977-80. General Chairman: four centennial celebrations, marking founding of Crown Colony of British Columbia in 1858, union of Crown Colonies of Vancouver Is. and British Columbia, 1866, Canadian Confedn, 1867, and joining into confedn by British Columbia in 1871. Past Chm., Inter-Provincial Lottery Corp.; Queen Elizabeth II Schol. Cttee, and Nancy Green Schol. Cttee; Hon. Trustee, British Columbia Sports Hall of Fame. Director: Duke of Edinburgh Awards Cttee; BC Forest Museum; Adv. Bd, Salvation Army; Canadian Council of Christians and Jews. Named British Columbia Man of the Year, 1958, and Greater Vancouver Man of the Year, 1967; Canadian Centennial Medal, 1967; Comdr Brother, OStJ, 1969; City of Victoria Citizenship Award, 1971; Queen's Jubilee Medal, 1977. Freeman of City of London, 1978. Hon. LLD, Univ. of British Columbia, 1978. Hon. Member: BC High Sch. Basketball Assoc.; BC Recreation Assoc. Hon. Chief: Alberni, Gilford and Southern Vancouver Is Indian Bands. *Recreations:* gardening, community activities.

Address: Parliament Buildings, Victoria, British Columbia V8V 4R3, Canada.

WALLACE, Reginald James, CMG 1979; OBE 1961; Financial and Development Secretary, Gibraltar, since 1979; *b* 16 Aug. 1919; *s* of James Wallace and Doris (*née* Welch); *m* 1st, 1943, Doris Barbara Brown, MD, FRCS, MRCOG (decd); one *d*; 2nd, 1973, Maureen Coady. *Educ:* John Gulson Sch., Coventry; Tatterford Sch., Norfolk; Leeds Univ. (BA); Queen's Coll., Oxford. Served War, 1939-46, 7th Rajput Regt, Indian Army (Major). Gold Coast/Ghana Admin. Service, 1947-58; Sen. District Comr, 1955; Asst Chief Regional Officer, Northern Region, 1957; Regional Sec., 1958; British Somaliland, 1958-60; Financial Sec.; War Office, 1961-66; HM Treasury, 1966-78; seconded to Solomon Is, as Financial Sec. (later Financial Adviser), 1973-76; seconded, as British Mem., Anglo/French Mission on Admin. Reform in the Condominium of the New Hebrides, 1977; Governor of Gilbert Is, 1978 to Independence, July 1979. *Recreations:* walking, gardening, music. *Address:* 6 Mount Road, Gibraltar. *Club:* Royal Commonwealth Society.

WALLACE, Robert, CBE 1970; BL; JP; Chairman, Highland Health Board, 1973-81; *b* 20 May 1911; *s* of late John Wallace, Glespin, Lanarkshire, and late Elizabeth Brydson; *m* 1940, Jane Maxwell, *d* of late John Smith Rankin, Waulkmill, Thornhill, Dumfriesshire and late Jane Maxwell; no *c*. *Educ:* Sanquhar Sch.; Glasgow University. Solicitor 1932; BL (Dist.) 1933. Private practice, 1932-40; Depute Town Clerk, Ayr Burgh, 1940-44; Civil Defence Controller, Ayr Burgh, 1941-44; Depute County Clerk and Treas., Co. Inverness, 1944-48; County Clerk, Treasurer and Collector of the County of Inverness, 1948-73; Temp. Sheriff, Grampian, Highland and Islands, 1976-. Hon. Sheriff at Inverness, 1967-. JP Co. Inverness, 1951-. *Recreations:* fishing, gardening. *Address:* Eildon, 29 Old Edinburgh Road, Inverness IV2 3HJ. *T:* Inverness 31969. *Club:* Caledonian (Edinburgh).

WALLACE, Walter Ian James, CMG 1957; OBE 1943; retired; *b* 18 Dec. 1905; *e s* of late David Wallace, Sandgate, Kent; *m* 1940, Olive Mary (*d* 1973), 4th *d* of late Col Charles William Spriggs, Southsea; no *c*. *Educ:* Bedford Modern School; St Catharine's College, Cambridge. Entered ICS 1928, posted to Burma; Dep. Commissioner, 1933; Settlement Officer, 1934-38; Dep. Commissioner, 1939-42; Defence Secretary, 1942-44; Military Administration of Burma (Col and Dep. Director Civil Affairs), 1944-45 (despatches); Commissioner, 1946; Chief Secretary, 1946-47. Joined Colonial Office, 1947, Asst Sec., 1949-62; Asst Under-Sec. of State, 1962-66, retired. *Publication:* Revision Settlement Operations in the Minbu District of Upper Burma, 1939. *Recreation:* local history. *Address:* 61 Windfield, Leatherhead, Surrey. *T:* Leatherhead 74022. *Club:* East India, Devonshire, Sports and Public Schools.

WALLACE, Walter Wilkinson, CVO 1977; CBE 1973 (OBE 1964); DSC 1944; Foreign and Commonwealth Office; *b* 23 Sept. 1923; *s* of late Walter Wallace and of Helen Wallace (*née* Douglas); *m* 1955, Susan Blanche, *d* of Brig. F. W. B. Parry, CBE; one *s* one *d*. *Educ:* George Heriot's, Edinburgh. Served War, Royal Marines, 1942-46 (Captain). Joined Colonial Service, 1946; Asst Dist Comr, Sierra Leone, 1948; Dist Comr, 1954; seconded to Colonial Office, 1955-57; Sen. Dist Comr, 1961; Provincial Comr, 1961; Develt Sec., 1962-64; Estabt Sec., Bahamas, 1964-67; Sec. to Cabinet, Bermuda, 1968-73; HM Commissioner, Anguilla, 1973; Governor, British Virgin Islands, 1974-78. *Recreation:* golf. *Address:* Becketts, Itchenor, Sussex. *T:* Birdham 512438; 20 Prince of Wales Terrace, W8. *T:* 01-937 7011. *Club:* Army and Navy.

WALLACE, William, CMG 1961; Assistant Comptroller of Patent Office and Industrial Property and Copyright Department, Department of Trade and Industry (formerly Board of Trade (Patent Office)), 1954-73, retired; *b* 8 July 1911; *s* of A. S. Wallace, Wemyss Bay, Renfrewshire; *m* 1940, Sheila, *d* of Sydney Hopper, Wallington, Surrey; one *s* one *d*. *Educ:* Mill Hill School; St Edmund Hall, Oxford. Barrister, Inner Temple, 1936-39. Served War of 1939-45, Royal Artillery with final rank of Major. Board of Trade legal staff, 1945-54. UK Delegate, Internat. Confs on Copyright and Patents; Chm. Intergovernmental Cttee on Rights of Performers, Record Makers and Broadcasting Orgns, 1967-69; Actg Chairman: Intergovernmental Copyright Cttee, 1970; Exec. Cttee, Berne Copyright Union, 1970; Vice-Chm., Whitford Cttee on Copyright and Designs, 1974. Jean Geiringer Meml Lectr, USA, 1971. *Address:* Weavers, Capel, Surrey. *T:* Dorking 711205.

WALLACE-HADRILL, Prof. John Michael, CBE 1982; DLitt; FBA 1969; Chichele Professor of Modern History, and Fellow of All Souls College, Oxford, since 1974; *b* 29 Sept. 1916; *e s* of late Frederic and Tamzin Norah Wallace-Hadrill, Bromsgrove, Worcs; *m* 1950, Anne, *e d* of late Neville Wakefield, DSO, and of Violet Wakefield (*née* Dewar); two *s*. *Educ:* Cheltenham College; Corpus Christi College, Oxford (Scholar, and Fellow). Lothian Prize, 1938. Served War of 1939-45, (latterly Major, Gen. Staff, attached to a dept of Foreign Office). Fellow and Tutor, 1947-55, Sen. Res. Fellow, 1961-74, Sub-Warden, 1964-66, Merton Coll., Oxford; Professor of Mediæval History, University of Manchester, 1955-61; Editor, English Historical Review, 1965-74. Lectures: Ford's, Oxford, 1969-70; Birkbeck, Cambridge, 1974; Stenton, Reading, 1974; Prothero, RHistS, 1974; Raleigh, British Acad., 1978; Kates, Stanford, 1979. Delegate, Oxford Univ. Press, 1971-82. Vice-Pres., Royal Hist. Soc., 1973-76; Publications Sec., British Academy, 1978-81. Vis. Distinguished Prof., Berkeley, Univ. of

California, 1979. Hon. Fellow, Merton Coll., Oxford, 1974. *Publications:* The Barbarian West, 400–1000, 1952; (with J. McManners) France, Government and Society, 1957; The Chronicle of Fredegar, 1960; The Long-Haired Kings, 1962; Early Germanic Kingship, 1971; Early Medieval History, 1976; (ed with R. H. C. Davis) The Writing of History in the Middle Ages, 1981. *Address:* All Souls College, Oxford. *Club:* Athenæum.

WALLEN, Ella Kathleen, MA (Oxon); Headmistress, St Mary's School, Wantage, 1977–80; *b* 15 Feb. 1914. *Educ:* Camden School for Girls; St Hugh's College, Oxford. History Mistress, Queen Victoria High School, Stockton-on-Tees, 1937–41; Senior History Mistress, High School for Girls, Gloucester, 1942–59; Headmistress: Queen Victoria High School, Stockton-on Tees, 1959–65; Bedford High Sch., 1965–76. *Address:* 15 Lynn Close, Marston Road, Oxford OX3 0JH.

WALLER, Gary Peter Anthony; MP (C) Brighouse and Spenborough, since 1979; *b* 24 June 1945; *s* of late John Waller and of Elizabeth Waller. *Educ:* Rugby Sch.; Univ. of Lancaster (BA Hons). Contested: Bor. Council Elections, Kensington, 1971 and 1974; GLC Elections, Leyton, 1973; Parly Election, Rother Valley, Feb. and Oct. 1974. Chairman: Lancaster Univ. Conservative Assoc., 1965; Spen Valley Civic Soc., 1978–80; Vice-Chm., Nat. Assoc. of Cons. Graduates, 1970–73 and 1976–77. Member: Exec. Cttee, Cons. Nat. Union, 1976–77; Management Cttee, Bradford and Dist Housing Assoc., 1976–. Exec. Sec., Wider Share Ownership Council, 1973–76; Secretary: Cons. Parly Sport and Recreation Cttee, 1979–81; Cons. Yorkshire Members, 1979–; All Party Wool Textile Gp, 1979–; Member: H of C Select Cttee on Transport, 1979–82; Jt Cttee on Consolidation Bills, 1982–; Treasurer, Parly Information Technology Cttee, 1981–; PPS to Sec. of State for Transport, 1982–. Pres., Brighouse Citizens Advice Bureau, 1979–; Vice-President: Newham S Cons. Assoc., 1979– (Chm., 1971–74); Bethnal Green and Bow Cons. Assoc., 1982–. Governor: George Green's Sch., Tower Hamlets, 1968–70; Isaac Newton Sch., N Kensington, 1971–73; Manager, Moorend C of E Primary Sch., Cleckheaton, 1977–80. *Recreations:* music, poetry, squash, football. *Address:* House of Commons, SW1A 0AA. *T:* 01-219 4010. *Clubs:* various local Conservative and Working Men's.

WALLER, George Mark, QC 1979; *b* 13 Oct. 1940; *s* of Rt Hon. Sir George Waller, qv; *m* 1967, Rachel Elizabeth, *d* of His Honour Judge Beaumont, qv; three *s*. *Educ:* Oundle Sch.; Durham Univ. (LLB). Called to the Bar, Gray's Inn, 1964. *Recreations:* tennis, golf. *Address:* Little Barfield, Chapel Row, Bucklebury, Berks. *T:* Woolhampton 2172; 2 Verulam Buildings, Gray's Inn, WC1. *T:* 01-242 9393. *Clubs:* Garrick, MCC.

WALLER, Rt. Hon. Sir George (Stanley), Kt 1965; OBE 1945; PC 1976; **Rt. Hon. Lord Justice Waller;** a Lord Justice of Appeal, since 1976; *b* 3 Aug. 1911; *s* of late James Stanley and late Ann Waller; *m* 1936, Elizabeth Margery, *d* of 1st Baron Hacking; two *s* one *d*. *Educ:* Oundle; Queens' Coll., Cambridge (Hon. Fellow 1974). Called to the Bar, Gray's Inn, 1934, Bencher, 1961, Treasurer, 1978. RAFO, 1931–36; served War of 1939–45, in RAFVR, Coastal Command; 502 Sqdn, 1940–41; Wing Comdr, 1943 (despatches). Chm., Northern Dist Valuation Bd, 1948–65; QC 1954; Recorder of Doncaster, 1953–54, of Sunderland, 1954–55, of Bradford, 1955–57, of Sheffield, 1957–61, and of Leeds, 1961–65; a Judge of the High Court, Queen's Bench Div., 1965–76; Presiding Judge, NE Circuit, 1973–76. Solicitor-General of the County Palatine of Durham, 1957–61; Attorney-General of the County Palatine of Durham, 1961–65; Member: Criminal Injuries Compensation Board, 1964–65; General Council of the Bar, 1958–62 and 1963–65; Parole Bd, 1969–72 (Vice-Chm., 1971–72); Adv. Council on the Penal System, 1970–73 and 1974–78; Criminal Law Revision Cttee, 1977–; Chm., Policy Adv. Cttee on Sexual Offences, 1977–. Pres., Inns of Court and Bar, 1979–80. *Address:* Hatchway, Hatch Lane, Kingsley Green, Haslemere, Surrey GU27 3LJ. *T:* Haslemere 4629. *Clubs:* Army and Navy; Hawks (Cambridge).
See also G. M. Waller.

WALLER, Sir (John) Keith, Kt 1968; CBE 1961 (OBE 1957); Secretary, Department of Foreign Affairs, Canberra, 1970–74, retired; *b* 19 Feb. 1914; *s* of late A. J. Waller, Melbourne; *m* 1943, Alison Irwin Dent; two *d. Educ:* Scotch Coll., Melbourne; Melbourne Univ. Entered Dept of External Affairs, Australia, 1936; Private Sec. to Rt Hon. W. M. Hughes, 1937–40; Second Sec., Australian Legation, Chungking, 1941; Sec.-Gen., Australian Delegn, San Francisco Conf., 1945; First Sec., Australian Legation, Rio de Janeiro, 1945; Chargé d'Affaires, 1946; First Sec., Washington, 1947; Consul-Gen., Manila, 1948; Officer-in-Charge, Political Intelligence Div., Canberra, 1950; External Affairs Officer, London, 1951; Asst Sec., Dept of External Affairs, Canberra, 1953–57; Ambassador to Thailand, 1957–60; Ambassador to USSR, 1960–62; First Asst Sec., Dept of External Affairs, 1963–64; Ambassador to US, 1964–70. Member: Australian Council for the Arts, 1973; Interim Film Board, 1974. Chm., Radio Australia Inquiry, 1975. *Address:* 17 Canterbury Crescent, Deakin, ACT 2600, Australia. *Club:* Commonwealth (Canberra).

WALLER, Sir John Stanier, 7th Bt, *cr* 1815; author, poet, and journalist; *b* 27 July 1917; *s* of Capt. Stanier Edmund William Waller (*d* 1923), and of Alice Amy (who *m* 2nd, 1940, Gerald H. Holiday), *d* of J. W. Harris, Oxford; *S kinsman* Sir Edmund Waller, 6th Bt, 1954; *m* 1974, Anne Eileen Mileham. *Educ:* Weymouth Coll.; Worcester Coll., Oxford (Exhibnr in History, 1936, BA in Eng. Lang. and Lit., 1939, OU DipEd (Teaching), 1940). Founder-Editor of Quarterly, Kingdom Come, first new literary magazine of war, 1939–41. Served 1940–46 with RASC (in Middle East, 1941–46); Adjt RASC,

HQ, Cairo Area; Capt. 1942; Features Editor, Brit. Min. of Inf., Middle East, 1943–45; Chief Press Officer, Brit. Embassy, Bagdad, 1945; News and Features Editor, MIME, Cairo, 1945–46. Dramatic Critic Cairo Weekly, The Sphinx, 1943–46; Founder-Mem. Salamander Soc. of Poets, Cairo, 1942; lectured in Pantheon Theatre, Athens, 1945; Greenwood Award for Poetry, 1947; Keats Prize, 1974; FRSL 1948; Lectr and Tutor in English and Eng. Lit. at Carlisle and Gregson (Jimmy's), Ltd, 1953–54; Asst Master, London Nautical Sch., May–June 1954; Information Officer, Overseas Press Services Div., Central Office of Information, 1954–59. Director: Literature Ltd, 1940–42; Richard Congreve Ltd, 1948–50; Export Trade Ships Ltd, 1956; Bristol Stone and Concrete Ltd, 1974; Mercantile Land and Marine Ltd, 1979. *Publications:* The Confessions of Peter Pan, 1941; Fortunate Hamlet, 1941; Spring Legend, 1942; The Merry Ghosts, 1946; Middle East Anthology (Editor), 1946; Crusade, 1946; The Kiss of Stars, 1948; The Collected Poems of Keith Douglas (Editor), 1951 and 1966; Shaggy Dog, 1953; Alamein to Zem Zem by Keith Douglas (Editor), 1966; Goldenhair and the Two Black Hawks, 1971; Return to Oasis (co-editor), 1980; contrib. to numerous anthologies and periodicals at home and abroad. *Recreations:* portrait photography, teaching. *Heir:* none. *Address:* 21 Lyndhurst Road, Hove, Sussex BN3 6FA. *T:* Brighton 734836. *Club:* Press.

WALLER, Rt. Rev. John Stevens; *see* Stafford, Bishop Suffragan of.

WALLER, Sir Keith; *see* Waller, Sir J. K.

WALLER, Sir Robert William, 9th Bt, *cr* 1780, of Newport, Co. Tipperary; employed by the General Electric Co. of America as an Industrial Engineer, since 1957; *b* 16 June 1934; *s* of Sir Roland Edgar Waller, 8th Bt, and Helen Madeline, *d* of Joseph Radl, Matawan, New Jersey, USA; *S* father 1958; is a citizen of the United States; *m* 1960 (marr. diss.); two *s* one *d* (and one *s* decd). *Educ:* St Peter's Prep. Sch.; Newark Coll. of Engrg; Fairleigh Dickinson University. *Heir: s* John Michael Waller, *b* 14 May 1962. *Address:* 5 Lookout Terrace, Lynnfield, Mass 01940, USA.

WALLER, Prof. Ross Douglas, CBE 1958 (MBE 1945); Director of Extra-Mural Studies, 1937–60, and Professor of Adult Education, 1949–66 (Professor Emeritus, 1966), Manchester University; *b* 21 Jan. 1899; *m* 1928, Isobel May Brown; three *s* one *d. Educ:* Manchester Central High School for Boys; Manchester University. Served European War, KOYLI, and NF, 1917–19. BA, 1920; MA 1921; post-graduate studies in Florence, 1921–22; Schoolmaster, 1922–24; Lecturer in English Literature, Manchester Univ., 1924–37. Chm. North-Western Dist, WEA, 1943–57; Pres., Educational Centres Association, 1948–65; OECD Consultant on Adult Educn in Sardinia, 1961–62. Cavaliere Ufficiale, Order of Merit, Italy, 1956. *Publications:* The Monks and the Giants, 1926; The Rossetti Family, 1932; Marlowe, Edward II (with H. B. Charlton), 1933; Learning to Live, 1947; Harold Pilkington Turner, 1953; Residential College, 1954; Design for Democracy (Introductory Essay), 1956. Articles in Adult Education, Highway, Times Educational Supplement, etc. *Recreations:* recorder playing, painting, and visiting Italy. *Address:* 61 Porchfield Square, St John's Gardens, Manchester M3 4FG. *T:* 061-832 7107.

WALLEY, Francis, CB 1978; consulting engineer; Consultant to the Ove Arup Partnership; Member, Standing Committee on Structural Safety, since 1977; *b* 30 Dec. 1918; *s* of late Reginald M. Walley and Maria M. Walley; *m* 1946, Margaret, *yr d* of late Rev. Thomas and Margaret J. Probert; two *d. Educ:* Cheltenham Grammar Sch.; Bristol Univ. MSc, PhD; FICE (Mem. Council, 1978–81); FIStructE (Vice-Pres., 1982–83; Hon. Treasurer, 1981; Hon. Sec., 1979–81). Entered Min. of Home Security as Engr, 1941; Min. of Works, 1945; Suptg Civil Engr, 1963; Dep. Dir of Building Develt, 1965; Dir of Estate Management Overseas, 1969; Dir of Post Office Services, 1971; Under-Sec., Dir of Civil Engineering Services, DoE, 1973–78. *Publications:* Prestressed Concrete Design and Construction, 1954; (with Dr S. C. C. Bate) A Guide to the Code of Practice CP 115, 1960; several papers to ICE and techn. jls. *Recreations:* gardening, furniture-making. *Address:* 13 Julien Road, Coulsdon, Surrey CR3 2DN. *T:* 01-660 3290.
See also Sir John Walley.

WALLEY, Sir John, KBE 1965; CB 1950; retired as Deputy Secretary, Ministry of Social Security, 1966 (Ministry of Pensions and National Insurance, 1958–66); *b* Barnstaple, Devon, 3 April 1906; *e s* of late R. M. Walley; *m* 1934, Elisabeth Mary, *e d* of late R. H. Pinhorn, OBE; two *s* two *d. Educ:* Hereford High Sch.; Hereford Cathedral Sch.; Merton Coll., Oxford; Postmaster, 1924–28; Hons Maths and Dip., Pol. and Econ. Sci. Ministry of Labour: Asst Principal, 1929; Sec., Cabinet Cttee on Unemployment, 1932; Principal, 1934; Asst Sec., Min. of Labour and National Service, 1941; Transf. Under-Sec., Min. of National Insurance, 1945; Chm., Dental Benefit Council, 1945–48. Chm., Hampstead Centre, National Trust, 1969–79, Pres., 1980–. *Publications:* Social Security–Another British Failure?, 1972; contribs to The Future of the Social Services, ed Robson and Crick, 1970; on Children's Allowances, in Family Poverty, ed David Bull, 1971; vol. in British Oral Archive of Political and Administrative History, 1980; articles in the press on Social Security matters. *Address:* 46 Rotherwick Road, NW11. *T:* 01-455 6528.
See also F. Walley.

WALLINGTON, Jeremy Francis; Chief Executive: Limehouse Productions Ltd, since 1982; Southern Pictures Ltd; Director of Programmes, Southern

Television Ltd, 1977–81; *b* 7 July 1935; *s* of Ernest Francis Wallington and Nell (*née* Howe); *m* 1955, Margaret Ivy Willment; three *s* one *d*. *Educ:* Royal Grammar Sch., High Wycombe, Bucks. Reporter on several Fleet Street newspapers, 1956–62; Managing Editor, Topic Magazine, 1962; Co-Founder of Insight, Sunday Times, 1963; Assistant Editor: Sunday Times, 1963–65; Daily Mail, 1965–67; Editor, Investigations Bureau, World in Action, Granada Television, 1967–68; Jt Editor, then Editor, World in Action, 1968–72; Head of Documentaries, Granada Television, 1972–77. *Publication:* (jtly) Scandal '63, 1963. *Recreation:* canal barges. *Address:* 6B Newell Street, E14. *T:* 01–987 8484. *Club:* British Academy of Film and Television Arts.

WALLIS, Captain Arthur Hammond, CBE 1952; RN (retired); *b* 16 Sept. 1903; *s* of late Harold T. Wallis; *m* 1940, Lucy Joyce (*d* 1974), *er d* of late Lt-Col L. E. Becher, DSO; one *s* one *d*. *Educ:* Wixenford; Osborne and Dartmouth. Entered Royal Navy as Cadet, 1917; specialised as Torpedo Officer, 1930; staff of Rear-Adm. Destroyers, 1936–38; Torpedo Officer, HMS Nelson, 1938–41; Comdr, 1941; i/c Torpedo Experimental Dept, HMS Vernon, 1941–43; Exec. Officer, HMS Illustrious, 1943–45; Captain, 1947; in command HM Underwater Detection Establishment at Portland, 1948–50; Sen. Naval Officer, Persian Gulf and in command HMS Wild Goose, 1950–51; Cdre, HMS Mauritius, 1951; UK Naval Delegate, Military Agency for Standardisation, NATO, 1952–53; Director of Under-water Weapons, Admiralty, 1953–56. Naval ADC to the Queen, 1956. Chief of Naval Information, Admiralty, 1957–64. *Recreations:* golf, gardening. *Address:* Compton's Barn, Woodstreet, near Guildford, Surrey. *T:* Worplesdon 235143. *Clubs:* Naval and Military; Worplesdon Golf.

WALLIS, Frederick Alfred John E.; *see* Emery-Wallis.

WALLIS, Col Hugh Macdonell, OC 1969; DSO 1919; OBE 1945; MC, VD, CD, KCLJ; *b* 7 Dec. 1893; *s* of John McCall Wallis, Peterborough, Ont, and Gertrude Thornton, *d* of Lt-Col Samuel Smith Macdonell, QC, LLD, DCL, Windsor, Ont; *m* 1st, 1935, Leslie (marr. diss., 1953), *d* of late Mr and Mrs K. K. Carson, London; 2nd 1969, Corinne de Boucherville (*d* 1981), *widow* of Hon. Jean Desy. *Educ:* Lakefield Preparatory Sch.; Toronto Univ. Enlisted 1st CEF, Sept. 1914; served France, Belgium, Germany, 1915–19; Bde Major 4th Can. Inf. Bde, 1918 (DSO, MC, despatches twice); Colonel Comdg The Black Watch, Royal Highlanders of Canada, then Permanent Active Militia, 1930; VD 1930; CD 1967; R of O, 1931; Hon. ADC to Earl of Bessborough, Gov.-Gen. of Canada, 1931–35; Active Service, Canadian Forces, 1940–45; Colonel Asst DAG Nat. Defence HQ (OBE); Hon. Lt-Col 3rd Bn The Black Watch of Canada, 1961–68. Chartered Accountant, with McDonald, Currie & Co., 1923. Past President: Canadian Citizenship Council, St Andrews Soc. of Montreal, Canadian Club of Montreal, Montreal Museum of Fine Arts. Man. Dir and Pres., Mount Royal Rice Mills Ltd, Montreal, 1924–53. Governor: Council for Canadian Unity; Lakefield College Sch.; Montreal General Hosp.; Montreal Children's Hosp. (Past Chm. of Exec.); l'Hôpital Marie Enfant; Chm., Adv. Bd, Canadian Centenary (1967) Council (past Chm. Org. and Exec. Cttees). Hon. Sponsor, Trent Univ., Ont., 1963; Associate, McGill Univ. and l'Univ. de Montréal. FRSA 1959. Kt Companion, Order of St Lazarus of Jerusalem. Outstanding Citizen Award, Montreal Citizenship Council, 1967. Canada Centennial Medal, 1967; Jubilee Medal, 1977. *Recreations:* travel, fine arts, Canadian books and history. *Address:* 131 Avenue de Breslay, Pointe Claire, PQ H9S 4M8, Canada. *Clubs:* Canadian, United Services (Montreal); Braeside Golf (Senneville).

WALLIS, Jeffrey Joseph; Managing Director, Eastoken, since 1981; *b* 25 Nov. 1923; *s* of Nathaniel and Rebecca Wallis; *m* 1948, Barbara Brickman; one *s* one *d*. *Educ:* Owen's; Coll. Aeronautical Engrg. Man. Dir, Wallis Fashion Group, 1948–80. Mem., Monopolies and Mergers Commn, 1981–. Formerly Member: CNAA; Clothing Export Council; NEDC (Textiles). Involved in art educn throughout career; various governorships. *Recreations:* motor racing, motor boating, industrial design. *Address:* 37 Avenue Close, NW8 6DA. *T:* 01-722 8665.

WALLIS, Peter Gordon; HM Diplomatic Service; Cabinet Office, since 1982; *b* 2 Aug. 1935; *s* of Arthur Gordon Wallis, DFC, BScEcon, and Winifred Florence Maud (*née* Dingle); *m* 1965, Delysia Elizabeth (*née* Leonard); three *s* one *d*. *Educ:* Taunton and Whitgift Schools; Pembroke Coll., Oxford (MA). Ministry of Labour and National Service, 1958–59; HM Customs and Excise, 1959–68 (Private Sec., 1961-64); HM Diplomatic Service, 1968; Tel Aviv, 1970; Nairobi, 1974; Counsellor (Econ. and Comm.), Ankara, 1977-81; RCDS, 1981. *Recreations:* reading, writing, music, children. *Address:* c/o Foreign and Commonwealth Office, SW1A 2AH.

WALLIS, Peter Ralph; Deputy Controller, Aircraft Weapons and Electronics, Ministry of Defence, since 1980; *b* 17 Aug. 1924; *s* of Leonard Francis Wallis and Molly McCulloch Wallis (*née* Jones); *m* 1949, Frances Jean Patricia Cowie; three *s* one *d*. *Educ:* University College Sch., Hampstead; Imperial Coll. of Science and Technology, London (BSc(Eng)). Henrici and Siemens Medals of the College, 1944. Joined Royal Naval Scientific Service 1944; work at Admty Signal and Radar Estab. till 1959, Admty Underwater Weapons Estab. till 1968; Asst Chief Scientific Advr (Research), MoD, 1968-71, Dir Gen. Research Weapons, 1971-75, Dir Gen. Guided Weapons and Electronics, 1975-78, Dir Gen. Research A (Electronics) and Dep. Chief Scientist (Navy), 1978-80. Marconi Award, IERE, 1964; ACGI, CEng, FIEE, FIMA. *Publications:* articles in Jl of IEE, IERE and Op. Res. Quarterly. *Recreations:* skiing, mountain walking, swimming, sailing, cycling, Gen. Sec.,

Hampstead Scientific Soc. *Address:* 22 Flask Walk, NW3 1HE. *Clubs:* Ski of GB; Eagle Ski.

WALLIS, Victor Harry; Assistant Under Secretary of State, Fire Department, Home Office, 1980-82; *b* 21 Dec. 1922; *s* of Harry Stewart Wallis, MBE, and Ada Elizabeth (*née* Jarratt); *m* 1948, Margaret Teresa (*née* Meadowcroft); one *s* three *d*. *Educ:* Wilson's Grammar School. Served Royal Scots and Indian Army (Major), 1941-47 (War, Burma and Defence medals); Territorial Army and TARO (Int. Corps), 1948-77. Entered Home Office, Immigration Service, 1947; Regional Officer, 1952; Policy Div., 1958; Chief Trng Officer, 1967; Establishments, 1972. Chm., various cttees, Fire Brigades Adv. Council, 1980-82. *Recreations:* philately, military history, painting. *Address:* 26 Lumley Road, Horley, Surrey RH6 7JL. *Club:* Civil Service.

WALLIS-JONES, Ewan Perrins; His Honour Judge Wallis-Jones; a Circuit Judge (formerly County Court Judge), since 1964; *b* 22 June 1913; *s* of late William James Wallis-Jones, MBE, and late Ethel Perrins Wallis-Jones; *m* 1940, Veronica Mary (*née* Fowler); one *s* two *d*. *Educ:* Mill Hill Sch.; University Coll. of Wales, Aberystwyth; Balliol Coll., Oxford. LLB Hons Wales, 1934; BA Oxon 1936; MA Oxon 1941. Qualified Solicitor, 1935; called to Bar, Gray's Inn, 1938. Chm., Carmarthenshire QS, 1966-71. ARPS. *Recreations:* music, reading and photography. *Address:* 25 Cotham Grove, Bristol BS6 6AN. *T:* Bristol 48908; 28 Quay Street, Carmarthen. *T:* Carmarthen 5106. *Club:* Royal Photographic Society.

WALLIS-KING, Maj.-Gen. Colin Sainthill, CBE 1975 (OBE 1971); retired; Director of Service Intelligence, 1977-80; *b* 13 Sept. 1926; *s* of late Lt-Col Frank King, DSO, OBE, 4th Hussars, and of Colline Ammabel, *d* of late Lt-Col C. G. H. St Hill; *m* 1962, Lisabeth, *d* of late Swan Swanstrøm, Oslo, Norway; two *d*. *Educ:* Stowe. Commissioned Coldstream Guards, 1945; Liaison Officer with Fleet Air Arm, 1954; Staff Coll., 1960; Regtl Adjutant, Coldstream Guards, 1961; seconded to Para. Regt, 1963; ACOS HQ Land Norway, 1965; Comdr 2nd Bn Coldstream Guards, 1969; Dep. Comdr 8 Inf. Brigade, 1972; Comdr 3 Inf. Brigade, 1973; BGS Intell., MoD, 1975. *Recreations:* equitation, sailing, music, cross-country skiing. *Address:* c/o Williams & Glyn's Bank, 19 Grosvenor Gardens, SW1. *Club:* Cavalry and Guards.

WALLOP, family name of **Earl of Portsmouth.**

WALLROCK, John; Chairman, Minet Holdings Ltd, since 1972; *b* 14 Nov. 1922; *s* of Samuel and Marie Kate Wallrock; *m* 1967, Audrey Louise Ariow; one *s* two *d*. *Educ:* Bradfield Coll., Berks. Cadet, Merchant Navy, 1939; Lieut RNR, 1943; Master Mariner, 1949; J. H. Minet & Co. Ltd, 1950, Dir, 1955-79, Chm., 1972-79; Underwriting Mem. of Lloyd's, 1951. Mem., Council of Management, White Ensign Assoc. Ltd, 1974-. FCIB, MNI. *Recreations:* yachting, shooting. *Address:* Cleeve Lodge, 42 Hyde Park Gate, SW7 5DU. *T:* 01-584 4476. *Clubs:* Boodle's; Royal London Yacht, Royal Southern Yacht, Lloyd's Yacht.

WALLS, Prof. Eldred Wright; Emeritus Professor of Anatomy in the University of London at Middlesex Hospital Medical School (Dean, Medical School, 1967-74); Hon. Consultant Anatomist, St Mark's Hospital; *b* 17 Aug. 1912; 2nd *s* of late J. T. Walls, Glasgow; *m* 1939, Jessie Vivien Mary Robb, MB, ChB, DPH, *o d* of late R. F. Robb and late M. T. Robb; one *s* one *d*. *Educ:* Hillhead High Sch.; Glasgow Univ. BSc, 1931; MB, ChB (Hons), 1934; MD (Hons), 1947, FRSE, FRCS, FRCSE; Struthers Medal and Prize, 1942. Demonstrator and Lectr in Anatomy, Glasgow Univ., 1935-41; Senior Lectr in Anatomy, University Coll. of S Wales and Monmouthshire, 1941-47; Reader in Anatomy, Middlesex Hospital Medical Sch. 1947-49, S. A. Courtauld Prof. of Anatomy, 1949-74; Lectr in Anatomy, Edinburgh Univ., 1975-82. Past President: Anatomical Soc. of GB and Ireland; Chartered Soc. of Physiotherapy. Lectures: Osler, Soc. of Apothecaries, 1967; Astor, Mddx Hosp., 1975; Gordon Taylor, RCS, 1976; Struthers, RCSE, 1978. *Publications:* (co-editor) Rest and Pain (by John Hilton) (6th edn), 1950; (co-author) Sir Charles Bell, His Life and Times, 1958; contrib. Blood-vascular and Lymphatic Systems, to Cunningham's Textbook Anat., 1981; contrib. to Journal of Anatomy, Lancet, etc. *Recreations:* golf and gardening. *Address:* Chesterhall, Ancrum, Jedburgh TD8 6UN. *T:* Ancrum 258. *Clubs:* MCC; New (Edinburgh).

WALLS, Henry James, BSc, PhD; Director, Metropolitan Police Laboratory, New Scotland Yard, 1964-68; *b* 1907; *s* of late William Walls, RSA, and late Elizabeth Maclellan Walls; *m* 1940, Constance Mary Butler; one *s* one *d*. *Educ:* George Watson's Boys' Coll., Edinburgh; Melville Coll., Edinburgh; Edinburgh Univ. BSc 1930; PhD 1933. Postgrad. research in physical chemistry, Munich, Edinburgh and Bristol, 1930-35; ICI (Explosives), 1935-36; Staff of Metropolitan Police Lab., 1936-46; Staff Chemist, Home Office Forensic Science Lab., Bristol, 1946-58; Director of Home Office Forensic Science Lab., Newcastle upon Tyne, 1958-64. *Publications:* Forensic Science, 1968; (with Alistair Brownlie) Drink, Drugs and Driving, 1969; Expert Witness, 1972; two books on photography; papers in journals dealing with forensic science. *Recreations:* reading, plays and films, talking, people, pottery. *Address:* 65 Marmora Road, SE22 0RY.

WALLS, Rev. Brother Roland Charles; Member, Community of the Transfiguration, since 1965; *b* 7 June 1917; *s* of late Roland William Walls and late Tina Josephine Hayward. *Educ:* Sandown Grammar Sch.; Corpus

Christi Coll., Cambridge; Kelham Theological Coll. Curate of St James', Crossgates, Leeds, 1940–42; Curate of St Cecilia's, Parson Cross, Sheffield, 1942–45; Licensed preacher, Diocese of Ely, 1945–48; Fellow of Corpus Christi Coll., Cambridge, 1948–62; Lecturer in Theology, Kelham Theological Coll., 1948–51; Chaplain and Dean of Chapel, Corpus Christi Coll., Cambridge, 1952–58; Canon Residentiary, Sheffield Cathedral, 1958–62; Chaplain of Rosslyn Chapel, Midlothian, 1962–68. Examining Chaplain to Bishop of Edinburgh. Lecturer at Coates Hall Theological Coll.; Lecturer in Dogmatics Dept, New Coll., Edinburgh, 1963–74. *Publication:* (contrib.) Theological Word Book (ed A. Richardson), 1950. *Recreations:* walking, music, etc. *Address:* Community House, 23 Manse Road, Roslin, Midlothian.

WALLWORK, John Sackfield, CBE 1982; Director, Daily Mail and General Trust PLC, since 1982; Managing Director, Northcliffe Newspapers Group Ltd, 1972–82 (General Manager, 1967–71); *b* 2 Nov. 1918; *s* of Peter Wallwork and Clara Cawthorne Wallwork; *m* 1945, Bessie Bray; one *s* one *d. Educ:* Leigh Grammar Sch., Leigh, Lancs. FCIS. General Manager, Scottish Daily Mail, Edinburgh, 1959–62; Asst Gen. Man., Associated Newspapers Gp Ltd, London, 1962–66, Dir, 1973–82. Chm., Press Association Ltd, 1973–74 (Dir, 1969–76); Dir, Reuters Ltd, 1973–76; Reuters Trustee, 1978–; Member Press Council, 1974–75; Newspaper Society: Mem. Council, 1967–; Jun. Vice-Pres.; Sen. Vice-Pres., 1976, Pres., 1977–78. Commander, Order of Merit, Republic of Italy, 1973. *Recreations:* golf, motoring. *Address:* Greenfield, Manor Road, Sidmouth, Devon EX10 8RR. *T:* Sidmouth 3489. *Clubs:* Wellington, Exeter Cricket.

WALLWORTH, Cyril; Assistant Under-Secretary of State, Ministry of Defence, 1964–76; Gwilym Gibbon Fellow, Nuffield College, Oxford, 1975–76; *b* 6 June 1916; *s* of Albert A. Wallworth and Eva (*née* Taylor); unmarried. *Educ:* Oldham High Sch.; Manchester Univ. BA (Hons) History, 1937. Asst Principal, Admiralty, 1939; Asst Private Secretary to First Lord, 1941–45, Principal, 1943; Asst Secretary, 1951; Under-Secretary, 1964. *Recreations:* music, wine, cooking, photography. *Address:* 134 Stein Road, Southbourne, Emsworth, Hants. *Club:* Hurlingham.

WALMESLEY WHITE, Brigadier Arthur, CBE 1972; Chairman, Palestine Exploration Fund, since 1973 (Member, Executive Committee, since 1949); *b* 10 Sept. 1917; *s* of late Walter Walmesley White, MA, and late Jessie Beswick; *m* 1951, Jocelyn Mary Beale, *d* of late Captain G. H. Beale, DSO, RN; one *s* three *d. Educ:* Eastbourne Coll.; Royal Military Academy; Pembroke Coll., Cambridge (MA). Commissioned, Royal Engineers, 1937; RE Field Units and Staff, 1939–45; Military Survey Staff and Units, 1946–49; Ordnance Survey, 1949–52; School of Military Survey, 1952–56 (Chief Instr, 1954–56); Directorate of Mil. Survey, 1956–59; CO, 42 Survey Engr Regt, Cyprus, 1959–62; Chief Survey Officer, Northern Army Gp/TWOATAF, Germany, 1962–63; Chief Geographic Officer, AFCENT, France, 1963–65; Ordnance Survey, 1965–69 (Dir of Map Publication, 1966–69). Brigadier 1966. Dir of Military Survey, and Chief of Geographical Section, Gen. Staff. MoD, 1969–72; retired, 1972. Planning Inspectorate, DoE, 1972–82. FRGS (Mem. Council, 1969–72); FRICS; MIOP. *Publications:* various papers on cartographic subjects in learned jls. *Recreations:* gardening, wood-working, hill-walking. *Address:* Old Barton, Whitestone, Exeter, Devon EX4 2LF. *T:* Longdown 232. *Club:* Army and Navy.

WALMSLEY, Arnold Robert, CMG 1963; MBE 1946; HM Diplomatic Service, retired; *b* 29 Aug. 1912; *s* of late Rev. Canon A. M. Walmsley; *m* 1944, Frances Councell de Mouilped. *Educ:* Rossall Sch.; Hertford Coll., Oxford. 1st Class Maths Mods, 1st Class Modern Greats. Private Sec. to Julius Meinl, Vienna, 1935–38; Foreign Office, 1939–45; established in Foreign Service, 1946; Foreign Office, 1946–50; British Consul in Jerusalem, 1950–54; Foreign Office, 1954–63; Head of Arabian Dept, 1961; Counsellor, Khartoum, 1963–65; Dir, Middle East Centre of Arab Studies, Lebanon, 1965–69. Order of the Two Niles (Sudan), 1965. *Publications:* (as Nicholas Roland) The Great One, 1967; Natural Causes, 1969; Who Came by Night, 1971. *Address:* Manor Farm, Dunmow Road, Bishop's Stortford, Herts. *Club:* Travellers'.

See also R. C. Walmsley.

WALMSLEY, Charles; *see* Walmsley, R. C.

WALMSLEY, Rt. Rev. Francis Joseph, CBE 1979; Bishop-in-Ordinary to HM Forces, since 1979; Titular Bishop of Tamalluma; *b* 9 Nov. 1926; *s* of Edwin Walmsley and Mary Walmsley (*née* Hall). *Educ:* St Joseph's Coll., Mark Cross, Tunbridge Wells; St John's Seminary, Wonersh, Guildford. Ordained, 1953; Asst Priest, Woolwich, 1953; Shoreham-by-Sea, Sussex, 1958; Chaplain, Royal Navy, 1960; Principal RC Chaplain, RN, 1975; retired from RN, 1979. Prelate of Honour to HH Pope Paul VI, 1975; ordained Bishop, 1979. *Recreations:* golf, photography, gardening.

WALMSLEY, Air Marshal Sir Hugh Sydney Porter, KCB 1952 (CB 1944); KCIE 1947; CBE 1943 (OBE 1937); MC 1918; DFC 1922; *b* 6 June 1898; 3rd *s* of late James Walmsley, Broughton, near Preston; *m* 1928, Audrey Maude, 3rd *d* of late Dr Pim, Sleaford; three *s. Educ:* Old Coll., Windermere; Dover Coll. 2nd Lieut, Loyal North Lancs Regt, 1915–16; seconded to RFC 1916; Captain, RFC, 1917; permanent commission RAF 1919 as Flying Officer; Flt Lt, 1921; Sqdn Ldr, 1931; Wing Comdr, 1937; Gp Capt., 1939; Air Cdre, 1942; Air Vice-Marshal, 1943; Acting Air Marshal, 1947–48; Air Marshal, 1949. 55 Sqdn, BEF, 1917–18 (MC); Iraq, 1921–23; OC 33 Sqdn Bicester, 1933–34, 8 Sqdn, Aden, 1935–37; War of 1939–45 (despatches 5

times); OC 71 Wing AASF, 1939–40; OC RAF Station, Scampton, 1940–41; HQ Bomber Command, 1941–42; AOC 91 Group, 1942–43; SASO, HQ Bomber Command, 1944–45; AOC 4 Group, Transport Command, 1945–46; Air Officer, Transport Command, SE Asia, 1946; AOC-in-C, Air HQ, India, 1946–47; Deputy Chief of the Air Staff, 1948–50; AOC-in-C, Flying Training Command, 1950–52; Retired from Active List, 1952. Managing Director of Air Service Training Ltd, 1952–59; Principal of College of Air Training, Hamble, 1960, resigned July 1960. *Recreations:* represented RAF Inter-Service Athletics in 1919, 1924 and 1926; all games; gardening, sailing. *Address:* Upwood, Tiptoe, Lymington, Hants. *Club:* Royal Air Force.

WALMSLEY, Nigel Norman; Managing Director, Capital Radio, since 1982; *b* 26 Jan. 1942; *s* of Norman and Ida Walmsley; *m* 1969, Jane Walmsley, broadcaster; one *d. Educ:* William Hulme's Sch.; Brasenose Coll., Oxford (BA English). Joined the Post Office, 1964; Asst Private Secretary to Postmaster General, 1967; Asst Director of Marketing, Post Office, 1973–75; Asst Sec., Industrial Planning Division of Dept of Industry, 1975–76; Director of Marketing, Post Office, 1977–81, Board Mem. for Marketing 1981–82. *Recreation:* intensive inactivity. *Address:* 26 Belsize Road, NW6 4RD. *T:* 01-586 1950.

WALMSLEY, Peter James, MBE 1975; Head of Petroleum Engineering Division, Department of Energy, since 1981; *b* 29 April 1929; *s* of George Stanley and Elizabeth Martin Walmsley; *m* 1970, Edna Fisher; three *s* one *d. Educ:* Caterham Sch., Surrey; Imperial Coll., London (BSc; ARSM). Geologist: Iraq Petroleum Co., 1951–59; BP Trinidad, 1959–65; BP London, 1965–72; Exploration Manager, BP Aberdeen, 1972–78; Dep. Chief Geologist, BP London, 1978–79; Regional Exploration Manager, BP London, 1979–81. Chairman, Petroleum Exploration Soc. of Gt Britain, 1971–72. *Publications:* contribs to various learned jls on North Sea geology. *Recreations:* home and garden. *Address:* Department of Energy, Thames House South, Millbank, SW1P 4QJ. *T:* 01-211 3000.

WALMSLEY, Prof. Robert, MD; DSc; FRCPE, FRCSE, FRSE; formerly Bute Professor of Anatomy, University of St Andrews, 1946–73; *b* 24 Aug. 1906; *s* of late Thomas Walmsley, Supt Marine Engr; *m* 1939, Isabel Mary, *e d* of James Mathieson, Aberdeen; two *s. Educ:* Greenock Acad.; Univ. of Edinburgh; Carnegie Inst. of Embryology, Baltimore, USA. MB, ChB (Edinburgh); MD (Edinburgh) with Gold Medal, 1937. Demonstrator, Lectr and Senior Lectr on Anatomy, Univ. of Edinburgh, 1931–46; Goodsir Fellowship in Anatomy, 1933; Rockefeller Fellowship, 1935–36; served as Pathologist in RAMC in UK and MEF, 1939–44. Struthers Lectr, Royal Coll. of Surgeons, Edinburgh, 1952; Fulbright Advanced Scholarship, 1960; Pres., Edinburgh Harveian Soc., 1963–64. Vis. Prof. of Anatomy: George Washington Univ., USA, 1960; Auckland, NZ, 1967. Formerly: Master, St Salvator's Coll.; Chm., Council St Leonard's and St Katherine's Schs; Hon. Pres., British Medical Students Assoc.; External Examiner in Anatomy, Cambridge, Edinburgh, Durham, Glasgow, Aberdeen, Liverpool, Singapore, Kingston (WI), Accra, etc. Life Mem. Anatomical Soc. Hon. Fellow, British Assoc. of Clinical Anatomists, 1980. Hon. DSc St Andrews, 1972. First Farquharson Award, RCSEd, 1974. *Publications:* Co-author Manual of Surgical Anatomy, 1964; (jtly) Clinical Anatomy of the Heart, 1978; co-reviser, Jamieson's Illustrations Regional Anatomy, 1981; contribs to various jls, on Heart, Bone and Joints, and on Whales. *Recreation:* gardening. *Address:* 45 Kilrymont Road, St Andrews, Fife. *T:* St Andrews 72879.

WALMSLEY, (Ronald) Charles, CB 1981; FRICS; Member of the Lands Tribunal, 1960–81; *b* 22 Jan. 1909; *s* of late Rev. Canon Alfred Moss Walmsley and Alice Jane (*née* Murgatroyd); *m* 1933, Joan Rosalind (*née* Hall); one *s* one *d. Educ:* Rossall Sch. FRICS 1941. Private practice as chartered surveyor, 1928–60. Vice-Pres., RICS, 1958–60. *Publications:* Walmsley's Rural Estate Management, 1948 (6th edn 1978); Walmsley's Agricultural Arbitrations, 1952 (3rd edn 1970). *Address:* 42 Tower House Close, Cuckfield, Haywards Heath, West Sussex RH17 5EQ.

See also A. R. Walmsley.

WALPOLE, family name of **Baron Walpole.**

WALPOLE, 9th Baron, of Walpole, *cr* 1723; 7th Baron Walpole of Wolterton, *cr* 1756; **Robert Henry Montgomerie Walpole,** TD; Captain, RA; *b* 25 April 1913; *s* of late Horatio Spencer Walpole and Dorothea Frances, *o d* of Frederick Butler Molyneux Montgomerie; *S* to baronies at the death of his cousin, 5th Earl of Orford, 1931; *m* 1937, Nancy Louisa, OBE, *y d* of late Frank Harding Jones, Housham Tye, Harlow, Essex; one *s* one *d* (and one *s* one *d* deced). *Educ:* Eton; South Eastern Agricultural Coll., Wye; Royal Agricultural Coll., Cirencester. *Recreations:* curling, shooting, golf. *Heir: s* Hon. Robert Horatio Walpole [*b* 8 Dec. 1938; *m* 1962, Judith (marr. diss. 1979), *yr d* of T. T. Schofield, Stockingwood House, Harpenden; two *s* two *d. Educ:* Eton; King's Coll., Cambridge]. *Address:* Wolterton Hall, Norwich NR11 7LY. *T:* Cromer 761210, Matlaske 274. *Club:* Norfolk (Norwich).

WALPOLE, Kathleen Annette, MA; Head Mistress of Wycombe Abbey School, Bucks, from 1948 until Dec. 1961; *b* Ootacamund, S India, 1899; *e d* of Major A. Walpole, RE. *Educ:* Southlands Sch., Exmouth; Westfield Coll., University of London. BA Hons London, 1921; History Mistress, The Church High Sch., Newcastle upon Tyne, 1922–27; Research Student, Westfield Coll., 1927–28; MA London, 1929; Alexander Prize of RHistSoc, 1931; History Mistress, The Royal Sch., Bath, 1928–34; Head Mistress, The

Red Maids Sch., Bristol, 1934-47. *Publications:* articles in the Trans. of Historic Society of Lancashire and Cheshire, and of the RHistSoc, 1929 and 1931, on Emigration to British North America. *Recreations:* gardening, walking, study of antiques. *Address:* 7 Springfield Place, Lansdown, Bath. *T:* Bath 317389. *Club:* Royal Commonwealth Society.

WALSER, Ven. David; Archdeacon of Ely, and Hon. Canon, since 1981; Rector of St Botolph's, Cambridge, since 1981; *b* 12 March 1923; *s* of William and Nora Walser; *m* 1975, Dr Elizabeth Enid Shillito. *Educ:* Clayesmore School; St Edmund Hall, Oxford (MA, DipTh); St Stephen's House, Oxford. Served RA and Royal Indian Mountain Artillery, 1942-46. Deacon 1950, priest 1951; Asst Curate, St Gregory the Great, Horfield, 1950-54; Vice-Principal, St Stephen's House, 1954-60; Asst Chaplain, Exeter Coll., Oxford, 1956-57; Junior Chaplain, Merton Coll., Oxford, 1957-60; Minor Canon, Ely Cathedral and Chaplain of King's School, 1961-71; Vicar of Linton, dio. Ely, 1971-81; Rector of Bartlow, 1973-81; RD of Linton, 1976-81. *Recreations:* hill walking, music, reading, camping, crosswords, hymn writing for local use. *Address:* St Botolph's Rectory, Summerfield, Cambridge CB3 9HE. *T:* Cambridge 350684.

WALSH, family name of **Baron Ormathwaite.**

WALSH, Sir Alan, Kt 1977; DSc; FRS 1969; Consultant Spectroscopist; *b* 19 Dec. 1916; *s* of late Thomas Haworth and Betsy Alice Walsh, Hoddlesden, Lancs; *m* 1949, Audrey Dale Hutchinson; two *s. Educ:* Darwen Grammar Sch.; Manchester Univ. BSc 1938; MSc (Tech.) 1946; DSc 1960. FAA 1958. British Non-Ferrous Metals Research Assoc., 1939-42 and 1944-46; Min. of Aircraft Production, 1943; Div. of Chemical Physics, CSIRO, Melbourne, 1946-77 (Asst Chief of Div., 1961-77). Einstein Memorial Lectr, Australian Inst. of Physics, 1967; Pres., Australian Inst. of Physics, 1967-69. Hon. Member: Soc. of Analytical Chemistry, 1969; Royal Soc. NZ, 1975. Foreign Mem., Royal Acad. of Sciences, Stockholm, 1969. Hon. FCS, 1973; Hon. FAIP, 1981; Hon. Mem., Japan Soc. of Analytical Chemistry, 1981. Hon. DSc Monash, 1970. Britannica Australia Science Award, 1966; Research Medal, Royal Soc. of Victoria, 1968; Talanta Gold Medal, 1969; Maurice Hasler Award, Soc. of Applied Spectroscopy, USA, 1972; James Cook Medal, Royal Soc. of NSW, 1975; Torbern Bergman Medal, Swedish Chem. Soc., 1976; Royal Medal, Royal Soc., 1976; John Scott Award, City of Philadelphia, 1977; Matthew Flinders Medal, Aust. Acad. of Science, 1980; Robert Boyle Medal, RSC, 1982. *Publications:* papers in learned jls. *Address:* 11 Dendy Street, Brighton, Victoria 3168, Australia. *T:* 03-592 4897. *Club:* Metropolitan Golf (Melbourne).

WALSH, Brian, QC 1977; a Recorder of the Crown Court, since 1972. Called to the Bar, Middle Temple, 1961. Prosecuting Counsel, DHSS. *Address:* 37 Park Square, Leeds LS1 2PD.

WALSH, Sir David (Philip), KBE 1962; CB 1946; retired as Deputy Secretary, Ministry of Housing and Local Government (1960-63). Formerly: Principal Asst Secretary (Director of Establishments), Admiralty; Under Secretary, Ministry of Town and Country Planning; Under-Secretary, Ministry of Housing and Local Government (formerly Min. of Local Government and Planning), 1951-60.

WALSH, Surgeon Rear-Adm. (retired) Dermot Francis, CB 1960; OBE 1952; FRCSE; *b* 21 Jan. 1901; *s* of Dr J. A. Walsh. *Educ:* Belvedere Coll., Dublin; Trinity Coll., Dublin. BA 1927; MB, BCh, BAO, 1928; FRCSE 1943, QHS 1958. CStJ 1958. *Recreations:* golf, gardening, music. *Address:* Latona, Torquay Road, Foxrock, Dublin 18. *T:* Dublin 893164.

WALSH, Maj.-Gen. Francis James, CBE 1948; CBE 1945; psc†; *b* 12 Jan. 1900; *s* of F. J. Walsh, Wexford, Eire; *m* 1931, Marjorie Olive Watney; two *s. Educ:* Clongowes Coll., Eire. RMC, Sandhurst, 1918; Royal Irish Regt, 1918-22; King's African Rifles, 1922-28; South Lancashire Regt, 1928-31; Indian Army, 1931-48; Staff Coll., Camberley, 1933-34; staff employment, India, Burma, Malaya, 1935-48; DA&QMG 33 Corps, 1943; DQMG 11 Army Group, 1943-44; DA&QMG 4 Corps and 14 Army, 1944-45; MGA N Comd, India, 1945-47. Maj.-Gen. (Temp.) 1945; Subst., 1947; retired, 1948. *Recreation:* sailing. *Address:* Orchard House, Turpins Lane, Frinton-on-Sea, Essex. *T:* 4472. *Club:* Naval and Military.

WALSH, Lt.-Gen. Geoffrey, CBE 1944; DSO 1943; CD; *b* 1909; *s* of late H. L. Walsh; *m* 1935, Gwynn Abigail Currie; one *s. Educ:* Royal Military Coll., Kingston; McGill Univ. (BEngEE). DSc(Mil) RMC, Kingston, 1971. Chief Engineer, 1st Canadian Army, 1944-45; DQMG, 1945-46; Comdr Northwest Highway System, 1946-48; Comdr Eastern Ontario Area, 1948-51; Comdr 27 Bde (Europe), 1951-52; DGMT 1953-55; QMG 1955-58; GOC, Western Command, 1958-61; Chief of the General Staff, Canada, 1961-64; Vice Chief of the Defence Staff, Canada, 1964-65. Col Comdt, Royal Canadian Army Cadets and Cadet Services of Canada, 1970-73. Legion of Merit (US); Comdr of Orange Order of Nassau (Netherlands). *Recreations:* golf, fishing, philately. *Address:* 201 Northcote Place, Rockcliffe Park, Ottawa, Canada. *Clubs:* RMC, Royal Ottawa Golf (Ottawa); USI (Ottawa and Edmonton).

WALSH, Ven. Geoffrey David Jeremy; Archdeacon of Ipswich, since 1976; *b* 7 Dec. 1929; *s* of late Howard Wilton Walsh, OBE and of Helen Maud Walsh (*née* Lovell); *m* 1961, Cynthia Helen, *d* of F. P. Knight, FLS, VMH,

and late H. I. C. Knight, OBE; two *s* one *d. Educ:* Felsted Sch., Essex; Pembroke Coll., Cambridge (MA Econ.); Lincoln Theological Coll. Curate, Christ Church, Southgate, London, 1955-58; Staff Sec., SCM, and Curate, St Mary the Great, Cambridge, 1958-61; Vicar, St Matthew, Moorfields, Bristol, 1961-66; Rector of Marlborough, Wilts, 1966-76; Rector of Elmsett with Aldham, 1976-80. Hon. Canon, Salisbury Cathedral, 1973-76. *Recreations:* gardening, golf, bird-watching. *Address:* 99 Valley Road, Ipswich IP1 4NF. *T:* Ipswich 218898.

WALSH, Graham Robert, FCA; Head of Corporate Finance Division, and Member, Management Committee, Morgan Grenfell Co. Ltd, since 1981 (Director, since 1973); *b* 30 July 1939; *s* of Robert Arthur Walsh and Ella Marian (*née* Jacks); *m* 1967, Margaret Ann Alexander; one *s* one *d. Educ:* Hurstpierpoint Coll., Sussex. Qualified as chartered accountant, 1962; joined Philip Hill Higginson Erlangers (now Hill Samuel & Co. Ltd), 1964; Director, Hill Samuel, 1970, resigned 1973; Director: Armitage Shanks Group Ltd, 1973-80; Phoenix Opera Ltd, 1970; Ward White Group plc, 1981. Dir Gen., Panel on Takeovers and Mergers, 1979-81; Dep. Chm., Issuing Houses Assoc., 1979. *Recreations:* opera, theatre, music, gardening, tennis. *Address:* 19 Alleyn Park, Dulwich, SE21 8AU. *T:* 01-670 0676.

WALSH, Henry George; HM Diplomatic Service; Counsellor (Economic), Washington, since 1980; *b* 28 Sept. 1939; *s* of James Isidore Walsh and Sybil Bertha Bazeley; *m* 1968, Janet Ann Grainger; two *d. Educ:* West Hill High Sch., Montreal; McGill Univ.; Churchill Coll., Cambridge. HM Treasury, 1966-74; Private Secretary to Chancellor of the Duchy of Lancaster, 1974-76; HM Treasury, 1976-78; Cabinet Office Secretariat, 1978-80. *Recreations:* golf, reading philosophical works, being taken for walks by Labrador retrievers. *Address:* c/o Foreign and Commonwealth Office, SW1; 3701 Leland Street, Chevy Chase, Md 20815, USA.

WALSH, James Mark, CMG 1956; OBE 1948; HM Diplomatic Service; Consul-General, Zürich, 1962-68; *b* 18 Aug. 1909; *s* of Mark Walsh and Emily (*née* Porter); *m* 1st, 1937, Mireille Loir (*d* 1966); one *s*; 2nd, 1967, Bertha Hoch. *Educ:* Mayfield Coll., Sussex; King's Coll., London; Lincoln's Inn, London. BA (Hons), 1929; LLB, 1932; Barrister, 1932; passed an examination and appointed to Foreign Service, 1932; Vice-Consul: Paris, 1932-33, Rotterdam, 1933-34; Judge of HBM Provincial Court, Alexandria, Egypt, 1934-38; Acting Consul-General, Barcelona, 1939; Vice-Consul, Philadelphia, 1939-44; Consul, Antwerp, 1944-45. First Secretary, British Legation: Helsinki, 1945-46, Budapest, 1946-48; Dep. Consul-General, New York, 1948-50; Counsellor (Commercial), Ankara, 1950-54, and Berne, 1954-59; Consul-General, Jerusalem, 1959-62. *Recreations:* painting, golf. *Address:* Fairfield, The Paddock, Farnham Lane, Haslemere, Surrey. *T:* Haslemere 52089.

WALSH, Dr John James; Consultant to Paddocks Private Clinic, Aylesbury Road, Princes Risborough; *b* 4 July 1917; *s* of Dr Thomas Walsh and Margaret (*née* O'Sullivan); *m* 1946, Joan Mary, *d* of Henry Teasdale and Nita Birks; three *s* one *d. Educ:* Mungret Coll.; University Coll., Cork. MB, BCh 1940; MD 1963; MRCP 1968, FRCP 1975; FRCS 1969. Various hospital appointments, including Medical Officer, Spinal Injuries Centre, Stoke Mandeville Hospital, Aylesbury, 1947; Deputy Director, National Spinal Injuries Centre, Stoke Mandeville Hospital, 1957-66, Dir, 1966-77. *Publications:* Understanding Paraplegia, 1964; a number of publications on subjects pertaining to paraplegia in medical journals. *Recreation:* shooting. *Address:* Wayside, Station Road, Princes Risborough, Bucks. *T:* Princes Risborough 3347.

WALSH, John P.; *see* Pakenham-Walsh.

WALSH, Sir John (Patrick), KBE 1960; Professor of Dentistry and Dean and Director, University of Otago Dental School, 1946-72; *b* 5 July 1911; *s* of John Patrick Walsh and Lillian Jane (*née* Burbidge), Vic, Australia; *m* 1934, Enid Morris; one *s* three *d. Educ:* Ormond Coll.; Melbourne Univ. BDSc 1st Cl. Hons Melbourne; LDS Victoria, 1936; MB, BS Melbourne, 1943; DDSc Melbourne, 1950; FDSRCS 1950; FDSRCS Edinburgh, 1951; MDS NUI, 1952; FRSNZ 1961; FACD 1962; Hon. FACDS, 1967; Hon. DSc Otago, 1975. Hosp. and teaching appointments in Melbourne till 1946. MO, RAAF, 1945-46. Consultant, WHO Dental Health Seminars: Wellington, 1954; Adelaide, 1959. Speaker: 11th and 12th Internat. Dental Congresses, London and Rome; Centennial Congress of Amer. Dental Assoc., New York, 1959; 12th, 14th and 15th Australian Dental Congresses. Chairman: Dental Council of NZ, 1956-72; Mental Health Assoc. of Otago, 1960. Dominion Pres., UNA, 1960-64. Member: MRC of NZ, 1950-72 (Chm. Dental Cttee, 1947-60); Scientific Commn; Fedn Dentaire Internat., 1954-61; Council, Univ. of Otago, 1958-63; Nat. Commn for UNESCO, 1961-69; Educn Commn, 1961-; Expert Panel on Dental Health, WHO, 1962; Nat. Council, Duke of Edinburgh's Award, 1963-68. CC, Dunedin, 1968-73. Pres., Dunedin Rotary Club, 1960, Governor Dist 298, 1966-67. Paul Harris Fellow, 1981. Hon. Mem., American Dental Assoc., 1969-; List of Honour, FDI, 1969-. Holds hon. degrees. *Publications:* A Manual of Stomatology, 1957; Living with Uncertainty, 1968; Psychiatry and Dentistry, 1976; numerous articles in scientific literature. *Recreation:* Retirement. *Address:* 108 Cannington Road, Dunedin, New Zealand. *T:* Dunedin 741083.

WALSH, Leslie; Stipendiary Magistrate, for Greater Manchester, 1974-75 (for Salford, 1951-74); *b* 6 May 1903; *s* of Rt Hon. Stephen and Anne Walsh; *m*

1934, Katharine de Hoghton Birtwell. *Educ:* Wigan Grammar Sch.; Victoria Univ., Manchester (LLB); St John's Coll., Oxford (BCL). Called to Bar, Gray's Inn, 1927; practised Northern Circuit. RAF, 1940-45. Deputy Licensing Authority NW Area, 1946-51; Chairman, Salford and District Rent Tribunal, 1946-51. Hon. MA Salford, 1976. *Address:* 4 Grange Road, Urmston, Manchester M31 1HU.

WALSH, Maj.-Gen. Michael John Hatley, CB 1980; DSO 1968; Chief Scout, since 1982; *b* 10 June 1927; *s* of Captain Victor Michael Walsh, late Royal Sussex, and Audrey Walsh; *m* 1952, Angela, *d* of Col Leonard Beswick; two *d*. *Educ:* Sedbergh Sch. Commnd, KRRC, 1946; served in Malaya, Germany, Cyprus, Suez, Aden, Australia and Singapore; Bde Maj. 44 Parachute Bde, 1960-61; GSO1 Defence Planning Staff, 1966; CO 1 Para Bn, 1967-69; Col AQ 1 Div., 1969-71; Comdr, 28 Commonwealth Bde, 1971-73; BGS HQ BAOR, 1973-76; GOC 3rd Armoured Div., 1976-79; Dir of Army Training, MoD, 1979-81. Hon. Col, 1st Bn Wessex Regt, TA, 1981-. *Recreations:* athletics, boxing (Pres., Army Boxing Assoc., 1980), parachuting (Pres., Army Parachute Assoc., 1979-81), sailing, Australian Rules football. *Address:* c/o Barclays Bank Ltd, James Street, Harrogate. *Club:* Royal Corinthian Yacht (Cowes).

WALSH, Lt-Col Noel Perrings; Under Secretary, and Director of Home Regional Services, Department of the Environment, 1976-79; *b* 25 Dec. 1919; *s* of late John and Nancy Walsh; *m* 1945, Olive Mary, *y d* of late Thomas Walsh, Waterford; three *s* one *d*. *Educ:* Purbrook Park Grammar Sch. Served Army, 1939-66; India, 1941-44; Arakan Campaign, 1944-45; DAQMG, 52 (L) Div., 1951-53; GSO2 RA, HQ BAOR, 1955-57; GSO1 PR, MoD Army, 1964-66; retired Lt-Col, RA, 1966. Entered Home Civil Service as Principal, MPBW, 1966; Regional Director: Far East, 1969-70; Midland Region, 1970-75. *Recreations:* gardening, squash, gauge O railway modelling. *Address:* 25 Oakfield Road, Selly Park, Birmingham B29 7HH. *T:* 021-472 2031. *Clubs:* Naval and Military; Edgbaston Priory (Birmingham).

WALSH, Walter; Member, Greater Manchester County Council (Chairman, 1978-79). Representative of Greater Manchester Council and Vice-Chairman, Manchester International Airport Authority. *Address:* 151 Park Road, Bolton, BL1 4RG. *T:* Bolton 24441; Greater Manchester County Council Offices, County Hall, Piccadilly Gardens, Portland Street, Manchester M60 3HP. *T:* 061-247 3111.

WALSH, Prof. William, FRSA; Professor of Commonwealth Literature, since 1972, Acting Vice-Chancellor, 1981-Sept. 1983, University of Leeds; Douglas Grant Fellow in Commonwealth Literature in the School of English, since 1969; Chairman, School of English, 1973-78; Director, Yorkshire Television, since 1967; *b* 23 Feb. 1916; *e s* of William and Elizabeth Walsh; *m* 1945, May Watson; one *s* one *d*. *Educ:* Downing Coll., Cambridge; University of London. Schoolmaster, 1943-51; Senior English Master, Raynes Park County Grammar Sch., 1945-51; Lecturer in Education, University Coll. of N Staffordshire, 1951-53; Lecturer in Education, Univ. of Edinburgh, 1953-57; Prof. of Education, and Head of Dept. of Education, Univ. of Leeds, 1957-72; Chm., Sch. of Education, 1969-72; Chm., Bd of combined Faculties of Arts, Economics, Social Studies and Law, Univ. of Leeds, 1964-66; Pro-Vice-Chancellor, Univ. of Leeds, 1965-67; Chm. Bd of Adult Educn, 1969-77; Member: IBA Adult Educn Cttee, 1974-76; IBA Educn Adv. Cttee, 1976-81; Bd of Foundn for Canadian Studies in UK, 1981-. Vis. Prof., ANU, 1968; Australian Commonwealth Vis. Fellow, 1970; Vis. Prof., Canadian Univs, 1974. FRSA 1970. *Publications:* Use of Imagination, 1959; A Human Idiom, 1964; Coleridge: The Work and the Relevance, 1967; A Manifold Voice, 1970; R. K. Narayan, 1972; V. S. Naipaul, 1972; Commonwealth Literature, 1973; Readings in Commonwealth Literature, 1973; D. J. Enright: poet of humanism, 1974; Patrick White: Voss, 1976; Patrick White's Fiction, 1977; F. R. Leavis, 1981; Introduction to Keats, 1981; R. K. Narayan, 1982; contributions to: From Blake to Byron, 1957; Young Writers, Young Readers, 1960; Speaking of the Famous, 1962; F. R. Leavis-Some Aspects of his Work, 1963; The Teaching of English Literature Overseas, 1963; Higher Education: patterns of change in the 1970s, 1972; Literatures of the World in English, 1974; Considerations, 1977; Indo-English Literature, 1977; Perspectives on Mulk Raj Anand, 1978; Awakened Conscience, 1978; The Study of Education, vol. 1, 1980; papers and essays on literary and educational topics in British and American journals. *Address:* 27 Moor Drive, Headingley, Leeds LS6 4BY. *T:* Leeds 755705.

WALSH, Prof. William Henry, FRSE 1979; FBA 1969; Emeritus Fellow, Merton College, University of Oxford, since 1979; Professor of Logic and Metaphysics in the University of Edinburgh, 1960-79, now Emeritus; Vice Principal, University of Edinburgh, 1975-79; *b* 10 Dec. 1913; *s* of Fred and Mary Walsh, Leeds; *m* 1938, Frances Beatrix Ruth (*née* Pearson); one *s* two *d*. *Educ:* Leeds Grammar Sch.; Merton Coll., Oxford. Class I, Classical Mods., 1934, Class I, Lit. Hum., 1936; Gaisford Greek Prose Prize, 1934; Junior Research Fellow, Merton Coll., 1936. Served War of 1939-45, Royal Corps of Signals, 1940-41; subsequently employed in branch of Foreign Office. Lecturer in Philosophy, Univ. Coll., Dundee (University of St Andrews), 1946; Fellow and Tutor in Philosophy, Merton Coll., Oxford, 1947-60, Emeritus Fellow, 1979; Sub-Warden, 1948-50, Senior Tutor, 1954-60; Lecturer in Philosophy, University of Oxford, 1947-60; Dean of Faculty of Arts, University of Edinburgh, 1966-68; Senatus Assessor, Univ. Ct, Edinburgh, 1970-73. Dawes Hicks Lecturer, British Academy, 1963. Visiting Professor: Ohio State Univ., USA, 1957-58; Dartmouth Coll., NH, USA,

1965; Univ. of Maryland, 1969-70; Rose Morgan Vis. Prof., Kansas Univ., 1980. Pres. Aristotelian Soc., 1964-65. Hon. DHL Rochester, 1979. *Publications:* Reason and Experience, 1947; An Introduction to Philosophy of History, 1951; Metaphysics, 1963; Hegelian Ethics, 1969; Kant's Criticism of Metaphysics, 1975; articles in philosophical periodicals. *Address:* 352 Banbury Road, Oxford OX2 7PP. *T:* Oxford 59328.

WALSH ATKINS, Leonard Brian, CMG 1962; CVO 1961; Honorary Consultant and Member, National Executive Committee, The Abbeyfield Society, since 1980, General Secretary, 1971, Consultant, 1975; *b* 15 March 1915; *o c* of late Leonard and Gladys Atkins; step *s* of late Geoffrey Walsh, CMG, CBE; *m* 1st, 1940, Marguerite Black (marr. diss. 1968); three *s*; 2nd, 1969, Margaret Lady Runcorn. *Educ:* Charterhouse (Scholar); Hertford Coll., Oxford (Scholar). BA, Lit. Hum., Class II, 1937. Asst Principal, India Office, 1937. Fleet Air Arm, Nov. 1940-July 1945; Lieut-Comdr (A), RNVR (despatches). Principal: Burma Office, 1945-47; Commonwealth Relations Office, 1947; Asst Secretary, 1949; Counsellor, British Embassy, Dublin, 1953-56 (sometime Chargé d'Affaires); Student, Imperial Defence Coll., 1957; Dep. High Comr, Karachi, 1959-61 (sometime Actg High Comr); Asst Under-Sec. of State, 1962; seconded to Civil Service Selection Bd, 1967; retired 1970. Member: Exec. Council, Nat. Assoc. of Voluntary Hostels, 1977-; Council, Nat. Fedn of Housing Assocs, 1978-. *Recreation:* sailing. *Address:* Berkeley Cottage, Mayfield, E Sussex.

WALSHAM, Rear-Adm. Sir John Scarlett Warren, 4th Bt, *cr* 1831; CB 1963; OBE 1944; RN, retired; Admiral Superintendent HM Dockyard, Portsmouth, 1961-64; *b* 29 Nov. 1910; *s* of Sir John S. Walsham, 3rd Bt, and Bessie Geraldine Gundreda (*d* 1941), *e d* of late Vice-Admiral John B. Warren; *S* father, 1940; *m* 1936, Sheila Christina, *o d* of Comdr B. Bannerman, DSO; one *s* two *d*. Rear-Admiral, 1961. *Heir: s* Timothy John Walsham [*b* 26 April 1939. *Educ:* Sherborne]. *Address:* Little Belcombe, Combe St Nicholas, Chard, Somerset.

WALSINGHAM, 9th Baron, *cr* 1780; **John de Grey**, MC 1952; Lieut-Colonel, Royal Artillery, retired, 1968; *b* 21 Feb. 1925; *s* of 8th Baron Walsingham, DSO, OBE, and Hyacinth (*d* 1968), *o d* of late Lt-Col Lambart Henry Bouwens, RA; *S* father, 1965; *m* 1963, Wendy, *er d* of E. Hoare, Southwick, Sussex; one *s* two *d*. *Educ:* Wellington Coll.; Aberdeen Univ.; Magdalen Coll., Oxford; RMCS. BA Oxon, 1950; MA 1959. Army in India, 1945-47; Palestine, 1947; Oxford Univ., 1947-50; Foreign Office, 1950; Army in Korea, 1951-52; Hong Kong, 1952-54; Malaya, 1954-56; Cyprus, Suez, 1956; Aden, 1957-58; Royal Military Coll. of Science, 1958-60; Aden, 1961-63; Malaysia, 1963-65. *Heir: s* Hon. Robert de Grey, *b* 21 June 1969. *Address:* Merton Hall, Thetford, Norfolk IP25 6QJ. *T:* Watton (Norfolk) 881226. *Clubs:* Army and Navy, Special Forces, Farmers'; Norfolk County (Norwich).

WALSTON, family name of **Baron Walston**.

WALSTON, Baron *cr* 1961 (Life Peer), of Newton; **Henry David Leonard George Walston**, CVO 1976; JP; farmer; *b* 16 June 1912; *o s* of late Sir Charles Walston, LittD, LHD, PhD, and Florence, *d* of David Einstein; *m* 1st, Catherine Macdonald (*d* 1978), *d* of late D. H. Crompton and late Mrs Charles Tobey; three *s* two *d* (and one *s* decd); 2nd, 1979, Mrs Elizabeth Scott. *Educ:* Eton; King's Coll., Cambridge (MA). Research Fellow in Bacteriology, Harvard, USA, 1934-35; Mem., Hunts War Agricultural Cttee, 1939-45; Dir of Agriculture, British Zone of Germany, 1946-47; Agricultural Adviser for Germany to FO, 1947-48; Counsellor, Duchy of Lancaster, 1948-54. Contested: (L) Hunts, 1945; (Lab) Cambridgeshire, 1951 and 1955; (Lab) Gainsborough, 1957 (by-election), and 1959. Parly Under-Sec. of State, FO, 1964-67; Parly Sec., BoT, Jan.-Aug. 1967; Member: UK Delegn to Council of Europe and WEU, 1970-75; European Parlt, 1975-77; joined SDP, 1981. HM Special Ambassador to inauguration of Presidents of Mexico, 1964, and of Columbia, 1966, and of Liberia, 1968. Crown Estate Comr, 1968-76; Chm., Inst. of Race Relations, 1968-71; Mem., Commonwealth Development Corp., 1975-, Dep. Chm., 1981-. Minister of Agriculture's Liaison Officer, 1969-70; Chairman: East Anglia Regional Planning Council, 1969-79; GB/East Europe Centre, 1974-; Centre of E Anglian Studies, 1975-79; Harwich Harbour Conservancy Bd, 1975-79; Member: Cambs Agricultural Cttee, 1948-50; Home Office Cttee on Experiments on Animals, 1961-62. Chm., Harlow Group Hosp. Management Cttee, 1962-64; Dep. Chm., Council, Royal Commonwealth Soc., 1963-64 (Vice-Pres., 1970-); Trustee, Rural Industries Bureau, 1959-64; Governor, Guy's Hosp., 1944-47. Hon. DCL East Anglia. JP Cambridge, 1944. *Publications:* From Forces to Farming, 1944; Our Daily Bread, 1952; No More Bread, 1954; Life on the Land, 1954; (with John Mackie) Land Nationalisation, for and against, 1958; Agriculture under Communism, 1961; The Farmer and Europe, 1962; The Farm Gate to Europe, 1970; Dealing with Hunger, 1976; contribs to Proc. of Experimental Biology and Medicine, Jl of Hygiene, Observer, Economist, New Statesman, Spectator. *Recreations:* shooting, sailing. *Address:* Town's End Springs, Thriplow, near Royston, Herts; A14 Albany, Piccadilly, W1; Marquis Estates, St Lucia, West Indies. *Clubs:* Brooks's, MCC; County (Cambridge); House of Lords Yacht.

WALTER, Hon. Sir Harold (Edward), Kt 1972; Barrister-at-Law; MLA 1959-82, Minister of External Affairs, Tourism and Emigration, 1976-82, Mauritius; *b* 17 April 1920; *e s* of Rev. Edward Walter and Marie Augusta Donat; *m* 1942, Yvette Nidza, MBE, *d* of James Toolsy; no *c*. *Educ:* Royal

Coll., Mauritius. Served in HM Forces, 1940-48, Mauritius Sub-Area; E Africa Comd, GHQ MELF. Called to Bar, Lincoln's Inn, 1951. Village Councillor, 1952; Municipal Councillor, Port Louis, 1956. Minister: of Works and Internal Communications, 1959-65; of Health, 1965-67 and 1971-76; of Labour, 1967-71; mem. numerous ministerial delegns. Chm., Commonwealth Med. Conf., 1972-74; Dep. Leader, UN General Assembly, NY, 1973, 1974, 1975; Pres., Security Council, UN, 1979; Mem. Exec. Bd, WHO, 1973-75, Pres., 1976-77. Chm., Council of Ministers, Organisation of African Unity, 1976-77. Commandeur de l'Ordre National Français des Palmes Académiques, 1974; Comdr de la Légion d'Honneur (France), 1980; Diplomatic Order of Merit (Korea), 1981. *Recreations:* shooting, fishing, swimming, gardening. *Address:* La Rocca, Eau Coulée, Mauritius. *T:* 860300. *Clubs:* Wings, Racing (Mauritius).

WALTER, Kenneth Burwood, CVO 1978; Full-time Member, British Airports Authority, 1975-77; *b* 16 Oct. 1918; *s* of late Leonard James Walter and of Jesse Florence Walter; *m* 1940, Elsie Marjorie Collett; two *s. Educ:* St Dunstan's Coll., SE6. Dept of Civil Aviation, Air Ministry, 1936. Served War, Royal Artillery (Anti Aircraft and Field), home and Far East, 1940-46. Ministries of: Civil Aviation; Transport and Civil Aviation; Aviation, 1946-66; British Airports Authority: Dep. Dir Planning, 1966; Dir Planning, 1972; Airport Dir, Heathrow, 1973-77. MCIT, ARAeS. *Publications:* various papers on airports. *Recreations:* music, swimming, fishing, gardening. *Address:* 7 Willersley Avenue, Orpington, Kent BR6 9RT.

WALTER, Captain Philip Norman, DSO 1940; RN; Commandant, Corps of Commissionaires, 1950-60; Director of The Times, 1958-64; *b* 12 Dec. 1898; *s* of Captain Philip Walter, RN, and *g s* of John Walter III, of The Times; *m* 1946, Sylvia (*d* 1976), *d* of J. C. M. Ogilvie-Forbes, Boyndlie, Aberdeenshire; one *s. Educ:* RN Colleges Osborne and Dartmouth. Served European War, 1914-18, Dardanelles and North Sea; Commander, 1932; Captain, 1940; War of 1939-45, Norway; commanded Inshore Squadron, N Africa, 1942; wounded, PoW; Assistant Chief of Staff to Allied Naval Commander-in-Chief, 1944; invalided, 1948. Chevalier of Légion d'Honneur, Croix de Guerre (France). *Address:* c/o Barclays Bank Ltd, 1 Pall Mall East, SW1.

WALTERS, Prof. Alan Arthur; Professor of Political Economy, Johns Hopkins University, Maryland, since 1976; on leave as Personal Economic Adviser to the Prime Minister, since 1981; *b* 17 June 1926; *s* of James Arthur Walters and Claribel Walters (*née* Heywood); *m* 1975, Margaret Patricia (Paddie) Wilson; one *d* of former marr. *Educ:* Alderman Newton's Sch., Leicester; University Coll. Leicester (BSc (Econ) London); Nuffield Coll., Oxford (MA). Lectr in Econometrics, Univ. of Birmingham, 1951; Visiting Prof. of Economics, Northwestern Univ., Evanston, Ill, USA, 1958-59; Prof. of Econometrics and Social Statistics, Univ. of Birmingham, 1961; Vis. Prof. of Economics, Massachusetts Inst. of Technology, 1966-67; Cassel Prof. of Economics, LSE, 1968-76; Vis. Fellow, Nuffield Coll., Oxford, 1982-83. Mem. Commission on Third London Airport (the Roskill Commission), 1968-70. Fellow, Econometric Soc., 1971. Hon. DLitt Leicester, 1981. *Publications:* Growth Without Development (with R. Clower and G. Dalton), 1966 (USA); Economics of Road User Charges, 1968; An Introduction to Econometrics, 1969 (2nd edn 1971); Economics of Ocean Freight Rates (with E. Bennathan), 1969 (USA); Money in Boom and Slump, 1970 (3rd edn 1971); Noise and Prices, 1974; (with R. G. Layard) Microeconomic Theory, 1977; (with Esra Bennathan) Port Pricing and Investment Policy for Developing Countries, 1979. *Recreations:* music, Thai porcelain. *Address:* 21 Victoria Square, SW1W 0RB. *Clubs:* Athenæum, Political Economy.

WALTERS, Dennis, MBE 1960; MP (C) Westbury Division of Wiltshire since 1964; *b* Nov. 1928; *s* of late Douglas L. Walters; *m* 1st, 1955, Vanora McIndoe (marr. diss. 1969); one *s* one *d*; 2nd, 1970, Hon. Celia (*née* Sandys) (marr. diss. 1979); one *s*; 3rd, 1981, Bridgett, *d* of J. Francis Shearer; one *d. Educ:* Downside; St Catharine's College (Exhibitioner), Cambridge (MA). War of 1939-45: interned in Italy; served with Italian Resistance Movement behind German lines after Armistice; repatriated and continued normal educn, 1944. Chm., Fedn of Univ. Conservative and Unionist Assocs, 1950; Personal Asst to Lord Hailsham throughout his Chairmanship of Conservative Party; Chm., Coningsby Club, 1959. Contested (C) Blyth, 1959 and Nov. 1960. Jt Hon. Sec., Conservative Parly Foreign Affairs Cttee, 1965-71, Jt Vice-Chm., 1974-78; Jt Chm., Euro-Arab Parly Assoc., 1978-81. Director: Cluff Oil Inc.; KCA International Ltd. Chm., Asthma Research Council, 1969-; Jt Chm., Council for Advancement of Arab British Understanding, 1970-82 (Jt Vice-Chm., 1967-70). Comdr, Order of Cedar of Lebanon, 1969. *Address:* 63 Warwick Square, SW1. *T:* 01-821 0377; Orchardleigh, Corton, Warminster, Wilts. *T:* Codford St Mary 369. *Club:* Boodle's.

WALTERS, Very Rev. Derrick; *see* Walters, Very Rev. R. D. C.

WALTERS, Geraint Gwynn, CBE 1958; Director for Wales, Ministry of Public Building and Works and Department of the Environment, 1966-72, retired; *b* in the Welsh Colony in Patagonia, 6 June 1910; *s* of Rev. D. D. Walters; *m* 1st, 1942, Doreena Owen (*d* 1959); 2nd, 1968, Sarah Ann Ruth Price; no *c. Educ:* various schools in Argentina and Wales; University Coll., Bangor (BA). Gladstone Prizeman, Foyle Prizeman. Schoolmaster, 1933-35; political organizer on staff of Rt Hon. David Lloyd George, 1935-40; Min. of Information, 1940-45; Dep. Regional Dir of Inf., Bristol and Plymouth,

1942-45; Principal, Min. of Works HQ, 1945-48; Dir for Wales, Min. of Works, 1948-63; Dir, Far East Region, Min. of Public Building and Works, 1963-66. Chm., Royal Inst. of Public Admin (S Wales Br.), 1960-61; Hon. Mem. of Gorsedd, 1961; Pres., St David's Soc. of Singapore, 1965; Leader of Welsh Overseas, at Nat. Eisteddfod of Wales, 1965; Chm., Argentine Welsh Soc., 1976-78, Pres., 1979-82. Chm., Civil Service Sports Council for Wales, 1970-72. Member: Welsh Bd for Industry, 1948-62; Housing Production Bd for Wales; Cttee of Inquiry on Welsh Television, 1963; Mem. Council, Univ. of Wales Inst. of Science and Technology; Govt Housing Comr for Merthyr Tydfil, 1972-73. *Recreations:* Rugby football, broadcasting, travel. *Address:* 29 The Rise, Llanishen, Cardiff. *T:* Cardiff 752070. *Clubs:* Civil Service; Cardiff and County (Cardiff).

WALTERS, Rear-Adm. John William Townshend; Assistant Chief of Defence Staff (Personnel and Logistics), since 1981; *b* 23 April 1926; *s* of William Bernard Walters and Lilian Martha Walters (*née* Hartridge); *m* 1949, Margaret Sarah Patricia Jeffkins; two *s* one *d. Educ:* John Fisher Sch., Purley, Surrey. Called to Bar, Middle Temple, 1956. Special Entry to RN, 1944; HMS King George V, 1944-46; HMS London, 1946-49; RN Air Station, Arbroath, 1949-51; Staff of C-in-C Mediterranean, 1951-53; Office of Vice Chief of Naval Staff, 1954-56; Sqdn Supply Officer, 8th Destroyer Sqdn, 1957-59; Staff of C-in-C Mediterranean, 1959-62; Secretary: to Flag Officer Middle East, 1962-64; to Naval Secretary, 1964-66; jssc 1967; Supply Officer, HMS Albion, 1967-69; Secretary to Chief of Fleet Support, 1969-72; Chief Naval Judge Advocate, 1972-75; Captain Naval Drafting, 1975-78; Director Naval Administrative Planning, 1978-80. *Recreations:* sailing, gardening; prison visitor. *Address:* Good Holding, 5 Hollycombe Close, Liphook, Hants GU30 7HR. *T:* Liphook 723222. *Clubs:* Army and Navy, Royal Naval Sailing Association.

WALTERS, Peter Ernest, CMG 1965; Group Staff Manager, Courage Ltd, 1967-78; Member, London (South) Industrial Tribunal, since 1978; *b* 9 Oct. 1913; *s* of Ernest Helm Walters and Kathleen Walters (*née* Farrer-Baynes); *m* 1943, Ayesha Margaret, *d* of Alfred and Winifred Bunker; three *d. Educ:* Windlesham House Sch. Emigrated to Kenya, 1931. Army Service, 1939-45; commissioned KAR, 1940; Major 1944. Cadet, Colonial Admin. Service, Kenya, 1945; Dist Comr, 1948; Provincial Comr, Northern Prov., 1959; Civil Sec., Eastern Region, Kenya, 1963-65; retd from Colonial Service, 1965. Principal, Min. of Aviation (London), 1965-67. Staff Manager, Courage, Barclay and Simonds Ltd, 1967. *Address:* Cherry Orchard, Ockley, near Dorking, Surrey RH5 5NS. *T:* Dorking 711119. *Club:* Nairobi (Kenya).

WALTERS, Peter (Hugh Bennetts) Ensor, OBE 1957; Public Relations and Fund Raising Consultant since 1959; *b* 18 July 1912; *yr s* of late Rev. C. Ensor Walters, a President of the Methodist Conference, and late Muriel Havergal, *d* of late Alderman J. H. Bennetts, JP, Penzance; *m* 1936, Marcia, *er d* of Percival Burdle Hayter; no *c. Educ:* Manor House Sch.; St Peter's Coll., Oxford. On staff of late Rt Hon. David Lloyd George, 1939; enlisted as volunteer in Army, 1940; commissioned in Royal Army Pay Corps, 1942; National Organizer, National Liberal Organization, 1944-51. General Sec., National Liberal Organization, Hon. Sec. and Treas., National Liberal Party Council, and Dir, National Liberal Forum, 1951-58. Vice-Chm., Nat. Liberal Club, 1972-74. *Recreation:* travel. *Address:* 2 North Lodge Mansions, Christchurch Road, Worthing, Sussex BN11 1JQ. *T:* Worthing 205678. *Club:* Union Society (Oxford).

WALTERS, Peter Ingram; Chairman, since 1981 and a Managing Director, since 1973, British Petroleum Co. Ltd; *b* 11 March 1931; *s* of Stephen Walters and Edna Walters (*née* Redgate); *m* 1960, Patricia Anne (*née* Tulloch); two *s* one *d. Educ:* King Edward's Sch., Birmingham; Birmingham Univ. (BCom). RASC, 1952-54; British Petroleum Co. Ltd, 1954-: Vice-Pres., BP North America, 1965-67; Chairman: BP Chemicals, 1976-81; BP Chemicals Internat., 1981; Dir, National Westminster Bank, 1981-; Member: Indust. Soc. Council, 1975-; Post Office Bd, 1978-79. President: Soc. of Chem. Industry, 1978-80; Gen. Council of British Shipping, 1977-78; Inst. of Manpower Studies, 1980- (Vice-Pres., 1977-80). Governor, London Business Sch., 1981-. *Recreations:* golf, gardening. *Address:* Britannic House, Moor Lane, EC2Y 9BU.

WALTERS, Very Rev. (Rhys) Derrick (Chamberlain); Dean of Liverpool, since 1983; *b* 10 March 1932; *s* of Ivor Chamberlain Walters and Rosamund Grace Walters (*née* Jackson); *m* 1959, Joan Trollope (*née* Fisher); two *s. Educ:* Gowerton Boys' Grammar School; London School of Economics; Ripon Hall, Oxford. BSc (Soc) Lond, 1955. Curate, Manselton, Swansea, 1957-58; Anglican Chaplain, University College, Swansea and Curate, St Mary's, 1958-62; Vicar of All Saints, Totley, 1962-67; Vicar of St Mary's, Boulton by Derby, 1967-74; Diocesan Missioner, Diocese of Salisbury, 1974-82; Vicar of Burcombe, 1974-79; Non-residentiary Canon of Salisbury, 1978; Residentiary Canon and Treasurer of Salisbury Cathedral, 1979-82. *Recreations:* escapist literature, croquet, classical music. *Address:* Liverpool Cathedral, L1 7AZ. *T:* 051-709 6271.

WALTERS, Sir Roger (Talbot), KBE 1971 (CBE 1965); BA; FRIBA; FIStructE; Architect and Controller of Construction Services, Greater London Council, 1971-78; *b* 31 March 1917; *3rd s* of Alfred Bernard Walters, Sudbury, Suffolk; *m* 1976, Claire Myfanwy Chappell. *Educ:* Oundle; Architectural Association School of Architecture; Liverpool University. Diploma in Architecture, 1939. Served in Royal Engineers, 1943-46. Office of Sir E. Owen Williams, KBE, 1936; Directorate of Constructional Design,

Min. of Works, 1941–43; Architect to Timber Development Assoc., 1946–49; Principal Asst Architect, Eastern Region, British Railways, 1949–59; Chief Architect (Development), Directorate of Works, War Office, 1959–62; Dep. Dir-Gen., R&D, MPBW, 1962–67; Dir-Gen., Production, 1967–69; Controller General, 1969–71. Hon. FAIA. *Address:* 46 Princess Road, NW1. *T:* 01-722 3740. *Club:* Reform.

WALTERS, Stuart Max, ScD; Director, University Botanic Garden, Cambridge, since 1973; *b* 23 May 1920; *s* of Bernard Walters and Ivy Dane; *m* 1948, Lorna Mary Strutt; two *s* one *d. Educ:* Penistone Grammar Sch.; St John's Coll., Cambridge. 1st cl. hons Pt I Nat. Scis Tripos 1940 and Pt II Botany 1946; PhD 1949. Research Fellow, St John's Coll., 1947–50; Curator of Herbarium, Botany Sch., Cambridge, 1948–73; Lectr in Botany 1962–73; Fellow of King's Coll., Cambridge, 1964–. *Publications:* (with J. S. L. Gilmour) Wild Flowers, 1954; (with J. Raven) Mountain Flowers, 1956; (ed, with F. H. Perring) Atlas of the British Flora, 1962; (with F. H. Perring, P. D. Sell and H. L. K. Whitehouse) A Flora of Cambridgeshire, 1964; (with D. Briggs) Plant Variation and Evolution, 1969; The Shaping of Cambridge Botany, 1981. *Address:* Cory Lodge, University Botanic Garden, Cambridge. *T:* Cambridge 358145.

WALTON, Anthony Michael, QC 1970; *b* 4 May 1925; *y s* of Henry Herbert Walton and Clara Martha Walton, Dulwich; *m* 1955, Jean Frederica, *o d* of William Montague Hey, Bedford; one *s. Educ:* Dulwich College (sometime Scholar); Hertford College, Oxford (sometime Scholar); pupil to W. L. Ferrar (maths) and C. H. S. Fifoot (law). BA 1946; BCL 1950; MA 1950. Pres., Oxford Union Society, Trinity Term 1945. Nat. Service as physicist. Called to the Bar, Middle Temple, 1950; Bencher, 1978; pupil to Lord Justice Winn. Interested in education. Liveryman, Worshipful Co. of Gunmakers. Freeman, City of London, 1968. *Publications:* (ed) (Asst to Hon. H. Fletcher-Moulton) Digest of the Patent, Design, Trade Mark and Other Cases, 1959; (ed) Russell on Arbitration, 17th edn, 1963 — 19th edn, 1979; (with Hugh Laddie) Patent Law of Europe and the United Kingdom, 1978. *Address:* 62 Kingsmead Road, SW2.

See also Hon. Sir Raymond Walton.

WALTON, Arthur Halsall, FCA; Partner in Lysons, Haworth & Sankey since 1949; *b* 13 July 1916; *s* of Arthur Walton and Elizabeth Leeming (*née* Halsall); *m* 1958, Kathleen Elsie Abram; three *s. Educ:* The Leys School. Articled in Lysons & Talbot, 1934; ACA 1940. Military Service, 1939–48: commnd Lancs Fusiliers, 1940. Inst. of Chartered Accountants: Mem. Council 1959; Vice-Pres., 1969; Dep. Pres. 1970; Pres. 1971. *Recreation:* reading. *Address:* Aldersyde, Prestbury Road, Wilmslow SK9 2LJ. *Club:* St James's (Manchester).

WALTON, Ernest Thomas Sinton, MA, MSc, PhD; Fellow of Trinity College, Dublin, 1934–74, Fellow emeritus 1974; Erasmus Smith's Professor of Natural and Experimental Philosophy 1947–74; *b* 6 October 1903; *s* of Rev. J. A. Walton, MA; *m* 1934, Winifred Isabel Wilson; two *s* two *d. Educ:* Methodist College, Belfast; Trinity College, Dublin; (Cambridge University). 1851 Overseas Research Scholarship, 1927–30; Senior Research Award of Dept of Scientific and Industrial Research, 1930–34; Clerk Maxwell Scholar, 1932–34; Awarded Hughes Medal by Royal Society, 1938. (With Sir John Cockcroft) Nobel prize for physics, 1951. Hon. DSc: Queen's Univ. of Belfast, 1959; Gustavus Adolphus Coll., Minn, USA, 1975. *Publications:* Papers on hydrodynamics, nuclear physics and micro-waves. *Address:* Trinity College, Dublin; 26 St Kevin's Park, Dartry Road, Dublin 6. *T:* 971328.

WALTON, Ven. Geoffrey Elmer; Archdeacon of Dorset, since 1982; *b* 19 Feb. 1934; *s* of Harold and Edith Margaret Walton; *m* 1961, Edith Mollie O'Connor; one *s. Educ:* St John's Coll., Univ. of Durham (BA); Queen's Coll., Birmingham (DipTh). Asst Curate, Warsop with Sookholme, 1961–65; Vicar of Norwell, Notts, 1965–69; Recruitment and Selection Sec., ACCM, 1969–75; Vicar of Holy Trinity, Weymouth, 1975–82; RD of Weymouth, 1980–82; Non-Residentiary Canon of Salisbury, 1981–. *Recreations:* conjuring, religious drama. *Address:* The Vicarage, Witchampton, Wimborne, Dorset BH21 5AP. *T:* Witchampton 840422.

WALTON, Prof. Sir John (Nicholas), Kt 1979; TD 1962; FRCP; Professor of Neurology, University of Newcastle upon Tyne, 1968–Sept. 1983; (from Oct. 1983) Warden, Green College, University of Oxford; *b* 16 Sept. 1922; *s* of Herbert Walton and Eleanor Watson Walton; *m* 1946, Mary Elizabeth Harrison; one *s* two *d. Educ:* Alderman Wraith Grammar Sch., Spennymoor, Co. Durham; Med. Sch., King's Coll., Univ. of Durham. MB, BS (1st Cl. Hons) 1945; MD (Durham) 1952; DSc (Newcastle) 1972; FRCP 1963 (MRCP 1950). Ho. Phys., Royal Victoria Inf., Newcastle, 1946–47; service in RAMC, 1947–49; Med. Registrar, Royal Vic. Inf., 1949–51; Research Asst, Univ. of Durham, 1951–56; Nuffield Foundn Fellow, Mass. Gen. Hosp. and Harvard Univ., 1953–54; King's Coll. Fellow, Neurological Res. Unit, Nat. Hosp., Queen Square, 1954–55; First Asst in Neurology, Newcastle upon Tyne, 1956–58; Cons. Neurologist, Newcastle Univ. Hosps, 1958–83; Dean of Medicine, Univ. of Newcastle upon Tyne, 1971–81. Mem. MRC, 1974–78; Mem., GMC, 1971– (Chm. Educn Cttee, 1975–82; Pres., 1982–); Pres., BMA, 1980–82; UK Rep., EEC Adv. Cttee, Med. Educn, 1975–83; Editor-in-Chief, Jl of Neurological Sciences, 1966–77; First Vice-Pres., World Fedn Neurol. (Chm., Res. Cttee), 1981–; Chm., Muscular Dystrophy Gp of GB, 1970–, etc. Col (late RAMC) and OC 1 (N) Gen. Hosp. (TA), 1963–66; Hon. Col 201 (N) Gen. Hosp. (T&AVR), 1971–77. Dr de l'Univ. (Hon.) Aix-Marseille, 1975; Hon. DSc: Leeds, 1979; Leicester, 1980. Hon. FACP 1980; Hon. FRCPE 1981. Hon. Corresponding For. Member: Amer. Neurological Assoc., Amer. Acad. of Neurology, and of French, German, Australian, Spanish, Polish, Venezuelan, Japanese and Brazilian Neurological Assocs. Numerous named lectureships and overseas visiting professorships. Hon. Freeman, Newcastle upon Tyne, 1980. *Publications:* Subarachnoid Haemorrhage, 1956; (with R. D. Adams) Polymyositis, 1958; Essentials of Neurology, 1961, 5th edn 1982; Disorders of Voluntary Muscle, 1964, 4th edn 1981; Brain's Diseases of the Nervous System, 7th edn 1969, 8th edn 1977, etc; numerous chapters in books and papers in sci. jls. *Recreations:* cricket, golf and other sports, reading, music. *Address:* (until Sept. 1983) Holmwood, 9 Beechfield Road, Gosforth, Newcastle upon Tyne NE3 4EP. *T:* Newcastle upon Tyne 858871; (from Sept. 1983) 1 Observatory Street, Oxford; (from Oct. 1983) Green College, Oxford OX2 6HG. *Clubs:* Athenæum, East India.

WALTON, Sir John Robert, Kt 1971; retired; Director, Waltons Ltd Group, Australia (Managing Director, 1951–72, Chairman, 1961–72); Chairman, FNCB-Waltons Corp. Ltd, Australia, 1966–75; *b* 7 Feb. 1904; *s* of John Thomas Walton; *m* 1938, Peggy Everley Gamble; one *s* one *d. Educ:* Scots Coll., Sydney. National Cash Register Co. Pty Ltd, 1930: NSW Manager, 1934, Managing Director in Australia, 1946–51. *Recreations:* gardening, swimming, golf, reading. *Address:* 9A Longwood, 5 Thornton Street, Darling Point, NSW 2027, Australia. *Clubs:* Rotary, Royal Sydney Golf, American National, Tattersall's (all in Sydney).

WALTON, John William Scott; Director of Statistics, Board of Inland Revenue, since 1977; *b* 25 Sept. 1925; *s* of late Sir John Charles Walton, KCIE, CB, MC, and late Nelly Margaret, Lady Walton, *d* of late Prof. W. R. Scott. *Educ:* Marlborough; Brasenose Coll., Oxford. Army (RA), 1943–47. Mutual Security Agency, Paris, 1952; Inland Revenue, 1954; Central Statistical Office, 1958, Chief Statistician, 1967, Asst Dir, 1972. *Publications:* (contrib. jtly) M. Perlman, The Organization and Retrieval of Economic Knowledge, 1977; articles in The Review of Income and Wealth, Economic Trends, Business Economist, Statistical News. *Address:* c/o Board of Inland Revenue, Somerset House, WC2R 1LB. *Club:* United Oxford & Cambridge University.

WALTON, Hon. Sir Raymond (Henry), Kt 1973; **Hon. Mr Justice Walton;** a Judge of the High Court of Justice, Chancery Division, since 1973; *b* 9 Sept. 1915; *e s* of Henry Herbert Walton and Clara Martha Walton, Dulwich; *m* 1940, Helen Alexandra, *e d* of Alexander Dingwall, Jedburgh; one *s* two *d. Educ:* Dulwich College; Balliol College, Oxford. Open Math. Schol., Balliol, 1933; BA 1937; MA 1942. Pres., Oxford Union Soc., Feb. 1938; BCL 1938. Called to Bar, Lincoln's Inn, 1939; Bencher, 1970. War service in Anti-Aircraft Artillery (including Instructor in Gunnery and Experimental Officer), 1940–46. Contested (L) North Lambeth, 1945. Returned to practice at Bar, 1946; QC 1963. Legal corresp., Financial Times, 1953–72. Mem., Lord Chancellor's Law Reform Cttee, 1959–; Chm., Insolvency Rules Adv. Cttee, 1977–. Church Comr for England, 1969–73; Dep. Chm., Boundaries Commn for England, 1973–. Hon. Fellow, Coll. of Estate Management, 1977. *Publications:* An introduction to the law of Sales of Land, 1949, 3rd edn 1969; (edited) Kerr on Receivers, 12th edn (with A. W. Sarson), 13th to 15th edns; Adkin's Law of Landlord and Tenant, 13th, 14th and (with Michael Essayan) 15th to 17th edns. *Recreation:* philately. *Address:* Royal Courts of Justice, WC2.

See also A. M. Walton.

WALTON, Sir William (Turner), OM 1967; Kt 1951; MusD; Composer; *b* 29 March 1902; *s* of Charles Alexander and Louisa Maria Walton; *m* 1949, Susana Gil Passo. *Educ:* Cathedral Choir School and Christ Church, Oxford. Hon. Student Christ Church, Oxford; Hon. MusD (Oxon, Dunelm, TCD, Manchester); Hon. DMus (Cantab, London); Hon. FRCM; Hon. FRAM; Gold Medal Royal Philharmonic Society, 1947; Gold Medal Worshipful Company of Musicians 1947; Benjamin Franklin Medal, RSA, 1972. Mem. Royal Swedish Acad. of Music; Accademico onorario di Santa Cecilia, Rome; Hon. Member: Amer. Acad. and Inst. of Arts and Letters, 1978; Royal Manchester Coll. of Music, 1972. *Compositions:* Pianoforte Quartet (Carnegie award), 1918, rev. 1974; String Quartet (unpublished), 1921; Façade (with Edith Sitwell), 1923 and 1926, Siesta for small orchestra, 1926; Portsmouth Point, 1926; Sinfonia Concertante for piano and orchestra, 1928; Viola Concerto, 1929; Belshazzar's Feast, 1931; Three Songs for Soprano, 1932; Symphony, 1935; Crown Imperial (Coronation March), 1937; In Honour of the City of London, 1937; Violin Concerto, 1939; Music for Children, 1940; Scapino (comedy overture), 1940; & (ballet), 1943; Henry V (film), 1945; Quartet, 1947; Hamlet (film), 1948; Sonata for Violin and Pianoforte, 1949; Te Deum, 1953; Orb and Sceptre (Coronation March), 1953; Troilus and Cressida (opera), 1954; Richard III (film), 1955; Johannesburg Overture, 1956; Violoncello Concerto, 1956; Partita, 1957; Anon in Love, 1960; Symphony No 2, 1960; Gloria, 1961; A Song for the Lord Mayor's Table, 1962; Prelude for Orchestra, 1962; Variations on a Theme by Hindemith, 1963; The Twelve (anthem), 1964; Missa Brevis, 1966; The Bear (comic opera) 1967; Capriccio Burlesco, 1968; Improvisations on an Impromptu by Benjamin Britten, 1970; Jubilate, 1972; Five Bagatelles (guitar), 1972; Sonata for String Orchestra, 1972; Cantico del Sole, 1974; Magnificat and Nunc Dimittis, 1974; Varii Capricci, 1976; Antiphon, 1977; Façade 2, 1979; Prologo e Fantasia, Passacaglia, 1982. *Address:* c/o Oxford University Press, 37 Dover Street, W1. *Clubs:* Athenæum, Savile, Garrick.

WALWYN, Rear-Adm. James Humphrey, CB 1964; OBE 1944; self-employed consultant, since 1975; Member, Central Arbitration Committee and Central Office of Industrial Tribunals, since 1978; *b* 21 Aug. 1913; *o s* of late Vice-Admiral Sir Humphrey Walwyn, KCSI, KCMG, CB, DSO and Lady Walwyn, DBE; *m* 1945, Pamela Digby Bell; one *s* two *d. Educ:* The Old Malthouse and RN College, Dartmouth. Entered RN, 1931; Lieut 1935; ADC to Governor of Newfoundland, 1936–37; specialised in Gunnery, 1938; HMS Renown, 1939–41; HMS Newcastle, 1942–44; Staff of C-in-C Home Fleet, 1945–47; Comdr 1948; Naval Staff Course, 1948; Admiralty, 1948–50; Comdg HMS Chevron, 1951–52; Captain 1953; Staff of SHAPE, Paris, 1954–56; Captain Inshore Flotilla, Mediterranean, 1956–58; Dir, RN Tactical School, 1958–59; Dir of Officer Appts, Admiralty, 1960–62; Rear-Adm. 1962; Flag Officer Flotillas, Mediterranean, 1962–65; retired, 1965. Chief Exec., Personnel, British Oxygen Co., 1965–75. FIPM. SBStJ 1972. *Recreations:* fishing, gardening. *Address:* 40 Jubilee Place, SW3. *T:* 01-352 7802. *Clubs:* Army and Navy, Hurlingham.

WALWYN, Peter Tyndall; racehorse trainer, since 1960; *b* 1 July 1933; *s* of late Lt-Col Charles Lawrence Tyndall Walwyn, DSO, OBE, MC, Moreton in Marsh, Glos; *m* 1960, Virginia Gaselee, *d* of A. S. Gaselee, MFH; one *s* one *d. Educ:* Amesbury Sch., Hindhead, Surrey; Charterhouse. Leading trainer on the flat, 1974, 1975; a new record in earnings (£373,563), 1975. Major races won include: One Thousand Guineas, 1970, Humble Duty; Oaks Stakes, 1974, Polygamy; Irish Derby, 1974, English Prince, and 1975, Grundy; King George VI and Queen Elizabeth Stakes, Ascot, 1975, Grundy; Epsom Derby, 1975, Grundy. *Recreations:* foxhunting, shooting. *Address:* Seven Barrows, Lambourn, Berks RG16 7UJ. *T:* Lambourn 71347. *Club:* Turf.

WANAMAKER, Sam; Actor; Director, Producer; *b* Chicago, 14 June 1919; *s* of Morris Wanamaker and Molly (*née* Bobele); *m* 1940, Charlotte Holland; three *d. Educ:* Drake University, Iowa, USA. Studied for the stage at Goodman Theatre, Chicago. Appeared in summer theatres, Chicago (acting and directing), 1936–39; joined Globe Shakespearian Theatre Group; first New York Appearance, Café Crown, 1941; Counter Attack, 1942. Served in United States Armed Forces, 1943–46. In several parts on New York stage, 1946–49; appeared in This, Too, Shall Pass, 1946; directed and played in: Joan of Lorraine, 1946–47; Goodbye My Fancy, 1948–49; directed: Caesar and Cleopatra, 1950; The Soldier and the Lady, 1954; created Festival Repertory Theatre, New York, 1950. First performance (also producer) on London stage as Bernie Dodd, in Winter Journey, St James's, 1952; presented and appeared in The Shrike, Prince's, 1953; produced: Purple Dust, Glasgow, 1953; Foreign Field, Birmingham, 1954; directed and appeared in One More River, Cat on a Hot Tin Roof, and The Potting Shed, 1957. In Liverpool, 1957, created New Shakespeare Theatre Cultural Center, where produced (appearing in some): Tea and Sympathy, A View from the Bridge, 1957; The Rose Tattoo, Finian's Rainbow, Bus Stop, The Rainmaker, and Reclining Figure (all in 1958). *Presented, prod and appeared in:* The Big Knife, Duke of York's 1954; The Lovers, Winter Garden, 1955; The Rainmaker, St Martin's 1956; A Hatful of Rain, Prince's, 1957; The Rose Tattoo, New, 1959; Iago, Stratford-on-Avon, 1959; Dr Breuer, in A Far Country, New York, 1961; The Watergate Tapes, Royal Court, 1974; *produced:* The World of Sholom Aleichem, Embassy, 1955; King Priam, Coventry Theatre and Royal Opera House, Covent Garden, 1962, 1967, and 1972; Verdi's La Forza del Destino, Royal Opera House, Covent Garden, 1962; John Player season, Globe, 1972–73; Southwark Summer Festival, 1974; Shakespeare Birthday Celebrations, 1974; *directed:* Children from their Games, New York, 1963; A Case of Libel, New York, 1963; A Murder Among Us, New York, 1964; Defenders, 1964; War and Peace (première), Sydney Opera House, 1973; The Ice Break, Royal Opera House, Covent Garden, 1977; Chicago Lyric Opera Gala, 1979; *acted and directed* Macbeth, Goodman Theater, Chicago, 1964; *acted (films):* Give Us This Day; Taras Bulba; Those Magnificent Men in Their Flying Machines, 1964; The Winston Affair, 1964; The Spy Who Came in from the Cold, 1964; Warning Shot; The Law, 1974; Spiral Staircase, 1974; The Sell-Out, 1975; The Voyage, 1975; Billy Jack goes to Washington, 1976; From Hell to Victory, 1978; Private Benjamin, 1980; The Competition, 1980; *films directed:* Hawk, 1965; Lancer, 1966; Custer, 1967; File of the Golden Goose, 1968; The Executioner, 1969; Catlow, 1970; Sinbad and the Eye of the Tiger, 1975; The Killing of Randy Webster, 1981; *directed (opera):* Aida, San Francisco, 1981; *directed (television):* Colombo, 1977; Hawaii 5-0, 1978; Dark Side of Love, Man Undercover, Mrs Columbo, Hart to Hart, 1979; *acted and directed (TV):* The Holocaust, 1977; The Return of the Saint, 1978; *acted (TV):* Blind Love, 1976; Charlie Muffin, 1979; The Family Business, 1981. Founder and Executive Director: Globe Playhouse Trust Ltd, 1971; World Centre for Shakespeare Studies Ltd. Directs and acts in TV productions, in UK and USA. *Address:* 99 Aldwych, WC2B 4JY.

WAND, Dr Solomon; Treasurer of British Medical Association, 1963–72 (Chairman of Council, 1956–61); *b* 14 January 1899; *s* of Louis and Jane Wand; *m* 1st, 1921, Claire Cohen (*d* 1951); one *s* one *d*; 2nd, 1960, Shaunagh Denison Crew, *o d* of Major Robert Douglas Crew and Irene Crew, Milford-on-Sea, Hants. *Educ:* Manchester Grammar School; Manchester University. Qualified 1921, MB, ChB (Manchester), with distinction in medicine; in general practice in Birmingham. FRCGP. Member of: Council BMA, 1935–72 (Pres. Midland Branch, 1969–70); Gen. Medical Council, 1961–71; Advertising Advisory Cttee of IBA (formerly ITA), 1961–75; Court of Governors, Univ. of Birmingham, 1969–70; Board, General Practice Finance Corporation, 1969–76; Chairman: Gen. Medical Services Cttee, BMA, 1948–52; Representative Body, BMA, 1951–54; Gold Medallist, BMA, 1961;

formerly Member Central Health Services Council, Medical Advisory Cttee of Min. of Health; formerly Mem. Health Education Cttee. Hon. Vice-Pres. British Medical Students Assoc., 1959; Chm., British Medical Students Trust, 1968–; formerly Examng MO, Dept of Health and Social Security; Member: Study Cttee of World Medical Assoc., 1959–; Management Cttee, Medical Insurance Agency, 1964–; Birmingham Central District Medical Cttee, 1974–; Chm., Med. Adv. Cttee, Allied Investments Ltd, 1973–78. Hon. DCL, Durham, 1957; Hon. LLD Queen's Univ., Belfast, 1962. *Publications:* contribs to Encyclopædia of General Practice. *Recreations:* travel, swimming, bridge. *Address:* D 5 Kenilworth Court, Hagley Road, Edgbaston, Birmingham B16 9NU. *T:* 021-454 3997.

WANDSWORTH, Archdeacon of; *see* Coombs, Ven. P. B.

WANGARATTA, Bishop of, since 1975; **Rt. Rev. Maxwell McNee Thomas,** ThD; *b* 23 Aug. 1926; *s* of Rev. Charles Elliot Thomas, ThL, and Elsie Frances Thomas (*née* McNee); *m* 1952, Elaine Joy Walker; two *s* one *d. Educ:* St Paul's Coll., Univ. of Sydney (MA, BD); General Theological Seminary, New York (ThD). Lectr in Theology and Greek, St John's Coll., Morpeth, NSW, 1950; deacon, 1950; priest, 1952; Curate: St Peter's, E Maitland, 1951–52; St Mary Magdalene, Richmond, Surrey, 1952–54; All Saints', Singleton, NSW, 1955. Priest-in-Charge and Rector, The Entrance, NSW, 1955–59; Fellow and Tutor, General Theol. Seminary, NY, 1959–63; Hon. Chaplain to Bishop of New York, 1959–63, Chaplain, 1963–64; Chaplain, Univ. of Melbourne and of Canterbury Fellowship, 1964–68; Consultant Theologian to Archbishop of Melbourne, Stewart Lectr in Divinity, Trinity Coll. and Chaplain of Canterbury Fellowship, 1968–75. Member: Gen. Synod's Commn on Doctrine, 1970– (Chm., 1976–); Faith and Order Commn, WCC, 1977–; Anglican-Orthodox Jt Doctrinal Discussion Gp, 1978. *Address:* Bishop's Lodge, Wangaratta, Victoria 3677, Australia. *T:* Wangaratta (057) 21.3643. *Clubs:* Melbourne, Royal Automobile of Victoria.

WANI, Most Rev. Silvanus; *see* Uganda, Archbishop of.

WANNAMETHEE, Phan; Ambassador of Thailand to the Court of St James's, since 1977; *b* 30 Jan. 1924; *s* of Mr and Mrs Puhn Wannamethee; *m* 1958, M. L. Hiranyika Ladawan; three *s* one *d. Educ:* Oberlin Coll., Ohio, USA (BA); Univ. of Calif at Berkeley (MA). Entered Foreign Min., Bangkok, 1942; attached Royal Thai Embassy, Washington, 1945; Third Sec., Cairo, 1956; Private Sec. to Prime Minister, 1957; First Secretary: Karachi, 1958; Saigon, 1959; (later Counsellor), London, 1964; Foreign Min., Bangkok: Dep. Under-Sec. of State, 1972; Dir-Gen., Polit. Dept, 1973; Under-Sec. of State for Foreign Affairs, 1973; Ambassador to Fed. Republic of Germany, 1976. *Recreation:* swimming. *Address:* Thaivilla, 28 Golfside, Cheam, Sutton, Surrey. *T:* 01-642 2131. *Clubs:* Athenæum, Travellers', Naval and Military, Special Forces, Hurlingham.

WANSTALL, Hon. Sir Charles Gray, Kt 1974; Chief Justice of Queensland, Australia, 1977–82; *b* 17 Feb. 1912; *m* 1938, Olwyn Mabel, *d* of C. O. John; one *d. Educ:* Roma and Gympie State Schs; Gympie High Sch., Queensland, Australia. Called to Queensland Bar, 1933. High Court, 1942. MLA (Liberal) for Toowong, 1944–50; Pres., Liberal Party of Australia (Qld Div.), 1950–53. QC 1956; Judge, Supreme Court, Qld, 1958; Sen. Puisne Judge, 1971. *Recreations:* reading, photography. *Address:* Chief Justice's Chambers, Supreme Court, Brisbane, Qld, Australia; 36 Jerdanefield Road, St Lucia, Brisbane, Queensland 4067, Australia. *Clubs:* Queensland (Brisbane); St Lucia Bowling.

WARBURTON, Col Alfred Arthur, CBE 1961; DSO 1945; DL; JP; Chairman, SHEF Engineering Ltd, 1970–75; Company Director since 1953; *b* 12 April 1913; *s* of late A. V. Warburton. *Educ:* Sedbergh. Served War of 1939–45, with Essex Yeomanry; Lt-Col comdg South Notts Hussars Yeomanry, 1953–58; Hon. Col 1966–76; Col DCRA 49th Inf. Div. TA, 1958–60; ADC to the Queen, 1961–66; Chm., Notts Cttee TA&VR Assoc. for E Midlands, 1970–78. Director, John Shaw Ltd, Worksop, 1953–66. President: East Midlands Area, Royal British Legion, 1976–77, 1981–82; Notts County Royal British Legion, 1979–. DL 1966, High Sheriff 1968, JP 1968, Notts. *Recreations:* shooting, fishing. *Address:* Wigthorpe House, near Worksop, Notts. *T:* Worksop 730357. *Club:* Cavalry and Guards.

WARBURTON, Dame Anne (Marion), DCVO 1979 (CVO 1965); CMG 1977; HM Ambassador to Denmark, since 1976; *b* 8 June 1927; *d* of Captain Eliot Warburton, MC and Mary Louise (*née* Thompson), US. *Educ:* Barnard Coll., Columbia Univ. (BA); Somerville Coll., Oxford (BA, MA); Hon. Fellow, 1977. Economic Cooperation Administration, London, 1949–52; NATO Secretariat, Paris, 1952–54; Lazard Bros, London, 1955–57; entered Diplomatic Service, Nov. 1957; 2nd Sec., FO, 1957–59; 2nd, then 1st Sec., UK Mission to UN, NY, 1959–62; 1st Sec., Bonn, 1962–65; 1st Sec., DSAO, London, 1965–67; 1st Sec., FO, then FCO, 1967–70; Counsellor, UK Mission to UN, Geneva, 1970–75; Head of Guidance and Information Policy Dept, FCO, 1975–76. Verdienstkreuz, 1st Class (West Germany), 1965; Grand Cross, Order of Dannebrog, 1979. *Recreations:* ski-ing, theatre, travel. *Address:* British Embassy, Kastelsvej 40, Copenhagen, Denmark; c/o Foreign and Commonwealth Office, SW1. *Clubs:* United Oxford & Cambridge University, Ski Club of Great Britain, English-Speaking Union.

WARBURTON, David; National Industrial Officer, General and Municipal Workers Union, since 1973; *b* 10 Jan. 1942; *s* of Harold and Ada Warburton; *m* 1966, Carole Anne Susan Tomney; two *d. Educ:* Cottingley Manor Sch., Bingley, Yorks; Coleg Harlech, Merioneth, N Wales. Campaign Officer, Labour Party, 1964; Educn Officer, G&MWU, 1964-66, Dist Officer/Reg. Officer, 1966-73. Secretary: Chemical Unions Council; Rubber Industry Jt Unions. Pres., Europ. Co-ord. Cttee, Chem., Rubber and Glass Unions. Chairman: Chem. and Allied Industries Jt Indust. Council; ICI Signatory Unions Cttee. Mem., Chemicals Econ. Develt Cttee. Mem. Bd, Commonwealth Develt Corp. *Publications:* Pharmaceuticals for the People, 1973; Drug Industry: which way to control, 1975; UK Chemicals: the way forward, 1977. *Recreations:* music, flicking through reference books. *Address:* 47 Hill Rise, Chorleywood, Rickmansworth, Herts. *T:* Rickmansworth 78726.

WARBURTON, Eric John Newnham, CBE 1966; a Vice-Chairman, Lloyds Bank Ltd, 1967-75; *b* 22 Nov. 1904; *o s* of late E. and H. R. Warburton, Bexhill-on-Sea, Sussex; *m* 1933, Louise, *er d* of late C. J. and L. R. Martin, Crowborough, Sussex; one *s* one *d. Educ:* Eastbourne Grammar School. Entered Lloyds Bank Ltd, 1922; Jt General Man., 1953; Dep. Chief Gen. Man., 1958; Chief Gen. Man., 1959-66; Dir, 1965-75; Dep. Chm., Lloyds Bank International Ltd, 1971-75; Director: Lloyds Bank Unit Trust Managers Ltd, 1966-75; First Western Bank Trust Co., Calif., 1974-75; Lewis's Bank Ltd, 1967-75; Intercontinental Banking Services Ltd, 1968-75. Chairman: Exec. Cttee, Banking Information Service, 1965-71; Bank Education Service, 1966-71; Dep. Chairman: City of London Savings Cttee, 1962-74; Exports Credit Guarantee Dept Adv. Council, 1968-71 (Member, 1966-71); Member: Decimal Currency Bd, 1967-71; Nat. Savings Cttee, 1963-74; Council, CBI, 1971-75. Member Board: Trinity Coll. of Music, 1968-; Management Cttee, Sussex Housing Assoc. for the Aged, 1970-; American Bankers Assoc. Internat. Monetary Conf., 1970-72. FRSA 1970; Hon. FTCL 1969. *Recreations:* golf, gardening, music. *Address:* 9 Denmans Close, Lindfield, Haywards Heath, West Sussex RH16 2JX. *T:* Lindfield 2351. *Club:* Oriental.

WARBURTON, Prof. Geoffrey Barratt; Professor of Applied Mechanics, University of Nottingham, since 1961; *b* 9 June 1924; *s* of Ernest McPherson and Beatrice Warburton; *m* 1952, Margaret Coan; three *d. Educ:* William Hulme's Grammar School, Manchester; Peterhouse, Cambridge. Cambridge: Open Exhibition in Mathematics, 1942; 1st cl. Hons in Mechanical Sciences Tripos, 1944; BA 1945; MA 1949; Junior Demonstrator, 1944-46. Asst Lecturer in Engineering, Univ. Coll. of Swansea, 1946-47; Dept of Engineering, Univ. of Edinburgh; Assistant, 1947-48, Lecturer, 1948-50 and 1953-56; ICI Research Fellow, 1950-53; Head of Post-graduate School of Applied Dynamics, 1956-61; PhD (Edinburgh) 1949. FRSE 1960; FIMechE 1968. Rayleigh Medal, Inst. of Acoustics, 1982. Associate Editor, Earthquake Engineering and Structural Dynamics; Member, Editorial Boards: Internat. Jl of Mechanical Sciences; Internat. Jl for Numerical Methods in Engineering; Jl of Sound and Vibration; Engineering Structures. *Publications:* The Dynamical Behaviour of Structures, 1964, 2nd edn 1976; research on mechanical vibrations, in several scientific journals. *Address:* University of Nottingham, Nottingham NG7 2RD.

WARBURTON, Richard Maurice; Director General, Royal Society for the Prevention of Accidents, since 1979; *b* 14 June 1928; *s* of Richard and Phylis Agnes Warburton; *m* 1952, Lois May Green; two *s. Educ:* Wigan Grammar Sch.; Birmingham Univ. (BA 1st Cl. Hons). Flying Officer, RAF, 1950-52. HM Inspector of Factories, 1952-79; Head of Accident Prevention Advisory Unit, Health and Safety Executive, 1972-79. *Recreations:* golf, gardening, fell walking. *Address:* 6 Assheton Road, Blackburn BB2 6SF. *T:* Blackburn 56824.

WARD, family name of **Earl of Dudley** and of **Viscounts Bangor** and **Ward of Witley.**

WARD OF WITLEY, 1st Viscount, *cr* 1960; **George Reginald Ward,** PC 1957; *b* 20 Nov. 1907; 4th *s* (twin) of 2nd Earl of Dudley; *m* 1st, 1940, Anne Capel (marr. diss., 1951); one *s* one *d* ; 2nd, 1962, Hon. Mrs Barbara Astor (who *m* 1st, 1942, Hon. Michael Langhorne Astor; she *d* 1980). *Educ:* Eton; Christ Church, Oxford. AAF, 1929; RAF, 1932-37 and 1939-45. MP (C) for Worcester City, 1945-60. Parly Under-Sec. of State, Air Min., 1952-55; Parly and Financial Sec., Admiralty, Dec. 1955-Jan. 1957; Secretary of State for Air, 1957-60. *Heir: s* Hon. Anthony Giles Humble Ward, *b* 10 June 1943. *Address:* 23 Queens Gate Gardens, SW7 5LZ. *Clubs:* White's, Pratt's.

WARD, Prof. Alan Gordon, CBE 1972 (OBE 1959); Procter Professor of Food and Leather Science, Leeds University, 1961-77, now Emeritus; *b* 18 April 1914; *s* of Lionel Howell Ward and Lily Maud Ward (*née* Morgan); *m* 1938, Cicely Jean Chapman; one *s* two *d. Educ:* Queen Elizabeth's Grammar Sch., Wimborne; Trinity Coll., Cambridge (schol.). BA (Cantab) 1935; MA (Cantab) 1940; FInstP 1946; FIFST 1966. Lectr in Physics and Mathematics, N Staffs Technical Coll., 1937-40; Experimental Officer, Min. of Supply, 1940-46; Sen. Scientific Officer, Building Research Station, 1946-48; Principal Scientific Officer, 1948-49; Dir of Research, The British Gelatine and Glue Research Assoc., 1949-59; Prof. of Leather Industries, Leeds Univ., 1959-61. Chm., Food Standards Cttee set up by Minister of Agriculture, 1965-79. Hon. EIFST 1979; Hon. FAIFST 1979. *Publications:* Nature of Crystals, 1938; Colloids, Their Properties and Applications, 1945; The Science and Technology of Gelatin, 1977; papers in Trans. Far. Soc., Jl

Sci. Instr, Biochem. Jl, etc. *Recreation:* music. *Address:* 35 Templar Gardens, Wetherby, West Yorkshire LS22 4TG. *T:* Wetherby 64177.

WARD, Albert Joseph Reginald; Chief Executive, London Docklands Development Corporation, since 1981; *b* 5 Oct. 1927; *s* of Albert E. and Gwendolene M. E. Ward, Lydbook, Glos; *m* 1954, Betty Anne Tooze; one *s* one *d. Educ:* East Dean Grammar Sch., Cinderford, Glos; Univ. of Manchester (BA Hons History). HM Inspector of Taxes, 1952-65; Chief Administrator, County Architects Dept, Lancashire CC, 1965-68; Business Manager, Shankland Cox & Associates, 1968-69; Corporation Secretary, Irvine New Town Development Corporation, 1969-72; Chief Executive: Coatbridge Borough Council, 1972-74; London Borough of Hammersmith, 1974-76; Hereford and Worcester CC, 1976-80. *Recreations:* walking, tennis, music, architecture and urban design. *Address:* 29 Pittville Lawn, Cheltenham, Glos GL52 2BH. *T:* Cheltenham 75632; Bridge House, Preston's Road, Isle of Dogs, E14 9TJ. *T:* 01-967 1160.

WARD, Mrs Ann Sarita; Chairman, Inner London Education Authority, 1981-82; Deputy Leader, London Borough of Southwark, since 1978; *b* 4 Aug. 1923; *d* of Denis Godfrey and Marion Phyllis Godfrey; *m* Frank Ward; one *s. Educ:* St Paul's Girls' Sch., Hammersmith. Professional photographer; photo journalist, Daily Mail, 1962-67, Daily Mirror, 1967-70; award winner, British Press Photographs of Year, 1967. Contested (Lab) Streatham, Gen. Election, 1970. *Recreations:* politics, community self-help printing, gardening. *Address:* 204 Peckham Rye, SE22 0LU. *T:* 01-693 4251.

WARD, Ven. Arthur Frederick, BA; Archdeacon of Exeter, 1970-81; Archdeacon Emeritus since 1981; Canon Residentiary of Exeter Cathedral, 1970-81, Precentor, 1972-81; *b* 23 April 1912; *s* of William and Annie Florence Ward, Corbridge, Northumberland; *m* 1937, Margaret Melrose, Tynemouth, Northumberland; two *d. Educ:* Durham Choir School; Newcastle upon Tyne Royal Grammar School; Durham University; Ridley Hall, Cambridge. Curate, Byker Parish Church, Newcastle, 1935-40; Rector of Harpurhey, North Manchester, 1940-44; Vicar of Nelson, 1944-55; Vicar of Christ Church, Paignton, 1955-62; Archdeacon of Barnstaple and Rector of Shirwell with Loxhore, Devon, 1962-70. *Recreations:* gardening, cricket, touring. *Address:* Melrose, Christow, Devon EX6 7LY. *T:* Christow 52498.

WARD, Sir Arthur (Hugh), KBE 1979 (OBE 1962); ACA; FNZIAS; Chancellor, Massey University, 1975-81 (Pro-Chancellor, 1970-75); *b* 25 March 1906; *s* of Arthur Ward and Ada Elizabeth Ward; *m* 1936, Jean Bannatyne Mueller; one *s* three *d. Educ:* Middlesbrough High Sch., Yorks. ACA (NZ); FNZIAS 1969. Sec., NZ Co-op. Herd Testing Assoc., 1929-36; Dir, Herd Improvement, NZ Dairy Bd, 1945-54; Gen. Man., Dairy Bd, 1954-70. Member: NZ Monetary and Econ. Council, 1970-79; Remuneration Authority, 1971-72; National Res. Adv. Council, 1970-72 (Chm., 1971-72); Council, Massey Univ., 1967-81. Marsden Medal for services to science, 1975; Queen's Silver Jubilee Medal, 1977. *Publications:* A Command of Co-operatives, 1975; articles on dairy cattle husbandry and dairy cattle breeding. *Recreations:* writing, reading, gardening, golf. *Address:* 17 Tui Crescent, Waikanae, New Zealand. *T:* Waikanae 6466; PO Box 56, Waikanae. *Club:* Wellington (Wellington, NZ).

WARD, (Arthur) Neville, RDI 1971; BArch; RIBA, FSIA; architect and designer; *b* 5 June 1922; *s* of Arthur Edward Ward and Winifred Alice Ward; *m* 1948, Mary Winstanley; one *s. Educ:* Wade Deacon Grammar Sch., Widnes; Sch. of Architecture, Univ. of Liverpool (BArch 1944); Edinburgh Coll. of Art. RIBA 1944; FSIA 1948. Mem., BoT Furniture Design Panel, 1946-48. Private practice, Ward and Austin, 1948-71, Ward Associates, 1972-; special concern in interiors, exhibns, ships accommodation, furniture; contrib. Britain Can Make It, 1946, and Festival of Britain, 1951. Pres., SIAD, 1967. Member: Nat. Adv. Cttee on Art Exams, 1952-57; Nat. Adv. Council on Art Educn, 1959-71; Council, RSA, 1965-70, and 1977-78; Council, RCA, 1968-72; Nat. Council for Diplomas in Art and Design, 1968-74. Master, Faculty of Royal Designers for Industry, 1977-78. *Publications:* (with Mary Ward) Living Rooms, 1967; (with Mary Ward) Home in the 20s and 30s, 1978; articles and essays in Arch. Rev., and Naval Arch. *Recreation:* jobbing. *Address:* Ward Associates, 68 Grafton Way, W1P 5LE. *T:* 01-387 0491.

WARD, Sir Aubrey (Ernest), Kt 1967; JP; DL; *b* 17 April 1899; *s* of Edward Alfred Ward; *m* 1919, Mary Jane Davidson Rutherford, MB, ChB (*d* 1979); one *d. Educ:* Royal Veterinary College, London. Served War of 1914-18; Night FO, RFC (now RAF). Veterinary Practice, 1923-66. Vice-Chm., Thames Conservancy Bd, 1964-74. Mayor of Slough, 1940-45, Hon. Freeman, 1961. JP 1957, DL 1963, Chm., CC, 1963-74, Buckinghamshire. *Address:* 54 Pound Lane, Marlow, Bucks. *T:* Marlow 5250.

WARD, Cecil; Town Clerk, Belfast City Council, since 1979; *b* 26 Oct. 1929; *s* of William and Mary Caroline Ward. *Educ:* Technical High Sch., Belfast; College of Technology, Belfast. Employed by Belfast City Council (formerly Belfast County Borough Council), 1947-; Asst Town Clerk (Administration), 1977-79. Mem. Arts Council of NI, 1981-. Dir, Ulster Orchestra Soc., 1980-. *Recreations:* music, reading, hill walking. *Address:* 24 Thornhill, Malone, Belfast, Northern Ireland BT9 6SS. *T:* Belfast 668950.

WARD, Rev. Canon Charles Leslie; Canon Treasurer of Wells and Prebendary of Warminster in Wells Cathedral, since 1978; *b* 11 June 1916;

s of Amos Ward and Maude Hazeldine Ballard; *m* 1943, Barbara, *d* of George and Alice Stoneman; two *s*. *Educ:* Mexborough Grammar Sch.; Lichfield Theological Coll. (Potter-Selwyn Exhibnr). Underground Surveyor, Cadeby Colliery, S Yorks, 1933-36. Assistant Curate: Parkgate, 1939; Rossington, 1940; Taunton, 1942; Bishop of Blackburn's Youth Chaplain and Succentor of Blackburn Cathedral, 1945; Vicar: St Michael, Ashton on Ribble, 1948; St Peter, Cheltenham, 1951; Northleach, Stowell, Hampnett, Yanworth and Eastington, 1960; Holy Trinity, Yeovil, 1964; Minehead, 1967. Life Governor, St Paul's and St Mary's Colls, Cheltenham, 1954-. *Recreations:* church spotting, driving motor cars, listening to music. *Address:* 23 Vicar's Close, Wells, Somerset BA5 2UJ. *T:* Wells 72360.

WARD, Christopher John; Editor, Daily Express, since 1981; *b* 25 Aug. 1942; *s* of John Stanley Ward and Jacqueline Law-Hume Costin; *m* 1971, Fanny Brown; one *s* two *d*. *Educ:* King's Coll. Sch., Wimbledon. Successively on staff of Driffield Times, 1959, and Newcastle Evening Chronicle, 1960-63; Daily Mirror: reporter, 1963-65; sub-editor, 1965-66; feature writer and columnist, 1966-76; Assistant Editor: Sunday Mirror, 1976-79; Daily Mirror, 1979-81. *Publications:* How to Complain, 1974; Our Cheque is in the Post, 1980. *Recreations:* competition pistol shooting, fell walking. *Address:* Daily Express, Fleet Street, EC4.

WARD, Christopher John Ferguson; solicitor; with Clark & Son, Reading, since 1965; *b* 26 Dec. 1942; *m* Janet Ward; two *s* one *d* by former marr. *Educ:* Magdalen College Sch.; Law Society Sch. of Law. MP (C) Swindon, Oct. 1969-June 1970; contested (C) Eton and Slough, 1979. Mem., Berks CC, 1965-81 (Leader of the Council and Chm., Policy Cttee, 1979-81). *Address:* Keys, Castle End, Ruscombe, near Reading, Berks RG10 9XG. *T:* Twyford 341347; (office) Reading 585321.

WARD, (Christopher) John (William); General Secretary, Association of First Division Civil Servants, since 1980; *b* 21 June 1942; *s* of Thomas Maxfield and Peggy Ward; *m* 1970, Diane Lelliott (separated). *Educ:* Oundle Sch.; Corpus Christi Coll., Oxford (BA LittHum); Univ. of East Anglia (Graduate DipEcon). Overseas and Economic Intelligence Depts, Bank of England, 1965; General Secretary, Bank of England Staff Organisation, 1973. Mem., Liberal Party Employment and Industrial Relations Panel, 1981-. *Recreations:* opera, theatre, watching football, playing village cricket. *Address:* Association of First Division Civil Servants, 17 Northumberland Avenue, WC2N 5AP. *Club:* Swindon Town Supporters.

WARD, David, CBE 1972; FRCM; opera singer; *b* 3 July 1922; *s* of James Ward and Catherine Bell; *m* 1960, Susan E. V. Rutherford; no *c*. *Educ:* St Patrick's School, Dumbarton; Royal College of Music. Royal Navy, 1940-43; Royal Indian Navy, 1943-46. Sadler's Wells, 1953-59; Covent Garden, 1960-64; now international free-lance singer, Germany, USA, Italy, France, etc. Hon. RAM 1973; FRCM 1973. Hon. LLD Strathclyde, 1974. *Recreation:* golf. *Address:* Kennedy Crescent, Lake Wanaka, New Zealand.

WARD, Rev. David Conisbee; Under Secretary, Management Support and Computers, Department of Health and Social Security, since 1981; *b* 7 Jan. 1933; *s* of late Sydney L. Ward and Ivy A. Ward; *m* 1958, Patricia Jeanette (*née* Nobes); one *s* one *d*. *Educ:* Kingston Grammar Sch.; St John's Coll., Cambridge (Scholar, MA). Asst Principal, Nat. Assistance Bd, 1956; Asst Private Sec. to Lord President of the Council and Minister for Science, 1960-61; Principal, Nat. Assistance Bd, 1961, Min. of Social Security, 1966, DHSS, 1968; Asst Sec., DHSS, 1970, Under Sec., 1976. Southwark Ordination Course, 1977-80; Deacon, 1980; Priest, 1981; Curate, St Matthew, Surbiton, 1980-. *Recreations:* philately, Chelsea FC, allotmenteering. *Address:* 5 St Matthew's Avenue, Surbiton, Surrey KT6 6JJ. *T:* 01-399 3323. *Club:* University Women's.

WARD, Sir Deighton (Harcourt Lisle), GCMG 1976; GCVO 1977; QC (Barbados) 1959; Governor-General, Barbados, since 1976; *b* 16 May 1909; *s* of Edmund Lisle Ward and Ellen Ward; *m* 1936, Audrey Doreen Ramsey; three *d*. *Educ:* Boys' Foundation Sch.; Harrison Coll., Barbados. Called to the Bar, Middle Temple, 1933; practised at Barbados Bar, 1934-63; Mem., Legislative Council of Barbados, 1955-58; Mem., House of Representatives, Fedn of West Indies, 1958-62; High Court of Barbados, 1963-76. Pres., Barbados Football Assoc., 1954-75. *Recreations:* reading, bridge, billiards. *Address:* Government House, Barbados. *T:* 92646. *Clubs:* Spartan (Barbados); (Hon.) Summerhays; (Hon.) Bridgetown; (Hon.) Barbados Turf.

WARD, Denzil Anthony Seaver, CMG 1967; Barrister, New Zealand; *b* Nelson, NZ, 26 March 1909; 3rd *s* of late Louis Ernest Ward, Civil Servant NZ Government and Secretary Geographic Board, and Theresa Ward (*née* Kilgour); *m* 1938, Mary Iredale Garland, *d* of late John Edwin Garland, Christchurch, NZ; three *d*. *Educ:* Christ's College and Cathedral Grammar Sch., Christchurch, NZ; Victoria Univ. of Wellington, NZ. BA 1928; LLB 1938; practised law as barrister and solicitor, 1938-42; Asst Law Draftsman, Law Drafting Office, 1942; First Asst, 1947; Law Draftsman, 1958-66; Counsel to Law Drafting Office and Compiler of Statutes, 1966-74. Lecturer in law subjects, Victoria Univ. of Wellington, NZ, 1944-45, 1949-55. Member: NZ Law Revision Commn, 1958-74; Public and Administrative Law Reform Cttee, 1966-80; Criminal Law Reform Cttee, 1971-; Vice-Patron, Legal Research Foundation, 1965-68. Mem. Otaki and Porirua Trusts Bd, 1952-71, Chm., 1965-71; Mem. Papawai and Kaikokirikiri Trusts Bd, 1965-81, Chm., 1972-81. Foundation mem. and mem. Council, NZ Founders Soc., 1939-42;

elected hon. life mem., 1941. Chm., Royal Wellington Choral Union, 1949-50; mem. Schola Cantorum, 1951-55. *Publications:* (jointly) Ward and Wild's Mercantile Law in New Zealand, 1947; (ed) NZ Statutes Reprint, 1908-57, vols 3-16; articles in legal periodicals. *Recreations:* music, reading, gardening, watching rugby and cricket. *Address:* 15 Plymouth Street, Karori, Wellington 5, New Zealand. *T:* 768-096.

WARD, Donald Albert; Secretary General, International Union of Credit and Investment Insurers (Berne Union), since 1974; *b* 30 March 1920; *s* of Albert and Rosie Ward; *m* 1948, Maureen Molloy; five *s*. *Educ:* Brewery Road Elementary Sch.; Southend-on-Sea High Sch.; The Queen's Coll., Oxford. BA(Hons)(Maths). Served War, Indian Army (RIASC), 10th Indian Div., Middle East and Italy, 1940-45 (despatches). Min. of Food, 1946-53; Export Credits Guarantee Dept, 1953-74 (Under-Sec., 1971-74). *Address:* Lindisfarne, St Nicholas Hill, Leatherhead, Surrey. *Club:* United Oxford & Cambridge University.

WARD, General Sir Dudley, GCB 1959 (KCB 1957; CB 1945); KBE 1953 (CBE 1945); DSO 1944; DL; *b* 27 Jan. 1905; *s* of L. H. Ward, Wimborne, Dorset; *m* 1st, 1933, Beatrice Constance (*d* 1962), *d* of Rev. T. F. Griffith, The Bourne, Farnham, Surrey; one *d*; 2nd, 1963, Joan Elspeth de Pechell, *d* of late Colonel D. C. Scott, CBE, Netherbury, Dorset. *Educ:* Wimborne Grammar Sch.; Royal Military Coll., Sandhurst. 2nd Lieut, Dorset Regt, 1929; Captain, The King's Regt, 1937. Served War of 1939-45 (DSO, CBE, CB); Director of Military Operations, War Office, 1947-48; Commandant, Staff Coll., Camberley, 1948-51; Commander of the 1st Corps, 1951-52; Deputy Chief of Imperial General Staff, 1953-56; Commander, Northern Army Group and Commander-in-Chief, British Army of the Rhine, 1957-Dec. 1959; Comdr in Chief, British Forces, Near East, 1960-62; Governor and Commander in Chief of Gibraltar, 1962-65. Colonel, King's Regt, 1947-57; Colonel Commandant, REME, 1958-63; ADC General to the Queen, 1959-61. DL Suffolk, 1968. *Recreation:* golf. *Address:* Wynney's Farmhouse, Dennington, Woodbridge, Suffolk. *T:* Badingham 663. *Club:* Army and Navy.

WARD, Edmund Fisher, CBE 1972; Architect; Member, Royal Fine Art Commission, since 1974; Consultant (formerly Partner), Gollins Melvin Ward Partnership. *Address:* White Cottage, The Street, Chipperfield, near King's Langley, Hertfordshire WD4 9BH.

WARD, Edward; *see* Bangor, 7th Viscount.

WARD, Edward Rex, CMG 1948; *b* 19 May 1902; *y s* of late Daniel Ward, FSI, Tavistock; *m* 1st, 1934, Mary Nell (from whom he obtained a divorce, 1941); 2nd, 1947, Molly Owen Jones, *née* Money (*d* 1971), widow of Flying Officer Owen Jones, RAF; one *s* two step *d*. *Educ:* King's Coll., Taunton; Coll. of Estate Management, Lincoln's Inn Fields, WC1. Colonial Administrative Service, Nigeria, 1926; transferred to The Gambia, 1942; Actg Governor on several occasions since 1945; Colonial Secretary, The Gambia, 1945-52; retired, 1952. *Recreation:* gardening. *Address:* Cameron House, 78 Pellhurst Road, Ryde, Isle of Wight. *Club:* Seaview Yacht.

WARD, Ven. Edwin James Greenfield, MVO 1963; Archdeacon of Sherborne since 1967; Rector of West Stafford since 1967; *b* 26 Oct. 1919; *er s* of Canon F. G. Ward, MC, lately of Canberra, Australia; *m* 1946, Grizell Evelyn Buxton; one *s* two *d*. *Educ:* St John's, Leatherhead; Christ's Coll., Cambridge (MA). Served King's Dragoon Guards, 1940; Reserve, 1946. Ordained 1948; Vicar of North Elmham, Norfolk, 1950-55; Chaplain to the Queen, 1955; Chaplain, Royal Chapel, Windsor Great Park, 1955-67. *Recreation:* fishing. *Address:* The Rectory, West Stafford, Dorchester, Dorset. *T:* Dorchester 64637.

WARD, Air Cdre Ellacott Lyne Stephens, CB 1954; DFC 1939; RAF, retired; *b* 22 Aug. 1905; *s* of late Lt-Col E. L. Ward, CBE, IMS; *m* 1929, Sylvia Winifred Constance Etheridge (*d* 1974), *d* of late Lt-Col F. Etheridge, DSO, IA, and late Mrs Etheridge; one *s* one *d*. *Educ:* Cranwell. No 20 Sqdn, India, 1926-30; Engineering Course, and Engineering duties, UK, 1930-34; student, Army Staff Coll., Quetta, 1936-37; comd No 28 Sqdn, RAF, 1938-39; MAP, 1940-42; Instructor, RAF Staff Coll., 1942-43; Bomber Comd, 1943-44; Dep. Head, RAF Mission to Chinese Air Force Staff Coll., Chengtu, China, 1945-46; SASO, Burma, 1946-47; Air Ministry, 1947-49; Flying Training Comd, 1949-52; Head of British Services Mission to Burma, 1952-54; AOC No 64 (N) Group, Royal Air Force, 1954-57. Chinese Cloud and Banner, 1946; Chinese Chenyuan, 1946. *Recreation:* bookbinding. *Address:* Carousel, 37 Brownsea Road, Sandbanks, Poole, Dorset BH13 7QW. *T:* Canford Cliffs 709455.

WARD, Francis Alan Burnett, CBE 1964; PhD; Keeper, Department of Physics, Science Museum, London, SW7, 1945-70; *b* 5 March 1905; *o s* of late Herbert Ward, CBE, and late Eva Caroline (*née* Burnett); *m* 1953, E. Marianne Brown, Ilkley. *Educ:* Highgate Sch.; Sidney Sussex Coll., Cambridge. MA, PhD (Cantab), 1931. Research on nuclear physics at Cavendish Laboratory, Cambridge, 1927-31; Asst Keeper, The Science Museum, 1931; seconded to Air Ministry (Meteorological Office), 1939. Flt-Lieut, RAFVR (Meteorological Branch), 1943-45. In charge of Atomic Physics and Time Measurement sections, Science Museum, 1931-70. FBHI; FInstP; FMA. *Publications:* official Science Museum Handbooks on Time Measurement, 1936 and 1937, and later edns; Catalogue of European Scientific

Instruments, British Museum, 1981. Various papers on atomic physics in Proc. Royal Society and Proc. Physical Soc. *Recreations:* bird-watching, gardening, photography, music. *Address:* Wendover, 8 Parkgate Avenue, Hadley Wood, Barnet, Herts EN4 0NR. *T:* 01-449 6880.

WARD, Frank D.; *see* Dixon Ward.

WARD, Frederick John; Under-Secretary, Department of the Environment (formerly Ministry of Housing and Local Government), 1968-76. *Address:* 29 Groveside, Great Bookham, Leatherhead, Surrey. *T:* Bookham 52282. *Club:* MCC.

WARD, Hubert, MA; JP; Headmaster of the King's School, Ely, since 1970; *b* 26 Sept. 1931; *s* of Allan Miles Ward and Joan Mary Ward; *m* 1958, Elizabeth Cynthia Fearn Bechervaise; one *s* two *d. Educ:* Westminster Sch.; Trinity Coll., Cambridge. Asst Master (Maths), Geelong C of E Grammar Sch., Victoria, 1955-66; Asst Master (Maths), Westminster Sch., London, 1966-69. JP Cambs. 1976. *Publication:* (with K. Lewis) Starting Statistics, 1969. *Recreations:* rowing, sailing, bird-watching. *Address:* The King's School, Ely, Cambridgeshire. *T:* Ely 2824.

WARD, Ivor William, OBE 1968; Deputy Managing Director, Associated Television (Network) Ltd, 1974-77, retired; *b* 19 Jan. 1916; *s* of Stanley James Ward and Emily Ward; *m* 1st, 1940, Patricia Aston; two *s* one *d* ; 2nd, 1970, Betty Nichols; one step *s. Educ:* Hoe Grammar Sch., Plymouth. Asst Engr, BBC Radio Plymouth, 1932; Technical Asst, BBC Experimental TV Service, Alexandra Palace, 1936; Maintenance Engr, BBC TV London, 1937. Instructor Radar, REME and Military Coll. of Science, 1939-45. Studio Manager, BBC TV, 1946; Producer, BBC TV, 1947-55; Head of Light Entertainment, ATV (Network) ITV, 1955-61; Production Controller, ATV, 1961-63; Executive Controller and Production Controller, ATV, 1963-67; Director of Programmes, ATV, 1968-76. Chm., ITV Network Sports Cttee, 1972-77; Head of Ops Gp, EBU: World Cup 1978, 1977-78; Moscow Olympics 1980, 1978-82. FRSA. *Recreations:* sport, golf, fishing, motor sport and motor cars, photography, music. *Address:* 50 Frith Street, W1.

WARD, John; *see* Ward, C. J. W.

WARD, Rt. Rev. John Aloysius; *see* Menevia, Bishop of, (RC).

WARD, Prof. John Clive, FRS 1965; Professor, Macquarie University, Sydney, NSW, since 1967; *b* 1 Aug. 1924; *s* of Joseph William Ward and Winifred Palmer. *Educ:* Bishops Stortford Coll.; Merton Coll., Oxford. Member, Inst. for Advanced Study, Princeton, 1951-52, 1955-56, 1960-61; Professor of Physics, Carnegie Inst. of Technology, Pittsburgh, 1959-60; The Johns Hopkins University, Baltimore, 1961-66. *Publications:* various articles on particle theory and statistical mechanics. *Recreations:* ski-ing, music. *Address:* School of Mathematics and Physics, Macquarie University, 171-7 Epping Road, North Ryde, NSW 2113, Australia; 16 Fern Street, Pymble, NSW 2073.

WARD, John Devereux, CBE 1973; BSc; CEng, FICE, FIStructE; MP (C) Poole, since 1979; *b* 8 March 1925; *s* of late Thomas Edward and Victoria Ward; *m* 1955, Jean Miller Aitken; one *s* one *d. Educ:* Romford County Technical Sch.; Univ. of St Andrews (BSc). Navigator, RAF, 1943-47; student, 1949-53. Employed, Consulting Engineers, 1953-58, Taylor Woodrow Ltd, 1958-79; Man. Dir, Taylor Woodrow Arcon, Arcon Building Exports, 1976-78. *Address:* 54 Parkstone Road, Poole, Dorset BH15 2PX. *T:* Poole 674771.

WARD, Sir John (Guthrie), GCMG 1967 (KCMG 1956; CMG 1947); *b* 3 March 1909; *o s* of late Herbert John Ward and Alice Ward (*née* Guthrie); *m* 1st, 1933, Bettine (*d* 1941), *d* of late Col Sydney Hankey; one *s* one *d* ; 2nd, 1942, Daphne, *d* of late Captain Hon. A. S. E. Mulholland and late Joan, Countess of Cavan; two *d. Educ:* Wellington Coll.; Pembroke Coll., Cambridge (History Schol.). BA 1929, Hon. Fellow 1976; Member of University Air Squadron. Entered Diplomatic Service, 1931; served Foreign Office and British Embassies, Baghdad (1932-34) and Cairo (1938-40); British Representative on League of Nations Cttee for settlement of Assyrians, 1935-37. Second Sec., 1936; First Sec., 1941; Mem. of UK Delegns to Moscow confs, 1943-44-45 and Potsdam conf., 1945; Counsellor and Head of UN Dept, Foreign Office, 1946; Counsellor, British Embassy, Rome, 1946-49; Civilian Member of Directing Staff of Imperial Defence Coll., London, 1950; Dep. UK High Comr in Germany, 1951-54; Dep. Under-Sec. of State, Foreign Office, 1954-56; British Ambassador to Argentina, 1957-61; British Ambassador to Italy, 1962-66; retired from HM Diplomatic Service, 1967. Chairman, British-Italian Soc., 1967-74. Mem. Council, RSPCA, 1970-75; Pres., ISPA. *Recreations:* history, gardening. *Address:* Lenox, St Margarets Bay, near Dover. *Club:* Royal Automobile.

WARD, Prof. John Manning, FASSA; FAHA; FRAHS; Vice-Chancellor and Principal, University of Sydney, since 1981; *b* 6 July 1919; *s* of Alexander Thomson Ward and Mildred Boughay Davis; *m* 1951, Patricia Bruce Webb; two *d. Educ:* Fort Street Boys' High Sch.; Univ. of Sydney (MA, LLB). FASSA 1954; FAHA 1969; FRAHS 1979. Challis Prof. of History, Sydney Univ., 1949-79; Dean, Faculty of Arts, 1962; Pro Dean, 1970-71; Chairman: Professorial Bd, 1974-75; Academic Bd, 1976-77; Dominion Fellow, St John's Coll., Cambridge, 1951; Vis. Prof., Yale Univ., 1963; Vis. Fellow, All Souls

Coll., Oxford, 1968; Smuts Vis. Fellow, Cambridge, 1972. Trustee, NSW Public Library, 1968-69; Mem., CL Libr., NSW, 1970-82; Chm., Archives Authority, NSW, 1979- (Mem. 1961-); Chm., NSW State Cancer Council, 1981-82; Mem., Parramatta Hosps Bd, 1982-. *Publications:* British Policy in the South Pacific, 1948, 3rd edn 1976; (jtly) Trusteeship in the Pacific, 1949; contrib. Australia (UN Series, Calif), 1947; Earl Grey and the Australian Colonies 1846-57, 1958; contrib. The Pattern of Australian Culture, 1963; Empire in the Antipodes, *c* 1840-1860, 1966; Changes in Britain 1919-1957, 1968; contrib. Historians at Work, 1973; Colonial Self-Government, The British Experience 1759-1856, 1976; James Macarthur: Colonial Conservative 1798-1867, 1981. *Recreations:* music, trains. *Address:* University of Sydney, New South Wales 2006, Australia. *T:* (02) 692 1122.

WARD, John Stanton, RA 1965 (ARA 1956); VPRP; *b* 10 Oct. 1917; *s* of Russell Stanton and Jessie Elizabeth Ward; *m* 1950, Alison Christine Mary Williams; four *s* twin *d. Educ:* St Owen's School, Hereford; Royal College of Art. Royal Engineers, 1939-46. Vogue Magazine, 1948-52. Has held exhibitions at Agnews Gallery and Maas Gallery. Hon. DLitt. *Recreation:* book illustration. *Address:* Bilting Court, Bilting, Ashford, Kent. *T:* Wye 812478. *Clubs:* Athenæum, Buck's, Harry's Bar.

WARD, Prof. (John Stephen) Keith; F. D. Maurice Professor of Moral and Social Theology in the University of London, since 1982; *b* 22 Aug. 1938; *s* of John George Ward and Evelyn (*née* Simpson); *m* 1963, Marian Trotman; one *s* one *d. Educ:* Universities of Wales and Oxford. BA Wales, BLitt Oxon; MA Cantab. Lecturer in Logic, Univ. of Glasgow, 1964-69; Lectr in Philosophy, Univ. of St Andrews, 1969-71; Lectr in Philosophy of Religion, Univ. of London, 1971-75; Dean of Trinity Hall, Cambridge, 1975-82. *Publications:* Ethics and Christianity, 1970; Kant's View of Ethics, 1972; The Divine Image, 1976; The Concept of God, 1977; The Promise, 1981; Rational Theology and the Creativity of God, 1982; Holding Fast to God, 1982. *Recreations:* music, walking. *Address:* 18 Leyborne Park, Kew, Richmond, Surrey TW9 3HA. *T:* 01-940 6667.

WARD, Joseph Haggitt; Under Secretary, Department of Health and Social Security, since 1976; *b* 7 July 1926; *s* of Joseph G. and Gladys Ward; *m* 1961, Anthea Clemo; one *s* one *d. Educ:* St Olave's Grammar School; Sidney Sussex College, Cambridge. Asst Principal, Min. of National Insurance, 1951; Private Sec. to Minister of Social Security, 1966-68; Asst Sec., 1968; Min. of Housing, later DoE, 1969-72; DHSS, 1972. *Recreations:* Eton fives, music. *Address:* 34 Uffington Road, SE27 0ND. *T:* 01-670 1732.

WARD, Sir Joseph James Laffey, 4th Bt *cr* 1911; *b* 11 Nov. 1946; *s* of Sir Joseph George Davidson Ward, 3rd Bt, and of Joan Mary Haden, *d* of Major Thomas J. Laffey, NZSC; *S* father, 1970; *m* 1968, Robyn Allison, *d* of William Maitland Martin, Rotorua, NZ. *Heir: b* Roderic Anthony Ward, *b* 23 April 1948.

WARD, Keith; *see* Ward, J. S. K.

WARD, Malcolm Beverley; His Honour Judge Malcolm Ward; a Circuit Judge, Midland and Oxford Circuit, since 1979; *b* 3 May 1931; *s* of Edgar and Dora Mary Ward; *m* 1958, Muriel Winifred, *d* of Dr E. D. M. Wallace, Perth; two *s* two *d. Educ:* Wolverhampton Grammar Sch.; St John's Coll., Cambridge (Open Mathematical Schol.; MA, LLB). Called to the Bar, Inner Temple, 1956; practised Oxford (later Midland and Oxford) Circuit; a Recorder of the Crown Court, 1974-79. Governor, Wolverhampton Grammar Sch., 1972- (Chm., 1981-). *Recreations:* golf, music, (in theory) horticulture. *Address:* 1 Fountain Court, Birmingham B4 6DR.

WARD, Martyn Eric; His Honour Judge Ward; a Circuit Judge since 1972; *b* 10 Oct. 1927; 3rd *s* of Arthur George Ward, DSM and Dorothy Ward (*née* Perkins); *m* 1st, 1957, Rosaleen Iona Soloman; one *d* ; 2nd, 1966, Rosanna Maria; two *s. Royal* Navy; Called to Bar, Lincoln's Inn, 1955. *Recreation:* ski-ing. *Address:* The House on the Heath, Fordham Heath, Colchester, Essex CO3 5TL. *T:* Colchester 240624.

WARD, Michael Jackson, CBE 1980; Controller, Home Division, British Council, since 1981; *b* 16 Sept. 1931; *s* of Harry Ward, CBE, and of late Dorothy Julia Ward (*née* Clutterbuck); *m* 1955, Eileen Patricia Foster; one *s* one *d. Educ:* Drayton Manor Grammar Sch.; University Coll. London (BA); Univ. of Freiburg; Corpus Christi Coll., Oxford. HM Forces, 1953-55; 2nd Lieut Royal Signals. Admin. Officer, HMOCS, serving as Dist Comr and Asst Sec. to Govt, Gilbert and Ellice Is; British Council, 1961-: Schs Recruitment Dept, 1961-64; Regional Rep., Sarawak, 1964-68; Dep. Rep., Pakistan, 1968-70; Dir, Appointments Services Dept, 1970-72; Dir, Personnel Dept, 1972-75; Controller, Personnel and Appts Div., 1975-77; Representative, Italy, 1977-81. *Recreations:* music, golf. *Address:* The British Council, 10 Spring Gardens, SW1A 2BN. *T:* 01-930 8466. *Club:* National Liberal.

WARD, Michael John; Public Relations Officer, London Borough of Lewisham, since 1980; *b* 7 April 1931; *s* of Stanley William Ward and Margaret Annie Ward; *m* 1953, Lilian Lomas; two *d. Educ:* Mawney Road Jun. Mixed Sch., Romford; Royal Liberty Sch., Romford; Bungay Grammar Sch.; Univ. of Manchester. BA (Admin). MIPR. Education Officer, RAF, 1953-57; Registrar, Chartered Inst. of Secretaries, 1958-60; S. J. Noel-Brown & Co. Ltd: O&M consultant to local authorities, 1960-61; Local Govt Officer to Labour Party, 1961-65; Public Relns consultant to local authorities,

1965-70; Press Officer, ILEA, 1970-74 and 1979-80. Contested (Lab) Peterborough, 1966, 1970, Feb. 1974; MP (Lab) Peterborough, Oct. 1974-1979; PPS to Sec. of State for Educn and Science, 1975-76, to Minister for Overseas Develt, 1976, to Minister of State, FCO, 1976-79. Sponsored Unfair Contract Terms Act, 1977. Councillor, Borough of Romford, 1958-61 and 1962-65; London Borough of Havering: Councillor, 1964; Alderman, 1971-; Leader of Council, 1971-74. Labour Chief Whip, London Boroughs Assoc., 1968-71; Member: Essex River Authority, 1964-71; Greenwich DHA, 1982-; Hon. Treas., Greater London Arts Assoc., 1969-71; Pres., London Govt Public Relations Assoc., 1977-79. *Recreations:* music, reading, travel. *Address:* 11A Morden Road Mews, SE3 0AE.

WARD, Michael Phelps, FRCS; FRGS; Consultant Surgeon: City and East London Area Health Authority (Teaching), since 1964; St Andrew's Hospital, Bow, since 1964; Lecturer in Clinical Surgery, London Hospital Medical College, since 1975; *b* 26 March 1925; *s* of late Wilfrid Arthur Ward, CMG, MC and Norah Anne Phelps; *m* 1957, Felicity Jane Ewbank; one *s. Educ:* Marlborough Coll., Wilts; Peterhouse, Cambridge (Ironmongers' Co. Exhibn); London Hosp. Med. Coll. BA Hons Cantab 1945, MA 1961; MB BChir 1949, MD 1968. FRCS 1955. Ho. Surg., Surgical Registrar, Sen. Surgical Registrar, London Hosp.; Asst Resident, Royal Victoria Hosp., Montreal, Canada; Consultant Surg., Poplar Hosp., E14, 1964-75; Hunterian Prof., RCS, 1954. Served RAMC, Captain, 1950-52. Fellow, Assoc. of Surgs of Gt Britain; FRSM. Member: Mount Everest Reconnaissance Expedn, 1951; Mount Everest Expedn, 1953 (1st Ascent); Scientific Expedn to Everest Region, 1960-61 (Leader, 1st Winter Ascents of Amadablam and other peaks); Leader: Scientific Expedns to Bhutan Himal, 1964 and 1965; scientific and mountaineering expedn to Mt Kongur, China, 1980-81. FRGS 1964. Dickson Asia Lectr, RGS, 1966; Cuthbert Peek Award, RGS, 1973; Founder's (Royal) Medal, RGS, 1982; Cullum Medal, Amer. Geog. Soc., 1954. Chm., Mount Everest Foundn, 1978-80. *Publications:* Mountaineers' Companion, 1966; In this Short Span, 1972; Mountain Medicine, 1975; many scientific and medical papers on the effects of great altitude, exposure to cold, and on exercise; also on exploratory journeys to the Nepal, Bhutan Himal and Chinese Central Asia. *Recreations:* mountaineering, ski-ing. *Clubs:* Athenæum, Alpine (Vice-Pres., 1968-69).

WARD, Neville; *see* Ward, A. N.

WARD, Air Vice-Marshal Peter Alexander; Deputy Chief of Staff (Operations), HQ Allied Air Forces Central Europe, since 1982; *b* 26 Jan. 1930; *s* of Arthur Charles Ward and Laura May (*née* Squires); *m* 1963, Patricia Louise (*née* Robertson); two *s. Educ:* Woking Grammar School. Joined RAF, 1947; Flying and Staff appointments; OC 511 Sqdn, 1968-70; jssc 1970; ndc 1971; Station Comdr, RAF Brize Norton, 1974-75; Senior Air Staff Officer, HQ 38 Group, 1976-79; rcds 1979; Dir Gen., RAF Training, 1980-82. *Address:* HQ AAFCE, Ramstein Air Base, BFPO 109. *Club:* Royal Air Force.

WARD, Maj.-Gen. Sir Philip (John Newling), KCVO 1976; CBE 1972; DL; Communar of Chichester Cathedral, since 1980; *b* 10 July 1924; *s* of George William Newling Ward and Mary Florence Ward; *m* ; two *s* two *d. Educ:* privately and at Monkton Combe School. Adjt, RMA Sandhurst, 1960-62; Bde Major, Household Bde, 1962-65; Comdg 1st Bn Welsh Guards, 1965-67; Comdr Land Forces, Gulf, 1969-71; GOC London Dist and Maj.-Gen. comdg Household Div., 1973-76; Comdt, RMA, 1976-79. Dir, Public Affairs, Internat. Distillers and Vintners (Home Trade), 1980-; Director: Gilbey Vintners; Morgan Furze. Chairman: Queen Alexandra Hosp. Home; Royal Soldiers Daughters School, 1980-83; Governor and Comdt, Church Lads and Church Girls Bde. Freeman, City of London, 1976. DL West Sussex, 1981. *Recreations:* gardening, fishing. *Address:* The Old Rectory, Patching, near Worthing, West Sussex. *Clubs:* Cavalry and Guards, Buck's.

WARD, Gen. Sir Richard (Erskine), GBE 1976; KCB 1971 (CB 1969); DSO 1943 and Bar, 1943; MC 1942; Chief of Personnel and Logistics, Ministry of Defence, 1974-76, retired; *b* 15 Oct. 1917; *o s* of late John Petty Ward and Gladys Rose Ward (*née* Marsh-Dunn); *m* 1947, Stella Elizabeth, 2nd *d* of late Brig. P. N. Ellis, RA, and Mrs Rachel Ellis; two *s* two *d. Educ:* Marlborough Coll.; RMC, Sandhurst. Commissioned Royal Tank Corps, 1937; served War of 1939-45 (despatches thrice); 5th Royal Tank Regt, 1939-43; Staff Coll., Camberley, 1944; Bde Major, 4th Armoured Bde, 1944; CO Westminster Dragoons, 1945; Korea with 1st Royal Tank Regt, 1952 (despatches); Lt-Col Chiefs of Staff Secretariat, 1955; CO 3 Royal Tank Regt, 1957; idc 1961; on staff of Chief of Defence Staff, 1962; comd 20 Armoured Bde, 1963; GOC 1st Division 1965-67; Vice-Adjutant-General, 1968-70; Cmdr British Forces, Hong Kong, 1970-73. Maj.-Gen., 1965; Lt-Gen., 1970; Gen., 1974. Col Comdt RTR, 1970-75. Dep. Commonwealth Pres., Royal Life Saving Soc., 1976-82. Croix de Guerre, with palm, 1940; Chevalier, Order of Leopold II, with palm, 1945. *Address:* Little Sheldons, Hook, Hants RG27 9LD. *Club:* Army and Navy.

WARD, Robin William; Director-General, West Yorkshire Passenger Transport Executive, since 1976; *b* 14 Jan. 1931; *s* of William Frederick and Elsie Gertrude Ward; *m* 1974, Jean Catherine Laird; one *s. Educ:* Colston's Sch., Bristol; University Coll. London. BScEcon, 1st Cl. Hons. Pilot Officer/Flying Officer, RAF Educn Br., 1954-55. Various posts, London Transport Exec., 1955-67; seconded to Brit. Transport Staff Coll. as mem. staff and latterly Asst Principal (incl. course at Harvard Business Sch.), 1967-70;

Industrial Relations Officer, London Transport Exec., 1970-74; Dir of Personnel, W Yorks Passenger Transport Exec., 1974-76. *Recreations:* Scottish country dancing; trying to learn the piano. *Address:* 1 Meadow Close, Hemsworth, Pontefract, West Yorkshire WF9 4PR. *T:* Hemsworth 613994.

WARD, Roy Livingstone, QC 1972; **His Honour Judge Roy Ward;** a Circuit Judge, since 1979; *b* 31 Aug. 1925; *m* 1972, Barbara Anne (*née* Brockbank); one *s* one *d. Educ:* Taunton Sch.; Pembroke Coll., Cambridge. BA(Hons). Served RAF, 1943-47. Called to Bar, Middle Temple, 1950. A Recorder of the Crown Court, 1972-79. *Address:* Tethers End, Shelsley Drive, Colwall, Worcs. *Club:* United Oxford & Cambridge University.

WARD, Rev. Canon Simon B.; *see* Barrington-Ward.

WARD, Sir Terence George, Kt 1971; CBE 1961 (MBE 1945); Dean of the Faculty of Dental Surgery, Royal College of Surgeons, 1965-68; *b* 16 Jan. 1906; *m* 1931, Elizabeth Ambrose Wilson (*d* 1981); one *s* one *d. Educ:* Edinburgh. Mem., SE Metropolitan Regional Hosp. Bd; Exmr, DSRCSEd, FDRCSIre. Pres., Internat. Assoc. Oral Surgeons; Past Pres., British Association of Oral Surgeons; Consulting Oral Surgeon to the Royal Navy; Consulting Dental Surgeon: to the British Army, 1954-71, Emeritus 1971; to the Royal Air Force; to Dept of Health and Social Security; to the Queen Victoria Hospital, East Grinstead. LRCP, LRCSEd 1928; LRFPS, 1930; LDS (Edinburgh) 1928; FDSRCS 1948; FACD (USA) 1959; FACDSurgeons; FFDRCS Ire., 1964; Hon. FDSRCSE, 1966; Hon. FRCCD, 1966. DDSc, Melbourne, 1963. Mem., SA Dental Assoc.; Hon. Member: Amer. Soc. Oral Surgeons; Dutch Soc. Oral Surgeons; Hon. Fellow: Scandinavian Assoc. Oral Surgeons; Spanish Assoc. Oral Surgeons. *Publication:* The Dental Treatment of Maxillo-facial Injuries, 1956. *Recreation:* golf. *Address:* 22 Marina Court Avenue, Bexhill-on-Sea, East Sussex. *T:* Bexhill-on-Sea 4760.

WARD, Thomas William, ARCA 1949; RE 1955; RWS 1957; sometime Course Director, Illustration, Harrow College of Technology and Art; painter in water colour and oil colour, draughtsman, engraver, illustrator; *b* 8 Nov. 1918; *s* of John B. Ward, Master Stationer, and Lilly B. Ward (*née* Hunt), Sheffield; *m* Joan Palmer, ARCA, *d* of F. N. Palmer, Blackheath; one *s* one *d. Educ:* Nether Edge Grammar Sch., Sheffield; Sheffield Coll. of Art (part-time); Royal Coll. of Art, 1946-49, Silver Medal, 1949, Postgrad. Scholarship, 1949-50. Cadet, Merchant Service, 1935-36; stationer, 1936-39; Military service, 1939-46: commissioned N Staffs Regt, 1942; GSO3 1944-46. *One Man Exhibitions include:* Walker Gall., 1957, 1960; Wakefield City Art Gall., 1962; Shipley Art Gall., 1962; Middlesbrough Art Gall., 1963; St John's Coll., York, 1965; Bohun Gall., Henley, 1974; Digby Gall., Colchester, 1981. *Group Exhibitions include:* Leicester Gall.; Kensington Gall.; Zwemmer Gall.; Bohun Gall. *Open Exhibitions include:* RA, RSA, NEAC, London Group, RSMA, and in Japan, USA, S Africa, NZ. *Important purchases include:* S London Art Gall.; V&A; Nat. Gall. of NZ; Leicester, Oxford and Durham Univs; Arts Council; Contemp. Art Soc.; Bowes Mus.; Graves Art Gall.; Rochdale Art Gall.; Lord Clark. *Illustrations include:* Colman Prentis Varley; Shell Mex; Editions Lausanne. Designer of theatre properties, Tom Arnold Ice Show. *Recreation:* sailing. *Address:* Hollydene, Ipswich Road, Holbrook, Ipswich IP9 2QT.

WARD, William Alan H.; *see* Heaton-Ward.

WARD, William Alec; HM Diplomatic Service, retired; *b* 27 Nov. 1928; *s* of William Leslie Ward and Gladys Ward; *m* 1955, Sheila Joan Hawking; two *s* two *d. Educ:* King's Coll. Sch., Wimbledon; Christ Church, Oxford. HM Forces, 1947-49. Colonial Office, 1952; Private Sec. to Permanent Under-Sec., 1955-57; Singapore, 1960-64; seconded to CRO, 1963; Karachi, 1964-66; Islamabad, 1966-68; joined HM Diplomatic Service, 1968; FCO, 1968-71; Salisbury, 1971-72; Dep. High Comr, Colombo, 1973-76; High Comr, Mauritius, 1977-81. *Recreations:* music, walking. *Address:* Nyewoods, Elm Road, Horsell, Woking, Surrey.

WARD, William Ernest Frank, CMG 1945; *b* 24 Dec. 1900; *s* of W. H. Ward, Borough Treasurer, Battersea; *m* 1926, Sylvia Grace, *d* of Arthur Clayton Vallance, Mansfield, Notts; no *c. Educ:* LCC elementary school; Mercers' Sch.; Dulwich Coll.; Lincoln Coll., Oxford (BLitt, MA); Ridley Hall, Cambridge (Diploma in Education). Master, Achimota Coll., Gold Coast, 1924; Director of Education, Mauritius, 1940; Deputy Educational Adviser, Colonial Office, 1945-56. Editor, Oversea Education, 1946-63. Member of UK delegation to seven general conferences of UNESCO and many other international meetings on education. *Publications:* History of Ghana, 1967 (originally published as History of the Gold Coast, 1948); Educating Young Nations, 1959; Fraser of Trinity and Achimota, 1965; The Royal Navy and the Slavers, 1969; various historical works and educational textbooks. *Recreations:* music, walking. *Address:* Flat 19, Ormsby, Stanley Road, Sutton, Surrey SM2 6TJ. *T:* 01-661 2878.

WARD, William Kenneth, CMG 1977; Under-Secretary, Department of Trade, 1974-78, retired; *b* 20 Jan. 1918; *e s* of late Harold and Emily Ward; *m* 1949, Victoria Emily, *d* of late Ralph Perkins, Carcavelos, Portugal; three *s* one *d. Educ:* Queen Elizabeth's Grammar Sch., Ashbourne; Trinity Coll., Cambridge. 1st class Hons Modern and Medieval Langs Tripos. Entered Ministry of Supply, 1939; Board of Trade, 1955; HM Principal Trade Commissioner, Vancouver, BC, 1959-63; Under-Sec., BoT, 1966-69, Min. of

Technology, later DTI and Dept of Trade, 1969–; Sec., BOTB, 1973. *Recreation:* gardening. *Address:* 31 Plough Lane, Purley, Surrey. *T:* 01-660 2462.

WARD-BOOTH, Maj.-Gen. John Antony, OBE 1971; Secretary, Eastern Wessex Territorial and Army Volunteer Reserve Association; *b* 18 July 1927; *s* of Rev. J. Ward-Booth and Mrs E. M. Ward-Booth; *m* 1952, Margaret Joan Hooper; two *s* two *d*. *Educ:* Worksop College, Notts. Joined Army, 1945; commnd into Worcestershire Regt in India, 1946; served India and Middle East, 1946–48; regular commn Bedfordshire and Hertfordshire Regt, 1948; served BAOR, Far East, Nigeria and Congo, 1950–63, trans. to Parachute Regt, 1963; commanded 3rd Bn, Parachute Regt, 1967–69; Hong Kong, 1969–70; Comdr, 16 Parachute Bde, 1970–73; Nat. Defence Coll., Canada, 1973–74; DAG, HQ BAOR, 1974–75; Dir, Army Air Corps, 1976–79; GOC Western District, 1979–82. Dep. Col, Royal Anglian Regt, 1982–. Governor, Enham Village Centre. *Recreations:* sailing, golf, squash, cricket. *Address:* Longthatch, Hurstbourne Priors, Whitchurch, Hants. *T:* Whitchurch 2461. *Club:* Army and Navy.

WARD-HARRISON, Maj.-Gen. John Martin Donald, OBE 1962; MC and bar 1945; Vice Lord-Lieutenant, North Yorkshire, since 1982; Manager, Thirsk Racecourse Ltd, since 1976; *b* 18 April 1918; *s* of Commander S. J. Ward-Harrison, Haughley House, Suffolk; *m* 1945, June Amoret, *d* of late Major C. A. Fleury Teulon, Inniskilling Dragoons; one *d* (one *s* decd). *Educ:* Shrewsbury Sch. Commnd Suffolk and Norfolk Yeomanry, 1936–39; 5th Royal Inniskilling Dragoon Guards, 1939–45; Staff Coll., S Africa, 1945; Staff appts and regimental duty, 1946–56; GSO1, 7 Armoured Div., 1956–58; comd 10th Royal Hussars (PWO), 1959–62; Col Gen. Staff, 1962–63; Brig., Royal Armoured Corps, E and S Commands, 1964; Imperial Defence Coll., 1965; Dep. Comdt, Staff Coll., Camberley, 1966–68; GOC Northumbrian District, 1968–70; COS, HQ Northern Comd, 1970–72; GOC NE District, 1973; retd 1973. Chm., York and Dist Br., CPRE. Hon. Dir, York Minster Fund, 1975–. DL North Yorks, 1978. *Recreations:* field sports. *Address:* Hazel Bush House, Stockton-on-the-Forest, York YO3 9TP. *T:* Flaxton Moor 239. *Club:* Army and Navy.

See also Sir I. G. Bosville Macdonald of Sleat, Bt.

WARD-JACKSON, Mrs (Audrey) Muriel; *b* 30 Oct. 1914; *d* of late William James Jenkins and Alice Jenkins (*née* Glyde); *m* 1946, George Ralph Norman Ward-Jackson (*d* 1982); no *c*. *Educ:* Queenswood, Hatfield, Herts; Lady Margaret Hall, Oxford (MA). Home Civil Service (Ministries of Works, Town and Country Planning, Housing and Local Government, and HM Treasury): Asst Principal, 1937; Principal, 1942; Asst Sec., 1946–55. A Director (concerned mainly with Finance), John Lewis Partnership, 1955–74; John Lewis Partnership Ltd: Dir, 1957–74; Dir, John Lewis Properties Ltd, 1969–74; Chm., John Lewis Partnership Pensions Trust, 1964–74. On Civil Service Arbitration Tribunal, 1959–64; Chm., Consumers Cttees (Agric. Marketing), 1971–75; Member: Nat. Savings Review Cttee, 1971–73; Royal Commn on Standards of Conduct in Public Life, 1974–76. A Governor, British Film Inst., 1962–65; Mem. Council, Bedford Coll., London Univ., 1967–72. *Recreations:* swimming, gardening. *Address:* Beacon Hill, Heddington, Calne, Wilts SN11 0PD. *T:* Bromham 850390. *Clubs:* Lansdowne, Naval and Military.

WARD THOMAS, Gwyn Edward, CBE 1973; DFC; Chairman since 1976 and Managing Director since 1970, Trident Television Ltd (Deputy Chairman, 1972–76); Chairman and Managing Director, Trident Casinos and Trident Bookmakers; Chairman: Trident Management Ltd; Trident Television Holdings (Australia) Pty Ltd; Trident Television Inc. (USA); Trident Television Associates Inc.; Trident Films Ltd; Trident Leisure Ltd; *b* 1 Aug. 1923; *o s* of William J. and Constance Thomas; *m* 1945, Patricia Cornelius; one *d*. *Educ:* Bloxham Sch.; The Lycée, Rouen. Served RAF, 1 Group Bomber Command and 229 Group Transport Command, 1941–46. Granada Television, 1955–61; Man. Dir, Grampian Television, 1961–67; Man. Dir, 1967–73, Dep. Chm., 1973–81, Yorkshire Television. Chairman: Castlewood Investments Ltd; Don Robinson Holdings Ltd; Watts & Corry Ltd; Pres., Trident Independent Television Enterprises SA, 1969–. British Bureau of Television Advertising: Dir, 1966; Chm., 1968–70; Mem. Council, Independent Television Companies Assoc., 1961–76 (Chairman: Labour Relations Cttee, 1967; Network Programme Cttee, 1971). *Recreations:* ski-ing, boats, photography. *Address:* Sefton, Old Avenue, St George's Hill, Weybridge, Surrey.

WARDALE, Sir Geoffrey (Charles), KCB 1979 (CB 1974); Second Permanent Secretary, Department of the Environment, 1978–80; *b* 29 Nov. 1919; *m* 1944, Rosemary Octavia Dyer; one *s* one *d*. *Educ:* Altrincham Grammar Sch.; Queens' Coll., Cambridge (Schol.). Army Service, 1940–41. Joined Ministry of War Transport as Temp. Asst Princ., 1942; Private Sec. to Perm. Sec., 1946; Princ., 1948; Asst Sec., 1957; Under-Sec., Min. of Transport, later DoE, 1966; Dep. Sec., 1972. Led inquiry into the Open Structure in the Civil Service (The Wardale Report), 1981. *Recreations:* transport history, painting, listening to music. *Address:* 4 Cranedown, Lewes, East Sussex. *T:* Lewes 3468; 6 Karen Court, Dilwyn, Herefordshire. *Club:* United Oxford & Cambridge University.

WARDE, John Robins; His Honour Judge John Warde; a Circuit Judge, since 1977; *b* 25 April 1920; (Guardian) A. W. Ormond, CBE, FRCS; *m* 1941, Edna Holliday Gipson; three *s*. *Educ:* Radley Coll., Abingdon, Berks;

Corpus Christi Coll., Oxford (MA). Served War, 1940–45: Lieut, RA; awarded C-inC's certif. for outstanding good service in the campaign in NW Europe. Member: Devon CC, 1946–49; Devon Agricl Exec. Cttee, 1948–53; West Regional Advisory Council of BBC, 1950–53. Admitted a solicitor, 1950; Partner in Waugh and Co., Solicitors, Haywards Heath and East Grinstead, Sussex, 1960–70. A Recorder of the Crown Court, 1972–77. Registrar of Clerkenwell County Court, 1970–77. *Recreations:* mountaineering, watching cricket, listening to music. *Address:* 20 Clifton Terrace, Brighton, East Sussex BN1 3HA. *T:* Brighton 26642. *Clubs:* Law Society, MCC, Forty.

WARDELL, Gareth Lodwig; MP (Lab) Gower, since Sept. 1982; *b* 29 Nov. 1944; *s* of John Thomas Wardell and Jenny Ceridwen Wardell; *m* 1967, Jennifer Dawn Evans; one *s*. *Educ:* London Sch. of Econs and Pol. Science (BScEcon, MSc). Geography Master, Chislehurst and Sidcup Technical High Sch., 1967–68; Head of Econs Dept, St Clement Danes Grammar Sch., 1968–70; Sixth Form Econs Master, Haberdashers' Aske's Sch., Elstree, 1970–72; Educn Lectr, Bedford Coll. of Physical Educn, 1972–73; Sen. Lectr in Geography, Trinity Coll., Carmarthen, 1973–82. *Publications:* articles on regional issues in British Econ. Survey. *Recreations:* cycling, cross-country running. *Address:* 67 Elder Grove, Carmarthen, Dyfed SA31 2LH. *T:* Carmarthen 4068.

WARDEN, Andrée, (Mrs Roy Warden); *see* Grenfell, A.

WARDER, John Arthur, CBE 1957; General Managing Director, Oil Operating Companies in Iran, 1963–67, retired; *b* 13 Nov. 1909; *s* of John William Warder and Blanche Longstaffe, Bournemouth; *m* 1936, Sylvia Mary Hughes; two *s* one *d*. *Educ:* Kent Coll., Canterbury. Joined Asiatic Petroleum Co., 1927; practical training in oilfields and refinery operations in Argentina. Pres. and Gen. Man., Cia. Mexicana de Petroleo El Aguila, 1950; Gen. Man., Shell Cos in Colombia, 1953; Vice-Pres., Cia. Shell de Venezuela, 1957, Pres., 1959; Shell's Regional Co-ordinator (Oil), Middle East, 1961–63; Dir, Shell Internat. Petroleum Co. Ltd, and Mem. of Bds, Iranian Oil Participants Ltd and Iraq Petroleum Co. Ltd, 1961–63. Officer, Order of Arts and Culture (France), 1966; Order of Taj, 3rd degree (Iran), 1966. *Recreations:* yachting, golf. *Address:* Byways, Village de Putron, Guernsey, CI. *T:* 36935. *Clubs:* American; Larchmont Yacht (New York); Chapultepec Golf (Mexico); Royal Channel Islands Yacht; Royal Guernsey Golf.

See also W. J. M. Shelton.

WARDINGTON, 2nd Baron, *cr* 1936, of Alnmouth in the County of Northumberland; **Christopher Henry Beaumont Pease;** *b* 22 Jan. 1924; *s* of 1st Baron and Hon. Dorothy Charlotte, *er d* of 1st Baron Forster; *S* father, 1950; *m* 1964, Margaret Audrey Dunfee, *d* of John and Eva White; one *s* two *d* (adopted). *Educ:* Eton. Served War of 1939–45, in Scots Guards, 1942–47, Captain. Partner in Stockbroking firm of Hoare Govett Ltd. Alderman of Broad Street Ward, City of London, 1960–63. Mem., Council of Foreign Bondholders, 1967–. Comr, Public Works Loan Bd, 1969–73. Trustee, Royal Jubilee Trusts. *Recreations:* cricket, golf, squash racquets. *Heir:* *b* Hon. William Simon Pease [*b* 15 Oct. 1925; *m* 1962, Hon. Elizabeth Jane Ormsby-Gore, *d* of 4th Baron Harlech, KG, PC, GCMG]. *Address:* Wardington Manor, Banbury, Oxon. *T:* Cropredy 202; 29 Moore Street, SW3. *T:* 01-584 5245. *Club:* Royal Automobile.

WARDLAW, Claude Wilson, PhD, DSc, MSc, FRSE; George Harrison Professor of Botany, University of Manchester, 1958–66, now Emeritus Professor; *b* 4 Feb. 1901; *s* of Major J. Wardlaw, HLI, and Mary Hood Wardlaw; *m* 1928, Jessie Connell (*d* 1971); two *s*. *Educ:* Paisley Grammar Sch.; Glasgow Univ. Demonstrator and Lecturer in Botany, Glasgow Univ., 1921–28; Pathologist and Officer-in-Charge, Low Temperature Research Station, Imperial College of Tropical Agriculture, Trinidad, BWI, 1928–40; Professor of Cryptogamic Botany, University of Manchester, 1940–58; wide travel in United States, Central and South America and in West Indies, Africa and East Indies. Prather Lecturer, Harvard Univ.; Hon. Foreign Mem., American Academy of Arts and Sciences; Hon. Foreign Correspondent, Académie d'Agriculture de la France; Hon. For. Associate, Royal Academy of Belgium; Corresp. Mem., American Botanical Soc., 1967; Sen. For. Scientist Fellowship, Nat. Sci. Foundation, Univ. of California, 1968. Vis. Prof., NY State Univ., Buffalo, 1967. Hon. DSc McGill. Pelton Award, Amer. Botanical Soc., 1970. Trinidad Volunteer Regt, 1937–40; Lt-Col TA, retired. *Publications:* Diseases of the Banana, 1935, rev. and greatly extended edns, as Banana Diseases, 1961, 1972; Green Havoc, 1935; Tropical Fruits and Vegetables: Storage and Transport, 1937; Phylogeny and Morphogenesis; Morphogenesis in Plants, 1952; Embryogenesis in Plants, 1955; Organization and Evolution in Plants, 1965; Morphogenesis in Plants: A Contemporary Study, 1968; Essays on Form in Plants, 1968; Cellular Differentiation in Plants and Other Essays, 1969; A Quiet Talent: Jessie Wardlaw, 1903–1971, 1971; Enchantment in Fern, 1974; obituary of F. W. Sansome, CBE, PhD, FRSE, FLS, in RSE Year Book 1982; scientific papers published in Phil. Trans. Royal Society Edinburgh, Royal Soc., Annals of Botany, Nature, etc; *Festschrift:* Trends in Plant Morphogenesis, ed E. G. Cutter, 1966. *Address:* 6 Robins Close, Bramhall, Stockport, Cheshire SK7 2PF.

WARDLAW, Sir Henry, 20th Bt of Pitreavie, *cr* 1631; *b* 30 Aug. 1894; *o s* of Sir Henry Wardlaw, 19th Bt, and Janet Montgomerie, *d* of James Wylie; *S* father 1954; *m* 1929, Ellen, *d* of John Francis Brady; four *s* one *d*. *Heir:* *s* Henry John Wardlaw, MB, BS [*b* 30 Nov. 1930; *m* 1962, Julie-Ann, *d* of late Edward Patrick Kirwan; five *s* two *d*]. *Address:* 82 Vincent Street, Sandringham, Vic 3191, Australia.

WARDLE, Air Cdre Alfred Randles, CBE 1945; AFC 1929; MRAeS; RAF, retired; *b* 29 Oct. 1898; *s* of William Wardle, Stafford; *m* 1926, Sarah, *d* of David Brindley, Cotes Heath; one *s* one *d*. Joined Hon. Artillery Co., 1916; RFC 1917; RAF 1918; Director of Operational Requirements, Air Ministry, 1943-46; AOC Ceylon, 1947-49; AOC No. 66 (Scottish) Group, 1950-52. Air Commodore, 1943; retired 1952. Secretary: Corby Develt Corp., 1954-67; Milton Keynes Develt Corp., 1967-68; Peterborough Develt Corp., 1968-69; Northampton Develt Corp., 1969; Central Lancs Develt Corp., 1971-72. *Address:* 88 Gipsy Lane, Kettering, Northants. *T:* Kettering 85780. *Club:* Royal Air Force.

WARDLE, (John) Irving; Drama Critic, The Times, since 1963; *b* 20 July 1929; *s* of John Wardle and Nellie Partington; *m* 1958, Joan Notkin (marr. diss.); *m* 1963, Fay Crowder (marr. diss.); two *s*; *m* 1975, Elizabeth Grist; one *s* one *d*. *Educ:* Bolton Sch.; Wadham Coll., Oxford (BA); Royal Coll. of Music (ARCM). Joined Times Educational Supplement as sub-editor, 1956; Dep. Theatre Critic, The Observer, 1960. Editor, Gambit, 1973-75. Play: The Houseboy, prod Open Space Theatre, 1974, ITV, 1982. *Publication:* biography: The Theatres of George Devine, 1978. *Recreation:* piano playing. *Address:* 51 Richmond Road, New Barnet, Herts. *T:* 01-440 3671.

WARDLE, Sir Thomas (Edward Jewell), Kt 1970; Lord Mayor of Perth, Western Australia, 1967-72; *b* 18 Aug. 1912; *s* of Walter Wardle and Lily Wardle (*née* Jewell); *m* 1940, Hulda May Olson; one *s* one *d*. *Educ:* Perth Boys' Sch., Western Australia. Member: King's Park Bd, 1970-81; Bd, Churchland Teachers Coll., 1973-78; Chairman: Trustees, WA Museum, 1973-82; Aboriginal Loans Commn, 1974-80; Pres., Nat. Trust of WA, 1971-82. Hon. LLD Univ. of WA, 1973. Commendatore, Order of Merit (Italy), 1970. *Recreations:* boating, fishing. *Address:* 3 Kent Street, Bicton, Western Australia 6157. *Clubs:* Returned Services League, Western Australian (both in Western Australia).

WARDS, Brig. George Thexton, CMG 1943; OBE 1935; late IA; Historian, Cabinet Office, 1951-69. *Educ:* Heversham Sch., Westmorland. Served European War, 1914-18, with 7 London Regt, France and Belgium, 1917-18; 2nd Lieut, Indian Army, 1918; attached to HM Embassy, Tokyo, 1923-28; NW Frontier of India, 1930; Bt Major, 1933; Staff Officer to British Troops in North China, 1932-36; Lt-Col and Asst Military Attaché, Tokyo, 1937-41; Brig., Military Attaché, Tokyo, 1941; GSO1, GHQ India, 1942; Commandant Intelligence Sch., India, 1943-45; Commandant Intelligence Corps, Training Centre, India, 1945-47. Lt-Col, 1944; Col, 1945. Official Interpreter in Japanese to Govt of India, 1928-32, 1936, and 1944-47. Information Officer, Min. of Food, 1949; Chief Enforcement Officer, Min. of Food, 1950. Chm., Nat. Anti-Vivisection Soc., 1954-57; Mem. Council, RSPCA, 1956-67; Official visit to Japan, 1966. *Publications:* Joint author, Official History, The War against Japan, Vol. I 1955, Vol. II 1958, Vol. III 1962, Vol. IV 1965, Vol. V 1969. *Club:* Army and Navy.

WARE, Cyril George, CB 1981; Under-Secretary, Inland Revenue, 1974-82; *b* 25 May 1922; *s* of Frederick George Ware and Elizabeth Mary Ware; *m* 1946, Gwennie (*née* Wooding); two *s* one *d*. *Educ:* Leyton County High Sch. Entered Inland Revenue as Tax Officer, 1939; Inspector of Taxes, 1949; Sen. Principal Inspector, 1969. *Recreations:* music, woodwork, gardening, swimming. *Address:* 86 Tycehurst Hill, Loughton, Essex. *T:* 01-508 3588.

WARE, Sir Henry (Gabriel), KCB 1972 (CB 1971); HM Procurator-General and Treasury Solicitor, 1971-75; *b* 23 July 1912; *o s* of late Charles Martin Ware and Dorothy Anne Ware (*née* Gwyn Jeffreys); *m* 1939, Gloria Harriet Platt; three *s* (and one *s* decd). *Educ:* Marlborough; St John's Coll., Oxford. Admitted solicitor, 1938; entered Treasury Solicitor's Dept, 1939; Dep. Treasury Solicitor, 1969-71. Served War of 1939-45 with Royal Artillery. *Recreations:* fly fishing, gardening. *Address:* The Little House, Tilford, Farnham, Surrey. *T:* Frensham 2151. *Clubs:* Athenæum; Frensham Fly Fishers (Frensham).

WARE, Martin, MB, MSc, FRCP; research student in micropalaeontology, University College of Wales, Aberystwyth, since 1975; *b* 1 Aug. 1915; *o s* of late Canon Martin Stewart Ware and late Margaret Isabel (*née* Baker, later Baker Wilbraham); *m* 1938, Winifred Elsie Boyce; two *s* three *d*. *Educ:* Eton; St Bartholomew's Hospital. MB, BS (London) 1939; MRCP 1945; FRCP 1967; MSc (Wales) 1978. Editor, St Bartholomew's Hosp. Jl, 1937-38. House-surgeon, St Bartholomew's Hosp., 1939; served with RAMC, attached to Royal W African Frontier Force (Captain, graded physician), 1940-45; Publications Officer, Medical Research Council, 1946-50; Asst Editor, British Medical Jl, 1950; Editor, 1966-75. Vice-President: BMA; Internat. Union of Med. Press, 1966-75; Member: Council of Res. Defence Soc., 1960-65; Med. Panel of British Council, 1966-75. *Recreations:* bird watching, reading. *Address:* 35 Rhos Hendre, Waun Fawr, Aberystwyth, Dyfed SY23 3PT. *T:* Aberystwyth 4059.

WARE, Michael John; barrister-at-law; Solicitor and Legal Adviser, Departments of the Environment and Transport, since 1982; *b* 7 May 1932; *s* of Kenneth George Ware and Phyllis Matilda (*née* Joynes); *m* 1966, Susan Ann Maitland; three *d*. *Educ:* Cheltenham Grammar Sch.; Trinity Hall, Cambridge (BA(Law), LLB). Called to Bar, Middle Temple. Nat. Service,

2/Lieut RASC, 1954-56. Board of Trade (later Dept of Trade and Industry): Legal Asst, 1957-64; Sen. Legal Asst, 1964-72; Asst Solicitor, 1972-73; Dir, Legal Dept, Office of Fair Trading, 1973-77; Under Secretary: Dept of Trade, 1977-81; DoE and Dept of Transport, 1982. *Recreation:* gardening. *Address:* 2 Marsham Street, SW1P 3EB.

WAREHAM, Arthur George; *b* 24 April 1908; *y s* of late George Wareham and of Elizabeth Wareham; *m* 1936, Kathleen Mary, *d* of H. E. and Mabel Tapley; one *s* one *d*. *Educ:* Queen's Coll., Taunton. Joined Western Morning News, 1926; Daily Mail, 1935; Editor, Daily Mail, 1954-59. Chm., Arthur Wareham Associates Ltd, 1961-77. *Address:* Three Corners, Forest Ridge, Keston, Kent. *T:* Farnborough (Kent) 53606.

WAREING, Prof. Philip Frank, PhD, DSc London; FRS 1969, FLS; Professor of Botany, University College of Wales, Aberystwyth, 1958-81, now Emeritus; *b* 27 April 1914; *e s* of late Frank Wareing; *m* 1939, Helen Clark; one *s* one *d* (and one *d* decd). *Educ:* Watford Grammar School; Birkbeck Coll., Univ. of London. Exec. Officer, Inland Revenue, 1931-41. Captain, REME, 1942-46. Lectr, Bedford Coll., Univ. of London, 1947-50; Lectr, then Sen. Lectr, Univ. of Manchester, 1950-58. Member: Nature Conservancy, 1965-68; Water Resources Board, 1968-71; Chm. Res. Adv. Cttee, Forestry Commn, 1972. Pres., Sect. K, British Assoc., 1970; Mem. Council, Royal Soc., 1972. Mem., Leopoldina Acad. of Science, 1971. *Publications:* Control of Plant Growth and Differentiation, 1970; various papers on plant physiology in scientific journals. *Recreations:* gardening, hill walking. *Address:* Bryn Rhedyn, Caemelyn, Aberystwyth, Dyfed SY23 3DA. *T:* Aberystwyth 3910.

WARHURST, Alan; Director, Manchester Museum, since 1977; *b* 6 Feb. 1927; *s* of W. Warhurst; *m* 1953, Sheila Lilian Bradbury; one *s* two *d*. *Educ:* Canon Slade Grammar Sch., Bolton; Manchester Univ. BA Hons History 1950. Asst, Grosvenor Museum, Chester, 1950-51; Asst Curator, Maidstone Museum and Art Gallery, 1951-55; Curator, Northampton Museum and Art Gallery, 1955-60; Director, City Museum, Bristol, 1960-70; Director, Ulster Museum, 1970-77. FSA 1958; FMA 1958. Pres., S Western Fedn Museums and Galleries, 1966-68; Chm., Irish Nat. Cttee, ICOM, 1973-75; President: Museums Assoc., 1975-76; N Western Fedn of Museums and Art Galls, 1979-80. *Publications:* various archaeological and museum contribs to learned jls. *Address:* The Manchester Museum, The University, Manchester M13 9PL. *T:* 061-273 3333.

WARING, Sir (Alfred) Holburt, 3rd Bt *cr* 1935; *b* 2 Aug. 1933; *s* of Sir Alfred Harold Waring, 2nd Bt, and of Winifred, *d* of late Albert Boston, Stockton-on-Tees; *S* father, 1981; *m* 1958, Anita, *d* of late Valentin Medinilla, Madrid; one *s* one *d*. *Educ:* Rossall School; Leeds College of Commerce. Director: SRM Plastics Ltd; Waring Investments Ltd; Rotaprint Ltd; Property Realisation Co. Ltd; Moor Park Golf Club Ltd; Moor Park (1958) Ltd. Governor, Med. Coll. of St Bartholomew's Hosp. Chm., Moor Park Lawn Tennis Club. *Recreations:* tennis, golf, squash, swimming. *Heir:* *s* Michael Holburt Waring *b* 3 Jan. 1964. *Address:* Earls Croft, 30 Russell Road, Moor Park, Northwood, Middlesex. *T:* Northwood 24570. *Clubs:* Moor Park Golf (Rickmansworth); Northwood Squash Centre (Northwood).

WARK, Sir Ian (William), Kt 1969; CMG 1967; CBE 1963; PhD (London); DSc (Melbourne); Hon. Consultant, CSIRO Institute of Earth Resources (formerly CSIRO Minerals Research Laboratories), since 1971; *b* 8 May 1899; *s* of William John Wark and Florence Emily (*née* Walton); *m* 1927, Elsie Evelyn, *d* of late W. E. Booth; one *d*. *Educ:* Scotch Coll., Melbourne; Univs of Melbourne, London and California (Berkeley). Exhibn of 1851 Science Research Scholarship, 1921-24; Lectr in Chemistry, Univ. of Sydney, 1925; Research Chemist, Electrolytic Zinc Co. of Australasia Ltd, 1926-39; CSIRO: Chief, Div. of Industrial Chemistry, 1940-58; Dir, Chemical Research Laboratories, 1958-60; Mem. Exec., 1961-65. Chm., Commonwealth Adv. Cttee on Advanced Educn., 1965-71. Gen. Pres., Royal Australian Chem. Inst., 1957-58; Treas., Australian Acad. of Science, 1959-63. FAA 1954; FTS 1976; Hon. Mem., Australasian Inst. of Mining and Metallurgy, 1960-; Fellow, UCL, 1965. Hon. DAppSc, Melbourne, 1977; Hon. DASc Victoria Inst. of Colls, 1979. ANZAAS Medal, 1973. *Publications:* (monograph) Principles of Flotation, 1938 (revised, with K. L. Sutherland, 1955); Why Research?, 1968; numerous papers in scientific jls. *Recreations:* golf, fishing. *Address:* 31 Linum Street, Blackburn, Victoria 3130, Australia. *T:* Melbourne 8772878. *Club:* Sciences (Melbourne).

WARMAN, Ven. Francis Frederic Guy; Archdeacon of Aston, 1965-77, Emeritus since 1977; Canon Residentiary of Birmingham, 1965-77, Emeritus since 1977; *b* 1 Dec. 1904; *er s* of Frederic Sumpter Guy Warman, one time Bishop of Manchester, and Gertrude Warman (*née* Earle); *m* 1932, Kathleen Olive, *d* of O. C. Phillips; one *s* one *d*. *Educ:* Weymouth Coll.; Worcester Coll., Oxford; Ridley Hall, Cambridge. Ordained as Curate of Radford, Coventry, 1927; Curate of Chilvers Coton, Nuneaton, 1930; Vicar of: St James, Selby, 1932; Beeston, Leeds, 1936; Ward End, Birmingham, 1943; Aston-juxta-Birmingham, 1946. Rural Dean of East Birmingham, 1948-65; Proctor in Convocation, 1945-75; Hon. Canon of Birmingham, 1948-65. *Recreations:* music, golf. *Address:* 76 Winterbourne Close, Lewes, Sussex BN7 1JZ. *T:* Lewes 2440.

WARMINGTON, Eric Herbert, MA; FRHistS; Professor Emeritus of Classics, University of London; Fellow of Birkbeck College; Vice-Master,

Birkbeck College, 1954–65, Vice-President, since 1966; Acting Master, 1950–51, 1965–66; *b* 15 March 1898; *s* of John Herbert Warmington, MA, and Maud Lockhart; *m* 1922, Marian Eveline Robertson, Kinsale, Co. Cork; one *s* two *d. Educ:* Perse School, Cambridge; Peterhouse, Cambridge (Scholar). Served in Garrison Artillery and King's Own Yorkshire Light Infantry, 1917–19; Cambridge University, 1919–22; First Class, Classical Tripos, Part I, 1921; First Class, Part II, 1922; BA 1922; Assistant master at Charterhouse, 1922–23; Classical Sixth Form master, Mill Hill School, 1923–25; Reader in Ancient History, University of London, 1925–35; Le Bas Prize, Cambridge University, 1925; MA 1925; FRHistS, 1928; Editor, Loeb Classical Library, 1937–74. Dean of Faculty of Arts, University of London, 1951–56; Member of Senate, University of London, 1956–66; Acting Director Univ. of London Inst. of Education, 1957–58; Chairman, Goldsmiths' College Delegacy, 1958–75; President London Branch Classical Assoc. 1963–66. *Publications:* The Commerce between the Roman Empire and India, 1928; Athens, 1928; The Ancient Explorers (with M. Cary), 1929; Greek Geography, 1934; Africa in Ancient and Medieval Times, in the Cambridge History of the British Empire, 1936; Remains of Old Latin, Vol. I, 1935; Vol. II, 1936; Vol. III, 1938, Vol. IV, 1940; articles in The Oxford Classical Dictionary, 1949; A History of Birkbeck College, University of London, during the second World War, 1939–1945, 1954; (ed) Great Dialogues of Plato (trans. by W. H. D. Rouse), 1956; various articles and reviews. *Recreations:* music, gardening and natural history. *Address:* 48 Flower Lane, Mill Hill, NW7. *T:* 01-959 1905.

WARMINGTON, Lt-Comdr Sir Marshall George Clitheroe, 3rd Bt, *cr* 1908; Royal Navy, retired; *b* 26 May 1910; *o s* of Sir Marshall Denham Warmington, 2nd Bt, and Alice Daisy Ing; *S* father, 1935; *m* 1st, 1933, Mollie (from whom he obtained a divorce, 1941), *er d* of late Capt. M. A. Kennard, RN (retired); one *s* one *d* ; 2nd, 1942, Eileen Mary (*d* 1969), *o d* of late P. J. Howes; two *s. Educ:* Charterhouse. *Heir: s* Marshall Denham Malcolm Warmington, *b* 5 Jan. 1934. *Address:* Swallowfield Park, near Reading, Berks RG7 1TG. *T:* Reading 882210. *Clubs:* Army and Navy; MCC.
See also Sir H. H. Trusted.

WARNE, (Ernest) John (David), CB 1982; Secretary, Institute of Chartered Accountants in England and Wales, since 1982; *b* 4 Dec. 1926; *m* 1953, Rena Wolfe; three *s. Educ:* Univ. of London (BA(Hons)). Civil Service Commission, 1953; Asst Comr and Principal, Civil Service Commn, 1953; BoT, later DTI and Dept of Industry: Principal, 1962; Asst Sec., 1967; Under-Sec., 1972; Dir for Scotland, 1972–75; Under-Sec.: Personnel Div., 1975–77; Industrial and Commercial Policy Div., 1977–79; Dep. Sec., Dep. Dir-Gen., OFT, 1979–82. *Recreations:* reading, collecting prints, languages. *Address:* 3 Woodville Road, Ealing, W5. *T:* 01-998 0215. *Club:* Reform.

WARNE, Rear-Adm. Robert Spencer, CB 1953; CBE 1945; retired; *b* 26 June 1903; *s* of E. S. Warne, London; *m* 1925, Dorothy Hadwen Wheelwright (*d* 1976); three *s. Educ:* RN Colleges, Osborne and Dartmouth. Joined Submarine Branch, 1925; Commander, 1936; Captain, 1941; Rear-Admiral 1951; Deputy Chief of Naval Personnel, Admiralty, 1951–53; Flag Officer, Germany and Chief British Naval Representative in the Allied Control Commission, 1953–55; retired 1955. *Recreations:* sailing, golf. *Address:* Tra Ley, 75 High Street, Prestwood, Bucks. *T:* Great Missenden 5158. *Club:* Royal Naval and Royal Albert Yacht (Portsmouth).

WARNER, Sir (Edward Courtenay) Henry, 3rd Bt, *cr* 1910; *m* ; three *s. Heir: s* Philip Courtenay Thomas Warner, *b* 3 April 1951.

WARNER, Sir Edward (Redston), KCMG 1965 (CMG 1955); OBE 1948; HM Diplomatic Service, retired; *b* 23 March 1911; *s* of late Sir George Redston Warner, KCVO, CMG, and Margery Catherine (*née* Nicol); *m* 1943, Grizel Margaret Clerk Rattray; three *s* one *d. Educ:* Oundle; King's College, Cambridge. Entered Foreign Office and Diplomatic Service, 1935; UK Delegation to OEEC, Paris, 1956–59; Minister at HM Embassy, Tokyo, 1959–62; Ambassador to Cameroon, 1963–66; UK Rep., Econ. and Social Council of UN, 1966–67; Ambassador to Tunisia, 1968–70. *Address:* The Old Royal Oak, High Street, Blockley, Glos GL56 9EX. *Clubs:* United Oxford & Cambridge University, Royal Commonwealth Society.
See also Sir N. A. Ramsay.

WARNER, Francis (Robert Le Plastrier); poet and dramatist; Fellow and Tutor in English Literature, St Peter's College, Oxford, since 1965; *b* Bishopthorpe, Yorks, 21 Oct. 1937; *s* of Rev. Hugh Compton Warner and Nancy Le Plastrier (*née* Owen); *m* 1958, Mary Hall (marr. diss. 1972); two *d. Educ:* Christ's Hosp.; London Coll. of Music; St Catharine's Coll., Cambridge (BA, MA). Supervisor St Catharine's Coll., Cambridge, 1959–63; Staff Tutor in English, Cambridge Univ. Bd of Extra-Mural Studies, 1963–65. Messing Internat. Award for distinguished contribns to Literature, 1972. *Publications:* poetry: Perennia, 1962; Early Poems, 1964; Experimental Sonnets, 1965; Madrigals, 1967; The Poetry of Francis Warner, USA 1970; Lucca Quartet, 1975; Morning Vespers, 1980; Spring Harvest, 1981; plays: Maquettes, a trilogy of one-act plays, 1972; Requiem: Pt 1, Lying Figures, 1972, Pt 2, Killing Time, 1976, Pt 3, Meeting Ends, 1974; A Conception of Love, 1978; Light Shadows, 1980; Moving Reflections, 1982; edited: Eleven Poems by Edmund Blunden, 1965; Garland, 1968; Studies in the Arts, 1968; contrib. Antios, TLS, etc; *relevant publications:* Francis Warner—Poet and Dramatist, ed Tim Prentki, 1977; Chess in the Mirror: a study of theatrical cubism in Francis Warner's Requiem and its Maquettes, by R. Jeffrey, 1980; Francis Warner and Tradition, by G. Pursglove, 1981. *Recreations:* children,

cathedral music, travel. *Address:* St Peter's College, Oxford OX1 2DL. *T:* Oxford 48436. *Club:* Athenæum.

WARNER, Sir Frederick Archibald, (Sir Fred Warner), GCVO 1975; KCMG 1972 (CMG 1963); HM Diplomatic Service, retired; Member (C) Somerset, European Parliament, since 1979; Director: Guinness Peat Group; Chloride Group Plc; Job Creation Ltd; Loral International Inc.; *b* 2 May 1918; *s* of Frederick A. Warner, Chaguanas, Trinidad, and Marjorie Miller Winants, New Jersey, USA; *m* 1971, Mrs Simone Georgina de Ferranti, *d* of late Col. Hubert Jocelyn Nangle; two *s* and one step *d. Educ:* Wixenford; RNC Dartmouth; Magdalen Coll., Oxford. Served War of 1939–45. Asst Principal, Foreign Office, Feb. 1946; Member of Foreign Service, April 1946; promoted 2nd Sec., May 1946; promoted 1st Sec., and transferred to Moscow, 1950; Foreign Office, Dec. 1951; Rangoon, 1956 (acted as Chargé d'Affaires, 1956); transferred to Athens, 1958; Head of South-East Asia Dept, Foreign Office, 1960; Imperial Defence College, 1964; Ambassador to Laos, 1965–67; Minister, NATO, 1968; Under-Secretary of State, FCO, 1969; Ambassador and Dep. Permanent UK Rep. to UN, 1969–72; Ambassador to Japan, 1972–75. Formerly Dir, Mercantile and General Reinsurance Co. Ltd. Order of the Chrysanthemum, 1st class (Japan). *Address:* Laverstock, Bridport, Dorset. *T:* Broadwindsor 543; 113 Fulham Road, SW1. *Clubs:* Beefsteak, Puffin's, Turf.

WARNER, Prof. Sir Frederick (Edward), Kt 1968; FRS 1976; FEng 1977; Emeritus Partner, Cremer and Warner; Visiting Professor, Bartlett School of Architecture, University College London, since 1970; *b* 31 March 1910; *s* of Frederick Warner; *m* 1st, Margaret Anderson McCrea; two *s* two *d* ; 2nd, Barbara Ivy Reynolds. *Educ:* Bancrofts Sch.; University Coll., London. Pres., Univ. of London Union, 1933. Chemical Engr with various cos, 1934–56; self-employed, 1956–. Joined Cremer and Warner, 1956, Senior Partner 1963–80. Inst. of Chemical Engrs: Hon. Sec., 1953; Pres., 1966; Mem. Council, Engrg Instns, 1962; President: Fedn Européenne d'Assocs nationales d'Ingenieurs, 1968–71; Brit. Assoc. for Commercial and Industrial Educn, 1977–; Pres., BSI, 1980– (Chm., Exec. Bd, 1973–76; Vice-Pres., 1968–80). Missions and Consultations in India, Russia, Iran, Egypt, Greece, France. Assessor, Windscale Inquiry, 1977. Chairman: Cttee on Detergents, 1970–74; Process Plant Working Party, 1971–77; Sch. of Pharmacy, Univ. of London, 1971–; Member: Royal Commn on Environmental Pollution, 1973–76; Adv. Council for Energy Conservation, 1974–79. Vis. Prof., Imperial Coll., 1970–78; Pro-Chancellor, Open Univ., 1974–79; Member Court: Cranfield Inst. of Technology; Essex Univ. Fellow UCL, 1967. Hon. Fellow, Sch. of Pharmacy, 1979. Ordinario, Accademia Tiberina, 1969. Hon. DTech, Bradford, 1969; Hon. DSc: Aston, 1970; Cranfield, 1978; Heriot-Watt, 1978; Newcastle, 1979; DUniv. Open, 1980. Gold Medal, Czecho-Slovak Soc. for Internat. Relations, 1969; Medal, Insinöö-riliitto, Finland, 1969; Leverhulme Medal, Royal Soc., 1978; Buchanan Medal, 1982. Hon. Mem., Koninklijk Instituut van Ingenieurs, 1972; Academico Correspondiente, AI Mexico, 1972. *Publications:* Problem in Chemical Engineering Design (with J. M. Coulson), 1949; Technology Today (ed de Bono), 1971; Standards in the Engineering Industries, NEDO, 1977; Risk Assessment, Royal Soc., 1982; papers on nitric acid, heat transfer, underground gasification of coal, air and water pollution, contracts, planning, safety, professional and continuous education. *Recreations:* monumental brasses, ceramics, gardens. *Address:* 140 Buckingham Palace Road, SW1. *T:* 01-730 0777. *Club:* Athenæum.

WARNER, Frederick Sydney, LDS RCS, 1926; LRCP, MRCS, 1928; FDS RCS, 1947; Dental Surgeon, Guy's Hospital, 1949–68, Emeritus since 1968; Sub-Dean, 1946–65; Lecturer in Oral Surgery, 1954–61, Guy's Hospital Dental School, SE1; Dean of Dental Studies, 1965–68; Member of Board of Examiners in Dental Surgery, Royal College of Surgeons of England, 1947–64, and University of London, 1953–57. *b* 14 April 1903; *s* of Frederick Watkin Warner; *m* 1937, Cicely Florence Michelson. *Educ:* Guy's Hospital Medical School. Asst Dental Surgeon, Guy's Hospital, 1936–49. Member of Board of Faculty of Dental Surgery, Royal College of Surgeons of England, 1946–65; Vice-Dean, 1954–55. *Recreations:* philately, photography. *Address:* Flat 11, 115A Ridgway, SW19.

WARNER, Gerald Chierici; HM Diplomatic Service; Counsellor, Foreign and Commonwealth Office, since 1976; *b* 27 Sept. 1931; *s* of Howard Warner and Elizabeth (*née* Chierici-Kendall); *m* 1956, Mary Wynne Davies, DMath, Lectr, City Univ; one *s* two *d. Educ:* Univ. of Oxford (BA). 3rd Sec., Peking, 1956–58; 2nd Sec., Rangoon, 1960–61; 1st Sec., Warsaw, 1964–66, Geneva, 1966–68; Counsellor, Kuala Lumpur, 1974–76. *Address:* c/o Foreign and Commonwealth Office, SW1A 2AH.

WARNER, Sir Henry; *see* Warner, Sir E. C. H.

WARNER, Hon. Sir Jean-Pierre Frank Eugene, Kt 1981; **Hon. Mr Justice Warner**; Judge of the High Court of Justice, Chancery Division, since 1981; a Judge of the Restrictive Practices Court, since 1982; *b* 24 Sept. 1924; *s* of late Frank Cloudesley ffolliot Warner and of Louise Marie Blanche Warner (*née* Gouet); *m* 1950, Sylvia Frances, *d* of Sir Ernest Goodale, *qv* ; two *d. Educ:* Sainte Croix de Neuilly; Ecole des Roches; Harrow; Trinity Coll., Cambridge (MA). Served in Rifle Bde, 1943–47, Actg Major, GSO2 (Ops) GHQ Far East. Called to Bar, Lincoln's Inn, 1950 (Cassel Schol.), Bencher 1966; Mem. Gen. Council of Bar, 1969–72. Junior Counsel: to Registrar of Restrictive Trading Agreements, 1961–64; to Treasury (Chancery), 1964–72; QC 1972; Advocate-Gen., Ct of Justice of European Communities, 1973–81.

Councillor: Royal Borough of Kensington, 1959-65 (Chm., Gen. Purposes Cttee, 1963-65); Royal Borough of Kensington and Chelsea, 1964-68. Dir, Warner & Sons Ltd and subsids, 1952-70. Vice-Pres., UK Assoc. for European Law, 1975-. Liveryman, Worshipful Co. of Weavers, 1957. Chevalier du Tastevin, 1952, Commandeur 1960. *Recreation:* sitting in the sun with a cool drink. *Address:* Royal Courts of Justice, WC2; 32 Abingdon Villas, W8 6BX. *T:* 01-937 7023.

WARNER, Rt. Rev. Kenneth Charles Harman, DSO 1919; DD (Edinburgh) 1950; Assistant Bishop in Diocese of Canterbury, since 1962; *b* 6 April 1891; *e s* of late Charles Edward Warner and Ethel Constantia Catharine Cornfoot, Tonbridge, Kent; *m* 1st, 1916, Constance Margaret (*d* 1968), 2nd *d* of Arnold F. Hills, Penshurst, Kent; two *s* two *d*; 2nd, 1970, Angela Morgan, *widow* of Rev. Edward Prescott-Decie. *Educ:* Tonbridge Sch.; Trinity Coll., Oxford; Cuddesdon Theological Coll. 2nd Cl. Jurisp., 1912; MA 1921; Solicitors' Articles, 1912; served European War, 1914-19; Major, Kent Cyclist Bn, 1917 (DSO); partner in firm of Warner Son and Brydone, Solicitors, Tonbridge, Kent, 1919-22; Cuddesdon, 1923; Deacon, 1923; Priest, 1924; Curate of St George's, Ramsgate, 1923-26; Chaplain Royal Air Force, 1927-33; Rector and Provost of St Mary's Cathedral, Glasgow, 1933-38; Archdeacon of Lincoln and 4th Canon in Lincoln Cathedral; Prebendary of Gretton, 1938-47; Bishop of Edinburgh, 1947-61, retired. Select Preacher: Cambridge University, 1939; Oxford University, 1950-51. *Address:* Perry Wood House, Sheldwich, near Faversham, Kent. *T:* Selling 263.

WARNER, Dr Michael Henry Charles; Head of ER3 Division, Ministry of Defence, since 1981; *b* 21 May 1927; *s* of Captain Herbert H. M. Warner, MA, RGA, and Mrs Jessie R. H. Warner; *m* 1971, Gillian Margaret (*née* Easby); one *s* (by previous *m*). *Educ:* Monkton Combe Sch., Bath; Queens' Coll., Cambridge (BA 1951, MA 1955); King's Coll., London (PhD 1973). Served RAF, 1945-48. Govt Communications HQ: Exec. Officer, 1952; Higher Exec. Officer, 1956; Deptl Specialist Officer, 1957; Min. of Defence: Principal, 1965; Asst Sec., 1974; Counsellor, FCO, 1979; Dep. Leader, UK Delegn to Comprehensive Test Ban Treaty Negotiations, Geneva, 1979-80. Leverhulme Fellow, 1971-72. *Publications:* contrib. Thomas Hardy Yearbook, Anglo-Welsh Rev., Envoi, and BBC 2. *Recreations:* tennis, bridge. *Address:* 62 Poulett Gardens, Twickenham, Mddx TW1 4QR. *T:* 01-892 1456. *Club:* Royal Victoria League.

WARNER, Rex; author; University Professor, University of Connecticut, 1964-74, retired 1974; *b* 9 March 1905; *s* of Rev. F. E. Warner and Kathleen Luce; *m* 1929, Frances Chamier Grove; two *s* one *d*; *m* 1949, Barbara, Lady Rothschild; one *d*; *m* 1966, Frances Chamier Warner. *Educ:* St George's Harpenden; Wadham College, Oxford (Open Classical Scholar, First Class Classical Hon. Mods, degree in English Literature); Hon. Fellow 1973. Schoolmaster in Egypt and in England; Director of The British Institute, Athens, 1945-47. Tallman Prof., Bowdoin Coll., 1962-63. Has written poems, novels, and critical essays; also has done work on films and broadcasting. Hon. DLitt Rider Coll., 1968. Comdr, Royal Order of Phœnix (Greece), 1963. *Publications:* Poems, 1937; The Wild Goose Chase, 1937; The Professor, 1938; The Aerodrome, 1941; Why was I killed?, 1943; Translation of the Medea of Euripides, 1944; English Public Schools, 1945; The Cult of Power, 1946; Translation of Aeschylus' Prometheus Bound, 1947; Xenophon's Anabasis, 1949; Men of Stones, 1949; John Milton, 1949; Translation of Euripides' Hippolytus, 1950; Men and Gods, 1950; Translation of Euripides' Helen, 1951; Greeks and Trojans, 1951; Views of Attica, 1951; Escapade, 1953; (with Martin Hürlimann) Eternal Greece, 1953 (new edn 1962); Translation of Thucydides, 1954; The Vengeance of the Gods, 1954; The Young Caesar, 1958; The Greek Philosophers, 1958; The Fall of the Roman Republic (trans. from Plutarch), 1958; Cæsar's War Commentaries (trans.), 1959; Poems of Seferis (trans.), 1960; Imperial Cæsar, 1960; Confessions of St Augustine (trans.), 1962; Pericles the Athenian, 1963; History of my Times (Hellenica), Xenophon (trans.), 1966; The Greek Style, by Seferis (trans.), 1966; The Converts, 1967; Athens at War, 1970; Plutarch: Moral Essays (trans.), 1971; Men of Athens, 1972. *Address:* Anchor House, St Leonard's Lane, Wallingford, Oxon. *Club:* Savile.

WARNOCK, Geoffrey James; Principal, Hertford College, Oxford, since 1971; Vice-Chancellor, University of Oxford, since 1981; *b* 16 Aug. 1923; *s* of James Warnock, OBE, MD; *m* 1949, Helen Mary Wilson (*see* Mrs H. M. Warnock); two *s* three *d*. *Educ:* Winchester Coll.; New Coll., Oxford, Hon. Fellow, 1973. Served War of 1939-45: Irish Guards, 1942-45 (Captain). Fellow by Examination, Magdalen Coll., 1949; Fellow and Tutor, Brasenose Coll., 1950-53; Fellow and Tutor in Philosophy, Magdalen Coll., 1953-71, Emeritus Fellow, 1972, Hon. Fellow, 1980. Visiting Lectr, Univ. of Illinois, 1957; Visiting Professor: Princeton Univ., 1962; Univ. of Wisconsin, 1966. *Publications:* Berkeley, 1953; English Philosophy since 1900, 1958, 2nd edn 1969; Contemporary Moral Philosophy, 1967; (ed with J. O. Urmson) J. L. Austin: Philosophical Papers, 2nd edn, 1970; The Object of Morality, 1971; articles in: Mind, Proc. Aristotelian Soc., etc. *Recreations:* golf, cricket. *Address:* Hertford College, Oxford. *T:* Oxford 42947.

WARNOCK, Mrs (Helen) Mary; Senior Research Fellow, St Hugh's College, Oxford, since 1976; *b* 14 April 1924; *d* of late Archibald Edward Wilson, Winchester; *m* 1949, Geoffrey James Warnock, *qv*; two *s* three *d*. *Educ:* St Swithun's, Winchester; Lady Margaret Hall, Oxford. Fellow and Tutor in Philosophy, St Hugh's Coll., Oxford, 1949-66; Headmistress, Oxford High Sch., GPDST, 1966-72; Talbot Res. Fellow, Lady Margaret Hall,

Oxford, 1972-76. Member: IBA, 1973-81; Cttee of Inquiry into Special Educn, 1974-78 (Chm.); Royal Commn on Environmental Pollution, 1979-; Adv. Cttee on Animal Experiments, 1979- (Chm.); SSRC, 1981-; UK Nat. Commn for Unesco, 1981-; Cttee of Enquiry into Human Fertilization, 1982- (Chm.). FCP 1979. DUniv. Open 1980. *Publications:* Ethics since 1900, 1960, 3rd edn 1978; J.-P. Sartre, 1963; Existentialist Ethics, 1966; Existentialism, 1970; Imagination, 1976; Schools of Thought, 1977; (with T. Devlin) What Must We Teach?, 1977; Education: a way forward, 1979. *Recreations:* music, gardening. *Address:* Hertford College, Oxford; St Hugh's College, Oxford; Brick House, Axford. *T:* Marlborough 54686.

See also Sir A. D. Wilson.

WARR, George Michael, CBE 1966; HM Diplomatic Service, retired; *b* 22 Jan. 1915; *s* of late Sir Godfrey Warr, and of Lady Warr; *m* 1950, Gillian Addis (*née* Dearmer); one *s* two *d* (and one step *s*). *Educ:* Winchester; Christ Church, Oxford. Entered Foreign Service, 1938; served in Chile, Germany, Soviet Union, Uruguay; Counsellor, British Embassy, Brussels, 1959-62; British Consul-General, Istanbul, Turkey, 1962-67; Ambassador to Nicaragua, 1967-70. *Recreations:* gardening, beekeeping. *Address:* Woodside, Frant, Tunbridge Wells TN3 9HW. *T:* Frant 496.

WARRACK, Guy Douglas Hamilton; Hon. ARCM; composer; conductor; *b* Edinburgh, 8 Feb. 1900; *s* of John Warrack, LLD, and Jean Hamilton (*née* Dunlop); *m* 1st, 1926, Jacynth Ellerton (marr. diss.); one *s* one *d*; 2nd, 1933, Valentine Clair Jeffrey; two *s*. *Educ:* Winchester; Magdalen College, Oxford; Royal College of Music. BA Oxon, 1923; Hon. ARCM, 1926. Teaching staff of RCM, 1925-35; Examiner for Associated Board of Royal Schools of Music, 1926-; Conductor: Oxford Orchestral Society and Oxford City Concerts for Children, 1926-30; Handel Society, 1934-35; BBC Scottish Orchestra, 1936-45; Musical Director, Sadler's Wells Theatre Ballet, 1948-51; Chairman: Composers' Guild of Great Britain, 1952, 1956; Sherlock Holmes Soc. of London, 1955-57; Intimate Opera Soc. Ltd, 1969-76; Conducted Concerts, Opera, Ballet, etc in London, Ceylon, New Zealand, South Africa and Provinces. Compositions include: Variations for Orchestra, 1924; Symphony in C minor (The "Edinburgh"), 1932; Divertimento Pasticciato, 1938; music for many films, including Theirs is the Glory, 1946; XIVth Olympiad, 1948; The Story of Time, 1949; A Queen is Crowned, 1953; also many arrangements. *Publications:* Sherlock Holmes and Music, 1947. Articles in The Times, Daily Telegraph, Music and Letters, Musical Times, etc. *Address:* 72 Courtfield Gardens, SW5. *T:* 01-370 1758. *Club:* New (Edinburgh).

WARRELL, Ernest Herbert; Organist, King's College, London, since 1980 (Lecturer in Music, KCL, 1953-80); *b* 23 June 1915; *er s* of Herbert Henry Warrell and Edith Peacock; *m* 1952, Jean Denton Denton; two *s* one *d*. *Educ:* Loughborough School. Articled pupil (Dr E. T. Cook), Southwark Cath., 1938; Asst Organist, Southwark Cath., 1946-54; Organist, St Mary's, Primrose Hill, 1954-57; Lectr in Plainsong, RSCM, 1954-59; Organist, St John the Divine, Kennington, SW9, 1961-68; Organist and Dir of Music, Southwark Cathedral, 1968-76; Musical Dir, Gregorian Assoc., 1969-82. Hon. FCTL 1977; FKC 1979. *Publications:* Accompaniments to the Psalm Tones, 1942; Plainsong and the Anglican Organist, 1943. *Recreation:* sailing. *Address:* 41 Beechhill Road, Eltham, SE9. *T:* 01-850 7800. *Clubs:* Special Forces, Little Ship; Royal Scots (Edinburgh).

WARREN, Very Rev. Alan Christopher; Provost of Leicester, since 1978; *b* 1932; *s* of Arthur Henry and Gwendoline Catherine Warren; *m* 1957, Sylvia Mary (*née* Matthews); three *d*. *Educ:* Dulwich College; Corpus Christi Coll., Cambridge (Exhibnr, MA); Ridley Hall, Cambridge. Curate, St Paul's, Margate, 1957-59; Curate, St Andrew, Plymouth, 1959-62; Chaplain of Kelly College, Tavistock, 1962-64; Vicar of Holy Apostles, Leicester, 1964-72; Coventry Diocesan Missioner, 1972-78; Hon. Canon, Coventry Cathedral, 1972-78; Proctor in Convocation, 1977-78, 1980-; Mem., Cathedral Statutes Commn, 1981-. *Publications:* Putting it Across, 1975; articles in Church Music and The Sign. *Recreations:* music, cricket, golf, steam trains. *Address:* Provost's House, St Martin's East, Leicester. *T:* Leicester 25294/5.

WARREN, Alastair Kennedy, TD 1953; Regional Editor, Scottish and Universal Newspapers Ltd, since 1974; Editor, Dumfries and Galloway Standard, since 1976; *b* 17 July 1922; *s* of John Russell Warren, MC, and Jean Cousin Warren; *m* 1952, Ann Lindsay Maclean; two *s*. *Educ:* Glasgow Acad.; Loretto; Glasgow Univ. (MA Hons). Served War of 1939-45: HLI, 1940-46; Major, 1946. Served 5/6th Bn HLI (TA) 1947-63. Sales Clerk, Stewarts & Lloyds Ltd, 1950-53; joined editorial staff of The Glasgow Herald as Sub-Editor, 1954; Leader Writer, 1955-58; Features Editor, 1958-59; Commercial Editor, 1960-64; City Editor, 1964-65; Editor, 1965-74. Provost of New Galloway and Kells Community Council, 1978-81. *Publications:* contribs to various periodicals. *Recreations:* swimming, hill walking. *Address:* Rathan, New Galloway, Kirkcudbrightshire. *T:* New Galloway 257.

WARREN, Sir Alfred Henry, (Sir Freddie Warren), Kt 1976; CBE 1970 (MBE 1957); Secretary to the Government Chief Whip, 1958-79; *b* 19 Dec. 1915; *s* of William Warren and Clara Wooff; *m* 1940, Margaret Ann; one *s* one *d*. *Educ:* Sir Walter St John's Grammar Sch., SW11. Asst Private Secretary to the Secretary to the Cabinet, 1951-58. *Address:* 93 South Eden Park Road, Beckenham, Kent. *T:* 01-658 6951.

WARREN, Dame (Alice) Josephine (Mary Taylor); see Barnes, Dame A. J. M. T.

WARREN, Rt. Rev. Alwyn Keith, CMG 1967; MC 1945; b 23 Sept. 1900; 2nd s of Major T. J. C. Warren, JP, Penlee House, Te Aute, Hawkes Bay, NZ, and Lucy, d of Ven. Samuel Williams, Archdeacon of Hawkes Bay, NZ; m 1928, Doreen Eda, d of Capt. C. F. Laws; one s two d. Educ: Marlborough College; Magdalen College, Oxford (BA 1922, Hons Nat. Sci.; MA 1926); Cuddesdon Theological College. Ordained, 1925; Curate of Ashford, Kent, 1925-29; Vicar of Ross and South Westland, NZ, 1929-32; Vicar of Waimate, South Canterbury, NZ, 1932-34; Vicar of St Mary's, Merivale, Christchurch, NZ, 1934-40; Archdeacon of Christchurch, 1937-44; Dean of Christchurch, 1940-51; Vicar-General, 1940-44 and 1946-51; Bishop of Christchurch, 1951-66. Chaplain to 2nd NZ Exped. Force (NZ Divisional Cavalry), Italy, 1944-45 (wounded, MC). Member Council, University Canterbury, 1946-73, Pro-Chancellor, 1961, Chancellor, 1965-69; Member Senate, University of New Zealand, 1948-61; Warden or Chm. Bds various colleges, schools and social service organisations. Chairman National Council of Churches of NZ, 1949-51; Member Central Committee of World Council of Churches, 1954-66. Chaplain and Sub-Prelate, Order of St John; Chaplain, Priory of St John in NZ, 1966-72; formerly Pres., Canterbury and West Coast Centre, St John Ambulance Assoc.; Pres., Christchurch Rotary Club; Vice-President: Christchurch Civic Music Council; Christchurch Harmonic Soc.; Pres., Royal Christchurch Musical Soc.; Trustee, NZ National Library. Publications: Prayers in Time of War, 1940; Christianity Today: section on Churches in NZ, 1947. Contrib. to Stimmen aus der ökumene, 1963 (Berlin). Recreations: formerly rowing, tennis, now people, reading biographies, music, gardening. Address: Littlecourt, 193 Memorial Avenue, Christchurch 5, New Zealand. Clubs: Leander; Christchurch, University of Canterbury, University Staff (Christchurch).

WARREN, Sir Brian; see Warren, Sir H. B. S.

WARREN, Sir Brian Charles Pennefather, 9th Bt cr 1784; b 4 June 1923; o s of Sir Thomas Richard Pennefather Warren, 8th Bt, CBE; S father, 1961; m 1976, Cola, d of Captain E. L. Cazenove, Great Dalby, Leics. Educ: Wellington College. Served War of 1939-45; Lt, 1943-45, 2nd Bn Irish Guards. Recreations: hunting, squash. Heir: cousin Patrick Vaughton Warren, Major RA, b 11 Jan. 1917. Address: The Wilderness, Castle Oliver, Kilmallock, Co. Limerick. T: Kilfinane 89. Club: Cavalry and Guards.

WARREN, Rt. Rev. Cecil Allan; see Canberra and Goulburn, Bishop of.

WARREN, Douglas Ernest, CMG 1973; b 8 June 1918; s of late Samuel Henry Warren; m 1945, Constance Vera (née Nix); two d. Educ: High Storrs Grammar Sch., Sheffield; Sheffield Univ. (BSc). FRICS. Royal Corps of Signals, 1940-46 (Captain): POW Thailand, 1942-45. Joined Colonial Service (later HMOCS), Tanganyika, as Surveyor, 1946: Supt of Surveys, 1955; transf. to Kenya as Asst Dir of Surveys, 1957; Dir of Survey of Kenya, 1961-65; retd from HMOCS, 1965; joined UK Civil Service as Dep. to Dir of Overseas Surveys, Min. of Overseas Develt, 1965, Dir of Overseas Surveys and Survey Adviser, 1968-80. Member: Land Surveyors Council, RICS, 1965-72; Council, RGS, 1968-71; various Royal Society cttees; Pres., Photogrammetric Soc., 1969-71. Recreations: travel, golf. Address: Brockstones, Bear's Den, Kingswood, Surrey. T: Mogador 2653. Club: Kingswood Golf.

WARREN, Hon. Sir Edward (Emerton), KCMG 1969 (CMG 1956); KBE 1959; MSM 1918; Member Legislative Council, New South Wales Parliament, 1954-78; b Broken Hill, NSW, 26 Aug. 1897; s of John T. Warren, Derbyshire, England; m 1926, Doris, d of Charles F. Schultz; two s. Educ: Broken Hill, NSW. Served European War, 1914-18: 18th Bn AIF, Gallipoli and France. Chairman: NSW Combined Colliery Proprietors' Assoc., 1949; Northern Colliery Proprietors' Assoc., 1949; Aust. Coal Assoc., 1956; Aust. Coal Assoc. (Research) Ltd, 1956; Aust. Coal Industry Research Laboratories Ltd, 1965; Brown's Coal Pty (Victoria); Coal & Allied (Sales) Pty Ltd; Dowsett Engineering (Australia) Pty Ltd. Man. Dir, The Wallarah Coal Co. Ltd; Governing Dir, Thomas Brown Ltd (Wellington, NZ). Director and Chief General Manager: Coal & Allied Industries Ltd; Coal & Allied Industries KK (Tokyo-Japan); J. & A. Brown & Abermain Seaham Collieries Ltd; Caledonian Collieries Ltd; Cessnock Collieries Ltd; Liddell Collieries Pty Ltd; Durham Coal Mines Pty Ltd; South Maitland Railways Pty Ltd; Hexham Engineering Pty Ltd; Jones Bros Coal Pty Ltd; Director: Westinghouse Brake (A/sia) Pty Ltd; McKenzie & Holland (Australia) Pty Ltd. Member: Coal Conservation Cttee, NSW Govt, 1951; C'wealth Govt Mission investigating overseas coal-mining methods, 1952; Dep. Chm., Aust. Nat. Cttee, World Power Conf., 1960; Vice-Chm., Internat. Exec. Council, World Power Conf., 1962; Chm., Coal Trades Section, Aust. Trade Mission to S America, 1962; Pres., Australia/Japan Business Co-operation Cttee, 1964-; rep. Aust. Employers, ILO, Geneva, 1964; Mem., Nat. Coal Research Adv. Cttee, 1965; launched Malaysia/Australia Business Co-operation Cttee, Kuala Lumpur, 1965; led Aust. Delegn, Hawaii, 1968 (resulted in Pacific Basin Econ. Co-op. Cttee); Australian Pres., 1970-71, and Internat. Pres., 1970-71, Pacific Basin Econ. Co-op. Council; Mem., C'wealth Govt Adv. Cttee, Expo 70, 1968; Pres., Australia/Korea Business Co-operation Cttee, 1969. Has travelled extensively. Member: Council, Univ. of NSW, 1965-; Med. Foundn, Univ. of NSW, 1968-. Rising Sun with Grand Cordon, Japan, 1967. Address: 16 Morella Road, Clifton Gardens, NSW 2088, Australia. T: (home) 969 4662;

(office) 27 8641. Clubs: American, Tattersall's, New South Wales, Royal Automobile of Australia, NSW Sports, Manly Golf (Sydney); Newcastle (Newcastle, NSW).

WARREN, Frederick Lloyd, MA, BSc (Oxon), PhD, DSc (London); Professor of Biochemistry, London Hospital Medical College, 1952-78, now Emeritus; b 2 Oct. 1911; s of Frederick James and Edith Agnes Warren; m 1st, 1949, Natalia Vera Peierls (née Ladan) (marr. diss., 1958); two s one d; 2nd, 1961, Ruth Natallé Jacobs. Educ: Bristol Grammar Sch.; Exeter Coll., Oxford. Demonstrator, Biochem. Dept, Oxford, 1932-34; Sir Halley Stewart Res. Fellow, Chester Beatty Research Institute, Royal Cancer Hospital, 1934-46; Laura de Saliceto Student, University of London, 1937-42; Anna Fuller Research Student, 1942-46; Senior Lecturer in Biochemistry, St Mary's Hospital Medical School, 1946-48; Reader in Biochemistry, University College, London, 1948-52. Publications: papers and articles in scientific journals. Address: 5 River View, Enfield, Mddx EN2 6PX. T: 01-366 0674.

WARREN, Sir (Harold) Brian (Seymour), Kt 1974; physician; b 19 Dec. 1914; er s of late Harold Warren, St Ives, Hunts and Marian Jessie Emlyn; m 1st, 1942, Dame Alice Josephine Mary Taylor Barnes, qv (marr. diss. 1964); one s two d; 2nd, 1964, Elizabeth Anne, y d of late Walter William Marsh, Wordsley, Staffs; two s. Educ: Bishop's Stortford Coll.; University Coll. London; University Coll. Hosp. MRCS, LRCP. Pres., Univ. of London Union, 1937-38. House Phys. and House Surg., UCH, 1942. War service with RAMC, RMO 1st Bn Gren. Gds and DADMS Gds Div., 1942-46 (despatches). Mem., Westminster City Council, 1955-64 and 1968-78; rep. West Woolwich on LCC, 1955-58, County Alderman 1961-62. Contested (C) Brixton Div. of Lambeth, 1959. Personal Phys. to Prime Minister, 1970-74. Mem., Westminster, Chelsea and Kensington AHA, 1975-77. Visitor and Mem. Emergency Bed Service Cttee; King Edward's Hosp. Fund for London, 1966-72; Mem. Governing Body, Westminster Hosp., 1970-74; Mem. Council, King Edward VII's Hosp. for Officers (Surg.-Apothecary, 1952-80). Pres., Chelsea Clinical Soc., 1955-56. Liveryman, Apothecaries Soc., 1950; Freeman, City of London. Publications: contrib. Encycl. Gen. Practice. Recreations: shooting, gardening, travel, listening to music. Address: Fairway House, Great Bedwyn, Marlborough, Wilts SN8 3LN. T: Marlborough 870870. Clubs: Boodle's, Pratt's.

See also M. G. J. Neary.

WARREN, Ian Scott; Master of the Supreme Court (Queen's Bench Division) since 1970; b 30 March 1917; er s of Arthur Owen Warren and Margaret Cromarty Warren (née Macnaughton); m 1st, 1943, Barbara (marr. diss.), er d of Walter Myrick, Tillsonburg, Ont.; four s one d; 2nd, Jeanne Hicklin, d of late Frederick and Lydia Shaw, Crosland Moor. Educ: Charterhouse (Exhbnr); Magdalene Coll., Cambridge (Exhbnr); BA 1938, MA 1950. Colonial Administrative Service, 1938-41, serving Gold Coast (Asst DC, 1940); RAF, 1942-46; Flying Badge and commissioned, 1943; Flt Lieut, 1944. Called to Bar, Lincoln's Inn, 1947, Bencher 1967; practised at Common Law Bar, London, 1947-70. Publication: Verses from Lincoln's Inn (jtly), 1975. Recreations: ski-ing, walking, poetry. Address: 7 Southwell Gardens, SW7. T: 01-370 2353. Clubs: Garrick, MCC.

WARREN, Jack Hamilton, OC 1982; banker; Vice-Chairman, Bank of Montreal, since 1979; b 10 April 1921; s of Tom Hamilton Warren and Olive Sykes (née Horsfall); m 1953, Hilary Joan Titterington; two s two d. Educ: Queen's Univ., Kingston, Ont, Canada (BA). Served War, with Royal Canadian Navy (VR) as Lieut (Exec.), 1941-45. Joined Dept of Extl Affairs, 1945; served at Canadian High Commn, London, 1948-51; transf. to Dept of Finance, 1954; Financial Counsellor, Canadian Embassy, Washington, 1954-57, and as alternate Canadian Dir of Internat. Bank for Reconstruction and Develt, and of Internat. Monetary Fund; returned to Extl Affairs and joined Canadian Delegn to Council of NATO and OEEC, 1957; apptd Asst Dep. Minister of Dept of Trade and Commerce, 1958; elected Chm. of GATT Contracting Parties, 1962-65; apptd Dep. Minister of Trade and Commerce, 1964; Dep. Minister of Dept of Industry, Trade and Commerce, 1968; High Comr for Canada in London, 1971-74; Ambassador to USA, 1975-77; Canadian Co-ordinator for the Multilateral Trade Negotiations, 1977-79. Hon. LLD Queen's, Ont, 1974. Outstanding Achievement Award, Public Service of Canada, 1975. Recreations: fishing, golf, skiing. Address: Vice-Chairman, Bank of Montreal, 3rd Floor, Head Office, 129 St James Street, Montreal, PQ H2Y 1L6, Canada. Clubs: Mount Royal, St Denis (Montreal); Rideau (Ottawa); White Pine Fishing, Larrimac Golf (Canada); Chevy Chase (Washington).

WARREN, Dame Josephine; see Barnes, Dame A. J. M. T.

WARREN, Kenneth Robin, CEng, FRAeS; FCIT; FRSA; MP (C) Hastings since 1970; Consultant in Engineering, Warren Woodfield Associates Ltd, since 1970; Director: Parsons, Tozer Newton Ltd, since 1971; Ventek Ltd, since 1972; Loral International, since 1980; b 15 Aug. 1926; s of Edward Charles Warren and Ella Mary Warren (née Adams); m 1962, Elizabeth Anne Chamberlain, MA Cantab; one s two d. Educ: Midsomer Norton; Aldenham; London Univ.; De Havilland Aeronautical Technical Sch. Research Engineer, BOAC, 1951-57; Personal Asst to Gen. Manager, Smiths Aircraft Instruments Ltd, 1957-60; Elliott Automation Ltd, 1960-69; Military Flight Systems: Manager, 1960-63; Divisional Manager, 1963-66; Marketing Manager, 1966-69. Former branch officer, G&MWU. Mem., Select Cttee on Science and

Technology, 1970-79; Mem., Council of Europe, 1973-80; Chm., WEU, Science, Technology and Aerospace Cttee, 1976-79; Chm., Cons. Parly Aviation Cttee, 1975-77; PPS to Sec. of State for Industry, 1979-81, to Sec. of State for Educn and Sci., 1981-. Liveryman, Coachmakers' Co.; Freeman, City of London. *Publications:* various papers to technical confs on aeronautical engineering and operations, in USA, UK, Netherlands and Japan. *Recreations:* mountaineering, flying, gardening. *Address:* Woodfield House, Goudhurst, Kent. *T:* Goudhurst 590.

WARREN, Prof. Michael Donald, MD, FRCP, FFCM; Director, Health Services Research Unit and Professor of Social Medicine, University of Kent, since 1971, jointly with Specialist in Community Medicine (Epidemiology and Health Services Research), South East Thames Regional Health Authority, since 1980; *b* 19 Dec. 1923; *s* of late Charles Warren and Dorothy Gladys Thornton Reeks; *m* 1946, Joan Lavina Peacock; one *s* two *d*. *Educ:* Bedford Sch.; Guy's Hosp.; London Sch. of Hygiene and Tropical Medicine. MB 1946, MD 1952; DPH 1952, DIH 1952; MRCP 1969, FRCP 1975; FFCM 1972. Sqdn Ldr RAF, Med. Branch, 1947-51; Dep. MOH, Metropolitan Borough of Hampstead, 1952-54; Asst Principal MO, LCC, 1954-58; Sen. Lectr and Hon. Consultant in Social Medicine, Royal Free Hosp. Sch., Royal Free Hosp. and London Sch. of Hygiene and Tropical Medicine, 1958-64; Sen. Lectr in Social Medicine, LSHTM, 1964-67; Reader in Public Health, Univ. of London, 1967-71; Prof. of Community Health, Univ. of London, 1978-80. Chm., Soc. of Social Medicine, 1982-83. Academic Registrar, Faculty of Community Medicine, Royal Colls of Physicians, 1972-77. Jt Editor, British Jl of Preventive and Social Medicine, 1969-72. *Publications:* (jt) Public Health and Social Services, 4th edn 1957, 6th edn 1965; (Jt Editor) Management and the Health Services, 1971; (jt) Physiotherapy in the Community, 1977; (jt) Physically Disabled People Living at Home, 1978; contribs to BMJ, Lancet, Internat. Jl of Epidemiology. *Recreations:* light gardening (crocuses, primroses, narcissi, irises and shrubs), genealogy, reading, listening to music. *Address:* 2 Bridge Down, Bridge, Canterbury, Kent CT4 5AZ. *T:* Bridge 830233. *Clubs:* Royal Society of Medicine; Kent County Cricket.

WARREN, Prof. Peter Michael, PhD; FSA; Professor of Ancient History and Classical Archaeology, University of Bristol, since 1977; *b* 23 June 1938; *s* of Arthur George Warren and Alison Joan Warren (*née* White); *m* 1966, Elizabeth Margaret Halliday; one *d*. *Educ:* Sandbach Sch.; Llandovery Coll.; University College of N Wales, Bangor (Ellen Thomas Stanford Schol.; BA 1st Cl. Hons Greek and Latin); Corpus Christi Coll., Cambridge (Exhibnr; BA Classical Tripos Pt II 1962; MA 1966; PhD 1966; Fellow, 1965-68); student, British Sch. at Athens, 1963-65. FSA 1973. Research Fellow in Arts, Univ. of Durham, 1968-70; Asst Director, British Sch. at Athens, 1970-72; University of Birmingham: Lectr in Aegean Archaeol., 1972-74; Sen. Lectr, 1974-76; Reader, 1976. Vis. Prof., Univ. of Minnesota, 1981. Dir of excavations, Myrtos, Crete, 1967-68; Debla, Crete, 1971; Knossos, 1971-73, 1978-. Member: Managing Cttee, British Sch. at Athens, 1973-77, 1978-79 (Chm., 1979-); Council, Soc. for Promotion of Hellenic Studies, 1978-81; Vice-Chm. Council, Bristol and Glos Archaeol Soc., 1980-81, Chm., 1981-. *Publications:* Minoan Stone Vases, 1969; Myrtos, an Early Bronze Age Settlement in Crete, 1972; The Aegean Civilizations, 1975; articles on Aegean Bronze Age, particularly Minoan archaeology, in archaeol and classical jls. *Recreations:* South Balkan travel and Greek village life. *Address:* Claremont House, Merlin Haven, Wotton-under-Edge, Glos GL12 7BA. *T:* Wotton-under-Edge 2290.

WARREN, Prof. Raymond Henry Charles, MusD; Stanley Hugh Badock Professor of Music, University of Bristol, since 1972; *b* 7 Nov. 1928; *m* 1953, Roberta Lydia Alice Smith; three *s* one *d*. *Educ:* Bancroft's Sch.; Corpus Christi Coll., Cambridge (MA, MusD). Music Master, Wolverstone Hall Sch., 1952-55; Queen's University Belfast: Lectr in Music, 1955-66; Prof. of Composition, 1966-72; Resident Composer, Ulster Orchestra, 1967-72. Compositions incl. 2 symphonies, 3 string quartets and 6 operas. *Publications: compositions:* The Passion, 1964; String Quartet No 1, 1967; Violin Concerto, 1967; Songs of Old Age, 1971. *Recreation:* walking. *Address:* 7 Redland Terrace, Redland, Bristol BS6 6TD. *T:* Bristol 37689.

WARREN, Robert Penn; writer; Member of: American Academy and Institute of Arts and Letters; American Philosophical Society; American Academy of Arts and Sciences; Professor of English, Yale University, 1962-73, now Emeritus; *b* 24 April 1905; *s* of Robert Franklin Warren and Anna Ruth Penn; *m* 1930, Emma Brescia (*d* 1951); *m* 1952, Eleanor Clark; one *s* one *d*. *Educ:* Vanderbilt University, Univ. of California; Yale University; Oxford University. Asst Professor: Southwestern Coll., Tennessee, 1930-31; Vanderbilt Univ., 1931-34; Assoc. Prof., Univ. of Louisiana, 1934-42; Founder and an editor Southern Review, 1935-42; Prof., Univ. of Minnesota, 1942-50; Prof. of Drama, Yale University, 1951-56. Houghton Mifflin Fellow (fiction), 1936; Guggenheim Fellow 1939, 1947; Shelley Memorial Award (poetry), 1942; Chair of Poetry, Library of Congress, 1944-45; Pulitzer Prize (fiction), 1947; Meltzer Award for screen play, 1949; Sidney Hillman Award for Journalism, 1957; Millay Prize (Amer. Poetry Society), 1958; National Book Award (Poetry), 1958; Pulitzer Prize (poetry), 1958, 1979; Irita Van Doren Award (Herald Tribune), 1965; Bollingen Prize for Poetry, 1967; Nat. Arts Foundn Award, 1968; Van Wyck Brooks Award for Poetry, 1969; Nat. Medal for Literature, 1970; Emerson-Thoreau Medal (Amer. Acad. of Arts and Sciences), 1975; Copernicus Award for Poetry, 1976; Harriet Monroe Poetry Award, 1977; Common Wealth Award, poetry, 1976; Pulitzer Prize,

poetry, 1979; Connecticut Council for the Arts Award, 1980. Chancellor, Acad. of American Poets, 1972; Jefferson Lectr, Nat. Endowment for Humanities, 1974. Hon. DLitt: University of Louisville, 1949; Kenyon College, 1952; Colby College, 1956; University of Kentucky, 1957; Swarthmore College, 1959; Yale University, 1960; Fairfield Univ., 1969; Wesleyan Univ., 1970; Harvard Univ., 1973; New Haven, 1973; Southwestern Coll., 1974; Univ. of the South, 1974; Johns Hopkins Univ., 1977; Monmouth Coll., 1979; Hon. LLD, Univ. of Bridgeport, 1965. MacArthur Prize Fellowship, 1981. Presidential Medal of Freedom, 1980. *Publications:* John Brown: Making of a Martyr, 1929; XXXVI Poems, 1936; Night Rider (novel), 1939; At Heaven's Gate (novel), 1943; Eleven Poems on Same Theme, 1942; Selected Poems, 1944; All the King's Men (novel), 1946, several editions (film, 1949); Coleridge's Ancient Mariner, 1947; Blackberry Winter (Novelette), 1947; Circus in the Attic (stories), 1947; World Enough and Time (novel), 1950, 2nd edn, 1974; Brother to Dragons (poem), 1953, rewritten version, 1979; Band of Angels (novel), 1955, (film, 1957); Segregation: The Inner Conflict of the South, 1956; Promises: Poems 1954-56, 1957; Selected Essays, 1958; The Cave (novel), 1959; You, Emperors, and Others: Poems 1957-60, 1960; Legacy of the Civil War: A meditation on the centennial, 1961; Wilderness (novel), 1961; Flood: a romance of our time (novel), 1964; Who Speaks for the Negro?, 1965; Selected Poems, Old and New, 1923-1966, 1966; Incarnations: Poems 1966-68, 1968; Audubon: a Vision (poems), 1969; Homage to Theodore Dreiser, 1971; Meet Me in the Green Glen (novel), 1971; Or Else—Poem/Poems, 1968-74, 1974; Democracy and Poetry, 1975; Selected Poems 1923-75, 1977; A Place to Come To (novel), 1977; Now and Then: Poems 1976-78, 1978; Being Here: Poetry 1977-79, 1980; Rumor Verified: Poems 1977-81, 1981; various collections and anthologies. *Recreations:* swimming, walking. *Address:* 2495 Redding Road, Fairfield, Conn, USA. *Club:* Century (New York).

WARREN, Stanley Anthony T., CEng, FRINA, FIMechE; RCNC; Director of Project Team (Submarines), Ministry of Defence (Procurement Executive), since 1979; *b* 26 Sept. 1925; *s* of Stanley Howard Warren and Mabel Harriett (*née* Ham); *m* 1950, Sheila Gloria May (*née* Rowe); two *s* one *d*. *Educ:* King's Coll., Univ. of London (BSc 1st Cl. Hons Engrg); RNC, Greenwich (1st Cl. Naval Architecture). FRINA 1967; FIMechE 1970. Sub-Lieut, RN, 1945-47; Constructor Lieut, RCNC, 1947-51; Royal Yacht Britannia design, 1951-54; frigate modernisations, 1954-57; Constructor, HM Dockyard, Malta, 1957-60; Admiralty Constructor Overseer, John Brown and Yarrow, 1960-64; Polaris Submarine design, 1964-67; Chief Constructor and Principal Naval Overseer, Birkenhead, 1967-72; Asst Dir and Through Deck Cruiser Proj. Manager, 1972-76; Dep. Dir of Submarines (Polaris), MoD (PE), 1976-79. *Publications:* contribs to learned societies. *Recreations:* golf, motoring, gardening. *Address:* 4 Kenton Drive, Trowbridge, Wilts. *T:* Trowbridge 5113.

WARREN, Dr Wilfrid, FRCP, FRCPsych; Physician, Bethlem Royal Hospital and the Maudsley Hospital, 1948-75, now Emeritus; *b* 11 Oct. 1910; *s* of Frank Warren, FSA, JP, and Maud Warren; *m* 1938, Elizabeth Margaret Park; one *s* one *d*. *Educ:* Sherborne Sch.; Sidney Sussex Coll., Cambridge (MA; MD 1948); St Bartholomew's Hosp., London. DPM 1946. FRCP 1972; FRCPsych 1971. Served War, 1939-45: Surgeon Lt Comdr, RNVR. Consultant Adviser, Child and Adolescent Psychiatry, DHSS (formerly Min. of Health), 1961-76; Hon. Consultant in Child Psych. to Army, 1969-75. President: Sect. of Mental Health, Soc. of Med. Officers of Health, 1962-63; Sect. of Psych., RSM, 1970-71. Treasurer, Royal Coll. of Psychiatrists (formerly Royal Medico-Psychol Soc.), 1962-79 (Vice-Pres., 1974-76). Distinguished Hon. Fellow, Amer. Psychiatric Assoc., 1968; Hon. FRCPsych, 1979. *Publications:* articles in learned jls on child and adolescent psychiatry. *Recreations:* gardening, literature, music. *Address:* 76 West Common Road, Hayes, Bromley, Kent BR2 7BY. *T:* 01-462 2676.

WARREN, William Phillip, CEng, FIEE, FInstPet; Executive Director, Welsh Development Agency, since 1976; *b* 7 Oct. 1924; *yr s* of Herbert U. Warren and Rebecca Warren (*née* Thomas); *m* 1956, Janice Mary, *er d* of James and Lilian Holloway; one *s* one *d*. *Educ:* Quakers Yard Grammar Sch.; Univ. of Wales, Cardiff (BSc). Post graduate trng and early appts, General Electric Co. Ltd, 1943-48; Asst Chief Commercial Engr, S Wales Electricity Board, 1948-54; Chief Executive, subsidiary co., Metal Industries Ltd, 1954-56; First Commercial Manager, UKAEA, 1956-59; Dir, several subsid. companies, Powell Duffryn Ltd, 1959-68; Director, Chief Executive of subsid. companies, Tube Investments Ltd, 1968-74; Man. Dir, Davy Water Engineering Ltd, Davy International Ltd, 1974-76. Governor, University of Wales, 1971-; Life Governor and Mem. Council, UWIST, 1968-; formerly Mem. Council: Industrial Assoc. of Wales and Mon. (now CBI, Wales); Brit. Manufrs of Petroleum Equipment. *Publications:* articles in learned jls include: UK Nuclear Power Programme; High Frequency Communications over EHT Circuits; Electronics in Industry. *Recreations:* gardening, occasional golf, charity fund raising. *Address:* Eastfield House, Cowbridge, S Glamorgan CF7 7EP. *T:* Cowbridge 2392. *Clubs:* Eccentric; Cardiff and County.

WARREN EVANS, (John) Roger, FCIOB; Director, Swansea Centre for Trade and Industry, since 1979; *b* 11 Dec. 1935; *s* of Thomas and Mary Warren Evans; *m* 1966, Elizabeth M. James; one *s* one *d*. *Educ:* Leighton Park Sch., Reading; Trinity Coll., Cambridge (BA History, 1st Cl.); London Sch. of Economics. Called to Bar, Gray's Inn, 1962. Television Interviewer, Anglia Television, 1960-61; Research Officer, Centre for Urban Studies, London, 1961; practice at Bar, 1962-69; Legal Correspondent, New Society, 1964-68;

general management functions with Bovis Gp, in construction and develt, 1969-74, incl. Man. Dir, Bovis Homes Southern Ltd, 1971-74; Under-Secretary, DoE, 1975; Industrial Advr on Construction, DoE, 1975-76; Man. Dir, Barratt Develts (London), Ltd, 1977-79. London Borough Councillor (Hackney), 1971-73. FIOB 1976. *Recreations:* golf, squash, talking, playing the guitar. *Address:* 23 St Peter's Road, Newton, Swansea. *T:* Swansea 68003.

WARRENDER, family name of **Baron Bruntisfield.**

WARRENDER, Col the Hon. John Robert, OBE 1963; MC 1943; TD 1967; DL; Chairman, Thistle Industrial Holdings Ltd, since 1973; *b* 7 Feb. 1921; *s* and *heir* of Baron Bruntisfield, *qv* ; *m* 1st, 1948, (Anne) Moireen Campbell (*d* 1976), 2nd *d* of Sir Walter Campbell, KCIE; two *s* two *d* ; 2nd, 1977, Shirley (*d* 1981) (former wife of J. J. Crawley, from whom she obtained a divorce 1977), *o d* of E. J. L. Ross; three step *s. Educ:* Eton; RMC, Sandhurst. Royal Scots Greys (2nd Dragoons), 1939-48; ADC to Governor of Madras, 1946-48; comd N Somerset Yeomanry/44th Royal Tank Regt, 1957-62; Dep. Brigadier RAC (TA), Southern and Eastern Commands, 1962-67. Brig., Queen's Body Guard for Scotland (Royal Co. of Archers), 1973. Knight of Malta. DL Somerset 1965. *Recreations:* shooting, fishing. *Address:* Whitelaws, Garvald, Haddington, East Lothian EH41 4LN. *Club:* Cavalry and Guards.
See also Hon. R. H. *Warrender.*

WARRENDER, Hon. Robin Hugh; Chairman and Chief Executive, Bain Dawes PLC, since 1973; *b* 24 Dec. 1927; 3rd *s* of Baron Bruntisfield, *qv; m* 1951, Gillian, *d* of Leonard Rossiter; one *s* two *d. Educ:* Eton; Trinity Coll., Oxford. Underwriting Member of Lloyd's, 1953; Tudor & Co. (Insurance) Ltd, 1958-62; Managing Director, Fenchurch Insurance Holdings Ltd, 1963-69; Dep. Chm., A. W. Bain & Sons Ltd, 1970; Chm., Bain Dawes Ltd and other group companies, 1973-. Director: Thistle Industrial Holdings Ltd, 1962-; Bishopsgate Insurance Co. Ltd, 1979-; Tosa Ltd (Canada), 1979-; Comindus S. A. (France), 1980-; Worms & Co., 1981-; Massey-Ferguson Ltd (Canada); Massey-Ferguson (Holdings) Ltd. Member: Lloyd's Insurance Brokers Cttee, 1979- (Chm., 1981); Lloyd's Investment Cttee, 1981-. Mem. Council, Bath Univ., 1979-; Hon. Treas., Governing Cttee, Royal Choral Soc., 1979-. *Recreations:* shooting, gardening, bridge. *Address:* Widcombe Manor, Bath, Avon. *T:* Bath 317116. *Clubs:* City of London, Portland, White's.
See also Baron Colgrain, Col the Hon. *J. R. Warrender.*

WARRINGTON, Bishop Suffragan of, since 1976; **Rt. Rev. Michael Henshall;** *b* 29 Feb. 1928; *m* Ann Elizabeth (*née* Stephenson); two *s* one *d. Educ:* Manchester Grammar Sch.; St Chad's Coll., Durham (BA 1954, DipTh 1956). Deacon 1956, priest 1957, dio. York; Curate of Holy Trinity, Bridlington and of Sewerby, 1956-59; Priest-in-charge, All Saints, Conventional District of Micklehurst, 1959-62; Vicar, 1962-63; Vicar of Altrincham, 1963-75; Proctor in Convocation, 1964-75; Mem., Terms of Ministry Cttee, General Synod, 1970-75; Hon. Canon of Chester, 1972-75; Secretary, Chester Diocesan Advisory Board for Ministry, 1968-75; Canon Emeritus of Chester Cathedral, 1979. Editor for 12 years of local newspaper, Spearhead. *Recreations:* military history, old battlefields, etc. *Address:* Martinsfield, Elm Avenue, Great Crosby, Liverpool, Merseyside L23 2SX. *T:* 051-924 7004; (office) 051-709 9722.

WARRINGTON, Archdeacon of; *see* Woodhouse, Ven. C. D. S.

WARRINGTON, Anthony; Company Secretary and Director, Policy Co-ordination, Rolls-Royce Ltd, initially on secondment from Department of Industry, since 1978; *b* 15 Aug. 1929; *s* of Stanley Warrington and Gladys (*née* Sutcliffe); *m* 1955, Lavinia Lord; three *s. Educ:* Welwyn Garden City Grammar Sch.; London School of Economics. Asst Statistician: Admiralty, 1953; British Electricity Authority, 1954-55; Economist, British Transport Commn, 1956-58; Statistician, Min. of Power, 1958-66; Asst Secretary: Petroleum Div., Min. of Power (later Min. of Technology), 1966-72; Atomic Energy Div., DTI, 1972-73; Under-Sec., DoI, 1973; Air Div., 1973-78; Dir-Gen., Concorde Div. DoI, 1976-77. *Recreations:* education, theatre, hockey. *Address:* 9 Fern Grove, Welwyn Garden City, Herts AL8 7ND. *T:* Welwyn Garden 26110.

WARSOP, Rear-Adm. John Charles; Port Admiral, Rosyth, since 1981; *b* 9 May 1927; *s* of John Charles Warsop and Elsie Lily Warsop; *m* 1958, Josephine Franklin Cotterell; two *d. Educ:* Gateway Sch., Leicester; RN Coll., Eaton Hall, Chester; RN Engineering Coll., Keyham, Plymouth, 1945-48. MIMechE. HM Ships Theseus and Gambia, 1949-50; RNC Greenwich, 1950-52; HMS Superb, 1952-54; Staff, RNEC, 1954-56; Min. of Defence, 1956-59; Sen. Engr, HMS Ark Royal, 1959-61; MoD, 1961-65; British Defence Staff, Washington, USA, 1965-68; MoD, 1968-70; Engr Officer, HMS Blake, 1970-72; MoD, 1972-75; CO, HMS Fisgard, 1975-77; MoD, 1977-81. Rear-Adm. 1981. *Publications:* papers for Instn of Marine Engineers. *Recreations:* offshore racing and cruising, Rugby. *Club:* Royal Naval Sailing Association.

WARTIOVAARA, Otso Uolevi, Hon. GCVO; Ambassador of Finland to the Court of St James's, 1968-74; *b* Helsinki, 16 Nov. 1908; *s* of J. V. Wartiovaara, Dir-Gen. of Finnish Govt Accounting Office, and Siiri Nystén; *m* 1936, Maine Alanen, three *s. Educ:* Helsinki Univ. Master of Law, 1932;

Asst Judge, 1934. Entered Foreign Service, 1934; Attaché, Paris, 1936-39; Sec. and Head of Section, Min. for For. Affairs, 1939-42; Counsellor, Stockholm, 1942-44; Consul, Haaparanta, Sweden, 1944-45; Head of Section, Min. for For. Affairs, 1945-49; Counsellor, Washington, 1949-52; Head of Admin. Dept, Min. for For. Affairs, 1952-54; Envoy and Minister, 1954; Head of Legal Dept, Min. for For. Affairs, 1954-56; Minister, Belgrade and Athens, 1956-58; Ambassador, Belgrade, and Minister to Athens, 1958-61; Ambassador to Vienna, 1961-68, and to Holy See, 1966-68, also Perm. Rep. to Internat. Atomic Energy Organization, 1961-68. Grand Cross, Order of Lion of Finland; Kt Comdr, Order of White Rose of Finland; Cross of Freedom; Silver Cross of Sport, Finland. Grand Gold Cross of Austria; Grand Cross, Orders of Phœnix (Greece), Pius IX, Flag (Yugoslavia); Comdr, Orders of Northern Star (Sweden) and Vasa (Sweden). *Recreations:* golf, shooting. *Address:* Lutherinkatn 6. A, 00100 Helsinki 10, Finland. *Club:* Travellers'.

WARTNABY, Dr John; Keeper, Department of Earth and Space Sciences, Science Museum, South Kensington, 1969-82; *b* 6 Jan. 1926; *o s* of Ernest John and Beatrice Hilda Wartnaby; *m* 1962, Kathleen Mary Barber, MD, MRCP, DPM; one *s* one *d. Educ:* Chiswick Grammar Sch.; Chelsea Coll. (BSc 1946); Imperial Coll. of Science and Technology (DIC 1950); University Coll., London (MSc 1967; PhD 1972). FInstP 1971. Asst Keeper, Dept of Astronomy and Geophysics, Science Museum, 1951; Deputy Keeper, 1960. *Publications:* Seismology, 1957; The International Geophysical Year, 1957; Surveying, 1968; papers in learned jls. *Recreations:* country walking, Zen, distance running. *Address:* 11 Greenhurst Lane, Oxted, Surrey RH8 0LD. *T:* Oxted 4461.

WARWICK; *see* Turner-Warwick.

WARWICK, 7th Earl of, *cr* 1759; **Charles Guy Fulke Greville;** Baron Brooke, 1621; Earl Brooke, 1746; DL; Lieut, Reserve of Officers, Grenadier Guards; *b* 4 March 1911, *e s* of 6th Earl and Marjorie (*d* 1943), *d* of Sir W. Eden, 7th Bt; *S* father, 1928; *m* 1st, 1933, Rose (from whom he obtained a divorce, 1938), *d* of late D. C. Bingham, Coldstream Guards, and Lady Rosabelle Brand; one *s* ; 2nd, 1942, Mary (from whom he obtained a divorce, 1949), *d* of P. C. Hopkinson, Kingston Gorse, Sussex; 3rd, 1963, Mme Janine Angele Josephine Detry de Marès. Merchant Navy, Admiralty Small Vessels Pool, 1943. Warwickshire CC, 1934-36; a Governor of Birmingham Univ.; Mayor of Warwick, 1951; Alderman 1952; DL, Warwickshire. Governor: Warwick Kings Schools; Royal Shakespeare Theatre. *Heir:* s Lord Brooke, *qv.*

WARWICK, Bishop Suffragan of, since 1980; **Rt. Rev. Keith Appleby Arnold;** *b* 1 Oct. 1926; *s* of Dr Frederick Arnold, Hale, Cheshire, and Alice Mary Appleby Arnold (*née* Holt); *m* 1955, Deborah Noreen Glenwright; one *s* one *d. Educ:* Winchester; Trinity Coll., Cambridge (MA); Westcott House, Cambridge. Served as Lieut, Coldstream Guards, 1944-48. Curate: Haltwhistle, Northumberland, 1952-55; St John's, Princes St, Edinburgh, 1955-61; Chaplain, TA, 1956-61; Rector of St John's, Edinburgh, 1961-69; Vicar of Kirkby Lonsdale, Cumbria, 1969-73; Team Rector of Hemel Hempstead, 1973-80. *Recreations:* voluntary housing, marriage guidance, etc; skiing, gardening. *Address:* Warwick House, 9 Armorial Road, Coventry CV3 6GH. *T:* Coventry 416200.

WARWICK, Cyril Walter; Chairman: Warwick & Esplen Ltd, since 1971; Houlder Bros & Co. Ltd, 1962-69 (President since 1970); *b* 30 Sept. 1899; 2nd *s* of late J. J. W. Warwick; *m* 1925, Dorothy Fitzgerald, *d* of late John Miller; one *s* one *d. Educ:* Tollington Sch.; King's Coll., London Univ. Served RFC and RAF, 1917-19. Joined Kaye Son & Co., shipbrokers, 1919; elected Baltic Exchange, 1920; joined Houlder Bros & Co. Ltd, 1938; Director Hadley Shipping Co. Ltd, 1938, Chm. 1962; Director: Houlder Line, 1944-69; Furness Withy & Co. Ltd, 1962-69; Royal Mail Lines Ltd, 1965-75; and various other shipping companies; Dep. Chairman, Houlder Bros, 1957; Director, Baltic Mercantile and Shipping Exchange, 1951; Vice-Chairman, 1959; Chairman, 1961-63; Hon. Mem., 1970. President: Cereals and Baltic Friendly Society, 1966-68; Baltic Exchange Benevolent Soc., 1973-77; Mem. Council, Chamber of Shipping of UK, 1949-75; Fellow, Inst. Chartered Shipbrokers; Liveryman, Worshipful Company of Shipwrights. Freight Market Rep. of Ministry of Transport, 1958-67. *Recreations:* riding, fishing. *Address:* Witley Court, Wormley, Godalming, Surrey. *T:* Wormley 2626. *Club:* Canning.

WARWICK, Prof. Roger; retired; Professor of Anatomy and Director of Department of Anatomy, Guy's Hospital Medical School, University of London, 1955-80. *Educ:* Victoria University of Manchester. BSc, 1935; MB, ChB, Manchester, 1937; MD (Gold Medal), 1952; PhD, 1955. House Physician and House Surgeon, Professorial Unit, Manchester Royal Infirmary, 1938-39; Surgeon Lieut, RNVR, 1939-45; Demonstrator and Lecturer in Anatomy, University of Manchester, 1945-55. Member: Anatomical Society of Great Britain (Symington Memorial Prize, 1953); Anatomical Socs of India and SA; Scientific Fellow of Zoological Society; Fellow, Linnean Soc.; Hon. Sec., Internat. Anat. Nomenclature Cttee; Member Society for Human Biology, etc. Sydney Renshaw Prize in Physiology, 1937. *Publications:* (co-ed) Gray's Anatomy, 35th edn, 1973, 36th edn, 1980; (ed) Wolff's Anatomy of the Eye and Orbit, 7th edn, 1977; contributions to Brain, Journal Anat., Journal Comp. Neurol., etc. *Recreations:* Natural history, especially Lepidoptera, radio communication, archæology. *Address:* c/o Department of Anatomy, Guy's Hospital Medical School, SE1 9RT.

WARWICK, Captain William Eldon, CBE 1971; RD, RNR retired; Commodore, Cunard Line Ltd, 1970-75; First Master, RMS Queen Elizabeth 2, 1966-72; *b* 12 Nov. 1912; *e s* of Eldon Warwick, architect and Gertrude Florence Gent; *m* 1939, Evelyn King (*née* Williams); three *s. Educ:* Birkenhead Sch.; HMTS Conway. Joined Merchant Service, 1928, serving in Indian Ocean and Red Sea; awarded Master Mariner's Certificate, 1936; joined Cunard White Star as Jun. Officer (Lancastria), 1937; commissioned in RNR, 1937. Mobilized in RN War Service, 1939, in Coastal Forces and Corvettes in North Atlantic, Russian Convoys and Normandy Landings, 1939-46 (despatches, 1946). First cargo command, Alsatia, 1954; first passenger command, Carinthia, 1958; followed by command of almost all the passenger liners in Cunard fleet. Promoted Captain RNR, 1960; retd RNR, 1965. Younger Brother of Trinity House; Liveryman, Hon. Co. of Master Mariners (Master, 1976-77); Freeman of City of London. *Recreations:* reading, music, walking. *Address:* Greywell Cottage, Callow Hill, Virginia Water, Surrey. *T:* Wentworth 3361. *Clubs:* Naval, Institute of Directors.

WASHBOURN, Rear-Admiral Richard Everley, CB 1961; DSO 1940; OBE 1950; Chief of Naval Staff, RNZN, 1963-65, retired; *b* 14 Feb. 1910; *s* of H. E. A. Washbourn, Nelson, NZ; *m* 1943, June, *d* of L. M. Herapath, Auckland, NZ; one *s* one *d. Educ:* Nelson Coll., New Zealand. Entered Royal Navy by Special Entry from New Zealand, 1927; HMS Erebus, 1928; HMS London, 1929-31; Courses, 1932; HMS Warspite, 1933; HMS Diomede, 1934-35; Specialised in Gunnery, 1936-37; HMS Excellent, 1938; HMS Achilles, 1939-42; Battle of the Plate, 13 Dec. 1939 (DSO); HMS Excellent, 1942; HMS Anson, 1943. Admiralty Gunnery Establishment, 1944-45; Exec. Officer, HMNZS, Bellona, 1946-48; Comdr Supt HMNZ Dockyard, Devonport, 1950; Dep. Director of Naval Ordnance, 1950-53; HMS Manxman, 1953; Chief Staff Officer to Flag Officer (Flotillas), Mediterranean, 1954-55; Director of Naval Ordnance, Admiralty, 1956-58; HMS Tiger, 1959; Director-General, Weapons, 1960-62; retired Royal Navy, 1962; entered RNZN, 1963; retired RNZN, 1965. *Recreation:* beachcombing. *Address:* Onekaka, RD2, Takaka, Golden Bay, Nelson, New Zealand.

WASS, Dr Charles Alfred Alan; Director of Safety in Mines Research Establishment, Sheffield, 1970-74; *b* 20 July 1911; *s* of William and Louise Wass, Sutton-in-Ashfield, Nottinghamshire; *m* 1936, Alice Elizabeth Carpenter; two *d. Educ:* Brunt's Sch., Mansfield; Nottingham Univ. Post Office Radio Research Station, 1934-46; Royal Aircraft Establishment, 1946-55; Safety in Mines Research Establishment, 1955-74. *Publications:* Introduction to Electronic Analogue Computers, 1955 (2nd edn, with K. C. Garner, 1965); papers on electrical communication subjects and mine safety. *Recreations:* music making, reed instruments. *Address:* The Old School House, Swine, Hull, North Humberside HU11 4JE. *T:* Hull 811227.

WASS, Sir Douglas (William Gretton), GCB 1980 (KCB 1975; CB 1971); Permanent Secretary to HM Treasury, 1974-83, and Joint Head of the Home Civil Service, 1981-83; *b* 15 April 1923; *s* of late Arthur W. and late Elsie W. Wass; *m* 1954, Dr Milica Pavičić; one *s* one *d. Educ:* Nottingham High Sch.; St John's Coll., Cambridge (MA; Hon. Fellow, 1982). Served War, 1943-46: Scientific Research with Admiralty, at home and in Far East. Entered HM Treasury as Asst Principal, 1946; Principal, 1951; Commonwealth Fund Fellow in USA, 1958-59; Vis. Fellow, Brookings Instn, Washington, DC, 1959; Private Sec.: to Chancellor of the Exchequer, 1959-61; to Chief Sec. to Treasury, 1961-62; Asst Sec., 1962; Alternate Exec. Dir, Internat. Monetary Fund, and Financial Counsellor, British Embassy, Washington, DC, 1965-67; HM Treasury: Under-Sec., 1968; Dep. Sec., 1970-73; Second Permanent Sec., 1973-74. Chm., British Selection Cttee of Harkness Fellowships; Dep. Chm., Council of Policy Studies Instt. Governor, Ditchley Foundn. *Address:* 6 Dora Road, SW19 7HH. *T:* 01-946 5556. *Club:* Reform.

WASSERMAN, Gordon Joshua; Under Secretary, Central Policy Review Staff, Cabinet Office, since 1981; *b* Montreal, 26 July 1938; *s* of late John J. Wasserman, QC, and Prof. Rachel Chait Wasserman; *m* 1964, Cressida Frances, *yr d* of late Rt Hon. Hugh Gaitskell, PC, CBE, MP, and of Baroness Gaitskell, *qv* ; two *d. Educ:* Westmount High Sch., Montreal; McGill Univ. (BA); New Coll., Oxford (MA). Rhodes Scholar (Quebec and New Coll.), 1959; Sen. Research Scholar, St Antony's Coll., Oxford, 1961-64; Lectr in Economics, Merton Coll., Oxford, 1963-64; Research Fellow, New Coll., Oxford, 1964-67; joined Home Office as Economic Adviser, 1967, Sen. Econ. Adviser, 1972, Asst Sec., 1977; Head, Urban Deprivation Unit, 1973-77; Civil Service Travelling Fellowship in USA, 1977-78. *Recreations:* gardening, walking, theatre. *Address:* c/o Cabinet Office, SW1. *Clubs:* Reform, Beefsteak.

WASSERSTEIN, Prof. Abraham; Professor of Greek, Hebrew University of Jerusalem, since 1969; *b* Frankfurt/Main, Germany, 5 Oct. 1921; *s* of late Berl Bernhard Wasserstein and late Czarna Cilla (*née* Laub); *m* 1942, Margaret Eva (*née* Ecker); two *s* one *d. Educ:* Schools in Berlin and Rome; privately in Palestine; Birkbeck Coll., London Univ. BA 1949, PhD 1951. Assistant in Greek, 1951-52, Lecturer in Greek, 1952-60, Glasgow Univ.; Prof. of Classics, Leicester Univ., 1960-69, and Dean of Faculty of Arts, 1966-69. Vis. Fellow, Centre for Postgraduate Hebrew Studies, Oriental Inst., Univ. of Oxford, 1973-74; Vis. Prof., Hochschule für Jüdische Studien, Heidelberg, 1980-81. Mem. Inst. for Advanced Study, Princeton, 1975-76. FRAS 1961; Pres., Classical Assoc. of Israel, 1971-74. *Publications:* Flavius Josephus, 1974; Galen, On Airs, Waters, Places (critical edn, with trans. and notes), 1982; contrib.

to learned journals. *Recreations:* theatre, travel. *Address:* Department of Classics, The Hebrew University, Jerusalem, Israel.

WASTELL, Cyril Gordon, CBE 1975; Secretary General of Lloyd's, 1967-76, retired; *b* 10 Jan. 1916; *s* of Arthur Edward Wastell and Lilian Wastell; *m* 1947, Margaret Lilian (*née* Moore); one *d. Educ:* Brentwood Sch., Essex. Joined Staff of Corporation of Lloyd's, 1932; apart from war service (Lieut Royal Corps of Signals), 1939-46, progressed through various depts and positions at Lloyd's, until retirement. *Recreations:* sailing, reading, gardening under duress. *Address:* Candys, Burgmann's Hill, Lympstone, Devon EX8 5HP.

WASTIE, Winston Victor, CB 1962; OBE 1946 (MBE 1937); Under-Secretary, Ministry of Public Building and Works, Scotland, 1959-62, retired; *b* 5 March 1900; *s* of H. Wastie; *m* 1924, Charmbury Billows; one *d. Educ:* Greenwich Secondary Sch. Civil Service, New Scotland Yard, 1915-42; Chief Licensing Officer, Civil Building Control, Ministry of Works, 1942-46; Assistant Secretary, Scottish HQ, Ministry of Works, 1946-59; Under-Secretary, 1959. *Recreations:* bridge, gardening and sport. *Address:* Dirleton, Hazelbank Close, Petersfield, Hants.

WATERFIELD, John Percival; company director and consultant; *b* Dublin, 5 Oct. 1921; *er s* of late Sir Percival Waterfield, KBE, CB; *m* 1950, Margaret Lee Thomas; two *s* one *d. Educ:* Dragon Sch.; Charterhouse (schol.); Christ Church, Oxford (schol.). Served War of 1939-45: 1st Bn, The King's Own Royal Rifle Corps (60th Rifles), Western Desert, Tunisia, Italy and Austria (despatches). Entered HM Foreign (subseq. Diplomatic) Service, 1946; Third Secretary, Moscow, 1947; Second Secretary, Tokyo, 1950; Foreign Office, 1952; First Secretary, Santiago, Chile, 1954; HM Consul (Commercial), New York, 1957; FO, 1960; Ambassador to Mali Republic, 1964-65, concurrently to Guinea, 1965; duties connected with NATO, 1966; Counsellor and Head of Chancery, New Delhi, 1966-68; Head of Western Organizations Dept, FCO, 1969; Man. Dir, BEAMA, 1971; Principal Estabs and Finance Officer, NI Office, 1973-79; on secondment to Internat. Military Services Ltd, 1979-80; retired from public service, 1980. *Address:* 17 Vincent Square Mansions, Walcott Street, SW1. *T:* 01-834 0800; 5 North Street, Somerton, Somerset. *T:* Somerton 72389. *Club:* Boodle's.

WATERFORD, 8th Marquess of, *cr* 1789; **John Hubert de la Poer Beresford;** Baron La Poer, 1375; Baronet, 1668; Viscount Tyrone, Baron Beresford, 1720; Earl of Tyrone, 1746; Baron Tyrone (Great Britain), 1786; *b* 14 July 1933; *er s* of 7th Marquess and Juliet Mary (who *m* 2nd, 1946, Lieut-Colonel John Silcock), 2nd *d* of late David Lindsay; *S* father, 1934; *m* 1957, Lady Caroline Wyndham-Quin, *yr d* of 6th Earl of Dunraven and Mount-Earl, CB, CBE, MC; three *s* one *d. Educ:* Eton. Lieut, RHG Reserve. *Heir: s* Earl of Tyrone, *qv. Address:* Curraghmore, Portlaw, Co. Waterford. *T:* Waterford 87102. *Club:* White's.

WATERHOUSE, Dr Douglas Frew, AO 1980; CMG 1970; FRS 1967; FAA 1954; FRACI 1948; Chief of Division of Entomology, Commonwealth Scientific and Industrial Research Organization, 1960-81, Honorary Research Fellow, since 1981; *b* 3 June 1916; *s* of late Prof. E. G. Waterhouse, CMG, OBE, and Janet Frew Kellie, MA; *m* 1944, Allison D., *d* of J. H. Calthorpe; three *s* one *d. Educ:* Sydney C. of E. Grammar Sch.; Universities of Sydney and Cambridge. BSc Hons, University Medal, MSc, DSc, Sydney. Served War of 1939-45, Captain, AAMC Medical Entomology. Joined Research Staff, CSIRO, 1938; Asst Chief, Div. of Entomology, 1953-59. Biological Secretary, Australian Acad. of Science, 1961-66; Chm. Council, Canberra Coll. of Advanced Educn, 1969-. Corresp. Mem., Brazilian Acad. of Sciences, 1974. Hon. For. Mem., All-Union Entomological Soc. of USSR, 1979; For. Mem., USSR Acad. of Science, 1982. Hon. FRES 1972. David Syme Research Prize, 1953; Mueller Medal, 1972; Farrer Medal, 1973. Hon. DSc, ANU, 1978. *Publications:* numerous articles on insect physiology, biochemistry, ecology and control of insects. *Recreations:* gardening, fishing, gyotaku. *Address:* 60 National Circuit, Deakin, ACT 2600, Australia. *T:* 731772. *Club:* Commonwealth (Canberra).

WATERHOUSE, Sir Ellis (Kirkham), Kt 1975; CBE 1956 (MBE 1943); FBA 1955; *b* 16 Feb. 1905; *s* of P. Leslie Waterhouse and Eleanor Margetson; *m* 1949, Helen, *d* of F. W. Thomas; two *d. Educ:* Marlborough; New Coll., Oxford (Scholar; MA; Hon. Fellow 1976). Commonwealth Fund Fellow (Department of Art and Archæology, University of Princeton, USA), 1927-29 (AM); Assistant, National Gallery, 1929-33; Librarian, British School at Rome, 1933-36; selected and catalogued pictures for RA Exhibition of 17th Century Art (1938), 1937; Fellow of Magdalen Coll., Oxford, 1938-47; served with Army and Foreign Office (mainly in Middle East), 1939-45; temp. editor, Burlington Magazine, 1946; Reader in History of Art, Manchester Univ., 1947-48; Director of National Galleries of Scotland, 1949-52; Slade Professor of Fine Art, University of Oxford, 1953-55; Clark Visiting Professor, Williams Coll., Mass, 1962-63; Mellon Visiting Professor, University of Pittsburgh, 1967-68; Barber Professor of Fine Arts and Dir of Barber Inst., Birmingham Univ., 1952-70; Dir of Studies, Paul Mellon Centre for Studies in British Art, 1970-73; Kress Prof. in Residence, Nat. Gallery of Art, Washington DC, 1974-75. Mem., Exec. Cttee, Nat. Art Collections Fund, 1972-. FRHistSoc. Hon. DLitt: Nottingham, 1968; Leicester, 1970; Birmingham, 1973; Oxon, 1976. Officer of Order Orange Nassau. Cavaliere ufficiale, Ordine al Merito della Repubblica italiana, 1961. *Publications:* El Greco's Italian Period, 1930; Roman Baroque Painting, 1937, rev. edn 1976;

Sir Joshua Reynolds, 1941; British Painting, 1530-1790, 1953; Gainsborough, 1958; Italian Baroque Painting, 1962; Jayne Lectures, 1964, 1965; Catalogue of Pictures at Waddesdon Manor, 1967; Reynolds, 1973; The Dictionary of British 18th Century Painters in Oils and Crayons, 1981; numerous articles and catalogues. *Address:* Overshot, Hinksey Hill, Oxford. *T:* Oxford 735320.

WATERHOUSE, Frederick Harry; tax and investment consultant, self employed, since 1982; *b* 3 June 1932; *m* 1954, Olive Carter; two *d. Educ:* King Edward's, Aston, Birmingham; London Univ. (BScEcon). Associate Mem. Inst. of Cost and Management Accountants. Chief Accountant, Copper Div., Imperial Metal Industries, 1967-70; Asst Chief Accountant, Agricl Div., ICI, 1970-72; Chief Accountant, Plant Protection Div., ICI, 1972-78; Dir, Société pour la Protection d'Agriculture (SOPRA), France, 1976-78; Dir, Solplant SA, Italy, 1976-78; Bd Member, Finance and Corporate Planning, The Post Office, 1978-79; Treasurer's Dept, ICI Ltd, Millbank, 1979-82. *Recreations:* golf, gardening, sailing. *Address:* 47 Grosvenor Road, Chichester PO19 2RT. *T:* Chichester 783745.

WATERHOUSE, Keith Spencer; writer; *b* 6 Feb. 1929; 4th *s* of Ernest and Elsie Edith Waterhouse; *m* 1951, Joan Foster (marr. diss. 1968); one *s* two *d. Educ:* Leeds. Journalist in Leeds and London, 1950-; Columnist with Daily Mirror, 1970-; Contributor to Punch, 1966-, Mem. Punch Table, 1979. Granada Columnist of the Year Award, 1970; IPC Descriptive Writer of the Year Award, 1970; IPC Columnist of the Year Award, 1973; British Press Awards Columnist of the Year, 1978; Granada Special Quarter Century Award, 1982. Films (with Willis Hall) include: Billy Liar; Whistle Down the Wind; A Kind of Loving; Lock Up Your Daughters. Plays (with Willis Hall) include: Billy Liar, 1960 (from which musical Billy was adapted, 1974); Celebration, 1961; All Things Bright and Beautiful, 1963; Say Who You Are, 1965; Whoops-a-Daisy, 1968; Children's Day, 1969; Who's Who, 1972; The Card (musical), 1973; Saturday, Sunday, Monday (adaptation from de Filippo), 1973; Filumena (adaptation from de Filippo), 1977; Worzel Gummidge, 1981. TV series: Budgie, Queenie's Castle, The Upper Crusts, Billy Liar, The Upchat Line, The Upchat Connection, Worzel Gummidge, West End Tales. *Publications: novels:* There is a Happy Land, 1957; Billy Liar, 1959; Jubb, 1963; The Bucket Shop, 1968; Billy Liar on the Moon, 1975; Office Life, 1978; Maggie Muggins, 1981; *plays:* (all with Willis Hall) include: Billy Liar, 1960; Celebration, 1961; All Things Bright and Beautiful, 1963; Say Who You Are, 1965; Who's Who, 1974; Saturday, Sunday, Monday (adaptation from de Filippo), 1974; Filumena (adaptation from de Filippo), 1977; *general:* (with Guy Deghy) Café Royal, 1956; (ed) Writers' Theatre, 1967; The Passing of The Third-floor Buck, 1974; Mondays, Thursdays, 1976; Rhubarb, Rhubarb, 1979; Daily Mirror Style, 1980. *Recreation:* lunch. *Address:* 29 Kenway Road, SW5. *Clubs:* Garrick, PEN.

WATERHOUSE, Mrs Rachel Elizabeth, CBE 1980; PhD; Chairman, Consumers' Association, since 1982 (Member Council, since 1966, Deputy Chairman, 1979-82); *b* 2 Jan. 1923; *d* of Percival John Franklin and Ruby Susanna Franklin; *m* 1947, John A. H. Waterhouse; two *s* two *d. Educ:* King Edward's High Sch., Birmingham; St Hugh's Coll., Oxford (BA 1944, MA 1948); Univ. of Birmingham (PhD 1960). WEA and Extra-mural tutor, 1944-47. Birmingham Consumer Group: Sec., 1964-65, Chm. 1966-68, Mem. Cttee, 1968-; Member: Nat. Consumer Council, 1975-; Consumers' Consultative Cttee of EEC Commn, 1977-; Price Commn, 1977-79; Council, Advertising Standards Authority, 1980-; NEDC, 1981-. Ministerial nominee to Potato Marketing Bd, 1969-81; Member: Home Office Working Party on Internal Shop Security, 1971-73; Adv. Cttee on Asbestos, 1976-79; Pres., Inst. of Consumer Ergonomics, Univ. of Loughborough, 1980- (Chm., 1970-80). Chm., Birmingham Gp, Victorian Soc., 1966-67, 1972-74. Hon. DLitt, Univ. of Technology, Loughborough, 1978. *Publications:* The Birmingham and Midland Institute 1854-1954, 1954; A Hundred Years of Engineering Craftsmanship, 1957; Children in Hospital: a hundred years of child care in Birmingham, 1962; (with John Whybrow) How Birmingham became a Great City, 1976. *Recreations:* conversation and sewing. *Address:* 252 Bristol Road, Birmingham B5 7SL. *T:* 021-472 0427. *Club:* Royal Commonwealth Society.

WATERHOUSE, Hon. Sir Ronald (Gough), Kt 1978; **Hon. Mr Justice Waterhouse;** Judge of the High Court of Justice, Family Division, since 1978; Judge, Employment Appeal Tribunal, since 1979; Presiding Judge, Wales and Chester Circuit, since 1980; *b* Holywell, Flintshire, 8 May 1926; *s* of late Thomas Waterhouse, CBE, and of Doris Helena Waterhouse (*née* Gough); *m* 1960, Sarah Selina, *d* of late Captain E. A. Ingram; one *s* two *d. Educ:* Holywell Grammar Sch.; St John's Coll., Cambridge. RAFVR, 1944-48. McMahon Schol., St John's Coll., 1949; Pres., Cambridge Union Soc., 1950; MA, LLB; called to Bar, Middle Temple, 1952 (Harmsworth Schol.); Wales and Chester Circuit; QC 1969; Bencher 1977. A Recorder of the Crown Court, 1972-77. Mem. Bar Council, 1961-65. Deputy Chairman: Cheshire QS, 1964-71; Flintshire QS, 1966-71. Contested (Lab) West Flintshire, 1959. Chairman: Inter-departmental Cttee of Inquiry on Rabies, 1970; Cttees of Investigation for GB and England and Wales, under Agricultural Mkting Act, 1971-78; Local Govt Boundary Commn for Wales, 1974-78. Mem. Council, Zoological Soc. of London, 1972-, a Vice-Pres., 1981-. *Recreations:* music, golf. *Address:* 12 Cavendish Avenue, NW8. *T:* 01-286 7609; Royal Courts of Justice, Strand, WC2. *Clubs:* Garrick, MCC; Cardiff and County (Cardiff).

WATERLOW, Sir Christopher Rupert, 5th Bt *cr* 1873; *b* 12 Aug. 1959; *s* of (Peter) Rupert Waterlow (*d* 1969) and Jill Elizabeth (*d* 1961), *e d* of E. T. Gourlay; *S* grandfather 1973. *Educ:* Stonyhurst Coll., Lancs. With Metropolitan Police. *Recreations:* music, shooting. Heir: great-uncle Derek Vaudrey Waterlow, *b* 19 Feb. 1902. *Address:* 36 Frewin Road, SW18. *Clubs:* Metropolitan Police Motor, Federation of British Police Motor Clubs, Stonyhurst Association.

WATERLOW, Sir (James) Gerard, 4th Bt *cr* 1930; Visiting Lecturer, Information Systems, London Business School, since 1979; *b* 3 Sept. 1939; *s* of Sir Thomas Gordon Waterlow, 3rd Bt, CBE and Helen Elizabeth (*d* 1970), *yr d* of Gerard A. H. Robinson; *S* father, 1982; *m* 1965, Diana Suzanne, *yr d* of Sir Thomas Skyrme, *qv* ; one *s* one *d. Educ:* Marlborough; Trinity College, Cambridge. Coordinator for Science Research Council Manufacturing Systems, 1980-; previously employed in the computer industry. *Recreations:* tennis, bridge. Heir: *s* (Thomas) James Waterlow, *b* 20 March 1970. *Address:* 12 Cliveden Place, SW1. *T:* 01-730 6595. *Clubs:* Lansdowne; Huntercombe; MCC.

WATERLOW, Prof. John Conrad, CMG 1970; MD, ScD; FRCP; FRS 1982; FRGS; Professor of Human Nutrition, London School of Hygiene and Tropical Medicine, since 1970; *b* 13 June 1916; *o s* of Sir Sydney Waterlow, KCMG, CBE, HM Diplomatic Service; *m* 1939, Angela Pauline Cecil Gray; two *s* one *d. Educ:* Eton Coll.; Trinity Coll., Cambridge (MD, ScD); London Hosp. Med. College. Mem., Scientific Staff, MRC, 1942; Dir, MRC Tropical Metabolism Research Unit, Univ. of the West Indies, 1954-70. *Publications:* numerous papers on protein malnutrition and protein metabolism. *Recreation:* mountain walking. *Address:* Oare, Marlborough, Wilts. *Club:* Savile.

WATERMAN, Fanny, OBE 1971; FRCM; Chairman of Committee, Leeds International Pianoforte Competition, since 1963, also Chairman of Jury, since 1981; *b* 22 March 1920; *d* of Myer Waterman and Mary Waterman (*née* Behrmann); *m* 1944, Dr Geoffrey de Keyser; two *s. Educ:* Allerton High Sch.; Royal College of Music, London (Mathilde Verne Schol.; ARCM 1943, FRCM 1972). Concert pianist, teacher of international reputation and experience. Vice-Pres., European Piano-Teachers Assoc., 1975-; Trustee, Edward Boyle Meml Trust, 1981-. Founded (with Marion Harewood) Leeds International Pianoforte Competition, 1961. Member of International Juries: Vienna, 1977; Terni, 1978; Munich, 1979; Leipzig, 1980; Leeds (Chm.), 1981; Calgary, Salt Lake City, Viña del Mar, 1982; Bolzano, 1983. 'Piano Playtime' series on ITV Channel 4. Hon. MA Leeds, 1966. *Publications:* (with Marion Harewood): series of Piano Tutors (8 vols), 1967-; 1st Year Piano lessons: 1st Year Repertoire; 2nd Year Piano lessons; 2nd Year Repertoire; 3rd Year Piano lessons: 3rd Year Repertoire; Duets and Piano Playtime, 1978; Recital Book for pianists, Book 1, 1981; Sonatina and Sonata Book, 1982; (with Paul de Keyser) 1st and 2nd Year Violinists Repertoire books, 1982. *Recreations:* travel, reading, voluntary work, cooking. *Address:* Woodgarth, Oakwood Grove, Leeds LS8 2PA. *T:* Leeds 655771.

WATERMAN, Rt. Rev. Robert Harold; *b* 11 March 1894; *s* of Canon Robert B. Waterman and Annabella Hughton; *m* 1921, Frances Isabel Bayne; two *s* two *d* (and two *s* decd). *Educ:* University of Bishop's Coll., Lennoxville, PQ. BA 1914, BD 1933, Deacon, 1920; priest, 1921; Curate of Bearbrook, 1920-21, Rector, 1921-27; Rector of Pembroke, 1927-33; Rector of Smith's Falls, 1933-37; Rector of Christchurch Cathedral, Hamilton, Diocese of Niagara, 1937-48; Dean of Niagara, 1938-48; Bishop Coadjutor of Nova Scotia, 1948-50; Bishop of Nova Scotia, 1950-63, retired. *Address:* Connaught Home, North Hatley, PQ J0B 2C0, Canada.

WATERPARK, 7th Baron *cr* 1792; **Frederick Caryll Philip Cavendish, Bt** 1755; Sales Director, CSE Aviation Ltd, since 1962; *b* 6 Oct. 1926; *s* of Brig.-General Frederick William Laurence Sheppard Hart Cavendish, CMG, DSO (*d* 1931) and Enid, Countess of Kenmare (she *m* 3rd, 1933, as his 3rd wife, 1st Viscount Furness, who *d* 1940; 4th, as his 2nd wife, 6th Earl of Kenmare), *d* of Charles Lindeman, Sydney, New South Wales, and widow of Roderick Cameron, New York; *S* uncle 1948; *m* 1951, Daniele, *e d* of Roger Guirche, Paris; one *s* two *d. Educ:* Eton. Lieut, 4th and 1st Bn Grenadier Guards, 1944-46. Served as Assistant District Commandant Kenya Police Reserve, 1952-55, during Mau Mau Rebellion. Heir: *s* Hon. Roderick Alexander Cavendish, *b* 10 Oct. 1959. *Address:* (office) CSE Aviation, Oxford Airport, Kidlington, Oxford; (home) 74 Elm Park Road, SW3. *Club:* Cavalry and Guards.

WATERS, Alwyn Brunow, CBE 1971 (MBE (mil.) 1943); GM 1944; Senior Partner, The Waters Jamieson Partnership, Architects and Engineers, London and Edinburgh, since 1977; *b* 18 Sept. 1906; *s* of Samuel Gilbert Waters and Gertrude Madeleine Brunow; *m* 1933, Ruby Alice Bindon; one *s* one *d. Educ:* Regent Street Polytechnic; Central Sch. of Arts and Crafts; Royal Academy Schs; Imperial College. ARIBA 1933; FRIBA 1945; FRIAS; FCIArb. War service, RE (bomb disposal), 1940-46 (Major). Asst in various London offices, 1927-32; teaching at LCC Hammersmith Sch. of Bldg and private practice, 1932-46; founded Llewellyn Smith & Waters, 1937, Senior Partner 1946-70; Senior Partner, A. B. Waters and Partners, 1970-76. Member: various cttees, RIBA, 1945-; Council, Inst. of Arbitrators, 1958-70 (Pres. 1965); Nat. Jt Consultative Cttee for Building, 1965-74 (Chm. 1972). Governor, Willesden Coll. of Technology, 1946-71; Chm., Jt Contracts Tribunal, 1960-73. Bossom Lectr, RSA, 1970. Master, Masons' Co., 1982-83; Asst, Arbitrators' Co., 1981-. *Publications:* Story of a House, 1948; contrib. Building, Architects Jl, etc, primarily on warehousing and distribution. *Recreations:* architecture, fly fishing. *Address:* Long Ridge, North Park, Gerrards Cross, Bucks. *T:* Gerrards Cross 82116. *Club:* Royal Automobile.

WATERS, Brig. Charles John, CBE 1981 (OBE 1977); Deputy Commander, Land Forces, Falkland Islands, since 1982; *b* 2 Sept. 1935; *s* of Patrick George Waters and Margaret Ronaldson Waters (*née* Clark); *m* 1962, Hilary Doyle Nettleton; three *s*. *Educ:* Oundle; Royal Military Academy, Sandhurst. Commissioned, The Gloucestershire Regt, 1955; GSO2, MO1 (MoD), 1970-72; Instructor, GSO1 (DS), Staff Coll., Camberley, 1973-74; Commanding Officer, 1st Bn, Gloucestershire Regt, 1975-77; Colonel General Staff, 1st Armoured Div., 1977-79; Comdr 3 Infantry Bde, 1979-81; RCDS 1982. *Recreations:* sailing, skiing, painting. *Address:* c/o National Westminster Bank, 4-6 Broad Street, Reading, Berks. *Clubs:* Army and Navy, Ski Club of Great Britain, Eagle Ski (c/o Alpine Club).

WATERS, David Watkin, Lt-Comdr RN; Caird Research Fellow, National Maritime Museum, 1979-82; *b* 2 Aug. 1911; *s* of Eng. Lt William Waters, RN, and Jessie Rhena (*née* Whitemore); *m* 1946, Hope Waters (*née* Pritchard); one step *s* one step *d*. *Educ:* RN Coll., Dartmouth. Joined RN, 1925; Cadet and Midshipman, HMS Barham, 1929; specialised in Aviation (Pilot), 1935. Served War of 1939-45: Fleet Air Arm, Malta (PoW, Italy, Germany, 1940-45). Admlty, 1946-50; retd, 1950. Admlty Historian (Defence of Shipping), 1946-60; Head of Dept of Navigation and Astronomy, Nat. Maritime Museum, 1960-76, and Sec. of Museum, 1968-71; Dep. Dir, 1971-78. Pres., British Soc. for Hist. of Sci., 1976-78 (Vice-Pres., 1972-74, 1978-81). Vis. Prof. of History, Simon Fraser Univ., Burnaby, BC, 1978; Regents' Prof., UCLA, 1979. Chm., Japan Animal Welfare Soc., 1972-80. Gold Medal, Admiralty Naval History, 1936, and Special Award, 1946; FRHistS 1951; FRInstNav 1959; Fellow, Inst. Internac. da Cultura Portuguesa, 1966; FSA 1970. *Publications:* The True and Perfect Newes of Syr Francis Drake, 1955; (with F. Barley) Naval Staff History, Second World War, Defeat of the Enemy attack on Shipping, 1939-1945, 1957; The Art of Navigation in England in Elizabethan and Early Stuart Times, 1958, 2nd edn 1978; The Sea—or Mariner's Astrolabe, 1966; The Rutter of the Sea, 1967; (with Hope Waters) The Saluki in History, Art, and Sport, 1969, 2nd edn 1982; (with G. P. B. Naish) The Elizabethan Navy and the Armada of Spain, 1975; Science and the Techniques of Navigation in the Renaissance, 1976; contrib.: Jl RIN; RUSI; Mariners' Mirror; American Neptune; Jl RN Scientific Service; Jl British Soc. of History of Science; Navy International. *Recreations:* living with and judging Salukis; growing apples; history of technology (especially in the Renaissance and Scientific Revolution, and Chinese sailing craft). *Address:* Robin Hill, Bury, near Pulborough, West Sussex. *T:* Bury (Sussex) 687. *Club:* English-Speaking Union.

WATERS, Mrs Frank; see Brown, D. L.

WATERS, Montague, QC 1968; *b* 28 Feb. 1917; *s* of Elias Wasserman, BSc, and Rose Waters; *m* 1940, Jessica Freedman; three *s*. *Educ:* Central Foundation Sch., City of London; London University. LLB (Hons) London, 1938. Solicitor of the Supreme Court, 1939. Military Service, KRRC, Intelligence Corps and Dept of HM Judge Advocate General, 1940-46 (Defence and Victory Medals, 1939-45 Star). Called to the Bar, Inner Temple, 1946; released from HM Forces with rank of Major (Legal Staff), 1946. Governor, Central Foundation Schools, 1968. Freeman, City of London, 1962. *Recreations:* theatre, sport. *Address:* Arlington, 20 The Bishops Avenue, N2. *T:* 01-883 3255.

WATERS, William Alexander, FRS 1954; Professor of Chemistry, Dyson Perrins Laboratory, Oxford University, 1967-70, now Professor Emeritus; Fellow, Balliol College, Oxford, 1945-70, now Fellow Emeritus; *b* Cardiff, 8 May 1903; *o s* of William Waters, schoolmaster, Cardiff; *m* 1932, Elizabeth, *y d* of William Dougall, Darlington; no *c*. *Educ:* Cardiff High Sch.; Gonville and Caius Coll., Cambridge. Rhondda Schol.; MA; PhD; ScD; MA Oxon (by incorporation). Lecturer in Chemistry, Durham Univ. (Durham Div.), 1928-45; University Demonstrator in Organic Chemistry, Oxford, 1945-60; Reader in Physical Organic Chemistry, 1960-67; Chemistry Tutor, Balliol Coll., 1945-67. Sir C. V. Raman Vis. Prof., Univ. of Madras, 1976-77. Leverhulme Research Fellow, 1939; Ministry of Supply: Scientific Officer, 1939-42; Senior Scientific Officer, 1942-44. Goldsmiths' Company's Exhibitioner (Chem.) 1923. FRIC (Member, Council 1968-71); Chem. Soc. Council, 1948-51, 1959-62; Member DSIR Road Tar Research Cttee, 1950-60. Hon. DSc Warwick, 1977. Chem. Soc. medal, 1973. *Publications:* Physical Aspects of Organic Chemistry, 5th edn, 1954; The Chemistry of Free Radicals, 2nd edn, 1948; (Editor and part author) Methods of Quantitive Micro-analysis, 1949, 2nd edn, 1955; (ed) Vistas in Free Radical Chemistry, 1959; Mechanisms of Oxidation of Organic Compounds, 1964; (ed) Free Radical Reactions, 1973, 1975; publications in Proc. Royal Society, Journal Chem. Society, Trans. and Discussions of Faraday Society. *Address:* 5 Field House Drive, Oxford. *T:* Oxford 55234.

WATERSON, Prof. Anthony Peter, MD, FRCP, FRCPath; Professor of Virology, Royal Postgraduate Medical School, London, 1967-81; *b* Hornsea, E Yorks, 23 Dec. 1923; *s* of Frederick Waterson and Frances (*née* Cooper); *m* 1958, Ellen Ware; one *s* two *d*. *Educ:* Epsom Coll.; Emmanuel Coll., Cambridge; London Hospital Medical Coll. MD (Cantab) 1954; MRCP 1950; FRCP 1970; FRCPath 1973. House appointments, London Hospital, 1947-48; MO, Headquarters Unit, BAFO, Germany, 1948-50; Ho. Phys. and Clin.

Pathologist, Addenbrooke's Hospital, Cambridge, 1950-52; Demonstrator in Path., 1953-58, Lecturer in Path., 1958-64, University of Cambridge; Fellow of Emmanuel Coll., 1954-64, Asst Tutor, 1957-64; Professor of Med. Microbiology, St Thomas's Hospital Medical Sch., 1964-67. Spent year 1962-63 on sabbatical leave at Max-Planck Institut für Virusforschung, Tübingen. Governor, Hampton Sch., 1977-. *Publications:* Introduction to Animal Virology, 1961, 2nd edn, 1968; (with Lise Wilkinson) An Introduction to the History of Virology, 1978; papers on viruses and virus diseases. *Recreations:* mountain walking; European history; gardens; browsing in Who's Who. *Address:* 17 Queen's Road, Richmond, Surrey. *T:* 01-940 2325.

WATERSTON, Dr Charles Dewar, FRSE, FGS; Keeper of Geology, Royal Scottish Museum, since 1963; *b* 15 Feb. 1925; *s* of Allan Waterston and Martha Dewar (*née* Robertson); *m* 1965, Marjory Home Douglas. *Educ:* Highgate Sch., London; Univ. of Edinburgh (BSc 1st Cl. Hons 1947; Vans Dunlop Scholar, PhD 1949; DSc 1980). FRSE 1958; FGS 1949. Asst Keeper, Royal Scottish Museum, 1950-63. Member: Scottish Cttee, Nature Conservancy, 1969-73; Adv. Cttee for Scotland, Nature Conservancy Council, 1974-82; Chairman's Cttee, 1978-80, Exec. Cttee, 1980-82, Council for Museums and Galleries in Scotland; Council, RSE, 1967-70 (Vice-Pres., 1980-); Hon. Sec., Edinburgh Geol Soc., 1953-58 (Pres., 1969-71). Keith Prize, RSE, 1969-71. *Publications:* (with G. Y. Craig and D. B. McIntyre) James Hutton's Theory of the Earth: the lost drawings, 1978; technical papers in scientific jls, chiefly relating to extinct arthropods and the history of geology. *Address:* 30 Boswall Road, Edinburgh EH5 3RN.

WATERSTON, David James, CBE 1972 (MBE 1940); FRCS; FRCSE; Hon. Consultant Surgeon, Hospital for Sick Children, Great Ormond Street; *b* 1910; *s* of late Prof. David Waterston, the University of St Andrews; *m* 1948, Anne, *widow* of Lieut H. C. C. Tanner, RN, and *d* of late Rt Rev. A. A. Markham, sometime Bishop of Grantham; one *s* two *d* (and one *s* decd). *Educ:* Craigflower Sch.; privately; Universities of St Andrews and Edinburgh. Ho. Surg., Royal Infirmary, Edinburgh, 1934; Ho. Surg., Surgical Registrar and Res. Medical Supt, Hospital for Sick Children, Great Ormond Street, London, 1934-38 and 1948-51, Consultant Surgeon, 1951-75. Hunterian Professor, RCS, 1961; President British Association Pædiatric Surgeons, 1961. Consulting Pædiatric Surgeon to the Army, to 1975. Served RAMC, 1939-45 (despatches twice, MBE); Captain, Field Ambulance and Field Transfusion Unit, Major (Surgical Specialist). Hon. MD: Genoa, 1970; Warsaw, 1977. *Publications:* chapters in: Paediatric Surgery, 2nd edn 1970; Operative Surgery, 2nd edn 1971; Surgery of the Oesophagus, 1972; articles in medical journals. *Address:* Richard Reynolds House, Old Isleworth, Middlesex. *T:* 01-560 2873. *Club:* Royal and Ancient (St Andrews).

WATERSTONE, David George Stuart; Chief Executive, Roth International; *b* 9 Aug. 1935; *s* of Malcolm Waterstone and Sylvia Sawday; *m* 1960, Dominique Viriot; one *s* two *d*. *Educ:* Tonbridge; St Catharine's Coll., Cambridge (MA). HM Diplomatic Service, 1959-70: Japan, 1959-64; Switzerland, 1968-70; Sen. Exec., RTC, 1970-71; BSC, 1971-81: Board Mem., 1976-81; Man. Dir, Commercial Affairs, 1972-77; Executive Chairman: BSC Chemicals, 1977-81; Redpath Dorman Long, 1977-81. *Recreations:* sailing, walking. *Address:* 45 Tabor Road, Hammersmith, W6. *T:* 01-741 7901. *Club:* Royal Harwich Yacht.

WATERTON, Sqdn Leader William Arthur, GM 1952; AFC 1942, Bar 1946; *b* Edmonton, Canada, 18 March 1916. *Educ:* Royal Military College of Canada; University of Alberta. Cadet Royal Military College of Canada, 1934-37; Subaltern and Lieut, 19th Alberta Dragoons, Canadian Cavalry, 1937-39; served RAF, 1939-46: Fighter Squadrons; Training Command; Transatlantic Ferrying Command; Fighter Command; Meteorological Flight; Fighter Experimental Unit; CFE High Speed Flight World Speed Record. Joined Gloster Aircraft Co. Ltd, 1946. 100 km closed circuit record, 1947; Paris/London record (618.5 mph), 1947; "Hare and Tortoise" Helicopter and jet aircraft Centre of London to Centre of Paris (47 mins), 1948. Chief Test Pilot Gloster Aircraft Co. Ltd, 1946-54. Prototype trials on first Canadian jet fighter, Canuck and British first operational delta wing fighter, the Javelin. *Publications:* The Comet Riddle, 1956; The Quick and The Dead, 1956; aeronautical and meteorological articles. *Recreations:* sailing, riding, photography, motoring, shooting. *Address:* c/o Williams & Glyn's Bank Ltd, Kirkland House, Whitehall, SW1. *Club:* Royal Military College of Canada (Kingston, Ont.).

WATES, Sir Ronald (Wallace), Kt 1975; JP; DL; President, Wates Ltd, since 1973 (Chairman, 1969-73); *b* 4 June 1907; *s* of Edward Wates and Sarah (*née* Holmes); *m* 1931, Phyllis Mary Trace; four *s*. *Educ:* Emanuel Sch. FRICS. Became a Director of Wates Ltd, 1931; Vice-Chm., 1937-69. Trustee, Historic Churches Preservation Trust; Chm., Royal Sch. for the Blind, 1971-82; Mem. Governing Body, Emanuel Sch., 1977-; Liveryman, Innholders' Co., 1945, Master, 1978-79; Hon. Liveryman, Bakers' Co., 1960. JP; DL Surrey, 1981. Hon. Fellow, University Coll. London, 1972. DUniv Surrey, 1975. *Address:* Manor House, Headley, near Epsom, Surrey KT18 6NA. *T:* Leatherhead 77346. *Clubs:* Royal Automobile, City Livery.

WATHEN, Julian Philip Gerard; Vice Chairman, Barclays Bank Ltd, since 1979; *b* 21 May 1923; *s* of Gerard Anstruther Wathen, CIE, and Melicent Louis (*née* Buxton); *m* 1948, Priscilla Florence Wilson; one *s* two *d*. *Educ:* Harrow. Served War, 60th Rifles, 1942-46. Third Secretary, HBM Embassy,

Athens, 1946–47. Barclays Bank DCO, 1948; Ghana Director, 1961–65; General Manager, 1966; Sen. Gen. Manager, Barclays Bank International, 1974; Vice Chm., 1976. Dep. Chm., Allied Arab Bank, 1977–; Vice-Chm. Cairo Barclays International Bank Ltd, 1976–; Director: Barclays Australia Ltd, 1973–; Mercantile & General Reinsurance Co., 1977–. Chairman: Royal African Soc., 1978–; Hall School Trust, 1972–. House Warden, Mercers' Co., 1982. *Address:* Woodcock House, Owlpen, Dursley, Glos GL11 5BY. *T:* Dursley 860214; 2 Markham Square, Chelsea, SW3 4UX. *T:* 01-589 3537. *Club:* Travellers'.

WATKIN, Rt. Rev. Abbot (Christopher) Aelred (Paul); titular Abbot of Glastonbury; Headmaster of Downside School, 1962–75; *b* 23 Feb. 1918; *s* of late Edward Ingram Watkin and Helena Watkin (*née* Shepheard). *Educ:* Blackfriars Sch., Laxton; Christ's Coll., Cambridge (1st class Parts I and II, historical Tripos). Housemaster at Downside Sch., 1948–62. Mayor of Beccles, 1979. FRHistS, 1946; FSA, 1950; FRSA, 1969. *Publications:* Wells Cathedral Miscellany, 1943; (ed) Great Chartulary of Glastonbury, 3 vols, 1946–58; (ed) Registrum Archidiaconatus Norwyci, 2 vols, 1946–48; Heart of the World, 1954; The Enemies of Love, 1958; Resurrection is Now, 1975; articles in Eng. Hist. Rev., Cambridge Hist. Journal, Victoria County History of Wilts, etc. *Address:* St Benet's, Grange Road, Beccles, Suffolk. *T:* Beccles 713179.

WATKIN, David John, MA, PhD; FSA; Fellow of Peterhouse, Cambridge, since 1970; University Lecturer in History of Art, Cambridge, since 1972; Member, Historic Buildings Council for England, since 1980; *b* 7 April 1941; *o s* of Thomas Charles and Vera Mary Watkin. *Educ:* Farnham Grammar Sch.; Trinity Hall, Cambridge (Exhibnr; BA (1st Cl. Hons Fine Arts Tripos); PhD). Librarian, Fine Arts Faculty, Cambridge, 1967–72. *Publications:* Thomas Hope (1769–1831) and the Neo-Classical Idea, 1968; (ed) Sale Catalogues of Libraries of Eminent Persons, vol. 4, Architects, 1970; The Life and Work of C. R. Cockerell, RA, 1974 (Alice Davis Hitchcock medallion, 1975); The Triumph of the Classical, Cambridge Architecture 1804–34, 1977; Morality and Architecture, 1977; The Rise of Architectural History, 1980; English Architecture, a Concise History, 1980; (with Hugh Montgomery-Massingberd) The London Ritz, a Social and Architectural History, 1980; (with Robin Middleton) Neo-Classical and Nineteenth-century Architecture, 1980; (jtly) Burke's and Savills Guide to Country Houses, vol. 3, East Anglia, 1981; The Buildings of Britain, Regency: a Guide and Gazetteer, 1982; Athenian Stuart, Pioneer of the Greek Revival, 1982; The English Vision: The Picturesque in Architecture, Landscape and Garden Design, 1982. *Address:* Peterhouse, Cambridge. *Clubs:* Athenæum, Travellers'; University Pitt (Cambridge).

WATKIN WILLIAMS, Sir Peter, Kt 1963; non-resident Chief Justice of Falkland Islands, since 1975; *b* 8 July 1911; *s* of late Robert Thesiger Watkin Williams, late Master of the Supreme Court, and Mary Watkin Williams; *m* 1938, Jane Dickinson (*née* Wilkin); two *d. Educ:* Sherborne; Pembroke Coll., Cambridge. Partner in Hansons, legal practitioners, Shanghai, 1937–40; served War of 1939–45, Rhodesia and Middle East, 1940–46. Resident Magistrate, Uganda, 1946–55; Puisne Judge, Trinidad and Tobago, 1955–58; Puisne Judge, Sierra Leone, 1958–61; Plebiscite Judge, Cameroons, 1961; Chief Justice of Basutoland, Bechuanaland and Swaziland, and President of the Court of Appeal, 1961–65; High Court Judge, Malawi, 1967–69; Chief Justice of Malawi, 1969–70. *Recreation:* fishing. *Address:* Lower East Horner, Stockland, Honiton, Devon.

WATKINS, family name of **Baron Watkins.**

WATKINS, Baron *cr* 1972 (Life Peer), of Glyntawe, Brecknock; **Tudor Elwyn Watkins;** Lieutenant of Powys, 1975–78; *b* 9 May 1903; *e s* of late County Councillor Howell Watkins, JP, Abercrave, Swansea Valley; *m* 1936, Bronwen R., 3rd *d* of late T. Stather, Talgarth; no *c. Educ:* local elementary schools; evening continuation classes; University Tutorial, WEA and NCLC classes; Coleg Harlech, N Wales (Bursary). Began working at local collieries at age of 13½; miner for 8 years; political agent for Brecon and Radnor, 1928–33; MP (Lab) Brecon and Radnor, 1945–70; PPS to Sec. of State for Wales, 1964–68. Alderman, Breconshire CC, 1940–74; Chm., Powys CC, 1974–77. General Secretary Breconshire Assoc. of Friendly Societies, 1937–48. Hon. Freeman, Brecon Borough; Chm., Brecon Beacons Nat. Park Cttee, 1974–78. *Recreations:* served as Secretary of Abercrave Athletic Club, Cricket Club, Ystalyfera Football League, Horticultural Society and Show. *Address:* Bronafon, Penyfan Road, Brecon, Powys. *T:* 2961.

WATKINS, Alan (Rhun); journalist; Political Columnist, Observer, since 1976; *b* 3 April 1933; *o c* of late D. J. Watkins, schoolmaster, Tycroes, Dyfed, and Violet Harris; *m* 1955, Ruth Howard (*d* 1982); one *s* two *d. Educ:* Amman Valley Grammar Sch.; Queens' Coll., Cambridge. Chm., Cambridge Univ. Labour Club, 1954. National Service, FO, Educn Br., RAF, 1955–57. Called to Bar, Lincoln's Inn, 1957. Research Asst, Dept of Govt, LSE, 1958–59; Editorial Staff, Sunday Express, 1959–64 (New York Corresp., 1961; Actg Political Corresp., 1963; Cross-Bencher Columnist, 1963–64); Political Corresp., Spectator, 1964–67; Script-Writer, BBC 3 and The Late Show, 1966–67; Political Corresp., New Statesman, 1967–76; Political Columnist, Sunday Mirror, 1968–69; Columnist, Evening Standard, 1974–75. Mem. (Lab) Fulham Bor. Council, 1959–62. Dir, The Statesman and Nation Publishing Co. Ltd, 1973–76. Chm., Political Adv. Gp, British Youth Council, 1978–81. Granada Award, Political Columnist of the Year, 1973. *Publications:* The Liberal Dilemma, 1966; (contrib.) The Left, 1966; (with A. Alexander) The

Making of the Prime Minister 1970, 1970; Brief Lives, 1982. *Recreations:* books, wine, cricket, Rugby. *Address:* 12 Battishill Street, N1 1TE. *T:* 01-359 7816. *Club:* Garrick.

WATKINS, Prof. Arthur Goronwy, CBE 1967; Professor of Child Health, Welsh National School of Medicine, 1950–68, Emeritus Professor, since 1968; Dean of Clinical and Post-Graduate Studies, 1947–68; *b* 19 March 1903; *s* of Sir Percy Watkins; *m* 1933, Aileen Llewellyn; one *s* three *d. Educ:* Sidcot Sch.; University Coll., Cardiff; University Coll. Hospital, London. BSc (Wales) 1925; MD (London) 1930; FRCP 1943. Res. Hosp. appts, University Coll. Hosp., 1927–29, West London Hosp., 1929, Hosp. for Sick Children, Gt Ormond Street, 1930; First Asst, Dept of Pædiatrics, University Coll. Hosp., 1930–32; Lectr In Pædiatrics, Welsh Nat. Sch. of Medicine, 1932–50; Cons. Pædiatrician, Royal Infirmary and Llandough Hosp., Cardiff, 1932. Former Mem. Bd of Govs, United Cardiff Hosps; Consultant and Adviser in Pædiatrics, Welsh Hosp. Bd; Hon. Treas. Brit. Pædiatric Assoc., 1958–63, Pres., 1966–67; Pres. Children's Sect., Roy. Soc. Med., 1953, Hon. Mem. 1970; Pres. Cardiff Div., BMA, 1953; Corr. Mem. Soc. de Pédiatrie, Paris; Hon. Fellow, Amer. Academy of Pediatrics, 1967; Mem. Albemarle Cttee on Youth Service; Mem. Central Coun. of Educ. (Wales), 1954–56; External Examr, Univs of Bristol, Birmingham, Manchester, Leeds; Colonial Office Visitor to W Indies, 1956 and Far East, 1959. President Cardiff Medical Soc., 1963–64. Hon. LLD Wales, 1981. *Publications:* (with W. J. Pearson) The Infant, 1932; Pædiatrics for Nurses, 1947; articles in BMJ, Lancet, Archives of Disease in Childhood, etc. *Recreation:* golf. *Address:* Maldwyn, 71 Danycoed Road, Cyncoed, Cardiff CF2 6NE. *T:* Cardiff 751262.

WATKINS, David John; MP (Lab) Consett since 1966; Engineer; *b* 27 Aug. 1925; *s* of Thomas George Watkins and Alice Elizabeth (*née* Allen); unmarried. *Educ:* Bristol. Member: Bristol City Council, 1954–57; Bristol Educn Cttee, 1958–66; Labour Party, 1950–; Amalgamated Union of Engineering Workers (formerly AEU), 1942–; Sec., AUEW Gp of MPs, 1968–77. Contested Bristol NW, 1964. Mem., House of Commons Chairmen's Panel, 1978–. Sponsored Employers Liability (Compulsory Insurance) Act, 1969, and Industrial Common Ownership Act, 1976 as Private Member's Bills; introd Drained Weight Bill, 1973, and Consett Steel Works Common Ownership Bill, 1980. Chm., Labour Middle East Council, 1974–; Jt Chm., Council for Advancement of Arab-British Understanding, 1979–. *Publications:* Labour and Palestine, 1975; Industrial Common Ownership, 1978; The World and Palestine, 1980. *Recreations:* reading, listening to music, swimming. *Address:* House of Commons, SW1. *T:* 01-219 3000.

WATKINS, Maj.-Gen. Guy Hansard, OBE 1974; Major General Royal Artillery and General Officer Commanding The Artillery Division, since 1982; *b* 30 Nov. 1933; *s* of Col A. N. M. Watkins and Mrs S. C. Watkins; *m* 1958, Sylvia Margaret Grant; two *s* two *d. Educ:* The King's Sch., Canterbury; Royal Military Academy, Sandhurst. Commissioned into Royal Artillery, 1953; CO 39 Medium Regt RA, 1973; Comd Task Force 'B'/Dep. Comd 1 Armd Div., 1977; Director, Public Relations (Army), 1980. *Recreations:* riding, fly fishing, skiing. *Address:* c/o National Westminster Bank PLC, 60 High Street, Bognor Regis, West Sussex. *Club:* Army and Navy.

WATKINS, Harold James; retired; Managing Director, Canusa Ltd, 1956–80; Director other subsidiaries (home and overseas) Montague L. Meyer Ltd; *b* 1914; *s* of late J. W. Watkins, Aberystwyth; *m* 1940, Jean, *d* of Frank Morris, OBE; one *s* (and one *s* decd). *Educ:* Ardwyn Grammar Sch., Aberystwyth; Univ. of Wales (BSc). Forestry and Forest Botany, 1935; Forest Products Research Laboratory, 1936. Joined Montague L. Meyer Ltd, 1937. Served War, 1940–45: India, Burma; Capt. 1st Royal Welch Fusiliers. Concerned with development of Malaysian Timber Industry, 1948–. A Forestry Comr, 1967–73; Mem., Nat. Cttee for Wales, Forestry Commn, 1967–73 (England, 1967–70). *Recreations:* poetry; the art of doing nothing. *Address:* Pen y banc, Cwmystwyth, Dyfed. *T:* Pontrhydygroes 219.

WATKINS, Lt-Col Hubert Bromley, OBE 1945; MC 1917; DCM 1916; DL; Vice-Lieutenant of Radnorshire, 1958–74; Chairman, Radnorshire Co. Ltd, 1966–70; Chairman, Bates & Hunt (Agric.) Ltd, 1952–70; *b* 9 July 1897; *s* of Hubert and Helen Watkins, Ludlow; *m* 1936, Mary (*née* Edwards); one *s* two *d. Educ:* Monmouth. King's Shropshire Light Infantry, 1914–19; Radnorshire Rifles (HG), 1940–45. Deputy Lieutenant, Powys (formerly Radnorshire), 1948; High Sheriff, 1952. President, National Assoc. Corn and Agricultural Merchants, 1949–50. *Recreations:* fishing, previously Rugby football and cricket. *Address:* Edgefield, Kingsland, Leominster, Herefordshire. *T:* Kingsland 571. *Club:* Cardiff and County (Cardiff).

WATKINS, Rt. Hon. Sir Tasker, Kt 1971; VC 1944; PC 1980; DL; **Rt. Hon. Lord Justice Watkins;** a Lord Justice of Appeal, since 1980; *b* 18 Nov. 1918; *s* of late Bertram and Jane Watkins, Nelson, Glam; *m* 1941, Eirwen Evans; one *d* (one *s* decd). *Educ:* Pontypridd Grammar Sch. Served War, 1939–45 (Major, the Welch Regiment). Called to Bar, Middle Temple, 1948, Bencher 1970; QC 1965; Deputy Chairman: Radnor QS, 1962–71; Carmarthenshire QS, 1966–71. Recorder: Merthyr Tydfil, 1968–70, Swansea, 1970–71; Leader, Wales and Chester Circuit, 1970–71; Judge of the High Court of Justice, Family Div., 1971–74, QBD, 1974–80; Presiding Judge, Wales and Chester Circuit, 1975–80. Counsel (as Deputy to Attorney-General) to Inquiry into Aberfan Disaster, 1966. Chairman: Mental Health Review Tribunal, Wales Region, 1966–71; Judicial Studies Bd, 1979–80. Hon. LLD Wales, 1979. DL

Glamorgan, 1956-. *Address:* Royal Courts of Justice, Strand, WC2A 2LL; Fairwater Lodge, Fairwater Road, Llandaff, Glamorgan. *T:* Cardiff 563558; 5 Pump Court, Middle Temple, EC4. *T:* 01-353 1993. *Clubs:* Army and Navy; Cardiff and County (Cardiff).

WATKINS, Thomas Frederick; Director, Chemical Defence Establishment, Porton, 1972-74; *b* 19 Feb. 1914; *s* of late Edward and late Louisa Watkins; *m* 1939, Jeannie Blodwen Roberts; two *d. Educ:* Cowbridge Grammar Sch.; Univ. of Wales, Cardiff. BSc Hons Wales 1935; MSc Wales 1936; FRIC 1947. Joined Scientific Staff of War Dept, 1936; seconded to Govt of India, 1939-44; seconded to Dept of Nat. Defence, Canada, 1947-49; Head of Research Section, CDRE, Sutton Oak and Min. of Supply CDE, Nancekuke, 1949-56; Supt Chemistry Research Div., CDE, Porton, 1956; Asst Dir Chemical Research, CDE, Porton, 1963; Dep. Dir, CDE, Porton, 1966. *Publications:* various papers on organic chemistry. *Recreation:* gardening. *Address:* 34 Harnwood Road, Salisbury, Wilts. *T:* Salisbury 5135.

WATKINS, Dr Winifred May, FRS 1969; Head of Division of Immunochemical Genetics, Clinical Research Centre, Medical Research Council, since 1976; *b* 6 Aug. 1924; *d* of Albert E. and Annie B. Watkins. *Educ:* Godolphin and Latymer Sch., London; Univ. of London. PhD 1950; DSc 1963. Research Asst in Biochemistry, St Bartholomew's Hosp. Med. Sch., 1948-50; Beit Memorial Research Fellow, 1952-55; Mem. of Staff of Lister Inst. of Preventive Medicine, 1955-76; Wellcome Travelling Research Fellow, Univ. of California, 1960-61; Reader in Biochemistry, 1965; Prof. of Biochemistry, Univ. of London, 1968-76; William Julius Mickle Fellow, London Univ. 1971. Landsteiner Memorial Award (jtly), 1967; Paul Ehrlich-Ludwig Darmstädter Prize (jtly), 1969. *Publications:* various papers in biochemical and immunological jls. *Address:* MRC Clinical Research Centre, Watford Road, Harrow, Middlesex HA1 3UJ.

WATKINS-PITCHFORD, Denys James, FRSA; ARCA; author and artist; *b* 25 July 1905; *s* of Rev. Walter Watkins-Pitchford, BA, and Edith Elizabeth (*née* Wilson); *m* 1939, Cecily Mary Adnitt (*d* 1974); one *d* (one *s* decd). *Educ:* privately; studied art in Paris, 1924, and at Royal Coll. of Art, London (Painting Schs), 1926-28. Asst Art Master, Rugby Sch., 1930-47. Served City of London Yeomanry RHA, 1926-29. Captain, Home Guard, 1940-46. Carnegie Medal, 1942. Broadcaster on natural history subjects. *Publications:* (under pseudonym 'BB'): Sportsman's Bedside Book, 1937; Wild Lone, 1939; Manka, 1939; Countryman's Bedside Book, 1941; Little Grey Men, 1941 (TV Serial, 1975); The Idle Countryman, 1943; Brendon Chase, 1944 (Radio Serial; TV Serial, Southern TV, 1981, shown in 14 countries); Fisherman's Bedside Book, 1945; The Wayfaring Tree, 1945; Down the Bright Stream, 1948; Shooting Man's Bedside Book, 1948; Meeting Hill, 1948; Confessions of a Carp Fisher, 1950; Letters from Compton Deverell, 1950; Tides Ending, 1950; Dark Estuary, 1952; The Forest of Boland Light Railway, 1955; Mr Bumstead, 1958; The Wizard of Boland, 1958; Autumn Road to the Isles, 1959; The Badgers of Bearshanks, 1961; The White Road Westwards, 1961; September Road to Caithness, 1962; Lepus the Brown Hare, 1962; The Summer Road to Wales, 1964; Pegasus Book of the Countryside, 1964; The Whopper, 1967; A Summer on the Nene, 1967; At the Back o' Ben Dee, 1968; The Tyger Tray, 1971; Pool of the Black Witch, 1974; Lord of the Forest, 1975; Recollections of a Longshore Gunner, 1976; A Child Alone (autobiog.), 1978; Ramblings of a Sportsman Naturalist, 1979; The Naturalist's Bedside Book, 1980; The Quiet Fields, 1981; contribs to Field, Country Life, Shooting Times. *Recreations:* natural history, fishing, shooting. *Address:* The Round House, Sudborough, Kettering, Northants. *T:* Thrapston 3215.

WATKINS-PITCHFORD, Dr John, CB 1968; Chief Medical Adviser, Department of Health and Social Security (formerly Ministry of Social Security and Ministry of Pensions and National Insurance), 1965-73; retired 1973; *b* 20 April 1912; *s* of Wilfred Watkins Pitchford, FRCS, first Director of South African Institute of Medical Research, and Olive Mary (*née* Nichol); *m* 1945, Elizabeth Patricia Wright; one *s. Educ:* Shrewsbury School; St Thomas's Hospital. MRCS, LRCP 1937; MB, BS 1939 (London); MD 1946 (London); DPH 1946; DIH 1949. Various hosp. appts War of 1939-45: served RAFVR, Sqdn Ldr. Med. Inspector of Factories, 1947-50; Sen. Med. Off., Min. of Nat. Insce, 1950. Mem., Industrial Injuries Adv. Council, 1975-. QHP 1971-74. *Publications:* articles on occupational medicine. *Recreation:* gardening. *Address:* Hill House, Farley Lane, Westerham, Kent. *T:* Westerham 64448. *Club:* Athenæum.

WATKINSON, family name of **Viscount Watkinson.**

WATKINSON, 1st Viscount *cr* 1964, of Woking; **Harold Arthur Watkinson,** PC 1955; CH 1962; President, Confederation of British Industry, 1976-77; Chairman of Cadbury Schweppes Ltd, 1969-74 (Group Managing Director, Schweppes Ltd, 1963-68); Director: British Insulated Callender's Cables, 1968-77; Midland Bank Ltd; *b* 25 Jan. 1910; *e s* of A. G. Watkinson, Walton-on-Thames; *m* 1939, Vera, *y d* of John Langman, West Sussex; two *d. Educ:* Queen's College, Taunton; King's College, London. Family business, 1929-35; technical and engineering journalism, 1935-39. Served War of 1939-45, active service, Lieut-Comdr RNVR. Chairman Production Efficiency Panel for S England, Machine Tool Trades Association, 1948; Chairman (first) Dorking Div. Conservative Assoc., 1948-49. MP (C) Woking Division of Surrey, 1950-64; Parliamentary Private Secretary to Minister of Transport and Civil Aviation, 1951-52; Parliamentary Secretary to Ministry of Labour and National Service, 1952-55; Minister of Transport

and Civil Aviation, Dec. 1955-59; Minister of Defence, 1959-62; Cabinet Minister, 1957-62. Mem., Brit. Nat. Export Council 1964-70; Chairman: Cttee for Exports to the United States, 1964-67; Nat. Advisory Cttee on the Employment of Older Men and Women, 1952-55; Companies Cttee, CBI, 1972-; a Vice-Pres., Council, BIM, 1970-73, Pres., 1973-78 (Chm. 1968-70). President: Grocers' Inst., 1970-71; Inst. of Grocery Distribution, 1972-73; Member: Council, RSA, 1972-77; NEDC, 1976-77; Falkland Islands Review Cttee, 1982-. President: RNVR Officers' Assoc., 1973-76; Weald and Downland Museum, 1982-. Chairman: Council, Cranleigh and Bramley Schools, 1973-; Recruitment Working Party, Duke of Edinburgh's 1974 Study Conf., 1972-74. *Publication:* Blueprint for Industrial Survival, 1976. *Recreations:* mountaineering, walking, sailing. *Heir:* none. *Address:* Tyma House, Bosham, near Chichester, Sussex. *Clubs:* Naval; Royal Southern Yacht (Southampton).

WATKINSON, John Taylor; barrister; Financial Reporter, BBC TV, since 1979; *b* 25 Jan. 1941; *s* of William Forshaw Watkinson; *m* 1969. *Educ:* Bristol Grammar Sch.; Worcester Coll., Oxford. Schoolmaster, 1964-71. Called to Bar, Middle Temple, 1971; practised, Midland Circuit, 1972-74. Contested (Lab) Warwick and Leamington, 1970; MP (Lab) Gloucestershire West, Oct. 1974-1979; PPS to Sec. of State, Home Office, 1975-79; Mem., Public Accounts Cttee, 1976-79; Hon. Sec., Anglo-Swiss Parly Gp, 1977. Former Member: Fabian Soc.; Soc. of Labour Lawyers; Mem. TGWU. Mem. and Rapporteur, Council of Europe and WEU, 1976-79. *Recreations:* theatre, cinema, opera, sport. *Address:* 10 Ulundi Road, Blackheath, SE3.

WATKISS, Ronald Frederick, CBE 1981; company director, since 1950; Leader, Conservative Party, Cardiff City Council, since 1973; Lord Mayor of Cardiff, 1981-82; *b* 21 May 1920; *o s* of Bertie Miles Watkiss and Isabella Watkiss; *m* 1941, Marion Preston; one *d* (one *s* decd). *Educ:* Howard Gardens High Sch., Cardiff. Served War, TA, 1939, Royal Corps of Signals, 1939-46; Burma, 1944-46 (1939-45 star, Burma star, Territorial medal). Elected to Cardiff City Council, 1960; Alderman, 1967-74; re-elected Councillor, 1973; Leader, 1973; Chm., Policy and Planning Cttees, 1976-79 (and of Planning Cttee, 1969-74). Member, Assoc. District Councils, 1976-79; Chm., Cardiff NW Conservative Constituency Assoc., 1978-81. Pres., Cardiff Credit Traders Assoc., 1953-54 and 1963-64; Pres., S Wales Dist Council Credit Traders, 1957-58. Queen's Silver Jubilee Medal, 1977. *Recreations:* Rugby and cricket (regret only as spectator now); relaxing at caravan whenever possible. *Address:* 21 Cefn Coed Gardens, Cyncoed, Cardiff CF2 6AX. *T:* Cardiff 752716. *Club:* Victory Services.

WATLING, (David) Brian, QC 1979; **His Honour Judge Watling;** a Circuit Judge, since 1981; *b* 18 June 1935; *o s* of late Vernon Russell Watling and late Edith Stella (*née* Ridley); *m* 1964, Second Officer Noelle Louise Bugden, WRNS. *Educ:* Charterhouse; King's Coll., London (LLB). Called to Bar, Middle Temple, 1957. Nat. Service, Sub-Lieut RNR, 1957. Temporary Dep. Chm., QS, 1969-71; Jun. Prosecuting Counsel: to Inland Revenue, 1970; Inner London Sessions, 1971; Prosecuting Counsel to the Crown, Mddx Sessions, 1972; Jun. Prosecuting Counsel to the Crown, Central Criminal Court, 1972, Sen. Prosecuting Counsel, 1975; Sen. Treasury Counsel, 1975-79; a Recorder of the Crown Court, 1979-81. Vis. Lectr in Law, Univ. Coll. at Buckingham, 1978-80, Vis. Prof. in Criminal Law, 1980-. Barrister and Advocate, Gibraltar. *Recreations:* sailing, fly fishing, cross country ski-ing, hill walking, theatre and ballet, fireside reading, the company of old friends. *Address:* Crown Court, Chelmsford, Essex. *Club:* Garrick.

WATSON, family name of **Baron Manton.**

WATSON, Adam; *see* Watson, John Hugh A.

WATSON, Alan; *see* Watson, W. A. J.

WATSON, Rear-Adm. Alan George, CB 1975. Joined Royal Navy as Dartmouth Cadet, 1941. Served War of 1939-45; HMS Jaguar, 1942; later HMS Dulverton and HMS Duke of York; joined HMS Swift, serving in Home Fleet, on Russian convoys and in Normandy, 1943-44; Dir-Gen., Personal Services and Training (Naval), MoD, Aug. 1972-74; Asst Chief of Naval Staff, 1974-77, retired. Chairman: Church of England Soldiers', Sailors' and Airmen's Clubs, 1979-; Church of England Soldiers', Sailors' and Airmen's Housing Assoc., 1979-.

WATSON, Alan John; Chief Executive, Charles Barker CBC Ltd, since 1980; Director: Charles Barker Group Ltd; IPC Video; *b* 3 Feb. 1941; *s* of Rev. John William Watson and Edna Mary (*née* Peters); *m* 1965, Karen Lederer; two *s. Educ:* Diocesan Coll., Cape Town, SA; Kingswood Sch., Bath, Somerset; Jesus Coll., Cambridge (Open Schol. in History 1959, State Schol. 1959) (MA Hons). Vice-Pres., Cambridge Union; Pres., Cambridge Univ. Liberal Club; Chm., Cambridge Univ. European Gp. Research Asst to Cambridge Prof. of Modern History on post-war history of Unilever, 1962-64. General trainee, BBC, 1965-66; Reporter, BBC TV, The Money Programme, 1966-68; Chief Public Affairs Commentator, London Weekend Television, 1968-69; Political and Economic Reporter, BBC TV: The Money Programme, Party Political Confs, Documentaries in UK and abroad, 1969-72; Reporter, Panorama, 1972-74; Presenter, The Money Programme, 1974-75; Head of TV, Radio, Audio-Visual Div., Directorate-Gen. Information, EC, Chief Exec., EC TV and Radio Studios, and Supervisory Editor, European Community Newsreel Service to Lomé Convention Countries, 1975-79. Contested (L) Richmond,

Oct. 1974 and 1979. Chm., City of London Br., European Movement. Member: Cttee, BFI; Liberal Party Council. Governor, Kingswood Sch. Grand Prix Eurodiaporama of European Community for Common Market coverage, 1974. *Publication:* Europe at Risk: an analysis of the politics and economics of European integration, 1972. *Recreation:* historical biography. *Address:* 2 Retreat Road, Richmond, Surrey TW9 1NN. *Clubs:* Reform, St James's, Royal Automobile.

WATSON, Sir Andrew; *see* Watson, Sir J. A.

WATSON, Maj.-Gen. Andrew Linton, CB 1981; Chief of Staff, Allied Forces, Northern Europe, 1980–82; *b* 9 April 1927; *s* of Col W. L. Watson, OBE, and Mrs D. E. Watson (*née* Lea); *m* 1952, Mary Elizabeth, *d* of Mr and Mrs A. S. Rigby, Warrenpoint, Co. Down; two *s* one *d*. *Educ:* Wellington Coll., Berks. psc, jssc, rcds. Commnd The Black Watch, 1946; served, 1946–66: with 1st and 2nd Bns, Black Watch, in UK, Germany, Cyprus and British Guiana; with UN Force, Cyprus; as GSO 2 and 3 on Staff, UK and Germany; GSO 1 HQ 17 Div./Malaya Dist, 1966–68; CO 1st Bn The Black Watch, UK, Gibraltar and NI, 1969–71; Comdr 19 Airportable Bde, Colchester, 1972–73; RCDS, 1974; Comdr British Army Staff, and Military Attaché, Washington, DC, 1975–77; GOC Eastern District, 1977–80. Colonel, The Black Watch, 1981–. *Recreations:* tennis, shooting, walking, classical music. *Address:* c/o Royal Bank of Scotland, 18 South Methven Street, Perth, Scotland. *T:* Perth 31441. *Clubs:* Army and Navy; Puffins (Edinburgh); Highland Brigade (Edinburgh).

WATSON, Anthony Heriot, CBE 1965; *b* 13 April 1912; *s* of William Watson and Dora Isabel Watson (*née* Fisher); *m* 1946, Hilary Margaret Fyfe. *Educ:* St Paul's Sch.; Christ Church, Oxford; University Coll., London. Statistical Officer, British Cotton Industry Research Assoc., 1936. Min. of Supply, 1940: Statistician; Asst Dir of Statistics; Min. of Aircraft Production, 1942; Statistician, Dept of Civil Aviation, Air Ministry, 1945; Chief Statistician: Min. of Civil Aviation, 1951; Min. of Transport and Civil Aviation, 1954; Min. of Aviation, 1959; Min. of Transport, 1964, Dir of Statistics, 1966; DoE, 1970; retired 1973. *Recreations:* music, garden. *Address:* 9 Kirk Park, Edinburgh EH16 6HZ. *T:* 031-664 7428.

WATSON, Arthur Christopher, CMG 1977; HM Diplomatic Service; High Commissioner in Brunei, since 1978; *b* 2 Jan. 1927; *s* of late Dr A. J. Watson and Dr Mary Watson, Kunming, China, and Chinnor; *m* 1956, Mary Cecil Candler (*née* Earl); one *d*; and one step *s* one step *d*. *Educ:* Norwich Sch.; St Catharine's Coll., Cambridge. Naval Service, 1945–48 (commissioned RNVR, 1946). Colonial Administrative Service, Uganda, 1951; District Commissioner, 1959; Principal Asst Sec., 1960; Principal, Commonwealth Relations Office, 1963; HM Diplomatic Service, 1965; Karachi, 1964–67; Lahore, 1967; FCO, 1967–71; HM Comr in Anguilla, 1971–74; Governor, Turks and Caicos Islands, 1975–78. *Recreations:* boats, birds. *Address:* c/o Foreign and Commonwealth Office, SW1. *Club:* Royal Commonwealth Society.

WATSON, (Daniel) Stewart, CB 1967; OBE 1958; *b* 30 Dec. 1911; *s* of Reverend Dr William Watson, DD, DLitt, and Mary Mackintosh Watson; *m* 1939, Isabel (*née* Gibson); one *s*. *Educ:* Robert Gordon's Coll.; Aberdeen University. Student Apprentice, British Thomson Houston, Rugby, 1933, Research Engr, 1936. Scientific Officer, Admiralty, 1938–; Dir, Admiralty Surface Weapons Establishment, 1961–68; Dep. Chief Scientist (Naval), MoD, 1968–72; Dir Gen. Establishments, Resources Programme A, MoD, 1972–73. *Publications:* contribs to IEEJ. *Recreations:* thoroughbred cars; caravanning. *Address:* The Cedars, Jumps Road, Churt, Surrey.

WATSON, Captain Sir Derrick William Inglefield Inglefield-, 4th Bt, *cr* 1895; TD 1945; 4th Battalion Queen's Own Royal West Kent Regimental Reserve of Officers (TA); Active List 3 Sept. 1939; now retired; *b* 7 Oct. 1901; *s* of Sir John Watson, 2nd Bt, and Edith Jane, *e d* of W. H. Nott, Liverpool; *S* brother, 1918; changed name by Deed Poll to Inglefield-Watson, Jan. 1946; *m* 1925, Margrett Georgina (who obtained a divorce, 1939), *d* of late Col T. S. G. H. Robertson-Aikman, CB; one *s* one *d*; *m* 1946, Terezia (Terry), *d* of late Prof. Charles Bodon, Budapest. *Educ:* Eton; Christ Church, Oxford. County Councillor, Kent (No 4 Tonbridge Division), 1931–37. *Heir: s* John Forbes Watson, Lt-Col Royal Engineers; *b* 16 May 1926. *Address:* Ringshill House, Wouldham, near Rochester, Kent. *T:* Medway 61514.

WATSON, Sir Duncan; *see* Watson, Sir N. D.

WATSON, Duncan Amos; Principal Assistant Treasury Solicitor, Common Law, since 1978; Chairman, Executive Council, Royal National Institute for the Blind, since 1975; *b* 10 May 1926; *m* 1954, Mercia Casey, Auckland, NZ. *Educ:* Worcester College for the Blind; St Edmund Hall, Oxford (BA). Solicitor. *Address:* 19 Great Russell Mansions, WC1B 3BE.

WATSON, Vice-Adm. Sir Dymock; *see* Watson, Vice-Adm. Sir R. D.

WATSON, Sir Francis (John Bagott), KCVO 1973 (CVO 1965; MVO 1959); BA Cantab; MA Oxon 1969, FBA 1969, FSA; Director, Wallace Collection, 1963–74; Surveyor of The Queen's Works of Art, 1963–72, retired; Advisor for Works of Art, since 1972; *b* 24 Aug. 1907; *s* of Hugh Watson, Blakedown, and Helen Marian Bagott, Dudley; *m* 1941, Mary Rosalie Gray (*d* 1969), *d* of George Strong, Bognor; one adopted *s*. *Educ:* Shrewsbury

School; St John's College, Cambridge. Registrar, Courtauld Inst. of Art, 1934–38; Asst Keeper (later Dep. Dir), Wallace Collection, 1938–63; Deputy Surveyor of The Queen's (until 1952 The King's) Works of Art, 1947–63; Trustee, Whitechapel Art Gallery, 1949–74; Chairman: Furniture History Society, 1966–74; Walpole Society, 1970–76; Slade Prof. of Fine Art, Oxford, 1969–70; Wrightsman Prof., NY Univ., 1970–71; Vis. Lectr, Univ. of California, 1970; Kress Prof., National Gallery, Washington DC, 1975–76. Uff. del Ord. al Merito della Repubblica Italiana, 1961. New York University Gold Medal, 1966. *Publications:* Canaletto, 1949 (rev. 2nd edn, 1954); (jtly) Southill, A Regency House, 1951; Wallace Collection: Catalogue of Furniture, 1956; Louis XVI Furniture, 1959 (rev. French edn, 1963); The Choiseul Gold Box (Charlton Lecture), 1963; (jtly) Great Family Collections, 1965; The Guardi Family of Painters (Fred Cook Memorial Lecture), 1966; (jtly) Eighteenth Century Gold Boxes, 1966; The Wrightsman Collection Catalogue, Vols 1 and 2: Furniture, 1966, Vols 3 and 4: Furniture, Goldsmith's Work and Ceramics, 1970, Vol. 5: Paintings and Sculpture; Giambattista Tiepolo, 1966; Fragonard, 1967; Chinese Porcelains in European Mounts, 1980; (jtly) Catalogue of the Mounted Oriental Porcelains in the J. Paul Getty Museum, 1983; numerous contribs to learned journals, in Europe, America and Asia. *Recreations:* sinology, Western Americana. *Address:* c/o 33 Whittingstall Road, SW6. *Club:* Beefsteak.

WATSON, George Hugh Nicholas; *see* Seton-Watson.

WATSON, Gerald Walter; Director, Central Computer and Telecommunications Agency, HM Treasury, 1978–82; *b* 13 Dec. 1934; *s* of Reginald Harold Watson and Gertrude Hilda Watson (*née* Ruffell); *m* 1961, Janet Rosemary (*née* Hovey); one *s* two *d*. *Educ:* King Edward VI, Norwich School; Corpus Christi Coll., Cambridge (MA). National Service, RAF Regt, 1953–55. War Office, 1958–64; MoD, 1964–69; Civil Service Dept, 1969–73; Northern Ireland Office, 1973–75; CSD, 1975–81. *Recreations:* opera and theatre going, gardening. *Address:* Topcroft Lodge, Bungay, Suffolk NR35 2BB. *T:* Woodton 435.

WATSON, Gilbert, CBE 1947; HM Senior Chief Inspector of Schools in Scotland, retired; *b* 28 Oct. 1882; *er s* of John Watson, Edinburgh; *m* 1st, 1911, Annie Macdonald (decd); 2nd, 1974, Christian M. Kennedy. *Educ:* Royal High School, Edinburgh; Edinburgh and Oxford Universities. Rector, Inverness Royal Academy, 1909; entered inspectorate of Scottish Education Department, 1910; HM Senior Chief Inspector, 1944. *Publications:* Theriac and Mithridatium: a study in Therapeutics (Wellcome Historical Medical Library), 1966; A Short History of Craigmillar Park Golf Club, Edinburgh, 1974; co-author of books on Latin Grammar and Latin prose composition. *Recreation:* golf. *Address:* 38 Granby Road, Edinburgh EH16 5NL. *T:* 031-667 5744.

WATSON, Henry, CBE 1969; QPM 1963; Chief Constable of Cheshire, 1963–74; *b* 16 Oct. 1910; *s* of John and Ann Watson, Preston, Lancs; *m* 1933, Nellie Greenhalgh; two *d*. *Educ:* Preston Victoria Junior Technical Coll. Admitted to Inst. of Chartered Accountants, 1934; joined Ashton-under-Lyne Borough Police, 1934; King's Lynn Borough Police, 1942; Norfolk County Constabulary, 1947; Asst Chief Constable, Cumberland and Westmorland, 1955, Chief Constable, 1959. CStJ 1973. *Recreation:* golf. *Address:* Gorgate Road, Hoe, Dereham, Norfolk.

WATSON, Maj.-Gen. (Henry) Stuart (Ramsay), CBE 1973 (MBE 1954); Executive Director, Institute of Directors, since 1977; *b* 9 July 1922; *yr s* of Major H. A. Watson, CBE, MVO and Mrs Dorothy Bannerman Watson, OBE; *m* 1965, Susan, *o d* of Col W. H. Jackson, CBE, DL; two *s* one *d*. *Educ:* Winchester College. Commnd 2nd Lieut 13th/18th Royal Hussars, 1942; Lieut 1943; Captain 1945; Adjt 13/18 H, 1945–46 and 1948–50; psc 1951; GSO2, HQ 1st Corps, 1952–53; Instr RMA Sandhurst, 1955–57; Instr Staff Coll. Camberley, 1960–62; CO 13/18 H, 1962–64; GSO1, MoD, 1964–65; Col GS, SHAPE, 1965–68; Col, Defence Policy Staff. MoD, 1968; idc 1969; BGS HQ BAOR, 1970–73; Dir Defence Policy, MoD, 1973–74; Sen. Army Directing Staff, RCDS, 1974–76. Col, 13th/18th Royal Hussars, 1979–. *Recreation:* golf. *Address:* The Glebe House, Little Kimble, Aylesbury, Bucks HP17 0UE. *T:* Stoke Mandeville 2200. *Club:* Cavalry and Guards.

WATSON, Herbert James, CB 1954; *b* 9 Aug. 1895; *s* of Thomas Francis Watson, Inverness; *m* 1929, Elsie May Carter; two *s* one *d*. *Educ:* Royal Naval College, Greenwich. Entered Royal Corps of Naval Constructors, 1918; Chief Constructor: Admiralty, 1940–43; Chatham, 1943–45; Manager: Malta, 1945–46; Devonport, 1946–47; Asst Director of Dockyards, 1947–49; Deputy Director of Dockyards, 1949–56. *Recreation:* sailing. *Address:* 106 Forrest Street, South Perth, WA 6151, Australia.

WATSON, Rev. Hubert Luing; retired as General Superintendent of the Baptist Union, North Western Area (1949–60); President of the Baptist Union of Great Britain and Ireland, 1963 (Vice-President, 1962); Chairman, Baptist Minister Fellowship, 1960–63; *b* 30 Nov. 1892; *s* of Austin and Margaret M. Watson; *m* 1914, Mercy (*née* Harwood); one *d*. *Educ:* Winslow School. Baptist Union Exams, External student, Manchester Coll. Pastor of: Milton and Little Leigh, 1918–23; Enon, Burnley, 1923–29; Ansdell, Lytham, 1929–35; Richmond, Liverpool, 1935–49. *Recreations:* gardening and motoring. *Address:* Cartref, Spurlands End Road, Gt Kingshill, High Wycombe, Bucks. *T:* High Wycombe 712062.

WATSON, Hugh Gordon; Barrister-at-Law; one of the Special Commissioners of Income Tax, 1952-76; *b* 3 Feb. 1912; *o s* of late Andrew Gordon Watson, Physician, 21 The Circus, Bath, and late Clementina (*née* Macdonald); *m* 1940, Winefride Frances (*d* 1973), *d* of late Clement Brand, Westfield, Reigate, and late Winefride Denise (*née* Casella); three *s. Educ:* Ampleforth College; Pembroke College, Oxford. Insurance Broker, 1935-39. Served War of 1939-45 in RNVR. Called to the Bar, Lincoln's Inn, 1947. *Address:* 24 Evesham Close, Reigate, Surrey.

WATSON, Sir (James) Andrew, 5th Bt, *cr* 1866; *b* 30 Dec. 1937; *s* of 4th Bt and Ella Marguerite, *y d* of late Sir George Farrar, 1st Bt; *S* father, 1941; *m* 1965, Christabel Mary, *e d* of K. R. M. Carlisle and Hon. Mrs Carlisle; two *s* one *d. Educ:* Eton. Barrister-at-law. Contested (L) Sutton Coldfield, Feb. and Oct. 1974. *Heir: s* Roland Victor Watson, *b* 4 March 1966. *Address:* Talton House, Newbold on Stour, Stratford-upon-Avon, Warwickshire. *T:* Alderminster 212.

WATSON, Prof. James Dewey; Director, Cold Spring Harbor Laboratory, since 1969; *b* 6 April 1928; *s* of James D. and Jean Mitchell Watson; *m* 1968, Elizabeth Lewis; two *s. Educ:* Univ. of Chicago (BS); Indiana Univ. (PhD); Clare Coll., Cambridge. Senior Res. Fellow in Biology, California Inst. of Technology, 1953-55; Harvard University: Asst Prof. of Biology, 1955-57; Associate Prof., 1958-61; Prof. of Molecular Biology, 1961-76. Member: US National Acad. Sciences, 1962-; Amer Acad. of Arts and Sciences, 1957; Royal Danish Acad. 1962; Amer. Philosophical Soc., 1976; Foreign Mem., Royal Soc., 1981. Hon. DSc: Chicago, 1961; Indiana, 1963; Long Island, 1970; Adelphi, 1972; Brandeis, 1973; Albert Einstein Coll. of Medicine, 1974; Hofstra, 1976; Harvard, 1978; Rockefeller, 1980; Hon. LLD Notre Dame, 1965. Hon. Fellow, Clare Coll., Camb., 1967. Nobel Award in Medicine and Physiology (jointly), 1962. Carty Medal, US National Acad. of Sciences, 1971; Presidential Medal of Freedom, 1977. *Publications:* Molecular Biology of the Gene, 1965, 3rd edn 1976; The Double Helix, 1968; scientific papers on the mechanism of heredity. *Recreation:* mountain walking. *Address:* Bungtown Road, Cold Spring Harbor, New York 11724, USA. *Clubs:* Athenæum; Piping Rock (New York).

WATSON, James Kenneth, FCA; Finance Director, National Freight Consortium, since 1982; *b* 16 Jan. 1935; *s* of James and Helen Watson; *m* 1959, Eileen Fay Waller; two *s* one *d. Educ:* Watford Grammar Sch.; Stanford Univ., California, USA. Baker Sutton & Co., Chartered Accountants, 1964; Financial Controller, Times Group, 1968; Finance Director: British Road Services Ltd, 1970-76; Nat. Freight Corp., later Nat. Freight Co., 1977-82. *Publications:* contribs to transport and financial press. *Recreations:* cricket, hockey, theatre, history. *Address:* Inglands, Lower Icknield Way, Buckland, Aylesbury, Bucks HP22 5LR. *Clubs:* Royal Automobile, MCC.

WATSON, Prof. James Patrick; Professor of Psychiatry, Guy's Hospital Medical School, since 1974; *b* 14 May 1936; *e s* of Hubert Timothy Watson and Grace Emily (*née* Mizen); *m* 1962, Dr Christine Mary Colley; four *s. Educ:* Roan Sch. for Boys, Greenwich; Trinity Coll., Cambridge; King's Coll. Hosp. Med. Sch., London. MA, MD; FRCP, FRCPsych, DPM, DCH. Qualified, 1960. Hosp. appts in Medicine, Paediatrics, Pathology, Neurosurgery, at King's Coll. Hosp. and elsewhere, 1960-64; Registrar and Sen. Registrar, Bethlem Royal and Maudsley Hosps, 1964-71; Sen. Lectr in Psychiatry, St George's Hosp. Med. Sch., and Hon. Consultant Psychiatrist, St George's Hosp., 1971-74. Member: Inst. of Group Analysis; British Assoc. for Behavioural Psychotherapy; British Psychological Soc. Mem., various bodies concerned with interfaces between counselling and psychotherapy, religion and medicine. *Publications:* papers on gp psychotherapy, treatment of phobic anxiety, psychiatry in gen. hosps, in BMJ, Lancet, British Jl of Psychiatry, British Jl of Med. Psychology, Behaviour Research and Therapy. *Recreations:* mountains; music, especially opera, especially Mozart. *Address:* 36 Alleyn Road, SE21 8AL. *T:* 01-670 0444.

WATSON, Prof. James Wreford; Professor of Geography, since 1954, and Convenor, Centre of Canadian Studies, since 1973, Edinburgh University; *b* 8 Feb. 1915; *s* of Rev. James Watson; *m* 1939, Jessie W. Black; one *s* one *d. Educ:* George Watson's College, Edinburgh; Edinburgh Univ. (MA); Toronto Univ. (PhD). Asst Lecturer in Geography, Sheffield Eng., 1937-39; Prof. of Geography, and founder of Geog. Dept, McMaster University, Canada, 1945-49; Chief Geographer, Canada, and Director of the Geographical Branch, Department of Mines and Technical Surveys, Canada, 1949-54; Prof. and founder of Geog. Dept, Carleton Univ., Ottawa, 1952-54; Edinburgh University: Head of Dept of Geography, 1954, Convenor, Sch. of Scottish Studies, 1956-59, Dean, Faculty of Social Science, 1964-68. Visiting Professor: Queen's Univ., Kingston, Ont, 1959-60; Univ. of Manitoba, 1968-69; British Columbia Univ., 1971; Simon Fraser Univ., BC, 1976-77; Calgary Univ., 1980-81. Editor: Scottish Studies, 1957-64; Atlas of Canada, 1949-54; Hon. Ed., Scot. Geog. Magazine, 1975-78. Member: Brit. Nat. Cttee for Geog., 1960-; Geog. Cttee, SSRC, 1965-68; Council SSRC, and Chm., Geog. Planning Jt Cttee, 1972-75; President: Geog. Section, Brit. Assoc. for Advancement of Science, 1971; British Assoc. for Canadian Studies, 1975-77; RSGS, 1977-82; Senior Vice-Pres., 1981, Pres., 1983-, IBG. Hon. LLD: McMaster Univ., 1977; Carleton Univ., Ottawa, 1979; Calgary Univ., 1981. Award of Merit, Amer. Assoc. of Geogrs, 1949; Murchison Award, RGS, 1956; Research Medal, RSGS, 1965; Special Award, Canadian Assoc. of Geographers, 1978; Governor General's Medal, Canada (literary), 1953. FRSC; FRSE. *Publications: geographical:* General Geography, 1957

(Toronto); North America: Its Countries and Regions, 1963 (London), 2nd edn 1968; A Geography of Bermuda, 1965 (London); Canada: Problems and Prospects, 1968 (Toronto); Geographical Essays (co-editor with Prof. R. Miller); (ed) The British Isles, A Systematic Geography, 1964 (London); (ed) Collins-Longmans Advanced Atlas, 1968; (ed with T. O'Riordan) The American Environment: perceptions and policies, 1975; (jtly with Jessie Watson) The Canadians: how they live and work, 1977; A Social Geography of the United States, 1978; The USA: habitation of hope, 1982; articles on historical and social geography in Geography, Scottish Geographical Magazine, Geographical Review, Jl of Geography, Canadian Jl of Economics and Political Science, etc; *literary:* Unit of Five, 1947; Of Time and the Lover, 1953; Scotland, the Great Upheaval, 1972; Cross-country Canada, 1979; verse in Canadian and British literary jls. *Address:* Centre of Canadian Studies, The University, Edinburgh.

WATSON, Prof. Janet Vida, (Mrs John Sutton), FRS 1979; Professor of Geology, Imperial College, University of London, since 1974; *b* 1 Sept. 1923; *d* of David Meredith Seares Watson, FRS, and Katharine Margarite (*née* Parker); *m* 1949, John Sutton, *qv. Educ:* South Hampstead High Sch.; Reading Univ.; Imperial Coll., London. BSc, PhD. Senior Studentship, Royal Commission for the Exhibition of 1851, 1949-52; Imperial College, London: Research and teaching, 1952-74; Personal Chair in Geology, 1974-. Member, National Water Council, 1973-76. Pres., Geol. Soc. of London, 1982-83. Bigsby Medal, 1965, Lyell Medal, 1973, Geological Soc. of London. *Publications:* (jtly with H. H. Read) Introduction to Geology, vol. 1, 1962, 2nd edn 1968, vol. 2, 1976; (jtly with H. H. Read) Beginning Geology, 1966. *Address:* Department of Geology, Imperial College, Prince Consort Road, SW7 2AZ.

WATSON, John, FRCS, FRCSE; Consultant Plastic Surgeon to: King Edward VII Hospital for Officers; London Hospital, 1963-82; Hon. Consultant Plastic Surgeon, Queen Victoria Hospital, East Grinstead; *b* 10 Sept. 1914; *s* of late John Watson; *m* 1941, June Christine Stiles; one *s* three *d. Educ:* Leighton Park, Reading; Jesus Coll., Cambridge; Guy's Hospital. MRCS, LRCP 1938; MA, MB, BChir (Cantab) 1939; FRCS(Ed.) 1946; FRCS 1963. Served as Sqdn Ldr (temp.) RAF, 1940-46 (despatches twice). Marks Fellow in Plastic Surgery, Queen Victoria Hosp., E Grinstead, 1947-50; Consultant Plastic Surgeon, Queen Victoria Hospital, East Grinstead, and Tunbridge Wells Gp of Hospitals, 1950-77. Exec. Trustee, E Grinstead Research Trust for Blond-McIndoe Research Centre; Gen. Sec., Internat. Confedn for Plastic and Reconstructive Surgery, 1971-75; Mem. Brit. Assoc. of Plastic Surgeons (Hon. Sec., 1960-62, Pres., 1969); Hon. FRSM. *Publications:* numerous articles on plastic surgery in techn. jls and scientific periodicals. Chapters in: Textbook of Surgery, Plastic Surgery for Nurses, Modern Trends in Plastic Surgery, Clinical Surgery. *Recreations:* fishing, astronomy. *Address:* Clock Court, Hartfield, East Sussex. *T:* 412.

WATSON, Rear-Adm. John Garth, CB 1965; BScEng; CEng, FICE, FIEE; Secretary, Institution of Civil Engineers, 1967-79; *b* 20 February 1914; *er s* of Alexander Henry St Croix Watson and Gladys Margaret Watson (*née* Payne); *m* 1943, Barbara Elizabeth Falloon; two *s* one *d. Educ:* Univ. Coll. School, Hampstead; Northampton Engineering Coll., Univ. of London. BSc (Eng.). MIEE 1948; AMICE 1944; MAmerIEE 1946; Amer. Soc. of Naval Engrs 1947. 2nd Lieut, 1st Bn Herts Regt (TA), 1932; resigned on joining Admiralty, 1939; Student and Asst Elec. Engr, Northmet Power Co.; HMS Vernon, 1939; Development of Magnetic Minesweepers, Dec. 1939; wounded, 1941; Warship Electrical Supt, London and SE Area, 1943; BJSM, Washington, DC, 1945; Admlty, 1948; transf. to Naval Elec. Branch, 1949; HMS Collingwood, 1950; 6th Destroyer Flot., HMS Broadsword, Battleaxe, Nov. 1950; Staff of Flag Officer, Flot., Home Fleet, HMS Superb, Switsure, 1951; Admlty, 1952; HM Dockyard Devonport, 1953; Capt. 1955; Staff of C-in-C Home Fleet, Fleet Elec. Officer, HMS Tyne, Maidstone, 1955; Suptg Elec. Engr, HM Dockyard Gibraltar, 1957; Sen. Officers' War Course, 1960; Admlty, 1961; Asst Dir of Elec. Engineering, Admlty, Nov. 1961; Adm. Superintendent, Rosyth, 1963-66; retired. ADC to the Queen, 1962. Mem., Smeatonian Soc. of Civil Engineers, 1968. Hon. Mem., Soc. of Civil Engrg Technicians, 1979. *Recreations:* sailing and light gardening. *Address:* Little Hall Court, Shedfield, near Southampton. *T:* Wickham 833216; 58 Iverna Court, W8. *T:* 01-937 2508. *Clubs:* Athenæum, Royal Thames Yacht; Royal Naval and Royal Albert Yacht (Portsmouth).

See also Vice-Adm. Sir P. A. Watson.

WATSON, John Grenville Bernard; MP (C) Skipton, since 1979; Director, John Waddington Ltd, since 1979; *b* 21 Feb. 1943; *s* of Norman V. Watson and Ruby E. Watson; *m* 1965, Deanna Wood; one *s* two *d. Educ:* Moorlands Sch., Leeds; Bootham Sch., York; College of Law, Guildford. Articled, 1962, qualified as solicitor, 1967; joined John Waddington Ltd as managerial trainee, 1968; Export Director, Plastona John Waddington Ltd, 1972; Marketing Dir, 1975, Man. Dir, 1977, Waddington Games Ltd; Director, John Waddington Ltd, Main Board, 1979-. Joined Young Conservatives, 1965; Chairman, Yorkshire YC, 1969; Personal Asst to Rt Hon. Edward Heath, 1970; Chm., Nat. YC, 1971; contested (C) York, general elections, Feb. and Oct. 1974; Chm., Conservative Candidates Assoc., 1975-79. Mem., Parly Select Cttee on Energy, 1980-82; PPS, NI Office, 1982-. Chm., British Atlantic Gp of Young Political Leaders, 1982-. Pres., British Youth Council, 1980-. *Recreations:* photography, fell walking, taking bets. *Address:* The Coach House, Carla Beck Lane, Carleton, Skipton, North Yorkshire BD23 3BU. *T:* Skipton 5759.

WATSON, (John Hugh) Adam, CMG 1958; Director General, International Association for Cultural Freedom, since 1974; Professor, Center for Advanced Studies, University of Virginia, since 1980; *b* 10 Aug. 1914; *er s* of Joseph Charlton Watson and Alice (*née* Tate); *m* 1950, Katharine Anne Campbell; two *s* one *d*. *Educ*: Rugby; King's Coll., Camb. Entered the Diplomatic Service, 1937; Brit. Legation, Bucharest, 1939; Brit. Embassy, Cairo, 1940; Brit. Embassy, Moscow, 1944; FO, 1947; Brit. Embassy, Washington, 1950; Head of African Dept, Foreign Office, 1956–59; appointed British Consul-General at Dakar, 1959; British Ambassador: to the Federation of Mali, 1960–61; to Senegal, Mauritania and Togo, 1960–62; to Cuba, 1963–66; Under-Secretary, Foreign Office, 1966–68; Diplomatic Adviser, British Leyland Motor Corp., 1968-73. Gwilym Gibbon Fellow, Nuffield Coll., Oxford, Oct. 1962–Oct. 1963. Vis. Fellow, ANU, 1973; Vis. Prof., Univ. of Virginia, 1978. *Publications*: The War of the Goldsmith's Daughter, 1964; Nature and Problems of Third World, 1968; (ed) The Origins of History, 1981; Diplomacy: the dialogue between States, 1982; various plays broadcast by BBC. *Address*: Sharnden Old Manor, Mayfield, East Sussex. *T*: Mayfield 2441; 53 Hamilton Terrace, NW8. *T*: 01-286 6330. *Club*: Brook's.

WATSON, John Parker, CBE 1972; TD 1945; partner, Lindsays, WS (formerly Lindsay Howe & Co., WS), 1935-79; *b* 22 Aug. 1909; *s* of John Parker Watson, WS, and Rachel Watson (*née* Henderson); *m* 1936, Barbara Parkin Wimperis; two *s* one *d*. *Educ*: Merchiston Castle Sch., Edinburgh; Corpus Christi Coll., Oxford (scholar); Edinburgh Univ. MA Oxon; LLB Edin. Served War, 1939-45, RA; Adjt, 94th (City of Edinburgh) HAA Regt; Staff Capt., JAG'S Dept; Bde Major, 12th AA Bde (8th Army); Staff Coll., Haifa; GSO2 HQ 9th Army. Admitted Mem., WS Soc., 1934. Lectr in Public Internat. Law, Edinburgh Univ., 1937-39. Chairman: Edinburgh Marriage Guidance Council, 1951-54; Scottish Marriage Guidance Council, 1962-65; Scottish Solicitors' Discipline Tribunal, 1974-78; Mem., SE Scotland Regional Hosp. Bd, 1952-55. Mem. Council, Law Soc. of Scotland, 1950-75 (Vice-Pres., 1957-58, Pres., 1970-72). *Recreations*: travel, hill walking, listening to music, golf. *Address*: 66 Murrayfield Gardens, Edinburgh EH12 6DQ. *T*: 031-337 3405. *Clubs*: Travellers'; New (Edinburgh).

WATSON, (John) Steven, MA; FRSE; FRHistS; Principal, University of St Andrews, since 1966; *b* Hebburn-on-Tyne, 20 March 1916; *o s* of George Watson and Elizabeth Layborn Gall, Newcastle upon Tyne; *m* 1942, Heba Sylvia de Cordova Newbery; two *s*. *Educ*: Merchant Taylors' Sch.; St John's Coll., Oxford (Andrew Schol.). 1st cl. hons Mod. Hist., 1939. Harmsworth Sen. Schol., Merton Coll., 1939-42, for research into Speakership of House of Commons; unfit, owing to loss of leg in road accident, for mil. service. Admin Asst to Controller-General, Min. of Fuel and Power, 1942; Private Sec. to Ministers of Fuel and Power, 1942-45; Lectr, Student and Tutor, Christ Church, Oxford, 1945-66 (Censor, 1955-61; Hon. Student, 1981); Chm. Bd of Modern History, Oxford, 1956-58; Editor, Oxford Historical series, 1950-66; Chm., Scottish Academic Press. Mem., British Library Bd, 1973-79. Wiles Lectr, 1968. Member: Franks Commission of University Inquiry, 1964-66; Cttee to examine operation of Section 2 of Official Secrets Act, 1971. Chm., ACU, 1978-79 (Vice-Chm., 1975-78). Hon. DLitt, DePauw, 1967; DHL: St Andrews, Laurinburg, NC, 1972; Philadelphia; DHum Simpson Coll., Iowa. Medal of City of Paris, 1967; Gold Medal, American Legion, 1978. *Publications*: (with Dr W. C. Costin) The Law and Working of the Constitution 1660-1914, 2 vols, 1952; The Reign of George III 1760-1815 (vol. XII, Oxf. Hist. of England), 1960; A History of the Salters' Company, 1963; essays in various collections and jls; TV scripts and performances. *Address*: University House, The Scores, St Andrews, Fife. *T*: (office) St Andrews 76161; 37 Flask Walk, NW3. *Clubs*: Caledonian; New (Edinburgh); Royal and Ancient (St Andrews).

WATSON, Rev. John T., BA (London); LTCL; General Secretary, British and Foreign Bible Society, 1960-69, retired; *b* 13 Jan. 1904; *s* of late F. Watson, Sutton Bridge, Lincs; *m* 1933, Gertrude Emily Crossley, Farsley, Leeds; two *s* one *d*. *Educ*: Moulton Grammar School; Westminster Training College, London; Didsbury Training College, Manchester. School-master, 1924-26. Missionary (under Methodist Missionary Soc.) in Dahomey, W Africa, 1929-34; Methodist Minister: Plymouth, 1935-38; Golders Green, 1938-46; Bible Society: Secretary for Schools and Colleges, 1946-49; Asst Home Sec., 1949-54; Asst Gen. Sec., 1954-60. Hon. DD, West Virginia Wesleyan Coll., 1966. *Publications*: Seen and Heard in Dahomey, 1934; Daily Prayers for the Methodist Church, 1951. *Recreation*: music. *Address*: 16 Beverington Road, Eastbourne, East Sussex. *T*: Eastbourne 29838.

WATSON, Joseph Stanley, MBE 1946; QC 1955; Social Security (formerly National Insurance) Commissioner, since 1965; *b* 13 Sept. 1910; *er s* of late Joseph Watson and late Gertrude Ethel (*née* Catton); *m* 1951, Elizabeth Elliston, *d* of late Col G. Elliston Allen, TD; four *d*. *Educ*: Rossall Sch.; Jesus Coll., Cambridge (MA). Barrister, Inner Temple, 1933. Served War of 1939-45 (MBE): RA (Field), UK, MEF, Force 281, Dodecanese in Unit and on G Staff (Greek Military Cross), rank of Major. No 7 (NW) Legal Aid Area Cttee, 1949-55. Mem. Gen. Council of the Bar, 1959-64; Master of the Bench, Inner Temple, 1961; Recorder of Blackpool, 1961-65. *Address*: 6 Grosvenor Gardens, SW1. *T*: 01-730 9236; The Old Dairy, Mickleham, Surrey. *T*: Leatherhead 74387.

WATSON, Leslie Michael Macdonald S.; *see* Saunders Watson.

WATSON, Air Cdre (retired) Michael, CB 1952; CBE 1945 (OBE 1942); *b* 12 Aug. 1909; *s* of late William Watson, Kew. *Educ*: St Paul's Prep. School; Saffron Walden School. Joined RAF 1929, and qualified as Pilot; trained as Signals Officer, 1933. Served War of 1939-45 (despatches twice); Air Min. Combined Ops Signals Plans 1942; HQ, AEAF, 1943; SHAEF 1944; HQ Middle East, 1946; Air Ministry, 1947; Comdg RAF Welford, 1949; HQ, Fighter Comd, 1950-53; Director of Signals, Air Ministry, 1953-54; retired from RAF at own request, 1954. Rolls Royce Representative with N American Aviation Inc., Calif., 1956-60; Asst Gen. Man., Sales and Service, Rolls Royce, Ltd, 1961-62; Space Div., N American Rockwell Inc., Calif, 1964-71, retired. Chevalier de la Légion d'Honneur, 1944; Officer US Legion of Merit, 1945. *Recreations*: fishing, sailing. *Address*: Box 5321, Big Bear Lake, Calif 92315, USA.

WATSON, Sir Michael M.; *see* Milne-Watson.

WATSON, Sir (Noel) Duncan, KCMG 1967 (CMG 1960); HM Diplomatic Service, retired; *b* 16 Dec. 1915; *s* of late Harry and Mary Noel Watson, Bradford, Yorks; *m* 1951, Aileen Bryans (*d* 1980), *d* of late Charles Bell, Dublin. *Educ*: Bradford Grammar School; New College, Oxford. Colonial Administrative Service: Admin. Officer, Cyprus, 1938-43; Assistant Colonial Secretary, Trinidad, 1943-45; Principal, Colonial Office (secondment), 1946; transferred to Home Civil Service, 1947; Principal Private Sec. to Sec. of State for the Colonies, 1947-50; Asst Sec.: CO, 1950-62, Cent. Af. Office, 1962-63; Under-Secretary, 1963; Asst Under-Sec. of State, CO and CRO, 1964-67; Political Adviser to C-in-C Far East, 1967-70; High Comr in Malta, 1970-72; Dep. Under-Sec. of State, FCO, 1972-74. *Address*: Sconce, Steels Lane, Oxshott, Surrey. *Clubs*: Travellers'; Royal Commonwealth Society; Leander.

WATSON, Sir Norman James, 2nd Bt, *cr* 1912; late Flying Officer, RAFVR; late KRRC and RAF; FRGS; *b* 17 March 1897; *er s* of Sir George Watson, 1st Bt, and Bessie, *d* of T. Atkinson; *S* father, 1930; *m* 1974, Lady (Beryl) Rose. *Educ*: Eton. Sheriff of Berkshire, 1940. *Publication*: (with Edward J. King) Round Mystery Mountain, 1935. *Heir*: none. *Address*: Flat 132, 55 Park Lane, W1. *Clubs*: Royal Air Force, Alpine.

WATSON, Vice-Adm. Sir Philip (Alexander), KBE 1976; MVO 1960; Chairman, Marconi Radar Systems Ltd, since 1981; Naval Consultant to GEC-Marconi Electronics Ltd, since 1977; Director, Marconi International Marine Co. Ltd, since 1977; *b* 7 Oct. 1919; *yr s* of A. H. St C. Watson; *m* 1948, Jennifer Beatrice Tanner; one *s* two *d*. *Educ*: St Albans School. FIEE 1963; FIERE 1965; CBIM 1973. Sub-Lt RNVR, 1940; qual. Torpedo Specialist, 1943; transf. to RN, 1946; Comdr 1955; HM Yacht Britannia, 1957-59; Captain 1963; MoD (Ship Dept), 1963; Senior Officers' War Course, 1966; comd HMS Collingwood, 1967; Dep. Dir of Engrg (Ship Dept), MoD, 1969; Dir Gen. Weapons (Naval), MoD, 1970-77; Chief Naval Engineer Officer, 1974-77. Rear-Adm. 1970; Vice-Adm. 1974. Mem. Council, IEE, 1975-78, Chm. South East Centre, 1982-83. Adm. Pres., Midland Naval Officers Assoc., 1979-. *Address*: Finchingfield House, Finchingfield, Braintree, Essex CM7 4JS. *T*: Great Dunmow 810289. *Club*: Army and Navy.

See also Rear-Adm. J. G. Watson.

WATSON, Dr Reginald Gordon Harry, CChem, FRSC; Director, Chemical Defence Establishment, Porton Down, since 1974; *b* 3 Nov. 1928; *s* of Gordon Henry and Winifred Catherine Watson; *m* 1951, Molly Joyce Groom; one *s* two *d*. *Educ*: Chislehurst and Sidcup Grammar Sch.; Imperial Coll., London (Royal Schol.). BSc (1st cl. Hons Chem.), PhD; DIC; ARCS. Res. Worker (Fuel Cells), Dept of Chemical Engrg, Univ. of Cambridge, 1951-56; joined Royal Naval Scientific Service, 1956, as Sen. Scientific Officer, Admty Materials Lab.; Head of Chemical Engrg Div., 1958-66; Naval Staff Course, 1962; Individual Merit Sen. Principal Scientific Officer, 1965; Director: Naval R&D Admin, 1967-69; Admty Materials Lab., 1969-74. *Publications*: papers on electrochemistry, chemical engineering and materials science. *Recreations*: photography, natural history, sailing. *Address*: 20 Merriefield Drive, Broadstone, Dorset BH18 8BP. *T*: Broadstone 692128. *Club*: Cambridge University Cruising.

WATSON, Rt. Rev. Richard Charles Challinor; *see* Burnley, Suffragan Bishop of.

WATSON, Richard (Eagleson Gordon) Burges; HM Diplomatic Service; Foundation for International Research and Studies, Florence, since 1981; *b* 23 Sept. 1930; *er s* of late Harold Burges Watson and Marjorie Eleanor (*née* Gordon); *m* 1966, Ann Rosamund Clarke; two *s* three *d*. *Educ*: King Edward VI Sch., Bury St Edmunds; St John's Coll., Cambridge (MA); École des Langues Orientales, Paris. RA, 1948-50 (2nd Lieut). Joined HM Foreign (subseq. Diplomatic) Service, 1954; Tokyo, 1954-60; FO, 1960-63; Bamako (Mali), 1963-66; British Delegn to OECD, 1966-69; FCO, 1969-71; Vis. Student, Woodrow Wilson Sch., Princeton, 1971-72; Counsellor (Economic), Tokyo, 1972-76; Counsellor (Commercial), Brussels, 1976-78; Head of Trade Relations and Exports Dept, FCO, 1978-81. *Recreations*: ski-ing, tennis, swimming, walking. *Address*: c/o Foreign and Commonwealth Office, SW1A 2AH. *Clubs*: Hurlingham, Travellers'.

WATSON, Vice-Adm. Sir (Robert) Dymock, KCB 1959 (CB 1956); CBE 1948; DL; *b* 5 April 1904; *e s* of Robert Watson, FRIBA, Farnham, Surrey; *m* 1st, 1939, Margaret Lois (*d* 1968), *d* of late Rev. F. R. Gillespy; one *s* three *d* ; 2nd, 1977, Elizabeth Evelyn Petronella, *widow* of Amyas Chichester, MC. *Educ:* Royal Naval Colls Osborne and Dartmouth. Captain; Asst Dir of Plans, Joint Planning Staff, Min. of Defence, 1944-46; Capt. (D) 1st Destroyer Flotilla Medit., 1947-48; idc, 1949; Dir of Plans, Admty, 1950-52; CO, HMS Illustrious, 1953; Rear-Adm., 1954; Flag Officer Flotillas, Medit., 1954-55, Vice-Adm. 1957; a Lord Commissioner of the Admiralty, Fourth Sea Lord, Chief of Supplies and Transport, 1955-58; Commander-in-Chief, South Atlantic and South America, 1958-60; retired, 1961. DL County of Brecknock, 1965, Powys 1974. *Address:* Manascin, Pencelli, near Brecon, Powys, Wales.

WATSON, Roderick Anthony, QC 1967; *b* 1920; *o s* of late O. C. Watson, CBE and Peggy (*née* Donnelly); *m* Ann, *o d* of late W. L. Wilson; three *s* one *d. Educ:* Christian Brothers, Beulah Hill; King's Coll., Univ. of London. Served War of 1939-45, Captain RASC. Called to the Bar, Lincoln's Inn, 1949, Bencher, 1975. *Address:* Merton House, The Promenade, Castletown, Isle of Man. *Clubs:* Army and Navy, Garrick; Isle of Man Yacht.

WATSON, Roy William; Director General, National Farmers' Union, since 1979; *b* 7 Feb. 1926; *s* of William and Eleanor Maud Watson; *m* 1st, 1947, Margaret Peasey; two *s* ; 2nd, 1977, Phyllis Frances Brotherwood (*née* Farrer). *Educ:* Alleyn's Sch., Dulwich. National Farmers' Union, 1948-: Asst Dir General, 1973-78; Dep. Dir General, 1978. *Recreations:* music, military history, golf, gardening. *Address:* Pinebrook, Offwell, Honiton, Devon. *T:* Wilmington 454.

WATSON, Steven; *see* Watson, J. S.

WATSON, Stewart; *see* Watson, D. S.

WATSON, Maj.-Gen. Stuart; *see* Watson, Maj.-Gen. H. S. R.

WATSON, Sydney, OBE 1970; MA; DMus; FRCO; FRCM; Student, Organist and Lecturer in Music, Christ Church, Oxford, 1955-70; Professor, Royal College of Music, 1946-71; Examiner, Royal Schools of Music; *b* Denton, Lancashire, 3 Sept. 1903; *s* of W. T. Watson. *Educ:* Warwick Sch.; Royal College of Music, Keble Coll., Oxford (Organ Scholar). Assistant music master, Stowe School, 1925-28; Precentor of Radley Coll., 1929-33; Conductor of Abingdon Madrigal Society, 1931-36; Organist of New Coll., Oxford, 1933-38; Organist of Sheldonian Theatre, Conductor of Oxford Harmonic Society, 1933-38; Oxford Orchestral Society, 1936-38; Director of Concerts, Balliol Coll., 1933-38, 1962-69; Choragus to Oxford Univ., 1963-68; Master of Music, Winchester Coll., and Conductor Winchester Music Club, 1938-45; Precentor and Director of Music, Eton Coll., 1946-55; Conductor Petersfield Festival, 1946-64, Slough Philharmonic Society, 1946-55; Windsor and Eton Choral Society, 1949-55; Conductor, Oxford Bach Choir, 1955-70; Oxford Orchestral Society, 1956-70. *Publications:* Church Music. *Address:* Aynhoe Park, Aynho, Banbury, Oxon. *Club:* Athenæum.

WATSON, Thomas Frederick, FCA; Governor, National Society for Epilepsy, since 1971 (Chairman, 1974-78); Chairman, Finance Committee, 1975-78, Vice Chairman, since 1978; *b* 18 April 1906; *s* of late Frederick Watson and Jane Lucy (*née* Britton); *m* 1932, Eveline Dorothy Strang; one *d. Educ:* Tiffins Sch., Kingston-on-Thames. FCIS 1957; FCA 1960. With Deloitte Co., Chartered Accountants, 1925-45; qual. as Chartered Sec., 1930; Incorporated Accountant, 1935. Exchange Telegraph Co. Ltd: Chief Acct, 1945; Secretary, 1949; Asst Man. Dir and Dep. Chm., 1954; Jt Man. Dir, 1958; Man. Dir, 1959; Chm. and Man. Dir, 1961-68. Mem. Council, Commonwealth Press Union, 1959-68. *Recreations:* gardening, bridge, theatre, charity work. *Address:* Rose Cottage, Hoggeston, Buckingham MK18 3LQ. *T:* Winslow 2251.

WATSON, Thomas Yirrell, CMG 1955; MBE 1943; *b* 27 May 1906; *s* of William Scott Watson and Edith Rose Watson (*née* Yirrell); *m* 1935, Margaret Alice, *d* of late J. J. Watson; one *d. Educ:* Aberdeen Grammar Sch.; Aberdeen Univ. (BSc); Cambridge Univ. (Diploma in Agricultural Science); Pretoria Univ., South Africa. Colonial Agricultural Scholar, 1929-31; Agricultural Officer, Kenya, 1931-43; Senior Agricultural Officer, Kenya, 1943-48; Dep. Director of Agriculture, Uganda, 1948-51; Director of Agriculture, Uganda, 1951-53; Secretary for Agriculture and Natural Resources, Uganda, 1954-55; Minister of Natural Resources, 1955-56. General Manager, Uganda Lint Cotton Marketing Board, 1951-53; MEC and MLC, Uganda, 1951-56. Member: Commission of Inquiry into Land and Population Problems, Fiji, 1959-60; Economic Development Commn, Zanzibar, 1961; Commission of Inquiry into Cotton Ginning Industry, Uganda, 1962; Commissioner, Burley Tobacco Industry Inquiry, Malawi, 1964. Coronation Medal, 1953. *Address:* Marchwood, 19 Seafield Road, Southbourne, Bournemouth, Dorset BH6 3JE.

WATSON, Victor Hugo; Chairman, John Waddington plc, since 1977; *b* 26 Sept. 1928; *s* of Norman Victor and Ruby Ernestine Watson; *m* 1952, Sheila May Bryan; two *d. Educ:* Clare Coll., Cambridge (MA). Served Royal Engineers (2nd Lieut), 1946-48. Joined John Waddington Ltd, 1951. *Recreations:* music, golf, sailing, shooting. *Address:* Moat Field, Moor Lane, East Keswick, Leeds LS17 9ET. *Club:* Eccentric.

WATSON, Sir William, Kt 1962; *b* 23 Nov. 1902; *s* of late Knight Watson, SSC; *m* 1929, Elizabeth Margaret Dods; two *s* one *d. Educ:* Melville College. Member of the Institute of Chartered Accountants of Scotland (Council, 1950-52). Partner Messrs Baillie Gifford & Co., 1930-47. Director: Bank of Scotland 1944-71 (Treasurer, 1952-66); Standard Life Assurance Co., 1941-75 (Chm., 1966-69); Member Edinburgh Southern Hospitals Group Board of Management, 1948, Chairman, 1950-52; Member Jenkins Cttee on Company Law Amendment, 1960; President Inst. of Bankers in Scotland, 1963-65; Member Academic Adv. Cttee, Universities of St Andrews and Dundee, 1964-66. *Recreation:* golf. *Address:* 1 Hope Terrace, Edinburgh EH9 2AP. *T:* 031-447 2752. *Clubs:* Caledonian; New (Edinburgh); Hon. Co. of Edinburgh Golfers.

WATSON, Prof. William, CBE 1982; MA; FBA 1972; FSA; Professor of Chinese Art and Archaeology in University of London, at the School of Oriental and African Studies, and Head of the Percival David Foundation of Chinese Art, since 1966; Trustee, British Museum, since 1980; *b* 9 Dec. 1917; *s* of Robert Scoular Watson and Lily Waterfield; *m* 1940, Katherine Sylvia Mary, *d* of Mr and Mrs J. H. Armfield, Ringwood, Hants; four *s. Educ:* Glasgow High Sch.; Herbert Strutt Sch.; Gonville and Caius Coll., Cantab (Scholar; tripos in Modern and Medieval Langs). Served Intelligence Corps, 1940-46, Egypt, N Africa, Italy, India, ending as Major. Asst Keeper, British Museum, first in Dept of British and Medieval Antiquities, then in Dept of Oriental Antiquities, 1947-66. Slade Prof. of Fine Art, Cambridge University, 1975-76. Pres., Oriental Ceramic Soc., 1981-. Sir Percy Sykes Meml Medal, 1973. *Publications:* The Sculpture of Japan, 1959; Archaeology in China, 1960; China before the Han Dynasty, 1961; Ancient Chinese Bronzes, 1961; Jade Books in the Chester Beatty Library, 1963; Cultural Frontiers in Ancient East Asia, 1971; The Genius of China (catalogue of Burlington House exhibn), 1973; Style in the Arts of China, 1974; L'Art de l'Ancienne Chine, 1980; contrib. to Jl RAS, Oriental Art, Burlington Mag., BM Quarterly, etc. *Recreations:* exploring Romanesque France and N Wales, opera, claret. *Address:* 54 St Augustine's Road, NW1. *T:* 01-485 4755.

WATSON, Prof. William Alexander Jardine; Professor of Law and Classical Studies, since 1979, Director of Center for Advanced Studies in Legal History, since 1980, University of Pennsylvania; *b* 27 Oct. 1933; *s* of James W. and Janet J. Watson; *m* 1958, Cynthia Betty Balls, MA, MLitt (marr. diss.); one *s* one *d. Educ:* Univ. of Glasgow (MA 1954, LLB 1957); Univ. of Oxford (BA (by decree) 1957, MA 1958, DPhil 1960, DCL 1973). Lectr, Wadham Coll., Oxford, 1957-59; Lectr, 1959-60, Fellow, 1960-65, Oriel Coll., Oxford; Pro-Proctor, Oxford Univ., 1962-63; Douglas Prof. of Civil Law, Univ. of Glasgow, 1965-68; Prof. of Civil Law, Univ. of Edinburgh, 1968-79. Visiting Professor of Law: Tulane Univ., 1967; Univ. of Virginia, 1970 and 1974; Univ. of Cape Town, 1974 and 1975; Univ. of Michigan, 1977. Mem. Council, Stair Soc., 1970-; Hon. Mem., Speculative Soc., 1975. *Publications:* (as Alan Watson): Contract of Mandate in Roman Law, 1961; Law of Obligations in Later Roman Republic, 1965; Law of Persons in Later Roman Republic, 1967; Law of Property in Later Roman Republic, 1968; Law of the Ancient Romans, 1970; Roman Private Law Around 200 BC, 1971; Law of Succession in Later Roman Republic, 1971; Law Making in Later Roman Republic, 1974; Legal Transplants, An Approach to Comparative Law, 1974; (ed) Daube Noster, 1974; Rome of the Twelve Tables, 1975; Society and Legal Change, 1977; The Nature of Law, 1977; The Making of the Civil Law, 1981; various articles. *Recreations:* Roman numismatics, shooting. *Address:* Law School, University of Pennsylvania, 3400 Chestnut Street, Philadelphia, Pa 19104, USA.

WATSON-ARMSTRONG, family name of **Baron Armstrong.**

WATT; *see* Gibson-Watt.

WATT, Sir Alan (Stewart), Kt 1954; CBE 1952; Hon. Fellow, Australian National University, since 1965; Director, The Canberra Times, 1964-72; *b* 13 April 1901; *s* of George Watt and Susan Stewart Robb Gray; *m* 1927, Mildred Mary Wait; three *s* one *d. Educ:* Sydney Boys' High Sch.; Sydney and Oxford Universities. Rhodes Scholar for NSW, 1921; practised as Barrister-at-Law, Sydney; appointed to Dept of External Affairs, Canberra, 1937; First Secretary, Australian Legation, Washington, 1940-45; Adviser, Australian Deleg. to San Francisco, UN Conf., 1945; Alternate Deleg., UN General Assembly, London, 1946; Asst Secretary (Political), Dept of External Affairs, 1946; Del. to UN Gen. Assemblies, New York, 1946 and 1947, Paris, 1948; Leader, Australian Deleg. to Conf. on Freedom of Information, Geneva, 1948. Australian Minister to USSR, 1947-48; Australian Ambassador to USSR, 1949-50; Secretary, Department of External Affairs, Canberra, ACT, 1950-53; Australian Commissioner in SE Asia, 1954-56; Australian Ambassador: to Japan, 1956-60; to Federal Republic of Germany, 1960-62. Australian Delegate, Colombo Plan Cons. Cttee Meeting, Sydney, 1950; Member Deleg. accompanying Prime Minister to Prime Ministers' Conf., London, 1951 and 1953; Member Australian Delegation to ANZUS Council Meeting, Honolulu, 1952, and Geneva, 1954; alternate Leader, Australian Deleg. to Conf. on Indo-China and Korea, Geneva, 1954, Manila Treaty Conf., Manila 1954. Bangkok 1955. Retired from Commonwealth Public Service, July 1962. Visiting Fellow, Australian National Univ., 1963-64; Dir, Australian Inst. of Internat. Affairs, 1963-69. *Publications:* Evolution of Australian Foreign Policy 1938-1965, 1967; Vietnam, 1968; Memoirs, 1972; United Nations, 1974. *Recreation:* lawn tennis. *Address:* 1 Mermaid Street,

Red Hill, Canberra, ACT 2603, Australia. *Club:* Commonwealth (Canberra).

WATT, Alexander Stuart, PhD; FRS 1957; retired as Lecturer in Forest Botany, Cambridge University (1933-59); *b* 21 June 1892; *s* of George Watt and Maggie Jean Stuart; *m* 1929, Annie Constable Kennaway; two *s* one *d*. *Educ:* Turriff Secondary Sch.; Robert Gordon's Coll., Aberdeen; Aberdeen and Cambridge Universities. BA 1919, PhD 1924, Cambridge. Lecturer in Forest Botany and Forest Zoology, 1915-29; Gurney Lecturer in Forestry, Cambridge, 1929-33. Visiting Lecturer, University of Colorado, 1963; Visiting Prof., University of Khartoum, 1965. *Publications:* papers in Journal of Ecology, New Phytologist, etc. *Recreation:* hill walking. *Address:* 38 Chesterton Hall Crescent, Cambridge. *T:* Cambridge 59371.

WATT, Very Rev. Alfred Ian; Rector of St Paul's, Kinross, since 1982; Convenor, Mission Board of the General Synod, since 1982; *b* 1934. *Educ:* Edinburgh Theological College. Deacon, 1960, priest 1961, Diocese of Brechin; Curate, St Paul's Cathedral, Dundee, 1960-63; Precentor, 1963-66; Rector of Arbroath, 1966-69; Provost of St Ninian's Cathedral, Perth, 1969-82. *Address:* The Rectory, Kinross.

WATT, Andrew, CBE 1963; Forestry Commissioner, 1965-69; *b* 10 Nov. 1909; 2nd *surv. s* of late James Watt, LLD, WS, and of late Menie Watt; *m* 1943, Helen McGuffog (*d* 1969); two *s* one *d*. *Educ:* Winchester; Magdalen Coll., Oxford. BA 1931. District Officer, Forestry Commn, 1934; Divisional Officer, 1940; Conservator, 1946; Director of Forestry for Scotland, 1957-63; Director of Forest Research, 1963-65. *Address:* Greenways, 4 Ravelston Dykes Lane, Edinburgh EH4 3NY. *T:* 031-337 7986.

WATT, Charlotte Joanne, (Mrs G. L. Watt); see Erickson, Prof. C. J.

WATT, David; Director, Royal Institute of International Affairs, since 1978; *b* Edinburgh, 9 Jan. 1932; *s* of Rev. John Hunter Watt and Helen Garioch Bryce; *m* 1968, Susanne, *d* of Dr Frank Burchardt; four *s*. *Educ:* Marlborough; Hertford Coll., Oxford. Dramatic Critic, Spectator, 1956-57; Diplomatic Corresp., Scotsman, 1958-60; Common Market Corresp., Daily Herald, 1960-61; Polit. Corresp., Spectator, 1962-63; Washington Corresp., Financial Times, 1964-67, Polit. Editor, 1968-77. Jt Editor, Political Qly, 1979-; regular contributor to The Times, 1981-. Vis. Fellow, 1972-73, Fellow, 1981-83, All Souls Coll., Oxford. Mem., Fisher Cttee on Self-regulation at Lloyd's, 1979-80. *Recreations:* music, chess, golf. *Address:* 18 Groveway, SW9 0AR. *T:* 01-582 9829. *Clubs:* Travellers', Beefsteak.

WATT, Prof. Donald Cameron; see Cameron Watt.

WATT, George Percival Norman, CMG 1957; CBE 1951; *b* 2 June 1890; *s* of Edmund J. Watt, Melbourne, Australia; *m* 1916, Nellie V. M. Hough (decd); one *s* one *d*. *Educ:* Wesley Coll., Melbourne, Victoria. Clerk, Victorian Railways and State Treasury, 1905-08; Navy Finance Branch, 1911; Accountant, Navy Department, 1917; Secretary, HMA Naval Establishments, Sydney, 1923; Commonwealth Public Service Inspector, 1928-40; First Assistant Secretary, Defence Division Treasury, Melbourne, 1940; Deputy Secretary, Treasury, Canberra, 1947-48; Secretary, Commonwealth Treasury, Canberra, 1948-51, retired. Chairman, Australian National Airlines Commission, 1950-57; Chairman, British Commonwealth Pacific Airlines, 1950-54; Director, Qantas Empire Airways, 1947-62; Chairman and Director, Volkswagen (Australasia) Ltd, 1959-66. *Recreation:* golf. *Address:* 23 Through Road, Burwood, Victoria 3125, Australia.

WATT, Sir G. S. H.; see Harvie-Watt.

WATT, Hamish; *b* 27 Dec. 1925; *s* of Wm Watt and Caroline C. Allan; *m* 1948, Mary Helen Grant; one *s* two *d*. *Educ:* Keith Grammar Sch.; St Andrews Univ. Engaged in farming (dairy and sheep). Subseq. company director, quarries. Contested (C), Caithness, 1966; contested (SNP), Banff, 1970; MP (SNP) Banff, Feb. 1974-79. *Address:* 21 Steinbeck Road, Buckie, Banffshire. *T:* Buckie 32882. *Clubs:* Farmers', Whitehall Court.

WATT, Ian Buchanan, CMG 1967; HM Diplomatic Service, retired; with Grindlays Bank, since 1977; *b* 3 Aug. 1916; *s* of John Watt and Margaret Gibson Watt, Perth; *m* 1963, Diana Susan, *d* of Captain R. A. Villiers, Royal Navy (retired) and late Mrs R. A. Villiers; two *s* one *d*. *Educ:* Perth Academy; St Andrews Univ. MA 1939. Asst Principal, Government of N. Ireland, 1939. Naval Service, 1942-46; Lieut, RNVR. Principal, Colonial Office, 1946; Asst Secretary, 1956; Dep. UK Commissioner, Malta, 1962; Dep. High Commissioner, Malta, 1964; transf. to Diplomatic Service, 1964; Counsellor, CRO, 1965; British High Commissioner, Lesotho, 1966-70; Counsellor, FCO, 1970-72; High Comr, Sierra Leone, 1972-76. *Recreation:* ornithology. *Address:* Kingswood House, 8 Lower Green Road, Esher, Surrey. *T:* 01-398 5728; Grindlay's Bank, 23 Fenchurch Street, EC3. *Club:* Travellers'.

WATT, Surgeon Vice-Adm. Sir James, KBE 1975; MS, FRCS; Medical Director-General (Navy), 1972-77; *b* 19 Aug. 1914; *s* of Thomas Watt and Sarah Alice Clarkson. *Educ:* King Edward VI Sch., Morpeth; Univ. of Durham. MB, BS 1938; MS 1949; FRCS 1955; MD 1972; FRCP 1975. Surgical Registrar, Royal Vic. Infirm., Newcastle upon Tyne, 1947; Surgical Specialist: N Ire., 1949; RN Hosp., Hong Kong, 1954; Consultant in Surgery,

RN Hospitals: Plymouth, 1956; Haslar, 1959; Malta, 1961; Haslar, 1963; Jt Prof. of Naval Surgery, RCS and RN Hosp., Haslar, 1965-69; Dean of Naval Medicine and MO i/c, Inst. of Naval Medicine, 1969-72. Chm., RN Clin. Research Working Party, 1969-77; Chm. Bd of Trustees, Naval Christian Fellowship, 1968-75; Pres., Royal Naval Lay Readers Soc., 1974. QHS 1969-77. Surg. Comdr 1956; Surg. Captain 1965; Surg. Rear-Adm. 1969; Surg. Vice-Adm. 1972. Mem., Environmental Medicine Res. Policy Cttee, MRC, 1974-77. Thomas Vicary Lectr, RCS, 1974. FICS 1964; Fellow: Assoc. of Surgeons of GB and Ire.; Med. Soc. of London (Mem. Council, 1976; Lettsomian Lectr, 1979; Pres., 1980-81; Vice-Pres., 1981-83); FRSM (Pres., 1982-); Hon. FRCSE; Member: Brit. Soc. for Surgery of the Hand; Internat. Soc. for Burns Injuries; Corr. Mem., Surgical Research Soc., 1966-77; Mem. Editorial Bd, Brit. Jl of Surgery, 1966-77. Hon. Freeman, Co. of Barbers, 1978. Hon. DCh Newcastle, 1978. Errol-Eldridge Prize, 1968; Gilbert Blane Medal, 1971. CStJ 1972. *Publications:* papers on: burns, cancer chemotherapy, peptic ulceration, hyberbaric oxygen therapy, naval medical history. *Recreations:* mountain walking, music. *Address:* 7 Cambisgate, Church Road, Wimbledon, SW19 5AL. *Club:* English-Speaking Union.

WATT, Richard Lorimer, CA; FBIM; Director, Trusthouses Forte Leisure Ltd, since 1981; *b* 20 June 1921; *s* of George Lorimer Watt and Sophia Fordyce Watt; *m* 1952, Elizabeth (*née* Hancock); one *s*. *Educ:* George Watson's Boys' Coll., Edinburgh; Edinburgh Univ. Brush Group (now part of Hawker Siddeley Group): various finance responsibilities, 1948-55; Planning Dir, 1955-57, Dir and Gen. Man., 1957-60, Mirrlees, Bickerton & Day Ltd; Dir and Gen. Man., National Gas Oil Engines Ltd, 1958-60; Booker Group: Exec. Dir, latterly Chm., Booker Industrial Holdings Ltd, 1960-70; Exec. Dir, latterly Dep. Chm., Booker Engineering Holdings Ltd, 1964-70; EMI Group: Gp Financial Controller, 1970-71; Gp Finance Dir, 1971-75; Asst Man. Dir, 1975-77; Gp Man. Dir, 1977-78; Vice-Chm., 1978-81. Director: Capitol Industries-EMI Inc., 1971-81; South Bank Theatre Bd, 1977-. *Recreations:* music, ballet, swimming. *Address:* Flat 12, 32 Bryanston Square, W1H 7FL. *T:* 01-723 8355. *Club:* Caledonian.

WATT, Robert; His Honour Judge Watt; County Court Judge since 1971; *b* 10 March 1923; *s* of John Watt, schoolmaster, Ballymena, Co. Antrim; *m* 1951, Edna Rea; one *d*. *Educ:* Ballymena Academy; Queen's Univ., Belfast (LLB). Called to Bar, Gray's Inn, 1946; called to Bar of Northern Ireland, 1946; QC (NI) 1964; subseq. Sen. Crown Prosecutor Counties Fermanagh and Tyrone. *Recreation:* sailing. *Address:* 12 Deramore Drive, Belfast BT9 5JQ. *Club:* Royal North of Ireland Yacht.

WATT, Robert Cameron; *b* 4 Aug. 1898; *s* of Rev. J. Gordon Watt; *m* 1925, Barbara (*d* 1977), *d* of late Rt Rev. E. J. Bidwell, former Bishop of Ontario; three *s*. *Educ:* Fettes Coll., Edinburgh; Oriel Coll., Oxford. Lecturer in History, Queen's Univ., Kingston, Ontario, 1922-24; Asst Master, Clifton Coll., 1924-26; Senior History Master, Rugby Sch., 1926-51, Housemaster, 1944-51; Rector, Edinburgh Acad., 1951-62; Assistant Master: St George's Sch., Newport, RI, 1963-66; Fettes Coll., 1967-78. *Recreations:* gardening, walking. *Address:* 9 Wardie Avenue, Edinburgh EH5 2AB.

See also D. Cameron Watt.

WATT, William, OBE 1969; FRS 1976; Senior Research Fellow, Department of Materials Science, University of Surrey, since 1975; *b* 14 April 1912; *o c* of Patrick Watt, Aberdeen, and Flora (*née* Corsar), Arbroath; *m* 1946, Irene Isabel Corps; two *d*. *Educ:* George Heriot's Sch., Edinburgh; Heriot-Watt Coll., Edinburgh BSc (1st Cl. Hons, Chem.); AH-WC. ARIC 1935. Research Chemist, Royal Aircraft Establishment, 1936-75, retiring as Sen. Principal Scientific Officer, (Merit). Hon. DSc Heriot-Watt, 1977. Gold Medal, Congrès des Matériaux Résistant à Chaud, Paris, 1951; (jtly) Civil Service Wolfe Award for Carbon Fibre Research, 1968; Silver Medal, RAeS, 1969; C. Pettinos Award for Res. and Innovation in Carbon, viz, Pyrolytic Graphite and Carbon Fibres, Amer. Carbon Cttee, 1971. *Publications:* (jtly) 57th Thomas Hawksley Lecture, IMechE (public lecture), 1970; Pettinos Award Lecture, Carbon Work at the RAE, 10th US Carbon Conf., Bethlehem (public lecture), 1971; many papers in Proc. of Confs and in scientific jls. *Recreations:* gardening, golf, continental travel. *Address:* 12 Barton End, Lenten Street, Alton, Hants GU34 1LD. *T:* Alton 88486. *Club:* North Hants Golf (Fleet, Hants).

WATT, Prof. W(illiam) Montgomery; Professor of Arabic and Islamic Studies, University of Edinburgh, 1964-79; *b* Ceres, Fife, 14 March 1909; *o c* of late Rev. Andrew Watt; *m* 1943, Jean Macdonald, *er d* of late Prof. Robert Donaldson; one *s* four *d*. *Educ:* George Watson's Coll., Edinburgh; University of Edinburgh; Balliol Coll., Oxford; University of Jena; Cuddesdon Coll. Warner Exhibition (Balliol), 1930; Ferguson Schol. in Classics, 1931; MA, PhD (Edinburgh); MA, BLitt (Oxon). Asst Lecturer, Moral Philosophy, University of Edinburgh, 1934-38; Curate: St Mary Boltons, London, 1939-41; Curate, Old St Paul's, Edinburgh, 1941-43; Arabic specialist to Bishop in Jerusalem, 1943-46; Lecturer, Ancient Philosophy, University of Edinburgh, 1946-47; Lectr, Sen. Lectr and Reader in Arabic, Univ. of Edinburgh, 1947-64. Visiting Professor: of Islamic Studies, University of Toronto, 1963; Collège de France, Paris, 1970; of Religious Studies, Univ. of Toronto, 1978; of Arab Studies, Georgetown Univ., 1978-79. Chairman, Assoc. of British Orientalists, 1964-65. Hon. DD Aberdeen, 1966. Levi Della Vida Medal, Los Angeles, 1981. *Publications:* Free Will and Predestination in Early Islam, 1949; The Faith and Practice of al-Ghazali, 1953; Muhammad at Mecca, 1953; Muhammad at Medina, 1956;

The Reality of God, 1958; The Cure for Human Troubles, 1959; Islam and the Integration of Society, 1961; Muhammad Prophet and Statesman, 1961; Islamic Philosophy and Theology, 1962; Muslim Intellectual, 1963; Truth in the Religions, 1963; Islamic Spain, 1965; Islam (in Propyläen Weltgeschichte, XI), 1965; A Companion to the Qur'an, 1967; What is Islam?, 1968; Islamic Political Thought, 1968; Islamic Revelation and the Modern World, 1970; Bell's Introduction to the Qur'ān, 1970; The Influence of Islam on Medieval Europe, 1972; The Formative Period of Islamic Thought, 1973; The Majesty that was Islam, 1974; Der Islam, i, 1980, ii, 1982; (ed) Islamic Surveys; contribs learned journals. *Address:* The Neuk, Dalkeith, Midlothian EH22 1JT. *T:* 031-663 3197.

WATT, Emeritus Prof. William Smith, MA (Glasgow and Oxon); Regius Professor of Humanity in the University of Aberdeen, 1952-79, Vice-Principal, 1969-72; *b* 20 June 1913; *s* of John Watt and Agnes Smith; *m* 1944, Dorothea, *e d* of R. J. Codrington Smith; one *s. Educ:* University of Glasgow; Balliol Coll., Oxford (Snell Exhibitioner and Hon. Scholar). First Class Hons in Classics, Glasgow Univ., 1933; Ferguson Schol., 1934; Craven Schol., 1934; First Class, Classical Moderations, 1935; Hertford Schol., 1935; Ireland Schol., 1935; First Class, Lit. Hum., 1937. Lecturer in Greek and Greek History, University of Glasgow, 1937-38; Fellow and Tutor in Classics, Balliol Coll., Oxford, 1938-52. Civilian Officer, Admiralty (Naval Intelligence Div.), 1941-45. Convener, Scottish Univs Council on Entrance, 1973-77. Governor, Aberdeen Coll. of Educn, 1958-75 (Chm. of Governors 1971-75). *Publications:* (ed) Ciceronis Epistulae ad Quintum fratrem, etc, 1958, 1965; (ed) Ciceronis Epistularum ad Atticum Libri I-VIII, 1965; (ed) Ciceronis Epistulae ad familiares, 1982; (ed with P. J. Ford) George Buchanan's Miscellaneorum Liber, 1982; articles and reviews in classical periodicals. *Address:* 38 Woodburn Gardens, Aberdeen AB1 8JA. *T:* Aberdeen 34369. *Club:* Business and Professional (Aberdeen).

WATTON, Rt. Rev. James Augustus, BA, DD; *b* 23 Oct. 1915; *s* of Geo. A. Watton and Ada Wynn; *m* 1941, Irene A. Foster; one *s* two *d. Educ:* Univ. of Western Ontario (BA); Huron Coll. (STh); Post graduate Univ. of Michigan. Deacon 1938; Priest 1939. Bishop of Moosonee, 1963-80; Archbishop of Moosonee and Metropolitan of Ontario, 1974-79; retired 1980. DD (*jure dig.*), 1955. *Address:* Box 803, Southampton, Ontario N0H 2LO, Canada.

WATTS, Arthur Desmond, CMG 1977; Deputy Legal Adviser, Foreign and Commonwealth Office, since 1982; *b* 14 Nov. 1931; *o s* of Col A. E. Watts, MA (Cantab); *m* 1957, Iris Ann Collier, MA (Cantab); one *s* one *d. Educ:* Haileybury and Imperial Service College; Royal Military Academy, Sandhurst; Downing Coll., Cambridge (Schol.). BA 1954; LLB (First Cl.) 1955; Whewell Schol. in Internat. Law, 1955; called to Bar, Gray's Inn, 1957; MA. Legal Asst, Foreign Office, 1957-59; Legal Adviser, British Property Commn (later British Embassy), Cairo, 1959-62; Asst Legal Adviser, FO, 1962-67; Legal Adviser, British Embassy, Bonn, 1967-69; Asst Solicitor, Law Officers Dept, 1969-70; Legal Counsellor, FCO, 1970-73; Counsellor (Legal Advr), Office of UK Permanent Rep. to EEC, 1973-77; Legal Counsellor, FCO, 1977-82. *Publications:* Legal Effects of War, 4th edn (with Lord McNair), 1966; contribs to: British Year Book of Internat. Law; Internat. and Comparative Law Quarterly; Egyptian Review of Internat. Law. *Recreation:* cricket (County Cap, Shropshire, 1955). *Address:* 61 Meriden Court, Chelsea Manor Street, SW1.

WATTS, Donald Walter, PhD; FRACI; Director, Western Australian Institute of Technology, since 1980; *b* 1 April 1934; *s* of late Horace Frederick Watts and of Esme Anne Watts; *m* 1960, Michelle Rose Yeomans; two *s. Educ:* Hale Sch., Perth; University of Western Australia (BSc Hons, PhD); University College London. FRACI 1967. Post-Doctoral Fellow, UCL, 1959-61; University of Western Australia: Sen. Lectr, 1962; Reader, 1969; Associate Prof., 1971; Personal Chair in Physical and Inorganic Chemistry, 1977-79. Vis. Scientist, Univ. of S California, 1967; Visiting Professor: Australian National Univ., 1973; Univ. of Toronto, 1974. *Publications:* Chemical Properties and Reactions (jtly) (Univ. of W Aust.), 1978; (jtly) Chemistry for Australian Secondary School Students (Aust. Acad. of Sci.), 1979; numerous papers on phys. and inorganic chemistry in internat. jls; several papers presented at nat. and internat. confs. *Recreations:* tennis (Mem. Interstate Tennis Team, 1952-53), squash (Mem. Interstate Squash Team, 1957-66), golf. *Address:* Western Australian Institute of Technology, Kent Street, Bently, WA 6102, Australia. *T:* (09) 350 7001; (private) 2 Minora Road, Dalkeith, WA 6009, Australia. *T:* (09) 386 3855. *Clubs:* Royal Kings Park Tennis (Perth); Nedlands Tennis (Nedlands); Lake Karrinyup Golf (Karrinyup).

WATTS, Helen Josephine, (Mrs Michael Mitchell), CBE 1978; Hon. FRAM; concert, lieder and opera singer (contralto); *b* 7 Dec. 1927; *d* of Thomas Watts and Winifred (*née* Morgan); *m* 1980, Michael Mitchell. *Educ:* St Mary and St Anne's Sch., Abbots Bromley; Royal Academy of Music (LRAM). Hon. FRAM 1961 (Hon. ARAM 1955). *Recreation:* gardening. *Address:* c/o Harold Holt Ltd, 31 Sinclair Road, W14 0NS. *Club:* English-Speaking Union.

WATTS, Colonel John Cadman, OBE 1959; MC 1946; FRCS 1949; Chairman, Armed Forces Committee, British Medical Association, 1978-82 (Chairman, North Bedfordshire Division, 1971; Member Council, 1972-74); *b* 13 April 1913; *s* of John Nixon Watts, solicitor, and Amy Bettina (*née* Cadman); *m* 1938, Joan Lillian (*née* Inwood); three *s* one *d. Educ:* Merchant Taylors' Sch.; St Thomas's Hospital. MRCS, LRCP, 1936; MB, BS, 1938. Casualty Officer, Resident Anæsthetist, House Surgeon, St Thomas's Hospital, 1937; Surgical Specialist, RAMC, 1938-60, serving in Palestine, Egypt, Libya, Syria, Tunisia, Italy, France, Holland, Germany, Malaya, Java, Japan, and Cyprus. Hunterian Professor, RCS, 1960; Professor of Military Surgery, RCS, 1960-64; Conslt Surgeon, Bedford Gen. Hosp., 1966-76. Co. Comr, St John Ambulance Brigade, 1970. Pres., Ipswich Div., BMA. OStJ 1970. *Publications:* Surgeon at War, 1955; Clinical Surgery, 1964; Exploration Medicine, 1964. *Recreations:* sailing, ski-ing, shooting. *Address:* Lowood Lodge, Hasketon, near Woodbridge, Suffolk. *T:* Grundisburgh 326. *Clubs:* Deben Yacht (Woodbridge); United Hospitals Sailing (Burnham-on-Crouch).

WATTS, John Francis, BA; Principal, Countesthorpe College, Leicestershire, 1972-81; Chairman, National Association for Teaching of English (NATE), 1974-76; *b* 18 Oct. 1926; *s* of John Weldon Watts and Norah K. Watts; *m* 1950, Elizabeth Hamilton; four *s* one *d. Educ:* West Buckland Sch.; Univ. of Bristol (BA). First Headmaster, Lue Quennevais Sch., Jersey, CI, 1964-69; Lectr, Univ. of London, 1969-72. *Publications:* Encounters, 1965; Contact, 1970 (Australia); Interplay, 1972; Teaching, 1974; The Countesthorpe Experience, 1977; Towards an Open School, 1980; contrib. to various publications. *Address:* 16 Highgate West Hill, N6 6NP.

WATTS, Maj.-Gen. John Peter Barry Condliffe, CBE 1979 (OBE 1972); MC 1960; Commander, Sultan of Oman's Land Forces, since 1979; *b* 27 Aug. 1930; *m*; seven *c. Educ:* Westminster Sch.; Andover Acad., USA; RMA Sandhurst. Commissioned, RUR, 1951 (Royal Irish Rangers, 1968); served Hong Kong, Malaya (despatches), Cyprus, Oman (MC), BAOR, Borneo and Saudi Arabia; 48 Gurkha Inf. Bde, 1967-69; CO 22 SAS Regt, 1970-72; Directing Staff, Staff Coll., 1972-74; MoD, 1974. *Address:* HQ Sultan's Armed Forces, Baît al Falaj, PO Box 602, Muscat.

WATTS, Ronald George, CBE 1962; *b* 15 May 1914; *m* 1940, Ruth Hansen (*d* 1970); one *s* two *d*; *m* 1972, Margit Tester. *Educ:* Latymer Sch., Edmonton; St John's Coll., Cambridge. Foreign Service from 1937; appointed Counsellor, Foreign Office, 1958; Consul-Gen., Osaka-Kobe, 1958-63; Head of Consular Dept, FO, 1963-65; Consul-Gen., Paris, 1966-67; FCO 1967-69, retired. *Recreation:* church organist.

WATTS, Roy, CBE 1978; Member, since 1974, Joint Deputy Chairman, since 1980, Group Managing Director, since 1982, British Airways Board; *b* 17 Aug. 1925; *m* 1951, Jean Rosaline; one *s* two *d. Educ:* Doncaster Grammar Sch.; Edinburgh Univ. (MA). FIMTA, FRAeS, FCIT. Army, 1944-47: commnd Sandhurst; 8th RTR. Accountant in local govt until 1955; joined BEA, 1955: Head of Systems Study Section (O&M Br.); Chief Internal Auditor; Area Man., Sweden and Finland; Fleet Planning Man.; Regional Gen. Man., North and East Europe; Dir, S1-11 Div; Chief Exec. BEA British Airways, 1972-74 (Chm., Jan.-March 1974); Chief Exec., European Div., British Airways, 1974-77; Dir, Commercial Operations, British Airways, 1977, Dir, Finance and Planning, 1978-79, Chief Exec., 1979-82. Chm., Assoc. of European Airlines, 1982. *Recreations:* squash, cricket. *Address:* Scotswood, Penn Road, Beaconsfield, Bucks. *T:* Beaconsfield 3755.

WATTS, Thomas Rowland, CBE 1978; Chartered Accountant; Chairman, Dental Rates Study Group, since 1982; Director, Jarrold & Sons Ltd, Norwich, since 1982; *b* 1 Jan. 1917; *s* of late Thomas William Watts and late Daisy Maud Watts (*née* Bultitude); *m* 1955, Hester Zoë Armistead; one *s* two *d. Educ:* Gresham's Sch., Holt. Articled to Price Waterhouse & Co., 1934-39, Partner, 1963-82 (ACA 1939, FCA 1960). Served War, TA, 1939-41, Royal Marines (Captain), 1941-46. Chm., Accounting Standards Cttee (UK and Ireland), 1978-82; Mem. Council, Inst. of Chartered Accountants in England and Wales, 1974-82; Mem. City EEC Cttee, 1974-82; Adviser to Dept of Trade on EEC company law, 1974-; Vice-Pres. d'honneur, Groupe d'Etudes des experts comptables de la CEE, 1979- (Vice-Pres., 1975-79). Chartered Accountants Founding Socs' Centenary Award, 1982. *Publications:* editor, various professional books; papers in professional jls. *Recreations:* travel, music, opera costume designs. *Address:* 13 Fitzwalter Road, Colchester, Essex CO3 3SY. *T:* Colchester 73520; 29 Capstan Square, Isle of Dogs, E14. *Club:* East India, Devonshire, Sports and Public Schools.

WATTS, Victor Brian; His Honour Judge Watts; a Circuit Judge, since 1980; *b* 7 Jan. 1927; *o s* of Percy William King Watts and Doris Millicent Watts; *m* 1965, Patricia Eileen (*née* Steer); one *s* one *d. Educ:* Colfe's Grammar Sch.; University Coll., Oxford. MA(Oxon); BCL. Called to the Bar, Middle Temple, 1950; subseq. Western Circuit; a Recorder of the Crown Court, 1972-80. Flying Officer, Royal Air Force, 1950-52. *Publications:* Landlord and Tenant Act, 1954; Leading Cases on the Law of Contract, 1955; occasional articles of a legal nature. *Recreations:* walking, tennis. *Address:* 28 Abinger Road, W4. *T:* 01-994 4435. *Club:* Hurlingham.

WATTS, William Arthur, MA, DSc; Provost, Trinity College, Dublin, since 1981; President, Royal Irish Academy, since 1982; *b* 26 May 1930; *s* of William Low Watts and Bessie (*née* Dickinson); *m* 1954, Geraldine Mary Magrath; two *s* one *d. Educ:* Trinity Coll., Dublin (MA, ScD). Lecturer in Botany, Univ. of Hull, 1953-55; Trinity College, Dublin: Lectr in Botany, 1955-65; Fellow, 1970; Professor of Botany, 1965-80; Prof. of Quaternary Ecology, 1980-81. Adjunct Prof. of Geology, Univ. of Minnesota, 1975-.

Governor: National Gallery of Ireland, 1982–; Marsh's Library, 1981–; Mem., National Board for Science and Technology, Ireland, 1978–; Board Member, Dublin Inst. for Advanced Studies, 1981–. Vice-Chm., Federated Dublin Voluntary Hosps, 1975–; Chm., Mercer's Hosp., 1975–. *Publications:* numerous articles on aspects of quaternary ecology. *Recreations:* walking, conservation studies, music. *Address:* Provost's House, Trinity College, Dublin 2. *T:* 772941, ext. 1558.

WATTS, William John, CBE 1979 (OBE 1969); HM Diplomatic Service, retired 1981; *b* 11 March 1923; *s* of William Thomas Watts and Beatrice (*née* Vickers); *m* 1949, Dr Anne Brown Watt; one *s* one *d*. RAF, 1941–46. HMOCS, Malaya, 1947–59: retd as Dep. Sec., Min. of Interior and Justice; HM Diplomatic Service, 1960–81: served in Colombo, Bangkok, Singapore and Nairobi. *Recreations:* tennis, reading, gardening. *Address:* 35 Gregories Road, Beaconsfield, Bucks. *Clubs:* Pathfinder; Royal Bangkok Sports (Thailand); Muthaiga (Nairobi, Kenya).

WAUCHOPE, Sir Patrick (George) Don–, 10th Bt, *cr* 1667; Horticulturist; *b* 7 May 1898; *o s* of late Patrick Hamilton Don–Wauchope (3rd *s* of 8th Bt) and late Georgiana Renira; *S* uncle 1951; *m* 1936, Ismay Lilian Ursula (marr. diss.), *d* of late Sidney Hodges, Edendale, Natal, South Africa; two *s. Educ:* The Edinburgh Academy. Served European War, 1914–18, with RFA, France and Belgium (wounded); War of 1939–46, Egypt and Italy. *Recreations:* cricket, golf. *Heir: s* Roger (Hamilton) Don–Wauchope [Chartered Accountant, S Africa; *b* 16 Oct. 1938; *m* 1963, Sallee, *yr d* of Lt-Col H. Mill Colman, OBE, AMICE, Durban; two *s* one *d*].

WAUD, Christopher Denis George Pierre; a Recorder of the Crown Court, since Dec. 1974; barrister-at-law; *b* 5 Dec. 1928; *s* of late Christopher William Henry Pierre Waud and Vera Constance Maria Waud; *m* 1954, Rosemary Paynter Bradshaw Moorhead; one *s* four *d* (and one *s* decd). *Educ:* Charterhouse; Christ Church, Oxford. Called to Bar, Middle Temple, 1956. Full-time Chm. of Industrial Tribunals, 1982 (Part-time, 1977–82). *Publication:* Redundancy and Unfair Dismissal, 1981, 1982–83. *Recreations:* sailing, walking. *Address:* Lamb Building, Temple, EC4Y 7AS; 93 Ebury Bridge Road, SW1W 8RE. *Clubs:* Royal Lymington Yacht (Lymington), Bar Yacht.

WAUGH, Auberon Alexander; Columnist: Private Eye, since 1970; The Spectator, since 1976; Chief Book Reviewer, Daily Mail, since 1981; *b* 17 Nov. 1939; *e s* of late Evelyn Waugh, writer, and late Laura Waugh, (*née* Florey House, Somerset; *m* 1961, Teresa, *o d* of 6th Earl of Onslow, KBE, MC, and *sister* of 7th Earl of Onslow, *qv* ; two *s* two *d. Educ:* Downside (schol. in Classics); Christ Church, Oxford (exhibn in English, read PPE). Editorial staff, Daily Telegraph, 1960–63. Commissioned Royal Horse Guards, 1957; served Cyprus; retd with wounds, 1958. Weekly Columnist, Catholic Herald, 1963–64; special writer, Mirror group, 1964–67; Political Correspondent: Spectator, 1967–70; Private Eye, 1970–; Weekly Columnist, The Times, 1970–71; Chief Fiction Reviewer: Spectator, 1970–73; Evening Standard, 1973–80; Weekly Columnist, New Statesman, 1973–76; monthly contributor, Books and Bookmen, 1973–80. Contested (Dog Lovers' Party) Devon North, 1979. Pres., British Croatian Soc., 1973–. Nat. Press 'Critic of the Year' commendations, 1976, 1978; 'What the Papers Say' Columnist of the Year, Granada TV, 1979. *Publications:* novels: The Foxglove Saga, 1960; Path of Dalliance, 1963; Who are the Violets Now?, 1966; Consider the Lilies, 1968; A Bed of Flowers, 1972; *non-fiction:* (with S. Cronje) Biafra: Britain's Shame, 1969; Four Crowded Years: the Diaries of Auberon Waugh, 1976; The Last Word: an Eyewitness Account of the Thorpe Trial, 1980; Auberon Waugh's Yearbook, 1981; *essays:* Country Topics, 1974; In The Lion's Den, 1978. *Recreation:* gossip. *Address:* Combe Florey House, near Taunton, Somerset; La Pesegado, 11320 Montmaur, France. *Club:* Beefsteak.

WAVERLEY, 2nd Viscount, *cr* 1952, of Westdean; **David Alastair Pearson Anderson;** Consultant Physician, Reading Group of Hospitals, since 1951; *b* 18 Feb. 1911; *s* of 1st Viscount Waverley, PC, GCB, OM, GCSI, GCIE, FRS, and Christina Anderson; *S* father, 1958; *m* 1948, Myrtle Ledgerwood; one *s* one *d* (and one *d* decd). *Educ:* Malvern Coll.; Universities of Frankfurt A/Main and Cambridge (Pembroke Coll.); St Thomas's Hospital, London. MB, BChir (Cantab), 1937; MRCP (London), 1946; FRCP (London), 1957. Appointments at St Thomas's Hospital, 1938–39. Served War of 1939–45, RAF Med. Br. Med. Registrar, Res. Asst Physician and Registrar Dept Clin. Pathology, St Thomas's Hospital, 1946–50. *Publications:* various communications to medical journals. *Recreations:* golf and fishing; formerly athletics and Association football (rep. Cambridge *v* Oxford, in Inter-Varsity Relays, etc). *Heir: s* Hon. John Desmond Forbes Anderson, *b* 31 Oct. 1949. *Address:* Chanders, Aldworth, Berks. *T:* Compton 377. *Clubs:* Travellers'; Hawks (Cambridge).

See also Brig. Hon. Dame Mary Pihl.

WAY, Sir Richard (George Kitchener), KCB 1961 (CB 1957); CBE 1952; Principal, King's College London, 1975–80; *b* 15 Sept. 1914; *s* of Frederick and Clara Way; *m* 1947, Ursula Joan Starr; one *s* two *d. Educ:* Polytechnic Secondary Sch., London. Joined Civil Service as Exec. Officer, 1933; Higher Executive Officer, 1940; Principal, 1942; Asst Secretary, 1946; Asst Under-Secretary of State, 1954; Deputy Under-Secretary of State, War Office, 1955–57; Dep. Secretary, Ministry of Defence, 1957–58; Dep. Secretary, Ministry of Supply, 1958–59; Permanent Under-Secretary of State, War Office, 1960–63; Permanent Secretary, Ministry of Aviation, 1963–66. Dep.

Chm., Lansing Bagnall Ltd, 1966–67, Chm. 1967–69; Chm., LTE, 1970–74. Chairman, EDC Machine Tool Industry, 1967–70; Member (part-time) Board of: BOAC, 1967–73; Dobson Park Industries Ltd, 1975–. Chm., Council of Roedean Sch., 1969–74; Mem. Council, London Zoological Soc., 1977– (Vice-Pres., 1979–); Chm., Royal Commn for the Exhibn of 1851, 1978–. FKC 1975. Coronation Medal, 1953. American Medal of Freedom (with bronze palm), 1946. CStJ 1974. *Address:* Manor Farm, Shalden, Alton, Hants. *T:* Alton 82383. *Clubs:* Brooks's, MCC.

WAYMOUTH, Charity, BSc (London), PhD (Aberdeen); Senior Staff Scientist, The Jackson Laboratory, Bar Harbor, Maine, 1963–81, now Emeritus; *b* 29 April 1915; *o d* of Charles Sydney Herbert Waymouth, Major, The Dorsetshire Regt, and Ada Curror Scott Dalgleish; unmarried. *Educ:* Royal School for Daughters of Officers of the Army, Bath; University of London; University of Aberdeen. Biochemist, City of Manchester General Hospitals, 1938–41; Research Fellow, University of Aberdeen, 1944; Beit Memorial Fellow for Medical Research, 1944–46; Member of scientific staff and head of tissue culture dept, Chester Beatty Research Institute for Cancer Research (University of London), 1947–52; British Empire Cancer Campaign-American Cancer Society Exchange Fellow, 1952–53; The Jackson Laboratory: Staff Scientist, 1952–63; Asst Dir (Training), 1969–72; Asst Dir (Research), 1976–77; Associate Dir (Scientific Affairs), 1977–80; Dir *ad interim*, 1980–81. Mem. Bd of Dirs, W. Alton Jones Cell Scis Center, 1979–82. Rose Morgan Vis. Prof., Univ. of Kansas, 1971. Member: Tissue Culture Association (President, 1960–62, Editor-in-Chief 1968–75; Mem. Council, 1980–); various British and American professional and learned societies. Hon. Life member and Hon. Director, Psora Society (Canada); Episcopal Church of the USA: Vice-Chm., Clergy Deployment Bd, 1971–79, and Exec. Council, 1967–70; Deputy, Gen. Convention, 1970, 1973, 1976, 1979, 1982; Member, Diocesan Council, Diocese of Maine, 1962–70, 1971–76; Chm., Cttee on the State of the Church, 1976–79. DD *hc* Gen. Theol Seminary, NY, 1979; Hon. ScD Bowdoin College, 1982. *Publications:* numerous papers in scientific journals, on nucleic acids and on tissue culture and cell nutrition. *Recreations:* reading, gardening. *Address:* 10 Atlantic Avenue, Bar Harbor, Maine 04609, USA. *T:* (207) 288-4008.

WAYNE, Sir Edward (Johnson), Kt 1964; MD, MSc, PhD, FRCP (London and Edinburgh); FRCP (Glasgow); Regius Professor of Practice of Medicine, Glasgow University, 1954–67; Physician to Western Infirmary, Glasgow; Hon. Physician to the Queen in Scotland, 1954–67; *b* 3 June 1902; *s* of late William Wayne, Leeds, Yorks, and late Ellen Rawding, Leadenham, Lincs; *m* 1932, Honora Nancy Halloran; one *s* one *d. Educ:* Leeds Univ. and Medical School (Akroyd Scholar and Sir Swire Smith Fellow); Manchester Univ. BSc Leeds (1st Class Hons Chemistry) 1923; MB, ChB (Leeds), 1st Class Hons, 1929; MD 1938; Hey Gold Medallist; Demonstrator in Physiology, University of Leeds, 1930–31; Assistant in Dept Clinical Research, University College Hospital, London, 1931–34; Professor of Pharmacology and Therapeutics, University of Sheffield, 1934–53 (formerly Physician to Royal Infirmary and Children's Hospital, Sheffield). Member Scottish Secretary of State's Advisory Cttee on Medical Research, 1958–67; Member of the Medical Research Council, 1958–62; Chairman, Clinical Research Board, 1960–64; Chairman, British Pharmacopœia Commn, 1958–63; Chairman, Advisory Cttee on Drug Dependence, 1967–69. Sims Commonwealth Travelling Professor, 1959. Bradshaw Lecturer, 1953; Lumleian Lecturer, RCP, 1959; Crookshank Lecturer and Medallist, Faculty of Radiol., 1966. Hon. DSc Sheffield, 1967. *Publications:* Papers in scientific and medical journals. *Address:* Lingwood Lodge, Lingwood, Norfolk NR13 4ES. *T:* Great Yarmouth 751370. *Club:* Athenæum.

WEARE, Trevor John, PhD; Director, Hydraulics Research Station, Department of the Environment, since 1981; *b* 31 Dec. 1943; *s* of Trevor Leslie Weare and Edna Margaret (*née* Roberts); *m* 1964, Margaret Ann Wright; two *s* two foster *d. Educ:* Aston Technical Coll.; Imperial College of Science and Technology (BSc Physics, PhD). Post-doctoral Research Fellow: Dept of Mathematical Physics, McGill Univ., Montreal, 1968–70; Dept of Theoretical Physics, Univ. of Oxford, 1970–72; Sen. Scientific Officer, Hydraulics Res. Station, 1972; Principal Scientific Officer, 1975; Sen. Principal Scientific Officer, Head of Estuaries Div., 1978. *Publications:* numerous contribs to scientific jls on theoretical High Energy Nuclear Physics, and on computational modelling in Civil Engineering Hydraulics; archaeological paper in Oxoniensia. *Recreations:* music, walking, archaeology. *Address:* 13 Blackstone Road, Wallingford, Oxon OX10 8JN. *T:* Wallingford 35759.

WEATHERALL, Prof. David John, MD, FRCP; FRS 1977; Nuffield Professor of Clinical Medicine, University of Oxford, since 1974; Fellow, Magdalen College, Oxford, since 1974; Hon. Director, Molecular Haematology Unit, Medical Research Council, since 1980; *b* 9 March 1933; *s* of Harry and Gwendoline Weatherall; *m* 1962, Stella Mayorga Nestler; one *s. Educ:* Calday Grange Grammar Sch.; Univ. of Liverpool. MB, ChB, MD, FRCP, FRCPath; MA Oxon 1974. Ho. Officer in Med. and Surg., United Liverpool Hosps, 1956–58; Captain, RAMC, Jun. Med. Specialist, BMH, Singapore, and BMH, Kamunting, Malaya, 1958–60; Research Fellow in Genetics, Johns Hopkins Hosp., Baltimore, USA, 1960–62; Sen. Med. Registrar, Liverpool Royal Infirmary, 1962–63; Research Fellow in Haematology, Johns Hopkins Hosp., 1963–65; Consultant, WHO, 1966–70; Univ. of Liverpool: Lectr in Med., 1965–66; Sen. Lectr in Med., 1966–69; Reader in Med., 1969–71; Prof. of Haematology, 1971–74; Consultant Physician, United Liverpool Hosps, 1966–74. Mem. Soc. of Scholars, and

Centennial Schol., Johns Hopkins Univ., 1976; Physician-in-Chief *pro tem.*, Peter Bent Brigham Hosp., Harvard Med. Sch., 1980. Pres., British Soc. for Haematology, 1980-. RSocMed Foundn Vis. Prof., 1981; Sims Commonwealth Vis. Prof., 1982; Phillip K. Bondy Prof., Yale, 1982; HM Queen Elizabeth the Queen Mother Fellow, Nuffield Prov. Hosps Trust, 1982. Watson Smith Lectr, RCP, 1974; Foundn Lectr, RCPath, 1979; Darwin Lectr, Eugenics Soc., 1979. Hon. Member: Assoc. of Physicians of GB and Ireland, 1968; Assoc. of Amer. Physicians, 1976. Ambuj Nath Bose Prize, RCP, 1980; Ballantyne Prize, RCPE, 1982; Stratton Prize, Internat. Soc. Haematology, 1982. *Publications:* The Thalassaemia Syndromes, 1965, 3rd edn 1981; Blood and its Disorders, 1973, 2nd edn 1981; (ed jtly) Oxford Textbook of Medicine, 1983; many papers on Abnormal Haemoglobin Synthesis and related disorders. *Recreations:* music, oriental food. *Address:* 8 Cumnor Rise Road, Cumnor Hill, Oxford. *T:* Oxford 862467.

WEATHERALL, Miles, MA, DM, DSc; FIBiol; consultant; Chairman of Council, Chelsea College, University of London, since 1970; *b* 14 Oct. 1920; *s* of Rev. J. H. and Mary Weatherall; *m* 1944, Josephine A. C. Ogston; three *d. Educ:* Dragon School and St Edward's School, Oxford; Oriel College, Oxford. BA, BSc 1941; BM 1943; MA 1945; DM 1951; DSc 1966. Open Schol. in Nat. Sci., Oriel Coll., 1938. Lecturer in Pharmacology, Edinburgh University, 1945; Head of Dept of Pharmacology, London Hosp. Med. Coll., 1949-66; Prof. of Pharmacology, Univ. of London, 1958-66; Wellcome Research Laboratories: Head, Therapeutic Res. Div., 1967-75; Dep. Dir, 1969-74; Dir of Estblt, 1974-79. Member: Adv. Cttee on Pesticides and other Toxic Chemicals, 1964-66; Council, Pharmaceutical Soc., 1966-70; Council, Roy. Soc. Med., 1972-82 (Hon. Sec. 1974-82); Comr, Medicines Commn, 1979-81. Hon. Lecturer: UCL, 1968-; KCL, 1979-. Mem. Cttee, Wine Soc., 1964-72. *Publications:* Statistics for Medical Students (jointly with L. Bernstein), 1952; Scientific Method, 1968; papers in scientific and medical journals. *Recreations:* writing, gardening, cooking. *Address:* Willows, Charlbury, Oxford OX7 3PX.

WEATHERHEAD, Alexander Stewart, TD 1964 and Bar 1973; solicitor; Partner in Tindal Oatts & Rodger, Solicitors, Glasgow, since 1960; *b* Edinburgh, 3 Aug. 1931; *er s* of Kenneth Kilpatrick Weatherhead and Katharine Weatherhead (*née* Stewart); *m* 1972, Harriett Foye, *d* of Rev. Dr Arthur Organ, Toronto, Canada; two *d. Educ:* Glasgow Acad.; Glasgow Univ. MA 1955, LLB 1958. Served in RA, 1950-52, 2nd Lieut, 1950. Solicitor, 1958; Mem. Council: Law Society of Scotland, 1971-; Soc. for Computers and Law, 1973- (Vice-Chm., 1973-82; Chm., 1982-); Mem., Royal Commn on Legal Services in Scotland, 1976-80. Trustee, Nat. Law Library Trust, 1979-. Joined TA, 1952; Lt-Col Comdg 277 (A&SH) Field Regt, RA (TA), 1965-67; The Lowland Regt (RA(T)), 1967 and Glasgow & Strathclyde Univs OTC, 1970-73; Col 1974; TAVR Col Lowlands (West), 1974-76; ADC (TAVR) to the Queen, 1977-81; Hon. Col, Glasgow and Strathclyde Univs OTC, 1982-. *Recreations:* sailing, reading, music. *Address:* 52 Partickhill Road, Glasgow G11 5AB. *T:* 041-334 6277. *Clubs:* Western, Royal Scottish Automobile (Glasgow); New (Edinburgh); Royal Highland Yacht (Oban); Royal Western Yacht (Hon. Sec., 1981-), Clyde Cruising (Glasgow).

WEATHERHEAD, Sir Arthur (Trenham), Kt 1960; CMG 1957; *b* 19 May 1905; *s* of late Canon A. S. Weatherhead; *m* 1938, Sylvia Mary, *d* of late A. Lace, Eastbourne; one *s* two *d. Educ:* St Bees School; Queen's College, Oxford. Sudan Plantations Syndicate, 1927; Colonial Administrative Service, Nigeria, 1930-60. Dep. Governor, Northern Region, Nigeria, 1958-60, retired. *Recreations:* gardening, chess. *Address:* Wood Rise, Amberley, Stroud, Glos. *T:* Amberley 2584.

WEATHERILL, Rt. Hon. (Bruce) Bernard, PC 1980; MP (C) Croydon North-East since 1964; Chairman of Ways and Means and Deputy Speaker, since 1979; *b* 25 Nov. 1920; *s* of late Bernard Weatherill, Spring Hill, Guildford, and Annie Gertrude (*née* Creak); *m* 1949, Lyn, *d* of late H. T. Eatwell; two *s* one *d. Educ:* Malvern College. Served War of 1939-45; commissioned 4/7th Royal Dragoon Guards, 1940; transferred to Indian Army, 1941 and served with 19th King George V's Own Lancers, 1941-45 (Captain). Man. Dir, Bernard Weatherill Ltd, 1957-70. First Chm., Guildford Young Conservatives, 1946-49; Chm., Guildford Cons. Assoc., 1959-63; Vice-Chm., SE Area Prov. Council, 1962-64; Member National Union of Cons. Party, 1963-64. An Opposition Whip, 1967; a Lord Comr of HM Treasury, 1970-71; Vice-Chamberlain, HM Household, 1971-72; Comptroller of HM Household, 1972-73; Treasurer of HM Household and Dep. Chief Govt Whip, 1973-74; Opposition Dep. Chief Whip, 1974-79. Freeman of City of London. *Recreations:* golf, tennis. *Address:* 98 Lupus Street, SW1. *T:* 01-828 6040.

WEATHERLEY, Prof. Paul Egerton, FRS 1973; Regius Professor of Botany in the University of Aberdeen, 1959-81, now Emeritus; *b* 6 May 1917; *o s* of late Leonard Roger Weatherley and late Ethel Maude (*née* Collin), Leicester; *m* 1942, Margaret Logan, *o d* of late John Pirie, JP, Castle of Auchry, Aberdeenshire; one *s* three *d. Educ:* Wyggeston School; Keble College (Open Schol.), Oxford. Final Sch. of Nat. Sci. (Hons Botany) 1939; Keble Research Schol., 1939-40, elected to Colonial Agric. Schol., 1940. Trained in RE, then Colonial Office cadet at Imperial Coll. of Tropical Agric. Trinidad, 1940-42. Govt Botanist in Dept of Agriculture, Uganda Protectorate, 1942-47; Asst Lectr, Univ. of Manchester, 1947-49; Lecturer in Botany, 1949-59 (Sen. Lectr 1956), Univ. of Nottingham. *Publications:* papers in (mainly) botanical

journals. *Recreations:* music, sketching. *Address:* Greystones, Torphins, Aberdeenshire AB3 4HP.

WEAVER, Sir Tobias Rushton, (Sir Toby Weaver), Kt 1973; CB 1962; *b* 19 July 1911; *s* of late Sir Lawrence Weaver, KBE, and late Lady Weaver (*née* Kathleen Purcell); *m* 1941, Marjorie, *d* of Rt Hon. Sir Charles Trevelyan, 3rd Bt, PC; one *s* three *d. Educ:* Clifton College; Corpus Christi College, Cambridge. Bank clerk, Toronto, 1932; teaching at Barking, 1935, Eton, 1936; Asst Director of Education: Wilts CC 1936, Essex CC 1939. Admiralty, 1941; War Office, 1942; Dept of Education and Science, 1946-73; Under-Secretary, 1956; Deputy Secretary, 1962. Visiting Professor of Education: Univ. of Southampton, 1973; Univ. of London Inst. of Educn, 1974; Open Univ., 1976-78. *Address:* 14 Marston Close, NW6. *T:* 01-624 4263.

WEBB, Anthony Michael Francis, CMG 1963; QC (Kenya) 1961; JP; a Chairman of Industrial Tribunals, since 1978; *b* 27 Dec. 1914; *s* of late Sir (Ambrose) Henry Webb; *m* 1948, Diana Mary, *e d* of late Capt. Graham Farley, Indian Army, and Mrs Herbert Browne (*née* Pyper); one *s* one *d. Educ:* Ampleforth; Magdalen Coll., Oxford (MA). Barrister-at-Law, Gray's Inn, 1939. Served War, 1939-46, Maj. GSO2, The Queen's Bays. Colonial Legal Service (HMOCS), 1947-64 (Malaya; Kenya; MLC 1958-63; Attorney-General and Minister for Legal Affairs, 1961-63); Sec., Nat. Adv. Council on Trng of Magistrates, and Trng Officer, 1964-73, Dep. Sec. of Commns, 1969-75, Head of Court Business, 1975-77, Lord Chancellor's Office; retd 1977. Member of Council of Kenya Lawn Tennis Association, 1957-63. JP, Kent, 1966. *Publication:* The Natzweiler Trial (ed). *Address:* Yew Tree Cottage, Speldhurst Road, Langton Green, Tunbridge Wells, Kent TN3 0JH. *T:* Langton 2779. *Club:* Special Forces.

WEBB, Rear-Adm. Arthur Brooke, CB 1975; retired; *b* 13 June 1918; *2nd s* of late Captain A. B. H. Webb and Mrs G. Webb; *m* 1949, Rachel Marian Gerrish; three *d. Educ:* St John's Coll., Southsea, Hants. Joined Royal Navy, 1936; served in Alexandria, 1939-42, HMS Howe, 1942-46, Egypt, 1946-48. Secretary: to Deputy Chief of Naval Personnel, (Manpower) Admiralty, 1951-53; to Flag Officer Germany, 1953-55; to Director of Naval Intell., 1955-58; HM Ships: Belfast, 1958-60; Hermes, 1962-64. Staff of Chief of Defence Staff, 1964-67; Chief Staff Officer (Administration) to Fleet Commander, Far East Fleet, 1967-69, and Flag Officer Plymouth, 1970-72; Flag Officer, Admiralty Interview Bd, 1973-75. Comdr 1954, Captain 1963, Rear-Adm. 1973. *Recreations:* DIY, gardening, camping, walking, sailing. *Address:* Sorrel Cottage, Burrell Way, Balsham, Cambridge CB1 6DY. *T:* West Wratting 810.

WEBB, Douglas Edward, CVO 1961; OBE 1947; Deputy Commissioner of Police of the Metropolis, 1961-66; retired; *b* 8 Oct. 1909; *yr s* of late Supt O. C. Webb, KPM, Metropolitan Police; *m* 1935, Mary McMillan, *yr d* of late Capt. J. S. Learmont, Trinity House; one *s* (one *d* decd). *Educ:* Bordon Grammar School; Devonport High School. Joined Metropolitan Police, 1929; Metropolitan Police Coll., Hendon, 1935-36 (Baton of Honour). Allied Commission, Italy and Austria, 1945-47. Chief Supt, Bow Street, 1952-53, West End Central, 1953-54; Dep. Commander, New Scotland Yard, 1954-55; Commander, No 3 District (E London), 1955-57; Asst Commissioner (Traffic), 1957-58; Assistant Commissioner, Administration and Operations (originated Special Patrol Gp), New Scotland Yard, Dec. 1958-61. Officer, Legion of Honour, 1961; Order of Merit, Chile, 1965. *Address:* Tanglewood, 5 Deer Park Close, Tavistock, Devon PL19 9HE. *T:* Tavistock 2377.

WEBB, Prof. Edwin Clifford; Vice-Chancellor, Macquarie University, since 1976; *b* 21 May 1921; *s* of William Webb and Nellie Webb; *m* 1942, Violet Sheila Joan (*née* Tucker); one *s* four *d* (and one *s* decd). *Educ:* Poole Grammar Sch.; Cambridge Univ. (BA, MA, PhD). FRACI 1968. Cambridge University: Beit Meml Res. Fellow, 1944-46; Univ. Demonstrator in Biochem., 1946-50; Univ. Lectr in Biochem., 1950-62; University of Queensland: Foundn Prof. of Biochem. and Head of Dept, 1962-70, now Emeritus Prof.; Dep. Vice-Chancellor (Academic), 1970-76. Hon. DSc Queensland, 1978. *Publications:* Enzymes, 1959, 3rd edn 1979; 56 scientific papers. *Recreations:* photography, music, motoring, coin collecting. *Address:* 3 Norfolk Street, Killara, Sydney, NSW 2071, Australia. *T:* Sydney 4981369.

WEBB, George Hannam, OBE 1974; HM Diplomatic Service; *b* 24 Dec. 1929; *s* of late George Ernest Webb, HM Colonial Service, Kenya, and Mary Hannam Webb (*née* Stephens); *m* 1956, Josephine, *d* of Richard Chatterton, Horncastle, Lincs; two *s* two *d. Educ:* Malvern Coll.; King's Coll., Cambridge (MA). Served 14/20th King's Hussars, 1948-49; Parachute Regt (TA), 1950-53. Joined Colonial Administrative Service, Kenya, 1953: District Officer, Central Nyanza, 1954-56; N Nyanza, 1956-57; District Commissioner, Moyale, 1958-60; MoD, Nairobi, 1960-62; joined Foreign Service, 1963: First Sec., Bangkok, 1964-67; FCO, 1967-69; Accra, 1969-73; FCO, 1973-77; Counsellor, Tehran, 1977-79, Washington, 1980-82. *Recreations:* books, mountains, travel; Hon. Editor, the *Kipling Journal*, succeeding Roger Lancelyn Green, 1980-. *Address:* c/o Foreign and Commonwealth Office, SW1A 2AH. *Clubs:* Travellers', Royal Commonwealth Society.

WEBB, James, CB 1978; Commissioner of Inland Revenue, 1968-78; *b* 11 Nov. 1918; *2nd s* of late James Webb and late Lucy Webb (*née* McGorrin); *m* 1957, Kathleen Veronica, *3rd d* of late Catherine Downey (*née* McDaid) and of late James Downey, Londonderry. *Educ:* St Francis Xavier's, Liverpool; King's Coll., London Univ. (LLB 1940, 1st Cl. Hons). Entered Inland Revenue Dept (Estate Duty Office), 1937. Served War of 1939-45: W Africa, India and Burma; HM Forces, South Lancashire Regt, 1940; Sandhurst, 1942; Nigeria Regt, 1942-45 (Temp. Major, 1945). Assistant Principal Inland Revenue, 1947; Principal Establishment Officer and Dir of Personnel, 1971-75. *Address:* 3 Avondale Avenue, Hinchley Wood, Esher, Surrey. *T:* 01-398 6330.

WEBB, Prof. John Stuart, FEng; Professor of Applied Geochemistry in the University of London, 1961-79, now Emeritus, and Senior Research Fellow, since 1979, Imperial College of Science and Technology; *b* 28 Aug. 1920; *s* of Stuart George Webb and Caroline Rabjohns Webb (*née* Pengelly); *m* 1946, Jean Millicent Dyer; one *s. Educ:* Westminster City School; Royal School of Mines, Imperial College of Science and Technology, BSc, ARSM, 1941. Served War of 1939-45, Royal Engineers, 1941-43. Geological Survey of Nigeria, 1943-44; Royal School of Mines, Imperial Coll., 1945-; Beit Scientific Research Fellow, 1945-47; PhD, DIC, in Mining Geology, 1947; Lecturer in Mining Geology, 1947-55; Reader in Applied Geochemistry, 1955-61. DSc, 1967. Mem., Home Office Forensic Science Cttee, 1969-75. Mem. Council, Instn of Mining and Metallurgy, 1964-71, and 1974-83, Vice Pres., 1971-73, Pres., 1973-74; Mem. Bd, Council Engineering Instns, 1973-74; Reg. Vice-Pres. (Europe), Soc. of Econ. Geologists, USA, 1979-81. Hon. Sec., Rowhook Medical Soc., 1975-; Hon. Mem., Assoc. Exploration Geochemists, USA, 1977; Hon. FIMM 1980. Consolidated Goldfields of SA Gold Medal, IMM, 1953; William Smith Medal, Geol. Soc. of London, 1981. *Publications:* (with H. E. Hawkes) Geochemistry in Mineral Exploration, 1962, 2nd edn (with A. W. Rose) 1979; (jtly) Geochemical Atlas of Northern Ireland, 1973; (jtly) Wolfson Geochemical Atlas of England and Wales, 1978; contrib. to scientific and technical jls. *Recreations:* fishing, amateur radio. *Address:* Stone Cottage, Lyons Road, Slinfold, Horsham, Sussex RH13 7QT. *T:* Slinfold 790243.

WEBB, John Victor Duncombe; Principal Clerk, Judicial Office, House of Lords, and Fourth Clerk at the Table (Judicial), since Aug. 1977; *b* 8 Nov. 1930; *s* of late John Arthur Webb and Idena Ann (*née* Kenroy); *m* 1st, 1960, Elizabeth Mary Cann (marr. diss.); one *d* ; 2nd, 1972, Elizabeth Ann McKee. *Educ:* Tonbridge Sch.; Wadham Coll., Oxford (Exhibnr; MA). Called to Bar, Lincoln's Inn (Cholmeley Scholar), 1955. Joined Parliament Office, House of Lords, 1958; Clerk, 1958-63; Chief Clerk, Cttee and Private Bill Office, 1963-71; Chief Clerk, Public Bill Office, 1971-77. *Publications:* Consolidation and Statute Law Revision (with Rt Hon. Lord Simon of Glaisdale) (in Public Law, 1975). *Recreations:* riding, walking. *Address:* 54a Onslow Square, SW7 3NX. *T:* 01-589 7688; 10 West Street, Aldbourne, Marlborough, Wilts. *T:* Marlborough 40270.

WEBB, Prof. Joseph Ernest, PhD (London) 1944, DSc (London) 1949; FIBiol; Professor of Zoology, 1960-80, and Vice-Principal, 1976-80, Westfield College, University of London, now Emeritus Professor; *b* 22 March 1915; *s* of Joseph Webb and Constance Inman Webb (*née* Hickox); *m* 1940, Gwenlilian Clara Coldwell; three *s. Educ:* Rutlish School; Birkbeck College, London. Research Entomologist and Parasitologist at The Cooper Technical Animals, 1939; Berkhampsted, Herts, 1940-46; Lecturer, Univ. of Aberdeen, 1946-48; Senior Lecturer, 1948-50, Professor of Zoology, 1950-60, University Coll., Ibadan, Nigeria. FIBiol. *Publications:* (jointly): Guide to Invertebrate Animals, 1975, 2nd edn 1978; Guide to Living Mammals, 1977, 2nd edn 1979; Guide to Living Reptiles, 1978; Guide to Living Birds, 1979; Guide to Living Fishes, 1981; Guide to Living Amphibians, 1981; various on insect physiology, insecticides, systematics, populations, tropical ecology and marine biology. *Recreations:* art, music, photography. *Address:* 43 Hill Top, NW11. *T:* 01-458 2571. *Club:* Athenæum.

WEBB, Kaye, MBE 1974; Director, Penguin Books Ltd; Chairman and Founder of Puffin Club (for children); Director, Unicorn Children's Theatre; Managing Director, Kaye Webb Ltd; *d* of Arthur Webb and Kathleen Stevens, journalists; *m* 1st, Christopher Brierley; 2nd, Andrew Hunter; 3rd, 1948, Ronald Searle, *qv* ; one *s* one *d.* Entered journalism via Picturegoer, 1931; joined Picture Post, 1938; Asst Editor, Lilliput, 1941-47; Theatre Corresp., The Leader, 1947-49; Feature Writer, News Chronicle, 1949-55; Editor of children's magazine Elizabethan, 1955-58; Theatre Critic to National Review, 1957-58; Children's Editor, Puffin Books, and Publishing Dir, Children's Div., Penguin Books Ltd, 1961-79; Editor, Puffin Post, 1967-. Children's Advisor, Goldcrest TV; Advisor, Internat. Centre for Child Studies; Mem. Exec. Cttee, PEN Club. Eleanor Farjeon Award for services to Children's Literature, 1969. *Publications:* (ed) C. Fry: Experience of Critics; (ed) Penguin Patrick Campbell; (ed) The Friday Miracle; (ed) The St Trinian's Story; (with Ronald Searle): Looking at London; Paris Sketchbook; Refugees 1960; (with Treld Bicknell) 1st and 2nd Puffin Annuals; Puffins Pleasure; I Like this Poem, 1979. *Recreations:* children and their interests, theatre, films. *Address:* 8 Lampard House, Maida Avenue, W2. *T:* 01-262 4695. *Clubs:* National Liberal, Puffin.

WEBB, Maysie (Florence), CBE 1979; BSc; Deputy Director, British Museum, since 1979 (Assistant Director 1968-71); *b* 1 May 1923; *d* of Charles and Florence Webb. *Educ:* Kingsbury County School; Northern Polytechnic. Southwark Public Libraries, 1940-45; A. C. Cossor Ltd, 1945-50; British Non-Ferrous Metals Research Assoc., 1950-52; Mullard Equipment Ltd, 1952-55; Morgan Crucible Co. Ltd, 1955-60; Patent Office Library, 1960-66;

Keeper, National Reference Library of Science and Invention, 1966-68. General Comr in England and Wales, 1976-. Mem. Council, RSA, 1971-76, 1978- (Chm., Membership Cttee, 1974-76, 1980-); Manager, Royal Instn, 1975-78. *Recreations:* family and friends, country life. *Address:* British Museum, Bloomsbury, WC1.

WEBB, Pauline Mary, AKC; Organiser, Religious Broadcasting, BBC World Service, since 1979; author; *b* 28 June 1927; *d* of Rev. Leonard F. Webb. *Educ:* King's Coll., London Univ. (BA, AKC); Union Theological Seminary, New York (STM). BA English Hons (King's), 1948; Teacher's Diploma, London Inst. of Educn, 1949. Asst Mistress, Thames Valley Grammar Sch., 1949-52; Editor, Methodist Missionary Soc., 1955-66; Vice-Pres., Methodist Conf., 1965-66; Dir, Lay Training, Methodist Church, 1967-73; Area Sec., Methodist Missionary Soc., 1973-79; Chm., Community and Race Relns Unit, BCC, 1976-79. Vice-Chm., Central Cttee, WCC, 1968-75. *Publications:* Women of Our Company, 1958; Women of Our Time, 1960; Operation-Healing, 1964; All God's Children, 1964; Are We Yet Alive?, 1966; Agenda for the Churches, 1968; Salvation Today, 1974; Eventful Worship, 1975; Where are the Women?, 1979. *Address:* Bush House, PO Box 76, Aldwych, WC2. *T:* 01-240 3456. *Club:* University Women's.

WEBB, Lt-Gen. Sir Richard (James Holden), KBE 1974 (CBE 1970, MBE 1952); CB 1972; Chairman, Local Government Commission, since 1978; *b* 21 Dec. 1919; *s* of late George Robert Holden Webb and Jessie Muriel Hair; *m* 1950, Barbara, *d* of Richard Griffin; one *s* one *d. Educ:* Nelson Coll., NZ; Royal Military Coll., Duntroon (Aust.); Staff Coll., Haifa; US Artillery School, Oklahoma; Joint Services Staff Coll., Latimer; Imperial Defence Coll. Commissioned NZ Army 1941. Served War, with Divisional Artillery, 2nd NZ Expeditionary Force, in Middle East and Italy, 1942-45, and Korea, 1950-51 (despatches twice). Quartermaster-Gen., NZ Army, 1967; Dep. Chief of Gen. Staff, NZ Army, 1969-70; Chief of Gen. Staff, NZ Army, 1970-71; Chief of Defence Staff, NZ, 1971-76. Comdr, Legion of Merit (US), 1971. *Recreation:* golf. *Address:* Pahangahanga, Waimate North, RD1 Ohaeawai, Bay of Islands, New Zealand. *Club:* Wellington (Wellington, NZ).

WEBB, Stella Dorothea; *see* Gibbons, S. D.

WEBB, Sir Thomas (Langley), Kt 1975; *b* 25 April 1908; *s* of Robert Langley Webb and Alice Mary Webb; *m* 1942, Jeannette Alison Lang; one *s* one *d. Educ:* Melbourne Church of England Grammar Sch. Joined Huddart Parker Ltd, 1926 (Man. Dir, 1955-61). Served War, AIF, 1940-45. Dir, Commercial Bank of Aust., 1960-78 (Chm., 1970-78); Director: Alliance Oil Development NL (Chm.); Bulkships Pty Ltd; Email Ltd; McIlwraith McEacharn Ltd (Vice-Chm.); Metals Exploration Ltd (Chm.); Trustees Executors & Agency Co. Ltd. Vice-Pres., Royal Victorian Eye and Ear Hosp. *Recreations:* golf, tennis. *Address:* 6 Yarradale Road, Toorak, Victoria 3142, Australia. *T:* Melbourne 2415259. *Clubs:* Australian, Melbourne, Royal Melbourne Golf, Royal South Yarra Tennis (all Melbourne).

WEBBER; *see* Lloyd Webber.

WEBBER, Fernley Douglas, CMG 1959; MC 1942; TD 1954; HM Diplomatic Service, retired; Secretary, Committee for Environmental Conservation, 1975-77; *b* 12 March 1918; *s* of Herbert Webber; *m* 1947, Veronica Elizabeth Ann, *d* of Major F. B. Richards, MC; two *s* two *d. Educ:* Cotham School, Bristol; Jesus College, Cambridge. Entered Colonial Office after open competition, 1939; Diplomatic Service, 1965. Served War of 1939-45, Burma, 1940-45; Comd 624 LAA Regt RA (RF) TA, 1952-54, Bt-Col, 1954. Principal, CO, 1946; Asst Sec. 1950; Establishment Officer, 1952-58; Head of E Af. Dept, 1958-63; idc 1964; Deputy High Commissioner in Eastern Malaysia during part of 1965; High Commissioner in Brunei, 1965-67; Minister, British High Commn in Canberra, 1967-68; FCO, 1969-70. *Address:* 6 Mills Lane, Bridge Corner, Long Melford, Suffolk. *Club:* Royal Commonwealth Society.

WEBBER, Lt-Col G. S. I.; *see* Incledon-Webber.

WEBBER, Roy Seymour, IPFA, FCCA; Town Clerk and Chief Executive, Royal Borough of Kensington and Chelsea, since 1979; *b* 8 April 1933; *s* of A. E. and A. M. Webber; *m* 1960, Barbara Ann (*née* Harries); one *s* three *d. Educ:* Ipswich School. Ipswich CBC, 1949-55; Coventry CBC, 1955-58; St Pancras BC, 1958-61; IBM (UK) Ltd, 1961-62; Woolwich BC, 1962-65; Greenwich LBC, 1965-68; Royal Borough of Kensington and Chelsea: Dep. Borough Treasurer, 1968-73; Director of Finance, 1973-79. *Recreations:* tennis, walking. *Address:* Woodland Cottage, Chelsfield Lane, Orpington, Kent BR6 7RP. *T:* Orpington 20935.

WEBER, (Edmund) Derek (Craig); editorial consultant; *b* 29 April 1921; 3rd *s* of late R. J. C. and of B. M. Weber; *m* 1953, Molly Patricia, *d* of the late R. O. and Ellen Podger; one *s* four *d. Educ:* Bristol Grammar School. Journalist on newspapers in Swindon, Bristol and Bath, and on magazines in London from 1937 until 1953, except for War Service in RAF, 1940-46. The Geographical Magazine: Art Editor, 1953; Assoc. Editor, 1965; Editor, 1967-81. Hon. Life Member: IBG, 1981; NUJ, 1981. Hon. FRGS 1980. Hon. MA Open, 1982. *Address:* 32 London Road, Maldon, Essex CM9 6HE. *T:* Maldon 52871. *Clubs:* Savage, Geographical.

WEBSTER, Very Rev. Alan Brunskill; Dean of St Paul's, since 1978; *b* 1918; *s* of Reverend J. Webster; *m* 1951, M. C. F. Falconer; two *s* two *d. Educ:* Shrewsbury School; Queen's College, Oxford. MA, BD. Ordained, 1942; Curate of Attercliffe Parishes, Sheffield, 1942; Curate of St Paul's, Arbourthorne, Sheffield, 1944; Westcott House, 1946; Vicar of Barnard Castle, 1953; Warden, Lincoln Theol Coll., 1959-70; Dean of Norwich, 1970-78. *Publications:* Joshua Watson, 1954; Broken Bones May Joy, 1968; Julian of Norwich, 1974. Contributor to The Historic Episcopate, 1954; Living the Faith, 1980. *Recreation:* writing. *Address:* The Deanery, 9 Amen Court, EC4M 7BU. *T:* 01-236 2827.

WEBSTER, Brian Mackenzie; Head of Defence Secretariat 8, Ministry of Defence, since 1982; *b* 25 Jan. 1938; *s* of Donald E. Webster and Muriel Webster; *m* 1967, Gillian Welland; one *s* two *d. Educ:* Durham Sch., Durham; St John's Coll., Cambridge (MA). Called to the Bar, Gray's Inn, 1965. Royal Air Force, 1956-58; Thos R. Miller and Son Ltd, Mutual Insurance, 1961-66; Ministry of Defence, 1966-71; Cabinet Office, 1971; Private Sec. to Secretary of the Cabinet, 1973; Northern Ireland Office, Belfast, 1974; Head of Internat. Procurement Policy Div., MoD, 1976; Counsellor, Defence Supply, Washington, 1979. *Recreations:* running, nineteenth century history. *Address:* Defence Secretariat, Ministry of Defence, Main Building, Whitehall, SW1.

WEBSTER, Maj.-Gen. Bryan Courtney, CBE 1981; Director of Army Quartering, since 1982; *b* 2 Feb. 1931; *s* of Captain H. J. Webster, Royal Fusiliers (killed in action, 1940) and late M. J. Webster; *m* 1957, Elizabeth Rowland Waldron Smithers, *d* of Prof. Sir David Smithers, *qv*; two *s* one *d. Educ:* Haileybury College; RMA Sandhurst. Commissioned Royal Fusiliers, 1951; ADC to GOC, 16 Airborne Div., 1953-55; served Korea, Egypt, Malta, Gibraltar, Hong Kong; Directing Staff, Staff Coll., 1969-70; Comd 1st Bn Royal Regt of Fusiliers, 1971-73; Comd 8th Inf. Brigade, 1975-77; Dep. Col, Royal Regt of Fusiliers (City of London), 1976; Nat. Defence Coll., India, 1979; Staff appts, Far East, MoD, incl. Dir of Admin Planning (Army), 1980-82. FBIM. *Recreations:* ornithology, shooting. *Address:* c/o Midland Bank, 69 High Street, Sevenoaks, Kent TN13 1LB. *Club:* Army and Navy.

WEBSTER, Charles, DSc; FBA 1982; University Reader in the History of Medicine, University of Oxford, since 1972; Director, Wellcome Unit for the History of Medicine, since 1972; Fellow of Corpus Christi College, Oxford, since 1972. *Publications:* The Great Instauration, 1975; From Paracelsus to Newton, 1982. *Address:* Wellcome Unit for the History of Medicine, 47 Banbury Road, Oxford OX2 6PE. *T:* Oxford 511730.

WEBSTER, Dr Cyril Charles, CMG 1966; Chief Scientific Officer, Agricultural Research Council, 1971-75 (Scientific Adviser, 1965-71); *b* 28 Dec. 1909; *s* of Ernest Webster; *m* 1947, Mary, *d* of H. R. Wimhurst; one *s* one *d. Educ:* Beckenham County Sch.; Wye Coll.; Selwyn Coll., Cambridge; Imperial Coll. of Tropical Agriculture, Trinidad. Colonial Agricultural Service, 1936-57: Nigeria, 1936-38; Nyasaland, 1938-50; Kenya (Chief Research Officer), 1950-55; Malaya (Dep. Dir of Agriculture), 1956-57; Prof. of Agriculture, Imperial Coll. of Tropical Agriculture, Univ. of W Indies, 1957-60; Dir, Rubber Research Inst. of Malaya, 1961-65; Dir-Gen., Palm Oil Research Inst. of Malaya, 1978-80. JMN, 1965. *Publications:* (with P. N. Wilson) Agriculture in the Tropics, 1966; scientific papers in agricultural jls. *Address:* 5 Shenden Way, Sevenoaks, Kent. *T:* Sevenoaks 453984.

WEBSTER, David; Director, United States, BBC, since 1981; Member of the Board of Management of the BBC, since 1977; *b* 11 Jan. 1931; *s* of Alec Webster and Clare Webster; *m* 1st, 1955, Lucy Law (marr. diss.), Princeton, NJ; two *s*; 2nd, 1981, Elizabeth Drew, author, Washington, DC. *Educ:* Taunton Sch.; Ruskin Coll., Oxford. British Broadcasting Corporation: Sub-Editor, External Services News Dept, 1953-59; Producer, Panorama, 1959-64; Exec. Producer, Enquiry, and Encounter, BBC-2, 1964-66; Dep. Editor, Panorama, 1966, Editor, 1967-69; Exec. Editor, Current Affairs Group, 1969, Asst Head, 1970; BBC Rep. in USA, 1971-76; Controller, Information Services, 1976-77; Dir, Public Affairs, 1977-80. Mem., Twentieth Century Fund Task Force on the Flow of the News, 1978-. Mem. Adv. Council, Ditchley Foundn of US, 1981-. Fellow, Internat. Council, National Acad. of Television Arts and Sciences, USA, 1980- (Chm., Internat. Council, 1974 and 1975). *Recreation:* coarse tennis. *Address:* BBC, 630 5th Avenue, New York, NY 10111, USA. *Clubs:* Savile; Century Association (NY). *See also* S. H. E. Kitzinger.

WEBSTER, David MacLaren, QC 1980; a Recorder of the Crown Court, since 1979; *b* 21 Dec. 1937; *s* of John MacLaren Webster and Winning McGregor Webster (*née* Rough); *m* 1964, Frances Sally McLaren, RE; three *s. Educ:* Hutchesons', Glasgow; Christ Church, Oxford (MA (Eng Lang and Lit)); Conservatoire d'Art Dramatique and Sorbonne (French Govt Schol. 1960-61). Radio and television work in drama and current affairs, Scotland, 1949-64; called to the Bar, Gray's Inn, 1964; joined Western Circuit; Member: Bar Council, 1972-74; Senate of Inns of Court and Bar, 1974-79, 1982- (Senate Representative, Commonwealth Law Conf., Edinburgh, 1977); Mem., Matrimonial Causes Rules Cttee, 1976-79; a Deputy Circuit Judge, 1976-79. Chm., Bar Theatrical Soc., 1976-; Mem., Western Circuit Univs Liaison Cttee, 1978-. Gold Medal, LAMDA, 1954; LRAM 1955. President, Oxford Univ. Experimental Theatre Club, 1958-59; Secretary, Mermaid's, 1958.

Recreations: theatre, sailing, cricket, Scottish literature. *Address:* 3 Pump Court, Temple, EC4. *T:* 01-353 0711. *Clubs:* Garrick, MCC, Bar Yacht; Hampshire.

WEBSTER, Derek Adrian, CBE 1979; Chairman and Editorial Director, Daily Record and Sunday Mail Ltd, since 1974; Member, Press Council, since 1981, Joint Vice-Chairman, since 1982; *b* 24 March 1927; *s* of James Tulloch Webster and Isobel Webster; *m* 1966, Dorothy Frances Johnson; two *s* one *d. Educ:* St Peter's, Bournemouth. Served RN, 1944-48. Reporter, Western Morning News, 1943; Staff Journalist, Daily Mail, 1949-51; joined Mirror Group, 1952; Northern Editor, Daily Mirror, 1964-67; Editor, Daily Record, 1967-72; Dir, Mirror Gp Newspapers, 1974-. Vice-Chm., Age Concern (Scotland), 1977-; Hon. Vice-Pres., Newspaper Press Fund. *Recreations:* boating, gardening. *Address:* Gateside, Blanefield, by Glasgow. *T:* Blanefield 70252. *Club:* Oil (Glasgow).

WEBSTER, Rev. Canon Douglas, MA, DD; Canon Residentiary of St Paul's Cathedral since 1969; Precentor, 1969-82, Chancellor since 1982; *b* 15 April 1920; *s* of Robert and Annie Webster; unmarried. *Educ:* Dulwich Coll.; St Peter's Coll., Oxford; Wycliffe Hall, Oxford. BA 1942, MA 1946. Curate: St Helens Parish Church, Lancs, 1943-46; Christ Church, Crouch End, London, 1946-47; Lectr, London Coll. of Divinity, 1947-52; Educn Sec., CMS, 1953-61; Theologian-Missioner, CMS, 1961-65; Chavasse Lectr in World Mission, Wycliffe Hall, Oxford, 1963-65; Prof. of Mission, Selly Oak Colls, Birmingham, 1966-69. Hon. Canon of Chelmsford, 1963-69; Exam. Chap. to Bp of Chelmsford, 1962-. Chm., Council of Christians and Jews, 1978-. Mem. Court, Worshipful Co. of Cutlers, Master 1974-76. Vis. Prof., Wycliffe Coll., Toronto, 1981. Lectures: Godfrey Day, Dublin, 1967; Moorhouse, Melbourne, 1969. Hon. DD Wycliffe Coll., Toronto, 1967. Sub-Chaplain 1977, Chaplain 1981, Order of St John of Jerusalem. Queen's Jubilee Medal, 1977. *Publications:* In Debt to Christ, 1957; What is Evangelism?, 1959; Local Church and World Mission, 1962; Pentecostalism and Speaking with Tongues, 1964; Unchanging Mission, 1965; Yes to Mission, 1966; Not Ashamed, 1970; Good News from John, 1974; contribs. to: Charles Simeon, Bicentenary Essays, 1959; The Parish Communion Today, 1962; Lambeth Essays on Ministry, 1968. *Recreations:* walking, gardening, music. *Address:* 1 Amen Court, EC4. *T:* 01-248 1817; The Moat House, Weston-sub-Edge, Chipping Campden, Glos. *T:* Evesham 840695. *Clubs:* United Oxford & Cambridge University, Royal Commonwealth Society.

WEBSTER, Henry George, CBE 1974; FSAE; Group Engineering Director, Automotive Products, since 1974; *b* Coventry, 27 May 1917; *s* of William George Webster; *m* 1943, Margaret, *d* of H. C. Sharp; one *d. Educ:* Welshpool County Sch.; Coventry Technical Coll. Standard Motor Co. Ltd: apprenticed, 1932; Asst Technl Engr, 1938-40; Dep. Chief Inspector, 1940-46; Asst Technl Engr, 1946-48; Chief Chassis Engr, 1948-55; Chief Engr, 1955-57; Dir and Chief Engr, Standard-Triumph Internat., 1957-68; Technical Dir, Austin Morris Div., British Leyland UK Ltd, 1968-74. Joined original Instn of Automobile Engrs, as a grad., 1937 (Sec. of Grad. Section, Coventry Br. of Instn, 1941-45); transf. to Associate Mem., 1946, Mem., 1964. MSAE, 1958; FSAE, 1976; FRSA. Freeman, City of Coventry. *Recreation:* golf. *Address:* The Old School House, Barrowfield Lane, Kenilworth, Warwickshire CV8 1EP. *T:* Kenilworth 53363.

WEBSTER, Ian Stevenson; His Honour Judge Webster; a Circuit Judge, since 1981; *b* 20 March 1925; *s* of late Harvey Webster and late Annabella Stevenson Webster (*née* McBain); *m* 1951, Margaret (*née* Sharples); two *s. Educ:* Rochdale Grammar Sch.; Manchester Univ. Sub. Lieut (A), RNVR, 1944. Called to the Bar, Middle Temple, 1948. Asst Recorder: of Oldham, 1970; of Salford, 1971; a Recorder of the Crown Court, 1972-76, 1981; Chm., Industrial Tribunals for Manchester, 1976-81. *Recreations:* golf, sailing. *Address:* Courts of Justice, Manchester. *T:* 061-832 8393; Moorside Cottage, 154 Syke Road, Rochdale, Lancs.

WEBSTER, John Alexander R.; *see* Riddell-Webster.

WEBSTER, John Lawrence Harvey, CMG 1963; *b* 10 March 1913; *s* of late Sydney Webster, Hindhead, and Elsie Gwendoline Webster (*née* Harvey); *m* 1st, 1940, Elizabeth Marshall Gilbertson (marr. diss., 1959); two *d*; 2nd, 1960, Jessie Lillian Royston-Smith. *Educ:* Rugby Sch.; Balliol College, Oxford (MA). District Officer, Colonial Administrative Service, Kenya, 1935-49; Secretary for Development, 1949-54; Administrative Sec., 1954-56; Sec. to Cabinet, 1956-58; Permanent Sec., Kenya, 1958-63; on retirement from HMOCS, with the British Council, 1964-80, in Thailand, Ceylon, Hong Kong, Istanbul and London. *Recreations:* travel, reading, swimming, golf. *Address:* Timbercroft, 11 Pevensey Road, West Worthing, Sussex. *Clubs:* Royal Commonwealth Society; Leander; Nairobi (Kenya).

WEBSTER, Rear-Adm. John Morrison; Flag Officer Sea Training, since 1982; *b* 3 Nov. 1932; *s* of Frank Martin Webster and Kathleen Mary (*née* Morrison); *m* 1962, Valerie Anne Villiers; one *s* two *d. Educ:* Pangbourne College. Joined RN, 1951; specialised navigation, 1959; Royal Australian Navy, 1959-61; HMS Lowestoft, 1961-63; BRNC, Dartmouth, 1963-65; HMS Dido, 1965-67; RN Tactical Sch., 1967-69; in command HMS Argonaut, 1969-71; MoD Navy, 1971-73; RNLO Ottawa, 1974-76; in command HMS Cleopatra and 4th Frigate Sqdn, 1976-78; MoD, Director Naval Warfare, 1980-82. Lt-Comdr 1963, Comdr 1967, Captain 1973, Rear-Adm. 1982. *Recreations:* painting, sailing. *Address:* c/o Royal Bank of

Scotland, 24 Lombard Street, EC3. *Clubs:* Royal Naval Sailing Association, Royal Naval of 1765 & 1785.

WEBSTER, Prof. John Roger, MA, PhD; DipEd; Professor of Education, and Dean of Faculty of Education, University College of Wales, Aberystwyth, since 1978; *b* 24 June 1926; *s* of Samuel and Jessie Webster; *m* 1963, Ivy Mary Garlick; one *s* one *d. Educ:* Llangefni Secondary Sch.; University College of Wales, Aberystwyth. Lectr, Trinity Coll., Carmarthen, 1948; Lectr in Educn, University Coll., Swansea, 1951; Director for Wales, Arts Council of GB, 1961–66; Prof. of Educn, University Coll. of North Wales, Bangor, 1966–78. Member: Lloyd Cttee on Nat. Film Sch., 1965–66; James Cttee on Teacher Educn and Trng, 1971;Venables Cttee on Continuing Educn, 1974–76; Council, Open Univ. (Chm., Educ. Studies Adv. Cttee), 1969–78; Chm., Standing Conf. on Studies in Educn, 1972–76; Member: CNAA, 1976–79; Post Office Users Nat. Council, 1981– (Chm., Wales, 1981–). *Publications:* Ceri Richards, 1961; Joseph Herman, 1962; contribs on educn and the arts to collective works and learned jls. *Address:* Bron y Glyn, Rhydyfelin, Aberystwyth, Dyfed SY23 4QD.

WEBSTER, Prof. Keith Edward, PhD; Professor of Anatomy, King's College, University of London, since 1975; *b* 18 June 1935; *e s* of Thomas Brotherwick Webster and Edna Pyzer; *m* 1959, Doreen Andrew; two *s. Educ:* UCL (BSc 1957, PhD 1960); UCH Med. Sch. (MB, BS 1962). University Coll. London: Lectr in Anatomy, 1962–66; Sen. Lectr in Anat., 1966–74; Reader in Anat., 1974–75. Symington Prize, British Anatomical Soc., 1966. *Publications:* A Manual of Human Anatomy, Vol. 5: The Central Nervous System (with J. T. Aitken and J. Z. Young), 1967; papers on the nervous system in Brain Res., Jl of Comp. Neurol., and Neurocytology. *Recreations:* Richard Wagner and myself. *Address:* Department of Anatomy, King's College London, Strand, WC2R 2LS. *T:* 01-836 5454.

WEBSTER, Michael George Thomas, DL; Chairman, Fitch Lovell Ltd, since 1977 (Vice-Chairman, 1976); Director: National Provident Institution, since 1973; Dickinson, Robinson Group Ltd, since 1976; *b* 27 May 1920; *s* of late J. A. Webster, CB, DSO, and late Constance A. Webster, 2nd *d* of late Richard and Lady Constance Combe; *m* 1947, Mrs Isabel Margaret Bucknill, *d* of late Major J. L. Dent, DSO, MC; three *d. Educ:* Stowe; Magdalen Coll., Oxford (MA). Commnd Grenadier Guards, 1940–46: NW Europe Campaign, 1944–45 (despatches); DAAG Guards Div., 1946. Joined Watney Combe Reid & Co. Ltd, 1946; Chm., Watney Combe Reid, 1963–68; Watney Mann Ltd: Vice-Chm., 1965–70; Chm., 1970–72; Deputy Chm., 1972–74; Chm., Watney Mann & Truman Holdings, 1974; Dir, Grand Metropolitan Ltd, 1972–74. Master of Brewers' Co., 1964–65. Chm., Aldenham School Governing Body, 1977–; a Vice-Pres., The Brewers' Soc. High Sheriff, Berks, 1971; DL Berks, 1975. *Recreations:* fishing, shooting, golf. *Address:* The Vale, Windsor Forest, Berks. *Clubs:* White's, Cavalry and Guards, MCC.
See also Viscount Torrington.

WEBSTER, Patrick; Barrister-at-Law; a Recorder of the Crown Court, since 1972; Chairman, Industrial Tribunals, Cardiff Region, since 1976 (a part-time Chairman, 1965–75); *b* 6 January 1928; *s* of Francis Glyn Webster and late Ann Webster; *m* 1955, Elizabeth Knight; two *s* four *d. Educ:* Swansea Grammar Sch.; Rockwell Coll., Eire; St Edmund's Coll., Ware; Downing Coll., Cambridge (BA). Called to Bar, Gray's Inn, 1950. Practised at bar, in Swansea, 1950–75; Chm., Medical Appeals Tribunal (part-time), 1971–75. *Recreations:* listening to music, watching rowing and sailing. *Address:* 103 Plymouth Road, Penarth, South Glam. *T:* Penarth 704758. *Clubs:* Penarth Yacht; Beechwood (Swansea).

WEBSTER, Hon. Sir Peter (Edlin), Kt 1980; **Hon. Mr Justice Webster;** a Judge of the High Court of Justice, Queen's Bench Division, since 1980; *b* 16 Feb. 1924; *s* of Herbert Edlin Webster and Florence Helen Webster; *m* 1955, Susan Elizabeth Richards (marr. diss.); one *s* two *d*; *m* 1968, Avril Carolyn Simpson, *d* of Dr John Ernest McCrae Harrisson. *Educ:* Haileybury; Merton Coll., Oxford (MA). RNVR, 1943–46 and 1950, Lieut (A). Imperial Tobacco Co., 1949; Lectr in Law, Lincoln Coll., Oxford, 1950–52; called to Bar, Middle Temple, 1952; Bencher, 1972; Standing Jun. Counsel to Min. of Labour, 1964–67; QC 1967; a Recorder of the Crown Court, 1972–80. Mem., Council of Justice, 1955–60, 1965–70; Mem., General Council of the Bar, 1967–74, and of Senate of the Inns of Court and the Bar, 1974–81 (Vice-Chm. 1975–76); Chm., 1976–77), Chm., London Common Law Bar Assoc., 1975–79; Mem., Judicial Studies Bd, 1979–, Chm., 1981–. Dir, Booker McConnell, 1978–79. *Address:* Royal Courts of Justice, Strand, WC2.

WEBSTER, Sir Richard James, Kt 1971; DSO 1945; Director of Organisation, Conservative Central Office, 1966–76; *b* 15 July 1913; *e s* of late Gerald Webster and late Violet Webster; *m* 1940, Sheila, *y d* of late Jack Marston and late Geraldine Marston; two *d. Educ:* Sandroyd Sch.; Shrewsbury Sch. Conservative Agent: West Willesden, 1946–47; Aldershot, 1948–57; Central Office Agent, North West Provincial Area, 1958–66. Dir, Inst. of Obst. and Gyn. Research Appeal, 1976–81. *Recreations:* all spectator sports, sunbathing. *Address:* Kennet Cottage, Kintbury, near Newbury, Berks. *Clubs:* Carlton (Hon.), St Stephen's Constitutional (Hon.).

WECK, Richard, CBE 1969; PhD; FRS 1975; FEng 1976; Visiting Industrial Professor, Imperial College of Science and Technology, 1968–74 and since 1975; *b* 5 March 1913; *s* of Francis and Katie Weck; *m* 1933, Katie (*née* Bartl). *Educ:* Tech. Univ., Prague (degree in Civ. Engrg). FICE, FIMechE, FInstW.

Site Engr, 1936–38 (Prague); Design Project Leader, 1938–43; Research Asst to Lord Baker, 1943–46; Head of Fatigue Laboratory, British Welding Research Assoc., 1946–51; Lectr in Engineering, Cambridge Univ., 1951–57; Dir of Research, British Welding Res. Assoc., 1957–68; Dir-Gen., Welding Inst., 1968–77. Bessemer Gold Medal, 1975. *Publications:* papers on welded structures, fatigue, res. stresses. *Recreations:* gardening, listening to music. *Address:* Abington Hall, Cambridge CB1 6AH. *T:* Cambridge 891339.

WEDD, George Morton; Under Secretary (Air, Noise and Waste), Department of the Environment; *b* 30 March 1930; *s* of Albert Wedd and Dora Wedd; *m* 1953, Kate Pullin; two *s* one *d. Educ:* various schs in Derbyshire; St John's Coll., Cambridge (BA 1951). Joined Min. of Housing and Local Govt (later DoE), 1951; Principal, 1957; Asst Sec., 1966; Under Sec., 1976. *Address:* Rowan Cottage, Herington Grove, Brentwood, Essex. *T:* Brentwood 224000; 1 Horsebrook Cottages, Avonwick, Devon.

WEDDELL, Prof. Alexander Graham McDonnell, MA (Oxon), MD, DSc (London); Professor of Anatomy, University of Oxford, 1973–1975; *b* 18 Feb. 1908; *s* of Alexander George Weddell and Maud Eileen McDonnell; *m* 1937, Barbara Monica Mills; two *d. Educ:* Cheltenham Coll.; St Bartholomew's Hosp. Med. Sch., London. Demonstrator in Anatomy, St Bart's, London, 1933–34; Commonwealth Fund Fellow in Neuroanatomy and Neurological Surgery, USA, 1935–37; Demonstrator in Anatomy, University Coll. London, 1937–39. Served War: Neurosurgery, RAMC, until 1943; then Anatomical Research for Royal Naval Personnel Cttee of MRC, 1943–45. Apptd Demonstrator in Human Anatomy, Univ. of Oxford, with leave of absence, 1945. Reader in Human Anatomy, Univ. of Oxford, 1947–73; Fellow and Med. Tutor, Oriel Coll., Oxford, 1947; Sen. Proctor, Univ. of Oxford, 1951; elected Mem., Hebdomadal Council, 1952. WHO study team investigating neurological rehabilitation in leprosy, 1960; Harold Chaffer Lectureship, Dunedin Univ., NZ, 1961; Mem., MRC Leprosy Sub-Cttee, 1967; Designated WHO Leprosy Ref. Lab. (under dir of Dr R. J. W. Rees), 1967. Pres., Anatomical Soc. of GB and Ire., 1973–75. *Publications:* papers in learned jls on cutaneous sensibility and leprosy. *Recreations:* photography, swimming. *Address:* 7 Mill Street, Islip, Oxford OX5 2SZ. *T:* Kidlington 6326.

WEDDERBURN; *see* Scrymgeour-Wedderburn.

WEDDERBURN, family name of **Baron Wedderburn of Charlton.**

WEDDERBURN OF CHARLTON, Baron *cr* 1977 (Life Peer), of Highgate; **Kenneth William Wedderburn,** FBA 1981; Cassel Professor of Commercial Law, London School of Economics, University of London, since 1964; *b* 13 April 1927; *o s* of Herbert J. and Mabel Wedderburn, Deptford; *m* 1st, 1951, Nina Salaman; one *s* two *d*; 2nd 1962, Dorothy E. Cole; 3rd, 1969, Frances Ann Knight; one *s. Educ:* Aske's Hatcham School; Whitgift School; Queens' College, Cambridge. BA 1948; LLB 1949 (Chancellor's Medallist); MA 1951. Royal Air Force, 1949–51. Called to the Bar, Middle Temple, 1953. Fellow, 1952–64, Tutor, 1957–60, Clare College, Cambridge; Asst Lectr, 1953–55, Lectr 1955–64, Faculty of Law, Cambridge University. Visiting Professor: UCLA Law Sch., 1967; Harvard Law Sch., 1969–70. Staff Panel Mem., Civil Service Arbitration Tribunal; Chm., Independent Review Cttee, 1976–; Mem., Cttee on Industrial Democracy, 1976–77; Independent Chm., London and Provincial Theatre Councils. Gen. Editor, Modern Law Review. *Publications:* The Worker and the Law, 1965, 2nd edn, 1971; Cases and Materials on Labour Law, 1967; (with P. Davies) Employment Grievances and Disputes Procedures in Britain, 1969; (ed) Contracts, Sutton and Shannon, 1956, 1963; Asst Editor: Torts, Clerk and Lindsell, 1982; Modern Company Law, Gower, 1969 (ed jtly 1979 edn); (ed with B. Aaron) Industrial Conflict, 1972; (with S. Sciarra *et al*) Democrazia Politica e Democrazia Industriale, 1978; (ed with Folke Schmidt) Discrimination in Employment, 1978; articles in legal and other jls. *Recreation:* Charlton Athletic Football Club. *Address:* London School of Economics, Aldwych, WC2. *T:* 01-405 7686.

WEDDERBURN, Sir Andrew John Alexander O.; *see* Ogilvy-Wedderburn.

WEDDERBURN, Prof. Dorothy Enid Cole; Principal, Bedford College, University of London, since 1981; *b* 18 Sept. 1925; *d* of Frederick C. Barnard and Ethel C. Barnard. *Educ:* Walthamstow High Sch. for Girls; Girton Coll., Cambridge (MA). Research Officer, subseq. Sen. Res. Officer, Dept of Applied Economics, Cambridge, 1950–65; Imperial College of Science and Technology: Lectr in Industrial Sociology, 1965–70, Reader, 1970–77, Prof., 1977–81; Dir, Industrial Sociol. Unit, 1973–81; Head, Dept of Social and Economic Studies, 1978–81, Senior Res. Fellow, 1981–. Vis. Prof., Sloan Sch. of Management, MIT, 1969–70. Mem. SSRC, 1976–82; Chm., SERC/SSRC Jt Cttee, 1980–82. Mem., Govt Cttee on the Pay and Condition of Nurses, 1974–75; part-time Mem., Royal Commn on the Distribution of Income and Wealth, 1974–78; Mem. Council, Advisory Conciliation and Arbitration Service, 1976–. *Publications:* White Collar Redundancy, 1964; Redundancy and the Railwayman, 1964; Enterprise Planning for Change, 1968; (with J. E. G. Utting) The Economic Circumstances of Old People, 1962; (with Peter Townsend) The Aged in the Welfare State, 1965; (jtly) Old Age in Three Industrial Societies, 1968; (with Rosemary Crompton) Workers' Attitudes and Technology, 1972; (ed) Poverty, Inequality and Class Structure, 1974; contrib. Jl of Royal Statistical Soc.; Sociological Review; New Society, etc. *Recreations:* politics, walking, cooking. *Address:* Flat 5, 65 Ladbroke Grove,

W11 2PD.
See also Professor G. A. Barnard.

WEDDERSPOON, Sir Thomas (Adam), Kt 1955; JP; b 4 August 1904; s of late Thomas and Margaret Wedderspoon; m 1936, Helen Catherine Margaret MacKenzie; one s two d. Educ: Seafield House, Broughty Ferry, Angus; Trinity College, Glenalmond, Perthshire; Trinity Hall, Cambridge. JP Angus, 1928. Address: Northfield, Keay Street, Blairgowrie, Perthshire PH10 6JD. T: Blairgowrie 2827.

WEDEGA, Dame Alice, DBE 1982 (MBE 1962); retired; b 20 Aug. 1905; d of Wedega Gamahari and Emma; Educ: Kwato Mission School, Milne Bay, PNG; trained in domestic arts, bookbinding, teaching and nursing. Missionary and teacher among head-hunting tribes of SE Papua during 1930s; first Papuan woman to attend internat. conf., Unesco/Pan Pacific, NZ, 1952; first Papuan Girl Guide Comr, 1956; welfare worker with Agric. Dept, helping village women upgrade land and crops, 1958; developed Ahioma Trng Centre, Milne Bay, for village women to learn domestic arts and child care, 1960-68; Mem., Legislative Council, 1961 (first Papuan woman); sent by Govt to assist women in Bougainville during copper mining dispute, 1969-70; as worker with Moral Re-Armament visited and lectured in Asia and Europe, incl. N Ireland, Sweden, Lapland; attended MRA internat. confs in Ceylon, India, Switzerland, Australia and PNG. Publication: Listen My Country (autobiog.), 1981. Recreation: swimming. Address: K.B. Mission, Box 32, Alotau, Milne Bay Province, Papua New Guinea.

WEDELL, Prof. (Eberhard Arthur Otto) George; Professor of Communications, University of Manchester and Director, European Centre for the Media, since 1982; b 4 April 1927; er s of late Rev. Dr H. Wedell and Gertrude (née Bonhoeffer); m 1948, Rosemarie (née Winckler); three s one d. Educ: Cranbrook; London School of Economics (BSc Econ., 1947). Ministry of Education, 1950-58; Sec., Bd for Social Responsibility, Nat. Assembly of Church of England, 1958-60; Dep. Sec., ITA, 1960-61, Secretary, 1961-64; Prof. of Adult Educn and Dir of Extra-Mural Studies, Manchester Univ., 1964-75; Vis. Prof. of Employment Policy, 1975-82; Senior Official, European Commn, 1973-82. Contested (L) Greater Manchester West, European Parly election, 1979; Chm., British Liberals in EEC, 1980-82. Mem. Council, European Centre for Vocational Trng, Berlin, 1980-82. Consultant: ABC, 1964-68; ODM, 1968; GPO, 1969; UNESCO, 1970-71; IBRD, 1971-72; Internat. Broadcast Inst., 1972-75. Trustee: William Temple Foundn, 1969-81; Beatrice Hankey Foundn, 1971-; Director, Royal Exchange Theatre Company, 1968-. FRSA; FRTS. Hon. MEd Manchester, 1968. Publications: The Use of Television in Education, 1963; Broadcasting and Public Policy, 1968; (with H. D. Perraton) Teaching at a Distance, 1968; (ed) Structures of Broadcasting, 1970; (with R. Glatter) Study by Correspondence, 1971; Correspondence Education in Europe, 1971; Teachers and Educational Development in Cyprus, 1971; (ed) Education and the Development of Malawi, 1973; (with E. Katz) Broadcasting in the Third World, 1977 (Nat. Assoc. of Educational Broadcasters of USA Book Award, 1978). Recreations: gardening, theatre, reading. Address: 18 Cranmer Road, Manchester M20 0AW. T: 061-445 5106; Vigneau, Lachapelle, 47350 Seyches, France. Clubs: Athenæum, Reform; Ski.
See also Ven. H. Lockley.

WEDGWOOD, family name of **Baron Wedgwood.**

WEDGWOOD, 4th Baron cr 1942, of Barlaston; **Piers Anthony Weymouth Wedgwood;** b 20 Sept. 1954; s of 3rd Baron Wedgwood and of Lady Wedgwood (Jane Weymouth, d of W. J. Poulton, Kenjockety, Molo, Kenya); S father, 1970. Educ: Marlborough College; RMA Sandhurst. Royal Scots, 1973-80. GSM for N Ireland, 1976. Heir: cousin John Wedgwood, MD, FRCP [b 28 Sept. 1919; m 1st, 1943, Margaret (marr. diss. 1971), d of A. S. Mason; three s two d; 2nd, 1972, Joan, d of J. Ripsher]. Address: Harewood Cottage, Chicksgrove, Tisbury, Wilts. T: Fovant 325.

WEDGWOOD, Dame (Cicely) Veronica, OM 1969; DBE 1968 (CBE 1956); FRHistS; FBA 1975; Hon. LLD Glasgow; Hon. LittD Sheffield; Hon. DLitt: Smith College; Harvard; Oxford; Keele; Sussex; Liverpool; Historian; b 20 July 1910; d of Sir Ralph Wedgwood, 1st Bt, CB, CMG. Educ: privately; Lady Margaret Hall, Oxford. 1st Class Mod. Hist. 1931. Mem., Royal Commn on Historical MSS, 1953-78. President: English Assoc., 1955-56; English Centre of Internat. Pen Club, 1951-57; Society of Authors, 1972-77; Member: Arts Council, 1958-61; Arts Council Literature Panel, 1965-67; Institute for Advanced Study, Princeton, 1953-68; Adv. Council, V&A Museum, 1960-69; Trustee, Nat. Gall., 1962-68, 1969-76; Hon. Member: American Academy of Arts and Letters, 1966; American Acad. of Arts and Scis, 1973. Special Lecturer, UCL, 1962-70. Hon. Fellow: Lady Margaret Hall, Oxford, 1962; UCL, 1965. Hon. Bencher, Middle Temple, 1978. Officer, Order of Orange-Nassau, 1946; Goethe Medal, 1958. Publications: Strafford, 1935 (revd edn, as Thomas Wentworth, 1961); The Thirty Years' War, 1938; Oliver Cromwell 1939, rev. edn 1973; Charles V by Carl Brandi (trans.), 1939; William the Silent, 1944 (James Tait Black Prize for 1944); Auto da Fé by Elias Canetti (translation), 1946; Velvet Studies, 1946; Richelieu and the French Monarchy, 1949; Seventeenth Century Literature, 1950; Montrose, 1952; The King's Peace, 1955; The King's War, 1958; Truth and Opinion, 1960; Poetry and Politics, 1960; The Trial of Charles I, 1964 (in USA as A Coffin for King Charles, 1964); Milton and his World, 1969; The Political Career of Rubens, 1975. Address: c/o Messrs Collins, 14 St James's Place,

SW1.
See also Sir John Wedgwood, Bt.

WEDGWOOD, Geoffrey H., RE 1934; ARCA; Artist Engraver; b 16 April 1900; s of Frank and Jane Wedgwood. Educ: Liverpool Institute; Liverpool School of Art; Royal College of Art; British School at Rome. ARE 1925; ARCA (London) 1925; awarded Rome Scholarship in Engraving; Member of The Chicago Society of Etchers 1926; Exhibitor Royal Academy since 1923; Exhibited Prague, Bucharest, Vienna and Empire Exhibition, South Africa, 1936; works in the following Permanent Collections: British Museum; Victoria and Albert Museum; Rutherston Collection, Manchester; Walker Art Gallery; Wakefield Collection; several English towns; Art Museum Boston, USA; Art Institute of Chicago, USA. Hon. Retired Fellow, Royal Soc. of Painter-Etchers and Engravers, 1971. Publications: Original Engravings. Address: Kingsley, 85 Rupert Road, Roby, Liverpool. Club: Sandon Society (Liverpool).

WEDGWOOD, John Alleyne, MA, FCIS; Chairman, Southern Electricity Board, since 1977; b 26 Jan. 1920; s of Rev. Charles Henry Wedgwood and Myrtle Winifred Perry; m 1st, 1942, Freda Mary Lambert (d 1963); 2nd, 1974, Lilian Nora Forey; one s. Educ: Monkton Combe Sch.; Queens' Coll., Cambridge (MA Hons Hist. Tripos). FCIS, CompIEE, FBIM. Served War, Lincs Regt and Durham LI, 1940-46 (Actg Major). Asst Principal, Min. of Fuel and Power, 1946-48; Admin. Officer, British Electricity Authority, 1948-55; Dep. Sec., London Electricity Bd, 1955-58; Dep. Sec., Electricity Council, 1958-65, Sec., 1965-74; Dep. Chm., S Eastern Elec. Bd, 1974-77. Pres., Inst. of Chartered Secs and Administrators, 1976. Chm. Bd of Management, Electrical and Electronics Industries Benevolent Assoc., 1977-. Member: Worshipful Co. of Scriveners, 1973-; SE Econ. Planning Council, 1975-79. First Master, Worshipful Co. of Chartered Secs and Administrators, 1978. Freeman, City of London, 1973. Recreations: gardening, music, railways, ornithology. Address: Pengethley, 16 Rotherfield Road, Henley-on-Thames, Oxon RG9 1NN. T: Henley-on-Thames 6804. Clubs: Royal Commonwealth Society; Phyllis Court (Henley).

WEDGWOOD, Sir John Hamilton, 2nd Bt, cr 1942; TD 1948; Deputy-Chairman of Josiah Wedgwood and Sons Ltd, until 1966; Member, British National Export Council, 1964-66; b 16 Nov. 1907; s of Sir Ralph L. Wedgwood, 1st Bt, CB, CMG, TD, and Iris, Lady Wedgwood (née Pawson) (d 1982); S father 1956; m 1st, 1933, Diana Mildred (d 1976), d of late Col Oliver Hawkshaw, TD; three s one d (and one s decd); 2nd, 1982, Dr Pamela Tudor-Craig, FSA, widow (née Wynn Reeves); one step d. Educ: Winchester College; Trinity College, Cambridge; and abroad. Served War of 1939-45, Major GSO2 (1b). Chm., Anglo-American Community Relations, Lakenheath Base, 1972-76. FRSA 1968; FRGS 1973. Liveryman, Worshipful Co. of Painter-Stainers, 1971. Hon. LLD Birmingham, 1966. Recreations: mountaineering, caving, foreign travel (Mem. Travelers' Century Club of California for those who have visited a hundred countries). Heir: s (Hugo) Martin Wedgwood [b 27 Dec. 1933; m 1963, Alexandra Mary Gordon Clark, er d of late Judge Alfred Gordon Clark, and Mrs Gordon Clark; one s two d. Educ: Eton; Trinity College, Oxford]. Address: c/o English-Speaking Union, 37 Charles Street, W1. Clubs: Alpine; British Pottery Manufacturers Federation (Stoke-on-Trent).
See also Dame C. V. Wedgwood.

WEDGWOOD, Dame Veronica; see Wedgwood, Dame C. V.

WEE CHONG JIN, Hon. Mr Justice; Chief Justice of the Supreme Court, Singapore; b 28 Sept. 1917; s of late Wee Gim Puay and Lim Paik Yew; m 1955, Cecilia Mary Henderson; three s one d. Educ: Penang Free Sch.; St John's Coll., Cambridge. Called to Bar, Middle Temple, 1938; admitted Advocate and Solicitor of Straits Settlement, 1940; practised in Penang and Singapore, 1940-57; Puisne Judge, Singapore, 1957, Chief Justice, 1963. Recreation: golf. Address: c/o Chief Justice's Chambers, Supreme Court, Singapore.

WEEDON, Dr Basil Charles Leicester, CBE 1974; DSc; PhD; FRS 1971; FRSC; Vice-Chancellor, Nottingham University, since 1976; b 18 July 1923; s of late Charles William Weedon; m 1959, Barbara Mary Dawe; one s one d. Educ: Wandsworth Sch.; Imperial Coll. of Science and Technology (ARCS; DIC). Research Chemist, ICI Ltd (Dyestuffs Div.), 1943-47; Lecturer in Organic Chemistry, Imperial Coll., 1947-55, Reader, 1955-60; Prof. of Organic Chemistry, QMC, 1960-76. Chm., Food Additives and Contaminants Cttee, 1968-; Mem., EEC Scientific Cttee for Food, 1974-81; Scientific Editor, Pure and Applied Chemistry, 1960-75. Mem., UGC, 1974-76. Tilden Lecturer, Chemical Society, 1966. Hon. DTech Brunel Univ., 1975. Meldola Medal, Roy. Inst. of Chemistry, 1952. Publications: A Guide to Qualitative Organic Chemical Analysis (with Sir Patrick Linstead), 1956; scientific papers, mainly in Jl Chem. Soc. Address: c/o Nottingham University, University Park, Nottingham NG7 2RD. T: Nottingham 56101.

WEEDON, Dudley William, BSc(Eng), CEng, FIEE; Formerly: Director, Cable & Wireless Ltd; Chairman, Energy Communications Ltd; retired 1982; b 25 June 1920; s of Reginald Percy and Ada Kate Weedon; m 1951, Monica Rose Smith; two s one d. Educ: Colchester Royal Grammar Sch.; Northampton Polytechnic. Marconi's Wireless Telegraph Co., 1937-48; Cable & Wireless Ltd, 1949-82. Recreation: sailing. Address: 103 Lexden Road, Colchester, Essex.

WEEKES, Rt. Rev. Ambrose Walter Marcus; *see* Gibraltar in Europe, Suffragan Bishop of.

WEEKES, Philip Gordon, OBE 1977; CEng, FIMinE; Area Director, South Wales Coalfield, since 1973; part time Member, National Coal Board, since 1977; *b* 12 June 1920; *s* of Albert Edwin and Gwladys Magdaline Weekes; *m* 1944, Branwen Mair Jones; two *s* two *d*. *Educ:* Tredegar Sch.; University Coll., Cardiff (BSc Hons; Fellow, 1982). Jun. official, Tredegar Iron & Coal Co., 1939. Served War, RAF, 1942-44. Manager: Wyllie Colliery, Tredegar (Southern) Colliery Co., 1946; Oakdale Colliery, 1948; seconded to Colonial Office, 1950; Colliery Agent, S Wales, 1951; HQ Work Study Engr, 1952; Gp Manager, Dep. Prod. Manager, Area Prod. Manager, in various areas in S Wales, 1954; Dir of Studies, NCB Staff Coll., 1964; Dep. Dir (Mining), S Midlands Area, 1967; Chief Mining Engr, Nat. HQ, 1970; Dir-Gen. of Mining, Nat. HQ, 1971. Dir, Develt Corp. for Wales, 1980-. Member: BBC Gen. Adv. Council, 1976-; St John's Priory for Wales, 1978-; Prince of Wales' Cttee, 1978-. OStJ 1977. *Publications:* articles in professional and techn. jls and transactions. *Address:* Hillbrow, Llantwit Major, South Glamorgan CF6 9RE. *T:* Llantwit Major 2125. *Club:* Cardiff and County.

WEEKS, Alan Frederick; Director, Sports Aid Foundation, since 1976; *b* 8 Sept. 1923; *s* of late Captain Frederick Charles Weeks, MN, and Ada Frances Weeks; *m* 1947, Barbara Jane (*née* Huckle); one *s* one *d* (and one *s* decd). *Educ:* Brighton, Hove and Sussex Grammar School. Served RNR, Midshipman to Lieut, 1939-46. PRO, Sports Stadium, Brighton, 1946-65; Sec., Brighton Tigers Ice Hockey Club, 1946-65; Dir, London Lions Ice Hockey Club, 1973-74. BBC Commentator: Ice Hockey, Ice Skating, 1951-; Football, 1956-78; Gymnastics, 1962-; Swimming, 1971-; Presenter: Summer Grandstand, 1959-62; Olympics, 1960, 1964; BBC Commentator: Winter Olympics: 1964, 1968, 1972, 1976, 1980; Olympics: 1968, 1972, 1976, 1980; World Cup: 1966, 1970, 1974, 1978; Commonwealth Games: 1970, 1974, 1978, 1982; Presenter, Pot Black, 1970-. *Recreation:* swimming. *Address:* c/o The Bagenal Harvey Organisation, 1a Cavendish Square, W1M 9HA.

WEEKS, Edward A.; Senior Editor and Consultant, Atlantic Monthly Press, since 1966; Trustee: University of Rochester (Hon.); United Negro College Fund; American Field Service (Croix de Guerre, 1918); Fellow American Academy Arts and Sciences; *b* 19 Feb. 1898; *s* of Edward Augustus Weeks and Frederika Suydam; *m* 1925, Frederica Watriss (decd); one *s* one *d* ; *m* 1971, Phœbe Adams. *Educ:* Pingry and Battin High School, Elizabeth, NJ; Cornell Univ.; BS Harvard, 1922; Camb. Univ. (Fiske Schol.). Hon. LittD: Northeastern Univ., Boston, 1938; Lake Forest Coll. (Illinois), 1939; Williams Coll., Mass., 1942; Middlebury College, Vt, 1944; University of Alabama, 1945; Dartmouth Coll., 1950; Bucknell Univ., 1952; Boston Univ., 1953; Hobart Coll., 1956; Univ. of Richmond, 1957; New York Univ. 1958; further hon. degrees from: Clark Univ., Massachusetts, 1958 (Humane Letters); Pomona Coll., Calif., 1958 (LittD); Univ. of Pittsburgh, 1959 (Humane Letters); Univ. of Akron, 1961 (LittD); Northwestern Univ., 1961 (Humane Letters); Rutgers, 1962 (Dr Letters); Union College, 1962 (DCL); Washington and Jefferson, 1962 (Dr Laws). Began as manuscript reader and book salesman with Horace Liveright, Inc., New York City, 1923; Associate Editor, Atlantic Monthly, 1924-28; Editor: Atlantic Monthly Press, 1928-37; Atlantic Monthly, 1938-66. Overseer, Harvard Coll., 1945-51. Henry Johnson Fisher Award, 1968; Irita Van Doren Award, 1970. *Publications:* This Trade of Writing, 1935; The Open Heart, 1955; In Friendly Candour, 1959; Breaking into Print, 1962; Boston, Cradle of Liberty, 1965; The Lowells and their Institute, 1966; Fresh Waters, 1968; The Moisie Salmon Club, a chronicle, 1971; My Green Age: a memoir, 1974; Myopia: 1875-1975, 1975; Writers and Friends, 1982; Editor: Great Short Novels (Anthology), 1941; Jubilee, One Hundred Years of the Atlantic (with Emily Flint), 1957; contrib. essays, articles, and book reviews to magazines. *Recreations:* fishing, preferably with a light rod; golf; poker. *Address:* 59 Chestnut Street, Boston, Mass 02108, USA; 8 Arlington Street, Boston, Mass 02116, USA. *Cable address:* Lanticmon. *Clubs:* Tavern (Boston); Century (New York).

WEEKS, Major-Gen. Ernest Geoffrey, CB 1946; CBE 1944; MC (and bar); MM (and bar); CD; retired; *b* Charlottetown, PEI, 30 May 1896; *s* of William Arthur and Fanny Weeks; *m* 1930, Vivian Rose Scott, Toronto, Canada; one *s*. *Educ:* Prince of Wales Coll., Charlottetown, PEI. Canadian Militia, 1910-14; European War, Belgium and France, 1915-19; Canadian Permanent Force from 1920; War of 1939-45, Italy; Maj.-Gen. i/c Administration Canadian Military, HQ, London, England, 1944-45; Adjutant-General Canadian Army, 1946-49; retired, 1949. *Recreations:* gardening, fishing. *Address:* 46 Prince Charles Drive, Charlottetown, PEI C1A 3C2, Canada.

WEEKS, Sir Hugh (Thomas), Kt 1966; CMG 1946; Chairman: Leopold Joseph Holdings Ltd, 1966-78; London American Finance Corporation Ltd, 1970-78; Electrical Industrial Securities, 1971-77; *b* 27 April 1904; *m* 1929; one *d* (and one *s* decd); *m* 1949, Constance Tomkinson; one *d*. *Educ:* Hendon Secondary and Kilburn Grammar Schools; Emmanuel College, Cambridge (MA). Research and Statistical Manager, Cadbury Bros, till 1939; Director of Statistics, Min. of Supply, 1939-42; Director-General of Statistics and Programmes and Member of Supply Council, 1942-43; Head of Programmes and Planning Division, Ministry of Production, 1943-45. Represented Ministries of Supply and Production on various Missions to N America, 1941-45; Managing Director J. S. Fry & Sons, 1945-47; Mem. Economic Planning Bd, 1947-48, 1959-61; Joint Controller of Colonial Development Corporation, 1948-51; Chm., NIESR, 1970-74. Director: Finance Corp. for

Industry, 1956-74; Industrial and Commercial Finance Corp., 1960-74. UK Representative, UN Cttee for Industrial Development, 1961-63. Dep. Chm., Richard Thomas & Baldwins, 1965-68; Dir, S Wales and Strip Mill Bds, BSC, 1968-72. Chairman: EDC for Distributive Trades, 1964-70; Econ. Cttees, FBI and CBI, 1957-72. Pres., British Export Houses Assoc., 1972-74. Medal of Freedom with Silver Palm (US). *Publications:* Market Research (with Paul Redmayne); various articles. *Address:* 8 The Grove, Highgate Village, N6. *T:* 01-340 9517.

WEETCH, Kenneth Thomas; MP (Lab) Ipswich, since Oct. 1974; *b* 17 Sept. 1933; *s* of Kenneth George and Charlotte Irene Weetch; *m* 1961, Audrey Wilson; two *d*. *Educ:* Newbridge Grammar Sch., Mon; London School of Economics. MSc(Econ), DipEd (London Inst. of Educn). National Service: Sgt, RAEC, Hong Kong, 1955-57; Walthamstow and Ilford Educn Authorities and Research at LSE, 1957-64; Head of History Dept, Hockerill Coll. of Educn, Bishop's Stortford, 1964-74. Contested (Lab) Saffron Walden, 1970. PPS to Sec. of State for Transport, 1976-78. *Recreations:* walking, reading, watching Association football, playing the piano in pubs. *Address:* 4 Appleby Close, Ipswich, Suffolk. *Club:* Silent Street Labour (Ipswich).

WEEVERS, Theodoor, LitD (Leyden); Officier in de Orde van Oranje-Nassau; Professor of Dutch Language and Literature, University of London, 1945-71; *b* Amersfoort, 3 June 1904; *e s* of Prof. Theodorus Weevers and Cornelia Jeannette, *d* of J. de Graaff; *m* 1933, Sybil Doreen, 2nd *d* of Alfred Jervis; two *s*. *Educ:* Gymnasia at Amersfoort and Groningen; Universities of Groningen and Leyden. Lecturer in Dutch at University College and Bedford College, London, 1931-36; Reader in Dutch Language and Literature in University of London, 1937-45; Lecturer in Dutch at Birkbeck College (Univ. of London), 1942-45. During War of 1939-45 Language Supervisor and Announcer-Translator in European News Service of BBC (Dutch Section), 1940-44. Corr. mem. Koninklijke Nederlandse Akademie van Wetenschappen te Amsterdam; hon. mem. Koninklijke Academie voor Nederlandse Taal en Letterkunde, Gent; mem. Maatschappij der Nederlandse Letterkunde. *Publications:* Coornhert's Dolinghe van Ulysse, 1934; De Dolinge van Ulysse door Dierick Volckertsz Coornhert, 1939; The Idea of Holland in Dutch Poetry, 1948; Poetry of the Netherlands in its European Context, 1170-1930, 1960; Mythe en Vorm in de gedichten van Albert Verwey, 1965; Albert Verwey's Portrayal of the Growth of the Poetic Imagination, in Essays in German and Dutch Literature, 1973; Droom en Beeld: De Poëzie van Albert Verwey, 1978; articles and reviews in Modern Language Review, Mededelingen Kon. Nederlandse Akademie van Wetenschappen, Tijdschrift v. Nederl. Taal en Letterkunde, De Nieuwe Taalgids, Neophilologus, Journal of English and Germanic Philology, German Life and Letters, Spiegel der Letteren, Publications of the English Goethe Society, English Studies. *Recreations:* music, walking. *Address:* 10 Devonshire Road, Harpenden, Herts.

WEIDENBAUM, Murray Lew, PhD; Mallinckrodt Distinguished University Professor, Washington University, 1971-81 and since 1982; *b* 10 Feb. 1927; *m* 1954, Phyllis Green; one *s* two *d*. *Educ:* City Coll., NY; Columbia Univ. (MA); Princeton Univ. (PhD 1958). Fiscal Economist, Budget Bureau, Washington, 1949-57; Corp. Economist, Boeing Co., Seattle, 1958-63; Sen. Economist, Stanford Res. Inst., 1963-64; Washington Univ., St Louis, 1964-81, 1982-, Prof. and Chm. of Dept of Econs, 1966-69; Asst Sec., Treasury Dept, Washington, 1969-71 (on secondment); Chairman, Council of Economic Advisers, USA, 1981-82. *Publications:* Federal Budgeting, 1964; Economic Impact of the Vietnam War, 1967; Modern Public Sector, 1969; Economics of Peacetime Defense, 1974; Government-Mandated Price Increases, 1975; The Future of Business Regulation, 1980; Business, Government, and the Public, 1981. *Address:* Center for the Study of American Business, Washington University, Campus Box 1208, St Louis, Missouri 63130, USA.

WEIDENFELD, family name of **Baron Weidenfeld.**

WEIDENFELD, Baron *cr* 1976 (Life Peer), of Chelsea; **Arthur George Weidenfeld,** Kt 1969; Chairman: Weidenfeld & Nicolson Ltd since 1948, and associated companies; *b* 13 Sept. 1919; *o s* of late Max and of Rosa Weidenfeld; *m* 1st, 1952, Jane Sieff; one *d* ; 2nd, 1956, Barbara Connolly (*née* Skelton) (marr. diss. 1961); 3rd, 1966, Sandra Payson Meyer (marr. diss. 1976). *Educ:* Piaristen Gymnasium, Vienna; University of Vienna (Law); Konsular Akademie (Diplomatic College). BBC Monitoring Service, 1939-42; BBC News Commentator on European Affairs on BBC Empire & North American service, 1942-46. Wrote weekly foreign affairs column, News Chronicle, 1943-44; Founder: Contact Magazine and Books, 1945; Weidenfeld & Nicolson Ltd, 1948. One year's leave as Political Adviser and Chief of Cabinet of President Weizmann of Israel. Vice-Chm., Bd of Governors, Ben Gurion Univ. of the Negev, Beer-Sheva; Governor: Univ. of Tel Aviv; Weizmann Inst. of Science. Mem., Royal Opera House Trust, 1974-. *Publication:* The Goebbels Experiment, 1943 (also publ. USA). *Recreations:* travel, opera. *Address:* 9 Chelsea Embankment, SW3. *T:* 01-351 0042.

WEIDLEIN, Edward Ray, MA, ScD, EngD, LLD; President Mellon Institute, 1921-56, retired; Technical Adviser of Rubber Reserve Company (now Synthetic Rubber Division of National Science Foundation), 1941-70; Director, Allegheny County Council West of the Boy Scouts of America; National Council of the Boy Scouts of America; Advisory Committee, Oakland Office, Mellon National Bank; President, Regional Industrial Develt

Corp. Fund, 1962-71; registered professional engineer in Pa; *b* Augusta, Kansas, 14 July 1887; *s* of Edward Weidlein and Nettie Lemon; *m* 1915, Hazel Butts; three *s. Educ:* University of Kansas. Developed processes for the use of sulphur dioxide in hydrometallurgy; Chief of Chemicals Branch War Production Board, 1940-42; Senior Consultant of Chemical Division of War Production Board, Feb. 1942-Mar. 1946; Head Technical Consultant in War Production Board, Mar. 1942-Mar. 1946; Technical Adviser, R&D Div., Quartermaster Corps, US Army, 1943-46; Member: Special Cttee for examination of enemy raw materials and supplies under War Metallurgy Cttee of Nat. Research Council and Nat. Acad. of Sciences; Research Cttee in Co-operation with Chemical Warfare Service of American Chemical Society; Cttee on Co-operation with National Defense Research Cttee of Office of Sc. Research and Development; Studies, Reports, and Seminars Cttee of Army Ordn. Assoc.; Nat. Engineers Cttee of Engineers Jt Council; Exec. Cttees, Allegheny Conf. on Community Develt and Pittsburgh Regional Planning Assoc.; Board of Directors Western Pennsylvania Hosp.; Bd of Trustees, Rolling Rock Club; Trustee (emer.) Univ. of Pittsburgh and of Shadyside Academy, Pittsburgh. Member, leading chemical and scientific societies. Various awards have been obtained for distinguished service in his field; Edward R. Weidlein Professorship established, 1967, by Bd of Trustees, Univ. of Pittsburgh. Holds numerous hon. degrees in Science, Laws and Engineering. *Publications:* (joint) Science in Action; Glances at Industrial Research; many articles on industrial research. *Recreations:* golf, hunting and fishing. *Address:* Weidacres, PO Box 45, Rector, Pennsylvania 15677, USA. *Clubs:* University, Pitt Faculty, Pittsburgh Golf, Rolling Rock, Duquesne, Authors' (Pittsburgh); Chemists' (New York); Chemists' (Pittsburgh).

WEIGALL, Peter Raymond; Managing Director, P. R. Weigall & Co. Ltd, since 1976; *b* 24 Feb. 1922; *s* of Henry Stuart Brome Weigall and Madeleine Bezard; *m* 1950, Nancy, *d* of Alexander Webster, CIE, and Margaret Webster; one *s* one *d. Educ:* Lycée Janson, Paris; Edinburgh Univ. (BSc). Served War, Captain, RE, 1942-46. Henry Wiggin & Co. Ltd, Birmingham, 1949-51; Petrochemicals Ltd, London, 1951-54; Chemical Industry Admin, Shell Petroleum Co., London, 1954-58; Chemicals Manager, Shell Sekiyu, Tokyo, 1958-63; Shell Internat. Chemical Co., London, 1964-69; Managing Dir, Monteshell, Milan, 1970-73; Industrial Advr to HM Govt, DTI, 1973-75. Member: Movement of Exports EDC, 1974-75; Chemicals EDC, 1974-75; Motor Vehicle Distribution and Repair EDC, 1974-75; Mergers Panel, Office of Fair Trading, 1974-75. *Recreations:* sailing, skiing. *Address:* 35 Cottenham Drive, SW20. *T:* 01-946 2905.

WEIGH, Brian, CBE 1982; Chief Constable of Avon and Somerset Constabulary, since 1979; *b* 22 Sept. 1926; *s* of late Edwin Walter Weigh and Ellen Weigh; *m* 1952, Audrey; one *d. Educ:* St Joseph's Coll., Blackpool, Lancs; Queen's Univ., Belfast. All ranks to Supt, Metrop. Police, 1948-67; Asst Chief Constable, 1967-69, Dep. Chief Constable, 1969-74, Somerset and Bath Constab.; Dep. Chief Constable, Avon and Somerset Constab., 1974-75; Chief Constable, Gloucestershire Constab., 1975-79. Mem., Royal Life Saving Soc. (Dep. Pres., UK Br.). *Recreations:* walking, gardening, golf, badminton. *Address:* Chief Constable's Office, Avon and Somerset Constabulary, Bristol BS99 7BH. *T:* Bristol 22022. *Club:* Royal Commonwealth Society.

WEIGHELL, Sidney; General Secretary, National Union of Railwaymen, 1975-82; Member, Trades Union General Council, since 1975; *b* 31 March 1922; *s* of John Thomas and Rose Lena Weighell; *m* 1st, 1949, Margaret Alison Hunter (killed, 1956); one *s* (one *d*, killed, 1956); 2nd, 1959, Joan Sheila Willets. *Educ:* Church of England Sch., Northallerton, Yorks. Joined LNER, Motive Power Dept, 1938. Elected to: NUR Exec., 1953; full-time NUR Official, 1954; Asst Gen. Sec., 1965. Labour Party Agent, 1947-52; Mem., Labour Party Exec., 1972-75. *Recreations:* trout fishing, swimming, gardening; professional footballer, Sunderland FC, 1945-47. *Address:* 7 The Chase, Bishop's Stortford, Herts CM23 3HT.

WEIGHILL, Air Cdre Robert Harold George, CBE 1973; DFC 1944; Secretary, Rugby Football Union, since 1973; *b* 9 Sept. 1920; *s* of late Harold James and Elsie Weighill, Heswall, Cheshire; *m* 1946, Beryl (*d* 1981), *d* of late W. Y. Hodgson, Bromborough, Cheshire; two *s* (one *d* decd). *Educ:* Wirral Grammar Sch., Bebington, Cheshire. Served War: RAF, 1941; No 2 F R Sqdn, 1942-44; No 19 F Sqdn, 1944-45. Sqdn Comdr, RAF Coll., Cranwell, 1948-52; Student, RAF Staff Coll., 1952; CO, No 2 FR Sqdn and 138 F Wing, 1953-57; Student, JSSC, 1959; Directing Staff, Imperial Defence Coll., 1959-61; CO, RAF, Cottesmore, 1961-64; Gp Captain Ops, RAF Germany, 1964-67; Asst Comdt, RAF Coll. of Air Warfare, 1967-68; Comdt, RAF Halton, 1968-73. ADC to the Queen, 1968-73. *Recreations:* Rugby (Harlequins, Barbarians, Cheshire, RAF, Combined Services, England), squash, swimming. *Address:* South View, Whitton Road, Twickenham, Mddx. *Clubs:* Royal Air Force, East India, Devonshire, Sports and Public Schools.

WEIGHT, Prof. Carel Victor Morlais, CBE 1961; RA 1965 (ARA 1955); Hon. RBA 1972 (RBA 1934); practising artist (painter); Hon. Fellow and Professor Emeritus, Royal College of Art, since 1973; Trustee RA, since 1975; *b* London, 10 Sept. 1908; *s* of Sidney Louis and Blanche H. C. Weight; British. *Educ:* Sloane School; Goldsmiths' Coll., Univ. of London (Sen. County Scholarship, 1933). First exhibited at Royal Acad., 1931; first one-man show, Cooling Galls, 1934; 2nd and 3rd exhibns, Picture Hire Ltd, 1936 and 1938. Official War Artist, 1945. Royal College of Art: Teacher of Painting, 1947;

Fellow, 1956; Prof. of Painting, 1957-73. One-man Shows: Leicester Galls, 1946, 1952, 1968; Zwemmer Gall., 1956, 1959, 1961, 1965; Agnew's, 1959; Russell Cotes Gall., Bournemouth, 1962; Fieldbourne Galleries, 1972; New Grafton Gall., 1974, 1976; exhibited in: 60 Paintings for 1951; (by invitation) exhibns of Contemporary British Art in provinces and overseas, incl. USSR, 1957; Retrospective Exhibns: Reading Museum and Art Gallery, 1970; RCA, 1973; Royal Acad., 1982. Work purchased by: Chantry Bequest for Tate Gall., 1955, 1956, 1957, 1963, 1968; Walker Art Gall., Liverpool; Southampton, Hastings and Oldham Art Galls, etc; Art Gall., Melbourne; Nat. Gall., Adelaide; Arts Council; New Coll., Oxford; Contemporary Art Soc.; V & A Museum. Mural for: Festival of Britain, 1951; Manchester Cathedral, 1963. Picture, Transfiguration, presented by Roman Catholics to the Pope. Member: London Group, 1950; West of England Acad.; Fine Arts Panel, Arts Council, 1951-57; Rome Faculty of Art, 1960. Mem., Cttee of Enquiry into the Economic Situation of the Visual Artist (Gulbenkian Foundn), 1978. *Recreations:* music, reading. *Address:* 33 Spencer Road, SW18. *T:* 01-228 6928. *Club:* Arts.

WEILER, Terence Gerard; *b* 12 Oct. 1919; *s* of Charles and Clare Weiler; *m* 1952, Truda, *d* of Wilfrid and Mary Woollen; two *s* two *d. Educ:* Wimbledon College; University College, London. Army (RA and Queen's Royal Regiment), 1940-45; UCL, 1937-39 and 1946-47; Home Office: Asst Principal, 1947; Principal, 1948; Asst Sec., 1958; Asst Under-Sec. of State, 1967-80; Mem., Prisons Board, 1962-66, 1971-80; Chm., Working Party: on Habitual Drunken Offenders, 1967-70; on Adjudication Procedures in Prisons, 1975. *Recreations:* cinema, crime fiction. *Address:* 372 Jersey Road, Osterley, Mddx. *T:* 01-560 7822.

WEINBERG, Mark Aubrey; Deputy Chairman, Hambro Life Assurance, since 1978 (Managing Director, 1971-78); *b* 9 Aug. 1931; *s* of Philip and Eva Weinberg; *m* 1st, 1961, Sandra Le Roith (*d* 1978); three *d*; 2nd, 1980, Anouska Hempel; one *s. Educ:* King Edward VII Sch., Johannesburg; Univ. of the Witwatersrand (BCom, LLB); London Sch. of Econs (LLM). Called to the Bar, South Africa, 1955. Barrister, S Africa, 1955-61; Man. Dir, Abbey Life Assurance Co., 1961-70. *Publication:* Take-overs and Mergers, 1962, 4th edn 1980. *Recreations:* riding, tennis. *Address:* 7 Old Park Lane, W1Y 3LJ. *T:* 01-499 0031.

WEINBERG, Prof. Steven, PhD; Higgins Professor of Physics, Harvard University, since 1973; concurrently Josey Regental Professor of Science, University of Texas, since 1982; Senior Scientist, Smithsonian Astrophysical Observatory, since 1973; *b* 3 May 1933; *s* of Fred and Eva Weinberg; *m* 1954, Louise Goldwasser; one *d. Educ:* Cornell Univ. (AB); Copenhagen Institute for Theoretical Physics; Princeton Univ. (PhD). Instructor, Columbia Univ., 1957-59; Research Associate, Lawrence Berkeley Laboratory, 1959-60; Faculty, Univ. of California at Berkeley, 1960-69; full prof., 1964; on leave: Imperial Coll., London, 1961-62; Loeb Lectr, Harvard, 1966-67; Vis. Prof., MIT, 1967-69; Prof., MIT, 1969-73; Vis. Prof. (on leave), Stanford Univ., 1976-77. Lectures: Richtmeyer, Amer. Assoc. of Physics Teachers, 1974; Scott, Cavendish Lab., 1975; Silliman, Yale Univ., 1977; Lauritsen, Calif. Inst. of Technol., 1979; Bethe, Cornell, 1979; Schild, Texas, 1979; de Shalit, Weizmann Inst., 1979; Henry, Princeton, 1981; Harris, Northwestern, 1981. Fellow, Amer. Acad. of Arts and Scis; Mem., US Nat. Acad. of Scis. For. Mem., Royal Soc. Hon. ScD: Knox Coll. 1978; Chicago, 1978; Rochester, 1979; Yale, 1979; City Univ. of New York, 1980; Clark, 1982. J. R. Oppenheimer Prize, 1973; Heinemann Prize in Mathematical Physics, 1977; Amer. Inst. of Physics—US Steel Foundn Science Writing Award, 1977; Elliott Cresson Medal of Franklin Inst., 1979; (jtly) Nobel Prize in Physics, 1979. *Publications:* Gravitation and Cosmology: principles and applications of the general theory of relativity, 1972; The First Three Minutes: a modern view of the origin of the universe, 1977; The Discovery of the Subatomic Particles, 1982; numerous articles in learned jls. *Recreation:* reading history. *Address:* Physics Department, University of Texas, Austin, Texas 78712, USA. *T:* (512) 471 4394. *Clubs:* Saturday (Boston, Mass); Cambridge Scientific (Cambridge, Mass).

WEINBERGER, Caspar Willard; Secretary of Defense, United States of America, since 1981; *b* San Francisco, Calif, 18 Aug. 1917; *s* of Herman and Cerise Carpenter (Hampson) Weinberger; *m* 1942, Jane Dalton; one *s* one *d. Educ:* Harvard Coll. (AB *magna cum laude*); Harvard Law Sch. (LLB). Member: Phi Beta Kappa; Amer. Bar Assoc.; State Bar of Calif. Served in Infantry, Private to Captain, AUS, 1941-45 (Bronze Star). Law Clerk to US Ct of Appeals Judge William E. Orr, 1945-47; with law firm Heller, Ehrman, White & McAuliffe, 1947-69, partner, 1959-69. Member, Calif Legislature from 21st Dist, 1952-58; Vice-Chm., Calif Republican Central Cttee, 1960-62, Chm. 1962-64; Chm., Commn on Calif State Govt Organization and Economy, 1967-68; Dir of Finance, Calif, 1968-69; Chm., Fed. Trade Commn, 1970; Dep. Dir, 1970-72, Dir 1972-73, Office of Management and Budget; Counsellor to the President, 1973; Sec., HEW, 1973-75. Gen. Counsel, Vice-Pres., Dir, Bechtel gp of companies, 1975-81; former Dir, Pepsi Co. Inc., Quaker Oats Co. Formerly staff book reviewer, San Francisco Chronicle; moderator weekly TV prog., Profile, Bay area, station KQED, San Francisco, 1959-68. Frank Nelson Doubleday (Smithsonian) Lectr, 1974; Chm., Pres.'s Commn on Mental Retardation, 1973-75; former Member: Trilateral Commn; Adv. Council, Amer. Ditchley Foundn; Bd of Trustees, St Luke's Hosp., San Francisco; former Nat. Trustee, Nat. Symphony, Washington, DC. *Publications:* contributed a semi-weekly column for a number of Calif newspapers. *Address:* The Pentagon, Washington, DC 20301,

USA. *T:* 202/695-5261. *Clubs:* Century (NY); Bohemian and Pacific-Union (San Francisco); Harvard (San Francisco/Washington DC); Burlingame Country.

WEINSTOCK, family name of **Baron Weinstock.**

WEINSTOCK, Baron *cr* 1980 (Life Peer), of Bowden in the County of Wiltshire; **Arnold Weinstock;** Kt 1970; BSc (Econ), FSS; Managing Director, General Electric Co. Ltd, since 1963; *b* 29 July 1924; *s* of Simon and Golda Weinstock; *m* 1949, Netta, *d* of Sir Michael Sobell, *qv*; one *s* one *d*. *Educ:* University of London. Degree in Statistics. Junior administrative officer, Admiralty, 1944–47; engaged in finance and property development, group of private companies, 1947–54; Radio & Allied Industries Ltd (later Radio & Allied Holdings Ltd), 1954–63 (Managing Director); General Electric Co. Ltd, Director 1961. Dir, Rolls-Royce (1971) Ltd, 1971–73. Hon. FRCR 1975. Hon. Fellow, Peterhouse, Cambridge, 1982; Hon. Bencher, Gray's Inn, 1982. Hon. DSc: Salford, 1975; Aston, 1976; Bath, 1978; Reading, 1978; Hon. LLD Leeds, 1978; Hon. DTech Loughborough, 1981. *Recreations:* racing and music. *Address:* 7 Grosvenor Square, W1.

WEIPERS, Prof. Sir William (Lee), Kt 1966; Director of Veterinary Education, 1949–68, Dean of the Faculty of Veterinary Medicine, 1968–74, University of Glasgow Veterinary School, retired 1974; *b* 21 Jan. 1904; *s* of Rev. John Weipers, MA, BD and Evelyn Bovelle Lee; *m* 1939, Mary MacLean; one *d*. *Educ:* Whitehill Higher Grade School, Dennistoun, Glasgow; Glasgow Veterinary College (MRCVS). General practice, 1925–27; on staff of Royal (Dick) Veterinary College, 1927–29. DVSM 1927; general practice, 1927–49. Dean of Faculties, Glasgow Univ., 1981-. Member Council of Royal College of Veterinary Surgeons, 1949–74, President, 1963–64. BSc (Glasgow), 1951; FRSE 1953; FRCVS 1958. DUniv Stirling, 1978; Hon. DVMS Glasgow, 1982. *Publications:* in professional papers. *Recreation:* tree culture. *Address:* The Snab, Duntocher, Dunbartonshire. *T:* Duntocher 73216. *Club:* Royal Scottish Automobile.

WEIR, family name of **Baron Inverforth** and **Viscount Weir.**

WEIR, 3rd Viscount *cr* 1938; **William Kenneth James Weir;** Vice Chairman, The Weir Group Ltd, since 1981 (Chairman and Chief Executive, 1972–81); Co-Chairman, RIT and Northern plc, since 1982; Director: BICC Ltd, since 1977; Esperanza plc; Member, Court of Bank of England, since 1972; *b* Nov 1933; *e s* of 2nd Viscount Weir CBE, and Lucy (*d* 1972), *d* of late James F. Crowdy, MVO; *S* father, 1975; *m* 1st, 1964, Diana (marr. diss.), *o d* of Peter L. MacDougall; one *s* one *d* ; 2nd, 1976, Mrs Jacqueline Mary Marr, *er d* of late Baron Louis de Chollet. *Educ:* Eton; Trinity Coll., Cambridge (BA). Dir, BSC, 1972–76. Dir, 1970, Chm., 1975–82, Great Northern Investment Trust Ltd. Mem., London Adv. Cttee, Hongkong & Shanghai Banking Corp. Mem., Scottish Econ. Council, 1972-. *Recreations:* shooting, golf, fishing. *Heir:* s Hon. James William Hartland Weir, *b* 6 June 1965. *Address:* Rodinghead, Mauchline, Ayrshire. *T:* Fiveways 233. *Club:* White's.

WEIR, Rear-Adm. Alexander Fortune Rose, CB 1981; JP; self-employed marine consultant; *b* 17 June 1928; *s* of late Comdr Patrick Wylie Rose Weir and of Minna Ranken Forrester Weir (*née* Fortune); *m* 1953, Ann Ross Hamilton Crawford, Ardmore, Co. Londonderry; four *d*. *Educ:* Royal Naval Coll., Dartmouth. FBIM 1979. Cadet, 1945–46; Midshipman, 1946–47; Actg Sub-Lieut under trng, HMS Zephyr, Portland, 1947; Sub-Lieut professional courses, 1947–48; Sub-Lieut and Lieut, HMS Loch Arkaig, Londonderry Sqdn, 1949–51; ADC to Governor of Victoria, Aust., 1951–53; HMS Mariner, Fishery Protection Sqdn, Home waters and Arctic, 1953–54; qual. as Navigating Officer, 1954; HMS St Austell Bay, WI, Navigating Officer, 1955–56; HMS Wave, Fishery Protection Sqdn, Home, Arctic and Iceland, 1956–58; Lt-Comdr, advanced navigation course, 1958; Staff ND Officer, Flag Officer Sea Trng at Portland, Dorset, 1958–61; HMS Plymouth, Staff Officer Ops, 4th Frigate Sqdn, Far East Station, 1961–62; Comdr 1962; Trng Comdr, BRNC Dartmouth, 1962–64; Comd, HMS Rothesay, WI Station, 1965–66; Staff of C-in-C Portsmouth, Staff Officer Ops, 1966–68; 2nd in Comd and Exec. Officer, HMS Eagle, 1968–69; Captain 1969; jssc 1969–70; Pres., Far East Comd Midshipman's Bd, 1970; Asst Dir Naval Operational Requirements, MoD(N), 1970–72; Captain (F) 6th Frigate Sqdn (8 ships) and HMS Andromeda, 1972–74; NATO Def. Coll., Rome, 1974–75; ACOS Strategic Policy Requirements and Long Range Objectives, SACLANT, 1975–77; Captain HMS Bristol, 1977–78; Dep. Asst Chief of Staff (Ops) to SACEUR, 1978–81. Member: Nautical Inst.; Royal Inst. of Navigation. Licenced Royal Naval Lay Reader, 1981; Licensed Lay Reader, Westbourne Parish, Dio. Chichester, 1982-. JP Chichester, 1982. *Recreations:* Rugby referee (RNRRU and RR Society of Virginia, USA); hockey, sailing, shooting, golf, squash. *Address:* Manor House, Aldsworth, Emsworth, Hampshire PO10 8QT. *T:* Emsworth 2973. *Clubs:* Naval and Military, Royal Navy 1765 and 1785, Institute of Directors; Royal Naval Sailing Association; Caravan (Sussex).

WEIR, Very Rev. Andrew John, MSc, DD; Clerk of Assembly and General Secretary, The Presbyterian Church in Ireland, since 1964; *b* 24 March 1919; *s* of Rev. Andrew Weir and Margaret Weir, Missionaries to Manchuria of the Presbyterian Church in Ireland. *Educ:* Campbell Coll., Belfast; Queen's Univ., Belfast; New Coll., Edinburgh; Presbyterian Coll., Belfast. Ordained, 1944; Missionary to China, 1945–51; Minister, Trinity Presbyterian Church,

Letterkenny, Co. Donegal, 1952–62; Asst Clerk of Assembly and Home Mission Convener, The Presbyterian Church in Ireland, 1962–64. Moderator of the General Assembly, The Presbyterian Church in Ireland, 1976–77. *Address:* (official) Church House, Belfast BT1 6DW. *T:* Belfast 222284; (home) 16 Harberton Drive, Belfast BT9 6PF. *T:* Belfast 667901.

WEIR, Rev. Cecil James Mullo, MA, DD, DPhil; Professor of Hebrew and Semitic Languages, University of Glasgow, 1937–68; *b* Edinburgh, 4 Dec. 1897; *e s* of late James Mullo Weir, SSC, FSAScot, Solicitor, Edinburgh; unmarried. *Educ:* Royal High School, Edinburgh; Universities of Edinburgh, Marburg, Paris and Leipzig; Jesus College, Oxford. Served European War, 1917–19, with Expeditionary Force in France, Belgium and Germany; Tutor in Hebrew, University of Edinburgh, 1921–22; MA Edinburgh with 1st Class Honours in Classics, 1923; 1st Class Honours in Semitic Languages, 1925; BD Edinburgh, 1926; DPhil Oxford, 1930; Minister of Orwell, Kinross-shire, 1932–34; Rankin Lecturer and Head of Department of Hebrew and Ancient Semitic Languages, University of Liverpool, 1934–37; Lecturer in the Institute of Archæology, Liverpool, 1934–37. President, Glasgow Archæological Soc., 1945–48; Dean of Faculty of Divinity, Univ. of Glasgow, 1951–54; Hon. DD (Edinburgh), 1959; FRAS, FSAScot. *Publications:* A Lexicon of Accadian Prayers in the Rituals of Expiation, 1934; contributed to A Companion to the Bible (ed Manson), 1939; Fortuna Domus, 1952; Documents from Old Testament Times (ed Thomas), 1958; Hastings's Dictionary of the Bible, 1963; A Companion to the Bible (ed Rowley), 1963; Archæology and Old Testament Study (ed Thomas), 1967; edited Transactions of Glasgow University Oriental Soc., Studia Semitica et Orientalia, Transactions of Glasgow Archæological Soc.; articles and reviews of books. *Recreations:* golf, travel. *Address:* 3 Inchgarry Court, North Berwick. *T:* North Berwick 2812.

WEIR, David Bruce, QC (Scot.) 1971; *b* 19 Dec. 1931; *yr s* of James Douglas Weir and late Kathleen Maxwell Weir (*née* Auld); *m* 1964, Katharine Lindsay, *yr d* of Hon. Lord Cameron, *qv* ; three *s*. *Educ:* Kelvinside Academy; Glasgow Academy; The Leys Sch., Cambridge; Glasgow Univ. (MA, LLB). Royal Naval Reserve, 1955–64, Lieut RNR. Admitted to Faculty of Advocates, 1959; Advocate Depute for Sheriff Court, 1964; Standing Junior Counsel: to MPBW, 1969; to DoE, 1970; Advocate Depute, 1979-. Chairman: Medical Appeal Tribunal, 1972–77; Pensions Appeals Tribunal, 1978-; Member: Criminal Injuries Compensation Bd, 1974–79; Transport Tribunal, 1979-. *Recreations:* sailing, music. *Address:* 9 Russell Place, Edinburgh EH5 3HQ. *T:* 031-552 2015. *Clubs:* New (Edinburgh); Royal Highland Yacht.

WEIR, Gillian; concert organist; *b* 17 Jan. 1941; *d* of Cecil Alexander Weir and Clarice M. Foy Weir. *Educ:* Royal College of Music, London. LRSM, LRAM, LTCL; Hon. FRCO. Winner of St Albans Internat. Organ Competition, 1964; Début, 1965: Royal Festival Hall, solo recital; Royal Albert Hall, concerto soloist, opening night of Promenade Concerts; since then, worldwide career solely as touring concert organist; concerto appearances with all major British orchestras, also with Boston Symphony, Seattle Symphony, Württemberg Chamber Orch., and others; solo appearances at leading internat. Festivals, incl. Bath, Aldeburgh, English Bach, Europalia, Europe and USA (AGO Nat. Conventions, RCCO Diamond Jubilee Nat. Convention, etc). Frequent radio and television appearances: BBC Third Prog., USA, Australasia, Europe; many first performances, incl. major works by Fricker, Connolly, Camilleri, Messiaen. Master-classes, adjudicator internat. competitions, UK, France, N America. Hon. FRCO and Mem. Council, RCO, 1977- (first woman Mem.); Pres., Incorp. Assoc. of Organists, 1981–83 (first woman Pres.). Internat. Performer of the Year Award, NY Amer. Guild of Organists, 1981; Internat. Music Guide's Musician of the Year Award, 1982. *Publications:* contributor to: Grove's Internat. Dictionary of Music and Musicians, 1980; musical jls and periodicals. *Recreation:* theatre. *Address:* c/o Clarion Concert Agency, 64 Whitehall Park, N19 3TN. *T:* 01-272 4413. *Club:* University Women's.

WEIR, Sir Michael (Scott), KCMG 1980 (CMG 1974); HM Diplomatic Service; Ambassador, Cairo, since 1979; *b* 28 Jan. 1925; *s* of Archibald and Agnes Weir; *m* 1953, Alison Walker; two *s* two *d* ; *m* 1976, Hilary Reid; two *s*. *Educ:* Dunfermline High School; Balliol College, Oxford. Served RAF (Flt Lt), 1944–47; subseq. HM Diplomatic Service; Foreign Office, 1950; Political Agent, Trucial States, 1952–54; FO, 1954–56; Consul, San Francisco, 1956–58; 1st Secretary: Washington, 1958–61; Cairo, 1961–63; FO, 1963–68; Counsellor, Head of Arabian Dept, 1966; Dep. Political Resident, Persian Gulf, Bahrain, 1968–71; Head of Chancery, UK Mission to UN, NY, 1971–73; Asst Under-Sec. of State, FCO, 1974–79. *Recreations:* golf, music. *Address:* c/o Foreign and Commonwealth Office, SW1.

WEIR, Peter Lindsay, AM 1982; film director, since 1969; *b* 21 Aug. 1944; *s* of Lindsay Weir and Peggy Barnsley Weir; *m* 1966, Wendy Stites; one *s* one *d*. *Educ:* Scots Coll., Sydney; Vaucluse High Sch.; Sydney Univ. Short Film: Homesdale, 1971; Feature Films: The Cars That Ate Paris, 1973; Picnic at Hanging Rock, 1975; Last Wave, 1977; The Plumber (for TV), 1979; Gallipoli, 1980; The Year of Living Dangerously, 1982. *Address:* c/o Palm Beach, NSW 2108, Australia.

WEIR, Richard Stanton; Secretary General (Chief Executive), Building Societies Association, since 1981; *b* 5 Jan. 1933; *o s* of Brig. R. A. Weir, OBE and Dr M. L. Cowan; *m* 1961, Helen Eugenie Guthrie; one *d*. *Educ:* Repton Sch., Derbys; Christ Church, Oxford (MA). Called to the Bar, Inner Temple,

1957. Commnd 3rd Carabiniers (Prince of Wales' Dragoon Guards), 1952. Head of Legal Dept, Soc. of Motor Mfrs and Traders Ltd, 1958-61; Exec., British Motor Corp. Ltd, 1961-64; Dep. Co. Sec., Rank Organisation Ltd, 1964-67; Head of Admin, Rank Leisure Services, 1967-69; Sec., CWS Ltd, 1969-74; Dir, The Retail Consortium, 1975-81. Mem., Consumer Protection Adv. Cttee set up under Fair Trading Act, 1973, 1973-76. *Recreations:* reading, walking, shooting. *Address:* 2 Lamont Road, SW10. *T:* 01-352 4809. *Club:* United Oxford & Cambridge University.

WEIR, Robert Hendry, CB 1960; Engineering Consultant; *b* Glasgow, 18 Feb. 1912; *s* of Peter and Malcolmina Weir; *m* 1934, Edna Frances Lewis; three *s*. *Educ:* Allan Glen's Glasgow; Glasgow University (BSc Hons). Engineering Apprenticeship, Wm Denny & Bros, Dumbarton, 1928-33; Royal Aircraft Establishment, 1933-39; Air Ministry HQ, 1939-40; Aircraft and Armament Experimental Establishment, 1940-42; Ministry of Aircraft Production and Ministry of Supply, 1942-; Asst Director, 1948-50; Director of Industrial Gas Turbines, 1950-52; Director of Engine Research and Development, 1952-53; Deputy Director-General, Engine Research and Development, 1954-59 (Min. of Supply); Dir-Gen. of Engine Research and Development 1959-60 (Min. of Aviation); Dir, Nat. Gas Turbine Establishment, Pyestock, near Farnborough, 1960-70; Dir, Nat. Engineering Laboratory, East Kilbride, 1970-74. FRAeSoc. Coronation Medal, 1953. *Publications:* various. *Recreations:* golf, painting; keen interest in Association Football. *Address:* 11 Broom Cliff, 30 Castleton Drive, Newton Mearns, Glasgow G77 5LG. *T:* 041-639 5388.

WEISKRANTZ, Lawrence, FRS 1980; Professor of Psychology, Oxford University, since 1967; Fellow, Magdalen College, Oxford; *b* 28 March 1926; *s* of Dr Benjamin Weiskrantz and Rose (*née* Rifkin); *m* 1954, Barbara Collins; one *s* one *d*. *Educ:* Girard College; Swarthmore; Univs of Oxford and Harvard. Part-time Lectr, Tufts University, 1952; Research Assoc., Inst. of Living, 1952-55; Sen. Postdoctoral Fellow, US Nat. Res. Coun., 1955-56; Research Assoc., Cambridge Univ., 1956-61; Asst Dir of Research, Cambridge Univ., 1961-66; Reader in Physiological Psychology, Cambridge Univ., 1966-67. Kenneth Craik Research Award, St John's Coll., Cambridge, 1975-76. Dep. Editor, Brain, 1981-. *Publications:* (jtly) Analysis of Behavioural Change, 1967; articles in Science, Nature, Quarterly Jl of Experimental Psychology, Jl of Comparative and Physiological Psychology, Animal Behaviour. *Recreations:* music, walking. *Address:* Department of Experimental Psychology, South Parks Road, Oxford OX1 3UD.

WEISMAN, Malcolm; Barrister-at-law; Assistant Commissioner of Parliamentary Boundaries, since 1976; a Recorder of the Crown Court, since 1980; *s* of David and Jeanie Pearl Weisman; *m* 1958, Rosalie, *d* of Dr and Mrs A. Spiro; two *s*. *Educ:* Harrogate Grammar Sch.; Parmiter's Sch.; London School of Economics; St Catherine's Coll., Oxford (MA). Blackstone Pupillage Prize. Chaplain (Sqdn Ldr), Royal Air Force, 1956; called to Bar, Middle Temple, 1961; Senior Chaplain, HM Forces, 1972. Religious advisor to small congregations, and Hon. Chaplain, Oxford and new universities, 1963-; Chm. and Sec.-Gen., Allied Air Forces in Europe Chief of Chaplains Cttee, 1981-. Member: Senior Common Room, Essex, Kent and Lancaster Univs, 1964-; Court of Univ. of Lancaster, 1970-; Governor, Parmiter's Sch., 1980-. *Recreations:* travelling, reading, doing nothing. *Address:* 1 Gray's Inn Square, WC1R 5AA. *T:* 01-405 8946.

WEISS, Mrs Althea McNish; *see* McNish, A. M.

WEISS, Sir Eric, Kt 1980; President, Foseco Minsep plc, since 1979 (Chairman, 1969-78); *b* 30 Dec. 1908; *s* of late Solomon Weiss and Ada Weiss; *m* 1934, Greta Kobaltzky; two *s* two *d*. *Educ:* Augustinus Gymnasium, Weiden, Germany; Neues Gym., Nurnberg, Germany. Founder, Foundry Services Ltd (original co. of Foseco Group), 1932; Chm., Minerals Separation Ltd, 1964; Chm., Foseco Minsep Ltd, 1969, when co. formed by merger of Foseco Ltd with Minerals Separation Ltd. Underwriting Mem., Lloyd's, 1976-79. United World Colleges: Dep. Pres., 1973-76; Mem., UK Commn of United World Colls Project, 1968-74; Mem., Internat. Council, 1969-76; Mem., Bd of Dirs, 1970-76; Mem. Bd Governors, United World Coll. of Atlantic, 1976-. Mem., Inst. of British Foundrymen. Trustee: Inst. for Archaeo-Metallurgical Studies, 1976-; Oakham Sch., 1963-. *Recreations:* golf, travel. *Address:* The Manor House, Little Marlow, Bucks SL7 3RZ. *T:* Marlow 2824. *Club:* Garrick.

WEISS, Robert Anthony, (Robin), PhD; Director, Institute of Cancer Research, since 1980; *b* 20 Feb. 1940; *s* of Hans Weiss and Stefanie Löwensohn; *m* 1964, Margaret Rose D'Costa; two *d*. *Educ:* University College London (BSc, PhD). Lecturer in Embryology, University Coll. London, 1963-70; Eleanor Roosevelt Internat. Cancer Research Fellow, Univ. of Washington, Seattle, 1970-71; Visiting Associate Prof., Microbiology, Univ. of Southern California, 1971-72; Staff Scientist, Imperial Cancer Research Fund Laboratories, 1972-80, Gustav Stern Award in Virology, 1973. *Publications:* RNA Tumour Viruses; various articles on cell biology, virology and genetics. *Recreations:* music, natural history. *Address:* Institute of Cancer Research, Chester Beatty Laboratories, Fulham Road, SW3 6JB.

WEISSKOPF, Prof. Victor Frederick; Professor of Physics at Massachusetts Institute of Technology, Cambridge, Mass, USA, since 1946 (on leave, 1961-65); Chairman, Department of Physics, MIT, 1967-73; *b* 19 Sept. 1908; *m* 1934, Ellen Margrete Tvede; one *s* one *d*. *Educ:* Göttingen, Germany. PhD 1931. Research Associate: Berlin Univ., 1932; Eidgenossiche Technische

Hochschule (Swiss Federal Institute of Technology), Zürich, 1933-35; Inst. for Theoretical Physics, Copenhagen, 1936; Asst Professor of Physics, Univ. of Rochester, NY, USA, 1937-43; Dep. Division Leader, Manhattan Project, Los Alamos, USA, 1943-45; Director-Gen., CERN, Geneva, 1961-65. Chm., High Energy Physics Adv. Panel, AEC, 1967-. Mem., Nat. Acad. of Sciences, Washington, 1954; Pres., Amer. Acad. of Arts and Sciences, 1976-79; Corresp. Member: French Acad. of Sciences, 1957; Scottish Acad. of Scis, 1959; Royal Danish Scientific Soc., 1961; Bavarian Acad. of Scis, 1962; Austrian Acad. of Scis, 1963; Spanish Acad. of Scis, 1964; Soviet Acad. of Scis, 1976; Pontifical Acad. of Scis, 1976. Hon. Fellow: Weizmann Inst., Rehovot, Israel, 1962; Inst. of Physics, France, 1980. Hon. PhD: Manchester, 1961; Uppsala, 1964; Yale, 1964; Chicago, 1967; Hon. DSc: Montreal, 1959; Sussex, 1961; Lyon, 1962; Basle, 1962; Bonn, 1963; Genève, 1964; Oxford, 1965; Vienna, 1965; Paris, 1966; Copenhagen, 1966; Torino, 1968. Cherwell-Simon Memorial Lecturer, Oxford, 1963-64. Planck Medal, 1956; Gamov Award, 1969; Prix Mondial Del Duca, 1972; Killian Award, 1973; Smoluchovski Medal, Polish Physical Soc., 1979; Nat. Medal of Science, 1979; Wolf Prize (Israel), 1981. Legion d'Honneur (France), 1959; Pour le Mérite Order, Germany, 1978. *Publications:* Theoretical Nuclear Physics, 1952; Knowledge and Wonder, 1962; Physics in the XX Century, 1972; papers on theoretical physics in various journals. *Address:* 36 Arlington Street, Cambridge, Mass 02140, USA.

WEISSMÜLLER, Alberto Augusto, FIB; Director, LITCO Bancorporation of New York (a subsidiary of Banca Commerciale Italiana), since 1982; *b* 2 March 1927; *s* of late Carlos Weissmüller and Michela Cottura; *m* 1976, Joan Ann Freifrau von Süsskind-Schwendi (*née* Smithson); one *s* one *d* by previous *m*. *Educ:* Univ. of Buenos Aires, Argentina; Illinois Inst. of Technol., Chicago, USA. Civil Engr, 1952; FIB 1977. The Lummus Co., New York, 1958-59; Office of Graham Parker, NY, 1960-62; Bankers Trust Co., NY, 1962-71: Edge Act subsid., 1962-64; Asst Treasurer, and mem., Bd of Corporation Financiera Nacional, Colombia, 1964-65; Asst Vice-Pres., 1965-67; Vice-Pres., 1967-71; Rome Rep., 1968-71; Crocker National Bank, San Francisco, seconded to United Internat. Bank (now Privatbanken Ltd), London, as Chief Exec., 1971-79; Chief Adviser, Bank of England, 1979-81; Chief Exec. (UK), Banca Commerciale Italiana, 1981-82; Chm., BCI Ltd, London, 1981-; Dir, Long Island Trust Co., 1982-. *Publication:* Castles from the Heart of Spain, 1977. *Recreations:* medieval fortified architecture, photography (architectural). *Address:* Banca Commerciale Italiana, 280 Park Avenue, New York, NY 10017, USA. *Clubs:* Overseas Bankers; Board Room (New York).

WEITNAUER, Dr Albert; *b* Brazil, 30 May 1916; *s* of Albert Weitnauer and Stephanie (*née* Hoeschl); unmarried. *Educ:* Basle Gymnasium; Basle Univ. (Dr of Laws). Entered Swiss Govt Service, 1941; Legal Adviser, later Dep. Head, Federal Office for War Economy, 1941-46; transf. to Commercial Div. Federal Dept of Public Economy, 1946; Head of Section I, 1951; attached to Swiss Legation in London, 1953-54 and in Washington, 1954-58 as Counsellor i/c Econ. Affairs; Delegate of Swiss Govt for Trade Agreements and Special Missions, 1959-71; Minister, 1961; Ambassador, 1966; Ambassador to the Court of St James's, 1971-76; State Secretary for Foreign Affairs, 1976-80, retired. *Publications:* articles on problems of Swiss foreign policy, European integration and world trade. *Recreations:* golf, reading, study of languages. *Address:* Jubiläumsstrasse 97, 3005 Berne, Switzerland.

WEITZ, Dr Bernard George Felix, OBE 1965; DSc; MRCVS; FIBiol; Chief Scientist, Ministry of Agriculture, Fisheries and Food, 1977-81; *b* London, 14 Aug. 1919; *m* 1945, Elizabeth Shine; one *s* one *d*. *Educ:* St Andrew, Bruges, Belgium; Royal Veterinary College, London. MRCVS 1942; DSc London 1961. Temp. Research Worker, ARC Field Station, Compton, Berks, 1942; Research Officer, Veterinary Laboratory, Min. of Agric. and Fisheries, 1942-47; Head of Serum Dept, 1952; Dir, Nat. Inst. for Res. in Dairying, Univ. of Reading, Shinfield, Berks, 1967-77. Vis. Prof., Dept of Agriculture and Horticulture, Univ. of Reading, 1980-. Member: ARC, 1978-81; NERC, 1978-81. Hon. FRASE, 1977. *Publications:* many contribs to scientific journals on Immunology and Tropical Medicine. *Recreations:* music, croquet. *Address:* Grazebrook, Brockhampton, Glos GL54 5XL.

WEITZMAN, David, QC 1951; Barrister-at-Law; *b* 18 June 1898; *s* of Percy Weitzman; *m* 1st, 1925 (wife *d* 1950); one *s* one *d*; 2nd, 1955, Lena (*d* 1969), widow of Dr S. H. Dundon, Liverpool; 3rd, 1972, Vivienne Hammond. *Educ:* Hutchesons' Grammar School, Glasgow; Manchester Central School; Manchester University. Private, 3rd Battalion Manchester Regiment, 1916; BA (History Honours), 1921; called to Bar (Gray's Inn), 1922; member of Northern Circuit. Member of Labour Party since 1923. Contested (Lab) Stoke Newington, 1935; MP (Lab) Stoke Newington, 1945-50, Hackney North and Stoke Newington, 1950-79. *Recreation:* golf. *Address:* Devereux Chambers, Devereux Court, Temple, WC2R 3JJ. *T:* 01-353 7534.
See also P. Weitzman.

WEITZMAN, Peter, QC 1973; a Recorder of the Crown Court, since 1974; *b* 20 June 1926; *s* of David Weitzman, *qv*, and late Fanny Weitzman; *m* 1954, Anne Mary Larkam; two *s* two *d*. *Educ:* Cheltenham Coll.; Christ Church, Oxford (MA). Royal Artillery, 1945-48. Called to Bar, Gray's Inn, 1952; Bencher, 1981. Mem., Senate of Inns of Court, 1980-81. *Recreations:* hedging and ditching. *Address:* 21 St James's Gardens, W11; Little Leigh, Kingsbridge, Devon.

WELANDER, Rev. Canon David Charles St Vincent; Canon Residentiary, Gloucester Cathedral, since 1975; *b* 22 Jan. 1925; *s* of late Ernest Sven Alexis Welander, Orebro and Uppsala, Sweden, and Louisa Georgina Downes Welander (*née* Panter); *m* 1952, Nancy O'Rorke Stanley; two *s* three *d*. *Educ:* Unthank Coll., Norwich: London Univ. (BD 1947, Rubie Hebrew Prize 1947); ALCD (1st Cl.) 1947; Toronto Univ., 1947–48 (Hon. Mem. Alumni, Wycliffe Coll., 1948). FSA 1981. Deacon 1948, Priest 1949; Asst Curate, Holy Trinity, Norwich, 1948–51; Chaplain and Tutor, London Coll. of Divinity, 1952–56; Vicar: of Iver, Bucks, 1956–62; of Christ Church, Cheltenham, 1963–75; Rural Dean of Cheltenham, 1973–75. Member: Council, St Paul's and St Mary's Colls of Educn, Cheltenham, 1963–78; Council, Malvern Girls' Coll., 1982–; Bishops' Cttee on Inspections of Theol Colls, 1967–; Sen. Inspector of Theol Colls, 1970–; Mem., Gen. Synod of C of E, 1970–; Trustee, Church Patronage Trust, 1969–78. Canon-Librarian of Gloucester, 1975–. *Publications:* History of Iver, 1954; Gloucester Cathedral, 1979; contrib. Expository Times, etc. *Recreations:* walking, sailing, church architecture, music. *Address:* 6 College Green, Gloucester GL1 2LX. *T:* Gloucester 21954. *Club:* Royal Commonwealth Society.

WELBORE KER, Keith R.; *see* Ker.

WELBOURN, Prof. Richard Burkewood, MA, MD, FRCS; Professor of Surgical Endocrinology, Royal Postgraduate Medical School, University of London, and Hon. Consultant Surgeon, Hammersmith Hospital, since 1979; *b* 1919; *y s* of late Burkewood Welbourn, MEng, MIEE, and Edith Welbourn, Rainhill, Lancs; *m* 1944, Rachel Mary Haighton, BDS, Nantwich, Cheshire; one *s* four *d*. *Educ:* Rugby School; Emmanuel College, Cambridge; Liverpool University. MB, BChir 1942; FRCS 1948; MA, MD Cambridge, 1953. War of 1939–45: RAMC. Senior Registrar, Liverpool Royal Infirmary, 1948; Research Asst, Dept of Surgery, Liverpool Univ., 1949. Fellow in Surgical Research, Mayo Foundation, Rochester, Minn., 1951. Professor of Surgical Science, Queen's University of Belfast, 1958–63; Surgeon, Royal Victoria Hospital, Belfast, 1951–63 and Belfast City Hosp., 1962–63; Prof. of Surgery, Univ. of London and Dir, Dept of Surgery, RPMS and Hammersmith Hosp., 1963–79. Consultant Adviser in Surgery to Dept of Health and Social Security, 1971–79. Member: Council, MRC, 1971–75; Council, Royal Postgraduate Med. Sch. Hunterian Professor, RCS of England, 1958. Member: Society of Sigma XI; British Medical Association. Formerly Mem. Council, British Soc. of Gastro-enterology and Assoc. of Surgeons; 58th Member King James IV Surgical Association Inc.; Fellow, West African Coll. of Surgeons; FRSM (Former Mem. Council, Section of Endocrinology, former Vice-Pres., Section of Surgery); Hon. Fellow Amer. Surgical Assoc.; Hon. Mem., Soc. for Surgery of the Alimentary Tract; formerly: Pres., Surgical Res. Soc.; Chm., Assoc. of Profs of Surgery; Mem., Jt Cttee for Higher Surgical Training; Examr in Surgery: Univ. of Liverpool; formerly Univs of Glasgow, Oxford, Sheffield, Edinburgh, and QUB; formerly Examr in Applied Physiology, RCS. Chm., Editorial Cttee, Journal of Medical Ethics; former Member: Editorial Cttee, Gut; Exec. Cttee, British Jl of Surgery. President: Internat. Surgical Gp; Vice-Chm., Soc. for the Study of Medical Ethics. Former Pres., Prout Club. Hon. MD Karolinska Inst., Stockholm, 1974; Hon. Mem., Roy. Coll. of Surgeons of Univs of Denmark, 1978. *Publications:* (with D. A. D. Montgomery): Clinical Endocrinology for Surgeons, 1963, rev. edn, Medical and Surgical Endocrinology, 1975; (with A. S. Duncan and G. R. Dunstan) Dictionary of Medical Ethics, 1977, 2nd edn 1980, American edn 1981; contrib. chaps to Textbook of British Surgery, ed Souttar & Goligher; Surgery of Peptic Ulcer, ed Wells & Kyle; Progress in Clinical Surgery, ed Rodney Smith; British Surgical Practice, ed Rock-Carling & Ross; Scientific Foundations of Surgery, ed Wells & Kyle; Scientific Foundations of Oncology, ed Symington and Carter; Scientific Foundations of Family Medicine, ed Fry, Gambrill & Smith; Recent Advances in Surgery, etc; papers, mainly on gastro-intestinal and endocrine surgery and physiology, in med. and surg. jls. *Recreations:* reading, writing, gardening, music. *Address:* 6 Broomfield Road, Kew Gardens, Richmond, Surrey TW9 3HR. *T:* 01-940 2906.

WELBY, Sir Bruno; *see* Welby, Sir R. B. G.

WELBY, Euphemia Violet, CBE 1944; JP; late Superintendent Women's Royal Naval Service; *b* 28 Sept. 1891; *d* of Admiral H. Lyon, CB; *m* 1917, Lt-Comdr R. M. Welby; two *s* one *d* (and one *d* decd). *Educ:* Private. Hon. Sec. SS&AFA Devonport, 1914–16; Red Cross Cook, Malta, 1916–19; later Hon. Sec. SS&AFA; served in WRNS, 1939–45; social work on committees in Plymouth and Chairman Astor Institute. JP Somerset, 1947. *Recreation:* riding. *Address:* College Farm, Tintinhull, near Yeovil BA22 8PQ. *T:* Martock 3536; Milton Lodge, Freshwater Bay, Isle of Wight. *T:* Freshwater 3139.

WELBY, Sir (Richard) Bruno (Gregory), 7th Bt *cr* 1801; *b* 11 March 1928; *s* of Sir Oliver Charles Earle Welby, 6th Bt, TD, and of Barbara Angela Mary Lind, *d* of late John Duncan Gregory, CB, CMG; *S* father, 1977; *m* 1952, Jane Biddulph, *y d* of late Ralph Wilfred Hodder-Williams, MC; three *s* one *d*. *Educ:* Eton; Christ Church, Oxford (BA 1950). *Heir:* *s* Charles William Hodder Welby [*b* 6 May 1953; *m* 1978, Suzanna, *o d* of Major Ian Stuart-Routledge, Harston Hall, Grantham; one *d*]. *Address:* Denton House, Grantham, Lincs.

WELBY-EVERARD, Maj.-Gen. Sir Christopher Earle, KBE 1965 (OBE 1945); CB 1961; DL; *b* 9 Aug. 1909; *s* of late E. E. E. Welby-Everard,

Gosberton House, near Spalding, Lincolnshire; *m* 1938, Sybil Juliet Wake Shorrock; two *s*. *Educ:* Charterhouse; CCC, Oxford. Gazetted The Lincolnshire Regt, 1930; OC 2 Lincolns, 1944; GSO1, 49 (WR) Inf. Div., 1944–46; GSO1 GHQ, MELF, 1946–48; OC 1 Royal Lincolnshire Regt, 1949–51; Comd 264 Scottish Beach Bde and 157 (L) Inf. Bde, 1954–57. BGS (Ops), HQ, BAOR, and HQ Northern Army Group, 1957–59; Chief of Staff, HQ Allied Forces, Northern Europe, 1959–61; GOC Nigerian Army, 1962–65; retd. DL Lincolnshire, 1966; High Sheriff of Lincolnshire, 1974. *Recreations:* shooting, cricket. *Address:* The Manor House, Sapperton, Sleaford, Lincolnshire NG34 0TB. *T:* Ingoldsby 273. *Clubs:* Army and Navy; Free Foresters.

WELCH, Anthony Edward, CB 1957; CMG 1949; formerly Under-Secretary, Board of Trade, 1946–66 (Ministry of Materials, 1951–54); *b* 17 July 1906; *s* of late Francis Bertram Welch; *m* 1946, Margaret Eileen Strudwick (*d* 1978); no *c*. *Educ:* Cheltenham College; New College, Oxford. *Address:* Brandon Lodge, Walberswick, Suffolk. *T:* Southwold 722582.

WELCH, Colin; *see* Welch, J. C. R.

WELCH, Air Vice-Marshal Edward Lawrence C.; *see* Colbeck-Welch.

WELCH, (James) Colin (Ross); Political Columnist, The Spectator, since 1982; *b* 23 April 1924; *s* of James William Welch and Irene Margherita (*née* Paton), Ickleton Abbey, Cambridgeshire; *m* 1950, Sybil Russell; one *s* one *d*. *Educ:* Stowe Sch. (schol.); Peterhouse, Cambridge (major schol., BA Hons). Commissioned Royal Warwickshire Regt, 1942; served NW Europe, twice wounded. Glasgow Herald, 1948; Colonial Office, 1949; Daily Telegraph: leader writer, columnist (Peter Simple, with Michael Wharton), Parliamentary sketch-writer, 1950–80; Dep. Editor, 1964–80; regular column, 1981–; Editor-in-Chief, Chief Executive magazine, 1980–82. Knight's Cross, Order of Polonia Restituta, 1972. *Publications:* (ed) Sir Frederick Ponsonby: Recollections of Three Reigns, 1951; (trans. with Sybil Welch) Nestroy: Liberty Comes to Krähwinkel, 1954 (BBC); articles in Encounter, Spectator, New Statesman, etc; contribs to symposia, incl. The Future that Doesn't Work, 1977 (New York). *Address:* 15 Lottage Cottage, Aldbourne, Wilts. *T:* Marlborough 40010.

WELCH, Sir John (Reader), 2nd Bt *cr* 1957; *b* 26 July 1933; *s* of Sir (George James) Cullum Welch, 1st Bt, OBE, MC, and Gertrude Evelyn Sladin Welch (*d* 1966); *S* father, 1980; *m* 1962, Margaret Kerry, *o d* of K. Douglass, Killara, NSW; one *s* twin *d*. *Educ:* Marlborough College; Hertford Coll., Oxford (MA). National service in RCS, 1952–54. Admitted a solicitor, 1960. Director, John Fairfax & Sons (Australia) Ltd. Ward Clerk of Walbrook Ward, City of London, 1961–74, Common Councilman, 1975–; Registrar of Archdeaconry of London. Liveryman, Haberdashers' Co., 1955 (Court of Assistants, 1973); Freeman, Parish Clerks' Co. (Master, 1967). Chm., Cttee of Management, London Homes for the Elderly. CStJ 1981. *Recreation:* piano. *Heir:* *s* James Douglass Cullum Welch, *b* 10 Nov. 1973. *Address:* Killara, The Glade, Kingswood, Tadworth, Surrey KT20 6LL; 16 Bedford Street, Covent Garden, WC2E 9HF. *T:* 01-379 7266. *Clubs:* City Livery, MCC, Surrey County Cricket.

WELCH, Robert Radford, MBE 1979; RDI 1965; FSIAD 1962; designer and silversmith, since 1955; *b* 21 May 1929; *m* 1959, Patricia Marguerite Hinksman; two *s* one *d*. *Educ:* Hanley Castle Grammar Sch.; Malvern Sch. of Art; Birmingham Coll. of Art; Royal Coll. of Art (DesRCA). FRSA 1967. Hon. Fellow RCA, 1972. Started own workshop in Chipping Campden, 1955; Design Consultant to Old Hall Tableware, 1955–. Vis. Lecturer: Central Sch. of Art and Design, 1957–63; RCA, 1963–71; visited India by invitation of All India Handicraft Bd, 1975. Silver commns for various clients, incl. civic plate, university colls, Goldsmiths' Hall, Canterbury Cathedral, V&A Museum, and British Govt Gift to St Lucia; tableware for British Ambassador's residence, Manila; design commns in Denmark, Germany, USA and Japan. Liveryman, Goldsmiths' Co., 1982. *Publication:* Design in a Cotswold Workshop (with Alan Crawford), 1973. *Recreations:* drawing, painting. *Address:* The White House, Alveston Leys, Alveston, Stratford-on-Avon, Warwicks. *T:* Stratford-on-Avon 4191.

WELCH, Rt. Rev. William Neville, MA; *b* 30 April 1906; *s* of Thomas William and Agnes Maud Welch; *m* 1935, Kathleen Margaret Beattie; two *s* two *d*. *Educ:* Dean Close Sch., Cheltenham; Keble Coll., Oxford; Wycliffe Hall, Oxford. Asst Curate: Kidderminster, 1929–32; St Michael's, St Albans, 1932–34; Organising Sec., Missions to Seamen, 1934–39; Vicar of Grays, 1939–43; Officiating Chaplain, Training Ship Exmouth, 1939–40; Vicar of Ilford, 1943–53; Rural Dean of Barking, 1948–53; Vicar of Great Burstead, 1953–56; Archdeacon of Southend, 1953–72; Bishop Suffragan of Bradwell, 1968–73. Proctor in Convocation, 1945 and 1950; Hon. Canon of Chelmsford, 1951–53. *Address:* 112 Earlham Road, Norwich. *T:* Norwich 618192.

WELD, Col Sir Joseph William, Kt 1973; OBE 1946; TD 1947 (two Bars); JP; Lord-Lieutenant of Dorset, since 1964; Chairman, Wessex Regional Health Authority (formerly Wessex Regional Hospital Board), 1972–75; *b* 22 Sept. 1909; *s* of Wilfrid Joseph Weld, Avon Dassett, Warwickshire; *m* 1933, Elizabeth, *d* of E. J. Bellord; one *s* six *d*. *Educ:* Stonyhurst; Balliol College, Oxford. Served with Dorset Regt, TA, 1932–41; Staff College, Camberley, 1941; GSO2, General Headquarters Home Forces, 1942; Instructor, Staff College, Camberley, 1942–43; GSO1, Headquarters SEAC, 1943–46;

commanded 4th Battalion Dorset Regt, 1947–51; Colonel, 1951. Hon. Colonel, 4th Battalion Dorset Regiment (TA). Chairman of Dorset Branch, County Landowners' Assoc., 1949–60; Chm. S Dorset Conservative Assoc., 1952–55 (Pres., 1955–59); Privy Chamberlain of Sword and Cape to Pope Pius XII. JP 1938, High Sheriff 1951, DL 1952, CC 1961, Dorset. KStJ 1967. *Address:* Lulworth Manor, East Lulworth, Dorset. *T:* West Lulworth 2352. *Club:* Royal Dorset Yacht.

WELD FORESTER, family name of **Baron Forester.**

WELDON, Sir Anthony (William), 9th Bt *cr* 1723; Managing Director, Bene Factum Press Ltd; *b* 11 May 1947; *s* of Sir Thomas Brian Weldon, 8th Bt, and of Marie Isobel, *d* of Hon. William Joseph French; *S* father, 1979; *m* 1980, Mrs Amanda Wigan, *d* of Major Geoffrey and Hon. Mrs North, Colleton Hall, Rackenford, Tiverton, Devon; one *d*. *Educ:* Sherborne. Formerly Lieutenant, Irish Guards. *Recreations:* stalking, fishing, antiquarian books and fine bindings. *Heir:* cousin Brig. Hamilton Edward Crosdill Weldon, *qv*. *Address:* The Fighting Cocks, West Amesbury, Salisbury, Wilts SP4 7BH. *Club:* White's.

WELDON, Fay; writer; *b* 22 Sept. 1935; *d* of Frank Birkinshaw and Margaret Jepson; *m* Ron Weldon; four *s*. *Educ:* Hampstead Girls' High Sch.; St Andrews Univ. *Publications:* The Fat Woman's Joke, 1969; Down Among the Women, 1972; Female Friends, 1975; Remember Me, 1977; Little Sisters, 1978; Praxis, 1979; Puffball, 1980; Watching Me, Watching You (short stories), 1981; The President's Child, 1982. *Recreation:* travel. *Address:* c/o Hodder & Stoughton, 47 Bedford Square, WC1B 3DP.

WELDON, Brig. Hamilton Edward Crosdill, CBE 1961 (OBE 1951); DL; Councillor, Waverley (Surrey) District Council, since 1979; *b* 14 September 1910; *s* of late Lt-Col Henry Walter Weldon, DSO, and Helen Louise Victoria Weldon (*née* Cowan); *heir-pres.* to Sir Anthony Weldon, Bt, *qv*; *m* 1st, 1935, Margaret Helen Katharine Passy (whom he divorced, 1946); one *d*; 2nd, 1948, Elwyne Priscilla Chaldecott; two *s* one *d*. *Educ:* Bilton Grange Preparatory School; Charterhouse; Royal Military Academy, Woolwich. Commissioned into RA as 2nd Lieut, 1930; Lieut 1933; Capt. 1938. Served War of 1939–45 (despatches, 1943, 1945): Adjutant, 1939–40; Bde Major, Malta, 1941; GSO1, RA Malta (Lt-Col), 1941–43. Staff Coll., Camberley, 1943–44; Lt-Col on Staff of SHAEF and 21 Army Group and various appointments in BAOR, 1944–47; AQMG (Lt-Col) HQ Southern Command, 1948; BAOR, 1951–52; Col on Staff of SHAPE, 1952–53; Command of 22 LAA Regt in Germany, 1953–55; Administrative Staff Coll., Greenlands, Henley, May–August 1955; Col at WO, 1955–58; Comdr, (Brig.) 33 AA Bde, 1958–60; Commandant, School of Artillery, Manorbier, 1960–62, retired. ADC to the Queen, 1961–62; Secretary, County of London T&AFA, 1962–68, Greater London TA&VRA, 1968–74. Croix-de-Guerre with Palm (Fr.), 1945. Hon. Col: 265 Light Air Defence Regt, RA (TA), 1965–67; London and Kent Regt, RA (T), 1967–69; London and Kent Regt RA Cadre, 1969–; a Dep. Hon. Col, 6th Bn Queen's Regt, T&AVR, 1971–72. Vice-Pres., Fedn of Old Comrades Assocs of London, 1963–; Pres., Windsor and District Gun Club, 1970–74; Hon. Treasurer, Nat. Canine Defence League, 1975–; Mem. Council, Nat. Artillery Assoc., 1976–; Regional Organiser, Army Benevolent Fund, 1975–79; Dir, Redgrave Theatre, Farnham, 1980–. DL Greater London, 1967–82. *Publications:* Drama in Malta, 1946; compiled Official Administrative History of 21 Army Group in NW Europe, 1945. *Recreations:* racing, shooting, theatre and writing. *Address:* 3 Burnt Hill Road, Wrecclesham, Farnham, Surrey GU10 4RU. *T:* Farnham 721783.

WELENSKY, Rt. Hon. Sir Roy, (Roland), PC 1960; KCMG 1959 (CMG 1946); Kt 1953; *b* Salisbury, Southern Rhodesia, 20 January 1907; *s* of Michael and Leah Welensky; *m* 1st, 1928, Elizabeth Henderson (*d* 1969); one *s* one *d*; 2nd, 1972, Valerie Scott; two *d*. *Educ:* Salisbury, S Rhodesia. Joined Railway service, 1924; Member National Council of the Railway Workers Union; Director of Manpower, Northern Rhodesia, 1941–46; formed N Rhodesia Labour Party, 1941; Member of Sir John Forster's commission to investigate the 1940 riots in Copperbelt; Chairman of various conciliation Boards and member of the Strauss (1943) and Grant (1946) Railway Arbitration Tribunals. Member of delegn to London to discuss Mineral Royalties (1949) and Constitution (1950 and 1951); Member of Northern Rhodesia delegation to Closer Association Conference at Victoria Falls, 1951. MLC, N Rhodesia, 1938, MEC 1940–53. Chm. Unofficial Members Assoc. 1946–53. Federation of Rhodesia and Nyasaland: Minister of Transport, Communications and Posts, 1953–56; Leader of the House and Deputy Prime Minister, 1955–56; Prime Minister and Minister of External Affairs, 1956–63 (also Minister of Defence, 1956–59). Heavy-weight boxing champion of the Rhodesias, 1926–28. *Publication:* Welensky's 4000 Days, The Life and Death of the Federation of Rhodesia and Nyasaland, 1964. *Relevant Publications:* The Rhodesian, by Don Taylor; Welensky's Story, by Garry Allighan. *Recreation:* gardening. *Address:* Shaftesbury House, Milldown Road, Blandford Forum, Dorset DT11 7DE. *Club:* Farmers'.

WELFORD, Prof. Walter Thompson, PhD, DSc; FRS 1980; Professor of Physics, Imperial College, University of London, since 1973; *b* 31 Aug. 1916; *s* of Abraham and Sonia Weinstein; *m* 1948, Jacqueline Joan Thompson (marr. diss. 1978); two *s*. *Educ:* LCC primary and technical schools; Univ. of London (BSc, PhD, DSc). Laboratory asst, 1933–42; R&D physicist in industry, 1943–48; Imperial College, 1948–; successively research asst, lectr, sen. lectr, reader and professor; Vis. Professor of Physics, Univ. of Chicago, 1980–.

Director, IC Optical Systems Ltd, 1970–. Thomas Young Medal, Inst. of Physics, 1973. *Publications:* Geometrical Optics, 1963; (with L. C. Martin) Technical Optics, Vol. 1, 1966; Aberrations of the Symmetrical Optical System, 1974; Optics (Oxford Phys. Series No 14), 1976, 2nd edn 1981 (Japanese edn 1976); (with R. Winston) The Optics of Non-Imaging Concentrators, 1978; numerous contribs dealing with all aspects of applied optics to learned jls. *Recreation:* surviving. *Address:* 8 Chiswick Road, W4 5RB. *T:* 01-995 2340.

WELLAND, Colin, (Colin Williams); actor, playwright; *b* 4 July 1934; *s* of John Arthur Williams and Norah Williams; *m* 1962, Patricia Sweeney; one *s* three *d*. *Educ:* Newton-le-Willows Grammar Sch.; Bretton Hall Coll.; Goldsmiths' Coll., London (Teacher's Dip. in Art and Drama). Art teacher, 1958–62; entered theatre, 1962; Library Theatre, Manchester, 1962–64; television, films, theatre, 1962–. Director: Radio Aire, 1981–; Fulham Rugby League Football Club. Films (actor): Kes; Villain; Straw Dogs; Sweeney; (original screenplay) Yanks, 1978; (original screenplay) Chariots of Fire, 1980 (won Oscar, Evening Standard and Broadcasting Press Guild Awards, 1982). Plays (author): Say Goodnight to Grandma, St Martin's, 1973; Roll on Four O'clock, Palace, 1981. Award winning TV plays include: Roll on Four O'clock, Kisses at 50, Leeds United, Your Man from Six Counties. Best TV Playwright, Writers Guild, 1970, 1973 and 1974; Best TV Writer, and Best Supporting Film Actor, BAFTA Awards, 1970; Broadcasting Press Guild Award (for writing), 1973. *Publications:* plays: Roomful of Holes, 1972; Say Goodnight to Grandma, 1973. *Recreations:* cricket, watching Rugby and soccer, films, dining out; enjoys travel. *Address:* c/o Anthony Jones, A. D. Peters Ltd, 10 Buckingham Street, WC2N 6BU.

WELLBELOVED, James; MP Bexley, Erith and Crayford, since 1974 (Erith and Crayford, Nov. 1965–1974) (Lab, 1965–81, SDP since 1981); Commercial Consultant; writer and broadcaster on foreign and domestic affairs; *b* 29 July 1926; *s* of Wilfred Henry Wellbeloved, Sydenham and Brockley (London), and Paddock Wood, Kent; *m* 1948, Mavis Beryl Ratcliff; two *s* one *d*. *Educ:* South East London Technical College. Boy seaman, 1942–46. Parly Private Secretary: Minister of Defence (Admin), 1967–69; Sec. of State for Foreign and Commonwealth Affairs, 1969–70; an Opposition Whip, 1972–74; Parly Under-Sec. of State for Defence (RAF), MoD, 1976–79. Dep. Chm., London MPs Parly Gp, 1970–81; Chairman: River Thames Gp; All Party Parly Camping and Caravanning Gp, 1967–74; Mem., Ecclesiastical Cttee, 1971–76. Member: RACS Political Purposes Cttee, 1973–; PLP Liaison Cttee, 1974–78; Vice Chm., Labour Party Defence Gp, 1970–81. Governor, Greenwich Hosp. Sch. *Publication:* Local Government, 1971. *Recreations:* camping, travel. *Address:* House of Commons, SW1. *T:* 01-219 4077.

WELLBY, Rear-Adm. Roger Stanley, CB 1958; DSO 1940; DL; Retired; lately Head of UK Services Liaison Staff in Australia and Senior Naval Adviser to UK High Commissioner, 1956–59; *b* 28 Apr. 1906; *o s* of Dr Stanley Wellby and Marian Schwann; *m* 1936, Elaine, *d* of late Sir Clifford Heathcote-Smith; three *s*. *Educ:* RNC, Dartmouth. Qualified as Torpedo Officer, 1931; Commander, 1939; Special Service in France, 1940 (DSO, Croix de Guerre); Captain, 1947; Imperial Defence College; Rear-Adm. 1956. Dep. Comr-in-Chief, St John Ambulance Brigade, 1963–71; Comr, St John Ambulance Brigade, Bucks, 1971–75. DL Bucks 1972. KStJ 1966. *Recreation:* hockey, for Navy. *Address:* Oakengrove, Hastoe, Tring, Herts. *T:* Tring 3233.

WELLER, Dr Thomas Huckle; Richard Pearson Strong Professor of Tropical Public Health, since 1954, and Head, Department of Tropical Public Health, 1954–81, Harvard; Director Center for Prevention of Infectious Diseases, Harvard School of Public Health, 1966–81; *b* 15 June 1915; *s* of Carl V. and Elsie H. Weller; *m* 1945, Kathleen R. Fahey; two *s* two *d*. *Educ:* University of Michigan (AB, MS); Harvard (MD). Fellow, Departments of Comparative Pathology and Tropical Medicine and Bacteriology, Harvard Medical School, 1940–41; Intern, Children's Hosp., Boston, 1941–42. Served War, 1942–45: 1st Lieut to Major, Medical Corps, US Army. Asst Resident in Medicine, Children's Hosp., 1946; Fellow, Pediatrics, Harvard Medical School, 1947; Instructor, Dept Tropical Public Health, Harvard School of Public Health, 1948; Assistant Professor, 1949; Associate Professor, 1950. Asst Director, Research Div. of Infectious Diseases, Children's Medical Center, Boston, 1949–55; Dir, Commission on Parasitic Diseases, Armed Forces Epidemiological Bd, 1953–59, Mem. 1959–72; Mem. Trop. Med. and parasitology study sect., US Public Health Service, 1953–56. Diplomate, American Board of Pediatrics, 1948; Amer. Acad. of Arts and Sciences, 1955; National Academy of Sciences, USA. Mead Johnson Award of Amer. Acad. of Pediatrics (jointly), 1954; Kimble Methodology Award (jointly), 1954; Nobel Prize Physiology or Medicine (jointly), 1954; Ledlie Prize, 1963; United Cerebral Palsy Weinstein-Goldenson Award, 1974; Bristol Award, Infectious Diseases Soc. of America, 1980. Hon. LLD Michigan, 1956; Hon. DSc Gustavus Adolphus Coll., 1975; Hon. LHD Lowell, 1977. *Publications:* numerous scientific papers on *in vitro* cultivation of viruses and on helminth infections of man. *Recreations:* gardening, photography. *Address:* (home) 56 Winding River Road, Needham, Mass 02192, USA; (office) 665 Huntington Avenue, Boston, Mass 02115. *Club:* Harvard (Boston).

WELLER, Walter; Principal Conductor, Royal Philharmonic Orchestra, since 1980; *b* 30 Nov. 1939; *s* of Walter and Anna Weller; *m* 1966, Elisabeth Samohyl; one *s*. *Educ:* Realgymnasium, Vienna; Akademie für Musik, Vienna (degree for violin and piano). Founder of Weller Quartet, 1958–69; Member,

Vienna Philharmonic, 1958-60. First Leader, 1960-69; Conductor, Vienna State Opera, 1969-75; Guest Conductor with all main European and American Orchestras, also in Japan and Israel, 1973-; Chief Conductor, Tonkünstler Orch., Vienna, 1974-77; Principal Conductor and Artistic Adviser, Royal Liverpool Philharmonic Orch., 1977-80, Guest Conductor Laureate, 1980-. Medal of Arts and Sciences, Austria, 1968. *Recreations:* magic, model railway, sailing, swimming, stamp-collecting, ski-ing. *Address:* Döblinger Hauptstrasse 40, 1190 Vienna, Austria. *T:* 34 01 64.

WELLES, (George) Orson; Director, Mercury Productions (films, theatre, radio, play publishing); Columnist; *b* Kenosha, Wisc., 6 May 1915; *s* of Richard Head Welles, inventor-manufacturer, and Beatrice Ives, pianist; *m* Virginia Nicholson, Chicago (whom he divorced, 1940); one *d*; *m* Rita Hayworth (who obtained a divorce, 1947); one *d*; *m* 1955, Paola Mori; one *d. Educ:* Todd School, Woodstock, Ill. Directed eight productions a year at Todd School, also doing some scene sketching; studied drawing at Chicago Art Inst., 1931; appeared at Gate Theatre, Dublin, 1931, in Trilby, Jew Suss, and Hamlet; returned to America, 1932; trip to Africa; toured US with Katharine Cornell, 1933; went into radio work as an actor, 1934; produced for Federal Theatre Macbeth with negro cast, Doctor Faustus and Horse Eats Hat; later formed Mercury Theatre, which produced The Cradle Will Rock, Heartbreak House, Shoemakers' Holiday, Danton's Death, Caesar and Five Kings; also made a series of Columbia educational recordings of Shakespearean plays for schoolroom use; came to Hollywood, 1939; produced, directed, wrote, and acted in his first picture, Citizen Kane; wrote, directed, and produced film, The Magnificent Ambersons; co-author, producer, and actor in Journey Into Fear. Produced Native Son in New York, 1939; co-starred Jane Eyre, 1943; appeared in Follow the Boys, 1943; produced, directed, starred in Mercury Wonder Show, a magic show for Army and Navy personnel, 1943; co-starred in Tomorrow is Forever, 1945; wrote, produced, acted and directed, The Lady From Shanghai, 1946; wrote screenplay, produced, directed and acted in screenplay, Macbeth, 1947; acted in Cagliostro (screenplay made in Italy), 1947; produced, and acted name-part in Othello, St James's, 1951; acted in film, Three Cases of Murder, 1955; adapted, produced, and acted in play, Moby Dick, Duke of York's, 1955; wrote, directed, and acted in film, Confidential Report, 1955; produced and acted name-part in King Lear, New York, 1956; adapted, directed and acted in film, Othello, 1956; acted in films: The Long, Hot, Summer, 1958, Compulsion, 1959, Ferry to Hong Kong, 1959, David and Goliath, 1961, The VIP's, 1963; (produced and acted) The Trial, 1963; Oedipus The King, 1968, Catch 22, 1970; The Kremlin Letter, 1970; Ten Days' Wonder, 1972; F for Fake, 1976; Butterfly, 1982. Directed The Immortal Story, 1968, Southern Star, 1969 (films); adapted and acted in play, Chimes at Midnight, 1960 (filmed 1966). Prod play, Rhinoceros, Royal Court Theatre, London, 1960. Associate Editor of Free World Magazine. Special Oscar Award, 1971. Life Achievement Award, American Film Institute, 1975. *Publications:* Illustrated edns of Macbeth, Julius Cæsar, Twelfth Night, and the Merchant of Venice with editing, illustrations, and stage directions (Mercury Shakespeare); Mr Arkadin, 1957. *Recreations:* prestidigitating, cartooning, swimming, reading. *Clubs:* Advertising, Lotos (New York); National Variety (Los Angeles).

WELLESLEY, family name of **Earl Cowley** and of **Duke of Wellington.**

WELLESLEY, Julian Valerian; Chairman, Charles Barker Group, since 1978; *b* 9 Aug. 1933; *s* of late Gerald Valerian Wellesley, MC, and Elizabeth Thornton Harvey; *m* 1965, Elizabeth Joan Hall; one *s* one *d*; three step *d. Educ:* Royal Naval Colleges, Dartmouth and Greenwich. Royal Navy, 1947-61: America and West Indies, 1955-56; Far East, 1957-58; Navigation Specialist Course, 1959. Joined Charles Barker, 1961; a Director of parent company, 1963, and Joint Managing Director, Ayer Barker Ltd, on its formation, 1971; Dep. Chm. of parent company, 1975, and Chm. of Ayer Barker, 1976. *Recreations:* family, music, reading, gardening, playing tennis, watching cricket. *Address:* Tidebrook Manor, Wadhurst, Sussex TN5 6PD. *T:* (office) 01-236 3011. *Clubs:* Brooks's; Sussex.

WELLINGS, Sir Jack (Alfred), Kt 1975; CBE 1970; Chairman and Managing Director, The 600 Group Ltd, since 1968; *b* 16 Aug. 1917; *s* of Edward Josiah and Selina Wellings; *m* 1946, Greta, *d* of late George Tidey; one *s* two *d. Educ:* Selhurst Grammar Sch.; London Polytechnic. Vice-Pres., Hawker Siddeley (Canada) Ltd, 1952-62; Dep. Man. Dir, 600 Group Ltd 1962. Mem., NEB, 1977-79; part-time Mem., British Aerospace, 1980-; non-exec. Dir, Clausing Corp., USA, 1982-. *Address:* Boundary Meadow, Collum Green Road, Stoke Poges, Bucks. *T:* Fulmer 2978.

WELLINGS, Victor Gordon, QC 1973; Member of the Lands Tribunal, since 1973; *b* 19 July 1919; *s* of late Gordon Arthur Wellings, solicitor, and Alice Adelaide Wellings (now Mrs Alice Adelaide Poole); *m* 1948, Helen Margaret Jill Lovell; three *s. Educ:* Reading Sch.; Exeter Coll., Oxford (MA). Called to Bar, Gray's Inn, 1949; practised 1949-73. War service, 1940-46; Captain Indian Army, 17th Dogra Regt; Intell. Corps, India; Captain, TARO, 1949-. *Publications:* Editor, Woodfall, The Law of Landlord and Tenant, 28th edn, 1978 (Jt Editor 26th and 27th edns, 1963 and 1968), and other works on same subject. *Recreations:* golf, fishing. *Address:* Cherry Tree Cottage, Whitchurch Hill, Pangbourne, Berks RG8 7PT. *T:* Pangbourne 2918. *Club:* United Oxford & Cambridge University.

WELLINGTON, 8th Duke of, *cr* 1814; **Arthur Valerian Wellesley,** MVO 1952; OBE 1957; MC; DL; Baron Mornington, 1746; Earl of Mornington, Viscount Wellesley, 1760; Viscount Wellington of Talavera and Wellington, Somersetshire, Baron Douro, 1809; Earl of Wellington, Feb. 1812; Marquess of Wellington, Oct. 1812; Marquess Douro, 1814; Prince of Waterloo, 1815, Netherlands; Count of Vimeiro, Marquess of Torres Vedras and Duke of Victoria in Portugal; Duke of Ciudad Rodrigo and a Grandee of Spain, 1st class; *b* 2 July 1915; *s* of 7th Duke of Wellington, KG, and Dorothy Violet (*d* 1956), *d* of Robert Ashton, Croughton, Cheshire; *S* father, 1972; *m* 1944, Diana Ruth, *o d* of Maj.-Gen. D. F. McConnel; four *s* one *d. Educ:* Eton; New Coll., Oxford. Served War of 1939-45 in Middle East (MC), CMF and BLA. Lt-Col Comdg Royal Horse Guards, 1954-58; Silver Stick-in-Waiting and Lt-Col Comdg the Household Cavalry, 1959-60; Comdr 22nd Armoured Bde, 1960-61; Comdr RAC 1st (Br.) Corps, 1962-64; Defence Attaché, Madrid, 1964-67, retired; Col-in-Chief, The Duke of Wellington's Regt, 1974-; Hon. Col 2nd Bn, The Wessex Regt, 1974-80. Director: Massey Ferguson Holdings Ltd, 1967; Massey Ferguson Ltd, 1973; Bodegas Internacionales, Madrid. President: Game Conservancy, 1976-81 (Dep. Pres., 1981-) Farm Management Assoc., 1976-; SE Branch, Royal British Legion, 1978-; BSJA, 1980-82; Vice-Pres., Docklands Settlements, 1978-. Member Council: Zool Soc., 1974- (Vice-Pres.); RASE, 1976-; St John of Jerusalem, Hampshire. Hampshire CC 1967-74; DL Hants, 1975. Governor of Wellington Coll., 1964-. OStJ. Officier, Légion d'Honneur (France). *Heir:* *s* Marquess of Douro, *qv. Address:* Stratfield Saye House, Reading; Apsley House, 149 Piccadilly, W1V 9FA. *Clubs:* Turf, Buck's.

WELLINGTON (NZ), Archbishop of, (RC), since 1979; **Most Rev. Thomas Stafford Williams,** DD; Metropolitan of New Zealand; *b* 20 March 1930; *s* of Thomas Stafford Williams and Lillian Maude Kelly. *Educ:* Holy Cross Primary School, Miramar; SS Peter and Paul Primary School, Lower Hutt; St Patrick's Coll., Wellington; Victoria University Coll., Wellington; St Kevin's Coll., Oamaru; Holy Cross Coll., Mosgiel; Collegio Urbano de Propaganda Fide, Rome (STL); University Coll., Dublin (BSocSc); Hon. DD. Assistant Priest, St Patrick's Parish, Palmerston North, 1963-64; Director of Studies, Catholic Enquiry Centre, Wellington, 1965-70; Parish Priest: St Anne's Parish, Leulumoega, W Samoa, 1971-75; Holy Family Parish, Porirua, NZ, 1976-79. *Recreations:* table tennis, tennis. *Address:* Viard, 21 Eccleston Hill, (PO Box 198), Wellington 1, New Zealand. *T:* 728-576.

WELLINGTON (NZ), Bishop of, since 1973; **Rt. Rev. Edward Kinsella Norman,** MC 1943; DSO 1945; *b* 1916. *Educ:* Univ. of New Zealand (BA 1939); St John's Coll., Auckland; Westcott House, Cambridge. Served War of 1939-45 (despatches, MC, DSO). Deacon 1947, priest 1948, Newcastle upon Tyne; Curate of Berwick-on-Tweed, 1947-49; Vicar of Waiwhetu, 1949-52; Levin, 1952-59; Tauranga, 1959-65; Karori, 1965-73; Chaplain to Samuel Marsden Coll. Sch., 1965-73; Chaplain to RNZNVR, 1966-73; Archdeacon of Wellington, 1969-73. Legion of Merit (US), 1945. *Address:* Bishopscourt, 28 Eccleston Hill, Wellington 1, New Zealand.

WELLINGTON, Sir Lindsay; *see* Wellington, Sir R. E. L.

WELLINGTON, Peter Scott, CBE 1981; DSC; PhD; ARCS; FLS; FIBiol; FRAgS; Director, National Institute of Agricultural Botany, 1970-81; Member, Governing Body, National Seed Development Organisation Ltd, since 1982; *b* 20 March 1919; *er s* of late Robert Wellington, MBE, MC; *m* 1947, Kathleen Joyce, *widow* of E. H. Coombe; one *s* one *d. Educ:* Kelly Coll.; Imperial Coll. of Science. BSc 1946. Observer, Fleet Air Arm, 1940-45 (Lt-Comdr (A) RNVR). Research Asst 1948-52, Chief Officer 1953-61, Official Seed Testing Stn for England and Wales; Asst Dir 1961-68, Dep. Dir 1968-69, Nat. Inst. of Agricultural Botany. Vice-Pres., Internat. Seed Testing Assoc., 1953-56 (Chm. Germination Cttee, 1956-70); Chief Officer, UK Variety Classification Unit, 1965-70; Chm., Technical Working Group, Internat. Convention for Protection of Plant Varieties, 1966-68. *Publications:* papers on germination of cereals and weeds, seed-testing and seed legislation. *Recreations:* gardening, walking, reading. *Address:* College Farm, 41 High Street, Teversham, Cambs. *T:* Teversham 2308.

WELLINGTON, Sir (Reginald Everard) Lindsay, Kt 1963; CBE 1944; Retired from BBC, 1963; *b* 10 August 1901; *s* of Hubert Lindsay Wellington and Nancy Charlotte Boughtwood; *m* 1st, 1928, Evelyn Mary Ramsay; one *s* one *d*; 2nd, 1952, Margot Osborn. *Educ:* Queen Elizabeth Grammar School, Wakefield; The Queen's College, Oxford. BBC Programme Staff since 1924; Director Broadcasting Division, Ministry of Information, 1940-41; N American Director, BBC, 1941-44; Controller (Programmes), BBC, 1944-45; Controller BBC Home Service, 1945-52; Director of Sound Broadcasting, BBC, 1952-63. *Recreations:* reading, music. *Address:* Witheridge, near Henley-on-Thames, Oxon. *T:* Nettlebed 641214. *Club:* Savile.

WELLS, Dean of; *see* Mitchell, Very Rev. P. R.

WELLS, Archdeacon of; *see* Thomas, Ven. C. E.

WELLS, Dr Alan Arthur, OBE 1982; FRS 1977; FEng 1978; Director-General, The Welding Institute, since 1977; *s* of Arthur John Wells and Lydia Wells; *m* 1950, Rosemary Edith Alice Mitchell; four *s* one *d. Educ:* City of London Sch.; Univ. of Nottingham (BScEng); Clare Coll., Cambridge (PhD). MIMechE, Hon. FWeldI. British Welding Res. Association: Asst Dir, 1956;

Dep. Dir (Scientific), 1963; Queen's Univ. of Belfast: Prof. of Struct. Science, 1964; Head of Civil Engrg Dept, 1970-77; Dean, Faculty of Applied Science and Technol., 1973-76. MRIA 1976. Hon. Dr, Faculty of Engrg, Univ. of Gent, 1972; Hon. DSc Glasgow, 1982. *Publications:* Brittle Fracture of Welded Plate (jtly), 1967; res. papers on welding technol. and fracture mechanics. *Recreation:* handyman about the house and garden. *Address:* The Welding Institute, Abington Hall, Abington, Cambs CB1 6AL. *T:* Cambridge 891162. *Club:* Athenæum.

WELLS, Bowen; MP (C) Hertford and Stevenage, since 1979; *b* 4 Aug. 1935; *s* of Reginald Laird Wells and Agnes Mary Wells (*née* Hunter); *m* 1975, Rennie Heyde; two *s. Educ:* St Paul's School; Univ. of Exeter (BA Hons); Regent St Polytechnic School of Management (Dip. Business Management). National Service, RN (promoted to Sub Lt), 1954-56. Schoolmaster, Colet Court, 1956-57; sales trainee, British Aluminium, 1957-58; Univ. of Exeter, 1958-61; Commonwealth Development Corporation, 1961-73: Personal Asst to Regional Controller and Ind. Relations Manager, 1962-65; Company Sec. and Ind. Relations Manager, Guyana Timbers, 1965-67; Manager, Guyana Housing and Develt Co., Guyana Mortgage Finance Co. and Cane Farming Develt Corp., 1967-71; Sen. Exec. for Subsidiary and Associated Develt Finance Co., 1971-73; Owner Manager, Substation Group Services Ltd, 1973-79. PPS to Min. of State for Employment, 1982-. Governor: Outward Bound Wales, 1979-; Inst. of Development Studies, 1980-. *Recreations:* music, walking, gardening, cooking, sailing. *Address:* 3 Farquhar Street, Bengeo, Hertford. *T:* Hertford 51229. *Club:* Naval.

WELLS, Charles Alexander, CBE 1963; SPk (Sitara-i-Pakistan) 1961; FRCS; Emeritus Professor of Surgery, University of Liverpool; Hon. Surgeon Royal Liverpool United Hospital and Consultant to Royal Prince Alfred, Sydney, NSW, and other hospitals; FRSocMed (President, Section of Surgery and Past President Section of Urology); Corresponding member Société Franc. d'Urologie; *b* 9 Jan, 1898; *o s* of late Percy M. and late Frances L. Wells, Liverpool; *m* 1928, Joyce Mary Rivett Harrington (*d* 1980); two *s. Educ:* Merchant Taylors', Crosby; Liverpool University (MB, ChB, 1st Hons). Active service, RFA, 1916-18. Lately surgeon and urologist to various hospitals; Resident Surgical Officer Ancoats Hospital, Manchester; Demonstrator in Anatomy McGill University, Montreal; Clinical Assistant St Peter's Hospital, London. Mem. Council RCS (Vice-Pres., 1965-66, Bradshaw Lectr, 1966); Mem. Med. Adv. Council, ODM, and Chm. Recruitment Panel; Chairman: Merseyside Conf. for Overseas Students; Cttee on Surgical Educn, Internat. Fedn Surgical Colls. Ex-Council of British Association of Urological Surgeons (Home and Overseas); Past President Liverpool Medical Institution; Pakistan Health Reforms Commn, 1960; Adrian Committee (Ministry of Health) on Radiation Hazards, 1958-; Medical Research Council's Committee, Pressure Steam Sterilisation. Litchfield Lectr, Oxford, 1953; Luis Guerrero Meml Lectr, Santo Tomas Univ., Manila, 1957; McIlraith Guest Prof., Univ. of Sydney, 1957; Murat Willis Orator, Richmond, Va, 1963. Hon. FACS 1968. Hon. LLD (Panjab), 1960. *Publications:* Surgery for Nurses, 1938; Text Book of Urology (ed Winsbury-White); Treatment of Cancer in Clinical Practice, 1960; contrib. to textbooks and symposia, various chapters, Prostatectomy (monograph), 1952; (with J. Kyle) Peptic Ulceration, 1960; (ed with J. Kyle) Scientific Foundations of Surgery, 1967, 2nd edn, 1974; numerous articles in scientific jls. *Recreations:* shooting, painting in oils. *Address:* 11 Curzon Road, Hoylake, Wirral, Merseyside L47 1HB. *T:* Hoylake 4326. *Club:* Carlton.

WELLS, Sir Charles Maltby, 2nd Bt *cr* 1944, TD 1960; *b* 24 July 1908; *e s* of 1st Bt, and Mary Dorothy Maltby (*d* 1956); *S* father, 1956; *m* 1935, Katharine Boulton, *d* of Frank Boteler Kenrick, Toronto; two *s. Educ:* Bedford School; Pembroke College, Cambridge. Joined RE (TA), 1933; Capt. 1939; served War of 1939-45: 54th (EA) Div., 1939-41; Lt-Col 1941; 76th Div., 1941-43; British Army Staff, Washington, 1943-45. *Heir:* s Christopher Charles Wells [*b* 12 Aug. 1936; *m* 1960, Elizabeth Florence Vaughan, *d* of I. F. Griffiths, Outremont, Quebec; two *s* two *d*]. *Address:* 37 Duggan Avenue, Toronto, Canada.

WELLS, Rear-Adm. David Charles, CBE 1971; farmer and grazier; *b* Inverell, NSW, Australia, 19 Nov. 1918; *s* of C. V. T. Wells; *m* 1940, J. Moira A., *d* of Rear-Adm. C. J. Pope, CBE; two *s* two *d. Educ:* St Peter's Coll., Adelaide, SA. Joined RAN, 1933. Served War of 1939-45: Atlantic, Mediterranean, Arctic, Indian and Pacific Oceans; HMAS Queenborough, 1953-56 (in comd); HMAS Cerberus, 1956-58; Dir of Plans, Navy Office, 1958-60; HMAS Voyager, 1960-62 (in comd); RN Exchange Service and Dep. Dir, RN Staff Coll., 1962-64; IDC 1965; HMAS Melbourne, 1965-66 (in comd); HMAS Albatross, 1967 (in comd); Rear-Adm. 1968; Flag Officer-in-Charge, E Australia Area, 1968-70; Dep. Chief of Naval Staff, Australia, 1970-71; ANZUK Force Comdr, Malaysia/Singapore, 1971-73; Flag Officer Comdg HM's Aust. Fleet, 1974-75, retired. *Address:* Pine Ridge, Leadville, NSW 2831, Australia.

WELLS, Doreen Patricia, (Marchioness of Londonderry); Ballerina of the Royal Ballet, 1955-74; *b* 25 June 1937; *m* 1972, 9th Marquess of Londonderry, *qv* ; two *s. Educ:* Walthamstow; Bush Davies School; Royal Ballet School. Engaged in Pantomime, 1952 and 1953. Joined Royal Ballet, 1955; became Principal Dancer, 1960; has danced leading roles in Noctambules, Harlequin in April, Dance Concertante, Sleeping Beauty, Coppelia, Swan Lake, Sylvia, La Fille mal Gardée, Two Pigeons, Giselle, Invitation, Rendezvous, Blood Wedding, Raymonda, Concerto, Nutcracker, Romeo and Juliet, Concerto

No 2 (Ballet Imperial); has created leading roles in Toccata, La Création du Monde, Sinfonietta, Prometheus, Grand Tour. Adeline Genée Gold Medal, 1954. *Recreations:* classical music, reading, theatre-going. *Address:* Wynyard Park, Billingham, Cleveland TS22 5NF. *T:* Wolviston 310.
See also Viscount Castlereagh.

WELLS, Prof. George Albert, MA, BSc, PhD; Professor of German, Birkbeck College, University of London, since 1968; *b* 22 May 1926; *s* of George John and Lilian Maud Wells; *m* 1969, Elisabeth Delhey. *Educ:* University College London (BA, MA German; PhD Philosophy; BSc Geology). Lecturer in German, 1949-64, Reader in German, 1964-68, University Coll. London. Director, Rationalist Press Assoc., 1974-. *Publications:* Herder and After, 1959; The Plays of Grillparzer, 1969; The Jesus of the Early Christians, 1971; Did Jesus Exist?, 1975; Goethe and the Development of Science 1750-1900, 1978; The Historical Evidence for Jesus, 1982; articles in Jl of History of Ideas, Jl of English and Germanic Philology, German Life and Letters, Question. *Recreation:* walking. *Address:* 35 St Stephen's Avenue, St Albans, Herts AL3 4AA. *T:* St Albans 51347.

WELLS, Prof. George Philip, FRS 1955; ScD; Emeritus Professor of Zoology in the University of London; *b* 17 July 1901; *er s* of Herbert George and Amy Catherine Wells; *m* 1927, Marjorie Stewart Craig (marr. diss., 1960); one *s* one *d. Educ:* Oundle; Trinity Coll., Cambridge. Temp. Asst, Dept of Zoology, University College, London, 1928; Lecturer, 1931; Reader, 1943; Professor, 1954-68. Hon. Associate, Dept of Zoology, British Museum (Natural History), 1953; Zoological Sec., Soc. for Experimental Biology, 1929-36, Hon. Member 1964; a Vice-Pres., Freshwater Biolog. Assoc., 1966-. *Publications:* (with H. G. Wells and Julian Huxley) The Science of Life, 1929-30 (in fortnightly parts); (various subseq. revisions); many scientific papers and popular writings and broadcasts. *Address:* University College, WC1E 6BT. *Club:* Savile.

WELLS, Lt-Col Herbert James, CBE 1958; MC 1918; FCA 1934; JP; DL; *b* 27 March 1897; *s* of late James J. Wells, NSW; *m* 1926, Rose Hamilton, *d* of late H. D. Brown, Bournemouth; no *c. Educ:* NSW. Chartered Accountant; Sen. Partner, Amsdon Cossart & Wells. Surrey CC: Alderman, 1960; Vice-Chm., 1959-62; Chm., 1962-65. JP Surrey 1952 (Chm., Magistrates' Ct, Wallington, 1960-70); DL 1962, High Sheriff 1965, Surrey. A General Comr for Income Tax. Freeman, City of London. Pres. Brit. Red Cross, Carshalton and Sutton Division; former Member, Surrey T&AFA, retired 1968; Chairman, Queen Mary's Hospital for Children, Carshalton, 1958-60; Member, Carshalton UDC, 1945-62 (Chm. 1950-52 and 1955-56). Served European War, 1914-18 with Aust. Inf. and Aust. Flying Corps in Egypt and France (MC); served War of 1939-45. DUniv Surrey, 1975. *Recreations:* football, hockey, tennis, squash, now golf. *Address:* 17 Oakhurst Rise, Carshalton Beeches, Surrey. *T:* 01-643 4125. *Club:* Royal Automobile.

WELLS, Jack Dennis; Assistant Director, Central Statistical Office, since 1979; *b* 8 April 1928; *s* of late C. W. Wells and of H. M. Wells (*née* Clark); *m* 1953, Jean Allison; one *s* one *d. Educ:* Hampton Grammar Sch.; Polytechnic of Central London. AIS 1955. Ministry of Fuel and Power, 1947; Royal Air Force, 1947-49; Min. of (Fuel and) Power, 1949-69; Private Secretary to Paymaster General, 1957-59; Chief Statistician, Dept of Economic Affairs, 1969; Min. of Technology, 1969; HM Treasury, 1970; Dept of (Trade and) Industry, 1971-79. Past Chairman, Old Hamptonians Assoc. *Publications:* contribs to Long Range Planning, Economic Trends, Statistical News, Review of Income and Wealth. *Recreations:* flying, cricket, badminton. *Address:* Central Statistical Office, Great George Street, SW1P 3AQ.

WELLS, John Julius; MP (C) Maidstone since October 1959; *b* 30 March 1925; *s* of A. Reginald K. Wells, Marlands, Sampford Arundel, Som; *m* 1948, Lucinda Meath-Baker; two *s* two *d. Educ:* Eton; Corpus Christi College, Oxford (MA). War of 1939-45: joined RN as ordinary seaman, 1942; commissioned, 1943, served in submarines until 1946. Contested (C) Smethwick Division, General Election, 1955. Chairman: Cons. Party Horticulture Cttee, 1965-71; Horticultural sub-Cttee, Select Cttee on Agriculture, 1968; Parly Waterways Group, 1974-; Vice-Chm., Cons. Party Agriculture Cttee, 1970; Mem., Mr Speaker's Panel of Chairmen, 1974. Master, Worshipful Co. of Fruiterers, 1977. Hon. Freeman, Borough of Maidstone, 1979. Kt Comdr, Order of Civil Merit (Spain), 1972. *Recreations:* country pursuits. *Address:* Mere House, Mereworth, Kent.

WELLS, Malcolm Henry Weston, FCA; London Representative, Bank in Liechtenstein, since 1981; *b* 26 July 1927; *s* of Lt-Comdr Geoffrey Weston Wells; *m* 1952, Elizabeth A. Harland, *d* of Rt Rev. M. H. Harland, *qv* ; one *s* one *d. Educ:* Eton Coll. ACA 1951, FCA 1961. Served RNVR, 1945-48. Peat, Marwick Mitchell Ltd, 1948-58; Siebe Gorman and Co. Ltd, 1958-63; Charterhouse Japhet, 1963-80 (Chm., 1973-80); Dir, Charterhouse Gp, 1971-80; Chm., Charterhouse Petroleum, 1977-82. Mem., CAA, 1974-77. Mem. Solicitors' Disciplinary Tribunal, 1975-81. *Recreation:* sailing. *Address:* Holmbush House, Findon, West Sussex. *T:* Findon 3630. *Clubs:* City of London, St James's, Overseas Bankers; West Wittering Sailing.

WELLS, Petrie Bowen; *see* Wells, B.

WELLS, Ronald Alfred, OBE 1965; BSc, FRSC, FIMM; Group Scientist, Turner & Newall, since 1981; Director, Salford University Industrial Centre

Ltd, since 1981; *b* 11 February 1920; *s* of Alfred John Wells and Winifred Jessie (*née* Lambert); *m* 1953, Anne Brebner Lanshe; two *s. Educ:* Birkbeck College, London; Newport Technical College. Service with Government Chemist, 1939-40; Royal Naval Scientific Service, 1940-47; Joined Nat. Chemical Laboratory, 1947; Mem. UK Scientific Mission, Washington, 1951-52; Head of Radio-chemical Group, 1956; Head of Div. of Inorganic and Mineral Chemistry, 1963; Deputy Director, Nov. 1963; Director of National Chemical Laboratory, 1964; Dir of Research, TBA Industrial Products Ltd, 1965-70, Jt Man. Dir, 1970-77; Man. Dir, AMFU Ltd (Turner & Newall), 1977-81; Dir, Rochdale Private Surgical Unit, 1975-81. Mem. Council, Royal Inst. Chemistry, 1965-68. *Publications:* numerous contribs to Inorganic Chromatography and Extractive Metallurgy. *Recreations:* gardening, golf. *Address:* Westbury, 19 First Avenue, Charmandean, Worthing, Sussex BN14 9NJ. *T:* Worthing 33844.

WELLS, Mrs Stanley; *see* Hill, S. E.

WELLS, Dr Stanley William; General Editor of the Oxford Shakespeare and Head of the Shakespeare Department, Oxford University Press, since 1978; Senior Research Fellow, Balliol College, Oxford, since 1980; *b* 21 May 1930; *s* of Stanley Cecil Wells and Doris Wells; *m* 1975, Susan Elizabeth Hill, *qv* ; one *d. Educ:* Kingston High Sch., Hull; University Coll., London (BA); Shakespeare Inst., Univ. of Birmingham (PhD). Fellow, Shakespeare Inst., 1962-77; Lectr, 1962; Sen. Lectr, 1971; Reader, 1973-77; Hon. Fellow, 1979. Consultant in English, Wroxton Coll., 1964-80. Dir, Royal Shakespeare Theatre Summer Sch., 1971-; Pres., Shakespeare Club of Stratford-upon-Avon, 1972-73. Member: Council, Malone Soc., 1967-; Exec. Council, Royal Shakespeare Theatre, 1976- (Governor, 1974-); Exec. Ctte, Shakespeare's Birthplace, 1976-78 (Trustee, 1975-81). Governor, King Edward VI Grammar Sch. for Boys, Stratford-upon-Avon, 1973-77. Guest lectr, British and overseas univs. Hon. DLitt Furman Univ., SC, 1978. Associate Editor, New Penguin Shakespeare, 1967-77; Editor, Shakespeare Survey, 1980-. *Publications:* (ed) Thomas Nashe, Selected Writings, 1964; (ed, New Penguin Shakespeare): A Midsummer Night's Dream, 1967, Richard II, 1969, The Comedy of Errors, 1972; Shakespeare, A Reading Guide, 1969 (2nd edn 1970); Literature and Drama, 1970; (ed, Select Bibliographical Guides): Shakespeare, 1973, English Drama excluding Shakespeare, 1975; Royal Shakespeare, 1977 (2nd edn 1978); Shakespeare: an illustrated dictionary, 1978; Shakespeare: the writer and his work, 1978; (ed with R. L. Smallwood) Thomas Dekker, The Shoemaker's Holiday, 1979; (with Gary Taylor) Modernizing Shakespeare's Spelling, with three studies in the text of Henry V, 1979; contrib. Shak. Survey, Shak. Qly, Shak. Jahrbuch, Theatre Notebook, Stratford-upon-Avon Studies, TLS, etc. *Recreations:* music, the countryside. *Address:* Midsummer Cottage, Church Lane, Beckley, Oxford. *T:* Stanton St John 252.

WELLS, Susannah, (Mrs Michael Wells); *see* York, S.

WELLS, Thomas Umfrey, MA; Headmaster, Wanganui Collegiate School, New Zealand, 1960-80; *b* 6 Feb. 1927; *s* of Athol Umfrey and Gladys Colebrook Wells; *m* 1953, Valerie Esther Brewis; two *s* one *d. Educ:* King's College, Auckland, New Zealand; Auckland University (BA); (Orford Studentship to) King's College, Cambridge. BA 1951; MA 1954. Assistant Master, Clifton College, 1952-60 (Senior English Master, 1957-60). Pres., NZ Assoc. of Heads of Independent Secondary Schs, 1972-75. Member: Univs Entrance Bd, 1972-80; HMC. *Recreations:* reading, theatre, cricket (Cambridge Blue, 1950), tennis, fishing; formerly Rugby football (Cambridge Blue, 1951). *Address:* PO Box 48, Owhango, King Country, New Zealand. *Clubs:* MCC; Hawks (Cambridge); Wanganui (NZ).

WELLS, William Henry Weston, FRICS; Partner, Chestertons, London, since 1965; Chairman, Frincon Holdings Ltd, since 1977; Chairman, Hampstead Health Authority, since 1982; *b* 3 May 1940; *s* of Sir Henry Wells, CBE, and Lady Wells; *m* 1966, Penelope Jean Broadbent; two *s* (and one *s* decd). *Educ:* Radley Coll.; Magdalene Coll., Cambridge (BA). Joined Chestertons, 1959; Chm., Land and House Property Corporation, 1977. Member: Board of Governors, Royal Free Hosp., 1968-74; Camden and Islington AHA, 1974-82; Chm., Special Trustees of Royal Free Hosp., 1979-; Mem. Council, Royal Free Hosp. Sch. of Medicine, 1977-. *Recreations:* family, philately, gardening. *Address:* 14 Brook Gardens, Kingston-upon-Thames, Surrey KT2 7ET. *Club:* Boodle's.

WELLS, William Thomas, QC 1955; Member, Magistrates Courts Rules Committee, since 1954; a Governor, Bedford College, since 1963; *b* 10 Aug. 1908; *s* of late William Collins Wells (formerly of Clare Coll., Cambridge, and Bexhill-on-Sea) and Gertrude Wells; *m* 1936, Angela, 2nd *d* of late Robert Noble, formerly of HM Colonial Legal Service; two *s* two *d. Educ:* Lancing Coll.; Balliol Coll., Oxford (BA 1930). Joined Fabian Society, 1930; called to Bar, Middle Temple, 1932, Bencher 1963. QC Hong Kong, 1968. Dep. Chm., Hertfordshire QS, 1961-71; Recorder of King's Lynn, 1965-71; a Recorder of the Crown Court, 1972-80. Formerly Mem., Internat. Adv. Committee of Labour Party and of Political Committee and Local Government Committee of the Fabian Society. Army, 1940-45: a General Staff Officer, 2nd grade, Directorate of Military Training, War Office, with temp. rank of Major, 1942-45. MP (Lab) Walsall, 1945-55, Walsall North, 1955-Feb. 1974; Member of Lord Chancellor's Ctte on Practice and Procedure of Supreme Court, 1947-53; Mem. of Chm.'s Panel, House of Commons, 1948-50; Mem. Departmental Cttee on Homosexual Offences and Prostitution, 1954-57; Chm., Legal and Judicial Gp (Parly Labour Party),

1964-70; a Chm. (part-time) of Industrial Tribunals, 1975-79. Governor, Polytechnic of North London, 1971-74 (formerly Northern Polytechnic, 1938-71). Hon. Freeman, Borough of Walsall, 1974. *Publications:* How English Law Works, 1947; contributor to journals, incl. the Tablet, and former contributor to The Fortnightly, Spectator, Times Literary Supplement, etc, mainly on legal, political and military subjects. *Address:* Pool Cottage, Melbourne, Derbys DE7 1AA. *T:* Melbourne 2382; 1 Gray's Inn Square, Gray's Inn, WC1R 5AA. *T:* 01-405 8946. *Club:* Athenæum.

WELLS-PESTELL, family name of **Baron Wells-Pestell.**

WELLS-PESTELL, Baron *cr* 1965 (Life Peer), of Combs in the County of Suffolk; **Reginald Alfred Wells-Pestell,** MA, LLD, FPhS; sociologist; Deputy Speaker, House of Lords and Deputy Chairman of Committees, since 1981; *b* 27 Jan. 1910; *o s* of Robert Pestell and Mary (*née* Manning); *m* 1935, Irene, *y d* of late Arthur Wells; two *s. Educ:* elementary and grammar schs; Univ. of London (Dip. in Econ. and Social Sciences). Formerly London Probation Service; Vice-Pres., Nat. Assoc. of Probation Officers, 1974-79. A Founder, Nat. Marriage Guidance Coun. (now a Vice-Pres.). Magistrate for London, 1946-; a Chm., Chelsea and E London Matrimonial Courts. Mem. LCC, 1946-52; Stoke Newington Borough, 1945-49 (Leader of Council, 1946; Mayor 1947-49); Mem. E Suffolk County Council, 1964-67. Contested (Lab) Taunton, 1955 and 1956, Hornsey, 1950 and 1951. Lord in Waiting (a Govt Whip), 1974-79; Spokesman in House of Lords for DHSS, 1974-79; Parly Under-Sec. of State, DHSS, 1979; Dep. Chief Opposition Whip, 1979-81. Member: Church of England Council for Social Aid (Vice-Chm.); Bridgehead Cttee (appointed by Home Office); Cttee and Council of Outcasts (providing help for the socially inadequate), and Chm. of Trustees; Wireless for the Bedridden (former Chm.); Pres., Handcrafts Adv. Assoc. for the Disabled; Pres. or Patron, other voluntary organisations; delegations to Far East, Africa and Israel, and to 5th Commonwealth Med. Conf., NZ, 1977. Captain KRRC, 9th Bn City of London HG, 1940-45. *Publications:* articles and pamphlets on marriage and family life, delinquency and social problems for press and jls. *Recreations:* music, opera. *Address:* 22 Vicarage Close, Oxford OX4 4PL. *T:* Oxford 771142.

WELMAN, Douglas Pole, CBE 1966; *b* 22 June 1902; *s* of late Col Arthur Pole Welman and late Lady Scott; *m* 1st, 1929, Denise, *d* of Charles Steers Peel; one *d* ; 2nd, 1946, Betty Marjorie, *d* of late Henry Huth. *Educ:* Tonbridge Sch.; Faraday House Engineering Coll. DFH, CEng, FIMechE, FIEE, CIGasE. Electrical and Mechanical Engineering career at home and abroad, West Indies, 1928-32; Consulting Practice, 1932-37; Man. Dir of Foster, Yates and Thom Limited, Heavy Precision Engineers, 1937-50; Chairman or Member of number of wartime committees in Lancashire including Armaments Production, Emergency Services Organisation, and Ministry of Production; went to Ministry of Aircraft Production at request of Minister as Director of Engine Production, 1942; Deputy Director-General, 1943; Control of Directorate-Gen. including Propeller and Accessory Production, 1944; Part Time Member North Western Gas Board, 1949, Chairman, 1950-64; Chairman, Southern Gas Board, 1964-67; Member, Gas Council, 1950-67; Chm. and Man. Dir, Allspeeds Holdings Ltd, 1967-72. Member, Ct of Govs, Univ. of Manchester Inst. of Sci. and Techn., 1956-64, 1968-72 (Mem. Coun., 1960-64, 1968-72). FRSA. StJ 1968 (OStJ 1964). *Publications:* articles and papers on company management. *Recreations:* sailing, fishing. *Address:* 11 St Michael's Gardens, St Cross, Winchester SO23 9JD. *T:* Winchester 68091. *Club:* Royal Thames Yacht.

WELSBY, Rev. Canon Paul Antony; Canon Residentiary and Vice-Dean of Rochester Cathedral, since 1966; Chaplain to the Queen, since 1980; *b* 18 Aug. 1920; *m* 1947, Cynthia Mary Hosmer; one *d. Educ:* Alcester Grammar Sch.; University Coll., Durham (MA); Lincoln Theological Coll.; Univ. of Sheffield (PhD). Curate at Boxley, Kent, 1944-47; Curate, St Mary-le-Tower, Ipswich, 1947-52; Rector of Copdock with Washbrook, 1952-66; Rural Dean of Samford, 1964-66. Director of Post-Ordination Training for Dio. of Rochester, 1966-; Examining Chaplain to Bp of Rochester, 1966-. Member, Church Assembly, 1964-70, General Synod, 1970-80; Chm., House of Clergy at Gen. Synod and Prolocutor of Convocation of Canterbury, 1974-80. *Publications:* A Modern Catechism, 1956; Lancelot Andrewes, 1958; How the Church of England Works, 1960; The Unwanted Archbishop, 1962; The Bond of Church and State, 1962; Sermons and Society, 1970; contrib. Theology. *Recreations:* grandchildren, walking, reading detective fiction, genealogy. *Address:* Southgate, The Precinct, Rochester, Kent ME1 1TH. *T:* Medway 45722.

WELSH, Andrew; Lecturer in Public Administration and Economics, Dundee College of Commerce, since 1979; *b* 19 April 1944; *s* of William and Agnes Welsh; *m* 1971, Sheena Margaret Cannon; one *d. Educ:* Univ. of Glasgow. MA (Hons) History and Politics; DipEd, 1980. Teacher of History, 1972-74. MP (SNP) South Angus, Oct. 1974-1979; SNP Party Chief Whip, 1978-79; SNP Spokesman on: Housing, 1974-78; Self Employed Affairs and Small Businesses, 1975-79; Agriculture, 1976-79; SNP Exec. Vice Chm. for Admin, 1979-. *Recreations:* music, horse riding, languages. *Address:* Olympia Buildings, Market Place, Arbroath, Angus DD11 1HR. *T:* Arbroath 74522. *Club:* Glasgow University Union.

WELSH, Brig. David, CBE 1959; DSO 1944; late Royal Artillery; Retired; *b* 10 April 1908; *s* of late Capt. Tom Welsh, Earlshaugh, Peeblesshire; *m* 1947, Maud Elinor Mitchell (*d* 1977), *d* of late Major M. I. M. Campbell, MC, of

Auchmannoch; one *s. Educ:* Winchester; RMA. Commissioned 2nd Lieut, RA, 1928. Served War of 1939-45 (DSO): with Royal Horse Artillery and Royal Artillery in France, N Africa and Italy. Lt-Col, 1950; Brigadier, 1958; Brigadier, RA, FarELF, 1957-60; retd, 1961. *Address:* 27 Manor House Lane, Walkington, Beverley, North Humberside. *Club:* Army and Navy.

WELSH, Frank Reeson; Director: Grindlays Bank Ltd, since 1971; Grindlay Brandts Insurance Ltd, since 1972; Underwriting Member of Lloyd's; *b* 16 Aug. 1931; *s* of F. C. Welsh and D. M. Welsh; *m* 1954, Agnes Cowley; two *s* two *d. Educ:* Gateshead and Blaydon Grammar Schools; Magdalene Coll., Cambridge (schol.; MA). With John Lewis Partnership, 1954-1958; CAS Group, 1958-64; Man. Dir, William Brandt's Sons & Co. Ltd, 1965-72; Chairman: Hadfields Ltd, 1967-79; Jensen Motors Ltd, 1968-72; Cox & Kings, 1972-76; Dir, Henry Ansbacher & Co., 1976-82. Member: British Waterways Board, 1975-81; Gen. Adv. Council, IBA, 1976-80; Royal Commn on Nat. Health Service, 1976-79; Health Educn Council, 1978-80. Vis. Lectr and Alcoa Schol., Graduate Sch. of Business Studies, Univ. of Tennessee, Knoxville, 1979-. CBIM. *Publications:* The Profit of the State, 1982; (contrib.) Judging People, 1982. *Recreation:* sailing. *Address:* Great Shelford, Cambridge. *Clubs:* Savile, United Oxford & Cambridge University.

WELSH, Prof. Harry Lambert, OC 1971; FRS 1962; FRSC 1952; Professor of Physics, University of Toronto, 1954-78, now Emeritus Professor; *b* 23 March 1910, Canadian; *s* of Israel Welsh and Harriet Collingwood; *m* 1942, Marguerite Hazel Ostrander; no *c. Educ:* University of Toronto; University of Göttingen. Demonstrator in Physics, Univ. of Toronto, 1935-42; Asst Professor, 1942-48; Assoc. Professor, 1948-54; Chm., Dept of Physics, 1962-68; Chm., Research Bd, 1971-73. Lt-Comdr, RCNVR (Operational Research at Navy HQ, Ottawa), 1944-45. Pres., Canadian Assoc. of Physicists, 1973; Medal of Cdn Assoc. of Physicists, 1961; Tory Medal, Royal Society of Canada, 1963. Hon. DSc: Univ. of Windsor, Ont., 1964; Memorial Univ., St John's, Newfoundland, 1968. Meggers Medal, Optical Soc. of America, 1974. *Publications:* many papers on infra-red and Raman spectroscopy and high-pressure physics in various scientific jls. *Recreation:* music. *Address:* 8 Tally Lane, Willowdale, Ontario M2K 1V4, Canada.

WELSH, Dame Mary; *see* Welsh, Dame R. M. E.

WELSH, Michael Collins; MP (Lab) Don Valley, since 1979; *b* 23 Nov. 1926; *s* of Danny and Winnie Welsh; *m* 1950, Brenda Nicholson; two *s. Educ:* Sheffield Univ. (Dept of Extramural Studies, Day Release Course, three years); Ruskin Coll., Oxford. Miner from age of 14 years. Member, Doncaster Local Authority, 1962-. *Address:* House of Commons, SW1A 0AA. *Club:* Carcroft Village Workingmen's (Carcroft, near Doncaster).

WELSH, Michael John; Member (C) Lancashire Central, European Parliament, since 1979; *b* 22 May 1942; *s* of Comdr David Welsh, RN, and Una Mary (*née* Willmore); *m* 1963, Jennifer Caroline Pollitt; one *s* one *d. Educ:* Dover Coll.; Lincoln Coll., Oxford (BA (Hons) Jurisprudence). Proprietors of Hays Wharf Ltd, 1963-69; Levi Strauss & Co. Europe Ltd, 1969-79 (Dir of Market Development, 1976). *Publication:* The Case for a Common Trade Policy, 1981. *Recreations:* amateur drama, sailing, rough walking. *Address:* Watercrook, 181 Town Lane, Whittle le Woods, Chorley, Lancs PR6 8AG. *T:* Chorley 76992. *Club:* Carlton.

WELSH, Dame (Ruth) Mary (Eldridge), DBE 1946; TD 1976; Legion of Merit, USA; *d* of late Dr William Dalzell; *m* 1922, Air Marshal Sir William Welsh, KCB, DSC, AFC (marr. diss. 1947; he *d* 1962); one *s.* Director WAAF, 1943-46. Air Chief Comdt, WRAF. *Address:* 3 Webb House, The Bury, Odiham, Hampshire.

WELTY, Eudora; Gold Medal for the Novel, Amer. Acad. and Inst. of Arts and Letters, 1972; National Medal for Literature, 1980; Presidential Medal of Freedom, 1980. *Publications:* A Curtain of Green, 1943; The Robber Bridegroom, 1944; The Wide Net, 1945; Delta Wedding, 1947; Golden Apples, 1950; The Ponder Heart, 1954; The Bride of Innisfallen, 1955; The Shoe Bird, 1964; Losing Battles, US 1970, UK 1982; One Time, One Place, 1971; The Optimist's Daughter, 1972 (Pulitzer Prize, 1973); The Eye of the Story, 1979; The Collected Stories of Eudora Welty, 1980. *Address:* 1119 Pinehurst Street, Jackson, Miss 39202, USA.

WEMYSS, 12th Earl of *cr* 1633, AND MARCH, 8th Earl of *cr* 1697; Francis David Charteris, KT 1966; Lord Wemyss of Elcho, 1628; Lord Elcho and Methil, 1633; Viscount Peebles, Baron Douglas of Neidpath, Lyne and Munard, 1697; Baron Wemyss of Wemyss (UK), 1821; Lord-Lieutenant of East Lothian since 1967; President, The National Trust for Scotland (Chairman of Council, 1947-69); Chairman, Royal Commission on Ancient and Historical Monuments and Constructions of Scotland; Lord Clerk Register of Scotland and Keeper of the Signet, since 1974; *b* 19 Jan. 1912; *s* of late Lord Elcho (killed in action, 1916) and Lady Violet Manners (she *m* 2nd, 1921, Guy Holford Benson (decd), and *d* 1971), 2nd *d* of 8th Duke of Rutland; *S* grandfather, 1937; *m* 1940, Mavis Lynette Gordon, BA, *er d* of late E. E. Murray, Hermanus, Cape Province; one *s* one *d* (and one *s* and one *d* decd). *Educ:* Eton; Balliol College, Oxford. Assistant District Commissioner, Basutoland, 1937-44. Served with Basuto Troops in Middle East, 1941-44. Lieutenant, Queen's Body Guard for Scotland, Royal Company of Archers; Lord High Comr to Gen. Assembly of Church of Scotland, 1959, 1960, 1977; Chairman: Scottish Cttee, Marie Curie Meml

Foundn; Scottish Churches Council, 1964-71; Pres., The Thistle Foundn; Former Mem., Central Cttee, WCC; Mem., Royal Commn on Historical Manuscripts, 1975-; Director, Wemyss and March Estates Management Co. Ltd; formerly Director: Standard Life Assurance Co. Ltd; Scottish Television Ltd. Hon. LLD St Andrews, 1953. *Heir: s* Lord Neidpath, *qv. Address:* Gosford House, Longniddry, East Lothian. *Club:* New (Edinburgh).
See also Baron Charteris of Amisfield.

WEMYSS, Rear-Adm. Martin La Touche, CB 1981; Clerk to the Brewers' Company, since 1981; *b* 5 Dec. 1927; *s* of Comdr David Edward Gillespie Wemyss, DSO, DSC, RN, and late Edith Mary Digges La Touche; *m* 1st, 1951, Ann Hall (marr. diss. 1973); one *s* one *d*; 2nd, 1973, Elizabeth Loveday Alexander; one *s* one *d. Educ:* Shrewsbury School. CO HMS Sentinel, 1956-57; Naval Intell. Div., 1957-59; CO HMS Alliance, 1959-60; CO Commanding Officers' Qualifying Course, 1961-63; Naval Staff, 1963-65; CO HMS Cleopatra, 1965-67; Naval Asst to First Sea Lord, 1967-70; CO 3rd Submarine Sqdn, 1970-73; CO HMS Norfolk, 1973-74; Dir of Naval Warfare, 1974-76; Rear-Adm., 1977; Flag Officer, Second Flotilla, 1977-78; Asst Chief of Naval Staff (Ops), 1979-81. *Recreations:* sailing, shooting, allotment cultivation. *Address:* 67 Chiswick Staithe, Hartington Road, W4. *T:* 01-994 2678. *Clubs:* White's, Army and Navy.

WENBAN-SMITH, William, CMG 1960; CBE 1957; *b* 8 June 1908; *o s* of Frederick Wenban-Smith, Worthing; *m* 1935, Ruth Orme, *e d* of S. B. B. McElderry, *qv*; three *s* two *d. Educ:* Bradfield; King's Coll., Cambridge (MA). Colonial Administrative Service, 1931-61: Cadet, Zanzibar, 1931; Administrative Officer, Grade II, 1933; Asst DO, Tanganyika, 1935; DO, 1943; Sen. DO, 1951 (acted on various occasions as Resident Magistrate, Comr for Co-op. Development, Provincial Comr, and Sec. for Finance); Dir of Establishments, 1953; Minister for Social Services, 1958; Minister for Education and Labour, 1959-61. Chairman, Public Service Commission and Speaker, Legislative Council, Nyasaland, 1961-63. HM Diplomatic Service, Kuala Lumpur, 1964-69. *Publication:* Walks in the New Forest, 1975. *Recreations:* music, gardening, walking. *Address:* Crossways, Milford on Sea, Lymington, Hants. *T:* Milford on Sea 3207. *Club:* Royal Commonwealth Society.
See also W. N. Wenban-Smith.

WENBAN-SMITH, William Nigel; HM Diplomatic Service; Head of East Africa Department, Foreign and Commonwealth Office, since 1982; *b* 1 Sept. 1936; *s* of William Wenban-Smith, *qv*; *m* 1st, 1961, Charlotte Chapman-Andrews; two *s* two *d*; 2nd, 1976, Charlotte Susanna Rycroft; two *s. Educ:* King's Sch., Canterbury; King's Coll., Cambridge (BA). National Service, RN. Plebiscite Supervisory Officer, Southern Cameroons, 1960-61; Asst Principal, CRO, 1961-65 (Private Sec. to Parly Under Sec., 1963-64); Second Sec., Leopoldville, 1965-67; First Sec. and (1968) Head of Chancery, Kampala, 1967-70; FCO, 1970-74; Dublin, 1975; Commercial Sec., Brussels, 1976-78; Commercial Counsellor, Brussels, 1978-80; on loan to Cabinet Office, 1980-82. *Recreations:* walking, squash, gardening. *Address:* c/o Foreign and Commonwealth Office, King Charles Street, SW1.

WENDT, Robin Glover; Chief Executive, Cheshire County Council and Clerk of Lieutenancy, since 1979; *b* 7 Jan. 1941; *er s* of William Romilly Wendt and late Doris May (*née* Glover), Preston, Lancs; *m* 1965, Prudence Ann Dalby; two *d. Educ:* Hutton Grammar Sch., Preston; Wadham Coll., Oxford Univ. (BA 1962). Asst Principal 1962, Principal 1966, Min. of Pensions and Nat. Insurance; Principal Private Sec. to Sec. of State for Social Services, 1970; Asst Sec., DHSS, 1972; Dep. Sec., Cheshire CC, 1975. Mem., Social Security Adv. Cttee, 1982-. *Recreations:* music, swimming, following sport. *Address:* Shiloh, Seahill Road, Saughall, Chester CH1 6BJ. *T:* Saughall 880322.

WENHAM, Brian George; Controller, BBC 2, since 1978; *b* 9 Feb. 1937; *s* of late George Frederick Wenham and of Harriet Wenham, London; *m* Elisabeth Downing, *d* of Keith and Margery Woolley; two *d. Educ:* Royal Masonic Sch., Bushey; St John's Coll., Oxon. Television journalist, Independent Television News, 1962-69; Editor, Panorama, BBC, 1969-71; Head of Current Affairs Gp, 1971-78. *Address:* Red Cottage, Wey Road, Weybridge, Surrey; BBC Television Centre, W12 7RJ. *T:* 01-743 8000.

WENNER, Michael Alfred; HM Diplomatic Service, retired; President, Wenner Trading Co.; Director, Micron Corporation, Houston; *b* 17 March 1921; *s* of Alfred E. Wenner and Simone Roussel; *m* 1950, Gunilla Cecilia Ståhle, *d* of Envoyé Nils K. Ståhle, CBE, and of Birgit Olsson; four *s. Educ:* Stonyhurst; Oriel College, Oxford (Scholar). Served E Yorks Regt, 1940; Lancs Fusiliers and 151 Parachute Bn, India, 1941-42; 156 Bn, N Africa, 1943; No 9 Commando, Italy and Greece, 1944-45. Entered HM Foreign Service, 1947; 3rd Sec., Stockholm, 1948-51; 2nd Sec., Washington, 1951-53; Foreign Office, 1953-55; 1st Sec., Tel Aviv, 1956-59; Head of Chancery, La Paz, 1959-61, and at Vienna, 1961-63; Inspector of Diplomatic Establishments, 1964-67; Ambassador to El Salvador, 1967-70. *Publication:* Advances in Controlled Droplet Application, Agro-Chemical Age, 1979. *Recreations:* fly-fishing, old maps. *Address:* 8277 Kingsbrook No 255, Houston, Texas 77024, USA; Laythams Farm, Slaidburn, Clitheroe, Lancs.

WENTWORTH, Maurice Frank Gerard, CMG 1957; OBE 1946; *b* 5 Nov. 1908; *s* of F. B. Wentworth, Finchley, N3; *m* 1962, Belinda Margaret, *d* of late B. S. Tatham and Mrs Tatham, Mickleham, Surrey; one *s* one *d. Educ:*

Haileybury; University Coll., London (BA). Military Service, 1939–46, Lieutenant-Colonel. Gold Coast: Inspector of Schools, 1930; Sen. Education Officer, 1945; Principal, Teacher Training Coll., Tamale, 1946; Administrative Officer Class I, 1951; Permanent Secretary, 1953; Establishment Secretary, 1954–57 (Ghana Civil Service); Chairman: Public Service Commission: Sierra Leone, 1958–61; E African High Commn, 1961–64; Appointments Officer, ODM, 1964–73. *Address:* Quarry Hill, Todber, Sturminster Newton, Dorset.

WERNER, Alfred Emil Anthony; Chairman, Pacific Regional Conservation Center, since 1975; *b* 18 June 1911; *o s* of late Professor Emil Alphonse Werner, Dublin; *m* 1939, Marion Jane Davies; two *d. Educ:* St Gerard's School, Bray; Trinity College, Dublin. MSc (Dublin Univ.) and ARIC 1936; MA (Dublin) and DPhil (Univ. of Freiburg im Breisgau) 1937; Hon. ScD (Dublin) 1971. Lecturer in Chemistry, TCD, 1937; Reader in Organic Chemistry, TCD, 1946; Research Chemist, National Gallery, 1948; Principal Scientific Officer, British Museum Research Laboratory, 1954, Keeper, 1959–75. Prof. of Chemistry, Royal Acad., 1962–75. FSA 1958; FMA 1959 (President, 1967); MRIA 1963. Pres., International Institute for the Conservation of Artistic and Historic Works, 1971 (Hon. Treasurer, 1962). *Publications:* The Scientific Examination of Paintings, 1952; (with H. Roosen-Runge) Codex Lindisfarnensis, Part V, 1961; (with H. J. Plenderleith) The Conservation of Antiquities and Works of Art, 1972; articles in scientific and museum journals. *Recreations:* chess, travelling. *Address:* Millwood House, Groton, Colchester, Essex. *T:* Boxford 210231; c/o Bishop Museum, PO Box 6037, Honolulu, Hawaii 96818, USA. *Club:* Athenæum.

WERNER, Louis Ronald, AM 1980; MSc, PhD; President, New South Wales Institute of Technology, since 1974; *b* 12 Sept. 1924; *s* of Frank Werner and Olive Maude Werner; *m* 1948, Valerie Irene (*née* Bean); two *s* one *d. Educ:* Univ. of New South Wales (BSc (1st Cl. Hons; Univ. Medal); MSc, PhD). FRACI. Sen. Lectr, 1954–60, Associate Prof., 1961–67, Head of Dept of Phys. Chemistry, 1964–67, Univ. of New South Wales; Dep. Dir, 1967–68, Director, 1968–73, NSW Inst. of Technology. Chm., NSW Advanced Educn Bd, 1969–71; Trustee, Mus. of Applied Arts and Scis, 1973– (Pres., Bd of Trustees, 1976–); Chm., Conf. of Dirs of Central Insts of Technology, 1975–; Member: Science and Industry Forum, Aust. Acad. of Science, 1971–76; Council for Tech. and Further Educn, 1970–; Hong Kong UPGC, 1972–; Governor, College of Law, 1972–76; Councillor, Nat. Roads and Motorists Assoc., 1977–. *Publications:* numerous papers in scientific jls. *Recreations:* yachting, golf. *Address:* 1 Crete Place, East Lindfield, NSW 2070, Australia. *T:* 467–1081. *Club:* Rotary (Sydney).

WERNHAM, Prof. Archibald Garden, MA Aberdeen, BA Oxford; Regius Professor of Moral Philosophy in the University of Aberdeen, 1960–81; *b* 4 March 1916; *e s* of Archibald Garden Wernham and Christina Noble; *m* 1944, Hilda Frances Clayton; two *s. Educ:* Robert Gordon's College, Aberdeen; Aberdeen University; Balliol College, Oxford. 1st Class Hons Classics, Aberdeen, 1938, Croom Robertson Fellow, Aberdeen, 1939; 1st Cl. Hons Classical Mods, Oxford, 1939, 1st Cl. Lit. Hum., Oxford, 1943. Served in RA, 1940–42. Lecturer in Moral and Political Philosophy, St Andrews Univ., 1945–53; Sen. Lecturer, 1953–59; Reader, 1959–60. *Publications:* Benedict de Spinoza-The Political Works, 1958; reviews and articles. *Recreations:* music, swimming, walking. *Address:* Ardil, Gladstone Place, Dyce, Aberdeen. *T:* Aberdeen 722489.

WERNHAM, Prof. Richard Bruce, MA Oxon; Professor of Modern History, Oxford University, 1951–72; Fellow of Worcester College, Oxford, 1951–72; now Professor and Fellow Emeritus; *b* 11 Oct. 1906; *o s* of Richard George and Eleanor Mary Wernham; *m* 1939, Isobel Hendry Macmillan, Vancouver BC; one *d. Educ:* Newbury Grammar School; Exeter College, Oxford. Research Asst, Inst. of Historical Research, London Univ., 1929–30; Temp. Asst, Public Record Office, 1930–32; Editor, PRO, State Papers, Foreign Series. 1933–; Lecturer in Modern History, University Coll., London, 1933–34; Fellow of Trinity College, Oxford, 1934–51, Senior Tutor, 1940–41 and 1948–51; University Lecturer in Modern History, Oxford, 1941–51; Examiner in Final Honour School of Modern History, Oxford, 1946–48. Vis. Professor: Univ. of S Carolina, 1958; Univ. of California, Berkeley, 1965–66; Una's Lectr, Berkeley, 1978. Served in RAF, 1941–45. *Publications:* Before the Armada: the Growth of English Foreign Policy 1485-1558, 1966; The Making of Elizabethan Foreign Policy, 1980; Calendars of State Papers, Foreign Series, Elizabeth; (ed) Vol III, New Cambridge Modern History: The Counter-Reformation and Price Revolution, 1559-1610, 1968. Articles in English Hist. Review, History, Trans Royal Hist. Soc., Encyclopædia Britannica. *Address:* 63 Hill Head Road, Hill Head, Fareham, Hants PO14 3JL.

WESIERSKA, Mrs George; see Walder, Ruth C.

WESIL, Dennis; *b* 18 Feb. 1915; *e s* of Jack and Polly Wesil, London; *m* 1941, Kathleen, *d* of H. S. McAlpine; two *d. Educ:* Central Foundation Sch.; University Coll., London. Entered London telephone service as Asst Supt of Traffic, 1937; PO Investigation Branch, 1941; Asst Postal Controller, 1947; Principal, PO Headqrtrs, 1953; Dep. Chief Inspector of Postal Services, 1961; Asst Sec. in charge of Postal Mechanisation Branch, 1963; Dep. Dir, NE Region (GPO), 1966; Director: NE Postal Region, 1967; London Postal Region, 1970–71; Sen. Dir, Posts, PO, 1971–75. Mem., PO Management Bd, 1975. *Recreations:* music, theatre, reading, open air. *Address:* 2 Stoneleigh,

Martello Road South, Poole, Dorset BH13 7HQ. *T:* Canford Cliffs 707304.

WESKER, Arnold; playwright; director; Founder Director of Centre 42, 1961 (dissolved 1970); Chairman, British Centre of International Theatre Institute, since 1978; *b* 24 May 1932; *s* of Joseph Wesker and Leah Perlmutter; *m* 1958, Dusty Bicker; two *s* two *d. Educ:* Upton House School, Hackney. Furniture Maker's Apprentice, Carpenter's Mate, 1948; Bookseller's Asst, 1949 and 1952; Royal Air Force, 1950–52; Plumber's Mate, 1952; Farm Labourer, Seed Sorter, 1953; Kitchen Porter, 1953–54; Pastry Cook, 1954–58. Former Mem., Youth Service Council. Author of plays: The Kitchen, produced at Royal Court Theatre, 1959, 1961 (filmed, 1961); Trilogy of plays (Chicken Soup with Barley, Roots, I'm Talking about Jerusalem) produced Belgrade Theatre (Coventry), 1958–60, Royal Court Theatre, 1960; Chips with Everything, Royal Court, 1962, Vaudeville, 1962 and Plymouth Theatre, Broadway, 1963; The Four Seasons, Belgrade Theatre (Coventry) and Saville, 1965; Their Very Own and Golden City, Brussels and Royal Court, 1966; The Friends, Stockholm and London, 1970 (also dir); The Old Ones, Royal Court, 1972; The Wedding Feast, Stockholm, 1974, Leeds 1977; The Journalists, Coventry (amateur), 1977, Yugoslav TV, 1978, Germany, 1981; The Merchant, Stockholm and Aarhus, 1976, Broadway, 1977, Birmingham, 1978; Love Letters on Blue Paper, Nat. Theatre, 1978 (also dir); Fatlips (for young people), 1978; Caritas (Scandinavian Project commission), 1980, Nat. Theatre, 1981; One More Ride on the Merry-Go-Round, 1981; Sullied Hand, 1981; Four Portraits (Japanese commn), 1982; Annie Wobbler; Lady Othello (film script), 1980. *Television:* (first play) Menace, 1963; Breakfast, 1981. *Publications:* Chicken Soup with Barley, 1959; Roots, 1959; I'm Talking about Jerusalem, 1960; The Wesker Trilogy, 1960; The Kitchen, 1961; Chips with Everything, 1962; The Four Seasons, 1966; Their Very Own and Golden City, 1966 (Marzotto Drama Prize, 1964); Fears of Fragmentation, 1970; The Friends, 1970; Six Sundays in January, 1971; The Old Ones, 1972; The Journalists, 1974 (in Dialog; repr. 1975); Love Letters on Blue Paper, 1974; (with John Allin) Say Goodbye! You May Never See Them Again, 1974; Words—as definitions of experience, 1976; The Wedding Feast, 1977; Journey Into Journalism, 1977; Said the Old Man to the Young Man, 1978; The Merchant, 1978; The Journalists, a triptych (with Journey into Journalism and A Diary of the Writing of The Journalists), 1979; Collected Plays, vols 1–4, 1980. *Address:* 27 Bishops Road, N6 4HR.

WESSEL, Robert Leslie, OBE 1969; *b* 21 Oct. 1912; *s* of late H. L. Wessel, Copenhagen, Denmark; *m* 1936, Dora Elizabeth, *d* of G. C. G. Gee, Rothley, Leics; two *s* two *d. Educ:* Malvern College. Entered N. Corah & Sons Ltd, 1932, Chm., 1957–69, retired. Served War of 1939–45, 44th Searchlight Regt RATA, 1939–41. Chairman: Nat. Youth Bureau, 1972–76; Youth Service Information Centre, 1968–72; Nat. Coll. for training Youth Leaders, 1960–70. Member: Council of Industrial Soc. (Chm., 1969–72); Cttee of Management, RNLI, 1974–82; Pro-Chancellor, Loughborough University of Technology, 1969–78; Group Chairman, Duke of Edinburgh's Conference, 1956. Mem., N and E Midlands Regional Bd, Lloyds Bank Ltd, 1962–78; Dir, Loughborough Consultants Ltd, 1970–78. FBIM; FIWM. Hon. DTech Loughborough, 1978. Mem., Worshipful Co. of Framework Knitters (Master, 1969–70). *Recreations:* painting, photography, music, travel. *Address:* Moult End, De Courcy Road, Salcombe, South Devon TQ8 8LQ. *T:* Salcombe 2641.

WEST, family name of **Baron Granville-West.**

WEST; *see* Sackville-West, family name of Baron Sackville.

WEST, Anthony Panther; author; *b* Hunstanton, Norfolk, 4 Aug. 1914; *m* 1936, Katharine Church; one *s* one *d*; *m* 1952, Lily Dulany Emmet; one *s* one *d. Educ:* in England. Became a breeder of registered Guernsey cattle and a dairy farmer, 1937. During war was with BBC's Far Eastern Desk, Home News Div., 1943–45, and then with their Japanese Service, 1945–47. Went to USA and joined staff of the New Yorker Magazine, 1950. Houghton Mifflin Fellow, 1947. *Publications:* Another Kind, (USA) 1949, (UK) 1951; One Dark Night, (UK) 1949, (as Vintage, USA, 1950); D. H. Lawrence (a critical biography), (UK) 1951, 2nd edn 1966; Gloucestershire, (UK) 1952; The Crusades, (USA) 1954 (as All About the Crusades, UK, 1967); Heritage, (USA) 1955; Principals and Persuasions, (USA) 1957, (UK) 1958, new edn 1970; The Trend Is Up, (USA) 1960; Elizabethan England, (USA) 1966, (UK) 1966; David Rees Among Others, (USA) 1970, (UK) 1970; Mortal Wounds, (USA) 1973, (UK) 1975. *Address:* c/o The New Yorker, 25 W 43rd Street, New York City, NY, USA.

WEST, David Arthur James; Assistant Under Secretary of State (Naval Personnel), Ministry of Defence, since 1981; *b* 10 Dec. 1927; *s* of Wilfred West and Edith West (*née* Jones). *Educ:* Cotham Grammar Sch., Bristol. Executive Officer, Air Ministry, 1946; Higher Executive Officer, 1955; Principal, 1961; Assistant Secretary, 1972; Asst Under Sec. of State, 1979. *Address:* 66 Denton Road, East Twickenham TW1 2HQ. *T:* 01-892 6890.

WEST, David Thomson, CBE 1982; Head of Economic Policy (Manpower) Branch, Department of Employment, since 1976; *b* 10 March 1923; *m* 1958, Marie Sellar; one *s* one *d. Educ:* Malvern Coll.; St John's Coll., Oxford. Served in RNVR, 1942–45; HM Diplomatic Service, 1946–76; served in Foreign Office, Office of Comr General for UK in SE Asia, HM Embassies, Paris, Lima, and Tunis; Counsellor, 1964; Commercial Inspector, 1965–68; Counsellor (Commercial) Berne, 1968–71; Head of Export Promotion Dept,

FCO, 1971-72; seconded to Civil Service Dept as Head of Manpower Div., 1972-76; transf. to Home Civil Service, 1976. *Address:* 7 St Paul's Place, N1. *T:* 01-226 7505; Lammas Cottage, Water Street, Lavenham, Suffolk. *T:* Lavenham 247873. *Club:* Garrick.

WEST, Prof. Donald James; Professor of Clinical Criminology since 1979, and Director since 1981, University of Cambridge Institute of Criminology; Fellow of Darwin College, Cambridge, since 1967; *b* 9 June 1924; *s* of John Charles and Jessie Mercedes West. *Educ:* Merchant Taylors' Sch., Crosby; Liverpool Univ. (MD). LittD Cambridge. MRCPsych. Research Officer, Soc. for Psychical Research, London, and pt-time graduate student in psychiatry, 1947-50; in hospital practice in psychiatry, 1951-59; Sen. Registrar, Forensic Psychiatry Unit, Maudsley Hosp., 1957-59; Inst. of Criminology, Cambridge, 1960-. Vice Pres., 1981-, and former Pres., British Soc. of Criminology; Vice Pres., 1965-, and former Pres., Soc. for Psychical Research. *Publications:* Psychical Research Today, 1954 (revd edn 1962); Eleven Lourdes Miracles (med. inquiry under Parapsych. Foundn Grant), 1957; The Habitual Prisoner (for Inst. of Criminology), 1963; Murder followed by Suicide (for Inst. of Criminology), 1965; The Young Offender, 1967; Homosexuality, 1968; Present Conduct and Future Delinquency, 1969; (ed) The Future of Parole, 1972; (jtly) Who Becomes Delinquent?, 1973; (jtly) The Delinquent Way of Life, 1977; Homosexuality Re-examined, 1977; (ed, jtly) Daniel McNaughton: his trial and the aftermath, 1977; (jtly) Understanding Sexual Attacks, 1978; Delinquency: its roots, careers and prospects, 1982; various contribs to British Jl of Criminology, Jl of Adolescence. *Recreations:* travel, parapsychology. *Address:* 32 Fen Road, Milton, Cambridge CB4 4AD. *T:* Cambridge 860308; Pilgrim's Place, 54 Rosslyn Hill, NW3 1ND. *T:* 01-435 6203.

WEST, Edward Mark; Deputy Director-General, Food and Agriculture Organization of the United Nations, since 1982; *b* 11 March 1923; *m* 1948, Lydia Hollander; three *s. Educ:* Hendon County Sch.; University Coll., Oxford (MA). Served RA (W/Lieut), 1943; ICU BAOR (A/Captain), 1945. Asst Principal, Colonial Office, 1947; Private Sec., PUS, Colonial Office, 1950-51, Principal, 1951-58; Head of Chancery, UK Commn, Singapore, 1958-61; Private Secretary to Secretary of State, Colonial Affairs, 1961-62; Private Secretary to Secretary of State for Commonwealth and Colonial Affairs, 1963; Asst Sec., ODM, 1964-70; Food and Agriculture Organization: Director, Programme and Budget Formulation, 1970; Asst Dir-Gen., Administration and Finance Dept, 1974; Asst Dir-Gen., Programme and Budget Formulation, 1976. *Address:* Food and Agriculture Organization of the UN, Terme di Caracalla, Rome, Italy.

WEST, Air Commodore Ferdinand, VC 1918; CBE 1945; MC; *b* London, 29 Jan. 1896; *s* of late Francis West and late Countess De la Garde de Saignes; *m* 1922, Winifred, *d* of John Leslie; one *s. Educ:* Xaverian Coll., Brighton; Lycée Berchet; Univ. of Genoa. 2nd Lieutenant, Lieutenant, and Acting Captain in the Royal Munster Fusiliers, 1914-17; attached to the Flying Corps, 1917-18; transferred to the Royal Air Force as a Captain, 1919 (wounded three times, MC, VC, despatches twice, Cavaliere Crown of Italy); Commanded 4 Squadron, RAF, Farnborough, 1933-36; Air Attaché, British Legations, Helsingfors, Riga, Tallin, Kovno, 1936-38; Commanded, RAF Station, Odiham, 1938-40; Air Attaché, British Embassy, Rome, 1940; Air Attaché, British Legation, Berne, 1940; retired from RAF, 1946. Man. Dir, J. Arthur Rank Overseas Film Distributors, 1947-58. Retired as Chairman: Hurst Park Syndicate, 1963-71; Continental Shipyard Agencies Ltd; Technical Equipment Supplies Ltd; Dir, Tokalon Ltd, 1963-73; Terravia Trading Services. Comdr Order of Orange Nassau, 1949; Chevalier Legion of Honour, 1958. First Class Army Interpreter (Italian) Second Class (French). *Address:* Zoar, Devenish Road, Sunningdale, Berks. *T:* Ascot 20579. *Club:* Royal Air Force.

WEST, Rt. Rev. Francis Horner, MA; *b* 9 Jan. 1909; *o s* of Sydney Hague and Mary West, St Albans, Herts; *m* 1947, Beryl Elaine, 2nd *d* of late Rev. W. A. Renwick, Smallbridge, Rochdale; one *s* one *d. Educ:* Berkhamsted School; Magdalene Coll. and Ridley Hall, Cambridge. Exhibitioner, Magdalene, Cambridge; MA 1934; Curate St Agnes, Leeds, 1933-36; Chaplain, Ridley Hall, Cambridge, 1936-38; Vicar of Starbeck, Yorks, 1938-42. Served War of 1939-45, as CF with BEF, MEF, CMF and SEAC, 1939-46 (despatches, 1945); Director of Service Ordination Candidates, 1946-47; Vicar of Upton, Notts, 1947-51; Archdeacon of Newark, 1947-62; Vicar of East Retford, 1951-55; Bishop Suffragan of Taunton, 1962-77; Prebendary of Wells, 1962-77; Rector of Dinder, Somerset, 1962-71. Select Preacher, Cambridge Univ., 1962. Visitor, Croft House School, 1968-79. *Publications:* Rude Forefathers, The Story of an English Village, 1600-1666, 1949; The Great North Road in Nottinghamshire, 1956; Sparrows of the Spirit, 1957; The Country Parish Today and Tomorrow, 1960; F. R. B.: a portrait of Bishop F. R. Barry, 1980. *Recreations:* writing, gardening. *Address:* 11 Castle Street, Aldbourne, Marlborough, Wilts. *T:* Marlborough 40630.

WEST, Lt-Col George Arthur Alston-Roberts-; Assistant Comptroller, Lord Chamberlain's Office, since 1981; an Extra Equerry to the Queen, since 1982; *b* 1937; *s* of Major W. R. J. Alston-Roberts-West, Grenadier Guards (killed in action 1940) and of Mrs W. R. J. Alston-Roberts-West; *m* 1970, Hazel, *d* of late Sir Thomas Cook and of Lady Cook. *Educ:* Eton Coll.; RMA, Sandhurst. Commissioned into Grenadier Guards, Dec. 1957; served in England, Northern Ireland, Germany and Cyprus; retired, 1980. *Address:* Stable House, St James's Palace, SW1. *Club:* Boodle's.

WEST, Rt. Hon. Henry William, PC (N Ire) 1960; Leader, Ulster Unionist Party, 1974-79; *b* 27 March 1917; *s* of late W. H. West, JP; *m* 1956, Maureen Elizabeth Hall; four *s* three *d. Educ:* Enniskillen Model School; Portora Royal School. Farmer. MP for Enniskillen, NI Parlt, 1954-72; Mem. (U), Fermanagh and S Tyrone, NI Assembly, 1973-75; Parly Sec. to Minister of Agriculture, 1958; Minister of Agriculture, 1960-67, and 1971-72; MP (UUUC) Fermanagh and South Tyrone, Feb.-Sept. 1974; Mem. (UUUC), for Fermanagh and South Tyrone, NI Constitutional Convention, 1975-76. N Ireland representative on British Wool Marketing Board, 1950-58; President, Ulster Farmers' Union, 1955-56. High Sheriff, Co. Fermanagh, 1954. *Address:* Rossahilly House, Enniskillen, Northern Ireland. *T:* Enniskillen 3060.

WEST, Mrs James; *see* McCarthy, Mary.

WEST, Prof. John Clifford, CBE 1977; PhD, DSc; CEng; FIEE; Vice-Chancellor and Principal, University of Bradford, since 1979; *b* 4 June 1922; *s* of J. H. West and Mrs West (née Ascroft); *m* 1946, Winefride Mary Turner; three *d. Educ:* Hindley and Abram Grammar School; Victoria Univ., Manchester. PhD 1953, DSc 1957. Matthew Kirtley Entrance Schol., Manchester Univ., 1940. Electrical Lieutenant, RNVR, 1943-46. Lecturer, University of Manchester, 1946-57; Professor of Electrical Engineering, The Queen's University of Belfast, 1958-65; University of Sussex: Prof. of Electrical and Control Engineering, 1965-78; Founder Dean, Sch. of Applied Scis, 1965-73, Pro-Vice-Chancellor, 1967-71; Dir, Phillips' Philatelic Unit, 1970-78. Director, A. C. E. Machinery Ltd, 1966-79. Member: UGC, 1973-78 (Chm., Technology Sub-Cttee, 1973-78); Science Res. Council Cttee on Systems and Electrical Engineering, 1963-67; Science Res. Council Engrg Bd, 1976-79; Vis. Cttee, Dept of Educn and Science, Cranfield; Civil Service Commn Special Merit Promotions Panel, 1966-72; Naval Educn Adv. Cttee, 1965-72; Crawford Cttee on Broadcasting Coverage, 1973-74; Inter-Univ. Inst. of Engrg Control, 1967- (Dir, 1967-70); Chm., Council for Educnl Technology, 1980-. Vice-Pres., IEE, 1980-; Chm., Automation and Control Div., IEE, 1970-71 (Vice-Chm., 1967-70). Member: Royal Philatelic Soc., 1960-; Sociedad Filatélica de Chile, 1970-; Chm., British Philatelic Council, 1980-81; FRPSL, 1970-. Hartley Medal, Inst. Measurement and Control, 1979. *Publications:* Textbook of Servomechanisms, 1953; Analytical Techniques for Non-Linear Control Systems, 1960; papers in Proc. IEE, Trans Amer. IEE, Brit. Jl of Applied Physics, Jl of Scientific Instruments, Proc. Inst. Measurement and Control. *Recreation:* philately. *Address:* 6 Park Crescent, Guiseley, Leeds LS20 8EL. *T:* Guiseley 72605. *Club:* Athenæum.

WEST, Martin Litchfield, DPhil; FBA 1973; Professor of Greek, Bedford College, University of London, since 1974; *b* 23 Sept. 1937; *s* of Maurice Charles West and Catherine Baker West (née Stainthorpe); *m* 1960, Stephanie Roberta Pickard; one *s* one *d. Educ:* St Paul's Sch.; Balliol Coll., Oxford. Chancellor's Prizes for Latin Prose and Verse, 1957; Hertford and de Paravicini Schols, 1957; Ireland Schol., 1957; Woodhouse Jun. Research Fellow, St John's Coll., Oxford, 1960-63; Fellow and Praelector in Classics, University Coll., Oxford, 1963-74; MA (Oxon) 1962, DPhil (Oxon) 1963; Conington Prize, 1965. Editor of Liddell and Scott's Greek-English Lexicon, 1965-81. *Publications:* Hesiod, Theogony (ed), 1966; Fragmenta Hesiodea (ed with R. Merkelbach), 1967; Early Greek Philosophy and the Orient, 1971; Sing Me, Goddess, 1971; Iambi et Elegi Graeci (ed), 1971-72; Textual Criticism and Editorial Technique, 1973; Studies in Greek Elegy and Iambus, 1974; Hesiod, Works and Days (ed), 1978; Theognidis et Phocylidis fragmenta, 1978; Delectus ex Iambis et Elegis Graecis, 1980; Greek Metre, 1982; articles in classical periodicals. *Recreations:* music, old Germanic languages. *Address:* Bedford College, Inner Circle, Regent's Park, NW1 4NS. *T:* 01-486 4400; 42 Portland Road, Oxford. *T:* 56060.

WEST, Michael Charles B.; *see* Beresford-West.

WEST, Morris (Langlo); novelist; *b* Melbourne, 26 April 1916; *s* of Charles Langlo West and Florence Guilfoyle Hanlon; *m* 1953, Joyce Lawford; three *s* one *d. Educ:* Melbourne Univ. (BA 1937). Taught modern langs and maths, NSW and Tas, 1933-39. Served, Lieutenant, AIF, South Pacific, 1939-43. Sec. to William Morris Hughes, former PM of Australia, 1943. FRSL; Fellow World Acad. of Art and Science. Hon. DLitt, Univ. of Santa Clara, 1969; Hon. DLitt Mercy Coll., NY, 1982. Internat. Dag Hammarskjold Prize (Grand Collar of Merit), 1978. *Publications:* Gallows on the Sand, 1955; Kundu, 1956; Children of the Sun, 1957; The Crooked Road, 1957 (Eng.: The Big Story); The Concubine, 1958; Backlash, 1958 (Eng.: The Second Victory); The Devil's Advocate, 1959 (National Brotherhood Award, National Council of Christians and Jews 1960; James Tait Black Memorial Prize, 1960; RSL Heinemann Award, 1960; filmed 1977); The Naked Country, 1960; Daughter of Silence, 1961; Daughter of Silence (play), 1961; The Shoes of the Fisherman, 1963; The Ambassador, 1965; The Tower of Babel, 1968; The Heretic, a Play in Three Acts, 1970; (with R. Francis) Scandal in the Assembly, 1970; Summer of the Red Wolf, 1971; The Salamander, 1973; Harlequin, 1974; The Navigator, 1976; Proteus, 1979; The Clowns of God, 1981 (Universe Literary Prize, 1981). *Address:* c/o Wiederkehr & Forster, Bahnhofstrasse 44, CH 8023 Zürich, Switzerland. *Clubs:* Wentworth Golf; Royal Prince Alfred Yacht (Sydney).

WEST, Peter; television and radio commentator/anchorman, since 1947; Rugby Football Correspondent of The Times, since 1971; Chairman, West Nally Group (sports marketing), since 1971; *b* 12 Aug. 1920; *s* of Harold William and Dorcas Anne West; *m* 1946, Pauline Mary Pike; two *s* one *d.*

Educ: Cranbrook Sch.; RMC, Sandhurst. Served War of 1939–45: Duke of Wellington's Regt. TV/Radio commentaries every year: on Test matches, 1952–; on Wimbledon, 1955–; on Rugby Union, 1950–; Olympics, 1948-60-64-68-72-76. TV shows: Chairman of: Why?, 1953; Guess my Story, 1953-54-55. Introduced: At Home, 1955; First Hand and It's Up to You, 1956-57; Box Office, 1957; Come Dancing, 1957-72 (incl.); Be Your Own Boss and Wish You Were Here, 1958; Get Ahead, 1958-62; Good Companions, 1958-62; First Years at Work (Schs TV), 1958-69 (incl.); Miss World, 1961-66 (incl.). Children's TV: introd.: Question Marks, 1957; Ask Your Dad, 1958; What's New?, 1962-63-64. Radio: introd.: What Shall We Call It?, 1955; Sound Idea, 1958; Morning Call, 1960-61; Treble Chance, 1962; Sporting Chance, 1964; Games People Play, 1975–. *Publications:* The Fight for the Ashes, 1953; The Fight for the Ashes, 1956. *Recreation:* gardening. *Address:* Coppings, 53 Tekels Avenue, Camberley, Surrey. *T:* Camberley 64630.

WEST, Prunella Margaret Rumney, (Mrs T. L. West); *see* Scales, Prunella.

WEST, Dame Rebecca, DBE 1959 (CBE 1949); CLit 1968; *b* Christmas, 1892; Cicily Isabel, *y d* of late Charles Fairfield, Co. Kerry; *m* 1930, Henry Maxwell Andrews (*d* 1968). *Educ:* George Watson's Ladies' College, Edinburgh. Joined Staff of Freewoman as reviewer, 1911; joined staff of The Clarion as political writer, 1912; has since contributed to many leading English and American newspapers as literary critic and political writer. Appeared in Warren Beatty's film, Reds, as one of the Witnesses, 1982. Fellow, Saybrook Coll., Yale Univ. Member American Academy of Arts and Sciences. Hon. DLitt: New York Univ., 1965; Edinburgh Univ., 1980. Benson Medal (RSL), 1966. Order of Saint Sava, 1937; Chevalier of the Legion of Honour, 1957. *Publications:* Henry James, 1916; The Return of the Soldier, 1918; The Judge, 1922; The Strange Necessity, 1928; Lions and Lambs (pseudonym Lynx in collaboration with Low); Harriet Hume, 1929; D. H. Lawrence, an Elegy, 1930; Ending in Earnest, 1931 (published in America only); St Augustine, 1933; The Rake's Progress (in collaboration with Low), 1934; The Harsh Voice, 1935; The Thinking Reed, 1936; Black Lamb and Grey Falcon (a book about Yugoslavia), 1942; The Meaning of Treason, 1949; A Train of Powder, 1955; The Fountain Overflows, 1957; The Court and the Castle, 1958; The Vassall Affair, 1963; The New Meaning of Treason, 1964; The Birds Fall Down, 1966; Rebecca West: A Celebration, 1977; 1900, 1982; The Young Rebecca: writings 1911-1917 (selected by Jane Marcus), 1982. *Address:* c/o Messrs Macmillan, 4 Little Essex Street, WC2R 3LF.

WEST, Prof. Richard Gilbert, FRS 1968; FSA; FGS; Fellow of Clare College, Cambridge, since 1954; Professor of Botany, University of Cambridge, since 1977, and Director, Subdepartment of Quaternary Research, since 1966; *b* 31 May 1926; *m* 1st, 1958; one *s*; 2nd, 1973, Hazel Gristwood; two *d. Educ:* King's School, Canterbury; Univ. of Cambridge. Univ. Demonstrator in Botany, 1957-60; Univ. Lecturer in Botany, 1960-67; Reader in Quaternary Research, 1967-75, Prof. of Palaeoecology, 1975-77, Univ. of Cambridge. Mem., Ancient Monuments Bd for England, 1980–. Darwin Lecturer to the British Association, 1959; Lyell Fund, 1961, Bigsby Medal, 1969, Geological Society of London. Hon. MRIA. *Publications:* Pleistocene Geology and Biology, 1968, 2nd edn 1977; (jtly) The Ice Age in Britain, 1972; The Pre-glacial Pleistocene of the Norfolk and Suffolk coasts, 1980. *Address:* Woodlands, 3A Woollards Lane, Great Shelford, Cambs. *T:* Cambridge 842578; Clare College, Cambridge.

WEST, Dr Thomas Summers, FRSE, FRSC; Director, Macaulay Institute for Soil Research, Aberdeen, since 1975; *b* 18 Nov. 1927; *s* of late Thomas West and of Mary Ann Summers; *m* 1952, Margaret Officer Lawson, MA; one *s* two *d. Educ:* Tarbat Old Public Sch., Portmahomack; Royal Acad., Tain; Aberdeen Univ. (BSc 1st Cl. Hons Chemistry, 1949); Univ. of Birmingham (PhD 1952, DSc 1962). FRSC (FRIC 1962); FRSE 1979. Univ. of Birmingham: Sen. DSIR Fellow, 1952-55; Lectr in Chem., 1955-63; Imperial Coll., London: Reader in Analytical Chem., 1963-65; Prof. of Analytical Chem., 1965-75. Pres., Analytical Div., 1977–, Asst Sec. Gen., 1982–, IUPAC; Pres., Soc. for Analytical Chem., 1969-71; Mem. Royal Society's British National Cttee for Chem. (Chm., Analytical Sub-cttee), 1965–; Hon. Sec., Chemical Soc., 1972-75 (Redwood Lectr, 1974). Meldola Medal, RIC, 1956; Instrumentation Medal, 1976, and Gold Medal, 1977, Chemical Soc.; Johannes Marcus Medal for Spectroscopy, Spectroscopic Soc. of Bohemia, 1977. *Publications:* Analytical Applications of Diamino ethane tetra acetic acid, 1958, 2nd edn 1961; New Methods of Analytical Chemistry, 1964; Complexometry with EDTA and Related Reagents, 1969. *Recreations:* gardening, motoring, reading, music, fishing. *Address:* 31 Bailliesewells Drive, Bieldside, Aberdeen AB1 9AT. *T:* Aberdeen 868294.

WEST, Timothy Lancaster; actor and director; *b* 20 Oct. 1934; *s* of Harry Lockwood West and Olive Carleton-Crowe; *m* 1st, 1956, Jacqueline Boyer (marr. diss.); one *d*; 2nd, 1963, Prunella Scales, *qv*; two *s. Educ:* John Lyon Sch., Harrow; Regent Street Polytechnic. Entered profession as asst stage manager, Wimbledon, 1956; first London appearance, Caught Napping, Piccadilly, 1959; Mem., RSC, 1964-66; Prospect Theatre Co., 1966-72: Dr Samuel Johnson, Prospero, Bolingbroke, young Mortimer in Edward II, King Lear, Emerson in A Room with a View, Alderman Smuggler in The Constant Couple, and Holofernes in Love's Labour's Lost; Otto in The Italian Girl, 1968; Gilles in Abelard and Heloise, 1970; Robert Hand in Exiles, 1970; Gilbert in The Critic as Artist, 1971; Sir William Gower in Trelawny (musical), Bristol, 1972; Falstaff in Henry IV Pts I and II, Bristol, 1973;

Shpigelsky in A Month in the Country, Chichester, 1974 (London, 1975); Brack in Hedda Gabler, RSC, 1975; Iago in Othello, Nottingham, 1976; with Prospect Co.: Harry in Staircase, 1976, Claudius in Hamlet, storyteller in War Music, and Enobarbus in Antony and Cleopatra, 1977; Ivan and Gottlieb in Laughter, and Max in The Homecoming, 1978; Beecham, Apollo, 1980; Uncle Vanya, Australia, 1982; with Old Vic Co.: Narrator in Lancelot and Guinevere, Shylock in The Merchant of Venice, 1980. *Directed:* plays for Prospect Co., Open Space, Gardner Centre, Brighton, and rep. at Salisbury, Bristol, Northampton and Cheltenham; own season, The Forum, Billingham, 1973; Artistic Dir, Old Vic Co., 1980-81. *Television includes:* Richard II, 1969; Edward II, and The Boswell and Johnson Show, 1970; Horatio Bottomley, 1972; Edward VII, 1973; Hard Times, 1977; Crime and Punishment, Churchill and the Generals, 1979 (Royal TV Soc. Award); Brass, 1982. *Films:* The Looking-Glass War, 1968; Nicholas and Alexandra, 1970; The Day of the Jackal, 1972; Hedda, 1975; Joseph Andrews, and The Devil's Advocate, 1976; William Morris, 1977; Agatha, and The 39 Steps, 1978; The Antagonists, 1980; Murder is Easy, and Oliver Twist, 1981. Compiled and dir. recital progs; sound broadcaster. Director: Apollo Society; Platforms Theatre Ltd; World Student Drama Trust. Member: Arts Council Drama Panel, 1974-76, and Touring Cttee, 1978-80; Council, LAMDA, 1980–; Director in Residence, Univ. of Western Australia, 1982. *Recreations:* theatre history, travel, music, old railways. *Address:* 46 North Side, Wandsworth Common, SW18 2SL.

WEST, Prof. William Dixon, CIE 1947; ScD, FGS, FNA (Geol.); Emeritus Professor of Applied Geology, Director of Ground Water Project, Madhya Pradesh, University of Saugar; *b* 1901; *s* of Arthur Joseph West. *Educ:* King's Sch., Canterbury; St John's Coll., Cambridge (BA; ScD). Former Director, Geological Survey of India; former Vice-Chancellor, Univ. of Saugar. Lyell Medal, Geological Soc. of London, 1950. *Address:* Department of Applied Geology University of Saugar, Madhya Pradesh, India.

WEST CUMBERLAND, Archdeacon of; *see* Hodgson, Ven. T. R. B.

WEST HAM, Archdeacon of; *see* Dawes, Ven. P. S.

WEST INDIES, Archbishop of, since 1980; **Most Rev. George Cuthbert Manning Woodroffe,** KBE 1980 (CBE 1973); MA, LTh; Bishop of the Windward Islands, since 1969; *b* 17 May 1918; *s* of James Manning Woodroffe and Evelyn Agatha (*née* Norton); *m* 1947, Aileen Alice Connell; one *s* one *d* (and one *s* decd). *Educ:* Grenada Boys' Secondary School; Codrington Coll., Barbados. Clerk in Civil Service, 1936-41; Codrington Coll. (Univ. of Durham), 1941-44; Deacon 1944; Priest 1945; Asst Priest, St George's Cath., St Vincent, 1944-47; Vicar of St Simon's, Barbados, 1947-50; Rector: St Andrew, 1950-57; St Joseph, 1957-62; St John, 1962-67; Rural Dean of St John, Barbados, 1965-67; Sub-Dean and Rector of St George's Cathedral, St Vincent, Windward Islands, 1967-69. Vice-Chm., Anglican Consultative Council, 1974. Mem., Bd of Educn, Barbados, 1964-67. Chm., Bd of Governors, Alleyne Sch., Barbados, 1951-57. Hon. DD Nashotah House, USA, 1980; Hon. LLD, Univ. of the West Indies, 1981. *Recreations:* music, driving, detective tales and novels, military band music. *Address:* Bishop's House, PO Box 128, St Vincent, West Indies. *T:* St Vincent 809-45-61895. *Club:* Royal Commonwealth Society.

WEST-RUSSELL, David (Sturrock); His Honour Judge West-Russell; Resident Judge, Southwark Crown Court, since 1983 (a Circuit Judge, since 1966; formerly Deputy Chairman, Inner London Quarter Sessions); *b* 17 July 1921; *o s* of late Sir Alexander West-Russell and late Agnes West-Russell; *m* Christine, *y d* of Sidney and Gladys Tyler; one *s* two *d. Educ:* Rugby; Pembroke Coll., Cambridge. Commissioned Queen's Own Cameron Highlanders, 1941; Parachute Regt, 1942-46; served in N Africa, Italy, France, Greece, Norway and Palestine (despatches, Maj.). Management Trainee, Guest Keen and Nettlefold, 1948-50; Harmsworth Law Scholar, 1952; called to Bar, Middle Temple, 1953; SE Circuit; Sen. Circuit Judge, Inner London Crown Court, 1979-82. Mem., Departmental Cttee on Legal Aid in Criminal Proceedings, 1964-65. Comr (NI Emergency Provisions Act), 1974–; Chm., Lord Chancellor's Adv. Cttee on Appts of Magistrates for Inner London, 1976–; Member: Inner London Probation and After-Care Cttee, 1979–; Lord Chancellor's Adv. Cttee on the Trng of Magistrates, 1980–; Judicial Studies Bd, 1980–; Parole Bd, 1980-82. Pres., Inner London Magistrates' Assoc., 1979–. *Recreations:* town gardening, country walking. *Address:* 24 Hamilton Terrace, NW8. *T:* 01-286 3718. *Club:* Garrick.

WESTALL, Gen. Sir John Chaddesley, KCB 1954 (CB 1952); CBE 1951; *b* 2 July 1901; *s* of late John Chaddesley Westall, Hawkes Bay, NZ; *m* 1st, 1930, Maud Marion Bushe (*d* 1971); two *s* one *d*; 2nd, 1977, Mrs Margaret Boyle. *Educ:* Dulwich College. Entered Royal Marines, Oct. 1919; Capt. 1930; Major 1939; Naval Staff College, 1938. Served War of 1939-45: Malaya, India and Burma; promoted Bt Lt-Col for War Service, 1944. Staff Officer Intelligence, South Africa, 1947. Comd Royal Marine Barracks, Plymouth, 1949; Comd Royal Marines, Deal, 1950; Maj.-Gen. 1951; Chief of Staff, Royal Marines, 1951; Commandant General, Royal Marines, 1952-55; retired, 1955. Col Comdt, Royal Marines, 1961-64. *Recreations:* fishing, shooting. *Address:* 95 Rugby Street, Christchurch, New Zealand.

WESTALL, Rupert Vyvyan Hawksley, MA Cantab; Lieutenant Commander RN (retired); Head Master, Kelly College, Tavistock, Devon, 1939-59; *b* 27 July 1899; *s* of late Rev. William Hawksley Westall and Adela

Clara Pope; *m* 1925, Sylvia G. D. Page (*d* 1979); two *s* three *d. Educ:* RN Colleges Osborne and Dartmouth; Queens' College, Cambridge. Royal Navy, 1912-22; served European War, 1914-18; served in HMS Goliath, HMS Canada, HMS Ure and four years in The Submarine Service; Service on East African Station and Gallipoli, 1914-15, Jutland, China Station; Queens' College, Cambridge, 1922-26 (Exhibitioner in History, MA 1926, 1st division 2nd class both parts History Tripos); Training College for Schoolmasters, Cambridge, 1925-26; VI form and Careers Master, Blundell's School, 1926-34; Head Master West Buckland School, 1934-38. *Address:* Penrose, Kimberley Place, Falmouth, Cornwall TR11 3QL. *T:* Falmouth 313238.

WESTBROOK, Eric Ernest, CB 1981; Arts Consultant, since 1980; *b* 29 Sept. 1915; *s* of Ernest James and Helen Westbrook; *m* 1st, 1942, Ingrid Nyström; one *d*; 2nd, 1964, Dawn Sime. *Educ:* Alleyn's Sch., Dulwich; various schools of art. Lecturer for Arts Council of Gt Britain, 1943; Director, Wakefield City Art Gallery, Yorks, 1946; Chief Exhibitions Officer, Arts Council of Gt Britain, 1949; Director: Auckland City Art Gallery, NZ, 1952-55; National Gallery of Victoria, Melbourne, Aust., 1956-73; Director (Permanent Head), Ministry for the Arts, Victoria, 1973-80, retired. Hon. LLD Monash, 1974. Chevalier de l'Ordre des Arts et Lettres (France), 1972. *Publications:* Birth of a Gallery, 1968; various articles and reviews in arts and museum pubns. *Recreations:* music, gardening. *Address:* Lot 52, Alma Road, Panton Hill, Victoria 3759, Australia. *T:* 719-7585.

WESTBROOK, Neil Gowanloch, CBE 1981; Chairman, Trafford Park Estates plc; *b* 21 Jan. 1917; *s* of Frank and Dorothy Westbrook; *m* 1945, Hon. Mary Joan Fraser, *o d* of 1st Baron Strathalmond, CBE; one *s* one *d. Educ:* Oundle Sch.; Clare Coll., Cambridge (MA). FRICS. Served War of 1939-45: Sapper, 1939; Actg Lt-Col 1945 (despatches). Treas., Manchester Conservative Assoc., 1964-73, Dep. Chm., 1973-74, Chm., 1974-, Chm., Greater Manchester Co-ordinating Cttee, 1977; Manchester City Council, 1949-70; Dep. Leader 1967-69; Lord Mayor 1969-70. Chm., North Western Art Galleries and Museums Service, 1965-68; Mem., Exec. Cttee, Museums Assoc., 1965-69. *Recreations:* football, fishing, horse racing. *Address:* White Gables, Prestbury, Cheshire. *T:* Prestbury 829337. *Clubs:* Carlton; Manchester Tennis and Racquets.

WESTBURY, 5th Baron, *cr* 1861; **David Alan Bethell,** MC 1942; DL; *b* 16 July 1922; *s* of Captain The Hon. Richard Bethell (*d* 1929; *o c* of 3rd Baron); *S* brother, 1961; *m* 1947, Ursula Mary Rose James; two *s* one *d. Educ:* Harrow. 2nd Lieut 1940, Capt. 1944, Scots Guards. Equerry to the Duke of Gloucester, 1946-49. DL N Yorks, formerly NR Yorks, 1973. KStJ 1977. *Heir: s* Hon. Richard Nicholas Bethell, MBE 1979 [*b* 29 May 1950; *m* 1975, Caroline Mary, *d* of Richard Palmer; one *d. Educ:* Harrow; RMA Sandhurst. Major Scots Guards, 1978]. *Address:* Barton Cottage, Malton, North Yorkshire. *T:* Malton 2293.

WESTBURY, (Rose) Marjorie; Singer and Actress; *b* 18 June 1905; *o d* of George and Adella Westbury, Langley, Near Birmingham. Won 4 year scholarship to RCM, London, 1927. Sang Gretel at Old Vic as operatic debut for Lilian Baylis, 1932. Began broadcasting (as singer), 1933; joined BBC Drama Repertory, 1942; Solveig in Peer Gynt; Ylena (Lorca); Miles and Flora in Turn of the Screw; Nora in The Doll's House; Elsa Strauss in the Henry Reed series (Emily Butter); Steve Temple in Paul Temple series; Susan Grantly in Barchester Chronicles. *Recreations:* gardening, cooking, sewing, croquet. *Address:* Copperdene, Budletts, Maresfield, E Sussex TN22 2EB. *T:* Uckfield 2806.

WESTCOTT, George Foss, MA, MIMechE; freelance, since 1957; *b* 6 Feb. 1893; *e s* of Rev. Arthur Westcott, 2nd *s* of Brooke Foss Westcott, Bishop of Durham; *m* 1938, Anne Esther Anderberg; two *d. Educ:* Sherborne; GNR Locomotive Works, Doncaster (Premium Apprentice); Queens' College, Cambridge (Exhibitioner). Served in European War, 1914-19, in ASC (MT) and RFC; Hons Mechanical Science Tripos, 1920; worked for Scientific and Industrial Research Department, 1920; Assistant at Science Museum, 1921; Keeper of Mechanical Engineering Collections, 1937; on loan to Admiralty Engineering Lab., 1939-41; Emergency Commn in RASC, 1941-42; Science Museum, 1942; Keeper of Dept of Land And Water Transport, 1950; retired 1953; re-engaged as Asst Keeper, 1953; finally retired from Civil Service, 1957; worked for Intercontinental Marketing Services Ltd, 1963; Reader, Acad. of Visual Arts, 1964; founded Basic Ideology Research Unit, 1967. *Publications:* Science Museum Handbooks; Pumping Machinery, 1932; Mechanical and Electrical Engineering, 1955 (new edn, revised by H. P. Spratt, 1960); The British Railway Locomotive, 1803-1853, 1958; various Historical Synopses of Events Charts, 1922-56; The Conflict of Ideas, 1967; Christianity, Freethinking and Sex, 1968; Towards Intellectual Freedom: the development of a basic ideology, 1972, rev. edn 1974; The Science of Man, 1975, rev. edn 1982. *Recreations:* sociological research, reading, writing. *Address:* 1 Netherlands Court, Eaton Road, Sutton, Surrey. *T:* 01-643 2837.

WESTCOTT, Prof. John Hugh, DSc(Eng), PhD, DIC, FEng, FIEE, FBCS, FInstMC; Professor of Control Systems, Imperial College of Science and Technology, since 1970; Chairman: Feedback plc; Churchill Controls Ltd; *b* 3 Nov. 1920; *s* of John Stanley Westcott and Margaret Elisabeth Westcott (*née* Bass); *m* 1950, Helen Fay Morgan; two *s* one *d. Educ:* Wandsworth Sch.; City and Guilds Coll., London; Massachusetts Inst. of Technology. Royal Commission for the Exhibition of 1851 Senior Studentship; Apprenticeship BTH Co., Rugby. Radar Research and Develt Estabt, 1941-45; Lectr,

Imperial Coll., 1951; Reader, 1956; Prof., 1961; Head of Computing and Control Dept, 1970-79. Control Commn for Germany, 1945-46. Consultant to: Bataafsche Petroleum Maatschappij (Shell), The Hague, Holland, 1953-58; AEI, 1955-69; ICI, 1965-69; George Wimpey & Son, 1975-. Chm., Control and Automation Div., Instn of Electrical Engrs, 1968-69. Mem., Exec. Council of Internat. Fedn of Automatic Control, 1969-75; Chm., United Kingdom Automation Council, 1973-79; Pres., Inst. of Measurement and Control, 1979-80; Governor, Kingston Polytechnic, 1974-80. *Publications:* An Exposition of Adaptive Control, 1962; monographs and papers, mainly on Control Systems and related topics. *Recreations:* gardening, reading. *Address:* Department of Electrical Engineering, Imperial College, SW7 2BT. *T:* 01-589 5111; (home) 3 Sharon Close, Long Ditton, Surrey KT6 5HD. *T:* 01-398 6808.

WESTENRA, family name of **Baron Rossmore.**

WESTERMAN, Sir (Wilfred) Alan, Kt 1963; CBE 1962 (OBE 1957); EdD; MAEcon; Chairman, Australian Industry Development Corporation, since 1971; *b* NZ, 25 March 1913; *s* of W. J. Westerman, Sydney, NSW; *m* 1969, Margaret, *d* of late B. H. White. *Educ:* Knox Grammar School; Universities of Tasmania, Melbourne and Columbia. Chairman, Commonwealth Tariff Board, 1958-60; Sec., Dept of Trade and Industry, Canberra, 1960-71. Director: Ampol Petroleum Ltd; Philips Industries Holdings Ltd; Chm., Stevedoring Industry Consultative Council, 1978-. *Recreation:* tennis. *Address:* Australian Industry Development Corporation, PO Box 1483, Canberra, ACT 2601, Australia. *Clubs:* Commonwealth (Canberra); Athenæum (Melbourne); Union (Sydney).

WESTLAKE, Prof. Henry Dickinson; Hulme Professor of Greek in the University of Manchester, 1949-72, now Professor Emeritus; *b* 4 Sept. 1906; *s* of C. A. Westlake and Charlotte M. Westlake (*née* Manlove); *m* 1940, Mary Helen Sayers; one *s* one *d. Educ:* Uppingham School; St John's College, Cambridge (Scholar). Strathcona Student, 1929; Assistant Lecturer, University College, Swansea, 1930-32; Fellow of St John's College, Cambridge, 1932-35; Assistant Lecturer, University of Bristol, 1936-37; Lecturer, King's College, Newcastle, 1937-46; Administrative Assistant, Ministry of Home Security, 1941-44; Reader in Greek, University of Durham, 1946-49; Dean of the Faculty of Arts, Univ. of Manchester, 1960-61; Pro-Vice-Chancellor, 1965-68. *Publications:* Thessaly in the Fourth Century BC, 1935; Timoleon and his relations with tyrants, 1952; Individuals in Thucydides, 1968; Essays on the Greek Historians and Greek History, 1969. Articles and reviews in learned periodicals. *Address:* West Lodge, Manor Farm Road, Waresley, Sandy, Bedfordshire SG19 3BX. *T:* Gamlingay 50877.

WESTLAKE, Peter Alan Grant, CMG 1972; MC 1943; *b* 2 Feb. 1919; *s* of A. R. C. Westlake, CSI, CIE, and late Dorothy Louise (*née* Turner); *m* 1943, Katherine Spackman; two *s. Educ:* Sherborne; Corpus Christi Coll., Oxford; Military College of Science. Served with 1st Regt RHA (Adjt 1942), and on the staff (despatches). HM Foreign Service (now Diplomatic Service), 1946-76: served in Japan and at Foreign Office; Joint Services Staff College, 1954; Israel, 1955; Japan, 1957; Administrative Staff Coll., 1961; Counsellor: Foreign Office, 1961; Washington, 1965; British High Commn, Canberra, 1967-71; Minister, Tokyo, 1971-76. Pres., Asiatic Soc. of Japan, 1972-74. UK Comr-General, Internat. Ocean Expo, Okinawa, 1975. BD Wales 1981, MSc Wales; Deacon, Church in Wales, 1981, Priest 1982. FRAS. Order of the Rising Sun, Japan. *Address:* 53 Church Street, Beaumaris, Anglesey.

WESTMEATH, 13th Earl of, *cr* 1621; **William Anthony Nugent;** Baron Delvin, by tenure temp. Henry II; by summons, 1486; Senior Master, St Andrew's School, Pangbourne; *b* 21 Nov. 1928; *s* of 12th Earl of Westmeath and Doris (*d* 1968), 2nd *d* of C. Imlach, Liverpool; *S* father, 1971; *m* 1963, Susanna Margaret, *o d* of J. C. B. W. Leonard, *qv* ; two *s. Educ:* Marlborough Coll. Captain, RA, retired. *Heir: s* Hon. Sean Charles Weston Nugent, *b* 16 Feb. 1965. *Address:* Farthings, Rotten Row Hill, Bradfield, Berks. *T:* Bradfield 744426.

WESTMINSTER, 6th Duke of, *cr* 1874; **Gerald Cavendish Grosvenor;** DL; Bt 1622; Baron Grosvenor, 1761; Earl Grosvenor and Viscount Belgrave, 1784; Marquess of Westminster, 1831; commissioned Queens Own Yeomanry, 1973, Captain 1980; *b* 22 Dec. 1951; *s* of 5th Duke of Westminster, TD, and of Viola Duchess of Westminster, *qv* ; *S* father, 1979; *m* 1978, Natalia, *d* of Lt-Col H. P. J. Phillips; two *d. Educ:* Harrow. Director: Hennell Ltd; Stuart Devlin Ltd; Claridge Hotel Ltd; Chester Grosvenor Hotel Co.; Sun Alliance & London Insurance Co. (West End); Marcher Sound Ltd. Governor: Internat. Students' Trust, 1977; Chester Teacher Training Coll., 1979; King's School, Chester, 1975; Court, Univ. of Manchester, 1980; Cawthorne's Endowed Sch., 1981; Cancer Res. Council, 1982. Chairman: NW Area Advisory Cttee on Agriculture, 1977-79; NW Industrialists' Council, 1979. Mem. of Select Cttee on European Communities Cttee, Sub-Cttee G-Rural Policy. President: London Tourist Bd, 1980-; Chester City Conservative Assoc., 1977-; Cheshire Young Conservatives. Patron: Worcs CCC; British Holstein Soc.; British Kidney Patients Assoc. Freeman: Chester, 1973; England, 1979; City of London, 1980. OStJ 1982. DL Cheshire, 1982. *Address:* Eaton Hall, Chester, Cheshire. *Clubs:* Brooks's, Cavalry, MCC; Royal Yacht Squadron.

WESTMINSTER, Viola Duchess of; Viola Maud Grosvenor; Lord Lieutenant of Co. Fermanagh, Northern Ireland, since 1979; *b* 10 June 1912;

d of 9th Viscount Cobham, KCB, TD, and Violet Yolande (*d* 1966), *y d* of Charles Leonard; *m* 1946, Lt-Col Robert George Grosvenor, later 5th Duke of Westminster (*d* 1979); one *s* (*see* Duke of Westminster) two *d. Educ:* privately. Served War in WAAF, 1939-46 (despatches). President for Co. Fermanagh: Girl Guides Assoc., Farming Soc., NSPCC, Salvation Army, British Legion (Women's Sect.), SJAB. Member Governing Body, Royal Acad. of Music. Nat. Vice-Pres., Women's Section, British Legion, Ulster, 1954-68. Former President of societies in Chester: Music Soc., Male Voice Choir, Operatic Soc., Ladies' Choir, BRCS, CPRE, Marriage Guidance Council, LEPRA. DStJ 1980. *Recreations:* music, trees, books, scrabble. *Address:* Ely Island, Enniskillen, Co. Fermanagh, N Ireland. *T:* Springfield 224.

WESTMINSTER, Archbishop of, (RC), since 1976; **His Eminence Cardinal (George) Basil Hume;** *b* 2 March 1923; *s* of Sir William Hume, CMG, FRCP. *Educ:* Ampleforth Coll.; St Benet's Hall, Oxford; Fribourg Univ., Switzerland. Ordained priest 1950. Ampleforth College: Senior Modern Language Master, 1952-63; Housemaster, 1955-63; Prof. of Dogmatic Theology, 1955-63; Magister Scholarum of the English Benedictine Congregation, 1957-63; Abbot of Ampleforth, 1963-76. Cardinal, 1976. President: RC Bishops' Conf. of England and Wales, 1979-; Council of European Bishops' Confs, 1979-; Mem. Council for Secretariat of Internat. Synod of Bishops, 1978-. Hon. Bencher, Inner Temple, 1976. Hon. DD: Cantab, 1979; Newcastle upon Tyne, 1979; London, 1980; Oxon, 1981; York, 1982; Hon. DHL: Manhattan Coll., NY, 1980; Catholic Univ. of America, 1980. *Publications:* Searching for God, 1977; In Praise of Benedict, 1981. *Address:* Archbishop's House, Westminster, SW1P 1QJ.

WESTMINSTER, Auxiliary Bishops of, (RC); *see* Butler, Rt Rev. B. C.; Guazzelli, Rt Rev. V.; Harvey, Rt Rev. P. J. B.; Konstant, Rt Rev. D. E.; Mahon, Rt Rev. G. T.; and O'Brien, Rt Rev. J. J.

WESTMINSTER, Dean of; *see* Carpenter, Very Rev. E. F.

WESTMINSTER, Archdeacon of; *see* Knapp-Fisher, Rt. Rev. and Ven. E. G.

WESTMORLAND, 15th Earl of *cr* 1624, **David Anthony Thomas Fane,** KCVO 1970; Baron Burghersh, 1624; late RHG; Master of the Horse, since 1978; Director, Sotheby Parke Bernet Group (Deputy Chairman, 1979, Chairman, 1980-82); *b* 31 March 1924; *e s* of 14th Earl of Westmorland and Hon. Diana Lister, *widow* of Capt. Arthur Edward Capel, CBE, and *y d* of 4th Baron Ribblesdale; *S* father 1948; *m* 1950, Jane, *d* of Lt-Col Sir Roland Lewis Findlay, 3rd Bt, and Barbara Joan, *d* of late Maj. H. S. Garrard; two *s* one *d.* Served War in 1939-45 (wounded); resigned from RHG with hon. rank of Captain, 1950. A Lord in Waiting to the Queen, 1955-78. *Heir: s* Lord Burghersh, *qv. Address:* Kingsmead, Didmarton, Glos; 23 Chester Row, SW1. *Clubs:* Buck's, White's.

WESTMORLAND AND FURNESS, Archdeacon of; *see* Attwell, Ven. A. H.

WESTOBY, Jack Cecil, CMG 1975; retired, 1974; *b* 10 Dec. 1912; *s* of John William Westoby and Rose Ellen Miles; *m* 1941, Florence May Jackson; two *s. Educ:* Wheeler Street Council Sch., Hull; Hymers Coll., Hull; University Coll., Hull, BScEcon (London); FSS; FIS. Railway clerk, LNER, 1936-45; Statistician, BoT, 1945-52. Food and Agriculture Organisation of United Nations: Economist/Statistician, 1952-58; Chief Forest Economics Br., 1958-62; Dep. Dir, Forestry Div., 1962-69; Dir of Program Co-ordination and Ops, Forestry Dept, 1970-74. Regents' Prof., Univ. of California, 1972. Foreign Member: Royal Agriculture and Forestry Acad. of Sweden, 1968; Italian Acad. of Forest Science, 1971; Finnish Forestry Soc., 1964; Soc. of Amer. Foresters, 1971; Hon. Life Mem., Commonwealth Forestry Soc. *Publications:* many studies and articles in official publications of FAO and in a wide variety of professional forestry jls. *Recreations:* music, theatre. *Address:* Calcioli, Via Collegalle 12, 50022 Greve-in-Chianti (FI), Italy. *T:* (055) 853.283.

WESTOLL, James, DL; *b* 26 July 1918; *s* of late James Westoll, Glingerbank, Longtown; *m* 1946, Sylvia Jane Luxmoore, MBE, *d* of late Lord Justice Luxmoore, Bilsington, Kent; two *s* two *d. Educ:* Eton; Trinity College, Cambridge (MA). Served War of 1939-45: Major, The Border Regiment (despatches). Called to Bar, Lincoln's Inn, 1952. Member, NW Electricity Board, 1959-66; a Deputy Chm., Cumberland Quarter Sessions, 1960-71; Cumberland County Council: CC 1947; CA 1959-74; Chm., 1958-74; Chm., Cumbria Local Govt Reorganisation Jt Cttee, 1973; Chm., Cumbria CC, 1973-76. DL 1963, High Sheriff 1964, Cumberland. Warden, Clothworkers' Company, 1973-75. CStJ 1977. *Recreations:* gardening, shooting. *Address:* Dykeside, Longtown, Carlisle, Cumbria CA6 5ND. *T:* Longtown 791235. *Clubs:* Boodle's, Farmers'; County and Border (Carlisle).

WESTOLL, Prof. Thomas Stanley, BSc, PhD Dunelm; DSc Aberdeen; FRS 1952; FRSE, FGS, FLS; J. B. Simpson Professor of Geology, University of Newcastle upon Tyne (formerly King's College, Newcastle upon Tyne, University of Durham), 1948-77, now Emeritus; Dean of Convocation, Newcastle upon Tyne University, since 1979; *b* W Hartlepool, Durham, 3 July 1912; *e s* of Horace Stanley Raine Westoll; *m* 1st, 1939, Dorothy Cecil Isobel Wood (marr. diss. 1951); one *s*; 2nd, 1952, Barbara Swanson McAdie. *Educ:* West Hartlepool Grammar School; Armstrong (later King's) Coll.,

Univ. of Durham; University College, London. Senior Research Award, DSIR, 1934-37; Lecturer in Geology, Univ. of Aberdeen, 1937-48. Leverhulme Emeritus Res. Fellow, 1977-79. Alexander Agassiz Visiting Professor of Vertebrate Paleontology, Harvard University, 1952; Huxley Lectr, Univ. of Birmingham, 1967. J. B. Tyrell Fund, 1937, and Daniel Pidgeon Fund, 1939, Geological Soc. of London. President: Palæontological Assoc., 1966-68; Section C, British Assoc. for Advancement of Science, Durham, 1970; Geological Soc., 1972-74; Mem. Council, Royal Soc., 1966-68. Corr. Mem., Amer. Museum of Natural History; Hon. Life Mem., Soc. of Vertebrate Paleontology, USA, 1976. Hon. LLD Aberdeen, 1979. Murchison Medal, Geol. Soc. London, 1967; Clough Medal, Geol Soc. of Edinburgh, 1977; Linnean Gold Medal (Zool.), 1978. *Publications:* (ed) Studies on Fossil Vertebrates, 1958; (ed, with D. G. Murchison) Coal and Coal-bearing Strata, 1968; (ed, with N. Rast) Geology of the USSR, by D. V. Nalivkin, 1973; numerous papers and monographs on vertebrate anatomy and palæontology and geological topics, in several journals. *Recreations:* photography and numismatics. *Address:* Department of Geology, The University, Newcastle upon Tyne NE1 7RU; 21 Osborne Avenue, Newcastle upon Tyne NE2 1JQ. *T:* 81-1622.

WESTON, Bertram John, CMG 1960; OBE 1957; retired from the public service; Estate Factor to British Union Trust Ltd, 1964-81; *b* 30 March 1907; *o s* of late J. G. Weston, Kennington, Kent; *m* 1932, Irene Carey; two *d. Educ:* Ashford Grammar School; Sidney Sussex College, Cambridge (MA); Pretoria University, SA (MSc, Agric); Cornell University, USA (Post Grad.). Horticulturist, Cyprus, 1931; Asst Comr, Nicosia (on secondment), 1937; Administrative Officer, 1939. War Service, 1940-43 (Major). Commissioner for development and post-war construction, Cyprus, 1943; Commissioner, 1946; Administrative Officer Class I, 1951; Senior Administrative Officer, 1954; Senior Commissioner, 1958; Government Sec., St Helena, 1960-63; acted as Governor and C-in-C, St Helena, at various times during this period. *Recreations:* lawn tennis, gardening, watching cricket and other sports. *Address:* 10 Westfield Close, Uphill, Weston-super-Mare BS23 4XQ. *Club:* Royal Commonwealth Society.

WESTON, Rear-Adm. Charles Arthur Winfield, CB 1978; Admiral President, RN College, Greenwich, 1976-78; Appeals Secretary, King Edward VII's Hospital for Officers, since 1979; *b* 12 July 1922; *s* of late Charles Winfield Weston and of Edith Alice Weston; *m* 1946, Jeanie Findlay Miller; one *s* one *d. Educ:* Merchant Taylors' Sch. Entered RN as Special Entry Cadet, 1940; HM Ships: Glasgow, 1940; Durban, 1942; Staff of C-in-C Mediterranean, as Sec. to Captain of the Fleet, 1944-45 (despatches 1945); Sec. to Cdre in Charge Sheerness, 1946-47, to Flag Captain Home Fleet, HMS Duke of York, 1947-48; Loan Service, RAN, 1948-50; HM Ships: St Vincent, 1952-53; Ceres, 1954-55; Decoy, 1956; Sec. to DCNP (Trng and Manning), 1957-58, to DG Trng, 1959; CO HMS Jufair, 1960; Supply Officer, St Vincent, 1961-62; Sec. to Fleet Comdr Far East Fleet, 1963-64, to Second Sea Lord, 1965-67; sowc 1968; Chief Staff Officer (Q) to C-in-C Naval Home Comd, 1969-70; DNPTS, 1971; Director Defence Admin Planning Staff, 1972-74; Dir of Quartering (Navy), 1975. ADC to the Queen, 1976. Rear-Adm. 1976. Liveryman, Shipwrights' Co., 1979-. FBIM. *Recreations:* cricket, golf, gardening, music. *Address:* Westacre, Liphook, Hants GU30 7NY. *T:* Liphook 723337. *Clubs:* MCC, Army and Navy.

WESTON, Christopher John; Chairman: Phillips Son & Neale, since 1972; Glendining & Co., and subsidiaries, since 1972; *b* 3 March 1937; *s* of Eric Tudor Weston and Evelyn Nellie Weston; *m* 1969, Josephine Annabel Moir; one *d. Educ:* Lancing Coll. FIA (Scot.). Director: Phillips, 1964-; Mornington Building Soc., 1973-. Chairman: Dowells, 1970-; Phillips Gp, 1972-; Soc. of Fine Art Auctioneers, 1973-; Bradford Peters & Co., 1978-; Cardinal Investment Trust plc, 1982-; General Investors and Trustees plc, 1982-. Liveryman, Painters-Stainers' Co. FRSA. *Recreations:* theatre, music. *Address:* 7 Blenheim Street, W1Y 0AS. *T:* 01-629 6602. *Club:* Oriental.

WESTON, Rt. Rev. Dom (David) Wilfrid (Valentine), OSB; Abbot of Nashdom, since 1974; *b* 8 Dec. 1937; *s* of late Rev. William Valentine Weston and late Mrs Gertrude Hamilton Weston. *Educ:* St Edmund's Sch., Canterbury. Entered Nashdom Abbey, 1960; deacon, 1967, priest, 1968; Novice Master, 1969-74; Prior, 1971-74. Chm., Communities Consultative Council, 1975-78; Vice-Pres., Church Union; Mem., Adv. Council for Religious Communities; Guardian, Shrine of Our Lady of Walsingham, 1980-. Freeman, City of London; Liveryman of Salters' Co. *Address:* Nashdom Abbey, Burnham, Slough SL1 8NL. *T:* Burnham 3176.
See also Ven. F. V. Weston.

WESTON, Ven. Frank Valentine; Archdeacon of Oxford and a Canon of Christ Church, Oxford, since 1982; *b* 16 Sept. 1935; *s* of William Valentine Weston and Gertrude Hamilton Weston; *m* 1963, Penelope Brighid, *d* of Marmaduke Carver Middleton Athorpe, formerly of Dinnington, Yorks; one *s* two *d. Educ:* Christ's Hospital; Queen's Coll., Oxford; Lichfield Theological Coll. BA 1960, MA 1964. Curate, St John the Baptist, Atherton, Lancs, 1961-65; Chaplain, 1965-69, Principal, 1968-76, College of the Ascension, Selly Oak, Birmingham; Vice-Pres., Selly Oak Colls, 1973-76; Principal and Pantonian Prof., Edinburgh Theological Coll., 1976-82. Liveryman, Salters' Co. *Publications:* (contrib.) Quel Missionnaire, 1971; contribs to Faith and Unity, Sobornost, Eglise Vivante. *Recreations:* wine, persons and song;

exploring the countryside. *Address:* Archdeacon's Lodging, Christ Church, Oxford OX1 1DP. *T:* Oxford 43847.
See also *Rt Rev. Dom D. W. V. Weston.*

WESTON, Galen; see Weston, W. G.

WESTON, Garfield Howard; Chairman: Associated British Foods, since 1967; Fortnum and Mason, since 1978; *b* 28 April 1927; *s* of late Willard Garfield Weston and Reta Lila Howard; *m* 1959, Mary Ruth, *d* of late Major-Gen. Sir Howard Kippenberger; three *s* three *d. Educ:* Sir William Borlase School, Marlow; New College, Oxford; Harvard University (Economics). Man. Director: Ryvita Co. Ltd, 1951; Weston Biscuit Co., Aust., 1954; Vice-Chairman, Associated British Foods Ltd, 1960; Chm., George Weston Holdings Ltd, 1978; Dir, Premier Milling Gp, S Africa, 1963. *Recreation:* gardening. *Address:* Weston Centre, Bowater House, 68 Knightsbridge, SW1X 7LR. *T:* 01-589 6363. *Club:* Lansdowne.

WESTON, Garry; see Weston, G. H.

WESTON, Geoffrey Harold, CBE 1975; FHA; retired; Deputy Health Service Commissioner for England, Scotland and Wales, 1977-82; *b* 11 Sept. 1920; *s* of George and Florence Mary Weston; *m* 1953, Monica Mary Grace Comyns; three *d. Educ:* Wolverhampton Sch. War Service, 1940-46. Gp Sec., Reading and Dist Hosp. Management Cttee, 1955-65; Board Sec., NW Metropolitan Regional Hosp. Bd, 1965-73; Regional Administrator, NW Thames RHA, 1973-76. Member: Salmon Cttee, 1965; Whitley Councils: Mem. Management side of Optical Council, 1955-65, and of Nurses and Midwives Council, 1966-76; Mem., Working Party on Collab. between Local Govt and Nat. Health Service, 1973-74. Inst. of Health Service Administrators: Mem., Nat. and Reg. Councils, 1959-78 (Vice-Chm. of Council, 1968; Chm. 1969, Pres. of Inst., 1970). Bd Mem., London and Provincial Nursing Services Ltd, 1973-; Trustee, 1978-; Chm., 1980-, Goring Day Centre. Parish Councillor, 1979-. *Recreations:* lawn tennis, gardening, travel, dining with friends. *Address:* Little Mead, Goring on Thames, near Reading, Berks. *T:* Goring on Thames 872881. *Club:* Royal Air Force.

WESTON, John; see Weston, P. J.

WESTON, Dr John Carruthers; General Manager, Northampton Development Corporation, 1969-77. *Educ:* Univ. of Nottingham. Admiralty Research, 1940-46; Plessey Co., 1946-47; Building Research Station, 1947-64; Chief Exec. Operational Div., Nat. Building Agency, 1964-65; Dir, Building Research Station, MPBW, 1966-69. *Recreations:* gardening, music, walking, reading and living.

WESTON, John Pix, BSc(Eng), BSc(Econ); CEng, FIEE, FBIM; Chief Administrative Officer and Clerk to the Governors, West Bromwich College of Higher Education, since 1979; *b* 3 Jan. 1920; *s* of John Pix Weston and Margaret Elizabeth (*née* Cox); *m* 1948, Ivy (*née* Glover); three *s. Educ:* King Edward's Sch., Birmingham; Univ. of Aston, 1946-50 (BSc(Eng), Hons); Univ. of London (LSE), 1954-57 (BSc(Econ), Hons). CEng 1953, FIEE 1966; FSS 1958; FREconS 1958; FBIM 1977. City of Birmingham: Police Dept, 1936-39; Electricity Supply Dept, 1939-48; Midlands Electricity Bd, 1948-50; English Electricity Co., 1950-51; NW Elec. Bd, 1951-58; Eastern Elec. Bd, 1958-60; Dep. Operating Man., Jamaica Public Services Co., 1960-61; Principal Asst Engr, Midlands Elec. Bd, 1961-64; Asst Ch. Commercial Officer, S of Scotland Elec. Bd, 1964-66; Sen. Econ. Adviser to Mrs Barbara Castle, MoT, 1966-69; Sen. Econ. and Chartered Engr, IBRD, 1968-70; Michelin Tyre Co., France, 1970-72; Dir of Post Experience Courses, Open Univ., 1972-75; Dir Gen., RoSPA, 1975-77; Gen. Sec., Birmingham Anglers' Assoc., 1977; Industrial Develt Officer, Argyll and Bute, 1977-79; Health, Safety and Welfare Officer, Newcastle Polytechnic, and Central Safety Advr, Northants CC, 1979. MIES 1963; Mem., Assoc. of Public Lighting Engrs, 1962. Page Prize, IEE, 1950; Rosebery Prize, Univ. of London, 1957. SBStJ 1962. *Publications:* papers, reports and other contribs on electricity, highways, educn (espec. function and progress of the Open University), safety, etc, to public bodies, congresses and conferences, UK and abroad. *Recreations:* cine photography, gardening, swimming, fell walking. *Address:* The Bungalow, Marlbrook Lane, Upper Marlbrook, Bromsgrove, Worcs. *T:* 021-445 2393. *Clubs:* Farmers', St John House; Birmingham Press.

WESTON, John William, CB 1979; Principal Assistant Solicitor, Board of Inland Revenue, 1967-80; *b* 3 Feb. 1915; *s* of Herbert Edward Weston, MA, and Emma Gertrude Weston; *m* 1943, Frances Winifred (*née* Johnson); two *s* one *d. Educ:* Berkhamsted Sch., Herts. Solicitor, 1937. Joined Inland Revenue, 1940; Sen. Legal Asst, 1948; Asst Solicitor, 1954. *Recreations:* tennis, golf. *Address:* 5 Dickerage Road, Kingston Hill, Surrey. *T:* 01-942 8130.

WESTON, Dame Margaret (Kate), DBE 1979; BScEng (London); MIEE; FMA; Director of the Science Museum, since 1973; *b* 7 March 1926; *o c* of late Charles Edward and Margaret Weston. *Educ:* Stroud High School; College of Technology, Birmingham (now Univ. of Aston). Engineering apprenticeship with General Electric Co. Ltd, followed in 1949 by development work, very largely on high voltage insulation problems. Joined Science Museum as an Assistant Keeper, Dept of Electrical Engineering and Communications, 1955; Deputy Keeper, 1962; Keeper, Dept of Museum Services, 1967-72. Mem., Ancient Monuments Bd for England, 1977-. Mem., SE Elec. Bd, 1981-. Trustee, Hunterian Collection, 1981-. Fellow, 1975, and

Mem. Governing Body, Imperial Coll. London. FMA 1976. Hon. DSc Aston, 1974. *Address:* 7 Shawley Way, Epsom, Surrey. *T:* Burgh Heath 55885.

WESTON, Michael Charles Swift, CVO 1979; HM Diplomatic Service; Counsellor (Information), Paris, since 1981; *b* 4 Aug. 1937; *s* of Edward Charles Swift Weston and Kathleen Mary Weston (*née* Mockett); *m* 1959, Veronica Anne Tickner; two *s* one *d. Educ:* Dover Coll.; St Catharine's Coll., Cambridge (Exhibitioner). BA, MA. Joined HM Diplomatic Service, 1961; 3rd Sec., Kuwait, 1962; 2nd Sec., FCO, 1965; 1st Secretary: Tehran, 1968; UK Mission, New York, 1970; FCO, 1974; Counsellor, Jedda, 1977; RCDS, 1980. *Recreations:* tennis, squash. *Address:* French Court, Pett, East Sussex TN35 4JA. *T:* Pett 2306.

WESTON, (Philip) John; HM Diplomatic Service; Head of Defence Department, Foreign and Commonwealth Office, since 1981; *b* 13 April 1938; *s* of late Philip George Weston and Edith Alice Bray (*née* Ansell); *m* 1967, Margaret Sally Ehlers; two *s* one *d. Educ:* Sherborne; Worcester Coll., Oxford. 1st Cl. Hons, Honour Mods Classics and Lit. Hum. Served with Royal Marines, 1956-58. Entered Diplomatic Service, 1962; FO, 1962-63; Treasury Centre for Admin. Studies, 1964; Chinese Language student, Hong Kong, 1964-66; Peking, 1967-68; FO, 1969-71; Office of UK Permanent Representative to EEC, 1972-74; Asst Private Sec. to Sec. of State for Foreign and Commonwealth Affairs (Rt Hon. James Callaghan, Rt Hon. Anthony Crosland), 1974-76; Counsellor, Head of EEC Presidency Secretariat, FCO, 1976-77; Vis. Fellow, All Souls Coll., Oxford, 1977-78; Counsellor, Washington, 1978-81. *Recreations:* running, chess, poetry. *Address:* c/o Foreign and Commonwealth Office, SW1.

WESTON, Rt. Rev. Dom Wilfrid; see Weston, Rt Rev. Dom D. W. V.

WESTON, W(illard) Galen; Chairman, since 1974, and President, since 1978, George Weston Ltd, Toronto; *b* England, 29 Oct. 1940; *s* of W. Garfield Weston and Reta Lila (*née* Howard). Chairman: Loblaw Companies Ltd; Loblaws Ltd; President: Wittington Investments Ltd; Wittington Leased Properties Ltd; Wittington Properties Ltd; Director: British Columbia Packers Ltd; GWH Developments Ltd; National Tea Co. (US); Peter J. Schmidt Inc. (US). Pres. and Governor, Garfield Weston Foundation. *Address:* Suite 2001, George Weston Ltd, 22 St Clair Avenue East, Toronto, Ont. M4T 2S3, Canada.

WESTON, Rear-Adm. William Kenneth, CB 1956; OBE 1945; RN retired; *b* 8 November 1904; *s* of late William Weston; *m* 1934, Mary Ursula Shine; one *s* two *d. Educ:* RNC Osborne and Dartmouth. RNEC Keyham; RNC Greenwich. Served on staff of Flag Officer Destroyers, Pacific, 1945-46; Admiralty District Engineer Overseer, NW District, 1951-54; Staff of C-in-C Plymouth, 1954-58; retired, 1958. Court of Assistants of the Worshipful Company of Salters, 1959, Master, 1963. *Address:* Brackleyways, Hartley Wintney, Hants. *T:* Hartley Wintney 2546. *Club:* Naval and Military.

WESTWELL, Alan Reynolds, CEng, MIMechE, MIProdE; FCIT; Director General, Strathclyde Passenger Transport Executive, since 1979; *b* 11 April 1940; *s* of Stanley Westwell and Margaret (*née* Reynolds); *m* 1967, Elizabeth Aileen Birrell; two *s* one *d. Educ:* Old Swan Coll.; Liverpool Polytechnic (ACT Hons). Liverpool City Transport Dept: progressively, student apprentice, Technical Asst, Asst Works Manager, 1956-67; Chief Engineer: Southport Corporation Transport Dept, 1967-69; Coventry Corp. Transport Dept, 1969-72; Glasgow Corp. Transport Dept, 1972-74; Director of Public Transport (responsible for bus/rail, airport, harbours), Tayside Regional Council, 1974-79. Vice-Pres., Scottish Council of Confedn of British Road Passenger Transport, 1981-82, Pres., 1982-83. *Publications:* various papers. *Recreations:* golf, swimming, tennis, music, modelling, reading. *Address:* 12 Glen Drive, Helensburgh, Dunbartonshire G84 9BJ. *T:* Helensburgh 71709. *Club:* Helensburgh Golf.

WESTWOOD, family name of **Baron Westwood.**

WESTWOOD, 2nd Baron, *cr* 1944, of Gosforth; **William Westwood;** Company Director; *b* 25 Dec. 1907; *s* of 1st Baron and Margaret Taylor Young (*d* 1916); *S* father 1953; *m* 1937, Marjorie, *o c* of Arthur Bonwick, Newcastle upon Tyne; two *s. Educ:* Glasgow; JP Newcastle upon Tyne, 1949. Dir of several private companies. Hon. Vice-Pres., Football Association, 1981 (Vice-Pres., 1974-81); Life Mem., Football League, 1981. FRSA; FCIS. *Recreations:* golf, football. *Heir: s* Hon. William Gavin Westwood [*b* 30 Jan. 1944; *m* 1969, Penelope, *er d* of Dr C. E. Shafto, Newcastle upon Tyne; two *s*]. *Address:* 12 Westfield Drive, Newcastle upon Tyne NE3 4XU.

WESTWOOD, Rt. Rev. William John; see Edmonton, Area Bishop of.

WETHERALL, Rev. Canon Theodore Sumner; *b* 31 May 1910; *s* of late Rev. A. S. Wetherall and Mrs G. V. M. Wetherall (*née* Bennett-Powell); *m* 1939, Caroline, 4th *d* of Dr Charles Milne; one *s* three *d. Educ:* St Edward's School, Oxford; Oriel College, Oxford. Exhibitioner at Oriel College, 1929; 1st Class Classical Mods, 1931; BA (2nd Class Lit. Hum.), 1933. Preparatory Schoolmaster, Wellesley House, Broadstairs, 1933-35; MA 1936; Liddon Student, 1936; Cuddesdon College, 1936-37; Asst Curate, St John's, Greengates, Bradford, 1937-39; Fellow and Chaplain, Corpus Christi College, Oxford, 1939-47, Dean, 1940-45, Vice-Pres., 1947; Principal of St Chad's

College, Durham, 1948–65. Vicar of St Edward the Confessor, Barnsley, 1965–69; Vicar of Huddersfield, 1969–76. Select Preacher to the Univ. of Oxford, 1945–47; Chaplain in the Univ. of Oxford to Bishop of Derby, 1940–47, Examining Chaplain to Bishop of Oxford, 1946–47, to Bishop of Durham, 1948–65, to Bishop of Bradford, 1949–55; to Bishop of Wakefield, 1969–76; Surrogate for Marriages, 1969–76; Rural Dean of Huddersfield, 1969–76. Hon. Canon: Durham, 1958–65, Wakefield, 1970–76; Hon. Canon Emeritus, Wakefield, 1976–. *Address:* 2 Lomas Cottages, Litton, Buxton, Derbyshire SK17 8QR. *T:* Tideswell 871042.

WETHERELL, Alan Marmaduke, PhD; FRS 1971; Division Leader, Experimental Physics Division, CERN (European Organisation for Nuclear Research), Geneva; *b* 31 Dec. 1932; *s* of Marmaduke and Margaret Edna Wetherell; *m* 1957, Alison Morag Dunn (*d* 1974); one *s. Educ:* Univ. of Liverpool (BSc, PhD). Demonstrator in Physics, Univ. of Liverpool, 1956–57; Commonwealth Fund Fellow, California Inst. of Technology, Pasadena, Calif., 1957–59; Physicist, CERN, 1959–63; Senior Physicist, 1963. Vis. Prof., Dept of Physics, Univ. of Liverpool, 1981–. *Publications:* scientific papers in: Proc. Phys. Soc. (London), Proc. Roy. Soc. (London), Physical Review, Physical Review Letters, Physics Letters, Nuovo Cimento, Nuclear Physics, Yadernaya Fizika, Uspekhi Fizicheski Nauk. *Recreations:* skiing, water skiing. *Address:* 27 Chemin de la Vendee, 1213 Petit Lancy, Geneva, Switzerland. *T:* 022 928742.

WETZEL, Dave; Member for Hammersmith North, Greater London Council, since 1981; Chairman of the Transport Committee, since 1981; *b* 9 Oct. 1942; *s* of Fred Wetzel and Ivy Donaldson; *m* 1973, Heather Allman; two *d. Educ:* Spring Grove Grammar Sch.; Southall Technical Coll., Ealing Coll., and the Henry George Sch. of Social Sciences (part-time courses). Student apprentice, 1959–62; Bus Conductor/Driver, 1962–65, Bus Official, 1965–69, London Transport; Br. Manager, Initial Services, 1969–70; Pilot Roster Officer, British Airways, 1970–74 (ASTMS Shop Steward); Political Organiser, Co-operative Soc., 1974–81. Hounslow Councillor, 1964–68. Editor, Civil Aviation News, 1978–81. *Recreations:* politics, Esperanto, camping. *Address:* County Hall, SE1 7PB. *T:* 01-633 7800. *Club:* Feltham Labour.

WEYER, Deryk Vander, FIB, CBIM; Group Deputy Chairman, Barclays Bank Ltd, since 1980; Chairman, Barclays Bank UK, since 1980; Director, Barclays Bank International Ltd, since 1977; *b* 21 Jan. 1925; *s* of Clement Vander Weyer and Harriet Weyer; *m* 1950, Marguerite (*née* Warden); one *s* one *d. Educ:* Bridlington Sch. FIB 1972; CBIM (FBIM 1976). Joined Barclays Bank Ltd, 1941: Asst Manager, Liverpool, 1956; Man., Chester Br., 1961; Local Dir, Liverpool, 1965; Asst Gen. Man., 1968; Gen. Man., 1969; Sen. Gen. Man., 1973; Vice-Chm., 1977–80; Chm., Barclays Merchant Bank Ltd, 1977–80. Pres., Institute of Bankers, 1979–81. Mem., Royal Commn on Distribn of Income and Wealth, 1977–79; part-time Mem., British Telecom. Corp., 1981–; Governor, Museum of London, 1978–. *Recreations:* painting, music. *Address:* 96 Old Church Street, Chelsea, SW3 6EP. *T:* 01-352 0312.

WEYMES, John Barnard, OBE 1975; HM Diplomatic Service, retired; Managing Director, Cayman Islands News Bureau, Grand Cayman, since 1981; *b* 18 Oct. 1927; *s* of William Stanley Weymes and Irene Innes Weymes; *m* 1978, Beverley Pauline Gliddon; three *c* (by a previous marr.). *Educ:* Dame Allan's Sch., Newcastle upon Tyne; King's Coll., Durham Univ., Newcastle upon Tyne. Served HM Forces, 1945–48. Foreign Office, 1949–52; 3rd Sec., Panama City, 1952–56; 2nd Sec., Bogotá, 1957–60; Vice-Consul, Berlin, 1960–63; Dep-Consul, Tamsui, Taiwan, 1963–65; 1st Sec., FCO, 1965–68; Prime Minister's Office, 1968–70; Consul, Guatemala City, 1970–74; 1st Sec., FCO, 1974–77; Consul-Gen., Vancouver, 1977–78; Ambassador to Honduras, 1978–81. *Recreations:* outdoor sport, partic. cricket; chess, reading. *Address:* Cayman Islands News Bureau, PO Box 1111, Grand Cayman, British West Indies. *T:* Cayman Islands 9-2742. *Clubs:* MCC, MCCC; Rodmell Cricket.

WEYMOUTH, Viscount; Alexander George Thynn; *b* 6 May 1932; *s* of Marquess of Bath, *qv* ; *m* 1969, Anna Gyarmathy; one *s* one *d. Educ:* Eton College; Christ Church, Oxford (BA, MA). Lieutenant in the Life Guards, 1951–52, and in Royal Wilts Yeomanry, 1953–57. Contested (Wessex Regionalist): Westbury, Feb. 1974; Wells, 1979; contested (Wessex Regionalist and European Federal Party) Wessex, European Election 1979. Pres., Verulam Inst., 1976–. Permanent exhibn of murals (painted 1964–69, opened to public 1973), in private apartments at Longleat House. Record, I Play the Host, singing own compositions, 1974. *Publications:* (as Alexander Thynn) (before 1976 Alexander Thynne) The Carry-cot, 1972; Lord Weymouth's Murals, 1974; A Regionalist Manifesto, 1975; The King is Dead, 1976; Pillars of the Establishment, 1980. *Heir:* *s* Hon. Ceawlin Henry Laszlo Thynn, *b* 6 June 1974. *Address:* Longleat, Warminster, Wilts. *T:* Maiden Bradley 300.

WHADDON, Baron *cr* 1978 (Life Peer), of Whaddon in the County of Cambridgeshire; **(John) Derek Page;** Director: Cambridge Chemical Co. Ltd, since 1962; Microautomatics Ltd; *b* 14 Aug. 1927; *s* of John Page and Clare Page (*née* Maher); *m* 1st, 1948, Catherine Audrey Halls (*d* 1979); one *s* one *d* ; 2nd, 1981, Angela Rixson. *Educ:* St Bede's College, Manchester; London University. External BSc (Soc.). MP (Lab) King's Lynn, 1964–70; contested (Lab) Norfolk NW, Feb. 1974. Mem., Council of Management, CoSIRA, 1975–; Mem., E Anglia Economic Planning Council, 1975–80.

Recreation: private pilot. *Address:* The Old Vicarage, Whaddon, Royston, Herts. *T:* Cambridge 207209. *Club:* Reform.

WHALE, Rev. John Seldon, MA (Oxon); DD (Glasgow); *b* 19 Dec. 1896; *s* of Rev. John Whale and Alice Emily Seldon; *m* Mary, *d* of Rev. H. C. Carter, MA; two *s* two *d* (and one *s* decd). *Educ:* Caterham School, Surrey; St Catherine's Society and Mansfield College, Oxford; 1st Class Hons Sch. of Mod. Hist. 1922; Magdalene College, Cambridge, 1933. Minister of Bowdon Downs Congregational Church, Manchester, 1925–29; Mackennal Professor of Ecclesiastical History, Mansfield College, Oxford, and Tutor in Modern History, St Catherine's, 1929–33; President of Cheshunt College, Cambridge, 1933–44; Headmaster of Mill Hill School, 1944–51; Visiting Professor of Christian Theology, Drew Univ., Madison, NJ, USA, 1951–53. Moderator of Free Church Federal Council, 1942–43; Select Preacher, Univ. of Cambridge, 1943, 1957; Warrack Lecturer, 1944; Russell Lecturer (Auburn and New York), 1936 and 1948; Alden Tuthill Lecturer, Chicago, 1952; Greene Lecturer, Andover, 1952; Currie Lecturer, Austin, Texas, 1953; Hill Lectr, St Olaf Coll., Minnesota, 1954; Visiting Lecturer, Univ. of Toronto, 1957; Danforth Scholar, USA, 1958; Sir D. Owen Evans Lectures, Aberystwyth, 1958. Visiting Professor, Univ. of Chicago, 1959; Senior Fellow of Council of Humanities, Princeton Univ., 1960. *Publications:* The Christian Answer to the Problem of Evil, 1936; What is a Living Church?, 1937; This Christian Faith, 1938; Facing the Facts, 1940; Christian Doctrine, 1941; The Protestant Tradition, 1955; Victor and Victim: the Christian doctrine of Redemption, 1960; Christian Reunion: historic divisions reconsidered, 1971; The Coming Dark Age, 1973 (Eng. trans. of Roberto Vacca's Il Medioevo Prossimo Venturo, 1972). *Address:* Wild Goose, Widecombe-in-the-Moor, Newton Abbot, S Devon TQ13 7TY. *T:* Widecombe-in-the-Moor 260.

WHALLEY, Richard Carlton; Chairman: Ewden Associates Ltd; F. & M. Ducker Ltd; A. Spafford & Co. Ltd; Pennine Plastics Ltd; *b* Quetta, India, 4 July 1922; *s* of Frederick Seymour Whalley, MC, FCGI, MIMechE, and Gwendolen, *d* of Sir William Collingwood; *m* 1945, Mary Christian Bradley; two *s* twin *d. Educ:* Shrewsbury Sch.; 151 OCTU, Aldershot. Served War: Private, Royal Berkshire Regt, 1940; commissioned 2nd Lieut, Royal Corps of Signals, 1942; Captain and Adjt, 2nd Div. Signals, India, Assam, Burma, 1942–45. War Office, AG II (O), 1945–48; GHQ Singapore, 1948–51. Vulcan Foundry Ltd: Asst Sec., 1952–58; Commercial Manager, 1958–60; Dep. Gen. Manager, 1960–65; Manager, English Electric Diesel Engine Div., 1965–67; Dir and Gen. Manager, Glacier Metal Co., 1968–70. 1970–78: Dep. Chm. and Managing Dir, Millspaugh Ltd; Chm. and Managing Dir, C. A. Harnden Ltd, Westbury Engrg Ltd, Hargreaves & Jennings Ltd, and T. Rowbottom Ltd; Director: Bertram-Scott Ltd; Sulzer Bros (UK) Ltd; Estridge & Ropner Ltd; Mem., Bd of British Shipbuilders (with special responsibility for personnel, indust. relations, and trng), 1978–82. *Recreations:* rowing, walking. *Address:* Sunnybank Farm, Bolsterstone, Sheffield S30 5ZL. *T:* Sheffield 883116. *Clubs:* Reform, London Rowing.

WHALLEY, Prof. William Basil; Professor of Chemistry and Head of Department of Pharmaceutical Chemistry, School of Pharmacy, University of London, 1961–82; *b* 17 Dec. 1916; *s* of William and Catherine Lucy Whalley; *m* 1945, Marie Agnes Alston; four *s* one *d. Educ:* St Edward's College, Liverpool; Liverpool University. BSc Hons 1938; PhD 1940; DSc 1952; FRIC 1950. MOS and ICI 1940–45. Lecturer, 1946–55, Sen. Lectr, 1955–57, Reader, 1957–61, in Organic Chemistry, at Liverpool University. *Publications:* contrib. on organic chemistry to several books: *eg* Heterocyclic Compounds, Vol. 7, Edited R. C. Elderfield, Wiley (New York); many pubns in Jl of Chem. Soc., Jl Amer. Chem. Soc., etc. *Recreations:* music and mountaineering. *Address:* 9 Peaks Hill, Purley, Surrey. *T:* 01-668 2244.

WHALLEY-TOOKER, Hyde Charnock, MA, LLM (Cantab), MA (Oxon); Emeritus Fellow of Downing College, Cambridge (Fellow, 1927–67, and Senior Tutor, 1931–47); University Lecturer in Law, 1931–67; *b* 1 Sept. 1900; *o s* of Edward Whalley-Tooker; *m* 1935, Frances, *er d* of late Thomas Halsted; one *d. Educ:* Eton; Trinity Hall, Cambridge; Balliol College, Oxford; Law Tripos Part I, Class I, 1921; Part II, Class I, 1922. *Address:* 5 Wilberforce Road, Cambridge. *T:* Cambridge 350073.

WHARNCLIFFE, 4th Earl of, *cr* 1876; **Alan James Montagu-Stuart-Wortley-Mackenzie;** Viscount Carlton, 1876; Baron Wharncliffe, 1826; *b* 23 March 1935; *o s* of 3rd Earl and late Lady Elfrida Wentworth Fitzwilliam, *d* of 7th Earl Fitzwilliam; *S* father 1953; *m* 1957, Aline Margaret, *d* of late R. F. D. Bruce, Wharncliffe Side, near Sheffield; one *d* (and one *d* decd). *Educ:* Eton. Joined RNVR, 1952; National Service, RN, 1953–55; RNSR, 1955–59. *Recreation:* shooting. *Heir:* cousin Alan Ralph Montagu-Scott-Wortley [*b* 27 July 1927; *m* 1952, Virginia Anne, *d* of W. Martin Claybaugh; two *s* one *d*]. *Address:* Wharncliffe House, Wortley, Sheffield S30 4DG. *T:* Sheffield 882331.
See also D. C. Mansel Lewis, Duke of Newcastle.

WHARTON, Barony *cr* 1544–5; in abeyance. Co-heiresses: Hon. Myrtle Olive Felix Robertson [*b* 20 Feb. 1934; *m* 1958, Henry MacLeod Robertson; three *s* one *d*]; Hon. Caroline Elizabeth Appleyard-List [*b* 28 Aug. 1935; *m* 1970, Commander Jonathon Cecil Appleyard-List, RN; one *d*].

WHARTON, Michael Bernard; author and journalist; 'Peter Simple' Columnist, Daily Telegraph, since 1960; *b* 19 April 1913; *s* of Paul Nathan and Bertha Wharton; *m* 1st, 1936, Joan Atkey (marr. diss. 1947); one *s* ; 2nd

1952, Catherine Mary Derrington (marr. diss. 1972); one *d* ; 3rd, 1974, Susan Moller. *Educ:* Bradford Grammar Sch.; Lincoln Coll., Oxford. Army service, Royal Artillery and General Staff, 1940-46. Scriptwriter and Producer, BBC, 1946-56; writer on Peter Simple column, Daily Telegraph, 1957-60. *Publications: as Michael Wharton:* (ed) A Nation's Security, 1955; Sheldrake (novel), 1958; editor and mainly writer of nine anthologies of Peter Simple column, 1963-80; *under pseudonym Simon Crabtree:* Forgotten Memories, 1941; Hector Tumbler Investigates, 1943. *Recreations:* walking, gardening, Celtic studies. *Address:* Forge Cottage, Naphill Common, High Wycombe, Bucks. *T:* Naphill 3454.

WHATELEY, Dame Leslie Violet Lucy Evelyn Mary, DBE 1946 (CBE 1943); TD 1951; *b* 28 Jan. 1899; *d* of late Ada Lilian Hutton and late Col Evelyn F. M. Wood, CB, DSO, OBE; *m* 1st, 1922, W. J. Balfour; one *s* ; 2nd, 1939, H. Raymond Whateley, Squadron-Leader, RAFVR. *Educ:* Convents of Society of HCJ, St Leonards-on-Sea and Cavendish Square. Private Secretary up to marriage, and then Social Welfare Work, including District Nursing Associations and Village Institutes. Director of Auxiliary Territorial Service, 1943-46; Hon. Col 668 (bn) HAA Regt RA (TA), 1948-53. Director World Bureau of Girl Guides/Girl Scouts, 1951-64; Administrator of Voluntary Services, Queen Mary's Hosp., Roehampton, 1965-74. Chevalier Légion d'Honneur, 1945; Order of Merit (USA), 1946. *Publications:* As Thoughts Survive, 1949; Yesterday, Today and Tomorrow, 1974. *Recreations:* gardening, writing. *Address:* c/o Lloyds Bank, 6 Pall Mall, SW1.

WHATLEY, Prof. Frederick Robert, FRS 1975; Sherardian Professor of Botany, Oxford University, since 1971; Fellow of Magdalen College, Oxford, since 1971; *b* 26 Jan. 1924; *s* of Frederick Norman Whatley and Maud Louise (*née* Hare); *m* 1951, Jean Margaret Smith Bowie; two *d. Educ:* Bishop Wordsworth's Sch., Salisbury; (Scholar) Selwyn Coll., Cambridge University (BA, PhD). Benn W. Levy Student, Cambridge, 1947. Sen. Lectr. in Biochemistry, Univ. of Sydney, 1950-53; Asst Biochemist, Univ. of California at Berkeley, 1954-58; Associate Biochemist, 1959-64; Guggenheim Fellowship (Oxford and Stockholm), 1960; Prof. of Botany, King's Coll., London, 1964-71. Vis. Fellow, ANU, 1979. *Publications:* articles and reviews in scientific jls. *Address:* Botany School, South Parks Road, Oxford OX1 3RA. *T:* Oxford 53391.

WHATLEY, William Henry Potts; General Secretary, Union of Shop Distributive and Allied Workers, since 1979; *b* 16 Dec. 1922; *s* of Arthur John and Ethel Whatley; *m* 1946, Margaret Ann Harrison. *Educ:* Gosforth Secondary School. Clerk, CWS, Newcastle upon Tyne, 1938; War Service, RAF, War of 1939-45; Area Organiser, USDAW, Bristol, 1948; National Officer, 1966; Chief Organising Officer, 1976; Member: TUC General Council, 1979; TUC Economic Cttee, 1979. *Recreations:* garden and reading. *Address:* 72 St Martin's Road, Ashton-on-Mersey, Sale, Cheshire. *T:* 061-973 3772.

WHEADON, Richard Anthony; Principal, Elizabeth College, Guernsey, since 1972; *b* 31 Aug. 1933; *s* of Ivor Cecil Newman Wheadon and Margarita Augusta (*née* Cash); *m* 1961, Ann Mary (*née* Richardson); three *s. Educ:* Cranleigh Sch.; Balliol Coll., Oxford. MA (Physics). Commissioned RAF, 1955 (Sword of Honour); Air Radar Officer, 1955-57; Asst Master, Eton Coll., 1957-66; Dep. Head Master and Head of Science Dept, Dauntsey's Sch., 1966-71. Mem., Wilts Educn Cttee's Science Adv. Panel, 1967-71. Member: HMC; SHA; NAHT; ASE. Rowed bow for Oxford, 1954, for GB in European Championships and Olympic Games, 1956; Captain RAF VIII, 1956 and 1957; Olympic Selector and Nat. Coach, 1964-66. Contingent Comdr, Dauntsey's Sch. CCF, 1969-70. *Publication:* The Principles of Light and Optics, 1968. *Recreations:* French horn, photography, electronics, singing, sailing, words. *Address:* Elizabeth College, Guernsey, Channel Islands. *T:* Guernsey 26544. *Club:* East India, Devonshire, Sports and Public Schools.

WHEATCROFT, George Shorrock Ashcombe; Professor of English Law, University of London, 1959-68, now Professor Emeritus; First Editor, British Tax Review, 1956-71, now Consulting Editor; first Editor of British Tax Encyclopedia, 1962-71, now Consulting Editor; Consulting Editor, Encyclopedia of Value Added Tax; Vice-Chairman, Hambro Life Assurance Ltd, 1971-79; Chairman, G. S. A. & M. Wheatcroft (Advisory Services) Ltd; Adviser to HM Customs and Excise on Value Added Tax, 1971-72; *b* 29 Oct. 1905; *s* of Hubert Ashcombe Wheatcroft and Jane (*née* Eccles); *m* 1930, Mildred Susan (*d* 1978), *d* of late Canon Walter Lock, DD, formerly Warden of Keble College, Oxford; two *s* one *d. Educ:* Rugby; New College, Oxford (MA). Qualified as Solicitor, 1929; partner in Corbin Greener and Cook, Solicitors, of 52 Bedford Row, London, 1930-51; Master of the Supreme Court (Chancery Division), 1951-59. Served as an officer in RASC, 1940-45; released in 1945 with hon. rank of Lt-Col (despatches twice). Mem., Payne Cttee on enforcement of civil debts. Past President British Chess Federation. Consulting Editor, Hambro Tax Guide, 1972-. Hon. Fellow: LSE, 1976; UC Buckingham, 1978. *Publications:* The Taxation of Gifts and Settlements, 1953 (3rd edn 1958); The Law of Income Tax, Surtax and Profits Tax, 1962; Estate and Gift Taxation, 1965; Capital Gains Tax, 1965; Wheatcroft on Capital Gains Taxes (with A. E. W. Park), 1967; Corporation Tax (with J. E. Talbot), 1968; Sweet & Maxwell's Guide to the Estate Duty Statutes, 1969 (2nd edn 1972); Whiteman and Wheatcroft on Income Tax and Surtax, 1971; (with G. D. Hewson) Capital Transfer Tax, 1975; titles Discovery, Execution, Judgments and Orders and Practice and Procedure in Halsbury's Laws of England (3rd edn); articles on taxation and legal procedure in periodicals. *Recreations:* golf, bridge, chess (represented England at Stockholm in 1937). *Address:* Brackenhill, Gravel Path, The Common, Berkhamsted, Herts HP4 2PJ. *Club:* Reform.

WHEATCROFT, Stephen Frederick, OBE 1974; Member, since 1972 and Director of Economic Development, since 1979, British Airways Board; Chairman: International Aeradio Ltd; British Airways Helicopter Ltd; British Airways Associated Companies Ltd; *b* 11 Sept. 1921; *s* of late Percy and Fanny Wheatcroft; *m* 1st, 1943, Joy (*d* 1974), *d* of late Cecil Reed; two *s* one *d* ; 2nd, 1974, Alison, *d* of late Arnold Dessau; two *s. Educ:* Latymer Sch., N9; London Sch. of Economics. BSc(Econ) 1942. Served War, Pilot in Fleet Air Arm, 1942-45. Commercial Planning Manager, BEA, 1946-53; Simon Research Fellow, Manchester Univ., 1953-55; private practice as Aviation Consultant, 1956-72; retained as Economic Adviser to BEA; Gp Planning Dir, British Airways, 1972-74; Commns for Govts of: Canada, India, W Indies, E African Community, Afghanistan; Consultant to World Bank; Assessor to Edwards Cttee on British Air Transport in the Seventies. Governor, London Sch. of Economics. Vis. Prof., Univ. of Surrey. FRAeS, FCIT (Pres., 1978-79); FAIAA. *Publications:* Economics of European Air Transport, 1956; Airline Competition in Canada, 1958; Air Transport Policy, 1966; articles in professional jls. *Recreation:* travel. *Address:* 20 Mallord Street, SW3. *T:* 01-351 1511. *Club:* Reform.

WHEATLEY, family name of **Baron Wheatley.**

WHEATLEY, Baron *cr* 1970 (Life Peer), of Shettleston, Glasgow; **Rt. Hon. Lord Justice-Clerk; John Wheatley,** PC 1947; one of the Senators of the College of Justice in Scotland since 1954; Lord Justice-Clerk since 1972; *b* 17 Jan. 1908; *s* of Patrick Wheatley and Janet Murphy; *m* 1935, Agnes Nichol; four *s* one *d. Educ:* St Aloysius Coll., Glasgow; Mount St Mary's Coll., Sheffield; Glasgow Univ. MA 1928; LLB 1930; called to Scottish Bar, 1932; Advocate-Depute, 1945-47 MP (Lab) East Edinburgh, 1947-54; Solicitor-General for Scotland, March-Oct. 1947; QC (Scotland) 1947; Lord Advocate, 1947-51. War of 1939-45, RA (Field) and later with Judge Advocate-General's Branch; Chm. Scottish Nurses' Salaries Cttee, 1945-47; Chm. Milk Enquiry in Scotland, 1946-47; Chm., Cttee on Teaching Profession (Scotland), 1961-63; Mem., Royal Commn on Penal Reform (England and Wales), 1964-66; Chairman: Exec. Cttee Royal Scottish Soc. for Prevention of Cruelty to Children, 1956-79; Royal Commn on Local Govt in Scotland, 1966-69; conducted enquiry into crowd safety at sports grounds, 1971-72. Hon. Pres., Age Concern (Scotland). Hon. LLD Glasgow, 1963; DUniv Stirling, 1976; Hon. FEIS. *Recreation:* golf. *Address:* 3 Greenhill Gardens, Edinburgh EH10 4BN. *T:* 031-229 4783.
See also T. Dalyell, Hon. John Wheatley.

WHEATLEY, Sir Andrew; *see* Wheatley, Sir G. A.

WHEATLEY, Very Rev. Arthur; Provost of St Andrew's Scottish Episcopal Cathedral, Inverness, since 1980; *b* 4 March 1931; *s* of George and Elizabeth Wheatley; *m* 1959, Sheena Morag Wilde; two *s* two *d. Educ:* Alloa Academy; Coates Hall Theol Coll., Edinburgh. Deacon 1970, priest 1970, Dio. Brechin; 1st Curate's title, St Salvador's with St Martin's, Dundee, 1970-71; Curate in Charge, St Ninian's Mission, Dundee, 1971-76; Rector of Holy Trinity, Elgin with St Margaret's Church, Lossiemouth, Dio. Moray, Ross and Caithness, 1976-80; Canon of St Andrew's Cathedral, 1978-80. *Recreations:* shooting, fishing, bee keeping and motor cycling. *Address:* St Andrew's Cathedral House, 15 Ardross Street, Inverness IV3 5NS. *T:* Inverness 33535.

WHEATLEY, Derek Peter Francis, QC 1981; Legal Adviser to Lloyds Bank; Member, Commercial Court Committee; Barrister-at-Law; *b* 18 Dec. 1925; 3rd *s* of late Edward Pearse Wheatley, company director, and Gladys Wheatley; *m* 1955, Elizabeth Pamela, *d* of John and Gertrude Reynolds; two *s* one *d. Educ:* The Leys Sch., Cambridge; University Coll., Oxford (MA). Served War of 1939-45, Army, 1944-47: (short univ. course, Oxford, 1944); commissioned into 8th King's Royal Irish Hussars, 1945, Lieut. University Coll., Oxford, 1947-49; called to the Bar, Middle Temple, 1951; Member: Senate of Inns of Court and the Bar, 1975-78, 1982-; Bar Council, 1982-. Deputy Coroner: to the Royal Household, 1959-64; for London, 1959-64; for Middlesex, 1960-64; Asst Dep.-Coroner for Surrey and for Essex, 1957-64; Recorder of the Crown Court, 1972-74. Chm., Bar Assoc. for Commerce, Finance and Industry, 1982-. *Publications:* articles in legal jls and The Times. *Recreation:* sailing. *Address:* 6 Pump Court, Temple EC4Y 7AR. *T:* 01-353 7242; Cheriton, Berwyn Road, Richmond, Surrey. *T:* 01-876 2182. *Clubs:* Athenæum, Bar Yacht, Little Ship.

WHEATLEY, Sir (George) Andrew, Kt 1967; CBE 1960; MA; BCL; Clerk of the Peace and Clerk of Hampshire County Council, 1946-67; *b* 1908; *s* of late Robert Albert Wheatley; *m* 1937, Mary Vera Hunt; three *s* two *d. Educ:* Rugby and Exeter Coll., Oxford. Asst Solicitor: Pembrokeshire CC, 1932-34; East Suffolk CC, 1934-36; N Riding, Yorks, 1936-39; Dep. Clerk of the Peace and Dep. Clerk of Cumberland CC, 1939-42; Clerk of the Peace and Clerk of the Cumberland CC, 1942-46. Hon. Sec., Society of Clerks of the Peace of Counties and of Clerks of County Councils, 1961; former Member: Local Government Advisory Panel, Dept of Technical Co-operation; Home Office Adv. Council on Child Care; Central Training Council in Child Care; Min. of Housing and Local Govt Departmental Cttee on Management in Local

Govt; Royal Commn on Assizes and Quarter Sessions; Mem., English Local Govt Boundary Commn, 1971-. DL Hants, 1967-70. *Clubs:* Royal Lymington Yacht, Royal Solent Yacht.

WHEATLEY, Hon. John Francis; Sheriff of Tayside Central and Fife at Perth, since 1980 (at Dunfermline, 1979-80); *b* 9 May 1941; *s* of Rt Hon. John Thomas Wheatley (Baron Wheatley), *qv*; *m* 1970, Bronwen Catherine Fraser; two *s*. *Educ:* Mount St Mary's Coll., Derbyshire; Edinburgh Univ. (BL). Called to the Scottish Bar, 1966; Standing Counsel to Scottish Develt Dept, 1971; Advocate Depute, 1975. *Recreations:* gardening, music. *Address:* Braefoot Farmhouse, Crook of Devon, Fossoway, Kinross-shire. *T:* Fossoway 212.

WHEATLEY, Maj.-Gen. Percival Ross, DSO 1943; late RAMC, retired; *b* Westbury, Wilts, 4 May 1909; *s* of late Rev. Percival Wheatley, Congregational Minister, and late Margaret Lettice Wheatley (*née* Wallis); *m* 1939, Dorothy Joan Fellows (*née* Brock); one *s*. *Educ:* St Dunstan's Coll., Catford; Guy's Hosp. Med. School. MB, BS (London), MRCS, LRCP, 1933; FRCS 1940. Commissioned Lieut RAMC, 1939; BEF as Surgical Specialist, Sept. 1939; 2nd in comd 16 Para. Field Ambulance, 1942, comdg, 1943; N Africa, 1942; Sicily and Italy, 1943; ADMS, 2nd Indian Airborne Div., 1944-46; Surgical Specialist, 1946-60: Catterick, Hamburg, Singapore, Japan, Millbank; seconded to Ghana Army, Surgical Specialist, 1960-61; Consultant Surgeon: FARELF, 1963-66; BAOR, 1966-67; Dir of Army Surgery and Consulting Surgeon to the Army, 1967-69. Surgeon, P&O Lines Ltd, 1969-77. FRSocMed; Senior Fellow: Brit. Orthopædic Assoc.; Assoc. of Surgeons of Great Britain and Ireland. QHS 1967-69. *Publication:* contrib. to Basic Surgery. *Recreation:* sailing. *Address:* Sherwood, High Park Avenue, East Horsley, Surrey. *T:* East Horsley 2151. *Club:* Army and Navy.

WHEATON, Rev. Canon David Harry; Principal, Oak Hill Theological College, since 1971; *b* 2 June 1930; *s* of Harry Wheaton, MBE, and Kathleen Mary (*née* Frost); *m* 1956, Helen Joy Forrer; one *s* two *d*. *Educ:* Abingdon Sch.; St John's Coll., Oxford (Exhibnr; MA); London Univ. (BD London Bible Coll.)); Oak Hill Theol Coll. NCO, Wiltshire Regt, 1948-49. Deacon, 1959; priest, 1960; Tutor, Oak Hill Coll., 1954-62; Rector of Ludgershall, Bucks, 1962-66; Vicar of St Paul, Onslow Square, S Kensington, 1966-71; Chaplain, Brompton Chest Hosp., 1969-71. Hon. Canon, Cathedral and Abbey Church of St Alban, 1976. *Publications:* (contrib.) Baker's Dictionary of Theology, 1960; (contrib.) New Bible Dictionary, 1962; (contrib.) New Bible Commentary (rev.), 1970. *Recreations:* walking, carpentry and do-it-yourself. *Address:* Oak Hill College, Southgate, N14 4PS. *T:* 01-441 0353.

WHEELDON, Rt. Rev. Philip William, OBE 1946; Hon. Assistant Bishop, Diocese of Wakefield, since 1977; *b* 20 May 1913; *e* *s* of late Alfred Leonard Wheeldon and late Margaret Proctor Wheeldon (*née* Smith); *m* 1966, Margaret Redfearn. *Educ:* Clifton Coll., Bristol; Downing Coll., Cambridge; Westcott House Theological Coll. BA 1935, MA 1942. Deacon, 1937; Priest, 1938; Farnham Parish Church, Dio. Guildford, 1937-39; Chaplain to the Forces, 1939-46; Chaplain, 1st Bn Coldstream Guards, 1939-42; Senior Chaplain, 79th Armoured Div., 1942-43; Dep. Asst Chaplain-Gen. 12th Corps, 1943-45; 8th Corps, 1945-46; Hon. Chaplain to the Forces, 1946-; Domestic Chaplain to Archbishop of York, 1946-49, Hon. Chaplain, 1950-54; General Sec., CACTM, 1949-54; Prebendary of Wedmore II in Wells Cathedral, 1952-54; Suffragan Bishop of Whitby, 1954-61; Bishop of Kimberley and Kuruman, 1961-65; resigned, 1965; an Asst Bishop, Dio. Worcester, 1965-68; Bishop of Kimberley and Kuruman, 1968-76. Hon. Asst Bishop, Diocese of Worcester, 1976-77. *Recreations:* music, sport, gardening. *Address:* Westgate Close, Clifton, Brighouse, West Yorks HD6 4HJ. *Club:* Brooks's.

WHEELER, Anthony; *see* Wheeler, H. A.

WHEELER, Arthur William Edge, CBE 1979 (OBE 1967); Commissioner for Law Revision, northern states of Nigeria, since 1980; *b* 1 Aug. 1930; *e* *s* of Arthur William Wheeler and Rowena (*née* Edge); *m* 1956, Gay (*née* Brady); two *s* one *d*. *Educ:* Mountjoy Sch.; Trinity Coll., Dublin (Reid Prof.'s Prize, MA, LLB). Called to the Irish Bar, King's Inns, 1953; called to the Bar, Gray's Inn, 1960. Crown Counsel, Nigeria, 1955; Legal Sec. (Actg), Southern Cameroons, and Mem. Exec. Council and House of Assembly, 1958; Principal Crown Counsel, Fedn of Nigeria, 1961; Northern Nigeria: Dep. Solicitor Gen., 1964; Dir of Public Prosecutions, 1966; High Court Judge, 1967; Chief Judge (formerly Chief Justice), Kaduna State of Nigeria, 1975; Chm., Commn of Inquiry into Ministries and Tenders Bd of Kano State, 1975. Mem., Body of Benchers, Nigeria, 1975; Associate Mem., Commonwealth Parly Assoc. *Recreations:* tennis, squash, golf. *Address:* Ministry of Justice, Kaduna, Nigeria. *Clubs:* Royal Commonwealth Society; Kildare Street & University (Dublin).

WHEELER, Charles (Cornelius-); journalist and broadcaster, since 1940; *b* 26 March 1923; *s* of late Wing-Comdr Charles Cornelius-Wheeler, RFC and RAFVR, and Winifred (*née* Rees); *m* 1961, Dip Singh; two *d*. *Educ:* Cranbrook School. Began journalism as tape-boy, Daily Sketch, 1940. Served War, Royal Marines, 1942-46; Captain 1944 (despatches NW Europe). Sub-editor, BBC Latin American Service, 1947-49; German Service Correspondent in Berlin, 1950-53; Talks writer, European Service, 1954-56; Producer, Panorama, 1956-58; S Asia Correspondent, 1958-62; Berlin Corresp., 1962-65; Washington Corresp., 1965-68; Chief Correspondent:

USA, 1969-73; Europe, 1973-76; BBC Television News, 1977; Panorama, 1977-79; Newsnight, 1980. Poynter Fellow, Yale Univ., 1973. *Publication:* The East German Rising (with Stefan Brant), 1955. *Recreations:* gardening, swimming, travel. *Address:* c/o Lloyds Bank Ltd, Cox's and King's Branch, 6 Pall Mall, SW1.

WHEELER, Prof. David John, FRS 1981; Professor of Computer Science, Cambridge University, since Oct. 1978; Fellow of Darwin College, Cambridge, since 1967; *b* 9 Feb. 1927; *s* of Arthur William Wheeler and Agnes Marjorie (*née* Gudgeon); *m* 1957, Joyce Margaret Blackler. *Educ:* Camp Hill Grammar Sch., Birmingham; Hanley High Sch., Stoke on Trent; Trinity Coll., Cambridge. Research Fellow, Trinity Coll., Cambridge, 1951-57; Visiting Asst Prof., Univ. of Illinois, USA, 1951-53; Asst Director of Research, Cambridge Univ., 1956-66; Reader in Computer Science, Cambridge Univ., 1966-78. *Publication:* The Preparation of Programs for an Electronic Digital Computer, 1951. *Address:* 131 Richmond Road, Cambridge CB4 3PS. *T:* Cambridge 351319.

WHEELER, Lt-Comdr Sir (Ernest) Richard, KCVO 1981 (CVO 1969; MVO 1965); MBE 1943; RN retd; Clerk of the Council and Keeper of Records, Duchy of Lancaster, 1970-81; *b* 21 July 1917; *s* of late Rev. Harold W. Wheeler, Burton Bradstock and Weston Turville, and Margaret Laura Wheeler; *m* 1st, 1939, Yvonne Burns (*d* 1973); one *d*; 2nd, 1974, Auriel Clifford. *Educ:* Marlborough Coll.; HMS Frobisher. Paymaster Cadet, RN, 1935; Lieut 1939; served: HM Ships Devonshire, Emerald, Office of C-in-C Med., 1940-42; Sec. to Chief of Staff, C-in-C Med., 1942-43; HMS Daedalus and Admty, 1944-47; Lt-Comdr 1947; retd (invalided), 1949. Asst Bursar, Epsom Coll., 1949-52; Chief Clerk, Duchy of Lancaster, 1952-70. *Address:* 40 The Street, Marden, Devizes, Wilts. *Club:* Army and Navy.

WHEELER, Frank Basil; Counsellor, HM Diplomatic Service; Head of Personnel Policy Department, Foreign and Commonwealth Office, since 1982; *b* 24 April 1937; *s* of late Harold Gifford Wheeler and Winifred Lucy Wheeler (*née* Childs); *m* 1959, Catherine Saunders Campbell (*d* 1979); one *s*. *Educ:* Mill Hill Sch. HM Forces, 1956-58. HM Foreign Service, 1958-: Foreign Office, 1958-61; Third Sec. (Commercial), Moscow, 1961-63; Asst Private Sec. to Minister of State, FO, 1963-65; Second Sec. (Commercial), Berne, 1965-67; First Sec., FO (later FCO), 1967-72; Wellington, 1972-75; FCO, 1975-77; Counsellor and Head of Chancery, Prague, 1977-79; Inspector, 1979-82. *Recreations:* music, modern art, tennis. *Address:* c/o Foreign and Commonwealth Office, SW1.

WHEELER, Sir Frederick (Henry), AC 1979; Kt 1967; CBE 1962 (OBE 1952); Director: Amatil Ltd, since 1979; Alliance Holdings Ltd, since 1979; Member, Commonwealth Government Defence Review Committee, since 1981; *b* 9 Jan. 1914; *s* of late A. H. Wheeler; *m* 1939, Peggy Hilda (*d* 1975), *d* of Basil P. Bell; one *s* two *d*. *Educ:* Scotch College; Melbourne University (BCom). State Savings Bank of Victoria, 1929-39; Treasury: Research Officer, 1939; Economist, 1944; Asst Sec., 1946; First Asst Sec., 1949-52; Treasurer Comptroller, ILO, Geneva, 1952-60; Chm., Commonwealth Public Service Bd, Canberra, 1961-71; Sec. to Treasury, Australia, 1971-79. Member: Aust. delegn to various British Commonwealth Finance Ministers' Conferences; Austr. Delegn Bretton Woods Monetary Conf.; UN Civil Service Adv. Bd, 1969-72. *Address:* 9 Charlotte Street, Red Hill, ACT 2603, Australia. *T:* 959 888. *Clubs:* (Pres. 1966-69) Commonwealth (Canberra); Royal Canberra Golf.

WHEELER, Geoffrey, CB 1952; *b* 22 Nov. 1909; *s* of late A. E. Wheeler; *m* 1937, Dorothy Mary Wallis; one *s* one *d*. *Educ:* Clay Cross School, Derbyshire; St John's Coll., Cambridge (Scholar). First Class Part I Historical Tripos, 1930; First Class Part II Historical Tripos, 1931. Entered Civil Service, 1932, and appointed to Board of Customs and Excise; Private Sec. to Sir Evelyn Murray, 1936; Principal, 1937; Assistant Secretary, 1943; Under-Secretary (Ministry of Defence), 1948; Under-Secretary: Min. of Aviation, 1964-67; Min. of Technology (Principal Estabt Officer), 1967-70; Min. of Aviation Supply, 1970-71; Asst Under Sec. of State (Personnel), Procurement Exec., MoD, 1971-72; Asst Dir, Civil Service Selection Bd, 1972-76. Pres., Groupe Statut EEC, 1977. Chm., London Derbyshire Soc., 1973-. *Recreations:* music; amateur theatre. *Address:* 57 Hillcrest Road, Purley, Surrey. *T:* 01-660 2858.

WHEELER, Lt-Col Geoffrey Edleston, CIE 1943; CBE 1948; Hon. MA University of Durham, 1955; Director of Central Asian Research Centre, 1953-68; *b* 22 June 1897; *s* of late Capt. Owen Wheeler, Leicestershire Regiment; *m* 1927, Irena Nicolaevna Boulatoff (*d* 1973); one *s*. *Educ:* Eastbourne Coll. Commissioned Queen's Regt 1915; served in France, 1915-17; transferred to Indian Army, 1918, 6th Gurkha Rifles; various Intelligence appointments in Turkey, Malta, and Palestine to 1925; Military Attaché, Meshed, 1926; Intelligence duties in Iraq, 1928-31; 7th Rajput Regt to 1936; General Staff, Army HQ, India, 1936-41; Director, Publications Division, Govt of India, 1941-46; Counsellor, British Embassy, Teheran, 1946-50. Sir Percy Sykes Memorial Medal, RCAS, 1967. *Publications:* Racial Problems in Soviet Muslim Asia; The Modern History of Soviet Central Asia; The Peoples of Soviet Central Asia. *Address:* 5 Sandown Lodge, Avenue Road, Epsom, Surrey.

WHEELER, Rt. Rev. Monsignor Gordon; *see* Wheeler, W. G.

WHEELER, (Harry) Anthony, OBE 1973; RSA, FRIBA; Senior Partner, Wheeler & Sproson, Architects, Town Planners, Edinburgh and Kirkcaldy, since 1954; *b* 7 Nov. 1919; *s* of Herbert George Wheeler and Laura Emma Groom; *m* 1944, Dorothy Jean Campbell; one *d*. *Educ:* Stranraer High Sch.; Royal Technical Coll., Glasgow; Glasgow School of Art; Univ. of Strathclyde (BArch). RIBA, DipTP, MRTPI. Glasgow Sch. of Architecture, 1937-48 (war service, Royal Artillery, 1939-46); John Keppie Scholar and Sir Rowand Anderson Studentship, 1948; RIBA Grissell Gold Medallist, 1948, and Neale Bursar, 1949. Assistant: to City Architect, Oxford, 1948; to Sir Herbert Baker & Scott, London, 1949; Sen. Architect, Glenrothes New Town, 1949-51; Sen. Lectr, Dundee Sch. of Arch., 1952-58; commenced private practice in Fife, 1952. Principal works include: Woodside Shopping Centre and St Columba's Parish Church, Glenrothes; Reconstruction of Giles Pittenweem; Redevelopment of Dysart and of Old Buckhaven; Town Centre Renewal, Grangemouth; Students' Union, Univ. of St Andrews; Hunter Building, Edinburgh Coll. of Art; St Peter's Episcopal Ch., Kirkcaldy. Member: Royal Fine Art Commn for Scotland; Scottish Housing Adv. Ctte, 1971-75; Trustee, Scottish Civic Trust; Pres., RIAS, 1973-75; Vice-Pres., RIBA, 1973-75. RSA 1975 (ARSA 1963); Treasurer, 1978-80; Sec., 1980-). 13 Saltire Soc. Awards for Housing and Reconstruction; 4 Civic Trust Awards. *Publications:* articles on civic design and housing in technical jls. *Recreations:* making gardens, sketching and water colours, fishing, music and drama. *Address:* Hawthornbank House, Dean Village, Edinburgh EH4 3BH. *T:* 031-225 2334. *Clubs:* Caledonian, Scottish Arts (Edinburgh).

WHEELER, Air Chief Marshal Sir (Henry) Neil (George), GCB 1975 (KCB 1969; CB 1967); CBE 1957 (OBE 1949); DFC 1941 (Bar 1943); AFC 1954; Director, Flight Refuelling Ltd, since 1977; *b* 8 July 1917; *s* of T. H. Wheeler, South African Police; *m* 1942, Elizabeth, *d* of late W. H. Weightman, CMG; two *s* one *d*. *Educ:* St Helen's College, Southsea, Hants. Entered Royal Air Force College, Cranwell, 1935; Bomber Comd, 1937-40; Fighter and Coastal Comds, 1940-45; RAF and US Army Staff Colls, 1943-44; Cabinet Office, 1944-45; Directing Staff, RAF Staff Coll., 1945-46; FEAF, 1947-49; Directing Staff, JSSC, 1949-51; Bomber Comd, 1951-53; Air Min., 1953-57. Asst Comdt, RAF Coll., 1957-59; OC, RAF Laarbruch, 1959-60; IDC, 1961; Min. of Defence, 1961-63; Senior Air Staff Officer, HQ, RAF Germany (2nd TAF), Sept. 1963-66; Asst Chief of Defence Staff (Operational Requirements), MoD, 1966-67; Deputy Chief of Defence Staff, 1967-68; Commander, FEAF, 1969-70; Air Mem. for Supply and Organisation, MoD, 1970-73; Controller, Aircraft, MoD Procurement Exec., 1973-75. ADC to the Queen, 1957-61. Dir, Rolls-Royce Ltd, 1977-82. FRAeS; CBIM. *Address:* Boundary Hall, Cooksbridge, Lewes, East Sussex. *Clubs:* Hurlingham, Royal Air Force, Flyfishers'.
See also Maj.-Gen. T. N. S. Wheeler.

WHEELER, John Daniel, JP; MP (C) City of Westminster, Paddington Division, since 1979; Director-General, British Security Industry Association, since 1976; *b* 1 May 1940; *s* of late Frederick Harry Wheeler and Constance Elsie (*née* Foreman); *m* 1967, Laura Margaret Langley; one *s* one *d*. *Educ:* county sch., Suffolk; Staff Coll., Wakefield. Home Office: Asst Prison Governor, 1967-74; Res. Officer, 1974-76. Prospective Parly Candidate, City of Westminster, Paddington, 1976-79. Dir, National Supervisory Council for Intruder Alarms, 1977-; Member: Home Office Standing Cttee on Crime Prevention, 1976-; Cons. Party National Adv. CPC Cttee, 1978-80; Home Affairs Select Cttee, 1979-; Chm., Home Affairs Sub-Cttee, Race Relations and Immigration, 1980-. Chm., Nat. Inspectorate of Security Guard Patrol and Transport Services, 1982-. JP Inner London, 1978. *Publications:* Who Prevents Crime?, 1980; (jtly) The Standard Catalogue of the Coins of the British Commonwealth, 1642 to present day, 1983. *Recreation:* enjoying life. *Address:* House of Commons, SW1A 0AA. *T:* 01-219 4615. *Club:* Carlton.

WHEELER, Sir John (Hieron), 3rd Bt *cr* 1920; formerly Chairman, Raithby, Lawrence & Co. Ltd, retired 1973; *b* 22 July 1905; 2nd *s* of Sir Arthur Wheeler, 1st Bt; *S* brother, Sir Arthur (Frederick Pullman) Wheeler, 1964; *m* 1929, Gwendolen Alice (*née* Oram); two *s*. *Educ:* Charterhouse. Engaged in Print. Served War of 1939-45, Trooper, RTR, 1941-45. After the war, returned to printing. *Recreations:* whittling, dry stone walling. *Heir: s* John Frederick Wheeler [*b* 3 May 1933; *m* 1963, Barbara Mary, *d* of Raymond Flint, Leicester; two *s* one *d*]. *Address:* 39 Morland Avenue, Leicester LE2 2PF. *Club:* Wig and Pen.

WHEELER, Hon. Sir Kenneth (Henry), Kt 1976; JP; Speaker of the Victorian Parliament, Australia, 1973-79; *b* 7 Sept. 1912; *s* of William Henry Wheeler and Alma Nellie Wheeler; *m* 1934, Hazel Jean Collins; one *s* one *d*. *Educ:* Mernda State Sch., Vic. Grazier and retail dairyman for 19 years. Municipal Councillor, 1950-59; Mayor, City of Coburg, Vic., 1955-56; elected to Parliament of Victoria for Essendon, 1958. *Recreations:* golf, football, exhibition of horses. *Clubs:* Essendon; Gisborne Golf; Royal-Park Golf; Royal Automobile of Victoria.

WHEELER, Michael Mortimer, QC 1961; *b* Westminster, 8 Jan. 1915; *o s* of late Sir Mortimer Wheeler, CH, CIE, MC, TD, and late Tessa Verney Wheeler, FSA; *m* 1939, Sheila, *e d* of late M. S. Mayou, FRCS; two *d*. *Educ:* Dragon School, Oxford; Rugby School; Christ Church, Oxford. Barrister; Gray's Inn, 1938; Lincoln's Inn, 1946 (Bencher 1967). Served throughout War of 1939-45, with RA (TA) in UK and Italy (Lt-Col 1945; despatches); TD

1961. *Address:* 114 Hallam Street, W1. *T:* 01-580 7284. *Clubs:* Garrick, MCC.

WHEELER, Sir Neil; *see* Wheeler, Sir H. N. G.

WHEELER, Maj.-Gen. Norman; *see* Wheeler, Maj.-Gen. T. N. S.

WHEELER, Sir Richard; *see* Wheeler, Sir E. R.

WHEELER, Maj.-Gen. (retd) Richard Henry Littleton, CB 1960; CBE 1953; *b* 2 Nov. 1906; *s* of Maj. Henry Littleton Wheeler, CB, DSO, and Vera Gillum Webb; *m* 1941, Iris Letitia Hope; one *d*. *Educ:* Uppingham; RMA, Woolwich. 2nd Lt RA, 1926. Served War of 1939-45, 50th Division. Lt-Col 1942; Brigadier 1950; HQ Northern Army Group, 1958-61; Maj.-Gen. 1959. Col Comdt RA, 1963-71. *Recreations:* riding, music. *Address:* Manor Farm, Knighton, Sherborne, Dorset DT9 6QU. *Club:* Army and Navy.

WHEELER, (Selwyn) Charles (Cornelius-); *see* Wheeler, C. C.

WHEELER, Maj.-Gen. (Thomas) Norman (Samuel), CB 1967; CBE 1964 (OBE 1958); Chairman, J. E. Beale Ltd, since 1980; *b* 16 June 1915; *e s* of late Thomas Henry Wheeler, S African Police; *m* 1939, Helen Clifford, *y d* of F. H. E. Webber, Emsworth, Hants; one *s* one *d*. *Educ:* South Africa; St Helen's College, Southsea; RMC Sandhurst. Commissioned Royal Ulster Rifles, 1935; Palestine Rebellion, 1937-39 (despatches). Served War of 1939-45 (despatches twice): Bde Major, 38 Irish Bde, 1941-42; MEF, 1942-43; British Military Mission to Albania, 1943-44; 2nd Bn Royal Ulster Rifles, 1944-45. AA & QMG 6th Airborne Div., 1945-46; Airborne Establishment, 1946-47; Mil. Asst to Adj.-Gen. to the Forces, 1949-50; UK Services Liaison Staff, Australia, 1951-52; GSO1 and Col GS, HQ Northern Army Group and HQ, BAOR, 1954-57; comd 1st Bn Royal Ulster Rifles Cyprus Rebellion, 1958-59 (despatches); comd 39 Inf. Bde Group, N Ireland, 1960-62; Chief of Staff 1st (British) Corps, BAOR, 1962-63; General Officer Commanding Second Division, 1964-66; Chief of Staff, Contingencies Planning, SHAPE, 1966-69; Chief of Staff, HQ, BAOR, 1969-71; retired, 1971. Dir and Sec., Independent Stores Assoc., 1971-76; Dep. Man. Dir, Associated Independent Stores Ltd, 1976-80. Independent Mem., Cinematograph Films Council, 1980-. *Recreations:* travel, tennis, water ski-ing. *Address:* Glebe House, Liston, Sudbury, Suffolk. *Clubs:* Army and Navy, Airborne, Special Forces.
See also Sir Neil Wheeler.

WHEELER, Rt. Rev. (William) Gordon; *see* Leeds, Bishop of, (RC).

WHEELER, William Henry, CMG 1959; PhD (London); Chairman, Mark Laboratories Ltd; *b* Petersfield, Hants, 5 March 1907; *s* of John William and Ellen Wheeler; *m* 1937, Mary Inkpen; no *c*. *Educ:* St Catharine's Coll., Cambridge (BA); Imperial Coll. of Science (DIC). Beit Memorial Research Fellow, Imperial Coll., 1931. Man. British Automatic Refrigerators, London, 1935; Government Scientific Service, 1937; Dir, Guided Weapons Research & Development, 1950; Head of UK Ministry of Supply Staff and Scientific Adviser to UK High Commission, Australia, 1955; Director of Explosives Research, Waltham Abbey, 1959. Man. Dir, 1961-82, and Dep. Chm., 1968-82, Urquhart Engineering Co. Ltd; Chm., Urquhart Engineering GmbH, to 1982; Dep. Chm., Steam and Combustion Engineering Ltd, to 1982; Chm., Process Combustion Corp., USA, to 1982. *Publications:* papers on Combustion and Detonation in Proc. and Trans. Royal Society, and on Rocket Propellants in Nature, Proc. of Inst. of Fuel and Instn of Chemical Engineers; papers on the Mechanism of Cavitation Erosion for DSIR and American Soc. of Mechanical Engineers. *Recreation:* private research laboratory. *Address:* Mark House, Ashmead Lane, Denham, Bucks.

WHEELER-BOOTH, Michael Addison John, MA; Principal Clerk, Overseas and European Office, House of Lords, since 1978; *b* 25 Feb. 1934; *s* of Addison James Wheeler and Mary Angela Wheeler-Booth (*née* Blakeney-Booth); *m* 1982, Emily Frances Smith. *Educ:* Leighton Park Sch.; Magdalen Coll., Oxford (Exhibnr; MA). Clerk, Parliament Office, House of Lords, 1960; seconded as Private Secretary to Leader of House and Government Chief Whip, 1965; seconded as Jt Sec., Inter-Party Conference on House of Lords Reform, 1967; Clerk of the Journals, 1970; Chief Clerk, Overseas and European Office, 1972. *Address:* Fir Tree Cottage, Sandford St Martin, Oxon OX5 4AG. *T:* Great Tew 632; 156 Lambeth Road, SE1. *T:* 01-633 0735.

WHEEN, Rear-Adm. Charles Kerr Thorneycroft, CB 1966; *b* 28 Sept. 1912; *s* of late F. T. Wheen, Holmbury, Chislehurst, Kent; *m* 1940, Veryan Rosamond, *d* of late William Acworth, Chobham; three *s* one *d*. *Educ:* RN College, Dartmouth. Entered RN as Cadet, 1926. Served War of 1939-45: China, The Nore, Admiralty, Normandy Landings, East Indies. Naval Attaché, Beirut, Amman and Addis Ababa, 1958-60; Director of Officers' Appointments (S), Admiralty, 1960-63; Flag Officer Admiralty Interview Board, 1964-66. Capt. 1956; Rear-Adm. 1964; retd 1966. Dir, Cement Makers Federation, 1967-79. Chm., Bd of Governors, Gordon Boys School, 1971-. *Recreations:* golf, fishing. *Address:* Willow House, Philpot Lane, Chobham, Surrey. *T:* Chobham 8118.

WHELAN, Air Cdre James Roger, CBE 1968; DSO 1944; DFC 1940 (Bar 1943); RAF retired; with Echo & Post Ltd, Hemel Hempstead, since 1969; *b* Saskatoon, Sask, Canada, 29 April 1914; *s* of James P. Whelan; *m* 1946, Irene, *d* of late P. Rennie, Bathurst, NB, Canada; two *d*. *Educ:* Bathurst High

School; Univ. of St Francis Xavier, Antigonish, NS, Canada. Commissioned, RAF, 1937. Served War of 1939-45: France, Egypt, Germany, Italy. Commanded RAF St Eval, 1957-58; Base Comdr, Christmas Island, 1959; Dir of Intelligence (B), Air Min., 1961-64; AO i/c A, HQ Coastal Command, 1965-68. RAF Staff Coll., 1949; jssc, 1952; idc, 1960. *Recreation:* photography. *Address:* 26 Laburnum Court, Dennis Lane, Stanmore, Mddx. *T:* 01-954 2255. *Club:* Royal Air Force.

WHELAN, Michael John, FRS 1976; MA, PhD, DPhil; Reader in the Physical Examination of Materials, Department of Metallurgy and Science of Materials, University of Oxford, since 1966; Fellow of Linacre College, Oxford, since 1967; *b* 2 Nov. 1931; *s* of William Whelan and Ellen Pound. *Educ:* Farnborough Grammar Sch.; Gonville and Caius Coll., Cambridge. FInstP. Fellow of Gonville and Caius Coll., 1958-66; Demonstrator in Physics, Univ. of Cambridge, 1961-65; Asst Dir of Research in Physics, Univ. of Cambridge, 1965-66. *Publications:* (co-author) Electron Microscopy of Thin Crystals, 1965; numerous papers in learned jls. *Recreation:* gardening. *Address:* 18 Salford Road, Old Marston, Oxford OX3 0RX. *T:* Oxford 244556.

WHELAN, Prof. Robert Ford, MD, PhD, DSc; FRCP, FRACP, FACE, FAA; Vice-Chancellor, University of Liverpool, since 1977; *b* Belfast, NI, 22 Dec. 1922; *s* of Robert Henry Whelan and Dorothy Ivy Whelan; *m* 1951, Helen Elizabeth Macdonald Hepburn; two *s* one *d. Educ:* private schs; QUB (MB, BCh, BAO 1946; MD 1951; PhD 1955; DSc 1960). MD Adelaide, 1958. FRACP 1962; FAA 1966; FACE 1974; FRCP 1980. RMO, Belfast City Hosp., 1947; Sen. Ship's Surg., Glen Line, Alfred Holt & Co., Far East and Australia, 1948; Jun. Lectr and Asst Lectr in Physiol., QUB, 1949-51; Res. Fellow, Sherrington Sch. of Physiol., St Thomas's Hosp. Med. Sch., 1951-52; Lectr in Physiol., QUB and NI Hosps Authority, 1952-57; Univ. of Adelaide: Prof. and Head of Dept of Human Physiol. and Pharmacol., 1958-71; Associate Dean, Faculty of Med., 1960 and 1961, Dean, 1964 and 1965; Mem., Educn Cttee, 1963-66, Chm., 1971; Hon. Cons. Physiologist, Royal Adelaide Hosp., 1959-71; Vice-Chancellor, Univ. of Western Australia, 1971-76. Member: EEC Adv. Cttee on Medical Trng, 1978-; Review Body on Higher Educn in N Ireland, 1979-81; Chm., Council for Postgraduate Medical Educn in England and Wales, 1980-; Vice-Chm., Cttee of Vice-Chancellors and Principals, 1981-; Mem. Council, ACU, 1981-. Vis. Prof., Sherrington Sch. of Physiol., St Thomas's Hosp. Med. Sch., 1962; Carnegie Trav. Fellow, USA, 1962; Vis. Prof., Dept. of Physiol., Univ. of Southern Calif, 1962; Vis. Lectr, Univ. of Queensland, 1964; (jtly) Demonstration, Royal Soc. Conversazione, 1966; Edward Stirling Lectr, Postgrad. Cttee, Univ. of Adelaide, 1967; Vis. Prof. of Physiol., Univ. of Singapore, 1970. Aust. Delegate, Internat. Congress of Pharmacology: Basle, 1969; San Francisco, 1972; Chm., Aust. Nat. Cttee, Internat. Union of Pharmacologists, 1968-75. Mem. Council, (new) Flinders Univ. of SA, 1966-71; Mem. Bd of Dirs, Walter and Eliza Hall Inst. for Med. Res., 1968-71; Mem. Bd of Governors: Collegiate Sch. of St Peter, Adelaide, 1967-71; Walford Sch. for Girls, Adelaide, 1969-71. Fellow: Royal Acad. of Med. in Ireland, 1953; Royal Soc. of SA, 1959. Member: Brit. Physiol Soc., 1951; Med. Res. Soc., 1953; Pharmacol Soc., 1956; Med. Sciences Club of SA, 1958 (Vice Pres. 1961, Pres. 1963); Extraord. Mem., Cardiac Soc. of Aust. and NZ, 1960; Foundn Mem. and Mem. Council, Aust. Physiol Soc., 1960. Hon. Member: Royal Adelaide Hosp. Med. Officers' Assoc., 1962; Aust. Soc. of Clin. and Expmtl Pharmacol., 1971 (first Pres., 1966); Aust. Physiol and Pharmacol Soc., 1972. Freeman, Apothecaries' Soc., 1981. *Publications:* Control of the Peripheral Circulation in Man, 1967; pubns in med. and sci. jls. *Address:* The Vice-Chancellor's Lodge, Sefton Park Road, Liverpool L8 3SL. *Club:* Athenæum.

WHELDON, Sir Huw (Pyrs), Kt 1976; OBE 1952; MC 1944; broadcaster; Chairman, Court of Governors, London School of Economics and Political Science, since 1975; Deputy Chairman, National Video Corporation, since 1981; consultant, NBC of America, since 1977; *b* 7 May 1916; *e s* of late Sir Wynn Wheldon KBE, DSO, LLD; *m* Jacqueline Mary (*née* Clarke); one *s* two *d. Educ:* Friars Sch., Bangor, Wales; London Sch. of Economics, BSc(Econ), 1938. Kent Educn Cttee staff, 1939. Commnd Royal Welch Fusiliers, 1940; served NW Europe and Middle East with 1st and 6th Airborne Divs (Major, 1st Bn Roy. Ulster Rifles), 1941-45. Arts Council Dir for Wales, 1946; Festival of Britain Directorate, 1949; BBC Television, 1952-77; producer, director, commentator, author; credits include: All Your Own, Opera for Everybody, Men in Battle, Portraits of Power, Orson Welles Sketchbook, 1952-57; Monitor, magazine of the arts, 1958-64; Royal Heritage, 1977. Head of Documentary Programmes, 1962; Head of Music and Documentary Programmes, 1963-65; Controller of Programmes, 1965-68; Man. Dir, BBC TV, 1968-75; Special Adviser, BBC, 1975-76. Special Adviser, Aspen Inst., 1977-. Pres., Royal TV Soc., 1979-; Trustee, Nat. Portrait Gall., 1976-; Governor, Nat. Film Sch., 1974-; Member: Youth Develt Council, 1959-62; Design Council, 1970-75; Council, Royal Coll. of Art, 1974-; Council, Brunel Univ., 1973-; Hon. Soc. of Cymmrodorion, 1950-. FRSA 1965. Hon. Fellow: LSE, 1973; Manchester Coll. of Art, 1969; British Kinematograph Soc., 1975; BAFTA, 1977; RCA 1980; Hon. DLitt Ulster, 1975; Hon. LLD Wales, 1978; DUniv Open, 1980. Gold Medal, Royal TV Soc., 1976 and 1978. *Address:* 120 Richmond Hill, Richmond, Surrey. *T:* 01-940 8119. *Clubs:* Garrick, Savile.

WHELER, Captain Sir Trevor Wood, 13th Bt, *cr* 1660; late Captain Royal Sussex Regiment, TF, 1914-20, and Royal Engineers, 1940-47; *b* 20 Sept. 1889; *s* of Lt-Col Sir Edward Wheler, 12th Bt, 1st Bn Royal Sussex Regt, and Mary Leontine, *d* of Sir Richard Wood, GCMG; *S* father, 1903; *m* 1915,

Margaret Idris, *y d* of late Sir Ernest Birch, KCMG; one *s* two *d.* Served War of 1914-18, 6th Bn, Royal Sussex Regt; Waziristan, NW Frontier, 1917; attached IA, 1918-20. A principal Game Farmer between the wars, and Pres., Gamefarmers' Assoc., throughout that period. War of 1939-45: Home Guard (LDV), 1940; recalled Army 1940; RE (Movement Control), Scottish Comd, and BAOR, 1940-46. CCG, 1947-50; served in Kenya Police Reserve throughout Mau Mau Emergency, 1953 (General Service Medal). *Heir: s* Edward Woodford Wheler, late Captain Royal Sussex Regt [*b* 13 June 1920; *m* 1945, Molly Ashworth, *e d* of Thomas Lever, Devon; one *s* one *d*]. *Address:* 5A Motcombe Court, Bedford Avenue, Bexhill-on-Sea, East Sussex. *T:* Bexhill 211333.

WHELON, Charles Patrick Clavell; a Recorder of the Crown Court, since 1978; *b* 18 Jan. 1930; *s* of Charles Eric Whelon and Margaret Whelon; *m* 1968, Prudence Mary (*née* Potter); one *s* one *d. Educ:* Wellington Coll.; Pembroke Coll., Cambridge (MA Hons). Called to Bar, Middle Temple, 1954. Liveryman of Vintners' Co., 1952-. *Recreations:* gardening, cartooning. *Address:* 2 Harcourt Buildings, Temple, EC4. *T:* 01-353 2112; Heatherside, Nately Scures, Basingstoke, Hants RG27 9JR. *T:* Hook 2233.

WHETSTONE, Rear-Adm. Anthony John, CB 1982; Assistant Chief of Naval Staff (Operations), since 1981; *b* 12 June 1927; *s* of Albert Whetstone; *m* 1951, Elizabeth Stewart Georgeson; one *s* two *d. Educ:* King Henry VIII School, Coventry. Joined RN, 1945; specialised in submarines, 1949; Commanded: HMS Sea Scout, 1956-57; HMS Artful, 1959-61; HMS Repulse, 1968-70; HMS Juno, 1972-73; HMS Norfolk, 1977-78; Flag Officer Sea Training, 1978-80. FBIM 1979. *Recreations:* hill walking, fishing, amateur dramatics. *Address:* 17 Anglesey Road, Alverstoke, Hants. *Clubs:* Naval; Hardway Sailing (Gosport).

See also N. K. Whetstone.

WHETSTONE, (Norman) Keith, VRD; Editor, Birmingham Evening Mail, since 1980; Editor-in-Chief, Evening Mail series, since 1980; Director, Birmingham Post & Mail Ltd, since 1980; *b* 17 June 1930; *yr s* of Albert and Anne Whetstone; *m* 1952, Monica Joan Clayton, Leamington Spa; three *s. Educ:* King Henry VIII Sch., Coventry. Served Royal Navy, 1949-50, 1951-52; Lt Comdr (S) RNVR, retired, 1965. Coventry Evening Telegraph, 1950-51; Western Morning News, 1952-55; Birmingham Post, 1955-58; Coventry Evening Telegraph, 1958-63; Editor, Cambridge Evening News, 1964-70; Editor, Coventry Evening Telegraph, 1970-80. Nat. Pres., Guild of British Newspaper Editors, 1976-77. Mem. Press Council, 1980-. *Recreations:* theatre, Rugby football, golf, squash. *Address:* Tudor Cottage, Benton Green Lane, Berkswell, Coventry CV7 7AY. *T:* Berkswell 32323. *Club:* Quadrant (Coventry).

See also A. J. Whetstone.

WHEWELL, Prof. Charles Smalley, PhD; Professor of Textile Industries, University of Leeds, 1963-77, Emeritus Professor 1977; (Professor of Textile Technology, 1954-63, Head of Department, 1963-75); *b* 26 April 1912; *m* 1937, Emma Stott, PhD; one *s. Educ:* Grammar School, Darwen, Lancs; University of Leeds (BSc, PhD). Research Chemist, Wool Industries Research Association, 1935-37. University of Leeds, 1937-77: Lecturer in Textile Chemistry; Lecturer in Textile Finishing; Senior Lecturer in Textile Chemistry; Reader in Textile Finishing; Pro-Vice-Chancellor, 1973-75. Pres., Textile Inst., 1977-79. Hon. Liveryman, Clothworkers' Company, 1970. Hon. Fellow: Huddersfield Polytechnic, 1977; Textile Inst., 1979. Textile Institute Medal, 1954; Warner Memorial Medal, 1960; Textile Institute Service Medal, 1971. *Publications:* contrib. to: Chambers's Encyclopædia; Encyclopædia Britannica; British Wool Manual; Waterproofing and Water-repellency; Chemistry of Natural Fibres, ed Asquith, 1977; Oxford History of Technology, ed Williams; Jl Soc. of Dyers and Colourists; Jl Textile Inst. *Recreations:* music (organ), travel. *Address:* Department of Textile Industries, The University of Leeds, Leeds LS2 9JT. *T:* Leeds 31751.

WHICKER, Alan Donald; television broadcaster (Whicker's World); writer; *b* 2 Aug. 1925; *o s* of late Charles Henry Whicker and late Anne Jane Cross. *Educ:* Haberdashers' Aske's Sch. Capt., Devonshire Regt; Dir, Army Film and Photo Section, with 8th Army and US 5th Army. War Corresp. in Korea, For. Corresp., novelist, writer and radio Broadcaster. Joined BBC TV, 1957: Tonight programme (appeared nightly in filmed reports from around the world, studio interviews, outside broadcasts, Eurovision, and Telstar, incl. first Telstar two-way transmission at opening of UN Assembly, NY, 1962); TV Series: Whicker's World, 1959-60; Whicker Down Under, 1961; Whicker on Top of the World!, 1962; Whicker in Sweden, Whicker in the Heart of Texas, Whicker down Mexico Way, 1963; Alan Whicker Report series: The Solitary Billionaire (J. Paul Getty), etc; wrote and appeared in own series of monthly documentaries on BBC 2, subseq. repeated on BBC 1, under series title, Whicker's World, 1965-67 (31 programmes later shown around the world); BBC radio programmes and articles for The Listener, etc; left BBC, 1968. Various cinema films, incl. The Angry Silence. Mem., successful consortium for Yorkshire Television, 1967. Contrib. a documentary series to ITV, 1968. Completed 16 Documentaries for Yorkshire TV during its first year of operation, incl. Whicker's New World Series, and Specials on Gen. Stroessner of Paraguay, Count von Rosen, and Pres. Duvalier of Haiti; Whicker in Europe; Whicker's Walkabout; Broken Hill—Walled City; Gairy's Grenada; documentary series, World of Whicker; Whicker's Orient; Whicker within a Woman's World, 1972; Whicker's South Seas, Whicker way out West, 1973; Whicker's World, series on cities, 1974-77; Whicker's World—Down

Under, 1976; Whicker's World: US, 1977 (4 progs); India, 1978 (7 progs); Indonesia, 1979; California, 1980 (6 progs); Around Whicker's World in 25 Years (3 retrospective progs), 1982; Whicker's World—the first million miles! (6 retrospective progs), 1982; Whicker's World aboard the Orient Express, 1982; Peter Sellers Meml programme. Various awards, 1963-, incl. Screenwriters' Guild, best Documentary Script, 1963; Guild of Television Producers and Directors Personality of the Year, 1964; Silver Medal, Royal Television Soc., 1968; Dumont Award, Univ. of California, 1970; Best Interview Prog. Award, Hollywood Festival of TV, 1973; Dimbleby Award, BAFTA, 1978; TV Times Special Award, 1978. FRSA 1970. *Publications:* Some Rise by Sin, 1949; Away—with Alan Whicker, 1963; Best of Everything, 1980; Within Whicker's World: an autobiography, 1982; Sunday newspaper columns; contrib. various internat. pubns. *Recreations:* people, photography, writing, travel, and reading (usually airline timetables). *Address:* Le Gallais Chambers, St Helier, Jersey.

WHIFFEN, David Hardy, MA, DPhil (Oxon), DSc (Birmingham); FRS 1966; FRSC; Professor of Physical Chemistry, since 1968, Head of School of Chemistry, since 1978, Pro-Vice-Chancellor, since 1980, University of Newcastle upon Tyne (Dean of Science, 1974-77); *s* of late Noël H. and Mary Whiffen; *m* Jean P. Bell; four *s. Educ:* Oundle School; St John's College, Oxford (Scholar). Sometime Commonwealth Fund Fellow, Sen. Student of Commn for 1851 Exhibition. Formerly: Lectr in Chemistry, Univ. of Birmingham; Supt, Molecular Science Div., NPL. Mem., Newcastle AHA, 1978-. Pres., Faraday Div., RSC, 1981-83. *Publications:* papers in scientific jls. *Address:* Department of Physical Chemistry, The University, Newcastle upon Tyne NE1 7RU. *T:* Newcastle 328511.

WHINNEY, Rt. Rev. Michael Humphrey Dickens; *see* Aston, Bishop Suffragan of.

WHIPPLE, Prof. Fred Lawrence; Senior Scientist, Smithsonian Astrophysical Observatory, since 1973; Director, Smithsonian Institution Astrophysical Observatory, 1955-73; Phillips Professor of Astronomy, Harvard University, 1968-77; *b* 5 Nov. 1906; *s* of Harry Lawrence Whipple and Celestia Whipple (*née* MacFarland); *m* 1st, 1928, Dorothy Woods (divorced 1935); one *s*; 2nd, 1946, Babette Frances Samelson; two *d. Educ:* Long Beach High School, Calif; UCLA; Univ. of California, Berkeley. Lick Observatory Fellow, 1930-31; Staff Member, Harvard Univ., 1931-; Instructor, 1932-38; Lecturer, 1938-45; Assoc. Prof., 1945-50; Professor, 1950-; Chm. Dept of Astronomy, 1949-56. US Nat. Cttee of Internat. Geophysical Year: Chm. Techn. Panel on Rocketry, 1955-59; Member: Techn. Panel on Earth Satellite Program, 1955-59; Working Group on Satellite Tracking and Computation, 1955-58; Scientific Advisory Bd to USAF, 1953-62; Cttee on Meteorology, Nat. Acad. of Sciences, Nat. Research Coun., 1958-; Special Cttees on Space Techn., Nat. Advisory Cttee for Aeronautics, 1958- (now NASA), US; Space Sciences Working Group on Orbiting Astronomical Observatories, Nat. Acad. of Sciences (Mem. Nat. Acad. of Sciences, 1959-); Advisory Panel to Cttee on Sci. and Astronautics of US House of Representatives, 1960-73; Amer. Philosophical Soc., Philadelphia; Amer. Acad. of Arts and Sciences, Boston; New York Acad. of Science, NY; several technical societies. Associate, Royal Astronomical Soc., 1970-. Benjamin Franklin Fellow, RSA, 1968-. Editor: Smithsonian Contributions to Astrophysics, 1956-73; Planetary and Space Science, 1958-. Hon. degrees: MA, Harvard Univ., 1945; DSc, Amer. Internat. Coll., 1958; DLitt, North-eastern Univ., 1961; DS, Temple Univ., 1961; LLD, CW Post Coll. of Long Island Univ., 1962. J. Lawrence Smith Medal of Nat. Acad. of Sciences, 1949; Donohue Medals, 1932, 1933, 1937, 1940, 1942 (received two medals that year); Presidential Certificate of Merit, 1948; Exceptional Service Award, US Air Force Scientific Adv. Bd, 1960; Space Flight Award, Amer. Astron. Soc., 1961; President's Award for Distinguished Federal Civilian Service, 1963; Space Pioneers Medallion, 1968; NASA Public Services Award, 1969; Kepler Medal, AAAS, 1971; Nat. Civil Service League's Civil Service Award, 1972; Henry Medal, Smithsonian Instn, 1973; Alumnus of the Year Award, UCLA, 1976; also has foreign awards. *Publications:* Earth, Moon and Planets, 1942, 3rd edn 1968. Many technical papers in various astronomical and geophysical journals and books; popular articles in magazines and in Encyclopædia Britannica. *Recreation:* cultivation of roses. *Address:* Smithsonian Astrophysical Observatory, 60 Garden Street, Cambridge, Mass 02138, USA. *T:* Boston University 4-7383.

WHISHAW, Anthony Popham Law, ARA 1980; *b* 22 May 1930; *s* of Robert Whishaw and Joyce (*née* Wheeler); *m* 1957, Jean Gibson; two *d. Educ:* Tonbridge Sch.; Chelsea Sch. of Art (Higher Cert); Royal College of Art (ARCA). Travelling Schol., RCA; Abbey Minor Schol.; Spanish Govt Schol. *One-Man Exhibns:* Libreria Abril, Madrid, 1957; Rowland Browse and Delbranco, London, 1960, 1961, 1963, 1965, 1968; ICA, 1971; New Art Centre, 1972; Folkestone Arts Centre, 1973; Hoya Gall., London, 1974; Oxford Gall., Oxford, 1974; ACME, London, 1978; Newcastle upon Tyne Polytech. Gall., 1979; (with Martin Froy) New Ashgate Gall., Farnham, 1979; Nicola Jacobs Gall., London, 1981. *Group Exhibns:* Gimpel Fils, AIA Gall., Café Royal Centen., Towards Art (RCA), Camden Arts Centre, London, Ashmoleum Mus., Oxford, 1957-72; Brit. Drawing Biennale, Teesside, 1973; British Landscape, Graves Art Gall., Sheffield, Chichester Nat. Art, 1975; Summer Exhibn, RA, 1974-81; British Painting, 1952-77, RA, 1977; London Group, Whitechapel Open, 1978, A Free Hand, Arts Council (touring show), 1978; The British Art Show, Arts Council (touring), Recent Arts Council Purchases and Awards, Serpentine Gall., First Exhibition, Nicola Jacobs Gall.,

Tolly Cobbold (touring), 55 Wapping Artists, London, 1979; Four Artists, Nicola Jacobs Gall., Sculpture and Works on Paper, Nicola Jacobs, Wapping Open Studios, Hayward Annual, Hayward Gall., Whitechapel Open, Whitechapel Gall., John Moore's Liverpool Exhibn 12, Walker Art Gall., Liverpool, 1980, London Gp, S London Art Gall., Wapping Artists, 1981. *Works in Collections:* Arts Council of Gt Britain, Coventry Art Gall., Leicester Art Gall., Nat. Gall. of Wales, Financial Times, Shell-BP, Museo de Bahia, Brazil, Nat. Gall. of Victoria, Melb., Seattle Mus. of Art, Bank of Boston, Chantrey Bequest, W Australia Art Gall., Bayer Pharmaceuticals, DoE, Nat. Westminster Bank. *Recreations:* chess, badminton. *Address:* 7a Albert Place, Victoria Road, W8 5PD. *T:* 01-937 5197.

WHISHAW, Sir Charles (Percival Law), Kt 1969; solicitor (retired); *b* 29 October 1909; 2nd *s* of late Montague Law Whishaw and Erna Louise (*née* Spies); *m* 1936, Margaret Joan, *e d* of late Col T. H. Hawkins, CMG, RMLI; one *s* two *d. Educ:* Charterhouse; Worcester College, Oxford. Called to Bar, Inner Temple, 1932; Solicitor, 1938; Partner in Freshfields, 1943-74. Trustee, Calouste Gulbenkian Foundn, 1956-81. Member: Iron and Steel Holding and Realisation Agency, 1953-67; Council, Law Soc., 1967-76. Comdr, Order of Prince Henry (Portugal), 1981. *Address:* Westcott Hill House, Westcott, Surrey RH4 3JY. *T:* Dorking 5315.

WHISTLER, Maj.-Gen. Alwyne Michael Webster, CB 1963; CBE 1959; retired, 1965; *b* 30 Dec. 1909; *s* of Rev. W. W. Whistler and Lilian Whistler (*née* Meade), Elsted, Sussex; *m* 1936, Margaret Louise Michelette, *d* of Brig.-Gen. Malcolm Welch, CB, CMG, JP, Stedham, Sussex; one *s* two *d. Educ:* Gresham's Sch., Holt; RMA Woolwich. 2nd Lt Royal Signals, 1929; served in India, 1932-44; War of 1939-45: Staff Coll., Camberley, 1944; Burma Campaign, 19 and 25 Indian Divs and XII Army, 1944-45 (despatches twice). ADPR, Berlin, 1946; GSO1 (Military Adviser), Military Governor of Germany, 1946-48; AQMG, War Office, 1949-50; JSSC 1950; Comdg Royal Signals, 3 Div., 1951-54; Col GS, War Office, 1955-57; Col Q Far ELF, 1957-58; Comdr Corps Royal Signals, 1 (British) Corps, BAOR, 1959-60; Signal Officer-in-Chief, War Office, 1960-62; Chairman, British Joint Communications Board, Ministry of Defence, 1962-64; Assistant Chief of the Defence Staff (Signals), 1964-65. Hon. Col Princess Louise's Kensington Regt (41st Signals) TA, 1963-66; Col Commandant, Royal Corps of Signals, 1964-68; Hon. Col 32nd (Scottish) Signal Regiment (V), 1967-72. Princess Mary Medal, Royal Signals Instn, 1978. Master of Fox Hounds, Nerbudda Vale Hunt, 1938-40. *Recreations:* field sports, particularly fishing. *Address:* Tigh-na-Leven, by Tarbert, Argyll. *T:* Tarbert 610.

WHISTLER, Laurence, CBE 1973 (OBE 1955); FRSL; engraver on glass; writer; *b* 21 Jan. 1912; *s* of Henry Whistler and Helen (*née* Ward); *yr b* of late Rex Whistler; *m* 1st, 1939, Jill (*d* 1944), *d* of Sir Ralph Furse, KCMG, DSO; one *s* one *d*; 2nd, 1950, Theresa, *yr sister* of Jill Furse; one *s* one *d. Educ:* Stowe; Balliol College, Oxford (Hon. Fellow 1974). BA Oxon. Chancellor's Essay Prize, 1934. Served War of 1939-45: private soldier, 1940; commissioned in The Rifle Brigade, 1941; Captain 1942. King's Gold Medal for Poetry, 1935 (first award); Atlantic Award for Literature, 1945. First Pres., Guild of Glass Engravers, 1975-80. *Work on glass includes:* goblets, etc, in point-engraving and drill, and engraved church windows and panels at: Sherborne Abbey; Moreton, Dorset; Checkendon, Oxon; Ilton, Som; Eastbury, Berks (window to Edward and Helen Thomas); Guards' Chapel, London; Stowe, Bucks; St Hugh's Coll., Oxford; Ashmansworth, Berks; Steep, Hants (windows to Edward Thomas); Hannington, Hants; Yalding, Kent (windows to Edmund Blunden); Thornham Parva, Suffolk. *Exhibitions:* Agnews, Bond Street, 1969; Marble Hill, Twickenham, 1972; Corning Museum, USA, 1974; Ashmolean, 1976. *Publications include:* Sir John Vanbrugh (biography), 1938; The English Festivals, 1947; Rex Whistler, His Life and His Drawings, 1948; The World's Room (Collected Poems), 1949; The Engraved Glass of Laurence Whistler, 1952; Rex Whistler: The Königsmark Drawings, 1952; The Imagination of Vanbrugh and his Fellow Artists, 1954; The View From This Window (poems), 1956; Engraved Glass, 1952-58; The Work of Rex Whistler (with Ronald Fuller), 1960; Audible Silence (poems), 1961; The Initials in the Heart: the story of a marriage, 1964, rev. edn 1975; To Celebrate Her Living (poems), 1967; Pictures on Glass, 1972; The Image on the Glass, 1975. *Address:* The Old Manor, Alton Barnes, Marlborough, Wilts. *T:* Woodborough 515.

WHISTON, Peter Rice, RSA 1977; ARIBA; FRIAS; Consultant Architect, since 1977; *b* 19 Oct. 1912; *s* of Thomas Whiston and Marie Barrett; *m* 1947, Kathleen Anne Parker; one *s* four *d. Educ:* Holy Cross Acad.; Sch. of Architecture, Edinburgh Coll. of Art. RIBA Silver Medallist for Recognised Schs, 1937. Served War, Staff Captain RE, 1940-45. Articled, City Architect, Edinburgh, 1930-35; Partner, Dick Peddie McKay & Jamieson, 1937-38; Chief Architect, SSHA, 1946-49; Sen. Lectr, Sch. of Architecture, ECA, 1950-69; Dir, Arch. Conservation Studies, at Heriot Watt Univ., 1969-77. Visiting Prof. at Internat. Centre for Conservation, Rome, 1971; Ecclesiological Practice, 1950-77. *Works include:* Cistercian Abbey at Nunraw; St Margaret's, St Mark's and St Paul's, Edin.; St Columba, Cupar; St Mary Magdalene's, Perth; St Ninian's and St Leonard's, Dundee. Awarded Papal Knighthood of St Gregory for Services to Architecture, (KSG), 1969. *Recreations:* travel, sketching, painting. *Address:* 14 Grange Court, Edinburgh. *T:* 031-668 2720.

WHITAKER, Benjamin Charles George; author; Director, Minority Rights Group, since 1971; *b* 15 Sept. 1934; 3rd *s* of late Maj.-Gen. Sir John Whitaker,

2nd Bt, CB, CBE, and late Lady Whitaker (*née* Snowden), Babworth, Retford, Notts; *m* 1964, Janet Alison Stewart; two *s* one *d*. *Educ:* Eton; New Coll., Oxford. BA (Modern History). Called to Bar, Inner Temple, 1959 (Yarborough-Anderson Scholar). Practised as Barrister, 1959-67. Extra-mural Lectr in Law, London Univ., 1963-64. MP (Lab) Hampstead, 1966-70; PPS to Minister of: Overseas Development, 1966; Housing and Local Govt, 1966-67; Parly Sec., ODM, 1969-70. Member: UN Human Rights Sub-Commn, 1975- (Vice-Chm., 1979); Goodman Cttee on Charity Law Reform, 1974-76; UK Nat. Commn for UNESCO, 1978-; Chairman: UN Working Gp on Slavery, 1976-78; Defence of Literature and Arts Soc., 1976-; City Poverty Cttee, 1971-. FRSA. *Publications:* The Police, 1964; (ed) A Radical Future, 1967; Crime and Society, 1967; Participation and Poverty, 1968; Parks for People, 1971; (ed) The Fourth World, 1972; The Foundations, 1974; The Police in Society, 1979; (contrib.) Human Rights and American Foreign Policy, 1979; UN Report on Slavery, 1982; Gen. Editor, Sources for Contemporary Issues series (7 vols), 1973-75. *Address:* 13 Elsworthy Road, NW3.
See also Sir James Whitaker, Bt.

WHITAKER, David Haddon; Editorial Director, since 1980 and Chairman, since 1982, J. Whitaker & Sons, Ltd; *b* 6 March 1931; *s* of late Edgar Haddon Whitaker, OBE and of Mollie Marian, *y d* of George and Louisa Seely; *m* 1st, 1959, Veronica Wallace (decd); two *s* two *d*; 2nd, 1976, Audrey Miller (marr. diss.). *Educ:* Marlborough; St John's Coll., Cambridge. Joined family firm of publishers, J. Whitaker & Sons, Ltd, 1955; Dir, 1966; Editor, The Bookseller, 1977-79. *Recreations:* reading, walking. *Address:* 30 Jenner House, Hunter Street, WC1. *T:* 01-837 8109. *Clubs:* Garrick, Thames Rowing; Leander (Henley-on-Thames).

WHITAKER, Frank Howard, CMG 1969; OBE 1946; Secretary of the Metrication Board, 1969-74; *b* 9 Jan. 1909; *er s* of late Frank Harold Whitaker and late Edith Whitaker, Bradford; *m* 1937, Marjorie Firth; no *c*. *Educ:* Thornton Grammar Sch.; Leeds University. LLB (1st cl. hons) 1929; Solicitor (1st cl. hons, D. Reardon and Wakefield and Bradford Prizeman), 1931. Legal Practice until 1939. Royal Air Force, 1940-46 (Sqdn Leader). Entered Civil Service as Principal, Board of Trade, 1946; Asst Sec., 1955; Export Credits Guarantee Dept, 1957, Under-Secretary, 1966. *Recreation:* mountaineering. *Address:* Tavistock, The Rowans, Gerrards Cross, Bucks.

WHITAKER, Sir James Herbert Ingham, 3rd Bt, *cr* 1936; Vice-Chairman, Halifax Building Society, since 1973, Chairman, London Advisory Board, since 1974; *b* 27 July 1925; *s* of late Maj.-Gen. Sir John Whitaker, 2nd Bt, CB, CBE, and Lady Whitaker (*née* Snowden); *S* father 1957; *m* 1948, Mary Elisabeth Lander Urling Clark (*née* Johnston), *widow* of Captain D. Urling Clark, MC; one *s* one *d*. *Educ:* Eton. Coldstream Guards, 1944. Served in North West Europe. Retired, 1947. Chm., The Moorside Trust; Chm., Governing Body, Atlantic College. High Sheriff of Notts, 1969-70. *Recreation:* shooting. *Heir:* s John James Ingham Whitaker, BSc, ACA [*b* 23 October 1952; *m* 1981, Janey, *d* of L. J. R. Starke, New Zealand]. *Address:* Babworth Hall, Retford, Notts. *T:* Retford 703454; Auchnafree, Dunkeld, Perthshire. *Club:* Boodle's.
See also B. C. G. Whitaker.

WHITAKER, Thomas Kenneth; Chancellor, National University of Ireland, since 1976; Member, Seanad Eireann (Irish Senate), 1977-82; *b* 8 Dec. 1916; *s* of Edward Whitaker and Jane O'Connor; *m* 1941, Nora Fogarty; five *s* one *d*. *Educ:* Christian Brothers' Sch., Drogheda; London Univ. (External Student; BScEcon, MScEcon). Irish CS, 1934-69 (Sec., Dept of Finance, 1956-69); Governor, Central Bank of Ireland, 1969-76; Dir, Bank of Ireland, 1976-. Dir, Arthur Guinness Son & Co. Ltd, 1976-. Chairman: Bord na Gaeilge, 1975-78; Agency for Personal Service Overseas, 1973-78. Pres., Econ. and Social Res. Inst.; Chm. Council, Dublin Inst. for Advanced Studies. MRIA. Hon. DEconSc National Univ. of Ireland, 1962; Hon. LLD: Univ. of Dublin, 1976; Queen's Univ. of Belfast, 1980. Commandeur de la Légion d'Honneur, France, 1976. *Publications:* Financing by Credit Creation, 1947; Economic Development, 1958. *Recreations:* fishing, golf, music. *Address:* 148 Stillorgan Road, Donnybrook, Dublin 4, Ireland. *T:* Dublin 693474.

WHITBREAD, Major Simon; Lord-Lieutenant and Custos Rotulorum for Bedfordshire, 1957-78; *b* 12 Oct. 1904; *s* of late Samuel Howard Whitbread, CB, JP, Southill, Biggleswade, Beds; *m* 1936, Helen Beatrice Margaret, *d* of Hon. Robert Trefusis, 27 Coleherne Court, SW7; one *s* one *d*. *Educ:* Eton; Trinity College, Cambridge. Joined KRRC, 1925; Captain, 1937; retired, 1937. Re-employed War of 1939-45, served in Africa and Italy (despatches). Dir, Whitbread & Co. Ltd, 1939-80; Gov. and mem. Bd of Management, Middlesex Hosp., 1937-79; Mem., General Nursing Council for England and Wales, 1958-65. DL 1946, JP 1939. County Councillor, 1938, CA 1949, Chm. CC 1967, Beds; High Sheriff of Beds, 1947. Pres., E Anglia TA&AFA, 1973-78. Hon. Col 286 Field Regt RA (TA) (The Hertfordshire and Bedfordshire Yeomanry), 1965-67. KStJ 1977 (OStJ 1941). *Recreations:* shooting and fishing. *Address:* The Mallowry, Riseley, Bedford. *T:* Riseley 248; 31 Egerton Gardens, SW3. *T:* 01-584 1763. *Clubs:* Buck's, MCC.

WHITBREAD, William Henry, TD; MA Cantab; President, Whitbread and Company, Ltd, 1972-79 (Chairman, 1944-71, Managing Director, 1927-68); Chairman, Whitbread Investment Co. Ltd, 1976-77; Vice-President of the Brewers' Society (Chairman, 1952-53); Past-Master, Brewers' Company; Vice-Pres. Inst. of Brewing (Chm. Res. Cttee, 1948-52); *b* 22 Dec. 1900; *s*

of late Henry William Whitbread, Norton Bavant, Wiltshire; *m* 1st, 1927, Ann Joscelyne (*d* 1936), *d* of late Samuel Howard Whitbread, CB, Southill, Beds; two *s* one *d*; 2nd, 1941, Betty Parr, *d* of Samuel Russell, ICS; one *s* two *d*. *Educ:* Eton; Corpus Christi College, Cambridge. Lovat Scouts, 1920-41; served War of 1939-45: Lovat Scouts, 1939-41; Reconnaissance Corps, 1941-45; Parachutist. Chm. Parliamentary Cttee, Brewers' Society, 1948-52. Director: Barclays Bank Ltd, 1958-73; Eagle Star Insurance Co., 1958-74. Member Governing Body Aldenham School, 1929-61 (Chairman, 1948-58). President: BSJA, 1966-68; Shire Horse Soc., 1971-72; Member: National Hunt Committee, 1956-68; Jockey Club, 1968-; Hurlingham Club Polo Committee, 1932-45; Master, Trinity Foot Beagles, 1921-23. *Recreations:* shooting, fishing and sailing. *Address:* Hazelhurst, Bunch Lane, Haslemere, Surrey; Letterewe, Ross-shire; Farleaze, Near Malmesbury, Wilts. *Clubs:* Brooks's, Pratt's, Royal Thames Yacht; Royal Yacht Squadron.
See also Sir H. T. Tollemache, Bt.

WHITBY, Bishop Suffragan of, since 1976; **Rt. Rev. Clifford Conder Barker,** TD 1970; *b* 22 April 1926; *s* of Sidney and Kathleen Alice Barker; *m* 1952, Marie Edwards (*d* 1982); one *s* two *d*. *Educ:* Oriel Coll., Oxford (BA 1950, MA 1955); St Chad's Coll., Durham (Dip. in Theol. 1952). Emergency Commn, The Green Howards, 1944-48; deacon 1952, priest 1953; Curate: All Saints', Scarborough, 1952-55; Redcar, 1955-57; Vicar: All Saints', Sculcoates, Hull, 1957-63; Rudby-in-Cleveland, 1963-70; RD of Stokesley, 1965-70; Vicar, St Olave with St Giles, York, 1970-76; RD of York, 1971-76; Canon of York, 1973-76. CF (TA), 1958-74. *Recreations:* golf, gardening, music. *Address:* 60 West Green, Stokesley, Middlesbrough, Cleveland TS9 5BD. *T:* Stokesley 710390.

WHITBY, Charles Harley, QC 1970; a Recorder of the Crown Court, Western Circuit, since 1972; *b* 2 April 1926; *s* of Arthur William Whitby and late Florence Whitby; *m* 1981, Eileen Scott. *Educ:* St John's, Leatherhead; Peterhouse, Cambridge. Open Schol., Peterhouse, 1943; served RAFVR, 1944-48; BA (History) 1st cl. 1949, MA 1951. Called to Bar, Middle Temple, 1952; Bencher, 1977; Mem. Bar Council, 1969-71, 1972-78. Mem., Criminal Injuries Compensation Bd, 1975-. Mem. Council, St John's Sch., Leatherhead. *Publications:* contrib. to Master and Servant in Halsbury's Laws of England, 3rd edn, Vol. 25, 1959 and Master and Servant in Atkin's Encyclopaedia of Court Forms, 2nd edn, Vol. 25, 1962. *Recreations:* golf, swimming, theatre, cinema. *Address:* 12 King's Bench Walk, Temple, EC4. *T:* 01-583 0811. *Clubs:* United Oxford & Cambridge University, Royal Automobile, Garrick.

WHITBY, Harry, CB 1965; Government-appointed Member, Potato Marketing Board, 1972-79; *b* 19 June 1910; *er s* of Edward Whitby, Hatfield, Herts, and Sarah Alice (*née* Booth); *m* 1937, Ruby Josephine, *yr d* of Charles J. Dyer, East Runton, Norfolk; two *s* two *d*. *Educ:* Ardingly College, Sussex; University of Manitoba. Student Asst, Agricultural Economics Research Institute, Univ. of Oxford, 1933-36; Asst to Advisory Officer in Agricultural Economics, Dept of Agriculture, Univ. of Leeds, 1936-38; Economist, Min. of Agriculture and Fisheries, 1938-47; Adviser on Farm Economics, 1947-50, Asst Sec. 1950-58, Under-Sec., 1958-68, Sec., 1968-71, Dept of Agriculture and Fisheries for Scotland. *Recreations:* gardening, cricket. *Address:* Cutlers Cottage, East Runton, Cromer, Norfolk.

WHITBY, Mrs Joy; Head of Children's Programmes, Yorkshire TV, since 1976; Director, Board of Channel 4, since 1980; *b* 27 July 1930; *d* of James and Esther Field; *m* 1954, Anthony Charles Whitby (*d* 1975); three *s*. *Educ:* St Anne's Coll., Oxford (BA Hons History). Schools Producer, BBC Radio, 1956-62; moved to BBC Television as Children's Producer, 1962-67; created Play School and Jackanory; Executive Producer, Children's Programmes, London Weekend Television, responsible for Catweazle, 1967-70; freelance producer and writer, 1970-76: work during this period incl. Grasshopper Island (film series for television, and novel, 1971); also children's book reviews for The Times. Responsible for television award-winning series The Book Tower; Eleanor Farjeon Award for Services to Children's Books, 1979. *Publications:* Grasshopper Island, 1971; articles on different aspects of children's television in The Spectator, The Listener, School Bookshop, The New Era. *Recreations:* books, theatre, gardening.

WHITBY, Professor Lionel Gordon, FRSE, FRCP, FRCPE, FRCPath; Professor of Clinical Chemistry, since 1963, Vice-Principal, since 1979, University of Edinburgh; *b* 18 July 1926; *s* of late Sir Lionel Whitby, CVO, MC, MD, FRCP, Regius Prof. of Physic and Master of Downing Coll., Cambridge; *m* 1949, Joan Hunter Sanderson; one *s* two *d*. *Educ:* Eton; King's Coll., Cambridge; Middlesex Hosp. MA, PhD, MD, BChir. Fellow of King's College, Cambridge, 1951-55; W. A. Meek Schol., Univ. of Cambridge, 1951; Murchison Schol., RCP, 1958; Rockefeller Trav. Res. Fellow, Nat. Insts of Health Bethesda, Md, USA, 1959. Registrar and Asst Lectr in Chem. Path., Hammersmith Hosp. and Postgrad. Med. Sch. of London, 1958-60; Univ. Biochemist to Addenbrooke's Hosp., 1960-63, and Fellow of Peterhouse, 1961-62, Cambridge; Dean of Faculty of Medicine, Univ. of Edinburgh, 1969-72; Curator of Patronage, Univ. of Edinburgh, 1978-. Member: Scientific Services Adv. Gp, SHHD, 1975-77; Laboratory Develt Adv. Group, DHSS, 1972-76; Screening Sub-Cttee of Standing Medical Adv. Cttee, 1975-81; Training Cttee RCPath, 1977-79. Guest Lectr, Amer. Chem. Soc., 1966; Vis. Prof. of Chemical Pathology, RPMS, 1974. Examr for RCPath and Univ. of London. *Publications:* (ed jointly) Principles and Practice of Medical Computing, 1971; (jointly) Lecture Notes on Clinical Chemistry, 1975, 2nd edn 1980; (jtly) Multiple Choice Questions on Clinical Chemistry,

1981; scientific papers on flavinglucosides, catecholamines and metabolites, several aspects of clin. chem., and early detection of disease by chemical tests. *Recreations:* gardening, photography. *Address:* 51 Dick Place, Edinburgh EH9 2JA. *T:* 031-667 4358; The Royal Infirmary, Edinburgh. *T:* 031-229 2477, ext. 2319.

WHITCOMBE, Maj.-Gen. Philip Sidney, CB 1944; OBE 1941; JP; *b* 3 Oct. 1893; *e s* of late Rt Rev. Robert Henry Whitcombe, DD, Bishop of Colchester; *m* 1919, Madeline Leila Brydges (*d* 1977), *d* of Canon Arthur Symonds, Over Tabley, Knutsford; two *s. Educ:* Winchester. Gazetted to ASC from Durham LI (Spec. Res.), June 1914; served with BEF in France and Flanders, Aug. 1914–18; DAD Transport, 1918–19; psc 1926; Bde Major, Madras, 1928–32; Bt Major, 1933; DAAG, N Comd, York, 1934–36; GSO 2 War Office, 1936–38; Bt Lt-Col 1939; served in France as ADS and T 1939–40 (despatches); AA and QMG 1940–41 (OBE); Gibraltar, Brig. i/c Admin., 1941–42; Col 1942; DA and QMG, BTNI, 1942–43; MGA Eastern Command, 1943–47; retired, 1947. JP for Wilts, 1948. *Recreations:* cricket, fishing. Played cricket for Essex, 1922, the Army, 1925, and Berkshire, 1925–32. *Address:* The Grange, Lake, Amesbury, Wilts. *T:* Amesbury 23175. *Clubs:* Army and Navy, MCC.

WHITE, family name of **Baron Annaly** and **Baroness White.**

WHITE, Baroness *cr* 1970 (Life Peer), of Rhymney, Monmouth; **Eirene Lloyd White;** Chairman, Select Committee on European Communities, and Principal Deputy Chairman of Committees, House of Lords, 1979–82; *b* 7 Nov. 1909; *d* of late Dr Thomas Jones, CH; *m* 1948, John Cameron White (*d* 1968). *Educ:* St Paul's Girls' Sch.; Somerville Coll., Oxford. Ministry of Labour officer, 1933–37 and 1941–45; Political Correspondent, Manchester Evening News, 1945–49; contested (Lab) Flintshire, 1945; MP (Lab) East Flint, 1950–70. Nat. Exec. Cttee of the Labour Party, 1947–53, 1958–72, Chm. 1968–69; Parly Secretary, Colonial Office, 1964–66; Minister of State for Foreign Affairs, 1966–67; Minister of State, Welsh Office, 1967–70. Mem., Royal Commn on Environmental Pollution, 1974–81. Governor: National Library of Wales; Brit. Film Inst. and National Film Theatre, 1959–64; Indep. Mem. Cinematograph Films Council, 1946–64. Chairman, Fabian Society, 1958–59; President: Nursery School Assoc., 1964–66; Nat. Council of Women (Wales); Council for Protection of Rural Wales; Lord President's nominee, Court of UCW, Aberystwyth and of UCNW, Bangor; Member: UGC, 1977–80; Council, UWIST, Cardiff, 1981–; Chairman: Internat. Cttee, Nat. Council of Social Service, 1973–77; Coleg Harlech; Adv. Cttee on Oil Pollution at sea, 1974–78; Land Authority for Wales, 1975–80; Dep. Chm., Metrication Bd, 1972–76; Vice-Pres.: Commonwealth Countries League; Commonwealth Youth Exchange Council, 1976–79. Hon. Fellow, Somerville College, Oxford, 1966. Hon. LLD: Wales, 1979; Queen's Univ., Belfast, 1981. *Address:* 36 Westminster Gardens, Marsham Street, SW1. *T:* 01-828 3320; Panteg, Ceinws, Machynlleth, Powys SY20 9HE. *T:* Corris 679. *Club:* Royal Commonwealth Society.

WHITE, Adrian N. S.; *see* Sherwin-White.

WHITE, Alan, OBE 1973; HM Diplomatic Service; Counsellor and Head of Chancery, Kuala Lumpur, since 1980; *b* 13 Aug. 1930; *s* of William White and Ida (*née* Hall); *m* 1st, 1954, Cynthia Maidwell; two *s* one *d* ; 2nd, 1980, Clare Corley Smith. WO, 1950; Germany, 1954–57; Hong Kong, 1959–63; MoD (Central), 1965; First Sec., FO (later FCO), 1966; Mexico City, 1969; First Sec., UK Disarmament Delegn, Geneva, 1974; Counsellor (Commercial), Madrid, 1976. *Recreations:* mountaineering, travel. *Address:* c/o Foreign and Commonwealth Office, SW1; c/o British High Commission, Kuala Lumpur, Malaysia. *Club:* Royal Automobile.

WHITE, Prof. Alan Richard, BA, PhD; Ferens Professor of Philosophy in the University of Hull, since 1961; *b* Toronto, Canada, 9 Oct. 1922; *s* of late George Albert White and Jean Gabriel White; *m* 1st, 1948, Eileen Anne Jarvis; one *s* two *d* ; 2nd, 1979, Enid Elizabeth Alderson. *Educ:* Midleton College and Presentation College, Cork; Trinity College, Dublin. Dublin: Schol. and 1st class Moderator in Classics, 1st class Moderator in Mental and Moral Science; Boxing Pink; President of the 'Phil'; Univ. Student in Classics and Dep. Lecturer in Logic, 1945–46; Asst Lecturer, Lecturer, Sen. Lecturer in Philosophy, Univ. of Hull, 1946–61; Visiting Professor: Univ. of Maryland, 1967–68, 1980; Temple Univ., 1974; Secretary, Mind Assoc., 1960–69, Pres., 1972. Pres., Aristotelian Soc., 1979–80. 42nd Dublin Rifles (LDF), 1941–45. *Publications:* G. E. Moore: A Critical Exposition, 1958; Attention, 1964; The Philosophy of Mind, 1967; (ed) The Philosophy of Action, 1968; Truth, 1970; Modal Thinking, 1975; The Nature of Knowledge, 1982; articles in philosophical journals. *Recreations:* dilettantism and odd-jobbery. *Address:* The University, Hull HU6 7RX. *T:* Hull 46311.

WHITE, Hon. Sir Alfred (John), Kt 1971; Tasmanian Agent-General in London, 1959-71; *b* 2 Feb. 1902; British; *m* 1939, Veronica Louisa Punch; two *s* two *d.* Elected to Tasmanian Parliament, 1941; Minister for Health and Chief Secretary, 1946–48, then Chief Secretary and Minister for Labour and Industry, Shipping and Emergency Supplies until Jan. 1959. JP since 1934, and Territorial JP for the State of Tasmania in London, 1959. Appointed Agent-General for Tasmania in London for period of 3 years, Jan. 1959, re-appointed for a further period of 3 years, Jan. 1962; re-appointed 1967; re-appointed 1970; resigned 1971 and retired. Granted title of "Honourable"

for life. *Recreations:* ski-ing, gardening, bowls and fishing. *Address:* 6 Clarke Avenue, Battery Point, Hobart, Tasmania 7000, Australia.

WHITE, Arthur John Stanley, CMG 1947; OBE 1932; *b* 28 Aug. 1896; *s* of A. R. White, DL, OBE, and of Minnie B. White, OBE (*née* Beauchamp); *m* 1932, Joan, *d* of R. O. Davies and *niece* of Lord Waring; four *s* one *d. Educ:* Marlborough College; Clare College, Cambridge (Scholar), MA 1930. Served European War, Wiltshire Regt, 1915–20, France and Ireland; Indian Civil Service, Burma, 1922; Under-Secretary, Home and Political Dept, 1924; Deputy Commissioner, 1928 (Burma Rebellion 1931-32, OBE); Secretary to Government of Burma, 1934; appointed to British Council as Dep. Sec.-Gen., 1937, Sec.-Gen. 1940–47, Controller, 1947–62. Retired 1962. Director, OPOS (Office for placing overseas boys and girls in British Schs), 1964–67. *Recreations:* hockey (International Trials, 1921 and 1922), cricket, tennis, shooting. *Address:* The Red House, Mere, Warminster, Wilts. *T:* Mere 860551. *Club:* East India, Devonshire, Sports and Public Schools.

WHITE, Arthur W.; *see* Walmesley White.

WHITE, Rev. Barrington Raymond; Principal, Regent's Park College, Oxford, since 1972; *b* 28 Jan. 1934; *s* of Raymond Gerard and Lucy Mildred White; *m* 1957, Margaret Muriel Hooper; two *d. Educ:* Chislehurst and Sidcup Grammar Sch.; Queens' Coll., Cambridge (BA Theol, MA); Regent's Park Coll., Oxford (DPhil). Ordained, 1959; Minister, Andover Baptist Church, 1959–63; Lectr in Ecclesiastical History, Regent's Park Coll., Oxford, 1963–72. First Breman Prof. of Social Relations, Univ. of N Carolina at Asheville, 1976. FRHistS 1973. *Publications:* The English Separatist Tradition, 1971; Association Records of the Particular Baptists to 1660, Part I, 1971, Part II, 1973, Part III, 1974; Authority: a Baptist view, 1976; Hanserd Knollys and Radical Dissent, 1977; contrib. Reformation, Conformity and Dissent, ed R. Buick Knox, 1977; The English Puritan Tradition, 1980; contribs to Baptist Qly, Jl of Theological Studies, Jl of Ecclesiastical History, Welsh Baptist Studies. *Recreation:* recorded music. *Address:* The Principal's Lodging, Regent's Park College, Oxford. *T:* Oxford 56093.

WHITE, Sir Bruce Gordon, KBE 1944 (CBE 1943; MBE 1919); FCGI; FICE; FIMechE; FIEE; Senior Partner, Sir Bruce White, Wolfe Barry & Partners, Chartered Civil and Consulting Engineers; *b* 5 Feb. 1885; *m* 1912, Margery Gertrude (*d* 1965), *d* of C. W. Hodson, CSI; one *s* one *d. Educ:* Marlborough. Served European War, 1914–18 (MBE); War of 1939-45 as Brig. Director of Ports and IWT, War Office (KBE). *Address:* Reydon, Midway, Walton-on-Thames, Surrey.

WHITE, Bryan Oliver; HM Diplomatic Service; Head of Mexico and Central America Department, Foreign and Commonwealth Office, since 1982; *b* 3 Oct. 1929; *s* of Thomas Frederick White and Olive May Turvey; *m* 1958, Helen McLeod Jenkins; one *s* two *d. Educ:* The Perse Sch.; Wadham Coll., Oxford (Lit.Hum.). HM Forces, 1948–49; FO, 1953; Kabul, Vienna, Conakry, Rio de Janeiro, the Cabinet Office, and Havana, 1953–79; Counsellor, Paris, 1980–82. *Recreation:* the Romance languages. *Address:* c/o Foreign and Commonwealth Office, SW1.

WHITE, Byron R(aymond); Associate Justice of the Supreme Court of the United States since 1962; *b* Fort Collins, Colorado, 8 June 1917; *s* of Alpha White, Wellington, Colorado; *m* 1946, Marion Lloyd Stearns, *d* of Dr Robert L. Stearns; one *s* one *d. Educ:* Wellington High Sch.; Univ. of Colorado; Oxford Univ. (Rhodes Scholar); Yale Univ. Law Sch (before and after War). Served War of 1939-45: USNR, Naval Intell., Pacific (two Bronze Stars). Law Clerk to Chief Justice of the United States, 1946–47; law practice in Denver, Colorado, 1947-60, with firm of Lewis, Grant, Newton, Davis and Henry (later Lewis, Grant and Davis). Dep. Attorney-Gen., 1961–62. Phi Beta Kappa, Phi Gamma Delta. As a Democrat, he was a prominent supporter of John F. Kennedy in the Presidential campaign of 1960. *Recreations:* ski-ing, paddle tennis, fishing. *Address:* US Supreme Court, 1 First Street NE, Washington, DC 20543, USA.

WHITE, Maj.-Gen. Cecil Meadows Frith, CB 1945; CBE 1943 (OBE 1941); DSO 1940; late Royal Signals; retired; Colonel Commandant, Royal Corps of Signals, 1950-60; *b* 29 Aug. 1897; *s* of late Herbert Meadows Frith White and late Annie Laura Borrett; *m* 1925, Elizabeth Rennie Robertson; one *d. Educ:* Eton College; RMA, Woolwich. Commissioned RFA 1915; served 1915–19 in Egypt, Serbia, Greece, and Palestine (despatches); transferred to Royal Signals, 1925; Brigade Major Signal Training Centre, 1934–36; Lt-Col 1939; served War of 1939-45 (despatches five times, DSO, OBE, CBE, CB); commanded 4th Indian Divisional Signals in Wavell's advance in Western Desert, 1940; CSO East Africa during East Africa Campaign, 1941; CSO 8th Army, 1941; Temp. Brig. 1941; Col 1943; acting Maj.-Gen. Jan. 1944 as SO in C 21 Army Group; Temp. Maj.-Gen. 1945; Maj.-Gen. 1949; CSO, GHQ, MELF, Nov. 1945–July 1949; GOC Catterick District, 1949-51; retired, 1951. Deputy Controller, Civil Defence, Southdown Group, 1958. Civil Defence Officer, County Borough of Brighton, 1960–65. *Recreations:* fishing, gardening; formerly polo and rugger, show-jumping, hunting, sailing. *Address:* Hansdown House, Maesbury, Wells, Somerset BA5 3HA. *TA* and *T:* Oakhill 840498.

WHITE, Prof. Cedric Masey, DSc(Eng.), PhD; Professor Emeritus, University of London, 1966; Consultant for River and Coastal projects; *b* 19 Oct. 1898; *s* of Joseph Masey White, Nottingham; *m* 1921, Dorothy F.

Lowe; 2nd, 1946, Josephine M. Ramage; one d. *Educ:* privately; University College, Nottingham. Served European War, in Tank Corps, 1917-19. Lecturer in Civil Engineering, Univ. of London, King's Coll., 1927-33; Reader in Civil Engineering, and Asst Prof. in Imperial Coll. of Science and Technology, 1933-45; Responsible for work of Hawksley Hydraulic Lab., 1933-66; Professor of Fluid Mechanics and Hydraulic Engineering, 1946-66. Completed various investigations for Admiralty, WO, MAP, etc, during War of 1939-45, and investigations of proposed river-structures for Hydro-Power here and abroad, 1946-56. Founder Member, Hydraulic Research Bd, 1946-51, 1959-67; sometime member of Research Committees of Instn of Civil Engineers; delegation on Hydrology to Internat. Union of Geodesy and Geophysics, 1939, 1948, 1951; Member: Council of British Hydromechanics Research Assoc., 1949-59; Internat. Assoc. for Hydraulic Research, 1947-59. Hon. ACGI, 1951. *Publications:* various engineering reports and scientific papers, chiefly on the motion of air and water. *Address:* 8 Orchard Close, East Budleigh, Devon. *T:* Budleigh Salterton 3559.

WHITE, Christopher John, PhD; Director of Studies, Paul Mellon Centre for Studies in British Art, since 1973, and Associate Director, Yale Center for British Art, New Haven, since 1976; Adjunct Professor of History of Art, Yale University, since 1977; *b* 19 Sept. 1930; *s* of Gabriel Ernest Edward Francis White, *qv; m* 1957, Rosemary Katharine Desages; one *s* two *d. Educ:* Downside Sch.; Courtauld Institute of Art, London Univ. BA (Hons) 1954, PhD 1970. Served Army, 1949-50; commnd, RA, 1949. Asst Keeper, Dept of Prints and Drawings, British Museum, 1954-65; Director, P. and D. Colnaghi, 1965-71; Curator of Graphic Arts, Nat. Gall. of Art, Washington, 1971-73. Dutch Govt Schol., 1956; Hermione Lectr, Alexandra Coll., Dublin, 1959; Adjunct Prof., Inst. of Fine Arts, New York Univ., 1973 and 1976; Conference Dir, European-Amer. Assembly on Art Museums, Ditchley Park, 1975; Visiting Prof., Dept of History of Art, Yale Univ., 1976. Reviews Editor, Master Drawings, 1967-80. *Publications:* Rembrandt and his World, 1964; The Flower Drawings of Jan van Huysum, 1965; Rubens and his World, 1968; Rembrandt as an Etcher, 1969; (jtly) Rembrandt's Etchings: a catalogue raisonné, 1970; Dürer: the artist and his drawings, 1972; English Landscape 1630-1850, 1977; The Dutch Paintings in the Collection of HM The Queen, 1982; film (script and commentary), Rembrandt's Three Crosses, 1969; various exhibn catalogues; contribs to Burlington Mag., Master Drawings, etc. *Address:* 14 South Villas, NW1 9BS. *T:* 01-485 9148; Shingle House, St Cross, Harleston, Norfolk IP20 0NT. *T:* St Cross 264; c/o Yale Center for British Art, Box 2120 Yale Station, New Haven, Conn 06520, USA.

WHITE, Sir Christopher (Robert Meadows), 3rd Bt *cr* 1937, of Boulge Hall, Suffolk; *b* 26 Aug. 1940; *s* of Sir (Eric) Richard Meadows White, 2nd Bt, and Lady Elizabeth Mary Gladys (*d* 1950), *o d* of 6th Marquess Townshend; *S* father, 1972; *m* 1st, 1962, Anne Marie Ghislaine (marr. diss. 1968), *yr d* of Major Tom Brown, OBE; 2nd, 1968, Dinah Mary Sutton (marr. diss. 1972), Orange House, Heacham, Norfolk; 3rd, 1976, Ingrid Carolyn Jowett, *e d* of Eric Jowett, Great Baddow; two step *s. Educ:* Bradfield Coll., Berks. Imperial Russian Ballet School, Cannes, France, 1961; schoolmaster, 1961-72; Professore, Istituto Shenker, Rome, and Scuola Specialisti Aeronauta, Macerata, 1962-63; Housemaster, St Michael's Sch., Ingoldisthorpe, Norfolk, 1963-69. Hon. Pres., Warnborough House, Oxford, 1973-. Lieutenant, TA, Norfolk, 1969. *Recreations:* dogs, vintage cars, antiques.

WHITE, Christopher Stuart Stuart-; *see* Stuart-White.

WHITE, David Harry; Group Managing Director: British Road Services Ltd, since 1976; Pickfords, since 1982; Director: National Freight Consortium; Freightliners Ltd; *b* 12 Oct. 1929; *s* of late Harry White, OBE, FCA, and Kathleen White; *m* 1971, Valerie Jeanne White; one *s* four *d. Educ:* Nottingham High Sch.; HMS Conway. Master Mariner's F. G. Certificate. Sea career, apprentice to Master Mariner, 1946-56; Terminal Manager, Texaco (UK) Ltd, 1956-64; Operations Manager, Gulf Oil (GB) Ltd, 1964-68; Asst Man. Dir, Samuel Williams Dagenham, 1968-70; Trainee to Gp Managing Director, British Road Services Ltd, 1970-76. FCIT; CBIM. *Recreations:* football supporter (Forest), walking. *Address:* Welton House, 15 Magdala Road, Mapperley Park, Nottingham NG3 5DE. *T:* Nottingham 608935. *Club:* Royal Automobile.

WHITE, Sir Dennis (Charles), KBE 1962 (OBE 1953); CMG 1959; Brunei Government Agent in the United Kingdom, since 1967; *b* 30 July 1910; unmarried. *Educ:* Bradfield College. Joined service of HH the Rajah of Sarawak, 1932. Civilian Prisoner of War, Dec. 1941-Sept. 1945. HM Overseas Civil Service: Senior Resident, 1955; British Resident, Brunei, 1958; HM High Comr for Brunei, 1959-63. Star of Sarawak (Officer) 1946. Esteemed Family Order of Brunei, 1st Class. *Recreations:* general. *Address:* Virginia Cottage, Emery Down, Lyndhurst, Hants. *Club:* Travellers'.

WHITE, Sir Dick (Goldsmith), KCMG 1960; KBE 1955 (CBE 1950; OBE 1942); formerly attached to Foreign and Commonwealth Office, retired 1972; *b* 20 Dec. 1906; *s* of Percy Hall White and Gertrude White (*née* Farthing); *m* 1945, Kathleen Bellamy; two *s. Educ:* Bishops Stortford Coll.; Christ Church, Oxford (Hon. Student, 1981); Universities of Michigan and California, USA. US Legion of Merit, Croix de Guerre (France). *Address:* The Leat, Burpham, near Arundel, West Sussex. *Club:* Garrick.
See also J. A. White.

WHITE, Edward George, OBE 1976; HM Diplomatic Service, retired; Chairman, Systemscribe Ltd, since 1979; *b* 30 June 1923; *s* of late George Johnson White, OBE, ISO, and Edith Birch; *m* 1st, 1945, Sylvia Shears; two *d* ; 2nd, 1966, Veronica Pauline (*née* Crosling). *Educ:* Bec Secondary Sch., London SW; London Univ. Served RAF, 1941-47. Various consular and diplomatic appts in Guatemala, USA, Madagascar, Burma, Thailand and India; Dep. Head of Finance Dept, FCO, 1976-78; Counsellor (Admin), Bonn, 1978-79. *Recreation:* fell walking. *Address:* 25 Edinburgh Way, East Grinstead, W Sussex RH19 4RT. *T:* East Grinstead 314375.

WHITE, Prof. Edwin George, PhD, DSc, BSc (Vet. Sci.), BSc (Physiol.), FRCVS; William Prescott Professor of Veterinary Preventive Medicine, University of Liverpool, 1950-76, now Emeritus; Pro-Vice-Chancellor, 1966-70; *b* 26 March 1911; *s* of Edwin White and Alice Maud White; *m* 1st, 1936, Grace Mary Adlington; two *d* ; 2nd, 1974, Winefred Wright. *Educ:* Newport (Mon.) High School; Royal Veterinary College, London (Kitchener Scholarship); University College, London. Studentship for Research in Animal Health, 1933-35, for postgraduate study in Germany and England; Lecturer in Pathology, Royal Veterinary College, London, 1935; Reader in Pathology, 1939; Principal Scientific Officer, Rowett Research Inst., Bucksburn, Aberdeenshire, 1946; Director of East African Veterinary Research Organisation, 1947-49; Dean of Faculty of Vet. Sci., Univ. of Liverpool, 1961-65. Pres., RCVS, 1967-68. Chm., Granada Schs Adv. Cttee. Chm. Governors, Birkenhead High Sch. *Publications:* articles in various scientific journals since 1934. *Recreation:* gardening. *Address:* Afton, Neston Road, Burton, South Wirral, Cheshire L64 5SY. *T:* 051-336 4210. *Club:* Royal Commonwealth Society.

WHITE, Elwyn Brooks; Contributor to The New Yorker; *b* 11 July 1899; *s* of Samuel T. White and Jessie Hart; *m* 1929, Katharine Sergeant Angell; one *s. Educ:* Cornell University, USA. Newspaper reporting, advertising, and editorial work as staff member of New Yorker Magazine, to which he has contributed verse, satirical essays, and editorials; wrote a monthly department for Harper's Magazine called One Man's Meat, 1938-43. Hon. degrees: Dartmouth Coll.; Univs of Maine, Yale, Bowdoin, Hamilton, Harvard, Colby. Fellow, Amer. Acad. of Arts and Sciences; Mem., AAAL, 1974. Gold Medal Nat. Inst. of Arts and Letters, 1960; Presidential Medal of Freedom, 1963; Laura Ingalls Wilder Award, 1970; Nat. Medal for Literature, 1971; Pulitzer Special Citation, 1978. *Publications:* The Lady is Cold, 1929; (with J. Thurber) Is Sex Necessary, 1929; Every Day is Saturday, 1934; The Fox of Peapack, 1938; Quo Vadimus?, 1939; One Man's Meat, 1942 (enlarged) 1944; Stuart Little, 1945; The Wild Flag, 1946; Here Is New York, 1949; Charlotte's Web, 1952; The Second Tree from the Corner, 1954; The Points of My Compass, 1962; The Trumpet of the Swan, 1970; Letters of E. B. White, 1976; Essays of E. B. White, 1977; Poems and Sketches of E. B. White, 1981; (ed, with Katharine S. White) A Subtreasury of American Humor, 1941; rev. and enl. Strunk, The Elements of Style, 1959. *Address:* North Brooklin, Maine, USA. *TA:* care The New Yorker Magazine, 25 W.43.

WHITE, Erica, FRBS (retired); Sculptor and Painter; *d* of Frederic Charles White, solicitor and Mildred S. Hutchings. *Educ:* St George's School, Harpenden; Slade School of Art (Sculpture Scholarship two years and Painting Prize); gained London University Diploma in Fine Arts; studied at Central School of Arts and Crafts; gained British Institution Scholarship in Sculpture; studied at Royal Acad. Schools (Silver and Bronze Medallist); awarded Feodora Gleichen Memorial Fund Grant; exhibited at Royal Academy and at Glasgow, Brighton, Bournemouth and other Art Galleries. *Recreations:* outdoor sports and music. *Address:* South Cliff Cottage, 3 South Cliff, Bexhill-on-Sea, Sussex TN39 3EJ. *T:* Bexhill 211013.

WHITE, Sir Ernest (Keith), Kt 1969; CBE 1967; MC; Chairman, R. J. White & Co. (Sydney) Pty Ltd, since 1935; *b* 1892; *s* of late Robert John White; *m* 1915, Pauline Marjory, *d* of J. J. Mason; one *s* two *d. Educ:* Gosford Public Sch., NSW. Served European War, 1914-18 (Sir Douglas Haig's despatches, MC): Captain 4th Bn AIF, in Egypt and France (Ypres, Somme, Broodsiend Ridge, Bullecourt, Sttrozeel). Pres., Liberal Democratic Party, Australia, 1943; Delegate to Prelim. and Plenary Conf. which founded Liberal Party of Australia, and apptd to Provisional State and Federal Council, 1943. Vice-Pres., Australian American Assoc. (Founder and 1st Federal Pres., 1936). *Address:* Baden House, Baden Road, Kurraba Point, Neutral Bay, NSW 2089, Australia. *T:* 90 5741. *Clubs:* Royal Commonwealth Society; Tattersall's; Australian Jockey; American National.

WHITE, Errol Ivor, CBE 1960; DSc, PhD (London); FRS 1956; FGS, FLS, FKC; Hon. Research Fellow, University of Reading; retired as Keeper of Department of Palæontology (formerly of Geology), British Museum (Natural History), 1955-66 (Deputy Keeper, 1938-55); *b* 1901; *y s* of late Felix E. White and Lilian Daniels; *m* 1st, 1933, Barbara Gladwyn Christian (marr. diss. 1940, she *d* 1969); 2nd, 1944, Margaret Clare (Jane), BCom (Leeds), *y d* of late T. C. Fawcett, Bolton Abbey, Yorks; one *s. Educ:* Highgate School (Senior Foundationer); King's Coll., London Univ. (Tennant Prizeman). BSc 1921; PhD 1927; DSc 1936. Entered British Museum (Natural History), 1922; Geological Expeditions to Madagascar, 1929-30, and Spitsbergen, 1939; temp. Principal, Min. of Health, 1940-April 1945; Hon. Sec. Ray Society, 1946-54, Vice-Pres., 1951-54, 1959-, Pres., 1956-59; Council, Geological Soc., 1949-53, 1956-60; Vice-Pres., 1957-60 (Murchison Medal, 1962); President, Linnean Soc., 1964-67 (Linnean Gold Medal, 1970); Chm. Systematics Assoc., 1955-58; Coun., Zool. Soc., 1959-63. *Publications:* Technical memoirs and papers in various scientific jls, chiefly relating to extinct agnatha and fishes. *Recreations:* ornithology, philately, bridge. *Address:* 19 Clevemede, Goring-on-Thames, Reading RG8 9BU. *T:* Goring-on-Thames 872525.

WHITE, Frank John; His Honour Judge White; a Circuit Judge, since 1974; *b* 12 March 1927; *s* of late Frank Byron White; *m* 1953, Anne Rowlandson, MBE, *d* of late Sir Harold Gibson Howitt, GBE, DSO, MC; two *s* two *d*. *Educ:* Reading Sch.; King's Coll., London. LLB, LLM (London). Sub-Lt, RNVR, 1945-47; called to the Bar, Gray's Inn, 1951; Mem., General Council of the Bar, 1969-73; Dep. Chm., Berkshire QS, 1970-72; a Recorder of the Crown Court, 1972-74. Mem., Lord Chancellor's Adv. Cttee on Legal Aid, 1977-. *Recreation:* photography. *Address:* 8 Queen's Ride, SW13 0JB. *T:* 01-788 8903; Blauvac, Vaucluse, France. *Clubs:* Athenæum, Roehampton.

WHITE, Frank Richard, JP; MP (Lab) Bury and Radcliffe, since Oct. 1974; industrial relations adviser; *b* Nov. 1939; *m* ; three *c*. *Educ:* Bolton Tech. Coll. Member: Bolton CC, 1963-74; Greater Manchester CC, 1973-75. Member: NUGMW; IPM; Inst. of Management Services. Contested (Lab) Bury and Radcliffe, Feb. 1974. PPS to Minister of State, Dept of Industry, 1975-76; Asst Govt Whip, 1976-78; Opposition Whip, 1980-82; opposition spokesman on church affairs, 1980-. Chm., All Party Paper Industry Gp, 1979-; Chm., NW Lab Gp, 1979-. *Address:* House of Commons, SW1A 0AA; 4 Ashdown Drive, Firwood Fold, Bolton, Lancs BL2 3AX.

WHITE, Sir Frederick William George, KBE 1962 (CBE 1954); PhD; FAA 1960; FRS 1966; Chairman, Commonwealth Scientific and Industrial Research Organization, 1959-70 (Deputy Chairman, 1957, Chief Executive Officer, 1949-57); *b* 26 May 1905; *s* of late William Henry White; *m* 1932, Elizabeth Cooper; one *s* one *d*. *Educ:* Wellington College, New Zealand; Victoria University College, Univ. of New Zealand (MSc 1928); Cambridge Univ. (PhD 1932). Postgrad. Schol. in Science, Univ. of NZ and Strathcona Schol., St John's Coll., Cambridge; Research in Physics, Cavendish Laboratory, 1929-31; Asst Lecturer in Physics, Univ. of London, King's Coll., 1931-36; Professor of Physics, Canterbury University Coll., NZ, 1937; Member, British Empire Cancer Campaign Soc., Canterbury Branch Cttee, 1938; Radio Research Cttee, DSIR NZ, 1937; Advisor to NZ Govt on radar research, 1939; seconded to Aust. CSIR, 1941; Chm., Radiophysics Adv. Bd, 1941; Chief, Div. of Radiophysics, 1942. Exec. Officer, 1945, Mem., Exec. Cttee, 1946, CSIR Aust. Radio Research Bd, 1942; Scientific Adv. Cttee, Aust. Atomic Energy Commn, 1953; FInstP; Fellow Aust. Instn of Radio Engrs. Hon. DSc: Monash Univ.; ANU; Univ. of Papua and New Guinea. *Publications:* scientific papers on nature of ionosphere over NZ and on propagation of radio waves; Electromagnetic Waves, 1934. *Recreation:* fishing. *Address:* 57 Investigator Street, Red Hill, Canberra, ACT 2603, Australia. *T:* 957424.

WHITE, Gabriel Ernest Edward Francis, CBE 1963; Director of Art, Arts Council of Great Britain, 1958-70; *b* 29 Nov. 1902; *s* of late Ernest Arthur White and Alice White; *m* 1st, 1928, Elizabeth Grace (*d* 1958), *d* of late Auguste Ardizzone; two *s* ; 2nd, 1963, Jane, *d* of late J. R. Kingdon and of Mrs Kingdon, Minehead; one *s* one *d*. *Educ:* Downside Sch.; Trinity Coll., Oxford. Staff Officer RE Camouflage, 1940-45; Asst Art Director, Arts Council of Great Britain, 1945-58. Order of the Aztec Eagle, 2nd class (Mexico). *Publications:* Sickert Drawings (in Art and Technics), 1952; Ardizzone, 1979. *Recreations:* drawing, painting. *Address:* 88 Holmdene Avenue, SE24. *T:* 01-274 9643.

See also C. J. White.

WHITE, Air Vice-Marshal George Alan, AFC 1973; Deputy Commander, Royal Air Force Germany, since 1982; *b* 11 March 1932; *s* of James Magee White and Evangeline (*née* Henderson); *m* 1955, Mary Esmé (*née* Magowan); two *d*. *Educ:* University of London (LLB). Pilot, 1956; served in RAF Squadrons and OCUs, 1956-64; RAF Staff College, 1964; HQ Middle East Command, 1966-67; 11 Sqn, 1968-70; 5 Sqn, 1970-72. Nat. Defence Coll., 1972-73; in command, RAF Leuchars, 1973-75; Royal Coll. of Defence Studies, 1976; Dir of Ops (Air Defence and Overseas), 1977-78; SASO No 11 Group, 1979-80; Air Cdre Plans, HQ Strike Comd, 1981-82. *Recreations:* sailing, riding, hill walking, music, archaeology, bridge. *Address:* c/o Williams & Glyn's Bank Ltd, Kirkland House, Whitehall, SW1A 2EB. *Club:* Royal Air Force.

WHITE, Sir George (Stanley Midelton), 3rd Bt, *cr* 1904; *b* 11 April 1913; *s* of 2nd Bt and late Kate Muriel, *d* of late Thomas Baker, Bristol; *S* father, 1964; *m* 1939, Diane Eleanor, *d* of late Bernard Abdy Collins, CIE; one *s* one *d*. *Educ:* Harrow; Magdalene College, Cambridge. Member of the firm of George White, Evans, Tribe & Co., Bristol (formerly George White, Evans & Co.). *Heir:* *s* George Stanley James White [*b* 4 November 1948; *m* 1974, Susan Elizabeth, *d* of late John Langmaid Ford; one *d* ; *m* 1979, Mrs Elizabeth J. Clinton (*née* Verdon-Smith)]. *Address:* Pypers, Rudgeway, near Bristol. *T:* Thornbury 412312.

WHITE, Maj.-Gen. Gilbert Anthony, MBE 1944; *b* 10 June 1916; *s* of Cecil James Lawrence White and Muriel (*née* Collins); *m* 1939, Margaret Isabel Duncan Wallet; two *d*. *Educ:* Christ's Hosp., Horsham. Member of Lloyd's, 1938. Joined TA Artists Rifles, 1937; TA Commn, E Surrey Regt, 1939; served BEF, 1940, N Africa, 1943-44, Italy, 1944-45; Staff Coll., 1944; Instructor, Staff Coll., Haifa, 1946; with UK Delegn to UN, 1946-48; served on Lord Mountbatten's personal staff in MoD, 1960-61; idc 1965; BAOR,

1966-69; Chief, Jt Services Liaison Orgn, Bonn, 1969-71; retd 1971. Mem. Council, Guide Dogs for the Blind, 1971-; Hon. Treasurer, S Regional Assoc. for the Blind, 1972-. *Recreations:* golf, racing. *Address:* Speedwell, Tekels Avenue, Camberley, Surrey. *T:* Camberley 23812. *Club:* Army and Navy.

WHITE, Sir Gordon; see White, Sir V. G. L.

WHITE, Harold Clare, MBE 1967; HM Diplomatic Service, retired; Consul-General, Seattle, 1976-79; *b* 26 Oct. 1919; *s* of Alfred John White and Nora White; *m* 1951, Marie Elizabeth Richardson; two *d*. *Educ:* Grammar Sch., Warrington. Served War, Royal Signals, 1939-45. GPO, 1937-39 and 1946; FO, 1947; Third Sec., Djakarta, 1951; FO, 1955; Vice-Consul, Piraeus, Kirkuk, San Francisco, and Durban, 1957-64; 1st Secretary: Kinshasa, 1964; Kuala Lumpur, 1968; FCO, 1972; Dep. Consul-Gen., Chicago, 1974. *Recreations:* cricket, golf. *Address:* 65 The Ridgeway, Tonbridge, Kent TN10 4NL. *T:* Tonbridge 359168. *Club:* Civil Service.

WHITE, Sir Harold (Leslie), Kt 1970; CBE 1962; MA; FLAA; FAHA; FASSA; National Librarian, National Library of Australia, Canberra, 1947-70; *b* Numurkah, Vic, 14 June 1905; *s* of late James White, Canterbury, Vic; *m* 1930, Elizabeth (MBE), *d* of Richard Wilson; two *s* two *d*. *Educ:* Wesley College, Melbourne; Queen's College, University of Melbourne. Commonwealth Parliamentary Library, 1923-67; National and Parliamentary Librarian, 1947-67. Visited US as Carnegie Scholar, 1939, and as first Australian under "Leaders and Specialists programme" of Smith Mundt Act, 1950. Represented Australia at various overseas Conferences, 1939-69. Chairman, Standing Cttee. Aust. Advisory Council on Bibliographical Services, 1960-70; Member: various Aust. cttees for UNESCO; Aust. Nat. Film Bd; UNESCO Internat. Cttee on Bibliography, Documentation and Terminology, 1961-64; Nat. Meml Cttee, 1975-; Chm., Adv. Cttee, Australian Encyclopaedia, 1970-; Governor, Australian Film Inst., 1958-77; Hon. Vice Pres., Library Assoc. of UK, 1970-. *Publications:* (ed) Canberra: A Nation's Capital; contribs to various jls. *Address:* 27 Mugga Way, Canberra, ACT 2603, Australia.

WHITE, Sir Henry Arthur Dalrymple D.; see Dalrymple-White.

WHITE, Air Vice-Marshal Hugh Granville, CB 1952; CBE 1944; CEng; FIMechE; retired; *b* 1 Mar. 1898; *s* of Herbert White, The Poplars, Maidstone, Kent; *m* 1926, Mabel Joyce Hickman; two *s* one *d*. *Educ:* HMS Conway; Eastbourne College; Royal Military College, Sandhurst; Jesus College, Cambridge. Commissioned in East Kent Regt, attached RFC, 1916; served as pilot in France, 1916-18; permanent commission on formation of RAF, 1918; comd Nos 29, 64 and 501 Squadrons; Staff appointments as Technical Officer, Royal Air Force College, Cranwell, 1930-33; HQ Air Defence, Gt Britain, 1933-35; STSO, HQ Far East, 1936-39; SASO No 24 Group, 1939-42; AOC Halton, 1942-46; STSO, HQ, BAFO, Germany, 1946-48; AOC No 43 Group, 1948-50; AOC No 41 Group, 1950-53; AOA HQ Maintenance Cmd, 1953-55; retired 1955. *Recreations:* played rugby for RAF, 1922-23; gardening. *Address:* 30 Hillside, Eastdean, Eastbourne, East Sussex BN20 0HE. *T:* Eastdean 3151. *Club:* Royal Over-Seas League.

WHITE, Prof. James, CEng; Dyson Professor of Refractories Technology, University of Sheffield, 1956-73, now Emeritus; Dean of Faculty of Metallurgy, 1958-62; *b* 1 April 1908; *s* of late John White and Margaret E. White (*née* Laidlaw), Langholm, Dumfriesshire; *m* 1936, Elizabeth Kelly, Glasgow; one *s*. *Educ:* Langholm Acad. (Dux Medallist); Dumfries Acad. (Science Dux); Glasgow University. BSc 1st Cl. Hons Physical Chemistry, 1931; PhD 1935; DSc 1939. DSIR Research Scholarship, Roy. Technical Coll., Glasgow, 1931; Dr James McKenzie Prize for Research, 1933; Research Asst in Metallurgy, Roy. Technical Coll., 1933; Associateship of Roy. Technical Coll., 1934; Lectr in Metallurgy, Roy. Tech. Coll., 1935; Andrew Carnegie Research Scholarship of Iron and Steel Inst., 1936-38; Andrew Carnegie Gold Medallist of Iron and Steel Inst., 1939; Research Technologist in Refractories Industry, 1943; Lectr in Refractory Materials, Sheffield Univ., 1946; Reader in Ceramics, Sheffield Univ., 1952. FIM 1952; Founder FICeram 1955; CEng 1977. FRSA 1972. Silver Jubilee Lectr, Glass and Ceramic Res. Inst., Calcutta. President: Sheffield Metallurgical Assoc., 1950; Refractories Assoc. of Great Britain, 1959-60; Chm. Clay Minerals Group, Mineralogical Society, 1959-61; First Chm. Basic Science Section, British Ceramic Soc.; Pres., British Ceramic Soc., 1961-62; Hon. Mem. Council, Iron and Steel Inst., 1961-62. Visiting Prof., Nat. Research Centre, Cairo, 1962; Student's Trust Fund Visiting Lectr, Univ. of the Witwatersrand, SA, 1964; Visiting Prof., Univ. of Illinois, 1966; Nat. Sci. Foundn Senior Foreign Scientist Fellowship, Univ. of Alfred, NY, 1968; R. B. Sosman Meml Lectr, Amer. Ceramic Soc., 1980. Fellow, Mineralogical Soc. of America, 1960; Hon. Mem., Iron and Steel Inst., 1973. Griffith Medal, Materials Science Club, 1971; (jtly) Al Allen Award, Amer. Ceramic Soc., 1982. *Publications:* numerous scientific papers on ferrous metallurgy and refractory materials (some jointly). *Recreations:* sketching, motor-cars, walking. *Address:* 1 Chequers Close, Ranby, Retford DN22 8JX.

WHITE, James; MP (Lab) Glasgow (Pollok) since 1970; Managing Director, Glasgow Car Collection Ltd, since 1959; *m* ; one *s* two *d*. *Educ:* Knightswood Secondary School. Served Eighth Army, War of 1939-45 (African and Italian Stars; Defence Medal). Mem. Commonwealth Parly Assoc. Delegns, Bangladesh, 1973, Nepal, 1981. *Address:* House of Commons, SW1; 23 Alder Road, Glasgow G43 2UU.

WHITE, James; Chairman, Irish Arts Council, since 1979; Professor of the History of Painting, Royal Hibernian Academy, since 1968; External Lecturer in the History of Art, University College, Dublin, since 1955; *b* 16 Sept. 1913; *s* of Thomas John White and Florence Coffey; *m* 1941, Agnes Bowe; three *s* two *d*. *Educ:* Belvedere Coll., Dublin; privately in European museums and collections. Art Critic: Standard, 1940-50; Irish Press, 1950-59; Irish Times, 1959-62. Curator, Municipal Gallery of Modern Art, Dublin, 1960-64; Director, Nat. Gallery of Ireland, 1964-80. Visiting Lectr in Univs and Socs in GB, Italy, USA, Canada. Pres., Friends of Nat. Collections of Ireland; Chairman: Internat. Council of Museums, Ireland; Irish Museums Assoc.; Irish Art Historians; Trustee, Chester Beatty Library of Oriental Art, Dublin. Radio and Television contribs: BBC, RTE, and in the USA. Irish Comr to Biennale at Venice and at Paris on various occasions; Organiser of Exhibns in Dublin, London, Paris, etc., incl. Paintings from Irish Collections, 1957. Corresp. Mem., Real Academia de Bellas Artes de San Fernando, 1975. Hon. LLD NUI, 1970. Arnold K. Henry Medal of RCS of Ireland. Chevalier, Légion d'Honneur, 1974; Order of Merit, Govt of Italy, 1977. *Publications:* Irish Stained Glass (with Michael Wynne), 1963; The National Gallery of Ireland, 1968; Jack B. Yeats, 1971; John Butler Yeats and the Irish Renaissance, 1972; Masterpieces of the National Gallery of Ireland, 1978; monographs on Louis Le Brocquy, George Campbell, Brian Bourke; contributor to: Apollo, Art News, Studio, Connoisseur, Blackfriars, Manchester Guardian, The Furrow, Doctrine and Life, Art Notes, Merian, Werk, Das Munster, Hollandsche Art, La Biennale, La Revue Française, Il Milione, Encyclopedia of Art, etc. *Recreations:* golf, swimming, gardening, bridge. *Address:* 15 Herbert Park, Ballsbridge, Dublin 4. *T:* 683723. *Club:* Kildare Street and University (Dublin).

WHITE, John Alan; Deputy Chairman, Associated Book Publishers Ltd, 1963-68 (Managing Director, 1946-62); former Director: British Publishers Guild Ltd; Eyre & Spottiswoode Ltd; Chapman & Hall Ltd; Book Centre Ltd; *b* 20 June 1905; *e s* of Percy Hall White and Gertrude (*née* Farthing); *m* 1st, Marjorie Lovelace Vincent (*d* 1958); two *s*; 2nd, Vivienne Rosalie Musgrave. *Educ:* Bishops Stortford College. President, Publishers' Association, 1955-57; Chairman, National Book League, 1963-65. *Recreations:* reading, gardening. *Address:* Hayfield House, College Road, Cork, Ireland. *T:* Cork 21519. *Club:* Garrick.

See also Sir Dick Goldsmith White.

WHITE, Lt-Col John Baker, TD 1950; JP; *b* West Malling, Kent, 12 Aug. 1902; *s* of late J. W. B. White, Street End House, Canterbury; *m* 1925, Sybil Irene Erica (*d* 1980), *d* of late C. B. Graham, Onslow Gardens, SW1; one *s* one *d*. *Educ:* Stubbington House, Fareham; Malvern College. Worked on farms in Kent and Sussex to gain a basic knowledge of agriculture, 1920-22; worked in a circus to gain a wider knowledge of human nature, 1922; studied the structure of industry and social science in London and various industrial centres, 1922-24; worked as a voluntary helper in canteens for the unemployed and among distressed ex-service men; employed in the coal industry, 1924-26; Director Economic League, 1926-45, Publicity Adviser, 1945-76. Joined Territorial Army, London Rifle Brigade, 1934; served in Army as regimental soldier, on War Office staff with Political Intelligence Dept of FO, and Political Warfare Mission in the Middle East, 1939-45; Lieut-Colonel 1941. MP (C) Canterbury division of Kent, 1945-53. JP Kent, 1954. Pres., E Kent Fruit Show Soc.; Vice Pres., Canterbury Soc. *Publications:* Red Russia Arms, 1934; It's Gone for Good, 1941; The Soviet Spy System, 1948; The Red Network, 1953; The Big Lie, 1955; Pattern for Conquest, 1956; Sabotage is Suspected, 1957; True Blue, 1970. *Address:* Street End Place, near Canterbury, Kent CT4 5NP. *T:* Petham 265.

WHITE, Hon. Sir John (Charles), Kt 1982; MBE (mil.) 1942; Judge of High Court of New Zealand, retired 1981, sitting as retired Judge since 1982; *b* 1 Nov. 1911; *s* of Charles Gilbert White and Nora Addison Scott White; *m* 1943, Dora Eyre Wild; one *s* three *d*. *Educ:* Wellesley Coll., Wellington; John McGlashan Coll., Dunedin; Victoria University Coll., Wellington; Univ. of New Zealand (LLM Hons). Barrister and Solicitor of Supreme Court of New Zealand. Judge's Associate, 1937-38; served War, Middle East, Greece, Crete, Italy, 1940-45, final rank Major; formerly Dominion Vice-Pres., New Zealand Returned Services Assoc.; Private practice as barrister and solicitor, Wellington, 1945-66; Pres., Wellington Law Soc., Vice-Pres., NZ Law Soc., 1966; QC and Solicitor General of New Zealand, 1966; Judge of the Supreme Court (now High Court), 1970, retd 1981; Judge Advocate General of Defence Forces, 1966-. Asst Editor, Sim's Practice & Procedure, 9th edn, 1955, and 10th edn 1966. *Recreations:* formerly Rugby, cricket, tennis. *Address:* 23 Selwyn Terrace, Wellington 1, New Zealand. *T:* 725-502. *Clubs:* Wellington; Dunedin; United Services Officers (Wellington).

WHITE, Prof. John Edward Clement Twarowski, FSA; Durning-Lawrence Professor of the History of Art, University College, London, since 1971; *b* 4 Oct. 1924; *s* of Brigadier A. E. White and Suzanne Twarowska; *m* 1950, Xenia Joannides. *Educ:* Ampleforth College; Trinity College, Oxford; Courtauld Institute of Art, University of London. Served in RAF, 1943-47. BA London 1950; Junior Research Fellow, Warburg Inst., 1950-52; PhD Lond. 1952; MA Manchester 1963. Lectr in History of Art, Courtauld Inst., 1952-58; Alexander White Vis. Prof., Univ. of Chicago, 1958; Reader in History of Art, Courtauld Inst., 1958-59; Pilkington Prof. of the History of Art and Dir of The Whitworth Art Gallery, Univ. of Manchester, 1959-66; Vis. Ferens Prof. of Fine Art, Univ. of Hull, 1961-62; Prof. of the History of Art and Chm., Dept of History of Art, Johns Hopkins Univ., USA,

1966-71. Member: Adv. Council of V&A, 1973-76; Exec. Cttee, Assoc. of Art Historians, 1974-81 (Chm., 1976-80); Art Panel, Arts Council, 1974-78; Vis. Cttee of RCA, 1977-; Chm., Reviewing Cttee on Export of Works of Art, 1976-82 (Mem., 1975-82). Trustee, Whitechapel Art Gall., 1976-. *Publications:* Perspective in Ancient Drawings and Painting, 1956; The Birth and Rebirth of Pictorial Space, 1957; Art and Architecture in Italy, 1250-1400, 1966; Duccio, 1980; articles in Burlington Magazine, Jl of Warburg and Courtauld Institutes, Art Bulletin. *Address:* Department of The History of Art, University College, Gower Street, WC1; (home) 25 Cadogan Place, SW1. *Club:* Athenæum.

WHITE, John Sampson, CMG 1970; Secretary to the Governor, South Australia, since 1976; *b* 9 June 1916; *s* of late W. J. White; *m* 1941, Dorothy G., *d* of late E. J. Griffin; one *s* one *d*. *Educ:* Black Forest Primary and Adelaide High Schs. AASA. Attorney-General's Dept, 1933-61. Served War, 2nd AIF, 1941-45, Captain. Asst Sec., Industries Develt Cttee, 1950, Sec., 1951-61; Sec., Land Agents' Bd, 1951-61; Sec. to Premier, SA, 1961-65; Mem., SA Superannuation Fund Bd, 1961-74; Sec., Premier's Dept, SA, 1965-74; Agent-Gen. for SA, 1974-76; Comr of Charitable Funds, 1964-74. Mem., Council of Governors, Presb. Girls' Coll., 1958-73. Freeman, City of London. *Recreations:* swimming, tennis. *Address:* Peppertree Cottage, Government House, North Terrace, Adelaide, SA 5000, Australia. *Clubs:* Adelaide, Naval, Military and Air Force, Sturt (Adelaide).

WHITE, John William, CMG 1981; DPhil; Fellow of St John's College, Oxford, since 1963; *b* Newcastle, Australia, 25 April 1937; *s* of late George John White and of Jean Florence White; *m* 1966, Ailsa Barbara, *d* of A. A. and S. Vise, St Lucia, Brisbane; one *s* three *d*. *Educ:* Newcastle High Sch.; Sydney Univ. (MSc); Lincoln Coll., Oxford (1851 Schol., 1959; MA, DPhil). ICI Fellow, Oxford Univ.; Research Fellow, Lincoln Coll., 1962; University Lectr, Oxford, 1963-, Assessor, 1981-82; Vice-Pres., St John's Coll., 1973. Neutron Beam Coordinator, AERE, Harwell, 1974; Asst Director, 1975, Director 1977-80, Institut Laue-Langevin, Grenoble. Tilden Lectr, Chemical Soc., 1975. Marlow Medal, Faraday Soc., 1969. *Publications:* various contribs to scientific jls. *Recreations:* family, squash, skiing. *Address:* 6 Benson Place, Oxford. *T:* Oxford 55685.

WHITE, Sir John (Woolmer), 4th Bt *cr* 1922; *b* 4 Feb. 1947; *s* of Sir Headley Dymoke White, 3rd Bt and of Elizabeth Victoria Mary, *er d* of late Wilfrid Ingram Wrightson; *S* father, 1971. *Educ:* Hurst Court, Hastings; Cheltenham College. *Heir:* uncle Lynton Stuart White, MBE, TD [*b* 11 Aug. 1916; *m* 1945, Phyllis Marie Rochfort, *d* of Sir Newnham Worley, KBE, and late Marie Forlong; four *s* one *d*]. *Address:* Salle Park, Norwich, Norfolk NR10 4SG.

WHITE, Lawrence John, CMG 1972; formerly Assistant Secretary, Board of Customs and Excise, 1961-75, retired; *b* 23 Feb. 1915; *s* of Arthur Yirrell White and Helen Christina White; *m* 1936, Ivy Margaret Coates; one *s*. *Educ:* Banbury Grammar Sch. Joined Customs and Excise, 1933; Commonwealth Relations Office, 1948-50; Customs and Excise, 1951-75. *Recreations:* reading, walking. *Address:* Peach Tree Cottage, Fifield, Oxon. *T:* Shipton under Wychwood 830806.

WHITE, Michael James Denham; FRS 1961; FAA; Visiting Fellow, Australian National University, since 1976; *b* 20 August 1910; *s* of James Kemp White and Una Theodora Chase; *m* 1938, Isobel Mary Lunn; two *s* one *d*. *Educ:* University College, London. Asst Lecturer, 1933-35, Lecturer, 1936-46, Reader, 1947, University Coll., London; Guest Investigator, Carnegie Instn of Washington, 1947; Professor of Zoology, Univ. of Texas, 1947-53; Senior Research Fellow, CSIRO, Canberra, Australia, 1953-56; Prof. of Zoology, Univ. of Missouri, 1957-58; Univ. of Melbourne: Prof. of Zoology, 1958-64; Prof. of Genetics, 1964-75. Pres., Genetics Soc. of Australia, 1971-73. Foreign Member: Amer. Acad. of Arts and Sciences; Amer. Philosophical Soc.; Accad. Nazionale dei Lincei; For. Associate, US Nat. Acad. of Sciences. Hon. Fellow, Linnean Soc. of London. Hon. Dr Sci. Biol Siena, 1979. Mueller Medallist, Aust. and NZ Assoc. for the Advancement of Science, 1965; Research Medal, Royal Soc. of Victoria, 1979. *Publications:* (Monograph) The Chromosomes, 1937, 6th edn 1973 (trans into French, Italian, Polish, Portuguese, and Spanish); Animal Cytology and Evolution, 1945, 3rd edn 1973; Modes of Speciation, 1978; many papers in learned journals. *Address:* Department of Population Biology, Australian National University, PO Box 475, Canberra City, ACT 2601, Australia.

WHITE, Air Vice-Marshal Michael William Langtry; Principal Medical Officer, RAF Support Command, 1973-74; retired 1974; *b* 6 March 1915; *s* of Frederick William White, solicitor, and Pauline Marie White; *m* 1940, Mary Seton Dury Arnould, Battle, Sussex; one *s* one *d*. *Educ:* Dauntsey's; St Bartholomew's Hosp. MFCM, MRCS, LRCP, DPH. Qualified as doctor, 1940. Served War, Mediterranean Theatre, 1942-45 (despatches 1943). Air Vice-Marshal, 1971; PMO RAF Training Comd, 1971-73. psc 1955. QHP 1972-74. *Recreations:* shooting, fishing, gardening. *Address:* Owl Cottage, Netheravon, Wilts. *T:* Netheravon 396. *Club:* Royal Air Force.

WHITE, Norman Arthur, PhD; CEng, FIMechE; Director and Managing Partner, Norman White Associates (specialists in international resources), since 1972; *b* 11 April 1922; *s* of late Charles Brewster White and Lillian Sarah (*née* Finch); *m* 1944, Joyce Marjorie Rogers (*d* 1982); one *s* one *d*. *Educ:* Luton Tech. Coll. (HNC 1943); Manchester Inst. of Sci. and Technol. (AMCT Hons

1948); London Univ. (BSc Eng (Hons) 1949); Univ. of Philippines (MSc 1955); Harvard Business Sch. (grad. AMP 1968); LSE (PhD 1973). CEng 1947; MRAeS 1947; FInstPet 1956; FInstE 1961; FIMechE 1964; FIMM 1979. Industrial apprentice, George Kent, and D. Napier & Son, 1936-43; Flight Test Engr, Mil. Aircraft develt, 1943-45. Joined Royal Dutch/Shell Gp, 1945; Petroleum Res. Engr, Thornton Res. Centre, 1945-51; Tech. Manager, Shell Co. of Philippines, 1951-55; Shell International Petroleum: Div. Hd, later Dep. Manager, Product Develt Dept, 1955-61; special assignments in various countries, 1961-63; Gen. Manager, Lubricants, Bitumen and LPG Divs, 1963-66; Dir of Marketing Develt, 1966-68; Chief Exec., New Enterprises Div., London and The Hague, 1968-72; Chm. and Dir, Shell oil and mining cos, UK and overseas, 1963-72. Energy Advr, Hambros Bank, 1972-76; Chairman: Exec. Cttee, Tanks Oil and Gas, 1974-; KBC Process Consultants, 1979-; American Oil Field Systems, 1980-; Dep. Chm., British Canadian Resources, Calgary, 1980-; Director: Environmental Resources, 1973-; Tesel Services, 1979-; Oil Field Systems Corp., NY, 1981-. Member: Parly and Scientific Cttee, House of Commons, 1977-; British Nat. Cttee, World Energy Conf., 1977-; World Energy Conf. Conservation Commn, 1979-; Dep. Chm., British Nat. Cttee, World Petroleum Congresses, 1977-; Member: Bd and World Council, Internat. Road Fedn, Geneva and Washington, 1964-72; UK CAA Cttee of Enquiry on Flight Time Limitations, 1972-73. Visiting Professor: Arthur D. Little Management Educn Inst., Boston, 1977-79; ASC, Henley, 1979- (Vis. Fellow 1976-79); Manchester Business Sch., 1981- (Vis. Industrial Dir 1971-81). Dep. Chm., Council of Management, Henley Centre for Forecasting, 1974-; London University: Member: Senate, 1974-; Governing Bd, Commerce Degree Bureau, 1975-; Academic Adv. Bd in Engrg, 1976-; Mem., Council of Mining and Metallurgical Instns, 1981-. Member Council: Inst. of Petroleum, 1975-81 (Vice-Pres., 1978-81); IMechE, 1980- (Chm., Engrg Management Div.). FRSA 1944; FBIM 1962; MRI 1974; Mem., RIIA, 1978; Founder Mem., British Inst. of Energy Econs, 1978. Associate, St George's House, Windsor Castle, 1972. Governor: King Edward VI Royal Grammar Sch., 1976-; Reigate Grammar Sch. *Publications:* Financing the International Petroleum Industry, 1978; contribs to professional jls in UK and Canada, on fluid mechanics, petroleum utilization, energy resources, R&D management, project financing and engrg management. *Recreations:* country and coastal walking, wild life, international affairs, comparative religions, domestic odd-jobbing. *Address:* 6 John Street, WC1N 2ES. *T:* 01-242 9921; Green Ridges, Downside Road, Guildford, Surrey GU4 8PH. *T:* Guildford 67523. *Club:* Athenæum.

WHITE, Patrick Victor Martindale; Author; *b* 28 May 1912; *s* of Victor Martindale White and Ruth Withycombe. *Educ:* Cheltenham Coll.; King's Coll., Cambridge. Brought up partly in Australia, partly in England. First published while living in London before War of 1939-45. Served War with RAF, as Intelligence Officer, mainly in Middle East. Returned to Australia after War. Nobel Prize for Literature, 1973. *Publications: novels:* Happy Valley, 1939; The Living and the Dead, 1941 (new edn 1962); The Aunt's Story, 1946; The Tree of Man, 1954; Voss, 1957 (1st annual literary award of £1000 from W. H. Smith & Son, 1959); Riders in the Chariot, 1961; The Solid Mandala, 1966; The Vivisector, 1970; The Eye of the Storm, 1973; A Fringe of Leaves, 1976; The Twyborn Affair, 1979; *plays:* The Ham Funeral, 1947; The Season at Sarsaparilla, 1961; A Cheery Soul, 1962; Night on Bald Mountain, 1962; Big Toys, 1977; Signal Driver, 1981; *short stories:* The Burnt Ones, 1964; The Cockatoos, 1974; *self-portrait:* Flaws in the Glass, 1981; *film:* The Night the Prowler, 1978. *Recreations:* friendship, cooking, gardening, listening to music, keeping dogs. *Address:* 20 Martin Road, Centennial Park, Sydney, NSW 2021, Australia.

WHITE, Adm. Sir Peter, GBE 1977 (KBE 1976; CBE 1960; MBE 1944); Consultant: Wilkinson Match Ltd, since 1978; The Industrial Society; Chief of Fleet Support, 1974-77; *b* 25 Jan. 1919; *s* of William White, Amersham, Bucks; *m* 1947, Audrey Eileen, *d* of Ernest Wallin, Northampton; two *s*. *Educ:* Dover College. Secretary: to Chief of Staff, Home Fleet, 1942-43; to Flag Officer Comdg 4th Cruiser Sqdn, 1944-45; to Asst Chief of Naval Personnel, 1946-47; to Flag Officer, Destroyers, Mediterranean, 1948-49; to Controller of the Navy, 1949-53; to C-in-C Home Fleet and C-in-C Eastern Atlantic, 1954-55; Naval Asst to Chm. BJSM, Washington, and UK Rep. of Standing Group, NATO, 1956-59; Supply Officer, HMS Adamant, 1960-61; Dep. Dir of Service Conditions and Fleet Supply Duties, Admty, 1961-63; idc 1964; CO HMS Raleigh, 1965-66; Principal Staff Officer to Chief of Defence Staff, 1967-69; Dir-Gen. Fleet Services, 1969-71; Port Admiral, Rosyth, 1972-74. Chm., Officers Pension Society. Mem. Foundn Cttee, Gordon Boys' Sch. *Address:* c/o Westminster Bank Ltd, 26 The Haymarket, SW1.

WHITE, Phyllis Dorothy; *see* James, Phyllis D.

WHITE, Raymond Walter Ralph, CMG 1982; Director: Alcan New Zealand, since 1982; Aurora Group, since 1982; BP New Zealand, since 1982; New Zealand South British Group, since 1982; New Zealand Advisory Board, Westpac Banking Corp., since 1982; *b* 23 June 1923; *s* of Henry Underhill White and Ethel Annie White; *m* 1946, Nola Colleen Adin; one *s* two *d*. *Educ:* Palmerston North Technical High Sch.; Victoria Univ. FCA 1981; FCIS 1968; FBINZ 1982. Dep. Governor, 1967-77, Governor, 1977-82, Reserve Bank of NZ. *Recreations:* golf, tennis, gardening. *Address:* 63 Chatsworth Road, Silverstream, New Zealand. *T:* Upper Hutt 82084. *Club:* Wellington (NZ).

WHITE, Captain Richard Taylor, DSO 1940 (Bars 1941 and 1942); RN retired; *b* 29 Jan. 1908; *s* of Sir Archibald White, 4th Bt and *heir-pres.* to Sir Thomas White, *qv*; *m* 1936, Gabrielle Ursula Style; three *s* two *d*. *Educ:* RN College, Dartmouth. Served War of 1939-45 (DSO and two Bars). Retired 1955. *Address:* Tilts House, Boughton Monchelsea, Maidstone, Kent ME17 4JE.

WHITE, Robin Bernard G.; *see* Grove-White.

WHITE, Roger Lowrey, JP; Managing Director, Research Information Services (Westminster) Ltd; Director: Williamson Tea Holdings Ltd, since 1972; Romai Tea Holdings Ltd, since 1977; *b* 1 June 1928; *o s* of late George Frederick White and Dorothy Jeanette White; *m* 1962, Angela Mary (*née* Orman), company director. *Educ:* St Joseph's Coll., Beulah Hill. National Vice-Chm., Young Conservatives, 1958-59; Founder Mem., Conservative Commonwealth Council; Mem. Council, London Borough of Bromley, 1964-68. MP (C) Gravesend, 1970-Feb. 1974. Mem., Asthma Research Council, 1973-. Freeman, City of London, 1953; Liveryman, Worshipful Co. of Makers of Playing Cards, 1975-; JP Inner London Area, 1965. *Recreations:* golf, fishing. *Address:* 74 Clifton Court, Aberdeen Place, NW8. *Club:* Carlton.

WHITE, Stephen Fraser; Senior Technical Adviser to National Water Council; *b* 13 May 1922; *s* of Robert and Iola White; *m* 1953, Judith Hamilton Cox; two *s* one *d*. *Educ:* Friars, Bangor; Nottingham Univ. BSc; FICE, MIWES, MIStructE. War Service in Indian Electrical and Mechanical Engineers, discharged 1947. G. H. Hill and Sons, Consulting Civil Engineers, 1947-59; Cardiff Corporation, 1959-62; Engineering Inspector, Min. of Housing and Local Govt, 1962-70; Dir of Water Engineering, Dept of the Environment, 1970-77. *Recreations:* golf, bridge. *Address:* 28 Biddenham Turn, Bedford. *T:* Bedford 53557.

WHITE, Terence de Vere, FRSL; *b* 29 April 1912; *s* of Frederick S. de Vere White, LLD, and Ethel (*née* Perry); *m* 1st, 1941, Mary O'Farrell (marr. diss. 1982); two *s* one *d*; 2nd, 1982, Victoria Glendinning (*née* Seebohm). *Educ:* St Stephen's Green Sch., Dublin; Trinity Coll., Dublin (BA, LLB). Admitted solicitor, 1933. Mem. Council, Incorporated Law Society, retd 1961. Literary Editor, The Irish Times, 1961-77. Vice-Chm., Board of Governors, National Gallery of Ireland; Trustee: National Library, 1946-79; Chester Beatty Library, 1959-80; Dir, Gate Theatre, 1969-81. Mem., Irish Academy of Letters, 1968; Hon. RHA 1968; Hon. Prof. of Literature, RHA, 1973; FRSL 1981. *Publications:* The Road of Excess, 1945; Kevin O'Higgins, 1948; The Story of the Royal Dublin Society, 1955; A Fretful Midge, 1957; A Leaf from the Yellow Book, 1958; An Affair with the Moon, 1959; Prenez Garde, 1962; The Remainder Man, 1963; Lucifer Falling, 1965; The Parents of Oscar Wilde, 1967; Tara, 1967; Leinster, 1968; Ireland, 1968; The Lambert Mile, 1969; The March Hare, 1970; Mr Stephen, 1971; The Anglo-Irish, 1972; The Distance and the Dark, 1973; The Radish Memoirs, 1974; Big Fleas and Little Fleas, 1976; Chimes at Midnight, 1977; Tom Moore, 1977; My Name is Norval, 1978; Birds of Prey, 1980; contribs to 19th Century, Cambridge Review, Horizon. *Recreation:* formerly riding. *Address:* c/o Allied Irish Banks, 100 Grafton Street, Dublin 2, Ireland. *Clubs:* Garrick; Kildare Street and University (Dublin).

WHITE, Thomas Anthony B.; *see* Blanco White.

WHITE, Sir Thomas Astley Woollaston, 5th Bt, *cr* 1802; JP; Hon. Sheriff for Wigtownshire, since 1963; *b* 13 May 1904; *s* of Sir Archibald Woollaston White, 4th Bt, and late Gladys Becher Love, *d* of Rev. E. A. B. Pitman; *S* father, 1945; *m* 1935, Daphne Margaret, *er d* of late Lt-Col F. R. I. Athill, CMG; one *d*. *Educ:* Wellington College. FRICS. JP Wigtownshire, 1952. *Heir:* *b* Capt. Richard T. White, *qv*. *Address:* Ha Hill, Wigtown, Wigtownshire. *T:* Wigtown 2238.

WHITE, Sir (Vincent) Gordon (Lindsay), KBE 1979; Chairman, Hanson International Management Services, since 1974; *b* 11 May 1923; *s* of late Charles White and Lily May (*née* Wilson); *m* 1974, Virginia Anne; one *s* (and two *d* by a former marriage). *Educ:* De Aston Sch., Lincs. Served War, 1940-46: Paranaval Section, Flying Duties, SOE, Force 136, Captain. Chairman, family publishing business, Welbecson Ltd, 1947-65; Dep. Chm., Hanson Trust Ltd, 1965-73; Chm., Hanson Internat. Management Services 1974-. Governor, BFI, 1982-. *Recreations:* flying (holder of helicopter licence), riding, skiing, tennis. *Address:* Sleepy Hollow, Warwick, Bermuda. *T:* (809 298) 1800. *Clubs:* Special Forces; Brook, Sky, Explorers' (New York); Travellers' (Paris); Mid-Ocean (Bermuda).

WHITE, Wilfrid H.; *see* Hyde White.

WHITE, William Kelvin Kennedy; HM Diplomatic Service; Deputy Chief Clerk and Chief Inspector, since 1982; *b* 10 July 1930; *y s* of Kennedy White, JP, Caldy, Cheshire, and late Violet White; *m* 1957, Susan Margaret, *y d* of late R. T. Colthurst, JP, Malvern, Worcs; three *s*. *Educ:* Birkenhead Sch.; Merton Coll., Oxford. HM Forces, 1949-50. Entered HM Foreign (later Diplomatic) Service, 1954; Foreign Office, 1954-56, attending UN Gen. Assemblies, 1954 and 1955; 3rd Sec., Helsinki, 1956-57; 2nd Sec., Commissioner-General's Office, Singapore, 1957-61; 2nd Sec., then 1st Sec., FO, 1961-66; 1st Sec. (Commercial), Stockholm, 1966-69; 1st Sec., then Counsellor, FCO, 1969-74; Counsellor, New Delhi, 1974-77; Head of South

Asian Dept, FCO, 1978-80; Minister, Canberra, 1980-81. *Address:* c/o Foreign and Commonwealth Office, SW1. *Clubs:* Travellers'; Moreton CC.

WHITE-THOMSON, Very Rev. Ian Hugh; Dean of Canterbury, 1963-76; *b* 18 December 1904; *m* 1954, Wendy Ernesta Woolliams; two *s* two *d. Educ:* Harrow; Oxford. Deacon, 1929; Priest, 1930; Curacy, St Mary's, Ashford, Kent, 1929-34; Rector of S Martin's with St Paul's, Canterbury, 1934-39; Chaplain to Archbishop of Canterbury, 1939-47; Vicar of Folkestone, 1947-54; Archdeacon of Northumberland and Canon of Newcastle, 1955-63; Chaplain to King George VI, 1947-52, to the Queen, 1952-63; Examining Chaplain to Bishop of Newcastle, 1955-63. Hon. Canon of Canterbury Cathedral, 1950. Governor, Harrow School, 1947-62, 1965-70. Hon. DCL Univ. of Kent at Canterbury, 1971. *Address:* Camphill, Harville Road, Wye, Ashford, Kent. *T:* Wye 812210.

WHITEHEAD, Edward Anthony; playwright, since 1971; theatre and film reviewer; *b* 3 April 1933; *s* of Edward Whitehead and Catherine Curran; *m* 1st, 1958, Kathleen Horton (marr. diss. 1976); two *d*; 2nd, 1976, Gwenda Bagshaw. *Educ:* Christ's Coll., Cambridge (MA). Military Service, King's Regt (Infantry), 1955-57. Bus conductor, copywriter, pharmaceutical salesman, and teacher, 1958-65; advertising exec., 1965-71. Evening Standard Award, and George Devine Award, 1971. *Publications:* The Foursome, 1972; Alpha Beta, 1972; The Sea Anchor, 1975; Old Flames, 1976; The Punishment (Hutchinson's Prompt series), 1976; Mecca, 1977; World's End, 1981. *Recreations:* soccer, pubs, music. *Address:* c/o Judy Daish Associates Ltd, 122 Wigmore Street, W1H 9FE. *T:* 01-486 5404.

WHITEHEAD, Frank Henry; Deputy Chairman, Macmillan Ltd, since 1980; *b* 25 Sept. 1918; *s* of William George Whitehead and Annie S. Whitehead; *m* 1941, Gwendolyn Heather (*née* Ross); one *s* two *d. Educ:* Harrow County Sch.; LSE; London Sch. of Printing. Served War, RA, 1939-46. Joined Macmillan, 1937; Dir, 1963; Gp Man. Dir, 1965-80. Liveryman, Stationers and Newspaper Makers Co. *Recreations:* reading, painting, music, gardening, photography. *Address:* 5 Briery Field, Chorleywood, Rickmansworth, Herts. *T:* Chorleywood 4721. *Clubs:* City Livery, Wig and Pen.

See also G. S. Whitehead.

WHITEHEAD, Garnet George Archie, DFC 1944; **His Honour Judge Whitehead;** a Circuit Judge, since 1977; *b* 22 July 1916; *s* of late Archibald Payne Whitehead and Margaret Elizabeth Whitehead; *m* 1946, Monica (*née* Watson); two *d. Educ:* Wisbech. Admitted Solicitor, 1949. Served War, 1939-45, RAF, Pilot, Bomber Comd and Transport Comd; demob. as Flt Lt, 1 Jan. 1947. Articled to Edmund W. Roythorne, MBE, Solicitor, Spalding. Formerly Senior Partner, Roythorne & Co., Solicitor, Boston, Lincs (Partner, 1950-77); a Recorder of the Crown Court, 1972-77. Formerly Alderman, Boston Borough Council; Mayor of Boston, 1969-70. *Recreations:* photography, walking. *Address:* 15 Burton Close, Boston, Lincs. *T:* Boston 64977.

WHITEHEAD, George Sydney, CMG 1966; MVO 1961; HM Diplomatic Service, retired; re-employed in Foreign and Commonwealth Office (Security Department), 1976-81; *b* 15 Nov. 1915; *s* of William George and Annie Sabina Whitehead; *m* 1948, Constance Mary Hart (*née* Vale); one *d* (and one step *d*). Educ: Harrow County Sch.; London Sch. of Economics. India Office, 1934. Armed Forces (Royal Artillery), 1940-45. Private Sec. to Parly Under-Sec. of State for India and Burma, 1945-46; British Embassy, Rangoon, 1947; CRO 1948-52; British High Commn, Canberra, 1952-55; Counsellor, British High Commn, Calcutta, 1958-61; Inspector, Commonwealth Service, 1961-64; Inspector, Diplomatic Service, 1965; Head of Asia Economic Dept, CO, 1966-67; Head of Commonwealth Trade Dept, CO, 1967-68; Head of Commodities Dept, FCO, 1968-69; Dep. High Comr and Minister (Commercial), Ottawa, 1970-72; Asst Under-Sec. of State, 1972-75, Dep. Chief Clerk, 1973-75, FCO. *Recreations:* gardening, reading, walking. *Address:* 399 Pinner Road, Harrow, Mddx. *T:* 01-427 5872. *Clubs:* Civil Service, Royal Commonwealth Society; Middlesex County Cricket.

See also F. H. Whitehead.

WHITEHEAD, Graham Wright, CBE 1977; President, Jaguar Rover Triumph Inc. (formerly BL Motors Inc.), NJ, since 1968; Chairman, Jaguar Rover Triumph Canada Inc., Ontario, since 1977; Director, Jaguar Cars Ltd, since 1982; *m* Gabrielle Whitehead, OBE; one *s* one *d*. Joined Wolseley Motors, 1945; moved to US, 1959. President: British-American Chamber of Commerce, NY, 1976-78; British Automobile Manufacturers Assoc., NY; Vice-Pres., St George's Soc. of NY. *Address:* 20 Meadow Place, Old Greenwich, Conn 06870, USA. *Club:* Riverside Yacht (Conn).

WHITEHEAD, Col James Buckley, CBE 1957; MC 1918; TD 1934 (four bars 1951); DL; JP; Cotton Spinner; *b* 1898; *s* of Edwin Whitehead, Oldham, Lancs; *m* 1926, Florence (*d* 1979); *d* of J. R. Thomason, Oldham; one *s* one *d. Educ:* Oldham High School. Served European War, 1916-19, in France and Flanders with 10th Manchester Regt; War of 1939-45 with Roy. Tank Regt and Yorkshire Hussars. Hon. Col 40/41 Royal Tank Regt. DL for Co. Lancaster, 1956; JP WR Yorks, 1948. *Address:* Staghurst, Grasscroft, near Oldham, Lancs. *T:* Saddleworth 2112.

WHITEHEAD, Dr John Ernest Michael, FRCPath; Director of Public Health Laboratory Service, since 1981; *b* 7 Aug. 1920; *s* of Dr Charles Ernest Whitehead and Bertha Whitehead; *m* 1946, Elizabeth Bacchus (*née* Cochran);

one *s* one *d. Educ:* Merchant Taylors' Sch.; Gonville and Caius Coll., Cambridge (MA); St Thomas's Hosp. Med. Sch. (MB BChir, DipBact). Jun. Ho. appts, St Thomas' Hosp., 1944-47; Lectr in Bacteriology, St Thomas's Hosp. Med. Sch., 1948-51; Travelling Fellowship, State Serum Inst., Copenhagen, 1949-50; Asst Bacteriologist, Central Public Health Laboratory, 1952-53; Dep. Dir, Public Health Lab., Sheffield, 1953-58; Dir, Public Health Lab., Coventry, 1958-75; Cons. Microbiologist, Coventry Hosps, 1958-75; Dep. Dir, Public Health Laboratory Service, 1975-81. Hon. Lecturer: Univ. of Sheffield, 1954-58; Univ. of Birmingham, 1962-75. Mem. Council, RCPath, 1981-; Mem., Adv. Cttee on Dangerous Pathogens, 1981-; Consultant Advr in Microbiol., DHSS, 1982-; Temporary Adviser and Chm., Working Gp on Safety Measures in Microbiology, WHO, 1976-; Chm., Working Gp on Organisation and Administration of Public Health Laboratory Services, Council of Europe, 1977-79. *Publications:* chapters in The Pathological Basis of Medicine, ed R. C. Curran and D. G. Harnden, 1974; papers and reviews in med. microbiology in various med. and scientific jls. *Recreations:* house and garden maintenance, skiing, modern languages. *Address:* Martins, Lee Common, Great Missenden, Bucks HP16 9JP. *T:* The Lee 492.

WHITEHEAD, John Stainton, CMG 1976; CVO 1978; HM Diplomatic Service; Minister, Tokyo, since 1980; *b* 20 Sept. 1932; *s* of late John William and Kathleen Whitehead; *m* 1964, Mary Carolyn (*née* Hilton); two *s* two *d. Educ:* Christ's Hospital; Hertford Coll., Oxford (MA). HM Forces, 1950-52; Oxford, 1952-55; FO, 1955-56; 3rd Sec., later 2nd Sec., Tokyo, 1956-61; FO, 1961-64; 1st Sec., Washington, 1964-67; 1st Sec. (Economic), Tokyo, 1968-71; FCO, 1971-76, Head of Personnel Services Dept, 1973-76; Counsellor, Bonn, 1976-80. *Recreations:* music, travel, tree-felling, walking, chess. *Address:* c/o Foreign and Commonwealth Office, SW1; British Embassy, No 1 Ichi Ban-Cho, Chiyoda-Ku, Tokyo, Japan. *T:* 265-5511.

WHITEHEAD, Phillip; MP (Lab) Derby North, since 1970; *b* 30 May 1937; adopted *s* of late Harold and Frances Whitehead; *m* 1967, Christine, *d* of T. G. Usborne; two *s* one *d. Educ:* Lady Manners' Grammar Sch., Bakewell; Exeter Coll., Oxford. President, Oxford Union, 1961. BBC Producer, 1961-67, and WEA Lecturer, 1961-65; Editor of This Week, Thames TV, 1967-70. Guild of TV Producers Award for Factual Programmes, 1969. Vice-Chm., Young Fabian Group, 1965; Chairman: Fabian Soc., 1978-79; Nat. Exec., RSPCA, 1980-; a founder of 76 Group for Broadcasting Reform, 1969; Mem., Annan Cttee on Future of Broadcasting, 1974-77. Contested (Lab) W Derbyshire, 1966; Front bench spokesman on higher educn, 1980- and on the arts, 1982-; Member: Procedure Cttee, 1977-79; Select Cttee on Home Affairs, 1979-81; PLP Liaison Cttee, 1975-79; Council of Europe Assembly, 1975-80. Member: NUJ; NUR. *Publication:* (jtly) Electoral Reform: time for change, 1982. *Recreations:* walking, cinema, old model railways. *Address:* Mill House, Rowsley, Matlock, Derbys. *T:* Darley Dale 2659; House of Commons, SW1.

WHITEHEAD, Sir Rowland (John Rathbone), 5th Bt, *cr* 1889; *b* 24 June 1930; *s* of Major Sir Philip Henry Rathbone Whitehead, 4th Bt, and 1st wife Gertrude, *d* of J. C. Palmer, West Virginia, USA; *S* father, 1953; *m* 1954, Marie-Louise, *d* of Arnold Christian Gausel, Stavanger, Norway; one *s* one *d. Educ:* Radley; Trinity Hall, Cambridge (BA). Late 2nd Lieutenant RA. Chm. of Trustees, Rowland Hill Benevolent Fund, 1982-. Governor, Appleby Grammar Sch. Liveryman, Fruiterers' Co.; Freeman, City of London. *Recreations:* poetry and rural indolence. *Heir: s* Lt Philip Henry Rathbone Whitehead [*b* 13 Oct. 1957. Welsh Guards.]. *Address:* Sutton House, Chiswick Mall, W4 2PR. *T:* 01-994 2710; Walnut Tree Cottage, Fyfield, Lechlade, Glos GL7 3NT. *Clubs:* Reform, Arts.

WHITEHEAD, Prof. Thomas Patterson, MCB, FRCPath, FRSC; Professor of Clinical Chemistry, University of Birmingham, since 1968; Consultant Biochemist, Queen Elizabeth Medical Centre, since 1960; Director of Wolfson Research Laboratories, since 1972; *b* 7 May 1923; *m* 1947, Doreen Grace Whitton; two *s* one *d. Educ:* Salford Royal Technical Coll.; Univ. of Birmingham (PhD). Biochemist to S Warwickshire Hospital Gp, 1950-60. Council Mem., Med. Research Council, 1972-76; Mem., Health Service Research Bd, 1973-75; Chairman: Div. of Path. Studies, Birmingham, 1974-80; Board of Undergraduate Med. Educn, Birmingham, 1982-; W Midlands RHA Res. Cttee, 1982-; DHSS Adv. Cttee on Assessment of Laboratory Standards, 1969-. Consultant to WHO, Geneva, 1974-. Pres., Assoc. of Clinical Biochemists, 1981-; Mem. Council, RCPath, 1982-. Wellcome Prize, 1972; Dade Award, Geneva, 1975. *Publications:* Quality Control in Clinical Chemistry, 1976; papers in med. and scientific jls. *Recreation:* growing and exhibiting sweet peas. *Address:* 70 Northumberland Road, Leamington Spa CV32 6HB. *T:* Leamington Spa 21974. *Club:* Athenæum.

WHITEHORN, John Roland Malcolm, CMG 1974; Director of Industry Affairs, Lilly Industries Ltd, since 1978; Director, Mitchell Cotts Group Ltd, since 1978; *b* 19 May 1924; *s* of late Alan and Edith Whitehorn; *m* 1st, 1951, Josephine (*née* Plummer) (marr. diss. 1973); no *c*; 2nd, 1973, Marion FitzGibbon (*née* Gutmann). *Educ:* Rugby Sch. (Exhbnr); Trinity Coll., Cambridge (Exhbnr). Served War, 1943-46, RAFVR (Flying Officer). Joined FBI, 1947; Dep. Overseas Dir, 1960; Overseas Dir, 1963; Overseas Dir, CBI, 1965-68; a Dep. Dir-Gen., CBI, 1966-78; Member: BOTB, 1975-78; Bd, British Council, 1968-82; Gen. Adv. Council, BBC, 1976-82. *Address:* 42 Ordnance Hill, NW8. *T:* 01-722 4665. *Clubs:* Reform, MCC.

See also Katharine Whitehorn.

WHITEHORN, Katharine Elizabeth, (Mrs Gavin Lyall); Columnist, The Observer, since 1960; *b* London; *d* of late A. D. and E. M. Whitehorn; *m* 1958, Gavin Lyall, *qv* ; two *s. Educ:* Blunt House; Roedean; Glasgow High School for Girls, and others; Newnham Coll., Cambridge. Publisher's Reader, 1950-53; Teacher-Secretary in Finland, 1953-54; Grad. Asst, Cornell Univ., USA, 1954-55; Picture Post, 1956-57; Woman's Own, 1958; Spectator, 1959-61. Member: Latey Cttee on Age of Majority, 1965-67; BBC Adv. Gp on Social Effects of Television, 1971-72; Board, British Airports Authority, 1972-77. *Publications:* Cooking in a Bedsitter, 1960; Roundabout, 1961; Only on Sundays, 1966; Whitehorn's Social Survival, 1968; Observations, 1970; How to Survive in Hospital, 1972; How to Survive Children, 1975; Sunday Best, 1976; How to Survive in the Kitchen, 1979; View from a Column, 1981. *Recreation:* gardening. *Address:* c/o The Observer, 8 St Andrew's Hill, EC4. *T:* 01-236 0202.
    See also J. R. M. Whitehorn.

WHITEHOUSE, Dr David Bryn; Director, British School at Rome, since Oct. 1974; *b* 15 Oct. 1941; *s* of Brindley Charles Whitehouse and Alice Margaret Whitehouse; *m* 1st, 1963, Ruth Delamain Ainger; one *s* two *d* ; 2nd, 1975, Elizabeth-Anne Ollemans; one *s* two *d. Educ:* King Edward's Sch., Birmingham; St John's Coll., Cambridge. MA, PhD; FSA; FRGS. Scholar, British Sch. at Rome, 1963-65; Wainwright Fellow in Near Eastern Archaeology, Univ. of Oxford, 1966-73; Dir, Siraf Expedn, 1966-73; Dir, British Inst. of Afghan Studies, 1973-74; Pres., Internat. Union of Institutes, 1980-; Mem. Council, Internat. Assoc. for Classical Archaeology. Corresp. Mem., German Archaeological Inst., 1980; Academician, Academia Fiorentina dell'Arte del Disegno; Fellow: Pontificia Accademia Romana di Archeologia; Accademia di Archeologia, Lettere e Belle Arti, Naples. *Publications:* (jtly) Background to Archaeology, 1973; (jtly) The Origins of Europe, 1974; (with Ruth Whitehouse) Archaeological Atlas of the World, 1975; (ed jtly) Papers in Italian Archaeology I, 1978; Siraf III: The Congregational Mosque, 1980; (with David Andrews and John Osborne) Papers in Italian Archaeology III, 1981; many papers in Iran, Antiquity, Med. Archaeol., Papers of Brit. Sch. at Rome, etc. *Address:* Accademia Britannica, Via Gramsci 61, 00197 Roma, Italy. *T:* 06-877 312.

WHITEHOUSE, Mary, CBE 1980; Honorary General Secretary, National Viewers' and Listeners' Association, 1965-80, President since 1980; free lance journalist, broadcaster; *b* 13 June 1910; *d* of James and Beatrice Hutcheson; *m* 1940, Ernest R. Whitehouse; three *s. Educ:* Chester City Grammar Sch.; Cheshire County Training Coll. Art Specialist: Wednesfield Sch., Wolverhampton, 1932-40; Brewood Grammar Sch., Staffs, 1943; Sen. Mistress, and Sen. Art Mistress, Madeley Sch., Shropshire, 1960-64. Co-founder, "Clean up TV campaign", 1964. *Publications:* Cleaning Up TV, 1966; "Who Does She Think She Is?", 1971; Whatever Happened to Sex?, 1977; A Most Dangerous Woman?, 1982. *Recreations:* reading, gardening, walking. *Address:* Blachernae, Ardleigh, Colchester, Essex. *T:* Colchester 230123.

WHITEHOUSE, Walter Alexander; Professor of Theology, University of Kent, 1965-77; Master of Eliot College, University of Kent, 1965-69, and 1973-75; *b* 27 Feb. 1915; *e s* of Walter and Clara Whitehouse, Shelley, near Huddersfield; *m* 1st, 1946, Beatrice Mary Kent Smith (*d* 1971); 2nd, 1974, Audrey Ethel Lemmon. *Educ:* Penistone Gram. Sch.; St John's Coll., Cambridge; Mansfield Coll., Oxford. Minister of Elland Congregational Church, 1940-44; Chaplain at Mansfield College, Oxford, 1944-47; Reader in Divinity, Univ. of Durham, 1947-65. Principal of St Cuthbert's Soc., Univ. of Durham, 1955-60; Pro-Vice-Chancellor of Univ., and Sub-Warden, 1961-64. Minister at High Chapel, Ravenstonedale, 1977-82. Hon. DD Edinburgh, 1960. *Publications:* Christian Faith and the Scientific Attitude, 1952; Order, Goodness, Glory (Riddell Memorial Lectures), 1959; The Authority of Grace, 1981. *Address:* 37 Cotswold Green, Stonehouse, Glos.

WHITELAW, Billie; actress; *b* 6 June 1932; *d* of Perceval and Frances Whitelaw; *m* Robert Muller, writer; one *s. Educ:* Thornton Grammar Sch., Bradford. Appeared in: *plays:* Hotel Paradiso, Winter Garden, 1954 and Oxford Playhouse, 1956; Progress to the Park, Theatre Workshop and Saville, 1961; England our England, Prince's, 1962; Touch of the Poet, Venice and Dublin, 1962; National Theatre, 1963-65: Othello, London and Moscow; Hobson's Choice; Beckett's Play; Trelawny of the Wells; The Dutch Courtesan; After Haggerty, Criterion, 1971; Not I, Royal Court, 1973 and 1975; Alphabetical Order, Mayfair, 1975; Footfalls, Royal Court, 1976; Molly, Comedy, 1978; Happy Days, Royal Court, 1979; The Greeks, Aldwych, 1980; Passion Play, Aldwych, 1981; Beckett, NY, 1981; Rockaby and Enough, NY, 1981; *films:* No Love for Johnny; Charlie Bubbles; Twisted Nerve; The Adding Machine; Start the Revolution Without Me; Leo the Last; Eagle in a Cage; Gumshoe; Frenzy; Night Watch; The Omen; Leopard in the Snow; The Water Babies; An Unsuitable Job for a Woman, 1982; *television:* No Trams to Lime Street; Lena Oh My Lena; Resurrection; The Skin Game; Beyond the Horizon; Anna Christie; Lady of the Camelias; The Pity of it all; Love on the Dole; A World of Time; You and I; Poet Game; Sextet (8 plays); Napoleon and Love (9 plays: Josephine); The Fifty Pound Note (Ten from the Twenties); The Withered Arm (Wessex Tales); The Werewolf Reunion (2 plays); Two Plays by Samuel Beckett; Not I; Eustace and Hilda (2 plays); The Serpent Son (dir. by Beckett); Private Schulz; The Badness Within Him; *radio plays:* The Master Builder; Hindle Wakes; Jane Eyre; The Female Messiah; Alpha Beta. Silver Heart Variety Club Award, 1961; TV Actress of Year, 1961, 1972; British Academy Award, 1968; US Film Critics

Award, 1968; Variety Club of GB Best Film Actress Award, 1977; Evening News Film Award as Best Actress, 1977. Hon. DLitt Bradford 1981. *Recreation:* pottering about the house. *Address:* c/o Joy Jameson, 7 West Eaton Place Mews, SW1X 8LY.

WHITELAW, Rt. Hon. William (Stephen Ian), PC 1967; CH 1974; MC; DL; MP (C) Penrith and the Border Division of Cumberland, since 1955; Home Secretary, since 1979; farmer and landowner; *b* 28 June 1918; *s* of late W. A. Whitelaw and Mrs W. A. Whitelaw, Monkland, Nairn; *m* 1943, Cecilia Doriel, 2nd *d* of late Major Mark Sprot, Riddell, Melrose, Roxburghshire; four *d. Educ:* Winchester Coll.; Trinity Coll., Camb. Reg. Officer, Scots Guards; Emergency Commn, 1939; resigned Commn, 1947. PPS to Chancellor of the Exchequer, 1957-58 (to Pres. of BOT, 1956); Asst Govt Whip, 1959-61; a Lord Comr of the Treasury, 1961-62; Parly Sec., Min. of Labour, July 1962-Oct. 1964; Chief Opposition Whip, Nov. 1964-70; Lord Pres. of Council and Leader, House of Commons, 1970-72; Secretary of State for: N Ireland, 1972-73; Employment, 1973-74; Chm., Conservative Party, 1974-75; Dep. Leader of the Opposition and spokesman on home affairs, 1975-79. Visiting Fellow, Nuffield Coll., Oxford, 1970-. DL Dunbartonshire, 1952-66; DL Cumbria, formerly Cumberland, 1967. *Recreations:* golf, shooting. *Address:* Ennim, Penrith, Cumbria. *Clubs:* White's, Carlton; Royal and Ancient (Captain 1969-70).
    See also Earl of Swinton.

WHITELEY, family name of **Baron Marchamley.**

WHITELEY, Maj.-Gen. Gerald Abson, CB 1969; OBE 1952; *b* 4 March 1915; *s* of late Harry Whiteley, Walton Park, Bexhill; *m* 1943, Ellen Hanna (*d* 1973). *Educ:* Worksop Coll.; Emmanuel Coll., Cambridge (MA). Solicitor, 1938. Commissioned, RA, 1940; Maj., DJAG's Staff, ME, 1942-45. AAG, Mil. Dept, JAG's Office, WO, 1945-48; Asst Dir of Army Legal Services: FARELF, 1948-51; WO, 1952-53; Northern Army Gp, 1953-54; MELF, 1954-57; BAOR, 1957-60; Dep. Dir of Army Legal Services, BAOR, 1960-62; Col, Legal Staff, WO, 1962-64; Dir of Army Legal Services, MoD, 1964-69. *Recreations:* photography, walking. *Address:* 8 Kemnal Park, Haslemere, Surrey. *T:* Haslemere 2803. *Club:* Army and Navy.

WHITELEY, Sir Hugo Baldwin Huntington-; see Huntington-Whiteley, Sir H. B.

WHITELEY, Gen. Sir Peter (John Frederick), GCB 1979 (KCB 1976); OBE 1960; Lieutenant-Governor and Commander-in-Chief, Jersey, since 1979; *b* 13 Dec. 1920; *s* of late John George Whiteley; *m* 1948, Nancy Vivian, *d* of late W. Carter Clayden; two *s* two *d. Educ:* Bishop's Stortford Coll.; Bembridge Sch.; Ecole des Roches. Joined Royal Marines, 1940; 101 Bde, 1941; HMS: Resolution, 1941; Renown, 1942; HMNZS Gambia, 1942; seconded to Fleet Air Arm, 1946-50; Adjt 40 Commando, 1951; Staff Coll., Camberley, 1954; Bde Major 3rd Commando Bde, 1957; Instructor, Staff Coll., Camberley, 1960-63; CO 42 Commando, 1965-66 (despatches, Malaysia, 1966); Col GS Dept of CGRM, 1966-68; Nato Defence Coll., 1968; Comdr 3rd Commando Bde, 1968-70; Maj.-Gen. Commando Forces, 1970-72; C of S, HQ Allied Forces Northern Europe, 1972-75; Commandant General, Royal Marines, 1975-77; C-in-C Allied Forces Northern Europe, 1977-79. Governor, Bembridge Sch. Liveryman, Fletchers' Co.; Mem. Ct of Assistants, Guild of Freemen of City of London. CBIM. KStJ 1980. *Publications:* contribs to Jane's Annual, NATO's Fifteen Nations, RUSI Jl, Nauticus. *Recreations:* music (Mem. Glyndebourne Festival Soc.), photography, painting, wood carving, sailing, dogs. *Address:* Government House, Jersey, Channel Islands. *T:* (office) Jersey 30906; (private) Jersey 35477. *Clubs:* Royal Yacht Squadron, Anchorites, Royal Marines Sailing, Royal Naval Sailing Assoc., Royal Norwegian Sailing.

WHITELEY, Samuel Lloyd; Deputy Chief Land Registrar, 1967-73; Legal Assistant to the Clerk to the Haberdashers' Company 1973-78, Freeman, 1978; *b* 30 April 1913; *s* of Rev. Charles Whiteley and Ann Letitia Whiteley; *m* 1939, Kathleen Jones; two *d. Educ:* George Dixon Sch.; Birmingham Univ. LLB (Hons) 1933. Admitted Solicitor, 1935; HM Land Registry, 1936; seconded Official Solicitor's Dept, 1939; RAF, 1940-46; HM Land Registry, 1946-73. *Recreations:* sport, as a reminiscent spectator; amateur theatre. *Address:* 8 Stonehaven Court, Knole Road, Bexhill, Sussex. *T:* Bexhill 213191.

WHITEMAN, Elizabeth Anne Osborn, DPhil; FRHistS, FSA; JP; Tutor in Modern History since 1946, Fellow since 1948, and Vice-Principal 1971-81, Lady Margaret Hall, Oxford; *b* 10 Feb. 1918; *d* of Harry Whitmore Whiteman and Dorothy May (*née* Austin). *Educ:* St Albans High Sch.; Somerville Coll., Oxford (MA 1945, DPhil 1951). FRHistS 1954; FSA 1958. Served War, WAAF, 1940-45: served in N Africa and Italy (mentioned in despatches, 1943). Rep. of Women's Colls, Oxford Univ., 1960-61. Member: Hebdomadal Council, Oxford Univ., 1968-; Academic Planning Bd, Univ. of Warwick, 1961-65; UGC, 1976-. Trustee, Ruskin Sch. of Drawing, 1974-77. JP City of Oxford, 1962. *Publications:* (contrib.) Victoria County History, Wilts, Vol. III, 1956; (contrib.) New Cambridge Modern History, Vol. V, 1961; (contrib.) From Uniformity to Unity, ed Chadwick and Nuttall, 1962; (ed with J. S. Bromley and P. G. M. Dickson, and contrib.) Statesmen, Scholars and Merchants: Essays in eighteenth-century History presented to Dame Lucy Sutherland, 1973; contrib. hist. jls. *Address:* Lady Margaret Hall, Oxford. *T:* Oxford 54353.

WHITEMAN, Peter George, QC 1977; barrister-at-law; Attorney and Counselor at Law, State of New York; Professor of Law, University of Virginia, since 1980; b 8 Aug. 1942; s of David Whiteman and Betsy Bessie Coster; m 1971, Katherine Ruth (née Ellenbogen); two d. Educ: Warwick Secondary Modern Sch.; Leyton County High Sch.; LSE (LLB, LLM with Distinction). Called to the Bar, Lincoln's Inn, 1967. Lectr, London Univ., 1966-70. Mem., Faculty of Laws, Florida Univ., 1977-; Visiting Professor: Virginia Univ., 1978; Univ. of California at Berkeley, 1980. FRSA. Publications: Whiteman and Wheatcroft on Capital Gains Tax, 1967, 3rd edn 1980; Whiteman and Wheatcroft on Income Tax, 1971, 2nd edn 1976; contrib. British Tax Encyc. Recreations: tennis, squash, mountain-walking, jogging, croquet. Address: 101 Dulwich Village, SE21 7BJ. T: 01-299 0858, (chambers) 01-353 9076.

WHITEMAN, William Meredith; MA; FRSA; writer, and consultant on caravanning and the countryside; Vice-President, Camping Club; b 29 May 1905; m 1931, Patricia Aileen Thornton (d 1954); three d; m 1965, Mary Moore (née Hall). Educ: St Albans School; St John's College, Cambridge. President National Picture Print Society, 1938. Founder National Caravan Council. Hon. Secretary, 1939-49, Hon. Director, 1949-52. Director, Caravan Club, 1938-60. Vice-Pres., British Caravanners Club, 1948-77. Organiser, Moveable Dwelling Conference, 1947-49. Editor, The Caravan, 1938-61. Man. Editor, Link House Publications Ltd, 1942-70; UK Mem., Internat. Caravan Commn, 1947-70, Pres., 1957-70; Countryside Commn transit site study group, 1969-70; Mem., Exec. Cttee, Hampshire Council of Community Service, 1971-. Served on more than 50 cttees, working parties etc, on caravanning and camping. Hon. Life Mem., Caravan Club; Hon. Mem., Fédération Internationale de Camping et de Caravanning. Publications: books on camping and caravanning. Address: Northfield Cottage, Steep, Petersfield, Hants GU32 2DQ. T: Petersfield 3915.

WHITESIDE, Dr Derek Thomas, FBA 1975; University Reader in History of Mathematics, Cambridge, since 1976; b 23 July 1932; s of Ernest Whiteside and Edith (née Watts); m 1962, Ruth Isabel Robinson; one s one d. Educ: Blackpool Grammar Sch.; Bristol Univ. (BA); Cambridge Univ. (PhD). Leverhulme Research Fellow, 1959-61; DSIR Research Fellow, 1961-63; Research Asst, 1963-72, Asst Dir of Research, 1972-76, Univ. of Cambridge. Médaille Koyré, Académie Internat. d'Histoire des Sciences, 1968; Sarton Medal, Amer. History of Sci. Soc., 1977. Publications: Patterns of Mathematical Thought in the later Seventeenth Century, 1961; (ed) The Mathematical Papers of Isaac Newton (8 vols), 1967-81; articles in Brit. Jl Hist. Science, Jl for Hist. of Astronomy, etc. Recreations: a diversity of things unenergetic. Address: Whipple Science Museum, Free School Lane, Cambridge.

WHITFIELD, family name of Baron Kenswood.

WHITFIELD, Adrian; a Recorder of the Crown Court, since 1981; b 10 July 1937; s of Peter Henry Whitfield and Margaret Mary Burns; m 1st, 1962, Lucy Caroline Beckett (marr. diss.); two d; 2nd, 1971, Niamh O'Kelly; one s one d. Educ: Ampleforth Coll.; Magdalen Coll., Oxford. BA Oxon. Called to the Bar, Middle Temple, 1964; Member of Western Circuit; Asst Parliamentary Boundary Commissioner, 1976; Deputy Circuit Judge, 1978. Publications: contribs on legal matters in medical and dental pubns. Recreations: reading, carpentry, country pursuits. Address: 47 Faroe Road, W14 0EL. T: 01-603 8982; Carpmael Building, Temple, EC4Y 7HT. T: 01-353 5537. Club: Hampshire.

WHITFIELD, Prof. Charles Richard, MD; FRCOG; FRCPGlas; Regius Professor of Midwifery in the University of Glasgow, since Oct. 1976; b 21 Oct. 1927; s of Charles Alexander and Aileen Muriel Whitfield; m 1953, Marion Douglas McKinney; one s two d. Educ: Campbell Coll., Belfast; Queen's Univ., Belfast (MD). House Surg. and Ho. Phys. appts in Belfast teaching hospitals, 1951-53; Specialist in Obstetrics and Gynaecology, RAMC (Lt-Col retd), 1953-64; Sen. Lectr/Ho. Reader in Dept of Midwifery and Gynaecology, Queen's Univ., Belfast, 1964-74; Consultant to Belfast teaching hosps, 1964-74; Prof. of Obstetrics and Gynaecology, Univ. of Manchester, 1974-76. Publications: papers on perinatal medicine, pregnancy anaemia and other obstetric and gynaec. topics in med. and scientific jls. Recreations: food, travel, sun-worship. Address: Redlands, 23 Thorn Road, Bearsden, Glasgow G61 4BS.

WHITFIELD, George; poet, artist, and (retired) journalist; former art critic, film critic, and sub-editor Liverpool Echo; b 1891; m Beatrix (d 1976), d of Jacob and Makrouhi Yanekian, Chanak, Dardanelles; one d. Educ: privately and at Jesuit College. Studied art under Fred V. Burridge, RE, in Liverpool. Political, sporting, and comic-strip cartoons in London, provincial and overseas papers; former correspondent motoring journals and film publicity, British and American companies. Served Royal Naval Air Service (aerial and service drawings). Founder-member of one-time Liverpool Pickwickians (their first Mr Pickwick) and Liverpool First-Nighters Society. On selection and hanging committees of World Cartoons Exhibn, first Liverpool Festival. Publications: poetry and signed articles on art, architecture, cinema, radio, boxing. Recreations: poetry, pictures, and people. Address: Rockley House, Rossett, Clwyd. Club: Press.

WHITFIELD, Rev. George Joshua Newbold; General Secretary, Church of England Board of Education, 1969-74; b 2 June 1909; s of late Joshua Newbold and Eva Whitfield; m 1937, Dr Audrey Priscilla Dence, d of late Rev. A. T. Dence; two s two d. Educ: Bede Gram. Sch., Sunderland; King's Coll., Univ. of London; Bishops' Coll., Cheshunt. BA 1st cl. Hons, Engl. and AKC, 1930 (Barry Prizeman); MA 1935. Asst Master, Trin. Sch., Croydon, 1931-34; Sen. Engl. Master: Doncaster Gram. Sch., 1934-36; Hymers Coll., Hull, 1937-43; Headmaster: Tavistock Gram. Sch., 1943-46; Stockport Sch., 1946-50; Hampton Sch., 1950-68. Chief Examr in Engl., Univ. of Durham Sch. Exams Bd, 1940-43. Deacon, 1962; Priest, 1963. Member: Duke of Edinburgh's Award Adv. Cttee, 1960-66; Headmasters' Conf., 1964-68; Corporation of Church House, 1974-; Pres., Headmasters' Assoc., 1967; Chm., Exeter Diocesan Educn Cttee, 1981-. Publications: (ed) Teaching Poetry, 1937; An Introduction to Drama, 1938; God and Man in the Old Testament, 1949; (ed) Poetry in the Sixth Form, 1950; Philosophy and Religion, 1955; (jtly) Christliche Erziehung in Europa, Band I, England, 1975. Recreations: gardening, photography. Address: Hampton House, 31 Foxholes Hill, Exmouth, Devon EX8 2DQ. T: Exmouth 74162. Club: Athenæum.

WHITFIELD, John Flett, JP, DL; Chairman, Surrey County Council, since 1981; b 1 June 1922; s of John and Bertha Whitfield; m 1946, Rosemary Elisabeth Joan Hartman; two d. Educ: Epsom Coll., Surrey. Served War, King's Royal Rifle Corps, 1939-46. HM Foreign Service, 1946-57; Director, Materials Handling Equipment (GB) Ltd, 1957-61; London Director, Hunslet Holdings Ltd, 1961-64. Director, Sunningdale Golf Club, 1973-77. Councillor: Berkshire CC, 1961-70; Surrey CC, 1970-. Contested (C) Pontefract, General Election, 1964. JP Berkshire 1971-, Chm. Windsor County Bench, 1978-80; DL Surrey 1982. Recreations: golf, foreign languages, bookbinding. Address: 4 Holiday House, Sunningdale, Berks SL5 9RW. T: Ascot 20997. Clubs: Royal and Ancient Golf of St Andrews; Royal Cinque Ports Golf; Sunningdale Golf; Rye Golf.

WHITFIELD, Professor John Humphreys; Serena Professor of Italian Language and Literature in the University of Birmingham, 1946-74; b 2 Oct. 1906; s of J. A. Whitfield; m 1936, Joan Herrin, ARCA; two s. Educ: Handsworth Grammar School; Magdalen College, Oxford. William Doncaster Scholar, Magdalen Coll., 1925-29; Double First Class Hons in Mod. Langs, 1928, 1929; Paget Toynbee Prizeman, 1933. Asst Master, King Edward VII School, Sheffield, 1930-36; University Lecturer in Italian, Oxford University, 1936-46; Awarder to Oxford and Cambridge Schools Examination Bd, 1940-68. Part-time Temporary Assistant Civil Officer, Naval Intelligence Department, 1943. Chairman, Society for Italian Studies, 1962-74; Senior editor of Italian Studies, 1967-74. President: Dante Alighieri Society (Comitato di Birmingham), 1957-75; Assoc. of Teachers of Italian, 1976-77. Barlow Lecturer on Dante, University College, London, 1958-59, Barlow Centenary Lecture, 1977; Donald Dudley Meml Lecture, Birmingham, 1980. Edmund G. Gardner Memorial Prize, 1959; Amedeo Maiuri Prize (Rome), 1965. Commendatore, Ordine al Merito della Repubblica Italiana, 1972 (Cavaliere Ufficiale, 1960). Publications: Petrarch and the Renascence, 1943 (NY, 1966); Machiavelli, 1947 (NY, 1966); Petrarca e il Rinascimento (tr. V. Capocci, Laterza), 1949; Dante and Virgil, 1949; Giacomo Leopardi, 1954 (Italian tr. 1964); A Short History of Italian Literature, 1962 (Pelican, 1960, 5th edn 1980); The Barlow Lectures on Dante, 1960; Leopardi's Canti, trans. into English Verse, 1962; Leopardi's Canti, ed with Introduction and notes, 1967; Discourses on Machiavelli, 1969; The Charlecote Manuscript of Machiavelli's Prince, facsimile edn with an Essay on the Prince, 1969; Castiglione: The Courtier, ed with introduction, 1974; Guarini: Il Pastor Fido, ed bilingual edn with introduction, 1976; articles and reviews contrib. to Modern Language Review, Italian Studies, History, Medium Aevum, Comparative Literature, Problemi della Pedagogia, Le parole e le Idee, Encyclopædia Britannica, Chambers's Encyclopædia, Hutchinson's Encyclopædia, Concise Encyclopædia of the Italian Renaissance, etc. Festschrift: Essays in Honour of John Humphreys Whitfield, 1975. Address: 2 Woodbourne Road, Edgbaston, Birmingham B15 3QH. T: 021-454 1035.

WHITFIELD LEWIS, Herbert John; see Lewis, H. J. W.

WHITFORD, Hon. Sir John (Norman Keates), Kt 1970; Hon. Mr Justice Whitford; a Judge of the High Court, Chancery Division, since 1970; b 24 June 1913; s of Harry Whitford and Ella Mary Keates; m 1946, Rosemary, d of John Barcham Green and Emily Paillard; four d. Educ: University College School; Munich University; Peterhouse, Cambridge. President, ADC. Called to the Bar: Inner Temple, 1935; Middle Temple, 1946 (Bencher 1970). Served with RAFVR, 1939-44: Wing Comdr, 1942; Chief Radar Officer and Dep. Chief Signals Officer, Air Headquarters Eastern Mediterranean; Advisor on patents and information exchanged for war purposes, HM Embassy, Washington, 1944-45. QC 1965. Member of Bar Council, 1968-70. Chm., Departmental Cttee on Law Relating to Copyright and Designs, 1974-76. Address: Royal Courts of Justice, WC2.

WHITHAM, Prof. Gerald Beresford, FRS 1965; Professor of Applied Mathematics, at the California Institute of Technology, Pasadena, Calif, since 1962; b 13 Dec. 1927; s of Harry and Elizabeth Ellen Whitham; m 1951, Nancy (née Lord); one s two d. Educ: Elland Gram. Sch., Elland, Yorks; Manchester University. PhD Maths, Manchester, 1953. Lectr in Applied Mathematics, Manchester Univ., 1953-56; Assoc. Prof., Applied Mathematics, New York Univ., 1956-59; Prof., Mathematics, MIT, 1959-62. FAAAS 1959. Publications: Linear and Nonlinear Waves, 1974; Lectures on Wave Propagation, 1979; research papers in Proc. Roy. Soc., Jl Fluid Mechanics,

Communications on Pure and Applied Maths. *Address:* Applied Mathematics 217-50, California Institute of Technology, Pasadena, California 91125, USA.

WHITING, Maurice Henry, OBE; MA, MB, BCh Cantab; FRCS; Consulting Surgeon, Royal London Ophthalmic Hospital; Emeritus Ophthalmic Surgeon, Middlesex Hospital; *b* 12 Oct. 1885; *s* of William Henry Whiting, CB; *m* 1st, 1916, Blanche Beatrice (*d* 1952), *d* of Edward Aggas; (*o s* killed in action, RAF, 1942); 2nd, 1953, Dorothy Miller, *d* of William Gilford. *Educ:* Mill Hill School; Downing College, Cambridge; The Middlesex Hospital, House Surgeon, Middlesex Hospital; House Surgeon and Pathologist, Royal London Ophthalmic Hospital; Capt. RAMC 1914-19; at Boulogne as Ophthalmic Specialist, 1915-19 (despatches); engaged in work in London as Ophthalmic surgeon since 1919; late Hon. Sec. Ophthalmological Soc. of the UK; late Ophthalmic Surgeon, Paddington Green Children's Hosp.; Member of Board of Governors Middlesex Hospital; President of Ophthalmological Society of UK, 1950-51; Pres. Old Millhillians Club, 1950-51; Pres. Downing College Assoc., 1953-54. *Publications:* Modern Developments in Cataract Extraction, Montgomery Lecture, RCSI, 1933; Ophthalmic Nursing; Concussion Changes in the Crystalline Lens; Technique of the Haab and Small Magnets, and other articles in medical and ophthalmic journals. *Address:* Top Meadow, Woodchurch Road, Tenterden, Kent. *T:* Tenterden 2752.

WHITING, Rev. Peter Graham, QHC 1981; Deputy Chaplain General to the Forces, Army, since 1981; *b* 7 Nov. 1930; *s* of Rev. Arthur Whiting and Mrs Olive Whiting; *m* 1960, Lorena Inns; two *s* three *d*. *Educ:* Yeovil Grammar Sch.; Irish Baptist Theol Coll., Dublin. Ordained into Baptist Ministry, 1956. Minister, King's Heath, Northampton, 1956-62; commnd RAChD, 1962; Regtl Chaplain, 1962-69 (Chaplain to 1st Bn The Parachutte Regt, 1964-66); Sen. Chaplain, BAOR, 1969-72; Staff Chaplain, HQ BAOR, 1973-74; Sen. Chaplain, 24 Airportable Bde, 1974-75; Dep. Asst Chaplain Gen., W Midland Dist, Shrewsbury, 1975-78 (Sen. Chaplain, Young Entry Units, 1976-78); Asst Chaplain Gen., 1st British Corps, BAOR, 1978-81. *Address:* Ministry of Defence Chaplains (A), Bagshot Park, Bagshot, Surrey GU19 5PL.

WHITLAM, Hon. (Edward) Gough, AC 1978; QC 1962; Fellow, University of Sydney Senate, since 1981; President, International Commission of Jurists, Australian Section, since 1982; Prime Minister of Australia, 1972-75; *b* 11 July 1916; *s* of late H. F. E. Whitlam, Australian Crown Solicitor and Aust. rep. on UN Human Rights Commission; *m* 1942, Margaret Elaine, *d* of late Mr Justice Dovey, NSW Supreme Court; three *s* one *d*. *Educ:* University of Sydney. BA 1938; LLB 1946. RAAF Flight Lieut, 1941-45. Barrister, 1947; MP for Werriwa, NSW, 1952-78; Joint Committee on Constitutional Review, 1956-59; Deputy Leader, Aust. Labor Party, 1960, Leader, 1967-77; Leader of the Opposition, 1967-72 and 1976-77; Minister for Foreign Affairs, 1972-73. Vis. Fellow, 1978-81, First Nat. Fellow, 1980-81, ANU. Vis. Prof., Harvard Univ., 1979. Hon. DLitt Sydney, 1981; Hon. LLD Philippines, 1974. Silver Plate of Honour, Socialist Internat., 1976. *Publications:* The Constitution *versus* Labor, 1957; Australian Foreign Policy, 1963; Socialism within the Constitution, 1965; Australia, Base or Bridge?, 1966; Beyond Vietnam: Australia's Regional Responsibility, 1968; An Urban Nation, 1969; A New Federalism, 1971; Urbanised Australia, 1972; Australian Public Administration and the Labor Government, 1973; Australia's Foreign Policy: New Directions, New Definitions, 1973; Road to Reform: Labor in Government, 1975; The New Federalism: Labor's Programs and Policies, 1975; Government of the People, for the People—by the People's House, 1975; On Australia's Constitution, 1977; Reform During Recession, 1978; The Truth of the Matter, 1979; The Italian Inspiration in English Literature, 1980; A Pacific Community, 1981; The Cost of Federalism, 1982; The Whitlam Government, 1983. *Address:* Westfield Towers, 100 William Street, Potts Point, Sydney, NSW 2011, Australia.

WHITLEY, Elizabeth Young, (Mrs H. C. Whitley); social worker and journalist; *b* 28 Dec. 1915; *d* of Robert Thom and Mary Muir Wilson; *m* 1939, Henry Charles Whitley (Very Rev. Dr H. C. Whitley, CVO; *d* 1976); two *s* two *d* (and one *s* decd). *Educ:* Laurelbank School, Glasgow; Glasgow University. MA 1936; courses: in Italian at Perugia Univ., 1935, in Social Science at London School of Economics and Glasgow School of Social Science, 1938-39. Ran Girls' Clubs in Govan and Plantation, Glasgow, and Young Mothers' Clubs in Partick and Port Glasgow; Vice-Chm. Scottish Association of Girls' Clubs and Mixed Clubs, 1957-61, and Chm. of Advisory Cttee, 1958-59. Broadcast regular programme with BBC (Scottish Home Service), 1953. Member: Faversham Committee on AID, 1958-60; Pilkington Committee on Broadcasting, 1960-62. Columnist, Scottish Daily Express. Adopted as Parly candidate for SNP by West Perth and Kinross, 1968. *Publications:* Plain Mr Knox, 1960; The Two Kingdoms: the story of the Scottish covenanters, 1977; descriptive and centenary articles for Scottish papers, particularly Glasgow Herald and Scotland's Magazine. *Recreations:* reading, gardening. *Address:* The Glebe, Southwick, by Dumfries. *T:* Southwick 276.

WHITLEY, Air Marshal Sir John R., KBE 1956 (CBE 1945); CB 1946; DSO 1943; AFC 1937, Bar, 1956; *b* 7 September 1905; *s* of late A. Whitley, Condette, Pas de Calais, France; *m* 1932, Barbara Liscombe (*d* 1965); three *s* (and one *s* decd); *m* 1967, Mrs Alison Russell. *Educ:* Haileybury. Entered Royal Air Force with a short-service commission, 1926; Permanent

Commission, 1931; served in India, 1932-37; served in Bomber Command, 1940-45, as a Squadron Comdr, Station Comdr, Base Comdr and AOC a Group; Director of Organisation (Establishments), Air Ministry, 1948 and 1949; Imperial Defence College, 1950; AOA, 2nd Tactical Air Force, 1951 and 1952; AOC No 1 (Bomber) Group, 1953-56; Air Member for Personnel, 1957-59; Inspector-General, RAF, 1959-62; Controller, RAF Benevolent Fund, 1962-68, retd. *Address:* 2 Woodside Close, Woodside Avenue, Lymington SO4 8FH. *T:* Lymington 76920. *Clubs:* Royal Air Force; Royal Lymington Yacht, Island Sailing (IoW).

WHITLEY, John Reginald; a Recorder of the Crown Court, since 1978; *b* 22 March 1926; *o s* of late Reginald Whitley and of Marjorie Whitley (*née* Orton); *m* 1966, Susan Helen Kennaway; one *d*. *Educ:* Sherborne Sch.; Corpus Christi Coll., Cambridge. Served War, Army, Egypt, Palestine, 1944-48; commissioned, KRRC, 1945. Called to the Bar, Gray's Inn, 1953; Western Circuit, 1953. *Recreation:* golf. *Address:* Kingsrod, Friday's Hill, Kingsley Green, near Haslemere, Surrey GU27 3LL. *T:* Haslemere 4582.

WHITLEY, Oliver John; Managing Director, External Broadcasting, British Broadcasting Corporation, 1969-72, retired; *b* 12 Feb. 1912; *s* of Rt Hon. J. H. Whitley, and Marguerite (*née* Marchetti); *m* 1939, Elspeth Catherine (*née* Forrester-Paton); four *s* one *d*. *Educ:* Clifton Coll.; New Coll., Oxford. Barrister-at-Law, 1935; BBC, 1935-41. Served in RNVR, 1942-46; Coastal Forces and Combined Ops. BBC 1946-: seconded to Colonial Office, 1946-49; Head of General Overseas Service, 1950-54; Assistant Controller, Overseas Services, 1955-57; Appointments Officer, 1957-60; Controller, Staff Training and Appointments, 1960-64; Chief Assistant to Dir-Gen., 1964-68. *Recreations:* reading and gardening. *Address:* Greenacre, Ganavan Road, Oban, Argyll PA34 5TU. *T:* Oban 62555.

WHITLOCK, William Charles; MP (Lab) Nottingham North since October 1959; *b* 20 June 1918; *s* of late George Whitlock and Sarah Whitlock, Sholing, Southampton; *m* 1943, Jessie Hilda, *d* of George Reardon of Armagh; five *s*. *Educ:* Itchen Gram. Sch.; Southampton Univ. Army Service, 1939-46. Apptd full-time Trade Union Officer, Area Organiser of Union of Shop, Distributive and Allied Workers, 1946. President, Leicester and District Trades Council, 1955-56; President, Leicester City Labour Party, 1956-57; President, North-East Leicester Labour Party, 1955-56, and 1958-59. Member East Midlands Regional Council of Labour Party, 1955-67, Vice-Chairman 1961-62, Chairman 1962-63. Opposition Whip, House of Commons, 1962-64; Vice-Chamberlain of the Household, 1964-66; Lord Comr of Treasury, March 1966-July 1966; Comptroller of HM Household, July 1966-March 1967; Dep. Chief Whip and Lord Comr of the Treasury, March-July 1967; Under Sec. of State for Commonwealth Affairs, 1967-68; Parly Under-Sec. of State, FCO, 1968-69. *Address:* House of Commons, SW1.

WHITMARSH, Gerald Edward Leaman, CBE 1972; DL; FCA; Vice-President, formerly Chairman, West Country Tourist Board, since 1974; Chairman: Poron Insulation Ltd; Capital Securities Ltd; Toptown Printers Ltd, since 1973; Director, Armada Investments Ltd, since 1976; *b* 10 Oct. 1908; *s* of Edward Whitmarsh, Plymouth; *m* 1938, Phyllis May, *d* of William T. Allchin, Charlton, SE; two *s* one *d*. *Educ:* Plymouth Coll.; Rippon Hall, Oxford. Contested (L): Truro, 1950; St Ives, 1959 and 1964. Chm., Devon CC, 1966-71 (Chm. Finance Cttee, 1965-67); Mem., SW Economic Planning Council, 1967-72. DL Co. Devon, 1969. Mem. Council, 1965-77, Finance Cttee, 1958-, Univ. of Exeter. Hon. MA, Exeter, 1965. *Recreation:* walking on Dartmoor. *Address:* South Winds, Crapstone, Yelverton, Devon. *T:* Yelverton 2316.

WHITMORE, Clive Anthony; Permanent Under-Secretary of State, Ministry of Defence, since 1983; *b* 18 Jan. 1935; *s* of Charles Arthur Whitmore and Louisa Lilian Whitmore; *m* 1961, Jennifer Mary Thorpe; one *s* two *d*. *Educ:* Sutton Grammar Sch., Surrey; Christ's Coll., Cambridge (BA). Asst Principal, WO, 1959; Private Sec. to Permanent Under-Sec. of State, WO, 1961; Asst Private Sec. to Sec. of State for War, 1962; Principal, 1964; Private Sec. to Permanent Under-Sec. of State, MoD, 1969; Asst Sec., 1971; Asst Under-Sec. of State (Defence Staff), MoD, 1975; Under Sec., Cabinet Office, 1977; Principal Private Sec. to the Prime Minister, 1979-82; Dep. Sec., 1981. *Recreations:* gardening, listening to music. *Address:* Ministry of Defence, Whitehall, SW1.

WHITMORE, Sir John (Henry Douglas), 2nd Bt *cr* 1954; *b* 16 Oct. 1937; *s* of Col Sir Francis Henry Douglas Charlton Whitmore, 1st Bt, KCB, CMG, DSO, TD, and of Lady Whitmore (*née* Ellis Johnsen); *S* father 1961; *m* 1st, 1962, Gunilla (marr. diss. 1969), *e d* of Sven A. Hansson, OV, KLH, Danderyd, and *o d* of Mrs Ella Hansson, Stockholm, Sweden; one *d*; 2nd, 1977, Diana Elaine, *e d* of Fred A. Becchetti, California, USA. *Educ:* Stone House, Kent; Eton; Sandhurst; Cirencester. Occupation: active in personal development and social change. *Recreations:* ski-ing, squash, motor cycling. *Address:* 200A West End Lane, NW6. *Club:* British Racing Drivers.

WHITNEY, John Norton Braithwaite; Director General, Independent Broadcasting Authority, since 1982; *b* 20 Dec. 1930; *s* of Willis Bevan Whitney and Dorothy Anne Whitney; *m* 1956, Roma Elizabeth Hodgson; one *s* one *d*. *Educ:* Leighton Park Friends' Sch., Reading, Berks. Radio producer, 1951-64; formed Ross Radio Productions Ltd, for making radio programmes, 1951, and Autocue Ltd 1955; opened Radio Antilles, 1963. Man. Dir, Capital Radio, 1973-82; Dir, Duke of York's Theatre, 1979-82; Dir,

Satellite Television PLC, March–May 1982. Chm. and co-founder, Local Radio Assoc., 1964; Chm., Assoc. of Indep. Local Radio Contractors, 1973, 1974, 1975, 1980. Wrote, edited and devised numerous television series, 1956–76. Founded Recidivists Anonymous Fellowship Trust, 1962; Member: Admin. Council, Royal Jubilee Trusts; Appeal Cttee, Nat. Council for Voluntary Orgns; Centenary Appeal Cttee, RCM; Welfare Cttee, Nat. Advertising Benevolent Soc.; Member Council: Royal London Aid Society; TV and Radio Industries Club; Operation Drake Fellowship; Intermediate Technol. Develt Gp; Trustee: Help a London Child; Soundaround; Venture Trust. Mem., RTS; FRSA. Barker, Variety Club of GB. *Recreations:* chess, photography, sculpture, looking at sunrises. *Address:* Independent Broadcasting Authority, 70 Brompton Road, SW3 1EY. *T:* 01-584 7011. *Clubs:* Garrick, Pilgrims, Whitefriars.

WHITNEY, Raymond William, OBE 1968; MP (C) Wycombe, Bucks, since April 1978; *b* 28 Nov. 1930; *o s* of late George Whitney, Northampton; *m* 1956, Sheila Margot Beswick Prince; two *s. Educ:* Wellingborough Sch.; RMA, Sandhurst; London Univ. (BA (Hons) Oriental Studies). Commnd Northamptonshire Regt, 1951; served in Trieste, Korea, Hong Kong, Germany; seconded to Australian Army HQ, 1960–63; resigned and entered HM Diplomatic Service, 1964; First Sec., Peking, 1966–68; Head of Chancery, Buenos Aires, 1969–72; FCO, 1972–73; Dep. High Comr, Dacca, 1973–76; FCO, 1976–78, Hd of Overseas Inf. Dept, 1977–78. Vice-Chm., Cons. Employment Cttee, 1980–; Chm., Cons. For. Affairs Cttee, 1981–; Mem., Public Accounts Cttee, 1981–. *Publications:* articles on Chinese and Asian affairs in professional jls. *Recreations:* theatricals (performing, producing and writing), tennis, bridge, walking. *Address:* The Dial House, Sunninghill, Berks SL5 0AG. *T:* Ascot 23164.

WHITSEY, Fred; Consultant Editor, Popular Gardening, since 1982; Gardening Correspondent, Daily Telegraph, since 1971; *b* 18 July 1919; *m* 1947, Patricia Searle. *Educ:* outside school hours, and continuously since then. Assistant Editor, Popular Gardening, 1948–64, Associate Editor, 1964–67, Editor, 1967–82. Gardening correspondent, Sunday Telegraph, 1961–71. Broadcaster on BBC and independent radio programmes. Gold Veitch Meml Medal, RHS, 1979. *Publications:* Sunday Telegraph Gardening Book, 1966; contribs to Country Life, Homes & Gardens, Woman's Realm, New York Times and The Garden. *Recreations:* gardening, music. *Address:* Avens Mead, 20 Oast Road, Oxted, Surrey RH8 9DU.

WHITSEY, Rt. Rev. Hubert Victor; *b* 21 Nov. 1916; *s* of Samuel and Rachel Whitsey, Blackburn, Lancs; *m* 1950, Jean Margaret Bellinger; two *s* one *d. Educ:* Queen Elizabeth's Grammar Sch., Blackburn; Technical Coll., Blackburn; St Edmund Hall, Oxford (MA); Westcott House, Cambridge. Midland Bank, 1933–39. Royal Regt Artillery (TA), 1938–46 (Lt Col 1945). Asst Curate, Chorley, Lancs, 1949–51; Vicar: Farington, Lancs, 1952–55; St Thomas, Halliwell, Bolton, 1955–60; Asst Rural Dean, Bolton, 1957–60; Vicar: All Saints and Martyrs, Langley, Manchester, 1960–68; Downham, Lancs, 1968–74; Hon. Canon, Manchester Cathedral, 1963, Emeritus, 1968; Bishop Suffragan of Hertford, 1971–74; Bishop of Chester, 1974–81. *Recreations:* idleness, practicality. *Address:* Hill Top, Twiston, Clitheroe, Lancs BB7 4DB.

WHITTAKER, Arnold, CSI 1947; CIE 1938; ICS, retired; Chairman Somerset County Council, 1956–59 (County Alderman, 1953); *b* 27 July 1900; *m* 1934, Hilda Lucy, *d* of late O. W. Street, MA; one *d. Educ:* Colne Grammar School; London School of Economics; Christ Church, Oxford. Joined ICS 1924; retired, 1939; Political Adviser to Indian Tea Association and Member, Assam Legislative Assembly; Secretary to Planting and Commerce Group, Assam Legislature, 1939–46. Dir, Bridgwater Building Society, 1961–79. *Address:* Hey House, Somerton, Somerset. *T:* Somerton 72447.

WHITTAKER, John Macnaghten, FRS 1949; MA, DSc, FRSE; Vice-Chancellor of Sheffield University, Sept. 1952–65, retired; *b* 7 March 1905; *s* of late Sir Edmund Whittaker, FRS; *m* 1933, Iona, *d* of J. S. Elliot; two *s. Educ:* Fettes; Edin. Univ.; Trinity College, Cambridge (Scholar). Wrangler, 1927; Smith's Prize, 1929; Adams Prize, 1949; Lecturer in Mathematics, Edinburgh Univ., 1927–29; Fellow and Lecturer, Pembroke Coll., Cambridge, 1929–33; Prof. of Pure Mathematics, Liverpool Univ., 1933–52. Senior Fellow, Birmingham University, 1965–66. Vis. Professor: Ain Shams Univ., Cairo, 1967; Inst. of Mathematics, Teheran, 1968–69; Univ. of West Indies, Barbados, 1970–71. Served in RA, 1940–45 (AA Command, Western Desert, Tunisia, and as GSO1, War Office); Lt-Col RA, 1944; Dep. Scientific Adviser to the Army Council, 1944. Chairman: Joint Standing Cttee of Universities and Accountancy Profession, 1953–64; Commn on Royal University of Malta, 1957. A Capital Burgess of the Town and Parish of Sheffield, 1956–70; Freedom of City of Sheffield, 1965. Hon. LLD (Sheffield). *Publications:* Interpolatory Function Theory, 1935; Les séries de base de polynomes quelconques, 1949; Memoirs in various journals. *Address:* 11B Endcliffe Crescent, Sheffield S10 3EB. *T:* Sheffield 663712.

WHITTAKER, Sir (Joseph) Meredith, Kt 1974; TD 1950; DL; Chairman of Scarborough and District Newspapers Ltd; *b* 28 Sept. 1914; *s* of late Francis Croyden Whittaker; *m* 1939, Gwenllian Enid, *d* of W. F. Allen, Scarborough; one *s* one *d. Educ:* Scarborough Coll.; Queen's Coll., Oxford (MA). Mem. NR Yorks CC, 1949–74, and North Yorkshire CC, 1973–81. Vice-Chm. of Exec. Council, County Councils Assoc., 1969–72; Chairman of Executive Council: County Councils Assoc., 1972–74; Assoc. of County Councils,

1973–76; President, British Sections of Internat. Union of Local Authorities and Council of European Municipalities. DL Yorks 1971. *Address:* High Dalby House, Thornton Dale, Pickering, North Yorkshire YO18 7LP. *T:* (home) Pickering 60214; (business) Scarborough 63631. *Club:* Anglo-Belgian.

WHITTALL, Harold Astley, CBE 1978; CEng; Chairman, B.S.G. International Ltd, since 1981; Director: Ransome, Sims & Jefferies Ltd, since 1977 (Deputy Chairman, since 1981); APV Holdings, since 1982; LRC International, since 1982; *b* 8 Sept. 1925; *s* of Harold and Margaret Whittall; *m* 1952, Diana Margharita Berner. *Educ:* Handsworth Grammar Sch., Birmingham; Aston and Birmingham Technical Colls. Gen. Manager, Belliss & Morcom, 1962; Managing Dir, Amalgamated Power Engineering, 1968, Chm., 1977–81. Pres., Engineering Employers' Fedn, 1976–78. *Address:* 26 Mead Rise, Edgbaston, Birmingham B15 3SD. *T:* 021-454 0890. *Clubs:* Royal Automobile, St James'.

WHITTALL, Michael Charlton, CMG 1980; OBE 1963; HM Diplomatic Service; Counsellor, Foreign and Commonwealth Office, since 1978; *b* 9 January 1926; *s* of Kenneth Edwin Whittall and Edna Ruth (*née* Lawson); *m* 1953, Susan Olivia La Fontaine; one *d. Educ:* Rottingdean; Rugby; Trinity Hall, Cambridge. Served RAF, 1944–48. Foreign Office, 1949; Salonika, 1949; British Middle East Office, 1952; Vice-Consul, Basra, 1953; FO, 1955; Second Secretary, Beirut, 1956; FO, 1958; First Secretary, Amman, 1959. *Recreations:* railways (GWR), birdwatching, walking, photography. *Address:* c/o Foreign and Commonwealth Office, SW1. *Club:* Royal Air Force.

WHITTAM, Prof. Ronald, FRS 1973; Professor of Physiology, University of Leicester, since 1966; *b* 21 March 1925; *e s* of Edward Whittam and May Whittam (*née* Butterworth), Oldham, Lancs; *m* 1957, Christine Patricia Margaret, 2nd *d* of Canon J. W. Lamb, Bridlington, Yorks; one *s* one *d. Educ:* Council and Technical Schools, Oldham; Univs of Manchester, Sheffield and Cambridge. BSc 1st Class Hons (Manchester); PhD (Sheffield and Cambridge). Served RAF, 1943–47. John Stokes Fellow, Dept of Biochem., Univ. of Sheffield, 1953–55; Beit Memorial Fellow, Physiological Lab., Cambridge, 1955–58; Mem. Scientific Staff, MRC Cell Metabolism Research Unit, Oxford, 1958–60; Univ. Lectr in Biochemistry, Oxford, 1960–66; Bruno Mendel Fellow of Royal Society, 1965–66; Dean of Fac. of Science, Leicester Univ., 1979–. Mem. Editorial Bd of Biochem. Jl, 1963–67; Hon. Sec., Physiological Soc., 1969–74; Mem. Biological Research Bd of MRC, 1971–74, Co-Chm., 1973–74; Member: Biological Sciences Cttee, UGC, 1974–; Educn Cttee, Royal Soc., 1979–; Chm., Biological Educn Cttee, Royal Soc. and Inst Biol., 1974–77. *Publications:* Transport and Diffusion in Red Blood Cells, 1964; scientific papers dealing with cell membranes. *Recreation:* walking. *Address:* Department of Physiology, The University, Leicester LE1 7RH. *T:* Leicester 551234.

WHITTAM SMITH, Andreas; City Editor, Daily Telegraph, since 1977; *b* 13 June 1937; *s* of Canon J. E. Smith and Mrs Smith (*née* Barlow); *m* 1964, Valerie Catherine, *d* of late Wing Comdr J. A. Sherry and Mrs N. W. H. Wyllys; two *s. Educ:* Birkenhead Sch., Cheshire; Keble Coll., Oxford (BA). With N. M. Rothschild, 1960–62; Stock Exchange Gazette, 1962–63; Financial Times, 1963–64; The Times, 1964–66; Dep. City Editor, Daily Telegraph, 1966–69; City Editor, The Guardian, 1969–70; Editor, Investors Chronicle and Stock Exchange Gazette, and Dir, Throgmorton Publications, 1970–77. Hon. Treasurer, Nat. Council for One Parent Families, 1982–. Wincott award, 1975. *Recreations:* music, history. *Address:* 31 Brunswick Gardens, W8 4AW. *Club:* Garrick.

WHITTEMORE, Ernest William, MM 1944 and Bar 1945; Under-Secretary, Department of Health and Social Security, 1973–76; *b* 31 Aug. 1916; *s* of late Ernest William Whittemore and Hilda Whittemore; *m* 1942, Irene Mollie Hudson; two *d. Educ:* Raine's Sch., Stepney; King's Coll., London. BA Hons English. Receiver's Office, New Scotland Yard, 1934–35; Min. of Health, 1935–45; Royal Artillery, 1942–46; Min. of Nat. Insce (and successor depts), 1945–76. *Recreations:* bibliomania, travel, sweet peas. *Address:* 39 Montalt Road, Woodford Green, Essex IG8 9RS. *T:* 01-504 7028.

WHITTERIDGE, Prof. David, FRS 1953; Waynflete Professor of Physiology, University of Oxford, 1968–79, now Emeritus Professor; *b* 22 June 1912; 2nd *s* of Walter and late Jeanne Whitteridge; *m* 1938, Gweneth, *d* of S. Hutchings; three *d. Educ:* Whitgift School, Croydon; Magdalen College, Oxford (1st cl. Physiology Finals, 1934); King's College Hospital. BSc 1936; BM, BCh 1937; DM 1945; Beit Memorial Fellowship, 1940; Schorstein Research Fellow, 1944; Fellow by Special Election, Magdalen College, Oxford, 1945–50; University Demonstrator in Physiology, Univ. of Oxford, 1944–50; Prof. of Physiology, Univ. of Edinburgh, 1950–68. Fellow of Magdalen Coll., Oxford, 1968–79, Hon. Fellow, 1979. Leverhulme Vis. Prof., Univ. Delhi, 1967 and 1973; Lectures: Sherrington, RSM, 1972; Victor Horsley Meml, BMA, 1972; Bowman, OSUK, 1977; Bayliss Starling, Physiolog. Soc., 1979; G. Parr Meml, EEG Soc., 1980. Mem. Bd of Trustees, Nat. Lib. of Scotland, 1966–70. Hon. Mem., Physiolog. Soc., 1982. Feldberg Prize, 1962. FRCP London, 1966. *Publications:* papers on physiological topics in Jl Physiol., Brain, etc. *Address:* Winterslow, Lincombe Lane, Boar's Hill, Oxford OX1 5DZ. *T:* Oxford 735211.

See also R. A. Furtado, Sir G. C. Whitteridge.

WHITTERIDGE, Sir Gordon (Coligny), KCMG 1964 (CMG 1956); OBE 1946; *b* 6 Nov. 1908; *s* of late Walter Randall and Jeanne Whitteridge, Croydon; *m* 1st, 1938, Margaret Lungley (*d* 1942; one *s* one *d* decd 1942); 2nd, 1951, Jane (*d* 1979), twin *d* of Frederick J. Driscoll, Brookline, Mass, USA; one *s*. *Educ*: Whitgift School, Croydon; University of Cambridge. Joined Consular Service, 1932; one of HM Vice-Consuls, Siam, 1933; Vice-Consul, Batavia, 1936; Acting Consul, Batavia, 1937, 1938, and 1939; Acting Consul, Medan, Sept. 1941–Feb. 1942. Employed at Foreign Office from June, 1942; promoted Consul (Grade II), Foreign Office, 1944, Consul, 1945. 1st Secretary, Moscow, 1948–49; Consul-General Stuttgart, 1949–51; Counsellor/Consul-Gen., 1950; Counsellor, Bangkok, 1951–56 (Chargé d'Affaires in 1952, 1953, 1954, 1955); Consul-Gen., Seattle, Wash, 1956–60; HM Consul-General, Istanbul, 1960–62; Ambassador: to Burma, 1962–65; to Afghanistan, 1965–68; retired, 1968. Chm., Anglo-Thai Soc., 1971–76; Hon. Treasurer, Soc. for Afghan Studies, 1972-. (Lay) Mem., Immigration Appeal Tribunal, 1970–81. *Recreation*: music. *Address*: 13 Grimwade Avenue, Croydon, Surrey. *Club*: Travellers'.
See also R. A. Furtado, Prof. D. Whitteridge.

WHITTET, Dr Thomas Douglas, CBE 1977; Chief Pharmacist, Department of Health and Social Security, 1967–78; *b* 4 Jan. 1915; *s* of late Thomas Douglas Whittet and Ellen Sloan Whittet (*née* Scott); *m* 1942, Doreen Mary Bowes; two *s*. *Educ*: Rosebank Sch., Hartlepool; Sunderland Polytechnic (Hon. Fellow 1980); University Coll., London (Fellow, 1979). PhC (now FPS) 1938; BSc (London) 1953; FRSC (FRIC 1955); CChem 1975; PhD (London) 1958. Mem., Coll. of Pharmacy Practice, 1982. Chief Chemist, Numol Ltd, 1939–41; hospital pharmacy, 1941–43; Chief Pharmacist and Lectr in Pharmacy: Charing Cross Hosp., 1943–47; University Coll. Hosp. and Med. Sch., 1947–65; Dep. Chief Pharmacist, Min. of Health, 1965–67. Member: Brit. Pharm. Codex Revis. Cttee, 1967–75; Joint Formulary Cttee, 1967–78; European Pharmacopoeia Commn, 1967–71; WHO Expert Adv. Cttee on Internat. Pharmacopoeia, 1948-; Council of Europe (Partial Agreement) Pharmaceutical Cttee, 1967–78; EEC Pharmaceutical Cttee and working parties, 1977–78. Consultant, UNIDO, 1978-. Master, Soc. of Apothecaries of London, 1982–83 (Sydenham Lectr, 1965; Delaune Lectr, 1977; Chm., Faculty of Hist. and Philos. of Medicine and Pharmacy, 1975–78; Court Visitor, 1978-). Wright Meml Lectr, Sydney, 1972; Winch Meml Lectr, 1973; Harrison Meml Lectr and Medallist, 1973; Todd Meml Lectr, 1980. Hon. Member: Royal Spanish Acad. of Pharmacy, 1958; Internat. Acad. of Pharmacy, 1965. Hon. DSc: Bath, 1968; Aston, 1974. Evans Gold Medal (Guild of Public Pharmacists), 1960; Charter Gold Medal, Pharm. Soc., 1978; Don Francke Medal, Amer. Soc. Hosp. Pharmacists, 1978. FRSocMed (Pres., Hist. of Medicine Section, 1981-). *Publications*: Hormones, 1946; Diagnostic Agents, 1947; Sterilisation and Disinfection, 1965; The Apothecaries in the Great Plague of London of 1665, 1971; many papers on medical and pharmaceutical history; numerous papers in Jl of Pharmacy and Pharmacology and in Pharmaceutical Jl on pyrogens and fever and on drug stability. *Recreations*: overseas travel, especially Commonwealth; medical and pharmaceutical history. *Address*: Woburn Lodge, 8 Lyndhurst Drive, Harpenden, Herts. *T*: Harpenden 4376. *Clubs*: Royal Commonwealth Society; MCC.

WHITTICK, Richard James; Assistant Under-Secretary of State, Home Office, 1967–72; *b* 21 August 1912; *s* of Ernest G. Whittick and Grace M. Shaw; *m* 1938, Elizabeth Mason; two *s*. *Educ*: George Heriot's School; Edinburgh University. British Museum (Natural History), 1936; Home Office, 1940; Principal Private Secretary to Home Secretary, 1952–53; Assistant Secretary, 1953. *Recreation*: gardening. *Address*: Coombe Cottage, Coombe, Sherborne, Dorset DT9 4BX. *T*: Sherborne 4488.

WHITTINGHAM, Charles Percival, BA, PhD Cantab; Head of Department of Botany, Rothamsted Experimental Station, since 1971; *b* 1922; *m* 1946, Alison Phillips; two *d*. *Educ*: St John's College, Cambridge. Professor of Botany, London University, at Queen Mary College, 1958–64; Head of Dept of Botany, 1967–71, and Prof. of Plant Physiology, 1964–71, Imperial Coll., Univ of London; Dean, Royal Coll. of Science, 1969–71; Hon. Dir, ARC Unit for Plant Physiology, 1964–71. Vis. Prof., Univ. of Nottingham, 1978-. *Publications*: Chemistry of Plant Processes, 1964; (with R. Hill) Photosynthesis, 1955; The Mechanism of Photosynthesis, 1974; contrib. to scientific journals. *Recreations*: music, travel. *Address*: Rothamsted Experimental Station, Harpenden, Herts.

WHITTINGHAM, Air Marshal Sir Harold (Edward), KCB 1945; KBE 1941 (CBE 1930); MB, ChB (Glasgow); FRCP; FRCPE; FRFPS; FRSTM&H; DPH, DTM&H; Director-General of RAF Medical Services, 1941–46; Medical Adviser, British Red Cross, 1946–48; Director of Medical Services, BOAC, 1948–57; Chairman: Air Ministry Flying Personnel Research Committee, 1949–67; IATA Medical Committee, 1950–57; Member, World Health Organisation Expert Advisory Panels on International Quarantine and on Environmental Sanitation, and Member, Expert Committee on Sanitation of International Airports, 1953–74; Medical Consultant to the Commonwealth Development Corporation, 1966–77 (Adviser, 1956–66); Hon. Civil Consultant in Aviation Medicine to RAF, since 1967; Consultant in Aviation Medicine to British Airways (formerly BEA), since 1957; *b* 1887; 2nd *s* of late Engineer Rear-Admiral Wm Whittingham, CB; *m* 1st, 1912, Agnes Kerr (*d* 1966), *d* of late William Seright, MD, FRFPS; one *s* one *d*; 2nd, 1966, Rita C. J., LRAM, *d* of late W. Harold White, MPS. *Educ*: Christ's Hosp.; Greenock Acad.; Glasgow Univ. Pathologist and Assistant Director of

Research, Royal Cancer Hosp., Glasgow, 1910–15; Pathologist, Scottish National Red Cross, 1914–15; served European War, 1915–18, with RAMC in India and Mesopotamia (despatches); attached Royal Flying Corps, 1917–18; transferred RAF, 1918, as Pathologist; in charge of RAF Sandfly Fever Commn, Malta, 1921–23; Director of Pathology, RAF, 1925–30; Lecturer, Bio-Chemistry, London School of Tropical Medicine, 1926–30; Pathologist, Royal Bucks Hosp., 1927–39; Consultant in Pathology and Tropical Medicine, RAF, 1930–35; OC RAF Central Medical Establishment, 1934–39; Consultant in Hygiene, Pathology and Tropical Medicine, RAF, 1935–39; Hon. Physician to the King, 1938–46; Director of Hygiene, Air Ministry, 1939–41; DGMS, RAF, 1941–46. Group Capt., 1932; Air Commodore, 1936; Air Vice-Marshal, 1940; Air Marshal, 1941. Hon. FRCSE; Hon. FRSM; Hon. FRIPHH. Royal Society of Tropical Medicine and Hygiene: Fellow, 1921; Mem. Council, 1924–43 and 1945–47; Vice-Pres., 1943–45; Pres., United Services Section, Roy. Soc. Med., 1938–39, 1958–60. Mem., Internat. Acad. of Astronautics; Hon. Fellow, Aerospace Med. Assoc.; Hon. Member: Assoc. Clinical Pathologists, 1921-; Soc. of Medical Consultants to the Armed Forces, USA; Assoc. Mil. Surgeons of USA. Harveian Lectr, RCS, 1946. Duncan and Lalcaca Medals, London Sch. of Tropical Medicine, 1920; N Persian Memorial Medallist, 1923; Chadwick Gold Medal, 1925; John Jeffries Award of Institute of Aeronautical Sciences, USA, 1944; Stewart Meml Award, 1970; Professorship of Aviation Med., RCP, named the Whittingham Professorship in recognition of his outstanding leadership in aviation med., 1973. KStJ 1945. Knight Grand Cross, Order of St Olaf of Norway, 1945; Commander of the Legion of Merit, USA, 1945; Cross and Star of the Order of Polonia Restituta, 1945; Czechoslovak Military Medal, 1st Class. Hon. LLD Glasgow. Hon. Freeman of Barber-Surgeon's Co. *Publications*: include numerous scientific papers and reports on aviation medicine, cancer, influenza, malaria, dysentery, sandfly fever, cerebrospinal fever, scarlet fever, diphtheria, tonsillitis and first aid. *Address*: 26 Marlborough Gardens, Lovelace Road, Surbiton, Surrey KT6 6NF. *T*: 01-399 8648. *Club*: Royal Air Force.

WHITTINGTON, Charles Richard, MC 1944; Chamberlain of London, 1964–1973; *b* 8 March 1908; *er s* of late Charles Henry Whittington, Stock Exchange, and Vera Whittington; *m* 1938, Helen Irene Minnie, *d* of late Lieutenant-Colonel J. E. Hance, RHA; one *s* four *d*. *Educ*: Uppingham School. Commissioned in Queen's Royal Regiment, TA, 1928; Captain, 1931; TARO, 1937. Served War of 1939–45 with Queen's, East Surrey, and Dorset Regts in Sicily, Italy, and NW Europe (D-Day landing, wounded, MC); demobilised with rank of Captain, 1945. Member of The Stock Exchange, London, 1931–64. Liveryman Mercers' Company, 1931; Mem. of Court of Common Council for Ward of Broad Street, 1939–64; one of HM Lieutenants, City of London, 1964–73. *Recreation*: gardening. *Address*: Wood Cottage, Brampton Bryan, Bucknell, Salop. *T*: Bucknell 291.

WHITTINGTON, Prof. Harry Blackmore, FRS 1971; Woodwardian Professor of Geology, Cambridge University, since 1966; *b* 24 March 1916; *s* of Harry Whittington and Edith M. (*née* Blackmore); *m* 1940, Dorothy E. Arnold; no *c*. *Educ*: Handsworth Gram. Sch.; Birmingham University. Commonwealth Fund Fellow, Yale Univ., 1938–40; Lectr in Geology, Judson Coll., Rangoon, 1940–42; Prof. of Geography, Ginling Coll., Chengtu, W China, 1943–45; Lectr in Geology, Birmingham Univ., 1945–49; Harvard Univ.: Vis. Lectr, 1949–50; Assoc. Prof. of Geology, 1950–58; Prof. of Geology, 1958–66. Trustee, British Museum (Nat. History), 1980-. Hon. AM, Harvard Univ., 1950. *Publications*: articles in Jl of Paleontology, Bulletin Geol. Soc. of Amer., Quarterly Jl Geol. Soc. London, etc. *Address*: 20 Rutherford Road, Cambridge CB2 2HH. *Club*: Geological.

WHITTINGTON, Joseph Basil, OBE 1981; HM Diplomatic Service, retired; HM Consul-General, Rotterdam, 1977–80; *b* 24 Oct. 1921; *s* of Joseph and Margaret Whittington; *m* 1947, Hazel Joan Rushton; two *s* one *d*. *Educ*: Cotton Coll., North Staffs; St Philip's Grammar Sch., Birmingham. Post Office, 1938–48. Served Army, 1940–46; Captain, Royal Artillery. Regional Boards for Industry, 1948–52; Bd of Trade, 1952–64; Asst Trade Commissioner, Jamaica, 1953–55; Bahamas and Bermuda, 1955–57 and Jamaica, 1957–58; Trade Commissioner, Johannesburg, 1958–62 and Toronto, 1963–67; transf. to Diplomatic Service, 1964; Head of Chancery, First Sec. (Commercial) and Consul, Liberia, 1968–70; First Sec. (Economic/Commercial), Zambia, 1970–73 and Malta, 1974–77. *Recreations*: gardening, golf, walking. *Address*: Heathcote, Darlington Road, Bath BA2 6NL. *T*: Bath 61697.

WHITTINGTON, Thomas Alan, CB 1977; Circuit Administrator, North Eastern Circuit, 1974–81; *b* 15 May 1916; *o s* of late George Whittington, JP and Mary Elizabeth Whittington; *m* 1939, Audrey Elizabeth, *y d* of late Craven Gilpin, Leeds; four *s*. *Educ*: Uppingham Sch.; Leeds Univ. (LLB). Commnd W Yorks Regt (Leeds Rifles) TA, 1937, serving War of 1939–45 in UK and 14th Army in India (Major). Solicitor of Supreme Court, 1945; Clerk of the Peace, Leeds, 1952–70; Senior Partner, Marklands, Solicitors, Leeds, 1967–70, Consultant, 1981-; Under-Sec., Lord Chancellor's Office, 1970; Circuit Administrator, Northern Circuit, 1970–74. *Recreations*: fishing, gardening, holiday golf. *Address*: The Cottage, School Lane, Collingham, Wetherby LS22 5BQ. *T*: Collingham Bridge 73881.

WHITTINGTON-SMITH, Marianne Christine, (Mrs C. A. Whittington-Smith); see Lutz, M. C.

WHITTLE, Dr Claude Howard, MA, MD Cantab; FRCP; Associate Lecturer in Clinical Medicine, University of Cambridge; Physician, and later Physician to the Skin Department of the United Cambridge Hospitals, 1930–61; Consultant Member, Medical Appeal Tribunal; Consultant Dermatologist, Ministry of Social Security, 1945–72; Hon. Consultant Physician; *b* 2 May 1896; *s* of Tom Whittle and Edith Annie Thompson; *m* 1923, Phyllis Lena Fricker, LRAM; three *s. Educ:* The Masonic School, Bushey, Herts; Queens' College, Cambridge (Foundation Scholar in Natural Science); King's Coll. Hosp., London. Clinical Pathologist, 1923. Pres. Dermatological Sec. RSM, 1961–62, Hon. Sec., 1945–6–7; Pres. British Assoc. of Dermatology, 1953–54, Hon. Mem. 1968; Member: Assoc. of Physicians; Path. Soc. of Gt Britain; British Allergy Soc.; Hon. Mem. British Soc. Mycopath., 1968, Pres., 1973–75. *Publications:* Vitamin A in psoriasis, Candida skin infections, Fungous infections in Cambridge, Paronychia, Kerato-acanthoma, in Brit. Jl Dermatology, Lancet, etc.; articles on skin diseases in Modern Treatment in General Practice, 1934 and 1938, and in Progress in Biological Sciences, 1960; many others in Proc. Roy. Soc. Medicine, Brit. Jl Dermatology, BMJ, Sabouraudia, Lancet, etc. *Recreations:* painting, sailing, music. *Address:* 41 Newton Road, Cambridge. *T:* 59237.

WHITTLE, Air Cdre Sir Frank, KBE 1948 (CBE 1944); CB 1947; Comdr, US Legion of Merit, 1946; FRS 1947; CEng; MA Cantab; RAF, retired; *b* 1 June 1907; *s* of M. Whittle; *m* 1930, Dorothy Mary Lee (marr. diss. 1976); two *s*; *m* 1976, Hazel S. Hall. *Educ:* Leamington Coll.; No 4 Apprentices' Wing, RAF Cranwell; RAF Coll., Cranwell; Peterhouse, Cambridge (Mechanical Sciences Tripos, BA 1st Cl. Hons). No 4 Apprentices' Wing, RAF Cranwell, 1923–26; Flight Cadet, RAF Coll., Cranwell, 1926–28 (Abdy-Gerrard-Fellowes Memorial Prize); Pilot Officer, 111 (Fighter) Sqdn, 1928–29; Flying Instructors' Course, Central Flying Sch., 1929; Flying Instructor, No 2 Flying Training Sch., RAF Digby, 1930; Test Pilot, Marine Aircraft Experimental Estab., RAF Felixstowe, 1931–32; RAF Sch. of Aeronautical Engrg, Henlow, 1932–34; Officer i/c Engine Test, Engine Repair Section, Henlow, 1934 (6 mths); Cambridge Univ., 1934–37 (Post-Graduate year, 1936–37); Special Duty List, attached Power Jets Ltd for devalt of aircraft gas turbine for jet propulsion, 1937–46; War Course, RAF Staff Coll., 1943; Technical Adviser to Controller of Supplies (Air), Min. of Supply, 1946–48; retd RAF, 1948. Hon. Technical Adviser: Jet Aircraft, BOAC, 1948–52; Shell Gp, 1953–57; Consultant, Bristol Siddeley Engines/Rolls Royce on turbo drill project, 1961–70. Mem. Faculty, US Naval Acad., Annapolis, Maryland, 1977–. Partnered late Flt-Lt G. E. Campbell in Crazy Flying RAF Display, Hendon, 1930; 1st flights of Gloster jet-propelled aeroplane with Whittle engine, May 1941. Freeman of Royal Leamington Spa, 1944. Hon. FRAeS; Hon. FAeSI; Hon. FIMechE; Founder Fellow, Fellowship of Engineering, 1976. Hon. Mem., Franklin Inst.; Hon. FAIAA; Hon. Mem., Société Royale Belge des Ingénieurs; Hon. Foreign Mem., Amer. Acad. Arts and Scis, 1976; For. Assoc., US Nat. Acad. of Engrg, 1978; Hon. Fellow, Soc. of Experimental Test Pilots, USA; Hon. MEIC. Hon. Fellow, Peterhouse. Hon. DSc: Oxon; Manchester; Leicester; Bath; Warwick; Exeter; Hon. LLD Edinburgh; Hon. ScD Cantab; Hon. DTech Trondheim. James Alfred Ewing Medal, ICE, 1944; Gold Medal, RAeS, 1944; James Clayton Prize, IMechE, 1946; Daniel Guggenheim Medal, USA, 1946; Kelvin Gold Medal, 1947; Melchett Medal, 1949; Rumford Medal, Royal Soc., 1950; Gold Medal, Fedn Aeronautique Internat., 1951; Churchill Gold Medal, Soc. of Engineers, 1952; Albert Gold Medal, Soc. of Arts, 1952; Franklin Medal, USA, 1956; John Scott Award, 1957; Goddard Award, USA, 1965; Coventry Award of Merit, 1966; International Communications (Christopher Columbus) Prize, City of Genoa, 1966; Tony Jannus Award, Greater Tampa Chamber of Commerce, 1969; James Watt Internat. Gold Medal, IMechE, 1977. *Publications:* Jet, 1953; Gas Turbine Aero-Thermodynamics, 1981.

WHITTLE, Kenneth Francis, CEng, FIEE; CBIM; Chairman, South Western Electricity Board, since 1977; *b* 28 April 1922; *s* of Thomas Whittle and May Whittle; *m* 1945, Dorothy Inskip; one *s* one *d. Educ:* Kingswood Sch., Bath; Faculty of Technol., Manchester Univ. (BScTech). Served War, Electrical Lieut, RNVR, 1943–46. Metropolitan Vickers Elec. Co. Ltd, 1946–48; NW Div., CEGB, 1948–55; North West Electricity Board: various posts, 1955–64; Area Commercial Officer, Blackburn, 1964–69; Manager, Peak Area, 1969–71; Manager, Manchester Area, 1971–74; Chief Commercial Officer, 1974–75; Dep. Chm., Yorks Elec. Bd, 1975–77. *Recreation:* golf. *Address:* 8 Cambridge Road, Clevedon, Avon BS21 7HX. *T:* Clevedon 874017.

WHITTLE, Prof. Peter, FRS 1978; FRSNZ 1981; Churchill Professor of Mathematics of Operational Research, University of Cambridge, since 1967; *b* 27 Feb. 1927; *s* of Percy Whittle and Elsie Tregurtha; *m* 1951, Käthe Hildegard Blomquist; three *s* three *d. Educ:* Wellington Coll., New Zealand. Docent, Uppsala Univ., 1951–53; employed New Zealand DSIR, 1953–59, rising to Senior Principal Scientifc Officer; Lectr, Univ. of Cambridge, 1959–61; Prof. of Mathematical Statistics, Univ. of Manchester, 1961–67. *Publications:* Hypothesis Testing in Time Series Analysis, 1951; Prediction and Regulation, 1963; Probability, 1970; Optimisation under Constraints, 1971; Optimisation over Time, 1982; contribs to Biometrika, Jl Roy. Statistical Soc., Proc. Camb. Phil. Soc., Proc. Roy. Soc. *Recreation:* guitar. *Address:* 268 Queen Edith's Way, Cambridge; Statistical Laboratory, University of Cambridge.

WHITTON, Cuthbert Henry; *b* 18 Feb. 1905; *s* of Henry and Eleanor Whitton; *m* 1938, Iris Elva Moody; one *d. Educ:* St Andrew's College,

Dublin; Dublin University. Malayan Civil Service, 1929; Colonial Legal Service, 1939; Puisne Judge, Federation of Malaya, 1951; Puisne Judge, Supreme Court, Singapore, 1954; Foreign Compensation Commn, Legal Dept, 1959–71. *Recreations:* golf, gardening. *Address:* 5 Marsham Lodge, Marsham Lane, Gerrard's Cross, Bucks. *T:* 85608. *Clubs:* Royal Commonwealth Society; Kildare Street and University (Dublin).

WHITTON, Prof. Peter William; Deputy Vice-Chancellor, University of Melbourne, since 1979; *b* 2 Sept. 1925; *s* of William Whitton and Rosa Bungay; *m* 1950, Mary Katharine White; two *s* three *d. Educ:* Latymer Upper Sch., London; Southampton Univ. (BScEng); Imperial College of Science and Technology, London (DIC, PhD). FIE(Aust). Engineering Cadet, English Electric Co., Preston, 1942–46; Wireless Officer, Royal Signals, Catterick and Singapore, 1946–48; Sen. Lectr in Mech. Engrg, Univ. of Melbourne, 1953–56; Head, Engrg Sect., ICI Metals Div. Research Dept, Birmingham, 1956–60; Foundation Prof. and Dean, Faculty of Engrg, Univ. of the West Indies, 1960–64; University of Melbourne: Prof. of Mech. Engrg, 1965–77, Emeritus Prof., 1977–; Dean, Faculty of Engrg, 1966; Principal, Royal Melbourne Inst. of Technology, 1977–78. ME Melbourne 1965. *Publications:* various papers on metal forming, in Proc. IMechE, London, and Jl of Inst. of Metals, London. *Recreations:* reading, golf. *Address:* University of Melbourne, Parkville, Victoria 3052, Australia; 425 Beach Road, Beaumaris, Victoria, Australia.

WHITTUCK, Gerald Saumarez, CB 1959; *b* 13 Oct. 1912; *s* of late Francis Gerald Whittuck; *m* 1938, Catherine McCrea; two *s. Educ:* Cheltenham; Clare Coll., Cambridge. Air Ministry, 1935; Private Secretary to Secretary of State, 1944–46; Asst Under-Secretary of State: Air Ministry, 1955–63; War Office, 1963–64; MoD, 1964–71; Dir, Greenwich Hosp., 1971–74. Mem., Royal Patriotic Fund Corp., 1971–74. *Address:* 15A Greenaway Gardens, NW3. *T:* 01–435 3742.

WHITWAM, Derek Firth, CEng, FRINA; RCNC; General Manager, HM Dockyard, Portsmouth, since 1981; *b* 7 Dec. 1932; *s* of Hilton and Marion Whitwam; *m* 1954, Pamela May (née Lander); one *s* one *d. Educ:* Royds Hall Sch., Huddersfield; Royal Naval Coll., Dartmouth; Royal Naval Engineering Coll., Manadon; Royal Naval Coll., Greenwich. Work on ship design, MoD (N) Bath, 1957–65; Rosyth Dockyard, 1965–68; Singapore Dockyard, 1968–70; DG Ships Bath, 1970–77; RCDS 1978; Productin Manager, Rosyth Dockyard, 1979–80. *Publications:* papers for Trans Royal Inst. of Naval Architects. *Recreations:* golf, music, walking. *Address:* General Manager, HM Dockyard, Portsmouth. *T:* Portsmouth 822351, ext. 22465.

WHITWELL, Stephen John, CMG 1969; MC; HM Diplomatic Service, retired; *b* 30 July 1920; *s* of Arthur Percy Whitwell and Marion Whitwell (née Greenwood). *Educ:* Stowe; Christ Church, Oxford. Coldstream Guards, 1941–47; joined HM Foreign Service (now Diplomatic Service), 1947; served: Tehran, 1947; FO, 1949; Belgrade, 1952; New Delhi, 1954; FO, 1958; Seoul, 1961. Polit. Adv. to C-in-C Middle East, Aden, 1964; Counsellor, Belgrade, 1965; Ambassador to Somalia, 1968–70; Head of East-West Contacts Dept, FCO, 1970–71. *Recreations:* reading, painting, looking at buildings. *Address:* Jervis Cottage, Aston Tirrold, Oxon. *Club:* Travellers'.

WHITWORTH, Clifford, MSc; PhD; FRSC; Vice-Chancellor of the University of Salford, 1967–74; *b* 6 Nov. 1906; *s* of late Joseph and Lucy Whitworth; *m* 1941, Ada Alice Belfit. *Educ:* Manchester Grammar School; Manchester University. Senior Research Assistant to Prof. H. S. Taylor, 1931–33; Industrial Research Chemist, 1933–35; Senior Lecturer in Chemistry, 1935–38, and Head of Dept of Pure and Applied Science, 1939–49, Loughborough College; Asst Education Officer for Further Education, Middlesex CC, 1949–57; Principal, Royal Coll. of Advanced Technology, Salford, 1959–67; Mem., Nat. Council for Technological Awards, 1955–60; Mem. Educn Cttee, Inst. of Fuel, 1951–73, Chm. 1968–73; Chm. NW Section, Inst. of Fuel, 1966–68; Vice-Pres., Inst. of Fuel, 1969–71. Mem. Council, Brit. Assoc. for the Advancement of Science, 1963–72; Chm., North-Western Regional Adv. Council Academic Bd, 1969–71. Member: Nat. Adv. Council on Educn for Industry and Commerce, 1970–72; Cttee for Industrial Technologies, DTI, 1972–74. Mem. Governing Body, Hornsey Coll. of Art, 1966–72; Vice-Pres., Union of Lancs and Cheshire Insts, 1967–. Hon. DSc Salford, 1971. *Publications:* contrib. to sci. jls. *Address:* 6 Highfield Road, Bramhall, Cheshire SK7 3BE. *Club:* Athenæum.

WHITWORTH, Francis John; Deputy Director-General, General Council of British Shipping, since 1980; Director, International Shipping Federation, since 1980; *b* 1 May 1925; *s* of late Captain Herbert Francis Whitworth, OBE, RNVR, and Helen Marguerite Whitworth (née Tait); *m* 1956, Auriol Myfanwy Medwyn Hughes; one *s* one *d. Educ:* Charterhouse (Jun. Schol.); Pembroke Coll., Oxford (Holford Schol.). MA Jurisprudence 1949). FBIM 1980 (MBIM 1967). Served War, Royal Marines, 1943–46. Called to Bar, Middle Temple, 1950. Joined Cunard Steam-Ship Co. as management trainee, 1950; service in USA and Canada, 1956–62; Personnel Director, 1965, Managing Dir Cunard Line, 1968, Group Admin Dir, 1969; joined British Shipping Fedn as Dep. Dir, Industrial Relations, 1972. Member, Nat. Maritime Board, 1962–; Chairman: Internat. Cttee of Passenger Lines, 1968–71; Atlantic Passenger Steamship Conf., 1970–71; Employers' Gp, Jt Maritime Commn of ILO, 1980; Mem., Industrial Tribunals for England and Wales, 1978–. Mem. Council, King George's Fund for Sailors, 1980–. Governor, Nat. Sea Trng Schs, 1966–71 (Chm., 1980–). *Recreations:* racing, opera, music, cricket. *Address:* The Old School House, Farley Chamberlayne, Romsey,

Hants SO5 0QR. *T:* Braishfield 68538. *Club:* United Oxford & Cambridge University.

WHITWORTH, Group Captain Frank, QC 1965; a Recorder of the Crown Court, since 1972; *b* 13 May 1910; *o s* of late Daniel Arthur Whitworth, Didsbury, Manchester; *m* 1st, 1939, Mary Lucy (*d* 1979), *o d* of late Sir John Holdsworth Robinson, JP, Bingley, Yorks; no *c*; 2nd, 1980, Mrs Irene Lannon. *Educ:* Shrewsbury Sch.; Trinity Hall, Cambridge. Served with RAFVR (Special Duties), 1940-45, retired. Called to Bar, Gray's Inn, 1934. Member of Dorking and Horley RDC, 1939-68. Contested (C) St Helens, 1945. Judge of Courts of Appeal of Jersey and Guernsey, 1971-80. Master, Clockmakers' Co., 1962 and 1971. Trustee, Whiteley Village Homes, 1963. *Publications:* miscellaneous verse and articles. *Recreation:* farming. *Address:* Little Manor House, Westcott, near Dorking, Surrey. *T:* Dorking 889966; 13 King's Bench Walk, Temple, EC4. *T:* 01-353 7204. *Club:* United Oxford & Cambridge University.

WHITWORTH, Hugh Hope Aston, MBE 1945; Lay Assistant to the Archbishop of Canterbury, 1969-78; *b* 21 May 1914; *s* of Sidney Alexander Whitworth and Elsie Hope Aston; *m* 1st, 1944, Elizabeth Jean Boyes (*d* 1961); two *s* one *d*; 2nd, 1961, Catherine Helen Bell. *Educ:* Bromsgrove Sch.; Pembroke Coll., Cambridge (BA). Indian Civil Service, Bombay Province, 1937-47; Administrator, Ahmedabad Municipality, 1942-44; Collector and District Magistrate, Nasik, 1945-46; Board of Trade, 1947-55; Scottish Home Dept, 1955; Asst Sec., 1957; Under-Sec., Scottish Home and Health Dept, 1968-69. *Recreations:* travel, theatre, gardening. *Address:* 47 Orford Gardens, Strawberry Hill, Twickenham, Mddx. *T:* 01-892 4672. *Club:* Royal Commonwealth Society.

WHITWORTH, Maj.-Gen. Reginald Henry, CB 1969; CBE 1963; MA; *b* 27 Aug. 1916; 2nd *s* of late Aymer William Whitworth and late Alice (*née* Hervey), Eton College; *m* 1946, June Rachel, *o d* of late Sir Bartle Edwards, CVO, MC, and of Daphne, MBE, *d* of late Sir Cyril Kendall Butler, KBE; two *s* one *d*. *Educ:* Eton; Balliol College, Oxford, 1st cl. Hons, Modern History, 1938; Laming Travelling Fellow, Queen's Coll., Oxford, 1938-39. 2nd Lt Grenadier Guards, 1940; GSO2, 78 Division, 1944; Bde Major, 24 Guards Brigade, 1945-46; GSO2, Staff College, Camberley, 1953-55; comdg 1st Bn Grenadier Guards, 1955-57; GSO1, SHAPE, 1958-59; Sen. Army Instructor, Jt Services Staff Coll., 1959-61; Comdr Berlin Infantry Bde Gp, 1961-63; DMS 1, Ministry of Defence, 1964-66; GOC: Yorkshire District, 1966-67; Northumbrian District, 1967-68; Chief of Staff, Southern Command, 1968-70. Bursar and Official Fellow, Exeter College, Oxford, 1970-81. Governor: Felsted Sch.; St Mary's, Wantage; Gordon Boys Sch. Chm., Army Museums Ogilby Trust. Bronze Star, USA, 1947. *Publications:* Field Marshal Earl Ligonier, 1958; Famous Regiments: the Grenadier Guards, 1974. *Recreations:* riding, fishing, military history. *Address:* The Old Manor, Letcombe Regis, Wantage, Oxon. *T:* Wantage 2259. *Club:* Army and Navy.

WHYTE, Gabriel Thomas; *b* 25 June 1925; *s* of Alexander and Margit Whyte; *m* 1951, Agnes Kalman; one *s*. *Educ:* Highgate Sch.; London Univ. (BSc Hon.). Founder and Man. Dir, Airfix Plastics Ltd, 1945-60; Dir, Airfix Industries, 1961-63; Man. Dir, Triumph Investment Trust, 1964-74; Pres., Atlantic Materials Ltd, 1975; Pres., Paget Agencies Ltd, 1975; Dir, Sangers Group PLC, London, 1982; Chm., Solidyne Inc., NY, 1982. *Recreations:* riding and dressage, hunting, shooting, fishing. *Address:* Queen's Cove, Pembroke, Bermuda; 910 Fifth Avenue, New York, NY 10021, USA.

WHYTE, Hamilton; *see* Whyte, W. E. H.

WHYTE, Rev. James Aitken; Professor of Practical Theology and Christian Ethics, University of St Andrews, since 1958; *b* 28 Jan. 1920; 2nd *s* of late Andrew Whyte, Leith, and late Barbara Janet Pittillo Aitken; *m* 1942, Elisabeth, *er d* of Rev. G. S. Mill, MA, BSc, Kalimpong, India; two *s* one *d*. *Educ:* Daniel Stewart's Coll., Edinburgh; University of Edinburgh (Arts and Divinity), MA 1st Cl. Hons Phil., 1942. Ordained, 1945; Chaplain to the Forces, 1945-48; Minister of: Dunollie Road, Oban, 1948-54; Mayfield, Edinburgh, 1954-58. St Andrews University: Dean, Faculty of Divinity, 1968-72; Principal, St Mary's Coll., 1978-82. Guest Lectr, Inst. for the Study of Worship and Religious Architecture, Birmingham, 1965-66; Lectures: Kerr, Univ. of Glasgow, 1969-72; Croall, Univ. of Edinburgh, 1972-73. Pres., Soc. for Study of Theol., 1983-. Hon. LLD Dundee, 1981. *Publications:* (ed jtly) Worship Now, 1972; contributor to Towards a Church Architecture, 1962; Preparing for the Ministry of the 1970's, 1965; A Dictionary of Christian Ethics, 1967; Duty and Discernment, 1975; articles in journals, etc. *Address:* 13 Hope Street, St Andrews, Fife. *Club:* New (Edinburgh).

WHYTE, John Stuart, CBE 1976; MSc(Eng); FEng 1980; FIEE; Engineer-in-Chief, Managing Director (major systems), and Member, Main Board, British Telecom, since 1981; *b* High Wycombe, 20 July 1923; *s* of late William W. Whyte and of Ethel K. Whyte; *m* 1951, E. Joan M. (*née* Budd); one *s* one *d*. *Educ:* The John Lyon Sch., Harrow; Northampton Polytechnic, London Univ. BSc(Eng) (Hons), MSc(Eng). Post Office Radio Laboratory, Castleton, Cardiff, 1949-57; PO Research Station, Dollis Hill: Sen. Exec. Engr, 1957-61; Asst Staff Engr, 1961-65. Asst Sec., HM Treasury, 1965-68; Dep. Dir of Engrg, PO, 1968-71; Dir, Operational Programming, PO, 1971-75; Dir of Purchasing and Supply, 1975-76, Sen. Dir of Develt, 1977-79, Dep. Man. Dir, 1979-81, PO Telecommunications; Dir, British

Telecommunications Systems Ltd, 1979-. Manager, Royal Instn, 1971-74 (Vice-Pres., 1972, 1973, 1974), Mem. Cttee of Visitors, 1975-78 (Chm., 1977-78), Chm., Membership Cttee, 1975-77. Mem., Nat. Electronics Council, 1977- (Mem. Exec. Cttee, 1977-; Dep. Chm., 1980-); Mem. Council, ERA, 1977-. President: Instn of PO Electrical Engrs, 1977-82; Instn of British Telecommunications Engrs, 1982-; Mem. Council, IEE, 1980- (Vice-Pres., 1981-; Chm. Professional Bd, 1981-). Liveryman, Scientific Instrument Makers' Co. Leader, British Hinku Expedn, 1979. *Publications:* various articles and papers in professional telecommunications jls. *Recreations:* mountaineering, photography, opera. *Address:* Wild Hatch, Coleshill Lane, Winchmore Hill, Amersham, Bucks HP7 0NT. *T:* Amersham 22663. *Clubs:* Alpine; Swiss Alpine (Berne).

WHYTE, (John) Stuart Scott; Under Secretary, Department of Health and Social Security, since 1978; *b* 1 April 1926; *er s* of late Thomas and Mysie Scott Whyte, Sandycove, Co. Dublin; *m* 1950, Jocelyn Margaret, *o d* of late George Hawley, CBE, Edinburgh; two *s* one *d*. *Educ:* St Andrew's Coll., Dublin; Trinity Coll., Univ. of Dublin. BA 1947; LLB 1948. Asst Principal, Dept of Health for Scotland, 1948; Principal, 1955; Principal Private Sec. to Sec. of State for Scotland, 1959; Asst Sec., Scottish Develt Dept, 1962; Asst Sec., Cabinet Office, 1969; Asst Under-Sec. of State, Scottish Office, 1969-74; Under Sec., Cabinet Office, 1974-78. *Address:* 26 Langley Hill, Langley, Herts. *T:* Kings Langley 64745; 26 Coppershell, Gastard, Corsham, Wilts. *T:* Corsham 713738.

WHYTE, Lewis Gilmour, CBE 1973; FFA; Chairman: London and Manchester Assurance Co. Ltd, 1961-78; New York & Gartmore Investment Trust Ltd, 1972-79; Welfare Insurance Co. Ltd, 1974-78; Director: Associated Commercial Vehicles Ltd, 1953-78; Broadstone Investment Trust Ltd, 1953-78; *b* 9 Oct. 1906; *s* of Robert Whyte and Florence Smith; *m* 1st, 1935, Ursula Frances Ware (marr. diss. 1971); one *s* three *d*; 2nd, 1971, Diana Mary Campbell. *Educ:* Trinity Coll., Glenalmond. FFA 1929. Investment Manager, later Dir, Equity & Law Life Assurance Company Ltd, 1940-1953; Dir, Save & Prosper Group Ltd, 1950-63; Member: NCB, 1963-66; NFC, 1971-74; Dep. Chm., British Leyland Motor Corporation Ltd, 1968-72; Chm., Transport Holding Company, 1971-73. Receiver-General, Order of St John of Jerusalem, 1955-68. GCStJ 1969. *Publications:* Principles of Finance and Investment, vol. 1, 1949, vol. 2, 1950. *Recreations:* golf, gardening. *Address:* Queen's Cottage, Somerford Keynes, Cirencester, Glos.

WHYTE, Stuart Scott; *see* Whyte, J. S. S.

WHYTE, William Erskine Hamilton, CMG 1979; HM Diplomatic Service; Ambassador and Deputy Permanent Representative to UN, since 1981; *b* 28 May 1927; *s* of late William Hamilton Whyte; *m* 1953, Sheila Annie Duck; three *d*. *Educ:* King's Sch., Bruton; The Queen's Coll., Oxford. Served, Royal Navy, 1945-48. Civil Asst, War Office, 1952-55; HM Foreign (later Diplomatic) Service, 1955; Vienna, 1956; Bangkok, 1959; UK Mission to UN, New York, 1963; Foreign Office, 1966; Counsellor, HM Embassy, Kinshasa, Democratic Republic of the Congo, 1970-71; Dir-Gen., British Information Services, and Dep. Consul-General (Information), NY, 1972-76; Head of News Dept, FCO, 1976-79; Minister (Economic and Social Affairs), UK Mission to UN, New York, 1979-81. *Recreations:* gardening, photography. *Address:* c/o Foreign and Commonwealth Office, SW1. *Club:* Century Association (New York).

WIBBERLEY, Prof. Gerald Percy, CBE 1972; Ernest Cook Professor of Countryside Planning in the University of London, University College/Wye College, 1969-82; *b* 15 April 1915; *m* 1st, 1943, Helen Yeomans (*d* 1963); one *d*; 2nd, 1972, Peggy Samways. *Educ:* King Henry VIII Grammar Sch., Abergavenny; Univs of Wales, Oxford, and Illinois, USA. BSc, MS, PhD. Asst Lectr, Univ. of Manchester, 1940-41; E Sussex Agricultural Cttee: Dist Officer, 1941-43; Asst Exec. Officer, 1943-44; Min. of Agriculture: Asst Rural Land Utilisation Officer, 1944-49; Research Officer, Land Use, 1949-54; Univ. of London, Wye Coll.: Head of Dept of Economics, 1954-69, also Reader in Agricultural Economics, 1958-62; Prof. of Rural Economy, 1963-69. Dir, CoSIRA, 1968-; Mem., Nature Conservancy Council, 1973-80; Pres., British Agricl Econs Soc., 1975-76. Chm., Rural Planning Services Ltd, 1972-82. Hon. Associate Mem. TPI, 1949-67; Hon. Mem., RTPI, 1967-. Hon. DSc Bradford, 1982. *Publications:* Agriculture and Urban Growth, 1959; (part author): The Agricultural Significance of the Hills, 1956; Land Use in an Urban Environment, 1960; Outdoor Recreation in the British Countryside, 1963; An Agricultural Land Budget for Britain 1965-2000, 1970; The Nature and Distribution of Second Homes in England and Wales, 1973; (jtly) Planning and the Rural Environment, 1976; Countryside Planning: a personal evaluation, 1982; contributor to Jls of: Agricl Economics, Land Economics, Town and Country Planning. *Recreations:* music, altering old houses, arguing about rural affairs. *Address:* Vicarage Cottage, 7 Upper Bridge Street, Wye, near Ashford, Kent. *T:* Wye 812377. *Club:* Farmers'.

WICKBERG, Gen. Erik E.; Comdr of the Order of Vasa (Sweden), 1970; General of the Salvation Army, 1969-74; *b* 6 July 1904; *s* of David Wickberg, Commissioner, Salvation Army, and Betty (*née* Lundblad); *m* 1929, Ens. Frieda de Groot (*d* 1930); *m* 1932, Captain Margarete Dietrich (*d* 1976); two *s* two *d*; *m* 1977, Major Eivor Lindberg. *Educ:* Uppsala; Berlin; Stockholm. Salvation Army Internat. Training Coll., 1924-25, and Staff Coll., 1926; commissioned, 1925; appts in Scotland, Berlin, London; Divisional Commander, Uppsala, 1946-48; Chief Secretary, Switzerland, 1948-53; Chief

Secretary, Sweden, 1953-57; Territorial Commander, Germany, 1957-61; Chief of the Staff, Internat. HQ, London, 1961-69; elected General of the Salvation Army, July 1969; assumed international leadership, Sept. 1969. Hon. LLD Choong Ang Univ., Seoul, 1970. Order of Moo-Koong-Wha, Korea, 1970; Commander, Order of Vasa, Sweden, 1970; Grosses Verdienstkreuz, Germany, 1971; The King's golden medal (Sweden), 1980. *Publications:* In Darkest England Now, 1974; Inkallad (autobiography, in Swedish), 1978; articles in Salvation Army periodicals and Year Book. *Recreations:* reading, fishing, chess. *Address:* c/o The Salvation Army, Ostermalmsgatan 71, Stockholm 5, Sweden.

WICKENDEN, Keith David; MP (C) Dorking, since 1979; Chairman: European Ferries Ltd, since 1972; Felixstowe Dock & Railway Co., since 1976; *b* 22 Nov. 1932; 3rd *s* of Joseph Robert Wickenden and Elsie Alice Wickenden (*née* Miller); *m* 1956, Brenda Paice; four *s. Educ:* East Grinstead Grammar Sch. FCA. Partner, Thornton Baker & Co., 1958. Jt Liquidator, Rolls Royce Ltd, 1971. Pres., Inst. of Freight Forwarders, 1979-80. *Recreations:* cricket, flying, being a Director of Brighton and Hove Albion Football Club. *Address:* House of Commons, SW1A 0AA. *Club:* Carlton.

WICKENS, Dr Alan Herbert, OBE 1980; FEng, FIMechE; Director of Research, British Rail, since 1978; *b* 29 March 1929; *s* of Herbert Leslie Wickens and Sylvia Wickens; *m* 1953, Eleanor Joyce Waggott; one *d. Educ:* Ashville Coll., Harrogate; Loughborough Univ. of Technol. (DLC Eng, BScEng London, 1951; DSc Loughborough, 1978). CEng, FIMechE 1971; MRAeS. Res. Engr, Sir W. G. Armstrong Whitworth Aircraft Ltd, Coventry, 1951-55; Gp Leader, Dynamics Analysis, Canadair Ltd, Montreal, 1955-59; Head of Aeroelastics Section, Weapons Res. Div., A. V. Roe & Co., Ltd, Woodford, 1959-62; British Rail: Supt, Res. Dept, 1962-67; Advanced Projs Engr, 1967-68; Dir of Advanced Projs, 1968-71; Dir of Labs, 1971-78. Industrial Prof. of Transport Technol., Loughborough Univ. of Technol., 1972-76. Pres., Internat. Assoc. of Vehicle System Dynamics, 1981-. Hon. DTech CNAA, 1978; Hon. Dr Open Univ. 1980. George Stephenson Res. Prize, IMechE, 1966; (jtly) MacRobert Award, 1975. *Publications:* papers on dynamics of railway vehicles and high speed trains publ. by IMechE, Amer. Soc. of Mech. Engrs, Internat. Jl of Solids and Structures, and Jl of Vehicle System Dynamics. *Recreations:* gardening, do-it-yourself, music. *Address:* Broomfields, 52 Broadway, Duffield, Derbyshire DE6 4BW. *T:* Derby 840341.

WICKHAM, Rt. Rev. Edward Ralph; Assistant Bishop, Diocese of Manchester, since 1982; *b* 3 Nov. 1911; *s* of Edward Wickham, London; *m* 1944, Dorothy Helen Neville Moss, *d* of Prof. Kenneth Neville Moss, Birmingham; one *s* two *d. Educ:* University of London (BD); St Stephen's House, Oxford. Deacon, 1938; Priest, 1939; Curate, Christ Church, Shieldfield, Newcastle upon Tyne, 1938-41; Chaplain, Royal Ordnance Factory, Swynnerton, 1941-44; Curate-in-charge, Swynnerton, 1943-44; Diocesan Missioner to Industry, Sheffield, 1944-59; Hon. Chaplain to Bishop of Sheffield, 1950-59; Canon Residentiary, Sheffield, 1951-59; Bishop Suffragan of Middleton, 1959-82. Sir H. Stephenson Fellow, Sheffield University, 1955-57. Chm. Working Party, Gen. Synod Industrial Cttee, 1977 (report: Understanding Closed Shops); Chairman, Bd for Social Responsibility Working Party: on Union Shop Agreements, 1977; on The Future of Work, 1980. Chm. Council, and Pro-Chancellor, Salford Univ., 1975-. Hon. DLitt Salford, 1973. *Publications:* Church and People in an Industrial City, 1957; Encounter with Modern Society, 1964; Growth & Inflation, 1975; contributions to: Theology, The Ecumenical Review, Industrial Welfare, etc. *Recreations:* mountaineering, rock-climbing. *Address:* 12 Westminster Road, Eccles, Manchester. *T:* 061-789 3144.

WICKHAM, Glynne William Gladstone; Professor of Drama, University of Bristol, since 1960; Dean of Faculty of Arts, 1970-72; *b* 15 May 1922; *s* of W. G. and Catherine Wickham; *m* 1954, Marjorie Heseltine (*née* Mudford); two *s* one *d. Educ:* Winchester College; New College, Oxford. Entered RAF, 1942; commissioned as Navigator, 1943; discharged as Flt Lt, 1946. BA, 1947; DPhil, 1948 (Oxon). President of OUDS, 1946-47. Asst Lecturer, Drama Dept, Bristol Univ., 1948; Senior Lecturer and Head of Dept, 1955. Worked sporadically as actor, script-writer and critic for BBC, from 1946; attended General Course in Broadcasting, BBC Staff Trg Sch., 1953. Travelled in America on Rockefeller Award, 1953. Visiting Prof., Drama Dept, State Univ. of Iowa, 1960; Ferens Vis. Prof. of Drama, Hull Univ., 1969; Vis. Prof. of Theatre History, Yale Univ., 1970; Killam Res. Prof., Dalhousie Univ., 1976-77. Lectures: G. F. Reynolds Meml, Univ. of Colorado, 1960; Judith E. Wilson, in Poetry and Drama, Cambridge, 1960-61; Festvortrag, Deutsche Shakespeare Gesellschaft, 1973; British Council, in Europe, annually 1969-79. Directed: Amer. première, The Birthday Party, for Actors' Workshop, San Francisco, 1960; world première, Wole Soyinka's Brother Jero's Metamorphosis, 1974. Consultant to Finnish National Theatre and Theatre School on establishment of Drama Department in Univ. of Helsinki, 1963. Governor of Bristol Old Vic Trust, 1963-. Consultant to Univ. of E Africa on establishment of a Sch. of Drama in University Coll., Dar-es-Salaam, Tanzania, 1965; Dir, Theatre Seminar, for Summer Univ., Vaasa, Finland, 1965; External Examr to Sch. of Drama in Univ. of Ibadan, Nigeria, 1965-68. Chairman: Nat. Drama Conf., Nat. Council of Social Service, 1970-76; Radio West plc (ILR Bristol), 1979-; Pres., Soc. for Theatre Research, 1976-; Member: English Panel, NCAA, 1968-72; Internat. Adv. Cttee, World Shakespeare Congress, Vancouver, 1971 (Chm. Elizabethan Theatre Panel); Adv. Cttee, British Theatre Museum, 1974-77; Edit. Cttee, Shakespeare

Survey, 1974-; Chm., Adv. Bd, Theatre Research International, 1975-. *Publications:* Early English Stages 1300-1660, Vol. I (1300-1576), 1959, 2nd edn 1980; Vol. II (1576-1660, Pt 1), 1962; Vol. II (Pt 2), 1972; Vol. III, 1981; Editor: The Relationship between Universities and Radio, Film and Television, 1954; Drama in a World of Science, 1962; Gen. Introd. to the London Shakespeare, 6 vols (ed J. Munro), 1958; Shakespeare's Dramatic Heritage, 1969; The Medieval Theatre, 1974, 2nd edn 1980; English Moral Interludes, 1975. *Recreations:* gardening and travel. *Address:* 6 College Road, Clifton, Bristol BS8 3JB. *T:* Bristol 34918. *Club:* Garrick.

WICKHAM, William Rayley; His Honour Judge Wickham; a Circuit Judge, since 1975; *b* 22 Sept. 1926; *s* of late Rayley Esmond Wickham and late Mary Joyce Wickham; *m* 1957, Elizabeth Mary (*née* Thompson); one *s* two *d. Educ:* Sedbergh Sch.; Brasenose Coll., Oxford (MA, BCL). Served War of 1939-45, Army, 1944-48. Called to Bar, Inner Temple, 1951. Magistrate, Aden, 1953; Chief Magistrate, Aden, 1958; Crown Counsel, Tanganyika, 1959; Asst to Law Officers, Tanganyika, 1961-63; practised on Northern Circuit, 1963-75; a Recorder of the Crown Court, 1972-75. *Recreations:* fell walking, music, amateur dramatics. *Address:* 115 Vyner Road South, Birkenhead. *T:* 051-652 2095.

WICKRAMASINGHE, Prof. Nalin Chandra, PhD, ScD; Professor and Head of Department of Applied Mathematics and Astronomy, University College, Cardiff, since 1973; Director, Institute of Fundamental Studies, Sri Lanka, since 1982; *b* 20 Jan. 1939; *s* of Percival Herbert Wickramasinghe and Theresa Elizabeth Wickramasinghe; *m* 1966, Nelum Priyadarshini Pereira; one *s* two *d. Educ:* Royal Coll., Colombo, Sri Lanka; Univ. of Ceylon (BSc); Univ. of Cambridge (MA, PhD, ScD). Commonwealth Scholar, Trinity Coll., Cambridge, 1960; Powell Prize for English Verse, 1961; Jesus College, Cambridge: Research Fellow, 1963-66; Fellow, 1967-73; Tutor, 1970-73; Staff Mem., Inst. of Theoretical Astronomy, Univ. of Cambridge, 1968-73. Visiting Professor: Vidyodaya Univ. of Ceylon, Univ. of Maryland, USA, Univ. of Arizona, USA, Univ. of Kyoto, Japan, 1966-70; Univ. of W Ontario, 1974, 1976; UNDP Cons. and Scientific Advisor to President of Sri Lanka, 1970-81. Collaborator with Prof. Sir Fred Hoyle, and propounder with Hoyle of the theory of the space origin of life and of microorganisms. *Publications:* Interstellar Grains, 1967; (with F. D. Kahn and P. G. Mezger) Interstellar Matter, 1972; Light Scattering Functions for Small Particles with Applications in Astronomy, 1973; The Cosmic Laboratory, 1975; (with D. J. Morgan) Solid State Astrophysics, 1976; (with F. Hoyle) Lifecloud: the Origin of Life in the Universe, 1978; (with F. Hoyle) Diseases From Space, 1979; (with F. Hoyle) The Origin of Life, 1980; (with F. Hoyle) Evolution From Space, 1981; (with F. Hoyle) Space Travellers, the Bringers of Life, 1981; over 250 articles and papers in astronomical and scientific jls; contributor to anthologies of Commonwealth Poetry, incl. Young Commonwealth Poets '65, ed P. L. Brent, 1965. *Recreations:* photography, poetry—both writing and reading, history and philosophy of science. *Address:* University College, PO Box 78, Cardiff CF1 1XL. *T:* Cardiff 44211. *Clubs:* Icosahedron Dining (Cardiff); Otters Aquatic (Colombo).

WICKREME, A. S. K.; *see* Kohoban-Wickreme.

WICKREMESINGHE, Dr Walter Gerald, CMG 1954; OBE 1949; *b* 13 Feb. 1897; *s* of Peter Edwin Wickremesinghe and Charlotte Catherine Goonetillaka; *m* 1931, Irene Amelia Goontilleka; two *s* two *d. Educ:* Royal College, Colombo; Ceylon Medical College; London University (the London Hospital); Harvard University (School of Public Health). Licentiate in Medicine and Surgery (Ceylon), 1921; MRCS, LRCP, 1923; Master of Public Health (Harvard), 1926; Dr of Public Health (Harvard), 1927. Director of Medical and Sanitary Services, Ceylon, 1948-53. Chief Delegate from Ceylon at WHO. Assembly and Executive board, Geneva, 1952; Mem. UN Health Planning Mission to Korea, 1952; WHO Consultant, Manila, 1965; Chairman, Committee of Inquiry into Mental Health Services, Ceylon, 1966. (Hon.) FAPHA 1952. OStJ. *Publications:* contributions to Brit. Med. Jl; Ceylon Med. Jl; Trans. Soc. of Med. Officers of Health, Ceylon; Amer. Jl of Public Health. *Recreations:* golf, tennis, riding, swimming. *Address:* 48 Buller's Lane, Colombo 7, Sri Lanka. *T:* Colombo 81374. *Clubs:* Otter Aquatic, Royal Colombo Golf (Colombo); Nuwara Eliya Golf, Nuwara Eliya Hill; (Life Mem.) Health Dept Sports.

WICKS, Allan; Organist, Canterbury Cathedral, since 1961; *b* 1923; *s* of Edward Kemble Wicks, Priest, and Nancie (*née* Murgatroyd); *m* 1955, Elizabeth Kay Butcher; two *d. Educ:* Leatherhead; Christ Church, Oxford. Sub-organist, York Minster, 1947; Organist, Manchester Cathedral, 1954. MusDoc Lambeth, 1974. *Address:* The Old Farm House, Lower Hardres, Canterbury, Kent. *T:* Petham 253.

WICKS, David Vaughan, RE 1961 (ARE 1950); Technical Artist, Bank of England Printing Works, 1954-79, retired, now Consultant; *b* 20 Dec. 1918; British; *m* 1948, Margaret Gwyneth Downs; one *s* one *d* (and one *s* decd). *Educ:* Wychwood, Bournemouth; Cranleigh School, Surrey. Polytechnic School of Art, 1936, silver medal for figure composition, 1938, 1939. Radio Officer, Merchant Navy, 1940-46. Royal College of Art, Engraving School, 1946-49, Diploma, ARCA Engraving. Taught Processes of Engraving at RCA, 1949-54. *Recreations:* archery and tennis.

WICKS, Hon. Sir James, Kt 1972; Chief Justice of Kenya, 1971-82 and of Court of Appeal, 1977-82; *b* 20 June 1909; *s* of late James Wicks and late Mrs

Wicks; *m* 1960, Doris Mary, *d* of late G. F. Sutton; no *c*. *Educ:* Royal Grammar Sch., Guildford; King's Coll., London (LLB); Christ Church, Oxford (MA, BLitt). Chartered Surveyor (PASI), 1931; called to the Bar, Gray's Inn, 1939; practised at Bar, 1939-40 and 1945-46. Served War: RAF (Sqdn Ldr), 1940-45 (despatches thrice). Crown Counsel Palestine, 1946-48; Magistrate, Hong Kong, 1948-53; Actg Additional Judge, Supreme Court, Hong Kong, 1948-49; Dist Judge, Hong Kong, 1953-58; Actg Puisne Judge, Hong Kong, 1953, 1955, 1957; High Court, Kenya: Puisne Judge, 1958-69; Sen. Puisne Judge, 1969-71. *Publication:* The Doctrine of Consideration, 1939. *Recreation:* golf. *Clubs:* Mombasa, Nairobi (Kenya).

WICKS, Sir James (Albert), Kt 1978; JP; Wanganui Computer Centre Privacy Commissioner, since 1978; Acting District Court Judge, 1980-81; *b* 14 June 1910; *s* of Henry James Wilmont Wicks and Melanie de Rohan Wicks (*née* Staunton); *m* 1942, Lorna Margaret de la Cour; one *s* one *d*. *Educ:* Christchurch Boys' High Sch.; Canterbury Univ., NZ. LLM (Hons) Univ. of New Zealand. Admitted Barrister and Solicitor of Supreme Court of NZ, 1932; Notary Public, 1951; Lectr in Trustee Law, Canterbury Univ., 1946-55; in practice as barrister and solicitor (in Christchurch), 1945-61; Mem. Council, Canterbury Dist Law Soc., 1954-61. Stipendiary Magistrate, 1961-78. JP 1963; Chairman: Magistrates' Courts' Rules Cttee, 1967-78; NZ Magistrates' Exec., 1973-78; Dept of Justice's Editorial Bd, 1968-78; Chairman: various Appeal Boards and Statutory Cttees, 1965-78; Teachers' Disciplinary Bd, 1978-; Cttee of Inquiry into the Administration of the Electoral Act, 1979-. *Publications:* papers to Australian Inst. of Criminology, Feb. 1974, and Commonwealth Magistrates' Conf., Kuala Lumpur, Aug. 1975; contribs to NZ Law Jl, Commonwealth Judicial Jl. *Address:* 29 Glen Road, Kelburn, Wellington 5, New Zealand. *T:* 759-204. *Club:* Canterbury (Christchurch, NZ).

WICKS, Nigel Leonard, CBE 1979; Assistant Secretary, Energy Division, HM Treasury, since 1978; *b* 16 June 1940; *s* of Leonard Charles and Beatrice Irene Wicks; *m* 1969, Jennifer Mary (*née* Coveney); three *s*. *Educ:* Beckenham and Penge Grammar Sch.; Univ. of Cambridge (MA); Univ. of London (MA). British Petroleum Co. Ltd, 1958-68; HM Treasury, 1968-75; Civil Service Dept, 1975-78. Mem. Bd, BNOC, 1980-82. *Address:* HM Treasury, Parliament Street, SW1P 3AG. *T:* 01-233 5806.

WICKS, Rt. Rev. Ralph Edwin, OBE 1982; ED 1964; Assistant Bishop of Brisbane, Australia, since 1973; *b* 16 Aug. 1921; *s* of Charles Thomas Wicks and Florence Maud Wicks (*née* White); *m* 1946, Gladys Hawgood; one *s* one *d*. *Educ:* East State Sch. and State High Sch., Toowoomba, Qld; St Francis Theological Coll., Brisbane, Qld (LTh). Mem., Qld Public Service (Educn Dept), 1936-41; Theological Student, 1941-44; Asst Curate: Holy Trinity Ch., Fortitude Valley, Brisbane, 1944-47; St James' Ch., Toowoomba, Qld, 1947-48; Rector: Holy Trinity Ch., Goondiwindi, Qld, 1949-54; Holy Trinity Ch., Fortitude Valley, Brisbane, 1954-63; St James' Church, Toowoomba, Qld, 1963-72. Hon. Canon of St John's Cath., Brisbane, 1968; Archdeacon of Darling Downs, Qld, 1973. Chaplain to the Australian Army, 1949-70. *Recreations:* reading, gardening, music. *Address:* Church House, Ann Street, Brisbane, Queensland 4001, Australia. *T:* Brisbane 294766.

WICKSTEAD, Cyril; Chairman, Eastern Electricity Board, 1978-82, retired; Member, Electricity Council, 1978-82; *b* 27 Sept. 1922; *s* of John William and Mary Caroline Wickstead; *m* 1948, Freda May Hill; two *s*. *Educ:* Rowley Regis Central Sch.; City of Birmingham Commercial Coll. FCIS; CBIM. Served War, Royal Navy (Lieut RNVR), 1942-46. Midland Electric Corporation for Power Distribution Ltd: various positions, 1937-42; Asst Sec., 1946-48; Midlands Electricity Board: Sec., S Staffs and N Worcs Sub-Area, 1948-59; Dep. Sec. of Bd, 1959-63; Sec., 1964-72; Dep. Chm., 1972-77. Freeman, City of London, 1979. *Recreations:* walking, music, gardening, sport. *Address:* Little Acre, Colchester Road, Dedham, Colchester, Essex CO7 6DH. *Club:* Naval.

WIDDAS, Prof. Wilfred Faraday, MB; BS; BSc; PhD; DSc; Professor of Physiology in the University of London, and Head of the Department of Physiology, Bedford College, 1960-81, now Professor Emeritus; *b* 2 May 1916; *s* of late Percy Widdas, BSc, mining engineer, and Annie Maude (*née* Snowdon); *m* 1940, Gladys Green; one *s* two *d*. *Educ:* Durham School; University of Durham College of Medicine and Royal Victoria Infirmary, Newcastle upon Tyne. MB, BS 1938; BSc 1947; PhD 1953; DSc 1958. Assistant in General Practice, 1938-39. Served in RAMC, 1939-47; Deputy Assistant Director-General Army Medical Services, War Office (Major), 1942-47. Research Fellow, St Mary's Hospital Medical School, 1947-49; Lecturer and Sen. Lecturer in Physiology, St Mary's Hospital Medical School, 1949-55; Senior Lecturer in Physiology, King's College, 1955-56; University Reader in Physiology at King's College, 1956-60. FRSocMed. Member: Royal Institution of Gt Britain; Physiological Society; Society of Experimental Biology. *Publications:* Membrane Transport of Sugars, chapter in Carbohydrate Metabolism and its Disorders; Permeability, chapter in Recent Advances in Physiology; also papers on similar topics in (chiefly) Jl of Physiology. *Recreations:* tennis, golf. *Address:* 67 Marksbury Avenue, Kew Gardens, Richmond, Surrey. *T:* 01-876 6374. *Club:* Queen's.

WIDDECOMBE, James Murray, CB 1968; OBE 1959; Director-General, Supplies and Transport (Naval), Ministry of Defence, 1968-70, retired; *b* 7 Jan. 1910; *s* of late Charles Frederick Widdecombe and late Alice Widdecombe; *m* 1936, Rita Noreen Plummer; one *s* one *d*. *Educ:* Devonport High Sch. Asst Naval Armament Supply Officer, Portsmouth, Holton Heath and Chatham,

1929-35; Dep. Naval Armt Supply Officer, Chatham, 1936; OC, RN Armt Depot, Gibraltar, 1936-40; Naval Armt Supply Officer: Admty, 1940-43; Levant, 1943-44. Capt. (SP) RNVR. Sen. Armt Supply Officer: Staff of C-in-C, Med., 1944-46; Admty, 1946-50; Asst Dir of Armt Supply, Admty, 1950-51, and 1956-59; Suptg Naval Armt Supply Officer, Portsmouth, 1951-53; Prin. Naval Armt Supply Officer, Staff of C-in-C, Far East, 1953-56; Dep. Dir of Armt Supply, Admiralty, 1959-61; Dir of Victualling, Admty, 1961-66; Head of RN Supply and Transport Service, MoD, 1966-68; special duties, Management Services, MoD, 1970-73. Gen. Sec., CS Retirement Fellowship, 1973-79. FBIM; FInstPS. *Recreations:* golf, gardening, amateur dramatics. *Address:* 1 Manor Close, Haslemere, Surrey GU27 1PP. *T:* Haslemere 2899. *Clubs:* Hindhead Golf, Navy Department Golfing Society.

WIDDICOMBE, David Graham, QC 1965; *b* 7 Jan. 1924; *s* of Aubrey Guy Widdicombe and Margaret (*née* Puddy); *m* 1961, Anastasia Cecilia (*née* Leech); two *s* one *d*. *Educ:* St Albans Sch.; Queen's Coll., Cambridge (BA 1st cl. Hons; LLB 1st cl. Hons; MA). Called to the Bar, Inner Temple, 1950, Bencher, 1973. Mem., Cttee on Local Govt Rules of Conduct, 1973-74; Chm., Oxfordshire Structure Plan Examination in Public, 1977. *Publication:* (ed) Ryde on Rating, 1968-. *Address:* 2 Mitre Court Buildings, Temple, EC4. *T:* 01-353 4844; Flat 6, 2 Albert Terrace, NW1. *T:* 01-586 3583. *Clubs:* Athenæum, Garrick.

WIDDOWS, Air Commodore Charles; *see* Widdows, Air Commodore S. C.

WIDDOWS, Roland Hewlett; Special Commissioner of Income Tax, since 1977; *b* 14 Aug. 1921; *s* of late A. E. Widdows, CB; *m* 1945, Diana Gweneth, *d* of late E. A. Dickson, Malayan Civil Service; two *s* one *d*. *Educ:* Stowe Sch.; Hertford Coll., Oxford (MA). Served in Royal Navy, Coastal Forces, 1941-45. Called to Bar, Middle Temple, 1948; entered Inland Revenue Solicitor's Office, 1951; Asst Solicitor, 1963; on staff of Law Commission, 1965-70; Lord Chancellor's Office, 1970-77; Under Secretary, 1972. *Recreation:* sailing. *Address:* 36 Gordon Road, Claygate, Surrey KT10 0PJ. *T:* Esher 62532.

WIDDOWS, Air Commodore (Stanley) Charles, CB 1959; DFC 1941; RAF retired; People's Deputy, States of Guernsey, 1973-79; *b* 4 Oct. 1909; *s* of P. L. Widdows, Southend, Bradfield, Berkshire; *m* 1939, Irene Ethel, *d* of S. H. Rawlings, Ugley, Essex; two *s*. *Educ:* St Bartolomew's School, Newbury; No 1 School of Technical Training, RAF, Halton; Royal Air Force College, Cranwell. Commissioned, 1931; Fighting Area, RAF, 1931-32; RAF Middle East, Sudan and Palestine, 1933-37; Aeroplane and Armament Experimental Estab., 1937-40; OC 29 (Fighter) Sqdn, 1940-41; OC RAF West Malling, 1941-42; Gp Capt., Night Ops, HQ 11 and 12 Gp, 1942; SASO, No 85 (Base Defence) Gp, 1943-44, for Operation Overlord; Gp Capt. Organisation, Supreme HQ, Allied Expeditionary Air Force, 1944; OC, RAF Wahn, Germany, 1944-46; RAF Instructor, Sen. Officers War Course, RNC, Greenwich, 1946-48; Fighter Command, 1948-54: SASO HQ No 12 Gp; Chief Instructor, Air Defence Wing, School of Land/Air Warfare; Sector Commander, Eastern Sector. Imperial Defence College, 1955; Director of Operations (Air Defence), Air Ministry, 1956-58. *Address:* Les Granges de Beauvoir, Rohais, St Peter Port, Guernsey, CI. *T:* Guernsey 20219.

WIDDOWSON, Dr Elsie May, CBE 1979; FRS 1976; Department of Medicine, Addenbrooke's Hospital, Cambridge, since 1972; *b* 21 Oct. 1906; *d* of Thomas Henry Widdowson and Rose Widdowson. *Educ:* Imperial Coll., London (BSc, PhD); DSc London 1948. Courtauld Inst. of Biochemistry, Mddx Hosp., 1931-33; KCH, London, 1933-38; Cambridge University: Dept of Exper. Medicine, 1938-66; Infant Nutrition Res. Div., 1966-72. President: Nutrition Soc., 1977-80; Neonatal Soc., 1978-81. Hon. DSc Manchester, 1974. *Publications:* (with R. A. McCance) The Composition of Foods, 1940 (2nd edn 1967); (with R. A. McCance) Breads White and Brown: Their Place in Thought and Social History, 1956; contrib. Proc. Royal Soc., Jl Physiol., Biochem. Jl, Brit. Jl Nut., Arch. Dis. Child., Lancet, BMJ, Nature, Biol. Neonate, Nut. Metabol., and Ped. Res. *Address:* Orchard House, 9 Boot Lane, Barrington, Cambridge. *T:* Cambridge 870219.

WIDDUP, Malcolm, CB 1979; retired 1980; Under-Secretary, HM Treasury, 1971-80; *b* 9 May 1920; *s* of John and Frances Ellen Widdup; *m* 1947, Margaret Ruth Anderson; one *s* one *d*. *Educ:* Giggleswick Sch.; Trinity Coll., Oxford (MA). Served War, Army, RA and Staff, 1940-45. Ministry of Food, 1946-53; HM Treasury, 1953-55; Cabinet Office, 1955-57; HM Treasury, 1957-60; Min. of Health, 1960-62; HM Treasury, 1962-66; UK Delegn to OECD, 1966-68; HM Treasury, 1968-80; Sen. Clerk, House of Lords, 1980-81. *Recreations:* sailing, gardening, music. *Address:* Cherry Tree Cottage, Manor Close, East Horsley, Leatherhead, Surrey.

WIESEL, Prof. Torsten Nils, MD; Robert Winthrop Professor of Neurobiology, since 1974, and Chairman, Department of Neurobiology, 1973-82, Harvard Medical School; *b* 3 June 1924; *s* of Fritz S. Wiesel and Anna-Lisa Wiesel (*née* Bentzer); *m* 1st, 1956, Teeri Stenhammar (marr. diss. 1970); 2nd, 1973, Ann Yee (marr. diss. 1981); one *d*. *Educ:* Karolinska Inst., Stockholm (MD 1954). Instructor, Dept of Physiol., Karolinska Inst., 1954-55; Asst, Dept of Child Psychiatry, Karolinska Hosp., Stockholm, 1954-55; Fellow in Ophthalmol., 1955-58, Asst Prof. of Ophthalmic Physiol., 1958-59, Johns Hopkins Univ. Med. Sch., Baltimore; Harvard Medical School:

Associate in Neurophysiol. and Neuropharmacol., 1959-60; Asst Prof., 1960-67; Prof. of Physiol., 1967-68; Prof. of Neurobiol., 1968-74. Lectures: Ferrier, Royal Soc., 1972; Grass, Soc. for Neurosci., 1976. Member: Amer. Physiol Soc.; AAAS; Amer. Acad. of Arts and Scis; Amer. Philosophical Soc.; Soc. for Neurosci. (Pres. 1978-79); Nat. Acad. of Scis; Swedish Physiol Soc.; Foreign Mem., Royal Soc. Hon. AM Harvard Univ., 1967; Hon. MD Linköping, 1982. Awards and Prizes: Dr Jules C. Stein, Trustees for Research to Prevent Blindness, 1971; Lewis S. Rosenstiel, Brandeis Univ., 1972; Friedenwald, Assoc. for Res. in Vision and Ophthalmology, 1975; Karl Spencer Lashley, Amer. Phil. Soc., 1977; Louisa Gross Horwitz, Columbia Univ., 1978; Dickson, Pittsburgh Univ., 1979; Ledlie, Harvard Univ., 1980; Soc. for Scholars, Johns Hopkins Univ., 1980; Nobel Prize in Physiology or Medicine, 1981. *Publications:* (contrib.) Physiological and Biochemical Aspects of Nervous Integration, 1968; (contrib.) The Organization of the Cerebral Cortex, 1981; contribs to professional jls, symposia and trans of learned socs. *Address:* 85 Pinckney Street, Boston, Mass 02114, USA. *T:* (617) 523-2503; Department of Neurobiology, Harvard Medical School, Boston, Mass 02115, USA. *T:* (617) 732-1657. *Club:* Harvard (Boston).

WIESNER, Dr Jerome Bert; Institute Professor, Massachusetts Institute of Technology, since 1980 (Provost, 1966-71; President, 1971-80); *b* 30 May 1915; *s* one *d. Educ:* University of Michigan, Ann Arbor, Michigan. PhD in electrical engineering, 1950. Staff, University of Michigan, 1937-40; Chief Engineer, Library of Congress, 1940-42; Staff, MIT Radiation Lab., 1942-45; Staff, Univ. of Calif Los Alamos Lab., 1945-46; Asst Prof. of Electrical Engrg, MIT, 1946; Associate Prof. of Electrical Engrg, 1947; Prof. of Electrical Engrg, 1950-64; Dir, Res. Lab. of Electronics, 1952-61. Special Assistant to the President of the USA, for Science and Technology, The White House, 1961-64; Director, Office of Science and Technology, Exec. Office of the President, 1962-64; Chm., Tech. Assessment Adv. Council, Office of Tech. Assessment, US Congress, 1976-78. Dean of Science, MIT, 1964-66. Member, Board of Directors: Celanese Corp.; Damon Corp.; Schlumberger Ltd. *Publications:* Where Science and Politics Meet, 1965; contrib.: Modern Physics for the Engineer, 1954; Arms Control, Disarmament and National Security, 1960; Arms Control, issues for the Public, 1961; Lectures on Modern Communications, 1961; technical papers in: Science, Physical Rev., Jl Applied Physics, Scientific American, Proc. Inst. Radio Engineers, etc. *Recreations:* photography, boating. *Address:* Massachusetts Institute of Technology, Cambridge, Mass 02139, USA. *T:* 253-2800. *Clubs:* Cosmos (Washington, DC); Commercial, St Botolph's (Boston); Century, Harvard Club of New York City (NY).

WIESNER, Prof. Karel František, OC 1975; FRS 1969; FRSC 1957; University Professor, University of New Brunswick, since 1976 (Research Professor, 1964-76); *b* 25 Nov. 1919; *s* of Karel Wiesner, industrialist, Chrudim, Czechoslovakia, and Eugenie Storová, Prague; *m* 1942, Blanka Pevná; one *s* (and one *d* decd). *Educ:* Gymnasium Chrudim; Charles Univ., Prague. Asst, Dept of Physical Chem., Charles Univ., Prague, 1945-46; Post-doctoral Fellow, ETH Zürich, 1946-48; Prof. of Organic Chem., Univ. of New Brunswick, 1948-62; Associate Dir of Research, Ayerst Laboratories, Montreal, 1962-64. Mem., Pontifical Acad. of Scis, 1978. Hon. DSc: New Brunswick, 1970; Western Ontario, 1972; Montreal, 1975. Order of Kyril and Method, 1st cl. (Bulgaria), 1981. *Publications:* about 185 research papers in various scientific periodicals. *Recreations:* tennis, ski-ing, hunting. *Address:* 814 Burden Street, Fredericton, New Brunswick E3B 4C4, Canada. *T:* 4544007.

WIGAN, Sir Alan (Lewis), 5th Bt *cr* 1898; *b* 19 Nov. 1913; second *s* of Sir Roderick Grey Wigan, 3rd Bt, and Ina (*d* 1977), *o c* of Lewis D. Wigan, Brandon Park, Suffolk; *S* brother, 1979; *m* 1950, Robina, *d* of Sir Iain Colquhoun, 7th Bt, KT, DSO; one *s* one *d. Educ:* Eton; Magdalen College, Oxford. Commissioned Suppl. Reserve, KRRC, 1936; served with KRRC, 1939-46; wounded and taken prisoner, Calais, 1940. Director, Charrington & Co. (Brewers), 1939-70. Master, Brewers' Co., 1958-59. *Recreations:* shooting, fishing, golf. *Heir: s* Michael Iain Wigan, *b* 3 Oct. 1951. *Address:* Badingham House, Badingham, Woodbridge, Suffolk. *T:* Badingham 664; Moorburn, The Lake, Kirkcudbright. *Club:* Army and Navy.

WIGDOR, Lucien Simon, CEng, MRAeS; Managing Director, L. S. Wigdor Ltd, since 1976; Director, Zambian Engineering Services Ltd, since 1979; Special Adviser on International Affairs, Bayerische Hypotheken- Und Wechsel- Bank AG, since 1981; Consultant, Lazard Bros, since 1982; *b* Oct. 1919; *s* of William and Adèle Wigdor; *m* 1951, Marion Louise, *d* of Henry Risner; one *s* one *d. Educ:* Highgate Sch.; College of Aeronautical Engineering. Served War, RAF, 1940-46; Operational Research, BEA: Research Engr, 1947-51; Manager, Industrial and Commercial Develt, Vertol Corp., USA, 1951-55; Managing Dir, Tunnel Refineries Ltd, 1955-69, Vice-Chm., 1969-72; Corporate Consultant, The Boeing Company, 1960-72; Dep. Dir-Gen., CBI, 1972-76; Chief Exec., Leslie & Godwin (Holdings) Ltd, 1977-78, Dir 1977-81; Chm., Weir Pumps Ltd, 1978-81; Director: The Weir Group, 1978-81; Rothschild Investment Trust, 1977-82; Rothschild Internat. Investments SA, 1981-82. *Publications:* papers to Royal Aeronautical Soc., American Helicopter Soc. *Recreations:* ski-ing, experimental engineering. *Address:* Wallingford, Leas Green, Chislehurst, Kent. *T:* 01-300 1519. *Clubs:* Carlton, Royal Air Force.

WIGG, family name of **Baron Wigg.**

WIGG, Baron *cr* 1967 (Life Peer), of the Borough of Dudley; **George Edward Cecil Wigg,** PC 1964; President, Betting Office Licensees' Association, since 1973; *b* 28 Nov. 1900; *m*; three *d. Educ:* Fairfields Council Schs and Queen Mary's Sch., Basingstoke, Hants. Served in Regular Army, 1919-37, 1940-46. MP (Lab) Dudley, 1945-67; PPS to Rt Hon. E. Shinwell when Minister of Fuel and Power, Sec. of State for War and Minister of Defence; an Opposition Whip, 1951-54; Paymaster-General, 1964-67. Member: Racecourse Betting Control Bd, 1957-61; Totalisator Bd, 1961-64; Chm., Horserace Betting Levy Bd, 1967-72. *Publication:* George Wigg, 1972. *Address:* 117 Newcastle Road, Trent Vale, Stoke-on-Trent.

WIGGIN, Alfred William, (Jerry Wiggin); TD 1970; MP (C) Weston-super-Mare since 1969; Parliamentary Under-Secretary of State for the Armed Forces, Ministry of Defence, since 1981; *b* 24 Feb. 1937; *e s* of late Col Sir William H. Wiggin, KCB, DSO, TD, DL, JP, and late Lady Wiggin, Worcestershire; *m* 1964, Rosemary Janet (marr. diss. 1982), *d* of David L. D. Orr; two *s* one *d. Educ:* Eton; Trinity Coll., Cambridge. 2nd Lieut, Queen's Own Warwickshire and Worcestershire Yeomanry (TA), 1959; Major, Royal Yeomanry, 1975-78. Contested (C), Montgomeryshire, Gen. Elections, 1964 and 1966. PPS to Lord Balniel, at MoD, later FCO, 1970-74, and to Ian Gilmour, MoD, 1971-72; Parly Sec., MAFF, 1979-81. Promoted Hallmarking Act, 1973. Jt Hon. Sec., Conservative Defence Cttee, 1974-75; Vice-Chm., Conservative Agricultural Cttee, 1975-79; Chm., West Country Cons. Gp, 1978-79. General Rapporteur, Economic Cttee, North Atlantic Assembly, 1976-79. *Address:* House of Commons, SW1. *T:* 01-219 4522; The Court, Axbridge, Somerset. *T:* Axbridge 732527. *Clubs:* Beefsteak, Pratt's; Royal Yacht Squadron.

WIGGIN, Jerry; see Wiggin, A. W.

WIGGIN, Sir John (Henry), 4th Bt *cr* 1892; MC 1946; Major, Grenadier Guards, retired; *b* 3 March 1921; *s* of Sir Charles Richard Henry Wiggin, 3rd Bt, TD, and Mabel Violet Mary (*d* 1961), *d* of Sir William Jaffray, 2nd Bt; *S* father, 1972; *m* 1st, 1947, Lady Cecilia Evelyn Anson (marr. diss. 1961; she *d* 1963), *yr d* of 4th Earl of Lichfield; two *s* ; 2nd, 1963, Sarah, *d* of Brigadier Stewart Forster; two *s. Educ:* Eton; Trinity College, Cambridge. Served War of 1939-45 (prisoner-of-war). High Sheriff Warwicks, 1976. *Heir: s* Charles Rupert John Wiggin, Major, Grenadier Guards [*b* 2 July 1949; *m* 1979, Mrs Mary Burnett-Hitchcock; one *s. Educ:* Eton]. *Address:* Honington Hall, Shipston-on-Stour, Warwicks. *T:* Shipston-on-Stour 61434.

WIGGINS, (Anthony) John; Under Secretary, Department of Energy, since 1981; *b* 8 July 1938; *s* of Rev. Arthur Wiggins and Mavis Wiggins (*née* Brown); *m* 1962, Jennifer Anne Walkden; one *s* one *d. Educ:* Highgate Sch.; The Hotchkiss Sch., Lakeville, Conn, USA; Oriel Coll., Oxford (BA). Assistant Principal, HM Treasury, 1961; Private Sec. to Permanent Under Sec., Dept of Economic Affairs, 1964-66; Principal: Dept of Economic Affairs, 1966-67; HM Treasury, 1967-69; Harkness Fellow, Harvard Univ., 1969-71 (MPA 1970); Asst Sec., HM Treasury (various posts in Domestic Economy Sector), 1972-79; Principal Private Sec. to Chancellor of the Exchequer, 1980-81. *Recreations:* mountain walking, skiing, opera. *Address:* St Anne's, Rowley Green Road, Arkley, Barnet, Herts EN5 3HH. *T:* 01-440 4072.

WIGGINS, David, FBA 1978; Fellow, and Praelector in Philosophy, University College, Oxford, since 1981; *b* 8 March 1933; *s* of Norman Wiggins and Diana Wiggins (*née* Priestley); *m* 1979, Jennifer Hornsby. *Educ:* St Paul's Sch.; Brasenose Coll., Oxford. BA 1955; MA 1958. Asst Principal, Colonial Office, London 1957-58. Jane Eliza Procter Vis. Fellow, Princeton Univ., 1958-59; Lectr, 1959, then Fellow and Lecturer, 1960-67, New College, Oxford; Prof. of Philosophy, Bedford Coll., Univ. of London, 1967-80. Visiting appointments: Stanford, 1964 and 1965; Harvard, 1968 and 1972; All Souls College, 1973; Princeton, 1980. Mem., Indep. Commn on Transport, 1973-74; Chm., Transport Users' Consultative Cttee for the South East, 1977-79. *Publications:* Identity and Spatio Temporal Continuity, 1967; Truth, Invention and the Meaning of Life, 1978; Sameness and Substance, 1980; philosophical articles in Philosophical Review, Analysis, Philosophy, Synthèse; articles on environmental and transport subjects in Spectator, Times, Tribune. *Address:* University College, Oxford.

WIGGINS, John; see Wiggins, A. J.

WIGGINS, Rt. Rev. Maxwell Lester; General Secretary, NZ Church Missionary Society, since 1982; *b* 5 Feb. 1915; *s* of Herbert Lester and Isobel Jane Wiggins; *m* 1941, Margaret Agnes (*née* Evans); one *s* two *d. Educ:* Christchurch Boys' High Sch., NZ; Canterbury University College, NZ (BA). Asst Curate, St Mary's, Merivale, NZ, 1938; Vicar of Oxford, NZ, 1941; CMS Missionary, Diocese Central Tanganyika, 1945; Head Master, Alliance Secondary Sch., Dodoma, 1948; Provost, Cathedral of Holy Spirit, Dodoma, 1949; Principal, St Philip's Theological Coll., and Canon of Cathedral of Holy Spirit, Dodoma, 1954; Archdeacon of Lake Province, 1956; Asst Bishop of Central Tanganyika, 1959; Bishop of Victoria Nyanza, 1963-76; Asst Bishop of Wellington, 1976-81. *Address:* 138A Hamilton Avenue, Christchurch 4, New Zealand.

WIGGLESWORTH, Gordon Hardy; Director: Turner Mansfield Associates (Development Consultants, Architects and Planners), since 1980; Quadrant Projects; Consultant, Alan Turner Associates, planning and development consultants; *b* 27 June 1920; *m* 1952, Cherry Diana Heath; three *d. Educ:*

Highgate; University Coll., London; Architectural Association. ARIBA; AADipl. Served War of 1939-45: Royal Engineers, 1941-46. Architectural Assoc., 1946-48; private practice and Univ. of Hong Kong, 1948-52; private practice: London, 1952-54; Hong Kong, 1954-56; London, 1956-57. Asst Chief Architect, Dept of Education and Science, 1957-67; Dir of Building Develt, MPBW, later DoE, 1967-72; Principal Architect, Educn, GLC (ILEA), 1972-74; Housing Architect, GLC, 1974-80. Address: 53 Canonbury Park South, N1 2JL. T: 01-226 7734.

WIGGLESWORTH, Sir Vincent (Brian), Kt 1964; CBE 1951; FRS 1939; MA, MD, BCh Cantab, FRES; Retired Director, Agricultural Research Council Unit of Insect Physiology (1943-67); Quick Professor of Biology, University of Cambridge, 1952-66; Fellow of Gonville and Caius College; b 17 April 1899; s of late Sidney Wigglesworth, MRCS; m 1928, Mabel Katherine, d of late Col Sir David Semple, IMS; three s one d. Educ: Repton; Caius Coll., Cambridge (Scholar); St Thomas' Hosp. 2nd Lt RFA, 1917-18, served in France; Frank Smart Student of Caius College, 1922-24; Lecturer in Medical Entomology in London School of Hygiene and Tropical Medicine, 1926; Reader in Entomology in University of London, 1936-44; Reader in Entomology, in University of Cambridge, 1945-52. Fellow, Imperial College, London, 1977. Hon. Member: Royal Entomological Soc.; Physiological Soc.; Soc. Experimental Biology; Assoc. Applied Biology; International Confs of Entomology; Soc. of European Endocrinologists; Royal Danish Academy of Science; Amer. Philosophical Soc.; US Nat. Academy of Sciences; American Academy of Arts and Sciences; Kaiserliche Deutsche Akademie der Naturforscher, Leopoldina; Deutsche Entomologische Gesellschaft; American Entomol. Soc.; USSR Acad. of Sciences; All-Union Entomol. Soc.; Entomol. Soc. of India; Société Zoologique de France; Société Entomologique de France, Société Entomologique d'Egypte; Entomological Society of the Netherlands; Schweizerische Entomologische Gesellschaft; Indian Academy of Zoology; Corresponding Member: Accademia delle Scienze dell' Istituto di Bologna; Société de Pathologie Exotique; Entomological Soc. of Finland; Dunham Lecturer, Harvard, 1945; Woodward Lecturer, Yale, 1945; Croonian Lecturer, Royal Society, 1948; Messenger Lecturer, Cornell, 1958; Tercentenary Lecturer, Royal Society, 1960. Royal Medal, Royal Society, 1955; Swammerdam Medal, Soc. Med. Chir., Amsterdam, 1966; Gregor Mendel Gold Medal, Czechoslovak Acad. of Science, 1967; Frink Medal, Zoological Soc., 1979. DPhil (hc) University, Berne; DSc (hc): Paris, Newcastle and Cambridge. Publications: Insect Physiology, 1934; The Principles of Insect Physiology, 1939; The Physiology of Insect Metamorphosis, 1954; The Life of Insects, 1964; Insect Hormones, 1970; Insects and the Life of Man, 1976; numerous papers on comparative physiology. Address: 14 Shilling Street, Lavenham, Suffolk. T: Lavenham 247293.

WIGHAM, Eric Leonard, CBE 1967; Labour Correspondent, The Times, 1946-69; b 8 Oct. 1904; s of Leonard and Caroline Nicholson Wigham; m 1929, Jane Dawson; one d. Educ: Ackworth and Bootham Schools; Birmingham University (MA). Reporter on Newcastle upon Tyne papers, 1925-32; Manchester Evening News, 1932-45; War Correspondent, The Observer and Manchester Evening News, 1944-45; Labour Correspondent, Manchester Guardian, 1945-46. Member, Royal Commission on Trade Unions and Employers' Associations, 1965-68. Order of King Leopold II (Belgium), 1945. Publications: Trade Unions, 1956; What's Wrong with the Unions?, 1961; The Power to Manage: a history of the Engineering Employers' Federation, 1973; Strikes and the Government 1893-1974, 1976, 2nd edn, 1893-1981, 1982; From Humble Petition to Militant Action: a history of the Civil and Public Services Association, 1903-1978, 1980. Recreation: gardening. Address: Link View, The Avenue, West Wickham, Kent. T: 01-776 0397. Club: National Liberal.

WIGHT, James Alfred, OBE 1979; FRCVS; practising veterinary surgeon, since 1939; author, since 1970; b 3 Oct. 1916; s of James Henry and Hannah Wight; m 1941, Joan Catherine Danbury; one s one d. Educ: Hillhead High Sch.; Glasgow Veterinary Coll. FRCVS 1982. Started in general veterinary practice in Thirsk, Yorks, 1940, and has been there ever since with the exception of war-time service with the RAF. Began to write at the ripe age of 50 and quite unexpectedly became a best-selling author of books on his veterinary experiences which have been translated into all European languages and many others, incl. Japanese. Hon. Mem., British Vet. Assoc., 1975. Hon. DLitt Heriot-Watt, 1979. Publications: (as James Herriot): If Only They Could Talk, 1970; It Shouldn't Happen to a Vet, 1972; All Creatures Great and Small, (USA) 1972; Let Sleeping Vets Lie, 1973; All Things Bright and Beautiful, (USA) 1973; Vet in Harness, 1974; Vets Might Fly, 1976; Vet in a Spin, 1977; James Herriot's Yorkshire, 1979; The Lord God Made Them All, 1981. Recreations: music, dog-walking. Address: Mire Beck, Thirlby, Thirsk, Yorks YO7 2DJ.

WIGHTWICK, Charles Christopher Brooke, MA; HM Inspector of Schools, since 1980; b 16 Aug. 1931; s of Charles Frederick Wightwick and Marion Frances Wightwick (née Smith); m 1955, Pamela Layzell; one s two d. Educ: St Michael's, Otford Court; Lancing Coll.; St Edmund Hall, Oxford. BA 1954, MA 1958. Asst Master, Hurstpierpoint Coll., 1954-59; Head of German, Denstone Coll., 1959-65; Head of Languages, then Director of Studies, Westminster Sch., 1965-75; Head Master, King's College Sch., Wimbledon, 1975-80. FRSA 1980. Publication: (co-author) Longman Audio-Lingual German, 3 vols., 1974-78. Recreations: photography, running, judo, language. Address: 45 Tonsley Place, SW18 1BG. T: 01-870 5993.

WIGLEY, Dafydd; MP (Plaid Cymru) Caenarfon since Feb. 1974; President, Plaid Cymru, since 1981; industrial economist; b April 1943; s of Elfyn Edward Wigley, former County Treasurer, Caernarfonshire CC; m Elinor Bennett (née Owen), d of Emrys Bennett Owen, Dolgellau; three s one d. Educ: Caernarfon Grammar Sch.; Rydal Sch., Colwyn Bay; Manchester Univ. Ford Motor Co., 1964-67; Chief Cost Accountant and Financial Planning Manager, Mars Ltd, 1967-71; Financial Controller, Hoover Ltd, Merthyr Tydfil, 1971-74. Vice-Pres., Nat. Fedn of Industrial Develt Authorities, 1981-. Member: Nat. Cttee for Electoral Reform; ASTMS. Member Merthyr Tydfil Borough Council, 1972-74. Sponsor, Disabled Persons Act, 1981. Publication: An Economic Plan for Wales, 1970. Address: House of Commons, SW1A 0AA.

WIGNER, Prof. Eugene P(aul); Thomas D. Jones Professor of Mathematical Physics of Princeton University, 1938-71, retired; b 17 Nov. 1902; s of Anthony and Elizabeth Wigner; m 1st, 1936, Amelia Z. Frank (d 1937); 2nd, 1941, Mary Annette Wheeler (d 1977); one s one d; 3rd, 1979, Eileen C. P. Hamilton. Educ: Technische Hochschule, Berlin, Dr Ing. 1925. Lectr, Princeton Univ., 1930, half-time Prof. of Mathematical Physics, 1931-36. Mem. Gen. Adv. Cttee to US Atomic Energy Commn, 1952-57, 1959-64; Director: Nat. Acad. of Sciences Harbor Project for Civil Defense, 1963; Civil Defense Project, Oak Ridge Nat. Lab., 1964-65. Pres., Amer. Physical Soc., 1956 (Vice-Pres., 1955); Member: Amer. Assoc. of Physics Teachers; Amer. Math. Soc.; Amer. Nuclear Soc.; Amer. Assoc. for Adv. of Scis; Sigma Xi; Franklin Inst.; German Physical Soc.; Royal Netherlands Acad. of Science and Letters, 1960; Foreign Mem., Royal Soc., 1970; Corresp. Mem. Acad. of Science, Göttingen, 1951; Austrian Acad. Sciences, 1968; Nat. Acad. Sci. (US); Amer. Philos. Soc.; Amer. Acad. Sci. Hon. Mem., Eötvös Lorand Soc., Hungary, 1976. Citation, NJ Sci. Teachers' Assoc., 1951. US Government Medal for Merit, 1946; Franklin Medal, 1950; Fermi Award, 1958; Atoms for Peace Award, 1960; Max Planck Medal of German Phys. Soc., 1961; Nobel Prize for Physics, 1963; George Washington Award, Amer. Hungarian Studies Assoc., 1964; Semmelweiss Medal, Amer. Hungarian Med. Assoc., 1965; US Nat. Medal for Science, 1969; Pfizer Award, 1971; Albert Einstein Award, 1972; Wigner Medal, 1978. Holds numerous hon. doctorates. Publications: Nuclear Structure (with L. Eisenbud), 1958; The Physical Theory of Neutron Chain Reactors (with A. M. Weinberg), 1958; Group Theory (orig. in German, 1931), English trans., NY, 1959; Symmetries and Reflections, 1967. Address: 8 Ober Road, Princeton, NJ 08540, USA. T: 609-924-1189. Club: Cosmos (Washington, DC).

WIGODER, family name of **Baron Wigoder.**

WIGODER, Baron cr 1974 (Life Peer), of Cheetham in the City of Manchester; **Basil Thomas Wigoder,** QC 1966; a Recorder of the Crown Court, since 1972; Liberal Chief Whip, House of Lords, since 1977 (Deputy Whip, 1976-77); Chairman, British United Provident Association, since 1981; b 12 Feb. 1921; s of late Dr P. I. Wigoder and of Mrs R. R. Wigoder, JP, Manchester; m 1948, Yoland Levinson; three s one d. Educ: Manchester Gram. Sch.; Oriel Coll., Oxford. Served RA, 1942-45. Pres. Oxford Union, 1946. Called to Bar, Gray's Inn, 1946, Master of the Bench, 1972; Mem., Gen. Council of the Bar, 1970-; Mem., Crown Court Rules Cttee, 1971-. BoT Inspector, Pinnock Finance (GB) Ltd, 1967. Chm., Health Services Bd, 1977-80; Mem., Council on Tribunals, 1980-. Chm., Liberal Party Exec., 1963-65; Chm., Liberal Party Organising Cttee, 1965-66. Contested (L): Bournemouth, 1945; Westbury, 1959 and 1964. Recreation: cricket. Address: House of Lords, SW1. Clubs: National Liberal, MCC.

WIGRAM, family name of **Baron Wigram.**

WIGRAM, 2nd Baron, cr 1935, of Clewer; **George Neville Clive Wigram,** MC 1945; JP; DL; b 2 Aug. 1915; s of Clive, 1st Baron Wigram, PC, GCB, GCVO, CSI, and Nora Mary (d 1956), d of Sir Neville Chamberlain, KCB, KCVO; S father 1960; m 1941, Margaret Helen, yr d of late General Sir Andrew Thorne, KCB, CMG, DSO; one s two d. Educ: Winchester and Magdalen College, Oxford. Page of Honour to HM King George V, 1925-32; served in Grenadier Guards, 1937-57: Military Secretary and Comptroller to Governor-General of New Zealand, 1946-49; commanded 1st Bn Grenadier Guards, 1955-56. Governor of Westminster Hospital, 1967. JP Gloucestershire, 1959, DL 1969. Heir: s Major Hon. Andrew (Francis Clive) Wigram, Grenadier Guards [b 18 March 1949; m 1974, Gabrielle Diana, y d of late R. D. Moore; two s]. Address: Poulton Fields, Cirencester, Gloucestershire. T: Poulton 250. Club: Cavalry and Guards.

WIGRAM, Rev. Canon Sir Clifford Woolmore, 7th Bt, cr 1805; Vicar of Marston St Lawrence with Warkworth, near Banbury, since 1945, also of Thenford, since 1975; Non-Residentiary Canon of Peterborough Cathedral, since 1973; b 24 Jan. 1911; er s of late Robert Ainger Wigram and Evelyn Dorothy, d of C. W. E. Henslowe; S uncle, 1935; m 1948, Christobel Joan Marriott, d of late William Winter Goode. Educ: Winchester; Trinity Coll., Cambridge. Asst Priest at St Ann's, Brondesbury, 1934-37; Chaplain Ely Theological College, 1937. Heir: b Maj. Edward Robert Woolmore Wigram, Indian Army [b 19 July 1913; m 1944, Viva Ann, d of late Douglas Bailey, Laughton Lodge, near Lewes, Sussex; one d. Educ: Winchester; Trinity Coll., Cambridge. Attached 2nd Batt. South Staffordshire Regt, Bangalore, 1935; Major, 19th KGO Lancers, Lahore, 1938]. Address: The Vicarage, Marston St Lawrence, Banbury, Oxon OX17 2DA.

WIGRAM, Derek Roland, MA, BSc (Econ.); Headmaster of Monkton Combe School, near Bath, 1946-68; *b* 18 Mar. 1908; *er s* of late Roland Lewis Wigram and of Mildred (*née* Willock); *m* 1944, Catharine Mary, *d* of late Very Rev. W. R. Inge, KCVO, DD, former Dean of St Paul's; one *s* one *d*. *Educ*: Marlborough Coll.; Peterhouse, Cambridge (Scholar). 1st Class Hons Classical Tripos, 1929; 2nd Class Hons Economics and Political Science, London, 1943; Assistant Master and Careers Master, Whitgift School, Croydon, 1929-36; House Master and Careers Master, Bryanston School, 1936-46. Hon. Associate Mem., Headmasters' Conf. (Chm., 1963-64); Vice-Pres., CMS (Chm., Exec. Cttee, 1956-58, 1969-72); Patron, Oxford Conf. in Education; Mem., Council of Lee Abbey; Mem. Adv. Council and Associate Consultant, Christian Orgns Research and Adv. Trust. Bishops' Inspector of Theological Colls (Mem. Archbishops' Commn, 1970-71); Governor, Walhampton Sch. (Chm. 1966-78). *Publication*: (Jt Editor) Hymns for Church and School, 1964. *Address*: Housels Field, Westwood, Bradford on Avon, Wilts. *T*: Bradford on Avon 2362.

WIKELEY, Thomas, CMG 1955; OBE 1944; *b* 9 Oct. 1902; *s* of late Col J. M. Wikeley (Indian Army, retired) and late Christine Wikeley (*née* Duns); unmarried. *Educ*: Loretto; Pembroke Coll., Cambridge. MA Mod. Langs. Levant Consular Service, 1926. Served at Alexandria, Cairo, Jedda, Rabat, Genoa, Harar, Addis Ababa, Port Said. Transferred to Foreign Office, 1944; Consul-General, Athens, Dec. 1946; Consul-General, Leopoldville, 1948-51; Consul-General, Tetuan (Spanish Morocco), 1952-54; Consul-General, Jerusalem, 1954-57; HM Minister and Consul-Gen., Guatemala, 1957-60; Foreign Office, 1962-69 (British Delegate to Internat. Exhibitions Bureau); retired 1969. *Publications*: trans. Eugène Pepin: The Loire and its Chateaux, 1971; trans. Jean Chesneaux: The Political and Social Ideas of Jules Verne, 1972. *Address*: 19 Cromwell Court, Hove, East Sussex BN3 3ÉF.

WILBERFORCE, family name of **Baron Wilberforce**.

WILBERFORCE, Baron, *cr* 1964 (Life Peer); **Richard Orme Wilberforce**, PC 1964; Kt 1961; CMG 1956; OBE 1944; a Lord of Appeal in Ordinary, 1964-82; Fellow, All Souls College, Oxford, since 1932; *b* 11 Mar. 1907; *s* of late S. Wilberforce; *m* 1947, Yvette, *d* of Roger Lenoan, Judge of Court of Cassation, France; one *s* one *d*. *Educ*: Winchester; New College, Oxford. Served War, 1939-46; returned to Bar, 1947; QC 1954; Judge of the High Court of Justice (Chancery Division), 1961-64; Bencher, Middle Temple, 1961. Chm. Exec. Council, Internat. Law Assoc.; Mem., Permanent Court of Arbitration; Pres., Fédération Internationale du Droit Européen, 1978. High Steward of Oxford University, 1967-; Chancellor, Univ. of Hull, 1978-; Visitor, Wolfson Coll., Oxford, 1974. Hon. Fellow, New Coll., Oxford, 1965. Hon. FRCM. Hon. Comp. Royal Aeronautical Society. Hon. Mem., Scottish Faculty of Advocates, 1978. Hon. DCL Oxon, 1968; Hon. LLD: London, 1972; Hull, 1973. Diplôme d'Honneur, Corp. des Vignerons de Champagne. US Bronze Star, 1944. *Publications*: The Law of Restrictive Trade Practices, 1956; articles and pamphlets on Air Law and International Law. *Recreations*: the turf, travel, opera. *Address*: House of Lords, SW1. *Club*: Athenæum.

WILBERFORCE, Robert, CBE 1924; retired; *b* 8 Dec. 1887; 2nd *s* of H. E. Wilberforce; *m* 1914, Hope Elizabeth (*d* 1970), *d* of Schuyler N. Warren, New York. *Educ*: Beaumont and Stonyhurst; Balliol College, Oxford. BA 1912, Honour School of Modern History; War Trade Intelligence Department, 1915-16; Attaché HM Legation to Holy See, 1917-19; called to Bar, Inner Temple, 1921; Member of British Delegation to Washington Disarmament Conference, 1921-22; Carnegie Endowment International Mission to Vatican Library, 1927; British Delegation to Geneva Disarmament Conference, 1932 and 1933; Director British Information Services, New York; retired 1952. *Publications*: The Church and Slavery; Meditations in Verse; Foreword to A Rug Primer, by Hope Elizabeth Wilberforce, 1979; articles and reviews in various periodicals. *Address*: St Teresa's, Corston, near Bath, Avon BA2 9AE. *T*: Saltford 2607.

WILBERFORCE, William John Antony, CMG 1981; HM Diplomatic Service; High Commissioner in Cyprus, since 1982; *b* 3 Jan. 1930; *s* of late Lt-Col W. B. Wilberforce and Cecilia (*née* Dormer); *m* 1953, Laura Lyon, *d* of late Howard Sykes, Englewood, NJ; one *s* two *d*. *Educ*: Ampleforth; Christ Church, Oxford. Army National Service, 2nd Lieut KOYLI, 1948-49. HM Foreign Service, 1953; served: Oslo, 1955-57; Berlin, 1957-59; Ankara, 1962-64; Åbidjan, 1964-67; Asst Head of UN (Econ. and Social) Dept, 1967-70, and of Southern European Dept, 1970-72; Counsellor, 1972-74, and Head of Chancery, 1974-75, Washington; Hd of Defence Dept, FCO, 1975-78; Asst Under-Sec., RCDS, 1979; Leader of UK Delegn to Madrid Conf. on Security and Cooperation in Europe Review Meeting, with rank of Ambassador, 1980-82. Hon. DHum Wilberforce, 1973. *Recreations*: the turf, travel, gardening. *Address*: c/o Foreign and Commonwealth Office, SW1; Markington Hall, Harrogate, N Yorks. *T*: Bishop Monkton 356. *Club*: Athenæum.

WILBRAHAM; *see* Bootle-Wilbraham, family name of Baron Skelmersdale.

WILBRAHAM, Sir Richard B.; *see* Baker Wilbraham.

WILBY, John Ronald William, CMG 1961; Professor of International Trade and Finance, Seattle University, 1967-81, now Emeritus; *b* 1 Sept. 1906; *s* of Thomas Wilby and Gertrude Snowdon; *m* 1944, Winifred Russell Walker; no *c*. *Educ*: Batley School; University of Leeds. Board of Inland Revenue, 1928-46; Board of Trade (Principal), 1946-49; First Secretary (Commercial), British Embassy, Washington, 1949-53; British Trade Commissioner, Ottawa, 1953-55; Principal British Trade Commissioner in Ontario, Canada, 1955-64; Consul-General in Seattle, 1964-67. *Recreations*: sailing, music. *Address*: 185 34th Avenue E, Seattle, Wash 98112, USA. *T*: EA5-6999.

WILCHER, Lewis Charles, CBE 1955; MA, BLitt; *b* 9 December 1908; *s* of L. G. Wilcher, Middle Swan, W Australia; *m* 1935, Vere Wylie; one *s* one *d*. *Educ*: St Peter's College, Adelaide; University of Adelaide; Balliol College, Oxford (Rhodes Scholar). Dean, Trinity College, Melbourne, 1934-37; Lecturer in Modern History, Univ. of Melbourne, 1935-40; AIF 1940-47; Lieut-Col; Asst Dir of Army Education, 1942-47; Principal, Univ. Coll., Khartoum, 1947-56; Warden, Queen Elizabeth House, Oxford, 1956-68. *Publication*: Education, Press, Radio, 1947. *Recreation*: walking. *Address*: 12 Staunton Road, Oxford OX3 7TW.

WILCOCK, Prof. William Leslie; Professor of Physics, University College of North Wales, Bangor, since 1965; *b* 7 July 1922. *Educ*: Manchester Univ. (BSc, PhD). Imperial Coll. of Science and Technology, London, 1956-65, Reader in Applied Physics, 1961-65. Mem., SERC, 1981-. *Publications*: Advances in Electronics and Electron Physics, vols 12-15 (ed jtly), 1960-61; numerous papers in scientific jls. *Address*: School of Physical and Molecular Sciences, University College of North Wales, Bangor LL57 2UW.

WILCOCKSON, Rear-Adm. Kenneth Dilworth East, CBE 1977; Director General of Naval Personal Services, Ministry of Defence (Navy), since 1981; *b* 22 Jan. 1927; *s* of William and Ivy Ruskin Wilcockson; *m* 1952, Stella Mary, *d* of Canon A. and Mrs Edgar, Ben Rhydding, Ilkley, Yorks; one *s* one *d*. *Educ*: Belle Vue High Sch., Bradford, Yorks. Joined RN as 'Hostilities Only' recruit, 1945; HMS Aurora, Duncansby Head and Tyne, 1945-47; HMS Phoenicia, Malta, 1947-49; HMS Ceres, Wetherby, Yorks, 1949-52; HMS Ganges, Shotley, 1952-54; Asst Sec., FO Second-in-Comd Far East, in HMS Newfoundland, Birmingham and Newcastle, 1954-55; RNAS, Lossiemouth, 1956-58; HMS Dainty, 1959-60; Asst Sec. and Fleet Legal Adviser to C-in-C Western Fleet, 1961-62; Dep. Fleet Supply Officer and Fleet Legal Adviser, Far East Fleet, 1962-65; HMS London, 1965-66; Chiefs of Staff Secretariat, 1967-68; Sec. to Chief of Allied Staffs NATO, Malta, 1969; Sec. to Admiral of the Fleet Sir Edward Ashmore, GCB, DSC, 1970-77, as VCNS, C-in-C Fleet and First Sea Lord; Staff of C-in-C Naval Home Comd, 1977-78; Captain HMS Pembroke, Chatham, 1979-81. Rear-Adm. 1981. *Recreations*: walking, gardening, golf. *Address*: c/o National Westminster Bank Ltd, 130 Commercial Road, Portsmouth, Hants. *Club*: Army and Navy.

WILCOX, Albert Frederick, CBE 1967; QPM 1957; Chief Constable of Hertfordshire, 1947-69, retired; *b* 18 April 1909; *s* of late Albert Clement Wilcox, Ashley Hill, Bristol; *m* 1939, Ethel, *d* of late E. H. W. Wilmott, Manor House, Whitchurch, Bristol; one *s* two *d*. *Educ*: Fairfield Grammar School, Bristol. Joined Bristol City Police, 1929; Hendon Police Coll., 1934; Metropolitan Police, 1934-43. Served Allied Mil. Govt, Italy and Austria (Lt-Col), 1943-46. Asst Chief Constable of Buckinghamshire, 1946. Cropwood Fellowship, Inst. of Criminology, Cambridge, 1969. Pres. Assoc. of Chief Police Officers, Eng. and Wales, 1966-67; Chm. of Management Cttee, Police Dependents' Trust, 1967-69. Regional Police Commander (designate), 1962-69. Member, Parole Board, 1970-73. Criminological Res. Fellowship, Council of Europe, 1974-76. Barrister-at-Law, Gray's Inn, 1941. Mem. Edit. Bd, Criminal Law Review. *Publication*: The Decision to Prosecute, 1972. *Address*: 34 Roundwood Park, Harpenden, Herts.

WILCOX, David John Reed; a Recorder of the Crown Court, since 1979; barrister-at-law; *b* 8 March 1939; *s* of Leslie Leonard Kennedy Wilcox and Margaret Ada Reed Wilcox (*née* Rapson); *m* 1962, Wendy Fay Christine Whiteley; one *s* one *d*. *Educ*: Wednesbury Boys' High Sch.; King's Coll., London (LLB Hons). Called to the Bar, Gray's Inn, 1962. Directorate, Army Legal Services (Captain): Legal Staff, 1962-63; Legal Aid, Far East Land Forces, Singapore, 1963-65. Crown Counsel, Hong Kong, 1965-68; Member, Hong Kong Bar, 1968. *Recreations*: reading, gardening. *Address*: The Garden House, 14a Park Terrace, Nottingham NG1 5DN. *T*: Nottingham 43960.

WILCOX, Rev. Canon David Peter; Principal of Ripon College, Cuddesdon, Oxford, and priest-in-charge, All Saints', Cuddesdon, since 1977; *b* 29 June 1930; *s* of John Wilcox and Stella Wilcox (*née* Bower); *m* 1956, Pamela Ann Hedges; two *s* two *d*. *Educ*: Northampton Grammar School; St John's Coll., Oxford (2nd cl. Hons Theol., MA); Lincoln Theological Coll. Deacon 1954, priest 1955; Asst Curate, St Peter's, St Helier, Morden, Surrey, 1954-56; Asst Curate, University Church, Oxford and SCM Staff Secretary in Oxford, 1956-59; Tutor, Chaplain, then Sub-Warden, Lincoln Theological Coll., 1959-64; USPG Missionary on staff of United Theological Coll., Bangalore, and Presbyter in Church of S India, 1964-70; Vicar of Great Gransden with Little Gransden, dio. Ely, 1970-72; Canon Residentiary, Derby Cathedral and Warden, E Midlands Joint Ordination Training Scheme, 1972-77; Proctor in Convocation, 1973-77; Canon Emeritus, Derby Cathedral, 1977. *Recreations*: walking, music. *Address*: The Old Vicarage, Cuddesdon, Oxford OX9 9HP. *T*: Wheatley 4368.

WILCOX, Desmond John; independent television producer/reporter; journalist and author; *b* 21 May 1931; *e s* of John Wallace Wilcox and Alice

May Wilcox; *m* 1st, (marr. diss.); one *s* two *d* ; 2nd, 1977, Esther Rantzen; one *s* two *d*. *Educ*: Cheltenham Grammar Sch.; Christ's Coll., London; Outward Bound Sea Sch. Sail training apprentice, 1947; Deckhand, Merchant Marine, 1948; Reporter, weekly papers, 1949; commissioned Army, National Service, 1949-51; News Agency reporter, 1951-52; Reporter and Foreign Correspondent, Daily Mirror, incl. New York Bureau and UN, 1952-60; Reporter, This Week, ITV, 1960-65; joined BBC 1965: Co-Editor/Presenter, Man Alive, 1965; formed Man Alive Unit, 1968; Head of General Features, BBC TV, 1972-80; Writer/Presenter, Americans, TV documentary, 1979; Presenter/Chm., Where it Matters, ITV discussion series, 1981; Producer/Presenter, The Visit, BBC TV, 1982. SFTA Award for best factual programme series, 1967; Richard Dimbleby Award, SFTA, for most important personal contrib. in factual television, 1971. *Publications*: (jtly) Explorers, 1975; Americans, 1978; (with Esther Rantzen) Kill the Chocolate Biscuit: or Behind the Screen, 1981. *Recreations*: offshore sail cruising, gardening, television. *Address*: 11 Lichfield Road, Kew Gardens, Surrey. *T*: 01-940 6722. *Clubs*: Arts, BBC.

WILCOX, Malcolm George, CBE 1979 (MBE (mil.) 1943); Director, Midland Bank plc, since 1974; Chairman: Forward Trust Group Ltd, since 1980; Director: Costain Group PLC, since 1981; European Investment Bank, since 1981; Crocker National Corp., since 1981; Crocker National Bank, since 1981; Jersey International Bank of Commerce Ltd, since 1982; Samuel Montagu & Co. (Holdings) Ltd, since 1982; appointed Member, British Technology Group, 1981; *b* 3 June 1921; *s* of late George Harrison and Edith Mary Wilcox; *m* 1958, Sheila Mary Hewitt; one *s* one *d*. *Educ*: Wallasey Grammar Sch. TA, 1939; served war 1939-45: RA, RHA and General Staff. Entered Midland Bank Ltd, Liverpool, 1938: Jt General Manager, 1967-72; Asst Chief General Manager, 1972-74; Chief General Manager, 1974-81; Managing Director, and later Vice Chm., Forward Trust Ltd, 1967-75; Chairman: Forward Trust Ltd, 1980-; Midland Montagu Leasing, 1980-; Midland Bank France SA, 1978-82; Midland Bank Finance Corp., 1980- (Dir, 1967-); Thomas Cook Gp Ltd, 1972-81 (Dep. Chm. 1972-75, 1980-81); European Banking Co. Ltd, 1974-78; Midland and International Banks Ltd, 1974-81; European Banks' International Co., 1975-81; European-American Banking Corp., 1975-81; European-American Bank and Trust Co. NY, 1975-81; Banque Européenne de Crédit, 1975-78; Standard Chartered Bank Ltd, 1975-79; Chartered Bank, 1975-79; Standard Bank Ltd, 1975-79; European-American Bancorp, 1976-81; Euro-Pacific Finance Corp. Ltd, 1975-77, alternate 1977-80; Bank of Bermuda Ltd, 1978-; Standard Chartered Overseas Hldgs Ltd, 1978-79; Samuel Montagu & Co., 1980-81 (Dir, 1970-81). Pres., Brit. Junior Chambers of Commerce, 1960-61; Chm., Finance Houses Assoc., 1970-72; Mem. Council, Inst. of Bankers, 1970-, Vice-Chm., 1976-77, Pres., 1977-79, Vice-Pres., 1979-; Mem., Export Guarantees Adv. Council, 1976-82, Dep. Chm., 1976-77; Chm., Liberalisation of Trade in Services Cttee, Cttee on Invisible Exports, 1982-. Member (part-time): NEB, 1981-; NRDC, 1981-; Member: Adv. Cttee, Ship Mortgage Finance Corp. Ltd, 1977-82; Presidential Council, City of Westminster Chamber of Commerce, 1977-; Adv. Bd, Brasilinvest, 1977-; Exec. Cttee, Hispanic and Luso Brasilian Council, at Canning Ho., 1979-; Adv. Council, European Management Forum, 1979-; BBC Consultative Gp on Industrial and Business Affairs, 1979-; Bd of Management, Royal Alexandra and Albert Sch., Reigate, 1972-; Adv. Panel to Graduate Business Centre, City Univ., 1971-77 (Chm.); Court and Council, City Univ., 1977-; Council, Oxford Centre for Management Studies, 1982-. Governor, RSC, 1979-. FIB, CBIM. *Publications*: contributor to banking jls. *Recreations*: theatre, gardening, reading, golf. *Address*: Woodland Chase, Blackhall Lane, Sevenoaks, Kent TN15 0HU. *T*: Sevenoaks 61215. *Club*: Wildernesse (Seal, Kent).

WILCOX, Dame Marjorie; *see* Neagle, Dame Anna.

WILD, David Humphrey; His Honour Judge Wild; a Circuit Judge (Crown Court, Cambridge) since 1972; *b* 24 May 1927; *s* of John S. Wild and Edith Lemarchand; *m* 1963, Estelle Grace Prowett, *d* of James Marshall, Aberdeen and Malaya; one *s*. *Educ*: Whitgift Middle Sch., Croydon. Served War of 1939-45, Royal Navy, 1944-48. Called to Bar, Middle Temple, 1951. Practised, London and SE Circuit, 1951-58, Midland Circuit, 1958-72. Councillor, Oundle and Thrapston RDC, 1968-72. *Publication*: The Law of Hire Purchase, 1960 (2nd edn, 1964). *Address*: 6 Pump Court, Temple, EC4; College Farm House, Fotheringhay, Peterborough. *Clubs*: Naval and Military, Savile; Northampton and County (Northampton); Luffenham Heath Golf.

WILD, Rt. Rev. Eric; Bishop Suffragan of Reading, 1972-82; *b* 6 Nov. 1914; *s* of R. E. and E. S. Wild; *m* 1946, Frances Moyra, *d* of late Archibald and Alice Reynolds; one *s* one *d*. *Educ*: Manchester Grammar School; Keble College, Oxford. Ordained deacon 1937, priest 1938, Liverpool Cathedral; Curate, St Anne, Stanley, 1937-40; Curate, St James, Haydock, 1940-42; Chaplain, RNVR, 1942-46; Vicar, St George, Wigan, 1946-52; Vicar, All Saints, Hindley, 1952-59; Director of Religious Education, Dio. Peterborough, 1959-62; Rector, Cranford with Grafton Underwood, 1959-62; Canon of Peterborough, 1961, Emeritus, 1962; Gen. Sec. of National Society and Secretary of C of E Schools Council, 1962-67; Rector of Milton, 1967-72; Archdeacon of Berks, 1967-73. *Publications*: articles in periodicals; reviews, etc. *Recreations*: gardening and walking. *Address*: 2 Speen Place, Speen, Newbury, Berks. *Club*: Army and Navy.

WILD, Captain Geoffrey Alan, CBE 1963; retired as Commodore, and Captain of Canberra, P&O Steam Navigation Company (1961-63); *b* 21 Feb.

1904; *s* of Rev. Harry Wild, formerly Vicar, St Annes, Clifton, near Manchester, and of Susan Wild (*née* Holt); *m* 1932, Dorothy Louisa Bickell; no *c*. *Educ*: St Bees, Cumberland; Nautical College, Pangbourne; Training Barquentine St George. Cadet, New Zealand Shipping Co., 1921. Joined P&O as 4th Officer, 1923; Staff Captain, 1949. First command in Shillong, 1951; commanded Iberia, 1956, also Strathnaver, Canton, Corfu, Chusan, Strathaird, Arcadia and Himalaya. *Recreation*: retaining interest in all sports. *Address*: 1 Valentine Court, South Street, Eastbourne, East Sussex.

WILD, Major Hon. Gerald Percy, AM 1980; MBE 1941; Company Director; Agent-General for Western Australia in London, 1965-71; *b* 2 Jan. 1908; *m* 1944, Virginia Mary Baxter; two *s* one *d*. *Educ*: Shoreham Gram. Sch., Sussex; Chivers Acad., Portsmouth, Hants. Served War of 1939-45 (despatches, MBE): Middle East, Greece, Crete, Syria, New Guinea and Moratai, Netherlands East Indies (Major). Elected MLA for Western Australia, 1947; Minister for Housing and Forests, 1950-53; Minister for Works and Water Supplies and Labour (WA), 1959-65. JP Perth (WA), 1953. *Recreations*: golf, tennis, cricket, football. *Address*: 2/41 Park Street, Como, WA 6152, Australia. *T*: 450.1910. *Clubs*: East India, Devonshire, Sports and Public Schools, MCC; Naval and Military, Western Australia, West Australian Turf (WA).

WILD, Very Rev. John Herbert Severn, MA Oxon; Hon. DD Durham, 1958; Dean of Durham, 1951-73, Dean Emeritus, since 1973; *b* 22 Dec. 1904; *e s* of Right Rev. Herbert Louis Wild and Helen Christian, *d* of Walter Severn; *m* 1945, Margaret Elizabeth Everard, *d* of G. B. Wainwright, OBE, MB. *Educ*: Clifton Coll.; Brasenose College, Oxford (Scholar); represented Oxford against Cambridge at Three Miles, 1927; Westcott House, Cambridge. Curate of St Aidan, Newcastle upon Tyne, 1929-33; Chaplain-Fellow of University College, Oxford, 1933-45; Domestic Bursar, 1936-45; Dean, 1939-42; Vice-Master, 1942-43; Pro-Master, 1945; Master, 1945-51; Hon. Fellow, 1951-; Select Preacher, Univ. of Oxford, 1948-49. Church Comr, 1958-73. ChStJ, 1966-. Chm. of Governors, Durham Sch., 1951-73. *Recreations*: fishing, walking. *Address*: Deacons Farmhouse, Rapps, Ilminster, Somerset TA19 9LG. *T*: Ilminster 3398. *Club*: United Oxford & Cambridge University.

WILD, Dr John Paul, CBE 1978; FRS 1970; FAA 1962; Commonwealth Scientific and Industrial Research Organization: Chairman, since 1979; Associate Member of Executive, 1977; Chief, Division of Radiophysics, 1971; *b* 1923; *s* of late Alwyn Howard Wild and late Bessie Delafield (*née* Arnold); *m* 1948, Elaine Poole Hull; two *s* one *d*. *Educ*: Whitgift Sch.; Peterhouse, Cambridge (Hon. Fellow 1982). ScD 1962. Radar Officer in Royal Navy, 1943-47; joined Research Staff of Div. of Radiophysics, 1947, working on problems in radio astronomy, esp. of the sun, later also radio navigation (Interscan aircraft landing system). For. Hon. Mem., Amer. Acad. of Arts and Scis, 1961; For. Mem., Amer. Philos. Soc., 1962; Corresp. Mem., Royal Soc. of Scis, Liège, 1969; For. Sec., Australian Acad. of Science, 1973-. Edgeworth David Medal, 1958; Hendryk Arctowski Gold Medal, US Nat. Acad. of Scis, 1969; Balthasar van der Pol Gold Medal, Internat. Union of Radio Science, 1969; Royal Medal, Royal Soc., 1980; Hale Medal, Amer. Astronomical Soc., 1982. Hon. DSc: ANU, 1979; Newcastle, 1982. *Publications*: numerous research papers and reviews on radio astronomy in scientific jls. *Address*: CSIRO, Limestone Avenue, Campbell, ACT 2602, Australia.

WILD, John Vernon, CMG 1960; OBE 1955; Colonial Administrative Service, retired; *b* 26 April 1915; *m* 1st, 1942, Margaret Patricia Rendell (*d* 1975); one *s* one *d* ; 2nd, 1976, Marjorie Mary Lovatt Robertson. *Educ*: Taunton School; King's College, Cambridge. Senior Optime, Cambridge Univ., 1937. Colonial Administrative Service, Uganda: Assistant District Officer, 1938; Assistant Chief Secretary, 1950; Establishment Secretary, 1951; Administrative Secretary, 1955-60; Chairman, Constitutional Committee, 1959. Teacher and Lectr in Mathematics, 1960-76. *Publications*: The Story of the Uganda Agreement; The Uganda Mutiny; Early Travellers in Acholi. *Recreations*: cricket (Cambridge Blue, 1938), golf, music. *Address*: Maplestone Farm, Broad Oak, Brede, near Rye, East Sussex TN31 6EP. *T*: Brede 882261. *Club*: Rye Golf.

WILDE, Derek Edward, CBE 1978; Vice Chairman, 1972-77, and Director since 1969, Barclays Bank Ltd; Deputy Chairman, Charterhouse Group, since 1980; *b* 6 May 1912; *s* of late William Henry Wilde and Ethel May Wilde; *m* 1940, Helen, *d* of William Harrison; (one *d* decd). *Educ*: King Edward VII School, Sheffield. Entered Barclays Bank Ltd, Sheffield, 1929; General Manager, 1961; Sen. General Manager, 1966-72. Dir, Yorkshire Bank Ltd, 1972-80; Chairman: Keyser Ullmann Holdings, 1975-81; Charterhouse Japhet, 1980-81. Governor, Midhurst Med. Res. Inst. Fellow, Inst. of Bankers (Hon. Fellow 1975). Hon. DLitt Loughborough, 1980. *Recreation*: gardening. *Address*: Ranmoor, Smarts Hill, Penshurst, Kent. *T*: Penshurst 870228,

WILDE, Peter Appleton; HM Diplomatic Service, retired; *b* 5 April 1925; *m* 1950, Frances Elisabeth Candida Bayliss; two *s*. *Educ*: Chesterfield Grammar Sch.; St Edmund Hall, Oxford. Army (National Service), 1943-47; Temp. Asst Lectr, Southampton, 1950; FO, 1950; 3rd Sec., Bangkok, 1951-53; Vice-Consul, Zürich, 1953-54; FO, 1954-57; 2nd Sec., Baghdad, 1957-58; 1st Sec., UK Delegn to OEEC (later OECD), Paris, 1958-61; 1st Sec., Katmandu, 1961-64; FO (later FCO), 1964-69; Consul-Gen., Lourenço Marques, 1969-71; Dep. High Comr, Colombo, 1971-73. Mem., Llanfihangel Rhosycorn Community Council, 1974-. Member: Management Cttee, Carmarthenshire

Pest Control Soc. Ltd, 1974-82; Council, Royal Forestry Soc., 1977-. *Recreation:* forestry. *Address:* Nantyperchyll, Gwernogle, Carmarthen, Dyfed SA32 7RR. *T:* Brechfa 241.

WILDENSTEIN, Daniel Leopold; art historian; President, Wildenstein Foundation Inc., since 1964; Chairman, Wildenstein & Co Inc., New York, since 1968 (Vice-President, 1943-59, President, 1959-68); *b* Verrières-le-Buisson, France, 11 Sept. 1917; *s* of Georges Wildenstein; *m* 1939, Martine Kapferer (marr. diss. 1968); two *s*; *m* 1978, Sylvia Roth. *Educ:* Cours Hattemer; Sorbonne (LèsL 1938). Gp Sec., French Pavilion, World's Fair, 1937; went to US, 1940; with Wildenstein & Co. Inc., New York, 1940-; Director: Wildenstein & Co. Inc., London, 1963-; Wildenstein Arte, Buenos Aires, 1963-. Dir, Gazette des Beaux Arts, 1963-; Dir of Activities, Musée Jacquemart-André, Paris, 1956-62; Musée Chaalis, Institut de France, Paris, 1956-62; organiser of art competitions (Hallmark art award). Mem., French Chamber of Commerce in US (Conseiller), 1942-; Founder (1947) and Mem, Amer. Inst. of France (Sec.). Mem., Institut de France (Académie des Beaux-Arts), 1971; Membre du Haut Comité du Musée de Monaco. *Publications:* Claude Monet, vol. 1, 1975, vols 2 and 3, 1979; Edouard Manet, vol. 1, 1976, vol. 2, 1977; Gustave Courbet, vol. 1, 1977, vol. 2, 1978. *Recreation:* horse racing (leading owner, 1976). *Address:* 48 avenue de Rumine, 1007 Lausanne, Switzerland; (office) 57 rue La Boétie, Paris 8ème, France. *T:* 563-01-00. *Clubs:* Brooks's; Turf and Field, Madison Square Garden (New York); Cercle de Deauville, Tir au Pigeon (Paris); Jockey (Buenos Aires).

WILDING, Richard William Longworth, CB 1979; Deputy Secretary, HM Treasury, since 1981 (Civil Service Department, 1976-81); *b* 22 April 1929; *er s* of late L. A. Wilding; *m* 1954, Mary Rosamund de Villiers; one *s* two *d. Educ:* Dragon Sch., Oxford; Winchester Coll.; New Coll., Oxford (MA). HM Foreign Service, 1953-59; transf. to Home Civil Service, 1959; Principal, HM Treasury, 1959-67; Sec., Fulton Cttee on Civil Service, 1966-68; Asst Sec., Civil Service Dept, 1968-70; Asst Sec., Supplementary Benefits Commn, DHSS, 1970-72; Under-Sec., Management Services, 1972-76, Pay, 1976, CSD. *Publications:* (with L. A. Wilding) A Classical Anthology, 1954; Key to Latin Course for Schools, 1966; articles in Jl Public Administration, Social Work Today, Studies. *Recreations:* music, gardening. *Address:* 16 Middleway, NW11. *T:* 01-455 6245. *Club:* Civil Service.

WILDISH, Vice-Adm. Denis Bryan Harvey, CB 1968; Director General of Personal Services and Training (Naval), 1970-72, retired; *b* 24 Dec. 1914; *s* of late Rear-Adm. Sir Henry William Wildish, KBE, CB; *m* 1941, Leslie Henrietta Jacob; two *d. Educ:* RNC Dartmouth; RNEC. Entered Royal Navy, 1928; Comdr 1948; Capt. 1957; Rear-Adm. 1966; Vice-Adm. 1970. Dir of Fleet Maintenance, 1962-64; Commodore Naval Drafting, 1964-66; Adm. Supt, HM Dockyard, Devonport, 1966-70. *Recreations:* cricket, painting. *Address:* Deans Farm, Weston, near Petersfield, Hants. *Clubs:* Army and Navy, MCC.

WILDSMITH, Brian Lawrence; artist and maker of picture books for young children; *b* 22 Jan. 1930; *s* of Paul Wildsmith and Annie Elizabeth Oxley; *m* 1955, Aurelie Janet Craigie Ithurbide; one *s* three *d. Educ:* de la Salle Coll.; Barnsley Sch. of Art; Slade Sch. of Fine Arts. Art Master, Selhurst Grammar School for Boys, 1954-57; freelance artist, 1957-. Production design, illustrations, titles and graphics for first USA-USSR Leningrad film co-production of the Blue Bird. Kate Greenaway Medal, 1962. *Publications:* ABC, 1962; The Lion and the Rat, 1963; The North Wind and the Sun, 1964; Mother Goose, 1964; 1; 2; 3;, 1965; The Rich Man and the Shoemaker, 1965; The Hare and the Tortoise, 1966; Birds, 1967; Animals, 1967; Fish, 1968; The Miller the Boy and the Donkey, 1969; The Circus, 1970; Puzzles, 1970; The Owl and the Woodpecker, 1971; The Twelve Days of Christmas, 1972; The Little Wood Duck, 1972; The Lazy Bear, 1973; Squirrels, 1974; Pythons Party, 1974; The Blue Bird, 1976; The True Cross, 1977; What the Moon Saw, 1978; Hunter and his Dog, 1979; Animal Shapes, 1980; Animal Homes, 1980; Animal Games, 1980; Animal Tricks, 1980; The Seasons, 1980; Professor Noah's Spaceship, 1980; Bears Adventure, 1981; The Trunk, 1981; Cat on the Mat, 1981; Pelican, 1982. *Recreations:* squash, tennis, music (piano). *Address:* 11 Castellaras, 06370 Mouans-Sartoux, France. *T:* (93) 75.24.11.

WILDY, Prof. (Norman) Peter (Leete); Professor of Pathology, and Fellow of Gonville and Caius College, University of Cambridge, since 1975; *b* 31 March 1920; *s* of late Eric Lawrence and Gwendolen Wildy; *m* 1945, Joan Audrey Kenion; one *s* two *d. Educ:* Eastbourne College; Caius Coll., Cambridge; St Thos Hosp., London. MRCS, LRCP 1944; MB, BChir 1948. RAMC, 1945-47. St Thomas's Hospital Medical School: Michael and Sydney Herbert and Leonard Dudgeon Res. Fellow, 1949-51; Lecturer in Bacteriology, 1952-57; Sen. Lectr in Bacteriology, 1957-58; Brit. Memorial Fellow in Virology, 1953-54; Asst Director, MRC Unit for Experimental Virus Research, Glasgow, 1959-63; Prof. of Virology, Univ. of Birmingham, 1963-75. FRSE 1962; FRCPath 1975. *Publications:* articles on bacteria and viruses. *Address:* The Old Parsonage, Hinxton, Cambs.

WILEMAN, Margaret Annie, MA; Honorary Fellow since 1973 (President (formerly Principal), 1953-73), Hughes Hall, Cambridge; *b* 19 July 1908; *e d* of Clement Wileman and Alice (*née* Brinson). *Educ:* Lady Margaret Hall, Oxford, and the University of Paris. Scholar of Lady Margaret Hall, Oxford, 1927; First in Hons School of Mod. Langs, 1930; Zaharoff Travelling Scholar, 1931; Assistant, Abbey School, Reading, 1934; Senior Tutor, Queen's College,

Harley Street, 1937; Lecturer, St Katherine's Coll., Liverpool, 1940; Resident Tutor, Bedford College, Univ. of London, 1944-53; Univ. Lectr. and Dir of Women Students, Dept of Educn, Cambridge Univ., 1953-73. *Address:* 5 Drosier Road, Cambridge CB1 2EY. *T:* Cambridge 51846. *Club:* University Women's.

WILES, Donald Alonzo, CMG 1965; OBE 1960; Executive Director, Barbados National Trust, since 1980; *b* 8 Jan. 1912; *s* of Donald Alonzo Wiles and Millicent Wiles; *m* 1938, Amelia Elsie Pemberton; two *d. Educ:* Harrison Coll., Barbados; Univs of London, Toronto, Oxford. Member of Staff of Harrison College, Barbados, 1931-45; Public Librarian, Barbados, 1945-50; Asst Colonial Secretary, Barbados, 1950-54; Permanent Secretary, Barbados, 1954-60; Administrator, Montserrat, 1960-64; Administrative Sec., Da Costa & Musson Ltd, 1965-79. *Recreations:* swimming, hiking, tennis. *Address:* Casa Loma, Pine Gardens, St Michael, Barbados. *T:* 66875. *Clubs:* Barbados Yacht, Bridgetown (Barbados).

WILES, Rev. Prof. Maurice Frank, FBA 1981; Canon of Christ Church, Oxford, and Regius Professor of Divinity, since 1970; *b* 17 Oct. 1923; *s* of late Sir Harold Wiles, KBE, CB, and of Lady Wiles; *m* 1950, Patricia Margaret (*née* Mowll); two *s* one *d. Educ:* Tonbridge School; Christ's College, Cambridge. Curate, St George's, Stockport, 1950-52; Chaplain, Ridley Hall, Cambridge, 1952-55; Lectr in New Testament Studies, Ibadan, Nigeria, 1955-59; Lectr in Divinity, Univ. of Cambridge, and Dean of Clare College, 1959-67; Prof. of Christian Doctrine, King's Coll., Univ. of London, 1967-70. FKC 1972. *Publications:* The Spiritual Gospel, 1960; The Christian Fathers, 1966; The Divine Apostle, 1967; The Making of Christian Doctrine, 1967; The Remaking of Christian Doctrine, 1974; (with M. Santer) Documents in Early Christian Thought, 1975; Working Papers in Doctrine, 1976; What is Theology?, 1976; Explorations in Theology 4, 1979; Faith and the Mystery of God, 1982. *Address:* Christ Church, Oxford.

WILES, Prof. Peter John de la Fosse; Professor of Russian Social and Economic Studies, University of London, since 1965; *b* 25 Nov. 1919; *m* 1st, 1945, Elizabeth Coppin (marr. diss., 1960); one *s* two *d* ; 2nd, 1960, Carolyn Stedman. *Educ:* Lambrook Sch.; Winchester Coll.; New Coll., Oxford. Royal Artillery, 1940-45 (despatches twice; mainly attached Intelligence Corps). Fellow, All Souls Coll., Oxford, 1947-48; Fellow, New Coll., Oxford, 1948-60; Prof., Brandeis Univ., USA, 1960-63; Research Associate, Institutet för Internationell Ekonomi, Stockholm, 1963-64. Vis. Prof.: Columbia Univ., USA, 1958; City Coll. of New York, 1964 and 1967. *Publications:* The Political Economy of Communism, 1962; Price, Cost and Output (2nd edn), 1962; Communist International Economics, 1968; (ed) The Prediction of Communist Economic Performance, 1971; Economic Institutions Compared, 1977. *Recreations:* simple. *Address:* 23 Ridgmount Gardens, WC1.

WILFORD, Sir (Kenneth) Michael, GCMG 1980 (KCMG 1976; CMG 1967); HM Diplomatic Service, retired; Director, Lloyds Bank International, since 1982; *b* Wellington, New Zealand, 31 Jan. 1922; *yr s* of late George McLean Wilford and late Dorothy Veronica (*née* Wilson); *m* 1944, Joan Mary, *d* of Captain E. F. B. Law, RN; three *d. Educ:* Wrekin College; Pembroke College, Cambridge. Served in Royal Engineers, 1940-46 (despatches). Entered HM Foreign (subseq. Diplomatic) Service, 1947; Third Sec., Berlin, 1947; Asst Private Secretary to Secretary of State, Foreign Office, 1949; Paris, 1952; Singapore, 1955; Asst Private Sec. to Sec. of State, Foreign Office, 1959; Private Sec. to the Lord Privy Seal, 1960; served Rabat, 1962; Counsellor (Office of British Chargé d'Affaires) also Consul-General, Peking, 1964-66; Visiting Fellow of All Souls, Oxford, 1966-67; Counsellor, Washington, 1967-69; Asst Under Sec. of State, FCO, 1969-73; Dep. Under Sec. of State, FCO, 1973-75; Ambassador to Japan, 1975-80. *Recreations:* golf, gardening. *Address:* Brook Cottage, Abbotts Ann, Andover, Hants. *T:* Abbotts Ann 509.

WILHELM, Most Rev. Joseph Lawrence, DD, JCD; former Archbishop of Kingston, Ontario, (RC); *b* Walkerton, Ontario, 16 Nov. 1909. *Educ:* St Augustine's Seminary, Toronto; Ottawa Univ., Ottawa, Ont. Ordained priest, Toronto, 1934. Mil. Chaplain to Canadian Forces, 1940-46 (MC, Sicily, 1943). Auxiliary Bishop, Calgary, Alberta, 1963-66; Archbishop of Kingston, Ont, 1967-82. Hon. DD Queen's Univ., Kingston, Ont, 1970. *Address:* The Anchorage, Belleville, Ont, Canada.

WILKES, Prof. Eric, OBE (civil) 1974 (MBE (mil.) 1943); FRCP, FRCGP, FRCPsych; Professor of Community Care and General Practice, Sheffield University, since 1973; *b* 12 Jan. 1920; *s* of George and Doris Wilkes; *m* 1953, Jessica Mary Grant; two *s* one *d. Educ:* Royal Grammar Sch., Newcastle upon Tyne; King's Coll., Cambridge (MA); St Thomas' Hosp., SE1 (MB, BChir). Lt-Col, Royal Signals, 1944. General Medical Practitioner, Derbyshire, 1954-73. High Sheriff of S Yorkshire, 1977-78; Chm., Sheffield and Rotherham Assoc. for the Care and Resettlement of Offenders, 1976-; Med. Director, St Luke's Nursing Home, Sheffield, 1971-; Chairman: Sheffield Council on Alcoholism, 1976-82; Prevention Cttee, Nat. Council on Alcoholism, 1980-83; Trinity Day Care Trust, 1979-. *Publications:* The Dying Patient, 1981; Long-Term Prescribing, 1982; various chapters and papers, mainly on chronic and incurable illness. *Recreations:* gardening, fishing, natural history. *Address:* Department of Community Medicine, The Medical School, Sheffield S10 2RX. *T:* Sheffield 26484; Grislow Field, Curbar, Sheffield. *T:* Baslow 2225.
See also Lyall Wilkes.

WILKES, Rev. John Comyn Vaughan, MA Oxon; Rector of Great Kimble, Aylesbury, 1967-72, retired; *b* 30 March 1902; *s* of L. C. Vaughan Wilkes, St Cyprian's, Eastbourne; *m* 1940, Joan, *y d* of late Very Rev. C. A. Alington, DD; six *s* one *d. Educ:* Fonthill, East Grinstead; St Cyprian's, Eastbourne; Eton Coll. (King's Schol.); Trinity Coll. Oxford (Classical Schol.). 1st Class Classical Moderations, 1923; 1st Class Lit. Hum., 1925; Half Blue for Golf (played *v* Cambridge, 1924, 1925); subsequently Assistant Master, Eton College 1925-37; Master in College, Eton College, 1930-37; Warden, Radley College, Abingdon, 1937-54; Vicar of Hunslet, Leeds, 1954-58; Vicar of Marlow, 1958-65; Rector of Preston Bissett, Buckingham, 1965-67. Ordained deacon (C of E) 1945; priest, 1945. *Recreations:* golf, gardening. *Address:* 29 Nelson Street, Hereford. *T:* Hereford 753565. *Clubs:* Sussex Martlets, Eton Ramblers, Oxford and Cambridge Golfing Society.
See also Baron Home of the Hirsel.

WILKES, Prof. John Joseph, FSA; Professor of Archaeology of the Roman Provinces, University of London, since 1974; *b* 12 July 1936; *s* of Arthur Cyril Wilkes and Enid Cecilia Eustance; *m* 1980, Dr Susan Walker. *Educ:* King Henry VIII Grammar Sch., Coventry; Harrow County Grammar Sch.; University Coll. London (BA); Univ. of Durham (St Cuthbert's Society) (PhD). FSA 1969. Research Fellow, Univ. of Birmingham, 1961-63; Asst Lectr in History and Archaeology, Univ. of Manchester, 1963-64; Lectr in Roman History, 1964-71, Sen. Lectr 1971-74, Univ. of Birmingham. Chm., Faculty of Archaeology, Hist. and Letters, British Sch. at Rome, 1979-. Vis. Fellow, Inst. of Humanistic Studies, Pennsylvania State Univ., 1971. Mem., Ancient Monuments Bd for Scotland, 1981-. Vice-Pres., Soc. for Promotion of Roman Studies, 1978; Pres., London and Middx Archaeological Soc., 1982-. Corresp. Mem., German Archaeol Inst., 1976. Governor, Mus. of London, 1981-. Editor, Britannia, 1980-. *Publications:* Dalmatia (Provinces of Roman Empire series), 1969; (jtly) Diocletian's Palace: joint excavations in the southeast quarter, Pt 1, Split, 1972; (ed jtly) Victoria County History of Cambridgeshire, vol. VII, Roman Cambridgeshire, 1978; papers, excavation reports and reviews in learned jls of Britain, Amer., and Europe. *Recreations:* listening to music, watching Association football. *Address:* Institute of Archaeology, 31-4 Gordon Square, WC1H 0PY. *T:* 01-387 6052.

WILKES, His Honour Lyall; a Circuit Judge (formerly Judge of the County Courts), 1964-82; *b* 19 May 1914; *e s* of George Wilkes, MBE and Doris Wilkes, Newcastle upon Tyne; *m* 1946, Margaret Tait; four *d. Educ:* Newcastle Grammar School; Balliol Coll., Oxford (MA). Secretary Oxford Union Society, 1937. Joined Middlesex Regiment 1940; served one year in the ranks; active service North Africa, Italy and German-occupied Greece, attached Force 133; Major, 1944 (despatches). Called to Bar, Middle Temple, 1947; practised North-Eastern Circuit, 1947-64; Dep. Chm., County of Durham QS, 1961-64; Asst Recorder, Sheffield and Newcastle upon Tyne, 1960-62; MP (Lab) for Newcastle Central, 1945-51, when did not stand for re-election. Jt Pres., HM Council of Circuit Judges, 1981. Pres., Friends of Laing Art Gall., Newcastle upon Tyne, 1981-. *Publications:* (with Gordon Dodds) Tyneside Classical: the Newcastle of Grainger, Dobson and Clayton, 1964; Tyneside Portraits: studies in Art and Life, 1971; Old Jesmond and other poems (limited edn), 1975; John Dobson: Architect and Landscape Gardener, 1980; (contrib.) Shell Book of English Villages, 1980; (contrib.) The Oxford Book of Death, 1983. *Recreation:* regretting the 20th century and avoiding its architecture. *Club:* Northern Counties (Newcastle-upon-Tyne).
See also Eric Wilkes.

WILKES, Maurice Vincent, MA, PhD; FRS 1956; FIEE; FBCS; Computer Engineer, Digital Equipment Corporation, USA, since 1980; Adjunct Professor of Computer Science and Electrical Engineering, Massachusetts Institute of Technology, since 1981; Head of the Computer Laboratory, Cambridge (formerly Mathematical Laboratory), 1970-80; Professor of Computer Technology, 1965-80, now Emeritus Professor; Fellow of St John's College, since 1950; *b* 26 June 1913; *s* of late Vincent J. Wilkes, OBE; *m* 1947, Nina Twyman; one *s* two *d. Educ:* King Edward's School, Stourbridge; St John's College, Cambridge. Mathematical Tripos (Wrangler). Research in physics at Cavendish Lab.; Univ. Demonstrator, 1937. Served War of 1939-45, Radar and Operational Research. Univ. Lecturer and Acting Dir of Mathematical Laboratory, Cambridge, 1945; Dir of Mathematical Laboratory, 1946-70. Member: Measurement and Control Section Committee, IEE, 1956-59; Council, IEE, 1973-76; First President British Computer Soc., 1957-60, Distinguished Fellow 1973. Mem. Council, IFIP, 1960-63; Chm. IEE E Anglia Sub-Centre, 1969-70; Turing Lectr Assoc. for Computing Machinery, 1967. Foreign Hon. Mem., Amer. Acad. of Arts and Sciences, 1974; Foreign Associate: US Nat. Acad. of Engrg, 1977; US Nat. Acad. of Scis, 1980. Hon. DSc: Newcastle upon Tyne, 1972; Hull, 1974; Kent, 1975; City, 1975; Amsterdam, 1978; Munich, 1978; Hon. DTech Linköping, 1975. Harry Goode Award, Amer. Fedn of Inf. Processing Socs, 1968; Eckert-Mauchly Award, Assoc. for Computing Machinery and IEEE Computer Soc., 1980; McDowell Award, IEEE Computer Soc., 1981; Faraday Medal, IEE, 1981; Pender Award, Univ. of Pennsylvania, 1982. *Publications:* Oscillations of the Earth's Atmosphere, 1949; (joint) Preparations of Programs for an Electronic Digital Computer, Addison-Wesley (Cambridge, Mass), 1951, 2nd edn 1958; Automatic Digital Computers, 1956; A Short Introduction to Numerical Analysis, 1966; Time-sharing Computer System, 1968, 3rd edn 1975; (jtly) The Cambridge CAP Computer and its Operating System, 1979; papers in scientific jls. *Address:* Digital Equipment Corporation, 77 Reed Road, Hudson, Mass 01749, USA. *T:* (617) 568-4000. *Club:* Athenæum.

WILKES, Richard Geoffrey, OBE 1969; TD 1959; DL; FCA; Partner, Price Waterhouse, Chartered Accountants, since 1969; *b* 12 June 1928; *s* of Geoffrey W. Wilkes and Kathleen (*née* Quinn); *m* 1953, Wendy Elaine, *d* of Rev. C. Ward; one *s* three *d. Educ:* Repton (Exhibnr). FCA 1952. Mem. Council, Inst. of Chartered Accountants in England and Wales, 1969- (Dep. Pres., 1979-80; Pres., 1980-81); Chm., UK Auditing Practices Cttee, 1976-78; UK Rep., Internat. Fedn of Accountants Auditing Practices Cttee, 1978-79. Governor, CARE for the Mentally Handicapped, 1972-. Commnd RHA, 1947; CO 4/5th Bn Royal Leics Regt (TA), 1966-69; Col TAVR E Midlands Dist, 1969-73; ADC (TAVR) to the Queen, 1972-77. Dep. Hon. Col, Royal Anglian Regt (Leics), 1981-. Comdt, Leics Special Constab., 1972-79; Chm., Leics Co. Cttee, E Midlands TA&VRA, 1980-. DL Leics, 1967. *Recreations:* shooting, sailing. *Address:* The Hermitage, Swingbridge Street, Foxton, Market Harborough, Leics LE16 7RH. *T:* East Langton 213. *Clubs:* Army and Navy; Leicestershire (Leicester).

WILKIE, Prof. Douglas Robert, FRS 1971; Jodrell Research Professor of Physiology, in the University of London, since 1979; *b* 2 Oct. 1922; *m* 1949, June Rosalind Hill; one *s. Educ:* Medical Student, University Coll. London, 1940-42 (Fellow, 1972); Yale Univ. (MD), 1942-43; University Coll. Hosp., MB, BS, 1944, MRCP 1945; FRCP 1972. Lectr, Dept of Physiology, UCL, 1948; Inst. of Aviation Medicine, Farnborough (Mil. Service), 1948-50; London University: Locke Research Fellowship (Royal Soc.), UCL, 1951-54; Readership in Experimental Physiology, UCL, 1954-65; Prof. of Experimental Physiology, 1965-69; Jodrell Prof., and Head of Physiology Dept, UCL, 1969-79. SRC Sen. Res. Fellowship, 1978. *Publications:* Muscle, 1968; contribs to learned jls, etc, mainly research on energetics of muscular contraction, and attempts to make thermodynamics simpler, recently, application of nuclear magnetic resonance in biology. *Recreations:* sailing, friends, photography. *Address:* 4 Grange Road, Highgate, N6. *T:* 01-348 0145.

WILKIE, James, MA, FRSE; Secretary Carnegie United Kingdom Trust, 1939-54; *b* Manchester, 1 June 1896; *er s* of late James Wilkie, Glasgow; *m* 1930, Ethel Susan, *er d* of late W. H. Moore, JP, Killough, Co. Down; three *d. Educ:* Whitgift School; Brasenose College, Oxford (Dist. Litt. Hum. 1920). Served European War, 1914-19 (Captain, Machine Gun Corps, despatches twice, wounded, Order of Crown of Rumania) and War of 1939-45 (Major, Home Guard). Entered Board of Education, 1921 (Asst Private Sec. to President, 1924-27), transferred to Empire Marketing Board, 1927-33; returned to Board of Education, 1933-39 (in charge of Metropolitan Div. and Sec. to Adult Education Cttee). Mem. Exec. Cttee: Newbattle Abbey Coll., 1939-54; Scottish Council of Social Service, 1944-54; Land Settlement Assoc., 1939-48; Nat. Central Library, 1939-50; Scottish Leadership Training Assoc., 1945-50; Member: NHS Executive Council for E Sussex, 1955-71; Advisory Council on Education in Scotland, 1948-51; Council of Nat. Federation of Young Farmers' Clubs, 1939-51; Vice-Pres.: Sussex Rural Community Council, Sussex Assoc. of Parish Councils; Irish Library Assoc., 1940-48; Pres., Library Assoc., 1951. *Address:* The Red Cottage, Fletching Common, Newick, Lewes, East Sussex BN8 4QS. *T:* Newick 2677.

WILKIN, (Frederick) John, CBE 1978 (OBE 1968); DFM 1943; Vice-Chairman, Hammersmith and Fulham District Health Authority, since 1982; *b* 15 Aug. 1916; *s* of late George Wilkin and Rosetta Christina Wilkin; *m* 1st, 1943, Marjorie Joan Wilson (*d* 1972); one *d*; 2nd, 1975, Laura Elizabeth Eason; one *s* one *d. Educ:* Southwark Central Sch.; Morley Coll., London. Served RAF, 1940-46: Navigator (12, 101 and 156 Sqdns); Permanent Award Pathfinder Badge. Asst Accountant, House of Commons, 1955, Chief Accountant, 1962-80; Secretary: House of Commons Members' Fund, 1962-81; Parliamentary Contributory Pensions Fund, 1965-80; Head of Admin Dept, House of Commons, 1980-81. Special Trustee, Charing Cross Hospital, 1979-; Mem. Council, Nat. Inc. Beneficent Soc., 1968-. Mem., Guild of Freemen of City of London. *Recreations:* gardening, watching sport; formerly cricket, cycling, table tennis. *Address:* 14 Forest Ridge, Beckenham, Kent BR3 3NH. *T:* 01-650 5261. *Club:* Pathfinder.

WILKINS, Frederick Charles, CB 1963; *b* 10 July 1901; *s* of Richard Charles Wilkins; *m* 1926, Winifred Bertha Denham; one *d. Educ:* Portsmouth. Entered Admiralty Service, 1917; Naval Store Officer, 1939 (Asst 1923; Dep. 1936); Asst Dir of Stores, 1942; Capt. RNVR (attached to Brit. Pacific Fleet, 1944-46); Dep. Dir of Stores, 1955; Dir of Stores, Admiralty, 1960-64. *Recreation:* reading (Theology). *Address:* 6 Spurwood Road, Turramurra, NSW 2074, Australia.

WILKINS, Sir Graham John, (Bob), Kt 1980; Chairman and Chief Executive, Beecham Group Ltd, since 1975; *b* 22 Jan. 1924; *s* of George William and Anne May Wilkins; *m* 1945, Daphne Mildred Haynes. *Educ:* Yeovil Sch.; University Coll., South West of England, Exeter (BSc). Dir and Vice-Pres., Beecham (Canada) Ltd, 1954-59; C. L. Bencard Ltd, and Beecham Research Labs Ltd: Asst Man. Dir, 1959; Man. Dir, 1960; Dir, Beecham Pharmaceutical Div., 1962-64; Beecham Group Ltd: Dir and Chm., Pharmaceutical Div., 1964-72; Man. Dir (Pharmaceuticals), 1972; Exec. Vice-Chm., 1974; Director: Beecham Inc., 1967-; Courtaulds Ltd, 1975-; Hill Samuel Gp Ltd, 1977-; THORN EMI (formerly Thorn Electrical Industries) Ltd, 1978-. Mem., Doctors' and Dentists' Remuneration Rev. Bd, 1980-. Vice-Chm., Proprietary Assoc. of GB, 1966-68; Pres., Assoc. of Brit. Pharmaceutical Industry, 1969-71 (Vice-Pres., 1968-69); Chm., Medico-Pharmaceutical Forum, 1971-73 (Vice-Chm., 1969-70); Pres., European Fedn of Pharmaceutical Industries Assoc., 1978-82; Mem., BOTB, 1977-80. *Publications:* various papers on pharmaceutical industry. *Recreations:* golf, theatre-going, motor yacht cruising. *Address:* Alceda, Walton Lane, Shepperton-on-Thames, Mddx TW17 8LQ. *T:* Walton 27714.

WILKINS, John Anthony Francis; Editor of The Tablet, since 1982; *b* 20 Dec. 1936; *s* of Edward Manwaring Wilkins and Ena Gwendolen Francis. *Educ:* Clifton Coll., Bristol (Scholar); Clare Coll., Cambridge (State Scholar, 1954; Major Scholar and Foundn Scholar; Classical Tripos 1959, Theol Tripos 1961; BA 1961). Served 1st Bn Glos Regt, 1955-57 (2nd Lieut). Planning Div., Marine Dept, Head Office of Esso Petroleum, London, 1962-63; Asst Editor: Frontier, 1964-67; The Tablet, 1967-72; features writer, BBC External Services, 1972-81; Producer, Radio 4, 1978. Ondas Radio Prize, 1973. *Recreation:* ornithology. *Address:* The Tablet, 48 Great Peter Street, SW1P 2HA. *T:* 01-222 7462.

WILKINS, Prof. Malcolm Barrett; FRSE 1972; Regius Professor of Botany, Glasgow University, since 1970; *b* 27 Feb. 1933; *s* of Barrett Charles Wilkins and Eleanor Mary Wilkins (*née* Jenkins); *m* 1959, Mary Patricia Maltby; one *s* (one *d* decd). *Educ:* Monkton House Sch., Cardiff; King's Coll., London. BSc 1955; PhD London 1958; AKC 1958; DSc 1972. Lectr in Botany, King's Coll., London, 1958-64; Rockefeller Foundn Fellow, Yale Univ., 1961-62; Research Fellow, Harvard Univ., 1962-63; Lectr in Biology, Univ. of East Anglia, 1964-65; Prof. of Biology, Univ. of East Anglia, 1965-67; Prof. of Plant Physiology, Univ. of Nottingham, 1967-70. Darwin Lectr, British Assoc. for Advancement of Science, 1967. Member: Biol. Sci. Cttee of SRC, 1971-74; Governing Body: Hill Farming Res. Orgn, 1971-80; Scottish Crops Research Inst, 1974-; Glasshouse Crops Res. Inst., 1979-; Exec. Cttee, Scottish Field Studies Assoc.; British Nat. Cttee for Biology, 1977-82; West of Scotland Sch. Co. Chm., Laurel ank Sch. Co. Ltd. Cons. Editor in Plant Biology, McGraw-Hill Publishing Co., 1968-80; Managing Editor, Planta; Editor, Plant Biology, 1981-. *Publications:* (ed) The Physiology of Plant Growth and Development; papers in Jl of Experimental Botany, Plant Physiology, Planta, Nature, Proc. Royal Soc. *Recreation:* sailing. *Address:* Department of Botany, The University, Glasgow G12 8QQ. *T:* 041-339 8855. *Club:* Caledonian.

WILKINS, Maurice Hugh Frederick, CBE 1963; MA, PhD; FRS 1959; Professor of Bio-physics, 1970-81, Emeritus Professor of Biophysics since 1981, and Fellow, since 1973, King's College, University of London; Director, Medical Research Council Cell Biophysics Unit, 1974-80 (Deputy Director, 1955-70, Director, 1970-72, Biophysics Unit; Director Neurobiology Unit, 1972-74); *b* 15 Dec. 1916; *s* of late Edgar Henry Wilkins and of Eveline Constance Jane (*née* Whittaker), both of Dublin; *m* 1959, Patricia Ann Chidgey; two *s* two *d*. *Educ:* King Edward's Sch., Birmingham: St John's College, Cambridge (Hon. Fellow, 1972). Research on luminescence of solids at Physics Department, Birmingham University, with Ministry of Home Security and Aircraft Production, 1938; PhD 1940; Manhattan Project (Ministry of Supply), Univ. of California (research on separation of uranium isotopes by mass spectrograph), 1944; Lectr in Physics, St Andrews Univ., 1945; MRC Biophysics Unit in Physics Department, King's College, London, 1946; Hon. Lecturer in the sub-department of Biophysics, 1958; Prof. of Molecular Biology, King's Coll., 1963-70. Pres., British Soc. for Social Responsibility in Science, 1969. Hon. Mem., Amer. Soc. of Biological Chemists, 1964; For. Hon. Mem., Amer. Acad. of Arts and Scis, 1970. Albert Lasker Award, Amer. Public Health Assoc., 1960. Hon. LLD Glasgow, 1972. (Jt) Nobel Prize for Medicine, 1962. *Publications:* papers in scientific journals on luminescence and topics in bio-physics, *eg* molecular structure of nucleic acids and structure of nerve membranes. *Address:* 30 St John's Park, SE3. *T:* 01-858 1817.

WILKINS, Maj.-Gen. Michael Compton Lockwood, OBE 1975; Major-General Commando Forces Royal Marines, since 1982; *b* 4 Jan. 1933; *s* of late Wilkins and Lucy (*née* Lockwood); *m* 1960, Anne Catherine (*née* Skivington); one *s* two *d*. *Educ:* Mill Hill School. Joined Royal Marines, 2nd Lieut, 1951; 40 Commando RM, 1954-56; Special Boat Sqdn, 1957-61; 41 Commando RM, 1961-62; RM Eastney, 1962-64; sc 1965; GSO2 (Ops) 17 Division, 1966-67; Plans Division, Naval Staff, 1968-69; Bde Major 3 Commando Bde, 1970-71; Directing Staff, Army Staff Coll., 1972-73; CO 40 Commando RM, 1974-75; NATO Defence Coll., 1976; Director of Drafting and Records, 1977-78; Comdr 3 Commando Bde, 1979-80; COS to Comdt Gen. RM, 1981-82. Commodore, Royal Marines Sailing Club. *Recreations:* sailing, riding. *Address:* c/o Barclays Bank, 20 High Street, Exeter, Devon.

WILKINS, Nancy; barrister-at-law; a Recorder of the Crown Court, since 1978; *b* 16 June 1932; three *s* one *d*. *Educ:* School of St Helen and St Katharine, Abingdon, Berkshire. Called to the Bar, Gray's Inn, Nov. 1962. *Publication:* An Outline of the Law of Evidence (with late Prof. Sir Rupert Cross), 1964, 5th edn 1980. *Address:* 50 High Pavement, Nottingham.

WILKINS, William Albert, CBE 1965; *b* 17 Jan. 1899; *m* 1923, Violet Florrie Reed; three *s* one *d*. *Educ:* Whitehall Elementary School, Bristol. Linotype operator; commenced work at 13½ as an errand boy. Apprenticed to Thos Goulding, Printer, 6 Nelson St, Bristol. Later employed by Bristol Evening Times and Echo and Bristol Evening World. Actively engaged in politics since 1922; MP (Lab) Bristol South, 1945-70; Assistant Govt Whip (unpaid), 1947-50; a Lord Comr of the Treasury, 1950-51. Member Typographical

Association (now National Graphical Association), 1919-. Past member of Typographical Association Nat. Executive, Past President Bristol Branch, Past Pres. South-Western Group TA. Member of Bristol City Council, 1936-46. *Address:* 37 King Street, Two Mile Hill, Kingswood, Bristol. *T:* 673779.

WILKINSON, Rev. Canon Alan Bassindale, PhD; Director of Training in the Diocese of Ripon, since 1978; *b* 26 Jan. 1931; *s* of late Rev. J. T. Wilkinson, DD; *m* 1975, Fenella Holland; two *s* one *d* of first marriage. *Educ:* William Hulme's Grammar Sch., Manchester; St Catharine's Coll., Cambridge; College of the Resurrection, Mirfield. MA 1958, PhD 1959 (Cambridge). Deacon, 1959; Priest, 1960; Asst Curate, St Augustine's, Kilburn, 1959-61; Chaplain, St Catharine's Coll., Cambridge, 1961-67; Vicar of Barrow Gurney and Lecturer in Theology, College of St Matthias, Bristol, 1967-70; Principal, Chichester Theol. Coll., 1970-74; Canon and Prebendary of Thorney, 1970-74, Canon Emeritus, 1975; Warden of Verulam House, Dir of Training for Auxiliary Ministry, dio. of St Albans, 1974-75; Lectr in Theology and Ethics, Crewe and Alsager Coll. of Higher Educn, 1975-78. Hulsean Preacher, 1967-68; Select Preacher, Oxford Univ., 1982. Mem., Bd of Educn, Gen. Synod, 1981-; Vice-Chm., Leeds Marriage and Personal Counselling Service, 1981-. Governor, SPCK, 1982-. *Publications:* The Church of England and the First World War, 1978; Would You Believe It?, 1980; contributor to: Cambridge Sermons on Christian Unity, 1966; Catholic Anglicans Today, 1968; also to: Faith and Unity, Sobornost, Preacher's Quarterly, London Quarterly Holborn Review, Theology, Clergy Review, New Fire. *Recreations:* gardening, walking, cinema, Victorian architecture. *Address:* 5 Adel Park Croft, Leeds LS16 8HT. *T:* Leeds 674221.

WILKINSON, Prof. Alexander Birrell; Professor of Private Law, since 1972 and Dean of the Faculty of Law, 1974-76, University of Dundee; *b* 2 Feb. 1932; *o s* of late Captain Alexander Wilkinson, MBE, The Black Watch and Isabella Bell Birrell; *m* 1965, Wendy Imogen, *d* of late Ernest Albert Barrett and of R. V. H. Barrett; one *s* one *d*. *Educ:* Perth Academy; Univs of St Andrews and Edinburgh. Walker Trust Scholar 1950, Grieve Prizeman in Moral Philosophy 1952, MA(Hons Classics) 1954, Univ. of St Andrews. National Service, RAEC, 1954-56. Balfour Keith Prizeman in Constitutional Law 1957, LLB (with distinction) 1959, Univ. of Edinburgh. Admitted to Faculty of Advocates, 1959; in practice at Scottish bar, 1959-69; Lecturer in Scots Law, Univ. of Edinburgh, 1965-69; Sheriff of Stirling, Dunbarton and Clackmannan at Stirling and Alloa, 1969-72. A Chm. of Industrial Tribunals (Scotland). Chancellor, Dio. of Brechin. Chairman: Central Scotland Marriage Guidance Council, 1970-72; Scottish Marriage Guidance Council, 1974-77; Legal Services Gp, Scottish Assoc. of CAB. *Publications:* (ed jtly) Gloag and Henderson's Introduction to the Law of Scotland, 8th edn 1980; articles in legal periodicals. *Recreations:* collecting books and pictures, reading, travel. *Address:* Invergowrie House, Dundee DD2 1UA. *T:* Dundee 68939. *Clubs:* New (Edinburgh); University (Dundee).

WILKINSON, Prof. Andrew Wood, CBE 1979; ChM (Edinburgh); FRCSE; FRCS; Emeritus Professor of Pædiatric Surgery, University of London; Surgeon, Hospital for Sick Children, Great Ormond Street, since 1958; Hon. Consultant Pædiatric Surgeon, Post-graduate Medical School, Hammersmith, and Queen Elizabeth Hospital for Children; Civilian Consultant in Pediatric Surgery to RN; *b* 19 April 1914; *s* of Andrew W. and Caroline G. Wilkinson; *m* 1941, Joan Longair Sharp; two *s* two *d*. *Educ:* Univ. of Edinburgh. MB, ChB, Edin., 1937; ChM; (1st cl. hons and gold medal for thesis), 1949; FRCS Edin. 1940; FRCS Eng. 1959. Surg. specialist, Lt-Col RAMC, 1942-46. Syme Surgical Fellowship, Univ. of Edinburgh, 1946-49; Senior University Clinical Tutor in Surgery, 1946-51; Lecturer in Surgery, University of Edinburgh and Assistant Surgeon, Deaconess Hosp., Edinburgh, 1951-53; Sen. Lectr in Surgery, Univ. of Aberd. and Asst Surg., Roy. Inf. and Roy. Aberd. Hosp. for Sick Children, 1953-58; Nuffield Prof. of Paediatric Surgery, Inst. of Child Health, 1958-79. Dir, Internat. Sch. of Med. Scis, Ettore Majorana Foundn, 1970-. Royal College of Surgeons of Edinburgh: Mem. Council, 1964-73; Vice-Pres., 1973-76; Pres., 1976-79; Founder and Mem., Appeal Cttee, 1978-. Member: Armed Forces Med. Adv. Bd; Nat. Med. Consultative Cttee. Examr Primary and Final FRCS Ed.; Past Examiner: Univ. Glasgow, DCH London; Primary FRCSEng. Lectures: Tisdall, Canadian Med. Assoc., 1966; Mason Brown Meml, 1972; Forshall, 1979; Simpson Smith Meml, 1980; Tan Sri Datu Ismail Oration, Kuala Lumpur, 1980. Hunterian Prof., RCS, 1965. Visiting Prof. Univ. of Alexandria, 1965, Albert Einstein Coll. of Medicine, 1967. Member: Bd of Governors, Hosp. for Sick Children, 1972-80; Cttee of Management, Inst. of Child Health, 1959-79. Founder Mem., Scottish Surgical Pædiatric Soc.; Hon. Mem., and Past Pres., British Assoc. of Pediatric Surgeons, 1970-72 (Denis Browne Gold Medal, 1981). FRSocMed (Pres. Open Section, 1974-76). Hon. FRCSI; Hon. FRACS; Hon. FCPS(Pakistan); Hon. FCPS (S Africa); Hon. Fellow: Brasilian Soc. Pædiatric Surgery; Greek Pædiatric Surgical Soc.; Amer. Acad. Pediatrics; Italian Pediatric Surgical Soc.; Pediatric Surgical Soc. of Ecuador; Hong Kong Surgical Soc.; Hon. Member: Neonatal Soc.; BPA; Peruvian Socs Pediatrics and Pædiatric Surgery; Hellenic Surgical Soc.; Corresp. Member: Scandinavian Pediatric Surgical Assoc.; Sicilian Calabrian Soc. of Pædiatric Surgery. *Publications:* Body Fluids in Surgery, 1955, 4th edn 1973 (Japanese edn, 1978); Recent Advances in Pædiatric Surgery, 1963, 3rd edn 1974 (Spanish edn, 1977); Parenteral Feeding, 1972; (jtly) Research in Burns, 1966; (ed jtly) Metabolism and the Response to Injury, 1976; Early Nutrition and Later Development, 1976; (jt) Placental Transport, 1978; Inflammatory Bowel Disease, 1980; Investigation of Brain Function, 1981; Immunology of Breast Feeding, 1981; chapters, articles and reviews in various books, and surgical and other jls. *Recreations:* fishing, gardening, cooking, eating. *Address:* Auchenbrae, Rockcliffe, Dalbeattie, Kirkcudbrightshire DG5 4QF. *Club:* New (Edinburgh).

WILKINSON, Christopher Richard; Head of Division of Industrial Economics, Directorate General for Internal Market and Industrial Affairs, Commission of the European Communities, since 1978; *b* 3 July 1941; *s* of Rev. Thomas Richard Wilkinson and Winifred Frances Wilkinson (*née* Steel); *m* 1965, Marie-Françoise Courthieu; one *s* one *d. Educ:* Hymers Coll., Kingston upon Hull; Heath Grammar Sch., Halifax; Selwyn Coll., Cambridge (MA). Commonwealth Economic Cttee, 1963-65; OECD, Paris, 1965-66; IBRD, Washington and Lagos, 1966-73; Head of Div., Directorate Gen. for Regional Policy, EEC, 1973-78. Vis. Fellow, Center for Internat. Affairs, Harvard Univ., 1982-83. Vice-Pres., European School Parents Assoc., Brussels, 1974, 1976-77. *Recreations:* mountain walking, gardening. *Address:* Avenue des Frères Legrain 23, 1150 Brussels, Belgium. *T:* 734-72-65; 81 Old Bank Road, Mirfield, West Yorkshire.

WILKINSON, Clive Victor; Leader of Labour Opposition, Birmingham City Council, 1976-80 and since 1982; *b* 26 May 1938; *s* of Mrs Winifred Jobson; *m* 1961, Elizabeth Ann Pugh; two *d. Educ:* Four Dwellings Secondary Sch., Quinton; Birmingham Modern Sch. Birmingham City Council: elected 1970; Leader, 1973-76 and 1980-82. Dir, Nat. Exhibn Centre, 1973-. Chm., CoSIRA, 1977-80; Dep. Chairman: AMA, 1974-76; Redditch Develt Corp., 1977-81. Member: Develt Commn, 1977-; Electricity Consumers Council, 1977-80; Council, Univ. of Birmingham, 1974-. *Recreations:* watching Birmingham City Football Club, playing squash. *Address:* 53 Middle Park Road, Birmingham B29 4BH. *T:* 021-475 1829. *Clubs:* Athol Social, Ley Hill Residents (Birmingham).

WILKINSON, Sir (David) Graham (Brook), 3rd Bt *cr* 1941; *b* 18 May 1947; *s* of Sir (Leonard) David Wilkinson, 2nd Bt, DSC, and of Sylvia Ruby Eva Anne, *d* of Professor Bosley Alan Rex Gater; *S* father, 1972; *m* 1977, Sandra Caroline, *d* of Dr Richard Rossdale; two *d. Educ:* Millfield; Christ Church, Oxford.

WILKINSON, David Lloyd; Chief Executive Officer and General Secretary, Cooperative Union, since 1975; *b* 28 May 1937; *m* 1960; one *s* one *d. Educ:* Royds Hall Grammar Sch. ACIS; CSD. *Address:* 29 Mountfield Road, Waterloo, Huddersfield HD5 8RA. *T:* Huddersfield 27419.

WILKINSON, Sir Denys (Haigh), Kt 1974; FRS 1956; Vice-Chancellor, University of Sussex, since 1976; *b* Leeds, Yorks, 5 September 1922; *o s* of Charles and Hilda Wilkinson; *m* 1st, 1947, Christiane Andrée Clavier (marriage dissolved, 1967); three *d*; 2nd, 1967, Helen Sellschop; two step *d. Educ:* Loughborough Gram. Sch.; Jesus Coll. Cambridge (Fellow, 1944-59, Hon Fellow, 1961). BA 1943, MA, PhD 1947, ScD 1961. British and Canadian Atomic Energy Projects, 1943-46; Univ. Demonstrator, Cambridge, 1947-51; Univ. Lecturer, 1951-56; Reader in Nuclear Physics, Univ. of Cambridge, 1956-57; Professor of Nuclear Physics, Univ. of Oxford, 1957-59; Prof. of Experimental Physics, Univ. of Oxford, 1959-76, Head of Dept of Nuclear Physics, 1962-76; Student, Christ Church, Oxford, 1957-76, Emeritus Student, 1976, Hon. Student, 1979. Dir, Internat. Sch. of Nuclear Physics, Erice, Sicily, 1975-. Mem. Governing Board of National Institute for Research in Nuclear Science, 1957-63 and 1964-65; Member: SRC, 1967-70; Wilton Park Acad. Council, 1979-; Council, ACU, 1980-; Chairman: Nuclear Physics Board of SRC, 1968-70; Physics III Cttee, CERN, Geneva, 1971-75; Radioactive Waste Management Adv. Cttee, 1978-; British Council Sci. Adv. Panel, 1977-; Pres., Inst. of Physics, 1980-. Lectures: Welch, Houston, 1957; Scott, Cambridge Univ., 1961; Rutherford Meml, Brit. Physical Soc., 1962; Graham Young, Glasgow Univ., 1964; Queen's, Berlin, 1966; Silliman, Yale Univ., 1966; Cherwell-Simon, Oxford Univ., 1970; Goodspeed-Richard, Pennsylvania Univ., 1973; Welsh, Toronto Univ., 1975; Tizard Meml, Westminster Sch., 1975; Lauritsen Meml, Cal. Tech., 1976; Herbert Spencer, Oxford Univ., 1976; Schiff Meml, Stanford Univ., 1977; Racah Meml, Hebrew Univ. Jerusalem, 1977; Cecil Green, Univ. of BC, 1978; Distinguished Lectr, Univ. of Alberta, 1979; Wolfson, Oxford Univ., 1980; Waterloo-Guelph Distinguished Lectr, 1981. Walker Ames Prof., Univ. of Washington, 1968; Battelle Distinguished Prof., Univ. of Washington, 1970-71.; For. Mem., Royal Swedish Acad. of Scis, 1980. Holweck Medal, British and French Physical Socs, 1957; Hughes Medal, Royal Society, 1965; Bruce-Preller Prize, RSE, 1969; Bonner Prize, American Physical Soc., 1974; Royal Medal, Royal Soc., 1980. Hon. DSc: Saskatchewan, 1964; Utah State, 1975; Guelph, 1981; Hon. FilDr Uppsala, 1980. Comm. Bontemps Médoc et Graves, 1973. *Publications:* Ionization Chambers and Counters, 1951; (ed) Isospin in Nuclear Physics, 1969; (ed) Progress in Particle and Nuclear Physics, 1978-; (ed jtly) Mesons in Nuclei, 1979; papers on nuclear physics and bird navigation. *Recreations:* mediæval church architecture and watching birds. *Address:* Gayles Orchard, Friston, Eastbourne, East Sussex BN20 0BA. *T:* East Dean 3333. *Clubs:* Athenæum, Achilles.

WILKINSON, Elizabeth Mary, PhD; FBA 1972; Professor of German, University College London, 1960-76, now Emeritus; *b* 17 Sept. 1909; *d* of Frank Wilkinson and Martha E. Gilleard, Keighley, Yorks. *Educ:* Whalley Range High Sch., Manchester; Bedford Coll., London. Prof.-at-Large of Cornell Univ., 1967-. President: English Goethe Soc., 1974-; Modern Language Assoc., GB, 1964; Hon. Mem., Modern Language Assoc. of America, 1965. Korresp. Mitglied, Akademie der Wissenschaften zu Göttingen, 1973; Deutsche Akad. für Sprache und Dichtung, 1976. Hon. LLD Smith Coll., Mass, 1966; Hon. DLitt Kent, 1971. Medaille in Gold des Goethe-Instituts, 1965; Preis für Germanistik im Ausland der Deutschen Akad. für Sprache und Dichtung, 1974. *Publications:* J. E. Schlegel: A German Pioneer in Aesthetics, 1945; (with L. A. Willoughby) Goethe: Poet and Thinker, 1962; with L. A. Willoughby) Schiller: On the Aesthetic Education of Man, 1967 (German edn 1977); Models of Wholeness, 1980. *Recreations:* housekeeping and scholarship at a civilized pace at last. *Address:* 33 Queen Court, Queen Square, WC1.

WILKINSON, Prof. Sir Geoffrey, Kt 1976; FRS 1965; Sir Edward Frankland Professor of Inorganic Chemistry, University of London; *b* 14 July 1921; *s* of Henry and Ruth Wilkinson; *m* 1951, Lise Sølver, *o d* of Rektor Prof. Svend Aa. Schou, Copenhagen; two *d. Educ:* Todmorden Secondary Sch (Royal Scholar, 1939); Imperial Coll., London; USA. Junior Scientific Officer, Nat. Res. Council, Atomic Energy Div., Canada, 1943-46; Research Fellow: Radiation Lab., Univ. of Calif, Berkeley, Calif, USA, 1946-50; Chemistry Dept, Mass Inst. of Technology, Cambridge, Mass, USA, 1950-51; Asst Prof. of Chemistry, Harvard Univ., Cambridge, Mass, 1951-56; Prof. of Inorganic Chemistry at Imperial Coll., Univ. of London, 1956, Sir Edward Frankland Prof. 1978. Arthur D. Little Visiting Prof., MIT, 1967; Lectures: William Draper Harkins' Meml, Univ. of Chicago, 1968; Leermakers, Wesleyan Univ., 1975; First Mond, Chem. Soc., 1980; John Simon Guggenheim Fellow, 1954. Foreign Member: Roy. Danish Acad. of Science and Arts (math.-phys section), 1968; Amer. Acad. of Arts and Sciences, 1970; Foreign Assoc., Nat. Acad. of Scis, 1975; Centennial Foreign Fellow, Amer. Chem. Soc., 1976. Hon. DSc: Edinburgh, 1975; Granada, 1976; Columbia, 1978; Bath, 1980. American Chem. Soc. Award in Inorganic Chemistry, 1965; Lavoisier Medal, Société Chimique de France, 1968; Chem. Soc. Award for Transition Metal Chemistry, 1972; (jtly) Nobel Prize for Chemistry, 1973; Consejero de Honor, Spanish Council for Scientific Res., 1974; Hiroshima Univ. Medal, 1978; Royal Medal, Royal Soc., 1981. *Publications:* (jtly) Advanced Inorganic Chemistry: a Comprehensive Text, 1962, 4th edn 1980; Basic Inorganic Chemistry, 1976; numerous in Physical Review, Journal of the American Chemical Society, etc. *Address:* Chemistry Department, Imperial College, SW7 2AY. *T:* 01-589 5111.

WILKINSON, Geoffrey Crichton, AFC; Chief Inspector of Accidents (Aircraft), since 1981; *b* 7 Nov. 1926; *s* of Col W. E. D. Wilkinson and Mrs E. K. Wilkinson; *m* 1958, Virginia Mary Broom; two *d. Educ:* Bedford Sch. Graduate, Empire Test Pilots Sch.; MRAES. Royal Indian Mil. Coll., 1943-44; served RN, 1944-47; aeronautical engrg course, 1948; served RAF, 1949-59 (Air Force Cross, 1956); Turner and Newall, 1959-61; Mercury Airlines, 1961-65; Accidents Investigation Br., 1965-. Air Medal, USA, 1953. *Recreations:* sailing, skiing, music. *Address:* Neatham Grange, Holybourne, Alton, Hants GU34 4NP. *T:* Alton 83842. *Clubs:* Royal Air Force; Royal Air Force Yacht (Hamble).

WILKINSON, Sir Graham Brook; *see* Wilkinson, Sir D. G. B.

WILKINSON, Sir Harold, Kt 1964; CMG 1946; retired as: Managing Director, The "Shell" Transport and Trading Co. Ltd; Director: The Shell Petroleum Co. Ltd; Shell Petroleum NV; Guinness Mahon Holdings; *b* 24 Feb. 1903; *s* of Charles Robert Wilkinson, MA Oxon, ICS, Ramsey, Isle of Man; *m* 1939, Marie Frances Elie; three *s* one *d* (and one step *d*). *Educ:* King William's Coll., Isle of Man. Joined Royal Dutch/Shell Group of Cos, 1922; formerly: Man. Dir and Dep. Chm., The "Shell" Transport and Trading Co. Ltd; Man. Dir, Shell Petroleum Co. Ltd; Principal Dir, Bataafse Petroleum Mij. NV; Pres., Asiatic Petroleum Corp., USA; Chm., Shell Caribbean Petroleum Co., USA; Pres., Canadian Shell; Chm., Shell Tankers; Dir, Shell Oil Co., USA; retd 1964. Petroleum Rep. in Washington of UK Govt, 1941-45. US Medal of Freedom with Bronze Palm, 1951; Kt Comdr Order of Merit, Ecuador; Comdr Order of Oranje-Nassau, 1964. *Recreations:* golf, sailing and shooting. *Address:* 9 avenue des Alpes, 1006 Lausanne, Vaud, Switzerland. *Clubs:* Hurlingham; Sunningdale; St Andrews; Royal Yacht Squadron; Royal Bermuda Yacht (Bermuda).

WILKINSON, Ven. Hubert Seed; Archdeacon of Liverpool, 1951-70; Archdeacon Emeritus, since 1971; Residentiary Canon, 1968-70; *b* 7 June 1897; *e s* of late Rev. John and Margaret Wilkinson; *m* Frances Elizabeth, 4th *d* of Dr J. Staveley Dick; two *d. Educ:* St John's Coll., Durham Univ. (Exhibnr). MA (2nd cl. Hons English Lit.; 2nd cl. Hons Modern Hist.). Served RA, 1916-18. Curate of Colne, 1925-29; Rector of Harpurhey, Manchester, 1929-36; Rector of Chester-le-Street, 1936-40; Rural Dean of Chester-le-Street, 1937-40; Vicar of Allerton, Liverpool, 1940-47; Canon Diocesan of Liverpool Cathedral, 1945-47, and 1951-68; Examining Chaplain to Bishop of Liverpool, 1945-47 and 1955-70; Vicar of Winster, 1947-48; Archdeacon of Westmorland, 1947-51; Vicar of Ambleside with Rydal, 1948-50; St Mary's, Grassendale, 1951-68; late Hon. Canon of Carlisle Cathedral and Director of Religious Education. *Address:* 89 Primrose Hill, Widmer End, High Wycombe, Bucks. *T:* High Wycombe 715649.

WILKINSON, James Hardy, MA Cantab, ScD; FRS 1969; Professor of Computer Science, Stanford University, since 1977; *b* 27 Sept. 1919; *s* of J. W. and K. C. Wilkinson; *m* 1945, Heather Nora Ware; one *s* one *d. Educ:* Sir Joseph Williamson's Mathematical Sch., Rochester; Trinity Coll., Cambridge. Major Scholar (Maths) Trinity Coll., 1935; Pemberton Prize, 1937; Mathison Prize, 1939; BA 1939, MA Cantab 1942; ScD 1962. War service: Mathematical Laboratory, Cambridge, 1940-43; Armament Research Dept, Fort Halstead, 1943-46. Mathematics Div., Nat. Physical Lab. (working on design, construction and use of electronic computers), 1946-80; DCSO, 1962-74; Individual Merit CSO, 1974-80. Visiting Professor: Univ. of Michigan, numerous occasions, 1957-73; Stanford Univ., 1961, 1967, 1969. Founder Fellow: Inst. of Mathematics and its Applications (Vice-Pres., 1973-75, Hon. Fellow 1977); British Computer Society (Distinguished FBCS, 1973). Mem. Council, Royal Soc., 1974-77. Visited USSR Academy of Sciences, as a leading scientist, 1968; Distinguished Lectr, Univ. of Waterloo, 1976; Sir Joseph Larmor Lectr, QUB, 1978; Distinguished Lectr, Yale, 1981; D. B. Gillies Meml Lectr, Illinois, 1981; Distinguished Lectr, Univ. of Minnesota, 1982. Hon. DTech Brunel, 1971; Hon. DSc Heriot-Watt, 1973; DUniv Essex, 1977; Hon. DMath Waterloo, 1978. A. M. Turing award, Assoc. for Computing Machinery, 1970; J. von Neumann award, Soc. for Applied Maths, 1970; Engineer of Distinction, Engineers Jt Council, 1974; G. E. Forsythe Award, Stanford Univ., 1977. Foreign Hon. Mem., Amer. Acad. of Arts and Sciences, 1974; Mem., Bavarian Acad. of Sciences, 1978. *Publications:* Rounding Errors in Algebraic Processes, 1963; The Algebraic Eigenvalue Problem, 1965; Linear Algebra, 1971; chapters in ten books on computers and numerical analysis; numerous papers in learned jls. *Recreations:* music, travel. *Address:* 40 Atbara Road, Teddington, Mddx. *T:* 01-977 1207.

WILKINSON, Jeffrey Vernon; Joint Group Managing Director, Lucas Industries plc, since 1980; *b* 21 Aug. 1930; *s* of late Arthur Wilkinson and Winifred May Allison; *m* 1955, Jean Vera Nurse; two *d*. *Educ:* Mathew Humberstone Foundation Sch.; King's Coll., Cambridge (MA); Sorbonne. FBCS, FBIM. Joined Joseph Lucas as graduate apprentice, 1954; Director, CAV, 1963; Director and General Manager, Diesel Equipment, CAV, 1967; Director: Simon Engineering, 1968; Joseph Lucas, 1974; Gen. Manager, Lucas Electrical, 1974; Divisional Man. Dir, Joseph Lucas Ltd, 1978. Liveryman, Wheelwrights Company, 1971-. *Recreations:* squash, water-skiing, swimming, reading, theatre, art. *Address:* Hillcroft, 15 Mearse Lane, Barnt Green, Birmingham B45 8HG. *T:* 021-445 1747.

WILKINSON, John Arbuthnot Ducane; MP (C) Hillingdon, Ruislip Northwood, since 1979; *b* 23 Sept. 1940; 2nd *s* of late Denys Wilkinson and Gillian Wilkinson, Eton College; *m* 1969, Paula Adey, *o d* of Joseph Adey, East Herrington, Co. Durham; one *d*. *Educ:* Eton (King's Scholar); RAF Coll., Cranwell; Churchill Coll., Cambridge (2nd cl. Hons Mod. Hist.; MA). Flight Cadet, RAF Coll., Cranwell, 1959-61 (Philip Sassoon Meml Prize, qualified French Interpreter); commnd 1961; Flying Instructor, No 8 FTS, Swinderby, 1962; resigned Oct. 1962. Churchill Coll., Cambridge, Oct. 1962-65. Trooper, 21st Special Air Service Regt (Artists'), TA, 1963-65; rejoined RAF 1965; Flying Instructor, RAF Coll., Cranwell, 1966-67; Tutor, Stanford Univ.'s British Campus, 1967; ADC to Comdr 2nd Allied Tactical Air Force, Germany, 1967; resigned RAF, 1967. Head of Universities' Dept, Conservative Central Office, 1967-68; Aviation Specialist, Cons. Research Dept, 1969; Senior Administration Officer (Anglo-French Jaguar Project), Preston Div., British Aircraft Corp., 1969-70; Tutor, Open Univ., 1970-71; Vis. Lectr, OCTU RAF Henlow, 1971-75; Chief Flying Instructor, Skywork Ltd, Stansted, 1974-75; Gen. Manager, General Aviation Div., Brooklands Aviation Ltd, 1975-76; PA to Chm., BAC, 1975-77; Senior Sales Executive, Eagle Aircraft Services Ltd, 1977-78; Sales Manager, Klingair Ltd, 1978-79. MP (C) Bradford W, 1970-Feb. 1974; Jt Sec., Cons. Parly Aviation Cttee, 1972-74; Sec., Cons. Parly Defence Cttee, 1972-74; Member Select Committee on: Race Relations and Immigration, 1972-74; Sci. and Technol., 1972-74; contested (C) Bradford W, Oct. 1974; PPS to Minister of State for Industry, 1979-80, to Sec. of State for Defence, 1981-; Vice-Chm., Cons. Parly Aviation Cttee, 1979; Chairman: Bow Group Standing Cttee on Defence, 1979-81; Anglo-Asian Cons. Soc., 1979-82; Anglo-Asian Cons. Parly Gp, 1980-82; Vice-Chm., Anglo-Somali Parly Gp, 1981-; Secretary: Anglo-Pakistan Parly Gp, 1972-74; Anglo-Bangladesh Parly Gp, 1979-; Treasurer, Anglo-Malaŵi Parly Gp, 1979-. Delegate to Council of Europe and WEU. *Publications:* (jtly) The Uncertain Ally, 1982; pamphlets and articles on defence and politics. *Recreation:* flying. *Address:* c/o House of Commons, SW1. *Club:* Royal Air Force.

WILKINSON, John Francis; Director, Public Affairs, BBC, since 1980; *b* 2 Oct. 1926; *s* of late Col W. T. Wilkinson, DSO, and Evelyn S. Wilkinson (*née* Ward); *m* 1951, Alison, *d* of late Hugh and Marian Malcolm; two *s* one *d*. *Educ:* Wellington Coll.; Edinburgh Univ. Naval Short Course, 1944-45; Cambridge and London Univs Colonial Course, 1947-48. Served Royal Navy (Fleet Air Arm trainee pilot, 1945), 1945-47; HM Colonial Service, N Nigeria, 1949; Asst District Officer, Bida, 1949; Asst Sec., Lands and Mines, Kaduna, 1950; Private Sec. to Chief Comr, N Nigeria, 1951; transf. to Nigerian Broadcasting Corp., 1952; Controller: Northern Region, 1952-56; National Programme, Lagos, 1956-58; joined BBC African Service as African Programme Organiser, 1958; East and Central African Programme Organiser, 1961; BBC TV Production Trng Course and attachment to Panorama, 1963; Asst Head, 1964, Head, 1969, BBC African Service; attachment to Horizon, 1972; Head of Production and Planning, BBC World Service, 1976; Secretary of the BBC, 1977-80. Chm. of Governors, Centre for Internat. Briefing, Farnham Castle, 1977-. Vice-Pres., Royal African Soc., 1978-82. *Publications:* Broadcasting in Africa, in African Affairs (Jl of Royal African Soc.), 1972; contrib. to Broadcasting in Africa, a continental survey of radio and television, 1974. *Recreations:* sailing, occasional golf. *Address:* Orchard House, Kingsley Green, Haslemere, Surrey GU27 3LG. *T:* Haslemere 3897. *Club:* Royal Commonwealth Society.

WILKINSON, Dr John Frederick, FRCP, MD (Gold Medal), ChB, BSc (1st Cl. Hons Chem.), MSc, PhD Manchester, DSc (Hon.) Bradford; CChem, FRSC; author; Consulting Physician; Consulting Physician, United Manchester Hospitals; late Director of Department of Hæmatology, University and Royal Infirmary of Manchester; late Reader in Hæmatology, and Lecturer in Systematic Medicine, Univ. of Manchester; late Hon. Consulting Hæmatologist, The Christie Cancer Hospital, Holt Radium Institute and The Duchess of York Hospital for Babies, Manchester; Hon. Fellow and Editor, Manchester Medical Society; formerly President, European Hæmatological Soc.; Life Councillor and Founder, International Hæmatological Soc.; *b* Oldham, 10 June 1897; *s* of John Frederick Wilkinson, Oldham and Stockport, and Annie, *d* of late Reverend E. Wareham, DD, Rector of Heaton Mersey; *m* 1964, Marion Crossfield, Major, WRAC. *Educ:* Arnold School, Blackpool; University of Manchester; Manchester Royal Infirmary. Served European War, 1916-19, RNAS, RN, and later attached Tank Corps, France; also served on Vindictive at Zeebrugge, 1918, and ballotted for Victoria Cross award; Chemical Research Manchester University, 1919-28; Medical Research since 1929; Regional Transfusion Officer, and Regional Adviser on Resuscitation, Ministry of Health, NW Region, 1940-46. Graduate Scholarship (Chemistry), 1920; Dalton Research Scholarship; Sir Clement Royds Research Fellowship; Medical (Graduate) Scholarship, 1923; Hon. Demonstrator in Crystallography; Research Asst in Physiology; Sidney Renshaw Physiology Prizeman; Gold Medal for Dissertation in Med., 1931, University of Manchester. RCP Lectures: Oliver Sharpey, 1948; Samuel Gee, 1977. Liveryman (and Osler Lectr, 1981), Worshipful Society of Apothecaries, London; Freeman City of London. Hon. DSc Bradford, 1976. *Publications:* scientific and medical publications since 1920 in English and foreign journals, etc. Sections on Blood Diseases, Anæmias and Leukæmias in British Encyclopædia of Medical Practice, 1936, 1950 and yearly supplements since 1951, and in Encyclopædia of General Practice, 1964; Section on Emergencies in Blood Diseases, in Medical Emergencies, 1948 to date; ed Modern Trends in Diseases of the Blood, 1955, 1975; The Diagnosis and Treatment of Blood Diseases, 1973; ed, Section in Clinical Surgery, 1967; articles on antiques, Old English and continental apothecaries' drug jars, etc, in miscellaneous medical and art jls, 1970-82. *Recreations:* motoring, antiques, travel, zoos, tropical fish keeping, lecturing. *Address:* Mobberley Old Hall, Knutsford, Cheshire WA16 7AB. *T:* Mobberley 2111; 5 Lorne Street, Manchester M13 0EZ. *T:* 061-273 4253. *Clubs:* Savage, Lansdowne.

WILKINSON, Kenneth Grahame, CBE 1979; Hon. DSc, BSc, FEng, FCGI, FRAeS, FCIT, FSLAET; FRSA; aviation consultant; Director, British Rail Engineering, since 1982; Director and Deputy Chairman, Airways Aero Associations Ltd; *b* 14 July 1917; *s* of Bertie and Dorothy Wilkinson; *m* 1941, Mary Holman Victory; one *s* one *d*. *Educ:* Shooter's Hill; Imperial Coll. (BSc, DIC). CBIM. Sen. Scientific Officer, RAE, Farnborough, 1945; Performance and Analysis Supt, BEA, 1946-52; Manager, Fleet Planning Br., BEA, 1960; Chief Engr, BEA, 1964; Mem. Bd, BEA, 1968-72; Dep. Chief Exec. and Man. Dir (BEA Mainline), BEA, 1971-72, Chm. and Chief Exec., BEA, Sept.-Nov. 1972; Mem. Bd, BOAC, 1972; Rolls Royce (1971) Ltd: Man. Dir, 1972-74; Vice-Chm., 1974-76; Engineering Dir, British Airways, 1976-79. Chm., Air Transport and Travel Industry Trng Bd, 1981-82; Mem., BAB, 1971-72 and 1976-81 (Dep. Chm., 1979-80). Chm., BGA Techn. Cttee, 1946-48; Chm., BGA, 1970, Vice-Pres., 1972; Pres. RAeS, 1972. Vis. Prof., Cranfield Inst. of Technology, 1981-. Member: Cranwell Adv. Bd, 1970-73; Council, Cranfield Inst. of Technology, 1971-. *Publications:* Sailplanes of the World (with B. S. Shenstone): Vol. 1, 1960; Vol. 2, 1963; articles and papers to: Jl of Royal Aeronautical Soc.; Aircraft Engineering. *Recreations:* gliding, swimming, gardening, travel. *Address:* Tanglin, Manor Road, Penn, Bucks HP10 8HY.

WILKINSON, (Lancelot) Patrick, MA; FRSL; Fellow, King's College, Cambridge; Lecturer in Classics, 1936-67, Reader in Latin Literature, 1967-69, Brereton Reader in Classics, 1969-74, Orator, 1958-74, Cambridge University; *b* 1 June 1907; *s* of late Lancelot George William and Kate Wilkinson; *m* 1944, Sydney Alix, *d* of late Sir Herbert Eason, CB, CMG; two *s*. *Educ:* Charterhouse; King's College, Cambridge, 1st Class Classical Tripos, Parts I and II; Craven Scholar, 1929; Chancellor's Classical Medallist, 1930; Craven Student, 1930; Fellow of King's College, Cambridge, 1932; Dean, 1934-45; attached to Foreign Office, GCHQ Bletchley Park, 1939-45; Asst Tutor, 1945-46; Senior Tutor, 1946-56; Vice-Provost, 1961-65. Chm., Cambridge Greek Play Cttee, 1973- (Sec., 1938-63); Dep. for Orator, 1950-51, 1957; Member of the Council of the Senate, 1952-56; Chm. of Classical Faculty, 1969, 1970; Foundation Mem. Council, New Hall, Cambridge, 1954-65; Governor, Queen Mary Coll., London, 1954-57; Mem. Governing Body, Charterhouse School, 1954-69. Mem. Conseil Consultatif of Fondation Hardt, Geneva, 1959-63. A Vice-Pres., Classical Assoc. (Pres., 1971-72). Lord Northcliffe Meml Lectr, UCL, 1976; Donald Dudley Meml Lectr, Univ. of Birmingham, 1976. Vis. Prof., Berkeley, Calif, Spring 1980. *Publications:* Horace and his Lyric Poetry, 1945; Letters of Cicero, 1949; Ovid Recalled, 1955 (abr. as Ovid Surveyed, 1962); Golden Latin Artistry, 1963; (with R. H. Bulmer) Register of King's College, Cambridge, 1919-58, 1963; words for Benjamin Britten's *Cantata Misericordium,* 1963; The Georgics of Virgil, 1969; The Roman Experience, 1974; (with R. H. Bulmer) Register of King's College, Cambridge, 1945-70, 1974; Classical Attitudes to Modern Issues, 1979; A Century of King's 1873-1972, 1980; Kingsmen of a Century

1873-1972, 1980; text for Le Keux's Engravings of Victorian Cambridge, 1981; articles in classical jls. *Recreations:* reading, travel. *Address:* King's College, Cambridge. *T:* 350411; 21 Marlowe Road, Cambridge. *T:* 63188.

WILKINSON, Sir Martin; see Wilkinson, Sir R. F. M.

WILKINSON, Hon. Sir Nicolas Christopher Henry B.; see Browne-Wilkinson.

WILKINSON, Patrick; see Wilkinson, L. P.

WILKINSON, Prof. Paul; Professor of International Relations, University of Aberdeen, since 1979; *b* 9 May 1937; *s* of Walter Ross Wilkinson and Joan Rosemary (*née* Paul); *m* 1960, Susan; two *s* one *d. Educ:* Lower School of John Lyon; University Coll., Swansea, Univ. of Wales (BA (jt Hons Mod. Hist. and Politics), MA). Royal Air Force regular officer, 1959-65. Asst Lecturer in Politics, 1966-68, Lectr in Politics, 1968-75, Sen. Lectr in Politics, 1975-77, University Coll., Cardiff; Reader, Univ. of Wales, 1978-79. Member, IBA Scottish Adv. Cttee, 1982-. Editorial Adviser, Contemporary Review, 1980-; Associate Editor, Terrorism: an international journal, 1980-; Mem., Editorial Board, Conflict Quarterly, 1980-. Civilian Consultant, Police Staff Coll., Bramshill, 1978-; External Examiner, Universities of: St Andrews, 1979-82; Edinburgh, 1979-81; Dublin, 1980-83. *Publications:* Social Movement, 1971; Political Terrorism, 1974; Terrorism versus Liberal Democracy, 1976; Terrorism and the Liberal State, 1977; (jtly) Terrorism: theory and practice, 1978; (ed) British Perspectives on Terrorism, 1981; The New Fascists, 1981; Defence of the West, 1983; contribs to wide range of jls in Britain, USA and Canada. *Recreations:* modern art, poetry, walking. *Address:* Edward Wright Building, Dunbar Street, Old Aberdeen, Aberdeen AB9 2UB. *T:* Aberdeen 40241.

WILKINSON, Sir Peter (Allix), KCMG 1970 (CMG 1960); DSO 1944; OBE 1944; HM Diplomatic Service, retired; *b* 15 April 1914; *s* of late Captain Osborn Cecil Wilkinson; *m* 1945, Mary Theresa, *d* of late Algernon Villiers; two *d. Educ:* Rugby; Corpus Christi Coll., Cambridge. Commissioned in 2nd Bn Royal Fusiliers, 1935; active service in Poland (despatches), France, Italy and Balkans; retired with rank of Lieut.-Colonel, 1946. Entered HM Foreign Service, appointed 1st Secretary at British Legation, Vienna, 1947; 1st Secretary at British Embassy, Washington, 1952; Secretary-General of Heads of Government Meeting at Geneva, 1955; Counsellor, HM Embassy, Bonn, 1955; Counsellor, Foreign Office, 1960-63; Under-Secretary, Cabinet Office, 1963-64; Senior Civilian Instructor at the Imperial Defence Coll., 1964-66; Ambassador to Vietnam, 1966-67; Under-Secretary, Foreign Office, 1967-68; Chief of Administration, HM Diplomatic Service, 1968-70; Ambassador to Vienna, 1970-71. Cross of Valour (Poland), 1940; Order of White Lion (IV Class) (Czechoslovakia), 1945. *Recreations:* gardening, sailing, fishing. *Address:* Mill House, Charing, Kent. *T:* Charing 2306. *Clubs:* White's, Army and Navy.

WILKINSON, Peter William, MC 1942; Director and General Manager, Anglia Building Society, since 1978; *b* 10 Dec. 1922; *s* of Frederic Walter Wilkinson, FCA, and Lillie Mary Wilkinson; *m* 1948, Cicely June (*née* Bettington); two *s* one *d. Educ:* Gresham's Sch., Holt. FCA; ACBSI. Served War of 1939-45 (MC). Joined Northampton Town and County Building Soc., 1963; Gen. Manager, Anglia Building Soc., 1970; Mem. Council, Building Socs Assoc., 1973-; Chm., Midland Assoc. of Building Socs, 1978-79. *Recreations:* fishing, sailing, golf. *Address:* Tharfield, East Haddon, Northampton NN6 8DE. *Club:* Naval and Military.

WILKINSON, Philip William, FIB; Director, since 1979, and Group Chief Executive, since 1983, National Westminster Bank PLC; Director, International Westminster Bank Ltd, since 1982; *b* 8 May 1927; *m* 1951, Eileen Patricia (*née* Malkin); one *s* two *d. Educ:* Leyton County High School. Joined Westminster Bank, 1943; Chief Executive, Lombard North Central Ltd, 1975; General Manager, Related Banking Services Division, 1978; a Director, National Westminster Bank Ltd, 1979; Dep. Group Chief Executive, 1980. *Recreations:* golf and watching sport. *Address:* 41 Lothbury, EC2P 2BP. *T:* 01-726 1266. *Club:* Royal Automobile.

WILKINSON, Sir (Robert Francis) Martin, Kt 1969; Chairman: the Stock Exchange, London, 1965-March 1973; the Stock Exchange, March-June 1973 (Deputy Chairman, 1963-65); Chairman, Federation of Stock Exchanges in Great Britain and Ireland, 1965-73; *b* 4 June 1911; *e s* of late Sir Robert Pelham Wilkinson and Phyllis Marion Wilkinson; *m* 1936, Dora Esme, *d* of late William John Arendt and late Mrs Arendt; three *d. Educ:* Repton. Member, Stock Exchange, 1933; Partner in de Zoete & Gorton, 1936; Senior Partner, de Zoete & Bevan, 1970-76; Member of Council, Stock Exchange, 1959. Chm., Altifund, 1976-81; Dir, City of London Brewery Trust (Chm., 1977-78). One of HM Lieutenants, City of London, 1973-. Served with RAF 1940-45. *Recreations:* cricket, gardening. *Address:* Hurst-an-Clays, Ship Street, East Grinstead, W Sussex RH19 4EE. *Club:* City of London.

WILKINSON, Sydney Frank, CB 1951; Director of Administration, National Research Development Corporation, 1955-65; *b* 14 Dec. 1894; *s* of Charles James Carey Wilkinson; *m* 1924, Gladys Millicent Boorsma; one *s. Educ:* Strand Sch.; King's Coll., London. Entered Civil Service, National Health Insurance Commission, 1913; Commissioned RFA, 1918; Private Secretary to Minister of Food, 1920; Secretary to Parliamentary Conference

on Reform of Licensing Law, 1921; Assistant Private Secretary to Sir Kingsley Wood, 1935; loaned to National Fitness Council, 1937; Private Secretary to Mr Walter Elliot and Mr Malcolm MacDonald, 1938-40; Security Executive, 1940-41; Director of Public Relations, Ministry of Health, 1941-43. Under-Secretary for Housing, Ministry of Housing and Local Government, 1951-54 (Ministry of Local Government and Planning, 1951; Ministry of Health, 1947-51). *Recreation:* golf. *Address:* 51 Cornwall Road, Cheam, Surrey SM2 6DU. *T:* 01-642 0374.

WILKINSON, Dr William Lionel; Deputy Director, British Nuclear Fuels Ltd, since 1979; Member, Science and Engineering Research Council, since 1981; *b* 16 Feb. 1931; *s* of Lionel and Dorothy Wilkinson; *m* 1955, Josephine Anne Pilgrim; five *s. Educ:* Christ's Coll., Cambridge. MA, PhD; CEng, FIChemE, FEng. Salters' Res. Schol., Christ's Coll., Cambridge, 1953-56; Lectr in Chem. Engrg, UC Swansea, 1956-59; UKAEA Production Gp, 1959-67; Prof. of Chem. Engrg, Univ. of Bradford, 1967-79. *Publications:* Non-Newtonian Flow, 1960; contribs to sci. and engrg jls on heat transfer, fluid mechanics, polymer processing and process dynamics. *Recreations:* sailing, fell-walking. *Address:* 2 Beechmount Close, Baildon, Shipley, W Yorks BD17 6JG. *T:* Bradford 584138.

WILKS, Jean Ruth Fraser, CBE 1977; Deputy Pro-Chancellor, Birmingham University, since 1979; *b* 14 April 1917; *d* of Mark Wilks. *Educ:* North London Collegiate Sch.; Somerville Coll., Oxford (MA). Assistant Mistress: Truro High Sch., 1940-43; James Allen's Girls' Sch., Dulwich, 1943-51; Head Mistress, Hertfordshire and Essex High Sch., Bishop's Stortford, Hertfordshire, 1951-64; Head Mistress, King Edward VI High Sch. for Girls, Birmingham, 1965-77. Pres., Assoc. of Head Mistresses, 1972-74; Member: Public Schools Commn, 1968-70; Council, Univ. of Birmingham, 1971- (Chm., Academic Staffing Cttee, Univ. of Birmingham, 1978-); Governing Council of Schools Council, 1972-75; Adv. Council on Supply and Trng of Teachers, 1973-78; Educn Cttee, Royal Coll. of Nursing, 1973-79; University Authorities Panel, 1982-. Pres., Somerville Coll. ASM, 1982-; Chm. Governors, Ellerslie, Malvern, 1982-. FCP 1978. *Address:* 4 Hayward Road, Oxford OX2 8LW. *Club:* Naval and Military.

WILKS, Jim; see Wilks, Stanley David.

WILKS, Stanley David, (Jim Wilks), CB 1979; MIEx; Associate of PA Management Consultants, since 1980; Director-General, Technology Transfer Group, since 1981; Director: Matthew Hall International Development, Ltd, since 1981; Hadson Petroleum International plc, since 1981; Chairman, BAMEXCO Ltd, since 1981; Associate Consultant, Strategy International, since 1981; *b* 1 Aug. 1920; *m* 1947, Dorothy Irene Adamthwaite; one *s* one *d. Educ:* Polytechnic Sch., London. Royal Armoured Corps, 1939-46; service with 48th Bn, Royal Tank Regt; 3rd Carabiniers, Imphal, 1944. Home Office, 1946-50; Board of Trade, later Dept of Trade, 1950-80: posts included 1st Sec., British Embassy, Washington, 1950-53; GATT, non-ferrous metals, ECGD, airports policy; Chief Exec., BOTB, 1975-80. Vice-Chm., Internat. Tin Council, 1968-69; Chm., Tech. Help for Exporters Management Cttee, BSI, 1982-. Chm., UK Wayfarer Assoc., 1982. MIEx 1981. *Recreations:* dinghy racing, backgammon, music. *Address:* 6 Foxgrove Avenue, Beckenham, Kent. *Clubs:* Eccentric, World Traders, Civil Service; Medway Yacht.

WILL, Ronald Kerr; Deputy Keeper of Her Majesty's Signet, since 1975; Senior Partner, Dundas & Wilson, CS, Edinburgh; *b* 22 March 1918; 3rd *s* of late James Alexander Will, WS and late Bessie Kennedy Salmon, Dumfries; *m* 1953, Margaret Joyce, *d* of late D. Alan Stevenson, BSc, FRSE; two *s. Educ:* Merchiston Castle Sch.; Edinburgh Univ. Commnd King's Own Scottish Borderers, 1940; served with 1st Bn and in Staff appts (despatches); psc; GSO2. Writer to the Signet, 1950. Director: Scottish Equitable Life Assce Soc. (Chm., 1980-); Scottish Investment Trust Co. Ltd and other companies; Mem. Council on Tribunals, 1971-76 and Chm. of Scottish Cttee, 1972-76. Governor, Merchiston Castle Sch., 1953-76. *Recreations:* shooting, fishing. *Address:* 3 Belgrave Place, Edinburgh EH4 3AN. *T:* 031-3328970. *Club:* New (Edinburgh).

WILLAN, Edward Gervase, CMG 1964; HM Diplomatic Service, retired; Ambassador to Czechoslovakia, 1974-77; *b* 17 May 1917; *er s* of late Captain F. G. L. Willan, RNR; *m* 1944, Mary Bickley Joy, *d* of late Lieut-Colonel H. A. Joy, IAOC. *Educ:* Radley; Pembroke Coll., Cambridge (Exhibitioner, MA). Indian Civil Service, 1939-47; 2nd Secretary (from 1948, 1st Secretary) on staff of UK High Commissioner, New Delhi, 1947-49; appointed to HM Diplomatic Service, 1948; Foreign Office, 1949-52; 1st Secretary, HM Embassy, The Hague, 1953-55; 1st Secretary, HM Legation, Bucharest, 1956-58 (Chargé d'Affaires, 1956, 1957 and 1958); Head of Communications Dept, FO, 1958-62; Political Adviser to Hong Kong Government, 1962-65; Head of Scientific Relations Dept, FO, 1966-68; Minister, Lagos, 1968-70; Ambassador at Rangoon, 1970-74. *Recreations:* travel, walking, gardening. *Address:* Cherry Tree Cottage, Shappen Hill, Burley, Hants. *Club:* United Oxford & Cambridge University.

WILLAN, Prof. Thomas Stuart, MA, BLitt, DPhil; Professor of Economic History, University of Manchester, 1961-73, now Emeritus; *b* 3 Jan. 1910; 3rd *s* of Matthew Willan and Jane (*née* Stuart); unmarried. *Educ:* Queen Elizabeth's Sch., Kirkby Lonsdale; The Queen's Coll., Oxford. Asst Lecturer, School of Economics and Commerce, Dundee, 1934-35; University of Manchester: Asst Lecturer in History, 1935-45; Lecturer in History, 1945-47;

Senior Lecturer in History, 1947–49; Reader in History, 1949–61. *Publications:* River Navigation in England, 1600–1750, 1936; The English Coasting Trade, 1600–1750, 1938; (ed with E. W. Crossley) Three Seventeenth-century Yorkshire Surveys, 1941; The Navigation of the Great Ouse between St Ives and Bedford in the Seventeenth Century, 1946; The Navigation of the River Weaver in the Eighteenth Century, 1951; The Muscovy Merchants of 1555, 1953; The Early History of the Russia Company, 1553–1603, 1956; Studies in Elizabethan Foreign Trade, 1959; (ed) A Tudor Book of Rates, 1962; The Early History of the Don Navigation, 1965; An Eighteenth-Century Shopkeeper, Abraham Dent of Kirkby Stephen, 1970; The Inland Trade, 1976; Elizabethan Manchester, 1980; articles in English Historical Review, Economic History Review, etc. *Address:* 3 Raynham Avenue, Didsbury, Manchester M20 0BW. *T:* 061-445 4771. *Club:* Penn.

WILLASEY-WILSEY, Maj.-Gen. Anthony Patrick, CB 1970; MBE 1948; MC 1956; Major-General, Commando Forces Royal Marines, Plymouth, 1968–70, retired; *b* 20 Sept. 1920; *e s* of late Colonel F. H. Willasey-Wilsey, MC, 8th Gurkha Rifles; *m* 1948, Dorothy, *y d* of Dr R. B. M. Yates, Market Drayton, Salop; two *s. Educ:* Repton Sch. Commissioned in RM, Jan. 1939; HMS Rodney, 1940–42; HMS Howe, 1943; 47 Commando, Belgium and Holland, 1944–45. Instructor, RMA, Sandhurst, 1948–50; 40 Commando, Malayan Emergency, 1951–52 (despatches); Staff Coll., Camberley, 1954; 40 Commando, Cyprus and Suez, 1956–58; DAA and QMG, HQ 3 Commando Bde, ME, 1958; jssc, 1961; CO, 43 Commando, 1962–63; G 1 Plans, MoD, 1964–65; Comdr, 3 Commando Bde, Far East, 1965–66. IDC, 1967. FBIM. *Address:* The Dun Cow Cottage, Market Drayton, Salop. *T:* Market Drayton 2360. *Club:* Army and Navy.

WILLATT, Sir Hugh, Kt 1972; Secretary General of the Arts Council of Great Britain, 1968–75 (Member, 1958–68); *b* 25 April 1909; *m* 1945, Evelyn Gibbs, ARE, ARCA, (Rome Scholar); no *c. Educ:* Repton; Pembroke Coll., Oxford (MA). Admitted a Solicitor, 1934; Partner, Hunt, Dickins and Willatt, Nottingham, and later Partner in Lewis, Silkin & Partners, Westminster. Served War of 1939–45, in RAF. Member BBC Midland Regional Adv. Council, 1953–58; Member Arts Council Drama Panel, 1955–68 (Chairman, 1960–68); (at various times) Member Board: National Theatre; Mercury Trust Ltd (Ballet Rambert); Nottingham Theatre Trust Ltd; Council, Royal Court Theatre (English Stage Co.), 1976–; Chairman: Nat. Opera Studio; Riverside Studios; Cttee of Visiting Arts Unit. FRSA 1974. Hon. MA, University of Nottingham. *Address:* 4 St Peter's Wharf, Hammersmith Terrace, W6. *Club:* Garrick.

WILLCOCK, Kenneth Milner, QC 1972; **His Honour Judge Willcock;** a Circuit Judge, since 1972. MA; BCL. Called to Bar, Inner Temple, 1950. Dep. Chm., Somerset QS, 1969–71; a Recorder of the Crown Court, 1972. *Address:* Queen Elizabeth Building, Temple, EC4Y 9BS.

WILLCOCK, Prof. Malcolm Maurice; Professor of Latin, University College London, since 1980; *b* 1 Oct. 1925; *s* of late Dr Maurice Excel Willcock and Evelyn Clarice Willcock (*née* Brooks); *m* 1957, Sheena Gourlay; four *d. Educ:* Fettes Coll.; Pembroke Coll., Cambridge (MA). Served Royal Air Force, 1944–47. Research Fellow, Pembroke Coll., Cambridge, 1951–52; Sidney Sussex College: Fellow, 1952–65; Sen. Tutor, 1962–65; University of Lancaster: first Professor of Classics, 1965–79; Principal, Bowland Coll., 1966–79; Pro-Vice-Chancellor, 1975–79. *Publications:* ed, Plautus Casina, 1976; Companion to the Iliad, 1976; ed, Iliad of Homer, Books I-XII, 1978; articles and reviews in classical jls. *Recreations:* squash, bridge. *Address:* 1 Lancaster Avenue, SE27. *T:* 01-761 5615.

WILLCOCKS, Sir David (Valentine), Kt 1977; CBE 1971; MC 1944; MA, MusB (Cantab), FRCO, FRCM, FRNCM, FRSAMD, FRSCM; Director, Royal College of Music, since 1974; Musical Director of the Bach Choir since 1960; General Editor, OUP Church Music, since 1961; *b* 30 Dec. 1919; *s* of late T. H. Willcocks; *m* 1947, Rachel Gordon, *d* of late Rev. A. C. Blyth, Fellow of Selwyn Coll., Cambridge; two *s* two *d. Educ:* Clifton Coll.; King's Coll., Cambridge. Chorister, Westminster Abbey, 1929–33; Scholar, Clifton Coll., 1934–38; FRCO, 1938; Scholar at College of St Nicolas (RSCM), 1938–39; Organ Scholar, King's Coll., Cambridge, 1939–40; Open Foundation Scholarship, King's Coll., Cambridge, 1940; Stewart of Rannoch Scholarship, 1940. Served War of 1939–45, 5th Bn DCLI, 1940–45. Organ Scholar, King's Coll., Cambridge, 1945–47; Fellow of King's Coll., Cambridge, 1947–51, Hon. Fellow, 1979; Organist of Salisbury Cathedral, 1947–50; Master of the Choristers and Organist, Worcester Cathedral, 1950–57; Fellow and Organist, King's Coll., Cambridge, 1957–73; Univ. Lectr in Music, Cambridge Univ., 1957–74; Univ. Organist, Cambridge Univ., 1958–74. Conductor: Cambridge Philharmonic Soc., 1947; City of Birmingham Choir, 1950–57; Bradford Festival Choral Soc., 1957–74; Cambridge Univ. Musical Soc., 1958–73. President: RCO, 1966–68; ISM, 1978–79; Old Cliftonian Soc., 1979–81; Nat. Fedn of Music Socs, 1980–. Fellow, St Michael's Coll., Tenbury; Hon. RAM; Hon. FTCL; Hon. GSM 1980; Hon. Fellow, Royal Canadian College of Organists, 1967. Hon. MA Bradford, 1973; Hon. DMus: Exeter, 1976; Leicester, 1977; Westminster Choir Coll., Princeton, 1980; Bristol, 1981; Hon. DLitt Sussex, 1982. *Recreation:* golf. *Address:* 2 Ennismore Gardens, SW7. *Clubs:* Athenæum, Arts.

WILLCOX, James Henry; Clerk of Private Bills, Examiner of Petitions for Private Bills and Taxing Officer, House of Commons, since 1977; *b* 31 March 1923; *s* of George Henry and Annie Elizabeth Willcox; *m* 1950, Winsome

Rosemarie Adèle Dallas Ross; one *s* one *d. Educ:* St George's Coll., Weybridge; St John's Coll., Oxford (Schol.; MA). Served RNVR, 1942–45. Assistant Clerk, House of Commons, 1947; Sen. Clerk, 1951; Clerk of Standing Committees, 1975–76; Clerk of Overseas Office, 1976–77. *Recreations:* walking, gardening, tennis. *Address:* Ridgemead, Shrubbs Hill Lane, Sunningdale, Berks SL5 0LD. *T:* Ascot 21144. *Club:* Garrick.

WILLEBRANDS, His Eminence Cardinal Johannes Gerardus Maria; President, Vatican Secretariat for Promoting Christian Unity, since 1969; Archbishop of Utrecht and Primate of Holland, since 1975; *b* Netherlands, 4 Sept. 1909. *Educ:* Warmond Seminary, Holland; Angelicum, Rome (Dr Phil.). Priest, 1934; Chaplain, Begijnhof Church, Amsterdam, 1937–40; Prof. of Philosophy, Warmond, 1940; Director, 1945; Pres., St Willibrord Assoc., 1946; organised Catholic Conf. on Ecumenical Questions, 1951; Sec., Vatican Secretariat for Promoting Christian Unity, 1960; Titular Bishop of Mauriana, 1964; Cardinal, 1969; Cardinal with the Title of St Sebastian, Martyr, 1975. Hon. Dr of Letters: Notre Dame Univ.; St Louis Univ.; St Olaf Coll., USA; St Thomas' Coll., St Paul's, Minn, 1979; Assumption Coll., Worcester, Mass, 1980; Hon. Dr of Theology: Catholic Univ. of Louvain; Leningrad Theological Acad. *Publications:* Oecuménisme et Problèmes Actuels; reports on the ecumenical situation and articles on inter-church relationships. *Address:* Via dell'Erba 1, Rome 00193, Italy; Maliebaan 40, PO Box 14019, 3508 SB Utrecht, Netherlands.

WILLESDEN, Area Bishop of; Rt. Rev. (Geoffrey) Hewlett Thompson; appointed Bishop Suffragan of Willesden, 1974; *b* 14 Aug. 1929; *o s* of Lt-Col R. R. Thompson, MC, RAMC; *m* 1954, Elisabeth Joy Fausitt, *d* of Col G. F. Taylor, MBE and late Dr Frances Taylor; two *s* two *d. Educ:* Aldenham Sch.; Trinity Hall, Cambridge (MA); Cuddesdon Theol College. 2nd Lieut, Queen's Own Royal West Kent Regt, 1948–49 (Nat. Service). Ordained 1954. Curate, St Matthew, Northampton, 1954; Vicar: St Augustine, Wisbech, 1959; St Saviour, Folkestone, 1966. Chm., Community and Race Relations Unit, BCC, 1980– (Vice-Chm., 1976–80). *Recreations:* fell walking, reading, gardening, music. *Address:* 173 Willesden Lane, NW6 7YN. *T:* 01-451 0189.

WILLESEE, Hon. Donald Robert; Member of Senate for Western Australia, 1949–75; *b* 14 April 1916; *m*; four *s* two *d. Educ:* Carnarvon, Western Australia. Special Minister of State, Minister assisting Prime Minister, Minister assisting Minister for Foreign Affairs and Vice-Pres. of Exec. Council, 1972–73; Minister for Foreign Affairs, 1973–75; Leader of Opposition in the Senate, 1966–67; Deputy Leader of Opposition in Senate, 1969–72; Deputy Leader of Govt in Senate, 1972. *Recreation:* swimming. *Address:* 5 Walton Place, Quinns Rock, WA 6030, Australia.

WILLETT, Archibald Anthony; Fellow and Bursar, St Antony's College, Oxford, since 1977; *b* 27 Jan. 1924; *s* of Reginald Beckett Willett and Mabel Alice (*née* Plaister); *m* 1948, Doris Marjorie Peat; one *s* one *d. Educ:* Oswestry High Sch.; Southall Grammar School. Lloyds Bank Ltd, 1940; Great Western Railway Co., 1941–42 and 1947–48; RAF (Signals Branch), 1942–47; Cable & Wireless Ltd, 1948–77; Dir, 1967–77; Dep. Man. Dir, 1971–72; Man. Dir, 1973–77. MA Oxon 1977; FCIS 1963; CBIM (FBIM 1975). *Recreations:* home and garden, walking. *Address:* St Antony's College, Oxford. *T:* Oxford 59651. *Clubs:* Royal Automobile; Exiles' (Twickenham).

WILLETT, Prof. Frank, FRSE 1979; Director and Titular Professor, Hunterian Museum and Art Gallery, Glasgow, since 1976; *b* 18 Aug. 1925; *s* of Thomas Willett and Frances (*née* Latham); *m* 1950, Mary Constance Hewitt; one *s* three *d. Educ:* Bolton Municipal Secondary Sch.; University Coll., Oxford. MA (Oxon); Dip. Anthropology (Oxon). War damage clerk, Inland Revenue, 1940; RAF Linguist, Japanese, 1943–44. Keeper, Dept of Ethnology and Gen. Archaeology, Manchester Museum, 1950–58; Hon. Surveyor of Antiquities, Nigerian Federal Govt, 1956–57, 1958; Archaeologist and Curator, Mus. of Ife Antiquities, Nigerian Fed. Govt, 1958–63; Supply Teacher, Bolton Educn Cttee, 1963–64; Leverhulme Research Fellow, 1964; Research Fellow, Nuffield Coll., Oxford, 1964–66; Prof. of Art History, African and Interdisciplinary Studies, Northwestern Univ., Evanston, Ill, USA, 1966–76; Vis. Fellow, Clare Hall, Cambridge, 1970–71. Hon. Corresp. Member, Manchester Literary and Philosophical Soc., 1958–. *Publications:* Ife in the History of West African Sculpture, 1967, rev. edn, Ife: une Civilisation Africaine, 1971; African Art: An Introduction, 1971, rev. 1977; (with Ekpo Eyo) Treasures of Ancient Nigeria, 1980; articles in Encyc. Britannica, Man, Jl of Afr. Hist., Afr. Arts, Africa, Jl of Nigerian Historical Soc., Odu, SA Archaeol Bull., Archæometry; many conf. reports and chapters in several books. *Recreation:* relaxing. *Address:* Hunterian Museum, University of Glasgow, Glasgow G12 8QQ. *T:* 041-339 8855 (ext. 285). *Club:* Royal Commonwealth.

WILLETT, Prof. Frederick John, DSC 1944; Vice-Chancellor, Griffith University, Queensland, since 1972; *b* 26 Feb. 1922; *s* of E. Willett; *m* 1949, Jane Cunningham Westwater; one *s* two *d. Educ:* Fitzwilliam House, Cambridge. MA (Cantab), MBA (Melb.). Observer, Fleet Air Arm, Atlantic, Mediterranean, Indian and Pacific theatres, 1939–46; served with British Naval Liaison Mission, Washington, 1942–43. Asst Director of Research in Industrial Management, Univ. of Cambridge, 1957–62; Sidney Myer Prof. of Commerce and Business Administration, Univ. of Melbourne, 1962–72, now Emeritus. Pro Vice-Chancellor, University of Melbourne, 1966–72. Mem., Aust.-China Council, 1979–82. Hon. LLD Melbourne 1973; FAIM. *Publications:* many articles and papers. *Address:* Griffith University, Nathan, Queensland 4111, Australia. *T:* Brisbane 275 7111. *Clubs:* Melbourne (Melbourne); Queensland (Brisbane).

WILLETT, Guy William; a Recorder of the Crown Court, 1971–76; *b* 10 June 1913; *y s* of late William and late Florence Mary Anne Willett; *m* 1945, Elizabeth Evelyn Joan Radford; one *s* two *d. Educ:* Malvern; Gonville and Caius Coll., Cambridge (BA). Called to Bar, 1937; Western Circuit, 1938; Head of Chambers, Francis Taylor Building, Temple, 1961–77. Chm., Halstead Sch., 1958–74. *Recreations:* cricket, sailing, golf. *Address:* Sundial House, 24A High Street, Alderney, CI. *T:* Alderney 2911. *Clubs:* Westfield and District Cricket (Pres. 1946–74), Admiralty Ferry Crew Assoc., Alderney Golf, Alderney Society, Bar Yacht, Bar Golf.

WILLETTS, Bernard Frederick, PhD; CEng, FIMechE, FIProdE; Deputy Chief Executive, Dubai Aluminium Company Ltd, since 1981; Director: Liverpool Daily Post and Echo, since 1976; Massey-Ferguson (Holdings) Ltd, since 1980; Telephone Rentals Ltd, since 1981; *b* 24 March 1927; *s* of James Frederick Willetts and Effie Hurst; *m* 1952, Norah Elizabeth Law; two *s. Educ:* Birmingham Central Grammar Sch.; Birmingham Univ. (BSc); Durham Univ. (MSc, PhD). Section Leader, Vickers-Armstrong (Engineers) Ltd, 1954–58; Massey-Ferguson (UK) Ltd: Chief Engineer, 1959; Director, Engineering, 1962; Director, Manufacturing, 1965; Dep. Managing Director, 1967; Plessey Co. Ltd: Group Managing Director, Telecommunications, 1968; Main Board Director, 1969; Dep. Chief Exec., 1975–78; Vickers Ltd: Asst Managing Director, 1978; Man. Dir, 1980. Dir (non-exec.), MEL, 1982–. Vice-Pres., Instn of Production Engineers, 1979–82. *Recreations:* gardening, squash, stamp collecting. *Address:* Suna Court, Pearson Road, Sonning-on-Thames, Berkshire. *T:* Reading 695050. *Clubs:* Lansdowne; Parkstone Yacht.

WILLEY, Rt. Hon. Frederick Thomas, PC 1964; MP (Lab) Sunderland North since 1950 (Sunderland, 1945–50); Vice-President, Save the Children Fund; Barrister; *b* 1910; *s* of late Frederick and Mary Willey; *m* 1939, Eleanor, *d* of late William and Elizabeth Snowdon; two *s* one *d. Educ:* Johnston Sch.; St John's Coll., Cambridge Univ. (Full blue Soccer; 1st Class Hons Law; Blackstone Prizeman, Harmsworth Studentship, McMahon Studentship, etc.). Called to Bar, Middle Temple, 1936. PPS to Rt Hon. J. Chuter Ede, 1946–50; Chm., Select Cttee on Estimates and Mem. Select Cttees on Statutory Instruments and Public Accounts until 1950; Parly Sec. to Ministry of Food, 1950–51; Dir, North-Eastern Trading Estates Ltd, until 1950; River Wear Commr until 1950; Former Mem., Consultative Assembly of the Council of Europe and Assembly of WEU; Minister of Land and Natural Resources, 1964–67; Minister of State, Ministry of Housing and Local Government, 1967; Member, Select Committee on: Privileges; Members' Interests (former Chm.); former Chairman, Select Committee on: Race Relations and Immigration; Selection; Abortion (Amendment) Bill; Parly and Scientific Cttee. Chm., PLP, 1979–81. Vice-Pres., Youth Hostels Trust of England and Wales. Hon. Fellow, Sunderland Polytechnic. *Publications:* Plan for Shipbuilding, 1956; Education, Today and Tomorrow, 1964; An Enquiry into Teacher Training, 1971; The Honourable Member, 1974; articles in various periodicals, legal and political. *Address:* 11 North Square, NW11.

WILLIAM-POWLETT, Vice-Admiral Sir Peveril (Barton Reibey Wallop), KCB 1953 (CB 1949); KCMG 1959; CBE 1945; DSO 1942; DL; RN retired; Governor of Southern Rhodesia, Nov. 1954–Dec. 1959; Vice-Chairman, Appledore Shipbuilders Ltd, 1974 (Chairman 1962–74); *b* 5 March 1898; 2nd *s* of Major Barton William-Powlett; *m* 1923, Helen Constance (*d* 1965), *d* of James Forbes Crombie, Aberdeen; three *d* ; *m* 1966, Mrs Barbara Patience William-Powlett, *d* of Sir Bernard Greenwell, 2nd Bt, MBE, and widow of Captain Newton William-Powlett, RN. *Educ:* Cordwalles Sch.; Osborne and Dartmouth. Midshipman, 1914; served European War, 1914–18, Gallipoli, Jutland; Lieut, 1918; specialised in signals; Commander 1931; Captain, 1938; commanded HMS Frobisher, 1938–39; Director of Manning, 1939–40; comd HMS Fiji, 1941 (DSO); Chief of Staff Force 'H', 1941–42; comd HMS Newcastle, 1942–44; Captain of Fleet, Home Fleet, 1944–45 (CBE); Captain in command of Royal Naval Coll., Dartmouth, 1946–48; Naval Secretary to First Lord of the Admiralty, 1948–50; Flag Officer (destroyers), Mediterranean Fleet, 1950–51; Commander-in-Chief, South Atlantic, 1952–54; retired, 1954; Rear-Admiral, 1948; Vice-Admiral, 1950. High Sheriff 1972, DL 1973, Devon. KStJ. *Recreations:* Rugby (played for England, 1922); golf, shooting, and fishing. *Address:* Cadhay, Ottery St Mary, Devon. *T:* Ottery St Mary 2432. *Clubs:* Naval and Military, Chelsea Arts. *See also Sir Michael Colman, Bt.*

WILLIAMS; *see* Garnons Williams.

WILLIAMS; *see* Rees-Williams, family name of Baron Ogmore.

WILLIAMS, Alan Frederick, PhD; Director, Medical Research Council Cellular Immunology Unit, since 1977; *b* 25 May 1945; *s* of Walter Alan and Mary Elizabeth Williams; *m* 1967, Rosalind Margaret Wright; one *s* one *d. Educ:* Box Hill High Sch., Melbourne; Melbourne Univ. (BAgrSc); Adelaide Univ. (PhD Biochem). Departmental Demonstrator, Biochemistry Dept, Oxford Univ., 1970–72; Jun. Research Fellow, Linacre Coll., Oxford, 1970–72; Staff Member, MRC Immunochemistry Unit, Oxford, 1972–77. *Publications:* contribs to biochemistry and immunology scientific jls.

Recreation: gardening. *Address:* Sir William Dunn School of Pathology, University of Oxford, Oxford OX1 3RE. *T:* Oxford 57321.

WILLIAMS, Prof. Alan Harold; Professor in the Department of Economics, University of York, since 1968; Member, National Water Council, since 1980; *b* 9 June 1927; *s* of Harold George Williams and Gladys May Williams (*née* Clark); *m* 1953, June Frances Porter; two *s* one *d. Educ:* King Edward's, Birmingham; Univ. of Birmingham (BCom). Lecturer, Exeter Univ., 1954–63; Sen. Lectr and Reader, Univ. of York, 1964–68. Visiting Lecturer: MIT, 1957–58; Princeton, 1963–64; Director of Economic Studies, HM Treasury Centre for Administrative Studies, 1966–68. Member: Yorkshire Water Authority, 1973–76; DHSS Chief Scientists Research Cttee, 1973–78; Royal Commission on the NHS, 1976–78; various SSRC Cttees and Panels, 1973–. Hon. DPhil Lund, 1977. *Publications:* Public Finance and Budgetary Policy, 1963; (with Robert Anderson) Efficiency in the Social Services, 1975; (with Robert Sugden) Principles of Practical Cost-Benefit Analysis, 1978; articles in Economica, Jl of Political Econ., Jl of Public Econs, Nat. Tax Jl, and elsewhere; numerous conf. papers on various aspects of public expenditure appraisal. *Recreations:* music, walking, teasing. *Address:* 8 Foxthorn Paddock, York YO1 5HJ. *T:* York 412249.

WILLIAMS, Rt. Hon. Alan John, PC 1977; MP (Lab) Swansea West since 1964; *b* 14 Oct. 1930; *m* 1957, Mary Patricia Rees, Blackwood, Mon; two *s* one *d. Educ:* Cardiff High Sch.; Cardiff College of Technology; University College, Oxford. BSc (London); BA (Oxon). Lecturer in economics, Welsh College of Advanced Technology; Free-lance Journalist. Joined Labour Party, 1950. Member: Association of Teachers at Technical Institutes, 1958–; Fabian Society; Co-operative Party; National Union of Students delegation to Russia, 1954. Contested (Lab) Poole, 1959. PPS to Postmaster General, 1966–67; Parly Under-Sec., DEA, 1967–69; Parly Sec., Min. of Technology, 1969–70; Opposition Spokesman on Consumer Protection, Small Businesses, Minerals, 1970–74; Minister of State: Dept of Prices and Consumer Protection, 1974–76; DoI, 1976–79; Opposition Spokesman on Wales, 1979–80; Shadow Minister for CS, 1980–. Chairman, Welsh PLP, 1966–67; Delegate, Council of Europe and WEU, 1966–67; Mem. Public Accts Cttee, 1966–67; Jt Chm., All-Party Minerals Cttee, 1979–. *Address:* House of Commons, SW1; Hill View, 96 Plunch Lane, Limeslade, Swansea. *Club:* Clyne Golf.

WILLIAMS, Alan Lee, OBE 1973; Director-General, English-Speaking Union, since 1979; *b* 29 Nov. 1930. *Educ:* Roan Sch., Greenwich; Ruskin Coll., Oxford. Freeman of Company of Watermen and Lightermen, 1945–51; National Service, RAF, 1951–53; Oxford, 1954–56; National Youth Officer, Labour Party, 1956–62; Dir, British Atlantic Cttee, 1972–74. MP (Lab) Hornchurch, 1966–70, Havering, Hornchurch, Feb. 1974–1979; PPS to Sec. of State for Defence, 1969–70, 1976; PPS to Sec. of State for NI, 1976–78. Chm., Parly Lab. Party Defence Cttee, 1976–79; Member: FO Adv. Cttee on Disarmament and Arms Control, 1975–79; Adv. Council of European Discussion Centre, Wilton Park, 1975–; Adv. Council on Public Records, 1977–; Chm., Delegn to 4th Cttee of UN, NY, 1966; Jt Editor, Labour Trades Union Press Service, 1975; Chairman: All Party Parly River Thames Group, 1974–79; Transport on Water Assoc.; Deputy Director, European Movement, 1970–71, Treasurer, 1972–79. Joined SDP, 1981. Member: Council, RUSI; Trilateral Commn, 1976; Council, Sea Cadet Assoc., 1976. Freeman, City of London. *Publications:* Radical Essays, 1966; Europe or the Open Sea?, 1971; Crisis in European Defence, 1973; UN Assoc. pamphlet, UN and Warsaw and Nato Pacts; Fabian Soc. pamphlet on East/West Détente. *Recreations:* reading, history and novels, walking, camping. *Address:* 6 North Several, Blackheath, SE3 0QR. *T:* 01-852 3188. *Clubs:* Reform, Travellers'.

WILLIAMS, (Albert) Clifford, BEM 1957; JP; Member: Welsh National Water Development Authority; Sports Council for Wales, 1972–75 (Vice-Chairman, Centre Committee; Chairman, Water Recreation Committee); *b* 28 June 1905; British; *s* of Daniel Williams, Blaina, Mon; *m* 1929, Beatrice Anne, *d* of Charles Garbett; one *d. Educ:* Primary Sch., Blaina, Mon. Trade Union Official, 1935–50. Mem. 21 years, Chm. 10 years, Usk Rivers Authority; Vice-Pres., former Assoc. of River Authorities. Administrator of Voluntary Hospitals, 40 years until 1969; Vice-Chm., N Monmouthshire HMC. County Councillor, Monmouthshire; Alderman, 1964–74; MP (Lab) Abertillery, April 1965–1970. *Recreations:* watching sports, Rugby football. *Address:* Brodawel, Abertillery Road, Blaina, Gwent NP3 3DZ. *T:* Blaina 379.

WILLIAMS, (Albert) Trevor; management scientist; *b* 7 April 1938; *s* of Ben and Minnie Williams; *m* 1st, 1970, Mary Lynn Lyster; three *s* ; 2nd, 1978, Deborah Sarah Fraser Duncan (*née* Milne); one *s. Educ:* King George V Sch., Southport; Queens' Coll., Cambridge (MA); Cranfield Institute of Technology (MSc). Rotary Foundation Fellow, Univ. of Ghana, 1961–62; Business Operations Research Ltd: Director, 1965–68; various academic appointments, 1968–78, including: Sen. Lectr and Vis. Professor, Graduate School of Business, Cape Town Univ.; Sen. Research Fellow, Sussex Univ.; Vis. Associate Prof., Wisconsin Univ.; Vis. Prof., INSEAD. Dir, Novy Eddison and Partners, 1971–74; Dep.-Dir for Futures Research, Univ. of Stellenbosch, 1974–78; Dep. Chief Scientific Officer, Price Commission, 1978–79; Advisor on Technology Projects, Scottish Development Agency, 1979; Dir, Henley Centre for Forecasting, 1980–81. *Publication:* A Guide to Futures Studies, 1976. *Recreations:* tennis, reading. *Address:* 2 Brookfield Park, NW5 1ER. *T:* 01-485 4265. *Club:* Institute of Directors.

WILLIAMS, Alexander, FInstP, FIQA; Under Secretary, Research and Technology Policy Division, Department of Industry, since 1981; *b* 30 March 1931; *s* of Henry and Dorothy Williams; *m* 1957, Beryl Wynne Williams (*née* Williams); one *s*. *Educ*: Grove Park Grammar Sch., Wrexham; University College of North Wales, Bangor (BSc). National Service, REME, 1953-55; Monsanto Chemicals, 1955-56; Southern Instruments, Camberley, 1956-59; National Physical Laboratory: Div. of Radiation Science, 1959-78; Head, Div. of Mechanical and Optical Metrology, 1978-81. *Publications*: A Code of Practice for the Detailed Statement of Accuracy (with P. J. Campion and J. E. Burns), 1973; numerous papers on measurements of radio-activity etc, to Internat. Jl of Applied Radiation Isotopes, Nucl. Instr. and Meth., etc. *Recreations*: bell-ringing, music, opera, walking. *Address*: c/o Department of Industry, Bressenden Place, SW1E 5DT.

WILLIAMS, Sir Alexander (Thomas), KCMG 1958 (CMG 1950); MBE 1936; *b* 13 July 1903; *s* of late John Williams and Mary Williams (*née* Kennedy); *m* 1931, Madeline O'Connor; two *s*. *Educ*: Bishop Foy Sch., Waterford; Trinity Coll., Dublin; Downing Coll., Cambridge. BA (Dublin). Cadet, Northern Rhodesia, 1928; District Officer, 1930; Assistant Chief Secretary, 1944; Administrative Secretary, 1947-52; Chief Secretary and Governor's Deputy, 1952-57; Governor and Commander-in-Chief of the Leeward Islands, 1957-59. Hon. LLD Dublin. KStJ 1958. *Recreation*: golf. *Address*: West Dormers, Cowes, Isle of Wight PO31 8BP. *T*: Cowes 293657. *Club*: Travellers'.

WILLIAMS, Alfred Martyn, CBE 1957; DSC; Commander RN retired; *b* 14 May 1897; *s* of J. C. Williams of Caerhays Castle, Cornwall; *m* 1920, Audrey Hester (*d* 1943), 2nd *d* of C. Coltman Rogers, Stanage Park, Radnorshire; two *s* one *d*; *m* 1945, Dorothea Veronica, widow of Major F. F. Robins and *yr d* of Colonel W. H. Carver; one *s*. *Educ*: RN Colleges, Osborne and Dartmouth. MP (U) North Cornwall, 1924-29; High Sheriff of Cornwall, 1938; DL Cornwall, 1956. *Address*: The Mount, Blackdown, Mary Tavy, Tavistock, Devon PL19 9QB. *Club*: Brooks's.
See also F. J. Williams.

WILLIAMS, Dr Alwyn, FRS 1967; FRSE, MRIA, FGS, PhD (Wales); Principal and Vice-Chancellor of University of Glasgow, since 1976; *b* 8 June 1921; *s* of D. D. and E. M. Williams; *m* 1949, E. Joan Bevan; one *s* one *d*. *Educ*: Aberdare Boys' Grammar Sch.; University College of Wales, Aberystwyth. Fellow, Univ. of Wales, 1946-48. Harkness Fund Fellow at US National Museum, Washington, DC, 1948-50; Lecturer in Geology in University of Glasgow, 1950-54; Prof. of Geology, 1954-74, Pro-Vice-Chancellor, 1967-74, Queen's Univ. of Belfast; Lapworth Prof. of Geology, and Head of Dept, Univ. of Birmingham, 1974-76. Pres., Palaeontological Assoc., 1968-70. Trustee, British Museum (Nat. History), 1971-79, Chm. of Trustees, 1974-79. Member: Equip. and Phys. Sci. sub-cttee, UGC, 1974-76; NERC, 1974-76; Adv. Council, British Library, 1975-77; Chm., Cttee on Nat. Museums and Galls in Scotland, 1979-81; Vice-Chm., Cttee of Vice-Chancellors and Principals, 1979-81. Hon. Fellow, Geol Soc. of America, 1970-; For. Mem., Polish Academies of Science. Hon. Associate, BM (Nat. Hist.), 1981-; Hon. FRCPS; Hon. DSc: Wales, 1974; Belfast, 1975; Edinburgh, 1979; Hon. LLD Strathclyde, 1982. Bigsby Medal, 1961, Murchison Medal, 1973, Geol Soc.; Clough Medal, Edin. Geol. Soc., 1976. *Publications*: contrib. to Trans Royal Soc., Jl Geological Society; Geological Magazine; Washington Acad. of Sciences; Geological Society of America; Palaeontology; Journal of Paleontology, etc. *Address*: The Principal's Lodging, 12 The University, Glasgow G12 8QG. *T*: 041-339 0383.

WILLIAMS, Anthony James, CMG 1971; HM Diplomatic Service; Leader of UK Delegation to Madrid Conference on Security and Cooperation in Europe Review Meeting, with rank of Ambassador, since 1982; *b* 28 May 1923; *s* of late Bernard Warren Williams, FRCS, and of Hon. Muriel B. Buckley; *m* 1955, Hedwig Gabrielle, Gräfin Neipperg; two *s* two *d*. *Educ*: Oundle; Trinity Coll., Oxford. Entered Foreign Service, 1945; served in: Prague; Montevideo; Cairo; UK Permanent Mission to UN, New York; Buenos Aires; UK Permanent Mission to 18 Nation Disarmament Conf., Western, United Nations and South East Asian Depts of Foreign Office. Counsellor, Head of Chancery, Moscow, 1965-67; IDC, 1968; Counsellor (Political), Washington, 1969-70; Ambassador at Phnom Penh, 1970-73; Minister, Rome, 1973-76; Ambassador to Libyan Arab Jamahariya, 1977-79, to Argentina, 1980-82. *Address*: c/o Foreign and Commonwealth Office, SW1. *Clubs*: Beefsteak, United Oxford & Cambridge University.

WILLIAMS, Arthur Vivian, CBE 1969; General Manager and Solicitor, Peterlee (New Town) Development Corporation, 1948-74, and of Aycliffe (New Town) Development Corporation, 1954-74; *b* 2 Jan. 1909; *s* of N. T. and Gwendolen Williams; *m* 1937, Charlotte Moyra, *d* of Dr E. H. M. Milligan; three *s* one *d*. *Educ*: William Hulme's Grammar Sch., Manchester; Jesus Coll., Oxford. BA (Oxon), Final Honour Sch. of Mod. Hist. Admitted as Solicitor, 1936; Dep. Town Clerk of Finchley, 1938-41; Town Clerk of Bilston, 1941-46; Town Clerk and Clerk of the Peace, Dudley, 1946-48. *Address*: Monks, Lindsey, Ipswich. *T*: Boxford 210039.

WILLIAMS, Rev. Austen; *see* Williams, Rev. S. A.

WILLIAMS, Bernard Arthur Owen, FBA 1971; Provost of King's College, Cambridge, since 1979; *b* 21 Sept. 1929; *s* of late O. P. D. Williams, OBE and of H. A. Williams; *m* 1955, Shirley Vivienne Teresa Brittain Catlin (*see*

Mrs S. V. T. B. Williams) (marr. diss. 1974); one *d*; *m* 1974, Patricia Law Skinner; two *s*. *Educ*: Chigwell Sch., Essex; Balliol Coll., Oxford. BA (Oxon) 1951; MA 1954. Fellow of All Souls Coll., Oxford, 1951-54; RAF (Gen. Duties Br.), 1951-53; Fellow of New Coll., Oxford, 1954-59; Vis. Lectr, Univ. Coll. of Ghana, 1958-59; Lectr in Philosophy, Univ. Coll., London, 1959-64; Professor of Philosophy, Bedford College, London, 1964-67; Knightbridge Prof. of Philosophy, Cambridge, and Fellow of King's Coll., Cambridge, 1967-79. Visiting Professor: Princeton Univ., USA, 1963; Harvard Univ., 1973; Vis. Fellow, Inst. of Advanced Studies, ANU, 1969; Sen. Vis. Fellow, Princeton, 1978. Mem., Institut International de Philosophie. Member: Public Schools Commn, 1965-70; Royal Commn on Gambling, 1976-78; Chm., Cttee on Obscenity and Film Censorship, 1977-79. Dir, English Nat. Opera (formerly Sadler's Wells Opera), 1968-. Hon. LittD Dublin, 1981. *Publications*: (ed with A. C. Montefiore) British Analytical Philosophy, 1966; Morality, 1972; Problems of the Self, 1973; A Critique of Utilitarianism, 1973; Descartes: The Project of Pure Enquiry, 1978; Moral Luck, 1981; (ed with A. K. Sen) Utilitarianism and Beyond, 1982; articles in philosophical jls, etc. *Recreation*: music, particularly opera. *Address*: Provost's Lodge, King's College, Cambridge CB2 1ST; Kent House, Swaffham Prior, Cambs. *T*: Newmarket 741443.

WILLIAMS, Betty; *see* Williams, Elizabeth.

WILLIAMS, Sir Brandon M. R.; *see* Rhys Williams.

WILLIAMS, Prof. Sir Bruce (Rodda), KBE 1980; Vice-Chancellor and Principal of the University of Sydney, 1967-81; Director, Technical Change Centre, since 1981; *b* 10 January 1919; *s* of late Reverend W. J. Williams; *m* 1942, Roma Olive Hotten; five *d*. *Educ*: Wesley College; Queen's College, University of Melbourne (BA 1939). MA Adelaide 1942; MA(Econ) Manchester, 1963. FASSA 1968. Lecturer in Economics, University of Adelaide, 1939-46 and at Queen's University of Belfast, 1946-50; Professor of Economics, University College of North Staffordshire, 1950-59; Robert Otley Prof., 1959-63, and Stanley Jevons Prof., 1963-67, Univ. of Manchester. Secretary and Joint Director of Research, Science and Industry Committee, 1952-59. Member, National Board for Prices and Incomes, 1966-67; Econ. Adviser to Minister of Technology, 1966-67; Member: Central Advisory Council on Science and Technology, 1967; Reserve Bank Board, 1969-81; Chairman: NSW State Cancer Council, 1967-81; Australian Vice Chancellors Cttee, 1972-74; Aust. Govt Cttee of Inquiry into Educn and Trng, 1976-79; Dep. Chm., Paramatta Hosps Bd, 1979-81. Editor, The Sociological Review, 1953-59, and The Manchester Sch., 1959-67. President Economics Section of British Assoc., 1964. Hon. DLitt: Keele, 1973; Sydney, 1982; Hon. DEcon Qld, 1980; Hon. LLD: Melbourne, 1981; Manchester, 1982; Hon. DSc Aston, 1982. *Publications*: The Socialist Order and Freedom, 1942; (with C. F. Carter): Industry and Technical Progress, 1957, Investment in Innovation, 1958, and Science in Industry, 1959; Investment Behaviour, 1962; Investment Proposals and Decisions, 1965; Investment, Technology and Growth, 1967; (ed) Science and Technology in Economic Growth, 1973; Systems of Higher Education: Australia, 1978; Education, Training and Employment, 1979. *Address*: 114 Cromwell Road, SW7 4ES. *T*: 01-370 5770. *Club*: Athenæum.

WILLIAMS, Campbell (Sherston); *see under* Smith, Campbell (Sherston).

WILLIAMS, Catrin Mary, FRCS; Consultant Ear, Nose and Throat Surgeon, Clwyd Health Authority (North), since 1956; *b* 9 May 1922; *d* of late Alderman Richard Williams, JP, Pwllheli, and Mrs Margaret Williams; unmarried. *Educ*: Pwllheli Grammar Sch.; Welsh National Sch. of Medicine (BSc 1942, MB, BCh 1945). FRCS 1948. Co-Chm., Women's National Commn, 1981-; Pres., Medical Women's Fedn, 1973-74; first Vice-Pres., Gymdeithas Feddygol Gymraeg (Welsh Med. Soc.), 1975-. *Recreations*: reading, embroidery. *Address*: Gwrych House, Abergele, Clwyd LL22 8EU. *T*: Abergele 822256.

WILLIAMS, Cecil Beaumont, CHB 1980; OBE 1963; Executive Director, Da Costa & Musson Ltd, Barbados, since 1980; *b* 8 March 1926; *s* of George Cuthbert and Violet Irene Williams; *m* 1952, Dorothy Marshall; two *s* one *d*. *Educ*: Harrison Coll., Barbados; Durham Univ.; Oxford Univ. BA, DipEd. Asst Master, Harrison Coll., 1948-54. Asst Sec., Govt Personnel Dept, and Min. of Trade, Industry and Labour (Barbados), 1954-56; Permanent Secretary: Min. of Educn, 1958; Min. of Trade, Industry and Labour, 1958-63; Dir, Economic Planning Unit, 1964-65; Manager, Industrial Develt Corp., 1966-67; High Comr to Canada, 1967-70; Permanent Sec., Min. of External Affairs, 1971-74; Ambassador to USA and Perm. Rep. to OAS, 1974-75; High Comr in UK, 1976-79. *Recreations*: music, tennis, reading, gardening. *Address*: Moonshine Hall, St George, Barbados.

WILLIAMS, Rear-Adm. Charles Bernard, CB 1980; OBE 1967; Flag Officer Medway and Port Admiral Chatham, 1978-80, retired; *b* 19 Feb. 1925; *s* of Charles Williams and Elizabeth (*née* Malherbe); *m* 1946, Patricia Mary, *d* of Henry Brownlow Thorp and Ellen Thorp; one *s* one *d*. *Educ*: Graeme Coll., Grahamstown, SA; Royal Naval Engineering Coll., Plymouth. Served in HM Ships Nigeria, Hornet, Triumph, 1946-53; in charge: Flight deck trials unit, 1953; Naval Wing, Nat. Gas Turbine Estabt, 1956; Sen. Engr, HMS Cumberland, 1958; in charge Admiralty Fuel Experimental Station, 1960; Comdr 1960; Engineer Officer, HMS London, 1962; Staff Engr, Flag Officer ME, 1964; Duty Comdr, Naval Ops MoD (N), 1967; Captain 1969; Dep.

Manager, Portsmouth Dockyard, 1969; Supt, Clyde Submarine Base, 1972; Captain, HMS Sultan, 1975; Rear-Adm. 1978. *Recreations:* sailing (Chm., Whitbread Round the World Race, 1981-), walking. *Address:* Green Shutters, Montserrat Road, Lee-on-Solent PO13 9LT. *T:* Lee-on-Solent 550816. *Clubs:* Royal Yacht Squadron; Royal Ocean Racing; Royal Naval Sailing Association.

WILLIAMS, Charles Cuthbert Powell, CBE 1980; Chief Executive, Henry Ansbacher Holdings PLC, since 1982; Chairman: Henry Ansbacher & Co. Ltd, since 1982; Berkeley Exploration and Production PLC, since 1982; *b* 9 Feb. 1933; *s* of late Dr Norman Powell Williams, DD, and Mrs Muriel de Lérisson Williams (*née* Cazenove); *m* 1975, Jane Gillian (*née* Portal); one step *s*. *Educ:* Westminster Sch.; Christ Church, Oxford (MA); LSE. British Petroleum Co. Ltd, 1958-64; Bank of London and Montreal, 1964-66; Eurofinance SA, Paris, 1966-70; Baring Brothers and Co. Ltd, 1970-77 (Man. Dir, 1971-77); Chm., Price Commn, 1977-79; Man. Dir, Henry Ansbacher & Co. Ltd, 1980-82. Parly Candidate (Lab), Colchester, 1964. Founder Mem., Labour Econ. Finance and Taxation Assoc. (Vice-Chm., 1975-77, 1979-). Director: Silvermines Ltd, 1979-; Foreign Anglican Church and Educn Assoc. Ltd; Schütz Choir Ltd; Mem. Council, The Friends of St John's, Smith Square. FRSA. *Recreations:* cricket (Oxford Univ. CC, 1953-55, Captain 1955; Essex CCC, 1953-59); music, real tennis. *Address:* 48 Thurloe Square, SW7 2SX. *T:* 01-581 1783. *Clubs:* Reform, Overseas Bankers', MCC.

WILLIAMS, Charles Frederick Victor, CIE 1944; late ICS; *b* 1898; Director, National Union of Manufacturers, 1953-56, retired Nov. 1956. *Educ:* Pembroke College, Oxford. Joined ICS 1923; Under-Sec. Madras Govt 1928; Sec., 3rd Round Table Conference, London, 1932; Under-Sec., Govt of India, 1933; Dep. Secretary, Govt of India, 1934; Secretary, Agent-General for India in South Africa, 1935; Home Secretary, Madras Govt, 1941; Jt Sec., Home Dept, Govt of India, 1945; Sec. to Governor-General (Public), 1947. *Address:* 16 Egerton Gardens, SW3. *T:* 01-584 3820. *Club:* East India, Devonshire, Sports and Public Schools.

WILLIAMS, Dr Cicely Delphine, CMG 1968; retired (except on demand); *b* 2 Dec. 1893; *d* of James Rowland Williams, Kew Park, Jamaica (Dir of Educn, Jamaica) and Margaret E. C. Williams (*née* Farewell). *Educ:* Bath High Sch. for Girls; Somerville Coll., Oxford (Hon. Fellow, 1977); King's Coll. Hosp. DM, FRCP, DTM&H. Colonial Med. Service: appts, 1929-48. WHO Adv. in Maternal and Child Health, 1948-51; Research on Vomiting Sickness, 1951-53; Sen. Lectr in Nutrition, London, 1953-55; consulting visits to various countries, 1955-59; Visiting Professor: of Maternal and Child Health, Amer. Univ. of Beirut, 1959-64; Tulane Sch. of Public Health, New Orleans, 1971-; Adv. in Trng Progrs, Family Planning Assoc., 1964-67. Lectures: Milroy, RCP, 1958; Blackfan, Harvard Med. Sch., 1973; Balgopal Oration, Paediatric Soc., Katmandu, Nepal, 1981; Speaker, Pakistan Paediatric Assoc., 1982. Emeritus Professor of Maternal and Child Health, Nursing and Nutrition, Tulane Sch. of Public Health, 1974. Hon. FRSM 1976; Hon. Fellow, King's Coll. Hosp. Medical Sch., 1978. Hon. DSc: Univ. of WI; Univ. of Maryland; Univ. of Tulane; Smith Coll., Northampton, Mass. James Spence Meml Medal, Br. Paed. Assoc., 1965; Goldberger Award in Clin. Nutrition, Amer. Med. Assoc., 1967; Dawson-Williams Award in Paediatrics, BMA (jt), 1973. Order of Merit, Jamaica, 1975. *Publications:* chapters in: Diseases of Children in the Tropics, 1954; Sick Children, 1956; The Matrix of Medicine, 1958; (with D. B. Jelliffe) Mother and Child Health: delivering the services, 1972; contrib. to: The Lancet, Archives of Diseases in Childhood, Tropical Pediatrics, etc. *Recreations:* people and solitude. *Address:* 24 Wyndham House, Plantation Road, Oxford OX2 6JJ. *T:* Oxford 50317. *Club:* Royal Commonwealth Society.

WILLIAMS, Clifford; *see* Williams, A. C.

WILLIAMS, Clifford; Associate Director, Royal Shakespeare Company, since 1963; *b* 30 Dec. 1926; *s* of George Frederick Williams and Florence Maud Williams (*née* Gapper); *m* 1st, 1952, Joanna Douglas (marr. diss. 1959); no *c* ; 2nd, 1962, Josiane Eugenie Peset; two *d*. *Educ:* Highbury County Grammar Sch. Acted in London (These Mortals, Larissa, Wolves and Sheep, Great Catherine), and repertory theatres, 1945-48; founded and directed Mime Theatre Company, 1950-53; Dir of Productions: at Marlowe Theatre, Canterbury, 1955-56; at Queen's Theatre, Hornchurch, 1957. Directed at Arts Theatre, London: Yerma, 1957; Radio Rescue, 1958; Dark Halo, Quartet for Five, The Marriage of Mr Mississippi (all in 1959); Moon for the Misbegotten, The Shepherd's Chameleon, Victims of Duty (all in 1960); The Race of Adam, Llandaff Festival, 1961. Joined Royal Shakespeare Company, 1961; Directed: Afore Night Come, 1962; The Comedy of Errors, 1963. Prods for RSC in Stratford and London: The Tempest, The Representative, The Comedy of Errors (revival), 1963; Richard II, Henry IV Pts I and II (co-dir), Afore Night Come (revival), The Jew of Malta, 1964; The Merchant of Venice, The Jew of Malta (revival), The Comedy of Errors (revival), 1965; The Meteor, Twelfth Night, Henry IV Pts I and II (co-dir, revivals), 1966; Doctor Faustus, 1968; Major Barbara, 1970; The Duchess of Malfi, 1971; The Comedy of Errors (revival), 1972; The Taming of the Shrew, A Lesson in Blood and Roses, 1973; Cymbeline, 1974; The Mouth Organ, Too True to be Good, 1975; Wild Oats, 1976, 1979; Man and Superman, 1977; The Tempest, 1978; The Love-Girl and the Innocent, 1981. Other productions include: Our Man Crichton, 1964, and The Flying Dutchman, 1966, in London; The Gardener's Dog, 1965, and The Merry Wives of Windsor, 1967, for the Finnish National Theatre; Volpone at Yale Univ., 1967; Othello, for Bulgarian Nat. Theatre,

1968; Soldiers, New York and London, 1968; Dido and Aeneas, Windsor Festival, 1969; Famine, English Stage Soc., 1969; As You Like It, 1967, and Back to Methuselah, 1969, both for the Nat. Theatre of GB; The Winter's Tale, 1969, for Yugoslav Nat. Theatre; Sleuth, London, NY and Paris, 1970; Oh! Calcutta!, London and Paris, 1970; Emperor Henry IV, New York, 1973; As You Like It (revival), New York, 1974; What Every Woman Knows, London, 1974; Emperor Henry IV, London, 1974; Murderer, London, 1975; Mardi-Gras, London, 1976; Carte Blanche, London, 1976; Stevie, The Old Country, Rosmerholm, London, 1977; The Passion of Dracula, London, 1978; Richard III, Mexican Nat. Theatre, 1979; Threepenny Opera, 1979, and The Love-Girl and the Innocent, 1980, Aalborg; Born in the Gardens, London, 1980; Overhead, Haymarket, 1981; To Grandmother's House We Go, NY, 1981; The Carmelites, Aalborg, 1981; Othello, Bad Hersfeld, 1982; Chapter 17, London, 1982. Also directed plays for the Arena Theatre, Triumph Theatre Co., Theatre Workshop, Guildford, Oxford, Coventry, Toronto, Los Angeles, Washington, Houston, Johannesburg, Edinburgh Festival; Malvern Festival. Mem. Welsh Arts Council, 1963-72; Chairman: Welsh Nat. Theatre Co., 1968-72; British Theatre Assoc., 1977-; Advisory Editor, Drama; Chm., British Children's Theatre Assoc., 1968-71; Governor, Welsh Coll. of Music and Drama, 1981-. Associate Artist of Yugoslav Nat. Theatre, 1969; FTCL. *Publications:* (ed) John O'Keeffe, Wild Oats, 1977; *plays:* The Disguises of Arlecchino, 1951; The Sleeping Princess, 1953; The Goose Girl, 1954; The Secret Garden, 1955; (with Donald Jonson) Stephen Dedalus, 1956; *translations:* Pirandello, As You Desire Me, 1981; Chekhov, The Cherry Orchard, 1981. *Recreations:* motor boating, water-ski-ing. *Address:* 43 Onslow Square, SW7 3NJ; The Vineyard, Domaine du Chateauneuf, 06560 Valbonne, France.

WILLIAMS, Colin; *see* Welland, C.

WILLIAMS, Colin Hartley; Executive Director: City Communications Centre, since 1979; Committee on Invisible Exports, since 1982; *b* 7 Dec. 1938; *s* of late Gwilym Robert Williams and Margaret (*née* Hartley); *m* 1964, Carolyn (*née* Bulman); one *s* two *d*. *Educ:* Grangefield Grammar Sch., Stockton-on-Tees; University College of Wales, Aberystwyth (BA). Journalist: Evening Gazette, Middlesbrough, 1960-63; Today Magazine, Odhams Press, 1964; Daily Sketch, 1964-66; Senior Lecturer, International Press Inst., Nairobi, 1967-68; Corporate and Public Relations Executive, 1969-74; Press Officer, Corporation of City of London, 1975-76; Asst Dir, City Communications Centre, 1977. *Publications:* articles on labour management, financial and communication topics. *Recreations:* writing, painting, tennis. *Address:* 84 Clare Road, Prestwood, near Great Missenden, Bucks HP16 0NU. *T:* Great Missenden 4464.

WILLIAMS, Cyril Herbert, CMG 1956; OBE 1949; *b* 27 Dec. 1908; *s* of T. E. Williams; *m* 1936, Patricia Joy Collyer; one *s* two *d*. *Educ:* Bedford Modern Sch.; Jesus Coll., Camb. (MA). Colonial Service, Kenya, 1931; Provincial Commissioner, Nyanza Province, Kenya, 1951-56, retd; farming in Kenya, 1956-65; Mem., Kenya Council of State, 1961-64; Chm., Naivasha CC, 1961-64; Mem., Nyandarua CC, 1963; Deputy Chairman Appeal Tribunal, 1962-63, apptd under the Public Security (Restriction) Regulations. Master: Westerleigh School, 1965-66; Great Sanders School, 1966-69; Claremont School, 1969-74, retired. *Recreations:* reading, watching sport. *Address:* Nortons Farm, New House, Sedlescombe, East Sussex. *Club:* East India, Devonshire, Sports and Public Schools.

WILLIAMS, Cyril Robert, CBE 1945; *b* 11 May 1895; *s* of Rev. F. J. Williams, MA; *m* 1928, Ethel Winifred Wise; two *d*. *Educ:* Wellington College, Berks; New College, Oxford. Dist Loco. Supt, Khartoum, Sudan Rlys, 1923; Asst Mech. Engineer (Outdoor), 1924; Loco. Running Supt, 1927; Works Manager, 1932; Asst Chief Mech. Engineer, 1936; Deputy General Manager, 1939; General Manager, 1941. JP Somerset, 1947-69. *Recreation:* philately. *Address:* Ballacree, Somerton, Somerset. *T:* Somerton 72408.

WILLIAMS, Dafydd Wyn J.; *see* Jones-Williams.

WILLIAMS, Prof. David; Professor of Mining Geology in the University of London (Imperial College), 1950-66, Emeritus Professor, since 1966; *b* 12 Oct. 1898; *s* of William and Laura Williams, Caernarvonshire, N Wales; *m* 1929, Dorothy Welland Shepard; two *d*. *Educ:* Holt Secondary School, Liverpool; University of Liverpool; Imperial College, London. DSc 1952, PhD 1925, MSc 1923, BEng 1921, Univ. of Liverpool; DIC. Geophysical Prospecting, N Rhodesia, 1926-28; Geologist, Rio Tinto Company, Spain, 1928-32; Lecturer in Geology, Imperial College, 1932-47, Reader in Mining Geology, 1947-50. Dean, Royal School of Mines, 1952-59. Secretary, Geological Society of London, 1942-51, Vice-Pres., 1951-53, 1964-65, Foreign Secretary, 1970-73; Council, Institution of Mining and Metallurgy, 1948-70, Vice-President, 1954-57, President, 1960-61; Pres., Geologists Assoc., 1958-60. Fellow, Imp. Coll. of Science and Technology, 1968. Hon. FIMM, 1969. Consolidated Gold Fields of SA Gold Medal, InstMM, 1934; Lyell Medal, Geological Soc. of London, 1959. *Publications:* (with W. R. Jones) Minerals and Mineral Deposits, 1948; scientific papers in geological and mining journals. *Address:* Downsway, 315 Fir Tree Road, Epsom Downs, Surrey. *T:* Burgh Heath 52655.

WILLIAMS, Adm. Sir David, GCB 1977 (KCB 1975); DL; Governor and Commander-in-Chief, Gibraltar, since 1982; a Gentleman Usher to The Queen, 1979-82, an Extra Gentleman Usher, since 1982; *b* 22 Oct. 1921; 3rd *s* of A. E. Williams, Ashford, Kent; *m* 1947, Philippa Beatrice Stevens; two *s. Educ:* Yardley Court Sch., Tonbridge; RN College, Dartmouth. Cadet, Dartmouth, 1935. Graduate, US Naval War Coll., Newport, RI. Served War of 1939-45 at sea in RN. Qual. in Gunnery, 1946; Comdr, 1952; Captain, 1960; Naval Asst to First Sea Lord, 1961-64; HMS Devonshire, 1964-66; Dir of Naval Plans, 1966-68; Captain, BRNC, Dartmouth, 1968-70; Rear-Adm. 1970; Flag Officer, Second in Command Far East Fleet, 1970-72; Vice-Adm. 1973; Dir-Gen. Naval Manpower and Training, 1972-74; Adm. 1974; Chief of Naval Personnel and Second Sea Lord, 1974-77; C-in-C Naval Home Comd, and ADC to the Queen, 1977-79, retired. Mem., Commonwealth War Graves Commn, 1980-. Pres., Ex Services Mental Welfare Soc., 1979-. DL Devon, 1981. *Recreations:* sailing, tennis, gardening. *Address:* The Convent, Gibraltar; Brockholt, Strete, Dartmouth, Devon. *Clubs:* Army and Navy; Royal Dart Yacht; RN Sailing Association; Royal Yacht Squadron; Royal Western Yacht.

WILLIAMS, Rear-Adm. David Apthorp, CB 1965; DSC 1942; *b* 27 Jan. 1911; *s* of Thomas Pettit Williams and Vera Frederica Dudley Williams (*née* Apthorp); *m* 1951, Susan Eastlake, 3rd *d* of late Dr W. H. Lamplough and *widow* of Surg. Cdr H. de B. Kempthorne, RN; one *s* two step *d. Educ:* Cheltenham College; Royal Naval Engineering College, Keyham. Joined RN, 1929. Served War, Engineer Officer, HMS Hasty, 1939-42 (DSC, despatches four times), 2nd Destroyer Flotilla, Med. Fleet, S Atlantic Stn, Home Fleet, E Med. Fleet; Sen. Engineer, HMS Implacable, 1942-45, Home Fleet, and 1st Aircraft Carrier Sqdn, British Pacific Fleet, Comdr (E) 1945; Capt. 1955; Rear-Adm. 1963; Dir Gen. Aircraft, Admiralty, 1962-64; Dir Gen., Aircraft (Naval), Ministry of Defence, 1964-65; retired list, 1965. CEng, MIMechE. *Recreations:* various. *Address:* 3 Ellachie Gardens, Alverstoke, Hants PO12 2DS. *T:* Gosport 83375. *Club:* Army and Navy.

WILLIAMS, David Barry, TD 1964; QC 1975; **His Honour Judge David Williams;** a circuit Judge, since 1979; *b* 20 Feb. 1931; *s* of Dr W. B. Williams and Mrs G. Williams, Garndiffaith, Mon; *m* 1961, Angela Joy Davies; three *s* one *d. Educ:* Cardiff High Sch. for Boys; Wellington Sch., Somerset; Exeter Coll., Oxford (MA). Served with South Wales Borderers, 1949-51, 2nd Bn Monmouthshire Regt (TA), 1951-67, retired (Major). Called to Bar, Gray's Inn, 1955; Wales and Chester Circuit, 1957. A Recorder of the Crown Court, 1972-79; Asst Comr, Local Govt Boundary Commn for Wales, 1976-79; Comr for trial of Local Govt election petitions, 1978-79. Chm., Legal Affairs Cttee, Welsh Centre for Internat. Affairs, 1980-; Member: Court, University Coll., Cardiff, 1980-; Council, UWIST, 1981-. *Recreations:* mountain walking, Rugby football. *Address:* 52 Cyncoed Road, Cardiff. *T:* Cardiff 498189. *Clubs:* Army and Navy; Cardiff and County (Cardiff).

WILLIAMS, David Carlton, PhD; retired; President and Vice-Chancellor, University of Western Ontario, 1967-77; *b* 7 July 1912; *s* of John Andrew Williams and Anna Williams (Carlton); *m* 1943, Margaret Ashwell Carson; one *s* one *d. Educ:* Gordon Bell and Kelvin High Schs; Univ. of Manitoba, Winnipeg (BA); Univ. of Toronto (MA, PhD, Psych.). Special Lectr in Psychology, Univ. of Toronto, 1946; Associate Prof. of Psychology, Univ. of Manitoba, 1947; Prof. and Head, Dept of Psychology, Univ. of Manitoba, 1948; Prof. of Psychology, Univ. of Toronto, 1949-58 (Cons. to Toronto Juvenile Ct Clinic, 1951-58); Dir of Univ. Extension, Univ. of Toronto, 1958; a Dir, John Howard Soc., Toronto, 1956-67; Mem., Royal Commn on Govt Organization, 1961; Chm., Ontario Commn on Freedom of Information and Individual Privacy, 1977. Vice-Pres., Univ. of Toronto, for Scarborough and Erindale Colls, 1963-67. Principal of Scarborough Coll., Univ. of Toronto, 1963; Principal of Erindale Coll., Univ. of Toronto, 1965. Chm., Council of Ontario Univs, 1970-73; Dir, Assoc. of Univs and Colls of Canada, 1970-. Hon. LLD: Univ. of Manitoba, 1969; Univ. Windsor, 1977; Univ. of Western Ontario, 1977; Toronto Univ., 1977. *Publications:* The Arts as Communication, 1963; University Television, 1965. *Recreations:* photography, music, swimming, fishing. *Address:* 252 Sydenham Street, London, Ontario, Canada N6A 1W5. *T:* 433-1436. *Clubs:* University, London, London Hunt and Country (all London, Ont); Arts and Letters, York (Toronto).

WILLIAMS, David Claverly, CVO 1970; CBE 1977; *b* 31 July 1917; *s* of late Rev. Canon Henry Williams, OBE, and late Ethel Florence Williams; *m* 1944, Elizabeth Anne Fraser; three *d. Educ:* Christ's Coll., Christchurch, NZ; Victoria Univ. of Wellington. Professional Exam. in Public Administration. Inland Revenue Dept, 1936-39. Served War, 2NZEF, Pacific and Middle East, 1939-46. NZ Forest Service, 1946-60; Official Sec. to the Governor-General of NZ, 1960-77; Sec./Manager, The Wellington Club (Inc.), 1978-82. *Address:* 4 Huia Road, Days Bay, Eastbourne, New Zealand. *Club:* United Services Officers' (Wellington).

WILLIAMS, David Glyndwr Tudor; President, Wolfson College, University of Cambridge, since 1980; Reader in Public Law, Cambridge University, since 1976; *b* 22 Oct. 1930; *s* of late Tudor Williams, OBE (Headmaster of Queen Elizabeth Grammar Sch., Carmarthen, 1929-55), and late Anne Williams; *m* 1959, Sally Gillian Mary Cole; one *s* two *d. Educ:* Queen Elizabeth Grammar Sch., Carmarthen; Emmanuel Coll., Cambridge (MA, LLB). LLM Calif. Called to the Bar, Lincoln's Inn, 1956. Commonwealth Fund Fellow of Harkness Foundn, Berkeley and Harvard, 1956-58; Lecturer: Univ. of Nottingham, 1958-63; Univ. of Oxford, 1963-67 (Fellow of Keble Coll.); Emmanuel College, Cambridge: Fellow, 1967-80; Sen. Tutor and Tutor for Admissions, 1970-76. Vis. Fellow, ANU, 1974.

Member: Council on Tribunals, 1972-80; Clean Air Council, 1971-79; Royal Commn on Environmental Pollution, 1976-; Commn on Energy and the Environment, 1978-81; Justice—All Souls Cttee on Administrative Law, 1978-; Special Advr to Home Affairs Cttee, H of C, 1980. *Publications:* Not in the Public Interest, 1965; Keeping the Peace, 1967; (ed jtly) Administrative Law, in Halsbury's Laws of England, Vol. 1, 4th edn 1973; articles in legal jls. *Address:* 29 Sedley Taylor Road, Cambridge. *T:* Cambridge 246232.

WILLIAMS, D(avid) Innes, MD, MChir Cambridge, FRCS; Director, British Post-graduate Medical Federation, University of London, since 1978; Chairman Council, Imperial Cancer Research Fund, since 1982 (Member, since 1975); Consulting Urologist: Hospital for Sick Children, Great Ormond Street (Urologist, 1952-78); St Peter's Hospital, London (Surgeon, 1950-78); Civilian Consultant Urologist to Royal Navy; *b* 12 June 1919; *s* of late Gwynne E. O. Williams, MS, FRCS; *m* 1944, Margaret Eileen Harding; two *s. Educ:* Sherborne Sch.; Trinity Hall, Cambridge; Univ. College Hospital. RAMC, 1945-48 (Major, Surg. Specialist). Urologist, Royal Masonic Hosp., 1963-72. Mem., Home Sec's Adv. Cttee on Cruelty to Animals, 1975-79. Member: GMC, 1979- (Chm., Overseas Cttee, 1981-); Council, RCS, 1974-. FRSocMed (Past Pres., Urology Sect.); Sen. Mem., British Assoc. Paediatric Surgeons (Denis Browne Medal, 1977). Hon. Member: British Assoc. Urological Surgeons (Past Pres.; St Peter's Medal, 1967); Assoc. Française d'Urologie; Amer. Surgical Assoc. *Publications:* Urology of Childhood, 1958; Paediatric Urology, 1968, new edn, 1982; Scientific Foundations of Urology, 1976, new edn, 1982; various contributions to medical journals. *Address:* (office) 33 Millman Street, WC1; 15c Heath Drive, NW3 7SN. *T:* 01-435 4926; The Old Rectory, East Knoyle, Salisbury, Wilts. *T:* 255.

WILLIAMS, Dr David Iorwerth, FRCP, FKC; Dean, King's College Hospital Medical School, 1966-77, now Dean Emeritus; former Consultant in Dermatology, King's College Hospital; Consultant to Kuwait Health Office, London; *b* 7 May 1913; *s* of William Tom Williams and Mabel Williams (*née* Edwards); *m* 1939, Ethel Margaret Wiseman; one *s* (one *d* decd). *Educ:* Dulwich Coll. (Jun. and Sen. Scholar); King's College Hosp. Med. Sch. Warneford and Raymond Gooch Scholar; MB, BS 1938; FRCP 1953; AKC 1934; FKC 1977. RAMC, 1940-46, Lt-Col. Member: BMA; Brit. Assoc. of Dermatology (Past Pres. and Past Sec., Hon. Mem. 1979); Royal Soc. of Med. (Past Pres. Dermatology Section); West Kent Medico-Chirurgical Soc. (Past Pres.); Hon. (or Foreign) Member: American, Austrian, Danish, French and S African Dermatological Socs. Gold Medal of Brit. Assoc. of Dermatology, 1965. *Publications:* articles in various med. jls over last 40 yrs. *Recreations:* golf, music. *Address:* 28 South Row, SE3 0RY. *T:* 01-852 7060.

WILLIAMS, David John; *b* 10 July 1914; *s* of late James Herbert Williams and of Ethel (*née* Redman); unmarried. *Educ:* Lancing College; Christ Church, Oxford (MA). Called to Bar, Inner Temple, 1939. Postgrad. Dip. in Social Anthropology, LSE, 1965. Served War of 1939-45, Royal Artillery. Practised as Barrister, Norwich, 1946-51; Resident Magistrate, Tanganyika, 1951-56; Senior Resident Magistrate, 1956-60; Judge of High Court of Tanganyika, 1960-62; Lord Chancellor's Office, 1966-79. FRAI 1966. *Recreations:* the arts and travelling. *Address:* Hillfield, 27 Crawley Hill, Camberley, Surrey GU15 2DA.

WILLIAMS, (David John) Delwyn; MP (C) Montgomery, since 1979; *b* 1 Nov. 1938; *s* of David Lewis Williams and Irena Violet Gwendoline Williams; *m* 1963, Olive Elizabeth Jerman; one *s* one *d. Educ:* Welshpool High School; University College of Wales, Aberystwyth. LLB. Principal, Porter & Williams, Solicitors; Consultant, Delwyn Williams & Co., Solicitors. Member: Select Cttee on Wales; Statutory Instruments Cttee; Jt Sec., All-Party Leisure and Recreation Industry Cttee. Mem., British Field Sports Soc. *Recreations:* race horse owner; cricket, golf, small bore shooting. *Address:* Frondeg, Guilsfield, Welshpool, Powys SY21 9NQ. *T:* Welshpool 3400; House of Commons, SW1A 0AA. *T:* 01-219 3505.

WILLIAMS, David Wakelin, MSc, PhD, FInstBiol; retired as Director, Department of Agriculture and Fisheries for Scotland, Agricultural Scientific Services, 1963-73; *b* 2 Oct. 1913; *e s* of John Thomas Williams and Ethel (*née* Lock); *m* 1948, Margaret Mary Wills, BSc, *d* of late Rev. R. H. Wills; one *s. Educ:* Rhondda Grammar School, Porth; University College, Cardiff. Demonstrator, Zoology Dept, Univ. Coll., Cardiff, 1937-38; Lectr in Zoology and Botany, Tech. Coll., Crumlin, Mon., 1938-39; research work on nematode physiology, etc. (MSc, PhD), 1937-41; biochemical work on enzymes (Industrial Estate, Treforest), 1942-43. Food Infestation Control Inspector (Min. of Food), Glasgow; Sen. Inspector, W Scotland, 1945; Scotland and N Ireland, 1946. Prin. Scientific Officer, Dept Agriculture for Scotland, 1948; Sen. Prin. Scientific Officer, 1961; Dep. Chief Scientific Officer (Director), 1963. Chairman, Potato Trials Advisory Cttee, 1963-; FInstBiol 1966 (Council Mem. Scottish Br., 1966-69). *Publications:* various papers, especially for the intelligent layman, on the environment, and on pest control and its side effects. *Recreations:* writing, music, Hi-Fi, photography. *Address:* 8 Hillview Road, Edinburgh EH12 8QN. *T:* 031-334 1108.

WILLIAMS, Delwyn; *see* Williams, D. J. D.

WILLIAMS, Dr Denis (John), CBE 1955; DSc; MD; FRCP; Hon. Consulting Neurologist: St George's Hospital; King Edward VII Hospital for Officers; Hon. Consulting Physician, National Hospital, Queen Square; Hon. Neurologist, Star and Garter Home, Richmond; Hon. Civil Consultant in

Neurology, RAF, British Airways; Civil Consultant in Electro-encephalography, RAF and Army; Chairman, Secretary of State's Hon. Medical Advisory Panel on Neurological Aspects of Safety in Driving, since 1967; *b* 4 Dec. 1908; *s* of Rev. Daniel Jenkin Williams, MA, BD, Aberayron and Elsie Leonora Edwards; *m* 1937, Joyce Beverley Jewson, MBE, JP, MB, BS, DPH; one *s* two *d* (and one *s* decd). *Educ:* Manchester Univ.; Harvard University. DSc (Physiol.), Manchester 1942 (MSc 1938, BSc 1929); MD (Gold Medal) Manchester 1935 (MB, ChB 1932); FRCP 1943 (MRCP 1937). After resident appts in Manchester and London, Prof. Tom Jones Mem. Fellow in Surgery; Halley Stewart Research Fellow, MRC; Rockefeller Travelling Fellow in Neurology. Hon. Research Fellow, Harvard Univ. Wing Comdr RAF; Air Crew Research and Clinical Neurology in Royal Air Force, 1939-45, and seconded to RN; Physician, Departments of Applied Electrophysiology, St George's and National Hosps. Consultant Advr in neurology, DHSS, 1966-73. Lectr in Neurology, London Univ., 1946-75; Chm., Academic Bd, Inst. of Neurology, 1965-74. Editor, Brain, and Modern Trends in Neurology, 1954-75. Bradshaw Lectr, RCP, 1955; Scott-Heron Lectr, Belfast, 1960; Guest Lectr, Canadian Medical Assoc., 1963; Hugh Cairns Lectr, Adelaide, 1965; Bruce Hall Lectr, Sydney, 1965; Guest Lectr, RACP, 1965; Richardson Lectr, Toronto, 1974. Visiting Professor: Univ. of Cincinnati, 1963, 1969; St Vincent's Hosp. Sydney (Hon. Phys.), 1965. Mem. Council, 1960-63, Vice-Pres., 1976, 1977, Royal Coll. of Physicians (Chm., Cttee on Neurology, 1965-74); Pres., Sect. of Neurology, Roy Soc Med, 1967; Pres., Assoc. of British Neurologists 1972-74 (Sec., 1952-60); Hon. Member: American, Canadian and German Neurological Assocs; EEG Soc. Examr, RCP and various Univs. Governor, Nat. Hosp.; Trustee, Brain Res. Trust. Gowers Medal, UC and Nat. Hosps, London, 1974. *Publications:* articles on brain function, epilepsy, abnormal behaviour and electro-encephalography, in Brain, Modern Trends in Neurology, and other journals; Neurology, in Price's Medicine; Contrib. to Handbook of Neurology. *Recreations:* farming, gardening. *Address:* 149 Harley Street, W1. *T:* 01-935 4444; 11 Frognal Way, Hampstead, NW3. *T:* 01-435 4030; Woodlands House, Mathry, Dyfed. *T:* St Nicholas 220. *Clubs:* Wayfarers', Royal Air Force.

WILLIAMS, Derek Alfred H.; *see* Hutton-Williams.

WILLIAMS, Derrick; *see* Williams, R. D.

WILLIAMS, Donald; *see* Williams, W. D.

WILLIAMS, Sir Donald Mark, 10th Bt *cr* 1866; *b* 7 Nov. 1954; *s* of Sir Robert Ernest Williams, 9th Bt, and of Ruth Margaret, *d* of Charles Edwin Butcher, Hudson Bay, Saskatchewan, Canada; *S* father, 1976. *Educ:* West Buckland School, Devon. *Heir: b* Barton Matthew Williams, *b* 21 Nov. 1956. *Address:* Upcott House, Barnstaple, N Devon.

WILLIAMS, Dorian (Joseph George), OBE 1978; Director, Pendley Centre of Adult Education, Tring, since 1945; BBC TV Equestrian Commentator, 1951-80; *b* 1 July 1914; *er s* of late Col Williams and Mrs V. D. S. Williams, Farnham Royal, Bucks; *m* 1st, 1938, Hon. Moyra Lubbock (marr. diss. 1946); 2nd, 1956, Jennifer Neale; one *s* one *d. Educ:* Harrow; Guildhall Sch. of Music and Drama. Schoolmaster, 1936-45. Founded Pendley Centre of Adult Education, Tring, 1945. MFH, Whaddon Chase, 1954-. Chairman: National Equestrian Centre, 1967-74; BHS, 1974-82, Pres., 1982-. Master, Farriers' Co., 1977-78. *Publications:* Clear Round, 1954; Pendley and a Pack of Hounds, 1956; Batsford Book of Horses, 1959; Every Child's Book of Riding, 1960; Show Pony, 1961; Pony to Jump, 1963; Working with Horses as a Career, 1963; Learning to Ride, 1964; The Horseman's Companion, 1967; Pancho, The Story of a Horse (novel), 1967; Famous Horse Stories, 1968; Kingdom for a horse (novel), 1971; Lost (novel), 1974; Great Riding Schools of the World, 1975; The Horse of the Year, 1976; Master of One, 1978; The Guinness Guide to Equestrianism, 1979. *Recreations:* riding, Shakespeare, study of Napoleon. *Address:* Foscote Manor, Buckingham. *T:* Buckingham 3152; (office) *T:* Buckingham 3981. *Clubs:* Buck's, Sportsman's.

WILLIAMS, Douglas, CB 1977; CVO 1966; Crown Agent, since 1978; *b* 14 May 1917; *s* of late James E. Williams and Elsie Williams; *m* 1948, Marie Jacquot; no *c. Educ:* Wolverhampton Sch.; Exeter Coll., Oxford. Served War, 1939-46 (despatches): Major, RA. Colonial Office, 1947; Principal, 1949; Colonial Attaché, Washington, 1956-60; Asst Sec., Colonial Office, 1961; transferred to ODM (later ODA), 1967, Under-Sec., 1968-73; Dep.-Sec., 1973-77. Member: EEC Econ. and Social Cttee, 1978-82; Governing Council, ODI, 1979-. *Publications:* articles on human rights and economic development, British colonial history. *Address:* 14 Gomshall Road, Cheam, Sutton, Surrey. *T:* 01-393 7306.

WILLIAMS, Sir Dudley; *see* Dudley-Williams, Sir Rolf Dudley.

WILLIAMS, Sir Edgar (Trevor), Kt 1973; CB 1946; CBE 1944; DSO 1943; DL; Emeritus Fellow, Balliol College, Oxford, since 1980; Chairman: Nuffield Provincial Hospitals Trust, since 1966; Nuffield Medical Benefaction, Oxford, since 1982; a Radcliffe Trustee, since 1960; a Freeman of Chester; *b* 20 Nov. 1912; *e s* of late Rev. J. E. Williams; *m* 1938, Monica, *d* of late Professor P. W. Robertson; one *d* ; *m* 1946, Gillian, *yr d* of late Major-General M. D. Gambier-Parry, MC; one *s* one *d. Educ:* Tettenhall College; KES, Sheffield; Merton College, Oxford (Chambers Postmaster, 1931-34; First Class, Modern History, 1934; Harmsworth Senior Scholar, 1934-35; Junior Research Fellow, 1937-39; MA 1938; Hon. Fellow, 1964-).

FRHistS 1947. Asst Lectr, Univ. of Liverpool, 1936. Served War of 1939-45 (despatches thrice); 2nd Lieut (SRO), 1st King's Dragoon Guards, 1939; Western Desert, 1941; GSO1, Eighth Army (North Africa, 1942-43, Sicily and Italy, 1943); Brig., Gen. Staff I, 21st Army Gp, 1944-45; Rhine Army, 1945-46; Officer, US Legion of Merit, 1945; UN Security Council Secretariat, 1946-47. Fellow, Balliol Coll., Oxford, 1945-80; a Pro-Vice-Chancellor, Oxford Univ., 1968-80.; Sec., Rhodes Trust, 1951-80. Editor, DNB, 1949-80. Mem., Devlin Nyasaland Commn, 1959; UK Observer, Rhodesian elections, 1980. DL Oxfordshire, 1964-. President, OUCC, 1966-68 (Sen. Treasurer, 1949-61); a Governor, St Edward's Sch., Oxford, 1960-. Hon. Mem., American Hosp. Assoc., 1971. Hon. Fellow: Queen Elizabeth House, Oxford, 1975; Wolfson Coll., Oxford, 1981. Hon. LLD: Waynesburg Coll., Pa, 1947; Univ. of Windsor, Ontario, 1969; Hon. LHD, Williams Coll., Mass, 1965; Hon. PdD, Franklin and Marshall Coll., Pa, 1966; Hon. DLitt: Warwick, 1967; Hull, 1970; Mt Allison, NB, 1980; Liverpool, 1982; Hon. LittD: Swarthmore Coll., Pa, 1969; Sheffield, 1981. *Festschrift:* Oxford and the Idea of Commonwealth (ed A. F. Madden and D. K. Fieldhouse), 1982. *Address:* 94 Lonsdale Road, Oxford OX2 7ER. *T:* Oxford 55199. *Clubs:* Athenæum, Savile; MCC; Vincent's (Oxford).

WILLIAMS, Maj.-Gen. Edward Alexander Wilmot, CB 1962; CBE 1958; MC 1940; DL; *b* 8 June 1910; *s* of late Captain B. C. W. Williams, DL, JP, Herringston, Dorchester and late Hon. Mrs W. M. Williams (*er d* of 2nd Baron Addington); *m* 1943, Sybilla Margaret, *er d* of late Colonel O. A. Archdale, MBE, late The Rifle Brigade, West Knighton House, Dorchester; one *s* three *d. Educ:* Eton; Royal Military College. 2nd Lieut 60th Rifles, 1930; Adjutant, 2nd Battalion (Calais), 1938-39. Served War of 1939-45; commanded 1st Bn 60th Rifles, 1944. Bt Lieut-Col, 1950; Directing Staff, Joint Services Staff College, 1950-52; commanded 2nd Bn 60th Rifles, 1954-55; Comdr 2nd Infantry Brigade, 1956-57; Imperial Defence College, 1958; Brigadier Author, War Office, 1959. GOC 2nd Div. BAOR, 1960-62; Chief of Staff, GHQ Far East Land Forces, May-Nov. 1962; General Officer Commanding Singapore Base District, 1962-63; Chairman, Vehicle Cttee, Min. of Defence, 1964; retired 1965; Colonel Commandant, 2nd Bn The Royal Green Jackets (The King's Royal Rifle Corps), 1965-70. DL Dorset, 1965; High Sheriff of Dorset, 1970-71. *Recreations:* fishing, shooting. *Address:* Herringston, Dorchester, Dorset. *T:* Dorchester 64122. *Clubs:* Army & Navy, Pratt's, Lansdowne; Royal Dorset Yacht.

WILLIAMS, Air Cdre Edward Stanley, CBE 1975 (OBE 1968); defence consultant; *b* 27 Sept. 1924; *s* of late William Stanley Williams and Ethel Williams; *m* 1947, Maureen Donovan; two *d. Educ:* Wallasey Central Sch.; London Univ. Sch. of Slavonic and E European Studies; St John's Coll., Cambridge (MPhil (Internat. Relations) 1982). Joined RAF, 1942; trained in Canada; service in flying boats, 1944; seconded BOAC, 1944-48; 18 Sqdn, Transport Comd, 1949; Instr, Central Navigation Sch., RAF Shawbury, 1950-52; Russian Language Study, 1952-54; Flying Appts MEAF, A&AEE, 216 Sqdn Transport Comd, 1954-61; OC RAF Element, Army Intell. Centre, 1961-64; Asst Air Attaché, Moscow, 1964-67; first RAF Defence Fellow, UCL, 1967-68; comd Jt Wing, Sch. of Service Intell., 1968-71; Chief, Target Plans, HQ Second ATAF, 1971-73; Chief Intell. Officer, HQ British Forces Near East, 1973-75; comd Jt Air Reconn. Intell. Centre, 1976-77; Defence and Air Attaché, Moscow, 1978-81, retired RAF, 1981. *Publications:* various articles in service jls. *Recreations:* Russian studies, walking, photography. *Address:* c/o Midland Bank, 104 Wallasey Village, Wallasey, Merseyside L45 3LS. *Club:* Royal Air Force.

WILLIAMS, Hon. Sir Edward (Stratten), KBE 1981; Justice of Supreme Court of Queensland, since 1971; *b* 29 Dec. 1921; *s* of Edward Stratten and Zilla Claudia Williams; *m* 1949, Dorothy May Murray; three *s* four *d* (and one *s* decd). *Educ:* Yungaburra State Sch., Qld; Mt Carmel Coll., Charters Towers, Qld; Univ. of London (LLB Hons). Served RAAF, UK and Aust., 1942-46. Barrister-at-Law, 1946; QC (Australia) 1965. Chairman, Parole Board of Qld, 1976-; Royal Commissioner, Aust. Royal Commn of Inquiry into Drugs, 1977-80; Member, Internat. Narcotics Control Board (UN), 1982-. Chairman, Commonwealth Games Foundn Brisbane (1982), 1976-. *Publications:* Report of Australian Royal Commission of Inquiry into Drugs and associated reports. *Recreations:* horse racing, gardening, golf. *Address:* 150 Adelaide Street East, Clayfield, Queensland 4011, Australia. *T:* 2624802. *Clubs:* Brisbane, United Services, Queensland Turf (Chairman, 1980-), Rugby Union, BATC, Tattersall's, Albion Park Trotting, Far North Queensland Amateur Turf (all Queensland).

WILLIAMS, Edward Taylor, CMG 1962; MICE; retired as General Manager, Malayan Railway; civil engineering railway consultant with Henderson, Hughes and Busby, consulting engineers and economists, since 1965; *b* Bolton, Lancashire, 15 October 1911; *s* of late Edward and Harriet Williams; *m* 1940, Ethel Gertrude Bradley; one step *s* one step *d. Educ:* Accrington Grammar School; Manchester College of Technology. LMS Rly, pupil engineer, 1929-36; Sudan Rly, Asst Civil Engr, 1936-38; Metropolitan Water Board, Civil Engr, 1939-41; Malayan Rly, 1941-62 (Gen. Man. 1959-62); Rly Advr, Saudi Govt Railroad, 1963-65. Interned in Singapore, in Changi and Sime Road, 1941-45. *Recreation:* travel. *Address:* Gatchell House, Trull, Taunton, Somerset. *T:* Taunton 83641.

WILLIAMS, Elizabeth, (Betty); working for peace, since 1976; *b* 22 May 1943; *m* 1961, Ralph Williams; one *s* one *d. Educ:* St Dominic's Grammar School. Office Receptionist. Leader, NI Peace Movement, 1976-78. Hon.

LLD, Yale Univ., 1977; Hon. HLD, Coll. of Sienna Heights, Michigan, 1977. Nobel Peace Prize (jtly), 1976; Carl-von-Ossietsky Medal for Courage, 1976. *Recreation:* gardening. *Address:* Orchardville Gardens, Finaghy, Belfast 10, N Ireland. *T:* Belfast 663465.

WILLIAMS, Emlyn, CBE 1962; MA; FRSL; *b* 1905; *m* Molly O'Shann (*d* 1970); two *s. Educ:* County School, Holywell; Geneva; Christ Church, Oxford (MA). Hon. LLD Bangor. *Plays:* A Murder has been Arranged; Glamour; Full Moon; Vigil; Vessels Departing; Spring, 1600; Night Must Fall; He Was Born Gay; The Corn is Green; The Light of Heart; The Morning Star; adaptation of A Month in the Country; The Druid's Rest; The Wind of Heaven; Trespass; Accolade; Someone Waiting; Beth; adaptation of The Master Builder. In addition to acting in most of these, has acted at the Old Vic, also in The Winslow Boy, Lyric, 1946; The Wild Duck, Saville, 1955; Season at Stratford-on-Avon, 1956. Shadow of Heroes, Piccadilly, 1958. As Charles Dickens (solo performance), Lyric (Hammersmith), Criterion, Duchess, 1951, Golden Theatre (New York), Ambassadors, 1952. As Dylan Thomas (A Boy Growing Up: solo performance), Globe, 1955 and 1958, Long Acre Theatre (New York), Oct. 1957, Ambassadors, 1980; as Saki (solo performance), Apollo, 1977. Acted in: Three, Criterion, 1961; Daughter of Silence, New York, 1961; A Man For All Seasons, New York, 1962; The Deputy, New York, 1964; World Tour as Dickens, 1964-65; as Charles Dickens, Globe, 1965, and Haymarket, 1975; acted in A Month in the Country, Cambridge, 1965; Forty Years On, Apollo, 1969. *Films include:* The Last Days of Dolwyn (author, co-director, and star), 1948; Ivanhoe, 1950; Deep Blue Sea, 1955; I Accuse, 1957; The Wreck of the Mary Deare, 1959; The L-Shaped Room, 1962; Eye of the Devil, 1966; The Walking-Stick, 1969; David Copperfield, 1969. *Publications:* (autobiog.) George, 1961; Beyond Belief, 1967; (autobiog.) Emlyn, 1973; (novel) Headlong, 1980. *Address:* 123 Dovehouse Street, SW3. *T:* 01-352 0208.

WILLIAMS, Eric, MC 1944; writer; *b* 13 July 1911; *m* 1st, 1940, Joan Mary Roberts (decd); 2nd, 1948, Sibyl Grain, MBE; no *c. Educ:* Christ's College, Finchley. Served War of 1939-45, RAF, 1940-46; shot down over Germany as Flt Lt Dec. 1942; captured, and imprisoned in Stalag-Luft III; escaped Oct. 1943; returned to England Dec. 1943. Book buyer Lewis's Ltd, 1946-49; Scriptwriter, Wessex Film Productions Ltd, 1949-50. Set out on slowest journey round the world, 1959. *Publications:* Goon in the Block, 1945; The Wooden Horse, 1949, rev. edn 1979; The Tunnel, 1951; The Escapers, 1953; Complete and Free, 1957; Great Escape Stories, 1958; Dragoman Pass, 1959 (rev. edn, Dragoman, 1970); The Borders of Barbarism, 1961; More Escapers, 1968; Great Air Battles, 1971. *Recreations:* travel, seafaring, fishing, shooting, fighting officiousness in all its forms. *Address:* Union Bank of Switzerland, Bern, Switzerland.

WILLIAMS, Brig. Eric Llewellyn Griffith G.; *see* Griffith-Williams.

WILLIAMS, Evelyn Faithfull M.; *see* Monier-Williams.

WILLIAMS, Sir Francis (John Watkin), 8th Bt *cr* 1798; QC 1952; *b* Anglesey, 24 Jan. 1905; *s* of Col Lawrence Williams, OBE, DL, JP (*d* 1958) (*gs* of 1st Bt); S brother, 1971; *m* 1932, Brenda, *d* of Sir John Jarvis, 1st Bt; four *d. Educ:* Malvern College; Trinity Hall, Cambridge. Barrister of Middle Temple, 1928. Served War of 1939-45; Wing Comdr, RAFVR. Recorder of Birkenhead, 1950-58; Recorder of Chester, 1958-71; Chm., Anglesey QS, 1960-71 (Dep. Chm., 1949-60); Chm., Flint QS, 1961-71 (Dep Chm., 1953-61); Dep. Chm., Cheshire QS, 1952-71; a Recorder of the Crown Court, 1972-74. JP Denbighshire, 1951-74; Chm. Medical Appeal Tribunal for N Wales Areas, 1954-57; High Sheriff: of Denbighshire, 1957, of Anglesey, 1963. Chancellor, Diocese of St Asaph, 1960. Freeman of City of Chester, 1960. *Heir:* half-*b* Lawrence Hugh Williams [*b* 25 Aug. 1929; *m* 1952, Sara Margaret Helen, 3rd *d* of Sir Harry Platt, Bt, *qv*; two *d*]. *Address:* Llys Meirchion, Denbigh, Clwyd. *T:* 69. *Clubs:* United Oxford & Cambridge University; Grosvenor (Chester).
See also Sir Charles Kimber, Bt.

WILLIAMS, Francis Julian, JP; DL; Member of Prince of Wales' Council, Duchy of Cornwall, since 1969; *b* 16 April 1927; 2nd *s* of Alfred Martyn Williams, *qv*; *m* Delia Fearne Marshall, *e d* of Captain Campbell Marshall; two *s. Educ:* Eton; Trinity Coll., Cambridge (BA). RAF, 1945-48. Chm., Cambridge Univ. Conservative Assoc;, 1950; Pres., Cambridge Union, 1951. Contested (C) All Saints Div. of Birmingham, 1955. Mem., Devon and Cornwall Cttee, Lloyds Bank, 1971-. Succeeded to Caerhays, 1955. Pres., Cornwall Cricket Club. Mem., Cornwall CC, 1967- (Vice-Chm., 1974; Chm., 1980). JP 1970, DL 1977, Cornwall. *Recreation:* gardening. *Address:* Caerhays Castle, Gorran, St Austell, Cornwall. *T:* Veryan 250. *Clubs:* Brooks's, White's.

WILLIAMS, Frank Denry Clement, CMG 1956; *b* 3 May 1913; *s* of Frank Norris Williams and Joanna Esther Williams; *m* 1941, Traute Kahn; no *c. Educ:* Leighton Park School, Reading; London School of Economics (BSc Econ.). Cadet, Colonial Administrative Service, 1946; Asst Financial Sec., Nigeria, 1952; Financial Secretary: Jamaica, 1954; Federation of Nigeria, 1956; Economic Adviser, Federation of Nigeria, 1957-58; Permanent Secretary, Prime Minister's Dept, Fedn of The W Indies, 1958-62; Financial Sec., The Gambia, 1962-65. *Recreations:* walking, languages. *Address:* 51 The Priory, London Road, Brighton, Sussex BN1 8QT.

WILLIAMS, Prof. Gareth Howel; Professor of Chemistry, University of London, and Head of Department of Chemistry, Bedford College, University of London, since 1967; *b* 17 June 1925; *s* of Morgan John and Miriam Williams, Treherbert, Glam; *m* 1955, Marie, BA, *yr d* of William and Jessie Mary Mitchell, Wanlockhead, Dumfriesshire; one *s* one *d. Educ:* Pentre Grammar Sch.; University Coll., London. BSc, PhD, DSc London; FRSC. Asst Lectr, then Lectr in Chemistry, King's Coll., Univ of London, 1947-60; Research Fellow, Univ. of Chicago, 1953-54; Reader in Organic Chemistry, Birkbeck Coll., Univ. of London, 1960-67. Vis. Lectr, Univ. of Ife, Nigeria, 1965; Rose Morgan Vis. Prof., Univ. of Kansas, 1969-70; Vis. Prof., Univ. of Auckland, NZ, 1977. External Examr: Univ. of Rhodesia, 1967-70; Univ. of Khartoum, 1967-73, 1976-80; City Univ., 1968-74; Univ. of Surrey, 1974-76; Brunel Univ., 1980-. *Publications:* Homolytic Aromatic Substitution, 1960; Organic Chemistry: a conceptual approach, 1977; (Editor) Advances in Free-Radical Chemistry, Vol. I, 1965, Vol. II, 1967, Vol. III, 1969, Vol. IV, 1972, Vol. V, 1975, Vol. VI, 1980; numerous papers in Jl Chem. Soc. and other scientific jls. *Recreation:* music. *Address:* Hillside, 22 Watford Road, Northwood, Mddx. *T:* Northwood 25297; Department of Chemistry, Bedford College, Regent's Park, NW1 4NS. *T:* 01-486 4400. *Club:* Athenæum.

WILLIAMS, Prof. Gareth Lloyd; Professor of Educational Planning, University of Lancaster, since 1973; *b* 19 Oct. 1935; *s* of Lloyd and Katherine Enid Williams; *m* 1960, Elizabeth Ann Peck; two *s* one *d. Educ:* Creeting St Mary; Framlingham; Cambridge Univ. (MA). Res. Officer, Agricl Econs Res. Inst., Oxford Univ., 1959-62; Res. Fellow, OECD, Athens, 1962-64; Principal Administrator, OECD, Paris, 1964-68; Associate Dir, Higher Educn Res. Unit, LSE, 1968-73. Specialist Adviser to Arts and Educn Sub-Cttee to House of Commons Cttee on Expenditure, 1972-76; Consultant to OECD, ILO, and UNESCO, 1968-. Member: Council, Policy Studies Inst., 1979-; Governing Council for Soc. for Res. into Higher Educn, 1970- (Chm., 1978-80). Mem. Bd, Red Rose Radio PLC, 1981-. FRSA 1982. *Publications:* (with Greenaway) Patterns of Change in Graduate Employment, 1973; (with Blackstone and Metcalf) The Academic Labour Market in Britain, 1974; Towards Lifelong Learning, 1978; (with Zabalza and Turnbull) The Economics of Teacher Supply, 1979; (with Woodhall) Independent Further Education, 1979. *Address:* Havercroft, Haverbreaks Road, Lancaster. *T:* Lancaster 66002.

WILLIAMS, Gareth Wyn, QC 1978; a Recorder of the Crown Court, since 1978; *b* 5 Feb. 1941; *s* of Albert Thomas Williams and Selina Williams; *m* 1962, Pauline Clarke; one *s* two *d. Educ:* Rhyl Grammar Sch.; Queens' Coll., Cambridge (Open Schol. (History) 1958; Univ. Prize, Jurisprudence 1962; Foundn Schol. 1964; LLB (1st Cl.) 1964; MA 1965). Called to the Bar, Gray's Inn, 1965; Standing Counsel, University Coll. of Swansea, 1975. *Address:* Southlake House, Shurlock Row, near Reading, Berks. *T:* Shurlock Row 617.

WILLIAMS, Geoffrey Guy; Deputy Chairman, J. Henry Schroder Wagg & Co. Ltd, since 1977; *b* 12 July 1930; *s* of late Captain Guy Williams, OBE, and Mrs Margaret Williams (*née* Thomas). *Educ:* Blundell's Sch.; Christ's Coll., Cambridge (MA, LLB). Slaughter and May, Solicitors, 1952-66, Partner 1961; Dir, J. Henry Schroder Wagg & Co. Ltd, 1966, Vice-Chm. 1974. Chm., National Film Finance Corp., 1976- (Dir, 1970-). Director: Bass Charrington Ltd, 1971-; Schroders Ltd, 1976-; John Brown and Co. Ltd, 1977-. Chm., Issuing Houses Assoc., 1979-81. *Recreations:* reading, theatre, cinema. *Address:* 18G Eaton Square, SW1W 9DD. *T:* 01-235 5212. *Club:* Brooks's.

WILLIAMS, (George Haigh) Graeme; barrister; a Recorder of the Crown Court, since 1981; *b* 5 July 1935; *s* of Leslie Graeme Williams and Joan Haigh Williams; *m* 1963, Anna Maureen Worrall; two *d. Educ:* Tonbridge Sch.; Brasenose Coll., Oxford (MA). Called to the Bar, Inner Temple, 1959. *Address:* 19 Murray Mews, NW1. *T:* 01-267 0817.

WILLIAMS, George Mervyn, CBE 1977; MC 1944; TD; DL; Chairman, Christie-Tyler Ltd, since 1959; Director, Lloyds Bank UK Management Ltd, since 1977 (Chairman, S Wales Regional Board); *b* 30 Oct. 1918; *yr s* of late Owain Williams and late Mrs Williams; *m* 1st, Penelope (marr. diss. 1946), *d* of late Sir Frank Mitchell, KCVO; 2nd, 1950, Grizel Margaretta Cochrane, DStJ, *d* of late Major Walter Stewart, DSO; one *s. Educ:* Radley Coll. Served War, Royal Fusiliers, N Africa and Italy, Major, 1939-46; British Military Mission to Greece, 1945. Great Universal Stores, 1946-49; Christie-Tyler Ltd: Sales Dir, 1949; Man. Dir. 1950-80. Governor, United World Coll. of Atlantic, 1980-. JP 1965-70, High Sheriff 1966, DL 1967-, Glamorgan. CStJ. *Address:* Llanharan House, Llanharan, Mid Glamorgan CF7 9NR. *T:* Llantrisant 226253; Craig y Bwla, Crickhowell, Powys NP8 1SU. *T:* Crickhowell 810413. *Clubs:* Brooks's; Cardiff and County (Cardiff).

WILLIAMS, George W.; *see* Wynn-Williams.

WILLIAMS, Gerald Wellington, JP; *b* 1903; *s* of Wellington Archbold Williams, JP, Shernfold Park, Frant, Sussex; *m* 1930, Mary Katharine Victoria (*d* 1981), *d* of Captain Joscelyn Heber-Percy, DL, JP, East Lympden, Ticehurst, Sussex; one *s* two *d. Educ:* Eton; Christ Church, Oxford (MA). RNVR, 1939 (Lt-Comdr 1942). MP (C) Tonbridge division of Kent, 1945-56, resigned. JP Tunbridge Wells, 1957; High Sheriff of Kent, 1968-69. *Address:* Crockham House, Westerham, Kent. *T:* Crockham Hill 215. *Clubs:* Carlton, MCC.

WILLIAMS, Gertrude, (Lady Williams), CBE 1963; Professor of Social Economics, University of London, 1955-64, Professor Emeritus since 1964; *b* 11 January 1897; *d* of I. Rosenblum; *m* 1919, Sir William Emrys Williams, CBE, DLitt; no *c. Educ:* Manchester University; London School of Economics. Apptd to Dept of Social Studies and Economics, Bedford Coll., Univ. of London, 1919, subseq. Special Lecturer in Economics, Reader in Social Economics, and Professor. Min. of Home Security and Min. of Labour and Nat. Service, 1940-42. Member of many Govt cttees of Enquiry. Member Central Training Council, 1964. *Publications:* The State and the Standard of Living, 1936; The Price of Social Security, 1946; Women and Work, 1946; Economics of Everyday Life (Pelican), 1950, rev. and enl. edn 1972, rev. and rewritten, 1976; Recruitment to Skilled Trades, 1957; Apprenticeship in Europe: The Lesson for Britain, 1963; The Coming of the Welfare State, 1967; articles in Economic Jl, etc. *Recreations:* travel, ballet, opera. *Address:* Grenville Paddock, Haddenham, Bucks. *T:* Haddenham 291464.

WILLIAMS, Prof. Glanmor, CBE 1981; Professor of History, 1957-82, University College of Swansea; *b* 5 May 1920; *s* of Daniel and Ceinwen Williams, Dowlais, Glam; *m* 1946, Margaret Fay Davies; one *s* one *d. Educ:* Cyfarthfa Grammar Sch., Merthyr Tydfil; Univ. Coll. of Wales, Aberystwyth. MA 1947; DLitt 1962. Univ. Coll. of Swansea: Asst Lectr in History, 1945; Sen. Lectr, 1952; a Vice-Principal, 1975-78. Nat. Governor, BBC, for Wales, 1965-71; Member: Royal Commn on Ancient and Historical Monuments in Wales, 1962-; Historic Bldgs Council for Wales, 1962-; British Library Bd, 1973-80 (Chm., Adv. Council, 1981-); Adv. Council on Public Records, 1974-82; Welsh Arts Council, 1978-81. Chm., Pantyfedwen Foundations, 1973-79; Pres., Cambrian Arch. Assoc., 1980. FRHistS 1954 (Vice-Pres., 1979-); FSA 1978. *Publications:* Yr Esgob Richard Davies, 1953; The Welsh Church, 1962; Owen Glendower, 1966; Welsh Reformation Essays, 1967; (ed) Glamorgan County History, vol. III 1971, vol. IV 1974, vol. V 1980; Religion, Language and Nationality in Wales, 1979; contrib. to: History, Welsh History Review, etc. *Recreations:* walking, gramophone, cine-photography. *Address:* 11 Grosvenor Road, Swansea. *T:* Swansea 204113. *Club:* National Liberal.

WILLIAMS, Glanville Llewelyn, QC 1968; FBA 1957; Fellow of Jesus College, Cambridge, 1955-78, Hon. Fellow, 1978, and Rouse Ball Professor of English Law in the University of Cambridge, 1968-78 (Reader, 1957-65; Professor, 1966); *b* 15 Feb. 1911; *s* of late B. E. Williams, Bridgend, Glam; *m* 1939, Lorna Margaret, *d* of late F. W. Lawfield, Cambridge; one *s. Educ:* Cowbridge; University College of Wales, Aberystwyth; St John's Coll., Cambridge. Called to the Bar, 1935; PhD (Cantab), 1936; Research Fellow of St John's Coll., 1936-42; LLD (Cantab), 1946; Reader in English Law and successively Professor of Public Law and Quain Professor of Jurisprudence, University of London, 1945-55; Carpentier Lecturer in Columbia Univ., 1956; Cohen Lecturer in Hebrew University of Jerusalem, 1957; first Walter E. Meyer Visiting Research Professor, New York Univ., 1959-60; Charles Inglis Thompson Guest Professor, University of Colorado, 1965. Special Consultant for the American Law Institute's Model Penal Code, 1956-58; Member: Standing Cttee on Criminal Law Revision, 1959-80; Law Commn's Working Party on Codification of Criminal Law, 1967; Cttee on Mentally Abnormal Offenders, 1972. Pres., Abortion Law Reform Assoc., 1962-. Hon. Bencher, Middle Temple, 1966. Fellow, Eugenics Soc. Ames Prize, Harvard, 1963; (joint) Swiney Prize, RSA, 1964. Hon. LLD: Nottingham, 1963; Wales, 1974; Glasgow, 1980. *Publications:* Liability for Animals, 1939; chapters in McElroy's Impossibility of Performance, 1941; The Law Reform (Frustrated Contracts) Act (1943), 1944; Learning the Law, 1st edn 1945, 11th edn 1982; Crown Proceedings, 1948; Joint Obligations, 1949; Joint Torts and Contributory Negligence, 1950; Speedhand Shorthand, 1952, 8th edn 1980; Criminal Law; The General Part, 1st edn 1953, 2nd edn 1961; The Proof of Guilt, 1st edn 1955, 3rd edn 1963; The Sanctity of Life and the Criminal Law, American edn 1956, English edn 1958; The Mental Element in Crime, 1965; (with B. A. Hepple) Foundations of the Law of Tort, 1976; Textbook of Criminal Law, 1978; articles in legal periodicals. *Address:* Merrion Gate, Gazeley Road, Cambridge CB2 2HB. *T:* Cambridge 841175.

WILLIAMS, Rev. Dr Glen Garfield; General Secretary, Conference of European Churches, since 1968; *b* 14 Sept. 1923; *s* of John Archibald Douglas Williams and Violet May (*née* Tucker); *m* 1945, Velia Cristina (*née* Baglio). *Educ:* Newport High Sch.; Universities of Wales (Cardiff), London, Tübingen. Military Service, 1943-47. Univ. studies, 1947-55. Minister, Dagnall Street Baptist Church, St Albans, 1955-59; European Area Secretary, World Council of Churches, Geneva, 1959-68. Hon. DTh Budapest, 1975; Hon. DD Bucharest, 1981. Order of St Vladimir, 1976, and St Sergius, 1979, Russian Orthodox Church; Order of St Mary Magdalene, 1980, Polish Orthodox Church. *Publications:* contrib. to Handbook on Western Europe, 1967, etc.; numerous articles, mainly in Continental journals. *Recreations:* travel, reading, archæology. *Address:* c/o 150 Route de Ferney, 1211 Geneva 20, Switzerland. *T:* (022)98.94.00. *Club:* Athenæum.

WILLIAMS, Graeme; *see* Williams, George H. G.

WILLIAMS, Rt. Rev. Gwilym Owen, DD Lambeth 1957; *b* 23 March 1913; *s* of Owen G. Williams; *m* 1941, Megan (*d* 1976), *d* of T. D. Jones; one *s. Educ:* Llanberis Gram. Sch.; Jesus Coll., Oxford, Hon Fellow, 1972. BA 1st Class Hons English, 1933; 1st Class Hons Theol. 1935; Gladstone Student at St Deiniol's Library, Hawarden, 1935; St Stephen's House, Oxford, 1936; MA 1937. Curate of Denbigh, 1937; Reader in Theology, St David's Coll.,

Lampeter, 1940; Warden of Church Hostel, Bangor; Lecturer in Theology, University Coll., Bangor; Canon of Bangor Cathedral, 1947; Warden and Headmaster, Llandovery Coll., 1948-56; Bishop of Bangor, 1957-82; Archbishop of Wales, 1971-82. Chaplain and Sub-Prelate of Order of St John of Jerusalem, 1965. *Publication:* The Church's Work, 1959. *Recreations:* fishing and walking. *Address:* Hafod-y-Bryn, Criccieth, Gwynedd. *Club:* Reform.

WILLIAMS, Sir Gwilym (Tecwyn), Kt 1970; CBE 1966; Director: Dalgety (UK) Ltd, since 1975; Dalgety Spillers, since 1980; *b* 1913; *s* of David and Margaret Williams; *m* 1936, Kathleen, *d* of John and Maria Edwards; two *s* one *d. Educ:* Llanfyllin CSS; Llysfasi Farm Inst.; Harper Adams Agric. Coll. Leader, Employers' side, Agricultural Wages Board, 1960-66; Director, FMC Ltd, 1962-75. Potato Marketing Board: Member, 1954-58; Chairman, 1955-58; Special Member, 1961-66. Member: Agric. NEDO, 1968-76; Econ. and Social Cttee, EEC, 1972-78; Adv. Council for Agriculture and Horticulture in England and Wales, 1973-. National Farmers' Union: Mem. Council, 1948- (Life Mem., 1977); Vice-Pres., 1953, 1954, 1960-62; Dep. Pres., 1955, 1963-65; Pres., 1966-70. Chm. Governors, Harper Adams Agric. Coll., 1977-. *Recreations:* trout fishing, shooting. *Address:* Red Gables, Longford, Newport, Salop. *T:* Newport (Salop) 810439. *Club:* Farmers'.

WILLIAMS, Very Rev. Harold Claude Noel; Provost of Coventry Cathedral, 1958-81; Provost Emeritus since 1981; *b* 6 Dec. 1914; *s* of Charles Williams and Elizabeth Malherbe, Grahamstown, S Africa; *m* 1940, Pamela Marguerite Taylor, Southampton; two *s* two *d* (and one *d* decd). *Educ:* Graeme Coll., S Africa; Durham Univ.; Southampton Univ. Ordained, 1938; Curate of Weeke, Winchester, 1938-40; Principal, St Matthew's Coll., S Africa, 1941-49; Vicar of Hyde, Winchester, 1950-54; Rector of St Mary's, Southampton, 1954-58. Hon. LLD Valparaiso Univ., USA. Grosse Verdienstkreuz des Verdienst Ordens, Federal Republic of Germany, 1967. *Publications:* African Folk Songs, 1948; (ed) Vision of Duty, 1963; Twentieth Century Cathedral, 1964; Coventry Cathedral and its Ministry, 1965; Nothing to Fear, 1967; Coventry Cathedral in Action, 1968; Basics and Variables, 1970; The Latter Glory, 1978; Order My Steps in Thy Way, 1982. *Recreations:* mountaineering and fishing. *Address:* 96 Stoney Road, Coventry CV3 6HY. *T:* Coventry 502561. *Club:* Alpine.

WILLIAMS, Air Vice-Marshal Harold Guy L.; *see* Leonard-Williams.

WILLIAMS, Harri Llwyd H.; *see* Hudson-Williams.

WILLIAMS, Rev. Harry Abbott; Community of the Resurrection, since 1969; *b* 10 May 1919; *s* of late Captain Harry Williams, RN, and Annie Williams. *Educ:* Cranleigh Sch.; Trinity Coll., Cambridge; Cuddesdon Coll., Oxford. BA 1941; MA 1945. Deacon, 1943; Priest, 1944. Curate of St Barnabas, Pimlico, 1943-45; Curate of All Saints, Margaret Street, 1945-48; Chaplain and Tutor of Westcott House, Cambridge, 1948-51; Fellow of Trinity Coll., Cambridge, 1951-69; Dean of Chapel, 1958-69, and Tutor, 1958-68; Exam. Chaplain to Bishop of London, 1948-69. Mem., Anglican delegation to Russian Orthodox Church, Moscow, 1956; Select Preacher, Univ. of Cambridge, 1950, 1958, 1975; Hulsean Preacher, 1962, 1975; Select Preacher, Univ. of Oxford, 1974. Licensed to officiate in Dio. of Ely, 1948-, Dio. of Wakefield, 1979-. *Publications:* Jesus and the Resurrection, 1951; God's Wisdom in Christ's Cross, 1960; The Four Last Things, 1960; The True Wilderness, 1965; True Resurrection, 1972; Poverty, Chastity and Obedience: the true virtues, 1975; Tensions, 1976; Becoming What I Am, 1977; The Joy of God, 1979; Some Day I'll Find You (autobiog.), 1982; contribs to: Soundings, 1962; Objections to Christian Belief, 1963; The God I Want, 1967. *Recreations:* idleness and religion. *Address:* House of the Resurrection, Mirfield, West Yorks.

WILLIAMS, Rev. Dr (Henry) Howard; Minister, Bloomsbury Central Baptist Church, since 1958; *b* 30 April 1918; *s* of Rev. Henry James Williams and Edith Gwenllian Williams; *m* 1950, Athena Mary (*née* Maurice); three *s* one *d. Educ:* Mountain Ash Grammar Sch.; Rawdon Coll.; Leeds Univ. BA, BD, PhD. Minister: Blenheim Baptist Church, Leeds, 1943-53; Beechen Grove, Watford, 1953-58; Member: Baptist Union Council, 1954-; Central Religious Advisory Council, BBC, 1962-65; Religious Advisory Panel, ITA, 1965-70. Pres., Baptist Union of Great Britain and Ireland, 1965; Director: Baptist Times Ltd; Central YMCA, London; Mem. Editorial Bd, New Christian, 1965-70. *Publications:* Down to Earth, 1964; Noughts and Crosses, 1965; Old Memories and New Ways, 1965; The Song of the Devil, 1972; My Word, 1973; contributor to Expository Times. *Recreations:* now reduced to viewing the activity of others. *Address:* 162 Hendon Way, NW2 2NE. *T:* 01-455 6628.

WILLIAMS, Ven. Henry Leslie; Archdeacon of Chester, since 1975; Vicar of Barnston, Wirral, since 1953; *b* 26 Dec. 1919; *m* 1949, Elsie Marie; one *s. Educ:* Bethesda Gram. Sch.; St David's Coll., Lampeter (BA); St Michael's Coll., Llandaff. Deacon 1943, priest 1944, Bangor; Curate of Aberdovey, 1943-45; St Mary's, Bangor, 1945-48; Chaplain, HMS Conway, 1948-49; Curate, St Mary-without-the-Walls, Chester, 1949-53. RD of Wirral North, 1967-75; Hon. Canon of Chester Cathedral, 1972-75. Mem., General Synod, 1978-80. CF (TA), 1953-62. *Recreations:* fly-fishing, bee-keeping. *Address:* The Vicarage, Barnston, Wirral, Merseyside. *T:* 051-648 1776.

WILLIAMS, Sir Henry Morton Leech, Kt 1961; MBE 1945; farmer; Managing Director, Guest, Keen, Williams Ltd, 1952-62; President, Bengal Chamber of Commerce and Industry, and President, Associated Chambers of Commerce, India, 1960; *b* 1913; *s* of late O. R. Williams; *m* 1945, Bridget Mary, *d* of late C. G. Dowding; two *s* two *d*. *Educ*: Harrow; Corpus Christi Coll., Cambridge. Served War of 1939-45 (despatches, MBE), becoming Major, REME. CC Berkshire, 1967. *Address*: Grounds Farm, Uffington, Oxon SN7 7RD. *Club*: Oriental.

WILLIAMS, Hilary a'Beckett E.; *see* Eccles-Williams.

WILLIAMS, Howard; *see* Williams, Henry H.

WILLIAMS, Hubert Glyn, AE 1944; a Recorder of the Crown Court, 1974-77; Senior Partner, Blake, Lapthorn, Rea & Williams, Solicitors, Portsmouth and District; *b* 18 Dec. 1912; *s* of John Christmas Williams and Florence Jane Williams (*née* Jones); *m* 1952, Audrey Elizabeth Righton; one *s* one *d*. *Educ*: Ruthin. Admitted solicitor, 1934 (2nd cl. Hons). Served War of 1939-45 (Sqdn Ldr; AE): AAF, 1939-41; RAFVR, 1941-45; UK, Egypt, E Africa, Palestine. Pres., Hampshire Inc. Law Soc., 1977-78. *Recreation*: cricket. *Address*: Twenty Nine, The Avenue, Alverstoke, Hants PO12 2JS. *T*: Gosport 83058. *Clubs*: MCC; Fareham and County (Fareham).

WILLIAMS, Hugo Mordaunt; writer; *b* 20 Feb. 1942; *s* of Hugh Williams, actor and playwright, and Margaret Vyner; *m* 1965, Hermine Demoriane; one *d*. *Educ*: Eton College. Asst Editor, London Magazine, 1961-70. Henfield Writer's Fellowship, Univ. of East Anglia, 1981. Awards (for poetry): Eric Gregory, 1965; Cholmondeley, 1970; Geoffrey Faber Memorial Prize, 1979. *Publications*: *poems*: Symptoms of Loss, 1965; Sugar Daddy, 1970; Some Sweet Day, 1975; Love-Life, 1979; *travel*: All the Time in the World, 1966; No Particular Place to Go, 1981. *Address*: 3 Raleigh Street, N1. *T*: 01-226 1655.

WILLIAMS, Ian Malcolm Gordon, CBE 1960 (OBE 1954; MBE 1945); *b* 7 May 1914; *s* of late Thomas and Mabel Williams. *Educ*: Tatterford Sch., Norfolk; Leeds Univ.; Gonville and Caius Coll., Cambridge. President, Leeds University Students' Union, 1939. Volunteered Military Service, Sept. 1939; Officer Cadet, 123 OCTU; Commnd Royal Regt of Artillery, March 1940; NW Frontier of India and Burma, 1940-45, as Major, RA, and Mountain Artillery, Indian Army (despatches, MBE). Staff Officer, Hong Kong Planning Unit, 1946; Adjutant, Hong Kong Defence Force, 1946. Entered Colonial Administrative Service, 1946; was District Officer and Asst Colonial Secretary, Hong Kong, 1946-49; at Colonial Office, 1949-51; Senior Asst Secretary, Secretariat, Cyprus, 1951-53; Commissioner of Paphos, 1953-55, of Larnaca, 1955-57, of Limassol, 1957-60; Chief Officer, Sovereign Base Areas of Akrotiri and Dhekelia, 1960-64; Member Administrator's Advisory Board; UK Chairman, Joint Consultative Board, 1960-64; Min. of Technology, 1965-67; DoE, 1967-71; Programme Dir, UN/Thai Programme for Drug Abuse Control in Thailand, 1972-79. Comdr, Most Noble Order of the Crown of Thailand, 1981. *Recreations*: art, Cypriot archæology, swimming. *Address*: White House, Adderbury, near Banbury, Oxfordshire. *Club*: East India, Devonshire, Sports and Public Schools.

WILLIAMS, (James) Vaughan, DSO 1942; OBE 1959; TD 1947; JP; HM Lieutenant for the County of West Glamorgan since 1974; *b* 25 Oct. 1912; *s* of James Vaughan Williams, Merthyr Tydfil; *m* 1938, Mary Edith Jones (*d* 1972), *d* of Bryn Jones, OBE, JP, Merthyr Tydfil; two *d*. Local Govt Service, 1930-39. Commnd RE (TA), 1934; served War of 1939-45, BEF, France, Egypt, Italy, Berlin (despatches 1942 and 1943); psc 1946; Lt-Col TA, 1947-59; Hon. Col 53rd (W) Div. RE, 1959-67. Mem. Wales TA&VRA, 1968; Vice-Chm. Glam TA&VR Cttee, 1968; President, Swansea Branch: Royal British Legion; Royal Engrs Assoc.; Dunkirk Veteran Assoc.; Scout Council West Glamorgan; West Glam Branch Red Cross Soc.; Mem., West Glam Council St John of Jerusalem. Past Chm., S Wales Assoc. ICE. Trustee, Wales and Border Counties TSB; Dir, Swansea Park Building Soc. DL Glam 1959, JP Glamorgan 1975. KStJ 1979. *Recreations*: travel, gardening. *Address*: 5 The Grove, Mumbles, Swansea, West Glamorgan. *T*: Swansea 68551. *Clubs*: Army and Navy; Bristol Channel Yacht.

WILLIAMS, John, OBE 1980; guitarist; *b* Melbourne, 24 April 1941. Studied with father, Segovia and at the Accademia Musicale Chigiana, Siena and RCM, London; since when has given many recitals and concerts, and made recordings of both solo guitar, and chamber and orchestral music. Mem., Sky, 1979-. *Recreations*: people, living, chess, table-tennis, music. *Address*: c/o Harold Holt Ltd, 31 Sinclair Road, W14.

WILLIAMS, John Brinley, FCIT; Joint Managing Director, British Transport Docks Board, since 1982 (Board Member since 1980); *b* 18 Aug. 1927; *s* of late Leslie Williams and of Alice Maud Williams; *m* 1951, Eileen (*née* Court); one *s* one *d*. *Educ*: Eveswell Sch., Newport. Asst Manager, Cardiff Docks, 1963-65; Commercial and Development Asst to Chief Docks Manager, South Wales Ports, 1965-67; Docks Manager: Cardiff and Penarth Docks, 1968-72; Hull Docks, 1972-75; Port Director: South Wales Ports, 1976-78; Southampton, 1978-82. *Recreations*: Rugby, open air pursuits. *Address*: Maes-y-Coed, Oakwood Road, Chandler's Ford, Hants. *T*: Chandler's Ford 69522. *Clubs*: Royal Southampton Yacht; Royal Southern Yacht (Hamble).

WILLIAMS, (John Bucknall) Kingsley; solicitor; Chairman, Wessex Regional Health Authority, 1975-82; *b* 28 July 1927; *s* of Charles Kingsley Williams and Margaret Elizabeth (*née* Bucknall); *m* 1961, Brenda (*née* Baldwin); two *s*. *Educ*: Kingswood Sch., Bath; Trinity Hall, Cambridge (MA, LLB). Partner, Dutton Gregory & Williams, Solicitors, Winchester, 1956-. Member: Winchester City Council, 1966-73; Hampshire CC (ex-officio Mem., Planning and Health Cttees, 1971-73); Assoc. of County Councils, 1973-75; NHS Supply Council, 1980-82; Vice-Chm., Council, Southampton Univ., 1976-. *Address*: Danesacre, Worthy Road, Winchester, Hants SO23 7AD. *T*: (home) Winchester 2594; (office) Winchester 66363.

WILLIAMS, Ven. John Charles; Archdeacon of Worcester, 1975-80, now Archdeacon Emeritus; Residentiary Canon of Worcester Cathedral, 1975-80; *b* 17 July 1912; *s* of William and Edith Williams; *m* 1940, Agnes Mildred Hutchings, MA; one *s* one *d*. *Educ*: Cowbridge Sch.; St David's University Coll., Lampeter; University College, Oxford. Asst Curate, Christ Church, Summerfield, Birmingham, 1937-39; Asst Curate, Hales Owen, in charge of St Margaret's, Hasbury, 1939-43; Vicar: Cradley Heath, Staffs, 1943-48; Redditch, Worcs, 1948-59. Surrogate, 1951-71; Rural Dean of Bromsgrove, 1958-59; Rector, Hales Owen, 1959-70; Archdeacon of Dudley, 1968-75; Vicar of Dodderhill, 1970-75. Hon. Canon, Worcester Cathedral, 1965-75; Examng Chaplain to Bishop of Worcester, 1965-80; Dir, Worcester Diocesan Central Services, 1974-75; Director of Ordination Candidates, 1975-79. *Publication*: One Hundred Years, 1847-1947; A History of Cradley Heath Parish. *Recreations*: history of architecture, sailing. *Address*: The Old Vicarage, Norton with Lenchwick, Evesham, Worcs WR11 4TL. *Clubs*: Oxford University Occasionals, United Oxford & Cambridge University.

WILLIAMS, John Eirwyn F.; *see* Ffowcs Williams.

WILLIAMS, Prof. John Ellis Caerwyn, FBA 1978; FSA; Professor of Irish, University College of Wales, Aberystwyth, 1965-79, now Professor Emeritus; Director of Centre for Advanced Welsh and Celtic Studies, Aberystwyth, since 1978; *b* 17 Jan. 1912; *s* of John R. Williams and Maria Williams; *m* 1946, Gwen Watkins. *Educ*: Ystalyfera Int. County Sch.; University Coll. of N Wales, Bangor (BA Hons: Latin 1933, Welsh 1934; MA); Nat. Univ. of Ireland, Dublin; TCD; United Theol Coll., Aberystwyth (BD 1944); Theol Coll., Bala. Research Lectr, UC of N Wales, Bangor, 1937-39; Fellow, Univ. of Wales, 1939-41; Lectr, 1945-51, Sen. Lectr, 1951-53, Prof. of Welsh, 1953-65, UC of N Wales. Leverhulme Fellow, 1963-64; Vis. Prof. Celtic, UCLA, 1968; Summer Sch., Harvard, 1968; O'Donnell Lectr in Celtic Studies, Oxford Univ., 1979-80. Chm., Welsh Acad., 1965-75; Cons. Editor, Univ. of Wales Welsh Dict. Fasc. xxiii-; Chm., Editorial Cttee, Welsh Acad. Dict., 1976-; Editor: Y Traethodydd, 1965-; Ysgrifau Beirniadol, i-xii; Studia Celtica, i-xv. Mem. Council for Name Studies in Gt Britain and Ireland, 1965-. FSA 1975; Hon. DLitt, Celt., Univ. of Ireland, 1967. *Publications*: trans., Ystoriau ac Ysgrifau Pádraic O Conaire, 1947; trans., Yr Ebol Glas, 1954; Traddodiad Llenyddol Iwerddon, 1958; trans., Aderyn y Gwirionedd, 1961; Edward Jones, Maes-y-Plwm, 1963; ed, Llên a Llafar Môn, 1963; trans., I. Williams, Canu Taliesin (Poems of Taliesin), 1968; The Court Poet in Medieval Ireland, 1972; Y Storïwr Gwyddeleg a'i Chwedlau, 1972; Beirdd y Tywysogion—Arolwg 1970, in Llên Cymru, and separately 1972; ed, Literature in Celtic Countries, 1971; trans. Jakez Riou, An Ti Satanazet (Diawl yn y Tŷ), 1972; Canu Crefyddol y Gogynfeirdd, 1976; Canu Crefyddol y Gogynfeirdd (Darlith Goffa Henry Lewis), 1976; The Poets of the Welsh Princes, 1978; Cerddi'r Gogynfeirdd i Wragedd a Merched, 1979; (with Máirín Ní Mhuiríosa Traidisiún Liteartha Na nGael, 1979; contribs to Bull. Bd of Celt. Studies, Celtica, Etudes Celt., Llên Cymru, etc. *Recreation*: walking. *Address*: University College of Wales, Aberystwyth SY23 2AX. *T*: Aberystwyth 3177; Iwerydd, 6 Pant-y-Rhos, Aberystwyth, Dyfed SY23 3QE. *T*: Aberystwyth 612959.

WILLIAMS, John Elwyn; His Honour Judge Williams; a Circuit Judge, since 1974; *b* 16 June 1921; *s* of Benjamin and Maria Williams; *m* 1st, Gwladys Margaret Vivian; two *s*; 2nd, Nancy Hilda. *Educ*: Cyfarthfa Castle Grammar Sch.; Aberystwyth University Coll.; University College London (LLB). Called to the Bar, Gray's Inn, 1950. *Recreations*: music, climbing. *Address*: Church Cottage, Belchamp Walter, Sudbury, Suffolk CO10 7AT.

WILLIAMS, Very Rev. John Frederick; *b* 9 March 1907; *s* of John Abraham and Lydia Miriam Williams; *m* Millicent Jones (JP 1951); one *d*. *Educ*: Friars' School, Bangor; University of Wales. Curate: Portmadoc, Caerns, 1930; Aberdare, Glam, 1933; Vicar: Miskin, Glam, 1937; Skewen, Glam, 1953; Rector, Neath, Glam, 1962; Canon, Llandaff Cathedral, 1963; Precentor, 1966; Archdeacon of Llandaff and Priest-in-Charge, Penmark, 1969-71; Dean of Llandaff, 1971-77. *Recreation*: calligraphy. *Address*: 3a Park Road, Barry, S Glam.

WILLIAMS, Rev. John Herbert; Deputy Chaplain General, Home Office Prison Department, since 1974; Priest-in-Ordinary to the Queen, since 1980; *b* 15 Aug. 1919; *s* of Thomas and Mary Williams; *m* 1948, Joan Elizabeth (*née* Morgan); one *s*. *Educ*: St David's Coll., Lampeter (BA Hons); Salisbury Theological Coll. Deacon 1943; priest 1944; Curate: Blaenavon (Gwent), 1943-46; Llanishen, Cardiff, 1946-48; Priest in Charge, Rogerstone (Gwent), 1948-51; Asst Chaplain, HM Prison, Manchester, 1951; Chaplain, HM Prison: Holloway, 1952; Birmingham, 1957; Wormwood Scrubs, 1964; South East Regional Chaplain, 1971. *Recreations*: Rugby, classical music/opera,

Francophile. *Address:* 121 Lynton Road, W3 9HN. *T:* 01-992 1448. *Clubs:* Zion College, City Livery.

WILLIAMS, (John) Kyffin, OBE 1982; RA 1974 (ARA 1970); *b* 9 May 1918; *s* of Henry Inglis Wynne Williams and Essyllt Mary Williams (*née* Williams). *Educ:* Shrewsbury Sch.; Slade Sch. of Art. Sen. Art Master, Highgate Sch., 1944–73. One-man shows: Leicester Galleries, 1951, 1953, 1956, 1960, 1966, 1970; Colnaghi Galleries, 1948, 1949, 1965, 1970; Thackeray Gall., 1975, 1977, 1979, 1981. Pres., Royal Cambrian Acad., 1969–76. Winston Churchill Fellow, 1968. Hon. MA Wales, 1973. *Publication:* Across the Straits (autobiog.), 1973. *Recreations:* the countryside, sport. *Address:* Pwllfanogl, Llanfairpwll, Gwynedd. *T:* Llanfairpwll 714693.

WILLIAMS, Sir (John) Leslie, Kt 1974; CBE 1970; Chairman, Civil Service Appeal Board, 1977–78 (Deputy Chairman, 1973–77); Secretary General, Civil Service National Whitley Council (Staff Side), 1966–73; *b* 1 Aug. 1913; *s* of Thomas Oliver Williams and Mary Ellen Williams; *m* 1937, Florrie Read Jones; one *s*. *Educ:* Grove Park Grammar Sch., Wrexham, N. Wales. Civil Servant, 1931–46. Society of Civil Servants: Asst Secretary, 1947–49; Dep. General Secretary, 1949–56; General Secretary, 1956–66. Royal Institute of Public Administration: Executive Council Member, 1955–74; Chairman, 1968; Vice-Pres., 1974–. Member Board of Governors: Nat. Hospitals for Nervous Diseases, 1962–82 (Chm., 1974–82); Hospital for Sick Children, 1976–81; Member: NW Metropolitan Regional Hospital Board, 1963–65; (part-time) UKAEA, 1970–80; Adv. Council, Civil Service Coll., 1970–76; (part-time) Pay Bd, 1974; Royal Commn on Standards of Conduct in Public Life, 1974–76; Armed Forces Pay Review Body, 1975–80; (part-time) Independent Chm., Conciliation Cttees NJC for Civil Air Transport, 1974–77; Standing Commn on Pay Comparability, 1979–80; London Adv. Gp on NHS, 1980–81. *Recreations:* cricket, gardening, music. *Address:* 26 Russell Green Close, Purley, Surrey. *T:* 01-660 9666.

WILLIAMS, John Melville, QC 1977; *b* 20 June 1931; *o s* of late Baron Francis-Williams and late Lady (Jessie Melville) Francis-Williams; *m* 1955, Jean Margaret, *d* of Harold and Hilda Lucas, Huddersfield; three *s* one *d*. *Educ:* St Christopher Sch., Letchworth; St John's Coll., Cambridge (BA). Called to the Bar, Inner Temple, 1955. Counsel to NUJ; a legal assessor to GMC. *Recreations:* mountain scrambling and walking, indifferent golf. *Address:* Deers Hill, Sutton Abinger, near Dorking, Surrey. *T:* Dorking 730331; 15 Old Square, Lincoln's Inn, WC2A 3UH. *T:* 01-831 7517.

WILLIAMS, John Peter Rhys, MBE 1977; FRCSEd; Senior Orthopaedic Registrar, St Mary's Hospital, London, since 1982; *b* 2 March 1949; *s* of Peter Williams, MB, BCh and Margaret Williams, MB, BCh; *m* 1973, Priscilla Parkin, MB, BS, DObst, RCOG; three *d*. *Educ:* Bridgend Grammar School; Millfield; St Mary's Hosp. Med. School. MB, BS London 1973; LRCP, MRCS, 1973; Primary FRCS 1976; FRCSEd 1980. University Hosp., Cardiff, Battle Hosp., Reading, St Mary's Hosp., London, 1973–78; Surgical Registrar, 1978–80, Orthopaedic Registrar, 1980–82, Cardiff Gp of Hosps. Played Rugby for Bridgend, 1967–68, 1976–79 (Captain, 1978–79), 1980–, for London Welsh, 1968–76; 1st cap for Wales, 1969 (Captain, 1978); British Lions tours, 1971, 1974; a record 55 caps for Wales, to 1981; won Wimbledon Lawn Tennis Junior Championship, 1966. *Publication:* JPR (autobiog.), 1979. *Recreations:* sport and music. *Address:* c/o St Mary's Hospital, Praed Street, W2 1NY; Llansannor Lodge, Llansannor, near Cowbridge, South Glamorgan. *Clubs:* Wig and Pen; Lord's Taverners'.

WILLIAMS, Captain Sir John (Protheroe), Kt 1967; CMG 1960; OBE 1950; *b* 1896; *m* 1st, 1921, Gladys Grieves (*d* 1962); one *s* three *d*; 2nd, 1964, Mrs Althea Florence Carr (widow). *Educ:* Queen Elizabeth's Grammar Sch., Carmarthen. Master Mariner; Chairman: Australian National Line, 1956–71; United Salvage Pty Ltd; City Ice & Cold Storage Pty Ltd; Penmore Pty Ltd; Snr Partner J. P. Williams & Associates, Penmore graziers; Underwriting Mem. of Lloyd's of London. Officer in Charge on behalf of Bank of England, Salvage Operations of RMS Niagara, sunk in 438 ft of water, 1941, when £2,396,000 worth of gold bullion weighing 8½ tons was recovered. *Publication:* So Ends This Day (autobiog.), 1982. *Address:* 77 St Georges Road, Toorak, Victoria 3142, Australia. *T:* 2412440; Penmore, Bolinda, Victoria. *Clubs:* Australian (Melbourne and Sydney); Melbourne (Melbourne).

WILLIAMS, Sir John (Robert), KCMG 1982 (CMG 1973); HM Diplomatic Service, retired; High Commissioner in Kenya, 1979–82; *b* 15 Sept. 1922; *s* of late Sydney James Williams, Australia; *m* 1958, Helga Elizabeth, *d* of Frederick Konow Lund, Bergen; two *s* two *d*. *Educ:* Sheen County School; Fitzwilliam House, Cambridge. Served War of 1939–45, with 1st Bn King's African Rifles in East Africa and Burma Campaign (Captain). Joined Colonial Office as Asst Principal, 1949; First Secretary, UK High Commission, New Delhi, 1956; Commonwealth Relations Office, 1958; Deputy High Commissioner in North Malaya, 1959–63; Counsellor, New Delhi, 1963–66; Commonwealth Office, 1966; Private Sec. to Commonwealth Secretary, 1967; Diplomatic Service Inspectorate, 1968; High Comr, Suva, 1970–74; Minister, Lagos, 1974–79 and concurrently Ambassador (non-resident) to Benin, 1976–79; Asst. Under-Sec. of State, FCO, 1979. Perm. British Rep. to UN Environment Prog. and to UN Centre for Human Settlements, 1979–82. *Recreations:* music, golf, gardening. *Address:* 3 York Avenue, SW14. *Clubs:* United Oxford & Cambridge University, Roehampton, Royal Commonwealth Society.

WILLIAMS, John Towner; composer of film scores; Conductor, Boston Pops Orchestra, since 1980; *b* 8 Feb. 1932. *Educ:* Juilliard Sch., NY. Hon. DMus: Berklee Coll. of Music, Boston, 1980; St Anselm Coll., Manchester, NH, 1981; Boston Conservatory of Music, 1982; Hon. DHL S Carolina, 1981; Hon. Dr of Fine Arts Northeastern Univ. (Boston), 1981. Awards include Oscars for: Fiddler on the Roof (filmscore arrangement), 1971; Jaws, 1976; Star Wars, 1978; 11 Grammies, 2 Emmys and many other awards; 16 Academy Award nominations. *Composer of film scores:* The Secret Ways, 1961; Diamond Head, 1962; None but the Brave, 1965; How to Steal a Million, 1966; Valley of the Dolls, 1967; The Cowboys, 1972; The Poseidon Adventure, 1972; Tom Sawyer, 1973; Earthquake, 1974; The Towering Inferno, 1974; Jaws, 1975; Jaws 2, 1976; The Eiger Sanction, 1975; Family Plot, 1976; Midway, 1976; The Missouri Breaks, 1976; Raggedy Ann and Andy, 1977; Black Sunday, 1977; Star Wars, 1977; Close Encounters of the 3rd Kind, 1977; The Fury, 1978; Superman, 1978; Dracula, 1979; The Empire Strikes Back, 1980; Raiders of the Lost Ark, 1981; E. T. (The Extra Terrestrial), 1982; many TV films. *Address:* c/o Boston Symphony Orchestra, 301 Massachusetts Avenue, Boston, Mass 02115, USA.

WILLIAMS, John Trevor; HM Diplomatic Service, retired; *b* 12 Nov. 1921; *yr s* of Dr Griffith Williams and Monica Johnson; *m* 1953, Ena Ferguson Boyd (*d* 1974); two *d*. *Educ:* St Paul's Sch.; Jesus Coll., Oxford. Joined Royal Armoured Corps, 1941; served with 14th/20th King's Hussars in Middle East and Italy, 1943–45. Home Civil Service, 1947–67; joined HM Diplomatic Service, 1967; Counsellor, High Commn, Wellington, NZ, 1967–69; Nato Defence Coll., Rome, 1970; Counsellor, Dublin, 1970–72; Head of Commodities Dept, FCO, 1972; seconded to: N Ireland Office, 1972–73; DoE, 1973–76. *Recreations:* riding, theatre, looking for good restaurants. *Address:* 29 Astell Street, Chelsea, SW3. *T:* 01-352 3945. *Club:* Hurlingham.

WILLIAMS, Maj.-Gen. John William C.; *see* Channing Williams.

WILLIAMS, Kenneth; *see* Williams, O. K.

WILLIAMS, Kenneth; actor; *b* 22 Feb. 1926; *s* of Charles George Williams and Louisa Alexandra (*née* Morgan). *Educ:* Lyulph Stanley Sch.; Bolt Court, London. Formerly lithograph draughtsman. Made first appearance on stage, Victoria Theatre, Singapore, playing the detective in Seven Keys to Baldpate, 1946, then Ninian in The First Mrs Fraser, Newquay Rep. Th., Cornwall, 1948; first London appearance as Slightly in Peter Pan, Scala, 1952; Dauphin in Saint Joan, Arts, 1954, transf. with this to St Martin's, 1955; Elijah in Orson Welles prodn of Moby Dick, Duke of York's, 1955; Montgomery in Sandy Wilson's The Buccaneer, Lyric, Hammersmith, 1955, subseq. Apollo, 1956; Maxime in Hotel Paradiso, Wintergarden, 1956; Kite in Wit to Woo, Arts, 1957; Green in Share My Lettuce, Lyric, Hammersmith, 1957, transf. to Comedy, 1957, and to Garrick, 1958; Portia in Cinderella, Coliseum, 1958. Starred in revue, Pieces of Eight, Apollo, 1959, and in One Over the Eight, Duke of York's, 1961. Played Julian in The Private Ear and the Public Eye, Globe, 1962; Jack in Gentle Jack, Queen's, 1963; Truscott in Loot, Arts, Cambridge, 1965; Bernard in Platinum Cat, Wyndham's, 1965; Drinkwater in Captain Brassbound's Conversion, Cambridge Th., 1971; Henry in My Fat Friend, Globe, 1972; Barillon in Signed and Sealed, Comedy, 1976; The Undertaking, Greenwich, later Fortune, 1979. Directed: Loot, Lyric Studio, 1980; Entertaining Mr Sloane, Lyric, Hammersmith, 1981. *Films:* Trent's Last Case; Beggar's Opera; The Seekers; Carry On series. *Television* series include: Hancock's Half Hour; International Cabaret; Kenneth Williams' Show; Whizz Kids Guide. Has broadcast regularly in Round the Horne, Stop Messing About, Just a Minute, etc. *Publication:* Acid Drops, 1980. *Recreations:* calligraphy, reading, music, walking. *Address:* ICM, 388/396 Oxford Street, W1N 9HE.

WILLIAMS, Kingsley; *see* Williams, J. B. K.

WILLIAMS, Kyffin; *see* Williams, John K.

WILLIAMS, Sir Leonard, KBE 1981; CB 1975; Director-General for Energy, Commission of the European Communities, 1976–81; *b* 19 Sept. 1919; *m* Anne Taylor Witherley; three *d*. *Educ:* St Olave's Grammar Sch.; King's Coll., London. Inland Revenue, 1938. War Service (RA), 1940–47. Ministry of Defence, 1948; NATO, 1951–54; Min. of Supply (later Aviation), 1954; Min. of Technology (later DTI), 1964; IDC 1966; Dep. Sec., 1973; Dept of Energy, 1974–76. *Address:* Blue Vines, Bramshott Vale, Liphook, Hants.

WILLIAMS, Leonard Edmund Henry, CBE 1981; DFC 1944; Chairman, Nationwide Building Society, since 1982 (Director, since 1975); *b* 6 Dec. 1919; *s* of William Edmund Williams; *m* 1946, Marie Harries-Jones; four *s* one *d*. *Educ:* Acton County Grammar School. FCA, FCBSI, IPFA; FRSA; CBIM. RAF, 1939–46. Acton Borough Council, 1935–39, Chief Internal Auditor 1946–49; Asst Accountant, Gas Council, 1949–53; Nationwide Building Society: Finance Officer, 1954–61; Dep. Gen. Man., 1961–67; Chief Exec., 1967–81. Director: Y. J. Lovell (Hldgs) plc, 1982–; Peachey Property Corp. plc, 1982–; Governor, BUPA Ltd, 1982–; Mem., Housing Corp., 1976–. Chairman: Metrop. Assoc. of Building Socs, 1972–73; Building Socs Assoc., 1979–81 (Dep. Chm., 1977–79); Mem. Council, Chartered Building Socs Inst. (Pres. 1969–70); Vice-Pres., Internat. Union of Building Socs and Savings Assocs. *Publication:* Building Society Accounts, 1966. *Recreations:* golf, reading. *Address:* The Romanys, Albury Road, Burwood Park, Walton-on-

Thames, Surrey KT12 5DY. *T:* Walton-on-Thames 42758. *Clubs:* Royal Air Force, City Livery.

WILLIAMS, Sir Leslie; *see* Williams, Sir J. L.

WILLIAMS, Ven. Leslie Arthur, MA; Archdeacon of Bristol, 1967-79; *b* 14 May 1909; *s* of Arthur and Susan Williams; *m* 1937, Margaret Mary, *d* of Richard Crocker; one *s* one *d. Educ:* Knutsford; Downing Coll., Cambridge. Curate of Holy Trinity, Bristol, 1934-37; Licensed to officiate, St Andrew the Great, Cambridge, 1937-40; Curate in Charge, St Peter, Lowden, Chippenham, 1940-42; Chaplain, RAFVR, 1942-46; Curate, Stoke Bishop, 1946-47; Vicar: Corsham, Wilts, 1947-53; Bishopston, Bristol, 1953-60; Stoke Bishop, Bristol, 1960-67. Rural Dean of Clifton, 1966-67; Hon. Canon of Bristol, 1958. *Recreation:* gardening. *Address:* 18 Reedley Road, Westbury on Trym, Bristol. *Clubs:* Hawks (Cambridge); Savage (Bristol).

WILLIAMS, Leslie Henry; Deputy Chairman, Imperial Chemical Industries Ltd, 1960-67; Chairman, ICI Fibres Ltd, 1965-67; *b* 26 Jan. 1903; *s* of late Edward Henry Williams; *m* 1930, Alice, *d* of late Henry Oliver Harrison; one *s. Educ:* Highbury County Sch.; London Univ. (BSc). Joined ICI Ltd, Paints Division, 1929; appointed Director, 1943; Managing Director, 1946; Chairman, 1947; Director of ICI Main Board, 1957, Dep. Chm., 1960; Director, British Nylon Spinners Ltd, 1957-64; Director Ilford Ltd, 1958-67. FRIC 1945; President, Royal Institute of Chemistry, 1967-70. Member, Monopolies Commission, 1967-73. Hon. FRIC 1978. Hon. DSc Salford, 1972. *Recreations:* golf, gardening, music. *Address:* Penny Green, West End Lane, Stoke Poges, Bucks. *T:* Farnham Common 3423.

WILLIAMS, Maxwell; *see* Williams, W. M. H.

WILLIAMS, Mrs Michael; *see* Dench, J. O.

WILLIAMS, Prof. Michael Maurice Rudolph, Professor of Nuclear Engineering, Queen Mary College, University of London, since 1970, Head of Department, since 1980; *b* 1 Dec. 1935; *s* of late M. F. Williams and G. M. A. Denton; *m* 1958, Ann Doreen Betty; one *s* one *d. Educ:* Ewell Castle Sch.; Croydon Polytechnic; King's Coll., London; Queen Mary Coll., London. BSc, PhD, DSc, CEng; Fellow, Instn Nuclear Engrs (Vice-Pres., 1971); FInstP. Engr with Central Electricity Generating Board, 1962; Research Associate at Brookhaven Nat. Lab., USA, 1962-63; Lectr, Dept of Physics, Univ. of Birmingham, 1963-65; Reader in Nuclear Engrg, Queen Mary Coll., London Univ., 1965-70. Chm. of Governors, Ewell Castle Sch., 1976-79. Exec. Editor: Annals of Nuclear Energy; Progress in Nuclear Energy. Fellow American Nuclear Soc. *Publications:* The Slowing Down and Thermalization of Neutrons, 1966; Mathematical Methods in Particle Transport Theory, 1971; Random Processes in Nuclear Reactors, 1974; contribs to Proc. Camb. Phil. Soc., Nucl. Science and Engrg, Jl Nuclear Energy, Jl Physics. *Address:* Nuclear Engineering Department, Queen Mary College, Mile End Road, E1. *T:* 01-980 4811.

WILLIAMS, Sir Michael O.; *see* Williams, Sir Osmond.

WILLIAMS, Sir Michael (Sanigear), KCMG 1968 (CMG 1954); HM Diplomatic Service, retired 1970; *b* 17 Aug. 1911; *s* of late Rev. F. F. S. Williams; *m* 1942, Joy Katharine Holdsworth Hunt (*d* 1964); two *d*; *m* 1965, Mary Grace Lindon (*née* Harding). *Educ:* Rugby; Trinity Coll., Cambridge. Entered Foreign Office, 1935; served at HM Embassy in Spain, 1938-39; Foreign Office, 1939-47; HM Embassy, Rome, 1947-50; HM Embassy, Rio de Janeiro, 1950-52; Foreign Office, 1952-56; Minister at Bonn, 1956-60; Minister to Guatemala, 1960-62; Ambassador to Guatemala, 1962-63; Assistant Under-Secretary of State, Foreign Office, 1963-65; Minister to the Holy See, 1965-70. *Recreations:* golf, gardening, motoring. *Address:* Wentways, Waldron, Heathfield, East Sussex.
See also Baron Dunboyne.

WILLIAMS, Nicholas James Donald; Managing Director and Chief Executive, Don Engineering, since 1977; President: Vintoil SA, since 1980; Vinton Oil and Gas Co., since 1980; *b* 21 Oct. 1925; *s* of late Nicholas Thomas Williams and Daisy Eustace (*née* Hollow); *m* 1st, 1947, Dawn Vyvyan (*née* Hill); one *s* one *d*; 2nd, 1955, Sheila Mary (*née* Dalgety); two *s* one *d. Educ:* St Erbyn's Sch., Penzance; Rugby Sch. (Scholar). Admitted Solicitor 1949. Served Royal Marines, 1943-47 (Captain). Partner, Nicholas Williams & Co., Solicitors, London, 1950; Senior Partner, Surridge & Beecheno, Solicitors, Karachi, 1955; Burmah Oil Co. Ltd: Legal Adviser, 1961; Co-ordinator for Eastern ops, 1963; Dir, 1965; Asst Man. Dir, 1967; Man. Dir and Chief Exec., 1969-75. Dir, Flarebay Ltd, 1978-. *Recreation:* sailing. *Address:* Charlton House, Tetbury, Glos. *Clubs:* Oriental, MCC, Royal Cornwall Yacht.

WILLIAMS, Nigel Christopher Ransome; HM Diplomatic Service; Head of United Nations Department, Foreign and Commonwealth Office, since 1980; *b* 29 April 1937; *s* of Cecil Gwynne Ransome Williams and Corinne Belden (*née* Rudd). *Educ:* Merchant Taylors' Sch.; St John's Coll., Oxford. Joined Foreign Service and posted to Tokyo, 1961; FO, 1966; Private Secretary: to Minister of State, 1968; to Chancellor of Duchy of Lancaster, 1969; UK Mission to UN, New York, 1970; FCO, 1973; Counsellor (Economic), Tokyo, 1976; Cabinet Office, 1980. *Address:* c/o Foreign and Commonwealth Office, SW1.

WILLIAMS, Noel Ignace B.; *see* Bond-Williams.

WILLIAMS, Norman; *see* Williams, R. N.

WILLIAMS, Sir Osmond, 2nd Bt, *cr* 1909; MC 1944; JP; *b* 22 April 1914; *s* of late Captain Osmond T. D. Williams, DSO, 2nd *s* of 1st Bt, and Lady Gladys Margaret Finch-Hatton, *o d* of 13th Earl of Winchilsea; *S* grandfather, 1927; *m* 1947, Benita Mary, *yr d* of late G. Henry Booker, and Mrs Michael Burn; two *d. Educ:* Eton; Freiburg Univ. Royal Scots Greys, 1935-37, and 1939-45; served Palestine, Africa, Italy and NW Europe. Chm., Quarry Tours Ltd, 1973-77. Vice-Chm., Amnesty Internat. (British Sect.), 1971-74. Trustee: Internat. Prisoners of Conscience Fund; Festiniog Rly Trust; Mem., Merioneth Park Planning Cttee, 1971-74. Governor, Rainer Foundn Outdoor Pursuits Centre, 1964-76. JP 1960 (Chairman of the Bench, Ardudwy-uwch-Artro, Gwynedd). Chevalier, Order of Leopold II with Palm; Croix de Guerre with Palm (Belgium), 1940. *Recreations:* music, travelling. *Heir:* none. *Address:* Borthwen, Penrhyndeudraeth, Gwynedd. *Club:* Travellers'.

WILLIAMS, (Owen) Kenneth, JP; Secretary, Commonwealth Magistrates' Association, since 1980; *b* 24 Dec. 1928; *m* 1956, Thelma Sanders; three *s* one *d. Educ:* Waterloo Grammar Sch.; Gordonstoun. Master Mariner; FIPM. Navigating Cadet, Deck Officer and Captain, 1945-56; commnd RNR, 1951; served on HMS Scorpion, retired Lieut, 1959; came ashore with Hicks, Parkes & Hoyle, Marine Surveyors, 1956; Dir and Partner, associated Consulting Engineers, J. Latta & Partners, 1958; joined Tate & Lyle Gp as a Marine Supt, Silvertown Services Shipping, 1962; Personnel Supt, Sugar Line, 1968; Gp Personnel & Trng Manager, United Molasses Co., 1973; Employee Relations Adviser, 1975, then on secondment to Industrial Participation Assoc. as Dir of Trng Services, 1977-80. Formerly: Chm. Dagenham Gp and Mem. IPM Nat. Cttee on Employee Relations; Councillor, London Bor. of Bromley, 1971-74; occasional Lectr, British Shipping Fedn; Mem., GCBS Management Development Working Party; Outside Examiner, NE London Polytechnic; Founder Mem. and Chm. of two schools' Parents' Assocs. Governor: The Ramsden Schs, 1975-; Orpington Coll. of Further Education, 1975-; Trustee, Orpington Village Hall Trust, 1976-. JP SE London Commission Area, 1976. *Publications:* Employment Legislation Guidance for Line Managers, 1978; Preparation and Training for Participation, 1979; latterly, contribs to Commonwealth Judicial Jl. *Recreations:* wine making, DIY home decorating, reading. *Address:* 96 Avalon Road, Orpington, Kent BR6 9BA. *T:* Orpington 23744.

WILLIAMS, Owen Lenn; retired; Regional Financial and Development Adviser, St Vincent, West Indies, 1976-78; *b* 4 March 1914; *s* of Richard Owen Williams and Frances Daisy Williams (*née* Lenn); *m* 1959, Gisela Frucht. *Educ:* St Albans Sch.; London University. Asst Principal, Export Credit Guarantee Dept, 1938; Asst Principal, Treasury, 1939; UK High Commn, Ottawa, 1941; Principal, Treasury, 1945; Asst Treasury Representative, UK High Commn, New Delhi, 1953; Treasury Rep., UK High Commn, Karachi, 1955; Economic and Financial Adviser, Leeward Islands, 1957; Perm. Sec., Min. of Finance, Eastern Nigeria, 1959; Asst Sec., Treasury, 1962; Counsellor, UK Delegn to OECD, 1968-73; Gen. Fiscal Adviser to Minister of Finance, Sierra Leone, 1974-75. *Recreations:* music, travel. *Address:* c/o National Westminster Bank Ltd, Caxton House, SW1; 75 Bayham Road, Sevenoaks, Kent. *Club:* Reform.

WILLIAMS, Paul; Chairman, Backer Electric Co. Ltd; Director: Minster Executive Ltd; Henry Sykes Ltd; *b* 14 Nov. 1922; *s* of late Samuel O. Williams and Esmée I. Williams (*née* Cail); *m* 1947, Barbara Joan Hardy (marr. diss. 1964); two *d*; *m* 1964, Gillian Foote, *e d* of A. G. Howland Jackson, Elstead, Surrey, and of Mrs E. J. Foote, and step *d* of late E. J. Foote, Cascais, Portugal; one *d. Educ:* Marlborough; Trinity Hall, Cambridge (MA). MP (C) Sunderland South, (C 1953-57, Ind. C 1957-58, C 1958-64). Chairman, Monday Club, 1964-69. FInstD; FBIM. *Address:* 6 Elm Park Road, SW3. *T:* 01-352 5527. *Clubs:* Boodle's, Institute of Directors.

WILLIAMS, Paul H.; *see* Hodder-Williams.

WILLIAMS, Penry Herbert, DPhil; Fellow and Tutor in Modern History, New College, Oxford, since 1964; *b* 25 Feb. 1925; *s* of late Douglas Williams and Dorothy Williams (*née* Murray); *m* 1952, June Carey Hobson, *d* of late George and Kathleene Hobson; one *s* one *d. Educ:* Marlborough Coll.; New Coll., Oxford, 1947-50; St Antony's Coll., Oxford, 1950-51. MA, DPhil Oxon. Served Royal Artillery, 1943-45, Royal Indian Artillery, 1945-47. Asst Lecturer in History, 1951-54, Lectr, 1954-63, Sen. Lectr, 1963-64, Univ. of Manchester; Fellow of Winchester Coll., 1978. Jt Editor, English Historical Review, 1982. *Publications:* The Council in the Marches of Wales under Elizabeth I, 1958; Life in Tudor England, 1963; The Tudor Régime, 1979, paperback 1981; (ed, with John Buxton) New College, Oxford 1379-1979, 1979; contribs to learned jls. *Address:* New College, Oxford OX1 3BN; 53 Park Town, Oxford OX2 6SL. *T:* Oxford 57613.

WILLIAMS, Peter F.; *see* Firmston-Williams.

WILLIAMS, Peter H.; *see* Havard-Williams.

WILLIAMS, Peter Keegan; HM Diplomatic Service; Counsellor, GATT, UK Mission, Geneva, since 1979; *b* 3 April 1938; *s* of William Edward Williams and Lilian (*née* Spright); *m* 1969, Rosamund Mary de Worms; two *d. Educ:*

Calday Grange Grammar Sch.; Collège de Marcq-en-Baroeul (Nord); Univ. de Lille; Pembroke Coll., Oxford (MA). Joined Diplomatic Service, 1962; language student, MECAS, Lebanon, 1962; Second Sec., Beirut, 1963, Jedda, 1964; Commonwealth Office, 1967; First Sec., FCO, 1969; Director, Policy and Reference Div., British Information Services, New York, 1970; First Sec., FCO, 1973; First Sec., Head of Chancery and Consul, Rabat, 1976 (Chargé d'Affaires, 1978 and 1979). *Recreations:* wine, walking. *Address:* c/o Foreign and Commonwealth Office, SW1. *Club:* United Oxford & Cambridge University.

WILLIAMS, Peter Lancelot, OBE 1971; editor, writer on ballet, designer; chairman of committees on dance; *b* 12 June 1914; *s* of Col G. T. Williams and Awdrie Elkington. *Educ:* Harrow Sch.; Central Sch. of Art and Design, London. Dress designer with own business, 1934-39; Head Designer, Jantzen Ltd, 1945-47; stage designer, 1947-. Arts Council of Great Britain, 1965-80: served on most panels with connections with ballet and music; resp. for ballet sect. on Opera and Ballet Enquiry, 1966-69 (led to develt of dance theatre throughout GB); Chm., Dance Advisory Cttee (formerly Dance Theatre Cttee), 1973-80. *Chairman:* Brit. Council's Drama Adv. Cttee, 1976-81; (also Founder), Dancers Pensions and Resettlement Fund, 1975-; Creative Dance Artists Ltd, 1979-; Vice-Chm., Royal Ballet Benevolent Fund; Mem., most cttees concerned with dance: Royal Acad. of Dancing, Cecchetti Soc. Asst Editor, Ballet, 1949-50; Founder Editor/Art Dir, Dance and Dancers, 1950-80; Ballet Critic, Daily Mail, 1950-53; Dance Critic, The Observer, 1982- (Deputy, 1970-). *Publications:* Masterpieces of Ballet Design, 1981; contrib. articles, mainly on dance and theatre, to newspapers and magazines in GB and internationally. *Address:* Tredrea, Perranarworthal, Truro, Cornwall; 1 St Albans Studios, St Albans Grove, W8.

WILLIAMS, Dr Peter Orchard, FRCP; Director: The Wellcome Trust, since 1965; Wellcome Institute for the History of Medicine, since 1981; *b* 23 Sept. 1925; *s* of Robert Orchard Williams, CBE, and Agnes Annie Birkinshaw; *m* 1949, Billie Innes Brown; two *d. Educ:* Caterham Sch.; Queen's Royal College, Trinidad; St John's Coll., Cambridge (MA); St Mary's Hospital Medical School. MB, BChir 1950; MRCP 1952; FRCP 1970. House Physician, St Mary's Hospital, 1950-51; Registrar, Royal Free Hospital, 1951-52; Medical Specialist, RAMC, BMH Iserlohn, 1954; Medical Officer, Headquarters, RAMC, 1955-60; Wellcome Trust: Asst and Dep. Scientific Secretary, 1960-64; Scientific Secretary, 1964-65. Vice-Pres., Royal Soc. of Tropical Med. and Hygiene, 1975-77; Member: Nat. Council of Soc. Services Cttee of Enquiry into Charity Law and Practice, 1974-76; BBC, IBA Central Appeals Adv. Cttee; Chairman: Foundations Forum, 1977-79; Assoc. of Med. Res. Charities, 1974-76, 1979-; Hague Club (European Foundns), 1981-. *Publications:* Careers in Medicine, 1952; papers in scientific journals. *Recreations:* gardening, travel, golf. *Address:* Ashley House, Wootton, Woodstock, Oxfordshire.

WILLIAMS, Sir Peter W.; *see* Watkin Williams.

WILLIAMS, Sir Philip; *see* Williams, Sir R. P. N.

WILLIAMS, Sir Ralph D. D.; *see under* Dudley-Williams, Sir Rolf (Dudley).

WILLIAMS, Prof. Raymond Henry; Fellow of Jesus College, Cambridge, since 1961; *b* 31 Aug. 1921; *s* of Henry Joseph Williams and Gwendolene Williams (*née* Bird); *m* 1942, Joyce Mary Dalling; two *s* one *d. Educ:* Abergavenny Grammar Sch.; Trinity Coll., Cambridge; MA, LittD. War service (ending as Captain), 21st Anti-Tank Regt, Guards Armoured Div., 1941-45; Staff Tutor in Literature, Oxford University Extra-Mural Delegacy, 1946-61; Univ. Reader in Drama, 1967-74, Professor of Drama, 1974-Sept. 1983, University of Cambridge. Mem., Arts Council, 1976-78. Vis. Prof. of Political Science, Stanford Univ., USA, 1973. DUniv Open, 1975; Hon. DLitt Wales, 1980. General Editor, New Thinkers' Library, 1962-70. Editor: Politics and Letters, 1946-47; May Day Manifesto, 1968. *Publications:* Reading and Criticism, 1950; Drama from Ibsen to Eliot, 1952; Drama in Performance, 1954 (rev. edn 1968); Culture and Society, 1958; Border Country, 1960; The Long Revolution, 1961; Communications, 1962 (rev. edn, 1976); Second Generation, 1964; Modern Tragedy, 1966; Public Inquiry, 1967; Drama from Ibsen to Brecht, 1968; The English Novel from Dickens to Lawrence, 1970; A Letter from the Country, 1971; Orwell, 1971; The Country and the City, 1973; Television: technology and cultural form, 1974; (ed) George Orwell, 1975; Keywords, 1976; Marxism and Literature, 1977; The Volunteers, 1978; (ed with Marie Axton) English Drama: forms and development, 1978; The Fight for Manod, 1979; Politics and Letters: interviews with New Left Review, 1979; Problems in Materialism and Culture, 1980; (ed) Contact: the history of human communications, 1981; Culture, 1981. *Recreation:* gardening. *Address:* Jesus College, Cambridge.

WILLIAMS, Raymond Lloyd, DPhil, DSc; CChem, FRSC; Director: Metropolitan Police Laboratory, since 1968; Visiting Professor in Chemistry, University of East Anglia, since 1968; *b* Bournemouth, 27 Feb. 1927; *s* of Walter Raymond Williams and late Vera Mary Williams; *m* 1956, Sylvia Mary Lawson Whitaker; one *s* one *d. Educ:* Bournemouth Sch.; St John's Coll., Oxford (schol.). Gibbs Univ. Schol. 1948, BA 1st Cl. Hons Nat Sci-Chem, MA, DPhil, DSc Oxon. Research Fellow, Pressed Steel Co., 1951-53; Commonwealth Fund Fellow, Univ. of California, Berkeley, 1953-54; progressively, Sen. Res. Fellow, Sen. Scientific Officer, Principal Sci.

Officer, Explosives R&D Estab., 1955-60; PSO, Admiralty Materials Lab., 1960-62; Explosives R&D Establishment: SPSO, 1962; Supt, Analytical Services Gp, 1962-65; Supt, Non-metallic Materials Gp, 1965-68. Jt Editor, Forensic Science International, 1978-. Hon. Mem., Assoc. of Police Surgeons of GB, 1980. *Publications:* papers in scientific jls on spectroscopy, analytical chemistry, and forensic science. *Recreations:* lawn tennis (played for Civil Service and Oxfordshire: representative colours), squash rackets, carpentry. *Address:* 9 Meon Road, Bournemouth, Dorset BH7 6PN. *T:* Bournemouth 423446.

WILLIAMS, (Reginald) Norman, CB 1982; Under Secretary, Department of Health and Social Security, since 1977; *b* 23 Oct. 1917; *s* of Reginald Gardnar Williams and Janet Mary Williams; *m* 1956, Hilary Frances West; two *s. Educ:* Neath Grammar Sch.; Swansea Univ. Served War: Captain RA and later Staff Captain HQ 30 Corps, 1940-46. Solicitor in private practice, 1947-48. Dept of Health and Social Security (formerly Min. of Nat. Insurance): Legal Asst, 1948; Sen. Legal Asst, 1959; Asst Solicitor, 1966; Principal Asst Solicitor, 1974. Member of Law Society. *Recreations:* golf, photography, reading. *Address:* Brecon, 23 Castle Hill Avenue, Berkhamsted, Herts HP4 1HJ. *T:* Berkhamsted 5291.

WILLIAMS, (Richard) Derrick, MA (Cantab); Principal, Gloucestershire College of Arts and Technology, since 1981; *b* 30 March 1926; *s* of Richard Leslie Williams and Lizzie Paddington; *m* 1949, Beryl Newbury Stonebanks; four *s. Educ:* St John's Coll., Cambridge. Asst Master, Lawrence Sherrif Sch., Rugby, 1950-51; Lectr, University Coll., Ibadan, Nigeria, 1951-52; Adult Tutor, Ashby-de-la-Zouch Community Coll., Leicestershire, 1952-54; Further Educn Organising Tutor, Oxfordshire, 1954-60; Asst Educn Officer: West Suffolk, 1960-65; Bristol, 1965-67; Dep. Chief Educn Officer, Bristol, 1967-73; Chief Educn Officer, County of Avon, 1973-76; Dir, Glos Inst. of Higher Educn, 1977-80. *Recreations:* cricket, music. *Address:* 7 Longs View, Avon Grange, Charfield, Glos. *T:* Wotton-under-Edge 3489.

WILLIAMS, Richard Hall; Under Secretary, Agriculture Department, Welsh Office, Cardiff, since 1981; *b* 21 Oct. 1926; *s* of Edward Hall Williams and Kitty Hall Williams; *m* 1949, Nia Wynn (*née* Jones); two *s* two *d. Educ:* Barry Grammar Sch., Glamorgan; University College of Wales, Aberystwyth (BScEcon Hons). Experience in university teaching, local government, industry and technical and management education before entering Civil Service, 1967; subsequent career within Welsh Office has included service in Health and Economic Planning Groups before entering Agriculture Dept on its establishment, 1978. *Recreation:* enjoying all things Welsh. *Address:* Argoed, Llyswen Road, Cyncoed, Cardiff CF2 6NG. *T:* Cardiff 752755.

WILLIAMS, Robert Emmanuel; *b* 1 Jan. 1900; *o s* of David Williams; *m* 1st, 1928, Rosamund May Taylor (*d* 1929); 2nd, 1938, Audrey Forbes Higginson; three *s* one *d. Educ:* Liverpool Institute; Liverpool Univ. (MSc); Brasenose Coll., Oxford (MA). Assistant Master: Ilkeston, Rugby, Lawrence Sheriff Sch., Repton, 1922-36; Lecturer, Oxford Univ. Department of Education, 1936-39; HM Inspector of Schools, 1939; Staff Inspector, 1945; Chief Inspector of Schools, Ministry of Education, 1952-61; Simon Senior Research Fellow, Manchester Univ., 1961-62; Lecturer in Education, London Univ. Institute of Education, 1962-67. *Publications:* contributions to School Science Review, Religion in Education. *Address:* Sea Crest, 10 Ryder's Avenue, Westgate-on-Sea, Kent. *T:* Thanet 33521.

WILLIAMS, Sir Robert (Evan Owen), Kt 1976; MD, FRCP, FRCPath; FFCM; Director, Public Health Laboratory Service, 1973-81; Chairman, Genetic Manipulation Advisory Group, since 1981; *b* 30 June 1916; *s* of Gwynne Evan Owen Williams and Cicely Mary (*née* Innes); *m* 1944, Margaret (*née* Lumsden); one *s* two *d. Educ:* Sherborne Sch., Dorset; University College, London and University College Hospital. Assistant Pathologist, EMS, 1941-42; Pathologist, Medical Research Council Unit, Birmingham Accident Hospital, 1942-46; on staff Public Health Laboratory Service, 1946-60 (Director, Streptococcus, Staphylococcus and Air Hygiene Laboratory, 1949-60); Prof. of Bacteriology, Univ. of London, at St Mary's Hosp. Med. Sch., 1960-73, Dean 1967-73. Mem. MRC, 1969-73. Pres., RCPath, 1975-78. Fellow, UCL, 1968. Hon. FRCPA, 1977; Hon. MD Uppsala, 1972; Hon. DSc Bath, 1977. *Publications:* (jt author) Hospital Infection, 1966; numerous publications in journals on bacteriological and epidemiological subjects. *Recreation:* horticulture. *Address:* Little Platt, Plush, Dorchester, Dorset DT2 7RQ. *T:* Piddletrenthide 320. *Club:* Athenæum.

WILLIAMS, Prof. Robert Joseph Paton, DPhil; FRS 1972; Royal Society Napier Research Professor at Oxford, since 1974; Fellow of Wadham College, Oxford, since 1955; *b* 25 Feb. 1926; *m* 1952, Jelly Klara (*née* Büchli); two *s. Educ:* Wallasey Grammar Sch.; Merton Coll., Oxford (MA, DPhil). FRSC. Rotary Foundn Fellow, Uppsala, 1950-51; Jun. Res. Fellow, Merton Coll., Oxford, 1951-55; Lectr, 1955-73, Reader in Inorganic Chemistry, 1973-74, Univ. of Oxford. Associate, Peter Bent Brigham Hosp., Boston, USA; Commonwealth Fellow, Mass, 1965-66. Liversidge Lectr, Chem. Soc., 1979; Bakerian Lectr, Royal Soc., 1981. For. Mem., Acad. of Science, Portugal. Hon. DSc Liège, 1980. Tilden Medal, Chem. Soc., 1970; Keilin Medal, Biochem. Soc., 1972; Hughes Medal, Royal Soc., 1979; Chaire Bruylants Medal, Louvain, 1979. *Publications:* (with C. S. G. Phillips) Inorganic Chemistry, 1965; (jtly) Nuclear Magnetic Resonance in Biology, 1977; (ed jtly) New Trends in Bio-Inorganic Chemistry, 1978; papers in Jl Chem. Soc., biochemical jls, etc. *Recreation:* walking in the country. *Address:* Wadham College, Oxford. *T:* Oxford 242564.

WILLIAMS, Robert Martin, CB 1981; CBE 1973; Chairman, State Services Commission, New Zealand, 1975-81; *b* 30 March 1919; *s* of late Canon Henry Williams; *m* Mary Constance, *d* of late Rev. Francis H. Thorpe; one *s* two *d. Educ:* Christ's Coll., NZ; Canterbury University College, NZ; St John's Coll., Cambridge. MA. 1st Class Hons Mathematics, Univ. Sen. Schol., Shirtcliffe Fellow, NZ, 1940; BA, 1st Class Hons Mathematics Tripos, Cantab, 1947; PhD Math. Statistics, Cantab, 1949. Mathematician at Radar Development Laboratory, DSIR, NZ, 1941-44; Member UK Atomic Group in US, 1944-45; Member, 1949-53, Director, 1953-62, Applied Mathematics Laboratory, DSIR, NZ; Harkness Commonwealth Fellow and Vis. Fellow, at Princeton Univ., 1957-58; State Services Commissioner, NZ Public Service, 1963-67; Vice-Chancellor: Univ. of Otago, Dunedin, 1967-73; ANU, 1973-75. Mem., NZ Metric Adv. Bd, 1969-73. Mem., Internat. Statistical Inst., 1961-. Chm., Cttee of Inquiry into Educnl TV, 1970-72. Carnegie Travel Award, 1969. Hon. LLD Otago, 1972. *Publications:* papers mainly on mathematical statistics and related topics. *Address:* 21 Wadestown Road, Wellington, New Zealand.

WILLIAMS, Sir (Robert) Philip (Nathaniel), 4th Bt *cr* 1915; *b* 3 May 1950; *s* of Sir David Philip Williams, 3rd Bt and of Elizabeth Mary Garneys, *d* of late William Ralph Garneys Bond; *S* father, 1970; *m* 1979, Catherine Margaret Godwin, *d* of Canon Cosmo Pouncey, Tewkesbury; one *s* one *d. Educ:* Marlborough; St Andrews Univ. MA Hons. *Heir: s* David Robert Mark Williams, *b* 31 Oct. 1980. *Address:* Bridehead, Dorchester, Dorset. *T:* Long Bredy 232. *Club:* MCC.

WILLIAMS, Sir Robin (Philip), 2nd Bt, *cr* 1953; Insurance Broker since 1952; Lloyd's Underwriter, 1961; 2nd Lieut, retired, RA; *b* 27 May 1928; *s* of Sir Herbert Geraint Williams, 1st Bt, MP, MSc, MEngAssoc, MInstCE; *S* father 1954; *m* 1955, Wendy Adèle Marguerite, *o d* of late Felix Joseph Alexander, London and Hong Kong; two *s. Educ:* Eton Coll.; St John's Coll., Cambridge (MA). 2nd Lieut, Royal Artillery, 1947. Vice-Chairman, Federation of Univ. Conservative and Unionist Assocs, 1951-52; Acting Chairman, 1952; Chairman of Bow Group (Conservative Research Society), 1954. Called to Bar, Middle Temple, 1954; Chm., Anti-Common Market League, 1969; Dir, Common Market Safeguards Campaign, 1973-76. Councillor, Haringey, 1968-74. *Publication:* Whose Public Schools?, 1957. *Heir: s* Anthony Geraint Williams, *b* 22 Dec. 1958. *Address:* 1 Broadlands Close, Highgate, N6.

WILLIAMS, Dr Roger Stanley, FRCP; Director, Liver Research Unit and Consultant Physician, King's College Hospital and Medical School, since 1966; Consultant, Liver Research Unit Trust, since 1974; *b* 28 Aug. 1931; *s* of Stanley George Williams and Doris Dagmar Clatworthy; *m* 1st, 1954, Lindsay Mary Elliott (marr. diss. 1977); two *s* three *d* ; 2nd, 1978, Stephanie Gay de Laszlo; one *s* one *d. Educ:* St Mary's Coll., Southampton; London Hosp. Med. Coll., Univ. of London. MB, BS (Hons), MD; MRCS, LRCP, MRCP, FRCP. House appointments and Pathology Asst, London Hospital, 1953-56; Jun. Med. Specialist, Queen Alexandra Hospital, Millbank, 1956-58; Medical Registrar and Tutor, Royal Postgrad. Med. Sch., 1958-59; Lectr in Medicine, Royal Free Hospital, 1959-65; Consultant Physician, Royal South Hants and Southampton General Hospital, 1965-66. Member: Adv. Gp on Hepatitis, DHSS, 1980-; Transplant Adv. Panel, DHSS, 1974-; WHO Scientific Gp on Viral Hepatitis, Geneva, 1972. Rockefeller Travelling Fellowship in Medicine, 1962; Legg Award, Royal Free Hosp. Med. Sch., 1964; Melrose Meml Lecture, Glasgow, 1970; Goulstonian Lectr, RCP, 1970; Searle Lecture, Amer. Assoc. for the Study of Liver Diseases, 1972; Sir Ernest Finch Vis. Prof., Sheffield, 1974; Fleming Lecture, Glasgow Coll. of Physicians and Surgeons, 1975; Sir Arthur Hurst Meml Lecture, British Soc. of Gastroenterology, 1975; Skinner Lecture, Royal Coll. of Radiologists, 1978; Albert M. Snell Meml Lecture, Palo Alto Med. Foundn, 1981. Member: European Assoc. for the Study of the Liver (Cttee Mem., 1966-70); Harveian Soc. of London (Sec., Councillor and Vice-Pres., 1963-70, Pres., 1974-75); Liver Club (Sec. and Treasurer, 1968-71); Royal Soc. of Medicine (Sec. of Section, 1969-71). *Publications:* Editor: Fifth Symposium on Advanced Medicine, 1969; Immunology of the Liver, 1971; Artificial Liver Support, 1975; Immune Reactions in Liver Disease, 1978; Drug Reactions and the Liver, 1981; (ed) Variceal Bleeding, 1982; author of over 500 scientific papers, review articles and book chapters. *Recreations:* tennis, sailing, opera. *Address:* Eaglehurst West, Stanswood Road, Calshot, Hants. *T:* Fawley 893090; 8 Eldon Road, W8. *T:* 01-937 5301. *Clubs:* Saints and Sinners; Royal Ocean Racing; Royal London Yacht (Cowes).

WILLIAMS, Sir Rolf D. D.; *see* Dudley-Williams.

WILLIAMS, Ronald William; Director, Office of Manpower Economics, since 1980; *b* 19 Dec. 1926; *yr s* of late Albert Williams and Katherine Teresa Williams (*née* Chilver). *Educ:* City of London Sch.; Downing Coll., Cambridge (BA, LLB). RN, 1945-48. Iraq Petroleum Co. Ltd, 1956-58; Philips Electrical Industries Ltd, 1958-64; Sen. Consultant, PA Management Consultants Ltd, 1964-69; Asst Sec., NBPI, 1969-71; Sen. Consultant, Office of Manpower Economics, 1971-73; Asst Sec., CSD, 1973-80; Under Sec. 1980. *Recreations:* history, music, things Italian. *Address:* c/o Office of Manpower Economics, 22 Kingsway, WC2B 6JY. *T:* 01-405 5944.

WILLIAMS, Roy; Under Secretary, Department of Trade, since 1979; *b* 31 Dec. 1934; *s* of Eric Williams and Ellen Williams; *m* 1959, Shirley, *d* of Captain and Mrs O. Warwick; one *s* one *d. Educ:* Liverpool Univ. (BA Econs). Asst Principal, Min. of Power, 1956; Principal, 1961; Harkness Commonwealth Fellow, Univs of Chicago and Berkeley, 1963-64; Principal Private Sec., Minister of Power and subseq. Paymaster Gen., 1969; Asst Sec., DTI, 1971; Principal Private Sec., Sec. of State for Industry, 1974; Under-Sec., DoI, 1976. *Address:* 4 The Glade, Sevenoaks, Kent. *T:* Sevenoaks 53369.

WILLIAMS, Rt. Hon. Shirley Vivien Teresa Brittain, PC 1974; MP (SDP) Crosby, since Nov. 1981; Professorial Fellow, Policy Studies Institute, since 1979; Co-founder, Social Democratic Party, 1981, President since 1982; broadcaster; *b* 27 July 1930; *d* of late Prof. Sir George Catlin, and late Mrs Catlin, (Vera Brittain); *m* 1955, Prof. Bernard Arthur Owen Williams (marr. diss. 1974), *qv* ; one *d. Educ:* eight schools in UK and USA; Somerville Coll., Oxford (MA), Hon. Fellow, 1970; Columbia Univ., New York. General Secretary, Fabian Soc., 1960-64 (Chm., 1980-81). Contested (Lab) Harwich, Essex, 1954 and 1955, and Southampton Test, 1959; MP (Lab) Hitchin, 1964-74, Hertford and Stevenage, 1974-79; Parliamentary Private Secretary, Minister of Health, 1964-66; Parly Sec., Min. of Labour, 1966-67; Minister of State: Education and Science, 1967-69; Home Office, 1969-70; Opposition spokesman on: Social Services, 1970-71, on Home Affairs, 1971-73; Prices and Consumer Protection, 1973-74; Sec. of State for Prices and Consumer Protection, 1974-76; Sec. of State for Educn and Science, 1976-79; Paymaster General, 1976-79. Chm., OECD study on youth employment, 1979. Mem., Labour Party Nat. Exec. Cttee, 1970-81. Visiting Fellow, Nuffield College, Oxford, 1967-75; Godkin Lectr, Harvard, 1980; Rede Lectr, Cambridge, 1980; Janeway Lectr, Princeton, 1981. Hon. DEd CNAA, 1969; Hon. Dr Pol. Econ.: Univ. of Leuven, 1976; Radcliffe Coll., Harvard, 1978; Leeds, 1980; Bath, 1980; Hon. LLD: Sheffield, 1980; Southampton, 1981; Hon. DLitt Heriot-Watt, 1980; Hon. DSc Aston, 1981. *Publications:* Politics is for People, 1981; Jobs for the 1980s; Youth Without Work, 1981. *Recreations:* music and walking. *Address:* c/o House of Commons, SW1; c/o Policy Studies Institute, 1 Castle Lane, SW1.

WILLIAMS, Rev. (Sidney) Austen, CVO 1980; Vicar of St Martin-in-the-Fields, since 1956; Chaplain to the Queen's Household, 1961-82, Extra Chaplain since 1982; a Prebendary of St Paul's Cathedral, since 1973; *b* 23 Feb. 1912; *s* of Sidney Herbert and Dorothy Williams; *m* 1945, Daphne Joan McWilliam; one *s* one *d. Educ:* Bromsgrove School; St Catharine's College, Cambridge (MA); Westcott House, Cambridge. Curate of St Paul, Harringay, 1937-40. Chaplain, Toc H, France and Germany (POW), 1940-48. Curate of: All Hallows, Barking by the Tower, 1945-46; St Martin-in-the-Fields, 1946-51; Vicar of St Albans, Westbury Park, Clifton, Bristol, 1951-56. Freeman of the City of London, 1977. *Recreations:* photography, ornithology. *Address:* 6 St Martin's Place, WC2N 4JJ. *T:* 01-930 0669.

WILLIAMS, Stanley; solicitor; Member, Mental Health Review Tribunal (Wales Region), since 1972; *b* 6 April 1911; *s* of Thomas and Sarah Elizabeth Williams; *m* 1948, Lily Ceridwen Evans; three *s* one *d. Educ:* Froncysyllte; Llangollen County Sch. (Schol.); Liverpool Univ. (LLB). Admitted Solicitor, 1934. Served War of 1939-45: ranks, 1940-43; commnd RAMC, 1943. Contested (Lab) Denbigh Division, 1959 and 1964. A Recorder of the Crown Court, 1972-75. Member: Bootle Corporation, 1934-38 and 1946-50; Denbighshire County Council, 1960-63; Wrexham Corporation, 1966-68; Noise Adv. Council, 1970. *Recreations:* music, walking, gardening. *Address:* Liddington, Wynnstay Lane, Marford, Wrexham, Clwyd. *T:* Gresford 2715.

WILLIAMS, Stuart Graeme, OBE 1949; Controller, Television Administration, BBC, 1956-74; Director of Studies, Royal Institute of Public Administration, since 1975; part-time Chairman, Civil Service Commission Appointment Boards; *b* 5 October 1914; *y s* of late Douglas Williams, author and journalist, and late Winifred Maud Williams (who *m* 2nd, late Sydney A. Moseley); *m* 1938, Catherine Anne, *d* of late Charles Thomas and Florence Hutchison; one *d. Educ:* Alleyn Court, Westcliff-on-Sea; Wallingbrook, Chulmleigh. Joined BBC as Programme Sub-Editor, Radio Times, 1931; particularly concerned with war-time and post-war develt, BBC Overseas, European and Monitoring Services, and with develt of BBC and Internat. TV. Principal appointments: Executive: Outside Broadcasting, 1938; Monitoring Service, 1939; Empire Service, 1940; Asst Head, Overseas Programme Admin., 1941; Admin. Officer, Overseas Services, 1942; visited Middle and Far East for negotiations concerning future of British Far Eastern Broadcasting Service, Singapore and Radio SEAC, Ceylon, 1947 and 1948; Head of External Broadcasting Admin., 1948; BBC Staff Admin. Officer, 1952; Asst Controller, Staff Admin., 1955; visited Nigeria to advise Nigeria Govt concerning incorporation of Nigeria Broadcasting Service, 1955; visited Malta as member of a BBC Working Party to report on possible introduction of television in Malta, 1959; advised on organisation of Broadcasting in Singapore, 1968; visited Nigeria for RIPA and Federal Govt to advise on Civil Service Management Trng, 1976. Dir, Visnews Ltd, the international Newsfilm Agency, 1957-74 (Dep. Chm., 1962-74); Chm., European Broadcasting Union Cost-Sharing Gp, 1965-74. Mem., Exec. Council, RIPA, 1951-68, Chm., 1957; Mem., Asian Broadcasting Union Finance Gp, 1971-74. World travel for BBC, and later EBU, 1947-74. *Address:* 92 Moor Lane, Rickmansworth, Herts WD3 1LQ. *T:* Rickmansworth 774271.

WILLIAMS, Mrs Susan Eva, MBE 1959; HM Lieutenant of South Glamorgan, since 1981; *b* 17 Aug. 1915; *d* of Robert Henry Williams and Dorothy Marie Williams; *m* 1950, Charles Crofts Llewellyn Williams. *Educ:* St James's, West Malvern. WAAF, 1939–45. JP 1961, High Sheriff 1968, DL 1973, Glamorgan. *Recreation:* National Hunt racing. *Address:* Caercady, Welsh St Donats, Cowbridge, S Glamorgan CF7 7ST. *T:* Cowbridge 2346.

WILLIAMS, Tennessee, (Thomas Lanier Williams); Playwright; *b* 26 March 1911; *s* of Cornelius Coffin Williams and Edwina Dakin. *Educ:* University of Missouri; University of Iowa; Washington University. Awarded Rockefeller Fellowship 1940 (playwriting); Grant from National Institute of Arts and Letters ($1000), 1943; New York Drama Critics Circle Award, 1944–45, 1947–48, 1955, 1960–61; Pulitzer Prize, 1948, 1955. Member Alpha Tau Omega. *Publications: plays:* Battle of Angels; The Glass Menagerie, 1944; (with Donald Windham) You Touched Me, 1945; A Streetcar Named Desire, 1947; Summer and Smoke, 1948; The Rose Tattoo, 1951; Camino Real, 1953; Cat on a Hot Tin Roof, 1955; Orpheus Descending, 1957; Garden District (2 plays: Suddenly Last Summer and Something Unspoken), 1958; Sweet Bird of Youth, 1959; Period of Adjustment, 1960 (filmed, 1963); The Night of the Iguana, 1961 (filmed, 1964); The Milk Train Doesn't Stop Here Any More, 1963 (revised, 1964; filmed, as Boom, 1968); Slapstick Tragedy, 1966; The Seven Descents of Myrtle, 1968; In the Bar of a Tokyo Hotel, 1969; Small Craft Warnings, 1972; Out Cry, 1973; The Red Devil Battery Sign, 1975; The Eccentricities of a Nightingale, 1976; Vieux Carré, 1977; A Lovely Sunday for Creve Coeur, 1979; Kirche, Küchen und Kinder, 1979; Clothes for a Summer Hotel, 1980; A House not Meant to Stand, 1981; Something Cloudy, Something Clear, 1981; *film:* Baby Doll, 1957; *screen plays for:* The Glass Menagerie, A Street Car Named Desire, The Rose Tattoo; (with Meade Roberts) The Fugitive Kind (Orpheus Descending); (with Gore Vidal) Suddenly Last Summer; Boom; *volumes:* volume of one-act plays, 1945; vols of short stories, 1948, 1960 (Three Players of a Summer Game); vol. of verse, 1944; Hard Candy and other Stories, 1954; Dragon Country (plays), 1970; Eight Mortal Ladies Possessed (short stories), 1975; *novels:* The Roman Spring of Mrs Stone, 1950; Moise and the World of Reason, 1976; *novella:* The Knightly Quest, 1966; *poems:* In the Winter of Cities, 1964; Androgyne, Mon Amour, 1977; *autobiography:* Memoirs, 1975. *Recreations:* swimming, travelling. *Address:* c/o Mitch Douglas, International Creative Management, 40 West 57th Street, New York, NY 10019, USA.

WILLIAMS, Sir Thomas; *see* Williams, Sir W. T.

WILLIAMS, Prof. Thomas Eifion Hopkins, CBE 1980; CEng; Professor of Civil Engineering, University of Southampton, since 1967; *b* 14 June 1923; *s* of David Garfield Williams and Annie Mary Williams (*née* Hopkins), Cwmtwrch, Brecon; *m* 1947, Elizabeth Lois Davies; one *s* two *d. Educ:* Ystradgynlais Grammar Sch.; Univ. of Wales (BSc, MSc); Univ. of Durham (PhD). FICE, MIStructE, FInstHE, FCIT, FRSA. Research Stressman, Sir W. G. Armstrong-Whitworth Aircraft, 1945; Asst Engr, Trunk Roads, Glam CC, 1946; Asst Lectr Civil Engrg, UC Swansea, 1947; Lectr in Civil Engrg, King's Coll., Univ. of Durham, 1948; Resident Site Engr, R. T. James & Partners, 1952; Post-doctoral Visitor, Univ. of California at Berkeley, 1955; Vis. Prof., Civil Engrg, Northwestern Univ., 1957; Sen. Lectr, Reader and Prof. of Civil and Transport Engrg, King's Coll., Univ. of Durham (subseq. Univ. of Newcastle upon Tyne), 1958–67. Chairman: Civil Engrg EDC, 1976–78; Standing Adv. Cttee on Trunk Rd Assessment, Dept of Transport, 1980– (Mem., Adv. Cttee, 1977–80); Member: EDC Civil Engrg, 1967–76; Transport Cttee, SRC; Roads Engrg Bd, ICE; British Nat. Cttee, PIARC; Council and Transp. Engrg Bd, Inst. Highway Engrs (Pres. 1979–80); Adv. Cttee on Traffic and Safety, TRRL, 1977–80. *Publications:* (Editor) Urban Survival and Traffic, 1961; Capacity, in Traffic Engineering Practice, 1963; Prediction of Traffic in Industrial Areas, 1966; Autostrade: Strategia, di sviluppo industriale e la vitalita delle nostre citta, 1965; Inter-City VTOL: Potential Traffic and Sites, 1969; Mobility and the Environment, 1971; (ed) Transportation and Environment: policies, plans and practice, 1973; Integrated Transport: developments and trends, 1976; Air, Rail and Road Inter-City Transport Systems, 1976; Land Use, Highways and Traffic, 1977; Motor Vehicles in a Changing World, 1978; Traffic Engineering 1960–81, 1981; contribs to Proc. ICE, Highway Engrs, IMunE, Road International, Traffic Engrg and Control, Segnalazioni Stradali, OTA/PIARC Confs. *Recreation:* music. *Address:* Willowdale, Woodlea Way, Ampfield, Romsey, Hants SO5 9DA. *T:* Chandler's Ford 3342. *Club:* Royal Automobile.

WILLIAMS, Thomas Lanier; *see* Williams, Tennessee.

WILLIAMS, Most Rev. Thomas Stafford; *see* Wellington (NZ), Archbishop of, (RC).

WILLIAMS, Thurston Monier, FRIBA; Managing Director, The National Building Agency, since 1977; *b* 3 March 1924; *s* of Frank Chauncy and Yvonne Williams; *m* 1955, Kirstine (*née* Uren); one *s* one *d. Educ:* Cranleigh Sch.; AA School of Architecture. AADip; ARIBA 1951, FRIBA 1968. Asst Architect, GLC, 1950–65; Borough Architect, London Borough of Hillingdon, 1965–77. RIBA: Hon. Sec., 1969–71, 1977–78; Vice-Pres., 1976–77. Pres., Assoc. of Official Architects, 1958–75. *Publications:* various papers in architectural and local govt jls. *Recreations:* walking, gardening. *Address:* NBA House, 7 Arundel Street, WC2R 3DZ. *T:* 01-836 4488.

WILLIAMS, Trevor; *see* Williams, A. T.

WILLIAMS, Trevor Illtyd, MA, BSc, DPhil, FRSC, FRHistS; scientific consultant and writer; *b* 16 July 1921; *s* of Illtyd Williams and Alma Mathilde Sohlberg; *m* 1st, 1945 (marriage dissolved, 1952); 2nd, 1952, Sylvia Irène Armstead; four *s* one *d. Educ:* Clifton College; Queen's College, Oxford. Nuffield Research Scholar, Sir William Dunn Sch. of Pathology, Oxford, 1942–45; Endeavour: Deputy Editor, 1945–54; Editor, 1954–74, 1977– (Consulting Scientific Editor, 1974–76); Editor, Outlook on Agriculture, 1982–. Academic Relations Advr, ICI Ltd, 1962–74. Chm., Soc. for the Study of Alchemy and Early Chemistry, 1967–; Jt Editor, Annals of Science, 1966–74; Chairman: World List of Scientific Periodicals, 1966–; Adv. Cttee on the Selection of Low-priced Books for Overseas, 1982–; Member: Adv. Council, Science Museum, 1972–; Council, University Coll., Swansea, 1965–. Vis. Fellow, ANU, 1981. Dexter Award, Amer. Chem. Soc., for contribs to the history of chemistry, 1976. *Publications:* An Introduction to Chromatography, 1946; Drugs from Plants, 1947; (ed) The Soil and the Sea, 1949; The Chemical Industry Past and Present, 1953; The Elements of Chromatography, 1954; (ed, jtly) A History of Technology, 1954–58; (with T. K. Derry) A Short History of Technology, 1960; Science and Technology (Ch. III, Vol. XI, New Cambridge Mod. History); (rev. edn) Alexander Findlay's A Hundred Years of Chemistry, 1965; (ed) A Biographical Dictionary of Scientists, 1968; Alfred Bernhard Nobel, 1973; James Cook, 1974; Man the Chemist, 1976; (ed) A History of Technology, Vols VI and VII: The Twentieth Century, 1978; A History of the British Gas Industry, 1981; A Short History of Twentieth Century Technology, 1982; numerous articles on scientific subjects, especially history of science and technology. *Recreations:* fishing, trade tokens. *Address:* 20 Blenheim Drive, Oxford. *T:* Oxford 58591. *Club:* Athenæum.

WILLIAMS, Vaughan; *see* Williams, J. V.

WILLIAMS, Walter Gordon Mason, FRICS; Deputy Chief Valuer, Valuation Office, Inland Revenue, since 1979; *b* 10 June 1923; *s* of Rees John Williams, DSO and Gladys Maud Williams; *m* 1950, Gwyneth Joyce Lawrence; two *d. Educ:* Cardiff High Sch. FRICS. Joined Valuation Office, 1947; Superintending Valuer (N Midlands), 1969–73; Asst Chief Valuer, 1973–79. *Address:* 33A Sydenham Hill, SE26 6SH. *T:* 01-670 8580.

WILLIAMS, Prof. William David, MA, DPhil; Professor of German, Liverpool University, 1954–80; *b* 10 March 1917; *s* of William Williams and Winifred Ethel Williams (*née* Anstey); *m* 1946, Mary Hope Davis; one *s* one *d. Educ:* Merchant Taylors' School; St John's Coll., Oxford (MA, DPhil). Served War of 1939–45, with Sudan Defence Force, Middle East, and as Liaison Officer with Polish Army in Italy; Asst Lecturer in German, Leeds Univ., 1946; Lecturer in German, Oxford Univ., 1948–54; Pro-Vice-Chancellor, Liverpool Univ., 1965–68. *Publications:* Nietzsche and the French, 1952; The Stories of C. F. Meyer, 1962; reviews, etc, in Modern Language Review, and Erasmus. *Recreation:* gardening. *Address:* Strangers Corner, 5 Summerfield Rise, Goring-on-Thames, near Reading, Berks. *T:* Goring-on-Thames 872603.

WILLIAMS, (William) Donald; *b* 17 Oct. 1919; 2nd *s* of Sidney Williams, Malvern; *m* 1945, Cecilia Mary (*née* Hirons); one *s. Educ:* Royal Grammar Sch., Worcester. Served War of 1939–45: Volunteer, 8th Bn Worcestershire Regt, May 1939; POW 1940 (Germany); escaped to Russia and was repatriated, 1945. Qualified as a Chartered Accountant, 1949. Partner in a Professional Practice, 1950–77, now on own account as Financial Consultant. Director: Fiesta Foods Ltd; Malvern Instruments Ltd; Kendalls of Malvern Ltd. Contested (C) Dudley, (Gen. Elec.), 1966; MP (C) Dudley, March 1968–1970. Contested (C) Dudley East, 1979. CC Hereford/Worcester, 1973–81. Governor, Abberley Hall and other schs. *Recreations:* reading, travelling. *Address:* Sexton Barns, 2 Cockshot Road, Malvern, Worcs. *T:* Malvern 5635.

WILLIAMS, (William) Maxwell (Harries); President, Law Society of England and Wales, since 1982; *b* 18 Feb. 1926; *s* of Llwyd and Hilary Williams; *m* 1951, Jenifer, *d* of late Rt Hon. E. L. Burgin, LLD, and Mrs Burgin, JP; two *d. Educ:* Nautical Coll., Pangbourne. Served 178 Assault Field Regt RA, Far East (Captain), 1943–47. Admitted Solicitor, 1950; Council of Law Society, 1962. Member: Royal Commission on Legal Services, 1976–79; Cttee of Management of Inst. of Advanced Legal Studies, 1980–. Vice-Pres., Law Society, 1981. Hon. Treasurer, Wildfowl Trust, 1974–80. *Recreation:* fishing. *Address:* 19 New Bridge Street, EC4V 6BY. *T:* 01-353 0211. *Club:* Garrick.

WILLIAMS, William Thomas, OBE 1980; ARCS; PhD, DSc (London); DIC; FIBiol; FLS; FAA 1978; with Australian Institute of Marine Science, Cape Ferguson, Townsville, since 1980; pianoforte teacher (LMus Australia), since 1973; *b* 18 Apr. 1913; *o s* of William Thomas and Clara Williams. *Educ:* Stationers' Company's School, London; Imperial College of Science and Technology. Demonstrator in Botany, Imperial College, 1933–36; Lecturer in Biology, Sir John Cass' College, 1936–40. Served War, 1940–46; RA (Sjt) RAOC (2/Lt), REME (T/Major). Lecturer in Botany, Bedford College, London, 1946–51; Professor of Botany, University of Southampton, 1951–65; CSIRO Division of Computing Research, Canberra, Australia, 1966–68; Div. of Tropical Pastures, Brisbane, 1968–73; Chief Res. Scientist, CSIRO, 1970–73; with Townsville Lab., CSIRO, 1973–80. Sometime Secretary of Society for Experimental Biology, and of Sherlock Holmes Society of London. Past Editor, Journal of Experimental Botany. Hon. DSc Queensland, 1973. *Publications:* The Four Prisons of Man, 1971; (ed) Pattern Analysis in Agricultural Science, 1976; over 150 papers on plant physiology, numerical taxonomy and statistical ecology in scientific journals. *Recreations:* music, drinking beer. *Address:* 10 Surrey Street, Hyde Park, Townsville, Qld 4812, Australia.

WILLIAMS, Sir (William) Thomas, Kt 1976; QC 1964; **His Honour Judge Sir Thomas Williams;** a Circuit Judge, since 1981; *b* 22 Sept. 1915; *s* of David John Williams, Aberdare, and Edith Williams; *m* 1942, Gwyneth, *d* of Rev. D. G. Harries, Aberdare; one *s* one *d*. *Educ:* University Coll., Cardiff; St Catherine's, Oxford; University of London; Lincoln's Inn. President, Students' Union, University of Wales, 1939. Baptist Minister, 1941-46; Chaplain and Welfare Officer, RAF, 1944-46; Tutor, Manchester College, Oxford, 1946-49. Called to the Bar, Lincoln's Inn, 1951, Bencher, 1972. Recorder: of Birkenhead, 1969-71; of the Crown Court, 1972-81. MP (Lab & Co-op) Hammersmith South, Feb. 1949-55, Barons Court, 1955-59, Warrington, 1961-81; Parliamentary Private Secretary: Minister of Pensions, 1950-51; Minister of Health, 1951; Attorney General, 1965-67. Chm., British Gp, IPU, 1974-76. Member: Advisory Council on Public Records, 1965-71; Adv. Council on Statute Law, 1974-81; SE Metropolitan Regional Hospital Board, 1965-71; Select Cttee for Parly Comr, 1974-81; Chm., Select Cttee on Parly Procedure, 1976-80; Pres., World Council IPU, 1976-80. Governor, King's Coll. Hosp., 1968-74; Chm., Cray Valley Hosp. Management Cttee, 1968-69. Fellow, University Coll. of South Wales, 1981. *Address:* Wickers Oake, Dulwich Wood Park, SE19.

WILLIAMS, Col William Trevor, FCIS; Director, Engineering Industries Association, since 1981; *b* 16 Oct. 1925; *s* of Francis Harold and Ethel Mabel Williams, Newton Manorbier; *m* 1951, Elizabeth, *d* of late Brig. Arthur Goldie; two *s* two *d*. *Educ:* Darwin Coll., Univ. of Kent (MA). FBIM, MCIT. Commissioned in Infantry, 1945; regimental service, India and Malaya, to 1949; seconded to Guyanese Govt, 1964, 1965; Commander, Maritime Air Regt, Far East, 1967-69; Project Officer, National Defence Coll., 1970-71; Adviser, Ethiopian Govt, 1971-72; Col Q BAOR, 1973-76 (Chm., Berlin Budget Cttee); Head of Secretariat, MoD, 1976-77; Director, SATRA, 1979-80. *Publications:* military. *Recreations:* golf, photography. *Address:* Mill Lane, Harbledown, Canterbury. *T:* Canterbury 68170.

WILLIAMS, Yvonne Lovat; Secretary, Monopolies and Mergers Commission, 1974-79; *b* 23 Feb. 1920; *d* of late Wendros Williams, CBE and Vera Lovat Williams. *Educ:* Queenswood Sch., Hatfield; Newnham Coll., Cambridge. BA History 1941, MA 1946. Temp. Civil Servant, BoT, 1941-46; Asst Principal, BoT, 1946-48, Principal 1948-56; Treasury, 1956-58; BoT, 1958-63; Asst Sec., BoT, Min. Tech., DTI, 1963-73. *Recreations:* visiting friends, theatres and old places. *Address:* Flat 16, The Limes, Linden Gardens, W2 4ET. *T:* 01-727 9851.

WILLIAMS-BULKELEY, Sir Richard Harry David, 13th Bt, *cr* 1661; TD; JP; Lord Lieutenant of Gwynedd, since 1974 (HM Lieutenant for the County of Anglesey, 1947-74); Member: Anglesey County Council, 1946-74 (Chairman, 1955-57); Mayor of Beaumaris, 1949-51; *b* 5 Oct. 1911; *s* of late Maj. R. G. W. Williams-Bulkeley, MC, and late Mrs V. Williams-Bulkeley, *S* grand-father, 1942; *m* 1938, Renée Arundell, *yr d* of Sir Thomas L. H. Neave, 5th Bt; two *s*. *Educ:* Eton. Served with 9th and 8th Bns Royal Welch Fusiliers, 1939-44, 2nd in Command of both Battalions and with Allied Land Forces South East Asia, specially employed, 1944-Sept. 1945, Lt-Col Comdt, Anglesey and Caernarvonshire Army Cadet Force, 1946-47 (resigned on appointment as HM Lieut). CStJ. *Recreations:* shooting, golf, hunting. *Heir:* *s* Richard Thomas Williams-Bulkeley [*b* 25 May 1939; *m* 1964, Sarah Susan, *er d* of Rt Hon. Sir Henry Josceline Phillimore, OBE; twin *s* one *d*]. *Address:* Plâs Meigan, Beaumaris, Gwynedd. *T:* Beaumaris 810345. *Club:* Boodle's.

WILLIAMS-ELLIS, Amabel, (Lady Williams-Ellis); Author and Journalist; *b* Newlands Corner, near Guildford; *d* of late J. St Loe Strachey, of the Spectator; *m* 1915, Sir Clough Williams-Ellis, CBE, MC, FRIBA (*d* 1978); (son killed in action, 1944) two *d*. *Educ:* home. Literary editor Spectator, 1922-23. *Publications:* An Anatomy of Poetry; The Pleasures of Architecture (with Clough Williams-Ellis); But We Know Better; Noah's Ark; The Wall of Glass; How You Began; The Tragedy of John Ruskin; The Beagle in S America; Men Who Found Out; How You Are Made; Volcano; What Shall I Be; To Tell the Truth; The Big Firm; Good Citizens; Learn to Love First; Women in War Factories; Princesses and Trolls; A Food and People Geography; The Art of being a Woman; Headlong down the Years; The Art of Being a Parent; Changing the World; Seekers and Finders; Modern Scientists at Work; Darwin's Moon (A Life of Alfred Russel Wallace); Life in England, a pictorial history; Gypsy Folk Tales; Out of This World (10 vols SF anthology); The Raingod's Daughter, 1977; The Story Spirits, 1980; Memoirs, 1983. *Recreation:* travel. *Address:* Plâs Brondanw, Llanfrothen, Gwynedd. *TA:* Penrhyndeudraeth.

WILLIAMS-THOMAS, Lt-Col Reginald Silvers, DSO 1940; TD; JP; DL; Commander of Crown (Belgium); Croix de Guerre; RA; Queen's Own Worcestershire Hussars; Glass Manufacturer; Director, Stevens and Williams Ltd; Lloyd's Underwriter; *b* 11 February 1914; *s* of late Hubert Silvers Williams-Thomas, Broome, Stourbridge, Worcestershire; *m* 1938, Esmée Florence Taylor; two *s* one *d*; *m* 1963, Sonia Margot Jewell, *d* of late Major

M. F. S. Jewell, CBE, DL, Birdham, near Chichester. *Educ:* Shrewsbury School. JP Staffs, 1947; DL Worcestershire, 1954. Freeman of the City of London; Mem., Worshipful Co. of Glass-Sellers. *Recreations:* shooting, archery, fishing, gardening. *Address:* The Tythe House, Broome, near Stourbridge, West Midlands. *T:* Kidderminster 700632.

WILLIAMS-WYNN, Col Sir (Owen) Watkin, 10th Bt, *cr* 1688; CBE 1969; FRAgSs 1969; Lord Lieutenant of Clwyd, 1976-79; *b* 30 Nov. 1904; *s* of Sir Robert William Herbert Watkin Williams-Wynn, 9th Bt, KCB, DSO; *S* father 1951; *m* 1st, 1939, Margaret Jean (*d* 1961), *d* of late Col William Alleyne Macbean, RA, and Hon. Mrs Gerald Scarlett; one *s* (and one *s* decd); 2nd, 1968, Gabrielle Haden Matheson, *d* of late Herbert Alexander Caffin. *Educ:* Eton; RMA, Woolwich. Commnd RA, 1925; RHA, Instructor at Equitation Sch., Weedon; Adj. 61st (Carnarvon and Denbigh Yeo.) Medium Regt RA (TA), 1936-40; Major, 1940. Served with Regt as 2nd in command, France and Dunkirk; served with 18th Division, Singapore (despatches twice); Prisoner of War, Siam and Burmah Railway; Lt-Col comdg 361st Med. Regt RA (TA), 1946; Hon. Col 361 Med. Regt RA (TA), 1952-57. Liaison Officer to Min. of Agriculture for N Wales, 1961-70; Mem., Nature Conservancy for Wales, 1963-66. Master Flint and Denbigh Foxhounds, 1946-61; Joint Master, Sir W. W. Wynn's Hounds, 1957. JP 1937, DL 1947, Denbighshire; High Sheriff of Denbighshire, 1954; Vice-Lieutenant, Denbighshire, 1957-66, Lord Lieutenant 1966-74; Lieutenant of Clwyd, 1974-76. KStJ 1972. *Heir:* *s* David Watkin Williams-Wynn [*b* 18 Feb. 1940; *m* 1968, Harriet Veryan Elspeth, *d* of Gen. Sir Norman Tailyour, KCB, DSO; two *s* twin *d*]. *Address:* Llangedwyn, Oswestry, Salop. *T:* Llanrhaiadr 269. *Club:* Army and Navy.

WILLIAMS-WYNNE, Col John Francis, CBE 1972; DSO 1945; JP; FRAgS; Vice Lord-Lieutenant of Gwynedd, since 1980 (Lieutenant, 1974-80; HM Lieutenant of Merioneth, 1957-74); Constable of Harlech Castle since 1964; *b* 9 June 1908; *s* of late Major F. R. Williams-Wynn, CB, and late Beatrice (*née* Cooper); *m* 1938, Margaret Gwendolen, *d* of late Rev. George Roper and late Mrs G. S. White; one *s* two *d*. *Educ:* Oundle; Magdalene College, Cambridge (MA Mech. Sciences). Commissioned in RA 1929; served NW Frontier, 1936; served War of 1939-45; psc Camberley; Brigade Major, RA 2 Div., 1940-41; 2 i/c 114 Fd Regt, 1942; GSO2 HQ Ceylon Comd, 1942; comd 160 Jungle Field Regt, RA, 1943-44; GSO1, GHQ India, 1945; GSO1, War Office, 1946-48; retd 1948; comd 636 (R Welch) LAA Regt, RA, TA, 1951-54; Subs. Col 1954. Hon. Col 7th (Cadet) Bn RWF, 1964-74. JP 1950, DL 1953, VL 1954, Merioneth. Chairman, Advisory Cttee, Min. of Agric. Experimental Husbandry Farm, Trawscoed, 1955-76. Part-time mem., Merseyside and N Wales Electricity Bd, 1953-65; National Parks Comr, 1961-66; Forestry Comr, 1963-65; Member: Regional Adv. Cttee N Wales Conservancy Forestry Commission, 1950-63; County Agric. Exec. Cttee, 1955-63 and 1967-71; Gwynedd River Board, 1957-63; Forestry Cttee of GB, 1966-76; Home Grown Timber Advisory Cttee, 1966-76; Prince of Wales's Cttee for Wales, 1970-79; President: Timber Growers Organisation, 1974-76; Royal Welsh Agric. Soc., 1968 (Chm. Council, 1971-77); Chairman: Agricl Adv. Cttee, BBC Wales, 1974-79; Flying Farmers' Assoc., 1974-. Pres., Merioneth Br., CLA, 1979-. Member: Airline Users Cttee, CAA, 1973-79; Sch. of Agric. Cttee, University Coll. N Wales, 1982. Chm. and Man. Dir, Cross Foxes Ltd. *Recreations:* farming, forestry and flying. *Address:* Peniarth, Tywyn-Merioneth, Gwynedd. *T:* Tywyn 710328. *Clubs:* Army and Navy, Pratt's.

See also Hon. D. A. C. Douglas-Home.

WILLIAMSON, family name of **Barons Forres** and **Williamson.**

WILLIAMSON, Baron *cr* 1962, of Eccleston (Life Peer); **Thomas Williamson,** Kt 1956; CBE 1950; JP; General Secretary National Union of General and Municipal Workers, 1946-61; a Director of Securicor Ltd since 1964; (part-time) member, Iron and Steel Board, 1960-67; Member of ITA, 1961-64; Chairman British Productivity Council, 1953-54; Director of the Daily Herald, 1953-62; *b* 2 September 1897; *s* of James and Selina Williamson; *m* 1925, Hilda Hartley, St Helens; one *d*. *Educ:* Knowsley Road, St Helens; Workers' Educational Association, Liverpool University. Member Liverpool City Council, 1929-35; Member National Executive British Labour Party, and Chm. of Finance and General Purposes Cttee, 1940-47; Mem. TUC General Council, 1947-62; Chm. TUC, 1956-57; MP (Lab) Brigg Div. of Lincoln and Rutland, 1945-48. Trustee: Thomson Foundn, 1962-78; Liverpool Vic. Friendly Soc., 1967-. Hon. Associate, College of Technology, Birmingham. Served as non-commissioned officer, Royal Engineers, 1915-19, two years' active service, France and Belgium. JP Liverpool, 1933. Hon. LLD (Cambridge), 1959. *Address:* 13 Hurst Lea Court, Alderley Edge, Cheshire.

WILLIAMSON, Air Commandant Dame Alice Mary, DBE 1958; RRC 1948 (ARRC 1941); retired as Matron-in-Chief, Princess Mary's Royal Air Force Nursing Service (1956-59); *d* of John William and Theodosia Williamson (*née* Lewis). *Educ:* Mells Girls Sch., near Frome, Somerset. Training Sch., Manchester Royal Infirmary, 1924-27; Post Graduate Courses, SCM, 1928-29; X-Ray Course, 1929-30; PMRAFNS, 1930-59. Promoted to Matron, Dec. 1944; Senior Matron, Wing Officer, 1951; Group Officer, 1952; Air Commandant, 1956; QHNS, 1956-59. Chief Nursing Officer, Kuwait Govt Nursing Service, 1959-62. *Recreations:* tennis, swimming, needlework. *Club:* United Nursing Services.

WILLIAMSON, Bruce, MD Edinburgh; FRCP; Hon. Consulting Physician: Royal Northern Hospital, N7; Prince of Wales General Hospital, N15; Barnet General Hospital; Enfield War Memorial Hospital; Brentwood and District Hospital; Hornsey Central Hospital; Ex-Member Medical Appeals Tribunal; Trustee Edinburgh University Club; *b* South Shields, 1893; 5th *s* of Captain David Williamson, Ladybank, and Jane Theresa Short, Edinburgh; *m* 1936, Margaret Stewart, *d* of William Gibson, Broughty Ferry; one *s* ; *m* 1959, Yvonne, *d* of Arthur Carlebach. *Educ:* Newcastle; Bruges; Royal Colleges and University of Edinburgh. Senior Pres., Royal Medical Society, Edinburgh, 1921; Hons MD Edinburgh University, 1925; Lt, Bucks Bn Oxford and Bucks LI, seconded Machine Gun Corps. Founder, Hon. Mem. and former Pres., Scottish Med. Golfing Soc. *Publications:* Text Books: Diseases of Children, 9th edn 1964; Vital Cardiology: A New Outlook on the Prevention of Heart Failure; Diastole (Honeyman Gillespie lecture, Edin. Univ.); The Autonomic Nervous System, 1972; The Executive and the Seventies (lay physiology), 1973; articles in medical journals; The Future and The Fighting General (political-economy); contrib. to The Statist. *Recreation:* golf. *Club:* Edinburgh Univ. of London.

WILLIAMSON, David Francis; Deputy Director General, Agriculture, European Commission, since 1977; *b* 8 May 1934; *s* of Samuel Charles Wathen Williamson and Marie Eileen Williamson (*née* Denney); *m* 1961, Patricia Margaret Smith; two *s*. *Educ:* Tonbridge Sch.; Exeter Coll., Oxford (MA). Entered Min. of Agriculture, Fisheries and Food, 1958; Private Sec. to Permanent Sec. and to successive Parly Secs, 1960-62; HM Diplomatic Service, as First Sec. (Agric. and Food), Geneva, for Kennedy Round Trade Negotiations, 1965-67; Principal Private Sec. to successive Ministers of Agric., Fisheries and Food, 1967-70; Head of Milk and Milk Products Div., Marketing Policy Div. and Food Policy Div., 1970-74; Under-Sec., Gen. Agricultural Policy Gp, 1974-76, EEC Gp, 1976-77; Dep. Sec., 1982. *Address:* 147 avenue des Statuaires, Uccle, 1180 Brussels, Belgium. *T:* 374 29 59.

WILLIAMSON, David Theodore Nelson, DSc; FRS 1968; Group Director of Engineering, Rank Xerox Ltd, 1974-76; Director, Xerox Research (UK) Ltd, 1975-76; retired; *b* 15 Feb. 1923; *s* of David Williamson and Ellie (*née* Nelson); *m* 1951, Alexandra Janet Smith Neilson; two *s* two *d*. *Educ:* George Heriot's Sch., Edinburgh; Univ. of Edinburgh. MO Valve Co. Ltd, 1943-46; Ferranti Ltd, Edinburgh, 1946-61; pioneered numerical control of machine tools, 1951; Manager, Machine Tool Control Div., 1959-61; Work on sound reproduction: Williamson amplifier, 1947, Ferranti pickup, 1949; collab. with P. J. Walker in develop't of first wide-range electrostatic loud-speaker, 1951-56; Dir of Res. and Develt, Molins Ltd, 1961-74. Member: NEL Metrology and Noise Control Sub cttee, 1954-57; NEL Cttee on Automatic Design and Machine Tool Control, 1964-66; Min. of Technology Working Party on Computer-Aided Design, 1967; Penny Cttee on Computer-Aided Design, 1967-69; Steering Cttee, IAMTACT, 1967-69; SRC Mech. and Prod. Engrg Cttee, 1965-69; SRC Control Panel, 1966-69; Mech. Engrg EDC, 1968-74; SRC Engrg Bd, 1969-75; Adv. Cttee for Mech. Engrg, 1969-71; Court, Cranfield Inst. of Technology, 1970-79; Council and Exec. Cttee, British Hydrodynamics Research Assoc., 1970-73; Design Council (formerly CoID) Engrg Design Adv. Cttee, 1971-75; Council for Scientific Policy, 1972-73; Science Mus. Adv. Cttee, 1972-79; SRC Manufrg Technology Cttee, 1972-75 (Chm.); Mech. Engrg and Machine Tool Requirements Bd, DTI subseq. DoI, 1973-76; Council, Royal Soc., 1977-78. *Publications:* contrib. to: Electronic Engineers' Reference Book, 1959; Progress in Automation, 1960; Numerical Control Handbook, 1968; papers and articles on engrg subjects; NEDO Discussion Paper No 1, 1971. James Clayton Lecture, IMechE, 1968. *Recreations:* music, photography. *Address:* Villa Belvedere, La Cima 10, Tuoro-sul-Trasimeno, 06069 Pg, Umbria, Italy. *T:* (075) 846285.

WILLIAMSON, Dame (Elsie) Marjorie, DBE 1973; MSc, PhD (London); Principal, Royal Holloway College, University of London, 1962-73; *b* 30 July 1913; *d* of late Leonard Claude Williamson and Hannah Elizabeth Cary. *Educ:* Wakefield Girls' High School; Royal Holloway College. Demonstrator in Physics, Royal Holloway College, University of London, 1936-39; Lecturer in Physics, University College of Wales, Aberystwyth, 1939-45; Lecturer in Physics, Bedford Coll., Univ. of London, 1945-55; Principal, St Mary's Coll., Univ. of Durham, 1955-62; Deputy Vice-Chancellor, Univ. of London, 1970-71, 1971-72. Fellow, Bedford Coll., Univ. of London, 1975. A Manager, The Royal Instn, 1967-70, 1971-74. Mem., Commonwealth Scholarship Commn, 1975-. *Publications:* Papers in various scientific periodicals. *Recreations:* music, gardening. *Address:* Forge Cottage, Pillerton Hersey, Warwick. *T:* Stratford on Avon 740243. *Club:* University Women's.

WILLIAMSON, Frank Edger, QPM 1966; *b* 24 Feb. 1917; *s* of John and late Mary Williamson; *m* 1943, Margaret Beaumont; one *d*. *Educ:* Northampton Grammar Sch. Manchester City Police, 1936-61; Chief Constable: Carlisle, 1961-63; Cumbria Constabulary, 1963-67; HM Inspector of Constabulary, 1967-72. OStJ 1967. *Address:* Eagle Cottage, Alderley Park, Nether Alderley, Macclesfield, Cheshire SK10 4TE. *T:* Alderley Edge 583135.

WILLIAMSON, Sir Hedworth; *see* Williamson, Sir N. F. H.

WILLIAMSON, Prof. James, FRCPE; Professor of Geriatric Medicine, University of Edinburgh, since 1976; *b* 22 Nov. 1920; *s* of James Mathewson Williamson and Jessie Reid; *m* 1945, Sheila Mary Blair; three *s* two *d*. *Educ:* Wishaw High Sch., Lanarkshire; Univ. of Glasgow (MB ChB 1943); FRCPE 1959 (MRCPE 1949). Training in general medicine, incl. two years in general

practice, later specialising in respiratory diseases, then in medicine of old age; Consultant Physician, 1954-73; Prof. of Geriatric Medicine in newly established Chair, Univ. of Liverpool, 1973-76. *Publications:* chapters in various textbooks; numerous articles in gen. med. jls and in jls devoted to subject of old age. *Recreations:* walking, reading. *Address:* 14 Ann Street, Edinburgh EH4 1PJ. *T:* 031-332 3568.

WILLIAMSON, Air Chief Marshal Sir Keith (Alec), GCB 1982 (KCB 1979); AFC 1968; Chief of the Air Staff, since 1982; Air ADC to the Queen, since 1982; *b* 25 Feb. 1928; *s* of Percy and Gertrude Williamson; *m* 1953, Patricia Anne, *d* of W/Cdr F. M. N. Watts; two *s* two *d*. *Educ:* Bancroft's Sch., Woodford Green; Market Harborough Grammar Sch.; RAF Coll., Cranwell. Commissioned, 1950; flew with Royal Australian Air Force in Korea, 1953; OC 23 Sqdn, 1966-68; Command, RAF Gütersloh, 1968-70; RCDS 1971; Dir, Air Staff Plans, 1972-75; Comdt, RAF Staff Coll., 1975-77; ACOS (Plans and Policy), SHAPE, 1977-78; AOC-in-C, RAF Support Comd, 1978-80; AOC-in-C, RAF Strike Command and C-in-C, UK Air Forces, 1980-82. *Recreation:* golf. *Address:* c/o Midland Bank Ltd, 25 Notting Hill Gate, W11. *Club:* Royal Air Force.

WILLIAMSON, Malcolm Benjamin Graham Christopher, CBE 1976; composer, pianist, organist; Master of the Queen's Music, since 1975; *b* 21 Nov. 1931; *s* of Rev. George Williamson, Sydney, Australia; *m* 1960, Dolores Daniel; one *s* two *d*. *Educ:* Barker Coll., Hornsby, NSW; Sydney Conservatorium. Composer-in-Residence, Westminster Choir Coll., Princeton, NJ, 1970-71. Pres., Royal Philharmonic Orch., 1977-82. *Compositions include: orchestral:* Sinfonietta; Concerto Grosso; Suite, Our Man in Havana; Sinfonia Concercante; Santiago de Espada Overture; Violin Concerto; three Piano Concertos; five Symphonies; *chamber music:* Partita on Themes of Walton; Epitaphs for Edith Sitwell; Serenade; Pas de Quatre; Concerto for Wind Quintet and Two Pianos; *ballets:* The Display; Sun into Darkness; Perisynthyon. *operas:* The English Eccentrics; The Violins of St. Jacques; Our Man in Havana; The Happy Prince; Julius Caesar Jones; Dunstan and the Devil; The Growing Castle; Lucky Peter's Journey; The Red Sea; The Moonrakers; Knights in Shining Armour; The Stone Wall; Genesis; The Winter Star; The Glitter Gang; The Snow Wolf; The Terrain of the Kings; *vocal:* Six English Lyrics; Ode to Music; From a Child's Garden; Three Shakespeare Songs; Pieta; Les Olympiques; *choral:* The Canticle of Fire; The World at the Manger; Symphony for Voices; In Place of Belief; Little Mass of St. Bernadette; The Mass of Christ the King (written for Silver Jubilee of the Queen); *piano:* two Sonatas; five Preludes; Travel Diaries; Sonata for two Pianos; *organ:* Organ Symphony; Vision of Christ-Phoenix; Peace Pieces; The Lion of Suffolk; Little Carols of the Saints. *Recreations:* reading, children. *Address:* Josef Weinberger Ltd, 10-16 Rathbone Street, W1P 2BJ.

WILLIAMSON, Dame Marjorie; *see* Williamson, Dame E. M.

WILLIAMSON, Sir (Nicholas Frederick) Hedworth, 11th Bt, *cr* 1642; *b* 26 Oct. 1937; *s* of late Maj. William Hedworth Williamson (killed in action, 1942) and Diana Mary, *d* of late Brig.-Gen. Hon. Charles Lambton, DSO (she *m* 2nd, 1945, 1st Baron Hailes, PC, GBE, CH); *S* uncle, 1946. *Address:* Abbey Croft, Mortimer, Reading, Berks RG7 3PE. *T:* Mortimer 332324.

WILLIAMSON, Nicol; actor; *b* Hamilton, Scotland, 14 Sept. 1938. Dundee Rep. Theatre, 1960-61; Royal Court: That's Us, Arden of Faversham, 1961; A Midsummer Night's Dream, Twelfth Night, 1962; Royal Shakespeare Company, 1962; Nil Carborundum, The Lower Depths, Women Beware Women; Spring Awakening, Royal Court, 1962; Kelly's Eye, The Ginger Man, Royal Court, 1963; Inadmissible Evidence, 1964, 1978, Royal Court, Wyndham's 1965 (Evening Standard Best Actor Award), NY 1965 (NY Drama Critics Award); A Cuckoo in the Nest, Waiting for Godot, Miniatures, 1964; Sweeney Agonistes, Globe, 1965; Diary of a Madman, Duchess, 1967; Plaza Suite, NY, 1968; Hamlet, Round House, 1969 (Evening Standard Best Actor Award), NY and US tour, 1969; Midwinter Spring, Queen's, 1972; Circle in the Square, Uncle Vanya, NY, 1973; Royal Shakespeare Company, 1973-75: Corialanus, Midwinter Spring, Aldwych, 1973; Twelfth Night, Macbeth, Stratford 1974, Aldwych 1975; dir and title role, Uncle Vanya, Other Place, Stratford, 1974; Rex, NY, 1975; Inadmissible Evidence, NY, 1981; Macbeth, NY, BBC Shakespeare series, 1982. *Films:* Inadmissible Evidence, 1967; The Bofors Gun, 1968; Laughter in the Dark, 1968; The Reckoning, 1969; Hamlet, 1970; The Jerusalem File, 1971; The Wilby Conspiracy, 1974; The Seven Per Cent Solution, 1975; The Cheap Detective, The Goodbye Girl, Robin and Marion, 1977; The Human Factor, 1979; Excalibur, Venom, 1980; I'm Dancing as Fast as I Can, 1981. *Television:* The Word, 1977. *Address:* c/o ICM, 388-396 Oxford Street, W1.

WILLIAMSON, Ven. Robert Kerr; Archdeacon of Nottingham, since 1978; *b* 18 Dec. 1932; *s* of James and Elizabeth Williamson; *m* 1956, Anne Boyd Smith; three *s* two *d*. *Educ:* Elmgrove School, Belfast; Oak Hill College, London. London City Missionary, 1955-61; Oak Hill Coll., 1961-63; Asst Curate, Crowborough Parish Church, 1963-66; Vicar: St Paul, Hyson Green, Nottingham, 1966-71; St Ann w. Emmanuel, Nottingham, 1971-76; St Michael and All Angels, Bramcote, 1976-79. *Recreations:* walking, tennis, reading and music. *Address:* 16 Woodthorpe Avenue, Woodthorpe, Nottingham NG5 4FD. *T:* Nottingham 267349; (office) Dunham House, Westgate, Southwell. *T:* Southwell 814331.

WILLIAMSON, Thomas Bateson; Assistant Secretary, Department of Health and Social Security, 1969-75, retired; *b* 17 April 1915; *y s* of late George Williamson and Dora May Williamson; *m* 1st, 1944, Winifred Mary Johnstone (decd); two *s*; 2nd, 1953, Pauline Mary Luard; four *d. Educ:* Barrow Gram. Sch.; Gonville and Caius Coll., Cambridge. 1st Cl. Hons, Mod. Langs Tripos, 1937. Entered War Office as Asst Principal, 1938. Served with HM Forces, 1940-45. Asst Principal, Min. of Health, 1945; Principal, 1946; Asst Secretary, 1954; Commonwealth Fund Fellowship, 1958-59; Under-Secretary, 1965; retired (health grounds), 1969; Asst Secretary, 1969; retired 1975. *Recreations:* fell-walking, music. *Address:* 1 St Mary's Grove, Barnes, SW13. *T:* 01-788 4274.

WILLINK, Sir Charles (William), 2nd Bt *cr* 1957; Assistant Master at Eton College, since 1954; *b* 10 Sept. 1929; *s* of Rt Hon. Sir Henry Urmston Willink, 1st Bt, MC, QC (*d* 1973), and Cynthia Frances (*d* 1959), *d* of H. Morley Fletcher, MD, FRCP; *S* father, 1973; *m* 1954, Elizabeth, *d* of Humfrey Andrewes, Highgate, London; one *s* one *d. Educ:* Eton College (scholar); Trinity College, Cambridge (scholar). MA Cantab. Assistant Master, Marlborough College, 1952-54; Housemaster, Eton College, 1964-77. *Publications:* articles on Euripidean drama in Classical Quarterly, 1966, 1968, 1971. *Recreations:* bridge, field botany, music (bassoon). *Heir: s* Edward Daniel Willink, *b* 18 Feb. 1957. *Address:* 22 High Street, Eton, Windsor SL4 6AZ. *T:* Windsor 62616.

WILLIS, family name of **Baron Willis.**

WILLIS, Baron, *cr* 1963, of Chislehurst (Life Peer); **Edward Henry Willis;** FRTS; FRSA; playwright (as Ted Willis); Director: World Wide Pictures, since 1967; Capital Radio Ltd, since 1974; 20th Century Security, since 1981; *b* London, 13 Jan. 1918; *m* 1944, Audrey Hale; one *s* one *d. Educ:* Tottenham Central School. *Plays include:* Hot Summer Night, New, 1957; God Bless the Guv'nor, Unity, 1959; Woman in a Dressing Gown, 1962; A Slow Roll of Drums, 1964; Queenie, 1967; Mr Polly, 1977; Doctor on the Boil, 1978; *Television scripts:* Dixon of Dock Green Series, 1953-75; Sergeant Cork, 1963-67; Knock on any Door, 1964; Crime of Passion, 1970; Hunter's Walk, 1973; Black Beauty, 1979; Buckingham Palace Connection, 1981; *Films include:* Woman in a Dressing Gown, 1958 (Berlin Award); Flame in the Streets (play, Hot Summer Night), 1961; Bitter Harvest, 1963; A Long Way to Shiloh, 1969; Maneater, 1979. President, Writers Guild of GB, 1958-68, 1976-79. Mem., Sports Council, 1971-73. *Publications:* Woman in a Dressing Gown and other TV plays, 1959; Whatever Happened to Tom Mix? (autobiography), 1970; *novels* Death May Surprise Us, 1974; The Left-Handed Sleeper, 1975; Man-eater, 1976; The Churchill Commando, 1977; The Buckingham Palace Connection, 1978; The Lions of Judah, 1979; The Naked Sun, 1980; The Most Beautiful Girl in the World, 1981; Spring at the Winged Horse, 1982. *Recreations:* tennis, Association football. *Address:* 5 Shepherds Green, Chislehurst, Kent BR7 6PB. *Club:* Garrick.

WILLIS, Charles Reginald; Director, Tiverton Gazette & Associated Papers Ltd, since 1971; Member, Press Council, 1967; *b* 11 June 1906; *s* of Charles and Marie Willis, Tiverton, Devon; *m* 1929, Violet Stubbs; one *d. Educ:* Tiverton Grammar Sch. Tiverton Gazette, 1922-27; North Western Daily Mail, 1927-29; Evening Chronicle, Newcastle upon Tyne, 1929-1935; Evening Chronicle, Manchester, 1935-42; Empire News, London, 1942-43; The Evening News, London, 1943 (Editor, 1954-66); Dir, Associated Newspapers Ltd, 1961-71; Editorial Dir, Harmsworth Publications, 1967-70. *Recreation:* cricket. *Address:* Howden Heyes, Ashley, Tiverton, Devon. *T:* Tiverton 254829. *Club:* Saints and Sinners.

WILLIS, Hon. Sir Eric (Archibald), KBE 1975; CMG 1974; Executive Secretary, Royal Australian College of Ophthalmologists, since 1978; *b* 15 Jan. 1922; *s* of Archibald Clarence Willis and Vida Mabel Willis (*née* Buttenshaw); *m* 1951, Norma Dorothy, *d* of L. E. Knight; two *s* one *d. Educ:* Murwillumbah High Sch., NSW; Univ. of Sydney (BA Hons). MLA (Liberal) for Earlwood, NSW, 1950-78; Dep. Leader, NSW Parly Liberal Party, 1959-75, Leader, 1976-77; Minister for Labour and Industry, Chief Secretary and Minister for Tourism, 1965-71; Chief Sec. and Minister for Tourism and Sport, 1971-72; Minister for Education, 1972-76; Premier and Treasurer, 1976; Leader of the Opposition, NSW Parlt, 1976-77. *Recreation:* reading. *Address:* 1/51 Upper Pitt Street, Kirribilli, NSW 2061, Australia. *T:* 929.9521.

WILLIS, Rt. Hon. Eustace George, PC 1967; *b* 7 March 1903; *s* of Walter Willis and Rose Jane Eaton; *m* 1929, Mary Swan Ramsay Nisbet; one *d. Educ:* City of Norwich Sch. Engine Room Artificer, Royal Navy, 1919-30. Served Royal Artillery, 1942-45. Political Organiser, 1930-32; Bookseller and Lecturer for NCLC, 1932-64. MP (Lab), North Edinburgh, 1945-50, East Edinburgh, April 1954-70. Member: Select Cttee on Estimates, 1945-50, 1954-59; Central Adv. Cttee to Min. of Pensions, 1945-50; Mineral Development Cttee, 1946-48. Chairman: Edinburgh City Labour Party, 1952-54; Scottish Labour Party, 1954-55; Scottish Parliamentary Labour Party, 1961-63. Parliamentary Deleg. to Atlantic Congress, 1959, NATO, 1960-62. Minister of State, Scottish Office, 1964-67. Gen. Comr, Bd of Inland Revenue, 1972-78; Mem., Scottish Parole Bd, 1975-80. *Recreations:* book-collecting, music. *Address:* 31 Great King Street, Edinburgh EH3 6QR. *T:* 031-556 6941.

WILLIS, Vice-Adm. Sir (Guido) James, KBE 1981; AO 1976; Chief of Naval Staff, Department of Defence, Australia, 1979-82, retired; *b* 18 Oct. 1923; *s* of late Jack Rupert Law Willis and Théa Willis; *m* 1st, 1949; one *s* two *d*; 2nd, 1976, Marjorie J. Rogers. *Educ:* Wesley Coll., Melbourne; Royal Australian Naval Coll. Imperial Defence Coll., 1967; Director General Operations and Plans, 1968-71; CO HMAS Melbourne, 1971-72; DDL Project Director, 1972-73; Chief of Naval Personnel, 1973-75; Chief of Naval Material, 1975-76; Asst Chief of Defence Force Staff, 1976-78; Flag Officer Commanding HMA Fleet, 1978-79. Commander 1956, Captain 1962, Rear-Adm. 1973, Vice-Adm. 1979. *Address:* 94 Endeavour Street, Red Hill, ACT 2603, Australia. *T:* 956 846.

WILLIS, Harold Infield, QC 1952; *b* 28 March 1902; *yr s* of late Sir Frederick James Willis, KBE, CB, and Lady Willis; *m* 1943, Eileen Burnett Murray; three *s. Educ:* Berkhamsted; New Coll., Oxford. Called to the Bar, 1926, Middle Temple; Bencher, Middle Temple, 1948, Treasurer, 1969. Served War of 1939-45, RAFVR, 1940-45. Dep. Chm., Hampshire QS, 1966-71. *Recreations:* gardening and fishing. *Address:* Homington House, Coombe Bissett, near Salisbury, Wilts.

WILLIS, Dr Hector Ford, CB 1960; Scientific Adviser, Ministry of Defence, 1962-70, retired; *b* 3 March 1909; *m* 1936, Marie Iddon (*née* Renwick). *Educ:* Howard Gardens High Sch.; University College, Cardiff; Trinity Coll., Cambridge. British Cotton Industry Research Association, 1935-38; Admiralty, 1938; Chief of the Royal Naval Scientific Service, 1954-62. US Medal of Freedom (Silver Palm), 1947. *Publications:* Papers in Proceedings of Royal Society, Philosophical Magazine, Proceedings of the Faraday Society. *Address:* Fulwood, Eaton Park, Cobham, Surrey.

WILLIS, Sir James; *see* Willis, Sir G. J.

WILLIS, His Honour John Brooke; a Circuit Judge (formerly County Court Judge), 1965-80; Barrister-at-Law; *b* 3 July 1906; *yr s* of William Brooke Willis and Maud Mary Willis, Rotherham; *m* 1929, Mary Margaret Coward (marr. diss., 1946); one *s* one *d*; *m* 1964, Terena Ann Steel (formerly Hood); two *d. Educ:* Bedford Modern Sch.; Sheffield Univ. Called to the Bar, Middle Temple, 1938, North Eastern Circuit. Served War of 1939-45. RAFVR, 1940-45, Sqdn Leader. Recorder, Rotherham, 1955-59, Huddersfield, 1959-65; Dep. Chm., W Riding of Yorks QS, 1958-71. Chairman, Medical Appeal Tribunal under the National Insurance (Industrial Injuries) Acts, 1953-65. *Address:* The Ivies, Etwall, near Derby DE6 6LR.

WILLIS, Maj.-Gen. John Brooker, CB 1981; retired 1981; *b* 28 July 1926; *s* of late William Noel Willis and of Elaine Willis; *m* 1959, Yda Belinda Jane Firbank; two *s* two *d. Educ:* privately, until 1941; Redhill Technical Coll. ptsc, jssc. Enlisted in Royal Navy (Fleet Air Arm) as Trainee Pilot; basic training in USA, 1944; returned to UK, transf. to Indian Army, attended Armoured OTS Ahmed Nagar, 1945; commnd 1947, joined 10th Royal Hussars; attended 13 Technical Staff Course, RMCS, 1958-60; Bt Lt-Col 1965, in comd 10th Hussars Aden; GSO1 (Armour) DS RMCS, 1968-69; Col GS MGO Secretariat, MoD, 1969-71; Dep. Comdt, RAC Centre, 1971-74; Sen. Officers' War Course, Greenwich, 1974; Dir Gen., Fighting Vehicles and Engr Equipment, 1977-81. *Recreations:* golf, horses and ponies, working on the land, wood carving. *Address:* c/o Lloyds Bank Ltd, 26 Hammersmith Broadway, W6 7AH.

WILLIS, John Henry, RBA, ARCA (London); artist; *b* Tavistock, 9 Oct. 1887; *s* of R. Willis, art dealer; *m* ; one *s. Educ:* Armstrong Coll., Durham Univ.; Royal College of Art, South Kensington. Portrait and Landscape Painter. *Principal works:* Kiwi Hut, on the line RA, 1921; 'Twixt Devon and Cornwall, on the line RA, 1923; The Nant Francon Pass, on the line RA, 1924; *portraits:* M. C. Oliver, RA, 1922; Stanley, son of E. J. Miles, RA, 1923. *Address:* 20 Titchfield Gardens, Paignton, Devon. *T:* Paignton 556850.

WILLIS, Sir John (Ramsay), Kt 1966; Judge of the High Court of Justice, Queen's Bench Division, 1966-80; *b* 1908; *s* of Dr and Mrs J. K. Willis, Cranleigh, Surrey; *m* two *s. Educ:* Lancing (Scholar); Trinity Coll., Dublin; BA, LLB (1st cl. Hons). Called to Bar, Gray's Inn, 1932; QC 1956. Royal Signals (TA), 1938-45; served War of 1939-45; GSO 1 14th Army. Bencher, Gray's Inn, 1953, Treasurer, 1969. Recorder of Southampton, 1965-66; Dep. Chairman, E Suffolk QS, 1965-71; Mem., Parole Bd, 1974-75. *Recreations:* mountaineering, gardening. *Clubs:* Garrick, Alpine.

WILLIS, John Trueman, DFM 1942; housing consultant; *b* 27 Oct. 1918; *s* of Gordon and Ethel Willis, Headington, Oxford; *m* 1947, Audrey Joan, *d* of Aubrey and Gertrude Gurden, Headington, Oxford; one *s* one *d. Educ:* Oxford High Sch., Oxford. Estates Management, Magdalen Coll., Oxford, 1935-36; Industrial Trng, Lockheed Hydraulic Brake Co., Leamington Spa, 1937-38. Served War of 1939-45: Pilot on 14 Sqdn RAF Middle East, 1940-42; PoW Stalag Luft III, Germany, 1943-45. Estates Management, 1946-64, Estates Sec., 1953-65, Magdalen Coll., Oxford; Rent Officer for Oxford, 1965-67; Sec. Housing Societies Charitable Trust, 1968-69; Director: Shelter, 1971-72 (Housing Dir, 1969-70); Liverpool Housing Trust, 1973-75; Castle Rock Housing Assoc., 1976-78. Mem., NEDO Housing Strategy Cttee, 1975-78. Vice-Chm., Housing Assocs Charitable Trust, 1980-. ICSA. *Publications:* Housing and Poverty Report, 1970; contrib. to architectural and housing jls as Dir of Shelter. *Recreations:* Rugby football, community action.

Address: 15 Manor Road, Hoylake, Wirral, Merseyside L47 3DE. *T:* 051-632 3873. *Club:* Oxford Sports.

WILLIS, Joseph Robert McKenzie, CB 1952; CMG 1946; Deputy Chairman, Board of Inland Revenue, 1957-71; *b* 18 March 1909; 2nd *s* of Charles Frederick Willis and Lucy Alice McKenzie; *m* 1945, Elizabeth Browning, *er d* of James Ewing; one *s* one *d. Educ:* Eton; Christ Church, Oxford. Entered Inland Revenue Dept, 1932; Under Secretary, Central Economic Planning Staff, Treasury, 1948-49; Commissioner of Inland Revenue, 1949; Student of Imperial Defence Coll., 1948. Professorial Res. Fellow and Vis. Prof., Bath Univ., 1972-79. Specialist advr to Select Cttee on Wealth Tax, 1975. *Publications:* (with C. T. Sandford and D. J. Ironside): An Accessions Tax, 1973; An Annual Wealth Tax, 1975; (with P. J. W. Hardwick) Tax Expenditures in the United Kingdom, 1978. *Address:* Bunbury, Lower Shiplake, Henley-on-Thames, Oxon. *T:* Wargrave 2726.

WILLIS, Rear-Adm. Kenneth Henry George, CB 1981; Chief of Staff to Commander-in-Chief, Naval Home Command, 1979-81; *m* ; three *d. Educ:* Royal Naval Engineering Coll.; Royal Naval Coll.; Jesus Coll., Cambridge (BA 1949). Joined RN 1944; served at sea and in shore weapons depts; Resident Officer, Polaris Executive, Clyde Submarine Base, 1965-68; i/c training, HMS Collingwood, 1969-70; Asst Dir, Underwater Weapon Dept, 1970; sowc 1974; Dep. Dir, RN Staff Coll., Greenwich, 1975-76, Dir, 1976; CO HMS Collingwood, 1976-79. FRSA. *Address:* c/o Barclays Bank Ltd, 1 Manvers Street, Bath, Avon.

WILLIS, Norman David; Deputy General Secretary, Trades Union Congress, since 1977 (Assistant General Secretary, 1974-77); *b* 21 Jan. 1933; *s* of Victor J. M. and Kate E. Willis; *m* 1963, Maureen Kenning; one *s* one *d. Educ:* Ashford County Grammar Sch.; Ruskin and Oriel Colls, Oxford. Employed by TGWU, 1949; Nat. Service, 1951-53; Oxford, 1955-59; Personal Research Asst to Gen. Sec., TGWU, 1959-70; Nat. Sec., Research and Educn, TGWU, 1970-74. Councillor (Lab) Staines UDC, 1971-74. *Recreations:* reading novels, watching television, going to jumble sales, looking at beautiful buildings, flowers, and canals. *Address:* 13 Links Road, Ashford, Mddx.

WILLIS, Lady; Olive Christine, CBE 1951; *b* 20 Nov. 1895; *d* of late Henry Edward Millar, Hampstead; *m* 1916, Lieut Algernon Usborne Willis (Admiral of the Fleet Sir Algernon U. Willis, GCB, KBE, DSO) (*d* 1976); two *d. Educ:* St Felix Sch., Southwold, Suffolk; Newnham Coll., Cambridge. Officer (Sister) Order of St John of Jerusalem, 1948. *Recreation:* gardening. *Club:* English-Speaking Union.

WILLIS, Robert William Gaspard, MA; Founder and Headmaster of Copford Glebe School, 1958-69, Principal, 1969-72 (now Copford College); *b* 22 Nov. 1905; *s* of Rev. W. N. Willis, founder and Headmaster for 38 years, of Ascham St Vincent's, Eastbourne, and Sophia Caroline Baker; *m* 1930, Ernestine Ruth Kimber; two *s* two *d. Educ:* Ascham St Vincent's, Eastbourne; Eton Coll. (Foundation Scholar); Corpus Christi Coll., Cambridge (Scholar). Assistant Master at Malvern Coll., Worcs, 1927-39 (Mathematics and Classics); Senior Mathematical Master at The King's School, Macclesfield, Cheshire, 1939-41; Headmaster of Sir William Turner's School (Coatham School), Redcar, 1941-53; Headmaster of English High School for Boys, Istanbul, Turkey, 1953-57. Hon. Fellow, Huguenot Soc. of London. Hon. Life Mem., Gainsborough's House Soc., Sudbury. *Recreation:* golf. *Address:* 8 Links View, Newton Green, Sudbury, Suffolk. *T:* Sudbury 72522. *Clubs:* Royal Over-Seas League; Newton Green Golf.

WILLIS, His Honour Roger Blenkiron, TD; a Circuit Judge (formerly County Court Judge), 1959-81; *b* 22 June 1906; *s* of late William Outhwaite Willis, KC, and Margaret Alice (*née* Blenkiron); *m* 1933, Joan Eleanor Amy Good; two *d. Educ:* Charterhouse School; Emmanuel Coll., Cambridge. Barrister, Inner Temple, Nov. 1930. Joined Middlesex Yeomanry (TA), 1938. Served War of 1939-45. *Recreation:* golf. *Address:* 18 Turners Reach House, 9 Chelsea Embankment, SW3. *Clubs:* Garrick, MCC.

WILLIS, Stephen Murrell; Partner, Pearless, de Rougemont & Co., East Grinstead, Sussex, Solicitors, since 1968; a Recorder of the Crown Court, since 1980; *b* 21 June 1929; *s* of late John Henry Willis and Eileen Marion (*née* Heard), Hadleigh, Suffolk; *m* 1st, 1953, Jean Irene Eve; one *s* three *d*; 2nd, 1975, Doris Florence Davies (*née* Redding); two step *d. Educ:* (chorister) Christ Church Cathedral, Oxford; Bloxham Sch. (scholar). National Service, Royal Signals, 1948-50. Admitted solicitor, 1955; Partner, Chamberlin Talbot & Bracey, Lowestoft and Beccles, Suffolk, 1955-63; a Deputy Circuit Judge, 1975. Founded The Suffolk Singers, 1960; Founder and Director, The Prodigal Singers and Gallery Band, 1964-; Chairman, The Renaissance Singers, 1969-. *Publications:* (composer of) mediaeval song settings for radio and theatre plays. *Recreations:* performing early music, sailing, travel. *Address:* 8 Church Lane, East Grinstead, West Sussex RH19 3BA. *T:* East Grinstead 23687. *Clubs:* Noblemen and Gentlemen's Catch, Law Society, Law Society Yacht; Rotary; Orford Sailing.

WILLIS, Ted; *see* Willis, Baron.

WILLISON, Lt-Gen. Sir David (John), KCB 1973; OBE 1958; MC 1945; Chief Royal Engineer, 1977-82; Consultant on International Affairs, National Westminster Bank Group, since 1980; *b* 25 Dec. 1919; *s* of Brig. A. C. Willison, DSO, MC; *m* 1941, Betty Vernon Bates; one *s* two *d. Educ:*

Wellington; RMA Woolwich. 2/Lt RE, 1939; OC 17 and 246 Field Cos, 1944-45; Staff Coll., Camberley 1945; Brigade Major, Indian Inf. Brigade, 1946; Malaya, 1947; WO, 1948-50; OC 16 Field Co., Egypt, 1950-52; GHQ MELF, 1952-53; OC, RE Troops, Berlin, 1953-55; Directing Staff, Staff Coll., Camberley, 1955-58; AQMG (Ops), HQ British Forces Aden, 1958-60; CO, 38 Engr Regt, 1960-63; Col GS MI/DI4, MoD, 1963-66; idc 1966; BGS (Intell.), MoD, 1967-70; BGS (Intell. and Security)/ACOS, G2, HQ NORTHAG, 1970-71; Dir of Service Intelligence, MoD, 1971-72; Dep. Chief Defence Staff (Int.), 1972-75; Dir Gen. of Intelligence, MoD, 1975-78. Col Comdt RE, 1973-82. Freeman, City of London, 1981. *Recreations:* sailing, ski-ing, shooting. *Address:* Long Barton, Lower Pennington Lane, Lymington, Hampshire. *Clubs:* Naval and Military; Royal Lymington Yacht.

WILLISON, Sir John (Alexander), Kt 1970; OBE 1964; QPM 1968; DL; *b* 3 Jan. 1914; *s* of John Willison Gow Willison and Mabel Willison, Dalry, Ayrshire; *m* 1947, Jess Morris Bruce. *Educ:* Sedbergh School. Joined City of London Police, 1933; served with RNVR, 1943-46; Chief Constable: Berwick, Roxburgh and Selkirk, 1952-58; Worcestershire Constabulary, 1958-67; West Mercia Constabulary, 1967-74. DL Worcs 1968. KStJ 1973. *Address:* Ravenhills Green, Lulsley, near Worcester.

WILLMER, Prof. Edward Nevill, ScD; FRS 1960; Emeritus Professor of Histology, University of Cambridge, since 1969; Fellow of Clare College since 1936; *b* 15 Aug. 1902; 5th *s* of Arthur W. Willmer, Birkenhead; *m* 1939, Henrietta Noreen (Penny), 2nd *d* of H. Napier Rowlatt; two *s* two *d. Educ:* Birkenhead Sch.; Corpus Christi Coll., Cambridge, since 1969; Fellow of Clare College. MA (Oxon) 1965; MSc (Manchester) 1927; ScD (Cambridge) 1944. Demonstrator and Assistant Lecturer in Physiology, Manchester, 1924-29; Lecturer in Histology, Cambridge, 1930-48; Reader, 1948-65, Prof., 1966-69. Editor, Biological Reviews, 1969-80. *Publications:* Tissue Culture, 1934; Retinal Structure and Colour Vision, 1946; Cytology and Evolution, 1960, 2nd edn 1970; (ed) Cells and Tissues in Culture, 1965; Old Grantchester, 1976; The River Cam, 1979; contrib. physiological and biological journals. *Recreations:* painting, gardening, walking. *Address:* Yew Garth, Grantchester, Cambridge. *T:* Cambridge 840360.

See also B. J. Davenport.

WILLMER, Rt. Hon. Sir (Henry) Gordon, PC 1958; Kt 1945; OBE 1945; TD; a Lord Justice of Appeal, 1958-Jan. 1969; *b* 1899; 4th *s* of late A. W. Willmer, JP, Birkenhead; *m* 1928, Barbara, *d* of late Sir Archibald Hurd; one *s* two *d. Educ:* Birkenhead Sch.; Corpus Christi Coll., Oxford. Hon. Fellow of Corpus Christi Coll., 1949. Called to Bar, 1924; KC 1939. Joined Territorial Army in 1925, and served with 53rd Medium Bde, RA (TA), till 1938, when retired on to TA Reserve of Officers, from which called up for service during the war; served with Coast Artillery, 1940-43, and with AMG, CMF, 1943-45. A Justice of the High Court. Probate, Divorce and Admiralty Division, 1945-58. President, Shipping Claims Tribunal, 1946; Member Supreme Court Cttee on Practice and Procedure, 1947; Member, General Claims Tribunal, 1950; Chm., NI Detention Appeals Tribunal, 1973-75. Chairman, Inns of Court Mission, 1950-63; Treasurer, Inner Temple, 1969; Chm., Statutory Cttee, Pharmaceutical Soc. of GB, 1970-80, Hon. Fellow 1980. Mem., London Maritime Arbitrators' Assoc., 1970. Chm. Marine Bd, Investigation into loss of Amoco Cadiz, 1978-80. Trustee, Thalidomide Children's Trust, 1973-81. Hon. LLD Liverpool, 1966. *Address:* Flat 1, 34 Arkwright Road, Hampstead, NW3 6BH. *T:* 01-435 0690.

See also J. F. Willmer.

WILLMER, John Franklin, QC 1967; *b* 30 May 1930; *s* of Rt Hon. Sir (Henry) Gordon Willmer, *qv*; *m* 1st, 1958, Nicola Ann Dickinson (marr. diss. 1979); one *s* three *d*; 2nd, 1979, Margaret Lilian, *d* of Chester B. Berryman. *Educ:* Winchester; Corpus Christi Coll., Oxford. National Service, 2nd Lieut, Cheshire Regt, 1949-50; TA Cheshire Regt, 1950-51; Middlesex Regt, 1951-57 (Captain). Called to Bar, Inner Temple, 1955, Bencher, 1975. Member: panel of Lloyd's Arbitrators in Salvage Cases, 1967; panel from which Wreck Commissioners appointed, 1967. *Recreation:* walking. *Address:* Flat 4, 23 Lymington Road, NW6 1HZ. *T:* 01-435 9245. *Club:* United Oxford & Cambridge University.

WILLMOTT, Prof. John Charles, PhD; Professor of Physics since 1964, Director of the Physical Laboratories since 1967, and a Pro-Vice-Chancellor since 1982, Manchester University; *b* 1 April 1922; *s* of Arthur George Willmott and Annie Elizabeth Willmott; *m* 1952, Sheila Madeleine Dumbell; two *s* one *d. Educ:* Bancroft's Sch., Woodford; Imperial Coll. of Science and Technol. (BSc, PhD). ARCS. Lectr in Physics, Liverpool Univ., 1948-58, Sen. Lectr, 1958-63. Mem., SERC (formerly SRC), 1978-. *Publications:* Tables of Coefficients for the Analysis of Triple Angular Correlations of Gamma-rays from Aligned Nuclei, 1968; Atomic Physics, 1975; articles on nuclear structure in learned jls. *Address:* 37 Hall Moss Lane, Bramhall, Cheshire SK7 1RB. *T:* 061-439 4169.

WILLMOTT, Peter; Head of Central Policy Unit, Greater London Council, since 1981; Visiting Professor, Bartlett School of Architecture and Planning, University College, London, since 1972; *b* 18 Sept. 1923; *s* of Benjamin Merriman Willmott and Dorothy Willmott (*née* Waymouth); *m* 1948, Phyllis Mary Noble; two *s. Educ:* Tollington Sch., London; Ruskin Coll., Oxford. BSc (Soc) (external) London. Research Asst, Labour Party, 1948-54; Institute of Community Studies: Res. Officer, 1954-60; Dep. Dir, 1960-64;

Co-Dir, 1964–78; Chm., 1978–. Dir, Centre for Environmental Studies, 1978–80. Vice-Chm., Planning Cttee, SSRC, 1971–74. Vis. Prof., Ecole Pratique des Hautes Etudes, Univ. of Paris, 1972; Chm., Organising Gp of Jt Working Party on Transmitted Deprivation (DHSS/SSRC), 1974–78. Regents' Lectr, Univ. of California, 1982. *Publications:* (with Michael Young) Family and Kinship in East London, 1957; (with Michael Young) Family and Class in a London Suburb, 1960; The Evolution of a Community, 1963; Adolescent Boys of East London, 1966; (with Michael Young) The Symmetrical Family, 1973; (ed) Sharing Inflation? Poverty Report, 1976; (with Graeme Shankland and David Jordan) Inner London: policies for dispersal and balance, 1977; (with Charles Madge) Inner City Poverty in Paris and London, 1981. *Address:* 27 Kingsley Place, N6 5EA. *T:* 01-348 3958.

WILLOCHRA, Bishop of, since 1970; **Rt. Rev. Stanley Bruce Rosier;** *b* 18 Nov. 1928; *s* of S. C. and A. Rosier; *m* 1954, Faith Margaret Alice Norwood; one *s* three *d. Educ:* Univ. of WA; Christ Church, Oxford. Asst Curate, Ecclesall, Dio. of Sheffield, 1954; Rector of: Wyalkatchem, Dio. of Perth, 1957; Kellerberrin, Dio. of Perth, 1964; Auxiliary Bishop in Diocese of Perth, Western Australia, 1967–70. *Recreation:* natural history. *Address:* Bishop's House, PO Box 96, Gladstone, SA 5473, Australia. *T:* (office) 086-62249; (home) 086-622057.

WILLOTT, Brian; *see* Willott, W. B.

WILLOTT, Lt-Col Roland Lancaster, DSO 1940; OBE 1945; TD 1946; BSc; CEng, FIMechE; *b* 1 May 1912; *s* of Frederick John Willott and Gertrude May Leese; *m* 1960, Elisabeth Petersen. *Educ:* Wellington Sch. (Somerset); University of Wales. College Apprentice Metropolitan Vickers Electrical Co., Trafford Park, Manchester; Mechanical Engineer Metropolitan Vickers Co., 1933–36; Major RE 1939–41; Lt-Col CRE 1941–45; Colonel Commander Army Group RE, 1945 (despatches, DSO, OBE, Order of Leopold of Belgium, Croix de Guerre). Chief Engineer, John Summers & Sons Ltd, 1945–69, Dir, 1965–71; Group Chief Engineer, Shotton Works, BSC, 1969–72. *Address:* Lea Croft, Yeld Lane, Kelsall Hill, Tarporley, Cheshire CW6 0TE. *T:* Kelsall 51344. *Club:* Army and Navy.

WILLOTT, (William) Brian, PhD; Chief Executive, British Technology Group (National Enterprise Board and National Research Development Corporation), since 1981; *b* 14 May 1940; *s* of Dr William Harford Willott and Dr Beryl P. M. Willott; *m* 1970, Alison Leyland Pyke-Lees; two *d. Educ:* Trinity Coll., Cambridge (MA, PhD). Research Associate, Univ. of Maryland, USA, 1965–67; Principal, Board of Trade, 1967–69; Principal: Shipping Policy, BoT, 1969–73; HM Treasury, 1973–75; Asst Sec., Dept of Industry, 1975–78; Secretary: Industrial Development Unit, DoI, 1978–80; NEB, 1980–81. *Recreations:* music, reading, ancient history, gardening. *Address:* Pembroke House, 11 Spencer Hill, Wimbledon, SW19 4PA. *T:* 01-946 1263. *Club:* Royal Automobile.

WILLOUGHBY, family name of **Baron Middleton.**

WILLOUGHBY; *see* Heathcote-Drummond-Willoughby, family name of Earl of Ancaster.

WILLOUGHBY, Rear-Admiral Guy; CB 1955; *b* 7 Nov. 1902; *s* of Rev. Nesbit E. Willoughby, Vicar of Bickington, Devon, and of Marjorie Helen Willoughby (*née* Kaye); *m* 1923, Mary, *d* of J. G. W. Aldridge, AMICE, Wimbledon; one *s* one *d. Educ:* Osborne and Dartmouth. Joined Osborne, 1916; Sub-Lieut, 1923; qualified as a naval pilot 1925, and thereafter flew as a pilot in Naval and RAF Squadrons, embarked in various Carriers until 1936; Commander, 1937; Commander (Air) in Glorious, 1938–39; served on naval staff, Admiralty, 1940–41; comd HM Carrier Activity, 1942–43; Captain, 1943; Chief Staff Officer to Admiral Comdg Carriers in Eastern Fleet, 1944; Director of Air Warfare and Training (Naval Staff, Admiralty), 1945–46; Imperial Defence Coll., 1947; 4th Naval Member of Australian Commonwealth Navy Board and Cdre (Air), 1948–50; comd HM Carrier Eagle, 1951–52; Rear-Admiral 1953; Flag Officer, Flying Training, 1953–56, retired, 1956. *Address:* High Croft, South Woodchester, near Stroud, Glos. *T:* Amberley 2594. *Club:* Naval and Military.

WILLOUGHBY, Maj.-Gen. Sir John (Edward Francis), KBE 1967 (CBE 1963; OBE 1953); CB 1966; *b* 18 June 1913; *s* of Major N. E. G. Willoughby, The Middlesex Regt, and Mrs B. A. M. Willoughby, Heytesbury, Wiltshire; *m* 1938, Muriel Alexandra Rosamund Scott; three *d.* Commissioned, Middlesex Regt, 1933. Served War of 1939–45 with Middlesex Regt, BEF, 1940–41; OC 2 Middlesex Regt, 1943; GSO 1 220 Military Mission, USA, Pacific, Burma and UK, 1943–44; OC 1 Dorsets Regt, NW Europe, 1944; served with Middlesex Regt, FARELF, Korea, 1950–51; GSO1, 3 Inf. Div., UK and MELF, 1951–53; OC 1 Middlesex Regt, British Troops Austria, UK and MELF, 1954–56; Colonel, The Middlesex Regt, 1959–65; Chief of Staff, Land Forces, Hong Kong, 1961; GOC, 48 Inf. Div. (TA) and W Midland District, 1963–65; GOC Land Forces ME Comd, Inspector-Gen. of Federal Regular Army of S Arabia and Security Comdr Aden State, 1965–67; Adviser on Defence to Fedn of Arab Emirates, 1968–71.

WILLOUGHBY, Kenneth James; *b* 6 Nov. 1922; *y s* of late Frank Albert Willoughby and late Florence Rose (*née* Darbyshire); *m* 1943, Vera May Dickerson; one *s* one *d. Educ:* Hackney Downs (Grocers') Sch.; Selwyn Coll., Cambridge. Tax Officer, Inland Revenue, 1939; Royal Engineers, UK,

Egypt, Italy, Austria, Greece, 1941–47 (despatches, Captain); Asst Auditor, Exchequer and Audit Dept, 1947; Asst Prin., Min. of Civil Aviation, 1949; Asst Private Sec. to Minister of Civil Aviation, 1950; Private Sec. to Perm. Sec., 1951; Principal, Min. of Transport (and later, Civil Aviation), 1951; Sec., Air Transport Adv. Council, 1957–61; Asst Sec., Min. of Aviation, 1962; Under-Secretary: Min. of Technology, 1968–70; DTI, 1970–74. *Recreations:* gardening, music, reading. *Address:* 84 Douglas Avenue, Exmouth, Devon EX8 2HG. *T:* Exmouth 71175.

WILLOUGHBY, Rt. Rev. Noel Vincent; *see* Cashel and Ossory, Bishop of.

WILLOUGHBY DE BROKE, 20th Baron, *cr* 1492; **John Henry Peyto Verney,** MC 1918; AFC 1940; AE; KStJ 1948; JP; Lord Lieutenant of Warwickshire, 1939–68; Air Commodore, Auxiliary Air Force, retired; *b* 21 May 1896; *o c* of 19th Baron and Marie Frances Lisette, OBE (*d* 1941), *y d* of C. A. Hanbury, Strathgarve, Ross-shire; *S* father, 1923; *m* 1933, Rachel, *d* of Sir Bourchier Wrey, 11th Bt, and Mrs Godfrey Heseltine; one *s* one *d. Educ:* Eton; Sandhurst. Served European War (MC); ADC to Governor of Bombay, 1919–22; late Captain, 17-21st Lancers; Adjutant, Warwickshire Yeomanry, 1925–29; Joint Master Warwickshire Hounds, 1929–35; commanded No. 605 (County of Warwick) AAF Squadron, 1936–39 (AFCAEA) Staff Officer 11 Fighter Group, 1940 (despatches); Deputy Director Public Relations, Air Ministry, 1941–44; Director Public Relations, 1945–46. Member: National Hunt Cttee, 1940 (Steward, 1942–44, 1950–53, and 1964–67); Jockey Club, 1941 (Steward, 1944–47 and 1954–56). Chm., Tattersall's Cttee, 1948–53. Chairman: Birmingham Racecourse Co. Ltd, 1952–65 (Dir, 1932–65); The Steeplechase Co. (Cheltenham) Ltd, 1953–71 (Dir, 1944–71); Wolverhampton Racecourse Co. Ltd, 1947–71; Race-Finish Recording Co. Ltd, later Racecourse Technical Services Ltd, 1959–70 (Dir, 1947–70). Mem., Bloodstock Industry Cttee, Animal Health Trust, 1944– (Chm., 1964–77). President: Hunters' Improvement Society, 1957–58; Warwickshire Association of Boys' Clubs; Scouts Association; Council for Order of St John, 1946–68. Hon. Colonel, Warwickshire Yeomanry, 1942–63. *Heir: s* Hon. Leopold David Verney [*b* 14 Sept. 1938; *m* 1965, Petra, 2nd *d* of Sir John Aird, 3rd Bt, MVO, MC; three *s*]. *Address:* 2 Upper Phillimore Gardens, W8 7HA. *T:* 01-937 8548. *Club:* Cavalry and Guards.

WILLS, family name of **Baron Dulverton.**

WILLS, Arthur William, DMus (Dunelm), FRCO (CHM), ADCM; composer; Organist, Ely Cathedral, since 1958; *b* 19 Sept. 1926; *s* of Violet Elizabeth and Archibald Wills; *m* 1953, Mary Elizabeth Titterton; one *s* one *d. Educ:* St John's Sch., Coventry. Sub. Organist, Ely Cathedral, 1949; Director of Music, King's School, Ely, 1953–65; Prof., Royal Academy of Music, 1964. Mem. Council, RCO, 1966–; Examr to Royal Schs of Music, 1966–. Recital tours in Canada, Europe, USA; recording artist. Hon. RAM, Hon. FLCM, FRSCM. *Publications:* The Art of Organ Improvisation, 1974; (contrib.) English Church Music, 1978; Organ, 1980; numerous musical compositions include: *organ:* Sonata, Trio Sonata, Christmas Meditations, Prelude and Fugue (Alkmaar), Tongues of Fire, Variations on Amazing Grace, Symphonia Eliensis, Concerto (organ, strings and timpani), The Fenlands (symphonic suite for brass band and organ); *guitar:* Sonata, Pavane and Galliard, Hommage à Ravel, Three Elizabethan Love Songs (alto and guitar), Moods and Diversions; *choral:* Missa Eliensis, The Child for Today (carol sequence), The Light Invisible (double choir, organ and percussion), Missa in Memoriam Benjamin Britten, An English Requiem. *Recreations:* travel, antique collecting, Eastern philosophy. *Address:* The Old Sacristy, The College, Ely, Cambs. *T:* Ely 2084. *Club:* Savage.

WILLS, Brian Alan, PhD; FPS, CChem, FRSC; Chief Pharmacist, Department of Health and Social Security, since 1978; *b* 17 Feb. 1927; *s* of William Wills and late Emily (*née* Hibbert); *m* 1955, Barbara Joan Oggelsby; one *d. Educ:* Univ. of Nottingham (BPharm); PhD (London). FPS 1972 (MPS 1949); FRSC (FRIC 1967, ARIC 1957); CChem 1975. Lecturer in Pharmaceutics, Sch. of Pharmacy, Univ. of London, 1951–57; Head of Research and Control Dept, Allen & Hanburys (Africa) Ltd, Durban, S Africa, 1957–62; Head of Control Div., Allen & Hanburys Ltd, London, E2, 1962–78. Member: British Pharmacopoeia Commn, 1973–; UK delegn to European Pharmacopoeia Commn, 1975–; WHO Expert Adv. Panel on Internat. Pharmacopoeia and Pharmaceutical Preparations, 1979–. Vis. Prof., Univ. of Bath, 1979–. Member: Bd of Studies in Pharmacy, London Univ., 1979–; Jt Formulary Cttee for British Nat. Formulary, 1979–; Council, Sch. of Pharmacy, London Univ., 1981–. *Publications:* papers on sterilisation and disinfection and on the preservation, stability and quality control of pharmaceutical preparations. *Address:* 1 Oakhill Drive, Welwyn, Herts AL6 9NW. *T:* Welwyn 4191.

WILLS, Sir David; *see* Wills, Sir H. D. H.

WILLS, Lt-Col Sir Edward; *see* Wills, Lt-Col Sir E. E. de W.

WILLS, Lt-Col Sir (Ernest) Edward (de Winton), 4th Bt, *cr* 1904, of Hazlewood and Clapton-in-Gordano; *b* 8 Dec. 1903; *s* of Sir Ernest Salter Wills, 3rd Bt, and Caroline Fanny Maud de Winton (*d* 1953); *S* father 1958; *m* 1st, 1926, Sylvia Margaret (*d* 1946), *d* of late William Barker Ogden; two *d* ; 2nd, 1949, Juliet Eve, *d* of late Captain John Eagles Henry Graham-Clarke, JP, Frocester Manor, Glos. *Educ:* Eton. Formerly Lieut, Scots Guards;

Lieut-Colonel late Middlesex Regt; Lieut-Colonel Comdg 5th Bn, Manchester Regt; served European War, 1939-45. Is a member of Lloyd's. *Recreation:* fishing. *Heir: nephew* David Seton Wills [*b* 29 Dec. 1939; *m* 1968, Gillian, twin *d* of A. P. Eastoe; one *s* three *d*]. *Address:* Lochs Lodge, Glenlyon, Perthshire PH15 2PU. *T:* Bridge of Balgie 200; Mount Prosperous, Hungerford, Berks RG17 0RP. *T:* Hungerford 2624. *Clubs:* Cavalry and Guards; Household Division Yacht.

See also Marquess of Ailesbury, A. C. N. Hopkins.

WILLS, Helen; *see* Roark, H. W.

WILLS, Sir (Hugh) David (Hamilton), Kt 1980; CBE 1971 (MBE 1946); TD 1964; DL; *b* 19 June 1917; 2nd *s* of late Frederick Noel Hamilton Wills and of Margery Hamilton Sinclair; *m* 1949, Eva Helen, JP, *d* of late Major A. T. McMorrough Kavanagh, MC; one *s* one *d. Educ:* Eton; Magdalen Coll., Oxford. Served War of 1939-45 with Queen's Own Cameron Highlanders (TA): France 1940, Aruba 1941; GSO 3 (Ops) GHQ Home Forces, 1942-43; GSO 2 (Ops) Southern Command, 1943-44. Chairman of Trustees, Rendcomb Coll., 1955-; Chm., Ditchley Foundation, 1972-; Mem. Governing Body, Atlantic Coll., 1963-73, 1980-. High Sheriff Oxfordshire 1961, DL 1967. *Recreations:* fishing, sailing. *Address:* Sandford Park, Sandford St Martin, Oxford OX5 4AJ. *T:* Great Tew 238. *Clubs:* Boodle's, Ends of the Earth.

WILLS, Sir John Spencer; Kt 1969; FCIT; Chairman, British Electric Traction Co. Ltd, 1966-82 (Director, 1939-82, Managing Director, 1946-73, Deputy Chairman, 1951-66); Director and Chairman: National Electric Construction Co. Ltd, since 1945; Birmingham and District Investment Trust Ltd, since 1946; Electrical & Industrial Investment Co. Ltd, since 1946; *b* 10 Aug. 1904; *s* of Cedric Spencer Wills and Cécile Charlotte; *m* 1936, Elizabeth Drusilla Alice Clare Garcke; two *s. Educ:* Cleobury Mortimer Coll., Shropshire; Merchant Taylors' Sch., London. Asst to Secs, British Traction Co. Ltd and British Automobile Traction Ltd, 1922-23; Sec., Wrexham and Dist Transport Co. Ltd, 1924-26; Gen. Manager, E Yorks Motor Services Ltd, 1926-31, Dir and Chm., 1931-65; Chm., Birmingham & Midland Motor Omnibus Co. Ltd, 1946-68; Dir, 1947-73, Dep. Chm., 1953-71, Monotype Corp. Ltd; Man. Dir, 1947-67, Chm., 1947-78, Broadcast Relay Service Ltd, later Rediffusion Ltd; Chm., Associated-Rediffusion Ltd, later Rediffusion Television Ltd, 1954-78; Director and Chairman: E Midland Motor Services Ltd, 1931-44; Yorks Woollen Dist Transport Co. Ltd, 1931-43; Hebble Motor Services Ltd, 1932-45; Yorks Traction Co. Ltd, 1932-46; Mexborough & Swinton Traction Co. Ltd, 1933-47; Western Welsh Omnibus Co. Ltd, 1933-60; Crosville Motor Services Ltd, 1933-41; Ribble Motor Services Ltd, 1942-47; N Western Road Car Co. Ltd, 1943-45; S Wales Transport Co. Ltd, Swansea Improvements & Tramways Co. Ltd, 1943-46; Devon Gen. Omnibus and Touring Co. Ltd, 1946-47; Man. Dir, British and Foreign Aviation Ltd and Great Western and Southern Air Lines Ltd, 1938-42; Director: Olley Air Service Ltd, Channel Air Ferries Ltd, West Coast Air Services Ltd, Air Booking Co. Ltd, 1938-42; Air Commerce Ltd, 1939-42; Yorks Electric Power Co. Ltd, 1942-48; Wembley Stadium Ltd, 1960-82 (Chm., 1965-82). Chm., Hull and Grimsby Sect., Incorp. Secs' Assoc. (now CIS), 1929-31; Member of Council: BET Fedn, 1933 (Pres., 1946-79); Public Road Transport Assoc. (formerly Public Transport Assoc.), 1943-68 (Chm., 1945-46; Hon. Mem., 1969), subseq. Confedn of British Road Passenger Transport Ltd (Hon. Mem., 1975); FCIT (Henry Spurrier Meml Lectr, 1946, Pres., 1950-51); Chairman: Omnibus Owners' Assoc., 1943-44; Nat. Council for Omnibus Industry, 1944-45 (Mem. 1940-66); Standing Cttee, Air Transport Sect., London Chamber of Commerce, 1953-65 (Mem. 1943; Dep. Chm. 1949). Governor, Royal Shakespeare Theatre, Stratford upon Avon, 1946-74; Mem. Council, Royal Opera House Soc., 1962-74; Trustee, LSO Trust, 1962-68; Vice-Patron, Theatre Royal Windsor Trust, 1965-. Member, UK Council, European Movement, 1966-. *Recreations:* complete idleness; formerly: flying, swimming, ski-ing, tennis, riding, shooting. *Address:* 1 Campden House Terrace, Kensington Church Street, W8 4BQ. *T:* 01-727 5981; Beech Farm, Battle, East Sussex. *T:* Battle 2950. *Clubs:* Naval and Military, East India, Devonshire, Sports, and Public Schools.

See also N. K. S. Wills.

WILLS, Sir John Vernon, 4th Bt, *cr* 1923; TD; FRICS; JP; Lord-Lieutenant and Custos Rotulorum of Avon, since 1974; Director: Bristol and West Building Society, since 1969 (Vice-Chairman, since 1982); Bristol Evening Post, since 1973 (Deputy Chairman, since 1978); Deputy Chairman, Bristol United Press, since 1980; Local Director, Barclays Bank, since 1981; *b* 3 July 1928; *s* of Sir George Vernon Proctor Wills, 2nd Bt, and Lady Nellie Jeannie, ARRC, JP, *y d* of late J. T. Rutherford, Abergavenny; *S* brother 1945; *m* 1953, Diana Veronica Cecil (Jane), *o d* of Douglas R. M. Baker, Winsford, Somerset; four *s. Educ:* Eton. Served Coldstream Guards, 1946-49; Lt-Col Comdg N Somerset and Bristol Yeomanry, 1965-67; Bt Col 1967; now TARO. Hon. Col, 37th (Wessex and Welsh) Signal Regt, T&AVR, 1975-. Dir, Bristol Waterworks Co., 1964-73; Chm., Wessex Water Auth., 1973-82; Mem., Nat. Water Council, 1973-82. Pro-Chancellor, Univ. of Bath, 1979-. Pres., Royal Bath and West Southern Counties Soc., 1980. Member of Somerset CC. JP 1962, DL 1968, High Sheriff, 1968, Somerset. KStJ 1978. *Heir: s* David James Vernon Wills, *b* 2 Jan. 1955. *Address:* Langford Court, near Bristol, Avon. *T:* Wrington 862338. *Club:* Cavalry and Guards.

WILLS, Joseph Lyttleton; Hon. Mr Justice Wills, CBE 1965; FSA; Judge, Supreme Court, Windward Islands and Leeward Islands, WI, since 1955; *b* 24 June 1899; *m* 1940, Dorothy Cather; one *d. Educ:* Middle School, Georgetown, British Guiana; Queen's Coll., British Guiana; King's Coll., London. Barrister-at-law, Inner Temple, 1928; admitted to practice as Barrister-at-Law, British Guiana, 1930; Magistrate, 1947; Additional Puisne Judge of Supreme Court of British Guiana, 1953-55. Councillor of Georgetown, 1933; Deputy Mayor, 1942-43; Hon. Member of Legislative Council, British Guiana, 1933; President, British Guiana Labour Union and British Guiana Workers League; Chairman and Member of several public committees; Member Judicial Service Commn, British Guiana, 1963; Chairman, Income Tax (Appeal) Board of Review, Guyana, 1966. Chairman of British Guiana Congregational Union, 1949-53 and 1974-75. Jubilee Medal, 1935; Coronation Medal, 1953. *Recreations:* horse-riding, motoring and cricket. *Address:* Lyttleton House, 57 Chalmers Place, Stabroek, Georgetown, Guyana. *Clubs:* Royal Commonwealth Society (West Indian); Guyana Cricket, Maltenoes Sports (Guyana); Castries (WI).

WILLS, Nicholas Kenneth Spencer, FCA; Managing Director: British Electric Traction Co. plc, since 1982; Birmingham & District Investment Trust plc, since 1970; Electrical & Industrial Investment plc, since 1970; National Electric Construction plc, since 1971; Chairman: Argus Press Holdings plc, since 1974; Boulton & Paul plc, since 1979; Electrical Press plc, since 1974; Initial plc, since 1979; *b* 18 May 1941; *s* of Sir John Spencer Wills, *qv* ; *m* 1973, Hilary Ann, *d* of N. C. Flood; two *s* two *d. Educ:* Rugby Sch.; Queens' Coll., Cambridge (MA). Binder Hamlyn & Co., 1963-67; Morgan Grenfell, 1967-70; Director: British Electric Traction Co. plc, 1975-; Bradbury, Agnew & Co. Ltd, 1974-; Globe Investment Trust plc, 1977-; National Mutual Life Assce Soc., 1974-; Drayton Consolidated, 1982-; St George Assce Co. Ltd, 1974-81; Colonial Securities Trust Co. Ltd, 1976-82; Cable Trust Ltd, 1976-77; Reg. Dir, City and Westminster, Nat. Westminster Bank, 1982-. Treasurer and Churchwarden, Church of St Bride, Fleet Street, 1978-; Asst, Worshipful Co. of Haberdashers', 1981-. *Recreations:* shooting, sailing, trying to farm in the Highlands. *Address:* Stratton House, Stratton Street, Piccadilly, W1X 6AS. *T:* 01-629 8886. *Clubs:* White's, Royal Automobile; Clyde Cruising.

WILLS, Peter Gordon Bethune, TD 1967; Partner, Sheppards and Chase, Stockbrokers, since 1960; *b* 25 Oct. 1931; *s* of P. L. B. Wills and E. W. Wills (*née* Stapleton). *Educ:* Malvern Coll.; Corpus Christi Coll., Cambridge, 1952-55 (MA). National Service with Royal Inniskilling Fusiliers, N Ireland and Korea, 1950-52; TA, London Irish Rifles, 1952-67. Joined Sheppards & Co. (later Sheppards and Chase), 1955. Member, Stock Exchange Council, 1973- (Dep. Chm., 1979-82). Director, George Wills and Sons (Holdings) Ltd, 1969, Vice-Chm., 1977. *Recreation:* collecting stamps. *Address:* 5/98 Elm Park Gardens, SW10 9PE. *T:* 01-352 5408.

WILLSON, Douglas James, CBE 1953; TD; *b* 30 Oct. 1906; *s* of late Ernest Victor Willson and late Mary Willson; *m* 1942, Morna Josephine, *d* of Stanley Hine; one *d. Educ:* Bishop's Stortford Coll., Herts. Admitted Solicitor, 1928; joined Customs and Excise, 1928. Served War, 1939-45, Lieut-Colonel, R.A. Solicitor for Bd of Customs and Excise, 1963-71. *Publications:* Titles Purchase Tax and Excise in Halsbury's Encyclopædia of Laws of England, 3rd edn; Willson & Mainprice on Value Added Tax. *Recreations:* gardening and bird watching. *Address:* Dove Cottage, West Farleigh, Kent. *T:* Maidstone 812203.

WILLSON, Prof. (Francis Michael) Glenn; Vice-Chancellor, Murdoch University, Western Australia, since 1978; *b* 29 Sept. 1924; *s* of late Christopher Glenn Willson and late Elsie Katrine (*née* Mattick); *m* 1949, Jean (*née* Carlyle); two *d. Educ:* Carlisle Grammar Sch.; Manchester Univ. (BA Admin); Balliol and Nuffield Colls, Oxford (DPhil, MA). Merchant Navy, 1941-42; RAF, 1943-46; BOAC 1946-47. Research Officer, Royal Inst. of Public Admin, 1953-60; Res. Fellow, Nuffield Coll., Oxford, 1955-60; Lectr in Politics, St Edmund Hall, Oxford, 1958-60; Prof. of Govt, UC Rhodesia and Nyasaland, 1960-64; Dean, Faculty of Social Studies, UC Rhodesia and Nyasaland, 1962-64; Univ. of California, Santa Cruz: Prof. of Govt/Politics, 1965-74; Provost of Stevenson Coll., 1967-74; Vice-Chancellor, College and Student Affairs, 1973-74; Warden, Goldsmiths' Coll., London, 1974-75; Principal of Univ. of London, 1975-78. *Publications:* (with D.N. Chester) The Organization of British Central Government 1914-56, 2nd edn 1914-64, 1968; Administrators in Action, 1961; contrib. Public Admin, Polit. Studies, Parly Affairs, etc. *Address:* 2 Park Road, Mount Pleasant, Western Australia 6153.

WILLSON, John Michael; HM Diplomatic Service; Counsellor, Bucharest, since 1980; *b* 15 July 1931; *e s* of late Richard and of Kathleen Willson; *m* 1954, Phyllis Marian Dawn, *o c* of late William and Phyllis Holman Richards, OBE; two *s* two *d. Educ:* Wimbledon Coll.; University Coll., Oxford (MA); Trinity Hall, Cambridge. National Service, 1949-51. HM Colonial Service, N Rhodesia, 1955-64; Min. of Overseas Development, 1965-70 (seconded to British High Commn, Malta, 1967-70); joined HM Diplomatic Service, 1970; British Consulate-General, Johannesburg, 1972-75; FCO (W Indian and N American Depts), 1975-78; Special Counsellor for African Affairs, 1978; Secretary-General, Rhodesian Independence Conf., 1979; Salisbury (on staff of Governor of Rhodesia), 1979-80. *Recreations:* gardening, photography, music. *Address:* c/o C. Hoare & Co., 37 Fleet Street, EC4P 4DQ. *Club:* Royal Commonwealth Society.

WILMERS, John Geoffrey, QC 1965; a Recorder of the Crown Court, since 1972; a Judge of the Court of Appeal of Jersey and Guernsey, since 1978; *b* 27 Dec. 1920; *m* 1946, June I. K. Mecredy; one *s* two *d. Educ:* Leighton Park Sch., Reading; St John's Coll., Cambridge. Called to the Bar, Inner Temple, 1948, Bencher, 1972. Dep. Chm., Hants QS, 1970-71. *Recreations:* travel, skiing, walking, gardening. *Address:* 1 Harcourt Buildings, Temple, EC4Y 9DA. *T:* 01-353 2214.

WILMINGTON, Joseph (Robert); JP; Chairman and Managing Director, Wilmington Employment Agencies Ltd, since 1966; *b* 21 April 1932; *s* of Joseph R. Wilmington and Magtilda Susanna Wilmington. *Educ:* Alsop High Sch., Liverpool; London Sch. of Economics. Mem., Liverpool City Council, 1962; Past Chm., Liverpool Liberal Party, 1965-67; Chairman: Personnel Cttee, Liverpool City Council; Markets Cttee, Liverpool City Council; Chief Whip; Lord Mayor of Liverpool, 1974-75. Chm., NW Fedn of Employment Consultants; Mem. Nat. Exec., Fedn of Employment Consultants; Mem. Inst. Employment Consultants. JP Liverpool, 1976. *Recreations:* football, music and the arts. *Address:* Jordaan, South Drive, Sandfield Park, Liverpool L12 1LH.

WILMOT, Air Vice-Marshal Aubrey S.; *see* Sidney-Wilmot.

WILMOT, Sir Henry Robert, 9th Bt *cr* 1759; *b* 10 April 1967; *s* of Sir Robert Arthur Wilmot, 8th Bt, and of Juliet Elvira, *e d* of Captain M. N. Tufnell, RN; *S* father, 1974. *Heir: b* Charles Sacheverel Wilmot, *b* 13 Feb. 1969. *Address:* Pitters Farmhouse, Sandy Lane, Chippenham, Wilts.

WILMOT, Sir John Assheton E.; *see* Eardley-Wilmot.

WILMOT, Robert William; Managing Director, International Computers Ltd, since 1981; *b* 2 Jan. 1945; *s* of Thomas Arthur William Wilmot and Frances Mary Hull; *m* 1969, Mary Josephine Sharkey; two *s. Educ:* Royal Grammar Sch., Worcester; Nottingham Univ. BSc (Hons) Electrical Engrg. Texas Instruments: Micro-electronics Design Engr, Bedford, 1966; Dept Manager, Advanced Technol. Products, Bedford, 1970; Tech. Dir, European Calculator Div., Nice, 1974; Manager, Professional Calculator Div., Dallas, 1975; Man. Dir, Bedford, 1978-81. *Recreations:* music, theatre, walking. *Address:* ICL House, Putney, SW15 1SW. *T:* 01-788 7272.

WILMSHURST, Michael Joseph; HM Diplomatic Service; UK Permanent Representative to International Atomic Energy Agency and to UN Organizations, Vienna, since 1982, with personal rank of Ambassador; *b* 14 Sept. 1934; *s* of Mr and Mrs E. J. Wilmshurst; *m* 1958, Mary Elizabeth Kemp; one *s* one *d. Educ:* Latymer Upper Sch.; Christ's Coll., Cambridge. BA 1959. Entered Foreign Service, 1953. 2nd Lieut, Royal Signals, 1953-55. Asst Private Sec. to Foreign Secretary, 1960-62; 2nd Sec., The Hague, 1962-65; 1st Sec. (Commercial), Bogota, 1965-67; Western European Dept, FCO, 1968-70; 1st Sec. (Commercial), Cairo, 1970-73; Asst Head of Energy Dept, FCO, 1974-75; Asst Head of Energy and Arms Control and Disarmament Depts, 1975-77; Counsellor and Head of Joint Nuclear Unit, FCO, 1977-78; Consul, Guatemala City, 1978-81; Sabbatical, Stiftung Wissenschaft und Politik, Ebenhausen. *Recreation:* reading. *Address:* c/o Foreign and Commonwealth Office, SW1. *Club:* Travellers'.

WILSEY, Maj.-Gen. Anthony Patrick W.; *see* Willasey-Wilsey.

WILSON; *see* McNair-Wilson.

WILSON, family name of **Barons Moran, Nunburnholme, Wilson, Wilson of Langside** and **Wilson of Radcliffe.**

WILSON, 2nd Baron, *cr* 1946, of Libya and of Stowlangtoft; **Patrick Maitland Wilson;** *b* 14 Sept. 1915; *s* of Field-Marshal 1st Baron Wilson, GCB, GBE, DSO, and Hester Mary (*d* 1979), *d* of Philip James Digby Wykeham, Tythrop House, Oxon; *S* father 1964; *m* 1943, Violet Storeen, *d* of late Major James Hamilton Douglas Campbell, OBE. *Educ:* Eton; King's College, Cambridge. Served War of 1939-45 (despatches). *Heir:* none. *Address:* c/o Barclays Bank Ltd, Cambridge.

WILSON OF LANGSIDE, Baron *cr* 1969 (Life Peer); **Henry Stephen Wilson,** PC 1967; QC (Scot.) 1965; *b* 21 March 1916; *s* of James Wilson, Solicitor, Glasgow, and Margaret Wilson (*née* Young); *m* 1942, Jessie Forrester Waters; no *c. Educ:* High School, Glasgow; Univ. of Glasgow (MA, LLB). Joined Army, 1939; Commd 1940; Regl Officer, HLI and RAC, 1940-46. Called to Scottish Bar, 1946; Advocate-Depute, 1948-51. Sheriff-Substitute: Greenock, 1955-56; Glasgow, 1956-65; Solicitor-General for Scotland, 1965-67; Lord Advocate, 1967-70; Dir, Scottish Courts Administration, 1971-74; Sheriff Principal of Glasgow and Strathkelvin, 1975-77. Contested (Lab) Dumfriesshire, 1950, 1955, W Edinburgh, 1951; Mem. SDP, 1981-. *Recreations:* hill walking, gardening. *Address:* Dunallan, Kippen, Stirlingshire. *T:* Kippen 210. *Club:* Western (Glasgow).

WILSON OF RADCLIFFE, Baron *cr* 1974 (Life Peer), of Radcliffe, Lancs; **Alfred Wilson;** *b* 10 June 1909; *s* of late William Barnes Wilson and Jane; *m* 1st, 1932, Elsie Hulton (*d* 1974); one *d* (one *s* decd); 2nd, 1976, Freda Mather. *Educ:* Technical Sch., Newcastle upon Tyne. CWS Ltd: Dep. Sec. and Exec. Officer, 1953; Sec., 1965; Chief Exec. Officer, 1969-74. FCIS.

Recreations: photography, walking, gardening. *Address:* 58 Ringley Road, Whitefield, Manchester.

WILSON, Rear-Adm. Alan Christopher Wyndham, CB 1972; retired, 1975; Senior Naval Member, Directing Staff, Royal College of Defence Studies, 1972-Jan. 1975; *b* 7 Sept. 1919; *s* of Alan Christopher Hill-Wilson and Nancy Green; *m* 1958, Joan Rhoda Landale, Deniliquin, Australia; one step *d. Educ:* St Bee's, Cumberland. Served at sea during War of 1939-45; Malta Dockyard, 1946-49; HMS Diamond, 1949-52; Admty, 1952-55; Australia, 1956-58; HMS Ark Royal, 1959-61; Admty, 1962-64; with Flag Officer, Aircraft Carriers, 1964-66; with Comdr, Far East Fleet, 1966-69; idc 1969; Hd of British Defence Liaison Staff, Canberra, 1970-72. *Recreations:* golf, fishing. *Address:* Church Farm House, Wellow, near Bath. *T:* Combe Down 832051. *Clubs:* Army and Navy, Royal Automobile.

WILSON, Prof. Alan Geoffrey; Professor of Urban and Regional Geography, University of Leeds, since 1970; *b* 8 Jan. 1939; *s* of Harry Wilson and Gladys (*née* Naylor); *m* 1965, Christine Diane Snow (marr. diss. 1978). *Educ:* Corpus Christi Coll., Cambridge (MA). Scientific Officer, Rutherford High Energy Lab., 1961-64; Res. Officer, Inst. of Econs and Statistics, Univ. of Oxford, 1964-66; Math. Adviser, MoT, 1966-68; Asst Dir, Centre for Environmental Studies, London, 1968-70. Mem., Kirklees AHA, 1979-82; Vice-Chm., Dewsbury HA, 1982-. Gill Meml Award, RGS, 1978. *Publications:* Entropy in Urban and Regional Modelling, 1970; Papers in Urban and Regional Analysis, 1972; Urban and Regional Models in Geography and Planning, 1974; (with M. J. Kirkby) Mathematics for Geographers and Planners, 1975, 2nd edn 1980; (with P. H. Rees) Spatial Population Analysis, 1977; (ed with P. H. Rees and C. M. Leigh) Models of Cities and Regions, 1977; Catastrophe Theory and Bifurcation: applications to urban and regional systems, 1981; (jtly) Optimization in Locational and Transport Analysis, 1981; Geography and the Environment: Systems Analytical Methods, 1981. *Recreations:* writing, dog walking, miscellaneous fads. *Address:* School of Geography, University of Leeds, Leeds LS2 9JT. *T:* Leeds 431751 ext 7176.

WILSON, Sir Alan (Herries), Kt 1961; FRS 1942; Part-time Member and Deputy Chairman, Electricity Council, 1966-76; *b* 2 July 1906; *o s* of H. and A. Wilson; *m* 1934, Margaret Constance Monks (*d* 1961); two *s. Educ:* Wallasey Gram. Sch.; Emmanuel College, Cambridge. Smith's Prize, 1928; Adams Prize, 1931-32; Fellow of Emmanuel College, Cambridge, 1929-33; Fellow and Lecturer of Trinity College, Cambridge, 1933-45; University Lecturer in Mathematics in the University of Cambridge, 1933-45; joined Courtaulds Ltd, 1945; Man. Dir, 1954; Dep. Chm., 1957-62. Dir, Internat. Computers (Hldgs) Ltd, 1962-72; Chm., Glaxo Group Ltd, 1963-73. Chairman: Committee on Coal Derivatives, 1959-60; Committee on Noise, 1960-63; Nuclear Safety Adv. Committee, 1965-66; Central Adv. Water Cttee, 1969-74; Member: Iron and Steel Board, 1960-67; UGC, 1964-66; President: Inst. of Physics and Physical Soc., 1963-64; Nat. Society for Clean Air, 1965-66; Aslib, 1971-73. Chm. Governing Body, Nat. Inst. of Agricultural Engrg, 1971-76; Chm., Bd of Governors, Bethlem Royal and Maudsley Hosps., 1973-80. Prime Warden, Goldsmiths Co., 1969-70. Hon. Fellow: Emmanuel College, Cambridge; St Catherine's College, Oxford; UMIST. Hon. FIChemE; Hon. FInstP; Hon. FIMA. Hon. DSc: Oxford; Edinburgh. *Publications:* The Theory of Metals, 1936, 2nd edition 1953; Semi-conductors and Metals, 1939; Thermo-dynamics and Statistical Mechanics, 1957; many papers on atomic physics. *Address:* 65 Oakleigh Park South, Whetstone, N20 9JL. *T:* 01-445 3030. *Club:* Athenæum.

WILSON, Alan Martin, QC 1982; a Recorder of the Crown Court, since 1979; *b* 12 Feb. 1940; *s* of Joseph Norris Wilson and late Kate Wilson; *m* 1st, 1966, Pauline Frances Kibart (marr. diss. 1975); two *d* ; 2nd, 1976, Julia Mary Carter; one *d. Educ:* Kilburn Grammar Sch.; Nottingham Univ. (LLB Hons). Called to the Bar, Gray's Inn, 1963; Dep. Circuit Judge, 1978. *Recreations:* rough shooting, boating, poetry. *Address:* The Old Off-Licence, Peopleton, near Pershore, Worcs WR10 2EE. *T:* Worcester 840511. *Clubs:* Union and County (Worcester); Bar Yacht.

WILSON, Alexander, FLA; Director General, British Library Reference Division, since 1980; *b* 12 Feb. 1921; *s* of late William Wilson and Amelia Wilson; *m* 1949, Mary Catherin Traynor; two *s. Educ:* Bolton County Grammar Sch. FLA 1950. Served War, RAF, 1941-46. Librarian at Bolton, Harrogate, Taunton, and Swindon, 1946-52; Dir of Library and Cultural Services, Dudley and later Coventry, 1952-72; Dir, Cheshire Libraries and Museums Service, 1972-79. Member: Library Adv. Council (England), 1971-74; British Library Bd, 1974-. *Publications:* contrib. books and periodicals on libraries and other cultural services. *Recreations:* walking, listening to music, lecturing and writing on professional subjects. *Address:* 1 Brockway West, Tattenhall, near Chester.

WILSON, Lt-Gen. Sir (Alexander) James, KBE 1974 (CBE 1966; MBE 1948); MC 1945; Chairman, Tobacco Advisory Council, since 1977; *b* 13 April 1921; *s* of Maj.-Gen. Bevil Thomson Wilson, CB, DSO, and of Florence Erica, *d* of Sir John Starkey, 1st Bt; *m* 1958, Hon. Jean Margaret Paul, 2nd *d* of 2nd Baron Rankeillour; two *s. Educ:* Winchester Coll.; New Coll., Oxford (BA, Law). Served War of 1939-45, North Africa and Italy, Rifle Bde (despatches); Adjt, IMA Dehra Dun, 1945-47; PS to C-in-C Pakistan, 1948-49; Co. Comdr, 1st Bn Rifle Bde, BAOR 1949 and 1951-52, Kenya 1954-55 (despatches); psc 1950; Bde Major 11th Armd Div., BAOR, 1952-54;

Instr, Staff Coll. Camberley, 1955-58; 2nd in comd 3rd Green Jackets, BAOR, 1959-60; GSO1 Sandhurst, 1960-62; CO 1st Bn XX Lancs Fus, 1962-64; Chief of Staff, UN Force in Cyprus, 1964-66 (Actg Force Comdr, 1965-66); Comdr, 147 Inf. Bde TA, 1966-67; Dir of Army Recruiting, MoD, 1967-70; GOC NW District, 1970-72; Vice Adjutant General, MoD, 1972-74; GOC SE District, 1974-77. Dep. Col (Lancashire), RRF, 1973-77, Col, 1977-82; Hon. Col, Oxford Univ. OTC, 1978-82. Col Commandant: Queen's Division, 1974-77; RAEC, 1975-79; Royal Green Jackets, 1977-81. Chm., Council, RUSI, 1973-75. Member: Sports Council, 1973-82; Council, CBI, 1977-; Pres., Army Cricket Assoc., 1973-76; Vice-Pres., Army Football Assoc., 1973-76, Chm., 1976-77, Pres., 1977-82; Hon. Vice-Pres., FA, 1976-82. Vice-Chm., NABC, 1977-; Chm., Crown and Manor Club, Hoxton, 1977-. Association Football Correspondent, Sunday Times, 1957-. *Publications:* articles and book reviews on mil. subjects and peacekeeping. *Recreations:* cricket, Association football. *Address:* Tobacco Advisory Council, Glen House, Stag Place, SW1; Flat 4, 33 Wilton Place, SW1; Goldhill Farm House, Edingley, near Newark, Notts. *T:* Southwell 813308. *Clubs:* Travellers', MCC; Notts CC.

WILSON, Alfred Harold, CB 1949; CBE 1946; *b* 9 March 1895; *er s* of late Alfred Henry Wilson; *m* 1925, Edythe Rose, *d* of late Philip Richard Snewin; no *c. Educ:* Tottenham Grammar School. Associate of Assoc. of Certified Accountants, 1922, FCCA 1980. Board of Trade, Central Office for Labour Exchanges, 1913; GPO, Accountant-General's Department, 1914. Served European War, Royal Marine Artillery, 1916-19. Assistant Surveyor, General Post Office, 1923; Principal, Air Ministry, Dept of Civil Aviation, 1937; Assistant Secretary, Air Ministry, i/c Organisation and Methods Division, 1941; Assistant Secretary (with title Director of Home Civil Aviation) Air Ministry, Dept of Civil Aviation, 1943; transferred to new Ministry of Civil Aviation on its formation and promoted Principal Asst Secretary, 1945; Under Secretary, Ministry of Civil Aviation, 1946; during this period was Chairman London Airport lay-out Panel, which was responsible for runway layout design of the Airport; Deputy Secretary, Ministry of Transport and Civil Aviation, 1956-58; Adviser on Commercial Air Transport to the Ministry of Transport and Civil Aviation, 1958-60; Member of the Air Transport Licensing Board, 1960-65. *Address:* c/o Barclays Bank, High Street, Guildford, Surrey.

WILSON, Rev. Canon Andrew; Canon Residentiary of Newcastle, and Director of Ordinands and Post-Ordination Studies, since 1964; Examining Chaplain to the Bishop of Newcastle, since 1969; *b* 27 April 1920; *o s* of late Stewart and Isobel Wilson. *Educ:* Salt's High School, Shipley; Univ. of Durham. Scholar of St Chad's Coll., Durham, 1939; BA Hons Mod. Hist., 1941; Lightfoot Scholar, 1941; Dip. Theol. (Dist.), 1943; MA 1944; Deacon, 1943; Priest, 1944. Asst Curate: of St Cuthbert's, Newcastle, 1943-45; of St John's, Wallsend, 1945-48; Priest-in-charge of Backworth, 1948-55; Vicar of Horton, 1955-58; Rector of St John's, Ballachulish, 1958-64. *Address:* 1 Mitchell Avenue, Jesmond, Newcastle upon Tyne NE2 3JY. *T:* Newcastle 812075.

WILSON, Andrew James; see Wilson, Snoo.

WILSON, Andrew N., FRSL; author; Literary Editor, The Spectator, since 1981; *b* 27 Oct. 1950; *s* of Lt-Col N. Wilson and Jean Dorothy (*née* Crowder); *m* 1971, Katherine, *d* of late Prof. Austin Duncan-Jones; two *d. Educ:* Rugby; New College, Oxford (MA). Chancellor's Essay Prize, 1971, and Ellerton Theological Prize, 1975. Asst Master, Merchant Taylors' Sch., 1974-76; Lecturer: New Coll., Oxford, 1976-80; St Hugh's Coll., Oxford, 1976-82. FRSL 1981. *Publications:* novels: The Sweets of Pimlico, 1977, 2nd edn 1982 (John Llewellyn Rhys Memorial Prize, 1978); Unguarded Hours, 1978; Kindly Light, 1979; The Healing Art, 1980 (Somerset Maugham Award, 1981; Arts Council National Book Award, 1981; Southern Arts Prize, 1981); Who was Oswald Fish?, 1981; Wise Virgin, 1982; *non fiction:* The Laird of Abbotsford, 1980 (John Llewellyn Rhys Memorial Prize, 1981); A Life of John Milton, 1983. *Recreations:* reading, chat. *Address:* 16 Richmond Road, Oxford. *T:* Oxford 511024. *Club:* Travellers'.

WILSON, Andrew Thomas, CMG 1982; Head, British Development Division in Southern Africa, since 1979; *b* 21 June 1926; *s* of John Wilson, farmer, and Gertrude (*née* Lucas); *m* 1954, Hilda Mary (*née* Williams); two *d. Educ:* Cowley Sch.; Leeds Univ. (BSc); St John's Coll., Cambridge (DipAg); Imperial College of Tropical Agriculture (DTA). Colonial Service/HMOCS, Northern Rhodesia/Zambia, 1949-66: Agricultural Officer, 1949; Chief Agricl Officer, 1959; Chief Agricl Research Officer, 1961; Dep. Director of Agriculture, 1963; ODM/ODA: Agricl Adviser, British Development Div. in the Caribbean, 1967; FCO: Agricl Adviser, Nairobi and Kampala, 1969; ODM/ODA: Agricl Adviser, E Africa Development Div., 1974; Agricl Adviser, Middle East Development Div., 1976. *Recreations:* sport, gardening. *Address:* c/o Foreign and Commonwealth Office, SW1; Bird in Hand, Hardingham, Norfolk. *T:* Hingham 517. *Clubs:* Farmers', Royal Commonwealth Society; Nairobi (Kenya).

WILSON, Sir Angus (Frank Johnstone), Kt 1980; CBE 1968; CLit 1972; FRSL 1958; author; Professor of English Literature, University of East Anglia, 1966-78, now Emeritus; *b* 11 Aug. 1913; *s* of William Johnstone-Wilson, Dumfriesshire, and of Maude (*née* Caney), Durban, Natal, South Africa. *Educ:* Westminster School; Merton College, Oxford. Foreign Office,

1942-46. Deputy to Superintendent of Reading Room, British Museum, 1949-55. Began to write in 1946. Lectr, Internat. Assoc. of Professors of English, Lausanne, 1959; Ewing Lectr, Los Angeles, 1960; Bergen Lectr, Yale Univ., 1960; Wm Vaughan Moody Lectr, Chicago, 1960; Northcliffe Lectrs, Lond., 1961; Leslie Stephen Lectr, Cambridge, 1962-63; Lectr, Sch. of Eng. Studies, E Anglia Univ., 1963-66; Beckman Prof., Univ. of California, Berkeley, 1967; John Hinkley Vis. Prof., Johns Hopkins Univ., Baltimore, 1974; Visiting Professor: Univ. of Delaware, 1977, 1980,1983; Univ. of Iowa, 1978; Georgia State Univ., 1979; Univ. of Michigan, 1979; Univ. of Minnesota, 1980; Univ. of Missouri, 1982; Andrew Mellon Vis. Prof., Univ. of Pittsburgh, 1981. Mem. Cttee, Royal Literary Fund, 1966. Mem. Arts Council, 1967-69; Chm., NBL, 1971-74. President: Powys Soc., 1970-80; Dickens Fellowship, 1974-75; Kipling Soc., 1981-. Foreign Hon. Mem., Amer. Acad. and Inst. of Arts and Letters, 1980. Hon. DLitt: Leicester, 1977; East Anglia, 1979; Sussex, 1981; Hon. LittD Liverpool, 1979. Chevalier de l'Ordre des Arts et des Lettres, 1972. *Publications:* (short stories, novels, etc); The Wrong Set, 1949; Such Darling Dodos, 1950; Emile Zola, 1950; Hemlock and After (novel), 1952; For Whom The Cloche Tolls, 1953, 2nd edn, 1973; The Mulberry Bush (play) (prod Bristol, 1955, Royal Court Theatre, London, 1956); Anglo-Saxon Attitudes (novel), 1956; A Bit off the Map, 1957; The Middle Age of Mrs Eliot (novel), 1958 (James Tait Black Meml Prize; Prix du Meilleur Roman Etranger, Paris); The Old Men at the Zoo (novel), 1961; The Wild Garden, 1963; Late Call (novel), 1964 (adapted for TV, 1975); No Laughing Matter (novel), 1967; The World of Charles Dickens, 1970 (Yorkshire Post Book of the Year, 1970); (with Edwin Smith and Olive Cook) England, 1971; As If By Magic (novel), 1973; The Naughty Nineties, 1976; The Strange Ride of Rudyard Kipling, 1977; Setting the World on Fire (novel), 1980; (with Tony Garrett) East Anglia in Verse, 1982. TV plays: After the Show (perf. 1959); The Stranger (perf. 1960); The Invasion (perf. 1963). *Recreations:* gardening, travel. *Address:* Felsham Woodside, Bradfield St George, Bury St Edmunds, Suffolk. *T:* Rattlesden 200. *Club:* Athenæum.

WILSON, Sir (Archibald) Duncan, GCMG 1971 (KCMG 1965; CMG 1955); HM Diplomatic Service, retired; Master of Corpus Christi College, Cambridge, 1971-80, Hon. Fellow, 1980; *b* 12 August 1911; *s* of late Archibald Edward Wilson and late Ethel Mary (*née* Schuster); *m* 1937, Elizabeth Anne Martin Fleming; two *d* (one *s* decd). *Educ:* Winchester; Balliol College, Oxford 1st Class Hon. Mods, Lit. Hum., Oxford; Craven schol., Oxford Univ., Jenkyns Exhibitioner, Balliol Coll.; Laming Fellow, Queen's Coll. Taught at Westminster School, 1936-37; Asst Keeper, British Museum, 1937-39; Min. of Economic Warfare, 1939-41; empl. FO, 1941-45; CCG, 1945-46; entered Foreign Service, 1947; served Berlin, 1947-49; Yugoslavia, 1951-53; Director of Research and Acting Librarian, 1955-57; Chargé d'Affaires, Peking, 1957-59; Assistant Under-Secretary, Foreign Office, 1960-64; Ambassador to: Yugoslavia, 1964-68; the USSR, 1968-71. Fellow, Center of International Affairs, Harvard Univ. (on Secondment, 1959-60). Hon. Vice-Pres., UK Council for Overseas Student Affairs. Mem., Standing Commn on Museums and Galls, 1973-78. Chm., Cttee of Enquiry into Public Records, 1978-80. Mem. Bd of Governors, King's Sch., Canterbury, 1972-80. *Publications:* Life and Times of Vuk Stefanović Karadzić, 1970; Leonard Woolf, a political biography, 1978; Tito's Yugoslavia, 1979. *Recreations:* music, golf, walking. *Address:* Cala Na Ruadh, Port Charlotte, Islay, Argyll. *Club:* Royal Commonwealth Society.

See also Mrs H. M. Warnock.

WILSON, Maj.-Gen. Arthur Gillespie, CBE 1955; DSO 1946; *b* 29 Sept. 1900; *s* of late Charles Wilson, originally of Glasgow, Scotland; *m* 1st, 1927, Edna D. L. Gibson (*d* 1940); no *c*; 2nd, 1953, Shirley H. Cruickshank, *d* of late Colin Campbell, Queenscliff, Victoria, Australia; no *c. Educ:* North Sydney Boys' High School, NSW, Australia; Royal Military College, Duntroon, Australia. Commissioned Aust. Staff Corps, 1921; served India with various Brit. and IA Artillery Units, 1924; commanded Roy. Aust. Artillery, Thursday Island, 1926-28; Staff College, Quetta, 1935-36; GSO3, AHQ 1938; continued to serve in various appts at AHQ until joined AIF 1940; GSO1 HQ AIF UK and then Assistant Mil. Liaison Officer, Australian High Commissioner's Office, UK, until 1943, when returned to Australia; served with AIF New Guinea Philippines and Borneo, 1943-45; DDSD(o) Land Headquarters, 1944-45; commanded British Commonwealth Base BCOF Japan, 1946-47; served various appts AHQ and HQ Eastern Command, 1947-52; Aust. Army Rep., UK, 1953-54; GOC, Central Command, Australia, 1954-57; retired 1957. *Address:* Leahurst Cottage, Crafers, South Australia 5152, Australia. *Club:* Naval, Military and Air Force (Adelaide).

WILSON, Prof. Arthur James Cochran, FRS 1963; Professor of Crystallography, Department of Physics, Birmingham University, 1965-82; *b* 28 November 1914; *o s* of Arthur A. C. and Hildegarde Gretchen (*née* Geldert) Wilson, Springhill, Nova Scotia, Canada; *m* 1946, Harriett Charlotte, BSc, PhD, Sociologist (*née* Friedeberg); two *s* one *d. Educ:* King's Collegiate School, Windsor, Nova Scotia, Canada; Dalhousie University, Halifax, Canada (MSc); Massachusetts Institute of Technology (PhD); Cambridge University (PhD). 1851 Exhibition Scholar, 1937-40. Res. Asst, Cavendish Lab., Cambridge, 1940-45; Lecturer, 1945, and Senior Lecturer, 1946, in Physics, University College, Cardiff; Professor of Physics, University College, Cardiff, 1954-65. Visiting Professor: Georgia Inst. of Technology, 1965, 1968, 1971; Univ. of Tokyo, 1972. Editor of Structure Reports, 1948-59; Editor of Acta Crystallographica, 1960-77; Assoc. Editor, Proc. Royal Society, 1978-; Editor of International Tables for Crystallography,

1982-. Member: Exec. Cttee, Internat. Union of Crystallography, 1954-60 and 1978-81 (Vice-Pres., 1978-81); ICSU Abstracting Bd, 1971-77, 1980- (Vice-Pres.). *Publications:* X-ray Optics, 1949 (Russian edn 1951, 2nd edn 1962); Mathematical Theory of X-ray Powder Diffractometry, 1963 (French edn 1964, German edn 1965); Elements of X-ray Crystallography, 1970; (with L. V. Azároff and others) X-ray Diffraction, 1974; (ed jtly) Crystallographic Statistics: Progress and Problems, 1982; numerous papers in Proc. Phys. Soc., Proc. Roy. Soc., Acta Cryst., etc. *Address:* The University of Birmingham, Birmingham B15 2TT. *Clubs:* Sierra (San Francisco); Swiss Alpine.

WILSON, Sir Austin (George), Kt 1981; OBE 1958; Chairman, Auckland Gas Co. Ltd, since 1963 (Director, since 1959); Director, NZ Insurance Co. Ltd, since 1961; *b* 6 Nov. 1906; *s* of George Wilson and Lydia Mary Wilson; *m* 1936, Ailsa Blanche (*née* Percy); one *s. Educ:* Auckland Grammar Sch. FCIS; FNZSocA; FInstD. Director, NZ Forest Products Co., 1959-79 (Chm., 1968-73 and 1977-79); Chm., NZ Insurance Co. Ltd, 1967-71; Chairman of Directors: Nissan Datsun Holdings Ltd, 1973-; Plessey (NZ) Ltd, 1970-; NZI Finance Corporation Ltd, 1972-. Member: Auckland Harbour Board, 1947-56 (Chm., 1953-55); Life Member: Auckland Chamber of Commerce, 1963; NZ Bureau of Importers, 1978; Gas Assoc. of New Zealand, 1978. *Recreation:* lawn bowls. *Address:* 3/19 Victoria Avenue, Remuera, Auckland 5, New Zealand. *T:* 549743. *Clubs:* Auckland, Northern, Rotary of Auckland (Auckland).

WILSON, Austin Peter; Assistant Under Secretary of State, since 1981; Head of Home Office Community Programmes and Equal Opportunities Department, since 1982; *b* 31 March 1938; *s* of Joseph and Irene Wilson; *m* 1962, Norma Louise, *y d* of D. R. Mill; one *s* two *d. Educ:* Leeds Grammar Sch.; St Edmund Hall, Oxford (BA). Entered Home Office, 1961; Private Secretary to Minister of State, 1964-66; Principal, 1966; Secretary, Deptl Cttee on Death Certification and Coroners (Brodrick Cttee), 1968-71; Asst Sec., 1974, Prison Dept; seconded to N Ireland Office, 1977-80; Asst Under Secretary of State, Criminal Justice Dept, 1981. *Recreations:* theatre, walking, exploring France. *Address:* Home Office, Queen Anne's Gate, SW1. *T:* 01-213 3000.

WILSON, Lt-Col Blair Aubyn S.; *see* Stewart-Wilson.

WILSON, Prof. Brian Graham; Vice-Chancellor, University of Queensland, since 1979; *b* 9 April 1930; *s* of Charles Wesley Wilson and Isobel Christie (*née* Ferguson); *m* 1st, 1959, Barbara Elizabeth Wilkie; two *s* one *d*; 2nd, 1978, Margaret Jeanne Henry. *Educ:* Queen's Univ., Belfast (BSc Hons); National Univ. of Ireland (PhD Cosmic Radiation). Post-doctoral Fellow, National Research Council, Canada, 1955-57; Officer in Charge, Sulphur Mt Lab., Banff, 1957-60, Associate Res. Officer, 1959-60; Associate Prof. of Physics, Univ. of Calgary, 1960-65, Prof., 1965-70, Dean of Arts and Science, 1967-70; Prof. of Astronomy and Academic Vice-Pres., Simon Fraser Univ., 1970-78. *Publications:* numerous, on astrophysics, in learned jls. *Recreations:* fishing, swimming. *Address:* 55 Walcott Street, St Lucia, Queensland 4067, Australia. *T:* (07)370 8757.

WILSON, Brian Harvey, CBE 1972 (MBE 1944); solicitor; Chairman, Metropolitan Housing Trust, since 1978; *b* 4 Sept. 1915; *o s* of Sydney John Wilson, MC, and Bessie Mildred (*née* Scott); *m* 1941, Constance Jane (*née* Gee); one *s. Educ:* Manchester Grammar Sch.; (Exhibitioner) Corpus Christi Coll., Cambridge (MA, LLB). Chief Asst Solicitor, Warrington, 1946-48; Dep. Town Clerk: Grimsby, 1948-53; Ilford, 1953-56; Town Clerk, Hampstead, 1956-65 (now Camden); Town Clerk and Chief Exec., London Borough of Camden, 1965-77; Hon. Clerk to Housing and Works Cttee, London Boroughs Assoc., 1965-79. Chm., Royal Inst. of Public Administration, 1973-75. Member: Uganda Resettlement Board, 1972-73; DoE Study Gp on Agrément, 1978. Chairman: Public Examn, Glos Structure Plan, 1980; Indep. Inquiry into death of Maria Mehmedagi, 1981. *Address:* Old Housing, Fifield, Oxon. *T:* Shipton-under-Wychwood 830695.

WILSON, Brian William John Gregg, MA; MBIM; Headmaster, Campbell College, Belfast, since 1977; *b* 16 June 1937; *s* of Cecil S. and Margaret D. Wilson; *m* 1969, Sara Remington (*née* Hollins); two *d. Educ:* Sedbergh Sch., Yorks; Christ's Coll., Cambridge (MA). NI short service commn, RIrF, 1955-57. Asst Master, Radley Coll., 1960-65; Housemaster, King's Sch., Canterbury, 1965-73; Dir of Studies, Eastbourne Coll., 1973-76. Mem., Central Religious Adv. Cttee, BBC/ITV, 1982. Hon. Sec., Ancient History Cttee, JACT, 1967-77. *Publications:* (with W. K. Lacey) Res Publica, 1970; (with D. J. Miller) Stories from Herodotus, 1973. *Recreations:* fives, squash, golf, cricket, hockey, etc; translating, theology, stock market, drama. *Address:* Headmaster's House, Campbell College, Belfast BT4 2ND. *T:* Belfast 63076.

WILSON, Brig. Charles Edward T.; *see* Tryon-Wilson.

WILSON, Sir Charles Haynes, Kt 1965; MA Glasgow and Oxon; Principal and Vice-Chancellor of University of Glasgow, 1961-76; *b* 16 May 1909; 2nd *s* of late George Wilson and Florence Margaret Hannay; *m* 1935, Jessie Gilmour Wilson; one *s* two *d. Educ:* Hillhead High School; Glasgow Univ.; Oxford Univ. Glasgow University Faulds Fellow in Political Philosophy, 1932-34. Lecturer in Political Science, London School of Economics, 1934-39; Fellow and Tutor in Modern History, Corpus Christi College, Oxford, 1939-52. Junior Proctor, 1945; Faculty Fellow, Nuffield College. Visiting

Professor in Comparative Government at Ohio State Univ., 1950; Principal, The University College of Leicester, 1952-57; Vice-Chancellor, Univ. of Leicester, 1957-61. Chairman: Commn on Fourah Bay Coll., Sierra Leone, 1957; Miners' Welfare Nat. Schol. Scheme Selec. Cttee, 1959-64; Acad. Planning Bd for Univ. of E Anglia, 1960; Member: Academic Planning Cttee and Council of UC of Sussex, 1958; Acad. Adv. Cttee, Royal Coll. of Science and Technology, Glasgow (now Univ. of Strathclyde), 1962; British Cttee of Selection for Harkness Fellowships of Commonwealth Fund, 1962-67; Heyworth Cttee on Social Studies, 1962; Acad. Planning Bd, Univ. of Stirling, 1964; Chairman, Cttee of Vice-Chancellors and Principals, 1964-67; Chm., Assoc. of Commonwealth Univs, 1966-67 and 1972-74. Mem., Museums and Galleries Commn (formerly Standing Commn on Museums and Galleries), 1976-. Hon. Fellow: Corpus Christi Coll., Oxford, 1963; LSE, 1965. Hon. LLD: Glasgow, 1957; Leicester, 1961; Rhodes Univ., 1964; Queen's Univ., Kingston, Ont, 1967; Ohio State Univ., 1969; Pennsylvania, 1975; Hon. DLitt: Strathclyde, 1966; NUU, 1976; Heriot-Watt, 1977; Hon. DCL East Anglia, 1966. Comdr, St Olav (Norway), 1966; Chevalier, Legion of Honour, 1976. *Address:* Whinnymuir, Dalry, Castle Douglas DG7 3TT. *T:* Dalry 218. *Club:* Royal Scottish Automobile.

WILSON, Prof. Charles Henry, CBE 1981; LittD; FBA 1966; Fellow of Jesus College, Cambridge, since 1938; Professor of Modern History, Cambridge University, 1965-79; *b* 16 Apr. 1914; *s* of Joseph Edwin Wilson and Louisa Wilson; *m* 1st 1939, Angela (marr. diss.), *d* of John Marshman; one *d*; 2nd, 1972, Alena, *d* of Dr Vladimir Kouril, Ostrava, Czechoslovakia. *Educ:* De Aston Grammar Sch., Lincs; Jesus Coll., Cambridge. DLitt Cambridge, 1976. Studied in Holland and Germany, 1937-38. Served in RNVR and Admiralty, 1940-45. Univ. Lecturer in History, 1945-64, Reader in Modern Economic History, 1964-65, Cambridge Univ.; Bursar of Jesus Coll., 1945-55. Ford Lecturer in English History, Oxford Univ., for 1968-69. Vis. Prof., Univ. of Tokyo, 1974. Prof. of History and Civilization, European Univ. Inst., Florence (seconded from Cambridge), 1976-79, Vis. Prof. 1980-81. Member: Lord Chancellor's Adv. Council on Public Records, 1972-77; Adv. Council, Business History Unit (LSE), 1981. Jt Ed., Econ. Hist. Review, 1960-67; Mem. Editorial Cttee, Jl of European Econ. Hist. (Rome), 1975-. Governor, British Inst. of Florence, 1979-; British Acad. deleg. to European Science Foundn, 1980. British Govt Representative, Anglo-Netherlands Cultural Commn, 1956. Corres. Fellow: Royal Danish Acad. of Arts and Science, 1970; Royal Belgian Acad., 1973. Manager, Istituto Datini, Prato, 1971. Hon. Vice-Pres., RHistS, 1981. LittD (*hc*) Univ. of Groningen, 1964; Univ. of Louvain, 1977. Comdr, Order of Oranje-Nassau, 1973. *Publications:* Anglo-Dutch Commerce and Finance in 18th Century, 1940; Holland and Britain, 1945; History of Unilever, 1954; Profit and Power, 1957; Mercantilism, 1958, 5th edn, 1971; (with William Reader) Men and Machines, 1958; A Memoir of Sir Ellis Hunter, 1962; A Man and His Times, 1962; England's Apprenticeship 1603-1763, 1965; Unilever, 1945-65, 1968; The Dutch Republic and the Civilization of the Seventeenth Century, 1968; Economic History and the Historian, 1969; Queen Elizabeth and the Revolt of the Netherlands, 1970; Parliaments, Peoples and Mass Media, 1970; The Relevance of History (Brussels), 1975; (chapter) Colonialism in Africa, Vol. 4 1975; The Transformation of Europe, 1976; (ed with N. G. Parker) The Sources of European Economic History, 1977; Il Cammino verso l'industrializzone (Bologna), 1979; Cambridge Economic History of Europe: (ed jtly with Prof. E. E. Rich, and contrib.) Vol. IV 1967, Vol. V 1977; New Cambridge Modern History: (chapters on economic history) Vol. VII 1957, Vol. XI 1962; numerous articles. *Recreation:* music. *Address:* Jesus College, Cambridge.

WILSON, (Christopher) David, CBE 1968; MC 1945; Chairman: Southern Television Ltd, 1976-81 (Managing Director, 1959-76); Southstar Television International, 1976-81; Beaumont (UK) Ltd, 1979-81; *b* 17 Dec. 1916; *s* of late Anthony James Wilson, Highclere, Worplesdon, Surrey; *m* 1947, Jean Barbara Morton Smith; no *c. Educ:* St George's Sch., Windsor; Aldenham. Served War of 1939-45: Captain RA, in India, Middle East and Italy. Business Manager, Associated Newspapers Ltd, 1955-57; Dir, Associated Rediffusion Ltd, 1956-57; Gen. Manager, Southern Television Ltd, 1957-59. Mem. Council, Southampton Univ.; Vice-Pres., Southern Arts Assoc.; Mem. Exec. Cttee, South East Arts Assoc.; Trustee: Chichester Festival Theatre Trust Ltd; Southampton and Wessex Med. Sch. Trust; Dir, Canterbury New Theatre Ltd. FCA 1947. *Recreations:* sailing, music. *Address:* Little Croft, Upham, Hants. *T:* Durley 204. *Clubs:* MCC; Royal Southern Yacht.

WILSON, Christopher Maynard, DIC, PhD; External Consultant, Logica Ltd, since 1981; *b* 19 Dec. 1928; *s* of late George Henry Cyril Wilson and of Adelaide Flora Marie Wilson; *m* 1953, Elizabeth Ursula Canning; one *s* two *d. Educ:* King Edward VII Sch., Sheffield; Worksop Coll., Notts; Imperial Coll., London Univ. (BSc, ARCS, DIC, PhD). National Service, RAF, 1947-49. Ferranti Computers, 1953-63; Ferranti merged with ICT, 1963, ICT merged with English Electric Computers to become ICL, 1968; Manager, UK Sales, 1968-70; Director: Marketing and Product Strategy, 1970-72; Internat. Div., 1972-77; Man. Dir, International Computers Ltd, 1977-81. *Recreations:* squash, tennis, gardening, sailing. *Address:* Tiles Cottage, Forest Road, Winkfield Row, near Bracknell, Berks. *Club:* Ascot Squash (Ascot).

WILSON, Clifford; Professor of Medicine, University of London, at the London Hospital and Director, Medical Unit, The London Hospital, 1946-71, now Emeritus Professor; *b* 27 Jan. 1906; *m* 1936, Kathleen Hebden; one *s* one *d. Educ:* Balliol College, Oxford. Brackenbury Scholar, Balliol Coll.,

Oxford, 1924; 1st Class Oxford Final Hons School of Nat. Sciences, 1928; House Physician, etc., London Hospital, 1931-34; Rockefeller Travelling Fellow, 1934-35; Research Fellow, Harvard Univ.; Asst Director, Medical Unit, London Hosp., 1938; Univ. Reader in Medicine, London Hosp., 1940; Major RAMC, Medical Research Section, 1942-45. President Renal Association, 1963-64. Examiner MRCP, 1960-; Censor, RCP, 1964-66; Senior Censor and Senior Vice-Pres., 1967-68. Dean, Faculty of Medicine, Univ. of London, 1968-71. *Publications:* sections on renal diseases and diseases of the arteries in Price's Text Book of Medicine; papers on renal disease, hypertension, arterial disease and other medical subjects, 1930-70. *Address:* The White Cottage, Woodgreen, Fordingbridge, Hants.

WILSON, Prof. Colin Alexander St John, FRIBA; Professor of Architecture, Cambridge University, since 1975; Fellow, Pembroke College, Cambridge, since 1977; Architect (own private practice); *b* 14 March 1922; *yr s* of late Rt Rev. Henry A. Wilson, CBE, DD; *m* 1st, 1955, Muriel Lavender (marr. diss. 1971); 2nd, 1972, Mary Jane Long; one *s* one *d. Educ:* Felsted Sch.; Corpus Christi Coll., Cambridge, 1940-42 (MA); Sch. of Architecture, London Univ., 1946-49 (Dip. Lond.). Served War, RNVR, 1942-46. Asst in Housing Div., Architects Dept, LCC, 1950-55; Lectr at Sch. of Architecture, Univ. of Cambridge, 1955-69; Fellow, Churchill Coll., Cambridge, 1962-71. Practised in assoc. with Sir Leslie Martin, 1955-64: on bldgs in Cambridge (Harvey Court, Gonville and Caius Coll.; Stone Building, Peterhouse); Univ. of Oxford, Law Library; Univ. of Leicester, Science Campus; Univ. of London, Royal Holloway Coll. In own practice Buildings include: Extension to Sch. of Architecture, Cambridge; Research Laboratory, Babraham; Extension to British Museum; Projects for Liverpool Civic and Social Centre, Group Headquarters and Research Campus for Lucas Industries Ltd, and The British Library, Euston Road. Vis. Critic to Yale Sch. of Architecture, USA, 1960 and 1964; Bemis Prof. of Architecture MIT, USA, 1970-72. Trustee: Tate Gall., 1973-80; Nat. Gall., 1977-80. *Publications:* articles in: The Observer; professional jls in UK, USA, France, Spain, Japan, Germany, Norway, Italy, Switzerland, etc. *Address:* 31A Grove End Road, NW8. *T:* 01-286 8306; 2 Grantchester Road, Cambridge. *T:* Cambridge 357776; (office) Colin St John Wilson & Partners, Northampton Lodge, 39A Canonbury Square, N1 2NH. *T:* 01-354 2030.

WILSON, Colin Henry; author; *b* Leicester, 26 June 1931; *s* of Arthur Wilson and Annetta Jones; *m* Dorothy Betty Troop; one *s*; *m* Joy Stewart; two *s* one *d. Educ:* The Gateway Secondary Technical School, Leicester. Left school at 16. Laboratory Asst (Gateway School), 1948-49; Civil Servant (collector of taxes), Leicester and Rugby, 1949-50; national service with RAF, AC2, 1949-50. Various jobs, and a period spent in Paris and Strasbourg, 1950; came to London, 1951; various labouring jobs, long period in plastic factory; returned to Paris, 1953; labouring jobs in London until Dec. 1954, when began writing The Outsider: has since made a living at writing. Visiting Professor: Hollins Coll., Va, 1966-67; Univ. of Washington, Seattle, 1967; Dowling Coll., Majorca, 1969; Rutgers Univ., NJ, 1974. Plays produced: Viennese Interlude; The Metal Flower Blossom; Strindberg. *Publications:* The Outsider, 1956; Religion and the Rebel, 1957; The Age of Defeat, 1959; Ritual in the Dark, 1960; Adrift in Soho, 1961; An Encyclopædia of Murder, 1961; The Strength to Dream, 1962; Origins of the Sexual Impulse, 1963; The Man without a Shadow, 1963; The World of Violence, 1963; Rasputin and the Fall of the Romanovs, 1964; The Brandy of the Damned (musical essays), 1964; Necessary Doubt, 1964; Beyond the Outsider, 1965; Eagle and Earwig, 1965; The Mind Parasites, 1966; Introduction to The New Existentialism, 1966; The Glass Cage, 1966; Sex and the Intelligent Teenager, 1966; The Philosopher's Stone, 1968; Strindberg (play), 1968; Bernard Shaw: A Reassessment, 1969; Voyage to a Beginning, 1969; Poetry and Mysticism, 1970; The Black Room, 1970; A Casebook of Murder, 1970; The God of the Labyrinth, 1970; Lingard, 1970; (jtly) The Strange Genius of David Lindsay, 1970; The Occult, 1971; New Pathways in Psychology, 1972; Order of Assassins, 1971; Tree by Tolkien, 1973; Hermann Hesse, 1973; Strange Powers, 1973; The Schoolgirl Murder Case, 1974; Return of the Lloigor, 1974; A Book of Booze, 1974; The Craft of the Novel, 1975; The Space Vampires, 1976; Men of Strange Powers, 1976; Enigmas and Mysteries, 1977; The Geller Phenomenon, 1977; Mysteries, 1978; Mysteries (play), 1979; The Quest for Wilhelm Reich, 1979; The War Against Sleep: the philosophy of Gurdjieff, 1980; Starseekers, 1980; Frankenstein's Castle, 1981; (ed with John Grant) The Directory of Possibilities, 1981; Poltergeist!, 1981; contribs to: The Spectator, Audio, Books and Bookmen, Hi-Fi News, Sunday Times, Sunday Telegraph, etc. *Recreations:* collecting gramophone records, mainly opera; mathematics. *Address:* Tetherdown, Trewallock Lane, Gorran Haven, Cornwall. *Clubs:* Savage; The Club (St Austell).

WILSON, Maj.-Gen. Dare; see Wilson, Maj.-Gen. R. D.

WILSON, David; see Wilson, C. D.

WILSON, Sir David, 3rd Bt *cr* 1920; solicitor; *b* 30 Oct. 1928; *s* of Sir John Mitchell Harvey Wilson, 2nd Bt, KCVO, and Mary Elizabeth (*d* 1979), *d* of late William Richards, CBE; *S* father, 1975; *m* 1955, Eva Margareta, *e d* of Tore Lindell, Malmö, Sweden; two *s* one *d. Educ:* Deerfield Acad., Mass., USA; Harrow School; Oriel Coll., Oxford (Brisco Owen Schol.). Barrister, Lincoln's Inn, 1954-61; admitted Solicitor, 1962; Partner in Simmons & Simmons, EC2, 1963-. *Heir: s* Thomas David Wilson, *b* 6 Jan. 1959. *Address:* Tandem House, Queen's Drive, Oxshott, Leatherhead, Surrey KT22 0PH. *Clubs:* Arts; Royal Southern Yacht.

WILSON, David Clive, PhD; HM Diplomatic Service; Head of Southern European Department, Foreign and Commonwealth Office, since 1981; *b* 14 Feb. 1935; *s* of Rev. William Skinner Wilson and Enid Wilson; *m* 1967, Natasha Helen Mary Alexander; two *s. Educ:* Trinity Coll., Glenalmond; Keble Coll., Oxford (schol., MA); PhD London 1973. National Service, The Black Watch, 1953-55; entered Foreign Service, 1958; Third Secretary, Vientiane, 1959-60; Language Student, Hong Kong, 1960-62; Second, later First Secretary, Peking, 1963-65; FCO, 1965-68; resigned, 1968; Editor, China Quarterly, 1968-74; Vis. Scholar, Columbia Univ., New York, 1972; rejoined Diplomatic Service, 1974; Cabinet Office, 1974-77; Political Adviser, Hong Kong, 1977-81. *Recreations:* mountaineering, ski-ing, reading. *Address:* c/o Foreign and Commonwealth Office, SW1. *Club:* Hurlingham.

WILSON, David Mackenzie, FBA 1981; Director of the British Museum, since 1977; *b* 30 Oct. 1931; *e s* of Rev. Joseph Wilson; *m* 1955, Eva, *o d* of Dr Gunnar Sjögren, Stockholm; one *s* one *d. Educ:* Kingswood Sch.; St John's Coll., Cambridge (LittD); Lund Univ., Sweden. Research Asst, Cambridge Univ., 1954; Asst Keeper, British Museum, 1954-64; Reader in Archaeology of Anglo-Saxon Period, London Univ., 1964-71; Prof. of Medieval Archaeology, Univ. of London, 1971-76; Jt Head of Dept of Scandinavian Studies, UCL, 1973-76. Mem., Ancient Monuments Bd for England, 1976-. Governor, Museum of London, 1976-81. Crabtree Orator 1966. Member: Royal Swedish Acad. of Sci.; Royal Acad. of Letters, History and Antiquities, Sweden; German Archaeological Inst.; Royal Gustav Adolf's Acad. of Sweden; Vetenskapssocieteten, Lund, Sweden; Royal Soc. of Sci. and Letters, Gothenburg; Royal Soc. of Sci., Uppsala; Royal Norwegian Soc. of Sci. and Letters; FSA; Hon. MRIA; Hon. Mem., Polish Archaeological and Numismatic Soc.; Sec., Soc. for Medieval Archaeology, 1957-77; Pres., Viking Soc., 1968-70; Pres., Brit. Archaeological Assoc., 1962-68. Hon. Fil.Dr Stockholm; Hon. Dr Phil Aarhus. Félix Neuburgh Prize, Gothenburg Univ., 1978. Order of Polar Star, 1st cl. (Sweden), 1977. *Publications:* The Anglo-Saxons, 1960, 3rd edn 1981; Anglo-Saxon Metalwork 700-1100 in British Museum, 1964; (with O. Klindt-Jensen) Viking Art, 1966; (with G. Bersu) Three Viking Graves in the Isle of Man, 1969; The Vikings and their Origins, 1970, 2nd edn, 1980; (with P. G. Foote) The Viking Achievement, 1970 (Dag Strömbäck Prize, Royal Gustav Adolf's Acad., 1975); Reflections on the St Ninian's Isle Treasure (Jarrow Lecture), 1970; (with A. Small and C. Thomas) St Ninian's Isle and its Treasure, 1973; The Viking Age in the Isle of Man, 1974; (ed) Anglo-Saxon Archaeology, 1976; Civil and Military Engineering in Viking Age Scandinavia, 1978; (ed) The Northern World, 1980, etc. *Address:* British Museum, WC1; The Lifeboat House, Castletown, Isle of Man. *Club:* Athenæum.

WILSON, Des; Chairman, CLEAR (Campaign for Lead-Free Air), since 1981; *b* 5 March 1941; *s* of Albert H. Wilson, Oamaru, New Zealand; *m* 1st, 1962, Rita Claire Williams (marr. diss. 1977); one *s* one *d*; 2nd, 1979, Fiona Thompson. *Educ:* Waitaki Boys' High Sch., New Zealand. Journalist-Broadcaster, 1957-67; Director, Shelter, Nat. Campaign for the Homeless, 1967-71; Head of Public Affairs, RSC, 1974-76; Editor, Social Work Today, 1976-79; Dep. Editor, Illustrated London News, 1979-81. Member: Nat. Exec., Nat. Council for Civil Liberties, 1971-73; Cttee for City Poverty, 1972-73; Bd, Shelter, 1982-. Columnist, The Guardian, 1968-70; Columnist, The Observer, 1971-75; regular contributor, Illustrated London News, 1972-. Contested (L) Hove, 1973, 1974; Mem., Liberal Party Council, 1973-74. *Publications:* I Know It Was the Place's Fault, 1970; Des Wilson's Minority Report (a diary of protest), 1973; So you want to be Prime Minister: a personal view of British politics, 1979. *Address:* 43 Sandy Bank, Bewdley, Worcs.

WILSON, Sir Duncan; see Wilson, Sir A. D.

WILSON, Ellis; see Wilson, H. E. C.

WILSON, Lt-Col Eric Charles Twelves, VC 1940; retired; *b* 2 October 1912; *s* of late Rev. C. C. C. Wilson; *m* 1943, Ann (from whom he obtained a divorce, 1953), *d* of Major Humphrey Pleydell-Bouverie, MBE; two *s*; *m* 1953, Angela Joy, *d* of Lt-Col J. McK. Gordon, MC; one *s. Educ:* Marlborough; RMC, Sandhurst. Commissioned in East Surrey Regt, 1933; seconded to King's African Rifles, 1937; seconded to Somaliland Camel Corps, 1939; Long Range Desert Gp, 1941-42; Burma, 1944; seconded to N Rhodesia Regt, 1946; retd from Regular Army, 1949; Admin Officer, HM Overseas Civil Service, Tanganyika, 1949-61; Dep. Warden, London House, 1962, Warden, 1966-77. Hon. Sec., Anglo-Somali Soc., 1972-77. *Recreation:* country life. *Address:* Woodside Cottage, Stowell, Sherborne, Dorset. *T:* Templecombe 70264.

WILSON, Frank Richard, CMG 1963; OBE 1946; Controller of Administration, Commonwealth Development Corporation, 1964-80; retired HMOCS Oct. 1963; *b* 26 Oct. 1920; *er s* of late Sir Leonard Wilson, KCIE and the late Muriel Wilson; *m* 1947, Alexandra Dorothy Mary (*née* Haigh); two *s. Educ:* Oundle Sch.; Trinity Hall, Cambridge (1939-40 only). Commnd Indian Army, 1941; retired as Lieut-Col, 1946. Joined Colonial Administrative Service (later HMOCS) in Kenya, 1947; District Comr, 1950-56; Private Sec. to the Governor, 1956-59; Provincial Comr, Central Province, 1959-63; Civil Sec., Central Region, 1963. *Address:* Old Brooklands, Moreton Pinkney, Northants.

WILSON, Geoffrey; Chairman, Wells, O'Brien & Co., since 1972; *b* 11 July 1929; *m* 1962, Philomena Mary Kavanagh; one *s* one *d. Educ:* Bolton County Grammar Sch.; Univ. of Birmingham; Linacre Coll., Oxford. PE Consulting Group, 1958-63; British Railways, 1963-71; Mem., BR Bd, 1968-71, Chief Exec. (Railways), 1971. Member: Council, Royal Inst. of Public Admin, 1970-71; Council, Inst. of Transport, 1970-71. *Recreations:* golf, gardening, painting. *Address:* 5 Lancaster Court, Well Place, Cheltenham, Glos.

WILSON, Maj.-Gen. Geoffrey Boyd, CB 1979; Regimental Comptroller, Royal Artillery, since 1982; Controller, Royal Artillery Institution, since 1982; Chairman, Board of Management, Royal Artillery Charitable Fund and Royal Artillery Association, since 1982; *b* London, 21 Jan. 1927; *s* of Horace Alexander Wilson and Hilda Evelyn (*née* Gratwicke); *m* 1952, Fay Rosemary Scott; five *d. Educ:* St Paul's Sch.; Edinburgh Univ. psc 1957, jssc 1963. Commnd RA, 1946; served Italy, Palestine, Egypt, N Africa, with 39 Medium Regt, 1946-50; 5 RHA, BAOR, 1951-54; GSO3 6 Armoured Div., BAOR, 1954-56; Brigade Major RA, 53 (Welsh) Div., 1958-60; Instr and GSO2, RMA Sandhurst, 1961-63; Batt. Comdr, 137 (Java) Bty, BAOR, 1964; 2 i/c and Ops Officer, 40 Light Regt, BAOR and Borneo, 1965-66; CO 20 Heavy Regt, BAOR, 1967-68; Asst Mil. Sec., Mil. Sec. (SB), MoD, 1969-71; CRA 3 Inf. Div., UK, 1971-73; RCDS, 1974; Dir, Def. Operational Plans, MoD, 1975-76; Maj.-Gen. RA, BAOR, 1976-77; GOC Artillery Div., 1977-79; C of S and Head of UK Delegn to Live Oak, SHAPE, 1979-82, retired 1982. A Col Comdt, Royal Regt of Artillery, 1982-. *Recreations:* gardening, music, reading. *Address:* c/o Artillery House, Connaught Barracks, Grand Depot Road, SE18 6SL. *T:* 01-855 9640. *Club:* Army and Navy.

WILSON, Hon. Geoffrey Hazlitt, FCA, FCMA; Chief Executive since 1981, and Chairman since 1982, Delta Group plc; *b* 28 Dec. 1929; *yr s* of 1st Baron Moran, MC, MD, FRCP, and of Lady Moran, MBE; *m* 1955, Barbara Jane Hebblethwaite; two *s* two *d. Educ:* Eton; King's Coll., Cambridge (BA Hons). JDipMA; CBIM. Articled to Barton Mayhew (now Ernst & Whinney), 1952; Chartered Accountant 1955; joined English Electric, 1956; Dep. Comptroller, 1965; Financial Controller (Overseas), GEC, 1968; joined Delta Group as Financial Dir, Cables Div., 1969; elected to Main Board as Gp Financial Dir, 1972; Jt Man. Dir, 1977; Dep. Chief Executive, 1980. Director: Blue Circle Industries plc, 1980-; English & International Trust Ltd, 1978-. Member: Council, Inst. of Cost and Management Accountants, 1972-78; Accounting Standards Cttee, 1978-79; Inflation Accounting Steering Gp, 1976-80; Chm., 100 Gp of Chartered Accountants, 1979-80. Mem. Management Bd, Engineering Employers Fedn, 1979-; Chm., EEF Cttee on Future of Wage Bargaining, 1980. Mem. Administrative Council, Royal Jubilee Trusts, 1979-, Hon. Treas., 1980-. *Recreations:* family, reading, vintage cars. *Address:* The Manor House, Newton Valence, near Alton, Hampshire GU34 3RB. *T:* Tisted 336; (office) 01-836 3535. *Clubs:* Boodle's, Royal Automobile.

WILSON, Sir Geoffrey Masterman, KCB 1969 (CB 1968); CMG 1962; Chairman, Oxfam, since 1977; *b* 7 April 1910; 3rd *s* of late Alexander Cowan Wilson and Edith Jane Brayshaw; *m* 1946, Julie Stafford Trowbridge; two *s* two *d. Educ:* Manchester Grammar School; Oriel College, Oxford. Chairman, Oxford Univ. Labour Club, 1930; Pres., Oxford Union, 1931. Harmsworth Law Scholar, Middle Temple, 1931; called to Bar, Middle Temple, 1934. Served in HM Embassy, Moscow, and Russian Dept of Foreign Office, 1940-45. Cabinet Office, 1947; Treasury, 1948; Director, Colombo Plan Technical Co-operation Bureau, 1951-53; Under-Secretary, Treasury, 1956-58; Deputy Head of UK Treasury Delegn and Alternate Exec. Dir for UK, Internat. Bank, Washington, 1958; Vice-President, International Bank, Washington, 1961; Deputy Secretary, ODM, 1966-68, Permanent Secretary, 1968-70; Dep. Sec.-Gen. (Economic), Commonwealth Secretariat, 1971. Chm., Race Relations Bd, 1971-77. Hon. Fellow, Wolfson Coll., Cambridge, 1971. *Address:* 4 Polstead Road, Oxford.

See also Prof. J. E. Meade, Prof. R. C. Wilson, S. S. Wilson.

WILSON, Geoffrey Studholme, CMG 1961; Commissioner of Police, Tanganyika Police Force, 1958-62; *b* 5 June 1913; *s* of late J. E. S. Wilson; *m* 1936, Joy Noel, *d* of Capt. C. St G. Harris-Walker; two *s. Educ:* Radley College. Joined Hong Kong Police, 1933; Commissioner of Police, Sarawak Constabulary, 1953-58. King's Police Medal, 1950. OStJ 1961. *Recreations:* golf, fishing, sailing. *Address:* c/o The Hong Kong & Shanghai Banking Corporation, 9 Waterloo Place, SW1Y 4BE. *Club:* Hong Kong (Hong Kong).

WILSON, George Pritchard Harvey, CMG 1966; JP; Chairman, Victorian Inland Meat Authority, 1973-77 (Deputy Chairman, 1970-73); *b* 10 March 1918; *s* of late G. L. Wilson; *m* 1945, Fay Hobart Duff; two *s* one *d. Educ:* Geelong Grammar School. Nuffield Scholar (Farming), 1952. Council Member, Monash University, 1961-69; Royal Agricultural Society of Victoria: Councillor, 1950; President, 1964-73; Trustee, 1968-. Member: Victoria Promotion Cttee, 1968-81; Victoria Economic Develt Corp., 1981-82. JP 1957. *Recreation:* fishing. *Address:* Wilson House, Berwick, Victoria 3806, Australia. *T:* Berwick 7071271. *Clubs:* Melbourne, Royal Automobile Club of Victoria (Melbourne).

WILSON, Gerald Robertson; Assistant Secretary, Scottish Office, since 1982; *b* 7 Sept. 1939; *s* of Charles Robertson Wilson and Margaret Wilson (*née* Early); *m* 1963, Margaret Anne, *d* of late John S. and Agnes Wight; one *s* one *d. Educ:* Holy Cross Academy, Edinburgh; University of Edinburgh. MA. Asst Principal, Scottish Home and Health Dept, 1961-65; Private Sec.

to Minister of State for Scotland, 1965-66; Principal, Scottish Home and Health Dept, 1966-72; Private Sec. to Lord Privy Seal, 1972-74, to Minister of State, Civil Service Dept, 1974; Asst Sec., Scottish Economic Planning Dept, 1974-77; Counsellor, Office of the UK Perm. Rep. to the European Communities, Brussels, 1977-82. *Recreation:* music. *Address:* c/o Scottish Office, New St Andrew's House, Edinburgh. *Club:* Royal Commonwealth Society.

WILSON, Gilbert; *b* 2 March 1908; *s* of J. E. Wilson; *m* 1934, Janet Joy Turner; two *d. Educ:* Auckland Grammar School. Served with 2nd NZEF, Middle East, 1940-43. Joined National Bank of New Zealand, 1924; joined Reserve Bank of New Zealand, 1935; Dep. Chief Cashier, 1948-53; Chief Cashier, 1953-56; Dep. Governor, 1956-62; Governor, 1962-67; also Alternate Governor for New Zealand of International Monetary Fund, 1962-67. *Recreations:* golf, gardening. *Address:* 41 Mere Road, Taupo, New Zealand. *Club:* Taupo Golf (NZ).

WILSON, Gordon; see Wilson, Robert G.

WILSON, Gordon Wallace; Under Secretary, Ministry of Agriculture, Fisheries and Food, since 1975; *b* 14 July 1926; *s* of late John Wallace Wilson and of Mrs Joyce Elizabeth Grace Sherwood-Smith; *m* 1951, Gillian Maxwell (*née* Wood); three *s. Educ:* King's Sch., Bruton; Queen's Coll., Oxford (BA PPE). Entered Civil Service (War Office), 1950; Principal Private Sec. to Sec. of State for War, 1962; Asst Sec., MoD, 1964; Dir, Centre of Admin Studies, HM Treasury, 1965; Asst Sec., DEA, 1968; HM Treasury, 1969. *Recreations:* tennis, carpentry, gardening, camping. *Address:* 61 Ottways Lane, Ashtead, Surrey. *T:* Ashtead 72898.

WILSON, Graeme McDonald, CMG 1975; British Civil Aviation Representative (Far East), 1964-81, retired; *b* 9 May 1919; *s* of Robert Linton McDonald Wilson and Sophie Hamilton Wilson (*née* Milner); *m* 1968, Yabu Masae; three *s. Educ:* Rendcomb Coll., Glos; Schloss Schule Salem, Germany; Lincoln Coll., Oxford; Gray's Inn, London. Served in Fleet Air Arm, 1939-46. Joined Home Civil Service, 1946. Private Sec. to Parly Sec., Min. of Civil Aviation, 1946-49; Planning 1, 1949-53; Dep. UK Rep. on Council of ICAO, 1953-56; Lt-Comdr (A) (Ö) (Ph) (q) RCNR, 1954; Internat. Relations 1, Min. of Transport and Civil Aviation, 1956-61; Asst Sec. Interdependence, Exports and Electronics, Min. of Aviation, 1961-64; seconded to Foreign Service as Counsellor and Civil Air Attaché, at twelve Far Eastern posts, 1964. Ford Foundn Fellow, Nat. Translation Center, Austin, Texas, 1968-69. *Publications:* Face At The Bottom Of The World: translations of the modern Japanese poetry of Hagiwara Sakutaro, 1969; (trans., with Ito Aiko) I Am a Cat, 1971; (trans., with Atsumi Ikuko) Three Contemporary Japanese Poets, 1972; (trans., with Ito Aiko) Ten Nights of Dream, 1973; Nihon no Kindaishi to Gendaishi no Dai Yon-sho: Hagiwara Sakutaro, 1974; (trans., with Ito Aiko) I Am a Cat II, 1979; (trans., with Ito Aiko) I Am a Cat III, 1983; articles on East Asian literature and poems (mostly Japanese, Chinese, Vietnamese and Korean trans). *Address:* 42 Cranford Avenue, Exmouth, Devon. *T:* Exmouth 4786. *Clubs:* Naval; PEN Club of Japan (Tokyo).

WILSON, Sir Graham (Selby), Kt 1962; MD, FRCP, DPH (London); FRS 1978; late Captain Royal Army Medical Corps (Special Reserve); Hon. Lecturer, Department of Bacteriology and Immunology, London School of Hygiene and Tropical Medicine, 1964-70; Director of the Public Health Laboratory Service, 1941-63; KHP, 1944-46; *b* 10 Sept. 1895; *m* Mary Joyce (*d* 1976), *d* of Alfred Ayrton, Chester; two *s. Educ:* Epsom College; King's Coll., London; Charing Cross Hospital, London; Governors' Clinical Gold Medal, Charing Cross Hospital, and Gold Medal, University of London, MB, BS; Specialist in Bacteriology, Royal Army Med. Corps, 1916-20; Demonstrator in Bacteriology, Charing Cross Hospital Medical School, 1919-22; Lecturer in Bacteriology, University of Manchester, 1923-27; Reader in Bacteriology, University of London, 1927-30; Prof. of Bacteriology as applied to Hygiene, London School of Hygiene and Tropical Medicine, 1930-47; William Julius Mickle Fellowship, University of London, 1939. Member: Council, RCP, 1938-40; of several cttees on tuberculosis, poliomyelitis and other infectious diseases; Weber-Parkes prize, RCP 1942; Milroy Lecturer, RCP, 1948; Hon. Fellow, Amer. Public Health Assoc., 1953; Hon. Fellow: Royal Soc. of Health, 1960; London Sch. of Hygiene and Tropical Medicine, 1976; Hon. FRSocMed, 1971; Hon. FRCPath, 1972. Czechoslovak Medical Society, Jan Evangelista Purkyně, 1963; Bisset Hawkins Medal, RCP, 1956; Marjory Stephenson Memorial Prize, 1959; Stewart Prize, 1960; Buchanan Medal, Royal Society, 1967; Harben Gold Medal, 1970; Jenner Meml Medal, 1975. Hon. LLD (Glasgow) 1962. *Publications:* The Principles of Bacteriology and Immunity (with late Professor W. W. C. Topley and Sir Ashley Miles), 6th edn 1975; The Hazards of Immunization, 1967; The Bacteriological Grading of Milk (with collaborators), 1935; The Pasteurization of Milk, 1942; The Brown Animal Sanatory Institution, 1979; numerous papers on bacteriological subjects. *Address:* 11 Morpeth Mansions, Morpeth Terrace, SW1P 1ER. *Club:* Athenæum.

WILSON, Rear-Adm. Guy Austen Moore, CB 1958; Breeder and Voluntary Organiser, Guide Dogs for the Blind Association; Chairman, Suffolk Old People's Welfare Association; *b* 7 June 1906; *s* of Ernest Moore Wilson, Buenos Aires, and Katharine Lawrence; *m* 1932, Dorothy, *d* of Sir Arthur Watson, CBE; two *s* three *d. Educ:* Royal Naval Colleges, Osborne and Dartmouth. Joined Royal Navy, 1920; Engineering Specialist Course, 1924-

28. Advanced Engineering Course, Royal Naval College, Greenwich, 1928-30; served War of 1939-45, at Admiralty and in HMS Berwick; Portsmouth Dockyard, 1946-49; Comdr, 1940; Captain, 1948; Dep. Director Aircraft Maintenance and Repair, Admiralty, 1950-52; Supt, RN Aircraft Yard, Fleetlands, 1952-55; Rear-Admiral, 1955; Deputy Engineer-in-Chief for Fleet Maintenance and Administration, 1955-57; Rear-Admiral Nuclear Propulsion and Deputy Engineer-in-Chief (Nuclear Propulsion), 1957-59, retired 1960; Chief Executive, Dracone Developments Ltd, 1960-63. *Recreations:* swimming, motoring, gardening. *Address:* Barn Acre, Saxstead Green, Woodbridge, Suffolk. *T:* Earl Soham 365.

WILSON, Rt. Hon. Sir Harold; see Wilson, Rt Hon. Sir J. H.

WILSON, Harold; His Honour Judge Wilson; a Circuit Judge, since 1981 (Midland and Oxford Circuit); *b* 19 Sept. 1931; *s* of late Edward Simpson Wilson; *m* 1973, Jill Ginever, *d* of late Charles Edward Walter Barlow; one step *s* one step *d* ; three *s* one *d* by previous marriage. *Educ:* St Albans Sch.; Sidney Sussex Coll., Cambridge (State Scholar; MA). Commnd service, RAF, RAFVR, RAuxAF, 1950-disbandment. Called to the Bar, Gray's Inn, 1958 (Holker Exhbr; runner-up, Lee Essay Prize, 1959); Oxford Circuit, 1960-70; Midland and Oxford Circuit, 1971-75; Dep. Chm., Monmouthshire Quarter Sessions, 1970; a Recorder, Midland and Oxford Circuit, 1971-75; Chm. of Industrial Tribunals, Birmingham, 1976-81. *Recreations:* rugby football, reading and listening to music. *Address:* 2 Harcourt Buildings, Temple, EC4Y 9DB. *T:* 01-353 8549.

WILSON, Harold Arthur Cooper B.; see Bird-Wilson.

WILSON, Harold Fitzhardinge Wilson; Solicitor and Parliamentary Officer, Greater London Council, 1970-77 (Dep. Solicitor and Dep. Parly Officer, 1965); *b* 6 Jan. 1913; *s* of Walter James Wilson and Aileen Wilson (*née* Scrivens), Broadway, Worcs; *m* 1939, Deb Buckland; one *s* one *d*. Law Clerk, LCC, 1935. Company Officer, then Senior Company Officer, Nat. Fire Service, 1939-45. Principal Asst, LCC, 1951; Asst Parly Officer, LCC, 1960. Hon. Solicitor, RoSPA, 1970-77. Liveryman, Glaziers' Co. *Recreations:* the theatre, travelling, gardening, reading. *Address:* 34 Victoria Drive, Bognor Regis, Sussex.

WILSON, Harry; see Wilson of Langside, Baron.

WILSON, (Harry) Ellis (Charter), MB, ChB; DSc; FRCPGlas; retired as Lecturer in Pathological Biochemistry at Royal Hospital for Sick Children, Glasgow; *b* 26 July 1899; *s* of Harry James and Margaret Williamina Wilson. *Educ:* Glasgow Academy and University. Carnegie Scholar, 1923; studied in Würzburg, 1926; Assistant in Institute of Physiology, Glasgow University, 1924; a Rockefeller Fellowship tenable in USA, 1926; carried out research in New York and the Mayo Clinic, Rochester; Carnegie Teaching Fellow in Institute of Physiology, Glasgow University, 1930; studied (research) in Germany, 1931; Professor of Biochemistry and Nutrition, The All-India Institute of Hygiene and Public Health, Calcutta, 1934-37, and Professor of Chemistry, The Medical College, Calcutta, 1935-37. *Publications:* papers on biochemical subjects in various journals. *Recreations:* golf, travel. *Address:* Redholm, 5 West Chapelton Avenue, Bearsden, Glasgow; The Royal Hospital for Sick Children, Yorkhill, Glasgow.

WILSON, Harry Lawrence L.; see Lawrence-Wilson.

WILSON, Henry Braithwaite; Assistant Under-Secretary of State, Home Office, 1963-71; *b* 6 Aug. 1911; *s* of Charles Braithwaite Wilson and Ellen Blanche Hargrove; *m* 1936, Margaret Bodden; two *s* two *d*. *Educ:* Leighton Park School; Lincoln College, Oxford. Editorial work for Joseph Rowntree Social Service Trust, 1933-40; Sub-Warden, Toynbee Hall, 1940-41; Home Office: Temp. Administrative Asst, 1941-44; Sec., Departmental Cttee on War Damaged Licensed Premises and Reconstruction, 1942-44; Principal, 1944 (estab. 1946); Asst Sec., 1956. *Recreations:* gardening, walking. *Address:* Arran, Yew Tree Road, Grange over Sands, Cumbria. *T:* Grange 3488.

WILSON, Col Henry James, CBE 1963 (OBE 1943); TD 1944; Farmer since 1949; Chairman: NFU Trust Co.; Trehane Trust; *b* 10 June 1904; *s* of late James Wilson; *m* 1930, Anita Gertrude Petley; three *s*. *Educ:* Mercers' School. Westminster Bank, 1921-39. Served London Scottish, 1923-44; Commanded 1st Bn London Scottish, 1941-44; AAG, 8th Army HQ, 1944; DDPS, AFHQ, 1944-45; War Office, 1945-49. Joined NFU, 1947; Council Member, 1954; Vice-Pres., 1958; Dep. Pres., 1959-62; Hon. Treasurer, 1971-81. Chairman: Bacon Consultative Council, 1957-64; Industry Panel, Bacon Mkt Council, 1964-72. *Recreations:* shooting, and fishing. *Address:* Hamsey, Caldbec Hill, Battle, East Sussex. *Clubs:* Farmers'; Highland Brigade.

WILSON, Henry James; Chief Chancery Registrar, 1979-82; *b* 3 Sept. 1916; *s* of Alfred Edgar and Margaret Ethel Wilson; *m* 1st, 1940, Felicity Sidney (*née* Daniels) (*d* 1971); one *s* two *d* ; 2nd, 1972, Peggy Frances (*née* Browne). *Educ:* Wrekin College. Territorial Army, Westminster Dragoons, 1936; embodied for war service, 1939; commissioned, later Captain Royal Tank Regt. Admitted Solicitor, 1938; joined Chancery Registrar's Office, 1946; Chancery Registrar, 1961. *Recreations:* gardening, opera. *Address:* Ingleside Ferbies, Speldhurst, Kent TN3 0NS. *T:* Langton 3172. *Club:* Sloane.

WILSON, Henry Moir, CB 1969; CMG 1965; MBE 1946; PhD, BSc, FRAeS; *b* 3 Sept. 1910; 3rd *s* of late Charles Wilson, Belfast; *m* 1937, Susan Eveline Wilson; one *s* three *d*. *Educ:* Royal Belfast Academical Institution, Queen's Univ., Belfast. Apprentice in Mech. Eng, Combe Barbour, Belfast, 1927-31; QUB, 1927-31 (part-time) and 1931-34 (full-time); BSc with 1st Class Hons in Elect. Eng, 1932; PhD 1934 (Thesis on High Voltage Transients on Power Transmission Lines). College Apprentice, Metropolitan-Vickers, Manchester, 1934-35. Joined RAF Educational Service, 1935; commissioned RAFVR, 1939; Senior Tutor, RAF Advanced Armament Course, Ft. Halstead, 1943-46; Senior Educ. Officer, Empire Air Armament School, Manby (Acting Wing Comdr), 1946-47. Joined Ministry of Supply, 1947, as Senior Principal Sci. Officer, Supt Servo Div., Guided Projectile Estab., Westcott, 1947; Supt Guidance and Control Div. Guided Weapons Dept, RAE, 1947-49; Head of Armament Dept, RAE, 1949-56. Dep. Chief Sci. Officer, 1952; Chief Scientific Officer, 1956; Director-General, Aircraft Equipment Research and Devel., Ministry of Aviation, 1956-62; Head, Defence Research and Development Staff, British Embassy, Washington, DC, 1962-65; Dep. Chief Scientist (Army), 1965-66, Chief Scientist (Army), 1967-70; Dir, SHAPE Tech. Centre, 1970-75. Hon. DSc QUB, 1971. *Recreations:* golf, gardening. *Address:* 7 Carlinwark Drive, Camberley, Surrey.

WILSON, Prof. Henry Wallace, PhD; FRSE, FInstP; Director, Scottish Universities' Research and Reactor Centre, since 1962; Personal Professor of Physics, Strathclyde University, since 1966; *b* 30 Aug. 1923; *s* of Frank Binnington Wilson and Janet (*née* Wilson); *m* 1955, Fiona McPherson Martin, *d* of Alfred Charles Steinmetz Martin and Agnes Mary (*née* McPherson); three *s*. *Educ:* Allan Glen's Sch., Glasgow; Glasgow Univ. (BSc, PhD Physics). AInstP 1949, FInstP 1962; FRSE 1963. Wartime work as Physicist, Explosives Res. Div., ICI, Ardeer. Asst Lectr, Natural Philosophy Dept, Glasgow Univ., 1947-51; post-doctoral Res. Fellow, Univ. of Calif, Berkeley, 1951-52; Lectr, Nat. Phil. Dept, Glasgow Univ., 1952-55; Leader of Physical Measurements Gp, UKAEA, Aldermaston, 1955-62 (Sen. Principal Scientific Officer, 1958). Inst. of Physics: Mem. Council, 1970-71; Chm., Scottish Br., 1969-71; mem. several cttees; Royal Soc. of Edinburgh: Mem. Council, 1966-69, 1976-79; Vice Pres., 1979-81. Member: Brit. Nuclear Energy Soc.; British Mass Spectrometry Soc. (Chm., 1977-79). *Publications:* Alpha, Beta and Gamma-ray Spectroscopy, ed K. Siegbahn, 1965; Activation Analysis, ed Lenihan and Thomson, 1965; Modern Aspects of Mass Spectrometry, ed R. I. Reed, 1968; Encyclopaedic Dictionary of Physics, ed J. Thewlis, 1973; papers on radioactivity, low energy nuclear physics, meson physics, mass spectrometry, isotope separation, effects of radiation, and reactor physics, in Phil. Mag., Nature, Phys. Rev., Proc. Phys. Soc., etc. *Recreations:* flying (light aircraft), sailing, hill-walking, industrial archaeology (esp. canal history). *Address:* Ashgrove, The Crescent, Busby, near Glasgow G76 8HT. *T:* 041-644 3107.

WILSON, Sir Hugh; see Wilson, Sir L. H.

WILSON, Ian D.; see Douglas-Wilson.

WILSON, Very Rev. Ian George MacQueen; Dean of Argyll and the Isles, since 1979; Rector of St John's, Ballachulish and St Mary's, Glencoe, since 1978; *b* 6 March 1920; *s* of Joseph and Mary Wilson; *m* 1952, Janet Todd Kyle. *Educ:* Edinburgh Theological College. Deacon 1950, priest 1951; Curate, St Margaret's, Glasgow, 1950-52; Priest-in-charge, St Gabriel's, Glasgow, 1952-57; Rector: Christ Church, Dalbeattie, 1957-61; St John's, Baillieston, 1961-64; St Paul's, Rothesay, 1964-75; Canon, St John's Cathedral, Oban, 1973; Priest-in-charge, St Peter's, Stornoway, 1975-78; Officiating Chaplain, RAF, Stornoway, 1975-78; Synod Clerk, Diocese of Argyll and the Isles, 1977-79. Hon. LTh, St Mark's Inst. of Theology, 1974. *Address:* The Rectory, Glencoe, Ballachulish, Argyll PA39 4HP. *T:* Ballachulish 335.

WILSON, Ian Matthew; Under Secretary, Scottish Education Department, since 1977; *b* 12 Dec. 1926; *s* of Matthew Thomson Wilson and Mary Lily Barnett; *m* 1953, Anne Chalmers; three *s*. *Educ:* George Watson's Coll.; Edinburgh Univ. (MA). Asst Principal, Scottish Home Dept, 1950; Private Sec. to Perm. Under-Sec. of State, Scottish Office, 1953-55; Principal, Scottish Home Dept, 1955; Asst Secretary: Scottish Educn Dept, 1963; SHHD, 1971; Asst Under-Sec. of State, Scottish Office, 1974-77. *Address:* 1 Bonaly Drive, Edinburgh EH13 0EJ. *T:* 031-441 2541. *Club:* Royal Commonwealth Society.

WILSON, Isabel Grace Hood, CBE 1961; MD, FRCP; Principal Medical Officer, Ministry of Health, retired; *b* 16 Sept. 1895; *d* of late Dr George R. Wilson and Susan C. Sandeman. *Educ:* privately; University of Edinburgh. MB, ChB, Edinburgh, 1921; DPM London, 1924; MD, Edinburgh, 1926; MRCP London, 1937, FRCP 1947. Formerly: Asst Medical Officer, Severalls Mental Hospital, Colchester; Physician, Tavistock Square Clinic for Functional Nervous Disorders; Medical Commissioner, Board of Control, 1931-49; Senior Medical Commissioner, Board of Control, 1949-60. Member BMA; President, Royal Medico Psychological Assoc., 1962-63. Founder Mem., Royal College of Psychiatrists. *Publications:* A Study of Hypoglycæmic Shock Treatment in Schizophrenia (Report), 1936; (jointly) Report on Cardiazol Treatment, 1938; various contributions to journals. *Recreations:* water-colour painting; travel. *Address:* 48 Redcliffe Gardens, SW10 9HB. *T:* 01-352 5707.

WILSON, James, JP; DSc, BCom, CEng, FIMechE; Industrial Training Consultant, retired; *b* 15 July 1899; *s* of late James Wilson, JP, Lugar and Glasgow; *m* 1930, Jesmar Smith, Clarkston, Glasgow; one *s* two *d. Educ:* Cumnock Academy; Kilmarnock Academy; Glasgow Univ.; Royal Technical Coll. Mech. and Electr. Engrg with Andrew Barclay Sons & Co. Ltd, Kilmarnock (sandwiched with University studies) and Gen. Electric Co., Coventry, 1914-21; Assistant and Lecturer: Royal Technical Coll., Glasgow, 1921, Glasgow Univ., 1921-35; part-time supervisor of science and technology classes, Corp. of Glasgow, 1931-35; Coventry Technical Coll., Vice-Principal, 1935-36; Principal, 1936-46; Principal, Birmingham College of Tech., 1946-56; Director of Education and Training, British Motor Corp. Ltd, 1962-65. OC engineer unit, Glasgow Univ., OTC, 1933-35; OC 71st LAA Battery (TAR), 122 LAA Regt, RA, 1939; Army Welfare Officer, Warwicks, TA, 1940-45; Chairman No. 84 (2nd City of Coventry) ATC, 1945-48; estab. Midland Theatre Company at College Theatre, Coventry, 1945 (in co-operation with Arts Council); founded Playgoers Circle. Member Anglo-American Prod. Assoc. Team "Education for Management", 1951; Mem. Council, Birmingham Productivity Assoc.; Mem., Jt Commn, Nat. Diplomas and Cert. in Business Studies. Ed. The Torch, Glasgow Education Cttee, 1932-35. Hon. MIPlantE; Hon. DSc Aston. *Publications:* (jointly) Gaining Skill; various on education and training, management education, humanism in tech. education. *Recreations:* golf, cinematography, magic. *Address:* 33 Dovehouse Lane, Solihull, West Midlands. *T:* 021-706 5333.

WILSON, Sir James; *see* Wilson, Sir A. J.

WILSON, Brig. James; Chief Executive, Livingston Development Corporation, since 1977; *b* 12 March 1922; *s* of late Alexander Robertson Wilson and Elizabeth Wylie Wilson (*née* Murray); *m* 1949, Audrie Veronica, *er d* of late A. W. and O. V. Haines; three *d. Educ:* Irvine Royal Academy; Edinburgh Academy; Aberdeen Univ. Commissioned RA, 1941; served War with 71 (West Riding) Field Regt, N Africa and Italy, 1941-45; Instructor, Sch. of Artillery, India, 1945-47; Adjt, Sussex Yeo., 1948-49; active service in Malaya and ME, 1950-53; psc 1954; DAQMG, War Office, 1955-57; Instructor, Staff Coll., 1959-61; CO, 439 (Tyne) Light Air Defence Regt, 1964-67; AQMG, Northern Comd, 1967-68; Col GS SD, HQ BAOR, 1969-71; AMA and DCBAS, Washington, 1972-73; DQMG, HQ UKLF, 1974-77. Mem. Executive Council, TCPA (Scotland), 1977-. Dir, Edinburgh Chamber of Commerce, 1979-82. FBIM 1980. *Recreations:* golf, sailing, bridge. *Address:* 10 Merchiston Avenue, Edinburgh EH10 4NY. *T:* 031-229 7017. *Clubs:* Army and Navy; New (Edinburgh).

WILSON, Rt. Hon. Sir (James) Harold, KG 1976; PC 1947; OBE 1945; FRS 1969; MP (Lab) Huyton Division of Lancs since 1950 (Ormskirk Division, 1945-50); Chancellor of Bradford University, since 1966; *b* 11 March 1916; *s* of late James Herbert and Ethel Wilson, Huddersfield, Yorks (formerly of Manchester); *m* 1940, Gladys Mary, *d* of Rev. D. Baldwin, The Manse, Duxford, Cambridge; two *s. Educ:* Milnsbridge Council Sch. and Royds Hall Sch. Huddersfield; Wirral Grammar Sch., Bebington, Cheshire; Jesus Coll., Oxford (Gladstone Memorial Prize, Webb Medley Economics Scholarship, First Class Hons Philosophy, Politics and Economics). Lecturer in Economics, New Coll., Oxford, 1937; Fellow of University Coll., 1938; Praelector in Economics and Domestic Bursar, 1945. Dir of Econs and Stats, Min. of Fuel and Power, 1943-44; Parly Sec. to Ministry of Works, 1945-March 1947; Sec. for Overseas Trade, March-Oct. 1947; Pres., BoT, Oct. 1947-April 1951; Chairman: Labour Party Exec. Cttee, 1961-62; Public Accounts Cttee, 1959-63; Leader, Labour Party, 1963-76; Prime Minister and First Lord of the Treasury, 1964-70, 1974-76; Leader of the Opposition, 1963-64, 1970-74. Chm., Cttee to Review the Functioning of Financial Instns, 1976-80. Pres., Royal Statistical Soc., 1972-73. An Elder Brother of Trinity House, 1968. Hon. Fellow, Jesus and University Colleges, Oxford, 1963. Hon. Freeman, City of London, 1975. Hon. Pres., Great Britain-USSR Assoc., 1976-. Pres., Royal Shakespeare Theatre Co., 1976-. Hon. LLD: Lancaster, 1964; Liverpool, 1965; Nottingham, 1966; Sussex, 1966; Hon. DCL, Oxford, 1965; Hon. DTech., Bradford, 1966; DUniv: Essex, 1967; Open, 1974. *Publications:* New Deal for Coal, 1945; In Place of Dollars, 1952; The War on World Poverty, 1953; The Relevance of British Socialism, 1964; Purpose in Politics, 1964; The New Britain (Penguin), 1964; Purpose in Power, 1966; The Labour Government 1964-70, 1971; The Governance of Britain, 1976; A Prime Minister on Prime Ministers, 1977; Final Term: the Labour Government 1974-76, 1979; The Chariot of Israel, 1981. *Recreation:* golf. *Address:* House of Commons, SW1.

WILSON, Dr James Maxwell Glover, FRCP, FRCPE, FFCM; Senior Principal Medical Officer, Department of Health and Social Security, 1972-76; *b* 31 Aug. 1913; *s* of late James Thomas Wilson and Mabel Salomons; *m* Lallie Methley; three *s. Educ:* King's College Choir Sch., Cambridge; Oundle Sch.; St John's Coll., Cambridge; University College Hosp., London. MA, MB, BChir (Cantab). Clinical appts, London and Cambridge, 1937-39. Served War, RAMC (Major, 6th Airborne Div.), 1939-45. Hospital appts, London and Edinburgh, 1945-54; medical work on tea estates in India, 1954-57; Medical Staff, Min. of Health (later DHSS), concerned with the centrally financed research programme, 1957-76; Sen. Res. Fellow, Inf. Services Div., Common Services Agency, Scottish Health Service, 1976-81. Lectr (part-time), Public Health Dept, London Sch. of Hygiene and Tropical Med., 1968-72. *Publications:* (with G. Jungner) Principles and Practice of Screening for Disease (WHO), 1968; contribs to med. jls, mainly on screening for

disease. *Recreations:* reading, walking, fishing. *Address:* Millhill House, Musselburgh, Midlothian EH21 7RP. *T:* 031-665 5829.

WILSON, James Noel, ChM, FRCS; Consultant Orthopædic Surgeon: Royal National Orthopædic Hospital, London, National Hospitals for Nervous Diseases, Queen Square and Maida Vale, since 1962; and Surgeon i/c of Accident Unit, RNOH, Stanmore, since 1955; Teacher of Orthopædics, Institute of Orthopædics, University of London; *b* Coventry, 25 Dec. 1919; *s* of Alexander Wilson and Isobel Barbara Wilson (*née* Fairweather); *m* 1945, Patricia Norah McCullough; two *s* two *d. Educ:* King Henry VIII Sch., Coventry; University of Birmingham. Peter Thompson Prize in Anatomy, 1940; Sen. Surgical Prize, 1942; Arthur Foxwell Prize in Clinical Medicine, 1943; MB, ChB 1943; MRCS, LRCP, 1943; FRCS 1948; ChM (Birmingham) 1949; House Surgeon, Birmingham General Hospital, 1943; Heaton Award as Best Resident for 1943. Service in RAMC, Nov. 1943-Oct. 1946, discharged as Captain; qualified as Parachutist and served with 1st Airborne Division. Resident surgical posts, Birmingham General Hospital and Coventry and Warwickshire Hospital, 1947-49; Resident Surgical Officer, Robert Jones and Agnes Hunt Orthopædic Hospital, Oswestry, 1949-52; Consultant Orthopædic Surgeon to Cardiff Royal Infirmary and Welsh Regional Hospital Board, 1952-55. President: World Orthopaedic Concern; Orthopaedic Section, RSocMed, 1982-83; former Mem. Brit. Editorial Bd, Jl of Bone and Joint Surgery; Fellow, and formerly Editorial Sec., British Orthopædic Assoc. (BOA Travelling Fellowship to USA, 1954); FRSocMed. *Publications:* Sections in Butterworth's Operative Surgery; (ed) Watson Jones Fractures and Joint Injuries, 6th edn, 1982; articles on orthopædic subjects to various journals. *Recreations:* golf, gardening and photography. *Address:* The Chequers, Waterdale, near Watford, Herts. *T:* Garston 72364. *Club:* Airborne.

WILSON, Air Vice-Marshal James Stewart, CBE 1959; Special Adviser in Epidemiology and Applied Entomology, Institute of Community Medicine, RAF Halton, since 1965; *b* 4 Sept. 1909; *s* of late J. Wilson, Broughty Ferry, Angus, and late Helen Fyffe Wilson; *m* 1937, Elizabeth Elias; one *s* (and one *s* decd). *Educ:* Dundee High Sch.; St Andrews Univ. (MB, ChB). DPH (London) 1948; FFCM(RCP) 1974. House Surgeon, Dundee Royal Infirmary, 1933; House Surgeon, Arbroath Infirmary, 1934; Commissioned Royal Air Force, 1935. Served North Africa, 1942-45. Director Hygiene and Research, Air Ministry, London, 1956-59; Principal Medical Officer, Flying Training Command, 1959-61; Director-General of Medical Services, Royal Australian Air Force, 1961-63. QHP 1961; Principal Medical Officer, Bomber Command, 1963-65, retired. *Publications:* articles (jointly) on respiratory virus infections, in medical journals. *Recreations:* golf, fishing, shooting. *Address:* Eucumbene, Buckland, Aylesbury, Bucks. *T:* Aylesbury 630062. *Club:* Royal Air Force.

WILSON, Sir John (Foster), Kt 1975; CBE 1965 (OBE 1955); Director, Royal Commonwealth Society for the Blind, since 1950; President, International Agency for the Prevention of Blindness, since 1974; *b* 20 Jan. 1919; *s* of late Rev. George Henry Wilson, Buxton, Derbys; *m* 1944, Chloe Jean McDermid, OBE 1981; two *d. Educ:* Worcester College for the Blind; St Catherine's, Oxford (MA Jurisprudence, Dipl. Public and Social Administration). Asst Secretary, Royal National Inst. for the Blind, 1941-49; Member, Colonial Office Delegation investigating blindness in Africa, 1946-47. Proposed formation of Royal Commonwealth Society for Blind; became its first Director, 1950; extensive tours in Africa, Asia, Near and Far East, Caribbean and N. America, 1952-67; world tours, 1958, 1963, 1978; formulated Asian plan for the Blind 1963, and African Plan for the Blind, 1966. Internat. Member of World Council for Welfare of Blind and World Braille Council; Founder Member, National Fedn of Blind (President, 1955-60). Helen Keller International Award, 1970; Lions Internat. Humanitarian Award, 1978; World Humanity Award, 1979; Albert Lasker Award, 1979. *Publications:* Blindness in African and Middle East Territories, 1948; Ghana's Handicapped Citizens, 1961; Travelling Blind, 1963; (ed) World Blindness and its Prevention, 1980; various on Commonwealth affairs, rehabilitation and blindness. *Recreations:* current affairs, travel, writing, tape-recording, wine-making. *Address:* 22 The Cliff, Roedean, Brighton, East Sussex. *T:* Brighton 607667. *Club:* Royal Commonwealth Society.

WILSON, Sir John Gardiner, Kt 1982; CBE 1972; Chairman, Australian Paper Manufacturers Ltd, since 1978; *b* 3 July 1913; *s* of J. S. Wilson; *m* 1944, Margaret Louise De Ravin; three *d. Educ:* Melbourne Grammar Sch.; Clare Coll., Cambridge (MA 1935). Served RAE, AIF, 1939-46, Col. With J. S. Wilson & Co., actuaries and sharebrokers, 1934-39; Mem., Melbourne Stock Exchange, 1935-47; joined Australian Paper Manufacturers, 1947: Dep. Man. Dir, 1953-59; Man. Dir, 1959-78. Director: Vickers Australia; Vickers Cockatoo Dockyard Pty; Qantas Airways. Mem., Aust. Science and Technology Council. *Address:* Australian Paper Manufacturers, GPO Box 1643N, South Gate, Melbourne, Vic 3001, Australia; 6 Woorigoleen Road, Toorak, Vic 3142, Australia. *Clubs:* Melbourne, Australian, Royal Melbourne Golf (Melbourne).

WILSON, Prof. John Graham; Cavendish Professor of Physics, 1963-76 (Professor, 1952-63), Pro-Vice-Chancellor, 1969-71, University of Leeds; now Emeritus Professor; *b* 28 April 1911; *er s* of J. E. Wilson, Hartlepool, Co. Durham; *m* 1938, Georgiana Brooke, *o d* of Charles W. Bird, Bisley, Surrey; one *s* one *d. Educ:* West Hartlepool Secondary Sch.; Sidney Sussex Coll., Cambridge. Member of Teaching staff, University of Manchester, 1938-52;

Reader in Physics, 1951. University of York: Member, Academic Planning Board, 1960-63; Member of Council, 1964-; Chairman, Joint Matriculation Board, 1964-67. DUniv York, 1975; Hon. DSc Durham, 1977. *Publications:* The Principles of Cloud Chamber Technique, 1951. Editor of Progress in Cosmic Ray Physics, 1952-71; (with G. D. Rochester), Cloud Chamber Photographs of the Cosmic Radiation, 1952. Papers on cosmic ray physics, articles in jls. *Recreations:* fell-walking, gardening. *Address:* 23 Newall Hall Park, Otley, West Yorks LS21 2RD. *T:* Otley 465184.

WILSON, J(ohn) Greenwood, MD, FRCP, DPH; Fellow of King's College, University of London; Group Medical Consultant, Health and Hygiene, FMC Ltd; formerly Medical Officer of Health, Port and City of London (first holder of dual appointment; MOH Port of London, 1954, MOH, City of London, in addition, 1956); *b* 27 July 1897; 2nd *s* of late Rev. John Wilson, Woolwich; *m* 1st, 1929, Wenda Margaret Hithersay Smith (marr. diss. 1941); one *s* two *d*; 2nd, 1943, Gwendoline Mary Watkins (*d* 1975); one *d. Educ:* Colfe Grammar Sch.; Westminster Hospital, University of London. Served European War, S. Lancashire Regt, RFC and RAF, 1916-19 (wounded). Various hospital appointments, London and provinces and some general practice, 1923-28; subseq. MOH and Sch. Medical Officer posts; then MOH City and Port of Cardiff, Sch. MO, Cardiff Education Authority, and Lecturer in Preventive Medicine, Welsh Nat. School of Medicine, 1933-54. President, Welsh Br. Society of Med. Officers of Health, 1940-45, Member Nat. Adv. Council for recruitment of Nurses and Midwives, 1943-56. Governor, St Bart's Hospital Medical College. Formerly Examiner in Public Health, RCPS (London); Vice-President (Past Chairman of Council) and Hon. Fellow, Royal Society of Health. Hon. Sec., Assoc. of Sea and Air Port Health Authorities of British Isles, 1936-43; Member, Central Housing Advisory Cttee, 1936-56; Member Royal Commission on Mental Health, 1954-57; Chairman, City Division, BMA, 1962-63; Vice-President (Past Chairman), National House-Building Council. Hon. Fellow American Public Health Association. OStJ 1953. *Publications:* Diptheria Immunisation Propaganda and Counter Propaganda, 1933; Public Health Law in Question and Answer, 1951; numerous contributions to med., scientific and tech. publications. *Recreations:* theatre, music, swimming. *Address:* Flat 2, 10 Beckenham Grove, Bromley BR2 0JU. *T:* 01-460 1532. *Club:* Wig and Pen.

WILSON, Ven. John Hewitt, CB 1977; Canon Emeritus of Lincoln Cathedral, since 1980; Rector of The Heyfords with Rousham and Somerton, diocese of Oxford, since 1981; *b* 14 Feb. 1924; 2nd *s* of John Joseph and Marion Wilson; *m* 1951, Gertrude Elsie Joan Weir; three *s* two *d. Educ:* Kilkenny Coll., Kilkenny; Mountjoy Sch., Dublin; Trinity Coll., Dublin. BA 1946, MA 1956. Curate, St George's Church, Dublin, 1947-50. Entered RAF, 1950: RAF Coll., Cranwell, 1950-52; Aden, 1952-55; RAF Wittering, 1955-57; RAF Cottesmore, 1957-58; RAF Germany, 1958-61; Staff Chaplain, Air Ministry, 1961-63; RAF Coll., Cranwell, 1963-66; Asst Chaplain-in-Chief: Far East Air Force, 1966-69; Strike command, 1969-73; Chaplain-in-Chief, RAF, 1973-80. QHC 1973-80. *Recreations:* Rugby football, tennis, driving, theatre. *Address:* Glencree, Philcote Street, Deddington, Oxford OX5 4TB. *T:* Deddington 38903. *Club:* Royal Air Force.

WILSON, Sir John (Martindale), KCB 1974 (CB 1960); a Vice-President, Civil Service Retirement Fellowship, since 1982; *b* 3 Sept. 1915; *e s* of late John and Kate Wilson; *m* 1941, Penelope Beatrice, *e d* of late Francis A. Bolton, JP, Oakamoor, Staffs; one *s* one *d. Educ:* Bradfield Coll.; Gonville and Caius Coll., Cambridge. BA (Cantab), 1st Class Law Trip., 1937; MA 1946. Asst Principal, Dept of Agriculture for Scotland, 1938; Ministry of Supply, 1939; served War, 1939-46 (despatches) with Royal Artillery in India and Burma; Private Sec. to Minister of Supply, 1946-50; Asst Sec., 1950; Under-Sec., 1954; Cabinet Office, 1955-58; MoD, 1958-60; Dep. Sec., Min. of Aviation, 1961-65; Dep. Under-Sec. of State, MoD, 1965-72; Second Permanent Under-Sec. of State (Admin), MoD, 1972-75. Chairman: Crown Housing Assoc., 1975-78; CS Appeal Bd, 1978-81 (Dep. Chm., 1975-78); Civil Service Retirement Fellowship, 1978-82. *Recreation:* gardening. *Address:* Bourne Close, Bourne Lane, Twyford, near Winchester, Hants. *T:* Twyford 713488. *Club:* Army and Navy.

WILSON, John Spark, CBE 1979 (OBE 1969); Assistant Commissioner, Traffic and Technical Support Department, Metropolitan Police, 1977-82, retired; *b* 9 May 1922; *s* of John Wilson and Elizabeth Kidd Wilson; *m* 1948, Marguerite Chisholm Wilson; two *s* one *d. Educ:* Logie Central Sch., Dundee. Joined Metropolitan Police, 1946; Special Branch, 1948-67; Detective Chief Supt, 1968; Comdr, 1969; went to Wales on Investiture of Prince of Wales, 1969; Dep. Asst Comr (CID), 1972; Asst Comr (Crime), 1975. *Recreations:* football, Rugby, boxing.

WILSON, Prof. John Stuart Gladstone, MA, DipCom; Professor of Economics and Commerce in the University of Hull, 1959-82, now Emeritus Professor; Head of Department, 1959-71, and 1974-77; *b* 18 Aug. 1916; *s* of Herbert Gladstone Wilson and Mary Buchanan Wilson (*née* Wylie); *m* 1943, Beryl Margaret Gibson, *d* of Alexander Millar Gibson and Bertha Noble Gibson; no *c. Educ:* University of Western Australia. Lecturer in Economics: University of Tasmania, 1941-43; Sydney, 1944-45; Canberra, 1946-47; LSE, 1948-49. Reader in Economics, with special reference to Money and Banking, Univ. of London, 1950-59; Dean, Faculty of Social Sciences and Law, Univ. of Hull, 1962-65; Chairman, Centre for S-E Asian Studies, Univ. of Hull, 1963-66. Hackett Research Student, 1947; Leverhulme Research Award, 1955.

Economic Survey of New Hebrides on behalf of Colonial Office, 1958-59; Consultant, Trade and Payments Dept, OECD, 1965-66; Consultant with Harvard Advisory Development Service in Liberia, 1967; headed Enquiry into Sources of Capital and Credit to UK Agriculture, 1970-73; Consultant, Directorate Gen. for Agric., EEC, 1974-75; Specialist Adviser, H of C Select Cttee on Nationalised Industries, 1976; Consultant, Cttee on Financial Markets, OECD, 1979-81; Dir, Centre for Jt Study of Economics, Politics and Sociology, 1980-82; SSRC Grant for comparative study of banking policy and structure, 1977-81; Cttee of Management, Inst. of Commonwealth Studies, London, 1960-77, Hon. Life Mem., 1980; Governor, SOAS, London, 1963-. Member: Yorkshire Council for Further Education, 1963-67; Nat. Advisory Council on Education for Industry and Commerce, 1964-66; Sec.-General, Société Universitaire Européenne de Recherches Financières, 1968-72, Pres., 1973-75, Vice-Pres., 1977-. Editor, Yorkshire Bulletin of Economic and Social Research, 1964-67; Mem., Editorial Adv. Bd, Modern Asian Studies, 1966-. *Publications:* French Banking Structure and Credit Policy, 1957; Economic Environment and Development Programmes, 1960; Monetary Policy and the Development of Money Markets, 1966; Economic Survey of the New Hebrides, 1966; (ed with C. R. Whittlesey) Essays in Money and Banking in Honour of R. S. Sayers, 1968, repr. 1970; Availability of Capital and Credit to United Kingdom Agriculture, 1973; (ed with C. F. Scheffer) Multinational Enterprises—Financial and Monetary Aspects, 1974; Credit to Agriculture—United Kingdom, 1975; The London Money Markets, 1976; (ed with J. E. Wadsworth and H. Fournier) The Development of Financial Institutions in Europe, 1956-1976, 1977; Industrial Banking: a comparative survey, 1978; contribs. to Banking in the British Commonwealth (ed R. S. Sayers), 1952 and to Banking in Western Europe (ed R. S. Sayers), 1962; A Decade of the Commonwealth, 1955-64, ed W. B. Hamilton and others, 1966; to International Encyclopaedia of the Social Sciences; Encyclopaedia Britannica, 15th edn; Economica, Economic Journal, Journal of Political Econ., Economic Record. *Recreations:* gardening, theatre, art galleries, photography. *Address:* Department of Economics and Commerce, The University, Hull, North Humberside. *Club:* Reform.

WILSON, John Tuzo, CC (Canada) 1974; OBE 1946; FRS 1968; FRSC 1949; Professor of Geophysics, University of Toronto, 1946-74, Emeritus Professor, 1977; Director-General, Ontario Science Centre, since 1974; *b* Ottawa, 24 Oct. 1908; *s* of John Armitstead Wilson, CBE, and Henrietta L. Tuzo; *m* 1938, Isabel Jean Dickson; two *d. Educ:* Ottawa; Universities of Toronto (Governor-General's medal, Trinity Coll., 1930; Massey Fellow, 1930), Cambridge (ScD), and Princeton (PhD). Asst Geologist, Geological Survey of Canada, 1936-46; Principal, Erindale Coll., Univ. of Toronto, 1968-74. Regimental service and staff appointments, Royal Canadian Engrs, UK and Sicily, 1939-43; Director, Opl. Research, Nat. Defence HQ, Ottawa (Colonel), 1944-46. President, International Union of Geodesy and Geophysics, 1957-60; Visiting Prof.: Australian Nat. Univ., 1950 and 1965; Ohio State Univ., 1968; California Inst. of Technology, 1976. Member Nat. Research Council of Canada, 1957-63; Member Defence Res. Board, 1958-64. Canadian Delegation to Gen. Ass., UNESCO, 1962, 1964, 1966. President: Royal Society of Canada, 1972-73; Amer. Geophysical Union, 1980-82. Overseas Fellow, Churchill Coll., Cambridge, 1965; Trustee, Nat. Museums of Canada, 1968-74. Hon. Fellow: Trinity Coll., University of Toronto, 1962; St John's Coll., Cambridge, 1981. Foreign Associate, Nat. Acad. of Sciences, USA, 1968; Foreign Hon. Mem., Amer. Acad. of Arts and Sciences; For. Mem., Royal Swedish Acad. of Sciences, 1981; Associé, Académie Royale de Belgique, 1981. Holds hon. doctorates and hon. or foreign memberships and medals, etc, in Canada and abroad. Vetlesen Prize, Columbia Univ., 1978. OC (Canada) 1970. *Publications:* One Chinese Moon, 1959; Physics and Geology (with J. A. Jacobs and R. D. Russell), 1959; IGY Year of the New Moons, 1961; (ed) Continents Adrift, 1972; Unglazed China, 1973; (ed) Continents Adrift and Continents Aground, 1976; scientific papers. *Recreations:* travel, sailing Hong Kong junk. *Address:* 27 Pricefield Road, Toronto M4W 1Z8, Canada. *T:* 923-4244. *Clubs:* Arts and Letters, York (Toronto).

WILSON, John Veitch D.; *see* Drysdale Wilson.

WILSON, John Warley; a Recorder of the Crown Court, since 1979; barrister-at-law; *b* 13 April 1936; *s* of John Pearson Wilson and Nancy Wade Wilson (*née* Harston); *m* 1962, Rosalind Mary Pulford. *Educ:* Warwick Sch.; St Catharine's Coll., Cambridge (MA). Called to the Bar, Lincoln's Inn, 1960, in practice, 1960-. Dep. Chairman, West Midlands Agricultural Land Tribunal, 1978-. *Recreations:* gardening, golf. *Address:* Victoria House, Farm Street, Harbury, Leamington Spa CV33 9LR. *T:* Harbury 612572.

WILSON, Joseph Albert; Secretary to the Cabinet, Sierra Leone Government, 1968; Barrister-at-Law; *b* 22 Jan. 1922; *e s* of late George Wilson; *m* 1947, Esther Massaquoi; two *s* four *d* (and one *s* decd). *Educ:* St Edward's Secondary Sch., Freetown, Sierra Leone; University of Exeter, (DPA); Middle Temple. Graded Clerical Service, Sierra Leone Government, 1941-47; family business, 1948-51; Secretary, Bonthe District Council, 1951-59; Administrative Officer, Sierra Leone Government, rising to rank of Cabinet Secretary, 1959-; High Comr from Sierra Leone to UK, 1967-68. Manager (Special Duties), SLST Ltd, 1959; Dir, National Diamond Mining Co. (Sierra Leone) Ltd. Mem., Court of Univ. of Sierra Leone. *Recreations:* tennis, golf. *Address:* 14 Syke Street, Brookfields, Freetown, Sierra Leone. *T:* 2590.

WILSON, Sir Keith (Cameron), Kt 1966; Member of House of Representatives for Sturt, South Australia, 1949-54, 1955-66; *b* 3 Sept. 1900;

s of Algernon Theodore King Wilson; *m* 1930, Elizabeth H., *d* of late Sir Lavington Bonython; two *s* one *d. Educ:* Collegiate School of St Peter, Adelaide; University of Adelaide. LLB 1922. Admitted to Bar, 1922. Served War of 1939-45: Gunner, 2nd AIF, 1940; Middle East, 1940-43; Major. Senator for South Australia, 1938-44. Chm., Aged Cottage Homes Inc., 1952-71; Past President: Blinded Welfare Fund; Good Neighbour Council of SA, 1968-72; Queen Elizabeth Hosp. Research Foundn; Legacy. *Publication:* Wilson-Uppill Wheat Equalization Scheme, 1938. *Address:* 79 Tusmore Avenue, Tusmore, SA 5065, Australia. *T:* 315578. *Club:* Adelaide (Adelaide).

WILSON, Sir (Leslie) Hugh, Kt 1967; OBE 1952; RIBA; FRTPI; Architect and Town Planner; Senior Partner, Hugh Wilson & Lewis Womersley, Chartered Architects and Town Planners, since 1962; *b* 1 May 1913; *s* of Frederick Charles Wilson and Ethel Anne Hughes; *m* 1938, Monica Chrysavye Nomico (*d* 1966); one *s* two *d. Educ:* Haberdashers' Aske's Sch. Asst Architect, private practices, 1933-39; Asst Architect, Canterbury, 1939-45; City Architect and Planning Officer, Canterbury, 1945-56; Chief Architect and Planning Officer, Cumbernauld New Town, 1956-62. Techn. Adviser on Urban Development to Min. of Housing and Local Government, 1965-67. Works include housing, churches, central area develt; Master Plans for Irvine, Skelmersdale, Redditch, and Northampton New Towns; central area plans for Oxford, Brighton, Exeter, Lewes, Cardiff, Torbay. Dir (part-time), Property Services Agency, DoE, 1973-74. Member: EDC for Building, NEDO, 1970-77; Royal Fine Art Commn, 1971-; Environmental Bd, 1975-79; Chm., London Docklands Jt Cttee, 1977-81; Mem., London Dockyards Develt Corp., 1981-. Vice-President, RIBA, 1960-61, 1962-64, Sen. Vice-President, 1966-67, President, 1967-69. DistTP 1956. Hon. FRAIC; Hon. FAIA; Hon. FIStructE; Hon. FICIOB; Hon. FCIBS; Hon. Mem., Akademie der Künste, Berlin. Hon. DSc Aston, 1969. *Recreations:* travel, music. *Address:* 2 Kings Well, Heath Street, Hampstead, NW3 1EN. *T:* 01-435 3637. *Club:* Athenæum.

WILSON, Canon Leslie Rule; Hon. Canon of Holy Cross Cathedral, Geraldton, since 1966; *b* 19 July 1909; *y s* of Rev. John and Mary Adelaide Wilson. *Educ:* Royal Grammar Sch., Newcastle upon Tyne; University College, Durham; Edinburgh Theological College. Asst Priest, Old St Paul's, Edinburgh, 1934-36; Rector of Fort William, 1936; Canon of Argyll and The Isles, 1940-42; Education Officer, 1942-45; Welfare Officer, SEAC (Toc H), 1945-46; Vicar of Malacca, Malaya, 1946-50; Principal Probation Officer, Federation of Malaya, 1950-52; Vicar of Kuching, Sarawak, 1952-55; Provost and Canon of St Thomas' Cathedral, Kuching, 1955-59; Rector of Geraldton, W Australia, 1960-64; Dean of Geraldton, 1964-66 (Administrator, Diocese of NW Australia, 1966); Archdeacon of Carpentaria, 1966-67; Rector of Winterbourne Stickland with Turnworth and Winterbourne Houghton, 1967-69; Vicar of Holmside, 1969-74. Founder and Chairman, Parson Woodforde Society, 1968-75 (Hon. Life Pres., 1975). *Recreations:* reading, genealogy. *Address:* Holmside, 12 Townsend Close, St Briavels, Lydney, Glos GL15 6TJ. *T:* Dean 530970.

WILSON, Leslie William, JP; Director-General, Association of Special Libraries and Information Bureaux (Aslib), 1950-78, retired; *b* 26 Sept. 1918; *s* of Harry Wilson and Ada Jane Wilson; *m* 1942, Valerie Jones; one *s* two *d. Educ:* Cambridgeshire High Sch.; Trinity Hall, Cambridge (Open Scholar, MA Mod. Langs). Army Service, India, 1940-46. Foreign Editor, Times Educnl Supplement, 1946-50. Hon. Fellow, Internat. Fedn for Documentation, 1978; Hon. Member: Inst. of Information Scientists, 1977; US Special Libraries Assoc., 1978; Aslib, 1978. JP Mddx, 1971. *Publications:* publ. extensively in scientific and library jls. *Recreations:* travel, gardening. *Address:* 29 St Peter's Road, St Margaret's-on-Thames, Mddx TW1 1QY. *T:* 01-892 6742.

WILSON, Rt. Rev. Lucian C. U.; *see* Usher-Wilson.

WILSON, Sir (Mathew) Martin, 5th Bt, *cr* 1874; *b* 2 July 1906; *s* of Lieut-Colonel Sir Mathew Richard Henry Wilson, 4th Bt, and Hon. Barbara Lister (*d* 1943), *d* of 4th Baron Ribblesdale; *S* father, 1958. *Educ:* Eton. *Heir: nephew* Brig. Mathew John Anthony Wilson, OBE, MC [*b* 2 Oct. 1935; *m* 1962, Janet Mary, *e d* of late E. W. Mowll, JP; one *s* one *d*]. *Address:* 1 Sandgate Esplanade, Folkestone, Kent.

WILSON, Sir Michael (Thomond), Kt 1975; MBE 1945; a Vice-Chairman: Lloyds Bank Ltd, 1973-81 (a Director, 1968-81; Chief General Manager, 1967-73); Lloyds & Scottish Ltd, 1976-81; Director: Lloyds Bank International Ltd, 1973-81; Yorkshire Bank Ltd, 1973-79; *b* 7 Feb. 1911; *e s* of late Sir Roy Wilson, Pyrford, near Woking; *m* 1933, Jessie Babette, *o d* of late John Winston Foley Winnington, Malvern, Worcs; two *s* one *d. Educ:* Rugby Sch.; Oriel Coll., Oxford. War Service with RA and on Staff in UK and India, 1939-45. Entered Lloyds Bank, 1932; Assistant General Manager, 1958; Dep. Chief General Manager, 1963. Chm., Export Guarantees Adv. Council, 1972-77. JP Berks, 1952-66. *Address:* Clytha, South Ascot, Berks. *T:* Ascot 20833.

WILSON, Nigel Guy, FBA 1980; Fellow and Tutor in Classics, Lincoln College, Oxford, since 1962; *b* 23 July 1935; *s* of Noel Wilson and Joan Lovibond. *Educ:* University Coll. Sch.; Corpus Christi Coll., Oxford (1st Cl. Classics (Mods) 1955; 1st Cl. Lit. Hum. 1957; Hertford Scholar 1955; Ireland and Craven Scholar 1955; Derby Scholar 1957). Lectr, Merton Coll., Oxford,

1957-62. Jt Editor, Classical Rev., 1975-. Ospite Linceo, Scuola normale superiore, Pisa, 1977. Gordon Duff Prize, 1968. *Publications:* (with L. D. Reynolds) Scribes and Scholars, 1968, 2nd edn 1974; An Anthology of Byzantine Prose, 1971; Medieval Greek Bookhands, 1973; St Basil on the Value of Greek Literature, 1975; Scholia in Aristophanis Acharnenses, 1975; (with D. A. Russell) Menander Rhetor, 1981; articles and reviews in various learned jls. *Recreations:* bridge, squash. *Address:* Lincoln College, Oxford. *T:* Oxford 241763.

WILSON, Norman George, CMG 1966; Commercial Director, ICI of Australia Ltd, 1972-73; Deputy Chairman, Fibremakers Ltd, 1972-73; *b* 20 Oct. 1911; *s* of P. Wilson; *m* 1939, Dorothy Gwen, *d* of late Sir W. Lennon Raws; one *s* two *d. Educ:* Melbourne University (BCE). Joined ICI Australia Ltd, 1935: Exec. positions, 1936-48; General Manager, Dyes and Plastics Group, 1949-54; Director, 1959-73; Managing Director: Dulux Pty Ltd, 1954-62; Fibremakers Ltd, 1962-72. Business Adviser to Dept of Air, and Dep. Chm. Defence Business Board, Commonwealth Government, 1957-76; Chairman Production Board, Dept of Manufacturing Industries, Commonwealth Government, 1960-76. Mem., Export Develt Council, Dept of Trade and Industry, Commonwealth Govt, 1966-72. Mem. Bd, Victorian Railways, 1973-; Dep. Chm., Victorian Conservation Trust, 1973-. FInstD, FAIM. *Recreations:* golf, farming. *Address:* Apartment 14, 18 Lansell Road, Toorak, Victoria 3142, Australia. *T:* Melbourne 24-4438; The Highlands, Kerrie, Romsey, Vic 3434, Australia. *T:* 054 270232. *Clubs:* Australian (Melbourne); Royal Melbourne Golf, Melbourne Cricket, Victoria Racing.

WILSON, Percy, CB 1955; Senior Chief Inspector of Schools for England and Wales, Department of Education and Science, 1957-65; Director of Education, Bank Education Service, 1965-79, Consultant, 1979-81; *b* 15 Dec. 1904; *s* of Joseph Edwin and Louisa Wilson; *m* 1st, 1929, Beryl Godsell (decd); 2nd, 1943, Dorothy Spiers; one *s* one *d. Educ:* Market Rasen Grammar Sch.; Jesus Coll., Cambridge. Schoolmaster, 1927-35; HM Inspector of Schools, 1935-45 (seconded to war duties, 1939-42); Staff Inspector for English, 1945-47; a Chief Inspector, Ministry of Education, 1947-57. Hon. FCP, 1965. A Governor, Wellington Coll., 1966-75. *Publication:* Views and Prospects from Curzon Street, 1964. *Recreation:* painting. *Address:* The Cottage, Walcot Lane, Drakes Broughton, Pershore, Worcs. *T:* Worcester 840265.

WILSON, Peter Cecil, CBE 1970; Director: Sotheby & Co., since 1938 (Chairman, 1958-80, Honorary Life President, since 1982); SPB Group, since 1977 (Chairman, 1977-80); *b* 8 March 1913; 3rd *s* of Sir Matthew Wilson, 4th Bt, CSI, DSO, Eshton Hall, Gargrave, Yorkshire; *m* 1935, Grace Helen Ranken (marr. diss.); two *s. Educ:* Eton; New Coll., Oxford. Benjamin Franklin Medal, RSA 1968. *Address:* Chateau de Clavary, 06810 Auribeau sur Siagne, France.
See also Sir M. M. Wilson.

WILSON, Peter Humphrey St John, CB 1956; CBE 1952; Deputy Under Secretary of State, Department of Employment and Productivity, 1968-69, retired (Deputy Secretary, Ministry of Labour, 1958-68); *b* 1 May 1908; *e s* of late Rt Rev. Henry A. Wilson, CBE, DD; *m* 1939, Catherine Laird (*d* 1963), *d* of late H. J. Bonser, London; three *d. Educ:* Cheltenham Coll. (Schol.); Corpus Christi Coll., Cambridge (Foundation Schol.). Assistant Principal, Ministry of Labour, 1930; Principal, 1936; Regional Controller, Northern Region, 1941; Controller, Scotland, 1944; Under Secretary, 1952. *Recreations:* reading, music, grand-children. *Address:* Thorntree Cottage, Blackheath, near Guildford, Surrey. *T:* Guildford 893758.

WILSON, Quintin Campbell, OBE 1975; HM Inspector of Constabulary for Scotland, 1975-79; *b* 19 Nov. 1913; *s* of William Wilson and Mary (*née* Cowan); *m* 1939, Adelia Campbell Scott; two *s. Educ:* Barr Primary Sch.; Girvan High Sch. Halifax Borough Police, April 1936; Ayrshire Constabulary, Nov. 1936; Chief Supt, Police Research and Planning Branch, Home Office, London, 1965; Dep. Chief Constable, Ayrshire, 1966; Chief Constable, Ayrshire, 1968-75. *Recreation:* golf. *Address:* 15 Portmark Avenue, Alloway, Ayr KA7 4DN. *T:* Alloway 43034.

WILSON, Prof. Raymond; Professor of Education, since 1968, Chairman of School of Education, 1969-76 and since 1980, University of Reading; *b* 20 Dec. 1925; *s* of John William Wilson and Edith (*née* Walker); *m* 1950, Gertrude Mary Russell; two *s* one *d. Educ:* London Univ. (BA English, 1st Cl.). Teacher, secondary schs, 1950-57; English Master, subseq. Chief English Master, Dulwich Coll., 1957-65; Lectr, Southampton Univ., 1965-68. *Publications:* numerous textbooks and anthologies; papers on English and related studies; occasional poet. *Address:* Roselawn, Shiplake, Henley-on-Thames, Oxon. *T:* Wargrave 2528. *Club:* Royal Commonwealth Society.

WILSON, Sir Reginald (Holmes), Kt 1951; BCom; FCIT; CBIM; Scottish Chartered Accountant; Director of business and finance companies; *b* 1905; *o s* of Alexander Wilson and Emily Holmes Wilson; *m* 1st, 1930, Rose Marie von Arnim; one *s* one *d* ; 2nd, 1938, Sonia Havell. *Educ:* St Peter's Sch., Panchgani; St Lawrence, Ramsgate; London Univ. BCom. Partner in Whinney Murray & Co., 1937-72; HM Treasury, 1940; Principal Assistant Secretary, Ministry of Shipping, 1941; Director of Finance, Ministry of War Transport, 1941; Under-Secretary, Ministry of Transport, 1945; returned to City, 1946; Joint Financial Adviser, Ministry of Transport, 1946; Member of Royal Commission on Press, 1946; Vice-Chairman, Hemel Hempstead

Development Corporation, 1946-56; Adviser on Special Matters, CCG, 1947. Comptroller BTC, 1947, Member BTC, 1953, Chm. E Area Board, 1955-60, Chm. London Midland Area Board, 1960-62; Dep. Chm. and Man. Dir, Transport Holding Co., 1962-67; Chairman: Transport Holding Co., 1967-70; Nat. Freight Corp., 1969-70; Transport Develt Gp, 1971-74 (Dep. Chm., 1970-71); Thos Cook & Son Ltd, 1967-76. Mem., Cttee of Enquiry into Civil Air Transport, 1967-69. Chm., Bd for Simplification of Internat. Trade Procedures, 1976-79. Award of Merit, Inst. Transport, 1953; President, Inst. Transport, 1957-58. Governor, LSE, 1954-58; Chairman, Board of Governors: Hospitals for Diseases of the Chest, 1960-71; National Heart Hospital, 1968-71; National Heart and Chest Hospitals, 1971-80; Chm., Cardiothoracic Inst., 1960-80; UK Rep., Council of Management, Internat. Hosp. Fedn, 1973-79. *Publications*: various papers on transport matters. *Recreations*: music, walking. *Address*: 49 Gloucester Square, W2 2TQ. *Clubs*: Athenæum, Oriental.

WILSON, Prof. Richard Middlewood; Professor of English Language, University of Sheffield, 1955-73; *b* 20 Sept. 1908; *e s* of late R. L. Wilson, The Grange, Kilham, Driffield, E Yorks; *m* 1938, Dorothy Muriel, *y d* of late C. E. Leeson, Eastgate House, Kilham, Driffield; one *d*. *Educ*: Woodhouse Grove School; Leeds University. Asst Lecturer, Leeds Univ., 1931, Lecturer, 1936; Senior Lecturer and Head of Dept of English Language, Sheffield Univ., 1946. *Publications*: Sawles Warde, 1939; Early Middle English Literature, 1939; (with B. Dickins) Early Middle English Texts, 1951; The Lost Literature of Medieval England, 1952; (with D. J. Price) The Equatorie of the Planetis, 1955; articles and reviews. *Recreation*: cricket. *Address*: 9 Endcliffe Vale Avenue, Sheffield S11 8RX. *T*: Sheffield 663431.

WILSON, Prof. Robert, CBE 1978; FRS 1975; Perren Professor of Astronomy and Director of the Observatories, University College London, since 1972; *s* of Robert Graham Wilson and Anne Wilson. *Educ*: King's Coll., Newcastle upon Tyne; Univ. of Edinburgh. BSc (Physics), Newcastle, 1948; PhD (Astrophysics), Edin., 1952. SSO, Royal Observatory, Edinburgh, 1952-57; Research Fellow, Dominion Astrophysical Observatory, Canada, 1957-58; Leader of Plasma Spectroscopy Gp, CTR Div., Harwell, 1959-61; Head of Spectroscopy Div., Culham Laboratory, 1962-68; Head of Science Research Council's Astrophysics Research Unit, Culham, 1968-72. Foreign Mem., Société Royale des Sciences, Liège; Vice-Pres., Internat. Astronomical Union. *Publications*: papers in many jls on: optical astronomy, plasma spectroscopy, solar physics, ultraviolet astronomy.

WILSON, Robert Andrew, CB 1962; Principal Keeper, Department of Printed Books, British Museum, 1959-66; *b* 18 July 1905; *s* of Robert Bruce Wilson; *m* 1967, Rosemary Ann, *d* of Sydney Joseph Norris. *Educ*: Westminster School; Trinity College, Cambridge. Assistant Keeper, Department of Printed Books, British Museum, 1929-48, Deputy Keeper, 1948-52; also Superintendent of the Reading Room, British Museum, 1948-52; Keeper, 1952-59. *Address*: 33 Denmark Avenue, Wimbledon, SW19.

WILSON, Robert Donald; farmer; Chairman: Mersey Regional Health Authority, since 1982; Electricity Consultative Council (North West), since 1981; *b* 6 June 1922; *s* of John and Kate Wilson; *m* 1946, E. Elizabeth. *Educ*: Grove Park Sch., Wrexham, Clwyd. Served RAF, 1940-46. Tyre industry, 1946-60; farming, 1954-; Director of various farming and property companies; Member of Lloyd's, 1970-; Board Mem. (part-time), North West Electricity Bd (NORWEB), 1981-; Vice-Chm. Governors, Cheshire College of Agriculture, 1980-; Chm., Cheshire Br. Country Landowners Assoc., 1980-. *Recreations*: fishing, shooting. *Address*: The Oldfields, Pulford, Chester, Cheshire CH4 9EJ. *T*: Rossett 570207.

WILSON, (Robert) Gordon; MP (SNP) Dundee East since Feb. 1974; Chairman, Scottish National Party, since 1979; formerly solicitor in private practice; *b* 16 April 1938; *s* of R. G. Wilson; *m* 1965, Edith M. Hassall; two *d*. *Educ*: Douglas High Sch.; Edinburgh Univ. (BL). Nat. Sec., SNP, 1963-71; Exec. Vice-Chm., 1972-73; Sen. Vice-Chm., 1973-74; Chm., 1979-. SNP Parly Spokesman: on Energy, 1974-; on Home Affairs, 1975-76; on Devolution (jt responsibility), 1976-79. Dep. Leader, SNP, 1974-79. *Recreations*: reading, sailing. *Address*: 48 Monifieth Road, Broughty Ferry, Dundee DD5 2RX. *T*: Dundee 79009; 01-219 3494/4474.

WILSON, Prof. Robert McLachlan, PhD; FBA 1977; Professor of Biblical Criticism, University of St Andrews, since 1978; *b* 13 Feb. 1916; *er s* of Hugh McL. Wilson and Janet N. (*née* Struthers); *m* 1945, Enid Mary, *d* of Rev. and Mrs F. J. Bomford, Bournemouth, Hants; two *s*. *Educ*: Greenock Acad.; Royal High Sch., Edinburgh; Univ. of Edinburgh (MA 1939, BD 1942); Univ. of Cambridge (PhD 1945). Minister of Rankin Church, Strathaven, Lanarkshire, 1946-54; Lectr in New Testament Language and Literature, St Mary's Coll., Univ. of St Andrews, 1954, Sen. Lectr, 1964, Prof., 1969-78. Vis. Prof., Vanderbilt Divinity Sch., Nashville, Tenn, 1964-65. Pres., Studiorum Novi Testamenti Societas, 1981-82. Hon. Mem., Soc. of Biblical Literature, 1972-. Associate Editor, New Testament Studies, 1967-77, Editor 1977-; Mem., Internat. Cttee for publication of Nag Hammadi Codices, and of Editorial Bd of Nag Hammadi Studies monograph series. Hon. DD Aberdeen, 1982. *Publications*: The Gnostic Problem, 1958; Studies in the Gospel of Thomas, 1960; The Gospel of Philip, 1962; Gnosis and the New Testament, 1968; (ed) English trans., Hennecke-Schneemelcher, NT Apocrypha: vol. 1, 1963 (2nd edn 1973); vol. 2, 1965 (2nd edn 1974); (ed) English trans., Haenchen, The Acts of the Apostles, 1971; (ed) English trans., Foerster, Gnosis:

vol. 1, 1972; vol. 2, 1974; (ed and trans., jtly) Jung Codex treatises: De Resurrectione, 1963; Epistula Jacobi Apocrypha, 1968; Tractatus Tripartitus, pars I, 1973, partes II et III, 1975; (ed) Nag Hammadi and Gnosis, 1978; (ed) The Future of Coptology, 1978; (ed jtly) Text and Interpretation, 1979; articles in British, Amer. and continental jls. *Recreation*: golf. *Address*: 10 Murrayfield Road, St Andrews, Fife. *T*: St Andrews 74331.

WILSON, Dr Robert Woodrow; Head, Radio Physics Research Department, Bell Laboratories, since 1976; *b* 10 Jan. 1936; *s* of Ralph Woodrow Wilson and Fannie May Willis; *m* 1958, Elizabeth Rhoads Sawin; two *s* one *d*. *Educ*: Rice Univ. (BA Physics, 1957); Calif Inst. of Technol. (PhD 1962). Post-doctoral Fellowship, Calif Inst. of Technol., 1962-63; Mem. Technical Staff, Bell Labs, Holmdel, NJ, 1963-76. Member: φβκ; Amer. Acad. of Arts and Sciences, 1978; US Nat. Acad. of Science, 1979. Hon. degrees: Monmouth Coll., 1979; Jersey City State Coll., 1979; Thiel Coll., 1980. Henry Draper Award, 1977; Herschel Award, RAS, 1977; (jtly) Nobel Prize for Physics, 1978. *Publications*: contrib. to Astrophys. Jl, Science, and Bell System Technical Jl. *Recreations*: running, skiing, playing the piano. *Address*: 9 Valley Point Drive, Holmdel, NJ 07733, USA. *T*: (201) 671-7807.

WILSON, Prof. Roger Cowan; Professor of Education, University of Bristol, 1951-71, Emeritus 1971; Visiting Professor: University of Malawi, 1966; Harvard University, 1968; *b* 3 August 1906; 2nd *s* of Alexander Cowan Wilson and Edith Jane Brayshaw; *m* 1931, Margery Lilian, *y d* of late Rev. C. W. Emmet, Fellow of University College, Oxford, and Gertrude Weir; one *s* one *d*. *Educ*: Manchester Grammar School; The Queen's College, Oxford (Exhibitioner); Manchester College of Technology. Chairman, OU Labour Club, 1927; President, Oxford Union, 1929; First Cl. in Philosophy, Politics and Economics, 1929. Apprentice in Cotton Industry, 1929-35; Talks Staff of BBC, 1935-40; dismissed from BBC as conscientious objector; General Secretary, Friends Relief Service, 1940-46; head of Dept of Social Studies, University College, Hull, 1946-51. Mem., Colonial Office and Min. of Overseas Develt adv. cttees and consultative missions, 1957-71. Senior Adviser on Social Affairs, United Nations Operation in the Congo, 1961-62. Chairman: Bd of Visitors, Shepton Mallet Prison, 1966-70; Council for Voluntary Action, South Lakeland, 1974-79; Cumbria Council on Alcoholism, 1979-81; Clerk, London Yearly Meeting of Society of Friends, 1975-78. JP Bristol, 1954-67. Médaille de la Reconnaisance Française, 1948. *Publications*: Frank Lenwood, a biography, 1936; Authority, Leadership and Concern, a study of motive and administration in Quaker relief work, 1948; Quaker Relief, 1940-48, 1952; The Teacher: instructor or educator, 1952; (with Kuenstler and others) Social Group Work in Great Britain, 1955; Difficult Housing Estates, 1963; Jesus the Liberator, 1981. *Recreations*: gardener's boy, walking, Quaker interests. *Address*: Peter Hill House, Yealand Conyers, near Carnforth, Lancs. *T*: Carnforth 733519.

See also D. M. Emmet, J. E. Meade, Sir Geoffrey Wilson *and* S. S. Wilson.

WILSON, Rt. Rev. Roger Plumpton, KCVO 1974; DD (Lambeth), 1949; Clerk of the Closet to the Queen, 1963-75; *b* 3 Aug. 1905; *s* of Canon Clifford Plumpton Wilson, Bristol, and Hester Marion Wansey; *m* 1935, Mabel Joyce Avery, Leigh Woods, Bristol; two *s* one *d*. *Educ*: Winchester Coll. (Exhibitioner); Keble Coll., Oxford (Classical Scholar). Hon. Mods in Classics 1st Class, Lit. Hum. 2nd Class, BA 1928; MA 1932. Classical Master, Shrewsbury Sch., 1928-30, 1932-34; Classical Master, St Andrew's Coll., Grahamstown, S Africa, 1930-32. Deacon, 1935; Priest, 1936; Curacies: St Paul's, Prince's Park, Liverpool, 1935-38; St John's, Smith Square, SW1, 1938-39; Vicar of South Shore, Blackpool, 1939-45; Archdeacon of Nottingham and Vicar of Radcliffe on Trent, 1945-49; also Vicar of Shelford (in plurality), 1946-49; Bishop of Wakefield, 1949-58; Bishop of Chichester, 1958-74. Chm., Church of England Schools Council, 1957-71; Mem., Presidium, Conf. of European Churches, 1967-74. *Recreations*: Oxford University Authentics Cricket Club, Oxford University Centaurs Football Club, golf. *Address*: Kingsett, Wrington, Bristol. *Club*: Royal Commonwealth Society.

WILSON, Sir Roland, KBE 1965 (CBE 1941); Kt 1955; Chairman: Commonwealth Banking Corporation, 1966-75; Qantas Airways Ltd, 1966-73; Wentworth Hotel, 1966-73; Director: The MLC Ltd, 1969-79; ICI Australia, 1967-74; economic and financial consultant; *b* Ulverstone, Tasmania, 7 April 1904; *s* of Thomas Wilson; *m* 1930, Valeska (*d* 1971), *d* of William Thompson; *m* 1975, Joyce, *d* of Clarence Henry Chivers. *Educ*: Devonport High School; Univ. of Tasmania; Oriel College, Oxford; Chicago University. Rhodes Scholar for Tasmania, 1925; BCom 1926, Univ. of Tasmania; Dipl. in Economics and Political Science 1926, and DPhil 1929, Oxon; Commonwealth Fund Fellow, 1928, and PhD 1930, Chicago. Pitt Cobbett Lecturer in Economics, Univ. of Tasmania, 1930-32; Director of Tutorial Classes, Univ. of Tasmania, 1931-32; Asst Commonwealth Statistician and Economist, 1932; Economist, Statistician's Branch, Commonwealth Treasury, 1933; Commonwealth Statistician and Economic Adviser to the Treasury, Commonwealth of Australia, 1936-40 and 1946-51; Sec. to Dept Labour and Nat. Service, 1941-46; Chairman Economic and Employment Commission, United Nations, 1948-49. Secretary to Treasury, Commonwealth of Australia, 1951-66; Member Bd: Commonwealth Bank of Australia, 1951-59; Reserve Bank of Australia, 1960-66; Qantas Empire Airways, 1954-73; Commonwealth Banking Corp., 1960-75. Hon. LLD Tasmania, 1969. *Publications*: Capital Imports and the Terms of Trade, 1931; Public and Private Investment in Australia, 1939; Facts and Fancies of

Productivity, 1946. *Address:* 64 Empire Circuit, Forrest, Canberra, ACT 2603, Australia. *T:* 95-2560. *Club:* Commonwealth (Canberra).

WILSON, Maj.-Gen. (Ronald) Dare, CBE 1968 (MBE 1949); MC 1945; MA Cantab; DL; retired; current interests farming, forestry and worldwide national park research; *b* 3 Aug. 1919; *s* of Sydney E. D. Wilson and Dorothea, *d* of George Burgess; *m* 1973, Sarah, *d* of Sir Peter Stallard, *qv* ; one *s. Educ:* Shrewsbury Sch.; St John's Coll. Cambridge (Pt I 1939, BA 1972). Commissioned into Royal Northumberland Fusiliers, 1939; served War, 1939-45: BEF 1940, ME and NW Europe (MC, despatches 1946); 6th Airborne Div., 1945-48; 1st Bn Parachute Regt, 1949; MoD, 1950; Royal Northumberland Fusiliers: Korea, 1951; Kenya, 1953; GSO2, Staff Coll., Camberley, 1954-56; AA&QMG, 3rd Div., 1958-59; comd 22 Special Air Service Regt, 1960-62; Canadian Nat. Defence Coll., 1962-63; Col GS 1(BR) Corps BAOR, 1963-65; comd 149 Infantry Bde (TA), 1966-67; Brig. 1966; Brig., AQ ME Comd, 1967; Maj.-Gen. 1968; Dir, Land/Air Warfare, MoD, 1968-69; Dir, Army Aviation, MoD, 1970-71. Exmoor Nat. Park Officer, 1974-78. Mem., UK Cttee for Internat. Nature Conservation; Consultant to Fedn of Nature and Nat. Parks of Europe. Church Warden, Church of St George, Morebath, Devon. Helicopter and light aircraft pilot; Mem., Army Cresta Run Team and Army Rifle VIII; captained British Free-Fall Parachute Team, 1962-65; Chm., British Parachute Assoc., 1962-65. FRGS. DL Somerset, 1979. Royal Aero Club Silver Medal, 1967. *Publications:* Cordon and Search, 1948; contribs to military jls. *Recreations:* country pursuits, travelling, winter sports. *Address:* Combeland, Dulverton, Somerset. *Club:* Flyfishers'.

WILSON, Hon. Sir Ronald (Darling), KBE 1979; CMG 1978; Justice of the High Court of Australia, since 1979; Chancellor, Murdoch University, since 1980; *b* 23 Aug. 1922; *s* of Harold Wilson and Jean Ferguson Wilson (*née* Darling); *m* 1950, Leila Amy Gibson Smith; three *s* two *d. Educ:* Geraldton State School; Univ. of Western Australia (LLB Hons; Hon. LLD 1980); Univ. of Pennsylvania (LLM). Assistant Crown Prosecutor, Western Australia, 1954-59; Chief Crown Prosecutor, WA, 1959-61; Crown Counsel, WA, 1961-69; QC 1963; Solicitor General, WA, 1969-79. Moderator, Presbyterian Church in Western Australia, 1965; Moderator, WA Synod, Uniting Church in Australia, 1977-79. *Address:* 88 Webster Street, Nedlands, WA 6009, Australia. *T:* 386 4500. *Club:* Weld (Perth).

WILSON, Ronald Marshall, CBE 1982; Partner, Bell-Ingram, Chartered Surveyors, since 1957; Director, Central Farmers Ltd, since 1971; *b* 6 March 1923; *s* of Marshall Lang Wilson and Margaret Wilson Wilson; *m* 1948, Marion Robertson Scobie; two *s. Educ:* Sedbergh; London Univ. (BSc Estate Management 1950). Served War of 1939-45; North Irish Horse; Court Orderly Officer, Wüppertal War Crimes Trial, 1946. Royal Institution of Chartered Surveyors: Mem. General Council, 1973—; President, 1979-80; Mem. Land Agency and Agricl Divisional Council, 1970-77 (Chm., 1974-75); Chm., Internat. Cttee, 1976-78. *Publications:* articles on technical and professional subjects, incl. Planning in the Countryside. *Recreations:* golf, fishing, shooting. *Address:* Baledgarno, Inchture, Perthshire PH14 9SH. *T:* Inchture 245. *Clubs:* Farmers'; Royal (Perth).

WILSON, Sheriff Roy Alexander, WS; Sheriff of Grampian, Highlands and Islands at Elgin and Aberdeen, since 1975; *b* 22 Oct. 1927; *s* of Eric Moir Wilson and Jean Dey Gibb; *m* 1954, Alison Mary Craig; one *s* one *d. Educ:* Drumwhindle Sch.; Aberdeen Grammar Sch.; Merchiston Castle Sch.; Lincoln Coll., Oxford Univ. (BA); Edinburgh Univ. (LLB); Thow Scholarship in Scots Law, 1952. WS; NP. Solicitor, 1953. Partner, subseq. Sen. Partner, Messrs Allan McNeil & Son, WS, Edinburgh, 1957-75. Chm., indust. relations tribunals, 1971-75. Rotarian; Pres., Moray Caring Assoc. Pres., Moray Rugby Club; Treasurer, Fochabers Curling Club. *Recreations:* golf, curling, spectator sports, reading. *Address:* Deansford, Bishopmill, Elgin, Moray. *T:* Elgin 7339. *Club:* Elgin.

WILSON, Roy Vernon, CEng, MICE; Director, Eastern Region, Property Services Agency, Department of the Environment, since 1980; *b* 23 July 1922; *s* of Alfred Vincent Wilson and late Theresa Elsie Wilson; *m* 1951, Elsie Hannah Barrett; three *s. Educ:* Cheadle Hulme Sch.; Manchester Univ. (BScTech Hons). Served Royal Engineers, 1942-44. Civil Engineer, local govt, 1945-51; Harlow Develt Corp., 1951-54; Air Ministry Works Directorate: Warrington, 1954-59; Newmarket, 1959-62; Germany, 1962-65; District Works Officer: Wethersfield, 1965-67; Mildenhall, 1967-72; Area Officer, Letchworth (PSA), 1972-76; Regional Director, Cyprus (PSA), 1976-79; Chief Works Officer, Ruislip, 1979. *Recreations:* lacrosse (earlier years), golf, tennis, badminton. *Address:* 12 Diomed Drive, Great Barton, Bury St Edmunds, Suffolk IP31 2TD. *Club:* Civil Service.

WILSON, Sandy; composer, lyric writer, playwright; *b* 19 May 1924; *s* of George Walter Wilson and Caroline Elsie (*née* Humphrey). *Educ:* Elstree Preparatory School; Harrow School; Oriel College, Oxford (BA Eng. Lit.). Contributed material to Oranges and Lemons, Slings and Arrows, 1948; wrote lyrics for touring musical play Caprice, 1950; words and music for two revues at Watergate Theatre, 1951 and 1952; (musical comedy) The Boy Friend for Players' Theatre, 1953, later produced in West End and on Broadway, 1954, directed revival (Comedy), 1967; (musical play) The Buccaneer, 1955; Valmouth (musical play, based on Firbank's novel), Lyric, Hammersmith and Savile Theatre, 1959, New York, 1960, revival, Chichester, 1982; songs for Call It Love, Wyndham's Theatre, 1960; Divorce Me, Darling! (musical

comedy), Players' Theatre, 1964, Globe, 1965; music for TV series, The World of Wooster, 1965-66; music for As Dorothy Parker Once Said, Fortune, 1969; songs for Danny la Rue's Charley's Aunt (TV), 1969; wrote and performed in Sandy Wilson Thanks the Ladies, Hampstead Theatre Club, 1971; His Monkey Wife, Hampstead, 1971; The Clapham Wonder, Canterbury, 1978; Aladdin, Lyric, Hammersmith, 1979. *Publications:* This is Sylvia (with own illustrs), 1954; The Boy Friend (with own illustrs), 1955; Who's Who for Beginners (with photographs by Jon Rose), 1957; Prince What Shall I Do (illustrations, with Rhoda Levine), 1961; The Poodle from Rome, 1962; I Could Be Happy (autobiog.), 1975; Ivor, 1975; Caught in the Act, 1976; The Roaring Twenties, 1977. *Recreations:* visiting the National Film Theatre and writing musicals. *Address:* 2 Southwell Gardens, SW7. *T:* 01-373 6172. *Club:* Players' Theatre.

WILSON, Snoo; writer, since 1969; *b* 2 Aug. 1948; *s* of Leslie Wilson and Pamela Mary Wilson; *m* 1976, Ann McFerran; one *s* one *d. Educ:* Bradfield Coll.; Univ. of East Anglia (BA English and American Studies). Associate Director, Portable Theatre, 1970-75; Dramaturge, Royal Shakespeare Co., 1975-76; Script Editor, Play for Today, 1976. Henfield Fellow, Univ. of E Anglia, 1978; US Bicentennial Fellow in Playwriting, 1981-82. *Publications: plays:* Layby (jtly), 1972; The Pleasure Principle, 1973; Pignight and Blowjob, 1974; Vampire, 1978; The Glad Hand, 1978; A Greenish Man, 1978; The Number of the Beast, 1982; Flaming Bodies, 1982, etc. *Recreations:* beekeeping, travel, tennis. *Address:* 41 The Chase, SW4 0NP.

WILSON, Stanley John, CBE 1981; FCIS; Managing Director, 1975-82 and Chief Executive, 1980-82, The Burmah Oil Co. Ltd; *b* 23 Oct. 1921; *s* of Joseph Wilson and Jessie Cormack; *m* 1952, Molly Ann (*née* Clarkson); two *s. Educ:* King Edward VII Sch., Johannesburg; Witwatersrand Univ. CA (SA); ASAA, ACMA; FCIS 1945; CBIM; FInst Pet. 1945-73: Chartered Accountant, Savory & Dickinson; Sec. and Sales Man., Rhodesian Timber Hldgs; Chm. and Chief Exec. for S Africa, Vacuum Oil Co.; Reg. Vice Pres. for S and E Asia, Mobil Petroleum; Pres., Mobil Sekiyu; Pres., subseq. Reg. Vice Pres. for Europe, Mobil Europe Inc.; Pres., Mobil East Inc., and Reg. Vice Pres. for Far East, S and SE Asia, Australia, Indian Sub-Continent, etc, 1973-75. Underwriting Mem. of Lloyd's. Freeman, City of London; Liveryman, Basketmakers' Co. FRSA. *Recreations:* golf, shooting, fishing. *Address:* Leigh Hill, Savernake, near Marlborough, Wilts SN8 3BH. *T:* Marlborough 810230. *Clubs:* City of London, Royal Automobile; Tidworth Garrison Golf; City (Cape Town); Rand (Johannesburg); Heresewentien (SA).

WILSON, Stanley Livingstone, CMG 1966; DSO 1943; Visiting Surgeon, Dunedin Hospital, 1937-66, Hon. Consulting Surgeon, Dunedin Hospital, since 1966; *b* 17 April 1905; *s* of Robert and Elizabeth Wilson; *m* 1930, Isabel, *d* of William Kirkland; two *s* one *d. Educ:* Dannevirke High School; University of Otago. Univ. Entrance Schol., 1923; MB, ChB 1928; FRCS 1932; FRACS 1937. Resident Surgeon, Dunedin Hosp., Royal Northern and St Mary's Hosps, London, 1929-37. NZ Medical Corps, Middle East; Solomons, 1940-44; OC 2 NZ Casualty Clearing Station, Pacific, 1943-44. President, Otago BMA, 1948; Council, RACS 1951-63 (President, 1961-62). Examiner in Surgery, Univ. of Otago, 1952-65; Court of Examiners, RACS, 1948-60; Mem., Otago Hosp. Bd, 1965-74. Hon. Fellow, American Coll. of Surgeons, 1963. Hon. DSc Otago, 1975. *Recreations:* golf, sheepfarming. *Address:* 27 Burwood Avenue, Dunedin, NW1, New Zealand. *T:* 741.061; Maypark, Middlemarch, Otago, New Zealand. *T:* 854. *Clubs:* Dunedin (Dunedin); Otago Officers' (Dunedin).

WILSON, Stephen Shipley, CB 1950; Keeper of Public Records, 1960-66; *b* 4 Aug. 1904; *s* of late Alexander Cowan Wilson and Edith Jane Brayshaw; *m* 1933, Martha Mott, *d* of A. B. Kelley and Mariana Parrish, Philadelphia, Pa; two *s* one *d. Educ:* Leighton Park; Queen's Coll., Oxford. Fellow, Brookings Inst., Washington, DC, 1926-27; Instructor, Columbia University, New York City, 1927-28; Public Record Office, 1928-29; Ministry of Transport, 1929-47; Ministry of Supply, 1947-50; Secretary, Iron and Steel Corporation of Great Britain, 1950-53, and Secretary, Iron and Steel Holding and Realisation Agency, 1953-60. Historical Section, Cabinet Office, 1966-77. *Address:* 3 Willow Road, NW3 1TH. *T:* 01-435 0148. *Club:* Reform.
See also J. E. Meade, Sir Geoffrey Wilson, R. C. Wilson.

WILSON, Prof. Thomas, CBE 1959; Professor of Tropical Hygiene, Liverpool School of Tropical Medicine, University of Liverpool, 1962-71; *b* 5 Nov. 1905; *s* of R. H. Wilson, OBE, Belfast; *m* 1930, Annie Cooley; two *s* one *d. Educ:* Belfast Royal Academy; Queen's Univ., Belfast. MB, BCh, BAO (Belfast) 1927; DPH (Belfast) 1929; DTM, DTH (Liverpool) 1930; MD (Belfast) 1952. MO, Central Health Bd, FMS 1930; Health Officer, Malayan Med. Service, 1931; Lieut and Capt., RAMC (POW in Malaya and Thailand), 1942-45; Sen. Malaria Research Officer, Inst. for Med. Res., Fedn of Malaya, 1949; Dir, Inst. for Med. Res., Fedn of Malaya, 1956; Sen. Lectr in Tropical Hygiene, Liverpool Sch. of Trop. Med., Univ. of Liverpool, 1959. *Publications:* (with T. H. Davey) Davey and Lightbody's Control of Disease in the Tropics, 1965, 4th edn 1971; contrib. to Hobson's Theory and Practice of Public Health, 3rd edn 1969, 5th edn 1979; articles in medical journals on malaria and filariasis. *Recreation:* golf. *Address:* 77 Strand Road, Portstewart, N Ireland.

WILSON, Prof. Thomas, OBE 1945; FBA 1976; FRSE 1980; Adam Smith Professor of Political Economy, University of Glasgow, 1958-82; Hon.

Fellow, London School of Economics, 1979; *b* 23 June 1916; *s* of late John Bright and Margaret G. Wilson, Belfast; *m* 1943, Dorothy Joan Parry; one *s* two *d*. *Educ*: Queen's University, Belfast; London School of Economics. Mins of Economic Warfare and Aircraft Production, 1940-42; Prime Minister's Statistical Branch, 1942-45. Fellow of University College, Oxford, 1946-58; Faculty Fellow of Nuffield College, Oxford, 1950-54; Vis. Fellow, All Souls Coll., Oxford, 1974-75; Editor, Oxford Economic Papers, 1948-58. Vice-Chm., Scottish Council's Cttee of Inquiry into the Scottish Economy, 1960-61; Nuffield Foundation Visiting Prof., Univ. of Ibadan, 1962. Economic Consultant to Govt of N Ireland, 1964-65, 1968-70; to Sec. of State for Scotland, 1963-64 and 1970-; Shipbuilding Industry Cttee, 1965. Mem., SSRC Economics Cttee, 1969-73. Dir, Scottish Mutual Assce Soc. (Chm., 1978-81). *Publications*: Fluctuations in Income and Employment, 1941; (ed) Ulster under Home Rule, 1955; Inflation, 1960; Planning and Growth, 1964; (ed) Pensions, Inflation and Growth, 1974; (ed with A. S. Skinner) Essays on Adam Smith, 1975; (ed with A. S. Skinner) The Market and the State, 1976; The Political Economy of Inflation (British Acad. Keynes Lecture), 1976; (with D. J. Wilson) The Political Economy of the Welfare State, 1982. *Recreations*: sailing and walking. *Address*: 8 The University, Glasgow G12 8QQ. *T*: 041-339 8344.

WILSON, Captain Sir Thomas (Douglas), 4th Bt, *cr* 1906; MC 1940; *b* (posthumous) 10 June 1917; *s* of Thomas Douglas Wilson (*s* of 1st Bt), 2nd Lieut 7th Bn Argyll and Sutherland Highlanders (killed in action, 1917), and Kathleen Elsie, *d* of Henry Edward Gray; *S* uncle, 1968; *m* 1947, Pamela Aileen, 2nd *d* of Sir Edward Hanmer, 7th Bt, and late Aileen Mary, *er d* of Captain J. E. Rogerson; one *s* three *d*. *Educ*: Marlborough and Sandhurst. Commissioned 15th/19th Hussars, 1937; served in France, 1939-40 (MC); Western Desert, 1942-43; retired, 1947. Contested (C) Dudley and Stourbridge, 1955. *Recreations*: hunting, racing. *Heir*: *s* James William Douglas Wilson, *b* 8 Oct. 1960. *Address*: Lillingstone Lovell Manor, Buckingham MK18 5BQ. *T*: Lillingstone Dayrell 237. *Club*: Cavalry and Guards.

WILSON, Thomas Marcus; Assistant Under-Secretary, Ministry of Defence (Procurement Executive), 1971-73; retired; *b* 15 April 1913; *s* of Reverend C. Wilson; *m* 1939, Norah Boyes (*née* Sinclair); no *c*. *Educ*: Manchester Grammar School; Jesus College, Cambridge. Asst Principal, Customs and Excise, 1936; Private Secretary: to Board of Customs and Excise, 1939; to Chm. Bd, 1940; Principal, 1941; lent to Treasury, 1942; lent to Office of Lord President of Council, 1946; Asst Sec., 1947; seconded: Min. of Food, 1949; Min. of Supply, 1953, Under-Sec., 1962, and Prin. Scientific and Civil Aviation Adv. to Brit. High Comr in Australia, also Head of Defence Research and Supply Staff, 1962-64; Under-Secretary: Min. of Aviation, 1964-67; Min. of Technology, 1967-70; Min. of Aviation Supply, 1970-71; MoD, 1971-73. *Recreations*: reading, music, painting and travel, especially in France. *Address*: Flat 6, 21 Queen Square, Bath.

WILSON, William; DL; MP (Lab) Coventry South East, since 1974 (Coventry South, 1964-74); *b* 28 June 1913; *s* of Charles and Charlotte Wilson; *m* 1939, Bernice Wilson; one *s*. *Educ*: Wheatley St Sch.; Cheylesmore Sch.; Coventry Jun. Technical School. Qual. as Solicitor, 1939. Entered Army, 1941; served in N Africa, Italy and Greece; demobilised, 1946 (Sergeant). Contested (Lab) Warwick and Leamington, 1951, 1955, March 1957, 1959. Member: Commons Select Cttee on Race Relations and Immigration, 1970-79; Warwicks CC, 1958-70 (Leader Labour Group), re-elected 1972. DL County of Warwick, 1967. *Recreations*: gardening, theatre, watching Association football. *Address*: Avonside House, High Street, Barford, Warwickshire. *T*: Barford 624278.

WILSON, Prof. William Adam; Lord President Reid Professor of Law, University of Edinburgh, since 1972; *b* 28 July 1928; *s* of Hugh Wilson and Anne Adam. *Educ*: Hillhead High Sch., Glasgow; Glasgow Univ. MA 1948, LLB 1951. Solicitor, 1951. Lectr in Scots Law, Edinburgh Univ., 1960, Sen. Lectr 1965. Dep. Chm., Consumer Protection Adv. Cttee, 1974-. *Publications*: (with A. G. M. Duncan) Trial Practice, Trustees and Executors, 1975; Introductory Essays on Scots Law, 1978; Law of Debt, 1981; articles in legal jls. *Address*: 2 Great Stuart Street, Edinburgh EH3 6AW. *T*: 031-225 4958.

WILSON, William Desmond, OBE 1964 (MBE 1954); MC 1945; DSC (USA) 1945; HM Diplomatic Service, retired; Deputy High Commissioner, Kaduna, Nigeria, 1975-81; *b* 2 Jan. 1922; *s* of late Crozier Irvine Wilson and Mabel Evelyn (*née* Richardson); *m* 1949, Lucy Bride; two *s*. *Educ*: Royal Belfast Acad. Instn; QUB; Trinity Coll., Cambridge. Joined Indian Army, 1941; served with 10 Gurkha Rifles, India and Italy, 1942-46 (Major). Colonial Admin. Service: Northern Nigeria, 1948-63 (MBE for Gallantry, 1954); retd as Permanent Sec.; joined Foreign (subseq. Diplomatic) Service, 1963; First Sec., Ankara, 1963-67; UN (Polit.) Dept, FO, 1967; First Sec. and Head of Chancery, Kathmandu, 1969-74; Counsellor, 1975; Sen. Officers' War Course, RNC Greenwich, 1975. *Recreations*: shooting, riding. *Address*: The Spinney, Forge Hill, Pluckley, Kent. *T*: Pluckley 300. *Clubs*: East India, St Stephen's Constitutional, Golfers'.

WILSON, William George, OBE 1960; Under Secretary and Controller, Newcastle Central Office, Department of Health and Social Security, 1979-81, retired; *b* 19 Feb. 1921; *s* of late William James Wilson and late Susannah Wilson; *m* 1948, Freda Huddleston; three *s*. *Educ*: Blaydon Secondary Sch.,

Co. Durham. Exec. Officer, Min. of Health, 1939. Served War, Army, in India and Ceylon, 1940-46. Higher Exec. Officer, Min. of Nat. Insurance, 1947; Asst Principal, Colonial Office, 1947; Principal, CO, 1950-57 (Adviser, UK Delegn to UN Gen. Assembly, 1951); Financial Sec., Mauritius, 1957-60; Principal, Dept of Technical Co-operation, 1960; Asst Sec., MoH, 1962; Consultant, Hosp. Design and Construction, Middle East and Africa, 1968-70; Asst Sec., DHSS, 1971; Under-Sec., DHSS, 1972-75; Asst Sec., DHSS, 1975-79. *Recreation*: book collecting. *Address*: Clarghyll Hall, Alston, Cumbria. *Clubs*: Wig and Pen, Royal Commonwealth Society.

WILSON, William Lawrence, CB 1967; OBE 1954; retired as Deputy Secretary, Department of the Environment, now Consultant; *b* 11 Sept. 1912; *s* of Joseph Osmond and Ann Wilson; *m* C. V. Richards; two *s*. *Educ*: Stockton on Tees Secondary School; Constantine College, Middlesbrough. BSc (London), FIMechE, Whitworth Prizeman. Apprentice, ICI Billingham 1928-33; Technical Asst, ICI, 1933-36; Assistant Engineer, HMOW, 1937; subsequently Engineer, 1939; Superintending Engineer, (MOW) 1945; Assistant Chief Engineer, 1954; Chief Engineer, 1962; Deputy Secretary, MPBW later DoE, 1969-73. Pres., Assoc. of Supervising Electrical Engineers. FRSA; Hon. FCIBS. Coronation Medal. *Publications*: papers on Radioactive Wastes; contrib. to World Power Conference, USSR and USA. *Recreations*: cricket, fishing, watching all forms of sport. *Address*: Oakwood, Chestnut Avenue, Rickmansworth, Herts. *T*: Rickmansworth 74419.

WILSON, William Napier M.; *see* Menzies-Wilson.

WILSON-HAFFENDEN, Maj.-Gen. Donald James, CBE 1945; *b* 26 November 1900; *s* of late Rev. L. A. Wilson-Haffenden, Seaford, Sussex; *m* 1923, Isabella Sutherland (*d* 1968); one *d* decd; *m* 1969, Ruth Lea Douglass (*d* 1978), late of CMS; *m* 1979, Annabella Khanna. *Educ*: Christ's Hosp.; Victoria Coll., Jersey. Commissioned 91st Punjabis (LI), 1920; served Waziristan, 1921-24; psc 1936; AA and QMG, 1st Division, 1941; DA and QMG 110 Force, 1941-42; DA and QMG 33 Corps, 1943; DQMG, GHQ, India, 1944. *Address*: 19 Hyde Park Gate, SW7. *Clubs*: Royal Commonwealth Society, Hurlingham.

WILSON JONES, Prof. Edward, FRCP, FRCPath; Professor of Dermatopathology since 1974, and Dean since 1980, Institute of Dermatology, University of London; *b* 26 July 1926; *s* of Percy George Jones and Margaret Louisa Wilson; *m* 1952, Hilda Mary Rees; one *s* one *d*. *Educ*: Oundle Sch.; Trinity Hall, Cambridge (MB, BChir 1951); St Thomas' Hosp., London. FRCP 1970; FRCPath 1975. National Service, Army, 1953-54. House Surgeon (Ophthalmic), St Thomas' Hosp., 1951; House Physician (Gen. Medicine), St Helier Hosp., Carshalton, 1951-52; House Physician (Neurology and Chest Diseases), St Thomas' Hosp., 1955; Registrar (Gen. Medicine), Watford Peace Meml Hosp., 1955-57; Registrar (Derm.), St Thomas' Hosp., 1957-60; Inst. of Dermatology, St John's Hosp. for Diseases of the Skin: Sen. Registrar (Derm.), 1960-62; Sen. Registrar (Dermatopath.), 1962-63; Sen. Lectr (Dermatopath.), 1963-74; Hon. Consultant, St John's Hosp. for Diseases of Skin, 1974-. *Publications*: (contrib.) Textbook of Dermatology, ed Rook, Wilkinson and Ebling, 3rd edn 1979; articles on dermatopath. subjects in British Jl of Derm., Arch. of Derm., Acta Dermatovenereologica, Dermatologica, Clin. and Exptl Derm., Histopath., and in Human Path. *Recreation*: art history. *Address*: Institute of Dermatology, St John's Hospital for Diseases of the Skin, 5 Lisle Street, WC2H 7BJ.

WILTON, 7th Earl of, *cr* 1801; **Seymour William Arthur John Egerton;** Viscount Grey de Wilton, 1801; *b* 29 May 1921; *s* of 6th Earl and Brenda (*d* 1930), *d* of late Sir William Petersen, KBE; *S* father, 1927; *m* 1962, Mrs Diana Naylor Leyland. *Heir*: (by special remainder) *kinsman* Baron Ebury, *qv*. *Address*: 27 Egerton Terrace, SW3. *Club*: White's.

WILTON, Sir (Arthur) John, KCMG 1979 (CMG 1967); KCVO 1979; MC 1945; HM Diplomatic Service, retired; Director, London House for Overseas Graduates, since 1979; Chairman, Arab-British Centre, since 1981; *b* 21 Oct. 1921; *s* of Walter Wilton and Annetta Irene Wilton (*née* Perman); *m* 1950, Maureen Elizabeth Alison Meaker; four *s* one *d*. *Educ*: Wanstead High School; Open Schol., St John's Coll., Oxford, 1940. Commissioned, Royal Ulster Rifles, 1942; served with Irish Brigade, N Africa, Italy and Austria, 1943-46. Entered HM Diplomatic Service, 1947; served Lebanon, Egypt, Gulf Shaikhdoms, Roumania, Aden, and Yugoslavia; Dir, Middle East Centre for Arabic Studies, Shemlan, 1960-65; Ambassador to Kuwait, 1970-74; Asst Under-Sec. of State, FCO, 1974-76; Ambassador to Saudi Arabia, 1976-79. *Recreation*: whatever is available. *Address*: London House, Mecklenburgh Square, WC1N 2AB. *T*: 01-837 8888; Wilmere Lodge, Middleton Stoney, Oxon.

WILTS, Archdeacon of; *see* Smith, Ven. B. J.

WILTSHIRE, Earl of; Christopher John Hilton Paulet; *b* 30 July 1969; *s* and *heir* of Marquess of Winchester, *qv*.

WILTSHIRE, Edward Parr, CBE 1965; HM Diplomatic Service, retired; *b* 18 Feb. 1910; 2nd *s* of late Major Percy Wiltshire and Kathleen Olivier Lefroy Parr Wiltshire, Great Yarmouth; *m* 1942, Gladys Mabel Stevens; one *d*. *Educ*: Cheltenham College; Jesus College, Cambridge. Entered Foreign Service, 1932. Served in: Beirut, Mosul, Baghdad, Tehran, Basra, New York (one of

HM Vice-Consuls, 1944); promoted Consul, 1945; transf. Cairo, 1946 (Actg Consul-Gen., 1947, 1948); transf. Shiraz (having qual. in Arabic, and subseq. in Persian); Consul, Port Said, 1952; 1st Sec. and Consul: Baghdad, 1952, Rio de Janeiro, 1957; promoted Counsellor, 1959; Political Agent, Bahrain, 1959-63; Consul-General, Geneva, 1963-67; Dir, Diplomatic Service Language Centre, London, 1967-68; worked for Council for Nature (Editor, Habitat), 1968-69; Consul, Le Havre, 1969-75. Hon. Associate, BM (Nat. Hist.), 1980. *Publications:* The Lepidoptera of Iraq, 1957; A Revision of the Armadini, 1979. *Recreations:* music, entomology. *Address:* Wychwood, High Road, Cookham, Berks SL6 9JS.

WILTSHIRE, Sir Frederick Munro, Kt 1976; CBE 1970 (OBE 1966); FTS 1976; Managing Director: Wiltshire File Co. Pty Ltd, Australia, 1938-77; Wiltshire Cutlery Co. Pty Ltd, 1959-77; Director: Repco Ltd, 1966-81; Australian Paper Manufacturers Ltd, since 1966; *b* 1911; *m* 1938, Jennie L., *d* of F. M. Frencham; one *d*. Chm., Dept of Trade and Industry Adv. Cttee on Small Businesses, 1968; Chm., Cttees of Inquiry, etc. Mem., Executive, CSIRO, 1974-78. Past Pres., Aust. Industries Develt Assoc.; Member, Manufacturing Industries Adv. Council, 1957-77 (Vice-Pres. 1972); Industrial Member, Science and Industry Forum of Aust. Acad. of Science, 1967-80; FAIM (Councillor, 1955-59). *Address:* 38 Rockley Road, South Yarra, Vic 3141, Australia. *Clubs:* Athenæum (Melbourne); Kingston Heath Golf (Aust.).

WIMALASENA, Nanediri; High Commissioner in London for Sri Lanka, 1977-80; *b* 22 March 1914; *m* 1938, Prema Fernando; one *s* two *d*. *Educ:* Ananda Coll., Colombo; Ceylon University Coll.; Ceylon Law Coll. Attorney-at-Law. Elected member, Kandy Municipal Council, 1946, remaining a member for an unbroken period of 21 years; Dep. Mayor of Kandy, 1946; Mayor of City of Kandy, 1963. Elected Member of Parliament for Senkadagala: March-July 1960; again, 1965, then re-elected 1970-May 1977; Dep. Minister of Finance, 1965-70. *Recreations:* tennis, hiking. *Address:* 55 Ward Place, Colombo 7, Sri Lanka.

WIMBERLEY, Maj.-Gen. Douglas Neil, CB 1943; DSO 1942; MC 1918; DL Dundee, 1947-75, Perthshire 1975; Hon. LLD Aberdeen, 1948, Dundee, 1967; *b* 15 Aug. 1896; *s* of late Colonel C. N. Campbell Wimberley, CMG, Inverness, and Lesmoir Gordon Wimberley; *m* 1925, E. Myrtle L., *d* of late Capt. F. L. Campbell, RN, Achalader, Perthshire, and Lady Dobell; one *s* one *d*. *Educ:* Alton Burn, Nairn; Wellington; Emmanuel College, Cambridge; RMC, Sandhurst. 2nd Lieut Cameron Highlanders, 1915; served European War as Regimental officer, France and Belgium, 1st and 51st Highland Divs, 1915-16 and 1917-18 (wounded, MC), including battles of Loos, Somme, Ypres, Cambrai and St Quentin; Acting and Temp. Major, 1918-19; North Russia, with MGC, 1919; Adjutant, 2nd Camerons, 1921; psc 1927; Bde Major 1st (Gurkha) Inf. Bde, 1929; Operations NWFP India, 1930; Brevet Major, 1933; DAAG and GSO II, WO, 1934-37; Brevet Lt-Col 1936; Lt-Col Commanding 1st Cameron Highlanders, 1938; France, 1939; GSO1 and Chief Instructor Senior Officers' School, 1940; Temp. Brigadier 1941; Temp. Major-General 1942; Major-General 1943; Brig. Comdr 13th and 152nd Seaforth and Cameron Bde, 1940-41; GOC 46th Div., 1941; Div. Comdr, 51st Highland Div., 1941-43; including battles Alamein, Mareth, Medinine, Akarit, Enfidaville and Adrano; 8th Army campaign N Africa, Sicily, 1942-43 (despatches, slightly wounded, DSO, CB), Comdt Staff Coll., Camberley, 1943-44; Dir of Infantry, WO, 1944-46; retd at own request; Principal of University College, Dundee, in the Univ. of St Andrews, 1946-54. Governor, Dundee Colls of Art and Technol., 1946-54; Founder Governor, Scottish Horticultural Res. Inst., 1952-62. Member Royal Company of Archers, Queen's Body Guard for Scotland; Gentleman Usher of the Scarlet Rod in the Order of the Bath, 1948-54; Registrar and Secretary, 1954-64. Hon. Col St Andrews Univ. OTC 1951-63; Col of the Queen's Own Cameron Highlanders, 1951-61. Chief, Gaelic Soc., Inverness, 1947; Pres., Royal Celtic Soc., 1971-74; Life Mem., British Legion (Scotland), 1950; Hon. Pres., Angus and Perthshire British Legion. *Publications:* military articles in service jls and Chambers's Encyclopædia; Army Quarterly prize essay, 1933. *Recreations:* once athletics (mem. Army AA; second, half mile, 1922); now genealogy. *Address:* Foxhall, Coupar Angus, Perthshire. *T:* 384. *Club:* Naval and Military (Hon. Mem.).

WIMBORNE, 3rd Viscount, *cr* 1918; **Ivor Fox-Strangways Guest;** Baron Wimborne, 1880; Baron Ashby St Ledgers, 1910; Bt 1838; *b* 2 Dec. 1939; *s* of 2nd Viscount and of Dowager Viscountess Wimborne; *S* father, 1967; *m* 1966, Victoria Ann (marr. diss. 1981), *o d* of late Col Mervyn Vigors, DSO, MC; one *s*. *Educ:* Eton. Chairman, Harris & Dixon Group of Cos, 1972-76 (Man. Dir, 1967-71). Jt Master, Pytchley Hounds, 1968-76. *Heir:* *s* Hon. Ivor Mervyn Vigors Guest, *b* 19 Sept. 1968. *Club:* Travellers' (Paris).

WIMBUSH, Rt. Rev. Richard Knyvet; Priest-in-charge of Etton with Dalton Holme, dio. York, since 1977; an Assistant Bishop, Diocese of York, since 1977; *b* 18 March 1909; *s* of late Rev. Canon J. S. Wimbush, Terrington, Yorks, and late Judith Isabel Wimbush, *d* of Sir Douglas Fox; *m* 1937, Mary Margaret, *d* of Rev. E. H. Smith; three *s* one *d*. *Educ:* Haileybury Coll.; Oriel Coll., Oxford; Cuddesdon Coll. 2nd cl. Classical Mods 1930; BA 1st cl. Theol. 1932; MA 1935. Deacon, 1934; Priest, 1935; Chaplain, Cuddesdon Coll., Oxon, 1934-37; Curate: Pocklington, Yorks, 1937-39; St Wilfrid, Harrogate, 1939-42. Rector, Melsonby, Yorks, 1942-48; Principal, Edinburgh Theological Coll., 1948-63; Bishop of Argyll and the Isles, 1963-77; Primus of the Episcopal Church in Scotland, 1974-77. Canon of St Mary's Cathedral,

Edinburgh, 1948-63; Exam. Chap. to Bp of Edinburgh, 1949-62; Select Preacher, Oxford Univ., 1971. *Recreations:* gardening, walking. *Address:* Etton Rectory, Beverley, Yorks HU17 7PQ. *T:* Dalton Holme 684. *Club:* New (Edinburgh).

WINCHESTER, 18th Marquess of, *cr* 1551; **Nigel George Paulet;** Baron St John of Basing, 1539; Earl of Wiltshire, 1550; Premier Marquess of England; *b* 23 Dec. 1941; *s* of George Cecil Paulet (*g g g s* of 13th Marquess) (*d* 1961), and Hazel Margaret (*d* 1976), *o d* of late Major Danvers Wheeler, RA, Salisbury, Rhodesia; *S* kinsman, 1968; *m* 1967, Rosemary Anne, *d* of Major Aubrey John Hilton; two *s* one *d*. *Heir:* *s* Earl of Wiltshire, *qv*. *Address:* Lydford Cottage, 19 Whyte Ladies Lane, Borrowdale, Harare, Zimbabwe.

WINCHESTER, Bishop of, since 1975; **Rt. Rev. John Vernon Taylor;** *b* 11 Sept. 1914; *s* of late Bishop J. R. S. Taylor and Margaret Irene Taylor (*née* Garrett); *m* 1940, Margaret Wright; one *s* two *d*. *Educ:* St Lawrence Coll., Ramsgate; Trinity Coll., Cambridge; St Catherine's Soc., Oxford; Wycliffe Hall, Oxford; Institute of Education, London. Curate: All Souls, Langham Place, W1, 1938-40; Curate in Charge, St Andrew's Church, St Helens, Lancs, 1940-43; Warden, Bishop Tucker College, Mukono, Uganda, 1945-54; Research Worker, Internat. Missionary Council, 1955-59; Africa Sec., CMS, 1959-63; Gen. Sec., CMS, 1963-74. Chm., Doctrinal Commn of C of E, 1978-. Examng Chap. to Bishop of Truro, 1974-75. Hon. Canon of Namirembe Cathedral, 1963-74. Hon. DD (Wycliffe Coll., Toronto), 1964. *Publications:* Man in the Midst, 1955; Christianity and Politics in Africa, 1957; The Growth of the Church in Buganda, 1958; African Passion, 1958; Christians of the Copperbelt, 1961; The Primal Vision, 1963; For All the World, 1966; Change of Address, 1968; The Go-Between God, 1972; Enough is Enough, 1975; *Recreations:* theatre, music. *Address:* Wolvesey, Winchester, Hants.

WINCHESTER, Dean of; *see* Stancliffe, Very Rev. M. S.

WINCHESTER, Archdeacon of; *see* Cartwright, Ven. E. D.

WINCHESTER, Ian Sinclair, CMG 1982; HM Diplomatic Service; Minister, Jedda, since 1982; *b* 14 March 1931; *s* of Dr Alexander Hugh Winchester, FRCS(Ed), and late Mary Stewart (*née* Duguid); *m* 1957, Shirley Louise Milner; three *s*. *Educ:* Lewes County Grammar Sch., Sussex; Magdalen Coll., Oxford. Foreign Office, 1953; Third Sec. (Oriental), Cairo, 1955-56; FO, 1956-60; Asst Political Agent, Dubai, 1960-62; Actg Political Agent, Doha, 1962; First Sec. (Inf.), Vienna, 1962-65; First Sec. (Commercial), Damascus, 1965-67; FO (later FCO), 1967-70; Counsellor, Jedda, 1970-72; Counsellor (Commercial), Brussels, 1973-76; FCO, 1976-81. *Address:* c/o Foreign and Commonwealth Office, SW1A 2AH.

WINCHILSEA, 16th Earl of, *cr* 1628, **and NOTTINGHAM,** 11th Earl of, *cr* 1675; **Christopher Denys Stormont Finch Hatton,** Bart 1611; Viscount Maidstone, 1623; Bart English, 1660; Baron Finch, 1674; Hereditary Lord of Royal Manor of Wye; *b* 17 Nov. 1936; *er s* of 15th Earl and Countess Gladys Széchényi (*d* 1978) (who obtained a divorce, 1946; she *m* 1954, Arthur Talbot Peterson), 3rd *d* of Count László Széchényi; *S* father, 1950; *m* 1962, Shirley, *e d* of late Bernard Hatfield, Wylde Green, Sutton Coldfield; one *s* one *d*. *Heir:* *s* Viscount Maidstone, *qv*. *Address:* South Cadbury House, Yeovil, Somerset.

WINCKLES, Kenneth, MBE 1945; business consultant; *b* 17 June 1918; *s* of Frank and Emily Winckles; *m* 1941, Peggy Joan Hodges; one *s* one *d*. *Educ:* Lower School of John Lyon, Harrow. FCA. Served War, Army, 1939-46, demobilised Lt-Col. Company Secretary, Scribbans-Kemp Ltd, 1947-48; Rank Organisation, 1948-67; Director and Gp Asst Managing Dir; Managing Dir, Theatre Div.; Dir, Southern Television Ltd; Dir, Rank-Xerox Ltd; Chm., Odeon Theatres (Canada) Ltd; Chm., Visnews Ltd. Chm. and Man. Dir, United Artists Corp, 1967-69; Man. Dir, Cunard Line Ltd, 1969-70; Dir, Hill Samuel Gp Ltd, 1971-80. Director: Horserace Totalisator Bd, 1974-76; CAA, 1978-80. An Underwriting Member of Lloyd's, 1977-. *Recreations:* golf, swimming, gardening, music. *Address:* Moor House, Fishers Wood, Sunningdale, Ascot, Berks SL5 0JF. *T:* Ascot 24800.

WINDER, Col John Lyon C.; *see* Corbett-Winder.

WINDEYER, Sir Brian (Wellingham), Kt 1961; FRCP, FRCS, FRCSE, FRSM, FRCR, DMRE; Vice-Chancellor, University of London, 1969-72; Professor of Radiology (Therapeutic), Middlesex Hospital Medical School, University of London, 1942-69; Dean, Middlesex Hospital Medical School, 1954-67; formerly Director: Meyerstein Institute of Radiotherapy, Middlesex Hospital; Radiotherapy Department, Mount Vernon Hospital; Cons. Adviser in Radiotherapy to Ministry of Health; *b* 7 Feb. 1904; *s* of Richard Windeyer, KC, Sydney, Australia; *m* 1st, 1928, Joyce Ziele, *d* of Harry Russell, Sydney; one *s* one *d*; 2nd, 1948, Elspeth Anne, *d* of H. Bowry, Singapore; one *s* two *d*. *Educ:* Sydney C of E Grammar Sch.; St Andrew's Coll., Univ. of Sydney. Sydney Univ. Rugby Team, 1922-27; combined Australian and NZ Univs Rugby Team, 1923; coll. crew, 1922-26. MB, BS Sydney; 1927; FRCSE 1930; DMRE Cambridge, 1933; FFR (now FRCR) 1940; FRCS (ad eundem) 1948; MRCP 1957. Formerly House Physician, House Surgeon and Radium Registrar, Royal Prince Alfred Hosp., Sydney; Asst, Fondation Curie, Paris, 1929-30; Middlesex Hospital: Radium Officer, 1931; MO i/c Radiotherapy Dept, 1936; Medical Comdt 1940-45; Dir, EMS Radiotherapy Dept, Mt Vernon Hosp., 1940-46; Dean, Faculty of Medicine, Univ. of London,

1964-68. Skinner Lectr, Faculty of Radiologists, 1943 (Pres. of Faculty, 1949-52); Hunterian Prof., RCS, 1951. Pres., Radiology Section, RSM, 1958-59. Chairman: Radio-active Substances Adv. Cttee, 1961-70; Nat. Radiological Protection Bd, 1970-78; Academic Council, Univ. of London, 1967-69; Matilda and Terence Kennedy Inst. of Rheumatology, 1970-77; Inst. of Educn, Univ. of London, 1974-; Council, RSA, 1973-78. Member: Royal Commn on Med. Educn; Grand Council and Exec. Cttee, British Empire Cancer Campaign; British Inst. of Radiology (late Mem. Council); Med. Soc. of London; MRC, 1958-62 and 1968-71; Clinical Research Bd, 1954-62 (Chm., 1968). Co-opted Mem. Council, RCS, to rep. radiology, 1948-53. Mem. Court, 1963-78, Master, 1972-73, Apothecaries' Soc. Hon. Mem., Amer. Radium Soc., 1948. Hon. FRACS, 1951; Hon. FCRA (now FRACR) 1955; Hon. FACR 1966. Hon. DSc: British Columbia, 1952; Wales, 1965; Cantab, 1971; Hon. LLD Glasgow, 1968; Hon. MD Sydney, 1979. *Publications:* various articles on cancer and radiotherapy. *Recreations:* golf, gardening. *Address:* 9 Dale Close, St Ebbe's, Oxford OX1 1TU. *T:* Oxford 42816; Upper Monynut, Cranshaws, Duns, Berwickshire TD11 3SR. *T:* Longformacus 250. *Club:* Athenæum.

WINDEYER, Rt. Hon. Sir (William John) Victor, PC 1963; KBE 1958 (CBE 1944); CB 1953; DSO (and bar), 1942; ED; Justice of the High Court of Australia, 1958-72, retired; *b* 28 July 1900; *s* of W. A. Windeyer, Sydney, NSW; *m* 1934, Margaret Moor Vicars; three *s* one *d. Educ:* Sydney Grammar Sch.; University of Sydney (MA, LLB). Admitted to Bar of NSW, 1925; KC (NSW) 1949; sometime lecturer in Faculty of Law, University of Sydney. Lieut AMF (Militia), 1922; War of 1939-45; Lieut-Colonel comdg 2/48 Bn, AIF, 1940-42 (including siege of Tobruk); Brig. comdg 20th Australian Inf. Bde, AIF, 1942-46 (El Alamein, New Guinea, Borneo); Major-General and CMF Member, Australian Military Board, 1950-53; Retired List, 1957. Trustee, Sydney Grammar Sch., 1943-70; Member of Senate, University of Sydney, 1949-59, Dep. Chancellor, 1953-58; Hon. Col, Sydney University Regiment, 1956-66; Member Council Australian National University, 1951-55. Director: Colonial Sugar Refining Co., 1953-58; Mutual Life and Citizens Assurance Co., 1954-58. Chairman Trustees, Gowrie Scholarship Fund, 1964-. Vice-President, Selden Society, 1965-; Pres., NSW Branch, Australian Scouts Assoc., 1970-78. Hon. Member, Society Public Teachers of Law; Hon. Bencher, Middle Temple, 1972-. Hon. Fellow, Royal Aust. Hist. Soc., 1976-. Hon. LLD Sydney, 1975. *Publications:* The Law of Wagers, Gaming and Lotteries, 1929; Lectures on Legal History, 1938, 2nd edn, 1949, rev. 1957; numerous articles and lectures on legal and historical subjects. *Address:* Peroomba, Harrington Avenue, Turramurra, NSW 2074, Australia. *Clubs:* Australian, Pioneers (Sydney); Elanora Country (Narrabeen).

WINDHAM, William Ashe Dymoke; General Manager, Runcorn Division, Arthur Guinness Son & Co. (Park Royal) Ltd, since 1972; Chairman, Skelmersdale Development Corporation, since 1979 (Deputy Chairman, 1977); *b* 2 April 1926; *s* of late Lt-Col Henry Steuart Windham and Marjory Russell Dymock; *m* 1956, Alison Audrey, *d* of late Maj. P. P. Curtis and Ellinor Kidston; two *s* one *d. Educ:* Bedford; Christ's Coll., Cambridge (MA). CEng, MIChemE. Mem., Runcorn Develt Corp., 1975-77. Mem., Cttee of Management, Henley Royal Regatta, 1973-; rowed for: Cambridge, 1947 and 1951; England, Empire Games, 1950; GB, European Championships, 1950 and 1951 (Gold Medal); Olympic Games, 1952. *Recreations:* shooting, fishing. *Address:* Crowley Lodge, Crowley, Northwich, Cheshire CW9 6NR. *T:* Arley 381. *Club:* Leander.

WINDHAM, Brig. William Russell S.; *see* Smijth-Windham.

WINDLESHAM, 3rd Baron, *cr* 1937; **David James George Hennessy,** CVO 1981; PC 1973; Bt 1927; Chairman, The Parole Board, since 1982; *b* 28 Jan. 1932; *s* of 2nd Baron Windlesham; *S* father, 1962; *m* 1965, Prudence Glynn, *qv* ; one *s* one *d. Educ:* Ampleforth; Trinity Coll., Oxford (MA; Hon. Fellow 1982). Chairman, Bow Group, 1959-60, 1962-63; Member, Westminster City Council, 1958-62. Minister of State, Home Office, 1970-72; Minister of State for Northern Ireland, 1972-73; Lord Privy Seal and Leader of the House of Lords, 1973-74. Mem., Cttee of Privy Counsellors on Ministerial Memoirs, 1975. Jt Man. Dir, 1974-75, Man. Dir, 1975-81, Chm., 1981, ATV Network; Dir, The Observer, 1981-. Vice-Pres., Royal Television Soc., 1977-82. Jt Dep. Chm., Queen's Silver Jubilee Appeal, 1977; Dep. Chm., The Royal Jubilee Trusts, 1977-80; Chm., Oxford Preservation Trust, 1979-; Trustee: Charities Aid Foundn, 1977-81; British Museum, 1981-; Community Service Volunteers, 1981-. *Publications:* Communication and Political Power, 1966; Politics in Practice, 1975; Broadcasting in a Free Society, 1980. *Heir:* s Hon. James Hennessy, *b* 9 Nov. 1968. *Address:* House of Lords, SW1A 0PW.

WINDSOR, Viscount; Ivor Edward Other Windsor-Clive; *b* 19 Nov. 1951; *s* and *heir* of 3rd Earl of Plymouth, *qv* ; *m* 1979, Caroline, *d* of Frederick Nettlefold and Hon. Mrs Juliana Roberts; one *s. Educ:* Harrow. Co-founder, and Dir, Centre for the Study of Modern Art, 1973. *Recreation:* cricket. *Heir:* s Hon. Robert Other Ivor Windsor-Clive, *b* 25 March 1981. *Address:* The Stables, Oakly Park, Ludlow, Shropshire.

WINDSOR, Dean of; *see* Mann, Rt Rev. M. A.

WINDSOR-AUBREY, Henry Miles; Puisne Judge, Supreme Court, Ghana, from 1949, retired; Chairman: Industrial Tribunal; Rent Tribunal; Rent Assessment Panel; *b* 1901; *m* 1928, Dorothy Dagmar Montrose; one *s. Educ:* Clifton College. Called to the Bar, Inner Temple, 1925. Served in Uganda,

1934-49. Magistrate, 1934-36; Crown Counsel, 1936-43; Solicitor-General, 1943-49. *Recreations:* golf and gardening. *Address:* 4 Grosvenor Court, Stanwix, Carlisle, Cumbria.

WINDSOR-CLIVE, family name of **Earl of Plymouth.**

WINDWARD ISLANDS, Bishop of; *see* West Indies, Archbishop of.

WINFIELD, Peter Stevens, FRICS; Senior Partner, Healey & Baker, London, Amsterdam, Brussels, New York, Paris, St Helier, Jersey, since 1975; *b* 24 March 1927; *s* of late Harold Stevens Winfield and Susan Cooper; *m* 1955, Mary Gabrielle Kenrick; four *s* two *d. Educ:* Sloane Sch., Chelsea; West London College of Commerce. Served Royal Artillery, 1944-48. Joined Healey & Baker, 1951. Governor, Guy's Hospital, 1973-74, Special Trustee, 1974-; Director, London Auction Mart Ltd, 1970-, Chairman, 1980-; Member: Lloyd's of London, 1978-; Property Investment Cttee of Save & Prosper Gp Ltd, 1980-; Horserace Totalisator Bd, 1981-. Liveryman: Worshipful Company of Farriers, 1967-; Worshipful Company of Feltmakers, 1972-, Asst to the Court, 1979-. *Recreations:* horseracing, cricket. *Address:* 29 St George Street, W1A 3BG. *T:* 01-629 9292. *Clubs:* Buck's, City Livery, United & Cecil, MCC, Turf.

WING, Prof. John Kenneth, MD, PhD; DPM; FRCPsych; Director, Medical Research Council Social Psychiatry Unit, since 1965; Professor of Social Psychiatry, Institute of Psychiatry and London School of Hygiene and Tropical Medicine, since 1970; *b* 22 Oct. 1923. *Educ:* Strand Sch.; University College London (MB, BS, MD, PhD). Served RNVR, 1942-46, Lieut (A). Hon. Consultant Psychiatrist, Maudsley and Bethlem Royal Hosp., 1960. Hon. MD Heidelberg, 1977. *Publications:* (ed) Early Childhood Autism, 1966, 2nd edn 1975 (trans. Italian 1970, German 1973); (with G. W. Brown) Institutionalism and Schizophrenia, 1970; (with J. E. Cooper and N. Sartorius) Description and Classification of Psychiatric Symptoms, 1974 (trans. German 1978, French 1980, Japanese 1981); Reasoning about Madness, 1978; ed, Schizophrenia: towards a new synthesis, 1978; ed (with R. Olsen), Community Care for the Mentally Disabled, 1979; (with J. Leach) Helping Destitute Men, 1979; (ed jtly) What is a Case?, 1981; (ed jtly) Handbook of Psychiatric Rehabilitation, 1981. *Address:* Institute of Psychiatry, de Crespigny Park, SE5 8AF. *T:* 01-703 5411.

WINGATE, Henry Smith; International Nickel Co. of Canada Ltd and International Nickel Co. Inc., New York: Director, 1942-75; Chairman of the Board and Chief Officer, 1960-72; Member, Advisory Committee, International Nickel Ltd, 1954-79; Director: Peoples' Symphony Concerts, Inc., New York; Société de Chimie Industrielle, Paris; *b* Talas, Turkey, 8 Oct. 1905; *s* of Henry Knowles Wingate and Jane Caroline Wingate (*née* Smith), US citizens; *m* 1929, Ardis Adeline Swenson; two *s. Educ:* Carleton Coll.; University of Michigan. BA Carleton Coll., 1927; JD Michigan 1929. Admitted to New York bar, 1931. Associated with Sullivan & Cromwell, NYC, 1929-35. Internat. Nickel Co. of Canada, Ltd: Asst Secretary, 1935-39; Secretary, 1939-49; Vice-President and Secretary, 1949-52; Vice-President, 1952-54; President, 1954-60. Assistant to the President, International Nickel Co., Inc., NY, 1935-54; President, 1954-60; former Director: Bank of Montreal; United States Steel Corporation; American Standard Inc.; Canadian Pacific Ltd; JP Morgan & Co., Inc.; Morgan Guaranty Trust Co. of New York (currently Mem. Adv. Council). Trustee: Seamen's Bank for Savings, NY; Foundn for Child Develt; Sen. Mem., The Conference Board; Member: The Business Council, Washington, DC; Canadian-American Cttee, National Planning Association, Washington, DC, and C. D. Howe Res. Inst., Montreal; Canadian Inst. of Mining and Metallurgy; Canadian Society of NY; Council on Foreign Relations, Inc., NY; Economic Club of NY; Mining and Metallurgical Society of America; Pilgrims of the United States; Vice-Pres., Amer. Friends of Canada Cttee, Inc. Formerly Trustee: US Steel Foundn Inc.; Legal Aid Soc. of NY; Public Health Inst., City of NY; Manhattan Eye, Ear and Throat Hosp.; Admiral Bristol Hosp., Constantinople, Turkey; US Council, Internat. Chamber of Commerce; Annuity Fund for Congregational Ministers; Retirement Fund for Lay Workers; Carleton Coll. Hon. LLD: Manitoba, 1957; Marshall, 1967; York, 1967; Laurentian, 1968; Colby Coll., 1970; Hon. LHD Carleton Coll., 1973. *Address:* (business) One New York Plaza, New York, NY 10004, USA. *T:* 742-4000; (home) 520 East 86th Street, New York, NY 10028. *T:* Regent 4-3568. *Clubs:* Recess, Union, Huntington Country, Lloyd Neck Bath, University (New York).

WINGATE, Captain Sir Miles (Buckley), KCVO 1982; FNI; Deputy Master and Chairman of the Board of Trinity House, London, since 1976; *b* 17 May 1923; *s* of Terrence Wingate and Edith Wingate; *m* 1947, Alicia Forbes Philip; three *d. Educ:* Taunton Grammar Sch.; Southampton and Prior Park Coll., Somerset. Master Mariner. Apprenticed to Royal Mail Lines Ltd, 1939; first Comd, 1957; elected to Bd of Trinity House, 1968. Vice-President: Internat. Assoc. of Lighthouse Authorities, 1980 (Mem., Exec. Cttee, 1976); Seamen's Hosp. Soc., 1980; Royal Alfred Seafarers Soc., 1980; Member: Gen. Council, King George's Fund for Sailors, 1976 (Hon. Sec., 1980); Cttee of Management, RNLI, 1976; Council, Missions to Seamen, 1982. Liveryman: Hon. Co. of Master Mariners, 1970; Worshipful Co. of Shipwrights, 1980. Governor, Pangbourne Coll., 1982. *Recreation:* golf. *Address:* Trinity House, Tower Hill, EC3N 4DH. *T:* 01-480 6601. *Clubs:* Royal Thames Yacht; Hove Deep Sea Anglers.

WINGATE, William Granville, QC 1963; **His Honour Judge Wingate;** a Circuit Judge (formerly a County Court Judge), since 1967; *b* 28 May 1911; *s* of Colonel George and Mary Ethel Wingate; *m* 1960, Judith Rosemary Evatt; one *s* one *d*. *Educ:* Brighton Coll.; Lincoln Coll., Oxford (BA). Called to Bar, Inner Temple, 1933; Western Circuit. Served Army, 1940-46. Dep. Chm., Essex QS, 1965-71. Member: Bar Council, 1961-67; County Court Rule Cttee, 1971-80; Lord Chancellor's Legal Aid Adv. Cttee, 1971-77; Lord Chancellor's Law Reform Cttee, 1974-. Chm., Brighton Coll. Council, 1978-. *Recreation:* sailing. *Address:* 2 Garden Court, Temple, EC4. *T:* 01-353 4741; Cox's Mill, Dallington, Heathfield, Sussex. *Clubs:* Royal Corinthian Yacht (Commodore, 1965-68), Bar Yacht (Commodore, 1972-76).

WINGFIELD, family name of **Viscount Powerscourt.**

WINGFIELD, Ven. John William; Archdeacon of Bodmin, 1979-81, now Emeritus; *b* 19 Dec. 1915; *s* of William and Gertrude Ann Wingfield; *m* 1940, Vera Francis; one *d*. *Educ:* Sheffield Pupil Teacher Centre; St Aidan's Theol College. Served RASC, 1940-46; retired with hon. rank of Captain. Ordained, Truro, 1947; Curate, Madron with Morvah, 1947-50; Rector, Perranuthnoe, 1950-59; Vicar, Budock, 1959-67; Asst Sec. and Sec., Truro Dio. Conf., 1961-70; RD, Carnmarth South, 1965-67; Vicar, Goran with St Michael Caerhays, 1967-70; Rector, Redruth, 1970-73; Hon. Canon, Truro Cathedral, 1970-81, Canon Emeritus, 1981; Sec., Truro Dio. Synod, 1970-80; Vicar, St Clement, Truro, 1973-79; Proctor in Convocation, 1977-80. *Recreations:* cricket, philately. *Address:* 16 Lanyon Road, Playing Place, Truro, Cornwall TR3 6HF. *T:* Devoran 864484.

WINGFIELD DIGBY; *see* Digby.

WINGFIELD DIGBY, Ven. Stephen Basil, MBE 1944; Archdeacon of Sarum, 1968-79; Canon Residentiary, 1968-79, and Treasurer, 1971-79, Salisbury Cathedral; *b* 10 Nov. 1910; *m* 1940, Barbara Hatton Budge; three *s* one *d*. *Educ:* Marlborough Coll.; Christ Church, Oxford; Wycliffe Hall, Oxford. Asst Master, Kenton Coll., Kenya, 1933-36; Curate, St Paul's, Salisbury, 1936-38; Priest-in-Charge, St George's, Oakdale, Poole, 1938-47. CF (temp.), 1939-45; SCF, 7th Armoured Div., 1943-45. Vicar of Sherborne with Castleton and Lillington, 1947-68. RD of Sherborne and Canon of Salisbury Cathedral, 1954-68. *Recreations:* fishing, shooting, cricket. *Address:* 77 Banks Road, Sandbanks, Poole, Dorset.

WINKS, Prof. Robin W(illiam Evert), MA, PhD; Professor of History, and Master of Berkeley College, Yale University, since 1957; *b* 5 Dec. 1930; *s* of Evert McKinley Winks and Jewell Sampson; *m* 1952, Avril Flockton, Wellington, NZ; one *s* one *d*. *Educ:* Univ. of Colorado (BA Hons 1952, MA 1953); Victoria Univ., NZ (MA Cert. 1952); Johns Hopkins Univ. (PhD 1957). Instructor, Yale Univ., 1957; Dir, Office of Special Projects and Foundns, Yale Univ., 1974-76. Chm., Council of Masters, Yale Univ., 1978-. Smith-Mundt Prof., Univ. of Malaya, 1962; Vis. Prof., Univ. of Sydney, 1963; Vis. Fellow, Inst. of Commonwealth Studies, 1966-67. Cultural Attaché, Amer. Embassy, London, 1969-71; Advisor to Dept of State, 1971-. Chm., Nat. Park Service Adv. Bd, 1981-. Mem. Council on For. Relations. FRHistS. Hon. MA Yale 1967; Hon. DLitt Univ. of Nebraska, 1976. *Publications:* Canada and the United States, 1960 (2nd edn 1973); The Cold War, 1964 (2nd edn 1977); Historiography of the British Empire-Commonwealth, 1966; Age of Imperialism, 1969; Pastmasters, 1969; The Historian as Detective, 1969; The Blacks in Canada, 1971; Slavery, 1972; An American's Guide to Britain, 1977; Other Voices, Other Views, 1978; The Relevance of Canadian History, 1979; Western Civilization, 1979; Detective Fiction, 1980; The British Empire, 1981; Modus Operandi, 1982; articles in Amer. Hist. Rev. *Recreations:* travel, old maps, detective fiction. *Address:* 403A Yale Station, New Haven, Conn 06520, USA. *Clubs:* Athenæum, Royal Commonwealth Society; Yale (NY).

WINLAW, Ashley William Edgell, OBE 1968; TD 1953; retired; *b* 8 Feb. 1914; *s* of Rev. G. P. K. Winlaw, Morden, Surrey, and Minnie Ashley, Kidlington, Yorks. *Educ:* Winchester Coll.; St John's Coll., Cambridge (MA). Master, Aldenham Sch., 1936-39; Master, Shrewsbury Sch., 1939-40; served War, 1940-46; Intelligence Corps, Special Forces, Airborne (Lt-Col; retired as Hon. Major). Master, Rugby Sch., 1946-54; Master, Kent Sch., Connecticut, USA, 1950-51; Headmaster, Achimota Sch., Accra, Ghana, 1954-59; Principal, Government Cadet Coll., Hasan Abdal, W Pakistan, 1959-65; Director of Studies, British Inst., Santiago, Chile, 1965-66; Principal, Federal Govt Coll., Warri, Nigeria, 1966-69; English Master: Bishops Senior Sch., Mukono, Uganda, 1969-72; Blantyre Secondary Sch., Blantyre, Malaŵi, 1972-75; Mangochi Secondary Sch., Mangochi, Malaŵi, 1975-78; Lectr in English, The Polytechnic, Univ. of Malaŵi, 1978-80. Tamgha-i-Pakistan (TPk), Pakistan, 1964. *Recreations:* sports, sailing, drama, painting. *Address:* Ann Page Cottage, 28 High Street, Aldeburgh, Suffolk IP15 5AG. *Clubs:* Special Forces, MCC, Free Foresters, I Zingari.

WINN, family name of **Barons Headley** and **St Oswald.**

WINN, Air Vice-Marshal Charles Vivian, CBE 1963; DSO 1945; OBE 1950; DFC 1941; AOC Scotland and Northern Ireland 1972-73; *b* 20 April 1918; *s* of C. A. Winn, Cardiff, Past Pres. of Shipping Fedn, and D. B. Winn (née Thomas); *m* 1946, Suzanne Patricia (née Baily); one *s* one *d*. *Educ:* St Peter's Sch., Weston-super-Mare; Wycliffe Coll. Station Comdr, Felixstowe, 1951 (Queen's Commendation for Bravery, 1953); DP2, Air Ministry, 1953;

Station Comdr: Weston Zoyland, 1955; Laarbruch, 1957; SASO, 38 Gp, 1960; Chief of Plans and Ops, Far East, Nov. 1962; Dir of Ops, MoD (Air), 1965; Air Comdr, Malta, 1968; Chief of Plans, SHAPE, 1971. Chief Recreation Officer, Anglian Water Authority, 1974. Vice-Chm., Ex-Services Mental Welfare Soc.; Mem., Air League. MBIM. *Address:* The Cottage, Green End, Great Stukeley, Huntingdon, Cambs. *Clubs:* Royal Air Force; Union (Malta).

WINNEKE, Hon. Sir Henry (Arthur), KCMG 1966; KCVO 1977; Kt 1957; OBE 1944; QC (Australia); Governor of Victoria, Australia, 1974-82; *b* 29 Oct. 1908; *s* of Henry Christian Winneke, Judge of County Courts, Victoria, and Ethel Janet Winneke; *m* 1933, Nancy Rae Wilkinson; two *s*. *Educ:* Ballarat Grammar Sch.; Scotch Coll., Melbourne; University of Melbourne. Master of Laws, 1st Class Hons, Melbourne, 1929; Hockey Blue, Melbourne Univ. Called to Victorian Bar, 1931. Served with Royal Australian Air Force, 1939-46, Group Captain, Director of Personal Services. Resumed practice Victorian Bar, 1946; KC 1949; Senior Counsel to Attorney-General and Prosecutor for the King, 1950; Solicitor-General of Victoria, 1951-64; Chief Justice, Supreme Court of Victoria, 1964-74; Lieutenant-Governor of Victoria, 1972-74. Member: Council Scotch Coll., Melbourne, 1947-56; Council Victoria Bar, 1948, 1949. President: Literary Council of Victoria, 1966; Boy Scouts Assoc., Victoria Br.; Victoria Law Foundn; Victorian Council Legal Educn. KStJ 1974. Hon. LLD: Melbourne, 1978; Monash, 1980. *Recreations:* golf, gardening, racing. *Address:* 4A The Pines, Kew, Vic 3101, Australia; 45 Lexington Avenue, Shoreham, Vic 3916, Australia. *Clubs:* Athenæum, Melbourne Cricket, Metropolitan Golf (Melbourne); Royal Autobobile, Victoria Racing, Moonee Valley Racing (Victoria).

WINNER, Dame Albertine (Louise), DBE 1967 (OBE 1945); Chairman, St Christopher's Hospice; *b* 4 March 1907; *d* of Isidore and Annie Winner, 4k Portman Mansions, W1. *Educ:* Francis Holland Sch., Clarence Gate; University College, London, and University College Hospital. BSc (Hons Physiology) 1929; MRCS, LRCP, 1932; MBBS London, 1933 (University Gold Medal); MD (London), 1934; MRCP (London) 1935; FRCP (London) 1959; FFCM 1973. Hon. Assistant Physician, Elizabeth Garrett Anderson Hospital, 1937; Hon. Physician, Mothers' Hospital, Clapton, 1937. Service with RAMC, 1940-46 (Lieut-Colonel). Service with Ministry of Health, 1947-67. Hon. Consultant for Women's Services to the Army, 1946-70. Visiting Lecturer, London School of Economics, 1951-63. Fellow, University College, London, 1965; Linacre Fellow, RCP, 1967-78. QHP 1965-68. *Publications:* articles in Lancet, Public Health, etc. *Recreations:* gardening, Japanese prints, music, people, opera. *Address:* 35 Gordon Mansions, Torrington Place, WC1. *T:* 01-636 1921. *Club:* University Women's.

WINNER, Prof. Harold Ivor, MA, MD, FRCP, FRCPath; Professor of Medical Microbiology (formerly of Bacteriology), University of London, at Charing Cross Hospital Medical School, since 1965; Consultant Bacteriologist, Charing Cross Hospital, since 1954; *b* 1 June 1918; *y s* of late Jacob Davis and Janet Winner; *m* 1945, Nina, *e d* of Jacques and Lily Katz; two *s*. *Educ:* St Paul's Sch.; Downing Coll., Cambridge (Maj. Schol.); University College Hospital Medical School. 1st class hons, Nat. Scis Tripos Cambridge, 1939. House Surgeon, Addenbrooke's Hospital, Cambridge, 1942; served RAMC, 1942-44; Asst Pathologist, EMS, 1945-48 and NW Group Laboratory, Hampstead, 1948-50; Lecturer, Sen. Lecturer, and Reader in Bacteriology, Charing Cross Hospital Medical Sch., 1950-64; Mem. School Council, 1967-69 and 1977-. Member: Univs' Cttee on Safety, 1981-; Adv. Cttee on Dangerous Pathogens, 1981-. Examiner: Examining Board in England, 1962-; Royal Coll. of Surgeons, 1971-76; Royal Coll. of Pathologists, 1975-; universities at home and overseas. Founder Fellow and Archivist, RCPath; formerly Pres. and Hon. Editor, Section of Pathology, and Vice-Pres., Sect. of Comparative Medicine, RSM; Chm., Med. Scis Historical Soc., 1982; Vis. Prof., Guest Lectr and corresp. Mem., various univs and medical insts at home and overseas. FRSA; FZS. *Publications:* Candida albicans (jointly), 1964; Symposium on Candida Infections (jointly), 1966; Microbiology in Modern Nursing, 1969; Microbiology in Patient Care, 1973, 2nd edn 1978; Louis Pasteur and Microbiology, 1974; chapters in medical books; papers in medical, scientific and nursing journals. *Recreations:* listening to music, looking at pictures and buildings, gardening, travel. *Address:* 48 Lyndale Avenue, NW2 2QA. *T:* 01-435 5959; Charing Cross Hospital Medical School, W6 8RF. *T:* 01-748 2050.

WINNER, Michael Robert; Chairman: Scimitar Films Ltd, Michael Winner Ltd, Motion Picture and Theatrical Investments Ltd, since 1957; *b* 30 Oct. 1935; *s* of George Joseph and Helen Winner. *Educ:* St Christopher's Sch., Letchworth; Downing Coll., Cambridge Univ. (MA). Film critic and Fleet Street journalist and contributor to: The Spectator, Daily Express, London Evening Standard, etc. Panellist, Any Questions, BBC radio. Entered Motion Pictures, 1956, as Screen Writer, Asst Director, Editor. Films include: Play It Cool, (Dir), 1962; The Cool Mikado (Dir and Writer), 1962; West Eleven (Dir), 1963; The System (Prod. and Dir), 1963; You Must Be Joking (Prod., Dir, Writer), 1965; The Jokers (Prod., Dir, Writer), 1966; I'll Never Forget What's 'isname (Prod. and Dir), 1967; Hannibal Brooks (Prod., Dir, Writer), 1968; The Games (Prod. and Dir), 1969; Lawman (Prod. and Dir), 1970; The Nightcomers (Prod. and Dir), 1971; Chato's Land (Prod. and Dir), 1971; The Mechanic (Dir), 1972; Scorpio (Prod. and Dir), 1972; The Stone Killer (Prod. and Dir), 1973; Death Wish (Prod. and Dir), 1974; Won Ton Ton The Dog That Saved Hollywood (Prod. and Dir), 1975; The Sentinel (Prod., Dir, Writer), 1976; The Big Sleep (Prod., Dir, Writer), 1977; Firepower (Prod.,

Dir), 1978; Death Wish Two (Prod., Dir, Writer), 1981; The Wicked Lady (Prod., Dir, Writer), 1982. Theatre productions: The Tempest, Wyndhams, 1974; A Day in Hollywood A Night in the Ukraine, 1978. *Recreations:* walking around art galleries, museums, antique shops. *Address:* 6/8 Sackville Street, W1X 1DD. *T:* 01-734 8385.

WINNICK, David Julian; MP (Lab) Walsall North, since 1979; *b* Brighton, 26 June 1933; *s* of late Eugene and Rose Winnick; *m* 1968, Bengi Rona, *d* of Tarik and Zeynep Rona. *Educ:* secondary school; London Sch. of Economics (Dip. in Social Admin). Army National Service, 1951-53. Branch Secretary, Clerical and Administrative Workers' Union, 1956-62 (now APEX); Mem. Exec. Council, APEX, 1978-. Advertisement Manager, Tribune, 1963-66. Employed by a voluntary organisation, 1970-79. Contested (Lab) Harwich, 1964; MP (Lab) Croydon South, 1966-70; contested (Lab): Croydon Central, Oct. 1974; Walsall N, Nov. 1976. Member: Willesden Borough Council, 1959-64; London Borough of Brent Council, 1964-66 (Chairman, Children Cttee, 1965-66). Contributor to socialist and trade union journals. *Recreations:* walking, cinema, theatre, reading. *Address:* House of Commons, SW1A 0AA.

WINNIFRITH, Sir (Alfred) John (Digby), KCB 1959 (CB 1950); *b* 16 Oct. 1908; *s* of Rev. B. T. Winnifrith; *m* 1935, Lesbia Margaret (*d* 1981), *d* of late Sir Arthur Cochrane, KCVO; two *s* one *d*. *Educ:* Westminster School; Christ Church, Oxford. Entered Board of Trade, 1932; transferred to HM Treasury, 1934; Third Secretary, HM Treasury, 1951-59; Permanent Secretary, Ministry of Agriculture, Fisheries and Food, 1959-67; Dir-Gen., National Trust, 1968-70. Trustee, British Museum (Natural History), 1967-72; Member: Royal Commn on Environmental Pollution, 1970-73; Commonwealth War Graves Commn, 1970-; Hops Marketing Board, 1970-78. Hon. ARCVS 1974. *Address:* Hallhouse Farm, Appledore, Kent. *T:* Appledore 264.

WINNING, Most Rev. Thomas J.; *see* Glasgow, Archbishop of, (RC).

WINNINGTON, Sir Francis Salwey William, 6th Bt, *cr* 1755; Lieut, late Welsh Guards; *b* 24 June 1907; *er s* of late Francis Salwey Winnington, *e s* of 5th Bt and Blanch, *d* of Commander William John Casberd-Boteler, RN; *S* grandfather, 1931; *m* 1944, Anne, *o d* of late Captain Lawrence Drury-Lowe; one *d*. *Educ:* Eton. Served War of 1939-45 (wounded, prisoner). Owns 4700 acres. *Heir: b* Colonel Thomas Foley Churchill Winnington, Grenadier Guards [*b* 16 Aug. 1910; *m* 1944, Lady Betty Marjorie Anson, *er d* of 4th Earl of Lichfield; two *s* two *d*]. *Address:* Brockhill Court, Shelsley Beauchamp, Worcs. *Club:* Cavalry and Guards.
See also Viscount Campden.

WINNINGTON-INGRAM, Prof. Reginald Pepys, FBA 1958; Professor of Greek Language and Literature in the University of London (King's College), 1953-71, now Professor Emeritus; Fellow of King's College, since 1969; *b* 22 Jan. 1904; *s* of late Rear-Admiral and late Mrs C. W. Winnington-Ingram; *m* 1938, Mary, *d* of late Thomas Cousins. *Educ:* Clifton Coll., Trinity Coll., Cambridge. BA 1925; MA 1929; Scholar of Trinity Coll., 1922, Fellow, 1928-32; 1st Class Classical Tripos, Part I, 1923; Waddington Schol., 1924; 1st Class Classical Tripos, Part II, 1925; Charles Oldham Classical Schol., 1926. Asst Lecturer and Lecturer, University of Manchester, 1928, 1930 and 1933; Reader in Classics, University of London (Birkbeck College), 1934-48. Temp. Civil Servant, Ministry of Labour and National Service, 1940-45 (Asst Secretary, 1944); Professor of Classics in the University of London (Westfield Coll.) 1948; J. H. Gray Lectures, Cambridge Univ., 1956. Vis. Prof., Univ. of Texas at Austin, 1971, 1973; Vis. Aurelio Prof., Boston Univ., 1975. President, Society for the Promotion of Hellenic Studies, 1959-62 (Hon. Secretary, 1963-82). Director, University of London Inst. of Classical Studies, 1964-67. Hon. DLitt Glasgow, 1969. *Publications:* Mode in Ancient Greek Music, 1936; Euripides and Dionysus, 1948; Sophocles: an interpretation, 1980; contribs to classical and musical journals, dictionaries, etc. *Recreation:* music. *Address:* 12 Greenhill, NW3 5UB. *T:* 01-435 6843. *Club:* Athenæum.

WINNIPEG, Archbishop of, (RC), since 1961; **His Eminence Cardinal George Bernard Flahiff,** CC (Canada) 1974; CSB, DD; *b* Paris, Ontario, 26 Oct. 1905; *s* of John James Flahiff and Eleanor (*née* Fleming). *Educ:* St Michael's Coll. (BA); St Basil's Seminary; University of Strasbourg; Ecole des Chartes and Ecole des Hautes Etudes, Paris, 1931-35; Professor of Mediæval History, University of Toronto Graduate School and Pontifical Institute of Mediæval Studies, 1935-54; Superior General, Basilian Fathers, 1954-61; Cardinal, 1969. Member: Sacred Congregation of Religious, Rome, 1969; Société de l'Ecole des Chartes (Paris); American Catholic Historical Society; Mediæval Academy of America. Hon. LLD: St John Fisher Coll., Rochester, NY, 1964; Seattle, 1965; Notre Dame, 1969; Manitoba, 1969; Windsor, 1970; Toronto, 1972; Hon. DD: Winnipeg, 1972; St Francis Xavier, 1973; Laval, 1974; Univ. of St Thomas, Houston, 1977. *Address:* 50 Stafford Street, Winnipeg, Manitoba R3M 2V7, Canada.

WINSER, (Cyril) Legh, CMG 1928; MVO 1927; Private Secretary to Governors of South Australia, 1915-40; *b* 27 Nov. 1884; *s* of Rev. C. J. Winser, MA; *m* 1912, Agnes Dorothy Mayura Langhorne; one *s* two *d*. *Educ:* Oundle. *Recreations:* cricket, golf. *Address:* Bostock Avenue, Barwon Heads, Victoria 3227, Australia. *Clubs:* Royal Adelaide Golf (Adelaide); Barwon Heads Golf.

WINSKILL, Air Commodore Sir Archibald (Little), KCVO 1980 (CVO 1973); CBE 1960; DFC 1941 and Bar 1943; AE; Captain of the Queen's Flight, 1968-82; Extra Equerry to The Queen, since 1968; *b* 24 Jan. 1917; *s* of late James Winskill; *m* 1947, Christiane Amilie Pauline, *d* of M. Baulieu, Calais, France; one *s* one *d*. War of 1939-45: Fighter Pilot: Battle of Britain; European and North African Theatres. Post-war: Air Adviser to Belgian Govt; Station Cmdr, RAF Turnhouse and Duxford; Gp Capt. Ops Germany; Air Attaché, Paris; Dir of Public Relations, MoD (RAF). MRAeS. *Recreations:* golf, sailing. *Address:* Anchors, Coastal Road, West Kingston Estate, East Preston, West Sussex. *T:* Rustington 75439. *Club:* Royal Air Force.

WINSTANLEY, family name of **Baron Winstanley.**

WINSTANLEY, Baron *cr* 1975 (Life Peer), of Urmston in Greater Manchester; **Michael Platt Winstanley;** TV and radio broadcaster, author, journalist, columnist, medical practitioner; Chairman, Countryside Commission, 1978-80; *b* Nantwich, Cheshire, 27 Aug. 1918; *e s* of late Dr Sydney A. Winstanley; *m* 1st, 1945, Nancy Penney (marr. diss. 1952); one *s* ; 2nd, 1955, Joyce M. Woodhouse; one *s* one *d*. *Educ:* Manchester Grammar Sch.; Manchester Univ. President, Manchester Univ. Union, 1940-41; Captain, Manchester Univ. Cricket Club, 1940-42; Captain Combined English Univs Cricket Team, 1941; Ed. University magazine, 1941-42. MRCS LRCP, 1944. Resident Surgical Officer, Wigan Infirmary, 1945; Surgical Specialist, RAMC, 1946; GP, Urmston, Manchester, 1948-66; MO, Royal Ordnance Factory, Patricroft, 1950-66; Treasury MO and Admiralty Surgeon and Agent, 1953-66; Member Lancs Local Med. Cttee, 1954-66; Member Lancs Exec. Council, 1956-65. Spokesman for Manchester Div. of BMA, 1957-65. Member Liberal Party Council, 1962-66. Contested (L) Stretford, 1964; MP (L) Cheadle, 1966-70; MP (L) Hazel Grove, Feb.-Sept. 1974. Chairman Liberal Party Health Cttee, 1965-66; Liberal Party Spokesman on health, Post Office and broadcasting. TV and radio broadcaster, 1957-; own series on Indep. TV and BBC. Member: BBC Gen. Adv. Council, 1967-70; Post Office Bd, 1978-80; Water Space Amenity Commn, 1980-. *Publications:* Home Truths for Home Doctors, 1963; The Anatomy of First-Aid, 1966; The British Ombudsman, 1970; Tell Me, Doctor, 1972; Know Your Rights, 1975; cricket columnist, Manchester Evening News, 1964-65; weekly personal column, Manchester Evening News, 1970-76; articles on current affairs, health, etc. *Recreations:* cricket; golf; playing the bagpipes. *Address:* Heather Hill, Broad Lane, Hale, Cheshire. *Clubs:* National Liberal, Authors'.

WINSTON, Charles Edward, CMG 1974; FRACS; Consulting Surgeon: Sydney Hospital, Australia, and Crown Street (Women's) Hospital, since 1958; Royal South Sydney Hospital, since 1963; *b* 3 June 1898; *s* of James Percival and Annie Elizabeth Winston; *m* 1933; one *d*. *Educ:* Sydney Boys' High Sch.; Univ. of Sydney. MB, ChM. Bd Dir, 1958, Vice Pres., 1968-, and Patron, Sydney Hosp.; Mem. Council, War Memorial Hosp., Sydney. *Publications:* papers on surgical problems to MJA. *Recreations:* golf, bowls, fishing. *Address:* 683 New South Head Road, Rose Bay, NSW 2029, Australia. *T:* 371-7728; 135 Macquarie Street, Sydney, NSW 2000, Australia. *T:* 27-1770. *Clubs:* Australian, Royal Sydney Golf (NSW).

WINSTON-FOX, Mrs Ruth, JP; Co-Chairman, Women's National Commission, 1979-81 (Member, since 1971); *b* 12 Sept. 1912; *d* of Major the Rev. Solomon Lipson, Hon. SCF, and Tilly Lipson (*née* Shandel); *m* 1st, 1938, Laurence Winston (*d* 1949); two *s* one *d* ; 2nd, 1960, Goodwin Fox (*d* 1974). *Educ:* St Paul's Sch.; London Univ. BSc Household and Social Sci.; Home Office Child Care Cert. Mental Hosps Dept and Child Care Dept, LCC, 1936-39; Dep. Centre Organiser, WVS, Southgate, 1941-45; Southgate Borough Council: Member, 1945-65; Alderman, 1955-65; Mayor of Southgate, 1958-59, Dep. Mayor, 1959-61; Sen. Officer, Adoptions Consultant, Social Services Dept, Herts CC, 1949-77. Member: London Rent Assessment Panel and Tribunals, 1975-; Review Cttee for Secure Accommodation, London Borough of Enfield, 1982-; Bd of Deputies of British Jews, 1960- (Chm. Educn Cttee, 1974-80; voluntary nat. organiser, exhibn Jewish Way of Life, 1978-); Vice-Pres., Internat. Council of Jewish Women, 1974- (Chairman: Status of Women Cttee, 1966-75; Inter-Affiliate Travel Cttee, 1975-81); Mem. Governing Body, World Jewish Congress, 1981-. Founder, one of first Day Centres for the Elderly in GB, Ruth Winston House, Southgate Old People's Centre, opened by Princess Alexandra, 1961, and again, 1972; Vice-President: Southgate Old People's Welfare Cttee, 1974-; Enfield Marriage Guidance Council; Southgate Horticultural Soc.; President: League of Jewish Women, 1969-72; First Women's Lodge, England, 1972-74. JP Mddx Area GLC, 1954-. *Publications:* articles only. *Recreations:* four grandchildren, travel, voluntary service. *Address:* 4 Morton Crescent, Southgate, N14 7AH. *T:* 01-886 5056. *Clubs:* University Women's, Bnai Brith.

WINSTONE, (Frank) Reece, FRPS; self employed, since 1925; illustrative photographer, since 1937; book designer, publisher and distributor, since 1957; *b* 3 Sept. 1909; *s* of John Ephraim Winstone and Lillian Kate (*née* Reece); *m* 1937, Dorothy Agnes Attrill; one *s*. *Educ:* Bristol Cathedral Sch. FRPS 1976. Partner, father's menswear business, 1925-36. *Publications:* Bristol As It Was, 1939-1914, 1957 (5th edn 1978); Bristol As It Was, 1914-1900, 1957 (3rd edn 1972); Bristol Today, 1958 (4th edn 1971); Bristol in the 1890's, 1960 (3rd edn 1973); Bristol in the 1940's, 1961 (2nd edn 1970); Bristol in the 1880's, 1962 (2nd edn 1978); Bristol As It Was, 1950-1953, 1964 (2nd edn 1970); Bristol As It Was, 1879-1874, 1965 (2nd edn 1968); Bristol As It Was, 1874-1866, 1966 (2nd edn 1971); Bristol As It Was, 1866-1860, 1967 (2nd edn

1972); Bristol Fashion, 1968; Bristol in the 1850's, 1968 (2nd edn 1978); Bristol As It Was, 1953-1956, 1969, (2nd edn 1979); Bristol's Earliest Photographs, 1970 (2nd edn 1975); Bristol Tradition, 1970; Bristol in the 1920's, 1971 (2nd edn 1977); Bristol As It Was, 1956-1959, 1972; Bristol Blitzed, 1973 (2nd edn 1976); Bristol's Trams, 1974; Bristol As It Was, 1913-1921, 1976; Bristol's Suburbs in the 1920's and 1930's, 1977; Bristol As It Was, 1928-1933, 1979; Bath As It Was, 1980; Bristol As It Was, 1960-1962, 1981; (ed) Bristol's History: Vol. 1, 1966 (3rd edn 1980); Vol. 2, 1975; (ed) Miss Ann Green of Clifton, 1974; (ed) History of Bristol's Suburbs, 1977. *Recreations:* local preservation societies, motoring, the gramophone, serious broadcast programmes, reading. *Address:* 23 Hyland Grove, Henbury Hill, Bristol BS9 3NR. *T:* Bristol 503646.

WINT, Dr Arthur Stanley, CD 1973; MBE 1954; FRCS; Doctor and Surgeon in charge, Linstead General Hospital, Jamaica, since 1978; *b* 25 May 1920; *s* of John Samuel Wint and Hilda Wint; *m* 1949, Norma Wint (*née* Marsh); three *d. Educ:* Calabar High School; Excelsior College, Jamaica; St Bartholomew's Medical School. MB BS; FRCS. Served RAF, 1942-47; Medical School, 1947-53. Participated in international athletics, 1936-53; Olympics 1948: Gold medal, 400 m; Silver medal, 800 m; Olympics 1952: Gold medal, 4x400 m Relay; Silver medal, 800 m. Medical Practitioner, 1953-73. Jamaican High Comr in the UK, 1974-78. FICS 1972; DMJ (Clin), 1975. *Recreations:* badminton, swimming, walking. *Address:* c/o Linstead General Hospital, Linstead, St Catherine, Jamaica, WI. *Club:* Polytechnic Harriers.

WINTER, Rt. Rev. Allen Ernest; *b* 8 Dec. 1903; *o s* of Ernest Thomas and Margaret Winter, Malvern, Vic; *m* 1939, Eunice Eleanor, 3rd *d* of Albert and Eleanor Sambell; three *s* two *d. Educ:* Melbourne C of E Grammar School; Trinity Coll., Univ. of Melbourne (BA 1926, MA 1928); University Coll., Oxford (BA 1932, MA 1951); Australian College of Theology (ThL 1927, ThD 1951 iur. dig.). Deacon, 1927, priest, 1928, Melbourne; Curate, Christ Church, S Yarra, 1927-29; on leave, Oxford, 1929-32; Curate, St James', Ivanhoe, 1932-35; Minister of Sunshine, 1935-39; Incumbent of St Luke's, Brighton, Melb., 1939-48; Chaplain, AIF, 1942-46; Incumbent of Christ Church, Essendon, 1948-49; Canon-Residentiary and Rector of All Saints' Cathedral, Bathurst, 1949-51; Bishop of St Arnaud, 1951-73; Chaplain, St John's Coll., Morpeth, NSW, 1974. *Address:* Lis Escop, 11 Bella Vista Road, North Caulfield, Vic 3161, Australia. *T:* 03-509-2554.

WINTER, Charles Milne, FIBScot; Managing Director, The Royal Bank of Scotland plc, since 1982; *b* 21 July 1933; *s* of David and Annie Winter; *m* 1957, Audrey Hynd; one *s* one *d. Educ:* Harris Acad., Dundee. FIBScot 1979. Served RAF, 1951-53. Joined The Royal Bank of Scotland, 1949; Director: The Royal Bank of Scotland, 1981-; The Royal Bank of Scotland Gp, 1981-; Williams and Glyn's Bank, 1982-. Pres., Inst. of Bankers in Scotland, 1981-. *Recreations:* golf, choral music. *Address:* 4 Charteris Park, Longniddry, East Lothian EH32 0NY. *T:* Longniddry 52340. *Club:* Caledonian.

WINTER, Frederick Thomas, CBE 1963; racehorse trainer since 1964; *b* 20 Sept. 1926; *s* of Frederick Neville Winter and Ann (*née* Flanagan); *m* 1956, Diana Pearson; three *d* (incl. twins). *Educ:* Ewell Castle. Served as Lieut, 6th Bn Para. Regt, 1944-47. Jockey, Flat, 1939-42; National Hunt jockey, 1947-64. *Recreations:* golf, gardening. *Address:* Uplands, Lambourn, Berks. *T:* Lambourn 71438.

WINTER, Keith, Novelist and Dramatist; *b* 22 Oct. 1906; *s* of Thomas Winter, Professor of Agriculture, Bangor University, N Wales, and Margaret Baron. *Educ:* Berkhamsted Sch.; Lincoln Coll., Oxford. After leaving school spent six months in the American Express Co., London; then became a preparatory school master for two and a half years; went to Oxford and published first novel while still there; has been writing ever since. *Publications: novels:* Other Man's Saucer; The Rats of Norway; Impassioned Pygmies; *plays:* The Rats of Norway; Ringmaster; The Shining Hour; Worse Things happen at Sea; Old Music; Weights and Measures; We at the Cross Roads; Miss Hallelujah; The Passionate Men; Round the Corner; *Musicals:* Nell; Say When! (with Arnold Goland); Pegasus (with Arnold Goland); *Films:* The Red Shoes, Above Suspicion, Devotion, Uncle Harry. *Recreations:* tennis, swimming, travel. *Address:* c/o Jo Stewart, International Creative Management, 40 West 57th Street, New York, NY 10019, USA.

WINTERBOTHAM, Group Captain Frederick William, CBE 1943; author; *b* 16 April 1897; *s* of late F. Winterbotham, Painswick, Gloucestershire; *m* 1st, 1921; one *s* two *d* ; *m* 1947; one *d. Educ:* Charterhouse; Christ Church, Oxon. Royal Gloucestershire Hussars, 1915; RFC and RAF, 1916-19; Pedigree Stock Breeder, 1920-29; Air Staff and Foreign Office, 1929-45; BOAC 1945-48. *Publications:* Secret and Personal, 1969; The Ultra Secret, 1974; The Nazi Connection, 1978. *Address:* Frittiscombe, Chillington, Kingsbridge, S Devon. *T:* Kingsbridge 580281. *Club:* Royal Air Force.

WINTERBOTTOM, family name of **Baron Winterbottom.**

WINTERBOTTOM, Baron, *cr* 1965 (Life Peer), of Clopton in the county of Northampton; **Ian Winterbottom;** Director, Dynavest Ltd; *b* 6 April 1913; *s* of G. H. Winterbottom, Horton House, Northants, and Georgina MacLeod; *m* 1st, 1939, Rosemary Mills (marr. diss. 1944); one *s* ; 2nd, 1944, Irene Eva, (Ira), Munk; two *s* one *d. Educ:* Charterhouse; Clare Coll., Cambridge. Worked in textile and engineering trades in Manchester, Derby,

and Bamberg and Cologne, Germany. Captain Royal Horse Guards; served War of 1939-45, NW European Campaign; ADC and subsequently Personal Assistant to Regional Commissioner, Hamburg, 1946-49. MP (Lab) Nottingham Central, 1950-55; Parly Under Sec. of State, Royal Navy, MoD, 1966-67; Parly Sec., MPBW, 1967-68; Parly Under-Sec. of State, RAF, MoD, 1968-70; opposition spokesman on defence, 1970-74; a Lord in Waiting (Govt Whip), 1974-78; spokesman on: defence, 1974-78; trade and industry, 1976-78; resigned from Govt, 1978; Founder Mem., SDP. Deleg., UN Trusteeship Council, 1974; Member: House of Lords All-Party Defence Study Gp; Parly and Scientific Cttee; CPA; Anglo-Nigerian Soc. Director: Winterbottom Bookcloth Co., 1955-57; Venesta Internat., 1957-66, 1970-74 (Chm., 1972-74); Chairman: Centurion Housing Association, 1980-; Nigeria Development Co. Ltd, 1980-; Hospital Products (Belmont) Ltd, 1980-; Collins Aircraft Co. 1980-; Consultant, C. Z. Scientific Instruments Ltd, 1980-. *Recreations:* birdwatching, music. *Address:* Woodland Place, St Briavels, Lydney, Glos GL15 6RT. *T:* Dean 530396. *Club:* Athenæum.

WINTERBOTTOM, Michael, MA, DPhil; FBA 1978; Fellow and Tutor in Classics, Worcester College, Oxford, since 1967; *b* 22 Sept. 1934; *s* of Allan Winterbottom and Kathleen Mary (*née* Wallis); *m* 1963, Helen Spencer; two *s. Educ:* Dulwich Coll.; Pembroke Coll., Oxford. 1st Cl. Hon. Mods and Craven Schol., 1954; 1st Cl. Lit. Hum. and Derby Schol., 1956; Domus Sen. Schol., Merton Coll., 1958-59; Research Lectr, Christ Church, 1959-62. MA 1959, DPhil 1964 (Oxon). Lectr in Latin and Greek, University Coll. London, 1962-67. *Publications:* ed Quintilian, 1970; (with D. A. Russell) Ancient Literary Criticism, 1972; Three Lives of English Saints, 1972; ed and trans., The Elder Seneca, 1974; ed (with R. M. Ogilvie) Tacitus, *Opera Minora,* 1975; ed and trans., Gildas, 1978; Roman Declamation, 1980; articles and reviews in jls. *Recreations:* Italy; travel, travel books and plans for travel. *Address:* Hill House, 65 Oxford Street, Woodstock, Oxford. *T:* Woodstock 811291.

WINTERBOTTOM, Sir Walter, Kt 1978; CBE 1972 (OBE 1963); retired; *b* 31 March 1913; *s* of James Winterbottom and Frances Holt; *m* 1942, Ann Richards; one *s* two *d. Educ:* Chester Coll. of Educn; Carnegie Coll. of Physical Educn. Schoolmaster, Oldham; Lectr, Carnegie Coll. of Phys. Educn; Wing Comdr, RAF, 1939-45; Dir of Coaching and Manager of England Team, Football Assoc., 1946-62; Gen. Sec., Central Council of Physical Recreation, 1963-72; Dir, The Sports Council, 1965-78. *Publications:* technical, on association football. *Recreations:* association football, cricket, squash rackets. *Address:* 15 Orchard Gardens, Cranleigh, Surrey. *T:* Cranleigh 271593.

WINTERSGILL, Dr William; Senior Principal Medical Officer, Department of Health and Social Security, since 1976; *b* 20 Dec. 1922; *s* of Fred Wintersgill and May Wintersgill; *m* 1952, Iris May Holland; three *d. Educ:* Barnsley Holgate Grammar Sch.; Leeds Medical Sch., Univ. of Leeds (MB, ChB). MRCGP, MFCM. House Surgeon, 1948, and Registrar, 1948-49, Pontefract Infirmary; Principal, Gen. Practice, Snaith, Yorks, 1950-66; Dept of Health and Social Security (formerly Min. of Health): Reg. MO, 1967-70; SMO, 1970-72; PMO, 1972-76; SPMO 1976. *Recreations:* gardening, antique collecting (silver especially), playing the piano, painting, old buildings. *Address:* Juniper Hill, Stoatley Rise, Haslemere, Surrey. *T:* Haslemere 51042.

WINTERTON, 7th Earl, *cr* 1766 (Ireland); **Robert Chad Turnour;** Baron Winterton, *cr* 1761 (Ireland); Viscount Turnour, 1766 (Ireland); Royal Canadian Air Force; *b* 13 Sept. 1915; *s* of Cecil Turnour (*d* 1953), Saskatoon, Sask.; *S* kinsman, 1962; *m* 1st, 1941, Kathleen Ella (*d* 1969), *d* of D. B. Whyte; 2nd, 1971, Marion Eleanor, *d* of late Arthur Phillips. *Educ:* Nutana Coll., Canada. Joined RCAF, 1940; with Canadian NATO Force Sqdn, Sardinia, 1957-58. *Heir: b* Noel Cecil Turnour, DFM, CD [*b* 11 Dec. 1919; *m* 1941, Evelyn Isobel, *d* of J. C. A. Oulton; three *s.* Formerly Flt Lieut, RCAF].

WINTERTON, Maj.-Gen. Sir John; *see* Winterton, Maj.-Gen. Sir (Thomas) John.

WINTERTON, Nicholas Raymond; MP (C) Macclesfield since Sept. 1971; *b* 31 March 1938; *o s* of late N. H. Winterton, Lysways House, Longdon Green, near Rugeley, Staffs; *m* 1960, Jane Ann, *e d* of J. R. Hodgson, Langley Gorse, Fox Hollies Road, Walmley, Sutton Coldfield, Warwicks; two *s* one *d. Educ:* Bilton Grange Prep. Sch.; Rugby Sch. Commnd 14th/20th King's Hussars, 1957-59. Sales Exec. Trainee, Shell-Mex and BP Ltd, 1959-60; Sales and Gen. Manager, Stevens and Hodgson Ltd, Birmingham (Co. engaged in sale and hire of construction equipment), 1960-71. Chairman: CPC Cttee, Meriden Cons. Assoc., 1966-68; Midland Branch, Contractors Mech. Plant Engrs Assoc., 1968-69. Member: W Midlands Cons. Council, 1966-69, 1971-72; Central Council, Nat. Union of Cons. and Unionist Assocs, 1971-72. Contested (C) Newcastle-under-Lyme, Oct. 1969, 1970; Jt Vice Chm., Anglo Danish Parly Gp; Chairman: All Party Parly Textile Gp; All Party Parly British Namibia Gp; Vice Chm., Cons. Parly Sports and Recreation Cttee; Sec., British South Africa Parly Gp; Sec. and Treasurer, UK Falkland Is Gp. County Councillor, Atherstone Div. Warwickshire CC, 1967-72. President: Macclesfield Boys Club; Poynton Community Centre; N Staffs Polytechnic Conservative Assoc.; Wigan Young Conservatives; Vice-President: NW Area Young Conservative Assoc.; Macclesfield and Congleton District Scout Council; Cheshire Scout Assoc.; Hon. Mem., Macclesfield Lions Club; Patron, Macclesfield and District Sheep Dog Trials Assoc. Liveryman, Weavers' Co.

Recreations: Rugby football, squash, hockey, tennis, swimming, horse riding. *Address:* Whitehall Farm, Mow Lane, Newbold Astbury, Congleton, Cheshire.

WINTERTON, Maj.-Gen. Sir (Thomas) John (Willoughby), KCB 1955 (CB 1946); KCMG 1950; CBE 1942 (OBE 1940); DL; retired; *b* 13 April 1898; *e s* of H. J. C. Winterton, Lichfield, Staffs; *m* 1921, Helen (*d* 1976), *d* of late H. Shepherd Cross, Hamels Park, Herts; three *s. Educ:* Oundle; RMA, Woolwich. Served European War, 1917-18; Burma, 1930-32; War of 1939-45; Dep. Comr Allied Commission for Austria, 1945-49; British High Commissioner and C-in-C in Austria, 1950; Military Governor and Commander, British/US Zone Free Territory of Trieste, 1951-54, retired Jan. 1955. ADC to the King, 1948-49. Colonel Comdt 1st Green Jackets 43rd and 52nd (formerly the Oxfordshire and Buckinghamshire Light Infantry), 1955-60. Formerly President, S Berks Conservative and Unionist Assoc. (Chairman, 1958-65). Formerly Member St John Council for Berkshire (Chairman, 1962-64); a Vice-Pres., Royal Humane Society, 1973- (Cttee Mem., 1962-73). DL, Berkshire, 1966. CStJ 1969. *Address:* Craven Lodge, Speen, Newbury, Berks. *T:* Newbury 40525. *Club:* Army and Navy.

WINTERTON, William Ralph, FRCS, FRCOG; Consultant Gynaecological Surgeon Emeritus, Middlesex Hospital; Surgeon, Hospital for Women, Soho Square; Obstetric Surgeon, Queen Charlotte's Maternity Hospital; Archivist to the Middlesex Hospital; *b* 24 June 1905; *o s* of late Rev. William Charles Winterton; *m* 1934, Kathleen Margaret, 2nd *d* of late Rev. D. Marsden; two *s* two *d. Educ:* Marlborough Coll.; Gonville and Caius Coll., Cambridge; Middlesex Hospital. MA; MB, BChir. House appointments, Middlesex Hospital, 1929-31; Gynæcological Registrar, Middlesex Hospital, 1934-36. Examr in Obstetrics to Universities of Cambridge, London, Glasgow, Ibadan, Dar-es-Salaam, and to Royal College of Obstetricians and Gynæcologists. Fellow of the Royal Society of Medicine, President Obstetric Section, 1960-61. Governor: Bancroft's Sch., Woodford Green, 1960-75; Howell's Sch., Denbigh (Vice-Chairman). Court of Assistants of the Drapers' Company (Master, 1964-65). Past President, Guild of Med. Bellringers. *Publications:* Aids to Gynæcology; (jointly) Queen Charlotte's Textbook of Obstetrics. Contributions to Medical Journals. *Recreations:* fishing, gardening, change ringing, and Do-it-yourself. *Address:* 95 Harley Street, W1N 1DF. *T:* 01-580 3733; 26 De Walden Street, W1; Youngloves, Rushden, Herts SG9 0SP. *T:* Broadfield 217.

WINTON, Frank Robert, MA, MD Cambridge, DSc London; FInstBiol, FIST; Emeritus Professor of Pharmacology, University of London, 1961; *b* 1894; *m* 1922, Bessie Rawlins; one *d. Educ:* Oundle Sch.; Clare Coll., Cambridge; St Bartholomew's and University College Hospitals. Assistant, Dept of Pharmacology, University College, London, 1924; Lecturer, Dept of Physiology, University College, London, 1927; Beit Memorial Research Fellow; Lecturer in Physiology, University of Cambridge, 1931; Reader in Physiology, University of Cambridge, 1933; Professor of Pharmacology, University College, London, 1938-61. Consultant, May and Baker Ltd, etc, 1961-71. Hon. Member, Harvey Society of New York. *Publications:* (joint) Human Physiology, 1930, 7th edn, 1979; Modern Views on the Secretion of Urine (ed F. R. Winton), 1956; Scientific Papers in Journal of Physiology, and other journals on the kidney, plain muscle, etc. *Recreations:* chamber music, wine. *Address:* 32 Arkwright Road, NW3 6BH. *T:* 01-435 2412.

WINTON, Walter; Keeper Department of Electrical Engineering, Telecommunications and Loan Circulation, Science Museum, 1976-80; *b* 15 May 1917; *m* 1942, Dorothy Rickard; two *s* one *d. Educ:* Glossop Grammar Sch.; Manchester Univ. (BSc and Teacher's Diploma). Royal Ordnance Factories, Chemist, 1940-45. Taught Science, Harrow County and Greenford, 1945-50; Assistant and Deputy Keeper, Science Museum, 1950-67; Keeper: Dept of Loan Circulation, Mining and Marine Technol., 1968-73; Dept of Museum Services, 1973; Dept of Mechanical and Civil Engrg and Loan Circulation, 1973-76. *Publications:* contrib. to journals. *Recreations:* Scottish dancing, sailing, fell-walking. *Address:* The Old Workhouse, Harefield, Middlesex. *T:* 01-420 2103.

WINTOUR, Charles Vere, CBE 1978 (MBE 1945); writer; Director, TV-am (News) Ltd, since 1982; *b* 18 May 1917; *s* of late Maj.-Gen. F. Wintour, CB, CBE; *m* 1st, 1940, Eleanor Trego Baker (marr. diss. 1979), *er d* of Prof. R. J. Baker, Harvard Univ.; two *s* two *d* (and one *s* decd); 2nd 1979, Mrs Audrey Slaughter. *Educ:* Oundle Sch.; Peterhouse, Cambridge. BA 1939; MA 1946. Royal Norfolk Regt, 1940; GSO2 Headquarters of Chief of Staff to the Supreme Allied Commander (Designate) and SHAEF, 1943-45 (despatches). Joined Evening Standard, 1946: Political Editor, 1952; Dep. Editor, 1954-57; Editor, 1959-76 and 1978-80; Managing Dir, 1978-79; Chm., 1968-80; Asst Editor, Sunday Express, 1952-54; Managing Editor, Daily Express, 1957-59, Managing Dir, 1977-78; Editor, Sunday Express Magazine, 1981-82; Director: Evening Standard Co. Ltd, 1959-82; Express (formerly Beaverbrook) Newspapers Ltd, 1964-82. Mem., Press Council, 1979-81. Croix de Guerre (France) 1945; Bronze Star (US) 1945. *Publication:* Pressures on the Press, 1972. *Recreations:* theatre-going, reading newspapers. *Address:* 5 Alwyne Road, N1 2HH. *Club:* Garrick.

WIRKKALA, Tapio; Knight of White Rose of Finland; designer; *b* 2 June 1915; *s* of Ilmari Wirkkala, artist, and Selma Wirkkala; *m* 1945, Rut Bryk, artist; one *s* one *d. Educ:* Sch. of Industrial Arts, Helsinki, 1933-36. Mil. rank

of Lt, Finnish Army. Glass designer for Karhula-Iittala, Finland, 1947-; designer for firms in Finland and abroad, 1955-. Art director, Sch. of Industrial Arts, Helsinki, 1951-54. *One-man exhibitions include:* Oslo, 1952; Smithsonian Instn Travelling Exhibn, USA, 1956-58 and 1971-73; England, Germany, Switzerland, Italy, 1962-64; Czechoslovakia, 1967-68; Montreal World Fair, 1967; Mexico Culture Olympics, 1968; Goldsmiths' Hall, 1972; Invitation Exhibn, Venice, 1976. *Exhibition architect:* Finnish Industrial Art Exhibn, Zurich and Gothenburg, 1951; Finnish Art and Industrial Arts Travelling Exhibn, GB, 1952 and USA, 1953; Finnish Glass Exhibn, Amsterdam, 1972; Friends of Finnish Handicraft Centenary Travelling Exhibn in 10 Towns in Finland, 1979-80. *Works included in:* Museum of Modern Art and Metropolitan Museum of Art, New York; Victoria and Albert Museum, London; Kunstgewerbemuseum, Zürich; National Museum, Stockholm; Nordenfjellske Museum, Trondheim; Stedelijk Mus., Amsterdam; Die Neue Sammlung, München; Nat. Gall. of Vic., Melbourne; Mus. Universitaria de Ciencias y Arte, Mexico City. Cross of Freedom (4th class; twice, once with oak leaves), Finland; Pro Finlandia Medal. SIA Medal, 1958; Cultural Foundn of Finland Honorary Prize, 1968; 7 Grande Premios at Milan Triennale and various other prizes and medals for design (ceramics, glass, wood, bank notes, stamps, etc); Academician, Helsinki, 1972; Hon. RDI (GB), 1964, Hon. Dr RCA 1971, and other foreign awards. *Recreation:* fishing. *Address:* Itäranta 24, Tapiola, Finland. *T:* 46 44 14.

WISBECH, Archdeacon of; *see* Patterson, Ven. W. J.

WISDOM, Prof. Arthur John Terence Dibben, MA; Professor of Philosophy, University of Oregon, 1968-72; Fellow of Trinity College, Cambridge; *b* 1904; *s* of Rev. H. C. Wisdom and Edith S. Wisdom. *Educ:* Aldeburgh Lodge School; Fitzwilliam House (now College), Cambridge (Hon. Fellow, Fitzwilliam Coll., 1978). BA 1924; MA 1934. Lecturer in Moral Sciences, Trinity Coll., Cambridge; Prof. of Philosophy, Cambridge Univ., 1952-68. DU Essex, 1978. *Publications:* Other Minds, 1952; Philosophy and Psycho-Analysis, 1952; Paradox and Discovery, 1966. Contributions to Mind and to Proceedings of the Aristotelian Society. *Address:* 154 Stanley Road, Cambridge.

WISDOM, Norman; Actor/Comedian; has starred regularly on stage and television since 1952. First film Trouble in Store, in 1953 (winning an Academy Award) since which has starred in 19 major films in both England and America; two Broadway awards for stage musical, Walking Happy; numerous Royal Performances, both film and stage. *Recreations:* all sports. *Address:* c/o Eric Glass Ltd, 28 Berkeley Square, W1X 6HD.

WISE, family name of **Baron Wise.**

WISE, 2nd Baron, *cr* 1951, of King's Lynn; **John Clayton Wise;** farmer; *b* 11 June 1923; *s* of 1st Baron Wise and of Kate Elizabeth, *e d* of late John Michael Sturgeon; *S* father, 1968; *m* 1946, Margaret Annie, *d* of Frederick Victor Snead, Banbury; two *s. Heir: s* Hon. Christopher John Clayton Wise, PhD, BSc Hons [*b* 19 March 1949. *Educ:* Norwich School; Univ. of Southampton. Plant Scientist]. *Club:* Farmers'.

WISE, Mrs Audrey; Member, National Executive Committee of the Labour Party, since 1982; *d* of George and Elsie Crawford Brown; *m* John Wise; one *s* one *d.* Shorthand typist. MP (Lab) Coventry South West, Feb. 1974-1979. Prospective Parly Cand. (Lab) Greenwich, Woolwich East, 1981-. *Publications:* Women and the Struggle for Workers' Control, 1973; Eyewitness in Revolutionary Portugal, 1975. *Recreations:* family life, camping, walking, reading. *Address:* 99 Wolverhampton Road, Stafford. *T:* Stafford 59490.

WISE, Derek; *see* Wise, R. D.

WISE, Prof. Douglass, OBE 1980; FRIBA; Director, Institute of Advanced Architectural Studies, University of York, since 1975; *b* 6 Nov. 1927; *s* of Horace Watson Wise and Doris Wise; *m* 1958, Yvonne Jeannine Czeiler; one *s* one *d. Educ:* King's Coll., Newcastle, Durham Univ. (BArch; DipTP). Lecturer in Architecture, 1959-65, Prof. of Architecture, 1965-69, Head of Dept of Architecture, 1969-75, Newcastle Univ. Principal, Douglass Wise & Partners, Architects, 1959-. RIBA: Chm., Moderators, 1969-75; Chm., Examinations Cttee, 1969-75; Mem. Council, 1976-79; Chm., Heads of Schools Cttee, 1971-73; Mem. Bd of Management, North Eastern Housing Assoc., 1967-76 (Vice-Chm., 1974-76); Mem. Council, Newcastle Polytechnic, 1974-77; past Mem. Council, Senate and Court, Newcastle Univ.; Governor, Building Centre Trust, London, 1976-. *Publications:* contribs to various technical jls on housing, continuing educn and architectural theory. *Recreations:* painting, natural history. *Address:* The Institute of Advanced Architectural Studies, The King's Manor, York YO1 2EP. *T:* York 24919.

WISE, Ernie; *see* Wiseman, Ernest.

WISE, Sir John (Humphrey), KCMG 1943; CBE 1939; Indian Civil Service, retired; *b* 11 March 1890; *s* of late William Wise, Ashbourne, Derbyshire, and St Servan, France; *m* 1918, Edith Frances Anne (*d* 1981), *d* of late Lt-Col L. G. Fischer, IMS; one *s* (one *d* decd). *Educ:* Christ's Hospital; University College, Oxford. Entered ICS, 1914; IARO, 1915-19, served in India, Mesopotamia, Egypt and Palestine (92nd Punjabis) (despatches); Deputy Commissioner, Toungoo, 1924; Secretary Public Service Commission, India,

1926; Deputy Commissioner, Pegu, 1931; Secretary to Govt of Burma, 1932-39; Member of Burma Railway Board, 1937; Controller of Supplies, Burma, 1939; Counsellor to Governor of Burma, 1940-46; Adviser to the Secretary of State for Burma, 1946-47; Leader of British Mission to Brazil, 1948; Deputy Chairman, Raw Cotton Commission, 1949-53. *Recreations:* chess, walking. *Address:* 5 Cressy House, Queen's Ride, SW13. *T:* 01-789 3745. *Club:* Roehampton.

WISE, Prof. Michael John, CBE 1979; MC 1945; PhD; FRGS; Professor of Geography in the University of London, at the London School of Economics and Political Science, since 1958; *b* Stafford, 17 August 1918; *s* of Harry Cuthbert and Sarah Evelyn Wise; *m* 1942, Barbara Mary, *d* of C. L. Hodgetts, Wolverhampton; one *s* one *d. Educ:* Saltley Grammar School, Birmingham; University of Birmingham. BA (Hons Geography) Birmingham, and Mercator Prize in Geography, 1939; PhD Birmingham, 1951. Served War, Royal Artillery, 80th LAA Regt, 1941-44, 5th Bn The Northamptonshire Regt, 1944-46, in Middle East and Italy; commissioned, 1941, Major, 1944. Assistant Lecturer, Univ. of Birmingham, 1946-48, Lecturer in Geography, 1948-51; Lecturer in Geography, London School of Economics, 1951-54; Sir Ernest Cassel Reader in Economic Geography, 1954-58. Chm., Departmental Cttee of Inquiry into Statutory Smallholdings, 1963-67; Mem., Min. of Transport Adv. Cttee on Landscape Treatment of Trunk Roads, 1971- (Chm., 1981-). Mem., UGC for Hong Kong, 1966-73; Recorder, Sect. E, Brit. Assoc. for Advancement of Science, 1955-60 (Pres., 1965); President: Inst. of British Geographers, 1974; IGU, 1976- (Vice-Pres., 1968-76); Geographical Assoc., 1976-77 (Hon. Treasurer, 1967-76); Mem., SSRC, 1976-; Chm., Council for Extra-Mural Studies, Univ. of London, 1976-; Mem. Council and Chm., Exec. Cttee, Assoc. of Agriculture; Hon. Sec., RGS, 1963-73, Vice-Pres., 1975-78, Hon. Vice-Pres., 1978-80, Pres., 1980-82. Governor, Birkbeck Coll., 1968-. Erskine Fellow, Univ. of Canterbury, NZ, 1970. Hon. Life Mem., Univ. of London Union, 1977. Hon. Mem., Assoc. of Japanese Geographers, 1980. DUniv Open, 1978; Hon. DSc Birmingham, 1982. Received Gill Memorial award of RGS, 1958; RGS Founder's Medal, 1977; Alexander Körösi Csoma Medal, Hungarian Geographical Soc., 1980; Tokyo Geographical Soc. Medal, 1981. *Publications:* Hon. Editor, Birmingham and its Regional Setting, 1951; A Pictorial Geography of the West Midlands, 1958; General Consultant, An Atlas of Earth Resources, 1979; numerous articles on economic and urban geography. *Recreation:* music. *Address:* 45 Oakleigh Avenue, N20. *T:* 01-445 6057. *Club:* Athenæum.

WISE, Peter Anthony Surtees; Assistant Commissioner (Commercial), Hong Kong Government Office, London, since 1978; also (non-resident) Counsellor (Hong Kong Trade Affairs), Helsinki, Oslo, Stockholm, Vienna, since 1980; *b* 26 June 1934; *s* of late J. A. S. (Tony) Wise and Lenore Dugdale; *m* 1956, Elizabeth Maryhead Odhams; two *s. Educ:* Royal Naval College, Dartmouth. Served Royal Navy, 1948-56 (invalided). Marconi Instruments Ltd, 1956-60; Vickers Ltd, 1961-74; First Secretary, later Counsellor (Hong Kong Affairs), UK Mission, Geneva, 1974-78. *Address:* Field House, Boxford, Berks RG16 8DN. *T:* Boxford 302. *Clubs:* MCC; Hong Kong (Hong Kong).

WISE, Very Rev. Randolph George, VRD 1964; Dean of Peterborough, since 1981; *b* 20 Jan. 1925; *s* of George and Agnes Lucy Wise; *m* 1951, Hazel Hebe Simpson; four *d. Educ:* St Olave's and St Saviour's Grammar School; Queen's Coll., Oxford (MA); Lincoln Theological Coll.; Ealing Technical Coll. (DMS). Served RNVR, 1943-47. Assistant Curate: Lady Margaret, Walworth, 1951-53; Stocksbridge, Sheffield, 1953-55; Vicar of Lady Margaret, Walworth, 1955-60; Vicar of Stocksbridge, 1960-66; Bishop of London's Industrial Chaplaincy, 1966-76; Guild Vicar, St Botolph, Aldersgate, 1972-76; Rector of Notting Hill, 1976-81. Member of Plaisterers' Company. *Recreations:* music, sculling. *Address:* The Deanery, Peterborough PE1 1XS. *T:* Peterborough 62780.

WISE, (Reginald) Derek, CBE 1977; Partner, Theodore Goddard, Paris, since 1957; *b* 29 July 1917; *s* of Reginald and Rita Wise; *m* 1957, Nancy Brenta Scialoya; two *s* one *d. Educ:* St Paul's Sch. Admitted solicitor, 1947. Served War of 1939-45, RA and Intell. Legal Adviser, British Embassy, Paris, 1962-. *Address:* 203 bis Boulevard St Germain, 75007 Paris, France. *T:* 222.07.94. *Club:* Travellers' (Paris).

WISEMAN, C. L., MA; Headmaster, Queen's College, Taunton, 1926-53; retired, 1953; *b* 20 April 1893; *s* of late Rev. F. L. Wiseman and Elsie Daniel; *m* 1946, Christine Irene, *d* of Sir William Savage, MD; *m* 1972, Patricia Joan Wragge, *d* of Prebendary R. Wragge-Morley. *Educ:* King Edward's School, Birmingham; Peterhouse, Cambridge (Scholar). Instructor Lt RN, 1915-19; Senior Mathematical Master, Kingswood School, Bath, 1921-26. *Recreation:* music. *Address:* 11 Park Lane, Milford-on-Sea, Lymington, Hants SO4 0PT.

WISEMAN, Gen. Clarence D., OC 1976; General of the Salvation Army, 1974-77; *b* Moreton's Harbour, Newfoundland; *m* Janet Kelly; one *s* one *d. Educ:* Salvation Army Officers Training Coll., Toronto, Canada (grad.). In comd chief Salvation Army evangelistic centres in Canada. Served overseas, War of 1939-45, as Chaplain, Canadian Forces; after 3 yrs directed all Salvation Army Welfare Services on various fighting fronts. After the war held some senior admin. posts in Canada. Transferred to E Africa to direct work of SA in Kenya, Tanzania and Uganda, 1960. Principal, Internat. Training Coll., London, Eng., 1962; Mem., General's Adv. Council, London; Head of Salvation Army in Canada and Bermuda, 1967-74. Holds hon.

doctorates. *Publications:* A Burning in My Bones, 1979; The Desert Road to Glory, 1981. *Address:* 170 Oakmeadow Boulevard, Scarborough, Ontario M1E 4H3, Canada.

WISEMAN, Prof. Donald John, OBE 1943; DLit; FBA 1966; FSA; Professor of Assyriology in the University of London since 1961; *b* 25 Oct. 1918; *s* of Air Cdre Percy John Wiseman, CBE, RAF; *m* 1948, Mary Catherine, *d* of P. O. Ruoff; three *d. Educ:* Dulwich College; King's College, London. BA (London); AKC, McCaul Hebrew Prize, 1939; FKC 1982. Served War of 1939-45, in RAFVR. Ops, 11 Fighter Group, 1939-41; Chief Intelligence Officer, Mediterranean Allied Tactical Air Forces with Rank of Group Capt., 1942-45. Heap Exhibitioner in Oriental Languages, Wadham Coll., Oxford, 1945-47; MA 1949. Asst Keeper, Dept of Egyptian and Assyrian, later Western Asiatic, Antiquities, British Museum, 1948-61. Epigraphist on archæological excavations at Nimrud, Harran, Rimah; Jt Dir of British School of Archæology in Iraq, 1961-65, Chm. 1970-. Pres., Soc. for Old Testament Studies, 1980. Corresp. Mem., German Archæological Inst., 1961. Ed. of Journal IRAQ, 1953-78; Joint Ed. of Reallexion der Assyriologie, 1959-. Bronze Star (USA), 1944. *Publications:* The Alalakh Tablets, 1953; Chronicles of Chaldaean Kings, 1956; Cuneiform Texts from Cappadocian Tablets in the British Museum, V, 1956; Cylinder-Seals of Western Asia, 1958; Vassal-Treaties of Esarhaddon, 1958; Illustrations from Biblical Archæology, 1958; Catalogue of Western Asiatic Seals in the British Museum, 1963; Peoples of Old Testament Times, 1973; Essays on the Patriarchal Narratives, 1980; contrib. to journals. *Address:* Low Barn, 26 Downs Way, Tadworth, Surrey KT20 5DZ. *T:* Tadworth 3536.

WISEMAN, Ernest, OBE 1976; (**Ernie Wise**); *b* 27 Nov. 1925; *s* of Harry and Connie Wiseman; *m* 1953, Doreen Blyth. *Educ:* Council School. Career in show business: radio, variety, TV, films. First double act (with E. Morecambe), at Empire Theatre, Liverpool, 1941; first broadcast, 1943; BBC and ITV television series, 1955- (Soc. of Film and Television Arts Best Light Entertainment Award, 1973); series sold to Time Life, USA, 1980. *Awards:* BAFTA (formerly SFTA), 1963, 1971, 1972, 1973, 1977; Silver Heart, 1964; Water Rats, 1970; Radio Industries, 1971, 1972; Sun Newspaper, 1973; Sun, 1974; Water Rats Distinguished Services, 1974; TV Times Hall of Fame Award, 1980-81; Commendation, 1981, Special Mention, 1982, HM Queen Mother's Award, Keep Britain Tidy. Freeman, City of London, 1976. *Films:* The Intelligence Men, 1964; That Riviera Touch, 1965; The Magnificent Two, 1966. *Publications:* (with E. Morecambe): Eric and Ernie: an autobiography of Morecambe and Wise, 1973; Scripts of Morecambe and Wise, 1974; Morecambe and Wise Special, 1977; There's No Answer to That, 1981. *Recreations:* boating, tennis, swimming, jogging. *Address:* Thames Television, Teddington Lock, TW11 9NT.

WISEMAN, Sir John William, 11th Bt, *cr* 1628; *b* 16 March 1957; *o s* of Sir William George Eden Wiseman, 10th Bt, and Joan Mary, *d* of late Arthur Phelps, Harrow; *S* father, 1962; *m* 1980, Nancy, *d* of Casimer Zylu, New Britain, Conn. *Educ:* Millfield Sch.; Univ. of Hartford, Conn, USA. *Heir: kinsman* Thomas Alan Wiseman [*b* 8 July 1921; *m* 1946, Hildemarie Domnik; (one *s* one *d* decd)]. *Address:* 32 Victoria Road, W8.

WISHART, Maureen; *see* Lehane, M.

WISTRICH, Enid Barbara, PhD; Principal Lecturer in Public Administration, Middlesex Polytechnic, since 1979; *b* 4 Sept. 1928; *d* of Zadik Heiber and Bertha Brown; *m* 1950, Ernest Wistrich, *qv* ; two *c* (and one *c* decd). *Educ:* Froebel Institute Sch.; Brackley High Sch.; St Paul's Girls' Sch.; London School of Economics (BScEcon, PhD). Research Asst, LSE, 1950-52; Instructor, Mt Holyoke Coll., Mass, USA, 1952-53; Research Officer, Royal Inst. of Public Administration, 1954-56; Sen. Res. Officer, LSE, 1969-72; NEDO, 1977-79. Councillor (Lab): Hampstead Metropolitan Bor. Council, 1962-65; London Bor. of Camden, 1964-68 and 1971-74; GLC, ILEA, 1973-77. Governor: Museum of London, 1974-77; British Film Inst., 1974-81 (also Actg Chm., 1977-78); National Film Sch., 1978-; Founder Trustee and Vice-Chm., Areopagitica Educnl Trust, 1980-; Chm. of Governors, Heathlands Sch. for Autistic Children, 1976-. *Publications:* Local Government Reorganisation: the first years of Camden, 1972; I Don't Mind the Sex, It's the Violence: film censorship explored, 1978; The Politics of Transport, 1983; articles in Political Qly, Local Government Studies, Jl of Media Law and Practice, Teaching Public Administration, etc. *Recreations:* experiencing the arts, admiring nature, fussing round the family. *Address:* 37B Gayton Road, NW3. *T:* 01-435 8796.

WISTRICH, Ernest, CBE 1973; Director, European Movement (British Council), since 1969; *b* 22 May 1923; *s* of Dr Arthur and Mrs Eva Wistrich; *m* 1950, Enid Barbara (*née* Heiber), *qv* ; two *c* (and one *c* decd). *Educ:* Poland; University Tutorial Coll., London. Served in RAF, 1942-46; Timber Merchant, 1946-67; Dir, Britain in Europe, 1967-69; Councillor, Hampstead Borough Council, 1959-65; Camden Borough Council, Alderman 1964-71, Councillor 1971-74; Chm., Camden Cttee for Community Relations, 1964-68; Mem., Skeffington Cttee on Public Participation in Planning, 1968-69. Contested (Lab): Isle of Thanet, 1964; Hendon North, 1966; Cleveland, European Parly election, 1979. Editor of various jls. *Publications:* contrib. Into Europe, Facts, New Europe and other jls. *Recreations:* music, walking, ski-ing. *Address:* 37B Gayton Road, NW3. *T:* 01-435 8796; (office) 01-839 3120. *Club:* National Liberal.

WITHALL, Maj.-Gen. William Nigel James, CB 1982; Director, Army Air Corps, since 1979; *b* 14 Oct. 1928; *s* of late Bernard Withall and Enid (*née* Hill); *m* 1952, Pamela Hickman; one *s* one *d. Educ:* St Benedict's; Birmingham Univ. (Civil Engrg degree). Commnd R.E, 1950; served in Hong Kong, Gulf States, Aden, Germany and India; Staff Coll., 1961; Sqdn Comd, 73 Fd Sqdn, 1964–66; Jt Services Staff Coll., Latimer, 1967; Mil. Asst to MGO, 1968–70; CO 26 Engr Regt, BAOR, 1970–72; Bde Comd, 11 Engr Bde, 1974–76; NDC, India, 1977; No 259 Army Pilots Course, 1978. Chm., Army Football Assoc., 1980–81; Pres., Army Cricket Assoc., 1981. Freeman, City of London, 1981; Liveryman, GAPAN, 1981. *Recreations:* cricket, squash, all games, reading, walking. *Address:* c/o Barclays Bank, High Street, Andover, Hants. *Clubs:* City Livery, MCC.

WITHERINGTON, Giles Somerville Gwynne; Chairman, Save the Children Fund, since 1982; *b* 7 June 1919; *s* of Iltid Gwynne Witherington and Alice Isabel Gage Witherington; *m* 1951, Rowena Ann Spencer Lynch; one *s* three *d. Educ:* Charterhouse; University Coll., Oxford (MA). War Service, Royal Artillery, UK, N Africa, Italy, 1939–46 (despatches). Joined Spicers Ltd, 1946, Jt Managing Director, 1960; joined Reed International Ltd: Director, 1963; Dep. Chm., 1976; retired, 1982. Mem. Council, Save the Children Fund, 1980. *Recreations:* shooting, gardening, modern art, travel. *Address:* Save the Children Fund, Grove Lane, Camberwell, SE5 8RD; Bishops, Widdington, Saffron Walden, Essex CB11 3SQ. *Club:* Arts.

WITHERS, Googie, (Mrs John McCallum), AO 1980; Actress since 1932; *b* Karachi, India, 12 March 1917; *d* of late Captain E. C. Withers, DMC, CIE, RIM, and late Lizette Catherine Wilhelmina van Wageningen; *m* 1948, John Neil McCallum, *qv*; one *s* two *d. Educ:* Fredville Park, Nonnington, Kent; Convent of the Holy Family, Kensington. Started as dancer in Musical Comedy. First film contract at age of 17; has acted in over 50 pictures, starring in 30. *Films include:* One of our Aircraft is Missing; The Silver Fleet; On Approval; Loves of Joanna Godden; It Always Rains on Sunday; White Corridors; Nickel Queen. *Plays include:* They Came to a City; Private Lives; Winter Journey; The Deep Blue Sea; Waiting for Gillian; Janus. Stratford on Avon Season, 1958: Beatrice in Much Ado About Nothing; Gertrude in Hamlet. The Complaisant Lover, New York, 1962; Exit the King, London, 1963; Getting Married, Strand, 1967; Madame Renevsky in The Cherry Orchard, Mrs Cheveley in An Ideal Husband, 1972; Lady Kitty in The Circle, Chichester Festival Theatre, 1976, Haymarket, 1977, Toronto, 1978; Lady Bracknell in The Importance of Being Earnest, Chichester, 1979. Tours: 1959, Australia and NZ with: Roar Like a Dove, The Constant Wife and Woman in a Dressing Gown; 1964, excerpts Shakespeare (Kate, Margaret of Anjou, Beatrice, Portia, Rosalind, Cleopatra); 1965, Australia and NZ, with Beekman Place; 1968, Australia, with Relatively Speaking; 1969–70, Australia and NZ, with Plaza Suite; 1978–80, Australia, NZ and Far East, with The Kingfisher; 1981, UK tour, The Cherry Orchard, The Skin Game, Dandy Dick. TV appearances in drama including The Public Prosecutor; Amphitryon 38; The Deep Blue Sea (Best Actress, 1954); Last Year's Confetti, Court Circular, 1971; Knightsbridge, 1972; The Cherry Orchard, 1973; series Within These Walls, 1974–76 (Best Actress of the Year, 1974). *Recreations:* music, travel, reading, interior decorating. *Address:* 1740 Pittwater Road, Bay View, NSW 2104, Australia; c/o Coutts & Co., 440 Strand, WC2.

WITHERS, John Keppel Ingold D.; *see* Douglas-Withers.

WITHERS, Senator Rt. Hon. Reginald (Greive), PC 1977; Senator (L) for Western Australia, since 1966; *b* 26 Oct. 1924; *s* of late F. J. Withers and I. L. Greive; *m* 1953, Shirley Lloyd-Jones; two *s* one *d. Educ:* Banbury; Univ. of WA (LLB). Barrister-at-law 1953. Served War, RAN, 1942–46. Councillor, Bunbury Municipal Council, 1954–56; Mem., Bunbury Diocesan Council, 1958–59, Treasurer, 1961–68. State Vice-Pres., Liberal and Country League of WA, 1958–61, State Pres., 1961–65; Mem., Federal Exec. of Liberal Party, 1961–65; Fed. Vice-Pres., Liberal Party, 1962–65. Govt Whip in Senate, 1969–71; Leader of Opposition in Senate, 1972–75; Special Minister of State, Minister for Capital Territory, Minister for Media, and Minister for Tourism and Recreation, Nov.–Dec. 1975; Vice-Pres. of Exec. Council, Leader of Govt in Senate, and Minister for Admin. Services, 1975–78. Sec., SW Law Soc., 1955–68. *Recreations:* swimming, reading, painting. *Address:* 23 Malcolm Street, West Perth, WA 6005, Australia. *T:* (09)3214608.

WITHERS, Rupert Alfred; Director, Dalgety Ltd (Deputy Chairman and Managing Director, 1969–71; Chairman, 1972–77); *b* 29 Oct. 1913; *o s* of late Herbert Withers, FRAM and Marguerite (*née* Elzy); *m* ; three *d. Educ:* University College School. Fellow Institute of Chartered Accountants, 1938. Secretary and Chief Accountant, Gloster Aircraft Co. Ltd, 1940–44; a Senior Partner of Urwick Orr & Partners Ltd until 1959; Man. Dir, Ilford Ltd, 1959–64; Chm. and Chief Executive, 1964–68. Mem. Council, Cheltenham Coll. 1964. *Recreations:* music, books, theatre. *Address:* Epwell Mill Cottage, Banbury, Oxon. *T:* Swalcliffe 327. *Clubs:* Savile, Buck's.

WITHY, George; Assistant Editor (night), Liverpool Echo, since 1972; *b* Birkenhead, 15 May 1924; *er s* of George Withy and Alma Elizabeth Withy (*née* Stankley); *m* 1950, Dorothy Betty, *e c* of Bertram Allen and Dorothy Gray, Northfield, Birmingham; two *d. Educ:* Birkenhead Park High Sch. Served War, Royal Artillery, Britain and NW Europe, 1942–47. Trainee and Reporter, Birkenhead News, 1940; Chief Reporter, Redditch Indicator, 1948; District Reporter, Birmingham Post and Mail, 1950; Editor, Redditch Indicator, 1952. Joined Liverpool Daily Post 1960: successively Sub-Editor,

Dep. Chief Sub-Editor, Asst News Editor, Chief Sub-Editor. Chief Sub-Editor, Liverpool Echo, 1970. Inst. of Journalists, 1962: successively Sec. and Chm., Liverpool District; Convenor, NW Region; Chm., Salaries and Conditions Bd, 1973–; Vice-Pres. and then Pres., 1975; Fellow 1975. Chm., Nat. Council for the Trng of Journalists, 1974, 1982 (Mem., 1970; Vice-Chm., 1973, 1981; Chm., North-West Adv. Trng Cttee, 1974–76); Mem., Newspaper Trng Cttee, Printing and Publishing Industry Trng Bd; Mem., Press Council, 1973–79. *Recreations:* writing on Rugby Union football, gardening, reading, philately. *Address:* 3 Woodside Road, Irby, Wirral, Merseyside L61 4UL. *T:* 051-648 2809.

WITNEY, Kenneth Percy, CVO; *b* 19 March 1916; *s* of late Rev. Thomas and of Dr Myfanwy Witney, S India; *m* 1947, Joan Tait; one *s* one *d. Educ:* Eltham Coll.; Wadham Coll., Oxford (Schol.). BA Hons Mod. History, 1938; MA 1975. Min. of Home Security, 1940; Private Sec. to Parly Under-Sec., 1942–44; Home Office, 1945; Asst Private Sec. to Home Sec., 1945–47; Colonial Office (Police Div.), 1955–57; Asst Sec., Home Office, 1957; Asst Under-Sec. of State, Home Office, 1969–76. Special Consultant to Royal Commn on Gambling, 1976–78. Chm., Kent Fedn of Amenity Socs, 1982. *Publications:* The Jutish Forest, 1976; The Kingdom of Kent, 1982. *Recreations:* local history, gardening. *Address:* 61 Hadlow Road, Tonbridge, Kent. *T:* Tonbridge 352971; 37 Paradise Row, Sandwich, Kent. *Club:* United Oxford & Cambridge University.

WITT, Rt. Rev. Howell Arthur John; *see* Bathurst, Bishop of.

WITT, Maj.-Gen. John Evered, CB 1952; CBE 1948; MC 1918; retired from Army, 1953; *b* 15 Jan. 1897; *s* of late Rev. A. R. Witt, Royal Army Chaplains' Department; *m* 1st, 1924, Kathleen Phyllis Outram (*d* 1968); one *s* 2nd, 1969, Mrs Cynthia Myrtle Margaret Reynolds (*d* 1982), *yr d* of late Dr Geoffrey Eden, FRCP. *Educ:* King's Sch., Canterbury. RMC Sandhurst, 1914; 2nd Lt ASC, Dec. 1914; BEF, 1915–19; BAOR, 1919–21; UK, 1921–23; BAOR, 1923–26; UK, 1926; India, 1927; Egypt, 1927–32; UK, 1932–46; Director of Supplies and Transport, BAOR, 1946–48; FarELF, 1948–49 (despatches); Director of Supplies and Transport, Middle East Land Forces, 1950–53. *Address:* c/o Barclay's Bank, Aldershot, Hants.

WITTE, Prof. William, FRSE; Professor of German in the University of Aberdeen, 1951–77; *b* 18 Feb. 1907; *o s* of W. G. J. and E. O. Witte; *m* 1937, Edith Mary Stenhouse Melvin; one *s* one *d. Educ:* Universities of Breslau, Munich, Berlin. MA, DLit (London); PhD (Aberdeen); FRSE 1978. Assistant, Department of German: Aberdeen, 1931–36; Edinburgh, 1936–37; Lecturer, Department of German, Aberdeen, 1937; Head of Dept, 1945; Reader in German, 1947. Gold Medal, Goethe Inst., 1971. Cross of the Order of Merit (Federal Republic of Germany), 1974. *Publications:* Modern German Prose Usage, 1937; Schiller, 1949; ed Schiller's Wallenstein, 1952; ed Two Stories by Thomas Mann, 1957; Schiller and Burns, and Other Essays, 1959; ed Schiller's Wallensteins Tod, 1962; ed Schiller's Maria Stuart, 1965; ed Goethe's Clavigo, 1973; contributions to collective works; articles in Modern Language Review, German Life and Letters, Oxford German Studies, Publications of the English Goethe Society, Publications of the Carlyle Soc., Aberdeen Univ. Rev., Wisconsin Monatshefte, Schiller-Jahrbuch, Forum for Modern Language Studies, Encyclopædia Britannica, etc. *Recreations:* gardening, motoring. *Address:* 41 Beechgrove Terrace, Aberdeen. *T:* 53799.

WITTEVEEN, Dr (Hendrikus) Johannes, Commander, Order of Netherlands Lion; Commander, Order of Orange Nassau; Board Member: Royal Dutch Petroleum Co., 1971–73 and since 1978; Thyssen-Bornemisza NV, since 1978; Robeco, 1971–73 and since 1979 (Adviser, 1971–73); Nationale-Nederlanden, since 1979; Chairman, Group of Thirty, since 1979; Adviser for International Affairs, Amro Bank, Amsterdam, since 1979; Member: International Council, Morgan Guaranty Trust Company of New York, since 1978; European Advisory Council, General Motors, since 1978; *b* Zeist, Netherlands, 12 June 1921; *m* 1949, Liesbeth de Vries Feyens; two *s* one *d. Educ:* Univ. Rotterdam (DrEcons). Central Planning Bureau, 1947–48; Prof., Univ. Rotterdam, 1948–63; Mem. Netherlands Parlt, First Chamber, 1959–63 and 1971–73, and Second Chamber, 1965–67; Minister of Finance, Netherlands, 1963–65 and 1967–71; First Deputy Prime Minister, 1967–71; Managing Director, IMF, 1973–78. Grand Cross, Order of Crown (Belgium); Order of Oak Wreath (Luxemburg); Order of Merit (Fed. Republic Germany). *Publications:* Loonshoogte en Werkgelegenheid, 1947; Growth and Business Cycles, 1954; articles in Economische Statistische Berichten, Euromoney. *Recreation:* hiking. *Address:* Wassenaar, Waldeck Pyrmontlaan 15, The Netherlands.

WITTIG, Prof. Georg, Dr Phil; *b* Berlin, 16 June 1897; *s* of Prof. Gustav Wittig and Martha (*née* Dombrowski); *m* 1930, Waltraut Ernst (*d* 1978); two *d. Educ:* Wilhelms-Gymnasium, Kassel; Marburg Univ. Lecturer, Marburg Univ., 1926–32; Division Director, Technische Hochschule, Braunschweig, 1932–37; Prof., Univs of Braunschweig, Freiburg and Tübingen, 1937–56; Prof., Heidelberg Univ., 1956–67, emeritus, 1967–. Member: Acad. of Sciences, Munich and Heidelberg; l'Acad. Française; Soc. Quimica del Perú; Leopoldina Halle; Hon. Member: Swiss Chem. Assoc.; New York Acad. of Scis; Chem. Soc., London; Soc. Chim. de France. Hon. doctorates, Sorbonne and Hamburg. Nobel Prize (jointly) 1979; many earlier awards, incl. Otto Hahn Prize, 1967; Karl Ziegler Prize, 1975. Ordens Grosses Verdienstkreuz, 1980. *Publications:* Textbook on Stereochemistry, 1930; numerous articles in jls on Metallorganic, Ylid and Carbanion Chemistry. *Recreations:* painting, music, hiking, mountain climbing. *Address:* Bergstrasse 35, 69 Heidelberg, Federal Republic of Germany. *T:* 40945.

WITTON-DAVIES, Ven. Carlyle; Archdeacon of Oxford and Canon of Christ Church, Oxford, 1957-82, now Archdeacon Emeritus; Sub Dean, 1972-82; Examining Chaplain to the Bishop of Oxford, 1965-82; *b* 10 June 1913; *s* of late Prof. T. Witton Davies, DD, and Hilda Mabel Witton Davies (*née* Everett); *m* 1941, Mary Rees, BA, *o d* of late Canon W. J. Rees, St Asaph, Clwyd; three *s* four *d. Educ:* Friars School, Bangor; University College of N Wales, Bangor; Exeter College, Oxford; Cuddesdon College, Oxford; Hebrew University, Jerusalem. Exhib., University Coll. of N Wales, Bangor, 1930-34; BA (Wales), 1st Cl. Hons Hebrew, 1934; BA (Oxon), 2nd Cl. Hons Theology, 1937; Junior Hall Houghton Septuagint Prize, Oxford, 1938, Senior, 1939; MA (Oxon), 1940; Deacon, 1937, Priest, 1938, St Asaph; Assistant Curate, Buckley, 1937-40; Subwarden, St Michael's College, Llandaff, 1940-44; Examining Chaplain to Bishop of Monmouth, 1940-44; Adviser on Judaica to Anglican Bishop in Jerusalem, 1944-49; Examining Chaplain to Bishop in Jerusalem, 1945-49; Canon Residentiary of Nazareth in St George's Collegiate Church, Jerusalem, 1947-49; Dean and Precentor of St David's Cathedral, 1949-57; Examining Chaplain to Bishop of St David's, 1950-57; Chaplain, Order of St John of Jerusalem, 1954-; Surrogate. Chairman: Council of Christians and Jews, 1957-78 (Vice-Pres., 1978-); Clergy Friendly Society, 1961-63. Mem., Archbishops' Commn on Crown Appointments, 1962-64; Censor Theologiae, Christ Church, 1972-75, 1978-80; Member, Convocation of Canterbury, and Church Assembly/General Synod of C of E, 1957-75, 1978-80. First recipient, Sir Sigmund Sternberg Award, 1979. *Publications:* Journey of a Lifetime, 1962; (part translated) Martin Buber's Hasidism, 1948; (translated) Martin Buber's The Prophetic Faith, 1949; contrib. to Oxford Dictionary of the Christian Church, 1957; contrib. to The Mission of Israel, 1963. *Recreations:* music, lawn tennis, swimming, travel. *Address:* 199 Divinity Road, Oxford.

WITTRICK, Prof. William Henry, FRS 1980; Beale Professor of Civil Engineering, University of Birmingham, 1969-82, now Professor Emeritus; *b* 29 Oct. 1922; *s* of late Frank Wittrick; *m* 1945, Joyce Farrington, *d* of late Arthur Farrington; two *d. Educ:* Huddersfield Coll.; St Catharine's Coll., Cambridge (Scholar). Mech. Scis Tripos 1942, Archibald Denny Prize. MA, ScD Cantab; PhD Sydney; FAA 1958; FRAeS; FEng 1981. Temp. Demonstrator in Engrg, Univ. of Cambridge, 1942-44; Scientific Officer, RAE, 1944-45; Univ. of Sydney: Sen. Lectr, 1945-54; Reader, 1954-56; Lawrence Hargrave Prof. of Aeronautical Engrg, 1956-64; Dean of Faculty of Engrg, 1962-63; Prof. of Structural Engrg, Univ. of Birmingham, 1964-69; Head of Dept of Civil Engineering, Univ. of Birmingham, 1969-80. Vis. Research Fellow, California Inst. of Technology, 1953; Vis. Prof., Coll. of Aeronautics, Cranfield, 1960; Pres., Australian Div. RAeS, 1961-62; Mem. 1956-61, Chm. 1961-64, Australian Aeronautical Research Cttee; Mem., Aeronautical Research Council, 1970-73. *Publications:* numerous contribs to theory of structures and mechanics of solids in learned jls. *Recreations:* bookbinding, carpentry, theatre. *Address:* The Old Forge, Ebrington, Chipping Campden, Glos GL55 6NL. *T:* Paxford 208.

WITTS, Leslie John, CBE 1959; MD Manchester; FRCP; DM Oxford; Hon. ScD Dublin; Hon. MD Bristol; Hon. DSc Belfast; Hon. DSc Manchester; Fellow of Magdalen College and Nuffield Professor of Clinical Medicine, Oxford, 1938-65; now Emeritus Fellow and Professor; *b* 1898; *s* of Wyndham John Witts, Warrington, Lancs; *m* 1929, Nancy Grace, *y d* of L. F. Salzman; one *s* three *d. Educ:* Boteler Grammar Sch., Warrington; Victoria Univ. of Manchester; Sidney Sussex Coll., Cambridge. Served with Inns of Court OTC and RFA, 1916-18; Dickenson Travelling Scholar, 1925; John Lucas Walker Student, 1926; Edmonds Research Fellow, 1929. Lectures: Goulstonian, RCP, 1932; Frederick Price, Dublin, 1950; Schorstein Meml, London Hosp., 1955; Sidney Watson Smith, Edinburgh, 1956; Gwladys and Olwen Williams, Liverpool, 1957; Shepherd, Montreal, 1959; Lumleian, RCP, 1961; Heath Clark, Univ. of London, 1966; Litchfield, Oxon, 1969; Harveian, RCP, 1971. Late Asst to Med. Unit, London Hospital; Director, Medical Professorial Clinic and Physician St Bartholomew's Hospital; Assistant Physician to Guy's Hospital; Member of Medical Research Council, 1938-42, 1943-47; Hon. Secretary and Treasurer Assoc. Physicians of Great Britain and Ireland, 1933-48; Second Vice-Pres. Royal Coll. of Physicians, 1965-66. Mem., Min. of Health Committee on Safety of Drugs, 1963-68. McIlrath Guest Professor, Sydney, 1956. Hon. Fellow, Royal Coll. of Physicians and Surgeons of Canada. Hon. Member, Assoc. of American Physicians, and Danish Soc. of Internal Med. *Publications:* Anæmia and the Alimentary Tract, 1956; The Stomach and Anaemia, 1966; Hypochromic Anaemia, 1969. Editor of Medical Surveys and Clinical Trials, 2nd edn, 1964. Contributions to medical and scientific journals. *Recreations:* walking, play-going. *Address:* 293 Woodstock Road, Oxford. *T:* 58843.

WITTY, (John) David; Chief Executive, Westminster City Council; Hon. Secretary, London Boroughs Association; *b* 1 Oct. 1924; *s* of late Harold Witty and Olive Witty, Beverley; *m* 1955, Doreen Hanlan; one *s. Educ:* Beverley Grammar Sch.; Balliol Coll., Oxford (MA). Served War, RN, 1943-46. Asst Town Clerk, Beverley, 1951-53; Asst Solicitor: Essex CC, 1953-54; Hornsey, 1954-60; Dep. Town Clerk: Kingston upon Thames, 1960-65; Merton, 1965-67; Asst Chief Exec., Westminster, 1967-77. Order of Infante D. Henrique (Portugal), 1978; Order of Right Hand (Nepal), 1980; Order of King Abdul Aziz (Saudi Arabia), 1981; Order of Oman, 1982.

Recreation: golf. *Address:* Westminster City Hall, Victoria Street, SW1E 6QP.

WIX, Ethel Rose; Special Commissioner of Income Tax, since 1977; *b* 1 Nov. 1921; *d* of Michael Wix and Anna Wix (*née* Snyder). *Educ:* Henrietta Barnett Sch.; Cheltenham Ladies' Coll.; University Coll. London (BA Hons 1942); Hull University Coll. (Cert Ed 1943). Special Operations Executive, 1944-45; lived in S Africa, 1948-54; work for S African Inst. of Race Relations, 1950-54; Africa Bureau, London, 1955-56; Solicitor of Supreme Court, 1960; Partner, Herbert Oppenheimer, Nathan & Vandyk, 1960-75; General Commissioner of Income Tax, 1976-78. *Publications:* papers on Cost of Living, 1951, and Industrial Feeding Facilities, 1953, for S African Inst. of Race Relations; summary of Royal Commn Report on E Africa, 1956, for Africa Bureau. *Recreations:* reading, cooking, theatre. *Address:* 5 Phillimore Gardens, W8 7QG. *T:* 01-937 8899. *Clubs:* Reform, University Women's, Special Forces.

WODEHOUSE, family name of **Earl of Kimberley.**

WODEHOUSE, Lord; John Armine Wodehouse; System Programmer, Glaxo, since 1979; *b* 15 Jan. 1951; *s* and *heir* of 4th Earl of Kimberley, *qv*; *m* 1973, Hon. Carol Palmer, MA (Oxon), *er d* of Baron Palmer, *qv*; one *s* one *d. Educ:* Eton; Univ. of East Anglia. BSc (Chemistry) 1973; MSc (Physical Organic Chemistry) 1974. FRSA. Research Chemist, Glaxo, 1977-79. Chm., UK Info Users Gp, 1981-. Associate Fellow, British Interplanetary Soc., 1981-. *Recreations:* interest in spaceflight, photography, computing, fantasy role playing games. *Heir:* s David Simon John Wodehouse, *b* 10 Oct. 1978. *Address:* Derry House, North End, Henley-on-Thames, Oxon RG9 6LQ.

WOLEDGE, Brian; Emeritus Professor of French Language and Literature, University of London; Fielden Professor of French, University College, London, 1939-71; Hon. Research Fellow, University College London; *b* 16 Aug. 1904; *m* 1933, Christine Mary Craven; one *s* one *d. Educ:* Leeds Boys' Modern School; University of Leeds. BA (Leeds) 1926; MA (Leeds) 1928; Docteur de l'Université de Paris, 1930; Asst Lecturer in French, University College, Hull, 1930-32; Lecturer in French, University of Aberdeen, 1932-39. Visiting Andrew Mellon Professor of French, University of Pittsburg, 1967. Docteur *hc* de l'Université d'Aix-Marseille, 1970. *Publications:* L'Atre périlleux; études sur les manuscrits, la langue et l'importance littéraire du poème, 1930; L'Atre périlleux, roman de la Table ronde (Les Classiques français du moyen âge 76), 1935; Bibliographie des romans et nouvelles en prose française antérieurs à 1500, 1954, repr. 1975, Supplement 1975; The Penguin Book of French Verse, Vol. 1, To the Fifteenth Century, 1961; Répertoire des premiers textes en prose française, 842-1210 (with H. P. Clive), 1964; La Syntaxe des substantifs chez Chrétien de Troyes, 1979. *Address:* 28a Dobbins Lane, Wendover, Aylesbury, Bucks. *T:* Wendover 622188.

WOLF, Prof. Peter Otto, FEng; FICE; FIWES; FRMetS; Professor, since 1966 and Head of Department of Civil Engineering, 1966-82, The City University, London; *b* 9 May 1918; *s* of Richard Wolf and Dora (*née* Bondy); *m* 1st, 1944, Jennie Robinson; two *s* one *d*; 2nd, 1977, Janet Elizabeth Robertson. *Educ:* University of London (BScEng). Assistant under agreement to C. E. Farren, Cons. Engr, 1941-44; Civilian Asst, a Dept of the War Office, 1944-45; Engineer (Chief Designer, Loch Sloy Project), under James Williamson, Cons. Engr, 1945-47; Engineer for Mullardoch Dam (Affric Project), John Cochrane & Sons Ltd, 1947-49; Imperial College of Science and Technology: Lectr in Fluid Mechanics and Hydraulic Engrg, 1949-55; Reader in Hydrology in Univ. of London, 1955-66. Private consultancy, London, 1950-. Visiting Professor: Stanford Univ., Calif, 1959-60, 1961-64; Cornell Univ., 1963. FASCE. *Publications:* trans. and ed, Engineering Fluid Mechanics, by Charles Jaeger, 1956; papers in Proc. ICE, Jl IWE, UNESCO Reports, UNESCO Nature and Resources, Proc. Internat. Water Resources Assoc., etc. *Recreations:* classical music, reading, ski-ing, sailing, walking. *Address:* 69 Shepherds Hill, N6 5RE. *T:* 01-340 6638. *Club:* Athenæum.

WOLFE, Prof. James Nathan; Professor of Economics, University of Edinburgh, since 1964; *b* 16 Sept. 1927; *s* of Jack Wolfe and Rose (*née* Segal); *m* 1954, Monica Anne Hart; one *d. Educ:* Westhill High Sch., Montreal; McGill Univ. (BA 1948, MA 1949); Glasgow Univ.; Queen's and Nuffield Colls, Oxford. BLitt (Oxon) 1952. Lecturer in Political Economy, Univ. of Toronto, 1952-60; Prof. of Economics, Univ. of California, Berkeley and Santa Barbara, 1960-64; Brookings Research Prof., 1963-64. Economic Consultant: to Nat. Economic Develt Office, 1963-64; to Sec. of State for Scotland, 1965-72; to Dept of Economic Affairs, 1965-69; Member, Interdeptl Cttee on Long Term Population Distribution, 1966-69. Visiting Scholar, Stanford Univ., 1982. *Publications:* ed, Government and Nationalism in Scotland, 1969; The Economics of Technical Information Systems, 1974; ed (with C. I. Phillips) Clinical Practice and Economics, 1977; (with M. Pickford) The Church of Scotland: an economic survey, 1980; articles in learned jls. *Recreations:* statistics, the novel, new ventures. *Address:* 3 St Margaret's Road, Edinburgh EH9 1AZ. *T:* 031-447 6645. *Clubs:* Athenæum; New, Scottish Arts, USC (Edinburgh).

WOLFE, William Cuthbertson; President, Scottish National Party, 1980-82; *b* 22 Feb. 1924; *s* of late Major Tom Wolfe, DD, and Katie Cuthbertson; *m* 1953, Arna Mary, *d* of late Dr Melville Dinwiddie, CBE, DSO, MC; two *s* two *d. Educ:* Bathgate Academy; George Watson's Coll., Edinburgh. CA.

Army service, 1942–47, NW Europe and Far East; Air OP Pilot. Hon. Publications Treas., Saltire Society, 1953–60; Scout County Comr, West Lothian, 1960–64; Hon. Pres. (Rector), Students' Assoc., Heriot-Watt Univ., 1966–69. Contested (SNP) West Lothian, 1962, 1964, 1966, 1970, Feb. and Oct. 1974, 1979; Chm., SNP, 1969–79. *Publication:* Scotland Lives, 1973. *Address:* Craigpark, Torphichen, Bathgate, West Lothian. *T:* Bathgate 52981.

WOLFENDALE, Prof. Arnold Whittaker, PhD, DSc; FRS 1977; FInstP, FRAS; Professor of Physics, University of Durham, since 1965; *b* 25 June 1927; *s* of Arnold Wolfendale and Doris Wolfendale; *m* 1951, Audrey Darby; twin *s. Educ:* Univ. of Manchester (BSc Physics 1st Cl. Hons 1948, PhD 1953, DSc 1970). FInstP 1958; FRAS 1973. Asst Lectr, Univ. of Manchester, 1951, Lectr, 1954; Univ. of Durham: Lectr, 1956; Sen. Lectr, 1959; Reader in Physics, 1963; Head of Dept, 1973–77. Chm., Northern Reg. Action Cttee, Manpower Services Commn's Job Creation Prog., 1975–78. Pres., RAS, 1981–. *Publications:* Cosmic Rays, 1963; (ed) Cosmic Rays at Ground Level, 1973; (ed) Origin of Cosmic Rays, 1974; (ed jtly and contrib.) Origin of Cosmic Rays, 1981; (ed) Gamma Ray Astronomy, 1981; (ed) Progress in Cosmology, 1982; original papers on studies of cosmic radiation. *Recreations:* fell walking, foreign travel. *Address:* Ansford, Potters Bank, Durham. *T:* Durham 45642.

WOLFENDEN, family name of **Baron Wolfenden.**

WOLFENDEN, Baron *cr* 1974 (Life Peer), of Westcott; **John Frederick Wolfenden,** Kt 1956; CBE 1942; *b* 26 June 1906; *s* of late G. Wolfenden, Halifax; *m* 1932, Eileen Le Messurier, 2nd *d* of late A. J. Spilsbury; one *s* two *d* (one *s* decd). *Educ:* Wakefield School; Queen's College, Oxford (Hastings Scholar, Akroyd Scholar; Hon. Fellow 1959); 2nd Class Classical Mods, 1926; 1st Class Literae Humaniores, 1928; Henry P. Davison Scholar Princeton University, USA, 1928–29; Fellow and Tutor in Philosophy, Magdalen College, Oxford, 1929–34; Headmaster of Uppingham School, 1934–44; Headmaster of Shrewsbury School, 1944–50; Vice-Chancellor of Reading University, 1950–63; Chm., UGC, 1963–68; Dir and Principal Librarian, British Museum, 1969–73. Director of Pre-Entry Training, Air Ministry, 1941; Chairman: Ministry of Education's Youth Advisory Council, 1942–45; Headmasters' Conference, 1945, 1946, 1948, 1949; Departmental Cttee on Employment of National Service Men, 1956; Secondary School Examinations Council, 1951–57; Departmental Cttee on Homosexual Offences and Prostitution, 1954–57; National Council of Social Service, 1953–60; CCPR Sport Enquiry, 1957–60; Family Service Units, 1957–63; National Association of Youth Clubs, 1958–63; Local Government Examinations Board, 1958–63; Councils for the Training of Health Visitors and for Training in Social Work, 1962–63; Carnegie UK Trust, 1969–74; Alleyn's Coll. of God's Gift, 1973–; Cttee on Voluntary Organisations, 1974–77. President: Section L British Association, 1955; Aslib, 1969–71; Chelsea Coll., Univ. of London, 1972–; Metropolitan Assoc. of Building Socs, 1978–; Chelsea Building Soc., 1978–; Nat. Children's Bureau, 1978–; Classical Assoc., 1979–80. Hon. DLitt: Reading, 1963; Warwick, 1977; Hon. LLD: Hull, 1969; Wales, 1971; Manchester, 1972; Williams Coll., Mass., 1973; Hon. LHD Hamilton Coll., NY, 1972; DUniv York, 1973. Oxford University Hockey XI, 1927, 1928, English Hockey XI, 1930–33. Provost, Order of the Buffalo Hunt (Manitoba). *Publications:* The Approach to Philosophy, 1932; The Public Schools To-Day, 1948; How to Choose Your School, 1952; Chapters in The Prospect Before Us, 1948; Education in a Changing World, 1951; Turning Points (memoirs), 1976; occasional articles, named lectures, and reviews. *Recreation:* learning to come to terms with arthritis, bi-focals and dentures. *Address:* The White House, Westcott, near Dorking, Surrey. *T:* Dorking 885475. *Clubs:* United Oxford & Cambridge University; Vincent's (Oxford).

WOLFF, Frederick Ferdinand, CBE 1975; TD 1945; Chairman, Rudolf Wolff & Co. Ltd, 1965–81; *b* 13 Oct. 1910; *s* of Philip Robert Wolff and Irma Wolff; *m* 1937, Natalie Winifred Virginia Byrne; two *s* three *d* (incl. twin *s* and *d*). *Educ:* Shirley House Prep. Sch., Watford, Herts; Beaumont Coll., Old Windsor, Berks. Oxfordshire and Bucks LI, 1939–45 (Captain). Joined Rudolf Wolff & Co., 1929; Partner, 1951. Chairman: London Metal Exchange Committee, 1970–77 (Mem. Cttee, 1961–77; Mem. Bd, 1963–); Fedn of Commodity Assocs, 1971–77; Mem., Cttee on Invisible Exports, 1971–. AAA Champion 440 yards, 1933; British Gold Medallist, 4 × 400 metres relay team, Olympic Games, Berlin, 1936. *Recreations:* golf, racing. *Address:* Parsonage Farm, Pauls Hill, Penn, Bucks. *T:* Penn 3349. *Clubs:* London Athletic, Gresham, Naval and Military; Beaconsfield Golf.

WOLFF, John Arnold Harrop, CMG 1963; *b* 14 July 1912; *er s* of late Arnold H. Wolff, Halebarns, Cheshire; *m* 1939, Helen Muriel McCracken, Howth, Co. Dublin; one *s* one *d. Educ:* Haileybury College; Peterhouse, Cambridge. Colonial Administrative Service, Kenya: District Officer, 1935–59; Provincial Commissioner, 1959–63; Civil Secretary, Rift Valley Region, 1963; retired, Nov. 1963. *Recreations:* gardening, golf. *Address:* Wallflowers, Bloxham, Oxon.

WOLFF, Michael, FSIAD; Founder and Director, Wolff Olins Ltd, since 1965; Director of the Hunger Project, since 1979; *b* 12 Nov. 1933; *s* of Serge Wolff and Mary (*née* Gordon); *m* 1976, Susan Kent; one *d. Educ:* Gresham Sch., Holt, Norfolk; Architectural Association Sch. of Architecture. Designer: Sir William Crawford & Partners, 1957–61; BBC Television, 1961–62; Main Wolff & Partners, 1964–65; with Wolff Olins Ltd as a founder, 1965–.

Recreation: seeing. *Address:* 9 Cumberland Gardens, WC1. *T:* 01-837 0991; (office) 22 Dukes Road, WC1H 9AB. *T:* 01-387 0891.

WOLFF, Prof. Otto Herbert, MD, FRCP; Nuffield Professor of Child Health, University of London, since 1965; Dean of the Institute of Child Health, since 1982; *b* 10 Jan. 1920; *s* of Dr H. A. J. Wolff; *m* 1952, Dr Jill Freeborough; one *s* one *d. Educ:* Peterhouse, Cambridge; University College Hospital, London. Lieut and Capt. RAMC, 1944–47. Resident Medical Officer, Registrar and Sen. Med. Registrar, Birmingham Children's Hospital, 1948–51; Lecturer, Sen. Lectr, Reader, Dept of Pædiatrics and Child Health, Univ. of Birmingham, 1951–64. Senator, London Univ.; Representative of London Univ. on GMC. Past Pres., British Pædiatric Assoc.; Member: Royal Society of Medicine; American Pædiatric Society; New York Academy of Sciences; Amer. Academy of Pediatrics; European Soc. for Paediatric Research; European Soc. for Paediatric Gastroenterology; Deutsche Akad. der Naturforscher Leopoldina. Corresp. Member: Société Française de Pédiatrie; Société Suisse de Pédiatrie; Osterreichische Gesellschaft für Kinderheilkunde; Società Italiana di Pediatria; Deutsche Gesellschaft für Kinderheilkunde; Fellow, Indian Acad. of Pediatrics. *Publications:* chapter on Disturbances of Serum Lipoproteins in Endocrine and Genetic Diseases of Childhood (ed L. I. Gardner); chapter on Obesity in Recent Advances in Paediatrics (ed David Hull); articles in Lancet, British Medical Journal, Archives of Disease in Childhood, Quarterly Jl of Medicine, etc. *Recreation:* music. *Address:* 53 Danbury Street, N1 8LE. *T:* 01-226 0748.

WOLFF, Rosemary Langley; Member, Police Complaints Board, since 1977; *b* 10 July 1926; *er d* of late A. C. V. Clarkson; *m* 1956, Michael Wolff, JP (*d* 1976); two *d. Educ:* Haberdashers' Aske's Sch. Mem., Community Relations Commn, 1973–77. Manager of various primary schs in North Kensington and Tower Hamlets, 1963–; Governor, City College; Chm., Conservative Contact Group, 1973–77; Mem., Managing Cttee, Working Ladies' Guild. *Address:* 13 Holland Park, W11 3TH. *T:* 01-727 9051.

WOLFSON, Geoffrey Mark; MP (C) Sevenoaks, since 1979; Director, Hambros Bank, since 1973; *b* 7 April 1934; *s* of Captain V. Wolfson, OBE, VRD, RNR, and Dorothy Mary Wolfson; *m* 1965, Edna Webb (*née* Hardman); two *s. Educ:* Eton Coll.; Pembroke Coll., Cambridge (MA). Served Royal Navy, 1952–54; Cambridge, 1954–57; Teacher in Canada, 1958–59; Warden, Brathay Hall Centre, Westmorland, 1962–66; Head of Youth Services, Industrial Soc., 1966–69; Head of Personnel, Hambros Bank, 1969–. *Recreations:* rowing (won Silver Goblets, Henley, 1956), rowing coaching, garden, travel. *Address:* The Manor House, Heverham, Sevenoaks, Kent.

WOLFSON, Sir Isaac, 1st Bt *cr* 1962; FRS 1963; Hon. Fellow: Weizmann Institute of Science, Israel; St Edmund Hall, Oxford; Jews' College; Lady Margaret Hall, Oxford; Founder Fellow, Wolfson College, Oxford; Chairman (since 1946), The Great Universal Stores Ltd; *b* 17 Sept. 1897; *m* 1926, Edith Specterman (*d* 1981); one *s. Educ:* Queen's Park School, Glasgow. Joined The Great Universal Stores Ltd, 1932. Member, Worshipful Company of Pattenmakers; Member, Grand Council, Cancer Research Campaign; Hon. Pres., Weizmann Institute of Science Foundation; Trustee, Religious Centre, Jerusalem; Patron, Royal College of Surgeons; Founder, and Pres., 1975– (formerly Chm.), and Trustee, Wolfson Foundation which was created in 1955 mainly for the advancement of health, education and youth activities in the UK and Commonwealth. Fellow, Royal Postgrad. Med. Sch., 1972; Hon. FRCP 1959; Hon. FRCS 1969; Hon. FRCP&S Glasgow. Hon. DCL Oxford, 1963; Hon. LLD: London, 1958; Glasgow, 1963; Cambridge, 1966; Manchester, 1967; Strathclyde, 1969; Brandeis Univ., US 1969; Nottingham, 1971; Hon. PhD Jerusalem, 1970. Einstein Award, US, 1967; Herbert Lehmann Award, US, 1968. Freeman, City of Glasgow, 1971. *Recreation:* golf. *Heir: s* Sir Leonard Gordon Wolfson, *qv. Address:* 74 Portland Place, W1.

WOLFSON, Sir Leonard (Gordon), Kt 1977; Chairman and a Founder Trustee, Wolfson Foundation; Managing Director, Great Universal Stores, since 1962 (Director, 1952); Chairman, Great Universal Stores Merchandise Corporation, since 1966; *b* 11 Nov. 1927; *s* of Sir Isaac Wolfson, 1st Bt, *qv* ; *m* 1949, Ruth, *d* of E. A. Sterling; four *d. Educ:* King's School, Worcester. Hon. Fellow: St Catherine's Coll., Oxford; Wolfson Coll., Cambridge; Wolfson Coll., Oxford; Worcester Coll., Oxford; Bar-Ilan Univ.; UCL. Patron, Royal College of Surgeons, 1976. Hon. FRCP, 1977. Hon. PhD: Tel Aviv, 1971; Hebrew Univ., 1978; Hon. DCL Oxon, 1972; Hon. LLD: Strathclyde, 1972; Dundee, 1979; Cantab, 1982; Hon. DSc Hull, 1977. *Recreations:* history, economics, golf. *Address:* Universal House, 251 Tottenham Court Road, W1A 1BZ.

WOLKIND, Jack, CBE 1978; Chief Executive (formerly Town Clerk), Tower Hamlets, since 1964; *b* 16 Feb. 1920; *s* of Samuel and Golda Wolkind; *m* 1945, Bena Sternfeld; two *s* one *d. Educ:* Mile End Central Sch.; King's Coll., London. LLB Hons, LLM (London). Admitted Solicitor, 1953. Army service to 1945. Dep. Town Clerk and Solicitor, Stepney Borough Council, 1952–65. Governor, QMC, Univ. of London. FRSA 1980. *Recreations:* reading, music. *Address:* 45 Gordon Avenue, Stanmore, Mddx HA7 3QQ. *Club:* City Livery.

WOLLASTON, Henry Woods; Standing Counsel to General Synod of the Church of England, since 1981; *b* 14 Nov. 1916; *s* of Sir Gerald Woods

Wollaston, KCB, KCVO; *m* 1944, Daphne Margaret Clark; one *s* two *d*. *Educ:* Harrow School; Cambridge Univ. (MA). Barrister-at-law. Served War, Captain, Grenadier Guards, 1940-46. Legal Adviser's Branch, Home Office, 1946; Principal Asst Legal Adviser, 1977-80. Master of the Haberdashers' Company, 1974-75. *Publications:* Jervis on Coroners, 9th edn, 1957; Court of Appeal, 1968; Parker's Conduct of Parliamentary Elections, 1970; Halsbury's Laws of England: 3rd edn, titles, Coroners, Elections, Police; 4th edn, title Elections; British Official Medals for Coronations and Jubilees, 1978. *Recreations:* real tennis, lawn tennis. *Address:* 2 Ashtead House, Ashtead, Surrey KT21 1LU.

WOLLEN, Sir (Ernest) Russell (Storey), KBE 1969 (CBE 1962; OBE 1953); retired; *b* 9 June 1902; *s* of Cecil Storey Wollen, Glengariffe, Torquay, Devon; *m* 1924, Maise, *d* of Robert Adamson, Neville's Cross, Co. Durham; two *s* two *d*. *Educ:* Marlborough. Coffee Planter, 1922-39; Chm., Coffee Bd of Kenya, 1933-40; Mem., Kenya Supply Bd, 1940-44; E African Manager, Dalgety & Co., 1944-55; Chm., Kenya Coffee Marketing Bd, 1955-67. Retired to reside in Western Australia, 1967. *Recreations:* sailing, riding, golf. *Address:* 24 Latham Street, Alfred Cove, WA 6153, Australia. *T:* Perth 3301335. *Clubs:* Farmers' (London); Muthaiga Country (Nairobi).

WOLLHEIM, Prof. Richard Arthur, FBA 1972; Professor of Philosophy, Columbia University, since 1982; *b* 5 May 1923; *s* of Eric Wollheim; *m* 1st, 1950, Anne, *yr d* of Lieutenant-Colonel E. G. H. Powell (marr. diss. 1967); two *s*; 2nd, 1969, Mary Day, *er d* of Robert S. Lanier, NYC; one *d*. *Educ:* Westminster School; Balliol College, Oxford (MA). Served in the Army, N Europe, 1942-45 (POW during Aug. 1944). Assistant Lecturer in Philosophy, University College, London, 1949; Lecturer, 1951; Reader, 1960; Grote Prof. of Philosophy of Mind and Logic in Univ. of London, 1963-82. Visiting Professor: Columbia Univ., 1959-60, 1970; Visva-Bharati Univ., Santiniketan, India, 1968; Univ. of Minnesota, 1972; Graduate Centre, City Univ. of NY, 1975; Univ. of California, Berkeley, 1981; Harvard Univ., 1982. Power Lectr, Univ. of Sydney, 1972; Leslie Stephen Lectr, Univ. of Cambridge, 1979; William James Lectr, Harvard Univ., 1982. Pres., Aristotelian Soc., 1967-68; Vice-Pres., British Soc. of Aesthetics, 1969-. Hon. Affiliate, British Psychoanalytical Soc. *Publications:* F. H. Bradley, 1959, rev. edn 1969; Socialism and Culture, 1961; On Drawing an Object (Inaugural Lecture), 1965; Art and its Objects, 1968, 2nd edn with suppl. essays, 1980; A Family Romance (fiction), 1969; Freud, 1971; On Art and the Mind (essays and lectures), 1973; The Good Self and the Bad Self (Dawes Hicks lecture), 1976; The Sheep and the Ceremony (Leslie Stephen lecture), 1979; edited: F. H. Bradley, Ethical Studies, 1961; Hume on Religion, 1963; F. H. Bradley, Appearance and Reality, 1968; Adrian Stokes, selected writings, 1972; Freud, a collection of critical essays, 1974; J. S. Mill, Three Essays, 1975; (with Jim Hopkins) Philosophical Essays on Freud, 1982; articles in anthologies, philosophical and literary jls. *Address:* 20 Ashchurch Park Villas, W12.

WOLMER, Viscount; William Lewis Palmer; *b* 1 Sept. 1971; *s* and *heir* of 4th Earl of Selborne, *qv*.

WOLPE, Berthold Ludwig, RDI 1959; graphic designer and teacher; *b* 29 Oct. 1905; *s* of Simon Wolpe and Agathe (*née* Goldschmidt); *m* 1941, Margaret Leslie Smith; two *s* two *d*. *Educ:* studied lettering and graphic design under Rudolf Koch, Offenbach Art Sch., 1924-27; goldsmith work under Theodor Wende, Pforzheim Art Sch., 1928. Assistant to Rudolf Koch, 1929-34; Teacher at Frankfurt Art Sch., 1930-33; worked with Ernest Ingham, Fanfare Press, London, 1935-40; joined Faber & Faber, designing and decorating books, book jackets and bindings, 1941; taught at Camberwell School of Art, 1949-53; Tutor, 1956-65, Vis. Lectr, 1965-75, Royal College of Art; teaching at City & Guilds of London Sch. of Art, 1975-. Lyell Reader in bibliography, Oxford Univ., 1981-82. Designed printing types: Hyperion, Albertus, Tempest, Sachsenwald, Pegasus, Decorata. Retrospective exhibn, V&A Mus., 1980. Hon. Member: Double Crown Club; Soc. of Scribes and Illuminators, 1977; Vice-Pres., Printing Historical Soc., 1977; Corresp. Mem., Bund Deutscher Buchkuenstler. Dr *hc* RCA 1968. *Publications:* Schriftvorlagen, 1934; (jtly) ABC Buechlein, 1934, 2nd edn 1977; Handwerkerzeichen, 1936; Marken und Schmuckstuecke, 1937; Fanfare Ornaments, 1938; A Newe Booke of Copies 1574, 1959, 2nd edn 1961; (jtly) Renaissance Handwriting, 1960; Vincent Figgins Type Specimens 1801 and 1815, 1967; Freedom of the Press: Broadsides, 1969; Steingruber Architectural Alphabet, 1972. *Recreations:* collecting material for studies of history of craftsmanship, of printing and calligraphy. *Address:* 140 Kennington Park Road, Lambeth SE11 4BZ. *T:* 01-735 7450.

WOLPERT, Prof. Lewis, DIC, PhD; FRS 1980; Professor of Biology and Head of Department of Anatomy and Biology as Applied to Medicine (formerly Department of Biology as Applied to Medicine), Middlesex Hospital Medical School, since 1966; *b* 19 Oct. 1929; *s* of William and Sarah Wolpert; *m* 1961; two *s* two *d*. *Educ:* King Edward's Sch., Johannesburg; Univ. of Witwatersrand (BScEng); Imperial Coll., London (DIC); King's Coll., London (PhD). Personal Asst to Director of Building Research Inst., S African Council for Scientific and Industrial Research, 1951-52; Engineer, Israel Water Planning Dept, 1953-54; King's College, London: Asst Lectr in Zoology, 1958-60; Lectr in Zoology, 1960-64; Reader in Zoology, 1964-66. Lectures: Steinhaus, Univ. of California at Irvine, 1980; van der Horst, Univ. of Witwatersrand, Johannesburg, 1981; Bidder, Soc. for Experimental Biology, Leicester, 1982. Scientific Medal, Zoological Soc., 1968. *Publications:* articles on cell and developmental biology in scientific jls.

Address: Department of Anatomy and Biology as Applied to Medicine, Middlesex Hospital Medical School, Cleveland Street, W1P 6DB.

WOLRIGE-GORDON, Patrick; *b* 10 Aug. 1935; *s* of late Captain Robert Wolrige-Gordon, MC and Joan Wolrige-Gordon; *m* 1962, Anne, *o d* of late Peter D. Howard and Mrs Howard; one *s* two *d*. *Educ:* Eton; New College, Oxford. MP (C) Aberdeenshire East, Nov. 1958—Feb. 1974. Liveryman Worshipful Company of Wheelwrights, 1966. *Recreations:* reading, walking, music. *Address:* Ythan Lodge, Newburgh, Aberdeenshire. *Club:* Royal Overseas League.
See also John MacLeod of MacLeod.

WOLSELEY, Sir Charles Garnet Richard Mark, 11th Bt, *cr* 1628; Partner, Smiths Gore, Chartered Surveyors, since 1979 (Associate Partner, 1974); *b* 16 June 1944; *s* of Capt. Stephen Garnet Hubert Francis Wolseley, Royal Artillery (*d* 1944, of wounds received in action), and of Pamela, *yr d* of late Capt. F. Barry and of Mrs Power, Wolseley Park, Rugeley, Staffs; *S* grandfather, Sir Edric Charles Joseph Wolseley, 10th Bt, 1954; *m* 1968, Anita Maria, *er d* of H. J. Fried, Epsom, Surrey; one *s* three *d*. *Educ:* St Bede's School, near Stafford; Ampleforth College, York. FRICS. *Recreations:* shooting, fishing, gardening. *Heir: s* Stephen Garnet Hugo Charles Wolseley, *b* 2 May 1980. *Address:* Wolseley Park, Rugeley, Staffs. *T:* Rugeley 2346; Hilliers, Petworth, West Sussex. *T:* Petworth 42414. *Clubs:* Farmers'; English XX Rifle (Bisley Camp, Brookwood).

WOLSELEY, Sir Garnet, 12th Bt, *cr* 1744-45 (Ireland); emigrated to Ontario, Canada, 1951; *b* 27 May 1915; *s* of late Richard Bingham and Mary Alexandra Wolseley; *S* cousin (Rev. Sir William Augustus Wolseley), 1950; *m* 1950, Lillian Mary, *d* of late William Bertram Ellison, Wallasey. *Educ:* New Brighton Secondary Sch. Served War of 1939-45, Northants Regt, Madagascar, Sicily, Italy and Germany. Boot Repairer Manager, 1946. *Address:* 73 Dorothy Street, Brantford, Ontario, Canada. *T:* 753-7957.

WOLSTENCROFT, Alan, CB 1961; Chairman, National Counties Building Society, since 1979; *b* 18 Oct. 1914; *yr s* of late Walter and Bertha Wolstencroft; *m* 1951, Ellen, *d* of late W. Tomlinson. *Educ:* Lancaster Royal Grammar Sch.; Caius Coll., Cambridge (MA 1st Cl. Classical Tripos). Assistant Principal, GPO, 1936. Served War of 1939-45: Royal Engineers (Postal Section), France and Middle East. Principal GPO, 1945; Assistant Secretary, GPO, 1949; Secretary, Independent Television Authority, 1954; General Post Office: Director of Personnel, 1955; Director of Postal Services, 1957; Director of Radio Services, 1960-64; Deputy Director General, 1964-67; Man. Dir Posts, 1967, Posts and GIRO, 1968; Adviser on Special Projects to Chm. of Post Office Corporation, 1969-70; Sec. to Post Office, 1970-73; retired. *Address:* Green Court, 161 Long Lane, Tilehurst, Reading RG3 6YW.

WOLSTENHOLME, Sir Gordon (Ethelbert Ward), Kt 1976; OBE (mil.) 1944; MA, MB, BChir; MRCS, FRCP, FIBiol; Harveian Librarian, Royal College of Physicians, since 1979; *b* Sheffield, 28 May 1913; *m* 1st; one *s* two *d*; 2nd; two *d*. *Educ:* Repton; Corpus Christi Coll., Cambridge; Middlesex Hosp. Med. Sch. Served with RAMC, 1940-47 (OBE); France, UK, ME and Central Mediterranean; specialist and advr in transfusion and resuscitation; OC Gen. Hosp. in Udine and Trieste; Dir, Ciba Foundn, 1949-78. Mem., GMC, 1973-83; Chm., Genetic Manipulation Adv. Gp, 1976-78. Founder Mem. 1954, Treasurer 1955-61, Mem. Exec. Bd 1961-70, UK Cttee for WHO; Organizer and Advr, Haile Selassie I Prize Trust, 1963-74; Advr, La Trinidad Med. Centre, Caracas, 1969-78. Royal Society of Medicine: Hon. Sec. 1964-70; Pres. Library (Sci. Res) Sect., 1968-70; Chm. Working Party on Soc's Future, 1972-73; Pres., 1975-77, 1978; Zoological Society: Scientific Fellow and Vice-Pres.; Member: Finance Cttee, 1962-69; Council, 1962-66, 1967-70, 1976-80; Chm., Nuffield Inst. for Comparative Medicine, 1969-70; Chm. Governors, Inst. for Res. into Mental and Multiple Handicap, 1973-77. Founder Mem. 1950, Hon. Treasurer 1956-69, Renal Assoc. of GB; Chm. Congress Prog. Cttee, 1962-64, Mem. Finance Cttee 1968-72, Internat. Soc. for Endocrinology; Trustee and Mem. Res. Bd, Spastics' Soc., 1963-67; Founder Chm., European Soc. for Clinical Investigation, 1966-67 (Boerhaave Lectr, 1976); Mem. Council 1969-75, Sponsor 1976-, Inst. for Study of Drug Dependence; Dir, Nuffield Foundn Inquiry into Dental Educn, 1978-80. Member: Council, Westfield Coll., London Univ., 1965-73; Planning Bd, University College at Buckingham, 1969-. Chm., Anglo-Ethiopian Soc., 1967-70. Mem. Ct of Assistants, Soc. of Apothecaries, 1969- (Master, 1979-80; Chm., Faculty of Hist. and Philosophy of Med. and Pharmacy, 1973-75; Visitor, 1975-78). Trustee: Foulkes Foundn; Tibble Trust; Lorch Foundn. Mem. Bd, Dahlem Konferenzen. Vice-Pres., ASLIB, 1979-82. Patron, FRAME. Hon. Life Governor, Middlesex Hosp., 1938. Hon. FACP, 1975; Hon. Fellow: Hunterian Soc., 1975 (Orator 1976); Royal Acad. of Med. in Ireland, 1976; European Soc. for Clinical Investigation, 1979; RSocMed, 1982. Hon. Member: Swedish Soc. of Endocrinology, 1955; Soc. of Endocrinology, 1959; Swiss Acad. of Med. Sciences, 1975; Assoc. Med. Argentina, 1977; Foreign Mem., Swedish Med. Soc., 1959; Hon. For. Mem., Amer. Acad. of Arts and Scis, 1981. Hon. LLD Cambridge, 1968; Hon. DTech Brunel, 1981; Hon. MD Grenada, 1982. Linnaeus Medal, Royal Swedish Acad. Sci., 1977; Pasteur Medal, Paris, 1982; Gold Medal: Perugia Univ., 1961; (class 1A) Italian Min. of Educn, 1961. Tito Lik, 1945; Chevalier, Légion d'Honneur, 1959; Star of Ethiopia, 1966. *Publications:* (ed) Ciba Foundation vols, 1950-78; Royal College of Physicians: Portraits, vol. I (ed with David Piper), 1964, vol. II (ed with John Kerslake), 1977; (ed with Valerie

Luniewska) Munk's Roll, vol. VI, 1982. *Recreations:* walking, photography. *Address:* 10 Wimpole Mews, W1M 7TF. *T:* 01-486 3884.

WOLTERS, Very Rev. Conrad Clifton; Chaplain to the Society of St Margaret, since 1976; Provost Emeritus of Newcastle, since 1976; *b* 3 April 1909; *e s* of Frederick Charles and Gertrude Elizabeth Wolters; *m* 1937, Joyce Cunnold; one *s. Educ:* privately; London College of Divinity; St John's College, Durham. ALCD 1932; LTh 1932; BA 1933; MA 1936. Curate: Christ Church, Gipsy Hill, SE19, 1933-37; Christ Church, Beckenham, 1937-41; Vicar, St Luke's, Wimbledon Park, 1941-49; Rector, Sanderstead, Surrey, 1949-59; Canon of Newcastle, 1959-62; Vicar of Newcastle and Provost of the Cathedral, 1962-76. *Publications:* (ed) Cloud of Unknowing, 1960; (ed) Revelations of Divine Love, 1966; (ed) The Fire of Love, 1971; (ed) The Cloud of Unknowing and Other Works, 1978; (ed) A Study of Wisdom, 1980. *Address:* The Cottage, St Margaret's Convent, East Grinstead, West Sussex RH19 3LD. *T:* East Grinstead 22406.

WOLTERS, Gwyneth Eleanor Mary; a Commissioner of Inland Revenue, 1971-78; *d* of late Prof. and Mrs A. W. Wolters. *Educ:* Abbey Sch., Reading; Reading Univ.; Newnham Coll., Cambridge. Entered Inland Revenue Dept, 1947. *Address:* 45 Albert Road, Caversham, Reading. *T:* Reading 472605.

WOLTON, Harry, QC 1982; *b* 1 Jan. 1938; *s* of late Harry William Wolton and of Dorothy Beatrice Wolton; *m* 1971, Julie Rosina Josephine Lovell (*née* Mason); three *s. Educ:* King Edward's Sch., Birmingham; Univ. of Birmingham. Called to the Bar, Gray's Inn, 1969. *Recreations:* family, reading. *Address:* Armscote Farm, Armscote, Stratford upon Avon, Warwickshire CV37 8DQ. *T:* Ilmington 234.

WOLVERHAMPTON, Bishop Suffragan of, since 1979; **Rt. Rev. Barry Rogerson;** *b* 25 July 1936; *s* of Eric and Olive Rogerson; *m* 1961, Olga May Gibson; two *d. Educ:* Magnus Grammar School; Leeds Univ. (BA Theology). Midland Bank Ltd, 1952-57; Leeds Univ. and Wells Theol Coll., 1957-62; Curate: St Hilda's, South Shields, 1962-65; St Nicholas', Bishopwearmouth, Sunderland, 1965-67; Lecturer, Lichfield Theological Coll., 1967-71, Vice-Principal, 1971-72; Lectr, Salisbury and Wells Theol Coll., 1972-75; Vicar, St Thomas', Wednesfield, 1975-79; Team Rector, Wednesfield Team Ministry, 1979. *Recreations:* cinema and stained glass windows. *Address:* 61 Richmond Road, Wolverhampton. *T:* Wolverhampton 23008.

WOLVERSON COPE, F(rederick); *see* Cope.

WOLVERTON, 5th Baron *cr* 1869; **Nigel Reginald Victor Glyn;** Captain RA, TA; *b* 23 June 1904; *o surv. s* of 4th Baron and Lady Edith Amelia Ward, CBE (*d* 1956), *o d* of 1st Earl of Dudley; *S* father, 1932. *Educ:* Eton. Heir: *kinsman* Jeremy Christopher Glyn [*b* 1 Oct. 1930; *m* 1956, Robina Elspeth, *o d* of Sir George Arthur Harford, 2nd Bt; one *d*]. *Address:* Queensberry House, Newmarket, Suffolk.

WOMBWELL, Sir George (Philip Frederick), 7th Bt *cr* 1778; *b* 21 May 1949; *s* of Sir (Frederick) Philip (Alfred William) Wombwell, 6th Bt, MBE, and late Ida Elizabeth, *er d* of Frederick J. Leitch; *S* father, 1977; *m* 1974, (Hermione) Jane, *e d* of T. S. Wrightson; one *s* one *d. Educ:* Repton. Heir: *s* Stephen Philip Henry Wombwell, *b* 12 May 1977. *Address:* Oulston Hall, Oulston, York.

WOMERSLEY, Denis Keith, CBE 1974; HM Diplomatic Service, retired; *b* 21 March 1920; *s* of late Alfred Womersley, Bradford, Yorks, and late Agnes (*née* Keighley); *m* 1955, Eileen Georgina, *d* of late George and Margaret Howe. *Educ:* Christ's Hospital; Caius Coll., Cambridge (Hons, MA). Served War, HM Forces, 1940-46. Entered Foreign (later Diplomatic) Service, 1946; Foreign Office, 1948, Control Commn Germany, 1952; Vienna, 1955; Hong Kong, 1957, FO, 1960; Baghdad, 1962; FO, 1963; Aden, 1966; Beirut, 1967; FCO, 1969-71; Bonn, 1971-74; Counsellor, FCO, 1974-77. FRSA 1976. *Recreations:* violin-playing, photography, Abbeyfield Soc. work. *Club:* Christ's Hospital (Horsham).

WOMERSLEY, J(ohn) Lewis, CBE 1962; RIBA; FRTPI; FRSA; Retired Consultant, Hugh Wilson and Lewis Womersley, Chartered Architects and Town Planners (Partner, 1964-77); *b* 12 Dec. 1910; *s* of Norman Womersley and Elizabeth Margaret Lewis; *m* 1936, Jean Roberts; two *s. Educ:* Huddersfield College. Asst Architect, private practices in London and Liverpool, 1933-46; Borough Architect and Town Planning Officer, Northampton, 1946-53; City Architect, Sheffield, 1953-64. Past Member Council, RIBA (Vice-President, 1961-62). Member: Central Housing Adv. Cttee, 1956-61, Parker Morris Cttee on Housing Standards, 1958-60, Min. of Housing and Local Govt; North West Econ. Planning Council, 1965-72; Manchester Conservation Areas and Historic Buildings Panel, 1970-77 (Chm., 1974-77); Chm., Manchester's Albert Meml Restoration Appeal Cttee, 1976-78. Works include housing, Manchester Education Precinct Plan, Huddersfield Polytechnic, Devolt Plan and Central Services Building, central area redevelopment. RIBA DistTP, 1956. Hon. LLD Sheffield, 1966; Hon. MA Manchester, 1978. *Publication:* Traffic Management in the Lake District National Park, 1972. *Recreations:* reading, gardening. *Address:* Wall Nook, Ferney Green, Bowness-on-Windermere, Cumbria. *T:* Windermere 3458.

WOMERSLEY, Sir Peter (John Walter), 2nd Bt *cr* 1945; Personnel Manager, Beecham Group; *b* 10 November 1941; *s* of Capt. John Womersley

(*o s* of 1st Bt; killed in action in Italy, 1944), and of Betty, *d* of Cyril Williams, Elstead, Surrey; *S* grandfather, 1961; *m* 1968, Janet Margaret Grant; two *s* two *d. Educ:* Aldro; Charterhouse; RMA, Sandhurst. Entered Royal Military Academy (Regular Army), 1960; Lt, King's Own Royal Border Regt, 1964, retd 1968. Heir: *s* John Gavin Grant Womersley, *b* 7 Dec. 1971. *Address:* Sunnycroft, The Street, Bramber, near Steyning, Sussex.

WONTNER, Sir Hugh (Walter Kingwell), GBE 1974; Kt 1972; CVO 1969 (MVO 1950); Chairman of The Savoy, Claridge's and Berkeley Hotels, London, and other undertakings associated with The Savoy, since 1948 (Managing Director, 1941-79); Clerk of the Royal Kitchens, since 1953, and a Catering Adviser in the Royal Household, since 1938; Underwriting Member of Lloyd's, since 1937; *b* 22 Oct. 1908; *er s* of Arthur Wontner, actor-manager; *m* 1936, Catherine, *o d* of Lieut T. W. Irvin, Gordon Highlanders (*d* of wounds, France, 1916); two *s* one *d. Educ:* Oundle and in France. On staff of London Chamber of Commerce, 1927-33; Asst Sec., Home Cttee, Associated Chambers of Commerce of India and Ceylon, 1930-31; Sec., London Cttee, Burma Chamber of Commerce, 1931; Gen. Sec., Hotels and Restaurants Assoc. of Great Britain, 1933-38; Asst to Sir George Reeves-Smith at The Savoy, 1938-41; Director, The Savoy Hotel Ltd, 1940; Sec., Coronation Accommodation Cttee, 1936-37, Chm., 1953; a British delegate, Internat. Hotel Alliance, 1933-38; Pres., Internat. Hotel Assoc., 1961-64, Mem. of Honour, 1965-. Chairman: Exec. Cttee, British Hotels and Rests Assoc., 1957-60 (Vice-Chm., 1952-57; Vice-Chm. of Council, 1961-68; Chm., London Div., 1949-51); Chm. of Council, British Hotels, Restaurants and Caterers Assoc., 1969-73; London Hotels Information Service, 1952-56; Working Party, Owners of Historic Houses open to the public, 1965-66; Historic Houses Cttee, BTA, 1966-77. Member: Historic Buildings Council, 1968-73; British Heritage Cttee, 1977-; Heritage of London Trust, 1980-; Barbican Centre Cttee, 1979-; Board of BTA, 1950-69; LCC Consultative Cttee, Hotel and Restaurant Technical School, 1933-38; Court of Assistants, Irish Soc., 1967-68, 1971-73; Vis. Cttee, Holloway Prison, 1963-68. Governor: University Coll. Hosp., 1945-53 (Chm., Nutrition Cttee, 1945-52); Christ's Hosp., 1963-. Trustee: College of Arms Trust; Southwark Cathedral Develt Trust; D'Oyly Carte Opera Trust; Morden Coll., Blackheath; Chm., Temple Bar Trustees; Vice Pres., The Pilgrims; Chairman: The Savoy Theatre, 1948-; Lancaster Hotel, Paris, 1973-; Eurocard International, 1964-78; Liveryman: Worshipful Co. of Feltmakers, 1934- (Master, 1962-63 and 1973-74); Clockmakers, 1967- (Warden, 1971-; Master, 1975-76); Hon. Liveryman: Worshipful Co. of Launderers', 1970; Plaisterers, 1975; Chancellor, The City Univ., 1973-74; one of HM Lieuts and a JP for the City of London, 1963-80, Chief Magistrate, 1973-74; Freeman of the City, 1934, Alderman for Broad Street Ward, 1963-79, Sheriff, 1970-71; Lord Mayor of London, 1973-74. Hon. Citizen, St Emilion, 1974; Freeman of the Seychelles, 1974. Order of Cisneros, Spain, 1964; Officer, L'Etoile Equatoriale, 1970; Médaille de Vermeil, City of Paris, 1972; Ordre de l'Etoile Civique, 1972; Officier du Mérite Agricole, 1973; Comdr, Nat. Order of the Leopard, Zaire, 1974; Knight Comdr, Order of the Dannebrog, 1974; Order of the Crown of Malaysia, 1974; Knight Comdr, Royal Swedish Order of the Polar Star, 1980. KStJ 1973 (OStJ 1971). Hon. DLitt 1973. *Recreations:* genealogy, acting. *Address:* 1 Savoy Hill, WC2. *T:* 01-836 1533. *Clubs:* Garrick, City Livery.

WOOD, family name of **Earl of Halifax** and **Baron Holderness.**

WOOD, Alan John, CBE 1971; Tan Sri (Malaysia) 1972; with Singer Sewing Machine Co., Stamford, Connecticut, USA; *b* 16 Feb. 1925; *s* of late Lt-Col Maurice Taylor Wood, MBE; *m* 1950 (marr. diss.); one *s* one *d* ; *m* 1978, Marjorie Anne (*née* Bennett). *Educ:* King Edward VI Royal Grammar Sch., Guildford, Surrey, UK. Served Army, 1943-47; demobilised rank Captain. Various exec. and managerial positions with Borneo Motors Ltd, Singapore and Malaya, 1947-64 (Dir, 1964); Dir, Inchcape Bhd, 1968-73, Exec. Dep. Chm. 1973-74; Exec. Vice Pres., Sowers, Lewis, Wood Inc., Old Greenwich, Conn, 1975-78. Pres., Malaysian Internat. Chamber of Commerce, 1968-72; Chm., Nat. Chambers of Commerce of Malaysia, 1968 and 1972. Panglima Setia Mahkota (Hon.), 1972. *Recreations:* golf, tennis. *Address:* 901 Stillwater Road, Stamford, Connecticut 06902, USA. *Clubs:* Oriental; Lake, Royal Selangor Golf (Kuala Lumpur); Penang (Penang); Burning Tree (Greenwich, Conn).

WOOD, Sir Alan Marshall M.; *see* Muir Wood.

WOOD, Alfred Arden, TD 1960; FRIBA, FRTPI; County Planner/Architect, West Midlands County Council, since 1973; *b* 8 Sept. 1926; *s* of late Henry Arden Wood, AMIMechE, and Victoria Wood (*née* Holt); *m* 1957, Dorinda Rae (*née* Hartley); one *s* one *d. Educ:* Ashville Coll., Harrogate; Harrogate Grammar Sch.; Hertford Coll., Oxford; Leeds Schs of Architecture and Town Planning. Dip. and Dip. with Dist. Served 8th Royal Tank Regt, Leeds Rifles TA and Westminster Dragoons TA, 1944-62. Architect, Stockholm CC, Harlow New Town, W Riding CC, Leeds CC, Glasgow Corp., partner in private practice, 1951-65; City Planning Officer, Norwich, 1965-72; County Planner, Hereford and Worcester CC, 1972-73. Member: Historic Buildings Council for England, 1969-; RTPI Council, 1969-75; UK Exec. European Architectural Heritage Year, 1975 (Chm., Heritage Grants Cttee); Preservation Policy Gp, 1967-70; Environmental Bd, 1975-78; Comr, Indep. Transport Commn, 1972-74. Prof., Centre for the Conservation of Historic Towns and Bldgs, Katholieke Univ., Leuven, Belgium, ex Coll. of Europe, Bruges, 1976; External Examiner, Manchester,

Birmingham, Aston univs; adviser, at various times, Council of Europe, Strasbourg, and OECD, Paris; lecture tours to N America, 1967, 1976, 1980; conf. addresses in Paris, Rome, Berlin, Amsterdam, Brussels, Zürich, London and elsewhere, 1965-81; occasional broadcaster. Civic Trust awards, 1969, 1971. *Publications:* contributor to jls of learned societies. *Recreations:* cities, buildings, travel, railways, music. *Address:* Broom House, Old Station Road, Bromsgrove, Worcestershire B60 2AF. *T:* Bromsgrove 71459.

WOOD, Sir Anthony John P.; *see* Page Wood.

WOOD, Ven. Arnold; Archdeacon of Cornwall and Canon Residentiary (Librarian), Truro Cathedral, since 1981; *b* 24 Oct. 1918; *s* of Harry and Annie Wood; *m* 1945, Dorothy Charlotte Tapper; two *d. Educ:* Holy Trinity School, Halifax; London Univ. (Dip. Economics). Commissioned, RASC, 1939-49. Legal Adviser and Man. Director, CMI Engineering Co. Ltd, 1949-63; student, Clifton Theological Coll., 1963-65; Curate, Kirkheaton, W Yorks, 1965-67; Vicar, Mount Pellon, W Yorks, 1967-73; Rector of Lanreath and Vicar of Pelynt, 1973-81; Rural Dean, West Wivelshire, dio. Truro, 1976-81. Gen. Comr of Income Tax, 1977-. *Recreations:* walking, bowls, music. *Address:* 22 Chainwalk Drive, Truro, Cornwall TR1 3ST. *T:* Truro 2866.

WOOD, Charles Gerald; writer for films, television and the theatre, since 1962; *b* 6 Aug. 1932; *s* of John Edward Wood, actor and Catherine Mae (*née* Harris), actress; *m* 1954, Valerie Elizabeth Newman, actress; one *s* one *d. Educ:* King Charles I Sch., Kidderminster; Birmingham Coll. of Art. Soldier, 1950-55; Factory worker, 1955-57; Stage Manager and Theatre Designer, 1957-59; Layout Artist, 1959-62. Consultant to Nat. Film Develt Fund, 1980-82. *Wrote plays:* Prisoner and Escort, John Thomas, Spare, (Cockade), Arts Theatre, 1963; Meals on Wheels, Royal Court, 1965; Don't Make Me Laugh, Aldwych, 1966; Fill the Stage with Happy Hours, Nottingham Playhouse, 1967; Dingo, Bristol Arts Centre, 1967; H, National Theatre, 1969; Welfare, Liverpool Everyman, 1971; Veterans, Lyceum, Edinburgh, 1972; Jingo, RSC, Aldwych, 1975; The Script, Hampstead Theatre, 1976; Has 'Washington' Legs?, Nat. Theatre, 1978. *Screenplays include:* The Knack (Grand Prix, Cannes, 1965; Best Comedy Award, Screenwriters Guild, 1965); Help!; How I Won the War; The Charge of the Light Brigade; The Long Day's Dying; Cuba; adapted: Bed Sitting Room (Peace Prize, Berlin Film Fest.); Wagner; Red Monarch. Numerous television plays; creator of Gordon Maple in series, Don't Forget to Write. Most Promising Playwright, 1963, Best Comedy, 1973, Evening Standard Awards. *Publications:* plays: Cockade, 1965; Fill the Stage with Happy Hours, 1967; Dingo, 1967; H, 1970; Veterans, 1972; Has 'Washington' Legs?, 1978. *Recreations:* military and theatrical studies; supporting Bristol Rovers FC. *Address:* The Manor House, Milton, near Banbury, Oxon. *Clubs:* Dramatists', British Playwrights' Mafia.

WOOD, David; actor, playwright, theatrical producer and director; *b* 21 Feb. 1944; *s* of Richard Edwin Wood and Audrey Adele Wood (*née* Fincham); *m* 1975, Jacqueline Stanbury; two *d. Educ:* Chichester High Sch. for Boys; Worcester Coll., Oxford. BA (Hons). Acted with OUDS and ETC at Oxford; first London appearance in ETC prodn, Hang Down Your Head and Die (also co-writer), Comedy, 1964; later performances include: A Spring Song, Mermaid, 1964; Dr Faustus (OUDS), 1966; Four Degrees Over, Edinburgh Festival and Fortune, 1966 (also contrib. lyrics and sketches); repertory, 1966-69; RSC's After Haggerty, Aldwych 1970, and Criterion 1971; A Voyage Round My Father, Greenwich, 1970, Toronto, 1972; Me Times Me, tour, 1971; Mrs Warren's Profession, 1972, and revue Just the Ticket, 1973, Thorndike, Leatherhead; The Provok'd Wife, Greenwich, 1973; Jeeves, Her Majesty's, 1975; Terra Nova, Chichester, 1980. Various revues in collaboration with John Gould; music and lyrics, The Stiffkey Scandals of 1932, Queen's, 1967; with John Gould formed Whirligig Theatre, touring children's theatre company, 1979. *Films include:* If . . . , 1968; Aces High, 1975; Sweet William, 1978; North Sea Hijack, 1979. *TV series include:* Mad Jack, Fathers and Sons, Cheri, Disraeli, The Avengers, Van der Valk, Danger UXB, Huntingtower, Enemy at the Door, Jackanory, Jim'll Fix It, When the Boat Comes In, The Brack Report. Screenplay, Swallows and Amazons, 1974. *Publications:* musical plays for children: (with Sheila Ruskin) The Owl and the Pussycat went to see . . . , 1968 (London productions); (with Sheila Ruskin) Larry the Lamb in Toytown, 1969 (London production); The Plotters of Cabbage Patch Corner, 1970 (London productions); Flibberty and the Penguin, 1971; The Papertown Paperchase, 1972; Hijack over Hygenia, 1973; Old Mother Hubbard, 1975; The Gingerbread Man, 1976 (London productions); Old Father Time, 1976; (with Tony Hatch and Jackie Trent) Rock Nativity, 1976; Nutcracker Sweet, 1977 (London production); Mother Goose's Golden Christmas, 1977; Tickle, 1978; Babes in the Magic Wood, 1978; There Was an Old Woman . . . , 1979; Cinderella, 1979; Aladdin, 1981; The Ideal Gnome Expedition (London production), 1982; (with Dave and Toni Arthur) Robin Hood, 1982; Dick Whittington and Wondercat, 1982; Meg and Mog Show (London production), 1982; various revues; articles in Drama, London Drama. *Recreations:* writing, conjuring, collecting old books. *Address:* c/o Margaret Ramsay Ltd, 14A Goodwin's Court, St Martin's Lane, WC2. *T:* 01-240 0691. *Club:* Green Room.

WOOD, Sir David (Basil) H.; *see* Hill-Wood.

WOOD, Maj.-Gen. Denys Broomfield, CB 1978; Secretary, Council of Engineering Institutions, since 1982 (Executive Secretary, 1978-82); *b* 2 Nov. 1923; *s* of late Percy Neville Wood and Meryl Broomfield; *m* 1948, Jennifer

Nora Page, *d* of late Air Cdre William Morton Page, CBE; one *s* two *d. Educ:* Radley; Pembroke Coll., Cambridge. MA, FIMechE. Commissioned into REME, 1944; war service in UK and Far East, 1944-47; Staff Captain, WO, 1948-49; Instructor, RMA, Sandhurst, 1949-52; Staff Coll., 1953; DAA&QMG, 11 Infantry Bde, 1955-57; OC, 10 Infantry Workshop, Malaya, 1958-60; jssc 1960; Directing Staff, Staff Coll., 1961-63; Comdr, REME, 3rd Div., 1963-65; Operational Observer, Viet Nam, 1966-67; Col GS, Staff Coll., 1967-69; idc 1970; Dir, Administrative Planning, 1971-73; Dep. Military Sec. (2), 1973-75; Dir of Army Quartering, 1975-78. Col Comdt, REME, 1978-. FRSA. *Recreations:* walking, gardening, reading. *Address:* Elmtree House, Hurtmore, Godalming, Surrey. *T:* Godalming 6936. *Club:* Army and Navy.

WOOD, Derek Alexander, QC 1978; *b* 14 Oct. 1937; *s* of Alexander Cecil Wood and Rosetta (*née* Lelyveld); *m* 1961, Sally Teresa Clarke, *d* of Lady Elliott and step *d* of Sir Norman Elliott, *qv* ; two *d. Educ:* Tiffin Boys' Sch., Kingston-upon-Thames; University Coll., Oxford (MA, BCL). Called to the Bar, Middle Temple, 1964. Dept of the Environment: Mem., Adv. Gp on Commercial Property Develt, 1975-78; Mem., Property Adv. Gp, 1978-; Mem., Working Party on New Forms of Social Ownership and Tenure in Housing, 1976. Dep. Chm., Soc. of Labour Lawyers, 1978-. Mem. Council, London Bor. of Bromley, 1975-78. *Recreation:* music. *Address:* Chatham House, Gosshill Road, Chislehurst, Kent BR7 5NS. *T:* 01-467 8475.

WOOD, Prof. Derek Rawlins, FIBiol; Dean of Faculty of Medicine and Professor of Applied Pharmacology, University of Leeds, since 1969; *b* 16 May 1921; *s* of Frederick Charles Wood and Ruth Dorothy (*née* Rawlins); *m* 1945, Mary Elizabeth Caldwell; two *s* two *d* (and one *s* decd). *Educ:* Wm Hulme's Grammar Sch., Manchester; Brasenose Coll. and Radcliffe Infirmary, Oxford. BM BCh, BSc, MA Oxford. House Physician, Radcliffe Inf., 1945; Demonstrator, Pharmacology, Oxford, 1945-46; Lectr 1946, Sen. Lectr 1952-57, Pharmacology, Univ. of Sheffield; J. H. Hunt Travelling Schol., 1949; J. H. Brown Fellow, Pharmacol., Yale, 1955-56; Associate Prof., Pharmacol., McGill Univ., 1957-60; Prof. and Head of Dept of Pharmacol., Univ. of Leeds, 1960-69. Hon. Sec., 1952-57, Hon. Treas., 1964-70, Brit. Pharmacol. Soc.; Member: Brit. Pharmacopoeia Commn, 1969-79; GMC, 1969-; Gen. Dental Council, 1971-; Leeds Reg. Hosp. Bd, 1969-74; Bd of Governors, United Leeds Hosps, 1969-74; Leeds AHA (T), 1974-82; Leeds DHA, W and E, 1982-. Chairman, University Hosps Assoc., 1978-81. Mem. Court: Univs of Bradford, 1970-, and Sheffield, 1966-79. Hon. MPS. *Publications:* Dental Pharmacology and Therapeutics (with L. E. Francis), 1961; contribs to Brit. Jl Pharmacol., Jl Physiol., and others. *Recreations:* gardening, music. *Address:* 27 Shire Oak Road, Leeds LS6 2DD. *T:* Leeds 752579; Faculty of Medicine, University of Leeds, Leeds LS2 9JT. *T:* Leeds 431751, ext. 7594.

WOOD, Prof. Edward James; Professor of Latin, University of Leeds, 1938-67, Professor Emeritus, 1967; Pro-Vice-Chancellor, University of Leeds, 1957-59; *b* 3 Sept. 1902; *s* of James M. A. Wood, Advocate in Aberdeen; *m* 1933, Marion Grace Chorley; one *s* one *d. Educ:* Aberdeen Grammar School; Aberdeen University; Trinity College, Cambridge. Lectr in Classics, Manchester University, 1928; Professor of Latin, Aberystwyth, 1932. *Publications:* contributions to: Classical Review, Gnomon. *Address:* 35 Barleyfields Road, Wetherby, West Yorks. *T:* Wetherby 62488.

WOOD, Eric; Finance Officer, University of Bristol, since 1979; *b* 22 Sept. 1931; *s* of Herbert Francis and Eva Wood; *m* 1955, Erica Twist; three *d. Educ:* West Hartlepool Grammar Sch.; Blandford Grammar Sch.; St Peter's Coll., Oxford (MA). IPFA. National Service, Army, 1950-51. Finance Depts, Cheshire, Durham and Notts County Councils, 1954-65; Finance Dept, London Transport, 1965-67; Asst Treasurer, GLC, 1967-73; Dir, CIPFA, 1973-79. *Publications:* articles in prof. accountancy press. *Recreations:* skiing, squash. *Address:* 32 Mariners Drive, Stoke Bishop, Bristol BS9 1QG. *T:* Bristol 681538.

WOOD, Sir Frederick (Ambrose Stuart), Kt 1977; Chairman since 1960, and Managing Director since 1953, Croda International Ltd; Chairman, British Technology Group (of National Research Development Corporation, since 1979 (Member, since 1973), and of National Enterprise Board, since 1981); *b* 30 May 1926; *s* of Alfred Phillip Wood, Goole, Yorkshire, and Patras, Greece, and Charlotte Wood (*née* Barnes), Goole, Yorkshire, and Athens, Greece; *m* 1947, J. R. (Su) King; two *s* one *d. Educ:* Felsted Sch., Essex; Clare Coll., Cambridge. Served War, Sub-Lt (A) Observer, Fleet Air Arm, 1944-47. Trainee Manager, Croda Ltd, 1947-50; Pres., Croda Inc., New York, 1950-53. Chm., Nat. Bus Co., 1972-78. Mem., Nationalised Industries Chms' Gp, 1975-78. Chm. British Sect., Centre Européen d'Entreprise Publique, 1976-78. *Address:* Plaster Hill Farm, Churt, Surrey. *T:* Headley Down 712134. *Club:* Carlton.

WOOD, Prof. Emer. Frederick Lloyd Whitfeld, CMG 1974; Professor Emeritus, Victoria University, 1969; *b* 29 Sept. 1903; *s* of Prof. G. A. Wood and Eleanor Madeline Wood (*née* Whitfeld), Sydney; *m* 1932, Joan Myrtle, *d* of E. L. Walter, Sydney; one *s* one *d* (and one *s* one *d* decd). *Educ:* Sydney Grammar Sch.; Univ. of Sydney (BA); Balliol Coll. Oxford (MA). Univ. Medals History and Philos., Sydney. Frazer Scholar, Univ. of Sydney, 1925; Goldsmith Sen. Student, Oxford, 1929; Lectr in History, Univ. of Sydney, 1930-34; Actg Lectr in History, Balliol Coll., 1929 and 1937; Prof. of History, Victoria Univ., Wellington, NZ, 1935-69. Carnegie Vis. Fellow, Royal Inst. of Internat. Affairs, London, 1952-53. Res. Dir, NZ Inst. of Internat. Affairs,

1974. *Publications:* The Constitutional Development of Australia, 1933; Concise History of Australia, 1935; New Zealand in the World, 1940; Understanding New Zealand, 1944; revised edns as This New Zealand, 1946, 1952 and 1958; The New Zealand People at War, Political and External Affairs, 1958; contrib. NZ Jl of History, DNB. *Recreation:* walking. *Address:* 4 Gladstone Terrace, Wellington, New Zealand. *T:* Wellington 726-818.

WOOD, Sir George (Ernest Francis), KBE 1975 (OBE 1946); ISO 1958; retired Director, Reserve Bank of New Zealand (1959-1964); *b* 13 July 1900; *s* of George Francis Wood and Margaret Wood (*née* Blewman); *m* 1928, Eileen Alice Oudaille; one *s* one *d. Educ:* Greymouth District High Sch.; Waitaki Boys' High Sch.; Victoria Univ., Wellington, NZ. MA Hons in Economics. Statistician, Dept of Statistics, Wellington, NZ, 1921-38; Govt Statistician: Palestine, 1938-45; New Zealand, 1946-58. Chm., Consumer Council, 1959-75. *Publications:* The Wordsmiths: a study of advertising, 1964; Consumers in Action, 1973. *Recreations:* gardening, reading, following Rugby football. *Address:* 116 Morningside Road, Whangarei, New Zealand. *T:* 87-274.

WOOD, Maj.-Gen. Harry Stewart, CB 1967; TD 1950; *b* 16 Sept. 1913; *e s* of late Roland and Eva M. Wood; *m* 1939, Joan Gordon, *d* of Gordon S. King; two *s* (and one *s* decd). *Educ:* Nautical Coll., Pangbourne. Civil Engineer (inc. articled trg), 1931-39. Commnd RA (TA), 1937. Served War of 1939-45: Regimental Service, Sept. 1939-June 1944; subseq. Technical Staff. Dep. Dir of Artillery, Min. of Supply (Col), 1958-60; Dep. Dir of Inspection (Brig.), 1960-62; Sen. Mil. Officer, Royal Armament Research and Development Estab. (Brig.), 1962-64; Vice-President, Ordnance Board, 1964-66, President, 1966-67. Maj.-Gen. 1964; retd, 1967. Legion of Merit, degree of Legionnaire (USA), 1947. *Recreations:* home and garden, motor sport. *Address:* Brook House, Faygate, near Horsham, Sussex. *T:* Faygate 342.

WOOD, Sir Henry (Peart), Kt 1967; CBE 1960; Principal, Jordanhill College of Education, Glasgow, 1949-71, retired; *b* 30 Nov. 1908; *s* of T. M. Wood, Bedlington, Northumberland; *m* 1937, Isobel Mary, *d* of W. F. Stamp, Carbis Bay, Cornwall; one *s* two *d. Educ:* Morpeth Grammar Sch.; Durham University. BSc 1930, MSc 1934, Durham; MA 1938, MEd 1941, Manchester. Lecturer, Manchester University, 1937-44; Jordanhill College of Education: Principal Lecturer, 1944-46; Vice-Principal, 1947-49. Part-time Lectr, Glasgow Univ., 1972-78; Assessor in Educn, Strathclyde Univ., 1972-82; Vis. Prof. in Educn, Strathclyde Univ., 1978-. Hon. LLD: Glasgow, 1972; Strathclyde, 1982. *Address:* 51 Whittingehame Drive, Glasgow G12 0YH. *T:* 041-334 3647.

WOOD, Sir Ian (Jeffreys), Kt 1976; MBE 1942; MD; FRCP, FRACP; Consultant Physician, Royal Melbourne Hospital, since 1963; *b* 5 Feb. 1903; *s* of Dr Jeffreys Wood and Mrs Isla Wood; *m* 1939, Edith Mary Cooke; two *d. Educ:* Melbourne C of E Grammar Sch.; Univ. of Melbourne (MD, BS). FRCP 1943; FRACP 1937. War Service, 1939-45: RAAMC, ME and Pacific Zone; Col Comdg 2/7 Aust. Gen. Hosp., New Guinea, 1944-45. Med. Supt, Children's Hosp., Melbourne, 1930-31; House Phys., Hosp. for Sick Children, Great Ormond Street, London, 1932; Royal Melbourne Hospital: Phys., 1939-63; Asst Dir, Walter and Eliza Hall Inst. of Med. Res., 1946-63. Neil Hamilton Fairley Medal, for Outstanding Contributions to Medicine, RCP and RACP, 1974; Stawell Oration, The Great and Glorious Masterpiece of Man, Melbourne, 1975. Univ. of Melbourne Blue for Cricket and Hockey, 1926; Victorian State Hockey Team, 1927. *Publications:* Diffuse Lesions of the Stomach (with Dr L. I. Taft), 1958; contribs in field of gastroenterology in BMJ, Lancet and Med. Jl of Aust. *Recreations:* book collecting, cricket and tennis. *Address:* Flat 1, 27 Tintern Avenue, Toorak, Vic 3142, Australia. *T:* 241 9622. *Clubs:* Melbourne, Melbourne Cricket.

WOOD, John; actor. *Educ:* Bedford Sch.; Jesus Coll., Oxford (Pres. OUDS). Old Vic Co., 1954-56; Camino Real, Phoenix, 1957; The Making of Moo, Royal Court, 1957; Brouhaha, Aldwych, 1958; The Fantasticks, Apollo, 1961; Rosencrantz and Guildenstern are Dead, NY, 1967; Exiles, Mermaid, 1970; joined Royal Shakespeare Company, 1971; Enemies, The Man of Mode, Exiles, The Balcony, Aldwych, 1971; The Comedy of Errors, Stratford, 1972; Julius Caesar, Titus Andronicus, Stratford, 1972, Aldwych, 1973; Collaborators, Duchess, 1973; A Lesson in Blood and Roses, The Place, 1973; Sherlock Holmes, Travesties (Evening Standard Best Actor Award, 1974; Tony Award, 1976), Aldwych, 1974, NY, 1974; The Devil's Disciple, Ivanov, Aldwych, 1976; Death Trap, NY, 1978; Undiscovered Country, Richard III, Nat. Theatre, 1979; Piaf, Wyndham's, 1980; The Provok'd Wife, Nat. Theatre, 1980. Television: A Tale of Two Cities, Barnaby Rudge, 1964-65; The Victorians, 1965; The Duel, 1966. Films: Nicholas and Alexandra, 1971; Slaughterhouse Five, 1972. *Address:* c/o Royal Shakespeare Company, Barbican Centre, Silk Street, EC2Y 8DS.

WOOD, John; Principal Assistant Director of Public Prosecutions, since 1981; *b* 11 Jan. 1931; *s* of Thomas John Wood and Rebecca Grand; *m* 1958, Jean Iris Wood; two *s. Educ:* King's College Sch., Wimbledon. Admitted Solicitor, 1955. Director of Public Prosecutions: Legal Assistant, 1958; Sen. Legal Asst, 1963; Asst Solicitor, 1971; Asst Director, 1977. *Recreations:* cricket, squash, music, theatre. *Address:* 4-12 Queen Anne's Gate, SW1. *T:* 01-213 5341.

WOOD, John Edwin, PhD; Head of Underwater Projects, British Aerospace DG, Bracknell Division (formerly Sperry Gyroscope); *b* 24 July 1928; *s* of late John Stanley Wood and Alice (*née* Hardy); *m* 1953, Patricia Edith Wilson

Sheppard (marr. diss. 1978); two *s* two *d. Educ:* Darlington Grammar Sch.; Univ. of Leeds (BSc, PhD). Joined Royal Naval Scientific Service at HM Underwater Countermeasures and Weapons Estabt, 1951; Admiralty Underwater Weapons Estabt, 1959; Head of Acoustic Research Div., 1968; Head of Sonar Dept, 1972; Admiralty Surface Weapons Establishment: Head of Weapons Dept, 1976; Head of Communications, Command and Control Dept, 1979; Chief Scientist (Royal Navy), and Director General Research (A), 1980, in rank of Under Secretary. Joined Sperry Gyroscope, 1981. *Publications:* Sun, Moon and Standing Stones, 1978, 2nd edn 1980; papers and book reviews in technical and archaeological jls. *Recreations:* archaeology, fell-walking. *Address:* 8 Marden Court, Copper Beech Drive, Farlington, Portsmouth PO6 1AZ. *T:* Cosham 377732. *Club:* Civil Service.

WOOD, Hon. Sir John (Kember), Kt 1977; MC 1944; **Hon. Mr Justice Wood;** a Judge of the High Court of Justice, Family Division, since 1977; *b* 8 Aug. 1922; *s* of John Roskruge Wood; *m* 1952, Kathleen Ann Lowe; one *s* one *d. Educ:* Shrewsbury Sch.; Magdalene Coll., Cambridge. Served War of 1939-45: Rifle Brigade, 1941-46. Magdalene Coll., 1946-48. Barrister (Lincoln's Inn), 1949, Bencher, 1977. QC 1969. A Recorder of the Crown Court, 1975-77. *Recreations:* sport, travel. *Address:* Royal Courts of Justice, WC2. *Clubs:* Garrick, MCC; Hawks (Cambridge).

WOOD, John Laurence; Keeper, Department of Printed Books, British Library, 1966-76; retired; *b* 27 Nov. 1911; *s* of J. A. Wood and Clara Josephine (*née* Ryan); *m* 1947, Rowena Beatrice Ross; one *s* one *d. Educ:* Bishop Auckland; Merton Coll., Oxford (BA); Besançon; Paris. Lecteur, Univ. of Besançon, 1934; Asst Cataloguer, British Museum, 1936; seconded to Foreign Office, 1941; Asst Keeper, British Museum, 1946; Deputy Keeper, 1959. Editor, Factotum, 1978-81. *Publications:* (trans.) The French Prisoner, Garneray, 1957; (trans.) Contours of the Middle Ages, Genicot, 1967. *Recreation:* bookbinding. *Address:* 88 Hampstead Way, NW11. *T:* 01-455 4395.

WOOD, John Peter; Editor, Amateur Gardening, since 1971; *b* 27 March 1925; *s* of Walter Ralph Wood and Henrietta Martin; *m* 1956, Susan Maye White; one *s* one *d. Educ:* Grove Park Grammar Sch.; Seale Hayne Agricultural Coll. (NDH and Dip. in Hort., of College). Served War, 1943-46. Horticultural studies, 1946-52; Amateur Gardening: Asst Editor, 1952-66; Dep. Editor, 1966-71. *Publications:* Amateur Gardening Handbook—Bulbs, 1957; Amateur Gardening Picture Book—Greenhouse Management, 1959. *Recreations:* gardening, music appreciation. *Address:* Lantern Cottage, Duck Street, Winterborne Kingston, Blandford Forum, Dorset. *T:* Bere Regis 265.

WOOD, Joseph Neville, (Johnnie), CBE 1978; Director General, The General Council of British Shipping, 1975-78; *b* 25 October 1916; *o s* of late Robert Hind Wood and Emily Wood, Durham; *m* 1st, 1944, Elizabeth Mary (*d* 1959); three *d*; 2nd, 1965, Josephine Samuel (*née* Dane). *Educ:* Johnston School, Durham; London School of Economics. Entered Civil Service (Board of Trade), 1935; Ministry of War Transport, 1940; jssc 1950; Ministry of Transport: Asst Sec., 1951; Far East Representative, 1952-55; Under-Sec., 1961; Chief of Highway Administration, 1967-68. Joined Chamber of Shipping of the UK, 1968, Dep. Dir, 1970, Dir, 1972-78. Mem., Baltic Exchange, 1968-; Director: Finance for Shipping Ltd, 1978-; Ship Mortgage Finance Co. Ltd, 1978-. Mem. Chichester DC, 1979-. Governor, Midhurst Grammar Sch. FCIT 1976. Freeman, City of London, 1978. Officier, Ordre de Mérite Maritime, 1950. *Recreation:* gardening. *Address:* Barbers Cottage, Heyshott, Midhurst, Sussex. *T:* Midhurst 4282.

WOOD, Kenneth Maynard; Chairman, Stocklands Equestrian Ltd; *b* 4 Oct. 1916; *s* of late Frederick Cavendish Wood and Agnes Maynard; *m* ; two *s* two *d. Educ:* Bromley County School. Cadet, Merchant Navy, 1930-34; electrical and mechanical engineering, 1934-37; started own company radio, television and radar development, 1937-39; sold business and joined RAF, transferred for development of electronic equipment, 1939-46; started Kenwood Manufacturing Co. Ltd, 1946; Managing Director, 1946 until take-over by Thorn Electrical Industries Ltd, 1968. Fellow, Inst. of Ophthalmology. *Recreation:* golf. *Address:* Dellwood Cottage, Wheatsheaf Enclosure, Liphook, Hants. *T:* Liphook 723108.

WOOD, Sir Kenneth (Millns), Kt 1970; FCA; *b* 25 April 1909; *s* of Sydney Wood and Edith Wood (*née* Barker); *m* 1939, Julia Mary, *d* of John and Mary Ambrose; one *d. Educ:* Barnstaple Grammar Sch.; Trinity Coll., Cambridge (BA). Wrangler in Maths Tripos, Trinity Coll., 1930. Chartered Accountant, 1933. Served War of 1939-45 (Lt-Col). Concrete Ltd (later Bison Group): Dir 1946; Man. Dir 1950; Chm. 1958-79. Seconded to Min. of Housing and Local Govt as Industrial Adviser on House-Building to Minister, 1966-67; Dir, National Building Agency, 1966-79. FBIM 1971-79. *Recreations:* golf, ski-ing, sailing, tennis. *Address:* Ridge End, Finchampstead, Berks. *T:* Eversley (Hants) 733294. *Club:* East Berks Golf.

WOOD, Leonard George, CBE 1978; Director of Parent Board, 1965-80, and Group Director of Music, 1966-78, EMI Ltd; *s* of Leonard George Wood and Miriam (*née* Barnes); *m* 1936, Christine Florence Reason (*d* 1978). *Educ:* Bishopshalt Sch., Hillingdon, Mddx; London Univ. (BCom). Served War, RAF: Sgt, Airfield Controller, 1943; commnd Flying Control Officer, 1944-46. Asst Record Sales Manager, UK, EMI Ltd, 1939, Record Sales Man., 1947; EMI Records Ltd: Gen. Man., 1957; Man. Dir, 1959-66; Chm., 1976-78;

EMI Ltd: Gp Divl Dir, 1961; Gp Asst Man. Dir, 1973-77. Internat. Fedn of Producers of Phonograms and Videograms: Chm. Council, 1968-73; Pres., 1973-76; Vice Pres. and Mem. Bd, 1967-81, Emeritus Vice-Pres., 1981-; Mem. Bd, IFPI (Secretariat) Ltd, 1979-81. Pres., Brit. Phonographic Industry, 1980- (Chm., 1973-80); Governor, Brit. Inst. of Recorded Sound, 1974-78; Dep. Chm., Phonographic Performance Ltd, 1967-80; Chm., Record Merchandisers Ltd, 1975-81; FRSA 1971. *Publication:* paper to RSA on growth and develt of recording industry. *Address:* Lark Rise, 39 Howards Thicket, Gerrards Cross, Bucks. *T:* Gerrards Cross 84233.

WOOD, Leslie Walter; General Secretary, Union of Construction, Allied Trades and Technicians, since 1978; Member, TUC General Council, since 1979; *b* 27 Nov. 1920; *s* of Walter William Wood and Alice Bertha Wood (*née* Clark); *m* 1945, Irene Gladys Emery; two *d. Educ:* Birmingham Central Technical Coll.; Ruskin Coll., Oxford. Apprenticed carpenter and joiner, 1935; RAF, 1939-45; Asst Workers' Sec., Cadbury's Works Council, 1948-49; full time employment in Union, 1953-; Asst Gen. Sec., Amalgamated Soc. of Woodworkers, 1962. Mem. Council, ACAS, 1980-. *Publication:* A Union to Build (history of Building Trades Unionism), 1979. *Recreations:* golf, swimming, bridge. *Address:* 67 Chestnut Grove, South Croydon, Surrey. *T:* 01-657 7852.

WOOD, Rt. Rev. Mark; *see* Wood, Rt Rev. S. M.

WOOD, Rt. Rev. Maurice Arthur Ponsonby; *see* Norwich, Bishop of.

WOOD, Norman, CBE 1965; Director: Co-operative Wholesale Society Ltd, 1942-64; Manchester Ship Canal Co., 1954-64; Associated British Foods Ltd, 1964-75, retired; *b* 2 Oct. 1905; *m* 1st, 1933, Ada Entwisle (*d* 1974); two *s* one *d*; 2nd, 1976, Nita Miller. *Educ:* Bolton Co. Grammar Sch.; Co-operative Coll. Nat. Exec. Co-operative Party, and Central Board of Co-operative Union, 1934; Ministry of Information, 1939; Chocolate and Sugar Confectionery War-time Assoc., 1942; British Tourist and Holidays Board (later BTA), 1947-70 (Dep. Chm., 1964-67); Plunkett Foundation, 1948- (Vice-Pres. 1972-); Cake and Biscuit Alliance, 1948; Wheat Commission, 1950; Domestic Coal Consumers Council, 1950; Coronation Accommodation Cttee, 1952. Member: British and Irish Millers, 1950-64; White Fish Authority, 1959-63; Food Res. Adv. Cttee, 1961-65; DTI Japan Trade Adv. Cttee, 1971-; Exec. Mem., British Food Export Council, 1970-75. Chairman: Food and Drink Cttee, British Week, Toronto, 1967, Tokyo, 1969; Chm., ten Food and Drink Missions to Hong Kong and Japan, 1968-76; Dir, Fedn of Agricl Co-ops (UK) Ltd, 1975-; Mem., Lab Party Study Gp on Export Services and Organisation, 1974. *Recreations:* walking, music. *Address:* 17 Wallace Fields, Epsom, Surrey; Treakles, Kettlebaston, Ipswich, Suffolk. *T:* 01-393 9052. *Club:* Oriental.

WOOD, Peter (Lawrence); theatrical and television director; Associate Director, National Theatre, since 1978; *b* 8 Oct. 1928; *s* of Frank Wood and Lucy Eleanor (*née* Meeson). *Educ:* Taunton School; Downing College, Cambridge. Resident Director, Arts Theatre, 1956-57; The Iceman Cometh, Arts, 1958; The Birthday Party, Lyric, Hammersmith, 1958; Maria Stuart, Old Vic, 1958; As You Like It, Stratford, Canada, 1959; Winter's Tale, Stratford, England, 1960; The Devils, Stratford, Aldwych, 1961; Hamlet, Stratford, England, 1961; The Private Ear and The Public Eye, Globe, 1962; The Devils, Aldwych, 1962; The Beggar's Opera, Aldwych, 1963; The Private Ear and The Public Eye, Morosco, New York, 1963; Co-Director, History Cycle, Stratford-on-Avon, 1964; The Master Builder, National Theatre, 1964; Carving a Statue, Haymarket, 1964; Poor Richard, Helen Hayes Theatre, New York, 1964; Love for Love, Moscow, and National Theatre, 1965; Incident at Vichy, Phoenix, 1966; The Prime of Miss Jean Brodie, Wyndham's, 1966; White Liars, and Black Comedy 1968; In Search of Gregory (film), 1968-69; Design for Living, Los Angeles, 1971; Jumpers, National Theatre, 1972, Burgtheater, Vienna, 1973; Billy Rose Theatre, NY, 1974; Dear Love, Comedy, 1973; Travesties, Aldwych, 1974, NY, 1975; Macbeth, LA, 1975; The Mother of Us All (opera), Santa Fé, 1976; Long Day's Journey into Night, LA, 1977; Cosi Fan Tutte, Santa Fé, 1977; The Guardsman, The Double Dealer, National Theatre, 1978; She Stoops to Conquer, Burgtheater, Vienna, 1978; Night and Day, Phoenix, 1978, NY, 1979; Undiscovered Country, Nat. Theatre, 1979; Il Seraglio, Glyndebourne, 1980; The Provok'd Wife, Nat. Theatre, 1980; Don Giovanni, Covent Garden, 1981; On the Razzle, Nat. Theatre, 1981; Macbeth, Staatsoper, Vienna, 1982. *Television:* Hamlet, USA, 1970; Long Day's Journey Into Night, USA, 1973; Shakespeare, episode I, ATV, 1976; Double Dealer, Granada, 1980. *Recreations:* swimming, sailing, travelling. *Address:* 11 Warwick Avenue, W9.

WOOD, Ralph; His Honour Judge Wood; a Circuit Judge since 1972; *b* 26 April 1921; *s* of Harold and Dorothy Wood, Wilmslow, Cheshire. *Educ:* Wilmslow Prep. Sch.; King's Sch., Macclesfield; Exeter Coll., Oxford. Served War of 1939-45: commissioned Somerset LI, and served in England, India and Manipur, 1941-46. Called to Bar, Gray's Inn, 1948; practised on Northern Circuit; JP Co. Lancs, 1970-; Dep. Chm., Lancashire QS, 1970-71. *Address:* 38 Hawthorn Lane, Wilmslow, Cheshire SK9 5DG. *T:* Wilmslow 522673.

WOOD, (René) Victor; Director: Coalite Group Ltd; Haslemere Estates Ltd; Wenham & Wemyss Ltd; Chandos Insurance Co. Ltd; Colbourne Insurance Co. Ltd; Falkland Islands Co. Ltd; Welbeck Finance Ltd; JLMB Investments Ltd; PM Associates Ltd; Multiple Health & Life Assurance Co. Ltd; Chairman: Lifeguard Assurance Ltd; Leonard Grouse Associates Ltd; *b* 1925. *Educ:* Jesus

Coll., Oxford (BA). FFA. Chief Exec., 1969-79, Chm. 1974-79, Hill Samuel Insurance and Shipping Holdings Ltd. Vice-Pres., British Insurance Brokers Assoc., 1981-. *Publications:* (with Michael Pilch): Pension Schemes, 1960; New Trends in Pensions, 1964; Pension Scheme Practice, 1967; Company Pension Schemes, 1971; Managing Pension Schemes, 1974; Pension Schemes, 1979. *Address:* Little Woodbury, Newchapel, near Lingfield, Surrey RH7 6HR. *T:* Lingfield 832054.

WOOD, Rt. Rev. Richard James; at St Mark's Theological College, Dar es Salaam, since 1979; *b* 25 Aug. 1920; *s* of Alexander and Irene Wood; *m* 1st, 1946, Elsa Magdalena de Beer (*d* 1969); one *s* one *d* (twins); 2nd, 1972, Cathleen Anne Roark; two *d. Educ:* Oldham Hulme Grammar School; Regent St Polytechnic; Wells Theological Coll. Electrical Officer, RAF, then with Ceylon Fire Insurance Assoc. Curate, St Mary's, Calne, 1952-55; Curate, St Mark's Cathedral, George, S Africa, 1955-58; Rector, Christ Church, Beaufort West, 1958-62; Vicar of St Andrew's, Riversdale, 1962-65; Chaplain, S African Defence Force, 1965-68; Asst, St Alban's, E London, 1968; Rector of St John's, Fort Beaufort, 1969-71; Rector of Keetmanshoop, dio. Damaraland, 1971; Priest-in-Charge of Grace Church and St Michael's, Windhoek and Canon of St George's Cathedral, 1972; Vicar Gen. and Suffragan Bishop of Damaraland, 1973-75; expelled by S Africa, 1975; Hon. Asst Bishop of Damaraland, 1976-; Sec. to The Africa Bureau, 1977; Priest-in-Charge of St Mary, Lowgate, Hull, Chaplain to Hull Coll. of Higher Education and Hon. Asst Bishop of York, 1978-79. Hon. Life Mem., Hull Univ. Student Union. *Recreations:* general home interests. *Address:* St Mark's Theological College, PO Box 25017, Dar es Salaam, Tanzania. *T:* Dar es Salaam 63182.

WOOD, Robert Eric, CBE 1972; Director, City of Leicester Polytechnic, 1969-73; *b* 6 May 1909; *e s* of Robert and Emma Wood; *m* 1935, Beatrice May Skinner; one *s* one *d. Educ:* Birkenhead Inst.; Liverpool Univ. BSc 1st cl. hons, MSc; FInstP. Lectr and Demonstrator, Liverpool Univ., 1930; Lecturer: Borough Road Trng Coll., 1931; Kingston Techn. Coll., 1934; Woolwich Polytechnic, 1939; Head of Physics Dept, Wigan Techn. Coll., 1942; Principal: Grimsby Techn. Coll., 1947; Leicester Regional Coll. of Technology, 1953. Assoc. of Principals of Technical Instns: Hon. Sec., 1960-65; Pres., 1965-66; Chm., Interim Cttee of Polytechnic Directors, 1969-70; Mem. Council, CNAA, 1964-70; Mem., Council for Techn. Educn and Trng in Overseas Countries, 1962-66; Vice-Chm., Nat. Adv. Council on Educn for Industry and Commerce, 1967-72. Hon. FBSI. *Address:* Capler, Peppers Lane, Burton Lazars, Melton Mowbray, Leics. *T:* Melton Mowbray 64576.

WOOD, Robert Noel; Director, Overseas Development Institute, 1974-82; *b* 25 Dec. 1934; *s* of Ernest Clement Wood, CIE and Lucy Eileen Wood; *m* 1962, Sarah Child; one *s* one *d. Educ:* Sherborne Sch.; New Coll., Oxford (BA Hons PPE); LSE (Rockefeller Student; Certif. in Internat. Studies). Nat. Service Commn, RHA, 1953-55. Dep. Res. Dir, Internat. Div., Economist Intelligence Unit Ltd, 1959-65; Inst. of Econs and Statistics, Oxford, 1965-70; Sen. Economist, Min. of Econ. Affairs and Develt Planning, Tanzania, 1966-69; Dir of Studies, Overseas Develt Inst., 1970-74; Adviser to House of Commons Select Cttee on Overseas Develt, 1973-74. *Publications:* contrib. Bull. Oxford Inst. of Econs and Statistics, ODI Rev. *Recreations:* Victorian painters and wood engravers, jazz, singing, swimming. *Address:* 19 Baalbec Road, N5 1QN.

WOOD, Roger L.; *see* Leigh-Wood.

WOOD, Rt. Rev. Roland Arthur; *see* Saskatoon, Bishop of.

WOOD, Prof. Ronald Karslake Starr, FRS; Professor of Plant Pathology, since 1964, and Head, Department of Pure and Applied Biology, Imperial College, University of London, since 1981; *s* of Percival Thomas Evans Wood and Florence Dix Starr; *m* 1947, Marjorie Schofield; one *s* one *d. Educ:* Ferndale Grammar Sch.; Imperial College. Royal Scholar, 1937; Forbes Medal, 1941; Huxley Medal, 1950. Research Asst to Prof. W. Brown, 1941; Directorate of Aircraft Equipment, Min. of Aircraft Production, 1942; Lectr, Imperial Coll., 1947; Commonwealth Fund Fellow, 1950; Univ. Reader in Plant Pathology, 1955; Research Fellow, Connecticut Agric. Experiment Stn, 1957. Mem. Council, British Mycological Soc., 1948; Sec., Assoc. of Applied Biologists; Mem., Parly and Sci. Cttee; Mem., Biological Council, 1949; Consultant, Nat. Fedn of Fruit and Potato Trades, 1955; Mem. council, Inst. of Biology, 1956; Chm., Plant Pathology Cttee, British Mycological Soc.; Mem. Governing Body, Nat. Fruit and Cider Inst., Barnes Memorial Lectr, 1962; Sec., First Internat. Congress of Plant Pathology, 1965; Mem. Governing Body, East Malling Research Stn, 1966 (Vice-Chm.); Pres., Internat. Soc. for Plant Pathology, 1968; Mem., Nat. Cttee for Biology, 1978; Chm., British Nat. Sub-Cttee for Botany, 1978; Dean, RCS, 1975-78. Scientific Dir, NATO Advanced Study Institute, Pugnochiuso, 1970, Sardinia, 1975, Cape Sounion, 1980; Consultant, FAO/UNDP, India, 1976. Fellow, Amer. Phytopathological Soc., 1972; Corres. Mem., Deutsche Phytomedizinische Gesellschaft, 1973. Otto-Appel-Denkmünster, 1978. Thurburn Fellow, Univ. of Sydney, 1979; Sir C. V. Raman Prof., Univ. of Madras, 1980; Regents' Lectr, Univ. of California, 1981. *Publications:* Physiological Plant Pathology, 1967; (ed) Phytotoxins in Plant Diseases, 1972; (ed) Specifity in Plant Diseases, 1976; (ed) Active Defence Mechanisms in Plants, 1981; numerous papers in Annals of Applied Biology, Annals of Botany, Phytopathology, Trans British

Mycological Soc. *Recreation:* gardening. *Address:* Pyrford Woods, Pyrford, near Woking, Surrey. *T:* Byfleet 43827.

WOOD, Russell Dillon, CVO 1979 (MVO 1975); VRD 1964; Lt-Comdr, RNR; Deputy Treasurer to the Queen since 1969; *b* 16 May 1922; *s* of William G. S. Wood, Whitstable, Kent, and Alice Wood; *m* 1948, Jean Violet Yelwa Davidson, *d* of Alan S. Davidson, Yalding, Kent; one *s* three *d*. *Educ:* King's Sch., Canterbury. Fleet Air Arm Pilot, 1940-46 (despatches twice). Qual. as Chartered Accountant, 1951; financial management career with major public companies, 1951-68. *Recreations:* private flying, sailing, shooting. *Address:* Cleves Cottage, Westleton, Suffolk. *T:* Westleton 325; 4 The Old Barracks, Kensington Palace, W8. *Clubs:* Army and Navy; East Anglian Flying, Aldeburgh Yacht.

WOOD, Sam, MSc; Director of Statistics and Business Research, Post Office, 1965-72, retired; *b* 10 Oct. 1911; *m* 1940, Lucy Greenhalgh Whittaker; two *d*. *Educ:* Glossop Grammar School, Derbyshire; University of Manchester. Gaskell Open Scholarship, Derbyshire Major Scholarship, 1929; BSc (1st cl. Hons) Maths; Bishop Harvey Goodwin Research Scholarship, 1932; MSc 1933. Civil Service: GPO, 1933-34; National Assistance Board, 1934-43; Min. of Aircraft Production, 1943-46; Treasury, 1946-50; GPO: Statistician, 1950; Chief Statistician, 1954. *Publications:* articles in Jl of Inst. of Statisticians, British Jl of Industrial Relations. *Address:* Boxhedge House, Astwood Road, Cranfield, Bedford. *T:* Bedford 750392.

WOOD, Rt. Rev. (Stanley) Mark; *see* Ludlow, Bishop Suffragan of.

WOOD, Terence Courtney; HM Diplomatic Service; Political Adviser and Head of Chancery, British Military Government, Berlin, since 1981; *b* 6 Sept. 1936; *s* of Courtney and Alice Wood; *m* 1st, 1962, Kathleen Mary Jones (marr. diss. 1981); one *s* one *d*; 2nd, 1982, Diana Humphreys-Roberts. *Educ:* King Edward VI Sch., Chelmsford; Trinity Coll., Cambridge. BA Hons 1960. RA, 1955-57 (2nd Lieut). Information Officer, FBI (later CBI), 1963-67; entered HM Diplomatic Service, 1968; Foreign Office, 1968-69; 1st Sec., Rome, 1969-73; FCO, 1973-77; Counsellor (Economic and Commercial), New Delhi, 1977-81. sowc, Royal Naval Coll., Greenwich, 1977. *Recreations:* music, painting. *Address:* c/o Foreign and Commonwealth Office, SW1. *Club:* Travellers'.

WOOD, Rev. Prof. Thomas; D. J. James Professor of Pastoral Theology, St David's University College, Lampeter, since 1957; Deputy Principal, 1971-77; Head of Department of Pastoral Theology, 1957-77, Department of Theology, since 1977; *b* 30 April 1919; *o s* of Willie Wood and Mabel (*née* Gaffey), Batley, Yorks; *m* 1945, Joan Ashley Pollard; three *s*. *Educ:* Batley Grammar Sch.; Univ. of Leeds (BA 1st Cl. Hons English 1941; BD 1945; MA with Dist. 1947); Coll. of the Resurrection, Mirfield. Deacon 1943, priest 1944. Asst Curate, St Anne's, Worksop, 1943-47; Sen. Asst Curate, Mansfield Parish Church, 1947-52; Vicar of Seascale, 1952-57. Chm., Ch. in Wales Working Party on Marriage and Divorce, 1972-75. Member: Southwell Dioc. Cttee for Post-ordination Trng, 1948-52; Social and Indust. Commn of Ch. Assembly, 1949-50; Churches' Council on Gambling, 1965-78; Doctrinal Commn of Ch. in Wales, 1969-; Ch. in Wales Adv. Commn on Ch. and Society, 1973-. An Ecclesiastical Judge, Provincial Ct of Ch. in Wales, 1976-. Bishop's Selector, CACTM, 1955-66; Select Preacher, Univ. of Cambridge, 1961. *Publications:* English Casuistical Divinity during the Seventeenth Century, 1952; The Pastoral Responsibility of the Church Today, 1958; Five Pastorals, 1961; Some Moral Problems, 1961; Chastity Not Outmoded, 1965; (contrib.) A Dictionary of Christian Ethics, 1967; articles and revs in Theol., Ch. Qtly Rev., Jl Theol Studies, Ch. in Wales Qtly, Trivium. *Address:* College House, St David's University College, Lampeter, Dyfed SA48 7ED.

WOOD, Victor; *see* Wood, R. V.

WOOD, Walter; Town Clerk, City of Birmingham, 1972-74; *b* Bolton, 11 Jan. 1914; *s* of Walter Scott Wood; *m* 1939, Hilda Maude, *d* of Albert Forrester; two *s*. *Educ:* Canon Slade Sch., Bolton; Victoria Univ., Manchester (LLB). Served with RAF, 1940-45. Admitted solicitor, 1937 (Daniel Reardon and Clabon premium); legal associate member, RTPI, 1948; Asst Solicitor, Bradford, 1937. Swansea, 1939; Dep. Town Clerk, Grimsby, 1947; Principal Asst Solicitor, Sheffield, 1948; Asst Town Clerk, Birmingham, 1952; Dep. Town Clerk, Birmingham, 1960. Panel Inspector, DoE, 1974. Governor, Solihull Sch., 1974. Pres., Birmingham Law Soc., 1976. Pres., West Midland Rent Assessment Panel, 1980-. *Recreations:* swimming, philately. *Address:* 43 Sandgate Road, Hall Green, Birmingham B28 0UN. *T:* 021-744 1195.

WOOD, Ven. Wilfred Denniston, JP; Archdeacon of Southwark, since 1982; Hon. Canon of Southwark Cathedral since 1977; *b* Barbados, WI, 15 June 1936; *s* of Wilfred Coward and Elsie Elmira Wood; *m* 1966, Ina Eileen, *d* of L. E. Smith, CBE, Barbadian MP; three *s* two *d*. *Educ:* Combermere Sch. and Codrington Coll., Barbados. Lambeth Dip. in Theol., 1962. Ordained deacon, St Michael's Cath., Barbados, 1961; ordained priest, St Paul's Cath., London, 1962. Curate of St Stephen with St Thomas, Shepherd's Bush, 1962-66, Hon. Curate, 1966-74; Bishop of London's Officer in Race Relations, 1966-74; Vicar of St Laurence, Catford, 1974-82; RD of East Lewisham, 1977-82. Chm., Martin Luther King Meml Trust. Mem., Royal Commn on Criminal Procedure, 1978-80. JP Inner London, 1971. *Publications:* (contrib.) The Committed Church, 1966; (with John Downing)

Vicious Circle, 1968. *Recreations:* reading, cricket; armchair follower of most sports. *Address:* 1A Dog Kennel Hill, East Dulwich Estate, SE22 8AA. *T:* 01-274 6767.

WOOD, Sir William (Alan), KCVO 1978; CB 1970; Second Crown Estate Commissioner, 1968-78; Chairman, London and Quadrant Housing Trust, since 1980; *b* 8 Dec. 1916; *m* 1943, Zoë, *d* of Rev. Dr D. Frazer-Hurst; two *s* two *d*. *Educ:* Dulwich Coll.; Corpus Christi Coll., Cambridge (Scholar). Ministry of Home Affairs, N. Ireland, 1939. Lieut, RNVR, 1942-46. Ministry of Town and Country Planning, 1946; Minister's Private Secretary, 1951; Principal Regional Officer (West Midlands), Ministry of Housing and Local Government, 1954; Asst Secretary, 1956; Under-Secretary, 1964-68. Chm. Council, King Alfred Sch., 1966-78, Pres. 1978-. *Address:* 654 Finchley Road, NW11. *T:* 01-458 2684. *Club:* Athenæum.

WOODALL, Alec; MP (Lab) Hemsworth since Feb. 1974; *b* 20 Sept. 1918; *m* 1950; one *s* one *d*. *Educ:* South Road Elementary School. Colliery official. PPS to Sec. of State for Trade, 1976-78. *Address:* 2 Grove Terrace, Hemsworth, West Yorkshire WF9 4BQ. *T:* Hemsworth 613897.

WOODALL, Lt-Gen. Sir John (Dane), KCMG 1959; KBE 1953 (OBE 1942; MBE 1919); CB 1947; MC 1917; Governor and Commander-in-Chief, Bermuda, 1955-60; *b* 19 April 1897; *s* of late Colonel F. Woodall, CMG; *m* 1st, 1920, Helen (Nischan-I-Schefakat), *o d* of late Sir Adam Block, KCMG; one *d*; 2nd, 1935, Marion, CStJ, *d* of late Alfred Aitkin Thom; one *s* two *d*. *Educ:* St Columba's; RMA, Woolwich; Staff Colleges, Camberley and RAF. Served European War, 1914-18, Major, Royal Artillery (despatches, MBE, MC); DAAG Turkey, 1922-24; Instructor in Gunnery; Brigade Major; commanded battery RA; Instructor RAF Staff College; commanded regt RA; GSO1; Brigadier, General Staff, 1940; DDSD, War Office; Director Man Power, War Office; served War of 1939-46 (despatches, CB, OBE); Vice-Adjutant-General to the Forces, 1949-52; GOC, N. Ireland, 1952-55; retired, 1955. Colonel Comdt, RA, 1954-62. KStJ 1958. *Recreations:* lawn tennis and squash. *Address:* Whitewell Lodge, near Whitchurch, Salop. *Club:* Army and Navy.

WOODALL, Mary, CBE 1959; PhD; DLitt; FSA; FMA; London Adviser to Felton Trust, Melbourne, 1965-75; *b* 6 March 1901. *Educ:* Cheltenham Ladies' Coll.; Somerville Coll., Oxford. Voluntary, British Museum Dept of Prints and Drawings. WRVS Regional Administrator, 1938-42; Temp. Principal, Ministry of Health and Ministry of Supply, 1942-45; Keeper, Dept of Art, 1945-56, Director, 1956-64, City Museum and Art Gallery, Birmingham. Trustee, Nat. Gallery, 1968-76. Fellow of University College, London, 1958. *Publications:* Gainsborough's Landscape Drawings, 1939; Thomas Gainsborough, 1949; The Letters of Thomas Gainsborough, 1962. *Recreations:* travelling, painting. *Address:* Red House, Clifton Hampden, Abingdon-on-Thames, Oxon. *Club:* University Women's.

WOODBINE PARISH, Sir David (Elmer), Kt 1980; CBE 1964; Chairman, City and Guilds of London Institute, 1967-79, Life Vice-President, 1979; *b* 29 June 1911; *o s* of late Walter Woodbine Parish and Audrey Makins; *m* 1939, Mona Blair McGarel, BA (Arch), ARIBA, *o d* of late Charles McGarel Johnston, Glynn, Co. Antrim; two *d*. *Educ:* Sandroyd; Eton; Lausanne, Switzerland. Chm. and Man. Dir, Holliday and Greenwood Ltd, 1953-59; Man. Dir, Bovis Holdings Ltd, 1960-66; Dep. Chm., Marine and General Mutual Life Assurance Soc., 1976- (Dir, 1971-). Chm., Jt Mission Hosp. Equip. Bd (ECHO), 1973-78. President: London Master Builders Assoc., 1952; Nat. Fedn of Building Trades Employers, 1960; Member: Regional Adv. Council for Technological Educn, London and Home Counties, 1952-69; Architects Registration Council, 1952-72; Nat. Adv. Council for Educn in Industry and Commerce, 1953-78; BIM Council, 1953-62, Bd of Fellows, 1966-72; Nat. Council for Technological Awards, 1955-61; Bd of Building Educn, 1955-66; Building Res. Bd, 1957-60; Industrial Training Council, 1958-64; Council, British Employers' Confedn, 1959-65; Council Foundn for Management Educn, 1959-65; British Productivity Council, 1961-70 (Chm., Educn and Trng Cttee, 1963-70); Human Sciences Cttee (SRC), 1963-66; Construction Industry Training Bd, 1964-70. Chairman: UK Nat. Cttee, Internat. Apprentice Competition, 1962; MPBW Working Party on Res. and Information, 1963; Nat. Examinations Bd for Supervisory Studies, 1964-73; Mem., Nat. Jt Consult. Cttee of Architects, Quantity Surveyors and Builders, 1958-70 (Chm. 1966-68); Chm., Dept of Health and Social Security Cttee of Inquiry on Hosp. Building Maintenance and Minor Capital Works, 1968-70; Member: Court, Russia Co., 1937-; Court, City Univ., 1967-72; Bd of Governors, The Polytechnic, Regent Street, 1967-70; Court, Polytechnic of Central London, 1970-76; Governing Body, Imperial Coll. of Science and Technology, 1971-81. Vice-Pres., Internat. Fedn of European Contractors of Building and Public Works, 1967-71. Vice-Chm., Bd of Governors, St Thomas' Hosp., 1967-74 (Chm., Rebuilding Cttee, 1968-76); Chairman: Council, St Thomas's Hosp. Med. Sch., 1970-; St Thomas' Dist Educn Adv. Council, 1974-81; Florence Nightingale Mus. Trust, 1982-; Member: Nightingale Fund Council, 1974-; Bd of Governors, Bethlem Royal Hosp. and Maudsley Hosp., 1975-78; Council of Governors, Utd Medical Schs of Guy's and St Thomas's Hosps, 1982-. Chm., Sussex Area, Royal Sch. of Church Music, 1981-. Master, Clothworkers' Co., 1974-75 (Warden, 1962-64; Chm., Angel Court Develt, 1969-80). Mem. Bd of Governors, Clothworkers' Foundation, 1977-. FCIOB (FIOB 1940); FRSA 1953; CBIM (FBIM 1957). Fellow, Imperial Coll., 1976; Hon. FCGI 1979. Hon. LLD Leeds, 1975. *Publications:* contribs to technical jls concerned with construction. *Recreations:* travel and music. *Address:* The Glebe Barn, Pulborough, West

Sussex RH20 2AF. *T:* Pulborough 2613; 5 Lurgan Mansions, Sloane Square, SW1W 8BH. *T:* 01-730 6512. *Club:* Boodle's.

WOODCOCK, Dr George, FRGS; Editor, Canadian Literature, 1959-77; author; *b* 8 May 1912; *s* of Samuel Arthur Woodcock and Margaret Gertrude Woodcock (*née* Lewis); *m* 1949, Ingeborg Hedwig Elisabeth Linzer. *Educ:* Sir William Borlase's Sch., Marlow. Editor, Now, London, 1940-47; freelance writer, 1947-54; Lectr in English, Univ. of Washington, 1954-56; Lectr, Asst Prof. and finally Associate Prof. of English, Univ. of British Columbia, 1956-63; Lectr in Asian Studies, Univ. of British Columbia, 1966-67. At the same time continued writing books and talks; also plays and documentaries for Canadian Broadcasting Corporation. Prepared a series of nine documentary films for CBC, on South Pacific, 1972-73. Hon. LLD: Victoria, 1967; Winnipeg, 1975; Hon. DLitt: Sir George Williams Univ., 1970; Univ. of Ottawa, 1974; Univ. of British Columbia, 1977. John Simon Guggenheim Fellow, 1950; Canadian Govt Overseas Fellow, 1957; Canada Council: Killam Fellow, 1970; Senior Arts Fellow, 1975. Governor-General's Award for Non-Fiction, 1967; Molson Prize, 1973; UBC Medal for Popular Biography, 1973 and 1976. FRSC 1968, FRGS 1971. *Publications:* William Godwin, 1946; The Anarchist Prince, 1950; Proudhon, 1956; To the City of the Dead, 1956; Selected Poems, 1967; Anarchism, 1962; Faces of India, 1964; The Greeks in India, 1966; The Crystal Spirit: a study of George Orwell, 1966; Canada and the Canadians, 1970; Dawn and the Darkest Hour, 1971; Gandhi, 1971; Rejection of Politics, 1972; Herbert Read, 1972; Who Killed the British Empire?, 1974; Gabriel Dumont, 1975; Notes on Visitations, 1975; South Sea Journey, 1976; Peoples of the Coast, 1977; Thomas Merton, Monk and Poet, 1978; Two Plays, 1978; The Canadians, 1980; The World of Canadian Writing, 1980; The George Woodcock Reader, 1980; The Mountain Road, 1981; Confederation Betrayed, 1981; also many articles. *Recreation:* travel. *Address:* 6429 McCleery Street, Vancouver, BC V6N 1G5, Canada. *T:* 604-266-9393. *Club:* Faculty (Vancouver).

WOODCOCK, Gordon, FCA, CIPFA; County Treasurer of Staffordshire, since 1973. Served War, Royal Navy, 1942-46. City Treasurer's Dept: Birmingham, 1937-42 and 1946-54; Stoke-on-Trent, 1954-73; City Treasurer of Stoke-on-Trent, 1971-73. *Address:* PO Box 10, County Buildings, Eastgate Street, Stafford ST16 2NF. *T:* Stafford 3121.

WOODCOCK, John, QPM 1976; CBIM; Chief Constable, South Wales Constabulary, since 1979; *b* 14 Jan. 1932; *s* of late Joseph Woodcock and of Elizabeth May Woodcock (*née* Whiteside); *m* 1953, Kathleen Margaret Abbott; two *s* one *d. Educ:* Preston, Lancs, elementary schs; Preston Technical Coll. Police cadet, Lancashire Constabulary, 1947-50; Army Special Investigation Branch, 1950-52; Constable to Chief Inspector, Lancashire Constabulary, 1952-65; Supt and Chief Supt, Bedfordshire and Luton Constabulary, 1965-68; Asst Chief Constable, 1968-70, Dep. Chief Constable, 1970-74, Gwent Constabulary; Dep. Chief Constable, Devon and Cornwall Constabulary, 1974-78; Chief Constable, N Yorkshire Police, 1978-79. Intermed. Comd Course, Police Coll., 1965, Sen. Comd Course, 1968; Study, Bavarian Police, 1977; European Discussion Centre, 1977; Internat. Police Course (Lectr), Sicily, Rome, 1978. FBI, Nat. Exec., Washington, 1981. Vice-Pres., Welsh Assoc. of Youth Clubs, 1981-; Chm., Welsh Adv. Cttee; King George Jubilee Trust; Member: Admin. Council, Royal Jubilee Trusts; Prince's Trust Cttee for Wales; Member, Governing Body: World College of the Atlantic, 1980; Police Staff Coll., Bramshill, Hants. OStJ 1981. *Recreations:* squash, badminton, walking. *Address:* Police Headquarters, Cowbridge Road, Bridgend, Mid Glamorgan CF31 3SR. *T:* Bridgend 55555. *Clubs:* Special Forces; Cardiff and County; United Services Mess; Cardiff Business (Vice-Pres.) (all Cardiff); Hon. Member, Swansea Lions.

WOODCOCK, John Charles; cricket writer; *b* 7 Aug. 1926; *s* of late Rev. Parry John Woodcock and Norah Mabel Woodcock (*née* Hutchinson). *Educ:* Dragon Sch.; St Edward's Sch., Oxford; Trinity Coll., Oxford (MA; OUHC *v* Cambridge, 1946, 1947). Manchester Guardian, 1952-54; Cricket Correspondent to The Times, 1954-, and to Country Life, 1962-; Editor, Wisden Cricketers' Almanack, 1980-; has covered 25 Test tours, 1950-, to Australia, 12 times, S Africa, W Indies, New Zealand, India and Pakistan. *Publications:* The Ashes, 1956; (with E. W. Swanton) Barclays World of Cricket, 1980. *Recreations:* the countryside, golf. *Address:* The Curacy, Longparish, near Andover, Hants SP11 6PB. *T:* Longparish 259. *Clubs:* MCC, Flyfishers'; Vincent's (Oxford); St Enodoc Golf.

WOODD WALKER, Geoffrey Basil, FRCS; retired as a Consultant Surgeon (West London Hospital, 1930-65); *b* 9 June 1900; *s* of Basil Woodd Walker, MD, and Margaret Jane Routledge; *m* 1932, Ulla Troili; two *s. Educ:* Rugby Sch.; King's Coll., Cambridge; St Mary's Hospital. MA Cambridge; MB, BCh; MRCS, LRCP London; FRCS 1928. *Recreation:* zoology (FZS). *Address:* 33 Lexden Road, Colchester, Essex CO3 3PX. *Club:* Athenæum.

WOODFIELD, Philip John, CB 1974; CBE 1963; Permanent Under-Secretary of State, Northern Ireland Office, since 1981; *b* 30 Aug. 1923; *s* of Ralph Woodfield; *m* 1958, Diana Margaret, *d* of Sydney Herington; three *d. Educ:* Alleyn's Sch., Dulwich; King's Coll., London. Served War of 1939-45: Royal Artillery, 1942-47 (captain). Entered Home Office, 1950; Asst Private Secretary to Home Secretary, 1952; Federal Government of Nigeria, 1955-57; Home Office, 1957-60; Private Secretary to the Prime Minister, 1961-65; Asst Sec. 1965-67, Asst Under-Sec. of State, 1967-72, Home Office; Deputy Sec., NI Office, 1972-74, Home Office, 1974-81. Secretary to

Commonwealth Immigration Mission, 1965; Secretary to Lord Mountbatten's inquiry into prison security, Nov.-Dec. 1966. *Recreation:* music. *Address:* Northern Ireland Office, Great George Street, SW1. *Clubs:* Garrick, Beefsteak.

WOODFIELD, Ven. Samuel Percy, MA; Rector of Waterval Boven (African and European), 1964-72 (Priest-in-charge, Waterval Boven Missions, 1959-72); Archdeacon of Barberton, 1960-63, Archdeacon Emeritus from 1964; Canon S Alban's Cathedral, Pretoria, South Africa, 1932-64; Hon. Canon, 1964; *b* 19 April 1889; *s* of Samuel Robinson Woodfield and Emma Utting. *Educ:* Great Yarmouth Grammar Sch.; Selwyn Coll., Cambridge. Asst Priest, St Mary's, Hitchin, 1915-19; Headmaster, Norton Sch., Letchworth, 1917-19; Asst Priest, Sawbridgeworth, 1919-21; Vice-Principal, Diocesan Training Coll., Pietersburg, N Transvaal, 1922-24, Principal, 1924-38, 1954-57; Priest-in-Charge, Pietersburg West Native Mission, 1936-38; Priest-in-charge, Pretoria Native Mission, 1938-53, and Coloured Mission, 1943-53; Archdeacon of Pretoria (City) Native Mission, 1945-53; Archdeacon of W Transvaal, 1953-60; Archdeacon of E Transvaal, 1958-60. Exam. Chaplain to Bishop of Pretoria, 1922-50; Member: Advisory Board for Native Education in the Transvaal, 1924-37, 1940-43, 1946-50; Chaplain Westfort Leper Inst., 1938-53; Div. Pathfinder Scout Commissioner for the Transvaal, 1931-50; Deputy Chief Scouts' African Commissioner for S Africa, 1943-53; Chief Scout's Commissioner for African Scouts, S Africa, 1953-61; Emeritus Comr, 1961. King George V Jubilee Medal; Coronation Medals, 1937, 1953. *Address:* Irene Homes, Irene, Transvaal, 1675, South Africa. *T:* 65116.

WOODFORD, Maj.-Gen. David Milner, CBE 1975; Senior Army Member, Royal College of Defence Studies, since 1982; *b* 26 May 1930; *s* of Major R. M. Woodford, MC, retd, and late Marion Rosa Woodford (*née* Gregory); *m* 1959, Mary E. Jones. *Educ:* Prince of Wales Sch., Nairobi; Wadham Coll., Oxford (BA). RCDS and psc. National Service, 1st Royal Fusiliers, Korea, 1953; Regtl service, Egypt, Sudan, UK, 1953-55; ADC/GOC Berlin, 1956-58; Adjt 1RF, Gulf, Kenya, 1958-60; Coy Comd 1RF, Malta, Cyprus, Libya, 1960-61; G3 Div./Dist, UK, 1962; sc Camberley, 1963; GSO2 MO 1, then MA/VCGS, 1964-66; Coy Comd 1RF, BAOR, UK, Gulf and Oman, 1966-68; GSO1 (DS) Staff Coll., 1968-70; CO 3 RRF, Gibraltar, UK, N Ireland, 1970-72; Col GS NEARELF (Cyprus), 1973-75; Comd 3 Inf. Bde (N Ireland), 1976-77; RCDS 1978; D Comd and COS SE Dist, UK, 1978-80; ACGS (Training and Combat Devel), 1981-82. Col RRF, 1982-. *Recreations:* literary, historical; passionate golfer. *Address:* c/o Royal College of Defence Studies, Seaford House, Belgrave Square, SW1X 8NS. *Clubs:* Army and Navy, New Zealand Golf.

WOODFORD, Brigadier Edward Cecil James, CBE 1946; DSO 1943; *b* 1901; *s* of late Major Edward Francis Woodford, York and Lancaster Regt; *m* 1949, Joanne Eileen, *d* of Peter Charles Mayer, Washington, DC, USA; one *s* two *d. Educ:* Bedford Sch.; RMC Sandhurst. 2nd Lieut, York and Lancaster Regt, 1920. Served War of 1939-45, N Africa, Iraq, Persia, Sicily, Italy, Burma, French Indo-China; Lieut-Colonel, 1942, Brigadier, 1945. Commander, Lubbecke District, BAOR, 1952-55, retired 1955. *Address:* 607 Ventura Place, Snee Farm, Mount Pleasant, SC 29464, USA.

WOODGATE, Joan Mary, CBE 1964; RRC 1959; Matron-in-Chief, Queen Alexandra's RN Nursing Service, 1962-66, retired; *b* 30 Aug. 1912; *d* of Sir Alfred Woodgate, CBE, and Louisa Alice (*née* Digby). *Educ:* Surbiton High Sch., Surrey. Trained at St George's Hospital, 1932-36, Sister, 1937-38; Queen Charlotte's Hospital, 1936. Joined QARNNS, 1938; served Middle East and Far East; HM Hospital Ship, Empire Clyde, 1945-47; HM Hospital Ship, Maine, 1953-54; Principal Matron: RNH Haslar, 1959-61; RNH Malta, 1961-62. OStJ 1959; QHNS, 1962-64. Member Commonwealth War Graves Commn, 1966-. *Recreations:* gardening, country pursuits. *Address:* Tiptoe, near Lymington, Hants. *Club:* English-Speaking Union.

WOODHALL, David Massey; Chief Executive, Commission for New Towns, since 1982; *b* 25 Aug. 1934; *s* of Douglas J. D. and Esme Dorothy Woodhall; *m* 1954, Margaret A. Howarth; two *s. Educ:* Bishop Holgate's Sch., Barnsley; Royds Hall, Huddersfield; Henley Administrative Staff Coll. Dip. Leeds Sch. of Architecture and Town Planning. West Riding CC, 1951-60; Cumberland CC, 1960-63; Northamptonshire CC, 1963-82: County Planning Officer, 1971-80; Asst Chief Executive, 1980-82. *Recreations:* motor-racing, fell walking, food and wine. *Address:* Manor Farm House, Easton Maudit, Wellingborough, Northants NN9 7NR. *T:* Wellingborough 664 851.

WOODHAM, Professor Ronald Ernest; Professor of Music, Reading University, 1951-77; *b* 8 Feb. 1912; *s* of Ernest Victor Woodham, Beckenham, Kent; *m* 1949, Kathleen Isabel, *d* of P. J. Malone; three *s. Educ:* Sherborne Sch.; Royal College of Music, London; Christ Church, Oxford. BA, DMus; FRCO, ARCM. Assistant Director of Music, Bradfield Coll., 1936. Served in RASC, in Middle East and Italy, 1939-45 (despatches). Acting Director of Music, Bradfield Coll., 1946; Director of Music, Sherborne Sch., 1946; Cramb Lecturer in Music, Glasgow Univ., 1947-51. *Address:* Lorien, Admoor Lane, Southend Bradfield, Reading RG7 6HT.

WOODHAMS, Ven. Brian Watson; Archdeacon of Newark, 1965-79, Archdeacon Emeritus since 1980; Hon. Canon of Southwell Minister, 1960-79; Rector of Staunton with Flawborough and Kilvington, 1971-79; *b* 16 Jan. 1911; *s* of Herbert and Florence Osmond Woodhams; *m* 1941, Vera Charlotte

White; one *s. Educ:* Dover Coll.; Oak Hill Theological Coll.; St John's Coll., University of Durham. LTh 1934, BA 1936, Durham. Deacon, 1936; Priest, 1937. Curate: St Mary Magdalene, Holloway, 1936-39; St James-the-Less, Bethnal Green, 1939-41; Christ Church, New Malden, i/c of St John, New Malden, 1941-43; Vicar: St Mark, Poplar, 1943-45; St James-the-Less, Bethnal Green, 1945-50; St Jude's, Mapperley, Nottingham, 1950-65; Farndon with Thorpe-by-Newark, 1965-71. Proctor in York Convocation, 1955-65. Chairman, Southwell Diocesan Board of Women's Work, 1966-79. *Recreations:* children's and refugee work (Chairman, Nottingham Branch Save the Children Fund); interested in sport (local FA football referee). *Address::* 2 Lunn Lane, Collingham, Newark, Notts. *T:* Newark 892207.

WOODHOUSE, family name of **Baron Terrington.**

WOODHOUSE, Ven. Andrew Henry, DSC 1945; MA; Archdeacon of Hereford and Canon Residentiary, Hereford Cathedral, since 1982; *b* 30 Jan. 1923; *s* of H. A. Woodhouse, Dental Surgeon, Hanover Square, W1, and Woking, Surrey, and Mrs P. Woodhouse; unmarried. *Educ:* Lancing Coll.; The Queen's Coll., Oxford. MA 1949. Served War, RNVR, 1942-46 (Lieut). Oxford, 1941-42 and 1946-47; Lincoln Theological Coll., 1948-50. Deacon, 1950; Priest, 1951; Curate of All Saints, Poplar, 1950-56; Vicar of St Martin, West Drayton, 1956-70; Rural Dean of Hillingdon, 1967-70; Archdeacon of Ludlow and Rector of Wistanstow, 1970-82. *Recreations:* photography, walking. *Address:* The Archdeacon's House, The Close, Hereford HR1 2NG. *T:* Hereford 272873. *Club:* Naval.

WOODHOUSE, Rt. Hon. Sir (Arthur) Owen, KBE 1981; Kt 1974; DSC 1944; PC 1974; **Rt. Hon. Mr Justice Woodhouse;** a Judge of the Supreme Court, New Zealand, since 1961; a Judge of the Court of Appeal, since 1974, President of the Court of Appeal, since 1981; *b* Napier, 18 July 1916; *s* of A. J. Woodhouse: *m* 1940, Margaret Leah Thorp; four *s* two *d. Educ:* Napier Boys' High Sch.; Auckland Univ. (LLB). Served War of 1939-45, Lt-Comdr in RNZNVR on secondment to RN; service in MTBs; liaison officer with Yugoslav Partisans, 1943; Asst to Naval Attaché, HM Embassy Belgrade, 1945. Joined Lusk, Willis & Sproule, barristers and solicitors, 1946; Crown Solicitor, Napier, 1953; appointed Judge of Supreme Court, 1961. Chm., Royal Commn on Compensation and Rehabilitation in respect of Personal Injury in NZ, 1966-67, and of inquiry into similar questions in Australia, 1973-74. Hon. LLD: Victoria Univ. of Wellington, 1978; Univ. of York, Toronto, 1981. *Recreations:* music, golf. *Address:* Judge's Chambers, Box 1606, Wellington, New Zealand. *Clubs:* Northern (Auckland); Hawkes Bay (Napier); Wellesley, Wellington (Wellington).

WOODHOUSE, Ven. (Charles) David (Stewart); Archdeacon of Warrington, since 1981; *b* 23 Dec. 1934; *s* of Rev. Hector and Elsie Woodhouse. *Educ:* Silcoates School, Wakefield; Kelham Theological College. Curate of St Wilfrid's, Halton, Leeds, 1959-63; Youth Chaplain, Kirkby Team Ministry, Diocese of Liverpool, 1963-66; Curate of St John's, Pembroke, Bermuda, 1966-69; Asst Gen. Secretary, CEMS, 1969-70; Gen. Sec., 1970-76; Rector of Ideford, Ashcombe and Luton and Domestic Chaplain to Bishop of Exeter, 1976-81. *Address:* The Vicarage, Wigan Road, Hindley WN2 3DF. *T:* Wigan 55505.

WOODHOUSE, Hon. (Christopher) Montague, DSO 1943; OBE 1944; MA (Oxon); *b* 11 May 1917; 2nd *s* of 3rd Baron Terrington, KBE; *b* and *heir-pres.* to 4th Baron Terrington, *qv ; m* 1945, Lady Davina, *d* of 2nd Earl of Lytton, KG, PC, GCSI, GCIE, and *widow* of 5th Earl of Erne; two *s* one *d. Educ:* Winchester; New Coll., Oxford (Craven and Hertford Schols, Gaisford Prizeman). First Cl. Hon. Mods, 1937; First Class Lit. Hum., 1939; MA 1947; Lord Justice Holker Schol. Gray's Inn, 1939; enlisted RA, 1939, commissioned 1940; Colonel, Aug. 1943, in command of Allied Military Mission to Greek Guerillas in German-occupied Greece (despatches twice, DSO, OBE, Officer of Legion of Merit (USA), Commander of Order of the Phoenix, with Swords (Greece). Served in HM Embassy, Athens, 1945, Tehran, 1951; Secretary-General, Allied Mission for Observing Greek Elections, 1946; worked in industry 1946-48; Asst Secretary, Nuffield Foundation, 1948-50; Foreign Office, 1952; Director-General, RIIA, and Dir. of Studies, 1955-59; MP (C) Oxford, 1959-66 and 1970-Sept. 1974; Parliamentary Secretary, Ministry of Aviation, 1961-62; Joint Under-Secretary of State, Home Office, July 1962-Oct. 1964. Dir, Educn and Training, CBI, 1966-70. President, Classical Assoc., 1968; Chm. Council, RSL, 1977-. Fellow of Trinity Hall, Cambridge, 1950; Visiting Fellow, Nuffield Coll., Oxford, 1956; Vis. Prof., King's Coll., London, 1978. FRSL 1951. Special Mem., Acad. of Athens, 1980. *Publications:* Apple of Discord, 1948; One Omen, 1950; Dostoievsky, 1951; The Greek War of Independence, 1952; Britain and the Middle East, 1959; British Foreign Policy since the Second World War, 1961; Rhodes (with late J. G. Lockhart), 1963; The New Concert of Nations, 1964; The Battle of Navarino, 1965; Post-War Britain, 1966; The Story of Modern Greece, 1968; The Philhellenes, 1969; Capodistria: the founder of Greek independence, 1973; The Struggle for Greece (1941-1949), 1976; Something Ventured, 1982; Karamanlis: the restorer of Greek democracy, 1982; numerous articles, translations, broadcasts. *Address:* Willow Cottage, Latimer, Bucks. *T:* Little Chalfont 2627.

WOODHOUSE, Ven. David; *see* Woodhouse, Ven. C. D. S.

WOODHOUSE, Henry, CB 1975; Principal Assistant Solicitor and Head of Transport Branch of Legal Directorate, Departments of the Environment and

Transport, until 1978, now retired; *b* 12 July 1913; *s* of Frank and Florence A. Woodhouse, Cradley Heath, Warley, W Midlands; *m* 1941, Eileen Mary, *d* of Harry and Florence C. Roach, Cradley Heath; two *d. Educ:* King Edward's Sch., Birmingham; St John's Coll., Oxford (MA). Solicitor, 1938; served in HM Forces, 1940-46: Lt-Col in Legal Div., Control Commn for Germany, 1945-46; entered Treasury Solicitor's Dept, 1946; Asst Treasury Solicitor, 1955-69; Principal Asst Treasury Solicitor, 1969-71; Principal Asst Solicitor, DoE, later Depts of the Environment and Transport, 1972-78. *Publications:* articles in The Conveyancer. *Recreations:* Methodist local preacher, photography, gardening. *Address:* Three Ways, Birchall, Leek, Staffs ST13 5RA. *T:* Leek 372814.

WOODHOUSE, James Stephen; Headmaster, Lancing College, since 1981; *b* 21 May 1933; *s* of late Rt Rev. J. W. Woodhouse, sometime Bishop of Thetford, and late Mrs K. M. Woodhouse; *m* 1957, Sarah, *d* of late Col Hubert Blount, Cley, Norfolk; three *s* one *d. Educ:* St Edward's Sch.; St Catharine's Coll., Cambridge. BA (English) Cantab, 1957; MA 1961. Nat. Service, 14th Field Regt RA, 1953. Asst Master, Westminster Sch., 1957; Under Master and Master of the Queen's Scholars, 1963; Headmaster, Rugby Sch., 1967-81. Chairman: NABC Religious Adv. Cttee, 1971; Bloxham Project, 1972-77; Head Masters' Conf., 1979; Vice-Chm., E-SU Schoolboy Scholarship Cttee, 1973-77. *Recreations:* sailing, music, hill walking. *Address:* The Old Farmhouse, Lancing College, Lancing, West Sussex BN15 0RW.

WOODHOUSE, Hon. Montague; *see* Woodhouse, Hon. C. M.

WOODHOUSE, Rt. Hon. Sir Owen; *see* Woodhouse, Rt Hon. Sir A. O.

WOODHOUSE, Ven. Samuel Mostyn Forbes; Archdeacon of London and Canon Residentiary of St Paul's, 1967-78, Archdeacon Emeritus and Canon Emeritus, 1978; Archdeacon to Retired Clergy, Bath and Wells, since 1978; Chairman, Retired Clergy Association, since 1980; *b* 28 April 1912; *s* of Rev. Major James D. F. Woodhouse, DSO, and Elsie Noel Woodhouse, Water, Manaton, Devon; *m* 1939, Patricia Daniel; two *s* one *d. Educ:* Shrewsbury; Christ Church, Oxford; Wells Theological Coll. BA 1934; MA 1942. Deacon, 1936, Priest, 1937, Diocese of Blackburn; Curate, Lancaster Priory, 1936-39. Chaplain to the Forces (Army), 1939-45 (despatches thrice). Vicar, Holy Trinity, South Shore, Blackpool, 1945-49; Vicar of Leominster, 1949-57; Rural Dean of Leominster, 1956-57; Rector of Bristol City Parish Church (St Stephen's), 1957-67. *Recreations:* golf, fishing, walking, painting, architecture. *Address:* Under Copse Cottage, Redhill, Wrington, Bristol BS18 7SH. *T:* Wrington 862711. *Clubs:* Leander; Vincent's (Oxford).

WOODIFIELD, Rear-Admiral Anthony, CB 1965; CBE 1961; MVO 1953; *b* 5 Aug. 1912; *s* of late Colonel A. H. Woodifield, CB, CMG, OBE, St Leonards-on-Sea, Sussex; *m* 1947, Elizabeth, *d* of late E. J. Stevens, Sutton, Surrey; two *s. Educ:* Cheltenham College. Joined RN, 1929. Served 1939-45 in Home Fleet and on East Indies Station. On Staff of Commander-in-Chief, Portsmouth and for Coronation Naval Review, 1951-53; Secretary to Flag Officer, Second-in-Command, Mediterranean, 1954-55; Secretary to Third Sea Lord and Controller of the Navy, 1956-61; Comdg Officer, HMS Phoenicia, 1961-63; Director General of Naval Personal Services and Officer Appointments, 1964-66. Comdr, 1947; Captain, 1955; Rear-Admiral, 1963; retired list, 1966. *Recreation:* fishing. *Address:* Stocks Cottage, Kington Langley, Chippenham, Wilts. *T:* Kington Langley 281. *Club:* Army and Navy.

WOODLAND, Austin William, CBE 1975; PhD; FGS; Hon. Professorial Fellow, University College of Swansea and Cardiff, since 1980; *b* Mountain Ash, Mid Glamorgan, 4 April 1914; *er s* of William Austin Woodland and Sarah Jane (*née* Butler); *m* 1939, Nesta Ann Phillips (*d* 1981); one *s* one *d. Educ:* Mountain Ash Co. Sch.; University Coll. of Wales, Aberystwyth (BSc Hons Geol., PhD). Lyell Fund, Geol Soc., 1947; FGS 1937. Temp. Asst Lectr in Geol., Manchester Univ., 1937; Demonstrator in Geol., QUB, 1937-39; Geologist, Geol Survey of GB (now incorp. in Inst. of Geol Sciences), 1939; Dist Geologist, 1957-62; Asst Dir (Northern England), 1962-71; Dep. Dir, 1971-75; Director: Inst. of Geol Sciences, 1976-79; Geol Survey of Northern Ireland, 1976-79; Geol Adv. to Minister of Overseas Develt, 1976-79. President: Yorks Geol Soc., 1966-68; Sect. C (Geol.), BAAS, Swansea, 1971 (Mem. Council, 1970-73; Mem. Gen. Cttee, 1973-); Vice-Pres., Geol Soc., 1968-70 (Mem. Council, 1967-70). Sec.-Gen., 6th Internat. Congress of Carboniferous Stratigraphy and Geol., Sheffield, 1967; Geol Adviser, Aberfan Disaster Tribunal, 1966-67. Major, Special Geol Sect., RE (AER), 1948-57. *Publications:* Geology of district around Pontypridd and Maesteg, 1964; (ed) Petroleum and the Continental Shelf of North West Europe, 1975; papers on geol aspects of manganese, coal, water supply, engrg applications. *Recreations:* golf, stamp collecting, gardening. *Address:* 60 Dan-y-Bryn Avenue, Radyr, Cardiff. *T:* Cardiff 843330.

WOODLOCK, Jack Terence; Under-Secretary, Department of Health and Social Security, 1969-79, retired; *b* 10 July 1919; *s* of late James Patrick and Florence Woodlock; *m* 1941, Joan Mary Taylor; three *s* one *d. Educ:* Bromley Grammar School. Entered Civil Service, 1936; served in Royal Artillery, 1939-45; Ministry of Health, 1945; Asst Principal 1946; Principal 1950; Principal Private Sec. to Minister, 1958-59; Asst Sec. 1959. *Recreations:* gardening, camping. *Address:* 9 Berens Way, Chislehurst, Kent. *T:* Orpington 22895.

WOODROFFE, Most Rev. George Cuthbert Manning; *see* West Indies, Archbishop of.

WOODROFFE, Jean Frances, (Mrs J. W. R. Woodroffe), CVO 1953; *b* 22 Feb. 1923; *d* of late Capt. A. V. Hambro; *m* 1st, 1942, Capt. Hon. Vicary Paul Gibbs, Grenadier Guards (killed in action, 1944), *er s* of 4th Baron Aldenham; one *d* (and one *d* decd); 2nd, 1946, Rev. Hon. Andrew Charles Victor Elphinstone (*d* 1975), 2nd *s* of 16th Lord Elphinstone, KT; one *s* (*see* 18th Lord Elphinstone) one *d*; 3rd, 1980, Lt-Col John William Richard Woodroffe. Lady-in-Waiting to the Queen as Princess Elizabeth, 1945; Extra Woman of the Bedchamber to the Queen, 1952-. *Address:* Maryland, Worplesdon, Guildford, Surrey. *T:* Worplesdon 232629.

WOODROOFE, Sir Ernest (George), Kt 1973; PhD, FInstP, FIChemE; Chairman, Leverhulme Trust, 1974-82; *b* 6 Jan. 1912; *s* of late Ernest George Woodroofe and Ada (*née* Dickinson); *m* 1st, 1938, Margaret Downes (*d* 1961); one *d*; 2nd, 1962, Enid Grace Hutchinson Arnold. *Educ:* Cockburn High Sch.; Leeds Univ. Staff of Loders & Nucoline Ltd, 1935-44; Staff of British Oil & Cake Mills Ltd, 1944-50; Mem., Oil Mills Executive of Unilever Ltd, 1951-55; Director of British Oil & Cake Mills Ltd, 1951-55; Head of Research Division of Unilever Ltd, 1955-61; Director: United Africa Co. Ltd, 1961-63; Unilever NV, 1956-74; Chm., Unilever Ltd, 1970-74 (Dir, 1956-74; Vice-Chm., 1961-70). President, International Society for Fat Research, 1962. Member Cttee of Enquiry into the Organisation of Civil Science, 1962-63; A Vice-Pres., Soc. of Chemical Industry, 1963-66; Member: Tropical Products Inst. Cttee, 1964-69; Council for Nat. Academic Awards, 1964-67; Cttee of Award of the Commonwealth Fund, 1965-70; Royal Commn for the Exhbn of 1851, 1968-; British Gas Corp., 1973-81. Director: Schroders Ltd, 1974-; Burton Group Ltd, 1974-; Guthrie Corp. Ltd, 1974-82. Chairman: Review Body on Doctors' and Dentists' Remuneration, 1975-79; CBI Research Cttee, 1966-69. Governor, London Business Sch., 1970-75 (Dep. Chm., 1973-75). Hon. ACT Liverpool, 1963; Hon. Fellow, University of Manchester Inst. of Science and Technology, 1968; Hon. LLD Leeds, 1968; DUniv Surrey, 1970; Hon. DSc: Cranfield, 1974; Liverpool, 1980. Vis. Fellow, Nuffield Coll., Oxford, 1972-80. Comdr, Order of Orange Nassau (Netherlands), 1972. *Recreations:* fishing, golf. *Address:* The Crest, Berry Lane, Worplesdon, Surrey. *T:* Worplesdon 232666. *Club:* Athenæum.

WOODROW, Maj.-Gen. (Albert) John, MBE 1949; *b* 3 June 1919; *s* of late Frederick Henry Woodrow, Portsmouth; *m* 1944, Elizabeth, *d* of late Major Sir John Theodore Prestige, Bourne Park, Bishopsbourne, Kent; two *s* one *d*. *Educ:* Nunthorpe. Commnd Royal Signals, 1940; served War of 1939-45 in NW Europe and Burma (despatches); British Mission to Burma, 1948-49; exchange duty Canada, 1954-56; CO 1 Div. Sigs, 1961-63; British Army Staff, Washington, 1963-65; Comdr Trng Bde Royal Signals, 1965-68; Dir of Public Relations Army, 1968-70; GOC Wales, 1970-73. Col Comdt, Royal Corps of Signals, 1970-77. Dir of Army Security, 1973-78, retired. *Address:* Hookers Green, Bishopsbourne, Canterbury, Kent. *Club:* Army and Navy.

WOODROW, David, CBE 1979; solicitor; *b* 16 March 1920; *s* of late Sydney Melson Woodrow and late Edith Constance (*née* Farmer); *m* 1950, Marie-Armande, *d* of late Benjamin Barrios, KBE, and late Lady Ovey; two *d*. *Educ:* Shrewsbury; Trinity Coll., Oxford (MA). Commnd Royal Artillery, 1940; served SE Asia; POW Java and Japan, 1942-45. Admitted Solicitor, 1949. Chairman: Reading and District HMC, 1966-72; Oxford Regional Hosp. Bd, 1972-74; RHA, 1973-78; NHS Nat. Staff Cttee, Administrative and Clerical Staff, 1975-79. *Recreation:* pottering (mainly making things). *Address:* King's Pool House, Ewelme, Oxon. *T:* Wallingford 39275. *Club:* Leander (Henley-on-Thames).

WOODROW, Gayford William; HM Diplomatic Service, retired; Consul, Algeciras, since 1982; *b* 21 Feb. 1922; *s* of William Alexander Woodrow and Charlotte Louise (*née* Ellis); *m* 1946, Janine Suzanne Marcelle Jannot; one *s*. *Educ:* Brockley County School. Served War, RAF, 1941-46. Foreign Office, 1946; Caracas, 1949; Vice Consul: Barcelona, 1952; Panama, 1954; Consul: Cairo, 1960; Alexandria, 1961; First Sec. and Consul, Warsaw, 1962; Consul: Valencia, 1965; Jerusalem, 1969; First Sec., Ottawa, 1976; Consul General, Tangier, 1978-80; Asst, Consular Dept, FCO, 1980-81. *Recreations:* walking, swimming, archaeology. *Address:* British Consulate, Avenida Francisco Franco II, Algeciras, Spain. *Club:* Surrey County Cricket.

WOODROW, Maj.-Gen. John; *see* Woodrow, A. J.

WOODRUFF, Prof. Alan Waller, CMG 1978; Professor of Medicine, University of Juba, Sudan, since 1981; Wellcome Professor of Clinical Tropical Medicine, London School of Hygiene and Tropical Medicine, 1952-81; Lecturer in Tropical Medicine, Royal Free Hospital School of Medicine, since 1952; Hon. Consultant in Tropical Diseases to: the Army, since 1956; British Airways, since 1962; *b* 27 June 1916; *s* of late William Henry Woodruff, Sunderland, and Mary Margaret Woodruff; *m* 1946, Mercia Helen, *d* of late Leonard Frederick Arnold, Dorking, and Amy Elizabeth Arnold; two *s* one *d*. *Educ:* Bede Collegiate Sch., Sunderland; Durham Univ. MB, BS 1939, MD 1941, Durham; DTM&H England, 1946; PhD London, 1952; FRCP 1953; FRCPE 1960. House Physician and House Surgeon, Royal Victoria Infirmary, Newcastle upon Tyne, 1939-40; MO and Med. Specialist, RAFVR, 1940-46; Med. Registrar, Royal Victoria Infirmary, Newcastle upon Tyne, 1946-48; Sen. Lectr in Clinical Tropical Medicine, London Sch. of Hygiene and Trop. Medicine, 1948-52; First Asst, 1948-52, Physician,

1952-81, Hosp. for Tropical Diseases, University Coll. Hosp., London; William Julius Mickle Fellow, Univ. of London, 1959. Lectures: Goulstonian, RCP, 1954; Lettsomian, Med. Soc. of London, 1969; Watson-Smith, RCP, 1970; Halliburton Hume, Newcastle-upon-Tyne, 1981. Orator, Reading Pathological Soc., 1976. Member: WHO Expert Adv. Panel on Parasitic Diseases, 1963-; Med. Cttee of Overseas Develt Administration; Visiting Professor at Universities: Alexandria, 1963; Ain Shams, Cairo, 1964; Baghdad, 1966, 1968, 1971, 1974; Mosul, 1977-79; Basrah, 1973-74; Makerere, 1973; Khartoum, 1974, 1978; Benghazi, 1976-80. Mem., Assoc. of Physicians of GB and Ireland; President: Durham Univ. Soc., 1963-73; Royal Soc. of Tropical Medicine and Hygiene, 1973-75; Medical Soc. of London, 1975-76; Section of History of Medicine, Royal Soc. Med., 1977-. Hon. Mem., Burma Med. Assoc., 1966; Hon. Mem., Société de Pathologie Exotique, Paris; Hon. Associate Mem., Soc. Belge de Médecine Tropicale, 1965; Hon. Mem., Brazilian Soc. of Tropical Medicine. Katherine Bishop Harman Prize, BMA, 1951. Hon. RE 1979. Gold Medal of Univ. of Pernambuco, Brazil, 1980. *Publications:* (with S. Bell) A Synopsis of Infectious and Tropical Diseases, 1968; (ed) Alimentary and Haematological Aspects of Tropical Disease, 1970; (ed) Medicine in the Tropics, 1974; sections in: Paediatrics for the Practitioner (ed Gaisford and Lightwood); Medicine (ed Richardson); contribs to BMJ, Lancet, Trans Royal Soc. Trop. Medicine and Hygiene, W African Med. Jl, E African Med. Jl, Newcastle Med. Jl, Practitioner, Clinical Science, Proc. Nutrition Soc., etc. *Recreation:* engraving. *Address:* 122 Ferndene Road, SE24. *T:* 01-274 3578; University of Juba, PO Box 82, Juba, Sudan. *Club:* Athenæum.

WOODRUFF, Harry Wells, CMG 1966; retired, 1972; *b* 31 Oct. 1912; *s* of Leonard Wells Woodruff and Rosina Woodruff; *m* 1938, Margaret Bradley; one *d*. *Educ:* Reigate Grammar Sch.; London Univ. Trade Comr, Johannesburg, 1946-51; Trade Comr and Economic Adviser to High Commissioner: Salisbury, 1951-55; Kuala Lumpur, 1957-61; Commercial Counsellor, Canberra, 1962-66; Economic Adviser to Foreign Office, 1966-68; Asst Sec., Dept of Trade and Industry (formerly Bd of Trade), 1968-72. *Publication:* (jointly) Economic Development in Rhodesia and Nyasaland, 1955. *Recreation:* painting. *Address:* 387 Sandbanks Road, Poole, Dorset.

WOODRUFF, Prof. Sir Michael (Francis Addison), Kt 1969; FRS 1968; FRCS; DSc, MS (Melbourne); Professor of Surgery (formerly of Surgical Science), University of Edinburgh, and Surgeon, Edinburgh Royal Infirmary, 1957-76; now Professor Emeritus; Director, Nuffield Transplantation Surgery Unit, Edinburgh, 1968-76; *b* 3 April 1911; *s* of late Prof. Harold Addison Woodruff and Margaret Ada (*née* Cooper); *m* 1946, Hazel Gwenyth Ashby; two *s* one *d*. *Educ:* Wesley Coll., Melbourne; Queen's Coll., University of Melbourne. MB, BS (Melbourne) 1937, MD 1940, MS 1941; FRCS 1946. Captain, Australian Army Medical Corps, 1940-46. Tutor in Surgery, Univ. of Sheffield, 1946-48; Lecturer in Surgery, Univ. of Aberdeen, 1948-52; Hunterian Prof., RCS, 1952; Travelling Fellow, WHO, 1949; Prof. of Surgery, Univ. of Otago, Dunedin, NZ, 1953-56. A Vice-Pres., Royal Soc., 1979. Associé Etranger, Académie de Chirurgie, 1964; Hon. Fellow American Surgical Assoc., 1965; Korrespondierendem Mitglied, Deutsche Gesellschaft für Chirurgie; Hon. FACS 1975; Hon. FRCPE 1982. Lister Medal, 1969; Gold Medal, Soc. of Apothecaries, 1974. *Publications:* (Joint) Deficiency Diseases in Japanese Prison Camps, 1951; Surgery for Dental Students, 1954; Transplantation of Tissues and Organs, 1960; (essays) On Science and Surgery, 1977; The Interaction of Cancer and Host, 1980; articles on surgical topics and on experimental tissue transplantation. *Recreations:* music, sailing. *Address:* The Bield, 506 Lanark Road, Juniper Green, Edinburgh EH14 5DH. *Clubs:* Athenæum; New (Edinburgh); Royal Forth Yacht.

WOODRUFF, Philip; *see* Mason, Philip.

WOODRUFF, William Charles, FRAeS; Assessor, Stansted Airport Public Inquiry; *b* 14 Aug. 1921; *s* of late Thomas and Caroline Woodruff; *m* 1946, Ethel May Miles; one *s* one *d*. *Educ:* St George's, Ramsgate. RAF, 1941-46: Navigator/Observer, 1409 Flight; POW Germany, 1943-45. Seconded Air Min., 1945, and later Min. of Civil Aviation for Air Traffic Control planning; various air traffic control appts at Hurn, Northolt, Southern Centre, Heston and MTCA Hdqrs, 1946-56; Air Traffic Control Officer i/c Heathrow, 1956-62; Sec. of Patch Long-term Air Traffic Control Planning Group, 1960-61; Dep. Dir, 1962-67, Dir, 1967-69, Civil Air Traffic Ops; National Air Traffic Services: Jt Field Comdr, 1969-74; Dep. Controller, 1974-77; Controller, 1977-81. Guild of Air Traffic Control Officers: Clerk, 1952-56; Master, 1956. *Publications:* articles on aviation subjects. *Address:* 25 Chichester Avenue, Ruislip, Mddx.

WOODS, Brian; His Honour Judge Woods; a Circuit Judge, since 1975; *b* 5 Nov. 1928; *yr s* of late E. P. Woods, Woodmancote, Cheltenham; *m* 1957, Margaret, *d* of late F. J. Griffiths, Parkgate, Wirral; three *d*. *Educ:* City of Leicester Boys' Sch.; Nottingham Univ. (LLB 1950). National Service, RAF, 1947-49. Called to the Bar, Gray's Inn, 1955; Midland Circuit; Dep. Chm., Lincs (Lindsey) QS, 1968. Chancellor, Diocese of Leicester, 1977-79; Reader, dio. of Leicester, 1970-79, dio. of Lichfield, 1978-. Mem. Council, S Mary and S Anne's Sch., Abbots Bromley, 1977-. Mem., Law Adv. Cttee, Nottingham Univ., 1979-. Fellow, Midland Div., Woodard Corp., 1979-. *Recreations:* daughters, musical music, taking photographs. *Address:* c/o Circuit Administrator, 2 Newton Street, Birmingham B4 7LU.

WOODS, Maj.-Gen. Charles William, CB 1970; MBE 1952; MC 1944; Chairman, Douglas Haig Memorial Homes, since 1975; *b* 21 March 1917; *s* of late Captain F. W. U. Woods and of Mrs M. E. Woods, Gosbrook House, Binfield Heath, Henley-on-Thames; *m* 1940, Angela Helen Clay; one *d* (one *s* decd). *Educ:* Uppingham Sch.; Trinity Coll., Cambridge (MA). Commnd into Corps of Royal Engineers, 1938; served War of 1939-45, N Africa, Sicily, Italy, NW Europe (D Landings with 50th Div.); Staff Coll., Camberley, 1946; served in Korea, 1951-52; comd 35 Corps Engineer Regt, BAOR, 1959-60; Dep. Military Secretary, 1964-67; Dir of Manning (Army), 1967-70. Col Comdt, RE, 1973-78. Chm., RE Assoc., 1971-77. *Recreations:* sailing, ski-ing. *Address:* Riversdale Cottage, Boldre, Lymington, Hants SO4 8PE. *T:* Lymington 73445. *Clubs:* Naval and Military, Royal Ocean Racing, Ski Club of Great Britain; Royal Lymington Yacht, Royal Engineer Yacht.

WOODS, Christopher Matthew, CMG 1979; MC 1945; HM Diplomatic Service; Counsellor, Foreign and Commonwealth Office, since 1977; *b* 26 May 1923; *s* of Matthew Grosvenor Woods; *m* 1954, Gillian Sara Rudd; four *s* one *d*. *Educ:* Bradfield Coll.; Trinity Coll., Cambridge. HM Forces, KRRC, 1942-47; Foreign Office, 1948; served Cairo, Tehran, Milan, Warsaw, Rome; First Secretary, 1965; FO, later FCO, 1967. *Address:* Barnardiston House, Chipping Hill, Witham, Essex.

WOODS, Sir Colin (Philip Joseph), KCVO 1977; CBE 1973; QPM 1980; Director and Consultant, Securicor and Securicor International, since 1982; *b* London, 20 April 1920; *s* of late Michael Woods, Sub-divisional Inspector, Metropolitan Police; *m* 1941, Gladys Ella May (*née* Howell); one *d*. *Educ:* LCC Primary and Secondary Schs; Finchley Grammar Sch. Served War, in 60th Rifles and RUR, 1939-46. Metropolitan Police: Constable, through ranks, to Dep. Comdr; Commander, Traffic Dept, 1966-67; Head of Management Services, 1968; Comdt, National Police Coll., 1969-70; Asst Comr (Traffic Dept), 1970; Asst Comr (Crime), 1972; Dep. Comr, 1975-77; HM Chief Inspector of Constabulary, 1977-79; Comr, Australian Federal Police, 1979-82. *Recreations:* walking, music, cabinet making, gardening. *Address:* Doversmead, Littleworth Road, The Sands, Farnham, Surrey GU10 1JW.

WOODS, Most Rev. Frank, KBE 1972; Archbishop of Melbourne, 1957-77; Primate of Australia, 1971-77; *b* 6 April 1907; *s* of late Rt Rev. E. S. Woods, DD, Bishop of Lichfield; *m* 1936, Jean Margaret Sprules; two *s* two *d*. *Educ:* Marlborough; Trinity Coll., Cambridge. Deacon, 1931; priest, 1932; Curate of Portsea Parish Church, 1932-33; Chaplain, Trinity Coll., Cambridge, 1933-36; Vice-principal, Wells Theological Coll., 1936-39; Chaplain to the Forces, 1939-45; Vicar of Huddersfield, 1945-52; Suffragan Bishop of Middleton, 1952-57. Proctor in Convocation, 1946-51; Chaplain to the King, 1951-52; Chaplain, Victoria Order of St John, 1962. Hon. Fellow, Trinity Coll., Melbourne, 1981. Hon. DD Lambeth, 1957; Hon. LLD Monash, 1979. *Recreation:* walking. *Address:* 2 Hughes Street, N Balwyn, Victoria 3104, Australia. *Clubs:* Melbourne, Australian (Melbourne).
See also Rt Rev. R. W. Woods.

WOODS, Maj.-Gen. Henry Gabriel, CB 1979; MBE 1965; MC 1945; General Officer Commanding North East District, 1976-80, retired; Head, Centre for Industrial and Educational Liaison (West and North Yorkshire), since 1980; *b* 7 May 1924; *s* of late G. S. Woods and F. C. F. Woods (*née* McNevin); *m* 1953, Imogen Elizabeth Birchenough Dodd; two *d*. *Educ:* Highgate Sch.; Trinity Coll., Oxford (MA 1st Cl. Hons Mod. History). FBIM. psc, jssc, rcds. Commnd 5th Royal Inniskilling Dragoon Guards, 1944; served NW Europe, 1944-45; Korea, 1951-52; Adjt, 1952-53; Sqdn Leader, 1954-55 and 1960-62; Army Staff Coll., 1956; Jt Services Staff Coll., 1960; Mil. Asst to Vice CDS, MoD, 1962-64; comd 5th Royal Inniskilling Dragoon Gds, 1965-67; Asst Mil. Sec. to C-in-C BAOR, 1968-69; Comdt, RAC Centre, 1969-71; RCDS, 1972; Mil. Attaché, Brit. Embassy, Washington, 1973-75. Chairman: SATRO Panel, 1982-83 (also a Dir, Standing Conf. on Schools' Science and Technology); W and N Yorks Regl Microelectronics Educn Programme, 1982-; Yorks and Humberside Industry/Educn Council, 1982-; Bradford and W Yorks Br., BIM, 1982-; N Yorks Scouts, 1982-; Member: Yorks Br. Exec. Cttee, Inst. of Dirs, 1982-; Yorks Br. Exec. Cttee, British Assoc. for Advancement of Sci., 1982-. Mem. Council, Univ. of Leeds, 1980-. Chm., 5th Royal Inniskilling Dragoon Guards Regtl Assoc. Officier, Ordre de Léopold, Belgium, 1965. *Publication:* Change and Challenge: the story of 5th Royal Inniskilling Dragoon Guards, 1978. *Recreations:* hunting, fencing, sailing, military history. *Address:* Grafton House, Tockwith, York YO5 8PY. *T:* Tockwith 735. *Clubs:* Cavalry and Guards; Ends of the Earth (UK section), Trinity Society.

WOODS, Ivan; see Woods, W. I.

WOODS, Very Rev. John Mawhinney; Rector of The Suttons with Tydd, since 1980; *b* 16 Dec. 1919; *s* of Robert and Sarah Hannah Woods. *Educ:* Edinburgh Theological College. Deacon 1958, for St Peter's, Kirkcaldy, Fife; priest, 1959; Rector of Walpole St Peter, Norfolk, 1960-75; Provost, St Andrew's Cathedral, Inverness, 1975-80. *Address:* The Rectory, Sutton St James, Spalding, Lincs.

WOODS, Prof. Leslie Colin, BE, MA, DPhil, DSc; Professor of Mathematics (Theory of Plasma), University of Oxford, and Fellow of Balliol College, Oxford, since 1970; *b* Reporoa, NZ, 6 Dec. 1922; *s* of A. B. Woodhead, Sandringham, NZ; *m* 1st, 1943; five *d*; 2nd, 1977, Dr Helen Troughton. *Educ:*

Auckland Univ. Coll.; Merton Coll., Oxford. Fighter pilot, RNZAF, Pacific Area, 1942-45. Rhodes Schol., Merton Coll., Oxford, 1948-51; Scientist (NZ Scientific Defense Corps) with Aerodynamics Div., NPL Mddx, 1951-54; Senior Lectr in Applied Maths, Sydney Univ., 1954-56; Nuffield Research Prof. of Engineering, Univ. of New South Wales, 1956-60; Fellow and Tutor in Engrg Science, Balliol Coll., Oxford, 1960-70; Reader in Applied Maths, Oxford, 1964-70. *Publications:* The Theory of Subsonic Plane Flow, 1961; Introduction to Neutron Distribution Theory, 1964; The Thermodynamics of Fluid Systems, 1975; many research papers in aerodynamics and plasma physics in Proc. Royal Soc., Physics of Fluids, etc. *Recreations:* music, sailing. *Address:* Balliol College, Oxford.

WOODS, Reginald Salisbury, (Rex Woods), MA; MD, BCh (Cantab); FRCS; Médaille d'Honneur de l'Education Physique et des Sports, République Française, 1946; in General Practice; Hon. Life Member, British Association of Sport and Medicine; Surgical Specialist to numerous insurance companies; Honorary Medical Officer: Cambridge University Boxing Club (also President); Cambridge University Point-to-Point and Cambridgeshire Point-to-Point; Cambridgeshire Warden King George's Jubilee Trust; Past Assistant of Glaziers' Company; a Patron of Cambridge Branch, Old Contemptibles and of British Legion; Past President, Downing College Association, 1962; *b* London, 15 Oct. 1891; *o s* of late H. T. Woods, Galway; *m* 1918, Irene, CBE, TD (*d* 1976), *y d* of late T. Pickering; one *s* two *d*. *Educ:* Dulwich Coll.; Downing Coll., Cambridge (Entr. Exh.); St George's Hospital (Senior Univ. Entrance Scholar, Research Exhib., etc.). HS, HP, and Surg. Registrar. Captain, RAMC, BEF, 1916-19 (despatches); late Surg. Spec. Ministry of Pensions; Surg. EMS (Cambridge County Hospital), 1939-43; Major, RAMC, 1943-45 (Surg. Spec. E Africa Command). Formerly: Pres., Cambridge Med. Soc., County Dir BRCS, and Chm., Nat. Playing Fields Assoc. and Cambs AAA. Co-Manager, 5 Oxford/Cambridge Athletic Tours *v* USA Univs, 1925-49. *Publications:* Cambridge Doctor, 1962; many contribs on sports injuries in British and US med. jls. *Recreations:* represented England 1914 and 1920-29; Great Britain at Olympic Games, 1924 and 1928, and British Empire *v* USA, 1924 and 1928, in Putting the Weight. President (1914), Hon. Treasurer (1919-39) and Chairman (1939-52), of CUAC. AAA Champion, 1924 and 1926; Captained Public Schools Past and Present at Rugby Football, 1919; golf, bridge. *Address:* 4 Manor Court, Grange Road, Cambridge; 40 Green Street, Cambridge. *Clubs:* British Sportsman's; Cambridge County, Hawks, Pitt, Cambridge, Achilles; Oxford and Cambridge Golfing Society.
See also Sir F. W. W. Pemberton.

WOODS, Rt. Rev. Robert Wilmer, KCVO 1971; MA; Prelate of the Most Distinguished Order of St Michael and St George, since 1971; *b* 15 Feb. 1914; *s* of late Edward Woods, Bishop of Lichfield, and Clemence (*née* Barclay); *m* 1942, Henrietta Marion (JP 1966), *d* of late K. H. Wilson; two *s* three *d*. *Educ:* Gresham's Sch., Holt; Trinity Coll., Cambridge. Asst Sec., Student Christian Movement, 1937-42; Chaplain to the Forces, 1942-46 (despatches, 1944); Vicar of South Wigston, Leicester, 1946-51; Archdeacon of Singapore and Vicar of St Andrew's Cathedral, 1951-58; Archdeacon of Sheffield and Rector of Tankersley, 1958-62; Dean of Windsor, 1962-70; Domestic Chaplain to the Queen, 1962-70; Register of the Most Noble Order of the Garter, 1962-70; Bishop of Worcester, 1970-81. Secretary, Anglican/Methodist Commn for Unity, 1965-74; Member: Council, Duke of Edinburgh's Award Scheme, 1968; Public Schools Commn, 1968-70; Governor, Haileybury Coll.; Pres, Queen's Coll., Birmingham, and Chm. Council, 1970-; Chairman: Windsor Festival Co., 1969-71; Churches Television Centre, 1969-79; Dir, Christian Aid, 1969. Chm., Birmingham and Hereford and Worcester Bd, MSC, 1976-. Visitor, Malvern Coll., 1970-81. *Recreations:* sailing, shooting, painting. *Address:* Torsend House, Tirley, Gloucester GL19 4EU. *T:* Tirley 327. *Club:* Brooks's.
See also Most Rev. F. Woods.

WOODS, Timothy Phillips, MA, DPhil; Headmaster, Gresham's School, since 1982; *b* 24 Dec. 1943; *s* of late Arthur Phillips Woods and of Katherine Isabella Woods; *m* 1969, Erica Lobb. *Educ:* Ranelagh Prep. Sch., Natal; Michaelhouse Sch., Natal; Rhodes Univ. (BA Hons, MA; UED); Oxford Univ. (DPhil). Cape Province Rhodes Scholar, 1968; Felsted School: Asst Master, 1971; Head of History, 1975. *Recreations:* cricket, hockey, squash, gardening, music, history and architecture of cathedrals. *Address:* The Headmaster's House, Gresham's School, Cromer Road, Holt, Norfolk NR25 6DZ. *T:* Holt 3739. *Club:* Vincent's (Oxford).

WOODS, (William) Ivan; 3rd *s* of late William and Anna Woods, Annaghmore, Co. Armagh; *m* (1st wife *d* 1965); one *s* one *d*; 2nd, 1966, Florence Margaret, *o d* of late William and Florence Sloan, Ach-na-mara, Donaghadee, Co. Down; one *s* two *d*. *Educ:* Mountjoy Sch., Dublin. Clerical Officer, Min. of Finance for N Ire., 1934; Accountant to Ministry, 1962; N Ire. Govt Liaison Officer in London, 1963; Dir of Office of Parliamentary Commissioner for Administration for Northern Ireland, 1969; Dir of Office of Commissioner for Complaints, Dec. 1969; Dep. Sec., Dept of Finance of NI, 1973-76. Sec., Milibern Trust, 1976-79. *Recreations:* golf, sailing. *Address:* 112 Warren Road, Donaghadee, Co. Down BT21 0PQ. *T:* Donaghadee 883568. *Clubs:* Donaghadee Golf, Portaferry Sailing, Mitchels GA (Co. Down).

WOODWARD, Hon. Sir (Albert) Edward, Kt 1982; OBE 1969; Judge of Federal Court of Australia, since 1977; *b* 6 Aug. 1928; *s* of Lt-Gen. Sir Eric

Winslow Woodward, KCMG, KCVO, CB, CBE, DSO, and Amy Freame Woodward (née Weller); m 1950, Lois Thorpe; one s six d. Educ: Melbourne C of E Grammar Sch.; Melbourne Univ. (LLM). Practising barrister, 1953-72; QC 1965; Judge, Commonwealth Industrial Court and Supreme Court of Australian Capital Territory, 1972-. Chairman, Armed Services Pay Inquiry, 1972; Royal Commissioner: Aboriginal Land Rights, 1973-75; into Australian Meat Industry, 1981-82; President, Trade Practices Tribunal, 1974-76; Director-General of Security, 1976-81. Chairman: Victorian Dried Fruits Bd, 1963-72; Nat. Stevedoring Industry Conf. and Stevedoring Industry Council, 1965-72; Australian Defence Force Academy Interim Council, 1982-. Address: 61 Park Street, South Yarra, Victoria 3141, Australia. T: (03) 267 5595.

WOODWARD, Prof. C(omer) Vann; Sterling Professor of History, Yale University, 1961-77, now Emeritus Professor; b 13 Nov. 1908; s of Hugh Allison Woodward and Bess (née Vann); m 1937, Glenn Boyd MacLeod; one s. Educ: Emory Univ. (PhB); Universities of Columbia (MA), North Carolina (PhD). Asst Professor of History, University of Florida, 1937-39; Visiting Asst Professor of History, University of Virginia, 1939-40; Assoc. Professor of History, Scripps Coll., 1940-43; Assoc. Professor of History, Johns Hopkins University, 1946; Professor of American History, Johns Hopkins Univ., 1947-61. Served with US Naval Reserve, 1943-46. Commonwealth Lecturer, UCL, 1954; Harold Vyvyan Harmsworth Professor of American History, University of Oxford, 1954-55; Literary Award, Nat. Inst. of Arts and Letters, 1954, etc. Corresp. Fellow: British Academy, 1972, RHistS, 1978. Member: American Academy of Arts and Sciences; American Philosophical Society; Nat. Inst. of Arts and Letters; American Historical Assoc. (President, 1969); Orgn of American Historians (President, 1968-69). Hon. degrees: MA Oxon, 1954; LLD: N Carolina, 1959; Arkansas, 1961; Michigan, 1971; LittD: Emory, 1963; William and Mary, 1964; Princeton, 1971; Columbia, 1972; DLitt Cambridge, 1975. Publications: Tom Watson: Agrarian Rebel, 1938; The Battle for Leyte Gulf, 1947; Origins of the New South (1877-1913), 1951 (Bancroft Prize, 1952); Reunion and Reaction, 1951; The Strange Career of Jim Crow, 1955; The Burden of Southern History, 1960; American Counterpoint, 1971; (ed) The Comparative Approach to American History, 1968; (ed) Mary Chesnut's Civil War, 1981 (Pulitzer Prize, 1982). Address: 104 Hall of Graduate Studies, Yale University, New Haven, Conn 06520, USA.

WOODWARD, Hon. Sir Edward; see Woodward, Hon. Sir A. E.

WOODWARD, Edward, OBE 1978; actor and singer, since 1946; b 1 June 1930; s of Edward Oliver Woodward and Violet Edith Woodward; m 1952, Venetia Mary Collett; two s one d. Educ: Kingston Coll.; RADA. Stage: Castle Theatre, Farnham, 1946; appeared for some years in rep. cos throughout England and Scotland; first appearance on London stage, Where There's a Will, Garrick, 1955; Mercutio in Romeo and Juliet, and Laertes in Hamlet, Stratford, 1958; Rattle of a Simple Man, Garrick, 1962; Two Cities (musical), 1968; Cyrano in Cyrano de Bergerac, and Flamineo in The White Devil, Nat. Theatre Co., 1971; The Wolf, Apollo, 1973; Male of the Species, Piccadilly, 1975; On Approval, Theatre Royal Haymarket, 1976; The Dark Horse, Comedy, 1978; starred in and directed Beggar's Opera, 1980; Private Lives, Australia, 1980; The Assassin, Greenwich, 1982; Richard III, Ludlow Fest., 1982; has appeared in 3 prodns in NY; films: Becket, 1966; File on the Golden Goose, 1968; Hunted, 1973; Sitting Target, Young Winston, The Wicker Man, 1974; Stand Up Virgin Soldiers, 1977; Breaker Morant, 1980; The Appointment, 1981; Who Dares Wins, Comeback, 1982. Over 200 TV prodns, inc. Callan (TV series and film, and in Wet Job, 1981), The Trial of Lady Chatterley, 1980, Churchill: The Wilderness Years, 1981; 12 long-playing records (singing) and 3 records (poetry). Many national and internat. acting awards. Recreations: boating, geology. Address: c/o Eric Glass Ltd, 28 Berkeley Square, W1X 6HD. T: 01-629 7162. Clubs: Green Room, Macreadys, Wellington.

WOODWARD, (Foster) Neville, CBE 1956; FRSE; FRSC; Technology Policy Adviser to government in developing countries; Chairman: Forth-Tech Services Ltd; Biotech Consultants Ltd; b 2 May 1905; s of Foster and Catherine Woodward; m 1932, Elizabeth Holme Siddall; one s one d. Educ: Bradford; University Coll., London (PhD, gold medallist). After ten years in industry, and two as Res. Asst (to Prof. Sir Robert Robinson, FRS), Oxford Univ., became Head of Res. and Develt Div., HM Chem. Defence Res. Establt, Sutton Oak, 1937-42. Officer in Charge, Min. of Supply Res. Establt, Leamington Spa, 1943; Dep. Sci. Adv. to Min. of Production, 1944-46; Dir, Inst. of Seaweed Research, 1946-56 (Mem. Bd Inst., 1956-69); seconded to FO as Dir UK Sci. Mission, Washington DC; Attaché for Sci. Questions, Brit. Embassy, Washington DC, and Sci. Adv. to UK High Comr in Canada, 1947-48; Hon. Sci. Adv. to Sec. of State for Scotland, 1951-56; Sci. Attaché to European Productivity Agency, OEEC, Paris, 1956-61; Sen. Sci. Counsellor, Directorate of Scientific Affairs, OECD, Paris, 1961-70. Dir, Arthur D. Little Res. Inst., 1956-70; Man. Dir, Arthur D. Little Ltd, 1963-68. Chm., Inveresk Res. Internat. Management Cttee, 1970-73. Mem., Council for Applied Science in Scotland, 1978-; Res. Policy Advr, Scottish Council: Develt and Industry, 1974-79. Vice-President: Soc. of Chemical Industry, 1968-71 (Jubilee Lectr, 1968-69); RIC, 1969-71; Chm., Assoc. of Consulting Scientists, 1967-69. Ramsay Meml Fellowship Trustee, 1969-. Publications: A Survey of Agricultural, Forestry and Fishery Products in the United Kingdom and their Utilisation (with J. Maxton and A. B. Stewart), 1953; Structure of Industrial Research Associations, 1964; (with T. S. Chung and R. D. Lalkaka) Guidelines for Development of Industrial Technology in Asia and the Pacific,

1976; about 50 publications in scientific press. Recreations: mountains, foreign travel, reading, writing. Address: St Margaret's Lodge, Gullane, East Lothian. T: Gullane 842210; Cuil Moss, Ardgour, Argyll. Clubs: New, Royal Society of Edinburgh, Edinburgh Research (Edinburgh).

WOODWARD, Geoffrey Frederick, RIBA; jssc; Director of Diplomatic and Post Office Services, Property Services Agency, Department of the Environment, since 1981; b 29 June 1924; s of Joseph Frederick and Edith Mary Woodward; m 1953, Elizabeth Marjory McCubbin; four s. Educ: Wirral Grammar School for Boys; Trinity College, Cambridge Univ.; School of Architecture, Liverpool Univ. (BArch). Architects' Dept: Hertfordshire CC, 1952-56; British Transport Commn, 1956-60; Directorate of Army Works, 1960-63; Directorate of Research & Development, Min. of Public Building and Works, 1963-67; Directorate of Works (Married Quarters), MPBW, 1967-70; Directorate of Works (Navy Home), PSA, 1970-71; Director of Works (Navy Home), PSA, 1971-75; Director, Directorate General of Design Services, Design Office, 1975-78; Under Sec., PSA, DoE, 1978; Dir of Architectural Services, 1978-81. jssc 1963. Recreations: motoring, walking and beer drinking in moderation. Address: Little Orchard, Cuddington Way, Cheam, Sutton, Surrey SM2 7JA. T: 01-643 1964.

WOODWARD, Geoffrey Royston; Under-Secretary, Ministry of Agriculture, Fisheries and Food, 1970-81; b 26 June 1921; o s of James Edward Woodward and Gwendolen May (née Dodridge); m 1st, 1947, Marjorie Beatrice Bishop (marr. diss. 1974); three s; 2nd, 1974, Doreen Parker, MBE. Educ: Bradford Grammar Sch. Entered Civil Service, 1938; served RAFVR, 1941-46 (Flt-Lt, despatches). Joined Min. of Agriculture and Fisheries, 1948. Recreation: armchair archaeology. Address: 3 Gilbert Court, Green Vale, W5 3AX. Club: Reform.

WOODWARD, Rear-Adm. Sir John Forster, KCB 1982; Flag Officer, First Flotilla, since 1981; b 1 May 1932; s of late T. Woodward and of M. B. M. Woodward; m 1960, Charlotte Mary McMurtrie; one s one d. Educ: Royal Naval College, Dartmouth. FINucE. Under training, Home Fleet, until 1953; Submarine Specialist, serving in HMS Sanguine, Porpoise, Valiant, and commanding HMS Tireless, Grampus and Warspite, from 1953; Min. of Defence and senior training posts, from 1971, plus comd HMS Sheffield, 1976-77; Director of Naval Plans, 1978-81. Recreations: sailing, philately, skiing. Address: c/o The Naval Secretary, Ministry of Defence, Old Admiralty Building, Whitehall, SW1. Clubs: Tamesis (Teddington); Hayling Island Sailing.

WOODWARD, Rev. Max Wakerley; Methodist Minister, retired 1973; b 29 Jan. 1908; s of Alfred Woodward, Methodist Minister, and Mabel Woodward; m 1934, Kathleen May Beaty; three s one d. Educ: Orme Sch., Newcastle; Kingswood Sch., Bath; Handsworth Coll., Birmingham. Missionary to Ceylon, 1929-42; Chaplain, Royal Navy, 1942-46; Minister: Leamington Spa, 1946-50; Finsbury Park, 1950-54; Harrow, 1954-58; Wesley's Chapel, London, 1958-64; Secretary, World Methodist Council, 1964-69; Minister, Bromley, Kent, 1969-73. Exchange Preacher, Univ. Methodist Church, Baton Rouge, La, 1957. Dir, Methodist Newspaper Co. Ltd, 1962. Publication: One At London, 1966. Recreations: gardening, stamp collecting. Address: 6a Field End Road, Pinner, Mddx HA5 2QL. T: 01-429 0608.

WOODWARD, Neville; see Woodward, F. N.

WOOF, Robert Edward; Member and official, National Union of Mineworkers; b 24 Oct. 1911; m Mary Bell (d 1971); one d. Educ: Elementary School. Began work in the mines at an early age, subsequently coal face worker. Member of the Labour Party, 1937-; MP (Lab) Blaydon, Co. Durham, Feb. 1956-1979. Member Durham County Council, 1947-56. Address: 10 Ramsay Road, Chopwell, Newcastle upon Tyne NE17 7AG.

WOOKEY, Eric Edgar, MC 1916; Dental Surgeon in private practice at Wimpole Street, 1933-68, retired, 1968; Senior Dental Surgeon, Royal Free Hospital, 1936-Sept. 1958, Hon. Consulting Dental Surgeon, since 1958; b 11 January 1892; s of Edgar Wookey, Shipham, Somerset, and Clara (née Davidson); m 1927, Doris Kathleen Fenner (d 1976); one s two d. Educ: Haverfordwest Grammar School; Clevedon College; Bristol University; Royal Dental Hospital, London. Bristol Univ. Student, medical and dental, 1909-14; Infantry commission in 4th Glos Regt TF, 1914; served overseas, France (wounded, despatches, MC); Italy, BEF (despatches twice); Bt Major, Comd 4th Glos Regt at Armistice, Nov. 1918. LDS, RCS 1919, and after a period of hospital practice commenced private practice at Hendon, 1920; Asst Dental Surgeon, Royal Free Hosp., 1921; full-time practice in Wimpole Street, 1933. During War of 1939-45, served in EMS. Member of Representative Bd, British Dental Assoc., 1946-54 and 1958-61; Pres. Metropolitan Branch, 1949-50; Founder Member, Past-President, and Past Chm. of Council, Brit. Soc. of Med. and Dental Hypnosis (formerly Dental and Med. Soc. for Study of Hypnosis); FRSocMed; Fellow Internat. Soc. of Clinical and Experimental Hypnosis (PP Brit. Section). Member: Council, Soc. for Psychical Research; British Archæological Soc. Liveryman, Tallow Chandlers' Co. Ecclesiological Soc. Silver Medal for Valour (Italy), 1918. Publications: articles in British Dental Jl and British Jl of Clinical Hypnosis. Recreations: music (piano), golf, numismatics, philately, horology. Address: 51 Lake View, Canons Park, Edgware, Middx. T: 01-958 6029.

WOOLDRIDGE, Ian Edmund; Sports Columnist, Daily Mail, since 1972; BBC Television documentary reporter and writer; *b* 14 Jan. 1932; *s* of late Edmund and Bertha Wooldridge; *m* 1st, Veronica Ann Churcher; three *s*; 2nd, Sarah Margaret Chappell Lourenço. *Educ:* Brockenhurst Grammar School. New Milton Advertiser, 1948; Bournemouth Times, 1953; News Chronicle, 1956; Sunday Dispatch, 1960; Daily Mail, 1961. Columnist of Year, 1975 and 1976; Sportswriter of Year, 1972, 1974, 1981, in British Press Awards. *Publications:* Cricket, Lovely Cricket, 1963; (with Mary Peters) Mary P, 1974; (with Colin Cowdrey) MCC: The Autobiography of a Cricketer, 1976; The Best of Wooldridge, 1978; Travelling Reserve, 1982. *Recreations:* travel, golf, Beethoven and dry Martinis. *Address:* 23 Montpelier Walk, SW7 1JF. *Club:* Scribes.

WOOLF, Harry, PhD; Director, Institute for Advanced Study, Princeton, USA, since 1976; *b* 12 Aug. 1923; *s* of Abraham Woolf and Anna (*née* Frankman); *m* 1961, Patricia A. Kelsh; two *s* two *d*. *Educ:* Univ. of Chicago (BS Physics and Maths 1948; MA Physics and History 1949); Cornell Univ. (PhD Hist. of Science 1955). Served US Army, 1943-46. Instructor: Boston Univ., Mass, 1953-54; Brandeis Univ., Waltham, Mass, 1954-55; Univ. of Washington, Seattle: Asst Prof., Associate Prof., Special Lectr, and Prof., 1955-61; Johns Hopkins University: Prof., Hist. of Science Dept, 1961-76 (Chm. of Dept, 1961-72); Provost, 1972-76. Pres., Chm. of Bd, Johns Hopkins Program for Internat. Educn in Gynecology and Obstetrics, Inc., 1973-76, Trustee 1976-; Mem. Adv. Bd, Smithsonian Research Awards, 1975-79; Member: Vis. Cttee Student Affairs, MIT, 1973-77; Corporation Vis. Cttee, Dept of Linguistics and Philosophy, MIT, 1977-; Nat. Adv. Child Health and Human Develt Council, NIH, 1977-80; Mem. Vis. Cttee, Research Center for Language Sciences, Indiana Univ., 1977-80; Trustee: Associated Universities Inc., Brookhaven Nat. Laboratories, Nat. Radio Astronomy Observatory, 1972-; Hampshire Coll., Amherst, Mass, 1977-81; Merrill Lynch Retirement Series Trust, 1982-; Trustee-at-Large, Univs Research Assoc. Inc., Washington, DC (Fermi Nat. Accelerator Lab.), 1978-, Chm. Bd 1979-. Member: Corp. Visiting Cttee for Dept. of Physics, MIT, 1979-; Council on Foreign Relations Inc., 1979-; Internat. Research and Exchanges Bd, NY, 1980-; Scientific Adv. Bd, Wissenschaftskolleg zu Berlin, 1981-; Adv. Bd, New Perspective Fund, Inc., Los Angeles, 1980-; Bd of Dirs, Alex. Brown Cash Reserve Fund, Inc., Baltimore, 1981-. Member: Académie Internat. d'Histoire des Sciences; Amer. Philosoph. Soc.; Phi Beta Kappa; Sigma Xi (also Bicentennial Lectr, 1976). Editor, ISIS Internat. Review, 1958-64; Associate Editor, Dictionary of Scientific Biog., 1970-80; Mem. Editl Bd, Interdisciplinary Science Revs, 1975-; Mem. Editl Adv. Bd, The Writings of Albert Einstein, 1977-. DSc *hc* Whitman Coll., 1979; Hon. DSc Amer. Univ., 1982. *Publications:* The Transits of Venus: a study in eighteenth-century science, 1959, repr. 1981; (ed) Quantification: essays in the history of measurement in the natural and social sciences, 1961; (ed) Science as a Cultural Force, 1964; (ed and contrib.) Some Strangeness in the Proportion: a centennial symposium to celebrate the achievements of Albert Einstein, 1980; (ed) The Analytic Spirit: essays in the history of science, 1981. *Address:* 97 Olden Lane, Princeton, NJ 08540, USA. *T:* (609) 734-8200. *Clubs:* Century Association (New York); Nassau (Princeton); Cosmos (Washington, DC).

WOOLF, Hon. Sir Harry (Kenneth), Kt 1979; **Hon. Mr Justice Woolf;** a Judge of the High Court of Justice, Queen's Bench Division, since 1979; Presiding Judge, South Eastern Circuit, since 1981; *b* 2 May 1933; *s* of Alexander Woolf and Leah Woolf (*née* Cussins); *m* 1961, Marguerite Sassoon, *d* of George Sassoon; three *s*. *Educ:* Fettes Coll.; University Coll., London (LLB; Fellow, 1981). Pres., University College Union Debating Soc., 1953. Called to Bar, Inner Temple, 1954; Bencher, 1976. Commnd (Nat. Service), 15/19th Royal Hussars, 1954; seconded Army Legal Services, 1955; Captain 1955. Started practice at Bar, 1956. A Recorder of the Crown Court, 1972-79. Jun. Counsel, Inland Revenue, 1973-74; First Treasury Junior Counsel (Common Law), 1974-79. Mem. Senate, Inns of Court and Bar, 1981-. *Address:* Royal Courts of Justice, Strand, WC2. *Club:* Garrick.

WOOLF, Sir John, Kt 1975; film and television producer; Chairman: Romulus Films Ltd; British & American Film Holdings PLC; Executive Director, Anglia TV Group PLC; *s* of Charles M. and Vera Woolf; *m* 1955, Ann Saville; two *s*. *Educ:* Institut Montana, Switzerland. War, 1939-45 (Bronze Star (USA), 1945): Asst Dir, Army Kinematography, War Office, 1944-45. Member: Cinematograph Films Council, 1969-79; Bd of Governors, Services Sound & Vision Corp. (formerly Services Kinema Corp.). Films produced by Romulus Group include: The African Queen, Pandora and the Flying Dutchman, Moulin Rouge, I am a Camera, Carrington VC, Beat the Devil, Story of Esther Costello, Room at the Top, Wrong Arm of the Law, The L-Shaped Room, Term of Trial, Life at the Top, Oliver!, Day of the Jackal, The Odessa File. Productions for Anglia TV include Tales of the Unexpected. Personal awards include: British Film Academy Award for Best Film of 1958: Room at the Top; Oscar and Golden Globe for Best Film of 1969: Oliver!; special awards for contribution to British film industry from Cinematograph Exhibitors Assoc., 1969, Variety Club of GB, 1974. *Address:* Brook House, 113 Park Lane, W1Y 4JN. *T:* 01-493 7741.

WOOLF, John Moss, CB 1975; Deputy Chairman of the Board of Customs and Excise, and Director-General (Customs and Establishments), 1973-78; *b* 5 June 1918; *o s* of Alfred and Maud Woolf; *m* 1940, Phyllis Ada Mary Johnson; one *d*. *Educ:* Drayton Manor Sch.; Honourable Society of Lincoln's Inn. Barrister-at-law, 1948. War Service, 1939-46 (Captain, RA). Inland Revenue, 1937. Asst Principal, Min. of Fuel and Power, 1948; HM Customs

and Excise, 1950: Principal, 1951; Asst Sec., 1960; Chm., Valuation Cttee, Customs Cooperation Council, Brussels, 1964-65; National Bd for Prices and Incomes, 1965; Under-Secretary, 1967; Asst Under-Sec. of State, Dept of Employment and Productivity, 1968-70; HM Customs and Excise: Comr, 1970; Dir of Establishments and Organisation, 1971-73. Advr on Price Problems, Govt of Trinidad & Tobago, 1969. Assoc. of First Div. Civil Servants: Mem. of Exec. Cttee, 1950-58 and 1961-65; Hon. Sec., 1952-55; Chm., 1955-58 and 1964-65; Mem., Civil Service National Whitley Council (Staff Side), 1953-55. Leader of Review Team to examine responsibilities of the Directors of the Nat. Museums and Galleries, 1978-79; Review of Organisation and Procedures of Chancery Div. of High Court, 1979-81; Overseas Adviser to CEGB, 1979-82. Commandeur d'Honneur, Ordre du Bontemps de Médoc et des Graves, 1973; Hon. Borgenerális (Hungary), 1974. *Publications:* Report on Control of Prices in Trinidad and Tobago (with M. M. Eccleshall), 1968; (with Lord Justice Oliver and R. H. H. White) Report of the Review Body on the Chancery Division of the High Court, 1981. *Recreations:* reading, gardening. *Address:* West Lodge, 113 Marsh Lane, Stanmore, Mddx HA7 4TH. *T:* 01-952 1373.

WOOLFORD, Harry Russell Halkerston, OBE 1970; Consultant, formerly Chief Restorer, National Gallery of Scotland; *b* 23 May 1905; *s* of H. Woolford, engineer; *m* 1932, Nancy Philip; one *d*. *Educ:* Edinburgh. Studied art at Edinburgh Coll. of Art (Painting and Drawing) and RSA Life School (Carnegie Travelling Scholarship, 1928), London, Paris and Italy; afterwards specialized in picture restoration. FMA; FIIC. Hon. MA Dundee, 1976. *Address:* Dean Park, Golf Course Road, Bonnyrigg, Midlothian EH19 2EU. *T:* 031-663 7949. *Club:* Scottish Arts.

WOOLFSON, Mark; Consultant and Director of Consortium, Pollution Control Consultants, since 1972; a Partner, Posford Parry & Partners, since 1976; *b* 10 Nov. 1911; *s* of Victor Woolfson and Sarah (*née* Kixman); *m* 1940, Queenie Carlis; two *d*. *Educ:* City of London. Student Engr, Lancashire Dynamo & Crypto, until 1936; Engr, ASEA Electric Ltd, 1936-40; War Service, RNVR, 1940-46 (Lt-Comdr); MPBW, later DoE, 1946-71, Chief Mech. and Electr. Engineer, 1969-71. FIMechE, FIEE. *Publications:* papers in Jls of Instns of Civil, Mechanical and Elect. Engrs. *Recreations:* tennis, gardening, golf. *Address:* 3 Runnelfield, Harrow, Mddx. *T:* 01-422 1599.

WOOLHOUSE, Prof. Harold William; Director, John Innes Institute, and Professor of Biological Sciences, University of East Anglia, since 1980; *b* 12 July 1932; *s* of William Everson Woolhouse and Frances Ella Woolhouse; *m* 1959, Leonie Marie Sherwood; two *s* one *d*. *Educ:* Univ. of Reading (BSc); Univ. of Adelaide (PhD). Lecturer and Sen. Lectr, Sheffield Univ., 1960-69; Professor of Botany, Leeds Univ., 1969-80. Vis. Professor, USC, Los Angeles, 1968. *Publications:* research papers on plant senescence photosynthesis, metal toxicity and tolerance, and physiology of adaptation. *Recreations:* poetry, music, poultry breeding, gardening. *Address:* 57 Damgate, Wymondham, Norfolk.

WOOLLAM, John Victor; Barrister-at-Law; *b* 14 Aug. 1927; *s* of Thomas Alfred and Edie Moss Woollam; *m* 1964, Lavinia Rosamund Ela, *d* of S. R. E. Snow; two *s*. *Educ:* Liverpool Univ. Called to the Bar, Inner Temple. Contested (C) Scotland Div. of Liverpool, 1950; MP (C) W Derby Div. of Liverpool, Nov. 1954-Sept. 1964; Parliamentary Private Sec. to Minister of Labour, 1960-62. *Recreation:* philately. *Address:* 3 South Hill Grove, Oxton, Merseyside.

WOOLLASTON, Sir (Mountford) Tosswill, Kt 1979; painter (abandoned other occupations, 1966); *b* 11 April 1910; *s* of John Reginald Woollaston and Charlotte Kathleen Frances (*née* Tosswill); *m* 1936, Edith Winifred Alexander; three *s* one *d*. *Educ:* Huinga Primary; Stratford (NZ) Secondary; brief brushes with art schools, Christchurch, 1931; King Edward Technical Coll., Dunedin, 1932. Member, The Group, Christchurch, 1935-; a few private but enthusiastic supporters; work featured in Art in New Zealand, 1937. Doldrums, 1950s; Auckland City Art Gallery began purchasing work, 1958, other galleries followed; overseas travel grant, NZ Arts Council, 1961; reputation increased. Govt purchases for embassies overseas, early sixties; Peter McLeavey, Dealer, Wellington, took over selling, 1967. *Publications:* The Faraway Hills (Auckland City Art Gall. Associates), 1962; ERUA (48 drawings of a boy, with text—Paul), 1966; Sage Tea (autobiog.), 1980. *Recreation:* gardening. *Address:* RD3, Motueka, New Zealand. *T:* Motueka 88425.

WOOLLCOMBE, Dame Jocelyn May, DBE 1950 (CBE 1944); *b* 9 May 1898; *d* of late Admiral Maurice Woollcombe and Ella Margaret Roberts; unmarried. *Educ:* Moorfield, Plymouth. Admiralty, NID as Clerk, 1916-19. Joined WRNS, enrolled as Chief Officer, Aug. 1939; Superintendent, 1940; Deputy Director, 1943-46; Director, 1946-50; Hon. ADC to the King, 1949. General Secretary, British Council for Aid to Refugees (Hungarian Section), 1957-58. Governor, The Sister Trust, 1956-65; Gov., WRNS Benevolent Trust, 1942-67; Pres., Assoc. of Wrens 1959-81. *Recreation:* drama. *Address:* 2 Thorn Park, Plymouth PL3 4TG.

WOOLLCOMBE, Rt. Rev. Kenneth John; a Canon Residentiary of St Paul's, since 1981; Precentor, since 1982; *b* 2 Jan. 1924; *s* of late Rev. E. P. Woollcombe, OBE, and Elsie Ockenden Woollcombe; *m* 1st, 1950, Gwendoline Rhona Vyvien Hodges (*d* 1976); three *d*; 2nd, 1980, Deaconess Juliet Dearmer; one *d*. *Educ:* Haileybury Coll., Hertford; St John's Coll.,

Oxford; Westcott House, Cambridge. Sub-Lieut (E) RNVR, 1945. Curate, St James, Grimsby, 1951; Fellow, Chaplain and Tutor, St John's Coll., Oxford, 1953, Hon. Fellow, 1971; Professor of Dogmatic Theology, General Theological Seminary, New York, 1960; Principal of Episcopal Theological Coll., Edinburgh, 1963; Bishop of Oxford, 1971–78; Asst Bishop, Diocese of London, 1978–81. Chm., SPCK, 1973–79. Mem., Central Cttee, World Council of Churches, 1975–83. Chm., Churches' Council for Covenanting, 1978–82. Hon. Chaplain, Glass Sellers' Co., 1978–. STD Univ. of the South, Sewanee, USA, 1963; Hon. DD Hartford, Conn, 1975. *Publications:* (contrib.) The Historic Episcopate, 1954; (jointly) Essays on Typology, 1957. *Address:* 5 Amen Court, EC4M 7BU.

WOOLLER, Arthur, CBE 1967; HM Diplomatic Service, retired; *b* 23 May 1912; *s* of Joseph Edward Wooller and Sarah Elizabeth (*née* Kershaw); *m* 1944, Frances, *e d* of Justice A. L. Blank, ICS; three *s*. *Educ:* Bradford Grammar School; Corpus Christi College, Oxford. ICS, Bengal, 1935; Indian Foreign and Political Service, 1939; UK Trade Comr, New Zealand, 1947; First Sec. (Commercial), Ottawa, 1953; UK Trade Comr, Toronto, 1959; British Trade Comr, Hong Kong, 1960; Principal British Trade Comr, Bombay, 1963; British Deputy High Commissioner in Western India, Bombay, 1965–68; High Comr in Mauritius, 1968–70; Economic Advr, FCO, 1970–72. *Recreation:* gardening. *Address:* c/o Midland Bank, High Street, Harpenden, Herts. *Club:* United Oxford & Cambridge University.

WOOLLETT, Maj.-Gen. John Castle, CBE 1957 (OBE 1955); MC 1945; MA Cantab; FICE; Principal Planning Inspector, Department of the Environment, 1971–81; *b* 5 Nov. 1915; *o s* of John Castle Woollett and Lily Bradley Woollett, Bredgar, Kent; *m* 1st, 1941, Joan Eileen Stranks (marr. diss., 1957); two *s* (and one *s* decd); 2nd, 1959, Helen Wendy Willis; two step *s*. *Educ:* St Benedict's Sch.; RMA Woolwich; St John's Coll., Cambridge. Joined RE, 1935; 23 Field Co., 1938–40 (BEF, 1939–40); 6 Commando, 1940–42; Major Comdg 16 Field Sqdn and 16 Assault Sqdn RE, 1942–45 (BLA, 1944–45); Student, Staff Coll., Camberley, 1946; DAAG and GSO2, Brit. Service Mission to Burma, 1947–50; Major Comdg 51 Port Sqdn RE, 1950; Instructor, Staff Coll., Camberley, 1950–53; Lt-Col Comdg 28 Field Engr Regt, 1954–55 (Korea); Bt Lt-Col 1955; Comdr Christmas Is, 1956–57; GSO1, Northern Army Gp, 1957–59; Col GS, US Army Staff Coll., Fort Leavenworth, 1959–61; DQMG (Movements), BAOR, 1962–64; Brig. Comdg Hants Sub District and Transportation Centre, RE, 1964–65; Sch. of Transport, 1965–66; Dep. Engr-in-Chief, 1966–67; Maj.-Gen., Chief Engineer, BAOR, 1967–70, retired. Col Comdt, RE, 1973–78. Pres., Instn of RE, 1974–79. *Recreations:* cruising, shooting. *Address:* 42 Rhinefield Close, Brockenhurst, Hants. *Clubs:* Army and Navy, Royal Ocean Racing, Royal Cruising; Island Sailing (Cowes), Royal Lymington Yacht.

WOOLLEY, family name of **Baron Woolley.**

WOOLLEY, Baron *cr* 1967 (Life Peer), of Hatton; **Harold Woolley,** Kt 1964; CBE 1958; DL; President of National Farmers' Union of England and Wales 1960–66; *b* 6 Feb. 1905; *s* of William Woolley, JP and Eleanor Woolley; *m* 1st, 1926, Martha Annie Jeffs (*d* 1936); four *s*; 2nd, 1937, Hazel Eileen Archer Jones (*d* 1975); two *d*. *Educ:* Woodhouse Grove School, Yorkshire. Farmer. Cheshire Deleg. to NFU Council, 1943; Chairman: NFU Parliamentary Cttee, 1947–57; Employers' Reps of Agricultural Wages Bd, 1947–57; Agricultural Apprenticeship Council for England and Wales, 1951–60. National Farmers' Union: Vice-Pres. 1948 and 1955; Dep. Pres., 1949–50 and 1956; Life Mem. Council; Director: NFU Mutual Insurance Society, 1965–80; NW Regional Adv. Bd, Abbey Nat. Building Soc. Member Nat. Jt Advisory Council to Ministry of Labour, 1950–58. President: Cheshire Agricl Soc.; Cheshire NFU. DL Cheshire, 1969. *Recreations:* racing, cricket, and all sports. *Address:* Hatton House Farm, Hatton Heath, Chester. *T:* Tattenhall 356. *Club:* MCC.
See also W. E. Woolley.

WOOLLEY, Rev. (Alfred) Russell; MA; Rector, St Lawrence, IoW, 1967–74; *b* 10 Sept. 1899; *e s* of late A. W. Woolley, Moseley, and Margaret A. Russell, Shrewsbury; *m* 1933, Lina Mariana, 3rd *d* of late Prof. Bertram Hopkinson, CMG, FRS, Fellow of King's College, Cambridge; four *s* three *d*. *Educ:* King Edward's Camp Hill Grammar School; Wadham College, Oxford (Symons Exhibitioner). 2nd Class Hons Modern History, 1922; incorporated MA Cantab. (Trinity College), 1929. Inns of Court OTC and 6th OC Bn, 1917–19. Bromsgrove School, 1922–26; Repton School, 1927–28; The Leys School (Chief History Master, House-Master, Librarian, OC, OTC), 1929–33; Headmaster of Scarborough Coll., 1933–37, and of Wellingborough Gram. Sch., 1937–45; Educnl Sec. to the Oxford Univ. Appts Cttee, 1945–62. Ordained 1960. Rector of Gestingthorpe, Essex, 1962–67. Mem. Coun. IAHM, 1945; of Oxfordshire Educn Cttee, 1955–62; of Govng Body of Milton Abbey Sch., 1955–74; of Lindisfarne Coll., 1961–77; ex-Sec. Oxford Union Soc. *Publications:* Oxford University and City, 1951; Clarendon Guide to Oxford, 1963, 5th edn 1983. *Recreations:* walking, travel. *Address:* Gestingthorpe Hall, Halstead, Essex CO9 3BB. *T:* Hedingham 60638.

WOOLLEY, David Rorie, QC 1980; barrister-at-law; a Recorder of the Crown Court, since 1982; *b* 9 June 1939; *s* of Albert and Ethel Woolley. *Educ:* Winchester Coll.; Trinity Hall, Cambridge (BA Hons Law). Called to the Bar, Middle Temple, 1962. *Publications:* Town Hall and the Property Owner, 1965; contribs to various legal jls. *Recreations:* opera, mountaineering, real tennis. *Address:* 2 Mitre Court Buildings, Temple, EC4. *T:* 01-583 1355. *Clubs:* MCC; Swiss Alpine.

WOOLLEY, John Maxwell, MBE 1945; TD 1946; Clerk, Merchant Taylors' Company, and Clerk to The Governors, Merchant Taylors' School, 1962–80; *b* 22 March 1917; *s* of Lt-Col Jasper Maxwell Woolley, IMS (Retd) and Kathleen Mary Woolley (*née* Waller); *m* 1952, Esme Adela Hamilton-Cole; two *s*. *Educ:* Cheltenham College; Trinity College, Oxford. BA (Oxon) 1938, MA (Oxon) 1962. Practising Solicitor, 1950–55; Asst Clerk, Merchant Taylors' Company, 1955–62. Governor, Wolverhampton Grammar Sch. *Address:* 26 Vallance Gardens, Hove, East Sussex BN3 2DD. *T:* Brighton 733200.

WOOLLEY, Richard; Consultant, Benn Brothers Ltd, since 1981 (Director, 1956, Deputy Chairman, 1972–76, Chairman, 1976–81); *b* 12 Jan. 1916; *s* of late John Woolley and Elizabeth Jane (*née* Scorgie); *m* 1940, Doreen Mary Walker; one *s*. *Educ:* Queen Elizabeth's Grammar Sch., Mansfield. Member, editorial staff, Benn Brothers Ltd, 1937; Editor: Newspaper World, 1939–53; Cabinet Maker, 1954–68. Nat. Pres., Furnishing Trades Benevolent Assoc., 1969–70. British Furniture Manufacturers Award of Merit, 1968. Junior Warden, 1979–80, Senior Warden, 1980–81, Master, 1981–82, Worshipful Co. of Furniture Makers. *Address:* Aberfoyle, Golf Side, Cheam, Surrey. *Clubs:* City Livery, Press.

WOOLLEY, Sir Richard (van der Riet), Kt 1963; OBE 1953; FRS 1953; Director, South African Astronomical Observatory, 1972–76; Hon. Fellow, University House, Australian National University, since 1955; Hon. Fellow, Gonville and Caius College, Cambridge, since 1956; *b* Weymouth, Dorset, 24 April 1906; *s* of Paymaster Rear-Admiral Charles E. A. Woolley, CMG, RN; *m* 1st, 1932, Gwyneth Jane Margaret (*née* Meyler) (*d* 1979); 2nd, 1979, Emily May Patricia Marples. *Educ:* Allhallows School, Honiton; University of Cape Town; Gonville and Caius College, Cambridge; MSc Cape Town; MA, ScD Cantab; Hon. LLD Melbourne. Commonwealth Fund Fellow, at Mt Wilson Observatory, California, 1929–31; Isaac Newton Student, Cambridge Univ., 1931–33; Chief Assistant, R Observatory, Greenwich, 1933–37; John Couch Adams Astronomer, Cambridge, 1937–39; Commonwealth Astronomer, 1939–55; Astronomer Royal, 1956–71. Hon. Professor of Astronomy in Australian National University, 1950–. Visiting Prof. of Astronomy, Univ. of Sussex, 1966–. Pres., Royal Astronomical Soc., 1963–65. Vice-Pres., International Astronomical Union, 1952–58; Pres., Australian and New Zealand Assoc. for the Advancement of Science, Melbourne meeting, 1955. Hon. DrPhil Uppsala, 1956; Hon. DSc Cape Town, 1969; Sussex, 1970. Corresp. Mem. de la Société Royale des Sciences de Liège, 1956. Master, Worshipful Co. of Clockmakers, 1969. Gold Medal, RAS, 1971. *Publications:* (with Sir Frank Dyson) Eclipses of the Sun and Moon, 1937; (with D. W. N. Stibbs) The Outer Layers of a Star, 1953. *Address:* 4 Myrtle Street, Somerset West, Cape, South Africa. *Club:* Athenæum.

WOOLLEY, Roy Gilbert; His Honour Judge Woolley; a Circuit Judge, since 1976; *b* 28 Nov. 1922; *s* of John Woolley and Edith Mary Woolley; *m* 1953, Doreen, *d* of Humphrey and Kathleen Morris; two *s* two *d*. *Educ:* Overton and Marchwiel Primary Schs; Deeside Secondary Sch.; UCL (LLB Hons 1949). Served War, 1939–45, Air Gunner, RAF. Christopher Tancred Student, Lincoln's Inn, 1948; called to the Bar, 1951; Wales and Chester Circuit; Recorder, 1975. Reader: Diocese of Chester, 1955–; Diocese of Lichfield, 1977–. *Recreations:* outdoor pursuits, incl. horse riding, gardening, shooting; interested in music, poetry, art and antique furniture. *Address:* Henlle Hall, St Martins, Oswestry, Salop SY10 7AX. *T:* Oswestry 61257.

WOOLLEY, Russell; see Woolley, A. R.

WOOLLEY, William Edward, CBE 1974; DL; Chairman, Cupal Ltd, since 1947; Director, Secto Co. Ltd, since 1947; *b* 17 March 1901; *s* of William Woolley, JP, and Eleanor Woolley; *m* 1929, Marion Elizabeth Aspinall; one *s* one *d*. *Educ:* Woodhouse Grove School, Yorkshire; Edinburgh University. MP (Nat L) for Spen Valley Division of Yorkshire, 1940–45; Parliamentary Private Secretary to Minister of Health, 1943, to Minister of Aircraft Production, 1945. JP; Chairman: Blackburn Borough Magistrates, 1956–72; Gen. Comrs Income Tax, Lancs Adv. Cttee, 1974–76; Gen Comrs Income Tax, Blackburn District, 1960–76; Blackburn and District Hosp. Management Cttee, 1952–74; Manchester Regional Hosp. Staff Cttee, 1966–74; Pres., Blackburn and District Council of Social Service. Contested (Nat L) Brighouse and Spenborough, General elections, 1950, 1951. DL Lancs, 1975. *Address:* Billinge Crest, Billinge End Road, Blackburn, Lancs BB2 6PY. *TA* and *T:* Blackburn 53449.
See also Baron Woolley.

WOOLMER, Kenneth John; MP (Lab) Batley and Morley, since 1979; *b* 25 April 1940; *s* of Joseph William and Gertrude May Woolmer; *m* 1961, Janice Chambers; three *s*. *Educ:* Gladstone Street County Primary, Rothwell, Northants; Kettering Grammar Sch.; Leeds Univ. (BA Econs). Research Fellow, Univ. of West Indies, 1961–62; Teacher, Friern Rd Sec. Mod. Sch., London, 1963; Lecturer: Univ. of Leeds (Economics), 1963–66; Univ. of Ahmadu Bello, Nigeria, 1966–68; Univ. of Leeds, 1968–79. Councillor: Leeds CC, 1970–78; West Yorkshire MCC, 1973–80 (Leader, 1975–77; Leader of Opposition, 1977–79). Chairman, Planning and Transportation Cttee, Assoc. of Metropolitan Authorities, 1974–77. Opposition spokesman on trade, shipping and aviation, 1981–; Mem., Select Cttee on Treasury and Civil Service, 1980–81; Chm., 1981, Vice-Chm., 1982, PLP Economics and Finance Gp. *Recreations:* all forms of sport, espec. soccer, Rugby Union and League, cricket and swimming. *Address:* House of Commons, SW1A 0AA.

WOOLNER, Maj.-Gen. Christopher Geoffrey, CB 1942; MC; *b* 18 Oct. 1893; *m* 1923, Anne, *d* of Sydney Pitt; two *d. Educ:* Marlborough; RMA, Woolwich. 2nd Lt RE, 1912; Captain, 1917; Bt Major, 1919; Major, 1928; Bt Lt-Col, 1933; Lt-Col, 1936; Col, 1939; Maj.-Gen., 1941. Survey Duty, Gold Coast, 1920–23; Officer Company of Gentlemen Cadets Royal Military Academy, 1924–27; GSO2 India, 1930–32; Bde Major, India, 1932–34; Deputy Inspector and Deputy Comdt School of Military Engineering, Aug.–Sept. 1939; GSO1, BEF, 1939–40; Bde Comdr, Feb.–Nov. 1940; Comdr, 1940. Served European War, 1914–18 (wounded, despatches twice, Bt Major, MC and two Bars); War of 1939–45 (despatches thrice, CB); Commander 81st (West African) Div.; Commander Mid-West District and 53 (Welsh) Infantry Division TA; retired, 1947. *Clubs:* Army and Navy, Naval and Military.

WOOLTON, 3rd Earl of, *cr* 1956; **Simon Frederick Marquis;** Baron Woolton, 1939; Viscount Woolton, 1953; Viscount Walberton, 1956; *b* 24 May 1958; *s* of 2nd Earl of Woolton and of Cecily Josephine (later Lady Forres, now Countess Lloyd George of Dwyfor), *e d* of Sir Alexander Gordon Cumming, 5th Bt; *S* father, 1969. *Educ:* Eton College; St Andrews Univ. (MA Hons). *Address:* 31 Tite Street, SW3; Glenogil, by Forfar, Angus. *Clubs:* Brooks's, Turf; New (Edinburgh); Royal and Ancient Golf.

WOOLVERTON, Kenneth Arthur; Head of British Development Division in the Caribbean, Overseas Development Administration of the Foreign and Commonwealth Office, since 1981; *b* 4 Aug. 1926; *s* of Arthur Eliott Woolverton and Lilian Woolverton; *m* 1957, Kathleen West; one *s. Educ:* Orange Hill Grammar Sch. Colonial Office, 1950–61; CRO, 1961–66 (2nd Sec., Jamaica); Min. of Overseas Development, 1966–79; Hd of Middle East Develt Div., ODA, 1979–81. *Recreations:* photography, archaeology, sailing. *Address:* British Development Division, PO Box 167, Bridgetown, Barbados; (home) 47 Durleston Park Drive, Great Bookham, Surrey. *T:* Bookham 54055.

WOOLWICH, Bishop Suffragan of, since 1975; **Rt. Rev. Michael Eric Marshall,** MA; *b* Lincoln, 14 April 1936. *Educ:* Lincoln Sch.; Christ's Coll., Cambridge (Tancred Scholar, Upper II: Hist. Pt 1 and Theol Pt 1a, MA); Cuddesdon Theological Coll. Deacon, 1960; Curate, St Peter's, Spring Hill, Birmingham, 1960–62; Tutor, Ely Theological Coll. and Minor Canon of Ely Cath., 1962–64; Chaplain in London Univ., 1964–69; Vicar of All Saints', Margaret Street, W1, 1969–75. Founder and Director: Inst. of Christian Studies, 1970; Internat. Inst. for Anglican Studies; Member: Gen. Synod, 1970, also Diocesan and Deanery Synods; Liturgical Commn; Anglican/Methodist Liaison Commn until 1974; SPCK Governing Body; USPG Governing Body. Exam. Chap. to Bp of London, 1974. Has frequently broadcast on BBC and commercial radio; also lectured, preached and broadcast in Canada and USA. *Publications:* A Pattern of Faith, 1966 (co-author); Glory under Your Feet, 1978; Pilgrimage and Promise, 1981; Renewal in Worship, 1982; Founder and co-editor, Christian Quarterly. *Recreations:* music, cooking. *Address:* 4 College Gardens, Dulwich, SE21 7BE. *Club:* Naval and Military.

WOOSTER, Clive Edward Doré, FRIBA; MBIM; consultant; *b* 3 Nov. 1913; *s* of Edward Doré Wooster; *m* ; two *s* ; *m* 1970, Patricia Iris (formerly Dewey). *Educ:* Private School, Southend-on-Sea. Private offices, 1930–40; War Service, Captain RA, 1940–46. Local Authority Offices and LCC, 1946–51; Ministry of Education, 1951–58; University Grants Cttee, 1958–59; Works Directorate, War Office, 1959–63; Dir of Building Management, MPBW, 1963–69; Dep. Chief Architect, Min. of Housing and Local Govt, 1969; Dir, Housing Develt, DoE, 1972–74, retired. RIBA Technical Standards Cttee, 1960–64; RIBA Building Controls Panel Chairman, 1960–63; RIBA Management Handbook Cttee, 1963–67; RIBA Council, 1970–72. *Publications:* Lectures on architectural and building management subjects; contrib. to professional journals. *Address:* 141 Harefield Road, Rickmansworth, Herts WD3 1PB. *T:* Rickmansworth 75401.

WOOTTON OF ABINGER, Baroness *cr* 1958 (Life Peer), of Abinger Common, **(Barbara Frances),** CH 1977; MA; holds Hon. Doctorates from Columbia (NY), Nottingham, Essex, Liverpool, Aberdeen, York, Hull, Aston in Birmingham, Bath, Southampton, Warwick, and London; *b* Cambridge, 1897; *d* of late Dr James Adam, Senior Tutor of Emmanuel Coll., Cambridge and Mrs Adam, sometime Fellow of Girton Coll., Cambridge; *m* 1st, 1917, John Wesley Wootton (*d* of wounds, 1917), Earl of Derby Research Student, Trinity College, Cambridge; 2nd, 1935, George Percival Wright (*d* 1964). *Educ:* Perse High School for Girls, Cambridge; Girton Coll., Cambridge (MA Cantab). Director of Studies and Lecturer in Economics, Girton Coll., 1920–22; Research Officer Trades Union Congress and Labour Party Joint Research Department, 1922–26; Principal, Morley College for Working Men and Women, 1926–27; Director of Studies for Tutorial Classes, University of London, 1927–44; Professor of Social Studies, University of London, 1948–52; Nuffield Research Fellow, Bedford College, University of London, 1952–57. A Governor of the BBC, 1950–56; a Deputy-Speaker in House of Lords, 1967–. Member: Departmental Cttee, Nat. Debt and Taxation, 1924–27; Royal Commission on Workmen's Compensation, 1938; Interdepartmental Cttee on Shop Hours, 1946–49; Royal Commn on the Press, 1947; UGC, 1948–50; Royal Commn on the Civil Service, 1954; Interdepartmental Cttee on the

Business of the Criminal Courts, 1958–61; Council on Tribunals, 1961–64; Interdepartmental Cttee on the Criminal Statistics, 1963–67; Royal Commn on Penal System, 1964–66; Penal Adv. Council, 1966–79; Adv. Council on Misuse of Drugs, 1971–74; Chm., Countryside Commn, 1968–70 (Nat. Parks Commn, 1966–68). JP in the Metropolitan Courts, 1926–70 (on the Panel of Chairmen in the Metropolitan Juvenile Courts, 1946–62). Hon. Fellow: Girton Coll., Cambridge, 1965–; Bedford Coll., London, 1964–; Royal Coll. of Psychiatrists, 1979. *Publications:* (as *Barbara Wootton*): Twos and Threes, 1933; Plan or No Plan, 1934; London's Burning, 1936; Lament for Economics, 1938; End Social Inequality, 1941; Freedom Under Planning, 1945; Testament for Social Science, 1950; The Social Foundations of Wage Policy, 1955; Social Science and Social Pathology, 1959; Crime and the Criminal Law, 1964; In a World I Never Made, 1967; Contemporary Britain, 1971; Incomes Policy: an inquest and a proposal, 1974; Crime and Penal Policy, 1978. *Recreation:* country life. *Address:* High Barn, Abinger Common, Dorking, Surrey. *T:* Dorking 730180.

WOOTTON, Godfrey; see Wootton, N. G.

WOOTTON, Gordon Henry; His Honour Judge Wootton; a Circuit Judge, since 1980; *b* 23 April 1927; *s* of William Henry Wootton and Winifred Beatrice Wootton; *m* 1st, 1953, Camilla Bowes (marr. diss. 1979); two *s* ; 2nd, 1979, Eileen Mary North. LLB Hons. Captain, RE, 1947. Called to the Bar, Middle Temple, 1952; Resident Magistrate, Uganda, 1954–62; a Recorder of the Crown Court, 1975–80. *Address:* Beech-Hurst, Abbotswood, Greenhill, Evesham, Worcs WR11 4NS.

WOOTTON, Harold Samuel, CMG 1942; FCIS; JP; Town Clerk of Melbourne, 1935–54, retired; *b* Ballan, Vic, 13 Dec. 1891; *s* of late John Richard Wootton, Tatura, Goulburn Valley, Victoria; *m* 1914, Anne, *d* of late Joseph Biggs; one *s* one *d. Educ:* State School, Waranga, Victoria; Central Business College, Melbourne. Junior Clerk, Melbourne Town Hall, 1909; Deputy Town Clerk, 1923. *Recreation:* bowls. *Address:* Unit 2, 11 Robert Street, Noosaville, Qld 4566, Australia. *Clubs:* St Kilda Bowling, Tewantin Bowling (Queensland).

WOOTTON, Ian David Phimester, MA, MB, BChir, PhD, FRSC, FRCPath, FRCP; Professor of Chemical Pathology, Royal Postgraduate Medical School, University of London, 1963–82; *b* 5 March 1921; *s* of D. Wootton and Charlotte (*née* Phimester); *m* 1946, Veryan Mary Walshe; two *s* two *d. Educ:* Weymouth Grammar School; St John's College, Cambridge; St Mary's Hospital, London. Research Assistant, Postgraduate Med. School, 1945; Lecturer, 1949; Sen. Lecturer, 1959; Reader, 1961. Consultant Pathologist to Hammersmith Hospital, 1952. Member of Medical Research Council Unit, Cairo, 1947–48; Major, RAMC, 1949; Smith-Mundt Fellow, Memorial Hosp., New York, 1951. Chief Scientist (Hosp. Scientific and Technical Services), DHSS, 1972–73. *Publications:* Microanalysis in Medical Biochemistry, 1964, ed 5th edn, 1974; Biochemical Disorders in Human Disease, 1970; papers in medical and scientific journals on biochemistry and pathology. *Recreations:* carpentry, boating, beekeeping. *Address:* Cariad Cottage, Cleeve Road, Goring, Oxon RG8 9DB. *T:* Goring 873050.

WOOTTON, (Norman) Godfrey; Stipendiary Magistrate for Merseyside, since 1976; *b* 10 April 1926; *s* of H. N. and E. Wootton, Crewe, Cheshire. *Educ:* The Grammar Sch., Crewe; Liverpool Univ. (LLB). Called to Bar, Gray's Inn, 1951. Joined Northern Circuit, 1951. A Recorder of the Crown Court, 1972. *Recreations:* travel, photography. *Address:* Magistrates' Court, Dale Street, Liverpool L2 2JQ. *Club:* Athenæum (Liverpool).

WOOZLEY, Prof. Anthony Douglas, MA; University Professor Emeritus of Philosophy and Law, University of Virginia, since 1983; *b* 14 Aug. 1912; *o s* of David Adams Woozley and Kathleen Lucy Moore; *m* 1937, Thelma Suffield (marr. diss. 1978), *e d* of late Frank Townshend, Worcester; one *d. Educ:* Haileybury College; Queen's College, Oxford. Open Scholar, Queen's College, 1931–35; 1st Cl. Class. Hon. Mods, 1933; 1st Cl. Lit. Hum., 1935; John Locke Schol., 1935. Served War, 1940–46 (despatches); commissioned King's Dragoon Guards, 1941; served N Africa, Italy, Greece, Egypt, Syria, Palestine; Major. Fellow of All Souls College, 1935–37; Fellow and Praelector in Philosophy, Queen's Coll., 1937–54; Librarian, 1938–54; Tutor, Queen's College, 1946–54; University Lecturer in Philosophy, 1947–54; Senior Proctor, 1953–54; Prof. of Moral Philosophy, Univ. of St Andrews, 1954–67; University of Virginia: Prof. of Philosophy, 1966; Commonwealth Prof. of Philosophy, 1974–77; Commonwealth Prof. and Univ. Prof. of Philosophy and Law, 1977–83. Editor of The Philosophical Quarterly, 1957–62; Editor, Home University Library, 1962–68. Visiting Professor of Philosophy: Univ. of Rochester, USA, 1965; Univ. of Arizona, 1972. *Publications:* (ed) Thomas Reid's Essays on the Intellectual Powers of Man, 1941; Theory of Knowledge, 1949; (with R. C. Cross) Plato's Republic: a Philosophical Commentary, 1964; (ed) John Locke's Essay Concerning Human Understanding, 1964; Law and Obedience, 1979; articles and reviews in Mind, etc. *Address:* 655 Kearsarge Circle, Charlottesville, Va 22901, USA.

WORCESTER, Bishop of, since 1982; **Rt. Rev. Philip Harold Ernest Goodrich;** *b* 2 Nov. 1929; *s* of Rev. Canon Harold Spencer Goodrich and Gertrude Alice Goodrich; *m* 1960, Margaret Metcalfe Bennett; four *d. Educ:* Stamford Sch.; St John's Coll., Cambridge (MA); Cuddesdon Theological Coll. Curate, Rugby Parish Church, 1954–57; Chaplain, St John's Coll., Cambridge, 1957–61; Rector of the South Ormsby Group of Parishes,

1961-68; Vicar of Bromley, 1968-73; Diocesan Director of Ordinands, Rochester, 1974-82; Bishop Suffragan of Tonbridge, 1974-82. *Recreations:* gardening, music, walking, looking at buildings. *Address:* Bishop's House, Hartlebury Castle, Kidderminster, Worcs DY11 7XX.

WORCESTER, Dean of; see Baker, Very Rev. T. G. A.

WORCESTER, Archdeacon of; see Coleman, Ven. Peter Everard.

WORDEN, Prof. Alastair Norman; Professor of Toxicology, University of Bath, since 1973; Chairman, Huntingdon Research Centre, 1951-78, Founder, since 1978; Hon. Professor of Toxicology, University of Surrey, since 1978; Chairman, Cambridge Applied Nutrition, Toxicology of Biosciences Group, since 1981; Senior Research Associate, Life Science Research, since 1981; Adjunct Professor of Toxicology, University of Lyon and Pasteur Institute, Lyon, since 1982; *b* 23 April 1916; *s* of Dr C. Norman and Elizabeth Worden; *m* 1st, 1942, Agnes Marshall Murray; one *s*; 2nd, 1950, Dorothy Mary Jensen (*née* Peel), MA (Fellow and Steward, Lucy Cavendish Coll., Cambridge); two *s* one *d. Educ:* Queen Elizabeth's Sch., Barnet; St John's Coll. and Sch. of Clinical Medicine, Cambridge (MA, MB, BChir, PhD); Royal Veterinary, Birkbeck and University Colls, London (DVetMed, DSc). DrVetMed Zurich; FRCPath; FRCVS; FACVT; FRIC; FIBiol; FLS, LSA, CChem. Research Student, Lister Inst. of Preventive Medicine and Univ. Cambridge, 1938-41; Res. Officer, Univ. Cambridge, 1941-45; Milford Res. Prof., and Jt Hd, Dept of Biochemistry, Univ. Wales, 1945-50; Fellow and Co-ordinator of Environmental Studies, Wolfson (formerly University) Coll., Cambridge, 1971-; Expert Pharmacologue-Toxicologue Specialisé du Ministère de la Santé Publique, France, 1974-. Member: ARC Tech. Cttees on Calf and Pig Diseases, 1944; Jt ARC Agricl Improvement Council Cttee on Grassland Improvement Station, 1946; ARC Res. (Frazer) Cttee on Toxic Chemicals, 1961; MAFF British Agrochemicals Jt Medical Panel, 1961; Zool Soc. Lond., Animal Husbandry and Welfare Cttee, 1954-, Hon. Res. Associate 1979-; Japan Pharmacol. Soc. 1970; Asociación Medica Argentina, 1974; Royal Society Study Gp on Long Term Toxic Effects, 1975-78; Sec., FRAME Toxicity Cttee, 1979-. Governor, Taverham Hall Educnl Trust, 1968; Mem. Papworth-Huntingdon HMC, 1970-74; Trustee: Lucy Cavendish Coll., Cambridge, 1975-; Cambridge Univ. Vet. Sch., 1981-. President: Hunts Br., Historical Assoc.; Hunts Fauna and Flora Soc., 1965-; Beds and Hunts Naturalist Trust; Chm., Mammal Soc. British Isles, 1953-54; Pres., Hunts Football League; Vice Pres., Hunts CCC, FA, and Referees' Assoc.; Life Member: CUCC; CURUFC. Mem. Worshipful Soc. Apothecaries, 1971. Freeman, City of London, 1974. Editor: Animal Behaviour, 1950-65; Toxicology Letters, 1977-. *Publications:* Laboratory Animals, 1947; (with Harry V. Thompson) The Rabbit, 1956; Animal Health, Production and Pasture, 1964; numerous papers on nutrition, biochemistry and toxicology. *Recreations:* history, natural history, sport, travel. *Address:* Cross Keys Orchard, Hemingford Abbots, Cambs PE18 9AE. *T:* Huntingdon 62434. *Clubs:* Athenæum, United Oxford & Cambridge University, Farmers', No 10; Sette of Odd Volumes; MCC, Lancashire CCC, Middlesex CCC, Surrey CCC, Plackpool FC.

WORDIE, Sir John (Stewart), Kt 1981; CBE 1975; VRD 1963; barrister-at-law; *b* 15 Jan. 1924; *s* of late Sir James Mann Wordie, CBE, Hon. LLD, and of Lady Wordie (*née* Henderson); *m* 1955, Patricia Gladys Kynoch, Keith, Banffshire, *d* of Lt-Col G. B. Kynoch, CBE, TD, DL; four *s. Educ:* Winchester Coll.; St John's Coll., Cambridge (MA; LLB). Served RNVR, 1942-46. Comdr RNR, 1967; Comdr London Div. RNR, 1969-71. Cambridge, 1946-49; Called to the Bar, Inner Temple, 1950; in practice at the Bar, 1951-. Chairman: Burnham, Pelham and Soulbury Cttees, 1966-; Wages Councils; Mem., Agricultural Wages Bd for England and Wales, 1974-; Dep. Chm. and Mem., Central Arbitration Cttee, 1976-. Mem. Court of Assistants, Salters' Co., 1971-, Master, 1975. *Recreations:* shooting, sailing and boating, athletics, tennis. *Address:* Shallows Cottage, Breamore, Fordingbridge, Hants. *T:* Breamore 432. *Clubs:* Travellers', RORC; Hawks (Cambridge); Royal Tennis Court, Clyde Corinthian Yacht.

WORDLEY, Ronald William; Managing Director, HTV Ltd, since 1978; *b* 16 June 1928; *s* of William Wordley and Elizabeth Anne Hackett; *m* 1953, Pamela Mary Offord; two *s* one *d* (and one *s* decd). *Educ:* Barnet Grammar Sch.; City of London Coll.; RMA, Sandhurst. Regular Army Officer: 2/Lieut RA, 1948; regtl duty, UK, Far East and Europe; Liaison Officer, RM Commando Bde, 1951, Captain; Air OP Pilot, 1953; Army Light Aircraft Sch., 1955; seconded Army Air Corps Cadre, 1957; resigned commn, 1958. Unilever (United Africa Co.), 1958-59; Anglia Television Ltd: Sales Exec., 1959; Gen. Sales Manager, 1962; Dep. Sales Controller, 1964; joined Harlech Consortium as Sales Controller, 1967; Sales Dir on bd of HTV Ltd, 1971. Director: Instock Ltd; Independent Television Publications Ltd; (also Mem. Council), Independent Television Cos Assoc. Ltd; HTV Gp plc; HTV Equipment Ltd; HTV Property Ltd. Mem., Inst. of Marketing. *Recreations:* music, travel, golf, swimming. *Address:* 6 Spring Leigh, Leigh Woods, Bristol, Avon. *T:* (office) Bristol 770271. *Clubs:* Clifton (Bristol); Crews Hill Golf (Mddx), Bristol and Clifton Golf, Burnham and Berrow Golf.

WORDSWORTH, Maj.-Gen. Robert Harley, CB 1945; CBE 1943; late IA; *b* 21 July 1894; *s* of W. H. Wordsworth; *m* 1928, Margaret Joan Ross-Reynolds; one *s* one *d*. Served European War, 1914-18, AIF (despatches); Waziristan, 1919-21; NW Frontier of India, 1930; Persia-Iraq, 1943 (CBE); Middle East, 1945 (CB); retired, 1947. Senator, Commonwealth Parlt of

Australia, 1949-59. Administrator, Norfolk Island, 1962-64. *Recreation:* trout fishing. *Address:* Malcombe Street, Longford, Tasmania 7301, Australia. *Club:* Launceston (Launceston, Tasmania).

WORKMAN, Charles Joseph, TD 1966; Secretary, Glasgow and North Argyll Legal Aid Committee, Law Society of Scotland, since 1982; *b* 25 Aug. 1920; *s* of Hugh William O'Brien Workman and Annie Shields; *m* 1949, Margaret Jean Mason; one *s* two *d. Educ:* St Mungo's Acad., Glasgow; Univ. of Glasgow (MA 1950, LLB 1952). Admitted solicitor, 1952. Served War, 1939-45: France, Belgium, Holland, Germany; commnd Second Fife and Forfar Yeomanry, RAC, 1942; Captain, 1945; served Intell. Corps TA and TAVR, 1954-69; Bt Lt-Col 1969; Hon. Col, Intell. and Security Gp (V), 1976. Entered Office of Solicitor to Sec. of State for Scotland as Legal Asst, 1955; Sen. Legal Asst, 1961; Asst Solicitor, 1966; Dep. Solicitor to Sec. of State, 1976; Dir, Scottish Courts Administration, 1978-82. Chm., Public Service and Commerce Gp, Law Soc. of Scotland, 1977-78. Founder Mem., Edinburgh Chamber Music Trust, 1977-. *Recreations:* hill walking, swimming, music. *Address:* 34 Queen's Crescent, Edinburgh EH9 2BA. *T:* 031-667 2060. *Clubs:* Army and Navy; New (Edinburgh).

WORKMAN, Robert Little, CB 1974; Under-Secretary, HM Treasury, 1967-74; *b* 30 Oct. 1914; *s* of late Robert Workman and Jesse Little; *m* 1940, Gladys Munroe Foord; two *d. Educ:* Sedbergh Sch.; Clare Coll., Cambridge. Economist, Export Credits Guarantee Dept, 1938-49; HM Treasury: Principal, 1949-59; Asst Secretary, 1959-66. Member, St Pancras Borough Council, 1945-49. *Recreations:* building and the visual arts. *Address:* Flatts Farm, Hawstead, Suffolk. *T:* Sicklesmere 497.

WORLOCK, Most Rev. Derek John Harford; see Liverpool, Archbishop of, (RC).

WORMALD, Brian Harvey Goodwin, MA; University Lecturer in History, Cambridge, 1948-79; Fellow of Peterhouse, 1938-79, Emeritus Fellow 1979; *b* 24 July 1912; *s* of late Rev. C. O. R. Wormald and Mrs A. W. C. Wormald (*née* Brooks); *m* 1946, Rosemary, *d* of E. J. B. Lloyd; four *s. Educ:* Harrow; Peterhouse, Cambridge (Scholar). BA 1934 (1st Class Hons Hist. Tripos, Parts I and II); Members Prize (English Essay), 1935; Strathcona Research Student, St John's College, 1936-38; Prince Consort Prize, 1938; MA 1938. Chaplain and Catechist, Peterhouse, 1940-48; Dean, 1941-44; Tutor, 1952-62. Select Preacher, Cambridge, 1945 and 1954. Junior Proctor, 1951-52. Received into Catholic Church, 1955. *Publication:* Clarendon: Politics, History and Religion, 1951. *Address:* c/o Peterhouse, Cambridge. *Club:* Travellers'.

WORMALD, Maj.-Gen. Derrick Bruce, DSO 1944; MC 1940, Bar 1945; Director-General of Fighting Vehicles and Engineer Equipment, Ministry of Defence, 1966-70, retired; *b* 28 April 1916; 2nd *s* of late Arthur and Veronica Wormald; *m* 1953, Betty Craddock; two *d. Educ:* Bryanston Sch.; RMA Sandhurst. Commnd into 13/18 Royal Hussars (QMO), 1936; served in India, 1936-38, BEF, 1939-40 and BLA, 1944-45; Comd, 25th Dragoons, India, 1945-47; Staff Coll., Quetta, 1947; War Office, 1948-50; Comdr, 1st Armoured Car Regt of Arab Legion, 1951-52; Comdr Arab Legion Armoured Corps, 1953-54; jssc 1955; GSO1, 11th Armoured Div., 1956; Comd, 3rd The King's Own Hussars, 1956, and The Queen's Own Hussars, 1958; Comdr, Aden Protectorate Levies, 1959-61; Comdr, Salisbury Plain Sub District, 1962-65. Col, 13th/18th Royal Hussars (QMO), 1974-79. Order of El Istiqlal (Jordan), 1953. *Recreations:* shooting, fishing, sailing. *Address:* Ballards, Wickham Bishops, Essex. *T:* Maldon 891218. *Club:* Cavalry and Guards.

WORMALD, Dame Ethel (May), DBE 1968; JP; DL; *b* 19 Nov. 1901; *d* of late John Robert Robinson, Journalist, Newcastle upon Tyne; *m* 1923, Stanley Wormald, MA, MEd, BSc (decd); two *s. Educ:* Whitley Bay High Sch.; Leeds Univ. (BA, DipEd). Liverpool City Councillor, 1953-67; Lord Mayor of Liverpool, 1967-68. President, Assoc. of Education Cttees, 1961-62; Chairman, Liverpool Education Cttee, 1955-61, and 1963-67; Governor: Liverpool Coll. of Higher Educn; Burton Manor Residential Coll. of Further Educn, Wirral; Mem. Court, Liverpool Univ. JP Liverpool, 1948-; DL Lancaster, 1970, Merseyside, 1974. *Address:* 26 Princes Park Mansions, Liverpool L8 3SA. *T:* 051-728 8670.

WORMALD, Peter John; Under Secretary, Department of Health and Social Security, since 1978; *b* 10 March 1936; *s* of Henry Rowland and Gladys Ada Wormald; *m* 1962, Elizabeth North; three *s. Educ:* Doncaster Grammar Sch.; The Queen's Coll., Oxford (MA). Assistant Principal, Min. of Health, 1958, Principal, 1963; HM Treasury, 1965-67, Asst Sec., 1970. *Recreations:* music, golf, contract bridge. *Address:* 31 Wilton Crescent, SW19 3QY. *T:* 01-540 5760. *Club:* United Oxford & Cambridge University.

WORMELL, Prof. Donald Ernest Wilson; Fellow Emeritus, Trinity College, Dublin; *b* 5 Jan. 1908; *yr s* of Thomas Wilson and Florence Wormell; *m* 1941, Daphne Dillon Wallace; three *s* one *d. Educ:* Perse School. Schol., St John's Coll., Cambridge, 1926; Sandys Student, 1930; Henry Fund Fellow, 1931; Sterling Research Fellow, Yale, 1932; PhD Yale, 1933. Fellow, St John's Coll., Cambridge, 1933-36; Asst Lecturer in Classics, University College, Swansea, 1936-39; employed by Air Ministry and Foreign Office, 1942-44; Fellow, TCD, 1939-78; Prof. of Latin, Univ. of Dublin, 1942-78, Public Orator, 1952-69; Vice-Provost, TCD, 1973-74. Leverhulme Res. Fellow, 1954. MRIA; Mem., Inst. for Advanced Study, Princeton, USA, 1967-68. *Publications:* (with H. W. Parke) The Delphic Oracle, 1956; (jtly) Ovid's

Fasti, 1978; articles on classical literature and ancient history in learned periodicals. *Recreation:* music. *Address:* 44 Seaview Park, Shankill, Co. Dublin. *T:* Dublin 823404.

WORRALL, Air Vice-Marshal John, CB 1963; DFC 1940; retired; Managing Director, The Advertising Agency Poster Bureau Ltd, 1964-65; *b* 9 April 1911; *o s* of late J. R. S. Worrall, Thackers, Bombay, India; *m* 1967, Barbara Jocelyne, *er d* of late Vincent Ronald Robb. *Educ:* Cranleigh; Royal Air Force Coll., Cranwell. Commission Royal Air Force, 1931; flying duties No 1 Sqdn, 1932, No 208 Sqdn, 1933-36; language study, Peking, 1936-39; commanded No 32 (F) Sqdn Biggin Hill, 1940; Fighter Control, Biggin Hill, 1940; Fighter and Transport Staff and Unit, 1941-45; RAF Staff Coll., 1945; Senior Personnel Staff Officer, HQ Transport Command, 1945-48; OC, RAF West Malling and Metropolitan Sector, 1948-49; OC, RAF Kai Tak, Hong Kong, 1949-51; HQ Home Command, 1952-53; Air Ministry, Organisation Branch, 1953-54; OC Eastern Sector, 1954-56; AOA, HQ Flying Training Command, 1956-58; Assistant Chief of Air Staff (Training), 1958-60; SASO, NEAF, 1960-63; retired from RAF, 1963. Chairman RAF Ski and Winter Sports Assoc., 1953-60, Vice-President, 1960-68; Chairman, Battle of Britain Fighter Assoc., 1958-60. *Recreations:* ski-ing, sailing. *Address:* Es Muli den Cosme, Calle Ramón Llull 49, Alqueria Blanca, Mallorca, Spain. *T:* Mallorca 65.38.73; *c/o* National Westminster Bank Ltd, 155 North Street, Brighton, East Sussex.

WORSFOLD, Reginald Lewis, CBE 1979; Member for Personnel, British Gas Corporation (formerly Gas Council), 1973-80, retired; *b* 18 Dec. 1925; *s* of Charles S. and Doris Worsfold; *m* 1952, Margot Kempell; one *s* one *d.* *Educ:* School of Technology, Art and Commerce, Oxford; London Sch. of Economics. MIPM. Served War of 1939-45: Lieut 44 Royal Marine Commandos, 1943-46. Organising Commissioner, Scout Council of Nigeria, 1947-49; Personnel Manager: British European Airways, 1953-65; W Midlands Gas Bd, 1965-69; Gas Council: Dep. Personnel Dir, 1969-70; Personnel Dir, 1970-72. *Recreations:* sailing, camping, music. *Address:* 59 Blenheim Gardens, Kingston Hill, Kingston-upon-Thames, Surrey. *T:* 01-549 2827.

WORSKETT, Prof. Roy, RIBA; MRTPI; Consultant Architect: Bath City Council, since 1979; Salisbury District Council, since 1980; Partner, Architectural Planning Partnership, Horsham, since 1982; *b* 3 Sept. 1932; *s* of Archibald Ellwood Worskett and Dorothy Alice Roffey; two *s* one *d.* *Educ:* Collyer's Sch., Horsham; Portsmouth Sch. of Architecture. MRTPI 1975; RIBA 1955. Architect's Dept, LCC, 1957-60; Architect, Civic Trust, London, 1960-63; Historic Areas Div., DoE (formerly MPBW), 1963-74; City Architect and Planning Officer, Bath City Council, and Prof. of Urban Conservation, Sch. of Architecture, Bath Univ., 1974-79; Consultant Head, Conservation Section, Crafts Council, 1979-82. Chm., Conservation Cttees, Crafts Adv. Cttee, 1974-79; Member: Heritage Educn Group, 1976-; Council for Urban Study Centres, TCPA, 1977-80; Council of Management, Architectural Heritage Fund, 1977-. Vis. Prof., Internat. Centre for Conservation, Rome, 1972-. *Publications:* The Character of Towns, 1968; articles in architect. and planning magazines. *Recreation:* looking and listening in disbelief. *Address:* 32 Smithbarn, Horsham, Sussex. *T:* Horsham 61781.

WORSLEY, Lord; Charles John Pelham; *b* 5 Nov. 1963; *s* and *heir* of 7th Earl of Yarborough, *qv.*

WORSLEY, Air Cdre G. N. E. T. C.; *see* Tindall-Carill-Worsley.

WORSLEY, Very Rev. Godfrey Stuart Harling; Dean Emeritus of Gibraltar, since 1969; *b* 4 Dec. 1906; *o s* of late Rev. A. E. Worsley, Rector of Georgeham; *m* 1933, Stella Mary, *o c* of late H. S. Church, Croyde Manor, N Devon; two *s* one *d.* *Educ:* Dean Close, Cheltenham; London College of Divinity. Deacon, 1929; Priest, 1931; Asst Curate, Croydon Parish Church, 1930-33; CF, Ireland, Malta, Catterick, 1933-43; SCF, W Africa, Greece, Cyprus, 1943-49; DACG, N Midland District and Malta, 1949-54; Rector of Kingsland, 1954-60; Rural Dean of Leominster, 1956-60; Prebendary of Cublington in Hereford Cathedral, and Proctor in Convocation, Diocese of Hereford, 1959-60; Dean of Gibraltar and Rural Dean of Southern Spain, and officiating chaplain RN, 1960-69; Rector of Pen Selwood, 1969-79. *Address:* Arrow Cottage, Eardisland, Leominster, Herefordshire.

WORSLEY, Lt-Gen. Sir John (Francis), KBE 1966 (OBE 1951); CB 1963; MC 1945; retired, 1968; *b* 8 July 1912; *s* of Geoffrey Worsley, OBE, ICS, and Elsie Margaret (*née* Macpherson); *m* 1942, Barbara Elizabeth Jarvis (*née* Greenwood); one *s* three *d* (and two step *d*). *Educ:* Radley; Royal Military Coll., Sandhurst. Unattached List, Indian Army (attached Queen's Own Cameron Highlanders), 1933; 3rd Bn 2nd Punjab Regt, 1934; served NW Frontier, India, 1935 and 1936-37; War of 1939-45, Middle East and SE Asia; Staff Coll., Quetta, 1941; Comd 2nd Bn 1st Punjab Regt, 1945; York and Lancaster Regt, 1947; Joint Services Staff Coll., 1951; Comd 1st Bn The South Lancashire Regt (Prince of Wales's Volunteers), 1953; Secretary, Joint Planning Staff, Ministry of Defence, 1956; Comd 6th Infantry Brigade Group, 1957; Imperial Defence Coll., 1960; General Officer Commanding 48 Division (Territorial Army) and West Midland District, 1961-63; Commandant, Staff Coll., Camberley, 1963-66; Commander, British Forces, Hong Kong, 1966-68. Mem., Nat. Army Museum Council. Pres., British Assoc. for Cemeteries in South Asia. *Address:* Castleton House, Sherborne, Dorset. *Club:* Army and Navy.

WORSLEY, Sir Marcus; *see* Worsley, Sir W. M. J.

WORSLEY, Gen. Sir Richard (Edward), GCB 1982 (KCB 1976); OBE 1964; joined Pilkington Bros, 1982; *b* 29 May 1923; *s* of H. H. K. Worsley, Grey Abbey, Co. Down; *m* 1st, 1959, Sarah Anne Mitchell; one *s* one *d* ; 2nd, 1980, Caroline, Duchess of Fife, *er d* of Baron Forteviot, *qv.* *Educ:* Radley Coll. Served War: commissioned into Rifle Bde, 1942, Middle East and Italian Campaigns, 1942-45. Instr, RMA Sandhurst, 1948-51; Malayan Emergency, 1956-57; Instr, Staff Coll., Camberley, 1958-61; CO, The Royal Dragoons, 1962-65; Comdr, 7th Armoured Bde, 1965-67; Imperial Defence Coll., 1968; Chief of Staff, Far East Land Forces, 1969-71; GOC 3rd Div., 1972-74; Vice-QMG, MoD, 1974-76; GOC 1 (Br) Corps, 1976-78; QMG, 1979-82. *Recreations:* shooting, ornithology. *Address:* c/o Barclays Bank Ltd, 27 Regent Street, SW1. *Club:* Cavalry and Guards.

WORSLEY, Sir (William) Marcus (John), 5th Bt *cr* 1838; JP; DL; *b* 6 April 1925; *s* of Colonel Sir William Arthington Worsley, 4th Bt, and Joyce Morgan (*d* 1979), *d* of Sir John Fowler Brunner, 2nd Bt; *S* father, 1973; *m* 1955, Hon. Bridget Assheton, *d* of 1st Baron Clitheroe, *qv* ; three *s* one *d.* *Educ:* Eton; New Coll., Oxford. Green Howards, 1943-47 (Lieut seconded to Royal West African Frontier Force). BA Hons (Oxford) Modern History, 1949. Programme Assistant, BBC European Service, 1950-53. Contested (C) Keighley, 1955; MP (C) Keighley, 1959-64, Chelsea, 1966-Sept. 1974; Parliamentary Private Secretary: to Minister of Health, 1960-61; to Minister without Portfolio, 1962-64; to Lord President of the Council, 1970-72. Second Church Estates Commissioner, 1970-74; a Church Commissioner, 1976-. Pres., Royal Forestry Soc. of England, Wales and N Ireland, 1980-82 (Vice-Pres., 1976-80); Chairman: Yorks Reg. Cttee, Nat. Trust, 1969-80; Nat. Trust Properties Cttee, 1980-. JP 1957, DL 1978, North Yorks; High Sheriff of North Yorks, 1982. *Recreations:* walking, reading. *Heir: s* William Ralph Worsley, ARICS, *b* 12 Sept. 1956. *Address:* Hovingham Hall, York YO6 4LU. *T:* Hovingham 206. *Clubs:* Boodle's; Yorkshire (York).

WORSTHORNE, Peregrine Gerard; Associate Editor, Sunday Telegraph, since 1976; *b* 22 Dec. 1923; *s* of Col Koch de Gooreynd, OBE (who assumed surname of Worsthorne by deed poll, 1921), and of Baroness Norman, *qv* ; *m* 1950, Claude Bertrand de Colasse; one *d.* *Educ:* Stowe; Peterhouse, Cambridge (BA); Magdalen Coll., Oxford. Commnd Oxf. and Bucks LI, 1942; attached Phantom, GHQ Liaison Regt, 1944-45. Sub-editor, Glasgow Herald, 1946; Editorial staff: Times, 1948-53; Daily Telegraph, 1953-61; Deputy Editor, Sunday Telegraph, 1961-76. *Publications:* The Socialist Myth, 1972; Peregrinations: selected pieces, 1980. *Recreations:* tennis, reading. *Address:* 6 Kempson Road, SW6 4PU; Westerlies, Wivenhoe, Essex. *T:* Wivenhoe 2886. *Clubs:* Beefsteak, Garrick.

See also S. P. E. C. W. *Towneley.*

WORSWICK, (George) David (Norman), CBE 1981; FBA 1979; Director, National Institute of Economic and Social Research, 1965-82; *b* 18 Aug. 1916; *s* of Thomas Worswick, OBE, and Eveline (*née* Green); *m* 1940, Sylvia, *d* of A. E. Walsh, MBE; one *s* two *d* (and one *s* decd). *Educ:* St Paul's Sch.; New Coll., Oxford (Scholar). 1st class Hon. Mods (Maths), 1935; 1st class Final Hons (Maths), 1937; Dipl. in Economics and Political Science (Distinction), 1938. Research staff, Oxford Univ. Institute of Statistics, 1940-60; Fellow and Tutor in Economics, Magdalen Coll., Oxford, 1945-65 (Sen. Tutor, 1955-57; Vice-President, 1963-65; Emeritus Fellow, 1969). Member UN Technical Assistance Mission to Turkey, 1954. Vis. Prof. of Economics, MIT, 1962-63. Mem., SSRC, 1966-70. President: Sect. F, British Assoc., 1971; Royal Econ. Soc., 1982-. Hon. DSc City, 1975. *Publications:* Joint Editor: The British Economy 1945-50, 1952; The British Economy in the 1950's, 1962; (ed) The Free Trade Proposals, 1960; (jt) Profits in the British Economy 1909-1938, 1967; (ed) Uses of Economics, 1972; (ed jtly) The Medium Term, 1974; (ed) The Concept and Measurement of Involuntary Unemployment, 1976; articles in Oxford Economic Papers, etc. *Recreation:* squash. *Address:* 25 Beech Croft Road, Oxford OX2 7AY. *T:* Oxford 52486. *Club:* United Oxford & Cambridge University.

WORTH, Abbot of; *see* Farwell, Rt Rev. G. V.

WORTH, George Arthur, MBE; JP; Farmer and Landowner; *b* 3 May 1907; *s* of late Arthur Hovendon Worth; *m* 1935, Janet Maitland, *d* of late Air Chief Marshal Sir A. M. Longmore, GCB, DSO; two *s* two *d.* *Educ:* Marlborough Coll.; Sidney Sussex Coll., Cambridge. Served War of 1939-45, RAF. JP Parts of Holland, Lincs, 1939; High Sheriff of Lincolnshire, 1948-49; DL Lincs, 1950-73. *Address:* 5 Church Lane, Manton, Oakham, Leics.

See also H. B. H. *Carlisle.*

WORTH, Irene, Hon. CBE 1975; actress; *b* 23 June 1916. *Educ:* University of California, Los Angeles (BE). Antoinette Perry Award for distinguished achievement in the Theatre, 1965. First appeared as Fenella in Escape Me Never, New York, 1942; debut on Broadway as Cecily Harden in The Two Mrs Carrolls, Booth Theatre, 1943. Studied for six months with Elsie Fogerty, 1944-45. Subsequently appeared frequently at Mercury, Bolton's, Q, Embassy, etc. Parts include: Anabelle Jones in Love Goes to Press, Duchess Theatre, 1946 (after Embassy); Ilona Szabo in The Play's the Thing, St James's, 1947 (after tour and Lyric, Hammersmith); Eileen Perry in Edward my Son, Lyric, 1948; Lady Fortrose in Home is Tomorrow, Cambridge Theatre, 1948; Olivia Raines in Champagne for Delilah, New, 1949; Celia Coplestone in The Cocktail Party, New, 1950 (after Edinburgh Festival, 1949; Henry Miller

Theatre, New York, 1950); Desdemona in Othello, Old Vic, 1951; Helena in Midsummer Night's Dream, Old Vic, 1952; Catherine de Vausselles in The Other Heart, Old Vic, 1952; Lady Macbeth in Macbeth, Desdemona in Othello, Helena in Midsummer Night's Dream, Catherine de Vausselles in The Other Heart, Old Vic tour of S Africa, 1952; Portia in The Merchant of Venice, Old Vic, 1953; Helena in All's Well That Ends Well and Queen Margaret in Richard III, First Season Shakespeare Festival Theatre, Stratford, Ont, Canada, 1953; Frances Farrar in A Day By The Sea, Haymarket, 1953–54; Alcestis in A Life in the Sun, Edinburgh Festival, 1955; leading rôles in: The Queen and the Rebels, Haymarket, 1955; Hotel Paradiso, Winter Garden, 1956; Mary Stuart, Phœnix Theatre, NY, 1957, Old Vic, 1958; The Potting Shed, Globe Theatre, London, 1958; Rosalind in As You Like It, Shakespeare Festival Theatre, Stratford, Ont, 1959; Albertine Prine in Toys in the Attic, Hudson Theatre, New York, 1960 (NY Newspaper Guild Page One Award); Season at Royal Shakespeare Theatre, Stratford, 1962; Goneril in King Lear, Aldwych, 1962; Doctor Mathilde von Zahnd in The Physicists, Aldwych, 1963; Clodia Pulcher in The Ides of March, Haymarket, 1963; World tour of King Lear for Royal Shakespeare Company, 1964; Alice in Tiny Alice, Billy Rose Theatre, New York, 1965 (Tony award 1965), Aldwych, 1970; Hilde in A Song at Twilight, Anne in Shadows of the Evening, Anna-Mary in Come into the Garden Maud (Noël Coward Trilogy), Queen's, 1966 (Evening Standard Award); Hesione Hushabye in Heartbreak House, Chichester and Lyric, 1967 (Variety Club of GB Award, 1967); Jocasta in Seneca's Oedipus, National Theatre, 1968; Hedda in Hedda Gabler, Stratford, Ont, 1970; worked with internat. Co. for Theatre Res., Paris and Iran, 1971; Notes on a Love Affair, Globe, 1972; Madame Arkadina, The Seagull, Chichester, 1973; Hamlet, Ghosts, The Seagull, Greenwich, 1974; Sweet Bird of Youth, Lake Forest, Washington, New York, 1975 (Tony Award, 1975; Jefferson Award, 1975); The Cherry Orchard, NY, 1977; Happy Days, NY, 1979; The Lady from Dubuque, NY, 1980; L'Olimpiade, Edinburgh Fest., 1982; Lake Forest, Ill, productions: Misalliance, 1976; Old Times, 1977; After the Season, 1978. Films: Order to Kill, 1957 (British Film Academy Award for Best Woman's Performance, 1958); The Scapegoat, 1958; King Lear (Goneril), 1970; Nicholas and Alexandra, 1971; Eye Witness, 1980. Daily Mail National Television Award, 1953–54, and has subseq. appeared on Television and acted with CBC Television in NY and Canada. Whitbread Anglo-American Award for Outstanding Actress, 1967. Recreation: music. Address: c/o ICM Sixth Floor, Milton Goldman, 40 West 57th Street, New York, NY 10019, USA.

WORTHINGTON, Edgar Barton, CBE 1967; MA, PhD; environmental consultant; b 13 Jan. 1905; s of Edgar Worthington and Amy E. Beale; m 1st, 1930, Stella Desmond Johnson (d 1978); three d; 2nd, 1980, Harriett Stockton, Cape Cod. Educ: Rugby; Gonville and Caius Coll., Cambridge. Expeditions to African Lakes, 1927–31; Balfour Student, 1930–33, and Demonstrator in Zoology, Cambridge Univ., 1933–37; Scientist for the African Research Survey, 1934–37; Mungo Park Medal, RSGS, 1939; Director of Laboratories and Secretary of Freshwater Biological Assoc., Windermere, 1937–46; Scientific Adviser to Middle East Supply Centre, 1943–45; Development Adviser, Uganda, 1946; Scientific Secretary to Colonial Research Council, 1946–49, to E Africa High Commission, 1950–51; Secretary-General to Scientific Council for Africa South of the Sahara, 1951–55; Deputy Director-General (Scientific) Nature Conservancy, 1957–65; Scientific Dir, Internat. Biological Programme, 1964–74; Pres., Cttee on Water Res. of Internat. Council of Scientific Unions, 1973–77. Order of Golden Ark (Netherlands), 1976; Member of Honour, IUCN, 1978. Publications: (with Stella Worthington) Inland Waters of Africa, 1933; Science in Africa, 1938; Middle East Science, 1946; Development Plan for Uganda, 1947; (with T. T. Macan) Life in Lakes and Rivers, 1951, rev. edn 1973; Science in the Development of Africa, 1958; (ed) Man-made Lakes: problems and environmental effects, 1973; Evolution of the IBP, 1975; (ed) Arid Land Irrigation: problems and environmental effects, 1976; The Nile, 1978; official reports and papers in scientific journals. Recreations: field sports and farming. Address: Colin Godmans, Furner's Green, Uckfield, East Sussex. T: Chelwood Gate 322. Clubs: Athenæum, Farmers'.

WORTHINGTON, Air Vice-Marshal (Retired) Sir Geoffrey (Luis), KBE 1960 (CBE 1945); CB 1957; idc; psa; Director-General of Equipment, Air Ministry, 1958–61, retired; b 26 April 1903; s of late Commander H. E. F. Worthington, RN; m 1931, Margaret Joan, d of late Maj.-Gen. A. G. Stevenson, CB, CMG, DSO; two s one d. Educ: HMS Conway; Eastbourne Coll. RAF Coll., Cranwell, 1921. Joined RAF, 1922; resigned 1924; re-joined, 1926, in Stores Branch; RAF Staff Coll., 1934. Served War of 1939–45 (despatches, DFE): HQ Maintenance Comd, 1939–43; Air Cdre, 1943; HQ AEAF, 1944; SHAEF, 1944–45; Air Comd, Far East, 1945–47; Director of Equipment B, Air Ministry, 1948–49; idc 1950; Director of Equipment D, Air Ministry, 1951–53; AOC No 42 Group, Maintenance Comd, 1954–55; Air Vice-Marshal, 1956; AOC No 40 Group, 1955–58. Comdr US Legion of Merit, 1955. Recreation: sailing. Address: Pear Tree House, Providence, Burnham-on-Crouch, Essex. T: Maldon 782388. Clubs: Royal Air Force; Royal Burnham Yacht.

WORTHINGTON, George Noel; His Honour Judge Worthington; a Circuit Judge, since 1979; b 22 June 1923; s of late George Errol Worthington and Edith Margaret Boys Worthington; m 1954, Jacqueline Kemble Lightfoot, 2nd d of late G. L. S. Lightfoot and Mrs Lightfoot, Carlisle; two s one d. Educ: Rossall Sch., Lancashire. Served War of 1939–45 in Royal Armoured Corps, 1941–46. Admitted a solicitor, 1949; a Recorder of the

Crown Court, 1972–79. Recreation: gardening. Address: 33 Cromwell Grove, W6 7RQ. T: 01-602 5965. Club: Cumberland County (Carlisle).

WORTLEY, Prof. Ben Atkinson, CMG 1978; OBE 1946; QC 1969; LLD (Manchester), LLM (Leeds); Hon. Docteur de l'Univ. de Rennes (1955); Strasbourg (1965); membre de l'Institut de droit international, 1967 (associe 1956); Professor of Jurisprudence and International Law, University of Manchester, 1946–75, now Emeritus; Barrister of Gray's Inn, 1947; b 16 Nov. 1907; o s of late John Edward Wortley and late Mary Cicely (née King), Huddersfield; m 1935, Kathleen Mary Prynne (d 1982); two s one d. Educ: King James's Grammar Sch., Almondbury; Leeds Univ.; France. Law Society Open Schol., 1925; 1st Class Hons LLB, 1928, and at Law Society's Final, 1929, also D. Reardon Prizeman. Practised full-time till 1931. Taught Law, London School Econ., 1931-33; Manchester Univ., 1933–34; Birmingham Univ., 1934–36; Manchester Univ., 1936–; visiting Prof. Tulane Univ., New Orleans, 1959. Ministry of Home Security, 1939–43; Instructor Commander RN (temp.), 1943–46. Member: Inst. Advanced Legal Studies, 1947–77; Council, UNIDROIT, 1950–; Society of Public Teachers of Law (President, 1964–65); an editor, Rev. Diritto Europeo and British Yearbook of International Law. Member Royal Netherlands Academy, 1960; Commendatore (Italy), 1961; Correspondent Hellenic Inst. for International and Foreign Law, and of Belgian Society for Comparative Law. Representative of HM Government at International Confs at The Hague, 1951, 1956, 1960, 1964, and at New York, 1955 and 1958. Sometime Mem., Lord Chancellor's Cttee on Conflict of Laws. Hon. DCL Durham, 1975. Hon. Brother, de la Salle Order, 1973; KSS, 1975. Publications: lectures, 1939, 1947, 1954 and 1958, published by Hague Academy of International Law; ed, 1961–, 13 vols Schill lecture series (inc. EEC Law 1972); Expropriation in Public International Law, 1959; Jurisprudence, 1967; part editor, Dicey's Conflict of Laws, 1949; (ed) UN, The First Ten Years, 1957; (ed) Law of the Common Market, 1974. Recreations: research on law of war, literature. Address: 24 Grave Lane, Wilmslow, Cheshire SK9 6LA. T: Wilmslow 522810. Club: Athenæum.

WOUK, Herman; author, US; b New York, 27 May 1915; s of Abraham Isaac Wouk and Esther Wouk (née Levine); m 1945, Betty Sarah Brown; two s (and one s dead). Educ: Townsend Harris High Sch.; Columbia Univ. (AB). Radio script writer, 1935–41; Vis. Professor of English, Yeshiva Univ., 1952–57; Presidential consultative expert to the United States Treasury, 1941. Served United States Naval Reserve, 1942–46, Deck Officer (four campaign stars). Member Officers' Reserve Naval Services. Trustee, College of the Virgin Islands, 1961–69. Columbia University Medal for excellence, 1952; Alexander Hamilton Medal, Columbia Univ., 1980. Hon. LHD, Yeshiva Univ., New York City, 1954; Hon. DLit: Clark Univ., 1960; American Internat. Coll., 1979. Publications: novels: Aurora Dawn (American Book of the Month), 1947; The City Boy, 1948; The Caine Mutiny (Pulitzer Prize), 1951; Marjorie Morningstar, 1955; Youngblood Hawke, 1962; Don't Stop The Carnival, 1965; The Winds of War, 1971; War and Remembrance, 1978; plays: The Traitor, 1949; The Caine Mutiny Court-Martial, 1953; Nature's Way, 1957; non-fiction: This Is My God, 1959, rev. edn 1973. Address: c/o BSW Literary Agency, 3255 N Street, NW, Washington, DC 20007, USA. Clubs: Cosmos, Metropolitan (Washington); Bohemian (San Francisco); Century (New York).

WRAGG, Prof. Edward Conrad; Director, Exeter University School of Education, since 1978; b 26 June 1938; s of George William and Maria Wragg; m 1960, Judith (née King); one s two d. Educ: King Edward VII Grammar Sch., Sheffield; Durham Univ. (BA Hons German Cl. 1; Postgrad. CertEd, Cl. 1); Leicester Univ. (MEd); Exeter Univ. (PhD). Asst Master, Queen Elizabeth Grammar Sch., Wakefield, 1960–64; Head of German, Wyggeston Boys' Sch., Leicester, 1964–66; Lectr in Education, Exeter Univ., 1966–73; Prof. of Educn, Nottingham Univ., 1973–78; Prof. of Educn and Dir of Sch. of Educn, Exeter Univ., 1978–. Pres., British Educnl Research Assoc., 1981–82; Specialist Adviser, Parliamentary Select Cttee, 1976–77; Chm., School Broadcasting Council for UK, 1981–. Publications: Teaching Teaching, 1974; Teaching Mixed Ability Groups, 1976; Classroom Interaction, 1976; A Handbook for School Governors, 1980; Class Management and Control, 1981; A Review of Teacher Education, 1982; Swineshead Revisited, 1982; frequent contributor to Guardian, Times Educnl Supp. (regular columnist), Times Higher Educn Supp. Recreations: football playing, watching and coaching; cooking, running, writing, music. Address: 14 Doriam Close, Exeter EX4 4RS. T: Exeter 77052.

WRAIGHT, Sir John (Richard), KBE 1976; CMG 1962; HM Diplomatic Service, retired; company consultant and company director, since 1976; b 4 June 1916; s of late Richard George Wraight; m 1947, Marquita Elliott. Served War of 1939–45 with Honourable Artillery Company and RHA, Western Desert and Libya; Ministry of Economic Warfare Mission in the Middle East, Cairo, 1944. Economic Warfare Adviser, HQ Mediterranean Allied Air Forces, Italy, June–Dec. 1944. Foreign Office, 1945; Special Assistant to Chief of UNRRA Operations in Europe, 1946. Entered Foreign (subseq. Diplomatic) Service, 1947; British Embassy: Athens, 1948; Tel Aviv, 1950; Washington, 1953; Asst Head of Economic Relations Dept, Foreign Office, 1957; Counsellor (Commercial): Cairo, 1959; Brussels and Luxembourg, 1962 (UK Comr on Tripartite Commn for Restitution of Monetary Gold, Brussels, 1962–68); Minister and Consul-General, Milan, 1968–73; Ambassador to Switzerland, 1973–76. Pres., Greater London SW Scout County, 1977–. Commander of the Order of the Crown (Belgium),

1966. *Recreations:* music, travel, gardening, birdwatching. *Address:* c/o Allied International Designers Group plc, 25 Wellington Street, WC2E 7DW.

WRAN, Hon. Neville Kenneth, QC (NSW) 1968; MP; Premier of New South Wales, since 1976; National President, Australian Labor Party, since 1980. *Educ:* Fort Street Boys' High Sch., Sydney; Sydney Univ. (LLB). Solicitor before admission to Bar of NSW, 1957. Joined Australian Labor Party, 1954: Branch and Electorate Council positions; Mem., Central Exec., NSW Br. Elected to Legislative Council, 1970; Dep. Leader of Opposition, 1971; Leader, Legislative Council, 1972; MLA for Bass Hill, Nov. 1973; Leader of Opposition, Dec. 1973-76. Is especially interested in law reform, civil liberties, industrial relations, conservation, art and cultural matters. Member: NSW Legal and Constitutional Cttee; Federal Legal and Constitutional Cttee; NSW Bar Assoc. *Recreations:* reading, walking, swimming. *Address:* Parliament House, Sydney, NSW, Australia. *Club:* Sydney Labor (Hon Life Mem.).

WRANGHAM, Sir Geoffrey Walter, Kt 1958; Judge of High Court of Justice, Family Division (formerly Probate, Divorce and Admiralty Division), 1958-73; retired; *b* 16 June 1900; *s* of late W. G. Wrangham and late E. A. F. Wilberforce; *m* 1925, Mary (*d* 1933), *d* of late S. D. Winkworth; one *s* one *d* ; *m* 1947, Joan, *d* of late Col W. Boyle; one *s* one *d. Educ:* Eton Coll.; Balliol Coll., Oxford. Called to Bar, 1923; joined North-Eastern Circuit; Gresham Lecturer in Law, 1925-33; Practised in London, 1923-33, thereafter in Bradford; Recorder of York, 1941-50; Judge of County Courts, Circuit 20, 1950-57, Circuit 16, 1957-58; Chm., N Riding QS, 1946-58, Dep. Chm. 1958-71; Master of the Bench, Inner Temple, 1958. Served KOYLI and RAC (Lt-Col), 1940-45. *Publications:* Edited (with W. A. Macfarlane) 8th Edition Clerk and Lindsell on Torts, 18th edition Chitty on Contracts. *Address:* Butlesdon House, Low Buston, Warkworth, Morpeth, Northumberland NE65 0XY. *T:* Alnwick 711300.

WRATTEN, Donald Peter; Senior Director, Post Office, 1970-81; *b* 8 July 1925; *er s* of late Frederick George and Marjorie Wratten; *m* 1947, Margaret Kathleen (*née* Marsh); one *s* one *d. Educ:* Morehall Elem. Sch. and Harvey Grammar Sch., Folkestone; London Sch. of Economics. Storehand, temp. clerk, meteorological asst (Air Min.), 1940-43; service with RAF Meteorological Wing, 1943-47. LSE, 1947-50. Joined Post Office, 1950; Private Sec. to Asst Postmaster Gen., 1955-56; seconded to Unilever Ltd, 1959; Private Sec. to Postmaster Gen., 1965-66; Head of Telecommunications Marketing Div., 1966-67; Director: Eastern Telecommunications Region, 1967-69; Exec. Dir, Giro and Remittance Services, 1969-74 (Sen. Dir, 1970-74); Sen. Dir Data Processing Service, 1974-75; Sen. Dir, Telecom Personnel, 1975-81. Member: Industrial Adv. Panel, City Univ. Business Sch., 1974-81 (Chm., 1977-81); Court, Cranfield Inst. of Technology, 1976-81; Business Educn Council, 1977-; Council, Intermediate Technology Develt Gp, 1982-. *Recreations:* travel, topography, photography, consumer affairs, do-it-yourself. *Address:* 10 Homefield Road, Radlett, Herts WD7 8PY. *T:* Radlett 4500.

WRAXALL, 2nd Baron, *cr* 1928, of Clyst St George, Co. Devon; **George Richard Lawley Gibbs;** DL; *b* 16 May 1928 (for whom Queen Mary was sponsor); *er s* of 1st Baron and Hon. Ursula Mary Lawley, OBE 1945, RRC (*d* 1979), *e d* of 6th Baron Wenlock; *S* father 1931. *Educ:* Eton, RMA Sandhurst. Coldstream Guards, 1948-53; Lieut North Somerset Yeomanry/44 Royal Tank Regt (TA), Dec. 1958; Captain, 1962; Major, 1965; retired 1967. Chairman: N Somerset Conservative Assoc., 1970-74; Avon County Scout Council, 1976-; Chm. Governors, St Katherine's Sch., Avon, 1976-81; Fellow, Woodard Schs (Western Div.), 1979-. DL Avon, 1974. *Heir: b* Hon. Eustace Hubert Beilby Gibbs, *qv. Address:* Tyntesfield, Bristol. *T:* Flax Bourton 2923. *Clubs:* Royal Automobile, Cavalry and Guards; Clifton (Bristol).

WRAXALL, Sir Charles (Frederick Lascelles), 9th Bt *cr* 1813; Trainee Auditor with Woolworths (Pty) Ltd, since 1980; *b* 17 Sept. 1961; *s* of Sir Morville William Lascelles Wraxall, 8th Bt, and of Lady (Irmgard Wilhelmina) Wraxall; *S* father, 1978. *Educ:* Archbishop Tenison's Grammar School, Croydon. *Recreations:* stamp and postcard collection, watching football. *Heir: b* Peter Edward Lascelles Wraxall, *b* 30 March 1967. *Address:* Flat 202, Mount Curtis, Main Road, Sea Point, Cape Town, 8001, South Africa.

WRAY, Sir Kenneth O. R.; *see* Roberts-Wray.

WRAY, Martin Osterfield, CMG 1956; OBE 1954; *b* 14 June 1912; *s* of late C. N. O. Wray; *m* 1938, Lilian Joyce, *d* of late R. W. Playfair, Nairobi, Kenya; one *s* two *d. Educ:* St George's Sch., Harpenden; Wadham Coll., Oxford. Colonial Administrative Service in Uganda, 1935; Administrative Secretary, Zanzibar, 1949; Administrative Secretary to High Commissioner for Basutoland, the Bechuanaland Protectorate and Swaziland, 1952; Resident Commissioner, Bechuanaland Protectorate, 1955-59; Chief Secretary, Northern Rhodesia, 1959-62. *Address:* Prospect House, East Knoyle, Wilts. *Club:* Royal Commonwealth Society.

WRENBURY, 3rd Baron, *cr* 1915; **John Burton Buckley;** Partner, Thomson Snell and Passmore, since 1974; *b* 18 June 1927; *s* of 2nd Baron and Helen Malise (*d* 1981), 2nd *d* of late His Honour John Cameron Graham of Ballewan, Stirlingshire; *S* father, 1940; *m* 1st, 1956, Carolyn Joan Maule (marr. diss., 1961), *o d* of Lt-Col Ian Burn-Murdoch, OBE, of Gartincaber,

Doune, Perthshire; 2nd, 1961, Penelope Sara Frances, *o d* of Edward D. Fort, The White House, Sixpenny Handley, Dorset; one *s* two *d. Educ:* Eton Coll.; King's Coll., Cambridge. Deputy Legal Adviser to the National Trust, 1955-56; Partner, Freshfield's, Solicitors, 1956-74. *Heir: s* Hon. William Edward Buckley, *b* 19 June 1966. *Address:* Oldcastle, Dallington, near Heathfield, East Sussex. *T:* Rushlake Green 830400. *Club:* Oriental.

WREY, Sir (Castel Richard) Bourchier, 14th Bt, *cr* 1628; *b* 27 March 1903; *s* of late Edward Castel Wrey and Katharine Joan, *d* of Rev. John Dene; *S* uncle, 1948; *m* 1946, Alice Sybil, *d* of Dr Lubke, Durban, S Africa; two *s. Educ:* Oundle. Served War of 1939-45; 2nd Lieut, RASC (Supp. Res.), France, 1939-40 (invalided); joined RN as ordinary seaman, 1940; Lieut, RNVR, 1942. *Heir: s* George Richard Bourchier Wrey [*b* 2 Oct. 1948; *m* 1981, Hon. Caroline Lindesay-Bethune, *d* of Viscount Garnock, *qv*]. *Address:* Hollamoor Farm, Tawstock, Barnstaple, N Devon; 145 Lambert Road, Durban, South Africa.

WRIGGLESWORTH, Ian William; MP Teeside, Thornaby, since Feb. 1974 (Lab and Co-op, 1974-81, SDP, since 1981); *b* Dec. 1939; *s* of Edward and Elsie Wrigglesworth; *m* Patricia Truscott; two *s. Educ:* Stockton Grammar Sch.; Stockton-Billingham Technical Coll; Coll. of St Mark and St John, Chelsea. Formerly: Personal Assistant to Gen. Sec., NUT; Head of Research and Information Dept of Co-operative Party; Press and Public Affairs Manager of National Giro. PPS to Mr Alec Lyon, Minister of State, Home Office, 1974; PPS to Rt Hon. Roy Jenkins, Home Secretary, 1974-76; Opposition spokesman on Civil Service, 1979-80; SDP spokesman on industry, 1981-. *Address:* House of Commons, SW1.

WRIGHT, Alan John; a Master of the Supreme Court, Supreme Court Taxing Office, since 1972; *b* 21 April 1925; *s* of late Rev. Henry George Wright, MA and Winifred Annie Wright; *m* 1952, Alma Beatrice Ridding; two *s* one d. *Educ:* St Olave's and St Saviour's Grammar Sch., Southwark; Keble Coll., Oxford. BA 1949, MA 1964. Served with RAF, India, Burma and China, 1943-46. Solicitor 1952; in private practice with Shaen Roscoe & Co., 1952-71; Legal Adviser to Trades Union Congress, 1955-71. *Recreations:* Germanic studies, walking, physical fitness training, travel, youth work, industrial law. *Address:* 21 Brockley Park, Forest Hill, SE23 1PT.

WRIGHT, Dr Alastair William, FRCPE; Consultant Physician, Bangour Hospital, retired; *b* 1 Dec. 1913; *s* of William Wright and Annie Elizabeth Wright; *m* 1939, Ethel Patricia Burnley; three *d. Educ:* Edinburgh Academy; Edinburgh Univ. (MB ChB, MD). FRCPE 1947. Served RAMC, Lt-Col/actg Col 1945. Consultant Physician, Bangour Hosp., 1947; Chairman, Bd of Management, Bangour Hosp., 1972. WHO Vis. Professor of Medicine, Baroda, India, 1967. Royal College of Physicians, Edinburgh: Mem. Council, 1960; Vice-Pres., 1979; General Nursing Council, Scotland: Member, 1968; Chm., Disciplinary Cttee, 1975; Member: Scottish Council, BMA (Chm., 1974-78); Scottish Council, Post Graduate Medical Educn, 1973-80; General Medical Council, 1974-78. *Recreation:* golf. *Address:* 36 Ormidale Terrace, Edinburgh EH12 6EF. *T:* 031-337 1810. *Club:* Edinburgh University Staff.

WRIGHT, Alec Michael John, CMG 1967; *b* Hong Kong, 19 Sept. 1912; *s* of Arthur Edgar Wright and Margery Hepworth Chapman; *m* 1948, Ethel Surtees; one *d. Educ:* Brentwood Sch. ARICS 1934; ARIBA 1937. Articled pupil followed by private practice in London. Joined Colonial Service, 1938; appointed Architect in Hong Kong, 1938. Commissioned Hong Kong Volunteer Defence Force, 1941; POW in Hong Kong, 1941-45. Chief Architect, Public Works Dept, Hong Kong, 1950; Asst Director of Public Works, 1956; Dep. Director, 1959; Director, 1963-69; Commissioner for Hong Kong in London, 1969-73. *Address:* 13 Montrose Court, Exhibition Road, SW7 2QG. *T:* 01-584 4293. *Club:* Hong Kong (Hong Kong).
See also Sir Denis Wright.

WRIGHT, Sir Allan Frederick, KBE 1982; farmer; Chairman of Directors, NZ Rural Banking and Finance Corporation; Director: Farmers' Mutual Insurance Group; Mair & Co.; NZ Railways Corporation; NZ Skin Pool Co-operative; *b* Darfield, 25 March 1929; *s* of Quentin A. Wright; *m* 1953, Dorothy June Netting; three *s* two *d. Educ:* Christ's Coll., Christchurch. Nat. Pres., Young Farmers' Clubs, 1957-58; President: N Canterbury Federated Farmers, 1971-74; Federated Farmers of NZ, 1977-81 (formerly Sen. Nat. Vice-Pres.). Mem., NZ Cricket Bd of Control, 1967-; Manager designate, NZ Cricket Team to England, 1983. Mem. Council, Lincoln Coll., 1974-. *Recreations:* cricket (played for N Canterbury), rugby, golf. *Address:* Annat, RD Sheffield, Canterbury, New Zealand.

WRIGHT, Arthur Francis Stevenson, MBE 1945; FRIBA, FRIAS; architect principal in private practice, since 1949; *b* 15 Feb. 1918; *s* of Arthur and Alice Wright; *m* 1946, Catherine Grey Linton; one *d. Educ:* Morgan Academy; College of Art, Dundee (DipArch 1948). Served War, Royal Engineers (Major), 1940-46. FRIBA 1956; FRIAS 1954 (Pres., 1975-77); FCIOB (FIOB 1974); FCIArb (FIArb 1976). *Recreations:* fishing, golf. *Address:* Hillside of Prieston, Tealing, Dundee DD4 0RG. *T:* Tealing 279.

WRIGHT, (Arthur Robert) Donald; Appointments' Secretary to the Archbishops of Canterbury and York, since 1975; Secretary, Crown Appointments Commission, since 1977; *b* 20 June 1923; *s* of late Charles North Wright and Beatrice May Wright; *m* 1948, Helen Muryell Buxton; two *s*

three *d*. *Educ*: Bryanston Sch.; Queens' Coll., Cambridge. Served War in France, Germany and India, 1942–46 (despatches). Taught at: University Coll. Sch., 1948–50; The Hill School, Pennsylvania, 1950; Leighton Park School, 1950–52; Marlborough College (Housemaster), 1953–62; Headmaster, Shrewsbury Sch., 1963–75. Chm., HMC, 1971. Served on BBC and IBA Adv. Councils and on Health Educn Council. Chm. Council, William Temple Foundn; Governor: King's Coll. Sch., Wimbledon; Benenden School (Chm.); Bishop Grosseteste Coll.; Mem. Court of Assistants, Corporation of Sons of Clergy. *Address*: Fielden House, Little College Street, Westminster, SW1P 3SH; 11 Station Road, Haddenham, Aylesbury, Bucks.
See also E. W. Wright.

WRIGHT, Basil Charles; Film Producer; *b* 12 June 1907; *s* of Major Lawrence Wright, TD, and Gladys Marsden. *Educ*: Sherborne; Corpus Christi Coll., Cambridge. Mawson Schol., CCC, 1926; BA (Hons), Classics and Economics. Concerned with John Grierson and others in development of Documentary Film, 1929–; directed, among many films: Song of Ceylon (Gold Medal and Prix du Gouvernement, Brussels), 1935; (with Harry Watt) Night Mail, 1936; Waters of Time, 1951; (with Paul Rotha) World Without End, 1953; (with Gladys Wright) took film expedition to Greece and made The Immortal Land, 1957 (Council of Europe Award, 1959) and Greek Sculpture (with Michael Ayrton), 1959; A Place for Gold, 1960; Visiting Lectr on Film Art, Univ. of Calif, Los Angeles, 1962 and 1968; Senior Lectr in Film History, Nat. Film Sch., 1971–73; Vis. Prof. of Radio, TV and Film, Temple Univ., Philadelphia, 1977–78. Producer, Crown Film Unit, 1945. Governor: Bryanston School, 1949–; British Film Institute, 1953; Fellow, British Film Academy, 1955; Council Mem., Roy. Coll. of Art, 1954–57. Gold Cross, Royal Order of King George I, Greece, 1963. *Publications*: The Use of the Film, 1949; The Long View, 1974. *Recreations*: opera, ballet, gardening. *Address*: Little Adam Farm, Frieth, Henley-on-Thames, Oxon. *Club*: Savile.

WRIGHT, Beatrice Frederika, (Lady Wright); Vice-President, Royal National Institute for the Deaf, since 1978; *b* New Haven, Connecticut; *d* of Mr and Mrs F. Roland Clough; *m* 1st, 1932, John Rankin Rathbone (Flight Lieut, RAFVR, MP, killed in action, 1940); one *s* one *d*; 2nd, 1942, Paul Hervé Giraud Wright (*see* Sir Paul Wright); one *d*. *Educ*: Ethel Walker School, Simsbury, Conn; Radcliffe College, Oxford. MP (U) Bodmin Div. of Cornwall, 1941–45. *Address*: 3 Ormonde Gate, SW3 4EU.
See also J. R. Rathbone.

WRIGHT, Billy; *see* Wright, W. A.

WRIGHT, Claud William, CB 1969; Research Fellow, Wolfson College, Oxford, 1977–July 1983; *b* 9 Jan. 1917; *s* of Horace Vipan Wright and Catherine Margaret Sales; *m* 1947, Alison Violet Readman; one *s* four *d*. *Educ*: Charterhouse; Christ Church, Oxford (MA). Assistant Principal, War Office, 1939; Private, Essex Regiment, 1940; 2nd Lieut, KRRC, 1940; War Office, rising to GSO2, 1942–45; Principal, War Office, 1944; Min. of Defence: Principal, 1947; Asst Sec., 1951; Asst Under-Sec. of State, 1961–68; Dep. Under-Sec. of State, 1968–71; Dep. Sec., DES, 1971–76. Mem. Cttee of Enquiry into conditions of service life for young servicemen, 1969–70; Chm., Cttee on Provincial Museums and Galleries, 1971–73. Lyell Fund, 1947, R. H. Worth Prize, 1958, Geological Society of London; Foulerton Award, Geologists Association, 1955; Stamford Raffles Award, Zoological Society of London, 1965. Phillips Medal, Yorks Geol. Soc., 1976. President, Geologists Assoc., 1956–58. Hon. Associate, British Museum (Nat. Hist.), 1973; fil.Dr *hc* Uppsala, 1979. *Publications*: (with W. J. Arkell *et al*) vol. on Ammonites, 1957, (with W. K. Spencer) on Starfish, 1966, in Treatise on Invertebrate Palaeontology; (with J. S. H. Collins) British Cretaceous Crabs, 1972; (with W. J. Kennedy) Ammonites of the Middle Chalk, 1981; papers in geological, palaeontological and archaeological journals. *Recreations*: palaeontology, natural history, gardening, archæology. *Address*: Old Rectory, Seaborough, Beaminster, Dorset DT8 3QY. *T*: Broadwindsor 68426. *Club*: Athenæum.

WRIGHT, Sir Denis (Arthur Hepworth), GCMG 1971 (KCMG 1961; CMG 1954); HM Diplomatic Service, retired; *b* 23 March 1911; *s* of late A. E. Wright, Hong Kong, and Margery Hepworth Chapman, York; *m* 1939, Iona Craig, Bolney, Sussex; no *c*. *Educ*: Brentwood School; St Edmund Hall, Oxford, Hon. Fellow 1972. Asst Advertising Manager to Gallaher & Co. (Tobacco Manufacturers), 1935–39. Employed from outbreak of war as Vice-Consul on economic warfare work at HM Consulate at Constantza (Roumania), 1939–41. Vice-Consul-in-charge of HM Consulate at Trebizond (Turkey), 1941–43; Acting-Consul-in-charge of HM Consulate, Mersin (Turkey), 1943–45; First Secretary (Commercial) to HM Embassy, Belgrade, 1946–48; Superintending Trade Consul at Chicago for Middle-Western Region of USA, 1949–51; Head of Economic Relations Department in the Foreign Office, 1951–53; appointed Chargé d'Affaires, Teheran, on resumption of diplomatic relations with Persia, Dec. 1953; Counsellor, HM Embassy, Teheran, 1954–55; Asst Under-Sec., FO, 1955–59; Ambassador to Ethiopia, 1959–62; Asst Under-Sec., FO, 1962; Ambassador to Iran, 1963–71. Governor, Oversea Service, Farnham Castle, 1972–; Mem. Council, British Inst. of Persian Studies, 1973– (Pres., 1978–); Chm., Iran Soc., 1976–79. Hon. Fellow St Antony's Coll., Oxford, 1976. *Publications*: Persia (with James Morris and Roger Wood), 1969; The English Amongst the Persians, 1977. *Address*: Duck Bottom, Haddenham, Aylesbury, Bucks. *Club*: Travellers'.
See also A. M. J. Wright.

WRIGHT, Desmond Garforth, QC 1974; *b* 13 July 1923; *s* of late Arthur Victor Wright and Doris Greensill; *m* 1952, Elizabeth Anna Bacon; one *s* one *d*. *Educ*: Giggleswick; Royal Naval Coll., Greenwich; Worcester Coll., Oxford (MA). Cholmondeley Scholar of Lincoln's Inn. Served War of 1939–45: RNVR, 1942–46. Staff of Flag Officer Malaya Forward Area, 1946. Called to Bar, Lincoln's Inn, 1950, Bencher, 1981. *Publication*: Wright on Walls, 1954. *Recreations*: cartology, conversation, skiing on snow. *Address*: 22 Old Buildings, Lincoln's Inn, WC2A 3UJ. *T*: 01-405 2072. *Club*: RNVR.

WRIGHT, Donald; *see* Wright, A. R. D.

WRIGHT, Prof. Donald Arthur, MSc, DSc; FInstP; FRAS; Honorary Research Fellow in Archaeology, University of Durham, since 1976; *b* Stoke-on-Trent, 29 March 1911; *m* 1937, Mary Kathleen Rimmer; one *s* one *d*. *Educ*: Orme School, Newcastle-under-Lyme; University of Birmingham. 1st Class Hons BSc 1932; MSc 1934; DSc Birmingham 1955. Research Physicist, GEC, Wembley, 1934–59; Head of Solid Physics Laboratory, Research Labs, GEC, Wembley, 1955–59; Prof. of Applied Physics, Univ. of Durham, 1960–76. Fellow Institute of Physics, 1946. Member of Board, Institute of Physics, 1957–64. Mem. of Council, Physical Society, 1955–58, Hon. Treasurer, 1958–60. *Publications*: Semiconductors, 1950 (revd edn 1965); Thermoelectric Cooling in Progress in Cryogenics, Vol. I, 1959; Thermoelectric Generation in Direct Generation of Electricity, 1965; many papers on electron emission and solid-state physics in learned journals. *Recreations*: tennis, music. *Address*: Museum of Archaeology, Fulling Mill, Durham; 16 St Mary's Close, Shincliffe, Durham. *T*: Durham 48408.

WRIGHT, Mrs Edmund Gordon; *see* Cross, H. M.

WRIGHT, (Edmund) Kenneth, MA, FCA; Chartered Accountant; Partner in Dearden and Co., 1940–76; *b* 10 Dec. 1909; *s* of late William Ameers Wright and late Martha Wright; *m* 1942, Daisy, *d* of late Rev. T. W. Thornton and Mrs Thornton; one *s* one *d*. *Educ*: preparatory schs in Southern Africa; Leighton Park Sch.; St Catharine's Coll., Cambridge (Engl. and Economics Triposes). ACA 1937, FCA 1945. London Ambulance Service, 1940–45. Chm., London and Dist. Soc. of Chartered Accountants, 1957–58; Mem. Council, Inst. of Chartered Accountants, 1959–76 (Dep. Pres., 1972, Pres., 1973). Governor, Leighton Park Sch., 1949–. *Publications*: numerous books and papers on fiscal and accountancy subjects in national and professional press, including: The Development of an Accounting Practice, 1965; Professional Goodwill and Partnership Annuities, 1967; Financial Planning for Individuals, 1970, 3rd edn 1979; (with Malcolm Penney) Capital Transfer Tax Planning, 1975, 3rd edn 1978. *Recreations*: gardening, philately, writing, civic amenities. *Address*: Old Orchard, Sevenoaks Road, Ightham, Kent. *T*: Borough Green 882374. *Club*: Reform.

WRIGHT, Sir Edward (Maitland), Kt 1977; MA, DPhil, LLD, DSc; FRSE; Research Fellow, University of Aberdeen, since 1976; *b* 1906; *s* of M. T. Wright, Farnley, 1910; *m* 1934, Elizabeth Phyllis, *d* of H. P. Harris, Bryn Mally Hall, N Wales; one *s*. *Educ*: Jesus Coll. and Christ Church, Oxford; Univ. of Göttingen. Master, Chard School, Somerset, 1923–26; Scholar, Jesus College, Oxford, 1926–30; Senior Scholar, Christ Church, 1930–33; Lecturer, King's College, London, 1932–33; Lecturer, Christ Church, 1933–35; Flt Lieut, RAFVR, 1941–43; Principal Scientific Officer, Air Ministry, 1943–45; Prof. of Mathematics, 1935–62, Vice-Principal, 1961–62, Principal and Vice-Chancellor, 1962–76, Univ. of Aberdeen. Member: Anderson Cttee on Grants to Students, 1958–60; Hale Cttee on Univ. Teaching Methods, 1961–64; Scottish Universities Entrance Bd, 1948–62 (Chm. 1955–62); Royal Commission on Medical Education, 1965–67. Vice-Pres., RUSI, 1969–72. Hon. LLD: St Andrews, 1963; Pennsylvania, 1975; Aberdeen, 1978; Hon. DSc Strathclyde, 1974. Hon. Fellow, Jesus College, Oxford, 1963. Macdougall-Brisbane Prize, RSE, 1952; Sen. Berwick Prize, London Math. Soc., 1978. Gold Medal of the Order of Polonia Restituta of the Polish People's Republic, 1978. *Publications*: Introduction to the Theory of Numbers (with Professor G. H. Hardy), 1938, 5th edn 1979; mathematical papers in scientific journals. *Address*: 16 Primrosehill Avenue, Cults, Aberdeen. *T*: Aberdeen 861185. *Club*: Caledonian.

WRIGHT, Edwin Walker, MBE 1945; Director, since 1953, Chairman, since 1979, Tarmac Ltd; *b* 7 July 1911; *s* of late Charles North Wright and Beatrice May Wright; *m* 1940, Maureen Auriol Francis Langley, *d* of late Cyril Owen Langley, DL; one *s* three *d*. *Educ*: Cheltenham Coll. Admitted Solicitor (Hons), 1935; Partner, Fowler Langley and Wright, Wolverhampton, 1938–. Commnd S Staffs Regt, 1939; DAAG (Major), N Command, 1943–45. Chm., House of Laity, Diocese of Lichfield, 1973–79. *Recreation*: music. *Address*: 19 Stockwell Road, Tettenhall, Wolverhampton. *T*: Wolverhampton 751479.
See also A. R. D. Wright.

WRIGHT, Eric; Under Secretary, Department of Industry, since 1979; *b* 17 Nov. 1933; *s* of Alec Wright and Elsie (*née* Worthington); *m* 1955, Pauline Sutton; three *s* (and one *s* decd). *Educ*: Wolstanton Grammar Sch.; Keble Coll., Oxford (BA 1st Cl. Hons Mod. Hist.). 2nd Lieut RASC, 1955–57. Ministry of Fuel and Power, 1957–65; Civil Service Commission, 1965–67; Min. of Technology, 1968–70; Sloan Fellow, London Business Sch., 1970–71; Principal Private Sec. to Secretary of State, DTI, 1971–72; Dept of Trade, 1972–77; Dept of Industry, 1977–. *Recreations*: music, tennis, chess. *Address*: 5 West Hill, South Croydon, Surrey CR2 0SB. *T*: 01-657 4569.

WRIGHT, Eric David, CB 1975; Member, Parole Board for England and Wales, since 1978; Deputy Under-Secretary of State, Home Office, and Director-General, Prison Service, 1973-77; *b* 12 June 1917; *s* of Charles Henry and Cecelia Wright; *m* 1944, Doris (*née* Nicholls); one *s*. *Educ:* Ealing County Grammar School. Joined War Office, 1935; Principal, 1945; seconded to Dept of the Army, Australia, 1951; Asst Secretary, 1955; Command Secretary, BAOR, 1955-58; Imperial Defence College, 1964; Asst Under-Sec. of State, MoD, 1965; on loan to Home Office, Police Dept, 1970-73. *Address:* 32 Valley Road, Rickmansworth, Herts WD3 4DS.

WRIGHT, Prof. Esmond; Director, Institute of United States Studies, and Professor of American History, London University, since 1971; Chairman, Border TV, since 1981 (Deputy Chairman, 1976-81); *b* 5 Nov. 1915; *m* 1945, Olive Adamson. *Educ:* University of Durham (Open Entrance Schol.); Univ. of Virginia (Commonwealth Fund Fellow). War Service, 1940-46, mainly in Middle East; demobilised as Lt-Col, 1946. Glasgow Univ., 1946-67; Prof. of Modern History, 1957-67. MP (C) Glasgow, Pollok, March 1967-1970. Founder-Mem., British Association for American Studies (Chm., 1965-68). Mem., Marshall Aid Commemoration Commn, 1966-; Vice-Chm. and Hon. Treas., AA, 1971-. FRHistS. *Publications:* A Short History of our own Times, 1951; George Washington and the American Revolution, 1957; The World Today, 1961, 4th edn 1978; Fabric of Freedom, 1961, 2nd edn 1978; (ed) Illustrated World History, 1964; Benjamin Franklin and American Independence, 1966; (ed) Causes and Consequences of the American Revolution, 1966; (ed) American Themes, 1967; American Profiles, 1967; (ed) Benjamin Franklin, a profile, 1970; A Time for Courage, 1971; A Tug of Loyalties, 1974; (with A. G. Nicolson) Europe Today, 1979; articles in periodicals. *Address:* 31 Tavistock Square, WC1. *T:* 01-387 5534. *Club:* Athenæum.

WRIGHT, Frederick Matthew, OBE 1976 (MBE 1945); General Manager, British Railways, Western Region and Member of British Railways (Western) Board, 1972-76; *b* 26 June 1916; *s* of Thomas Bell Wright and Ethel Johnson; *m* 1940, Claire Agnes (*née* Cook); one *s* one *d*. *Educ:* Rutherford Coll., Newcastle upon Tyne. FCIT; FInstM. Joined LNER, 1933. Served with Royal Engrs in France, Madagascar, Africa and India, 1939-45. British Railways: posts in traffic depts, 1945-61; Eastern Region: Commercial Supt, Great Northern Line, 1961; Divisional Man., Doncaster, 1964; Asst Gen. Man., York, 1968; Mem., BR (Eastern) Bd, 1969; Dep. Gen. Man., York, 1970. Chm., Bournemouth Helping Services Council, 1978; Vice Chm., E Dorset Community Proj. Agency, 1981-. Dorset County Dir, St John Ambulance Assoc., 1976-81. OStJ 1975, CStJ 1980. *Recreations:* gardening, soccer, Rugby, cricket (critic). *Address:* 6 Chaucer Road, Canford Cliffs, Poole, Dorset BH13 7HB. *Club:* Parkstone Yacht (Parkstone).

WRIGHT, Georg Henrik von, GCVO (Hon.); MA; Research Professor in the Academy of Finland, since 1961; *b* Helsingfors, 14 June 1916; *s* of Tor von Wright and Ragni Elisabeth Alfthan; *m* 1941, Maria Elisabeth von Troil, CVO (Hon.); one *s* one *d*. *Educ:* Svenska Normallyceum, Helsingfors; Helsingfors Univ. Helsingfors University: Lectr and Acting Prof. of Philosophy, 1943-46; Prof. of Philosophy, 1946-61 (also in Univ. of Cambridge, 1948-51); Prof. at Large, Cornell Univ., 1965-77; Chancellor of Abo Academy, 1968-77; Visiting Professor: Cornell Univ., 1954 and 1958; Univ. Calif., Los Angeles, 1963; Univ. Pittsburg, 1966; Univ. Karlsruhe, 1975; Lectures: Shearman Meml, University Coll., London, 1956; Gifford, Univ. of St Andrews, 1959-60; Tarner, Trinity Coll., Cambridge, 1969; Woodbridge, Columbia Univ., 1972; Nellie Wallace, Univ. of Oxford, 1978. President: Internat. Union of History and Philosophy of Science, 1963-65; Acad. of Finland, 1968-69; Philosophical Soc. of Finland, 1962-73; Institut International de Philosophie, 1975-78. Fellow: Finnish Soc. of Sciences (Pres., 1966-67, Hon. Fellow 1978); New Soc. of Letters, Lund; Royal Swedish Academy of Sciences; Royal Soc. of Letters, Lund; British Academy; Royal Swedish Academy of Letters, History and Antiquities; Finnish Acad. of Sciences; Royal Danish Acad. of Sciences and Letters; Royal Acad. of Arts and Sciences, Uppsala; Norwegian Acad. of Science and Letters; Royal Acad. of Science, Trondheim; Hon. Foreign Mem., Amer. Acad. of Arts and Sciences. Sometime Fellow, Trinity College, Cambridge. Hon. degrees: Helsingfors Univ. (doctor of pol. sci.); Univ. of Liverpool (DLitt); Univ. of Lund (doctor of philosophy); Turku Univ. (doctor of philosophy). Wilhuri Foundn Internat. Prize, 1976. *Publications:* The Logical Problem of Induction, 1941, rev. edn 1957; Den logiska Empirismen, 1943; Uber Wahrscheinlichkeit, 1945; A Treatise on Induction and Probability, 1951; An Essay in Modal Logic, 1951; Logical Studies, 1957; The Varieties of Goodness, 1963; The Logic of Preference, 1963; Norm and Action, 1963; An Essay in Deontic Logic, 1968; Time, Change, and Contradiction, 1969; Explanation and Understanding, 1971; Causality and Determinism, 1974; Freedom and Determination, 1980; Wittgenstein, 1982. *Address:* 4 Skepparegatan, Helsingfors, Finland.

WRIGHT, George Henry, MBE 1977; Regional Secretary, Wales, Transport and General Workers Union, since 1972; General Secretary, Wales, Trades Union Congress, (part-time), since 1974; *b* 11 July 1935; *s* of William Henry and Annie Louisa Wright; *m* 1956, Margaret Wright; two *d*. *Educ:* Tinkers Farm Sch., Birmingham. Car worker, 1954-65. T&GWU: District Officer, West Bromwich, 1966-68; District Secretary, Birmingham, 1968-72. Member: Co-operative Develt Agency, 1981-; Adv. Cttee, BBC. *Recreations:* fishing, gardening. *Address:* 5 Kidwelly Court, Caerphilly, Mid Glamorgan, Wales. *T:* Caerphilly 885434.

WRIGHT, George Paul; Chief Superintendent, Royal Signals and Radar Establishment, Ministry of Defence, Baldock, 1976-80; *b* 27 April 1919; *s* of late George Maurice Wright, CBE, and of late Lois Dorothy Wright (*née* Norburn); *m* 1957, Jean Margaret Reid, *d* of Lt-Col Charles Alexander Reid Scott, DSO and Marjorie Reid Scott (*née* Mackintosh); one *s* one *d*. *Educ:* Bishops Stortford Coll.; Magdalen Coll., Oxford. BA 1948, MA 1951; FInstP. Admty Signal Estabt, 1939-45; Services Electronics Research Lab., 1945-57; Dept of Physical Research, Admty, 1957-63; Services Electronics Research Lab., 1963-76 (Dir, 1972-76). *Recreations:* music, sailing, gardening. *Address:* Tilekiln Farmhouse, Earls Colne, Colchester, Essex. *T:* Earls Colne 2432. *Clubs:* United Oxford & Cambridge University, Civil Service; Blackwater Sailing.

WRIGHT, Gerard, QC 1973; *b* 23 July 1929; *s* of Leo Henry and Catherine M. F. Wright; *m* 1950, Betty Mary Fenn; one *s* two *d*. *Educ:* Stonyhurst Coll.; Lincoln Coll., Oxford (BA, BCL). Served in Army, 1947-49, rank T/Captain. Called to Bar, Gray's Inn, 1954 (Arden Scholar, Barstow Scholar); Northern Circuit. KHS 1974; KCHS 1979; Auxiliaire de l'Hospitalité de Notre Dame de Lourdes, 1982. *Recreations:* skiing, sailing, squash. *Address:* Pine Lodge, Coral Ridge, Noctorum, Birkenhead, Merseyside L43 7XE. *T:* 051-652 4138; Melbourne House, 21 North John Street, Liverpool L2 5QU. *T:* 051-236 0718. *Club:* Racquet (Liverpool).

WRIGHT, Prof. H(enry) Myles; FRIBA; FRTPI; Lever Professor of Civic Design, University of Liverpool, 1954-75; now Emeritus Professor; University Planning Consultant, 1957-77; *b* 9 June 1908; *s* of H. T. Wright, Gosforth, Newcastle upon Tyne; *m* 1939, Catharine Noble (*d* 1981), *y d* of Very Rev. H. N. Craig, Dean of Kildare; two *d*. *Educ:* Fettes College, Edinburgh (Foundationer); King's College, Newcastle upon Tyne; St John's College, Cambridge. Assistant in various private offices, 1930-35; Asst Editor, The Architects' Journal, and in private practice, 1935-40; Partner in firm of Sir William Holford, 1948-54; principally engaged on planning proposals for Cambridge and Corby New Town. Member British Caribbean Federal Capital Commn, 1956. *Publications:* The Planner's Notebook, 1948; Cambridge Planning Proposals, 1950, and Corby New Town (with Lord Holford), 1952; Land Use in an Urban Environment (Editor and contributor), 1961; The Dublin Region: Preliminary and Final Reports, 1965 and 1967; other technical publications. *Recreations:* walking, reading. *Address:* 9 Pine Hey, Parkgate, Cheshire L64 3TJ.

WRIGHT, Prof. Jack Clifford, MA, BA; Professor of Sanskrit in the University of London, at the School of Oriental and African Studies since 1964; Head, Department of Indology and Modern Languages and Literatures of South Asia, School of Oriental and African Studies, since 1970; *b* 5 Dec. 1933; *s* of Jack and Dorothy Wright, Aberdeen; *m* 1958, Hazel Chisholm (*née* Strachan), Crathes, Banchory; one *s*. *Educ:* Robert Gordon's Coll., Aberdeen; Univ. of Aberdeen (MA Hons in French and German, 1955); University of Zürich; Univ. of London (BA Hons in Sanskrit, 1959). Lectr in Sanskrit, Sch. of Oriental and African Studies, Univ. of London, 1959-64. *Address:* School of Oriental and African Studies, University of London, WC1.

WRIGHT, Adm. Jerauld, DSM (US) (twice); Silver and Bronze Star Medals; Legion of Merit (US); USN retired; US Ambassador to Nationalist China, 1963-65; *b* Amherst, Mass., 4 June 1898; *s* of Gen. William Mason Wright and Marjorie R. (Jerauld) Wright; *m* 1938, Phyllis B. Thompson; one *s* one *d*. *Educ:* US Naval Academy. Ensign, USN, 1917; promoted through grades to Admiral, 1954, Executive Staff of US Naval Academy; operational staff appointments for N African, Sicilian and Italian landings; Mem., Gen. Mark Clark's Expedition to North Africa, 1942; Comd British Sub. HMS Seraph in evacuation of Gen. Henri Giraud from S France to Gibraltar, 1942; Staff Adv. to Sir Andrew B. Cunningham, RN, in N African invasion, 1942; Staff Comdr, 8th Fleet in Sicily and Salerno landings, 1943. Comdr, USS Santa Fe, Pacific, 1943-44; Comdr Amphibious Group Five, 1944-45; Comdr Cruiser Div. Six, 1945; Asst Chief of Naval Operations for Fleet Readiness, 1945-48; Comdr. Amphibious Force, US Atlantic Fleet, 1949-51; US Rep. NATO Standing Group, Washington, 1951-52; C-in-C US Naval Forces, E Atlantic and Medit., 1952-54; Supreme Allied Commander, Atlantic, and C-in-C Western Atlantic Area, NATO, 1954-60; C-in-C Atlantic (US Unified Command), and C-in-C Atlantic Fleet, 1954-60. Pres. US Naval Inst., 1959. Holds Hon. doctorates in Laws and Science. Awarded foreign decorations. *Address:* (home) 2706 36th Street NW, Washington, DC 20007, USA. *Clubs:* Metropolitan, Alibi, Chevy Chase (Washington); Knickerbocker, Brooke (New York).

WRIGHT, Joe Booth, CMG 1979; HM Diplomatic Service, retired; Ambassador to Ivory Coast, Upper Volta and Niger, 1975-78; *b* 24 Aug. 1920; *s* of Joe Booth Wright and Annie Elizabeth Wright; *m* 1st, 1945, Pat (*née* Beaumont); one *s* two *d*; 2nd, 1967, Patricia Maxine (*née* Nicholls). *Educ:* King Edward VI Grammar Sch., Retford; Univ. of London. BA Hons, French. GPO, 1939-47. Served War, HM Forces: RAOC, Intelligence Corps, 1941-46. Entered Foreign Office, 1947; FO, 1947-51; Vice-Consul, Jerusalem, 1951; Consul, Munich, 1952, and Basra, 1954; Dep. Consul, Tamsui, 1956; FO, 1959-64; Consul, Surabaya, 1964; Consul, Medan, 1965-67; First Sec. (Information), Nicosia, 1968; Head of Chancery and Consul, Tunis, 1968-71; Consul-General: Hanoi, 1971-72; Geneva, ████-75. *Publication:* Francophone Black Africa Since Independence, 1981. *Recreations:* cricket, film-going, music, writing. *Address:* 29 Brittany Road, St Leonards-on-Sea, East Sussex TN38 0RB. *Club:* Royal Over-Seas League.

WRIGHT, Captain John, DSC 1944; RN (retd); Assistant Managing Director and General Manager, Marconi Underwater Systems Ltd, Portsmouth, since 1982; *b* 30 April 1921; *s* of Percy Robert and Lucy Ada Wright; *m* 1946, Ethel Lumley Sunderland; one *s* two *d. Educ:* Liverpool Univ. (Part I for BSc). MIEE; Silver Medal, City and Guilds. Served War: RNVR, 1942; 16th Destroyer Flotilla, 1942; HMS Birmingham, 1943; HMS Diadem, 1943. Devonport Gunnery Sch., 1946; HMS Collingwood, 1948; BJSM, USA, 1951; Admiralty Surface Weapons Estabt, 1952; HMS Cumberland, 1956; Naval Ordnance Div., 1958; British Naval Staff, USA, 1960; Polaris Technical Dept, 1964; HM Dockyard, Chatham, 1968; RN retd 1972; Gen. Manager, HM Dockyard, Devonport, 1972-77; Gen. Man., Marconi Space and Defence Systems Ltd, Portsmouth, 1981-82. *Recreations:* fishing, gardening. *Address:* Oakdene, 21 Blackbrook Park Avenue, Fareham, Hants PO15 5JN. *T:* Fareham 280512.

WRIGHT, John Henry, CBE 1964; HM Diplomatic Service, retired; with Government Communications HQ, 1970-77; *b* 6 Dec. 1910; *s* of John Robert Wright and Margaret Leadbetter; *m* 1939, Joan Harvey; two *s. Educ:* Barrow Grammar Sch.; Trinity Coll., Cambridge. Vice-Consul, Genoa, 1934; Addis Ababa, 1937; Havana, 1939; 2nd Sec., Quito, 1943; 1st Sec., 1945; transf. to Foreign Office, 1948; 1st Sec. (Commercial), Helsinki, 1950; 1st Sec. (Commercial), Santiago, 1953; Counsellor, at Shanghai, of HM Chargé d'Affaires in China, 1958-60; Counsellor, temporarily employed in Foreign Office, Dec. 1960-61; HM Consul-General at Rotterdam, 1961-63; Ambassador to Honduras, 1963-69. *Recreations:* reading, walking, music. *Address:* Horse Inn House, Bourton-on-the-Hill, Moreton-in-Marsh, Glos. *Club:* United Oxford & Cambridge University.

WRIGHT, John Hurrell C.; *see* Collier-Wright.

WRIGHT, John Keith; Under Secretary, Overseas Development Administration, Foreign and Commonwealth Office (formerly Ministry of Overseas Development), since 1971; *b* 30 May 1928; *s* of late James Wright and of Elsie Wright, Walton-on-Thames, Surrey; *m* 1958, Thérèse Marie-Claire, *er d* of René Aubenas, Paris. *Educ:* Tiffins' Sch.; King's Coll., Cambridge (MA Hist., 1950; Dipl. in Economics, 1954; Gladstone Memorial Prize, 1954); Yale Univ. OEEC, Paris: Economics and Statistics Directorate, 1951-52; Agriculture and Food Directorate, 1954-56; UK Atomic Energy Authority, 1956-61; Chief Scientific Adviser's staff, MoD, 1961-66 (UK Delegn to 18 Nation Disarmament Conf., 1962-64); Sen. Econ. Adviser, CRO, 1966-68; Head of Economists Dept and subseq. Dir (Economic), FCO, 1968-71. Chm., Economists' Panel, First Division Assoc., 1973-75; Member: Court of Governors, London Sch. of Hygiene and Tropical Medicine, 1979-81; Council, Queen Elizabeth Coll., Univ. of London, 1982-. Has exhibited at Royal Academy. *Publications:* articles on economic subjects. *Recreations:* economic and military history, piano-playing, opera, amateur radio (G4IOL). *Address:* 47 Brunswick Gardens, W8; Bowling Corner, Sandwich, Kent. *Clubs:* Athenæum, Beefsteak.

WRIGHT, (John) Michael, QC 1974; a Recorder of the Crown Court, since 1974; *b* 26 Oct. 1932; *s* of Prof. John George Wright, DSc, MVSc, FRCVS, and Elsie Lloyd Razey; *m* 1959, Kathleen, *er d* of F. A. Meanwell; one *s* two *d. Educ:* King's Sch., Chester; Oriel Coll., Oxford. BA Jurisprudence 1956, MA 1978. Served Royal Artillery, 1951-53. Called to Bar, Lincoln's Inn (Tancred Student), 1957; Leader, SE Circuit, 1981-; Vice-Chm. of the Bar, 1982-83. Member: Bar Council, 1972-; Senate of the Four Inns of Court, 1973-74; Senate of the Inns of Court and the Bar, 1975-. Mem. Supreme Court Rules Cttee, 1973-74. *Recreations:* books, music. *Address:* 2 Crown Office Row, Temple, EC4Y 7HJ. *T:* 01-353 9337; White Friars, St Albans Road, Reigate, Surrey. *T:* Reigate 47792.

WRIGHT, Sir (John) Oliver, GCMG 1981 (KCMG 1974; CMG 1964); GCVO 1978; DSC 1944; HM Diplomatic Service, retired; re-appointed, Ambassador to Washington, since 1982; *b* 6 March 1921; *m* 1942, Lillian Marjory Osborne; three *s. Educ:* Solihull School; Christ's College, Cambridge (MA; Hon. Fellow 1981; pre-elected Master, May 1982, resigned July 1982). Served in RNVR, 1941-45. Joined HM Diplomatic Service, Nov. 1945; served: New York, 1946-47; Bucharest, 1948-50; Singapore, 1950-51; Foreign Office, 1952-54; Berlin, 1954-56; Pretoria, 1957-58. Imperial Defence College, 1959. Asst Private Sec. to Sec. of State for Foreign Affairs, 1960; Counsellor and Private Sec., 1963; Private Sec. to the Prime Minister, 1964-66 (to Rt Hon. Sir Alec Douglas-Home, and subseq. to Rt Hon. Harold Wilson); Ambassador to Denmark, 1966-69; seconded to Home Office as UK Rep. to NI Govt, Aug. 1969-March 1970; Chief Clerk, HM Diplomatic Service, 1970-72; Dep. Under-Sec. of State, FCO, 1972-75; Ambassador to Federal Republic of Germany, 1975-81. Director: Siemens Ltd, 1981-82; Amalgamated Metal Corp., April-July 1982; Bd Mem., British Council, 1981-82. Grand Cross, German Order of Merit, 1978. *Recreations:* theatre, gardening. *Address:* c/o Foreign and Commonwealth Office, SW1; Burstow Hall, near Horley, Surrey. *T:* Horley 3494. *Club:* Travellers'.

WRIGHT, Joseph, OBE 1978; FPS; FCIS; Secretary (Chief Executive), National Pharmaceutical Association (formerly National Pharmaceutical Union), 1961-81; *b* 7 Jan. 1917; *s* of late Thomas Wright and Margaret (*née* Cardwell); *m* 1942, Margaretta May Hart Talbot, BA, MPS; two *s* two *d. Educ:* Blackpool Boys' Grammar Sch.; Chelsea Polytechnic. Dip., Chem. and Druggist and PhC examinations. Called to the Bar, Middle Temple, 1952. In retail pharmacy, 1933-47, incl. 4 years apprenticeship in Blackpool, with

subseq. experience in London. Served war, RAF, commnd wireless navigator, Coastal Comd. On staff, Pharm. Section, Min. of Health, 1947-48; joined NPU, 1948: Asst Sec., 1949, Dep. Sec., 1955, Sec. and Manager, 1961; Dir, NPA Gp, 1971 (Gp comprises Nat. Pharm. Assoc. Ltd, Chemists' Def. Assoc. Ltd, Pharmacy Mutual Insce Co. Ltd, Pharm. and Gen. Prov. Soc., NPU Ltd (t/a NPA Sces), NPU Holdings Ltd). Director: NPU Holdings Ltd, 1965-81; NPU Ltd, 1971-81; Indep. Chemists Marketing Ltd, 1972-81; NPU Marketing Ltd, 1966-81; Member: Standing Pharm. Adv. Cttee, 1964-82; Poisons Bd, 1963-; Panel of Fellows of Pharm. Soc., 1965-82; Gen. Practice Sub-Cttee, PSGB, 1963-81; Bd, Nat. Chamber of Trade, 1973-82; Trade & Professional Alliance, 1975-81; Legislation & Taxation Cttee, Nat. Ch. of Trade, 1964-81; Adviser to Pharm. Services Negotiating Cttee, 1977-81. Hon. Life Mem., S African Retail Chem. and Druggists Assoc., 1974; Distinguished Service Award, Pharmacy Guild of Aust., 1978. Charter Gold Medal of Pharmaceutical Soc. of GB, 1980. Liveryman, Worshipful Soc. of Apoth. of London, 1978-. Freedom of City of London. *Recreations:* reading, travel and—intermittently—pharmaceutical education. *Address:* 116 Wynchgate, Winchmore Hill, N21 1QU. *T:* 01-886 1645.

WRIGHT, Judith, (Mrs J. P. McKinney); writer; *b* 31 May 1915; *d* of late Phillip Arundel Wright, CMG, and Ethel Mabel (*née* Bigg); *m* J. P. McKinney; one *d. Educ:* NSW Correspondence Sch.; New England Girls' Sch.; Sydney Univ. Secretarial work, 1938-42; Univ. Statistician (Univ. of Queensland), 1945-48. Creative Arts Fellow, ANU, 1974; Australia Council Senior Writers' Fellowship, 1977. Dr of Letters (Hon.): Univ. of Queensland, 1962; Univ. of New England, 1963; Univ. of Sydney, 1976; Monash Univ., 1977; ANU, 1981. Encyclopædia Britannica Writer's Award, 1965; Robert Frost Medallion, Fellowship of Australian Writers, 1975. FAHA 1970. *Publications:* verse: The Moving Image, 1946; Woman to Man, 1950; The Gateway, 1953; The Oxford Book of Australian Verse, 1954; The Two Fires, 1955; Birds, 1960; Five Senses, 1963; The Other Half, 1966; Collected Poems, 1971; Alive, 1972; Fourth Quarter, 1976; The Double Tree, 1978; *prose:* The Generations of Men, 1955; New Land New Language, 1956; Preoccupations in Australian Poetry, 1964; The Nature of Love, 1966; Because I Was Invited, 1975; Charles Harpur, 1977; The Coral Battleground, 1977; The Cry for the Dead, 1981; four books for children; also critical essays and monographs. *Recreation:* gardening. *Address:* c/o Post Office, Braidwood, NSW 2622, Australia.

WRIGHT, Kenneth; *see* Wright, E. K.

WRIGHT, Kenneth Campbell, OBE 1973; PhD; HM Diplomatic Service; Counsellor, Paris, since 1982; *b* 31 May 1932; *s* of James Edwin Wright and Eva Rebecca Wright (*née* Sayers); *m* 1958, Diana Yolande Binnie; one *s* two *d. Educ:* George Heriot's Sch., Edinburgh; Univs of Edinburgh (MA 1st Cl. Hons Mod Langs, PhD) and Paris (LèsL). Short-service commission, Royal Air Force, 1957-60. Lecturer, Inst. Politique Congolais and Lovanium Univ., Congo (Zaire), 1960-63; Lectr, later Sen. Lectr, Dept of Modern Languages, Univ. of Ghana, 1963-65; entered HM Diplomatic Service, 1965; FO, 1965-68; First Sec., Bonn, 1968-72; FCO, 1972-75; First Sec., later Counsellor, UK Permanent Representation to the European Communities, Brussels, 1975-79; FCO, 1979-82. *Recreations:* people, places, books. *Address:* c/o Foreign and Commonwealth Office, SW1. *Club:* Athenæum.

WRIGHT, Lance Armitage, RIBA; Associate Director, International Committee of Architectural Critics, since 1978; *b* 25 Dec. 1915; *s* of Edmund Lancelot Wright and Elizabeth Helen (*née* Bonser); *m* 1942, Susan Melville Foster; two *s* two *d. Educ:* Haileybury; University Coll. London; Architectural Assoc. Sch. Architect in private practice, 1946-73; Registrar, Royal West of England Academy Sch. of Architecture, 1950-53; Technical Editor, The Architects Journal, 1954; Editor, The Architectural Review, 1973-80. Chevalier, Order of St Gregory the Great, 1971. *Publication:* (with D. A. C. A. Boyne) Architects Working Details, vols 4-15, 1953-69. *Address:* 18 Holly Hill, Hampstead, NW3 6SE.

WRIGHT, Louis Booker; Hon. OBE 1968; historian, writer; consultant in history, National Geographic Society, since 1971; Director, Folger Shakespeare Library, 1948-68; *b* 1 March 1899; *s* of Thomas Fleming Wright and Lena Booker Wright; *m* 1925, Frances Black; one *s. Educ:* Wofford College; University of North Carolina. AB 1920, Wofford Coll.; MA 1924, PhD 1926, N Carolina. Service in US Army, 1918; newspaper corres. and editor, 1918-23; instructor and associate Prof. of Eng., University of North Carolina, 1926-32; visiting scholar, Huntington Library, 1931-32; member permanent research group, Huntington Library, also Chm., Cttee on Fellowships and Mem. Exec. Cttee, 1932-48; Vis. Professor: Univs of Michigan 1935, Washington 1942, Calif. at Los Angeles 1934-48; Pomona Coll., 1941-48; Calif. Inst. of Technology, 1932-48; Univ. of Minnesota, 1946; Indiana Univ. on the Patten Foundation, 1953. Chm. Advisory Bd, John Simon Guggenheim Memorial Foundation; Vice-Chm., Council on Library Resources, Inc.; Mem. Bd of Directors H. F. du Pont Winterthur Museum and Harry S. Truman Library Inst. for Nat. and Internat. Affairs. Trustee, Shakespeare Birthplace Trust; Mem. Research Cttee and Trustee, National Geographic Society. Hon. LittD: Wofford, 1941; Mills College, 1947; Princeton, 1948; Amherst, 1948; Occidental College, 1949; Bucknell, 1951; Franklin and Marshall, 1957; Colby Coll., 1959; Univ. of British Columbia, 1960; Leicester Univ., 1965; Winthrop Coll., 1980; Hon. LLD: Tulane, 1950; George Washington, 1958; Chattanooga, 1959; Akron, 1961; St Andrews, 1961; Washington and Lee, 1964; Mercer, 1965; LHD: Northwestern, 1948;

Univ. of N Carolina, 1950; Yale, 1954; Rockford Coll., 1956; Coe Coll., 1959; Georgetown Univ., 1961; California State Coll., 1966; Univ. of California, 1967; Brown Univ., 1968; Univ. of S Carolina, 1972; Lander Coll., 1974; Hon. DLitt, Birmingham, England, 1964. FRSA (Benjamin Franklin Medal, 1969); FRSL; FRHistS; Mem., Amer. Philosophical Soc. and other learned socs. Cosmos Club award for distinction in hist. and letters, 1973. *Publications:* Middle-Class Culture in Elizabethan England, 1935; Puritans in the South Seas, 1936; The First Gentlemen of Virginia, 1940; Religion and Empire, 1942; The First Americans in North Africa, 1945; The Atlantic Frontier, 1947; Culture on the Moving Frontier, 1955; The Cultural Life of the American Colonies, 1957; Shakespeare for Everyman, 1964; Everyday Life in Colonial America, 1965; The Dream of Prosperity in Colonial America, 1965; The History of the Thirteen Colonies, 1967; Everyday Life on the American Frontier, 1968; Gold, Glory and the Gospel, 1970; Barefoot in Arcadia: memories of a more innocent era, 1974; Tradition and the Founding Fathers, 1975; South Carolina: a Bicentennial History, 1976; Magna Carta and the Tradition of Liberty, 1976; Of Books and Men, 1976; The John Henry County Map of Virginia 1770, 1977. Edited: Letters of Robert Carter, 1940; The Secret Diary of William Byrd of Westover, 1709-12, 1941; Quebec to Carolina in 1785-1786, 1943; An Essay Upon the Government of the English Plantation on the Continent of America, 1701, 1945; The History and Present State of Virginia, 1705 (by Robert Beverley), 1947; The Historie of Travell into Virginia Britania, 1612, (by William Strachey) 1953; The Folger Library General Reader's Shakespeare, 1957-68; William Byrd of Virginia: The London Diary 1717-1721, and Other Writings, 1958; The Elizabethans' America, 1965; The Prose Works of William Byrd of Westover, 1966; West and by North: North America seen through the eyes of its seafaring discoverers, 1971; The Moving Frontier, 1972. *Recreation:* fishing. *Address:* 3702 Leland Street, Chevy Chase, Md 20815, USA. *T:* 652-5509. *Clubs:* Cosmos (Washington); Century (New York).

WRIGHT, Prof. Margaret S.; *see* Scott Wright.

WRIGHT, Martin; Director, Howard League for Penal Reform, 1971-81; *b* 24 April 1930; *s* of late Clifford Kent Wright and Rosalie Wright, Stoke Newington; *m* 1957, Louisa Mary Nicholls; three *s* two *d*. *Educ:* Repton; Jesus Coll., Oxford. Librarian, Inst. of Criminology, Cambridge, 1964-71. Mem. Council, The Cyrenians, 1969-80 (Chm., Cambridge Cyrene Community (formerly Cambridge Simon Community), 1965-71). ALA 1960. *Publications:* (ed) The Use of Criminological Literature, 1974; Making Good: Prisons, Punishment and Beyond, 1982. *Recreation:* suggesting improvements. *Address:* 107 Palace Road, SW2. *T:* 01-671 8037.

WRIGHT, Michael; *see* Wright, J. M.

WRIGHT, Michael Thomas; Editor since 1973, Editor and Publisher since 1980, Country Life; Editorial Consultant, Country Life Books, since 1978; Editor in Chief and Publisher, Antique Dealer and Collectors' Guide, since 1982; *b* 10 Dec. 1936; *o c* of Thomas Manning Wright and Hilda Evelyn Wright (*née* Whiting); *m* 1964, Jennifer Olga Angus, 2nd *d* of C. B. Angus, Singapore; two *s*. *Educ:* Bristol Grammar Sch.; Gonville and Caius Coll., Cambridge (MA); Trinity Coll., Dublin. Member, Honourable Society of Gray's Inn. Churchwarden, St Michael's Parish Church, Highgate, 1974-79. Judge, RICS/The Times Conservation Awards, 1976, 1977, 1978, 1979, 1980, 1981, 1982. Mem., DoE Working Party on Rural Settlements. Formerly: Financial Analyst, Ford Motor Co. Asst Sec., Town Planning Inst.; Editor, Town Planning Inst. Jl; Asst Editor, Country Life; Managing Editor, Journal of Royal Inst. of British Architects; Dep. Editor, Country Life. FRSA 1980. *Publications:* contrib. articles to: TPI Jl, RIBA Jl; Water Space; Country Life. *Recreations:* music, tennis, walking; participation in local amenity society work. *Address:* 7 Fitzwarren Gardens, Highgate, N19 3TR. *T:* 01-272 2971. *Club:* Travellers'.

WRIGHT, Sir Oliver; *see* Wright, Sir J. O.

WRIGHT, Patrick Richard Henry, CMG 1978; HM Diplomatic Service; Deputy Under-Secretary of State, Foreign and Commonwealth Office, since 1982; *b* 28 June 1931; *s* of late Herbert H. S. Wright and of Rachel Wright (*née* Green), Chetwode, Bucks; *m* 1958, Virginia Anne Gaffney; two *s* one *d*. *Educ:* Marlborough; Merton Coll. (Postmaster), Oxford (MA). Served Royal Artillery, 1950-51; joined Diplomatic Service, 1955; Middle East Centre for Arabic Studies, 1956-57; Third Secretary, British Embassy, Beirut, 1958-60; Private Sec. to Ambassador and later First Sec., British Embassy, Washington, 1960-65; Private Sec. to Permanent Under-Sec., FO, 1965-67; First Sec. and Head of Chancery, Cairo, 1967-70; Dep. Political Resident, Bahrain, 1971-72; Head of Middle East Dept, FCO, 1972-74; Private Sec. (Overseas Affairs) to Prime Minister, 1974-77; Ambassador to: Luxembourg, 1977-79; Syria, 1979-81. *Recreations:* music, philately, walking. *Address:* c/o Foreign and Commonwealth Office, King Charles Street, SW1. *Club:* United Oxford & Cambridge University.

WRIGHT, Sir Paul (Hervé Giraud), KCMG 1975 (CMG 1960); OBE 1952; FRSA; HM Diplomatic Service, retired; Special Representative of the Secretary of State for Foreign and Commonwealth Affairs, since 1975; Chairman, Irvin Great Britain Ltd, since 1979; Governor, Westminster Cathedral Choir School, since 1981; Hon. Secretary General, London Celebrations Committee for the Queen's Silver Jubilee, 1977; *b* 12 May 1915; *o s* of late Richard Hervé Giraud Wright; *m* 1942, Beatrice Frederika

Rathbone (*see* Beatrice Wright), *widow* of Flt-Lt J. R. Rathbone, MP; one *d*. *Educ:* Westminster. Employed by John Lewis Partnership Ltd, 1933-39. Served HM Forces, War of 1939-45; Major, KRRC; HQ 21 Army Group, 1944-45 (despatches). Contested (L) NE Bethnal Green, 1945. Asst Dir, Public Relations, National Coal Bd, 1946-48; Dir, Public Relations, Festival of Britain, 1948-51. HM Foreign Service: Paris and New York, 1951-54; Foreign Office, 1954-56; The Hague, 1956-57; Head of Information, Policy Dept in FO, 1957-60; Cairo, 1960-61; UK Delegn to N Atlantic Council, 1961-64; Minister (Information), Washington, 1965-68, and Dir-Gen., British Inf. Services, NY, 1964-68; Ambassador to Congo (Kinshasa) and to Republic of Burundi, 1969-71; Ambassador to the Lebanon, 1971-75. *Address:* 3 Ormonde Gate, SW3 4EU. *Club:* Garrick.

WRIGHT, Peter Harold, VC 1944; late Company Sergeant-Major, Coldstream Guards; farmer; *b* 10 Aug. 1916, British; *m* 1946, Mollie Mary Hurren, Wenhaston; one *s* two *d*. *Educ:* Brooke, Norfolk (elementary school). Left school at 14 and worked on father's farm up to the age of 20. Joined Coldstream Guards, 1936; sailed for Egypt, 1937. Served in Egypt, Palestine, Syria and throughout the Libyan campaign and North Africa, took part in the landing at Salerno, Italy, Sept. 1943; demobilised, 1945. *Address:* Poplar Farm, Helmingham, Stowmarket, Suffolk.

WRIGHT, Peter Robert; Director, Sadler's Wells Royal Ballet, since 1977; *b* 25 Nov. 1926; *s* of Bernard and Hilda Mary Wright; *m* 1954, Sonya Hana; one *s* one *d*. *Educ:* Bedales School. Dancer: Ballet Jooss, 1945-47, 1951-52; Metropolitan Ballet, 1947-49; Sadler's Wells Theatre Ballet, 1949-51, 1952-56; Ballet Master, Sadler's Wells Opera, and Teacher, Royal Ballet Sch., 1956-58; freelance choreographer and teacher, 1958-61; Ballet Master and Asst Dir, Stuttgart Ballet, 1961-63; BBC Television Producer, 1963-65; freelance choreographer, 1965-69; Associate Dir, Royal Ballet, 1964-77. *Creative Works:* Ballets: A Blue Rose, 1957; The Great Peacock, 1958; Musical Chairs, 1959; The Mirror Walkers, 1962; Quintet, 1962; Namouna, 1963; Designs for Dancers, 1963; Summer's Night, 1964; Danse Macabre, 1964; Variations, 1964; Concerto, 1965; Arpege, 1974; El Amor Brujo, 1975; Summertide, 1976; own productions of classics: Giselle: Stuttgart, 1966; Cologne, 1967; Royal Ballet, 1968; Canadian National Ballet, 1970; Munich, 1976; Dutch National Ballet, 1977; Houston, Texas, 1979; Frankfurt, 1980; Rio de Janeiro, Brazil, 1982; Winnipeg, 1982; The Sleeping Beauty: Cologne, 1968; Royal Ballet, 1968; Munich, 1974; Dutch National Ballet, 1981; Coppelia: Royal Ballet, 1976; Swan Lake: Sadler's Wells Royal Ballet, 1981. Evening Standard Award for Ballet, 1982. *Recreations:* potter, gardener. *Address:* c/o Royal Opera House, Covent Garden, WC2E 7QA. *T:* 01-240 1200.

WRIGHT, Hon. Sir Reginald Charles, Kt 1978; *b* Tasmania, 10 July 1905; *s* of John and Emma Wright; *m* 1930, Evelyn Arnett; two *s* four *d*. *Educ:* Devonport St High Sch., Tasmania; Univ. of Tasmania. BA, LLB. Admitted Tasmanian Bar, 1928; Lectr in Law, Univ. of Tasmania, 1931-46; Captain, Aust. Field Artillery, AIF, 1941-44; Pres., Liberal Party, Tasmania, 1945-46; MHA for Franklin, Tasmania, and Leader of Opposition, Tasmanian House of Assembly, 1946-49; Senator (Lib) for Tasmania, 1949-78; Minister for Works and Minister assisting Minister for Trade and Industry and in charge of Tourist Activities, 1968-72. *Address:* Wallys Farm, Central Castra, Tasmania, Australia. *Clubs:* Naval and Military, Ulverstone.

WRIGHT, Maj.-Gen. Richard Eustace John G.; *see* Gerrard-Wright.

WRIGHT, Sir Richard (Michael) C.; *see* Cory-Wright.

WRIGHT, Robert Anthony Kent, QC 1973; *b* 7 Jan. 1922; *s* of Robert and Eva Wright; *m* 1956, Gillian Elizabeth Drummond Hancock. *Educ:* Hilton Coll., Natal, S Africa; St Paul's Sch., London; The Queen's Coll., Oxford (MA). Indian Army, 1942-46. Major. Oxford, 1946-48. Called to Bar, Lincoln's Inn, 1949, Bencher 1979. *Recreations:* music, sailing, golf, walking. *Address:* 24 Old Buildings, Lincoln's Inn, WC2A 3UJ. *T:* 01-242 5532. *Clubs:* National Liberal; Bosham Sailing (Bosham); Royal Wimbledon Golf (Wimbledon).

WRIGHT, Very Rev. Ronald (William Vernon) Selby, CVO 1968; TD; DD; FRSE; FSA Scotland; JP; Minister Emeritus of the Canongate (The Kirk of Holyroodhouse), Edinburgh, and of Edinburgh Castle (Minister, 1936-77); Extra Chaplain to the Queen in Scotland, 1961-63 and since 1978 (Chaplain, 1963-78); Chaplain to The Queen's Bodyguard for Scotland, Royal Company of Archers, since 1973; *b* 12 June 1908; *s* of late Vernon O. Wright, ARCM, and late Anna Gilberta, *d* of Major R. E. Selby; unmarried. *Educ:* Edinburgh Academy; Melville Coll.; Edinburgh Univ. (MA; Hon. DD 1956); New Coll. Edinburgh. Warden, St Giles' Cathedral Boys' Club, 1927-36, and Canongate Boys' Club (formerly St Giles'), 1937-78. Cadet Officer, The Royal Scots, 1927-31; Student-Asst at St Giles' Cathedral, 1929-36; Asst Minister of Glasgow Cathedral, 1936; Warden of first Scottish Public Schools' and Clubs' Camp, 1938; Chaplain to 7th/9th (Highlanders) Bn The Royal Scots, 1938-42 (France, 1940), 1947-49; Senior Chaplain to the Forces: 52nd (Lowland) Div., 1942-43; Edinburgh Garrison, 1943; Middle East Forces, 1943-44; NE London, 1944; 10th Indian Div., CMF, 1944-45 (despatches); Hon. SCF, 1945-. Special Preacher, Oxford Univ., 1944; Select Preacher, Cambridge Univ., 1947; Visiting Preacher: Aberdeen Univ., 1946, 1953, 1965, 1973; St Andrews Univ., 1951, 1956, 1967, 1973; Glasgow Univ., 1955, 1973; Edinburgh Univ., 1959; Birmingham Univ., 1959; Hull Univ., 1967; Dundee Univ., 1973. Chaplain to, the Lord High Comr, 1959, and 1960. Conducted numerous series of religious broadcasts for BBC as Radio Padre, toured for War Office and BBC all Home Comds in 1942 and 1943 and MEF, 1943-44; toured transit camps etc in Italy, Austria, S Germany, etc, 1945; toured, for Church of Scotland: India, 1972; for HM Forces: Hong Kong 1973; Singapore, 1973. Moderator, Presbytery of Edinburgh, 1963; Moderator, Gen. Assembly of the Church of Scotland, 1972-73. Chm., Edinburgh and Leith Old People's Welfare Council, 1956-69; Extraordinary Dir, The Edinburgh Academy, 1973-; Hon. Chaplain to: Fettes Coll., 1957-60, 1979-82; Loretto Sch., 1960-83 (Hon. Old Lorettonian, 1976); Edinburgh Acad., 1966-73; Merchant Co. of Edinburgh, 1973-; Governor of Edinburgh Castle, 1959-; ChStJ 1976; President: Scottish Church Soc., 1971-74; Scottish Assoc. of Boys Clubs; Vice-Pres., Old Edinburgh Club; Hon. Pres. Scottish Churches FA; Patron, Lothian Amateur FA. Mem. Edinburgh Educn Cttee, 1960-70. JP Edinburgh, 1963. Cross of St Mark, 1970. *Publications:* Asking Why (with A. W. Loos), 1939; The Average Man, 1942; Let's Ask the Padre, 1943; The Greater Victory, 1943; The Padre Presents, 1944; Small Talks, 1945; Whatever the Years, 1947; What Worries Me, 1950; Great Men, 1951; They Looked to Him, 1954; Our Club, 1954; The Kirk in the Canongate, 1956; The Selfsame Miracles, 1957; Our Club and Panmure House, 1958; Roses in December, 1960; The Seven Words, 1964; An Illustrated Guide to the Canongate, 1965; Take up God's Armour, 1967; The Seven Dwarfs, 1968; Haply I May Remember, 1970; In Christ We Are All One, 1972; Seven Sevens, 1977; Another Home, 1980; edited and contributed to Asking Them Questions, 1936; A Scottish Camper's Prayer Book, 1936; I Attack, 1937; Asking Them Questions-Second Series, 1938; Front Line Religion, 1941; Soldiers Also Asked, 1943; Asking Them Questions-Third Series, 1950; Asking Them Questions (a Selection), 1953; The Beloved Captain: Essays by Donald Hankey, 1956; (with L. Menzies and R. A. Knox) St Margaret, Queen of Scotland, 1957; A Manual of Church Doctrine (with T. F. Torrance), 1960; Fathers of the Kirk, 1960; Asking Them Questions, a new series, 1972, 1973; contrib. to Chambers's Encyclopædia, DNB, etc. Editor, Scottish Forces' Magazine (quarterly), 1941-76. *Recreations:* trying to run Boys' Clubs and Camps since 1927, history of Edinburgh. *Address:* The Queen's House, 36 Moray Place, Edinburgh EH3 6BX. *T:* 031-226 5566. *Clubs:* Athenæum; New (Hon. Mem.), Puffins (Edinburgh).

WRIGHT, Sir Rowland (Sydney), Kt 1976; CBE 1970; Chairman, Blue Circle Industries PLC, since 1978; *b* 4 Oct. 1915; *s* of late Sydney Henry Wright and Elsie May; *m* 1940, Kathleen Mary Hodgkinson, BA; two *s* one *d. Educ:* High Pavement Sch., Nottingham; UC Nottingham. BSc London; FRSC. Joined ICI Ltd, Dyestuffs Div., 1937; Production Dir, Imperial Chemical (Pharmaceuticals) Ltd, 1955-57; Production Dir, Dyestuffs Div., 1957-58; Research Dir, 1958-61; Jt Man. Dir, ICI Ltd Agricultural Div., 1961-63, Chm. 1964-65; Personnel Dir, ICI Ltd, 1966-70; Dep. Chm., ICI Ltd, 1971-75, Chm., 1975-78; Director: AE&CI Ltd, 1970-75 (Dep. Chm., 1971-75); Royal Insurance Co., 1973-79; Barclays Bank Ltd, 1977-; Hawker Siddeley Group, 1979-; Shell Transport & Trading Co. Ltd, 1981-. Chm., Reorganisation Commn for Eggs, 1967-68; Past Mem. Council, Foundn for Management Educn; Mem. Council, Chemical Industries Assoc., 1968-73; Pres. Inst. of Manpower Studies, 1971-77, Hon. Pres., 1977-; Vice-Pres., Soc. of Chemical Industry, 1971-74; Mem., British Shippers' Council, 1975-78; Trustee, Civic Trust, 1975-78. Governor, London Graduate School of Business Studies, 1975-78. FRSA 1970-; CBIM 1975; FIChemE; Mem., Royal Instn, 1971-. Hon. LLD: St Andrews, 1977; Belfast, 1978; Nottingham, 1978. *Recreations:* gardening, photography. *Address:* Portland House, Stag Place, SW1E 5BJ. *Club:* Athenæum.

WRIGHT, Roy Kilner; Deputy Editor, The Standard (formerly London Evening Standard), since 1979; *b* 12 March 1926; *s* of Ernest Wright and Louise Wright; *m* 1st (marr. diss.); two *d*; 2nd, 1969, Jane Barnicoat (*née* Selby). *Educ:* elementary sch., St Helens, Lancs. Jun. Reporter, St Helens Reporter, 1941; Army Service; Sub-Editor: Middlesbrough Gazette, 1947; Daily Express, Manchester, 1951; Daily Mirror, London, 1952; Features Editor, Daily Express, London; Dep. Editor, Daily Express, 1976, Editor, 1976-77; Dir, Beaverbrook Newspapers, 1976-77; Senior Asst Editor, Daily Mail, 1977. *Address:* 25 Foskett Road, SW6. *T:* 01-736 0403; Girards, Broadchalke, Wilts. *T:* Broadchalke 385.

WRIGHT, Roy William, CBE 1970; MIEE; Director, since 1957, Deputy Chairman and Deputy Chief Executive, 1965-75, The Rio Tinto-Zinc Corporation; Director: Davy Corporation Ltd, since 1976; A. P. V. Holdings Ltd, since 1976; Transportation Systems and Market Research, since 1978; *b* 10 Sept. 1914; *s* of late Arthur William Wright; *m* 1939, Mary Letitia, *d* of late Llewelyn Davies; two *d. Educ:* King Edward VI Sch., Chelmsford; Faraday House Coll., London. Served War of 1939-45, S African Navy and RN in S Atlantic, N Atlantic and Arctic; Lt-Comdr 1944. Joined Rio Tinto Co. Ltd, 1952; Man. Dir, Rio Tinto Canada, 1956; Director: Rio Tinto Co. Ltd, 1957; Lornex Mining Co., Vancouver, 1970-79; Rio Algom Ltd, Toronto, 1960-80; Palobra Mining Co., Johannesburg, 1963-80; Rio Tinto South Africa Ltd, Johannesburg, 1960-79. Chairman: Process Plant Expert Cttee, Min. of Technology, 1968; Econ. Develt Cttee for Electronics Industry, NEDO, 1971-76. *Address:* Cobbers, Forest Row, East Sussex. *T:* Forest Row 2009. *Clubs:* Royal Automobile; Toronto (Toronto).

WRIGHT, Sewall; Professor Emeritus of Genetics, University of Wisconsin, since 1960; *b* 21 Dec. 1889; *s* of Philip Green Wright and Elizabeth Quincy Sewall; *m* 1921, Louise Lane Williams; two *s* one *d. Educ:* Lombard Coll.; University of Illinois; Harvard Univ. BS Lombard Coll., 1911; MS Illinois,

1912; ScD Harvard, 1915. Senior Animal Husbandman, US Dept of Agriculture, 1915-25; University of Chicago: Assoc. Professor of Zoology, 1926-29; Professor of Zoology, 1930-37; Ernest D. Burton Distinguished Service Professor, 1937-54; Leon J. Cole Professor of Genetics, University of Wisconsin, 1955-60; Hitchcock Professor, University of California, 1943; Fulbright Professor, University of Edinburgh, 1949-50. Hon. Member, Royal Society of Edinburgh; Foreign Member: Royal Society, London (Darwin Medal 1980); Royal Danish Acad. of Sciences and Letters. Hon. ScD: Rochester, 1942; Yale, 1949; Harvard, 1951; Knox Coll., 1957; Western Reserve, 1958; Chicago, 1959; Illinois, 1961; Wisconsin, 1965; Hon. LLD, Michigan State, 1955. Nat. Medal of Science, 1966. *Publications:* Evolution and the Genetics of Populations, vol. 1, 1968, vol. 2, 1969, vol. 3, 1977, vol. 4, 1978; numerous papers on genetics of characters of guinea pig, population genetics, theory of evolution and path analysis. *Recreation:* travel. *Address:* 3905 Council Crest, Madison, Wisconsin 53711, USA. *Club:* University (Madison).

WRIGHT, Sheila Rosemary Rivers; MP (Lab) Birmingham, Handsworth, since 1979; *b* 22 March 1925; *d* of Daniel Rivers Wright and Frances Grace Wright; *m* 1949, Ronald A. Gregory; two *c.* Social Science Cert. 1951; BScSoc London External 1956. Personnel Officer, 1951-57; Social Worker, 1957-74. Councillor: Birmingham CC, 1956-78; West Midlands CC, 1973-81. Member, Birmingham Reg. Hosp. Bd and W Midlands RHA, 1966-80. *Address:* 42 Beaudesert Road, Birmingham B20 3TQ.

WRIGHT, Shirley Edwin McEwan; industrial consultant; *b* 4 May 1915; *s* of Alfred Coningsby Wright and Elsie Derbyshire; *m* 1939, Dora Fentem; one *s* three *d. Educ:* Herbert Strutt Sch., Belper; Coll. of Technology, Manchester; Univ. of Sheffield. BEng, CEng, FIMechE. Metropolitan Vickers, 1932, ICI Explosives Div., 1938; Asst Chief Engr, ICI Nobel Div., 1955; Dir, Irvine Harbour Bd, 1962; Engrg and Techn Dir, ICI Nobel Div., 1965; Pres., Philippine Explosives Corp., 1970; Chief Exec., Livingston Develt Corp., 1972-77; Dir, Premix-Fibreglass, 1978-80. *Recreations:* cricket, golf. *Address:* Hazeldene, West Kilbride, Ayrshire. *T:* West Kilbride 822659.

WRIGHT, Stanley Harris; Chairman: International Commercial Bank PLC, since 1981; Wolstenholme Rink PLC, since 1982 (Director, since 1980); *b* 9 April 1930; *er s* of John Charles Wright and Doris Wright; *m* 1st, 1957, Angela Vivien Smith (marr. diss. 1973); one *s*; 2nd, 1973, Alison Elizabeth Franks. *Educ:* Bolton Sch.; Merton Coll., Oxford (Postmaster): 1st cl. hons PPE. Asst Principal, BoT, 1952-55; 2nd Sec., UK Delegn to OEEC, Paris, 1955-57; Principal, HM Treasury, 1958-64; 1st Sec. (Financial), British Embassy, Washington, 1964-66; Asst Sec., HM Treasury, 1966-68; Lazard Bros & Co. Ltd, 1969 and 1970 (Man. Dir 1969); Under-Sec., HM Treasury, 1970-72. Director: Lazard Bros & Co. Ltd, 1972-81; Wilkinson Match Ltd, 1974-81; Scripto Inc., 1977-81. Member: Layfield Cttee on Local Government Finance, 1974-76; Armstrong Cttee on Budgetary Reform, 1979-80; Chm., British Bankers Assoc. Fiscal Cttee, 1974-80. Dir, Law Land Co., 1979-81. Mem. Council, Westfield Coll., 1977-. *Recreations:* various. *Address:* 6 Holly Place, NW3. *Clubs:* Reform, MCC.

WRIGHT, Thomas Erskine, MA; Supernumerary Fellow, Queen's College, Oxford, since 1953; *b* 15 Sept. 1902; *s* of Rev. Thomas Wright, MA, Stirling, and Isabel Hamilton Ritchie; unmarried. *Educ:* Stirling High Sch.; Univ. of Glasgow; Balliol Coll., Oxford (Snell Exhibitioner and Hon. Scholar). 1st Class Hons in Classics, Univ. of Glasgow, 1924; Hertford and Craven Scholarships, Chancellor's Prize (Latin Prose), Ferguson Scholarship in Classics, 1925; 1st Class Hons Mods, Chancellor's Prize (Latin Verse), Ireland Scholarship, 1926; 1st Class Lit Hum, 1928. Official Fellow of the Queen's Coll., Oxford, and Praelector in Classics, 1928-48; became Tutor and Senior Tutor and held various other college offices. Professor of Humanity, Univ. of St Andrews, 1948-62, Dean of the Faculty of Arts, 1951-54; Member of the University Grants Cttee, 1954-63; Sec. and Treas., Carnegie Trust for Univs of Scotland, 1962-69. *Publications:* The Latin Contribution to a Liberal Education, 1949; contributions to Oxford Classical Dictionary, *Veterum Laudes*, Fifty Years of Classical Scholarship, and periodicals. *Address:* 10 Gladstone Place, Stirling. *T:* Stirling 2681. *Club:* Stirling and County (Stirling).

WRIGHT, Prof. Verna, FRCP; Professor of Rheumatology, University of Leeds, since 1970; *b* 31 Dec. 1928; *s* of Thomas William and Nancy Eleanor Wright; *m* 1953, Esther Margaret Brown; five *s* four *d. Educ:* Bootle Sch.; Univ. of Liverpool (MB ChB 1953, MD 1956). FRCP 1970 (MRCP 1958). House Officer, Broadgreen Hosp., Liverpool, 1953-54; Sen. Ho. Officer, Stoke Mandeville Hosp., 1954-56; Research Asst, Dept of Clin. Medicine, Univ. of Leeds, 1956-58; Research Fellow, Div. of Applied Physiology, Johns Hopkins Hosp., Baltimore, 1958-59; Lectr, Dept of Clin. Med., Univ. of Leeds, 1960-64; Sen. Lectr, Dept of Medicine, Univ. of Leeds, 1964-70. Adv. Fellow to World Fedn of Occupational Therapists. President: Heberden Soc., 1977; British Assoc. for Rheumatology and Rehabilitation, 1978-80; Soc. for Research in Rehabilitation, 1978; Soc. for Back Pain Research, 1977-79. Member, Johns Hopkins Soc. for Scholars, USA, 1978-. *Publications:* Lubrication of Joints, 1970; Seronegative Polyarthritis, 1976; Clinics in Rheumatic Diseases: Osteoarthrosis, 1976; Rheumatism for Nurses and Remedial Professions, 1977; Evaluation of Artificial Joints, 1977; Introduction to the Biomechanics of Joints and Joint Replacement, 1981; Applied Drug Therapy in Rheumatic Diseases, 1982. *Recreation:* interdenominational

Christian youth work. *Address:* Inglehurst, Park Drive, Harrogate HG2 9AY. *T:* Harrogate 502326.

WRIGHT, Prof. William, MA; ScD; BSc, PhD, CEng, FICE, FIProdE; FIEI; FRSE; SFTCD; Professor of Engineering, Trinity College, Dublin, since 1957; Director, Graduate School of Engineering Studies since 1963; Dean, Faculty of Mathematical and Engineering Sciences, 1969-79; *b* 3 Dec. 1918; *s* of late Rev. James Wright, DD; *m* 1st, 1944, Mildred Anderson (*d* 1959), *d* of James Robertson, MA; two *s* one *d* ; 2nd, Barbara Robinson, MA, PhD, LLB, FTCD, Chevalier de l'Ordre National du Mérite, *d* of W. Edward Robinson; one *s. Educ:* Inverness Royal Academy; George Watson's Coll.; Glasgow Univ. Civil Engineer with LMSR and Min. of Transport, 1935-39. Served War, 1939-46, Captain, Royal Engineers, Middle East, Italy and Germany. Consulting Engineer, 1946-49. Glasgow Univ., 1938-39 and 1946-49 (John Oliphant Bursar) 1st Class Hons Civil Engineering. Lecturer in Civil Engineering, Aberdeen Univ., 1949-54; Head of Dept of Civil Engineering, Southampton Univ., 1954-57. UNESCO Consultant, 1981. Mem. Council, Instn of Production Engineers, 1964; Pres., Instn of Engineers of Ireland, 1977-78. AMICE 1949; PhD Aberdeen, 1952; MICEI 1957; MICE 1958; MA Dublin, 1960; ScD Dublin, 1963. *Publications:* papers in learned journals in Britain and America. *Recreations:* fishing, mountaineering. *Address:* Les Trembles, 35 Palmerston Road, Rathmines, Dublin 6. *T:* Dublin 978619.

WRIGHT, William Alan, CIE 1945; AFC; *b* 27 Nov. 1895; *s* of Rev. Thomas Wright and Annie Pedley; *m* 1948, Elizabeth Ada, *d* of A. E. Garrott, Launceston, Tasmania; one *s* one *d. Educ:* Oundle. 2nd Lieut, Leicestershire Regt, Jan, 1915; joined the Royal Flying Corps, Sept. 1916; Captain about July 1917 (Chevalier of Crown of Belgium and Belgian Croix de Guerre); transferred to RAF on its formation (AFC); joined Indian Civil Service, 1921, and served in Burma, acting Judge Rangoon High Court in 1939; with Government of India, War Dept, 1942-45, as Deputy Secretary, and then as officiating Joint Secretary; Deputy Director of Civil Affairs, Burma, Brig. 1945; Judge Rangoon High Court, 1945-48. *Address:* Salween, 10 Smithers Street, Lorne, Victoria 3232, Australia.

WRIGHT, William Ambrose, (Billy Wright), CBE 1959; Controller of Sport, Central Independent Television Ltd, since 1982 (Head of Sport and Outside Broadcasts, ATV Network Ltd, 1966-81); *b* 6 Feb. 1924; *m* 1958, Joy Beverley; two *d,* and one step *s. Educ:* Madeley Secondary Modern Sch. Professional Footballer; became Captain, Wolverhampton Wanderers Football Club; played for England 105 times; Captain of England 90 times; Manager of Arsenal Football Club, 1962-66. FA Cup Winners medal; 3 Football League Winners Medals. *Publications:* Captain of England; The World's my Football Pitch. *Recreations:* golf, cricket. *Address:* 87 Lyonsdown Road, New Barnet, Herts.

WRIGHT, Prof. William David, ARCS, DIC, DSc; Professor of Applied Optics, Imperial College of Science and Technology, 1951-73; *b* 6 July 1906; *s* of late William John Wright and Grace Elizabeth Ansell; *m* 1932, Dorothy Mary Hudson; two *s. Educ:* Southgate County Sch.; Imperial Coll. Research engineer at Westinghouse Electric and Manufacturing Co., Pittsburgh, USA, 1929-30; research and consultant physicist to Electric and Musical Industries, 1930-39. Lecturer and Reader in Technical Optics Section, Imperial Coll., 1931-51. Chm. Physical Soc. Colour Group, 1941-43; Vice-Pres., Physical Soc., 1948-50; Sec., International Commn for Optics, 1953-66; Chairman: Physical Soc. Optical Group, 1956-59; Colour Group (GB), 1973-75; Pres., International Colour Assoc., 1967-69. Hon. DSc City Univ., 1971. *Publications:* The Perception of Light, 1938; The Measurement of Colour, 4th edn, 1969; Researches on Normal and Defective Colour Vision, 1946; Photometry and the Eye, 1950; The Rays are not Coloured, 1967. About 80 original scientific papers, mainly dealing with colour and vision. *Address:* 68 Newberries Avenue, Radlett, Herts WD7 7EP. *T:* Radlett 5306.

WRIGHT, Most Rev. William Lockridge, DD, DCL, LLD; *b* 8 Sept. 1904; *s* of Rev. Canon J. de Pencier Wright and Lucy Lockridge; *m* 1936, Margaret Clare, BA; two *s* two *d. Educ:* Queen's University, Kingston, Ontario; Trinity College, Toronto. LTh 1927. Curate St George's, Toronto, 1926-28; Incumbent St James', Tweed, 1928-32; Curate Christ's Church Cathedral, Hamilton, 1932-36; Rector St George's Church, Toronto, 1936-40; Rector St Luke's Cathedral, Sault Ste Marie, 1940-44; Dean St Luke's Cathedral, 1941-44; Bishop of Algoma, 1944; Archbishop of Algoma and Metropolitan of Ontario, 1955-74; Acting Primate of the Anglican Church of Canada, Aug. 1970-Jan. 1971. DD (juris dig.) 1941; DCL (Bishop's Univ. Lennoxville), 1953; DD (*hc*): Wycliffe Coll., Toronto, 1956; Huron Coll., 1957; Montreal Diocesan Coll., 1958; LLD (*hc*) Laurentian University of Sudbury, Ont, 1964. *Recreations:* ice hockey, rugby football. *Address:* Box 637, Sault Ste Marie, Ontario P6A 5N2, Canada.

WRIGHTSON, Sir John (Garmondsway), 3rd Bt; *cr* 1900; TD 1948; DL; Hon. Treasurer, Smeatonian Society of Civil Engineers, 1949-79; *b* 18 June 1911; *s* of 2nd Bt and Gwendolin Cotterill (*d* 1964), *d* of G. Harding Neame; *S* father, 1950; *m* 1939, Hon. Rosemary Dawson, *y d* of 1st Viscount Dawson, PC, GCVO, KCB, KCMG; one *s* three *d. Educ:* Eton. Late Major, Durham LI (TA). Served War of 1939-45, 6th Airborne Div., France and Germany (despatches). Chm., Head, Wrightson & Co., 1960-76, retired. Hon. Col, 7th Bn, The Light Infantry (V), T&AVR, 1975-79. High Sheriff, Durham, 1959, DL 1960. Hon. DCL Durham, 1971. *Heir: s* Charles Mark Garmondsway Wrightson [*b* 18 Feb. 1951; *m* 1975, Stella Virginia, *d* of late George Dean;

two *s*]. *Address:* Neasham Hall, near Darlington. *T:* Darlington 720333. *Club:* Carlton.
See also Oliver Wrightson.

WRIGHTSON, Oliver; His Honour Judge Wrightson; a Circuit Judge, since 1978; *b* 28 May 1920; *y s* of Col Sir Thomas Garmondsway Wrightson, 2nd Bt, TD. *Educ:* Eton; Balliol Coll., Oxford. Served with Coldstream Guards, 1942-46, Captain. Called to Bar, Lincoln's Inn, 1950. A Recorder of the Crown Court, 1972-78. *Recreations:* lawn tennis, music. *Address:* The Bridge House, Eryholme, Darlington, Yorks. *Club:* Northern Counties (Newcastle upon Tyne).
See also Sir John Wrightson, Bt.

WRIGLEY, Arthur Joseph, CBE 1965; MD (London) Gold Medal; FRCS; FRCOG; retired as Obstetric Physician, St Thomas' Hospital, London; *b* 5 May 1902; *er s* of late Canon Joseph Henry Wrigley, Clitheroe, Lancs; *m* 1930, Ann (*d* 1976), *d* of late Colonel J. W. Slater, CMG, Dunscar, Lancs; one *s* one *d. Educ:* Rossall Sch.; St Thomas' Hospital. Hon. FCOG S Africa. *Publications:* many medical. *Address:* Green Garth, Elm Grove, Alderley Edge, Cheshire SK9 7PD. *T:* Macclesfield 582194.

WRIGLEY, Prof. Edward Anthony, PhD; FBA 1980; Professor of Population Studies, London School of Economics and Political Science, since 1979; Fellow of Peterhouse, Cambridge, since 1958; *b* 17 Aug. 1931; *s* of Edward Ernest Wrigley and Jessie Elizabeth Wrigley; *m* 1960, Maria Laura Spelberg; one *s* three *d. Educ:* King's Sch., Macclesfield; Peterhouse, Cambridge (MA, PhD). William Volker Res. Fellow, Univ. of Chicago, 1953-54; Lectr in Geography, Cambridge, 1958-74; Tutor, Peterhouse, 1962-64, Sen. Bursar, 1964-74; Co-Dir, SSRC Cambridge Gp for History of Population and Social Structure, 1974-. Mem., Inst. for Advanced Study, Princeton, 1970-71; Hinkley Vis. Prof., Johns Hopkins Univ., 1975; Tinbergen Vis. Prof., Erasmus Univ., Rotterdam, 1979. Pres., British Soc. for Population Studies, 1977-79. *Publications:* Industrial Growth and Population Change, 1961; (ed) English Historical Demography, 1966; Population and History, 1969; (ed) Nineteenth Century Society, 1972; (ed) Identifying People in the Past, 1973; (ed with P. Abrams) Towns in Societies, 1978; (with R. S. Schofield) Population History of England, 1981. *Recreations:* gardening, violin making. *Address:* 13 Sedley Taylor Road, Cambridge CB2 2PW. *T:* Cambridge 247614.

WRIGLEY, Air Vice-Marshal Henry Bertram, CB 1962; CBE 1956; DL; Senior Technical Staff Officer, Royal Air Force Fighter Command, 1960-64, retired; Sales Manager Air Weapons, Hawker Siddeley Dynamics, 1964-76; *b* 24 Nov. 1909; *s* of Frederick William Wrigley and Anne Jeffreys, Seascale, Cumberland; *m* 1935, Audrey, *d* of C. S. Boryer, Portsmouth; one *d. Educ:* Whitehaven Grammar Sch.; RAF Coll., Cranwell. 33 Squadron, 1930; HMS Glorious 1931; HMS Eagle, 1933; long Signals Course, 1934; various signals appointments until 1937; RAF Signals Officer, HMS Glorious, 1938; served War of 1939-45, X Force, Norway, 1940; Fighter Command, 1940-43; HQ South East Asia, 1943-46; RAF Staff Coll., 1946; comd Northern Signals Area, 1947-50; jssc 1950; Inspector, Radio Services, 1950-52; Chief Signals Officer, 2nd TAF, 1952-54; Director of: Signals (I), Air Ministry, 1954-57; Guided Weapons (Air), Min. of Aviation, 1957-60. DL, Hertfordshire, 1966. *Recreation:* gardening. *Address:* Boonwood, Turpin's Chase, Oaklands Rise, Welwyn, Herts. *T:* Welwyn 5231. *Club:* Royal Air Force.

WRIGLEY, Dame Isobel; *see* Baillie, Dame Isobel.

WRIGLEY, Prof. Jack, CBE 1977; Professor of Education, since 1967 and Deputy Vice-Chancellor, since 1982, University of Reading; *b* 8 March 1923; *s* of Harry and Ethel Wrigley; *m* 1946, Edith Baron; two *s. Educ:* Oldham High Sch.; Manchester Univ. BSc, MEd (Manch.); PhD (Queen's, Belfast). Asst Mathematics Teacher: Stretford Grammar Sch., 1946-47; Chadderton Grammar Sch., 1948-50; Research Asst, Manchester Univ., 1950-51; Lectr in Educn: Queen's Univ., Belfast, 1951-57; Univ. of London Inst. of Educn, 1957-62; Research Adviser, Curriculum Study Gp in Min. of Educn, 1962-63; Prof. of Educn, Univ. of Southampton, 1963-67; Dir of Studies, Schools Council, 1967-75. Member: Bullock Cttee on Teaching of Reading and other uses of English, 1972-74; SSRC, Mem. Council and Chm. Educnl Res. Bd, 1976-81. *Publications:* (ed) The Dissemination of Curriculum Development, 1976; Values and Evaluation in Education, 1980; contrib. learned jls. *Recreations:* chess (Ulster Chess Champion, 1957), theatre, foreign travel. *Address:* 68 Grosvenor Road, Caversham, Reading, Berks RG4 0ES. *T:* Reading 471812.

WRIGLEY, Michael Harold, OBE 1971; HM Diplomatic Service; retired; *b* 30 July 1924; *e s* of Edward Whittaker Wrigley and Audrey Margaret Wrigley; *m* 1950, Anne Phillida Brewis; two *s* two *d. Educ:* Harrow; Worcester Coll., Oxford. Served War of 1939-45: Rifle Brigade, 1943-47. HM Diplomatic Service, 1950; served HM Embassies: Brussels, 1952-54; Bangkok, 1956-59; Office of Commissioner-Gen. for South-East Asia, Singapore, 1959-60; HM Embassy, Bangkok (again), 1961-64 and 1966-71; Counsellor, Kuala Lumpur, 1971-74; Counsellor, FCO, 1974-76. Mem., North Yorkshire CC, 1977-. *Recreations:* shooting, racing. *Address:* Ganton Hall, Scarborough, N Yorks. *T:* Sherburn 223. *Clubs:* Turf; Royal Bangkok Sports (Bangkok).

WRINTMORE, Eric George; Regional Chairman of Industrial Tribunals, since 1976; a Deputy Circuit Judge, since 1980; *b* 11 June 1928; *s* of Rev. F. H. and Muriel Wrintmore; *m* 1951, Jean Blackburn; two *s* one *d. Educ:* Stationers' Company's Sch.; King's Coll. London (LLB Hons). Called to Bar, Gray's Inn, 1955; full-time Chm., Industrial Tribunals, 1971. *Recreations:* sailing, squash, golf. *Address:* Regional Office of the Industrial Tribunals, 19/29 Woburn Place, WC1H 0LU. *T:* 01-632 4921/5. *Clubs:* Chichester Yacht; Ifield Golf and Country.

WRIXON-BECHER, Major Sir William F.; *see* Becher.

WROATH, John Herbert; a Recorder of the Crown Court, since 1978; County Court Registrar, since 1965; *b* 24 July 1932; *s* of Stanley Wroath and Ruth Ellen Wroath; *m* 1959, Mary Bridget Byrne; two *s* one *d. Educ:* Ryde Sch., Ryde, IoW. Admitted Solicitor, 1956; private practice, 1958-66; Registrar, Isle of Wight County Court, 1965; County Prosecuting Solicitor, 1966; full-time County Court Registrar, 1972. *Recreations:* sailing, bowling, reading, painting. *Address:* 25 Consort Road, Cowes, Isle of Wight. *T:* Cowes 292677. *Clubs:* Royal London Yacht; Cowes Island Sailing (Cowes).

WRONG, Henry Lewellys Barker; General Administrator, Barbican Centre for Arts and Conferences, since 1970; *b* Toronto, Canada, 20 April 1930; *s* of Henry Arkel Wrong and Jean Barker Wrong; *m* 1966, Penelope Hamilton Norman; two *s* one *d. Educ:* Trinity Coll., Univ. of Toronto (BA). Stage and business administration, Metropolitan Opera Assoc., New York, 1952-64; Director Programming, National Arts Center, Ottawa, 1964-68; Director, Festival Canada Centennial Programme, 1967. Centennial Medal, Govt of Canada, 1967. *Address:* Yew Tree House, Much Hadham, Herts SG10 6AJ. *T:* Much Hadham 2106; 12 Brandon Mews, Barbican, EC2. *Clubs:* Mark's; Badminton and Rackets (Toronto).

WROTH, Prof. Charles Peter, MA, PhD, DSc; FEng, MICE; FGS; Professor of Engineering Science, University of Oxford, since 1979; Fellow of Brasenose College, Oxford, since 1979; *b* 2 June 1929; *s* of Charles Wroth and of late Violet Beynon Wroth (*née* Jenour); *m* 1954, Mary Parlane Wroth (*née* Weller); two *s* two *d. Educ:* Marlborough Coll.; Emmanuel Coll., Cambridge (MA, PhD). Schoolmaster, Felsted Sch., 1953-54; Research Student, Univ. of Cambridge, 1954-58; Engineer, G. Maunsell & Partners, London, 1958-61; University of Cambridge: Lectr in Engineering, 1961-75; Reader in Soil Mechanics, 1975-79; Fellow of Churchill Coll., 1963-79. Chairman, British Geotechnical Soc., 1979, 1980, 1981. *Publications:* (with A. N. Schofield) Critical State Soil Mechanics, 1968; contribs to learned jls on soil mechanics and foundation engineering. *Recreations:* golf, Real tennis. *Address:* Department of Engineering Science, Parks Road, Oxford OX1 3PJ. *Clubs:* MCC; Hawks, Jesters.

WROTTESLEY, family name of Baron Wrottesley.

WROTTESLEY, 6th Baron *cr* 1838; **Clifton Hugh Lancelot de Verdon Wrottesley;** Bt 1642; *b* 10 Aug. 1968; *s* of Hon. Richard Francis Gerard Wrottesley (*d* 1970) (2nd *s* of 5th Baron) and of Georgina Anne (who *m* 1982, Lt-Col Jonathan L. Seddon-Brown), *er d* of Lt-Col Peter Thomas Clifton, *qv* ; *S* grandfather, 1977. *Heir: uncle* Hon. Mark Wrottesley, *b* 21 June 1951. *Address:* Dummer House, Basingstoke, Hants.

WUTTKE, Hans A., Dr jr; German banker; Executive Vice President, International Finance Corporation (World Bank Group), since 1981; *b* Hamburg, 23 Oct. 1923; *m* 1st, 1957, Marina M. Schorsch (marr. diss. 1976); two *s* two *d* ; 2nd, 1982, Jagoda M. Buíc. *Educ:* Univs of Cologne and Salamanca. Dresdner Bank AG, 1949-54; Daimler-Benz AG, 1954-61; Partner, M. M. Warburg-Brinckmann, Wirtz and Co., Hamburg, 1961-75; Executive Director, S. G. Warburg and Co. Ltd, London, 1962-75; Man. Dir, Dresdner Bank AG, Frankfurt, 1975-80; Chm., Deutsch-Süd-Amerikanische Bank AG, 1975-80. Mem. Board several European companies; Mem. Bd, German Development Co., Cologne, 1962-80; Chairman: East Asia Assoc., 1963-73; Comité Européen pour le Progrès Economique et Social (CEPES). *Address:* 1818 H Street NW, Washington, DC 20433, USA. *T:* (202) 676-0381.

WYATT, Arthur Hope, CMG 1980; HM Diplomatic Service; Counsellor (Economic and Commercial), Ankara, since 1981; *b* 12 Oct. 1929; *s* of Frank and Maggie Wyatt, Anderton, Lancs; *m* 1957, Barbara Yvonne, *d* of Major J. P. Flynn, late Indian Army; two *d. Educ:* Bolton School. Army, 1947-50; FO, 1950-52; 3rd Sec., Ankara, 1952-56; 2nd Sec., Phnom Penh, 1956-58; 2nd Sec., Ankara, 1958-61; FO, 1962-66; 1st Sec., Bonn, 1966-70; FCO, 1970-72; Counsellor and Head of Chancery, Lagos, 1972-75; Dep. High Comr, Valletta, 1975-76; Diplomatic Service Inspector, 1977-79; Counsellor (Econ. and Comm.) and Consul-Gen., Tehran, 1979. *Recreations:* golf, football, bridge, stamp collecting. *Address:* c/o Foreign and Commonwealth Office, SW1A 2AH. *T:* 01-839 7010.

WYATT, (Christopher) Terrel, FEng, FICE, FIStructE; Chairman, Costain Group Ltd, since 1980; *b* 17 July 1927; *s* of Lionel Harry Wyatt and Audrey Vere Wyatt; *m* 1970, Geertruida; four *s. Educ:* Kingston Grammar Sch.; Battersea Polytechnic (BScEng); Imperial Coll. (DIC). FICE 1963; FIStructE 1963; FEng 1980. Served RE, 1946-48. Charles Brand & Son Ltd, 1948-54; Richard Costain Ltd, 1955-: Dir, 1970-; Gp Chief Exec., 1975-80; Dep. Chm., 1979-80. *Recreation:* sailing. *Address:* 4 Martingales Close, Ham, Richmond, Surrey. *T:* 01-940 8614.

WYATT, David Joseph, CBE 1977; HM Diplomatic Service; Under Secretary on loan to Home Civil Service, since 1979; *b* 12 Aug. 1931; *s* of late Frederick Wyatt and of Lena (*née* Parr); *m* 1957, Annemarie Angst (*d* 1978); two *s* one *d. Educ:* Leigh Grammar Sch. National Service, RAF, 1950-52. Entered Foreign Service, 1949; Berne, 1954; FO, 1957-61; Second Sec., Vienna, 1961; First Sec., Canberra, 1965; FCO, 1969-71; First Sec., Ottawa, 1971; Counsellor, 1974; seconded Northern Ireland Office, Belfast, 1974-76; Counsellor and Head of Chancery, Stockholm, 1976-79. *Address:* c/o Foreign and Commonwealth Office, SW1.

WYATT, Gavin Edward, CMG 1965; Consultant; *b* 12 Jan. 1914; *s* of Edward A. Wyatt and Blanche M. Muller; *m* 1950, Mary Mackinnon, *d* of John Macdonald, Oban; one *s* one *d. Educ:* Newton Abbot Grammar Sch. CEng, FIEE 1951; FIMechE 1962. Engineer and Manager, East African Power & Lighting Co. Ltd, Tanganyika and Kenya, 1939-57; Chief Exec. Officer and General Manager, Electricity Corp. of Nigeria, 1957-62; Man. Director, East Africa Power & Lighting Co. Ltd, 1962-64; World Bank, 1965-76, retired as Dir, Projects Dept, Europe, Middle East and North Africa Region. *Recreations:* gardening, sailing, farming. *Address:* Holne Bridge Lodge, Ashburton, South Devon.

WYATT, Terrel; *see* Wyatt, C. T.

WYATT, Woodrow Lyle; Chairman, Horserace Totalisator Board, since 1976; *b* 4 July 1918; *y s* of late Robert Harvey Lyle Wyatt and Ethel Morgan; *m* 1957, Lady Moorea Hastings (marr. diss., 1966), *e d* of 15th Earl of Huntingdon, *qv* ; one *s* ; *m* 1966, Veronica, *widow* of Dr Laszlo Banszky; one *d. Educ:* Eastbourne Coll.; Worcester Coll., Oxford, MA. Served throughout War of 1939-45 (despatches for Normandy); Major, 1944. Founder and Editor, English Story, 1940-50; Editorial Staff, New Statesman and Nation, 1947-48; Weekly Columnist: Reynolds News, 1949-61; Daily Mirror, 1965-73; Sunday Mirror, 1973-. Began Panorama with Richard Dimbleby, 1955; under contract BBC TV, 1955-59; introduced non-heat-set web offset colour printing to England, 1962. MP (Lab), Aston Div. of Birmingham, 1945-55, Bosworth Div. of Leicester, 1959-70; Member of Parly Delegn to India, 1946; Personal Asst to Sir Stafford Cripps on Cabinet Mission to India, 1946; Parly Under-Sec. of State, and Financial Sec., War Office, May-Oct. 1951. Contested (Lab) Grantham Div. of Lincolnshire, 1955. Mem. Council, Zoological Soc. of London, 1968-71, 1973-77. *Publications:* The Jews at Home, 1950; Southwards from China, 1952; Into the Dangerous World, 1952; The Peril in Our Midst, 1956; Distinguished for Talent, 1958; Turn Again, Westminster, 1973; The Exploits of Mr Saucy Squirrel, 1976; The Further Exploits of Mr Saucy Squirrel, 1977; What's Left of the Labour Party?, 1977; To the Point, 1981. *Address:* 19 Cavendish Avenue, NW8. *T:* 01-286 9020.

WYBURN, Prof. George McCreath; Regius Professor of Anatomy, Glasgow University, 1948-72; *b* 11 March 1903; *s* of Robert Wyburn, Solicitor; *m* 1935, Jean Sharp; four *s* two *d. Educ:* High Sch., Glasgow; University of Glasgow. Graduated from Glasgow Univ., 1925; appointed to staff of Anatomy Dept, University of Glasgow, 1930; Senior Lecturer, Anatomy Dept, 1935. *Publications:* scientific publications in Journal of Anatomy, Proc. and Trans. of Royal Society of Edinburgh, Journal of Endocrinology, Journal of Surgery, Journal of Obstetrics and Gynecology, etc. *Address:* 7 Woodvale Avenue, Bearsden, Glasgow G61 2JS. *Club:* Glasgow Golf.

WYETH, Andrew Newell; artist; landscape painter; *b* 12 July 1917; *s* of Newell and Caroline Wyeth; *m* 1940, Betsy Merle James; two *s. Educ:* privately. First one man exhibn, William Macbeth Gall., NY, 1937; subsequent exhibitions include: Doll & Richards, Boston, 1938, 1940, 1942, 1944; Cornell Univ., 1938; Macbeth Gall., 1938, 1941, 1943, 1945; Art Inst. of Chicago, 1941; Museum of Modern Art, NYC, 1943; Dunn Internat. Exhibn, London, 1963; one man exhibns: M. Knoedler and Co., NYC, 1953, 1958; MIT, Cambridge, 1966; The White House, Washington DC, 1970; Tokyo, 1974; retrospectives: Metropolitan Museum, NY, 1976; RA, 1980 (1st by living American artist); Tokyo, 1974, 1979. Member: Nat. Inst. of Arts and Letters (Gold Medal, 1965); Amer. Acad. of Arts and Sciences; Amer. Acad. of Arts and Letters (Medal of Merit, 1947); Académie des Beaux-Arts, 1977; Hon. Mem., Soviet Acad. of the Arts, 1978. Presidential Medal of Freedom, 1963; Einstein Award, 1967. Hon. AFD: Colby Coll., Maine, 1954; Harvard, 1955; Dickinson, 1958; Swarthmore, 1958; Nasson Coll., Maine, 1963; Temple Univ., 1963; Maryland, 1964; Delaware, 1964; Northwestern Univ., 1964; Hon. LHD Tufts, 1963. *Address:* Chadds Ford, Pa 19317, USA.

WYFOLD, 3rd Baron, *cr* 1919, of Accrington, **Hermon Robert Fleming Hermon-Hodge;** 3rd Bt, *cr* 1902; Director, Robert Fleming Holdings, and other companies; *b* 26 June 1915; *s* of 2nd Baron and Dorothy (*d* 1976), *e d* of late Robert Fleming, Joyce Grove, Oxford; *S* father, 1942. *Educ:* Eton; Le Rosey, Switzerland. Captain, Grenadier Guards (RARO), 1939-65. *Heir:* none. *Address:* Sarsden House, Churchill, Oxfordshire. *T:* Kingham 226. *Clubs:* Carlton, Pratt's; Metropolitan (New York).

WYKEHAM, Air Marshal Sir Peter, KCB 1965 (CB 1961); DSO 1943 and Bar 1944; OBE 1949; DFC 1940 and Bar 1941; AFC 1951; technical consultant, since 1969; *b* 13 Sept. 1915; *s* of Guy Vane and Audrey Irene Wykeham-Barnes; family changed name by Deed Poll, 1955, from Wykeham-Barnes to Wykeham; *m* 1949, Barbara, *d* of J. B. Priestley, *qv* ;

two s one d. Educ: RAF Halton. Commissioned, 1937; served with fighter sqns, 1937–43 (commanded Nos 73, 257 and 23 sqns); commanded fighter sectors and wings, 1943–45; Air Ministry, 1946–48; Test Pilot, 1948–51; seconded to US Air Force, Korea, 1950; commanded fighter stations, 1951–53; NATO, 1953–56; staff appointments, 1956–59; AOC No 38 Gp, RAF, 1960–62; Dir, Jt Warfare Staff, Min. of Defence, Aug. 1962–64. Comdr, FEAF, 1964–66; Dep. Chief of Air Staff, 1967–69. FRAeS 1968; Fellow, Guild of Air Pilots and Air Navigators; FBIM. Chevalier, Order of Dannebrog, 1945; US Air Medal, 1950. Publications: Fighter Command, 1960; Santos-Dumont, 1962. Recreations: sailing, writing. Address: South Bank, 112 Lower Ham Road, Kingston-on-Thames, Surrey. Club: Royal Automobile.

WYKES, James Cochrane, MA (Cantab); b 19 Oct. 1913; m 1938, Cecile Winifred Graham, e d of J. Graham Rankin; one s one d. Educ: Oundle Sch.; Clare Coll., Cambridge (Open Exhibn in Classics). Asst Master, Loretto Sch., 1935–51; Headmaster, St Bees Sch., 1951–63; Head of Educational Broadcasting, ATV Network, 1963–66; Inner London Education Authority: Dir of Television, 1966–75; Television Adviser, 1975–78. Chm., Nat. Educnl Closed Circuit Television Assoc., 1970–72. Served War of 1939–45: Black Watch (RHR), 1940–44. Publication: Caesar at Alexandria, 1951. Recreations: walking, fishing, ornithology, music. Address: 20 Grosvenor Crescent, Edinburgh. T: 031-337 6585. Clubs: New (Edinburgh); MCC.

WYLD, Martin Hugh; Chief Restorer, National Gallery, since 1979; b 14 Sept. 1944; s of John Wyld and Helen Leslie Melville; one d. Educ: Harrow School. Assistant Restorer, National Gallery, 1966. Recreation: travel. Address: 21 Grafton Square, SW4 0DA. T: 01-720 2627. Clubs: Colony Room, MCC.

WYLDBORE-SMITH, Maj.-Gen. Sir (Francis) Brian, Kt 1980; CB 1965; DSO 1943; OBE 1944; General Officer Commanding, 44th Division (TA) and Home Counties District, 1965–68; Director, Conservative Board of Finance, since 1970; b 10 July 1913; s of Rev. W. R. Wyldbore-Smith and Mrs D. Wyldbore-Smith; m 1944, Hon. Molly Angela Cayzer, d of 1st Baron Rotherwick; one s four d. Educ: Wellington Coll.; RMA, Woolwich. Served Middle East, Italy, France and Germany, 1941–45; Military Adviser to CIGS, 1947–49; GSO1, 7 Armoured Div., 1951–53; Comd 15/19 King's Royal Hussars, 1954–56; IDC 1959; BGS Combat Development, 1959–62; Chief of Staff to Commander-in-Chief, Far East Command, 1962–64. Col, 15/19 Hussars, 1970–77. Recreations: hunting, shooting. Address: Grantham House, Grantham, Lincs. T: Grantham 4705. Clubs: Buck's, Naval and Military.

WYLIE, Rt. Hon. Lord; Norman Russell Wylie, PC 1970; VRD 1961; a Senator of the College of Justice in Scotland, since 1974; b 26 Oct. 1923; o s of late William Galloway Wylie and late Mrs Nellie Smart Wylie (née Russell), Elderslie, Renfrewshire; m 1963, Gillian Mary, yr d of late Dr R. E. Verney, Edinburgh; three s. Educ: Paisley Grammar Sch.; St Edmund Hall, Oxford (Hon. Fellow, 1975); Univs of Glasgow and Edinburgh. BA (Oxon) 1948; LLB (Glasgow) 1951. Admitted to Faculty of Advocates, 1952; QC (Scotland) 1964. Appointed Counsel to Air Ministry in Scotland, 1956; Advocate-Depute, 1959; Solicitor-General for Scotland, April–Oct. 1964. MP (C) Pentlands Div., Edinburgh, Oct. 1964–Feb. 1974; Lord Advocate, 1970–74. Trustee, Carnegie Trust for Univs of Scotland, 1976–; Chm., Scottish Nat. Cttee, English-Speaking Union of the Commonwealth, 1978–. Served in Fleet Air Arm, 1942–46; subseq. RNR; Lt-Comdr, 1954. Recreations: shooting, sailing. Address: 30 Lauder Road, Edinburgh EH9 2JF. T: 031-667 8377. Clubs: New (Edinburgh); Royal Highland Yacht.

WYLIE, Sir Campbell, Kt 1963; ED; QC; b NZ, 14 May 1905; m 1933, Leita Caroline Clark; no c. Educ: Auckland Grammar Sch.; Univ. of New Zealand. LLM 1st Class hons (Univ. of New Zealand), 1928; Barrister and Solicitor (New Zealand), 1928; Barrister-at-law, Inner Temple, 1950. Was in private practice, New Zealand, until 1940. War service, 1940–46 (despatches). Crown Counsel, Malaya, 1946; Senior Federal Counsel, 1950; Attorney-General: Barbados, 1951; British Guiana, 1955; The West Indies, 1956; Federal Justice, Supreme Court of The West Indies, 1959–62; Chief Justice, Unified Judiciary of Sarawak, N Borneo and Brunei, 1962–63; Chief Justice, High Court in Borneo, 1963–66; Law Revision Commissioner, Tonga, 1966–67; Chief Justice, Seychelles, 1967–69; Comr for Law Revision and Reform, Seychelles, 1970–71. QC 1952 (Barbados), 1955 (British Guiana). Address: River Lodge, 53 Stanhill Drive, Chevron Island, Surfers Paradise, Queensland 4217, Australia. T: 385532.

WYLIE, Derek; see Wylie, W. D.

WYLIE, Rt. Hon. Norman Russell; see Wylie, Rt Hon. Lord.

WYLIE, (William) Derek, FRCP, FRCS, FFARCS; Consulting Anaesthetist, St Thomas' Hospital, SE1; Consultant Anaesthetist, The Royal Masonic Hospital, 1959–82; Dean, St Thomas's Hospital Medical School, 1974–79; Adviser in Anaesthetics to the Health Service Commissioner, since 1974; b 24 Oct. 1918; s of Edward and Mabel Wylie, Huddersfield; m 1945, Margaret Helen, 2nd d of F. W. Toms, Jersey, CI (formerly Dep. Inspector-Gen., Western Range, Indian Police); two s two d. Educ: Uppingham Sch.; Gonville and Caius Coll., Cambridge (MA; MB, BChir); St Thomas's Hosp. Med. Sch. MRCP 1945, FFARCS 1953, FRCP 1967, FRCS 1972. Resident posts at St Thomas' Hosp., 1943–45. Served RAFVR, 1945–47, Wing Comdr. Apptd Hon. Staff, St Thomas' Hosp., 1946; Consultant, 1948; Sen. Cons.

Anaesthetist, 1966–79; Cons. Anaesthetist, The National Hosp. for Nervous Diseases, 1950–67. Examiner: FFARCS, 1959–72; FFARCSI, 1966–78. Mem., Bd of Faculty of Anaesthetists, RCS, 1960–70 (Dean, 1967–69; Vice-Dean, 1965–66; Bernard Johnson Adviser in Postgraduate Studies, 1959–67); Mem. Council, RCS, 1967–69; FRSM (Mem. Council, 1962–72; Hon. Treas., 1964–70; Pres., Section of Anaesthetics, 1963); Mem., Bd of Governors, St Thomas' Hosp., 1969–74; elected Mem. Council, Med. Defence Union (Vice-Pres., 1962–). Jenny Hartmann Lectr, Basle Univ., 1961; Clover Lectr and Medallist, RCS(Eng), 1974. Pres., Assoc. of Anaesthetists of GB and Ireland, 1980–82. Hon. Citizen of Dallas, USA, 1963; Hon. FFARCSI, 1971. Publications: The Practical Management of Pain in Labour, 1953; A Practice of Anaesthesia, 3rd edn, 1972 (jtly with Dr H. C. Churchill-Davidson); papers in specialist and gen. med. jls. Recreations: reading, travel, philately. Address: Court in Holmes, Forest Row, Sussex. T: Forest Row 3076. Club: Royal Automobile.

WYLLIE, Robert Lyon, CBE 1960; DL; JP; FCA; b 4 March 1897; s of Rev. Robert Howie Wyllie, MA, Dundee; m 1924, Anne, d of Thomas Rutherford, Harrington, Cumberland; two d. Educ: Hermitage Sch., Helensburgh; Queen's Park Sch., Glasgow. Served European War, 1914–18, with Lothians and Border Horse (France). Chartered Accountant, 1920; FCA 1949. Dir, Ashley Accessories Ltd; Life Vice-President, Cumberland Development Council Ltd. Formerly Chairman: W Cumberland Industrial Develt Co. Ltd; W Cumberland Silk Mills Ltd; Cumberland Develt Council Ltd; Whitehaven & Dist Disablement Advisory Cttee, and Youth Employment Cttee; Vice-Chm. W Cumberland Hosp. Management Cttee; Hon. Treas., NW Div., YMCA. JP 1951; DL 1957, Cumbria, formerly Cumberland. OStJ 1976. Recreation: fishing. Address: The Cottage, Papcastle, Cockermouth, Cumbria. T: Cockermouth 823292.

WYLLIE, William Robert Alexander; Chairman and Chief Executive, Asia Securities Ltd, Hong Kong, since 1981; Chairman, BSR, since 1982; b 9 Oct. 1932; s of Robert Wyllie and Marion Margaret Rae (née McDonald); m 1959, Ann Helena Mary (née Lewis); two s one d. Educ: Scarborough State Sch., Perth, W Australia; Perth Technical Coll. (qual. Automobile and Aeronautical Engrg). MIRTE. Sen. Exec./Br. Manager, Wearne Bros Ltd, Malaysia/Singapore, 1953–64; Man. Dir, Harpers Internat. Ltd, Hong Kong, 1964–73; Chm. and Chief Exec., China Engineers Holdings Ltd, Hong Kong, 1973–75; Deputy Chairman and Chief Executive: Hutchison Internat. Ltd, Hong Kong, 1975-Dec. 1977; Hutchison Whampoa Ltd, Hong Kong, Jan. 1978-June 1979 (Chm. and Chief Exec., 1979–80). FInstD 1980. Recreations: power boating, water skiing, Scuba diving, motor racing, restoration of vintage cars. Address: Asia Securities Ltd, Suite 1506, 15th Floor, Hutchison House, Hong Kong. T: (office) 5-264616; (home) 5-94946. Clubs: British Racing Drivers, Bentley Owners; Hong Kong, American, Australian, Shek O Country, Royal Hong Kong Jockey, Royal Hong Kong Yacht (Hong Kong).

WYMAN, John Bernard, MBE 1945; FRCS; FFARCS; Consultant Anaesthetist, Westminster Hospital, 1948–81; Dean, Westminster Medical School, 1964–81 (Sub-Dean, 1959–64); b 24 May 1916; s of Louis Wyman and Bertha Wyman; m 1948, Joan Dorothea Beighton; three s one d. Educ: Davenant Foundn Sch., London; King's Coll., London (Fellow 1980); Westminster Med. Sch. MRCS, LRCP 1941; DA 1945; FFARCS 1953; FRCS 1981. Military Service, 1942–46: Major RAMC; N Africa, Italy and India. Cons. Anaesthetist, Woolwich War Memorial Hospital Hosp., 1946–64; formerly Hon. Anaesthetist, Italian Hosp. Hunterian Prof., RCS, 1953. Member: Bd of Governors, Westminster Hosp., 1959–74; Sch. Council, Westminster Med. Sch., 1959–81; Croydon AHA, 1974–75; Kensington and Chelsea and Westminster AHA, 1975–81. Publications: chapters in med. text books and papers in gen. and specialist jls on anaesthesia and med. educn. Recreation: gardening. Address: Chilling Street Cottage, Sharpthorne, Sussex. T: Sharpthorne 810281. Club: Savage.

WYNDHAM, family name of **Baron Egremont and Leconfield.**

WYNDHAM, Sir Harold (Stanley), Kt 1969; CBE 1961; retired from Department of Education, New South Wales; b Forbes, NSW, Australia, 27 June 1903; s of late Stanley Charles Wyndham; m 1936, Beatrice Margaret, d of Rt. Rev. A. C. Grieve; three s. Educ: Fort Street Boys' High Sch.; Univ. of Sydney (MA Hons, Cl. I); Stanford Univ. (EdD). Lectr, Sydney Teachers' Coll., 1925-27 and 1934; Teacher, NSW Dept of Educn, 1928-32; Carnegie Fellow, Stanford, 1932–33; Head of Research and Guidance, NSW Dept of Educn, 1935–40; Inspector of Schools, 1940–41. Flt Lt (A&SD Br.), RAAF, 1942–43; Commonwealth Dept of Post-War Reconstruction, 1944–46 (Leader, Aust. Delegn, Constituent Meeting for UNESCO, London, 1945); Sec., NSW Dept of Educn, 1948–51; Dep. Dir-Gen. of Educn, 1951–52; Dir-Gen. and Permanent Head, Dept of Education, 1952–68, Macquarie Univ., Professorial Fellow, 1969–75, Hon. Professorial Fellow, 1976–. Mem. Aust. Delegn to: UNESCO, 1958 and 1966; Commonwealth Educn Conf., Oxford, 1959. Vis. Fellow to Canada, 1966; Fellow and Past-Pres., Aust. Coll. of educn; Mem., Nat. Library Council of Australia, 1962–73; Chm., Soldiers' Children Educn Bd, Repatriation Dept and Dept of Veterans' Affairs, 1964–. Publications: Class Grouping in the Primary School, 1932; Ability Grouping, 1934; articles in a number of professional jls. Recreations: music, gardening. Address: 3 Amarna Parade, Roseville, NSW 2069, Australia. T: 406-4129. Club: University (Sydney).

WYNDHAM-QUIN, family name of **Earl of Dunraven.**

WYNDHAM-QUIN, Captain Hon. Valentine Maurice; RN (retired); *b* 1890; *yr s* of 5th Earl of Dunraven, CB, DSO; *u* and *Heir-Pres.* of 7th Earl of Dunraven and Mount-Earl, *qv*; *m* 1919, Marjorie Elizabeth (*d* 1969), *d* of late Rt Hon. E. G. Pretyman; three *d. Educ:* Eton; HMS Britannia. Served European War, 1914-19, in command of destroyers of the Patrol Flotillas, Grand Fleet and Harwich Force; retired 1934; returned to Active Service, 1939-44, in command of HM Ships in Home Waters, the South Atlantic and Mediterranean Fleet (despatches 5 times); Naval Attaché, Buenos Aires, 1944-47; retired 1948. Chairman, Royal National Life Boat Institution, 1964-68. *Recreations:* hunting and shooting. *Clubs:* White's; Royal Yacht Squadron (Cowes).
See also Baron Egremont, Marquess of Salisbury.

WYNFORD, 8th Baron, *cr* 1829; **Robert Samuel Best;** MBE 1953; DL; Lt-Col Royal Welch Fusiliers; *b* 5 Jan. 1917; *e s* of 7th Baron and Evelyn (*d* 1929), *d* of late Maj.-Gen. Sir Edward S. May, KCB, CMG; *S* father, 1943; *m* 1941, Anne Daphne Mametz, *d* of late Maj.-Gen. J. R. Minshull Ford, CB, DSO, MC; *one s* two *d. Educ:* Eton; RMC, Sandhurst. 2nd Lieut, RWF, 1937; served BEF; GHQ Home Forces; North Africa (Croix de Guerre); Egypt; Italy; wounded, 1944; Instructor, Staff College, 1945-46; War Office, 1947-49; OC Depot, RWF, 1955-57; Instructor Joint Service Staff Coll., 1957-60; RARO 1960. DL Dorset, 1970. *Heir: s* Hon. John Philip Best [*b* 23 Nov. 1950; *m* 1981, Fenella Christian Mary, *o d* of Arthur Reginald Danks]. *Address:* Wynford House, Wynford Eagle, Dorchester, Dorset DT2 0ET. *TA* and *T:* Maiden Newton 20241. *Club:* Army and Navy.

WYNN, family name of **Baron Newborough.**

WYNN, Arthur Henry Ashford; Adviser on Standards, Department of Trade and Industry (formerly Ministry of Technology), 1965-71; *b* 22 Jan. 1910; *s* of late Prof. William Henry Wynn, MD, MSc; *m* 1938, Margaret Patricia Moxon; three *s* one *d. Educ:* Oundle Sch.; Trinity Coll., Cambridge (Entrance Scholar, Nat. Science and Mathematics; MA). Barrister-at-Law, Lincoln's Inn, 1939; Director of Safety in Mines Research Establishment, Ministry of Fuel and Power, 1948-55; Scientific Member of National Coal Board, 1955-65; Member: Advisory Council on Research and Development, Ministry of Power, 1955-65; Safety in Mines Research Advisory Board, 1950-65; Exec. Cttee, British Standards Institution, 1966-71; Advisory Council on Calibration and Measurement, 1967-71; Chairman: Standing Joint Cttee on Metrication, 1966-69; Adv. Cttee on Legal Units of Measurement, 1969-71. *Publications:* (with Margaret Wynn): The Protection of Maternity and Infancy in Finland, 1974; The Right of Every Child to Health Care in France, 1974; Nutrition Counselling in Canada, 1975; Prevention of Handicap of Perinatal Origin in France, 1976; Prevention of Preterm Birth, 1977; Prevention of Handicap and Health of Women, 1979; Prevention of Handicap of Early Pregnancy Origin, 1981; Lead and Human Reproduction, 1982. *Address:* 9 View Road, N6. *T:* 01-348 1470.

WYNN, Sir (Owen) Watkin W.; *see* Williams-Wynn.

WYNN, Terence Bryan; Editor, Liberal News, and Head of Liberal Party Organisation's Press Office, since 1977; *b* 20 Nov. 1928; *o s* of late Bernard Wynn and Elsie Wynn (*née* Manges); unmarried. *Educ:* St Cuthbert's Grammar Sch., Newcastle upon Tyne. Started as jun. reporter with Hexham Courant, Northumberland, 1945; Blyth News, 1947-48; Shields Evening News, 1948-50; Sunderland Echo, 1950-53; Reporter with Daily Sketch, 1953-58; News Editor, Tyne Tees Television, 1958, then Head of News and Current Affairs, 1960-66; Editorial Planning, BBC Television News, 1966-67; Sen. Press and Information Officer with Land Commn, 1967-71; Sen. Inf. Officer, HM Customs and Excise, 1971-72; Editor, The Universe, 1972-77. Helped to found and first Editor of Roman Catholic monthly newspaper, Northern Cross. Chm., Catholic Writers' Guild, 1967-70 (Hon. Vice-Pres., 1970); Judge for British Television News Film of the Year Awards, 1961-64; Mem. Mass Media Commn, RC Bishops' Conf. of England and Wales. *Publication:* Walsingham, a modern mystery play, 1975. *Recreations:* reading, writing, talking. *Address:* (office) 1 Whitehall Place, SW1A 2HE; Bosco Villa, 30 Queen's Road, South Benfleet, Essex. *T:* South Benfleet 2033. *Club:* Press.

WYNN-WILLIAMS, George, MB, BS London; FRCS; FRCOG; Surgeon, Chelsea Hospital for Women; Consulting Obstetrician to City of Westminster; Consulting Gynæcologist, Chelsea Hospital for Women; Consulting Obstetric Surgeon, Queen Charlotte's Hospital; Consulting Gynæcologist to the Civil Service; Teacher in Gynæcology and Obstetrics, London University; *b* 10 Aug. 1912; *er s* of William Wynn-Williams, MRCS, LRCP, and Jane Anderson Brymer, Caernarvon, N Wales; *m* 1943, Penelope, *o d* of 1st and last Earl Jowitt of Stevenage, PC, and Lesley McIntyre; two *s* one *d. Educ:* Rossall; King's Coll.; Westminster Hospital. MRCS, LRCP 1937; MB, BS (London) 1938; MRCOG 1941; FRCS 1943; FRCOG 1967. Alfred Hughes Anatomy Prize, King's Coll.; Chadwick Prize in Clinical Surgery, Forensic Medicine and Public Health Prizes, Westminster Hospital. Various appointments 1937-41; Chief Asst and Surgical Registrar and Grade I Surgeon, EMS, 1941-45; Acting Obst. and Gynæcol. Registrar, Westminster Hosp., 1941-46; Surgeon-in-Charge, Mobile Surg. Team to Portsmouth and Southampton, June-Oct. 1944; Chief Asst, Chelsea Hosp. for Women, 1946-47; Obst. Registrar, Queen Charlotte's Hosp., 1946-50; Cons.

Obstetrician, Borough of Tottenham; Cons. Gynæcologist, Weir Hosp. Surgical Tutor, Westminster Hosp., 1941-46; Obst. and Gynæcol. Tutor, Westminster Hosp., 1941-48; Lectr and Demonstrator to Postgrad. Students, Queen Charlotte's Hosp., 1946-50; Lectr to Postgrad. Students, Chelsea Women's Hosp., 1946-; Examiner, Central Midwives' Board; Recognized Lectr of London Univ.; Assoc. Examiner in Obst. and Gynæcol., Worshipful Co. of Apothecaries. Woodhull Lectr, Royal Instn, 1978. Member: BMA; Soc. for Study of Fertility; The Pilgrims. FRSM. *Publications:* (jtly) Queen Charlotte's Text Book of Obstetrics; contributions to medical journals, including Human Artificial Insemination, in Hospital Medicine, 1973; Infertile Patients with Positive Immune Fluorescent Serum, 1976; Spermatazoal Antibodies treated with Condom Coitus, 1976. *Recreations:* tennis, shooting, fishing. *Address:* 48 Wimpole Street, W1M 7DG. *T:* 01-487 4866; 39 Hurlingham Court, SW6; The Hall, Wittersham, Isle of Oxney, Kent. *Clubs:* Hurlingham, Chelsea Arts, English-Speaking Union, Oriental; Rye Golf.

WYNNE, Prof. Charles Gorrie, FRS 1970; BA, PhD; Senior Research Fellow, Imperial College, London, since 1978 (Director, Optical Design Group, 1960-78); Professor of Optical Design, University of London, 1969-78, now Emeritus; Consultant to the Royal Greenwich Observatory, Herstmonceux Castle, Sussex; *b* 18 May 1911; *s* of C. H. and A. E. Wynne; *m* 1937, Jean Richardson; two *s* one *d. Educ:* Wyggeston Grammar Sch., Leicester; Exeter Coll., Oxford (Scholar). Optical Designer, Taylor Taylor & Hobson Ltd, 1935-43; Wray (Optical Works) Ltd, 1943-60, latterly Director. Hon. Sec. (business), Physical Soc., 1947-60; Hon. Sec., Inst. of Physics and Physical Soc., 1960-66. Editor, Optica Acta, 1954-65. Thomas Young Medal, Inst. of Physics, 1971; Gold Medal, Royal Astronomical Soc., 1979; Rumford Medal, Royal Soc., 1982. *Publications:* scientific papers on aberration theory and optical instruments in Proc. Phys. Soc., Mon. Not. RAS, Astrophys. Jl, Optica Acta, etc. *Address:* Morar, Boreham Street, near Hailsham, Sussex. *T:* Herstmonceux 832234.

WYNNE, David; sculptor, since 1949; *b* Lyndhurst, Hants, 25 May 1926; *s* of Comdr Charles Edward Wynne and Millicent (*née* Beyts); *m* 1959, Gillian Mary Leslie Bennett (*née* Grant); two *s,* and one step *s* one step *d. Educ:* Stowe Sch.; Trinity Coll., Cambridge. FZS; FRSA. Served RN, 1944-47: minesweepers and aircraft carriers (Sub-Lieut RNVR). No formal art training. First exhibited at Leicester Galls, 1950, and at Royal Acad., 1952. One-man Exhibitions: Leicester Galls, 1955, 1959; Tooth's Gall., 1964, 1966; Temple Gall., 1964; Findlay Galls, New York, 1967, 1970, 1973; Covent Garden Gall., 1970, 1971; Fitzwilliam Museum, Cambridge, 1972; Pepsico World HQ, New York, 1976; retrospective, Cannizaro House, 1980; also various mixed exhibns. Large works in public places: Magdalen Coll., Oxford; Malvern Girls' Coll.; Civic Centre, Newcastle upon Tyne; Lewis's, Hanley; Ely Cathedral; Birmingham Cath.; Church of St Paul, Ashford Hill, Berks; Ch. of St Thomas More, Bradford-on-Avon; Mission Ch., Portsmouth; Fountain Precinct, Sheffield; Bowood House, Wilts; London: Albert Bridge; British Oxygen Co., Hammersmith; Cadogan Place Gardens and Cadogan Sq.; Crystal Palace Park; Guildhall; Longbow House; St Katharine-by-the-Tower; Taylor Woodrow; Wates Ltd, Norbury; also London Road, Kingston-upon-Thames; Elmsleigh Centre, Staines; IPC HQ, Sutton; USA: Ambassador Coll., Texas, and Ambassador Coll., Calif; Atlantic Richfield Oil Co., New Mexico; Lakeland Meml Hosp., Wis; First Fed. Savings, Mass; Pepsico World HQ, Purchase, NY; Playboy Hotel and Casino, Atlanta City, NJ; Sarasota, Fla; also Perth, WA. Bronze portrait heads include: Sir Thomas Beecham, 1956; Sir John Gielgud, 1962; Yehudi Menuhin, 1963; The Beatles, 1964; Kokoschka, 1965; Sir Alec Douglas-Home, 1966; Robert, Marquess of Salisbury, 1967; The Prince of Wales, 1969; Lord Baden-Powell, 1971; Virginia Wade, 1972; The Queen, 1973; King Hassan of Morocco, 1973; Air Chief Marshal Lord Dowding, 1974; The Begum Aga Khan, 1975; Pele, 1976; Lord Hailsham, 1977; Prince Michael of Kent, 1977; Earl Mountbatten of Burma, 1981; Paul Daniels, 1982; Jackie Stewart, 1982. Designed: Common Market 50 pence piece of clasped hands, 1973; the Queen's Silver Jubilee Medal, 1977 (with new effigy of the Queen wearing St Edward's Crown). *Relevant publications:* T. S. R. Boase, The Sculpture of David Wynne 1949-1967, 1968; Graham Hughes, The Sculpture of David Wynne 1968-1974, 1974; David Wynne, The Messenger, 1982. *Recreations:* active sports, poetry, music. *Address:* 12 South Side, SW19. *T:* 01-946 1514. *Clubs:* Garrick, Hurlingham; Leander (Henley-on-Thames); 1st and 3rd Trinity Boat; St Moritz Tobogganing; The Royal Tennis Court (Hampton Court Palace).

WYNNE, Col J. F. W.; *see* Williams-Wynne.

WYNNE-EDWARDS, Vero Copner, CBE 1973; MA, DSc; FRS 1970; FRSE, FRSC; Regius Professor of Natural History, University of Aberdeen, 1946-74, Vice Principal, 1972-74; *b* 4 July 1906; 3rd *s* of late Rev. Canon John Rosindale Wynne-Edwards and Lilian Agnes Streatfeild; *m* 1929, Jeannie Campbell, *e d* of late Percy Morris, Devon County Architect; one *s* one *d. Educ:* Leeds Grammar Sch.; Rugby Sch.; New Coll., Oxford. 1st Class Hons in Natural Science (Zoology), Oxford, 1927; Senior Scholar of New Coll., 1927-29; Student Probationer, Marine Biological Laboratory, Plymouth, 1927-29; Assistant Lecturer in Zoology, Univ. of Bristol, 1929-30; Asst Prof. of Zoology, McGill Univ., Montreal, 1930-44; Associate Prof., 1944-46. Canadian representative, MacMillan Baffin Island expedition, 1937; Canadian Fisheries Research Board expeditions to Mackenzie River, 1944, and Yukon Territory, 1945; Baird Expedition to Central Baffin Island, 1950. Visiting Prof. of Conservation, University of Louisville, Kentucky, 1959,

Commonwealth Universities Interchange Fellow New Zealand, 1962; Leverhulme Emeritus Fellowship, 1978-80. Jt Editor, Journal of Applied Ecology, 1963-68. Member: Nature Conservancy, 1954-57; Red Deer Commn (Vice-Chm.), 1959-68; Royal Commn on Environmental Pollution, 1970-74; President: British Ornithologists' Union, 1965-70; Scottish Marine Biological Assoc., 1967-73; Section D, British Assoc., 1974; Chairman: NERC, 1968-71; DoE and Scottish Office Adv. Cttees on Protection of Birds, 1970-78; Scientific Authority for Animals, DoE, 1976-77. For. Mem., Societas Scientiarum Fennica, 1965; Hon. Mem., British Ecological Soc., 1977. FIBiol 1980. Hon. DUniv Stirling, 1974; Hon. LLD Aberdeen, 1976. Godman-Salvin Medal, British Ornithologists' Union, 1977; Neill Prize, RSE, 1977; Frink Medal, Zoological Soc., 1980. *Publications:* Animal Dispersion in relation to social behaviour, 1962; scientific papers on ornithology (esp. oceanic birds), animal populations. *Recreation:* ski-ing. *Address:* Ravelston, William Street, Torphins, Via Banchory, Aberdeenshire AB3 4JR. *Club:* Naval and Military.

WYNNE-JONES, family name of **Baron Wynne-Jones.**

WYNNE-JONES, Baron, *cr* 1964, of Abergele (Life Peer); **William Francis Kenrick Wynne-Jones;** Pro-Vice-Chancellor, 1965-68, Professor of Chemistry, Head of the School of Chemistry, 1956-68, University of Newcastle upon Tyne; Chancellor, Newcastle upon Tyne Polytechnic, since 1976; *b* 8 May 1903; *y* s of late Rev. T. J. Jones, Shaistaganj, India; *m* 1st, 1928, Ann Drummond (*d* 1969); two *d*; 2nd, 1972, Rusheen Preston, *d* of Mrs Neville Preston. *Educ:* Monkton Combe Sch., Bath; University College of Wales, Aberystwyth; Balliol Coll., Oxford. Research Asst and Lectr in Physical Chemistry, Univ. of Bristol; International Research Fellow, Univ. of Copenhagen; Lectr in Chemistry, Univ. of Reading; Leverhulme Research Fellow, Princeton Univ.; Prof. of Chemistry, University College, Dundee; Head of Chemistry Div., Royal Aircraft Establishment, Farnborough. Chm., Scientific and Technical Cttee, N Atlantic Assembly, 1973-77. Chm. of Governors, Newcastle upon Tyne Polytechnic, 1973-76. Coal Carbonisation Science Lectr and Medallist, 1972. Hon. DSc Bristol, 1968. *Publications:* articles in scientific journals. *Address:* Carlyle House, 16 Chelsea Embankment, SW3.

WYNNE MASON, Walter, CMG 1967; MC 1941; *b* 21 March 1910; *y* s of late George and Eva Mason, Wellington, NZ; *m* 1945, Freda Miller, *d* of late Frederick and Lilian Miller, Woodford, Essex; two *s* one *d*. *Educ:* Scots Coll., NZ; Victoria University College, NZ (MA). NZ Govt Education Service 1934-39; served NZ Army, 1939-46; NZ War Histories, 1947-48; NZ Diplomatic Service, 1949-54; Chief, Middle East, Commonwealth War Graves Commission, 1954-56, Dir of External Relations and Deputy to Dir-Gen., 1956-70; Mem., Sec. of State for Environment's panel of independent Inspectors, 1972-77. *Publication:* Prisoners of War, 1954. *Recreations:* lawn tennis, theatre, music. *Address:* Keene House, Hillier Road, Guildford, Surrey. *T:* Guildford 572601.

WYNTER, Sir Luther (Reginald), Kt 1977; CBE 1966 (OBE 1962, MBE 1950); MD; FICS; private medical practitioner, Antigua, since 1927; *b* 15 Sept. 1899; *s* of Thomas Nathaniel Wynter and Pauline Jane Wynter; *m* 1927, Arah Adner Busby. *Educ:* Wolmers High Sch., Jamaica; Coll. of City of Detroit, USA; Dalhousie Univ. (MD, ČM); Moorfields Hosp. (DOMS). FICS (Ophthalmology) 1969. Gen. med. practitioner, Hamilton, Ont, Canada, 1925-27; actg govt radiologist, Antigua, 1937-51; ophthalmologist, Antigua, 1953-64, hon. consulting ophthalmologist, 1966-. Nominated Mem., Antigua Govt, 1956-66; Senator and Pres. of Senate, 1967-68 (often acting as Governor or Dep. to Governor). Hon. LLD: Univ. of the West Indies, 1972; Dalhousie, 1975. *Recreation:* learning to play bridge. *Address:* PO Box 154, St John's, Antigua, West Indies. *T:* (office) St John's 22027, (home) Hodges Bay 22102. *Clubs:* (Hon. Life Mem.) Mill Reef, (Hon. Mem.) Lions (Antigua).

WYSS, Sophie; Concert Singer; *b* 1897; 2nd *d* of Oscar and Helène Wyss, La Neuveille, Switzerland; *m* 1925, Captain Arnold Gyde; two *s*. *Educ:* Conservatoires de Genève et Bâle. Operatic debut, Geneva, 1922; recitals and chamber concerts for BBC, 1927-64; concerts throughout Great Britain, in Europe and in Australia. First performances include: Britten's Les Illuminations, Our Hunting Fathers; all Roberto Gerhard's vocal works; works of Lennox Berkeley, Alan Rawsthorne, Elizabeth Maconchy, Racine Fricker, Matyas Seiber, William Wordsworth and many other composers. Inspired many of these composers to write French as well as English songs and to re-arrange innumerable folk songs into modern idiom. *Address:* Foley House, 18 Upper Bognor Road, Bognor Regis, West Sussex PO21 1JD.

Y

YALE, David Eryl Corbet, FBA 1980; Reader in English Legal History, Cambridge University, since 1969; Fellow, Christ's College, since 1950; *b* 31 March 1928; *s* of Lt-Col J. C. L. Yale and Mrs Beatrice Yale (*née* Breese); *m* 1959, Elizabeth Ann, *d* of C. A. B. Brett, Belfast; two *s*. *Educ:* Malvern Coll., Worcs; Queens' Coll., Cambridge (BA 1949, LLB 1950, MA 1953).

Called to the Bar, Inner Temple, 1951; Asst Lectr and Lectr in Law, Cambridge Univ., 1952-69. Literary Dir, Selden Soc. *Publications:* various, mainly in field of legal history. *Recreation:* fishing. *Address:* Christ's College, Cambridge. *T:* Cambridge 67641.

YALOW, Rosalyn Sussman, PhD; Senior Medical Investigator, Veterans Administration, since 1972; *b* 19 July 1921; *d* of Simon Sussman and Clara (*née* Zipper); *m* 1943, Aaron Yalow; one *s* one *d*. *Educ:* Hunter Coll., NYC (AB Physics and Chemistry, 1941); Univ. of Ill, Urbana (MS Phys. 1942, PhD Phys. 1945). Diplomate, Amer. Bd of Radiol., 1951. Asst in Phys., Univ. of Ill, 1941-43, Instr, 1944-45; Lectr and Temp. Asst Prof. in Phys., Hunter Coll., 1946-50. Veterans Admin Hospital, Bronx, NY: Consultant, Radioisotope Unit, 1947-50; Physicist and Asst Chief, Radioisotope Service, 1950-70 (Actg Chief, 1968-70); Chief, Nuclear Medicine Service, 1970-80; Dir, Solomon A. Berson Res. Lab., 1973-; Chief, VA Radioimmunoassay Ref. Lab., 1969-. Consultant, Lenox Hill Hosp., NYC, 1952-62. Res. Prof., Dept of Med., Mt Sinai Sch. of Med., 1968-74, Distinguished Service Prof., 1974-79; Distinguished Prof.-at-Large, Albert Einstein Coll. of Med., Yeshiva Univ., NY, 1979-. Chm., Dept of Clin. Sciences, Montefiore Hosp. and Med. Centre, Bronx, NY, 1980-. IAEA Expert, Instituto Energia Atomica, Brazil, 1970; WHO Consultant, Radiation Med. Centre, India, 1978-; Sec., US Nat. Cttee on Med. Physics, 1963-67. Member: President's Study Gp on Careers for Women, 1966-; Med. Adv. Bd, Nat. Pituitary Agency, 1968-71; Endocrinol. Study Sect., Nat. Insts of Health, 1969-72; Cttee for Evaluation of NPA, Nat. Res. Council, 1973-74; Council, Endocrine Soc., 1974- (Koch Award, 1972; Pres., 1978); Bd of Dirs, NY Diabetes Assoc., 1974-. Member: Editorial Adv. Council, Acta Diabetologica Latina, 1975-77; Ed. Adv. Bd, Encyclopaedia Universalis, 1978-; Ed. Bd, Mt Sinai Jl of Medicine, 1976-79; Ed. Bd, Diabetes, 1976-79. Fellow: NY Acad. of Sciences (Chm., Biophys. Div., 1964-65; A. Cressy Morrison Award in Nat. Sci., 1975); Radiation Res. Soc.; Amer. Assoc. of Physicists in Med.; Biophys. Soc.; Amer. Diabetes Assoc. (Eli Lilly Award, 1961; Banting Medal, 1978); Amer. Physiol Soc.; Soc. of Nuclear Med. Associate Fellow in Phys., Amer. Coll. of Radiol. Member: Nat. Acad. of Sciences; Amer. Acad. Arts and Sciences; Foreign Associate, French Acad. of Medicine. Hon. DSc and Hon. DHumLett from Amer. univs and med. colls. Nobel Prize in Physiology or Medicine, 1977; VA Exceptional Service Award, 1975 and 1978. Has given many distinguished lectures and received many awards and prizes from univs and med. socs and assocs. *Publications:* over 300 papers and contribns to books, research reports, proceedings of conferences and symposia on radioimmunoassay of peptide hormones and related subjects, since 1944. *Address:* 3242 Tibbett Avenue, Bronx, NY 10463, USA. *T:* (212) KI 3-7792.

YAMEY, Prof. Basil Selig, CBE 1972; FBA 1977; Professor of Economics, University of London, since 1960; Member (part-time), Monopolies and Mergers Commission, 1966-78; *b* 4 May 1919; *s* of Solomon and Leah Yamey; *m* 1948, Helen Bloch (*d* 1980); one *s* one *d*. *Educ:* Tulbagh High Sch.; Univ. of Cape Town; LSE. Lectr in Commerce, Rhodes Univ., 1945; Senior Lectr in Commerce, Univ. of Cape Town, 1946; Lectr in Commerce, LSE, 1948; Associate Prof. of Commerce, McGill Univ., 1949; Reader in Economics, Univ. of London, 1950. Trustee: National Gall., 1974-81; Tate Gall., 1979-81; Mem. Council, National Trust, 1979-81; Member: Cinematograph Films Council, 1969-73; Cttee of Management, Courtauld Inst., 1981-; Cttee of Management, Warburg Inst., 1981-. *Publications:* Economics of Resale Price Maintenance, 1954; (jt editor) Studies in History of Accounting, 1956; (with P. T. Bauer) Economics of Under-developed Countries, 1957; (jt editor) Capital, Saving and Credit in Peasant Societies, 1963; (with H. C. Edey and H. Thomson) Accounting in England and Scotland, 1543-1800, 1963; (with R. B. Stevens) The Restrictive Practices Court, 1965; (ed) Resale Price Maintenance, 1966; (with P. T. Bauer) Markets, Market Control and Marketing Reform: Selected Papers, 1968; (ed) Economics of Industrial Structure, 1973; (jt editor) Economics of Retailing, 1973; (jt editor) Debits, Credits, Finance and Profits, 1974; (with B. A. Goss) Economics of Futures Trading, 1976; Essays on the History of Accounting, 1978; (jt editor) Stato e Industria in Europa: Il Regno Unito, 1979; articles on economics, economic history and law in learned journals. *Address:* 36 Hampstead Way, NW11. *T:* 01-455 5810.

YANG, Chen Ning; physicist, educator; Einstein Professor and Director, Institute for Theoretical Physics, State University of New York at Stony Brook, New York, since 1966; *b* Hofei, China, 22 Sept. 1922; *s* of Ke Chuen Yang and Meng Hwa Lo; *m* 1950, Chih Li Tu; two *s* one *d*. Naturalized 1964. *Educ:* National Southwest Associated Univ., Kunming, China (BSc), 1942; University of Chicago (PhD), 1948. Institute for Advanced Study, Princeton, NJ: Member, 1949-55; Prof. of Physics, 1955-65; several DSc's from universities. Member of Board: Rockefeller Univ., 1970-76; AAAS, 1976-80; Salk Inst., 1978-; Ben Gurion Univ.; Member: Amer. Phys. Soc.; Nat. Acad. Sci.; Amer. Philos. Soc., Sigma Xi; Brazilian, Venezuelan and Royal Spanish Acads of Sci. Nobel Prize in Physics, 1957; Einstein Commemorative Award in Sciences, 1957; Rumford Prize, 1980. *Publications:* contrib. to Physical Review, Reviews of Modern Physics. *Address:* (home) 14 Woodhull Cove, Setauket, New York 11733, USA; (office) State University of New York at Stony Brook, New York 11790, USA.

YANG, Ti-Liang; Hon. Mr Justice Yang; Justice of Appeal, Hong Kong, since 1980; Judge of the High Court, Hong Kong, since 1975; *b* 30 June 1929; *s* of late Shao-nan Yang and Elsie (*née* Chun); *m* 1954, Eileen Barbara (*née* Tam); two *s*. *Educ:* The Comparative Law Sch. of China; Soochow Univ.,

Shanghai; UCL (LLB Hons 1953). Called to the Bar, Gray's Inn, 1954. Magistrate, Hong Kong, 1956; Sen. Magistrate, 1963; Rockefeller Fellow, London Univ., 1963-64; District Judge, Dist Court, 1968; Puisne Judge, Supreme Court, 1975. Chairman: Kowloon Disturbances Claims Assessment Bd, 1966, Compensation Bd, 1967; Commn of Inquiry into the Rainstorm Disasters, 1972; Commn of Inquiry into the Leung Wing-sang Case, 1976. Mem., Chinese Lang. Cttee (Chm. Legal Sub-cttee), 1970. Former Vice Chm., Bd of Trustees, Chung Chi Coll. Vice Chm., Hong Kong Sea Cadet Corps; Hon. President: Hong Kong Scouts Assoc.; Hong Kong Discharged Prisoners' Aid Soc.; Soc. Against Child Abuse. Adviser, Hong Kong Juvenile Care Centre. Former Council Member: Univ. of Hong Kong; Chinese Univ. of Hong Kong; Hong Kong Baptist Coll.; Chairman: University and Polytechnic Grants Cttee; Chief Justice's Working Party on Voir Dire Proceedings and Judges' Rules, 1979. Past Member: Law Reform Commn (Chm., Sub-Cttee on law relating to homosexuality), 1980; Commn of Inquiry into the MacLennan Case, 1980. *Publications:* contrib. Internat. and Comparative Law Qly. *Recreations:* philately, reading, walking, oriental ceramics, travelling, music. *Address:* Supreme Court, Hong Kong. *T:* Hong Kong 5-239728. *Clubs:* Hong Kong, Hong Kong Country, Royal Hong Kong Jockey, Hong Kong Gun (Hong Kong).

YANKOV, Alexander; Professor of International Law, Sofia State University, since 1968; Deputy Minister for Foreign Affairs, Bulgaria, since 1976; *b* 22 June 1924; *m* 1949, Eliza; one *s* one *d. Educ:* Sofia State Univ. Law Sch. (PhD Internat. Law); Hague Acad. of Internat. Law. Asst Prof. of Internat. Law, 1951-54, Associate Prof. 1957-64, Sofia State Univ. Sec., Internat. Union of Students, Prague, 1954-57; Counsellor, Perm. Mission of Bulgaria to UN, mem. delegns to sessions of UN Gen. Assembly, 1965-68; Vice-Chm., UN Cttee on Peaceful Uses of Sea-bed, 1968-73; Ambassador of Bulgaria to Court of St James's, 1972-76; Ambassador and Perm. Rep. to UN, 1977-80. Mem., Perm. Court of Arbitration at The Hague, 1971; Mem. Court of Arbitration to Bulgarian Chamber of Commerce, 1970-. Pres., 8th Assembly, IMCO, 1973-75; Head of Bulgarian Delegn, 3rd UN Conf. on Law of the Sea; Chm., 3rd Cttee, UN Conf. on Law of the Sea, NY 1973, Caracas 1974, Geneva 1975, NY 1976, 1977, 1982; Chm., 4th Cttee, London Conf. on Marine Pollution by Ships, 1973; Member: Exec. Council, Internat. Law Assoc., 1973-; Internat. Law Commn, 1977-. Order 9 Sept. 1944, 1959; Order of Freedom of the People, 1960; Order of Cyril and Methodius, 1962; Order of People's Republic of Bulgaria, 1974 (all Bulgaria). *Publications:* The European Collective Security System, 1958; Reservations to the Declaration of Acceptance of Compulsory Jurisdiction of the International Court of Justice, 1961; The Peace Treaty with the Two German States and its Legal Effects, 1962; Principles of International Law as Applied to the Treaty Practice of Bulgaria, 1964; The United Nations: Legal Status and International Personality, 1965; Exploration and Uses of the Sea-bed: a new legal framework, 1970; United Nations Declaration on Principles of Friendly Relations and Progressive Development of International Law, 1971; United Nations and Development of International Trade Law, 1971, etc. *Recreations:* theatre, swimming. *Address:* Sofia State University, Ruski 15, Sofia, Bulgaria.

YAPP, Sir Stanley Graham, Kt 1975; Leader, West Midlands County Council, 1973-77; Member, Birmingham City Council, later Birmingham District Council, 1961-77 (Leader, 1973); *s* of late William and of Elsie Yapp; *m* Carol Ann; one *s* one *d.* Member, West Midlands Economic Planning Council (Chm., Transport Cttee); Member many bodies both local and national, inc.: Vice-Chm. LAMSAC; Member: Local Govt Trng Board; Nat. Jt Councils on pay and conditions; AMA; BR Adv. Bd, Midlands and N Western Reg., 1977-79; Chm., West Midlands Planning Authorities Conf., 1973-75, Vice-Chm. 1975-77. Governor, BFI, 1977-79. *Publications:* contribs to Local Government Chronicle, Municipal Journal, Rating and Valuation. *Recreations:* astronomy, vintage public transport, brass-banding.

YARBOROUGH, 7th Earl of, *cr* 1837; **John Edward Pelham;** Baron Yarborough, Baron Worsley, 1794; Major Grenadier Guards, retired 1952; Vice Lord-Lieutenant (formerly Vice-Lieutenant), Lincolnshire, since 1964; JP; *b* 2 June 1920; *s* of 6th Earl of Yarborough; *S* father, 1966; *m* 1957, Mrs Ann Duffin, *d* of late John Herbert Upton, Ingmire Hall, Yorkshire; one *s* three *d. Educ:* Eton; Trinity College, Cambridge. Contested (C) Grimsby, 1955. President: Midland Area, British Legion, 1959-60, East Midland Area, 1960-62; Nat. Exec. Council, British Legion, 1962-73; Patron, E Midlands Area, 1974-. High Sheriff of Lincolnshire, 1964; Hon. Col, 440 Light AD Regt, RA (TA), 1965-69, Humber Regt, RA T&AVR, 1969-71; Dep. Hon. Col, 2nd Bn, Yorkshire Volunteers, 1971-72. JP, Parts of Lindsey, 1965. *Recreations:* shooting, sailing. *Heir: s* Lord Worsley, *qv. Address:* Brocklesby Park, Habrough, South Humberside DN37 8PL. *T:* Roxton 60242. *Clubs:* Cavalry and Guards, Boodle's; Royal Yacht Squadron.

YARBURGH-BATESON; *see* de Yarburgh-Bateson, family name of Baron Deramore.

YARDE, Air Vice-Marshal Brian Courtenay, CVO 1953; CBE 1949; psa; *b* 5 September 1905; *s* of late John Edward Yarde, Crediton, Devon, and Bedford; *m* 1927, Marjorie, *d* of late W. Sydney Smith, Bedford; two *d. Educ:* Bedford School; RAF College, Cranwell (Sword of Honour), 1926. Served War of 1939-45 in France, Malaya, Middle East, UK (despatches thrice); Deputy Director of Bomber Operations, Air Ministry, 1945; Senior Director, RAF Staff College, 1946-47; Station Commander, Gatow, 1947-49 (Berlin

Airlift); Provost Marshal and Chief of the Royal Air Force Police, 1951-53; Air Officer Commanding No. 62 Group, 1953-54. Air Commodore, 1951; Acting Air Vice-Marshal, 1954; Commandant-General of the Royal Air Force Regiment and Inspector of Ground Combat Training, 1954-57, retired. Chairman, Courtenay Caterers Ltd, Andover. Officer American Legion of Merit. *Address:* Wiremead, East Cholderton, Andover, Hants SP11 8LR. *T:* Weyhill 2265.

YARDE-BULLER, family name of **Baron Churston.**

YARDLEY, Prof. David Charles Miller; Chairman, Commission for Local Administration in England, since 1982; *b* 4 June 1929; *s* of Geoffrey Miller Yardley and Doris Woodward Yardley (*née* Jones); *m* 1954, Patricia Anne Tempest Olver; two·s two *d. Educ:* The Old Hall Sch., Wellington; Ellesmere Coll., Shropshire; Univ. of Birmingham (LLB); Univ. of Oxford (MA, DPhil). Called to Bar, Gray's Inn, 1952. RAF Flying Officer (nat. service), 1949-51. Bigelow Teaching Fellow, Univ. of Chicago, 1953-54; Fellow and Tutor in Jurisprudence, St Edmund Hall, Oxford, 1953-74; CUF Lectr, Univ. of Oxford, 1954-74; Sen. Proctor, Univ. of Oxford, 1965-66; Barber Prof. of Law, Univ. of Birmingham, 1974-78; Head of Dept of Law, Politics and Economics, Oxford Poly., 1978-80; Rank Foundn Prof. of Law, University Coll. at Buckingham, 1980-82. Visiting Prof. of Law, Univ. of Sydney, 1971. Constitutional Consultant, Govt of W Nigeria, 1956; Chm., Thames Valley Rent Tribunal, 1963-; Vice-Pres., Cambs Chilterns and Thames Rent Assessment Panel, 1966-; Oxford City Councillor, 1966-74; Chm. of Governors, St Helen's Sch., Abingdon, 1967-81; Chm., Oxford Area Nat. Ins. Local Appeal Tribunal, 1969-. *Publications:* Introduction to British Constitutional Law, 1960, 5th edn, 1978; A Source Book of English Administrative Law, 1963, 2nd edn, 1970; The Future of the Law, 1964; Geldart's Elements of English Law, 7th edn, 1966, 9th edn, 1983; Hanbury's English Courts of Law, 4th edn, 1967; Hanbury and Yardley, English Courts of Law, 5th edn, 1979; Principles of Administrative Law, 1981; (with I. N. Stevens) The Protection of Liberty, 1982. *Recreations:* lawn tennis, squash racquets, theatre, cats. *Address:* 9 Belbroughton Road, Oxford OX2 6UZ. *T:* Oxford 54831.

YARMOUTH, Earl of; Henry Jocelyn Seymour; *b* 6 July 1958; *s* and *heir* of 8th Marquess of Hertford, *qv.*

YARNOLD, Rev. Edward John, SJ; DD; Tutor in Theology, Campion Hall, Oxford, since 1964 (Master, 1965-72; Senior Tutor, 1972-74); *b* 14 Jan. 1926; *s* of Edward Cabré Yarnold and Agnes (*née* Deakin). *Educ:* St Michael's Coll., Leeds; Campion Hall, Oxford (MA); Heythrop College (STL). Taught classics at St Francis Xavier's Coll., Liverpool, 1954-57; ordained, 1960; taught classics at St Michael's Coll., Leeds, 1962-64. Sarum Lectr, Univ. of Oxford, 1972-73. Assoc. Gen. Sec., Ecumenical Soc. of Blessed Virgin Mary, 1975-; Mem., Anglican-Roman Catholic Internat. Commn, 1970-81. Lectr (part-time), Heythrop Coll., London, 1978-80. Order of St Augustine, 1981. *Publications:* The Theology of Original Sin, 1971; The Awe-Inspiring Rites of Initiation, 1972; The Second Gift, 1974; (with H. Chadwick) Truth and Authority, 1977; (ed jtly and contrib.) The Study of Liturgy, 1978; They are in Earnest, 1982; articles in learned jls. *Recreation:* opera. *Address:* Campion Hall, Oxford. *T:* Oxford 726811 or 40861.

YARNOLD, Patrick; HM Diplomatic Service; Counsellor (Economic and Commercial), Brussels, since 1980; *b* 21 March 1937; *s* of late Leonard Francis Yarnold and Gladys Blanche Yarnold (*née* Merry); *m* 1961, Caroline, *er d* of Andrew J. Martin; two *d. Educ:* Bancroft's School. HM Forces, 1955-57. Joined HM Foreign (now Diplomatic) Service, 1957; served: FO, 1957-60; Addis Ababa, 1961-64; Belgrade, 1964-66; FO (later FCO), 1966-70; 1st Sec., Head of Chancery, Bucharest, 1970-73; 1st Sec. (Commercial), Bonn, 1973-76; FCO, 1976-79. *Recreations:* travel, photography, walking, genealogy, local history, reading, etc. *Address:* c/o Foreign and Commonwealth Office, SW1. *Club:* Cercle Gaulois (Brussels).

YARROW, Dr Alfred, FFCM; Senior Principal Medical Officer, Department of Health and Social Security, since 1977; *b* 25 May 1924; *s* of Leah and step *s* of Philip Yarrow; *m* 1953, Sheila Kaufman; two *d. Educ:* Hackney Downs Grammar Sch.; Edinburgh Univ. (MB, ChB); London Sch. of Hygiene and Trop. Medicine (Hons DPH). Foundn FFCM 1972. Dep. Area MO, Tottenham and Hornsey, 1955-60; Area MO, SE Essex, 1960-65; MOH, Gateshead, 1965-68; Dir, Scottish Health Educn Unit, 1968-73; SMO, DHSS, 1973-77. Temp. Consultant, WHO, 1975-76. Brit. Council Lectr, 1975; Council of Europe Fellow, 1978. *Publications:* So Now You Know About Smoking, 1975; scientific papers on demography, epidemiology, preventive medicine and health educn. *Recreations:* walking, travelling, reading. *Address:* 67 Wychwood Avenue, Edgware, Mddx HA8 6TQ. *T:* 01-952 1979.

YARROW, Sir Eric Grant, 3rd Bt, *cr* 1916; MBE (mil.) 1946; DL; Chairman: Yarrow & Co. Ltd, since 1962; Yarrow-Admiralty Research Department Ltd, since 1969; Y-ARD (Australia) Pty Ltd, since 1968; Yarrow Africa Maritime Consultancy (Pty) Ltd, since 1969; Director: Standard Life Assurance Co., since 1958; Yarrow (Africa) (Holdings) (Pty) Ltd, since 1949; Clydesdale Bank Ltd, since 1962 (Joint Deputy Chairman, since 1975); Croftinloan (Holdings) Ltd, since 1959; *b* 23 April 1920; *o s* of Sir Harold Yarrow, 2nd Bt and 1st wife, Eleanor Etheldreda (*d* 1934); *S* father, 1962; *m* 1st, 1951, Rosemary Ann (*d* 1957), *yr d* of H. T. Young, Roehampton, SW15; one *s*; 2nd, 1959, Annette Elizabeth Françoise (marr. diss. 1975), *d* of late A. J. E.

Steven, Ardgay; three s (including twin s); 3rd, 1982, Mrs Joan Botting, d of R. F. Masters, Piddinghoe, Sussex. *Educ:* Marlborough Coll.; Glasgow Univ. Served apprenticeship, G. & J. Weir Ltd. Served Burma, 1942-45; Major RE, 1945. Asst Manager Yarrow & Co., 1946; Dir, 1948; Man. Dir, 1958-67. Mem. Council, RINA, 1957-; Vice-Pres., 1965; Hon. Vice-Pres., 1972. Mem., General Cttee, Lloyd's Register of Shipping, 1960; Prime Warden, Worshipful Co. of Shipwrights, 1970; Deacon, Incorporation of Hammermen of Glasgow, 1961-62; Retired Mem. Council, Institution of Engineers & Shipbuilders in Scotland. Pres., Scottish Convalescent Home for Children, 1957-70; Mem. Exec. Cttee Princess Louise Scottish Hospital at Erskine (Chm., 1980-). OStJ. DL Renfrewshire, 1970. *Recreations:* golf, shooting. *Heir: e s* Richard Grant Yarrow, *b* 21 March 1953. *Address:* Cloak, Kilmacolm, Renfrewshire PA13 4SD. *T:* Kilmacolm 2067. *Clubs:* Army and Navy; Royal Scottish Automobile.

YARWOOD, Dame Elizabeth (Ann), DBE 1969; JP; DL; *b* 25 Nov. 1900; *d* of Henry and Margaret Gaskell; *m* 1918, Vernon Yarwood; two *s. Educ:* Whitworth Street High Sch., Manchester. Councillor, Manchester City Council, 1938-74, Alderman, 1955-74; Lord Mayor of Manchester, 1967-68. Director: Manchester & Salford Co-operative Society Ltd, 1955; Manchester Ship Canal, 1964. Vice-Pres., Manchester County Girl Guides Assoc. Freeman of the City of Manchester, 1974. Hon. MA Manchester, 1978. JP Manchester, 1945; DL Lancs, 1974. *Recreation:* reading. *Address:* 80 Yew Tree Lane, Manchester M23 0DR. *T:* 061-998 3179.

YATES, Alfred, FBPsS; Director, National Foundation for Educational Research in England and Wales, since 1972; *b* 17 Nov. 1917; *s* of William Oliver Yates and Frances Yates; *m* 1943, Joan Mary Lawrence-Fellows; one *s* one *d. Educ:* Farnworth Grammar Sch.; Sheffield Univ. (BA); Oxford Univ. (MA); QUB (MEd). FBPsS 1957. Served War, Army, 1940-46: Captain, REME. Schoolmaster, Launceston Coll., Cornwall, 1939-40; Lectr, QUB, 1946-51; Sen. Res. Officer, NFER, 1951-59; Sen. Tutor, Dept of Educnl Studies, Oxford Univ., 1959-72. FCP 1981. *Publications:* Admission to Grammar Schools, 1957; Grouping in Education, 1966; An Introduction to Educational Measurement, 1968; The Role of Research in Educational Change, 1971; The Organisation of Schooling, 1971. *Recreations:* reading, theatre, watching Association football and cricket. *Address:* 46 London Road, Wheatley, Oxford. *T:* Wheatley 3315.

YATES, Anne; see Yates, E. A.

YATES, (Edith) Anne, (Mrs S. J. Yates), CBE 1972; Vice-Chairman, East Midlands Airport, since 1977; *b* 21 Dec. 1912; *d* of William Blakeman and Frances Dorothea (*née* Thacker); *m* 1935, Stanley James Yates; two *s* one *d. Educ:* Barrs' Hill Girls' Sch., Coventry. County Councillor, 1955, County Alderman, 1966, Notts; Chm., Notts CC, Feb. 1968-March 1974. Chairman: E Midlands Sports Council, 1972-77; Midlands Tourist Bd, 1971-76; Indep. Chm., Nat. Cttee on Recreation Management Trng, 1976-; Member: Sports Council, 1971-74; E Midlands Council of Sport and Recreation, 1977-; MSC, 1974-76; East Midlands Regional MSC, 1977-; English Tourist Bd, 1975-78; Nat. Water Council, 1973-79 (Chm., Water Training Cttee, 1973-79). *Recreations:* reading, music, theatre. *Address:* Manor Close, Rolleston, Newark, Notts. *T:* Southwell 813362.

YATES, Frank, CBE 1963; ScD; FRS 1948; Honorary Scientist, Rothamsted Experimental Station, since 1968 (formerly Head of Statistics Department and Agricultural Research Statistical Service, and Deputy Director); *b* 1902; *s* of Percy and Edith Yates, Didsbury, Manchester; *m* 1939, Pauline (*d* 1976), *d* of Vladimir Shoubersky; *m* 1981, Ruth Hunt, *d* of William James Hunt, Manchester. *Educ:* Clifton; St John's Coll., Cambridge. Research Officer and Mathematical Adviser, Gold Coast Geodetic Survey, 1927-31; Rothamsted Experimental Station, 1931, Dept of Statistics, 1933, Agric. Res. Statistical Service, 1947, Dep. Dir, 1958; Scientific Adviser to various mins, UNO, FAO, 1939-; Wing Comdr (Hon.) RAF, 1943-45; Mem. UN Sub-Commn on Statistical Sampling, 1947-52. Sen. Res. Fellow, Imperial Coll., 1969-74; Sen. Vis. Fellow, Imperial Coll., 1974-77. Pres., British Computer Society, 1960-61; Pres., Royal Statistical Society, 1967-68. Royal Medal of the Royal Society, 1966. Hon. DSc London, 1982. *Publications:* Design and Analysis of Factorial Experiments, 1937; (with R. A. Fisher) Statistical Tables for Biological, Medical and Agricultural Research, 1938 (6th edn 1963); Sampling Methods for Censuses and Surveys, 1949 (4th edn 1981); Experimental Design: Selected Papers, 1970. Numerous scientific papers. *Recreation:* mountaineering. *Address:* Stackyard, Rothamsted, Harpenden, Herts. *T:* Harpenden 2732. *Club:* Athenæum.

YATES, Ian Humphrey Nelson; General Manager and Chief Executive, The Press Association Ltd, since 1975; *b* 24 Jan. 1931; *s* of James Nelson Yates and Martha (*née* Nutter); *m* 1956, Daphne J. Hudson, MCSP; three *s. Educ:* Lancaster Royal Grammar Sch.; Canford Sch., Wimborne. Royal Scots Greys, Germany and ME (National Service Commn), 1951-53. Management Trainee, Westminster Press Ltd, 1953-58 (Westmorland Gazette, and Telegraph & Argus, Bradford);Asst to Man. Dir, King & Hutchings Ltd, Uxbridge, 1958-60; Bradford and District Newspapers: Asst Gen. Man., 1960; Gen. Man., 1964; Man. Dir, 1969-75; Dir, Westminster Press Planning Div., 1969-75. President: Young Newspapermen's Assoc., 1966; Yorks Newspaper Soc., 1968. Member: Council, Newspaper Soc., 1970-75; Council, Commonwealth Press Union, 1977-. *Recreations:* walking, reading, theatre. *Address:* Woodbury, 11 Holmwood Close, East Horsley, Surrey. *T:* East Horsley 3873.

YATES, Rt. Rev. John; see Gloucester, Bishop of.

YATES, William; business consultant; Administrator of Christmas Island, Indian Ocean, since 1982; *b* 15 September 1921; *er s* of late William Yates and of Mrs John T. Renshaw, Burrells, Appleby, Westmorland; *m* 1st, 1946, Hon. Rosemary (marr. diss. 1955), *yr d* of 1st Baron Elton; two *d* (one *s* decd); 2nd, 1957, Camilla, *d* of late E. W. D. Tennant, Orford House, Ugley, Bishop's Stortford; four *s. Educ:* Uppingham; Hertford Coll., Oxford. Served War, 1940-45, North Africa and Italy; Captain The Bays, 1945. Shropshire Yeomanry, 1956-67. Appointed Legal Officer to report on State lands in Department of Custodian's Office in Tripoli, Libya, 1951. MP (C) The Wrekin Division of Shropshire, 1955-66. Myron Taylor Lectures in International Affairs, Cornell Univ., USA, 1958 and 1966. MP (L) Holt, Vic, Aust. Commonwealth, 1975-80; Mem. Liberal Party Parly Cttee for Defence and Foreign Affairs, 1975-80; Mem., Cttee of Privileges, House of Representatives, 1977-80. Mem., Inst. of Internat. Affairs, Victoria. *Address:* Administrator's Residence, Christmas Island, Australia 6798; 17 Cypress Grove, Dandenong, Victoria 3175, Australia. *Clubs:* Cavalry and Guards, St Stephen's Constitutional; Commonwealth (Canberra).

YATES-BELL, John Geoffrey, FRCS; retired; Consultant Urologist to King's College Hospital; *b* 6 Dec. 1902; *s* of John Bell, FRCVS, and Matilda Bell, London; *m* 1932, Winifred Frances Hordern (*née* Perryman) (*d* 1979); one *s* one *d. Educ:* St Dunstan's College; King's College, London. MB, BS London 1926; FRCS 1930. King's College Hospital: House Surgeon, 1926-28; Surgical Registrar, 1928-29; Junior Urological Surgeon, 1930; Hon. Urological Surgeon, 1937. Emeritus Urological Surgeon, Epsom and Leatherhead Hosps. President, Urological Section, RSM, 1952 (Vice-Pres. 1939); Fellow Internat. Soc. of Urology, 1934; Founder Member, British Assoc. of Urological Surgeons (Hon. Treas., 1954-56). *Publications:* Kidney and Ureter, Stone (British Surgical Practice), 1950; Mythology of Greece and Rome, 1980; articles in British Jl of Urology, Jl of Urology, Medical Press, Lancet, etc. *Recreation:* lawn tennis. *Address:* Westane, Tyrrells Wood, Leatherhead, Surrey KT22 8QJ. *T:* Leatherhead 73170.

YEABSLEY, Sir Richard Ernest, Kt 1950; CBE 1943; FCA; *b* 16 May 1898; *m* 1923, Hilda Maude Willson; one *d. Educ:* Alperton School. Served European War, 3rd Bn (City of London Regiment) Royal Fusiliers, 1914-19. Independent member of Hosiery Working Party, 1945; Member: Committee to examine the organisation and methods of distribution of Building Materials, 1946; Committee to enquire into the resources of Minerals in the United Kingdom, 1946; Supreme Court Cttee on Practice and Procedure, 1947; Cttee on Resale Price Maintenance, 1947; Monopolies and Restrictive Practices Commn, 1949-56. Accountant Adviser to BoT, 1942-68; formerly Sen. Partner, Hill, Vellacott & Co., and Hill, Vellacott & Bailey, Chartered Accountants, retd March 1963; Pres. Society of Incorporated Accountants, 1956-57. *Address:* 9 Alverton Hall, West Cliff Road, Bournemouth. *T:* Bournemouth 766293. *Club:* Royal Automobile.

YEATES, W(illiam) Keith, MD, MS; FRCS; Consultant Urologist, Newcastle University Hospitals, since 1951; Hon. Lecturer in Urology, Newcastle University, since 1974; Consultant Adviser in Urology to Department of Health, since 1978; Hon. Senior Lecturer, Institute of Urology, University of London, since 1981; *b* 10 March 1920; *s* of William Ravensbourne Yeates and Winifred (*née* Scott); *m* 1946, Jozy McIntyre Fairweather; one *s* one *d. Educ:* Glasgow Academy; Whitley Bay Grammar Sch.; King's Coll., Newcastle, Univ. of Durham. Visiting Professor: Universities of: Baghdad, 1974, 1978; California, LA, 1976; Texas, Dallas, 1976; Delhi, 1977; Cairo, 1978; Kuwait, 1980; Guest Prof., New York section, Amer. Urolog. Assoc., 1977; Principal Guest Lectr, Urolog. Soc. of Australasia, 1977; Guest Lecturer: Italian Urolog. Assoc., 1978; Yugoslavian Urolog. Assoc., 1980; Vis. Lectr, Rio de Janeiro, 1975; Mem., Internat. Soc. of Urology, 1958-; Foundation Mem., European Assoc. of Urology, 1974; Hon. Member: Urolog. Soc. of Australasia, 1977; Canadian Urological Assoc., 1981; President: N of England Surgical Soc., 1971-72; British Assoc. of Urological Surgeons, 1980-82 (Vice-Pres., 1978-80). Editor, British Journal of Urology, 1973-78 (Chm., Editorial Cttee, 1978-). *Publications:* various chapters in text books on Urology, particularly on bladder dysfunction and male infertility. *Recreation:* urology. *Address:* 22 Castleton Grove, Jesmond, Newcastle upon Tyne NE2 2HD. *T:* Newcastle upon Tyne 814030.

YEEND, Sir Geoffrey (John), Kt 1979; CBE 1976; Secretary, Department of the Prime Minister and Cabinet, since 1978 and Secretary to Cabinet, since 1976, Australia; *b* 1 May 1927; *s* of Herbert J. Yeend and Ellen Yeend; *m* 1952, Laurel Mahoney; one *s* one *d. Educ:* Canberra High Sch.; Canberra University Coll., Melbourne Univ. (BCom). Served War, RAE, AIF, 1945-46. Dept of Post War Reconstruction, 1944-49; Prime Minister's Dept, 1950; Private Sec. to Prime Minister, 1952-55; Asst Sec., Aust. High Commn, London, 1958-60; Prime Minister's Dept: Asst Sec., 1961; First Asst Sec., 1967; Dep. Sec., 1972; Under Sec., Dept of the Prime Minister and Cabinet, 1976. Aust. Eisenhower Fellow, 1971. Internat. Hockey Fedn: Councillor, 1959-66; Vice-Pres., 1967-76; Member of Honour, 1979. *Recreations:* golf, fishing. *Address:* 1 Loftus Street, Yarralumla, ACT 2600, Australia. *T:* 062 732066. *Clubs:* Commonwealth (Canberra); Royal Canberra Golf.

YELLOWLEES, Sir Henry, KCB 1975 (CB 1971); Chief Medical Officer, Department of Health and Social Security, Department of Education and Science and Home Office, since 1973; *b* 1919; *s* of late Henry Yellowlees,

OBE, Psychiatrist of Bath. *Educ:* Stowe Sch.; University Coll., Oxford. MA, BM, BCh Oxon 1950. FRCP 1971 (MRCP 1966, LRCP 1950), MRCS Eng., FFCM 1972. Pilot, RAF, 1941-45. Resident Med. Officer, Mddx Hosp., London, 1951-54; Asst Senior Med. Officer, South West Regional Hosp. Bd, 1954-59; Dep. Sen. Admin. Med. Officer, North West Metropolitan Regional Hosp. Bd, 1959-63; Principal Med. Officer, Min. of Health, 1963-65 (seconded); Senior Principal Med. Officer, 1965-67 (established); Dep. Chief Med. Officer, 1967-72, 2nd Chief Med. Officer, 1972-73, Dept of Health and Social Security. Member: Medical Research Council, 1974-; Gen. Medical Council, 1979-. Hon. FRCP Glasgow, 1974; Hon. FRCPsych, 1977; Fellow Brit. Inst. of Management, 1974. *Address:* Alexander Fleming House, Elephant and Castle, SE1 6BY.

YEMM, Prof. Edmund William, BA, DPhil Oxon; Melville Wills Professor of Botany, University of Bristol, 1955-74, Emeritus Professor 1974; *b* 16 July 1909; *s* of William H. Yemm and Annie L. Brett; *m* 1935, Marie Solari; one *s* three *d. Educ:* Wyggeston School, Leicester; Queen's College, Oxford. Foundation, Schol., Queen's Coll., 1928; Christopher Welch Schol., 1931. Major, REME, 1942-45. Research Fellow, Queen's Coll., 1935-38; Lecturer, Univ. of Bristol, 1939-49; Reader in Botany, Univ. of Bristol, 1950-55; Pro-Vice-Chancellor, Bristol Univ., 1970-73. Fellowship, Rockefeller Foundation, 1954; Vis. Prof., Western Reserve Univ., 1966-67. *Publications:* scientific papers in Proc. Royal Soc., New Phytologist, Biochemical Jl, Jl of Ecology, Jl of Experimental Botany. *Recreations:* cricket, gardening; formerly football (Oxford Univ. Assoc. Football Blue, 1929-31). *Address:* The Wycke, 61 Long Ashton Road, Bristol BS18 9HW. *T:* Long Ashton 2258.

YENDELL, Rear-Adm. William John, CB 1957; RN, retired; *b* 29 Dec. 1903; *e s* of late Charles Yendell; *m* 1937, Monica Duncan; one *d. Educ:* RN Colleges Osborne and Dartmouth. Qualified Gunnery Officer, 1929; commanded HM Ships: Bittern, 1938; Shah, 1943-45; Glasgow, 1950; Superb, 1950. Director of Naval Ordnance, 1951-54; Assistant Chief of Naval Staff (Warfare), 1954-57. Naval ADC 1954-. Comdr, 1937; Captain, 1945. *Recreations:* painting and most games. *Address:* The Bell Cottage, Newtonmore, Inverness-shire. *T:* Newtonmore 344. *Club:* Royal Naval and Royal Albert Yacht (Portsmouth).

YEO, Douglas; Director, Shell Research Ltd, Thornton Research Centre, since 1980; *b* 13 June 1925; *s* of Sydney and Hylda Yeo; *m* 1947, Joan Elisabeth Chell; two *d. Educ:* Secondary Sch., St Austell; University Coll., Exeter (BSc London). Expedn on locust control, Kenya, 1945. HMOCS, 1948-63; Tropical Pesticides Research Inst., Uganda and Tanzania, 1948-61 (Scientific Officer, 1948-51, Sen. Scientific Officer, 1951-57, Prin. Scientific Officer, 1957-61). Internat African Migratory Locust Control Organisation, Mali: on secondment, 1958, 1960; Dir and Sec. Gen., 1961-63. Shell Research Ltd: Research Dir, Woodstock Agricultural Research Centre, 1963-69, Dir, 1969-76; Dir, Biosciences Lab., Sittingbourne, 1976-80. FIBiol. *Publications:* papers in Bulletin Ent. Res., Bull. WHO, Anti-Locust Bull., Qly Jl Royal Met. Soc., Jl Sci. Fd. Agric., Plant Protection Confs, etc. *Recreations:* sailing, fishing. *Address:* Shell Research Ltd, Thornton Research Centre, PO Box No 1, Chester, Cheshire CH1 3SH. *Club:* Royal Corinthian Yacht (Burnham or Crouch).

YEO, Kok Cheang, CMG 1956; MD; MB; BS; DPH; DTM&H; *b* 1 April 1903; *s* of Yeo Kim Hong; *m* Florence, *d* of late Sir Robert Ho-tung, KBE; one *s* two *d. Educ:* Hong Kong University; Cambridge University; London School of Hygiene and Tropical Medicine. MB, BS, Hong Kong, 1925, MD, 1930; DTM&H (England) 1927; DPH, Cambridge, 1928. Assistant Medical Officer of Health, Hong Kong, 1928; Lecturer and Examiner in public health, Hong Kong University, 1936-37; Official JP 1938; Chinese Health Officer, senior grade, 1939-47; Deputy Director of Health Services, and Vice-Chairman of Urban Council, 1947-50; Deputy Director of Medical and Health Services, 1950-52; member of Legislative Council, Hong Kong, 1951-57; Director of Medical and Health Services, Hong Kong, 1952-58; Professor of Social Medicine, Hong Kong University, 1953-58; retd 1958. *Address:* 25 Beverley Gardens, Woodmancote, Cheltenham, Glos GL52 4QD. *T:* Bishops Cleeve 4674.

YEO, Timothy Stephen Kenneth; Director, Spastics Society, since 1980; *b* 20 March 1945; *s* of late Dr Kenneth John Yeo and Norah Margaret Yeo; *m* 1970, Diane Helen Pickard; one *s* one *d. Educ:* Charterhouse; Emmanuel Coll., Cambridge. Director, Worcester Engineering Co. Ltd, 1975-. Hon. Treasurer, International Voluntary Service, 1975-78. Trustee, African Palms, 1970-. *Recreation:* skiing. *Address:* 12 Park Crescent, W1N 4EQ. *T:* 01-636 5020. *Club:* Royal St George's (Sandwich).

YEOMAN, Prof. Michael Magson, PhD; FRSE; Regius Professor of Botany, University of Edinburgh, since 1978; Dean of the Faculty of Science, Edinburgh University, since 1981; *b* 16 May 1931; *s* of Gordon Yeoman and Mabel Ellen (*née* Magson), Newcastle upon Tyne; *m* 1962, Erica Mary Lines; two *d. Educ:* Gosforth Grammar Sch.; King's Coll., Univ. of Durham (BSc 1952, MSc 1954, PhD 1960); FRSE 1980. National Service, Royal Corps of Signals, 1954-56. Demonstrator in Botany, King's Coll., Newcastle upon Tyne, 1957-59; Edinburgh University: Lectr in Botany, 1960; Sen. Lectr, 1968; Reader, 1973. Member: Governing Bodies, Nat. Vegetable Res. Stn and Scottish Plant Breeding Stn; Editorial Bds of Jl of Experimental Botany, Plant Science Letters, and New Phytologist. *Publications:* (ed) Cell Division in

Higher Plants, 1976; contrib. scientific jls; chapters, articles and revs in books. *Recreations:* military history, photography, gardening, walking. *Address:* 9 Glenlockhart Valley, Edinburgh EH14 1DE. *T:* 031-443 8540.

YERBURGH, family name of **Baron Alvingham.**

YERBY, Frank Garvin; Novelist; *b* 5 September 1916; *s* of Rufus Garvin Yerby and Wilhelmina Smythe; *m* 1956, Blanca Calle Pérez; two *s* two *d* of former marriage. *Educ:* Haines Institute; Paine College; Fisk Univ.; Univ. of Chicago. Teacher, Florida Agricultural and Mechanical Coll., 1939; Southern Univ. (Baton Rouge, Louisiana), 1940-41; War work: laboratory technician, Ford Motor Company, Detroit, 1941-44; Ranger Aircraft, New York, 1944-45; writer since 1944; O. Henry Award for short story, 1944. *Publications:* The Foxes of Harrow, 1946; The Vixens, 1947; The Golden Hawk, 1948; Pride's Castle, 1949; Floodtide, 1950; A Woman Called Fancy, 1951; The Saracen Blade, 1952; The Devil's Laughter, 1953; Benton's Row, 1954; The Treasure of Pleasant Valley, 1955; Captain Rebel, 1956; Fairoaks, 1957; The Serpent and the Staff, 1958; Jarrett's Jade, 1959; Gillian, 1960; The Garfield Honor, 1961; Griffin's Way, 1962; The Old Gods Laugh, 1964; An Odor of Sanctity, 1965; Goat Song, 1967; Judas, My Brother, 1968; Speak Now, 1969; The Man from Dahomey, 1970; The Girl from Storyville, 1972; The Voyage Unplanned, 1974; Tobias and the Angel, 1975; A Rose for Ana Maríia, 1976; Hail the Conquering Hero, 1977; A Darkness at Ingraham's Crest, 1978. *Recreations:* photography, painting. *Address:* c/o Wm Morris Agency, 1350 Avenue of the Americas, New York, NY 10019, USA. *Clubs:* Authors Guild (New York); Real Sociedad Hipica Española (Madrid).

YOCKLUNN, Sir John (Soong Chung), KCVO 1977; Kt 1975; National Librarian of Papua New Guinea, since 1975; *b* Canton, China, 5 May 1933; *s* of late Charles Soong Yocklunn and Wui Sin Yocklunn, formerly of W Australia; *m* 1981, Patricia Ann Mehegan. *Educ:* Northam High Sch., W Australia; Univ. of W Australia (BA); Aust. Nat. Univ. (BA); Univ. of Sheffield (MA). ALA; ALAA. Dept of the Treasury, Canberra, 1959-63; Nat. Library of Australia, Canberra, 1964-67; Librarian-in-Charge, Admin Coll. of Papua New Guinea, Port Moresby, 1967-69; Exec. Officer, Public Service Board of Papua New Guinea, 1969-70; Librarian, Admin Coll., 1970-72; Principal Private Sec. to Chief Minister, 1972-73; study in UK, under James Cook Bicentenary Schol., 1973-74; on return, given task of organising a national library; Chm., PNG Honours and Awards Cttee, 1975-. Vice-Pres., Pangu Pati, 1968-72; Nat. Campaign Manager for Pangu Pati for 1972 general elections in Papua New Guinea; Treasurer, Pangu Pati, 1973-79. Asst Dir, Visit of Prince of Wales to PNG, 1975; Dir, Visits of the Queen and Prince Philip to PNG, 1977 and 1982. *Publications:* The Charles Barrett Collection of Books relating to Papua New Guinea, 1967, 2nd edn 1969; articles on librarianship and politics in various jls and encyclopedias. *Recreations:* book collecting, languages, cooking. *Address:* PO Box 1821, Boroko, Papua New Guinea. *T:* (office) Port Moresby 256200; (home) Port Moresby 258998.

YOFFEY, Joseph Mendel, DSc, MD, FRCS; Visiting Professor, Hebrew University of Jerusalem, since 1969; Professor of Anatomy, University of Bristol, 1942-67, now Professor Emeritus; *b* 10 July 1902; *s* of Rabbi Israel Jacob Yoffey and Pere Jaffe; *m* 1940, Betty Gilfis, LLB; three *d. Educ:* Manchester Grammar School; Univ. of Manchester. Leech Research Fellow, University of Manchester, 1926-27; Research Scholar, BMA, 1928-29; House Surgeon, Manchester Royal Infirmary, 1929-30; Asst Lectr in Anatomy, Univ. of Manchester, 1930; Senior Lectr in Anatomy, University College of South Wales and Monmouthshire, Cardiff; Hunterian Prof., RCS England, 1933 and 1940; Fellow of Rockefeller Foundn, 1937-39. Visiting Professor: Univ. of Washington, 1958; Univ. of Calif., San Francisco, 1967-68; John Curtin Sch. of Medical Research, ANU, 1968-69. Hon. Life Mem., Reticulendotheliol Soc., 1978; Hon. Mem., Amer. Assoc. of Anatomists, 1980. John Hunter Triennial Medal, RCS, 1968. Hon. LLD Manchester, 1973. Knight First Class of the Order of the Dannebrog (Denmark), 1959. *Publications:* Quantitative Cellular Hæmatology, 1960; Bone Marrow Reactions, 1966; (with Dr F. C. Courtice) Lymphatics, Lymph and the Lymphomyeloid Complex, 1970; Bone Marrow in Hypoxia and Rebound, 1973; numerous scientific papers. *Recreations:* music, walking, modern Hebrew. *Address:* 1 Rehov Degania, Beth Hakerem, Jerusalem, Israel. *T:* Jerusalem 525738.

YONG NYUK LIN; Member, Presidential Council for Minority Rights, Singapore; *b* Seremban, Malaya, 24 June 1918; *s* of late Yong Thean Yong and Chen Shak Moi; *m* 1939, Kwa Geok Lan; two *d. Educ:* Raffles Coll., Singapore. Science Master, King George V Sch., Seremban, Malaya, 1938-41; with Overseas Assurance Corp., Singapore, 1941 (resigned, as Gen. Manager, 1958). Legislative Assemblyman, Singapore, 1959-65, MP 1965-79; Minister for Educn, 1959-63; Chm., Singapore Harbour Bd, 1961-62; Minister for: Health, 1963-68; Communications, 1968-75; Minister without Portfolio, 1975-76; High Comr in London, 1975-76. Dir, Metal Box Singapore Ltd; Exec. Chm., Singapore Land/Marina Centre Development Private Ltd. *Address:* 50 Oei Tiong Ham Park, Singapore 1026.

YONGE, Sir (Charles) Maurice, Kt 1967; CBE 1954; FRS 1946; FRSE; DSc(Ed.); Hon. Fellow in Zoology, University of Edinburgh; *b* 9 Dec. 1899; *s* of John Arthur Yonge, MA, JP, and Sarah Edith Carr; *m* 1st, Martha Jane (*d* 1945), *d* of R. T. Lennox, Newmilns, Ayrshire; one *s* one *d* ; 2nd, Phyllis Greenlaw, *d* of Dr D. M. M. Fraser, Eastry, Kent; one *s. Educ:* Silcoates School, Wakefield; Edinburgh Univ. Baxter Natural Science Scholar, 1922-24; Carnegie Research Scholar, 1924-25. Temporary Asst Naturalist, Marine

Biological Assoc., Plymouth, 1925-27; Balfour Student, Univ. of Cambridge, 1927-29; leader, Great Barrier Reef Expedition, 1928-29; Physiologist, Marine Biological Assoc., Plymouth, 1930-32; Prof. of Zoology, Univ. of Bristol, 1933-44; Regius Prof. of Zoology, Univ. of Glasgow, 1944-64, Research Fellow in Zoology, 1965-70. Visiting Prof., Univ. of California, 1949; Prather Lecturer, Harvard Univ., 1957; Visiting Prof., Univ. of Washington, 1959, 1969; Royal Soc. Vis. Prof., Univ. of Hong Kong, 1978. Mem., Advisory Cttee on Fishery Research to the Development Commission, 1937-56; UK Representative, Pacific Science Council; Pres. and Chm. of Council, Scottish Marine Biological Assoc., 1944-67; Chairman: Supervisory Cttee, Brown Trout Lab., Pitlochry, 1949-59; Colonial Fisheries Adv. Cttee; Mem., Audio-Visual Aids Cttee of Univ. Grants Cttee; Mem., Natural Environment Research Council, 1965-70; Vice-President and Hon. Member: Marine Biological Assoc. UK; Scottish Marine Biological Assoc.; Vice-Pres. Royal Soc. of Edinburgh, 1953-56 (Makdougall-Brisbane Prize, 1957), Pres., 1970-73; Pres., Section D, British Assoc., 1961; Mem. Council, Royal Society, 1952-54, 1968-70. Hon. Life Fellow, Pacific Science Assoc.; Mem., Royal Danish Acad. of Science and Letters; Hon. Member: Malac. Soc. London; California Academy of Sciences; Royal Soc. of NZ. Hon. DSc: Bristol, 1959; Heriot-Watt, 1971; Manchester, 1975. Darwin Medal, Royal Society, 1968. *Publications:* (with F. S. Russell) The Seas, 1928, 4th edn 1975; A Year on the Great Barrier Reef, 1930; British Marine Life, 1944; The Sea Shore, 1949; (with J. Barrett) Guide to the Seashore, 1958; Oysters, 1960; (ed, with K. M. Wilbur) Physiology of Mollusca, vol. i, 1964, vol. ii, 1967; (with T. E. Thompson) Living Marine Molluscs, 1976; (ed, with F. S. Russell) Advances in Marine Biology; numerous scientific papers in standard scientific journals, since 1923. *Recreations:* travel, reading of history, woodwork. *Address:* 13 Cumin Place, Edinburgh EH9 2JX. *T:* 031-667 3678.

YONGE, Dame (Ida) Felicity (Ann), DBE 1982 (MBE 1958); Special Adviser in Government Chief Whip's Office, since 1979; *b* 28 Feb. 1921; *d* of Comdr W. H. N. Yonge, RN, and Kathleen Yonge. *Educ:* Convent of the Holy Child, St Leonard's-on-Sea. Served WRNS (2nd Officer), 1940-46. Assistant Purser, P&OSNCo., 1947-50; Private Secretary: to Chairman of the Conservative Party, 1951-64; to Leader of the Opposition, 1964-65; to Opposition Chief Whip, 1965-70 and 1974-79; to Leader of House of Commons, 1970-74. *Recreations:* gardening, bridge. *Address:* 58 Leopold Road, Wimbledon, SW19 7JF.

YORK, Archbishop of, since 1975; **Most Rev. and Rt. Hon. Stuart Yarworth Blanch**, PC 1975; *b* 1918; *s* of late William Edwin and of Elizabeth Blanch; *m* 1943, Brenda Gertrude, *d* of late William Arthur Coyte; one *s* four *d. Educ:* Alleyns Sch., Dulwich; Oxford (BA 1st cl. Theo. 1948, MA 1952). Employee of Law Fire Insurance Soc. Ltd, 1936-40; Navigator in RAF, 1940-46; St Catherine's Coll., Oxford, 1946-49 (Hon. Fellow, 1975); Curate of Highfield, Oxford, 1949-52; Vicar of Eynsham, Oxon, 1952-57; Tutor and Vice-Principal of Wycliffe Hall, Oxford, 1957-60 (Chm. 1967-); Oriel Canon of Rochester and Warden of Rochester Theological Coll., 1960-66; Bishop of Liverpool, 1966-75. Sub-Prelate, OStJ, 1975-. Mem. Council, York Univ., 1976-. Pro-Chancellor: Hull Univ., 1975-; York Univ., 1977-. Hon. LLD Liverpool, 1975; Hon. DD: Hull, 1977; Wycliffe Coll., Toronto, 1979; DUniv York, 1979. *Publications:* The World Our Orphanage, 1972; For All Mankind, 1976; The Christian Militant, 1978; The Burning Bush, 1978; The Trumpet in the Morning, 1979; The Ten Commandments, 1981; Living by Faith, 1983. *Recreations:* squash, walking, music. *Address:* Bishopthorpe, York YO2 1QE. *Club:* Royal Commonwealth Society.

YORK, Dean of; *see* Jasper, Very Rev. R. C. D.

YORK, Archdeacon of; *see* Stanbridge, Ven. L. C.

YORK, Christopher, DL; *b* 27 July 1909; *s* of late Col Edward York; *m* 1934, Pauline Rosemary, *d* of late Sir Lionel Fletcher, CBE; one *s* three *d. Educ:* Eton; RMC Sandhurst. Joined The Royal Dragoons, India, 1930; retired, 1934, on to Supplementary Reserve; rejoined Regt, 1939, rank Major; joined Land Agents Soc., 1934, and passed examinations, acting as Land Agent until elected MP; MP (U) Harrogate Division, 1950-54 (Ripon Division of the West Riding, 1939-50); DL West Riding of Yorkshire, Later N Yorkshire, 1954; High Sheriff of Yorkshire, 1966. Pres., RASE, 1979. Hon. Fellow, Royal Veterinary Coll., 1971. *Recreation:* shooting. *Address:* South Park, Long Marston, York. *TA* and *T:* Rufforth 357. *Clubs:* Boodle's, Carlton; Yorkshire (York).

YORK, Susannah, (Mrs Michael Wells); actress and writer; *b* 9 Jan. 1942; *d* of William Fletcher and Joan Bowring; *m* 1960, Michael Wells; one *s* one *d. Educ:* Marr Coll., Troon, Scotland; RADA, London. *Films* include: The Greengage Summer, 1961; Freud, 1962; Tom Jones, 1963; A Man for All Seasons, 1966; The Killing of Sister George, 1968; They Shoot Horses, Don't They, 1969; Zee and Co., 1971; Images, 1972. *Theatre* includes: Wings of a Dove, 1964; A Singular Man, 1965; The Maids, 1974; Peter Pan, 1977; The Singular Life of Albert Nobbs, 1978; Hedda Gabler, New York 1981, London 1982. TV series We'll Meet Again, 1982. *Publications:* In Search of Unicorns, 1973; Larks Castle, 1975. *Recreations:* family, writing, gardening, reading, houses, riding, languages, travelling, theatre, cinema, walking. *Address:* c/o ICM, 388-396 Oxford Street, W1N 9HE.

YORKE, family name of **Earl of Hardwicke.**

YORKE, Richard Michael, QC 1971; a Recorder of the Crown Court, since 1972; *b* 13 July 1930; *e s* of Gilbert Victor Yorke, Civil Engineer. *Educ:* Solihull Sch., Warwickshire; Balliol Coll., Oxford (MA). Commissioned 2nd Lt, RA, July 1949 (Prize of Honour, Best Officer Cadet); Lieut, Honourable Artillery Company, 1951; Captain, 1953. Asst to Sec., British Road Services, 1953-56. Called to Bar, Gray's Inn, 1956 (Lee Prizeman), Bencher 1981; started practice in Oct. 1956; joined Inner Temple, 1968; Barrister, Supreme Court of NSW and High Court of Australia, 1972; QC NSW 1974. Consultant, Bodington & Yturbe, Paris, 1973-. Contested (C): Durham, 1966; Loughborough, Feb. and Oct. 1974. Pres., Civil Aviation Review Bd, 1972-75. Vice-Chm., Senate/Law Soc. Jt Working Party on Banking Law, 1975-; Mem. Special Panel, Transport Tribunal, 1976. Voluntary Governor, Bart's Hospital, 1974. *Recreations:* flying, skiing, ocean racing. *Address:* 4 and 5 Gray's Inn Square, Gray's Inn, WC1R 5AY. *T:* 01-404 5252. *Telex:* 895 3743 Gralaw; *Cables:* Graylegal; Selborne Chambers, 174 Philip Street, Sydney, NSW 2000. *T:* 25 2181; 9 rue d'Anjou, 75008 Paris, France; (home) 5 Cliveden Place, SW1W 8LA. *T:* 01-730 6054; Eden Roc, Rue de Ransou, 1936 Verbier, Switzerland. *T:* (026) 76504. *Clubs:* Cavalry and Guards, Royal Ocean Racing, St Stephen's Constitutional; County (Durham); Island Sailing (Cowes).

YORKSHIRE, EAST RIDING, Archdeacon of; *see* Vickers, Ven. M. E.

YORSTON, Sir (Robert) Keith, Kt 1969; CBE 1962 (OBE 1960); FCA, FASA, FCIS; Hon. FAIM; *b* 12 Feb. 1902; *s* of late R. Yorston, Shetland Is; *m* 1934, Gwendolen C., *d* of late F. A. Ridley; one *s* one *d. Educ:* Caulfield Public Sch.; Univ. of Melbourne (BCom). Principal, Aust. Accountancy Coll., Sydney, 1933-66. In practice as a Chartered Acct, in Sydney, 1933-70. Federal Pres., Australian-American Assoc., 1960, 1962-64, 1966-67, 1972; NSW Pres., Australian-American Assoc., 1957-63, 1965-74; Pres., Aust. Soc. of Accts, NSW, 1959. Rep. Australia at: Internat. Congress of Accts, 1957, 1962; Internat. Congress of Inst. of Management, 1957. Member: Adjudicating Panel for best Annual Report in Australia (since inception of Annual Report Award); Bd, Scottish Hosp., Sydney. Mem. Adv. Bd, Presbyterian Foundation. Chm., The Presbyterian Church (NSW) Property Trust, 1964-75. Annual Research Lecturer, Aust. Soc. of Accts: Univ. Sydney, 1951; Univ. WA, 1952; Univ. Tas, 1953; Univ. Melb., 1959; Edgar Sabine Memorial Lecture, Adelaide Univ., 1959; Guest Lectr, Jubilee Convention of NZ Soc. of Accts, 1960. *Publications:* (several books reproduced in other countries, such as UK, India and New Zealand; numerous standard text books (some jointly) on accounting, law and company practice (mostly with 2-6 edns) including: Australian Company Director, 1932; Australian Shareholders Guide, 1958, 3rd edn 1971; Australian Commercial Dictionary, 1945, 5th edn 1972; Limited Liability Companies in Australia, 1956; Twentieth Century Commerce and Book-keeping, 12th edn 1960; Costing Procedures, 1951, 5th edn 1976; Advanced Accounting, 1948, 8th edn 1978; Elementary Accounting, 1952, 5th edn 1975; Company Law in New South Wales, 1947, 3rd edn 1968; Company Law in Victoria, 1955, 2nd edn 1959; Accounting Fundamentals, 1949, 7th edn, rev. 1980; Australian Mercantile Law, 1939, 16th edn 1981; Annual Reports of Companies, 1958; Australian Secretarial Practice, 1936, 6th edn 1978; Company Secretary's Guide (NSW), 1946, 2nd edn 1950; Company Secretary's Guide (Victoria), 1948, 2nd edn 1952; Company Secretary's Guide (Queensland), 1947; Company Law, 1962, 3rd edn 1968; Proprietary and Private Companies in Australia, 1939, 2nd edn 1952. *Address:* 29 Trafalgar Avenue, Roseville, NSW 2069, Australia.

YOUDE, Sir Edward, KCMG 1977 (CMG 1968); MBE 1949; HM Diplomatic Service; Governor and Commander-in-Chief, Hong Kong, since 1982; *b* 19 June 1924; *m* 1951, Pamela Fitt; two *d. Educ:* Sch. of Oriental Studies, Univ. of London. RNVR, 1943-46. Joined Foreign Office, 1947; Third Sec., Nanking and Peking, 1948; Foreign Office, 1951; Second Sec., Peking, 1953; First Secretary: Washington, 1956-59; Peking, 1960-62; Foreign Office, 1962-65; Counsellor and Head of Chancery, UK Mission to UN, 1965-69; a Private Secretary to the Prime Minister, 1969-70; IDC, 1970-71; Head of Personnel Services Dept, FCO, 1971-73; Asst Under-Sec. of State, FCO, 1973-74; Ambassador to China, 1974-78; Dep. Under-Sec. of State (Chief Clerk), FCO, 1978; Dep. to Permanent Under-Sec. of State, and Chief Clerk, FCO, 1980-82. *Recreations:* walking, theatre, music. *Address:* Government House, Hong Kong.

YOUDS, Edward Ernest; His Honour Judge Youds; a Circuit Judge, Bedford, since 1972; *b* 21 Nov. 1910; *s* of late Edward Youds. *Educ:* Birkenhead Sch.; Magdalene Coll., Cambridge. BA, LLB (Hons) Cantab. Called to Bar, Gray's Inn, 1936. Practised on Northern Circuit as Barrister-at-law. Served 1940-45, France and Germany (despatches, 1945). Dep. Chm., Lancs County Sessions, 1961-66; County Court Judge, 1966-69; Puisne Judge, High Court, Uganda, 1969-72. *Address:* Bedford County Court, May House, Goldington Road, Bedford.

YOUELL, Rev. Canon George; *b* 23 Dec. 1910; *s* of late Herbert Youell, Beccles; *m* 1936, Gertrude Barron (*d* 1982), *d* of late J. Irvine, West Hartlepool; two *s* three *d. Educ:* Beccles; St Michaels; Hartley Coll., Manchester; St Stephen's House, Oxford; Univ. of Keele (MA 1969). Ordained, 1933; Curate, St John's, Chester, 1933; Clerical Dir of Industrial Christian Fellowship, 1937; chaplain attached to 2nd Bn Grenadier Guards (BEF and Guards Armoured Div.), 1939; Sen. Chaplain to Forces: Nigeria, 1942; Woolwich and SE London, 1944; Nigeria and Gold Coast, 1945; Rector of Ightfield with Calverhall, Salop, 1947; Rural Dean of Leek, 1952-56; Vicar of Leek, 1952-61; Archdeacon of Stoke-upon-Trent, 1956-70; Vicar of Horton, Leek, 1968-70; Chaplain, Univ. of Keele, 1961-68; Hon. Canon, Lichfield Cathedral, 1967-70; Canon Residentiary of Ely Cathedral, 1970-81; Vice-Dean and Treas., 1973-81. *Publications:* Africa Marches, 1949; contributor on colonial and sociological affairs to the Guardian, 1947-51. *Recreation:* fell walking. *Address:* Stranton Cottage, Wattisfield Road, Walsham le Willows, near Bury St Edmunds, Suffolk. *T:* Walsham le Willows 888.

YOUENS, Ven. Archdeacon John Ross, CB 1970; OBE 1959; MC 1946; Chaplain to the Queen since 1969; Senior Treasurer, Corporation of the Sons of the Clergy, since 1982; *b* 29 Sept. 1914; *e s* of late Canon F. A. C. Youens; *m* 1940, Pamela Gordon Lincoln (*née* Chandler); one *s* (two *d* decd). *Educ:* Buxton Coll.; Kelham Theological Coll. Curate of Warsop, Notts, 1939-40. Commissioned RA Chaplains' Dept, 1940; Aldershot and SE Comd, 1940-42; Sen. Chaplain: 59 Inf. Div., 1942; Chatham, 1943; 2nd Army Troops, June 1944; Guards Armd Div., Nov. 1944-45; 3rd Inf. Div. in Egypt and Palestine, 1945-48; 7th Armd Div. in Germany, 1948-50; Aldershot, 1950-51; DACG, Egypt, 1951-53; Tripoli, 1953-54; Sen. Chaplain, RMA Sandhurst, 1955-58; DACG, Gibraltar, 1958-60; ACG War Office, 1960-61, Rhine Army, 1961-66; Chaplain General to the Forces, 1966-74; Archdeacon Emeritus, 1974. Dep. Chairman, Keston Coll., Centre for the Study of Religion and Communism (Mem. Council, 1975-). *Recreation:* golf. *Address:* Bulfigs, Hook Heath, Woking, Surrey GU22 0QE. *T:* Woking 68031. *Clubs:* Army and Navy, Cavalry and Guards (Hon. Mem.), MCC.

YOUENS, Sir Peter (William), Kt 1965; CMG 1962; OBE 1960; *b* 29 April 1916; 2nd *s* of late Canon F. A. C. Youens; *m* 1943, Diana Stephanie, *d* of Edward Hawkins, Southacre, Norfolk; two *d*. *Educ:* King Edward VII's School, Sheffield; Wadham College, Oxford. MA (Oxon), 1938. Joined Colonial Administrative Service; naval service, 1939-40. Sub-Lt, Cadet S. L., 1939; Asst Dist Comr, 1942; Dist Comr, 1948; Colony Comr and Member, Sierra Leone Legislative Council, 1950; Asst Sec., Nyasaland, 1951; Dep. Chief Sec., 1953-63; Secretary to the Prime Minister and to the Cabinet, Malawi, 1964-66 (Nyasaland, 1963-64); Mem., Nyasaland Legislative Council, 1954-61. Retired, 1966. Exec. Dir, Lonrho Ltd, 1966-69, Non-Exec. Dir, 1980-81, Exec. Dir, 1981-; Partner, John Tyzack & Partners Ltd, 1969-81; Dir, Oxford Playhouse Company (Anvil Productions Ltd), 1978-. *Address:* The Old Parsonage, Hurstborne Priors, Whitchurch, Hants. *Clubs:* East India, Devonshire, Sports and Public Schools; Vincent's (Oxford).

YOUNG, family name of **Baron Kennet, Baroness Young** and **Baron Young of Dartington.**

YOUNG; *see* Hughes-Young, family name of Baron St Helens.

YOUNG; *see* Mackworth-Young.

YOUNG, Baroness *cr* 1971 (Life Peer), of Farnworth in the County Palatine of Lancaster; **Janet Mary Young;** PC 1981; Lord Privy Seal, since 1982; Leader of the House of Lords, since 1981; *b* 23 Oct. 1926; *d* of John Norman Leonard Baker and Phyllis Marguerite Baker (*née* Hancock); *m* 1950, Geoffrey Tyndale Young; three *d*. *Educ:* Dragon School Oxford, Headington School, and in America; St Anne's Coll., Oxford; MA (Politics, Philosophy and Economics); Hon. Fellow, 1978. Baroness in Waiting (Govt Whip), 1972-73; Parly Under-Sec. of State, DoE, 1973-74; Minister of State, DES, 1979-81; Chancellor, Duchy of Lancaster, 1981-82. A Vice-Chm., Cons. Party Organisation, 1975-, Dep. Chm., 1977-79. Co-Chm., Women's Nat. Commn, 1979-. Councillor Oxford City Council, 1957; Alderman, 1967-72; Leader of Conservative Group, 1967-72. Dir, UK Provident Instn, 1975-79. Mem., BR Adv. Bd, Western Reg., 1977-79. Hon. FIMunE. *Recreation:* music. *Address:* House of Lords, SW1A 0PW.

YOUNG OF DARTINGTON, Baron *cr* 1978 (Life Peer), of Dartington in the County of Devon; **Michael Young,** BSc (Econ), MA, PhD; Director, Institute of Community Studies since 1953; Deputy Chairman, Dartington Hall, since 1980 (Trustee, since 1942); *b* 9 Aug. 1915; father a musician, mother a writer; *m* 1st, 1945, Joan Lawson; two *s* one *d*; 2nd, 1960, Sasha Moorsom; one *s* one *d*. *Educ:* Dartington Hall Sch.; London Univ. Barrister, Gray's Inn. Dir of Political and Economic Planning, 1941-45; Sec., Research Dept, Lab. Party, 1945-51. Chairman: Social Science Research Council, 1965-68; Dartington Amenity Research Trust, 1967-; Internat. Extension Coll., 1970-; Nat. Consumer Council, 1975-77; Mutual Aid Centre, 1977-; Dir, Mauritius Coll. of the Air, 1972; Member: Central Adv. Council for Education, 1963-66; NEDC, 1975-78; Policy Cttee, SDP, 1981-; President: Consumer's Assoc., 1965- (Chm., 1956-65); National Extension Coll., 1971- (Chm., 1962-71); Adv. Centre for Educn, 1976- (Chm., 1959-76). Chm., Tawney Soc., 1982-. Fellow, Churchill Coll., Cambridge, 1961-66; Vis. Prof. of Extension Educn, Ahmadu Bello Univ., Nigeria, 1974. Hon. LittD Sheffield, 1965; DUniv Open, 1973; Hon. DLitt Adelaide, 1974; Hon. LLD Exeter, 1982. Hon. Fellow: LSE, 1978; Plymouth Polytechnic, 1980. *Publications:* Family and Kinship in East London (with Peter Willmott), 1957; The Rise of the Meritocracy, 1958; Family and Class in a London Suburb (with Peter Willmott), 1960; Innovation and Research in Education, 1965; Learning Begins at Home (with Patrick McGeeney), 1968; (ed) Forecasting and the Social Sciences, 1968; The Symmetrical Family (with Peter Willmott), 1973; (ed) The Poverty Report, 1974 and 1975; (with Marianne Rigge) Mutual Aid in a Selfish Society, 1979; (with others) Distance Teaching for the Third

World, 1980; The Elmhirsts of Dartington—the creation of an Utopian Community, 1982. *Recreation:* painting. *Address:* 18 Victoria Park Square, E2.

YOUNG, Prof. Alec David, OBE 1964; MA; FRS 1973; FEng, FRAeS; AFAIAA; Professor and Head of the Department of Aeronautical Engineering, Queen Mary College, London University, 1954-78, now Emeritus; Vice-Principal, Queen Mary College, 1966-78; *b* 15 Aug. 1913; *s* of Isaac Young and Katherine (*née* Freeman); *m* 1st, 1937, Dora Caplan (*d* 1970); two *s* one *d*; 2nd, 1971, Rena Waldmann (*née* Szafer). *Educ:* Caius Coll., Cambridge. Wrangler, Mathematical Tripos, 1935. Research Student in Aeronautics, Cambridge, 1935-36; Mem. of staff, Aerodynamics Dept, Royal Aircraft Estab., 1936-46; College of Aeronautics: Senior Lectr and Dep. Head of Dept of Aerodynamics, 1946-50; Prof. and Head of Dept of Aerodynamics, 1950-54. Dean, Faculty of Engineering, Univ. of London, 1962-66; Mem. Senate, Univ. of London, 1970-78. Mem. various Cttees of Aeronautical Research Council, Chm. of Council, 1968-71. Chm., Bd of Direction, Von Karman Institute for Fluid Dynamics, 1964; Mem., Advisory Bd, RAF Coll., Cranwell, 1966. Gold Medal, 1972, Royal Aeronautical Soc. (Past Chm., Aerodynamics Data Sheets Cttee); FRAeS, 1951; FEng 1976. Ludwig Prandtl Ring, Deutsche Gesellschaft für Luft-und Raumfahrt, 1976; Von Karman Medal, AGARD, 1979. Commandeur de l'Ordre de Leopold, 1976. Fellow QMC, 1980. *Publications:* various, of Aeronautical Research Council, Coll. of Aeronautics Reports series; articles in Aeronautical Quarterly and Jl of Royal Aeronautical Soc., Quarterly Jl of Mechanics and Applied Mathematics, and Aircraft Engineering. Co-author of An Elementary Treatise on the Mechanics of Fluids, 1960, 2nd edn 1970; Aircraft Excrescence Drag, 1981. *Recreations:* drama, sketching. *Address:* 26 Rotherwick Way, Cambridge CB1 4RX. *T:* Cambridge 249703.

YOUNG, Maj.-Gen. Alexander, CB 1971; *b* 22 Feb. 1915; *s* of late Alexander and Mary M. K. G. Young, Edinburgh; *m* 1942, Joan Madeline, *d* of late John N. Stephens, London; one *s*. *Educ:* Daniel Stewart's Coll., Edinburgh. Served, BEF, 1940; WO, 1942-46; HQ, Caribbean Area, 1947-50; WO, 1950-52; HQ Middle East Comd, Egypt and Cyprus, 1954-57; Bt Lt-Col 1955; Comdr RAOC, 4 Inf. Div., 1957-59; HQ, BAOR, 1959-61; WO, 1961-64; Dep. Dir, Ordnance Services, Eastern Comd, 1964-65; Comd COD, Bicester, 1965-67; Comd UK Base Org., 1967-68; Dir of Ordnance Services, MoD, 1968-71. Col Comdt, RAOC, 1971-75. FBIM. *Recreations:* travel, golf. *Address:* Gaddons Cottage, Seaward Drive, West Wittering, Sussex. *T:* West Wittering 2118. *Club:* Army and Navy.

YOUNG, Alexander; free-lance concert and opera singer; Head of Department of Vocal Studies, Royal Northern College of Music, Manchester, since 1973; *b* London; *m* 1948, Jean Mary Prewett; one *s* one *d*. *Educ:* secondary; (scholar) Royal Coll. of Music, London; studied in London with late Prof. Pollmann, of Vienna State Academy. FRNCM 1977. Served War, HM Forces, 1941-46. Has regular engagements with the BBC and has sung in the USA, Canada, and most European countries, as well as frequently in Britain. First operatic rôle (tenor), as Scaramuccio in Strauss' Ariadne, Edin. Fest., with Glyndebourne Opera, 1950; parts at Glyndebourne, and began broadcasting for BBC, 1951 (subseq. incl. opera, oratorio, recitals, light music, etc). First appearances: with English Opera Group, world Première of Lennox Berkeley's opera, A Dinner Engagement, 1954; also appeared at Royal Festival Hall, several times with Sir Thomas Beecham, in Mozart Requiem; at Sadler's Wells Opera, as Eisenstein in Die Fledermaus, 1959, and subsequently in many roles such as: Ramiro in La Cenerentola; title role in Count Ory; Almaviva in The Barber of Seville; notable roles include: Tom in Stravinsky's Rake's Progress (which he created for British audiences); David in Die Meistersinger; title role in Mozart's Idomeneo. At Covent Garden sang in: Strauss's Arabella; Britten's A Midsummer Night's Dream. Oratorio roles include: Evangelist in Bach Passions; Elgar's Dream of Gerontius; Britten's War Requiem. Is regularly engaged by Welsh National Opera and Scottish Opera. Many commercial recordings, especially of Handel oratorios and operas, as well as The Rake's Progress conducted by the composer. Lieder recitals a speciality. *Recreation:* photography. *Address:* Royal Northern College of Music, 124 Oxford Road, Manchester M13 9RD.

YOUNG, Andrew; Mayor of Atlanta, Georgia, since 1981; *b* New Orleans, La, 12 March 1932; *s* of Andrew J. Young and Daisy Fuller; *m* 1954, Jean Childs; one *s* three *d*. *Educ:* Howard Univ., USA; Hartford Theological Seminary. Ordained, United Church of Christ, 1955; Pastor, Thomasville, Ga, 1955-57; Associate Dir for Youth Work, Nat. Council of Churches, 1957-61; Admin. Christian Educn Programme, United Church of Christ, 1961-64; Mem. Staff, Southern Christian Leadership Conf., 1961-70; Exec. Dir, 1964-70; Exec. Vice-Pres., 1967-70; elected to US House of Representatives from 5th District of Georgia, 1972 (first Black Congressman from Georgia in 101 years); re-elected 1974 and 1976; US Ambassador to UN, 1977-79. Chairman: Atlanta Community Relations Commn, 1970-72; National Democratic voter registration drive, 1976; during 1960s organized voter registration and community devel programmes. Holds numerous hon. degrees and awards. *Address:* The Office of the Mayor, 68 Mitchell Street SW, Atlanta, Georgia 30303, USA.

YOUNG, Bertram Alfred, OBE 1980; dramatic critic, since 1964, and arts editor, 1971-77, The Financial Times; *b* 20 Jan. 1912; *y* (twin) *s* of Bertram William Young and Dora Elizabeth Young (*née* Knight); unmarried. *Educ:* Highgate. Served with Artists Rifles, 1930-35, and Lancs Fusiliers, KAR and

Staff, 1939–48; Asst Editor, Punch, 1949–62; Dramatic Critic, Punch, 1962–64. Mem., British Council Drama Adv. Cttee, 1973–; Pres., Critics' Circle, 1978–80. Hon. Kentucky Col, 1980. *Publications:* Tooth and Claw, 1958; How to Avoid People, 1963; Bechuanaland, 1966; Cabinet Pudding, 1967; Colonists from Space, 1979; The Mirror up to Nature, 1982; author of about 20 radio plays broadcast 1938–49. *Recreation:* music (consumer only). *Address:* Clyde House, Station Street, Cheltenham GL50 3LX. *T:* Cheltenham 581485. *Club:* Garrick.

YOUNG, Air Vice-Marshal Brian Pashley, CB 1972; CBE 1960 (OBE 1944); Commandant General, Royal Air Force Regiment, 1968–73, retired; *b* 5 May 1918; *s* of Kenneth Noel Young and Flora Elizabeth Young, Natal, S Africa; *m* 1942, Patricia Josephine, *d* of Thomas Edward Cole, Bedford; three *s* two *d. Educ:* Michaelhouse, Natal, SA; RAF Coll., Cranwell. Fighter Comd, UK and France, 1938–40 (wounded); Hosp., 1941–42; Coastal Comd, N Ire and Western Isles, 1942–43; Aden and Persian Gulf, 1944; Staff Coll., Haifa, 1945; Middle East, 1946–47; Air Min., 1948–50; Bomber Comd HQ No 1 Gp, Hemswell/Gaydon, 1951–57; HQ Bomber Comd, 1958–60; NATO, Fontainebleau, Asst Chief of Staff, Intelligence, 1960–62; IDC 1963; AOC, Central Reconnaisance Estabt, 1964–67. Rep. RAF: athletics, 1939, Rugby, 1947–48. *Address:* Chapel Walk House, The Street, Didmarton, Glos. *Club:* Royal Air Force.

YOUNG, Sir Brian (Walter Mark), Kt 1976; MA; Director-General, Independent Broadcasting Authority (formerly Independent Television Authority), 1970–82; *b* 23 Aug. 1922; *er s* of late Sir Mark Young, GCMG; *m* 1947, Fiona Marjorie, *o d* of late Allan, 16th Stewart of Appin; one *s* two *d. Educ:* Eton; King's College, Cambridge. Served in RNVR, mainly in destroyers, 1941–45. First class hons in Part I, 1946, and Part II, 1947, of Classical Tripos; Porson Prize, 1946; Winchester Reading Prize, 1947; BA 1947; MA 1952. Assistant Master at Eton, 1947–52; Headmaster of Charterhouse, 1952–64; Dir, Nuffield Foundn, 1964–70. Member: Central Advisory Council for Education, 1956–59 (Crowther Report); Central Religious Adv. Cttee of BBC and ITA, 1960–64; Arts Council of GB, 1982–. A Managing Trustee, Nuffield Foundn, 1978–. Hon. DLitt Heriot-Watt, 1980. *Publications:* Via Vertendi, 1952; Intelligent Reading (with P. D. R. Gardiner), 1964. *Recreations:* music, travel, history, problems. *Address:* Hill End, Woodhill Avenue, Gerrards Cross, Bucks. *T:* Gerrards Cross 87793.

YOUNG, Carmichael Aretas, MD, FRCP; Hon. Consulting Physician and Physician i/c Diabetic Clinic, St Mary's Hospital, London, W2; *b* Adelaide, S Australia, 19 Aug. 1913; *e s* of Aretas Henry Young, Adelaide, SA and Isabelle Wilson, Parattah, Tas; *m* 1939, Marie, 2nd *d* of W. H. Lewry, Botley, Hants; three *s* one *d. Educ:* Carey Grammar Sch., Kew, Vic.; St Mary's Hosp. Medical Sch., Univ. of London. MRCS, LRCP 1936, FRCP 1950; MB, BS (London), 1936, MD 1940. House Phys. and House Surg., St Mary's Hosp., 1936–37; House Phys., Asst Resident MO, Brompton Hosp., 1938; Asst, Professorial Medical Unit, St Mary's, 1939; Phys., EMS, 1940–41; Medical Specialist 10th (Brit.) CCS, 1942–43 (despatches); No 1 Gen. Hosp., 1944; Lt-Col RAMC O i/c Medical Div. 43 Gen. Hosp., 1945; OC 43 Gen. Hosp., Beirut, 1946. Medical Registrar, Prince of Wales' Gen. Hosp., 1946–47; Consultant in Chest Diseases, Min. of Pensions, 1948; St Mary's Hosp., 1948–78; Sub-Dean, St Mary's Hosp. Medical School, 1952–53; Examiner: Soc. of Apothecaries, Medicine, 1964–70; Univ. London, Therapeutics, Medicine, 1957–62; Conj. Bd, Pathology, Medicine (Chm., 1970–71); Pro-Censor, 1973–74, Censor, 1974–75, RCP. Mem., Bd of Governors, St Mary's Hosp., 1958–61. Hon. Colonel No 4 Gen. Hosp. AER, 1961. *Publications:* History of the Otter Swimming Club, 1869–1969, 1969; short articles in medical jls. *Recreations:* swimming, water-polo, golf, gardening. *Address:* The Tile House, Billingshurst Road, Ashington, W Sussex. *T:* Ashington 892544. *Clubs:* Otter Swimming (Pres. 1964–67); West Sussex Golf.

YOUNG, Rev. Canon (Cecil) Edwyn; Chaplain, The Queen's Chapel of the Savoy, and Chaplain of the Royal Victorian Order, since 1974; Chaplain to the Queen since 1972; *b* 29 April 1913; *er s* of Cecil Morgan Young and Doris Edith Virginia Young, Colombo, Ceylon; *m* 1944, Beatrice Mary, *e d* of Percy Montague Rees and Beatrice Rees; two *s* one *d. Educ:* Radley Coll.; Dorchester Missionary College. Curate, St Peter's, London Docks, 1936–41; Priest in Charge, St Francis, N Kensington, 1941–44; Rector of Broughton with Ripton Regis, 1944–47; Vicar of St Silas, Pentonville, 1947–53; Rector of Stepney, 1953–64, and Rural Dean of Stepney, 1959–64; Prebendary of St Paul's, 1959–64; Rector and Rural Dean of Liverpool, 1964–73; Canon Diocesan, 1965–73. Commissary, Diocese of North Queensland, 1959–, Canon to the Ordinary, 1974–. Chaplain: Worshipful Co. of Distillers, 1974–; Weavers' Co., 1977–; to Chm., Freight Forwarders Inst., 1974–. Pres., Sion College, 1963–64. Hon. Chaplain, HCIMA. *Publications:* No Fun Like Work, 1970; (contrib.) Father Groser, East End Priest, 1971. *Recreations:* meeting people; wild flowers; the theatre, especially music hall; watching cricket. *Address:* The Queen's Chapel of the Savoy, Strand, WC2; 18 Coombe Lane West, Kingston on Thames. *T:* 01-942 1196. *Clubs:* Greenroom, City Livery.

YOUNG, (Charles) Kenneth, FRSL; Political and Literary Adviser to Beaverbrook Newspapers since 1965, and formerly, Editor of the Yorkshire Post; *b* 27 Nov. 1916; *o s* of late Robert William Young, Iron Founder, Middlestown, Wakefield, and late Alice Jane Young (*née* Ramsden); *m* 1949, Elizabeth Constantinou (*d* 1950); one *d*; *m* 1951, Phyllis, *d* of late Lt-Col and Mrs J. A. Dicker; three *s* one *d. Educ:* Queen Elizabeth's Grammar Sch.

(Junior Dept), Wakefield; Coatham Sch., Redcar; Leeds Univ. BA (1st Cl. Hons Eng. Lang. and Lit.), 1938. Served War of 1939–45. Royal Corps of Signals, 1940; Intelligence Corps, 1941 (Algeria, Italy, Greece); Foreign Office, 1944. BBC European Service, 1948; Daily Mirror, 1949; Daily Mail, 1950; Permanent Under-Sec. Dept, Cabinet Office, 1950; Daily Telegraph, 1952–60; Editor of The Yorkshire Post, 1960–64; Political Commentator, Birmingham Evening Mail, 1978–. FRSL 1964. Broadcaster; Editor, Television series, The Book Man, 1960. Governor, Welbeck College, 1963–73. *Publications:* D. H. Lawrence, 1952; John Dryden (critical biography), 1954; Ford Madox Ford, 1958; (ed) The Bed Post, 1962; (ed) The Second Bed Post, 1965; A. J. Balfour, authorised biography, 1963; Churchill and Beaverbrook: a study in friendship and politics, 1966; Rhodesia and Independence: a study in British colonial policy, 1967, 2nd edn 1969; Sir Compton Mackenzie, an essay, 1967; Music's Great Days in the Spas and Watering-places, 1968; The Greek Passion: a study in people and politics, 1969; Sir Alec Douglas-Home, 1970; Chapel, 1972; (ed) Diaries of Sir Robert Bruce Lockhart, vol. I, 1973, vol. II, 1980; H. G. Wells, an essay, 1974; Life of 6th Earl of Rosebery, 1974; Arnold Bennett, an essay, 1975; Baldwin: a biography, 1976; Lord Macaulay, an essay, 1977; J. B. Priestley, an essay, 1978; A Neighbourhood of Writers, 1981. *Recreations:* being with family, listening to music, talk. *Address:* Beaufort House, Oxenden Street, Herne Bay, Kent. *T:* Herne Bay 5419. *Clubs:* Beefsteak, Wig and Pen, East India.

YOUNG, Christopher Godfrey; His Honour Judge Young; a Circuit Judge, since 1980; *b* 9 Sept. 1932; *s* of the late Harold Godfrey Young, MB, ChB, and Gladys Mary Young; *m* 1969, Jeanetta Margaret, *d* of Halford and Dorothy Vaughan; one *s. Educ:* Bedford Sch.; King's Coll., Univ. of London (LLB Hons 1954). Called to the Bar, Gray's Inn, 1957; Midland and Oxford Circuit, 1959; a Recorder of the Crown Court, 1975–79. Chm., Maidwell with Draughton Parish Council, 1973–76. *Recreations:* natural history, gardening. *Address:* School Farm House, Maidwell, Northants. *T:* Maidwell 682. *Club:* Northampton and County (Northampton).

YOUNG, Colin, OBE 1976; Director, National Film School of Great Britain, since 1970; *b* 5 April 1927; *s* of Colin Young and Agnes Holmes Kerr Young; *m* 1960, Kristin Ohman; two *s. Educ:* Bellahouston Academy, Glasgow; Univs of Glasgow, St Andrews and California (Los Angeles). Theatre and film critic, Bon Accord, Aberdeen, 1951; cameraman, editor, writer, director, 1953–; producer, 1967–; UCLA (Motion Pictures): Instructor, 1956–59; Asst Prof., 1959–64; Assoc. Prof., 1964–68; Prof., 1968–70, Head, Motion Picture Div., Theater Arts Dept, UCLA, 1964–65; Chm., Dept of Theater Arts, 1965–70. Vice-Chm., 1972–76, Chm., 1976–, Edinburgh Film Festival; Governor, BFI, 1974–80. Member: Arts Council Film Cttee, 1972–76; Public Media Panel, Nat. Endowment for Arts, Washington, 1972–77; Gen. Adv. Council, BBC, 1973–78; Council of Management, BAFTA, 1974–81; Exec. Cttee, Centre International de Liaison des Ecoles de Cinéma et de Télévision, 1974– (Pres., 1980–); Nat. Film Finance Corp., 1979–. FBKS 1975. Chm., Cttee on Educational Policy, UCLA, 1968–69. Los Angeles Editor, Film Quarterly, 1958–68. *Publications:* various articles in collections of film essays (including Principles of Visual Anthropology, 1975), 1961–; experimental film essay for Unesco, 1963; ethnographic film essay for Unesco, 1966; contribs to Film Quarterly, Sight and Sound, Jl of Aesthetic Education, Jl of the Producers Guild of America, Kosmorama (Copenhagen), etc. *Address:* National Film School, Beaconsfield, Bucks. *Club:* Savile.

YOUNG, David Edward Michael, QC 1980; *b* 30 Sept. 1940; *s* of George Henry Edward Young and Audrey Young; *m* 1968, Ann de Bromhead; two *d. Educ:* Monkton Combe Sch.; Hertford Coll., Oxford (MA). Called to the Bar, Lincoln's Inn, 1966; practising at Chancery Bar, specialising in indust. property work (patents, trade marks, copyright and restrictive trade practices). *Publication:* (co-ed) Terrell on the Law of Patents, 12th edn 1971. *Recreations:* field sports, tennis, ski-ing. *Address:* Gussage House, Gussage All Saints, Wimborne, Dorset BH21 5ET.

YOUNG, David Ivor; Chairman, Manpower Services Commission, since 1982; *b* 27 Feb. 1932; *s* of Joseph and Rebecca Young; *m* 1956, Lita Marianne Shaw; two *d. Educ:* Christ's Coll., Finchley; University Coll., London (LLB Hons). Admitted solicitor, 1956. Exec., Great Universal Stores Ltd, 1956–61; Chairman: Eldonwall Ltd, 1961–75; Manufacturers Hanover Property Services Ltd, 1974–; Dir, Town & City Properties Ltd, 1972–75. Chairman: British ORT, 1975–80, Pres., 1980–82; Admin. Cttee, World ORT Union, 1980–; Dir, Centre for Policy Studies, 1979–82 (Mem., Management Bd, 1977); Mem., English Industrial Estates Corp., 1980–82. Industrial Adviser, 1979–80, Special Adviser, 1980–82, DoI. Mem., NEDC, 1982–. Chm., Internat. Council of Jewish Social and Welfare Services, 1981–. Hon. FRPS, 1981. *Recreations:* fishing, sailing, computing. *Address:* 28 York Terrace West, NW1 4QA; Fairacres, Graffham, W Sussex GU28 0NZ. *Club:* Carlton.

YOUNG, Rt. Rev. David Nigel de Lorentz; *see* Ripon, Bishop of.

YOUNG, Lt-Gen. Sir David (Tod), KBE 1980; CB 1977; DFC 1952; GOC Scotland and Governor of Edinburgh Castle, 1980–82; *b* 17 May 1926; *s* of late William Young and Davina Tod Young; *m* 1950, Joyce Marian Melville; two *s. Educ:* George Watson's Coll., Edinburgh. Commissioned, The Royal Scots (The Royal Regt), 1945 (Col, 1975–80). Attached Glider Pilot Regt, 1949–52; Bt Lt-Col, 1964; Mil. Asst to Dep. Chief of Gen. Staff, MoD, 1964–67; commanded 1st Bn The Royal Scots (The Royal Regt), 1967–69; Col Gen. Staff, Staff Coll., 1969–70; Comdr, 12th Mechanized Bde, 1970–72;

Dep. Mil. Sec., MoD, 1972-74; Comdr Land Forces, NI, 1975-77; Dir of Infantry, 1977-80. Col Comdt, Scottish Div., 1980-82. *Recreations:* golf, shooting, spectator of sports. *Address:* c/o Royal Bank of Scotland plc, 83 Princes Street, Edinburgh EH2 2ER. *Club:* Royal Scots (Edinburgh).

YOUNG, David Wright; MP (Lab) Bolton East, since Feb. 1974; teacher; *b* Greenock, Scotland, 12 Oct. 1930. *Educ:* Greenock Academy; Glasgow Univ.; St Paul's Coll., Cheltenham. Head of History Dept; subseq. insurance executive. Joined Labour Party, 1955; contested: South Worcestershire, 1959; Banbury, 1965; Bath, 1970. PPS to Sec. of State for Defence, 1977-79. Formerly Alderman, Nuneaton Borough Council; Councillor, Nuneaton District Council. Chm., Coventry East Labour Party, 1964-68. Member, Transport and General Workers Union; Member, Fabian Society. Is especially interested in comprehensive educn, defence, pensions, economics. *Recreations:* reading, motoring. *Address:* House of Commons, SW1A 0AA.

YOUNG, Dr Edith Isabella, CBE 1964; *b* 7 March 1904; *d* of William Ross Young and Margaret Ramsay Young (*née* Hill). *Educ:* High School of Stirling; Univ. of Glasgow. BSc 1924, MA (1st cl. Hons Mathematics and Natural Philosophy) 1925. HM Inspector of Schools, Scottish Educn Dept, 1935-64; HM Inspector, in charge of Dundee and Angus, 1946-52; HM Chief Inspector, Highland Div., 1952-64. UNESCO expert on the teaching of science in Yugoslavia, Oct. 1956-Feb. 1957; UK Deleg., UNESCO Conf., Belgrade, 1960; Mem. Council for Technical Educn and Trg for Overseas Countries, 1964-68 (Chm., Women's Gp); UK Deleg. to Commonwealth Conf. on Trg of Technicians in Huddersfield, 1966; Co-Chm., Women's Nat. Commn, 1971-73; Pres., British Fedn of Univ. Women, 1967-70. Chairman: Northern Area Nurse Trng Cttee, 1967-81; Inverness Hosp. Bd, 1968-74. Hon. LLD Southampton, 1967. *Recreations:* sundry. *Address:* 36 Broadstone Park, Inverness. *T:* Inverness 33216. *Clubs:* Royal Over-Seas League, University Women's.

YOUNG, Edward Preston, DSO 1944; DSC 1943; writer and retired book designer; *b* 17 Nov. 1913; *m* 1st, 1945, Diana Lilian Graves (marr. diss.); two *d*; 2nd, 1956, Mary Reoch Cressall. *Educ:* Highgate Sch. Served War, 1940-45: RNVR; entered submarine service 1940 (despatches, DSC); first RNVR officer to command operational submarine, 1943 (DSO, Bar to DSC); temp. Commander RNVR, 1945. Man. Dir, Rainbird Publishing Gp Ltd, 1970-73. *Publications:* One of Our Submarines, 1952; Look at Lighthouses, 1961; The Fifth Passenger, 1962; Look at Submarines, 1964. *Address:* c/o Barclays Bank Ltd, 19 Great Cumberland Place, W1.

YOUNG, Rev. Canon Edwyn; *see* Young, Rev. Canon C. E.

YOUNG, Eric, OBE 1976; HM Diplomatic Service; High Commissioner to Seychelles, since 1980; *b* 16 Nov. 1924; *s* of late Robert Young, MBE, and Emily Florence Young, Doncaster; *m* 1949, Sheila Hutchinson; three *s* one *d*. *Educ:* Maltby Grammar Sch.; Sheffield Univ. (BA 1948). Served War, RN, 1943-46. Editorial staff: Sheffield Telegraph, 1948; Western Morning News, 1951; Daily Dispatch, 1952; Manchester Guardian, 1957; PRO, NCB, Manchester, 1958; Dep. Dir, UK Inf. Office, Tanganyika and Zanzibar, 1960; First Secretary: (Inf.), Dar es Salaam, 1961; (Aid), Kaduna, 1963; Commonwealth Office (later FCO), 1967; Madras, 1969; Head of Chancery, Reykjavik, 1973 (Hd of Brit. Interests Section, French Embassy, during breach of diplomatic relations, 1976); Dep. High Comr, Bombay, 1977. *Recreations:* music, books, living in England. *Address:* c/o Foreign and Commonwealth Office, SW1. *Clubs:* Royal Over-Seas League, Royal Commonwealth Society.

See also Air Vice-Marshal G. Young.

YOUNG, Eric Edgar; HM Diplomatic Service, retired; *b* 1 July 1912; *yr s* of late Frank E. Young, Dulwich; *m* 1938, Aurora Corral, San Sebastian, Spain; two *d*. *Educ:* Alleyn's Sch., Dulwich; Jesus Coll., Oxford. Asst Master, Haberdashers' Aske's Hatcham Boys Sch., 1935-40. Served Army, 1940-46 (Major, RAC). Diplomatic (formerly Foreign) Service, 1946-70; Served at: Buenos Aires, 1946-49; Montevideo, 1950-52; Mexico City, 1952-55; FO, 1955-58; Rangoon, 1958-60; HM Consul, Tamsui (Formosa), 1960-62; FO, 1962-64; Adv. to Kenya Min. of Foreign Affairs, Nairobi, 1964-67; HM Consul-General, Paris, 1967-70. Mem. Adv. Cttee, Nat. Art-Collections Fund, 1977-; Nat. Art-Collections Fund Lecture, 1979. *Publications:* Four Centuries of Spanish Painting, Barnard Castle, 1967; The Bowes Museum, Barnard Castle, Catalogue of Spanish and Italian Paintings, 1970; Bartolomé Bermejo: The Great Hispano-Flemish Master, 1975; Francisco Goya, 1978; Bartolomé Murillo Werkverzeichnis, 1980; contrib. to: Apollo, The Burlington Magazine, The Connoisseur, Archivo Español de Arte, Goya, Revista de Arte, Art Bulletin (NY), Museum Studies (Chicago), J. Paul Getty Museum Jl, Actas del XXIII Congreso Internacional de Historia del Arte (Granada), Pantheon (Munich), Fenway Court (Boston, Mass), Arte Veneta, Boletín de la Institución Fernán González (Burgos). *Recreation:* art history. *Address:* 19 Hyde Park Gardens Mews, W2 2NU.

See also Sir F. G. Young.

YOUNG, Eric William, BEng (Hons); MIMechE, MIEE; *b* 26 March 1896; 2nd *s* of Colonel C. A. Young, CB, CMG; *m* 1936, Mrs Olive Bruce. *Educ:* Epsom Coll.; Shrewsbury Sch.; Liverpool Univ. (BEng Hons, 1922). Served RE (T) (Lieut) 1913-19. Metropolitan Vickers Ltd, 1922-26; Technical Manager, Electrolux Ltd, 1926-39; Rootes Ltd: General Manager, Aero Engine Factories, 1939-45; Director and General Manager, Sunbeam Talbot

Ltd, 1945-46; Director, Rootes Export Co. Ltd, 1946-47; Sales Director, Harry Ferguson Ltd, 1947-53; Managing Director, Eastern Hemisphere Division, Massey-Ferguson Ltd, 1953-56; Vice-Chm., Massey-Ferguson Holdings Ltd, 1956-65, Chm., 1965-70. *Recreations:* golf, gardening. *Address:* Childerstone, Liphook, Hampshire GU30 7AP. *T:* Liphook 722125. *Club:* Liphook Golf.

YOUNG, Sir Frank (George), Kt 1973; DSc, PhD (London), MA (Cantab); FRS 1949; CChem, FRSC; Sir William Dunn Professor of Biochemistry, University of Cambridge, 1949-75; now Professor Emeritus; Master of Darwin College, Cambridge, 1964-76, Hon. Fellow 1977; Hon. Fellow of Trinity Hall, Cambridge, since 1965 (Fellow, 1949-64); Fellow of University College, London; *b* 25 March 1908; *er s* of late Frank E. Young, Dulwich; *m* 1933, Ruth (MB, BS, MRCPsych), *o c* of Thomas Turner, Beckenham, Kent; three *s* one *d*. *Educ:* Alleyn's Sch., Dulwich; University Coll., London. Beit Memorial Fellow at University Coll., London, University of Aberdeen and University of Toronto, 1932-36; Member of Scientific Staff, Medical Research Council, 1936-42; Professor of Biochemistry, University of London, 1942-49. Syndic, CUP, 1951-64; Mem. Council of Senate, Cambridge, 1965-68; Chm., Clinical Sch. Planning Cttee, Univ. of Cambridge, 1969-76. Vice Pres. and Hon. Mem., British Diabetic Assoc., 1948-; Member: Medical Res. Council, 1950-54; Commission on Higher Educ. for Africans in Central Africa, 1952; Inter-University Council for Higher Education Overseas, 1961-73; Commission on new Chinese University in Hong Kong, 1962-63; Medical Sub-Cttee, UGC, 1964-73; Board of Governors of United Cambridge Hospitals, 1964-68; Royal Commn on Medical Educn, 1965-68; Council, British Nutrition Foundn, 1967-80; Council of Nestlé Foundn, Lausanne, 1972-80. Trustee, Kennedy Memorial Trust, 1964-76. President: European Assoc. for the Study of Diabetes, 1965-68, Hon. Mem., 1973; British Nutrition Foundn, 1970-76; Internat. Diabetes Fedn, 1970-73 (Hon. Pres., 1973-); Vice-Pres. and Mem. of Exec. Bd, Internat. Council of Scientific Unions, 1970-73. Chairman: Smith Kline and French Trustees (UK), 1963-77; Clinical Endocrinology Cttee (MRC), 1965-72; Adv. Cttee on Irradiation of Food (UK), 1967-80; Mem. Executive Council, Ciba Foundation, 1954-67, Chm. 1967-77, Trustee, 1967-. Croonian Lecturer, Royal Society, 1962. Named lectureships held abroad: Renziehausen, Pittsburg, 1939; Sterling, Yale, 1939; Jacobæus, Oslo, 1948; Dohme, Johns Hopkins, 1950; Banting, Toronto, 1950; Banting, San Francisco, 1950; Richardson, Harvard, 1952; Hanna, Western Reserve, 1952; Woodward, Yale, 1958; Brailsford Robertson, Adelaide, 1960; Upjohn, Atlantic City, 1963. Hon. Member: Consejo Superior de Investigaciones Científicas, Madrid; Biochemical Soc. and Soc. for Endocrinology, and Hon. or corresp. member of many foreign medical and scientific bodies. Hon. FRCP. Hon. LLD Aberdeen; Hon. DSc Zimbabwe; Doctor *hc* : Catholic University of Chile; Univ. Montpellier. Coronation Medal, 1953. *Publications:* scientific papers in Biochemical Journal and other scientific and medical journals on hormonal control of metabolism, diabetes mellitus, and related topics. *Address:* 11 Bentley Road, Cambridge CB2 2AW. *T:* Cambridge 352650. *Club:* Athenæum.

See also E. E. Young.

YOUNG, Frederick Trestrail Clive, CBE 1937; *b* 19 March 1887; *y s* of late James Young, Calcutta, and of late L. Z. Young, Rockmount, Helensburgh, Dunbartonshire; *m* 1920, Hope MacLellan Fulton, Findhorn, Helensburgh; two *s* one *d*. *Educ:* Merchiston Castle, Edinburgh (School Captain); Pembroke Coll., Cambridge. BA (Hons Classical Tripos, 1909); Sudan Political Service, 1910, District Commissioner; Commissioner Nomad (Beja) Administration, 1926; Assistant Civil Secretary, 1929-32; Governor: Kassala Province, 1932-34; Blue Nile Province, 1934-36; Retired, 1936; Order of Nile 4th class, 1920, 3rd class, 1930; King George V Jubilee Medal, 1935. *Recreations:* golf, tennis, sailing. *Address:* West Down House, Budleigh Salterton, Devon. *T:* Budleigh Salterton 2762. *Club:* Royal Commonwealth Society.

YOUNG, Frieda Margaret, OBE 1969; HM Diplomatic Service, retired; *b* 9 April 1913; *d* of Arthur Edward Young. *Educ:* Wyggeston Grammar Sch., Leicester; Wycombe Abbey Sch., Bucks; and in France and Germany. Home Office, 1937-39; Min. of Home Security, 1939-41; MOI 1941-44; Paris 1944-48; Tehran 1948-51; Vienna 1951-54; FO 1954-57; First Secretary and Consul, Reykjavik, 1957-59; Consul, Cleveland, 1959-62; FO 1962-65; Consul, Bergen, 1965-68; Consul-General, Rotterdam, 1968-73. *Recreations:* travel, photography, bird-watching. *Address:* 6 Lady Street, Lavenham, Suffolk. *Club:* Royal Commonwealth Society.

YOUNG, Gavin Neil B.; *see* Barr Young.

YOUNG, George Bell, CBE 1976; Managing Director, East Kilbride Development Corporation, since 1973 (and Stonehouse, 1973-77); *b* 17 June 1924; *s* of late George Bell Young and late Jemima Mackinlay; *m* 1946, Margaret Wylie Boyd (decd); one *s*; *m* 1979, Joyce Marguerite McAteer. *Educ:* Queens Park, Glasgow. MIEx 1958; MInstM 1969; FBIM 1982. RNVR, 1942-45, Lieut (destroyers and mine-sweepers). Journalist and Feature Writer, Glasgow Herald, 1945-48; North of Scotland Hydro-Electric Board, 1948-52; Chief Exec. (London), Scottish Council (Development and Industry), 1952-68; Gen. Man., E Kilbride Develt Corp., 1968-73. Mem. Council, Nat. Trust for Scotland, 1974-79; Dir, Royal Caledonian Schools, 1957-; Chm., East Kilbride and District National Savings Cttee, 1968-78; Trustee, Strathclyde Scanner Campaign; Scottish Chm., British Heart Foundn, 1975-79 (Mem., East Kilbride Cttee, 1970-; Pres., Scottish Appeal, 1980-); Chm., E Kilbride Cttee, Order of St John (CStJ 1979). FRSA 1968. Member:

Saints and Sinners Club of Scotland (Hon. Sec., 1982-); Royal Glasgow Inst. of the Fine Arts; The Merchants House of Glasgow; Cttee of 20 Nat. Children's Homes for Scotland. *Recreations:* golf, fishing. *Address:* 4 Newlands Place, East Kilbride, Lanarkshire. *T:* East Kilbride 30094. *Clubs:* Caledonian; Royal Scottish Automobile (Glasgow).

YOUNG, George Kennedy, CB 1960; CMG 1955; MBE 1945; *b* 8 April 1911; *s* of late George Stuart Young and Margaret Kennedy, Moffat, Dumfriesshire; *m* 1939, Géryke, *d* of late Dr M. A. G. Harthoorn, Batavia, Dutch EI. *Educ:* Dumfries Acad.; Univs of St Andrews, Giessen, Dijon, Yale, MA (First Class Hons Mod. Langs) 1934; Commonwealth Fund Fellowship, 1934-36; MA (Political Science), Yale, 1936; Editorial staff The Glasgow Herald, 1936-38; British United Press, 1938-39. Served War of 1939-45; commissioned KOSB 1940 (despatches, E Africa, 1941); specially employed list, Italy and W Europe, 1943-45. Berlin correspondent, British United Press, 1946. Joined HM Foreign Service, 1946; Vienna, 1946; Economic Relations Dept, FO, 1949; British Middle East Office, 1951; Ministry of Defence, 1953-61; Under-Secretary, 1960. Kleinwort, Benson Ltd, 1961-76; Pres., Nuclear Fuel Finance SA, 1969-76. Medal of Freedom (Bronze Palm), 1945. *Publications:* Masters of Indecision, 1962; Merchant Banking, 1966; Finance and World Power, 1968; Who Goes Home?, 1969; Who is my Liege?, 1972. *Recreations:* music, reading, swimming, walking. *Address:* 37 Abbotsbury House, W14. *T:* 01-603 8432.

YOUNG, Sir George (Samuel Knatchbull), 6th Bt, *cr* 1813; MP (C) Ealing, Acton, since Feb. 1974; Parliamentary Under Secretary of State, Department of the Environment, since 1981; *b* 16 July 1941; *s* of Sir George Young, 5th Bt, CMG, and Elisabeth (*née* Knatchbull-Hugessen); *S* father 1960; *m* 1964, Aurelia Nemon-Stuart, *er d* of Oscar Nemon, *qv*, and of Mrs Nemon-Stuart, Boar's Hill, Oxford; two *s* two *d. Educ:* Eton; Christ Church, Oxford (Open Exhibitioner); MA Oxon, MPhil Surrey. Economist, NEDO, 1966-67; Kobler Research Fellow, University of Surrey, 1967-69; Economic Adviser, PO Corp., 1969-74. Councillor, London Borough of Lambeth, 1968-71; Mem., GLC, for London Borough of Ealing, 1970-73. An Opposition Whip, 1976-79; Parly Under Sec. of State, DHSS, 1979-81. Chm., Acton Housing Assoc., 1972-79. *Publications:* Accommodation Services in the UK 1970-1980, 1970; Tourism, Blessing or Blight?, 1973. *Recreations:* squash, bicycling. *Heir: s* George Horatio Young, *b* 11 Oct. 1966. *Address:* House of Commons, SW1A 0AA.

YOUNG, Gerard Francis, CBE 1967; JP; CEng, FIMechE; HM Lord-Lieutenant and Custos Rotolurum, for South Yorkshire, since 1974; President, Tempered Group Ltd; *b* 5 May 1910; *s* of Smelter J. Young, MICE, and Edith, *d* of Sir John Aspinall, Pres. ICE and Pres. IMechE; *m* 1937, Diana Graham Murray, MA, BSc, JP, *d* of Charles Graham Murray, MD; two *s* three *d. Educ:* Ampleforth College. Engrg Apprentice, LNER, Doncaster. Entered family firm, The Tempered Spring Co. Ltd (later Tempered Group Ltd), 1930; Dir, 1936; Man. Dir, 1942; Chm., 1954-78. Dir, 1958, Chm., 1967-80, Sheffield Area Board, Sun Alliance & London Insurance Group; Dir, National Vulcan Engineering Group, 1962-79. Member: Nat. Bd for Prices and Incomes, 1968-71; Top Salaries Review Body, 1971-74; Armed Forces Pay Review Body, 1971-74; Gen. Comr of Income Tax, 1947-74 (Chm., Don Div., 1968-74). Dir, Crucible Theatre Trust Ltd, 1967-75; Sec., Assoc. of Christian Communities in Sheffield, 1940-46; Chm., Radio Hallam Ltd, 1973-79; Trustee, Sheffield Town Trust (Town Collector, 1978-81); Chm., J. G. Graves Charitable Fund, 1974-; Chm., Freshgate Foundn, 1979-; President: Council of St John, South and West Yorks, 1979-; Yorks Volunteers Council, 1980-81. Univ. of Sheffield: Mem. Council, 1943; Treas., 1947-51; Pro-Chancellor, 1951-67; Chm., 1956-67. Mem. Bd of Govs, United Sheffield Hosps, 1948-53 (Chm. of Finance Cttee, 1948-50); Chm., Royal Hosp., 1951-53. Master, Company of Cutlers in Hallamshire, 1961-62. JP Sheffield, 1950. High Sheriff of Hallamshire, 1973-74; DL West Riding of Yorks, 1974. Hon. LLD Sheffield, 1962. KStJ 1976; GCSG 1974. *Recreations:* gardening, 12 grandchildren. *Address:* 69 Carsick Hill Crescent, Sheffield S10 3LS. *T:* Sheffield 302834. *Clubs:* Carlton; Sheffield (Sheffield).
See also H. J. S. Young.

YOUNG, Air Vice-Marshal Gordon, CBE 1963; retired; *b* 29 May 1919; *s* of late Robert Young, MBE, and late Emily Florence Young, Doncaster; *m* 1943, Pamela Doris Weatherstone-Smith; two *d. Educ:* Maltby Grammar School; Sheffield Univ. Served War of 1939-45, Flying Boat Ops S Atlantic and Western Approaches (despatches); Air Min., 1945-47; Asst Air Attaché, Moscow, 1949-52; OC No 204 Sqdn, 1954-55; RAF Staff Coll., 1956; OC Flying Wing, RAF St Mawgan, 1958-60; Asst Chief, Comdrs-in-Chief Mission to Soviet Forces in Germany, 1960-63; OC RAF Wyton, 1963-65; Air Attaché, Bonn, 1966-68; SASO Coastal Command, 1968-69; COS No 18 (M) Gp, 1969-71. *Recreation:* bird-watching (MBOU 1969). *Address:* 703-185 Ontario Street, Kingston, Ont K7L 2Y7, Canada. *T:* 613-549-2461. *Clubs:* Royal Air Force; Royal Scottish Automobile (Glasgow).
See also Eric Young.

YOUNG, Most Rev. Sir Guilford; see Hobart, Archbishop of, (RC).

YOUNG, Maj.-Gen. Hugh A., CB 1946; CBE 1945; DSO 1944; CD 1954; Vice-President, Central Mortgage and Housing Corporation since 1947; *b* 3 April 1898; *s* of Andrew and Emily Young, Winnipeg; *m* 1927; one *s* one *d. Educ:* Winnipeg Collegiate; University of Manitoba (BSc Elec. Engineering, 1924). RC Signals, 1924; Staff Coll., Camberley, England,

1933-34; various General Staff appointments during the war; commanded Inf. Bde, operations Normandy, 1944; QMG Canadian Army, 1944-47; retired, 1947. Dep. Minister of Department of Resources and Development, and Comr of NW Territories, Canada, 1950-53; Dep. Minister, Dept of Public Works, 1953-63. *Address:* Apt 104, Plaza Towers, 465 Richmond Road, Ottawa, Canada.

YOUNG, Hugo John Smelter; Political Editor since 1973, and Joint Deputy Editor since 1981, The Sunday Times; *b* 13 Oct. 1938; *s* of Gerard Francis Young, *qv*; *m* 1966, Helen Mason; one *s* three *d. Educ:* Ampleforth Coll.; Balliol Coll., Oxford (Ba Jurisprudence). Yorkshire Post, 1961; Harkness Fellow, 1963; Congressional Fellow, US Congress, 1964; The Sunday Times, 1965-: Chief Leader Writer, 1966-77. Columnist of the Year, British Press Awards, 1980. *Publications:* (jtly) The Zinoviev Letter, 1966; (jtly) Journey to Tranquillity, 1969; The Crossman Affair, 1974; (jtly) No, Minister, 1982. *Address:* The Sunday Times, 200 Gray's Inn Road, WC1X 8EZ.

YOUNG, Jimmy; see Young, L. R.

YOUNG, John Allen, CBE 1975; Chairman and Managing Director, Young & Co.'s Brewery, since 1962; *b* 7 Aug. 1921; *e s* of late William Allen Young and of Joan Barrow Simonds; *m* 1951, Yvonne Lieutenant, Liège; one *s. Educ:* Nautical Coll., Pangbourne; Corpus Christi Coll., Cambridge (BA Hons Econs). Served War, 1939-45: Lt-Comdr (A) RNVR; comd 888 Naval Air Sqdn (despatches). Runciman Ltd, 1947; Moor Line, 1949; Young & Co.'s Brewery, 1954-. Director: Foster-Probyn Ltd; Cockburn & Campbell; Chm., RI Shipping Ltd. Gen. Comr of Taxes, 1965-. President: London Carthorse Parade Soc., 1957-68; Shire Horse Soc., 1963-64 (Treas., 1962-73); Greater London Horse Show, 1972-74; Battersea Scouts, 1974-. Chm., Bd of Governors, Nat. Hosps for Nervous Diseases, 1982- (Mem. Bd, 1972-; Chm. Finance, 1974-82); Dep. Chm., Inst. of Neurology, 1982- (Chm., Jt Res. Adv. Cttee, 1973-82). *Recreations:* music, sailing. *Address:* Moonsbrook Cottage, Wisborough Green, West Sussex. *T:* Wisborough Green 355. *Club:* Royal Yacht Squadron (Cowes).

YOUNG, Major John Darling, JP; Lord-Lieutenant of Buckinghamshire, since 1969; *b* 4 Jan. 1910; *o s* of late Sir Frederick Young; *m* 1934, Nina (*d* 1974), *d* of late Lt-Col H. W. Harris; three *d. Educ:* Eton and Oxford (BA). Commissioned The Life Guards, 1932-46; Middle East and Italy, 1940-44. Member Bucks Agricultural Executive Cttee, 1947-58. Pres., Eastern Wessex TA&VRA, 1976-78. DL 1958, High Sheriff, 1960, JP 1964, CC 1964-77, CA 1969-74, Buckinghamshire. KStJ 1969. *Recreation:* shooting. *Address:* Thornton Hall, Thornton, Milton Keynes MK17 0HB. *T:* Buckingham 3234. *Clubs:* Turf, Cavalry and Guards.

YOUNG, Sir John (Kenyon Roe), 6th Bt *cr* 1821; Purchasing Analyst; *b* 23 April 1947; *s* of Sir John William Roe Young, 5th Bt, and Joan Minnie Agnes (*d* 1958), *d* of M. M. Aldous; *S* father, 1981; *m* 1977, Frances Elise, *o d* of W. R. Thompson. *Educ:* Hurn Court; Napier College. Joined RN, 1963; transferred to Hydrographic Branch, 1970; qualified Hydrographic Surveyor, 1977; retired from RN, 1979; attended Napier Coll., 1979-80. Mem. Hydrographic Soc. *Recreations:* Rugby, golf. *Heir: uncle* Patrick Elliott Young [*b* 6 March 1917; *m* 1946, Sadie Reid, *o d* of Laurence Beattie; one *s* three *d*]. *Address:* 8 Morar Place, Kinross, Tayside KY13 7YX.

YOUNG, Hon. Sir John (McIntosh), KCMG 1975; Hon. Mr Justice Young; Lieutenant-Governor of Victoria and Chief Justice of the Supreme Court of Victoria, Australia, since 1974; *b* Melbourne, 17 Dec. 1919; *s* of George David Young, Glasgow, and Kathleen Mildred Young, Melbourne; *m* 1951, Elisabeth Mary, *yr d* of late Dr Edward Wing Twining, Manchester; one *s* two *d. Educ:* Geelong Grammar Sch.; Brasenose Coll., Oxford (MA); Inner Temple; Univ. of Melbourne (LLB). Served War: Scots Guards, 1940-46 (Captain 1943); NW Europe (despatches), 1945. Admitted Victorian Bar, 1948; Associate to Mr Justice Dixon, High Court of Australia, 1948; practice as barrister, 1949-74; Hon. Sec., Victorian Bar Council, 1950-60; Lectr in Company Law, Univ. of Melbourne, 1957-61; Hon. Treas., Medico Legal Soc. of Vic., 1955-65 (Vice-Pres., 1966-68; Pres., 1968-69). QC (Vic.) 1961; admitted Tasmanian Bar, 1964, QC 1964; NSW Bar, 1968, QC 1968; Consultant, Faculty of Law, Monash Univ., 1968-74. Mem., Bd of Examiners for Barristers and Solicitors, 1969-72; Mem. Council, Geelong Grammar Sch., 1974; Pres., Victorian Council of Legal Educn and Victoria Law Foundn, 1974-. Pres., Victorian Br., Scout Assoc. of Australia, 1974-; Pres., St John Council for Victoria, 1975-; KStJ 1977; Chancellor, Order of St John in Australia, 1982-. Hon. Col, 4th/19th Prince of Wales's Light Horse, 1978-. *Publications:* (co-author) Australian Company Law and Practice, 1965; articles in legal jls. *Recreations:* riding, golf. *Address:* 17 Sorrett Avenue, Malvern, Victoria 3144, Australia. *Clubs:* Cavalry and Guards; Melbourne, Australian (Melbourne).

YOUNG, John Richard Dendy; Advocate of Supreme Court, South Africa, since 1971, Senior Counsel, South Africa, since 1979; *b* 4 Sept. 1907; 5th *s* of James Young and Evelyn Maud Hammond; *m* 1946, Patricia Maureen Mount; four *s* two *d. Educ:* Hankey, Cape Province, SA; Humansdorp, CP, SA; University, South Africa (External). Joined Public Service, S Rhodesia, 1926; resigned to practise at Bar, 1934; joined Military Forces, 1940; active service, North Africa, Sicily and Italy; commissioned in the field; demobilised, 1945. QC 1948; MP Southern Rhodesia, 1948-53; Member Federal Assembly, 1953-56; Judge of the High Court of Rhodesia, 1956-68; Chief Justice,

Botswana, 1968-71. *Recreations:* swimming, walking. *Address:* 8 Tulani Gardens, Greenfield Road, Kenilworth, Cape, 7700, South Africa. *Club:* Salisbury (Zimbabwe).

YOUNG, John Zachary, MA; FRS 1945; Professor of Anatomy, University College, London, 1945-74, now Emeritus, Hon. Fellow, 1975; *b* 18 March 1907; *s* of Philip Young and Constance Maria Lloyd. *Educ:* Wells House, Malvern Wells; Marlborough Coll.; Magdalen Coll., Oxford (Demy). Senior Demy, Magdalen Coll., 1929, Christopher Welch Scholar, 1928, Naples Biological Scholar, 1928, 1929; Fellow of Magdalen Coll., Oxford, 1931-45 (Hon. Fellow, 1975); University Demonstrator in Zoology and Comparative Anatomy, Oxford, 1933-45; Rockefeller Fellow, 1936. Fullerton Professor of Physiology, Royal Institution, 1958-61. Pres., Marine Biol Assoc., 1976-. Foreign Member: Amer. Acad. of Arts and Scis; Amer. Philosophical Soc.; Accademia dei Lincei. Hon. DSc: Bristol, 1965; McGill, 1967; Durham, 1969; Bath, 1973; Duke, 1978; Oxford, 1979; Hon. LLD: Glasgow, 1975; Aberdeen, 1980. Royal Medal, Royal Society, 1967. *Publications:* The Life of Vertebrates, 1950, 3rd edn 1981; Doubt and Certainty in Science, 1951; The Life of Mammals, 1957; A Model of the Brain, 1964 (lectures); The Memory System of the Brain, 1966; An Introduction to the Study of Man, 1971; The Anatomy of the Nervous System of *Octopus vulgaris*, 1971; Programs of the Brain, 1978; scientific papers, mostly on the nervous system. *Address:* 166 Camden Road, NW1. *T:* 01-485 0498.

YOUNG, Kenneth; *see* Young, C. K.

YOUNG, Kenneth Middleton, CBE 1977; Member of Board (Personnel and Industrial Relations), Post Office Corporation, since 1972; *b* 1 Aug. 1931; *s* of Cyril W. D. Young and Gwladys Middleton Young; *m* 1958, Brenda May Thomas; one *s* one *d. Educ:* Neath Grammar Sch.; University Coll. of Wales, Aberystwyth; Coll. of Science and Technology, Univ. of Manchester. BA (Hons) 1952. Pilot Officer/Navigator, General Duties (Aircrew), RAF, 1952-54. Asst Personnel Manager, Elliott-Automation Ltd, 1955-59; Collective Agreements Manager, later Salary Administration Manager, Massey-Ferguson (UK) Ltd, 1959-64; Personnel Adviser, Aviation Div., Smiths Industries Ltd, 1964-66; Group Personnel Manager, General Electric Company Ltd, and Dir, GEC (Management) Ltd, 1966-71. Member: Management Bd, Engineering Employers Fedn, 1971; CBI Employment Policy Cttee; Council, Inst. of Manpower Studies. MIPM. *Recreations:* photography; Chelsea Football Club. *Address:* Ingleton, Main Drive, Gerrards Cross, Bucks. *T:* Gerrards Cross 85422.

YOUNG, Leslie, DSc (London), PhD, FRSC; Professor of Biochemistry in the University of London, and Head of the Department of Biochemistry, St Thomas's Hospital Medical School, London, SE1, 1948-76, now Professor Emeritus; Hon. Consultant, St Thomas' Hospital; *b* 27 Feb. 1911; *o c* of John and Ethel Young; *m* 1939, Ruth Elliott; one *s. Educ:* Sir Joseph Williamson's Mathematical Sch., Rochester; Royal College of Science, London; University College, London. Sir Edward Frankland Prize and Medal of Royal Institute of Chemistry, 1932; Bayliss-Starling Memorial Scholar in Physiology, University Coll., London, 1933-34; Asst Lectr in Biochemistry, University College, London, 1934-35; Commonwealth Fund Fellow in Biochemistry at Washington Univ. Medical School and Yale Univ., USA, 1935-37; Lectr in Biochemistry, University Coll., London, 1937-39; Assoc. Prof. of Biochemistry, Univ. of Toronto, 1939-44; chemical warfare research for the Dept of Nat. Defence, Canada, 1940-46; Prof. of Biochemistry, Univ. of Toronto, 1944-47; Reader in Biochemistry, University Coll., London, 1947-48. Hon. Sec., The Biochemical Soc., 1950-53; Vice-Pres., The Royal Institute of Chemistry, 1964-66; Mem., Bd of Governors, St Thomas' Hosp., 1970-74; Chm. of Council, Queen Elizabeth Coll., London Univ., 1975-80, Hon. Fellow, 1980. *Publications:* (with G. A. Maw) The Metabolism of Sulphur Compounds, 1958; papers on chem. and biochem. subjects in various scientific journals. *Address:* 23 Oaklands Avenue, Esher, Surrey KT10 8HX. *T:* 01-398 1262. *Club:* Athenæum.

YOUNG, Leslie Clarence, CBE 1980; Chairman, J. Bibby & Sons Ltd, since 1979; Chairman, Merseyside Development Corporation, since 1981; *b* 5 Feb. 1925; *s* of late Clarence James Young and of Ivy Isabel Young; *m* 1949, Muriel Howard Pearson; one *s* one *d. Educ:* London School of Economics (BScEcon). Courtaulds Ltd: held range of senior executive appts, incl. chairmanship of number of gp companies, 1948-68; J. Bibby & Sons Ltd, 1968: Managing Director, J. Bibby Agriculture Ltd, 1968; Chm. and Man. Dir, J. Bibby Food Products Ltd, 1970; Gp Man. Dir, J. Bibby & Sons Ltd, 1970; Dep. Chm. and Man. Dir, J. Bibby & Sons Ltd, 1977. Chairman: NW Regional Council, CBI, 1976-78; NW Industrial Development Board, 1978-81; Trustee, Civic Trust for the North West, 1978-. Regional Dir, N Regional Bd, National Westminster Bank Ltd, 1979-; Non-Exec. Dir, Granada Television Ltd, 1979-. Member Council: N of England Zoological Soc., 1979-; Royal Liverpool Philharmonic Soc., 1980-. *Recreations:* golf, fly-fishing, walking. *Address:* Orchard House, Haddon Lane, Ness, South Wirral L64 8TA. *T:* 051-336 5224. *Club:* Carlton.

YOUNG, Leslie Ronald, (Jimmy Young), OBE 1979; Presenter, Jimmy Young Programme, BBC Radio Two, since 1973 (Radio One, 1967-73); *b* 21 Sept.; *s* of Frederick George Young and Gertrude Woolford; *m* 1st, 1946, Wendy Wilkinson (marr. diss.); one *d*; 2nd, 1950, Sally Douglas (marr. diss.). *Educ:* East Dean Grammar Sch., Cinderford, Glos. RAF, 1939-46. First BBC radio broadcast, songs at piano, 1949; pianist, singer, bandleader, West End,

London, 1950-51; first theatre appearance, Empire Theatre, Croydon, 1952; regular theatre appearances, 1952-; first radio broadcast introd. records, Flat Spin, 1953; BBC TV Bristol, Pocket Edition series, 1955; first introd. radio Housewives' Choice, 1955; BBC radio series, incl.: The Night is Young, 12 o'clock Spin, Younger Than Springtime, Saturday Special, Keep Young, Through Till Two, 1959-65; presented progs, Radio Luxembourg, 1960-68. BBC TV: series, Jimmy Young Asks, 1972; The World of Jimmy Young, 1973. First live direct BBC broadcasts to Europe from Soviet Union, Jimmy Young Programme, 16 and 17 May 1977; Jimmy Young Programmes broadcast live from Egypt and Israel, 9 and 12 June 1978, from Zimbabwe-Rhodesia, 9 and 10 Aug. 1979; Host for Thames TV of first British Telethon, 2nd and 3rd Oct. 1980; Jimmy Young Programme live from Tokyo, 26th, 27th and 28th May 1981. ITV series: Whose Baby?, 1973; Jim's World, 1974. Hit Records: 1st, Too Young, 1951; Unchained Melody, The Man From Laramie, 1955 (1st Brit. singer to have 2 consec. no 1 hit records); Chain Gang, More, 1956; Miss You, 1963. Weekly Column, Daily Sketch, 1968-71. Variety Club of GB Award, Radio Personality of the Year, 1968. *Publications:* Jimmy Young Cookbook: No. 1, 1968; No. 2, 1969; No 3, 1970; No 4, 1972; (autobiogs) JY, 1973, Jimmy Young, 1982; contrib. magazines, incl. Punch, Woman's Own. *Recreation:* worrying. *Address:* c/o Broadcasting House, Portland Place, W1A 1AA. *Clubs:* Wig and Pen; Wigan Rugby League Social.

YOUNG, Mark; General Secretary, British Air Line Pilots' Association, since 1974; *b* 7 June 1929; *s* of Arnold Young and Florence May (*née* Lambert); *m* 1st, 1952, Charlotte Maria (*née* Rigol) (*d* 1978); two *s* two *d*; 2nd, 1979, Marie-Thérèse, (Mollie) (*née* Craig); one *s. Educ:* Pendower Technical Sch., Newcastle upon Tyne. Electrician, 1944-61; Head of Res., ETU, 1961; National Officer, ETU, 1963-73. *Recreations:* flying, ballooning, golf, tennis. *Address:* 81 New Road, Harlington, Hayes, Mddx.

YOUNG, Mary Lavinia Bessie, OBE 1967; Matron of the Westminster Hospital, SW1, 1951-66, retired; Mayor of Shaftesbury, Dorset, 1971-72; *b* 15 Nov. 1911; *d* of late Bennett and Rosalind Young. *Educ:* Girls' High Sch., Shaftesbury, Dorset. SRN, RSCN, SCM. Belgrave Hospital for Sick Children, SW9, 1929-32; KCH, SE5, 1933-36; Chiswick and Ealing Maternity Hospital, 1937; private nursing, 1938. King's College Hospital: Night Sister, 1938-40; Home Sister, 1940-41; Sister, Private Patients' Wing, 1941-44. Asst Matron, Royal Hospital, Richmond Surrey, 1944-45; Asst and Dep. Matron, Westminster Hospital, SW1, 1945-51. *Recreation:* gardening. *Address:* St Martins, Angel Square, Shaftesbury, Dorset. *T:* Shaftesbury 2020.

YOUNG, Sir Norman (Smith), Kt 1968; Chairman: Pipelines Authority of South Australia, since 1967; South Australian Brewing Co. Ltd; South Australian Oil and Gas Corporation Pty Ltd; *b* 24 July 1911; *s* of Thomas and Margaret Young; *m* 1936, Jean Fairbairn Sincock; two *s* one *d. Educ:* Norwood High Sch.; University of Adelaide. Member: Adelaide City Council, 1949-60; Municipal Tramways Trust, 1951-67 (Dep. Chairman); Royal Commn on Television, 1953-54; Bankruptcy Law Review Cttee, 1956-62. Chairman: News Ltd, 1971-81; Elder Smith Goldsbrough Mort Ltd, 1975-81; Bradmill Ltd, 1979-82. Fellow, Inst. of Chartered Accountants, 1933; FASA, 1932; Associate in Commerce, University of Adelaide, 1930. *Publication:* Bankruptcy Practice in Australia, 1942. *Address:* 256 Stanley Street, North Adelaide, South Australia 5006, Australia. *T:* 2673688.

YOUNG, Brig. Peter, DSO 1942; MC 1942 and two Bars 1943; military historian; Captain-Generall, The Sealed Knot Society of Cavaliers and Roundheads, since 1968; *b* 28 July 1915; *s* of Dallas H. W. Young, MBE, and Irene Barbara Lushington Mellor; *m* 1950, Joan Duckworth; no *c. Educ:* Monmouth Sch.; Trinity Coll., Oxford. 2nd Lieut, Bedfordshire and Hertfordshire Regt, 1939. Served War of 1939-45: BEF Dunkirk (wounded), 1940; No 3 Commando, 1940; raids on Guernsey, 1940; Lofoten and Vaagso, 1941, Dieppe, 1942, Sicily and Italy, 1943; comd No 3 Commando, 1943-44; Normandy, 1944; Arakan, 1944-45; comd 1st Commando Bde, 1945-46. Commanded 9th Regt Arab Legion, 1953-56. Reader in Military History, Royal Military Acad., Sandhurst, 1959-69. Gen. Editor, Military Memoirs series, 1967-; Editor, Purnell's History of First World War, 1970-72; Editor in Chief, Orbis' World War II, 1972-74; TV Consultant: Churchill and the Generals, 1980; 1798, The Year of the French, 1981. Vice-President: Commando Assoc.; Naseby Preservation Soc.; Military Historical Soc.; Chm., Cheriton 1644 Assoc. FSA 1960; FRGS 1968. Order of El Istiqlal (Jordan) 3rd Class, 1954. *Publications:* Bedouin Command, 1956; Storm from the Sea, 1958; The Great Civil War (with late Lt-Col Alfred H. Burne, DSO), 1959; Cromwell, 1962; Hastings to Culloden (with John Adair), 1964; World War 1939-45, 1966; Edgehill, 1642: The Campaign and the Battle, 1967; The British Army, 1642-1970, 1967; The Israeli Campaign, 1967, 1967; (ed) Decisive Battles of the Second World War, 1967; Charge (with Lt-Col J. P. Lawford), 1967; (jt editor) The Civil War: Richard Atkyns and John Gwyn, 1967; Oliver Cromwell, 1968; Commando, 1969; Cropredy Bridge, 1644 (with Margaret Toynbee), 1970; Marston Moor, 1644, 1970; (ed with Lt-Col J. P. Lawford) History of the British Army, 1970; Chasseurs of the Guard, 1971; The Arab Legion, 1971; George Washington's Army, 1972; (ed) John Cruso, Militarie Instructions for the Cavall'rie, 1972; Blücher's Army, 1973; Armies of the English Civil War, 1973; (with Lt-Col J. P. Lawford) Wellington's Masterpiece, 1973; (ed and contrib.) The War Game, 1973; (ed and contrib.) The Machinery of War, 1973; (with R. Holmes) The English Civil War, 1974; Atlas of the Second World War, 1974; (with M. Toynbee)

Strangers in Oxford, 1974; (with W. Emberton) The Cavalier Army, 1974; (ed with Brig. M. Calvert) A Dictionary of Battles: 1816-1976, 1977; 1815-1915, 1977; 1715-1815, 1978; (with W. Emberton) Sieges of the Great Civil War, 1642-1646, 1978; Civil War England, 1981; The Fighting Man, 1981; numerous articles in Army Historical Research Journal and Chambers's Encyclopædia. *Recreations:* equitation, wargaming. *Address:* Flat 3, Twyning Manor, Tewkesbury, Glos. *Clubs:* Savage, The Sette of Odd Volumes.

YOUNG, Ven. Peter Claude; Archdeacon Emeritus of Cornwall and Canon Emeritus of Truro Cathedral; *b* 21 July 1916; *s* of Rev. Thomas Young and of Mrs Ethel Ashton Young; *m* 1944, Marjorie Désirée Rose; two *s. Educ:* Exeter Sch.; Exeter Coll., Oxford; Wycliffe Hall, Oxford. BA 1938, BLitt 1940, MA 1942, MLitt 1980, Oxon. Asst Curate of Ottery St Mary, 1940-44; Asst Curate of Stoke Damerel, i/c of St Bartholomew's, Milehouse, Plymouth, 1944-47; Rector of Highweek, Newton Abbot, 1947-59; Vicar of Emmanuel, Plymouth, 1959-65; Archdeacon of Cornwall and Canon Residentiary of Truro Cathedral, 1965-81; Examining Chaplain to Bishop of Truro, 1965-81. *Recreations:* motoring, fishing, reading. *Address:* 31 Princes Road, Cheltenham, Glos. *T:* Cheltenham 39955.

YOUNG, Pierre Henry John, FRS 1974; Deputy Engineering Director, Rolls Royce Ltd, since 1978; *b* 12 June 1926; *s* of late David Hunter Young and late Jeanne (*née* Barrus); *m* 1953, Lily Irène (*née* Cahn); one *s* one *d. Educ:* Lycée Condorcet,Paris; Westminster Sch.; Trinity Coll., Cambridge (BA). FRAeS, FIMechE. Joined Bristol Siddeley Engines Ltd, 1949; i/c Concorde Olympus 593 engine programme from 1962; Engrg Dir, Olympus 593, Rolls Royce Ltd, 1966-70, Techn. Dir 1970-73; Dep. Company Technical Dir, Rolls Royce (1971) Ltd, 1973-76; Dir, Advanced Engineering, Rolls Royce Ltd, 1976. *Publications:* contrib. Jl RAeS. *Recreation:* mountain-walking. *Address:* 5 Rockleaze Avenue, Bristol BS9 1NG; PO Box 3, Filton, Bristol BS12 7QE.

YOUNG, Priscilla Helen Ferguson, CBE 1982; Director, Central Council for Education and Training in Social Work, since 1971; *b* 25 Nov. 1925; *d* of Fergus Ferguson Young and Helen Frances Graham (*née* Murphy). *Educ:* Kingsley Sch., Leamington Spa; Univ. of Edinburgh (MA). Social Worker: London Family Welfare Assoc., 1947-51; Somerset CC Children's Dept, 1951-53; Oxford City Children's Dept, 1953-58 (Dep. Children's Officer); Child and Family Services, Portland, Me, USA, 1958-61; Lectr/Sen. Lectr, Sch. of Social Work, Univ. of Leicester, 1961-71. Hon. Fellow, Sheffield City Polytechnic, 1977. *Publication:* The Student and Supervision in Social Work Education, 1967. *Recreations:* growing plants, clay modelling. *Address:* Derbyshire House, St Chad's Street, WC1H 8AD. *T:* 01-278 2455.

YOUNG, Sir Richard (Dilworth), Kt 1970; BSc, FIMechE; CBIM; Chairman, Boosey & Hawkes Ltd, since 1979 (Deputy Chairman, 1978-79); Director: Ingersoll Engineers Inc., since 1976; Rugby Portland Cement Co., since 1968; Commonwealth Finance Development Corp. Ltd, since 1968; *b* 9 April 1914; *s* of Philip Young and Constance Maria Lloyd; *m* 1951, Jean Barbara Paterson Lockwood, *d* of F. G. Lockwood; four *s. Educ:* Bromsgrove; Bristol Univ. Joined Weldless Steel Tube Co. Ltd, 1934; served with various Tube Investments companies in production and engineering capacities until 1944; Representative of TI in S America and Man. Dir of Tubos Britanicos (Argentina) Ltda, 1945-50; Man. Dir of TI (Export) Ltd, 1950-53; Sales Dir of TI Aluminium Ltd, 1953-56; Asst to Chm. of Tube Investments Ltd, 1957-60; Dir, 1958; Asst Man. Dir, 1959; Man. Dir, 1961-64; Chairman: Park Gate Iron & Steel Co., 1959-64; Raleigh Industries Ltd, 1960-64; Alfred Herbert Ltd: Dep. Chm., 1965-66; Chm., 1966-74; Man. Dir, 1969-70; Dir, Ingersoll Milling Machine Co., USA, 1967-71. Member: Council BIM, 1960-65; Council, IMechE, 1969-76; Adv. Cttee on Scientific Manpower, 1962-65; SSRC, 1973-75; Council, Warwick Univ., 1966-; Central Adv. Council on Science and Technol., 1967-70; SRC Engineering Bd, 1974-76. *Address:* Bearley Manor, Bearley, near Stratford-on-Avon, Warwickshire. *T:* Stratford-on-Avon 731220. *Club:* Athenæum.

YOUNG, Robert Henry; Consultant Orthopædic Surgeon, St George's Hospital, SW1, since 1946; Hon. Consultant, St Peter's Hospital, Chertsey, since 1939; *b* 6 Oct. 1903; *s* of James Allen Young and Constance Barrow Young; *m* 1st, 1929, Nancy Willcox; 2nd, 1961, Norma, *d* of Leslie Williams; two *s. Educ:* Sherborne Sch.; Emmanuel Coll., Cambridge; St Thomas' Hospital, SE1. *Publications:* numerous articles in leading medical journals. *Address:* 111 Harley Street, W1. *Clubs:* United Oxford & Cambridge University, Buck's.

YOUNG, Robert S.; Play Producer and Adjudicator; retired; *b* near Manchester, 28 May 1891; *s* of late Alexander Young, Manchester, merchant, and Elizabeth Stevenson, both from Sligo, Ireland; *m* 1923, Doris Lillian Hill, Salisbury; no *c. Educ:* Manchester Grammar Sch. Travelled in South America, South Africa, seven years in New Zealand; invited to stand for NZ Parliament for Labour; joined NZ Forces when war broke out in 1914; saw service at Anzac and in France (twice wounded); after the war joined Sir Frank Benson on the stage, founded the County Players Repertory Theatre at Tonbridge, Kent. MP (Lab) Islington North, 1929-31; actively interested in Labour movement for past 60 years. *Publication:* Cricket on the Green. *Recreations:* lacrosse, keen cricketer. *Address:* Ham Cottage, Albourne Road, Hurstpierpoint, Hassocks, Sussex.

YOUNG, Roger William, MA; STh, LHD, FRSE; Principal of George Watson's College, Edinburgh, since 1958; Scottish Governor of the BBC, since 1979; *b* 15 Nov. 1923; *yr s* of Charles Bowden Young and Dr Ruth Young, *qv* ; *m* 1950, Caroline Mary Christie; two *s* two *d. Educ:* Dragon Sch., Oxford; Westminster Sch. (King's Scholar); Christ Church, Oxford (Scholar). Served War of 1939-45, RNVR, 1942-45. Classical Mods, 1946, Lit Hum 1948. Resident Tutor, St Catharine's, Cumberland Lodge, Windsor, 1949-51; Asst Master, The Manchester Grammar Sch., 1951-58. 1st Class in Archbishop's examination in Theology (Lambeth Diploma), 1957. Participant, US State Dept Foreign Leader Program, 1964. Member: Edinburgh Marriage Guidance Council, 1960-75; Scottish Council of Christian Educn Movement, 1960-81 (Chm., 1961-67; Hon. Vice-Pres., 1981-); Management Assoc., SE Scotland, 1965-; Educational Research Bd of SSRC, 1966-70; Court, Edinburgh Univ., 1967-76; Public Schools Commn, 1968-70; Consultative Cttee on the Curriculum, 1972-75; Adv. Cttee, Scottish Centre for Studies in Sch. Administration, 1972-75; Royal Soc. of Edinburgh Dining Club, 1972-; Scottish Adv. Cttee, Community Service Volunteers, 1973-78; Edinburgh Festival Council, 1970-76; Independent Schs Panel of Wolfson Foundn, 1978-; Gen. Adv. Council of BBC, 1978-79; Scottish Council of Independent Schs, 1978-; Royal Observatory Trust, Edin., 1981-; Hon. Sec., Headmasters' Assoc. of Scotland, 1968-72, Pres., 1972-74; Chairman: HMC, 1976; BBC Consult. Gp on Social Effects of TV, 1978-79; Bursary Bd, Dawson International Ltd, 1977-; Council of Royal Soc. of Edinburgh, 1982-. Conducted Enquiry on Stirling Univ., 1973. Hon. LHD, Hamilton Coll., Clinton, NY, 1978. *Publications:* Lines of Thought, 1958; Everybody's Business, 1968; Everybody's World, 1970; Report on the Policies and Running of Stirling University 1966-1973, 1973. *Recreations:* gardening, photography, climbing, golf. *Address:* 27 Merchiston Gardens, Edinburgh EH10 5DD. *T:* 031-337 6880.

YOUNG, Ruth, CBE 1941 (MBE 1928); MB, ChB; retired; *b* 26 Jan. 1884; *d* of William B. Wilson, Flax Merchant, Dundee; *m* 1917, C. B. Young, sometime Reader in English, Delhi Univ.; two *s* one *d. Educ:* High Sch., Dundee; St Andrews Univ. BSc 1907, MB, ChB 1909; Postgraduate Study, Vienna and Dresden. Lecturer, Women's Christian Medical Coll., Ludhiana, Punjab, India, 1910-16; Professor of Surgery, Lady Hardinge Medical Coll., Delhi, 1916-17; voluntary work till 1925, chiefly in Maternity and Child Welfare; Personal Assistant to Chief Medical Officer, Women's Medical Service of India, 1925-31; Director, Maternity and Child Welfare Bureau, Indian Red Cross Society, 1931-35; Principal, Lady Hardinge Medical Coll., New Delhi, 1936-40; Rockefeller Fellowship to study Public Health Nursing in China, Japan, Canada and USA, 1934. In Ethiopia, to advise Ethiopian Women's Work Association on Welfare Work, 1943. Medical Adviser, Women's Foreign Mission, Church of Scotland, retired, 1951. Kaisar-i-Hind Gold Medal, 1936; Silver Jubilee and Coronation Medals. *Publications:* The Work of Medical Women in India (with Dr M. I. Balfour), 1929; The Science of Health, 1932; Handbook for Health Visitors (Indian Red Cross Society), 1933; numerous pamphlets on Maternity and Child Welfare, Health, etc., relating to India. *Address:* 220 Bruntsfield Place, Edinburgh EH10 4DE. *T:* 031-229 3103.

See also Roger William Young.

YOUNG, Sir Stephen Stewart Templeton, 3rd Bt, *cr* 1945; advocate; *b* 24 May 1947; *s* of Sir Alastair Young, 2nd Bt, and Dorothy Constance Marcelle (*d* 1964), *d* of late Lt-Col Charles Ernest Chambers, and *widow* of Lt J. H. Grayburn, VC, 43rd LI; *S* father, 1963; *m* 1974, Viola Margaret Nowell-Smith, *d* of Prof. P. H. Nowell-Smith, *qv* and Perilla Thyme (she *m* 2nd, Lord Roberthall, *qv*); two *s. Educ:* Rugby; Trinity Coll., Oxford; Edinburgh Univ. Voluntary Service Overseas, Sudan, 1968-69. *Heir: s* Charles Alastair Stephen Young, *b* 21 July 1979. *Address:* Glen Rowan, Shore Road, Cove, Dunbartonshire G84 0NU.

YOUNG, Stuart, FCA; Senior Partner, Hacker Young, Chartered Accountants, since 1960; a Governor of the BBC, since 1981; *b* 23 April 1934; *s* of Joseph Young and Betty (*née* Sterling); *m* 1956, Shirley (*née* Aarons); two *d. Educ:* Woodhouse, Finchley. FCA 1956; Mem., Certified Public Accountants of Israel, 1976. Director: Caledonian Airways Ltd, 1973-; Waring & Gillow (Holdings) Ltd, 1969-; Bank Leumi (UK) Ltd, 1975-; Jewish Chronicle Newspapers Ltd, 1982-; Tesco Stores (Holdings) plc, 1982-. Formerly: Chm., Beautility Ltd; Dir, Drages Ltd, Gamages Ltd, and Anglo-Portuguese Bank Ltd. Jt Pres., Jt Israel Appeal, 1977- (Treasurer, 1968-75; Chm., 1975-77). Appeal Chm., UK European Heritage, 1973-75; Chm., Central Council of Jewish Social Services, 1978. Member: Historic Bldgs Council, 1976-; Finance and Investment Cttee, Wolfson Coll., Cambridge, 1977-; British Overseas Trade Gp for Israel, 1979-. Appeals Treasurer, Bd of Deputies of British Jews, 1979-82. Trustee: Architectural Heritage Fund, 1973-; Nat. Gallery, 1980-. Governor, Tel-Aviv Univ. Freeman, City of London, 1977. *Recreations:* golf, chess, historic buildings. *Address:* Fourth Floor, St Alphage House, 2 Fore Street, EC2Y 5DH. *T:* 01-628 9771. *Clubs:* Carlton; Coombe Hill Golf; Potters Bar Golf; Hampstead Golf.

YOUNG, Wayland; *see* Kennet, Baron.

YOUNG, William Hilary, CMG 1957; HM Diplomatic Service, retired; Ambassador to Colombia 1966-70; *b* 14 Jan. 1913; *s* of late Rev. Arthur John Christopher Young and Ethel Margaret (*née* Goodwin); *m* 1946, Barbara Gordon Richmond, *d* of late Gordon Park Richmond; one *s* one *d. Educ:* Marlborough Coll.; Emmanuel Coll., Cambridge. Entered Consular Service,

1935; served HM Legation, Tehran, 1938–41; Foreign Office, 1941–45; 1st Secretary, 1945; Berlin (Political Division, Control Commission), 1945–48; HM Legation, Budapest, 1948–50; attached to IDC, 1951; Counsellor: UK High Commn, New Delhi, 1952–54; Foreign Office, 1954–57; Minister, Moscow, 1957–60; Senior Civilian Instructor, IDC, 1960–62; Minister, British Embassy, Pretoria and Cape Town, 1962–65; Fellow, Harvard University Center for Internat. Affairs, 1965–66. *Address:* Blackmoor, Four Elms, Edenbridge, Kent.

YOUNG, Hon. William Lambert, JP; High Commissioner for New Zealand in UK, since 1982; concurrently High Commissioner in Nigeria; *b* 13 Nov. 1913; *s* of James Young and Alice Gertrude Annie Young; *m* 1946, Isobel Joan Luke; one *s* four *d. Educ:* Wellington Coll. Commenced work, 1930; spent first 16 yrs with farm servicing co., interrupted by War Service, N Africa with Eighth Army, 1940–43; took over management of wholesale distributing co. handling imported and NZ manufactured goods; Gen. Man. of co. manufg and distributing radios, records, electronic equipment and owning 32 retail stores, 1956; purchased substantial interest in importing and distributing business, 1962. MP (National) Miramar, 1966–81; Minister of Works and Develt, 1975–81. Formerly Chairman: National Roads Bd; National Water and Soil Authority; NZ Fishing Licensing Authority. Formerly: Director: Johnsons Wax of NZ Ltd (subsid. of USA Co.); Howard Rotovator Co. Ltd; AA Mutual Insurance Co.; J. J. Niven Ltd; NZ Motor Bodies Ltd; Trustee, Wellington Savings Bank. Life Mem., AA of Wellington (Mem. Council). JP 1962. *Address:* New Zealand High Commission, New Zealand House, Haymarket, SW1Y 4TQ. *T:* 01-930 8422. *Club:* Wellington (Wellington, NZ).

YOUNG, Sir William Neil, 10th Bt, *cr* 1769; Managing Director, KBIM (Pacific) Ltd; Director, Kleinwort Benson (Hong Kong) Ltd; *b* 22 Jan. 1941; *s* of Captain William Elliot Young, RAMC (killed in action 27 May 1942), and Mary, *d* of late Rev. John Macdonald; *S* grandfather, 1944; *m* 1965, Christine Veronica Morley, *o d* of R. B. Morley, Buenos Aires; one *s* one *d. Educ:* Wellington Coll.; Sandhurst. Captain, 16th/5th The Queen's Royal Lancers, retired 1970. *Recreations:* ski-ing, sailing, tennis, shooting. *Heir: s* William Lawrence Elliot Young, *b* 26 May 1970. *Address:* 39 Tung Tau Wan Road, Stanley, Hong Kong.

YOUNG-HERRIES, Sir Michael Alexander Robert; *see* Herries.

YOUNGER, family name of Viscount Younger of Leckie.

YOUNGER OF LECKIE, 3rd Viscount, *cr* 1923; **Edward George Younger;** OBE 1940; 3rd Bt of Leckie, *cr* 1911; Lord-Lieutenant, Stirling and Falkirk (formerly of County of Stirling), 1964–79; Colonel, Argyll and Sutherland Highlanders (TA); *b* 21 Nov. 1906; *er s* of 2nd Viscount and Maud (*d* 1957), *e d* of Sir John Gilmour, 1st Bt; *S* father 1946; *m* 1930, Evelyn Margaret, MBE (1963), *e d* of late Alexander Logan McClure, KC; three *s* one *d. Educ:* Winchester; New Coll., Oxford. Served War of 1939–45 (OBE). *Heir: s* Hon. George (Kenneth Hotson) Younger, *qv. Address:* Leckie, Gargunnock, Stirling. *T:* Gargunnock 281. *Club:* New (Edinburgh).

See also Hon. R. E. G. Younger.

YOUNGER, Maj.-Gen. Allan Elton, DSO 1944; OBE 1962; MA; Director-General, Royal United Services Institute for Defence Studies, 1976–78; *b* 4 May 1919; *s* of late Brig. Arthur Allan Shakespear Younger, DSO, and late Marjorie Rhoda Younger (*née* Halliley); *m* 1942, Diana Lanyon; three *d. Educ:* Gresham's; RMA Woolwich; Christ's Coll., Cambridge. Commnd RE, 1939; France and Belgium, 1940; France, Holland and Germany, 1944–45; Burma, 1946–47; Malaya, 1948; Korea, 1950–51; RMA Sandhurst, 1954–57; Bt Lt-Col 1959; comd 36 Corps Engineer Regt in UK and Kenya, 1960–62; Instructor US Army Comd and Gen. Staff Coll., Fort Leavenworth, 1963–66; Programme Evaluation Gp, 1966–68; Chief Engr, Army Strategic Comd, 1968–69; COS, HQ Allied Forces Northern Europe, Oslo, 1970–72; Sen. Army Mem., Directing Staff, RCDS, 1972–75. Col Comdt, RE, 1974–79. Member Council: British Atlantic Cttee; Lord Kitchener Nat. Meml Fund. Silver Star (US), 1951. *Publications:* contribs to RUSI Jl, Military Review (USA). *Recreations:* ski-ing, writing. *Address:* Southern Haye, Heath Rise, Camberley, Surrey. *T:* Camberley 21214. *Club:* Army and Navy.

YOUNGER, Charles Frank Johnston, DSO 1944; TD 1952; *b* 11 Dec. 1908; *s* of late Major Charles Robert Johnston Younger, King's Dragoon Guards; *m* 1935, Joanna, *e d* of late Rev. John Kyrle Chatfeild, BD, MA, LLB; one *d. Educ:* Royal Naval Coll., Dartmouth. Served Royal Navy, 1926–37. Served War of 1939–45 (despatches, DSO); RA (Field), 15th Scottish Division, 1939–41; 17th Indian Light Div., Burma, 1942–45; commanded 129th Lowland Field Regt, RA, 1942–45 and 278th Lowland Field Regt RA (TA), 1946–52 (Lt-Col). Joined William Younger & Co. Ltd, 1937, Dir 1945–73; Dir, Scottish & Newcastle Breweries Ltd, 1946–73; Dir, Bank of Scotland, 1960–79. Vice Pres., Brewers' Soc. (Chm., 1964–45); Chm., Scottish Union & National Insurance Co., 1954–57, 1966–68, Dep. Chm., 1968–79; Dir, Norwich Union and Associated Cos, 1966–79, Vice-Chm., 1976–79. Chm., Scottish Adv. Bd, 1976–80. UK deleg. to EFTA Brewing Ind. Council, 1964–73; Mem. Council, CBI, 1965–73. Mem., Worshipful Company of Brewers. Mem., Royal Company of Archers (Queen's Body Guard for Scotland). Freeman of the City of London. *Recreations:* country pursuits. *Address:* Painsthorpe Hall, Kirby Underdale, York. *T:* Bishop Wilton 342.

Clubs: Boodle's, Pratt's.
See also Earl of Halifax.

YOUNGER, Rt. Hon. George (Kenneth Hotson), TD 1964; PC 1979; DL; MP (C) Ayr, since 1964; Secretary of State for Scotland, since 1979; *b* 22 Sept. 1931; *e s* and *heir* of 3rd Viscount Younger of Leckie, *qv* ; *m* 1954, Diana Rhona, *er d* of Captain G. S. Tuck, RN, Little London, Chichester, Sussex; three *s* one *d. Educ:* Cargilfield Sch., Edinburgh; Winchester Coll.; New Coll., Oxford. Commnd in Argyll and Sutherland Highlanders, 1950; served BAOR and Korea, 1951; 7th Bn Argyll and Sutherland Highlanders (TA), 1951–65; Hon. Col, 154 (Lowland) Transport Regt, RCT, T&AVR, 1977–. Director: George Younger & Son Ltd, 1958–68; J. G. Thomson & Co. Ltd, Leith, 1962–66; Maclachlans Ltd, 1968–70; Tennant Caledonian Breweries Ltd, 1977–. Contested (U) North Lanarkshire, 1959; Unionist Candidate for Kinross and West Perthshire, 1963, but stood down in favour of Sir A. Douglas-Home. Scottish Conservative Whip, 1965–67; Parly Under-Sec. of State for Develt, Scottish Office, 1970–74; Minister of State for Defence, 1974. Chm., Conservative Party in Scotland, 1974–75 (Dep. Chm., 1967–70). Member of Queen's Body Guard for Scotland (Royal Company of Archers). DL Stirlingshire, 1968. *Recreations:* music, tennis, sailing, golf. *Address:* Easter Leckie, Gargunnock, Stirlingshire. *T:* Gargunnock 274. *Clubs:* Caledonian; Highland Brigade.

See also Hon. R. E. G. Younger.

YOUNGER, Maj.-Gen. Sir John William, 3rd Bt *cr* 1911; CBE 1969 (MBE 1945); Commissioner-in-Chief, St John Ambulance Brigade, since 1980; *b* 18 Nov. 1920; *s* of Sir William Robert Younger, 2nd Bt, and of Joan Gwendoline Johnstone (later Mrs Dennis Wheatley; she *d* 1982); *S* father, 1973; *m* 1st, 1948, Mrs Stella Jane Dodd (marr. diss. 1952), *d* of Rev. John George Lister; one *s* one *d* ; 2nd, 1953, Marcella Granito, Princess Pignatelli Di Belmonte, *d* of Prof. Avv. R. Scheggi. *Educ:* Canford Sch.; RMC Sandhurst. Served War 1939–45, Middle East (PoW) (MBE); 2nd Lt, Coldstream Gds, 1939; Lt Col 1959; AQMG, HQ London Dist, 1961–63; Col 1963; AAG, War Office, 1963–65; Brig. 1967; Dep. Dir, Army Staff Duties, MoD, 1967–70; Dir of Quartering (A), MoD, 1970–73; Maj.-Gen. 1971; Dir, Management and Support of Intelligence, 1973–76. Mem., various Civil Service Commn and Home Office Interview Bds. Dep. Comr, St John Ambulance Bde, London (Prince of Wales's) Dist, 1978. KStJ 1980. *Recreations:* golf, photography, travel. *Heir: s* Julian William Richard Younger, *b* 10 Feb. 1950. *Address:* 23 Cadogan Square, SW1X 0HU. *Club:* Boodle's.

YOUNGER, Maj.-Gen. Ralph, CB 1957; CBE 1954; DSO 1945; MC 1941; JP; DL; *b* 12 July 1904; *e s* of late William Younger, Ravenswood, Melrose; *m* 1938, Greta Mary, *d* of late A. W. Turnbull, Clifton, Maybank, Yeovil; one *s* one *d. Educ:* Charterhouse, Trinity Coll., Cambridge. 2nd Lieut, 7th Hussars, 1926; served War of 1939–45 (MC, DSO), 7th Hussars, Western Desert, 1940–41; Burma, 1942; 3rd Carabiniers, India, 1942–43; Burma, 1944; Comdr 255 Ind. Tank Bde, Burma, 1945; Lieut-Colonel comdg Royal Scots Greys, 1947–48; Commander: 30 Lowland Armoured Bde, TA, 1949–50; 7th Armoured Bde, 1950–53; Royal Armoured Corps Centre, 1953–54; GOC North Midland District and Commander 49th Armoured Division, TA, 1954–57; retired, 1958. Colonel, 7th Queen's Own Hussars, 1952–58, of Queen's Own Hussars, 1958–62; Commandant, Army Cadet Force (Scotland), 1959–65; Chairman, T&AFA, Roxburgh, Berwick and Selkirk, 1966–68; Member Royal Company of Archers (Queen's Body Guard for Scotland); Col, The Royal Scots Dragoon Guards (Carabiniers and Greys), 1971–74. JP Roxburghshire, 1961; DL Roxburgh, 1962; Ettrick and Lauderdale, 1975. Joint Master Duke of Buccleuch's Foxhounds, 1960–66. *Recreations:* hunting, fishing, and shooting. *Address:* Ravenswood, Melrose, Roxburghshire. *T:* St Boswells 2219. *Clubs:* Cavalry and Guards, Army and Navy, MCC.

YOUNGER, Hon. Robert Edward Gilmour; Sheriff of Glasgow and Strathkelvin at Glasgow, since 1979; *b* 25 Sept. 1940; third *s* of 3rd Viscount Younger of Leckie, *qv* ; *m* 1972, Helen Jane Hayes; one *s* one *d. Educ:* Cargilfield Sch., Edinburgh; Winchester Coll.; New Coll., Oxford (MA); Edinburgh Univ. (LLB); Glasgow Univ. Advocate, 1968. *Recreation:* out of doors. *Address:* Old Leckie, Gargunnock, Stirling, Scotland FK8 3BN. *T:* Gargunnock 213.

See also Rt. Hon. G. K. H. Younger.

YOUNGER, Sir William McEwan, 1st Bt, *cr* 1964, of Fountainbridge; DSO 1942; DL; Chairman: Scottish & Newcastle Breweries Ltd, 1960–69 (Managing Director, 1960–67); The Second Scottish Investment Trust Company Ltd, 1965–75; *b* 6 Sept. 1905; *y s* of late William Younger, Ravenswood, Melrose; *m* 1936, Nora Elizabeth Balfour (marr. diss., 1967); one *d. Educ:* Winchester; Balliol Coll., Oxford. Served War of 1939–45 (despatches, DSO); Western Desert, 1941–43; Italy, 1943–45; Lt-Col, RA. Hon. Sec., Scottish Unionist Assoc., 1955–64; Chm., Conservative Party in Scotland, 1971–74. Mem. Queen's Body Guard for Scotland. Director: British Linen Bank, 1955–71; Scottish Television, 1961–71; Chm., Highland Tourist (Cairngorm Development) Ltd, 1966–78. DL Midlothian, 1956. *Recreations:* mountaineering and fishing. *Heir:* none. *Address:* 29 Moray Place, Edinburgh. *T:* 031-225 8173. *Clubs:* Carlton, Alpine; New (Edinburgh).

YOUNGSON, Prof. Alexander John; Director, Research School of Social Sciences, Australian National University, since 1974; *b* 28 Sept. 1918; *s* of Alexander Brown, MA, MB, ChB and Helen Youngson; *m* 1948, Elizabeth

Gisborne Naylor; one *s* one *d. Educ:* Aberdeen Grammar Sch.; Aberdeen Univ. Pilot, Fleet Air Arm, 1940-45. MA Aberdeen Univ., 1947; Commonwealth Fellow, 1947-48. Lecturer, University of St Andrews, 1948-50; Lecturer, University of Cambridge, 1950-58; Prof. of Political Economy 1963-74, and Vice-Principal, 1971-74, Univ. of Edinburgh. Mem., Royal Fine Art Commn for Scotland, 1972-74. DLitt Aberdeen Univ., 1952. *Publications:* The American Economy, 1860-1940, 1951; Possibilities of Economic Progress, 1959; The British Economy, 1920-1957, 1960; The Making of Classical Edinburgh, 1966; Overhead Capital, 1967; After the Forty-Five, 1973; Beyond the Highland Line, 1974; Scientific Revolution in Victorian Medicine, 1979; contrib. to various journals devoted to economics and economic history. *Recreations:* gardening, fishing. *Address:* Box 4 PO, Canberra, ACT 2600, Australia.

YOUNIE, Edward Milne, OBE 1978; HM Diplomatic Service, retired; Consultant, Control Risks Ltd, since 1982; *b* 9 Feb. 1926; *s* of Mary Dickie and John Milne Younie; *m* 1st, 1952, Mary Groves (*d* 1976); 2nd, 1979, Mimi Barkley. *Educ:* Fettes Coll. (Scholar); Gonville and Caius Coll., Cambridge (Scholar) (BA Hons). RN, 1944-46. HM Colonial Service, Tanganyika, 1950-62; FCO, 1963; Johannesburg, 1964-67; Blantyre, 1967-69; First Secretary: Lagos, 1972-76; Nairobi, 1977-79; Salisbury, 1979-81 (Counsellor, 1980); FCO, 1981-82. *Recreations:* golf, tennis, music. *Address:* 31 Burton Lodge, Portinscale Road, SW15; Glebe House, Kippen, Stirling.

YOUNSON, Maj.-Gen. Eric John, OBE 1952; BSc; CEng, FRAeS, FBIM, FIIM, FRSA; Industrial Consultant; Clerk to the Worshipful Company of Scientific Instrument Makers, since 1976; *b* 1 March 1919; *o s* of late Ernest M. Younson, MLitt, BCom, Jarrow; *m* 1946, Jean Beaumont Carter, BA; three *d. Educ:* Jarrow Grammar Sch.; Univ. of Durham; Royal Military Coll. of Science. Served War of 1939-45: commissioned, RA, 1940; UK and NW Europe (despatches). Directing Staff, RMCS, 1953-55; Atomic Weapons Research Estab., 1957-58; Attaché (Washington) as rep. of Chief Scientific Adviser, 1958-61; Head of Defence Science 3, MoD, 1961-63; Dep. Dir of Artillery, 1964-66; Dir of Guided Weapons Trials and Ranges, Min. of Technology, 1967-69; Vice-Pres., Ordnance Board, 1970-72, Pres., 1972-73, retired 1973; Sen. Asst Dir, Central Bureau for Educnl Visits and Exchanges, 1973-74; Dep. Dir, SIMA, 1974-78. Freeman, City of London, 1981. *Publications:* articles on gunnery and scientific subjects in Service jls; occasional poetry. *Recreations:* photography, electronics. *Address:* 9 Montague Close, SE1. *T:* 01-403 3300; 7 Pondwick Road, Harpenden, Herts. *T:* Harpenden 5892. *Club:* Army and Navy.

YOXALL, Harry Waldo, OBE 1966; MC 1916 and Bar 1917; JP; Chairman, The Condé Nast Publications Ltd, 1957-64; President, Periodical Proprietors' Association, 1956-59 (Vice-President, 1959-65); Vice-President, International Federation of the Periodical Press, 1960-65; *b* 4 June 1896; *o s* of late Sir James Yoxall, MA, MP, JP, and late Lady Yoxall, JP (*née* Coles); *m* 1918, Josephine Fairchild Baldwin (*d* 1970); one *s* one *d. Educ:* St Paul's Sch. (captain of the school); Balliol Coll., Oxford (scholar). Served KRRC, 1915-19; British Military Mission to US, 1917-18. Joined The Condé Nast Publications Inc., 1921; appointed Business Manager and Director, The Condé Nast Publications Ltd, 1924; Managing Director, 1934. Comr of Income Tax for Elmbridge Div. of Surrey, 1944-50. Chairman, General Periodicals' Council, Periodical Proprietors' Assoc., 1947-51. Member Council of Royal College of Art, 1951-54; a Governor of the Star and Garter Home for Disabled Sailors, Soldiers and Airmen, 1943-76, Vice-Pres., 1976- (Chairman, Finance Cttee, 1964-68). Chm., Internat. Wine and Food Soc., 1972-75, Vice-Pres., 1975-81, Pres., 1981-82. JP Richmond, Surrey, 1941- (Past Chairman of Bench and of Juvenile Court). Grand Officier, Confrérie des Chevaliers du Tastevin, 1977 (Prix Littéraire, 1979). *Publications:* Modern Love, 1927; All Abroad, 1928; A Respectable Man, 1935; Journey into Faith, 1963; Forty Years in Management, 1964; A Fashion of Life, 1966; The Wines of Burgundy, 1968, rev. edn 1978; Retirement a Pleasure, 1971; The Enjoyment of Wine, 1972. *Recreations:* wine, reading. *Address:* 10 Campden House Court, W8. *T:* 01-937 3847. *Clubs:* Savile, Saintsbury; Richmond Golf (Richmond, Surrey).

YPRES, 3rd Earl of, *cr* 1922; Viscount, *cr* 1916; of Ypres and of High Lake; **John Richard Charles Lambart French;** *b* 30 Dec. 1921; *o s* of 2nd Earl and Olivia May (*d* 1934), *d* of Maj.-Gen. Thomas John; *S* father, 1958; *m* 1st, 1943, Maureen Helena (marr. diss. 1972), *d* of Major H. John Kelly, US Foreign Service (retd), and of Mrs Kelly, Stow Bedon Hall, Attleborough, Norfolk; three *d*; 2nd, 1972, Deborah, *d* of R. Roberts, Liverpool; one *d. Educ:* Winchester; Trinity Coll., Dublin. Served War of 1939-45 as Captain, King's Royal Rifle Corps. *Heir:* none.

YUDKIN, John, MA, PhD, MD, BCh (Cambridge); BSc (London); FRCP, FRSC, FIBiol; Professor of Nutrition, University of London, at Queen Elizabeth College, 1954-71, Emeritus Professor, since 1971; *b* 8 August 1910; 3rd *s* of Louis and Sarah Yudkin, London; *m* 1933, Emily Himmelweit; three *s. Educ:* Hackney Downs (formerly Grocers' Company) School, London; Chelsea Polytechnic; Christ's Coll., Cambridge; London Hospital. Research in Biochemical Laboratory, Cambridge, 1931-36; Research in Nutritional Laboratory, Cambridge, 1938-43; Benn Levy Research Student, 1933-35; Grocers' Company Research Scholar, 1938-39; Sir Halley Stewart Research Fellow, 1940-43; Dir of Medical Studies, Christ's Coll., Cambridge, 1940-43; Prof. of Physiology, Queen Elizabeth Coll., 1945-54; Fellow, Queen Elizabeth Coll., London, 1976. William Julius Mickle Fellow, 1961-62.

Publications: This Slimming Business, 1958; The Complete Slimmer, 1964; Changing Food Habits, 1964; Our Changing Fare, 1966; Pure, White and Deadly, 1972; This Nutrition Business, 1976; A-Z of Slimming, 1977; numerous articles on biochemistry and nutrition in scientific and medical journals. *Address:* 16 Holly Walk, Hampstead, NW3. *T:* 01-794 3023.

YUKAWA, Morio, Hon. GCVO; Japanese diplomatist; *b* 23 Feb. 1908; *m* 1940, Teiko Kohiyama; two *s. Educ:* Tokyo Imperial Univ. (Law Dept). Joined Diplomatic Service, and apptd Attaché, London, 1933; Dir, Trade Bureau of Economic Stabilization Bd (Cabinet), 1950; Dir, Econ. Affairs Bureau (For. Min.), 1951; Counsellor, Paris, 1952; Dir, Internat. Co-op. Bureau (For. Min.), 1954; again Dir, Econ. Affairs Bureau, 1955; Ambassador to The Philippines, 1957-61; Dep. Vice-Minister (For. Min.), 1961-63; Ambassador to Belgium, 1963-68; concurrently Ambassador to Luxembourg and Chief of Japanese Mission to European Economic Community, 1964-68; Ambassador to Court of St James's, 1968-72. Grand Master of Ceremonies, Imperial Household, Tokyo, 1973-79. First Order of Sacred Treasure and many other decorations, inc. Hon. GCVO 1971. *Publications:* articles and brochures, principally on historical subjects. *Recreations:* golf, theatre, history and biography. *Address:* Sanbancho Hilltop, 5-10 Sanbancho, Chiyoda-ku, Tokyo, Japan. *Clubs:* Tokyo, Nihon, Gakushikai (Tokyo); Hodogaya Country (Yokohama).

YUKON, Bishop of, since 1981; **Rt. Rev. Ronald Curry Ferris;** *b* 2 July 1945; *s* of Herald Bland Ferris and Marjorie May Ferris; *m* 1965, Janet Agnes (*née* Waller); one *s* four *d. Educ:* Toronto Teachers' Coll. (diploma); Univ. of W Ontario (BA); Huron Coll., London, Ont. (MDiv). Teacher, Pape Avenue Elem. School, Toronto, 1965; Principal Teacher, Carcross Elem. School, Yukon, 1966-68. Incumbent, St Luke's Church, Old Crow, Yukon, 1970-72; Rector, St Stephen's Memorial Church, London, Ont., 1973-81. Hon. DD, Huron Coll., London, Ont., 1982. *Address:* 21 Tatchun Road, Whitehorse, Yukon Y1A 3P1, Canada.

Z

ZACHARIAH, Joyce Margaret; Secretary of the Post Office, 1975-77; *b* 11 Aug. 1932; *d* of Robert Paton Emery and Nellie Nicol (*née* Wilson); *m* 1978, George Zachariah. *Educ:* Earl Grey Sch., Calgary; Hillhead High Sch., Glasgow; Glasgow Univ. (MA 1st cl. Hons French and German, 1956). Post Office: Asst Principal, 1956; Private Sec. to Dir Gen., 1960; Principal, 1961; Asst Sec., 1967; Dir, Chairman's Office, 1970. *Address:* Vårflodsgatan 17, 41712 Gothenburg, Sweden.
See also E. J. Emery.

ZACHAROV, Prof. Vasilii, (Basil), PhD, DSc; Director, University of London Computing Centre, since 1978, and Professor of Computer Systems, since 1979; *b* 2 Jan. 1931; *s* of Viktor Nikiforovich Zakharov and Varvara Semyenovna (*née* Krzak); *m* 1959, Jeanne (*née* Hopper); one *s* one *d. Educ:* Latymer Upper Sch.; Univ. of London (BSc: Maths 1951, Phys 1952; MSc 1958; PhD 1960; DIC 1960; DSc 1977). MInstP. Research in Computer systems and applications, Birkbeck Coll., 1953-56; digital systems development, Rank Precision Instruments, 1956-57; Research Fellow, Imperial Coll., 1957-60; Physicist, European Organisation for Nuclear Res. (CERN), Geneva, 1960-65; Reader in Experimental Physics, Queen Mary Coll., London, 1965-66; Head of Computer Systems and Electronics Div., as Sen. Principal Sci. Officer, SRC Daresbury Laboratory, 1966-69, Dep. Chief Sci. Officer, 1970-78; Vis. Scientist: JINR Dubna, USSR, 1965; CERN, 1971-72; Consultant to AERE Harwell, 1965; Vis. Prof. of Physics, QMC London, 1968; Vis. Prof., Westfield Coll., 1974-78. Member, SRC Comp. Sci. Cttee, 1974-77. *Publications:* Digital Systems Logic, 1968; scientific papers in professional jls on photoelectronics, computer systems, elementary particle physics and computer applications. *Recreations:* collecting Russian miscellanea, skiing, shooting; grape growing, wine making, wine drinking. *Address:* 5 Addison Place, Holland Park, W11 4RJ. *T:* 01-603 7614.

ZAFRULLA KHAN, Hon. Chaudhri Sir Muhammad, KCSI 1937; Kt 1935; BA (Hons, Punjab), LLB (Hons, London); Hon. Bencher, Lincoln's Inn; Barrister-at-Law, Lincoln's Inn; President, International Court of Justice, 1970-73 (Member, 1954-61, 1964-73); *b* 6 Feb. 1893. *Educ:* Government College, Lahore; King's Coll. and Lincoln's Inn, London. Advocate, Sialkot, Punjab, 1914-16; practised in Lahore High Court, 1916-35; Editor, "Indian Cases", 1916-32. Member, Punjab Legislative Council, 1926-35; Deleg. Indian Round Table Confs, 1930, 1931 and 1932; Deleg. to Joint Select Cttee on Indian Parliamentary Reforms, 1933; Pres. All-India Muslim League; 1931; Mem. Viceroy's Exec. Council, 1935-41; Leader Indian Delegn to Session of Assembly of League of Nations, Dec. 1939; Agent-General to Government of India in China, 1942; Judge, Indian Fedl Court, Oct. 1941-June 1947; Constitutional Adviser to Nawab of Bhopal, June-Dec. 1947; Minister of Foreign Affairs and Commonwealth Relations, Pakistan, 1947-54; Leader Pakistan Delegn: to Annual Sessions of Gen. Assembly of UN, 1947-54; to Security Council of UN, on India-Pakistan dispute, 1948-51; Permanent Rep. of Pakistan at UN, 1961-64; Pres., UN Gen. Assembly, 1962. Hon. LLD:

Cantab; Columbia; Denver; California; Hon. FKC London; Hon. Fellow, LSE. *Publications:* Indian Cases; the Criminal Law Journal of India; Reprints of Punjab Criminal Rulings, Vol. IV; Fifteen Years' Digest; Islam: Its Meaning for Modern Man, 1962; (ed and trans.) The Quran, 1970. *Address:* 16 Gressenhall Road, SW18.

ZAHEDI, Ardeshir; Ambassador of Iran to the United States, 1959-61 and 1973-79; Ambassador of Iran to Mexico, 1973-76; *b* Tehran, 16 Oct. 1928; *s* of General Fazlollah and Khadijeh Zahedi; *m* 1957, HIH Princess Shahnaz Pahlavi (marr. diss., 1964); one *d. Educ:* American Coll. of Beirut; Utah State Univ. (BS). Treasurer, Jt Iran-American Commn, and Asst to Dir of Point 4 Program, 1950; took part in revolution led by Gen. Zahedi which overthrew Mossadegh, 1953; Special Adviser to Prime Minister, 1953; Chamberlain to HIM the Shahanshah of Iran, 1954-59; Head of Iranian Students Program, 1959-60; Head of Mission representing Iran at 150th Anniv. Celebrations in Argentina, 1960; Ambassador of Iran to the Court of St James's, 1962-66; Foreign Minister of Iran, 1967-71. Represented Iranian Govt: at signing of Treaty banning Nuclear Tests, London, 1963; at Independence Celebrations, Bahamas, 1973. Hon. Doctorates: Utah State Univ., 1951; Chungang Univ. of Seoul, 1969; East Texas State, 1973; Kent State Univ., 1974; St Louis Univ., 1975. Holds decorations from Iran and 23 other countries incl. Iranian Taj with Grand Cordon First Class, 1975. *Recreations:* hunting, shooting.

ZAHIRUDDIN bin Syed Hassan, Tun Syed, SMN, PSM, DUNM, SPMP, JMN, PJK; Governor of Malacca, since 1975; *b* 11 Oct. 1918; *m* 1949, Toh Puan Halimah, *d* of Hj. Mohd. Noh; five *s* five *d. Educ:* Malay Coll., Kuala Kangsar; Raffles Coll., Singapore (Dip.Arts). Passed Cambridge Sch. Cert. Malay Officer, Tanjong Malim, etc, 1945-47; Dep. Asst Dist Officer, 1948; Asst Dist Officer, 1951-54; 2nd Asst State Sec., Perak, 1955; Registrar of Titles and Asst State Sec. (Lands), Perak, 1956; Dist Officer, Batang Padang, Tapah, 1957; Dep. Sec., Public Services Commn, 1958; Principal Asst Sec. (Service), Fedn Estabt Office, Kuala Lumpur, 1960; State Sec., Perak, 1961; Permanent Sec.: Min. of Agric. and Co-operatives, Kuala Lumpur, 1963; Min. of Educn, Kuala Lumpur, 1966; Dir-Gen., Public Services Dept, Kuala Lumpur, 1969; retd, 1972. High Comr for Malaysia in London, 1974-75. Chm., Railway Services Commn, Kuala Lumpur, 1972-. Chairman: Special Cttee on Superannuation in the Public Services, 1972, and Statutory Bodies; Bd of Governors, Malay Coll., Kuala Kangsar; Interim Council of Nat. Inst. of Technology; Central Bd. Vice-Pres., Subang Nat. Golf Club, 1972-74. Hon. GCVO 1974. *Recreation:* golf. *Address:* Seri Melaka, Malacca, Malaysia.

ZAIDI, Bashir Husain, Syed, CIE 1941; Padma Vibhushan 1976; Member: Court, Aligarh University; Executive Council, Jamia Millia University, New Delhi; Director of several industrial concerns; *b* 1898; *s* of Syed Shaukat Husain Zaidi; *m* 1937, Qudsia Abdullah (*d* 1960); two *s* one *d. Educ:* St Stephen's College, Delhi; Cambridge University. Called to Bar, Lincoln's Inn, 1923; served Aligarh Univ., 1923-30; entered Rampur State service, 1930; Chief Minister Rampur State, UP, 1936-49; Member: Indian Constituent Assembly, 1947-49, Indian Parliament, 1950-52; Indian Delegation to Gen. Assembly of UN, 1951; Indian Parliament (Lok Sabha), 1952-57; (Rajya Sabha) 1964-70; Govt of India's Commn of Inquiry on Communal Disturbances, 1967-69. Chm., Associated Journals Ltd, 1952-77. Vice-Chancellor, Aligarh Muslim University, 1956-62. Leader, Good Will Mission to 9 Afro-Asian countries, 1964; Leader, Cultural Delegn to participate in Afghan Independence Week celebrations, 1965. Trustee, Youth Hostels Assoc. of India. DLitt *hc:* Aligarh 1964; Kanpur 1974. *Address:* Zaidi Villa, Jamianagar, New Delhi, India.

ZAMBIA, CENTRAL, Bishop of, since 1979; **Rt. Rev. Robert Selby Taylor;** *b* 1 March 1909; *s* of late Robert Taylor, Eden Bank, Wetheral, Cumberland; unmarried. *Educ:* Harrow; St Catharine's Coll., Cambridge; Cuddesdon Coll. Ordained deacon, 1932; priest, 1933; served as a curate at St Olave's, York; went out to Diocese of Northern Rhodesia in 1935 as a Mission priest; Principal of Diocesan Theological Coll., 1939; Bishop of Northern Rhodesia, 1941-51; Bishop of Pretoria, 1951-59; Bishop of Grahamstown, 1959-64; Archbishop of Cape Town, 1964-74. Hon. Fellow, St Catharine's Coll., Cambridge, 1964. DD (Hon.) Rhodes Univ., 1966. *Address:* Box 174, Ndola, Zambia; Seaspray, Main Road, Kalk Bay, CP, South Africa. *T:* 8-5588. *Clubs:* Royal Commonwealth Society; Civil Service (Cape Town).

ZAMBONI, Richard Frederick Charles, FCA; Managing Director, Sun Life Assurance Society plc, since 1979; *b* 28 July 1930; *s* of Alfred Charles Zamboni and Frances Hosler; *m* 1960, Pamela Joan Marshall; two *s* one *d. Educ:* Monkton House Sch., Cardiff. Gordon Thomas & Pickard, Chartered Accountants, 1948-54; served Royal Air Force, 1954-56; Peat Marwick Mitchell & Co., 1956-58; British Egg Marketing Board, 1959-70, Chief Accountant, from 1965; Sun Life Assurance Society plc, 1971-, Director, 1975-. Member, Management Cttee, Life Offices' Assoc., 1981-; Hon. Treasurer, Insurance Institute of London, 1982-. Member, Management Cttee, Effingham Housing Assoc. Ltd, 1980-; Director, Worldtech Ventures Ltd, 1981-. *Recreations:* ornithology, gardening, tennis. *Address:* Long Meadow, Beech Avenue, Effingham, Leatherhead, Surrey KT24 5PH. *T:* Bookham 58211.

ZANDER, Prof. Michael; Professor of Law, London School of Economics, since 1977; Legal Correspondent of The Guardian, since 1963; *b* 16 Nov. 1932; *s* of Dr Walter Zander and Margaret Magnus; *m* 1965, Betsy Treeger; two

c. Educ: Royal Grammar Sch., High Wycombe; Jesus Coll., Cambridge (BA Law, double 1st Cl. Hons; LLB 1st Cl. Hons; Whewell Scholar in Internat. Law); Harvard Law Sch. (LLM). Solicitor of the Supreme Court. National Service, RA, 1950-52, 2nd Lieut. Cassel Scholar, Lincoln's Inn, 1957, resigned 1959; New York law firm, 1958-59; articled with City solicitors, 1959-62; Asst Solicitor with City firm, 1962-63; London Sch. of Economics: Asst Lectr, 1963; Lectr, 1965; Sen. Lectr, 1970; Reader, 1970. *Publications:* Lawyers and the Public Interest, 1968; (ed) What's Wrong with the Law?, 1970; (ed) Family Guide to the Law, 1971 (2nd edn 1972); Cases and Materials on the English Legal System, 1973 (3rd edn 1980); (with B. Abel-Smith and R. Brooke) Legal Problems and the Citizen, 1973; Social Workers, their Clients and the Law, 1974 (3rd edn 1981); A Bill of Rights?, 1975 (2nd edn 1979); Legal Services for the Community, 1978; (ed) Pears Guide to the Law, 1979; The Law-Making Process, 1980; The State of Knowledge about the English Legal Profession, 1980; articles in Criminal Law Rev., Mod. Law Rev., Law Soc.'s Gazette, New Law Jl, Solicitors' Jl, Amer. Bar Assoc. Jl, New Society, etc. *Recreations:* reform, the cello. *Address:* 12 Woodside Avenue, N6 4SS. *T:* 01-883 6257.

ZANGWILL, Prof. Oliver Louis, FRS 1977; Professor of Experimental Psychology, University of Cambridge, 1952-81, now Emeritus; *b* 29 Oct. 1913; *yr s* of Israel Zangwill, author and dramatist, and Edith Ayrton Zangwill; *m* 1st, 1947, Joy Sylvia, BEd (marr. diss. 1976), *d* of late Thomas Moult; one *s* decd; 2nd, 1976, Shirley Florence Tribe, BDS (Edin.); one *s* (adopted). *Educ:* University College School, London; King's College, Cambridge (BA 1935, MA 1939). Natural Science Tripos, Part I, Class 2, 1934; Moral Science Tripos, Part II, Class 1, with special distinction, 1935. Research Student, Cambridge Psychological Laboratory, 1935-40; Psychologist, Brain Injuries Unit, Edinburgh 1940-45; Asst Director, Institute of Experimental Psychology, Oxford, 1945-52; Senior Lecturer in General Psychology, Univ. of Oxford, 1948-52. Visiting Psychologist, Nat. Hosp. for Nervous Diseases, Queen Square, London, 1947-79, Hon. Res. Fellow, 1979; Hon. Consulting Psychologist to United Cambridge Hospitals, 1969-. Editor, Quart. Jl Exper. Psychology, 1958-66. President: Sect. J. Brit. Assoc. Adv. Sci., 1963; Experimental Psychology Soc., 1962-63; British Psychological Soc., 1974-75. Mem., Biological Research Board, Medical Research Council, 1962-66. Professorial Fellow, 1955-, Supernumerary Fellow, 1981-, King's Coll., Cambridge. Mem., Assoc. of British Neurologists, 1973. Hon. For. Mem., Soc. Française de Neurologie, 1971. Sir Frederic Bartlett Lectr, 1971; Stolz Lectr, Guy's Hosp., 1979. Kenneth Craik Award, St John's Coll., Cambridge, 1977-78. DUniv Stirling, 1979; ScD St Andrew's, 1980. Hon. FRCPsych 1980. *Publications:* An Introduction to Modern Psychology, 1950; Cerebral Dominance and its relation to psychological function, 1960; Jt Author and Jt Editor: Current Problems in Animal Behaviour, 1961; Amnesia, 1966, 2nd edn 1977; Lateralisation or Language in the Child, 1981; Handbook of Psychology, vol. 1, General Psychopathology, 1982; papers in psychological and medical journals. *Recreations:* reading, natural history. *Address:* 247 Chesterton Road, Cambridge. *T:* Cambridge 65750.

ZARNECKI, Prof. George, CBE 1970; MA, PhD; FSA; FBA 1968; Professor of History of Art, University of London, 1963-82 (Reader, 1959-63); Deputy Director, Courtauld Institute of Art, 1961-74; *b* 12 Sept. 1915; *m* 1945, Anne Leslie Frith; one *s* one *d. Educ:* Cracow Univ. MA Cracow Univ., 1938; PhD Univ. of London, 1950. Junior Asst, Inst. of History of Art, Cracow Univ., 1936-39. Served war of 1939-45 as lance-corporal in Polish Army; in France, 1939-40 (Polish Cross of Valour and Croix de Guerre, 1940); prisoner of war, 1940-42; interned in Spain, 1942-43; in Polish Army in UK, 1943-45. On staff of Courtauld Institute of Art, Univ. of London, 1945-. Slade Professor of Fine Art, Univ. of Oxford, 1960-61. Vice-President: Soc. of Antiquaries of London, 1968-72; British Soc. of Master Glass Painters, 1976-; British Archaeol Assoc., 1979-; Member: Corpus Vitrearum Medii Aevi Cttee, British Acad., 1956-; Conservation Cttee, Council for Places of Worship, 1969-75; Royal Commn on Historical Monuments, 1971-; Arts Sub-Cttee of UGC, 1972-77; Publications Cttee, British Acad., 1978-; Sub-Cttee for Higher Doctorates, CNAA, 1978-82; Chm., Corpus of Anglo-Saxon Sculpture Cttee, British Acad., 1979-. Inst. for Advanced Study, Princeton, 1966. Hon. DLitt: Warwick, 1978; East Anglia, 1981. Gold Medal of Merit (Poland), 1978. *Publications:* English Romanesque Sculpture 1066-1140, 1951; Later English Romanesque Sculpture 1140-1210, 1953; English Romanesque Lead Sculpture, 1957; Early Sculpture of Ely Cathedral, 1958; Gislebertus, sculpteur d'Autun, 1960 (English edn, 1961); Romanesque Sculpture at Lincoln Cathedral, 1964; La sculpture a Payerne, Lausanne, 1966; 1066 and Architectural Sculpture (Proceedings of Brit. Acad.), 1966; Romanik (Belser Stilgeschichte, VI), 1970 (English edn, Romanesque Art, 1971); The Monastic Achievement, 1972; (contrib.) Westminster Abbey, 1972; Art of the Medieval World, 1975; Studies in Romanesque Sculpture, 1979; articles in archaeological journals. *Address:* 22 Essex Park, N3 1NE. *T:* 01-346 6497.

ZEALLEY, Christopher Bennett; Director since 1970 and Trustee since 1976, Dartington Hall Trust; Chairman, Dartington & Co. Ltd; *b* 5 May 1931; *s* of Sir Alec Zealley and Lady Zealley (*née* King); *m* 1966, Ann Elizabeth Sandwith; one *s* one *d. Educ:* Sherborne Sch.; King's Coll., Cambridge (MA Law). Commnd RNVR, 1953; ICI Ltd, 1955-66; IRC, 1967-70. Chairman: Public Interest Research Centre, 1972-; Social Audit Ltd, 1972-; Consumers' Assoc., 1976-81; Charities Aid Foundn, 1982-. Director: JT Group Ltd; Good Food Club Ltd. *Recreation:* music. *Address:* Culverwood, Rattery, South Brent, Devon. *Club:* Naval.

ZEEMAN, Prof. Erik Christopher, FRS 1975; Professor, Director of Mathematics Research Centre, University of Warwick, since 1964; Senior Fellow, Science Research Council, since 1976; *b* 4 Feb. 1925; *s* of Christian Zeeman and Christine Zeeman (*née* Bushell); *m* 1960, Rosemary Gledhill; three *s* two *d. Educ:* Christ's Hospital; Christ's Coll., Cambridge (MA, PhD). Commonwealth Fellow, 1954; Fellow of Gonville and Caius Coll., Cambridge, 1953-64; Lectr, Cambridge Univ., 1955-64. Visiting Prof. at various institutes, incl.: IAS; Princeton; IHES, Paris; IMPA, Rio; also at various univs, incl.: California, Florida, Pisa. Hon. Dr, Strasbourg. *Publications:* numerous research papers on topology, dynamical systems, and applications to biology and the social sciences, in various mathematical and other jls. *Recreation:* family. *Address:* 40 Warwick New Road, Leamington Spa. *T:* Leamington 26997.

ZEFFIRELLI, G. Franco (Corsi); opera, film and theatrical producer and designer since 1949; *b* 12 February 1923. *Educ:* Florence. Designer: (in Italy): A Streetcar Named Desire; Troilus and Cressida; Three Sisters. Has produced and designed numerous operas at La Scala, Milan, 1952-, and in all the great cities of Italy, at world-famous festivals, and in UK and USA; *operas include:* Lucia di Lammermoor, Cavalleria Rusticana, and Pagliacci (Covent Garden, 1959, 1973); Falstaff (Covent Garden, 1961); L'Elisir D'Amore (Glyndebourne, 1961); Don Giovanni, and Alcina (Covent Garden, 1962); Tosca, Rigoletto (Covent Garden, 1964, 1966, 1973); Don Giovanni (Staatsoper-Wien, 1972); Otello (Metropolitan, NY, 1972); Antony and Cleopatra (Metropolitan, NY, 1973); Otello (La Scala, 1976); La Bohème (Metropolitan, NY, 1981); *stage:* Romeo and Juliet (Old Vic, 1960); Othello (Stratford-on-Avon), 1961; Amleto (National Theatre), 1964; After the Fall (Rome), 1964; Who's Afraid of Virginia Woolf (Paris), 1964, (Milan), 1965; La Lupa (Rome), 1965; Much Ado About Nothing (National Theatre), 1966; Black Comedy (Rome), 1967; A Delicate Balance (Rome), 1967; Saturday, Sunday, Monday (Nat. Theatre), 1973; Filumena, Lyric, 1977; *films:* The Taming of the Shrew, 1965-66; Florence, Days of Destruction, 1966; Romeo and Juliet, 1967; Brother Sun, Sister Moon, 1973; Jesus of Nazareth, 1977; The Champ, 1979; Endless Love, 1981. Produced Beethoven's Missa Solemnis, San Pietro, Rome, 1971. *Address:* Via due Macelli 31, Rome.

ZEHETMAYR, John Walter Lloyd, VRD 1963; FIFor; Senior Officer for Wales and Conservator South Wales, Forestry Commission, 1966-81, retired; Appointed Member, Brecon Beacons National Park Committee, since 1982; *b* 24 Dec. 1921; *s* of late Walter Zehetmayr and late Gladys Zehetmayr; *m* 1945, Isabell (Betty) Neill-Kennedy; two *s* one *d. Educ:* St Paul's, Kensington; Keble Coll., Oxford (BA). Served RNVR, 1942-46 (despatches); now Lt Cdr RNR retired. Forestry Commission: Silviculturist, 1948-56; Chief Work Study Officer, 1956-64; Conservator West Scotland, 1964-66. Mem. Prince of Wales' Cttee, 1970-81. *Publications:* Experiments in Tree Planting on Peat, 1954; Afforestation of Upland Heaths, 1960. *Recreations:* garden, conservation, skiing. *Address:* The Haven, Augusta Road, Penarth, S Glam CF6 2RH.

ZEIDLER, Sir David, Kt 1980; CBE 1971; FRACI; FIChemE; Chairman and Managing Director, ICI Australia, 1973-80, retired; *s* of Otto William and Hilda Maude Zeidler; *m* 1943, June Susie Broadhurst; four *d. Educ:* Scotch Coll., Melbourne; Melbourne Univ. (MSc). CSIRO, 1941-52; joined ICI Australia, 1952: Research Manager, 1953; Development Manager, 1959; Controller, Dyes and Fabrics Gp, 1962; Dir, 1963; Man. Dir, 1971; Dep. Chm., 1972. Chm., Metal Manufacturers Ltd, 1981-; Director: Amatil Ltd, 1979-; Broken Hill Prop. Co. Ltd, 1978-; Commercial Bank of Australia Ltd, 1974-; past Director: ICI New Zealand Ltd; IMI Australia Ltd. Mem. Board, Science Mus. of Victoria, 1964-82; Hon. Treasurer, Walter and Eliza Hall Inst. of Med. Res., 1972-; Dep. Chm., Queen's Silver Jubilee Trust, 1977-. Chm., Govt Inquiry into Elec. Generation and Power Sharing in SE Aust., 1980-81; Member, or past Mem., cttees concerned with prof. qualifications, defence industry, educn and trng, internat. business co-operation. Member: Aust.-Japan Businessmen's Co-operation Cttee, 1978-80; Aust.-NZ Businessmen's Council Ltd, 1978-80; Sir Robert Menzies Meml Trust, 1978-; Council, Aust. Acad. of Technol. Scis, 1979-; Inst. of Dirs; Royal Society, Victoria; Royal Soc. for Encouragement of Arts Manuf. and Commerce in London; Cook Society. *Recreations:* tennis, ski-ing, golf. *Address:* 45/238 The Avenue, Parkville, Victoria 3052, Australia. *T:* 387 5720. *Clubs:* Melbourne, Australian (Melb. and Sydney), Commonwealth (Canberra), Sciences.

ZELLICK, Prof. Graham John, JP; PhD; Professor of Public Law in the University of London at Queen Mary College, since 1982; Public Public Law, since 1981; *b* 12 August 1948; *s* of R. H. and B. Zellick; *m* 1975, Jennifer Temkin, LLM, Barrister, Lectr in Law, LSE; one *s* one *d. Educ:* Christ's Coll., Finchley; Gonville and Caius Coll., Cambridge (MA, PhD); Stanford Univ. Ford Foundn Fellow, Stanford Law Sch., 1970-71; Lectr, 1971-78, Reader in Law, 1978-82, QMC, London Univ. Vis. Fellow, Centre of Criminology, 1978-79, and Vis. Prof. of Law, 1975, 1978-79, Toronto Univ. Member: Council and Exec. Cttee, Howard League for Penal Reform, 1973-; Jellicoe Cttee on Bds of Visitors of Prisons, 1973-75; Chm., Sub-Cttees on Discipline and Complaints, Justice Cttee on Prisoners' Rights, 1981-. Governor, Pimlico Sch., 1973-77; Mem. Ct of Governors, Polytechnic of Central London, 1973-77. JP Inner London (N Westminster), 1981. Assessor, Howard Jl of Penology, 1978-; Editor, European Human Rights Reports, 1978-82; Mem. Editl Bd, British Jl of Criminology, 1980-. *Publications:* (contrib.) Halsbury's Laws of England, 4th edn 1922; contribs to collections of essays, pamphlets, the national press, and professional and learned periodicals incl. British Jl of Criminology, Criminal Law Rev., Modern Law Rev., Public Law, Univ. of Toronto Law Jl. *Address:* Faculty of Laws, Queen Mary College, E1 4NS. *T:* 01-980 4811.

ZEMAN, Prof. Zbyněk Anthony Bohuslav; Research Professor in European History, Oxford University, since 1982; *b* Prague, 18 Oct. 1928; *s* of late Jaroslav and Růžena Zeman; *m* 1956, Sarah Anthea Collins (separated); two *s* one *d. Educ:* London and Oxford Universities. BA (Hons) London, DPhil Oxon. Research Fellow, St Antony's Coll., Oxford, 1958-61, and Mem. editorial staff, The Economist, 1959-62; Lectr in Modern History, Univ. of St Andrews, 1963-70; Head of Research, Amnesty International, 1970-73; Director, East-West SPRL (Brussels) and European Cooperation Research Gp, 1974-76; Prof. of Central and SE European Studies and Dir, Comenius Centre, Lancaster Univ., 1976-82. *Publications:* The Break-up of the Habsburg Empire 1914-1918, 1961; Nazi Propaganda, 1964; (with W. B. Scharlau) The Merchant of Revolution, A Life of Alexander Helphand (Parvus), 1965; Prague Spring, 1969; A Diplomatic History of the First World War, 1971; The Masaryks, 1976. *Recreations:* skiing, squash, cooking. *Address:* Modern History Faculty, Indian Institute, Broad Street, Oxford OX1 3BQ. *Clubs:* Beefsteak, Czechoslovak National House.

ZETLAND, 3rd Marquess of; Lawrence Aldred Mervyn Dundas; Bt 1762; Baron Dundas, 1794; Earl of Zetland, 1838; Earl of Ronaldshay (UK), 1892; DL; Temporary Major Yorkshire Hussars (TA); *b* 12 Nov. 1908; *er s* of 2nd Marquess of Zetland, KG, PC, GCSI, GCIE, FBA, and Cicely, *d* of Colonel Mervyn Archdale; *S* father, 1961; *m* 1936, Penelope, *d* of late Col Ebenezer Pike, CBE, MC; three *s* one *d. Educ:* Harrow; Trinity Coll., Cambridge. ADC on Staff of Viceroy of India, 1930-31. DL, North Yorks, 1965. *Heir:* *s* Earl of Ronaldshay, *qv. Address:* Aske, Richmond, North Yorks DL10 5HJ. *T:* Richmond (Yorks) 3222; 59 Cadogan Place, SW1. *T:* 01-235 6542. *Clubs:* All England Lawn Tennis, Jockey.

ZETTER, Paul Isaac, CBE 1981; Chairman: Zetters Group Ltd, since 1972; Sports Aid Foundation Ltd, since 1976; *b* 9 July 1923; *s* of late Simon and Esther Zetter; *m* 1954, Helen Lore Morgenstern; one *s* one *d. Educ:* City of London Sch. Army, 1941-46. Family business, 1946-; became public co., 1965. Mem., Glovers' Co., 1981-; Freeman, City of London, 1981. *Publication:* It Could Be Verse, 1976. *Recreations:* varied water sports, walking, trout breeding, member of the Test and Itchen Fishing Association Ltd. *Address:* 86 Clerkenwell Road, EC1. *Club:* Royal Automobile.

ZETTERLING, Mai Elizabeth; Actress, films and stage, film director, writer; *b* 24 May 1925; *d* of Joel and Lina Zetterling; *m* 1st, 1944, Tutte Lemkow; one *s* one *d* ; 2nd, 1958, David John Hughes (marr. diss. 1977). *Educ:* Stockholm, Sweden. Graduate of Royal Theatre School of Drama, Stockholm. First appeared as Cecilia in Midsummer Dream in the Workhouse, Blanche Theatre, Stockholm, Oct. 1941. Stage successes (all at Royal Theatre, Stockholm) include: Janet in St Mark's Eve; Agnes in The Beautiful People; Brigid in Shadow and Substance; Maria in Twelfth Night; Nerissa in Merchant of Venice; Electra in Les Mouches; Adela in House of Bernarda. First appearance in London, as Hedwig in The Wild Duck, St Martin's, Nov. 1948; subsequently Nina in The Seagull, Lyric, Hammersmith, and St James's, 1949; Eurydice in Point of Departure, Lyric, Hammersmith and Duke of York's, 1950; Karen in The Trap, Duke of York's, 1952; Nora Helmer in A Doll's House, Lyric, Hammersmith, 1953; Poppy in The Count of Clérambard, Garrick, 1955; Thérèse Tard in Restless Heart, St James's, 1957; Tekla in Creditors, Lyric, Hammersmith, 1959, etc. *Swedish films* include: Frenzy, Iris, Rain Follows Dew, Music in the Dark, A Doll's House, Swinging on a Rainbow. *English films* include: Frieda, The Bad Lord Byron, Quartet, Portrait from Life, Lost People, Blackmailed, Hell is Sold Out, Tall Headlines, Desperate Moment, Faces in the Dark, Offbeat, The Main Attraction, and Only Two Can Play, Scrubbers. *United States films* include: Knock on Wood, Prize of Gold, and Seven Waves Away. Director of documentary films for BBC; Dir and Prod and co-writer with David Hughes of short film The War Game; 1st Award at Venice for Narrative Shorts, 1963; Director: Swedish full-length films, Alskande Par, (Eng.) Loving Couples, 1965; Night Games, 1966 (and *see infra*); Dr Glas, 1968; Flickorna, 1968; The Girls, 1968; Writer and Director: Visions of Eight (Olympics film), USA, 1972; Vincent the Dutchman, (award 1973); We Have Many Names (and actress), Sweden, 1975; The Moon is a Green Cheese, Sweden, 1976; The Native Squatter (for Canadian TV), Sweden, 1977; Lady Policeman (Granada TV documentary), 1979; Of Seals and Men (with Greenland trade dept), 1979; Love, Canada, 1980; Love and Marriage (Canadian TV documentary). Dir and Deviser, Playthings, Vienna English Theatre, New Half Moon Theatre, 1980. *Publications:* The Cat's Tale (with David Hughes), 1965; Night Games (novel), 1966; Shadow of the Sun (short stories), 1967; Bird of Passage (novel), 1976; Rains Hat (children's book), 1979; Ice Island (novel), 1979; The Women Who Did . . . Who Dares (autobiog.), 1983. *Recreations:* gardening, cooking, philosophical esp, alchemy. *Address:* c/o Douglas Rae Management Ltd, 28 Charing Cross Road, W1.

ZHUKOV, Georgi Alexandrovich; Hero of Socialist Labour (1978); Orders of: Lenin (2); Red Banner of Labour (2); Red Star; Joliot-Curie Medal; Columnist of Pravda, since 1962; Alternate Member, Central Committee, CPSU, since 1976; MP since 1962; Member, Foreign Relations Committee, USSR Supreme Soviet, since 1966; Chairman, Soviet-French parliamentary group, since 1966; Vice-President, Soviet Committee of Peace, since 1965, Member Presidium, World Peace Council, since 1974; Vice-President, Soviet-

American Institute, since 1961; President, Society USSR-France, since 1958; Secretary, Moscow writing organization, since 1970; *b* 1908. *Educ:* Lomonosov Inst., Moscow. Corresp.: local papers in Lugansk, Kharkov, 1927-32; Komsomolskaya Pravda, 1932-46 (Mem. Editorial Bd); Pravda, 1946-47; Pravda in Paris, 1947-52; Foreign Editor of Pravda, 1952-57; Chairman, USSR Council of Ministers' State Committee for Cultural Relations with Foreign Countries, 1957-62. Mem., Central Auditing Cttee of CPSU, 1956-76, elected by XX, XXII, XXIII and XXIV Congresses of CPSU. Prizes: Lenin (for Journalism); Vorovsky; Union of Soviet Journalists; internat. organization of journalists. *Publications:* Border, 1938; Russians and Japan, 1945; Soldier's Life, 1946; American Notes (essays), 1947; The West After War, 1948; Three Months in Geneva, 1954; Taming Tigers, 1961; Japan, 1962; Meetings in Transcarpathia, 1962; One MIG from a Thousand, 1963, 2nd edn 1979; These Seventeen Years, 1963; Silent Art, 1964; The People of the Thirties, 1964; Vietnam, 1965; America, 1967; The People of the Forties, 1968, 2nd edn 1975; From Battle to Battle: letters from the ideological struggle front, 1970; Chilean Diary, 1970; The USA on the Threshold of the Seventies, 1970; The People in the War (about Vietnam), 1972; 33 Visas, 1972; Times of Great Changes, 1973; Alex and others, 1974; Poisoners, 1975; The War: the beginning and the end, 1975; Letters from Rambouillet, 1975; European Horizons, 1975; Thirty Conversations with TV Viewers, 1977; Town's Beginning, 1977; Thoughts of Unthinkable, 1978; Society without Future, 1978; The Tale of Dirty Tricks, 1978. *Address:* 24 Pravda Street, Moscow, USSR.

ZIEGLER, Henri Alexandre Léonard, Ingénieur Général Air; Grand Officier, Légion d'Honneur; Croix de Guerre (1939-45); Rosette de la Résistance; Hon. CBE; Hon. CVO; Legion of Merit (US); French Aviation Executive; *b* Limoges, 18 Nov. 1906; *s* of Charles Ziegler and Alix Mousnier-Buisson; *m* 1932, Gillette Rizzi; three *s* one *d. Educ:* Collège Stanislas, Paris; Ecole Polytechnique (Grad.); Ecole Nationale Supérieure de l'Aéronautique. Officer-Pilot in French Air Force, 1928 (5000 hours); Tech. Officer, Min. of Aviation, 1929; Dep. Dir of Flight Test Centre, 1938; Foreign Missions: Gt Britain, USA, Germany, Poland, USSR. War of 1939-45: Dep. Buying Mission, USA, Dec. 1939; French Resistance, 1941-44; Col and Chief of Staff, Forces Françaises de l'Intérieur (London), 1944. Dir-Gen., Air France, 1946-54. Dir of Cabinet: of J. Chaban-Delmas (Min. of Public Works, Transport and Tourism), 1954; of Gen. Cormiglion-Molignier (Min. of Public Works), 1955-56; Admin. Dir-Gen., Ateliers d'aviation Louis Breguet, 1957-67. Pres. Dir-Gen., Sud Aviation, 1968; Pres. Dir-Gen., Soc. Nationale Industrielle Aérospatiale, 1970-73; Pres., Airbus Industrie, 1970-74. Pres., Air Alpes, 1961-76; Pres., Forum Atomique Européen, 1956-60; Admin. Inst. du Transport Aérien, 1969-77; Pres., Union Syndicale des Industries Aérospatiales, 1971-74. Mem., Amicale des anciens des essais en vol. Hon. Fellow, Soc. of Experimental Test Pilots; Hon. FRAeS. *Publication:* La Grande Aventure de Concorde, 1976. *Recreation:* alpinism. *Address:* 55 boulevard Lannes, 75116 Paris, France. *T:* 504.61.53. *Club:* Aéro-Club de France (Paris).

ZIEGLER, Philip Sandeman; Director and Editor, William Collins and Sons; *b* 24 Dec. 1929; *s* of Major Colin Louis Ziegler, DSO, DL, and Mrs Dora Ziegler (*née* Barnwell); *m* 1st, 1960, Sarah Collins; one *s* one *d* ; 2nd, 1971, Mary Clare Charrington; one *s. Educ:* Eton; New Coll., Oxford (1st Cl. Hons Jurisprudence; Chancellor's Essay Prize). Entered Foreign Service, 1952; served in Vientiane, Paris, Pretoria and Bogotá; resigned 1967; joined William Collins and Sons Ltd, 1967, Editorial Dir 1972, Editor-in-Chief, 1979-80, resigned when apptd to write official biog. of Earl Mountbatten of Burma. Chm., The London Library, 1979-. FRSL 1975; FRHS 1979. *Publications:* Duchess of Dino, 1962; Addington, 1965; The Black Death, 1968; William IV, 1971; Omdurman, 1973; Melbourne, 1976 (W. H. Heinemann Award); Crown and People, 1978; Diana Cooper, 1981. *Address:* 22 Cottesmore Gardens, W8 5PR. *T:* 01-937 1903; Picket Orchard, Ringwood, Hants. *T:* Ringwood 3258. *Club:* Brooks's.

ZIENKIEWICZ, Prof. Olgierd Cecil, FRS 1979; Professor, and Head of Civil Engineering Department, University of Wales at Swansea, since 1961; *b* Caterham, 18 May 1921; *s* of Casimir Zienkiewicz and Edith Violet (*née* Penny); *m* 1952, Helen Jean (*née* Fleming), Toronto; two *s* one *d. Educ:* Katowice, Poland; Imperial Coll., London. BSc (Eng); ACGI; PhD; DIC; DSc (Eng); DipEng; FICE; FASCE. Consulting engrg, 1945-49; Lectr, Univ. of Edinburgh, 1949-57; Prof. of Structural Mechanics, Northwestern Univ., 1957-61. Naval Sea Systems Comd Res. Prof., Monterey, Calif, 1979-80. Hon. Founder Mem., GAMNI, France. Chairman: Cttee on Analysis and Design, Internat. Congress of Large Dams; Jt Computer Cttee, Instn of Civil Engineers. Mem. Council, ICE, 1972-75 (Chm., S Wales and Mon. Br.); Telford Premium, ICE, 1963-67. General Editor, Internat. Jl Numerical Methods in Engineering; Member Editorial Board: Internat. Jl Solids and Structures; Internat. Jl Earthquakes and Structural Mechanics; Internat. Jl Rock Mechanics, Numerical and Analytical Methods in Geomechanics. James Clayton Fund Prizes, IMechE, 1967, 1973. For. Associate, US Nat. Acad. of Engrg, 1981. Hon. Dr, Lisbon, 1972; Hon. DSc NUI, 1975; Hon. DSci Free Univ., Brussels, 1982. FEng 1979; FCGI 1979. James Alfred Ewing Medal, ICE, 1980; Newmark Medal, ASCE, 1980; Worcester Reed Warner Medal, ASME, 1980. *Publications:* Stress Analysis, 1965; Rock Mechanics, 1968; Finite Element Method, 1967, 3rd edn 1977; Optimum Design of Structures, 1973; Finite Elements in Fluids, 1975; Numerical Methods in Offshore Engineering, 1977; numerous papers in Jl ICE, Jl Mech. Sci., Proc. Royal Soc., Internat. Jl of Num. Methods in Engrg, etc. *Recreations:* sailing, skin-diving.

Address: 29 Somerset Road, Langland, Swansea. *T:* Swansea 68776. *Clubs:* Rotary (Mumbles); Bristol Channel Yacht, Mumbles Yacht.

ZIJLSTRA, Jelle; Central Banker; President, Netherlands Bank, 1967-81; *b* 27 Aug. 1918; *s* of Ane Zijlstra and Pietje Postuma; *m* 1946, Hetty Bloksma; two *s* three *d. Educ:* Netherlands Sch. of Economics. Asst, Netherlands Sch. of Economics, 1945; Prof., Theoretical Economics, 1948-52; Prof., Public Finance, 1963-66, Free Univ. of Amsterdam; Minister of Economic Affairs, 1952-58; of Finance, 1959-63; Prime Minister, 1966-67. Mem., Chm. Board, and Pres., BIS, 1967-82; Governor, IMF, 1967-. *Publications:* Planned Economy, 1947; The Velocity of Money and its Significance for the Value of Money and for Monetary Equilibrium, 1948; Economic Order and Economic Policy, 1952. *Recreations:* sailing, ski-ing. *Address:* Bavoylaan 14, The Hague, Netherlands.

ZILKHA, Selim Khedoury; Director, Habitat Mothercare Group, since 1982 (Chairman and Managing Director, Mothercare Ltd and associated cos, 1961-82); *b* 7 April 1927; *s* of Khedoury Aboodi Zilkha and Louise (*née* Bashi); *m* (marr. diss.); one *s* one *d. Educ:* English Sch., Heliopolis, Egypt; Horace Mann Sch. for Boys, USA; Williams Coll., USA (BA Major Philos.). Chairman: Amerfin Co. Ltd, GB, 1955-68; Spirella Co. of Great Britain Ltd, 1957-62; Chm./Jt Man. Dir, Lewis & Burrows Ltd, 1961-64; Dir, Zilkha & Sons Inc., USA, 1947-. *Recreations:* bridge, backgammon, golf, tennis, horse racing. *Address:* 30 Rockefeller Plaza, New York, NY 10112, USA. *T:* (212) 765-8661. *Clubs:* Portland; Sunningdale Golf; Travellers' (Paris).

ZIMAN, Herbert David; Literary Editor of The Daily Telegraph, 1956-68; *b* Hampstead, 21 March 1902; *s* of late David Ziman, Reefton, New Zealand and Lena (*née* Cohen); *m* 1928, Jean Ritchie, *d* of late C. J. Macalister, MD, FRCP, TD, of Liverpool and Bourton-on-the-Water; two *d* (and one *s* decd). *Educ:* Rugby (Scholar and Senior Leaving Exhibitioner) and University College, Oxford (Senior Scholar). Leader-writer and Asst Literary Editor, Liverpool Daily Post, 1925-26; Film critic of Liverpool Daily Post, 1926-29, and of Glasgow Herald, 1927-29; Museum, Library and Archæological Correspondent, The Times, 1930-33; Leader-writer, Daily Telegraph, 1934-39, and 1946-55. Served in Artists' Rifles, Middlesex Regt and Intelligence Corps (GSO3 South-Eastern Command and Southern Command) and in Political Intelligence Dept, 1939-44. Daily Telegraph War Correspondent in France, Belgium, Holland and Germany with 1st Canadian, 2nd British and 1st US Armies, 1944-45. Special Correspondent of Daily Telegraph subsequently in Western Europe, Greece, Turkey, USSR, Israel, China, Uganda, Kenya, Congo, United States, Canada, Mexico, Chile, Brazil and New Zealand. Hon. Secretary, Friends of the National Libraries, 1931-37, Exec. Cttee FNL, 1937-82; Council, Anglo-Belgian Union, 1957-82. Officier, Ordre de Léopold II (Belgium), 1979. *Address:* 10 Eton Road, NW3. *T:* 01-722 5526. *Club:* Reform.

ZIMAN, Prof. John Michael, FRS 1967; Visiting Professor in Departments of Science and Economic Studies and Humanities, Imperial College of Science and Technology, since 1982; *b* 16 May 1925; *s* of late Solomon Netheim Ziman, ICS, retired, and Nellie Frances Ziman (*née* Gaster); *m* 1951, Rosemary Milnes Dixon; two adopted *s* two adopted *d. Educ:* Hamilton High Sch., NZ; Victoria University Coll., Wellington, NZ; Balliol Coll., Oxford. Junior Lectr in Mathematics, Oxford Univ., 1951-53; Pressed Steel Co. Ltd Research Fellow, Oxford Univ., 1953-54; Lectr in Physics, Cambridge Univ., 1954-64; Fellow of King's Coll., Cambridge, 1957-64; Editor of Cambridge Review, 1958-59; Tutor for Advanced Students, King's Coll., Cambridge, 1959-63; Prof. of Theoretical Physics, 1964-69, Melville Wills Prof. of Physics, 1969-76, Dir, H. H. Wills Physics Lab., 1976-81, Henry Overton Wills Prof. of Physics, 1976-82, Univ. of Bristol. Rutherford Memorial Lectr in India and Pakistan, 1968. Chm., Council for Science and Society; Mem., Scientific Council, Internat. Centre for Theoretical Physics, Trieste, 1970-79. *Publications:* Electrons and Phonons, 1960; Electrons in Metals, 1963; (with Jasper Rose) Camford Observed, 1964; Principles of the Theory of Solids, 1965; Public Knowledge, 1968; Elements of Advanced Quantum Theory, 1969; The Force of Knowledge, 1976; Reliable Knowledge, 1978; Models of Disorder, 1979; Teaching and Learning about Science and Society, 1980; Puzzles, Problems and Enigmas, 1981; numerous articles in scientific jls. *Address:* Imperial College of Science and Technology, Department of Social and Economic Studies, 53 Prince's Gate, Exhibition Road, SW7 2PG. *T:* 01-589 5111.

ZIMBALIST, Efrem; Violinist; Director of The Curtis Institute of Music, Philadelphia, 1941-68, retired; *b* Russia, 1889; *m* 1st, 1914, Alma Gluck, singer; one *s* one *d* ; 2nd, 1943, Mary Louise Curtis Bok. Musical training Imperial School, St Petersburg, under Leopold Auer. Has concertized continuously since debut in 1907 in Berlin. Composer of works for orchestra: American Rhapsody; Concerto for violin and orchestra (1st performance with Philadelphia Orchestra, 1947); Landara (Opera Premiere, Acad. of Music, Phila, 1957); Concerto for piano and orchestra (1st perf. with New Orleans Symph. Orch., 1959); String Quartet in E minor; Violin Sonata; many minor works for voice, violin and piano. *Address:* 100 North Arlington Avenue, Reno, Nevada 89501, USA.

ZIMMERN, Archibald, CBE 1982; Justice of Appeal, Supreme Court of Hong Kong, 1981-82; *b* 15 Aug. 1917; *s* of late Adolph and Mary Zimmern; *m* 1950, Cicely, *d* of Sir Robert Kotewall, CMG, LLD; one *s* one *d. Educ:*

Diocesan Boy's School, Hong Kong. Called to the Bar, Inner Temple, 1958; QC (Hong Kong), 1973. Judge of the High Ct, Hong Kong, 1977-81. *Recreations:* cricket, golf, horse racing. *Address:* B7 Woodbury Court, 137 Pokfulam Road, Hong Kong. *T:* 5-8184034. *Clubs:* Royal Wimbledon Golf; Hong Kong; Royal Hong Kong Golf, Hong Kong Cricket.

ZINN, Major William Victor, CEng, FICE, FIStructE; MEIC (Canada), MSCE (France); retired; Principal of W. V. Zinn & Associates, International Consulting Civil and Structural Engineers, 1934-80; *b* 7 July 1903; *s* of late Roman Reuben Zinn and Bertha Zinn (*née* Simon); *m* 1st, 1934, Laure (*d* 1960), *d* of Chaim and Fleur Modiano, London; one *s* one *d*; 2nd, 1963, Monica, *d* of late Alan Ribton-Turner and Josephine Ribton-Turner (*née* Carey). *Educ:* University College Sch. and University Coll., London. BSc (Eng), MConsE London. War Service, 14th Army Burma, Major RE (retd) 1939-45. Sen. Partner: Haigh Zinn & Associates, Haigh Zinn & Humphreys, and Airport Development Consultants; New Steelworks, Guest Keen & Nettlefolds, Cardiff, 1932-35; Consultant assisting UKAEA and Min. of Works on Atomic Power Stations at Harwell, Windscale, Capenhurst, Calder Hall, Chapel Cross and Dounreay, 1952-56. *Works:* London Hilton Hotel and Royal Garden Hotel; London Govt Offices: Min. of Transport, Min. of Housing, Min. of Works, Dept of Postmaster-Gen., Central Electricity Authority and Min. of Civil Aviation; County Halls: Devon, Gloucester, Norfolk, Lanarkshire, 1954-66; Housing Projects for UK Local Authorities, totalling over 53,000 dwellings, 1934-69; overseas: Princes Bldg and Mandarin Hotel, also Brit. Mil. Hosp., Hong Kong, 1965; Feasibility Reports for World Bank: Teesta Barrage, and Chandpur Irrigation Project (East Pakistan), 1960-62; Ceylon Water Supplies and Drainage for World Health Organisation of the UNO, 1968; development of new techniques for deep underground city excavations, 1960-66; Engineering Consultant for Livingston New Town, Scotland, 1968; Tsing Yi Bridge (2,000 ft), Hong Kong, 1973; underground car park, Houses of Parliament, Westminster, 1974. *Publications:* Economical Construction of Deep Basements, 1968; Detailing by Computer, 1969; Phenomena and Noumena, 1980; Global Philosophy, 1981. *Recreation:* Theravada Buddhism. *Address:* High Trees, Mont Sohier, St Brelades Bay, Jersey, Channel Islands.

See also Rt Hon. J. D. Mabon.

ZINNEMANN, Fred; Film Director since 1934; *b* Austria, 29 April 1907; *s* of Dr Oskar Zinnemann, Physician and Anna F. Zinnemann; *m* 1936, Renée Bartlett; one *s*. *Educ:* Vienna Univ. (Law School). First film, The Wave (documentary) directed for Mexican Govt, 1934; initiated, with others, school of neo-realism in American cinema, directing among other films: The Seventh Cross, 1943; The Search, 1948; The Men, 1949; Teresa, 1950; High Noon, 1951; Member of the Wedding, 1952; From Here to Eternity, 1953. Later films include: Oklahoma!, 1956; The Nun's Story, 1959; The Sundowners, 1960; Behold a Pale Horse, 1964; A Man for All Seasons, 1966; The Day of the Jackal, 1973; Julia, 1977; Five Days One Summer, 1982. Member: Amer. Film Inst.; Acad. of Motion Picture Arts; Directors' Guild of America. Fellow, BAFTA, 1978. Awards include: Academy Award, Los Angeles, 1951, 1954, 1967; Film Critics' Award, NY, 1952, 1954, 1960, 1967; Golden Thistle Award, Edinburgh, 1965; Moscow Film Festival Award, 1965; D. W. Griffith Award, 1970; Donatello Award, Florence, 1978. Gold Medal of City of Vienna, 1967. *Publication:* article on directing films, Encyclopædia Britannica. *Recreations:* mountain climbing, chamber music. *Address:* 128 Mount Street, W1. *T:* 01-499 8810. *Club:* Sierra (San Francisco).

ZOBEL de AYALA, Jaime; Executive Vice-President and Vice-Chairman, Ayala Corporation; *b* 18 July 1934; *s* of Alfonso Zobel de Ayala and Carmen Pfitz y Herrero; *m* 1958, Beatriz Miranda; two *s* five *d*. *Educ:* La Salle, Madrid; Harvard Univ. (BA, Arch. Scis). Major, Philippine Air Force (Res.). First Pres., Cultural Center of Philippines, 1969-70. Philippine Ambassador to the Court of St James's and concurrently to Scandinavian countries, 1971-74. Comendador de la Orden del Merito Civil, Spain, 1968; Chevalier des Arts et des Lettres, 1980. *Recreation:* horseback riding. *Address:* Ayala Corporation, PO Box 259, Commercial Centre, Makati, Metro Manila, D-708, Philippines. *Clubs:* White's; Fox (Harvard).

ZOUCHE, 18th Baron, *cr* 1308, of Haryngworth; **James Assheton Frankland;** Bt 1660; company director; President, Multiple Sclerosis Society of Victoria, since 1981; *b* 23 Feb. 1943; *s* of Major Hon. Sir Thomas William Assheton Frankland, 11th Bt, and Mrs Robert Pardoe (*d* 1972), *d* of late Captain Hon. Edward Kay-Shuttleworth; *S* to father's Btcy 1944; *S* grandmother, 17th Baroness Zouche, 1965; *m* 1978, Sally Olivia, *y d* of R. M. Barton, Diss, Norfolk. *Educ:* Lycée Jaccard, Lausanne. Served 15/19th the King's Royal Hussars, 1963-68. *Heir: u* Hon. Roger Nathaniel Frankland [*b* 11 April 1909; *m* 1st, 1931 (marr. diss., 1947); two *s*; 2nd, 1947, Olivia, *d* of Rev. Hon. Nigel Campbell and *widow* of Major S. J. R. Bucknill, Irish Guards]. *Address:* 7 St Vincent's Place, Albert Park, Victoria 3206, Australia. *Clubs:* Cavalry and Guards; Melbourne (Melbourne).

ZSÖGÖD, Géza B. G.; *see* Grosschmid-Zsögöd, G. B.

ZUCKER, Kenneth Harry, QC 1981; a Recorder of the Crown Court, since 1982; *b* 4 March 1935; *s* of Nathaniel and Norma Zucker; *m* 1961, Ruth Erica, *y d* of Dr H. Brudno; one *s* one *d*. *Educ:* Westcliff High Sch.; Exeter Coll., Oxford, 1955-58 (MA). Served in Royal Air Force, 1953-55. Bacon Scholar, Gray's Inn, 1958; Called to Bar, Gray's Inn, 1959; Atkin Scholar, Gray's Inn,

1959. *Recreations:* reading, walking, photography. *Address:* 60 Gurney Drive, N2 0DE. *T:* 01-458 1556.

ZUCKERMAN, family name of Baron Zuckerman.

ZUCKERMAN, Baron *cr* 1971 (Life Peer), of Burnham Thorpe, Norfolk; **Solly Zuckerman,** OM 1968; KCB 1964 (CB 1946); Kt 1956; MA, MD, DSc; MRCS, FRCP; FRS 1943, FIBiol, Hon. FRCS, Hon. FPS; President: Zoological Society of London, since 1977; British Industrial Biological Research Association, since 1974; Visitor, Bedford College, since 1968; *b* Cape Town, 1904; *m* 1939, Lady Joan Rufus Isaacs, *er d* of 2nd Marquess of Reading; one *s* one *d*. *Educ:* S African College Sch.; Univ. of Cape Town (Libermann Scholar); University Coll. Hosp., London (Goldsmid Exhibnr). Demonstrator of Anatomy, Univ. of Cape Town, 1923-25; Union Res. Scholar, 1925; Res. Anatomist to Zoological Soc. of London and Demonstrator of Anatomy, UCL, 1928-32; Res. Associate and Rockefeller Res. Fellow, Yale Univ., 1933-34; Beit Meml Res. Fellow, 1934-37, Univ. Demonstrator and Lectr in Human Anatomy, 1934-45, Oxford Univ.; William Julius Mickle Fellow, Univ. of London, 1935; Hunterian Prof., Royal Coll. of Surgeons, 1937; Sands Cox Prof. of Anatomy, Univ. of Birmingham, 1943-68; Professor-at-Large, Univ. of E Anglia, 1969-74. Scientific Adviser, Combined Operations HQ; Scientific Advr on planning, AEAF, MAAF, SHAEF, 1939-46 (Gp Capt. (Hon.) RAF, 1943-46); Member: Min. of Works Sci. Cttee, 1945-47; Cttee on Future Sci. Policy (Barlow Cttee), 1946-48; Min. of Fuel and Power Sci. Adv. Cttee, 1948-55; Dep. Chm., Adv. Council on Sci. Policy, 1948-64; Mem., Agricl Res. Council, 1949-59; Chairman: Cttee on Sci. Manpower, 1950-64; Natural Resources (Technical) Cttee, 1951-64; Hon. Sec., Zoological Soc. of London, 1955-77; UK Delegate, Nato Science Cttee, 1957-66; Mem., BBC Gen. Adv. Council, 1957-62; Chairman: Cttee on Management and Control of Research and Develt, 1958-61; Defence Research Policy Cttee, 1960-64; Chief Scientific Adviser: to Sec. of State for Defence, 1960-66; to HM Govt, 1964-71; Chm., Central Adv. Cttee for Science and Technology, 1965-70; UK Delegate on UN disarmament working gps, 1966-71; Trustee, British Museum (Natural History), 1967-77; Chm., Hosp. Sci. and Tech. Services Cttee, 1967-68; Mem., Royal Commn on Environmental Pollution, 1970-74; Chm., Commn on Mining and the Environment, 1971-72; Mem., WHO Adv. Cttee on Med. Research, 1973-77. President: Parly and Sci. Cttee, 1973-76; Assoc., of Learned and Professional Soc. Publishers, 1973-77; Fauna Preservation Soc., 1974-81; Bath Inst. of Med. Engrg, 1980-82. Lectures: Gregynog, UC Wales, 1956; Mason, Univ. of Birmingham, 1957; Caltech Commencement, 1959; Lees Knowles, Cambridge, 1965; Maurice Lubbock, Oxford, 1967; Maurice Bloch, Glasgow, 1969; Trueman Wood, RSA, 1969; Compton, MIT, 1972; Edwin Stevens, RoySocMed, 1974; Romanes, Oxford, 1975; Rhodes, S Africa, 1975. Medal of Freedom with Silver Palm (USA); Chevalier de la Légion d'Honneur. Fellow, University College, London; Fellow Commoner, Christ's College, Cambridge; Gold Medal, Zoological Soc. of London, 1971; Hon. Mem., Academia das Ciencias, Lisboa; Foreign Member: Amer. Philosophical Soc., Amer. Acad. of Arts and Sciences; Professor Emeritus: Univ. of Birmingham, Univ. of E Anglia. Dr *hc* Bordeaux, 1961; Hon. DSc: Sussex, 1963; Jacksonville, USA, 1964; Bradford, 1966; Hull, 1977; Columbia, USA, 1977; East Anglia, 1980; Hon. LLD: Birmingham, 1972; St Andrews, 1980. *Publications:* The Social Life of Monkeys and Apes, 1932, 2nd edn 1981; Functional Affinities of Man, Monkeys and Apes, 1933; (ed, anonymous) Science in War, 1940; A New System of Anatomy, 1961, 2nd edn, 1981; (ed) The Ovary, 2 vols, 1962, 2nd edn 1977; Scientists and War, 1966; Beyond the Ivory Tower, 1970; From Apes to Warlords (autobiography), 1978; (ed) Great Zoos of the World, 1980; Science Advisers, Scientific Advisers and Nuclear Weapons, 1980; Nuclear Reality and Illusion, 1982; contribs to scientific jls since 1925. *Address:* University of East Anglia, Norwich NR4 7TJ. *Clubs:* Beefsteak, Brooks's.

ZUKERMAN, Pinchas; concert violinist; *b* Tel Aviv, Israel, 16 July 1948; *s* of Jehuda and Miriam Zukerman; *m* 1968, Eugenia Rich, flautist; two *d*. *Educ:* Juilliard School of Music. Début, USA, 1969; Europe, 1970. Violin soloist with every major orchestra in USA and Europe; tours of USA, Europe, Israel, Scandinavia, Australia; extensive recordings. Music Director: South Bank Festival, 1978-80; St Paul Chamber Orch., 1980-81, 1981-82. First prize, Leventritt Internat. Violin Competition, 1967. *Recreations:* tennis, horseback riding. *Address:* c/o Sheldon Gold, ICM Artists Ltd, 40 West 57th Street, New York, NY 10019, USA. *T:* (212) 556-5600.

ZULU, Rt. Rev. Alphaeus Hamilton; *b* 29 June 1905; *m* 1929, Miriam Adelaide Magwaza; one *s* six *d*. *Educ:* St Chad's Coll., Ladysmith (qual. teacher); Univ. of S Africa. BA (dist. Soc. Anthrop.) 1938; LTh 1940. Deacon, 1940; Priest, 1942. Curate of St Faith's Mission, Durban, 1940-52, Priest-in-charge, 1952-60; Suffragan Bishop of St John's, (formerly St John's, Kaffraria), 1960-66; Bishop of Zululand, 1966-75. Jt Pres., World Council of Churches, 1968-75. Hon. PhD Natal, 1974. *Recreation:* tennis. *Address:* PO Box 177, Edendale, Natal 4505, S Africa.

ZULUETA, Sir Philip Francis de, Kt 1963; Chairman, Tanks Consolidated Investments Ltd, since 1983 (Director, since 1969); Director: Union Minière, since 1969; Banque Belge Ltd, since 1981; Imperial Continental Gas Association, since 1982; *b* 2 Jan. 1925; *o s* of late Professor Francis de Zulueta; *m* 1955, Hon. Marie-Louise, *e d* of 2nd Baron Windlesham; one *s* one *d*. *Educ:* Beaumont; New College, Oxford (Scholar). MA. Welsh Guards, NW Europe, 1943-47 (Capt., 1945). Foreign Service, 1949: Moscow, 1950-52;

Private Sec. to successive Prime Ministers (Lord Avon, Mr Macmillan, Sir A. Douglas-Home), 1955-64. Asst Sec., HM Treasury, 1962. Resigned from Foreign Service and joined Philip Hill-Higginson, Erlangers, 1964; Dir, Hill Samuel & Co., 1965-72; Chief Exec., 1973-76, Chm., 1976-81, Antony Gibbs Holdings Ltd.; Special Adviser to Bd of Hongkong and Shanghai Banking Corp., 1981. Member: Adv. Council, BBC, 1967-71; Franco-British Council, 1972- (Chm., British Section, 1981-); Exec. Cttee, Trilateral Commn, 1973-; Council, CBI, 1982-; Zoological Soc., 1982-. Chm., Corporate Affairs Cttee, Inst. of Dirs, 1981-. Kt of Honour and Devotion, SMO Malta, 1965. *Address:* 3 Westminster Gardens, Marsham Street, SW1P 4JA. *T:* 01-828 2448. Eastergate House, Eastergate, West Sussex PO20 6UT. *T:* Eastergate 2108. *Clubs:* Beefsteak, Pratt's, White's; Jockey (Paris).

ZUNTZ, Prof. Günther, FBA 1956; DrPhil (Marburg); Emeritus Professor, Manchester University; Professor of Hellenistic Greek, 1963-69; *b* 28 Jan. 1902; *s* of Dr Leo Zuntz and Edith (*née* Bähring); *m* 1947, Mary Alyson Garratt; two *s* one *d. Educ:* Bismarck-Gymnasium, Berlin-Wilmersdorf; Berlin, Marburg, Göttingen and Graz Universities. Teacher, Odenwaldschule, 1924-26; Teacher, Marburg Gymnasium and Kassel Gymnasium, 1926-32; worked for Monumenta Musicae Byzantinae, in Copenhagen, 1935-39, in Oxford, 1939-47; Librarian, Mansfield College, Oxford, 1944-47; Senior Lecturer, Manchester University, 1947-55 (Reader, 1955-63). Korresp. Mitglied, Oesterreich. Akad. der Wissenschaften, 1974. *Publications:* Hölderlins Pindar-Übersetzung, 1928; (with C. Höeg) Prophetologium, i-vi, 1939-71; The Ancestry of the Harklean New Testament, 1945; The Text of the Epistles, 1953; The Political Plays of Euripides, 1955, corrected repr., 1963; The Transmission of Plays of Euripides, 1965; Persephone, 1971; Opuscula Selecta, 1972; Ein griechischer Lehrgang, 1982. Articles in many learned journals. *Recreation:* music. *Address:* 1 Humberstone Road, Cambridge. *T:* 357789.

ZURENUO, Rt. Rev. Sir Zurewe (Kamong), Kt 1981; OBE 1971; Head Bishop of Evangelical Lutheran Church of Papua New Guinea, 1973-82; *b* 5 July 1920; *s* of Zurenuo and Kbasung (previously the people took only one name and were known by none other); *m* 1941, Eleju; two *s* three *d* (and one *s* decd). *Educ:* Lutheran Mission schools (8 years in formal schools and 2 years teacher trng). Began teaching in Lutheran Schools, 1939, interrupted by illness, 1946; also did pastoral work; became Church Secretary of Sattelberg Circuit of Lutheran Church, 1953, and was elected General Secretary of Evangelical Lutheran Church of New Guinea, 1962; ordained, 1966. Instrumental in leading the church from mission status to indigenous church status; played a leading role in writing the constitution of the church; active in community affairs and inter-church relations; Chairman, Melanesian Council of Churches, 1970-73; established Lae City Christian Council, 1972 (Chm., 1972-82). *Address:* Evangelical Lutheran Church of Papua New Guinea, PO Box 80, Lae, Papua New Guinea.